Who'sWho of American Women

Biographical Titles Currently Published by Marquis Who's Who

Who's Who in America
Who's Who in America derivatives:
  Geographic/Professional Index
  Supplement to Who's Who in America
  Who's Who in America Classroom Project Book
Who Was Who in America
  Historical Volume (1607-1896)
  Volume I (1897-1942)
  Volume II (1943-1950)
  Volume III (1951-1960)
  Volume IV (1961-1968)
  Volume V (1969-1973)
  Volume VI (1974-1976)
  Volume VII (1977-1981)
  Volume VIII (1982-1985)
  Index Volume (1607-1985)
Who's Who in the World
Who's Who in the East
Who's Who in the Midwest
Who's Who in the South and Southwest
Who's Who in the West
Who's Who in American Law
Who's Who of American Women
Who's Who of Emerging Leaders in America
Who's Who in Entertainment
Who's Who in Finance and Industry
Index to Who's Who Books
Directory of Medical Specialists
Supplement to Directory of Medical Specialists

Who'sWho of American Women®

16th edition
1989-1990

MARQUIS
Who'sWho

Macmillan Directory Division
3002 Glenview Road
Wilmette, Illinois 60091 U.S.A.

 For information, contact Marquis Who's Who, 3002 Glenview Road, Wilmette, Illinois 60091, 312/ 256-6067, (effective November, 1989: 708/ 256-6067).

Library of Congress Catalog Card Number 58–13264
International Standard Book Number 0–8379–0416–1
Product Code Number 030514

James J. Pfister—President
Paul E. Rose—Executive Vice President
Timothy J. Sullivan—Vice President, Finance
A. Robert Weicherding—Vice President, Publisher
Sandra S. Barnes—Group Vice President, Product Manager
Jill F. Lazar—Product Manager

Distributed in Asia by
United Publishers Services Ltd.
Kenkyu-Sha Bldg.
9, Kanda Surugadai 2-Chome
Chiyoda-ku, Tokyo, Japan

Manufactured in the United States of America

Table of Contents

Preface vi

Board of Advisors vii

Standards of Admission viii

Key to Information ix

Table of Abbreviations x

Alphabetical Practices xvi

Biographies 1

Preface

The sixteenth edition of *Who's Who of American Women* marks the thirtieth anniversary of publication of this reference book. As women have entered a variety of professions in greater numbers since 1958, when the first edition was published, there has been an increasing interest in and need for their biographical data.

In the first volume of *Who's Who of American Women*, volunteer workers in civic, religious, and club activities constituted almost sixteen percent of the biographees. While the proportion of women in these areas has declined, increasing prominence has been achieved in many other fields. This directory includes women who are moving up in professional areas to which they are relatively new, as well as those at high levels in fields traditionally accessible to women. For example, the volume contains considerable representation of women in all areas of government: federal officials, high-level state positions, mayors, and judges. Outstanding women are found in many sectors of business, such as advertising, banking, insurance, and publishing. In addition, women entrepreneurs constitute an important segment of the biographees. As always, women are prominent in the performing arts—dance, theater, opera—with increasing representation in music as, for example, players in symphony orchestras.

In preparing the contents of this edition—more than 25,000 sketches—the Marquis researchers have drawn on a variety of contemporary sources: newspapers, periodicals, professional associations, and other information. The result has been coverage of personal and professional biographical information about women in virtually every important field of endeavor.

In most cases, biographees have furnished their own data, thus assuring a high degree of accuracy. In some cases where individuals of high reference interest failed to supply information, Marquis staff members compiled the data through careful, independent research. Sketches compiled in this manner are denoted by an asterisk. As in previous editions, biographees were given the opportunity to review prepublication proofs of their sketches to make sure they were correct.

Selection of a name for inclusion in *Who's Who of American Women* is based on one fundamental principle: reference value. Some women are eligible for listing because of position, while others have distinguished themselves by noteworthy achievements in their fields. Many listees qualify by virtue of both position and accomplishment.

In the editorial evaluation that resulted in the ultimate selection of the names in this directory, an individual's desire to be listed was not sufficient reason for inclusion; rather it was the person's achievement that ruled. Similarly, wealth or social position was not a criterion; only occupational stature or achievement influenced selection.

In assembling this comprehensive reference source on outstanding American women, Marquis Who's Who editors and researchers have exercised diligent care in the preparation of each biographical sketch. Despite all precautions, errors occasionally occur. Users of this directory are invited to draw the attention of the publisher to any errors found so that corrections can be made in a subsequent edition.

The sixteenth edition of *Who's Who of American Women* continues the tradition of excellence established in 1899 with the publication of the first edition of *Who's Who in America*. The essence of that tradition is the continuing effort at Marquis Who's Who to produce reference works that are responsive to the needs of their users.

Board of Advisors

Marquis Who's Who gratefully acknowledges the following distinguished individuals who have made themselves available for review, evaluation, and general comment with regard to the publication of the sixteenth edition of *Who's Who of American Women*. The advisors have enhanced the reference value of this edition by the nomination of outstanding individuals for inclusion. However, the Board of Advisors, either collectively or individually, is in no way responsible for the final selection of names appearing in this volume, nor does the Board of Advisors bear responsibility for the accuracy or comprehensiveness of the biographical information or other material contained herein.

Jean Dalrymple
Theater Producer and Director

Mildred S. Dresselhaus
Institute Professor
Electrical Engineering and Physics
Massachusetts Institute of Technology

Joseph J. Ellis
Dean of Faculty
Mount Holyoke College

Margaret Hillis
Director
Chicago Symphony Chorus

Jill Krementz
Author and Photographer

Beatrice Laufer
Composer

Jan Keene Muhlert
Director
Amon Carter Museum

Sylvia Porter
Chairman
The Sylvia Porter Organization, Inc.

Catharine R. Stimpson
Dean and Vice Provost for Graduate Education
The Graduate School-New Brunswick
Rutgers University

Barbara S. Uehling
Chancellor
University of California-Santa Barbara

Standards of Admission

The major criterion for determining who will be included in *Who's Who of American Women* is the extent of a woman's reference value. Such reference interest is judged on either of two factors: 1) the position of responsibility held, or 2) the level of achievement attained by the individual.

Admission based on the factor of position includes the following examples:

- High-level federal officials
- Specified elected and appointed state officials
- Mayors of major cities
- Principal officers of selected businesses
- Outstanding educators from major universities and colleges
- Principal figures of cultural and artistic institutions
- Heads of major women's organizations
- Recipients of major awards and honors
- Members of selected honorary organizations
- Other women chosen because of incumbency or membership

Admission for individual achievement is based on objective qualitative criteria. To be selected, a woman must have attained conspicuous achievement. The biographee may scarcely be known in the local community but may be recognized in some field of endeavor for noteworthy accomplishment.

Key to Information

[1] CHAMBERS, ELIZABETH BATES, [2] lawyer; [3] b. Mitchell, S.D., July 19, 1940; [4] d. Oscar William and Judith (Strait) Bates; [5] m. Richard T. Chambers, Dec. 11, 1967; [6] children: Christopher Dwight, Mary Beth. [7] BA, U. Okla., 1962, MA, 1967; JD, Rice U., 1970. [8] Bar: Tex. 1970, S.D. 1973, U.S. Dist. Ct. S.D. 1982, U.S. Supreme Ct. 1982. [9] Assoc. Newman, Calvin & Swain, Houston, 1967-73, ptnr., 1973-74; ptnr. Hadley, Ellis, Chambers & Gonzalez, Amarillo, Tex., 1974-78; sole practice, Rapid City, S.D., 1978-82; ptnr. Chambers & Costner, Rapid City, 1982-85, sr. ptnr., 1985—; lectr. Black Hills State Coll., Spearfish, S.D., 1987; mem. Gov.'s Task Force on Constl. Revision, Pierre, S.D., 1988—; bd. dirs. Custer Nat. Bank. [10] Contbr. articles to profl. jours. [11] Trustee The Grove Sch., Rapid City, 1982—; active Pennington County United Way. [12] Served with WAC, 1962-63. [13] Named Outstanding Woman of Yr., Amarillo C. of C., 1975; Lincoln Found. grantee, 1980. [14] Mem. ABA, S.D. Bar Assn., S.D. Assn. Def. Counsel, Pennington County Bar Assn., World Wildlife Fedn. [15] Democrat. [16] Lutheran. [17] Clubs: Rushmore Hills Country, Noontime (Rapid City). [18] Lodge: Order Eastern Star. [19] Avocations: golf, photography, quilting. [20] Home: 5237 Woodbine Way Rapid City SD 57702 [21] Office: Chambers & Costner 964 N Omaha St Rapid City SD 57701

KEY

[1]	Name
[2]	Occupation
[3]	Vital statistics
[4]	Parents
[5]	Marriage
[6]	Children
[7]	Education
[8]	Professional certifications
[9]	Career
[10]	Writings and creative works
[11]	Civic and political activities
[12]	Military
[13]	Awards and fellowships
[14]	Professional and association memberships
[15]	Political affiliation
[16]	Religion
[17]	Clubs
[18]	Lodges
[19]	Avocations
[20]	Home address
[21]	Office address

Table of Abbreviations

The following abbreviations and symbols are frequently used in this book.

*An asterisk following a sketch indicates that it was researched by the Marquis Who's Who editorial staff and has not been verified by the biographee.

AA, A.A. Associate in Arts
AAAL American Academy of Arts and Letters
AAAS American Association for the Advancement of Science
AAHPER Alliance for Health, Physical Education and Recreation
AAU Amateur Athletic Union
AAUP American Association of University Professors
AAUW American Association of University Women
AB, A.B. Arts, Bachelor of
AB Alberta
ABA American Bar Association
ABC American Broadcasting Company
AC Air Corps
acad. academy, academic
acct. accountant
acctg. accounting
ACDA Arms Control and Disarmament Agency
ACLU American Civil Liberties Union
ACP American College of Physicians
ACS American College of Surgeons
ADA American Dental Association
a.d.c. aide-de-camp
adj. adjunct, adjutant
adj. gen. adjutant general
adm. admiral
adminstr. administrator
adminstrn. administration
adminstrv. administrative
ADP Automatic Data Processing
adv. advocate, advisory
advt. advertising
AE, A.E. Agricultural Engineer
A.E. and P. Ambassador Extraordinary and Plenipotentiary
AEC Atomic Energy Commission
aero. aeronautical, aeronautic
aerodyn. aerodynamic
AFB Air Force Base
AFL-CIO American Federation of Labor and Congress of Industrial Organizations
AFTRA American Federation of TV and Radio Artists
agr. agriculture
agrl. agricultural
agt, agent
AGVA American Guild of Variety Artists
agy. agency
A&I Agricultural and Industrial
AIA American Institute of Architects
AIAA American Institute of Aeronautics and Astronautics
AID Agency for International Development
AIEE American Institute of Electrical Engineers
AIM American Institute of Management
AIME American Institute of Mining, Metallurgy, and Petroleum Engineers
AK Alaska
AL Alabama
ALA American Library Association
Ala. Alabama
alt. alternate
Alta. Alberta
A&M Agricultural and Mechanical
AM, A.M. Arts, Master of
Am. American, America
AMA American Medical Association
A.M.E. African Methodist Episcopal
Amtrak National Railroad Passenger Corporation
AMVETS American Veterans of World War II, Korea, Vietnam
anat. anatomical
ann. annual
ANTA American National Theatre and Academy
anthrop. anthropological
AP Associated Press
APO Army Post Office
apptd. appointed
Apr. April
apt. apartment
AR Arkansas
ARC American Red Cross
archeol. archeological
archtl. architectural
Ariz. Arizona
Ark. Arkansas
ArtsD, ArtsD. Arts, Doctor of
arty. artillery
AS American Samoa
AS Associate in Science
ASCAP American Society of Composers, Authors and Publishers
ASCE American Society of Civil Engineers
ASHRAE American Society of Heating, Refrigeration, and Air Conditioning Engineers
ASME American Society of Mechanical Engineers
assn. association
assoc. associate
asst. assistant
ASTM American Society for Testing and Materials
astron. astronomical
astrophys. astrophysical
ATSC Air Technical Service Command
AT&T American Telephone & Telegraph Company
atty. attorney
Aug. August
AUS Army of the United States
aux. auxiliary
Ave. Avenue
AVMA American Veterinary Medical Association
AZ Arizona

B. Bachelor
b. born
BA, B.A. Bachelor of Arts
BAgr, B.Agr. Bachelor of Agriculture
Balt. Baltimore
Bapt. Baptist
BArch, B.Arch. Bachelor of Architecture
BAS, B.A.S. Bachelor of Agricultural Science
BBA, B.B.A. Bachelor of Business Administration
BBC British Broadcasting Corporation
BC, B.C. British Columbia
BCE, B.C.E. Bachelor of Civil Engineering
BChir, B.Chir. Bachelor of Surgery
BCL, B.C.L. Bachelor of Civil Law
BCS, B.C.S. Bachelor of Commercial Science
BD, B.D. Bachelor of Divinity
bd. board
BE, B.E. Bachelor of Education
BEE, B.E.E. Bachelor of Electrical Engineering
BFA, B.F.A. Bachelor of Fine Arts
bibl. biblical
bibliog. bibliographical
biog. biographical
biol. biological
BJ, B.J. Bachelor of Journalism
Bklyn. Brooklyn
BL, B.L. Bachelor of Letters
bldg. building
BLS, B.L.S. Bachelor of Library Science
Blvd. Boulevard
bn. batallion
B.& O.R.R. Baltimore & Ohio Railroad
bot. botanical
BPE, B.P.E. Bachelor of Physical Education
BPhil, B.Phil. Bachelor of Philosophy
br. branch
BRE, B.R.E. Bachelor of Religious Education
brig. gen. brigadier general
Brit. British, Brittanica

Bros. Brothers
BS, B.S. Bachelor of Science
BSA, B.S.A. Bachelor of Agricultural Science
BSD, B.S.D. Bachelor of Didactic Science
BST, B.S.T. Bachelor of Sacred Theology
BTh, B.Th. Bachelor of Theology
bull. bulletin
bur. bureau
bus. business
B.W.I. British West Indies

CA California
CAA Civil Aeronautics Administration
CAB Civil Aeronautics Board
Calif. California
C.Am. Central America
Can. Canada, Canadian
CAP Civil Air Patrol
capt. captain
CARE Cooperative American Relief Everywhere
Cath. Catholic
cav. cavalry
CBC Canadian Broadcasting Company
CBI China, Burma, India Theatre of Operations
CBS Columbia Broadcasting Company
CCC Commodity Credit Corporation
CCNY City College of New York
CCU Cardiac Care Unit
CD Civil Defense
CE, C.E. Corps of Engineers, Civil Engineer
cen. central
CENTO Central Treaty Organization
CERN European Organization of Nuclear Research
cert. certificate, certification, certified
CETA Comprehensive Employment Training Act
CFL Canadian Football League
ch. church
ChD, Ch.D. Doctor of Chemistry
chem. chemical
ChemE, Chem.E. Chemical Engineer
Chgo. Chicago
chirurg. chirurgical
chmn. chairman
chpt. chapter
CIA Central Intelligence Agency
CIC Counter Intelligence Corps
Cin. Cincinnati
cir. circuit
Cleve. Cleveland
climatol. climatological
clin. clinical
clk. clerk
C.L.U. Chartered Life Underwriter
CM, C.M. Master in Surgery
CM Northern Mariana Islands
C.&N.W.Ry. Chicago & North Western Railway
CO Colorado
Co. Company
COF Catholic Order of Foresters
C. of C. Chamber of Commerce
col. colonel
coll. college
Colo. Colorado
com. committee
comd. commanded
comdg. commanding
comdr. commander
comdt. commandant
commd. commissioned
comml. commercial
commn. commission
commr. commissioner
condr. conductor
Conf. Conference
Congl. Congregational, Congressional
Conglist. Congregationalist
Conn. Connecticut
cons. consultant, consulting
consol. consolidated
constl. constitutional
constn. constitution
constrn. construction
contbd. contributed
contbg. contributing
contbn. contribution
contbr. contributor
Conv. Convention
coop. cooperative
CORDS Civil Operations and Revolutionary Development Support
CORE Congress of Racial Equality
corp. corporation, corporate
corr. correspondent, corresponding, correspondence
C.&O.Ry. Chesapeake & Ohio Railway
C.P.A. Certified Public Accountant
C.P.C.U. Chartered Property and Casualty Underwriter
CPH, C.P.H. Certificate of Public Health
cpl. corporal
C.P.R. Cardio-Pulmonary Resuscitation
C.P.Ry. Canadian Pacific Railway
C.S. Christian Science
CSB, C.S.B. Bachelor of Christian Science
C.S.C. Civil Service Commission
CT Connecticut
ct. court
ctr. center
CWS Chemical Warfare Service
C.Z. Canal Zone

D. Doctor
d. daughter
DAgr, D.Agr. Doctor of Agriculture
DAR Daughters of the American Revolution
dau. daughter
DAV Disabled American Veterans
DC, D.C. District of Columbia
DCL, D.C.L. Doctor of Civil Law
DCS, D.C.S. Doctor of Commercial Science
DD, D.D. Doctor of Divinity
DDS, D.D.S. Doctor of Dental Surgery
DE Delaware
Dec. December
dec. deceased
def. defense
Del. Delaware
del. delegate, delegation
Dem. Democrat, Democratic
DEng, D.Eng. Doctor of Engineering
denom. denomination, denominational
dep. deputy
dept. department
dermatol. dermatological
desc. descendant
devel. development, developmental
DFA, D.F.A. Doctor of Fine Arts
D.F.C. Distinguished Flying Cross
DHL, D.H.L. Doctor of Hebrew Literature
dir. director
dist. district
distbg. distributing
distbn. distribution
distbr. distributor
disting. distinguished
div. division, divinity, divorce
DLitt, D.Litt. Doctor of Literature
DMD, D.M.D. Doctor of Medical Dentistry
DMS, D.M.S. Doctor of Medical Science
DO, D.O. Doctor of Osteopathy
DPH, D.P.H. Diploma in Public Health
DPhil, D.Phil. Doctor of Philosophy
D.R. Daughters of the Revolution
Dr. Drive, Doctor
DRE, D.R.E. Doctor of Religious Education
DrPH, Dr.P.H. Doctor of Public Health, Doctor of Public Hygiene
D.S.C. Distinguished Service Cross
DSc, D.Sc. Doctor of Science
D.S.M. Distinguished Service Medal
DST, D.S.T. Doctor of Sacred Theology
DTM, D.T.M. Doctor of Tropical Medicine
DVM, D.V.M. Doctor of Veterinary Medicine
DVS, D.V.S. Doctor of Veterinary Surgery

E. East
ea. eastern
E. and P. Extraordinary and Plenipotentiary
Eccles. Ecclesiastical
ecol. ecological
econ. economical
ECOSOC Economic and Social Council (of the UN)
ED, E.D. Doctor of Engineering
ed. educated

EdB, Ed.B. Bachelor of Education
EdD, Ed.D. Doctor of Education
edit. edition
EdM, Ed.M. Master of Education
edn. education
ednl. educational
EDP Electronic Data Processing
EdS, Ed.S. Specialist in Education
EE, E.E. Electrical Engineer
E.E. and M.P. Envoy Extraordinary and Minister Plenipotentiary
EEC European Economic Community
EEG Electroencephalogram
EEO Equal Employment Opportunity
EEOC Equal Employment Opportunity Commission
E.Ger. German Democratic Republic
EKG Electrocardiogram
elec. electrical
electrochem. electrochemical
electrophys. electrophysical
elem. elementary
EM, E.M. Engineer of Mines
ency. encyclopedia
Eng. England
engr. engineer
engring. engineering
entomol. entomological
environ. environmental
EPA Environmental Protection Agency
epidemiol. epidemiological
Episc. Episcopalian
ERA Equal Rights Amendment
ERDA Energy Research and Development Administration
ESEA Elementary and Secondary Education Act
ESL English as Second Language
ESSA Environmental Science Services Administration
ethnol. ethnological
exec. executive
exhbn. exhibition
expdn. expedition
expn. exposition
expt. experiment
exptl. experimental

F.A. Field Artillery
FAA Federal Aviation Administration
FAO Food and Agriculture Organization (of the UN)
FBI Federal Bureau of Investigation
FCA Farm Credit Administration
FCC Federal Communications Commission
FCDA Federal Civil Defense Administration
FDA Food and Drug Administration
FDIA Federal Deposit Insurance Administration
FDIC Federal Deposit Insurance Corporation
FE, F.E. Forest Engineer
FEA Federal Energy Administration
Feb. February
fed. federal
fedn. federation
FERC Federal Energy Regulatory Commission
fgn. foreign
FHA Federal Housing Administration
fin. financial, finance
FL Florida
Fla. Florida
FMC Federal Maritime Commission
FOA Foreign Operations Administration
found. foundation
FPC Federal Power Commission
FPO Fleet Post Office
frat. fraternity
FRS Federal Reserve System
FSA Federal Security Agency
Ft. Fort
FTC Federal Trade Commission

G-1 (or other number) Division of General Staff
GA, Ga. Georgia
GAO General Accounting Office
gastroent. gastroenterological
GATT General Agreement of Tariff and Trades
gen. general
geneal. genealogical
geod. geodetic
geog. geographic, geographical
geol. geological
geophys. geophysical
gerontol. gerontological
G.H.Q. General Headquarters
G.N.Ry. Great Northern Railway
gov. governor
govt. government
govtl. governmental
GPO Government Printing Office
grad. graduate, graduated
GSA General Services Administration
Gt. Great
GU Guam
gynecol. gynecological

hdqrs. headquarters
HEW Department of Health, Education and Welfare
HHD, H.H.D. Doctor of Humanities
HHFA Housing and Home Finance Agency
HHS Department of Health and Human Services
HI Hawaii
hist. historical, historic
HM, H.M. Master of Humanics
homeo. homeopathic
hon. honorary, honorable
Ho. of Dels. House of Delegates
Ho. of Reps. House of Representatives
hort. horticultural
hosp. hospital
HUD Department of Housing and Urban Development
Hwy. Highway
hydrog. hydrographic

IA Iowa
IAEA International Atomic Energy Agency
IBM International Business Machines Corporation
IBRD International Bank for Reconstruction and Development
ICA International Cooperation Administration
ICC Interstate Commerce Commission
ICU Intensive Care Unit
ID Idaho
IEEE Institute of Electrical and Electronics Engineers
IFC International Finance Corporation
IGY International Geophysical Year
IL Illinois
Ill. Illinois
illus. illustrated
ILO International Labor Organization
IMF International Monetary Fund
IN Indiana
Inc. Incorporated
Ind. Indiana
ind. independent
Indpls. Indianapolis
indsl. industrial
inf. infantry
info. information
ins. insurance
insp. inspector
insp. gen. inspector general
inst. institute
instl. institutional
instn. institution
instr. instructor
instrn. instruction
internat. international
intro. introduction
IRE Institute of Radio Engineers
IRS Internal Revenue Service
ITT International Telephone & Telegraph Corporation

JAG Judge Advocate General
JAGC Judge Advocate General Corps
Jan. January
Jaycees Junior Chamber of Commerce
JB, J.B. Jurum Baccalaureus
JCB, J.C.B. Juris Canoni Baccalaureus
JCD, J.C.D. Juris Canonici Doctor, Juris Civilis Doctor
JCL, J.C.L. Juris Canonici Licentiatus

JD, J.D. Juris Doctor
jg. junior grade
jour. journal
jr. junior
JSD, J.S.D. Juris Scientiae Doctor
JUD, J.U.D. Juris Utriusque Doctor
jud. judicial

Kans. Kansas
K.C. Knights of Columbus
K.P. Knights of Pythias
KS Kansas
K.T. Knight Templar
KY, Ky. Kentucky

LA, La. Louisiana
lab. laboratory
lang. language
laryngol. laryngological
LB Labrador
lectr. lecturer
legis. legislation, legislative
LHD, L.H.D. Doctor of Humane Letters
L.I. Long Island
lic. licensed, license
L.I.R.R. Long Island Railroad
lit. literature
LittB, Litt.B. Bachelor of Letters
LittD, Litt.D. Doctor of Letters
LLB, LL.B. Bachelor of Laws
LLD, L.L.D. Doctor of Laws
LLM, L.L.M. Master of Laws
Ln. Lane
L.&N.R.R. Louisville & Nashville Railroad
LS, L.S. Library Science (in degree)
lt. lieutenant
Ltd. Limited
Luth. Lutheran
LWV League of Women Voters

M. Master
m. married
MA, M.A. Master of Arts
MA Massachusetts
mag. magazine
MAgr, M.Agr. Master of Agriculture
maj. major
Man. Manitoba
Mar. March
MArch, M.Arch. Master in Architecture
Mass. Massachusetts
math. mathematics, mathematical
MATS Military Air Transport Service
MB, M.B. Bachelor of Medicine
MB Manitoba
MBA, M.B.A. Master of Business Administration
MBS Mutual Broadcasting System
M.C. Medical Corps
MCE, M.C.E. Master of Civil Engineering
mcht. merchant
mcpl. municipal
MCS, M.C.S. Master of Commercial Science
MD, M.D. Doctor of Medicine
MD, Md. Maryland
MDip, M.Dip. Master in Diplomacy
mdse. merchandise
MDV, M.D.V. Doctor of Veterinary Medicine
ME, M.E. Mechanical Engineer

ME Maine
M.E.Ch. Methodist Episcopal Church
mech. mechanical
MEd., M.Ed. Master of Education
med. medical
MEE, M.E.E. Master of Electrical Engineering
mem. member
meml. memorial
merc. mercantile
met. metropolitan
metall. metallurgical
MetE, Met.E. Metallurgical Engineer
meteorol. meteorological
Meth. Methodist
Mex. Mexico
MF, M.F. Master of Forestry
MFA, M.F.A. Master of Fine Arts
mfg. manufacturing
mfr. manufacturer
mgmt. management
mgr. manager
MHA, MH.A. Master of Hospital Administration
M.I. Military Intelligence
MI Michigan
Mich. Michigan
micros. microscopic, microscopical
mid. middle
mil. military
Milw. Milwaukee
mineral. mineralogical
Minn. Minnesota
Miss. Mississippi
MIT Massachusetts Institute of Technology
mktg. marketing
ML, M.L. Master of Laws
MLA Modern Language Association
M.L.D. Magister Legnum Diplomatic
MLitt, M.Litt. Master of Literature
MLS, M.L.S. Master of Library Science
MME, M.M.E. Master of Mechanical Engineering
MN Minnesota
mng. managing
MO, Mo. Missouri
moblzn. mobilization
Mont. Montana
M.P. Member of Parliament
MPE, M.P.E. Master of Physical Education
MPH, M.P.H. Master of Public Health
MPhil, M.Phil. Master of Philosophy
MPL, M.P.L. Master of Patent Law
Mpls. Minneapolis
MRE, M.R.E. Master of Religious Education
MS, M.S. Master of Science
MS, Ms. Mississippi
MSc, M.Sc. Master of Science
MSF, M.S.F. Master of Science of Forestry
MST, M.S.T. Master of Sacred Theology
MSW, M.S.W. Master of Social Work
MT Montana
Mt. Mount
MTO Mediterranean Theatre of Operations
mus. museum, musical
MusB, Mus.B. Bachelor of Music
MusD, Mus.D. Doctor of Music
MusM, Mus.M. Master of Music
mut. mutual
mycol. mycological

N. North
NAACP National Association for the Advancement of Colored People
NACA National Advisory Committee for Aeronautics
NAD National Academy of Design
N.Am. North America
NAM National Association of Manufacturers
NAPA National Association of Performing Artists
NAREB National Association of Real Estate Boards
NARS National Archives and Record Service
NASA National Aeronautics and Space Administration
nat. national
NATO North Atlantic Treaty Organization
NATOUSA North African Theatre of Operations
nav. navigation
NB, N.B. New Brunswick
NBC National Broadcasting Company
NC, N.C. North Carolina
NCCJ National Conference of Christians and Jews
ND, N.D. North Dakota
NDEA National Defense Education Act
NE Nebraska
NE Northeast
NEA National Education Association
Nebr. Nebraska
NEH National Endowment for Humanities
neurol. neurological
Nev. Nevada
NF Newfoundland
NFL National Football League
Nfld. Newfoundland
NG National Guard
NH, N.H. New Hampshire

NHL National Hockey League
NIH National Institutes of Health
NIMH National Institute of Mental Health
NJ, N.J. New Jersey
NLRB National Labor Relations Board
NM New Mexico
N.Mex. New Mexico
No. Northern
NOAA National Oceanographic and Atmospheric Administration
NORAD North America Air Defense
Nov. November
NOW National Organization for Women
N.P.Ry. Northern Pacific Railway
nr. near
NRC National Research Council
NS, N.S. Nova Scotia
NSC National Security Council
NSF National Science Foundation
N.T. New Testament
NT Northwest Territories
numis. numismatic
NV Nevada
NW Northwest
N.W.T. Northwest Territories
NY, N.Y. New York
N.Y.C. New York City
NYU New York University
N.Z. New Zealand

OAS Organization of American States
ob-gyn obstetrics-gynecology
obs. observatory
obstet. obstetrical
Oct. October
OD. O.D. Doctor of Optometry
OECD Organization of European Cooperation and Development
OEEC Organization of European Economic Cooperation
OEO Office of Economic Opportunity
ofcl. official
OH Ohio
OK Oklahoma
Okla. Oklahoma
ON Ontario
Ont. Ontario
ophthal. ophthalmological
ops. operations
OR Oregon
orch. orchestra
Oreg. Oregon
orgn. organization
ornithol. ornithological
OSHA Occupational Safety and Health Administration
OSRD Office of Scientific Research and Development
OSS Office of Strategic Services
osteo. osteopathic
otol. otological
otolaryn. otolaryngological

PA, Pa. Pennsylvania
P.A. Professional Association
paleontol. paleontological
path. pathological
P.C. Professional Corporation
PE Prince Edward Island
P.E.I. Prince Edward Island
PEN Poets, Playwrights, Editors, Essayists and Novelists (international association)
penol. penological
P.E.O. women's organization (full name not disclosed)
pfc. private first class
PHA Public Housing Administration
pharm. pharmaceutical
PharmD, Pharm.D. Doctor of Pharmacy
PharmM, Pharm.M. Master of Pharmacy
PhB, Ph.B. Bachelor of Philosophy
PhD, Ph.D. Doctor of Philosophy
PhM, Ph.M. Master of Philosophy
Phila. Philadelphia
philharm. philharmonic
philol. philological
philos. philosophical
photog. photographic
phys. physical
physiol. physiological
Pitts. Pittsburgh
Pkwy. Parkway
Pl. Place
P.&L.E.R.R. Pittsburgh & Lake Erie Railroad
P.O. Post Office
PO Box Post Office Box
polit. political
poly. polytechnic, polytechnical
PQ Province of Quebec
PR. P.R. Puerto Rico
prep. preparatory
pres. president
Presbyn. Presbyterian
presdl. presidential
prin. principal
proc. proceedings
prod. produced (play production)
prodn. production
prof. professor
profl. professional
prog. progressive
propr. proprietor
pros. atty. prosecuting attorney
pro tem pro tempore
PSRO Professional Services Review Organization
psychiat. psychiatric
psychol. psychological
PTA Parent-Teachers Association
ptnr. partner
PTO Pacific Theatre of Operations, Parent Teacher Organization
pub. publisher, publishing, published
pub. public
publ. publication
pvt. private

quar. quarterly
qm. quartermaster
Q.M.C. Quartermaster Corps
Que. Quebec

radiol. radiological
RAF Royal Air Force
RCA Radio Corporation of America
RCAF Royal Canadian Air Force
RD Rural Delivery
Rd. Road
REA Rural Electrification Administration
rec. recording
ref. reformed
regt. regiment
regtl. regimental
rehab. rehabilitation
Rep. Republican
rep. representative
Res. Reserve
ret. retired
rev. review, revised
RFC Reconstruction Finance Corporation
RFD Rural Free Delivery
rhinol. rhinological
RI, R.I. Rhode Island
RN, R.N. Registered Nurse
roentgenol. roentgenological
ROTC Reserve Officers Training Corps
R.R. Railroad
Ry. Railway

S. South
s. son
SAC Strategic Air Command
SALT Strategic Arms Limitation Talks
S.Am. South America
san. sanitary
SAR Sons of the American Revolution
Sask. Saskatchewan
savs. savings
SB, S.B. Bachelor of Science
SBA Small Business Administration
SC, S.C. South Carolina
SCAP Supreme Command Allies Pacific
ScB, Sc.B. Bachelor of Science
SCD, S.C.D. Doctor of Commercial Science
ScD, Sc.D. Doctor of Science
sch. school
sci. science, scientific
SCLC Southern Christian Leadership Conference
SCV Sons of Confederate Veterans
SD, S.D. South Dakota
SE Southeast
SEATO Southeast Asia Treaty Organization
SEC Securities and Exchange Commission
sec. secretary

sect. section
seismol. seismological
sem. seminary
Sept. September
s.g. senior grade
sgt. sergeant
SHAEF Supreme Headquarters Allied Expeditionary Forces
SHAPE Supreme Headquarters Allied Powers in Europe
S.I. Staten Island
S.J. Society of Jesus (Jesuit)
SJD Scientiae Juridicae Doctor
SK Saskatchewan
SM, S.M. Master of Science
So. Southern
soc. society
sociol. sociological
S.P. Co. Southern Pacific Company
spl. special
splty. specialty
Sq. Square
S.R. Sons of the Revolution
sr. senior
SS Steamship
SSS Selective Service System
St. Saint, Street
sta. station
stats. statistics
statis. statistical
STB, S.T.B. Bachelor of Sacred Theology
stblzn. stabilization
STD, S.T.D. Doctor of Sacred Theology
subs. subsidiary
SUNY State University of New York
supr. supervisor
supt. superintendent
surg. surgical
SW Southwest

TAPPI Technical Association of the Pulp and Paper Industry
Tb. Tuberculosis
tchr. teacher
tech. technical, technology
technol. technological
Tel. & Tel. Telephone & Telegraph
temp. temporary
Tenn. Tennessee
Ter. Territory
Terr. Terrace
Tex. Texas
ThD, Th.D. Doctor of Theology
theol. theological
ThM, Th.M. Master of Theology
TN Tennessee
tng. training
topog. topographical
trans. transaction, transferred
transl. translation, translated
transp. transportation
treas. treasurer
TT Trust Territory
TV television
TVA Tennessee Valley Authority
twp. township
TX Texas
typog. typographical

U. University
UAW United Auto Workers
UCLA University of California at Los Angeles
UDC United Daughters of the Confederacy
U.K. United Kingdom
UN United Nations
UNESCO United Nations Educational, Scientific and Cultural Organization
UNICEF United Nations International Children's Emergency Fund
univ. university
UNRRA United Nations Relief and Rehabilitation Administration
UPI United Press International
U.P.R.R. United Pacific Railroad
urol. urological
U.S. United States
U.S.A. United States of America
USAAF United States Army Air Force
USAF United States Air Force
USAFR United States Air Force Reserve
USAR United States Army Reserve
USCG United States Coast Guard
USCGR United States Coast Guard Reserve
USES United States Employment Service
USIA United States Information Agency
USMC United States Marine Corps
USMCR United States Marine Corps Reserve
USN United States Navy
USNG United States National Guard
USNR United States Naval Reserve
USO United Service Organizations
USPHS United States Public Health Service
USS United States Ship
USSR Union of the Soviet Socialist Republics
USV United States Volunteers
UT Utah

VA Veterans' Administration
VA, Va. Virginia
vet. veteran, veterinary
VFW Veterans of Foreign Wars
VI, V.I. Virgin Islands
vice pres. vice president
vis. visiting
VISTA Volunteers in Service to America
VITA Volunteers in Technical Service
vocat. vocational
vol. volunteer, volume
v.p. vice president
vs. versus
VT, Vt. Vermont

W. West
WA Washington (state)
WAC Women's Army Corps
Wash. Washington (state)
WAVES Women's Reserve, US Naval Reserve
WCTU Women's Christian Temperance Union
we. western
W. Ger. Germany, Federal Republic of
WHO World Health Organization
WI Wisconsin
W.I. West Indies
Wis. Wisconsin
WSB Wage Stabilization Board
WV West Virginia
W.Va. West Virginia
WY Wyoming
Wyo. Wyoming

YK Yukon Territory
YMCA Young Men's Christian Association
YMHA Young Men's Hebrew Association
YM & YWHA Young Men's and Young Women's Hebrew Association
yr. year
YT, Y.T. Yukon Territory
YWCA Young Women's Christian Association

zool. zoological

Alphabetical Practices

Names are arranged alphabetically according to the surnames, and under identical surnames according to the first given name. If both surname and first given name are identical, names are arranged alphabetically according to the second given name. Where full names are identical, they are arranged in order of age—with the elder listed first.

Surnames beginning with De, Des, Du, however capitalized or spaced, are recorded with the prefix preceding the surname and arranged alphabetically under the letter D.

Surnames beginning with Mac and Mc are arranged alphabetically under M.

Surnames beginning with Saint or St. appear after names that begin Sains, and are arranged according to the second part of the name, e.g. St. Clair before Saint Dennis.

Surnames beginning with Van, Von or von are arranged alphabetically under letter V.

Compound hyphenated surnames are arranged according to the first member of the compound. Compound unhyphenated surnames are treated as hyphenated names.

Parentheses used in connection with a name indicate which part of the full name is usually deleted in common usage. Hence Abbott, W(illiam) Lewis indicates that the usual form of the given name is W. Lewis. In such a case, the parentheses are ignored in alphabetizing. However, if the name is recorded Abbott, (William) Lewis, signifying that the entire name William is not commonly used, the alphabetizing would be arranged as though the name were Abbott, Lewis.

Who'sWho of American Women

AADALEN, SHARON PRICE, nursing educator, researcher; b. Manchester, N.H., June 26, 1940; d. Trevor Alaric Pryce and Beatrice (Dinsmore) Price; m. Richard Jerome Aadalen, July 27, 1963; children: Richard Andrew, Kirk Jeremy, Lora Elizabeth. BA magna cum laude, Radcliffe Coll., 1962; BS in Nursing, Western Res. U., 1967; MS in Pub. Health, U. Minn., 1979, PhD in Edn., 1983; cert. Reflective Leadership Program Hubert Humphrey Inst. Pub. Affairs, 1984. RN, cert. pub. health nursing, Minn. Staff nurse pub. health Vis. Nurse Assn., Roxbury Dist. Boston, 1964-65; staff and charge nurse, Lakeside Hosp., Univ. Hosps., Cleve., 1965-66; staff and charge nurse neurol. rehab. Benjamin Rose Hosp., Univ. Hosps., Cleve., 1966; staff nurse coronary rehab., coronary ICU, Mt. Sinai Hosp., Mpls., 1974-76; instr. Sch. Nursing SUNY-Plattsburgh, 1967-69; instr. Sch. Pub. Health, U. Minn., Mpls., 1979-82, adj. faculty, 1982-86, adj. asst. prof. maternal child health program Sch. Pub. Health, 1986—, adj. asst. prof. Sch. Nursing, 1986—; community faculty mem. nursing edn. program Met. State Univ., Mpls., 1986—; prin. investigator Minn. Sudden Infant Death Ctr., 1978-85; dir. nursing edn. and research United Hosp., St. Paul, 1985—; cons. div. nursing and health scis. mgmt. Minot State Coll. (N.D.), 1982; workshop coordinator dept. family social sci. U. Minn., St. Paul, 1983, cons., 1983; instr. sch. nurse achievement program U. Colo., 1983; mem. maternal and child health external grants rev. com. Minn. Dept. Health, 1983; bd. dirs., exec. com. Midwest Alliance in Nursing, 1982-83; mem. task force Gov.'s White House Conf. on Family Stress and Work, 1981; speaker profl. confs. U.S.; invited speaker USSR, 1983. Contbr. chpts. to books, articles to profl. jours. Bd. dirs. YWCA, Cleveland Heights, Ohio, 1969-73; speakers bur. Minn. affiliate Am. Heart Assn., 1975-77; mem. Citizens League, 1979—; mem. subcom. Citizens Adv. Task Force on Edn., Edina, Minn., 1975-77; v.p. Edina Community Lutheran Ch., 1983-84, pres. 1984-85, mem. Council of Ministers; mem. allocation and evaluation panels United Way Mpls., 1983-86; mem. Edina Health Adv. Bd., 1985-87, chmn., 1985-86; mem. State Community Health Services Adv. Com., 1985-86. Thompson scholar, 1960-61, Mass. Gen. Hosp. Sch. Nursing scholar, 1962-64; Ruth Sherman fellow, 1962; trainee div. nursing USPHS, HEW, Frances Payne Bolton Sch. Nursing, Western Res. U., 1966-67, Sch. Pub. Health, U. Minn., 1977-78; scholar reflective leadership seminar Hubert H. Humphrey Inst. Pub. Affairs, U. Minn., 1983-84. Mem. Am. Nurses Assn. (council nurse researchers, council continuing edn., council on computer applications), Minn. Nurses Assn., Am. Pub. Health Assn., Minn. Pub. Health Assn. (future directions task force 1980-81), Am. Assn. Adult and Continuing Edn., Am. Assn. Nurse Execs., Minn. Assn. Nurse Execs. (edn. com. 1985—, chmn. 1986—), Twin Cities Assn. Nurse Execs., Midwest Nursing Research Soc., Minn. Mental Health Assn., World Futures Soc., U. Minn. Alumni Assn. (interim bd. dirs. Constituent Soc. Sch. Pub. Health), Sigma Theta Tau (bd. dirs. 1980-82, research award 1984, distinguished lectr. 1988—), Phi Delta Kappa, Phi Kappa Phi. Home: 4924 Dale Dr Edina MN 55424 Office: United Hosp Nursing Edn and Research Dept 333 N Smith Ave Saint Paul MN 55102

AARON, CHLOE WELLINGHAM, television executive; b. Santa Monica, Calif., Oct. 9, 1938; d. John Rufus and Grace (Lloyd) Wellingham; m. David Laurence Aaron, Aug. 11, 1962; 1 child, Timothy Wellingham. BA, Occidental Coll., 1961; MA, George Washington U., 1966; HHD, Occidental Coll., 1987. Freelance journalist 1965-70; dir. pub. media program Nat. Endowment for Arts, Washington, 1970-76; sr. v.p. programming Pub. Broadcasting Service, Washington, 1976-81; pres. Chloe Aaron Assocs., 1981—; dir. cultural and children's programs KQED-TV, San Francisco, 1987—. Producer: TV film The Soldier's Tale, PBS (Emmy award 1984), 1984. Mem. trustee com. on film Mus. Modern Art, N.Y.C.; mem. bd. pub. devel. Corp. of N.Y.C., Ctr. Visual History, Nancy Hanks Ctr., Am. Jazz Orchestra. Recipient Alumni Seal award Occidental Coll., 1983. Office: 500 8th St San Francisco CA 94103

AARON, SHIRLEY MAE, tax consultant; b. Covington, La., Feb. 28, 1935; d. Morgan and Pearl (Jenkins) King; m. Michael A. Aaron, Nov. 27, 1976; m. Richard L. King, Feb. 16, 1952 (div. Feb. 1965); children—Deborah, Richard, Roberta, Keely. Adminstrv. asst. South Central Bell, Covington, La., 1954-62; acct. Brown & Root, Inc., Houston, 1962-75; timekeeper Alyeska Pipeline Co., Fairbanks, Alaska, 1975-77; adminstrv. asst. Boeing Co., Seattle, 1979—; pres. Aaron Enterprises, Seattle, 1977—. Bd. dirs. Burien 146 Homeowners Assn., Seattle, 1979—, pres., 1980-83. Mem. Nat. Assn. Female Execs. Avocation: singing.

AARONSON, BRENDA CARYL, educator; b. Pittsfield, Mass., Nov. 13, 1938; d. Jacob Solon and Sally (Golden) A. BMus, U. N.C., 1960; MA, NYU, 1967, cert., 1979. Asst. to coordinator and film prodn. NYU Med. Ctr., N.Y.C., 1961-62; asst. to advt. and prodn. mgr. Mills Music, Inc., N.Y.C., 1962-63; music librarian NYU, N.Y.C., 1963-65; music educator Union Free Sch. Dist. No. 10, Commack, N.Y., 1965-66; music educator, acting chmn. George Washington High Sch., Bd. Edn. City N.Y., 1966-71; music educator, asst. chmn. Adlai E. Stevenson High Sch., 1971-78; music educator, dean students Martin L. King Jr. High Sch., 1978—; examining asst. Bd. Exams Bd. Edn. City N.Y., 1986—. Composer mus. comedy: Extension H., 1959, secular and sacred works, 1962—; author children's texts and musicol. articles, 1964—; conductor, 1960—. Lectr. State of Israel Bonds, N.Y.C., 1980-82, bd. dirs. new leadership div., 1980-82; pres. Aviv chpt. B'nai B'rith Women, N.Y.C., 1983-85; v.p., exec. offices Gotham unit B'nai B rith, N.Y.C., 1979-82; v.p. Golda Meir group Hadassah, N.Y.C., 1980-82. Recipient Outstanding Service and Bull. awards B'nai B'rith Women, N.Y.C., 1979-86, Outstanding Service awards Hadassah, 1980-82, Israel leadership award State of Israel Bonds, 1982. Mem. Nat. Band Assn., Nat. Sch. Orch. Assn., N.Y. State Sch. Music Assn. Democrat. Jewish. Home: 170 W End Ave New York NY 10023 Office: King High Sch 122 Amsterdam Ave New York NY 10023

ABAD, ROSARIO DALIDA, elementary educator; b. Ilocos Norte, Philippines, Apr. 23, 1936; came to U.S., 1966; d. Primitivo Agoo and Adelaida (Cacal) Dalida; m. Domingo Abad, June 8, 1969; children: Eric, Jon, Jenny. Grad., Philippine Normal Coll., 1954; BA in Edn., Far Eastern U., Manila, 1961; MA in Edn., Far Eastern U., 1966. Educator Rizal Pub. Schs., Philippines, 1955-58, Manila Pub. Schs., 1958-66; instr. Mindoro Coll., Philippines, 1964-66; tchr. Sudbury (Ont., Can.) Schs., 1966-67, St. Bernard (La.) Schs., 1967-68, Jefferson Parish (La.) Schs., 1968-73, New Orleans Sch. Bd., 1973—. Contbr. articles to profl. jours.; free-lance writer. V.p. Philippine-Am. Sports Assn. New Orleans, 1987—, Kapit-Bahay Assn., 1984—. Recipient Recognition award Kapit-Bahay Assn., 1984. Mem. Internat. Reading Assn., Nat. Assn. Female Execs., Am. Fedn. Tchrs., United Tchrs. New Orleans, Philippine-Am. Womens' Assn. La. (v.p. 1985-87, Recognition award 1986). Democrat. Roman Catholic. Home: 2612 Mercedes Blvd New Orleans LA 70114

ABADIE, ROBELYNN HOOD, insurance executive; b. Denham Springs, La., Nov. 11, 1950; d. Robin Sr. and Ernestine Aubrey (Facundus) Hood; children: Melissa Anne, Jason Matthew. Grad., St. Louis Inst. Music, 1969. Clk. bank card dept. La. Nat. Bank, Baton Rouge, 1970-71, analyst real estate, 1976-77; owner, mgr. Water Bros., Inc., Baton Rouge, 1971-73; owner, distbr. Seyforth Labs., Inc., Dallas, 1977-79; sales agt. Southwestern Life Ins. Co., Baton Rouge, 1979-82; mgr. sales Mut. Security Life Ins. Co., Baton Rouge, 1982-84; mgr. agy. Am. Gen. Life Ins. Co., Baton Rouge, 1984-86; gen. agt. Fidelity Union Life Ins. Co., Baton Rouge, 1986—; mem. task force on credit life State of La., Baton Rouge, 1985; speaker in field. Contbr. articles to profl. jours. Dir. tng. union Parkview Bapt. Ch., Baton Rouge, 1980-81, tchr. Sunday sch., leader Bible study, 1982-83, chmn. ins. com., 1982-84, mem. fin. com., 1985-86, outreach dir., 1986-87; mem. leadership com. local chpt. YWCA, 1987—. Named Rookie of Yr. Baton Rouge Gen. Agts. and Mgrs. Assn., 1980. Fellow Life Underwriters Tng. Council; mem. Nat. Assn. Life Underwriters (Nat. Quality award 1979-81), La. Assn. Life Underwriters, Baton Rouge Assn. Life Underwriters (chmn. pub. service 1979-80, chmn. house com. 1980-83, chmn. legis. com. 1983-86, bd. dirs. 1980-86, 88—), Baton Rouge Gen. Agts. and Mgrs. Assn. (sec., treas. 1988—, Rookie of Yr. 1980), Women Life Underwriters Conf. (bd. dirs. 1983-85, charter chmn., parliamentarian 1986, treas. 1986-87), Women Life Underwriters Confederation (v.p. 1987-88, pres.-elect 1988—), Baton Rouge C. of C. Clubs: Century (Baton Rouge) (polit. action com. 1979—), Ambassador. Office: Abadie Fin Services 8748 Quarters Lake Rd Baton Rouge LA 70809

ABAJIAN, WENDY ELISSE, instructional design specialist; b. Selma, Calif., Mar. 16, 1955; d. Mesik Nishon and Blanche Peggy (Emerzian) A. AA, Kings River Community Coll., 1975; BA, Calif. State U., Fresno, 1978; MS, U. So. Calif., 1981, EdD, 1986. Instr., tchr. various sch. dists., Burbank and Fresno, Calif., 1981-82; free-lance writer various corps., Los Angeles area, 1984-86; pres., ind. producer Abhawk Prodns., Inc., Long Beach, Calif., 1986—; cons. multi-media projects. Contbr. articles to profl. jours. Mem. Rep. Nat. Com., Washington, 1983—, Statue of Liberty Ellis Island Found., 1984—, Women Appointees Council, Sacramento, 1988, Burbank Ctr. for Retarded; foster parent Foster Parent Plan, R.I., 1979—; pres., chairwoman Brighton Home Care, Inc. Mem. Nat. Assn. for Female Execs., Ednl. Grad. Orgn., Am. Film Inst., Farm Bur. Fedn., Calif. Tchrs. Assn. Armenian Apostolic. Office: Abhawk Prodns Inc PO Box 8654 Long Beach CA 90808-0654

ABARBANEL, GAIL, social service administrator, educator; b. Los Angeles, Apr. 17, 1944; d. Sam and Sylvia (Cramer) A.; m. Stephen P. Klein, Jan. 31, 1975. BA magna cum laude, UCLA, 1966; MSW, U. So. Calif., 1968. Lic. clin. social worker. Clin. social worker Mental Health Agy., Los Angeles, 1968-74; founder, dir. Rape Treatment Ctr. and Dept. Social Services Santa Monica (Calif.) Hosp. Med. Ctr., Los Angeles, 1974—; cons., educator in field. Contbr. articles to profl. jours.; author successful legislation to change rape laws. Bd. dirs. Clare Found., 1975-77; active Am. Cancer Soc., 1975-79; Child Trauma Council, 1978-81; Sr. Health Ctr., 1981-87. Recipient Gov.'s Victim Services award, 1985, Coro Found. Pub. Affairs award, 1985, Woman of Year Leadership award YWCA, 1980, 82, Status of Women award AAUW, 1978, Nat. Outstanding Achievement award Am. Cancer Soc., 1977, Disting. Citizen award Los Angeles County Bar Assn., 1988, Humanitarian award Nat. Conf. Christians and Jews, 1987; named Outstanding Alumni, U. So. Calif., 1979. Fellow Soc. for Clin. Social Work; mem. Nat. Assn. Social Workers (Agy. of Yr. award 1977), Nat. Orgn. for Victim Assistance (Exemplary Program award 1985), Women in Health, Phi Beta Kappa, Pi Gamma Mu. Office: Santa Monica Hosp 1225 15th St Santa Monica CA 90404

ABARBANEL, JUDITH EDNA, marketing executive; b. N.Y.C., Jan. 26, 1956; d. Albert Brandt and Dorothy Irene (Fennell) A.; m. Christopher George Lucas, June 17, 1984. BA, UCLA, 1977; MBA, MA, Ohio State U., 1980. Accredited pub. relations profl., 1988. Sales mgr. Columbus Magic, Ohio, 1979; account mgr. Mktg. Centre, St. Petersburg, Fla., 1980-82; asst. mktg. dir. MBI, Inc., Golden, Colo., 1983; dir. mktg. Colo. Outward Bound Sch., Denver, 1983—; owner A Sporting Proposition, Boulder, Colo., 1984—. Adv. bd. Learning Unltd. Mem. Denver Advt. Fedn., Pub. Relations Soc. Am. Avocations: mountain biking, race organizing, teaching. Office: Colo Outward Bound Sch 945 Pennsylvania St Denver CO 80203

ABARBANELL, GAYOLA HAVENS, financial advisor, consultant; b. Chgo., Oct. 21, 1939; d. Leonard Milton and Lillian Love (Leviten) Havens; m. Burton J. Abarbanell, June 1, 1965 (div. 1972); children: Jeffrey J. and Dena Reddick. Student, UCLA, 1975; student, San Joaquin Coll. Law, 1976-77. Lic. real estate broker, Calif.; lic. life ins. broker, Calif., Wash., Nev., N.Y., Ill.; lic. securities broker, all states. Postal clk. Van Nuys, Calif., 1966-69; regional mgr. Niagara Cyclo Massage, Fresno, Calif., 1969-72; owner, mgr. AD Enterprises, Fresno, Calif., 1970-72; agt., field supr. Equitable of Iowa, Fresno, Calif., 1972-73; rep. Ciba Pharms., Fresno, Calif., 1973-75; owner, operator Creativity Unltd., Fresno, Calif., 1975-76; fin. advisor Univ. Securities Corp., Los Angeles, Calif., 1976-83, Fin. Network Investment Corp., Los Angeles, Calif., 1983—; lectr. seminars for civic orgns.; mem. adv. bd. Fin. Network, Torrance, Calif., 1985-88. Co-author: Guidelines to Feminist Consciousness Raising, 1985. Past nat. CR coordinator NOW. Recipient award Women in Ins., 1972, Top Achievers award Fin. Network Investment Corp., 1978-88, Top Producer award Univ. Club-Univ. Securities, 1980, 81, 82; named No. 1 Producer, 1982, 83, Top Producer Fin. Network Investment Corp., 1983, 84, 85, 86. Mem. Bus. and Profl. Assn. Los Angeles, Central Calif., Bus. and Profl. Assn., Internat. Assn. Fin. Planners, So. Calif. Socially Responsible Investment Profls., ACLU, NOW (nat. coordinator 1975-76), So. Calif. Women for Understanding, Gay Acad. Union, Nat. Gay Task Force. Democrat. Jewish. Office: G Abarbanell Inc 9724 Washington Blvd #203 Culver City CA 90232-2722

ABARE, MARION LAVALETTE, media specialist; b. Malden, Mass., Aug. 16, 1927; d. Ray Emerson Lavalette and Pauline (Augusta) Dow; m. Robert E. Abare, July 6, 1947 (div. 1979); children: Susan, Jacqueline Dotson, Lianne, Tim, Julie Gardner, Robert, John, Michael, Michele Cole. Student, Acad. Aero., 1945-46, Johnson County Community Coll., 1974, U. Kans., 1974-77; BA, Rockhurst Coll., 1984; postgrad., U. Mo., 1986—. Dir. news and publicity Rockhurst Coll., Kansas City, Mo., 1977-83; specialist media and publicity U. Mo. Conservatory of Music, Kansas City, 1983—. Contbr. articles to profl. jours. Mem. Pub. Relations Soc. Am. (v.p. 1985-86, 3 Prism awards), Internat. Assn. Bus. Communicators (bd. dirs. 1982), Founder Arts Communicators. Republican. Roman Catholic. Home: 9617 Outlook Dr Overland Park MO 66207 Office: U Mo Conservatory Music 4949 Cherry St Kansas City MO 66207

ABBATE, SUSAN MARY, incentive travel agency executive; b. Chgo., July 4, 1958; d. Carl Albert and Joanne Joan (Bellanca) A. BS, Ill. State U., 1980. Asst. recreation dir. Playboy Resort and Country Club, Lake Geneva, Wis., 1980, recreation dir., 1980-81; travel dir. S & H Motivation and Travel, Hillside, Ill., 1981-83, sr. travel dir., 1981-84, mgr. spl. accounts, 1984-85, travel accounts mgr., 1986-87, sr. travel accounts mgr., 1987—. Office: S & H Motivation and Travel 5999 Butterfield Rd Hillside IL 60162

ABBEY, PATRICIA ANN, banker, cattle rancher; b. Coleman, Tex., Sept. 7, 1955; d. Charlie Ray and Betty Jeane (Traylor) Abbey. BBA, Tex. Tech. U., 1977. With Countywide Ins., Coleman, Tex., 1973-74; student asst. Tex. Tech. U., Lubbock, 1975-77; asst. field supr. Employers Ins. Tex., Dallas, 1978-81; project mgr. Tex. Commerce Bank, Houston, 1982-84, sr. v.p., cashier Tex. Commerce Bank, Midland, 1984—; ptnr. Abbey Polled Herefords, Coleman, Tex., 1978—. Recipient Tunnell award Tex. Tech. Rodeo Assn., 1977. Mem. Am. Bankers Assn., Nat. Assn. Female Execs., Tex. Polled Hereford Assn. (adv. dir. 1984—), Tex. Poll-Ettes (v.p. 1983-84, pres. 1984-85 , dir. 1982—, treas. 1986—, Miss Tex. Poll-Ette 1976-77), Phi Gamma Nu. Methodist. Club: Pilot. Home: PO Box 3294 Midland TX 79702 Office: Tex Commerce Bank PO Box 3905 Midland TX 79701

ABBOTT, FRANCES ELIZABETH DOWDLE, journalist, civic worker; b. Rome, Ga., Mar. 21, 1924; d. John Wesley and Lucille Elizabeth (Field) Dowdle; student Draughon's Bus. Coll., Columbia, S.C.; m. Jackson Miles Abbott, May 15, 1948; children—Medora Frances, David Field, Elizabeth Stockton, Robert Jackson. Feature writer, Mt. Vernon corr. Alexandria Gazette, Va., 1967-75; librarian, research assoc. Gadsby's Tavern Mus., Alexandria, 1977—. Chmn. ann. George Washington Birthnight Ball, Mt. Vernon, 1974-82; sec. 250th Washington Birthday Celebration Commn., 1979-82; chmn. publicity Waynewood Woman's Club, Waynewood Citizens Assn.; treas. Mt. Vernon Citizens Assn., 1967-82; dist. chmn. Mt. Vernon March of Dimes, 1960-62; sec. Waynewood Sch. P.T.A., 1962-64; tchr. 1st aid Girl Scouts U.S.A., 1964-65; den mother Cub Scouts, 1966; registrar DAR, 1968-77; chmn. publicity Mt. Vernon Women's Republican Club, 1955. Named Mrs. Waynewood by Community Vote, 1969. Mem. Audubon Naturalist Soc., Nat. Trust Historic Preservation. Episcopalian. Home: 8501 Doter Dr Alexandria VA 22308 Office: 135 N Royal St Alexandria VA 22314

ABBOTT, JENNIFER, marketing professional; b. Los Angeles, July 5, 1957; d. Norman and Nancy (Van Cott) A.; m. Howard Bulka, Sept. 1985. BA, U. San Francisco, 1980, MA, 1982. Office: 1905 Pierce St San Francisco CA 94115

ABBOTT, KIM MARIE, sales executive; b. Groton, Mass., Aug. 3, 1962; d. Gordon Howard and Marjorie Joyce (White) A. AS in Mgmt., Mt. Ida Jr. Coll., 1982; BS in Bus. Mgmt., U. Lowell, 1985. Accounts receivable supr. Frequency Sources, Inc., Chelmsford, Mass., 1984-85; mktg. adminstr. S & S Electronics, Inc., Lowell, Mass., 1985-87, sales mgr., 1987; telesales mgr. Mesa Tech., Inc., Lowell, 1987—. Recipient Alumnae award Mt. Ida Jr. Coll., Newton Center, Mass, 1982. Home: 13 Lucille Ave Westford MA 01886 Office: MESA Tech Corp 150 Industrial Ave E Lowell MA 01852

ABBOTT, MABEL KESTER, food products executive, consultant; b. Phila., June 13, 1920; d. Charles Leland and Ethel Thomas (Walton) K.; m. Arthur Cobb Abbott Sept. 1, 1942 (dec. 1975); children: Adelle Abbott Webb, Arthur Cobb Jr. BS in Home Econs., Drexel U., 1941. Cert. secondary edn. tchr. Foods demonstrator Great A&P Tea Co., Phila. and N.Y.C., 1941-42; tchr. Bd. Edn. City of Phila., 1942; exec. v.p. Abbott & Cobb, Inc., Feasterville, Pa., 1975—; pres. Charles L. Kester Funeral Home, Phila., 1980—; bd. dirs. Food and Energy Systems, Inc., Phila. Named Woman of Yr. Phila. Fashion Group, 1961. Mem. Alumnae Assn. Drexel U. (bd. dirs. Phila. chpt. 1978—). Republican. Episcopalian. Club: Frankford Arsenal Women's. Lodge: Zonta (2d v.p. Phila. club1982-84). Office: Abbott & Cobb Inc PO Box 307 Feasterville PA 19047

ABBOTT, MARY ANN, tobacco company executive; b. Indpls., Sept. 29, 1955; d. Elwood L. and Shirley (Kirch) McElhiney; m. Theodore L. Abbott, Sept. 4, 1982; 1 child, Lindsey. BS, Ball State U., 1977; postgrad., Eastern Mich. U., 1984-85. Tchr. Northview Jr. High Sch., Indpls., 1977-79; sales rep. Brown & Williamson Tobacco Co., Indpls., 1979-80; field sales asst. Brown & Williamson Tobacco Co., Columbus, Ohio, 1980-81; div. sales mgr. Brown & Williamson Tobacco Co., Peoria, Ill., 1981-82; key accounts mgr. Brown & Williamson Tobacco Co., Detroit, 1982—. Mem. Tobacco Action Network. Republican. Roman Catholic. Office: Brown & Williamson Tobacco 17197 N Laurel Park Dr Suite 107 Livonia MI 48152

ABBOTT, ROSEMARY KENDALL, corporation executive; b. Chgo., May 13, 1951; d. Jesse Ray and Shirley Ruth (Pohl) Kendall; m. Gary Peter Abbott, Feb. 4, 1978. A.A., Kendall Jr. Coll., 1971; B.S. in Indsl. Psychology, U. Ill., 1973, M.A. in Indsl. Relations, 1974. Tng. and devel. rep. Union Carbide Corp., Texas City, Tex., 1974-76, employment assoc., 1976-77, non-exempt employee relations adminstr., 1977-79, labor relations adminstr., 1979-81, mgr. employment and salary adminstrn., 1981-86, mgr. employment, tng. and salary adminstrn., 1986-87, mgr. human resources solvents and coatings materials div., Danbury, Conn., 1987—. Mem. Am. Compensation Assn., Indsl. Relations Research Assn. Club: Houstonian (Houston). Office: Union Carbide Corp 39 Old Ridgebury Rd Office #K441 Danbury CT 06817-0001

ABBOTT, SHELLEY (ABOUDÉ), writer, business consultant; b. Glens Falls, N.Y., Aug. 10, 1954; d. Samuel and Betty Emma (Rock) Abbott; children: Timothy Abbott, Samantha Abbott. Grad. high sch., Glens Falls. Editor, mgr. TV Data Inc., Glens Falls, 1974-76; computer data entry Off Track Betting, Schenectady, N.Y., 1976-77; columnist United Media Syndicate, N.Y.C., 1974-86, UPI, N.Y.C., 1975—; owner, pres. The Enterprise, Glens Falls, 1974—; lectr. schs. and orgns., N.Y., 1980—; advt. cons. to bus., N.Y., 1984—; cons. Psychic Research Library, Lake George, N.Y., 1985-87, various bus. orgns. Contbr.: (cartoons) Harness Horseman Internat., 1978-81, There Ought To Be a Law, 1980-85; columnist Off Track Betting Newsletter, 1978—; writer short stories, also articles for newspapers and mags.; hostess numerous city homeshows, N.Y., 1985. Mem. Cornell U. Feline Health Ctr. Mem. Nat. Assn. Female Execs. Smithsonian Assocs., Assn. for Retarded Children, New Eng. Anti-Vivesect. Soc., Nat. Humane League, State Humane League. Democrat. Roman Catholic. Avocations: breeding Siamese cats, international travel. Office: The Enterprise PO Box 905 Glens Falls NY 12801

ABBOTT, SUSAN LEIGH, lawyer; b. Buffalo, Apr. 20, 1955; d. James Addison and Marguerite Louise (Hutchcraft) Abbott; m. Joseph A. Barbknecht, Nov. 1984. B.A., U. Okla., 1977, J.D., 1980. Bar: Okla. 1980, Tex. 1981. Assoc. Rex K. Travis, Oklahoma City, 1978-81, Shank, Irwin & Conant, Dallas, 1981-84, Baker, Mills & Glast, Dallas, 1984—. Mem. Young Republicans Dallas County, Dallas Mus. Art. Fellow Tex. Bar Assn.; mem. State Bar Okla., Dallas County Bar Assn., Dallas Assn. Young Lawyers (vol. counselor 1981—, sec.-newsletter editor 1985-86, membership chmn. 1986-87), Tex. Assn. Young Lawyers (bd. dirs. Dallas 1987—), Phi Beta Kappa. Methodist.

ABBOTT, VIRGINIA MILLER, speech and language pathologist, educator; b. Washington, Dec. 25, 1942; d. Edward Donald and Virginia Augusta (Grohs) Miller; m. Henry L. Abbott Jr., Aug. 30, 1966; 1 child, Benjamin Henry. BA, George Washington U., 1964; MEd, Fitchburg State Coll., 1972. Dir. speech and hearing clinic Burbank Hosp., Fitchburg, Mass., 1968-72; cons. tchr. Leominster (Mass.) Pub. Schs., 1972-76; chmn. evaluation team, spl. needs dept. Lunenburg (Mass.) Pub. Schs., 1977-81; speech-lang. pathologist Groton-Dunstable (Mass.) Pub. Schs., 1982-87, elem. supr., 1984-87. Mem. N.H. Lang., Speech and Hearing Assn., Fla. Lang., Speech and Hearing Assn., Columbian Women, Com. on Lang., Speech and Hearing Services in the Schs., Am. Speech and Hearing Assn. Home: 498 Valley Rd Mason NH 03048

ABBOTT-YOUNG, MARY GAY, foundation administrator; b. Pitts., Dec. 1, 1952; d. Thomas W. And Gaynell H. (Barrett) Abbott; m. James R. Young, Dec. 27, 1974; children: Barrett Thomas, Carrie Ann. BS, Calif. State U., 1973; MEd, Temple U., 1978. Alcoholism counselor Guiffre Med. Ctr., Phila., 1975-78; various Rescue Mission of Trenton (N.J.) Inc., 1978—, exec. dir., 1986—; founder Non-profits Serving Hungry and Homeless of Mercer County, Trenton, 1987—; chmn. subcom. Mayors Task Force on Hungry, Trenton, 1987—. Bd. dirs. YWCA, Trenton, 1987—. Mem. Phi

Gamma Mu. Roman Catholic. Office: Rescue Mission of Trenton Inc PO Box 617 Trenton NJ 08604

ABDELLAH, FAYE GLENN, government association official; b. N.Y.C., Mar. 13, 1919; d. H.B. and Margaret (Glenn) A. BS in Teaching, Columbia U., 1945, MA in Teaching, 1947, EdD, 1955; LLD (hon.), Case Western Res. U., 1967, Rutgers U., 1973; DSc (hon.), U. Akron, 1978, Cath. U. Am., 1981, Monmouth Coll., 1982, Ea. Mich U., 1987, U. Bridgeport, 1987; D of Pub. Service, Am. U., 1987. RN. Commd. officer USPHS, Rockville, Md., 1949, advanced through grades to rear adm., 1970, asst. surgeon gen., chief nurse officer, 1970-87, dep. surgeon gen., 1981—, chief nursing edn. br., div. nursing, 1949-59; chief research grants br. Bur. Health Manpower Edn., NIH, HEW, Rockville, 1959-69, dir. Office Research Tng. Nat. Ctr. for Health Services Research and Devel., Health Services Mental Health Adminstrn., Rockville, 1969; acting dep. dir. Nat. Ctr. for Health Services Research and Devel., Rockville, 1971, Bur. Health Services Research and Evaluation, Health Resources Adminstrn., Rockville, 1973; dir. Office Long-Term Care, Office Asst. Sec. for Health, HEW, Rockville, 1973-80. Author: Effect of Nurse Staffing on Satisfactions with Nursing Care, 1959, Patient Centered Approaches to Nursing, 1960, Better Patient Care Through Nursing Research, 1965, 2d edit., 1979, 3d edit., 1986, Intensive Care, Concepts and Practices for Clinical Nurse Specialists, 1969, New Directions in Patient Centered Nursing, 1972; Contbr. articles to profl. jours. Recipient Mary Adelaide Nutting award, 1983, hon. recognition award Am. Nurses Assn., 1986, Outstanding Leadership award U. Pa., 1987. Charter fellow Am. Acad. Nursing (v.p., pres.); mem. Am. Psychol. Assn., AAAS, Assn. Mil. Surgeons U.S., Sigma Theta Tau, Phi Lambda Theta. Home: 3713 Chanel Rd Annandale VA 22003 Office: 5600 Fishers Ln Rm 18-67 Rockville MD 20852

ABDOO, ANGELA FONTANA, small business owner; b. Bklyn., June 24, 1941; d. Louis and Mary (Acciarito) Fontana; m. Charles David Abdoo, Jan. 17, 1979 (div. 1984). Student, Bklyn. Coll., 1960-62. Adminstrv. asst. North Am. Rockwell, Anaheim, Calif., 1965-67; psychiat. technician Fairview State Hosp., Costa Mesa, Calif., 1967-68; typographer Wells Graphics, Bklyn., 1978-80, Down to Bus. Advt., Bklyn., 1980-82; owner Taurus Typesetters, Bklyn., 1982—. Recipient 1st Place award Columbia Scholastic Press Assn., N.Y.C., 1986, 87. Republican. Roman Catholic. Office: Taurus Typesetters 5009 Ave M Brooklyn NY 11234

ABEBE, TEGEST GORFE, dentist; b. Addis Abeba, Ethiopia, July 8, 1956; came to U.S., 1974; d. Gorfe Abebe and Tshai Molla; married. BS, McKendree Coll., 1978; D of Dental Medicine, So. Ill. U., 1984. Cert. dentist, Tex. Dentist Dallas Pub. Health, 1985-86; gen. practice dentistry Austin, Tex., 1986—; instr. Tex. Coll. Med. Dental Assts., Dallas, 1985-86; instr. dental edn. numerous grade schs., high schs. and pvt. groups, Austin, 1986—. Bd. dirs. Ethiopian Community Orgn., Austin, 1986—, Tex. Mental Rehab. Program, Austin, 1987—; vol. commmunity orgns., Dallas and Austin, 1986—. Recipient Honors award Ethiopian Community Famine Outreach, Houston, 1984-85. Mem. ADA, Tex. Dental Assn., Dallas County Dental Soc., Acad. Gen. Dentistry, Am. Soc. Dentistry for Children (Plaque award 1985), Tex. Assn. Women Dentists. Home: 2120 Gaston Pl Austin TX 78723 Office: Family Dentistry 2113 E Martin Luther King Suite 105 Austin TX 78702

ABEL, FLORENCE CATHERINE HARRIS, social worker; b. Phila., Dec. 28, 1941; d. Wilber Fiske and Melda Elizabeth (Beitzel) Harris; m. David Lynn Abel, Jan. 22, 1983. B.S., High Point (N.C.) Coll., 1963; M.S.W., U. Md., 1972. Diplomate in Clin. Social Work. Social work asst. Calvert County (Md.) Dept. Social Services, Prince Frederick, 1964-69; social work asst. Prince George's County (Md.) Dept. Social Service, Hyattsville, 1969-71; social worker Md. Children's Aid and Family Service, Towson, Md., 1972-80, Crownsville (Md.) Hosp. Center, 1980-86; field instr. U. Md. Sch. Social Work, 1985-86; chairperson Social Work Peer Rev. Com., 1982-83; cons. Contact Balt., 1974-79; counselor Family Life Center, Columbia, Md., 1974-80; mem. citizens adv. council N.W. Mental Health Balt. County, 1977-78. sec. bd. dirs. Christian Counseling Assocs., Columbia, 1978—, family therapist, 1980—; mem. Faith at Work Team, Columbia, 1973-75, Calvert County Commn. on Aging, 1967-68, Evang. Women's Caucus, Washington, 1976—, N.W. Coalition Social Agys., Balt. County, 1978; Author: The Beitzel Family a History of hte Descendants of John George Beitzel, 1986. cons. Nursing Home Ministry Evang. Presbyn. Ch., Annapolis, Md., 1978. Vice pres., treas. bd. dirs. Wheaton Animal Hosp., Inc., Kensington, Md. Lic. cert. social worker, Md. Mem. Nat. Assn. Social Workers, Register Clin. Social Workers, Assn. Certified Social Workers, Md. Conf. Social Concern, Christian Assocs. for Psychol. Studies. Democrat. Presbyterian. Home: 120 Hedgewood Dr Greenbelt MD 20770 Office: Stevens Forest Profl Bldg 9630 Santiago Rd Suite 101 Columbia MD 21045

ABEL, JUDY SOMMER, speech pathologist; b. N.Y., Feb. 14, 1942; d. Sidney and Freda (Anfag) Sommer; 1 child, Erik. BA in Speech Pathology, Queens Coll., 1963, MS in Speech Pathology, 1966. Speech pathologist Montefiore Hosp, Brinx, N.Y., 1968-69, Beth Israel Hosp., N.Y., 1969-71, Mt. Sinai Hosp., N.Y., 1971-75, Casa Colina Rehab. Hosp., Pomona, Calif., 1975; dir., owner, speech pathologist Abel Ctr. for Speech, Hearing & Counseling, Cottage Grove, Oreg., 1975—; owner Abel Ctr. Rehab. Therapies, Cottage Grove, 1975—. Mem. Am. Speech Lang. Hearing Assn., Oreg. Speech and Hearing Assn., Nat. Assn. Female Execs., Inc. Home: 43 N H St Cottage Grove OR 97424 Office: The Abel Ctr for Speech Hearing and Counseling 1137 E Main St Cottage Grove OR 97424

ABELAR, INA MAE, equipment technician; b. Jay Em, Wyo., July 18, 1926; d. Merritt Lyle and Leeta May (Worthen) Cameron; B.A., Calif. State Poly. U., 1978; m. Michael Sandoval Abelar, Nov. 17, 1951 (div. 1966); children—Debora Jean, Michelle Elaine, Randolph Lee. Lumber estimator Keith Brown Bldg. Supply, Salem, Oreg., 1946-48; with Whiting-Mead Bldg. Supply, Vernon, Calif., 1949-51, Trojan Lumber Co., Burbank, Calif., 1952-55; bookkeeper Jerry Kalior Bookkeeping Systems, North Hollywood, Calif., 1959-66; with Calif. State Poly. U., Pomona, 1967—, supervising equip. technician II dept. physics, 1979—, mem. campus staff council, 1970—, chmn., 1977-78. Recipient outstanding staff award Calif. State Poly U., 1983-84. Deaconess, Upland Christian Ch., 1978-81; mem. chancellery choir Bethany Bapt. Ch., 1984—. Mem. Mu Phi Epsilon. (chpt. pres. 1983-86). Democrat. Home: 1833 Benedict Way Pomona CA 91767 Office: 3801 W Temple St Rm 8-238 Pomona CA 91768

ABEL-CHRISTIAN, STACEY LYNN, educator; b. New Brunswick, N.J., Feb. 5, 1960; d. Clarence Wallace and Laura Lee (Wilkinson) Abel; m. James Carroll Christian; 1 child, Mark Andrew. BA, U. Ariz., 1982, MEd, 1986. Cert. elem. tchr., Ariz. Elem. tchr. Flowing Wells Schs., Tucson, 1983—; pension adminstr. Karabinas and Assocs., Tucson, 1986; counselor pvt. practice, Tucson, 1986—; leader parent study group, Tuscon, 1986-87, behavioral intervention team Homer Davis Elem. Sch., Tucson, 1986-87. Counselor Las Familias, Tucson, 1985-86. Mem. Ariz. Counselors Assn., Pi Lambda Theta, Phi Delta Kappa. Republican. Baptist.

ABELES, GINA LEE, psychologist, research writer; b. Evanston, Ill., Apr. 29, 1936; d. Harry Easton and Nancy Penelope (Marsh) Godwin; m. Sigmund M. Abeles, June 5, 1961 (div. 1971); children: David Paul, Shoshanna Lynn. AB, Ind. U., 1957; postgrad., U. Heidelberg, Fed. Rep. Germany, 1959; MA, Boston U., 1973, PhD, 1975. Clin. psychology trainee Blockton Va. Hosp., Mass., 1971-72; predoctoral fellow Boston U., 1969-71, instr. abnormal psychology, 1972-74, research assoc. in sociology, mental health, 1975-79; freelance editor and research writer 1974—. NIMH fellow, 1977-79. Mem. Am. Psychol. Assn. Episcopalian. Home and Office: 128 Cabot St Newton MA 02158

ABEL HOROWITZ, MICHELLE SUSAN, advertising agency executive; b. Detroit, Mar. 31, 1950; d. Martin Louis and Phyllis (Berkowitz) A.; m. H. Jay Abel Horowitz, July 11, 1976; children—Jordan Michael, Stefanie Jennifer. Student Goucher Coll., 1967-70; B.A. in Econs., U. Mich., 1971; postgrad. in econs. U. Calif.-San Diego, 1973; M.A. in Econs., U. Detroit, 1974-76. Planning group supr. Hill Holliday Connors, Cosmopolus, Mass., 1976-78; econ. analyst Data Resources, Boston, 1978-79; v.p., media dir. Barkley & Evergreen, Southfield, Mich., 1979-80; v.p., dir. mktg. and media Yaffe/Berline, Southfield, Mich., 1980-82; exec. v.p., dir. client services, corp. treas. Berline Group, Birmingham, Mich., 1982—; instr. Oakland U., Rochester, Mich., 1982; trustee, chairperson mktg. com. Harbinger Dance Co., Farmington, Mich., 1983—. Named Advt. Woman of Yr., Women's Ad Club Detroit, 1982. Mem. Adcraft Club Detroit, Women in Communications. Democrat. Jewish. Office: The Berline Group 31600 Telegraph Rd #100 Birmingham MI 48010-3439

ABELL, LERON EVELYN, retired medical technologist; b. Tifton, Ga., Dec. 31, 1912; d. Elbert David and Mary Elvira (Willis) Paulk; m. C. Stanley Abell, Oct. 6, 1935; 1 child, James Gerald. Student in med. tech., U. Houston, 1952-56, U. Ga., 1960, Ga. State U., 1967. Chief med. technologist Diagnostic Hosp., Houston, 1956-59; with bacteriology and mycology dept. Tching. Hosp., U. Fla., Gainesville, 1959; program developer No. Ga. Vocat. Sch., Clarksville, 1960-62, Med. Diagnostic and Research Labs., Atlanta, 1962-66; pub. health instr. Ctr. for Disease Control, Atlanta, 1966-78. Author: Simple Technique for Blood Cholesterol, 1959, (with Wallace and Woodcock) Medical Technology Retraining in Six Months, 1970; mem. steering com. Look, Listen, and Learn program, 1973. Assisted in home and field courses in various state health depts. in U.S., 1974-78. Mem. DAR (local rec. sec. 1984-86), UDC (local pres. 1984-86), Am. Soc. Clin. Pathologists (cert.), Nat. Assn. Retired Fed. Employees, Am. Legion Aux. Republican. Baptist. Club: Pine Garden. Lodge: Order Ea. Star. Home: 2507 Cedar Falls San Antonio TX 78232

ABELLA, MARISELA CARLOTA, business executive; b. Havana, Cuba, Feb. 5, 1943; d. Carlos and Angela (Acosta) Abella; m. Alberto Herrera Nogueira, Apr. 6, 1968 (div. Apr. 1986); 1 child, Carlos Alberto Herrera Abella. Asst. to v.p and gen. mgr. bonding dept. Manuel San Juan (P.R.) Co. Inc., 1962-64; asst. corp. sec. and exec. sec. to pres. and stockholder Interstate Gen. Corp., Hato Rey, P.R., 1964-72, corp. sec. and pvt. sec. to corp. pres., 1972-79; sec.-treas., dir. A. H. Enterprises Inc., Caparra Heights, P.R., 1979-86; v.p., sec., bd. dirs. El Viajero Inc.; bd. dirs. A. H. Enterprises Inc., San Juan; pres. Marisela Abella Mktg. and Selling Promotional Items and Ideas, Caparra Heights, 1986—. Roman Catholic. Clubs: Caribe Hilton Swimming and Tennis, Barry U. Alumnae Assn. Home: 909 Borinquen Towers 2 Caparra Heights PR 00920 Office: PO Box 10510 Caparra Heights PR 00922

ABERCROMBIE, JOYCE REHBURG, dairy and nutrition council director; b. Sewickley, Pa., Feb. 13, 1939; d. William Max and Agnes Marion (Rumsey) Rehburg; m. Donald H. Abercrombie, Aug. 18, 1962. BS, Ind. State Coll., 1961; postgrad., Pa. State U., 1963-65, Carnegie-Mellon U., 1963-65; MEd, Ind. U. of Pa., 1974. Home service rep. Peoples Natural Gas Co., Pitts., 1961-62; tchr. home econs. Avalon Sch. Dist., Pitts., 1962-71; grad. asst. Ind. U. Pa., 1971-72; tchr. home econs. Blairsville (Pa.)-Saltsburg Sch. Dist., 1972-73; program dir. Dairy and Nutrition Council-Mid-East, Pitts., 1973-80, area dir., 1980—; adj. staff Health Edn. Ctr., Pitts., 1978-83; mem. curriculum devel. team Nat. Dairy Council, Chgo., 1976-77. Mem. exec. com. United Mental Health, Inc., Pitts., 1980-86, bd. dirs., 1978-86; participant Big Bros./Big Sisters, Pitts., 1986—. Presch. Nutrition Edn. grantee Pa. Dept. Edn., 1980-81. Mem. Am. Home Econs. Assn., Pa. Home Econs. Assn. (chmn. subject matter 1987—), Pa. Nutrition Council (chmn. pub. relations 1986—, pres.-elect 1988—), Soc. for Nutrition Edn., Nutrition Council Southwestern Pa. (steering com. 1978-84), Soc. Pub. Heath Educators (sec. 1976-77). Home: 403 Sutton Pl Wexford PA 15090 Office: Dairy and Nutrition Council-Mid East 9370 McKnight Rd Suite 306 Pittsburgh PA 15237

ABERCROMBIE, VIRGINIA TOWNSEND, writer; b. Houston, Dec. 24, 1927; d. F. Lee and Yvonne (Burghard) Townsend; m. John B. Abercrombie, Apr. 1, 1950; children: Virginia Lee, John B. Jr., Gilchreas T. BA, U. Tex., 1950. Founder Brown Rabbit Press, Houston, 1979—. Poetry published in Mississippi Arts and Letter, Poem, Roanoke Rev., Sam Houston Lit. Rev., Bluegrass Lit. Rev., Pudding, Midway Rev. 5, Rising Star, Madison Rev., others; co-author: Catering in Houston, 1977, Places to Take a Crowd in Houston, 1979, Catering to Houston, 1981, Party File, 1986; co-editor: (poem anthology) Christmas in Texas, 1979. Social dir. women's aux. Houston Bar Assn., 1975-76, pres., 1976-77. Recipient Honorable Mention Houston Poetry Festival, 1988. Clubs: Houston Country, Jr. League (puppet chmn.). Avocations: painting, sculpture. Home: 3 Smithdale Ct Houston TX 77024

ABERNATHY, BARBARA EUBANKS, counselor; b. Mobile, Ala., Aug. 28, 1963; d. Hardy Millard and Sarah Louise (Pate) Eubanks; m. James Abernathy Jr., Dec. 15, 1984. BS, Northwestern U., 1984; MS, U. South Ala., 1986. Mental health worker 11 Charter Southland Hosp., Mobile, 1985-86; counselor Indian River Community Mental Health, Ft. Pierce, Fla., 1986-87; family counselor Youth Service Bur., Palm Beach County, Fla., 1987—; behavior mgmt. cons. Okeechobee (Fla.) Sch. System, 1987. Counselor Rape Crisis Ctr., Mobile, 1985-86, Contact Mobile, 1985-86; troop leader Girl Scouts of Chgo., 1982-84. Named one of Outstanding Young Women of Am., 1987. Mem. Am. Psychol. Assn., Am. Assn. Counseling and Devel., Kappa Delta Pi. Office: Palm Beach County Youth Service Bur 4210 Australian Ave West Palm Beach FL 33407

ABNEY, BOBBIE JEAN, financial administrator; b. Ft. Worth, Jan. 3, 1933; d. Joe M. and Minnie M. (Mead) Williams; m. Louis E. Castell, Feb. 24, 1951 (div. 1963); children: Teresa Castell Little, Louis E.; m. Paul M. Abney, Oct. 9, 1964. Student, Victoria Jr. Coll., 1950-52, Durham Bus. Coll., 1963-64, LaSalle Coll., 1968-70. Acct. Sage Investments, Corpus Christi, Tex., 1970-71; comptroller Barshop Hotel, Inc., Houston, 1971-78; fin. mgr. Charter Oil Co., Livingston, Tex., 1978-84; br. mgr. Security Fin. Corp. Tex., Livingston, 1985—. Active Girl Scouts U.S., Livingston, 1986—, Livingston Parent-Tchr. Orgn., 1986—. Mem. Nat. Assn. Female Execs., Bus. and Profl. Women's Club (treas. 1986-88, Woman of Yr. 1986-87, Am. Legion Aux. Democrat. Mem. Ch. of Christ. Home: PO Box 1359 Livingston TX 77351 Office: Security Fin Corp 613 N Washington St Livingston TX 77351

ABORN, CARLENE MELLO, media specialist, consultant; b. Fall River, Mass., Jan. 2, 1932; d. Joseph Richard and Henrietta (Aragao) Mello; m. Dale Humphrey Aborn, Aug. 1, 1953; children: Roni, Scott, Keith. BA in Edn., Avila Coll., Kansas City, Mo., 1964; MA, U. South Fla., 1969. Tchr. Mo. Sch. Bd., Lee's Summit, 1964-69; media specialist Pinellas County Sch. Bd., Clearwater, Fla., 1970-78; media dir. Sch. Bd. Pinellas County, Clearwater, 1980—; Washington corr. Nat. Opinion Mag., San Jose, Calif., 1977-80; cons. Wollensak div. 3M, St. Paul, 1978-81; cons. Fla. Dept. Edn., Tallahassee, 1975-78, Griffin (Ga.) County Sch. Bd., 1987. Editor: Fla. Media Quar., 1978-80; contbr. articles to ednl. jours. and mag. Vol. ARC, Pinellas County, Fla., 1984. Recipient John Cotton Dana P.R. award ALA and H.W. Wilson Co., 1975, 85; named Outstanding Educator Pinellas County, Fla., 1976, 86. Mem. ALA (John Cotton Dana award 1975, 85), Fla. Assn. Media Educators (publs. bd. 1969—), Pinellas County Tchr.'s Assn., Pinellas County Assn. Library Media Educators, Assn. Ednl. Communication Tech. Home: 9425 Blind Pass Rd #908 Saint Petersburg Beach FL 33706 Office: Osceola High Sch 9751 98th St Seminole FL 34647

ABRAHAM, ANDREA RUTH, data processing professional; b. New Hyde Park, N.Y., Mar. 28, 1961; d. Andrew J. and Diane (Kern) May; m. Andrew Charles Abraham, Feb. 8, 1985. BS, San Diego State U., 1983. Computer operator Warren Henry Motors, Miami, 1977-79; analyst materials Topaz Electronics Co., San Diego, 1982-83; dir. info. resource ctr. Midwest Pacific Fin. Inc., San Diego, 1985-88; mgr. info. services LandGrant Devel., San Diego, 1988—; cons. local small businesses, San Diego, 1983—. Mem. Women Computing Professionals (chmn. 1987), San Diego St. Alumni., Data Processing Mgmt. Assn., Nat. Assn. Female Execs. Office: LandGrant Devel 12625 High Bluff Dr Suite 212 San Diego CA 92130

ABRAHAM, RITA BETTY, architectual company executive; b. N.Y.C., Apr. 27, 1951; d. Joseph Abraham and Rose (Fabritz) Sokolik; m. Michael Jay Yurow, Jan. 11, 1987. AB in Am. Studies, George Washington U., 1973, MA in Urban Regional Planning, 1979; Cert. French Studies, Sorbonne, Paris, 1980. Program officer NEH, Washington, 1973-76; dir. pub. relations Pa. Ave. Devel. Corp., Washington, 1976-80; freelance writer Paris, 1980; dir. mktg. Georgetown Park Mall, Washington, 1980-82; dir. corp. affairs and congl. relations Pa. Ave. Devel. Corp., 1982-85, Swanke Hayden Connell Architects, Washington, 1985-88; dir. bus. devel. and sales Washington region PHH Neville Lewis, Washington, 1988—; cons., lectr. in field. Com. mem. The Greater Washington Bd. Trade, The Ballston Ptnrship. Mem. Comml. Real Estate Women, The Real Estate Group, The D.C. Downtown Ptnrship. Democrat. Office: PHH Neville Lewis 1615 L Street NW Washington DC 20036

ABRAHAMSON, SHIRLEY SCHLANGER, state justice; b. N.Y.C., Dec. 17, 1933; d. Leo and Ceil (Sauerteig) Schlanger; m. Seymour Abrahamson, Aug. 26, 1953; 1 son, Daniel Nathan. A.B., NYU, 1953; J.D., Ind. U., 1956; S.J.D., U. Wis., 1962. Bar: Wis. 1962. Asst. dir. Legis. Drafting Research Fund, Columbia U. Law Sch., 1957-60; since practiced in Madiso; mem. firm LaFollette, Sinykin, Anderson & Abrahamson, 1962-76; justice Supreme Ct. Wis., Madison, 1976—; prof. U. Wis. Sch. Law, 1966—, currently on leave; Mem. Wis. Bd. Bar Commrs.; mem. adv. bd. Nat. Inst. Justice, U.S. Dept. Justice, 1980-82; mem. Mayor's Adv. Com., Madison, 1968-70, Gov.'s Study Com. on Jud. Orgn., 1970-72; bd. visitors Ind. U. Sch. Law, 1972—, U. Miami Sch. Law, 1982—, Brigham Young U. Sch. Law, 1986—; bd. dirs. LWV, Madison, 1963-65; Union council Wis. Union, U. Wis., 1970-71. Editor: Constitutions of the United States (National and State) 2 vols, 1962. Bd. dirs. Wis. Civil Liberties Union, 1968-72, chmn. Capital Area chpt., 1969. Mem. ABA (council, sect. of legal edn. and admissions to the bar 1976-86, mem. commn. on undergrad. edn. in law and the humanities 1978-79), Wis. Bar Assn., Dane County Bar Assn., 7th Cir. Bar Assn., Nat. Assn. Women Judges, Am. Law Inst. (council), Order of Coif, Phi Beta Kappa. Home: 2012 Waunona Way Madison WI 53713 Office: Wis Supreme Ct PO Box 1688 Madison WI 53701

ABRAMS, ANNE, publicist; b. Bklyn., May 11, 1953; d. Sidney and B. Hilda (Langweber) A.; m. Mark Timothy Farmer, May 19, 1985. BA, SUNY-Fredonia, 1974; MA, U. Kans., 1976. Program coordinator Hashinger Arts Ctr., Lawrence, Kans., 1974-77; artistic/mng. dir. Crown Uptown Theatre, Wichita, Kans., 1977-79; dir. student activities Dickinson Coll., Carlisle, Pa., 1979-80; asst. gen. mgr. Am. Theatre Prodns., N.Y.C., 1980-81; account exec., publicist Fred Nathan Co., N.Y.C., 1981-88; dir., founder Women's Resource Ctr., Carlisle, 1979-80; theatrical cons. and dir. Com. mem. Women in Bus. Against Cancer, Am. Cancer Soc., N.Y.C., 1983; bd. dirs. AIDS Resource Ctr., N.Y.C., 1986-87; ptnr. Browne-Abrams Pub. Relations, 1988—. Democrat. Avocations: cooking, antiques, swimming, writing.

ABRAMS, MARGARET SMITH, lawyer; b. Neptune, N.J., Sept. 8, 1954; d. Thomas Joseph and Jeanne Marie (Hanlon) Smith; m. Douglas Breen Abrams, May 15, 1976; children: Noah Breen, Elliot Sol. BA cum laude Wake Forest U., 1976, postgrad., 1976-77; postgrad. Duke U., 1979-80; J.D., Wake Forest U., 1980. Bar: N.C., 1980. Research asst. N.C. Ct. Appeals, Raleigh, 1980-82; assoc. Blanchard, Tucker, Twiggs & Abrams, P.A., Raleigh, 1982—. Active Wake County Democratic Women, Raleigh, 1980—, N.C. Consumer's Council, 1981—, Wake County YWCA, Raleigh, 1983—; bd. dirs. Infant-Toddler Ctr., Raleigh. Hankins scholar Wake Forest U., 1972-76, tuition scholar, 1976-77, 77-79; Am. Jurisprudence award in contracts and criminal law, 1977; Corpus Juris Secundum award in contracts, 1977. Mem. Assn. Trial Lawyers Am., N.C. Acad. Trial Lawyers (mem. edn. com., lectr.), N.C. Bar Assn., Wake County Bar Assn., N.C. Assn. Women Attys. Home: 5421 Huntingwood Dr Raleigh NC 27606

ABRAMS, ROBERTA BUSKY, nursing administrator; b. Bklyn., Feb. 16, 1937; d. Albert H. and Gladys Busky; m. Robert L. Abrams, June 28, 1959 (div. 1977); children: Susan Abrams Federman, David B. BSN, U. Rochester, 1959; MA, Fairfield U., 1977. Asst. head nurse Jewish Hosp., Bklyn., 1959-60; instr. medicine/surgery The Bklyn. Hosp., 1960-62, U. Rochester, N.Y., 1963-64; instr. ob-gyn Malden Hosp. Sch. Nursing, Mass., 1965-66; instr. prospective parents ARC, San Rafael, Calif., 1968-69; instr. ob-gyn SUNY, Farmingdale, 1970-71; instr. maternal/child health Stamford (Conn.) Hosp., 1971-75; clinician maternal/child health Lawrence Hosp., Bronxville, N.Y., 1975-78; asst. prof. nursing Ohio Wesleyan U., Delaware, 1981-84; dir. The Elizabeth Blackwell Hosp. at Riverside Meth., Columbus, Ohio, 1978-86; dir. nursing Henry Ford Hosp., Detroit, 1986-87, assoc. adminstr. nursing, 1988—; cons. maternal/child nursing currents Ross Labs, 1984-88; lectr. in field. Contbr. articles to profl. jours. Mem. LWV, NAACOG (vice chmn. Ohio 1984-87), Am. Sco. Psychoprophylaxsis, Greater Detroit Orgn. Nurse Execs., Sigma Theta Tau. Home: 32478 Dunford Farmington Hills MI 48018 Office: Henry Ford Hosp 2799 W Grand Blvd Detroit MI 48202

ABRAMS, ROSALIE S., state agency official; b. Balt.; d. Isaac and Dora (Rodbell) Silber; R.N., Sinai Hosp.; postgrad. Columbia U.; B.S., Johns Hopkins U., 1963, M.A. in Polit. Sci.; 1 child, Elizabeth Joan Herlich. Public health nurse, 1941-43; bus. mgr. Sequoia Med. Group, Calif., 1946-47; asst. bus. mgr. Silber's Bakery, Balt., 1947-53; mem. Md. Ho. of Dels., 1967-70; mem. Md. Senate, 1970-83, majority leader, 1978-82; chmn. Dem. Party of Md., 1978-83, chmn. fin. com., 1982-83; dir. Office on Aging, State of Md., 1983—; host Outlook TV show, 1983—; guest lectr., witness before congl. coms. Platform com. on nat. health care Dem. Nat. Com., 1979—; chmn. Md. Humane Practices Commn., 1978-83, mem., 1971-74; mem. New Coalition, 1979-83, State-Fed. Assembly Com. on Human Resources, 1977-83, Md. Comprehensive Health Planning Agency, 1972-75, Md. Commn. on Status of Women, 1968—, Am. Jewish Com.; bds. dirs. Sinai Hosp., Balt., 1973—, Balt. Jewish Council, Cross Country Improvement Assn., 1969—, Fifth Dist. Reform Democrats, 1967—; chmn. legis. com. Balt. Area Council on Alcoholism, 1973-75. Served with Nurse Corps USN, 1944-46. Recipient Louise Waterman Wise Community Service award, 1969, award Am. Acad. Comprehensive Health Planning, 1971, Balt. News Am. award, Women of Distinction in Medicine, 1971, traffic safety award, Safety First Club of Md., 1971, Ann London Scott Meml. award for legis. excellence, Md. Chpt. NOW, 1975, Md. Nurses Assn., 1975, service award Balt. Area Council on Alcoholism, 1975. Md. Order Women Legislators (pres., 1973-75), Nat. Conf. State Legislatures (human resources and urban affairs steering com. 1977-83), Nat. Legis. Conf. (human resources task force, intergovt. relations com. 1975-83). Jewish. Office: 301 W Preston St Suite 1004 Baltimore MD 21201

ABRAMS, RUTH IDA, state justice; b. Boston, Dec. 26, 1930; d. Samuel and Matilda A. B.A., Radcliffe Coll., 1953; LL.B., Harvard U., 1956; hon. degree, Mt. Holyoke Coll., 1977, Suffolk U., 1977, New Eng. Sch. Law, 1978. Bar: Mass. 1957. Ptnr. firm Abrams, Abrams & Abrams, Boston, 1957-60; asst. dist. atty. Middlesex County, Mass., 1961-69; asst. atty. gen. Mass., chief appellate sect. criminal div. 1969-71; spl. counsel Supreme Jud. Ct. Mass., 1971-72; assoc. justice Superior Ct. Commonwealth of Mass., 1972-77, Supreme Jud. Ct. Mass., Boston, 1977—; mem. Gov.'s Commn. on Child Abuse, 1970-71, Mass. Law Revision Commn. Proposed Criminal Code for Mass., 1969-71; trustee Radcliffe Coll., from 1981. Editor: Handbook for Law Enforcement Officers, 1969-71. Recipient Radcliffe Coll. Achievement award, 1976, Radcliffe Grad. Soc. medal, 1977. Mem. ABA (com. on proposed fed. code from 1977), Mass. Bar Assn., Am. Law Inst., Am. Judicature Soc. (dir. 1978), Am. Judges Assn., Mass. Assn. Women Lawyers. Office: Mass Supreme Ct 1412 New Courthouse Pemberton Sq Boston MA 02108 *

ABRAMS, SANDRA JEAN, social worker, researcher; b. St. Louis, Nov. 8, 1947; d. Harold Joseph and Leah Janet (Rosen) A. BA, U. Cin., 1970; MSW, St. Louis U., 1972; D of Social Work, Columbia U., 1986. Dir. social services Bio-Med. Corp., Bronx, N.Y., 1973-79; program devel. coordinator HEW Sickle-Cell Disease Study at Columbia U. Presbyn. Med. Ctr., N.Y.C., 1979-86; community planner Assoc. Jewish Charities and Welfare Fund, Balt., 1986-88; dir. Inst. Gerontol. Research Edn. N.Mex. State U., Las Cruces, 1988—; cons. Chinese Immigration Services, 1983-85, Sickle Cell Self Help Orgn., Inc., 1980-86; lectr. in field. Contbr. articles, research reports to profl. jours. Bd. dirs. Young Audiences of Md., Balt., 1987, Health Edn. Ctr., Las Cruces, 1988—. Grantee Nat. Kidney Found., 1974, Chem. Bank, 1983-86. Mem. Nat. Assn. Social Workers, Assn. Clin. Social Workers, Assn. Cert. Social Workers, Patients on Hemodialysis and Transplant (bd. dirs. N.Y. chpt. 1975-78), Am. Soc. on Aging, Nat. Council on Aging, Gerontol. Soc. Am. Democrat. Jewish. Office: N Mex State U Inst Gerontol Research and Edn PO Box 30001 Dept 3TG Las Cruces NM 88003

ABRAMS, SHIRLEY ANN, educator; b. Vincent, Ala., Nov. 4, 1945; m. David E. Abrams, Sept. 5, 1970; 1 child, Duane. BS, Ala. A&M U., 1968; MEd, U. Alaska, 1977. Tchr. Shelby County Bd. Edn., Vincent, Ala., 1970-72, Anchorage Sch. Dist., 1973-86; pres. Anchorage Edn. Assn., 1986—. Recipient Edn. Awareness award Alaska State Assn. of Colored Women's Club, 1987. Mem. Nat. Alliance Black Sch. Educators (recipient cert. appreciation, 1986), NEA, Anchorage Edn. Assn. (pres. 1986-87, 87-88), Nat. Black Child Devel. Inst., Cook Inlet Delta Kappa, Zeta Beta (recipient outstanding service in edn. award, 1987). Address: PO Box 111421 Anchorage AK 99511 Home: 6243 Green Tree Circle Anchorage AL 99516 Office: Anchorage Edn Assn 1411 W 33rd St Anchorage AL 99516

ABRAMS, TERRY SALMON, management consultant; b. Washington, Apr. 15, 1943; d. Joseph Harold and Virginia Louise (McCormick) Salmon; m. Yale Abrams, Sept. 6, 1969; children: Kim Evan, Dale Robin. BA, Pa. State U., 1964. Various secretarial positions San Francisco, 1964-74; account and media coordinator Mark/West Internat., Santa Rosa, Calif., 1987—; v.p. Yale Abrams Assocs., Inc., Santa Rosa, 1981—. Bd. dirs. Santa Rosa Symphony Found., 1986—, pres., v.p. Extended Child Care, Santa Rosa, 1984-87; pres. sch. site council Mark West Sch. Dist., Santa Rosa, 1980-84. Mem. Santa Rosa C. of C. (mem. steering com. 1985-87). Republican. Office: Yale Abrams Assocs Inc PO Box 5318 Santa Rosa CA 95402

ABRAMSON, ROCHELLE SUSAN, violinist; b. Detroit, Jan. 1, 1953; d. Seymour I. and Mayme (Tureck) A.; B.Mus., U. Mich., 1973; M.Mus., Juilliard Sch. Music, 1975, Profl. Studies degree, 1976. Founding mem. Trio N.Y., 1975-78, Muse-Arts Ensemble, Los Angeles, 1978—; 1st violin N.Y.C. Ballet Orch., 1976-78; 1st violin Los Angeles Philharmonic Orch., 1978—; founding mem. Trio Candide, 1984—. Recipient awards Artists Internat. Young Musicians Auditions, 1977, Nat. Fedn. Music Clubs Biennial String Competition, 1973, Stillman-Kelly String Competition, 1968, Nat. Arts Club, 1976, Palm Beach Flagler-Matthews Competition, 1974, Charleston Symphony Competition, 1976, Kingsport Symphony Competition, 1975, Talman Prize, Soc. Am. Musicians, 1975, Young Artist award Music Study Club Detroit, 1978. Home: 1231 N Ogden Dr Los Angeles CA 90046-4726 Office: c/o Los Angeles Philharm 135 N Grand Ave Los Angeles CA 90012

ABREU, DAISY, electronics company executive; b. Havana, Cuba, Nov. 14, 1962; came to U.S., 1962; d. Luis and Esther (Martinez) Sire; m. Alejandro Javier Abreu, Aug. 16, 1985; 1 child, Alejandro Javier Jr. Degree, Chgo. Conservatory, 1976; tchr.'s degree, 1977. Adminstr. Universal Electronics Corp., Miami, Fla., 1984-86, pres., 1986—. Mem. pub. relations staff, sec. State Rep., Miami, 1982—, Better Bus. Bur., 1987—. Recipient Recognition award Miami Crush Park, 1986. Mem. Nat. Assn. Female Execs. Republican. Roman Catholic. Club: Kendale Lake Assn. (Miami). Home: 14829 SW 80th St 202 Miami FL 33193 Office: Universal Electronic Corp 4333 SW 75th Ave Miami FL 33155

ABREU, JUDITH ANN, broadcasting company executive; b. Franklin, Pa.; d.Dorothy Mozelle (Cast) Snyder; m. Ralph Francis Abreu, Nov. 16, 1974 (dec. 1980); children—Jennifer, Jessica. B.A., U. Tex., 1966, M.A., 1967; postgrad. NYU, 1978. Systems engr. IBM, Poughkeepsie, N.Y., 1968-70; sr. programmer Morgan Guaranty Co., N.Y.C., 1970-72; mgr. systems CBS, N.Y.C., 1972-76, dir. mgmt. info. systems edn., 1976-79, dir. systems assurance, 1979-83, dir. advanced office systems, 1983—; cons. Vol. Urban Cons. group, N.Y.C., 1979—; bd. dirs. Berkeley Enterprises, Computers and People. Instr. English, Internat. Club, N.Y.C., 1970-74; speaker Open Doors, N.Y.C. Pub. Schs., 1981—; bd. dirs. Berkeley Enterprises; leader Hudson County council Girl Scouts U.S.A., 1985. Recipient Outstanding Community award Am. Biographical Inst., 1975. Mem. Office Info. Systems Forum (pres. 1983-84), Office Products Exchange Network (communications officer 1986-87, treas. 1988-89), Assn. for Women in Computing, Office Products Exchange Network (treas. 1988—), U. Tex. Alumni Assn., Phi Mu (pres. 1978-80). Club: 500 (N.Y.C.). Home: 1004 Palisade Ave Union City NJ 07087 Office: CBS Inc 51 W 52d St New York NY 10019

ABREU, SUE HUDSON, physician, army officer; b. Indpls., May 24, 1956; d. M.B. Hudson and Wilma Hudson (Jones) Black; m. Michael H. Abreu, Dec. 24, 1979. B.S. in Engring., Purdue U., 1978; M.D., Uniformed Services U., 1982. Commd. 2d lt. U.S. Army, 1978, recommd. capt., 1982; med. officer candidate, Bethesda, Md., 1978-82; intern Walter Reed Army Med. Ctr., Washington, 1982-83, resident in diagnostic radiology, 1983-85, fellow in nuclear medicine, 1985-87, staff nuclear medicine physician, 1987-88, med. research fellow, 1988-89. Mem. Soc. Nuclear Medicine, Am. Coll. Nuclear Physicians, Soc. Women Engrs., Am. Med. Women's Assn., Am. Assn. Women Radiologists, Tau Beta Pi, Omicron Delta Kappa, Phi Kappa Phi. Avocations: calligraphy; sports. Home: 3520 Nimitz Rd Kensington MD 20895-1714 Office: Walter Reed Army Med Ctr Nuclear Medicine Service Washington DC 20307-5001

ABSHIER, SHIRLEY ANN, geologist; b. Vernon Center, N.Y., Oct. 19, 1936; d. Harry E. and Anna (Cuomo) Sauerhafer; BS, U. Tex., El Paso, 1969; m. Jon F. Abshier, Nov. 5, 1964; children: Debrah, Gerald, Thomas, Patricia. Social services welfare caseworker N.Mex. Health and Social Service Dept., Grants, 1969-72; petroleum geologist Mobil Oil Corp., Denver, 1973-80, editor Mobil Denver E & P Newspaper, 1979-80, mem. speakers' bur., 1979-80; sr. geologist Sunmark Oil Co., Denver, 1980-81; dist. geologist Trans-Tex. Energy, Inc., 1981 82; geol. cons., 1982-86; v.p. A-W Systems, Ltd., 1986—; pres., cons., indsl. hygienist Abshier & Assocs., 1986—. Chmn., N.Mex. Crippled Childrens Assn., 1970-72; charter mem. Grants Boys Ranch, 1970-72; mem. N.Mex. Gov.'s Com. on Mental Health, 1970-72; Jefferson County rep. to Republican County Conv., 1976—. Mem. Am. Assn. Petroleum Geologists, Rocky Mountain Assn. Geologists, Profl. Geologist, Clear Creek County Mining and Metals Assn. Republican. Episcopalian. Editor: RMAG Guidebook, 1979; editor Mobil Messenger, 1979. Home and Office: 524 NE Malibu Dr Lee's Summit MO 64064

ABT, SYLVIA HEDY, dentist; b. Chgo., Oct. 7, 1957; d. Wendel Peter and Hedi Lucie (Wieder) A. Student, Loyola U., Chgo., 1975-77; cert. dental hygiene, Loyola U., Maywood, Ill., 1979, DDS, 1983. Registered dental hygienist. Dental asst. Office Dr. Baran and Dr. O'Neill, DDS, Chgo., 1977-78; dental hygienist Drs. Spiro, Sudakoff, Kadens, Weidman, DDS, Skokie, Ill., 1979-83, Dr. Laudando, DiFranco, Rosemont, Ill., 1980-83; gen. practice dentistry Chgo., 1983—. Vol. Community Health Rotations, VA Hosps., grammar schs., convalescent ctrs., mental health ctrs., Maywood, Ill. and Chgo., 1978-82. Recipient 1st Place award St. Apollonia Art Show, Loyola U., 1982. Mem. ADA, Ill. State Dental Soc., Chgo. Dental Soc., Loyola Dental Alumni Assn. (golf outing registration chair 1987, awards in golf and tennis 1987), Psi Omega (historian, editor). Office: 6509 W Higgins Chicago IL 60656

ABT, VICKI, sociologist, educator; b. N.Y.C., Dec. 9, 1942; d. Harold and Sylvia (Marcus) A.; student (tuition scholar) Mich. State U., 1960-61; B.A., Hofstra U., 1963; M.A., Pa. State U., 1966; Ph.D. (Univ. fellow), Temple U., 1972; 1 dau., Andrea Abt Jones. Teaching asst., research fellow Temple U., 1967-71; instr. Pa. State U. Ogontz Campus, 1966-71, assoc. prof. sociology, advisor women's studies, 1971—; research cons. Phila. Dept. Mental Health and Retardation. Chmn. Bucks County Community Devel. Citizens Com., 1975-82. Recipient Outstanding Teaching award Amoco, 1986. Mem. Am. Sociol. Assn., Am. Psychol. Assn., Popular Culture Assn., Assn. Anthrop. Study of Play, Soc. Psychol. Study Social Issues, Soc. Advancement of Field Theory, Nat. Council Compulsive Gambling, NOW. Jewish. Club: B'rith Sholom. Author: (with others) The Business of Risk: Commercial Gambling in Mainstream America, 1985. Contbr. articles to profl. jours., chpts. to books. Home: 1617 Graham Rd Meadowbrook PA 19046 Office: Pa State Univ Ogontz Campus Sutherland Bldg Abington PA 19001

ACAR, SUZANNE, computer systems analyst; b. Pitts., Dec. 6, 1956; d. Halil Ibrahim and Mildred (Byrd) A. BA, James Madison U., 1978. Clk.-typist USN Naval Air Systems Command, Washington, 1978-80, sec., 1980-82, intern computer programming, 1982-83, computer programmer, 1983-85; systems analyst USIA Voice of Am., Washington, 1985-87, counselor EEO, 1986-87; systems analyst USIA, Washington, 1987—; cons. Christian Stewardship Ministries, Fairfax, Va., 1984. V.p. Clusters at Woodlawn Homeowners Assn., Alexandria, Va., 1985-86. Mem. Assn. for Fed. Info. Resources Mgmt., Nat. Assn. Female Execs., Nat. Wildlife Fedn. Club: Crystal Gateway Racquet (Crystal City, Va.). Home: 5375D Bedford Terr Alexandria VA 22309 Office: USIA 400 4th St SW Room 336 Washington DC 20547

ACE, MAUREEN RITA, entrepreneur; b. Syracuse, N.Y., Nov. 24, 1948; d. F. Joseph and M. Eileen (Hyland) Quinn; m. Robert Charles Ace, July 14, 1984; 1 child, William Patrick Morrissey. Student, Wm. Paterson Coll., 1966-69. Sr. buyer Mennen, Morris Plains, N.J., 1978-83; purchasing mgr. Monet Jewelers, N.Y.C., 1984-86; ptnr. The Wooddale Group, East Stroudsburg, Pa., 1986—; distbr. Success Motivation Inst. Editor: The Beacon, 1967, (with others) Valdosta (Ga.) State News, 1969; judge Point of Purchase Advt. Inst. Active com. Rep. Senatorial, Washington, 1986-87; chmn. Joint Alanon Conv., Somerville, N.J. Served with USNR, 1981-87. Mem. N.J. Packaging Exec. Club (treas. 1985), Nat. Assn. Female Execs. Republican. Roman Catholic.

ACEITUNO, MARIA A., psychotherapist; b. Dec. 10, 1957; d. Andres A. and Rosamaria (Franklin) A. BA in Psychology, U. Md., 1980; MA in Psychology, Bowie (Md.) State Coll., 1982. Cert. family counseling, psychotherapy Nat. Bd. Pvt. practice psychotherapy Bowie, 1980—; cons. in field. Leader Bowie Youth Group, 1984—. Mem. Internat. Soc. Hypnosis, Am. Soc. Clin. Hypnosis, N.Am. Soc. Adlerian Psychology, Am. Assn. for Counseling and Devel., Nat. Council Hispanic Women, Assn. Exec. Women, Nat. Honor Soc. in Psychology. Home: 4420 Olando Ln Bowie MD 20715 Office: 3231 Superior Ln A-28 Bowie MD 20715

ACHESON, ALICE BREWEN, publicist; b. Indiana, Pa., July 26, 1936; d. Stewart F. and Anna M.J. (Mohr) Brewen; A.B., Bucknell U., 1958; M.A., CUNY, 1963; m. Donald H. Acheson, Dec. 12, 1970 (dec.). Tchr. English and Spanish, Mt. Vernon (N.Y.) High Sch., 1958-69; exec. sec., then exec. asst. Media Medica, Inc., N.Y.C., 1969-71; with McGraw Hill Book Co., N.Y.C., 1971-78, asso. editor, 1971-76, publicity asso., 1977-78; asso. publicity dir. Simon & Schuster, N.Y.C., 1979-80, Crown Publishers Inc., N.Y.C., 1980-81; ind. publicist, prin. Alice B. Acheson, N.Y.C., 1981—; mem. faculty Willamette Writers' Conf., 1981, Folio Pub. Week, 1983, 84, Face to Face Pub. Conf. and Expn., 1977, 79, 81, Howard U. Press Book Pub. Inst., 1984, NYU Pub. Inst., 1985, Nat. Writers Union seminar, 1985, Small Press Expo, 1987, 88; mem. publishing bd. Aperture Found., 1987—. Recipient Partner-in-Edn. award N.Y.C. Bd. Edn., 1977, 78. Mem. Publishers Publicity Assn. (program com. 1979-83), Nat. Assn. Female Execs., Am. Soc. Profl. and Exec. Women. Address: 136 E 36th St New York NY 10016

ACHTEN, ESTHER (MRS. ALFRED FRIEDMAN), physician; b. Dchurin, Russia, Nov. 27, 1919; d. Jacob and Lifsa (Lernerman) Achten; M.S., Escuela Preparatoria de Mexico, 1937; M.D. cum laude, Nat. U. Mex., 1943; m. Alfred Friedman, Dec. 3, 1944: children—Jack, Frank, Stanley, Melvin. Came to U.S., 1944, naturalized, 1950. Intern, Orange County Gen. Hosp., Orange, Calif., 1947-49; mem. Ross-Loos Med. Group, Los Angeles, 1951—, ptnr.; 1969—, historian, 1969—; practice medicine specializing in family pratice, Los Angeles, 1951—. Active Pioneer Women for Israel. Recipient plaque as clinician of yr. Cigna Health Plans, 1985. Fellow Am. Acad. Family Physicians; mem. AMA, Am. Israel, Calif., Los Angeles County med. assns. Home: 1222 S Genesee Ave Los Angeles CA 90019 Office: Ross-Loos Med Ctr 1711 W Temple St Los Angeles CA 90026

ACKEN, BRENDA THOMAS, business executive; b. Princeton, W.Va., Mar. 16, 1947; d. Murl Price and Pauline Farmer (Woolwine) Thomas; B.S. in Bus. Adminstrn., Concord Coll., Athens, W.Va., 1968. Sr. acct. Higgins & Gorman, attys. and C.P.A.s, Beckley, W.Va., 1968-74; sec.-treas., dir. South Atlantic Coal Co., Inc., Permac, Inc., REP Aviation, Inc., Bakertown Coal Co., Inc., REP Sales, Inc., Tri-States Sales Co., Bluefield, W.Va., 1974—; vice chmn. Bluefield Health Systems, Inc., 1987—; sec., treas. dir. Race Fork Coal Corp., South Atlantic Fuels Devel., Inc.; chmn. bd. dirs. Bluefield Community Hosp., 1987—, vice chmn. bd. dirs., 1981—; adv. bd. Bluefield Salvation Army, 1979-85; mem. mus. subcom. Pocahontas Coalfield Centennial Celebration, 1981-82; mem. adv. bd. Concord Coll., 1984-85; mem. Selective Service Bd., Selective Service Bd. Appeals. C.P.A., W.Va. Mem. Am. Inst. C.P.A.s (mem. at large council 1985—, chmn. Upward mobility of women com. 1985-87), Nat. Assn. Accts., W.Va. Soc. C.P.A.s (pres. So. chpt. 1976-77, state dir. 1978-81, v.p. 1981-82 pres. 1983-84, Outstanding Chpt. Pres. award, 1977, Outstanding Com. Chmn. award 1979, Pub. Service award 1983). Mem. Ch. of God. Clubs: Fincastle Country, Quota Internat. (pres. Bluefield 1978-79, dist. gov. 1980-81, bd. dirs. East area 1983-85, treas. 1985-86).Mem. West Va. Soc. CPA's (bd.dirs 1978-85), Am. Inst. CPA's (chmn. upward mobility of women com. 1985-88). Republican. Home: 628 Parkway Bluefield WV 24701 Office: South Atlantic Coal Co Inc 127 North St Bluefield WV 24740

ACKER, PHYLLIS ANN, executive, consultant; b. Mpls., Sept. 15, 1939; d. Glenn Kirt and Ruth Winnifred (Cropper) A. B.A., Augsburg Coll., 1961; postgrad. Columbia U. Sch. Social Work, 1962-63. Social worker Luth. Child Welfare Assn., N.Y.C., 1963-65, Ramsey County, St. Paul, 1965-69; vol. service coordinator, Ramsey County, Koochiching County, Dakota County, 1969-74; exec. dir. Info. and Vol. Ctr., Rochester, Minn., 1974-77; chief vol. service State Minn., St. Paul, 1977-83; sr. assoc. Energize Assocs., Phila./St. Paul, 1983-84; cons., trainer, vol. coordinator Cit of Bloominton, 1985-86. . Author/editor: Guidelines for Volunteer Transportation, 1980; contbr. articles to profl. jours. Del. Minn. Women's Consortium, 1982—, Interclub Council, 1982—, Gavel Club, St. Paul, 1982—, Joint Service Club Planning Com., St. Paul, 1980-82; active Luth. Women's Caucus, Twin Cities, 1983—; cons. Courage Ctr., Golden Valley, Minn., 1983-85, Battered Women's Shelter, Rochester, 1976-77; bd. dirs. YWCA, Rochester, 1975-77; cons., trainer, bd. dirs. Nat. Ctr. Vol. Action, Washington, 1973-78; chmn. Community Service Coordinating Council, Rochester, 1975-76; dir. Office of Vol. Services, St. Paul Red Cross, 1987—; bd. dirs. Women's Resource Ctr., 1986-87; exec. com. Charities Rev. Council of Minn., 1987. Mem. Minn. Assn. Vol. Dirs. (pres. 1970-73), Assn. Vol. Adminstrn. (treas. 1979-80, pub. policy chair 1977-78). Democrat. Lutheran. Club: Zonta Internat. (pres. 1982-84, area dir. 1986-87). Office: St Paul Chpt ARC 100 S Robert St Saint Paul MN 55107

ACKER, VIRGINIA MARGARET, nursing educator; b. Madison, Wis., Aug. 11, 1946; d. Paul Peter and Lucille (Klein) A. Diploma in Nursing, St. Mary's Med. Ctr., Madison, 1972; BS in Nursing, Incarnate Work Coll., San Antonio, 1976; MS in Health Professions, S.W. Tex. State U., 1980. RN, Wis., Tex. Staff nurse St. Mary's Hosp., Milw., 1972-73, Kenosha Meml. Hosp., Wis., 1973-74, S.W. Tex. Meth. Hosp., San Antonio, 1974-75, Met. Gen. Hosp., San Antonio, 1975-76; instr. Bapt. Meml. Hosp. System Sch. Nursing, San Antonio, 1976-83; dir. nursing Meml. Hosp., Gonzales, Tex., 1983-84; instr., dir. nursing Victoria Coll., Ceuro, Tex., 1984-86; dir. nursing Rocky Knoll Health Care Facility, Plymouth, Wis., 1986-87, Unicare Health Facilities, Milw., 1987—. Mem. Tex. Assn. Vocat. Nurse Educators, Nat. Assn. Female Execs., AAUW. Roman Catholic. Avocations: cross-stiching, reading, camping, fishing. Home: 102 1/2 Forest Ave Plymouth WI 53073 Office: Unicare Health Facilities Milwaukee WI 53208

ACKERLY, WENDY S., engineer; b. Chgo., July 23, 1960; d. Robert S. Jr. and Linda (Loucks) A.; m. Curtis William Johnson, Sept. 4, 1982. BS in Atmospheric Sci., U. Calif., Davis, 1982. Programmer U. Calif, Davis, 1982-83; cons. software Tesco, Sacramento, 1983; software engr. Bently Nev. Corp., Minden, Nev., 1984-85; mgr. computer scis. Jensen Electric Co., Reno, 1985-86; software engr. Jensen Electric Co., Cameron Park, Calif., 1986—. Mem. Am. Meteorol. Soc. Republican. Office: Jensen Electric Co 140 Jensen St Reno NV 89502

ACKERMAN, DIANA FELICIA, philosophy educator; b. Bklyn., June 23, 1947; d. Arthur and Zelda (Sondack) A.; A.B. summa cum laude, Cornell U., 1968; Ph.D., U. Mich., 1976. Asst. prof. philosophy Brown U., Providence, 1974-79, assoc. prof., 1979—; vis. asst. prof. philosophy UCLA, 1976; vis. hon. lectr. in logic and metaphysics U. St. Andrews, Scotland, 1983; sr. Fulbright lectr. Hebrew U., 1985; fellow Ctr. for Advanced Study in the Behavioral Scis. Mem. ACLU, Am. Philos. Assn., NAACP. Author articles in field. Office: Brown U Dept Philosophy Providence RI 02912

ACKERMAN, JACQUELINE KAY, assistant principal; b. Wisconsin Rapids, Wis., May 12, 1943; d. Jack Vernon and Elizabeth Josephine (Johnson) A. BS, Wis. State U., 1966; MS, U. Wis., 1968, PhD, 1971, MS in Curriculum, 1980, MS in Sch. Adminstrn., 1982. Cert. secondary tchr. Tchr., student tchr. supt. Manitowoc County (Wis.) Tchr.'s Coll., 1970-71; tchr., chair Dept. Edn. and Psychology Lakeland Coll., Sheboygan, Wis., 1971-76; tchr., dean students Menominee Indian High Sch., Keshena, Wis., 1976-81; asst. prin. Shawano (Wis.) High Sch., 1981-86, Bay Port High Sch., Green Bay, Wis., 1986—; coordinator, JOM Summer High Sch., Keshena, 1977-80; cons. CESA #3, Gillette, Wis., 1980-81; presenter, author Wis. Dept. Pub. Instruction AODA Programs and Pamphlet, 1983-86, presenter Sch.-Human Service Liaison, 1985-86. Contbr. articles to sci. jours. Musician Shawano Mcpl. Band, 1982-86; bd. dirs. Positive Youth Devel., Shawano, 1983-86. Mem. Assn. Curriculum and Supervision, Nat. Assn. Biology Tchrs., Wis. Entomol. Soc., Assn. Wis. Sch. Adminstrs. (asst. prin. commn. 1981-83, 87—), Nat. Assn. Secondary Sch. Prins. (regional dir. 1983-84), LWV (v.p. 1985-86), Bus. and Profl. Women, Howard-Suamico Bus. and Profl. Assn., Howard-Suamico Lioness Assn. (sec. 1988—). Methodist. Office: Bay Port High Sch 1217 Cardinal Ln Green Bay WI 54303

ACKERMAN, LOUISE MAGAW, writer, civic worker; b. Topeka, July 9, 1904; d. William Glenn and Anna Mary (Shaler) Magaw; BS, Kans. State U., 1926; MA, U. Nebr., 1942; m. Grant Albert Ackerman, Dec. 27, 1926; children—Edward Shaler, Anita Louise. Free lance writer, 1930—. Mem. Nat. Soc. Daus. Colonial Wars (nat. pres. 1977-80), Daus. Am. Colonists (regent Nebr. 1970-72), DAR (past v.p. gen.), Americans of Armorial Ancestry (sec. 1976-82), Nat. Huguenot Soc. (2d v.p. 1977-81), Nebr. Writers Guild (past sec.-treas.), Nat. League Am. Pen Women, Colonial Lords in Am., Nat. Gavel Soc., Soc. Descs. of Founders of Hartford, Conn., Phi Kappa Phi. Republican. Club: Nat. Writers. Lodge: Order Eastern Star. Home: Eastmont Towers III Apt 428 6335 O St Lincoln NE 68510

ACKERMAN, MARIAN JAMES, advocacy organization executive; b. N.Y.C., June 8, 1938; d. Felix John and Mary (Wozniak) James; m. Richard Peter Ackerman, Aug. 27, 1960; children: Mary Lynn, Richard. BA in Polit. Sci., Hofstra U., 1960; postgrad., Adelphi U., Brown U. Cert. tchr., Mass. Asst. to dir. fin. pension Gen. Motors Corp., N.Y.C., 1960-61; tchr. Brentwood (N.Y.) Pub. Schs., 1963-66; curriculum planner Ford Found., Brentwood, 1963-66; pres. Council on Status of Women, Winston-Salem, N.C., 1979-80, exec. dir., 1981—; founder, dir. Job Strategy Ctr. for Women, 1984—; project dir. Hampton Schs., Pitts., 1977-78, Women's Leadership Conf., Winston-Salem, 1982-83. Group chairperson Family Services, Winston-Salem, 1986-87; employment discrimination adv. human relations, City of Winston-Salem, 1986-87; community leader Salem Coll., Winston-Salem, 1987. Mem. Am. Soc. Tng. and Devel., Women's Network (pres. 1982-83). Roman Catholic. Home: 2825 Bartram Rd Winston-Salem NC 27106 Office: Council on Status of Women 660 W 5th St Winston-Salem NC 27106

ACKERMAN, MONA RIKLIS, foundation administrator; b. Tel-Aviv, Israel, May 22, 1946; d. Meshulam and Judith (Stern) Riklis; m. Irwin Ackerman, Dec. 18, 1966 (div. 1977); children: Ari, Gila. BA, NYU, 1968; MA, Yeshiva U., 1984, PhD, 1987. Story editor Frank Yablans Prodns., N.Y.C., 1975-77; editor Dell Publishing, N.Y.C., 1978-79; sr. editor Jove Books, N.Y.C., 1979-80; dir. Rapid Am. Corp., N.Y.C., 1976—; pres. Riklis Family Found., N.Y.C., 1981—. Bd. govs. United Jewish Appeal of Greater N.Y., 1984-86; bd. dirs. United Jewish Appeal-Fedn. Jewish Philanthropies, 1986—, Bd. Jewish Edn., N.Y.C., 1983-84, Am. Friends of Rechov Sumsum, 1984—, Hayeled Found., 1987—, Am. Friends of Israel Mus., 1987—; internat. bd. govs. Weizmann Inst. of Sci., 1985—, Tel Aviv Mus., 1987; mem. exec. com. Nat. Jewish Coalition, 1987—; mem. painting and sculpture com. Mus. Modern Art, 1985—; mem. Rockefeller U. Council, 1986—, Com. for Yr. 2000, NYU, 1986—, overseer faculty arts and scis., 1987. Republican. Office: Riklis Family Found 595 Madison Ave New York NY 10022

ACKERMAN, SANDRA J., editor; b. Plainfield, N.J., Aug. 16, 1957; d. Bernard and Nancy (Bernstein) A. BA, Yale U., 1979. Mng. editor Am. Scientist, New Haven, 1985—. Contbr. articles to profl. jours.

ACKERMAN, SUSAN JANE, advt. agency exec.; b. Utica, N.Y., Oct. 10, 1941; d. Richard James and Annette Louise (Gardner) A.; B.A. cum laude, Harvard U., 1964, postgrad., 1963-64. Research project dir. Young and Rubicam Inc., N.Y.C., 1964-67; dir. of research Bresnick Co., Inc., Boston, 1967-69, Cambridge Mktg. Group Inc., N.Y.C., 1969-72; dir. mktg. Muir Cornelius Moore Inc., N.Y.C., 1973-75; assoc. dir. mktg. and research Grey Advt. Inc., N.Y.C., 1975-77, v.p. and sr. assoc. dir. mktg. and research, internat. research coordinator, 1978-83, dir. mktg. and research, Americas/Pacific, 1984—. Republican. Episcopalian. Office: Grey Advt Inc 777 3rd Ave New York NY 10017

ACKLES, JANICE VOGEL, fundraising executive, writer; b. Pasadena, Calif.; d. Roy George August and Genevieve Irene (Hunter) Vogel; m. David Thomas Ackles, Dec. 9, 1972; 1 child, George Arthur Vogel. BA in Art History, Calif. State U., Los Angeles, 1970; postgrad., U. So. Calif., 1970, 75. Social worker Los Angeles County Dept. Pub. Social Services, 1970-73; free-lance writer 1972—; asst. editor Am. Jour. Physiology, Los Angeles, 1980-84; dir. devel. research World Vision, Monrovia, 1985-88, Childrens Hosp., Los Angeles, 1988—. Contbr. articles to nat. mags. and newspapers. Vol. researcher Los Angeles County Mus. Art, 1973-75; mem. Assistance League So. Calif., Los Angeles, East African Wildlife Soc., Mus. Contemporary Art, Los Angeles, Greater Los Angeles Zoo Assn., Natural History Mus. Mem. Am. Prospect Research Assn., Nat. Soc. Fund Raising Execs., Nat. Assn. Female Execs., Ind. Writers So. Calif., Calif. Press Women, Inc. Democrat. Congregationalist.

ACKLEY, SUZANNE MARIE, orthopedic surgeon; b. Bklyn., Jan. 29, 1950; d. James Aloysius and Marie Bertha (Lahey) A. BA, Hofstra U., 1971, postgrad., 1972-76; MD, Albany Med. Coll., 1980. Intern in surgery U. Md. Hosp., Balt., 1980-81, resident in orthopedics, 1981-85; fellow in hand surgery Rush-Presbyn. St. Lukes Med. Ctr., Chgo., 1985-86; attending surgeon orthodpedic and hand surgery Kaiser-Permanente Med. Group, Anaheim, Calif., 1987—; attending hand surgeon U. Calif. Med. Ctr., Orange, 1986—. Home: 835 Seagull Lane Apt C103 Newport Beach CA 92663 Office: Kaiser Permanente Med Group 411 Lakeview Ave LMO II Anaheim CA 92807

ACORD, BARBARA BURROWS RADDATZ, educator; b. Los Angeles, Dec. 26, 1928; d. Harry and Sophia (Dittman) Burrows; m. Benjamen Raddatz, June 11, 1949 (div. Dec. 1970); children: Randolph, Marjorie, Thomas, Deborah; m. William A. Acord, Feb. 26, 1974 (dec.). AA, Riverside City Coll., 1956; BA, Calif. State U., San Bernardino, 1970; MA, Pacific Oaks Coll., 1974; postgrad., Claremont Coll., 1976-81. Cert. marriage, family, child counselor, Calif., 1974. Dir. pvt. Nursery Sch. and High Sch., Riverside, Calif., 1964-56; career devel., coordinator Riverside County Head Start and Corono Norco Sch. Dist., Riverside, 1966-72; instr. Chaffey Community Coll., Alta Loma, Calif., 1971-82; class room coordinator, family counselor Casa Colina Hosp., Pomona, Calif., 1973-79; counselor LaVerne (Calif.) Ctr. for Edn. Counseling, 1976-82; social worker III San Andreas Regional Ctr., Salinas, Calif., 1984-87; practice family and individual counseling Medford, 1987—; cons. Pomona U. Sch. Dist., Calif., 1973-80, San Gabriel Valley Regional Ctr., Covina, Calif., 1976-82, Nat. Council Alcoholism, Covina, 1980-82; instr. U. LaVerne, 1976-82. Author: On Learning and Growing, 1974; co-author: Parent Advocacy Training, 1977, Creative Competency, 1978. Vol. Day Springs Hospice, Medford, 1987—; bd. dirs. Gold Coast Arab Horse Assn., Santa Clara County, Calif., 1983-85. Riverside County Headstart scholar, 1970, Ednl. Profl. Devel. Act scholar, 1971-74. Mem. Am. Assn. Marriage and Family Therapists, Calif. Asssn. Marriage and Family Therapists. Democrat. Presbyterian. Clubs: Arab Horse Assn. (So. Oreg.), (bd. dirs. 1988) , Region III Arab Horse Assn. (bd. mem. 1983-85). Home: 4373 Tami Ln Central Point OR 97502

ACOSTA, ANNEMARIE, lawyer, district attorney; b. Groton, Conn., Apr. 13, 1953; d. Joseph Francis and Aloha Fern (Alexander) A. BA, St. Mary's Coll., Moraga, Calif., 1975; JD, Southwestern U., Los Angeles, 1985. Bar: Calif., 1986; cert. tchr., Calif. Substitute tchr. Ventura (Calif.) County Sch. Dist., 1975-76; adminstrv. asst. The Rainbow Jean Co., Ltd., Torrance,

Calif., 1977-78, Brentwood Assocs., Los Angeles, 1978-80, Jetcopters, Inc., Van Nuys, Calif., 1980-82; law clk. to presiding justice U.S. Ct. Appeals, Los Angeles, 1984; law clk. Los Angeles County Dist. Atty., 1985-86, dep. dist. atty., 1986—. Mem. Los Angeles Jr. C. of C., 1979-85; vol. Los Angeles Spl. Olympics, 1980-82; area chmn. golf tournament Los Angeles Open Championship, 1980-86; asst. vice chmn. Los Angeles Watts Summer Games, 1980-83. Served as ensign U.S.N. Res., 1987—. Keck Found. scholar, 1983, Themis Soc. scholar, 1984. Mem. ABA, Los Angeles County Bar Assn., Assn. Dep. Dist. Attys. Republican. Roman Catholic. Home: 6610 Orange St Apt 1 Los Angeles CA 90048 Office: Los Angeles County Dist Atty 210 W Temple St Room 18000 Los Angeles CA 90012

ACTON, ANN, financial aid administrator; b. Kankakee, Ill., June 7, 1942; d. Lawrence Donald and Yvonne Marie (Dionne) Boudreau; m. William Arden Acton, Aug. 26, 1961; children: Cory Francis, Michaek Arden, Gregory Lee. Student Coll. St. Francis, Joliet, Ill., 1959-61; BA in Psychology cum laude, So. Ill. U., Carbondale, 1971, MPA, 1983. Asst. dir. human resources Shawnee Community Coll., Ullin, Ill., 1973-74; health planner, adminstrv. asst. Miss.-Ohio Valley Regional Planning Commn., Mounds, Ill., 1974-75; health planner, planning coordinator, field dir., assoc. dir. Comprehensive Health Planning in So. Ill., Carbondale, 1975-81; dir. planning and devel. Franklin Hosp., Benton, Ill., 1981-82; pres. Acton Assocs., West Frankfort, Ill., 1982-88; dir. fin. aid Shawnee Community Coll., Ullin, Ill., 1987—; bd. dirs. Franklin-Williamson Counties Mental Health Assn. Adv. com. Lions of Ill. Hearing Services, Ill. Com. Definitional Study of Devel. Disabilities; policy adv. com. Coal Miners Respiratory Disease Program; mem. Regional 208 Water Quality Com.; pres. Comprehensive Health Planning in So. Ill.; chairperson Greater Egypt Health Council. Mem. Am. Pub. Health Assn., Midwest Assn. Student Fin. Aid Adminstrs., Assn. Student Fin. Aid Adminstrs., Am. Soc. Pub. Adminstrn., Nat. Assn. Female Execs., Phi Kappa Phi. Democrat. Roman Catholic. Lodge: Elks. Home: 108 N Horrell St West Frankfort IL 62896 Office: Shawnee Community Coll Ullin IL 62992

ACTON, CONSTANCE FOSTER, university administrator, consultant; b. Fall River, Mass., July 12, 1947; d. Foster Southworth and Constance Norton (McIntyre) A. BS with honors, Mich. Tech. U., 1968; PhD, U. Pa., 1973; postdoctoral fellow, Yale U., 1975; postgrad., Golden Gate U., 1985—. Asst. prof. Mich. Tech. U., Houghton, 1975-76; engrng. specialist Olin Corp., New Haven, Conn., 1976-78; dir. research C.A. Metals Refining, Inc., New Haven, 1978-79; sr. process engr. Davy McKee Corp., San Mateo, Calif., 1979-82; engrng. specialist Bechtel Group, Inc., San Francisco, 1982-84; project mgr. research and devel. U. Calif. Lawrence Livermore Lab., 1984—; mem. research adv. council U.S. Bur. Mines, 1982-85; cons. Jensen Industries, Inc., New Haven, 1978-79, NASA, La Jolla, Calif., 1985, First Capital Group, Inc., San Rafael, Calif., 1985-87, Davy McKee Corp., San Mateo, Calif., 1985-87; pub. Graphos Press, 1987—. Tech. writer for Mayor of Needles, Calif., 1987; patentee in field; contbr. articles to profl. jours. NDEA fellow, 1972; Research grantee NSF, 1975. Mem. Am. Soc. of Metals, Internat. Precious Metals Inst. (pub. com. 1982-85), Am. Inst. Metall. Engrs., San Francisco Gem and Mineral Club, Sigma Xi. Club: Macintosh. Home: 463 Green Glen Way Mill Valley CA 94941 Office: U Calif PO Box 1528 Mill Valley CA 94942

ACTON, PATRICIA NASSIF, lawyer, educator; b. Cedar Rapids, Iowa, June 7, 1949; d. M. Morey and Barbara (Lindsey) Nassif; m. Richard Gerald Lyon-Dalberg-Acton, Mar. 19, 1988. B.A. in history with honors, U. Iowa, 1971, J.D., 1974. Admitted to Iowa bar, 1974; assoc. atty. Simmons, Perrine, Albright & Ellwood, Cedar Rapids, 1974-78; sole practice, Cedar Rapids 1978-80; Bigelow teaching fellow, lectr. law U. Chgo. Law Sch., 1980-81; vis. assoc. prof. Coll. Law, U. Iowa, 1981-84, clin. assoc. prof., 1984-85, clin. prof., 1985—; vis. prof. U. Fla. Coll. Law, 1985. Mem. Iowa Bar Assn., Order of Coif, Phi Beta Kappa. Editor notes and comments The Iowa Law Rev. 1973-74; contbr. articles to profl. jours. and books on lit. and entertainment law. Office: U Iowa College of Law Iowa City IA 52242

ACUNA, REBECCA ANNE, administrative operations manager; b. Corpus Christi, Tex., July 8, 1961; d. Miguel Lara and Candelaria (Villa) A. BBA, North Tex. State U., 1983. Acct. adminstr. IBM Corp., Dallas, 1983-86; adminstrv. ops. mgr. IBM Corp., El Paso, Tex., 1987—. Vol. Casa de Amigos, Dallas, 1984, Family Place, Dallas, 1985, Cary Jr. High Sch., Dallas, 1986; tchr. Holy Trinity Bible Sch., Dallas, 1985-86; tchr. Jr. Achievement Project Bus., El Paso, 1988. Recipient North Tex. 40 award Office of the Pres., 1982; leadership scholar Southwestern Life Ins., 1982. Mem. Exec. Women Internat., Chi Omega (v.p. 1981-82), Delta Sigma Pi, Order of Omega. Office: IBM 4191 N Mesa El Paso TX 79902

ACZEL, SUSAN KENDE, mathematician; b. Budapest, Hungary, June 22, 1927; d. Lajos and Iren Kende; came to Can., 1965, naturalized, 1972; m. Janos D. Aczel, Dec. 14, 1946; children—Catherina Aczel Boivie Julie Aczel More. BS, U. Budapest, 1948; MS, U. Szeged, 1950. Teaching asst. U. Szeged, 1949-50; asst. prof. Tech. U. Miskolc, 1950-52; head cultural dept. City of Debrecen, 1953-55; research assoc. U. Waterloo, Ont., Can., 1965-71. Author bibliographies on math. books in Hungary and on works on functional equations, 1964—. Home: 97 McCarron Crescent, Waterloo, ON Canada N2L 5M9

ADAIR, JOAN, retail executive, school official; b. Spokane, Wash., Jan. 18, 1935; d. John Sherman and Laura Georgina (Barnes) Harris; student Santa Ana (Calif.) Coll., 1970-72; children—Laurie Gaye, Marcus Paul. Personnel asst. City of Tustin (Calif.), 1972-77; office mgr. Santa Ana Coll., 1977-78; agy. N.Y. Life Ins. Co., 1978-79; exec. sec. Tchrs. Mgmt. & Investment Co., Newport Beach, Calif., 1979-80, regional mgr., 1980-84; exec. sec. to dir. and bd. trustees Idyllwild (Calif.) Sch. Music and Arts, 1983-85; personnel asst. Shepard Ambulance, Inc., 1987—; co-owner The Pony Shop, 1983-85 . Mem. Nat. Assn. Securities Dealers, Am. Soc. Profl. and Exec. Women, Nat. Assn. Bus. and Indsl. Saleswomen, Internat. Assn. Fin. Planners, Nat. Assn. Female Execs. Home: 2229 S 111th Pl Seattle WA 98168 Office: 1140 12th Ave Seattle WA 98122

ADAMCHEK, JANICE LYNN, personnel director; b. Seattle, Sept. 11, 1949; d. Vernon Wayne and Hazel Kathleen (Butcher) Beranek; m. Stacy Richard Mattox, July 8, 1967 (div. Oc. 1972); 1 child, Michael Sean; m. Thomas Bruce Adamchek, Aug. 4, 1979. Student, Montgomery Coll. and U. Md., 1971-78. Adminstrv. aide Dept. Transpn. Montgomery County, Silver Spring, Md., 1967-74; adminstrv. aide to asst. Community Service Ctr. Program Montgomery County, Silver Spring, 1974-79; various positions John Brown Engrs. & Constructors Inc. Trafalgar House Co., Stamford, Conn., 1979—; mgr. personnel John Brown Engrs. & Constructors Inc. Trafalgar House Co., Stamford, 1983—; rep. Coll. Placement Council, Bethlehem, Pa., 1982—. Active United Way, Silver Spring and Stamford 1968—. Mem. Nat. Constructors Assn. (employee relations com. 1982-85), Engring. Assocs. (exec. com. 1986-87). Home: 5 Boulder Ct Norwalk CT 06854 Office: John Brown E&C Inc 17 Amelia Pl PO Box 1432 Stamford CT 06904

ADAMOVICH, SHIRLEY GRAY, librarian, state official; b. Pepperell, Mass., May 8, 1927; d. Willard Ellsworth and Carrie (Shattuck) Gray; m. Frank Walter Adamovich, Aug. 31, 1960; children: Carrie Rose, Elizabeth Maude. B.A., U. N.H., 1954; M.S., Simmons Coll., Boston, 1955. Cons. Vt. State Library, Montpelier, 1955-58; head cataloger Bentley Coll., Waltham, Mass., 1958-60; tchr. U. N.H. System, Durham, 1965-79; asst. state librarian N.H. State Library, Concord, 1979-81, state librarian, 1981-85; commr. N.H. Dept. Libraries, Arts and Hist. Resources, Concord, 1985—. Editor: A Reader in Library Technology, 1975. Served in USAF, 1949-53. Mem. ALA, New Eng. Library Assn., N.H. Library Assn., N.H. Library Trustees Assn., N.H. Ednl. Media Assn. Office: NH State Library 20 Park St Concord NH 03301

ADAMS, ALICE, writer; b. Fredericksburg, Va., Aug. 14, 1926; d. Nicholson Barney and Agatha Erskine (Boyd) A.; 1 son, Peter Adams Linenthal. A.B., Radcliffe Coll., 1946. Author: novels Careless Love, 1966, Families and Surviviors, 1975, Listening to Billie, 1978, Rich Rewards, 1980, Superior Women, 1984, Second Chances, 1988; (short story collections) Beautiful Girl, 1979; To See You Again, 1982, Return Trips, 1985; contbr. short stories to: New Yorker, others. Guggenheim fellow, 1978-79; NEA grantee, 1976; recipient Best Am. Short Stories award, 1976, O. Henry awards 1971-82, 84—. Mem. PEN. Democratic Socialist. Office: care Press Relations Alfred A Knopf Inc 201 E 50th St New York NY 10022

ADAMS, ALICE PATRICIA, sculptor; b. N.Y.C., Nov. 16, 1930; d. Charles P. and Loretto G. (Tobin) A.; m. William D. Gordy, Feb. 7, 1969; 1 dau., Katherine Adams Gordy. Student, Adelphi Coll., 1948-50; BFA, Columbia U., 1953; postgrad. (French Govt. fellow), 1953-54; postgrad. Fulbright Travel grantee, L'Ecole Nat d'Art Decoratif, Aubusson, France, 1953-54. Lectr. Manhattanville Coll., Purchase, N.Y., 1960-79; instr. sculpture Sch. Visual Arts, 1980-87. One-woman shows, N.Y.C., 1972, 74, 75, Hal Bromm Gallery, N.Y.C., 1979, 80, group shows include, Whitney Museum Am. Art, N.Y.C., 1971, 73, Indpls. Mus. Art, 1974, Nassau County Mus. Fine Arts, Roslyn, N.Y., 1977, Wave Hill, Riverdale, N.Y., 1979, Mus. Modern Art, N.Y.C., 1984; represented in permanent collections, Weatherspoon Gallery U. N.C., Greensboro, U. Nebr., Everson Mus., Syracuse, N.Y., Haags Gemetemuseum, The Hague, Netherlands; pub. commissions include Crosby Gardens, Toledo, Ohio, Design Team Seattle Transit Project, Workers' Place Park, Lawrence, Mass. Creative Artists Pub. Service grantee, 1973-74, 76-77; Nat. Endowment for Arts Artists grantee, 1978-79; Guggenheim fellow, 1981-82. Home: 3370 Ft Independence St Bronx NY 10463

ADAMS, ANNE MAYO, social worker; b. Cleve., Mar. 25, 1931; d. Edward L. and Kate S. (Hammond) Mayo; student Skidmore Coll., 1949-51; B.A. in Sociology, U. Wis., 1953; postgrad. Bridgewater State Tchrs. Coll., 1965-66; m. Charles B. Adams, Mar. 17, 1979; children by previous marriage—Michelle Morel Taylor, Catherine Morel Zanartu, Jean Pierre Morel. Social worker with aged, blind, disabled and children, Akron and Medina, Ohio, 1969-72; social worker, West Palm Beach, Fla., 1972-73; social worker adult protective service State of Fla., West Palm Beach, 1972-80, social and rehabilitative counsellor II, 1980—; public speaker in field; participant seminars in law, psychology and counselling techniques. Founder gerontology program Meml. Presbyn. Ch., West Palm Beach, 1982; mem. session, choir, Christian edn. com. Lakewood Congl. Ch.; mem. Fla. Council on Aging, 1984—; chmn. screening com. Adopt-A-Family of the Palm Beaches; sec. women's aux. Salvation Army of Palm Beaches. Mem. Fla. Assn. for Health and Social Services, Alpha Chi Omega. Republican. Club: Cotillion of Palm Beaches (pres.). Home: 2287 Carambola Rd West Palm Beach FL 33406 Office: State of Fla Unit 2 Health and Rehab Services 3 3801 S Congress Ave Lake Worth FL 33460

ADAMS, ANNE PATRICK, marketing coordinator; b. Dallas, Oct. 18, 1954; d. Carol Anne (Patrick) Adams. BA, Tex. Tech U., 1976; student, Jane Jones Sch. Art, 1978-84; postgrad, So. Meth. U., 1986-88. Girl friday Newman Graphics Corp., Dallas, 1977-78; reservations sales rep. Delta Air Lines, Dallas, 1978-84, computer instr., 1984-86, coordinator mktg. automation, 1986—. Exhibited at Tex. State Fair, 1981, 82 (1st place), 83 (3rd place), 84 (2d place), 85 (2d place), 86 (2d place). Publicity chmn. Park Cities Bapt. Ch., Dallas, 1983—; mem. Dallas Mus. Art, 1987—; leader Young LIfe, 1982; bd. dirs. 500 Inc. Civic Club, Dallas, 1981-84; vol. Kent Hance for State Senate, Lubbock, 1976, Tom Carter for Senate, Dallas, 1986, Campaign to Re-Elect Gov. Bill Clements, Dallas, 1986. Recipient Delta Air Lines Sales Excellence award, 1978, 83; named one of Outstanding Young Women of Am., 1984; Am. Bus. Women Assn. Scholar, 1976. Mem. Nat. Assn. Female Execs., Delta ProTeam, S.W. Watercolor Soc., Zeta Tau Alpha. Republican. Methodist. Club: Chimeras Social Orgn. Home: 5916 Birchbrook #225 Dallas TX 75206 Office: Delta Air Lines 8700 Stemmons Freeway Dallas TX 75247

ADAMS, AUDREY LEE, physician, anesthesiologist, educator; b. Sioux Falls, S.D., Mar. 27, 1952; d. James Robert and Louise (Lewis) A.; m. Edward Lee Schumann, Dec. 9, 1983. BS in Medicine, U. S.D., 1975; MD, Northwestern U., 1976. Diplomate Am. Bd. Anesthesiology; cert. spl. competence in critical care medicine ABA. Intern Northwestern-McGraw Med. Ctr., Chgo., 1977, resident in anesthesiology, 1978-79, fellow, 1980; asst. prof. anesthesiology Pritzker Sch. Medicine, U. Chgo., 1981-82; asst. prof. U. Calif., Irvine, 1982-85, assoc. prof., 1986—; dir. surg. intensive care, Long Beach VA Med. Ctr., Calif., 1982-85. Named Outstanding Tchr., U. Chgo. Med. House Officers, 1982. Mem. Am. Soc. Anesthesiology, Soc. Critical Care Medicine, Internat. Anesthesia Research Soc., Am. Med. Women's Assn. Office: PO Box 6565 Orange CA 92613

ADAMS, AUNDREA JASMINE KAYE, nurse, small business owner; b. Longview, Tex., Sept. 29, 1954; d. George Marion and Lena (Epps) A. BS in Psychology, Tex. Woman's U., 1976, BS in Nursing, 1977. Registered nurse, Tex. Med., surgical staff nurse Good Shepherd Med. Ctr., Longview, 1978-79; asst. dir. nurses, cons., coordinator in-service edn. Cleaver Meml. Convalescent, Longview, 1979-81; profl. rehab. nurse Dallas Rehab. Inst., 1981-82, Baylor Inst. for Rehab., Dallas, 1982-87; owner, exec. dir. Reality Book Co., Dallas, 1987—; model Kurl Keeper Hair Products. Author: Welcome to Reality!, Is This the One?. Vol. Service Program for Aging Needs, Denton, Tex., 1975, health service for mentally and physically handicapped Denton State Sch., 1976; panel judge for Miss Black Tex. Pageant, Tyler, 1978. Recipient Merit Cert. Longview Greek Council, 1981; presented as 1981 Bachelorette Ebony Mag., 1981. Mem. Am. Bookdealers Exchange, Nat. Assn. for Female Execs., Alpha Kappa Alpha (Epsilon Zeta Omega chpt.). Democrat. Baptist.

ADAMS, BARBARA, English language educator, poet, writer; b. N.Y.C., Mar. 23, 1932; d. David S. Block and Helen (Taxter) Block Tyler; m. Elwood Adams, June 6, 1952; children—Steven, Amy, Anne, Samuel. BS, SUNY-New Paltz, 1962, MA, 1970; PhD, NYU, 1981. Adj. instr. Orange County Community Coll., Middletown, N.Y., 1970-77; grad. asst. NYU, N.Y.C., 1974-77; adj. lectr. SUNY-Albany, 1977-81; instr. Mt. St.Mary Coll., Newburgh, N.Y., 1980-81; asst. prof. SUNY-Cobleskill, 1981-83; adj. assoc. prof. Pace U., N.Y.C., 1983-84, assoc. prof. English, 1984—, dir. bus. communications, 1984—; poet in residence Cape Cod Writers' Conf., 1988. Author: Double Solitaire, 1982. Contbr. poems, stories, articles to various mags. and jours. Recipient 1st prize for poetry NYU and Acad. Am. Poets, 1975; Penfield fellow NYU, 1977. Mem. MLA, Assn. Bus. Communication, Poets and Writers. Home: 57 Cooch Ln Newburgh NY 12550 Office: Pace U Pace Plaza New York NY 10038

ADAMS, BARBARA (BOBBI) JEAN, painter; b. Plainfield, N.J., July 30, 1939; d. Robert Jr. and Georgeola (Whipple) A.; m. Hal Carnes Austin Jr., Dec. 25, 1976. BS magna cum laude, Wheaton Coll., 1961; postgrad., Art Students League, 1970-74, Nat. Acad., 1973-74. Artist-in-residence S.C. Arts Commn., Columbia, 1982—. Prin. works include (murals) School Days, 1982, Images, 1983, We Are The Children, 1986, The Food Factory, 1987, Journey 'Round the World, 1987. Chmn. Environ. Commn., Fanwood, N.J., 1970-76; pres. Lee County Council Garden Clubs, Bishopville, S.C., 1982; emergency med. technician Intermediate Bishopville Rescue Squad, 1982-87. Recipient Purchase award S.C. Mus. Commn., 1982, Purchase award Nat. Bank S.C., 1982, Cert. Distinction Columbia Mus. Art, 1983. Mem. Artists' Equity, Art Student's League (life, Awards of Merit 1975-76), Guild of S.C. Artists (v.p., treas. 1982-83), Artists' Guild Columbia, Allied Artists Am. (assoc.). Club: Iris Garden (Bishopville) (treas. 1986—). Home and Office: 215 S Heyward St Bishopville SC 29010

ADAMS, BETTIE SHERRY, entertainment facility executive; b. Richmond, Va., July 17, 1935; d. Edgar Allen and Dorothy (Shobe) Sherry; m. Raymond Alexander Adams, Sept. 5, 1953 (div.); children: Sherrie Lynne, Valerie Lee. Sec. athletics dept. U. Richmond, 1953-56; box office mgr. Coll. of William and Mary, Williamsburg, Va., 1968-87, asst. dir. William and Mary Hall, 1971-86, dir., 1986—. Mem. Internat. Assn. Auditorium Mgrs. (cert. facility exec., past conf. speaker, editor assn. history 1975), Nat. Assn. Female Execs., Nat. Entertainment Conf., Country Music Assn., Am. Mgmt. Assn., Am. Heart Assn. (sec. bd. dirs. 1986-87), Va. Council Garden Clubs (sec. 1974). Republican. Episcopalian. Club: Kingswood Garden (Williamsburg) (pres. 1973). Home: 5416 Skalak Dr Williamsburg VA 23185 Office: William and Mary Hall PO Box HC Williamsburg VA 23187

ADAMS, BETTY VIRGINIA, petroleum products company executive; b. Butler, Ga., Jan. 6, 1925; d. William Burton and Martha William (Duckworth) A.; B.A., U. N.C., 1946; B.A., Va. Intermont Coll., 1944. Chmn. Fuel Oil & Equipment Co., Inc., Roanoke, Va., 1949—. Methodist. Clubs: Roanoke Country; Yacht and Country (Stuart, Fla.). Office: PO Box 12626 Roanoke VA 24027

ADAMS, BEVERLY JOSEPHINE, data processing executive; b. Kansas City, Kans., Nov. 29, 1951; d. Cecil and Eula Laverne (Lynch) Brown; m. Theodore Lavern Adams, Sept. 20, 1969; children: Theodore Lavern Jr., Terry Levar. AA in Data Processing, Kansas City Kans. Community Coll., 1980; BS in Mgmt. and Computers, Park Coll., Parkville, Mo., 1986. Sr. data processor AT&T Communications, Kansas City, Mo., 1984-86, computer programmer, 1987—; lectr. in field. Editor: (newspaper) Courier, 1969, (newsletter) Kansas City Link, 1987. Cons. Youth of Am., Kansas City, 1983; mem. Kansas City Chiefs Football, 1968-72, Coalition Labor Union Women, Washington, 1984, AFL-CIO City Labor Council, Kansas City, 1984; dir. ch. adult and youth choir, Kansas City, 1982—. Recipient Outstanding Community Services award AT&T Techs., 1984; named one of Outstanding Young Women of Am., 1981. Mem. Nat. Assn. Female Execs, Alliance AT&T Employees (chairperson 1987), Profl. Women's Fedn., Young People's Willing Workers, Gamma Mu Gamma (program chmn. 1985). Republican. Penacostal. Clubs: Wecomo (Services award 1983), Young Adults Action (bd. dirs., Leadership award 1980), YWCA (Kansas City). Home: 2635 N 22d St Kansas City KS 66104 Office: AT&T Communications 2121 E 63d St Kansas City MO 64130

ADAMS, CAROL ANN, accountant; b. Louisville, Jan. 16, 1963; d. Oscar L. and Antonette M. (Chingari) McCamant; m. Phillip D. Adams, Feb. 6, 1983 (div. 1985). Student, Anchorage Community Coll., 1981-84. Ops. officer Alaska Nat. Bank of the North, Anchorage, 1981-85; accounting rep. Enstar Natural Gas Co., Anchorage, 1985—; model, tchr. Rising Star Modeling, Anchorage, 1986—. Mem. Nat. Assn. Female Execs. Democrat. Roman Catholic. Home: 4015 E 20th St Apt 95 Anchorage AK 99508 Office: Enstar Natural Gas Co 3000 Spenard Rd Anchorage AK 99503

ADAMS, CAROLINE J. H., magazine classified advertising sales manager; b. Dallas, June 15, 1951; d. Bill G. and Anita N. (Murrah) Hickey. BFA, So. Methodist U., 1973. Office mgr., media planner Jim Leslie & Assocs., Dallas, 1973; continuity dir. Sta. KZEW-FM, Dallas, 1973-75; sec. Neiman-Marcus Co., Dallas, 1975-77; exec. sec. Harris Corp., Dallas, 1979-80; mgr. classified sales, circulation ADWEEK/Southwest Mag., Dallas, 1980—. Editor Dallas Advt. League newsletter, 1987—. Mem. Mag. Adv. Sales Tex., Am. Business Women's Assn. Republican. Methodist. Home: 5902 E University Blvd Dallas TX 75206 Office: ADWEEK 2909 Cole Ave Suite 220 Dallas TX 75204

ADAMS, CHRISTIE TEWKSBURY, marketing and public relations consultant; b. San Diego, Dec. 27, 1949; d. Henry Jackson and Lillian B. Adams, Jr.; student Am. Coll. Switzerland, Leysin, 1968-69; BA in Art History, Stanford U., 1972; postgrad. U. Hawaii, 1972-73. Advance publicist NBC Entertainment Corp., NBC TV/RCA, Burbank, Calif., 1974; advance rep. Ice Capades, Hollywood, Calif., 1974-76; asst. v.p. Pioneer Fed. Savs. and Loan, Honolulu, 1976-78; dir. public relations Kapiolani/Children's Med. Center, Honolulu, 1979-83; dir. pub. relations Hyatt Regency Waikiki, 1983; exec. dir. Hawaii Soc. AIA, 1984-86; founder Christie Adams & Assocs., mktg. and pub. relations, 1986—; site coordinator for Hawaii Health Fair '81. Author, photographer various internal and external corp. publs., reports, brochures, bus. lit., newsletters. Judge, publicist Hawaii's Jr. Miss Scholarship Program, 1978; mem. Liberty House Consumer Bd., Honolulu, 1978, working women panel Glamour mag., 1979, cast Honolulu Press Club's Gridiron Shows, 1980, 81, Air & Space Mus., Jan Charlot Found.; TV hostess Friends of Hawaii Public TV's Festival Nights membership/fund-raising dr., 1981. Named to Mademoiselle mag. Coll. Bd., 1971; named 2d runner-up Miss Internat. Beauty Pageant, Honolulu, 1972; recipient awards including Galley award Hawaii Communicators Assn., 1979, 80, 1st place award for instl. newspapers and mags. Hawaii Med. Assn., 1980, cert. of appreciation YWCA, 1980, citation for 1st place in internal publs. div. splty. hosps. Acad. Hosp. Pub. Relations' ann. MacEachern Awards Competition, 1981; named 1 of 5 winners Hosp. Forum jour. Photography Contest, 1980. Mem. Internat. Assn. Bus. Communicators (2d v.p., dir. and program co-chairperson Hawaii chpt. 1982), Australian-Am. C. of C., Counselors Acad. of Pub. Relations Soc. Am., Nat. Fedn. Ind. Bus., Screen Actors Guild, Small Bus. Hawaii, Bishop Mus. Assn., Friends of Hawaii Pub. Radio, Pub. Relations Soc. Am., Arts Council Hawaii (charter), Daus. Hawaii, Friends of Iolani Palace, Hist. Hawaii Found. (charter), Honolulu Acad. Arts, Inventors Council Hawaii (charter; sec., dir. and publicist 1978-79, v.p., dir. 1979-80), Stanford Alumni Assn., Nat. Trust Hist. Preservation. Club: Stanford of Hawaii (sec. 1979-80, dir. 1979-81). Office: 6254 Kawaihae Pl Honolulu HI 96825-1904

ADAMS, CYNTHIA D., health sciences educator; b. Detroit, Sept. 10, 1946; d. Walter Norbert Tokarz and Eugenia W. (Czastkiewicz) Tokarz; m. Charles Richard Adams, Feb. 18, 1978; children—Erik, Jessica, Kerensa. B.S., Wayne State U., 1968, Ed.D., 1973; M.A., Eastern Mich. U., 1970. Instr., Wayne State U., Detroit, 1970-71; chief technologist, ednl. coordinator Detroit Macomb Hosp. Assn., 1971-74; dir., asst. prof. health adminstrn. program Mercy Coll., Detroit, 1974-76; assoc. prof., chmn. dept. med. tech. Univ. of Health Scis., Chgo. Med. Sch., North Chicago, Ill., 1976-80, prof., dean, 1980—; dir. workshops Profl. Seminars Cons., N.Y.C., 1985—. Contbr. articles to profl. jours. Mem. adv. bd. Coll. Lake County, Grayslake, Ill., 1979-84; sci. fair judge Ill. Jr. Acad. Sci., 1980—; adv. bd. Lake County Urban League, Waukegan, Ill., 1980—; yearbook advisor Lake Bluff Jr. High Sch., Ill., 1983—; adv. bd. Lake County YWCA, Waukegan, 1984—. Recipient Cert. of Achievement for Outstanding Women in Edn., YWCA, Lake County, 1983, 84. Mem. Am. Assn. Allied Health Professionals, Am. Soc. Med. Technologists (cert. Omicron Sigma award 1980), Am. Soc. Clin. Pathologists (dir. workshops 1976—), Am. Soc. Allied Health Profls. (chmn. women's interest sect. 1984—), Am. Midwest Assn. Allied Health Deans, Ill. Med. Technology Assn. (chmn. sci. assembly 1979-80), Chgo. Soc. Med. Technologists (co-chmn. by-laws com. 1984-85, bd. dirs., 1984—). Home: 340 E Scranton Ave Lake Bluff IL 60044 Office: The Univ of Health Scis Sch of Related Health Scis North Chicago IL 60064

ADAMS, EDA ANN FISCHER, nursing educator; b. Montclair, N.J., Jan. 27, 1943; d. Otto Gustav and Theresa (Yannotta) Fischer; m. Bruce Leonard Adams, June 12, 1970. Diploma, Mountainside Hosp. Sch. Nursing, Montclair, 1963; B.S.N., Fairleigh Dickinson U., 1969; M.A.T., Tchrs. Coll., Columbia U., 1977; Ed.M., 1979. Staff nurse Mountainside Hosp., Montclair, 1963-65, St. Barnabus Med. Ctr., Livingston, N.J., 1965-66; asst. head nurse Mountainside Hosp., 1967-71, head nurse, 1971-73, instr. Sch. Nursing, 1973-79; instr. Seton Hall U., South Orange, N.J., 1979-81; asst. prof. Bergen Community Coll., Paramus, N.J., 1983—; researcher Nationwide Survey Faculty Clin. Practice. Vol., Hospice, Inc., Montclair, 1981—. Mem. Mountainside Hosp. Alumnae Assn., Sigma Theta Tau. Republican. Baptist. Home: 18 Holmehill Ln Roseland NJ 07068 Office: Bergen Community Coll Paramus Rd Paramus NJ 07652

ADAMS, EENA J. CARLISLE, dietitian, educator; b. Mt. Hope, Kans.; d. Alfred George and Nora Agnes (Kissick) Carlisle; B.S. in Home Econs., Kans. State U., 1939; M.S. in Foods and Nutrition, 1970; student Ohio U., 1954-61; m. Lawrence D. Adams, Dec. 11, 1940: children—Karen Jean Adams McCarthy, Maureen Janet Adams Mitchell. Tchr., Leonardville, Kans., 1939-40, Jan'es Pvt. Sch., Front Royal, Va., 1949-52, Forestdale Sch., McCracken County, Ky., 1952-53, Jackson (Ohio) County and City Schs., 1953-68, Head Start, Jackson, 1965-68; grad. teaching asst. Kans. State U., Manhattan, 1969-70; asst. prof. home econs. Wayne (Nebr.) State Coll., 1970-76; asst. prof. home econs. and dietetics Morehead (Ky.) State U., 1976-82, coordinator energy mgmt. asst. program, 1979-80; cons. dietitian, 1982—. Mem. Front Royal (Va.) Recreation Council. Delta Kappa Gamma Annie Webb Blanton scholar, 1968. Mem. Am. Dietetic Assn. (registered dietitian), Nutrition Today Soc., Soc. Nutrition Edn., Am. Home Econs. Assn., Inst. Food Tech., W.Va.-Ohio-Ky. Dietetic Assn., Ohio Dietetic Assn., Ky. Dietetic Assn., Ohio Edn. Assn., Chi Omega, Delta Kappa Gamma (pres.), Alpha Lambda Delta. Office: Crique Side Apt 4 Morehead KY 40351

ADAMS, HAZEL GREENLEE REDFEARN (MRS. PAYTON F. ADAMS II), educator; b. Monroe, N.C., Nov. 12, 1905; d. Ephraim Eugene and Rebecca (Laney) Redfearn; student Radford Coll., 1924; A.B., U. Ky.,

1940, M.A., 1953; postgrad. U. Nebr., 1955; m. Payton F. Adams II, July 11, 1928; children—Payton F. III, Juliette Greenlee (Mrs. J. B. Hawk). Elementary tchr. Larchmont Sch., Norfolk, Va., 1924-28, Winchester City Schs. (Ky.), 1943-53; supr. Clark County Schs. (Ky.), 1953-61; supr. student tchrs. Ky. Wesleyan Coll., 1945-48; instr. Wesleyan Coll., Macon, Ga., 1960; asst. and assoc. prof. edn. Dakota Wesleyan U., Mitchell, S.D., 1961-69; assoc. prof. early childhood edn. Pfeiffer Coll., Misenheimer, N.C., 1969—, supr. student tchrs., 1969-73. Chmn., Clark County Community Council, 1950-52, Clark County Recreation Bd., 1955-60; supr. Teen-Town Winchester, 1954-60; mem. adv. council Southeastern Christian Coll., Winchester, Ky., 1973-79; aide Clark County Hosp. Aux. 1980-88. Mem. AAUW, AAUP, NEA, S.D. Edn. Assn., DAR (treas. chpt. 1975-80), Assn. Supervision Curriculum Devel., Assn. for Childhood Edn., Assn. Childhood Edn. Internat. (adviser Pfeiffer Coll. chpt. 1972-73), N.C. Assn. Supervisory Educators. Mitchell Bus. and Profl. Women Club, Albemarle Bus. and Profl. Women (pres. 1972-73), Ky. Hist. Soc., Nat. Trust Hist. Preservation, Phi Kappa Phi (pres. 1964-66), Delta Kappa Gamma (pres. 1964-66), Pi Gamma Mu. Methodist. Clubs: Irvine (Ky.) Garden, Daniel Boone Music, Christian Women's, Order Eastern Star. Home and Office: 136 College St Winchester KY 40391

ADAMS, JANET LOUISE, state legislator, educator; b. Vincent, Iowa, Aug. 30, 1937; d. Wilbur A. and Verda A. (Larson) Jeanblanc; m. Ronald D. Adams, Dec. 28, 1957; children: Kathy Adams Graeve, Cindy Adams Ernst, Tim, Terry, Suanne Adams Willman, Joe, Dan. BA, Buena Vista Coll., 1984. Tchr. Corwith (Iowa) Community Sch., 1957-58; office mgr. Adams Trucking Inc., Webster City, Iowa, 1965-83; tchr. Webster City Community Sch., 1985—; mem. Iowa Ho. of Reps., 1986—; mem. Dem. Central Com., 1970—. Mem. Iowa State Edn. Assn., LWV (state pres. 1982-84), Bus. Profl. Women, Am. Assn. Univ. Women. Roman Catholic. Home: 1102 Division Webster City IA 50595

ADAMS, JEAN RUTH, entomologist; b. Edgewater Park, N.J., Aug. 17, 1928; d. Herbert Raymond and Gertrude Gladys (Budd) A.; B.S., Rutgers U., 1950, Ph.D. (Trubeck fellow), 1962. Lab. technician Rohm & Haas Co., Bristol, Pa., 1951-57; postdoctoral fellow U. Pa., Phila., 1961-62; research entomologist U.S. Dept. Agr., Agr. Research Center, Beltville, Md., 1962—; cons. insect pathology, electron microscopy, 1958—. Mem. nominating com. D.C. Bapt. Conv., 1977-79, dir. Acteens, Mission Youth Orgn., D.C. Bapt. Conv., 1972-87, 88—, Sunday sch. tchr. 1st Bapt. Ch., Hyattsville, Md., 1962—, chmn. Christian edn. bd., 1973-74, mem. nominating com., 1974-77, mem. bd. missions, 1977-80, ch. treas., 1973-74, mem. choir, 1979—, diaconate, 1980-86, vice chmn., 1981-82, chmn., 1982-84, trustee Bapt. Home, 1982—, sec., 1985—; editorial bd. Journal of Invertebr. Pathol, 1986—. Registered profl. entomologist. Mem. Electron Microscopy Soc. Am. (chmn. sci. exhibits ann. meeting 1982), Entomol. Soc. Am., Am. Soc. for Cell Biology, Soc. for Invertebrate Pathology (sec. 1982-84), Washington Soc. for Electron Microscopy (council 1976-83, sec.-treas. 1976-78, sec. 1980-82), Washington Entomol. Soc., Md. Entomol. Soc., Sigma Xi, Sigma Delta Epsilon. Contbr. articles to profl. jours. Home: 6004 41st Ave Hyattsville MD 20782 Office: US Dept Agr Agr Research Ctr W Insect Pathology Lab Bldg 011A Room 214 Beltsville MD 20705

ADAMS, JENNIFER A., solar designer, technical writer; b. Rochester, N.H., Sept. 15, 1952; d. Richard O. and Janice (Cooper) A. BA in English Lit., U. N.H., 1974; Assoc. Degree in Engring. Technology, N.H. Tech. Inst., 1977; MCE, U. Colo., 1984. Designer, tech. writer Total Environ. Action, Harrisville, N.H., 1977-81; bldg. editor Solar Age Mag., Harrisville, N.H., 1981-82; engring. editor Solar Age mag., Harrisville, N.H., 1984-85; editor Brick House Pub., Andover, Mass., 1985-86, Yankee Books, Dublin, N.H., 1986; designer John Jordon Architect PA, Hancock, N.H., 1986—; real estate broker Harrisville, N.H., 1981—; journalist designer The Write Design, Harrisville, N.H., 1985—. Author: The Solar Church, 1982, Building Details for Energy Conservation, 1984; (with others) Solar Heating: A Construction Manual, 1982; Editor: Solar Energy Handbook 2nd Edition, 1983, Yankee Ghosts, 1986, The New Solar Home Book, 1986; contbr. articles to profl. jours. Bd. dirs. Northeast Solar Energy Assn. 1986—. Democrat. Congregational. Office: The Write Design PO Box 116 Harrisville NH 03450

ADAMS, KAYE HALL, mortgage broker; b. DeKalb, Tex., Sept. 26, 1943; s. J. Roscoe and Minnie Rebecca (Shafer) Hall; m. Carl E. Adams, Oct. 8, 1960; children: Brentley Dean, Rebecca Adams Davidson. Lic. real estate broker, Tex. Owner, mgr. Sq. One Real Estate, Bonham, Tex., 1980-85; v.p. Supreme Mortgage Inc., Sherman, Tex., 1985-86; owner, mgr. Adams First Fin., Inc. (formerly Adams Fin. Resources), Sherman, 1986—; sec., mem. Pvt. Industry Council, Denison, Tex., 1981-87; pres. Texoma Housing Fin. Corp., Denison, 1981—; chair Bid Procurement Research Com., Sherman, 1987. Mem. Nat. Assn. Realtors, Tex. Assn. Realtors, Grayson County Bd. Realtors (affiliate), Dallas Assn. Profl. Mortgage Women, Sherman C. of C. Republican. Mem. Ch. of Christ. Office: Adams First Fin Inc One Grand Ctr Suite 210 Sherman TX 75090

ADAMS, LAURIE MARIE, art historian, psychoanalyst, educator; b. N.Y.C., Sept. 29, 1941; d. Daniel Edward and Helen Louise (Nelson) Schneider; B.A., Newcomb Coll., 1962; M.A. in Psychology, Columbia U., 1963, Ph.D. in Art History, 1967; m. John Brett Adams, July 24, 1970; children: Alexa, Caroline. Prof. art history John Jay Coll., City U. N.Y., 1966—; vis. asst. prof. U. Fla., Gainesville, 1967, Sarah Lawrence Coll., Bronxville, N.Y., 1967, Mt. Holyoke Coll., 1972; lectr. Columbia U., N.Y.C., 1968, instr. Sch. of Visual Arts, N.Y.C., 1976; pvt. psychoanalytic practice N.Y.C., 1978—. Recipient CUNY summer travel grantee, 1967, 68; Columbia summer travel grantee, 1966. Mem. Am. Psychol. Assn. (assoc.), Coll. Art Assn., N.Y. Center for Psychoanalytic Tng. Author children's books. Editor: Giotto in Perspective, 1974, Source: Notes in the History of Art; author: Art Cop, 1974; Art on Trial, 1976; contbr. articles to profl. jours. Office: 444 W 56th St New York NY 10019

ADAMS, MARGARET DIANE, association director; b. St. Paul, Oct. 31, 1937; d. William Frank and Margaret Mary (O'Donnell) Rudolph; BA, Met. State U., 1976; m. Ronald Earl Adams, Feb. 25, 1976; children: Margaret, Michelle and Mark (triplets); children by previous marriage: Roberta, Barbara, William, John, Dana. Bookkeeper, Universal CIT Credit Corp., 1956-59; clk. U. Minn., 1963-65; sec. Granville House, St. Paul, 1965-67, adminstrv. asst., 1967-72; adminstrv. asst. Assn. of Halfway House Alcoholism Programs of N.Am., Inc., St. Paul, 1972, project coordinator, 1973-74, project dir., 1974-78, acting dir., 1978-79, exec. dir., 1979-81; pres. Adams Enterprises, 1981-82; owner Adams Taxi, 1981-85; community faculty mem. Met. State U., 10986—. Asst. chem. dependency counseling program, Conceptual Counseling, St. Paul, 1984-87; vol. counselor Whole Life Ctr., St. Paul, 1987-88; mem. team ministry Shakopee Prison for Women, Minn., 1985—; program dir. Sarah Family Programs (ministry for women and children), St. Paul, 1987—; cons. Nat. Center for Alcohol Edn.; lectr., adviser Lakewood Community Coll. Mem. Nat. Assn. Female Execs. (network dir. 1979-81), Nat. Assn. Alcoholism Counselors, Minn. Assn. Alcoholism Counselors, Ind. Assn. Alcoholism and Drug Abuse Counselors (cert. alcoholism and drug counselor), Nat. Coalition for Adequate Alcoholism Programs, N. Am. Indian Women's Council on Chem. Dependency. Author: Women: On Women in Recovery, 1976; mem. editorial bd. Do It Now Found., 1978-79. Office: Sarah Family Programs 771 Randolph Ave Saint Paul MN 55102

ADAMS, MARIANNE KATHRYN, management consultant; b. Albany, N.Y., Jan. 10, 1924; d. Harold James and Marion Stern (Schwartzman) A. BA, N.Y. State Coll. for Tchrs., Albany, 1945, MA, 1946. Sr. personnel technician N.Y. State Dept. Civil Services, Albany, 1958-62; sr. adminstrv. analyst N.Y. State Dept. Health, Albany, 1962-63, assoc. adminstrv. analyst, 1965-68, dir. health manpower resources, 1968-69, dir. adminstrv. analysis, 1969-74, cons. pub. health planning and grants, 1974-80; asst. dir. personnel N.Y. State Dept. Social Services, Albany, 1963-65; exec. sec. N.Y. State Pub. Health Council; lectr. procedures and communications Russell Sage Coll. (evening div.), Albany, 1972-76. Editor: N.Y. State Preretirement Counseling Guide, 1962. Vice chmn., chmn. state agy. campaign United Fund, Albany, 1965, 73, 74; campaign worker Albany Symphony Orch.-Saratoga Performing Arts Ctr., 1970-80, San Diego Symphony Orch.; vice chmn. Rancho Bernardo Aux., 1986—; chair, council on ministries, mem. adminstrv. bd. Hope United Meth. Ch., San Diego, 1984-88; mem. residential com., asst. sec. Rancho Bernardo Community Planning Bd., San Diego, 1985-86; co-chair of membership Bernardo Home Owners Corp., 1988—. Recipient Cert. for Outstanding Contbn. SUNY-Albany Alumni Bd. Dirs., 1978, Citation Gov. Hugh L. Carey, State of N.Y., 1980. Mem. Am. Soc. for Pub. Adminstrn. (bd. dirs. Capital dist. chpt. 1972-74), Am. Pub. Health Assn., AAUW (treas. Rancho Bernardo chpt. 1981-83, v.p. program 1983-84, pres. 1984-85, sec., treas. San Diego Imperial Interbranch chpt. 1985-87, chair legis. 1987—), Bus. and Profl. Womens Club. Club: Cornell of N.Y. Home: 12417 Lomica Dr San Diego CA 92128

ADAMS, MARLYS, real estate broker; b. Ashland, Wis., July 16, 1931; d. Asa Earl and Vera Genevieve (Beck) Rhodes; m. Rodger Gustav Benson, Mar. 8, 1952 (div. Feb. 1967); children—Scott R., Jeffrey R., Valerie L.; m. Charles William Adams, Nov. 24, 1967. Student Eau Claire State Coll., 1950-51; grad. X-ray Technician, Fairview Hosp., Mpls., 1952. Grad. Realtors Inst.; cert. residential specialist. Real estate agt. Spring Co., Mpls., 1963-66, Bermel-Smaby Realty, Mpls., 1966-68; real estate agt. Charles W. Adams, Inc., Mpls., 1969-73, pres., broker, mgr., 1973—; bd. dirs. Realtors Credit Union, Mpls., 1971—, pres., 1978. Commr., City of Golden Valley, Minn., 1980-84; fund raiser Realtors Polit. Action Com., Mpls., 1983-84. Named Woman of Achievement, Twin West C. of C., Mpls., 1984; recipient Appreciation award Realtors Credit Union, 1978; Good Neighbor award Radio Sta. WCCO, Mpls., 1984. Mem. Nat. Assn. Realtors, Minn. Assn. Realtors (bd. dirs. 1983—, mem. exec. com. 1983—), Mpls. Bd. Realtors (bd. dirs., mem. exec. com. 1983—, pres 1984, Realtor of Yr. 1984). Republican. Baptist. Avocations: reading, travel. Home: 1410 Mayland Ave N Golden Valley MN 55427 Office: Adams Assocs Realtors 7711 Country Club Dr Golden Valley MN 55427

ADAMS, MYRA NELLE, personnel relations supervisor; b. Russellville, Ark., Aug. 21, 1936; d. Robert William and Gladys Lucille (Campbell) Lee; m. John C. Adams, May 28, 1961; children: John Scott, Robert Alan. Student, U. Ark., 1974-88. Clk. personnel relations Westinghouse Electric Corp., Little Rock, 1957-68, sec. personnel relations, 1968-74, asst. personnel relations, 1974-79, supr. personnel relations, 1979-83; supr. personnel relations N.Am. Philips Lighting Corp., Little Rock, 1983—. Mem. Ark. Personnel Assn. (chair membership com. 1982). Republican. Mem. Ch. of Nazarene. Home: 24 Tallyho Ln Little Rock AR 72209 Office: Philips Lighting Co 2701 W Roosevelt Rd Little Rock AR 72204

ADAMS, PEGGY HOFFMAN, county agency administrator; b. Mpls., July 21, 1936; d. Donald Brooks and Margaret Jane (Gruber) Hoffman; BS Cedar Crest Coll., 1958; m. Harry C. Adams, Dec. 26, 1968; children: Frank, Harry, Edward, Irene. Tchr. Allentown (Pa.) Sch. Dist., 1958-69; sales rep., reporter Quakertown (Pa.) Free Press, 1974-76; advt. cons. Media Dynamics, Bedminster, Pa., 1973-76; dir. Bucks County Consumer Protection and chief sealer weights and measures, Doylestown, Pa., 1976—. Editor, co-pub.: History of Bedminster, 1976, Richland, The Manor, The Township, Quakertown, 1978. Sec.-treas. Bedminster Bicentennial Com., 1976-78, Bedminster Hist. Commn., 1978-82, Bedminster Hist. Soc., 1982—; active Opera Guild of Opera of Phila., 1970—; Rep. committeewoman, Pa., 1974—; alt. del. Rep. Nat. Conv., 1972; co-chmn. fin. Bucks County Rep. Com., 1975—; chmn. pub. relations United Way of Bucks County; bd. dirs. Blue Cross Greater Phila., 1977—, Planned Parenthood Bucks County, 1983—. Mem. Upper Bucks C. of C. (bd. dirs. 1979—, Community Service award 1986), Am. Standard Testing Materials, Soc. Consumer Affairs Profls. (treas. Delaware Valley chpt. 1981-84), Pa. Assn. Weights and Measures (sec. 1983—), Nat. Conf. Weights and Measures (nat. chmn. W/M Week, liaison com. 1983—, task force on commodity requirements 1984—, task force on energy allocations 1988—), NE Conf. Weights and Measures (sec. 1984—, Man of Yr. 1987), Nat. Assn. Consumer Agy. Adminstrs., Bucks County Fedn. Women's Clubs (legis. chmn.), Cedar Crest Coll. Alumni Assn. (class corr. 1966—). Ch. of Christ. Club: Quakertown Women's (past pres.). Home: Edge Hill Rd Bedminster PA 18910 Office: Court House Annex Broad and Union Sts Doylestown PA 18910

ADAMS, RUTH SALZMAN, foundation executive; b. Los Angeles, July 25, 1923; d. George Thomas and Josephine Amanda (Benson) Salzman; m. Mark F. Skinner, 1946 (div. 1951); children—Gail, Beth, Megan; m. Robert McCormick Adams, Jr., July 24, 1953. B.A., U. Minn., 1946. Editorial sec. Econometrics of Cowles Commn., U. Chgo., 1953-55; mng. editor, then editor Bull. of Atomic Scientists, Chgo., 1955-68, editor, 1978-84; dir. internat. security program John D. and Catherine T. MacArthur Found., Chgo., 1985—; research assoc. Am. Acad. Arts and Scis., Cambridge, Mass., 1969-78. Editor: Contemporary China, 1965; (with William McNeill) Human Migrations: Policies and Implications, 1979; (with S. Cullen) The Final Epidemic: Scientists and Physicians on Nuclear War, 1981. Exec. dir. Ill. div. ACLU, 1971-74; governing bd. Internat. Centre of Insect Physiology and Ecology, Nairobi, Kenya, 1971-79; bd. dirs. Council for a Livable World, Washington, 1962—, Chgo. Women's Network, 1981—, Washington Com. for Nat. Security, 1983-85; participant Internat. Pugwash Confs. on Sci. and World Affairs, 1957—; mem. adv. bd. on sci. and tech. devel. Nat. Acad. Scis., 1973-78. Recipient Adlai Stevenson award for human understanding UN Assn., Chgo., 1978, award Forum on Physics and Soc. of Am. Phys. Soc., 1983. Fellow Am. Acad. Arts and Scis.; mem. Council on Fgn. Relations, AAAS. Office: J D & C T MacArthur Found 140 S Dearborn Chicago IL 60603

ADAMS, SARAH VIRGINIA, family counselor; b. San Francisco, Oct. 23, 1955; d. Marco Tulio and Helen (Jorge) Zea; m. Glenn Richard Adams, Mar 22, 1980; children: Mark Vincent, Elena Giselle, Johnathan Richard. BA, Calif. State U., Long Beach, 1978, MS, 1980. Lic. marriage, family, child counseling. Tutor math. and sci. Montebello, Calif., 1979-82; behavioral specialist Cross Cultural Psychol. Corp., Los Angeles, 1979-80; psychol. asst. Legal Psychology, Los Angeles, 1980-82, Eisner Psychol. Assocs., Los Angeles, 1982-83; assoc. dir. Legal Psychodiagnosis and Forensic Psychology, Los Angeles, 1982-83; adminstrv. dir. Diagnostic Clinic of West Covina, Calif., 1983-85, dir., 1985—; owner Adams Family Counseling Inc. (name formerly Diagnostic Clinic of West Covina), Calif., 1987—; tchr. piano, Montebello, 1973-84; ins. agent Am. Mut. Life Ins., Des Moines, 1982-84. Fellow Am. Assn. Marriage and Family Therapists, Calif. Assn. Marriage and Family Therapists, Calif. State Psychol. Assn., Calif. Soc. Indsl. Medicine and Surgery, Los Angeles County Psychol. Assn., Nat. Assn. Female Execs., Psi Chi, Pi Delta Phi. Republican. Roman Catholic. Home: 3402 Sunset Hill Dr West Covina CA 91791 Office: Adams Family Counseling Inc 260 S Glendora #101 West Covina CA 91790

ADAMS, SHIRLEY LUCILE, nurse; b. Marshall, Tex., Feb. 22, 1941; d. Gerald Hugo and Ella Mary (Hodges) Adams; BS, Howard U., 1962; grad. Los Angeles County Sch. Nursing, 1975; children: Sherilyn Marie Lum-Bird, E. Gerald Steven Lum, Michael J. Premmer. former adminstrv. student asst. Eldorado Coll., West Covina, Calif.; staff nurse spl. care nurseries, newborn intensive care unit Los Angeles-U. So. Calif. Med. Center Women's Hosp., 1975-81, critical care nurse neonatology, 1976-81, clin. instr. nursing; staff nurse Queen of Valley Hosp. Nursery. Social vice chmn. Young Democrats Am., Washington, 1962. Mem. Nat. Assn. Negro Women, Nat. Assn. Female Execs., Philathias Soc., ACLU, Psi Chi. Roman Catholic. Home: 3513 Millbury Ave Baldwin Park CA 91706

ADAMS, SHIRLEY MAE, college administrator; b. Iowa City, Nov. 10, 1946; d. Andrew Thomas and Lillian Mary (Hinek) Norman; m. James A. Kolner, June 22, 1968 (div. Oct. 1985); 1 child, Brian Alan; m. David Chase Adams, May 23, 1987. BA, U. No. Iowa, 1968; MA, U. Iowa, 1973, PhD, Iowa State U., 1983; postdoctoral, Harvard U. Inst. for Mgmt. of Lifelong Edn., 1987. Coordinator Norfolk (Va.) Pub. Schs., 1969-73; assoc. head Kirkwood Community Coll., Cedar Rapids, 1973-76; cons. adult edn. Iowa Dept Pub. Instrn., Des Moines, 1976-83; asst. dean Drake U. Coll. Continuing Edn., Des Moines, 1983-84, acting dean, 1984-86; dean U. Scranton (Pa.) Dexter Hanley Coll., 1986—; mem. Vocat. Edn. Coordinating Council, Scranton, 1987. Editor: (newsletter) Iowa Adult Educator, 1976-80; (booklet) Requirements of Iowa Licensing Boards, 1979, 81; co-editor: (booklet) Continuing Education Guidelines, State of Iowa, 1978, 85. Mem. gov.'s task force on literacy State of Iowa, 1985, Scranton Council for the Advancement of Literacy, 1986—, Lucan Ctr. for the Arts, Scranton, 1987—, Hill Neighborhood Assn., Scranton, 1986—; active Pa. State Planning Task Force Adult Edn., 1987—. Named Adult Educator of Yr., Mo. Valley Adult Edn. Assn., 1981, Woman of Yr., Am. Bus. Women's Assn., 1983. Mem. Am. Assn. Adult and Continuing Edn. (chair Nat. Adult Edn. Week), Assn. Continuing Higher Edn., Pa. Adult and Continuing Edn. Assn., Nat. Assn. Women Deans, Council for Advance of Experiential Learning, Cross Keys (hon.), Leadership Lackawana, Pi Lambda Theta. Democrat. Episcopalian. Office: U Scranton Dexter Hanley Coll Scranton PA 18510

ADAMS, SUSAN ALEXANDRIA STIERHEIM, small business owner; b. Houston, Nov. 18, 1947; d. Walter Alexander and Ruth (Ragsdale) Stierheim; m. John A Adams, June 21, 1944; children: J. Scott, S. Mark, W. Matthew, Jennifer. AB, La. Tech U., 1984. Sales mgr. Playhouse Co., Inc., Lafayette, La., 1976-79; acct. Bank of La., New Orleans, 1977-79; chief acct. Leau Claire Systems, Kenner, La., 1979-80; acctg./computer mgr. Jefferson Door Co., Harvey, La., 1984-86; owner, mgr. Adam's Wholesalers and Susan's Bargain Box, Sunset, La., 1986—; cons. Woman's Missionary Union, La., 1980—. Author: Jongleur, 1984. Mem. Baptist Women, Baptist Young Women, Assn. Women's Missionary Union (conf. leader, 1966—), State La. Women's Missionary Union (conf. leader 1980—). Republican. Home and Office: Susan's Bargain Box PO Box 198 Sunset LA 70584

ADAMS, SUSAN RAE, small business owner; b. Baker, Oreg., Aug. 25, 1939; d. Raymond Peter and Marian Edith (Hayden) Donovan; children: Michael Charles, Teresa Michelle. Student, Coll. Idaho, 1958-61, Anchorage Community Coll., 1980-83. Mgr. Aim Constrn., Anchorage, 1974-78; owner Tax & Bookkeeping, Anchorage, 1974-79; coordinator Arco Alaska, Inc., Anchorage, 1978-86; owner Adams Bus. Coordinator, Anchorage, 1986—. Pres. Texwilliger Sch., Portland, Oreg., 1969; mem. ARCO Civil Action Program, Alaska, 1978-86; vol. Scottish Rite Aphasia Found., Alaska, 1984—, Shrine Masons, Alaska, 1984—. Mem. Assn. Desk and Derrick Clubs (bd. dirs. 1979-81), Alaska Music Guild. Libertarian. Home and Office: 4711 Kupreanof St Anchorage AK 99507

ADAMS, TERRI ROSENBLATT, educational foundation director, consultant; b. N.Y.C., Nov. 27, 1951; d. George Leopold and Stephanie (Gumpel) Rosenblatt; m. John Jay Adams, May 3, 1986. Student, Dartmouth Coll., 1971-72; BA, Mt. Holyoke Coll., 1973; M in Internat. Adminstrn., Sch. for Internat. Tng., Brattleboro, Vt., 1978. Assoc. dir. programs Fgn. Student Service Council, Washington, 1976-78; asst. dir. internat. and govtl. affairs Am. Assembly Collegiate Schs. of Bus., Washington, 1978-80; dir. programs/services/alumni affairs Internat. House, N.Y.C., 1980-82; dir. NASA Tchr. in Space Project Council of Chief State Sch. Officers, Washington, 1983-86; exec. dir. Tchr. in Space Edn. Found., Washington, 1986-87; founding dir. Mobility Internat. U.S.A., Chgo., 1976-79; pres. Resources Internat., Washington, 1980—. Editor: Whole World Handbook, 1974. Bd. dirs. Lisle Fellowship, N.Y.C., 1978-81. Mem. Nat. Assn. Fgn. Student Affairs (chair com. on women internat. 1978-84), Nat. Assn. for Female Execs. Club: Mt. Holyoke. Home: 2365 Glade Bank Way Reston VA 22091

ADAMS, VICTORIA ELEANOR, realty company executive; b. San Francisco, Feb. 8, 1941; d. George Mulford and Sarah Louise (Dearborn) A.; m. Gene M. Richardson, 1965 (div. 1972); 1 child, Raymond; m. Franklin Carlisle Boosman, May 13, 1972; 1 child, Eric. AA, Palomar Coll., 1976; BBA summa cum laude, Nat. U., 1978. Sales adminstr. Evergreen Internat. Airlines, McMinnville, Oreg., 1983; corp. adminstr. N.N. Jaeschke, Inc., San Diego, 1984—; adminstrv. mgr. Tomlinson Agy., Inc., Spokane, Wash., 1980-86; v.p. Champion Realty Inc., Spokane, 1987—; publishing dir. Champion Pubs., 1987—; bd. dirs. Feline Enterprises, Spokane, Noevir Inc. Editor: Bravura, 1976; (text) Science Among Us, 1965; designer Astrology game, 1974. Contbr. articles to profl. jours. Solicitor, Am. Heart Assn., 1985. Recipient Cert. Real Estate Sales Achievment, 1978, 1982, 85, 86; Cert. Outstanding Contbn. to Real Estate Edn., 1980. Mem. Internat. Platform Assn., AAUW, Adminstrv. Mgmt. Soc. (publicity com. 1980), Exec. Womens Network, Nat. Assn. Female Execs., Nat. Assn. Realtors, Spokane Bd. Realtors (edn. officer 1979-80), Inohomish County Bd. Realtors (edn. coms. 1988—). Avocations: writing, educational research, fishing, camping, traveling. Home: N 7205 Cincinnati Spokane WA 99208 Office: Advance Properties 3405 188th St SW Lynnwood WA 98037

ADAMS-CURTIS, MICHELLE ELAINE, marketing professional; b. Springfield, Ill., Apr. 12, 1953; d. Wendell Leon and Juanita Estella (Anderson) Adams; children: Jade, Leslie, Linzy Anne. Student, Ill. State U., 1971-72, Lincoln Land Community Coll., 1972-73, Sangamon State U., 1987. Sec. Ill. Bur. of the Budget, Springfield, 1973-77; adminstrv. asst. Office Gov. State Ill., Springfield, 1978-83; asst. to gov. State of Ill., Springfield, 1978-87; spl. asst. to dir. Ill. Housing Devel. Authority, Chgo., 1988; mktg. asst. Weiss, Peck & Greer Investments, Chgo., 1988—. Home: 302 North Oak Park Ave Apt Oak Park IL 60302

ADAMS-ENDER, CLARA LEACH, nurse; b. Willow Springs, N.C., July 11, 1939; d. Otha and Caretha (Sapp) Leach; m. F. Heinz Ender; 1 child, Sven Ingo. BS, N.C. Agrl. and Tech. State U., 1961; MS, U. Minn., 1969; M in Mil. Art and Sci., Command and Gen. Staff Coll., 1976; Diploma Internat. in Mgmt. Relations and Leadership, U.S. Army War Coll., 1982. Reg. nurse. Commd. 2d lt. U.S. Army, 1961, advanced through grade to brigadier gen.; staff nurse intensive care Walson Army Hosp., Ft. Dix, N.J., 1961-63; staff nurse surg. intensive care 121st Evacuation Hosp., Seoul, Korea, 1963-64; nurse instr. U.S. Army Med. Tng. Ctr., Ft. Sam Houston, Tex., 1965-67; asst. prof. U. Md. Sch. Nursing, Balt., 1969-74; asst. chief nurse Kimbrough Army Hosp., Ft. Meade, Md., 1974-75; nurse inspector gen. Hdqrs. Health Services Command, Ft. Sam Houston, 1976-78; chief nurse 97th Gen. Hosp. Frankfurt (Fed. Republic of Germany) Army Med. Ctr., 1978-81, U.S. Army Recruiting Command, Ft. Sheridan, Ill., 1981-84, Walter Reed Army Med. Ctr., Washington, 1984-87; chief army nurse corps staff Surgeon Gen. of the Army, Falls Church, 1987—; vis. com. Care-Western Res. U., Cleve., 1984—; cons. Children's TV Workshop, N.Y.C., 1971-73, 7th Med. Command Europe, Heidelberg, Germany, 1978-81, Chief Army Nurse Corps, Washington, 1972-75. Contbr. articles to profl. jours. V.p. Rocks, Inc., Washington, 1987—; bd. dirs. Boy Scout of Am., Lake Forest, Ill, 1983-84. Recipient Presdl. Sports award, 1980, Legion of Merit award U.S. Army, 1987. Mem. Am. Nurses Assn. (mem. com. 1984—), Nat. League for Nursing (lectr. 1973—), U.S. Army Med. Dept. (Profl. Designator award 1985), NAACP, Am. Orgn. Nurse Execs., Chi Eta Phi (sec., Outstanding Com. Mem. award 1987), U.S. Army War Coll. Alumni Assn. Roman Catholic. Clubs: Walter Reed Officers Wives (chair ways and means com. 1985-86), Washington Area 500. Home: 2003 Gatewood Place Silver Spring MD 20903 Office: HQ DA (DASG-CN) 5111 Leesburg Pike Falls Church VA 22041-3528

ADAMSON, ANN LENHARDT, political consultant, real estate investor; b. Toccoa, Ga., Sept. 18, 1934; d. Edwin Bernard Lenhardt and Adeline (Henderson) Foster; m. Charles L. Adamson, Nov. 27, 1953; children: Lisa Adamson Bell, Alis Adamson Albritton. Student, DeKalb Coll., Decatur, Ga., 1972, Ga. State U., 1975. With Ga. Sec. State Office, Atlanta, 1952-79; real estate agt. Ga., 1972—; asst. sec. state State of Ga., 1973-79; pvt. practice polit. cons. Atlanta, 1979—, 1984; lay mem. on com. to rewrite Canons of Judicial Ethics, Atlanta, 1982-84; designer flag for Jekyll Island, Ga., 1958, seals of Ga. Senate, Ho. Reps. and Gen. Assembly, 1958. Active Oakland Cemetery Hist. Soc., Atlanta Zoo Soc., Gov's. Club, Ga. State Dems., Ga. Fedn. Dem. Women, Landmark Home Owners Assn. Mem. DeKalb Bd. Realtors, Ga. State Career and Retired Employees, Nat. Assn. Fed. Execs. Methodist. Home: 2160 East Lake Rd NE Atlanta GA 30307

ADAMSON, LUCILE FRANCES, infosystems specialist; b. Chetopa, Kans., Nov. 10, 1926; d. Truby Herbert and Anna Helen (Gail) A.; BS, Kans. State U., 1948; MS, State U. Iowa, 1950; PhD, U. Calif., Berkeley, 1956. Asst. prof. nutrition Hawaii Agrl. Expt. Sta., 1956-60; asst. prof. dept. pediatrics U. Mo., Med. Center, Columbia, 1960-64; research asso., dir. Core Lab., Harvard U. clin. research unit Thorndike Meml. Lab., 1964-70; sr. research assoc. dept. biochemistry Monash U., Melbourne, Australia, 1970-72; staff scientist Environ. Def. Fund, Washington, 1972-74; prof., program adminstr. program macroenviron. and population studies Howard U., Washington, 1974-81. Contbr. articles to profl. jours. Research on hormonal effects on amino acid transport and protein/mucopolysaccharide synthesis in vitro.

ADAMSON, MARY ANNE, geographer, systems engineer; b. Berkeley, Calif., June 25, 1954; d. Arthur Frank and Frances Isobel (Key) Adamson; m. Richard John Harrington, Sept. 20, 1974. BA with highest honors and great distinction U. Calif.-Berkeley, 1975, M.A., 1976, postgrad., 1978—. Cert. tchr. earth scis., Calif.; cert. cave rescue ops. and mgmt., Calif.; lic. emergency med. technician, Contra Costa (Calif.) County. Teaching asst. dept. geography U. Calif., Berkeley, 1976; geographer, environ. and fgn. area analyst Lawrence Livermore Nat. Lab., Livermore, Calif., 1978-83, cons., 1983-86; systems engr. ESL, Sunnyvale, Calif., 1986—. Staff mem. ARC/Am. Trauma Soc/Sierra Club Urgent Care and Mountain Medicine seminars, 1983-86. Asst. editor Vulcan's Voice, 1982. Mem. Assn. Am. Geographers, Assn. Pacific Coast Geographers, Nat. Speleol. Soc. (geology, geography sects., sec., editor newsletter Diablo Grotto chpt. 1982-86), Calif. Res. Peace Officers Assn., Walnut Creek Disaster Response Group, U. Calif. Alumnae Assn., Phi Beta Kappa. Contbr. articles to profl. jours. Home: 4603 Lakewood St Pleasanton CA 94566 Office: ESL Inc 495 Java Dr Sunnyvale CA 94088

ADAMSON, NOVA JAN, accountant; b. Kilgore, Tex., Aug. 23, 1958; d. Sammy Edwards and Drucilla Ilene (DeRamus) A. AS, Kilgore Coll., 1978; BBA, North Tex. State U., 1980; MBA, Tex. Woman's U., 1987. Cost acct. Mostek, Carrollton, Tex., 1980-83; planning analyst United Techs./Mostek, Carrollton, 1983-85; inventory acct. Cable & Wireless, Dallas, 1985-86; acct. Motorola, Dallas, 1986—. Vol. Spl. Olympics, Dallas, 1984-87. Mem. Nat. Assn. Female Execs., Phi Chi Theta. Home: 1229 Amherst Denton TX 76201-1701

ADAMSON, RHONDA LEE, computer engineer; b. Arlington, Va., Oct. 25, 1957; d. Robert Lee and Margie Janet (Harrell) A. BS in Elec. Engring., Rutgers U., 1980, MS in Computer Sci., 1983. Assoc. mem. tech. staff RCA Astro Electronics, Princeton, N.J., 1983-86; field engr. Summa Technologies, Inc., Fairfield, Conn., 1986; coordinator data processing Housatonic Community Coll., Bridgeport, Conn., 1986—. Active N.J. Group Against Smoking Pollution, Summit, 1979—. Mem. IEEE, Conn. Community Colls. Data Processing Coordinators Group (chair 1987-88), Mensa, Astrological Soc. of Princeton. Home: 92 Kaye Vue Dr Apt C Hamden CT 06514 Office: Housatonic Community Coll 510 Barnum Ave Bridgeport CT 06608

ADAMS-SLONE, RITA DIANE, physician; b. Portsmouth, Ohio, Apr. 29, 1949; d. Roy Harrison and Sally Ann (Chinn) Adams; m. Roy Henderson Slone, May 29, 1966; children: Duke Edward, Stacy Diane. AS, Ohio U., 1974, BA, 1979, DO, 1984. Lic. physician, Ohio, Ky. Staff nurse Pike County Community Hosp., Waverly, Ohio, 1974; continuing care nurse Scioto Meml. Hosp., Portsmouth, 1975-76, ICU nurse, 1976-77; nurse Scioto County Health Dept., Portsmouth, 1977; physician Adams Clinic, Minford, Ohio, 1985-86; family practice medicine Portsmouth, 1986—; med. dir. U.S. Health Facilities, Jackson, Ohio, 1988—. Mem. Ky. Hist. Soc. Mem. Am. Osteopathic Assn., Portsmouth Acad. Family Physicians, Nat. Assn. Female Execs., Ducks Unlimited, Nat. Ruffed Grouse Soc., Nat. Rifle Assn., United Meth. Women. Republican. Home: 3532 Gallia St New Boston OH 45662 Office: US Health So Ohio Med Office Bldg 336 E Main St Jackson OH 45640

ADCROFT, PATRICE GABRIELLA, editor; b. Scranton, Pa., Apr. 15, 1954; d. Joseph Raymond and Patricia Ann (Ryan) A. BA In Mag. Journalism and Creative Writing, Syracuse U., 1976. Editor-in-chief Carbondale (Pa.) Miner Mid Valley Gazette, 1976-77; staff writer Good Housekeeping Mag., N.Y.C., 1978-80; mng. editor Family Media/Alive and Well, N.Y.C., 1980-81; freelance writer, editor N.Y.C., 1981-82; sr. editor CBS Mags. Family Weekly, N.Y.C., 1982-84; sr. editor Omni Mag., N.Y.C., 1984-85, exec. editor, 1985-86, editor, 1986—. Editor-in-chief Omni Future Medical Almanac, 1987; contbr. writer Arthur C. Clarke's 2019, 1986, Omni Book of Continuum, 1982. Roman Catholic. Office: Omni Mag 1965 Broadway New York City NY 10023

ADDELSON, KATHRYN PYNE, philosophy educator, writer; b. Providence, Apr. 22, 1932; d. Joseph Abraham and Catherine (Newton) Etchells; m. Terence Parsons, June 10, 1967 (div.); children: Catherine Casey Pyne, Shawn Pyne; m. 2d Richard Ullman Addelson, Oct. 31, 1980. A.B., Ind. U., 1961; Ph.D., Stanford U., 1968. Lectr. Bryn Mawr Coll., (Pa.), 1965-66, CCNY, N.Y.C., 1966-67; asst. prof. philosophy U. Ill., Chgo., 1967-72; prof. philosophy Smith Coll., Northampton, Mass., 1972—; assoc. editor Feminist Studies. Contbr. writings to anthologies and jours. Nat. Endowment for Humanities grantee, 1978-79; Nat. Endowment for Humanities fellow, 1978-79. Mem. Soc. for Women in Philosophy (exec. sec. Eastern div.). Office: Smith College Northampton MA 01060 *

ADDIS, SARA ALLEN, franchise executive; b. El Paso, Tex., May 15, 1930; d. Waldo Rufus and Cordelia Dean (Kerr) Allen; m. Bobby Joe Addis, June 5, 1949; children—Craig Dell, Alan Blake, Neil Clark, Sara Kathleen. Sec. to adminstr. Southwestern Gen. Hosp., El Paso, 1948-49; sec. to dir. of personnel U. Tex., El Paso, 1964-65; pres., founder Sara Care Franchise Corp., El Paso, 1978—. Named Small Bus. Person of Yr., Small Bus. Adminstrn., 1986, 87. Mem. Internat. Franchise Assn., Nat. Fedn. Ind. Businesses, Presidents Assn. Am. Mgmt. Assn., El Paso Better Bus. Bur., El Paso C. of C., Assn. Pioneer Women. (Entrepreneur of Yr.), Bus. and Profl. Women El Paso (Small Bus. Person of Yr. 1983, 85, 86, 87), Exec. Forum, Profl. Women's Network U. Tex. El Paso. Republican. Club: Lower Valley Women's. Lodge: Order Eastern Star. Avocations: oil painting; music; travel. Home: 8417 Parkland St El Paso TX 79925 Office: Sara Care Franchise Corp 1200 Golden Key Circle Suite 368 El Paso TX 79925

ADDISON, MARY JANE, civic worker; b. Beaumont, Tex.; d. Henry Davis and Corinne (Carter) Pond; R.N., Jefferson Davis Sch. Nursing, 1945; student U. Houston; m. Eugene Morse Addison, Mar. 10, 1946; children—Eugene Morse, Paul Davis. Mem. choir First Bapt. Ch.; den mother Cub Scouts, 6 years, recipient Den Mothers award, 1961; pres. Huntsville (Tex.) PTA, 1955-56, v.p. dist. bd., 1956-57, state life mem. PTA, 1967; pres. Women's Missionary Union, First Bapt. Ch., 1965-68, also Sunday Sch. tchr.; chmn. heritage com. Mayor's Bicentennial Com., 1974-76; chmn. city beautification com. Tex. Sesquicentennial Celebration, 1982-86; pres. Woman's Forum, Tex. Fedn. Womens Clubs, 1972-74, 80-81, named Woman of Year, 1974; charter and life mem. Hosp. Aux., pres., 1971-72; pres. Walker County Cancer Soc., 1983-84; bd. dirs. Cultural Arts Center, 71-72; chmn. bd. dirs. Sam Houston Meml. Mus. 1983-87; bd. dirs. Walker County Hist. Commn.; mem., dir., sponsor Community Choir; mem. mayors com. Bicentennial of the Constn. of U.S. Celebration, 1987—. Decorated Grand Peiory of Am. Order St. John of Jerusalem, dame Knights Hospitaller; recipient Cert. of Commendation, Heritage Com., 1980, 81. Mem. Daus. Republic of Tex. (pres. Houston chpt. 1970-75, 79-81, registrar 1975—, state rec. sec. gen. 1973-75, state 1st v.p. gen. 1975-77, pres. gen. 1977-79 library bd. 1981-83, Alamo bd. 1983-85, 87—), DAR (regent Mary Martin Elmore Scott chpt. 1972-74, 82-86), Daus. Am. Colonists (regent Capt. John Utie chpt., state corr. sec. 1977-79, state rec. sec. 1983-85, state 1st vice regent 1985-87), UDC (dist. rec. sec. 1974-76, dist. chmn. 1981-83, state historian 1984-86, pres. chpt. 1983-85), Colonial Dames Am., Dames of Ct. of Honor, Tex. Hist. Found. (dir., cert. of commendation 1980, 81, mem. state heritage com.), Walker County Geneal. Soc., San Jacinto Mus. History Assn., Lone Star Drama Hist. Assn. (state adv. bd.), Victorian Soc. (charter mem. Tex. chpt.), Am., Tex. (pres. 38th Dist. 1977-83) nurses assns., AMA, Spain and Tex. Soc., Tex., Tri-County (past pres.) med. auxs., Tex. Acad. Family Physicians (charter; state parliamentarian 1983-84), Beautify Tex. Council, Nat. Soc. Magna Charta Dames (state sec. 1988—), Daus. War of 1812, Colonial Dames of XVII Century.. Clubs: Garden (past pres. chmn. city beautification com.); Univ. Women Sam Houston State U. (charter).

ADDY, JO ALISON PHEARS, economist; b. Ger., May 2, 1951; d. William and Paula (Lee) Phears; B.A., Smith Coll., 1973; M.B.A., Adelphi U., 1975; postgrad. Stanford U., 1975-78; m. Tralance Obuama Addy, May 25, 1979; children—Mantse, Miishe, Dwetri. Economic analyst Morgan Guaranty, N.Y.C., 1973-75; econ. con. Nat. Planning Assn., Washington, 1976; economist Rand Corp., 1978; economist World Bank, Washington, 1979-80; asst. v.p., internat. economist Crocker Bank, San Francisco, 1980-85; asst. v.p., economist, money markets 1st RepublicBank, Dallas, 1985-87, prin. SEGI Internat., Dallas, 1987—; lectr. in field. NSF fellow, 1976-79. Mem. Am. Econ. Assn., Dallas Economist Club, Dallas Women's Found. Home: 1904 Rockcliff Ct Arlington TX 76012

ADELMAN, SANDIE SLOTKIN, educational administrator; b. Bkyn., Sept. 5, 1931; d. Sam and Ann (Kotick) Slotkin (dec.); m. Joseph Adelman, July 15, 1951 (dec.); children—Todd Fred, Beth Heidi. B.A., SUNY-Albany, 1952; M.A., Bklyn. Coll., 1954; M.S., L.I. U., Greenvale, N.Y., 1984. With N.Y.C. Bd. Edn., 1952—, city-wide supr. curriculum and evaluation, 1972-75, coordinator tng. and testing, 1975-76, dir. job tng. program Rikers Island, 1976-82, coordinator adult basic edn./high sch. equivalency services, Queens, 1983-86; dir. Queens Adult Learning Ctr., 1986—; cons. in field; guest lectr. Fordham U., L.I. U., 1972-74. Producer documentary: Manpower Training, the Next Decade, 1973. Sec. Nat. Council Jewish Women, Queens, 1959-66, v.p., 1960-62, pres., 1963-65; den mother, trainer Queens council Boy Scouts Am., 1963-67; treas. Queens Council Jewish Women, 1964; mem. exec. council Campfire Girls, Queens, 1965-70. Mem. Am. Vocat. Assn., Nat. Assn. female Execs. (network leader 1981—), N.Y. State Community/Continuing Edn., Women Adminstrs. in Vocat. Edn. (Who's Who award 1983), Am. Corrections Assn. (profl.), Internat. Corrections Assn. (profl.), Correctional Edn. Assn. Home: 89-51 208th St Queens NY 11427

ADILETTA, DEBRA J. OLSON, infosystems specialist; b. Gloucester, Mass., Oct. 1, 1959; d. Melvin Porter Jr. and Ruth Margaret (Dahlmer) Olson; m. Mark Anthony Adiletta, Aug. 25, 1984. BA, Coll. of Holy Cross, Worcester, Mass., 1981; MBA, U. Rochester, 1986. Systems analyst Eastman Kodak Co., Rochester, N.Y., 1981-85, infosystems specialist, 1985-86, personal computer area mgr., 1986-87, bus. anlayst, cons., 1987—. seminar instr., Rochester, 1987. Fin. advisor Sts. Peter and Paul Ch., Rochester, 1985-86; div. chairperson United Way, Rochester, 1987. Mem. Assn. Systems Mgmt., Holy Cross Alumni Assn. (sec. 1983-84, treas. 1984—). Office: Eastman Kodak Co 343 State St Rochester NY 14650

ADKINS, BETTY A., state legislator; b. Mpls., June 4, 1934; d. John Edward and Barbara (Graff) Whalen; m. Wally Adkins, 1956; children—Patrick, Susan, Michael, Kathleen, Caroline, Nancy. Student North Hennepin Community Coll.; student U. Minn., 1952-53. Formerly dep. clk. Otsego Twp., vice chmn. Wright County Bd. Adjustment, Minn.; mem. Minn. Senate, St. Paul, 1982—. Formerly chmn. Wright County Democratic-Farmer-Labor Party. Office: State Capitol Saint Paul MN 55155 also: 550 Central Ave E Saint Michael MN 55376 *

ADKINS, DONNA MARIA, publicist; b. Gary, Ind., Dec. 28, 1945; d. Fred and Sadie (Lamar) Anderson; 1 dau., Tamara. Student, Ind. U.-Gary, 1962-63, Hammond Bus. Coll., 1964-65. Reader service mgr. Kiver Pubs., Inc., Chgo., 1969-70; collections mgr. Contemporary Books, Inc., Chgo., 1973-78, publicity dir., 1978—. Mem. Black Ind. Polit. Orgn., Chgo., 1983—. Mem. Chgo. Women in Pub. Democrat. Baptist. Home: 7819 S Kimbark Ave Chicago IL 60619 Office: Contemporary Books Inc 180 N Michigan Ave Chicago IL 60601

ADKINS, ELIZABETH ANNE, clin. social worker; b. Danville, Ill., Apr. 8, 1941; d. Albert William and Elizabeth Adele (Bahnke) A.; B.A., So. Ill. U., 1963; M.S.W., San Diego State U., 1969. Tchr., Clarence (N.Y.) Cen. Jr. High Sch., 1963-64; asst. adminstr. D'Youville Coll., 1964; caseworker Erie County Welfare Dept., Buffalo, N.Y., 1964-65; child welfare worker Los Angeles County Dept. Adoptions, 1965-72; pub. health social worker Los Angeles County Pub. Health Dept., 1972-74; corp. sec. Health Adv. Group, Inc., Los Angeles, 1978-80; social work supr. Los Angeles County-U. So. Calif. Med. Ctr., Los Angeles, 1974—; clin. instr. Sch. Medicine U. So. Calif, 1986—. Mem. Los Angeles County Commn. on Life Support Policies, 1979-81; mem. adv. council bio-ethics NCCJ, 1977-78; mem. Santa Monica Symphony, 1970—. Lic. clin. social worker. Mem. Acad. Cert. Social Workers, Nat. Assn. Social Workers (chmn. pub. relations com.), Los Angeles County Bar Assn. Com. on Legal Aspects of Bioethics, Hastings Ctr. of Soc. Ethics and the Life Scis., Mensa, DAR. Home: 2700 N Cahuenga Blvd E #2207 Los Angeles CA 90068 Office: 1200 N State St Room 6433 Los Angeles CA 90033

ADKINS, MARILYN BIGGS, lawyer, consultant; b. East Greenwich, R.I., July 3, 1945; d. John Elmer and Merle Bonita (Irish) Biggs; m. John C. Adkins, Oct. 12. 1965 (div. Feb. 1978). BA, U. Denver, 1967, JD, 1982. Bar: Colo. 1982, U.S. Dist. Ct. Colo. 1982, U.S. Ct. Appeals (10th cir.) 1982. Owner Texaco Service Stas., Denver, 1971-78; legal asst., paralegal Law Offices of Hubert M. Safran, Denver, 1974-82; pvt. practice bookkeeping Denver, 1978-81; ptnr. Safran & Adkins, Denver, 1982—; leg. dir. Colo. Trial Lawyers Assn., Denver, 1982-87; mem. Dist. Atty.'s Arbitration Panel, Denver, 1976; active Colo. Supreme Ct. Pub. Edn. Com., 1984—. Contbr. chpt. on torts to Law in Colorado, 1987, articles to profl. jours. Instr. Denver Inner City Parish, 1970-75; mem. Anti-Defamation League Civil Rights Commn., Denver, 1983—; del. Democratic County Convs., Denver, 1975-78, 86; advisor U.S. Senate Com., Washington, 1978; trustee Temple Sinai, Denver, 1986-88. Mem. ABA, Colo. Bar Assn., Denver Bar Assn., Assn. Trial Lawyers Am., Colo. Trial Lawyers Assn. (bd. dirs. 1983—), Trial Lawyers for Pub. Justice, U. Denver Alumni Assn. Democrat. Jewish. Office: Safran & Adkins 1832 Clarkson St Denver CO 80218

ADLER, JANE EVE, internationally syndicated columnist, cartoonist and illustrator; b. Providence, Oct. 8, 1944; d. Frank Kozlov and Ruth Cohen; m. Edwin I. Adler, Feb. 19, 1961; children—Lindsay, Steven. B.A., U. R.I., 1971. Art dir. Trinity Sq. Theatre, 1971-72; T.V. talk show hostess, writer, artistic dir. original plays PBS 1971-72; weekly columnist/illustrator Boston Herald, Providence Journal, National Observer, 1972-77; N. Am. Syndicate syndicated columnist/illustrator, 1977—; tchr., lectr., TV and radio guest in horticulture and writing. Author monthly nat. mag. columns; writer of books on children (with Hank Ketchum of Dennis the Menace), 1982—; columnist for Boston Herald on child healthcare, 1984—; travel writer for Whitegate News Syndicate, 1987—. Participant in numerous one woman and group art shows, 1965—. Organizer of free painting course for women at U. R.I.; active in numerous charity and cultural activities. Recipient awards for writing from various groups such as R.I. Fed. Garden Clubs. Mem. R.I. Horticulture Soc. (organizer), Garden Writers of Am., N.Y. Art Dirs. Club, Childhood and Adult Devel. Resources Inst. (founder, bd. dirs.) Jewish. Lodges: Masons, B'nai Brith. Office: 71 Faunce Dr Providence RI 02906

ADLER, JOAN LEE, communication company executive; b. Syracuse, N.Y., Apr. 13, 1953; d. Daniel K. and Rosamond (Small) A. BA, Ithaca (N.Y.) Coll., 1975; MS in Communications, Syracuse U., 1976. Asst. to producer Sta. WCNY-TV, Syracuse, 1975-76; prodn. asst. various prodn. cos., Los Angeles, 1976-78; sec. Off-Line Inc., Burbank, Calif., 1977-78; ops. scheduler The Post Group, Hollywood, Calif., 1978-80; dir. ops. The Post Group, Hollywood, 1980-81, v.p. ops., 1981—; adj. lectr. Syracuse U., 1987—; redruiter Stephens Coll., Columbia, Mo., 1987—; cons. in field. Mem. Acad. TV Arts and Scis., Am. Women in Radio and TV, Nat. Assn. Female Execs. Democrat. Jewish. Office: The Post Group 6335 Homewood Ave Hollywood CA 90028

ADLER, LEONORE LOEB, psychologist; b. Karlsruhe, W. Ger., May 2, 1921; d. Leo and Elsie (Laemle) Loeb; m. Helmut E. Adler, May 22, 1943; children—Barry Peter, Beverly Sharmaine, Evelyn Renée. B.A. cum laude, Queens Coll., CUNY, 1968; Ph.D., Adelphi U., 1972. Research asst. Am. Mus. Natural History, N.Y.C., 1956-84; adj. asst. prof. psychology Coll. S.I., CUNY, 1974-80; research assoc. Mystic Marinelife Aquarium (Conn.), 1976-85; assoc. prof. dept. psychology, dir. Inst. for Cross-Cultural and Cross-Ethnic Studies, Molloy Coll., Rockville Centre, N.Y., 1980—; chmn. internat. and nat. confs. Author book chpts.; translator: This is the Dachshund, 1966, 2d rev. edit., 1975; co-editor: Comparative Psychology at Issue, 1973, Language, Sex and Gender: Does "la Différence" Make a Difference, 1979; editor: Issues in Cross-Cultural Research, 1977; Cross-Cultural Research at Issue, 1982; contbr. articles and chpts. to handbooks, profl. jours. and encys. Mem. to gov.'s com. on women N.Y. State Women's Com., 1977. Recipient Disting. Contbr. of Decade award, Internat. Orgn. Study Group Tensions, 1981. Fellow N.Y. Acad. Scis.; mem. Am. Psychol. Assn. (network of reps. of com. on women in psychology 1982—), Eastern Psychol. Assn. (bd. dirs. 1985-86, 87—), N.Y. State Psychol. Assn. (pres. div. social psychology 1978-79, 80-82, 84-85; pres. div. acad. psychology 1982-83, 88—; mem. council reps. 1981-84, 86-87; chmn. com. women's issues 1982-84, plaque for outstanding achievement from women's com. 1984, medallion from social div. 1984, Kurt Lewin award 1985), Internat. Assn. Cross-Cultural Psychology, Soc. Cross-Cultural Research, Internat. Orgn. Study Group Tensions (mng. editor Internat. Jour. Group Tensions, 1978-84, assoc. editor 1984-85), Animal Behavior Soc., Internat. Soc. Comparative Psychology, Assn. Women in Sci., Soc. Advancement Social Psychology, Internat. Council Psychologists (treas. 1983-85), Cheiron, the Internat. Soc. for History of Behavioral and Social Scis., Queens County Psychol. Assn. (pres.-elect 1985-87, pres. 1987-88), Psi Chi (faculty adviser Molloy Coll., 1980—), Alpha Sigma Lambda, Zeta Epsilon Gamma. Jewish. Home: 162-14 86th Ave Jamaica NY 11432 Office: Molloy Coll Inst Cross Cultural and Cross Ethnic Studies 1000 Hempstead Ave Rockville Centre NY 11570

ADOLPH, MARY ROSENQUIST, financial company executive; b. Springfield, Mass., Oct. 7, 1949; d. Jesse Woodson and Doris May (Marquette) Rosenquist; m. Earl Anthony Soares, Mar. 18, 1972 (div. 1982); m. Joseph Edward Adolph, Oct. 3, 1986. Student San Domenico Sch., 1966-68, Dominican Coll., San Rafael, 1967-69, Calif., San Francisco Conservatory of Music, 1968-70; A.A., Coll. of Marin, 1969. Asst. v.p. Western Travelers Life Ins. Co./Putnam Fin. Services, San Rafael, 1970-80; v.p. Unimarc, Ltd., Novato, Calif., 1980-83; v.p. mktg. Western States Monetary Planning Services, Inc., Newhall, Calif., 1983—. Mem. exec. com. San Marin Valley Homeowners Assn., 1979-81. Mem. Internat. Assn. Fin. Planners, Life Underwriters Assn. Democrat. Roman Catholic. Home: 14710 Burbank Blvd #102 Van Nuys CA 91411 Office: Western States Monetary Planning Services Inc 23030 Lyons Ave Suite 209 Newhall CA 91321

ADONAYLO, RAQUEL, pianist, singer; b. Uruguay; came to U.S., 1975; d. Ruben and Felicia (Bornstein) A.; grad. W. Kolischer Conservatory of Music, Uruguay, 1944; student of E. Casal-Chapi and Lazare-Levy, France; vocal student of Ninon Vallin, 1951-56; m. Ziszko Peniazek, Apr. 26, 1952; children—Pablo, Eduard, Ana. Concert pianist, 1941—; soprano, appearances in opera and oratorio, also recitalist, performing throughout world, 1952—, including numerous contemporary world premieres; voice instr. Curtis Inst. Music, Phila., 1975—; pvt. piano tchr., Uruguay, 1947-62, Israel, 1963-75, Rosemont, Pa., 1976—; dir. Ninon Vallin Sch. Singing, 1953-58; faculty Rubin Acad., Jerusalem, 1963-64; vocal coach, 1956—; chamber music coach, dir. seminars, throughout world; rec. artist Columbia Records. Recipient Grand prize as soloist with orch. Record Circle of Critics, 1966. Address: 439 N Ithan Ave Rosemont PA 19010

ADREON, BEATRICE MARIE RICE, pharmacist; b. Huntington, W.Va., July 23, 1929; d. Lloyd Emerson and Beatrice (Odell) Rice; student Mary Washington Coll., 1947-49; B.S. in Pharmacy, Med. Coll. Va., 1952; M.A. in Spl. Studies and Women's Studies, George Washington U., 1976; m. Harry Barnes Adreon, Jr., Dec. 27, 1952. Summer vol. worker pharmacies De Paul Hosp., Norfolk, Va., 1949, U.S. Marine Hosp., Norfolk, 1950; pharmacist Washington Clinic, 1954-71; counselor George Washington U., 1976-77, cons. gerontology health scis. dept., 1977—; cons. medicine control traffic patterns nursing homes Cross & Adreon, Washington, 1962—; founder, pres. Pharmacy Counseling Services, Inc., 1978—. Instr. advanced first aid ARC, 1952—, civil def. instr., 1952—; vol. Spanish Edn. Devel. Center, Washington, 1972; mem. Arlington (Va.) Community Services Bd., chmn. com. substance abuse. Recipient Arnold and Marie Schwartz award in pharmacy, 1980. Mem. Acad. Pharmacy Practice, Am. Pharm. Assn., Va. Pharm. Assn., Potomac Pharmacists Assn., AAAS, Am. Inst. History of Pharmacy, Nat. Council Patient Info. and Edn. (task force pub. info.), Panhellenic Assn., Kappa Epsilon. Episcopalian (mem. bishop's com. neighborhood services 1967-69, chmn. services for aged div. 1967-69). Contbr. articles in field to profl. jours. Home: 4524 N 19th Rd Arlington VA 22207

ADRI (ADRIENNE STECKLING), fashion designer; b. St. Joseph, Mo.. Ed., Sch. Fine Arts, Washington U., St. Louis, Parson Sch. Design. Owner, pres. Adri Clotheslab Inc., N.Y.C. Recipient Coty award, 1982. Office: Adri 143 W 20th New York NY 10011§

ADRIAN, PATRICIA LEE GRIMSHAW, association executive; b. Reliance, S.D., July 20, 1938; d. Walter George and Dorthy Veronica (Zastrow) Grimshaw; student Sinte Gleska U., 1973; m. Robert Earl Adrian, Oct. 12, 1957; children—James Robert, Thomas Edward, Kevin Patrick, David Duane. Sec., Cherry Todd Electric, 1956-57; tchr. White River (S.D.) Ind. Sch. Dist., 1970-71; dir. S.D. Beef Industry Council, 1970-73, pres., 1972-73, exec. v.p., 1973—; exec. sec., lobbyist S.D. Livestock Assn., part-time 1977—; pres. Mktg. Internat., Inc., 1981—; ptnr. Prairie Press; dir. Nat. Livestock and Meat Bd. Gov.'s rep. to nutrition symposium Old West Regional Commn., 1979-80; elected chmn. Beef Industry Council of Nat. Livestock and Meat Bd., 1986—; mem. S.D. Indsl. Devel. Commn., 1979-82; mem. S.D. Agrl. Mktg. Commn., 1980-82; mem. adv. com. S.D. Vocat. Tech. Edn. Commn. for Agr.; bd. dirs. S.D. Livestock Expansion Found., 1981—; vice-chmn. Cattleman's Beef Promotion and Research Bd. Operating com., 1986—. Recipient Disting. Service award S.D. Stockgrowers Assn., 1974, S.D. State U., 1976, S.D. State U. Alumni Assn., 1987. Mem. Nat. Fedn. Press Women, Am. Soc. Assn. Execs., Nat. Cattlemen's Assn., S.D. Livestock Assn., Am. Agri-Women, U.S. Meat Export Fedn. (dir. 1980-82), S.D. Press Women's Assn., S.D. CowBelles (pres.). Republican. Roman Catholic. Home: Star Route Box 222 White River SD 57579 Office: SD Beef Industry Council 110 W Capitol St Pierre SD 57501

ADVINCULA, MARIETTA MAGSAYSAY, college dean, real estate broker; b. Manila, May 4, 1939; came to U.S., 1961, naturalized, 1978; d. Gregorio and Rosalia (Peralta) Magsaysay; m. Ronaldo C. Advincula, Dec. 4, 1965; children: Monica Rose, Ronna Marisse, Melanie Rhoda. BS in Home Econs., U. Philippines, 1959; MS, U. Kans., 1965; cert. in hosp. adminstrn. U. Ill., 1980-81. Dietetic intern Philippine Gen. Hosp., Manila, 1960, U. Minn. Hosp., Mpls., 1962; reviewer/lectr. Bd. Exam. for Dietitians, Philippines, 1967-71; nutritionist YWCA, Philippines, 1971; tng. specialist applied nutrition program in Philippines, UNICEF, 1970-71; instr. food and nutrition Coll. Home Econs., U. Philippines, 1965-71; supr. menu selection West Suburban Hosp., Oak Park, Ill., 1971-72; clin. dietitian/teaching dietitian Weiss Meml. Hosp., Chgo., 1972-73, chief therapeutic dietitian, 1973-76; devel. specialist Malcolm X Coll., City Colls. of Chgo., 1976-78; reviewer/lectr. Northside Traineeship Council/U. Ill., 1974-81; clin. asst. prof. U. Ill. Sch. Associated Med. Scis., Med. Dietetics Curriculum, 1975-79; asst. dir. dept. dietetics U. Ill. Hosp., Chgo., 1976-79; asst. prof. dept. nutrition and med. dietetics U. Ill. Coll. Associated Health Professions, Chgo., 1979-81; asst. dean adult continuing edn. dept. Truman Coll., City Colls. Chgo., 1981—, dir. vol. services office, 1987—; cons. food service and nutrition education Intervention, 1979-80; cons., instr. inquiry edn. Augustana Hosp. Sch. Nursing, 1980; preceptor Am. Dietetic Assn. Traineeship, Weiss Hosp., 1973-76, Hosp. and Ednl. Food Service Suprs., 1973-76, Am. Dietetic Assn., U. Ill. Hosp., 1976-77; assoc. Nat. Inst. Edn. Inquiry, 1976-78; coordinator staff devel., continuing edn. seminars Weiss Hosp., 1973-76, U. Ill. Hosp., 1976-79; coordinator interviewing, counseling and med. recording skills workshop Am. Dietetic Assn., 1979-81; lectr. dept. nutrition and med. dietetics Coll. Associated Health Profs., U. Ill., 1979-80; cons. nutrition program Mayor's Office Sr. Citizen and the Handicapped, Chgo City Wide Coll., 1981, Nutrition Edn. Tng. Program, Ctr. Urban Program, Bd. Edn., Chgo., 1981; founding pres. Lakambini (Filipino) Performing Arts, 1975—; pres.-elect Networking Together, Inc., 1987-88; bd. dirs. Midwest Women's Ctr.; mem. adv. bd. Alderman Schiller's Social Service Com. Author videotape program: Sociocultural Aspect of Food Behavior Slide, 1981; chmn. revision com. Manual of Clinical Dietetics, 1981; author: Nutrition of Children, Mothers, and the Aged, 1973. Editor: The Home Economist, 1968-70. Contbr. articles to profl. jours. Mem. Arts and Humanities Task Force; organizer, liaison Filipino Community of OLM Parish, 1979-85; chmn. Ill. Minority Women's Caucus, 1986-87; bd. mem. Mother's Club, Our Lady of Mercy Sch., 1980-82; treas. Eugene Civic Neighborhood Assn., 1982-83, v.p., 1981-82; mem. sch. bd. Our Lady of Mercy Sch., 1982-85, pres., 1983-85; mem. Archdiocesan Pastoral Council, 1984-88; chmn. Task Force on Consolidation and Expansion, 1986; mem. adv. bd. Assn. Chinese from Indochina. U. Philippines scholar, 1955-59; named Most Outstanding New Citizen, Nutrition Care Adminstrn., Met. Chgo. Citizenship Council, 1979; recipient Certs. of Recognition, Filipino Spiritual Community Action, Philippines Week, 1983, Truman Coll. Student Govt., 1984-86; named Most

Outstanding Filipino in the Midwest in the Field of Edn., Cavite Assn. Am., 1987; recipient Disting. Women's award Women's Network to Re-elect Mayor Harold Washington, Outstanding award in Field of Edn. Networking Together, Inc., 1987. Mem. Am. Assn. Philippines Dietitians (chmn. 1985-87), Am. Dietetic Assn., Ill. Adult and Continuing Educators, Ill. Dietetic Assn., Soc. Nutrition Edn., Women in Mgmt., Chgo. Nutrition Assn., Food and Instn. Systems Mgmt. Edn. Council, Filipino Am. Women's Network, Philippine Educators Assn., Chgo. Dietetic Assn., Ill. Consultation Ethnicity in Edn., Nutrition Today, Ill. Council Women's Programs, Am. Assn. Diabetes Eduors, Nat. Assn. Female Execs., Cons. Dietitians in Health Care Facilities, Asian/Pacific Womens' Network, Northside Realty Bd., Minority Women's Caucus, Phi Kappa Phi. Roman Catholic. Avocations: sewing, gardening, cooking, reading, swimming. Home: 5021 N Monticello Chicago IL 60625 Office: Truman Coll 1145 W Wilson St Chicago IL 60640

AERY, SHAILA ROSALIE, state educational administrator; b. Tulsa, Dec. 4, 1938; d. Silas Cleveland and Billie (Brewer) A. B.S., U. Okla., 1964; M.S., Okla. State U., 1972, Ed.D., 1975. Spl. asst., chancellor Okla. Regents for Higher Edn., Oklahoma City, 1977; spl. asst., chancellor U. Mo., Columbia, 1978-80, asst. provost acad. affairs, 1980-81; dep. commr. higher edn. State of Mo., Jefferson City, 1981, commr., 1982—; dir. Mo. Higher Edn. Loan Authority, St. Louis, 1982—; commr. Edn. Commn. of the States, Denver, 1983—; mem. exec. bd. State Higher Edn. Offices, Denver, 1983—. Contbr. articles to profl. jours. Mem. AAUW. Democrat. Episcopalian. Office: Higher Edn Coordinating Bd 101 Adams St Jefferson City MO 65101

AFRIDI, PARVEEN NIAZ, psychiatrist; b. Farrukhabad, India, June 20, 1944; came to U.S., 1972; d. Niaz Mohammed and Zakia Sultana Khan-Afridi; M.D. (Merit scholar), S.M.S. Med. Coll., Japiur, India, 1968; m. Mohammed Kalimi, Apr. 26, 1970 (div. Nov. 1975); 1 son, Omar. Rotating intern S.M.S. Med. Coll. Hosp., Jaipur, 1968-69; attending med. officer dept. ob-gyn, Kota and Meerut, India, 1969-72; postdoctoral research Inst. Cancer Research, Columbia U., N.Y.C., 1972-73; resident in psychiatry N.Y. U.-Bellevue Med. Center, N.Y.C., 1974-77; attending psychiatrist Manhattan Psychiat. Center, N.Y.C., 1977-80; clin. instr. psychiatry Albert Einstein Med. Center, N.Y.C. and attending psychiatrist Jacobi Hosp., 1980-81; clin. instr. psychiatry Downstate Med. Center, N.Y.C. and sr. attending psychiatrist Kings County Hosp., N.Y.C., 1981-83, clin. asst. prof SUNY-Health Sci. Ctr., Bklyn., 1983—, sr. attending psychiatrist Kings County Hosp., 1983—. Named one of best psychiat. residents Manhattan Psychiat. Center, 1974-75; recipient Physicians Recognition award AMA, 1977, 83. Mem. Am. Psychiat. Assn., Menninger Found., N.Y. Acad. Scis., Am. Psychiatrists from India (life), N.Y. U.-Bellevue Psychiat. Soc., Assn. Indians in Am., Assn. Asian and Indian Women in Am. Home: Gramercy Spire 142 E 16th St Apt 6D New York NY 10003 Office: 451 Clarkson Ave Brooklyn NY 11203

AFTERGOOD, LILLA, biochemist, nutritionist; b. Krakow, Poland, Jan. 10, 1925; came to U.S., 1949, naturalized, 1956; d. Jacob and Zofia (Selzer) Anisfeld; B.S., Sorbonne U., 1948; M.S., U. So. Calif., 1951, Ph.D., 1956; m. Edgar Aftergood, Aug. 17, 1949; children—David, Steven, Annette. Sr. research asso. dept. biochemistry U. So. Calif., 1956-59; asso. research biochemist Sch. Public Health, UCLA, 1959-80. Mem. Am. Inst. Nutrition, Am. Heart Assn., Council on Arteriosclerosis, AAAS, Sigma Xi. Co-author: Nutrition for Today, 1973; Nutrition and Motherhood, 1982; mem. editorial bd. Nutrition and the MD; contbr. numerous articles to sci. jours.

AGARD, EMMA ESTORNEL, psychotherapist; b. Bronx, N.Y.; m. John Victor Agard, Feb. 25, 1968. BA, Queens Coll.; MSW, Fordham U., 1962; cert. in Psychoanalytic Psychotherapy, Tng. Inst. for Mental Health, 1979; cert. in Child and Adolescent Psychotherapy, Postgrad. Ctr. for Mental Health, 1982. Supr. social work Foster Care Div., N.Y.C., 1968-72; asst. dir. Henry St. Settlement Urban Family Ctr., N.Y.C., 1972-74; supr. Tng. Inst. for Mental Health, N.Y.C., 1974—; pvt. practice psychotherapist N.Y.C., 1974—; lectr. social work Columbia U., N.Y.C., 1977-80; adj. asst. prof. NYU, 1978-80; field instr. N.Y.C. Housing Authority, 1974-80; dist. dir., cons. Am. Consultation Ctrs., Bklyn. and N.Y.C., 1985—. Mem. Albemarle-Kenmore Neighborhood Assn., Bklyn., 1974—. Fellow N.Y. State Soc. Clin. Social Work Psychotherapists (pres. Bklyn. chpt. 1988—); mem. Profl. Soc. of Tng. Inst. for Mental Health (sec.), Nat. Assn. Social Workers (diplomate), Acad. Cert. Social Workers, Nat. Coalition 100 Black Women, Delta Sigma Theta. Address: 221 E 21st St Brooklyn NY 11226

AGARD, KATHRYN ANN, hospital administrator; b. Muskegan, Mich., Mar. 1, 1949; d. Adolph William and Lucille Kathryn (Bohland) Ross; m. Hans Hewitt Agard, Feb. 25, 1972; children: Corey Joel, Kelly Erin. BA, Albion Coll., 1971; MPA, Western Mich. U., 1976, postgrad., 1982—. Life cons. Ottawa Mental Health, Holland, Mich., 1972-73, Muskegan Mental Health, 1974-77; chief exec. officer Muskegan Planned Parenthood, 1974-77; community service dir. Muskegan Community Coll., 1977-78; Great Lake regl. dir. Planned Parenthood Fedn. Am., Detroit, 1978-79; chief ops. officer Planned Parenthood Southeastern Pa., Phila., 1979-81, chief exec. officer, 1981-83; mgr. community relations Hackley Hosp., Muskegan, 1983-85, dir. planning and mktg., 1985-88; found. developer Council Mich. Founds., Grand Haven, 1988—; founder Compass, Muskegan, 1983—; v.p. Advanced Health Services, Grand Rapids, Mich., 1986-87; chmn. health care curriculum, Grand Valley State Coll., Allendale, Mich., 1987—. Contbr. articles to profl. jours. cons. Girl Scouts USA, 1986, Planned Parenthood Hospitality, 1985, Mich. Domestic Violence Coalition, 1986. Mem. New Muskegan (nominating com. chmn. 1987—), Muskegan C. of C. (cons., Recognition award 1986). Office: Council Mich Founds PO Box 599 Grand Haven MI 49417

AGATE, CAROL, law adminstrator, lawyer; b. Providence, Mar. 10, 1934; d. William S. and Matilda Orkin; divorced; children: James, Marjorie. AB, Brown U., 1955; postgrad., UCLA, 1974; JD, U. Conn., 1974. Bar: Calif. 1974. Dep. city atty. City of Los Angeles, 1975-77; sole practice Los Angeles, 1977-80, 85-87; clin. prof. Loyola Law Sch., Los Angeles, 1980-84; law clk. to presiding justice High Ct. of Am. Samoa, Pago Pago, 1984-85; adminstrv. law judge State of Calif., 1988—.

AGBAYANI, MARY ALLEN, travel company executive, educator; b. The Philippines, Aug. 8, 1946; came to U.S. 1968; d. Constancio and Benita (Cagaanan) Arbotante; m. Randolph Agbayani, Sept. 6, 1973. BS in Edn., Philippine Normal Coll., 1965; MEd, Northeastern U., 1973. Cert. travel cons. Travel cons. Winters World Travel, LaGrange, Ill., 1979-83; instr. phys. edn. Chgo. Bd. Edn., 1971-83; instr. Ill. Inst. Tech., Chgo., 1980-81, Triton Coll., River Grove, Ill., 1981—; pres. Berkeley Travel, Ill., 1983-86; mgr. Cardel Travel, Stone Park, Ill., 1986—; dir. Mary Allen Travel Sch., Berkeley, 1984—; cons. M.A. & Assocs., Berkeley, 1985—, Cragin Travel, Chgo., 1987—. Author: Passport to a New Horizon, 1985. Mem. Philippine Educators Assn. (sec. 1979), Am. Soc. Travel Agts., Am. Retail Travel Agts., Inst. Cert. Travel Agts. Roman Catholic. Avocations: tennis, travel. Office: Cardel Travel 1522 N Mannheim Rd Stone Park IL 60165

AGEE, NELLE HULME, art history educator; b. Memphis, May 22, 1940; d. John Eulice and Nelle (Ray) Hulme; m. Bob R. Agee, June 7, 1958; children: Denise, Robyn. Student Memphis State U., 1971-72, postgrad., 1978; BA, Union U., Jackson, Tenn., 1978; postgrad. Jackson State U., 1978, Seminole Okla. Coll., 1982, Okla. Bapt. U., 1984. Cert. tchr. art, history, Ky., Tenn. Offices services supr. So. Bapt. Theol. Sem., Louisville, 1961-64; kindergarten tchr. Shively Heights Bapt. Ch., Louisville, 1965-70; editorial asst. Little Publs., agrl. mags., Memphis, 1973-75; tchr. art Humboldt High Sch., Tenn., 1978-82; vis. artist-in-schs. Tenn. Arts Commn., Nashville, 1978, 81, 82; adj. prof. art history Seminole Coll., Okla., 1985-86, 87—; frequent speaker art orgns., ch. groups; tchr. art workshops Humboldt City Sch. system; tchr. Cultural Arts Day Camp, Jackson, Tenn., 1982; nat. pres. ministers' wives conf. So. Bapt. Conv., 1987-88; vol. Mabee-Gerrer Mus., Shawnee. Exhibited art in various shows. Active Salvation Army Aux., Shawnee; v.p. Union U. Woman's Club, 1976-77, pres., 1978. Recipient Disting. Classroom Tchr. award Tenn. Edn. Assn., 1982. Mem. Univ. Alliance, Okla Bapt. U., Alpha Delta Kappa. Democrat. Baptist. Avocations: stained glass, pottery making, travel. Home: 616 University Pkwy Shawnee OK 74801

AGGER, CAROLYN E., lawyer; b. N.Y.C., May 27, 1909. A.B., Barnard Coll., 1931; M.A., U. Wis., 1932; LL.B. cum laude, Yale U., 1938. Bar: D.C. 1938, U.S. Tax Ct. 1943, U.S. Supreme Ct. 1950, U.S. Ct. Claims 1956, U.S. Ct. Appeals (6th cir.) 1958. Atty., NLRB, 1938-39; atty. tax div. U.S. Dept. Justice, Washington, 1939-43; now ptnr. Arnold & Porter, Washington. Mem. Order of Coif. Office: Arnold & Porter Thurman Arnold Bldg 1200 New Hampshire Ave NW Washington DC 20036

AGLIO, SUSAN MARY, computer consultant; b. Springfield, Mass., Apr. 24, 1957; d. Anthony M. and Sophie A. (Starzyk) A.; m. Pablo O. Serritella, Sept. 24, 1983. BS in Info. Systems, George Mason U., 1985. Personnel asst. Sperry Inc., Reston, Va., 1982-84, programming asst., 1984, assoc. mem. program staff, 1984-86; computer cons. Arthur Andersen and Co., Washington, 1986-87; systems analyst Advanced Technology Systems, Falls Church, Va., 1987—; instr. Microcomputer Software, No. Va. Community Coll., Alexandria, 1987. Mem. Nat. Assn. Female Execs. Home: 3006 Virginia Dare Ct Chantilly VA 22021

AGUILAR, ISABEL (CHAVELA), counselor, academic administrator; b. Calexico, Calif., Nov. 5, 1936; d. Silbestre Macias and Petra (Soria) Badajós; m. Ruben Aguilar, Apr. 7, 1956; children: Ruben Anthony, John Xavier. AA, Imperial Valley Coll.; BA, San Diego State U., MS. Cert. community coll. counselor, adminstr., instr., personnel worker, Calif. Receptionist, interpreter Imperial County Hosp., El Centro, Calif., 1955-58; clerk typist Immigration and Naturalization Service, Calexico, 1958-60; med. clinic mgr. M.P. Ajalat Clinic, Calexico, 1961-72; admissions and records clk. San Diego State U.-Imperial Valley Campus, Calexico, 1972-77, admissions officer, 1977-80, admissions counselor and vet., 1980-83, outreach coordinator, counselor, alumni dir., scholarship coordinator,campus staff senator disabled students services, student info. coordinator, student life advisor, new student orientation coordinator, supr. high schs., student counselors, student's info., San Diego campus, outreach coordinator for local area, chmn., coordinator ann. Women's Non-traditional Conf. for High Sch. Women, 11 years.; Campus test coordinator, 1977—; campus liaison Imperial Valley Coll., Imperial, Calif., 1980—; mem. Instructionally Related com., Commencement com.; advisor Associated Student Council. Chmn. City Beautification Com., Calexico, 1980—; chmn. Affirmative Action Adv. Cons. to Bd. of Suprs., El Centro, 1983—. Recipient San Diego State U. Annual Alumna award, 1980; Delta Kappa Gamma scholar, 1978. Mem. Advocated for Women in Academia, Imperial Valley Guidance Assn. (sec. 1985-86), Raza Advocates for Calif. Higher Edn., Western Assn. of Ednl. Opportunity Personnel. Democrat. Roman Catholic. Lodge: Soroptimists (pres. Calexico club 1983-84, v.p. 1982-83, sec. 1984-85, publicity mgr. 1981-82, alternate del. 1985-86). Home: 814 Rockwood Ave Calexico CA 92231 Office: San Diego State U Imperial Valley 720 Heber Ave Calexico CA 92231

AGUILAR, OLIVIA, association executive; b. Phoenix, May 2, 1952; d. Carlos Ramirez and Frances (Soto) A. BA in Edn., Ariz. State U., 1975. Lic. elem. tchr. Elem. librarian Glendale (Ariz.) Sch. Dist., 1975-79, Tillamook (Oreg.) Sch. Dist. #9, 1979-84; organizer Oreg. Edn. Assn., Eugene, 1984; mem. field staff Alaska div. NEA, Anchorage, 1984-86; human and civil rights specialist NEA, Washington, 1987—; arbitrator auto line Better Bus. Bur., Washington, 1987. Fellow NEA Staff Orgn. Democrat. Office: NEA 1201 16th St NW Washington DC 20036

AHART, MARY KATHLEEN, battery manufacturing company executive; b. Elgin, Ill., Dec. 19, 1953; d. Frances George and Rosebud Marie (Attardo) Cumpata; m. Steve A. Ahart, July 25, 1975; children: William Cody, Joseph Charles. BS in Edn., No. Ill. U., 1975; postgrad. in bus. adminstrn., Lewis U., 1986—. Mgmt. trainee Southland Corp., Chgo., 1975-76; sales rep. Duracell, U.S.A., Oakbrook, Ill., 1976-80; sales mgr. Duracell, U.S.A., Oakbrook, 1980—. Mem. Nat. Assn. Female Execs. Home: 767 Medford Dr Carol Stream IL 60188 Office: Duracell USA 1211 W 22d St Suite 708 Oak Brook IL 60521

AHERN, MARGARET ANN, nun, nurse, educator; b. Manchester, N.H., Nov. 23, 1931; d. Timothy Joseph and Helen Bridget (Kearns) Ahern; R.N., Sacred Heart Hosp. Sch. Nursing, 1952; BS in Nursing, Mt. St. Mary Coll., 1957; MS in Nursing, Cath. U. Am., 1965. Entered Sisters of Mercy, Roman Cath. Ch., 1953; staff nurse Sacred Heart Hosp., Manchester, 1954-57, operating room supr., 1957-62, med.-surg. nursing instr., 1962-66, dir. Sch. Nursing, 1966-75; dir. Sch. Nursing, Cath. Med. Center, Manchester, N.H., 1975-79, dir. dept. edn. and mem. sr. mgmt., 1979-87; pres. Cath. Med. Ctr Networks, Inc., 1987—. Chmn. bd. dirs. Health Edn. Consortium, 1977—; bd. dirs. Vis. Nurse Assn., 1981-87; adv. bd. Hesser Coll., 1980—, N.H. Voc-Tech. Coll., 1979—; mem. United Health Systems Agy., 1977-83; mem. adv. council on continuing edn. St. Anselm Coll., 1978—; mem. gen. chpt. Sisters of Mercy, 1968-70, 79-81, chmn. fin. bd., 1981-86, chmn. Bd. Conciliation and Arbitration, 1982-87. Recipient Distinguished Women Leaders award YMCA, 1986. Mem. Am. Nurses Assn., N.H. Nurses Assn., Nat. League for Nursing, New Eng. Cath. Hosp. Assn., New Eng. Edn. and Research Orgn., N.H. Heart Assn., Sigma Theta Tau. Democrat. Roman Catholic. Contbr. articles to profl. jours. Home: 647 Canal St Manchester NH 03104 Office: Cath Med Ctr Network 228 Maple St Manchester NH 03103

AHERN, MARY MARGARET, art director; b. N.Y.C., Aug. 12, 1940; d. Maurice Francis and Marie Hanora (Tonry) A. Cert., Cooper Union Art Sch., 1961, BFA (hon.), 1976; BS in Edn., NYU, 1968. Asst. art dir., The Viking Press, N.Y.C., 1961-62; book designer Mus. Modern Art, N.Y.C., 1962-66; sr. book designer Random House, N.Y.C., 1968-71; juvenile art dir. Atheneum Pubs., N.Y.C., 1975-87. Mem. The Typophiles, Am. Inst. Graphic Arts, Type Dirs. Club, Am. Printing History Assn. Home: 35-11 85 St Jackson Heights NY 11372 Office: Simon and Schuster Juveniles 1230 Avenue of the Americas New York NY 10020

AHLE, PATTI ADAIR, management analyst; b. Enid, Okla., May 20, 1953; d. Richard Baxter Jr. and Mildred Louella (Youngblood) Adair; m. Michael James Ahle, Apr. 4, 1987. BA in History, U. Okla., 1976. Program analyst Tng. Doctrine Cmmd., U.S. Army, Ft. Sill, Okla., 1978-83; mgmt. analyst Tng. Doctrine Cmmd., U.S. Army, Anniston, Ala., 1983-85, U.S. Army C.E., Sacramento, 1985—; pvt. practice cons., Sacramento, 1986—. Co-author: Productivities Improvement Techniques, 1986. Mem. Am. Soc. Mil. Comptrollers, U. Okla. Alumni Assn., Alpha Chi Omega. Home: 2650 Stonecreek Dr Apt 222 Sacramento CA 95833

AHNEMAN, PATRICIA MAE, pilot; b. Parkersburg, W.Va., Oct. 29, 1951; d. Theodore John and Patricia Mae (Godman) A. Student, Wagner Coll., 1969-73, Embry-Riddle U., 1987—. Cert. airline transport pilot CW46, comml. pilot, flight instr., ground instr., aircraft dispatcher. Standardbred trainer Saddle Rock Stables, Westbury, N.Y., 1975-78; flight instr., flight sch. mgr. D.R. Aviation, Inc., Ft. Lauderdale, Fla., 1978-80; co-pilot CW46, DC 3,4,6, CV440 Am. Flyers Co., Inc., Ft. Lauderdale, 1978-85; capt. CW46, office mgr. Miami (Fla.) Air Lease, Inc., 1985-86; FAA liaison Millon Air, Inc., Miami, 1986-87; capt. CW46, co-pilot Am. Flyers Co., Inc., Miami, 1987—. Vol. Sr. Citizens Assisting, Coconut Grove, Fla., 1985—. Recipient Vol. Service award Am. Cancer Soc., 1968, 69, Vol. Service award St. Brigid's Ch., Westbury, N.Y., 1975, 76; named Outstanding Vol. Southside Hosp., Bay Shore, N.Y., 1966-70, Outstanding Vol. March of Dimes, Westbury, 1974. Mem. Aircraft Owners and Pilots Assn., Nat. Assn. Female Execs., Alpha Eta Phi. Republican. Methodist. Home: 3201 Aviation Ave #3 Coconut Grove FL 33133 Office: PO Box 330089 Coconut Grove FL 33233

AHR, DEIRDRE O'MEARA, lawyer; b. N.Y.C., June 2, 1946; d. Thomas Francis and Mary Veronica (Meehan) O'Meara; m. Paul Robert Ahr, June 8, 1968 (div.); children—Thomas Brady, Andrew Travers. B.A. cum laude, Trinity Coll., 1968; M.Ed., Va. Commonwealth U., 1976; J.D., U. Mo., 1982. Bar: Mo. 1982, U.S. Dist. Ct. (we. dist.) Mo. 1982. Tchr. Prince George's County Schs., Md., 1968-70, St. Michael's Sch., Richmond, Va., 1976-78; staff lawyer Mo. Supreme Ct., Jefferson City, 1981-83; gen. counsel State of Mo. Detention Facilities Commn., Jefferson City, 1983; gen. counsel State of Mo. Jud. Fin. Commn., Jefferson City, 1983-85; clk. of the ct. Mo. Ct. Appeals Eastern Dist., St. Louis, 1985—. Recipient Acad. Excellance award in environ. law U. Mo. Sch. Law, 1981. Mem. ABA, Mo. Bar Assn., St. Louis County Bar Assn., Lawyers Assn. St. Louis, Met. St. Louis Bar Assn., Am. Judicature Soc., Phi Delta Phi. Roman Catholic. Office: Mo Ct Appeals 111 N 7th St Saint Louis MO 63101

AHRENS, WENDY JOAN, data processing executive; b. Glen Cove, N.Y., Aug. 4, 1950; d. Thomas J. and Isabelle Taylor; student U. Md., Augsburg, W.Ger., 1969-71, SUNY, Farmingdale, 1972-74; m. Kent E. Ahrens, May 9, 1969; 1 son, Kenneth K. Sales rep. Met. Life Ins. Co., Huntington, N.Y., 1974-76, sales mgr., Flushing, N.Y., 1976-79; asst. dir. market devel. J. C. Penney Life Ins. Co., Dallas, 1979-81, dir. employment, 1981-82; mktg. cons. Informatics, Gen., Dallas, 1982-84, Incepts Inc., Dallas, 1984—; instr. ins. mktg. S. La. U., Lafayette, 1980. Chmn. recruiting Industry Task Force on Women and Minorities, Washington, 1980-83; mem. Plano Civic Com. Task Force, 1983—; chmn. United Way, L.I., N.Y., 1977; mem. telethon com. Easter Seals, N.Y.C., 1978. Recipient Pres.'s Conf. award Met. Life Ins. Co., 1974, 75; Nat. Quality award Nat. Assn. Underwriters, 1974, 75, Nat. Sales Achievement award, 1974, 75. Mem. Soc. Ins. Researchers, Nat. Assn. Life Underwriters, Gen. Agts. and Mgrs. Conf., Women's Life Underwriters Conf. Contbr. articles in field to profl. publs. Home: 4105 Early Morn Plano TX 75075

AICHINGER, BARBARA PARSONS, electrical engineer; b. Cleve., Apr. 3, 1960; d. Richard James and Marie (McMahon) Parsons; m. Edward W. Aichinger Jr., Jan. 8, 1983. BSEE, U. Akron, 1983; MSEE, U. Lowell, 1987. Software engr. Digital Equipment Corp., Maynard, Mass., 1983-84; sr. design engr. Digital Equipment Corp., Littleton, Mass., 1984—. Mem. So. Women Engrs., IEEE., Nat. Honor Soc. Office: Digital Equipment Corp Codman Hill Rd Boxborough MA 01719

AIELLO, BARBARA, educational company executive, puppeteer; b. Pitts., Nov. 6, 1947; d. Antonio and Helen Ruth (Kaupiek) A.; m. Richard Laurie Dolph, June 8, 1985; 1 child, Rosanna Forrest. BS in Edn., Indiana U. of Pa., 1968; MA in Edn., George Washington U., 1971; postgrad., Harvard U., 1974-75. spl. edn. tchr. pub. schs., Washington, 1969-74; editor Teaching Exceptional Children, Council for Exceptional Children, Reston, Va., 1975-77; edn. cons. Learning mag., Palo Alto, Calif., 1977-78; pres., founder, script writer The Kids On The Block, Inc., Columbia, Md., 1978—; mem. adv. bd. Inst. for Mental Health Initiatives, Washington, 1985-88, Ctr. for Children of Div., Washington, 1986-88. Corr. N.Y. Times, 1974-85. Recipient One To One Media award N.Y. State Advocacy Bd. for Mentally Retarded, 1979, On Behalf of Youth award Camp Fire, Inc., 1980, Instr. Mag. award for The Invisible Children article, 1980, Outstanding Achievement award Epilepsy Found. Am., 1982, Outstanding Pub. Service award Easter Seal Soc., 1984, Margaret Pope Hovey award People-To-People Com., 1984, Disting. Service award Pres.'s Com. on Employment Handicapped, 1985. Mem. Council for Exceptional Children, Nat. Assn. Female Execs. Avocations: cross country skiing, running, reading biographies, cycling. Office: The Kids On the Block Inc 9385-C Gerwig Ln Columbia MD 21046

AIGEN, BETSY PAULA, psychotherapist; b. N.Y.C., Sept. 13, 1938; d. Abraham H. and Gertrude (Rosenblum) Wasserman; m. Ronald Aigen, Dec. 7, 1957 (div. Jan. 1979); m. Isadore Schumukler, June 20, 1982; 1 child, Jennifer Loren. BA, New Sch. Social Research, 1971; MA, Columbia U., 1972; D of Psychology, Rutgers U., 1980. Group co-leader, asst. psychotherapist Inst. Rational Psychotherapy, N.Y.C., 1967-72; asst. course instr. Columbia U., N.Y.C., 1971-72; psychotherapist Mt. Carmel Guild, Englewood, N.J., 1980-82, SELF Edn. Learning and Feeling, N.Y.C., 1982—; founder, dir. Surrogate Mother Program, N.Y.C., 1985—; cons. Police Chief Tng. Community Workshops Assn., N.Y.C., 1973-74, Richmond Fellowship Mental Health Halfway Houses, Eng. and U.S., 1970-75. Contbr. articles to profl. jours. Chmn. Tenants Com., N.Y.C., 1975-85; active Profl. Theatre, 1956-67. Mem. Nat. Orgn. Women, RESOLVE, Adoptive Parents Com., Am. Psychol. Assn., N.Y. St. Psychol. Assn., N.J. St. Psychol. Assn., N.Y. Assn. Feminist Therapists. (co-founder, charter), Am. Orgn. Surrogate Parenting Practitioners (founder, charter). Democrat. Jewish. Home: 640 W End Ave #3D New York NY 10024 Office: Surrogate Mother Program 640 W End Ave Suite 3D New York NY 10024

AIKEN, LINDA HARMAN, nurse sociologist; b. Roanoke, Va., July 29, 1943; d. William Jordan and Betty Philips (Warner) Harman; married; children: June Elizabeth, Alan James. B.S. in Nursing, U. Fla., 1964, M.Nursing, 1966; Ph.D. in Sociology, U. Tex., 1973. Nurse Med. Ctr. U. Fla., Gainesville, 1964-65, instr. Coll. Nursing, 1966-67; instr. Sch. of Nursing, U. Mo., Columbia, 1967-70, clin. nurse specialist, 1967-70; program officer Robert Wood Johnson Found., Princeton, N.J., 1974-76, dir. research, 1976-79, asst. v.p., 1979-81, v.p., 1981-87; trustee prof. nursing and sociology, assoc. dir. for nursing affairs Leonard Davis Inst. Health Econs., U. Pa., Phila., 1988—; mem. task force on long-term health care policies U.S. Dept. Health and Human Services, 1986-87, Sec's. Commn. on Nursing, 1988; mem. panel on quality med. care for consumers Office Tech. Assessment, 1986-88. Assoc. editor: Jour. Health and Social Behavior, 1979-81, Transaction Soc., 1985—; mem. editorial bd.: Evaluation Quar., 1979-80, Med. Care, 1983—; author: Health Policy and Nursing Practice, 1981, Nursing in the 1980's, 1982, Applications of Social Science to Clinical Medicine and Health Policy, 1986, Evaluation Studies Rev. Ann., 1985; contbr. articles to profl. jours. Mem. Adv. Council Social Security, 1982-83. Recipient Joint Secretarial commendation U.S. Dept. Health and Human Services and HUD, 1987; NIH Nurse Scientist fellow, 1970-73. Mem. Inst. Medicine, Nat. Acad. Scis., Am. Acad. Nursing (pres. 1979-80), Am. Sociol. Assn. (chair med. sociology sect. 1983-84), Council Nurse Researchers, Am. Nurses Assn. (Jessie M. Scott award 1984), Sigma Theta Tau, Phi Kappa Phi. Home: 242 Prospect Ave Princeton NJ 08540 Office: U Pa 420 Service Dr Philadelphia PA 19104-6096

AIKENS, MARTHA BRUNETTE, national park service administrator, consultant, educator; b. Jayess, Miss., Aug. 23, 1949; d. Walter and Elnora La Doris (Bridges) A. B.S. in Social Sci., Alcorn State U., 1971; postgrad. George Williams Coll., 1974, Fla. Internat. U., 1977, George Washington U., 1979, Pa. State U., 1979, U. So. Calif.-D.C. Ext., 1980. Social worker Pearl River County Devel. Corp., Picayune, Miss., 1971-72; environ. ednl. specialist Nat. Park Service, Homestead, Fla., 1973-76, environ. ednl. coordinator, 1976-78, communications specialist, 1976-78, park mgr., Bklyn., 1978-79, St. Augustine, Fla., 1979-83, Washington, 1983—; instr., cons. Coll. African Wildlife Mgmt., Tanzania, Africa, 1980, Mather Tng. Ctr., Harpers Ferry, W.Va., 1977—, Fed. Law Enforcement Tng. Ctr., Glynco, Ga., 1983—, Office of Internat. Affairs, Nat. Park Service, Washington, 1980—. Author tchrs. guides on Everglades Nat. Park, 1973-76, park brochure, 1977. Contbr. chpts. to books. Mem. Strategic Planning Task Force, Atlanta, 1981-83, Southeast Regional Equal Opportunity Commn., Atlanta, 1982-83, Dept. Interior's Partnership in Edn. Commn., Washington, 1983—, Fed. Interagy. Commn. on Edn., Washington, 1983—, Nat. Park Service Employee Relations Task Force, Washington, 1983—.

AILLONI-CHARAS, MIRIAM C., interior designer; b. Veere, The Netherlands, July 31, 1935; came to U.S., 1958; d. Maurits and Elzina (De Groot) Taytelbaum; m. Dan Ailloni-Charas, Oct. 8, 1957; children: Ethan Benjamin, Orrin, Adam. Degree in interiors, Pratt Inst., 1962; BSc, SUNY, Albany, 1978. Interior designer S.J. Miller Assocs., N.Y.C., 1960-63; free-lance interior designer Rye Brook, N.Y., 1963—. treas. Temple Guild, Congregation Emanu-El, Rye, N.Y., 1979—, trustee, 1986—. Recipient cert. of merit U.S. Jr. C. of C., 1962. Mem. Am. Soc. Interior Designers, Allied Bd. Trade, Westchester Assn. Women Bus. Owners, Nat. Trust for Hist. Preservation. Home and Office: 23 Woodland Dr Rye Brook NY 10573

AIMÉE, JOYCE, entertainment company executive; b. Bklyn., May 4, 1930; d. David Joseph and Jessica (Ganz) Geronimus; m. Harold L. Epstein, Oct. 16, 1949 (div. 1962); 1 child, Matthew Bruce Epstein; m William McPeck Titchnell, Nov. 2, 1966; 1 child, David Langland Titchnell. Grad. high sch., N.Y.C. Child performer ABC Network, N.Y.C., 1938-44; musician various nightclubs, hotels, Las Vegas, Nev. and N.Y., 1945-57; film actress Fla., Calif., Europe, S.Am., and Reno, Nev., 1945-57; sub-agent George B. Hunt and Assocs., Los Angeles, 1957-62; pres., owner Aimee Entertainment Assn., Los Angeles, 1962—; founder, exec. dir. Americana Dance Theater, Inc., Van Nuys, Calif., 1972—. Producer (film documentary) De Mille Dynasty, 1985, as an exhibition, 1986 (Angel award 1987), TV documentary Americana at Penny Lane, 1988 (Angel award). Dir. Cultural Found., Woodland

Hills, Calif., 1979—; pres. San Fernando Valley Arts Council, Woodland Hills, 1978—; commr. Los Angeles County Music and Performing Arts, 1987—. Named Leading Accordionist of Yr. World Accordion Review, London, 1956, 57, 58, 59. Mem. Am. Fed. Musicians, Screen Actors Guild, AFTRA, Writers Guild Am., Am. Guild Mus. Artists. Republican. Clubs: Child Help USA (Los Angeles, v.p. 1972-78), San Fernando Cultural Valley Soc. (v.p. 1974-76). Office: Aimee Entertainment Assn 13743 Victory Blvd Van Nuys CA 91401

AINGWORTH, JANET LYNN BOND, controller; b. Weatherford, Okla., Sept. 16, 1955; d. Lester Wayne and Ila L. (Anglin) Bond; m. Dennis Thomas Aingworth, May 24, 1980 (Apr. 1986). BS in Acctg., S.W. Okla. State U., Weatherford, 1977. Cost acct., controller Comac, Oklahoma City, 1977-81; supr. gen. acctg. Diners Club, Englewood, Colo., 1981-82; controller DSI, Inc., Denver, 1982—. Democrat. Lutheran. Home: 7264 S Crescent Dr Littleton CO 80120 Office: DSI Inc 1440 S Lipan St Denver CO 80223

AINLEY, REBECCA EARLENE, sales professional; b. Santa Ana, Calif., Nov. 8, 1959; d. James Reuben and Clara Lenore (Walker) Talley; m. Calvin Matthew Ainley, June 17, 1978; children: Timothy Martin, Jessica Dannielle. Student, Rancho Santiago Community Coll., Santa Ana, 1977-78, 80, 85-86. Sec., receptionist Athletes in Action, Fountain Valley, Calif., 1980; sales clk. Fresno (Calif.) Bible House, 1980-81; sec., receptionist Hume Lake Christian Camps, Fresno, 1981; sales rep. Selman Chevrolet, Orange, Calif., 1986; sales rep., cons. Infometrics, Brea, Calif., 1986-87; salesperson, fundraiser Team West Promotions, Newport Beach, Calif., 1987—; cons. interviewer Hume Lake Christian Camps, 1987—. Mem. Nat. Assn. Female Execs. Republican. Club: Lead's (Orange). Home: 422 E 22d St Santa Ana CA 92706 Office: Team West Promotions Box 5808 Newport Beach CA 92662

AINSLEY, LUCY ELIZABETH, educational adminstrator; b. Bad Axe, Mich., June 29, 1942; d. Kenneth Sylvester and Mildred (Grekowicz) Smith; m. Alan Kent Ainsley, Sept. 9, 1967 (div. 1977). BS in Edn., Cen. Mich. U., 1964; MA, Mich. State U., 1969; MLS, Wayne State U., 1975, EdD, 1987. Speech tchr. MacArthur High Sch., Saginaw, Mich., 1964-66, librarian, 1966-67; media cons. Saginaw Intermediate Schs., 1967-68; media dir. Waterford (Mich.) Mott High Sch., 1968-73; coordinator media services Birmingham (Mich.) Pub. Schs., 1973-85, dir. instructional tech., 1985—; lectr. in field; cons. Lenawee Intermediate Schs., Adrian, Mich., 1985. Editor Media Mgmt. Jour., 1986; author: Sch. Library Media Annual, 1985; contbr. articles to profl. jours. Mem. adv. bd. Children's Com. for TV, Detroit, 1984—; ad hoc advisor Birmingham Cablecasting Bd., 1980—; chmn. Bloomfield Cable Access Com., 1985. Mem. LWV (cable coordinator 1987—), Nat. Assn. for Edn. Communications and Tech. (bd. dirs. 1983-86, pres.-elect 1989, Edgar Dale award 1978), Mich. Assn. for Media in Edn. (chpt. pres. 1974), Phi Delta Kappa (newsletter editor), Assn. for Supervision and Curriculum Devel. Office: Birmingham Pub Schs 1525 Covington Rd Birmingham MI 48010

AIRTH, MISKIT, video production, programming executive; b. Live Oak, Pa., May 29, 1939; d. George Edward and Dorothy A. A.B., Randolph-Macon Woman's Coll., 1961; M.A., Dallas Theatre Ctr., Baylor U., 1963. Mem. repertory theater, tchr.-dir. Children's Theater Dallas Theater Ctr., 1961-63; with touring children's theater Nat. Theater Co., 1963-64; with Phoenix Theater, 1964-69, Am. Place Theater, 1964-69, Shakespeare-in-the-Park, N.Y.C., 1964-69; producer Sta. WPIX-TV, N.Y.C., 1969-75; assoc. producer Good Morning America ABC-TV, N.Y.C., 1975-76; producer A Woman Is—With Bess Myerson Sta. WCBS-TV, N.Y.C., 1976-77; exec. producer Sta. WABC-TV, N.Y.C., 1977-80; dir. program devel. for East Coast Viacom Enterprises, N.Y.C., 1980-81; dir. programming and studio ops. Warner Amex Cable Communications, 1981-84, M.B.A. Video Projects/Quality Value Convenience Home Shopping Network, Phila., 1984—; vis. scholar Boston U. Communications Inst.; lectr. Womanschool, N.Y.C., Randolph-Macon Woman's Coll., Lynchburg, Va., New Sch. for Social Research, N.Y.C., Inst. New Cinema Artist, N.Y.C. Producer: weekly film documentary New York Closeup, Sta. WPIX-TV, 8 N.Y. areas, 1969-73 (Emmy awards, 2 personal awards); documentary series WABC Spl. Reports, 1977-80; WABC You! show (Emmy for pilot show); instant spl. Life Was Worth Living, WABC, N.Y.C.; You Can't Get There From Here (Emmy), The Town That Build N.Y. (Emmy), Elvis-Love Him Tender with Joel Siegel (Emmy); (on location) prodns. Studio 30, QUBE Cable; Cincinnati Alive (Emmy), Swordquest (Ace award), (others). Mem. adv. com. So. Ohio Coll.; mem. planning com. Nat. Cancer Communications Conf., Houston; mem. allocation com. United Way, Phila., 1985; bd. dirs. Women's Soc. for Prevention Cruelty to Animals, Phila., 1985—. Recipient 2 Silver medals Internat. Film Festival, N.Y.C., 1979, 80; recipient Emmy award for outstanding documentary, 1971, 72, 80, Emmy award for outstanding mag., 1980, Emmy award for outstanding entertainment, 1980, 2 awards of excellence Communications Excellence for Black Audiences, 1979, 80, Bd. Govs. award Nat. Acad. TV arts and Scis., 1983, award Nat. Cable TV Assn., 1982, 4 nominations 1983 Ace Awards, 1983 Emmy Awards. Mem. Nat. Acad. TV Arts and Scis. (gov. N.Y.C. chpt.), Am. Women in Radio and TV (dir. N.Y.C. chpt.), Women in Cable (founder, 1st pres. Cin. Tri-State chpt.), Phi Beta Kappa. Office: MBA Video Projects 624 S 10th St Philadelphia PA 19147

AITCHISON, BEATRICE, transportation economist; b. Portland, Oreg., July 18, 1908; d. Clyde Bruce and Bertha (Williams) Aitchison; AB, Goucher Coll., 1928, ScD (hon.), 1979; AM, Johns Hopkins, 1931; PhD in Math., 1933; MA with honors in Econs., U. Oreg., 1937. Asso. prof. math. U. Richmond, 1933-34; lectr. statistics Am. U., 1934-44; instr. econs. U. Oreg., 1939-41; jr. statistician advancing to sr. statistician ICC, 1938-48, prin. transport economist, 1948-51; dir. transport econs. div. Office Transp., Dept. Commerce, 1951-53; dir. transp. research Post Office Dept., Washington, 1953-58, dir. transp. research and statistics, 1958-67, dir. transp. rates and econs., 1967-71; transp. cons., 1971—. Cons. Traffic Analysis and Forecasting Office Def. Transp., 1942-45; cons. mil. traffic. service U.S. Dept. Def., 1950-53. Recipient Alumnae Achievement citation Goucher Coll., 1954; First Ann. Fed. Woman's award, 1961, Career Service award Nat. Civil Service League, 1970. Fellow Am. Statis. Assn., AAAS; mem. Am. Econ. Assn., Am. Soc. Trans and Logistics, Phi Beta Kappa, Sigma Xi, Pi Lambda Theta, Phi Delta Gamma. Episcopalian. Contbr. to numerous govt. publs. Home and Office: 3001 Veazy Terr NW Apt 534 Washington DC 20008-5402

AITKEN, LEA ELIZABETH, accountant, computer consultant; b. McCook, Nebr., Apr. 27, 1947; d. Robert Brown and Lowell Elaine (Joslyn) A.; m. Raymond Marion Moncier, Dec. 30, 1972. MusB, Fresno State Coll., 1969, postgrad., 1969-70; postgrad., U. Ky., 1982-83; MBA, U. Denver, 1988. Tour guide Fresno (Calif.) Zoo Soc., 1967-70; tchr. Teague Elem. Sch. Dist., Fresno, 1970-76, asst. compensatory edn. dir., 1976-79; headmistress St. Aidans Episcopal Sch., Fresno, 1978-80; office mgr. Episcopal Theol. Seminary, Lexington, Ky., 1980-83; acctg. supr. Thorsen and Co., Denver, 1984-85; acct., cons. Holben, Dennis, and Co., Aurora, Colo., 1985—. Office mgr. Students for Robert Kennedy, Fresno, 1968; vestrywoman St. Stephen's Ch., Aurora, 1986—. Mem. Nat. Assn. Female Execs., Data Processing Mgrs. Assn., Mu Phi Epsilon. Democrat. Episcopalian. Office: Holben Dennis and Co 3001 S Jamaica Ct Aurora CO 80014

AITKEN, MOLLY BENNETT, foundation administrator; b. Hollywood, Calif., July 25, 1944; d. Mervyn Dreux Bennett and Valré (Czech) Vasilas; m. Alvin M. Marks, Aug. 25, 1965 (div. 1976); children: Bridget Grace, Sean Christopher, Frederick Peter, Jacqueline Lee; m. Gerard James Aitken III, Dec. 26, 1977 (dec.); children: Gerard James IV, Mary Hannah. BA, Nev. So. U., 1962; MA, NYU, 1968. Hostess, singer Rounders Club Show, Sta. KLAS-TV, Las Vegas, Nev., 1962-63; actress, singer Ed Sullivan Show, Copacabana, Joe Franklin Show, 1962-65; fundraiser U.S. Equestrian Team, 1972-76; spl. asst. to pres. Marks Polarized Corp., N.Y.C., 1965-82; mgr. horse show Assn. for the Help of Retarded Children, 1973-74; mgr. Century Horse Show, N.Y.C., 1974-75; pres. World Energy Found., N.Y.C, 1982—; bd. dirs. Phototherm, Inc., Amherst, N.H. Contbg. editor North Shore Club Life mag., 1971-75, Horsemen's Yankee Peddler Mag., 1970-78; contbr. numerous articles on horses to jours. Pres. United Cerebral Palsy Aux., Long Island, N.Y., 1970-74; founder Riding for the Handicapped, Long Island, 1972; campaign organizer Edward M. Kennedy for Pres., Athol, Mass., 1979-80. Recipient Disting. Service award United Cerebral Palsy, 1973, numerous horsemanship awards; recieved papal blessing Pope Paul VI, 1964; U.S. flag flown in honor of Mr. and Mrs. Aitken over the Capitol, Washington, 1985. Mem. Am. Horse Shows Assn. (life), N.E. Right to Life Assn., Screen Actors Gulid, Am. Guild of Variety Artists. Roman Catholic. Home: Green Gables Farm Athol MA 01331 Office: World Energy Found 360 E 72d Suite A1011 New York NY 10021

AIUPPA, GERALDINE FRANCES, career planning and placement director; b. Melrose Park, Ill., June 30, 1944; d. Anna Lucy (Dizonno) A. BA, Northeastern Ill. U., 1973, MA, 1978. Career placement Oakton Community Coll., Des Plaines, Ill., 1973—; adj. faculty Triton Coll., River Grove, Ill., 1981-82, part-time faculty Oakton Community Coll., Des Plaines, 1984—, co-founder, program planner, cons. Work Edn. Adv. Council, 1984—. Producer cable TV video prodn. Ability is Ageless, 1981. Promoter Adventures in the Automated Workplace, Oakton Community Coll., Des Plaines, 1981. Served with USN, 1962-63. Mem. Women in Mgmt., Midwest Coll. Placement Assn., Council on Women's Programs, Govt. Coll. Relations Council, World Future Soc. Roman Catholic. Club: Toastmasters (Oak Park, Ill.) (pres. 1984). Office: Oakton Community Coll 1600 E Golf Rd Des Plaines IL 60016

AKERS, CATHAYANNE MARIE, manufacturing executive, chemist; b. San Jose, Calif., Aug. 13, 1952; d. Charles Marshall Sr. and Georgia Irene (Miller) A.; m. James Floyd Dorris, Jan. 4, 1969 (dec. Nov. 1974); 1 child, Cindy Lee Anne Dorris. Diploma in gen. edn., Clackamas Community Coll.; AAS, Lower Columbia Coll., 1977; student, Monroe County (Mich.) Community Coll., 1986, U. Toledo, 1987—. Inventory clk., receptionist Hood River County Abundant Food Stores, Dalles, Oreg., 1970; guard Lawrence Security, Portland, Oreg., 1971-72; store detective Lipman & Wolfe, Portland, Oreg., 1972-74; exptl. technician I Weyerhaeuser Paper Co., Longview, Wash., 1977-79; water shed technician Wash. State Dept. Agri., Kelso, 1979; chemist Indsl. Chems. div. Am. Cyanamid Co., Longview, 1979-82; lab. technician City of Monroe (Mich.) Wastewater Treatment Plant, 1984-85; electrician apprentice Geal Electric, Monroe, 1985; product engr. intern Monroe Auto Equipment Div. of Tenneco Automatic, 1986; pres., chief exec. officer Gap Plumbing, Inc., Monroe, 1987—, bd. dirs.; lab. analyst Lower Columbia Coll., 1976; plumber's apprentice Plumbers, Pipe Fitters and Refrigeration Joint Apprenticeship and Tng. Com., Tacoma, 1982-84. Participant Hands Across Am., Toledo, 1986; team leader March of Dimes-Walk Am., Monroe, 1988. Pell grantee U. Toledo, 1987-88. Mem. Soc. Women Engrs. (student), VFW Aux., Nat. Safety Council (defensive driving campaign 1977). Democrat. Roman Catholic. Home: 237 White Oak Ct Monroe MI 48161 Office: Gap Plumbing Inc 121 N Roessler St Monroe MI 48161

AKERS, F. ANNIE, small business owner; b. Charlotte, N.C., Oct. 7, 1951; d. James Jones Akers and Frances Laura (King) Akers Davis. BA, Greenbrier Coll., 1971, U. N.C., Charlotte, 1974. Mktg. rep. Roger La Viale, Ltd., N.Y.C., 1971-81; pres. Akers Clothiers, Ltd., Pitts., 1981—. Mem. Pitts. Jr. League, 1981—. Mem. Nat. Assn. Women Bus. Owners, Referral Group Greater Pitts. Democrat. Office: Akers Clothiers Ltd 345 Fourth Ave Suite 300 Pittsburgh PA 15222

AKIN, MARY JANE, computer consultant; b. Charles City, Iowa, Mar. 18, 1948; d. George Joseph and Esther Alice (Lawless) Naumann; m. Alfred Kenneth Akin, June 16, 1973; children: Ned Theron, Zara Maria. BA in Sociology, SUNY, Buffalo, 1972; postgrad., U. Md., 1972-73, U. Iowa, 1975. Cert. in data processing. Programmer Fireman's Fund Am., San Francisco, 1969-70; methods analyst Blue Cross of Western N.Y., Buffalo, 1970-71; programmer/analyst Group Hospitalization, Inc., Washington, 1972; mem. tech. staff Computer Scis. Corp., Falls Ch., Va., 1973-74; systems analyst Westinghouse Learning Corp., Iowa City, 1974-76; programmer/analyst Network Data Processing, Cedar Rapids, Iowa, 1976-77, Control Data Corp., Plymouth, Minn., 1977-79; systems programmer Apache Corp., Mpls., 1979-80; mgr. Northwestern Nat. Life Ins. Co., Mpls., 1980-85; pvt. practice computer cons. Rogers, Minn., 1985—. NWNL rep. SHARE, Mpls., 1980-85; mem. DFL Feminist Caucus, Mpls., 1985, 87. Mem. Assn. Women in Computing (nat. bd., TC pres. 1978-79), Ind. Computer Cons. Assn., Computer Measurement Group. Democrat. Episcopalian. Home and Office: 23405 County Rd 10 Rogers MN 55374-9304

AKOS, CATHERINE, voice educator; b. Budapest, Hungary, Apr. 8, 1925; came to U.S., 1954, naturalized, 1957; d. Ignatz and Berta (Zilzer) A.; m. Ernest White, Sept. 6, 1946; 1 child, George. Grad. opera and concert artist Lisst Ferencz Acad. Music, Budapest, 1944. Soloist with Budapest, Bucarest, Cluj Opera Romania, from 1945; mem. Radio Diffusion Francaise, Paris, 1947-52; soloist with Swiss Romande Orch., Switzerland, 1952; soloist in Israel, Germany, Can. Opera, Toronto, 1953-57, soloist with Boston Symphony, NBC, CBS, 1954-57; assoc. prof. voice So. Methodist U., Dallas, 1957—. Played leading role on Broadway in Menotti's opera The Saint of Bleeker Street, 1954; recs. RCA Records. Mem. Nat. Assn. Tchrs. of Singing, AAUP, Am. Guild Musical Artists, Dallas Goethe Soc. (bd. dirs.), Pi Kappa Lambda. Home: 3518 Gillon Ave Dallas TX 75205

ALAUPOVIC, ALEXANDRA VRBANIC, artist, educator; b. Slatina, Yugoslavia, Dec. 21, 1921; d. Joseph and Elizabeta (Papp) Vrbanic; student Bus. Sch., Zagreb, Yugoslavia, 1940-41, Acad. Visual Arts, Zagreb, Yugoslavia, 1944-48; postgrad. Acad. Visual Arts, Prague, Czechoslovakia, 1949, Art Sch., U. Ill., 1959-60; MFA, U. Okla., 1966; m. Peter Alaupovic, Mar. 22, 1947; children—Betsy, H. Clark Hyde. Came to U.S., 1958. Sec., Arko Liquer & Yeast Factory and Distillery, Zagreb, 1941-44; instr. U. Okla., Norman, 1964-66; instr. three dimensional design sculpture Oklahoma City U., 1969-77, Okla. Sci. Found., Oklahoma City, 1969-75; one-woman shows at Okla. Art Ctr., Oklahoma City, U. Okla. Mus. Art, Norman, La Mandragore Internat. Galerie d'Art, Paris, 1984; exhibited art in group shows retrospective 50 yrs. Struggle, Growth and Whimsy, 1987-88, Okla. Art Ctr., Springfield (Mo.) Art Mus., Okla. U. Mus., Norman, 7th Ann. Temple Emanuel Brotherhood Arts Festival, Dallas, Salon des Nation, Paris, 1983; represented in permanent collections Okla. U. Art Mus., Okla. State Art Collection, Okla. Art Ctr., Mercy Health Ctr. Recipient Jacobson award U. Okla., 1964; hon. mention in sculpture Philbrook Art Ctr., Tulsa, 1967; 1st sculpture award Philbrook Art Ctr., Tulsa, 1970; biography included in Virginia Watson Jones' Contemporary American Women Sculptors, 1986. Mem. Internat. Sculpture Center. Home: 11908 N Bryant St Oklahoma City OK 73111 Office: Route 1 Box 167A Oklahoma City OK 73111

ALBERGA, ALTA WHEAT, artist; b. Ala.; d. James Richard and Leila Savannah (Sullivan) Wheat; B.A., M.A., Wichita State U., 1954; B.F.A., Washington U., St. Louis, 1961; M.F.A., U. Ill., 1964; m. Alvyn Clyde Alberga, Dec. 3, 1930. Mem. faculty Wichita (Kans.) State U., 1955-56, Webster Coll., St. Louis, 1962, Presbyn. Coll., Clinton, S.C., 1969-74; pvt. art tchr., Greenville, S.C., 1974—; substitute tchr. Greenville County Schs.; tchr. painting Tempo Gallery Sch., Greenville, 1974—, Greenville County Mus. Sch., 1975—; one-woman shows: Greenville County Mus., 1979, Greenville Artists Guild Gallery, 1979, 83, Wichita State U., 1954, St. Louis Artists Guild, 1956, N.C. State U., 1965; group shows include: Pickens County Mus., 1979, Inter/Art 81, Washington 1981, Greenville Artists Guild, 1982, Art/7, Washington, 1983; represented in pvt. collections; bd. dirs. Greenville Artists Guild, 1977-79, pres., 1985; bd. dirs. Guild Gallery, 1978, Guild Greenville Symphony, 1982-83. Recipient Richard K. Weil award St. Louis Mus., 1957; Purchase prize S.C. Arts Commn., 1972. Mem. Artists Equity (pres. St. Louis chpt. 1962), Internat. Platform Assn. (life), Art Students League, Guild Greenville Artists (pres. 1984-85), S.C. Artists Guild, Southeastern Council Printmakers, Greenville Symphony Guild, Kappa Pi, Kappa Delta Pi. Democrat. Home: 11 Overton Dr Greenville SC 29609

ALBERGO, REBECCA MERYL, advertising agency executive; b. N.Y.C., Apr. 27, 1961; d. Norman Albin and Ann (Flaster) Hollander; m. Joseph Michael Albergo, Aug. 12, 1982. B.S. in Biology summa cum laude, Pace U., 1981, postgrad. in mktg., 1986. Account coordinator Rowland Co., N.Y.C., 1982-83; v.p. account supr. AC&R/DHB & Bess Advt., N.Y.C., 1983—. Mem. Nat. Assn. Female Execs. Republican. Jewish. Office: AC&R/DHB & Bess Advt 16 E 32d St New York NY 10016

ALBERS, SUSAN L., grants coordinator; b. Indpls., Mar. 15, 1956; d. Robert L. and Mary K. (Hensley) A. BA, Lincoln Christian Coll., 1978. Office adminstr. English dept. Indiana U. and Purdue U., Indpls., 1979-83; paralegal Richard P. Tinkham Jr., P.C., Indpls., 1983-85; pres. Planamics, Ltd., Indpls., 1985-88; grants coordinator Indpls. Mus. Art, 1988—. Dir. choir Chapel Rock Christian Ch., Indpls., 1986-87. Mem. Network Women in Bus., Nat. Assn. Female Execs., Indpls. C. of C. Republican. Home: 3021 Pebble Point Dr 1B Indianapolis IN 46214 Office: Inpls Mus Art 1200 W 38th St Indianapolis IN 46208

ALBERSHEIM, RENEE, information center manager; b. Boston, Mar. 13, 1961; d. Peter and Joyce Elizabeth (Johnson) A. B.A. in Psychology, U. Colo., 1983, M.B.A. in Info. Systems, 1985. Sec. Joint Inst. Lab. Astrophysics, U. Colo., Boulder, 1981-83, film series dir. Program Council U. Colo., 1982-83, dir. Trivia Bowl, 1983-84; mgr. Diners Club Info. Facility, Citicorp/Diners Club, Denver, 1985-86 ; mgr. info. ctr. Teepak, Inc., Danville, Ill., 1986—. Vice chmn. U. Meml. Ctr. Bd., U. Colo., Boulder, 1983-85. Mem. Assn. M.B.A. Execs., Nat. Assn. Female Execs., Am. Film Inst., Nat. Trust for Hist. Preservation, Colo. Mountain Club. Republican. Avocations: mountain climbing; backpacking; stamp collecting; reading; drawing. Home: 5664 S Walnut Ave #2-A Downers Grove IL 60616 Office: Teepak Inc 1211 W 22d St Suite 1100 Oak Brook IL 60521

ALBERT, BEVERLY FOIT, architect; b. Buffalo, Apr. 28, 1938; d. Franklin and Ruth Marie (Fix) Foit; B.Arch., Cornell U., 1961; M.Arch., SUNY, Buffalo, 1975; Ph.D., Saybrooke Inst., 1978; m. James T. Albert, Dec. 28, 1963; children—James T., Jeffrey J., Richard A. Partner Foit, Baschnagel, Maharan & Albert, Buffalo, 1966-69; assoc. firm Castle, Hamilton, Houston & Lownie, Buffalo, 1970-71; prin. firm Foit-Albert and Assos., Buffalo, 1976—; assoc. prof. Sch. Architecture and Environ. Design, Buffalo, 1969—. Recipient Research award Progressive Architecture mag., 1975. Mem. Soc. Archtl. Historians, Constrn. Specifications Inst., Assn. Bus. and Profl. Women in Constrn., Assn. Minority Enterprises N.Y. Contbr. articles to profl. publs. Home: 10 Maple Dr Orchard Park NY 14127 Office: 700 Main St Buffalo NY 14202

ALBERT, CECELIA ANNE, editor; b. Balt., Sept. 22, 1954; d. Joseph Kenneth and Marion Cecelia (Frederick) A.; m. Thomas Dale Reeg, Dec. 18, 1982. BA in Philosophy, U. Calif., Santa Barbara, 1976. Editor Clio Books, ABC-Clio Info. Services Inc., Santa Barbara, 1979-85; mng. editor ABC Polit. Sci., 1980-82; copy editor Coastlines, U. Calif., Santa Barbara, 1982-85; assoc. editor ABC-Clio, 1985-88; dir. promotions/fgn. rights, Sun and Moon Press, Los Angeles, 1988—. Editor: World Economic Data: A Compendium of Current Economic Information for All Countries of the World, Santa Barbara, 1987; contbg. author: An Encyclopedic Handbook of American Womens' History, 1988. Recipient Clio award, 1987. Democrat. Home: 1970 Mission Ridge Rd Santa Barbara CA 93103 Office: ABC-Clio 2040 Alameda Padre Serra Santa Barbara CA 93103

ALBERT, ELIZABETH ANNA, data processing executive, systems software specialist; b. N.Y.C., Nov. 5, 1953; d. Tuhan M. and Stephanie (Halczak) Kuziw; m. Mounir Albert, Nov. 17, 1978. BS in Math. and Stats., CUNY, 1977; postgrad., Ill. Inst. Tech., 1986, Chgo. Kent Sch. Law. Tech. rep. Xerox Corp., N.Y.C., 1975-76; programmer Palm Beach County Sch. Bd., West Palm Beach, Fla., 1976-77; systems analyst J.C. Penney, N.Y.C., 1977-78; sr. communications specialist Am. Express, N.Y.C., 1978-80; computer facilities analyst Standard Oil Ind., Chgo., 1980-82; dir. tech. services Dials Automation, Inc., Chgo., 1982-85; mgr. tech. ops. Goldman Sachs., Chgo., 1985-86; pres. Am. Computer Techs., Schaumburg, Ill., 1986—; speaker Guide, Anaheim, Calif., 1982; cons. Arthur Anderson & Co., Chgo., 1985-86; subject matter expert S.R.A., Inc., Chgo., 1986—. N.Y. State Regents scholar, 1971, Ill. Inst. Tech. scholar, 1986. Mem. Soc. Women in Law, ABA, Chgo. Bar Assn. Republican. Office: Am Computer Techs Inc 999 Plaza Dr Suite 400 Schaumburg IL 60173

ALBERT, JANYCE LOUISE, banker; b. Toledo, July 27, 1932; d. Howard C. and Glenola Mae (Masters) Blessing; m. John R. Albert, Aug. 7, 1954; children: John R., James H. Student Ohio Wesleyan U., 1949-51; BA, Mich. State U., 1953; MS, Iowa State U., 1980. Asst. personnel mgr./tng. supr. Sears, Roebuck & Co., Toledo, 1953-56; tchr. adult edn. Tenafly Pub. Schs. (N.J.), 1966-70; personnel officer, tng. officer, tng. and edn. mgr. Iowa Dept. Transp., Ames, 1974-77; coll. recruiting coordinator Rockwell Internat., Cedar Rapids, Iowa, 1977-79; engring. adminstrn. mgr., 1979-80; employee relations and job evaluation analyst Phillips Petroleum Co., Bartlesville, Okla., 1980-81; v.p., dir. personnel Republic Bancorp, Tulsa, 1981-83; v.p. and dir. human resources First Nat. Bank, Rockford, Ill., 1983—; advisor to Nat. Profl. Secs. Assn. Mem. employee services com. Rockford Bd. Edn.; bd. dirs. Rocvale Children's Home, United Way of Ames, 1976-77; mem. adv. council Rockford br. Ill. Job Service; publicity chmn. Tenafly 300th Ann. Celebration, 1969; bd. deacons Presbyn. Ch., Ames, 1972 75; mem adv. council Rockford YWCA, bd. dirs., 1986; co-chmn. YWCA Leader Luncheon, 1985; advisor Rockford chpt. ARC; mem. Mayor's Task Force for Rockford Project Self-Sufficiency. Pres.'s scholar, 1951-53; recipient YWCA Kate O'Connor award for Women in Labor Force 1984. Mem. Rockford Network (past chairperson 1985, pres. 1986), Rockford C. of C. (transp. com.), Rockford Personnel Assn. (co-chmn. programs 1985-86, adv. council), Am. Soc. Personnel Adminstrn., Rockford Personnel Assn., Employee Benefits Assn. No. Ill. (membership chmn.), Rockford Council Affordable Health Care, Rockford Personal and Profl. Power Coalition, P.E.O., Sigma Epsilon, Alpha Gamma Delta, Phi Kappa Phi. Home: 5587 Thunderidge Dr Rockford IL 61107 Office: First Nat Bank Rockford 401 E State St Rockford IL 61110

ALBERTI, RITA ADELINE, lawyer; b. Bklyn., Mar. 8, 1951; d. Pasquale and Luise (Scheeff) A. BA, CUNY, 1972, MS, 1974; Profl. Diploma, Hofstra U., 1978; JD, St. John's U., 1985. Bar: N.Y. 1986, D.C. 1986; cert. tchr. N.Y.C., N.Y. Tchr. Rose Milett County Day Sch., East Rockaway, N.Y., 1973-80; housing mgr. NAVSTA N.Y. Navy Family Housing, East Meadow, N.Y., 1980-86; dep. county atty. Family Ct. Bureau, Westbury, N.Y., 1986—; div. head Camp Milett, East Rockaway, summers 1973-79. Sec. Long Beach (N.Y.) Rep. Club, 1987—. Served to lt. col. Civil Air Patrol, 1974—. Named N.Y. State Regent scholar, 1968-72. Mem. ABA, N.Y. State Bar Assn., D.C. Bar Assn., Nassau County Bar Assn., Nassau Women's Bar, Colombian Lawyers Assn. Republican. Roman Catholic. Home: 329 E State St Long Beach NY 11561 Office: Family Ct Bur 1200 Old Country Rd Westbury NY 11590

ALBERTINE, ANNE MARIE CESARE, retail executive; b. Scranton, Pa., July 25, 1949; d. Sette James and Josephine (Azzarelli) Cesare; m. James Joseph Albertine, May 12, 1979; 1 child, James Joseph Jr. BS, Coll. Misericordia, Dallas, Pa., 1971; postgrad., Am. U., 1987—. Mgmt. trainee Sears, Roebuck and Co., New Brunswick, N.J., 1971; div. mgr. Sears, Roebuck and Co., Greece, N.Y., 1972; tng. dir. Sears, Roebuck and Co., Neptune, N.J., 1972-74; asst. personnel mgr. Sears, Roebuck and Co., Paramus, N.J., 1974-75; personnel mgr. Sears, Roebuck and Co., Union City, N.J., 1975-77; mdse. mgr. Sears, Roebuck and Co., Wayne, N.J., 1977-78, Hagerstown, Md., 1978-80; asst. store mgr. Sears, Roebuck and Co., Frederick, Md., 1981-84; regional systems mgr. regional officer Sears, Roebuck and Co., Bethesda, Md., 1984-87, regional mktg. mgr. home improvements category, 1988—; bd. dirs. Nat. Capital Assn. for Cooperative Edn., Washington, 1986—, Columbia Hosp. for Women Services Corp., 1987—. Mem. Nat. Assn. Female Execs., Kappa Gamma Pi, Sigma Phi Sigma. Democrat. Roman Catholic. Home: 5707 Springfield Dr Bethesda MD 20816 Office: Sears Roebuck and Co 10301 Westlake Dr Bethesda MD 20817

ALBIN, MAJORIE ANN, banker; b. Tuscola, Ill., Aug. 8, 1930; d. George David and Mae L. (Perry) Martin; student Eastern Ill. U., 1948, 49, Wharton Sch., U. Ill., m. John S. Albin, Sept. 10, 1949; children—Perry S., Martin L., David A. Tax acct. Longview, Ill., 1963—; v.p., chief exec. officer Longview State Bank, 1978—, also dir.; v.p. State Bank of Chrisman; dir. Newman Manor, Inc., Plant Pals, Inc., Longview Capitol Corp., Albi Pork Farm, Inc. Bd. dirs. Jarman Hosp., Tuscola, Continental Manor Nursing Home, Newman, Ill. Office: Longview State Bank Box 37 Longview IL 61852

ALBRECHT, GEORGENE LEE, science writer, graphic illustrator, editor; b. Pitts., Oct. 13, 1941; d. Harvey Howard and Effie Caroline (Ishman) Hetrick; m. Lawrence John Albrecht, Aug. 24, 1963; children—Brian James, Christopher Alan. Student in grahic art Inst. Pitts., 1959-61. Illustrator B K & T Advt., Pitts., 1961-63; free-lance artist, 1970-80; hort. columnist Gesneriad Saintpaulia News, Greenwood, Ind., 1981—, contbg. editor, illustrator, 1981—, assoc. editor, Greenwood, Ind., 1985—; docent Phipps Conservatory, Pitts. Bd. dirs. Saintpaulia Internat. Knoxville, 1982-88, Cons., mem. Pitts. Civic Garden Ctr., 1984. Recipient Best in Show award Gesneriad Soc. Internat. Show, Indpls., 1983, Louisville, 1984, French Lick, Ind., 1985, Springfield, Ohio, 1986, King, Prince of Show Pitts. Rose Soc., 1987. Mem. Am. Orchid Soc. (highly commended cert. 1986), Am. Gloxinia and Gesneriad Soc., Orchid Soc. Western Pa. (dir. 1983-84). Democrat. Home: 101 Oak Heights Dr Oakdale PA 15071

ALBRECHT, JANE KATHERINE, lawyer; b. St. Louis, Aug. 31, 1952; d. Edgar Samuel and Geraldine (Hendricks) A. B.S. magna cum laude, Regis Coll., 1974; J.D., Georgetown U., 1980. Bar: D.C. 1980, U.S. Ct. Appeals (fed. cir.) 1981, U.S. Ct. Internat. Trade 1981, U.S. Dist. Ct. D.C. 1982, U.S. Ct. Appeals (D.C. cir.) 1987. Tax auditor IRS, St. Louis, 1975-77; law clk. Solicitor's Office, Gen. Legal Services, Dept. Interior, Washington, 1979; research asst. Georgetown U. Law Ctr., Washington, 1978-80; atty. Office Gen. Counsel, U.S. Internat. Trade Commn., Washington, 1980-84; assoc. Verner, Lippert, Bernhard & McPherson, Washington, 1984-85, Dewey, Ballantine, Bushby, Palmer and Wood, 1985—. Mem. Internat. Bar Assn., Women in Govtl. Relations.

ALBRECHT, KAY MONTGOMERY, educator, consultant, child advocate; b. Lafayette, La., Jan. 29, 1949; d. Michael H. and Imogene (McCallum) M.; m. Larry Steven Albrecht, June 23, 1973. BA, U. Southwestern La., 1970; MS in Child Devel., U. Tenn., 1972, PhD in Family Studies, 1984. Head Start coordinator U. Tenn., Knoxville, 1972-75; instr. Incarnate Word Coll., San Antonio, 1976-77; instr. Southwest Tex. State U., San Marcos, 1977-80; tng. dir. Daybridge Learning Ctrs., Houston, 1984-85, v.p., 1985-86; v.p. Child Care Mgmt. Assocs., 1986—; founder Hearts Home Early Learning Ctrs., Inc., 1986—; cons. Adminstrn. for Children, Youth and Families, HHS, Washington, 1982-83, Binney & Smith (author Crayola Creativity Program), Mervyn's, Angeles Toys, Houston Ind. Sch. Dist., Houston Mayor's Office; adv. bd. Nat. Acad. Early Childhood Programs, 1986—. Author staff orientation manual and consumer curriculum guide, 1980, 85, quality assurance manual for child care ctrs., 1987, School-Age Child Care Manual, Infant-Toddler Child Care, Crayola Creativity Program Manual. Mem. Hayes County Child Welfare Bd. San Marcos, 1979-81, Houston Com. for Pvt. Sector Initiatives Child Care; vol. Initiatives for Children, 1988—; coordinator Child Care Am. Campaign, 1988; pres. bd. dirs. Big Bros.-Big Sisters, Knoxville, 1981-83; vol. cons. Head Start, San Marcos and Knoxville, 1978-84; mem. com. Mayor's Task Force on Children, Houston, 1985. Nat. Inst. Edn. fellow, 1982-83. Fellow Am. Psychol. Assn.; mem. Am. Home Econs. Assn. (treas. 1984-86), Nat. Assn. for Edn. Young Children, Nat. Council Family Relations, Nat. Acad. Early Childhood Programs (adv. bd. 1987—), Houston Assn. Edn. Young Children (bd. dirs. 1984-86, Child Care Am. coordinator 1988), Internat. Council on Women's Health Issues (bd. dirs. 1987—). Democrat. Methodist. Avocations: water skiing, hiking, cooking, wild flower identification. Office: Child Care Mgmt Assocs PO Box 820687 Houston TX 77282

ALBRECHT, SUSAN ELAINE, organization development consultant; b. Denver, Oct. 11, 1958; d. Duane Taylor and Elinor (Gaylord) A. BA in Urban Affairs, U. Pacific, 1980; postgrad., Pepperdine U., 1987—. Asst. mgr. maintenance installation Pacific Bell, San Francisco, 1980-83, mgr. installation ctr., 1983-84; planner Pacific Bell, San Francisco and San Ramon, Calif., 1984-86; communication recognition specialist Pacific Bell, San Ramon, 1986-87; mgr. corp. communications Bellcore, Livingston, N.J., 1987—. Sec. Telegraph Hill Neighborhood Assn. Aux., San Francisco, 1985, 86, 87; mem. San Francisco Heritage, 1980—, Hist. Denver, 1980—. Mem. San Francisco Planning and Urban Research Assn., Orgn. Devel. Network, Bay Area Orgn. Devel. Network. Republican. Episcopalian. Office: Bellcore 290 W Mt Pleasant Ave Rm 2C326 Livingston NJ 07039

ALBRIGHT, BARBARA JOY, editor; b. Fremont, Neb., July 2, 1955; d. Arthur William and Ruth Ann (Walther) A. BS in Food and Nutrition cum laude, U. Nebr., 1977; MS in Nutrition Communications, Boston U., 1980. Registered dietitian. Dietetic intern San Diego VA Hosp., 1977-78; clin. dietitian Independence (Mo.) Hosp., 1978-79; nutritionist Mktg. Sci. Inst., Cambridge, Mass., 1980; asst. food editor Redbook mag., N.Y.C., 1980-81; free-lance writer, home economist N.Y.C., 1981-82; assoc. food editor Woman's World mag., Englewood, N.J., 1982-83; home economist, dietitian Dudley Anderson Yutzy Pub. Relations, N.Y.C., 1983-85; from food editor to editor in chief Chocolatier mag., N.Y.C., 1985—. Co-author: Mostly Muffins, 1984, Simply Scones, 1988, Wild About Brownies, 1985; contbr. articles to Los Angeles Times Syndicate, Country Living, other mags. Named Master U. Nebr., 1986. Mem. Am. Dietetic Assn., Soc. for Am. Cuisine, Home Economists in Bus. (editor newsletter 1986), N.Y. Women's Culinary Alliance (contbg. editor newsletter 1985-87), Conn. Women's Culinary Alliance, N.Y. Soc. for Nebr. (bd. dirs.), Chi Omega (sec./treas. 1976-77). Republican. Lutheran. Club: Nebr. Soc. N.Y. (N.Y.C.) (steering com., coordinator Tast of Nebr. 1985). Home: 885 Post Rd #2B Darien CT 06820 Office: Chocolatier Mag 45 W 34th St Suite 500 New York NY 10001

ALBRIGHT, JUDITH ANN, travel company executive; b. Winfield, Kans., Sept. 1, 1940; d. Chester Earl and Ada Emma (Beaman) Harris; m. Daniel H. Hibdon, Sept. 9, 1961 (div. June 1979); children: Carolyn Dianne, Stephanie Lynn; m. John N. Albright, Nov. 17, 1979. BFA summa cum laude, U. Denver, 1969; MA, U. Colo., 1973. Counselor travel Am. Express/Travel Assocs., Denver, 1961-68; tchr. art Jefferson County Schs., Denver, 1969-70; owner Artisans Around Town, Denver, 1973-79; dir. sales Denver West Tours, Golden, Colo., 1979-82; owner, gen. mgr. Customtours, Inc., Denver, 1982-85; adminstr. travel State of Colo., Denver, 1984-87; pres. Travel Mgmt. Cons., Inc., Littleton, Colo., 1985—; instr. travel SST Travel Schs., Aurora, Colo., 1985-86. Author: The Travel Arranger's Notebook, 1987; (with others) Government Contractors Handbook, 1987, Transportation Refund Guide, 1987. Researcher Lakewood (Colo.) Bi-Centennial Com., 1976; bd. dirs. Am. Indian Travel Commn., Denver, 1980-83. Mem. Rocky Mountain Bus. Travel Assn., Soc. Govt. Meeting Planners, Soc. Travel Agts. in Govt. Democrat.

ALBRIGHT, LAURIE JO, school psychologist; b. Toledo, Jan. 14, 1952; d. Lawrence Ray and Josephine Amelia (Knott) A.; m. Brian Lee Larson, Sept. 24, 1983; children: Timothy Martin, Bradley Roy. BA in Psychology magna cum laude, Cleve. State U., 1973, MA in Psychology, 1975. Lic. sch. psychologist, Ohio. Staff sch. psychologist Positive Edn. Program Early Intervention Ctr. East, Cleve., 1975-80, program coordinator, 1980—. Mem. Nat. Assn. Sch. Psychologists, Am. Psychol. Assn., Am. Orthopsychiat. Assn., Ohio Sch. Psychologist Assn., Cleve. Assn. Sch. Psychologists (pres. 1983-84), Sch. Psychol. Ohio polit. action com. (co-pres. 1987—). Office: Early Intervention Ctr East 5443 Rae Rd Lyndhurst OH 44124

ALBRIGHT, LINDA LEECH, business machines company executive; b. Columbus, Ind., Aug. 21, 1942; d. Kenneth Myers Leech and Velma Bernice (Lowry) Gagnon; m. William E. Albright (div. Jan. 1985); children: Kimberly E., Bridget B., Gwyndolyn F. BA, Lindenwood Coll., 1964; MBA, Rochester Inst. Tech., 1976. Cartographer Aero. Chart & Info. Ctr., St. Louis, 1965-68; service engr. Xerox Corp., Rochester, N.Y., 1976-78, product planner, 1978-80, sr. fin. analyst, 1980-81, planning mgr., 1981-83; mgr. product devel. Konica Bus. Machines, Windsor, Conn., 1983-88, dir., 1988—. Treas. United Ch. of Christ, Fairport, N.Y., 1982. Mem. AAUW (bd. dirs. 1976). Republican. Club: Toastmasters (Rochester) (named Toastmaster of the Yr. 1976). Office: Konica Bus Machines 500 Day Hill Rd Windsor CT 06095

ALBRIGHT, LOVELIA FRIED, art importing executive; b. N.Y.C., Dec. 13, 1934; d. George and Hilda (Lazanov) Fried; m. Lee Albright, Nov. 30, 1958; children: Gregre Scott, Glenn Keith, Todd Cameron. Student, Bennington Coll., 1952-55, Grad. Sch. Internat. Studies, Geneva. Publicist Doubleday & Co., N.Y.C., 1960-63; pres., owner Design Cons. for Industry, N.Y.C., 1964-72, Lovelia Enterprises, Inc., N.Y.C., 1972—. Monthly columnist home furnishings N.Y. Antique Guide, 1972. Office: Lovelia Enterprises Inc 356 E 41st Pl New York NY 10017

ALBRIGHT, MADELEINE, political scientist; b. Prague, Czechoslovakia, May 15, 1937; d. Josef and Anna (Speeglova) Korbel; m. Joseph Medill Patterson Albright, June 11, 1959 (div. 1983); children: Anne Korbel, Alice Patterson, Katharine Medill. B.A. with honors, Wellesley Coll., 1959; M.A., Columbia U., 1968; cert., Russian Inst., 1968, Ph.D., 1976. Washington coordinator Maine for Muskie, 1975-76; chief legis. asst. to U.S. Senator Muskie 1976-78; mem. staff NSC, 1978-81; fellow Woodrow Wilson Internat. Ctr. for Scholars, Washington, 1981-82; Donner prof. internat. affairs, dir. women in fgn. service Sch. Fgn. Service Georgetown U., 1982—, sr. fellow in Soviet and Eastern European Affairs Ctr. for Strategic and Internat. Studies,, 1981; fgn. policy coordinator Mondale for Pres. campaign, 1984, to Geraldine A. Ferraro, 1984; vice chmn. Nat. Dem. Inst. for Internat. Affairs, Washington, 1984—. Author: Poland: The Role of the Press in Political Change, 1983; contbr. articles to profl. jours., chpts. to books. Bd. dirs. Beauvoir Sch., Washington, 1968-76, chmn., 1978-83; trustee Black Student Fund, 1969-78, 82—, Democratic Forum, 1976-78, Williams Coll., 1978-82, Wellesley Coll., 1983—; mem. exec. com. D.C. Citizens for Better Pub. Edn., 1975-76; bd. dirs. Washington Urban League, 1982-84, Atlantic Council, 1984—, Ctr. for Nat. Policy, 1985—, Chatham House Fedn., 1986—; sr. fgn. policy advisor Dukakis for Pres. Campaign, 1988. Mem. Council Fgn. Relations, Am. Polit. Sci. Assn., Czeckoslovak Soc. Arts and Scis. Am., Atlantic Council U.S. (dir.), Am. Assn. for Advancement Slavic Studies. Office: Georgetown U Sch Fgn Service Washington DC 20007

ALBRIGHT, MICHELLE LOUISE, real estate executive; b. Nome, Alaska, Dec. 28, 1961; d. Wayne Paul and Elizabeth Louise (Cavota) A. BA, The Catholic U. Am., 1984; BBA, George Washington U., 1988. Real estate appraisers U.S. Dept. Interior, Washington, 1985-86, Urquhart & Assocs., Kensington, Md., 1986-88, Coldwell Banker, Washington, 1988—. Recipient Am. Ind. Am. scholar U.S. Dept. Edn., Washington, 1985. Mem. Am. Indian Soc. Republican. Roman Catholic. Home: 13701-13 Modrad Way Sinver Spring MD 20904 Office: Urquhart & Assocs 10605 Concord St #203 Kensington MD 20895

ALBRIGHT, SANDRA KAY, health center facility administrator; b. Bloomington, Ind., Dec. 17, 1945; d. Warren Edward and Adele Joan (Barr) A. BA, St. Mary's Coll., South Bend, Ind., 1967; MSW, U. Mich., 1969; cert. advanced mgmt., Radcliffe Coll., 1984. Lic. social worker. Social worker Boston State Hosp., 1969-71; clin. dir. The Little House, FDNH, Dorchester, Mass., 1971-74, exec. dir., 1974-84; mgmt. fellow Med. East Community Health Plan, Braintree, Mass., 1985-86; div. exec. dir. Med. East Community Health Plan, Peabody, Mass., 1986—. Mem., bd. dirs. Shepherd House, Dorchester, 1981—, Bay Cove Human Services, Dorchester, 1982—; pres. Andrew Corp., Dorchester, 1983—. Mem. Nat. Assn. Social Workers. Democrat. Roman Catholic. Home: 10 Roberts Ave Newton MA 02160 Office: Med East Community Health Plan North Shore Shopping Ctr Peabody MA 01961

ALBRO, PATRICIA JANE, civil engineer; b. Balt., Mar. 1, 1960; d. Walter Arthur and Doris (Freeberger) A. BS, Va. Polytech. Inst. and State U., 1983. Lic. land surveyor, Va. Design team leader Paciulli, Simmons & Assocs., Ltd., Fairfax, Va., 1983—. Mem. ASCE (assoc.), Am. Congress Surveying and Mapping, Va. Assn. Surveyors, Inc. (assoc.), Forum for Women in Surveying. Democrat. Methodist. Home: 2459 Glengyle Dr Vienna VA 22180 Office: Paciulli Simmons & Assocs Ltd 11130 Main St Fairfax VA 22030

ALCON, SONJA LEE DE BEY RYAN, medical social worker; b. Orange City, Iowa, Aug. 2, 1937; d. Albert Lee Gerard and Clarice Victoria (Brown) deBey; B.A., Western Md. Coll., 1959; M.S.W., U. Md., 1973; m. Richard J. Gebhardt, June 6, 1959; children—Russell, Cheryl, KurtGebhardt Ryan; m. George W. Ryan, Dec. 28, 1968; 1 dau., Alanna (dec.); m. David E. Alcon, July 20, 1985. Caseworker, Springfield State Hosp., Sykesville, Md., 1959-61; dir. social work dept. Hanover (Pa.) Gen. Hosp., 1966—; clin. assoc. prof. sch. social work and social planning U. Md., 1987—; cons. Golden Age Nursing Home, Hanover, 1973-76, Carlisle (Pa.) Hosp., 1974-78, Hanover Vis. Nurse Assn., 1977-83; chmn. profl. adv. com. Vis. Nurse Assn. of Hanover and Spring Grove, Inc., 1986-89; mem. social work adv. council Western Md. Coll., 1979, 80. Bd. dirs. Hospice of York, 1980-82, Hanover chpt. ARC, 1976-79, Adams-Hanover Mental Health, 1973-76; pres. Human Services Orgn., 1980, v.p., 1985-86; mem. adv. council Hanover Hospice, 1982-85; treas. Hanover Community Progress Com., 1976-80; mem. Adams-Hanover Sheltered Workshop Com., 1968-70; bd. dirs. Hanover Community Players, 1974-77, sec., 1982; organizer local chpt. Make Today Count and Preemie Parent Support Group, 1979; initiator Children's Cardiac Fund, 1979; mem. Hanover Oratorio Soc., 1964-85; active YWCA, 1979-84; co-organizer Adams-Hanover chpt. Compassionate Friends, 1983; mem. vestry All Saints Episcopal Ch., 1973-74, 76-79, 83-86, vestry sec., 1975, diocesan del. Central Pa., 1978, 80-86, mem. altar guild, 1968-86, treas. ch. women, 1979-83. Recipient York Daily Record Exceptional Citizen award, 1979, Spl. Recognition cert. Col. Richard McAllister chpt. DAR, 1980; finalist YWCA Salute to Women, 1986, 87. Mem. Nat. Assn. Social Workers, Acad. Cert. Social Workers, Am. Hosp. Assn. Soc. Hosp. Social Work Dirs., Central Pa. Hosp. Social Workers (treas. 1981-85, v.p. 1987, pres. 1988), Hosp. Assn. of Pa. Soc. for Hosp. Social Work Dirs., U. Md. Alumni Assn. (bd. dirs. 1983). Lodges: Order Eastern Star (worthy matron 1985-86), Order of Amaranth (worthy patron 1988—), White Shrine (adv. bd., Commandery Aux., Elks Aux. (v.p. local 1986-88), Internat Order of the Rainbow for Girls (adv. bd. Hanover Assembly). Home and Office: RD #3 3305-M Tamarind Dr Spring Grove PA 17362

ALCOTT, AMY STRUM, professional golfer; b. Kansas City, Mo., Feb. 22, 1956; d. Eugene Yale and Leatrice (Strum) A. Profl. golfer Ladies Profl. Golf Assn., 1975—; dir. Women's Golf Devel. Elizabeth Arden, Inc.; asst. golf coach UCLA Women's Golf Team; host Amy Alcott Golf Classic for Multiple Sclerosis Soc., 1980—; dir. Youth Golf Devel., Sunkist. Named Rookie of Year Ladies Profl. Golf Assn., 1975, Player of Yr. Ladies Profl. Golf Assn., 1980; Player of Year Golf mag., 1980; Jewish Athlete of Year, 1980; Calif. Golf Writers Hall of Fame, 1987; recipient Seagrams Seven Crown of Sports award, 1980, Vare Trophy, 1980, Ladies Pro Golf Assn. Founders Cup award, 1986. Office: Ladies Pro Golf Assn 4675 Sweetwater Blvd Sugar Land TX 77479

ALCOTT, MARGARET ANN, corporate real estate administrator; b. N.Y.C., Jan. 26, 1943; d. John Peter and Angela Sara (Corliss) McGuire; m. Robert John Alcott, April 20, 1963; children: Kevin Keith, Scott Patrick. BA, Rutgers U., 1978; M in Urban Planning, Princeton U., 1981. Lic. real estate broker, N.J. Office mgr., salesperson Stults Realty Co., Cranbury, N.J., 1972-75; lectr. Rider Coll., Lawrence, N.J., 1981-82; asst. mgr. real estate N.J. Bell, Orange, 1982-83; dir. real estate Doubleday & Co., Inc., N.Y.C., 1984-85; mgr. real estate BASF Corp., Parsippany, N.J., 1985-87, Consumers Distbg. Corp., Edison, N.J., 1987-88; owner, broker Alcott Agy., Princeton Junction, N.J., 1975-84 88—; adj. prof. Fairleigh Dickinson U., Rutherford, N.J., 1982. Author: Recreational Development of Urban Waterfronts, 1981. Garden State fellow, 1979-81, Princeton U. fellow, 1979-81. Mem. Nat. Assn. Corp. Real Estate Execs., Nat. Council Shopping Ctrs., Employee Relocation Council. Republican. Home: 53 N Mill Rd Princeton Junction NJ 08550

ALCOTT, SUSAN, writer, editor, public relations specialist; b. Los Angeles, June 7, 1940; d. William Kenneth and Hazel Stella (Pearson) Allin; student Los Angeles Harbor Coll., 1958-59, El Camino Coll., 1959-61, Calif. State U., 1961-64, Writers Guild Am. West, Inc., 1970-74, Arthur Alsberg's Advanced Screenwriting Workshop, 1980-81; div. Teaching asst., lab. technician Calif. State U., Los Angeles, 1963-64; with Musifon, Inc., Los Angeles, 1965-69; with Mickey Garrett & Assos., Public Relations, Los Angeles, 1967-68; freelance reader Screen Gems TV, Burbank, Calif., 1972; corp. sec.-treas., adminstrv. asst., dir. Don Perry Enterprises, Inc., Los Angeles, 1969-80; free-lance bus. and public relations writing service Susan Alcott's Scribe Services Ltd., Sherman Oaks, Calif., 1981—; pub. relations adminstr., editor, feature writer the Spl. Friends of Kenny Rogers Kenny Rogers Prodns. Inc., Los Angeles, 1981-87; with music pub. amd copyright dept. Cooper Epstein & Hurewitz, 1988—; actress theatres So. Calif.; actress films, TV, commls.; poetry published Poetry Parade mag., Writers Guild Am. West Inc, newspapers; contbr. Ellery Queen Mystery Mag.;lyricist Nobody's Child. Recipient Writers Guild Found. award, 1972, cert., 1974. Mem. ASCAP, Screen Actors Guild, Am. Film Inst., Nat. Assn. Female Execs., Planetary Soc. Editor: Patterns, 1982.

ALCOZER, ROMALDA FRANCESCA, health system administrator; b. Austin, Tex., July 19, 1950; d. Manuel and Romalda (Gonzales) Vallez; m. Jan D. Rumberger, Dec. 19, 1970 (div. Sept. 1977). BS in Nursing, U. Mary Hardin-Baylor, 1972; MS in Nursing, Pa. State U., 1981. Charge nurse Santa Fe Meml. Hosp., Temple, Tex., 1972; staff nurse VA Ctr., Temple, Tex., 1972-73, head nurse, 1980-81; staff nurse Pitts., 1981; head nurse Phila., 1981-83; pub. health nurse Pa. Dept. Health, Harrisburg, 1973-78; grad. asst. Pa. State U., University Park, 1979; dir. Scott & White Meml. Hosp., Temple, 1983-85, Holy Cross Hosp. Home Health, Austin, 1985-87; project coordinator Daus. Charity Nat. Home Health System, Austin, 1987—. Candidate Miss Hope Am. Cancer Soc., Harrisburg, 1977. U. Mary Hardin-Baylor scholar, 1969. Mem. Am. Nurses Assn. (cert. med.-surg. nurse), Nat. Assn. for Female Execs., Tex. Nurses Assn. (recording sec. 1987—), Am. Diabetes Assn., Oncology Soc., Hispanic C. of C., Zachary Scott Theatre (vol. 1985—). Democrat. Roman Catholic. Home: 1504 Hether St Austin TX 78704 Office: Holy Cross Hosp Home Health 2600 E Martin Luther King Austin TX 78702

ALDAVE, BARBARA BADER, educator, lawyer; b. Tacoma, Dec. 28, 1938; d. Fred A. and Patricia W. (Burns) Bader; m. Ralph Theodore Aldave, Apr. 2, 1966; children—Anna Marie, Anthony John. B.S., Stanford U., 1960; J.D., U. Calif.-Berkeley, 1966. Bar: Oreg. 1966, Tex. 1982. Assoc. law firm Eugene, Oreg., 1967-70; asst. prof. U. Oreg., 1970-73; vis. prof. U. Calif.-Berkeley, 1973-74; vis. prof., asst. prof. to prof. U. Tex., Austin, 1974—, co-holder James R. Dougherty chair for faculty excellence, 1981-82, Piper prof., 1982, Joe A. Worsham centennial prof., 1984—; vis. prof. Northeastern U., 1985—. Mem. women's com. Travis County Democratic Orgn.; pres. NETWORK; bd. dirs. Austin Council on Fgn. Affairs, Women's Advocacy Project. Recipient Teaching Excellence award U. Tex. Student Bar Assn., 1976, appreciation awards Thurgood Marshall Legal Soc. of U. Tex., 1979, 81, 85, 87, Teaching Excellence award Chicano Law Students Assn. of U. Tex., 1984, Hermine Tobolowsky award Women's Law Caucus of U. Tex., 1985. Mem. ABA (com. on corp. laws sect. corp., banking and bus. law), Travis County Women Lawyers Assn., Stanford Alumni Assn., Bread for the World, Gray Panthers, Pax Christi, United Campuses To Prevent Nuclear War, Lawyers Alliance for Nuclear Arms Control, Amnesty Internat. USA, Fellowship of Reconciliation, Nat. IMPACT, Nat. Lawyers Guild, Order of Coif, Phi Delta Phi, Iota Sigma Pi, Omicron Delta Kappa. Roman Catholic. Club: Stanford (Austin). Home: 803 Cedar Park Dr Austin TX 78746 Office: U Tex 727 E 26th St Austin TX 78705

ALDEA, PATRICIA, architect; b. Bucharest, Romania, Mar. 18, 1947; came to U.S., 1976; d. Dan Jasmin Negreanu and Sonia (Friedgant) Philip-Negreanu; m. Val O. Aldea, Feb. 17, 1971; 1 child, Donna-Dana. MArch, Ion Mincu, Bucharest, 1970. Registered architect, N.Y. Architect, project. mgr. The Landmark Preservation Inst., Bucharest, 1971-76; architect Edward Durell Stone Assn., N.Y.C., 1977-79; assoc. architect, project mgr. Alan Lapidus P.C., N.Y.C., 1980—. Columnist Contemporanul art jour., 1969-73. Hist. landmarks study fellow Internationes Fed. Republic of Germany, 1974. Office: Alan Lapidus PC 2112 Broadway New York NY 11023

ALDER, ALTHEA ALICE, marketing service agency executive; b. Wilmore, Kans., Jan. 4, 1933; d. Lloyd Lewis and Margaret Mae (Baldwin) A.; student Ft. Hays State U., 1952-55. Owner, operator 2 beauty shops, 1961-67; quality control mgr., supr. women Solo Cup Co., 1967-70; v.p. purchasing, prodn. and premiums William A. Robinson, Inc., Northbrook, Ill., 1970-79; pres. A-three Services Agy., Ltd., Northbrook, Ill., 1980—, Lake Forest Tng. Salon, Ltd., 1979-80. Served with U.S. Army, 1951-53, 55-61, Korea. Decorated Army Commendation medal. Mem. Am. Legion. Lodge: Eastern Star. Home: 1116 Greenwood Ave Deerfield IL 60015 Office: A-three Services 3125 Commercial Ave Northbrook IL 60062

ALDERDICE, SUNNY PURL, newspaper editor; b. Dallas, Dec. 21, 1930; d. George Clark Purl and Bernice (Dillard) Purl Blanton; m. Barham Alderdice, Dec. 21, 1948; children—Barbara Emily Alderdice Anthony. Grad. Midlothian High Sch., 1948. Writer, editor Midlothian Mirror (Tex.), 1969—. Recipient various awards Texas Press, 1972—. Mem. park bd. Midlothian, Tex., 1975-79; mem. community edn. adv. bd., Midlothian, 1979-82; mem. sr. citizen adv. bd., Midlothian, 1979—; mem. home rule charter com., Midlothian, 1980; founder Midlothian Ch. Women, 1980—; life mem. Midlothian PTA, 1972. Sunny Alderdice Day proclaimed by City of Midlothian, 1973. Mem. Midlothian Cemetery Assn. Presbyterian. Club: Ladies of Leaf. Office: Midlothian Mirror 214 W Ave F PO Box 70 Midlothian TX 76065

ALDERMAN, MINNIS AMELIA, psychologist, educator, small business owner; b. Douglas, Ga., Oct. 14, 1928; d. Louis Cleveland Sr. and Minnis Amelia (Wooten) A. AB in Music, Speech and Drama, Ga. State Coll., Milledgeville, 1949; MA in Supervision, Murray State U., 1960; postgrad. in psychology and fine arts, Columbia Pacific U., Los Angeles, 1987—. Tchr. music Lake County Sch. Dist., Umatilla, Fla., 1949-50; instr. vocal and instrumental music, dir. band, orch. and choral Fulton County Sch. Dist., Atlanta, 1950-54; instr. English, speech, debate, vocal and instrumental music, dir. drama, band, choral and orch. Elko County Sch. Dist., Wells, Nev., 1954-59; tchr. English and social studies Christian County Sch. Dist., Hopkinsville, Ky., 1960; instr. psychology, guidance counselor Murray (Ky.) State U., 1961-63, U. Nev., Reno, 1963-67; owner Minisizer Exercising Salon, Ely, Nev., 1969-71, Knit Knook, Ely, 1969—, Minimimeo, Ely, 1969—, Gift Gamut, Ely, 1977—; prof. dept. fine arts Wassuk Coll., Ely, 1986—, assoc. dean, 1986-87, dean, 1987—; counselor White Pine County Sch. Dist., Ely, 1960-68; supr. testing Ednl. Testing Service, Princeton, N.J., 1960-68, Am. Coll. Testing Program, Iowa, 1960-68, U. Nev., Reno, 1960-68; chmn. bd. White Pine Sch. Dist. Employees Fed. Credit Union, Ely, 1961-69; psychologist mental hygiene div. Nev. Personnel, Ely, 1969-75, dept. employment security, 1975-80; sec.-treas. bd. dirs. Great Basin Enterprises, Ely, 1969-71; pvt. instr. piano, violin, voice and organ, Ely, 1981—; dir. band Sacred Heart Sch., Ely, 1982—. Author various news articles, feature stories, pamphlets, handbooks and grants in field. Pres. White Pine County Mental Health Assn., 1960-63, 78—; mem. Gov.'s Mental Health State Commn., 1963-65; bd. dirs. White Pine County Sch. Employees Fed. Credit Union, 1961-68, pres., 1963-68; 2d v.p. White Pine Community Concert Assn., 1965-67, pres., 1967, 85—, treas., 1975—, dr. chmn., 1981—; dir. Community Choir, 1975—; bd. dirs. White Pine chpt. ARC, 1978-82; mem. Nev. Hwy. Safety Leaders Bd., 1979-82; mem. Gov.'s Commn. on Status Women, 1968-74; sec.-treas. White Pine Rehab. Tng. Ctr. for Retarded Persons, 1973-75; mem. Gov.'s Commn. on Hwy. Safety, 1979-81; dir. Ret. Sr. Vol. Program, 1973-74; vice chmn. Great Basin Health Council, 1973-75, Home Extension Adv. Bd., 1977-80; sec.-treas. Great Basin chpt. Nev. Employees Assn.; bd. dirs. United Way, 1970-76; vice chmn. White Pine Council on Alcoholism and Drug Abuse, 1975-76, chmn., 1976-77; grants author, originator Community Tng. Center for Retarded People, 1972, Ret. Sr. Vol. Program, 1974, Nutrition Program for Sr. Citizens, 1974, Sr. Citizens Center, 1974, Home Repairs for Sr. Citizens, 1974, Sr. Citizens Home Assistance Program, 1977, Creative Crafters Assns., 1976; bd. dirs. Sacred Heart Parochial Sch., 1982—, dir. band, 1982—; candidate for diaconal ministry, 1982—. Precinct reporter ABC News 1966. Fellow Am. Coll. Musicians, Nat. Guild Piano Tchrs.; mem. NEA (life), Nat. Fedn. Ind. Bus. (dist. chair 1971-85, nat. guardian council 1985—, state guardian council 1987—), AAUW (pres. Wells br. 1957-58, pres. White Pine br. 1965-66, 86-87, bd. dirs. 1965-87, rep. edn. 1965-67, implementation chair 1967-69, area advisor 1969-73), Nat. Fedn. Bus. and Profl. Women (1st v.p. Ely chpt. 1965-66, pres. Ely chpt. 1966-68, 74-76, 85—, bd. dirs. Nev. chpt. 1966—, 1st v.p. Nev. chpt. 1970-71, pres. Nev. chpt. 1972-73, nat. bd. dirs. 1972-73), Mensa (supr. testing 1965—), Delta Kappa Gamma (chpt. pres. 1968-72, state bd. 1967—, chpt. parliamentarian 1974-78, state 1st v.p. 1967-69, state pres. 1969-71, nat. bd. 1969-71, state parliamentarian 1971-73). Club: White Pine Knife and Fork (Ely) (1st v.p. 1969-70, pres. 1970-71, bd. dirs. 1979—). Home: 945 Ave H PO Box 457 East Ely NV 89315 Office: 1280 Ave F PO Box 457 East Ely NV 89315

ALDERSON, MARGARET NORTHROP, arts administrator, educator, artist; b. Washington, Nov. 28, 1936; d. Vernon D. and Margaret (Lloyd) Northrop; m. Donald Marr Alderson, Jr., June 4, 1955; children— Donald Marr III, Barbara Lynn Hennesy, Brian, Graham. Student George Washington U., 1954-55; A.A., Monterey Peninsula Jr. Coll., 1962. Staff, tchr. Galerie Jaclande, Springfield, Va. 1972-73; artist/tchr. Studio 7, Torpedo Factory Art Ctr., Alexandria, 1974—, dir. ctr., 1979-85; tchr. Fairfax County Recreation, 1972-73, Art League Schs., Alexandria, 1978—, ann. Feb. workshop, Accapulco, Mex.; cons. in field; project supr. City of Alexandria for Torpedo Factory Art Ctr., 1978-83; ptnr. Soho Hubris Art Gallery (N.Y.), 1977-78; one woman shows at Way Up Gallery, Livermore, Calif., 1971, Lynchburg Coll. (Va.), 1978, Farm House Gallery, Rehobeth, Del., 1979, Art League Gallery, Alexandria, Va., 1980, 86, Lyceum Mus., Alexandria, 1987, Alexandria Mus., 1987-88, William Ris Gallery, Stone Harbor, N.J., 1988; exhibited in group shows at Art League Gallery, Alexandria, 1972—; represented in permanent collections Phillip Morse Collection, United Va. Bank, CSX Corp., Office U.S. Atty. Gen., Office of Ins. Gen. EPA, Aerospace Corp. Festival chmn. City Festival Cultural Arts, Livermore, Calif., 1971; bd. dirs., Cultural Alliance Greater Washington, 1982—; bd. dirs. Torpedo Factory Art Ctr., 1978—; mem. Partners for Liveable Places, 1979—. Recipient 1st Place Awards in Watercolor, Art League, 1975, 76, 77, 82, also numerous purchase awards, Jane Morton Norman award Ky. Nat. Watercolor Show, 1986, adrirondack Nat. Watercolor Show, 1987, 3d award Catherine Lorillard Show, N.Y.C., 1987. Mem. Fed. Nat. Mortgage Assn., Va. Watercolor Soc. (pres. 1982, 1st place awards ann. exhibit 1980, 82), Potomac Valley Watercolorists (pres. 1978), Torpedo Factory Artists Assn. (pres. 1977-78), Springfield Art Guild (pres. 1977), Artists Equity, Am. Council on Arts, Am. Watercolor Soc., Am. Council of Univ. and Community Arts Ctrs., Nat. League Am. PEN Women, Am. Mgmt. Assn., Nat. Historic Trust. Republican. Home: 2204 Windsor Rd Alexandria VA 22307 Studio: Studio 7 Torpedo Factory Art Ctr 105 N Union St Alexandria VA 22314

ALDREDGE, THEONI VACHLIOTIS, costume designer; b. Athens, Greece, Aug. 22, 1932; d. Gen. Athanasios and Meropi (Gregoriades) Vachliotis; m. Thomas E. Aldredge, Dec. 10, 1953. Student, Am. Sch., Athens, 1949-53, Goodman Theatre, Chgo.; LHD, De Paul U., 1985. Mem. design staff Goodman Theatre, 1951-53; head designer N.Y. Shakespeare Festival, 1962—. Designer numerous Broadway and off Broadway shows, ballet, opera, TV spls.; films include Girl of the Night, You're a Big Boy Now, No Way To Treat a Lady, Uptight, Last Summer, I Never Sang for My Father, Promise at Dawn, The Great Gatsby (Brit. Motion Picture Acad. award 1976), Network, The Cheap Detective, The Fury, The Eyes of Laura Mars, The Champ, Semi-Tough, The Rose, Monsignor, Annie, Ghostbusters; Broadway shows include A Chorus Line (Theatre World award 1976), Annie (Tony award 1977), Barnum (Tony award 1979), Dream Girls, Woman of the Year, Onward Victoria, La Cage Aux Folles (Tony award 1984), 42nd Street, A Little Family Business, Merlin, Private Lives, The Corn Is Green, The Rink, Blithe Spirit, Chess, Ziegfeld. Recipient Obie award for Disting. Service to Off Broadway Theatre Village Voice, Maharam award for Peer Gynt, N.Y.C. Liberty medal, 1986, numerous Drama Desk and Critics awards. Mem. United Scenic Artists, Costume Designers Guild, Acad. Motion Picture Arts Scis. (Oscar award Great Gatsby 1975). Office: 330 East 39 St New York NY 10016

ALDRICH, ANN, federal judge; b. Providence, June 28, 1927; d. Allie C. and Ethel M. (Carrier) A.; m. Chester Aldrich, 1960 (dec.); children: Martin, William; children by previous marriage: James, Allen; m. John H. McAllister III. BA cum laude, Columbia U., 1948; LLB cum laude, NYU, 1950, LLM, 1964, JSD. Bar: D.C. bar, N.Y. bar 1952, Conn. bar 1966, Ohio bar 1973, Supreme Ct. bar 1956. Research asst. to mem. faculty N.Y. U. Sch. Law; asso. firm Samuel Nakasian, Washington, 1952-53; mem. gen. counsel's staff FCC, Washington, 1953-60; U.S. del. to Internat. Radio Conf., Geneva, 1959; practice law Darien, Conn.; asso. prof. law Cleve. State U., 1968-71, prof., 1971-80; judge U.S. Dist. Ct. (no. dist.) Ohio, 1980—; bd. govs. Citizens' Communications Center, Inc., Washington; mem. litigation com.; guest lectr. Calif. Inst. Tech., Pasadena, summer 1971. Mem. Fed. Bar Assn., Nat. Assn. of Women Judges, Fed. Communications Bar Assn., Fed. Judge Assn. Episcopalian. Office: US Dist Ct 210 US Courthouse 201 Superior Ave NE Cleveland OH 44114 *

ALDRICH, LYNNE MERRILL, university administrator; b. Detroit, July 23, 1946; d. Claude E. and Irene (Suzanne) (Keil) Gardner; AB in Polit. Sci., W. Va. U., 1969; postgrad. Wayne State U. Asst., then acting area mgr. Fotomat Corp., Detroit, 1969-70; acad. service officer dept. biol. scis. Wayne State U., 1970-83; exec. asst. to sr. v.p. univ. relations Wayne State U., 1983-86; confidential asst. to pres., 1986— . Bd. dirs., sec. LaSalle Townhouse Coop. Assn., 1978-82. Recipient Humanitarian award Wayne State U., 1980, 81, bd. govs. Recognition Award Wayne State U., 1982. Mem. Nat. Assn. Female Execs., Mich. Advancement Council, Council for Advancement and Support Edn., AAUW (dir. Mich. div. bd., pres. Detroit 1986-90), Leadership Detroit VI. Club: Wayne State U. Faculty, Women's Econ. (Detroit). Office: Wayne State U Office of Pres Detroit MI 48202

ALDRICH, MICHELE L., historian, archivist, data processing executive; b Seattle, Oct. 6, 1942; d. Jean and Marion (Deasy) La Clergue; m. Mark Aldrich, Sept. 4, 1965. BA, U. Calif., Berkeley, 1964; PhD, U. Tex., 1974. Lectr. Smith Coll., Northampton, Mass., 1969-70; staff mem. Valley Women's Ctr., Northampton, 1970-73; asst. editor Henry Papers, Smithsonian Instn., Washington, 1974-75; field worker Women's History Survey, Mpls., 1976-77; archivist, project dir., mgr. computer services AAAS, Washington, 1977—; cons. Aaron Burr Papers, N.Y.C., 1975-76; research assoc. Calif. Acad. Scis., San Francisco, 1980—. Editor: (with N. Reingold, A. Molella) Joseph Henry Papers, 1975, (with A. Leviton, P. Rodda, E. Yochelson) Frontiers of Geology, 1982; author: (with P.Q. Hall) Programs in Science for Women, 1980, (with A. Leviton) John Anderson's Herpetology of Arabia, 1984; contbr. articles to profl. jours. Mem. Forum For History of Sci. in Am. (cordinating com. 1987—). Fellow U. Tex., Austin, 1965-66, NSF, 1967-68. Fellow AAAS; mem. Soc. Am. Archivists, Geol. Soc. Am. (chair history div. 1979-80, sec.-treas. 1984-88), History Sci. Soc. (publicity officer 1978-83, co-chmn. women's com. 1984-86). Democrat. Home: 24 Elm St Hatfield MA 01038 Office: AAAS 1333 H St NW Washington DC 20005

ALDRICH, NANCY ARMSTRONG, psychotherapist; b. Taylorville, Ill., Oct. 4, 1925; d. Guy L. and Alice Irene (Hicks) Armstrong; m. Paul Harwood Aldrich, Sept. 30, 1949; children: Gregory Paul, Mark Douglas, Alice Ann Aldrich White, Ruth Lynne. AB with highest honors, U. Ill., 1947, BS in Chemistry, 1948, MS in Chemistry, 1949; MSS, Bryn Mawr Coll., 1986. Lic. clin. social worker. Parole bd. mem. State of Del., Dover, 1970-74; instr. continuing edn. U. Del., Newark, 1976-78, program specialist, 1978-83; v.p. Aldrich Assocs. Inc., Landenberg, Pa., 1983—, psychotherapist, 1987—; psychotherapist Family Community Service Del. County, Media, Pa., 1986, Tressler Ctr. for Human Growth, Wilmington, Del., 1987—; coordinator human resources devel. program Tressler Ctr. for human Devel., 1983-84. Pres. YWCA New Castle County, Wilmington, 1974-76; mem. Statewide Health Coordinating Council, Del., 1978-79; bd. dirs., com. mem. United Way Del., Wilmington, 1975-84. Mem. Del. Soc. Lic. Clin. Social Workers, Del. Assn. Alcohol and Drug Counselors, Nat. Assn. Social Workers, Del. Gerontological, Am. Assn. Univ. Women (pres. Wilmington br. 1968-70, nat. resolutions com. mem. 1971-72,, fellowship award named in honor 1970), Phi Beta Kappa, Phi Kappa Phi, Iota Sigma Pi. Unitarian. Home: 625 Chambers Rock Rd Landenberg PA 19359

ALDRICH, NANCY COOK, engineer, administrator; b. Ogden, Utah, Oct. 16, 1944; d. William Burford and Margaret (Spilker) Cook; m. Ralph E. Aldrich, Aug. 10, 1968. BA in Physics, Scripps Coll., 1966; MS in Physics, Tufts U., 1969. Physicist Naval Underwater Weapons Sta., Newport, R.I., 1966; engr. Microwave Assn., Burlington, Mass., 1967; assoc. engr. Honeywell Electro Optics (formerly Honeywell Radiation Ctr.) div. Honeywell Corp., Lexington, Mass., 1969-70, engr., 1970-71, sr. engr, 1971-72, prin. engr., 1972-75, sr. prin. engr., 1975-78, program mgr., 1978-81, bus. mgr., 1981-82, engring. mgr., 1982-84, sect. head, 1984-86, chief engr., 1986—. Leader Girl Scouts U.S., Acton, Mass., 1972. Recipient Ed Lund Mgmt. award, 1987; named Disting. Alumna Scripps Coll., 1984. Mem. Profl. Council. Office: Electro-Optics div Honeywell Corp 2 Forbes Rd Lexington MA 02173

ALDRICH, NANCY WELZ, airline pilot; b. Houston, Dec. 9, 1939; d. Robert Wesley and Vivian Beulah (Attaway) Welz; children: Christopher Robin Alexandre, Dawn Venise Alexandre Meyer. Instr. flight Ellsworth Aviation, Longmont, Colo., 1978-80; instr. ground King Accelerated Ground Schs., San Diego, 1980-82; contract pilot Denver, 1982-83; tng. prog. developer United Airlines, Denver, 1983-84, flight ops. instr., 1984-85, airline pilot, 1985—; aviation cons. AvCon., Inc., Broomfield, Colo., 1982-88; accident prevention counselor FAA, Denver, 1981—; safety chmn. Colo. Ninety Nines, Inc., Denver, 1982—. Author: Flying--For Nervous Birds, 1987, various study guides; lectr. Flight Without Fear, 1982—; contbr. articles to profl. jours. Mem. Aircraft Owners and Pilots Assn., Internat. Ninety Nines. Republican. Episcopalian.

ALDRICH, STEPHANIE RAE HEGEDUS, chemist; b. Akron, Ohio, June 26, 1944; d. Stephen Paul and Fannie Alberta (Beck) Hegedus; student Purdue U., South Bend (Ind.) Campus, evenings 1972-74; grad. Varian Inst. Chromotography, 1981; children—Todd Clifton, Robert LeRoy. Charge nurse LaGrange Nursing Home, Ind., 1972-73; tchr. reality therapy, activities dir. Rehab. Center, Michigan City, Ind. 1973-75; metallurgy, sand control apprentice Josam Mfg. Co., Michigan City, 1978-79; mgr. quality control labs. Manley Bros. div. Brit. Indsl. Sands, Ltd., U.K., 1979-81, mgr. quality control and research and devel. labs., 1981-82, analytical chemist for plants in Mich. and Ill., 1982—. Mem. AAAS, Nat. Assn. Female Execs., Am. Chem. Soc., Chem. Engrin. Product Research Panel. Democrat. Lutheran. Contbr. poetry to various publs. Home: 1215 Earl Rd Michigan City IN 46360 Office: Manley Bros 128 S 15th St Chesterton IN 46304

ALDRIDGE, RITA MARY, university financial administrator; b. N.Y.C., July 4, 1926; d. Howard and Helen Valentine (Maune) Dougherty; 1 dau., Jane Kathryn Aldridge Cooper. PhB summa cum laude with honors Fordham U., 1987. Exec. asst. Real Estate, N.Y.C., 1959-62; adminstrv. asst. Cornell U. Med. Coll., N.Y.C., 1964-72, adminstrv. mgr., 1972-77, fin. mgr., 1977-87, fin. dir., 1987—, mem. grievance panel, 1974—. Mem. Nat. Assn. Female Execs., Coll. Art Assn., Alpha Sigma Lambda, Phi Kappa Phi, Alpha Sigma Nu. Office: Cornell U Med Coll 1300 York Ave New York NY 10021 Mailing Address: 104 Haynes Dr Williamsburg VA 23185

ALEANDRI, EMELISE FRANCESCA, producer, television personality, actress; b. Riva del Garda, Italy; came to U.S., 1948; d. John Baptist and Elodia (Lutterotti) A. AB in French, Coll. of New Rochelle, N.Y., 1965; MA in Theater, Hunter Coll., N.Y.C., 1975; MPhil in Theater, CUNY, 1976, PhD in Theater, 1983. Drama instr. Hunter Coll., N.Y.C., 1971-73, Borough of Manhattan City Coll., N.Y.C., 1973-74, N.Y.C. Tech. Coll., Bklyn., 1971-84; dir. Ctr. Italian-Am. Studies, Bklyn. Coll., 1984-87; producer Italics Mag. Show CUNY-TV, N.Y.C., 1987—. Author: Italian-American Theatre, 1983; translator various plays from Italian to English; contbr. articles to profl. jours. Recipient N.Y. State Hist. award, 1961; NEA grantee Bklyn. Coll., 1970. Mem. Actor's Equity Assn., Screen Actor's Guild, Dramatists Guild, Soc. Stage Dirs. and Choreographers, AFTRA. Office: Italian-American Inst 33 W 42d St New York NY 10036

ALEMAN, MINDY R., advertising and public relations executive, freelance writer; b. N.Y.C., Nov. 23, 1950; d. Lionel and Jocelyn (Cohen) Luskin; m. Gary Aleman, Aug. 27, 1983. BA, U. Akron, 1972, MA, 1975. Instr. speech U. Akron, 1973-83; car salesperson Dave Towell Cadillac, Akron, 1977-79, mgr. fin. and ins., 1979; account exec., pub. relations dir. Loos, Edwards & Sexauer, Akron, 1980-82; mktg. services coordinator Century Products, Stow, Ohio, 1982-83; mgr. advt., pub. relations Century Products, Gerber Furniture Group, Stow, 1983-86, Macedonia, Ohio, 1986—. Playwright Danny's Choice, 1972. Mem. Am. Mktg. Assn., Pub. Relations Soc. Am. (accredited), Akron Advt. Club (various awards 1983-88), Akron Women's Network, Sales and Mktg. Execs. of Cleve. Office: Gerber Furniture Group Inc 9600 Valley View Rd Macedonia OH 44056

ALENIER, KARREN LALONDE, management analyst, poet; b. Cheverly, Md., May 7, 1947; d. Rona Lee (Bass) Keenan; 1 child, Ivan Ascher. BA with honors, U. Md., 1969. Computer programmer Fed. Power Commn., Washington, 1969-71; computer systems analyst Labor Dept., Washington, 1972-77; computer specialist Energy Dept., Washington, 1977-82; mgmt. analyst Justice Dept., Washington, 1982—; bd. dirs. Word Works, Inc., Washington, 1984—, pres., chair bd., 1987; bd. dirs. Poetry Com. Greater Washington, 1985—, pres., chair bd., 1987; bd. dirs. Folger Shakespeare Library. Author: Wandering on the Outside, 1975, The Dancer's Muse, 1981, Whose Woods These Are, 1983. Recipient Dellbrook awards Shenandoah Coll., Va., 1978, 79, Billee Murray Denny award Lincoln Coll., Ill., 1981. Mem. Poetry Soc. Am. Jewish. Avocations: photography, gourmet cooking, foreign travel, cycling. Home: 4601 N Park Ave #1212 Chevy Chase MD 20815 Office: The Word Works PO Box 42164 Washington DC 20015

ALESCHUS, JUSTINE LAWRENCE, land broker; b. New Brunswick, N.J., Aug. 13, 1925; d. Walter and Mildred Lawrence; student Rutgers U.; m. John Aleschus, Jan. 23, 1949; children—Verdene Jan, Janine Kimberley, Joanna Lauren. Dept. sec. Am. Baptist Home Mission Soc., N.Y.C., 1947-49; claims examiner Republic Ins. Co., Dallas, 1950-52; broker Damon Homes, L.I., 1960-72; exclusive broker estate of Kenneth H. Leeds, L.I., 1980—; pres. Justine Aleschus Real Estate. Past-pres. Nassau-Suffolk Council of Hosp. Aux., 1981-82; hon. mem. aux. of St. John's Episcopal Hosp., Smithtown, N.Y., also past pres., mem. hosp. adv. bd.; pres. L.I. Coalition for Sensible Growth, Inc.; mem. Smithtown Industry Adv. Bd.; exec. bd. dirs. Suffolk County council Boy Scouts Am.; mem. adv. bd. Suffolk County council Girl Scouts U.S. Mem. Suffolk County Real Estate Bd. (pres.), L.I. Mid-Suffolk Businessmen's Assn., Eastern L.I. Execs. (sponsor-trustee), Smithtown Bus. and Profl. Women's Network, L.I. Assn., JEI Com., Hauppauge Indsl. Assn. Advancement Commerce & Industry. Republican. Lutheran. Office: 300 Hawkins Ave Lake Ronkonkoma NY 11779

ALESSI, DANA LOUISE, publishing company executive; b. Colorado Springs, Colo., Sept. 2, 1943; d. Fred and Louise Winifred (Hall) Bennett; m. Paul Thomas Alessi, Aug. 27, 1966 (div. Mar. 1988). Student, Knox Coll., Galesburg, Ill., 1961-62; BA, U. Colo., 1965; MA, Ind. U., 1966, U. Mo., 1972. Cataloger Stephens Coll., Columbia, Mo., 1972-73; librarian Mo. Sch. of Religion, Columbia, 1972-73; pub. services librarian Wartburg Coll., Waverly, Iowa, 1973-74, dir., 1974-75; asst. head. acquistions and procurement U. Houston, 1975-76, head acqusitions, 1977-78; regional sales mgr. Blackwell No. Am., Houston, 1978-83; div. sales mgr. Blackwell No. Am., Kansas City, Mo., 1983-86; dir. monographic and selection services Blackwell No. Am., Lake Oswego, Ore., 1987-88; dir. service devel. Blackwell No. Am., Blackwood, N.J., 1988—. Mem. Friends of the Library, Rice U., Houston, 1987—, U. Iowa, Iowa City, 1982—, U. Colo., Boulder, 1983—. Mem. Am. Library Assn., Tex. Library Assn., Phi Beta Kappa, Beta Phi Mu. Democrat.

ALEXA, NANCY ANN, financial analyst; b. Yonkers, N.Y., July 9, 1954; d. Harry and Mae (Poirier) Alexa; B.S. in Mgmt., Rutgers U., 1985. With Holland Am. Line (USA) Inc., N.Y.C., 1982-83, Rothschild Inc., N.Y.C., 1983-84, Kelso & Co. (investment bankers), N.Y.C., 1984-87, Citicorp N.Am., Iselin, N.J., 1987—. Office: Citicorp North Am 100 Wood Ave S Iselin NJ 08830

ALEXANDAR, WENDY ELIZABETH, engineer; b. Bklyn., Dec. 3, 1957; d. Ira Arthur and Paula Schwartz; m. Jonathan Robert Strong, Aug. 23, 1978 (div. 1984); m. Iskandar Ra Alexandar, May 25, 1985. BSEE, U. Pa., 1981. Mem. engring. staff RCA Missle and Surface Radar div., Moorestown, N.J., 1981-83; mem. tech. staff Formation, Inc., Mt. Laurel, N.J., 1983-85; sr. mem. tech. staff Concurrent Computer Corp., Tinton Falls, N.J., 1985—. Mem. IEEE, Soc. Creative Anachronism (chronicler 1984), Medieval Studies and Restoration. Democrat. Jewish. Office: Concurrent Computer Corp 106 Apple St Tinton Falls NJ 07724

ALEXANDER, ANNETTE, sales executive; b. Santa Barbara, Calif., Apr. 6, 1949; d. Ezra Milton and Rosamond (Tudor) A.; 1 child, Sarin Delana. Student, U. Calif., Santa Barbara, 1973-78. Dir. personnel Mfr. div. Am. Hosp., Santa Barbara, 1971-79; co-owner irrigation systems co., Santa Barbara, 1979-84; mfr. mgr. Aquatic Systems, Santa Barbara, 1984-87, nat. sales mgr., 1987—; personnel cons. Alexander Enterprises, Santa Barbara, 1979—; past pres. AEA Credit Union. Fundraiser Mothers Against Drunk Driving, Santa Barbara, 1979—; vol. CALM, Santa Barbara, 1985—; active Single Parents Alliance, 1983—. Recipient Outstanding Achievement award City of Santa Barbara, 1973, 74, 75. Mem. Am. Compensation Assn., Profl. Women in Horticulture. Home: 1510 Sinaloa St Santa Barbara CA 93108 Office: Aquatic Systems div Waterman Industries Inc 1900 N 25th Dr Phoenix AZ 85009

ALEXANDER, BARBARA LEAH SHAPIRO, psychiatric social worker; b. St. Louis, May 6, 1943; d. Harold Albert and Dorothy Miriam (Leifer) Shapiro; m. Richard E. Alexander. B in Music Edn., Washington U., St. Louis, 1964; postgrad., U. Ill., 1964-66; MSW, Smith Coll., 1970; postgrad., Inst. Psychoanalysis, Chgo., 1971-73, grad., child therapy program, 1976-80; cert. therapist Sex Dysfunction Clinic, Loyola U., Chgo., 1975. Diplomate in Clin. Social Work. Research asst., NIMH grantee Smith Coll., 1968-70; probation officer Juvenile Ct. Cook County, Chgo., 1966-68, 70; therapist Madden Mental Health Center, Hines, Ill., 1970-72; supr., therapist, field instr. U. Chgo., U. Ill. Grad. Schs. Social Work, also Pritzker Children's Hosp., Chgo., 1972—; therapist, cons., also pvt. practice, 1973—; instr. tng. and advanced tng. Effectiveness Tng. Assocs., Chgo., 1974; instr. psychology Northeastern U., Chgo., 1975; intern Divorce Conciliation Service, Circuit Ct. Cook County, 1976-77. Contbr. articles to profl. jours. Bd. dirs., Grant Park Concerts Soc.; Cathedral Counseling; sec. Art Resources in Teaching. Recipient Sterling Achievement award Mu Phi Epsilon, 1964. Mem. Acad. Cert. Social Workers (cert.), Nat. Assn. Social Workers (pres. 1987—), Ill. Soc. Clin. Social Work (pres., bd. dirs., chmn. services to mems. com., dir. pvt. practitioners' referral service), Am. Assn. Marriage and Family Therapy, Assn. Child Psychotherapists, Am. Assn. Sex Educators and Counselors, Amateur Chamber Music Players Assn., Jewish Geneal. Soc., Smith Coll. Alumni Assn. (bd. dirs.). Democrat. Home: 179 E Lake Shore Dr Chicago IL 60611 Office: 919 N Michigan Ave #3012 Chicago IL 60611

ALEXANDER, BARBARA LYNNE, film producer, literary agent; b. Los Angeles, Jan. 6, 1942; d. Henry and Esther (Weiss) Alexander; m. Shirl Hendryx, July 24, 1983. Student U. Calif., Berkeley, 1960-61; B.A., UCLA, 1963. Tchr., Culver City (Calif.) Unified Sch. Dist., 1963-67; producer, dir., writer Comprenetics, Inc., Los Angeles, 1970-74; asso. producer Sutherland Prodns., Los Angeles, 1974-75; partner/producer Snow Prodns., Los Angeles, 1976-81; v.p. theatrical devel. Odyssey Communication, Inc., Culver City, 1977-81; v.p. prodn. Inst. for Career and Vocat. Tng., Culver City, 1979-81; ind. producer, Los Angeles, 1981-84; partner Pettit & Alexander Prodns., Los Angeles, 1984; lit. agt. The Wallerstein Co., Los Angeles, 1985-88; lit. agt., producer The Barbara Alexander Co., Los Angeles, 1988—. Recipient Info. Film Producers of Am. Bronze award, 1972, 76, 79; Am. Indian Film Festival Spl. Achievement award, 1978, 80, Bronze and Silver award Internat. Film and TV Festival of N.Y., 1978, 80; Columbus Film Festival Bronze award, 1979; U.S. Indsl. Film Festival Gold Camera award, 1979; Film Adv. Bd. award of excellence, 1976, others. Mem. Acad. TV Arts and Scis., Women in Film (bd. dirs. 1978-80), Los Angeles Cinematheque (founding mem., bd. dirs. 1976-78). Address: 12310 Dorothy St Los Angeles CA 90049

ALEXANDER, BARBARA TOLL, investment banker; b. Little Rock, Dec. 18, 1948; d. Lawrence Jesser and Geraldine Best (Proctor) Toll; m. Lawrence Allen Alexander, Jan. 25, 1969 (div. 1980); m. Thomas Beveridge Stiles, II, Mar. 7, 1981; stepchildren: Thomas B. Stiles III, Jonathan E. Stiles. BS, U. Ark., 1969, MS, 1970. Asst. v.p. Wachovia Bank & Trust Co., Winston-Salem, N.C., 1972-76; security analyst Investors Diversified Services, Mpls., 1976-78; 1st v.p. Smith Barney Inc., N.Y.C., 1978-84; v.p. Salomon Bros., N.Y.C., 1984-86, dir., 1986, mng. dir., 1987. Named No. 1 housing analyst in U.S., Instl. Investor, 1983, 86, 87. Mem. Inst. Chartered Fin. Analysts, Fin. Analysts Fedn., N.Y. Soc. Security Analysts, Constrn. and Bldg. Materials Analysts Group (pres. 1984-85), Acad. Women Achievers. Presbyterian. Home: 18 Tuttle Ave Spring Lake NJ 07762 Office: Salomon Bros Inc 1 New York Plaza New York NY 10004

ALEXANDER, BEVERLY MOORE, mechanical engineer; b. Portsmouth, Va., Apr. 11, 1947; d. Julian Morgan and Ezefferlee (Griffin) Moore; m. Ronald Lee Rutherford, Dec. 21, 1969 (div. Dec. 1977); m. Larry Ray Alexander, Mar. 4, 1978. BS, Aero. Engring., Va. Poly. Inst. and State U., 1969; postgrad., U. New Orleans. Registered profl. engr., La. Assoc. engr. McDonnell Douglas Corp., St. Louis, 1969-74; design engr. Bell Aerospace Textron, New Orleans, 1974-81; supr. systems integration, New Orleans, 1981-83, chief interface activities, 1983-84; chief engr. Bell Aerospace Textron, New Orleans, 1984-85, dir. engring. planning and control, 1985-86, chief engr. engring. services, 1986—. Mem. La. Engring. Soc., Nat. Assn. Female Execs., ASNE, SNAME. Republican. Episcopalian. Home: 313 Margon CT Slidell LA 70458 Office: Textron Marine Systems 6800 Plaza Dr New Orleans LA 70127

ALEXANDER, CHERYL YVETTE, probation officer; b. Waco, Tex., Feb. 8, 1958; d. L.C. and Dorothy Lee (Howard) Christman; m. Michael Jerome Alexander, Apr. 23, 1983; children: Veronica Nicole, Michelle Janiece. BS, S.W. Tex. State U., 1979, postgrad. in sch. psychology. Childcare worker Meridell Achievement Ctr., Austin, Tex., 1979-81; correctional officer Travis County Jail, Austin, 1981-82, Fed. Correctional Inst., Bastrop, Tex., 1982-83; probation officer Travis County Adult Probation, Austin, 1984—. Mem. Tex. Adult Probation Assn., Exec. Female Assn., Nat. Assn. Sch. Psychology. Mem. Ch. of Christ. Home: 12009 Capt Baily's Ct Austin TX 78753 Office: Travis County Adult Probation PO Box 1748 Austin TX 78767

ALEXANDER, DONNA THOMPSON, health science facility administrator, dietitian; b. Chgo., Nov. 16, 1939; d. Harvey George and Hilma Elvina (Johnson) Thompson; divorced; children: David Scott, Stephen Risdon, James William Henry. BA in Liberal Arts, Northwestern U., 1962; MPH, U. Mich., 1977. Registered dietitian. Clin. dietitian Evanston (Ill.) Hosp., 1961-63; instr. Forsythe Intermediate Sch., Ann Arbor, Mich., 1975, Cen. Ariz. Community Coll., Coolidge, 1979; nutritionist Gila River Indian Community, Sacaton, Ariz., 1977-81; dir. dietary services Phoenix Meml. Hosp., 1981-85; assoc. dir. nutritional services Moses H. Cone Meml. Hosp., Greensboro, N.C., 1985-88, St. Elizabeth's Med. Center, Dayton, Ohio, 1988—. Author: (edn. module) Clin. Dietetics, 1981. Pres. Huron River Heights Civic Assn., Ann Arbor, 1973-75; mem. multi-ethnic bd. Ann Arbor Pub. Schs., 1974-75, Old Battle Corest Homeowners Assn. Bd., 1987-88; nutrition vol. Washtenaw County Coop. Extension, Ann Arbor, 1974-77; mem. devel. com. 4-H Mich., Lansing, 1976-77; hospice vol., Greensboro, 1986-88. HEW grantee, 1976. Mem. Soc. for Hosp. Food Service Adminstrs. (N.C. chpt., program com. Ariz. chpt.), Am. Dietetic Assn., LWV (fin. com., edn. com. 1974), Alpha Chi Omega.

ALEXANDER, ELAINE HARRIETT, purchasing manager; b. Phila., Oct. 18, 1949; d. Gregory Peter and Cleopatra (Coste) A. AB, Hood Coll., Frederick, Md., 1971; Cert. in Secondary Edn., Villanova (Pa.) U., 1975; MBA, Temple U., 1985. Cert. purchasing mgr. Purchasing agt. Cen. Pa. Nat. Bank div. Meridian Bancorp, Phila., 1976-79; sr. buyer electronics space systems div. Gen. Electric Corp., Valley Forge, Pa., 1979-85; mgr. purchasing govt. systems div. RCA Corp., Camden, N.J., 1985-86; asst. mgr. contracts Bell of Pa. and the Diamond State Telephone Cos., Phila., 1987-88; corp. contract mgr. No. Telecom, Inc., Nashville, 1988—; guest lectr. exec.-in-residence program Hood Coll., 1982. Grant proposal reviewer Consortium for Advancement of Pvt. Higher Edn., Washington, 1985-86; trustee Hood Coll., 1983—. Mem. Purchasing Mgmt. Assn. Phila. (pub. relations com. 1979-87), Hood Coll. Alumni Assn. Phila. (v.p., pres. 1980-82), Phila. Jaycees (bd. dirs. 1978-79, v.p. 1979-80). Republican. Eastern Orthodox. club: Hellenic Univ. of Phila. (bd. dirs. 1974-75). Home: 541 Overview Ln Franklin TN 37064 Office: Northern Telecom Inc Northern Telecom Plaza 200 Athens Way Nashville TN 37228

ALEXANDER, ELIZABETH POPE, hospital administrator, consultant; b. South Pittsburg, Tenn., Nov. 2, 1937; d. Franklin and Virginia Lee (Stubbs) Pope; m. John Benard Furey, Nov. 12, 1968 (div. 1970); 1 child, Stephanie Elizabeth; m. Edward George Alexander, July 26, 1975. BA, Bennett Coll., 1961; MSW, Atlanta U., 1963; postgrad., Tulane U., 1964. Group worker Orleans Neighborhood Ctrs., New Orleans, 1963-65; community organizer

Anti-Poverty Agy., New Orleans, 1965-67; dir. ctr. Anti-Poverty Desire Neighborhood, New Orleans, 1967-69; specialist community relations U.S. Dept. Justice, Washington, 1970-72; coordinator fed. women's program Materiel Command U.S. Army, Alexandria, Va., 1972-75; outreach worker City of New Orleans Housing Authority, 1975-76; adminstrv. officer, coordinator employee assistance program VA Med. Ctr., New Orleans, 1976—; cons. Alexander, Cooper and Assocs. Ltd., New Orleans, v.p. 1985—; field instr. So. U., 1983—, Tulane U., 1980-85, Xavier U., 1985—; investigator EEO. Mem. Gov.'s Adv. Council Drug Abuse, New Orleans, 1986—. Mem. Nat. Assn. Female Execs., Nat. Council Negro Women, Federally Employed Women, VA Hosp. Fed. Credit Union (supervisory chmn. 1980-85), La. Assn. Substance Abuse Counselors and Trainers (cert., sec.-treas. 1979-84). Democrat. Baptist. Home: 5300 St Bernard Ave New Orleans LA 70122

ALEXANDER, ELIZABETH THOMAS, marketing executive; b. Phoenix, Nov. 7, 1939; d. John Francis and Alice Marie (Hanson) Thomas; m. Thomas Jack Alexander, June 6, 1960; children: John, Stephen, Thomas. BA, U. Ariz., 1961. Tchr. Tucson Sch. Dist. #1, 1961-63; pres. L&C Gourmet Products, Inc., Tucson, 1982—. Advisor Jr. League of Tucson, 1986-87; trustee Tucson Psychiat. Inst., 1981-84; v.p., trustee Tucson Community Found., 1983—, U.S. of Am. Found., 1986—; sec., bd. dirs. Pima Council on Aging, 1979-84. Mem. Am. Mktg. Assn., Nat. Assn. Specialty Food Trade, Nat. Assn. Female Execs., Key Group. Republican. Episcopalian. Club: Silver & Turquoise (Tucson) (chairperson 1985-86). Home: 4133 E Poe St Tucson AZ 85711 Office: L&C Gourmet Products Inc PO Box 12607 Tucson AZ 85732

ALEXANDER, ETHEL SKYLES, state legislator; b. Chgo., Jan. 16, 1925. Ed., Chgo. Loop Jr. Coll. Formerly mem. Ill. Ho. of Reps.; now mem. Ill. Senate. Democrat. Address: 610 E 61st St Chicago IL 60637 *

ALEXANDER, INEZ DELORIS, educator, computer consultant; b. Ocala, Fla., Nov. 29, 1941; d. Aaron and Margaret (Daniel) Manoney; m. James Roosevelt Alexander, June 12, 1966; children: Antoinette Yvonne, James Roosevelt Jr. BS, Morris Brown Coll., 1964; MEd, Ga. State U., Atlanta, 1976. Tchr. Atlanta Bd. Edn., 1963-66, Cin. Pub. Schs., 1966-72, DeKalb County Schs., Decatur, Ga., 1973—. Mem. Am. Bus. Women Assn., DeKalb Assn. Educators, Nat. Appleworks User Group, DeKalb Adminstr. Assn., Delta Sigma Theta. Baptist. Home: 3011 Katherine Valley Rd Decatur GA 30032

ALEXANDER, JACQUELINE PETERSON, librarian; b. N.Y.C., Aug. 28, 1928; d. Stephen Edgar and Anna (Boehm) Peterson; A.B., Hunter Coll., 1949; M.L.S., U. R.I., 1972; m. Lewis McElwain Alexander, Dec. 30, 1950; children—Louise, Lance. Asst. editor Law of the Sea Inst. Procs., 1966-71; reference librarian U. R.I., Kingston, 1971; research librarian Internat. Center Marine Resource Devel., 1973-79; regional librarian U.S. Naval Edn. and Tng. Support Center, Groton, Conn., 1979-81; asst. chief acquisitions sect. Dept. Transp., 1983-84; librarian Edwards & Angell, Providence, 1984—; tech. librarian, head books, periodicals div. Nav. Underwater Systems Center, Newport, R.I., 1971-72. Pres. South County Sr. Citizens Housing, 1974-82; bd. dirs., sec. South County Housing Improvement Found., 1966-83; bd. dirs. Washington County Vis. Nurse Assn., 1968-71; mem. South Kingstown Citizens Adv. Bd., 1965-71. Mem. Am. Assn. Law Librarians, Law Librarians of New Eng., Beta Phi Mu. Home: 66 Beech Hill Rd Peace Dale RI 02879 Office: Edwards & Angell One Hospital Trust Plaza Providence RI 02903

ALEXANDER, JANE, actress; b. Boston, Oct. 28, 1939; d. Thomas Bartlett and Ruth (Pearson) Quigley; m. Robert Alexander, July 23, 1962 (div. 1969); 1 child, Jason; m. Edwin Sherin, Mar. 29, 1975. Student, Sarah Lawrence Coll., 1957-59, U. Edinburgh, 1959-60. Ind. television, film and theatrical actress 1962—. Appeared in prodns.: Charles Playhouse Boston, 1964-65, Arena Stage, Washington, 1965-68, 70—, Am. Shakespeare Festival; plays include Major Barbara, Mourning Becomes Electra, Merry Wives of Windsor, Stratford, Conn., summers 1971-72; Broadway prodns. include The Great White Hope, 1968-69 (Tony award 1969, Drama Desk award, Theatre World award), 6 Rms Riv Vu, 1972-73 (Tony nomination), Find Your Way Home, 1974 (Tony nomination), Hamlet, 1975, The Heiress, 1976, First Monday in October, 1978 (Tony nomination), Goodbye Fidel, 1980, Monday After the Miracle, 1982; also appeared in plays The Time of Your Life, Present Laughter, 1975, The Master Builder, 1977, Losing Time, 1980, Antony and Cleopatra, 1981, Hedda Gabler, 1981, Old Times, 1984; appeared in films The Great White Hope, 1970 (Acad. award nomination), A Gunfight, 1970, The New Centurions, 1972, All the President's Men, 1976 (Acad. award nomination), The Betsy, 1978, Kramer vs. Kramer, 1979 (Acad. award nomination), Brubaker, 1980, Night Crossing, 1981, Testament, 1983 (Acad. award nomination), City Heat, 1984, Sweet Country, 1986, Square Dance, 1987; appeared in TV films: Welcome Home Johny Bristol, 1971, Miracle on 34th Street, 1973, Death Be Not Proud, 1974, Eleanor and Franklin, 1976, Eleanor and Franklin: The White House Years (Emmy nomination), 1977 (TV Critics Circle award), Lovey, 1977, A Question of Love, 1978, Playing For Time, 1980 (Emmy award 1980), Calamity Jane: The Diary of a Frontier Woman, 1981, Dear Liar, 1981, Kennedy's Children, 1981, In the Custody of Strangers, 1982, In Love and War, 1987, Open Admissions, 1987; appeared in TV spl. A Circle of Children, 1977, Blood and Orchids, 1986, Calamity Jane, 1984 (Emmy nomination), Malice in Wonderland, 1985 (Emmy nomination), In Love and War, 1987, Open Admissions, 1987; author: (with Greta Jacobs) The Bluefish Cookbook, 1979-83; translator: (with Sam Engelstad) The Master Builder (Henrik Ibsen), 1978. Bd. dirs. Nat. Stroke Assn., Denver, 1985—. Recipient Achievement in Dramatic Arts award St. Botolph Club, 1979; Israel Cultural award, 1982; Western Heritage Wrangler award, 1985; Helen Caldicott Leadership award, 1984. Mem. Womens Action for Nuclear Disarmament (bd. dirs. 1981—), Wildlife Conservation Internat. (bd. dirs. 1984—), Film Forum (bd. dirs. 1985—). Office: care William Morris Agy 1350 Ave of the Americas New York NY 10019

ALEXANDER, JOYCE MARY, illustrator; b. Pepin, Wis., Mar. 31, 1927; d. Colonel and Martha (Varnum) Yochem; m. Don Tocher, June 27, 1955 (div. 1962); m. Dorsey Potter Alexander, Nov. 1, 1963. Student, Coll. Arts and Crafts, 1946, Acad. of Art, 1961-62. Co-founder, owner Turtle's Quill Scriptorium Publishers, Berkeley, Calif., 1963—. Author: Thaddeus, 1972, Happy Bird Day, 1980; illustrator numerous books including: California Farm and Ranch Law, 1967, Chinatown, A Legend of Old Cannery Row, 1968, The Sea: Excerpts from Herman Melville, 1970, Of Mice, 1970, David: Psalm Twenty-Four, 1970, Shakespeare: Selected Sonnets, 1974, Psalm One Hundred Four, 1978, Messiah: Choruses from Handel's Messiah, 1985, A Flurry of Angels, Angels in Literature, 1986, Soil and Plant Analysis, A Practical Guide for the Home Gardener; The Blue-Jay Yarn; work represented in permanent collections Hunt Botan. Library at Carnegie-Mellon U. Republican. Office: Turtle's Quill Scriptorium PO Box 643 Mendocino CA 95460

ALEXANDER, JUDITH ANN, bank consultant; b. Fort Sill, Okla., Oct. 14, 1940; d. James Buchanan and Gerry Lee (Gibbs) Permenter; m. Robert Miles Turner, Oct. 28, 1962 (div. 1972); m. Clarence Withers Alexander, Dec. 19, 1975 (div. Jan. 1987). Student, U. Okla., 1958-59; B.A. in English, U. Tulsa, 1962; M.B.A., U. Okla., 1969; postgrad., U. St. Thomas, 1975-78. Asst. cashier So. Nat. Bank of Houston, 1971-73, asst. controller, 1973-74, asst. v.p. and asst. controller, 1974, v.p., controller, 1974-77, sr. v.p., controller, 1977-79; cons. 1979—. Mem. NOW, Nat. Audubon Soc., Beta Gamma Sigma, Gamma Phi Beta. Republican. Office: 4144 Greystone Way #607 Sugar Land TX 77479

ALEXANDER, LENORA COLE, educator, former government official; b. Buffalo, Mar. 9, 1935; d. John L. and Susie (Stamper) Cole; m. T.M. Alexander Sr., June 22, 1976. BS, SUNY, Buffalo, 1957, MEd, 1969, PhD, 1974. Lic. elem. tchr., elem. sch. prin. Tchr. pub. schs. Chgo. and Lancaster, N.Y., 1957-68; v.p. student life Am. U., Washington, 1974-77; v.p. student affairs U. D.C., 1978-81; dir. Women's Bur. Dept. Labor, Washington, 1981-86; Commonwealth prof. George Mason U., Fairfax, Va., 1986—; pres. LCA and Assocs., Inc., Washington, 1986—; cons. div. student affairs U. Calif. Irvine, 1971, CCNY, 1972, Temple U., 1973; advisor regional and city planning colloquium U. Pa., 1973; panel on selection fellow HEW, 1976-77; cons. advanced instrl. devel. program Dillard U., 1977-81; mem. mayor's blue ribbon panel on reorgn. Dept. Human Resources, Washington, 1977; mem. selection com. fellows program Am. Council on Edn., 1982; lectr. in field. Author tech. reports for U.S. Govt. Printing Office. Trustee Wider Opportunities for Women, 1975-77; del. Internat. Commn. on Status Women, 1982, Columbia, 1983, Women in World Prep. Conf., 1983; apptd. del. Decade for Women in World Conf., UN, Vienna, Austria, 1984, Kenya, 1986; U.S. rep. on role women on economy Orgn. Econ. Devel., Paris, 1982—; mem. adv. com. on women vets VA, 1983; participant Jerusalem Internat. Forum, Am.-Israel Friendship League, 1986; mem. D.C. Bd. Elections and Ethics, 1986—; bd. dirs. Legal Aid Soc., Washington, 1975-77, D.C. Rental Accommodations Commn., 1978-79, Found. for Exceptional Children, Reston, Va., 1987—, McAuley Inst., Silver Spring, Va., 1987—. SUNY grad. fellow, 1968; recipient Disting. Alumnus award SUNY-Buffalo, 1983, Pauline Weeden Maloney award in nat. trends and Services The Links, Phila., 1984, Disting. Service Citation Nat. MBA Assn., 1984, Outstanding Woman award DC chpt. Federally Employed Women, Washington, 1984, Outstanding Polit. Achievement award Nat. Assn. Minortiy Polit. Women, 1985, Outstanding Career Woman award women's activities com. Alpha Phi Alpha, Washington, 1986, Woman of Achievement award Women's City Club Cleve., 1986. Mem. Delta Sigma Theta. Republican. Home: 3020 Brandywine St NW Washington DC 20008

ALEXANDER, LINDA DIANE (GRAHAM), lawyer, educator; b. Winchester, Va., May 10, 1953; d. Kenneth A. and Edna Frances (Whitlow) Graham; m. Patrick B. Alexander, May 8, 1975. B.A. in Govt., George Mason U., 1975, B.A. in Philosophy, 1975; J.D., U. Okla., 1978. Bar: Okla. 1978, U.S. Dist. Ct. (we. dist.) Okla. 1979, U.S. Ct. Claims 1980, U.S. Ct. Appeals (10th cir.) 1980, U.S. Ct. Appeals (8th cir.) 1984, U.S. Ct. Appeals (5th cir.) 1987. Legal intern Foliart, Mills & Niemeyer, Oklahoma City, 1976-79, assoc., 1979-81; sole practice law, Oklahoma City, 1981-84; ptnr. firm Niemeyer, Noland & Alexander, Oklahoma City, 1984—; prof. Sch. Law, Oklahoma City U., 1981-83. Mem. Okla. Bar Assn., Oklahoma County Bar Assn., Assn. Trial Lawyers Am. Democrat. Mem. Ch. of Christ. Office: Niemeyer Noland & Alexander 300 N Walker St Oklahoma City OK 73102

ALEXANDER, MARGARET LOUISE STRACHAN, writer; b. Phila., Nov. 13, 1908; d. Frank Russel and Margaret (Marcus) Pitcairn; m. John E. Strachan, Dec. 15, 1928 (dec. Oct. 1958); children: Jacqueline McCarthy, Bruce Pitcairn, John; m. Jack M. Alexander, Feb. 9, 1963 (dec. July 1986). Student, U. Pa., 1929-31, U. Wash., 1946-48. Staff feature writer Seattle Times Newspaper, 1945-51, Long Beach (Calif.) Press Telegram, 1952; dir. publicity Sheraton-Gibson Hotel, World Affairs Inst., and Better Housing League, Cin., 1949-59, Ford Found. Workshops, Berea (Ky.) Coll., 1959; asst. to Dorothy Neighbors Seattle Times, 1961-64; instr. creative writing Northshore Sch. Dist., Bothell, Wash., 1966; moderator juvenile writing panel Pacific NW Writers Conf., 1966—, pres., 1970—; instr. Writers Digest, 1983-86. Author (under name Margaret Pitcairn Strachan): numerous children's and young adult novels, including: Class President, 1959, Mennonite Martha, 1961, Dolores and the Gypsies, Patience and the Mulberry Leaf, 1962, Summer in El Castillo, A Batch of Trouble, 1963, Cabins with Window Boxes, 1964, The Hop Ranch Mystery, 1965, Maria Takes a Fancy, 1966, Trouble at Torrent Creek, 1967, Chinese Scroll Mystery, 1967, Winds of Fate, 1968, Two Families Make One, 1969, Mystery of Blue Barn Stables, 1970, Volunteering: A Practical Guide for Teenagers, 1971; contbr. stories and articles to periodicals. Recipient 3d pl. award for juvenile books Nat. Press Women, 1972; Wash. State Gov.'s award, 1960. Mem. Mystery Writers of Am. (pres. Seattle chpt. 1988), Authors Guild, Seattle Freelancers, Pacific NW Writers Conf. (hon., past pres.), Wash. State Press Women (award 1967), Nat. League Am. Pen Women (award 1965, 1st award teen category 1975), Women in Communications. Home and Office: 119 Madison House 12215 NE 128th Kirkland WA 98034

ALEXANDER, MARGO, nutrition and food service executive; b. Bklyn., May 10, 1952; d. Al and Ethel (Levinson) Isaacs; m. Robert Robinson, Dec. 1984. B.A., Bklyn. Coll., 1974; M.A., NYU 1977; postgrad. Pace U., 1980-81. Clin. dietitian Brookdale Med. Center, Bklyn., 1974-77; supervising dietitian Beth Israel med. Center, N.Y.C., 1977-78; assoc. dir. food service L.I. Coll. Hosp., Bklyn., 1978-82, dir., 1982—; Registered dietitian; accomplished health care food adminstr. Mem. Am. Hosp. Assn. (bd. dirs., regional dir. Am. Soc. Hosp. Food Service Adminstrs., pres. 1984), Am. Dietetic Assn. (Young Dietitian of Yr. award 1983), Greater N.Y. Dietetic Assn. (past chmn. legis. and public policy com.), Greater N.Y. Hosp. Assn. (chairperson Dietary Purchasing Shared Services Com. 1986-87). Office: LI Coll Hosp Food Service 340 Henry St Brooklyn NY 11201

ALEXANDER, MARY E., lawyer; b. Chgo., Nov. 16, 1947; d. Theron and Marie (Bailey) A.; m. Lyman Saunders Faulkner, Jr., Dec. 1, 1984; 1 child, Michelle. B.A., U. Iowa, 1969; M.P.H., U. Calif.-Berkeley, 1975; J.D., U. Santa Clara, 1982. Bar: Calif. 1982. Researcher, U. Cin., 1969-74; dept. dir., sr. environ. health scientist Stanford Research Inst., Menlo Park, Calif., 1975-80; cons. Alexander Assocs., Ambler, Pa., 1980-82; assoc. Caputo, Liccardo Rossi Sturges & McNeil, San Jose, Calif., 1982-84; assoc. Cartwright, Slobodin, Bokelman, et al, San Francisco, 1984—. Com. mem. Cancer Soc., San Jose, 1983. Nat. Inst. Occupational Safety and Health scholar U. Calif.-Berkeley, 1975. Democrat. Home: 967 Clinton Rd Los Altos CA 94022 Office: Cartwright Slobodin Bokelman et al 101 California 26th Floor San Francisco CA 94111

ALEXANDER, MARY LOUISE, financial planner; b. St. Cloud, Minn., Mar. 5, 1950; d. Thomas E. and Jean E. (Wichman) A.; B.F.A., Stephens Coll., 1972. Registered health underwriter; registered rep. Riding dir. Hidden Valley Farms, Newton, N.J., 1974, El Dorado Ranch, Westtown, N.Y., 1974; riding instr. Frances Reker Sch. of Horsemanship, Rockford, Minn., 1975; instr. Area Learning Center, Dist. 742, St. Cloud, 1976, asst. dean of boys, 1976; sales rep. N.W. Nat. Life Ins. Co., St. Cloud, 1977-78; prin. Mary Alexander Ins. Agy., Cold Spring, Minn., 1978-88; mgr. fin. planning dept., Garnsey Bros., Inc., Sanford, Maine, 1988—; pres. M. Alexander & Assocs., Contempory Ins. Concepts, Maxi-Mktg. Inc., 1980—; sales rep. Berkshire LIfe, Portland; owner, mgr. Bay Hill Farm. Mem. Nat. Assn. Health Underwriters, Minn. Assn. Health Underwriters, Nat. Fedn. Ind. Bus. Owners, Greater Twin Cities Chow Chow Club, Am. Quarter Horse Assn., Maine Quarter Horse Assn. Lutheran. Home: Chadbourne Ridge Rd Rural Rt F02 PO Box 322 West Buxton ME 04093 Office: Garnsey Bros Inc 845 Main St Sanford ME 04073

ALEXANDER, MARY LOUISE, biology educator; b. Ennis, Tex., Jan. 15, 1926; d. Emmett F. and Florence (Hill) Alexander; B.A., U. Tex., 1947, M.A., 1949, Ph.D., 1951. Instr., research asst. Genetics Found., U. Tex., 1944-51; postdoctoral fellow biology div. AEC, Oak Ridge, 1951-52; postdoctoral research fellow U. Tex., 1952-55; research asso. U. Tex.-M.D. Anderson Hosp. and Tumor Inst., Houston, 1956-58, asst. biologist, 1959-62; research scientist Genetics Found. U. Tex., Austin, 1962-67; research cons. Brookhaven Nat. Lab., Upton, N.Y., 1955; research participant Oak Ridge Inst. Nuclear Studies, 1951-77; asso. prof. biology S.W. Tex. State U., San Marcos, 1966-69, prof., 1970—. Nat. Cancer Inst. fellow Inst. Animal Genetics, Edinburgh, Scotland, 1960-61. Mem. Genetics Soc. Am., Radiation Research Soc., Am. Soc. Human Genetics, Sigma Xi, Gamma Phi Beta, Phi Sigma, Alpha Epsilon Delta. Home: Hunter's Glen Route 2 Box 119 San Marcos TX 78666

ALEXANDER, NANCY NICHOLS, veterinarian; b. Brookhaven, Miss., Oct. 24, 1955; d. Mack and Mary Alice (Cooke) Nichols; m. William Brent Alexander, Dec. 29, 1978. B.A., U. Tenn., 1977; D.V.M., 1980. Veterinarian Farragut Animal Clinic, Knoxville, 1980—, Cedar Bluff Animal Clinic, 1980—; vet. cons. Gifted Talented program, Knoxville, 1983—. Mem. AVMA, Tenn. Vet. Med. Assn., Knoxville Acad. Vet. Medicine, Alpha Epsilon Delta, Phi Beta Kappa, Chi Omega. Republican. Baptist. Home: 2115 Bishop's Bridge Rd Knoxville TN 37922 Office: Cedar Bluff Animal Clinic 9049 Middlebrook Pike Knoxville TN 37923

ALEXANDER, SHANA, journalist, author, lecturer; b. N.Y.C., Oct. 6, 1925; d. Milton and Cecelia (Rubenstein) Ager; m. Stephen Alexander, 1951 (div.); 1 dau., Katherine. Student, Vassar Coll., 1942-45. With PM, 1944-46, Harper's Bazaar, 1946-47; with Flair, 1950; reporter Life mag., 1951-61, staff writer, 1961-64; writer twice monthly column The Feminine Eye, 1964-69; editor McCall's mag., N.Y.C., 1969-71; v.p. Norton Simon Communications, Inc., 1971-72; radio and TV commentator Spectrum CBS News, 1971-72; columnist, contbg. editor Newsweek, 1972-75; commentator CBS 60 Minutes, 1975-79; Bd. dirs. Am. Film Inst. Author: The Feminine Eye, 1970, Shana Alexander's State-by-State Guide to Women's Legal Rights, 1975, Talking Woman, 1976, Anyone's Daughter, 1979, Appearance of Evil: The Trial of Patty Hearst, Nutcracker: Money, Madness, Murder—A Family Album, 1985, Very Much a Lady: The Untold Story of Jean Harris and Dr. Herman Tarnower, 1983, Dangerous Games: The Pizza Connection Trial, 1988. Recipient Sigma Delta Chi and U. So. Cal. Nat. Journalism award, 1965, Los Angeles Times Woman of Year award, 1967, Golden Pen award Am. Newspaper Womens Club, 1969, Front Page award Newswomen's Club N.Y., 1973, Matrix award N.Y. Women in Communications, 1973-74, Spirit of Achievement award Albert Einstein Coll. Med., 1976; Creative Arts award Nat. Women's div. Am. Jewish Congress. Address: care Doubleday & Co Inc 245 Park Ave New York NY 10017 *

ALEXANDER, SUSAN REED, economic analyst; b. Charleston, W.Va., Mar. 3, 1941; d. Andrew Stirling and Betsy Reed (Miller) A.; A.B. in Math., Sweet Briar Coll., 1963; M.B.A. in Fin., U. Houston, 1983. Adminstrv. asst. Earl and Wright, Cons. Engrs., San Francisco, 1965-72; programmer/analyst Bechtel, Inc., San Francisco, 1972-79, econ. analyst Bechtel Petroleum, Inc., Houston, 1979-81, study mgr., econ. analyst, 1981-83; bus. project mgr. ETSI Pipeline Project, San Francisco, 1984; study mgr., econ. analyst Bechtel, Inc., Houston, 1985-87; cons. energy-transp. planning, 1987—. Contbr. articles to profl. jours. Mem. Jr. League San Francisco, Am. Contract Bridge League (lifemaster 1974). Beta Gamma Sigma. Mailing Address: PO Box 460614 Houston TX 77056-8614

ALEXANDER, SUSAN (SANDY), author; b. Queens, N.Y., Apr. 30, 1927; d. Louis and Sally Ann (Antler) A. Student, Columbia U. Feature writer L.I. Reporter, Corona, N.Y.; feature writer Antler Pub. Co., Tucson, editor; instr. creative writing Tucson Open U., 1982-87, Elder Hostel Program, U. Ariz., 1987—. Author: William the Whalehunter, Herpes Handbook, 1986; (with others) Kick the Drug Habit, 1986, rev. edit., 1988; editor, feature columnist Franchise Jour. mag.; author How to... series; contbr. articles to popular mags. Mem. Soc. Southwestern Authors (awards com. 1987). Office: Antler Pub Co PO Box 43394 Tucson AZ 85733

ALEXANDER, VICKI LYNN, quality assurance specialist; b. Waterloo, Iowa, Jan. 21, 1956; d. Donald Raymond and Mavis L. (Nichols) Lemons; m. Steve Otero, Nov. 15, 1974 (div. Oct. 1979); m. David Mark Alexander, July 1, 1983; 1 child, Sarah Lynn. Student, Hawkeye Inst. Tech., 1973-74, Tidewater Community Coll., 1978-79, Kirkwood Community Coll., 1980-81. Cable technician Northwestern Bell, Waterloo, Iowa, 1979-80; quality assurance specialist Def. Contract Adminstrn. Services Mgmt. Area, Dept. of Def., Cedar Rapids, Iowa and Denver, 1980-86; indsl. property mgmt. specialist Def. Logistics div. Def. Contract Adminstrn. Services Mgmt. Area, Denver, 1986-87; quality assurance specialist USAF Contract Mgmt. Div., Denver, 1987—; vice chair Fed. Women's Program, Denver, 1986—. Served with USN, 1974-78. Mem. Nat. Assn. Female Execs. Methodist. Office: AFPRO Det 10/QAX Martin Marietta Ops PO Box 179 Denver CO 80201-0179

ALEXANDER-WILLIAMS, VYNESSA, bank executive; b. Chgo., May 14, 1957; d. Silas James Alexander and Geraldine Ozella (Reese) Dantzler; m. Matthew Bernard Williams, Oct. 18, 1986. BBA, U. Wis., Whitewater, 1980. Mgmt. trainee Continental Ill. Bank, Chgo., 1981, supr. bankers acceptance, 1981-83, supr. export letters of credit, 1983-85, asst. mgr., ops. officer, 1986—. Mem. fin. com. Grant A.M.E. Ch., Chgo., 1983-84; bd. dirs. Akarama Found., Chgo., 1983—, treas., fin. sec., 1988—; bd. dirs. Nia Comprehensive Ctr., Chgo., 1986—; mem. Metro Bd. of Chgo. Urban League, 1984-85. Named one of Outstanding Young Women of Am., 1983, 86. Mem. Urban Bankers Forum, Nat. Assn. Bank Women, Soc. Advancement Mgmt. (mem. dir. 1979-80), Mid.-Am. Council in Internat. Banking (collection com. 1985-87), Women in Internat. Trade, Chgo. Vocat. Alumni Assn. (chmn. 1982—), Metro Bd.-Urban League, Alpha Kappa Alpha (treas. 1986-87). Home: 5219 S Greenwood Chicago IL 60615 Office: Continental Ill Bank 231 S LaSalle Chicago IL 60693

ALEXANDRE, JUDITH LEE, social services administrator; b. N.Y.C., Dec. 14, 1944; d. Jerome Jacob and Dorothy Dale (Locks) A. BA, U. Calif., Santa Barbara, 1966; MSW, U. Denver, 1970; PhD, U.S. Internat. U., 1983. Lic. clin. social worker, Calif.; diplomate clin. social work. Social worker II Aid to Families with Dependent Children, 1968-70; social worker IV Protective Services and Intake, 1970-72; social worker dir. New Life Homes, 1972-79; supr. Foster Care Placement, 1973-74; counselor Bible Fellowship Ch., Ventura, Calif., 1976-80; asst. prof. sociology Westmont Coll., 1976-83, assoc. prof. sociology, 1983—; coordinator counseling and outreach Bible Fellowship Ch. Counseling Ctr., 1980-86, dir., 1980—; instr. Calif. Luth. Coll. Grad. Program Clin. Psychology, Thousand Oaks, 1988—; instr. grad. sch. marriage and family counseling Azusa Pacific U., 1982—, human services Ventura Coll., 1974-77; social work supr. II Protective Services Placement, 1974-76; liaison Foster Parents Assn., 1973-76; cons. Coalition Agy. Household Violence, Ventura, 1985—, pub. health dept. Ventura Adolescent Parent Program, 1986—; bd. dirs. Child Abuse and Neglect, Ventura, 1985—, mem. program com. 1985-86, v.p., pres. elect, 1987-88, pres. 1988—; lectr. confs. and sems. Contbr. articles to profl. jours. and mags. Bd. trustees Ventura (Calif.) Unified Sch. Dist., 1986—; tchr., active leader Sunday sch. Bible Fellowship Ch., Ventura, 1970—; mem. allocations panel United Way; group leader in-patient Vista Del Mar, 1986—. Mem. Nat. Assn. Social Workers, Nat. Assn. Social Workers Referral Service (v.p. 1986-87), Bus. and Profl. Women (chmn. spl. program 1984, Channel Island Woman of Yr. award 19861st v.p. 1987-88), Nat. Assn. Christian Social Workers (so. Calif. chpt.), Nat. Council on Social Work Edn., Am. Humane Soc. (children's div.). Democrat. Office: Bible Fellowship Ch Counseling Ctr 1788 Johnson Dr Ventura CA 93003

ALEXIOU, MARINA S., business management company executive; b. N.Y.C., Feb. 12, 1940; d. Stanley and Mary S. (Couloumbi) A. Cert. in bus. mgmt. U. N.C., 1959; student bus. mgmt. Ctr. for Degree Studies, Scranton, Pa. Legal sec. Jordan, Wright, Henson & Nichols, attys., Greensboro, N.C., 1959-60; with North Am. Philips Co., 1961— (company mergered with Consol. Electronics 1969 then became North Am. Philips Corp.), adminstrv. asst. to pres. and dir., 1965-69, adminstrv. asst. to chmn., chief exec. officer, pres. and dir., 1969-77, adminstrv. asst to chmn., chief exec. officer and dir., 1978-80, adminstrv. asst. to chmn. and dir., chmn. governing com. U.S. Philips Trust, 1981-84, adminstrv. asst. to dir., chmn. governing com. U.S. Philips Trust, 1985-86, mgr. corp. purchasing, 1985—. Mem. U.S. Senatorial Bus. Adv. Bd. and Steering Com., Washington; adv. bd. Am. Security Council, Washington. Asst. chmn. fund raising Am. Cancer Soc., 1978—, mem. exec. com., 1985—. Dep. chmn. exec. Republican Com. of Bronxville (N.Y.), 1980—; mem. Rep. Presdl. Task Force, Washington, Rep. Senatorial Inner Circle. Mem. Nat. Assn. Exec. Sec., Nat. Assn. Female Execs., Am. Soc. Profl. and Exec. Women, Internat. Platform Assn., UN We Believe (exec. planning com.), Smithsonian Nat. Assocs., N.Y. Philharm. Soc. Republican. Greek Orthodox. Lodge: Toastmasters (charter). Home: Northgate Alger Ct Bronxville NY 10708 Office: N Am Philips Corp 100 E 42nd St New York NY 10017

ALFONSO, JACQUELINE T., social service consultant; b. Northfield, Minn., Apr. 4, 1945; d. John Edward and Lois Marie (Holmes) Tripp; m. Delio Patricio Alfonso, Mar. 26, 1966 (div. 1971); 1 child, Yanaba Nehesi. BA in Philosophy, U. Minn., 1981, MA in Philosophy, 1984. Adminstrv. fellow Minn. Women's Ctr., Mpls., 1980-83; coordinator Neighborhood Employment Network, Mpls., 1984-87; exec. dir. United Handicapped Fedn., St. Paul, 1987—; instr. St. Catherine Coll., St. Paul, 1984—; cons. in field. Contbr. articles to profl. jours. Bd. dirs. West Bank Community Devel. Corp., Mlps., 1986, 87, Corcoran Neighborhood Assn., Mlps., 1986, 87. Office: United Handicapped Fedn 1821 University Ave #281S Saint Paul MN 55104

ALFORD, HELEN JOHNSON, lawyer; b. Murfreesboro, Tenn., July 3, 1951; d. Jack Ewing and Beulah Lee (Carter) Johnson; m. Woodrow Ellis Alford, June 27, 1975; 1 dau., Jacqueline Cecile. B.S. in Bus. Law, U. New Orleans, 1980; J.D., Tulane U., 1982. Bar: Ala. 1982, Miss. 1983. Office mgr.

Brown Constrn. Co., Marrero, La., 1976-79; legal sec. Scariano & McCranie, Metairie, La., 1975-76, Billy F. Brown, Biloxi, Miss., 1973-75; assoc. Hand, Arendall, Bedsole, Greaves & Johnston, Mobile, Ala., 1982—. Mem. Ala. Bar, Miss. Bar, Ala. Def. Lawyers Assn. Republican. Presbyterian. Home: 1909 LaPine Dr Mobile AL 36618 Office: Hand Arendall Bedsole Greaves & Johnston 3000 First Nat Bank Bldg Mobile AL 36601

ALFORD, JOAN FRANZ, entrepreneur; b. St. Louis, Sept. 16, 1940; d. Henry Reisch and Florence Mary (Shaughnessy) Franz; m. Charles Hebert Alford, Dec. 28, 1978; stepchildren: Terry, David, Paul. BS, St. Louis U., 1962; postgrad. Consortium of State Univ., Calif., 1975-77; MBA, Pepperdine U., 1987. Head user services Lawrence Berkeley Lab., Calif., 1977-78, head software support and devel. Computer Ctr., 1978-82, dep. head, 1980-81; regional site analyst mgr. Cray Research, Inc., Pleasanton, Calif., 1982-83; owner, pres. Innovative Leadership, Oakland, Calif., 1983—. Contbr. articles to profl. jours. Bd. dirs., sec. Vol. Ctrs. of Alameda, Oakland, 1985, bd. dirs., 1984—; campaign mem. Marge Gibson for County Supr., Oakland, 1984; mem. Oakland Piedmont Rep. Orgn., Alameda County Apt. Owners Assn., 1982. Mem. Assn. Computing Machinery, Spl. Interest Group on Computer Personnel Research. (past chmn.), Internat. Platform Assn., Small Owners for Fair Treatment. Republican. Clubs: Claremont Pool and Tennis, Lakeview, San Francisco Opera Guild. Avocations: swimming, skiing, opera, horseback riding, gardening. Home: 2605 Beaconsfield Pl Oakland CA 94611 Office: Innovative Leadership 2605 Beaconsfield Pl Oakland CA 94611

ALFSEN, LOIS JEAN, home economist; b. Waupaca, Wis., Aug. 9, 1934; d. Allan William and Sara Margaret (Plowman) Schroeder; B.S., U. Wis., Stevens Point, 1956; m. George W. Alfsen, June 12, 1960; children—Geoffrey Wayne, Gregg Allan. Cert. home economist. Tchr. home econs. Hortonville (Wis.) High Sch., 1956-58, Preble High Sch., Green Bay, Wis., 1958-60, Waupaca High Sch., 1960-61; tchr. consumer edn. Gateway Tech. Inst., Kenosha and Racine, Wis., 1974-76; consumer info. coordinator consumer services Johnson Wax, Racine, 1975—; mem. home econs. vocat. edn. adv. com. Racine Unified Sch. Dist., 1981-84, Preservation Racine, Racine Zool. Assn. Rep., Racine Women's Civic Council, 1967-68, 78-79; lay del. to state conf. Wis. United Meth. Conf., 1981-84. Mem. Internat. Fedn. Home Econs., Am. Home Econs. Assn., AAUW, Home Economists in Bus. (nat. public relations com. 1981-82), NOW, Nat. Consumer League, Wis. Home Economists in Homemaking (chmn. 1967-68), Wis. Rural Homemaking Instrs., Wis. Home Econs. Assn. (newsletter asst. editor, dist. meeting reservations chmn., exec. com., state council, state v.p.), Wis. Home Economists in Bus. (ways and means chmn., mem. exec. bd.), Wis. Women's Network, Wis. PTA, Racine-Kenosha Home Econs. Assn. (pres. 1967-68, 78-79), Preservation Racine, Racine Zool. Assn., Phi Upsilon Omicron. Home: 1128 Shorecrest Dr Racine WI 53402 Office: 1525 Howe St Racine WI 53403

ALGARY, RUTH WILKINS, community volunteer; b. Asheville, N.C., Apr. 10, 1938; d. William Fellows and Elizabeth (Russell) Wilkins; m. William Page Algary, Sept. 6, 1958; children: Kathryn Algary Tarleton, John Page, Sarah Price. Student, U. N.C., 1956-58. Treas. Sara Collins Elem. PTA, Greenville, S.C., 1971-76; community vol. Greenville Jr. League, 1973-74; children's ch. leader Westminster Presby. Ch., Greenville, 1975; council mem. Sara Collins Elem. Sch., Greenville, 1976-77; program devel. coordinator, bd. dirs. Greenville YWCA, 1976-77; substitute tchr. Sch. Dist. of Greenville County, 1984—, devel. team, 1986; sec. Beck Middle Sch. PTA, Greenville, 1979-80; pres. S.E. area PTA Council, Greenville, 1979-80; v.p. Dist. 1 PTA, Greenville, 1980-83. Sr. high youth leader Westminster Presby. Ch., Greenville, 1984-85; pres. Greenville Little Theatre League, 1987-88; chmn. ways and mean com. Greenville County Med. Aux., 1979; pres. Colonial Dames XVII Centennial, 1980. Mem. S.C. PTA (Life Mem. award 1983). Club: J.L. Mann Athletic (Greenville) (treas. 1981-86). Home and Office: 20 Stonehaven Dr Greenville SC 29607

ALI, NILOFAR (JAMALI), pathologist; b. Peshawar, Pakistan, Mar. 24, 1945; came to U.S., 1972; d. Ahamad Hussain and Shafqat Jamali; m. Azhar Asghar Ali, Feb. 29, 1970; 1 child, Saira Ali. Degree, Frontier Coll., Peshawar, 1963; MBBS, Khyber Med. Coll., Peshawar, 1968. Diplomate Am. Bd. Pathology. Resident in pathology Stamford (Conn.) Hosp., 1973078; pathologist Derrick & Assocs., Orlando, Fla., 1980—. Republican. Moslem. Club: Sweet Water. Home: 518 Spring Creek Dr Longwood FL 32779

ALI, PERVEEN KHAN, communications company executive; b. Karachi, Pakistan, Jan. 1, 1957; came to U.S., 1972; d. Riaz Ahmed and Jamila (Begum) Khan; m. Ahmed Ali, Sept. 24, 1982; children: Subhan Mustafa Ali, Kamran Ahmed. B.S., U. Southwestern La., 1977. Programmer analyst Ohio Nat. Life Ins., Cin., 1977-79; programmer analyst AT & T Communications, Cin., 1979-82, system analyst, Los Angeles, 1982-86; v.p. Geo-Etka Inc. Geo-Etka, Inc., Orange, Calif., 1985—. Republican. Moslem. Avocations: reading. travelling; music. Home: 1944 Peaceful Hills Rd Diamond Bar-Walnut CA 91789 Office: Geo-Etka Inc 739 N Main St Orange CA 92668

ALLANACH, ELAINE JACQUELINE, nurse, army officer; b. San Jose, Calif., Mar. 26, 1954; d. William Burt and Edith Gwendolyn (Schindler) Moreland; m. Bruce Carlton Allanach, Oct. 8, 1976; stepchildren: Dawn Louise, Christopher Bruce, Jeffrey Scott, Sean Michael. BS in Nursing, U.Md., 1976; MS in Nursing, Med. Coll. Ga., 1988. Registered nurse, Ga., Md. Commd. 2d lt. Nurse Corps, U.S. Army, 1972, advanced through grades to maj., 1978; staff nurse gen. medicine-oncology Walter Reed Army Med. Ctr., Washington, 1976-78, team leader gen. medicine-oncology, 1978-79, head nurse med. splty. ward, 1979-80; asst. head nurse gynecol. oncology unit Tripler Army Med. Ctr., Honolulu, 1980-81, head nurse med. splty. clinic, 1981-83; staff nurse orthopedics Eisenhower Army Med. Center, Ft. Gordon, Ga., 1983-84, patient edn. coordinator, 1984-85, head nurse recovery room, 1985-86; lectr. in field. Contbr. articles to nursing, mil., and med. publs. Mem. pub. edn. com. Am. Cancer Soc., Honolulu, 1982. Decorated Meritorious Service medal. Mem. Am. Diabetes Assn., Am. Assn. Diabetic Educators, Grad. Student Nurses Assn. (sec. 1986-87), Am. Nurses Assn., Mensa, Sigma Theta Tau. Avocations: bible studies, jogging, movies, breeding chow-chows. Home: 7 Woodbridge Way Evans GA 30809 Office: Med Coll Ga Sch Nursing Dept Nursing Adminstrn Augusta GA 30912

ALLANSMITH, MATHEA REUTER, ophthalmologist; b. Santa Barbara, Calif., May 31, 1930; d. Harry and Mary (Benthall) Reuter; children: Lynn, Lauren, Kathryn, Carolyn, Andrew, Jennifer. MD, U. Calif., San Francisco, 1955. Diplomate Am. Bd. Pediatrics, Am. Bd. Ophthalmology. Intern San Francisco Hosp., 1955-56; resident in ophthalmology Stanford Hosp., San Francisco, 1957; resident in pediatrics Stanford Hosp., 1958-59, U. Calif. Hosp., San Francisco, 1957-58; fellow in pediatric allergy U. Calif. Hosp., 1959-60; postdoctoral fellow in immunology dept. med. microbiology Stanford U., 1960-63, resident in ophthalmology, 1969-72, research asso. depts. med. microbiology, surgery and ophthalmology, 1963-67, acting asst. prof. surgery and ophthalmology, 1967-68, asst. prof., 1968-74; head Stanford Eye Bank, 1970-75; assoc. prof. ophthalmology Harvard Med. Sch., 1975—; inst. sr. scientist Eye Research Inst., 1975—. Mem. editorial bd. Am. Jour. Ophthalmology, 1973-87, Ophthalmology, 1979—. Fellow Am. Acad. Allergy; mem. Am. Assn. Immunology, Assn. Research in Vision and Ophthalmology, Phi Beta Kappa, Sigma Xi. Office: 20 Staniford St Boston MA 02114

ALLARD, ANN HELMUTH, infosystems specialist; b. Cleve., Oct. 10, 1950; d. Donovan Edward and Ruth Irma (Walter) Helmuth; m. Thomas M. Shimko, June 19, 1971 (div. Dec. 1981); m. James Kay Allard, Apr. 8, 1984. BS, Case Inst. of Case Western Res. U., 1971; MLS, Case Western Res. U., 1973, MS in Health Sci. Edn., 1975, PhD in Info. Sci., 1977. Assoc. analyst Republic Steel Corp., Cleve., 1976-81; sr. analyst Nat. Acme, Cleve., 1982-83, Picker Internat., Highland Heights, Ohio, 1983-84; systems cons. Systemation, Inc., Beachwood, Ohio, 1984—. Mem. Assn. Systems Mgmt, Assn. Computing Machinery, The Computer Soc. Office: Systemation Inc 23200 Chagrin Blvd Beachwood OH 44122

ALLARD, JEAN, lawyer; b. Trenton, Mo., Dec. 16, 1924; d. Ben J. and Marion (Watson) McGuire; 1 son, John Preston. A.B., Culver-Stockton Coll., 1945, LL.D. (hon.), 1977; A.M., Washington U., St. Louis, 1947; J.D., U. Chgo., 1953; LL.D. (hon.), Elmhurst Coll., 1979. Bar: Ill. 1953, Ohio 1959. Dept. counselor, psychology dept. U. Chgo., 1948-51, research asso. Law Sch., 1953-58, asst. dean, 1956-58; asso. firm Fuller, Harrington, Seney & Henry, Toledo, 1958-59, Lord, Bissell & Brook, Chgo., 1959-62; sec., gen. counsel Maremont Corp., Chgo., 1962-72; v.p. for bus. and finance U. Chgo., 1972-75; partner firm Sonnenschein Carlin Nath & Rosenthal, Chgo., 1976—; bd. dirs. Commonwealth Edison Co., La Salle Nat. Bank, A. Johnson & Co. Inc. Trustee Culver-Stockton Coll., 1976-87; bd. dirs. Chgo. Sch. Fin. Authority, 1980—. Mem. Am., Ill., Chgo. bar assns., Am. Law Inst., Chicagoland Enterprise Ctr. (chair), Leadership Gr. Chgo. (dir.), Latino Inst. (bd. dirs.). Clubs: Economic, Commercial, Law, Chicago. Home: 5844 Stony Island Ave Chicago IL 60637 Office: 8000 Sears Tower Chicago IL 60606

ALLBRIGHT, KARAN ELIZABETH, psychologist, consultant; b. Oklahoma City, Okla., Jan. 28, 1948; d. Jack Gahnal and Irma Lolene (Keesee) A. BA, Oklahoma City U., 1970, MAT, 1972; PhD, U. So. Miss., 1981. Cert. sch. psychologist, Ga.; cert. psychometrist, Ga.; lic. psychologist, Okla., Ark. Psychol. technician Donald J. Bertoch, Ph.D., Oklahoma City, 1973-76; asst. adminstr. Parents' Assistance Ctr., Oklahoma City, 1976-77; psychology intern Burwell Psycho-ednl. Ctr., Carrollton, Ga., 1980-81; staff psychologist Griffin Area Psychoednl. Ctr., Ga., 1981-85; clinic dir. Sequoyah County Guidance Clinic, Sallisaw, Okla., 1985-88; psychologist Baker Psychiatric Clinic, Ft. Smith, Ark., 1988—; cons. Harbor View Mercy Hosp., 1988—; lectr. various orgns.; dir. workshops. Mem. Task Force to Prevent Child Abuse, Fayette County, Ga., 1984-85, Task Force on Family Violence, Spalding County, Ga., 1983-85; cons. Family Alliance (Parents Anonymous) Sequoyah County, Okla., 1985-88. Named Outstanding Young Women in Am., 1980. Mem. Am. Psychol. Assn., Southeastern Psychol. Assn., Nat. Assn. Sch. Psychologists, Nat. Council for Exceptional Children, Okla. Psychol. Assn., Okla. Pub. Health Assn., Nat. Assn. Health Service Profiders in Psychology, Psi Chi, Delta Zeta (chpt. dir. 1970-72). Democrat. Presbyterian. Home: 2100 Brooken Hill Dr Apt 3-C Fort Smith AR 72903 Office: Baker Psychiat Clinic 2112 S Greenwood Fort Smith AR 72901

ALLBRIGHT, MARTHA PHILLIPS, lawyer; b. Muscatine, Iowa, Sept. 12, 1952; d. Sherwood Roy and Ruth (Vetter) Phillips; m. Edwin T. Allbright, July 10, 1982. B.A., U. Denver, 1974, J.D., 1977. Bar: Colo. 1978. Atty., Saunders Snyder Ross & Dickson, Denver, 1978-83; spl. counsel Atler, Zall & Haligman, Denver, 1983-85; with Allbright and Buchanan, P.C., 1986—; real estate broker Centerline Properties, Denver, 1983—; v.p. mktg. Centerline Sports, Denver, 1982—; lobbyist water and environ. legislation, 1981—. Contbr. articles to profl. jours. Mem. Denver Bar Assn. (exec. council young lawyers sect.), Colo. Bar Assn. (exec. council young lawyers sect., chmn. environ. law com.), ABA, Colo. Water Congress, Colo. Groundwater Assn. Gamma Phi Beta. Republican. Presbyterian. Club: P.E.O. Home: 5944 S Meadowbrook Dr Morrison CO 80465

ALLDREDGE, ALICE LOUISE, biology educator; b. Denver, Feb. 1, 1949. BA in Biology, Carleton Coll., 1971; PhD in Ecology, U. Calif., Davis, 1975. NATO postdoctoral fellow Australian Inst. Marine Sci., Townsville, Queensland, 1975-76; asst. prof. biology U. Calif., Santa Barbara, 1976-82, assoc. prof., 1982-86, prof., 1986—. Author: Tunicata: Yearbook of Science and Technology, 1979; contbr. articles to profl. jours. NSF grad. fellow. Mem. Phi Beta Kappa, Sigma Xi. Office: U Calif Dept Biol Scis Santa Barbara CA 93106

ALLEMAN, AURELIA RUSHTON (LEA), business executive; b. Fortville, Ind., Sept. 30, 1928; d. Frank M. and Mary M. (Davis) Rushton; m. Zachary T. Bunch, June 5, 1950; children—Zachary Taylor, Tanja Flame, Freeman Enmeier, Olivia Cutcher; m. 2d Ralph J. Alleman, May 7, 1973; children—Stephanie Miller, Bruce, Mark. Student Fortville, Ind. pub. schs. Owner, pres. Be Wise, Inc., Indpls., 1956-62, Miracles Happen, Inc., 1963-67, 20th Century Computer Matching, 1965-73; v.p. Dip-Er-Do Plane Co., Fort Lee, N.J., 1976-77; adminstr. Mgmt. Cleaning Controls, Inc., Chgo., 1981-84; dir. ASQ Clubs; chmn. Lee Parker Enterprises, Inc. Active LWV. Mem. Am. Bus. Women (ednl. com. mem., 1973-74). Author: How to Happily Kiss the Singles Scene Goodbye, 1979. Home: 5100 North Marine Dr Chicago IL 60640 Office: Berman Sales Co Inc 1728 S Michigan Ave Chicago IL 60616

ALLEN, ADRIENNE LYNN, advertising executive; b. Chattanooga, Oct. 16, 1950; d. Roscoe Bryant and Helen Earlene (Hamilton) A. BFA, So. Meth. U., 1972. Mech. artist Taylor Pub. Co., Dallas, 1972; designer Image Plus Design Studio, Dallas, 1972-73, Bob Knight & Assocs., Dallas, 1973-74; asst. art dir. Comml. Prodns., Inc., Dallas, 1974-76; co-owner, art dir. And Assocs., Inc., Dallas, 1976-77; proprietor, creative dir. Adrienne Allen and Assocs., Dallas, 1977—; creative cons. March of Dimes Gourmet Gala, Dallas, 1986—, Dallas Epilepsy Assn., 1986—, The CoCo Awards, Dallas, 1986—, Treescape Dallas, 1984-85. Designer various advt. campaigns, 1981—. Pub. Awareness Service award Dallas Epilepsy Assn., 1987. Mem. Alpha Delta Pi (v.p. 1970-71). Republican. Home: 9706 Summerwood Circle Dallas TX 75243 Office: Adrienne Allen and Assocs 5494 La Sierra Dr Dallas TX 75231

ALLEN, ALICE CATHERINE TOWSLEY, public relations professional, writer, consultant; b. N.Y.C., July 26, 1924; d. George Everett and Alice Sophia (Kunkeli) Goldsmith; m. Harold Dulmage Towsley, Jan. 4, 1940 (div. 1942); m. Charles Kissam Allen, Jan. 20, 1973. Student, U. Hawaii, 1941-42. Writer Honolulu Advertiser, 1942-47; advt. mgr. Paterson Morning Call, Paterson, N.J., 1949-52; publ. cons. N.Y. (N.Y.C.) Herald Tribune, 1953; assoc. editor Mayfair, Travel, Fashion mags., N.Y.C., 1953-54; pub. editor Assoc. Jr. Leagues, Inc., N.Y.C., 1954-59; editor, asst. pub. Doctor's Wife mag., N.Y.C., 1959-65; pub. relations dir., editor Am. Field Service Internat., N.Y.C., 1967-72; free-lance writer, pub. cons. N.Y.C., 1973—. Club: Overseas Press. Home: 325 E 41st St New York NY 10017

ALLEN, ANNA JEAN, chiropractor; b. Henderson, Ky., Apr. 6, 1955; d. Harold D. and Aiko (Nakashima) Allen. A.S., U. Ky., 1973, B.S., 1976; Dr.Chiropractic, Palmer U., 1980; postgrad. Pan Am. U., 1981, San Antonio Coll., 1983. Health instr. Nautilus, Davenport, Iowa, 1978-80; dir. chiropractic, Harlington, Tex., 1980-81, Handley Chiropractic, San Antonio, 1982-83, NE Chiropractic Ctr., El Paso, Tex., 1983-84, Viscount Chiropractic, El Paso, 1984—. Mem. Am. Bus. Woman's Assn., Nat. Assn. Female Execs., Nat. Fedn. Ind. Bus., Chiropractic Orthopedist Assn., Christian Chiropracticc Assn., Found. for Chiropractic Research, Found. for Chiropractic Research, Tex. Palmer Alumni Assn., Palmer Alumni Assn., Am. Chiropractic Assn., Tex. Chiropractic Assn. (dist. dir. 1986). Avocations: scuba diving; weight lifting; running; bicycling; painting. Office: Viscount Chiropractic Health Ctr 8838 Viscount Suite 0 El Paso TX 79925

ALLEN, BEATRICE, piano educator; b. N.Y.C., June 30, 1917; d. Samuel and Rose (Krell) Hyman; m. Eugene Murray Allen, Jan. 23, 1937; children: Marlene Allen Galzin, Julian Lewis. Student NYU, 1933-36; diploma (scholar), Inst. Musical Arts, N.Y.C., 1939, postgrad. (scholar), 1939-40; diploma (fellow, letter commendation), Juilliard Grad. Sch., N.Y.C., 1943; BA magna cum laude Cedar Crest Coll., 1980. Mem. faculty prep. div. Juilliard Sch. Music, 1957-69, Moravian Coll., 1967-68, Northampton County Area Community Coll., 1968-70, Manhattan Sch. Music, 1969—; mem. founding faculty Community Music Sch., Allentown, Pa., 1982—; artist-in-residence, condr. Tchrs. Workshop, Antioch Coll., Yellow Springs, Ohio, 1966; Bach lectr., recitals various univs.; concert appearances Town Hall, N.Y.C., Chautauqua, N.Y., others. Winner N.J. Artists contest, 1936. Mem. Music Tchrs. Nat. Assn. (program chmn. Lehigh Valley chpt. 1981-82), Pa. Music Tchrs. Assn. Address: 2100 Main St Bethlehem PA 18017

ALLEN, BESSIE CLYDE, home economics educator; b. Sumter, S.C., Aug. 10, 1942; m. Robert E. Gist, Sept. 12, 1964 (div. 1978); children: Antoinette, Bernadette; m. Frederick D. Allen, June 28, 1980; stepchildren: Fred, Stephney, Glenn, Leslie, Cynthia. B.S. in Home Econs., S.C. State Coll., 1964; MS in Home Econs., SUNY, Buffalo, 1974; MA in Ednl. Adminstrn., Kean Coll., 1984. Cert. tchr., prin.-supr. Tchr. Wagner (S.C.) Bd. Edn., 1964-65; home economist Clemson (S.C.) U., 1965-68; tchr. Lackawanna (N.Y.) Bd. Edn., 1968-75; tchr. Neptune (N.J.) Twp. Bd. Edn., 1975-87, chmn. dept., 1987-88; coordinator Adult Evening Sch., Neptune, 1987—; adv. bd. Perth Amboy (N.J.) Drop-out Project, 1986—, Montivale (N.J.) Drop-out Project, 1986—, N.J. State Vocat. Edn., 1987—. Author: Metrics, 1979, Nutrition Education, 1985. Named Outstanding Young Educator, N.Y. Jaycees, 1971. Mem. NEA (rep. bldg. 1978), Am. Home Econs. Assn. (Tchr. Yr. N.J. chpt., Top Ten Home Econs. Tchrs. U.S. 1987), Am. Vocat. Assn., Prins./Suprs. Assn., Nat. Assn. Females Execs., Monmouth County Jack and Jill, Kappa Delta Pi. Democrat. Presbyterian. Club: Ocean Drifters (N.J.) (v.p. 1985-87, elder 1984-87). Home: 19 Hartshorne Rd Wayside NJ 07712

ALLEN, CARMEN DENISE, nurse; b. Newark, N.J., Sept. 24, 1962; d. Luther Clarence Sr. and Hilda Mae (Allen) Allen. BS in Nursing, Seton Hall U., 1984; postgrad., Upsala Coll., 1988. R.N. N.J. Home health aide Patient Care, W. Orange, N.J., 1982-83; student nurse Newark (N.J.) Beth Israel Med. Cen., 1983-84, staff nurse, 1984—. Mem. U.S. Tennis Assn. Democrat.

ALLEN, CATHERINE BRYANT, denominational executive, writer; b. Birmingham, Ala., Mar. 26, 1942; d. Leonard P. and Betty Lou (Durham) Bryant; m. Lee Norcross Allen, Aug. 24, 1963; children: Leland Norcross III, Leslie Catherine. BA, Samford U., 1964; MBA, Emory U., 1984. Editor Sunbeam Activities mag. Woman's Missionary Union So. Bapt. Conv., Birmingham, 1964-67, pub. relations dir., 1967-74, asst. to exec., 1974-83, dir. pub. and employee relations, assoc. exec. dir., 1983—; instr. journalism Samford U., Birmingham, 1970-71; bd. dirs. Ministers Life, Mpls. Author: The New Lottie Moon Story, 1980, A Century to Celebrate: History of Woman's Missionary Union, 1987, Laborers Together with God, 1987; (with Alma Hunt) History of Woman's Missionary Union, revised edition, 1976, (with Lee N. Allen) Courage to Care, 1988; also contbr. numerous articles and phamphlets. Mem. Horizon 280 Assn., Birmingham, 1983-84. Named Alumna of Yr., Samford U., 1980. Mem. Women in Communication, Bapt. Pub. Relations Assn. (pres. 1971-72), Phi Kappa Phi, Chi Omega. Office: Woman's Missionary Union PO Box C-10 Birmingham AL 35283

ALLEN, DEBORAH RUDISILL, clinical psychologist, educator, university administrator; b. Port Chester, N.Y., Oct. 31, 1951; d. Stewart Ellwood and Sarah Louise (Rudisill) A.; m. Howard Schein, Nov. 24, 1984; 1 dau., Stevie Scarlett. BA in Psychology summa cum laude, U. Vt., 1972; MA in Clin. Psychology, Mich. State U., 1974, PhD in Clin. Psychology, 1977. Lic. psychologist, Ill. Asst. prof. psychology Olin health services and counseling ctr. Mich. State U., East Lansing, 1977-78; clin. counselor U. Ill., Urbana, 1978—, asst. dir. counseling ctr., 1981-84, assoc. dir. counseling ctr., 1984—; pvt. practice psychology, Urbana, 1979—; cons. employee assistance program Control Data Inc., Urbana, 1984—. Contbr. articles to profl. jours.; co-author: (book) Giving Advice to Students: A Roadmap for College Professionals, 1987, (brochures) numerous self-help publs. , 1984—. Mem. Am. Psychol. Assn., Am. Assn. Counseling and Devel., Am. Coll. Personnel Assn., Phi Beta Kappa, Phi Kappa Phi, Psi Chi. Home: 608 W Nevada St Urbana IL 61801 Office: U Ill Counseling Ctr 610 E John St Champaign IL 61820

ALLEN, DIANA UPTAIN, geriatric services director; b. Guntersville, Ala., Mar. 3, 1948; s. Mann and Ruth (Bearden) Uptain; B.S. in Human Services, U. Tenn., Chattanooga, 1975; M.S.S.W., U. Tenn.-Knoxville, 1986; m. Charles Clay Allen, June 10, 1978; 1 son, Matthew Clay. Cert. master social worker, Tenn. Med. sec. Team Evaluation Center, Chattanooga, 1967-72; dir. social service Hamilton County (Tenn.) Nursing Home, Chattanooga, 1975-80, Meml. Hosp., Chattanooga, 1980-85; case mgr. Sr. Adult Assessment and Counseling Service, Chattanooga, 1986-87; exec. dir. Older Adult Services, Inc., Chattanooga, 1987—; Sarah Key Patten scholar, 1974. Mem. Nat. Assn. Social Workers, Nat. Council on Aging, Tenn. Conf. on Social Welfare, Nat. Soc. Fund Raising Execs., Pi Gamma Mu. Home: 923 Dunsinane Rd Signal Mountain TN 37377

ALLEN, DONNA, association executive, author; b. Petoskey, Mich., Aug. 19, 1920; d. Caspar and Louise (Densmore) Rehkopf; m. Russell Allen, Sept. 8, 1942 (div. 1970); children: Dana, Indra, Martha, Mark. AB, Duke U., 1943; MA, U. Chgo., 1953; PhD, Howard U., 1971. Extension tchr. Indsl. and Labor Relations Cornell U., Ithaca, N.Y., 1953-55; legis. asst. Congressman William H. Meyer, Washington, 1960; Washington rep. Nat. Com. Against Repressive Legis., 1965-74, vice-chmn., 1975—; pres. Women's Inst. for Freedom of Press, Washington, 1972—; editor, Media Report to Women, 1972-87; past dir. Datline Copenhagen, Dateline Nairobi; dir., organizer annual confs. on planning nat. and internat. communication system for women, Washington, 1978-84. Author: Fringe Benefits, 1964; co-author: Communications at the Crossroads: The Gender Gap Connection, 1988. Recipient Broadcast Preceptors award Broadcast Communication Arts Dept., 1978, Headliner award Women in Communications, Inc., 1979, Wonder Woman Found. award, 1983. Mem. Nat. Women's Polit. Caucus, Nat. Women's Party (bd. dirs. 1978-86, 4th v.p. 1985-87), Nat. Orgn. for Women. Home and Office: 3306 Ross Pl NW Washington DC 20008

ALLEN, FRANCES ELIZABETH, computer scientist; b. Peru, N.Y., Aug. 4, 1932; d. John Abram and Ruth Genevieve (Downs) A.; m. Jacob T. Schwartz, July 22, 1972. B.S., State U. N.Y., Albany, 1954; M.A., U. Mich., 1957. Research computer scientist IBM Research Lab., Yorktown Heights, N.Y., 1957—; adj. asso. prof. N.Y. U., 1970-72; mem. computer sci. adv. bd. NSF, 1972-75, cons., 1975-78; lectr. Chinese Acad. Scis., 1973, 77; IEEE disting. visitor, 1973-74; cons. prof. Stanford U., 1977-78. Mem. Assn. Computing Machinery (nat. lectr. 1972-73), Programming Systems and Langs. (Paper award 1976), Nat. Acad. Engring. (elected 1987). Home: Finney Farm Croton-on-Hudson NY 10520 Office: IBM Corp PO Box 704 Yorktown Heights NY 10598

ALLEN, GINA, author; b. Trenton, Nebr.; d. R.V. and Osa (Hanel) Hunkins; 1 dau., Ginita Allen Wall. B.A., Northwestern U., 1940. Exec. sec. Youth Commn. 3d Jud. Dist., N.Mex., 1955-60; mem. bd. Golden Gate chpt. NOW, 1970—; pres. Humanist Assn. San Francisco, 1976-85; sec. Am. Humanist Assn., 1973-77, sr. humanist counselor, 1972—, founding chmn. feminist caucus, 1977—, founder feminist caucus, 1977—, chmn. div. humanist counseling, 1982—, v.p., 1979-83. Author: Prairie Children, 1941, On the Oregon Trail, 1942, Rustics for Keeps, 1948, (with R.V. Hunkins) Tepee Days, 1941, Trapper Days, 1942, Sod-House Days, 1945, The Forbidden Man, 1961 (Anisfield-Wolf award 1962), Gold!, 1964, Gold Is, 1969, Intimacy, 1971; also short stories, articles in popular mags.; editorial bd. Humanist mag., 1983—. Chairwoman N.Mex. Democratic Central Com., 1956-59. Recipient Pioneer award Am. Humanist Assn., 1983. Unitarian.

ALLEN, ISABEL ELAINE, biostatistician, educator; b. N.Y.C., Oct. 18, 1948; d. John Thomas and Claire Isabel (Meldrum) Allen; BA, Skidmore Coll., 1970; MA, U. Evansville, 1975; PhD, Cornell U., 1979; m. Jeffrey Richard Seaman, Jan. 21, 1978; children: Christopher Allen, Julia Elizabeth. Statis. cons. Hist. New Harmony, Inc. (Ind.), 1975; research/teaching asst. dept. econs. and social stats. Cornell U., Ithaca, N.Y., 1976-78; asst. prof. stats. Wharton Sch., U. Pa., Phila., 1978-83, adj. assoc. prof., 1983-85, research assoc. in population studies, 1980—; sr. biostatistician, supr. clin. trials Wyeth Labs., Radnor, Pa., 1983-86; project leader Centocor, Inc., Malvern, Pa., 1986-88, asst. dir. biomed. ops., head biometry, 1988—; research assoc. prof. Med. Coll. Pa., Phila., 1985—; chmn. sci. adv. com. Stat Systems, Inc., 1986-88; cons. Dept. Revenue, Commonwealth of Pa., 1979-81, Def. Logistics Agy. Dept. Def., 1980-81. Bd. dirs. Parent-Infant Ctr., Phila., 1980-81, treas., 1980-81. Cornell fellow, 1977, research fellow in population, 1976; U. Pa. faculty summer fellow and grantee, 1979; Prudential fellow for inflation research, 1981-82. Mem. Am. Statis. Assn., Am. Soc. Quality Control. Contbr. articles to profl. jours. Home: Jug Hollow Rd Phoenixville PA 19460 Office: Centocor Inc 244 Great Valley Pkwy Malvern PA 19355

ALLEN, JESSIE LEE, nurse; b. Clarke County, Miss., Mar. 8, 1925; d. Roosevelt and Margie (Collins) Harper; G.E.D., Emily Griffith Opportunity Sch., Denver, 1963; A.A.S. in Mental Retardation Tech., Angelina Jr. Coll., 1972; L.P.N., Meridian Jr. Coll., 1976; m. Lawrence Allen, Oct. 26, 1974; 1 son, Renard Williams. Attendant, then head attendant and relief attendant supr. Ridge State Home and Tng. Sch., Denver, 1962-66; attendant, then attendant supr. I Tex. Research Inst. of Mental Scis., Houston, 1968-70;

therapist asst. Lufkin (Tex.) State Sch., 1970-72; nurse Watkins Meml. Hosp., Quitman, Miss., 1976-77, staff nurse, 1981—; nurse Archusa Convalescent Center, 1977—. Mem. Am. Assn. Mental Deficiency, Nat. Fedn. L.P.N.'s. Baptist. Home: Route 3 Box 176 Vossburg MS 39366 Office: HC Watkins Meml Hosp Quitman MS 39355

ALLEN, JOYCE SMITH, medical librarian; b. Englewood, N.J., Aug. 1, 1939; d. Harold Willard and Mary Elizabeth Smith; m. Jim Frank Allen, Mar. 1974 (div. 1984); 1 child, Shani Jamilla. BA, Howard U., 1961; MLS, Atlanta U., 1966; cert. in advanced studies, U. Ill., 1974. Reference librarian Howard U., Washington, 1966-73; mgr. library Meth. Hosp. Ind., Indpls., 1977—; instr. Ind. Vocat. Tech. Coll., 1979, 85, Med. Library Assn., 1982—, Martin Ctr. Coll., Indpls., 1983-84. Author career materials. Vol. Indpls. Police Dept. Library, 1977, Children's Mus., Indpls., 1987—. Recipient Minority Bus. and Profl. Achiever award Ctr. for Leadership Devel., Indpls., 1981. Mem. ALA, Internat. Tng. and Communication Soc., Med. Library Assn., Council on Library Technicians, Greater Midwest Regional Med. Library Network. Democrat. Home: 3815 N Bolton Ave Indianapolis IN 46226 Office: Meth Hosp Ind 1701 N Senate Blvd Indianapolis IN 46201

ALLEN, JUDITH GIBSON, financial services marketing executive; b. Summit, N.J., Mar. 30, 1957; d. Gordon E. and Sally (Sprague) A. AB in History, Brown U., 1979; MBA, Harvard U., 1983. News producer Sta. WJAR-TV, Providence, R.I., 1979-81; mktg. asst. Merrill Lynch, Pierce, Fenner & Smith, N.Y.C., 1983-84, mgr. cash mgmt. account nat. sales, 1984-86, dir. mktg. strategy and services group fin. services, 1986; dir. mktg. Merrill Lynch Internat. Bank, N.Y.C., 1986—. Vol. Com. to Re-Elect Congressman Green, N.Y.C., 1984, 86; usher Fifth Avenue Presbyn. Ch., N.Y.C., 1985—. Mem. Media Educators Assn., Brown U. Assn. Class Officers (v.p. 1979—), Brown U. Nat. Alumni Schs. Program (interviewer 1979—), Harvard Club of N.Y.C., Harvard Bus. Sch. Club. Republican. Home: 470 West End Ave Apt 7D New York NY 10024 Office: Merrill Lynch Internat Bank World Financial Ctr South Tower New York NY 10080-1711

ALLEN, JUDY ADAMS, social counselor; b. Nashville, Nov. 11, 1946; d. Ernest Bradley and Elsie Mai (Griffith) Adams; divorced; children: Ricky Wayne, Lisa Ann. Student, George Peabody Coll., 1965; AS summa cum laude, Volunteer State Coll., 1980; BS, Tenn. State U., 1984. Office mgr. Town & Country Hardware, Nashville, 1966-74; rehab. counselor Nationwide Therapeutics, Nashville, 1983-84; social counselor Tenn. Dept. Human Services, Nashville, 1985—. Author poetry Horse Swapper, Nary a Thing on Me, 1976, An Old Man's Lament, 1978, The Chrysanthemums, 1980; contbr. articles to profl. jours. Mem. ch. and soc. com. Arlington Meth. Ch., 1984-86, Prison Fellowship Emmaus Movement, Nashville, 1979-84. Mem. Tenn. State Employees Assn. Democrat. Methodist. Home: 1020 Iverson Ave Nashville TN 37216 Office: Tenn Dept Human Services 1000 Second Ave N Nashville TN 37202

ALLEN, LEATRICE DELORICE, psychologist; b. Chgo., July 15, 1948; d. Burt and Mildred Floy (Taylor) Hawkins; m. Allen Moore, Jr., July 30, 1965 (div. Oct. 1975); children—Chandra, Valarie, Allen; m. Armstead Allen, May 11, 1978. A.A. in Bus. Edn., Olive Harvey Coll., Chgo., 1975; B.A. in Psychology cum laude, Chgo. State U., 1977; M.Clin. Psychology, Roosevelt U., 1980. Clk., U.S. Post Office, Chgo., 1967-72; clin. therapist Bobby Wright Mental Health Ctr., Chgo., 1979-80; clin. therapist Community Mental Health Council, Chgo., 1980-83, assoc. dir., 1983—; cons. Edgewater Mental Health, Chgo., 1984—, Project Pride, Chgo., 1985—; victim services coordinator Community Mental Health Council, Chgo., 1986-87; mgr. youth family services Mile Square Health Ctr., Chgo., 1987—. Scholar Chgo. State U., 1976, Roosevelt U., 1978; fellow Menninger Found., 1985. Mem. Nat. Orgn. for Victim Assistance, Ill. Coalition Against Sexual Assault (del. 1985—), Soc. Traumatic Stress Studies (treatment innovations task force). Avocations: aerobics; reading; theatre; dining. Home: 16603 S Paulina St Markham IL 60426

ALLEN, LISA JANE, television reporter, lawyer; b. Willimantic, Conn., Apr. 29, 1956; d. Myron and Nancy Lois (Sussman) A. B.A. summa cum laude, Tufts U., 1978; J.D., Emory U., 1982. Bar: Ga. 1982. News writer sta. WEEI-CBS Radio, Boston, 1977-78; anchor, reporter sta. WHYN-TV, Springfield, Mass., 1978-79; producer, reporter sta. WGBY-TV, Springfield, 1979; anchor, reporter sta. WGST, Atlanta, 1979-81; assignment editor, reporter sta. WSB-TV, Atlanta, 1981-82; TV corr. Cox Communications, Washington, 1983-85; med. reporter Sta. KTVI-TV, St. Louis, 1985—; mem. House/Senate Radio and TV News Galleries, Washington, 1983-85. Mem. ABA, Phi Beta Kappa.

ALLEN, LISA KATHLEEN, fashion consultant; b. Camp Le Jeune, N.C., Mar. 1, 1958; d. Terence Michael Allen and June Elizabeth (Goeke) Axness. BS in Bus. Adminstrn., N.Mex. State U., 1981. Spokesperson Pub. Service Co. of N.Mex., Albuquerque, 1983; dir. mktg. research Lovelace Med. Ctr., Albuquerque, 1983-84; sales mgr. Alan's Clothier, Albuquerque, 1984-85; wardrobe planner, owner Allen Wardrobe Planning, Albuquerque, 1985—; wardrobe cons. Broadway Southwest, Albuquerque, 1987, N.Mex. Bd. of Realtors, Albuquerque, 1987, First Nat. Bank of Belen, N.Mex., 1987. Columnist: Dress to Fit Role Increases Odds for Success, 1987; designer Packet for Men and Women, 1987. youth advisor Irick for Gov., Albuquerque, 1982. Named Miss N.Mex., 1982-83, Hon. Citizen Country of Costa Rica, 1982, City of Matamoros, Mexico, 1982. Mem. Delta Sigma Pi. Address: 7544 Lantern NE Albuquerque NM 87109

ALLEN, LOUISE, writer, educator; b. Alliance, Ohio, Sept. 21, 1910; d. Earl Wayne and Ella Celesta (Goodall) A.; m. Benjamin Yukl, June 27, 1936; children: Katherine Anne Yukl Johnston, Kenneth Allen, Richard Lee, Margaret Louise Yukl Border. Student, Cleve. Coll. Western Res. U., 1963, Lakeland Community Coll., 1981-84. Co-founder Sch. Writing, Cleve., 1961-62; founder, dir. Allen Writers' Agy., Wickliffe, Ohio, 1963-84; editorial assoc. criticism service Writer's Digest mag., 1967-69; instr. Cuyahoga Community Coll., 1965-81, Lakeland Community Coll., Mentor, Ohio, 1973-81, Scottsdale Community Coll., 1984-88. Contbr. articles to mags. Mem. Mensa, Assn. Mundial de Mujures Periodistas y Escritoras, Women in Communications, Nat. League Am. Pen Women, DAR, Textile Arts Club of Cleve. Mus. Art. Republican. Congregationalist. Clubs: Shore Writers (founder), Euclid Three Arts; Women's City (Cleve.). Lodge: Altrusa. Address: 2609 W Southern #11 Tempe AZ 85282

ALLEN, LUNELLE SPENCER, nurse; b. Cherokee County, S.C., Oct. 3, 1931; d. William E. and Nancy Anna (Wilson) Spencer; m. Karl H. Zerbst, Oct. 16, 1955 (div. Feb. 1970); children: Karl H. Zerbst Jr., Chris Anthony Zerbst; m. Raymond D. Allen, Jan. 23, 1973. Diploma in Nursing, Columbia (S.C.) Hosp. Sch. Nursing, 1952. RN, S.C. Staff nurse Columbia Hosp., 1952-54; staff nurse Roper Hosp., Charleston, S.C., 1955, supr. obgyn, 1955-62; staff nurse Westvaco Corp., Charleston, 1962-77, head nurse, 1977—. Mem. North Charleston (S.C.) Citizen's Adv. Council, 1976-80; pres. Pepperhill Neighborhood Council, North Charleston, 1983; active PTA. Mem. S.C. Occupational Health Nurses Assn. (numerous coms. 1963—). Lutheran. Clubs: Antique Auto of Am., Coastal Carolina (Charleston) (sec.). Lodges: Daus. of Nile, Milcah Temple. Home: 7631 Hillandale Rd North Charleston SC 29418 Office: Westvaco Corp PO Box 29411 North Charleston SC 29411-2905

ALLEN, MARIA GEORGINA QUEVEDO, social worker; b. Camaguey, Cuba, Oct. 30; came to U.S. 1961, naturalized, 1970; d. Pedro Manuel and Dolores (Peralta) Quevedo; m. Wilfredo O. Allen, Sept. 8, 1950; children: Wilfredo, Jorge A. Doctora en Leyes, U. La Habana, Cuba, 1943; MSW, Fla. State U., 1969. Social worker Cuban refugee program Fla. State Dept. Welfare, 1962-67; caseworker Health and Rehab. Services, 1969-71; supr. social services U. Miami Comprehensive Health Care Program, 1971-74; social worker, supr. evaluation unit Goodwill Industries, Miami, 1974-79; regional social services supr. dept. youth and family devel. Met. Dade County Fla., 1974—; asst. prof., field instr. Barry Coll., 1974—. Recipient Miami City Commn. for Vol. Services in Child Day Care award, 1977. Mem. Nat. Assn. Social Workers, Coalition for Spanish Am. Women.Acad. Cert. Social Workers, Cuban Bar in Exile, Fla. State U. Alumni Assn. Roman Catholic. Club: Cuban Women's. Office: 11025 SW 84th St Miami FL 33173

ALLEN, MARILYN MYERS POOL, theater director, video producer; b. Fresno, Calif., Nov. 2, 1934; d. Laurence B. and Asa (Griggs) Myers; B.A., Stanford U., 1955, postgrad., 1955-56; postgrad. U. Tex., 1957-60, W. Tex. State U. summers 1962, 63; m. Joseph Harold Pool, Dec. 28, 1955; children—Pamela Elizabeth, Victoria Anne, Catherine Marcia; m. Neal R. Allen, Apr. 1982. Pvt. tchr. drama, speech, acting, directing, speech correction, Amarillo, Tex., 1960-82, Midland, Tex., 1982—; free-lance radio and TV actress; asst. mng. dir. Amarillo Little Theatre, 1964-66, mng. dir., 1966-68; mng. dir. Horsehoe Players, touring profl. theater, 1969-73; actress, multimedia prodn. Palo Duro Canyon, 1971; dir. touring children's theatre, 1978-79 guest actress in Medea, Amarillo Coll., 1981; guest reciter Midland-Odessa Symphony, 1984. Pres. Tex. Non-Profit Theatres, 1972-74, 75-77, bd. dirs., 1988—; 1st v.p. High Plains Center for Performing Arts, 1969-73; adv. mem. dept. fine arts Amarillo Coll., 1980-82. Adv. mem. Tex. Constnl. Revision Commn., 1973-75; mem. adv. council U. Tex. Coll. Fine Arts, 1969-72; community adv. com. for women Amarillo Coll., 1975-79; conv. program com. Am. Theatre Assn., 1978, program participant 1978-80, bd. dirs., 1980-83; bd. dirs. Amarillo Found. Health and Sci. Edn., 1976-82, program v.p., 1979-81; bd. dirs. Domestic Violence Council, 1979-82, March of Dimes, 1979-81, Tex. Panhandle Heritage Found., 1964-82, Friends of Fine Arts, W. Tex. State U., 1980-82, Amarillo City Library, 1980-82, Amarillo Symphony, 1981-82; publicity chmn. Midland Community Theatre, 1984—, bd. govs., 1986—, sec., 1987. Recipient cert. of appreciation Woman of Year, Amarillo Bus. and Profl. Women's Club, 1966; Best Actress award for Hedda Gabler role Amarillo Little Theatre 1965, Best Dir. award for Rashomon, 1967; named Woman of Yr., Beta Sigma Pi, 1980; Travel fellow AAUW, 1973, 78. Mem. Am. Community Theatre Assn. (dir. 1969-72, 82-84, v.p. planning and devel. 1985-87), S.W. Theatre Conf. (dir. 1973-76, 82-84, exec. com. 1982-84), Tex. Theatre Council (dir. 1974-81, exec. com., pres. 1975-76), AAUW (br. pres. 1973-75, state chmn. cultural interests 1975-77, state bd. dirs. 1984-88, program v.p. Midland 1988—), DAR, (chpt. chaplain 1971-75, historian 1975-77), C. of C. (fine arts council), U.S. Judo Assn., Symphony Guild, Amarillo Art Assn., Midland Symphony Guild (arrangements chmn. 1983-84), Act IX, Amarillo Law Wives Club (pres. 1976-77), Hamhocks (v.p. 1985-86). Episcopalian.

ALLEN, MARYON PITTMAN, former senator, journalist, lecturer, interior and clothing designer; b. Meridian, Miss., Nov. 30, 1925; d. John D. and Tellie (Chism) Pittman; m. Joshua Sanford Mullins, Jr., Oct. 17, 1946 (div. Jan. 1959); children: Joshua Sanford III, John Pittman, Maryon Foster; m. James Browning Allen, Aug. 7, 1964 (dec. June 1978). Student, U. Ala., 1944-47, Internat. Inst. Interior Design, 1970. Office mgr. for Dr. Alston Callahan, Birmingham, Ala., 1959-60; bus. mgr. psychiat. clinic U. Ala. Med. Center, Birmingham, 1960-61; life underwriter Protective Life Ins. Co., Birmingham, 1961-62; women's editor Sun Newspapers, Birmingham, 1962-64; v.p., partner Pittman family cos., J.D. Pittman Partnership Co., J.D. Pittman Tractor Co., Emerald Valley Corp., Mountain Lake Farms, Inc., Birmingham; mem. U.S. Senate (succeeding late husband James B. Allen), 1978; dir. public relations and advt. C.G. Sloan & Co. Auction House, Washington, 1981; feature writer: Birmingham News,, 1964; writer syndicated column Reflections of a News Hen, Washington, 1969-78; feature writer, columnist Maryon Allen's Washington, Washington Post, 1979-81; owner The Maryon Allen Co. Cliff House (Restoration/Design). Mem. Ladies of U.S. Senate unit ARC, Former Mems. of Congress, Ala. Hist. Commn., Blair House Fine Arts Commn.; charter mem. Birmingham Com. of 100 for Women; trustee Children's Fresh Air Farm; trustee, elder Ind. Presbyn. Ch., Birmingham; Democratic Presdl. elector, Ala., 1968; bd. dirs. Positive Maturity, Birmingham. Recipient 1st place award for best original column Ala. Press Assn., 1962, 63, also various press state and nat. awards for typography, fashion writing, food pages, also several awards during Senate service. Mem. Fashion Group Birmingham. Clubs: Washington Press, 1925 F Street, 91st Congress, Congressional, Birmingham Country. Home: Cliff House 3215 Cliff Rd Birmingham AL 35205

ALLEN, MICHELLE JOANNE, advertising executive; b. Dearborn, Mich., Aug. 29, 1960; d. Edward Norman Durocher and Norma Fannie (Wheatley) Burdett; m. Brian Henry Allen, Oct. 5, 1984; 1 child, Paul James. Grad. high sch., Dearborn. Office clk., switchboard operator Dearborn Press and Guide, 1978, coordinator retail sales, 1978-81, asst. dir. advt., 1981-82, dir. advt., 1982—. Designer advt. section Fairlane Town Ctr., 1983. Mem. Dearborn C. of C. (women's div.). Home: 24133 Carlysle Dearborn MI 48126 Office: Dearborn Press and Guide 15340 Michigan Ave Dearborn MI 48126

ALLEN, NANCY KACHELRIESS, judicial agency executive; b. Irvington, N.J., July 12, 1951; m. Roger Warren Allen, May 10, 1986. BA in Sociology with honors, Russell Sage Coll., 1974. Sr. probation officer Middlesex County Probation Dept., New Brunswick, N.J., 1974-80, tng. officer, 1980-86; prin. tng. technician Adminstrv. Office of the Cts., Trenton, N.J., 1986—; program coordinator State Law Enforcement Planning Agy., Trenton, 1982. Mem. Am. Probation and Parole Assn., Probation Assn. of N.J., Middlesex County Probation Officers' Assn., Tng. Adv. Council Adminstrv. Office of Cts., Mid Atlantic States Correction Assn. Office: Adminstrv Office of Cts CN-037 Trenton NJ 08625

ALLEN, PAMELA KATHERINE, information systems manager; b. Barre, Vt., June 5, 1947; d. Edward Joseph and Katherine Louise (Cook) Coughlin; m. Jonathan Dwight Allen, June 14, 1969 (div. 1981); 1 child, Sarah Elizabeth; m. Thomas Dudley Bethea, Dec. 18, 1982. BA in Math., SUNY-Plattsburgh, 1969. Computer programmer Addressograph-Multigraph, Cleve., 1970-73; programmer-analyst Canal Bank, Portland, Maine, 1973-76; sr. programmer-analyst L.L. Bean Co., Freeport, Maine, 1976-77; systems and program mgr. L.L. Bean Co., Freeport, 1977-87, mgr. info. and systems and program mgr., 1987-88, mgr. info. mgmt. and productivity, 1988—. Mem. Assn. Systems Mgmt. (pres. 1980-83), Assn. Women in Computing, Maine Women's Lobby, Maine Audubon Soc., Portland Landmarks, Maine Hist. Soc., Island Inst. Home: 18 Cushman St Portland ME 04101 Office: LL Bean Co Casco St Freeport ME 04032

ALLEN, PAULINE VIRGINIA, accountant; b. Guntown, Miss., Feb. 7, 1909; d. Henry James and Madia Jane (Kennedy) A.; student Southwestern U., Memphis, 1927-29, 32-33, U. Miss., 1933-34; A.B., Duke U., 1935. Math. tchr. high sch., Pleasant Grove, Miss., 1936-37; clk. ins. agy., Tunica, Miss., 1940-48; bookkeeper, Tunica, 1952-56; accountant Tunica County Hosp., 1956—. Mem. Hosp. Fin. Mgrs. Assn. Democrat. Methodist. Club: Order Eastern Star. Home: Box 96 Tunica MS 38676

ALLEN, RANDY LEE, management consulting executive; b. Ithaca, N.Y., June 24, 1946; d. Richard Hallstead and Mary Elizabeth (Howe) Hallstead Baker; m. John James Meehan, Apr. 24, 1983 (div. Aug. 1987); 1 child, Scott Hallstead. BA in Physics, Cornell U., 1968; postgrad. Syracuse U., 1968, Seattle U., 1973-74. Cert. mgmt. cons., cert. systems profl. Programmer, IBM, Endicott, N.Y., 1968-69; product and industry mgr. Boeing Computer Service, Seattle, 1969-74; dir. mktg. Androcor subs. Boeing Computer, Calumet City, Ill., 1974-76; ptnr. Touche Ross & Co., Newark, 1976—; trustee N.J. Inst. Tech., Newark, 1984-87, bd. of overseers N.J. Inst. Tech., 1988—. mem. adv. bd. computer info. scis. dept. Author: OCR-A Cost/Benefit Guide; Pos Trends in the '80's; Bottom Line Issues in Retailing; Pos Current Trends and Beyond, 1987; also articles. Regional fund raiser Cornell U., 1983-84, 87-88; chmn. long range plan United Meth. Ch. Bishop Janes, Basking Ridge, N.J., 1983. Recipient Acad. Women Achievers award YWCA, 1984. Mem. Inst. Mgmt. Cons. (nominating com.), Am. Mgmt. Assn., Am. Arbitration Assn., Exec. Women N.J. (pres. 1979-81, dir. 1981-85). Clubs: Cornell; Basking Ridge Golf. Avocations: skiing, tennis, stamp collecting, symphony, art, swimming, boating, reading. Office: Touche Ross & Co One Gateway Ctr Newark NJ 07102

ALLEN, RAYE VIRGINIA, cultural historian; b. Temple, Tex., May 27, 1929; d. Irvin and Vivian (Arnold) McCreary; m. Henry Kiper Allen, June 9, 1951; children—Henry Kiper, Irvin McCreary, Rave Virginia. B.A., U. Tex.-Austin, 1951, M.A. in Am. Civilization, 1975, Ph.D. candidate. Mem. Am. Folklife Ctr. in Library of Congress, Washington, 1976-84, chmn., 1978-79; trustee, sec. Future Homemakers of Am. Found., 1983—; bd. dirs. Future Homemakers Am., 1978-85; trustee U.S.-N.Z. Arts Found.; coordinator com. for Restoration of Ellis Island; mem. Centennial Commn. of U. Tex.-Austin and chmn. continuing edn. com., 1981-84, bd. visitors U. Tex. astronomy dept. and McDonald Obs., 1984—; adv. council Inst. Texan Cultures; mem. Am. Revolution Bicentennial Commn. of Tex., 1971-75; co-founder, 1st pres. Cultural Activities Ctr. of Temple, Tex., 1957-59; bd. dirs. Tex. State Soc. of Washington, 1980-83, Tex. Cultural Alliance, Inst. Humanities, Salado, Tex., Tex. Folklife Resources. Recipient Outstanding Citizen of Temple award, 1973; Raye Virginia Allen State Pres. scholarship established in her honor Future Homemakers Am., 1986. Episcopalian. Home: 1513 30 St NW Washington DC 20007 also: Green Oaks Farm #19 Hartrick Bluff Rd Temple TX 76502

ALLEN, SALLIE KAY, medical sales representative; b. Lake Charles, La., June 8, 1949; d. Henry Grady and Margaret (Nelson) A. BA in English, McNeese State U., 1971. Educator Dallas (Tex.) Ind. Schs., Vermilion Parish Sch. Bd., 1971-73; bookstore mgr. Southwestern Med. Sch., Dallas, 1974-78; profl. med. rep. Abbott Pharm., Lake Charles and Monterey, Calif., 1979-84; med. sales rep. Norwich Eaton Pharm., Los Angeles, 1984-86, Seton Products, Inc., Los Angeles, 1986—. Mem. Nat. Assn. Female Execs., Tri-County Pharm. Assn. Republican. Home and Office: 3623 Kalsman Dr #1 Los Angeles CA 90016

ALLEN, SARAH FRANCES, contractor; b. Tampa, Fla., Sept. 2, 1943; d. Ralph Walter and Allie Rebecca (Stafford) Overman; student U. South Fla., 1962, BS, SUNY; postgrad. George Mason U.; children: William Kennon, Heather. Founder, pres. Sarah Allen Homes, Inc., 1974—. With Peace Corps, Jamaica. Bd. dirs. Asolo Theater. Mem. Fla. Bd. Realtors, Sarasota-Manatee Contractors Assn., Nat. Assn. Home Builders, Fla. Assn. Home Builders, Sarasota Bd. Realtors, Fla. Bd. Realtors, DAR. Republican. Episcopalian. Home: 5053 Ocean Blvd Suite 98 Sarasota FL 34242 Office: Sarah Allen Homes Inc 5053 Ocean Blvd Suite 98 Sarasota FL 34242

ALLEN, SHARON AMERINE, educational administrator; b. Alexandria, La., Apr. 22, 1942; B.A. in Speech Therapy, Northwestern State U., Natchitoches, La., 1965, M.A. in Speech Pathology, 1968; children—Lisa, Brooke. Speech therapist public schs., La., 1965-73; speech and hearing cons. Nicholls State U., Thibodaux, La., 1973-78; prin. TARC Houma, La., 1978-87, exec. dir. 1987—. Cert. tchr., La. Mem. Am. Speech, Lang. and Hearing Assn. (cert.), La. Speech and Hearing Assn., Am. Assn. Mental Deficiency, LAC Parents Anonymous. Home: 202 Lynwood Houma LA 70360 Office: 1 McCord Rd Houma LA 70360

ALLEN, SHEILA HILL, nursing executive, counselor, consultant; b. Imperial, Nebr., Sept. 28, 1935; d. Roger William and Lois Marion (Clayton) Hill; children—Lee-Ann Hill, Todd Everett, Andrew James. R.N., St. Lukes Sch. Nursing, 1958; B.S., U. Denver, 1959. Asst. head nurse St. Lukes Hosp., Denver, 1959-62; dir. nursing Ridge Vista Mental Health, San Jose, Calif., 1973-75; primary care nurse O'Connor Hosp., 1981; dir. nursing services Westwood Mental Health Facility, Fremont, Calif., 1975—Bd. dirs., sec. Health Acctg. Services, Calif., 1984—; ptnr., owner Health Acctg. Services, Fremont, 1984—, owner Westwood Mental Health, 1984—. Contbr. articles to profl jours. Mem. Am. Nurses Assn., Calif. Assn. Health Facilities, Mental Health Com. on Dual Diagnosis, Delta Gamma, Sigma Theta Tau, Alpha Sigma Chi. Home: 6513 Trinidad Ct San Jose CA 95120 Office: 4303 Stevenson Blvd Fremont CA 94538

ALLEN, SUSAN BURDETTE, consultant; b. Durham, N.C., Nov. 18, 1951; d. Malcolm Burdette and Louise (Lloyd) A.; m. David A. Searcy, 1987. B.S. in Interior Design, U. N.C., Greensboro, 1973. Mgr., designer Intra, Greensboro, 1973-75; designer Priba Interiors, Fed. Republic Germany, 1976-78, Comml. Office Furniture, Washington, 1978-79; owner, mgr. Phasedesign, Greensboro, 1979-83; creator, v.p., co-owner Funnybusiness, Inc., Greensboro and Winston-Salem, N.C., 1979-87; owner Funny U., Greensboro, 1982-87; pres. Allen Resource Group (cons., program speaker The Tech. of Enthusiasm on morale and team building strategies), Greensboro, 1984—; pres., editor G/Golden Triad Mag., div. Piedmont Impressions, Inc., Greensboro, 1985-87. Bd. dirs. Old Greensborough Preservation Soc., U. N.C.-Greensboro Sch. Home Econs. Found., 1983-87. Mem. Women's Profl. Forum, Nat. Speakers Assn. (chmn. ea. workshop, pub. relations com.) Carolina Speakers Assn. (officer, bd. dirs. 1987—). Home and Office: PO Box 6841 Duke Campus Station Durham NC 27708

ALLEN, VIRGINIA ANN, military officer; b. Phoenixville, Pa., Sept. 29, 1953; d. Eugene Womack and Claire Ruth (Reno) A.; m. Timothy Jackson Northcut, June 1, 1985. B in Music Edn., Catholic U., 1976, MusM, 1977. Commd. 2d lt. U.S. Army, 1977, advanced through grades to capt., 1981; adminstrv. office U.S. Army Element, Sch. of Music, Norfolk, 1978, student company cmdr., 1978-79, tng. officer, 1979; cmdr. and conductor U.S. Army Forces Command Band, Ft. McPherson, Ga., 1979-82; pub. relations officer U.S. Army Field Band, Ft. Meade, Md., 1982-84, assoc. conductor, 1982-85; pub. affairs officer Dept. of Army, The Pentagon, Washington, 1985-86; staff band officer U.S. Forces Command, Ft. McPherson, 1986—; advanced through grades to major U.S. Army, 1987. Mem. Women Band Dirs. Nat. Assn., Nat. Band Assn., Nat. Assn. Female Execs., Assn. of U.S. Army. Office: Hdqrs US Forces Command Fort McPherson GA 30330

ALLENBAUGH, BEVERLY MARIE, county official; b. Kellogg, Idaho, July 16, 1935; d. Harry and L. Ethel (Simmons) Farmer; m. Andrew A. Clarke, Aug. 31, 1957 (dec.); children: Terry, Brian, Arthur, Brigid, Teresa; m. William J. Allenbaugh, Mar. 18, 1980; stepchildren: Diana, Robin, Bill Jr., J.J. BA in Edn., Cen. Wash. U., 1958, postgrad., 1960-70. Tchr. Reecer Creek Sch., Ellensburg, Wash., 1958-60, St. Andrew's Cath. Sch., Ellensburg, 1960-61; bookkeeper Fisher Mills Feed Store, Ellensburg, 1974-77; county auditor Kittitas County, Wash., 1977—, also co-chmn. voter outreach, co-chmn. recording com., 1987-88; chmn. Kittitas County Computer User Group, 1981—; sec. fin. com. Kittitas County, 1977—; mem. bus. adv. council, Ellensburg High Sch., 1981-84. Leader, Wash. 4-H Extension Service, 1979-85; state chmn. Citizen Bee, 1986-88; sec. County Centennial Com.; co-chmn. edn. com. Com. for Handicapped Accessibility for Voters in Wash. State, 1985-86. Mem. Wash. County Auditor's Assn. (sec. treas. 1983-84, co-chmn. edn. com. 1983-84, pres. 1984-85, planning com. Crossroads '85), Internat. Assn. Clks., Recorders, Election Ofcls. and Treasurers, Nat. Assn. County Ofcls., Cowbells (sec.-treas.) Ellensburg Grange, Wash. Assn. County Ofcls. (adv. bd. 1987—, bd. dirs.), Ellensburg Homemakers Club, Ellensburg Horse Club, Cen. Wash. U. Assn. Students in Religious Edn. (chmn. 1956, treas. 1956-57). Club: Soroptimists. Lodge: Moose Aux. Avocations: horse backpacking, fishing, sewing, children's activities, 4-H. Home: Route 4 Box 254 C Ellensburg WA 98926 Office: Kittitas County Auditor Room 105 Courthouse Ellensburg WA 98926

ALLENTUCK, MARCIA EPSTEIN, English language and art history educator; b. Manhattan, N.Y., June 8, 1928; m. 1949; 1 dau. B.A., NYU, 1948; Ph.D., Columbia U., N.Y.C., 1964. Lectr. English Columbia U., 1955-57, Hunter Coll., 1957; from lectr. to prof. English, CCNY, 1959—; prof. history of art Grad. Ctr. CUNY, 1974—. Author: The Works of Henry Needler, 1961; Henry Fuseli; The Artist as Critic and Man of Letters, 1964; Isaac Bashevis Singer, 1969; John Graham's System and Dialectics of Art, 1971; contbr. articles to profl. jours. Morrison fellow AAUW, 1958-59; Howard fellow Brown U., 1966-67, Huntington Library fellow, 1968, 77; fellow Nat. Translation Ctr. U. Tex., 1968-69, Chapelbrook Found., 1970-71, Dumbarton Oaks Harvard U., 1972-73; sr. fellow NEH, 1973-74; vis. fellow Wolfson Coll. Oxford U., 1974—; fellow Brit. Acad. Newberry Library, 1980; Murray research fellow Radcliffe Coll., Harvard U., 1982; fellow Inst. Advanced Studies in the Humanities, Edinburgh U. (Scotland), 1984; Am. Philos. Soc. grantee, 1966-67; recipient Sussman Meml. medal N.Y.U., 1946. Fellow Royal Soc. Arts London; mem. Brit. Soc. Archtl. Historians, MLA, Milton Soc. Am., Augustan Reprint Soc., Soc. Archtl. Historians, Coll. Art Assn., Phi Beta Kappa.

ALLERS, MARLENE ELAINE, law office business manager; b. Crosby, Minn., Dec. 29, 1931; d. Robert Prudent and Tressa Ida May (Hiller) Huard; m. Herbert Dodge Allers, Aug. 29, 1950 (dec. Aug. 1977); children—Melanie Lynn, Geoffrey Brian. B.S. in Math., U. Minn.-Mpls., 1966, B.A. in Acctg., 1968, M.B.A. in Personnel and Fin. Mgmt., 1972. Bus. mgr., Earl Clinic, St. Paul, 1959-68, Lindquist & Vennum, Mpls., 1968-79, Stacker, Ravich & Simon, Mpls., 1979-82, Wagner, Johnston & Falconer, Ltd., Mpls., 1983—; lectr. Inst. of Continuing Legal Edn., Mpls., 1977. Recipient Outstanding Achievement award in Bus. Young Women's Christian Assn., Mpls., 1978.

Mem. Minn. Legal Adminstrs. Assn., Mensa. Avocations: bridge; reading. Home: 608 Queen Ave S Minneapolis MN 55405

ALLEY, CAROL SCOTT, senator's aide, communications specialist; b. Pitts., Apr. 12, 1932; d. Frank Joseph and Ruth Scott (McCracken) Carlson; m. Rembert Caven Alley, Jr., Apr. 29, 1961 (div. Apr. 1984); children: Rembert Caven III, Daniel Carlson. BA, Muskingum Coll., 1954. Prodn. editor Together Mag., Chgo., 1956-61; editor Mus. N.Mex., Santa Fe, 1964-68; news dir., host KKAT, KSWS Radio, Roswell, N.Mex., 1970-75; producer, host KBIM-TV, Roswell, 1975-79; pub. info. dir. Eastern N.Mex. U., Roswell, 1981-83; senator's aide Senator Jeff Bingaman, Albuquerque, 1983—; mem. Talent Bank, Profl. Presbyn. Communicators, N.Y.C., 1986—. Editor El Palacio, 1964-68. Bd. dirs. N.Mex. Repertory Theatre, Albuquerque Pub. Access TV. Recipient Best Documentary award N.Mex. Broadcasters, 1972. Mem. Women in Communications. Democrat. Avocations: archaeology, reading, walking. Home: 1200 Marquette NW Albuquerque NM 87102 Office: Senator Jeff Bingaman 500 Gold SW Room 9017 Dennis Chavez Fed Bldg Albuquerque NM 87102

ALLINGTON, GLORIA JEAN HAM, educational administrator; b. Northwood, N.D., May 21, 1945; d. John Henry Ham and Selma Tina (Haabak) Thorson; m. Gary Francis Allington, June 6, 1966 (div. May 1986). Student, U. N.D., 1963-66; ADN, Miami Dade Community Coll., 1968; BCS, U. Miami, 1976, MS in Edn., 1987. RN, Fla.; cert. meeting profl. Staff nurse Jackson Meml. Hosp., Miami, Fla., 1969-71, asst. head nurse, 1971-73; nurse educator U. Miami Sch. Medicine, 1973-75, adminstrv. asst., 1975-81, asst. dir. div. continuing med. edn., 1981, dir. div. continuing med. edn., 1981—. Contbr. articles to profl. jours. Exec. bd. dirs. Project Newborn, Miami, 1977-86; bd. dirs. Ronald McDonald House of So. Fla., Miami, 1977-82; mem. Zool. Soc. of South Fla., Miami, 1986—. Recipient James W. Colbert, Jr., M.D. award, Health Edn. Media Assn., 1977. Mem. Soc. Med. Coll. Dirs. of Continuing Med. Edn., Alliance for Continuing Med. Edn., Meeting Planners Internat. (internat. dir. 1986-88). Democrat. Roman Catholic. Office: U Miami Sch Medicine PO Box 016960 D23-3 Miami FL 33101

ALLISON, JANE LEA, telemarketing executive; b. Oskaloosa, Iowa, July 17, 1953; d. Melvin Eldred and Jeneane Lucille (Maughan) Dykstra. B.S. in Bus., N.E. Mo. State U., 1974; Cert., Coll. Fin. Planning, Denver, 1976. Regional sales mgr. Great Western Fin., Newport Beach, Calif., 1974-77, Continental Ins. Co., Newport Beach, 1977-78; account exec., br. mgr. Equitec, Newport Beach, 1978-81; sales rep. Security First, Century City, Calif., 1981-83; br. mgr. BretCourt Fin., Santa Ana, Calif., 1983-84; ins. sales specialist Johnson & Higgins, Des Moines, 1984-86; gen. mgr., Securities Mktg. Group, Inc, Costa Mesa, Calif, 1987; dir. mktg., Choate, Collins, Devereaux and Mazelli, 1987—. Mem. Internat. Assn. Fin. Planning, Nat. Assn. Exec. Women, Nat. Assn. Security Dealers, Alpha Sigma Alpha. Democrat. Roman Catholic. Avocations: horseback riding; snow skiing; water skiing; bowling; racquetball. Home: 17266 Nisson #C Tustin CA 92680 Office: Securitech Mktg 3303 N Harbor Blvd C-12 Costa Mesa CA 92696

ALLISON, JANE SHAWVER, medical school administrator, management consultant; b. San Angelo, Tex., Dec. 29, 1938; d. Floyd McKinzie and Bertha J. (Hicks) Shawver; m. Cecil Wayne Allison, June 22, 1957; children: Jana Lea, David Wayne, Don McKinzie. Student U. Denver, 1954, Northwestern U., 1955, Tex. Tech. U., 1956-57, Midwestern U., Wichita Falls, Tex., 1958. Continuity writer, Sta. KFDX-TV, Wichita Falls, Tex., 1957-58; sec. Wichita Falls Symphony, Tex., 1968-70; adminstrv. asst. Coll. of Bus. Tex. Tech U., Lubbock, 1971-74, coordinator programs dept. family medicine Health Sch. Ctr., 1974-77, adminstr. dept. family medicine, 1978-87, clin. adminstrv. dir. dept. family medicine, 1987—; cons. Family Practice Residency, Amarillo, Tex., 1984, Temple, Tex., 1984-85. Bd. dirs. Lubbock Symphony Orch., Inc., 1976—, mem. nominating com., 1986, exec. com., 1987-88, v.p. 1988—; bd. dirs. Helen A. Hodges Charitable Trust, Lubbock, 1983—; mem. Tex. Tech U. Coll. Bus. Adminstrn. Lubbock Council, 1988—. Recipient Superior Achievement award Tex. Tech U. Health Scis. Ctr., 1987, HSC award of Excellence Tex. Tech. U. Health Scis. Ctr., 1987; honoree 75th Birthday Celebration, Caprock Council Girl Scouts USA. Mem. Med. Group Mgmt. Assn., Acad. Practice Assembly, Assn. Family Practice Adminstrs. (bd. dirs. 1985, 87, charter pres. 1984, chmn. steering com. 1983). Mem. Disciples of Christ. Club: Soroptimist Internat. (pres. 1986-87, regional parlimentarian, 1986-88). Office: Tex Tech U Health Sci Ctr Dept Family Medicine Lubbock TX 79430

ALLISON, LOYETTE E., construction company executive; b. Delano, Calif., July 7, 1946; d. Dempsey Willard and Billie Wanda (Fink) Bogard; m. Robert Lee, Nov. 30, 1963; children—Cindy Kay, Ann Rena. Student Pima Coll., 1979, U. Denver, 1983. Sales mgr. K-Mart, Tucson, 1975-78; clk.-typist Fairfield Green Valley, Ariz., 1978-81; purchasing agt. Tobin Homes, Tucson, 1981-83; constrn. mgr. Fairfield La Cholla Hills, Tucson, 1983-86; v.p., ops. mgr. Fairfield Pusch Ridge, 1986—. Notary public State of Ariz. Mem. Nat. Assn. Female Execs., Am. Bus. Inst. (2000 notable women, Disting. Service award). Baptist. Avocations: stock car racing; aerobics, modern dance. Home: 2151 W Felicia Pl Tucson AZ 85741 Office: Fairfield La Cholla Hills 8700 N La Cholla Blvd Tucson AZ 85741

ALLISON, MARY ANN, financial company executive, author; b. Orange, N.J., Sept. 27, 1949; d. David S. and Mary (McNaughton) Burnet; m. Eric William Allison, July 17, 1971. B.A., Shimer Coll., 1971; M.B.A., L.I. U., 1977. Various position Avis Rent-A-Car, Garden City, N.Y., 1971-80, v.p. Citicorp N.Y.C., 1980—. Co-author: Through the Valley of Death, 1983; Managing Up, Managing Down, 1984; contbr. articles to profl. publs. and nat. mags. Mem. Am. Soc. for Tng. and Devel., Am. Soc. Personnel Adminstrn., Authors Guild, Mystery Writers Am., Japan Soc. Episcopalian. Office: OLDS 666 Fifth Ave 5th Floor New York NY 10103

ALLISON, PAMELA SUSAN, nurse; b. Chattanooga, Nov. 21, 1950; d. William Kenneth Jones and Helen Katie (Garner) Jones Allison; adopted d. William B. Allison; m. Larry Wayne Thomas, July 6, 1968 (div. Mar. 31, 1981; 1 child, William Forrest; m. Michael Sean O'Flaherty, Oct. 1, 1983. Cert. critical care RN. Nursing, Baptist Coll. at Charleston, 1978. R.N., S.C. Cardiothoracic clinician surg. ICU, Med. U. S.C., Charleston, 1978-82; nurse intensive care and cardiac care Trident Regional Med. Ctr., Charleston, 1982-85; instr. advanced cardiac life support Am. Heart Assn., Charleston, 1983—; clin. applications specialist, cons., Baxter-Am. Edwards Critical Care Div., 1987—; cons. Area Health Edn. Consortium, Walterboro, S.C., 1983—. Mem. Am. Assn. Critical Care Nurses. Home: 2430 Pristine View Charleston SC 29407 Office: Baxter American Critical Care div 17221 Red Hill Ave Irvince CA 92714-5686

ALLISON, SHIRLEY ELLEN KREIDLER, educator; b. Lock Haven, Pa., July 22, 1940; d. Clarence E. and Mary Louise (Laubach) Kreidler; m. Ronald David Allison, Jan. 21, 1960; children: Kirk DuMond, Shanna K., Kristopher Todd. BS, Lock Haven State Coll., 1962; M of Pub. Adminstrn., Pa. State U., Middletown, 1985; postgrad., Shippensburg U., 1988—. Cert. tchr., Pa., Md. Tchr. South Williamsport (Pa.) Sch. Dist., 1962-64, Bellefonte (Pa.) Area Sch. Dist., 1965-67, State College (Pa.) Sch. Dist., 1968-69, Frederick (Md.) County Sch. Dist., 1969-70, Howard County Sch. Dist., Waterloo, Md., 1970-71, Lower Dauphin Sch. Dist., Hummelstown, Pa., 1971—; mem. curriculum and instrn. council Lower Dauphin Sch. Dist., 1985—, inservice council, 1985—. Chmn. East Hanover Twp. Park and Recreation Bd., Grantville, Pa., 1981—, park bldg. com., 1985—. Mem. NEA, AAUW, Pa. State Edn. Assn., Pa. Recreation and Park Soc., Inc., Sigma Kappa. Republican. Home: Shady Ln RD 2 Hummelstown PA 17036 Office: Lower Dauphin Sch Dist 201 S Hanover St Hummelstown PA 17036

ALLISON, SUSAN KATHERINE, materials management consultant; b. Hollywood, Calif., June 10, 1955; d. Carroll Wood and Barbara Lee (Pierce) A. AA in Liberal Arts, Glendale Coll., 1987; student, Calif. State U., Los Angeles, 1987—. Dept. supr. Wal Mart, Hot Springs, Ark., 1972-73; personal asst. Elizabeth King and Assocs., Hot Springs, 1972-73; customer service rep. GAF Photo Service, Los Angeles, 1974-75; purchasing asst. Joy Mfg. Co., Los Angeles, 1975-78; buyer ops. dept. CBS TV Network, Los Angeles, 1978-84; contract negotiator Los Angeles Olympic Orgn. Commn., 1984-85; cons. in materials mgmt. Glendale, Calif., 1985—; promotional news radio hostess Sta. KNX-CBS Inc., Los Angeles, 1985—. Editor Torchlight newspaper, 1972, Historical Tour guide book, 1986. Mem. Glendale Hist. Soc., 1986—; cons. Women's Council Verdugo Hills Hosp., Glendale, 1985-86. Mem. Olympic Alumni Assn., Los Angeles Women's Entertainment League, Los Angeles Advt. Softball League, Nat. Trust Hist. Preservation, Alpha Gamma Sigma. Republican. Episcopalian. Office: PO Box 9013 Glendale CA 91206

ALLMAND, LINDA F(AITH), library director; b. Port Arthur, Tex., Jan. 31, 1937; d. Clifton James and Jewel Etoile (Smith) A. B.A., North Tex. State U., 1960; M.A., U. Denver, 1962. Clerical asst. Gates Meml. Library, 1953-55; library asst. Houston Pub. Library, 1955-58; children's librarian Denver Pub. Library, 1960-63; children's coordinator Anaheim Pub. Library, Calif., 1963-65; br. mgr. Dallas Pub. Library, 1965-71; instr. North Tex. State U., Denton, 1967—; chief br. services Dallas Pub. Library, 1971-81; dir. Ft. Worth Pub. Library, 1981—; instr. Dallas County Community Coll., 1981; bldg. cons. Jacksonville Pub. Library, Tex., 1976-79, Haltom City Pub. Library, 1983-85, Carrollton Pub. Library, 1979-81, Hurst Pub. Library, 1977-78, Dallas Pub. Library, 1974-80. Author: 1981-2000, Ft. Worth Public Library—Facilities and Long-Range Planning Study, 1982; contbr. chpts. to books, articles to profl. jours. Bd. dirs. City of Dallas Credit Union, 1973-81; com. chmn. Goals for Dallas, 1967-69; mem. Forum Ft. Worth, 1983; bd. dirs. Sr. Citizen's Centers, Inc., 1982. Pilot Club of Port Arthur scholar, 1954; Library Binding Inst. scholar, 1958; recipient Disting. Alumnus award North Tex. State U., 1983, Leadership Ft. Worth, 1982-83, named Tarrant County Newsmaker of Yr., 1984. Mem. ALA, Tex. Library Assn. (pres. pub. library div. 1980-81, chmn. planning com. 1982-84, Librarian of Yr. award 1985; pres.-elect 1985-86, pres. 1986-87), Tarrant Regional Librarians Assn., Am. Mgmt. Assn., Dallas County Librarians Assn. (pres. 1968-69), Freedom to Read Found. Home: 701 Timberview Ct N Fort Worth TX 76112 Office: Fort Worth Pub Library 300 Taylor St Fort Worth TX 76102

ALLOWAY, ANNE MAUREEN SCHUBERT, industrial waste administrator; b. Martinez, Calif., Oct. 19, 1954; d. James Benjamin and Mariel Ann (Phillips) Schubert; m. William Glenn Alloway, Apr. 27, 1974; children: Joseph Benjamin, Odinn Glenn, Aaron Dean. AS in Life Sci., Allan Hancock Coll., 1982, AA in Liberal Arts, 1982. Cert. indsl. waste insp., 1984. Indsl. waste insp. City of Santa Maria, Calif., 1982-86; mgr. indsl. pretreatment program, collection systems Simi Valley (Calif.) County Sanitation Dist., 1986—; sect. chmn. Tri-Counties Pub. Edn. Mem. State Pub. Edn. Com., Ventura county Hazardous Waste Mgmt.(adv. com. bd. supr), Tri Counties Voluntary Cert. Com (sec. chmn.), State Voluntary Cert. Com., Tri Counties Pub. Edn. (sec. chmn.), Calif. Water Pollution Control Assn. indsl./ hazardous waste com., pub. edn. com.), Water Pollution Control Fedn., Ventura County Hazardous Waste Mgmt. (adv. com.). Recipient Merit award Industrial Waste Inspection Tech., 1986. Republican. Roman Catholic. Club: Coast and Valley Health. Lodge: Keepers of the Flame. Avocations: painting, writing, sports, reading. Home: 1753 Cochran #G Simi Valley CA 93065 Office: Simi Valley County Sanitation Dist 500 W Los Angeles Ave Simi Valley CA 93065

ALLRED, RITA REED, artist; b. Davenport, Iowa, Apr. 12, 1935; d. Edward Platt and Delia Marie (Quinn) Reed; m. Glenn Charles Scott, June 9, 1956 (div. Nov. 1977); children—Sheryl Marie, Laura Ann; m. Robert Yates Allred, Dec. 9, 1977. Student Marycrest Coll., Davenport, 1953-56; BS in Art Edn., Drake U., 1958. Art tchr. Fayetteville City Schs., N.C., 1961-64, Charlotte-Mecklenburg Schs., N.C., 1967-71; cons., project dir. PCA Internat., Matthews, N.C., 1981; artist, art cons. Rita Reed Allred & Assocs., Charlotte, 1972—, dir. workshops, 1976—; civilian artist USCG, 1981—; instr. portrait painting Cen. Piedmont Community Coll., 1986—; painter in oils; recent commns. include paintings for U.S. Army, USCG, portraits for ABCO Industries, U.S. Naval Inst. Service Head Portrait Series; pres. Willow Reed Studios, 1986—. Bd. dirs. Internat. House, Charlotte, 1985-86; mem. Sister Cities Com., Charlotte, 1984-85. Recipient George Gray award USCG, 1983. Democrat. Club: Cedarwood Country (Matthews, N.C.). Avocations: golf, art. Home and Studio: 7217 Quail Meadow Ln Charlotte NC 28210 Office: Willow Reed Studios 10811 Pineville Rd Pineville NC 28134

ALLRED, VERNICE HARRIS, personnel director; b. Evadale, Tex., July 11, 1941; d. Ennis Harris and Lorraine (Garsee) Lucky; m. Travis Lee Allred Sr., May 16, 1966 (div. Mar. 1974); children: Travis Allred Jr., Travise DeEtte. BA, Eckerd Coll., St. Petersburg, Fla., 1983. With general office B.T. Morris Auto Repair, Tampa, Fla., 1970-74; bookkeeper Calvin Steel Erectors, Tampa, 1974-76, Group Enterprises, Tampa, 1976-79; sr. personnel rep. Unisys Corp., Oldsmar, Fla., 1979—. Author: (newspaper) Unisys Corp. Coordinator March of Dimes, Clearwater, Fla., 1987. Mem. Nat. Assn. Female Execs., Pinellas Personnel Assn. Democrat. Home: 7601 W Caracas St Tampa FL 33615 Office: Unisys Corp SR 584 Oldsmar FL 33518

ALLRICH, LOUISE BARCO, art dealer; b. Ft. Monroe, Va., Feb. 16, 1947; d. Ernest Terrill and Margaret Louise (Nicklason) Barco; m. Theodre C. Allrich, June 18, 1966 (div. 1973). BS, U. Calif., Davis, 1968. Trainee Peace Corps., 1968; office mgr. Knoll Internat., San Francisco, 1968-69; design asst. Western Contract Furnishings, San Jose, Calif., 1969; sales person Los Robles Gallery, Palo Alto, Calif., 1970; owner, pres. The Allrich Gallery, San Francisco, 1971—; lectr. Fine Art Mus., Houston, 1979, Los Angeles County Mus., 1979, Portland Art Mus., 1983, Sch. Art Inst., Chgo., 1983, Cranbrook Acad. Art, Bloomfield Hills, 1986, Coll. Art Assn., Boston, 1987; panelist Oakland (Calif.) Mus., 1981, Nat. Sculpture Conf., 1987; mem. steering com. Art Culture Future, Am. Craft Council, 1985-86; bd. dirs. Old Pueblo Mus., Tucson, 1988—. Trustee The Old Pueblo Mus., Tuscon. Mem. Soc. for Encouragement of Contemporary Art, Am. Craft Council (steering com. Art Culture Future 1985-86, collectors circle), San Francisco Art Dealers Assn. (v.p. 1979). Office: The Allrich Gallery 251 Post St San Francisco CA 94108

ALMOND, JOAN, chemistry instructor; b. Bklyn., May 19, 1934; d. Harry Christian Nintzel and Helen Pauline (Diviak) Levesen; m. Randall Leroy Field Sr., Nov. 15, 1952 (div. Feb. 1972); children: Randall Leroy Jr., Roland, Gary, Brian, Lorraine, Thomas; m. Bransford Wayne Almond, Dec. 9, 1986. Grad. high sch., Bklyn. Sec. Fulton Savs. Bank, Bklyn., 1952-53; mgr. reprodn. Air Pre-heater Corp., Wellsville, N.Y., 1958; chemistry technician fibers div. Allied Chem., Hopewell, Va., 1963-76; chemistry technician Va. Power Co.-North Anna Power Sta., Mineral, 1976-86, assoc. instr., 1987—. Roman Catholic. Lodge: Women of Moose (chair Moosehart Hopewell com. chpt. 1971). Office: Va Power Co-North Anna Power Sta Box 402 Mineral VA 23114

ALMOND, JONNA DEE, sales executive; b. St. Charles, Ill., Nov. 5, 1961; d. Thomas Lee Almond and Jacqueline Dee (Crorkin) Runyan. BS in Mgmt. and Mktg. cum laude, U. Scranton, 1983. Br. administr. Hamilton-Avnet Cos., Santa Clara, Calif., 1983-84; acct. mgr. Western Micro Systems, Mountain View, Calif., 1984-86; distbn. mgr. Corvus Systems, San Jose, Calif., 1986-88; sr. account mgr. Novell Inc., Santa Ana, Calif., 1988—. Named Race For The Top Winner Keytronic Corp., Tahiti, 1985-86; recipient Western Regional Sales award Corvus Systems, 1986. Mem. Soc. Christian Businesswomen. Republican. Home: 21661 Brookhurst Apt 279 Huntington Beach CA 92646

ALPAUGH, REVELYN KAY, image consultant; b. Wichita, Kans., Aug. 17, 1947; d. Louis Eugene and Evelyn Lucille (Gray) Satterlee; m. Donald Robert Alpaugh, Aug. 19, 1967; children: Lance Derek, Brook Danielle. BSE, Emporia (Kans.) State U., 1969; MS, Kans. State U., 1984. Cert. tchr., Kans. Tchr. Indian Creek Jr. High Sch., Overland Park, Kans., 1969-71; with Gaslight Real Estate, Overland Park, 1971-73; instr. Johnson County Community Coll., Overland Park, 1978-84; image cons. BeautiControl, Leawood, Kans., 1983—; also bd. dirs. BeautiControl, Leawood. Mem. Nat. Assn. Female Execs., Phi Kappa Phi, Sigma Sigma Sigma. Home and Office: 8004 Ensley Ln Leawood KS 66206

ALPER, CAROLYN, artist; b. Oct. 1, 1927; d. Albert and Lillian (Friedlander) Small; m. Morton O. Alper, Sept. 11, 1948 (div. Sept. 1972); children: Richard Small, Patricia Alper Sargis. Studied with Morris Louis, 1953-57; BA, Am. U., 1968; studied with Gene Davis, 1969-71. Founder Foundry Gallery, 1972-76, v.p., 1976; founder Patchwork Table, Giftshop, Washington, 1973; designer Assoc. Designers, 1979-81; prin. Carolyn Alper Enterprises, Design Studio, Washington, 1981—; instr. drawing Chevy Chase (Md.) Community Ctr., 1972-76, Inst. for Learning In Retirement, Dept. Continuing Edn. Am. U., Washington, 1984. Works exhibited locally in group shows, 1970-80; sculptor Corcoran Day Sch., 1981. Bd. dirs. acquisitions com. Friends of Corcoran Gallery Art, Washington, 1971-76, mem. 15th anniversary drawing exhbn. com., 1976, chmn. membership, 1978-80, trustee, 1987—; v.p. Jewish Hist. Soc.; bd. dirs., design com. Watergate West, 1979-85; active Nat. Symphony, Friends of Kennedy Ctr.; trustee Washington Project for the Arts, 1979-85. Mem. Washington Women's Art Profl. Soc., Artists Equity, Allied Bd. Trade. Club: Woodmont Country. Office: Carolyn Alper Enterprises 2700 Virginia Ave NW Washington DC 20037

ALPER, JOANNE FOGEL, lawyer; b. N.Y.C., Sept. 16, 1950; d. Ben R. and Florence D. (Schneider) Fogel; m. Paul Edward Alper, Aug. 4, 1973; children—Michael Ian, Brooke Lauren. BA, Syracuse U., 1972; JD, George Washington U., 1975. Bar: Va. 1975, U.S. Dist. Ct. (ea. dist.) Va. 1975, D.C. 1976, U.S. Dist. Ct. D.C. 1976, U.S. Ct. Appeals (4th and D.C. cirs.) 1978, U.S. Supreme Ct. 1980. Assoc. Leonard, Cohen & Gettings, Arlington, Va., 1975-79; ptnr. Cohen, Gettings, Alper & Dunham, Arlington, 1979—. Mem. Arlington County Fair Housing Bd., 1984-88, mem. Commn. on Arlington's Future, 1986. Fellow Am. Acad. Matrimonial Lawyers; mem. Arlington Bar Assn. (pres. 1982-83), Va. State Bar (pres. conf. local bar assns. 1984-85 , chmn. family law sect. 1985-86), Va. Trial Lawyers Assn. (dist. gov. 1983-87, gov. at large 1987—), No. Va. Young Lawyers Assn. (pres. 1979, v.p. Arlington County 1978). Home: 5601 Little Falls Rd Arlington VA 22207 Office: Cohen Gettings Alper & Dunham 1400 N Uhle St Arlington VA 22201

ALPERIN, GOLDIE GREEN, consulting librarian, lawyer; b. Des Moines, Aug. 16, 1905; d. Morris and Bessie (Miliwer) Green; LL.B., Drake U., 1927; m. Moses Alperin, Dec. 25, 1930 (dec. 1950); children—Herschel Burton, Judith Miriam. Admitted to Iowa bar, 1927, U.S. Supreme Ct. bar, 1959; practice in Des Moines, 1927-30; law librarian Chgo. Bar. Assn., 1951-63; dir. Def. Information Office, Chgo., 1963-65; librarian book selections Northwestern U. Law Sch. Library, 1966-72; ret., 1972. Named one of 20 rep. U.S. women lawyers of various phases practice Women's Adjustment Bd., London, Eng., 1957; One of Outstanding Women of Am. Bicentennial, Austin (Tex.) Bicentennial Com., 1976; cert. religious sch. tchr. Bd. Jewish Edn., Chgo., 1951. Mem. Am. (sec. 1960-65), Chgo. (past exec. bd., editor 1958-59) assns. law libraries, Nat. Assn. Women Lawyers (regional) dir. 1960-64). Jewish religion. Asst. editor Women Lawyers Jour., 1961-67, exec. bd., 1961-67. Home: 3100 Lake Shore Dr #1512 Chicago IL 60657

ALPER KRAMER, LORRAINE, advertising executive; b. N.Y.C., Feb. 15, 1949; d. Sidney M. Alper and Evelyn Roslyn (Bercowitz) Opat; m. Bruce Kramer; children: Casey, Jeremy. BA, Hofstra U., 1970. Adminstrv. asst. Kenyon & Eckhardt, N.Y.C., 1970-71; asst. to pres. Storck & Fitzgerald, N.Y.C., 1971-72; mgr. advt. Kayser-Roth, N.Y.C., 1972-74; mgr. print prodn. The Advt. Agy., Los Angeles, 1974-76, D'Arcy MacManiusz Masius, Los Angeles, 1976-81; v.p., dir. print prodn. and traffic BBDO, Los Angeles, 1981—. Mem. Advt. Prodn. Assn. So. Calif. Democrat. Jewish. Office: BBDO West 10960 Wilshire Blvd Los Angeles CA 90024

ALPERN, LINDA LEE WEVODAU, health agency administrator; b. Harrisburg, Pa., July 16, 1949; d. William Irvin Wevodau and Maretia Christine (Mills) Staley; m. Neil Stephen Alpern, Apr. 12, 1985; 1 child, Philip Wevodau. BS in Edn., Shippensburg (Pa.) U., 1971. Unit program coordinator Pa. Div. Am. Cancer Soc., Harrisburg, 1973-75, unit exec. dir., 1975-76, div. service dir., 1976-81; div. med. affairs dir. Pa. Div. Am. Cancer Soc., Hershey, 1981-83; div. crusade dir. Md. Div. Am. Cancer Soc., Balt., 1983-84, div. v.p. for field ops., 1984-87, div. dep., exec. v.p. for field ops., 1987—, v.p. ops., 1988%. Mem. AAUW (publicity chair 1983). Democrat. Methodist. Home: 4108 Colonial Rd Baltimore MD 21208 Office: Am Cancer Soc 1840 York Rd Timonium MD 21093

ALPERN, MILDRED, history educator, consultant; b. Boston, Sept. 10, 1931; d. Samuel and Mary (Poncewicz) Rosoff; m. Hale Nissen Alpern, Aug. 27, 1954; children—Merry, Spenser. BA, Boston U., 1953; MA summa cum laude, Columbia U., 1966. Cert. tchr. social studies. Tchr. history Spring Valley (N.Y.) Sr. High Sch., 1966—; adj. instr. Rockland Community Coll., Suffern, N.Y., 1973-76; instr. Manhattan Coll., Riverdale, N.Y., summers 1983, 84, 85, 87; mem. advanced placement European history test devel. com., Coll. Bd. 1979-82, chmn. 1982-86, mem. Coll. Bd. history and social scis. adv. com., 1983—, chmn., 1985—, chmn. acad. adv. council, 1987; master tchr. summer inst. Sarah Lawrence Coll., Bronxville, N.Y., 1984; mem. faculty Coll. Bd. Project Equality Inst., 1986, 87. Co-editor (history column) Am. Hist. Assn. Perspectives, 1982—; co-author (teaching guide) Household and Kin, 1981; contbr. articles to profl. publs. Recipient award for contbns. in edn. Rockland County Women's Network, 1984; Fulbright Commn. study grantee, Italy, 1980, NEH grantee Tufts U., 1983. Mem. Orgn. Am. Historians (chmn. teaching div. 1982-83), Am. Hist. Assn. (teaching div.), Nat. Council for Social Studies, Women in Hist. Profession (coordinating com.), Phi Beta Kappa, Pi Gamma Mu. Democrat. Home: 13 Cragmere Rd Suffern NY 10901 Office: Spring Valley Sr High Sch Rt 59 Spring Valley NY 10977

ALPERT, JANET A(NNE), title insurance company executive; b. Peoria, Ill., Dec. 6, 1946; d. Charles Albert and Betty Jane (Kopp) Nutter; m. Steven Alpert, Mar. 9, 1969 (div. July 1975); m. Calvin D. Beltman, May 14, 1978. BA, U. Calif., Santa Barbara, 1968; MBA, U. Conn., 1978. With Lawyers Title Ins. Corp., Los Angeles, 1969-73, nat. div. mgr., 1974-78; v.p. Lawyers Title Ins. Corp., Richmond, Va., 1979-83, sr. v.p., nat. div. mgr., 1984-88, sr. v.p. ops. NE region, 1988—. Advisor Jr. Achievement, Richmond, 1981-83. Mem. Geneol. Research Inst. of Va. (bd. dirs. 1986—), Indsl. Devel. Research Corp. (assoc. dir. 1986—), Beta Gamma Sigma. Democrat. Methodist. Office: Lawyers Title Ins Corp 6630 W Broad St Richmond VA 23112

ALSBERG, EVERYL PARKER, consultant; b. Springhill, Okla., Oct. 14, 1921; d. Airy Lasker and Pearl Ellen (Collinsworth) Snelson; student U. So. Calif., 1943; B.S., U. Tulsa, 1953; postgrad. UCLA, 1953-58, Occidental Coll., 1958-62; M.A. in Adminstrn., Calif. State U., Los Angeles, 1962, postgrad., 1962-74; Ph.D., Walden U., 1979; m. Willis Parker, Jr., 1942 (dec.); children—Richard, Pennye Ellen; m. 2d, Harold Alsberg, 1969. Tchr., Fairfax, Va., 1953-55, Los Angeles City Schs., 1956-57; tchr. La Canada (Calif.) Unified Sch. Dist., 1957-62, prin. Paradise Canyon Elem. Sch., 1962-76, dir. instrn. K-8, 1976-78; cons. ednl. adminstrn., 1978-81; mgr. Peck & Peck, Annapolis, Md., 1981-84; cons. Mary Kay Cosmetics, Inc. dir. PDQ Bus. Services, 1979-81, v.p., 1980. Dir. jr. high fellowship Presbyterian Ch., 1960-62; pres. Annapolis Bon Haven Community Assn., 1981-88. bd. dirs. Colonial Players Annapolis, 1979-82, sec., 1981-84, chmn., 1984-87. Mem. Assn. Supervision and Curriculum Devel., Elementary Sch. Sci. Assn. (past sec., v.p., pres.), Profl. Educators Group, NEA, PTA (life), Mortar Bd., Kappa Delta Pi, Delta Kappa Gamma (pres. 1980-82, 2d v.p. 1982-84, membership chmn. 1984-86), Epsilon Gamma (past pres.), Phi Mu (past chpt. adviser, pres. Glendale alumna club, nat. pub. relations dir., nat. membership dir., nat. pledge dir., dist. alumnae dir.), Democrat. Club: Annapolis Panhellenic (scholarship chmn., pres. 1986-87). Home: 778 Bon Haven Dr Annapolis MD 21401

ALSTON, LELA, Ariz. state senator; b. Phoenix, June 26, 1942; d. Virgil Lee and Frances Mae Koonse Mulkey; B.S., U. Ariz., 1967; M.S., Ariz. State U., 1971; children—Brenda Susan, Charles William. Tchr. high sch., 1968—; mem. Ariz. State Senate, 1977—. Named Disting. Citizen, U. Ariz. Alumni Assn., 1978. Mem. NEA, Ariz. Edn. Assn., Am. Home Econs. Assn., Ariz. Home Econs. Assn., Am. Vocat. Assn. Methodist. Office: Office of the State Senate State Capitol Phoenix AZ 85007

ALT, JANE EILEEN STONER, hospital executive; b. Salt Lake City, Oct. 20, 1956; d. Donald Lawrence and Alice Marie (Zeyen) Stoner; m. Gary J. Alt, Oct. 12, 1985. BS in Bus. Adminstrn., Calif. State U., 1982. With Chico Med. Group, Calif., 1974-76, Robert S. Johnson, MD, Chico, Calif.,

1977; with N.T. Enloe Meml. Hosp., Chico, 1979-80, bus. office sec., 1980-81, collection clk./dept. sec., 1981-83, with telecommunications, 1983—. Mem. Nat. Notary Assn., Nat. Assn. Female Execs. Lodge: Soroptimist (pres. 1988—). Home: 153 Worthy Ave Oroville CA 95965 Office: N T Enloe Meml Hosp W 5th Ave and the Esplanade Chico CA 95926

ALTER, ELEANOR BREITEL, lawyer; b. N.Y.C., Nov. 10, 1938; d. Charles David and Jeanne (Hollander) Breitel; children: Richard B. Zabel, David B. Zabel. B.A. with honors, U. Mich., 1960; postgrad., Harvard U., 1960-61; LL.B., Columbia U., 1964. Bar: N.Y. 1965. Atty., office of gen. counsel, ins. dept. State of N.Y., 1964-66; assoc. Miller & Carlson, N.Y.C., 1966-68, Marshall, Bratter, Greene, Allison & Tucker, N.Y.C., 1968-74; mem. firm Marshall, Bratter, Greene, Allison & Tucker, 1974-82, Rosenman & Colin, 1982—; fellow U. Chgo. Law Sch., 1988; adj. prof. law NYU Sch Law, 1983-87; lectr. in field. Editorial bd.: N.Y. Law Jour. Contbr. articles to profl. jours. Trustee Clients' Security Fund State of N.Y., 1983—, chmn., 1985—; bd. visitors U. Chgo. Law Sch., 1984-87. Mem. Am. Law Inst., Am. Bar Assn., N.Y. State Bar Assn., Assn. Bar City N.Y. (library com. 1978-80, com. on matrimonial law 1977-81, 87—, judiciary com. 1981-84, Exec. com. 1988—), N.Y. County Lawyers Assn. (chmn. com. on matrimonial law 1980-82), Am. Acad. Matrimonial Lawyers. Office: Rosenman & Colin 575 Madison Ave New York NY 10022

ALTER, LUCILE L(EVINE), publisher, editor; b. N.Y.C., Dec. 13, 1931; d. Harold Joseph and Sylvia (Moskowitz) Levine; m. Robert H. Alter, Aug. 21, 1954; children—Deborah, Amy, Marjorie. B.F.A., Ithaca Coll., 1953. Sec., CBS-TV, N.Y.C., 1953-54; editor The Enterprise, Hastings/Dobbs Ferry, N.Y., 1979-84, editor, pub. Hastings/Dobbs Ferry, Ardsley and Irvington, N.Y., 1982-84. Editor in-depth reporting Cable TV Franchise in Hastings, 1979 (award N.Y. State Press Assn. 1980). Mem. community adv. bd. St. Cabrini Nursing Home, Dobbs Ferry, 1983—, Group Home for Retarded Adults, Hastings, 1981—; mem. adv. bd. Young Adult Inst., N.Y.C., 1983—; mem. community adv. bd. Graham/Windham Home, Hastings, 1982-85; village trustee Hastings-on-Hudson, N.Y., 1986—. Recipient Editor award Sr. Citizen Edit., N.Y. Press Assn., 1984. Home: 18 Terrace Dr Hastings-on-Hudson NY 10706

ALTER, LYNNE, comptroller; b. Miami Beach, Fla., Dec. 24, 1953; d. Irwin Stanley Alter and Barbara (Messinger) Gottfried; 1 child, Jessica Reneé. Cert. emergency med. technician, Miami-Dade Coll., 1981. Exec. asst. Ecol. Devel. Corp., Miami, Fla., 1972-73; asst. coordinator outreach program Miami-Dade Coll., 1973-74; editor music book Columbia Pictures Publs., Miami, 1974-75; corp. sec., comptroller MAC Parking, Inc., Miami, 1978-81; emergency med. technician Randle-Ea. Ambulance, Miami, 1980-81; comptroller Bay Rag & Grading, Inc., Miami, 1981—. Guardian ad litem Guardian Ad Litem Program, Miami, 1983—. Mem. Nat. Assn. for Female Execs. Democrat. Office: Bay Rag & Grading Inc 59 NW 14 St Miami FL 33136

ALTER, MARGARET GRAMATKY, marriage and family counselor, educator; b. Pasadena, Calif., Oct. 12, 1937; d. Ferdinand Gunner and Margaret (Ganssle) Gramatky; m. Donald Leslie Alter, July 31, 1959; children: Sutia Kim, David Mark. BA in English, U. Calif., Berkeley, 1959; postgrad., Berkeley Bapt. Div. Sch., 1966, Coll. Holy Names, 1968, Calif. State U., Hayward, 1969-70; MA in Psychology, Counseling, Pacific Sch. Religion, 1974, M of Div., 1976; PhD, Grad. Theol. Union, 1985. Lic. marriage, family, child counselor, parent effectiveness tng. instr.; cert. tchr., Calif. Tchr. English lang. King Jr. High Sch., Oakland, Calif., 1969-61, Woodstock Sch., India, 1961-65, Albany (Calif.) Evening Sch., 1966-67; tchr. English lang., psychology Oakland Adult Day Sch., 1967-72, 1973-77; pvt. practice counseling Berkeley, 1976—; research asst. dept. human relations Coop. Extension U. Calif., Berkeley, 1977-78; instr. marriage counseling Pacific Sch. Religion, Berkeley, 1977, 78, 80, adj. prof., 1983; instr. Vista Comm. Coll., Berkeley, 1978-83; counselor Ctr. Ministry, Berkeley, 1982-84, Ctr. Experiential Theol., Berkeley, 1984-85; supr. Unitas Counseling Ctr., Berkeley, 1985-88; developer-instr. parenting classes, Calif., Oreg., 1972-80; cons. McClymonds High Sch., 1972-73, St. Benedict's Sch., Oak Knoll Naval Hosp., Oakland Recreation Dept., 1977-79; adj. prof. Am. Bapt. Sem. West, Berkeley, 1984, New College, Berkeley, 1988. Author: (with Robert C. Leslie) Sustaining Intimacy, 1978; contbr. articles to profl. jours. Sch. supt. Montclair Presbyn. Ch., Oakland, 1975-76, chmn. edn., 1975-77, elder, 1982-84; mem. Family Life Council YMCA, 1978-80. Pacific Sch. Religion fellow, 1979-80. Mem. Am. Assn. Pastoral Counselors (chmn. theol. social concerns com., pacific region, 1987—), Calif. Assn. Marriage Family Therapists, Inst. Logotherapy (bd. dirs. 1977-80). Home: 998 Euclid Ave Berkeley CA 94708

ALTHAUS, BARBARA DONALSON, realtor, insurance underwriter; b. Fort Worth, Mar. 20, 1937; d. Thomas Kyle and Lucille (Martin) Donalson; student U. Tex., 1955-57; m. Dudley Nolin Althaus, Dec. 25, 1969. Legal exec. sec. firm McCully & Christensen, Houston, 1959-64; office mgr. H.A. Bornefeld, Jr., Houston, 1964-69; owner, sec./treas. Althaus Acres Realtors and Auctioneers, Inc., Fredericksburg, Tex., 1969—. Chmn. Damenfest, 1977; Tex. Auctioneers Assn. Aux., 1977, pres., 1981-84. Mem. Nat. Auctioneers Assn. Aux., (bd. dirs. 1983-86), DAR (organizing regent 1974-76, state chmn. jr. Am. citizens 1976-79, registrar 1980-82, state parliamentarian 1985-88, pres. 1987—), Daus. Am. Colonists (state chmn. colonial heritage 1981-83), vice regent 1983-86), Fredericksburg C. of C. (ambassador 1980-84), Magna Charta Dames, Daus. of Republic Tex., Alpha Phi. Democrat. Methodist. Home: Althaus Ranch Fredericksburg TX 78624 Office: 1906 N Llano St PO Box 312 Fredericksburg TX 78624

ALTHER, VICTORIA SCHIEBEL, accountant; b. Seattle, Wash., Sept. 25, 1957; d. Joseph Schiebel and Patricia Alice (Shaughnessy) Howard; children: Jeffrey, Matthew. BSBA, Georgetown U., 1979, MS in Fin., Am. U., 1983. CPA. Mgr. Snyder Newrath & Co., Inc., Bethesda, Md., 1980-86, Coopers & Lybrand, Washington, 1987—. Recipient Carl C. Conway Scholarship, 1975. Mem. Am. Assn. Individual Investors, Internat. Assn. for Fin. Planning (chmn. bd. nat. capital chpt. 1987—). Republican. Home: 8610 Grant St Bethesda MD 20817

ALTHOFF, CECILIA CONNOLE, sales executive; b. Denison, Tex., Jan. 3, 1948; d. William Henry and Mary Liston (Scully) A. BS, Spring Hill Coll., 1969. Research asst. Health and Welfare Planning Council, Memphis, 1970; probation officer Memphis Juvenile Ct., 1970-74; dir. patient rep. services St. Joseph Hosp. East, Memphis, 1974-78; communication specialist So. Poison Ctr., Memphis, 1979-82; area program rep. Lifeline Systems, Inc., Watertown, Mass., 1982-85, dist. mgr., 1985-86, regional mgr., 1986-87; sales exec. securities, investments N.Y. Life Fin. Services, 1988—; cons. job search, resume writing, outplacement counseling. Founder Germantown Animal Welfare League, Tenn., 1979—, parliamentarian, 1980, chmn. nominating com. 1980, 81, 82, Humane Soc. U.S. Mem. Am. Assn. Female Execs., Memphis Network. Republican. Roman Catholic. Club: Summit (Memphis). Office: Crescent Ctr Suite 200 6075 Poplar Ave Memphis TN 38119

ALTIERI, JEANNETTE CORVINO, accountant; b. Bridgeport, Conn., May 8, 1937; d. Christopher C. and Julia Marie (Carbonara) Corvino; m. Mario Dominic Altieri, Mar. 29, 1954; children: Jeanmarie, Michael, Lisa Ann, John Christopher. Student, U. New Haven, 1975, Air Traffic Controller Sch., 1976, Housatonic Community Coll. Office mgr. Sportsmen Accessories, Inc., Bridgeport, Conn., 1972-76, New Haven Travel Service, Inc., 1976-79; acct. mgr. Warnaco Outlet Stores div., Warneco Inc., Bridgeport, 1977-87; mgr. Internat. Acctg. Warnaco, Inc., Bridgeport, 1979—; mgr. internat. acctg. Warnaco, Inc., Bridgeport, 1987—; execc. adviser Jr. Achievement, 1980—. Mem. Nat. Assn. Female Execs., Am. Soc. Profl. and Exec. Women. Home: 43 Bunting Rd Seymour CT 06483 Office: 325 Lafayette St Bridgeport CT 06602

ALTLAND, MARILOU, social agency administrator; b. Pitts., Aug. 31, 1955; d. Theodore Louis and Mary Cecilia (Turnley) Gross; m. David F. Altland, Oct. 11, 1980 (div. Jan. 1987). BA, Wheeling (W.Va.) Coll., 1977; postgrad. in human services adminstrn., Villanova U., 1985—. Juvenile counselor Three Rivers Youth, Pitts., 1977-80; social worker John J. Kane Hosp., Pitts., 1978-80, supr., 1979-80; residential supr. Wordsworth Acad., Ft. Washington, Pa., 1981-82, administrator community living arrangement, 1982-84, foster care dir., 1984—. Vol. coordinator Am. Family Inst., Valley Forge, Pa., 1980—; co-chairperson judiciary com. Graterford (Pa.) Prison, 1984-86, vol., 1986—. Recipient Disting. Service award Am. Family Inst., 1985, Award of Honor Am. Family Inst., 1986; named Vol. of Yr., Lifers, Inc. Graterford Prison, 1985. Fellow AAUW (grantee 1986-87); mem. Nat. Assn. Female Execs. Democrat. Roman Catholic. Office: Wordsworth Acad 509 Ashbourne Rd Elkins Park PA 19117

ALTMAN, ADELE ROSENHAIN, physician; b. Tel Aviv, Israel, June 4, 1924; came to U.S., 1933, naturalized, 1939; d. Bruno and Salla (Silberzweig) Rosenhain; m. Emmett Altman, Sept. 3, 1944; children: Brian R., Alan L., Karen D. Diplomate Am. Bd. Radiology. Intern Queens Gen. Hosp., N.Y.C., 1949-51; resident Hosp. for Joint Diseases, N.Y.C., 1951-52, Roosevelt Hosp., N.Y.C., 1955-57; clin. instr. radiology Downstate Med. Ctr., SUNY, Bklyn., 1957-61; asst. prof. radiology N.Y. Med. Coll., N.Y.C., 1961-65, assoc. prof., 1965-68; assoc. prof. radiology U. Okla. Health Sci. Ctr., Oklahoma City, 1968-78; assoc. prof. dept. radiology U. N.Mex. Sch. Medicine, Albuquerque, 1978-85. Author: Radiology of the Respiratory System: A Basic Review, 1978; contbr. articles to profl. jours. Fellow Am. Coll. Angiology, N.Y. Acad. Medicine; mem. Am. Coll. Radiology, Am. Roentgen Ray Soc., Assn. Univ. Radiologists, Radiol. Soc. N.Am. Clubs: Hadassah, B'nai B'rith Women.

ALTMAN, ELLEN, librarian, educator; b. Pitts., Jan. 1, 1936; d. William and Catherine (Wall) Conley. A.B., Duquesne U., 1957; M.L.S., Rutgers U., 1965, Ph.D., 1971. Instr., asst research prof. Rutgers U., 1965-67, 70-72; asst. prof. U. Ky., 1972-73, U. Toronto, 1974-76; assoc. prof. Ind. U., 1976-79; prof. Grad. Library Sch., U. Ariz., Tucson, 1979—; cons. various research orgns., state libraries. Active Exec. Women's Council So. Ariz., 1980—. Author: Performance Measures in Pub. Libraries, 1973, A Data Gathering and Instructional Manual for Performance Measures in Public Libraries, 1976, Local Public Library Administration, 1980. Fulbright-Hayes sr. lectr., 1978. Mem. ALA, AAUP, Am. Mgmt. Assn. Office: 1515 E 1st St Tucson AZ 85721

ALTMAN, KATHRYN ANN, school system administrator; b. Mantorville, Minn., Apr. 1, 1933; d. Ross Emanuel and Margaret (Goodhue) Ensminger; children: Sandra Ann McIntyre, Stephen Ross McIntyre. BA, Blackburn Coll., 1954; MS, Fla. State U., 1963; Phd, U. S.C., 1973. Tchr. Harbor View Elem. Sch., Charleston, S.C., 1960-62; counselor St. Andrews High Sch., Charleston, 1963-70, U. S.C., Columbia, 1971-72; coordinator of guidance Charleston County Sch. Dist., Charleston, 1972-83, dir. pupil and personnel services, 1983—; adj. prof. Coll. of Charleston, 1984-86, The Citadel, Charleston, 1983—; v.p. S.C. State Bd. Examiners of Profl. Counselors and Therapists, 1986—. Recipient Tribut to Women in Industry award, Charleston YWCA, 1987. Mem. Am. Assn. Counseling and Devel. (bd. dirs. 1980-83), S.C. Assn. Counseling and Devel. (pres. 1976-77, Outstanding Adminstr. 1986), Charles Adlerian Soc. (pres. 1975-76), Florence Crittenton Bd. (v.p. 1986-87). Home: 758 Arcadian Way Charleston SC 29407

ALTOBELLO, MILDRED FRANCES, realtor; b. West Palm Beach, Fla., Mar. 3, 1953; d. Francis Anthony and Ethel Hamner (Martin) A. BA, U. Ala., 1975; MBA, Samford U., 1977. Ter. mgr. Burroughs Corp., Miami, Fla., 1978-80; mgmt. trainee Coral Gables Fed. Savs. and Loan (Fla.), 1981; realtor-assoc. Keyes Co., Coral Gables, 1981-88; mem. Keyes Million Dollar Sales Club, Keyes Inner Circle, 1986; active Coral Gables Bd. of Realtors (realtor-lawyer com., communications com. 1985—, realtors polit. action com. 1987—), Civic Opera of Palm Beaches, 1969—; chmn. liturgical com. U. of Ala., Tuscaloosa, 1973. Mem. Soc. Profl. Journalists, Women in Communications, Inc., Sunset Jaycees, Coral Gables C. of C. Democrat. Roman Catholic.

ALTOM, RHODA LYNN, real estate developer, construction executive; b. Vancouver, Wash., Feb. 26, 1957; d. Alford Woodrow and Sharon Thora (Mattson) Baines; d. Cory Alan Carlson, July 26, 1986. BS in Engring., Wash. State U., 1980; postgrad. in bus. adminstrn., U. Wash. Engr. H.S. Wright Constrn. Co., Seattle, 1980, project engr., 1980-83; owner, gen. contractor Star Constrn., Seattle, 1980-83; project mgr. Wright, Runstad Devel. Co., Seattle, Anchorage, 1983-85; owner, developer Altom-Dickerman Properties, Seattle, 1982—; facilities mgr. King Broadcasting Co., Seattle, 1985—. Bd. dirs., v.p. facilities, mem. exec. com. YWCA, Seattle, King County, 1985—. Recipient scholarship Women in Cpmstrn., 1978, 79. Club: City (charter, membership com. 1983-85). Office: King Broadcasting Co 333 Dexter Ave North Seattle WA 98109

ALTON, ANN LESLIE, lawyer; b. Pipestone, Minn., Sept. 10, 1945; d. Howard Robert, Jr. and Camilla Ann (DeMong) Alton; m. Gerald Russell Freeman Sr.; children: Matthew Alton (dec.), Brady Michael Alton. BA Smith Coll., 1967; JD U. Minn., 1970. Bar: Minn. 1970, U.S. Dist. Ct. Minn. 1972, U.S. Supreme Ct. 1981. Asst. county atty., Hennepin County, Mpls., 1970—, felony prosecutor, criminal div., 1970-75, acting chief citizen protection div., 1975-76, chief citizen protection/econ. crime div., 1976-79, chief econ. crime unit, 1979-85, sr. atty. civil div. handling labor and employment, 1985—; instr. Hamline U. Law Sch., St. Paul, 1973-76; adj. prof. law William Mitchell Coll. Law, St. Paul, 1977—; adj. prof. U. Minn. Law Sch., 1978-82; lectr. in field, 1970—; bd. dirs. Pan-O-Gold Realty Co., Alton Realty Co. Vice chmn. bd. dirs. Minn. Program on Victims of Sexual Assault, 1974-76; bd. dirs. Physician's Health Plan, Health Maintenance Orgn., 1976-80, exec. com. 1977-80; mem. legal drug abuse subcom. Gov. Minn. Adv. Com. Drug Abuse, 1972-74; bd. visitors U. Minn. Law Sch., 1979-85; mem. child abuse project coordinating com. Hennepin County Med. Soc., 1982-83, chmn. corp., labor, ins. subcom. 1982. Mem. ABA (criminal law, labor and employment law, civil litigation sects., chmn. criminal law com.), Minn. Bar Assn., Hennepin County Bar Assn. (ethics com. 1973-76, criminal law com. 1973—, vice chmn. 1979-80, unauthorized practice law com. 1977-78, individual rights and responsibilities com. 1977-78, labor and employment law com. 1985—), Nat. Dist. Attys. Assn., Minn. County Attys. Assn., Minn. Trial Lawyers Assn., Am. Judicature Soc., Minn. Women Lawyers, U. Minn. Law Sch. Alumni Assn. (dir. 1979-85). Author articles, pamphlet, manual. Home: 2105 Xanthus Ln Plymouth MN 55447 Office: 2000 Hennepin County Govt Center Minneapolis MN 55487

ALTSCHUL, BJ, public relations counselor; b. Norfolk, Va., Jan. 28, 1948; d. Lemuel and Sylva (Behr) A. Student, Goucher Coll., 1965-67; B.A., U. South Fla., 1970, postgrad., 1980-84. Reporter St. Petersburg Times, Fla., 1973-74; dir. pub. relations Valkyrie Press, Inc., St. Petersburg, 1974-77; founding editor Bay Life, Clearwater, Fla., 1977-79, Tampa Bay Monthly, Clearwater, 1977-79; mng. editor Fla. Tourist News, Tampa and Orlando, 1981; founder Capital Communications of Tampa, 1981, since owner, prin., name changed to b j Altschul & Assocs., 1985; mgr. editorial and info. services Va. Port Authority, Norfolk, 1985—; adj. faculty Old Dominion U., Norfolk, 1986—. Author: Cracker Cookin' & Other Favorites, 1984; editor: The Underground Gourmet, 1983; contbg. author: Virginia: A Commonwealth Comes of Age, 1988. Bd. dirs. Pinellas County Big Bros.-Big Sisters, 1980-82, Fla. Folklore Soc., 1984-85. Grant rev. panelist Fla. Fine Arts Council, 1981. Mem. Fla. Motion Picture and Television Assn. (treas. 1976-78), Fla. Freelance Writers Assn., Hampton Rds. C. of C. (co-chmn. pub. relations Internat. Azalea Festival 1986, chmn. publications 1987), Hampton Rds. Fgn. Commerce Club, World Affairs Council, Va. Conf. on World Trade (chmn. pub. relations com.), Downtown Norfolk Devel. Corp. (chmn. urban living com.), Mensa, Pub. Relations Soc. Am. (chmn. Mid-Atlantic Dist. 1988, chmn.-elect govt. sect., bd. dirs. accreditation chmn. Hampton Rds. chpt. 1985—). Avocations: sailing, classical music, folk music, jazz. Home: 9300-H Silver Stream Ln Richmond VA 23229 Office: Va Port Authority 600 World Trade Ctr Norfolk VA 23510

ALTSHUL, SARA BETH, literary agent, producer; b. Chgo., Feb. 3, 1954; d. Alex Abraham and Amy Jasmine (Reibman) A. BA in Art History, UCLA, 1975. Sec. United Artists Corp., Los Angeles, 1975-76; agt. trainee Ziegler/Roth Agy., Los Angeles, 1976-77; exec. story editor Orion Pictures Corp., Los Angeles, 1978-79; v.p. prodn. Ladd Co., Los Angeles, 1979-84, RKO Pictures, Los Angeles, 1985-86; producer New Star Entertainment, Los Angeles, 1986-87; lit. agt. Agy. Performing Arts, Los Angeles, 1988—. Democrat. Buddhist.

ALTWIES, DIANE CARMELLA, financial project administrator; b. Wayne, N.J., June 15, 1963; d. Louis Gene and Constance Jean (Fusco) Macri; m. Michael Andrew Altwies, Aug. 24, 1985. BS cum laude, U. South Fla., 1983, postgrad., 1983-88. Computer operator NCNB Nat. Bank, Tampa, Fla., 1981-83; program adminstr. Harris Corp., Palm Bay, Fla., 1984, ABA Industries, Pinellas Park, Fla., 1984-85; program mgr. ABA Industries, Pinellas Park, 1984-85; program adminstr. Computer Systems div. Unisys, Oldsmar, Fla., 1985—. Republican. Roman Catholic. Club: Unisys Golf League. Office: Unisys Corp 3655 SR 584 Oldsmar FL 33557

ALUMBAUGH, MARSHA MARIE, food service executive; b. Hayward, Calif., Apr. 5, 1952; d. Herbert H. Honey and Evelyn (Erickson) Hailstone; m. Kevin L. Alumbaugh, Nov. 30, 1980 (div. Jan. 1986). AA, Grossmont Jr. Coll., 1973; BA, San Diego State U., 1975; MBA, Rockhurst Coll., 1987. Tchr. Day Care Ctr., San Diego, 1976-77; with Ky. Fried Chicken, various locations, 1970—, from sales hostess to dist. tng. mgr., 1970-83; area mgr. Ky. Fried Chicken, Kansas City, Mo., 1983-88; area supr. Long John Silver's, Overland Park, Kans., 1988—. Mem. Nat. Orgn. Female Execs., DAR. Home: 7602 E 134th Terr Grandview MO 64030

ALUSEO, ALICE RUTH, infosystems specialist; b. New Brighton, Pa., June 4, 1958; d. Sam and Shirley (Mate) A. BS in Mgmt., Computer Sci., Calif. (Pa.) State U., 1979. Analyst internat. systems Eastman Kodak Co., Rochester, N.Y., 1980—; programmer Dan Mar Enterprises, Rochester, 1986-88; instr. computer programming Bryant & Stratton Sch. Bus., Rochester, 1985-86, dean continuing edn. Founder Worldwide Bus. Info. Systems newsletter, Eastman Kodak Co., Rochester. Mem. Rochester's Women's Network. Home: 418 Carter St Rochester NY 14621 Office: Eastman Kodak Co 343 State St Rochester NY 14650

ALVARADO, DONNA M., government administrator; b. Washington, Nov. 8, 1948; d. Ricardo and Rita A. B.A., Ohio State U., 1969, M.A., 1970. Asst. dir. U.S. Senate Com. on Judiciary, Washington, 1980-81, counsel, 1981-83; dep. asst. sec. for Equal Opportunity and Safety Policy, Office of Sec. of Def., Washington, 1983-85; dir. ACTION, Washington, 1985—; asst. dir. Office of Policy Coordination Office of Pres.-Elect.; profl. staff mem. House Select com. on Narctics Abuse and Control. Mem. Pres.'s Task Force on Legal Equity for Women, 1985—; mem. Commn. on Internat. Migration and Cooperative Econs. Devel., 1987-88; mem. prevention com. White House Conf. for a Drug Free Am., 1987-88; mem. U.S. Del. to UN Conf. on Decade for Women, Nairobi, 1985; mem. Republican Nat. Hispanic Assembly, 1985—. Recipient Dept. Def. Medal, Eagle award Nat. Guard Bur., 1985. Mem. Mexican-Am. Women's Nat. Assn. (exec. v.p. 1983), Am. Soc. Pub. Adminstrn. Office: Adminstrvt Agys ACTION Office of Dir 806 Connecticut Ave NW Washington DC 20525

ALVARE, ANITA MARIE, public relations consultant; b. Phila., Dec. 31, 1952; d. Louis John and Rosemary Audrey (Cosgrove) A.; art student Rosemont Coll., 1970-71. With Certain Teed Corp., Valley Forge, Pa., 1972-81, asst. mgr. communications, 1976-78, pub. relations mgr., 1978-81; owner, pres. Alvare Assocs., Wayne, Pa., 1981—; ptnr., sec. Executive Sports, Wayne, Pa., 1985—. Republican. Roman Catholic. Club: Publicity. Home: 28th & Pennsylvania Ave Philadelphia PA 19130 Office: 409 E Lancaster Ave Wayne PA 19087

ALVARIÑO DE LEIRA, ANGELES (ANGELES ALVARIÑO), biologist, oceanographer; b. El Ferrol, Spain, Oct. 3, 1916; came to U.S., 1958, naturalized, 1966; d. Antonio Alvariño-Grimaldos and Carmen Gonzalez Diaz-Saavedra; m. Eugenio Leira-Manso, Mar. 16, 1940; 1 child, Angeles. B.S. and Letters summa cum laude, U. Santiago de Compostela (Spain), 1933; M. Natural Scis., U. Madrid, 1941, cert. Doctorate, 1951, D.Sc. summa cum laude, 1967. Cert. Biologist-Oceanographer, Spanish Inst. Oceanography, 1952. Prof. biology Coll. El Ferrol, Spain, 1941-48; fishery research biologist dept. Sea Fisheries Spain, 1948-52; histologist Superior Council Sci. Research, 1948-52; biologist, oceanographer Spanish Inst. Oceanography, 1950-57; biologist Scripps Inst. Oceanography, U. Calif.-LaJolla, 1958-69; fishery research biologist Nat. Marine Fisheries Service Southwest Fisheries Ctr., NOAA, U.S. Dept. Commerce, La Jolla, 1970-87, emeritus scientist, 1987—; assoc. prof. U. Nat. Autonomous Mexico, 1976, U. San Diego, 1982—; research assoc. San Diego State U., 1979-82; vis. prof. Poly. Tech. Mexico, 1982—, U. Parara, Brazil, 1982. Contbr. numerous articles to profl. jours., chpts. to sci. books; discovered 22 new species of animals. Brit. Council fellow, 1953-54; Fulbright fellow, 1956-57; NSF grantee, 1961-69; U.S. Office Navy grantee, 1958-69; Calif. Coop. Oceanic Fishery Investigation grantee, 1958-69; UNESCO grantee, 1979. Fellow Am. Inst. Fishery Research Biologists, San Diego Soc. Natural History; mem. Assn. Natural History Soc., Western Naturalists Soc., Calif. Acad. Scis., Biol. Soc. Washington, Hispano-Am. Assn. Researchers on Marine Scis., Marine Biol. Assn. U.K., Sigma Xi. Home: 7535 Cabrillo Ave La Jolla CA 92037 Office: Nat Marine Fisheries Service PO Box 271 La Jolla CA 92038

ALVERIO-GIROT, CARMEN ENID, occupational therapist; b. San Lorenzo, P.R., Sept. 13, 1960; d. Emilio and Carmen (Laureano) Alverio; m. Jose Manuel Girot, Oct. 17. BS in Occupational Therapy magna cum laude, U. P.R., 1982. Registered occupational therapist. Staff occupational therapist Nuestra Senora de Los Angeles Hosp., Rio Piedras, P.R., 1982, Brooke Army Med. Ctr., San Antonio, 1982-84; occupational therapist, asst. health care adminstr. U.S. Army Health Clinic, San Juan, P.R., 1984-85; occupational therapist, clin. supr. Letterman Army Med. Ctr., San Francisco, 1986; occupational therapist advisor USA Humanitarian Med. Team, El Salvador, Cen. Am., 1986-87, Martin Army Community Hosp., Columbus, Ga., 1987—. Contbr. articles to profl. jours. Vol. Am. Muscular Dystrophy Summer Camp, P.R., 1979, 2d Ann. Internat. Amputee Soccer Tournament, Seattle, 1987; registration com. Army Med. Dept. Biathon Race, Ft. Benning, Ga., 1987; asst. rescue team Earthquake Nat. Disaster, El Salvador, 1987. Mem. Am. Occupational Therapists Assn., Tex. Occupational Therapists Assn., World Fedn. of Occupational Therapists, Mil. Surgeons of U.S. Club: Officers. Home: 3912 Ashmore Dr Columbus GA 31909 Office: Occupational Therapy Clinic Martin Army Community Hosp Fort Benning GA 31905

ALVEY, DORIS MAY GIORDANO, hypnotherapist, nurse; b. N.Y.C., Nov. 1, 1945; d. Dominic Louis Giordano and Agnes (Victoria) Johnson; m. Lorenzo Marcello Margini, June 5, 1974 (div. 75); m. Clifford Charles Alvey, Apr. 11, 1981. RN, Queens Gen. Hosp. Sch. Nursing, 1966; BA in Psychology, Marymount Manhattan Coll., 1973; MS, CUNY, 1978; PhD in Hypnotherapy, Am. Inst. Hypnotherapy, Santa Ana, Calif., 1985. Cert. Hypnotherapist, psychiatric, mental health nurse. Nurse in charge Phoenix House Therapeutic Ctr., N.Y.C., 1968-70; research coordinator N.Y. Med. Coll., N.Y.C., 1971-74; pvt. practice psychotherapy N.Y.C., 1974-84; research coordinator UCLA Harbor Gen. Hosp., Torrance, Calif., 1985-86; dir., owner South Ctr. for Hypnosis and Health Edn., Costa Mesa, Calif., 1984—; psychiatric, alcohol cons. Comp Care, Tustin, Calif., 1984-85; home care cons. Med. Home Coll., Los Angeles, 1986; psychiatric nursing supr. Coll., Cerritos, Calif., 1986—. Watercolor painter exhibited in group show's including Madison Sq. Garden Art Show, 1981. Vol. Laguna Art Mus., Costa Mesa; active Save the Children Found., 1983—. Named THerapist Who Cares Bayview Manor Home for Adults, Bklyn., 1980. Mem. Calif. Council Hypnotherapy, Milton H. Erickson Soc., Am. Women in Bus. (Irvine, Calif.), Costa Mesa C. of C. Episcopalian. Club: GLAZA (Los Angeles). Home: 357 Grenoble Ln Costa Mesa CA 92627 Office: South Coast Ctr of Hypnosis and Health Edn 666 Baker St Costa Mesa CA 92626

ALVIN, BETTIE LEOLA, project director and mental health professional; b. Landstuhl, Federal Republic of Germany, Mar. 4, 1956; came to U.S., 1956; d. John Edward and Mildred (Ivy) A. BS in Psychology, Ill. State U., 1977, MS in Clin. Psychology, 1980. Registered social worker, Ill. Therapist II Comprehensive Mental Health Ctr. of St. Clair County, Inc., East St. Louis, Ill., 1980-82, outpatient coordinator, 1982-87; project dir. ill. Dept. Children and Family Services, East St. Louis, 1987—. Co-author children's books, 1986. dir. christian edn. Morning Star Missionary Bapt. Ch., East St. Louis, 1985—. Ill. State scholar, 1978-80. Mem. Nat. Orgn. Female Execs., Headstart Policy Bd., Parents Too Soon Adv. Bd., Council Integrated Youth Services. Democrat. Home: 4901 Lake Dr Centerville IL 62205

ALVINO, SYLVIA MARIE, reading educator, corporate executive, consultant; b. Chicago Heights, Ill., Oct. 17, 1948; d. John Joseph and Diana

(Urbinati) A. BA in English, Loyola U., Chgo., 1970, MEd in Reading, 1977. Reading specialist Project Upward Bound, Loyola U., Chgo., 1972—; v.p. fin., cons. Assn. for Career Devel., Inc., Chgo., 1980—, The Phoenix Group, Inc., Chgo., 1982—, mgr. High Sch. Renaissance Program, Chgo. Bd. Edn., 1984-86, learning specialist chpt. I program E.C.I.A., 1986—. Author: (with others) Tutorial Supervisor's Manual, 1977; Cable TV Training Manual, 1981; editor Vineyard, 1971-73. Recipient plaques Rush Med. Ctr., 1982, Loyola U. Upward Bound Program, 1982, Calumet High Sch., 1978. Mem. Mid-Am. Equal Ednl. Opportunity Program Personnel, Assn. Supervision and Curriculum Devel.; Ind. Voters Ill., Ill. Guidance and Personnel Assn., Internat. Reading Assn., Nat. Council Tchrs. of English, Phi Delta Kappa, Phi Chi Theta (officer Beta Psi chpt.). Roman Catholic. Home: 2252 Sherman Ave Evanston IL 60201 Office: Loyola U Project Upward Bound 1041 W Loyola Ave Chicago IL 60626 Office: 6101 N Sheridan Rd Chicago IL 60660

ALWINE, JANET DARLENE, corporate executive; b. Covington, Va., Jan. 30, 1952; d. Bennie Hilston and Edna Darlene (Phillips) Burkholder; m. David Lynn Snyder, Sr., Jan. 31, 1970 (div. 1975); 1 child, David Lynn, Jr.; m. Thomas Samuel Alwine, June 7, 1986. Student, Dabney S. Lancaster Community Coll., Clifton Forge, Va., 1973-77. Owner, operator The Hair Sta., Covington, 1974-77; with Alleghany/Covington Dept. Social Services, 1977-81; adminstr. Tanglewood Manor Home for Adults, Covington, 1981-86; bus. mgr. Country Comfort Chimney Services, Inc., York, Pa., 1987—. Mem. Nat. Assn. Females Execs., Beta Sigma Phi (pres. 1981-82, treas. 1984-85). Methodist. Lodge: Women of the Moose. Home: 72 W Hoke St Spring Grove PA 17362

AMACHER, KATHRYN MARIE, physician; b. Cleve., Feb. 24, 1957; d. Richard Donald and Rosemarie Jean (Divoky) A. BS, U. Ill., 1979; DO, Chgo. Coll. Osteopathic Medicine, 1983. Commnd. 2d lt. USAF, 1983, advanced through grades to capt., 1983—; osteopathy internship Malcolm Grow Med. Ctr., Andrews AFB, Md., 1983-84; dir. urgent care USAF, McClellan AFB, Calif., 1984-88; internal medicine resident USAF, Travis AFB, Calif., 1988—. Bd. dirs. Womankind, Sacramento, Calif, 1983—; program Sacramento NOW, 1986-87. Mem. Am. Osteopathic Assn., Osteopathic Physicians and Surgeons of Calif., Am. Med. Women's Assn., Assn. Military Osteopathic Physicians and Surgeons, Sacramento Orgn. Women. Democrat. Episcopal.

AMADIO, BARI ANN, metal fabrication executive; b. Phila., Mar. 26, 1949; d. Fred Deutscher and Celena (Lusky) Garber; m. Peter Colby Amadio, June 24, 1973; children: P. Grant, Jamie Blair. BA in Psychology, U. Miami, 1970; diploma in Nursing, Thomas Jefferson U., 1973, Johnston-Willis Sch. Nursing, 1974; BS in Nursing, Northeastern U., 1977; MS in Nursing, Boston U., 1978; JD, U. Bridgeport, 1983. Faculty Johnston-Willis Sch. Nursing, Richmond, Va., 1974-75; staff, charge nurse Mass. Gen. Hosp., Boston, 1975-78; faculty New England Deaconess, Boston, 1978-80, Lankenau Hosp. Sch. of Nursing, Phila., 1980-81; pres. Original Metals, Inc., Phila., 1985—, also bd. dirs.; owner Silver Carousel Antiques, Rochester, Minn. Treas. Women's Assn. Minn. Orch., Rochester, 1986-87, pres., 1987—, newsnotes editor, 1985-87; mem. mayor's coms. All. Am. City Award Com., Rochester, 1984—, Mayor's coms. Entertainment League, Rochester, 1987—; bd. dirs. Rochester Civic League, 1988—. Mem. Am. Soc. Law and Medicine, Zumbro Valley Med. Soc. Aux. (Rochester) (fin. chmn. 1986—, treas. 1988—), Nat. Assn. Female Execs., Nat. Assn. Food Equipment Manufacturers, Friends of Mayowood, Phi Alpha Delta, Sigma Theta Tau. Home: 816 9th Ave SW Rochester MN 55902

AMARA, LUCINE, opera and concert singer; b. Hartford, Conn., Mar. 1, 1927; d. George and Adrine (Kazanjian) Armaganian; Jan. 7, 1961 divorced June 1964. Student, Music Acad. of West, 1947, U. So. Calif., 1949-50. Appeared at Hollywood Bowl, 1948, soloist, San Francisco Symphony, 1949-50, with Met. Opera, N.Y.C., 1950—, appeared on Met. Opera: In Performance, 1982, 83, 84; recorded Pagliacci, 1951, 60; singer with New Orleans, Hartford, Pitts., Central City operas, 1952-54, appeared Glyndebourne Opera, 1954, 55, 57, 58, Edinburgh Festival, 1954, singer, Aida, Terme Di Caracalla, Rome, 1954, also Stockholm Opera, N.Y. Philharm., St. Louis Civic Light Opera, 1955-56; has appeared in leading or title roles in several operas including: Tosca, Aida, Amelia in Un Ballo in Maschera, others; appeared with St. Petersburg (Fla.) Opera; opera and concert tour, Russia, 1965, Manila, 1968, Paris, Mex., 1966, Hong Kong and China, 1983; rec. artist, Columbia, RCA, Victor, Angel records, Met. Opera Record Club; albums include: Beethoven's Symphony No. 9, Leon Cavallo, I Pagliacci, La Bohème, Verdi's Requiem. Recipient 1st prize Atwater-Kent Radio Auditions, 1948. Mem. Sigma Alpha Iota. Office: Metropolitan Opera New York NY 10023

AMARAL, MARY ELLEN, lawyer; b. Kenosha, Wis., Aug. 5, 1946; s. Nestor Johnson and Mary Louise (Parker) Thompson; m. Donald Earl Mielke, Apr. 27, 1968 (div. Jan. 1978); m. Charles Patrick Amaral, Aug. 31, 1980; children—Maura Patricia, Brian Patrick. B.A. in Journalism, U. Mich., 1968; postgrad. Temple U., 1968-69; M.S. in Mgmt., Pace U., 1979; J.D., U. Denver, 1973. Bar: Colo. 1974. With Mountain Bell, Denver, 1970-76; with regulatory matters AT&T, N.Y.C., 1976-79, regulatory matters dist. mgr., 1981-83, regional atty. govt. relations, Denver, 1983-87; assoc. Davis, Graham & Stubbs, Denver, 1987—; Senate banking-internat. fin. minority staff mem. Conf. Bd. Congl. Asst., Washington, 1980. Mem. Gotham Bus and Profl. Women (legis. chmn. 1978-80, Outstanding Profl. Woman of Yr. 1982), ABA, Denver Bar Assn., Colo. Bar Assn., Colo. Women's Bar Assn., Alliance Profl. Women. Lodge: Zonta (N.Y. chpt. pres. 1983, Denver chpt. chmn. internat. and community relations com. 1984-86, 2d v.p. membership com. 1986-87). Home: 1725 Fillmore Ct Louisville CO 80027 Office: Davis Graham & Stubbs 370 17th St Suite 4700 Denver CO 80201-0185

AMATO, CAMILLE JEAN, manufacturing executive; b. N.Y.C., Aug. 6, 1942; d. William and Mary Carmela (Lombardi) Tuorto; m. Thomas Amato, June 1, 1963; children—Dawn, Thomas. Assoc. Sci., SUNY-Albany, 1981, B.S., 1983; B.S., Empire State Coll., 1983, M. Bus. and Policy, 1986. Lic. realtor, notary, N.Y. Controller, owner Island Marine Inc., Bellmore, N.Y., 1977—; account mgr. L.I. Luth. Assn., Brookville, N.Y., 1983-84, Borden Inc. Chem., Glen Cove, N.Y., 1984-85; real estate agt. N. of 25A R.E. Inc., Locust Valley, N.Y., 1986—; owner, v.p. Penn Yan (N.Y.) Marine Mfg. Inc., 1986—; pres., owner Camille Properties, Inc., Penn Yan, 1986—; cons. various areas. Cons. sub-com. edn. and safety N.Y. State Senate, 1976-77. Mem. Nat. Assn. Female Execs., L.I. Bd. Realtors. Roman Catholic. Avocation: classical piano. Home: Woodstock Manor Muttontown Oyster Bay NY 11771

AMATO, PAULA ANN, accountant; b. Manchester, N.H., Sept. 15, 1962; d. Richard J. and Marlene A. (Remillard) McInnis; m. Joseph A. Amato Jr., Sept. 29, 1984; 1 child, Meghan R. BS, N.H. Coll., 1984, postgrad., 1984—. Acct. Erin Food Services, Manchester, 1984-85; supervisory acct. AI Network Corp., Manchester, 1985—. Mem. acad. planning and rev. bd. Hesser Coll., 1988—. Fellow Nat. Assn. Female Execs.; mem. Nat. Assn. Accts. (bd. dirs. 1984—), Nat. Assn. Exec. Females. Home: 44 Gold St Manchester NH 03103 Office: AI Network Corp Two Wall St Manchester NH 03103

AMATO, ROSEMARIE HELEN, design company executive, educator; b. Cleve., July 20, 1950; d. August Martin and Helen (Kovanes) A.; m. Richard Adam Damiani, July 3, 1978. BS, Ohio State U., 1972; MS, Cleve. State U., 1978. Educator Lorain (Ohio) City Schs., 1972-74, Cuyahoga Heights Local Schs., Cleve., 1974-81; pres., owner Western Reserve Design Studio, Inc., Cleve., 1980—. Advisor Sohio Riverfest for City of Cleve., Cleveland Flats, 1986, Community Design for Cleveland Flats, 1985-86; community rep. Woman Space, Cleve., 1984-85. Named Outstanding Sr. Woman Leader, Ohio State U., 1972, Outstanding Pace Setter Greater Cleve. Enterprising Women, Directory of Enterprising Women of Greater Cleve., 1985. Mem. Am. Soc. Interior Designers, Greater Cleve. Growth Assn., Cleve. Bus. and Profl. Women's Club (2nd v.p. 1983-86, 1st v.p. 1986-87), Woman Bus. Owners Assn.(mem. at large rep. to bd. dirs. 1986-87, mem. chmn. 1986-87), Order Sons of Italy in Am. (local trustee 1981-85, local fin. sec. 1985-87, state scholarship chmn. 1982, 83, 86, Italian awareness in USA state chmn., 1985), Flats Oxbow Assn. (sec. 1985-86), Cleve. Women's City Club, Alpha Delta Kappa (corresponding sec. 1983-85). Republican. Roman Catholic. Home: 1900 Grove Ct Cleveland OH 44113 Office: Western Reserve Design Studio Inc 30014 Detroit Rd Westlake OH 44145

AMATO, ROSEMARY MARCELLA, shoe company executive; b. Cleve., May 17, 1952; d. Sam Anthony and Elizabeth Barbara (Cherney) A.; BSBA, John Carroll U., 1974; postgrad. Ga. State U., 1976, Samford U., 1981. Asst. to controller Mr. Coffee, Cleve., 1973-75; staff acct. Luria Bros., Cleve., 1975-76; capital acctg. mgr. Reliance Electric Co., Cleve., 1976-77, cost acct., Gainesville, Ga., 1977-79, modernization controller, Cleve., 1979-80, regional controller, Birmingham, Ala., 1980-85; asst. corp. controller, bus. systems analyst Pic 'N Pay Stores, Inc., Charlotte, N.C., 1985—; controller Your Choice Inc., Charlotte, 1988—. Mem. AAUW, Nat. Assn. Female Execs., Nat. Assn. Accts., Assn. Info. and Image Mgmt. Republican. Roman Catholic. Office: Your Choice Inc PO Box 34000 Charlotte NC 28261

AMBROE, MARY ELLEN, educator; b. Charleroi, Pa., Oct. 10, 1945; d. Peter and Mary Ann (Ruby) Didik; m. Stanley Ambroe, Dec. 16, 1967; children: Mary Michelle, Rebecca Anne. BS, Ind. U., 1967. Home econs. tchr. Sr. Hign Sch. Dist., Sidman, Pa., 1982—. Advisor, coach Scholastic Quiz Team, Sidman, Pa., 1983—, Trivial Pursuit Club, 1984—; mem. Cen. Western Scholastic Quiz League, spring 1981—, commr., 1986—; co-advisor Forest Hills Nat. Honor Soc., 1984—; judge clothing constrn. 4-H Club, Cambria County, Ebensburg, Johnstown, Loretto (Pa.), 1970-80; judge local newspaper's recipe contest, 1981. Mem. Pa. State Edn. Assn., NEA. Democrat. Roman Catholic. Office: Forest Hills Sr High Sch PO Box 158 Sidman PA 15955

AMBURGEY, VALERIA, mathematics and information sciences educator; b. Lexington, Ky., Feb. 22, 1952; d. Eugene and Glenna Compton Amburgey; m. Thomas Alexander Wark, May 20, 1972 (div. 1981). EdB, Stephen F. Austin State U., 1972; EdM, U. Houston, 1979, Ed.D., 1984. Resident hall asst. Stephen F. Austin State U., 1971-72; tchr. Galveston (Tex.) Ind. Sch. Dist., 1973-76, Aldine Ind. Sch. Dist., Houston, 1976-81; teaching asst., lectr. U. Houston, 1979-82, 84-85; cons. Region IV, Edn. Service Ctr., Houston, 1982-85; pres. VEGA Ventures, Inc.; v.p. Trinity-Brazos River Valley Council Tchrs. Math., 1987-88. Contbr. book rev., software revs. to Arithmetic Tchr., 1983. Sec., bd. dirs. Pine Village North Homeowner's Assn., Houston, 1983. Mem. Nat. Council Tchrs. Math., Tex. Council Tchrs. Math., Tex. Assn. Suprs. Math., Math. Assn. Am., Trinity-Brazos River Valley Council Tchrs. Math. (v.p. 1987-88, pres. 1988-89), Research Council Diagnostic and Prescriptive Math., Tex. Computer Edn. Assn., Pi Mu Epsilon, Kappa Delta Pi. Home: 2404 Ave P Huntsville TX 77340 Office: Sam Houston State U Div Math and Info Scis Huntsville TX 77341

AMBURGEY-LEHMAN, VICKI LYNETTE, medical technologist, specialist; b. Fleming, Ky., Sept. 16, 1958; d. Claude and Dalma (Hale) Amburgey; m. Ronald L. Lehman Jr., Sept. 30, 1986. BS in Med. Technology, Ind. U., 1980. Microbiology technologist St. Joseph's Hosp., Ft. Wayne, Ind., 1979-80; med. technologist Ft. Wayne Med. Lab., 1980-81, chemistry supr., 1981-83; tech. specialist Roche Diagnostic Systems, Nutley, N.J., 1983—. Mem. Am. Soc. Clin. Pathologists (cert.), Am. Assn. Clin. Chemists, Nat. Assn. Female Execs. Republican. Baptist. Home: 107 Carol Ann Ln Streamwood IL 60107

AMENDT, MARILYN JOAN, personnel director; b. Marshalltown, Iowa, June 21, 1928; d. Floyd Wilford and Helen Mary (Scheid) Peterson; m. Virgil E. Amendt, Sept. 4, 1949 (div. Aug. 1971); children: Gregory F., Scott R., Brad A. AA, Stephens Coll., Columbia, Mo., 1948; postgrad., U. Mich., 1978, U. Wis., Superior, 1980-83. Cert. personnel mgr. Office mgr. S&O Products, Inc., Marshalltown, Iowa, 1961-71; life underwriter Lincoln Liberty Life Ins. Co., Marshalltown, Iowa, 1971-72; retail store mgr. Amy's Fashions, Marshalltown, Iowa, 1972-74, Maurices, Inc., Marshalltown, Iowa, 1974-76; corp. personnel dir. Maurices, Inc., Duluth, Minn., 1976-84; sr. v.p., dir. human resources Ohrbach's, Inc., N.Y.C., 1984-87; dir. personnel adminstrn. AMCENA Corp., N.Y.C., 1987—; lectr. U. Wis, Superior, 1981-82, U. Minn., Duluth, 1981-82. Founder, pres., bd. dirs. Mid-Iowa Sheltered Workshop, Marshalltown, 1968-76; mem. Hostess com., Duluth (Minn.) Day Luncheon, 1983; keynote speaker, Am. Bus. Women's Day, Mpls, Duluth, 1984, 85, 86. Mem. Am. Bus. Women's Assn. (dist. v.p. 1982, nat. v.p. 1983, nat. pres. 1984, woman of the yr. 1978), Am. Soc. Exec. and Profl. Women. Home: 121 Brush Hollow Crescent Rye Brook NY 10573

AMENTA, CAROLINE, travel agency executive; b. Tarrytown, N.Y., Sept. 30, 1928; d. Carmelo John and Rosaria (Cavalieri) Malandrino; m. Sebastian Amenta, Dec. 27, 1952; children—Paul, John, Frank. Student Wood Bus. Sch., N.Y.C., 1946-47. Office sec. Westinghouse Internat., N.Y.C., 1947-49, Polychrome Co. Inc., Yonkers, N.Y., 1949-52, N.Y. State Regional Health Office, White Plains, 1952-55; travel cons. McGregor Travel, White Plains, 1967-70; pres. ATC Travel, Inc., Tarrytown, 1970—; sec. PJF Properties Ltd., Tarrytown, 1984—. Fellow Profl. Bus. Women (v.p. 1983-85). Roman Catholic. Avocations: swimming, reading, travel. Office: ATC Travel Inc 239 N Broadway Suite 3 North Tarrytown NY 10591

AMERINE, ANNE FOLLETTE, aerospace engineer; b. San Francisco, Sept. 27, 1950; d. William T. and Wilma (Carlson) F.; m. Jorge Armando Verdi D'Eguia, July 4, 1970 (div.); m. Donald Amerine, Dec. 18, 1983. AA, Coll. Marin, 1977; BA in Math. with honors, Mills Coll., 1979. Sr. computer operator Bank of Am. Internat. Services, San Francisco, 1972-74; mathematician Pacific Missile Test Ctr., Pt. Mugu, Calif., 1979-80; engr. Grumman Aerospace Corp., Pt. Mugu, 1979-83; engr. Litton Guidance and Control Systems, 1984-86, product support and assurance dept. project mgr., 1986—. Chmn. Marina West Neighborhood Council, 1982-84; mem. NOW; chmn. subcom. Ventura County Community Coll. Dist. Citizen's Adv. Com. on Status of Women, 1983-84. Aurelia Henry Reinhart scholar, 1978-79; recipient Project Sterling award Grumman Aerospace Corp., 1982. Mem. Nat. Assn. Female Execs., Soc. Women Engrs. (chmn. career guidance com. and speaker Ventura County sect.), Litton Women's Enhancement Orgn. (founder, v.p. and chmn. info. and edn. com. 1985-86, editor newsletter 1986-87), Assn. Old Crows, Mills Coll. Alumni, Alpha Gamma Sigma (life). Office: Litton Guidance & Control Systems 5500 Canoga Ave MS 80 Woodland Hills CA 91367-6698

AMERY, KATHY OLSEN, design engineer; b. Colorado Springs, Aug. 12, 1960; d. Fred and June (Olsen) A. BS in Elec. Engring., U. Colo., 1983. Test engr. Honeywell Corp., Phoenix, 1983-86, design automation engr., 1986-87, software engr., 1987—. Republican. Office: Honeywell Corp 13430 N Black Canyon Phoenix AZ 85029

AMES, KATHRYN ANN ECKSTAM, academic administrator; b. Monroe, Wis., June 15, 1956; d. Eugene Emanuel and Evelyn Olga (Urben) E.; m. Carl W. Ames, Mar. 5, 1988. BA in Eng., Spanish, and Hispanic Studies, St. Olaf Coll., 1978; MEd, N. Texas State U., 1981; postgrad., Lutheran Theol. Sem., 1988—. Residence hall dir. Tex. Christian U., Ft. Worth, 1978-79; grad. asst. to dir. N. Tex. State U., Denton, 1979-81; salesperson Iverson's Scandinavian Imports, Edina, Minn., 1983-84; adviser for fgn. students, study abroad and internat. careers U. Ala., Birmingham, 1984-88; cons. Friendship Force, Birmingham, 1986—. Liaison with internat. students Shades Valley Luth. Ch., Birmingham, 1985—. Recipient Excellence in Service Internat. Students award Moslem Student Assn., Birmingham, 1985, 86, 87. Mem. Nat. Assn. Fgn. Student Affairs (Ala. sec. 1986-87), Internat. Soc. Intercultural Edn., Tng. and Research, Am. Soc. Notaries, Ala. Assn. Collegiate Registrars and Admissions Officers, AAUW, Sierra Club (vice chmn. calendar sales coordinator Cahaba Group, 1987—). Club: B'Ham (com. fgn. relations).

AMES, LOUISE BATES, child psychologist; b. Portland, Maine, Oct. 29, 1908; d. Samuel Lewis and Annie Earle (Leach) Bates; m. Smith Whittier Ames, May 22, 1930 (div. 1937); 1 child, Joan Ames Chase. A.B., U. Maine, 1930, M.A., 1933, Sc.D., 1957; Ph.D., Yale U., 1936; D.Sc., Wheaton Coll., 1967. Cert. psychologist, Conn. Research sec., personal asst. to Dr. Gesell Yale Linc Child Devel., Yale Med. Sch., 1933-36, instr., 1940-44, asst. prof., 1944-50; curator Yale Films of Child Devel., 1944-50; co-founder Gesell Inst. Child Devel., dir. research, sec.-treas., 1950-65, asso. dir., chief psychologist, 1968, co-dir., 1971-77, acting dir., 1978, pres., 1978-88. Author: daily syndicated newspaper column Parents Ask; weekly TV broadcast on child behavior, WBZ, Boston, 1952-55; author 32 books, including: (with Arnold Gesell and others) The Gesell Institute's Child from One to Six; editorial bd. Jour. Learning Disabilities, Jour. Genetic Psychology. Mem. Conn. Psychol. Soc., Am. Psychol. Assn., Soc. Research Child Devel., Internat. Council Psychologists (dir. 1945-47), Soc. Projective Techniques (pres. 1970), Sigma Xi. Home: 283 Edwards St New Haven CT 06511 Office: 310 Prospect St New Haven CT 06511

AMES, SANDRA PATIENCE, sales office executive; b. Quincy, Calif., May 23, 1947; d. Bruce Ray Richards and Margaret Elizabeth (Steiner) Richards Johnson; m. Martin P.M. Bettenhausen, Dec. 10, 1965 (div. 1972); m. Thomas William Ames, Nov. 28, 1975. Student Yuba City Jr. Coll., 1965-66. Sales corr. Nat. Can Corp. (now known as Am. Nat. Can Co.), Seattle, 1974-76, Lehigh Valley, Pa., 1976-79, nat. account sales corr., Chgo., 1979-81, dist. sales office mgr., 1981-82, sales analyst I, Oakbrook, Ill., 1982-84, regional sales office mgr., 1984-86; mgr. regional sales office, Oakbrook, 1987—. Mem. Nat. Assn. Female Execs. Republican. Office: Am Nat Can Corp 915 Harger Rd Oak Brook IL 60521

AMEY, RAE, media administrator; b. Shreveport, La., Sept. 26, 1947; d. Bruce Harold and Genevieve (Amey) Gentry; m. John E. Scarborough, Dec. 18, 1971 (div. Nov. 1979). Student, La. State U., 1968-70, U. Houston, 1972-74; BA in Liberal Arts, Antioch U., 1985. Free-lance photographer Houston, 1973—; adminstrn. coordinator Y.E.S. Inc., Sta. KCET-TV, Los Angeles, 1980-83; free-lance cdnl. TV writer, cons. Los Angeles, 1983-84; asst. to pres. prodn. So. Calif. Consortium, Cypress, 1984, project mgr., dir. devel., project dir. The Human Condition, 1985-87; pres. Video Nexus, San Pedro, Calif., 1987—. Editor TV guide book, 1985; photography exhbns. include: Contemporary Art Mus., Houston, 1973, Galveston (Tex.) Arts Ctr., 1975, Cameravision Gallery, Los Angeles, 1980. Mem. Women in Communications (chmn. scholarship and ednl. fund 1986—, v.p. campus services 1987—). Democrat. Home: 703 W 28th St San Pedro CA 90731 Office: Video Nexus 703 W 28th St San Pedro CA 90731

AMICE, CAROL RIZZARDI, marketing manager, copywriter; b. Chambersburg, Pa., Aug. 11, 1955; d. Carl J. and Angela A. (Zagrosky) Rizzardi; m. Thierry Thymen Amice, June 12, 1980. Student U. Ill.-Chgo., 1983, U. Md., Munich, 1979-80; B.S.J., Northwestern U., 1978, student Simpson Coll., 1987—. Staff reporter Dayton (Ohio) Jour.-Herald, 1977, Pottsville (Pa.) Republican, 1976; asst. personnel and logistics U. Md., 1979-80; copy editor Stars and Stripes, Griesheim, W.Ger., 1980; asst. advt. mgr., pub. relations specialist Chas. Levy Circulating Co., Chgo., 1981-83; copywriter, mktg. and merchandising mgr. Better Homes and Gardens mag., Des Moines, 1983-87, promotion mgr., Better Homes and Gardens Books, 1987—; instr. part-time Drake U., 1987—; copy editor Comparative Law Yearbook, 1978; contbr. article to Women's mag. Recipient Internat. Relations award Holzkirchen Internat. Volkssport Festival, Ministry of Fgn. Affairs, Fed. Republic Germany, 1985. Vol. internat. exchange program Youth for Understanding. Recipient German Ministry of Foreign Affairs award Holzkirchen Internat. Volkssport Festival, 1985. Mem. Women in Communications (v.p. membership/communications chpt. 1984-85, pres. 1986, mem. nat. First Amendment com. 1986-87, regional meeting planning com. 1988, Cora award 1987), Advt. Profls. Des Moines (Gridiron producer 1985, sec.-treas. 1986-87, recipient of Addy award 1984-86), ACLU, Iowa Civil Liberties Union, greater Des Moines Volkssport Assn. (founder 1984, pres. 1985-86), Am. Volkssport Assn. (pub. relations and spl. events com. 1986), Amnesty Internat., Democrat. Home: 9009 Maplecrest Dr Norwalk IA 50211 Office: Better Homes and Gardens Books 17th and Locust Sts Des Moines IA 50336

AMICK, CAROL CAMPBELL, state legislator; b. Cleve.; d. Charles L. and Janet (Campbell) A.; m. William S. Moonan. B.S., Iowa State U.; M.P.A., Harvard U. Mem. Mass. Ho. of Reps., 1975-77, Mass. Senate, 1977—; mem. Mass. Gov.'s Commn. on Status of Women, 1975-82; state senate chmn. Mass. Legis. Water Policy Commn., 1978—. Recipient Legislator of Yr. award Mass. Pub. Health Assn., 1985, Legislator of Yr. award Mass. Audubon Soc., 1986. Mem. Mass. Caucus Women Legislators, 1975—, chmn., 1976; active Friends of Bedford Pub. Library, Mass. Mem. LWV, Alpha Lambda Delta, Sigma Kappa. Democrat. Office: Mass Senate State Capitol Boston MA 02133 Other Address: 18 Crescent Ave Bedford MA 01730 *

AMICK, LINDA CLAMP, textile executive; b. Leesville, S.C., Oct. 20, 1947; d. James Belton Clamp and Louise (Anderson) Waits; m. James Elton Eargle Sr., Sept. 4, 1965 (div. Aug. 1981); children: James Jr., Christopher, Katrina; m. Ronald Westley Amick, Apr. 2, 1983; children: Ronda, Tonja, Tessa, Jane. Weaver J.B. Martin Co., Leesville, S.C., 1963-77, supr., 1977-87, dept. mgr., 1987—. Democrat. Methodist. Home: 102 Circle Dr Batesburg SC 29070 Office: JB Martin Co Pond Branch Leesville SC 29006

AMICONE, PATRICIA WEIGEL, corporate executive, educator; b. Cleve., Mar. 13, 1938; d. John Thurman and Opal O'Berry (Page) Weigel; m. Jerry Dale Bibles, July 4, 1957 (div. Nov. 1972); children: Opal, Jeri Sue, Lawrence, James; m. Stephen Joseph Amicone, July 27, 1984. AA, San Bernardino Valley Coll., 1972; BA, Immaculate Heart Coll., 1976; MEd, Calif. State U., 1983. Cert. early childhood tchr., Calif. Psychiatric technician State of Calif., Patton, 1970-72, tng. coordinator, 1979-80; therapist Child Psych in-Patient Unit, Riverside, Calif., 1972-75; asst. program dir. Children's Therapeutic Group Home Services, 1975-77; program dir. Family Treatment Deseret Ctr., Inc., 1977-79; instr. Calif. State U., 1980-82; program dir. Valleyview Children's Hosp., Beaumont, Calif., 1982-83; dir. A Spl. Pl., Hermosa Beach, Calif., 1983-84; pres. Seapsrites, Inc., Hermosa Beach, 1984—; cons. Children and Youth Interagy. Com., Riverside, 1973-79, Senate Select Subcom. on Children, Sacramento, Calif., 1977-80, Sex Edn. and Family Planning Commn. Patton State Hosp., 1979-81; mem. adv. bd. early childhood edn. El Camino Coll., Calif., 1986—, Calif. Regional Occupational Programs, 1987—. Youth rep. Human Relations Com., Corona, claif., 1968-72, Womans Adv. Commn., Patton, 1979-81, St. John's Episc. Ch., Corona, 1968-71; area coordinator youth programs Episc. Diocese Los Angeles, 1968-71; pres. Episc. Ch. Women, Corona, 1968-69. Mem. Nat. Assn. for Edn. Young Children, Am. Assn. Psychiatric Services for Children, Forensic Mental Health Assn. of Calif. (sec. 1979-82), Calif. Childrens Lobby. Democrat. Home: 12152 Aaron Dr Moreno Valley CA 92388 Office: Seasprites Inc 417 25th St Hermosa Beach CA 90252

AMIEL, KAREN BAGGETT, art dealer, consultant; b. Alexander City, Ala., July 13, 1950; d. Clifford Ansel and Margaret Eloise (Howell) Baggett. BA, Am. U., 1971. Curator Arts Council of Great Britain, 1973-78; dir. Waddington Gallery, N.Y.C., London, 1979-80; cons. Congreve Pub. Co., N.Y.C., 1980-81; assoc. Multiples Inc./Marian Goodman Gallery, N.Y.C., 1980-81; ind. dealer, art cons. N.Y.C., 1981-82; dir. Delahunty, N.Y.C., 1982-84; ind. artist rep., art cons. N.Y.C., 1984—; art history slide librarian Am. U., Washington, 1969-71; mus. asst. Dunbarten Oaks, Washington, 1971; illustrator, graphic designer Dinosaur Pubs., Cambridge, Eng., 1971; exhibition organizer Englische Kusnt Geganenwart Palais Thurn and Taxis, Bregenz, Austria, 1977. Office: 225 E 73d St New York NY 10021

AMIEVA, MARTA Z(ENAIDA), investment banker; b. Havana, Cuba, Oct. 11, 1945; came to U.S., 1961, naturalized, 1969; d. Jose and Alsina (Felipe) Ferreira; m. Carlos Amieva, Nov. 25, 1961. BS in Commerce, Corazon de Maria, Havana, 1961; student N.Y. Inst. Tech., Commack, 1973—. Clk. Phoenix of London, N.Y.C., 1963-65; mgr. A.M.C., N.Y.C., 1965-70, Gambit Mgmt., N.Y.C., 1970-75; v.p. Republic Bank N.Y., N.Y.C., 1975-81; pres. AMK Systems, Inc., N.Y.C., 1981-88; v.p. Investment Bank, 1988—; cons. to fin. insts. Active Thirteen, N.Y.C., Nat. Cancer Inst. and Ptnrs. in Courage; mem. Rep. Presdl. Task Force, Washington, 1986-87. Named Woman of Yr., N.Y.C. YMCA, 1980. Mem. Women in Communications, N.Y. Acad. Scis., Women in Computing, Nat. Assn. Female Execs., Smithsonian Assocs., Nat. Mus. Women in Arts (charter), NOW (charter). Club: Centurion.

AMIN, JAMILLAH MAARIJ (JOYCE MARIE JOSEPH), food technologist, real estate agent; b. Lake Charles, La., Jan. 11, 1947; d. Anthony Armo and Edna (LeMelle) Joseph; m. Yusuf D. Amin Sr., Aug. 31, 1968 (div. Dec. 1981); children—Laval Vallare, Yusuf, Ishmael, Harun,

Caliph; m. Guy R. Grant, July 27, 1985. Student San Jose City Coll., 1965-67, San Jose State Coll., 1967-68, Calif. Poly. Inst., 1970-71; A.A., Yuba Coll., 1970; B.S., Calif. State U.-Fresno, 1973. Quality control technician Adolph Coors Co., Golden, Colo., 1979, food technologist, 1979-80; asst. mgr. food service Am. River Coll., Sacramento, 1982-83; food service mgr. U. Calif., Davis, 1983-84; pub. service dir. KMFO Broadcasting, Aptos, Calif., 1984-85; real estate agt. Cornish and Carey Realtors, Hollister, Calif., 1985-87; agt., property mgr. IFS Inc., Hollister, 1987—. Planning Commr. City of Hollister, 1987—. Recipient Outstanding Service award Sabin Sch., 1977; Outstanding Service award Gold Oak Sch., 1981. Mem. Inst. Food Technologists, San Benito County Bd. Realtors (sec. 1988). Republican. Avocations: writing poetry; gardening; hiking. Home: 1481 Versailles Dr Hollister CA 95023 Office: IFS Inc 996 San Benito St Hollister CA 95023

AMNEUS, D.A., English language educator; b. Beverly, Mass., Oct. 15, 1919; d. Nils A. and Harriet S. (Anchersen) A.; divorced; children: Paul, Pamela. AB, U. Calif. Berkeley, 1941; MA, U. So. Calif., 1947, PhD, 1953. From asst. prof. to prof. Calif. State U., Los Angeles, 1950—; prof. emeritus Calif. State U. Author: Back to Patriarchy, 1979, The Mystery of MacBeth, 1983, The Three Othellos, 1986; contbr. articles to profl. jours. Mem. NOW. Republican. Home: 2131 S Primrose Ave Alhambra CA 91803 Office: U Calif English Dept 5151 State Univ Dr Los Angeles CA 90032

AMONSON, JOHANNE LESLIE, barrister, solicitor; b. Edmonton, Alta., Canada, Mar. 28, 1949; d. Leslie Earl an Trudy Johanna (Fritz) A.; married, Mar. 6, 1981; 1 child: Matthew Charles Arthur. BA, U. Oreg., 1970; LLB, U. Alta., 1977. Bar: Alta. 1978. Assoc. Weeks Joyce, Edmonton, 1978-85; ptnr. Peterson Ross, Edmonton, 1985—; tchr. Bavarian, Ministry Edn. Fed. Republic Germany, 1972-73,; tchr. and lectr. on legal edn. Contbr. papers to legal publs. Exhbns. registrar Glenbow Mus. Calgary, 1973-74. Named to Dean's List, U. Ore., 1969-70, U. Alta. Law Rev., 1975-77; recipient of fgn. student scholarship, U. Ore., 1967-70. Mem. Law Soc. Alta., Can. (mentor), Can. Bar Assn. (panelist, nat. council and provincial exec. mem., coordinator no. sects.; chairperson, wills and trusts sect.), Internat. Bar Assn., Edmonton Bar Assn. Conservative. Lutheran. Office: Peterson Ross, 2700 CN Tower, 10004 104th Ave, Edmonton, AB Canada T5J 0K1

AMOROSO, MARIE DOROTHY, EEG technologist; b. Phila., Jan. 16, 1924; d. Salvatore and Clorinda (Gaudio) A. Med. Lab. Tech., Hahnemann Hosp., Phila., 1943; postgrad., Temple U., Phila., 1945-48, U. Pa., Phila., 1947-48, 1950. EEG technician Hahnemann Med. Coll., Phila., 1943-53, Phila. Gen. Hosp., 1953-62; histology technician Temple Med. Coll. Temple U., Phila., 1962-63; allergy technician Harry Rogers, M.D., Phila., 1963; EEG technologist Haverford (Pa.) State Hosp., 1963—; instr. EEG Osteopathic Med. Ctr Sch. Allied Health, Phila., 1978-85. Editor: The Eastern Breeze, 1977-79; contbr. articles to profl. jours.; patentee in field. Mem. Am. Soc. Electroneurodiagnostic Technologists, Inc., Clin. EEG Technicians Technologists Soc., The Western Soc. Electrodiagnostic Technologists, So. Soc. EEG Technicians, Inc., Eastern Soc. EEG and Neurodiagnostic Technicians (sec. 1977-79), Phila. Regional EEG Technician's Assn. (exec. bd. 1967, sec. 1969), Electro-Physiological Technologists Assn. Gt. Britain. Home: 477 Brookfield Rd Drexel Hill PA 19026 Office: Haverford State Hosp 3500 Darby Rd Haverford PA 19041

AMOS, JACQUELYN VEAL, child care center administrator; b. Miami, Fla., Dec. 1, 1939; d. Jack Haskell Veal and Dolores (Neidecken) Baker; m. Robert W. Amos, 1959 (div. Mar. 1970); children: Pamela Anne, Laurie Anne. Grad. high sch., Miami. Owner, operator McNatt's Nursery, 1964-67, Neighborhood Kids Preschool, 1969—, Jamos Mgmt. Co., Inc., Sunrise, Fla., 1986—; owner, operator Margate Day Care Ctr., 1971-76, Plantation West Day Care Ctr., 1972-76, Coral Springs Country Day Sch., 1972-79, Lauderdale North Park Day Care Ctr., 1973-76, The Little Place in West Palm Beach, 1973-79, Neighborhood Kids Preschool Wellington, 1979—; active Today's Children Preschool Program, 1972-82. Mem. Plantation C. of C. Republican. Roman Catholic. Office: Jamos Mgmt Co Inc 6196 NW 11th St Sunrise FL 33313

AMOS, JOAN MARIE, insurance agency executive; b. Leominster, Mass., Nov. 22, 1935; d. Louis Adelard and Cecelia Irene (Lamoreux) LaBelle; m. Charles Clinton Amos, Feb. 2, 1962; 1 child, Jonathan Ashley. Cert. in Acctg., LaSalle U., Chgo., 1968; charter property and casualty underwriting courses Boston U., 1968-69. Sec., treas. Henry Leblanc Inc., Fitchburg, Mass., 1969-74, Marsolais Ins. Agy., Ayer, Mass., 1970-74, Aanco Underwriters, Inc., St. Petersburg, Fla., 1973—, Countryside Insurors, Inc., Tarpon Springs, Fla., 1982-85; pres. Ins. Premium Acceptance Corp., St. Petersburg, 1986—; pres. Gulfport Mini-Warehouse, Inc., Fla., 1986—. owner, operator Jomar Charter & Properties, St. Petersburg, 1973—. Bd. dirs. Fla. Orch., St. Petersburg, 1981-83, bd. govs., 1984-87; fund raising chmn. Pinellas Assn. for Retarded Children, St. Petersburg, 1982; life mem. Arthritis Found., Family Services. Am. Nat. Novice Ladies Figure Skating Champion, Roller Skating Rink Operators Assn. Am., 1953. Mem. Nat. Assn. Ins. Women, Ins. Women of St. Petersburg, Nat. Assn. Ins. Agts., Am. Cancer Soc. (life), Arthritis Found. (Sword of Hope chpt.), Nat. Notary Assn., Nat. Assn. Female Execs. Roman Catholic. Clubs: Cross of Lorraine Soc., Infinity, Boley's Angels. Home: 300 Rafael Blvd NE Saint Petersburg FL 33704 Office: Aanco Underwriters Inc 10033 9th St Saint Petersburg FL 33716

AMOS, MARGARET, educational program director; b. Stuart, Va., Oct. 25, 1942; d. Wade Russell and Annie Sue (Nelson) A. BSEd, Radford U., 1964; MSEd, Va. Poly. Inst. and State U., 1977. Tchr. home econs. Franklin County High Sch., Rocky Mount, Va., 1964-66; tchr. home econs. Chatham (Va.) High School, 1966-68, 73-74, tchr. sci., 1968-73; extension agt. Va. Coop. Extension Service, Pittsylvania County, 1974-78, Giles County, 1978-81, Botetourt County, 1981-85; program leader, west cen. dist. Va. Coop. Extension Service, Roanoke, 1985—. Bd. dirs. Giles County Multi-Discipline Team, Pearisburg, Va., 1979-81, West Cen. 4-H Ednl. Ctr., Wirtz, Va., 1985—; fund raiser Am. Heart Assn., Botetout County, 1984-85; mem. adminstrv. bd. Fincastle (Va.) United Meth. Ch., 1984-86. Fellow NSF, 1968, 69. Mem. Va. Assn. Extension Home Economists (pres. 1984-86), Nat. Assn. Extension Home Economists, Va. Home Econs. Assn., Am. Home Econs. Assn., Va. Assn. 4-H Agts., Nat. Assn. 4-H Agts., Giles County Arts and Crafts Guild (bd. dirs. 1980-81), Phi Kappa Phi. Clubs: Quota Internat. (Roanoke), Cedars Country (bd. dirs. 1976-78) (Chatham). Home: RT 1 Box 138 Troutville VA 24175 Office: Va Coop Extension Service 5369 Peters Creek Rd NW Roanoke VA 24019

AMOWITZ, GEORGETTE WEISZ, choreographer, educator; b. Paris, Oct. 26, 1929 (parents Am. citizens); d. Bela and Margaret (Goldman) Weisz; B.A., U. Wis., 1951; postgrad. Juilliard Sch., 1951-53; tchrs. cert. Labanotation, Dance Notation Bur., Inc., 1956, advanced cert. Labanotation, 1960; m. J. David Amowitz, Jan. 30, 1954 (dec. 1979); children—Michael Bennett, Steven Paul, Susan Lynn; m. 2d Nathaniel T. Gorchoff, Sept. 4, 1983. Choreographer, Va. Grass Roots Opera Theatre, Lynchburg, 1955-58, Briar Patch Summer Theatre, Sweet Briar, Va., 1956, Lynchburg Little Theatre, 1955, 60, 67, 76, Lynchburg Coll. Opera Theatre, 1958, 63, Lynchburg Fine Arts Center, 1969, 74, Randolph-Macon Woman's Coll. Dance Concerts, Lynchburg, 1958-74; instr. dance Randolph-Macon Woman's Coll., 1956, 58, 59-62, 63, 64-65, 70-71, lectr. dance 76-77, 78-79, 82; lectr. dance Hollins Coll., 1977, U. Wis.-Milw., 1981-82; reconstructor dance works Lynchburg Fine Arts Center, 1958, 59, 62, 70, 71, 75, Hollins (Va.) Coll., 1976, 77, 80, Sweet Briar Coll., 1963, U. Wis.-Milw., 1981, Dance Theatre of Central Va., 1983-84; Talent Trust instr. Lynchburg City Schs., 1974-75, Fine Arts Center, 1974-75; v.p. Dance div. Fine Arts Center, 1973-74, asso. dir., 1974-75, dir. Dance Players, 1969; dir. Jr. Dansnotators of Lynchburg, 1958-66, Little Dance Theatre, 1959-63, Lynchburg Dance Theatre Workshop, 1966-76; chmn. dance dept. Nat. Fedn. Music Clubs, 1975-77; pvt. tchr. technique and Labanotation, Lynchburg, 1958-76. Fellow Internat. Council Kinetography Laban; mem. Dance Notation Bur. (dir. 1956-57, 61-64), U. Wis. Alumni Assn. (life). Choreography registered for copyright includes Shepherds Dance from Amahl and the Night Visitors, 1959; And After the Journey, 1984.

AMPARAN, MARIA ELENA, personnel executive; b. Los Angeles, Aug. 19, 1945; d. John S. and Concepcion (Mendez) A. AA, East Los Angeles Coll., 1967; BA in Journalism, Calif. State U., Los Angeles, 1969. Sec., coordinator press and publicity Sta. KNBC, 1969-70; prin. public relations rep. Model Cities Program East N.E. neighborhood City of Los Angeles, 1970-72; pub. info. aide Housing Authority, Los Angeles, 1972; editor So. Calif. Rapid Transit Dist., 1972-73; coordinator Dept. Community Services County of Los Angeles, 1973-76; employment specialist Kaiser Permanente Med. Care Program, Los Angeles, 1976-79; personnel supr. McDonald's Corp., Denver, 1979-85; personnel supr. Foster Farms, South El Monte, Calif., 1986—. Vol., coordinator Youth Motivation Task Force, 1976-79; mem. employer adv. com. Career Planning Ctr., Inc., 1978-79; bd. dirs. Denver Pvt. Industry Council, 1984-85; mem. Denver Mayor's Task Force on Youth, 1984-85. Recipient commendation award Los Angeles County Bd. Supervisors. Mem. Personnel Mgmt. Assn. San Diego, Personnel Mgmt. Assn. of Aztlan (chairperson ad hoc placement com., pres. San Diego chpt. 1982-84, nat. publicity chmn. 1982-84, Profl. Women's Journalism Soc., Beta Phi Gamma. Democrat. Roman Catholic. Home: 2110 India St Los Angeles CA 90039 Office: 1913 Frank Stiles Rd PO Box 3247 South El Monte CA 91733

AMSTER, KAREN ALICE, computer store owner; b. Cin., June 24, 1957; d. Earl Leroy and Katherine Elizabeth (Zeis) Jurma; m. Robert Koerner Amster, June 7, 1979. BA, Williams Coll., 1979. Substitute tchr. Ft. Bragg (N.C.) Sch. System, 1980-82; computer instr. Fayetteville (N.C.) Tech. Inst., 1982; owner Complete Computer Ctr., Fort Bragg, N.C., 1982-84, Computer Works, Petersburg, Va., 1984—; tchr. St. Joseph Elem. Sch., Petersburg, 1986-87; instr. John Tyler Community Coll., 1984—. Asst. editor newsletter Ft. Lee Officers' Wives' Club, 1984; editor Computer Club newsletter, Petersburg, 1985-86. Vol. ACS, Ft. Bragg, 1980-83, N.C. Tech. Inst., 1984, Ft. Lee, Va., 1984-86; chmn. vol. com. Army Community Service Annex, Ft. Lee, 1984-85; v.p. Downtown Petersburg, Inc., 1986-88. Mem. Hist. Petersburg Found., Dowtonw Petersburg, Inc. (v.p. 1986-88), Old Towne Merchants Assn. (v.p. 1986-87), Petersburg C. of C., Va. C. of C. Presbyterian. Home: 314-C Exchange Petersburg VA 23803 Office: Computer Works 314 Exchange Petersburg VA 23803

AMSTER, LINDA EVELYN, newspaper executive, consultant; b. N.Y.C., May 21, 1938; d. Abraham and Belle Shirley (Levine) Meyerson; m. Robert L. Amster, Feb. 18, 1961 (dec. Feb. 1974). B.A., U. Mich., 1960; M.L.S., Columbia U., 1968. Tchr. English Stamford High Sch., Conn., 1961-63; research librarian The Detroit News, 1965-67; research librarian The N.Y. Times, N.Y.C., 1967-69, supr. news research, 1969-74, news research mgr., 1974—; bd. dirs. Council for Career Planning, N.Y.C., 1982—. Contbr. articles to books, N.Y. Times and other publs. Mem. Spl. libraries Assn. Club: Coffee House. Home: 336 Central Park W New York NY 10025 Office: The NY Times 229 W 43d St New York NY 10036

AMUNDSON, EVA DONALDA, civic worker; b. Langdon, N.D., Apr. 23, 1911; d. Elmer Fritjof and Alma Julia (Nelson) Hultin; m. Leif Amundson, Mar. 1, 1929 (dec. 1974); children—Constance, Eleanor, Ardis, Priscilla. Bd. dirs. Opportunity Workshop, Missoula, Mont., 1950—, Rockmont Group Homes, Missoula, 1976—, Bethany L'Arche (group home for girls), 1976—; mem. Missoula Sr. Citizen's Ctr., 1980-82, pres., 1982-85; tchr. Norwegian cooking and baking, 1954-56, Norweigan Rosemaling, 1975-79; treas. Sacakawea Homemakers Club, 1979-81; mem. Am. Luth. Ch. Women St. Pauls' Lutheran Ch., 1951—; active Easter Seal Program, Heart Fund, March of Dimes, United Way, Campfire Girls; mem. adv. council Area Agy. on Aging, Missoula, 1984—. Recipient Outstanding Sr. award Missoula Jr. C. of C., 1984. Mem. Sons. of Norway. Club: Orchard Homes Country (mem. art judging com.). Lodges: Order of Eastern Star, Elks. Avocations: rosemaling; oil painting; poetry. Home: 324 Kensington Ave Missoula MT 59801

AMUSO, JEAN ELIZABETH FRANKEL, social services administrator; b. Brookville, Pa., Jan. 6, 1943; d. Joseph Louis Lackovic and Anita Elizabeth Walters Munson; m. Philip T. Amuso. BA, U. Tampa, 1965; MSW, Fla. State U., 1974. Social worker Dept. Pub. Welfare, Tampa, Fla., 1965-67; supr. Div. Family Services, Tampa, 1967-72, dist. supr. child support enforcement, 1974-76; dist. supr. client support Dept. Health and Rehab. Services, Tampa, 1976-85, dist. programs mgr., 1985—; vice chair program devel. com. Pvt. Industry Council, Tampa, 1981-84, 87; chairperson human services adv. com. Hillsborough Community Coll., 1981-85; MSW adv. com. U. South Fla., 1982—. Chairperson admissions com. United Way Greater Tampa, 1985—; adv. bd. Fla. Diagnostic Learning Resources Ctr., 1982—; bd. dirs. Edn. and Tng. Council, Tampa, 1981-84, Vol. Ctr. Hillsborough County, 1982—. Recipient Appreciation plaque Sch. Social Work U. South Fla., 1987. Mem. Nat. Assn. Female Execs., Bus. and Profl. Women, Athena Soc., Fla. Assn. Health and Social Services (pres. 1974-75), Zeta Tau Alpha Alumnae Assn. (pres. 1985-86). Home: 3418 Hunters Run Ln Tampa FL 33614 Office: Dept Health Rehab Services 4000 W Buffalo Ave Tampa FL 33614

AMYOTTE, SHERRY JO, chemical company technician; b. Grand Rapids, Mich., Jan. 22, 1956; d. George Alex and Joan Pauline (Harrison) A. BA in Biology, U. N.C., Charlotte, 1985. Lab. tech. U. N.C., Charlotte, 1983-85, research tech., 1985—; quality control tech. Unocal Chems.-Mallard Creek, Charlotte, 1986—. Contbr. articles to profl. jours. Mem. Am. Soc. Zoologists, N.C. Acad. Sci., Wilderness Soc. Democrat. Methodist. Club: Piedmont Adventure (Concord, N.C.). Lodge: Order Eastern Star. Home: 798 Davis St Concord NC 28025 Office: Unocal Chems Div 14800 Mallard Creek Rd Charlotte NC 28213

ANABLE, ANNE CURRIER STEINERT, journalist; b. Boston, Feb. 18; d. Robert Shuman and Lucy Pettingill (Currier) Steinert; grad. West Hill Jr. Coll., Boston, 1951; m. Anthony Anable, Jr., 1962 (div. 1965); m. Robert C. Henriques, 1973 (div. 1980). Reporter women's pages N.Y. Jour. Am., N.Y.C., 1961-66, World Jour. Tribune, N.Y.C., 1966-67; fashion editor Cleve. Plain Dealer, 1967-73; fashion and beauty editor New Woman mag., Ft. Lauderdale, Fla., 1973-75, 78-79; contbg. editor Conn. sect. N.Y. Times, 1977-81; beauty editor L'Officiel/USA, 1979, New Woman mag., 1982; fashion editor Am. Salon, 1984-87; contbg. editor Playbill, N.Y.C., 1985—, Harris Publs., 1987—. Recipient Fashion Reporting award N.Y., 1970. Mem. Soc. Profl. Journalists, Fashion Group, Fashion's Inner Circle. Home: 7 Flower Hill Pl Port Washington NY 11050

ANAGNOS, THALIA, civil engineering educator; b. Santa Monica, Calif., Nov. 20, 1956; d. Aris Anagnos and Lorraine (Pritchard) Oshins; m. Jeffrey Russell Koseff, July 4, 1986. BA, U. Calif., San Diego, 1979; MS, Stanford U., 1980, PhD, 1985. Asst. prof. dept. civil engring. San Jose (Calif.) U., 1984—. Contbr. articles to profl. jours. Mem. ASCE, Am. Seismol. Soc., Earthquake Engring. Research Inst., Structural Engrs. Soc. No. Calif., Soc. Women Engrs., Sigma Xi, Phi Kappa Phi. Office: San Jose State U Dept Civil Engring San Jose CA 95192-0082

ANAGNOST, MARIA ATHENA, surgeon; b. Chgo., Oct. 21, 1943; d. Themis John and Catherine (Cook) A.; B.A., Northwestern U., 1965; M.D., U. Ill., 1973. Resident in surgery U. Chgo. Hosps. and Clinics, 1973-74; gen. surgery resident Michael Reese Med. Center, Chgo., 1975-79, chief resident, 1979-80; practice medicine specializing in surgery; surg. staff Oak Park (Ill.) Hosp., Westlake Community Hosp., Melrose Park, Ill., Gottlieb Meml. Hosp., Melrose Park, St. Anne's Hosp., Chgo., St. Anne's Hosp. West (past sec.-treas.), Northlake, Ill., Good Samaritan Hosp., Downers Grove, Ill., Ravenswood Hosp. Chgo.; chmn. dept. surgery, mem. surg. staff Loretto Hosp. Chgo.Candidate for alderman, Chgo., 1964. Diplomate Nat. Bd. Med. Examiners; cert. Am. Bd. Surgery. Recipient Physicians' Recognition award AMA. Fellow ACS, Internat. Coll. Surgeons; (vice-regent); mem. AMA, Ill. Med. Soc., Chgo. Med. Soc., Am. Soc. Abdominal Surgeons, Hellenic Med. Soc., U. Ill. Alumni Assn., Northwestern U. Alumni Assn. Contbr. articles to profl. jours. Office: 1545 Clinton Pl River Forest IL 60305 also: 3825 Highland Ave Downers Grove IL 60515 also: 11 S LaSalle St Chicago IL 60603

ANANKO, JAIME ALLYN, nurse practitioner, health care consultant; b. Newark, Sept. 6, 1949; d. Stanley Thomas and Alexandria (Ananko) Chmielewski. A.A.S., County Coll. Morris, Randolph, N.J., 1975; B.S.N., Seton Hall U., 1977, M.S.N., 1979, with broadcast communications dept. Luzerne County Coll., Nanticoke, Pa., 1986—. Cert. nurse practitioner. ind. nurse practitioner, Wilkes-Barre, 1983—; primary health care cons.; free-lance indsl. video writer, editor, photographer; Robert Wood Johnson Found. trainee, 1978-79. Mem. Am. Assn. Critical Care Nurses, Am. Nurses Assn. (cert. adult nurse practitioner). Democrat. Roman Catholic. Office: PO Box 2016 Wilkes Barre PA 18703

ANASTASI, ANNE (MRS. JOHN PORTER FOLEY, JR.), psychology educator; b. N.Y.C., Dec. 19, 1908; d. Anthony and Theresa (Gaudiosi) A.; m. John Porter Foley, Jr., July 26, 1933. A.B., Barnard Coll., 1928; Ph.D., Columbia U., 1930; Litt.D. (hon.), U. Windsor, Can., 1967; Sc.D. (hon.), Cedar Crest Coll., 1971, La Salle Coll., 1979, Fordham U., 1979; Paed.D. (hon.), Villanova U., 1971. Instr. psychology Barnard Coll., N.Y.C., 1930-39; asst. prof., chmn. dept. Queens Coll., N.Y.C., 1939-46; assoc. prof. psychology Fordham U., N.Y.C., 1947-51; prof. Fordham U., 1951-79, prof. emeritus, 1979—, chmn. dept. psychology, 1968-74; mem. NRC, 1952-55; pres. Am. Psychol. Found., 1965-67. Author: Differential Psychology, 1937, rev. edit., 1949, 58, Psychological Testing, 1954, 6th edit., 1987, Fields of Applied Psychology, 1964, 2d edit., 1979; also articles in field.; editor: Individual Differences, 1965, Testing Problems in Perspective, 1966; Contributions to Differential Psychology, 1982. Recipient award for disting. service to measurement Ednl. Testing Service, 1977, award disting. contbns. to research Am. Ednl. Research Assn., 1983, Gold medal Am. Psychol. Found., 1984, Nat. Medal of Science, 1987. Mem. Am. Psychol. Assn. (rec. sec. 1952-55, pres. div. gen. psychology 1956-57, bd. dirs. 1956-59, 68-70, pres. div. evaluation and measurement 1965-66, pres. 1971-72, Disting. Sci. award 1981, E. L. Thorndike medal div. ednl. psychology 1984), Ea. Psychol. Assn. (pres. 1946-47, dir. 1948-50), Psychonomic Soc., Phi Beta Kappa, Sigma Xi.

ANASTOLE, DOROTHY JEAN, electronics company executive; b. Akron, Ohio, Mar. 26, 1932; d. Leonard L. and Helen (Sagedy) Dice; student De Anza Jr. Coll., Cupertino, Calif., spring 1969; children—Kally, Dennis, Christopher. Various secretarial positions in mfg., 1969-75; office mgr. Sci. Devices Co., Mountain View, Calif., 1975-76; exec. adminstrv. sec. corp. office Cezar Industries, Palo Alto, Calif., 1976-77; office and personnel mgr. AM Bruning Co., Mountain View, 1977-81; dir. employee relations Consol. Micrographics, Mountain View, 1981-83; personnel mgmt. cons., 1983-84; mgr. adminstrn./employee relations Mitsubishi Electronics Am., Inc., Sunnyvale, Calif., 1984—. Bd. dirs. Agnew State Hosp., San Jose, Calif., 1966-72, div. chmn. program mentally retarded, 1966-72, staff tutor, 1966-72. Recipient Service award Agnew State Hosp., 1972. Mem. Am. Soc. Profl. and Exec. Women, Am. Soc. Personnel Adminstrn. Office: Mitsubishi Electronics Am 1050 E Argues Ave Sunnyvale CA 94086

ANCELL, BARBARA BIBEN, public relations executive; b. Seneca Falls, N.Y., Feb. 26, 1943; d. David Hugh and Hilda (Zeitlin) Rubinstein; student Eastman Sch. Dental Hygiene, 1961-63; m. Nathan S. Ancell, Nov. 3, 1984; children—Matthew Lee Biben, Douglas Ross Biben. Dir. Germanow Art Gallery, Rochester, N.Y., 1973-75; free-lance artist, Rochester, 1972-80; producer-host Pub. TV Arts Show, Rochester, 1977; pub. service mgr. Gannett Rochester Newspapers, 1978, dir. public service and promotion, 1979-84, mgr. community relations, 1984-85 ; pres. Ancell Assocs.; mem. N.Y. State Pubs. Newspaper in Edn. Commn., 1979-82. Bd. dirs. United Way, 1980-86 ; Rochester Bus. Opportunities, 1979-83, GEVA Theatre, 1979-85; v.p. Lend-A-Hand Charity; mem. Monroe Community Coll. Advisory Com., for Community Services, 1980—; dir. Ad Council, 1980-85; bd. dirs. Jr. League, 1976-78, Arts for Greater Rochester, 1980-86, Women's Career Ctr., 1978-80, Ctr. Ednl. Devel., 1985-86; campaign mgr. Robert L. Dey for N.Y. State Senate, 1978; bd. dirs. Bus. Commn. ; commr. Brighton Cable Commn.; bd. dirs. Highland Hosp., chmn. Women's Health Source Adv. Bd. Recipient Lantern award for pub. service, Nat. Frank Trip award for pub. service. Mem. Internat. Newspaper Promotion Assn. (pres. Eastern region), Women in Communication (dir.), Greater Rochester Women's Fund Adv. Bd., (hon. lifetime mem.) Advt. Council. Home: 110 Runnymede Rd Rochester NY 14618

ANCKER, CAROLYN ROSE, real estate sales associate, community service volunteer; b. Phila., Nov. 4, 1919; d. Laurence Loeb and Theresa (Rothenberg) A. BA, Randolph-Macon Woman's Coll., Lynchburg, Va., 1941. Receptionist, Travelers Aid Soc., Phila., 1946; exec. sec. Women's com. Red Cross Drive, Phila., 1947; sales assoc. John J. McGroarty, Elkins Park, Pa., 1952-56, Century 21 Langsdorf-Adler, Elkins Park, 1977-87, Century-21 Einhorn-Adler, 1987—. Pa. rep. U.S. Com. for UNICEF; v.p. spl. events Greater Phila. Area Com. for UNICEF; vice chmn. spl. gifts United Way; sec., membership campaign chmn. disaster blood services Am. Red Cross; mem. Southeastern Pa. Chpt. Bd. Am. Red Cross; exec. com. mem., chmn. vols. Friends of Scheie Eye Inst., 1972—; bd. dirs., chmn. inter-faith com. Keneseth Israel Sisterhood, 1986—; chmn. scholarship benefit Beaver Coll., 1987—, exec. com. mem., sec. women's bd., v.p., 1987—; pres. Phila. Fed. of Women's Clubs and Allied Orgns., Inc., 1984-86; v.p. membership Women for Greater Phila., 1977—, chmn. women's history week opening, 1987, chmn. hostesses for We The People-200 events, 1987—; v.p. Citizen's Action for Better TV, 1985—; mem. World Affairs Council; mem. women's leadership bd. Fedn. Jewish Agys. Mem. AAUW (bd. dirs. Phila. br., pres. Phila. br. 1960-62, program chmn. ednl. found. 1987—, Outstanding Woman award 1987, Pa. state chmn. nat. hdqrs. bldg. fund 1958-62, internat. fellow 1962, del. to nat. conv. 1987), Ea. Montgomery County Bd. Realtors, Nat. Assn. Realtors (women's council realtors), Pa. Assn. for Voluntarism (conf. com. 1987), Phila. Art Alliance, Friends Independence Nat. Hist. Park (various coms.), Colonial Phila. Hist. Soc. (bd. dirs.), Phila. Mus. Art, Pa. Acad. Fine Arts, Phila. Orch. Soc. (Old York Rd. com. 1980—, past treas.), Cheltenham Twp. Hist. Commn., Randolph Macon Woman's Coll. Alumnae Assn. (1st v.p. 1966-69), Republican. Clubs: Philmont Country, Altrusa (pres. 1976-78, exec. com. 1987—) (Phila.).

ANCKER-JOHNSON, BETSY, physicist, automotive company executive; b. St. Louis, Apr. 29, 1927; d. Clinton James and Fern (Lalan) A.; m. Harold Hunt Johnson, Mar. 15, 1958; children: Ruth P. Johnson, David H. Johnson, Paul A. Johnson, Martha H. Johnson. B.A. in Physics with high honors (Pendleton scholar), Wellesley Coll., 1949; Ph.D. magna cum laude, U. Tuebingen, Germany, 1953; D.Sc. (hon.), Poly. Inst. N.Y., 1979, Trinity Coll., 1981, U. So. Calif., 1984, Alverno Coll., 1984; LL.D. (hon.), Bates Coll., 1980. Instr., jr. research physicist U. Calif., 1953-54; physicist Sylvania Microwave Physics Lab., 1956-58; mem. tech. staff RCA Labs., 1958-61; research specialist Boeing Co., 1961-70, exec., 1970-73; asst. sec. commerce for sci. and tech. 1973-77; dir. phys. research Argonne Nat. Lab., Ill., 1977-79; v.p. environ. activities staff Gen. Motors Tech. Center, Warren, Mich., 1979—; affiliate prof. elec. engring. U. Wash., 1964-73; dir. Gen. Mills; mem. Energy Research Adv. Bd. Dept. Energy. Author over 70 sci. papers; patentee in field. Mem. staff Inter-Varsity Christian Fellowship, 1954-56; mem. visiting com. elec. and computer div. MIT, U. Wash.; mem. bd. visitors Oakland U., Dept. Def. Sci. Bd.; mem. adv. bd. Stanford U. Sch. Engring., Fla. State U., Fla. A&M U., Congrl. Caucus for Sci. and Tech.; trustee Wellesley Coll., 1972-77. AAUW fellow, 1950-51; Horton Hollowell fellow, 1951-52; NSF grantee, 1967-72. Fellow Am. Phys. Soc. (councillor-at-large 1973-76), IEEE, AAAS; mem. Nat. Acad. Engring., World Environ. Ctr., Air Pollution Control Assn., Soc. Automotive Engrs. (bd. dirs. 1979-81), Phi Beta Kappa, Sigma Xi. Office: Gen Motors Corp Environ Activities Staff 30400 Mound Rd Warren MI 48090-9015

ANCTIL, JOANNE CAMERON, reading consultant, coordinator; b. Manchester, N.H., Nov. 22, 1947; d. John and Anna Francis (Annis) Cameron; m. Gerard Roger Anctil; June 24, 1967; children: Jennifer, John. BS in Edn., U. Lowell, 1969, MEd in Reading and Lang., 1984. Tchr. elem. sch. Nashua (N.H.) Sch. Dist., 1969-75, tchr. remedial reading, 1975-84, reading specialist, 1984-86; reading cons. Amherst (N.H.) Supervisory Union, 1986—; tchr. remedial reading Title I Summer Sch., Nashua, 1966-74; facilitator Jr. Great Books, Amherst and Nashua, 1985—; chairperson Young Author's Program, Nashua, 1984-86, Spring Fling Week, Nashua, 1986, I Love to Read and Write, Amherst, 1987. Author lit. guides Anctil's Literature Packets, 1987. Mem. child care com. Bd. of Christian Edn. First Ch., Nashua, 1985—; chairperson Ann. Ch. Fair Children's Toy Room First Ch., Nashua, 1983—. Mem. Internat. Reading Assn., New Eng. Reading Assn., Granite State Reading Council. Rockhill Reading Council (publicity chairperson 1978-80), Pi Lambda Theta. Republican. Office: Amherst Sch Dist Wilkins Sch Boston Post Rd Amherst NH 03031

ANDERA, KATHERINE ANNE, county government official; b. San Antonio, Nov. 11, 1949; d. Joseph John and Amira (Andary) A. B in Bus.,

U. Tex., 1975. Dep. assessor Bexar County Tax Office, San Antonio, 1973-74, supr., 1974-76, mgr., 1976-80; mgr. records Bexar Appraisal Dist., San Antonio, 1981—. Active Tex. Folklife Festival, San Antonio, 1971—, League of United Latin Am. Council, San Antonio, 1985; bd. dirs. Nat. Apostolate of Maronites, N.Y.C., 1984—. Mem. Am. Records Mgmt., Bus. Forms Mgmt., Tex. Assn. Assessing Officers. Maronite Catholic. Club: AMELEB (San Antonio). Office: Bexar Appraisal Dist 535 S Main San Antonio TX 78204

ANDERS, BARBARA LYNNE, lyric soprano; b. Jackson, Miss., Sept. 4, 1938; d. William Reid Gainey and Eunice Jeannette (Simmons) Gainey-Ferguson; m. Dan Raney Anders, Mar. 9, 1957; children: Melissa Lynne Dickers, Laurie Nan Anders Campbell. Student Belhaven Coll., 1956-57. Appeared as Marsinah in Kismet at Am. Light Opera Co., Washington, 1967; with opera chorus Washington Opera, 1971-78, Wolf Trap Opera Co., Vienna, Va., 1972-79; appeared at Kennedy Ctr., Washington, 1981, Piccolo Spoleto Festival, Charleston, S.C., 1981; soloist with numerous coll. performances, nationwide; rep. People to People Goodwill Tour, Nat. Music Council, Scandinavia and USSR. Rec. soloist Golden Age Rec., 1978. Pres. Am. Opera Scholarship Soc., Washington, 1980-81, Friday Morning Music Club, Washington, 1983-84, performed at the 12th Internat. Biog. Congress, Budapest, Hungary, 1985. Mem. Internat. Platform Assn., Nat. Fedn. Music Clubs (nat. opera chmn. 1983-87, Marie Morrisey Keith Vocal award 1956), D.C. Fedn. Music Clubs (chairperson jr. festivals 1977-78, pres. 1978-80), Am. Guild Mus. Artists, Internat. League Women Composers, Nat. Alliance of Profl. and Exec. Women's Network, Delta Omicron.

ANDERS, SUSAN BETH, accountant; b. Toledo, Nov. 1, 1956; d. Hal Frederick and Janet Agnes (Jacobs) Anders. B.B.A., So. Methodist U., 1978; M.S., North Tex. State U., 1986. C.P.A., Tex. Staff acct. Philip Vogel & Co., Dallas, 1978-80, Sharp, Bausch & Co., Dallas, 1980-83, Dohm & Wolff, Dallas, 1984-87, Touche Ross & Co., 1987—. Nat. Merit scholar, Roper Corp., 1974-78; recipient Sr. award in acctg., So. Methodist U., 1978. Mem. Am. Inst. C.P.A.s, Tex. Soc. C.P.A.s, Am. Women's Soc. C.P.A.s, Beta Alpha Psi, Beta Gamma Sigma. Republican. United Methodist. Clubs: Am. Mensa Ltd., Intertel. Home: 7340 Skillman #1114 Dallas TX 75231 Office: Touche Ross & Co 2001 Bryan Tower Suite 2400 Dallas TX 75201

ANDERSEN, CAROLYN ANNETTE PEREZ, marketing consulting company executive; b. Winthrop, Mass., June 12, 1948; d. Antonio Fernandez Perez and Priscilla Carolyn (Willson) Perez Logan; m. Gary Howard Andersen, Apr. 23, 1977; 1 child, Metian Allana. BA, Winthrop Coll., 1969; JD, U. Puget Sound, 1980. Prodn. asst. J. Ned Block Prodns., Seattle, 1970-72; mktg. analyst, v.p. Ilium Assocs., Inc., Seattle, 1972-80; chief exec. officer Ilium Assocs., Inc., Bellevue, Wash., 1980—; sec. Forum Communications, Inc., Bellevue, 1980—. Mem. Nat. Assn. Female Execs., Phi Delta Phi. Office: Ilium Assocs Inc 500-108th Ave NE Suite 2450 Bellevue WA 98004

ANDERSEN, DORIS EVELYN, real estate broker; b. Christian County, Ky., Oct. 30, 1923; d. William Earl and Blanche Elma (Withers) Johnston; m. Roger Lewis Shirk, July 9, 1944 (div. 1946); 1 child, Vicki Lee Shirk Sanderson; m. DeLaire Andersen, July 6, 1946; children: Craig Bryant, Karen Rae, Kent DeLaire, Chris Jay, Mardi Lynn. Diploma, South Bend Coll. Commerce, 1942; diploma in banking Notre Dame U., 1946; student Ind. U., 1942-44. Tng. dir. First Nat. Bank, Portland, Oreg., 1963-69; assoc. broker Stan Wiley, Inc., Portland, 1969-79; prin. Doris Andersen & Assocs., Portland, 1979—; speaker at seminars; mem. Gov.'s Task Force Council on Housing, Salem, Oreg., 1985-86. Contbr. articles to profl. jours. Mem. task force Oreg. Dept. Energy, Salem, 1984-85. Mem. Nat. Assn. Realtors (dir. 1983—, regional v.p. Northwest region 1988), Oreg. Assn. Realtors (dir. 1979—, pres. 1986—), Portland Bd. Realtors (pres. 1982), Women's Council Realtors (local pres. 1977, state pres. 1978, gov. nat. orgn. 1979), Internat. Platform Assn., Internat. Biog. Assn. Avocations: reading, travel. Home and Office: PO Box 1169 Shady Cove OR 97539

ANDERSEN, MARIANNE SINGER, clinical psychologist; b. Baden nr. Vienna, Austria, June 18, 1930; came to U.S., 1940, naturalized, 1946; d. Richard L. and Jolanthe (Garda) Singer; 1 son, Richard Esten. BA, CUNY, 1950, MA, 1974; PhD, Fla. Inst. Tech., 1980. Book editor specializing in psychology and psychiatry various pub. firms including W.W. Norton Co., Sterling Pub. Co., E.P. Dutton Co., N.Y.C., 1950-71; research assoc. Inst. for Research in Hypnosis, N.Y.C., 1974-76, fellow in clin. hypnosis, 1976, dir. seminars, 1978-82, dir. edn., 1982—; psychotherapist specializing in hypnotherapy Morton Prince Ctr. for Hypnotherapy, 1976—, dir. weight control clinic, 1980—, dir. clin. services, 1981-82; dir. adminstrn. Internat. Grad. U., N.Y.C., 1974-77; pvt. practice psychotherapy, 1977—; adminstrv. coordinator Internat. Grad. Sch. Behavior Sci., Fla. Inst. Tech., 1978; co-dir. The Melbourne Group, 1983—; lectr. hypnosis and hypnotherapy to mental and phys. health profls., 1977—. Author: (with Louis Savary) Passages: A Guide for Pilgrims of the Mind, 1972; research on treatment obesity with hypnotherapy. Mem. Soc. for Clin. and Exptl. Hypnosis, Internat. Soc. for Clin. and Exptl. Hypnosis, Am. Psychol. Assn., Am. Soc. Bariatric Physicians (affiliate), N.Y. Acad. Scis.

ANDERSON, ALICE MACLAREN, writer; b. Worcester, Mass., Jan. 18, 1938; d. Edward Wallace and Phyllis A. (Batcheller) MacLaren; m. Donald M. Anderson, Dec. 15, 1956 (dec. June 1977); children: Julie T. Fournier, Cathie Jeanne, Jonathan D. Student, Framingham Tchrs. Coll., 1955-58; student in English and journalism, Clark U., 1968, Brown U., 1972; student in travel and tourism, Quinsigamond Community Coll., 1986-87. Journalist Worcester Telegram and Evening Gazette, Worcester, 1955—. Recipient Outstanding Journalism and Responsible Pub. Community Service award Gen. Fedn. Women's Clubs and Whitinsville Woman's Club, 1976, Feature Writing award New Eng. Associated Press News Execs. Assn., 1986. Club: Sutton (Mass.) Young Women's. Home: 65 Hartness Rd Sutton MA 01527 Office: Worcester Telegram and Evening Gazette 20 Franklin St Worcester MA 01608

ANDERSON, ALLAMAY EUDORIS, health educator, home economist; b. N.Y.C., July 18, 1933; d. John Samuel and Charlotte Jane (Harrigan) Richardson; B.A., Queens Coll., CUNY, 1975; profl. mgmt. cert. Adelphi U., 1978; M.S. in Edn., Fordham U., 1984; m. Edgar Leopold Anderson, Jr., Apr. 14, 1957; 1 son, David Lancelot. Mem. staff sch. food service, dietitian Bd. Edn., N.Y.C., 1968-88; tchr. home econs., Louis Armstrong Middle Sch., 1988—. profl. devel. cons., N.Y.C., 1978—; ptnr. Masiba Bldg. Corp., Corona, N.Y., 1975-82; adj. lectr. Home Econs. Queens Coll., 1987. Devel. coordinator League for Better Community Life, Inc., 1977—, treas. exec. bd., 1970-76; officer N.Y.C. Community Devel. Agy., 1980-83; mem. adv. council home econs. dept. Queens Coll.; mem. Kwanzaa Adv. Com. (P.R.) Urban Coalition, 1983; vestry mem. youth ministries Grace Episcopalian Ch., 1982—. Mem. NAACP, Nat. Soc. Fund Raising Execs., Langston Hughes Library Action Com. (bd. dirs. 1987—, treas. 1988), Queens Coll. Home Econs. Alumni Assn. (v.p., chmn. bylaws com. 1982), Assn. Supervision and Curriculum Devel. Office: 100-13 34th Ave Corona NY 11368

ANDERSON, ANNELISE GRAEBNER, economist; b. Oklahoma City, Nov. 19, 1938; d. Elmer and Dorothy (Zilisch) Graebner; m. Martin Anderson, Sept. 25, 1965. B.A., Wellesley Coll., 1960; M.A., Columbia U., 1965, Ph.D., 1974. Assoc. editor McKinsey and Co., Inc., 1963-65; researcher Nixon Campaign Staff, 1968-69; project mgr. Dept. Justice, 1970-71; assoc. dir. U.S. Office Mgmt. and Budget, Washington, 1981-83; from asst. prof. bus. adminstrn. to assoc. prof. Calif. State U.-Hayward, 1975-80; sr. policy adviser Reagan Presdl. campaign and transition, Washington, 1980; assoc. dir. econs. and govt. Office Mgmt. and Budget, Washington, 1981-83; sr. research fellow Hoover Instn., Stanford U., Calif., 1983—; mem. Nat. Sci. Bd., 1985—; bd. dirs. Fin. Corp. Am. Author: The Business of Organized Crime: A Cosa Nostra Family, 1979, Illegal Alines and Employer Sanctions: Solving the Wrong Problem, 1986; contbr. articles to profl. jours., chpts. to books. Mem. bd. overseers Rand/UCLA Ctr. for Study Soviet Internat. Behavior, Los Angeles, 1987—. Mem. Am. Econ. Assn., Western Econ. Assn., Beta Gamma Sigma. Office: Stanford U Hoover Instn Stanford CA 94305-6010

ANDERSON, BETH, composer; b. N.Y.C., Jan. 3, 1950; d. Sydney Hart and Marjorie Celeste (Hoskins) A.; m. Michael Scott Cooper, June 27, 1976 (div. Mar. 1978). Student, U. Ky., 1966-68; BA in Music, U. Calif., Davis, 1971; MFA in Piano Performance, Mills Coll., 1973, MA in Composition, 1974; postgrad. NYU, 1977-78. Cert. music tchr., N.Y., Ky.; cert. coll. instr., Calif. Instr. Coll. New Rochelle, N.Y., 1970-86; accompanist schs., colls. Composer: (quartet) Skaters' Suite, 1980, The Eighth Ancestor, 1980; (voice and piano) Twinkle Tonight, 1980, Womanrite, 1980, Time Stands Still, 1980, Beauty Runs Faster, 1980; (film score) World Honeymoon, 1980; (radio) Poetry Is Music, 1980; Revel, 1984, (orchestral) Pennyroyal Swale, 1985, (string quartetes) Rosemary Swale, 1986, others. Mem. Am. Composers Alliance (bd. dirs., admissions com.), Broadcast Musicians Inc., Poets and Writers, League Women Composers, Am. Music Ctr. Home: 26 2d Ave #2B New York NY 10003

ANDERSON, CAROL, banker; b. Boston, Feb. 15, 1946; d. John Daniel and Mary (Esther) Wentworth; m. Stephen D. Anderson, June 4, 1966; 1 child, Kim Marie. Student, Bridgewater (Mass.) State Coll., 1963-66, Mass. Bay Community Coll., 1985—. With acctg. dept. Reed & Barton, Taunton, Mass., 1966-69; from teller to v.p. Bank of Taunton, 1970—; past pres. Credit Profls., Brockton, Mass., 1981-83. Bd. dirs. Taunton United Way, 1986. Mem. Inst. Fin. Edn. (v.p. 1984—). Roman Catholic. Clubs: Young Execs. (Boston); Easton (Mass.) Country. Home: 227 King St Raynham MA 02767 Office: Bank of Taunton 33 Weir St Box 791 Taunton MA 02780

ANDERSON, CAROL ELAINE, elementary educator, resource specialist; b. Genoa, Colo., May 21, 1933; d. Owen Henderson and Ruth (Bruch) Self; m. Kenneth Lee Anderson, Mar. 21, 1959; children: Kelly Lea Anderson Salery, Charles Anthony. AA, Graceland Coll, Lamoni, Iowa, 1951-53; BA, No. Colo. U., 1957-60; MA, Calif. State U., Hayward, 1977. Cert. tchr., Calif. Jr. high tchr. Denair (Calif.) Unified Sch. Dist., 1962-64; elem. tchr. Modesto (Calif.) City Schs., 1967-76, resource specialist, spl. day class tchr., 1977-81, counselor Alternat Sch., 1988—; head tchr. Fairview Elem. Sch., Modesto, 1978-80. Mem. Modesto LWV, 1982—. Mem. Council for Exceptional Children (sec. 1986-87), Stanislaus County Assn. Resource Specialists (v.p. 1986-87, pres.1987—), Modesto Tchrs. Assn. (state council rep. 1975-76, 2d v.p. 1986-87). Democrat. Mem. Reorganized Ch. of Jesus Christ of Latter Day Saints. Home: 1111 Wellesley Ave Modesto CA 95350

ANDERSON, CAROL JUNE, systems analyst; b. Milw., Dec. 14, 1942; d. George Walter and Juanita June (Albers) A.; m. Frederick C. Haberland, May 4, 1963 (div. Apr. 1973); children: Christina Louise Haberland, Heather Noel Haberland; m. Kenneth James Ryan, Oct. 5, 1984. Student, Ripon Coll., 1962-63, Boston Coll., 1973-74; BA in Applied Behav. Scis., Nat. Coll. Edn., McLean, Va., 1987. Sec. Corning Med., Medfield, Mass., 1972-76, supr. word processing, 1976-77; customer support rep. Itek Graphic Products, Waltham, Mass., 1977-78; sr. market support rep. Micom Data Systems, Inc., Boston, 1978-79, sales rep., 1979-80; supr. word processing Fidelity Data Systems, Inc., Boston, 1981-82; methods analyst Arkwright-Boston Ins. Co., Waltham, 1982-83; gen. mgr. WordSystems, Inc., Washington, 1983-84; sr. analyst ASI Systems Internat., Falls Church, Va., 1984—; guest lectr. Johnston-Wales Coll., Providence, 1975; instr. Needham (Mass.) Adult Edn., 1981-83; mem. adv. com. Occupational Career Edn., Needham, 1982-83. Bd. dirs. Needham Theater Group, 1981-83. Mem. Assn. Info. Systems Profls. (bd. dirs. 1981-83), Women in Info. Processing, DAR. Home: 5300 Holmes Run Pkwy #1516 Alexandria VA 22304 Office: ASI Systems Internat 520 N Washington St Falls Church VA 22046

ANDERSON, CAROL MCMILLAN, lawyer; b. Malone, Fla., Aug. 7, 1938; d. Fillmore Allen and Ernestine (Dickson) McMillan; m. Philip Sloan Anderson, Oct. 9, 1965; 1 child, Courtney Beth. BS, Fla. Atlantic U., 1969; JD, Cumberland Sch. Law, 1971. Bar: Fla. 1971. Asst. U.S. atty. Office of U.S. Atty., Miami, Fla., 1971-74; ptnr. Anderson & Anderson, Ft. Lauderdale, Fla. 1974—; mem. jud. nominating com. 4th dist. ct. appeals, 1987—. Pres. Hospice Hundred, 1988—; mem. Thousand Plus, Mus. Art; bd. dirs. Ft. Lauderdale Philharm. Soc.; asst. sec., trustee Royal Dames Cancer Research. Recipient Alumnae Achievement award Katharine Gibbs Sch., Boston, 1973. Mem. ABA, Assn. Trial Lawyers Am., Fed. Bar Assn., Fla. Assn. Trial Lawyers, Fla. Bar, Broward County Bar Assn., Broward County Women Lawyers (v.p. 1981), Gold Circle Nova U. Presbyterian. Clubs: 110 Tower, Coral Ridge Yacht. Home: 32 Isla Bahia Dr Fort Lauderdale FL 33316 Office: Anderson & Anderson PA 1313 S Andrews Ave Fort Lauderdale FL 33316

ANDERSON, CAROLE ANN, educator; b. Chgo., Feb. 21, 1938; m. Clark Anderson, Feb. 14, 1973; 1 child, Julie. Diploma, St. Francis Hosp., 1958; BS, U. Colo., 1962, MS, 1963, PhD, 1977. Group psychotherapist Dept. Vocat. Rehab., Denver, 1963-72; psychotherapist Prof. Psychiatry and Guidance Clinic, Denver, 1970-71; asst. prof., chmn. nursing sch. U. Colo., Denver, 1971-75; therapist, coordinator The Genessee Mental Health, Rochester, N.Y., 1977-78; assoc. dean U. Rochester, N.Y., 78-86; dean, prof.coll. of nursing Ohio State U., Columbus, 1986—; lectr. nursing sch. U. Colo., Denver, 1970-71; cons. The Piton Found., Denver, 1977; prin. investigator biomed. research support grant, 1986, clin. research facilitation grant, 1981-82; program dir. profl. nurse traineeship, 1978-86, advanced nurse tng. grant, 1982-85. Author: (with others) Women as Victims, 1986, Violence Toward Women, 1982, Substance Abuse of Women, 1982. Pres., bd. dirs. Health Assn., Rochester, 1984-86; mem. north sub area council Finger Lakes Health Systems Agy., 1983-86, longrange planning com., 1981-82. Am. Acad. Nursing fellow. Mem. Am. Sociological Assn., Am. Nurses Assn., Ohio Nurses Assn., Sigma Theta Tau. Home: 406 West Sixth Ave Columbus OH 43201 Office: Ohio State Univ Coll of Nursing 1585 Neil Ave Columbus OH 43210

ANDERSON, CAROLE LEWIS, investment banker; b. East Stroudsburg, Pa., Oct. 7, 1944; d. William A. and Rosamonde (Lewis) A.; m. John Mason Lee Sweet, Apr. 9, 1983; children: John Mason Lee Anderson-Sweet, Dunn Lewis Anderson-Sweet. B.A. in Polit. Sci., Pa State U., 1966; M.B.A. in Fin., NYU, 1976. Securities analyst PaineWebber, Jackson & Curtis, N.Y.C., 1971-73, assoc. v.p., 1973-75, v.p. research, 1975-77; v.p. PaineWebber, Inc., N.Y.C., 1977-82, mng. dir., 1982-85; sr. v.p. corp. devel. Hasbro, Inc., N.Y.C., 1985-87; also dir. Hasbro, Inc., Pawtucket, R.I.; mng. dir. Md. Nat. Investment Banking Co., Washington, 1987-88, pres., chief exec. officer, 1988—; bd. dirs. Master Media Ltd., Forum for Women Dirs., N.Y.C. County com. person Democratic Party, Manhattan, N.Y., 1975-82; chmn. Hasbro Children's Found., 1985-87, exec. com. and trustee, 1985—; mem. N.Y. com. U.S. Commn. on Civil Rights, 1980-84; trustee Mary Baldwin Coll., Staunton, Va., 1987—, Penn State Alumni Council, 1987—. Named to Acad. Women Achievers, YWCA, N.Y.C., 1982; recipient Disting. Alumna award Pa. State U., 1987. Mem. N.Y. Soc. Security Analysts, Pa. State U. Alumni Council. Office: Md Nat Investment Banking Co 7474 Greenway Ctr Dr Greenbelt MD 20770

ANDERSON, CAROLYN JOYCE, business development executive; b. Mishawaka, Ind., Mar. 14, 1947; d. Ebon Clayton and Maxine Ruth (Haag) Angel; m. Thomas Anderson (dec.); children: Charmien, Andrew, Paul. BS in Bus., Ind. U., 1978. CPA, Ind. Staff acct. Holdeman, Fulmer and Chiddister CPA's, Elkhart, Ind., 1974-78; comml. lender Midwest Commerce Bank, Elkhart, 1978-81; corp. controller Bivouac Industries, Inc., Vandalia, Mich., 1981-84; dir. Small Bus. Devel. Ctr., South Bend, Ind., 1984—. Methodist. Lodge: Kiwanis. Office: Small Bus Devel Ctr 300 N Michigan South Bend IN 46601

ANDERSON, CATHERINE J(EAN), sales representative; b. Cleve., Aug. 8, 1952; d. John Joseph and Edith Mary (De French) Corrado; m. Donald R. Anderson, Sept. 18, 1982 (Dec. 1984). BA, U. Toledo, 1974. Asst. pub. relations dir. Toldeo Area C. of C., 1974-75; pub. and employee info. coordinator The Andersons, Maumee, Ohio, 1975-77; realtor, assoc. owner Century 21 Embassy, Toledo, 1977-81; pub. relations and mktg. dir. Bostleman Corp., Toledo, 1981-82; v.p. Anderson Tool & Machine Co., Toledo, 1982-85; acct. exec. Amerestate, Inc., Cin., 1985-87; sales rep. Nestlé-Beich, Bloomington, Ill., 1987—. Author: Style Book (Toledo area C. of C.), 1975; designer brochure Jr. Achievement of N.W. Ohio. Mem. Toledo Opera Guild. Mem. Press Club of Toledo. Republican. Roman Catholic. Home: 6808 Woodlake Dr Toledo OH 43617 Office: Nestlé-Beich 101 S Lumber St Bloomington IL 61701

ANDERSON, CHERYL, government affairs adviser; b. Camp Campbell, Ky.; d. Edward Gustav and Virginia Leona (Case) A.; B.A., U. Wash., 1969; m. Richard T. Ney, July 4, 1975; children—Alexander Case, Justin Anderson. Asst. press sec. Senator Warren G. Magnuson, Washington, 1969-71; parliamentarian officer Australian Senate, Canberra, Australia, 1971-72; administrv. asst. Richard Ney Assocs., Inc., Washington, 1972-73, account rep., 1973-74, v.p., 1974—, sec., dir., v.p. Advocacy Internat. Ltd., Washington, 1977—; dir. Bellhouse Med., Inc., Washington, 1986-87; mgr. Haemonetics Corp., Braintree, Mass., 1987-88; prin. assoc. Advocacy Services Group, Washington, 1988—. Contbr. articles to profl. jours. Mem. Am. Assn. Med. Instrumentation, Am. Assn. of Blood Banks, Regulatory Affairs Profls. Assn. Home: 5121 Yuma St NW Washington DC 20016 Office: Advocacy Internat Ltd 1825 Eye St NW Suite 400 Washington DC 20006

ANDERSON, CHRISTINE PIDGEON, engineering manager; b. St. Louis, Sept. 26, 1955; d. Vernon Wesley and Norma Jane (Adams) Pidgeon; m. Wayne Michael Anderson, Feb. 18, 1955; 1 child, Heather Michelle. BS, Duke U., 1976; M Engring., U. Va., 1979, PhD, 1982. Design engr. Intermedics, Inc., Freeport, Tex., 1981-84, program mgr., 1984—. Contbr. articles to profl. jours.; inventor in field. U. Va. fellow, 1976-79. Mem. IEEE, Project Mgmt. Inst. Democrat. Methodist. Home: 20 Holly Chase Richwood TX 77531 Office: Intermedics Inc PO Box 617 Freeport TX 77541

ANDERSON, CLAUDIA SMITH, lawyer; b. Peoria, Ill., Mar. 21, 1953; d. Lester Berry and June Edda (Kopal) Smith; m. Curtis A. Anderson, Aug. 26, 1972. Student, Stephens Coll., 1971-72; BS in Elem. Edn., Rockford Coll., 1976; JD cum laude, Gonzaga U., 1979. Bar: Ill. 1979, U.S. dist. ct. (cen. dist.) Ill. 1980. Assoc. Acton, Acton, Meyer & Smith, Danville, Ill., 1979-83; ptnr. Acton, Meyer, Smith, Miller & Anderson, Danville, 1984-86, Anderson & Anderson, 1987—. Apptd. mem. Danville Plan Commn., 1984—; bd. dirs. YWCA, Danville, 1984—; adv. bd. dirs. St. Elizabeth Hosp., 1987—. Recipient Am. Jurisprudence award, 1979. Mem. AAUW (life), Ill. Bar Assn., Vermilion County Bar Assn. (pub. relations chmn. 1984—), Assn. Trial Lawyers Am., Ill. Trial Lawyers Assn., Danville C. of C. (bd. dirs. 1984—), DAR. Republican. Roman Catholic. Club: Executive (Danville) (pres. 1981-82). Office: 923 N Vermilion St Danville IL 61832

ANDERSON, CYNTHIA ELAINE, account administrator; b. Waco, Tex., Feb. 8, 1958; d. Elroy and Catherine Elizabeth Danforth; 1 child, Cheree LaShaun. Student, Tex. Women's U., 1981. Acctg. administr. IBM Corp., Dallas. Math tutor Community Service, Dallas, 1983—; vol. Community in Schs. Program, Dallas, 1984—. Mem. Nat. Assn. Female Execs. Club: IBM Running (treas.). Home: 4817 N O'Connor #334 Las Colinas TX 75062 Office: IBM Corp 1605 LBJ Freeway Dallas TX 75234

ANDERSON, CYNTHIA FINKBEINER SJOBERG, speech and language pathologist; b. Hastings, Mich., Dec. 7, 1949; d. Charles Lavern and Lois Mae (Kenyon) Finkbeiner; m. Peter Carl Sjoberg, Sept. 6, 1974 (div. Dec. 1981); 1 child, Hilary Kenyon; m. Donald Anderson, Sept. 16, 1985. BS, Western Mich. U., 1972, MA, 1974. Dir. speech Hackley Hosp., Muskegon, Mich., 1974-75; speech pathologist Grand Haven Pub. Schs., Mich., 1975—; dir. Ambucs Summer Lang. Clinic, Grand Haven, 1984—. Creator summer lang. program. Pres. Kiddie Carousel, Grand Haven, 1983-86; Stephen minister Christ Community Ch., Spring Lake, Mich., 1984—, elder, 1986—; big sister Grand Haven, 1975-80. Named Ambucs Nat. Therapist of Yr., 1985; recipient Excellence in Service award Grand Haven Pub. Schs., 1987. Mem. Am. Speech/Hearing/Lang. Assn. (cert.). Democrat. Home: 2102 Jane Ct Grand Haven MI 49417 Office: Grand Haven Pub Schs 1415 Beechtree Grand Haven MI 49417

ANDERSON, DAUN ROBIN, computer professional; b. Winchester, Mass., Oct. 15, 1950; d. Ernest Lawrence and Muryle Caroline (Sandgren) A. BA in Modern Langs., Coll. William and Mary, 1972; MA in French, Pa. State U., 1975; MBA, Boston Coll., 1987. Teaching asst. Pa. State U., 1972-73; info. analyst to tech. research analyst GTE Labs., Waltham, Mass., 1977-80; software specialist Comml. Union Assurance Cos., Boston, 1980-81; systems engr. Nixdorf Computer Corp., Waltham, Mass., 1981-83; sr. hardware communications analyst Cullinet Software, Westwood, Mass., 1983-87, project leader network services, mgr. network services, 1986-87; program mgr. Wang Labs. Inc., Lowell, Mass., 1987—. Mem. Assn. Systems Mgmt., Am. Mgmt. Assn. Home: 126 Windsor Rd Waban MA 02168

ANDERSON, DEBORAH GAIL COOK, educator; b. San Antonio, Dec. 26, 1956; d. Clarence Edward and Dorothy Mae (Colvin) Cook; m. Dwight Edward Anderson, June 22, 1980 (div. Sept. 1981). BS, Tex. Woman's U., 1979; postgrad. U. Houston, 1982—. Spl. edn. tchr. Ashford Elem., Sch., Houston Ind. Sch. Dist., 1979-80, resource tchr., 1981—, sec. hospitality com., 1982—; substitute tchr. Marshall Elem. Sch., Detroit, 1980-81; spl. edn. pvt. tutor, Houston, 1982—; tutor Denton Assn. Student Helpers (Tex.), 1977; vol. behavior technician North Tex. State U. Ctr. Behavioral Studies, Denton, 1976-77; vol. Spl. Olympics, Denton, 1978, Lowry Hall, Denton, 1978. Mem. Young Women's Aux., Mt. Calvery Bapt. Ch., Denton, 1977-79, pres., 1978-79, mem. usher bd., 1977-79, youth worker, 1978-79; youth worker, Sunday sch. tchr., mem. outreach com., Christian debutante com. Liberty Bapt. Ch.; mem. Houston Council Edn., 1981—. Mem. Council Exceptional Children, Assn. Childhood Edn. Internat., NEA, NAACP (named most prominent black woman Tex. Woman's U. chpt. 1979), Nat. Assn. Black Social Workers, Tex. State Tchrs. Assn., Houston Tchrs. Assn., Mortar Bd., Sarah Circle, Alpha Chi, Delta Sigma Theta. Democrat. Home: 2020 Bentworth St Apt 414 Houston TX 77077 Office: Ashford Elem Sch 1815 Shannon Valley Houston TX 77077

ANDERSON, DORIS EHLINGER, lawyer; b. Houston, Dec. 1; d. Joseph Otto and Cornelia Louise (Pagel) Ehlinger; m. Wiley Newton Anderson, Jr., Aug. 26, 1946; children—Wiley Newton III, Joe E. Permanent high sch. tchr.'s cert. U. Houston, 1948; BA, Rice U., 1946; JD, U. Tex., 1950; MLS in Museology U. Okla. Bar: Tex. 1950, U.S. Supreme Ct. Assoc. Ehlinger & Anderson, Houston, 1950-52, ptnr., 1965—; assoc. Price, Guinn, Wheat & Veltmann, Houston, 1952-55, Wheat, Dyche & Thornton, Houston, 1955-65; life mem. Rice Assocs., Houston, 1984—; dir. Houston Bapt. Mus. Am. Architecture and Decorative Arts, 1980—, curator costume, 1980; hist. lectr. Editor, author Houston, City of Destiny, 1980. Contbr. articles to hist. publs. Partliamentarian Harris County Flood Control Task Force, Houston, 1975—; docent Bayou Bend Mus. Fine Arts, Houston. Recipient best interpretive exhibit award Tex. Hist. Commn., 1983, Outstanding Woman of Yr. award YWCA, Houston, 1983; named adm. Tex. Navy, 1980. Mem. ABA, Women Attys. Houston, UDC (pres. Jefferson Davis chpt.) Daus. Republic Tex. (parliamentarian gen.), Am. Mus. Soc. (bd. dirs. Houston 1981—), Harris County Heritage Soc. (librarian), Kappa Beta Pi. Episcopalian. Home: 5556 Cranbrook Houston TX 77056 Office: Ehlinger & Anderson 5556 Sturbridge Houston TX 77056

ANDERSON, DORIS ELAINE, lawyer; b. Elkhart, Ind., Nov. 6, 1934; d. Frederick John and Hazel Elizabeth (Bergman) A. B. in Mus., U. Mich., 1956; J.D., U. Calif.-Berkeley, 1964. Bar: Calif. 1968 Atty., Fibreboard Corp., San Francisco, 1965-79; gen. counsel Internat. Diamond Corp., San Rafael, Calif., 1980-82; legal counsel Kaiser-Crebs Mgmt. Corp., Oakland, Calif., 1983-85; asst. sec., atty. Amfac, Inc., San Francisco, 1985—. Mem. Am. Soc. Corp. Secs., Inc. Avocations: tennis, golf, music. Home: 1079 Cragmont Ave Berkeley CA 94708 Office: Amfac Inc 44 Montgomery St San Francisco CA 94104

ANDERSON, EDITH HELEN, nursing school administrator; b. N.J., June 3, 1927. B.S., Manhattanville Coll., 1951; M.A., N.Y. U., 1958, Ph.D., 1963. Staff nurse Halloran VA Hosp., S.I., N.Y., 1948-49; camp nurse Ten Mile River camp Boy Scouts Am., N.Y., 1949; pub. health nurse Vis. Nurse Assn., Elizabeth, N.J., 1950-54, Community Service Soc., N.Y.C., 1954-56; instr. practical nursing program Elizabeth (N.J.) Bd. Edn., 1956-58; teaching fellow grad. program in parent-child nursing N.Y. U., 1958-60, asst. prof., dir. grad. program in parent-child nursing, 1960-64; acting chief nursing sect. Children's Bur., Social and Rehab. Service, HEW, Washington, 1967-68; nursing edn. cons. Nursing Sect. Children's Bur., Welfare Adminstrn., 1964-69; dean Sch. Nursing, Coll. Health Scis. and Social Welfare, U. Hawaii, Honolulu, 1969-76; dean coll. nursing U. Del., Newark, 1976—; Cons. P.R. Dept. Health, U. P.R., 1963, V.I. Dept. Health, 1964, Inst. Tech. Interchange East-West Center, U. Hawaii; tchr./trainer field tng. program Provincial Health Dept., Republic of China, Taiwan, 1969, tchr./trainer Tb control, Ryukya Islands; tchr./trainer Tb control Inst. Tech. Interchange, East-West Center, Lyndon B. Johnson Tropical Med. Center, Am. Samoa, 1970, 71; mem. med. adv. bd. VA Hosp., Elsmere, Del., 1977-87; mem. Del. State Coordinating Health Council, 1978-84, Health Resource Mgmt. Council, 1988—. Author: Commitment to Child Health, 1967, (with others) Maternity Care in the United States: Gains and Gaps, 1966, Current Concepts in Clinical Nursing, Vol. I, 1967, Vol. II, 1969, Vol. III, 1971, Vol. IV, 1973. Fellow Am. Acad. Nursing; mem. Am. Nurses Assn., Hawaii Nurses Assn. (editor mag. 1973-75, chmn. publicity com. 1973-75), Nat. League Nursing (chmn. maternal child nursing sect. So. region 1965, chairperson bd. rev. of accreditation 1980-81), Hawaii League Nursing (1st v.p. 1973), Mid-Atlantic Regional Nursing Assn. (1st governing bd. 1981, v.p. 1982-83), Pi Lambda Theta, Sigma Theta Tau. Home: 1403 Shallcross Ave Hamilton House Apt 502 Wilmington DE 19806

ANDERSON, ELISABETH MADGE KEHRER, physician, state administrator; b. Aberdeen, S.D.; d. Robert Ewald and Oriole (Johnston) Kehrer; m. Page Morris Anderson, Jan. 6, 1951; children: Bruce Statham, Catherine Mercer, Mary Elisabeth. BA, U. Louisville, 1946, MD, 1949; MPH, U. Hawaii, 1971. Intern Queen's Hosp., Honolulu, 1949-50, resident, 1950-51; physician, dir. research Pacific Inst. Rehab. Medicine, Honolulu, 1960-69; asst. to pres. Hawaii Med. Assn., Honolulu, 1972-75; chief med. health services div. Hawaii Dept. Health, Honolulu, 1980—; mem. Hawaii Cancer Commn., 1984—; mem. adv. bd. Hawaii Cancer Research Ctr., 1986—; mem. staff Queen's Hosp. Contbr. articles to profl. jours. Sec., bd. trustees Hawaii Loa Coll., Kaneohe, 1966-75; mem. exec. bd. Community Scholarship Program, Honolulu, 1966-71; mem. Stanford Biol. Preserve Docent Council (Calif.), 1978—; chmn. bd. Hawaii Nature Ctr., Honolulu, 1983—; past vice chmn., trustee Multiple Sclerosis Found. Hawaii; mem. exec. bd. Health and Community Service Council Hawaii, Jr. League of Honolulu. Mem. Yosemite Nat. History Assn., Am. Coll. Preventive Medicine, Am. Pub. Health Assn., Hawaii Med. Assn., Honolulu County Med. Soc., Sierra Club, Honolulu Acad. Arts, Outdoor Circle, Hawaii Bot. Soc. Clubs: Punahou Tennis, Trail and Mountain, Outrigger Canoe. Office: Hawaii Dept Health 1250 Punchbowl St Honolulu HI 96813

ANDERSON, ELIZABETH JANE, lawyer; b. Woodstock, Va., Apr. 9, 1955; d. Robert Homer, Jr. and Betty S. A. AB, Duke U., 1977; JD, T.C. Williams Sch. Law, 1982. Bar: Va. 1983. Staff atty. S.W. Va. Legal Aid Soc., Marion, 1983-84; assoc. Greer and Greer, P.C., Rocky Mount, Va., 1984-85; asst. commonwealth's atty., Norfolk, Va., 1986-87; sole practice, Norfolk, 1987—. Chmn. Students for Ford, Durham, N.C., 1976; del. N.C. Student Legislature, Durham, 1974-76; v.p. Coll. Reps., Durham, 1975-76; active Norfolk City Dem. Com., LWV. Recipient Book award for Evidence, Am. Jurisprudence, 1982. Mem. ABA, ACLU, Assn. Trial Lawyers Am., Va. Trial Lawyers Assn., Va. State Bar, Va. Bar Assn., Va. Women Attys. Assn., Delta Theta Phi. Democrat. Lutheran. Office: St Paul Bldg 125 St Paul's Blvd Suite 200 Norfolk VA 23510

ANDERSON, ERICA SUE, copper mine supervisor, landscape and irrigation contractor; b. Tucson, May 18, 1949; d. Kent Jerome and Mary Louise (Fox) A.; 1 child, Erik S. Young. Student, U. Ariz., 1967-69; BS cum laude, Springfield Coll., 1971; MBA summa cum laude, U. Phoenix, 1983. Laborer Duval Corp., Sahuarita, Ariz., 1974-77, supr., 1977-86, reclamationist, 1977-86; packaging supr. Cyprus Minerals, Cyprus Sierrita Mine, Sahuarita, 1986-87, molybdenum mktg. services supr., 1987—; pres. Green Valley Plants and Landscapes, Sahuarita, 1986. Vol. Therapeutic Riding of Tucson, 1979-81; sec. Ams. Concerned About Tomorrow, Tucson, 1981-82. Mem. Nat. Assn. Female Execs. Avocations: landscaping, skiing, horses, swimming, reading. Home: 16900 S LaCanada Sahuarita AZ 85629

ANDERSON, ETHEL AVARA, retail executive; b. Meridian, Miss.; s. Thomas Franklin and Annie Ethel (Jones) Avara.; m. Theron Young Anderson, Aug. 2, 1940 (dec. Aug. 1964); 1 child, Brenda Anderson Jackson. Grad. high sch., Meridian. Owner, mgr. Med. and Merchants Collections, Meridian, 1977—. Mem. exec. bd., sec. United Way of Meridian, 1983-87; mem. exec. bd., dir. Miss. Industries for Developmentally Disabled, Meridian, 1984-87, Lauderdale Assn. Retarded Children, Meridian, 1983-87. Mem. Meridian C. of C. (liaison 1985-87), Xi Gamma, Beta Sigma Phi. Methodist. Lodge: Civitan (bd. dirs. Meridian club 1984-87). Home: 3400 20th St Meridian MS 39301 Office: Med Merchants and Collection 906 20th Ave Suite 205 Meridian MS 39301

ANDERSON, FRANCES JANE, communications company owner; b. Freeport, Ill., Oct. 1, 1931; d. Lillian Rose A.; A.B., Millikin U., 1953; student Salvation Army Sch. for Officers Tng., 1953; M.S., Northwestern U., 1970. Ordained minister, Salvation Army, 1953; editor youth publs. Salvation Army, Chgo., 1956-75; asst. dir. public relations for central states, 1975-77; writer, editor bd. communications Bapt. Gen. Conf., Arlington Heights, Ill., 1977-81, editorial mgr., public affairs, 1981-82; writer/producer Domain Communications, 1982-84; owner Anderson Communications, Inc., 1984—; mem. faculty Olivet Coll., Kankakee, Ill., 1981—; prof. communications Salvation Army Sch., Chgo., 1981—. Mem. Salvation Army Com. for White House Conf. on Children and Youth, 1960, 70. Mem. Women in Communications (rec. sec. 1980, newsletter editor 1981, treas. 1982, pres. North Shore chpt. 1983-84), Conf. Editors Ch. Mags. for Children and Youth, Northwest Suburban Assn. Commerce and Industry, MacDowell Artists Assn. Contbr. articles to religious jours. Home: 3925 Triumvera Dr #9G Glenview IL 60025 Office: Anderson Communications Inc 1699 E Woodfield Rd #A3 Schaumburg IL 60173

ANDERSON, FRANCES SWEM, nuclear medical technologist; b. Grand Rapids, Mich., Nov. 27, 1913; d. Frank Oscar and Carrie (Strang) Swem; student Muskegon Sch. Bus., 1959-60; cert. Muskegon Community Coll., 1964; m. Clarence A.F. Anderson, Apr. 9, 1934; children—Robert Curtis, Clarelyn Christine (Mrs. Roger L. Schmelling), Stanley Herbert. X-ray file clk., film librarian Hackley Hosp., Muskegon, Mich., 1957-59; student refresher course in nuclear med. tech. Chgo. Soc. Nuclear Med. Techs., 1966; radioisotope technologist and sec. Hackley Hosp., 1959-65; nuclear med. technologist Butler Meml. Hosp., Muskegon Heights, Mich., 1966-70, Mercy Hosp., Muskegon, 1970-79; ret., 1979. Mem. Muskegon Civic A Capella choir, 1932-39; mem. Mother-Tch. Singers, PTA, Muskegon, 1941-48, treas. 1944-48; with Muskegon Civic Opera Assn., 1950-51, office vol. Alive '88 Crusade, mem. com. for 60th High Sch. class reunion. Soc. Nuclear Medicine Cert. nuclear medicine technologist Soc. Nuclear Medicine. Mem. Am. Registry Radiologic Technologists. Mem. Forest Park Covenant Ch. (mem. choir 1953-79, 83—, choir sec. 1963-69, Sunday sch. tchr. 1954-75, supt. Sunday sch. 1975-78, treas. Sunday sch. 1981-86, chmn. master planning council, coordinator centennial com. to 1981, ch. sec. 1982-84, 87); co-chmn. Jackson Hill Old Timers Reunion, 1982, 83, 85; mem. Muskegon Body Building Assn. Health and Wellness Ctr. (permanent, member of month Mar., 1985). Home: 5757 E Sternberg Rd Fruitport MI 49415

ANDERSON, GERALDINE LOUISE, laboratory scientist; b. Mpls., July 7, 1941; d. George M. and Viola Julia-Mary (Abel) Havrilla; m. Henry Clifford Anderson, May 21, 1966; children—Bruce Henry, Julie Lynne. BS, U. Minn., 1963. Med. technologist Swedish Hosp., Mpls., 1963-68; hematology supr. Glenwood Hills Hosp. lab., Golden Valley, Minn., 1968-70; assoc. scientist dept. pediatrics U. Minn. Hosps., Mpls., 1970-74; instr. health occupations and med. lab. asst. Suburban Hennepin County Area Vocat. Tech. Ctr., Brooklyn Park, Minn., 1974-81, St. Paul Tech. Vocat. Inst., 1978—; research med. technologist Miller Hosp., St. Paul, 1975-78; research assoc. Children's and United Hosps., St. Paul, 1979—; mem. health occupations adv. com. Hennepin Tech. Ctrs., 1975—, chairperson, 1978-79; mem. hematology slide edn. rev. bd. Am. Soc. Hematology, 1976—. Contbr. articles to profl. jours. Mem. Med. Lab. Tech. Polit. Action Com., 1978—; resource person lab. careers Robbinsdale Sch. Dist., Minn., 1970-79; del. Crest View Home Assn., 1981—; mem. sci. and math. subcom. Minn. High Tech. Council. Recipient service awards and honors Omicron Sigma. Mem. Minn. Soc. Med. Tech. (sec. 1969-71), Am. Soc. Profl. and Exec. Women, Am. Soc. Med. Tech. (del. to ann. meetings 1972—, chmn. hematology sci. assembly 1977-79, nomination com. 1979-81, bd. dirs. 1985-88), Twin City Soc. Med. Technologists, Twin City Hosp. Assn. (speakers bur. 1968-70), Assn. Women in Sci., World Future Soc., AAAS, AAUW, Minn. Med. Tech. Alumni, Am. Soc. Hematology, Soc. Analytical Cytology, Nat. Assn. Female Execs., Sigma Delta Epsilon (corr. sec. Xi chpt. 1980-82, pres. 1982-84), Alpha Mu Tau. Lutheran. Office: United Hosps Inc Harris Cancer Research Lab 333 Smith Ave N Saint Paul MN 55102

ANDERSON, HELEN SHARP, civic worker; b. Ennis, Tex., June 10, 1916; d. John H. and Eula (King) Sharp; A.B., U. Tex., 1937; m. Thomas Dunaway Anderson, Feb. 21, 1938; children—John Sharp, Helen Shaw, Lucille Streeter. Mem. Mt. Vernon Ladies Assn. of the Union, vice regent, 1967—, regent, 1982-86; bd. dirs. Nat. Cathedral Assn., Washington, 1971-75, also mem. various spl. coms.; mem. Garden Club Am., 1945—, zone vice-chmn., 1959-62, nat. dir., 1975-77, nat. v.p., 1977-79, nat. chmn. long-range planning, 1979-80; bd. dirs. Japan Am. Soc. Houston, 1974-78; mem. fine arts adv. com. U. Tex., Austin, 1963—; mem. Bayou Bend adv. com., 1988—; chmn. Jr. Gallery, Mus. Fine Arts, Houston, 1953-54, docent, 1964-70; bd. dirs. Houston and Harris County council Girl Scouts U.S.A., 1966-67, Sheltering Arms, 1964-67; bd. trustees Winedale Hist. Ctr., 1987—; bd. dirs. Harris County Heritage Soc., 1963-65, v.p., 1965-66; mem. River Oaks Garden Club, Houston, 1945—, pres., 1958, 59; mem. coms. Christ Ch. Cathedral, Houston; mem. Houston Jr. League, Bayou Bend Adv., 1988—, Winedale Hist Ctr. Council, 1987. Republican. Episcopalian. Clubs: Sulgrave (Washington); River Oaks Garden (Houston); Assembly; Colony (N.Y.); Bolero. Address: 3925 Del Monte Dr Houston TX 77019

ANDERSON, JACQUELINE JONES, educator; b. Hartford, Conn., July 13, 1935; d. Ella B. (Jones) Anderson; B.A., N.H. Coll., 1979; cert. Hartford U., 1971, Hartford Coll. for Women, 1971, U. Conn., 1978; children—Wilfred, Gregory, Kevin, Kyle. With Community Renewal Team, CAP Agy., Hartford, 1966-69; freelance tng. cons., Hartford, 1974—; dir. Health Care Dept., Hartford Hosp., 1969—. Bd. dirs. Ambulatory Health Care Planning, Inc., 1970-71, PIT I Drugs, 1972-75, YMCA, 1973—, Toward an Allied Health Career Today, 1973-77, Get the Lead Out, 1974—, Child Guidance Center, 1974-78, AMISTAD Group Home for Girls, 1977—, Upper Albany Community Orgn., 1977—, Health Systems Agy., 1977—, Bergdorf Health Planning Com., 1977-79, Black Coalition on Health Issues, 1978—, Elderly Crisis Intervention, 1979—; mem. Conn. Stroke Program, 1972, Blue Hills Clinic task force on drugs, 1972-73, Mayor's Health Services Com., 1973-77, Community Health Adv. Com., City of Hartford, 1978—; resource person Planned Parenthood, 1972-77; Justice of the Peace, Hartford County, 1972-75; mem. Republican Town Com., 1973—; councilwoman Hartford Ct. of Common Council, 1975-77, many others. Recipient Cert. of Merit, CRT of Greater Hartford, 1972; Outstanding Woman of Yr. award Conn. Women's Soc., 1979; Cert. of Appreciation, Health Systems Agy. of N.C. Conn., 1980; Upper Albany Community Orgn. Service to Community award, 1981; others. Mem. Am. Public Health Assn., Conn. Hosp. Assn., New Eng. Public Health Assn., Soc. for Patient Reps., Alliance of Black Social Workers. Republican. Methodist. Contbr. articles to profl. jours. Home: 101 Tower Ave Hartford CT 06120 Office: 80 Seymour St Hartford CT 06115

ANDERSON, JANE LOUISE BLAIR, librarian, horse breeder, poet; b. Wilkinsburg, Pa., Nov. 6, 1948; d. Francis Preston and Mary Louise (Maxwell) Blair; m. Russell Karl Anderson Jr., Apr. 20, 1973; children: Christina Lynn, Melissa Jane. BS in Edn., Clarion State Coll., 1971; MS in Library Sci., Duquesne U., 1974. Cert. pub. librarian, Pa. Substitute tchr. Wilkinsburg Schs., 1971, tchr. Head Start, 1971; librarian Franklin Regional Schs. Intermediate High Sch., Murrysville, Pa., 1971—; breeder quarter horses, Fenelton, Pa., 1978—. Contbr. poems to various anthologies. Vol. mem. Rescue 5 Ambulance, Murrysville, 1974-76, Medic I ambulance, 1976-78; sec. Franklin Area REACT, 1976-78; first aid instr. ARC, Murrysville, 1975-80; instr. CPR, Am. Heart Assn., Westmoreland County, 1976-80; vol. worker with deaf, 1978-83; vol. United Cerebral Palsey, Butler, Pa., 1981—. Mem. Westmoreland County Library Assn., Pa. Library Assn., Am. Quarter Horse Assn., Pa. Quarter Horse Assn., Butler County C. of C., Am. Boarding Kennel Assn. Methodist. Home: Fern Valley Farm PO Box 12 Fenelton PA 16034 Office: 3220 School Rd Murrysville PA 15668

ANDERSON, JANELLE MARIE, account executive; b. Beloit, Wis., Mar. 28, 1954; d. Lyle Kenneth Anderson and Helen Catherine (Hammer) Hughes; adopted d. Hilary William Hughes. AA, U. Wis., Fond du Lac, 1976; postgrad., Arnie DeLuca Sem., Chgo., 1983, Women's Bus. Inst., Neenah, Wis., 1986. Legal sec. Nugent & Nugent, Attys., Waupun, Wis., 1976-80; salesman Modern Motors, Fond du Lac, 1980-82; clk., technician Old World Stained Glass, Fond du Lac, 1982-83; mgr. classifieds Pub.'s Devel. Services Inc., Fond du Lac, 1983-86, account mgr. nat. sales, 1985—; cons. Decra-Led Corp. Am., Portage, Wis., 1985. Mem. Milw. Advt. Club, Wis. Advt. Pubs. Assn. (chmn. bd. 1987-88), Milw. Grocery Mfrs. Reps. (bd. dirs. 1988—), Milw. Food Brokers Assn., Fond du Lac Jaycees (Wis. program del. Outstanding Young Adult and Wisconsinite awards 1987-88, v.p. individual devel. 1985-86, 1st woman pres. 1986—, numerous awards). Roman Catholic. Home: 136 1/2 E Merrill Ave Fond du Lac WI 54935 Office: Pubs Devel Services Inc 101 S Main St Fond du Lac WI 54935

ANDERSON, JANET CONRAD, psychologist; b. Pitts., June 29, 1926; d. Kenneth Russell and Susan Elizabeth (Elk) Conrad; m. Robert Reeser Seidel, June 7, 1949 (div.); children: Suzanne Elizabeth, Cynthia Ruth, Robert Conrad; m. William Bryan Anderson, Oct. 15, 1983. BS in Retail Mgmt., Drexel U., 1947; MEd in Counseling, West Chester U., 1969; EdD in Psychology and Devel., Temple U., 1972. Lic. psychologist, Pa. Asst. publicity dir. Giubel Bros., Phila., 1947-49; asst. buyer Bon Marche, Seattle, 1965; grad. asst. West Chester U., 1968-69, assof. prof. criminal justice, 1973-75, chmn., graduate advisor, 1975-83; pvt. practice psychologist, cons., custody and marital counselor West Chester, 1983—; cons. Eranda-Evaluator fed. program, West Chester; instr. Drexel U., Pa. State U., 1969 73, Thomas Jefferson U., 1972-79. Mem. Am. Psychol. Assn. Office: 326 W Union St West Chester PA 19380

ANDERSON, JANICE CAROLYN, nurse, cardiac sonographer; b. Savannah, Ga., Aug. 27, 1939; d. James Carswell and Lois Elizabeth (Robbins) Milligan; m. James Mixon Anderson, Sr., Sept. 5, 1959; children—James Mixon, Joseph, Jill. Diploma nursing U. Sch. Nursing, Augusta, Ga., 1966; B.S., Med. Coll. Ga., 1977. Staff nurse U. Hosp., Augusta, Ga., 1966; staff nurse coronary care unit St. Joseph Hosp., Augusta, 1967, head nurse coronary care unit, 1968, adminstrv. supr. coronary care unit, 1969-73, nurse instr. coronary care tng. program, 1970-73; nurse coordinator Augusta area cardiovascular facility Univ. Hosp., Augusta, 1972-73; inservice ednl. instr., coordinator continuing nursing edn. Hosp. and Clinics, Med. Coll. Ga., Augusta, 1973-75; cardiovascular nurse cons. Meml. Hosp. Washington County, Sandersville, Ga., 1974-75; cardiovascular nurse clinician Paul E. Cundey, Jr., M.D., cardiologist, Augusta, Ga., 1975-85; cardiac sonographer cardiac diagnostic lab., Cardiovascular Assocs. of Augusta, 1987—; cons. ultrasound and sonography, cardiovascular resource nurse, Stephens County Hosp., Tocca, 1987—; prin. JMA Communications; co-owner Alpine Video, Helen, Ga. Contbr. articles to profl. ultrasound jours. Chmn. nursing edn. com. Am. Heart Assn., Ga. affiliate, 1973-74; bd. dirs. Am. Heart Assn., Ga. affiliate, Richmond County unit, 1973-85, co-chmn. high blood pressure com. Recipient Bronze Service medallion, Ga. affiliate, Am. Heart Assn., 1971, Silver Service medallion, 1973, Gold Service medallion, 1975. Mem. Am. Heart Assn., Am. Soc. Echocardiography. Home: PO Box 388 Helen GA 30545 Office: PO Box 569 Helen GA 30545

ANDERSON, JANICE LARAE ALDEN, telecommunications executive; b. Frederic, Wis., Dec. 1, 1935; d. Clifford Oscar and Kathleen Harriet (Streed) Alden; m. Thomas Anderson Roden, Jr., Aug. 31, 1957 (div. July 20, 1971); children—Jacquelyn Lee, Thomas Alden; m. 2d, Robert William Anderson, July 29, 1973. Exec. sec. Pillsbury Co., Mpls., 1953-60; water safety instr., trainer ARC, Mpls., Rocky River, Ohio and Shoreview, Minn., 1962-70; supervising analyst-forecasting Continental Telephone Co., Mpls., 1971—. Vol. dir. ARC vision-hearing screening program, St. Paul, 1968-71; sec. dist. 55, chair precinct 4 Ind. Republicans, 1978-85. Named Toastmaster of Yr., Woodbury, Minn., 1981. Mem. United Ch. of Christ. Clubs: St. Paul-Mpls. Heathkit Computer Users Group (treas. 1982-83), Monterey Jacks Toastmasters (Bloomington, Minn.) (pres. 1984). Home: 1265 Kolff Ct Newport MN 55055 Office: Continental Telecom Inc 1300 Mendota Hts Rd PO Box 50770 Saint Paul MN 55150

ANDERSON, JANICE LINN, real estate broker; b. Paris, Tenn., Sept. 2, 1943; d. Orel Vernon and Rosie Elizabeth (Brockwell) L.; m. David James Anderson, June 11, 1965 (div. Oct. 1973). Entertainer, recording artist 4-Sons Record Co., Paris, Tenn., 1958-73; med. transcriptionist The Paris Clinic, 1965-73; computer operator, asst. to v.p. Medicare Adminstrn./Equitable, Nashville, 1973-74; property mgmt. asst. Dobson & Johnson, Inc., Nashville, 1974-76; dir. leasing and mgmt. Fortune-Nashville Co., 1976-78; real estate brokerage asst. J.G. Martin, Jr./Caudill Properties, Inc., Nashville, 1978—; pvt. practice resume preparation, Nashville, 1982—. Active Girl Scouts U.S.A., Paris, 1967-69; mem. ARC, Nashville, 1978, Am. Inst. for Cancer Research, Washington, D.C., 1985, Christian Appalachian Project, Lancaster, Ky., 1986. Mem. Nat. Assn. Female Execs., Bus. and Profl. Womens Club (Pres. 1965-73), Profl. Musicians Union, Womens Missionary Union (bd. dirs. Paris chpt. 1970-71), Internat. Platform Assn., Realtors' Secs. Assn., Am. Biographical Inst., Inc. Baptist. Home: 812 Elissa Dr Nashville TN 37217 Office: J G Martin Jr/Caudill Properties Inc American Trust Bldg 15th Fl Nashville TN 37201

ANDERSON, JEAN LORRAINE, nursing educator; b. Halifax, N.S., Apr. 22, 1945; d. Colin Francis and Elizabeth Florence (MacDonald) Livingstone; m. Alexander Michael Anderson; children: Colin Henry Michael, Sheena Margaret Isabel, Laura Mary Catherine, Sarah Christina Ann. Diploma in Nursing, St. Martha's Hosp. Sch. Nursing, Antigonish, N.S., 1966; BS in Nursing, St. Francis Xavier U., Antigonish, N.S., 1970. Nurse, surgery St. Martha's Hosp., Antigonish, N.S., 1966-67; clin. instr. St. Martha's Hosp., Antigonish, 1981—; staff nurse ICU St. Joseph's Hosp., Victoria, B.C., 1967-68, nurse, 1967-68; nurse in charge Ranklin Inlet (N.W.T.) Nsg. Sta., 1970-76; staff nurse, maternity St. Martha's Hosp., Antigonish, 1979-81; nursing instr. St. Martha's Hosp. Sch. of Nursing, Merigomish, Can., 1981—. Roman Catholic. Home: RR 1 Merigomish, Pictou County, NS Canada B0K 1G0

ANDERSON, JO ANNE ROCHELLE, educator; b. Willmar, Minn., June 12, 1938; d. Alexander and Elsie (Johnson) Everson; m. Edward L. Anderson, June 4, 1960; children: Jennifer Rochelle, Lisa Jo. BA, Ariz. State U., 1960; MEd, U. Ariz., 1964. Instr. Tucson Unified Sch. Dist., 1960-69, instr. adult evening program, 1960-72; instr. Am. Banking Inst. U. Ariz., Tucson, 1967; assoc. instr. Pima Community Coll., Tucson, 1967-76, instr., specialist office productivity, 1977—; instr., dir. personnel dept. Pima Community Coll., 1969-72; cons., owner Bus. Extra-ordinaire Inc., Tucson; cons., instr. IBM Corp., Tucson, 1986, 87; speaker, seminar leader for various orgns. Sunday sch. instr. Our Saviors Lutheran Ch., Tucson, 1974—; chairperson adv. com. Pima Community Coll. Office Edn., Tucson, 1977—; producer, editor handbook Salpointe Catholic High Sch., Tucson, 1983—, organizer, supr. athletic banquets, 1986—. Mem. NEA, Ariz. Educators Assn., Pima Community Coll. Educators Assn., Ariz. Bus. Educators Assn. (historian 1968), Nat. Assn. Female Execs. Republican. Lutheran. Home: 1501 N Indigo Dr Tucson AZ 85745

ANDERSON, JOAN SCHEUERMANN, psychologist, educator; b. New Orleans, Mar. 17, 1933; d. Leonhard Naef and Margaret Scheuermann; B.A., Sophie Newcomb Coll., 1954; Ph.D., U. Houston, 1969; m. Frank Clayton Anderson, Jr., Apr. 30, 1954; children—Frank Clayton III, Mollie Elise. Pvt. practice clin. psychology, Houston, 1969—; clin. assoc. prof. Baylor Coll. Medicine, Houston; chmn. Tex. Bd. Examiners of Psychologists, 1982. Bd. dirs. Living Bank, 1965—, Children's World, 1970-75, Homes of St. Mark, 1977—. Mem. Am. Psychol. Assn., Tex. Psychol. Assn. (pres. 1977), Houston Psychol. Assn. (pres. 1979). Episcopalian. Office: 1535 W Loop S Suite 222 Houston TX 77027

ANDERSON, JOAN WELLIN FREED, public relations executive, consultant, freelance journalist; b. Shreveport, La., Aug. 18, 1945; d. Cyril and Rose (Friedman) F.; m. Steven G. Rapfogel, 1966 (div. 1984); children—Lisa L., Robert B.; m. J. Warren Anderson, July 21, 1984. B.A. in Gen. Studies, Tex. Christian U. Freelance reporter Sta. KERA-TV, Dallas, 1979-80, Fort Worth Star-Telegram, 1980-83, Fort Worth bur. Dallas Morning News, 1980-82; pub. relations coordinator Amon Carter Mus., Fort Worth, 1982; med. writer Tex. Coll. Osteo. Medicine, Fort Worth, 1982-85; freelance writer, 1985—; producer video programs for pub. access cable channel. Bd. dirs. Am. Cancer Soc., 1982-84, active Cancer Hotline; facilitator for fair housing edn. and info. for Community Housing Resource Bd., Ft. Worth; bd. dirs. Women's Haven of Tarrant County (Tex.) Inc., 1987—, chmn. community relations com., 1988; mem. Court Apptd. Spl. Adv. for Foster Children, 1986-88; mem. mktg. com. Circle Theater. Mem. Women in Communications, Inc. (past dir.), Internat. Assn. Bus. Communicators, Sigma Delta Chi. Contbr. articles to popular mags.

ANDERSON, JOANN MORGAN, counselor; b. Detroit, Dec. 25, 1933; d. Verbon Anthony and Wanda Joan (Hutchison) Morgan; m. Robert Arthur Anderson; children: Carol Sue, Douglas Ross, Paul William. BA, U. Wash., 1957; MA, Fielding Inst., 1977. Self employed counselor Edmonds, Wash., 1976-78; dir. High Point Counseling Service, Edmonds, 1978-80, Woodway Counseling Assn., Edmonds, 1980-86; mem. clin staff Northwest Health Assocs., Edmonds, 1986—; cons. Edmonds Sch. Dist. 15, 1979-82, Wash. Edn. Assn., 1980, Non-Profit Bds. Dirs., Seattle, 1985-87. vol. various agencies, 1957-76; pres. Stevens Meml. Hosp. Aux., Edmonds, 1964-65. Mem. Internat. Transactional Analysis Assn. (cert.), Am. Assn. Counseling and Devel., AAUW, Assn. Transpersonal Psychology, Mortar Bd., Beta Gamma Sigma. Republican. Methodist. Lodge: Soroptomist. Office: Northwest Health Assn 21727 76th W #107 Edmonds WA 98020

ANDERSON, JOLENE SLOVER, publisher; b. Tulare, Calif.; d. James P. Sr. and Helen B. (Walters) Slover; ed. Victor Valley Coll., Riverside City Coll.; m. Douglas R. Anderson, June 14, 1975; 1 dau. by previous marriage—Sabrina Jo. Model, Connor Sch. Modeling, Fresno, Calif., 1955-65; actress M. Kosloff Studios, Hollywood, Calif., 1965; nat. sales mgr. Armed Services Publs., 1966-68; pres., dir. Sullivan Publs., Inc., Riverside, Calif., 1970-82; pres., chief exec. officer Heritage House Publs., 1983-87; pres. Jolene S. Anderson Pub. Cons., Inc., 1987—. Mem. Riverside Tourist and Conv., 1981, public relations com. YWCA, 1981; mem. City Councils Cultural Heritage Bd.; treas. DeAnza Verde Homeowners, 1978; active Rape Crisis Center. Mem. Riverside C. of C. Club: Soroptimists (chmn. 1981). Office: PO Box 7453 Riverside CA 92513

ANDERSON, JOYCE, management consultant; b. Shelby, N.C., Feb. 27, 1958; d. Charles Ernest and Patsy (Dycus) A. BA in Eng., Purdue U., W. Lafayette, Ind., 1980. Adminstrv. asst. AIT, Inc., W. Hartford, Conn., 1980-81, v.p. ops., 1981-82; project mgr. Comarco, Inc., Anaheim, Calif., 1983, br. office mgr., 1983-86, dir. mktg., 1986-87; pres., cons. Anderson Bus. Services, Inc., Shelby, N.C., 1987—; assoc. cons. The Quest Group, McLean Va., 1987—. Mem. Soc. Logistics Engrs., Data Processing Mgmt. Assn., Soc. Tech. Communications (treas. 1984). Democrat. Baptist. Office: Anderson Bus Services Inc 1820 Kings Rd Shelby NC 28150

ANDERSON, JUDITH ANN, academic administrator; b. Evansville, Ind., Aug. 28, 1948; d. Elmer and Edna Irene (Kinney) Jaggers; m. Haldon L. Anderson, Nov. 29, 1969; children: Ryan Jason, Renee Michelle. BS, Ind. State U., 1970, MA, 1972, PhD, 1977. Registered psychologist, Ill. Asst. prof. Fla. State U., Tallahassee, Fla., 1977-78; dir. career devel. UCP Fla., Tallahassee, 1979-80; psychologist Human Services Ctr., Toledo, 1981-82; pvt. practice psychology Charleston, Ill., 1982—; dir. affirmative action Eastern Ill. U., Charleston, Ill., 1982—; cons. Dept. Rehab. Services, mattoon, Ill., 1982-86; Dept. Children and Family Services, Charleston, Ill., 1982—. Contbr. articles to profl. jour. Pres. bd. dirs. Coalition Against Domestic Violence, several counties, Ill., 1985-86. Fla. Dept. Labor grantee, 1979-81; Univ. scholar Bryn Mawr Inst., 1984. Mem. Am. Psychol. Assn., Am. Assn. Affirmative Action, Am. Assn. U. Adminstrs., Am. Assn. Higher Edn. Democrat. Home: 513 Ashby Dr Charleston IL 61920 Office: Eastern Ill U 108 Old Main Charleston IL 61920

ANDERSON, JUDITH MAXINE, judicial education specialist; b. Olympia, Wash., July 20, 1958; d. Donald Richard and Lena (Gaviorno) A. BA in Edn., Western Wash. U., 1981; MBA, Seattle Internat. U., 1986. Job counselor Dist. #113 Ednl. Services, Olympia, 1977-84; jud. edn. specialist Adminstr. for Cts., Olympia, 1984—; sec. crisis clinic Thurston and Mason County, Olympia, 1985—, bd. dirs., Olympia. Mem. Nat. Assn. Jud. Educators. Episcopalian. Home: 3128 59th Ct SE Olympia WA 98501 Office: Adminstr for Cts 1206 S Quince St MS EZ-11 Olympia WA 98504

ANDERSON, KAREN ANN, sail maker; b. Cin., Jan. 30, 1954; d. Richard Fredrick and Ann (Neugent) Anderson; m. David Alan Weiniger, Aug. 26, 1976 (div. 1987). Service rep., salesperson Ulmer Kolius Sails, Oakland, Calif., 1981-88; salesperson Marion Sailmakers, Inc., Almeda, Calif., 1988—. Home: 2232 Ptarmigan Ct Union City CA 94587 Office: Marion Sailmakers Inc 2035 Clement Ave Alameda CA 94501

ANDERSON, KAREN LEE, microscopy company specialist; b. Cleveland Heights, Ohio, May 28, 1951; d. Emmett E. and Frances U. (Unkefer) A. BS, Wilmington Coll., 1973. Histology technician Clinton Meml. Hosp., Wilmington, Ohio, 1973-74; supr. histology Bethesda Hosp., Cin., 1974-75; histology technician Meml. City Gen. Hosp., Houston, 1975-77; research asst. U. Tex. Health Sci. Ctr., Houston, 1977-80; sales rep. Am. Optical Corp., Houston, 1980-82; field product specialist microscopy Carl Zeiss, Inc., Houston and Cin., 1982-83, 86—; tech. support mgr. Thornwood, N.Y., 1983-86. Mgr. participation The Holiday Project, Cin., 1986, mgr. pub. relations, 1987; mem. cin. May Festival Chorus, 1987—. Mem. Am. Assn. for Clin. Pathologists (cert. histology technican), Nat. Assn. Female Execs., Nat. Mus. for Women in the Arts, Sierra Club (leader scenic rivers program 1986—). Democrat.

ANDERSON, KARYN DAWN, banker; b. Salt Lake City, Oct. 30, 1945; d. Terence William and Fern Mildred (Jensen) A.; m. Robert Anderson, June 5, 1964 (div. 1978); children—Michael, Sherrie, Brett, Tammy, Brandon. Student, U. Utah, 1964-65. Office mgr. Pacific Leasing Co., Salt Lake City, 1978-80, Pacific Mortgage Co., Salt Lake City, 1978-80; v.p. CD Mortgage Inc., Salt Lake City, 1980-83; div. liaison City Consumer Service, Salt Lake City, 1983-85; br. mgr. First Union Mortgage Co., Salt Lake City, 1985-87; pres., owner Mortgage Lending Ctr., Inc., 1988—. Author: Crystal Chandeliers, 1978; (children's book) Freddie Frog, 1984; contbr. articles to profl. jours., mags. Bd. dirs. Utah State Elem. Sch. Poison Prevention Com., 1975-76; pres. Utah State Pharm. Aux., Salt Lake City, 1975-76; pres. Boulton Elem. Sch. PTA, 1977-78. Recipient Pres.'s award Utah State Pharm. Aus., 1976, Utah State PTA, 1978, award Loan Officer Assn. Mem. Credit Profls., Utah Profl. Saleswomen Assn., Nat. Assn. Female Execs., Women's Council Realtors, Assn. Profl. Mortgage Women, Women in Bus. Republican. Mormon. Avocations: reading; writing; music; boating; skiing. Office: Mortgage Lending Ctr 637 E 400 South Salt Lake City UT 84102

ANDERSON, KAY CLIFTON, manufacturing company executive; b. Washington, Dec. 8, 1952; d. Ernest Ridley and Marjorie (Bowyer) Clifton; m. LeRoy E. Anderson, Nov. 26, 1978; children: LeRoy, Eric, David. BE, Pittsburg (Kans.) State U., 1974. Cost estimator labor and material Cessna Aircraft Co., Wichita, Kans., 1974-78; subcontract buyer Boeing Mil. Airplane Co., Wichita, 1978—. Home: 327 W 58th St S Wichita KS 67217 Office: Boeing Mil Airplane Co PO Box 7730 Wichita KS 67277

ANDERSON, KAYE WEST, educator; b. Salt Lake City, Apr. 3, 1944; d. John Alva and Ellen Jessie (Koskie) W.; m. Ernest Allen Stephens, June 5, 1965 (div. 1971); m. James Arthur Anderson, Sept. 9, 1973 (div. 1978). BS in Elem. Edn., Phillips U., 1966; MS in Edn., So. Ill. U., Edwardsville, 1970; PhD in Reading and Language Arts, So. Ill. U., Carbondale, 1980. Tchr. Highland (Ill.) Community Schs., 1966-69, Edwardsville Community Schs., 1969-70, Chgo. Bd. Edn., 1971-73; staff mem. The Ecumenical Inst., Chgo., 1971-74; instr., coordinator field experience U. Ill., Chgo., 1974-75; asst. prof., ctr. coordinator So. Ill. U., Carbondale, 1975-81; assoc. prof. tchr. edn. S.E. Mo. State U., Cape Girardeau, 1981—; cons. Chgo. Bd. Edn., 1974-75; coordinator of reading inservice program, tng. modules devel. Chgo. Consortium of Colls. and Univs., 1974-75; mem. planning com. Southeast Mo. Children/Young Adults Lit. Festival, Cape Girardeau, 1982—; fgn. expert Shanghai Tchrs. U., People's Republic of China, 1987. Author Cold Feet: How to Get Them Dancing, 1982; contbr. articles to profl. jours. Named Outstanding Educator in Ill. Chgo. Area Reading Assn., 1980; So. Ill. U. scholar, 1980. Mem. Internat. Reading Assn. (coordinator Mo. State council poster contest 1984-86, program coordinator 18th annual conf. 1985, sec. children's lit. and reading group 1985—, editor newsletter 1985-87, editor The Missouri Reader 1985-88, Research in Reading award 1986, chair various coms. 1983—, sponser SE Mo. council 1983—, editor newsletter 1983-84), Nat. Council Tchrs. of English (mem. com. 1981-87). Disciple of Christ. Club: Roll-A-Ways Square Dance (cuer 1985—) (Cape Girardeau). Home: PO Box 127 Jackson MO 63755 Office: SE Mo State U Dept Tchr Edn Cape Girardeau MO 63701

ANDERSON, KELLY ELIZABETH, marketing professional; b. Oakland, Calif., June 7, 1957; d. Frank Stoakes Anderson and Emily Elizabeth (Wright) Kimlinger. BA in Math., BA in Environ. Studies, U. Calif., Santa Cruz, 1979, BA in Sci. Communications, 1980. Staff writer Charlotte (N.C.) Observer, 1980; sci. writer, editor Frank Porter Graham Child Devel Ctr., U. N.C., Chapel Hill, 1980-81; coordinator communications Sea Grant Coll. Program, U. Calif., San Diego, 1981-84; mgr. tech. publs. Loral Instrumentation, San Diego, 1984-87, mgr. mktg. communications, 1987—; acting dir. tech. services, Loral Instrumentation, San Diego, 1986. Contbr. more than 200 articles to profl. jours. Mem. Desktop Pub. Adv. Com. Grossmont Coll., San Diego, 1986—. AAAS fellow, 1980; recipient Excellence in Writing award Internat. Assn. Bus. Communicators, 1981, Council for Advancement and Support of Edn., 1984. Mem. Nat. Mgmt. Assn. (v.p. 1986), Soc. for Tech. Communication (awards of Excellence and Achievement 1981-84), Computer and Electronics Mktg. Assn. (officer 1987-88). Office: Loral Instrumentation 8401 Aero Dr San Diego CA 92123

ANDERSON, KIM COX, sales executive; b. Louisville, Feb. 6, 1958; d. Gilbert Harris Cox and Lyda Marion (Klinglesmith) Lewis; m. Gary Wayne Anderson, June 4, 1977 (div. July 1981). Radiologic technologist St. Vincent Hosp., Indpls., 1980-81, cardiovascular radiologic technologist, 1981-85; sales rep. Elecath, Cin., 1985-86; clin. specialist Advanced Cardiovascular Systems, Austin, Tex., 1986-87; sales rep. Advanced Cardiovascular Systems, Forest Hills, N.Y., 1987—. Mem. Am. Registry of Radiologic Technologist, 1979-88. Republican.

ANDERSON, LINDA CAROL, lawyer; b. Los Angeles, May 25, 1955; d. Adrian Campbell Anderson and Laura Ann (Kroencke) Harvey. Student U. Utah, 1977; B.A. in English cum laude, high honors with distinction, Brigham Young U., 1978; postgrad. U. Tex., 1980; J.D. cum laude, Brigham Young U., 1981. Bar: Tex. 1981. Adminstrv. aide Brigham Young U. Honors Program, Provo, Utah, 1976-78; legal intern Oppenheiner, Rosenberg, Kelleher & Wheatley, San Antonio, summer 1980; briefing atty. Tex. Ct. Appeals, San Antonio, 1981-82, ct. clerk, 1982-83; asst. criminal dist. atty. Bexar County Dist. Atty.'s Office, San Antonio, 1983-84; assoc. atty. litigation sect. Fulbright & Jaworski, 1984-86; trial atty. Environ. Enforcement Sect. U.S. Dept. Justice, 1986—; chmn. Tex. State BAr Com. on Child Abuse, 1985-1986, chmn. legal com., chmn. writing com. Dist. Atty.'s Task Force Child Abuse, San Antonio, 1984-86; chmn. writing com. Dist. Atty.'s Task Force Domestic Violence, 1983; atty. provider Pro Bono Legal Services, San Antonio, 1983-86. Contbr. chpt. to book, articles to profl. jours. Recipient Fine Arts scholarship La Canada Town and Country Assn., 1973-77; Calif. State scholar, 1973; Soroptimist scholar, 1973-77; Heppe Meml. Found. scholar, 1973-77; Univ. scholar Brigham Young U., 1978. Mem. ABA (2d pl. regional client counselling competition 1980), Am. Judicature Soc., Tex. Bar Assn. (chmn. com. on child abuse and neglect 1985-86), NOW, Amnesty Internat. Democrat. Clubs: Italian, English Circle, Job's Daus. (musician 1969-71). Office: Dept Justice 10th and Pennsylvania NW Washington DC 20530

ANDERSON, LOUISE ELLEN, municipal administrator; b. Detroit, Aug. 6, 1939; d. Reuben Andrew and Bertha Angeline (Mayer) Henderson; children: Guy Marc, Renee Helen. BS in Edn., Wayne State U., 1962, M in Pub. Adminstrn., 1978. Program adminstr. Detroit Dept. Health, 1965-79; govt. analyst Detroit Water & Sewerage Dept., 1979-85; adminstrv. analyst Orange County, Santa Ana, Calif., 1985-86; asst. to gen. mgr. Mission Viejo (Calif.) Community Services Dist., 1987—. Arbitrator Nat. Panel Consumer Arbitrators, Detroit, 1981-85; bd. dirs. Town Sq. Coop., Detroit, 1984-85. Recipient Spirit of Detroit award Detroit City Council, 1985. Mem. Am. Pub. Health Assn., Am. Soc. for Pub. Adminstrn. (program planning com. Detroit chpt. 1980, Orange County chpt.), Assn. Profl. and Tech. Employees (bd. dirs. Detroit chpt. 1981-85), Mun. Mgmt. Assts. So. Calif. (program planning com. 1986-87). Office: Don Greek and Assocs Civil Engrs-Cons 1102 N Tustin Orange CA 92629

ANDERSON, LYNN COOVER, veterinarian, biotechnology manager, b. Erie, Pa., Jan. 4, 1954; d. Kenneth Oliver and Martha Claire (Coover) Anderson; m. John F. Carpenter, June 12, 1982. D.V.M., Iowa State U., 1977. Diplomate Am. Coll. Lab. Animal Medicine Clinician Lisle Emergency Vet. Service, Lisle, Ill., 1978-79, Boone Animal Hosp., Western Springs, Ill., 1977-79; postdoctoral fellow U. Mich. Med. Sch., Ann Arbor, 1979-81; asst. prof. lab. medicine U. Minn. Med. Sch., Mpls., 1981-83; supr. lab. animal medicine Riker Labs., Inc., 3M, St. Paul, 1983-86; mgr. Amgen, Inc., Thousand Oaks, Calif., 1987—; adj. asst. prof., vice chmn. adv. council Animal Health Tech., U. Minn.-Waseca, 1984-86. Editor Iowa State U. Veterinarian mag., 1976-77; author profl. meeting presentations and profl. audio-visual program; contbr. chpts. to books, articles to profl. jours.; referee profl. jours. Mem. Jr. League of Mpls., 1982-86. Mem. AVMA, Am. Soc. Lab. Animal Practitioners (bd. dirs. 1985-87), Am. Assn. Lab. Animal Sci. (regional examining bd. 1981-86, com. on lab. animal techs. 1984-87, pubs. com. 1986-88, council on edn. 1986-88), Minn. Assn. Lab. Animal Sci. (bd. dirs. 1982-86), So. Calif. Assn. Lab. Animal Sci. (bd. dirs. 1987-88), 3M Circle Tech Excellence, Assn. for Women Vets (sec. 1986-88), Am. Assn. for Accreditation of Lab. Animal Care (ad hoc cons. 1987—), Mortar Bd., Phi Zeta, Kappa Alpha Theta (dir. Mpls. alumnae chpt. 1982-84). Republican. Congregationalist. Office: Amgen Inc 1900 Oak Terrace Ln Thousand Oaks CA 91320

ANDERSON, MARGARET POMEROY, small business owner; b. San Francisco; d. William Arthur Pomeroy and Margaret C. Guittard; m. F.H. Hoover, Dec. 20, 1966 (div. 1981); children: Laura, Cleveland; m. Derby Ferris Anderson, May 22, 1982. BA, U. Calif., Berkeley, 1965. Asst. dir. Pomeroy Galleries, San Francisco, 1965-69; owner, officer Hoover Gallery, San Francisco, 1969-82, Pomeroy-Anderson, Southport, Conn., 1983—; lectr. continuing edn. Fairfield (Conn.) U., 1984—. Contbr. articles on art and antiques to profl. jours.; N.Y. corr. Antiques West, 1986—. Mem. women's bd. San Francisco Art Inst., 1977; dir. San Francisco Opera Guild, 1969-79; chair support com. Archives Am. Art , San Francisco, 1978-80, mem. com., N.Y.C., 1983—. Mem. Am. Soc. Appraisers (sr.), Conn. Soc. Appraisers (treas. 1985-86, 2d v.p. 1986-87, 1st v.p. 1987—). Club: Town and Country (San Francisco). Office: PO Box 787 Southport CT 06490

ANDERSON, MARGRET ELIZABETH, lawyer; b. Port Chester, N.Y., Oct. 2, 1949; d. Samuel Glover and Evelyn (Oliver) A.; m. Robert T. McDonald, May 16, 1980; children: Christina Anderson-McDonald, Meredith Anderson-McDonald. Student, Wellesley Coll., 1967-69; BA, Yale U., 1971; JD, U. Pa., 1974. Bar: Pa. 1974, U.S. Dist. Ct. (ea. dist.) Pa. 1975, U.S. Ct. Appeals (3rd cir.) 1976. Intern Pub. Defender, Phila., 1972-73, U.S. Civil Rights Commn., Washington, 1973; legal writing instr. U. Pa. Sch. Law, Phila., 1973-74; asst. atty. gen. Pa. Dept. of Justice, Phila., 1974-79; sr. atty. Merck & Co., Inc., West Point, Pa., 1979—. Mem. Zoning Hearing Bd., Abington, Pa., 1985—. Mem. Nat. Bar Assn., Pa. Bar Assn. Episcopalian. Office: Merck & Co Inc Sumneytown Pike West Point PA 19486

ANDERSON, MARIAN, contralto; b. Phila., Feb. 27, 1902; d. John Berkeley and Anna Anderson; ed. Phila. pub. schs.; mus. edn. pvt. study in Phila., N.Y. and abroad; hon. degrees 23 Am. ednl. instns., 1 Korean; m. Orpheus H. Fisher, July 24, 1943. As child sang in Union Bapt. Ch. choir, Phila.; a fund raised through a church concert enabled her to take singing lessons under an Italian instr.; won 1st prize in competition with 300 others at N.Y. Lewisohn Stadium, 1925; began singing career, 1924; debut in Un Ballo in Maschera, Met. Opera, 1955; has made many concert tours of the U.S. and Europe; one of the leading contraltos in world; appearances in all famous concert halls, stadia, now ret. U.S. del. to UN, 1955, also 13th Gen. Assembly. Recipient Bok Award, 1940, Congl. Medal of Honor, 1977, Nat. Medal of Arts, 1986; awarded Finnish decoration "probenignitate humana", 1940; decorations from Sweden, Philippines, Haiti, Liberia, France, numerous states and cities in U.S.; Yokus Lo medal (Japan). Mem. Alpha Kappa Alpha. Author: My Lord, What a Morning. Home: Danbury CT 06810 Office: care ICM Artists Ltd 40 W 57th St New York NY 10019

ANDERSON, MARTHA ALENE, environmental health and safety executive, academic administrator; b. Monessen, Pa., June 15, 1945; d. Jesse Lee and Helen Frances (Daugherty) Cain; m. James O. Anderson, Sept. 9, 1966; 1 child, Heather Linn. BS in Biology, Calif. State Coll., 1967. Research asst. W.Va. U., Morgantown, 1967-72; tchr. Hokkaido Internat. Sch., Sapporo, Japan, 1972-73; research asst. Pa. State U., 1974-76 research assoc. U. Ariz., Tucson, 1976-80; mgr. chem. waste Dept. Risk Mgmt., U. Ariz., Tucson, 1980-81, asst. dir., 1981-85, dir., 1985-87; dir. environ. health and safety Thomas Jefferson U., Phila., 1987—. Named Woman of Yr., Tucson Bus. and Profl. Women, 1985, Woman on Move, Tucson YWCA, 1985. Mem. Am. Soc. Safety Engrs. (sec. 1985-86, v.p. 1986—), Am. Indsl. Hygiene Assn., Am. Soc. Hosp. Engrs., Bus. and Profl. Women of Thomas Jefferson U. (pres. 1988—), Campus Safety Assn. Avocations: Japanese literature, sewing. Office: Thomas Jefferson U Dept Environ Health and Safety Edison 1620 Philadelphia PA 19107

ANDERSON, MARTHA GAIL, chemical company executive; b. Bakersfield, Calif., Aug. 27, 1951; d. Charles and Jerline (James) Alford; m. Jan Philip Anderson, Oct. 28, 1969; children: Charles Philip, Bryan Christopher. Cert., Cypress Jr. Coll., 1973-74, Mesa Jr. Coll., 1984-85. Owner ACCO Chem. Co., Chula Vista, Calif. Mem. Beta Sigma Phi (v.p. 1979-82).

ANDERSON, MARTHA J., credit union administrator; b. Kansas City, Kans., June 21, 1938; d. William C. and Irene A. (Ramsey) Kloiber; m. Carl R. Anderson, Aug. 23, 1959; children: Sheryl R., Steven R. Grad. high sch., Kansas City. Mgr., treas. Wyandotte County Tchrs. Credit Union, Kansas City, 1962-67; gen. mgr. Okla. State Univ. Employees' Fed. Credit Union, Stillwater, 1971—; sec. Credit Union Chpt. Kansas City, 1962-63. Mem. Okla. Credit Union League (bd. dirs. 1980-86, treas. 1983-84), Credit Union Nat. Assn. (nat. dir. 1980-86), Stillwater C. of C. Republican. Baptist. Lodge: Order Eastern Star. Office: Okla State U Employees Fed Credit Union 350 Student Union Building Stillwater OK 74078

ANDERSON, MARY ANN, flight attendant; b. Torrance, Calif., Apr. 5, 1943; d. Clifford Eugene and Thresa Marie (Hammond) King; m. Karl Mantei, April 15, 1973 (div. 1977); 1 child, Annette Marie; m. David Jerome Anderson, Dec. 10, 1984; children: Lisa Marie, Angela Eve. BS, Portland (Oreg.) State U., 1972, MS, 1975. Cert. tchr., Oreg., Wash. Prin. the Beginning Sch., Oreg. Episc. Schs., Portland, 1972-74; tchr. curriculum devel. Tigard (Oreg.) Sch. Dist., 1974-75; owner, prin. Mt. Park Learning Tree Day Sch., Lake Oswego, Oreg., 1976-83; flight attendant internat. United Air Lines, Seattle, 1984—. Author: Tracey: A Mother's Journal of Teenage Addiction, 1988. Adminstrv. asst. Joyce Cohen for State Senate Campaign, Lake Oswego, 1982. Mem. Alpha Chi Omega. Roman Catholic. Home: PO Box 2022 Friday Harbor WA 98250

ANDERSON, MARY ELLEN, risk/insurance coordinator; b. Liberty, S.C., June 25, 1940; d. William Robert and Ruby Irene (Trammell) Murphy; m. Howard Eugene Anderson, Sept. 8, 1956 (div. Jan. 1987); children: Howard Eugene Jr., Sterling Craig. Student, Polk Community Coll., 1980. Sec. H. Lamar Stewart Ins. Agy, Frostproof, Fla., 1962-64; accounts payable clk. Ben Hill Griffin, Inc., Frostproof, 1964-65; agt. Bullard Ins. Agy., Inc., Lake Wales, Fla., 1966-79; risk/ins. coordinator Coca-Cola Foods, Auburndale, Fla., 1979—; dir. Fla. Girls State, Inc., Orlando, 1988—. City chmn. March of Dimes, Frostproof, 1964; campaign worker Tom Wheeler for Sheriff, Winter Haven, Fla., 1988. Mem. Risk and Ins. Mgmt. Soc., Inc., VFW., Am. Legion, DAV. Democrat. Baptist. Lodge: Polk Bus. Women's Sertoma. Office: Coca-Cola Foods PO Box 247 Auburndale FL 33823

ANDERSON, MARY JANE, newsletter publisher, public relations specialist; b. Richmond, Va., May 27, 1930; d. Francis W. and Margaret G. (Esbrook) A.; B.A. in Journalism, Wayne State U., 1951. Staff writer Skyline mag. and Mich. Motor Carrier, Detroit, 1952-54; reporter Fairchild Publs., Detroit, 1954-57, Home Furnishings Daily/Footwear News, Chgo., 1957-67; food service editor Vend Mag., Billboard Publs., N.Y.C., 1967-72; owner Anderson Publs. (pubs. The Anderson Report, Foods By Mail); prin. MJA Pub. Relations, Chgo., 1979—. Active local Republican campaigns; broadcaster Chgo. Radio Info. Services for blind and print handicapped; vol. Rec. for the Blind, N.Y.C. Named Food Editor of Yr., Nat. Assn. Coll. and Univ. Food Services. Mem. Women in Communications (past pres.), Internat. Food Editorial Council (past v.p.). Office: Anderson Publs 320 N Michigan Suite 1305 Chicago IL 60601

ANDERSON, MARY JORGENSEN, mathematician; b. Winchester, Tex., Oct. 31, 1937; d. Roy Lewis and Nellie Joyce (Hart) Jorgensen; B.S., La. State U., 1965, M.S., 1968, Ph.D., 1979; m. Edmund Hughes Anderson, Oct. 10, 1975; children—Carolyne Gail Calvert, Gary Steven Calvert, Christopher Lewis Calvert. Engring. technician La. Dept. Hwys., Baton Rouge, 1957-60; grad. asst. La. State U., 1965-68, 76-78; instr. in math. Miss. State U., 1970-76, asst. prof. math., 1978-81; mathematician Superior Oil Co., Midland, Tex., 1981-85; info. systems mgr. Mobil Oil Corp., Denver, 1985—. Mem. Am. Math. Soc., Assn. Women in Math., Miss. Acad. Scis., Pi Mu Epsilon, Phi Delta Kappa. Episcopalian. Contbr. articles to profl. jours.; reviewer Math. Revs., 1984—. Office: Mobil Oil Corp PO Box 5444 Denver CO 80217

ANDERSON, MARY LOU, educator; b. Mt. Pleasant, Iowa, Aug. 29, 1949; d. Carl Marion and Hazel Lucile (Mitchell) A. B.S. in Edn., Northeast Mo. State U., 1971, M.S. in Elem. Guidance, 1974. Lic. elem. tchr., Mo. Elem. tchr. Waynesville pub. schs., Mo., 1971-73, Hannibal pub. schs., Mo., 1973-79, Bel Ridge Elem. Sch., St. Louis, 1979-86; counselor Bel Ridge Elem. Sch., 1986-87; counselor Lincoln Elem. Sch., 1987—; ERA cons. ERAmerica, Washington, 1980-81, NEA, Washington, 1980-82; state conf. workshop leader NEA, 1979-83; co-founder, chmn. Mo. NEA Women's Caucus, 1975-78. Pres. Mo. ERA Coalition, 1980-82; pres. Polit. Action Com. St. Louis Women's Polit. Caucus, 1984-85, endorsement com. chair, 1987; campaign worker Mo. Democratic Orgn., 1982—. Mem. NEA (LEAST discipline cons. 1981—, Lorna Bottger Polit. Action award 1982), St. Louis Suburban Tchrs. Assn. (bd. dirs. 1983-87), Normandy Tchrs. Assn. (chmn. instrn. and profl. devel. com., mem. negotians com. 1985—), St. Louis Internat. Reading Assn., Mo. Sch. Counselors Assn., St. Louis Suburban Counselors Assn., NOW, ACLU, Phi Delta Kappa. Mem. United Ch. of Christ. Avocations: playing piano; aerobics; reading; plays and movies. Home: 4497 Pershing St Apt 107 Saint Louis MO 63108 Office: Bel Ridge Elem Sch 8930 Boston Ave Saint Louis MO 63121

ANDERSON, MEGAN BOTHWELL, cultural exchange consultant, educator; b. Salt Lake City, Sept. 10, 1944; d. Vernon Edward and Elizabeth (Bothwell) Anderson; m. Marvin L. Friedland, Apr. 1, 1967 (div. 1970); 1 child, Michael. BS, U. Utah, 1966, MS, 1971, postgrad. Research asst. U. Utah, Salt Lake City, 1962-71; environmental geographer Dept. Trans. Environ. Council Utah, Salt Lake City, 1971-74; cons. Utah State U. Found, Salt Lake City, 1974; asst. st. planning coordinator St. Utah, Salt Lake City, 1974-79; pres. M.T. Enterprises and Cons., Salt Lake City, 1979—; cons. Utah Dept. Transp., Salt Lake City 1986; liaison paleontological, U. Utah, 1968-71, sci. and tech. com., Utah St. Gov. 1979. Author: Utah Resource Information System, 1979, The Multiple Use and Joint Development, 1975. St. rep. Fed. Emergency Mgmt. Agy, Los Angeles, Washington 1976; sch. rep. ARC, Logan1961. Mem. Utah Sect. Am. Cong. Surveying and Mapping (hospitality chmn. 1974, sec. 1973-74, editor newsletter 1972, speaker 1973 Washington). Episcopalian. Home: 3939 St Francis Cir Salt Lake City UT 84124 Office: MT Enterprises and Cons 3939 St Francis Cir Salt Lake City UT 84124

ANDERSON, MELODY TAYLOR, accountant; b. Berea, Ky., June 23, 1959; d. Melvin Monroe and Patricia Ann (Bronson) Taylor; divorced; 1 child, Jeffrey Lee. Cert. real estate. Office mgr. T&M Coal Corp., Harlan, Ky., 1978-82; personnel dir. Harlan County Solid Waste Dept., 1982-83; asst. mgr., bookkeeper Eastern Food Mart, Harlan, 1984-85; exec. sec. agrl. stabilization and conservation USDA, Harlan, 1983-86; real estate assoc. Bert Ed Pollitte Real Estate, Harlan, 1985-86; realtor Don Foster & Assocs./Better Homes and Gardens, Richmond, Ky., 1986-87; office mgr. Lowell D. Land, CPA, Richmond, 1986-87, East Gate Supply, Richmond, %; acct., cons. MTA & Assocs., Richmond, Ky., 1987—; office mgr. Dal-Tex Constrn. Co. and Will-Shard Building Products, Orlando, Fla., 1987—. Sec. Harlan County rural devel. com., 1985. Mem. Nat. Assn. Female Execs., Nat. Bd. Realtors, Madison Bd. Realtors, Ky. Bd. Realtors, U.S. Jaycees, Ky. Jaycees, Madison County Jaycees (exec. advisor 1986). Republican. Office: 5545 Devonbriar Way #101 Orlando FL 32822

ANDERSON, MERLINE POWELL, fund raiser; b. Indianola, Miss., Jan. 7, 1946; d. Aruator and Catherine (Bishop) Powers; m. James A. Anderson, May 28, 1966 (div. 1968); 1 dau., Tracy Sherra. Student Forest Park Community Coll., St. Louis, 1964-65; B.S. in Bus. Adminstrn., Lindenwood Coll., St. Charles, Mo., 1978, postgrad., 1978-79. Sec., adminstrv. asst. Mo. State Agys., St. Louis, 1965-70; legal asst. Atty. Forriss D. Elliott, St. Louis, 1970-77; dir. devel. Central Med. Ctr., St. Louis, 1977-83; freelance fund raising cons., St. Louis, 1983—; mem. Nat. Health Screening Council, St. Louis, 1985—; sec., ptnr. United Entertainment & Investment Corp. Treas. St. Louis Urban Affairs Council, 1978—; bd. dirs. Nat. Urban Affairs Council, St. Louis, 1978—; v.p. Rosary High Sch. PTA, St. Louis, 1983-85; treas. Campaign for Eddie Davis for Bd. Edn., St. Louis, 1983. Mem. Nat. Soc. Fund Raising Execs. (sec. 1980-82), Nat. Assn. Hosp. Devel., Nat. Assn. Female Execs. Democrat. Baptist.

ANDERSON, MICHAEL LARSEN, human resources administrator; b. Nashville, Feb. 19, 1941; d. Ralph Michael and Vee (Allen) Larsen; m. William J. Anderson, III, June 4, 1958 (div. 1984); children—Alicia Sayle, William Joseph, Ralph Michael Larsen, Mollie Blair. Student, Vanderbilt U., 1958-60, Xavier Coll., 1977-78. Asst. dir. human resources PEDCo. Inc., Cin., 1979-81, human resources dir., 1981-83. Pres. Nashville area chpt. Lupus Found. Am. Inc., 1987-88, 88—; bd. dirs. Nashville Mental Health Assn., 1968-71; founding bd. dirs. Children's Hosp., Nashville; child advocacy chmn. Jr. League, Huntington, W.Va., 1974-75; child advocacy co-chmn. Jr. League Cin., 1977-78. Appeared on cover of Time mag., July 1965, Town & Country, 1974. Episcopalian.

ANDERSON, PAMELA LYNNE, communications executive; b. Sioux Falls, S.D., Dec. 16, 1959; d. Kenneth Wayne and Pearl Daisey (Sumption) A. B of Secondary Edn., Augustana Coll., 1982. Secondary tchr. West Allis (Wis.) Sch. Dist., 1982-83; network adminstr. Republic Telcom, Inc., Bloomington, Minn., 1983-85; telecommunications analyst Honeywell, Inc., Mpls., 1985-86, telecommunications specialist, 1986-87, supr. voice services, 1988—. Vol. Spl. Olympics, Mpls., 1985-87, Minn. Freeze Campaign, St. Paul, 1987; mentor Mpls. Bus. Mentor Program, 1986-87. Mem. Minn. Telecommunications Assn., Honeywell Women's Council, Kappa Delta Phi. Avocations: travel, reading, sailing, golfing, biking. Office: Honeywell Inc Honeywell Plaza MN26-4201 Minneapolis MN 55408

ANDERSON, PEGGY JEAN, university administrator, linguist; b. Fargo, N.D., Mar. 28, 1945; d. Walter Raymond and Elizabeth (Snider) A.; B.S. in Edn., Emporia State U., 1967; M.A. in Linguistics, U. Kans., 1979; m. Richard John Robinson, Apr. 18, 1981. Tchr. spl. edn., English, Kansas City (Kans.) Public Schs., 1967-68; tchr. Somerdale (N.J.) Public Schs., 1968-73; dir. fgn. staff, instr. YMCA Japan, Fukuoka, 1973-77; instr. Applied English Center, U. Kans., Lawrence, 1977-79; coordinator English as Second Lang. Programs, U. Iowa, 1979-81; curriculum coordinator Intensive English Lang. Center, Wichita State U., 1981-82, asso. dir. center, 1982—; reviewer Scott-Foresman Pub. Co.; cons. to community groups, public schs., internat. bus. Nat. Assn. Fgn. Student Affairs grantee, 1980—. Mem. TESOL, Mid-Am. TESOL (1st v.p., pres.), Nat. Assn. Fgn. Student Affairs, Linguistic Soc. Am., Mid-Am. MLA, Wichita Handweaver's Guild (pres.). Democrat. Episcopalian. Research in second lang. acquisition, teaching methodology, curriculum design. Home: 2410 Bromfield Circle Wichita KS 67226 Office: Wichita State U Intensive Lang Tng Ctr Wichita KS 67208

ANDERSON, PEGGY JEAN, career counseling administrator; b. Coffeyville, Kans., Nov. 3, 1943; d. James Franklin and Norma Jacquelyn (Garrett) Edwards; m. James D. Anderson, Nov. 30, 1962 (div. 1980); children: Mark Donald, Charles Michael. Grad. high sch., Alaska. Sec. Upland Industries, Omaha, 1974-75; statistician Union Pacific Railroad, Omaha, 1975-79; sales rep. Bus. Services & Equipment Co., Omaha, 1979-80; v.p.

Word and Data Processing Products, Omaha, 1980-84; pres., owner Anderson Data Service, Omaha, 1984-86; cons., v.p. mktg. Career Design, Inc., Omaha, 1986—. Judge Jr. Achievement, Omaha, 1985-87. Mem. Omaha Network (sec.), Sales and Mktg. Execs., Adminstrv. Mgmt. Soc. (several awards). Republican. Methodist. Office: Career Design 12020 Shamrock Plaza Suite 300 Omaha NE 68154

ANDERSON, PHYLLIS REINHOLD, business executive, management consultant, engineer; b. Denver, July 29, 1936; d. Floyd Reinhold and Minerva Eva (Needham) A.; children: Kristin Elizabeth, Michele Ann. Metall. Engr., Colo. Sch. Mines, 1962; MBA, U. Chgo., 1968. Mill metallurgist, supr. U.S. Steel Corp., 1962-66; research and devel. sr. metallurgist, supr., planner Continental Can Co., 1966-73; mgr. corp. planning B.F. Goodrich Co., 1973-76; regional assoc. Strategic Planning Inst., Cambridge, Mass., 1975-76; project mgr. corp. planning, sales engring., then project mgr. corp. devel. Signode Corp., Glenview, Ill., 1976-80; mgmt. cons., 1974—; pres., prin. cons. Corp. Devel. Assocs., Inc., mgmt. cons. in strategic planning, mktg., product and systems devel., CAD/CAM/CAE, Oak Brook, Ill., 1980—; assoc. Strategic Planning Inst., 1982—, initial exec. com., chmn. membership com., 1975-76; bd. dirs. Quest Assocs. Mgmt. and Quality Cons.; instr. bus. analysis methods. Author: Corporate Strategic Planning: An Integrated Approach, 1981; contbr. articles to profl. jours. Active psychiat. support services, career counseling women's groups and individuals. Recipient Leadership award Chgo. YWCA, 1977. Mem. Am. Soc. Metals, Soc. Women Engrs., Am. Mktg. Assn., N.Y. Acad. Scis., Women in Mgmt., Nat. Assn. Women Bus. Owners, AAAS, Mensa. Clubs: Execs. of Chgo., Whitehall. Home: 2201 S Highland Ave Lombard IL 60148 Office: 55 W 22nd St Suite 111 Lombard IL 60148

ANDERSON, SANDRA WOOD, data processing executive; b. Lugoff, S.C., Mar. 9, 1949; d. Sam Jr. and Eloise (Wood) Wright; m. James Edward Anderson, Sept. 20, 1974 (div. 1985). BS in Bus. Edn., Benedict Coll., Columbia, S.C., 1970; cert. in data processing, Midland Tech. Coll., Columbia, 1983; cert. Electronics, Kershaw County Vocat. Sch., Camden, S.C., 1985. Accounts receivable clk. Rollins, Inc., Atlanta, 1970-72, Watkins Motor Lines, Atlanta, 1972-75; recapping clk. Nat. Linen Service, Columbia, 1976; proof operator S.C. Nat. Bank, Columbia, 1976-77, accounts payable clk., 1977-81, computer operator, scheduler, tape librarian, 1981-86, shift mgr., data processing officer, 1986—. Mem. S.C. Polit. Action Com., Columbia, 1986-87, Roundtop Bapt. Ch., Blythewood, S.C. Mem. Am. Inst. Banking (basic and standard cert., 1978, 81), Greater Columbia Tennis Club, Zeta Phi Beta. Home: 418 Eskie Dixon Rd Elgin SC 29045 Office: SC Nat Bank 1628 Browning Rd Room 115 Columbia SC 29226

ANDERSON, SAUNDRA LEE, recreation therapist; b. Salt Lake City, Feb. 9, 1951; d. Arthur Ray and Betty Jane (Griffith) Carlston; m. Michael Thomas Anderson, Jan. 5, 1980; 1 child, Matthew Thomas. B.S., U. Utah, 1975. Cert. therapeutic recreation specialist. Recreation therapist Utah State Tng. Sch., Salt Lake City, 1974-75, West Jordan Care Ctr., Salt Lake City, 1976-78, Wyo. State Tng. Sch., Lander, 1978-87 . Treas. Lander Dist. Recreation Bd., 1983-85; bd. dirs. Wyo. Spl. Olympics, 1987—. Mem. Ch. of Jesus Christ of Latter Day Saints. Avocations: traveling, camping, cross country skiing, gardening. Home: PO Box 119 Hudson WY 82515

ANDERSON, SHARON A., gas company executive. d. DeWayne C. and Edith (Walker) A. BSBA, U. Tulsa, 1977. CPA, Okla. With Okla. Natural Gas Co., Tulsa, 1965—, asst. mgr. corp. responsibility and community affairs, 1979-80, asst. mgr. fin. reporting, 1980-83, mgr. fin. reporting., 1983—. Mem. Skiatook Reservoir Authority, Tulsa, 1980-84. Mem. Am. Inst. CPA's, Okla. Soc. CPA's, Nat. Assn. Female Execs., LWV (treas. Met. Tulsa chpt. 1987—), Okla. Heritage Assn. Republican. Club: Toastmasters. Office: Okla Natural Gas Co 100 W 5th St Tulsa OK 74103

ANDERSON, SHARON LEE MUTH, food service executive; b. Monterey, Calif., Jan. 21, 1957; d. Arnold John and Mardell Mary (Behler) Muth; m. William Vance Erik Anderson, June 28, 1953. AA in Bus., Monterey Peninsula Coll., 1983; BS in Bus. cum laude, Golden Gate U., 1984, MBA, 1985. Prodn. scheduler Graco/LTI Corp., Monterey, Calif., 1979-81, mgr. purchasing, 1981-84; v.p. distbn. Pentagram Corp., Honolulu, 1985—. Served to 2d lt. USAR, 1986—. Mem. Nat. Purchasing Assn., Hawaii Purchasing Assn., Nat. Rifle Assn. Republican. Roman Catholic. Office: Pentagram Corp 1056 Fort St Mall Honolulu HI 96813

ANDERSON, SHIRLEY JEAN, home economist; b. Vermillion, S.D., Jan. 10, 1950; d. Ronald James and Dorothy Adeline (Hofland) A. BS in Home Econs. Edn., S.D. State U., 1972, MS in Home Econs., Child Devel., 1984. Home econs., family living agent Lyon County Extension Service, Marshall, Minn., 1973—, dir., 1980—; mem. exec. com. extension faculty cons. com. Lyon County Extension Service, St. Paul, 1983—. Bd. dirs. Marshall/Lyon County Library, 1986—, Marshall United Way, 1986—. Mem. Am. Home Econs. Assn., Minn. Home Econs. Assn. (1987—), Nat. Assn. Extension Home Econs. (Disting. Service award 1983), Minn. Assn. Extension Home Econs. (Disting. Service award 1983), Minn. Assn. Extension Agts. Lutheran. Club: Linc/Lyon Home Econs (Marshall). Office: Lyon County Extension Service 1400 E Lyon St Marshall MN 56258

ANDERSON, TAMMY BETH, communications manager; b. Queens, N.Y., Sept. 1, 1960; d. David Abraham and Diane Lois (Herman) Schulman; m. Kurt James Anderson, Sept. 14, 198 6; 1 stepchild, Jason Richard Weidner. Degree in comml. art, Hennepin County Vocat.-Tech., Eden Prairie, Minn., 1978; postgrad., Coll. St. Catherine, St. Paul, 1985—. Correspondence sec. Ross Investment Co., Edina, Minn., 1980; quality control rep. Hubbard Milling Co., Minnetonka, Minn., 1980-81; ins. inspector Underwriters Service Co., Hopkins, Minn., 1982-83; dir. publs., communications mgr. Lifetouch Nat. Sch. Studios, Mpls., 1984—. Author, editor: Versatile Beans, 1978, Exposure mag., 1986—. Tutor Glenwood-Lyndale Community Ctr., Mpls., 1982; women's advocate Sojourner Shelter, Minnetonka, 1984—; active Sta. KFAI-Radio, Mpls., Simon Weisenthal Ctr., Mpls., 1985-86. Mem. Nat. Assn. Female Execs., Women in Communications Inc. Democrat. Jewish. Club: Minnesota Sword. Office: Lifetouch Nat Sch Studios 7800 Picture Dr Minneapolis MN 55435

ANDERSON, THELMA KAY, pharmaceutical company official; b. Sims, Ill., Nov. 2, 1938; d. Henry Audry and Leota Zelma (Wells) Linder; BS, McKendree Coll., 1961; student Sch. Med. Tech., Meth. Hosp. of Central Ill., 1962; MBA, Rutgers U., 1975; m. Raymond Francis Anderson, Apr. 18, 1964. Lab. asst. McKendree Coll., 1959-61; med. technologist Methodist Hosp. Central Ill., 1962-63; hematology supr. and instr. USAF Hosp., Scott AFB, Ill., 1963-65; hematology supr. VA Hosp., East Orange, N.J., 1965-66; teaching supr. Perth Amboy (N.J.) Gen. Hosp., 1966-69, chief technologist, lab. mgr., 1969-72; adj. faculty Middlesex Coll., 1972-73; gen. supr., adminstrv. dir. lab. ops. Center for Lab. Medicine, Metuchen, N.J., 1972-73; med lab. supr., dir. tng. Schwarz-Mann div. Becton-Dickinson & Co., Orangeburg, N.Y., 1973-74; nat. ednl. coordinator, tech. cons. services specialist Roche Diagnostics, Nutley, N.J., 1974-76, product sales mgr., 1976-80, product mktg. mgr., 1980-87, mgr. project devel., 1987—; adj. faculty Middlesex County Coll., med. tech. adv. council. Chair McKendree Coll. Alumni Jamboree, 1986, bd. trustees, 1986—, acad. affairs com., 1986—. Recipient P. Akers Alumni award, 1987. Mem. Clin. Ligand Assay Soc., N.J. Soc. Med. Tech. (dir., past pres. 1972-73, chmn. membership com. 1979-80), Am. Soc. Med. Tech. (asso. ed. Jour. 1979-81), N.J. Blood Bank Assn., Am. Soc. Microbiologists, Alpha Mu Tau. Home: 732 Van Nest Dr Martinsville NJ 08836 Office: 1 Sunset Ave Montclair NJ 07042

ANDERSON, VEDA LEONE, educator; b. Exeter, Calif., Aug. 29, 1932; d. Raymond Leon and Fern (Hough) Hurst; m. Horace Stanley Dennis, June 13, 1954 (div. 1963); children: Deborah E. Laws, Sharon L. Coble, Jeanette E. Davis; m. Gerald Eugene Anderson, Sept. 25, 1971; adopted children: Keely J. Sheehey, Tina M. Anderson, Gerald E. Anderson II. BS in Edn., N.Mex. State U., 1954, postgrad., 1970—; MA in Edn., Western N.Mex. U., 1969, postgrad., 1970—; postgrad., U. Tex., El Paso, 1968, San Jose State U., 1970. Tchr. Las Cruces (N.Mex.) Pub. Schs., 1954-55, 1958-59, Ft. Smith (Ark.) Pub. Schs., 1957-58, Deming (N.Mex.) Pub. Schs., 1963—; tchr. ednl. TV, Deming; dir. workshops pub. schs., 1968, state conv., 1969, local tchrs., 1975-77, 1980-82. Chmn. Rep. Women's Activities, 1980-84; tchr. Bible class Ch. Christ, Deming, 1963—. Mem. Internat. Fedn. Bus. and Profl. Women (Outstanding Educator 1982, Outstanding Young Woman Am. 1969), NEA (sec. Deming chpt., bldg. rep.), N.Mex. Edn. Assn., Beta Sigma Phi (sec.-treas. 1987, pres. v.p.). Office: Meml Sch 1000 S 10th St Deming NM 88031

ANDERSON-IMBERT, ANA ISABEL, rheumatologist, health care facility administrator; b. Buenos Aires, Aug. 21, 1940; d. Enrique and Margot (Di Clerico) Anderson Imbert; m. Jack Joseph Himelbau, May 30, 1965; children: Robert, Vanessa. BA, U. Mich., 1960, MS, 1963, MD, 1968. Diplomate Am. Bd. Internal Medicine. Resident Columbia Presbyn. Hosp., 1969-70; rheumatologist Permanente Med. Group Kaiser, Hayward, Calif., 1973—; asst. chief medicine Kaiser-Permanente Med. Ctr., Hayward, Calif., 1976-79; chief medicine Kaiser-Permanente Med. Ctr., Fremont, Calif., 1979-86, chief legal medicine, 1983-86, asst. physician in charge, 1986-87, physician in charge, 1987—. Recipient fellow Cornell U., 1970-71, U. Calif. Med. Sch. fellow, 1971-72. Mem. Am. Rheumation Assn. Home: 909 Paramount Rd Oakland CA 94610 Office: Kaiser-Permanente Med Ctr 39400 Paseo Padre Pkwy Fremont CA 94538

ANDERSON OLIVO, MARGARET ELLEN, physiologist, educator; b. Omaha, June 17, 1941; d. Clarence Lloyd and Anita Emma (Kruse) Anderson; B.A., Augustana Coll., Sioux Falls, S.D., 1963; Ph.D. (NSF predoctoral fellow), Stanford U., 1967; m. Richard F. Olivo, Sept. 4, 1971. NIH postdoctoral fellow Harvard U., 1968-70; research asso. Lab. of Neurobiology U. P.R., 1970-71; vis. asst. prof. Clark U., 1972; asst. prof. Bennington (Vt.) Coll., spring 1973; asst. prof. Smith Coll., Northampton, Mass., 1973-79, asso. prof. dept. biol. scis., 1979-85, prof., 1985—. NIH research grantee, 1974-86. Mem. Soc. for Neuro-sci., Soc. Gen. Physiologists, Biophys. Soc. Office: Smith Coll Dept Biol Sci Northampton MA 01063

ANDES, JOAN KEENEN, information processing company executive; b. Clarksburg, W.Va., Apr. 23, 1930; d. Ree Martin and Mary Ruth (Pyle) Groghan; m. William Anderson Keenen, Oct. 15, 1949 (div. 1969); children—Paula Annette Keenen Skelton, William Ree Keenen; 1 foster child, Donald Monroe Dreyer; m. Ralph Paul Andes, Sept. 29, 1976. Pvt. sec. State Capitol, Charleston, W.Va., 1948-49; statis. typist various acctg. offices, Beaumont, Tex., 1949-60; owner Machine Acctg. and Computing, Beaumont, 1960-70, Automated Enterprises Keypunch Sch., 1962-72; pres. Applied Data Processing, Beaumont, 1970-83; owner Applied Info. Processing, Beaumont, 1983—. Active Better Bus. Bur., Beaumont C. of C., Democratic Party, Westgate Youth Group, 1985-88. Mem. Data Processing Mgmt. Assn. (pres. 1972-73, 80, awards chmn. 1985-86), Nat. Assn. Female Execs., Nat. Fedn. Ind. Bus. Republican. Mem. Ch. of Christ. Avocations: counted cross stitch, collecting Coke memorabilia; coin collecting; skiing. Home: 1410 Marshall Pl Beaumont TX 77706 Office: Applied Info Processing 855 IH 10 South Suite 135 Beaumont TX 77701

ANDREA, ELMA WILLIAMS, retail executive; b. Carroll County, Va.; d. Preston and Macy (Goad) Williams; m. Mario I. Andrea, Nov. 29, 1986; AB with spl. honors, George Washington U., 1953; MA in Public Adminstrn., Am. U., 1961. Asst. program dir., asst. dir. ops. WTOP, CBS-Radio and TV, 1947-51; mem. pub. relations staff George Washington U., 1951-52; registrar Washington Sch. for Secs., 1953; exec. sec. Joint Econ. Com. of U.S. Congress, 1956-59; legis. info. specialist NEA, Washington, 1960-84; asst. mgr. Gem Tree Jewelry Store, Bethesda, Md., 1984—. Bd. dirs. Edn. Assocs. Fed. Credit Union, 1973-83, pres., 1975-77; bd. dirs. Met. Area Credit Union Mgmt. Assn., 1977-82, sec., 1977-82; bd. dirs. Kenwood Beach (Md.) Citizens Assn., 1981-84. Recipient Alumni Service award George Washington U., 1970. Mem. AAUW (br. publicity chmn. 1956-59), Am. News Women's Club, NEA (life), Columbian Women George Washington U. (pres. 1965-67), George Washington U. Alumni Assn. (dir. 1965-67, 69-70), Edn. Writers Assn., Gemological Inst. Am., Women's Joint Congressional Com. (chmn. 1974-76), Phi Delta Gamma (chpt. pres. 1973-74, nat. conv. chmn. 1980, nat. treas. 1980-84, nat. pres. 1984-86 , trustee 1980-86, nat. bylaws 1986—), Pi Sigma Alpha. Mem. Nat. Woman's Party, Woman's Nat. Dem. Club, Twentieth Century Club. also: Il Bel Tramonto White Sands MD 20814 Office: Gem Tree 7720 Wisconsin Ave Bethesda MD 20814

ANDREACCHI, LINDA MARIE, real estate counselor; b. San Francisco, July 20, 1949; d. Betty Delcina (Gresh) A.; children: Shannon Renee Fischer, Kelly Amber Fischer. Grad. high sch., Burlingame, Calif. Real estate counselor Trotter Realty, Millbrae, Calif.; real estate agt. Lam & Buchsbaum, Elkins Park, Pa. Mem. Nat. Assn. Realtors, Calif. Assn. Realtors (mem. ethics com.), North San Mateo County Bd. Realtors (chmn. spl. events), Pa. Assn. Realtors, Willow Grove C. of C., Holy Redeemer's Aux. Home: 7 Hermosa Ln South San Francisco CA 94080-3159 Office: Trotter Realty 200 Broadway Millbrae CA 94030

ANDREEN, LINDA SAXON, contract administrator; b. Chgo., Oct. 28, 1948; d. George William and Shirlee Joan (Francioni) Simpson; m. David John Andreen, Feb. 17, 1940; children: Susan Lynn Wise, Jeffrey Scott. Student, Roosevelt U. Purchasing official Baxter Travenol Labs, Deerfield, Ill.; purchasing agt. Valley Nat. Bank, Phoenix, Ariz.; contract adminstr. Arizona Bank, Phoenix; profl. rep. to Minority and Women-Owned Bus. Council. Chairperson exec. com., pub. relations com. Ariz. Minority Supplier Devel. Council. Mem. Purchasing Mgmt. Assn. Ariz. (editor Ariz. Purchaser 1985-86, bd. dirs. 1986—, pub. relations chmn. 1987—), Purchasing Mgmt. Assn. Chgo. Republican. Home: 3012 W Sierra St Phoenix AZ 85029 Office: Arizona Bank 34 W Monroe Phoenix AZ 85002

ANDREEN-SALKIN-PENN, AVIVA LOUISE, academic administrator, educator; b. Frankfurt, Fed. Republic Germany, Jan. 6, 1952; d. Robert Benjamin Andreen and Margie Corinne (LaPointe) Marshall; m. Merrill R. Penn, Nov. 8, 1987; 1 child, Robert Morton Salkin. BA, NYU, 1975; postgrad., Laser Inst. Am., 1980. Cert. Mobile Laser Operator, N.Y. Tchr. Kibbutz Regavim, D.N. Menasche, Israel, 1975-76; account rep. Traveler's Ins. Co., N.Y.C., 1976; spl. projects coordinator Sapan Engring. Co., N.Y.C., 1976-78; sec., treas. founder J. Sapan Holographic Studios, N.Y.C., 1979; owner, pres. Universal Media Cons., White Plains, N.Y., 1980-84; dir. edn. Am. Ctr. for Laser Edn., White Plains, 1980-84; dir. edn., owner Am. Ctr. for Laser Edn., Riverdale, N.Y., 1984—; lectr. Hudson River Mus., Yonkers, N.Y., 1986-87, producer laser light show, Andrus Planetarium. Curator Holography A New Dimension White Plains Mus. Gallery, Hudson River Mus., Yonkers, Troster Hall Sci.; bd. dirs. Westchester Women of Chabad, White Plains, 1986-87. Mem. Laser Inst. Am., N.Y. Acad. Scis., Nat. Assn. Female Execs., Mus. Holography. Club: Courage to Change (White Plains) (chmn. 1987); Rosh Pina of Yonkers. Office: Am Ctr for Laser Edn 5642 Mosholu Ave Riverdale NY 10471

ANDREOLI, KATHLEEN GAINOR, nurse, educator, administrator; b. Albany, N.Y., Sept. 22, 1935; d. John Edward and Edmunda Elizabeth (Ringlemann) Gainor; children: Paula Kathleen, Thomas Anthony, Karen Marie. B.S.N., Georgetown U., 1957; M.S.N., Vanderbilt U., 1959; D.S.N., U. Ala., Birmingham, 1979. Staff nurse Albany Hosp. Med. Ctr., 1957; instr. St. Thomas Hosp. Sch. Nursing, Nashville, 1958-59, Georgetown U. Sch., Nursing, 1959-60, Duke U. Sch. Nursing, 1960-61, Bon Secours Hosp. Sch. Nursing, Balt., 1962-64; ednl. coordinator, physician asst. program, instr. coronary care unit nursing inservice edn. Duke U. Med. Ctr., Durham, N.C., 1965-70; ednl. dir. physician asst. program dept. medicine U. Ala. Med. Ctr., Birmingham, 1970-75; clin. assoc. prof. cardiovascular nursing Sch. Nursing U. Ala. Med. Ctr., 1970-77, asst. prof. nursing dept. medicine, 1971, assoc. prof., 1972—, assoc. prof. nursing Sch. Pub. and Allied Health, 1973—; assoc. dir. Family Nurse Practitioner Program, 1976, assoc. prof. community health nursing Grad. Program, 1977-79, assoc. prof. dept. pub. health, 1978-79; prof. nursing, spl. asst. to pres. for ednl. affairs U. Tex. Health Sci. Ctr., Houston, 1979-87; v.p. for ednl. services, interdisciplinary edn., internat. programs U. Tex. Health Sci. Ctr., 1987; v.p. nursing affairs Rush-Presbyn.-St. Lukes's Med. Ctr., Dean Rush U. Coll. Nursing, Chgo., 1987—; acting dean Sch. Allied Health Scis.; exec. dir. acad. services, prof. nursing, 1987; cons. in field. Author, editor: (with others) Comprehensive Cardiac Care, 1983; editor: Heart and Lung, Jour. of Total Care, 1971; contbr. articles to profl. jours. Recipient Founder's award N.C. Heart Assn., 1970, Disting. Alumni award Vanderbilt U. Sch. of Nursing, 1984, Leadership Tex. award, 1985. Fellow Am. Acad. Nursing; mem. Inst. Medicine, Am. Nurses Assn., Nat. League Nursing, Am. Assn. Critical Care Nurses, Ala. Heart Assn., Council Family Nurse Practitioners and Clinicians, Am. Heart Assn. Council Cardiovascular Nursing, Sigma Theta Tau, Alpha Eta, Phi Kappa Phi. Roman Catholic. Office: Rush Presbyn-St Lukes Med Ctr VP of Nursing Affairs 1753 W Congress Pkwy Chicago IL 60612

ANDRES, MARIAN GAIL, educator, business owner, choreographer, dancer; b. San Diego, Sept. 18, 1944; d. Giles Xavier and Rose Annette (Landsberger) Adrian; m. Frederick S. Andres, Apr. 12, 1963 (div. Feb. 1976); 1 child, Michael Adrian Andres. Student, San Jose State U., 1962-64, West Valley Jr. Coll., 1968-70. Dir., owner Marian Andres Dance Studio, San Jose, Calif., 1972-85, Branham Dance Ctr., San Jose, Calif., 1985—; founder, dir. Valley Dance Tchrs., San Jose, 1972-82; reg. dir. Dance Troupe, 1974-77. Designer: (computer program) Dance Sch. Organizer, 1986. Mem. Nat. Assn. Dance and Affiliated Artists (chpt. pres. 1970-72), Dance Educators of Am. (cert. 1981-88). Office: Branham Dance Ctr 1088 Branham Ln San Jose CA 95136

ANDRESS, CHARLOTTE FRANCES, emerita social work executive; b. Birmingham, Ala., Apr. 22, 1910; d. Francis Samuel and Tommie (Daniel) Andress; B.S., Birmingham-So. Coll., 1932; A.M. in Social Service Adminstrn., U. Chgo., 1943. Asst. dir. Girl Scouts Am., Birmingham, 1932-35, exec. dir., Nashville, 1935-41; instr. Loyola U., Chgo., 1942-45; dir. U.S.O., Augusta, Ga., 1945-48; asst. dir. YWCA, Chgo., 1948-50, exec. dir., St. Louis, 1950-53; dir. group work, youth service Fedn. Protestant Welfare Agys., N.Y.C., 1953-59; exec. dir. Inwood House, N.Y.C., 1959-82, exec. dir. emerita, 1982—. Chmn. adv. bd. Jefferson Park Center, 1959-65; nat. camp com. Camp Fire Girls, 1959-68; bd. Social Work Vocat. Bur., 1961-66; dir. Trail Blazer Camps, 1957-83, chmn. personnel com., 1982-83; mem. Camp Sharparoon com. N.Y.C. Mission Soc., 1960-76, mem. personnel com., 1962-66; adv. bd. social welfare Meth. Ch., 1958-63; mem. United Meth. Bd. Missions, 1964-72; bd. Bethel Meth. Home, 1965-72, sec. bd., 1966-72; women's com. Japan Internat. Christian U. Found., 1969—, exec. com., 1983—; adv. bd. Isabella Thoburn Coll., 1967-75; chmn. nat. com. Wesleyan Service Guild, 1970-72; trustee Christ United Meth. Ch., 1975-84; trustee Martha Mertz Found., 1979—, sec., 1981—, v.p., 1983—; bd. United Meth. City Soc., 1980-86. Named Disting. Alumna Birmingham So. Coll., 1981. Cert. social worker, N.Y. Mem. Nat. Assn. Social Workers (sec. bd. N.Y.C. chpt. 1958-60, chmn. personnel standards and practices 1960-69, 73-74), Acad. Cert. Social Workers, Nat. Conf. on Social Welfare, Bethany Deaconess Soc. (dir. 1971—, sec. 1974-76, pres. 1976—), Internat. Conf. Social Welfare, N.Y. Deaconess Assn. (dir. 1969—, sec. 1971—), Soc. Women Geographers, 1982—, Gamma Phi Beta. Democrat. Club: Cosmopolitan. Home: 3030 Park Ave Bridgeport CT 06604

ANDRESS, KATHRYN J., nursing coordinator; b. Hartley, Iowa, May 27, 1946; d. Paul Martin Purintun and Pearl Eleanor (Arnold) Messerer. Diploma, Allen Meml. Sch. Nursing, Waterloo, Iowa, 1967; BS in Health Edn., Calif. State U., Long Beach, 1975. Staff nurse U. Minn. Hosps., Mpls., 1967-68; head nurse transplant unit U. Minn. Hosps., 1968-70; asst. head nurse Long Beach Community Hosp., 1971-76; hemodialysis clin. nurse specialist St. Mary's-Bauer Hosp., Long Beach, 1976-79; asst. nurse mgr. Providence Hosp., Anchorage, Alaska, 1979-85; dialysis coordinator Providence Hosp., 1981—; organ procurement coordinator-Alaska Northwest Organ Procurement Agy., Seattle, 1981—; RN; cert. hemodialysis nurse Bd. Nephrology Examiners, Nurses and Technicians. Mem. Am. Assn. Critical Care Nurses (critical care RN, pres. Anchorage chpt. 1987-88), Am. Nephrology Nurses Assn., Sigma Theta Tau. Democrat. Methodist. Office: Providence Hosp 3200 Providence Dr Anchorage AK 99519

ANDREW, JANE HAYES, ballet company executive; b. Phila., Jan. 1, 1947; d. David Powell and Vivian Muriel (Saeger) Hayes; m. Brian David Andrew, June 14, 1977; 1 child, Kevin Hayes. AB, Barnard Coll., 1968, grad., Harvard Arts Adminstrn. Instit., 1972. Mgr. theater Minor Latham Playhouse, Barnard Coll., N.Y.C., 1970-74; co. mgr. Houston Ballet, 1974-77, Ballet West, Salt Lake City, 1978-83; gen. mgr. Pacific N.W. Ballet, Seattle, 1983-87; organizer non-profit consortium nat. ballet cos. and nat. presenting orgns., 1987; pres., exec. dir. Ballet/Am., 1988; panelist NEA Dance Program Presentors, 1987-88; pres., exec. dir. Ballet/Am., 1988—; cons. Ariz. Arts Commn., Phoenix, 1985-86; com. mem. 25th Anniversary of World's Fair, Seattle, 1986-87; panelist NEA Local Programs, 1987. Editor (directory) Philadelphia Cultural Organizations, 1977. Bd. dirs. Good Shepherd Adv. Bd., Seattle, 1985-87. Recipient Dorothy D. Spivack award Barnard Coll., N.Y.C., 1972. Mem. Dance/USA (chmn. Mgrs. Council 1986). Home and Office: Ballet/Am 807 NW 56th St Seattle WA 98107

ANDREW, VALERIE JANE, electronics company executive; b. Mpls., Dec. 4, 1961; d. David L. and Jane E. (Wilson) A. BA in Econs., Internat. Relations, Knox Coll., 1984. Product mktg. specialist Bicc-Vero Electronics, Hamden, Conn., 1985-86; mgr. electronic products Rittal Corp., Bristol, Conn., 1986—. Vol. Waterbury (Conn.) Renewal and Econ. Devel., 1986. Mem. VMEbus Internat. Trade Assn., Nat. Assn. Female Execs. Office: Rittal Corp 30 Cross St Bristol CT 06010

ANDREWS, CAROL CORDER, political scientist, educator; b. Wilmington, Del.; d. Kenneth Wilson and Aurelia Moreland (Speer) Corder; B.A. (Gen. Motors nat. scholar), Duke U., 1960; Certificat d'Etudes Politiques, Institut d'Etudes Politiques, U. Paris (France), 1961; M.A. (East Asian Inst. fellow), Columbia U., 1964, Ph.D., 1978; postgrad. Inter-Univ. Program for Chinese Lang. Tng., Taipei, Taiwan, 1966-67; div.; 1 son, Ethan Andrews. Research contract for study Taiwanese-Mainlander polit. relations Brookings Instn., Washington, 1967; research Kuomintang Party Archives, Taichung, Taiwan, 1967-68; asst. prof. polit. sci. Holy Names Coll., Oakland, Calif., 1970-79, assoc. prof., 1979-81, chairperson dept. history and polit. sci., 1979-80; editor, writer, researcher, 1982—. Bd. dirs. Alameda County chpt. UN Assn. U.S.A., World Without War Council, 1979—. Recipient Contemporary China Studies Com. award, 1967-70. Nat. Def. Fgn. Lang. fellow, 1962-64, 65-67. Mem. Am. Polit. Sci. Assn., Women's Caucus for Polit. Sci., Assn. for Asian Studies, AAUP, Internat. Platform Assn., Phi Beta Kappa. Democrat. Episcopalian. Club: Commonwealth of Calif. Contbr. articles to profl. jours. Home: 612 Vincente Ave Berkeley CA 94707

ANDREWS, GAYLE MARIE, marketing consultant; b. Caldwell, Idaho, Oct. 24, 1946; d. Oral Frederick and Margaret Eleanor (Sheehan) A.; m. Capers Lowry Bohler, Aug. 11, 1973 (div. Nov. 1978). BA in Journalism, Gonzaga U., 1967; MBA, Harvard U., 1982. Recreational worker ARC, Korea, Fed. Republic Germany, Boston and Phila., 1967-73; sales rep. Boise Cascade Corp., Atlanta, 1974-77, asst. regional mgr., 1977; gen. mgr. Boise Cascade Corp., Jacksonville, Fla., 1977-79, Boston, 1979-80; asst. to v.p. Boise Cascade Corp., Portland, 1982-84; mktg. mgr. Boise Cascade Corp., Itasca, Ill., 1984; v.p., gen. mgr. Midwest Dist. Group, Arlington Heights, Ill., 1985-87; v.p. mktg. and adminstrn. Capitol Hardware Mfg. Co., Inc., Chgo., 1987—; cons. distbn., Arlington Heights, 1987—. Vol. ARC, Portland, 1982-83, Mus. of Sci. and Industry, Chgo., 1985. Republican. Roman Catholic. Club: HBS of Chgo. Home: 705 Ascot Ct Hoffman Estates IL 60194

ANDREWS, JULIE, actress, singer; b. Walton-on-Thames, Eng., Oct. 1, 1935; d. Edward C. and Barbara Wells; m. Tony Walton, May 10, 1959 (div.); 1 dau., Emma; m. Blake Edwards, 1969. Studied with pvt. tutors, studied voice with Mme. Stiles-Allen. Debut as singer, Hippodrome, London, 1947; appeared in pantomime Cinderella, London, 1953; appeared: Broadway prodn. The Boy Friend, N.Y.C., 1954, My Fair Lady, 1956-60 (N.Y. Drama Critics award 1956), Camelot, 1960-62; films include Mary Poppins, 1964 (Acad. award for best actress 1964), The Americanization of Emily, 1964, Torn Curtain, 1966, The Sound of Music, 1966, Hawaii, 1966, Thoroughly Modern Millie, 1967, Star!, 1968, Darling Lili, 1970, The Tamarind Seed, 1973, 10, 1979, Little Miss Marker, 1980, S.O.B, 1981, Victor/Victoria, 1982, The Man Who Loved Women, 1983, That's Life!, 1986, Duet For One, 1986; TV debut in High Tor, 1956; star TV series The Julie Andrews Hour, 1972-73; also spls.; Author: (as Julie Edwards): Mandy, 1971, The Last of the Really Great Whangdoodles, 1974. Recipient Golden Globe award Hollywood Fgn. Press Assn., 1964, 65; named World Film Favorite (female), 1967. Office: care Greengage Prodns 11777 San Vincente Blvd #501 Los Angeles CA 90049 also: Hanson & Schwam 9200 Sunset Blvd Los Angeles CA 90069

ANDREWS, KAREN ELIZABETH, marketing executive; b. Ft. Lauderdale, Fla., Apr. 24, 1954; d. Harold Shibboleth and Aileen Gee (Toney) Lee; m. Robert Luverne Moore II, Apr. 19, 1971 (div. Aug. 1974); 1 child, Crystal Dawn Moore; m. Dennis Blaine Andrews, June 27, 1981; 1 child, Shawna Michele. Student, West Va. U.; BSW, W. Va. State Coll., 1979. Social worker II, econ. service worker III W. Va. Dept. Welfare, Charleston, 1975-80; delivery person Caman Auto Parts, Ft. Myers, Fla., 1980-81; comml. fisherman Ft. Myers Beach, Fla., 1981-82; 1st mate Island Bell, Sanibel Island, Fla., 1982-85; mng. dir. Research Data Services, Inc., Ft. Myers, 1986—. Tour guide Thomas Alva Edison's Winter Home, Ft. Myers, Fla. Mem. Nat. Assn. Social Workers, Nat. Assn. Female Execs., Am. Legion, DAR, Daughters of the American Confederacy. Republican. Baptist. Lodge: Eastern Star. Home: 1504 Ransom St Fort Myers FL 33901 Office: Research Data Services Inc 2271 McGregor Blvd Suite A Fort Myers FL 33901

ANDREWS, KATHRYNE CONSTANTINE, art director; b. Haverhill, Mass., Jan. 24, 1945; d. Constantine John and Joy (Seferlis) A. BA, Wheaton Coll., Norton, Mass., 1967; MA, Columbia U., 1970; PhD, Union Grad. Sch., Yellow Springs, Ohio, 1977. Chief edn. The Bklyn. Mus., 1973-84; chief art and design United Nations Chidrens Fund Greeting Card Operation, N.Y.C., 1984—; adj. prof. Bankstreet Coll.-Mus. Edn. Program, N.Y.C., 1975-78; founding mem. 22 Wooster Gallery, N.Y.C., 1979. Recipient NEH grant, 1978, 80, Nat. Mus. Act grant, 1979. Mem. Am. Assn. Mus. Greek Orthodox. Office: UNICEF Greeting Card Operation 331 E 38th St 8th Fl New York NY 10016

ANDREWS, MARY ELLEN, civic organization executive; b. Corning, N.Y., Nov. 10, 1931; d. Edwin Hardy and Edith Marie (Lowe) Ober; B.A., Mt. Holyoke Coll., 1953; postgrad. Syracuse U., 1974-75; m. James A. Reynolds, Jan. 28, 1962; m. 2d, Richard Hale Andrews, July 14, 1970; 1 dau., Amy Elizabeth; stepchildren—R. Hale, D. Gage, Philadelphia M. French/English translator Les Ateliers de Construction Electrique de Charleroi, N.Y.C., 1954-55, French Nat. R.R., N.Y.C., 1955-56; public relations asst. Steuben Glass, N.Y.C., 1956-64; French/English translator Corning (N.Y.) Internat. Corp., 1964-67; research asst. Corning Glass Wks. Found., 1967-70; French/English translator Corning Internat. Corp., 1972-75; office mgr. Beak Assos., Ithaca, N.Y., 1975-77; corporate relations staff, devel. office, Cornell U., Ithaca, 1977-79; staff asst. evening programs, Elmira Coll., N.Y., 1979-80, dir. public relations, 1980-84, advisor student newspaper, The Octagon, 1980-84; exec. dir. Schuyler County C. of C., 1984—. Bd. dirs. Elmira Symphony and Choral Soc., 1982-84, Chemung Valley Arts Council, 1984-87. Mem. LWV (Schuyler County), N.Y. State Council of Chamber Execs. Democrat. Presbyterian. Editor-in-chief Campus Mag., 1980-84. Home: RD 2 Old Corning Rd Watkins Glen NY 14891 Office: Schuyler County C of C 1000 N Franklin St Watkins Glen NY 14891

ANDREWS, MARY GIBSON DUFFY, military officer; b. New Bern, N.C., Nov. 1, 1949; d. Richard Nixon and Mary Hazel (Brock) Duffy. BS in Edn., Biology, U. Tenn., 1971; diploma, U.S. Army Command and Gen. Staff Coll., 1986, Defense Info. Sch., 1984. Commd. 2d lt. U.S. Army, 1972, advanced through grades to maj., 1984; intelligence staff officer 9th Infantry Div., Ft. Lewis, Wash., 1973-74; recruiter U.S. Army Aviation Ctr., Ft. Rucker, Ala., 1974-75; adm.'s aide and protocol officer Pacific Command, Hawaii, 1976-78; equal opportunity officer Ft. Devens, Mass., 1979-80; sec. recorder Army Discharge Review Bd. Pentagon, Washington, 1982-84; pub. affairs officer Army Pub. Affairs Pentagon, Washington, 1984-85; cmdr. 228th Adj. Gen. Co. (Postal), Frankfurt, Fed. Republic of Germany, 1986—. Mem. Frankfurt Singles Ch. Group, 1987—. Mem. Assn. of the U.S. Army, Nat. Assn. Female Execs., Alpha Chi Omega. Republican. Presbyterian. Office: 228 Postal Co Box 256 APO New York NY 09082

ANDREWS, OLA JEAN, office administrator; b. El Dorado, Ark., Dec. 9, 1929; d. Joseph Henry and Leceola (Tobin) A. Sec., Oakland Dept. Health Service, 1958-69, supr. Dept. Social Services, 1968-78; music. dir. Christliches Zentrum, Berlin, Germany, 1978-81; exec. sec. Harsh Investment Co., Oakland, 1981-82; Wang system adminstr. San Francisco Dept. Treasury, 1982—; pres. Believers, Inc., Oakland, 1971—, fund raiser, 1972-78; disc jockey Sta. KRE, Berkeley, Calif., 1973-78; instr. Prison Fellowship, Washington, 1983—; office mgr. Mass. Indemnity & Life Ins. Co., Atlanta, 1985—. Recipient awards KQED-TV, San Francisco, 1974, San Francisco Dept. Treasury, 1985. Grantee Sta. KDIA, Oakland, 1962-65. Mem. Exec. Females, Encore. Democrat. Avocations: travel, piano.

ANDREWS, SUSAN CAROL, comptroller; b. Oakland, Calif., Jan. 14, 1943; d. John Parish and Dorothy Sophia (Sharkey) A. BA, Northwestern U., 1964. Social worker Alameda County Dept. Human Resources, Oakland, 1965-67; founder Animal Transport Service, Oakland, 1968—; bookkeeper Checker Van and Storage Co., Oakland, 1968-72; supr. acctg. Checker Van and Storage Co., 1972-79, comptroller, 1979—; ptnr. Pet Transfer Unltd., Oakland, 1979—. Democrat. Office: Checker Van and Storage Co 1199 Pine St Oakland CA 94607

ANDREWS, SUSAN LYNN, insurance agent, marketing specialist; b. Los Angeles, Feb. 1, 1962; d. John Morton Machunka-Andrews and Charmaine Mary (Wells) Andrews Gordon. Student U. Colo., Boulder, 1980-83. Dir. Gordon Gen. Ins., Los Angeles, 1978-84; mortgage specialist Am. Internat. Group, Los Angeles and N.Y.C., 1984-86; U.S. agt. confidential program Bayly Martin and Fay, Los Angeles, 1986-87; sr. account exec., Safeguard Health Enterprises, Inc., Anaheim (Calif.) and Los Angeles, 1986—; pres., Infinity Ins. Agy., Beverly Hills, Calif., 1987—. Vol. City of West Hollywood City Hall, Calif., 1986; mem. Lupus Found., Los Angeles, Multiple Schlerosis Soc. of Los Angeles, AIDS Project, Los Angeles. Mem. Am. Mgmt. Assn., Hispanic Acad. of Media Arts and Scis., Calif. Assn. of Affiliated Agys., Am. Film Inst., Women in Mgmt. (bd. dirs. Los Angeles chpt.), Art Deco Soc. Los Angeles, Nat. Assn. Female Execs., Amnesty Internat., Los Angeles Jr. C. of C., Kappa Kappa Gamma. Avocations: tennis; nordic skiing; travel; art deco; theatre. Mailing Address: PO Box 10986 Beverly Hills CA 92013-3986

ANDREWS, THEODORA ANNE, librarian; b. Carroll County, Ind., Oct. 14, 1921; d. Harry Floyd and Margaret Grace (Walter) Ulrey; B.S. with distinction, Purdue U., 1953; M.S., U. Ill., 1955; m. Robert William Andrews, July 18, 1940 (div. 1946); 1 son, Martin Harry. Asst. reference librarian Purdue U., West Lafayette, Ind., 1955-56, pharmacy librarian, instr., 1956-60, pharmacy librarian, asst. prof., 1960-65, pharmacy librarian, assoc. prof. library sci., 1965-71, prof. library sci., pharmacy librarian, 1971-79, prof. library sci., pharmacy, nursing and health scis. librarian, 1979—. Mem. Purdue Women's Caucus, 1973—, v.p., 1975-76, pres., 1976-77; mem. Internat. Women's Yr. Regional Planning Com., 1977; del. Ind. Gov.'s Conf. Libraries and Info. Services, 1978. U. Ill. grad. fellow, 1954-55. Mem. Spl. Libraries Assn. (John H. Moriarty award Ind. chpt. 1972), ALA, Med. Library Assn., AAUP, Am. Assn. Colls. Pharmacy, Kappa Delta Pi, Delta Rho Kappa. Baptist. Author: A Bibliography of the Socioeconomic Aspects of Medicine, 1975; A Bibliography of Drug Abuse Including Alcohol and Tobacco, 1977; A Bibliography of Drug Abuse, Supplement 1977-1980, 1981; Bibliography on Herbs, Herbal Remedies and Natural Foods, 1982; Substance Abuse Materials for School Libraries, an Annotated Bibliography, 1985; Guide to the Literature of Pharmacy and the Pharmaceutical Sciences, 1986; sect. editor Advances in Alcohol and Substance Abuse, 1981—; contbr. articles to profl. jours. Office: Pharmacy Bldg Purdue U West Lafayette IN 47907

ANDREWS ZEICHNER, ROBIN DAWN, publishing company executive; b. Morristown, N.J., Aug. 17, 1962; d. Robert David and Mary Ann T. (Stames) Andrews; m. Craig Zeichner, Oct. 18, 1987. BS, N.Y.U., 1984. Dir. subscription C.C. Pub. Inc., N.Y.C., 1985—; mgr. fulfillment, analyst circulation Family Computing div. Scholastic Inc., N.Y.C., 1984-85, Instl. Investor, N.Y.C., 1985; mgr. circulation Sports Assocs. Inc., N.Y.C., 1986-86, Billboard Publ. Inc., N.Y.C., 1087—. Mem. Direct Mktg. Assn. Democrat. Unitarian. Home: 615 Westminster Rd #3B Brooklyn NY 11230 Office: Billboard Publ 1515 Broadway New York NY 10036

ANDRIES, ELOISE DELORES GOMÉZ, Spanish educator; b. Sacramento, Jan. 14, 1942; d. Juventino F. and Angelita E. (Navarro) Gómez; m. Ronald D. Andries, Aug. 24, 1939; children: Monya, Lauren. BA, Northwestern State U., 1967; MEd, La. State U., 1973. Instr. Rapides Parish Sch. System, Alexandria, La., 1967-74; instr., counselor La. State U., Alexandria, 1974—. Mem. AAUW (chair com., pres. 1987—), La. Assn. Coll. and Univ. Students (coll. rep. 1986—), La. Assn. of Women Deans, Adminstrs. and Counselors (pres. 1985—), La. Assn. Fgn. Language Tchrs. (cons. 1984—), Alexandria C. of C. (chair sect. 1986), Phi Beta Kappa, Phi Kappa Phi. Roman Catholic. Office: La State U Rm 112 Avoyella Hall Alexandria LA 71302

ANDRIOTAKIS, TINA MARIE, manufacturing importer; b. Detroit, Feb. 6, 1958; d. Theodore James and Antigone (Goutes) A.; m. Antoine Jacques Heintz, Nov. 15, 1985. Cert., Parsons Sch. of Design, N.Y.C., 1975; BA in French, Kalamazoo Coll., 1980; studied with, Pierre Cardin Haute Couture, Paris, 1979. Sales clk. Saks Fifth Ave., Detroit, 1977-78; orientation asst. Fgn. Study Office Kalamazoo Coll., 1980; adminstrv. asst. Eurextil Import/Export Corp., N.Y.C., 1981; internat. prodn. mgr. Robert Lippman, Inc., N.Y.C., 1981-86; trade dir. Deo Resourcing Internat., Ltd., N.Y.C., 1986—. Mem. Nat. Assn. Female Execs. Greek Orthodox.

ANDRISAN, LINDA SUE, journalist; b. Detroit, Sept. 24, 1956; d. Titus and Virginia (Krivak) A.; m. David Briggs Pinson, June 21, 1980. BA in English Literature, Wheaton Coll., 1978; MA, Emory U., 1987, PhD in Comparative Lit., 1987. Tchr. English and Spanish Gwinnett County Bd. Edn., Atlanta, 1978-79; teaching asst. of Spanish Emory U., Atlanta, 1979-82; Spanish instr. Suzuki Internat. Learning, Atlanta, 1982-83; instr. English as secondary language DeKalb Community Coll., Clarkston, 1985-86; reporter Covington (Ga.) Newspaper, 1984-85, Rockdale Neighbor Newspaper, Conyers, Ga., 1985-86; assoc. editor, s.w. editor Adweek/ Abernathy Publs., Atlanta, 1986-87; freelance journalist Atlanta, Washington, 1987—. Contbr. articles to Marietta Daily Jour., Gwinnett Dailey News, The Atlanta Mag., Bus. Atlanta Mag., Southline, CreativeLoafing. Fulbright scholar U.S. Dept. State, Washington, 1983-84. Mem. MLA, The Soc. Profl. Journalists, League of Women Voters (bd. officers 1986), Fulbright Alumni Assn. Evangelical. Clubs: DeKalb County Dem. Breakfast, Atlanta Press. Home and Office: 3230 S Utah St Arlington VA 22206

ANDRITSCH, MARIANNE FELDMAN, communication consultant; b. Milw., Apr. 24, 1954; d. Marvin and Joan (Dizon) Feldman; m. James Michael Andritsch, Nov. 20, 1976; 1 child, Sarah M. BA, U. Wis., 1976. Dir. communications Mental Health Assn. in Milw. County, 1976-81; dir. pub. affairs Alverno Coll., Milw., 1981; dir. community relations Family Service Milw., 1982-87; communications cons. Milw., 1987—. V.p. Milw. Human Relations Radio-TV Council, 1976-85; bd. dirs. S.W. Milw. br. YMCA, 1981-84. Recipient United Way Communicators award United Way Greater Milw., 1987. Mem. Nat. Assn. Mental Health Info. Officers (Communicators award 1978, 86), Pub. Relations Soc. Am.

ANDRLA, VALERIE ETTA, manufacturing company executive; b. Wichita, Kans., June 27, 1948; d. William Francis and Barbara June (Ballance) A.; m. James Edward Baxter, Aug. 4, 1968 (div. Apr. 1975); 1 child, Janell Renee. Student, Wichita State U., 1969-71; BSME, U. Kans., 1978; MBA in Fin. and Internat. Bus., U. Chgo., 1982. Registered EIT engr., Kans., Ill. Meat packer Cudahy Co., Wichita, 1968-75; mgr. AB Sand & Rock Co., Wichita, 1975-76; plant engr. Food, Machinery & Chem. Co., Inc., Lawrence, Kans., 1976-78; engring. liaison Internat. Harvester Corp. (name changed to Navistar), Chgo., 1979-80, purchasing engr., 1981-82, supr. purchasing research, 1983-84, corp. buyer, 1985-87, product mgr., 1988—; pres. Three Wooden Horses, Inc., Schaumburg, Ill., 1988—. Contbr. Kans. Engineer mag., 1976-78. Tutor math. Community Service Ctr., Rolling Meadows, Ill., 1982-86; council mem. Sister Cities, Rolling Meadows, 1984-87. Mem. ASME, Soc. Mfg. Engrs., Chgo. Rubber Group, AAUW (chair ways and means com. 1984-86, newsletter editor 1984-87, pres. 1988—), U. Chgo. Women's Bus. Group. Republican. Methodist. Home: 2554 Barkwood Apt 208 Schaumburg IL 60173 Office: Navistar Internat Corp 600 Woodfield Dr Schaumburg IL 60196

ANDRUS, JOYCELON MARIE, art educator, nun; b. Duluth, Minn., June 21, 1939; d. James W. and Rufina C. (Appert) A.; adopted children: Kimberly, Lisandra, Theresa, Tamara, Young Soo, Jacqueline, Cecilia, Michella, Antonya, Stephanie, Chandler, Michael, Kenneth, Austin, Halistin, Valerie, Kalanthe, Anton. BA in Art, Mont. State U., 1964; MA in Art, U. Mont., 1966. Cert. elem. and secondary tchr., Washington. Tchr. 7th grade St. Joseph's Sch., Mandan, N.D., 1960-61, tchr. 7th and 8th grades, 1964-65; tchr. elem. art sch. dist. 405, Bellevue, Wash., 1966-71; tchr. art Stevens Jr. High Sch., Port Angeles, Wash., 1971-76, Port Angeles High Sch., 1976—; nun Sisters for Christian Community, 1979. Chmn. Port Angeles art com., 1976-86. Mem. NEA, Wash. Edn. Assn., Port Angeles Edn. Assn. Republican. Roman Catholic. Home: 3012 Porter PO Box 95 Port Angeles WA 98362 Office: Port Angeles High Sch 304 E Park Port Angeles WA 98362

ANDRUS-OVERLEY, MARY EVELYN, social worker; b. Abbeville, La., Sept. 10, 1943; d. Homer Webb and Evelyn Belle (Andrus) Overley; m. Clarence John Rosa, Sept. 11, 1965 (div. Feb. 1985); 1 child, Simone Alexis Rosa. BA, U. Southwestern La., 1965; MSW, Tulane U., 1977. Visitor welfare La. Dept. Pub. Welfare, New Orleans, 1965; caseworker, group worker City of New Orleans, 1966-74; asst. psychol. testing New Orleans Mental Health Ctr., 1974-76; dir. adult programs Kingsley House, New Orleans, 1978-83, mgr. vol. resources, 1983-84; assoc. social justice Dept. Social Justice Unitarian Universalist Assn., Boston, 1984—; mem. bd. and steering com. Religious Network Equality Women, 1984—, social advocacy com. Family Service Greater Boston, 1985—. Co-editor: Resolutions and Resources: A Social Responsibility Handbook, 1985; contbr. articles to profl. jours. Mem. Nat. Assn. Social Workers. Democrat. Unitarian. Home: 658 Tremont St 9 Boston MA 02118 Office: Unitarian Universalist Assn 25 Beacon St Boston MA 02108

ANDRUZZI, ELLEN ADAMSON, nurse, marital and family therapist; b. Colon, Panama, Dec. 15, 1917 (parents Am. citizens); d. Charles and Annie Isabel (Grinder) Adamson; m. Francis Victor Andruzzi, May 28, 1941; children—Barbara F., Francis C., Judith E., Antonette T., John J. BS in Pub. Health Nursing, Cath. U. Am., 1947, MS in Nursing, 1951. Cert. clin. specialist, psychiat. nurse. Pub. health nurse Washington Health Dept., 1942-44; instr. psychiat. nursing St. Elizabeth's Hosp., Washington, 1948-57; dir. nursing Glenn Dale Hosp., Md., 1961-67; chief mental health nurse dept. human resources D.C. Govt., 1967-73; cons. NIMH, HHS, Rockville, Md., 1973-81; marital and family therapist TA Assocs., Camp Springs, Md., 1973—; assoc. GWITA, Rockville, 1975-79; instr. Charles County Community Coll., LaPlata, Md., 1976-78, Prince George Community Coll., Largo, Md., 1973-81; assoc. Ctr. for Study of Human Systems, Chevy Chase, Md., 1976—. Author chpts. in books. Dist. co-capt. Prince Georgians for Glendening, Prince George County, Md., 1985-86; chmn. plan devel. com. So. Md. Health Systems Agy., Clinton, 1984—, sec. governing body, 1978-80; chmn. Mental Health Adv. Com. Prince George County, Cheverly, Md., 1983-85. Recipient Disting. Nurse award St. Elizabeths Hosp., 1985, Paula Hamburger Vol. award Mental Health Assn. Md., 1985, Recognition of Service award Md. Nurses Assn., 1983. Fellow Am. Acad. Nursing, Am. Orthopsychiat. Assn.; mem. Internat. Transactional Analysis Assn. (clin.), Am. Nurses Assn., World Fedn. for Mental Health, Am. Assn. for Marriage and Family Therapy (clin.), Nat. Mental Health Assn. (v.p. 1984-87), Mental Health Assn. Prince George County (pres. 1974-76, 87-88), Sigma Theta Tau (Kappa chpt., Excellence in Nursing award 1984). Democrat. Roman Catholic. Avocations: theatre, ballet, swimming, foreign travel.

ANEMA, CHERYL LYNN, nurse; b. Chgo., Oct. 21, 1958; d. Kenneth John and Bertha (Schaap) Anema. R.N., Wesley-Passavant Sch. Nursing, 1979; B.S. in Nursing, DePaul U., 1983; MS in Nursing, Loyola U., Chgo., 1987. R.N., Ill. Unit sec. Northwestern Meml. Hosp., Chgo., 1978-79, staff nurse, 1979-83; team supr. Ingall's Meml. Hosp., Harvey, Ill., 1984-86; nursing instr., St. Xavier's Coll, Chgo., 1988—; real estate sales assoc., Naughton Realtors, Lansing, 1988—. Mem. Am. Nurses Assn., Ill. Nurses Assn., Chgo. Nurses Assn. Republican. Home: 16525 S Park Ave South Holland IL 60473

ANGEL, CAROL MAE, accountant, financial planner; b. Newberg, Ore., Apr. 7, 1941; d. Leo A. and Hilda A. (Schneider) Blanchette; m. Rexford E. Angel, Apr. 22, 1961; 1 child, Shawn M. B in Mgmt., Marylhurst Coll., Portland, Ore., 1986. CPA, Ore. Staff acct. Jarrard, Siebert, Simpson, Portland, 1970-72; Prin. Carol Angel & Co., Portland, 1972-84, 1987—; ptnr. Angel, Crouse, & Co., Portland, 1984-87. Columnist for Progressive Woman mag. Mem. Am. Soc. CPA's, Ore. Soc. CPA's, Am. Soc. CLU/ChFC's. Republican. Office: Carol Angel & Co 2061 NW Hoyt Portland OR 97209

ANGEL, PHYLLIS JEAN, financial executive; b. North Platte, Nebr., Aug. 10, 1947; d. Ralph Henry and Lucille (Bussell) Shinn; m. Lewis Worth Angel, Jan. 11, 1969 (div. 1975). A.A., North Eastern Jr. Coll., 1967; student cosmetology Mile Hi Beauty Sch., 1969. Office rep. Standard Quarter Horse Assn., Lakewood, Colo., 1967-69; info. operator Mountain Bell, Denver, 1967; sec. King Soopers Bakery, Denver, 1973, Prudential Ins. Co., Denver, 1973-76; owner/operator Phyl's Styling Salon, Sedalia, Colo., 1976-77; fin. adminstr. Martin Marietta, Denver, 1978—; cons. Self Images, Denver, 1973-79, Frisbie & Frisbie, Denver, 1973-80; owner A & B Enterprises, Denver, 1974-76; owner Shaklee Product Distbn., Denver, 1982—. Author: A Wolf Pup Was Born, 1983; Grandma, 1984; Wax Doll, 1984. Coach, Wagon Wheel Softball Team, Champion, Nebr., 1963-65; active Muscular Dystrophy Telethon, Littleton, Colo., 1974, Multiple Sclerosis Ride-A-Thon, Cheyenne, Wyo., 1975; sponsor Little League Baseball Team, Sedalia, 1976. Recipient Grand Cross of Colors, Rainbow Girls, 1965; Golden Poet award, 1985, Silver Poet award, 1986. Mem. Career Womens Assn., Internat. Platform Assn., Nat. Mus. Women in Arts Club: Square Dance. Methodist. Clubs: 4-H, Rodeo. Lodges: Order Eastern Star. Home: PO Box 620215 Littleton CO 80162

ANGELASTRO, JANE ELLEN, corporate librarian, biochemist; b. N.Y.C., May 14, 1942; d. George Christain and Edna Frances (Byrnes) Schofield; m. Michael Angelo Angelastro, Jan. 21, 1967; children: Terese, Pat George, Karen. BS, Coll. of Mt. St. Vincent, 1964; MLS, L.I. U., 1985. Biochemist Merck Inst., Rahway, N.J., 1964-67; sr. library asst. L.I. Univ. Grad. Library, Sparkill, N.Y., 1981-85; library dir. Halcon Research div. Tex. Eastern Corp., Montvale, N.J., 1985-86; assoc. mgr. AT&T Tech. Info. Ctr., White Plains, N.Y., 1986—. Sr. librarian St. Anthony Elem. Sch., Nanuet, N.Y., 1974-84; officer various town and ch. youth orgns., Nanuet, 1975-85. Mem. Spl. Libraries Assn., Assn. Computing Machinery, Internat. Network of UNIX Users. Home: 13 Glen Rose Ct West Nyack NY 10994 Office: AT&T NOG 18th Floor 1 N Lexington Ave White Plains NY 10601

ANGELINI, SHERRY LARAINE (CRUZ), research laboratory administrator; b. Springfield, Mo., Aug. 23, 1945; s. Robert Eugene and Juanita Maxine (Budd) Ballew; m. Lawrence James Cruz (div. 1981); children: Corey Allen, Wade Lawrence, Lundyn Laraine. Grad. high sch., San Lorenzo, Calif. Material services analyst Sandia Nat. Labs., Livermore, Calif., 1978-81, alt. nuclear material rep., 1981-83, nuclear material rep., 1983-86, project leader, security, 1986—, coordinator ops. security, 1987—; rep. to Trade Adv. Council for Word Processing, Oakland, Calif., 1979-81; co-owner Angelini's Italian Restaurant, Modesto, Calif., 1988—. Judge Alameda County Vocat. Olympics, Pleasanton, Calif., 1979; speaker Sonoma Sch. Career Day, Livermore, 1978, Healds Bus. Day, Concord, 1981. Mem. Nat. Assn. Female Execs. Office: Sandia Nat Labs PO Box 969 Livermore CA 94550-0096

ANGELL, BETTY ELLEN, interior designer; b. Centralia, Mo., Mar. 16, 1927; s. Robert Loren and Margaret Amanda Jane (Smith) A. Cert., N.Y. Sch. Design, 1946. Interior designer Denver Dry Goods, 1946-49; cons. home furnishings Barker Bros., Los Angeles, 1950-52; interior designer Joske's, Houston, 1952-55, Showroom Finer Furniture, Corpus Christi, Tex., 1955-66, Braslau's, Corpus Christi, 1966-70, Browning Bros., Corpus Christi, 1970—; lectr. in field. Author: The Layman's Handbook of Interior Design, 1972. Mem. Am. Soc. Interior Designers (long range planning nat. com. 1987—, nat. bd. dirs. 1975—, regional v.p., Medalist award 1984, Commendation for Outstanding Service 1986), Am. Inst. Interior Designers (v.p., sec., chmn., bd. dirs. Tex. chpt. 1959-75, Outstanding Interior Designer 1974). Democrat. Home: 346 Southern Corpus Christi TX 78404 Office: Browning Bros 2001 S Staples Corpus Christi TX 78404

ANGELO, GAYLE-JEAN, mathematics and physical science educator; b. Winchester, Mass., Nov. 27, 1951; d. John William and Josephine Marie (Tavano) A.; B.A. in Physics with honor, Northeastern U., 1975, M.Ed. in Curriculum and Instrn. of Sci. and Math., 1978; M.S. in Applied Statis., Columbia U., 1984, postgrad., 1984—. Clin. chemist Boston Med. Lab., Inc., 1971-73; exptl. physicist Northeastern U., 1975-76; tchr. natural scis., head sci. dept. Girls Cath. High Sch., Malden, Mass., 1977-78; research and teaching asst. Columbia U., N.Y.C., 1978-80, research assoc., 1982-83; research scientist Air Force Rocket Propulsion Lab., Edwards AFB, Calif., 1980-82; research and devel. analyst, engr. Varian-Extrion Div., Gloucester, Mass., 1984-86; instr. math. Golden Gate U., Cerro Coso Community Coll., 1981-82, Columbia U., N.Y.C., 1982-83; instr. chemistry North Shore Community Coll., 1985-86; instr. math., physics Imperial Valley Coll., Imperial, Calif., 1986—. Served with USAF, 1980-82; mem. Air N.G., 1982-85. Decorated Air Force Commendation; cert. secondary tchr., Mass.; cert. community coll. tchr., Calif. Mem. Am. Assn. Physics Tchrs., Am. Phys. Soc., Mathematical Assn. of Am., Nat. Council Tchrs. Math., Nat. Sci. Tchrs. Assn., Soc. Coll. Sci. Tchrs., Mensa, Sigma Xi, Phi Delta Kappa, Sigma Pi Sigma, Sigma Delta Epsilon, Kappa Delta Pi. Home: 310 Lariat Ln Imperial CA 92251 Office: Imperial Valley Coll Math Sci Engring Dept 380 E Aten Rd Imperial CA 92251

ANGELO, SANDRA ANN, management consultant; b. Chgo., June 19, 1952; d. Michael Raymond and Rose Josephine (Manago) A.; foster child, Leslee Tornabeni. BS, Purdue U., 1974; MA, U. Md., 1979; PhD, Purdue U., 1981. Tchr. 7th grade Dunbar Jr. High Sch., St. Charles, Ill., 1974-76; instr. graphic arts U. Md., College Park, 1976-77; instr. materials and process beginning electricity/electronics Purdue U., West Lafayette, Ind., 1977-81; asst. mgr. HappyGrams, Inc., Algonquin, Ill., 1981-83; asst. prof. electricity, English, communications, basic math. DeVry Inst. Tech., Lombard, Ill., 1982-84; asst. mgr. Ameritech Services, Inc., Schaumburg, Ill., 1984-86; pres. Mgmt. Strategies, Bartlett, Ill., 1986—. Mem. Mt. Prospect (Ill.) Community Band, 1982—; vol. Friends In Service Here, Bartlett, 1986—; bd. dirs. Horizen Townhouse Assn., Bartlett, 1986, 87,88; yoga instr. Medinah (Ill.) Park Dist., 1986, 87, 88. Recipient fellowship U.S. Office Edn., 1977-78. Mem. IEEE, Am. Soc. Profls. and Exec. Women, Nat. Assn. Female Execs., Kappa Delta Pi, Epsilon Pi Tau. Roman Catholic. Office: Mgmt Strategies PO Box 8076 Bartlett IL 60103-8076

ANGELONE, CATHERINE, federal agency administrator; b. Queens, N.Y., May 24, 1946; d. Dominick Anthony and Italia Marie (Masone) A.; children: Garrett Keith and Eric Joseph Gorton. Assoc. Applied Sci., Fashion Inst. Tech., 1965; BSW, Adelphi U., 1977; MSW cum laude, 1978. Asst. regional dir. Nassau County Youth Bd., Mineola, N.Y., 1979-81, coordinator community devel., 1983-86; asst. program dir. Nassau County Dept. Mental Health, Mineola, 1981-83; special asst. to regional adminstr. U.S. Small Bus. Adminstrn., N.Y.C., 1986—. Vol. various Island Park (N.Y.) youth orgns., 1961—, Office of First Lady Mrs. Nancy Reagan, 1982—; tchr. religion Sacred Heart Ch., 1974-76, 83-84; sec. Island Park Rep. Club, 1984-86. Mem. Assn. Cert. Social Workers. Roman Catholic. Home: 31 Waterford Rd Island Park NY 11558 Office: US Small Bus Adminstrn 26 Federal Plaza New York NY 10278

ANGLIN, DANA FORTNER, television executive; b. Birmingham, Ala., Sept. 17, 1952; d. Arthur Cowan and Marilyn Yvonne (Marsh) Fortner; m. Forrest Lehjeune Anglin, Jan. 29, 1977 (div. 1985); 1 child, Andrea Nicole. BS, Auburn U., 1974. Work study intern Frederick Atkins, N.Y.C., 1974; sales rep. Xerox Corp., Birmingham, Ala., 1975-79; account exec. WERC/WKXX Radio Mooney Broadcasting, Birmingham, 1982-83; account exec. WVTM-TV Times Mirror Broadcasting, Birmingham, 1983—; mem. alumni devel. bd. Sch. Human Scis. Auburn U., 1985—. State Field Dir. Miss Am. Scholarship Pageant, Ala. 1982—; dir. Queen's Pageant All American Bowl, Ala., 1985—. Mem. Am. Advt. Fedn., Am. Women Radio & TV Treas. Republican. Home: 718 Rockbridge Rd Birmingham AL 35216 Office: WVTM-TV PO Box 10502 Birmingham AL 35202

ANGOFF, MARION BRENDA, advertising executive, educator; b. Cambridge, Mass., Mar. 23, 1939; d. Nathan Robert and Evelyn (Kanter)

A. BA, Wellesley Coll., 1961; MEd, Tufts U., 1962. Cert. English and History tchr., Mass. Assoc. editor Harvard Med. Alumni bulletin, Boston, 1962; tchr. English Lexington (Mass.) Pub. Schs., 1963—; acct. exec. New Eng. Times Jobfinder, Norwood, Mass., 1987—. Lexington Pub. Schs. grantee, 1979. Mem. Lexington Edn. Assn., Mass. Tchrs. Assn., Nat. Council Tchrs. Englis, New. Eng. Poetry Club (organizer readings 1984—). Home: 25 Bothfeld Rd Newton MA 02159

ANGOTTI, CATHERINE MARIE, consulting nutritionist; b. Arlington, Va., Nov. 9, 1946; d. Frank William and Catherine Jeannette (Kolakoski) Poos; B.S., James Madison U., 1968; R.D., Med. Coll. Va., 1969; postgrad. Va. Poly. Inst. and State U., 1975; m. John Joseph Angotti, Sept. 15, 1973; 1 dau., Heather Jeannette. Home economist Washington Gas Light Co., 1968; clin. dietitian Fairfax Hosp., Fairfax, Va., 1969-73; pvt. practice as nutrition cons., Va., 1972—; nutrition cons. Manassas (Va.) Manor Nursing Home, 1973-74, Bio-Tech., Inc., Falls Church, Va., 1977-78; nutrition surveyor JWK Internat., Annandale, Va., 1980-81; nutrition cons. NASA, Washington, 1977—; pres. Nutrition Cons., Inc., 1980—; nutrition lectr. state and nat. meetings. Del. for Va. Dietetic Assn. to Va. Council on State Legis., 1974-76; mem. Com. for Pub. of Regional Diet Manual, 1971-73. Food Service Execs. awards scholar, 1967; Mem. Am. Dietetic Assn. (named Recognized Young Dietitian of Yr. 1975, state rep. for nutrition services payment system 1984-87), Va. Assn. Allied Health Profls. (del. 1974-79, bd. dirs. 1975-77), Cons. Nutritionists (Va. state coordinator 1976-79), D.C. Dietetic Assn., Va. Dietetic Assn. (exec. bd. 1974-76, 82—, legis. chmn. 1974-76, mem. nominating com. 1982-84, mem. licensure com. 1983—, chmn. nutrition services payment system bd. 1984—, del.), No. Dist. Dietetic Assn. (exec. bd. 1970-86, 88—, treas. 1980-82, pres. 1983-84, chmn. nominating com. 1984-85, dietetic appreciation award, 1987, mem. awards com. 1988), Fairfax County Nutrition Com., Cons. Nutritionists of the Chesapeake Bay Area (nominating com. 1983, sec. 1986-87), Nat. Assn. Female Execs., Soc. for Nutrition Edn. Democrat. Roman Catholic. Contbr. articles to profl. jours. Home: 2727 Oak Valley Dr Vienna VA 22180 Office: 10721 Main St Fairfax VA 22030

ANGUIANO, LUPE, business executive; b. La Junta, Colo., Mar. 12, 1929; d. Jose and Rosario (Gonzalez) A.; student Ventura (Calif.) Jr. Coll., 1948, Victory Noll Jr. Coll., Huntington, Ind., 1949-52, Marymount Coll., Palos Verdes, Calif., 1958-59, Calif. State U., Los Angeles, 1965-67; M.A., Antioch-Putney-Yellow Springs, Ohio, 1978. S.W. regional dir. NAACP Legal Def. and Ednl. Fund, Los Angeles, 1965-69; civil rights specialist HEW, Washington, 1969-73; S.W. regional dir. Nat. Council Catholic Bishops, Region X, San Antonio, 1973-77; pres. Nat. Women's Employment and Edn., Inc., San Antonio, 1978-81; pres. Lupe Anguiano & Assocs., 1981—; cons. Tex. Dept. Human Resources, Dept. Labor, Women's Bur.; proposal reader U.S. Office Edn.-Women's Equity Act; mem. Tex. Adv. Council on Tech.-Vocat. Edn. Calif. del. White House Conf. on Status Mexican-Ams. in U.S., 1967; founding mem. policy council Nat. Women's Polit. Caucus, from 1971; Tex. and nat. del. Internat. Women's Year, 1976-77; chmn. Nat. Women's Polit. Caucus Welfare Reform Task Force, from 1977; co-chmn. Nat. Peace Acad. Campaign, 1977-81; founder, bd. dirs. Nat. Chicana Found., Inc., 1971-78; bd. dirs. Calif. Council Children and Youth, 1967, Rio Grande Fedn. Chicano Health Centers, S.W. Rural States, 1974-76, Women's Lobby, Washington, 1974-77, Rural Am. Women, Washington, from 1978, Small Bus. Council Greater San Antonio; mem. Pres.'s Council on Pvt. Sector Initiatives, 1983. Recipient Community award Coalition Mexican-Am. Orgns., 1967, Outstanding Service award Washington, 1968, Thanksgiving award Boys' Club, 1976, Outstanding Service award Tex. Women's Polit. Caucus, 1977, Liberty Bell award San Antonio Young Lawyers, 1981, Vista award for exceptional service to end poverty, 1980, Headliner award San Antonio Women in Communications, 1978, Woman of Year award Tex. Women's Polit. Caucus, 1978; named Outstanding Woman of Yr., Los Angeles County, 1972; Woman of the 80s Ms. mag., 1980; Wonder Woman Found. award, 1982; Advocate of Yr., San Antonio SBA, 1984. Mem. Assn. Female Execs., Pres.'s Assn., Am. Mgmt. Assn. Democrat. Roman Catholic. Author: (with others) U.S. Bilingual Education Act, 1967, Texas A.F.D.C. Employment and Education Act, 1977; manuals Women's Employment and Education Model Program.

ANISE-LEVINE, ZAHRA MUSA, personnel specialist; b. N.Y.C., Aug. 18, 1947; m. Barry Richard Levine, Mar. 9, 1980. AA, City Coll. San Francisco, 1969; BA, San Francisco State Coll., 1971; MA, San Francisco State U., 1974; postgrad., Inst. for Applied Linguistics, France, 1974. Cert. adult edn. educator, Calif.; cert. community coll. instr., Calif. Instr. Skyline Community Coll., San Bruno, Calif., 1973-74; tax technician IRS, San Francisco, 1974-75; with personnel dept. Dept. of Army, San Francisco, 1975-76; specialist personnel mgmt. Puget Sound Naval Shipyard Dept. of Navy, Bremerton, Wash., 1976-77; assoc. dir. Mgmt. & Communications Inst. Office of Personnel Mgmt., San Francisco, 1977-80; specialist employee devel. Def. Logistics Agy., Def. Contract Adminstrn. Services Region Dept. Def., El Segundo, Calif., 1980—; team leader community coll. program Def. Contract Adminstrn. Services Region div. Dept. Def., El Segundo, Calif., 1986—. Mem. Arab-Am. Anti-Defamation League, Los Angeles, 1980—. Mem. Am. Soc. for Tng. and Delivery, Nat. Soc. for Performance and Instrn., Assn. Arab-Am. Univ. Grads. Office: DCASRLA-KW 222 N Sepulveda Blvd El Segundo CA 90245-4320

ANKROM, BARBARA BURKE, journalist; b. Upper Darby, Pa., May 30, 1943; d. Joseph Anthony and Teresa Gertrude (Smart) Burke; A.B., Wheeling Coll., 1965; children—Joseph Burke Nied, Laura Ann Nied, Michele Marie Nied; m. 2d, Robert W. Ankrom, Sr. Asst. editor Jones & Laughlin Steel Corp., Pitts., 1965-66; reporter/photographer Democrat Messenger, Waynesburg, Pa., 1976-77; corr. McGraw-Hill & World News Pubs., N.Y.C., 1976—; writer Pitts. Bus. Times, 1981-82; tech editor, writer JWK Internat. Corp., Pitts., 1982-84; writer-editor W.Va. U. Energy and Water Research Ctr., 1985-88; writer, editor W.Va. U. Mining Extension Service, 1988—; freelance writer, 1984—. Public relations dir. Boy Scouts Am., Greene County, Pa., 1977-84; editor, reporter, pub. Democrat Messenger, 1976. Mem. AAUW. Democrat. Roman Catholic. Asst. editor Men and Steel mag., 1965-66; editor Pa. chpts. Pan American's U.S.A. Guide Book, 1979, 80. Home: RD 1 Box 234A Clarksville PA 15322 Office: WVa U Mining Extension Service Morgantown WV 26505

ANNS, ARLENE EISERMAN, pub. co. exec.; b. Pearl River, N.Y.; d. Frederick Joel and Anna (Behnke) E.; student Bergen Jr. Coll., 1946-48; B.S., Utah State U., 1950; postgrad. Traphagen Sch. Design, 1957, N.Y. U., 1958, Hunter Coll., 1959-60. Research and promotion asst. Archtl. Record, N.Y.C., 1952-56; asst. research dir. Esquire Mag., N.Y.C., 1956-62; research mgr. Am. Machinist, publ. McGraw-Hill, Inc., N.Y.C., 1962-67, mktg. service mgr., 1967-69, 1969-71, sales mgr., 1976-77, dir. mktg., 1977-78; v.p. mktg. services Morgan-Gramplan, Inc., N.Y.C., 1971-72; mktg. dir. Family Health & Diversion mag., 1972-74; dist. sales mgr. Postgrad. Medicine, 1974-76; advt. sales mgr. Contemporary Ob/Gyn, 1976-78; dir. profl. devel., 1978-80; pub. Graduating Engr. and dir. classified advt., McGraw, Inc., N.Y.C., 1980—. Mem. Am. Mktg. Assn., Pharm. Advt. Club, Advt. Women N.Y., Advt. Club N.Y., Sales Exec. Club, Employment Mgmt. Assn., Am. Soc. Personnel Adminstrs., Coll. Placement Council, Am. Assn. Energy Edn., Pi Sigma Alpha. Home: 101 Brianwood Ct Lakes Quinton VA 23141

ANOFF, JEAN S., advertising company executive; b. Chgo., Sept. 25, 1937; d. Authur H. and Gwendolyn M. (Straus) Schoenstadt; m. Philip R. Anoff, July 16, 1964; children: Carol Marie Jennings, Donald William, Cathy Jane. Student, Pomona Coll., Clairmont, Calif.; BA, U. Mich. Cert. Master Advt. Specialist, 1988. Legal sec. Chgo., 1958-60; v.p. H. Schoenstadt & Sons, Inc., Chgo., 1960-64; pres. Sesco, Inc., Charlotte, N.C., 1975—; chairperson Women Bus. Owners, Charlotte, 1986—. Leader Jewish Family Service Task Force on Sustance Abuse, Charlotte, 1987; vol. Sr. Women's Group, Charlotte, 1987; pres. B'nai B'rith Women, Charlotte, 1970; v.p. Temple Beth'El, 1968; bd. dirs., charter mem. Temple Beth Shalom, 1971-76, Jewish Community Ctr., 1977-78; neighborhood chairperson Hornet's Net Girls Scouts of Am., Charlotte, 1972; v.p. Young Dems., Chgo., 1958. Recipient Clio award, 1981, 82, 83, Community Service award, B'nai B'rith Internat., 1979. Mem. Specialty Advt. Assn. Internat., Charlotte C. of C. Club: Women's Variety of Ill. (pres. 1962-64). Home: 1635 Cavendish Ct Charlotte NC 28211 Office: Sesco Inc 5208 Monroe Rd Charlotte NC 28205

ANSELL, MARYLEE, real estate executive; b. White Hall, Ill., Mar. 29, 1936; d. Ellsworth and Harriett (Rhodes) a. BS, So. Ill. U., 1958. Exec. sec. The May Dept. Stores Co., St. Louis, 1958-62; sec., treas. Danter Assocs., St. Louis, 1962-68; exec. asst. Shure Mfg., St. Louis, 1968-72; from trainee to asst. div. mgr. The Equitable Life Assurance Soc. of the U.S., St. Louis, 1972-83; dir. ops. Linclay Corp., St. Louis, 1983—. Presbyterian. Office: Linclay Corp PO Box 27316 Saint Louis MO 63141

ANTAL, EMOKE, accountant; b. Budapest, Hungary, June 6, 1944; came to U.S., 1962; d. George and Ilona (Melczer) A.; m. Steven C. Scheer, June 14, 1962 (div. 1972). BA, Loyola Coll., Balt., 1979. CPA, Md. Acctg. asst. L.I.G. Bus. Bur., Lakewood, Ohio, 1962-64; head bookkeeper Pacific Builders Supply Co., Cleve., 1964-67; office mgr. Geltman Sponging Co., Cleve., 1967-68; staff acct. Naron & Wagner, CPA's, Balt., 1968-73; office mgr. Security Ford Tractor, Balt., 1973; chief fin. officer Avon Am., Ltd., Garrison, Md., 1973-86; pvt. practice acctg. Glen Arm, Md., 1986—. Mem. Am. Inst. CPA's, Md. Assn. CPA's. Republican. Roman Catholic. Club: Holiday Health. Home and Office: 12003 Deer Bit Ln Glen Arm MD 21057

ANTANAITIS, CYNTHIA EMILY, lawyer; b. Bridgeport, Conn., Oct. 16, 1954; d. George Alexander and Stella Marie (Bernius) A. BS magna cum laude, Western Conn. State U., 1976; JD, SUNY, Amherst, 1980. Bar: Conn. 1983, U.S. Dist. Ct. Conn. 1983. Legis. and regulations specialist State of Conn. Dept. of Banking, Hartford, 1981-83, asst. counsel, 1983-86, sr. adminstrv. atty., 1986—. Mem. ABA, Conn. Bar Assn., N.Am. Securities Administrators Assn., Inc. (ad hoc com. on arbitration 1988—, fin. planners and investment advisers com. 1984—, legis. com. 1981-84, vice chmn. 1982-84). Roman Catholic. Office: State of Conn Dept of Banking 44 Capitol Ave Hartford CT 06106

ANTHONISEN, LOIS JOANN, financial planning executive; b. Minot, N.D., Dec. 28, 1941; d. Victor L. and Bernice O. (Strathe) Pommier; m. Martin W. Anthonisen; 1987; 1 child, Ashley I. Student, Jamestown Coll., 1960-61. With 1st Nat. Bank, Minot, 1963-67; exec. sec. Burlington No. Railway, Minot, 1967-82; owner, mgr. Ottmann Tax and Bus. Service, Minot, 1971-86; pres. Lois J. Ottmann and Assocs., Fin. Planning, Minot, 1983-86; prin. AFC Adv. Corp., Homewood, Ill., 1986—; dir. compliance and edn., gen. securities prin., prin. fin. planner FSC Securities Corp., Homewood, 1985-88—, product selection bd. north cen. region, 1985-87; with Integraded Resources Equity Corp., 1988—. Chairperson fundraising Miss N.D. Pageant, 1981-85, traveling companion, 1981-83. Mem. Internat. Assn. Fin. Planning (bd. dirs. ethics and pub. relations, v.p. programs Chgo. south suburban chpt. 1986-88), Quota Internat. (bd. dirs. 1984-85), Minot C. of C. (bus. and mil. affairs coms. 1983-85). Republican. Office: Integrated Resources Equity Corp 17450 S Halsted St Suite 25E Homewood IL 60430

ANTHONY, BETTY ARLENE, medical center executive; b. Jacksonville, Fla., July 14, 1926; d. Glessner Earl and Florence Claudine (Smyth) Pratt; m. Yancey Lamar Anthony, II, Sept. 13, 1983. Student Jones Bus. Coll., Jacksonville, 1944, New Orleans Bapt. Theol. Sem., 1952, U. Fla., 1953-54, Tampa U., 1956. Promotion sec. Fla. Bapt. Conv., Jacksonville, 1945-53; sec. First Bapt. Ch., Tampa, 1955-59; sec. to asst. adminstr. Bapt. Med. Ctr., Jacksonville, 1960-65, sec. to exec. dir., 1966-80, corp. sec., 1980—; asst. sec., treas. Bapt. Health, Inc., Jacksonville, 1983—; sec. Bapt. Health Found., Inc., Jacksonville, 1983—, exec. com., 1988—; Bapt. Health Properties, Inc., Jacksonville, 1983—, Bapt. Med. Ctr. of Port St., Inc., Jacksonville, 1981—; sec. and treas. Bapt. Med. Ctr. of Ga., Inc., Jacksonville, 1980—; asst. sec. N.E. Fla. Breast Ctr., Inc., Jacksonville, 1984—; sec. Healthcare Mgmt. Services, Inc., Jacksonville, 1980—; asst. sec., treas. So. Bapt. Hosp. of Fla. Inc., Jacksonville, 1985—; sec.-treas. Southbank Advt. Inc., 1987; asst. sec. The Pavilion Developer Inc., 1987. Mem. Fla. Hosp. Exec. Secs. Assn. (dir. 1973-76, pres. 1975-76, program chmn. 1974-75), Am. Soc. Corp. Secs., Nat. Assn. Female Execs. Avocations: jogging, creative writing, church activities, oil painting/drawing, gardening. Office: Baptist Health Inc 1300 Gulf Life Dr Suite 303 Jacksonville FL 32207

ANTHONY, GERALDINE CECILIA, educator; b. Bklyn., Oct. 5, 1919; d. William and Agnes Josephine (Murphy) A.; B.A., Mt. St. Vincent U., 1951; M.A. in Philosophy, St. Johns U., N.Y.C., 1956, Ph.D. in English, 1963. Joined Congregation of Sisters of Charity of Halifax, Roman Cath. Ch., 1939; tchr. jr. and sr. high schs., Boston, N.Y., 1942-62; prof. English, Mt. St. Vincent U., Halifax, N.S., 1965-87, now prof. emeritus. Recipient cert. in 17th Century poetry Exeter Coll., Oxford U., Eng., 1964; fellow in journalism U. Minn., 1965. Mem. Assn. Can. Univs. Tchrs. English, Assn. Canadian Theatre History. Author: John Coulter, 1976; Gwen Pharis Ringwood, 1981; editor: (series) Profiles in Canadian Drama, 1977; Stage Voices, 1978. Home: 51 Marlwood Dr, Halifax, NS Canada B3M 3H4 Office: 51 Marlwood Dr, Wedgewood Park, Halifax, NS Canada B3M 3H4

ANTHONY, GRETCHEN WILHELMINA HAUSER, architect, consultant on accessibility for disabled; b. Mpls., Nov. 13, 1936; d. Theodor Emmanuel and Margrete Alice (Norman) Hauser; m. John Duncan Anthony, June 17, 1961 (div. Jan. 1980); children—Caitlin Anharad, Ian David. Student Pa. State U., 1954-59; B.Arch., U. Mich., 1961. Registered profl. architect, Pa. Draftswoman, designer Todd & Giroux AIA, Rochester, N.Y., 1961-62, Michaell DeAngelis AIA, Rochester, 1962-63, John M. Puskar AIA, Pitts., 1963-66; ptnr. Puskar & Anthony, Pitts., 1968-70; self-employed architect, 1970—, Fairmont, W.Va., 1974—; cons. Washington County Planning Commn., Pa., 1966-67, 1970-73. Draftswoman, designer and specifications writer on variety of construction and remodeling projects. Organizer, past pres. Marion County High Spirit MS Com., Fairmont, W.Va., 1973—; del. Gov. of W.Va. Conf. on Handicapped Individuals, Charleston, 1976; alt. White House Conf. on Handicapped Individuals, 1976; mem. W.Va. Adv. Council on Edn. of Exceptional Children, Charleston, 1978-81; organizer Handicapped United of W.Va., Fairmont, pres., 1982—; bd. dirs. greater W.Va. chpt. Nat. M.S. Soc., Charleston, 1983-87 ; past vice chmn. consumer adv. com. Clarksburg Dist. div. W.Va. Vocat. Rehab., 1983—; trustee Coordinating Council for Ind. Living, Morgantown, W.Va., 1984—; mem. consumer adv. com. W.Va. Client Assistance Program, Charleston, 1984—, W.Va. Ind. Living Council, 1987, W.Va. U. Social Justice Council, 1987—, W.Va. U. Handicapped Accessibility Com., 1987—. Recipient award W,va, Adv. Com on Edn. of Exceptional Children, Merit award W.Va. Rehab. Assn. Avocations: reading; knitting. Home and Office: Access Unltd 6 Diana Dr Fairmont WV 26554

ANTHONY, JOAN CATON, lawyer; writer; b. South Bend, Ind., July 28, 1939; d. Joseph Robert and Margaret Catherine (McMeel) Caton; m. Robert Armstrong Anthony, Jan. 3, 1980; 1 child, Peter. BA, Marquette U., 1961; MA, Northwestern U., 1963; JD, Catholic U. Am., 1979. Bar: D.C. 1980, Va. 1982. Instr. English, Marquette U., Milw., 1963-65; instr. English, George Washington U., Washington, 1965-69, asst. prof., 1969-70; spl. asst. student affairs HEW, Washington, 1970-72; dir. Office Student and Youth Affairs, U.S. Office Edn., Washington, 1972-74, legis. specialist, 1974-78; chief mgmt. ops. br. Fed. Wildlife Permit Office, U.S. Fish and Wildlife Service, Washington, 1978-81; assoc. firm Cate and Goodbread, Washington, 1981-86; mem. U.S. del. to 2d meeting Conf. Parties to Conv. on Internat. Trade in Endangered Species of Wild Flora and Fauna, San Jose, Costa Rica, 1979. Contbr. lit. revs., essays and articles on univ.-community relations, western settlement and internat. negotiations to various publs. Bd. dirs. McLean Citizens Assn., 1982-83, Fairfax County Humane Soc., 1983; pres. Franklin Forest Frolickers, 1985-86; treas. Greater McLean Rep. Women's Club, 1987-88. Recipient spl. achievement award U.S. Fish and Wildlife Service, 1981. Mem. ABA, D.C. Bar Assn., Va. Bar Assn. Roman Catholic. Home: 2011 Lorraine Ave McLean VA 22101

ANTHONY, MARGARET ALICE, photographer, educator; b. Memphis, July 8, 1944; d. Charles Thomas and Marguerite (McGaha) Wellons; m. Murray Stephen Anthony, Oct. 14, 1967. BS, Memphis State U., 1966; med. technologist, Memphis Bapt. Hosp., 1967; MFA, East Tenn. State U., 1987. Med. technologist Pineview Gen. Hosp., Valdosta, Ga., 1967-68, U. Mo., Columbia, 1968-72; grad. asst. photographer East Tenn. State U., Johnson City, 1985-87, instr. photography, 1987—. Photographer: one-woman exhibits include Tenn. Tchrs. Credit Union, East Tenn. State U. Slocumb Gallery, Western Carolina U. Chelsea Gallery, Ralston Fine Art; group exhibits include Women in Photography, U. Ala., Huntsville, 1985, Nat. Aperture, Winston-Salem, N.C., 1986, The Print Club, Phila., 1987, Illuminance, Lubbock, Tex., 1987-88, and various other galleries; represented in permanent collections Brooks Mus. Art, Memphis; contbg. photographer: Appalachia Now and Then, 1986-88, Mockingbird, 1981-85, Photo Rev., 1985, 88. Asst. Acteen dir. Holston Bapt. Assn., Johnson City 1979-88; vol. Johnson City Bapt. Ctr. Recipient Juror's Photography award Phila. Print Club, 1987; named Vol. of Yr. Holston Bapt. Assn., 1987. Mem. Am. Soc. Clin. Pathologists (registered med. technologist, assoc. 1967-87), Memphis Zool. Soc., Phi Kappa Phi, Gamma Beta Phi. Republican. Baptist. Home: 6 Mistletoe Ct Johnson City TN 37604

ANTHONY, SHARON LYNN, nurse; b. Wyandotte, Mich., May 4, 1955; d. Howard William and Dorothy Mae (Ashland) A. BA in Biology, Hiram (Ohio) Coll., 1978; AD in Nursing, Lakeland Coll., Mentor, Ohio, 1980; postgrad. in bus., U. Phoenix, 1987—. Head nurse perinatal clin. research ctr. Cleve. Met. Gen. Hosp., 1983-87; clin. dir. birthing ctr. Phoenix Meml. Hosp., Apr.-Dec. 1987; clin. dir. maternal child health Desert Smaritan Hosp., Phoenix, 1988—. Mem. Nat. Assn. Research Nurses and Dieticians, Northeastern Ohio Educators, Greater Cleve. Diabetes Assn., Nurses Assn. of Am. Coll. Obstetricians and Gyncologists. Home: 5038 S Hardy Dr #2005 Tempe AZ 85282 Office: Desert Samaritan Hosp Phoenix AZ

ANTIN, ELEANOR, artist; b. N.Y.C., Feb. 27, 1935; d. Sol and Jeanette (Efron) Fineman; m. David Antin, Dec., 1961; 1 son, Blaise. B.A., CCNY, 1958; student, Tamara Daykarhanova Sch. for Stage, N.Y.C., 1954-56. Prof. visual arts U. Calif., San Diego. Artist, producer videotapes Little Match Girl Ballet, 1975, Adventures of a Nurse, 1976, The Nurse and the Hijackers, 1977, The Angel of Mercy, 1980, from the Archives of Modern Art, 1987; (film) Loves of a Ballerina, 1986; one-woman shows include Mus. Modern Art, N.Y.C., 1973, Whitney Mus. Film and Video Program, N.Y.C., 1978, Long Beach Mus. Art, Calif., 1979, Ronald Feldman Gallery, N.Y.C., 1977, 79, 80, 83, 86; group shows include, Sâo Paulo Biennal, Brazil, 1975, Phila. Mus. Fine Arts, 1978, Hirschhorn Mus., Washington, 1979, 84, Santa Barbara Mus. Art, Calif., 1979, performances include Battle of the Bluffs, 1975, 80, The Angel of Mercy, 1977, 80, Before the Revolution, 1979, Recollections of My Life with Diaghiler, 1980, 86, El Desdichado (The Unlucky One), 1983, Help! I'm in Seattle, 1986, 87, Who Cares About a Ballerina?, 1987, 88, (videotape) From the Archives of Modern Art, 1987; represented in permanent collections, Long Beach Mus. Art, San Francisco Mus. Modern Art, Wadsworth Atheneum, Hartford, Conn., Mus. Modern Art, N.Y.C.; artist performer at Venice Bienale, 1976, Mus. Contemporary Art, Chgo., 1978, Houston, 1978, 80; author: book Being Antinova, 1983. Nat. Endowment for Arts grantee, 1979; recipient Vesta award, Los Angeles, 1985. Office: U Calif at San Diego Visual Arts Dept La Jolla CA 92093

ANTMAN, LORI LINETTE, chiropractor; b. Hackensack, N.J., June 25, 1960; d. Frank James and Ninette Dorothee (Mercier) A. BS in Biochemistry, Tex. A&M U., 1982; D. Chiropractic, Tex. Chiropractic Coll., 1986. Diplomate Nat. Bd. Chiropractic. Small bus. office mgr. Seabrook, Tex., 1986; owner Chirpractic Health Ctr., Galveston, Tex., 1987—; clin. staff asst. Tex. Chiropractic Coll., Pasadena, Tex., 1985-86. Mem., sec. Galveston Police Appreciation Com., 1987-88; mem. service com. Student Y Assn., College Station, Tex., 1978-82. Mem. Am. Chiropractic Assn., Tex. Chiropractic Assn., Tex. Chiropractic Coll. Alumni Assn., Galveston Republican Womans Club, Alpha Phi Omega, Gamma Sigma Delta. Home: 3428 Cove View Blvd #809 Galveston TX 77554 Office: Chiropractic Health Ctr 4603 Fort Crockett Blvd PO Box 3367 Galveston TX 77552

ANTON, CHERYL LYNN, sales manager; b. Toledo, Nov. 3, 1953; d. Ralph Herbert and Coletta Marie (Nickerson) Snyder; student U. Toledo, 1971-73; 1 son, John Daniel. With Kroger Co., Toledo, 1972-80, dept. supr. merchandising; sales dir. Growth Unltd., Toledo, 1979-80; owner CJ's Bar, Toledo, 1980-82; sales rep. Armour Food Co., Orlando, Fla., 1983-85; dist. sales mgr. Jones Dairy Farm, 1985-87; regional sales mgr. Southland Corp., 1987—. Mem. Nat. Assn. Female Execs. (network dir. 1979—), Nat. Assn. for Women. Democrat. Home: 6105 Luzon Dr Orlando FL 32809 Office: Southland Corp Fla 1970 Sand Lake Rd Orlando FL 32859

ANTONACCI, LORI (LORETTA MARIE), marketing and promotion consultant; b. Riverton, Ill., Mar. 31, 1947; d. Antonio and Gena Marie A. B.A., Bradley U., 1969. Broadcast copywriter Sta. WIRL-TV, Peoria, Ill., 1969; communications specialist Walgreen Co., Chgo., 1970-72; creative supr. Nat. Assn. Realtors, Chgo., 1973; creative dir., producer Steve Sohmer, Inc., N.Y.C., 1974-77; owner, exec. producer Antonacci Prodns., N.Y.C., 1977-79; promotion specialist Ziff-Davis Publs., 1979-80; promotion mgr. Psychology Today, 1980-81; pres. Antonacci & Assocs., N.Y.C., 1982—; adj. prof. Gallatin Div. NYU, 1986—. Bd. dirs. Artists Talk on Art, Inc., Artists Community Fed. Credit Union; founder Artists Talk on Art Panel series, 1974. Recipient Golden Eagle award CINE, 1976; award U.S. Indsl. Film Festival, 1977; CEBA award, 1979; Bronze medal Internat. Film and TV Festival N.Y., 1979. Mem. Advt. Women N.Y. (profl. devel. com. 1983-85, career council com. 1984-86, program com. 1986—), Women in Communications, Media Marketers, Assn. Am. Women in Radio and TV. Address: 15 E 10th St New York NY 10003

ANTONE, KAREN ANN, real estate executive; b. Mpls., Jan. 21, 1947; d. Carl Harry and Mildred Marion (Johnson) Olson. Student U. Minn., 1966-68. Mortgage closer F&M Bank, Mpls., 1968-73; mortgage dept. coordinator Guarantee Title, Inc., Mpls., 1973-74; real estate closer Bermel Smaby Realtors, Mpls., 1974-75; real estate assoc. Edina Realty, Inc., Mpls., 1976—, sales adv. council, 1986-88, chmn. 1987. Active Minn. Real Estate Polit. Action Com., 1982. Mem. Greater Mpls. Area Bd. Realtors, Minn. Assn. Realtors, Nat. Assn. Realtors, Nat. Assn. Female Execs. Avocations: arts; jogging; reading, traveling. Office: Edina Realty Inc 4015 W 65th St Edina MN 55435

ANTONE, LINDA ANN, educational program developer, director; b. Mpls., Aug. 31, 1947; d. Richard and Mary Antone. BA in Internat. Relations, U. Minn., Mpls., 1969; postgrad. in broadcast communications, 1977-80. Advt. prodn. mgr. Hoffman Press, Mpls., 1972-73; advt. dir. Medallion Pub., Inc., Mpls., 1974-75; assoc. producer Wilson Learning Corp., Eden Prairie, Minn., 1976-79, producer, dir., 1979-82, dir. video dept., 1982-83; producer, dir. video programs for firms including AT&T, Ford Motor Co., Consol. Freightways. Producer, dir. tng. program ARC, 1982-83, v.p. prodn., 1983-86, product mgr., 1986-87; mem. Mpls. chpt. ARC pub. relations com., 1983; producer, dir. pub. service announcements Minn. Women's Network, Mpls., 1982-83. Recipient JVC Video award, 1984, N.Y. Internat. Film & Video award, 1985. Mem. Internat. Television Assn. (judge Golden Reel awards 1982), Am. Film Inst., Women in Communications (program com. Mpls.), NOW, Minn. Entrepreneurs Club, Women's Internat. League for Peace and Freedom (newsletter editor Mpls. 1975-77). Home: 4700 Ewing Ave S Minneapolis MN 55410 Office: Wilson Learning Corp 6950 Washington Ave S Eden Prairie MN 55344

ANTONELLI, PATTIE ELLEN, public relations executive; b. Cambridge, Mass., Nov. 1, 1953; d. Mary Frances (Keane) Collins; m. Joseph F. Antonelli, May 22, 1983. BS in Journalism, Suffolk U., 1975. Pub. relations dir. Foodmaster Supermarkets, Cambridge, 1975-77; pub. info. specialist Somerville (Mass.) Community Devel., 1978-80; adminstrv. asst. Middlesex County, Cambridge, 1980; dir. pub. affairs and vols. J.B. Thomas Hosp., Peabody, Mass., 1980—; bd. dirs. Bay Colony Devel. Corp., Newton. Bd. dirs. ACR, Lynn, Mass., 1981-83. Recipient Excellence in Pub. Relations award Pub. Relations Casebook, 1983, Merit award Healthcare Mktg. Report, 1985. Mem. Pub. Relations Soc. Am. (accredited, award 1985), New England Hosp. Pub. Relations Assn. (Excellence award 1983, 86, First Place 1984), Am. Soc. of Hosp. Pub. Relations and Mktg., New England Devel. Assn., New England Assn. of Hosp. Vol. Dirs. Roman Catholic. Home: 1A Summit Rd Medford MA 02155 Office: JB Thomas Hosp 15 King St Peabody MA 01960

ANTONELLIS, CHARLENE ADELE, human resources executive; b. Springfield, Mass., June 6, 1948; d. Joseph and Dorothy A. (Pederzoli) A. BS, Springfield Coll., 1970, MEd, 1971; MBA, Boston Coll., 1979. Dir. personnel Springfield Coll., 1971-73, New Eng. Bapt. Hosp., Boston, 1974; mgr. affirmative action dept. Raytheon, Waltham, Mass., 1974-75; personnel officer Boston Coll., Chestnut Hill, Mass., 1975-77; cons. Costello, Erdlen & Co., Westwood, Mass., 1977-81; sr. human resources rep. Computervision

Corp., Bedford, Mass., 1981-82, mgr. human resources dept. research and devel. div., 1982-83, dir. human resources dept. research and devel. div., 1983-84, v.p. human resources dept. research and devel. div., 1984—. Home: 23 Ivy Ln Milford MA 01757 Office: Computervision Corp 14 Crosby Dr Bedford MA 01757

ANTONIO, MARLENE JOAN, commission administrator; b. Moose Jaw, Sask., Can., Apr. 24, 1936; d. John Ewan and Ruby Irene (Bagg) Lauder; m. Harry Antonio, Apr. 27, 1957; 1 child, Jolaine Ann. B of Edn., U. Sask., 1956, BS, 1957; M of Edn., U. Calgary, Alta., Can., 1969. Geologist, Texaco Exploration Co., Calgary, 1957-58; tchr. Calgary Bd. Edn., 1966-70, 79-80; instr. Mt. Royal Coll., Calgary, 1970-74, U. Calgary, 1976-78; chmn. Alta. Human Rights Commn., Edmonton, 1979-85; mem. gov. council geol., geophy. Assn. Profl. Engrs., 1986—; mem. Minister's Consultative Com. on Tolerance and Understanding, Alta., 1983-84. Sec.-treas. Calgary Home and Sch. Assn., 1976-78. Recipient Good Servant award Can. Council Christians and Jews, 1984. Nat. Council Jewish Women scholar, Saskatoon, Sask., 1955-57. Mem. Alta. Tchrs. Assn., Can. Assn. Statuatory Human Rights Agys. (pres. 1984-85), Assn. Profl. Engrs., Geologists and Geophysicists of Alta. (hon. 1986-87, practice rev. bd. 1987—, governing council). Office: Assn Profl Engrs, 1500 Scotia Place Tower One, 10060 Jasper Ave, Edmonton, AB Canada T5J4A2

ANTOUN, SISTER M. LAWREACE, college president emerita; b. Meadville, Pa., Dec. 30, 1927; d. George K. and Freda (Habib) Antoun; B.S. Villa Maria Coll., 1954; M.S., Notre Dame U., 1959, postgrad. (doctoral candidate). Instr. chemistry Villa Maria Coll., Erie, Pa., 1955-61, asst. prof. chemistry, 1965-66, pres. 1966-88; past mem. Pa. Commn. on Financing of Higher Edn.; mem. exec. com. Commn. Ind. Colls. and Univs.; evaluator Middle States Assn./Commn. Higher Edn.; trustee Middle States Assn.; mem. Erie Conf. on Community Devel.; past chmn. Pa. Postsecondary Planning Commn.; chmn. Council Higher Edn.; past mem. adv. com. edn. Pa. Bd. Edn.; bd. dirs. Sisters of St. Joseph. Mem. Commonwealth Jud. Council; chairperson adv. council McMannis Ednl. Trust Fund; past mem. Home Rule Charter Com.; adv. bd. human ecology Cornell U.; bd. incorporators St. Vincent Health Center; bd. dirs. Hamot Med. Ctr., Erie Conf. on Community Devel., chmn. Pa. State Bd. of Edn. Mem. Am. Assn. Ind. Colls. and Univs., Pa. Assn. Coll. and Univs., Pa. Assn. Ind. Colls. and Univs.

ANTRIM, MINNIE FAYE, residential care facility administrator; b. Rochester, Tex., June 30, 1916; d. Charles C. Montandon and Myrtle Caldona (Brown) Montandon Taylor; m. Cecil C. Antrim, Jan. 1, 1938; children—Linda Faye Antrim Hathway, Cecil C. Student Central State Tchrs. Coll., Edmond, Okla., 1937. Asst. purchasing agt. Scenic Gen. Hosp., Modesto, Calif., 1955-68, Health Dept., Probation Dept., Stanislaus, Calif., 1955-68; owner, adminstr. Sierra Villa Retirement Home, Fresno, Calif., 1968-77, Mansion Home, Fresno, 1977—. Mem. Am. Coll. Health Care Adminstrs., Calif Bus. and Profl Club. Methodist. Club: Garden. Avocation: glee clubs. Home: 6070 E Townsend Fresno CA 93727

AONA, GRETCHEN MANN, artist, photographer; b. Omaha, June 25, 1933; d. Albert Paul and Gladys Louise (Mann) Andersen; A.B., San Jose State U., 1951, M.A. in Art, 1966; m. Daniel Kaleikoa Aona, Jr., June 16, 1979. Textbook illustrator math. and stats. dept. Stanford U., 1960-63; sci. illustrator Melabs, Mountain View, Calif., 1967; instr. art, crafts, and photography Kapiolani Community Coll., Honolulu, 1967-88, chmn. humanities dept., 1978-79; one-woman shows in photography include: Fantasy Images, Queen Emma Gallery, Honolulu, 1977, Foyer Gallery, Leeward Community Coll., Honolulu, 1980; group exhbns. include: Photo '70, '71, '72, Sixty Yrs. World in Color, Hague, Netherlands, 1973, Honolulu, Art Hawaii One, Honolulu Acad. Art, 1974, 75, Gt. Hawaiian Open Art Exhbn., 1981, Artists of Hawaii, Honolulu Acad. Arts, 1981, Honolulu Printmakers 55th Ann. Exhbn., 1983, 60th Ann. Exhbn., 1988, Windward Artists Easter Art Show, 1984, 85, 88, Hawaii Watercolor Soc. Exhibit, 1985, 86, Image 13 Hawaii, 1987; invitational exhbns. include Koa Gallery, Kapiolani Community Coll., 1987, Florals and Nature Scenes, Ho'omaluhia Botanical Garden, 1987, Aloha Ho'omaluhia, 1988. Represented by South Shore Gallery, Honolulu. Recipient Purchase award Honolulu Acad. Art, 1981, Hawaii State Found. Culture and Arts, 1987 (2). Mem. Hawaii Watercolor Soc., Pacific Handcrafters Guild. Democrat. Roman Catholic. Author: Creative Exploration in Crafts, 1976. Home: 45-453 B Mokulele Dr Kaneohe HI 96744

APELIAN, SYLVA, investment banker; b. Beirut, Apr. 1, 1943; d. George and Marie (Jules) A. AB, San Francisco State U., 1965; MA Internat. Law, Columbia U., 1967; MBA, U. Chgo., 1978. V.p. fin. ops. Blue Cross Blue Shield of Ill., Chgo., 1974-78; dir. planning analysis Singer Co., Stamford, Conn., 1978-80; mgr. bus. strategy cons. Gen. Electric Co., Fairfield, Conn., 1980-82; v.p. corp. fin. Becker Paribas, N.Y.C., 1982-84; first v.p. E.F. Hutton and Co., Inc., N.Y.C., 1984-86, sr. v.p., 1986—. Bd. govs. Health Systems Agy., Chgo., 1976-77. Named Woman of Influence Office of Mayor N.Y.C., N.Y. Woman, 1986. Republican. Club: Econ. Home: 50 Central Park W New York NY 10023 Office: E F Hutton and Co Inc 31 W 52d St New York NY 10019

APICHINO, MICHELLE CAPAGLI, overseas manpower manager; b. Sacramento, Jan. 23, 1950; d. Stanford Austin and Thelma Elvira (Berger) Petersen; m. David Michael Apichino, April 24, 1984; 1 stepchild, Anthony David. Grad. high sch., Sacramento, 1967. Pharm. technician Tallac Village Pharmacy, Sacramento, 1969-73; mgr. Concession Contract Foley & Burke, Redwood City, Calif., 1973-76; supr. billing Pharmacare Services, Sacramento, 1976-78; mgr. office G.E. Langsjoen, MD, Sacramento, 1978-81; adminstr. fin. H.E. Internat., Inc., Sacramento, 1982-85, mgr., bd. dirs., U.S. rep., 1985—. Republican. Mormon.

APPEL, NINA S., university dean; b. Prague, Czechoslovakia; d. Leo and Nora (Thein) Schick; m. Alfred Appel Jr., Sept. 1, 1957; children: Karen Oshman, Richard. Student, Cornell U.; JD, Columbia U. Mem. faculty Loyola U. Sch. Law, Chgo., assoc. dean, now dean. Jewish. Office: Loyola U Law Sch 1 E Pearson Chicago IL 60611

APPELBAUM, JUDITH PILPEL, editor, consultant, educator; b. N.Y.C., Sept. 26, 1939; d. Robert Cecil and Harriet Florence (Fleischl) Pilpel; B.A. with honors, Vassar Coll., 1960; m. Alan Appelbaum, Apr. 16, 1961; children—Lynn Stephanie, Alexander Eric. Editor, Harper's Mag., N.Y.C., 1960-74; mng. editor Harper's Weekly, 1974-76; sr. cons. Atlas World Press Rev., 1977; mng. editor Publishers Weekly, 1978-81; founder Sensible Solutions, Inc., 1979; contbg. editor Publishers Weekly, 1981-82; columnist N.Y. Times Book Rev., 1982-84; mng. dir. Sensible Solutions, Inc., 1984—; assoc. dir. Ctr. for Book Research, U. Scranton, 1985-88; book rev. editor Book Research Quar., 1984-86, editor in chief, 1986-88; mem. faculty Pub. Inst. of U. Denver, 1981—, CUNY edn. in pub. program, 1982—; editorial adv. Book Industry Study Group Newsletter, 1980-83; mem. stats. com. Book Industry Study Group, 1984—; adv. bd. Coordinating Council of Lit. Mags., 1980—. Mem. Authors Guild, Women's Media Group, PEN, Com. Small Mag./Press Editors and Publishers. Author: How to Get Happily Published, 1978, 3d edit., 1988; editor: (with Tony Jones and Gwyneth Cravens) The Big Picture: A Wraparound Book, 1976; The Question of Size in the Book Industry Today, 1978; Getting a Line on Backlist, 1979; Paperback Primacy, 1981; Small Publisher Power, 1982. Office: Sensible Solutions Inc 6 E 39th St New York NY 10016

APPELBAUM, MARILYN M(ARY), non-profit child care educational center executive, educator; b. Cleve., Dec. 21, 1941; d. Manny and Renee (Goldstein) Slomovits; m. Sanford J. Appelbaum, June 19, 1959 (div. 1986); children: Tobi Carole Appelbaum Chapman, Martin Howard. BA in Psychology summa cum laude, Cleve. State U., 1970; Montessori diploma Nat. Ctr. Montessori Edn., Washington, 1979; MA in Edn., Am. U., 1980; MA in Behavioral Sci., U. Houston, 1980, postgrad., 1982—. Dir., owner Oak Point Acad., Houston, 1973-87; exec. dir., editor, writer Nat. Ctr. Montessori Edn., 1979-81, dir., 1979—; exec. dir. Nat. Ctr. for Child Care Profls., Houston, 1980—; mem. proprietary sch. adv. commn. Tex. commr. edn., 1983; specialist speaker Criminal Investigations Task Force, Los Angeles, 1984; mem. day care standards devel. com. Tex. Dept. Human Resources, 1984; lectr. in field. Author: Do it Right, A positive Approach to Discipline, 1980, Let's Cook It Right, 1982, Practical Life and Home Living Skills, 1982, Reading and Writing Manual, 1983, Ground Rules for the Classroom, A Step-By-Step Approach, 1983, Child Care Professional Training Course, 1984; also articles. Mem. Nat. Assn. Child Care Mgmt., Nat. Ctr. Montessori Edn. (bd. dirs.), Am. Montessori Soc., Assn. Children with Learning Disabilities, Phi Delta Kappa. Jewish. Avocations: boating, reading, travel, research, writing.

APPELL, KATHLEEN M., management consultant; b. Phila., Apr. 20, 1943; d. Joseph F. and Catherine (Laing) Hudson; m. Vincent M. Mandes (div. Apr. 1968); children: Carren Lee, Vincent, Lori. Cert., Phila. Modeling Sch., 1960-61, Horsham Found., 1979-81, Behavioral Acad., 1981, Fashion Acad., 1984. Adminstr. Phila. Modeling and Career Sch., 1965-68; pres. K.M. Appell Enterprises Ltd., Warwick, Pa., 1968-76, 1984—; exec. asst. Horsham Psychiat. Hosp., Ambler, Pa., 1976-84, cons., 1976-84; dir. admissions Career Inst., Phila., 1986-87; cons. Resource Spectrum, Ambler, 1979-82, Horsham Mgmt. Corp., Ambler, 1978-84. Contbr. articles to profl. jours. Mem. Republican Task Force Com., Washington, 1981. Mem. Women's Econ. Devel., Assn. Fashion and Image Cons., Profl. and Exec. Women. Mem. Dutch Reformed Ch. Home: 1005 Gates Pl Warminster PA 18974

APPLE, DAINA DRAVNIEKS, management, administrative systems designer; b. Kuldiga, Latvia, USSR, July 6, 1944; came to U.S., 1951; d. Albins Dravnieks and Alina A. (Bergs) Zelmenis; divorced; 1 child, Almira Moronne; m. Martin A. Apple, Sept. 2, 1986. BS, U. Calif., Berkeley, 1977, MA, 1980. Economist U.S. Forest Service, Berkeley, 1974-84; mgmt. analyst U.S. Forest Service, San Francisco, 1984—. Author: Public Involvement In the Forest Service-Methodologies, 1977, Public Involvement-Selected Abstracts for Natural Resources, 1979, The Management of Policy and Direction in the Forest Service, 1982, An Analysis of the Forest Service Civil Rights Program, 1984, Organization Design-Abstracts for Natural Resources Users, 1985. Mem. AAUW, Am. Forestry Assn., Sigma Xi, Phi Beta Kappa (nat. sec. 1985—, pres. No. Calif. chpt. 1982-84, 1st v.p. 1981), Phi Beta Kappa Assocs. Club: Commonwealth of Calif. (100 Leaders of Tomorrow). Home: PO Box 26155 San Francisco CA 94126 Office: US Forest Service Planning and Budgeting Office 630 Sansome St San Francisco CA 94111

APPLE, RITA ELLEN, real estate broker; b. Grand Haven, Mich., Aug. 11, 1949; d. Roland Bertram and Margaret Elizabeth (Engel) Lloyd; m. Thomas Bernard Hanley, Apr. 11, 1970 (div. Sept. 1983); children—Kevin Michael Hanley, Shannon Marie Hanley; m. Richard Pierce Apple, Oct. 12, 1983. Student Muskegon Jr. Coll., 1967-68, West Shore Coll., Ludington, Mich., 1968-70; B.A. in Acctg., Grand Valley State Coll., 1971; student Real Estate Sch. Edn., Chgo., 1981. Design cons. Harris Internat., Chgo., 1976-77; staff acct. Angel, Kaplan, Gomberg, C.P.A.s, Chgo., 1977-81; broker cons. Brannigar, Inc., Geneva, Ill., 1981-83; broker of record Regency Realty, Itasca, Ill., 1983-85; mng. broker Century 21SNS Realty, Chgo., 1985—; owner Hobby Horse Farm, Benton Harbor, Mich., 1987—. Troop leader Chgo. council Girl Scouts U.S.A., 1977-80; founder Golden Triangle Civic Orgn., Chgo., 1981-84, pres., 1982, editor newsletter, 1982-84; participant Chgo. Neighborhood Media Group, 1984; chairperson Women for Alderman Gerald McLaughlin, Chgo., 1984, 85; hostess, interviewer Mayor of Chgo. Presentation, 1984. Mem. North Side Real Estate Bd., NW Suburban Real Estate Bd., Nat. Assn. Female Execs., NW Suburban Women in Sales. Democrat. Roman Catholic. Club: Lakeshore (Chgo.). Avocations: golf; riding and training Arabian horses; old house renovation; painting and drawing; reading. Address: Hobby Horse Farm 2155 Maple Ln Benton Harbor MI 49022 also: 3030 Lakeshore Ave Benton Harbor MI 49022 Office: Century 21 SNS Realty Inc 2714 W Touhy Ave Chicago IL 60645 also: 5707 N Major Chicago IL 60646

APPLEGATE, EDNA (KAY), civic worker; b. Las Vegas, N.Mex., May 15, 1919; d. George Washington and Dora Maude (Bearce) Howell; m. George Edward Applegate, Nov. 30, 1945 (dec. 1980); 1 child, Nancy Kay. R.N., Hotel Dieu Sch. Nursing, 1942; B.S., Columbia U., 1956, M.S., 1963. Sch. nurse tchr. Garden City Pub. Sch., N.Y., 1960-73; pub. health nurse Nassau County Dept. Health, Garden City, 1953-60. Author: Breakfast Book, 1976; Little Book of Baby Foods, 1979. Bd. dirs. Maternal and Child Health Ctr., Santa Fe, 1978-80, Myasthenia Gravis Found. N.Mex. chpt., 1986—, LWV, Santa Fe, 1974-80, Vol. Involvement Service, Santa Fe, 1977-83, Santa Fe Opera Guild, 1981-82, Santa Fe Cancer Soc., 1983-84; mem. steering com. March of Dimes Birth Defects Found., Santa Fe, 1979-85, vol. coordinator N.Mex. chpt., 1985-86; mem. adv. bd. women's unit Charter Sunrise Hosp., Albuquerque, 1985—; mem. fin. com. St. John's Coll., Santa Fe, 1978-83, mem. fine arts com., 1979-83; co-founder The Gilbert & Sullivan Soc., Santa Fe, 1984; charter mem. Compadres del Palacio, 1986; chmn. N.Mex. com. to restore the Montezuma (N.Mex.) Hotel, 1986—. Served as 2d lt. Army Nurse Corp, 1942-44. Fellow Am. Sch. Health Assn., Royal Soc. Health; mem. N.Y. Mental Health Assn. Democrat. Mailing Address: PO Box 2688 Santa Fe NM 87504

APPLEMAN-VASSIL, NANCI, research administrator; b. Oceanside, N.Y., Apr. 25, 1953; d. Mitchell Appleman and Zelda (Schuster) Goldstein; m. John Nicholas Vassil, Oct. 18, 1980; 1 child, Michael Alexander. BA in Psychology, U. Denver, 1975; MA in Counseling, U. Colo., 1978. Head clk. Safeway Stores, Inc., Denver, 1974-78; mgr. Best Western Washington-Duke U., Durham, N.C., 1978-80, Holiday Inn Hotel, College Park, Md., 1980; asst. mgr. of programs NTL Inst., Arlington, Va., 1981—; freelance cons., Arlington, 1983—. Mem. Assn. of Psychol. Type, Am. Assn. for Counseling and Devel. Home: 1224 S Frederick St Arlington VA 22204 Office: NTL Inst 1240 N Pitt Stvd #1000 Alexandria VA 22209

APPLETON, DOLOROS MAXINE, real estate executive; b. Utica, Nebr., Dec. 27, 1929; d. John Wesley and Anna Elizabeth (Moravec) Vrana; m. Richard J. Elliott, Nov. 24, 1950 (div. 1952); m. 2d, Thomas Ellis Appleton, May 21, 1955; 1 dau., Jane Emily. Student U. Nebr., 1947-48, U. Ill., 1954, Belleville Coll., 1977-78. Tchr. Portland Heights Sch. Dist., Superior, Nebr., 1948-50; asst. supt. schs. Champaign County, Urbana, Ill., 1951-57; organizer, tchr. Horstmann Sub-Primary Sch., Loring AFB, Maine, 1957-59; salesman Smiley Homes, Inc., O'Fallon, Ill., 1963-69, First Nat. Holding Corp., 1970-82, Fulford Realty, Inc., 1982-86, Realty World Stein and Assoc., 1986—. Mem. Nat. Assn. Realtors, Ill. Assn. Realtors, Belleville Bd. Realtors (dir. 1975-79, 83—), Nat. Women's Council Realtors, Ill. Women's Council Realtors (chpt. pres. 1983-84). Republican. Methodist. Home: 200 Fontainebleau St O'Fallon IL 62269 Office: Realty World Stein and Assocs 1001 S Lincoln Ave O'Fallon IL 62269

APPLETON, MARINA CATHERINE, military officer, management consultant; b. New Brunswick, N.J., July 31, 1956; d. Adam John Ambrogi and Dolores Ann (Motisko) Naylor; m. Martin David Appleton, Oct. 25, 1985. BS in Biochemistry, U. Scranton, Pa., 1978; MA in Adminstrv. Sci., George Washington U., 1984; postgrad. in law, Cath. U. Am., 1987—. Research chemist Litton Industries, Scranton, 1979-80; commd. ensign USN, 1980, advanced through grades to lt., 1984; admiral's aide Office of the Chief of Naval Research, Arlington, Va., 1981-83; chemist Naval Research Lab., Washington, 1983-84; mgmt. analyst Office of the Chief of Naval Ops., Washington, 1984-87; tech. cons. Scicon Corp., Scranton, 1985—. Assoc. mem. Smithsonian Instn., Washington, 1981-87; coordinator ARC, Arlington, 1981-83, Navy Relief Soc., Washington, 1985-86. Mem. Nat. Assn. Female Execs., Am. Chem. Soc., AAAS, Phi Lambda Upsilon, Sigma Xi. Home: 8318 Tobin Rd #12 Annandale VA 22003 Office: Office Chief of Naval Ops Arlington Naval Annex Washington DC 20350

APPLETON, MYRA, magazine editor, writer; b. Phila., Dec. 21, 1934; d. Joseph and Sylvia (Pouls) Magid; m. John Johnston Appleton, July 29, 1962. B.A., Temple U., 1955. Researcher TV Guide, Phila., 1956-61; assoc. editor Show Bus. Illustrated, Chgo., 1961-62; contbg. editor Show mag., N.Y.C., 1962-64; free-lance writer N.Y.C., 1964-68; sr. editor Cosmopolitan mag., N.Y.C., 1968-88; editor Lear's mag., N.Y.C., 1988—. Author various mag. articles, film scripts. Mem. Womens Media Group. Office: Lear's Mag 505 Park Ave New York NY 10022

APURVO, MA PUJA, musician, writer; b. Orlando, Fla., Aug. 18, 1954; d. Matthew Louis and Rose Ann (Bogash) Cohen. BA, Brown U., 1975. Mus. dir. various theater companies, N.Y.C., 1975-80; improvisational keyboard composer Satsang, various, 1981-86; pres. Soundless Sound Recordings, Boulder, Colo., 1986—; tchr. music pvt. practice, N.Y.C., 1974-78; composer, keybd. player Children's Theatres, N.Y.C., 1975-80, Heart to Heart Mus. Duo, Boulder, Colo., 1986—; composer N.Y.C. Modern Dance Co., 1980-82.; musician We The People, Boulder,1987—, Healing Our World, Boulder, 1987—. Contbg. editor New Frontier, Music of the Spheres, Harmonic Times mags., 1987—; editor The Word of Harmony mag., 1988; contbr. articles to Mighty Natural Directory. Home: 1705 14th St #283 Boulder CO 80302 Office: Soundless Sound PO Box 8005 Suite 283 Boulder CO 80306

ARAKAWA, MARY K., systems analyst; b. Inglewood, Calif., Dec. 23, 1961; d. Tadashi Tom and Mitsuko A. BS in Bus. Adminstrn., Calif. State U., Long Beach, 1985. Installation cons. Profl. Hosp. Services div. Am. Med. Internat., Los Angeles, 1985-86; system and documentation analyst Info. Systems Group of Am. Med. Internat., Los Angeles, 1986-87; systems analyst mgmt. and info. systems Douglas Aircraft, Long Beach, Calif., 1987—. Mem. Los Angeles County Mus. Art., 1986—. Data Processing Mgmt. Assn., Assn. for Women in Computing, Women in Mgmt. Republican. Office: Douglas Aircraft 1755 Ximeno Ave Long Beach CA 90815

ARANETA, MYRNA ROBERTA HIPOLITO, consultant; b. Manila, June 7, 1949; came to U.S., 1984; d. Artemio and Asuncion A. BA in Psychology, St. Paul Coll., Manila, 1968; MA in Clin. Psychology, U. St. Tomas, Manila, 1973; postgrad., U. Philippines, Dilliman, 1976-78. Tchr. kindergarten St. Paul Coll., Manila, 1968-70; guidance counselor U. St. Tomas, Manila, 1970-71; with guidance dept. Loyola Heights, Quezon City, Philippines, 1975—, guidance counselor Ateneou U.; assoc. cons., with mgmt. devel. services Economic Devel. Found., Makati, Philippines, 1976-78; orgn. devel. tng. mgr. Procter & Gamble, PMC, Manila, 1979-81, mgr. orgn. and employee devel., 1981-84; orgn. devel. cons. Procter & Gamble, PMC, Makati, 1986-87; mgr. human resources devel. Norwich (N.Y.) Eaton Pharms., Inc. subs. Procter & Gamble Co., 1984-86; organization effectiveness cons. Internat. Personnel div. Procter & Gamble Co., Cin., 1987—. Fellow Psychol. Assn. Philippines; mem. Am. Soc. Tng. Devel., orgn. Devel. Network, World Futurist Soc., Nat. Assn. Female Execs. Office: The Procter & Gamble Co 299 Sycamore St E Cincinnati OH 45201

ARANT, PATRICIA M., educator; b. Mobile, Ala., Dec. 2, 1930. B.A., Ala. Coll., 1952; A.M., Radcliffe Coll., 1957; Ph.D., Harvard U., 1963. Researcher U.S. Govt., Washington, 1952-56; asst. prof. Russian Vanderbilt U., Nashville, 1963-65; asst. prof., assoc. prof., prof. Slavic langs. and lits. Brown U., Providence, 1965—, also assoc. dean Grad. Sch., 1981—. Author: Russian for Reading, 1981. Grantee Am. Council Learned Socs.-Social Scis. Research Council, 1969, Internat. Research and Exchanges, 1973. Mem. Am. Assn. Tchrs. Slavic and East European Langs., Am. Folklore Soc. Home: 5 D Squire Ln East Providence RI 02915 Office: Brown U Box E Providence RI 02912

ARAYA, ROSE MARIE, scientific affairs associate; b. Lewiston, Idaho, Feb. 25, 1944; d. Ralph Henry and Rose M. (Friedman) Schotzko; m. M. Araya; children: Hanna, Petros. BA, Ft. Wright Coll., 1966. Cataloger Haile Selassie I Univ. Library, Addis Ababa, Ethopia, 1966-72, Inst. Ethiopian Studies, Addis Ababa, 1972-73; adminstrv. asst., paralegal Am. Home Products Corp. Law Dept., N.Y.C., 1975-80; sci. affairs assoc. Whitehall Labs. Med. Library, N.Y.C., 1980—. Mem. AAAS, Spl. Libraries Assn., Associated Info. Mgrs., Am. Soc. Info. Sci., Am. Council Sci. and Health. Democrat. Office: Whitehall Labs 685 3d Ave New York NY 10017

ARBUCKLE, JILL HESTER GRENFELL, infosystems company owner, operator, treasurer; b. Lockerbie, Scotland, May 19, 1932; came to U.S., 1955.; d. Herbert Arthur and Joy Lillian (Grenfell) Kelly; m. Timothy Arbuckle, May 26, 1962 (div. Sept. 1986); 1 child, Alexander. BA with honors, Cambridge U., 1954. From programmer to analyst Computer Usage Co., N.Y.C., 1955-67; analyst Data Stas. Corp., N.Y.C., 1967-69; prin. Donovan Data, N.Y.C., 1969-71; founder, ptnr., treas. Trewhella, Cohen & Arbuckle, N.Y.C., 1971—. Club: Appalachian Mountain. Home: 40 Kingwood Dr Little Falls NJ 07424 Office: Trewhella Cohen & Arbuckle 500 Fifth Ave New York NY 10110

ARBUTHNOT, NANCY PROTHRO, educator; b. Jacksonville, Fla., Mar. 8, 1950; d. Randell Hunt and Nancy (Wilde) Prothro; m. Stephen Kimber Arbuthnot, Oct. 12, 1984; children: Margaret, Charles. BA, U. Md., 1973, MA, 1976; PhD, U. Va., 1981. Assoc. prof. U.S. Naval Acad., Annapolis, Md., 1981—; editor Sibyl Child Press, Hyattsville, Md., 1981—. Mem. Wallace Stevens Soc., Western Am. Literature Assn. Home: 709 Dahlia St NW Washington DC 20012 Office: US Naval Acad English Dept Annapolis MD 21402

ARCAROLI, JEANETTE, nurse; b. Jersey City, July 28, 1945; d. Phillip Alexander Arcaroli and Marie (Terranova) Immediate. Diploma in nursing, Harlem Valley State Hosp., 1970; BA in Psychology, U. Okla., 1975; MS in Nursing, U. Okla., Oklahoma City, 1980. Head nurse N.Y. State Dept. Mental Health, Wingdale, 1970-71; supr. Okla. State Dept. Mental Health, Norman, 1974-79; head nurse VA Med. Ctr., Oklahoma City, 1980-87; dir. nursing and elderly services Taliaferro Community Mental Health Ctr., Lawton, Okla., 1987—; clin. asst. prof., adj. faculty U. Okla. Coll. Nursing, 1982—; cons. Okla. Health Dept., 1981-82, Hospice Orgn., 1985-86, Community Mental Health Ctrs., 1985-86, Med. Help, Inc., Santa Ana, Calif., 1984-86. Served to lt. USAF, 1971-73, capt. Res. Named one of Outstanding Young Women of Am., 1980. Mem. Gerontol. Soc. Am., Coll. Health Care Execs., Am. Nurses Assn. (cert.), Nat. League for Nursing, Assn. Mental Health Adminstrs. (cert.), Sigma Theta Tau. Home: 7210 NW Eisenhower Dr Lawton OK 73505

ARCHBOLD, RONNA RAE, college administrator; b. Duluth, Minn., Sept. 22, 1947; d. Wilton Reuden and Georgia Adeline (Smith) A. B.A., Walla Walla Coll., 1969; M.Ed., Worcester State Coll., 1981; postgrad. Boston Coll., 1983-86. Registrar Monterey Bay Acad., Watsonville, Calif., 1969-72; from asst. to assoc. dean women Walla Walla Coll., College Place, Wash., 1972-76; from asst. to assoc. dir. admissions Atlantic Union Coll., South Lancaster, Mass., 1976-80, chief exec. officer pub. relations and recruitment, 1980-84, chief exec. officer fund raising and pub. relations, 1984-85, asst. to pres., 1985-86, asst. prof. speech communication dept. English; pvt. practice salesperson, 1986—. Thayer Conservatory Orch., South Lancaster, 1981-83; organist, dir. choirs First Ch., Sterling, Mass., 1983—, St. Patrick's Ch., Rutland, Mass., 1977-83. Mem. Am. Guild Organists, Choisters Guild.

ARCHER, MARY JANE, state agency administrator; b. Oakland, Calif., Aug. 23, 1949; d. Francis Evert and Doris Marlene (Howard) W.; m. Bradley Eugene Archer; Nov. 10, 1984. BS in Acctg., Calif. State U., Hayward, 1971, MBA in Acctg., 1977. Auditor Calif. State Controller's Office, Sacramento, 1972-81, supr., 1981-84, asst. chief, 1984—; mem. exec. women's com. Calif. State Controller's Office, Sacramento, 1984—. Mem. Calif. Assn. Mgmt., Nat. Assn. for Female Execs. Republican. Office: Calif State Controller's Office PO Box 942850 Sacramento CA 94250-0588

ARCHER, MARY JANE, physical therapist; b. Bethany, Mo., June 7, 1950; d. Ralph Edward and Edna Mae (Golliher) A. Student, Northwestern Mo. State U., 1968-71; BS, U. Mo., 1973; MA in Rehab. Adminstrn., So. Ill. U., 1981. Lic. physical therapist. Staff physical therapist St. John's Hosp., Anderson, Ind., 1973—; staff physical therapist Community Hosp., Indpls., 1975-76, edn. coordinator physical and occupational therapy, 1976-78; acad. clin. coordinator, instr. sch. medicine Ind. U., Indpls., 1978-80; acad. clin. coordinator, asst. prof. U. Indpls., 1980-85; pres., staff Cen. Physical Therapists, Inc., Indpls., 1985—. Mem. Ind. Chpt. Polit. Action Com., Indpls., 1985-87; mem. Ch. at the Crossing. Mem. Nat. Assn. for Female Execs., Am. Nursing Care (adv. bd. 1986—), Am. Physical Therapy Assn. (treas. state dist. 1980-82, Ind. chpt. 1987, del. to nat. 1979, 82-87). Mem. Ch. of God. Home: 8633 El Rico Dr Indianapolis IN 46240 Office: Cen Physical Therapists Inc 8060 Knue Rd Suite 206 Indianapolis IN 46240

ARCHER, ROBERTA RUTH, court interpreter; b. Rupert, Idaho, Oct. 8, 1930; d. James Willis and Sibyl Mae (Sadue) A.; children—Charlotte Dianne Kellum Gandy, Belita Earline Kellum, H. Armando Kellum, James Willis

Kellum. B.A., Dallas Sem., 1950; postgrad. Puebla, Mexico City, 1974. Cert. U.S. ct. interpreter. Supervisory tchr. Am. Sch., Puebla, Mexico, 1969-74; instr. English Preparatory Bus. Sch., 1969-74; insp., coordinator, prof. Autonomous U. Puebla, 1969-74; lang. coordinator, founding mem., tchr. Hist. Instn. IPECYT, Puebla, 1969-74; pres. Archer Profl. Translating Service, El Paso, 1975—; sr. staff ofcl. U.S. Ct. Interpreter, El Paso, 1981—. Contbg. writer Puebla daily, 1969-74. Mem. Internat. Assn. Constructive Christian Profl. Women (founder), Nat. Assn. Female Execs. Avocations: reading; camping; swimming; hiking. Home: 203 Fountain St El Paso TX 79912 Office: US Courts 511 E San Antonio Suite 142 El Paso TX 79912

ARCHIBALD, CLAUDIA JANE, parapsychologist; b. Atlanta, Nov. 14, 1939; d. Claud Bernard and Doris Evelyn (Linch) A. B in Psychology, Georgia State U., 1962; BTh., Emory U., 1964; DD, Stanton Coll., 1969. Pvt. practice psychio-spiritual counselor Atlanta, 1960—; minister Nat. Spiritualist Assn., Atlanta, 1969-72; parapsychologist Ctr. for Life, Atlanta, 1985-86; parapsychologist Inst. of Metaphysical Inquiry, Atlanta, 1980—, also bd. dirs., founder, 1980—. Author: (book) Quantitative Symbolism, 1980; dir. Phoenix Dance Unltd., 1984—; choregrapher (dance) Phoenix Rising, 1985. Vol. Aid Atlanta, 1987—. Recipient City Grant award Bur. Cultural Affairs, Atlanta, 1985, 86. Mem. Am. Psychical Research Assn., Soc. Metaphysicians (corr. Eng. chpt.), Am. Assn. Parapsychology, N.Am. Ballet Assn. Home: 2638 Valmar Dr Atlanta GA 30340

ARCHIE, VICTORIA ESTHER, social worker; b. N.Y.C., June 4, 1960; d. James Lee and Marjorie Ann (Booth) A. Student, New York U., 1978-79, Andrews U., 1979-81; BA with honors, L.I. U., 1983. With home health care mgmt. Richmond Home Need Services, S.I., N.Y., 1985-86; case worker N.Y.C. Spl. Services for Children, 1986—; child care mgmt. worker Pam O'Neill, N.Y.C., 1983—; home health care mgmt. Richmond Home Need Services, S.I., 1985-86. Prin. works exhibited at L.I. U. Mem. Nat. Assn. Female Execs. Democrat. Seventh Day Adventist. Home: 61-15 98th St Rego Park NY 11374 Office: NYC Spl Services for Children 165-15 Archer Ave Jamaica NY 11433

ARDELEAN, DIANE MARIE, human resources executive; b. Indpls., June 6, 1951; d. Aurel and Christine (Normant) A. BA, Ind. U., 1974, MBA, 1986. Personnel relations rep. Westinghouse Electric Corp., Bloomington, Ind., 1977-80, sr. personnel relations rep., 1980-81, supr. human resources, 1981-87, mgr. personnel relations, 1987—. Bd. dirs. Bloomington North High Sch. Office Labs, 1977-84, chair, 1984; bd. dirs. Evang. Community Ch., Bloomington, 1987; personnel bd. Girl Scouts U.S., Bloomington, 1981-82; mem. self sufficiency task force City of Bloomington, 1982; div. chair United Way Fund Drive, Bloomington, 1984, city-wide major corp. chair, 1985. Mem. Network Career Women (founder, bd. dirs. 1985-86), S. Cen. Ind. Personnel Assn. (sec. 1980). Home: Rural Rt 1 Box 78 Solsberry IN 47459 Office: Westinghouse Electric 300 N Curry Pike Bloomington IN 47402

ARDOLF-THOMPSON, DORIS LEONE, consultant radio; b. Sherburn, Minn., July 23, 1958; d. Leo Albert and Gladys (Popelka) Ardolf; m. Theodore Francis Stecker, Sept. 19, 1981. BA, Coll. St. Benedict, 1977; MA, West Georgia Coll., 1986; postgrad., U. Tex., San Antonio, 1986-87. On-air personality Sta. KNIA, Knoxville, Iowa, 1980; on-air personality, engr. Sta. KIOZ, Laramie, WY, 1980; on-air personality, music dir., asst. program dir. Stas. KHYS/KPAC, Port Arthur, Tex., 1981-82; program dir. Stas. WSAI/WKXF, Cin., 1983-84; v.p. Stecker-Thompson Assocs., San Antonio, 1984-88; pres., Arlington (Tex.) and Ft. Worth, 1988—. Vol. various animal protection groups, San Antonio, 1985—. Mem. ACLU, NOW, Mensa. Democrat. Roman Catholic. Club: Intertel (San Antonio). Home and Office: Stecker-Thompson Assocs 5206 Independence Ave Arlington TX 76017

ARDREY, ELIZABETH S., television producer; b. N.Y.C., Sept. 22, 1963; d. Rushton Leigh Jr. and Sally (David) A. Grad. cum laude, Choate Rosemary Hall, Wallingford, Conn., 1981; student, Carnegie Mellon U., 1982-83; BA, Tulane U., 1985. Editorial asst. Rolling Stone Mag., N.Y.C., 1984; asst. assignment editor Sta. WDSU-TV, New Orleans, 1984; prodn. asst. Fairbanks Films, N.Y.C., 1985; asst. casting dir. McCaffrey and McCall Advt., N.Y.C., 1986, asst. producer, 1987; asst. producer, sales rep. The Ptnrs.'/USA, N.Y.C., 1988—. Contbr. Meml. Sloan Kettering, 1985—; exec. com. Madison Sq. Boys Club, 1986—, Youth Counseling League, 1985—, N.Y.C. Republican. Episcopalian. Home: 333 E 89th St New York NY 10028 Office: The Partners'/USA 23 W 26th St New York NY 10010

ARE, LISA DARRYL, accountant; b. Evanston, Ill., Oct. 19, 1950; d. Leon Herman Schreiner and Georgene Virginia (Issitt) Schreiner Raymond; m. Sam Edwards Marsh, Dec. 20, 1970 (div. 1979); 1 child, Kylan Cameron; m. Andi Are, Jan. 6, 1983; 1 child, Anna-Liisa. Student, New Eng. Conservatory, 1968-69, Colo. State U., 1970-71, 74; BS in Bus. magna cum laude, U. Colo., 1981. CPA, Colo. Computer operator Williams Chevrolet, Colorado Springs, Colo., 1976-77; head bookkeeper Penkhus Volvo-Mazda, Colorado Springs, 1977-79; staff acct. Auld, Loetscher & Meyers, CPA's, Colorado Springs, 1979-81; sr. supr. acct. Steven R. Covalt & Assocs., P.C., Colorado Springs, 1981-83; prin. Lisa D. Are CPA, P.C., Colorado Springs, 1983—. Violinist Ft. Collins (Colo.) Symphony Orch., 1970-76; violist Colorado Springs Symphony Orch., 1977-87, mem. budget com., 1987—, adviser Symphony Players Com., 1985; asst. campaign mgr. Renny Fagan for state legislature, Colorado Springs, 1986; mem. loan Rev. Com. Colorado Springs City Council, 1986—; mem. mortgage revenue bond bd. El Paso County, Colorado Springs, 1987—; treas. Jerry Buchholz for state legislature, 1988; mem. El Paso County Citizen's budget rev. com., 1987; vol. speaker tax and fin. matters, 1983—. Mem. Bus. and Profl. Women (treas. Pikes Peak chpt. 1983-84), Nat. Assn. Female Execs. (Network Exchange Women chpt. treas. 1983-85), Am. Inst. CPA's, Colo. Soc. CPA's, Am. Women's Soc. CPA's, Nat. Assn. Pub. Accts., C. of C. (city and county affairs councils 1987—), Beta Gamma Sigma. Democrat. Unitarian. Club: Toastmasters.

ARENDT, KATHERINE LOCKHART, economist; b. Washington, Sept. 23, 1952; d. Luther Bynum and Betty Jane (Brodnan) Lockhart; B.A., Duke U., 1974; M.A., Tufts U., 1975; postgrad. U. Va., 1976-78; m. Douglas M. Arendt, May 9, 1981; 1 son: Dustin Lockhart Arendt. Economist developing nations U.S. Dept. Treasury, Washington, 1978-79, Export-Import Bank U.S., Washington, 1979-86; contracts administrator, Gen. Atomics, San Diego, 1987—. Va. Gov.'s fellow, 1976-78. Office: Gen Atomics PO Box 85608 San Diego CA 92138-5608

ARENSON, KAREN WATTEL, journalist; b. Long Beach, N.Y., Jan. 3, 1949; d. Harold Louis and Sara (Gordon) Wattel; m. Gregory Keith Arenson, Sept. 4, 1970; 1 child, Morgan Elizabeth. S.B., MIT, 1970; M.Pub. Policy, Harvard U., 1972. Assoc. dir. Nat. Affiliation of Concerned Bus. Students, Chgo., 1972-73; corr. Bus. Week Mag., 1973-77, editor, 1977-78; reporter N.Y. Times, N.Y.C., 1978-84, asst. fin. editor, 1985-86; editor Sunday Bus. Sect. N.Y. Times, 1987—; mem. vis. com. dept. econs., edni. counselor MIT. Author: The New York Times Guide to Making the New Tax Law Work for You, 1981. Recipient Matrix award Women in Communications, 1982; recipient Journalism award Washington Monthly, 1981. Mem. MIT Alumni Assn. (bd. dirs. 1986—). Home: 125 W 76th St New York NY 10023 Office: NY Times 229 W 43d St New York NY 10036

ARENT-GRIFFITH, JUDITH MARY, manufacturing official, writer, media consultant; b. Wausau, Wis., Aug. 15, 1952; d. David and Ruth Mary (Goetzman) Arent; m. T. David Griffith, Dec. 27, 1975. B.A. in Broadcast Journalism, U. Wis., 1974, M.A. in Consumer Affairs and Pub. Relations, 1976. Lic. media specialist-pub. info., Wis. Tech. writer pub. relations Minuteman, Inc., Waterloo, Wis., 1976; press sec. to Bud Stewart for Congress, Muskogee, Okla., 1976; mgr. mktg. Met. Tulsa Transit Authority, 1977-80; mktg. coordinator John Zink Co., Tulsa, 1980—; adj. prof. U. Tulsa, 1981-82; freelance writer, media cons. Community Relations, Unltd., Tulsa, 1980, Phillips & Johnson Advt., 1982—; editor, cons. John Cegielski, 1983—. Mem. Women in Communications (pres. Tulsa chpt. 1982-83, Margaret Garner Winston award 1974), Meeting Planners Internat. Home: 7617 S Urbana St Tulsa OK 74136 Office: John Zink Co 4401 S Peoria St PO Box 702220 Tulsa OK 74170

ARESON, SALLY RYMAN, purchasing specialist; b. Upper Montclair, N.J., Jan. 13, 1954; d. Robert H. and Lois (Ryman) Areson. BA, U. Hartford, 1976; MBA, Fairleigh Dickinson U., 1987. Social worker So. Fla. State Hosp., Hollywood, 1978; research asst. Riverside Hospice, Boonton, N.J., 1979-81; purchasing agt. Wagner div. Cooper Industries, Parsippany, N.J., 1982-86; purchasing mgr. Vital Signs, Inc., Totowa, N.J., 1986-87; sourcing mgr. Allied Aftermarket div. Allied Signal, East Providence, R.I., 1987-88, 1988—. Mem. Nat. Assn. Purchasing Mgmt., Nat. Assn. Female Execs. Democrat. Episcopalian. Home: Rural Rt #2 10 Maple St Hope Valley RI 02832 Office: Allied Aftermarket div Allied Signal 105 Pawtucket Ave East Providence RI 02916

ARESTY, ESTHER BRADFORD, author, scriptwriter; b. Syracuse, N.Y.; d. Jacob and Bertha (Levin) Bradford; m. Jules Aresty, June 24, 1936; children—Robert Joseph, Jane Aresty Silverman. Student DePaul U., 1929-31. Radio commentator Sta.-WJJD, Chgo., 1931-35; advt. mgr. Mandel Bros., Chgo., 1934-36; free-lance radio advt. writer, Chgo., 1936-41; radio scriptwriter Elsa Maxwell Show, Mut. Broadcasting Corp., N.Y.C., 1945-47; free-lance radio scriptwriter, N.Y.C., 1947—. Author: (young adult novels) The Grand Venture, 1963, (as Elaine Arthur) Romance in store, 1983; (cookbook) The Delectable Past, 1964 (Cookbook Guild choice 1964); (etiquette history) The Best Behavior, 1970; (French gastronomy) The Exquisite Table, 1980. Contbr. articles on cookbooks, Careme, Fanny Farmer, Etiquette, Escoffier, Cordon Bleu to Ency. Americana. Bd. dirs. Trenton Community Found., 1960-72, pres., 1962-64; bd. dirs. Mercer County Guidance Ctr., Trenton, 1965-80, McCarter Theatre Assocs., Princeton, N.J., 1972-83. Mem. Authors Guild, PEN, Am. Inst. Wine and food (adv. bd.). Avocations: collecting rare cookbooks; piano; painting; chamber music.

ARGO, DINAH LOUISE, sales professional; b. Nevada City, Calif., Sept. 26, 1940; d. Arthur Crozier and Mary Louise Davisson; m. E. Bradford Bush, Apr. 1, 1958 (div. Mar. 1974); children: Deborah Ann, Michelle, Renne, Bradford Lynn; m. Floyd Eldon Argo, Feb. 4, 1978. A in Mid. Mgmt. cum laude, San Antonio Coll., 1983; B in Applied Arts and Scis., SW (Tex.) State U., 1987. Market researcher Handy Andy, San Antonio, 1967-76; sales rep. Nelson Brokerage Co., San Antonio, 1976-81; account rep. Quaker Oats Co., San Antonio, 1981-82, account supr., 1982-84, account mgr., 1984—. Mem. PTA Lackland City Elem. Sch., San Antonio, 1965-76, sec., 1968, Devine PTA, Devine Athletic Boosters Club, Devine Band Boosters; community vol. Mem. Nat. Assn. Sales Women, Gold Key Soc. Republican. Methodist.

ARIAS, SAUNDRA MCGEE, physician; b. Sandpoint, Idaho, Nov. 17, 1951; d. Carl Fred and Hazel Louise (Burks) McGee; m. Jim Richard Arias, Oct. 7, 1978. BA, Walla Walla Coll., 1975; MD, Loma Linda U., 1978. Diplomate Nat. Bd. Med. Examiners. Intern Valley Med. Ctr. of Fresno (Calif.), 1978-79; med. dir. Fairfield Family Med. Ctr., Winnsboro, S.C., 1979-81; staff physician S.C. State Penitentiary, Columbia, 1981-82; gen. practice medicine, Ridgeway, S.C., 1981-82, Atwater, Calif., 1982—; med. dir. Bloss Hosp. Preventive Med. Ctr., Atwater, 1983; med. adv. bd. Merced Hospice, 1983-84; med. advisor Sweatshop, Merced, Calif., 1983; assoc. clin. prof. family practice U. Calif., Davis, 1985-86; vice chief of staff Bloss Meml. Hosp., 1986, chief of staff, 1987. Dir. choir Seventh Day Adventist Ch., Merced, 1983—. Named Woman of Yr., Soroptomists, 1986, 87. Mem. Merced County Found. for Med. Care, Merced-Mariposa Med. Soc., Calif. Med. Soc., Am. Women Med. Assn., Am. Acad. Family Physicians, AMA, Atwater C. of C. Home: 2452 E Olive Ave Merced CA 95340 Office: Ridgeway Med Assocs 1550 Winton Way Atwater CA 95301

ARMACOST, JULIE DIANE, makeup artist, hair stylist; b. Chgo., Sept. 17, 1952; d. Demosthenes S. and Athens (Chiochios) Balodimas; m. William G. Armacost, Sept. 12, 1954 (div. Sept. 1983). BA in Art cum laude, No. Ill. U., 1973; student, U. Grenoble (France), 1971, Fashion Inst. Tech., N.Y.C., 1982. Graphic designer Arthur Andersen & Co., Chgo., 1973-75; graphic artist Masonite Corp., Chgo., 1975-77; makeup sales cons. Marilyn Miglin, Ltd., Chgo., 1977-78; mem. hair and makeup team Armacost Assocs., N.Y.C. and Cin., 1978-82; fitness instr. The Molly Fox Studios, Inc., N.Y.C., 1985-87; beauty specialist Julie Armacost & Co., N.Y.C., 1983—; cons. in field. Mem. Nat. Assn. Female Execs. Home and Office: 142 E 16th St Apt 14F New York NY 10003

ARMAO, VERONICA ANNE, psychologist; b. S. Stefano Camastra, Messina, Italy, Apr. 22, 1915; came to U.S., 1919; d. Felice and Rosaria (Presti) A. BS in Edn., Mt. St. Joseph Tech. Coll., 1942; MA, Cath. U. Am., 1950; postgrad., Marywood Coll., 1955-56, Harvard U., 1976. Lic. psychologist, N.Y. Tchr. Catholic Diocese, Buffalo, 1941-42; nursery sch. tchr. Our Lady Victory Infant Home, Lackawanna, N.Y., 1942-50, psychologist, 1950-67, administr., 1967-69, dir. children services, 1969-83, child psychologist, 1983-85; cons. O.L.V. Infant Home, Lackawanna, N.Y., 1985—, Assn. Retarded Children, Buffalo, 1986—. Trustee St. Mary's Sch. Deaf, Buffalo, 1983—; mem. adv. council Trocaine Coll. Buffalo, 1987. Named Humanitarian Year, Human Rights Commn., Lackawanna, 1980, recipient Service Mankind award, Sertoma Clubs Western N.Y., 1983. Mem. Am. Psychol. Assn., N.Y. State Psychol. Assn., Psychol. Assn. Western N.Y. Democrat. Roman Catholic.

ARMBRECHT, CAROL ANN, nurse; b. Youngstown, Ohio, Mar. 4, 1950; d. Albert A. and Angeline M. (Ciarniello) Salata; B.S. in Nursing, Case Western Res. U., 1972; M.S., Tex. Woman's U., 1979; m. Karl James Armbrecht, May 26, 1972; children—Abby Lyn, Karly Ann. Staff nurse Univ. Hosps. Cleve., 1972-73, 74-75, St. Elizabeth Hosp. Med. Center, Youngstown, 1973-74, clin. coordinator, 1976-79; instr. nursing Youngstown State U., 1975-76, Pa. State U., Sharon and Monaca, Pa., 1980-85; grad. asst. Kent (Ohio) State U., 1979-81, asst. prof. nursing, 1981-83; asst. prof., dir. continuingedn. U. Akron, Ohio, 1983-86; pvt. practice as clin. nurse specialist, Youngstown, 1985—; psychology intern Towne Sq. Psychol. Services, Canfield, Ohio, 1981-82. Recipient Cushing-Robb award Case Western Res. U., 1973; research grantee Case Western Res. U. Nursing Alumni Assn., 1979. Mem. Am. Nurses Assn., Nurses Assn. Am. Coll. Ob-Gyn, Ohio Nurses Assn., Tex. Woman's U. Alumni Assn., Phi Delta Kappa, Sigma Theta Tau. Roman Catholic. Author articles in field. Home: 58 Overhill Rd Youngstown OH 44512 Office: 3040 Belmont Youngstown OH 44504

ARMBURG, ANTONINA, marketing professional; b. Hann Münden, Fed. Republic of Germany, Oct. 19, 1946; came to U.S., 1952; d. Antoni and Wanda (Ciula) Marko; m. Walter W. Armburg Jr., Aug. 22, 1966 (div.); children: Christine Marie, Jennifer Lee. BS, Southeastern Mass. U., 1982. Research technologist Goodyear Research, Akron, Ohio, 1967-69; med. technologist Morton Hosp., Taunton, Mass., 1969-80, supr. blood bank, 1980-83; rep. mktg. Ortho Diagnostic Systems, Inc. div. Johnson & Johnson, Raritan, N.J., 1983—. Mem. Am. Soc. Clin. Pathologists (cert.). Roman Catholic. Home: 75 Lawrence St Swansea MA 02777

ARMENTO, MARIANNE, state official; b. Hampton, Iowa, Mar. 21, 1948; d. Ervin John Ernest and Margaret Wilma Caroline (Bessman) Meyer; B.A., Kalamazoo Coll., 1970; m. Paul A. Armento, III, Aug. 16, 1975. Personnel asst. Central Nat. Bank, Chgo., 1970, personnel adminstr., 1971-74, human resources officer, 1974-75; personnel analyst Ill. Dept. Personnel, Springfield, 1975-76, lead personnel analyst, 1976-78, supr. reconsiderations and appeals, div. tech. services, 1978-84, mgr. class standards and reconsiderations, 1984—. Asso. mem. and choir mem. 1st Congregational Ch., Springfield, 1977—. Mem. Am. Mgmt. Assn., Nat. Assn. Female Execs. Mem. United Ch. Christ. Office: Ill Dept Cen Mgmt Services 504 Stratton Bldg Springfield IL 62706

ARMIJO, JACQULYN DORIS, interior designer; b. Gilmer, Tex., July 2, 1938; d. Jack King and Iris Adele (Cook) Smith; children—John, Christy, Mike. Student North Tex. State Coll., U. N.Mex. Profl. model, 1961-75; sec. State Farm Ins., Albuquerque, 1965-71; life ins. agt. Mountain States, Albuquerque, 1980; owner Interiors by Jacqulyn, Albuquerque, 1961—; cons., lectr. in field. Mem. Alby Little Theatre, Friends of Little Theatre, Symphony Women; fund raiser for Old Town Hist. Com., Arthritis Fund. Mem. Am. Soc. Interior Design (chmn. historic restoration Albuquerque), Internat. Soc. Interior Design, Internat. Platform Assn., Civil War Club (pres. local chpt.) Republican. Roman Catholic. Clubs: Albuquerque Jr. Women's, Los Amapolas Garden. Home and Office: 509 Chamiso Ln NW Albuquerque NM 87107

ARMISTEAD, KATHERINE KELLY (MRS. THOMAS B. ARMISTEAD III), travel consultant, interior designer, civic worker; b. Pitts., Apr. 14, 1926; d. Joseph Anthony and Katherine Arnold (Manning) Kelly; grad. Finch Jr. Coll., 1946; m. Thomas Boyd Armistead, III, Nov. 29, 1952; children—Katherine Kelly (Mrs. W. Michael Roark), Thomas Boyd IV. Editor news Sta. WOR, N.Y.C., 1946-51; with Dumont TV, 1951-52; editor Social Service Rev., 1956-57; interior designer, Los Angeles, 1963—; travel cons. Gilner Internat. Travels, Beverly Hills, Calif., 1980—. Editorial bd. Previews Mag., 1984—. Pres. Jrs. Social Service, Los Angeles, 1962-64; nat. chpt. chmn. Associated Alumnae of Sacred Heart, 1960-66; pres. La Floristas, 1967-68, Los Angeles Orphanage Guild, 1969-70; coordinator Jr. Mannequin Assisteens, Assistance League So. Calif., 1971-72; mem. patroness com. Hollywood Bowl; pres. docent council Los Angeles County Mus. Art, 1976-77, pres. decorative arts council, 1977-80, chmn. Am. antiques conf., 1979-81, mem. costume council, mem. past pres.' council, 1981—, mem. capital gifts campaign com.; bd. dirs. Los Angeles Orphanage Guild, 1970—; Cert. travel cons. Recipient Eve award Assistance League So. Calif. Mem. Am. Soc. Travel Agents. Republican. Roman Catholic. Clubs: Beach (Santa Monica, Calif.), Birnam Wood Golf (Santa Barbara, Calif.), Bel Air Garden.

ARMITAGE, ROSETTA ALBA, financial executive; b. Thomaston, Conn., May 12, 1928; d. Frank and Rose Marie (D'Andrea) Franzoso; divorced; children: Thomas J., Joyce C. McNeeley. AA, Post Coll., 1947; student, San Diego City Coll., 1955-62, South Cen. Community Coll., 1981. Asst. treas. Foodmaker, Inc., San Diego, 1957-71; treas., controller Cookes' Equipment Co. Inc., et al, Wallingford, Conn., 1971—. Mem. Rep. town com., Branford, Conn., 1982—. Mem. Am. Mgmt. Assn. Republican. Roman Catholic. Home: 14 Featherbed Ln Branford CT 06405 Office: Cooke's Equipment Co Inc 346 Quinnipial St Wallingford CT 06492

ARMSTRONG, ANNA MARIA EDUARDA (MIEKE), landscape designer; b. Stavoren, Netherlands, June 14, 1937; came to U.S., 1961; d. Sybrand Marinus and Marca Eduarda (Van Heloma) Van Haersma Buma; m. John Kremer Armstrong, Apr. 27, 1963; children—Marca Carine van Heloma, Jeb Stuart. Horticulturist, Huis te Lande, The Hague (Netherlands), 1960. Landscape designer, Leeuwarden, Netherlands, 1961; teaching fellow Bklyn. Botanic Garden, 1961-62; bookkeeper, mcpl. bond dealer Chas. E. Weigold & Co., N.Y.C., 1964-66; landscape designer, Bronxville, N.Y., 1970—; lectr. and instr. in field; researcher in field. Bd. dirs., asst. treas. Jr. League of Bklyn., 1965-68; transfer chmn., com. mem. Jr. League of Bronxville, N.Y., 1970-77; bd. dirs. Brookwood Child Care, Bklyn., 1965-68, Musica Sacra, N.Y.C., 1977-80. Mem. Am. Horticulture Soc., Bronxville Working Gardeners (pres. 1981-84). Episcopalian. Clubs: Netherlands (N.Y.C.); Bronxville Field. Avocations: sailing; swimming; speed skating; cross-country skiing.

ARMSTRONG, ANNE LEGENDRE (MRS. TOBIN ARMSTRONG), former ambassador, corporate director, educator; b. New Orleans, Dec. 27, 1927; d. Armant and Olive (Martindale) Legendre; m. Tobin Armstrong, Apr. 12, 1950; children: John Barclay, Katharine A., Sarita S., Tobin and James L. (twins). Grad., Vassar Coll., 1949. Trustee Kenedy County (Tex.) Sch. Bd., 1968-74; mem. Rep. Nat. Com. from Tex., 1968-73, co-chmn., 1971-73; del. Rep. Nat. Conv., 1964-84; counsellor to U.S. Pres., 1973-74; U.S. ambassador Gt. Britain, No. Ireland, 1976-77; chmn. adv. bd. Ctr. for Strategic and Internat. Studies (formerly affiliated with Georgetown U.), 1981-87, chmn. bd. trustees, 1987—; chmn. Pres.'s Fgn. Intelligence Adv. Bd., 1981—; Pres. Nat. Thanksgiving Commn., 1986—; bd. dirs. Gen. Motors Corp., Halliburton Co., Boise Cascade Corp., Am. Express Co. Bd. regents Smithsonian Instn., 1978—; bd. overseers Hoover Instn., 1978—; co-chmn. Reagan-Bush Campaign, 1980; pres. Blair House Restoration Fund, 1985—; mem. nat. council Dallas Mus. Art, 1986—. Recipient Rep. Woman of Yr. award, 1979, Texan of Yr. award, 1981, Presdl. Med. of Freedom award, 1987; named Tex. Women's Hall Fame, 1986. Mem. English-Speaking Union (chmn. 1978-80), Council Fgn. Relations, Tex. Womens Alliance (chmn. 1985—), Am. Assocs. of Royal Acad. Trust (trustee 1985—), Phi Beta Kappa. Clubs: Econ, N.Y; F St. (Washington).

ARMSTRONG, CLARA JULIA EVERSHED (MRS. ROLLIN S. ARMSTRONG), retired college administrator; b. Murray, Utah, Aug. 25, 1911; d. Elmer B. and Lenora K. (Tripp) Evershed; student Henager Bus. Coll., 1936-37; m. Rollin S. Armstrong, Sept. 29, 1956; foster children—Maxwell Rollin, Ruth Elizabeth, Robert Neil, Philip Samuel. Office mgr., credit mgr. D.N. & E. Walter & Co., Salt Lake City, 1937-48; with Latter Day Saints Bus. Coll., Salt Lake City, 1948-77, sec., 1948-52, fgn. student adviser, 1952-55, vet. coordinator, 1952-55, rehab. counselor, 1952-55, registrar, 1955-62, sec.-treas., 1962-76; vol. worker, 1976—. Mem. Ch. of Jesus Christ of Latter-day Saints (pres. Ward Mut. Improvement Assn. 1941-45). Home: 475 East 900 South Box 27 Salt Lake City UT 84111 Office: 411 E South Temple Salt Lake City UT 84111

ARMSTRONG, DENISE GRACE, association executive. Diploma, Briarcliffe Secretarial Sch., L.I., N.Y., 1974. Sec., Klar, Klar & Tifford, law office, East Meadow, N.Y., 1974-76; exec. sec. Nassau Acad. Medicine and Nassau County Med. Soc., Garden City, N.Y., 1976-80; exec. dir. Suffolk County Dental Soc., Hauppauge, N.Y., 1980-88, exec. dir., 1988—. Mem. Am. Soc. of Assn. Execs., Assn. of Component Soc. Execs. of ADA, Nat. Assn. for Female Execs., Smithtown Bus. and Profl. Women's Network. Office: Suffolk County Dental Soc 850 Veterans Memorial Hwy Hauppauge NY 11788

ARMSTRONG, JANE BOTSFORD, sculptor; b. Buffalo; d. Samuel Booth and Edith (Pursel) Botsford; m. Robert Thexton Armstrong, July 3, 1960. Student, Middlebury Coll., 1939-40, Pratt Inst., 1940-41, Art Students' League, 1962-64. One-man shows Frank Rehn Gallery, N.Y.C., 1971, 73, 75, 77, Columbus (Ohio) Gallery Fine Arts, 1972, Columbia (S.C.) Mus. Art, 1975, New Britain (Conn.) Mus. Am. Art, 1972, Johnson Gallery, Middlebury Coll., 1973, Mary Duke Biddle Gallery for Blind N.C. Mus. Art, 1974, J.B. Speed Art Mus., Louisville, 1975, Buffalo State U., 1975, Marjorie Parr Gallery, London, 1976, Ark. Art Center, 1977, Dallas Mus. Fine Art, 1978, Wichita (Kans.) Art Mus., 1978, 82, Wadsworth Atheneum, 1979, Harmon Gallery, 1979, 81, Washington County (Md.) Mus. Fine Arts, Hagerstown, 1979, Chautauqua (N.Y.) Nat. Exhbn. Am. Art, 1980, Southeastern Center Contemporary Art, Winston-Salem, N.C., 1980, Rollins Coll., Winter Park, Fla., 1981, The Sculpture Center, N.Y.C., 1981, Sid Deutsch Gallery, N.Y.C., 1983, Boca Raton Mus. (Fla.), 1983, Burchfield Ctr., Buffalo, 1985, Glass Art Gallery, Toronto, 1985, Schiller-Wapner Galleries, N.Y.C., 1987, St. Gaudens Gallery, St. Gaudens Nat. Hist. Site, 1988; exhibited in USIA group exhbn., Europe, 1975-76, Artists of Am., Denver, 1981, 82, 83, 84, 85, 86, 87; represented in numerous acad., indsl., pub. and pvt. collections. Recipient Pauline Law prize Allied Artists Am., 1969, 70, Gold medal, 1976, Ralph Fabri medal honor, 1978, Chaim Gross Found. award, 1980; cert. merit NAD, 1973; Council Am. Artists' Socs. prize Nat. Sculpture Soc., 1973; Porton award, 1981. Fellow Nat. Sculpture Soc. (Bronze medal 1976, Tallix Foundry award 1985, Percival Dietsch prize 1986); Mem. Nat. Arts Club (gold medal for sculpture 1968, 69, 71, best in show 1973, Edith W. Macguire award 1975, Plaque Honor 1977, Alexander Saltzman award 1983), Audubon Artists (medal of honor 1972), Sculptors Guild, Allied Artists Am., Nat. Assn. Women Artists (Charles N. Whinston Meml. prize 1973, Anonymous Mem. award. 1975, 77, Mrs. C. D. Murphy Meml. prize 1979, Elizabeth S. Blake prize 1980, Amelia Peabody award 1986), Knickerbocker Artists (Elliot Liskin award 1979, Knickerbocker award 1982, Marian Weisberg award 1985, Gold medal for disting. achievement in sculpture 1986), Catharine Lorillard Wolfe Art Club (Liskin award 1981, Anna Hyatt Huntington award 1982). Home and Studio: High Meadow Way Manchester Center VT 05255

ARMSTRONG, NAOMI YOUNG, retired educator; b. Dermott, Ark., Oct. 17, 1918; d. Allen Wesley and Sarah Elizabeth (Fluker) Young; B.S., Northwestern U., 1961; L.H.D. (hon.), U. Libre, Karachi, Pakistan, 1974; Ph.D. (hon.), World U., Tucson, 1979; D.LiH. (hon.), Universal Orthodox Coll., Iperu-Remo, Ogun State, Nigeria, 1980; Litt.D. (hon.) World Acad. Arts and Culture, Taipei, Taiwan, 1981; m. Joe Leslie Armstrong, July 17, 1938; 1 dau., Betty-Jo Armstrong Dunbar. Actress, Skyloft Players, also

Center Aisle Players, Chgo., 1945-59; silk dress operator Rue Ann Originals Chgo., 1947-55; clk. Bur. Pub. Debt, 1955-56, IRS, 1956-59; caseworker Cook County Dept. Pub. Aid, Chgo., 1961-62; tchr. Chgo. pub. schs., 1962-83, creative writing instr., 1975-77, instr. Social Center, 1965-67; dramatic instr. Crerar Meml. Presbyn. Ch., Chgo., 1972; real estate salesman Century 21 Maner, 1978—; pres., dir., founder Chrysopoets, Inc., 1987. Mem. exec. bd., membership chmn. Northwestern U. Young Alumni Council, 1971-72; trustee World U., 1973-74. Recipient Hon. Gold diploma, spl. award 3d World Congress Poets, 1976, Silver cup and Silver medallion 9th World Congress Poets, 1986; named Internat. Woman of 1975, United Poets Laureate Internat. others; lic. real estate salesman. Mem. United Poets Laureate Internat. (exec. bd.), Internat. Platform Assn. (life; bd. govs.; 3d Preview winner 1976), World Poets Resource Center, Poetry Soc. London, Centro Studi e Scambi Internat., Intercontinental Biog. Assn. (life), World Poetry Soc. (life), Internat. Poets Acad. (Internat. Eminent Poet 1987), NAACP (life, chpt. chmn. edn. com. 1983), Sigma Gamma Rho. Author: A Child's Easter, 1971; Expression I, 1973; Expression III, 1976; Naomi's Two Line Sillies (A Guide for Living) Expression IV, 1985. Address: 9257 S Burnside Ave Chicago IL 60619

ARMSTRONG, PAMELA GAYLE, psychologist; b. Tulsa, Sept. 17, 1945; d. Bernard Charles and Julia Helen (Spillman) A.; m. John D. Wills, Aug. 10, 1968 (div. Oct. 1980); 1 child, Megan Armstrong. A.B. in Psychology, George Washington U., 1967; M.Ed., Advanced Grad. Specialist in Counseling, U. Md., 1970, Ph.D. in Counseling, 1981. Cert. rehab. counselor. Dir. out-patient rehab., supervisory rehab. therapist Psychiat. Inst., Washington, 1970-76; regional child devel. coordinator Tenn. Office Child Devel., Jackson, 1978-79; intern psychologist Prince George's County Directorate of Mental Health, Cheverly, Md., 1981-82, psychologist and vocat. coordinator, 1982—; pvt. practice psychology and rehab. cons. Rehab. Services Adminstrn. grantee, 1968-70. Mem. Am. Psychol. Assn., Md. Psychol. Assn., Prince George's County Mental Health Assn., Alliance for the Mentally Ill of Md., Assn. Employee Assistance Program Practitioners. Home: 5553 Eaglebeak Row Columbia MD 21045 Office: Prince George's County Health Dept 6100 Jost St Fairmount Heights MD 20743 also: Stevens Forest Profl Ctr 9650 Santiago Rd Suite 103 Columbia MD 21045

ARMSTRONG, SYNETTA SILVERSTEIN ANDERSON, communications professional; b. St. Louis, June 7, 1953; d. Clarence and Florine (Jackson) Anderson; children—Ebony C., Charles R. B.S., Northwestern U., 1975. Producer, host Sta. KPLR-TV, St. Louis, 1975-77; promotion dir., account exec. Belleville (Ill.) News-Democrat, 1977-79; communications coordinator Brown Group, Inc., St. Louis, 1979-80, communications mgr., 1980-85; staff mgr. pub. relations Southwestern Bell Publs., St. Louis, 1985—; producer video program 60-minutes/month, Brown Group-United Way (Emmy nomination), 1982; copywriter Jan Matzlinger-Yes I Can (Flair nomination), 1983. Recipient 1st place award Editor's Communication Competition, 1982, 83. Mem. Internat. Assn. Bus. Communicators. Office: Southwestern Bell Publs Inc 12800 Publications Dr Saint Louis MO 63131

ARMSTRONG-POPPELBAUM, SYLVIA FINCH, personnel executive; b. Jamestown, N.Y., Sept. 28, 1939; d. Charles Leslie and Josephine Van Vliet (Phillips) Finch; m. Thomas L. Poppelbaum, June 16, 1979; children by previous marriage: Ronald C. Armstrong, Andrew D. Armstron. AB cum laude, Syracuse U., 1961, MBA, 1987. Tchr. secondary social studies, Williamsville, N.Y., 1961-64; dir. Oneida County Youth Bur., Utica, N.Y., 1976-77; asst. for contract mgmt. Oneida County CETA Program, Utica, 1977-79; exec. dir. Planned Parenthood of the Mohawk Valley, Utica, 1979-85; mgr. personnel Jay-K Ind. Lumber Corp., New Hartford, N.Y., 1985—. Chair budget panel United Way of Greater Utica. Mem. Cen. N.Y. Personnel Mgrs. Assn., Utica Met. Bus. and Profl. Women, Mohawk Valley Bus. and Indsl. Health Care Coalition. Home: 30 Hamilton Pl Clinton NY 13323 Office: Jay-K Ind Lumber Corp Seneca Twp New Hartford NY 13413

ARNDT, CYNTHIA, educator; b. N.Y.C., Sept. 27, 1947; d. Charles Joseph and Pura Maria (Rios) A.; B.A., Hunter Coll., 1971, M.A., 1975; profl. diploma in adminstrn. Fordham U., 1981. Adminstrv. asst. to asst. registrar Hunter Coll., N.Y.C., 1968-69; cataloguer asst. Finch Coll. Library, N.Y.C., 1974; tchr. N.Y. Bd. Edn., N.Y.C., 1974-82; bilingual coordinator Jr. High Sch. 143, 1982—. Mem. Am. Artist Soc., Center Inter-Am. Relations, Hispanic Am. Hist. Soc., Nat. Council Social Studies, N.Y. Assn. Curriculum Devel., Puerto Rican Edn. Assn., Assn. Curriculum Devel., Nat. Travel Club, Kappa Delta Pi, Phi Delta Kappa. Democrat. Roman Catholic. Reviewer Booklist, 1981. Home: 50 W 97th St New York NY 10025

ARNDT, DIANNE JOY, artist, photographer; b. Springfield, Mass., Dec. 20, 1939; d. Samuel Vincent and Carrie Lillian Annino; student Art Students League, 1965-71; B.F.A. with honors in Painting, Pratt Inst., 1974; student journalism, Columbia U., 1979-80, 86; MFA, Hunter Coll., 1981; m. Joseph Vincent Bower, June 16, 1979; 1 dau. by previous marriage—Christabelle Nita Arndt. Photojournalist, photo cons. to mags. and bus., N.Y.C., 1978—; artist, filmmaker, 1962—; recent exhbns. include: Pyramid Arts Ctr., Rochester, N.Y., 1986, Food Stamp Gallery, N.Y.C., 1988, ABC No Rio, 1986, Storefront for Art and Architecture, N.Y.C., 1986, Post Machina Group, Bologna, Italy, 1986, Postaes, Brazil, 1987, Am. Cultural Ctr., U.S., New Delhi and Bombay, 1987, Bathurst Arms Installation, Eng., 1987, Cuando, N.Y.C., 1987, Camden Arts, London, 1987, Nat. Inst. of Archtl. Edn., 1988, Phillip Morris Traveling Photo Exhibit, 1988, Centennial Library Gallery, Isca Graphics, Edmonton, Alta., Can., 1988. Recipient Exptl. Writing award Columbia U., 1967, 1st prize in show Springfield (Mass.) Mus. Fine Art, 1967. Mem. AIA (art and architecture com.), Am. Soc. Mag. Photographers, Artists Talk on Art (bd. dirs., exec. dir.), Profl. Women Photographers, West Side Arts Coalition, The Nat. Mus. of Women in the Arts, Found. for Community of Artists.

ARNDT, JOAN MARIE, librarian, educator; b. Stillwater, Minn., Sept. 7, 1945; d. Clarence Joseph and Harriet Joan (Richert) A. BA, Coll. of St. Catherine, St. Paul, 1967; MA, U. Minn., 1970, degree in media specialty, 1973. Cert. librarian, elem. educator. Media generalist, librarian Roseville (Minn.) Area Schs., 1967—; instr. continuing edn. Hamline U., St. Paul, 1981—; guest lectr. U. Wis., Eau Claire, 1985, Upper Mississippi Media Conf., 1988; book reviewer U. Minn., Mpls., 1988—, Five Owls, Mpls., 1988—. Mem. Minn. Edn. Media Orgn., Minn. Reading Assn., Am. Fed. Tchrs., Minn. Fedn. Tchrs, Friends of Ramsey County Library. Roman Catholic. Home: 5730 Donegal Dr Shoreview MN 55126 Office: Central Park Media Ctr 535 W County Rd B2 Roseville MN 55113

ARNDT, KELLIE BIRDGETT, interior designer; b. Detroit, Sept. 15, 1964; d. Glenn Earl and Phyllis Karen (Paulson) A.; m. Robert Preston Cole, June 11, 1988. Student, Stetson U., 1982-83, Internat. Acad. Merchandising and Design, 1983-86. Interior designer Roberts' Interior Design, Inc., Largo, Fla., 1984—; cons. in field. Mem. Tampa Bay Interior Design Assn., Am. Soc. for Prevention of Cruelty to Animals, People for Ethical Treatment of Animals, Humane Soc. U.S., Greenpeace. Republican. Lutheran. Home: 690 Harbor Island Clearwater FL 34630

ARNEACH, CHARLOTTE CLEVELAND, data processing consultant, high tech. entrepreneur; b. Morris, Ill., Aug. 1, 1943; d. George Lindsay and Florence Arline (Kramer) Cleveland; m. Lloyd Knowles Arneach, Apr. 13, 1964; children: Lloyd Knowles Jr., Dawn Marie. BA, U. N.C., Asheville, 1967; MA, W. Ga. Coll., 1976. Mgr. AT&T, Atlanta, 1969-76; project mgr. Lasker-Goldman Co., N.Y.C., 1976-77; mgr. tech. support Mgmt. Control Systems, Marietta, Ga., 1977-78; sr. systems analyst Consol. Computers Internat., Atlanta, 1978-79; mgr. customer support Computer Usage Co., Norcross, Ga., 1979-80; mgr. Control Data Corp., Atlanta, 1980-83; group mgr. Intec Systems, West Palm Beach, Fla., 1983-85; pres. Comprehensive Data Solutions, Roswell, Ga., 1986-88; pres. Bus./Technology Inc., Alpharetta, Ga., 1988—, also bd. dirs.; bd. dirs. CDS, Inc., Marietta, Ga. Co-pres. Kennesaw (Ga.) PTA, 1970; troop leader Kennesaw area Girl Scouts U.S., 1970-73; active Gwinnett Festival Singers, Norcross, Ga., Cumming (Ga.) Choral. Mem. Women in Info. Processing, Info. Systems Cons. Assn. Republican. Episcopalian. Office: Bus/Technology Inc 301 Fernbank Ct Alpharetta GA 30201

ARNOLD, BARBARA EILEEN, state legislator; b. N. Adams, Mass., Aug. 3, 1927; d. Lester Flemming and Sarah (Van Hagen) Smith; m. William E. Arnold, Dec. 5, 1946; children—Wynn, Jeffrey, Gayle, Christopher. B.A. in Psychology, U. Mass., postgrad. Keene State Coll. Spl. Edn. Clinic tchr. Keene State Coll., N.H., 1964-67; spl. edn. tchr. Easter Seal Rehab. Ctr., Manchester, N.H., 1967-74; state legislator N.H., 1982—, now Republican floor leader Ho. of Reps.; mem. N.H. Council Vocat. Tech. Edn., 1986—; mem. Ways and Means com., State and Fed. Relations commn.; chmn. Manchester Rep. Del.; Del. Bd. dirs. ARC, 1975—, chmn. bd. dirs., 1977-80; Manchester campaign chmn. Warren Rudman for U.S. Senate, 1980, 86; mem. adv. bd. Greater Manchester Federated Women's Club; mem. vestry, registered lay leader, mem. diocesan commns., del. gen. conv. Episcopal Ch.; mem. com. for children, families, social services on the Nat. Conf. of State Legislatures, State Adv. Com. for Vocat. Child Care Programs. Mem. Kappa Kappa Gamma. Address: 374 Pickering St Manchester NH 03104

ARNOLD, BARBARA LENORE, school district business manager; b. Worland, Wyo., Oct. 21, 1941; d. William T. and Georgia (Garroutte) A. BA in Bus. Edn., U. Wyo., 1964, MEd in Bus. Edn., 1970. Tchr. bus. edn. Sweetwater County Sch. Dist. #2, Green River, Wyo., 1964-72, bus. mgr., 1972—; tchr. bus., acctg., ethics Western Wyo. Community Coll., Rock Springs, 1980—, Westminster Coll., Salt Lake City, 1981-82. Campaign chmn. United Way Green River, 1986, bd. dirs., 1987; mem. membership com. YWCA Sweetwater County, 1987. Named Sweetwater County Bus. Woman of Yr., Bus. and Profl. Women, 1979. Mem. Assn. Sch. Bus. Officials, Wyo. assn. Sch. Bus. Officials, Green River C. of C. (bd. dirs. 1973). Republican. Christian Scientist. Office: Sweetwater County Sch Dist #2 400 N 1st E Green River WY 82935

ARNOLD, BEVERLY MCGOVN, management consultant; b. Harrisburg, Pa., Dec. 24, 1961; d. John Appleby and Barbara (Montgomery) A. Cert. Internat. Econs., Oxford (Eng.) U., 1982; BBA, Grove City (Pa.) Coll., 1983; M in Mass Communications, Boston U., 1985. Account exec. Arnold Fuel Co., Harrisburg, Pa., 1981; temp. press sec. U.S. Congressman Gekas, Washington, 1983, video cons., 1984; econs. researcher Ted Heath, London, Eng., 1984; pres. Beverly Prodns., Inc., Boston, 1985; cons. Nissen-Lie, Oslo, Norway, 1985—; cons. Norwegian Caribbean Lines, Oslo, 1985—, Norwegian Defense Dept., 1986-87, Royal Viking Line, San Francisco, 1986-87, Airbus Indsl., Oslo, 1987—, Norwegian Fgn. Ministry, Oslo, 1987, Cruise Industry News, N.Y.C., 1987, Pepsi-Cola, Scandanavia, 1987—, Wartsila Shipyards, Finland, 1987—, Veritec Offshore Engring., Oslo, 1987—, SAS Airlines, Oslo, 1987—, Sheraton Hotel, Oslo, 1987—. Mem. Women in Communications, Internat. TV Assn., Norwegian Am. C. of C., Exec. Female. Republican. Home: 215 W 95th St Apt 12C New York NY 10025

ARNOLD, BRENDA ANN, nursing administrator; b. Morristown, N.J., May 8, 1958; d. Wiley Allen and Beverly Ann (Riebel) A. BS in Nursing, W.Va. Wesleyan Coll., 1981. RN, N.J. Staff nurse Morristown Meml. Hosp., 1981-82; clinician A in psychiatry Med. Coll. Va. Hosp., Richmond, 1984-85; charge nurse King James Care Ctr., Chatham Twp., N.J., 1985-86; charge nurse Cheshire Home, Florham Park, N.J., 1982-83, asst. dir. nursing, 1986-87; asst. dir. nursing N.J. Eastern Star Home, Bridgewater, 1987—. Mem. Assn. Nursing Adminstrs. (assoc. LTC facilities N.J. area), Alpha Gamma Delta. Home: 11 Garfield Ave Madison NJ 07940 Office: N J Eastern Star Home 111 Finderne Ave Bridgewater NJ 08807

ARNOLD, FLORENCE MILLNER, artist; b. Prescott, Ariz., Sept. 16, 1900; d. George Thomas and Cora Grace (Paxton) Millner; diploma Mills Coll., 1923; B.S. in Edn., U. So. Calif., 1937; postgrad. Claremont Coll., 1938-40; m. Archibald Adrian Arnold, Aug. 14, 1925; 1 dau., Adrienne (Mrs. Jonathon Chakerian). Supr. music Placentia (Calif.) schs., 1924-41; tchr. music Fullerton (Calif.) High Sch., 1941-48, Buena Park (Calif.) schs., 1948-66; one-woman shows Long Beach Mus. Art, 1961, 69, 70, Calif. State U. at Fullerton, 1967; retrospective Fullerton Arts Commn., 1974; numerous group shows including Esther Robles Gallery, Los Angeles, 1965, Laguna Beach Mus. Art, 1966-68, Women U.S.A., 1973; represented in permanent collections at Long Beach Mus. Art, Laguna Beach Mus. Art, Fullerton Coll., Mills Coll. Art, U. Calif., Fullerton. Cons. program for gifted children Buena Park Schs., 1973-74. Mem. goals com. City Fullerton, 1970. Bd. dirs. Muckenthaler Cultural Center, 1964-78; pres. Art Alliance Calif. U. Calif., Fullerton, 1976-77; bd. trustees Fullerton Sci. Mus., 1971-74. Named Woman of Year Fullerton C. of C., 1973. Mem. Los Angeles County Mus. Art, Laguna Beach Mus. Art (dir. 1967-69), Orange County Art Assn. (pres. 1960-62, 1968-69), Smithsonian Inst. (Archives Am. Art), Delta Kappa Gamma. Address: 1136 Valencia Mesa Dr Fullerton CA 92633

ARNOLD, GAIL WALLACE, construction consultant; b. Oneida, N.Y., June 3, 1946; d. Earl Jay and Edith Evelyn (Allen) Devendorf; student Onondaga Community Coll., 1977-79; m. Claude Arnold, July 29, 1963 (div. Nov. 1969); children—Joseph Todd, Thomas Edwin. Restaurant owner, Chittenango, N.Y., 1974-76; asst. constrn. super Taylor Woodrow Blitman, Lowell, Mass., 1979; asst. contract adminstr. Cambridge (Mass.) Housing Authority, 1980-81; constrn. supt. Boston Housing Authority, 1981-82; cons. Drug abuse counselor, Chittenango, 1976-79; mem. Millis Alcohol and Drug Abuse Assn.; mem., sec. council on aging Millis Town Bd.; bd. dirs. King Phillip Elderly Services, Norfolk County; chmn. Chittenango chpt. March of Dimes, 1974. Mem. New Eng. Song Writers Assn. Democrat. Roman Catholic. Clubs: Fin, Fur and Feather Hunt. Home: 171 Plain St Millis MA 02054

ARNOLD, HARRIETT ANN BROWN, academic administration educator; b. Lake Charles, La., June 19, 1945; d. Harold Brown and Rebecca (Jones) Brown; m. John H. Arnold, Feb. 14, 1970; 1 child, Jason Christopher. BA, San Francisco State U., 1968; MA, San Jose State U., 1974; EdD, U. San Francisco, 1984. Cert. tchr., teaching adminstr. Calif.,. Social worker YMCA, Oakland, Calif., 1968-70; classroom tchr. Alum Rock Sch. Dist., San Jose, 1970-74, adminstrv. asst., 1974-75; vice-prin. Franklin McKinley Sch. Dist., San Jose, 1975-79; prin. Berryessa Sch. Dist., San Jose, 1979-84; dir. staff devel. Sequoia Sch. Dist., Redwood City, Calif., 1984-86; prof. Calif. State U., Hayward, 1986-87, San Jose State U., 1987—. Former commr. White House Conf. on Comms. on Status of Women. Recipient Outstanding Program Practices SDE, Sacramento, 1973, Exemplary Teaching award Santa Clara County League of Friends, 1987, Key to City of El Paso, Mayor's Office, El Paso, 1987. Mem. Assn. Curriculum and Devel. (bd. dirs. 1988-91), Calif. Affiliate of Assn. Curriculum and Devel. (bd. dirs. 1984-87), Women Leaders in Edn. (bd. dirs. 1981-84), Women's Leadership Council (v.p.), NAACP, Nat. Women's Polit. Caucus, Alpha Kappa Alpha. Democrat. Baptist. Club: Links, Inc. (Santa Clara County). Office: Sequoia Union High Sch Dist 480 James Ave Redwood City CA 94062

ARNOLD, JANET NINA, health care consultant; b. Poughkeepsie, N.Y., Apr. 23, 1933; d. Paul Dudley and Pauline Katherine (Board) Bartram; A.B., Vassar Coll., 1955; postgrad. Sch. Med. Tech., Albany Med. Center, 1955-56; M.S., Vassar Coll., 1963; M.H.S.M., Webster Coll., 1981; m. Robert William Arnold, Dec. 19, 1954; children—Paul Dudley, Janet Elizabeth. Research asst., med. technologist H. Aird Boswell, M.D., Troy, N.Y., 1956-59; teaching supr., adminstrv. cons. Vassar Bros. Hosp., Poughkeepsie, N.Y., 1959-69; adv. to med. lab., lectr. med. mycology Vassar Coll., Poughkeepsie, 1961-66; asst. lab. mgr. Boulder (Colo.) Meml. Hosp., 1975-80; cons. hosp. planning Mercy Med. Center, Denver, 1981-82; lab. dir. Valley View Hosp. and Med. Ctr., Thornton, Colo., 1982-85; cons. health care mgmt. MRI, 1985—; acad./adminstrv. cons. U. Guam, Vassar Coll., Boulder Community Hosp., others. Sec., bd. dirs. Sanitas Fed. Credit Union, 1977-78, pres., 1979-82. Vassar Coll. teaching fellow, 1961-63; NSF research fellow, 1960-62. Mem. Am. Acad. Microbiology, Soc. for Gen. Microbiology, Am. Soc. Med. Technologists, Colo. Public Health Assn., Med. Mycological Soc. of the Ams. Republican. Episcopalian. Asso. editor Am. Jour. Med. Tech., 1980—; contbr. articles to profl. jours. Home: 4195 Chippewa Dr Boulder CO 80303

ARNOLD, JANET ONSTAD, corporate professional; b. Warroad, Minn., July 11, 1932; d. Emmet Alphonso and Virginia Mernie (Reagin) Onstad; m. Tomas Burton Arnold (div. 1975); children: Pamela, Thomas, Virginia. RN, Mpls. Gen. Hosp., 1953, BS, 1981. Asst. head nurse Mpls. Gen. Hosp., 1953-56, coordinator of chemical dependency aftercare programs, 1976-82; v.p. D'Odor Co. div. Rowell of Fla., Leesburg, 1984-86; pres. Arnold Technologies, Leesburg, 1986—, Companion Magic, Inc., Leesburg, 1986—. Vol. Rep. Party, Mpls., 1968-75, Heart Assn., Mpls., 1968-72; Coordinator N.I.P. Orgn., Mpls., 1965-76. Mem. Bus. and Profl. Women (v.p. 1984-86, pub. relations com. 1987—), Exec. Female Orgn. (ways and means com. 1985-86). Clubs: Mpls. Women's (civic contribution com.), Leesburg Womens. Home: PO Box 968 Lady Lake FL 32659

ARNOLD, JEANNE GOSSELIN, communications executive; b. Rutland, Vt., Dec. 19, 1917; d. Eugene Arthur and Eleanor (Ranberg) Gosselin; children: Eugene Van Rensselaer Arnold, Linda Krull Beattie. Student, SUNY, Albany, 1935-38, 45-47, Russel Sage Coll., Troy, N.Y., 1964-65. Reporter, women's editor, columnist, feature writer Albany Times Union, N.Y., 1945-79; dir. Media Services Unltd., Westerlo, N.Y., 1979—. Author: (poetry) The Flesh Recalls, 1956, Ballad of Witches Hill, 1987; (biography) A Man of Faith, 1983. Chmn. Westerlo Planning Bd., 1978-86. Recipient ann. Justice award N.Y. State Bar Assn., 1975, Outstanding Woman award Coll. St. Rose, Albany, 1976, Albany YMCA, 1977. Mem. The Newspaper Guild. Roman Catholic. Home: Rte 1 Box 265 Westerlo NY 12193

ARNOLD, JOAN DEAN, publisher; b. Marshall, Mo., Jan. 12, 1944; d. Alfred Douglas and Imogene Devonia (Simmons) Kidd; m. John Gerald Arnold (div.); children: John Douglas, Christopher Alan. Owner, mgr. Harbor Shopping Ctr., Harbor Landing, Mile Sq. Plaza and Garfield Plaza, Huntington Beach, Calif., 1975-83; designer, owner The Dream Factory, Huntington, 1974—; founder, owner Huntington Pacific Thrift and Loan, 1982—; owner, pub. Mauian mag., Lahaina, Hawaii, 1984—; developer, owner Double Gemini Corp., Huntington, 1978-83. Mem. archtl. com. Orangewood Home for Battered Children, Orange, Calif., 1980; dist. chmn. Maui County Reps.; bd. dirs. W. Maui Youth Ctr., Lahaina, Lahaina Salvation Army. Mem. Hawaii Pub. Assn., Small Mag. Pub. Assn., Hawaii Visitors Assn., Maui C. of C. (bd. dirs.), Hotel Assn. Hawaii. Lodge: Soroptimist. Home: 31 Kai Pali Pl Lahaina HI 96761 Office: 505 Front St Suite 213 Lahaina HI 96761

ARNOLD, JOANNE EASLEY, journalism educator, university official; b. Hutchinson, Kans., June 18, 1930; d. Orland Royce and Bernice Anna (Daugherty) Easley; B.A., U. Colo., 1952, M.A., 1965, Ph.D., 1971; m. Sanders Gibson Arnold, June 7, 1952 (div. 1983); 1 son, Sanders Gibson. Reporter, mem. editorial staff Boulder (Colo.) Daily Camera, 1955-56; tchr. journalism, speech and English, Boulder High Sch., 1956-71, dir. publs., 1958-69, chmn. dept. English, 1967-69; asst. dir. Nat. Center for Higher Edn. Mgmt. Systems, Western Interstate Commn. for Higher Edn., Boulder, 1971-74; asso. prof. journalism U. Colo., Boulder, 1974—, asso. dean Sch. Journalism, 1974-75, 82—, asso. vice chancellor for acad. affairs, 1975-80; adviser Elem. and Secondary Edn. Act, Title III, Colo., 1972-75; cons. Bur. Communications, U. Colo., 1970-71; cons. elementary and secondary edn., organizational communication, lectr.; mem. Western Interstate Commn. for Higher Edn., 1975-84. . Commr., vice chmn. Boulder Public Libraries, 1973-76; mem. com. on fiscal policy City of Boulder, 1972-73; mem. Boulder Valley Sch. Dist. Re-2 Bd. Edn., 1975-79; mem. nat. adv. council Girl Scouts Am., 1977-84; trustee Boulder Library Found., 1974-76, Boulder Meml. Hosp. Newspaper Fund fellow Wall St. Jour., 1961; named Nat. Woman of Achievement, Women in Communication Inc., 1987, Nat. Fedn. Press Women, 1979. Mem. Nat. Soc. for the Study of Communication, Speech Assn. Am., Kappa Tau Alpha, Theta Sigma Phi, Alpha Delta Kappa, Phi Kappa Delta, Pi Beta Phi. Club: U. Colo. Alumni (dir. 1954) (Boulder). Editor: Higher Edn. Mgmt., 1971-74. Contbr. articles to profl. jours. Home: 815 Park Ln Boulder CO 80302

ARNOLD, KATHLEEN SPELTS, state senator; b. Miami, Fla., Oct. 25, 1941; d. John Keith and Mary Fay (Webber) Shay; m. Harold G. Arnold, Jan. 31, 1982; children by previous marriage—Melinda Kathleen, Meghan Shay, Richard John. B.A., U. Colo., 1963. Tchr., Bear Creek High Sch., Jefferson County, Colo., 1963-64, 65-67; asst. prodn. control mgr. Fordwerke, Cologne, Fed. Republic Germany, 1964-65; state rep. Colo. Gen. Assembly, Denver, 1978-83, state senator, 1983-87, chmn. judiciary com., 1980-83, state affairs com., 1985-86;candidate for regent U. Colo., 1988; del. Nat. Conf. State Legislatures, 1980-83; candidate for Lt. Gov., 1986. Bd. dirs. U. Colo. Alumni Bd., Denver, 1987—, United Bank, 1988—; chmn. Chatfield YMCA Fund Drive, Colo. Council of Chs.; mem. curriculum council Jefferson County Schs.; sec. Littleton Fire Bd. Mem. South Jeffeo-Kalewood C. of C. Republican. Presbyterian. Office: Lane House 6436 W Frost Dr Littleton CO 80123

ARNOLD, KIMBALL CLARK, volunteer; b. Chgo., Mar. 13, 1950; d. Donald Wrigley and Helen (Hardin) Clark; m. Thomas Eads Arnold Jr., April 8, 1972; children: Betsy, Thomas III, Charles. Student. No. Ariz. U., 1968-70. Bd. dirs. Desert Bot. Garden, 1983-86; volunteer COMPAS, 1982-84; adminstrv. community v.p. placement chmn., rummage chmn. membership council dir., 1972—, bd. dirs. 1987—, Jr. League of Phoenix, 1982—; room mother coordinator, pres. All Saint's Episcopal Day Sch., 1981-83, pres. bd. govs., 1987; pres. All Saints Parent Assn., 1987-88, bd. govs. 1987-88; various positions including bd. dirs. St. Luke's Service League, Phoenix, 1982—, pres. 1984-85, trustee 1986—; active Poison Mgmt. Ctr., Phoenix, 1985-86; bd. trustees St. Luke's Med. Ctr., 1984-85; mem. Ariz. Community Found. Distbrn. Com., 1988—. Recipient Leadership in Volunteerism award St. Luke's Med. Ctr., 1985; named Vol. of the Yr. Dirs. of Vols. in Agys., 1985. Republican. Episcopalian. Home: 7020 N Wilder Rd Phoenix AZ 85021

ARNOLD, LORNA JEAN, insurance agencies owner; b. N.Y.C., Oct. 20, 1945; d. George B. and Constance (Wiseman) A. AB in Am. Studies, Syracuse U., 1966; student, New Paltz State Tchrs. Coll., 1967. CLU; chartered fin. cons. Tchr. Wappingers Falls (N.Y.) Cen. Sch., 1968-69; personnel cons. M.D. Lowe Agy., Houston, 1969; real estate agt. Jim West Real Estate, Houston, 1970; sales rep. Traveler Ins. Co., Houston, 1973-77; pres. Carey C. Shaw, Inc., Houston, 1981—; owner Arnold & Assocs., Houston, 1977—; asst. moderator Life Underwriters Tng. Council, Houston, 1973-75. Mem. various council coms. Girl Scouts U.S., Houston, 1976-81; vol. chair Depelchen Faith Home, Houston, 1982-83; head bookstores outreach program Unity Ch. Christianity, Houston, 1983-85. Mem. Nat. Assn. Life Underwriters, Am. Soc. Chartered Life Underwriters, Am. Soc. Chartered Fin. Cons., Cert. Profl. Ins. Agts., Golden Key Soc. Club: Fondren Tennis. Office: Arnold & Assocs PO Box 770665 Houston TX 77215-0665

ARNOLD, MAGDA B(LONDIAU), psychologist, author; b. Mi-Trebova, Czechoslovakia, Dec. 22, 1903; came to Can., 1928; d. Rudolf and Rosa Marie (Blondiau) Barta; divorced; children: Joan, Margaret, Katherine. BA, U. Toronto, 1939, MA, 1940, PhD, 1942. Lctr. U. Toronto, Ont., Can., 1942-47; dir. research and tng. Vet.'s Affairs Dept. Sunnybrook Hosp., Toronto, 1946-47; vis. lectr. Wellesley (Mass.) Coll., 1947-48; assoc. prof., dept. head Dept. Psychol. Bryn Mawr (Pa.) Coll., 1948-50; vis. lectr. Harvard U., Cambridge, Mass., 1947-48 summers; prof., head dept. Dept. Psychol. Barat Coll., Lake Forest, Ill.; prof. Dept. Psychology Loyola U. Chgo., 1952-72, dir. behavior lab., 1961-70, dir. exptl. div., 1965-72; Reilly Disting. prof. psychology Xavier U., Cin., 1970-72; prof., chair Div. Social Scis. Spring Hill Coll., Mobile, Ala., 1972-75; dir. project NSF Grant Div. Social Scis. Spring Hill Coll., Mobile, 1972-75. Author: The Human Person, 1954, Emotion and Personality, 1960, Story Sequence Analysis, 1962, The Nature of Emotion: Selected Readings, 1968, Emocion Y Personalidad, 1969, Feelings and Emotions: The Loyola Symposium, 1970, Memory and the Brain, 1984; contbr. articles to profl. jours. Fellow Helen Putnam Advanced Research, 1952-54, Guggenheim, 1957-58, Fulbright Research, 1962-63. Fellow Am. Psychol. Assn.; mem. Sigma Xi. Republican. Roman Catholic.

ARNOLD, MARY ANN, military officer; b. Pitts., Feb. 12, 1939; d. John Albert and Julia Christina (Wenzel Hartley) Hopper; m. Anthony Ray Arnold, Dec. 11, 1973. RN, Allegheny Gen. Hosp., Pitts., 1960; BS in Nursing, U. R.I., 1969; MA, Pepperdine U., 1976. RN, Calif., Pa.; cert. quality assurance profl. Staff, head nurse Allegheny Gen. Hosp., Pitts., 1960-62; commd. USN, 1962, advanced through grades to capt.; head nurse Naval Hosp. USN, Bethesda, Md., 1962-65; basic instr. Naval Sch. Health Scis. San Diego, 1970-73, med. supr., staffing cons. Naval Hosp., 1973-76; med. supr. Naval Hosp. Camp Pendleton, Calif., 1976-79; officer spl. projects, coordinator intensive care Bethesda, 1979-83; sr. nurse Station Hosp. Keflavick, Iceland, 1983-84; coordinator quality assurance Naval Hosp. Camp Pendleton, 1984—. Bd. dirs. YWCA, San Diego, 1987—. Named in Tribute to

Women in Industry YWCA, 1986. Mem. Nat. Assn. Quality Assurance Profls., Calif. Assn. Quality Assurance Profls., Allegheny Gen. Hosp. Alumnae Assn., Phi Kappa Phi. Republican. Presbyterian. Home: 2407 Jacaranda Ave Carlsbad CA 92008 Office: USN Naval Hosp Camp Pendleton CA 92055

ARNOLD, MARY BERTUCIO, pediatric endocrinologist; b. Fitchburg, Mass., Sept. 29, 1924; d. George and Louise (Byrolly) Bertucio; AB, Vassar Coll., 1945; MD cum laude, U. Vt., 1950; MA, Brown U., 1974; m. John Hampton Arnold, July 28, 1956 (dec. Apr. 1972); children—John, Mark, Matthew. Intern, resident Hartford (Conn.) Hosp., 1950-52; asst./sr. pediatric resident Babies' Hosp., Columbia-Presbyn. Med. Center, N.Y.C., 1952-54; pediatric endocrinology research fellow Mass. Gen. Hosp., Boston, 1954-57; asst. in pediatrics Harvard U. Sch. Medicine, Boston, 1955-57; instr. pediatrics/asst. prof. U. N.C. Sch. Medicine, Chapel Hill, 1959-65; lectr. med. sci./assoc. prof. pediatrics Brown U., Providence, 1966-74, assoc. prof., 1974—; chmn. dept. pediatrics, dir. pediatric endocrinology Roger Williams Gen. Hosp., Providence, 1971—. Chmn., Heart Health in the Young Com., Am. Heart Assn., R.I. Affiliate, Inc., 1979-82; mem. adv. com. New Eng. Regional Hypothyroidism Screening Program, 1976—; mem. subcom. pediatric planning rev. guidelines Hosp. Assn. R.I., 1976—; mem. program com. R.I. Clin. Diabetes Assn., 1975-80. Recipient Carrbee award U. Vt. Sch. Medicine, 1950, Excellence in Teaching award Brown U., 1978. Mem. Endocrine Soc., Lawson Wilkins Pediatric Endocrine Soc. (founding mem.), Am. Fedn. Clin. Research, AAAS, Am. Med. Women's Assn., Am. Acad. Pediatrics, AMA, New Eng. Pediatric Soc., R.I. Clin. Diabetes Assn. (pres. 1975-77), Sigma Xi. Episcopalian. Contbr. articles to profl. jours. Office: 825 Chalkstone Ave Providence RI 02908

ARNOLD, MARY PAMELA, mental health counselor; b. Ft. Wayne, Ind., Nov. 30, 1949; d. Charles Stanton and Marjorie Ann (Davis) A. Cert. in psycho-trauma tng., Centralia (Ill.) Hosp., 1970; student, Purdue U., 1975-77; BS in Spl. Edn., Ball State U., 1981; postgrad., Nat. Coll. Edn., 1986-89. Counselor child guidance Hoyleton (Ill.) Children's Home, 1970-72; owner, adminstr. Miss Pam's Nursery Sch., Michigan City, Ind., 1973-75; spl. edn. cons. Michigan City Sch. System, 1975-78; instr. Ind. Vocat. Tech. Coll., Indpls., 1979-86; asst. activity dir. Normandy House Nursing Home, Wilmette, Ill., 1986-87; evening adminstr. Normandy Hall Retirement Residence, Evanston, Ill., 1986-87; Research adminstr. Jack Tanzman (Assn. of Cert. Social Workers), Evanston, 1987—; mgmt. cons. Gen. Motors, Indpls., 1982-86; cons. counselor Parents Without Partners, Valparaiso, Ind., 1984-85; tng. cons. Houston Corp., Indpls., 1984; founder, coordinator Play Therapy for Abused Children, Michigan City, 1977; presenter, organizer Displaced Homemaker Seminar, Muncie, Ind., 1980. Vol. Muscular Dystrophy Telethon, Michigan City, 1985; counselor Battered Women, Muncie, 1979-81. Nat. Coll. Edn. fellow, 1986-89; Parents' Group for Spl. Student scholar, 1978. Mem. AAUW, Nat. Orgn. Human Service Edn. (asst. to pres. 1986-87, conf. coordinator 1986-87), NOW. Mem. Ch. of Christ. Club: Women's (Michigan City).

ARNOLD, NAOMI ANNETTE (ANNE), foundation administrator; b. Poplar Bluff, Mo., Jan. 13, 1954; d. Austin Warner and Naomi E. (Clark) A. A, Crowleys Ridge Coll., 1974. Legis. asst. Congressman Bill Alexander, Washington, 1974-80; office mgr., exec. dir. Democrat. Party of Ark., Little Rock, 1980-85; campaign mgr. Hampton Roy for Lt. Gov., Little Rock, 1985-86; adminstrv. asst. The Salvation Army, Ft. Worth, 1986—. Legis. chmn. Tarrant County Dem. Women, Ft. Worth, 1987—; mem. Ark State Dem. com., Little Rock, 1986, Pulaski County Dem. com., Little Rock, 1982-86; mem. exec. com. Pulaski County Dem., Little Rock, 1986; pres. Pulaski County Young Dem., Little Rock, 1984. Mem. Nat. Assn. Female Execs., Inst. Politics and Govt. (cert.). Episcopalian. Home: 166 Coventry Place Fort Worth TX 76107

ARNOLD, OLINDA DIAS, insurance agency executive; b. Santa Barbara, Portugal, Aug. 12, 1945; came to U.S., 1967; d. Manuel Machado and Olinda Da Conceicão (Bretao) Dias; m. Henry Stuart Arnold, Nov. 6, 1966; 1 child, Belinda D. AA, Coll. of the Sequoias, 1965. Legal sec. Grimes & Warwick, San Diego, 1972-75; legal asst. Law Offices of John A. Harin, San Diego, 1975-79; v.p., treas. Henry S. Arnold & Co., San Diego, 1979—. Bd. dirs. Azorean Alliance, San Diego, 1979, Spirit of '76, 1983— (1st Worn and Torn award 1986); mem. San Carlos Area Council, San Diego, 1987. Mem. Nat. Notary Assn., Nat. Assn. Female Execs. Roman Catholic. Office: 3444 Camino Del Rio #201 San Diego CA 92108

ARNOLD, SANDRA ASUNCION, Spanish educator; b. Cienfuegos, Las Villas, Cuba, Aug. 15, 1949; came to U.S., 1961; d. Mario and Justa (Denis) Martin; m. Philip Cowley Arnold, July 17, 1971; 1 child, Monica Martin. BA, UCLA, 1972, MA, 1977; MBA, Pepperdine U., 1980. Cert. Spanish tchr., Calif. Tchr. Spanish John Adams Jr. High Sch., Santa Monica, Calif., 1973-81; instr. Spanish Calif. State U., Northridge, 1981-86; owner For the Love of Spanish, Van Nuys, Calif., 1982—; instr. Oakwood Sch., North Hollywood, Calif., 1984-85, Coll. Canyons., Valencia, Calif., 1985—; tng. instr. UCLA, 1975-81. Contbr. articles to children's mags. Calif. Fedn. scholar, 1968. Mem. Soc. children's Book Writer (chairperson event com.). Democrat. Roman Catholic.

ARNOLD, SHEILA, state legislator; b. N.Y.C., Jan. 15, 1929; d. Michael and Eileen (Lynch) Keddy; coll. courses; m. George Longan Arnold, Nov. 12, 1960; 1 son, Peter; 1 son by previous marriage, Michael C. Young; stepchildren—Drew, George Longan, Joe. Mem. Wyo. Ho. of Reps., 1978—, mem. com. on appropriations, com. on rules and procedures; dir. First Interstate Bank of Laramie. Former mem., sec. Wyo. Land Use Adv. Coms.; past pres. Dem. Women's Club, Laramie; past vice-chmn. Albany County Dem. Cen. Com.; past mem. Dem. State Com.; mem. Nat. Conf. State Legislatures Com. on Fiscal Affairs and Oversight. Recipient Spl. Recognition award from Developmentally Disabled Citizens of Wyo., 1985. Mem. Laramie Area C. of C. (pres. 1982; Top Hand award 1977), LWV, Internat. Platform Assn. Clubs: Faculty Women's (past pres.), Zonta, Laramie Women's, Cowboy Joe. Office: Capitol Bldg Cheyenne WY 82002

ARNOLD, SUSAN BIRD, safety education training, consulting and products company executive; b. Reading, Pa., Feb. 28, 1951; d. Frank Edward and Esther (Savidge) Bird; B.A., Mercer U., Macon, Ga., 1972; m. Robert Melvin Arnold, Jr., Mar. 18, 1972; children—Jennifer Michelle, Amelia Michelle, Stephanie Michelle, Elizabeth Michelle. Audio-video technician Internat. Safety Acad., 1971; with Internat. Loss Control Inst., 1974—, mgr. ednl. products div., 1978-82, v.p. adminstrv. services, v.p. press div., Loganville, Ga., 1982-85, exec. dir., gen. mgr., 1985—. Contbr. to Risk Control Rev. Mem. adv. com. Inst. Safety, Health and Rehab. for the Exceptional, 1978-84; bd. dirs. Bluesprings Day Camp for Handicapped. Mem. AVMA Aux. Methodist. Home: PO Box 609 Loganville GA 30249 Office: Internat Loss Control Inst Hwy 78 Loganville GA 30249

ARNOLD, VERNA ALINE, educator, administrator; b. Haskell, Tex., Apr. 7, 1931; d. Bert W. and Juanita V. (Brooks) Marchbanks; m. Walter Eugene Arnold, Sept. 6, 1969; 1 dau., Teresa Anderson. A.A., Eastfield Coll., 1973; B.B.A., N.Tex. State U., 1975, M.B.A., 1976, Ph.D., 1978. Asst. adminstr. Doctors Hosp., Dallas, 1959-60; adminstrv. asst. Baylor U. Med. Ctr., Dallas, 1960-66; hosp. adminstr. Ennis Mcpl. Hosp. (Tex.), 1966-70; asst. prof. mgmt. N.Tex. State U., Denton, 1979-85, exec. asst. to chancellor, 1982-84; v.p. Arnold Assocs., Plainview, Tex., 1985—; chairperson div. bus. Wayland Bapt. U., Plainview, 1985—. Contbr. articles to profl. jours. Mem. AAWU, Am. Pub. Health Assn., Am. Hosp. Assn., Am. Acad. Mgmt., Tex. Hosp. Assn., SW Acad. Mgmt., Bus. and Profl. Women's Club (v.p. 1968-70), Beta Gamma Sigma, Sigma Iota Epsilon, Phi Theta Kappa. Republican. Baptist. Office: Wayland Bapt U 1900 W 7th Plainview TX 79072

ARNONE, JAYNE ELIZABETH, territory manager; b. St. Louis, Aug. 10, 1956; d. John S. and Audrey E. (Eime) A. Student, U. Bologna (Italy), 1977-78; BA, U. Mo., 1979. Sales rep. Riverfront Times, St. Louis, 1980-81, St. Louis Blues Hockey Club, St. Louis, 1982; mktg. rep. West Travel Ltd., St. Louis, 1982-83; advt. mgr. Colman's Grant Village, St. Louis, 1984-85; instr. Italian Shaw Community Sch., St. Louis, 1979—; ter. mgr. Carter-Wallace, Inc., Cranbury, N.J., 1985—; interpreter for Italian lang., St. Louis, 1979—. Mem. Student Adv. Council Dept. Romance Lang., Carter's Master Club, Phi Sigma Iota. Club: Italian (pres. Columbia club 1978-79). Home and Office: 5015 Bancroft Saint Louis MO 63109

ARNOT, SUSAN EILEEN, publishing company director; b. East Orange, N.J., Aug. 10, 1957; d. Robert B. and Mae (Cockcroft) A. BA, Coll. William and Mary, 1979; student, Cambridge U., 1977; cert., NYU, 1979. Promotion asst. Viking Press/Penguin Books, N.Y.C., 1979-82; mgr. promotion Rizzoli Internat. Publs., N.Y.C., 1982-83; mgr. advt. promotion USA Today, N.Y.C., 1983-85; promotion dir. Whitney Communications Co. (name now Retirement LIving Pub Co.), N.Y.C., 1985—; career adv. Coll. William and Mary, 1980—. Writer/editor quar.: (newsletter) 50 Plus Market Update, 1985—. Vol. cook, fundraiser Cathedral Soup Kitchen, St. John the Divine Cathedral, 1983-85. Recipient Best of N.Y. Addy award for advt., 1986. Mem. Women in Communications Inc. (chpt. publicity com. 1985-86, fin. com. 1986—, spl. events com. 1986—), NOW, Coll. William and Mary Alumni Soc. (chpt. pres. 1986—, exec. bd. 1983-86), AAUW (chpt. corr. sec. 1983-86, chair com. on women's work 1984-86), Mag. Marketers Assn. Methodist. Avocations: travel, music, theater, reading. Home: 230 W 107th St Apt 3J New York NY 10025 Office: Retirement Living Pub Co Inc 850 3d Ave New York NY 10022

ARNOULD, SIMONNE MARCELLE, optician; b. Fort-De-France, Martinique, Apr. 25, 1930; came to U.S., 1959; d. Etienne St. Ange and EmiLienne Noëmie Huyghues-Lacour; m. Andre Jacques Arnould; 1 child, Nicole. Student, Coll. of Optometry, Paris, 1948-49; diploma, Dispensing Optician Sch., Montreal, 1954. Diplomate Nat. Contact Lens Examiner. Stylist, dispensing optician, contact lens fitter various opticians, Calif., 1960-75; lectr. in field. Fellow Nat. Acad. Opticianry, Contact Lens Soc. Am.; mem. Am. Bd. Opticianry (cert. 1965, master optician 1972), Calif. Soc. Ophthalmic Dispensers, (v.p. 1973), Pacific Coast Contact Lens Soc. (treas. 1981), Nat. Assn. Female Execs. (pres. Escondido chpt. 1985-87), Escondido C. of C. Roman Catholic. Club: Lead's. Lodge: Soroptimist (past pres. Escondido chpt.). Office: Apropos Optical 675-D N Broadway Escondido CA 92025 Also: Foothill Optical 345 W Foothill Blvd Glendora CA 91740

ARNSTEIN, CAREN P., marketing executive; b. Alexandria, Va., Aug. 12, 1955; d. Saul Robert and Joanne (Willens) Arnstein. BS in Environ. Sci., U. Mass., 1977; MS in Communications Mgmt., Simmons Coll., 1987. Field technician BCI, Geonetics, Laconia, 1977-78; pub. relations copywriter Metcalf & Eddy, Inc., Wakefield, Mass., 1979-85; mktg. writer WSI, Bedford, Mass., 1985-86; mgr. mktg. communications ERT, Inc., Concord, Mass., 1986—. Mem. Nat. Assn for Female Execs., Pub. Relations Soc., NOW. Democrat. Jewish. Office: ERT Inc 696 Virginia Rd Concord MA 01742

ARNSTEIN, SHERRY PHYLLIS, health care executive; b. N.Y.C., Jan. 11, 1930; m. George E. Arnstein, June 26, 1951; B.S., UCLA, 1951; M.S. in Communications, Am. U., 1963; postgrad. in systems dynamics MIT, summer 1976. Washington editor Current Mag., 1961-63; staff cons. Pres. Com. on Juvenile Delinquency, 1963-65; spl. asst. to asst. sec. HEW, 1965-67; chief citizen participation advisor Model Cities Adminstrn., HUD, 1967-68; pub. policy cons., Washington, 1968-75; sr. research fellow HHS, Washington, 1975-78; v.p. govt. relations Nat. Health Council, Inc., Washington, 1978-85; exec. dir. Am. Assn. Colls. Osteo. Medicine, 1985—. Bd. dirs. Youth Policy Inst. Author: (with Alexander Christakis) Perspectives on Technology Assessment, 1975; editor: Government Relations Handbook Series, 1979-85, Washington Report Series, 1985. mem. editorial bd. Tech. Assessment Update, 1975-78, The Bureaucrat, 1975-83, Pub. Adminstrn. Rev., 1978-83, Health Mgmt. Quar., 1985. Contbr. articles to profl. jours. Office: Am Assn Colls Osteo Medicine 6110 Executive Blvd Suite 405 Rockville MD 20852

ARNTSON, JUDITH CHRISTINE, nurse; b. Los Angeles, Mar. 5, 1938; d. Lloyd Calvin and Christine Elizabeth (Eisenbach) Sharpe; m. Joseph R. Fernandez, Oct. 6, 1959 (div. June 1985); children: Tina, Marie Beam; m. David Arnold Arntson, May 24, 1986. BSN, Calif. State U., Fullerton, 1976; MSN, Calif. State U., Los Angeles, 1978. RN, Calif.; cert. trainer mgmt. of assaultive behavior, interaction mgmt. instr. Staff nurse Los Angeles County/U. So. Calif. Med. Ctr., 1969-71, City of Hope Nat. Med. Ctr., Duarte, Calif., 1971-77; asst. prof. nursing Calif. State U., Fullerton, 1977-78; dir. emergency and referral services Ingleside Hosp., Rosemead, Calif., 1979-84; inservice dir. Ingleside Hosp., Rosemead, 1979-85, dir. edn. dept., 1985-87; dir. nursing Brea (Calif.) Hosp. and Neuropsychiat. Ctr., 1987—; instr. in nursing San Antonio Coll., Walnut, Calif., 1977-78, U. Calif. Irvine Med. Ctr., 1976, Golden West Coll., 1976, Calif. State U., Fullerton, 1979; guest lectr. Lincoln Tng. Ctr., 1984; speaker on AIDS to various orgns. Chair psychiat. inservice com. Inservice and Health Edn. Council of Los Angeles, 1980-81. Mem. Calif. State U. Nursing Alumni Assn. (pres. 1980), San Gabriel Valley Nursing Consortium. Office: Brea Hosp Neuropsychiat Ctr 875 N Brea Blvd Brea CA 92621

ARON, TRUDY MCDERMOTT, professional association executive; b. Denver, Jan. 25, 1946; d. Michael and Virginia Mae (Holtman) McD.; m. Karl Joseph Aron, Dec. 24, 1985. Student, Met. State Coll., Denver, 1967-69. Front office mgr. Hyatt House Hotel, Des Moines, 1967-70; asst. to dir. Continuing Legal Edn. In Colo., Inc., Denver, 1975-80; exec. dir. Colo. AIA, Denver, 1980—. Mem. Am. Soc. Assn. Execs., Colo. Soc. Assn. Execs., Soc. Archtl. Adminstrs. (hon.), Downtown Denver Bus. and Profl. Women. Democrat. Home: 3811 W 29th Ave Denver CO 80211 Office: AIA of Colo Carriage House 1459 Pennsylvania Denver CO 80203

ARONHALT, BETTE LOUISE, health care administrator; b. Cumberland, Md., Aug. 5, 1947; d. Gover Owens LeMoins and Dorothy Alice (Gilbert) A. AS, U. Md., 1982; BS, W.Va. U., 1970; PhD, London Inst. Art, 1970. cons. Goodwill Mennonite Nursing Home, Grantsville, Md., 1982—, med. adminstrn. free mktg. services. Editor (newspaper) Stethescoop, 1980-82. Vol. Am. Heart Assn., Am. Cancer Assn., Hospice, Cumberland, Md., Rep. Com., Allegany County. Mem. Am. Coll. Utilization Rev. Physicians (affiliate), Am. Med. Records Assn., Nat. Assn. Females Execs., North Am. Med. Dental Assn., Mini-Board, Smithsonian Assn., We. Md. Med. Record Assn. (pres.), Md. Med. Record Assn., Am. Med. Record Assn., Va. Assn. Durable Med. Equipment Cos. (chmn. hosp. liaison com.), Med. Equipment Dealers Assn. Md., Kappa Delta Psi (pres. Keyser, W. Va. chpt.). Republican. Lutheran. Clubs: Cumberland Tennis (treas.), Cumberland Golf Assn., Bedford Springs Golf Assn. Home: 608 Hilltop Dr Cumberland MD 21502 Office: Oxytec Inhalation Therapy 15401 McMullen Hwy Cumberland MD 21502

ARONNE-AMESTOY, LIDA BEATRIZ, Spanish educator; b. Mendoza, Argentina, Jan. 26, 1940; d. Oswaldo Pascual José and Lida Rosa (Massei) Aronne; m. Ricardo Roberto Amestoy, Apr. 10, 1965 (dec. June 1984); children: Marcelo Daniel, Laura Ariadna; m. Larry Lee Kreis, July 1987. MA in English Lit., U. Cuyo, Argentina, 1963; PhD in Spanish Am. Lit., U. Conn., 1982. Tchr. ESL A. Schweitzer High Sch., Mendoza, 1964-65; prof. English, English lit. Sarmiento U., San Juan, Argentina, 1965-67, U. Cuyo, Mendoza, 1967-75; prof. Spanish-Am. lit. Córdoba (Argentina) Nat. U., 1976-78; teaching asst. Spanish U. Conn., 1980-82; asst. prof. Spanish U. Cin., 1984-85; asst. prof. Spanish Providence (R.I.) Coll., 1982-84, assoc. prof. Spanish, 1985—; vis. prof., Mexico, 1976, 78, 83; lectr. in field, 1974-87; dir. literary workshops, Providence, 1986-87, Hispanic Arts workshops, Providence, 1986—; cons. R.I. State Council on Arts, 1987—. Author: Cortázar: La Novela Mandala, 1972, América en la Encrucijada de Mito y Razón, 1976, Utopía Paraíso e Historia: Inscripciones del mito en G. Márquez, Rulfo y Cortázar, 1986; author (short stories) Camino a Damasco, 1966; editor Hispanic Jour. of Arts and Culture, Providence, 1987. U. Cuyo grantee, 1973-75; U. Conn. fellow, 1980-82, First Whetten fellow, 1981-82. Mem. MLA, New Eng. Ctr. for Latin Am. Studies, Sigma Delta Pi. Methodist. Office: Providence Coll Dept Modern Languages Eaton and River Ave Providence RI 02918

ARONSON, REBECCA, clothing designer; b. Lima, Ohio, Oct. 17, 1941; d. Walter Gilbert Everett and Marian Marciel (Evans) Pearce; m. Niels R. Keiper, Dec. 23, 1968 (div. Apr. 1975); m. Douglas Ira Battenberg, May 19, 1979. Student, Bowling Green (Ohio) State U., 1959-61. Pvt. sec. Chem. Abstracts, Columbus, Ohio, 1961-63; flight attendant Am. Airlines, Chgo., Washington, 1963-69; booking agt. Nat. Concert Bur., Lawrence, Kans., 1969-72; owner The Village Jewel, Columbus and Cin., 1972-75; territory rep. Reynolds Metals Co., Columbus, 1973-75; project coordinator Holland & Lyons, Inc., Washington, 1976-78; dir. mktg. Mid. States Constrn., Rockville, Md., 1978-79; asst. dir. condominium devel. Charles E. Smith Cos., Arlington, Va., 1980-81; pres., designer Aronson Enterprises, Inc., Washington, 1982—. Dir. Edn. Foundry Meth. Ch., Washington, 1978-81; rep. Real Estate Developers Task Force, Washington, 1981. Mem. Assn. for Research and Enlightenment, Nat. Assn. Female Execs. Club: KIWI's. Home and Office: Aronson Enterprises Inc 4628 Sedgwick St NW Washington DC 20016

AROVA, SONIA, ballet educator, administrator; b. Sofia, Bulgaria, June 20, 1928; came to U.S., 1954; d. Albert and Rene (Melamedoff) Errio; m. Thor Sutowski, Mar. 11, 1965. Grad. Fine Arts Sch., Paris, 1940, Eng., 1944. Ballerina Internat. Ballet, London, 1944-47, Rambert Ballet, London, 1947-50, Royal Ballet, London, 1961, Festival Ballet, London, 1951-54, Ballet deChamps-Elysees, Paris, 1950-51, Am. Ballet Theater, N.Y.C., 1956-58; artistic dir. Nat. Ballet, Oslo, 1964-70, Hamburg Ballet, Fed. Republic Germany, 1970-71; co-dir. San Diego Ballet, 1971-75; dir. State of Ala. Ballet, Birmingham, 1981—, instr. Sch. Fine Arts, 1975—. Recipient World Championship of Dance award Ballet Jury, Paris, 1939; decorated knight of First Order, King Olav of Norway, 1971.

ARP, CLAUDIA STEMBRIDGE, social services administrator, consultant; b. Commerce, Ga., July 26, 1942; d. Joel Eugene and Catherine (Rice) Stembridge; m. David Hayden Arp Jr., Dec. 28, 1962; children: David Jarrett, Joel Hayden, Jonathan Eugene. BS in Home Econs., U. Ga., 1964. Cert. tchr. home econs., Ga. Cons. Campus Crusade for Christ, Atlanta, 1970-71, Knoxville, Tenn., 1971-73, 82—, Fed. Republic of Germany, 1973-76, Vienna, Austria, 1977-82; co-founder, co-dir. Marriage Alive, Internat., Knoxville, 1983—; co-host The Family Workshop radio program Sta. WIVK/WRJZ, Knoxville, 1984—; speaker in field. Author: Sanity in the Summertime, 1981, Ten Dates for Mates, 1983, Almost 13, 1986, (cassette tape) Making Your Marriage Live, 1985. Bd. dirs. Mom's Support Group, Knoxville, 1984—. Mem. Assn. Couples for Marriage Enrichment, Phi Kappa Phi. Presbyterian. Club: Knoxville Racquet. Home: 8624 Dovefield Dr Knoxville TN 37923

ARRINGTON, NELLIE WEBB, marketing executive, consultant; b. Balt., Oct. 16, 1952; d. Elbert C. and Margaret Virginia (Webb) Arrington; m. Robert Stacy Evans, Jan. 3, 1981; 1 child, Elyse Anne. AB, Western Md. Coll., 1974; MS, Johns Hopkins U., 1980. Reporter, editor Stromberg Publs., Ellicott City, Md., 1974-79; mktg. exec. Henry Adams, Inc., Balt., 1980-84, Edmunds & Hyde, Inc., Balt., 1984-85; realtor Long & Foster Realtors, Inc., Columbia, Md., 1986—; mktg./mgmt. cons., Ellicott City, 1977—. Author news feature series The Crime of Rape (2d pl. award Md.-Del.-D.C. Press Assn. 1975); contbr. articles to profl. jours. Pres., Lawyer's Hill-Rockburn Area Assn., Elk Ridge, Md., 1975-77. Mem. Soc. Mktg. Profl. Services (founding pres. Chesapeake chpt. 1981-83, jury chmn. 1981-82, nat. conv. speaker 1984, sr. roundtable 1984), Nat. Assn. Realtors, Homebuilders Assn. Md. (bd. dirs. Howard County chpt. 1988—, chmn. com. polit. affairs), Howard County Bd. Realtors, Columbia Jaycees (internal v.p. 1980-81, Officer of Yr. award 1981). Democrat. Episcopalian. Club: Md. Press (pres. 1981), Long and Foster Dirs.

ARRINGTON, VICTORIA ROBINSON, mortgage company executive; b. Melrose Park, Ill., Nov. 4, 1956; d. Henry Lee and Ernestine (Horton) Robinson; m. Terry Arrington, Sept. 26, 1981; 1 child, Andrew Alexander. AS in Bus. and Acctg., Triton Coll., 1976; BS in Bus. and Fin., Ea. Ill. U., 1978. Quality control rep. Fed. Nat. Mortgage Assn., Chgo., 1978-85; mgr. conventional underwriting Lyons Mortgage Corp., Rolling Meadows, Ill., 1985-87; asst. treas., credit officer Chase Home Mortgage Co., Oak Brook, Ill., 1987—. Sec. Hayden Meml. Ednl. Com., Maywood, Ill., 1973; bd. dirs. Maple Tree Child Care Ctr., 1981; former sec. mem. Maywood Youth Commn., 1973. Named one of Outstanding Young Women in Am., 1983. Mem. Nat. Assn. Negro Bus. and Profl. Women's Club, Inc. (treas. 1982-86), Phi Gamma Nu, Delta Mu Delta. Home: 637 S 24th Ave Bellwood IL 60104 Office: Chase Home Mortgage Corp 1 S 660 Midwest Rd Oak Brook Terr IL 60181

ARROWSMITH, MARIAN CAMPBELL, educator; b. St. Louis, Nov. 12, 1943; d. William Rankin and Elizabeth (Mitchell) Arrowsmith; m. William Earl Schroyer, July 23, 1983; stepchildren: Carey Jo, Amy Lynn. BS, La. State U., 1961; MEd, Southeastern La. U., 1978. Lic. tchr., La.; cert. practicum supr. Inst. for Reality Therapy. Tchr. 1st grade McDonough #26, Jefferson Parish Sch. Bd., Gretna, La., 1966; 2nd grade tchr. Woodlawn High Sch., Baton Rouge, 1966-67; kindergarten tchr. Univ. Terrace Elem. Sch., Baton Rouge, summer 1967; 1st grade tchr. Westminster Elem. Sch., Baton Rouge, 1967-72, Elm Grove Elem. Sch., Harvey, La., 1972-73; kindergarten tchr. Westminster Elem. Sch., Baton Rouge, summers 1968, 69, 70, 71, Elm Grove Elem. Sch., summer 1973; 1st grade tchr. St. Andrews Episcopal Sch., New Orleans, 1973-74; kindergarten tchr. St. Tammany Parish Sch. Bd., Folsom, La., 1974-77; early childhood specialist St. Tammany Parish Sch. Bd., Covington, La., 1977-87; prin. Woodlake Elementary Sch., 1987—; off-campus coordinating asst. St. Tammany Parish for Dept. Continuing Edn., Southeastern La. U., 1985-87; condr. workshops in field; selected ofcl. pres. Sunbelt Region of Reality Therapists, 1983; regional dir. La. and Miss. Reality Therapists, Sunbelt Bd. of Reality Therapists, 1983. Author: Helping Your Child at Home, 1982-83; Handbook for Early Childhood Tutorial Program, 1983-84. Mem. AAUW, Friends of Audubon Zoo, Vols. of Am., La. Assn. on Children Under Six, So. Assn. on Children Under Six, La. Assn. Sch. Execs., Nat. Assn. Female Execs., Sunbelt Assn. Reality Therapists (regional bd. 1982—, pres. and internat. bd. dirs. 1986—), Internat. Assn. Reality Therapists, Assn. Tchr. Educators, Delta Kappa Gamma (v.p. 1986), Alpha Delta Kappa (v.p.). Democrat. Presbyterian. Club: Basset Hound Club of Greater New Orleans (dir.). Avocations: horticulture, reading, fishing, showing dogs, racquetball. Home: 2327 Livingston St Mandeville LA 70448

ARSENAULT, LEONA MARIE, financial executive; b. Saratoga Springs, N.Y., May 6, 1954; d. Joseph Abel and Elva M. (Gallant) A. Student Seminole Community Coll., 1982-85, Otterbein Coll., 1987—. Asst. to mng. editor Orlando Sentinel, Fla., 1973-78; asst. to gen. mgr. Cardinal Industries, Inc., Sanford, Fla., 1979-81, asst. v.p., 1981-84, v.p. corp. fin., 1984-86, corp v.p. corp. fin., Columbus, Ohio, 1987—. Republican. Roman Catholic. Office: Cardinal Industries 2255 Kimberly Pkwy E Columbus OH 43232

ARTAZ, JEANNINE FORD, radio and television personality, fashion designer; b. San Antonio, May 22, 1929; d. Grady Carlton and Volahelen (Latham) Ford; m. Ches T. Von Baronofjski-Childres, Sept. 9, 1946 (dec. May 1964); children—Ginger Dona Watts, Honey Dawn Johnson, Carlton Ford Childres-Artaz, Grady Baron Childres-Artaz; m. Souvenir James Artaz, Jan. 24, 1968; stepchildren—Soundra Lee Crabtree, Bob Gene, Cheri Ann Bleyeu, Danny Joe, Bonnie Lynn Harris, Marlene Denise Halstad. Illustration degree Paris Art Inst., 1946; B.A., Tex. Christian U., 1949; student radio engring. Colo. State U., 1972-74; B.A. in Comml. Art, Art Inst. Chgo., 1949; student Coco Chanel's Studios, Paris, 1947-48. Designer, Originals by Jeannine, San Antonio, also Denver and Glenwood Springs, Colo., 1942—; disc jockey, announcer Stas. WOAI and KTSA, San Antonio, 1944-50; air personality Stas. KOA/KBTV and KIMN, Denver, 1951-68; women's program dir., announcer Radio Sta. KGLN, Glenwood Springs, Colo., 1970-82; dir. Tails Ranch, Garfield County Humane Assn., Glenwood Springs, 1982—; weather watcher Sta. KCNC-TV, Denver, 1982—; host talk show Everybody's Talkin' Sta. KDNK-Radio, Carbondale, Colo., 1986—; also mem. bd. dirs. humane assn., 1982—; tchr. radio/TV, J.F. Modeling Agy., Denver, 1956-60; owner, operator Just Me Designs, Aspen, Colo., 1987—. Author, editor: (children's plays) Play Time, 1976 (Illustrating award 1976). Designer Gidetts household appliance covers (Am. Design award 1980). Leader, 4-H Club, Glenwood Springs, 1972-83; active Valley View Hosp. Aux., 1966—; chmn. Am. Hosp. Aux., Denver, 1963-64; mem. Glenwood Springs Parks and Recreation Commn., 1973—; counselor Children Against Drugs, Glenwood Springs, 1982—; advisor Parent Adv. Bd., Glenwood Springs, 1970-83. Named Vol. of Yr., Garfield Sch. Dist., Glenwood Springs, 1973; Woman Broadcaster of Yr., Am. Broadcasting System, N.Y.C., 1956, 58; recipient award for multiple sclerosis work Borden Co., 1980; Ford Found. grantee, 1984. Mem. Colo. Women Broadcasters Assn. (Colo. Woman Broadcaster of Yr. 1956, 58), Airplane Pilots and Owners Assn., Am. Weather Observers Assn., Am. Designers Inc. (Coty award 1959), Am. Design Assn. (sec. Denver 1955-57), Am. Humane Assn. (founding mem., local dir. 1982—). Avocations: flying, needlework, gardening, reading, drawing. Home: 509 W 12th St Glenwood Springs CO 81601

ARTERS, LINDA BROMLEY, public relations consultant, writer; b. Phila., Dec. 18, 1951; d. Edward Pollard and Rosalyn Irene (Bromley) A. BA, Thiel Coll., 1973. Dir. customer relations Artmann Devel. Corp. Inc., Media, Pa., 1973-74; with S.E. Nat. Bank, Malvern, Pa., 1974-78, coordinator pub. relations, 1976-78; pvt. practice pub. relations consultant Media, 1978-84, Tempe, Ariz., 1984—; lectr. in field; past mem. pvt. industry council County De. (Pa.) CETA Program. free lance writer for local, regional and nat. mags. and newspapers. Past chmn. Emergency Dept. Vols. Chandler Regional Hosp; past bd. dirs. South Chester County Advanced Life Support Inc., United Cerebral Palsy of Del County; mem. Phila. Indoor Tennis Corp., 1977-82. Mem. Internat. Assn. Bus. Communicators, Nat. Fedn. Ind. Bus., Nat. Assn. Female Execs., Pub. Relations Soc. Am. (eligibility com. Phoenix chpt., mem. counselors group), U.S. Tennis Writers Assn., Phoenix C. of C. (communications council), Tempe C. of C. (chmn. communications council), Cen. Ariz. Mountain Rescue Assn. (chmn. pub. relations). Republican. Presbyterian. Office: Arters & Assocs 4630 E Elwood St Suite 1 Phoenix AZ 85040

ARTHUR, BRENDA KAY, financial consultant; b. Charleston, W.Va., May 28, 1951; d. Earl Washington and Martena (Miller) A. BA in Sociology, W.Va. U., 1972; MS in Edn., U. Dayton, 1975. Lic. ins. rep., Calif., Ariz. Field underwriter N.Y. Life Ins. Co., Long Beach, Calif., 1981-85; registered rep. N.Y. Life Securities Corp., Long Beach, Calif., 1984-85; fin. planner CIGNA Individual Fin. Services Corp., Irvine, Calif., 1985-87; registered rep. CIGNA Securities, Irvine, 1985-87; fin. cons., planner Fin. Services Inc., Newport Beach, Calif., 1987—; registered rep. Southmark Securities, 1987—. Mem. ARC, Santa Ana, Calif. 1982—, Adam Walsh Resource Ctr. Named Distinguished West Virginian, gov. W.Va., 1986. Mem. Nat. Assn. Life Underwriters, Orange County Charitable Giving Council, Planned Giving Roundtable Los Angeles, Orange County Planned Giving Com., Internat. Assn. Fin. Planning. Lodge: Zonta Internat. (v.p. 1985-86, bd. dirs. 1986—). Home: 1737 N Oak Knoll Dr Anaheim CA 92807 Office: Fin Services UnlimitedLtd 1601 Dove St Suite270 Newport Beach CA 92660

ARTHURS, ALBERTA BEAN, foundation executive; b. Framingham, Mass., Dec. 20, 1932; d. Maurice and Eleanor Irene (Levenson) Bean; m. Edward Arthurs, Dec. 20, 1960; children: Lee Michael, Daniel Jacob, Madeleine Hope. B.A., Wellesley Coll., 1954; Ph.D., Bryn Mawr Coll., 1972. Editor Liberty Mut. Ins. Co. Mag., Boston, 1954-56; dir. admissions Eliot-Pearson Sch.-Tufts U., Medford, Mass., 1957-59, instr. English, 1958-62; instr., lectr. Rutgers U., New Brunswick, N.J., 1964-72, asst. prof., 1972-73; dean Radcliffe Coll., Cambridge, Mass., 1973-75, Harvard U., Cambridge, 1975-77; pres., prof. English Chatham Coll., Pitts., 1977-82; dir. arts and humanities Rockefeller Found., N.Y.C., 1982—; bd. dirs. Culbro Corp., Techo-Serve, The Equitable Funds. Bd. dirs. Harbridge House, 1980-82, Salzburg Seminar in Am. Studies, Presbyn.-Univ. Hosp., Pitts, 1979-82, Pitts. Symphony Soc., 1980-82; trustee Dalton Sch., Hotchkiss Sch., 1975-83, Pine Manor Coll., 1976-81, Ellis Sch., 1977-82. Mem. Council on Fgn. Relations. Clubs: Duquesne (Pitts.); Harvard (N.Y.C.); Signet Soc. (Cambridge). Office: The Rockefeller Found 1133 Ave of Americas New York NY 10036

ARTHURS, CAROLE N., financial executive; b. Dover, Ohio, Oct. 10, 1934; d. Edward Stanley and Marjorie Elizabeth (Allison) Marks; m. Jim Arthurs, Aug. 31, 1953; children: Scott, Jamie, Kelly, Andrew, Shawn. Student, Edison Community Coll.; grad., Bert Rodgers Real Estate Sch., 1970; student, Valencia Community Coll., 1985. Mgr. housing sales adminstrn. GAC Properties, Cape Coral, Fla., 1970-73; contract adminstr. GAC Properties, Kissimmee, Fla., 1973-74; creative writer Dart Industries, Kissimmee, 1974-82; adminstr. Resort Ownership Market, Kissimmee, 1982-84; trust assoc. Pan Am. Bank, Orlando, Fla., 1984-86; editor Sr. Citizens News & Views, Orlando, 1986—. Editor Poinciana newspaper, 1975; contbr. articles to profl. jours. Mem. disaster team ARC, Kissimmee, 1985; corp. bd. dirs. Casselberry Sr. Ctr.; mem. adv. com., pub. speaker Older Ams., Orlando; mem. sr. adv. bd. Kissimmee Meml. Hosp.; Sunday sch. tchr., mem. ch. council, worship chmn. All Sts. Luth. Ch., Orlando. Recipient Community Service award Poinciana Youth Activities, 1975, Poinciana Pioneer newspaper, 1975, 4-H Club, 1976, others. Fellow Fla. Free-lance Writers Assn., Nat. Assn. for Female Execs. Republican. Home: 2500 Paradise Circle Kissimmee FL 32741 Office: Sr Citizens News & Views 723 E Colomial Dr Orlando FL 32803

ARUNDEL, GERALDINE PATTON, retired educator; b. Fremont, Nebr., Aug. 25, 1914; d. Guy Gerald and Lillian Armstrong (Spencer) Patton; B.A., Calif. State U., Long Beach, 1956; M.S., U. So. Calif., 1966, Ed.D., 1973; m. Frank Henry Arundel, July 2, 1935; children—Frank Gerald, Paul Henry. Tchr. elementary sch., Torrance and Long Beach, Calif., 1956-58; tchr. orthopedically handicapped Norwalk-La Mirada (Calif.) Sch. Dist., from 1963; substitute tchr., Compton, Bellflower and Paramount, Calif., 1958-63; home tchr., Norwalk, 1961-63; chmn. woman's com. for affirmative action policy statement by Bd. Edn., Norwalk-La Mirada Unified Sch. Dist., 1975. Grantee Crippled Children's Soc., 1962. Mem. Am. Assn. Mental Deficiency, Council Exceptional Children, AAUW, Calif. Ret. Tchrs. Assn. (dir. scholarship found.), Pi Lambda Theta, Phi Delta Gamma, Delta Epsilon. Democrat. Roman Catholic. Author: (transparency series and text) Mainstreaming a Physically Handicapped Student; (cassette with Helen Brown) Problems of Mainstreaming a Physically Handicapped Student. Home: 1888 Blackhawk St Oceanside CA 92056

ARVANITES, MARGHERITA JESSIE, engineer; b. Ipswich, Mass., Apr. 29, 1955; d. Jessie Agnes (Shaw) A. BA in Econs. and Bus. Adminstrn., Pfeiffer Coll., Misenheimer, N.C., 1978. Field service rep. Gen. Electric, Evendale, Ohio, 1979-80, evaluation engr., 1980-82, tech. forecaster mil. products, 1982-84; customer service rep. Gen. Electric, Ontario, Calif., 1984-85, power plant engr. propulsion engring. dept., 1985, mgr. engine testing propulsion engring. dept., 1985-87, mgr. engine testing and large engine engring. propulsion engring. dept., 1987—. Named one of Outstanding Young Women of Yr., 1986. Republican. Greek Orthodox. Home: 4143 Tenango Rd Claremont CA 91711

ARVAY, NANCY JOAN, insurance company executive; b. Pitts., Aug. 27, 1952; d. William John and Cornelia (Prince) A. BA in History, Duke U., 1974; postgrad., Columbia U., 1974-75. Polit. and internat. communications specialist U.S. Senate Fgn. Relations Com., Washington, 1975-77; broadcast media relations rep. Am. Petroleum Inst., Washington, 1977-79; broadcast media relations rep. Chevron U.S.A., San Francisco, 1979-82, coordinator electronic news media relations, 1982-85; sr. media relations rep. Chevron Corp., San Francisco, 1985-87; dir. pub. relations Fireman's Fund Corp., Novato, Calif., 1987—; lectr. Dept. Interior-Park Service, Beckley, W.Va., 1983; chmn. pub. relations Internat. Oil Spill Conf., Washington, 1984-85. Author, coordinator: Research Studies in Business and the Media, 1980-83; contbg. author This Is Public Relations, 1985. Founding mem. San Francisco chpt. Overseas Edn. Group; mem. pub. relations com. World Affairs Council San Francisco. Mem. Pub. Relations Soc., Radio/TV News Dirs. Assn. (assoc.), San Francisco Women in Bus. Office: Fireman's Fund Corp 777 Marin Dr Novato CA 94998

ARVEDON, MAELYN NORMA SIGAL, former bank security official; b. Boston, Nov. 21, 1954; d. Samuel and Sandra (Levin) Sigal; m. David K. Arvedon, June 3, 1979; children: Andrew Lowell, Amy Melissa. AB magna cum laude, Boston Coll., 1976; MBA, Boston U., 1981. Cert. in life ins. Mass. Successively teller, asst. head teller, research analyst, head teller, customer service rep., audit asst. Mut. Bank for Savs. and predecessor, Boston, 1976-81, loss prevention specialist, 1981-84. Adv. Com. to Elect Frank Rich Gov. of Mass., 1981; adv. Jr. Achievement, 1982-83. Recipient ins. sales awards. Mem. Nat. Assn. Female Execs., Old Girls Network, Savs. Bank Women of Mass., Mass. Police Fraudulent Check Assn. Jewish.

ARZT, ANNETTE M., psychologist; b. Chgo., Jan. 14, 1939; d. Salvatore and Winifred (Asciutto) Tagliavia; m. Thomas Ladendorf Arzt; Aug. 27, 1960; children: Tom Leonard, Ann Marie. AA, Oakton Community Coll., 1978; BA, Northeastern Ill. U., 1980; MS, Ill. Inst. Technology, 1982, PhD, 1985. Therapist Maryville Acad., Des Plaines, Ill., 1979, Skokie (Ill.) Valley Hosp., 1981-82, Ill. Inst. Technology Counseling Ctr., Chgo., 1982, Ravenswood Hosp., Chgo., 1982-83; tchr. Oakton Community Coll., Des Plaines, 1983; therapist Neuropsychiat. and Psychotherapy Assocs., Vernon Hills, Ill., 1983-87, 1983-87; researcher, coordinator Ill. State Psychiat. Inst., Chgo., 1983-84, research cons., 1984-85; clin. psychology intern VA Hosp., North Chgo., 1984-85; therapist, cons. Baum & Assocs., Elgin, Ill., 1985-87; sr. psychologist, assoc. dir. Dr. Robert R. Newsome Clinics, Palos Heights and Des Plaines, 1985—. Bd. dirs. alumni relations council Oakton Community Coll., Des Plaines, 1982-85. Mem. Am. Psychol. Assn. Home: 8421 N Oriole Niles IL 60648 Office: Dr Robert R Newsome Clinics 6600 College Dr Suite #1A Palos Heights IL 60463

ASA, ALICE EVELYN, real estate broker; b. Long Pine, Nebr., June 25, 1932; d. Shelley Theodore and Minnie Margueretta (West) Moore; m. Leland Forrest Asa, June 25, 1952; children—Sandra Jayne Asa Lundberg, Bert Forrest. B.A. in Edn., Northwestern Coll., Mpls., 1955, M.Ed., Macalester Coll., St. Paul, 1957; postgrad. U. Wyo.-Laramie, 1963-64. Cert. tchr., Nebr., Ill., B.C.; lic. real estate broker Calif., B.C. Tchr. rural sch., Bassett, Nebr., 1949-52; tchr. Bensenville Pub. Schs. (Ill.), 1956-57, Omaha Pub. Schs., 1957-60; instr. edn. Trinity Western Coll., Langley, B.C., Can., 1962-67, 69-72; saleswoman Block Bros. Realty, Langley, 1972-75; saleswomen, broker Sunset Co. Realtors, Santa Barbara, Calif., 1976-85; owner, broker ASA Realty, Santa Barbara, 1985—. Author: (geneology) The Moore and West Families, 1983. Charter mem. Westbrook Evangelical Free Ch., Omaha, 1957-63; guide Pioneer Girls Club Evangelical Free Ch., Kearney, Nebr., 1967-69. Recipient numerous awards. Mem. Santa Barbara County Bd. Realtors (chairperson 1978-79, recipient plaque for disting. service 1979, Howard Gates award 1981). Republican. Home and Office: 1460 Las Positas Pl Santa Barbara CA 93105

ASAI-SATO, CAROL YUKI, lawyer; b. Osaka, Japan, Oct. 22, 1951; came to U.S., 1953; d. Michael M. and Sumiko (Kamei) Asai; 1 child, Ryan Makoto Sato. BA cum laude, U. Hawaii, 1972; JD, Willamette Coll. Law, 1975. Bar: Hawaii 1975. Assoc. firm Ashford & Wriston, Honolulu, 1975-79; counsel Bank of New Eng., Boston, 1979-81; assoc. counsel Alexander & Baldwin, Honolulu, 1981-83, sr. counsel, 1984—; bd. dirs. Hawaii Mother's Milk, Inc.; mem. Med. Claims Conciliation Panel, 1983—. Willamette Coll. Law Bd. Trustees scholar, 1972-73. Mem. ABA, Hawaii Bar Assn., Hawaii Women Lawyers, Phi Beta Kappa, Phi Kappa Phi. Democrat. Office: Alexander & Baldwin Inc 822 Bishop St Honolulu HI 96813

ASATO, SUSAN PEARCE, corporate professional, educator; b. Dallas, Dec. 29, 1949; d. Joe Camp and Sue (Dickey) Pearce; m. Morris T. Asato, Apr. 1, 1973. Student, U. Internat., Saltillo, Mex., 1968; BE, U. Tex., 1973; MBA, Calif. State U., San Bernardino, 1981. Tchr. Austin (Tex.) Ind. Sch. Dist., 1972-73; research assoc. U. Tex., Austin, 1973-77; dir. Tairyu (Japan) English Ctr., 1977-78; agt. purchasing U. Calif., Riverside, 1978-83; gen. mgr. corp. purchasing ABC-TV, Hollywood, Calif., 1983—; instr., lectr. U. Calif., Riverside, 1981-83. mem. Nat. Assn. Purchasing Mgrs., Nat. Assn. Ednl. Buyers, Nat. Contract Mgmt. Assn., Purchasing Mgmt. Assn. Los Angeles, Calif. Assn. Pub. Purchasing Officials. Episcopalian. Office: ABC-TV 4151 Prospect Ave Hollywood CA 90027

ASBILL, PAULINE PORTER (MRS. DAVID ST. PIERRE ASBILL), office manager; b. Royston, Ga., Sept. 19, 1906; d. James Alexander and Ophelia Kathryn (Fowler) Porter; R.N., Med. Coll. S.C. Sch. Nursing, 1926; m. David St. Pierre Asbill, Feb. 9, 1928; 1 son, David St. Pierre. Nurse charge pediatrics dept. Roper Hosp., Charleston, S.C., 1926-28; nurse obstet. dept. N.Y. Polyclinic Med. Sch. and Hosp., N.Y.C., 1928-29; mgr. physician's office, Columbia, S.C., 1934—. State civil def. nurse Richland County Civil Def. Council, S.C., 1953—. Mem. Woman's Aux. Assn. Surgeons So. Ry. and Seaboard Air Line R.R. Systems; woman's aux. Columbia Med. Soc. (chmn. decorations 1948-55, v.p. 1942); S.C. Med. Assn. (charge decorations 1952-55). Mem. Columbia Art Assn. (art com. 1935-36), Delphian Soc., Internat. Platform Assn. Episcopalian. Clubs: Columbia Woman's (publicity chmn. 1940; decorations com. 1939), Forest Lake Country, Altrusa (Columbia). Home: 1551 Sam Rittenberg Blvd Apt 234 Charleston SC 29407 Office: 1417 Barnwell St Columbia SC 29201

ASBURY, ROBENA ISABEL, retired nurse; b. Kansas City, Kans., Aug. 16, 1928; d. Joseph William and Lucy Helen (Nason) Berg; m. Faye Smith, June 11, 1950; children—Joseph Ernest, Denise Earlene, Mark Edwin. Diploma Bethany Hosp., 1949; certs. U. Kans. Coll. Nursing, 1981, 84, Brigham Young U., 1982. Nurse, Cushing Hosp., Leavenworth, Kans., 1949; rehab. nurse Vets. Hosp., Wadsworth, Kans., 1950-52; relief nurse Bethany Hosp., Kansas City, Kans., 1953-54; staff nurse recovery room St. Margaret's Hosp., Kansas City, 1954-61; internist office nurse J. Warren Manley, M.D., Kansas City, 1961-69; occupational health nurse Fairbanks Morse Pump div. Colt Industries, Kansas City, 1969-85; dist. rep. Kans. State Nurses Assn., Topeka, 1966; nursing rep. Pres.'s Roundtable City Kansas City, Kans., 1961-62. Author: Orthopedic Nursing, 1950; relief nurse Mut. Benefit Life Ins. Co., Kansas City, Mo., 1988—. Coordinator, editor History Bethany Hospital School of Nursing, 1964. Leader, organizer Blue Birds, 1960-62; project leader 4-H Club; counselor Boy Scouts Am.; mem. missionary couple Australia Melbourne Mssion, 1985-87, Liberty Stake, 1987-88. Mem. Greater Kansas City Occupational Health Nurses Assn., Am. Assn. Occupational Health Nurses, Inc., Bethany Alumnae Assn. (pres. 1966-67). Republican. Mem. Ch. of Jesus Christ of Latter-day Saints.

ASCHER, AMALIE ADLER, author, journalist, columnist; b. Balt.; d. Charles and Alene (Steiger) Adler; B.A., Goucher Coll., 1949; m. Eduard Ascher, May 18, 1954; children—Kenneth Charles Weinberg, Cynthia Cecille. Garden columnist Balt. Sunday Sun, 1976—, feature writer, 1968—, contbr. Sunday Sun mag., 1968—; hostess, writer The Flower Show, Md. Center for Public Broadcasting, 1973—; lectr. numerous states and fgn. countries, 1965—; columnist Los Angeles Times-Washington Post Wire Service. Recipient Quill and Trowel award Garden Writers Assn. Am., 1980; Cert. of Merit for hort. lit. Nat. Council State Garden Clubs, Inc., 1975, named Flower Arranger of Year, 1973; Garden Writers award Bedding Plants, Inc., 1984. Mem. Garden Writers Assn. Am. (dir. 1975-76), Indoor Gardening Nat. Council State Garden Clubs, Inc. (dir., chmn. 1977-79), Authors Guild, Authors League, Am. Hort. Soc. Republican. Jewish. Author: The Complete Flower Arranger, 1974. Contbr. numerous articles to various mags. and newspapers. Home and Office: 610 W 40th St Baltimore MD 21211

ASCHER, GEORGIA B., real estate executive; b. N.Y.C., Oct. 10, 1948; d. Erwin George and Geneva Winona (Groth) A. AA, Madison (Wis.) Area Tech. Coll., 1968; cert., U. Wis., 1977. From payroll to accounts payable acct. C.A. Hooper Co., Madison, 1968-72; fashion, photo model Beautiful People, Madison, 1972-74; acct., property mgr. Am. United Inc./Richard Roberts Co., Madison, 1975-77; property mgr. Midwest Mgmt. Co., Madison, 1978-81; owner, mgr. Accredited Realty Mgmt., Madison, 1982-84; nat. property mgr. Verex Assurance Inc., Madison, 1985—. Author: Arm's Resident Information Handbook, 1984 (Gold award Inst. Real Estate Mgmt. 1985). Mem. Madison Area Tech. Coll. (adv. com. real estate 1984—, instr. 1984-87), Inst. Real Estate Mgmt. (chpt. sec.-treas. 1982-83, v.p. 1983-84, pres. 1984-85, instr. 1984—, governing council 1986—, nominee regional v.p. 1987, Most Improved Chpt of Yr. award 1984, Bronze award 1985, Silver award 1986), Greater Madison Bd. Realtors, Madison Area Tech. Coll. Alumni Assn. Republican. Lutheran. Office: Verex Assurance Inc 150 E Gilman St Madison WI 53703

ASCHER-NASH, FRANZI, writer; b. Vienna, Austria, Nov. 28, 1910; came to U.S., 1938, naturalized, 1944; d. Luise Frankl and Leo Ascher; grad. cum laude, Humanistisches Maedchengymnasium, Vienna, 1928; student Vienna Acad. Music, 1929-31; m. Edgar R. Nash, Nov. 21, 1960. Free-lance short story writer, Vienna, 1934-38; after arrival in U.S., lectr. women's clubs under auspices of N.Y. Herald Tribune; music reviewer Neue Volkszeitung weekly, N.Y.C.; monthly light essay Austro-Am. Tribune; writer radio playlets German-Am. Writers Assn.; host short German lang. radio programs Sta. WBNX; tchr. New Sch. Social Research, N.Y.C.: writer annotations for classical records; host radio program The Story of the Art Song, Sta. WFUV-FM; appearances on Spoken Words Program Sta. WNYC; lectr. on the art song; lectr. music CUNY, York (Pa.) Coll., others; contbr. essays and poems to German-Am. Studies mag., Lyrik und Prosa mag., Lyrica Germanica mag., Inspiré, Swiss mag., Schatzkammer; author: (novella) Das Zwoelftonwunder, 1952; (novella) Confession in the Twilight (1st prize The Villager mag.), 1948; (books) Bilderbuch aus der Fremde, 1948, Gedichte eines Lebens, 1976, others; also poetry anthologies pub. in U.S., India, Germany and Austria. Founder Leo Ascher Award program Millersville U. Recipient citation Soc. German-Am. Studies, 1973. Mem. Assn. German Lang. Authors in Am., Soc. German-Am. Studies, Literarische Union (W. Ger.), Tagore Inst. of Creative Writing (India). Club: B'nai B'rith. Home: 118 N George St Millersville PA 17551

ASCHOFF, LORRAINE MARIE, computer information scientist; b. N.Y.C., Feb. 14, 1950; d. Edward William and Marie Louise (Marshall) A.; m. John Morgan Roquemore III, Feb. 23, 1973 (div. June 1976). BA in Art History, U. Fla., 1971; MBA in Fin., NYU, 1984, advanced profl. cert. in cpouter applications and info. systems, 1988. Sales rep. VIP Fabrics, N.Y.C., 1978-81; asst. to v.p. mktg. RAM Data, N.Y.C., 1981-82; sales agt. Equitable Life Assurance Soc., N.Y.C., 1982; programmer/analyst Drexel Burnham Lambert, N.Y.C., 1984-86, sr. programmer/analyst, 1986—. Clin. assoc. Suicide and Crisis Prevention Ctr., Gainesville, Fla., 1972. Mem. Mensa, Phi Beta Kappa (sec. 1985-87, pres. 1987— L.I. Alumnae and Alumni), Alpha Lambda Delta. Democrat. Home: 95-24 115 St Richmond Hill NY 11419 Office: Drexel Burnham Lambert 25 Broadway New York NY 10004

ASH, MARY KAY WAGNER, cosmetics company executive; b. Hot Wells, Tex., May 12; d. Edward Alexander and Lula Vember (Hastings) Wagner; m. Melville Jerome Ash, Jan. 6, 1966 (dec.); children: Marylyn Theard, Ben Rogers, Richard Rogers. Student, U. Houston, 1942-43. Mgr. Stanley Home Products, Houston, 1939-52; nat. tng. dir. World Gift Co., Dallas, 1952-63; founder, chmn. May Kay Cosmetics, Inc., Dallas, 1963—; speaker to various orgns. Bd. dirs. Wadley Inst. Molecular Medicine; chmn. bldg. fund. Prestonwood Bapt. Ch., Dallas; hon. chmn. Tex. Breast Screening Project, Am. Cancer Soc. Mem. Bus. and Profl. Women's Club. Office: Mary Kay Cosmetics Inc 8787 Stemmons Freeway Dallas TX 75247

ASH, SHARON KAYE, real estate company executive; b. Altus, Ark., July 21, 1943; d. William Clyde and Odus Marie (Drew) Cline; m. J.W. Ash, June 1, 1966 (div. Oct. 1978); 1 child, Brian Edward. B.S., S.W. Mo. State U., 1985. Lic. real estate broker, Mo. Personal lines asst. Squibb Ins., Springfield, Mo., 1967-69; bookkeeper Hood-Rich, Architects and Engrs., Springfield, 1969—; owner Ash Computer Service, Springfield, 1985—; owner, broker Ash Real Estate, Springfield, 1985—. Mem. Mo. Assn. Realtors, Nat. Assn. Realtors, Springfield Area C. of C., Million Dollar Sales Club, Nat. Assn. Female Execs. Democrat. Episcopalian. Avocations: golf; boating; reading; collecting clowns; jogging. Home: 712 McCann Springfield MO 65804 Office: Ash Real Estate 1722W S Glenstone Springfield MO 65804

ASH, VIRGINIA MARIA, piano educator; b. Rigby, Idaho, Apr. 22, 1918; d. Hugh Hastings and LaVera Maria (Jensen) Judd; student Colo. Woman's Coll., Denver, 1936-37, Coll. So. Idaho, 1981-84; m. Henry Woodrow Ash, June 1, 1938; children—Anthony Woodrow, Fredric Judd, Rosalie Marie, David Charles. High sch. tchr., Moore, Idaho, 1946-47, Richfield, Idaho, 1947-49; newspaper reporter Buhl (Idaho) Herald, 1955-57, Citizen Record, Filer, Idaho, 1957-60; pvt. piano tchr., 1947-84. Candidate for Mayor of Buhl, 1979; bd. dirs. Twin Falls Community Concert Assn., 1962-72; precinct committeewoman Buhl Democratic Com.; mem. Buhl City Planning and Zoning Commn., 1985—; elder Presbyn. Ch.; mem. campaign Peace Acad. Recipient award Senator Len Jordan short story contest, 1960's. Mem. Idaho Writers League, Common Cause, LWV, ACLU, NAACP, Fellowship of Reconciliation. Lodge: Order Eastern Star (past matron). Author various articles, poetry. Address: 809 11th St Buhl ID 83316

ASHBAUGH, ANN MARIE, air force officer, nurse administrator; b. Wilkes-Barre, May 11, 1945; d. Valentine and Stella Theresa (Byczek) Kompinski; m. George Eric Ashbaugh, Nov. 9, 1972; children: Anita Louise, Aimee Susan. RN, Mercy Hosp., Wilkes Barre, Pa., 1967; BS, Wilkes Coll., 1972; diploma Air Command and Staff Coll., 1984. Commd. 2d lt. U.S. Army, 1968; commd. 1st. lt. USAF, 1972, advanced through grades to maj., 1984; dir. nursing Vista Grande Hosp., Perris, Calif., 1975, Extended Care Hosp., Riverside, Calif., 1976; staff nurse Jerry L. Pettis Meml. VA Med. Ctr., Loma Linda, Calif., 1978; officer-in-charge phys. exams 452d Air Refeuling Wing, March AFB, Calif., 1979; charge nurse USAF Hosp., Loring, Maine, 1979-84, asst. chief nurse, 1984-85; chief nurse USAF Air Transportable Hosp. 554th Med. Group, Nellis AFB, Nev., 1985—. Mem. So. Nev. Allied Arts Council. Mem. AAUW, Am. Nurses Assn. (cert., council nursing adminstrn. 1982—), Nev. Nurses Assn., Assn. Mil. Surgeons U.S., Nat. Assn. Female Execs., Am. Orgn. Nurse Execs., N.Am. Nursing Diagnosis Assn., Air Force Hist. Found., Polish Geneal. Soc., Polish Inst. Arts and Scis. Am., Wilkes Coll. Alumni. Avocations: genealogy, opera, needlepoint. Home: PSC Box 2364 APO New York NY 09179-5367 Office: SGN USAF Regional Hosp Lakenheath NV 89191

ASHBURN, SHIRLEY SMITH, nursing educator; b. Anderson, Ind., May 11, 1945; d. Ollie J. and Audrey Jeanette (Chandler) S.; 1 child. BSN, Ohio State U., 1967, MS, 1970. Instr., Ohio State U., Columbus, 1970-76; asst. prof. Capital U., Bexley, Ohio, 1976-80; inservice instr. Children's Hosp.-Orange County, Orange, Calif., 1980-82; prof. Cypress (Calif.) Coll., 1982—; cons. central lines Kaiser Permanente, So. Calif., 1983-86; growth and devel. cons. Columbus Tech. Inst., 1977-78. Author: The Process of Human Development, 1980, 2d edit., 1986. Leader, Brownie Scouts, Saddleback Valley, Calif., 1981-82; v.p. cheerleading Pop Warner Football, Saddleback Valley, 1984-86; advisor Red Cross Youth Council, Columbus, Ohio, 1976. Named Outstanding Tchr., Nursing Students at Ohio State U., Columbus, 1972-76. Mem. Am. Nurses Assn., Calif. Tchrs. Assn., Mortar Board, Sigma Theta Tau. Democrat. Office: Cypress Coll 9200 Valley View St Cypress CA 90630

ASHBY, NORMA RAE BEATTY, broadcaster; b. Helena, Mont., Dec. 27, 1935; d. Raymond Wesley Beatty and Ella Mae (Lamb) Beatty Watson Mehmke; m. Shirley Carter Ashby, Sept. 5, 1964; children—Ann, Tony. B.A., U. Mont.-Missoula, 1957. Reporter, Helena Ind. Record, 1953-56; picture dept. Life Mag., N.Y.C., 1957-58; picture researcher MD Med. Newsmag., N.Y.C., 1959-61; producer, hostess TV Show Today in Mont., Sta. KRTV, Great Falls, 1962-85; editor Noon News, Sta. KRTV, 1985—; producer Great Falls Centennial program, 1984. Author: What Is A Montanan?, 1971; Montana Woman, 1977; Montanans, 1982; scriptwriter: Last Chance Gulch, 1964, Gentle Giants, 1969, Our Latchstring is Out, 1979; Paris Gibson, 1983; Martha, Pioneer Woman, 1984. Co-chmn. Cascade County Bicentennial Com., Great Falls, 1974-76; founder, chmn. C.M. Russell Auction, Great Falls, 1979; bd. dirs. Mont. Physicians Service, Helena, 1980-87; co-chmn. Great Falls Centennial Com., 1982-84; chair Mont. Jefferson awards; pres. Cascade County Mental Health Assn., 1980-82; bd. dirs. Cascade County Hist. Soc., 1987—, Mental Health Assn. Mont., also editor. Recipient TV Program of Yr. award Greater Mont. Found. 1982-88; Communication and Leadership award Mont. Toastmasters Internat., 1983; Tribune Most Influential Woman in Great Falls, 1984; hon. mem. Blackfeet Tribe Blackfeet Reservation, Browning, Mont., 1981; named Mont. TV Broadcaster Yr., 1985. Mem. Women in Communications, Great Falls Advt. Fedn. (dir., Silver medal 1980), AWRT (founder, pres. Mt. Big Sky chpt. 1967, recipient cert. of commendation 1982). Club: PEO, Broadcast Pioneers. Office: KRTV PO Box 1331 Great Falls MT 59403

ASHBY, ROSEMARY GILLESPY, college president; b. Farnham, Surrey, Eng., May 16, 1940; came to U.S. 1967; d. Robert Dymock and Margaret Lois (Gillespy) Watson; m. John Hallam Ashby, June 17, 1967. B.A., U. Capetown, S. Africa, 1960; B.A., Cambridge U., 1963, M.A., 1967, M.Litt., 1972. Head resident Radcliffe Coll., Cambridge, Mass., 1968-70, asst. dir. career planning, 1969-70; dir. residence, instr. French Pine Manor Coll., Chestnut Hill, Mass., 1970-71, dean students, 1971-75, acting pres., 1975-76, pres., 1976—; pvt. tutor Sao Paulo, Brazil, 1963-65; teaching asst. U. Capetown, 1959-60; panelist N.E. Assn. Schs. and Colls., Boston, 1983, Nat. Assn. Ind. Schs., Boston, 1985. Author chpt. in book. Adv. bd. Keimei Fund for Internat. Edn., N.Y.C., 1978—. Nat. Endowment of Humanities fellow, 1984. Mem. Mass. Commn. on Post-secondary Edn., Assn. Am. Colls. (exec. com. 1977-78), Assn. Ind. Colls. and Univs. in Mass. (exec. com. 1977-80), Women's Coll. Coalition (exec. com. 1985—), Am. Inst. Fgn. Study (bd. acad. advisors 1986—). Home: 41 Crafts Rd Chestnut Hill MA 02167 Office: Pine Manor Coll 400 Heath St Chestnut Hill MA 02167

ASHDOWN, MARIE MATRANGA (MRS. CECIL SPANTON ASHDOWN, JR.), writer, lecturer; b. Mobile, Ala.; d. Dominic and Ave (MAllon) Matranga; m. Cecil Spanton Ashdown Jr., Feb. 8, 1958; children: Cecil Spanton III, Charles Coster; children by previous marriage: John Stephen Gartman, Vivian Marie Gartman. Student Maryville Coll. Sacred Heart, Springhill Coll.Feature artist, women's program dir. daily program Sta. WALA, also WALA-TV, Mobile, 1953-58; v.p., dir. Met. Opera Guild, N.Y.C., 1970-78; opera instr. in-service program Met. Opera Guild, N.Y.C., 1970-80, Marymont Coll., N.Y.C., 1979-85; exec. dir. Musicians Emergency Fund Inc., N.Y.C., 1985—; cons. No. Ill. U. Coll. of Visual and Performing Arts, 1985—; lectr. in field. Author: Opera Collectables, 1979, contbr. articles to profl. jours. Recipient Extraordinary Service award March of Dimes, 1958, Medal of Appreciation award Harvard Bus. Sch. Club N.Y.C., 1974, Cert. Appreciation, Kiwanis Internat., 1975, Arts Excellence award N.J. State Opera, 1986. Mem. Successful Meetings Directory, Nat. Inst. Social Scis., Com. for China Relations. Avocations: collecting art, antique ceramics and porcelains, bookbinding. Home: 25 Sutton Pl S New York NY 10022 Office: Musicians Emergency Fund Inc 16 E 64th St New York NY 10021

ASHE, CAROLYN HENLEY, business educator, management consultant, entrepreneur; b. Belton, Tex., Feb. 13, 1947; d. Adolphus Isaac and Alva Evelyn (Weaver) Henley; m. Roy L. Ashe, Feb. 11, 1975; 1 dau., Alva Madelaine. B.B.A., N. Tex. State U., 1969, M.B.A., 1971; Ed.D., U. Houston, 1983. Teaching fellow Sch. Bus. Adminstrn., N. Tex. State U., Denton, 1969-70; with bookkeeping dept. So. Union Gas Co., Galveston, Tex., 1970-72; fin. analyst comml. loan dept. U.S. Nat. Bank, Galveston, 1972-74; instr., mgmt. coordinator Galveston Coll., 1974-76; prof., coordinator mgmt. devel. dept. San Jacinto Coll., Pasadena, Tex., 1976-83; prof. Coll. Bus., Prairie View A&M U., Prairie View, Tex., 1983-84; pres. Love Arc, Inc. dba Happy Tots Day Care Ctr., 1984-85; sole proprietor Ashe & Assocs., Mgmt. Cons., 1983—; adjunct prof. U. Houston Downtown, 1985-88. Bd. dirs. Planned Parenthood of Houston and S.W. Tex.; budget rev. panel and allocations com. United Way. Mem. Nat. Assn. Female Execs., Nat. Bus. Edn. Assn., Delta Pi Epsilon, Delta Sigma Theta. Office: Ashe & Assocs 1300 Main St Suite 642 Houston TX 77002

ASHFORD, CAROLYN KAY, publishing executive; b. Kansas City, Mo., July 1, 1946; d. Milton Jennings and Virginia Caroline (Ford) Marquette; m. John Edward Ashford, Aug. 11, 1973 (div. Aug. 1983). BA in Polit. Sci., BJ, U. Mo., 1968, MA in Journalism, 1969. Dir. Mo. Dept. Natural Resoruces, Jefferson City, 1976-77; chief staff Gov. State Govt., Jefferson City, 1977-81; corp. dir. communications Payless Cashways, Kansas City, Mo., 1981-84; pub. Bus. First, Columbus, Ohio, 1984-1985; v.p. ops. Am. City Bus. Jours., Kansas City, 1985-87, exec. v.p., chief operating officer, 1987—. Democrat. Mem. Unity Sch. of Christianity. Home: 8329 Northern Blvd Kansas City MO 64138 Office: Am City Bus Jours 3535 Broadway Kansas City MO 64111

ASHFORD, JANET ISAACS, editor, writer; b. Los Angeles, Feb. 9, 1949; d. John P. and Alice (Munro) Isaacs; m. Victor A. Ashford; children: Rufus, Florence, Molly. BA, UCLA, 1974. Freelance writer 1979—; editor, pub. Childbirth Alternatives Quarterly, 1979—; lectr. in field. Author: The Whole Birth Catalog, 1983, (script/slide set) Sitting, Standing, Squatting, 1985, Mothers and Midwives: A History of Traditional Childbirth, 1988; editor Birth Stories, 1984. Co-founder L.I. Childbirth Alternatives; community video producer, 1987—. Mem. Internat. Childbirth Edn. Assn., Am. Soc. for Psychoprophylaxis in Obstetrics, Midwives Alliance of No. Am., Calif. Assn. Midwives, The Authors' Guild. Home: 327 Glenmont Dr Solana Beach CA 92075

ASHFORD, MARGUERITE KAMEHAOKALANI, librarian; b. Honolulu, Feb. 4, 1953; d. Clinton Rutledge and Joan Beverly (Schumm) A.; m. Ronald K. Hirano, Aug. 2, 1986. BA with honors, Stanford U., 1974; postgrad., U. Otago, Dunedin, New Zealand, 1975; MLS, U. Hawaii, 1976. Title searcher Title Guaranty of Hawaii, Honolulu, 1974-76; reference librarian Bernice P. Bishop Mus., Honolulu, 1976-83, assoc. librarian, 1983-87, head librarian, 1987—; cons. in field. Contbr. articles to profl. jours. Mem. Office of Hawaiian Affairs Culture and Edn. Com., Honolulu, 1984-86. Rotary Internat. fellow, 1974-75. Mem. Am. Library Assn., Am. Mus. Assn., Soc. of Am. Archivists, Hawaiian Hist. Soc., Hawaii Library Assn. (exec. bd. dirs. 1985-86, chair various coms.), Beta Phi Mu. Home: 44-509 Kaneohe Bay Dr Kaneohe HI 96744 Office: Bernice P Bishop Mus PO Box 19000-A Honolulu HI 96817

ASHINOFF, SUSAN JANE, menswear manufacturing company executive; b. N.Y.C., Dec. 7, 1949; d. Lawrence Lloyd and Thelma B. (Rubens) A.; m. Robert Beier Mintz, June 18, 1983; 1 child, Geoffrey Harrison. A.A., Dean Jr. Coll., 1969; B.A., Finch Coll., 1971; M.P.A., N.Y.U., 1977. Menswear advt. asst. New Yorker Mag., N.Y.C., 1971-72; assoc. Staub, Warmbold & Assocs., Inc., exec. search co., N.Y.C., 1972-80; exec. v.p. Muhammad Ali Sportswear, Ltd., N.Y.C., 1980-81; pres. Forum Sportswear, Ltd., N.Y.C. and Portsmouth, Va., 1981—; dir. Coronet Casuals, Inc. Trustee Dean Jr. Coll. Named to Outstanding Young Women Am., U.S. Jaycees, 1980. Mem. Nat. Assn. Men's Sportswear Buyers, Men's Apparel Guild Calif. Club: N.Y.U.

ASHKIN, ROBERTA ELLEN, lawyer; b. N.Y.C., July 1, 1953. BA magna cum laude, Hofstra U., 1975; JD, St. John's U., N.Y.C., 1978. Bar: N.Y., 1979, U.S. Dist. Ct. (ea. and so. dists.), 1980. Assoc. editor Matthew Bender, N.Y.C., 1975-79; assoc. Morris & Duffy, N.Y.C., 1979-81, Lipsig, Sullivan & Liapakis, N.Y.C., 1981-84, Julien & Schlesinger, P.C., N.Y.C., 1984—. Mem. N.Y. State Bar Assn., Assn. Trial Lawyers Am., N.Y. Trial Lawyers Assn., Phi Beta Kappa.

ASHKINAZE, CAROLE LYNNE, columnist, editorial writer, educator; b. N.Y.C., Jan. 20, 1945; d. Harry M. and Rose (Goldstein) A. French lang. cert., U. Rouen, Caen, France, 1964-65; A.B. with honors, St. Lawrence U., Canton, N.Y., 1966; M.S. in Journalism, Columbia U., 1967. Reporter Newsday, Garden City, N.Y., 1967-74; reporter Denver Post, 1974-75; producer Sta. WXIA-TV, Atlanta, 1975-76; columnist Atlanta Constn., 1976—, mem. editorial bd., 1982—; host weekly TV talk show, newspaper video edit; instr. Emory U., Atlanta, 1976—; radio commentator sta. WGST-Ga. Network, Atlanta, 1982-86; trustee St. Lawrence U., 1987—. Editor: Saturday Night, Sunday Morning: Singles & The Church, 1978. Atlanta chmn. Holiday Project, 1984-87, mem. nat. com. 1987—; mem. Mayor's Task Force on the Handicapped.; grad. Leadership Atlanta, 1983, Leadership Ga., 1986; trustee St. Lawrence U., 1987—; nat. mgr. corp. fundraising The Holiday Project, 1987—. Recipient George Polk Meml. award L.I. U., 1967; Pub. Service award N.Y. State Pubs. Assn., 1967, 70; Pulitzer prize, 1970; Media award for Econ. Understanding, Amos Tuck Sch. Bus. Adminstrn., Dartmouth Coll., 1979; first place for best editorial Ga. Press Assn., 1984; named Woman of Yr. Ga. Women's Polit. Caucus, 1983; St. Lawrence U. Alumni Citation, 1987. Mem. Soc. Profl. Journalists (dir. 1976-84, v.p. 1983-84, chmn. 1st Amendment Congress 1980, chmn. profl. devel. 1983; recipient 1st place award in criticism 1976), Columbia Journalism Alumni Assn. (regional v.p. 1985—), Nat. Kidney Found. Ga. (bd. dirs. 1985-86 , v.p. 1986). Jewish. Club: Sporting (Atlanta). Office: Atlanta Constn 72 Marietta St Atlanta GA 30303

ASHLEY, ANN KNIGHT, wine company administrator; b. Asheville, N.C., Oct. 31, 1953; d. Edward Hines and Ruby Francis (Jones) Knight; m. Monroe Maston Ashley, Jr., Oct. 18, 1961. BFA in Art Edn., U. N.C., Greensboro, 1975. Head cultural arts dept., instr. Charles D. Owen Sr. High Sch., Buncombe County Schs., Swannanca, N.C., 1976-79; regional trainer Steak & Ale Corp., Dallas, 1980-83; mgr. Biltmore Estate Wine Co., Asheville, 1984—; cons. Traveler's Mgmt. Corp., Winston-Salem, N.C. Author: Stokes County Art Curriculum, 1975; tng. manuals. Mem. bd. adjustments town council, Montreat, N.C., 1987. Mem. Nat. Restaurant Assn., Wine Educators Soc., Nat. Assn. for Female Execs. Presbyterian. Lodges: Zonta (charter mem. Asheville chpt.), Rotary. Office: Biltmore Wine Co Biltmore Estate Asheville NC 28757

ASHLEY, ELIZABETH, librarian; b. Waycross, Ga., July 8, 1943; d. James Bryant and Henrietta (Hargreaves) Lewis; m. Rhett Ashley, Sept. 9, 1973 (div. July 1977); m. Stefan Mellin, June 21, 1978 (div. Feb. 1986). AA Stephens Coll., 1963; BA, U. Fla., 1965; MS, Fla. State U., 1969; MA, Ariz. State U., 1975. Cataloging librarian Columbia U., N.Y.C., 1967; circulation librarian Fla. State U., Tallahassee, 1968-69; acquisitions librarian Ariz. State U., Tempe, 1969-76, No. Ariz. U., Flagstaff, 1977-78; approval librarian Baker & Taylor Co., Somerville, N.J., 1979-80; dir. tech. services Golden Gate Sem., Mill Valley, Calif., 1981-87; dir. tech. services Windward Community Coll., Kaneohe, Hawaii, 1988—. Author: A Midsummer Madness, 1979, Abraham Steele, 1981, The Skull, 1982. Founder, exec. dir. Friends of Trees Soc., 1983—. Mem. ALA, Calif. Library Assn., Am. Theol. Library Assn., Phi Theta Kappa, Phi Kappa Phi, Beta Phi Mu. Presbyterian. Office: Windward Community Coll 45-720 Keaahala Rd Kaneohe HI 96744

ASHLEY, KATHY LITTLEFIELD, county official; b. Woodruff, S.C., Apr. 10, 1945; d. William Edwin and Elsie Dorothy (Campbell) Littlefield; m. William Lowry Ashley, July 25, 1981. BS, Lander Coll., 1967; MS, Winthrop Coll., 1982. Extension home economist Clemson U. Extension, Aiken, S.C., 1967-73; county extension agt. Clemson U. Extension, Spartanburg, S.C., 1974-76, Abbeville, S.C., 1976—; asst. dir., dir. food services Wofford Coll., Spartanburg, 1973-74; cons. George W. Park Seed Co., Greenwood, S.C., 1986—. Author: (slide set) Country Decorating for City Living, 1986 (Nat. Assn. Extension Home Economists award 1986). Named Outstanding Eggucator S.C. Egg Bd., 1986, 87. Mem. Smocking Arts Guild of Am., Am. Home Econs. Assn. (cert.), S.C. Home Econs. Assn. (Best of Show award 1987), S.C. Assn. Extension Home Economists (sec. 1984-86, 1st v.p. 1986—, Outstanding Home Economist award 1977, Comml. awards 1984-86), Nat. Assn. Extension Home Economists (Disting. Service award), Epsilon Sigma Phi. Presbyterian. Home: Rt 2 Box 85 Honea Path SC 29654 Office: Clemson U Extension PO Box 640 Abbeville SC 29620

ASHLEY, LORI JEAN, financial planner; b. Port Huron, Mich., Dec. 28, 1960; d. Don Ralph and Barbara Jean (Heston) A. A in Bus. Adminstrn., St. Clair County Community Coll., 1981; BS in Mgmt., Oakland U., 1983. With sales staff Met. Ins. Co., Bloomfield Hills, Mich., 1983-84; cert. fin. planner Provident Mut. Co., Bloomfield Hills, 1984—; pres. bd. dirs. Diversified Fin. Concepts, Bloomfield Hills. Mem. Inst. Cert. Fin. Planners, Nat. Assn. Life Underwriters (Nat. Quality award 1986), Nat. Assn. Female Execs. Republican. Methodist. Office: Provident Mut 1471 S Woodward Ave Suite 270 Bloomfield Hills MI 48013

ASHLEY, MERRILL, ballerina; b. St. Paul; m. Kibbe Fitzpatrick. Student, Sch. Am. Ballet. Joined N.Y.C. Ballet, 1967, prin. dancer, 1977—. Prin. roles in: Balanchine's Ballo della Regina and Ballade, Jerome Robbins' Four Chamber Works, Robbins'/Tharp's Brahms/Handel Author: Dancing for Balanchine, 1984. Recipient Dance Mag. award, 1987. Address: care NYC Ballet Lincoln Ctr Plaza New York NY 10023

ASHLING, PAMELA, marketing executive; b. Faribault, Minn., July 31, 1950; d. Frederick Dexter and Marian Katherine (Krenske) Orne; m. Lloyd William Ashling, Nov. 4, 1977; children: Ryan Lloyd, Granville Peterson. Asst. office mgr. Southdale Ford, Mpls., 1972-79; service writer Bloomington (Minn.) Honda, 1979-81; claims adjuster American Warranty Corp., Edina, Minn., 1981-83; mktg. rep. Solitaire, Bloomington, 1983-86; exec. v.p. mktg. Chase Bernard Fin. Service, Bloomington, 1987—. Mem St. Patrick's Ch. Altar Guild, Bloomington, 1982-86, long-range planning com., 1984. Episcopalian. Home: 2255 Overlook Circle Bloomington MN 55431

ASHMORE, CARRIE MAE, educator; b. Springfield, Tenn., Mar. 5, 1923; d. James Dean and Vera Louvenia (Osborne) Barbee; student Tenn. State U., 1941-43; B.S., Wilberforce U., 1946; postgrad. Atlanta U., 1957-60, Chgo. State U., 1965, 70, 71, Roosevelt U., 1967, 68, 73; m. Edward Travis Ashmore, July 23, 1945; children—Travis Dean and Edward Lane (twins), Juanita Sherri, Angela Jean and Angelo Gene (twins), Andre Bernard. Tchr., Bransford High Sch., Springfield, Tenn., 1946-48; sec. Murrays Superior Products, Chgo., 1948-49; adminstrv. asst. Atlanta U., 1949-60; tchr. Atlanta Public Schs., 1960-62, Gary (Ind.) Public Schs., 1962-64, Wendell Phillips High Sch., Chgo., 1964-68; tchr. Hyde Park Career Acad., Chgo., 1969—; mem. tchr. corps project of Hyde Park Career Acad. and Roosevelt U. Recipient Am. Legion medal, 1941. Mem. Chgo. Assn. of Mentally Retarded, Lambda Eta Sigma, Zeta Sigma Pi. Methodist. Home: 422 W 98th St Chicago IL 60628 Office: 6220 S Stony Island Ave Chicago IL 60637

ASHMORE, KARLA LYNN, computer training coordinator; b. West Point, N.Y., Nov. 3, 1956; d. Fred D. and Margaret Erika (Buckmann) Spinks; m. David Jefferson Ashmore, Feb. 19, 1977 (div. Dec. 17, 1979); 1 child, Erika Margaret Augusta. BA, Ind. U.-Purdue U. at Indpls., 1982; MS, Ind. U., 1986. Mgr. Eastside Chiropractic Clinic, Indpls., 1978-80; English tutor univ. div. Ind. U.-Purdue U. at Indpls., 1980-82, composition instr. English dept., 1982-83, tech. writer computing services, 1983-84; tech. writer Ind. U. Adminstrv. Computing, 1984-87; computer tng. coordinator Melvin Simon and Assocs., Inc., Indpls., 1987—. Author 4 articles, 5 book revs. and 20 pub. poems; editor: Literary Jour., Genesis, All-Am. Mag., Am. Collegiate Press Assn., 1983. Mem. Indpls. Nuclear Weapons Freeze, Inc. Mem. Soc. Tech. Communication (Cert. of Achievement 1985), Soc. Profl. Journalists, Writer's Ctr. of Indpls., Ind. U. Alumni Assn., Sigma Delta Chi, Pi Lambda Theta. Democrat. Unitarian. Office: Melvin Simon & Assocs Inc 2 West Washington Indianapolis IN 46207

ASHTON, BETSY FINLEY, broadcast journalist, author, lecturer; b. Wilkes-Barre, Pa., May 13, 1944; d. Charles Leonard Hancock Jones and Margaretta Betty (Hart) Jones Layton; m. Arthur Benner Ashton, Nov. 5, 1966 (div. 1972); m. Robert Clarke Freed, May 18, 1974 (div. 1981); m. Jacob B. Underhill III, Oct. 17, 1987. BA, Am. U., 1966, postgrad. in fine arts, 1969-71; student in painting Corcoran Sch. Art, 1968. Tchr. art Fairfax County (Va.) Pub. Schs., 1967-70; reporter, anchor Sta. WWDC, Washington, 1972-73, Sta. WMAL-AM-FM, Washington, 1973-75; corr. Sta. WTTG-TV, Washington, 1975-76, Sta. WJLA-TV, Washington, 1976-82; consumer corr. CBS News and Sta. WCBS-TV, N.Y.C., 1982-86; sr. corr. Today's Bus., 1986-87; personal fin. contbr. CBS Morning Program, 1987, Lifetime Cable TV, 1988—; bd. dirs. Lowell E. Mellett Fund for a Free and Responsible Press, Washington, 1979-82; courtroom artist numerous trials, Washington, 1978-81. Reporter TV news report Caffeine, 1981 (AAUW award 1982); reporter spot news 6 P.M. News, 1979 (Emmy award); author: Betsy Ashton's Guide to Living on Your Own, 1988. Concert master of ceremonics Beethoven Soc., Washington, 1979-82. Recipient Laurel award Columbia Journalism Rev., 1984, Outstanding Alumna award Am. U., 1985, Outstanding Media award Am. U., 1986, Best Consumer Journalism citation Nat. Press Club, 1983. Mem. Sigma Delta Chi (pres. Washington chpt. 1980-81), Alpha Chi Omega (v.p. chpt. 1964-66). Methodist. Club: The Liberty (N.Y.C.). Avocations: painting, drawing, skiing, golf.

ASHTON, DORE, author, educator; b. Newark; d. Ralph N. and Sylvia (Ashton) Shapiro; m. Adja Yunkers, July 8, 1952 (dec. 1983); children—Alexandra Louise, Marina Svietlana; m. Matti Megged, 1985. B.A., U. Wis., 1949; M.A., Harvard, 1950; Ph.D. honoris causa, Moore Coll., 1975, Hamline U., 1982. Asso. editor Art Digest, 1951-54; asso. critic N.Y. Times, 1955-60; lectr. Pratt Inst., 1962-63; head humanities dept. (Sch. Visual Arts), 1965-68; prof. Cooper Union, 1968—; art critic, lectr., dir. exhbns. Bd. dirs. Found. for Edn. in Arts; adv. bd. John Simon Guggenheim Found., Smithsonian Instn.; mem. exec. bd. of P.E.N. Author: Abstract Art Before Columbus, 1957, Poets and the Past, 1959, Philip Guston, 1960, The Unknown Shore, 1962, Rauschenberg's Dante, 1964, Modern American Sculpture, 1968, Richard Lindner, 1969, A Reading of Modern Art, 1970, Pol Bury, 1971; Cultural Guide for New York, 1972; Picasso on Art, 1972, The New York School: A Cultural Reckoning, 1973, A Joseph Cornell Album, 1974, Yes, But, A Critical Biography of Philip Guston, 1976, A Fable of Modern Art, 1980, American Art Since 1945, 1982, About Rothko, 1983, Jacobo Borges, 1984, 20th Century Artists on Art, 1985, Out of the Whirlwind, 1987, Fragonard in the Universe of Painting, 1988; co-author: (with Denise Browne Hare) Rosa Bonheur, A Life and Legend, 1981; co-editor: Redon, Moreau, Bresdin, 1961; N.Y. contbg. editor Studio Internat, 1961-74, Opus Internat, 1968-74, XXième Siècle, 1955-70; assoc. editor Arts, 1974—; Contbr. to: Vision and Value series (Gyorgy Kepes), 1966, The New Art Anthology (Gregory Battcock), 1966. Adv. bd. Swann Found., Guggenheim Found., PEN. Recipient Mather award for art criticism Coll. Art Assn., 1963; Guggenheim fellow, 1964; Graham fellow, 1963; Ford Found. fellow, 1960; Nat. Endowment for Humanities grantee, 1980. Mem. Internat. Assn. Art Critics, Coll. Art Assn., Phi Beta Kappa. Home: 217 E 11th St New York NY 10003

ASHTON, SISTER MARY MADONNA, state health commissioner; b. St. Paul; d. Avon B. and Ruth (Fehring) A. B.A., St. Catherine's Coll., St. Paul, 1944; M.S., St. Louis U., 1946; M.H.A., U. Minn., 1958. Mem. Congregation of Sisters St. Joseph of Carondelet; dir. med. social service dept. St. Joseph's Hosp., St. Paul, 1949-56; dir. out-patient dept. St. Mary's Hosp., Mpls., 1958-59; asst. adminstr. St. Mary's Hosp., 1959-62, adminstr., 1962-68, exec. v.p., 1968-72, pres., 1972-82; commr. health State of Minn., 1983—; dir. Nat. City Bank, Mpls., St. Catherine's Coll., St. Paul; Bush summer fellow Harvard Sch. Bus., 1976. Recipient Sabra Hamilton award Program in Hosp. Adminstrn. U. Minn., 1958; Minn. Health Citizen of Yr. award, 1977, Gaylord Anderson Leadership award, 1988. Fellow Am. Coll. Healthcare Execs.; mem. Nat. Catholic Health Assn. (sec.), Assn. State Territorial Health Officers (sec.-treas.). Home: 5101 W 70th St #120 Minneapolis MN 55435 Office: Dept Health State of Minn 717 SE Delaware St Minneapolis MN 55440

ASHTON, NANCY LYNN, psychology educator; b. New Brunswick, N.J., Apr. 20, 1950; d. Louise Kenyon Wickware; 1 child, Hilarie Chanda. BA, Smith Coll., 1972; MA, U. Fla., 1974, PhD, 1976. Asst. prof. psychology Kearney (Neb.) State Coll., 1976-77; asst. prof. psychology Stockton State Coll., Pomona, N.J., 1977-82, assoc. prof., 1982—, coordinator psychology program, 1987—; chmn. proposal rev. com., mem. exec. com. Atlantic County (N.J.) Human Services Adv. Council, 1987—. Contbr. articles to profl. jours., chpts. to books. Mem. Nat. Women's Polit. Caucus, Washington, 1980—. Sloan fellow, 1971; research and profl. devel. grants Stockton State Coll., 1979, 81, 83, 88. Mem. Am. Psychol. Assn., Nat. Women's Studies Assn., Ea. Psychol. Assn., Soc. Advancement Social Psychology, NOW (treas. Atlantic County chpt. 1986-88), Sigma Xi, Psi Chi. Club: Alliance (founder 1982), (Atlantic County). Office: Stockton State Coll Jim Leeds Rd Pomona NJ 08240

ASHTON, PATRICIA LEE, business consultant; b. Santa Monica, Calif., Oct. 1, 1945; d. Newton Curtis Ashton and Betty (White) Shorter; m. Larry A. Austin (div. Sept. 1972); m. L. Ray Polvadore (div. Dec. 1981). BA, Hastings Coll., 1967; postgrad., U. S.C., 1970. Tchr. Dewitt (Mich.) High Sch., 1967-68, Anderson County Schs., Norris, Tenn., 1968-71; TV program dir., program host Santa Fe Cablevision, 1972-73; asst. cashier, head teller Bank of Santa Fe, 1974-79; office mgr. Drs. Landmann and Greenfield, Santa Fe, 1981-83; pres., chief exec. officer Cyrano's, Inc., Santa Fe; free-lance writer, Santa Fe, 1979—; dir. devel. The Life Link, 1988—. Actor, vol. Santa Fe Community Theatre, 1982—; actor , bd. dirs. West End Prodns., Santa Fe, 1983—; spl. coordinator United Way of Santa Fe County, 1987. Mem. Santa Fe C. of C. (fine arts task force 1983-84). Republican. Presbyterian. Club: Santa Fe Country (bd. dirs. 1980-81). Office: Cyrano's Inc 236 Montezuma St Santa Fe NM 87501

ASHWORTH, ELINOR GENE, financial analyst; b. Phoenix, Dec. 12, 1942; d. Arvid Wick and Erma Gene (Grant) Cooper; m. Monroe Alfred Ashworth III, Aug. 1, 1964 (div. Aug. 1977); children: Leslie, Monroe. AA, Del Mar Coll., 1963; BA, U. Houston, 1978, MBA, 1980. Adminstrv. asst. audit dept. Houston Nat. Bank (now Rep. Bank of Houston), 1976-78; analyst, portfolio mgr. Investment Advisors, Inc., Houston, 1978-87, exec. v.p., 1980—, dir. research, 1988—, also bd. dirs. Trustee Sch. Woods., Houston, 1974-77; pres., bd. dirs. New Neighbors League, Houston, 1968-73; mem. Mus. Fine Arts, Houston, 1987—. Fellow Fin. Analyst Fedn. (chartered); mem. Houston Soc. Fin. Analysts (treas. 1986—, v.p. 1987, pres. 1988), Investment Counsel Assn. Am. Republican. Methodist. Office: Investment Advisors Inc 1100 Louisiana Suite 2600 Houston TX 77002

ASHWORTH, KATHRYN FORSYTH, lawyer; b. Seattle, Nov. 19, 1941; d. Albert John Chisholm and Mary Catherine (Fickes) Forsyth; m. Thomas Ashworth III, Aug. 31, 1963; children—Sara Elizabeth, James Chisholm, Michael Stephen. B.A., Mills Coll., 1963; J.D., U. San Diego, 1981. Bar: Calif. 1981. Ptnr. Shea & Ashworth, San Diego, 1982—. Bd. dirs. Voices for Children, 1982—, pres., 1982-84; mem. foster care policy bd. Calif. Children's Lobby, 1980—; mem. San Diego County Delinquency Prevention Commn., 1980-87. Mem. ABA, Calif. Bar Assn., San Diego County Bar Assn. (chmn. law week 1984, state bar meeting 1985), Lawyers Club San Diego, San Diego Bar Assn. Aux. (dir. 1968-74, 83-84). Republican. Roman Catholic. Club: Jr. League San Diego (dir. 1974-78, 80-81, mem. area VI council 1978-79). Office: Shea & Ashworth 1855 1st Ave San Diego CA 92101

ASIYO, JUNI AWITI, software engineer; b. Nairobi, Kenya, June 8, 1958; came to U.S. in 1978; d. B. Richard and Phoebe Muga (Omer) A. BS, BA, E. Stroudsburg (Pa.) U., 1981; MS, Pa. State U., 1984. Engr. Telex Corp., Raleigh, N.C., 1984—. Mem. Nat. Assn. Exec. Women. Democrat. Home: Tower Box 16012 Raleigh NC 27610

ASKINS, NANCY PAULSEN, hospital training administrator; b. St. Paul, Nov. 2, 1948; d. Charles A. and Stasia (Sawicki) Paulsen; m. Arthur J. Askins, Apr. 28, 1979. B.S.H.Ec., U. Cin., 1970; B.S.Ed., 1971, M.Ed., 1972; postgrad. SUNY-Buffalo, 1974-76, Temple U., 1976; student C.L.U. program, 1979-81, Inst. Fin. Edn., 1982-85; cert. in mgmt. Am. Mgmt. Assn./Monmouth Coll., 1984. Asst. aquatic supr. Cin. Recreation Commn., 1969-72; student affairs adminstr., mem. faculty U. Cin., 1970-72, Tex. Luth. Coll., 1972-73, SUNY-Geneseo, 1974-76, Temple U., 1976-78; tchr. drug awareness coordinator Harlandale Schs., San Antonio, 1973-74; career life ins. agt., fin. planning cons. Phoenix Mut. Life Ins. Co., Phila., 1978-81; registered rep., securities agt. Phoenix Equity Planning Corp., Phila., 1980-81; owner Paulsen-Askins Fin. Services, Somers Point, N.J., 1980-81; mem. women's task force Phoenix Cos., 1980-81; tng. services coordinator Collective Fed. Savs. & Loan Assn., Egg Harbor City, N.J., 1981-82, asst. v.p., tng. dir., 1982-84; tng. mgr. Shore Meml. Hosp., 1984-86, dir. edml. devel., 1986—, adj. prof. Atlantic Community Coll, Mays Landing, N.J., 1986—; owner Nancy's Exquisite Creations, Somers Point, N.J., 1987—; also part-time instr. wellness program; facilitator Assertiveness Tng. Group, Interpersonal Communications Group; owner, cons. Nancy P. Askins, MEd; instr. Inst. Fin. Edn., 1982-85; adj. prof. bus. and social scis. Atlantic Community Coll., Mays Landing, N.J., 1986—; owner Nancy's Exquisite Creations, Somers Point, N.J., 1987—. Agy. chmn. United Way Campaign, Phila., 1979, 80; bd. dirs. South Jersey Regional Theater, 1983-86, chmn., 1983-84; active ann. Muscular Dystrophy Telethon, Phila.; active Girl Scouts U.S.A., 1956-74, 84—; mem. Parish council, parish enrichment com., 1984—, cantor St. Joseph Roman Cath. Ch., Somers Point, N.J., 1979—; bd. dirs. Holly Shores Council Girl Scouts U.S.A., 1984-85; host fgn. exchange students Am. Scandinavian Student Exchange Program, 1985—; mem. Somers Point Bd. Edn., 1986. Recipient Brotherhood-Sisterhood Achievers award NCCJ, 1985. Mem. Greater Camden Assn. Life Underwriters (chmn. Life Ins. Week for South Jersey 1978-79, dir. 1979-81, pub. relations chmn. 1979-81, chmn. state edn. 1981), Am. Soc. Tng. and Devel. (treas. S. Jersey chpt. 1983—, nat. dir. hosps. and healthcare industry group 1984-86, nat. conf. speaker 1984—), AAUW, Am. Hosp. Assn., Am Soc. Health Edn. and Tng., Greater Mainland C. of C. (v.p., treas., membership coordinator 1979—, recipient 1983 Pres. award), U. Cin. Alumni of Greater Phila. Area (pres. 1980—), Club: Alliance/The Women's Network (dir. 1983-84). Democrat. Home: PO

Box 398 Somers Point NJ 08244-0398 Office: Shore Meml Hosp New York Ave and Shore Rd Somers Point NJ 08244-2389

ASLANI, CAROLE SUE, public policy educator, training company executive; b. Big Rapids, Mich., Oct. 22, 1943; d. Dwaine Charles and Eula Ferne (Crysler) Voss; m. Iraj Aslani, Mar. 20, 1981. B.S., Mich. State U., 1965; M.P.A., Western Mich. U., 1984. Tchr., Marysville Pub. Schs. (Mich.), 1965-67; social worker Berrien County Dept. Social Services, Benton Harbor, Mich., 1967-72, casework supr., 1972-76; pub. policy educator Mich. Dept. Social Services, Lansing, Mich., 1976—; owner Human Resource Devel. Tng. Co. Home Extension Service scholar, 1961. Mem. Mid-Mich. Landlords Assn., Am. Soc. Tng. and Devel., Am. Pub. Welfare Assn. Methodist. Home: 315 Richard Ave Lansing MI 48917

ASLANIAN, SHARON C., employment service company executive; b. Cortland, N.Y., Mar. 8, 1943; d. John E. and Helen (Ambrose) Morgia; m. Paul Scire (div. 1983); m. Paul Aslanian, Apr., 13, 1985; children: Carmen Alberts, Rudolf Giessen. Grad. high sch., Cortland. Area mgr. AAA Employment Service, Coral Springs, Fla., 1973-83; pres., owner Ameribiz Employment Co., Bedford, N.H., 1983—. Mem. The Bus. Group, Nashua C. of C., Manchester C. of C. Office: Ameribiz Inc 167 S River Rd Bedford NH 03102

ASMUSSEN-SPOFFORD, GAYLE MARIE, accountant; b. Jamaica Plain, Mass., June 16, 1948; d. Fredrick Augustos and Gertrude May (Thompson) Asmussen; m. William J. Mackilligan, Aug. 14, 1970 (div. Mar. 1986); children: Kellsy Amanda, Courtney Alicia; m. David Hugh Spofford, May 17, 1986. BS, U. Maine, 1977. Sales clk. Foxmoor Casuals, Portland, Maine, 1971-72; supr. sales Casual Corner, Portland, 1972-73; pvt. practice acctg. Ogunquit, Maine, 1979-81; ptnr. Boone Assocs., Wells, Maine, 1981—; tchr. acctg. Wells-Ogunquit Adult Edn., Wells, 1986—. Chmn. Wells Capitol Improvements Com., 1985—; mem. sch. improvement com. Wells-Ogunquit Sch. Dist., 1986. Mem. Nat. Assn. Accts., Wells C. of C. Office: Boone Assocs RR 1 Box 270-1 Wells ME 04090

ASSELIN, MAXINE MARIE, educator; b. Little Falls, N.Y., Apr. 28, 1938; d. Norman Alfred and Lydia Helen (Senft) A. B in Music, Eastman Sch. Music, 1960; M in Music, Manhattan Sch. Music, 1962; PhD, U. Conn., 1972. Profl. vocal soloist and chorister Bach Aria Soc., Schola Cantorum, Fifth Ave. Presbyn. Ch., N.Y.C., 1960-65; prof. music Bridgewater (Mass.) State Coll., 1973—; dir. Jubilate Chorale, Inc., Brockton, 1982—, Phoenix Choir, Inc., Bridgewater, 1982-85. Mem. Music Educators Nat. Conf. (Mass. exec. bd. dirs. 1985-87), Am. Choral Dirs. Assn. (pres. Mass. state 1983-85, eastern div. pres. elect 1986-88, pres. 1988-90). Home: 3 Holly Rd Taunton MA 02780 Office: Bridgewater State Coll Bridgewater MA 02324

ASSELTA, CAROLYN ANN, human resource director; b. Phila., Sept. 7, 1945; d. Frank and Caroline (Rotondo) Gallo; m. Thomas N. Asselta, Dec. 25, 1938; chilren: Thomas K., Kevin G. AA, Pierce Jr. Coll., 1972; BA, Glassboro State Coll., 1977; MS, Rutgers U., 1987. Data processer Kerr Glass, Millville, N.J., 1964-72; mgr. human resources Clevepak Corp., White Plains, N.Y., 1972-84, Wheaton Glass Co., Millville, 1984-87; corp. dir. human resources Wheaton Industries, Millville, 1987-88, Lenox China, Pomona, N.J., 1988—; adj. faculty Glassboro State Coll., 1978-83, Cumberland County Coll., Vineland, 1980-81. Mem. Mgmt. Inst. (bd. dirs. 1976—, Leadership award 1980), Personnel Mgmt. Assocs. (pres. 1978-80, chair employer legisl. com. 1980-82), Am. Soc. Personnel Adminstrn., Internat. Mgmt. Council (sec. 1987—), Am. Soc. Tng. and Devel. Home: Box 165A Catawba Ave Newfield NJ 08344 Office: Wheaton Glass Cos 220 G St Millville NJ 08344

ASTARITA, SUSAN GALLAGHER, communications company executive; b. Wilmington, Del., Oct. 6, 1941; d. Hugh Francis and Alice Clara (Pepper) Gallagher; AB in Polit Sci., Randolph-Macon Woman's Coll., 1963; MA in Comparative Govt., Georgetown U., 1973; postgrad. U. So. Calif., 1973-75; m. Bruce Thomas Astarita, May 24, 1969; 1 child, Alice Catherine. Adminstrv. asst. George Washington U., Washington, 1964, Ford Found., Nat. Assn. Edn. Broadcasters, Washington, 1965-66; asst. producer Youth Wants To Know, Theodore Granik Enterprises, Washington, 1966-68; community and public relations dir. Del. Tech. and Community Coll., Georgetown, 1968-72; writer-editor Inst. Indsl. Relations, UCLA, 1975-77; prin. Astarita Communications, Rolling Hills Estates, Calif., 1977—; lectr. Harbor Coll. Bd. dirs. The Assocs. (Palos Verdes Community Arts Assn.), 1977-79, Palos Verdes Symphony, 1978-79; mem. peninsula com. Calif. State U., Dominguez Hills; mem. Palos Verdes Transit Adv. Com. Mem. Women in Communications (dir. Los Angeles chpt. 1980-83), Torrance C. of C., Community Assn. of Peninsula (multi-cultural affairs com.). Democrat. Episcopalian. Office: 777 Silver Spur Rd Suite 233 Rolling Hills Estates CA 90274

ASWAD, BETSY (BECKER), writer, educator; b. Binghamton, N.Y., Feb. 10, 1939; d. George Marrinan and Jane (Sprout) Becker, B.A. with high honors in English, Harpur Coll., Binghamton, 1961; M.A., SUNY, Binghamton, 1965, Ph.D. with distinction, 1973; m. Richard N. Aswad, Sept. 22, 1962; children—Jem, Kristin. Mem. film editing staff Sta. WNBF-TV, Binghamton, 1957; apprentice So. Tier Playhouse, summers 1957, 58; asst. editor Link Log, 1962-63; teaching asst., then instr. English, SUNY, Binghamton, 1963-74, mem. adj. faculty, 1974-83, fellow Coll.-in-the Woods, 1973. Sec., Friends of Binghamton Public Library, 1977-78; co-program chmn. Tappan Circle, First Presbyn. Ch., Binghamton, 1979-80; vol. Probe, Binghamton Gen. Hosp., 1978-79, Meals on Wheels, 1979-82, St. Mary's Soup Kitchen, 1983—, Binghamton Downtown Forum, 1986—. Author: Winds of the Old Days (Edgar Allan Poe spl. award Mystery Writers Am.), 1980, paperback edit., 1983; Family Passions, 1985. Home: 192 Deyo Hill Rd Binghamton NY 13905

ATALAY, ANDREA SWERLING, software consulting manager; b. Lorain, Ohio, May 20, 1956; d. Richard Henry and Renee (Newman) Swerling; m. Carlos Tomas Atalay, Oct. 9, 1983; stepchildren—Estela, Carlos I. B.A., Notre Dame Coll., Cleve., 1981. Data processing cons., Cleve., 1973-80; fin. control mgr. Gould, Inc., Cleve., 1980-82; cons. mgr. Deltak, Inc., Pitts., 1982; br. mgr. Info. Builders, Inc., Chgo., 1983-87; area mgr. On-Line Software Internat., Inc., Rolling Meadows, Ill., 1987—. Mem. Am. Mgmt. Assn. Avocations: reading; interior design, golf, animals. Office: On-Line Software Internat Inc 3315 Algonquin Rd Suite 620 Rolling Meadows IL 60008

ATAMIAN, SUSAN, nurse; b. Cambridge, Mass., Sept. 14, 1950; d. Raymond H. and Alice (Chakerian) A. BA, Simmons Coll., Boston, 1972. RN, Mass. Staff nurse Mass. Gen. Hosp., Boston, 1972-74, pvt. duty nurse, 1975-76, staff nurse, 1976-77, research study nurse, 1977-80, sr. research study nurse, 1984-87, dir. clin. research nurse group, 1985—, research study nurse, study coordinator, 1987-88, infection control nurse, 1988—; research asst. III U. Cinn. Hosp., 1980-81; staff nurse Kimberly Nurses, Orange, Calif., 1982; instr. nursing Mass. Gen. Hosp., Boston, 1980-81; cons. nutrition and liver diseases, McGaw Labs, Santa Ana, Calif., 1980-81; chmn. faculty dev. library com. Shepard Gill Sch., Boston, 1983-84. Mem. Am. Nurses Assn., Mass. Nurses Assn., Am. Nurses Found. Century Club, Nat. Assn. Reserve Nurses and Dietitians. Armenian Apostolic. Club: Simmons (Boston). Office: Mass Gen Hosp 15 Parkman St ACC 730 Boston MA 02114

ATCHLEY, LYDONNA ROSE, accountant; b. Farmington, N.Mex., Sept. 24, 1957; d. Raymond Leon and Lela Earnestine (Dearman) Cheek; m. Phillip Henshaw, June 29, 1974 (div. Feb. 1983); m. Joseph Peter Atchley, Aug. 22, 1983; children: April Dawn, Jennifer Reahine. Diploma in tax, Federated Sch., 1985, Internat. Correspondence Sch. Courses, 1985. CPA, Okla. Pres. Atchley Tax Acctg., Okemah, Okla., 1985—; advisor Contempo Fashions, Kansas City, Kans., 1986—. Author poetry. Brownie leader U.S. Girl Scouts, Okemah, 1983-84; vol. Okfuskee 4-H Orgn, OKemah, 1984-87; chmn. St. Judes Bike-a-thon, Okemah, 1987. Recipient Appreciation award OKale. Head Start, 1981, Appreciation award Girl Scout U.S., 1983. Mrm. Okla. Jaycees. Democrat. Baptist. Home and Office: 415 N 4th Okemah OK 74859

ATHEN, JOAN IVERSEN, small business owner; b. Washington, May 8, 1944; d. Charles Soren and Eleanor (Desale) Iversen; m. Larry Deane Athen, Aug. 28, 1965 (div. 1980); children: Scott Carl, Eric Soren; m. Garth V. Davis, Dec. 27, 1987. AA, Stephens Coll., Columbia, Mo., 1964. Store mgr., asst. buyer Woodward & Lothrop, Washington, 1964-70; advt. dir. Columbia (Md.) Assn., 1978-80; gen. ptnr. Eagle Video Ltd. Partnership, Columbia, 1980—; pres. Plaza Vending Corp., Columbia, 1980—, Plaza Telecommunications, Inc., Columbia, 1987—. Alt. del. Rep. Nat. Conv., Kansas City, Mo. and Detroit, 1976, 80, del., Dallas, 1984, rules com., Md., 1988; chmn. Howard County Rep. Cen. Com., 1983—. Named Outstanding Businesswoman, Columbia Jaycees, 1980, Patuxent Bus. and Profl. Women Assn., 1985. Mem. Nat. Automatic Merchandising Assn., Md. Vending Assn., D.C. Vending Assn., Va. Vending Assn., Am. Bus. Women Assn., Amusement and Music Operators Assn., Columbia Bus. Exchange, N.Am. Riding for the Handicapped Assn., Md. Therapeutic Horsemanship Assn. (founding, pres. 1975—), Howard County C. of C. (chmn. 1987, Outstanding Businesswoman award 1986-87). Home: 6380 Barefoot Boy Columbia MD 21045

ATHEY, SUELLEN MARIE, data processing executive; b. Mandan, N.D., Dec. 23, 1955; d. Joseph and Joan Marie (Gartner) Steckler; m. G. Richard Athey, Aug. 14, 1976; children: Melissa Marie, Mark Ryan. BS in Computer Sci., U. N.D., 1977; MBA, East Carolina U., 1984. Programmer Hallmark Cards, Inc., Kansas City, Mo., 1977-78; instr. Pitt Community Coll., Greenville, N.C., 1978-79; analyst, programmer East Carolina U., Greenville, 1979-80; programmer III Burroughs Wellcome Co., Greenville, 1980-82, systems analyst programmer, 1982-84, data base analyst, 1984-86, sr. data base adminstr., 1986-87; data base adminstr. Champion Internat. Corp., Hamilton, 1987—; co. chmn. CSP com. SHARE, Chgo., 1986-87; facilitator Quality Circles Burroughs Wellcome, Greenville, 1984-87. Sec. Lake Ellsworth Civic Assn., Greenville, 1981-82, pres., 1983-84, v.p., 1985-86. Mem. Nat. Assn. for Female Execs., AMA Aux., Beta Gamma Sigma. Republican. Roman Catholic. Club: Commerce (Greenville). Office: Champion Internat Corp Knightsbridge Hamilton OH 45020

ATKINS, CANDI, management consultant, small business owner; b. Chgo., Aug. 19, 1946; d. Norman R. and Catherine Kay (Coughlin) Wolfe; children: James N., Amanda Kate Arzoomanian. Assoc. in Edn., Thornton Community Coll., 1968. Chief exec. officer Candi Atkins & Assocs., San Francisco, Calif., 1981—; owner, ptnr. Big Wonderful Me, Pittsburg, Calif. and Hinsdale, Ill., 1986—; faculty Diablo Valley Community Coll., Pleasant Hill, Calif., 1982-85; nat. trainer Nan McKay & Assocs., San Diego, 1984-87. Author: Shopping For Big Wonderful Me, 1988. Candi Atkins Day named in her honor Mayor of San Francisco, 1982. Mem. Inst. Real Estate mgmt. (exec. com. San Francisco chpt. 1980-84, instr. 1981—, accredited resident mgr., cert. property mgr., Accredited Resident Mgr. of Yr. 1980), Nat. Speakers Assn., Nat. Assn. for Female Execs. Roman Catholic. Home and Office: 1427 26th Ave San Francisco CA 94122

ATKINS, HANNAH D., state official. M. Charles N. Atkins; 3 children: Edmund, Charles, Valerie. Grad., St. Augustine's Coll., grad., U. Chgo. Library Sch.; LHD (hon.), Benedict Coll., Columbia, S.C. Okla. state rep. 1968-79, commr., U.S. Commn. to UNESCO, 1979-82; asst. dir. Okla. Dept. Human Services, 1983-87; Okla. sec. of state Okla. City, 1987—; del. to UN Gen. Assembly, 1980; former nat. committeewoman, Dem. Nat. Com.;pres., Okla. chpt., Am. Soc. Public Adminstrn.; bd. dirs., Women Execs. in State Govt., ACLU; former chmn., Okla. Advisory Com., US Commn. on Civil Rights. Mem. NAACP, Urban League, Phi Beta Kappa, Alpha Kappa Alpha. Office: Office of Sec of State 101 State Capitol Bldg Oklahoma City OK 73105 *

ATKINS, JEANNE SMITH, business manager for child care center corporation; b. Trinity, Tex., Oct. 27, 1946; d. Henry Franklin and Mary Amelia (Whitten) Smith; m. Allen Brann Atkins, Feb. 13, 1979. BBA, Sam Houston State U., Huntsville, Tex., 1969; MBE, Stephen F. Austin State U., Nacogdoches, Tex., 1981. Lic. tchr., Tex.; lic. in real estate sales. Tchr. Pasadena (Tex.) Ind. Sch. Dist., 1969-70, Deer Park (Tex.) Ind. Sch. Dist., 1970-79; tchr., head dept. bus. Nacogdoches (Tex.) Ind. Sch. Dist., 1979-83; instr. acctg. MacCormac Jr. Coll., Chgo., 1983-84; bus. mgr. Supreme Ct. Racquet Club, Inc., Austin, Tex., 1984-85; v.p., bus. mgr. Kids Komputing, Inc., Austin, 1985-87; dir., bus. mgr. Hatch-Kinderworld, Inc., Austin, 1987—. Author microcumputer course: Accounting Principles, 1983. Mem. NEA, Tex. Tchrs. Assn., Chgo. Bus. Educators Assn. Republican. Mem. Unity ch. Home: 6016 Belfast St Austin TX 78723 Office: Kinderworld Inc 3200 Hatch Ln Cedar Park TX 78613

ATKINS, JERILYN HORNE, podiatrist; b. Pitts., Feb. 2, 1954; d. John Bernard and Isabelle Priscilla (Carter) Horne; m. Floyd Lee Atkins Jr., July 29, 1979 (div. Nov. 1986); children: Floyd Lee III, Marcus Alan. BS, Spelman Coll., 1976; DPodiatric Medicine, Ohio Coll., 1980. Dr. Podiatric Medicine. Resident podiatrics Kirkwood Gen. Hosp., Detroit, 1980-81, staff podiatrist, 1981-82; practicing medicine specializing in podiatry Detroit, 1982—; cons. Western Med. Co., Detroit, 1986-87; mem. bd. Mich. Dept. Licensing and Regulation, 1988—. Commr., bd. dirs. Highland Park (Mich.) Parks and Recreation Dept., 1984-88; mem. Detroit Area council Boy Scouts Am., 1988; soccer coach Southfield (Mich.) Parks and Recreation Dept. Mem. Am. Podiatric Med. Assn., Nat. Podiatric Med. Assn., Mich. Podiatric Med. Assn., Spelman Coll. Alumni Assn., Mich. Recreation and Park Assn., NAACP, Nat. Assn. Female Execs. Democrat. Office: Advanced Podiatric Ctrs PC 15800 W McNichols St Suite 113 Detroit MI 48235

ATKINS, KAREN ANN, information systems manager; b. Saginaw, Mich., Jan. 15, 1937; d. Chester Everett and Mary Jane (Newhouse) Hoyt; m. George P. Atkins Jr.; children: Tracey Lynn, George Poole III, Sharyn Leigh. AA, Brevard Community Coll., 1978; BBA, Barry U., 1987. Tchr. Clearlake Middle Sch., Cocoa, Fla., 1974-75; exec. sec. Brevard Community Coll., Cocoa, 1975-78, dir. Word Processing Ctr., 1978-84, sec. adv. com., 1979-80, mem. office tech. adv. com., 1984—, chmn., 1984; owner, mgr. Answerphone of Titusville, Fla., 1970—; mgr. info. support services Shuttle Processing Contract Brown and Assocs. Mgmt. Services, Kennedy Space Ctr., Fla., 1984—. Mem. Nat. Mgmt. Assn., Assn. Info. Systems Profl. (honor sec. achievement awards 1984-86), Nat. Assn. Female Execs., Cen. Brevard Profl. Women's Network, Beta Sigma Phi. Democrat. Methodist. Club: Toastmasters. Office: Brown and Assocs Mgmt Services PO Box 21187 Kennedy Space Center FL 32815

ATKINS, PATRICIA BOWEN, legal services executive, lawyer; b. Trenton, N.J., Apr. 2, 1944; d. William and Marie (Reeves) Bowen; m. Richard Leonard, June 15, 1963 (div. 1973); 1 dau., Victoria; m. Robert Martin Atkins, July 7, 1973; children—Leeanne, Robert. B.A., Trenton State Coll., 1966; M.A., Kean Coll., 1970; J.D., Rutgers U., 1979. Bar: N.J. 1979, Pa. 1984. Tchr., Bd. Edn., Trenton, N.J., 1966-68, guidance counselor, 1968-70; instr. Mercer County Community Coll., Trenton, 1970-72; spl. dept. atty. gen., asst. prosecutor Mercer County Prosecutor's Office, Trenton, 1979-80; chief hearings and adminstrv. procedure N.J. Dept. Agr., Trenton, 1980-82; mng. atty. Burlington office Camden Regional Legal Services, 1982-83, exec. dir., 1983—. Recipient award for achievement in field of law, Met. Civic League, Trenton, 1980. Mem. Nat. Bar Assn., N.J. Bar Assn., N.J. Assn. Black Women Lawyers, South Jersey Lawyers Assn., Camden County Bar Assn., Burlington County Bar Assn., Salem County Bar Assn., Cumberland County Bar Assn., Tri-County Women Lawyers Assn., Alpha Kappa Alpha. Roman Catholic. Club: Jack and Jill of Am. Home: 319 Mimosa Pl Cherry Hill NJ 08003 Office: Camden Regional Legal Services Inc 530 Cooper St Camden NJ 08102

ATKINS-MIKE, DEBORAH DENISE, computer analyst, realtor; b. Norfolk, Va., Oct. 19, 1959; d. William A. and Mophecia (Cook) Brickhouse; m. Peter Oswald Mike, Oct. 24, 1987. BA in Math., U. Va., 1981; postgrad., Johns Hopkins U., 1982-83. Primary systems engr. GTE Govt. Systems Corp., Vienna, Va., 1985-87; computer analyst Info. Systems and Networks Corp., Arlington, Va., 1987—; realtor Mount Vernon Realty, Chevy Chase, Md., 1988. Active Smithsonian Pres. Assoc. Program, 1988. Mem. Nat. Assn. Realtors, Md. Assn. Realtors, Montgomery County Bd. Realtors, Nat. Assn. Female Execs. (dir. Reston, Va. chpt. 1986).

ATKINSON, JEANNE B., clothing executive; b. Chgo., Feb. 27, 1932; d. John William and Lempi Marie (Erickson) Pagliucco; m. Bill Atkinson, Dec. 5, 1969 (div. June 1986); children: Robert James Blinken Jr., Rachel Jeanne Blinken. BA, Oberlin (Ohio) Coll., 1953. V.p., owner Bill Atkinson Ltd., N.Y.C., 1974-82; ptnr. Presentation, N.Y.C., 1974-86; dir. fashion mktg. Scovill Apparel Fasteners, N.Y.C., 1986, mktg., merchandising cons., 1986—; adj. prof. Fashion Inst. Tech., N.Y.C., 1980-87; v.p. Anne French Inc., N.Y.C., 1982-83, Adri Internat. Ltd., N.Y.C., 1984-85. Mem. Oberlin Coll. Devel. Program Com., 1986-87. Mem. Fashion Group Inc. (chairwoman membership com. 1988), John Frederick Oberlin Soc. Office: 32 W 40th St New York NY 10018

ATKINSON, JUNE WALLACE, lawyer; b. Taneyville, Mo., June 15, 1940; d. Robert Lee Wallace and Viva Frances (Hicks) Clas; m. Virgil Lee Conner, Jan. 1, 1959 (div. Nov. 1960); 1 child, Robin Abrams; m. Paul Edward Atkinson, Oct. 31, 1964 (div. Aug. 1973); 1 child, Lisa Michelle. Student, Santa Monica (Calif.) Coll., 1978; JD, U. West Los Angeles, 1982. Bar: Calif., 1982. Assoc. Daniel C. Olney, Wilmington, Calif., 1982—. Mem. ABA, Fed. Bar Assn., Calif. Bar Assn., Los Angeles Trial Lawyers Assn., Calif. Trial Lawyers Assn., Assn. Trial Lawyers Am. Republican. Presbyterian. Home: 1830 11th St Santa Monica CA 90404 Office: 1448 15th St #107 Santa Monica CA 90404

ATKINSON, LINDA MAE, chiropractor; b. Detroit, May 20, 1953; d. Ray and Mary (Paich) Elwart; D.C., Palmer Coll. Chiropractic, Davenport, Iowa, 1975; m. Warren Bernard Atkinson, Dec. 28, 1978; children—Devin Patrick, Derek Benjamin; stepchildren—Jenny T.M., Warren D. Exec. coordinator Romulus (Mich.) Chiropractice Clinic, 1968-78; Exec. coordinator Arbor Vitae Chiropractic Centre, Chelsea, Mich., 1978-81, dir., chiropractor, v.p., sec.-treas., 1979-84; pvt. practice, Jackson, Mich., 1984—; speaker Parker Sch. Profl. Success. Mem. Internat. Chiropractic Assn., Women Doctors of Chiropractice, Mich. Chiropractic Council. Republican. Roman Catholic. Address: 2397 Shirley Dr Jackson MI 49202

ATKINSON, REGINA ELIZABETH, medical social worker; b. New Haven, May 13, 1952; d. Samuel and Virginia Louise Griffin; B.A., U. Conn., Storrs, 1974; M.S.W., Atlanta U., 1978. Social work intern Atlanta Residential Manpower Center, 1976-77, Grady Meml. Hosp., Atlanta, 1977-78; med. social worker, hosp. coordinator USPHS, Atlanta, Palm Beach County (Fla.) Health Dept., West Palm Beach, 1978-81; dir. social services Glades Gen. Hosp., Belle Glade, Fla., 1981—; instr. Palm Beach Jr. Coll.; participant various work shops, task forces. Vice pres. Community Action Council South Bay, 1978-79. Whitney Young fellow, 1977; USPHS scholar, 1977. Mem. Am. Hosp. Assn., Soc. Hosp. Social Work Dirs., Assn. State and Territorial Pub. Health Social Workers, Nat. Assn. Black Social Workers, Nat. Assn. Social Workers, Soc. for Hosp. Social Work Dirs., Fla. Public Health Assn., Fla. Assn. Health and Social Services, Glades Area Assn. for Retarded Citizens. Home: 525 1/2 SW 10th St Belle Glade FL 33430 Office: 1201 S Main St Belle Glade FL 33430

ATTARD, ADELAIDE, gerontologist, educator; b. N.Y.C., June 2, 1930; d. Consiglio and Elizabeth (Bonnici) Spitery; children—Ronald, Gary. B.A., Empire State Coll., 1974; post masters cert. in gerontology Adelphi U., 1976; M. Profl. Studies, New Sch. for Social Research, 1978. Asst. dir. sr. citizens unit Nassau County Dept. Recreation, 1966-68, recreation supr., 1968-69; supr. community services Dept. Recreation and Community Activities, Oyster Bay, N.Y., 1970-71; adj. prof. Adelphi U., Garden City, N.Y., 1975-77, New Sch. for Social Research gerontological services adminstrn., N.Y.C., 1979—; commr. Nassau County Dept. Sr. Citizen Affairs, Mineola, N.Y., 1971—; dir. Am. Assn. for Internat. Aging, Washington; chairperson Fed. Council on Aging, Washington, 1981-86; chairperson Committee on Family and Community Support Systems, mem. nat. adv. com. White House Conf. on Aging, Washington, 1981; del. to UN World Assembly on Aging, Vienna, 1982, White House Conf. on Aging, 1971, 81; mem. County Exec.'s Task Force on Status of Women, Mineola, 1977-80, mem. Gov.'s Task Force on Aging, Albany, N.Y., 1977-78; mem. adv. council N.Y. State Community Services for Elderly, Albany, 1987. Contbr. articles to profl. jours. Bd. dirs. Welfare Research, Inc., N.Y.C., 1982—, Health and Welfare Council of Nassau County, N.Y., 1981—; mem. Nat. and Regional Tng. and Edn. Task Force Adminstrn. on Aging, Washington, 1971-73; mem. policy/adv. council for Columbia U. Ctr. for Geriatrics and Gerontology Long-Term Care Gerontology Ctr., N.Y.C., 1980—; adv., mem. curriculum com. dept. nursing SUNY, Farmingdale, 1982-83; mem. adv. com. on gerontol. services adminstrn. New Sch. for Social Research, 1976—; mem. Nassau County Criminal Justice Coordinating Council, 1982—; mem. Nassau County Republican Com., 1969—. Named Boss of Yr., Nat. Sec.'s Assn., Long Island chpt., 1971; Recipient Congl. award for Meritorious Service, 1981; Long Island Women Achievers' award 110 Ctr. for Bus. and Profl. Women, 1977, cert. of Leadership, L.I. Assn. Commerce and Industry, 1978; Pacemaker award St. Francis Hosp., 1975, Woman of Yr. award Long Beach Rep. Com., 1986; Cert. of Excellence, New Sch. Social Research, 1978-79, Disting. Contbns. in Field of Pub. Mgmt. award L.I. chpt. Am. Soc. Pub. Adminstrn., 1984. Mem. Nat. Assn. Area Agys. on Aging (bd. dirs. 1976-78), N.Y. State Assn. Area Agys. on Aging (pres. 1976-77), Am. Assn. Retired Persons (assoc. mem.), N.Y. Conf. on Aging. Republican. Office: Nassau County Dept Sr Citizen Affairs 222 Willis Ave Mineola NY 11501

ATTEE, JOYCE VALERIE JUNGCLAS, artist; b. Cin., Apr. 4, 1926; d. LeRoy Francis and Clara Marie (Becker) Jungclas; B.A., Rollins Coll., 1948; postgrad. U. Cin., 1952, 54, Art Acad. Cin., 1962-64, Edgecliff Coll., 1967; m. William Robert Attee III, Oct. 25, 1952; children—Robin Wilson, Wendy Ann. One-man shows: Loring Andrews Rattermann Gallery, 1964, Town Club, 1966, 69, 72, 75, 78, 81, 82, 83, 84, Jr. League Office, 1975, Court Gallery, 1969, Bissingers', 1970, 76, Cin. Nature Center, 1974, 78, Cin. Country Day Sch., 1974; 2 woman show: Town Club Cin., 1984, Bissinger's, 1984; group shows include: Cin. Art Mus., 1962, Zoo Arts Festival, 1961, 62, 66, Town Club Cin., 1973-75, 77-79, 80-84, 85, Palm Beach (Fla.) Galleries, 1974, Showcase of Arts, 1976, Ursuline Center, 1976, Court Galleries, 1977, Indian Hill Artists, 1957-76, 82, 83, regional and local shows Nat. League Am. Pen Women, 77, 78, also nat. biennial art exhibit, 1970, Nat. Bicentennial Show, Washington, 1976, James H. Barker Gallery, Palm Beach, Fla., 1979, 80, 81, 82, Nantucket, 1982, Cin. Women's Club Show, 1979, Cin. Nature Ctr., 1983; represented in permanent collections: Bissingers, Cin. Recipient 1st prize in still life or flowers Cin. Womans Art Club, 1965, 69; Marjorie Ewell Meml. award, 1975. Mem. Nat. League Am. Pen Women (past pres. Cin. br., past state art chmn. 1st prize graphics 1975), Women's Art Club Cin. (past v.p.), Jr. League Cin., Jr. League Garden Circle (pres. 1974-75). Episcopalian. Clubs: Town, University, Indian Hill. Author: Elbey Jay, 1964. Home: 8050 Indian Hill Rd Cincinnati OH 45243

ATTIAS, SHEILA TELANOFF, educational administrator; b. Phila., Nov. 8, 1935; d. Rudolph M. and Gertrude (Rudolph) Telanoff; m. William Attias, June 19, 1960; children: Erik, Lori. BS in Edn., Temple U., 1957, MEd equivalency, 1960; normal sch. degree, Gratz Coll., 1957. Cert. tchr., Pa. Tchr. Wissahickon Sch. Dist., Ambler, Pa., 1957-61, Fairfax County Sch. Dist., McLean, Va., 1961-63, Sch. Dist. Phila., 1963-64; owner, dir. Hawthorne Country Day Sch., Wyndmoor, Pa., 1973-81; office mgr. Germantown Window Cleaning Co., Glenside, Pa., 1981-83; admissions officer McCarrie Sch., Phila., 1983; fin. aid adminstr., registrar Gordon Phillips Beauty Sch., Phila., 1983-86; dir. student fin. services Art Inst. Phila., 1986; ops. mgr. Career Inst., Phila., 1987—. Mem. Nat. Assn. Female Execs., Nat. Assn. Student Fin. Adminstrs. Democrat. Jewish.

ATTWOOD, CHRISTINE ALISON, controller; b. Auckland, New Zealand, Aug. 13, 1954; d. Reginald James and Betty Fay (Ross) A. MACPA chartered accountant, New Zealand. Auditor Assocs. of Arthur Young & Co., New Zealand, 1976; bank loan officer Devel. Fin. Corp. of New Zealand, 1977-78; fin. cons. Coopers & Lybrand, Los Angeles, 1978-81; fin. analyst Chrysler Corp., Detroit, 1981-82, mgr. acctg., 1982-84, mgr. product and fin., 1984-85, mgr. procurement, 1985-86; asst. controller-fin. Chrysler Can., Ltd., Windsor, Ont., 1986—; speaker Chrysler Speakers Bur., Detroit, 1984—; officer Chrysler Can., Windsor, 1986—. Mem. Leadership Detroit VII, 1985-86. Mem. New Zealand Soc. Chartered Accts., Mich. Assn. CPA's, Investment Club. Republican. Episcopalian. Home: 1470 Sodon Ct

Bloomfield Hills MI 48013 Office: Chrysler Canada Ltd, PO Box 1621, Windsor, ON Canada N9A 4H6

ATTWOOD, CYNTHIA LOU, lawyer; b. Chgo., Dec. 12, 1946; d. John Gordon and M. Louise (Crenshaw) A.; B.A., Oakland U., 1969; J.D., U. Minn., 1973. Admitted to D.C. bar, 1973; atty. employment sect. civil rights div. U.S. Dept. Justice, Washington, 1973-74, atty. appellate sect., civil rights div., 1974-79; counsel appellate litigation mine safety and health div. Office of Solicitor, U.S. Dept. Labor, Arlington, Va., 1979-80, dep. assoc. solicitor, 1980-81, assoc. solicitor, 1981-86, assoc. solicitor occupational safety and health, 1986—. Mem. Women's Equity Action League, Women's Legal Def. Fund, Audubon Soc., Women's Bar Assn., D.C. Bar. Office: Room S-4004 Office of Solicitor US Dept Labor 200 Constitution Ave NW Washington DC 20210

ATWATER, EVELYN LOUISE LOWE (MRS. VERNE S. ATWATER), record company executive; b. Akron, Ohio, Aug. 21, 1921; d. Alvin Sylvis and Mary (Marcum) Lowe; B.A., Heidelberg Coll., 1943; m. Verne Stafford Atwater, May 29, 1943; children—Lynda Mary Atwater Pyfrin, Louise Christine Atwater Reinhart. Tchr. Kittery (Maine) Sch., 1944, Seaside (Oreg.) High Sch., 1944-45; co-founder Sing'N Do Co., Inc., Midland Park, N.J., 1955, pres., 1964—; rec. artist pub. Children's songs. Pres. YWCA, Ridgewood, N.J., 1968-70, bd. dirs., 1957-70, bd. dirs., 1957-70; trustee Ridgewood Library, 1971-75; mem. Ridgewood Choral, 1966-82; contralto soloist Ridgewood Meth. Ch., 1951-68; v.p. nat. bd. YWCA, 1977—, chmn. tribute to women and industry project YWCA, Ridgewood, 1974-77, nat. bd. dirs., 1980-83; bd. dirs. United Way of Bergen County, 1983—; adviser TWIN mgmt. Forum, chmn. Internat. Twin. Recipient Heidelberg Citation Heidelberg Coll., 1988. Mem. NEA, ASCP, N.J. Library Trustee Assn. Presbyterian (elder). Clubs: Ridgewood College (program chmn. 1964-66), Ridgewood Women's (chmn. music dept. 1963-65, 72—), Am. Woman's (Buenos Aires, Argentina) (program chmn. 1962-63); Arcola Country; Cosmopolitan (N.Y.C.). Home: 500 Clinton Ave Wyckoff NJ 07481 Office: Sing 'N Do Co Inc PO Box 149 Midland Park NJ 07432

ATWATER, TANYA MARIA, marine geophysicist, educator; b. Los Angeles, Aug. 27, 1942; d. Eugene and Elizabeth Ruth (Ransom) A.; 1 child, Alyosha Molnar. Student, MIT, 1960-63; BA, U. Calif., Berkeley, 1965; PhD, Scripps Inst. Oceanography, 1972. Vis. earthquake researcher U. Chile, 1966; research assoc. Stanford U., 1970-71; asst. prof. Scripps Inst. Oceanography, 1972-73; U.S.-USSR Acad. Scis. exchange scientist 1973; asst. prof. MIT, 1974-79, assoc. prof., 1979-80, research assoc., 1980-81; prof. dept. geoscis. U. Calif., Santa Barbara, 1980—; chairperson ocean margin drilling Ocean Crust Planning Adv. Com., mem. public adv. com. on law of sea U.S. Dept. State, 1979-83; Sigma Xi lectr., 1975-76; keynote speaker 1st Iberian-Latin Am. Congress on Frontiers of Geophysics. Sci. cons.: Planet Earth: Continents in Collision (R. Miller), 1983; contbr. articles to profl. jours. Sloan fellow, 1975-77; recipient Newcomb Cleveland prize AAAS, 1980; named Scientist of Yr. World Book Ency., 1980. Fellow Am. Geophys. Union (fellows com. 1980-81, Ewing award subcom. 1980), Geol. Soc. Am. (Penrose Conf. com. 1978-80); mem. AAAS, Assn. Women in Sci, Am. Geol. Inst., Phi Beta Kappa, Eta Kappa Nu. Office: U Calif Dept Geoscis Santa Barbara CA 93106

ATWOOD, GENEVIEVE, geologist; b. LaJolla, Calif., May 4, 1946; d. Eugene and Margaret (Fisher) A. B.A., Bryn Mawr Coll., 1968; M.A., Wesleyan U., Middleton, Conn., 1973. Field geologist Lamont Doherty/Honduras, Minas de Oro, 1971-72; staff geologist Nat. Acad. Scis., Washington, 1972-74; mem. Utah Ho. of Reps., 1974-80; sr. geologist Ford Bacon and Davis Utah, Salt Lake City, 1975-81; state geologist, dir. Utah Geol. and Mineral Survey, Salt Lake City, 1981—; dir. Salt Lake City Water and Sewer Bd., 1978—, Central Utah Project, Orem, 1981-84, Network Mag., Salt Lake City, 1983—. Editor: 3 books; contbr. articles to profl. jours. Bd. dirs. U. Utah Hosp., Salt Lake City, 1978—. Recipient Legislator of Yr. award Utah Assn. Social Workers, 1977, Jim Bridger award Utah State U., 1978, John F. Kennedy fellow Harvard U., 1978. Mem. Geol. Assn. Am., Utah Geol. Assn. Republican. Episcopalian. Clubs: Town (Salt Lake City); Wadawanuck (Stonington, Conn.). Office: Utah Geol & Mineral Survey 606 Black Hawk Way Salt Lake City UT 84108

ATWOOD, MARGARET ELEANOR, author; b. Ottawa, Ont., Can., Nov. 18, 1939; d. Carl Edmund and Margaret Dorothy (Killam) A. BA, U. Toronto, 1961; AM, Radcliffe Coll., 1962; postgrad., Harvard U., 1962-63, 65-67; LittD (hon.), Trent U., 1973, Concordia U., 1980, Smith Coll., Northampton, Mass., 1982, U. Toronto, 1983, U. Waterloo, 1985, U. Guelph, 1985, Mt. Holyoke Coll., 1985, Victoria Coll., 1987; LLD (hon.), Queen's U., 1974. Lectr. in English U. B.C., 1964-65, Sir George Williams U., 1967-68, U. Alta., 1969-70; asst. prof. English York U., Toronto, 1971-72; writer-in-residence U. Toronto, 1972-73, U. Ala., Tuscaloosa, 1985; Berg Chair NYU, 1986; writer-in-residence Macquarie U., Australia, 1987. Author: (poetry) Double Persephone, 1961, The Circle Game, 1967, The Animals in That Country, 1968, The Journals of Susanna Moodie, 1970, Procedures for Underground, 1970, Power Politics, 1973, Poems for Voices, 1970, You Are Happy, 1975, Selected Poems, 1976, (Am. edit., 1978), Two-Headed Poems, 1978, True Stories, 1981, Interlunar, 1984, Selected Poems II, 1985; (novel) The Edible Woman, 1969, (Am. edit.), 1970, Surfacing, 1972, (Am. edit.), 1973, Lady Oracle, 1973, Life Before Man, 1979, Bodily Harm, 1981, Murder in the Dark, 1983, The Handmaid's Tale, 1985; short stories Dancing Girls, 1977, Bluebeard's Egg, 1983; (juvenile) Up in the Tree, 1978, Anna's Pet, 1980; non-fiction Survival: A Thematic Guide to Canadian Literature, 1972, Second Words: Selected Critical Prose, 1982; author: (TV scripts) The Servant Girl, Can. Broadcasting Co., 1974—, (with Peter Pearson) Heaven On Earth, Can. Broadcasting Co., 1986; contbr. poems, short stories, revs. and articles to scholarly jours. Recipient E.J. Pratt medal, 1961, Pres.'s medal U. Western Ont., 1965, YWCA Women of Distinction award, Gov. Gen.'s award, 1966, 1st pl. Centennial Commn. Poetry Competition, 1967, Union Poetry prize Chicago, 1969, Bess Hoskins prize of Poetry Chicago, 1974, City of Toronto Book award, 1977, Can. Booksellers Assn. award, 1977, award for short fiction Periodical Distbr. Can., 1977, St. Lawrence award for Fiction, 1978, Radcliffe Grad. medal, 1980, Molson award, 1981, Internat. Writer's prize Welsh Arts Council, 1982, Book of Yr. award Periodical Distbrs. of Can. and Found. for Advancement Can. Letters, 1983, Los Angeles Times Fiction award, 1986, Gov. Gen.'s Lit. award, 1986, Ida Nudel Humanitarian award, 1986, Toronto Arts award, 1986, Arthur C. Clarke award for Best Sci. Fiction, 1987, Commonwealth Lit. Prize regional award, 1987, Silver medal for Best Article of Yr. Council for Advancement and Support of Edn., 1987; Guggenheim fellow, 1981; decorated companion Order of Can., 1981; named Woman of Yr. Ms. Mag., 1986. Fellow Royal Soc. of Can., Am. Acad. Arts and Secs. (fgn. hon. lit. mem. 1988). Office: care Oxford Univ Press, 70 Wynford Dr, Don Mills, ON Canada M3C 1J9

ATWOOD, MARY DEAN, clinical psychologist; b. Cushing, Okla., Aug. 8, 1939; d. Delbert Cecil and Mildred Louise (Manire) Anglin; m. Chester Francis Dean, Sept. 3, 1969 (div. 1974); children: Denise Dean Johnson, Douglas Chester; m. John Thomas Atwood, June 25, 1976. BS in Edn., U. Okla., 1959; MA in Guidance, Counseling, U. N.Mex., 1965, PhD in Clin. Psychology, 1974. Lic. clin. psychologist, Okla. Tchr. Okla. City Pub. Schs., 1960-61; counselor Tenn. Vocat. Sch. Girls, Tullahoma, 1962; tchr. N.Mex. Pub. Schs., 1964, N.Mex. Girls Home, 1965; psychologist Tenn. State Sch. Girls, Tullahoma, 1968; psychologist, coordinator Moore (Okla.) Health Ctr., 1974-76; clinical psychologist Atwood and Atwood Clin. Psychologists P.C., Oklahoma City, 1976—; health cons. researcher Okla. Inst. Natural Health, Oklahoma City, 1986-88; pres. Medicine Man Co., 1988—. Contbr. articles profl. jours. Group leader NOW, 1982-83; chmn. Hosp. Hospitality House charity Wimbledon Tennis Tournament, 1984-85; lectr. Planned Parenthood, Oklahoma City, 1984-85. NIMH fellow, 1973-74. Mem. Iridologists Internat., Am. Psychology Assn., Nat. Health Fedn., Assn. Advancement Psychologists, Southwestern Psychology Assn., Okla. Psychologist Assn., Okla. Psychol. Assn. (chmn. social issues 1976, bd. dirs. 1983-84), Kappa Delta Pi. Club: Quail Creek Golf and Country. Office: Medicine Man Co 2911 NW 122d Suite 122 Oklahoma City OK 73120

ATWOOD, MARY SANFORD, author; b. Mt. Pleasant, Mich., Jan. 27, 1935; d. Burton Jay and Lillian Belle (Sampson) Sanford; B.S., U. Miami, 1957; m. John C. Atwood, III, Mar. 23, 1957. Author: A Taste of India, 1969. Mem. San Francisco/N. Peninsula Opera Action, Hillsborough-Burlingame Newcomers, Suicide Prevention and Crisis Center, DeYoung Art Mus., Internat. Hospitality Center, Peninsula Symphony, San Francisco Art Mus., World Affairs Council, Mills Hosp. Assos. Mem. AAUW, Suicide Prevention Aux. Republican. Club: St. Francis Yacht. Address: 40 Knightwood Ln Hillsborough CA 94010

ATWOOD, ROSLYN IRENE, underwriter; b. Buffalo, Apr. 22, 1945; d. George Edward Alwood and Lorraine Charlotte (Winkleman) Gibson. BA, Chapman Coll., 1971; MA, Pacific Luth. U., 1976, Pacific Luth. U., 1974; postgrad., Ball State U., 1978-79, Western State Coll. at Law, 1985, U.S. Internat. U., 1988. Commd. capt.. U.S. Army, 1975, served to maj. res., 1981—; ind. field underwriter Calif., 1981—; instr. Columbia Coll., 1976-77; registered rep. Ins. Industry Series #6, 1985—. Mem. Nat. Assn. Life Underwriters of North San Diego County (treas., mem. v.p. 1988—), Nat. Assn. Female Execs, Nat. Notary Assn. Republican. Clubs: Toastmasters (adminstrv. v.p., v.p. membership Vista Chpt.). Home: 123 Mayfair St Oceanside CA 92054

ATWOOD, THERESA ANN, nursing educator, artist; b. Richmond Ind., Feb. 13, 1944; d. Richard Albert and Marie Ange (Roy) Wickens; m. James Phillip Atwood, May 20, 1972; children: Jerold Lee, Jody Marie. B of Health Sci., Ball State U., 1972; MEd, Purdue U., 1982, BS in Nursing, 1986. RN. Staff nurse St. John's Hosp., Anderson, Ind., 1965-68; nursing educator St. Elizabeth Med. Ctr., Lafayette, Ind. and St. Joseph's Coll., Rensselaer, Ind., 1972—. Mem. Right to Life, ARC, Am. Heart Assn., Nat. League for Nursing, Ind. Square Dance Caller's Assn. Republican. Roman Catholic. Clubs: Rhinestone Rustlers Square Dancing (Kokomo, Ind.). Home: 1801 Maple St Lafayette IN 47904 Office: St Elizabeth Sch Nursing Lafayette IN 47904

AU, ALICE MAN-JING, chemist; b. Canton, People's Republic of China; d. Ying-Tak and Yeuk-Suet Au. BS, U. Calif., Riverside, 1972, PhD, 1976. Postdoctoral scholar U. Calif., San Diego, 1976-78; postgrad. researcher U. Calif., San Francisco, 1978-80, research biochemist, 1980-81; pub. health chemist Calif. State Dept. Health Service, Berkeley, 1981-84, pub. health chemist III, 1984—; dir. EEO adv. com. Sacramento, 1986-87; cons. Sci. Innovations, San Francisco, 1983—. Contbr. articles to profl. jours. dir. adv. com. Calif. State Dept. Health Services EEO Com., Sacramento, 1986. Fellow NSF, 1972; DAR scholar 1970; Disting. Acad. scholar U. Calif., Riverside, 1972-76. Mem. AAAS, Am. Chem. Soc., N.Y. Acad. Scis., Phi Beta Kappa.

AUER, CATHERINE ANN, systems analyst; b. Anderson, Ind.; d. Charles Anthony and Edeltraut Ann (Hartwig) A. BA, Miami U., Oxford, Ohio, 1974, MA, 1976. Fin. aid. officer Miami U., 1976-83, systems analyst, 1983—. Mem. Soc. Tech. Communication (cert. systems profl., program chair SW Ohio chpt. 1984), Nat. Assn. Female Execs., Assn. Women Faculty and Profl. Staff, IBM PC User Group (editor newsletter 1983-84). Office: Miami U Computing Ctr Oxford OH 45056

AUER, MARILYN MILLS, banker; b. Port Huron, Mich., Apr. 30, 1936; d. James Carleton and Eunice Margaret (Foster) Mills; m. James Matthew Auer, Feb. 1, 1964; 1 child, Charles William. BS, Northwestern U., 1960; MS, U. Wis., 1964. Tchr. Rockridge High Sch., Edgington, Ill., 1960-62; teaching asst. U. Wis., Madison, 1962-64; legal sec. Atty. Edmund P. Arpin, Neenah, Wis., 1964-66; lending asst. Republic Realty Mortgage Corp., Wauwatosa, Wis., 1972-79; editor Creative Homeowner Press, Milw., 1979-82; adminstrv. sec., asst. to govt. lending dept. 1st Bank, N.A., Milw., 1982-87, adminstrv. specialist, 1987—. Editor: The Baton of Phi Beta, 1964-70; freelance reviewer The Milw. Jour., 1972-84; contbr. to books by Creative Home Press. Mem. Milw. Symphony Chorus, 1975-86. Mem. Milw. Met. Assn. Profl. Mortgage Women (officer, editor newsletter, 1986—), Phi Beta. Office: 1st Bank NA 201 W Wisconsin Ave Milwaukee WI 53259-1000

AUER, RUTH ANN, financial planner; b. St. Louis, Jan. 23, 1959; d. Adolph Charles and Emma Ella (Gruber) A. AS, Belleville Area Coll., 1979; BSBA, Washington Un, St. Louis, 1981; MBA, St. Louis U., 1982. Cert. fin. planner First Fin. Group of St. Louis, Inc., 1982—. Mem. Inst. Cert. Fin. Planners (cert.), Internat. Assn. Fin. Planners. Republican. Roman Catholic. Office: First Fin Group of St Louis Inc 14 Park Place Profl Ctr Belleville IL 62221

AUERBACH, ANITA L., clinical psychologist; b. Flushing, N.Y., Dec. 23, 1946; d. Ben and Gussie (Zuckerman) Weiss; B.A. cum laude, SUNY, Buffalo, 1968, M.A., 1970; Ph.D. (N.Y. State Regents fellow 1970-72), George Washington U., 1977; m. Steven Miles Auerbach, May 25, 1969. Chief research youth crime control project D.C. Dept. Corrections, 1970-74; intern clin. psychology No. Va. Tng. Center, Fairfax, 1974-75, staff psychologist, then chief psychol. services, 1975-79; pvt. practice clin. psychology, dir. Commonwealth Psychol. Assocs., McLean, Va., 1979—; lectr. Washington Tech. Inst., 1972-74, George Mason U., 1978—; cons. in field. Adv. bd. family edn. project Joseph P. Kennedy, Jr. Found., 1977-79; mem. regional appeals bd. No. Va. Public Sch. System, 1977-79. Recipient N.Y. State Scholar Incentive award, 1969; diplomate Am. Bd. Med. Psychotherapists, Internat. Acad. Behavioral Medicine. Mem. Am. Psychol. Assn., Am. Soc. Clin. Hypnosis, Va. Acad. Clin. Psychologists, Va. Psychol. Assn., No. Va. Soc. Clin. Psychologists, Washington Soc. Study Clin. Hypnosis, Psi Chi, Alpha Lambda Delta. Author articles in field. Office: 1449 Dolly Madison Blvd McLean VA 22101

AUERBACH, NINA JOAN, English language educator; b. N.Y.C., May 24, 1943. B.A., U. Wis., 1964; M.A., Columbia U., 1967, Ph.D., 1970. Instr. English Cleve. State U., 1968; asst. prof. Calif. State U., Los Angeles, 1970-72; asst. prof. U. Pa., Phila., 1972-77, assoc. prof., 1977-83, prof., 1983—. Author: Communities of Women: An Idea in Fiction, 1978; Woman and the Demon: The Life of A Victorian Myth, 1982; Romantic Imprisonment: Women and Other Glorified Outcasts, 1985, Ellen Terry, Player in Her Time, 1987. Contbr. articles to profl. jours. Ford Found. research fellow, 1975-76; fellow Radcliffe Inst., Cambridge, Mass., 1975-76; Guggenheim fellow, 1979-80. Mem. MLA, Coll. English Assn., Northeast Victorian Soc. Office: Dept English U Pa Philadelphia PA 19174

AUERBACK, SANDRA JEAN, social worker; b. San Francisco, Feb. 21, 1946; d. Alfred and Molly Loy (Friedman) A.; m. Joseph Gauthier, June 10, 1968 (div. Aug. 1978). BA, U. Calif., Berkeley, 1967; MSW, Hunter Sch. Social Work, 1972. Diplomate clin. social work. Case aide Spaulding Youth Ctr., Tilton, N.H., 1968-69; case worker Lakeside Sch., Spring Valley, N.Y., 1969-70; clin. social worker Jewish Family Services, Bklyn., 1972-73, Hackensack, N.J., 1973-78; pvt. practice psychotherapy San Francisco, 1978—; dir. intake adult day care Jewish Home for the Aged, San Francisco, 1979—. Bd. dirs. Demarest (N.J.) Little Theater, 1977-78. Mem. Nat. Assn. Social Workers (cert., bd. dirs. Bay Area Referral Service 1983-87, chmn. referral service 1984-87, state practice com. 1987—, rep. to Calif. Council Psychiatry, Psychology, Social Work and Nursing 1987—), Mental Health Assn. San Francisco (trustee 1987—), Am. Group Psychotherapy Assn., Am. Soc. Aging, Spouses of Gays (founder). Home: 1100 Gough St Apt 8C San Francisco CA 94109 Office: 450 Sutter San Francisco CA 94108

AUER CONNOR, ALICE MARIE, executive business service operator, consultant; b. Denver, June 23, 1948; d. Michael John and Virginia (Grout) Auer; m. John Busto, July 16, 1966 (div. Sept. 1972); children: John Joseph Jr., Stephen Michael; m. Kenneth Francis Connor; Feb. 21, 1986. AA in Sci., Community Coll. of Denver, 1972; BS in Edn., U. Colo., Boulder, 1975. Career developer Singer Career Systems, Denver, 1975-77; writer, editor Singer Career Systems, Rochester, N.Y., 1977-80; mgr. Environ. Research and Tech., Ft. Collins, Colo., 1980-85, Exec. Suites, Ltd., Ft. Collins, 1985-87; owner, operator Colony Plaza Corp. dba Exec. Suites Ltd., Ft. Collins, 1987—; free-lance writing, editing, Denver, Ft. Collins, 1980—; cons. Gold Suite Layout & Design, Cheyenne, Wyo., 1986-87, Secretarial Services, Madison, Wis., 1986. Editor jours., tech. text. Bd. dirs. Mile High Child Care, Denver, 1972-77, Multiple Sclerosis of Ft. Collins, 1986—. Mem. C. of C., Nat. Assn. Profl. and Secretarial Services, Nat. Assn. Female Execs. Democrat. Roman Catholic. Home: 201 S Grant Fort Collins CO 80521 Office: Exec Services Corp 19 Old Town Sq #238 Fort Collins CO 80524

AUFDENKAMP, JO ANN, librarian, lawyer; b. Springfield, Ill, Mar. 22, 1926; d. Erwin C. and Johanna (Ostermeier) A.; B.A., MacMurray Coll. for Women, 1945; B.L.S., U. Ill., 1946; postgrad. U. Chgo., 1964-66; J.D., John Marshall Law Sch., 1976. Asst. librarian Commerce Library U. Ill., 1946-48; librarian Fed. Res. Bank of Chgo., 1948-80; adminstr. info. services legal dept. Lincoln Nat. Life Ins. Co., Ft. Wayne, Ind., 1980-81; asst. trust officer Central Trust and Savs. Bank, Geneseo, Ill., 1981-83; practice law, 1983-84; cons. Ill. Valley Library System, 1984-87, Harvey (Ill.) Pub. Library, 1987—; with Office Nat. Planning, Liberia, 1963. Mem. Ill. Bar Assn., ALA, Spl. Libraries Assn., Ill. Library Assn. Republican. Lutheran. Home: 601 Rose Hill Springfield IL 62704 Office: Harvey Pub Library 155th and Turlington Harvey IL 60426

AUFDERHAAR-KING, SUSAN, commercial professional services consulting company executive; b. Celina, Ohio, Feb. 14, 1951; d. Norman Robert and Eleanor Belle (Shook) Aufderhaar; B.G.S., U. Nebr., Omaha, 1978; cert. MIT, 1980; M.B.A., Webster U., 1985; 1 dau., Laura Michelle. Programmer/systems analyst Dept. Def., U.S. Air Force, 1969-75; sr. programmer, analyst, mgr. quality assurance Majers Market Research, 1978-79; staff mgr. bus. systems Northwestern Bell Telephone Co., Omaha, 1979-82; mgr. area consultative staff AT&T Info. Systems, 1982-83; sr. dir. mktg. Datapoint Corp., 1983-85; sr. exec. data processing cons., mgr. exec. cons. services Boeing Computer Services, Seattle, 1985—. Served with USAF, 1969-75; Vietnam. Decorated Air Force Commendation medal. Mem. Assn. Computing Machinery (past sec.), Data Processing Mgrs. Assn. (exec. bd., sec.), Nat. Assn. Female Execs., Am. Mgmt. Assn., Smithsonian Instn., Cousteau Soc., Women Data Processing, Nat. Honor Soc. Republican. Mem. United Ch. of Christ. Club: Eastern Star. Office: 104 Heritage Ln Madison AL 35758

AUGELLO, NINA CATHERINE, personnel services administrator; b. N.Y.C., July 5, 1954; d. Angelo and Rose (Cirlincione) Augello; m. Steven Scott Miller, Apr. 24, 1983. BA, CUNY 1975; postgrad. Cornell U., 1975; MA in English, NYU, 1976. Instr. Hunter Coll. CUNY, N.Y.C., 1976-79; paralegal asst. firm Proskauer, Rose, N.Y.C., 1979-80; account mgr. Career Blazers Law Services Div. (subs. Personnel Pool 1983), N.Y.C., 1980-81, area account mgr., 1981-82, mgr. law services, 1982-85; dir. corp. devel. Career Blazers, 1985—, now v.p. Contbr. articles to profl. jours. Recipient Blanche Colton Williams award, Hunter Coll., 1975, Irene Steinman award, 1975; Jewish Found. Edn. of Girls grad. scholar, 1975. Mem. Sales Exec. Club N.Y., Women in Sales (v.p., program chmn. N.Y. chpt. 1982-83), Nat. Assn. Female Execs., Herbert F. Johnson Art Mus., NYU Alumni Assn., Assn. Personnel Cons. N.Y., Mus. Modern Art, Met. Mus. Art, Phi Beta Kappa. Home: Apt 14F 425 W 23d St New York NY 10011 Office: Career Blazers 500 Fifth Ave New York NY 10110

AUGUSTYNIAK, MARY ANN ELIZABETH, social worker; b. Bklyn., July 12, 1952; d. Allen L. and Helen R. Brown (foster parents). Student, U. New Haven, 1970-72; BS, So. Conn. State Coll., 1975. Co-founder, dir. Marivon Sch., Inc., Hamden, Conn., 1975-79; social worker, admission/discharge coordinator Winthrop Continuing Care Ctr., New Haven, 1980-82; med. coordinator Med. Personnel Pool, Inc., New Haven, 1982-86; social worker Vets. Home and Hosp., Rocky Hill, Conn., 1986—. Co-founder SIGNONYMOUS performance group, 1986—. Vol. Community Tng. Home, New Haven, 1979—; active New Haven YWCA, 1986. Emblem club scholar, 1972; grantee Jewish Community Ctr., 1975. Mem. Nat. Soc. Autistic Citizens, Social Work Oncology Group, Conn. Hosp. Assn. Social Work Conf. Democrat. Roman Catholic. Home: 451 George St New Haven CT 06511 Office: Rocky Hill Veterans Home and Hosp 281 West St Rocky Hill CT 06067

AUL, GRETA RUTH, lawyer; b. Olean, N.Y., Nov. 19, 1949; d. Edward Leroy and Marilyn Holmes (Rubin) A.; m. Kent Dixon Mikus, Oct. 22, 1972 (div. Nov. 1984); 1 child, Clark Clifford Mikus-Aul. BS, Carnegie-Mellon U., 1972; JD, Dickinson Sch. Law, 1977. Bar: Pa., 1977. Asst. atty. gen. Pa. Commn. for Women, Harrisburg, 1977-80; assoc. Minney, Mecum & Kohr, Lancaster, Pa., 1980-82; ptnr. Mikus & Aul, Lancaster, Pa., 1983-84; assoc. Appel, Yost & Sorrentino, Lancaster, Pa., 1984—. Author: (with others) Pennsylvania Matrimonial Practice, 1980. V.p. program Lancaster YWCA, 1984-86, treas., 1986-87; bd. dirs. Hamilton Park Playground Assn., Lancaster, 1985—. Named Citizen of Yr. Lancaster YWCA, 1987. Mem. Pa. Bar Assn. (chair equal rights com. 1986—, chair spouse abuse com. family law sect. 1986—). Democrat. Episcopalian. Club: Lancaster Recorder Consort. Office: Appel Yost & Sorrentino 33 N Duke St Lancaster PA 17602

AULD, LINDA SUE, insurance company executive; b. McPherson, Kans., July 13, 1945; d. Gilbert Eugene and Lucille Beatrice (Lindquist) Yowell; m. Jarrell Duane Auld, Dec. 27, 1967 (Nov. 1976); children: Jason Jeremy, Malia Carin. BS, U. Kans., 1968. Cert. occupational therapist. Psychiat. occupational therapist Med. Coll. Ga., Augusta, 1968-69, Kaneohe (Hawaii) State Hosp., 1969; rehab. respiratory therapist Meth. Hosp., Dallas, 1974-76; policy writer The Alliance Ins. Cos., McPherson, 1976, automobile ins. rater, 1976, work mgmt. analyst, 1976, work mgmt. coordinator, 1976-83, work mgmt. mgr., asst. v.p., 1983-85, policy services mgr., asst. v.p., 1985-88, policy services mgr., v.p., 1988—; occupational therapist cons. The Cedars, McPherson, 1976, Northview Nursing Home, McPherson, 1976; speaker various confs., 1978, 81. Contbr. articles to profl. jours. Mem. Supporting Our Children's Edn., McPherson, 1982—; vol. archeol. fieldworker Kans. State Hist. Soc., Topeka, 1986—. Mem. Kans. Anthrop. Assn. Republican. Office: The Alliance Ins Cos 1122 N Main McPherson KS 67460

AULENTI, LYNDA JOY, computer programmer; b. Quincy, Mass., Jan. 28, 1961; d. Harold Glen and Lois Ada (Bratton) Keener; m. James Vito Aulenti, Jan. 21, 1955. Student, Pillsbury Coll., 1979-80, Tunxis Community Coll., 1980; student in computer technology, Cen. N.Eng. Coll. Technology. Computer coordinator and trainer Northwestern Mutual Life, Bloomfield, Conn., 1980-84; office automation analyst Barclay's Am./Bus. Credit, East Hartford, Conn., 1984-86; computer programmer, cons. The Constell Group, Inc., Concord, Mass., 1986-87; software engr. Mediqual Systems, Inc., Westborough, Mass., 1988—. Author, editor computer handbook, 1986. Mem. Focus Users Group of Boston, Nat. Assn. Female Execs. Home: 3 Wallace Terrace Auburn MA 01501 Office: Mediqual Systems Inc 1900 West Park Dr Westborough MA 01581

AULETTA, NANCY ELLEN, corporate professional; b. Passaic, N.J., June 11, 1954; d. Fred and Helen (Arena) Mier; m. Edward John Auletta, July 22, 1978. Student, Montclair State Coll., 1972-75, Fairleigh Dickinson U., 1987—. Customer service rep. Scheck Bros., Secaucus, N.J., 1974-77; supr. packaging dept. Howmedica, Rutherford, N.J., 1977-82; mgr. prodn. control Foods Plus, Moonachie, N.J., 1982-84; mgr. customer service Osteonics Corp., Allendale, N.J., 1984-87; mgr. distbn. services Osteonics Corp., Allendale, 1987—. Mem. Internat. Customer Service Assn. Democrat. Roman Catholic. Office: Osteonics 59 Rt 17 Allendale NJ 07401

AULETTA-ANZILOTTI, LORI LYNN, controller; b. Bronx, N.Y., Mar. 8, 1959; d. Nicholas Michael and Rose (Troiano) Auletta; m. Robert Dominick Anzilotti, June 14, 1981; children: Christina Lynn, Paula Ann. BBA in Acctg., Iona Coll., 1981, MBA in Fin., 1986. Acct. S & A Concrete Co., Inc., N.Y.C., 1981-84, controller, 1985—; cons. Glen Island Casino, New Rochelle, N.Y., 1983—. Treas. fund raising N.Y.C. chpt. St. Jude's Childrens Research Hosp., 1985-86, exec. com., 1985-88, dinner com., 1985-88. Republican. Roman Catholic. Home: 1073 Grant Ave Pelham Manor NY 10803

AULT, LINDA CAE, educator, learning disabilities specialist; b. Dallas, Aug. 10, 1954; d. Carlos Desmond and Carol Beth (Yarborough) Wier; m. Gary Cecil Ault, Apr. 24, 1976; 1 child, Grant Clayton. B.S., U. Tex.-Austin, 1975, M.S. with honors U. Tex.-Dallas, 1981. Resource tchr. Richardson Ind. Sch. Dist. (Tex.), 1977—. Active 500, Inc., Dallas, 1982—; vol. Young Republicans, Dallas, 1980, Variety Club Tex. Mem. U. Tex.-Austin Ex-Students Assn., Council for Learning Disabilities, Richardson Assn. Children with Learning Disabilities, Richardson Edn. Assn., Delta Zeta. Baptist. Clubs: Daus. of Nile, Masons.

AUMILLER, LINDA LOUISE, health science facility administrator; b. Frederick, Md., July 20, 1954; d. Raymond Chapman and Marie (Louise) Beall; m. Roy Edward Aumiller, June 10, 1972; children: Lisa Marie, Roy Anthony. BS in Nursing, Spalding U., 1980; MS in Nursing, Widener U., 1986. RN. Nurse aide Nortons-Children's Hosp., Louisville, 1977-78; nurse operating room Norton-Children's Hosp., Louisville, 1980-81; nurse technician VA Med. Ctr., Louisville, 1979, nurse, 1982; nurse ARC, Louisville, 1981, U. Louisville, 1981-82; nurse Phila. VA Med. Ctr., 1982-83, head nurse, surgery, 1983-85, coordinator DRG, 1985—. Mem. Nursing Orgn. of the VA, Am. Nurses Assn. (cert. med.-surg. nurse), Sigma Theta Tau. Democrat. Unitarian.

AUMOND-STRICK, SANDRA, diversified company corporate administrator; b. Holyoke, Mass., Sept. 1, 1937; d. George Raymond and Helen Mary (Shaker) Aumond; m. Benjamin T. Strick, Sept. 3, 1979; 1 child, Joan. Student, Mt. Holyoke Coll., 1950; BA in History, Marymount Coll., Los Angeles, 1953. Various secretarial positions 1954-70; with Swedlow, Inc. & Pilkington, Garden Grove, Calif., 1970—; spl. asst. to chmn. bd., exec. asst. to pres. and chmn. bd. Swedlow, Inc. & Pilkington, Garden Grove, Calif. and Eng., 1979-82; corp. adminstr., mgr. spl. projects, bd. dirs. CES Corp., 1982—, Spec-Comm, Inc., 1982—. Mem. vol. bd. Children's Hosp., Santa Ana, Calif., 1970-79; fundraiser City of Hope. Mem. Am. Mgmt. Assn., Women in Mgmt. Clubs: Balboa Bay, Coto de Caza. Home: 20 Crest Circle Corona Del Mar CA 92625 Office: 12122 Western Ave Garden Grove CA 92645

AURELIAN, LAURE, medical sciences educator; b. Bucharest, Romania, June 17, 1939; came to U.S., 1963, naturalized, 1971; d. George I. and Stella (Ben-Joseph) A.; M.S., Tel-Aviv U., 1962; Ph.D., Johns Hopkins U., 1966; m. I.I. Kessler, Nov. 24, 1970; 1 dau., Amalia D. Asst. prof. dept. lab. animal medicine and microbiology Johns Hopkins U. Sch. Medicine, Balt., 1969-74, assoc. prof. dept. biophysics and biochemistry, 1975-82, asso. prof. dept. comparative medicine and biophysics, 1974-82, prof. div. biophysics, 1982—; prof. dept. pharmacology U. Md., 1982—, dir. vinology/immunology labs., 1984—; mem. NIH study sects. internat. teaching, 1973; mem. sci. adv. com. Internat. Biomed. Inst. UNESCO, 1987—. ACS grantee, 1970-74; NIH grantee, 1969—; WHO grantee, 1980—; others; named Disting. Young Scientist, Md. Acad. Sci., 1970. Mem. David Boyes Soc. Gynecol. Oncology, Brit. Coll. Can. (hon.) Am. Soc. Microbiology, AAAS, Am. Assn. Immunologists, Soc. Exptl. Biology and Medicine, Md. Acad. Sci., N.Y. Acad. Sci., Am. Assn. Cancer Research, Reticuloendothelial Soc. Editor Jour. Soviet Oncology, 1980-86, European Jour. Gynecol. Oncology, 1982—; contbr. articles to profl. jours. Home: 3404 Bancroft Rd Baltimore MD 21215

AUSMAN, PATRICIA JANE, osteopathic physician; b. Darby, Pa., Oct. 16, 1949; d. Edward Francis and Pauline Ausman. BA in Biology, Rosemont (Pa.) Coll., 1971; DO, Phila. Coll. Osteo. Medicine, Phila., 1975. Intern Lancaster (Pa.) Osteo. Hosp., 1975-76; resident in family practice Phila. Coll. Osteo. Med., 1976-77; staff physician Pennhurst Ctr., Spring City, Pa., 1977-80; asst. prof. N.Y. Coll. Osteo. Medicine, Old Westbury, 1980-86; practice medicine specializing in family practice and osteo. manipulative therapy Hempstead, N.Y., 1986—; staff med. cons. Hofstra Health Dome, Hempstead, 1986—; speaker Am. Cancer Soc., L.I., 1986—; mem. Personal Dynamics, Hempstead, 1986—; cons./physician adv. panel of patient care, 1983—; presenter many workshops; lectr. on nutrition, stress and osteo. medicine. Author: Introduction to Osteopathic Medicine; co-editor: Osteopathic Approach to Diagnosis and Treatment; contbr. articles to profl. jours., newspapers. Mem. Am. Osteo. Assn., Am. Acad. Osteopathy, Am. Holistic Med. Assn., Am. Assn. for History of Medicine, N.Y. Acad. Scis., Nat. Assn. Female Execs. Office: 160 Atlantic Ave Hempstead NY 11550

AUSTIN, AURELIA, author; b. Decatur, Ga.; d. Herbert O. and Virgil Mary (Wells) A.; ed. So. Bus. U., Mpls. Sch. Art, Atlanta Conservatory of Music; pvt. organ studies. Pvt. sec. to pres. Ashcraft-Wilkinson, Atlanta, 1952-71, Duval Corp., Houston, 1972-77; author: Bright Feathers (award as best book of poems by a Georgian), 1958; Georgia Boys with Stonewall Jackson (award Ga. Writers Assn.), 1968; (anthology) Wind Across the Plain, 1983, Christmas is Beauty, 1983, Capt. Nathaniel (Nathan) Austin of Gilder Plantation, S.C. and His Sons in the American Revolution, 1986, rev. edit., 1987, 3d rev. edit., 1988 (Nat. League Am. Pen Women award for excellence); editor: Poetry Prisms, 1956; Leaves of Life, 1964; contbr. articles to mags.; columnist 13 Ga. newspapers. Mem. Nat. League Am. Pen Women (award 1970, pres. Atlanta br. 1980-82, state pres. Ga. 1982-84), Ga. Poetry Soc., Atlanta Writers Club (pres. 1967-68). Baptist. Home: 526 Hardendorf Ave Atlanta GA 30307

AUSTIN, GAYLE CAROL CATES, graphic artist; b. Washington, Jan. 2, 1939; d. Lawrence Cates and Margarete (Roberts) Kise; m. James H.C. Austin, Aug. 25, 1962 (div. Oct. 1978); 1 child, Melinda C. Student, George Washington U., 1958; AA, Sullins Jr. Coll., 1959; student, U. Va., Fairfax, 1960, Am. U., 1960-62. Illustrator office of emergency planning Exec. Office of Pres., White House, Washington, 1961-62; illustrator office sec. Dept. Commerce, Washington, 1963; illustrator math and computers dept. U.S. Army Engr., McLean, Va., 1967-69; illustrator U.S. Geol. Survey, Reston, Va., 1973-75; artist Kappie Originals, Bethesda, Md., 1976-78; illustrator bur. land mgmt. U.S. Dept. Interior, Washington, 1982—; v.p. Fed. Design Council, Washington, 1983-85, exec. council, 1985-86. With publicity dept. Am. Indian Inter-Tribal Cultural Orgn., 1985-87. Mem. Women in the Arts Nat. Mus. Assn., Soc. Am. Profl. Women. Lodges: Jobs Daughters, Bethel 5. home: 13506 Chevy Chase Ct Chantilly VA 22021 Office: US Dept Interior Bur Land Mgmt 18 & C Sts NW Washington DC 20240

AUSTIN, GRACE BALIUNAS, periodontist, educator; b. Vilnius, Lithuania, May 22, 1940; d. Adolph and Anna Catherine (Savage) Baliunas; B.S., U. Chgo., 1963; D.D.S., Northwestern U., 1967; cert. periodontics N.J. Dental Sch., 1976; m. Nov. 28, 1970. Diplomate Am. Bd. Periodontology. Asst. prof. Northwestern U. Dental Sch., Chgo., 1967-69; sr. clin. scientist Warner Lambert Co., Morris Plains, N.J., 1969-71; clin. assoc. prof. periodontics N.J. Dental Sch., Newark, 1977-84; pvt. practice periodontics, Berkeley Heights, N.J., 1978—; mem. staff Overlook Hosp., Summit, N.J., 1979—. Ill. State scholar, 1959; grantee Coll. Medicine and Dentistry N.J. Found., 1976. Mem. Am. Acad. Periodontology, ADA, N.J. Dental Assn., Central Dental Soc., Internat. Assn. Dental Research, N.J. Soc. Periodontists (pres.-elect 1985-87), Psi Omega. Contbr. articles to profl. jours. Home: 15 Dominick Ct Short Hills NJ 07078 Office: 576 Springfield Ave Berkeley Heights NJ 07922

AUSTIN, IRMA CAROLINE, magazine publishing company official; b. Dothan, Ala., Oct. 29, 1941; d. Frank A. and Irma (Rocker) Marshall; m. Joseph H. Austin, May 20, 1972 (dec. Mar. 1975). BA, Trenton State Coll., 1963; MA, Columbia U., 1968. Tchr., Dutch Neck, N.J., 1963-66, El Monte, Calif., 1966-67, West New York, N.J., 1968-79; bus. and personnel mgr. Hal Publs. Inc. (pub. Working Woman and Success! mags.), N.Y.C., 1979-86; group mgr. human resources Working Woman/McCall's Group, N.Y.C., 1987—. Bd. govs. Palisades Gen. Hosp., North Bergen, N.J. Mem. Adminstrv. Mgmt. Soc., Am. Soc. Personnel Adminstrn., Women in Communication, Working Woman Speakers Bureau, NOW, Nat. Women's Polit. Caucus. Office: Working Woman Mag 230 Park Ave New York NY 10169

AUSTIN, JOANN CLARK, lawyer; b. Balt., Oct. 15, 1939; d. Thomas Winder Young and Aurie Austin Clark; A.B., Earlham Coll., 1961; M.A.T., Johns Hopkins U., 1965; J.D. with honors, U. Md., 1978; 1 son, Lawan Tarn Petty. Research biologist Nat. Cancer Inst., Bethesda, Md., 1961-63; tchr. Brookline (Mass.) Public Schs., 1965-67; sr. computer programmer Computer Usage Co., Inc., Boston, Los Angeles, 1967-70; bookkeeper, bus. mgr. Koinonia Found., Balt., 1974-76; admitted to Maine bar, 1979; individual practice law, South China, Maine, 1979—; staff atty. Legal Services for the Elderly, Augusta, Maine, 1980-82. Bd. dirs. Sch. of Living, York, Pa., treas., 1975-79; trustee Balt. Monthly Meeting of Friends Homewood, 1976-79, clk. Vassalboro Quar. Meeting, 1981—; bd. dirs. Oak Grove-Coburn Sch., Vassalboro, 1982—; mem. permanent bd. New Eng. Yearly Meeting of Friends; mem. exec. com. Am. Friends Service Com., 1977-78; bd. dirs. Sam Ely Community Land Trust, 1981—; bd. dirs. Maine Women's Lobby, 1981-82; selectman Town of China, 1981—; chmn. China Republican Town Com., 1982-86; mem. exec. com. Kennebec County Extension Service, 1985-87. Mem. ABA, Maine Bar Assn., China Area C. of C. (pres. 1988), Vassalboro Grange, NOW, Natural Resources Council. Address: PO Box 150 Rt 32 N South China ME 04358

AUSTIN, JOANNE MYERS, quality assurance engineer; b. Covington, Va., Jan. 16, 1931; d. Forrest Leon and Ruth Elizabeth (Hite) Myers; m. Edward I. Austin, Aug. 5, 1955 (div. Oct. 1978); 1 child, Timothy Edward. Student, Georgetown Coll., 1950-51, Dabney Lancaster Coll., 1975. Sec. Westvaco Research Lab., Covington, Va., 1953-55; exec. sec., city clk. City of Covington, 1970-78; supr. personnel Bath County Hydro Project Daniel Constn. Co., Warm Springs, Va., 1978-79; inspector quality control V.C Summer Nuclear Site Daniel Constn. Co., Jenkinsville, S.C., 1979; inspector quality control, technician Wolf Creek Nuclear Project Daniel Constrn. Co., New Strawn, Kans., 1979-81; engr. quality assurance Washington Supply System, Hanfor, Wash., 1981, Va. Power Co., Richmond, 1981—; lead auditor in quality assurance engring and quality control specialist N. Anna Power Sta., Va. Power Co., Mineral, 1986—. Recording sec. PTA Covington 1962-68. Mem. Covington Bus. and Profl. Women's Assn. (chmn. music, 1963-68, recording sec.), Am. Soc. Quality Control. Methodist. Home: PO Box 1239 Louisa VA 23093 Office: Va Power North Anna Power Sta Mineral VA 23090

AUSTIN, LOIS ANN LOEHR, academic administrator; b. Mt. Vernon, Ind., Aug. 15, 1939; d. Charles Alois and Golda (Baldwin) Loehr; m. Clyde W. Render Nov. 21, 1956 (div. May 1983); children: Teresa Greathouse, Kimberly Render, Jeffrey Render, Shawn Render (dec.). BS, U. So. Ind., 1977; MS, Ind. State U., 1983; postgrad., Ind. U.-Purdue U., Indpls., 1987—. Mgr. office Miss. Valley Steel Co., Mt. Carmel, Ill., 1976-78; coordinator fin. aid Ind. Vocat. Tech. Coll., Evansville, 1978-85; mgr. fin. aid Bloomington, 1985-86; asst. dir. fin. aid Indpls., 1986-87; mgr. fin. aid State of Ind., 1987—. Leader 4-H, Mt. Vernon, 1965-69, mem. Posey County (Ind.) council, 1969; sec. Diocesan Council, Evansville, 1968; coordinator Women in Networking, Evansville, 1985. Mem. Nat. Assn. Student Fin. Aid, Midwest Assn. Student Fin. Aid, Ind. Assn. Student Fin. Aid (sec. 1987—), Ind. Assn. Women Deans, Adminstrs. and Counselors, AAUW, VFW Aux. Democrat. Unitarian Universalist. Club: Homemakers (Posey County). Home: 80 N Ritter St Indianapolis IN 46219 Office: Ind Vocat Tech Coll 1 W 26th St Box 7034 Indianapolis IN 46207-7034

AUSTIN, MARGARET SCHILT, lawyer; b. Buffalo, June 5, 1950; d. Earl Alfred and Mary Margaret (Belk) Schilt; children: Emily Jean, Nathan Earl. BA, U. Mich., 1972, JD, 1979; MA, Northwestern U., 1973. Bar: Mich. 1979. Ptnr. Dobson, Griffin, Austin and Berman, Ann Arbor, Mich., 1979—; bd. dirs. Ann Arbor Student Bldg. Industry Program, Inc. Mem. ABA, Mich. Bar Assn., Am. Bus. Women's Assn. Home: 930 Duncan Ann Arbor MI 48103 Office: Dobson Griffin Austin & Berman PC 500 City Center Bldg Ann Arbor MI 48104

AUSTIN, MINNIE RUTH, college program administrator; b. Paulding, Miss., Apr. 19, 1945; d. Isom and Viola (Clayton) Harrison; m. Ronald Lawrence Austin, Dec. 25, 1969; children: Roland Lamar, Rodrick Lavelle. BS, Rust Coll., 1967; postgrad., U. So. Miss., 1980, 87. Cert. tchr., Miss. Tchr. Monroe County Schs., Aberdeen, Miss., 1967-72, East Jasper Pub. Schs., Heidelberg, Miss., 1972-75, Hattiesburg (Miss.) Pub. Schs., 1975-80; asst. dir. union and student activities U. So. Miss., Hattiesburg, 1980-87, adviser union programming bd., 1981—; counselor Hattiesburg Pub. Schs., 1987—. Mem. exec. bd. U. So. Miss. United Way, 1984-85. Mem. Nat. Assn. Female Execs., Civitan Club, Pi Tau Chi. Democrat. Baptist. Home: 304 1/2 Tuscan Ave Hattiesburg MS 39401

AUSTIN, PAGE INSLEY, lawyer; b. Balt., May 1, 1942; d. John Webb and Sallie Byrd (Massey) Insley; m. William H. Austin, June 10, 1967. BA in Philosophy, Valparaiso U., 1962; MA in Philosophy, Washington U., St. Louis, 1963; postgrad., Yale U., 1963-66; JD, U. Tex., 1977. Bar: Tex. 1977, U.S. Dist. Ct. (so. dist.) Tex. 1978, U.S. Ct. Appeals (10th cir.) 1980, U.S. Ct. Appeals (5th cir.) 1981, U.S. Supreme Ct. 1986. Instr. Yale U., New Haven, 1966-67, U. Houston, 1967-73; assoc. Vinson & Elkins, Houston, 1977-84, ptnr., 1984—. Mem. ABA, Tex. Bar Assn., Houston Bar Assn., Order of Coif, Chancellors. Home: 7510 Prestwick Houston TX 77025 Office: Vinson & Elkins 1001 Fannin 3300 First City Tower Houston TX 77002

AUSTIN-LETT, GENELLE, educator; b. Chgo.; d. Howard Joseph and Evelyn Gene (Reynolds) Blomquist. B.A., U. Ill., Chgo., 1969; M.A., No. Ill. U., 1972. Teaching and research asst. No. Ill. U., 1970-71; TV prodn. asst. Nat. Coll. Edn. High Sch. Workshop, 1972; prof. mass media and critical consumer Principia Coll., summer 1975; reviewer in interpersonal communication, media and behavioral scis. Houghton Mifflin, Harper & Row, William C. Brown, and Wadsworth Pub., 1972—, also asso. prof. speech communication and media Ill. Central Coll., East Peoria, 1971-79; editorial cons. Concordia Pub. House, 1978-82; program dir. Clayton (Mo.) U., 1978-82; tchr. English, Principia Upper Sch., 1983—; asst. prof. communications Meramec Community Coll.; coordinator performing arts multimedia presentations, publicity and recruitment; lectr. media consumerism, psychopolitics and advt.; instr. communications, cons. crisis intervention Fed. Police Tng., 1974-75. Group leader Community Devel. Council, 1974; organizer 9th Ward Teenage Republicans, Chgo., 1963, coordinator, 1967-69; adviser to Ill. Central Coll. Young Reps., 1971-75; clk., dir. exec. bd., chmn. bd. 1st Ch. of Christ, Scientist, Peoria; nat. advisory bd. Am. Security Council; mem. Rep. Nat. Com. Recipient Honors Day recognition U. Ill., 1968, hon. mention Nat. Arts and Letters playwriting contest, 1972; lic. life ins. agt., Mo. Mem. Ill. Speech and Theatre Assn., Speech Communication Assn., Central States Speech Assn., Internat. Data Speak. Clubs: U.S. Senatorial, Bible Investigation, Racquet. Author: (with others) Instructor's Manual for Mass Communication and Human Interaction, 1977; (with Jan Sprague) Talk to Yourself, 1976; contbr. articles to Christian Sci. periodicals.

AUTHORS, MARY VERONICA, economist; b. Bklyn., Apr. 6, 1922; d. Daniel Emmanuel and Mary Agnes (Love) Guggenheim; m. James Hubert Authors, Sept. 8, 1951 (dec. 1982). BS, Fordham U., 1949, MBA, 1971. Info. specialist Fed. Reserve Bank of N.Y., N.Y.C., 1941-45, econ. analyst, 1945-51; econ. analyst, freelance statistician various, 1951-56; research economist AM Star Corp., N.Y.C., 1956-68; statistician Union Camp Corp., Wayne, N.J., 1969-73, mkt. research analyst, 1973-82, sr. economist, 1982-86, economist, 1986—. Bd. dirs. Friends of Bloomingdal Library, N.J., 1982-87, Boque Pond Townhouse Assn., Bloomingdale, 1986-87, pres. 1981-83; vol. Clarence Dillon Library, Bedminster, N.J., 1975-80. Mem. Nat. Assn. Bus. Economists (treas. N.J. chpt. 1984-86, v.p. 1986-87, treas. 1984-86, pres. 1987-88), Am. Statistician Assn., Met. Economists Assn., Women's Econ. Roundtable. Roman Catholic. Office: Union Camp Corp 1600 Valley Rd Wayne NJ 07470

AUTREY, MADELYN PAULETTE, software engineer; b. Atmore, Ala., Feb. 10, 1963; d. Eddie Lee and Thelma Lee (Brown) A. Student, Lansing Community Coll., 1980-81; BS in Computer Sci., Ala. A & M, 1985. Software engr. Harris Corp., Syosset, N.Y., 1985-87, Allied-Signal Areospace Co. div. Bendix Tests Systems, Teterboro, N.J., 1987—. Mem. NAACP, Am. Soc. for Quality Control, Zeta Phi Beta. Baptist. Home: Evergreen at Clifton Condos 18 Evergreen Dr Apt 27 Clifton NJ 07014 Office: Allied-Signal Aerospace Co Bendix Test Systems Div Teterboro NJ 07608

AUTRY, GWYNNE WHEELER, banker, realtor; b. Temple, Tex., Mar. 3, 1933; d. Walter L. and Lois (Chancellor) Wheeler; m. D. Alessio, 1950 (div.); children: Ric, Chris; m. Thomas O. Cardwell, 1962 (dec. 1975); 1 child, Heather; m. King Autry, 1980. AA in French and English, Temple Jr. Coll., 1954; BBA in Mktg., So. Meth. U., 1958. Cert. real estate salesperson, Tex., Colo. Sales mgr., trainer Tecon Corp., Dallas, Denver, 1975-78; savs. and investment officer Dallas Fed. Savings and Loan, 1977-80; v.p. money market ops. Nat. Mortgage Corp. Am., Dallas, 1980-83; sr. v.p. nat. funds and money market ops. dept. Commodore Savs. and Loan, Dallas, 1983—. Mem. Sales and Mktg. Execs. Internat., Nat. Assn. Female Execs., Delta Zeta. Republican. Home: 6611 Harvest Glen Dallas TX 75248 Office: Commodore Savings and Loan 1845 Woodall-Rodgers Freeway Dallas TX 75201

AUVENSHINE, ANNA LEE BANKS, educator; b. Waco, Tex., Nov. 27, 1938; d. D.C. and Lois Elmore Banks; B.A., Baylor U., 1959, M.A., 1968, Ed.D., 1978, postgrad. Colo. State U., 1970-71, U. No. Colo., 1972; m. William Robert Auvenshine, Dec. 21, 1963; children—Karen Lynn, William Lee. Tchr. math. and English, Lake Air Jr. High Sch., Waco Ind. Sch. Dist., 1959-63, Ranger (Tex.) Ind. Sch. Dist., Ranger High Sch., 1964, Canyon (Tex.) Ind. Sch. Dist., Canyon Jr. High Sch., 1964-66; instr. English, Baylor U., 1963; tchr. math. Canyon Ind. Sch. Dist., Canyon High Sch., 1968-70; tchr. math. and English, St. Vrain Sch. Dist., Erie (Colo.) High Sch., 1970-71; tchr. English and reading Thompson Sch. Dist., Loveland (Colo.) High Sch., 1971-72; instr., reading program dir. Ranger Jr. Coll., 1972-84, chmn. humanities div., 1978-82; tchr. math. Hillsboro High Sch., 1984-85, adminstr. Hillsboro Ind. Sch. Dist., 1985—. Trustee, Ranger (Tex.) Ind. Sch. Dist., 1979-84, v.p. bd. trustees, 1980-82, pres., 1982-84; community chmn., publicity chmn., troop leader Ranger Girl Scout Assn., 1974-77; sec. Eastland County Heart Assn., 1975-77; ch. sch. supt. First United Meth. Ch., Ranger, 1979-81, organist, 1974-77, mem. adminstrv. bd., 1979-84. Mem. Internat. Reading Assn., Assn. Supervision and Curriculum Devel., Western Coll. Reading Assn., Tex. Assn. Sch. Adminstrs., Tex. Assn. Gifted and Talented, Tex. Jr. Coll. Tchrs. Assn. (cert. of appreciation 1979, mem. profl. devel. com. 1974-79, vice chmn. 1976-77, mem. resolutions com. 1979-80), Ranger PTA (parliamentarian 1978-79), Ranger Jr. Coll. Faculty Orgn. (pres. 1980-81), Baylor Alumni Assn. (life), Delta Kappa Gamma (pres. Beta Upsilon chpt. 1978-80, pres. Gamma Delta chpt. 1986—, achievement award 1980). Methodist. Clubs: 1947 (pres. 1977-78) (Ranger); Baylor Bear (Waco). Home: 412 Corsicana St Hillsboro TX 76645 Office: Hillsboro Ind Sch Dist Box 459 Hillsboro TX 76645

AVELAR, CARMEN MARIA, journalist, editor; b. San Francisco, Oct. 11, 1923; d. Miguel and Victoria Simon; grad. Merritt Bus. Coll., Oakland, Calif., 1943; m. Alfred J. Avelar, Jan. 19, 1946 (dec.); children—Richard M., Diana Avelar Kewell. Advt. copywriter Jackson Furniture Co., Oakland, Calif., 1942-46; women's feature writer Sparks Newspapers, Hayward, Calif., 1963-79, columnist, food editor, 1979-85; dir. Spectrum Inc. Service Agy., Hayward, Calif. Active Hayward Sister City com. Mem. Women in communications. Past mem. bd. dirs. Children's Hosp. Med. Center Aux., Oakland, Calif.; bd. dirs. Eden Hosp. Found., Castro Valley, Calif.

AVERELL, LOIS HATHAWAY, speech and language pathologist, audiologist; b. Boston, Apr. 8, 1917; d. Merle Leon and Mildred Hathaway (Allen) A.. Diploma, Wheelock Coll., 1941; BS in Edn., Boston U., 1942, EdM, 1953, postgrad., 1963-65. Cert. tchr., Mass. Tchr. kindergarten Dana Hall Schs., Wellesley, Mass., 1942-44; head tchr., pre-sch. program Brimmer and May Sch., Boston, 1944-52; speech therapist United Cerebral Palsy of South Shore, Inc., Quincy, Mass., 1952-53; dir. speech and hearing Meeting St. Sch. Children's Rehab Ctr., Providence, 1953-57; head speech and hearing pathologist Children's Hosp. Med. Ctr., Boston, 1957-63; teaching fellow Boston U., 1963-64; dir. speech, hearing and cleft palate clinic North Shore Children's Hosp. Med. Ctr., Salem, Mass., 1966-76; speech pathologist, audiologist South Shore Mental Health Assn., Quincy, 1977-78; speech-alng. pathologist, audiologist Mayflower House Child Care Ctr., Plymouth, Mass., 1978-85. Mem. Am. Speech-Lang. and Hearing Assn. (dual cert. clin. competence), Mass. Speech and Hearing Assn., Am. Auditory Soc., Am. Assn. Clin. Counselors (diplomate, sec. 1968-75), Nat. Acad. Counselors and Family Therapists, Internat. Soc. for Augmentative and Alternative Communication, NE Communication Enhancement Group, Pi Lambda Theta, Alpha Sigma Alpha. Republican. Baptist. Club: Women's Garden of Whitman (pres.). Lodge: Zonta (1st v.p. 1975-77 Salem club). Home: 815 Washington St Whitman MA 02382

AVERSA, DOLORES SEJDA, educational administrator; b. Phila., Mar. 26, 1932; d. Martin Benjamin and Mary Elizabeth (Esposito) Sejda; B.A., Chestnut Hill Coll., 1953; m. Zefferino A. Aversa, May 3, 1958; children—Dolores Elizabeth, Jeffrey Martin, Linda Maria. Owner, Personal Rep. and Public Relations, Phila., 1965-68; ednl. cons. Franklin Sch. Sci. and Arts, Phila., 1968-72; pres., owner, dir. Martin Sch. of Bus., Inc., Phila., 1972—; mem. ednl. planning com. Ravenhill Acad., Phila., 1975-76. Active Phila. Mus. of Art, Phila. Drama Guild. Mem. Nat. Bus. Edn. Assn., Pa. Bus. Edn. Assn., Am. Bus. Law Assn., Pa. Sch. Counselors Assn., Am.-Italy Soc., Phila. Hist. Soc., World Affairs Council Phila., Hist. Soc. Pa. Mem. ASTA (sch. div.). Roman Catholic. Home: 2111 Locust St Philadelphia PA 19103 Office: 2417 Welsh Rd Philadelphia PA 19114

AVERY, CHRISTINE ANN, pediatrician; b. Bklyn., Mar. 30, 1951; d. Basil Steven and Mary P. Goerner; B.S. summa cum laude, U. Houston, 1972; M.D., U. Tex. Health Sci. Ctr., 1976; m. Henry Jakob Wachtendorf, June 7, 1973; 1 son, Henry James. Resident in pediatrics U. Tex. Health Sci. Ctr., San Antonio, 1976-79, asst. prof. pediatrics and otorhinolaryngology; dir. Otitis Media Study Ctr., NIH, San Antonio, 1980-87 , now prof. pediatrics Cornell Med. Ctr., 1987—. Recipient Physician Recognition award, 1979, 82, 85. Mem. Am. Acad. Pediatrics, Tex. Pediatric Soc., San Antonio Pediatric Soc. Republican. Roman Catholic. Contbr. articles to profl. jours. Office: Cornell Med Ctr Dept Pediatrics 515 E 68th St New York NY 10128

AVERY, CYNTHIA GAIL, health care consultant; b. Jacksonville, Fla., Sept. 11, 1948; d. Henry and Mary Ruth (Halverson) Avery. B.A., Boston U., 1970; M.S.W., U. Pitts., 1976. Lic. social worker, S.C. Community bd. trainer United Mental Health, Inc., Pitts., 1971-73; cons. specialist St. Joseph's Hosp., Pitts., 1973-77; dir. South Hills Health System, Pitts., 1977-80, 80-81; health care cons. Dept. Health and Environ. Control, Greenville and Anderson, S.C., 1981—; trainer Pa. State U., 1976-77; field instr. U. Pitts. Sch. Social Work, 1977-81; cons. Continuum of Care for Emotionally Disturbed Children, Anderson, 1986—. Editor-co-pub. Greenville's Gold, 1984; copywriter: Greenville Pleasure Guide, 1985; editor Communiqué, 1985. Mem. Gov.'s Task Force on Veneral Disease Prevention, Harrisburg, Pa., 1972, Gov.'s Council on Drug and Alcohol Abuse, 1977. Gov.'s Council on Drug and Alcohol Abuse grantee, 1979. Mem. Nat. Assn. Female Execs., Nat. Assn. Social Workers, Creative Bus. Exchange (dir.), S.C. Soc. Clin. Social Work, NOW, AAUW, LWV (v.p.), Boston U. Alumni Assn., Nat. Mus. of Women in Arts, Friends of the Library. Avocations: ink drawing; Chinese brush painting; tennis; travel.

AVERY, JANE CAROLYN, public relations executive; b. Wolfeboro, N.H., July 29, 1946; d. Howard Clifton and Elvira (Zulauf) A. BA, Simmons Coll., 1968; JD, George Washington U., 1973. Editor Lawyers Coop. Pub. Co., Rochester, N.Y., 1973-76; opinion editor Mass. Lawyer's Weekly, Boston, 1976-81, editor, 1981-86; pub. Va. Lawyers Weekly, Richmond, 1986-88; pres. J.C. Avery & Assocs., Inc., Richmond, 1988—; chmn. bd. J. Clifton Avery Agy. Inc., Wolfeboro, N.H., 1976—; mem. Va. State Bar Traditions of Excellence Com., 1986-88. Contbr. articles to profl. jours. Trustee Simmons Coll., Boston, 1984—, chmn. nat. planned giving fund, 1979-86; mem. Lakes Region Conservation Trust, N.H., 1985—, Va. Mus. Fine Arts. Mem. Nat. Trust for Historic Preservation, Smithsonian Assocs., N.H. Real Estate, Internat. Assn. Bus. Communicators, George Washington U. Alumni Assn. Republican. Club: Boston Simmons (pres. 1985-86). Home and Office: JC Avery & Assocs Inc 31 James Falls Dr Richmond VA 23221

AVERY, LEE ANN, accounting administrator; b. Hartford, Conn., Feb. 21, 1957; d. William Kenneth and Anna Beatrice (Kerr) A. AA, Holyoke (Mass.) Community Coll., 1978; BBA, U. Mass., 1980; postgrad., Fordham U., 1988—. CPA, Conn. Sr. acct. Coopers & Lybrand, Hartford, 1980-83; with fin. mgmt. program The Dexter Corp., Windsor Locks, Conn., 1983-85; mgr. fin. analysis Alpha/Mercer div. The Dexter Corp., Newark, 1985-87; mgr. acctg. research Gen. Pub. Utilities, Parsippany, N.J., 1987—. Trustee, treas. The Master's Sch., Simsbury, Conn., 1982-85; del. People to People Citizen Ambassador Program, Peoples Republic of China, 1986. Arthur H. Carter Found. scholar. Mem. Am. Inst. CPA's, Nat. Assn. for Female Execs. Home: 195 Jacoby St Maplewood NJ 07040

AVERY, MARY ELLEN, pediatrician, educator; b. Camden, N.J., May 6, 1927; d. William Clarence and Mary (Miller) A. AB, Wheaton Coll., Mass., 1948, DSc, 1974; MD, Johns Hopkins U., 1952; DSc (hon.), Trinity Coll., 1976, U. Mich., 1975, Med. Coll. Pa., 1976, Albany Med. Coll., 1977, Med. Coll., Wis., 1978, Radcliffe Coll., 1978; MA (hon.), Harvard U., 1974; LHD, Emmanuel Coll., 1979, Northeastern U., 1981, Russell Sage Coll., 1983.

Intern Johns Hopkins Hosp., 1953-54, resident, 1954-57; research fellow in pediatrics Boston, 1957-59, Balt., 1959-69; assoc. prof. pediatrics Johns Hopkins U., 1964-69; prof., chmn. dept. pediatrics McGill U. Med. Sch., 1969-74; prof. pediatrics Harvard U., 1974—; physician-in-chief Montreal Children's Hosp., 1969-74, Children's Hosp. Med. Center, Boston, 1974-85; mem. council Med. Research Council Can.; mem. study sect. NIH, 1967—. Author: The Lung and Its Disorders in the Newborn Infant, 4th edit., 1981, (with A. Schaffer) Diseases of the Newborn, 1971, 5th edit. (with H.W. Taeusch), 1984; (with G. Litwack) Born Early, 1984; author, editor: Pediatric Medicine, 1988; also articles; mem. editorial bd. Pediatrics, 1965-71, Am. Rev. Respiratory Diseases, 1969-73, Am. Jour. Physiology, 1967-73, Jour. Pediatrics, 1974-84, Clin. and Investigative Medicine, 1977—, Medicine, 1985—, Johns Hopkins Med. Jour, 1978-82, Clin. and Investigative Medicine, 1978—, Medicine, 1985. Trustee Wheaton Coll. (1965-85), Radcliffe Coll., Johns Hopkins U., 1982-88. Recipient Mead Johnson award in pediatric research, 1968, Trudeau medal Am. Thoracic Soc., 1984; Markle scholar in med. scis., 1961-66. Fellow Am. Acad. Pediatrics, Am. Acad. Arts and Scis., Royal Coll. Physicians and Surgeons Can.; mem. Can. Pediatric Soc., Am. Physiol. Soc., Soc. Pediatric Research (pres. 1972-73), Brit. Pediatric Assn. (hon.), Inst. Medicine (council 1987—), Assn. Med. Sch. Dept. Chairmen (1969-85), Am. Pediatric Soc., Phi Beta Kappa, Alpha Omega Alpha. Office: 221 Longwood Ave Boston MA 02115

AVINA, DONNA MARTIN, small business owner; b. Madera, Calif., Oct. 5, 1944; d. Randolph Fred and Tressie Mae (Chambers) Martin; m. Nestor Joseph Avina, July 13, 1963; children: Michael, David, Jody Ann. BA in Journalism, San Jose State U., 1976, MS in Mass Communications, 1984. Asst. pub. relations Santa Clara County Govt., San Jose, Calif., 1974-75; legis. aide Calif. State Assembly, Sacramento, 1975-76; specialist pub. relations Gavilan Community Coll. Dist., Gilroy, Calif., 1976-86; instr. mass communications Gavilan Community Coll. Dist., Gilroy, 1985—; owner, mgr. Bare Furniture, Gilroy, 1983—; owner, chief exec. mktg. dir. Creative Woods, Gilroy, 1985—; pvt. practice cons. pub. relations Gilroy, 1986—. Contbr. articles to profl. jours. Founding mem. Gilroy Community Theatre, 1970; bd. dirs. Santa Clara County Social Services Commn., San Jose, 1974-75; precinct coordinator Supervisorial Campaign, County Govt., Gilroy area, 1977. Mem. Gilroy C. of C. (mem. tourism com. 1986—), Nat. Assn. Self-Employed, AAUW (chmn. Teen Pregnancy Prevention Project, Gilroy, 1986, chmn. edn. com. 1986—), Nat. Assn. Unfinished Furniture Retailers, Calif. St. Employees Assn. (mem. pub. relations com. 1977-79). Democrat. Protestant. Home: 7334 Ticonderoga Pl Gilroy CA 95020 Office: Creative Woods 7511 Railroad St Gilroy CA 95020

AVINA-RHODES, NINA ALVARADO, health facility director; b. Alamo, Tex., Nov. 29, 1944; d. Pedro Vasques Avina and Enriqueta Alvarado-Avina; m. James Lamar Rhodes Jr., Feb. 14, 1977; children: James Lamar III, Aaron Abraham, David Isaiah. BS in Bus. Adminstrn., Calif. State U., San Jose, 1973, postgrad., 1973-75; postgrad., La Salle U., 1987—. Cert. tchr., Ariz.; cert. adult basic educator, Calif.; cert. ESL tchr., Calif. Instr. Ctr. for Employment Tng., Santa Clara, Calif., 1976-80; pres. Avina Bros. Trucking Co., Fresno, Calif., 1982-84; writer grants Quechan Nation Indian Tribe, Yuma, Ariz., 1984-86; exec. dir. Western Ariz. Health & Edn. Ctr., Yuma, Ariz., 1986—. Co-host program Sta. KTEH-TV, San Jose, 1983. Co-facilitator Vietnam Vets. Outreach Ctr., San Jose; bd. dirs. Ctr. for Employment Tng., Yuma, 1984—; mem. Milpitas Unified Sch. Bd., 1981-82. Recipient Humanitarian award VA, 1983, Humanitarian award Vietnamese Community of Santa Clara County, 1983, Citizen of Honor award Vietnam Combat Vets., Ltd., 1983; named Woman of Achievement Santa Clara County Bd. Suprs., 1983. Mem. AMVETS (pres. aux. Yuma chpt. 1986—). Baha'i. Home: 1740 W 24th Ln Yuma AZ 85364 Office: Western Ariz Health & Edn Ctr 281 W 24th St Suite 136 Yuma AZ 85364

AVINO-BARRACATO, KATHLEEN, construction manager, consultant; b. Bklyn., Nov. 30, 1956; d. Charles and Rosanna (Scarlota) A.; m. Joseph Moran Olague (div. Jan. 1985); m. Joseph Louis Barracato Jr., Aug. 23, 1986. B in Architecture, Pratt Inst., 1978; postgrad., U. Tex., 1984; cert. in constrn. mgmt., NYU, 1985—. Draftsperson Michael Harris Spector and Assocs., Great Neck, N.Y., 1974-78; designer Brodsky & Adler, Architects and Engrs., N.Y.C., 1978-79, Emery Roth and Son, Architects, N.Y.C., 1979; borough design mgr., urban park designer N.Y.C. Dept. of Parks and Recreation, Queens, 1979-81; project mgr. Lawrence D. White, Assocs., Austin, Tex., 1981; pvt. practice cons., educator Austin, 1981-85; drafting dept. head Durham Nixon-Clay Coll., Austin, 1982-84; asst. supt. constrn., constrn. mgr. N.Y.C. Dept. Social Services, 1985-87; project mgr. Racal-Chubb Security Systems, East Rutherford, N.J., 1987—. Mem. Nat. Assn. Female Execs. Republican. Roman Catholic. Club: Columbian. Home: 8701 Shore Rd Brooklyn NY 11209 Office: Racal-Chubb Security Systems 1 Madison St East Rutherford NJ 07073

AVISE, ANNE LOUISE, banker; b. Des Moines, Sept. 28, 1948; d. Buris Ortis and Rosemary Agnes (Lowther) A. BA, Mundelein Coll., 1970. Acctg. mgr. Stouffer's, Atlanta and Oak Brook, Ill., 1972-74, McGregor Swire Air Services, Ltd., Bensenville, Ill., 1974-76; budget and audit analyst Life Care Services, Des Moines, 1976-78; mgmt. analyst State of Iowa, Des Moines, 1978-81; asst. v.p., mgr. adminstrv. services Bankers Trust, Des Moines, 1981—. Served to 1st lt. WAC, U.S. Army, 1970-72. Mem. Assn. Info. Systems Profls. (v.p. programs, v.p. membership, treas., pres., bd. dirs.), Assn. Records Mgrs. and Adminstrs. (treas., bd. dirs.), Inst. Cert. Records Mgrs., Nat. Assn. Bank Women.

AVRAM, HENRIETTE DAVIDSON, government official, information systems specialist; b. N.Y.C., Oct. 7, 1919; d. Joseph and Rhea (Olsho) Davidson; m. Herbert Mois Avram, Aug. 23, 1941; children: Lloyd, Marcie, Jay. Student, Hunter Coll., N.Y.C., George Washington U.; Sc.D. (hon.), So. Ill. U., 1977. Systems analyst, methods analyst, programmer Nat. Security Agy., 1953-59; systems analyst Am. Research Bur., 1959-61, Datatrol Corp., 1961-65; supervisory info. systems specialist Library of Congress, Washington, 1965-67; asst. coordinator info. systems Library of Congress, 1967-70; chief MARC Devel. Office, 1970-76; dir. Network Devel. Office, 1976-80, dir. processing systems, network and automation planning, 1980-83, asst. librarian for processing services, 1983—, chmn. network adv. com., 1981—; chair subcom. 2 sectional com. Z39 Am. Nat. Standards Inst., 1966-80; chair RECON Working Task Force, 1968-73, Internat. Relations Round Table, 1986-87; chair subcom. 4 working group 1 on character sets Internat. Orgn. for Standardization, 1971-80; lectr. dept. library sci. Cath. U. Am., Washington, 1973—, mem. strategies for 80's com. Sch. Library and Info. Sci., 1980-81; mem. Com. for Coordination of Nat. Bibliog. Control, 1976-79, Linked Systems Project Policy Com., 1985—; mem. steering com. MARC Internat. Network Study, 1975—; bd. visitors Library and Learning Resources Com., 1980—; mem. internat. standards coordinating com. Info. Systems Standards Bd., 1983-86; del. to U.S. nat. com. UNESCO/Gen. Info. Program, 1983—; chair internat. relations com. Nat. Info. Standards Orgn., 1983—. Bd. editors: Jour. Library Automation, 1970-72; contbr. articles to profl. jours. Recipient Superior Service award Library of Congress, 1968, Margaret Mann citation in cataloging and classification, 1971, Fed. Woman's award, 1974; award for achievement in library and info. tech. ALA-Library Info. Tech. Assn., 1980; co-recipient ACRL Acad./Research Librarian of Year award, 1979. Fellow Internat. Fedn. Library Assns. and Instns. (chair working group on content designators 1972-77, mem. program mgmt. com. 1983—, mem. exec. bd. 1983-87, 1st v.p. 1985-87); mem. ALA (bd. dirs., past pres. info. sci. and automation div., Melvil Dewey award 1981, Lippincott award 1988), Am. Soc. Info. Sci. (spl. interest group on library automation and networks 1965—), Assn. Library and Info. Sci. Edn., Assn. Bibliog. Agys. Britain, Australia, Can. and U.S. (del. 1977—). Home: 1776 Elton Rd Silver Spring MD 20903 Office: Library of Congress Washington DC 20540

AVRIL, LAURA DELYNN, corporate professional; b. Detroit, Mar. 28, 1960; d. J. Kevin and Marilyn (Doyle) Smith; m. Paul J. Avril, June 9, 1984. BBA, Loyola U., Chgo., 1983. CPA, Ill. With Price Waterhouse, Chgo., 1983-85; treasury analyst HAVI Corp., Westmont, Ill., 1985-86, adminstrv. mgr., 1986-88, mgr. fin. planning, 1988—. Fellow Am. Inst. CPA's; mem. Ill. Soc. CPA's, Beta Alpha Psi (pres. 1982-83). Home: 4456 Brittany Dr Lisle IL 60532 Office: HAVI Corp 777 Oakmont Ln Westmont IL 60559

AWL, CHARLOTTE JANE, nursing educator; b. St. Louis, Apr. 28, 1935; d. Herbert Vincent and Elizabeth Edwards (White) Pate; diploma Presbyn. Hosp. Sch. Nursing, Phila., 1956; student U. Pa., 1957-58; B.S. with distinction in Gen. Nursing, U. Ind., 1960, M.S. in Nursing Edn., 1961; postgrad. (Ada Belle Clark Welsh scholar), Ill. State U., 1978—; cert. CPR instr.; m. Richard Allen Awl, Sept. 2, 1962; children—Deborah Jane, David Allen, Stephen Scott. Team leader Presbyn. Hosp., Phila., 1956-57, head nurse women's surg. ward, 1957-58; staff nurse Bloomington (Ind.) Hosp., part-time 1958-60; pvt. duty nurse Robert Long Hosp., Indpls., spring 1960, Nursing Service Bur. Dist. 5, Ind. State Nurses Assn., Indpls., summer 1962; instr. med.-surg. nursing De Pauw U. Sch. Nursing, Greencastle and Indpls., 1961-63; instr. Meth. Med. Center Sch. Nursing, Peoria, Ill., 1963-64, part-time staff nurse Meth. Med. Center of Ill., 1964-66; cons. dept nursing Bradley U., Peoria, 1966-67, asst. prof., 1967-74, asso. prof., 1974—, assoc. chmn. dept. nursing, 1972-78, assoc. dir. div. nursing, 1978—, standard first aid instr. Am. Red Cross Multimedia. Mem. AAUP, Am. Nurses Assn., Nat. League Nursing, Assn. Operating Room Nurses, Council on Grad. Edn. for Adminstrn. in Nursing, Sigma Theta Tau, Pi Lambda Theta, Kappa Delta Pi, Phi Kappa Phi. Presbyterian. Office: Bradley Univ Div Nursing Peoria IL 61625

AWTRY-SMITH, MARILYN JOAN, psychic research consultant; b. Amityville, N.Y., Feb. 11, 1933; d. William Arthur and Bertha Eliza (Wheland) Jackson; student N.Y. Inst. Applied Arts and Scis., 1950-51; grad. Morris Pratt Inst., Wis., 1972; m. Jack Awtry, Apr. 27, 1952 (div. 1963); children—Jacalyn Susan, Nancy Jean Awtry Harmon; m. Henry Donald Smith, Apr. 2, 1984. Procurement asst. U.S. Air Force, Patrick AFB, Fla., 1963-66; contract negotiator/adminstr. NASA, 1966-72; contracting officer U.S. Coast Guard, Washington, 1972-83; ordained minister and medium Nat. Spiritualist Assn. of Chs., 1973—, trustee, 1983—; pres. SAM, Inc., Arlington, Va., 1979-82; co-founder Harmonial Philosophy Assn., 1973-86, trustee, 1983-87; ordained minister of Harmonial Pholosophy Assn., 1987, dean Harmonial Philosophy Inst., pastor Ch. Harmonial Fellowship, Deland, Fla., 1988— lectr. in field; counsellor-medium in parapsychology, 1965—, monthly columnist The Spotlight, The Nat. Spiritualist, Speakout, Harmonial Philosophy Assn. quarterly jour. . Recipient Outstanding Performance awards U.S. Govt., 1961, 63, 65, 76, 81, 82. Mem. South Cassadaga Spiritualist. Assn., Assn. for Research and Enlightenment, Nat. Contract Mgmt. Assn., Morris Pratt Inst., Ednl. Bur. Spiritualism, Lily Dale Assembly. Democrat. Clubs: Nat. Spiritualist Tchrs. and Ministerial Assn. Author: (pamphlet) You and a Way, 1977; The History of the National Spiritualist Assn. of Churches; A Spiritualist View of the Bible; co-author: Educational Course in Modern Spiritualism, 1981; Brighten Your Way - A Daily Devotional, Natural Law; Contemporary Definitions of Psychic Phenomena and Related Subjects; The Sunflower, An Introductory Approach to Natural Law. Home: 447 Lake St Cassadaga FL 32706

AXELROD, LEAH JOY, tour company executive; b. Milw., Sept. 7, 1929; d. Harry J. and Helen Janet (Ackerman) Mandelker; m. Leslie Robert Axelrod, Mar. 10, 1951; children—David Jay, Craig Lewis, Harry Besser, Garrick Paul, Bradley Neal, Nell Anne. B.S., U. Wis., 1951. Creative drama specialist Highland Park Parks & Recreation Dept., Ill., 1962-82; program specialist Pub. Library, Highland Park, 1972-82; ednl. cons. Bd. Jewish Edn., Chgo., 1973-80; children's edn. specialist Jewish Community Ctr., Chgo., 1975-82; tour cons. My Kind of Town Tours, Highland Park, 1975-79, pres., 1979—. Editor: Highland Park: All American City, 1976. Co-author: Highland Park By Foot or By Frame, 1980; Highland Park: American Suburb, 1982. Bd. dirs. Midwest Fedn. Temple Sisterhoods, 1975-79; pres. B'nai Torah Sisterhood, 1982-84; founding mem., v.p. Highland Park Hist. Soc., pres. 1987—; founder, bd. dirs. Chgo. Jewish Hist. Soc.; mem. Highland Park Historic Preservation Commn. Mem. Am. Theatre Assn., Ill. Theatre Assn. (dir. creative dramatics 1977-79); bd. dirs. Midwest Zionist Youth Commn. Club: Hadassah (Highland Park). Home: 2100 Linden Ave Highland Park IL 60035 Office: My Kind of Town Tours Inc PO Box 924 Highland Park IL 60035

AYDELOTTE, MYRTLE KITCHELL, nursing administrator, educator, consultant; b. Van Meter, Iowa, May 31, 1917; d. John J. and Larava Josephine (Gutshall) Kitchell; m. William O. Aydelotte, June 22, 1956; children—Marie Elizabeth, Jeannette Farley. B.S., U. Minn., 1939, M.A., 1947, Ph.D., 1955; postgrad., Columbia U. Tchrs. Coll., summer 1948. Head nurse Charles T. Miller Hosp., St. Paul, 1939-41; supr. surg. teaching St. Mary's Hosp. Sch. Nursing, Mpls., 1941-42; instr. U. Minn., 1945-49; dir., dean State U. Iowa Coll. Nursing, 1949-57, prof., 1957-62; asso. chief nurse VA Hosp. Research for Nursing, Iowa City, 1963-64; chief nursing research VA Hosp. Research for Nursing, 1964-65; prof. U. Iowa Coll. Nursing, 1964-77, 82-88; exec. dir. Am. Nurses Assn., 1977-81; dir. nursing U. Iowa Hosps. and Clinics, 1968-76; mem. sci. adv. bd. Center for Health Research, Wayne State U., 1972-76, Inst. Medicine, 1973—; cons. U. Minn., 1970, 82, U. Rochester, 1971, U. Mich., 1970, 73, U. Colo., 1970-71, U. Hawaii, 1972-73, Ariz. State U., 1972, U. Nebr., 1972-73. Contbr. articles to profl. jours.; editorial bd.: Nursing Forum, 1969—, Jour. Nursing Adminstrn, 1971. Mem., v.p. Iowa City Library Bd., 1961-67; mem. Johnson County Bd. Health, 1967-70; mem. adv. com. on family living courses Iowa City Bd. Edn., 1970-72. Served with Army Nurse Corps, 1942-46. Mem. Am. Nurses Assn., Am. Hosp. Assn., Am. Acad. Nursing, Sigma Theta Tau (research com. 1968-72). Home: 201 N 1st Ave Iowa City IA 52240 also: 149 Oswegatchie Rd Waterford CT 06385

AYERLE, SUSAN ANN, real estate executive; b. Ventura, Calif., Mar. 18, 1958; d. Karl H. and Lydia (Haupt) A.; m. Paul Gordon Atwood, Oct. 8, 1978 (div. Mar. 1980). Aircraft ins. underwriter Omni Aviation, Inc., Van Nuys, Calif., 1976-79; escrow coordinator Met. Devel. Corp., Beverly Hills, Calif., 1979-82; sales dir. Met. Devel. Corp., Las Vegas, 1982-85; v.p. sales, mktg. Green Valley Homes, Inc., Las Vegas, 1985—. Mem. Southern Nev. Sales & Mktg. Council, Southern Nev. Homebuilders Assn. (recipient 4 HOMER awards 1987). Democrat. Roman Catholic.

AYERS, ANNE LOUISE, education specialist; b. Albuquerque, Oct. 22, 1948; d. F. Ernest and Gladys Marguerite (Miles) A. BA, U. Kans., 1970; MEd, Seattle Pacific U., 1971. Staff cons. in student devel. Cen. Wash. State U., Ellensburg, 1971-72; dir. recruitment for N.D. and Mont. Chapman Coll., Orange, Calif., 1972-74; instr. psychology Hampton (Va.) Inst., 1973-78; edn. service specialist Gen. Ednl. Devel. Ctr., Fort Monroe, Va., 1975-77; edn. specialist U.S. Army Transp. Sch., Ft. Eustis, Va., 1977-79, Nat. Mine Health and Safety Acad., Beckley, W.Va., 1979—; pres. Appalachian Love Arts, Daniels, W.Va., 1983—. Inventor decorative pen holder, psychedelic ring product. Mem. Nat. Soc. for Performance and Instrn., Am. Ednl. Research Assn., Nat. Assn. Women Deans of Adminstrn. and Counselors, Internat. Platform Assn., Am. Fedn. Govt. Employees (union steward). Methodist. Home: PO Box 233 Daniels WV 25832 Office: Nat Mine Safety and Health Acad PO Box 1166 Beckley WV 25802

AYERS, SANDRA MILLER, accountant; b. Orlando, Fla., Nov. 13, 1958; d. John W. and Mildred Levonia (Phillips) Miller; m. Marcus Stephen Ayers, Jan. 10, 1987. BBA, U. Ga., 1979, M in Acctg., 1980. CPA, Fla. Tax staff Price Waterhouse, Tampa, Fla., 1981-82, tax sr., 1982-83; tax acct. Questor Corp., Tampa, 1983-84; tax sr. Peat Marwick Main, Tampa, 1984-85, tax mgr., 1985-87; v.p. Atlantic Coast Securites Corp., Tampa, 1986—; owner, mgr. real estate investment co. Tampa, 1986—; co-owner real estate investment co., 1987—. cons. Girl Scouts USA, Tampa, 1984-87, Tampa Ballet, 1987—; acct. Holiday Festival, Tampa, 1987; bd. dirs. Artist Alliance Inc., 1987; mem. Race and Religion Com. Hyde Park United Meth. Ch., 1988—. Mem. Fla. Inst. CPA's, Nat. Assn. Female Execs. (treas., charter mem. Tampa Bay Network 1987). Republican. Methodist. Office: Atlantic Coast Securities Corp One Urban Ctr 4830 W Kennedy Blvd Suite 330 Tampa FL 33609

AYERS, TAMMY LYNN, purchasing agent; b. LaFollette, Tenn., Oct. 12, 1961; d. Manuel Ray and Gladys (Miller) A. BBA in Acctg., Ohio State U., 1984. Purchasing agent Sensotec, Inc., Columbus, Ohio, 1984—. Mem. Nat. Assn. Purchasing Mgrs. (treas., bd. dirs. 1987—). Methodist. Office: Sensotec Inc 1200 Chesapeake Ave Columbus OH 43212

AYLOUSH, CYNTHIA MARIE, personnel director, corporate treasurer; b. Jackson, Mich., July 2, 1950; d. Leonard Edward and Violet Caroline (Kroeger) Ullrich; m. Abbott Selim Ayloush, June 21, 1980; children: Sasha Christine, Nadia Marie. AA, Fullerton Coll., 1970; diploma in fashion mdse., Brooks Coll., 1975; BS, Pepperdine U., 1980. Receptionist, Hydraflow, Commerce, Calif., 1968-74, personnel mgr., Cerritos, Calif., 1979—, treas., 1979—, corp. sec., 1985—; with sales dept. Robinson's, Cerritos, Calif., 1974-75, dept. mgr., 1975-79. Mem. Am. Soc. Personnel Adminstrs., Personnel Indsl. Relations Assn., Merchants and Mfrs. Assn., Cerritos C. of C. (dir. 1983—). Republican. Roman Catholic. Clubs: Soroptimist (sec. 1979—), Century, Pepperdine Univ. Office: Hydraflow 13259 E 166th St Cerritos CA 90701

AYRAULT, MARGARET WEBSTER, emeritus educator; b. Tonawanda, N.Y., Sept. 8, 1911; d. Miles and (Maud) Eleanor (Webster) A.; A.B., Oberlin Coll., 1933; B.S. in L.S., Drexel Inst. Tech., 1934; M.S. in L.S., Columbia U., 1940. Gen. asst. Drexel Inst. Tech. Library, Phila., 1934; cataloger Pratt Free Library, Balt., 1934-38; asst. reference dept. library Columbia U., 1939-40; head cataloger Carnegie Endowment for Internat. Peace Library, Washington, 1941-43; chief processing sect. library U.S. Dept. Agr., Washington, 1943-50; chief bibliog. control sec. Tech. Library, Naval Ordnance Test Sta., Inyokern, Calif., 1950-51; asst. librarian Bur. Budget, Washington, 1952-54; head cataloging dept. library U. Mich., Ann Arbor, 1954-65; prof. Grad. Sch. Library Studies, U. Hawaii, Honolulu, 1965-75, prof. emeritus, 1976—. Mem. Friends of Library of Hawaii, bd. dirs., 1979-85; chmn. library com. Arcadia Retirement Residence. Mem. ALA (past counselor, exec. bd. resources and tech. services div. 1958-62, orgn. com. 1968-70, Margaret Mann citation 1975), Hawaii Library Assn. (hon.; pres. 1974-75), U. Hawaii Library Assn., AAUP, Phi Beta Kappa, Beta Phi Mu. Contbr. articles to profl. jours. Home: 1434 Punahou St Apt 729 Honolulu HI 96822 Office: U Hawaii Grad Sch Library Studies Honolulu HI 96822

AYRES, LINDA L., art historian, curator; b. Berlin, Md., May 25, 1947; d. John Pershing and Hilda Margaret (Smallwood) A.; m. David Emmert Brewster, Apr. 21, 1977. BA, Washington Coll., 1969; MA, Tufts U., 1973. Bicentennial coordinator Fogg Art Mus., Cambridge, Mass., 1974-75, asst. to dir., 1975-76; research asst. Nat. Portrait Gallery, Washington, 1977-78, asst. curator Am. art, 1978-84; acting curator Am. art Nat. Gallery, 1983; curator painting and sculpture Amon Carter Mus., Ft. Worth, 1984—. Author exhbn. catalogue: Harvard Divided, 1976; Thomas Moran's Watercolors of Yellowstone, 1984; co-author exhbn. catalogue: An American Perspective, 1981; Bellows: Boxing Pictures, 1982, George Bellows: The Artist and His Liethographs (1916-1924), 1988; American Paintings, Watercolors and Drawings from the Collection of Rita and Daniel Fraad, 1985; contbg. author: John Hay Whitney Collection, 1983; co-author: John Singer Sargent, 1986, American Paintings: Selections from the Amon Carter Museum, 1986, American Frontier Life: Early Western Painting and Prints, 1987; contbr. Three Centuries of Am. Painting, 1988. Recipient New Eng. Book award, 1976. Mem. Coll. Art Assn. Democrat. Episcopalian. Office: Amon Carter Mus Art Fort Worth TX 76113

AYRES, MARILYN COINER, college dean; b. Garden City, Kans., Jan. 11, 1937; d. Melvin Cleatis and Blanche Leota (Kemper) Coiner; m. Monroe Upton Ayres, Dec. 27, 1958; 1 child, Marc Coiner. BS in Bus. Edn., Okla. State U., 1955-58, MS in Bus. Edn., 1960-61. Instr. secretarial adminstrn. Okla. State U., Stillwater, 1964-66; prof. office systems County Coll. Morris, Randolph, N.J., 1972—, office systems dept. chmn., 1983-87, dean div. sci., tech. and math., 1987—. Co-editor: The Observer, 1976-78. Named one of Outstanding Young Women of Am., 1967. Mem. Nat. Bus. Edn. Assn., Ea. Bus. Edn. Assn., Assn. Info. System Profls., Am. Soc. for Engring. Edn., Delta Pi Epsilon, Phi Kappa Phi, Kappa Alpha Theta. Home: 10 Larch Dr Chester NJ 07930 Office: County Coll of Morris Rt 10 and Center Grove Rd Randolph NJ 07869

AYSCUE, FREDA JEAN, investment/insurance company executive; b. Winston-Salem, N.C., June 13, 1950; d. Fred Jennings and Bessie Elizabeth Hauser; B.S. in Family Studies and Consumer Sci. (FS/CS scholar, Stokeley Van Camp Outstanding Achievement award 1974), San Diego State U., 1974; m. John H. Ayscue, Jr., Sept. 12, 1970. Sales coordinator Norris Industries, Los Angeles, 1974-75; ind. sales rep., So. Calif., 1975-78; regional mgr. Geno Designs, Atlanta, 1978-79; div. supt. Roosevelt Nat. Investment Co., New Orleans, 1979-83; exec. conf. dir. Fin. Services div. Am. Guaranty, Atlanta, 1983-87; asst. agys., exec. mktg. staff Fin. Services Network, Atlanta, 1986-87; nat. dir. license tng. Liberty One Corp., Atlanta, 1987-88, v.p. mktg., 1988—; cons. F.J. Ayscue & Assocs., 1980—; speaker in field. Mem. cons. council New Orleans/Bayou Health Systems Agy., 1981-82. Bd. dirs. Rehoboth Womens Ministry, chair Outreach. Mem. Bus. and Profl. Women, Am. Soc. Profl. and Exec. Women, Nat. Assn. Female Execs., Home Economists in Bus., Womens Equity Action League, Women's Polit. Caucus, NOW (chpt. public relations chmn. 1979-81, del. nat. conv. 1980-81). Office: PO 1009 Stone Mountain Atlanta GA 30086

AZA, CARMEN, steamship company executive; b. Bilbao, Spain, Apr. 4, 1937; came to U.S., 1970; d. Gerardo Aza and Pilar Ortega; m. Guillermo A. Martinez-Colon, Aug. 23, 1972 (dec. Jan. 1978); 1 child, Begonia. Student French lit., Sorbonne, Paris, 1958-60; student socio-econ. scis., U. Deusto, Bilbao, 1965-70. Exec. sec. Naviera Artola, Bilbao, S.Am., 1960-70; adminstrv. officer Spanish Consulate, N.Y.C., 1971; exec. v.p. Caravel Fashions Spain, Inc., N.Y.C., 1971-72; pres. Bur. Comml. Services, Inc., N.Y.C., 1972-85, Internat. Trading and Shipping Agy., Inc., N.Y.C., 1978—; designated agt. and rep. for Spain, Italy, Portugal, Mex., and Greece for fgn. fisheries before U.S. Govt., 1978—. Decorated Lazo de Dama de la Orden del Merito Civil (Spain). Mem. Spain-U.S. C. of C. Roman Catholic. Club: N.Y. Athletic (hon.). Office: Internat Trading & Shipping Agy Inc 19 Rector St Ste 1115 New York NY 10006-2380

AZAMA, GWENDOLYN JOYCE, city clerk; b. Orange City, Fla., Jan. 7, 1949; d. James William and Willie Belle (Taylor) Frazier; m. Curtis Lee Azama, May 31, 1971 (div. Mar. 1984); children: Curtis Lee Jr., Anthony James. BA, Stetson U., 1970, MA, 1983. From employment interviewer to supr. employment counseling Fla. State Employment Services, Daytona Beach, 1971-80; job service mgr. State of Fla., 1980-85; regional mgr. Fla. Dept. Labor, Lakeland, 1985-87; city clk. City of Daytona Beach, 1987—. Bd. dirs. Volusia-Flagler County United Way, Daytona Beach, 1987—; mem. Community Leadership com. Polk Community Coll., Lakeland, 1986-87. Mem. Fla. Assn. City Clerks Regional Coordinating Council 1988—, Fla. Employment Counselors Assn. (past officer, Citation), NAACP (Disting. Service award 1984), Excelsior Bus. and Profl. Women's Club (pres. 1981-83)., Assn. Records Mgrs. and Adminstrs. Baptist. Home: 1147 Edith Dr Daytona Beach FL 32017

AZCUENAGA, MARY L., government official; AB, Stanford U., 1967; JD, U. Chgo., 1973. Atty. FTC, Washington, 1973-75, asst. to gen. counsel, 1975-76, staff atty. San Francisco regional office, 1977-80, asst. regional dir., 1980-81, asst. to exec. dir., 1981-82, litigation atty. Office of Gen. Counsel, 1982, asst. gen. counsel for legal counsel, 1983-84, commr., Washington, 1984—. Office: FTC Office of the Chmn 6th St & Pennsylvania Ave NW Washington DC 20580

AZCUY, ANA MARIA, news anchor; b. Havana, Cuba, Nov. 23, 1955; d. Aracelio Rafael and Aida Luz (Andreu) A. AA in Broadcasting, Miami Dade Community Coll., 1974; BA in Communications, Fla. Atlantic U., 1976; MA in Journalism, Columbia U., N.Y.C., 1977. News reporter Sta. WTVJ-TV, Miami, Fla., 1977-79, news anchor, 1983—; reporter, anchor Sta. WPLG-TV, Miami, Fla., 1979-81; news anchor Sta. KSAT-TV, San Antonio, 1982-83. Bd. dirs. Parent Resource Ctr., Miami, 1986—, Am. Heart Assn., 1985-86. Mem. Nat. Assn. Hispanic Journalists, NATAS, Sigma Delta Chi, Phi Kappa Phi. Roman Catholic. Office: Sta WTVJ-TV 316 N Miami Ave Miami FL 33128

AZNAVORIAN, KATHLEEN DUL, manufacturing executive; b. Detroit, May 12, 1947; d. Alexander Stanley and Estelle Catherine (Obloj) Dul; m. Michael A. Aznavorian, July 3, 1982; children: Jeffrey, Jennifer. BS in Acctg., U. Detroit, 1968; MA in Polit. Sci., Fla. Atlantic U., 1971. CPA, Mich. Sr. acct. Laventhol & Horwath, Southfield, Mich., 1972-75; treas. Mortgage Co., Dearborn, Mich., 1975-78; asst. mgr. fin. reporting K-Mart Corp., Troy, Mich., 1978-82; pres., treas. Fox Hills Country Club, Plymouth, Mich., 1982—; also bd. dirs. Fox Hills Country Club, Plymouth; pres., treas.

Clips and Clamps Industries, Plymouth, 1987—, also bd. dirs.; bd. dirs. Clips and Clamps, Inc., Plymouth. Treas. Plymouth Symphony Orch., 1986-87; vol. VISTA, Boston, 1968-69. Mem. Am. Inst. CPA's, Mich. Assn. CPA's, Internat. Assn. Hospitality Accts., Gamma Pi Epsilon, Theta Phi Alpha (treas. 1967-68). Avocations: golf, piano. Office: Clips & Clamps Industries 15050 Keel St Plymouth MI 48170

AZZARELLO, JANET LUCILLE, health services administrator; b. Muskegon, Mich., May 27, 1957; d. Joseph and Mary Francis (Pawlowski) A. AA, Muskegon Community Coll., 1977; BS, Western Mich. U., 1980; M in Rehab. Adminstrn., De Paul U. Staff occupational therapist MacNeal Hosp., Berwyn, Ill., 1981-87, HomeCare Med. Services, LaGrange, Ill., 1982-87; mgr. occupational therapy, communicative disorders St. Joseph Hosp., Chgo., 1987—. Vol. Am. Cancer Soc., Chgo., 1986. Mem. Am. Occupational Therapy Assn., Ill. Occupational Therapy Assn. (chairperson 1986-87), Chgo. Area Council of Occupational Therapy Dirs., Clin. Educators Group, Hand Study Specialty Group. Office: St Joseph Hosp 2900 N Lake Shore Dr Chicago IL 60657

AZZATO, JUDITH ANNE, social worker; b. Floral Park, N.Y., Dec. 23, 1946; d. John August and Eleanor (Buckley) Rissmeyer; BA, Queens Coll., Flushing, N.Y., 1967; MSW, Fordham U., 1971; m. Michael J. Azzato, Jr., Aug. 19, 1967 (div. Aug. 1974). Caseworker, community organizer Suffolk County Dept. Social Services, Bay Shore, N.Y., 1967-73; lectr. Cornell U. Coll. Human Ecology, Ithaca, N.Y., 1974; social worker Northport-East Northport (N.Y.) Community Council, 1974-75; project dir. YMCA Outreach Project, Bay Shore, 1976-77; therapist Luth. Community Services, 1978-79; social worker L.I. Devel. Ctr., Melville, N.Y., 1978—. Bd. dirs. Econ. Opportunity Council of Suffolk, Inc., Patchogue, N.Y., 1974-77; mem. 2d Congl. Dist. Com. on Youth, 1976; bd. dirs. Suffolk County Youth Bd., 1974-75; mem. Suffolk County Conf. Juvenile and Criminal Justice, Inc., 1976-80; founding mem. Day Care Council of Suffolk, 1971-74, N.Y. State Assn. Child Day Care Councils, Inc., 1972-74; fundraiser Women's Polit. Caucus, 1973; mem. Youth Services Coordinating Council of Suffolk, 1975-77; chair ELAN N.Y. state Legislation Com., 1987-88. Qualified cert. social worker N.Y.; recipient award Suffolk County Community Service, 1977; N.Y. State-Suffolk County Dept. Social Services scholar, 1969-71. Mem. Nat. Assn. Social Workers (del. 1977, 79, 81, 84, treas. Suffolk div. 1978-81, sec. Suffolk div. 1986-90, editor newsletter 1971-75, sec. N.Y. State council 1973-75, Clin. Register Social Workers (diplomate 1978, 82, 85, 87), Queens Coll. Alumni Orgn., Alpha Sigma Alpha. Contbg. author: First Directory of Child Day Care Centers in Suffolk County, 1972; founding social worker Victims Info. Bur. of Suffolk, Inc., 1975-76.

BAACKE, MARGARETA IRMGARD, German educator; b. Berlin, July 10, 1923; d. Willibald Ludwig and Irmgard Karla (Zinke) B. Ph.D., Philipps U., 1953. Translator NYU Med. Ctr., 1954; instr. German, U. Ill., 1955; asst. prof. German, French, English lit. Western State Coll., Gunnison, Colo., 1955-57; asst. prof. German, Purdue U., West Lafayette, Ind., 1957-65; assoc. prof. German, Knox Coll., Galesburg, Ill., 1965—; instr. Ind. Fgn. Lang. Inst. for High Sch. Tchrs., Bloomington, Ind., summer 1963, NDEA Inst., Scranton, Pa., summer 1968, German Grad. Sch., Millersville, Pa., summers 1969, 70; dir., leader classes to Western and Eastern Germany, 1974, 79. Mem. MLA, Am. Assn. Tchrs. of German. Lutheran. Home: Rural Route 1 Box 170 Knoxville IL 61448 Office: Knox Coll South St Galesburg IL 61401

BAADH, VALERIE, choreographer, producer, designer; b. Burbank, Calif., Sept. 16, 1952; d. Uffe and Shirley (Goldberg) B.; m. Michael Earl Garrett, May 20, 1979; children—John David Garrett, Rose Kaiulani Garrett. B.F.A., Calif. Inst. Arts, 1973. Choreographer Dancers' Group, San Francisco, 1981-83; ind. choreographer, San Francisco, 1984—; dir. Kadeka Dances for Kids, San Francisco, 1982-84, Dancers Group/Footwork, San Francisco, 1983. Choreographer: Half Past Eight, 1981, White Dance, 1982, Spy in the House of Love, 1983, Mother Goose Suite, 1984; producer: Bay Area Theatre Week, 1986, Event of the Year, San Francisco, 1986; prodn. designer: An Evening of Comedy and Dance with Robin Williams and Friends, San Francisco, 1985; producer Nina Watt Solos, 1986, Rosa Montoya Bailes Flamencos, 1987. Mem. Nat. Assn. Law Firm Mktg. Adminstrs., Internat. Platform Assn. Home: 120 Solano St Brisbane CA 94005

BAAS, JACQUELYNN, art historian, museum administrator; b. Grand Rapids, Mich., Feb. 14, 1948. BA in History of Art, Mich. State U.; Ph.D. in History of Art, U. Mich. Registrar U. Mich. Mus. Art, Ann Arbor, 1974-78, asst. dir., 1978-82; editor Bull. Museums of Art and Archaeology, U. Mich., 1976-82; chief curator Hood Mus. Art, Dartmouth Coll., Hanover, N.H., 1982-84, dir., 1985—. Contbr. articles to jours. and catalogues. NEH fellow, 1972-73; Nat. Endowment Arts fellow, 1973-74, 87-88. Mem. Coll. Art Assn. Am., Print Council Am., Am. Assn. Museums, Assn. Art Mus. Dirs.. Home: 69 Lebanon St Hanover NH 03775 Office: Hood Mus Art Dartmouth Coll Hanover NH 03755

BABA, MARIETTA LYNN, university official, anthropologist, b. Flint, Mich., Nov. 9, 1949; d. David and Lillian (Joseph) Baba; m. David Smokler, Feb. 14, 1977 (div. 1982); 1 child, Alexia Baba Smokler. BA with highest distinction, Wayne State U., 1971, MA in Anthropology, 1973, Ph.D. in Phys. Anthropology, 1975. Asst. prof. sci. and tech. Wayne State U., Detroit, Mich., 1975-80, assoc. prof. anthropology, 1980-88, prof., 1988—, spl. asst. to pres., 1980-82, asst. devel. officer, 1982-83, asst. provost, 1983-85; assoc. provost, 1985—, dir. Internat. Programs and Interim Assoc. Dean of Grad. Sch., 1988; founder, corp. officer Applied Research Teams Mich., Inc., Detroit, Intelligent Techs., Inc., Detroit; evolution researcher Wayne State U., 1975-82; cons. Gen. Motors Research Labs., 1988; lectr. nat. and internat. symposia, profl. conferences. Contbr. numerous papers and abstracts to tech. jours; patentee in field. Bd. dirs. City-Univ. Consortium, Detroit, 1980-83; v.p. Neighborhood Service Orgn., Detroit, 1980-85; mem. State Research Fund Feasibility Rev. Panel, 1982-86; active Leadership Detroit Class IV, 1982-83; dir. Mich. Tech. Council (SE div.), 1984-85. Job Partnership Tng. Act grantee, 1981-88; NSF grantee, 1982, 84-85. Issued letters patent for method to map joint ventures and maps produced thereby; Fellow Am. Anthrop. Assn. (bd. dirs. 1986-88, exec. com. 1986-88), Nat. Assn. Practice Anthropology (pres. 1986-88), Soc. Applied Anthropology, Phi Beta Kappa, Sigma Xi. Office: Wayne State U 1050 Mackenzie Hall Detroit MI 48202

BABAKANIAN, VIVIAN, accountant; b. Tehran, Iran, Mar. 16, 1961; came to U.S., 1962; d. Nick and Lilly (Ovrahi) B. BS, NYU, 1983. Mgr. Ernst and Whinney, N.Y.C., 1983-85, Irvine, Calif., 1986-88; div. controller Trammell Crow Co., Los Angeles, 1988—. Home: 307 E Bay #2 Newport Beach CA 92661 Office: Trammell Crow Co 5701 S Eastern Ave Suite 400 Los Angeles CA 90040

BABB, CAROL ELIZABETH, marketing researcher; b. Port Lavaca, Tex., July 27, 1958; d. Leon and Marian B. BA, Memphis State U., 1980, MA, 1983. Instr. Memphis State U., 1982; research analyst Bapt. Meml. Hosp., Memphis, 1983-84; mgr. market research Le Bonheur Children's Med. Ctr., Memphis, 1985—. Mem. Am. Mktg. Assn., Nat. Assn. for Female Execs., Phi Kappa Phi. Home: 610 Shotwell Memphis TN 38111 Office: Le Bonheur Children's Med Ctr Mktg Dept One Children's Plaza Memphis TN 38103

BABB, SANORA, writer; b. Leavenworth, Kans., Apr. 21, 1907; d. Walter Lacy and Jennie Anna (Parks) B.; student Kans. U., 1924; A.A., Garden City Jr. Coll., 1925; m. James Wong Howe, Sept. 18, 1949 (dec. 1976). Editor, The Clipper, 1940-41, Calif. Quar., 1951-52 (both Los Angeles); instr. short story UCLA Extension, 1959; novel; The Lost Traveler, 1958, Brit. edit., 1958, The Dark Earth, 1987; memoir: An Owl On Every Post, 1970, Brit. edit., 1971; contbr. short stories to anthologies (including Best American Short Stories 1950, 60), texts, mags., poems to mags. Mem. Authors Guild Am. Democrat. Office: care McIntosh & Otis 475 Fifth Ave New York NY 10017

BABBAGE, JOAN DOROTHY, journalist; b. Montclair, N.J., Jan. 10, 1926; d. Laurence Washburn and Dorothy A. (Davenport) Babbage; B.A. in English, Mt. Holyoke Coll., 1948; postgrad. Art Students League, New Sch. for Social Research; m. Vernon H. Ellsworth, Mar. 6, 1971. Publicist Paramount Internat. Films, N.Y.C., 1952-58; reporter Newark News, 1960-67, food editor, 1967-72; feature writer, reporter Star-Ledger, Newark, 1972—. Vice pres. jr. group Women's Nat. Republican Club, N.Y.C., 1955. Recipient recommendation award N.J. br. Humane Soc. U.S., PICA Club N.J. award, 1980, Community Media award Assn. Retarded Citizens, Morris County Unit, N.J., 1987, Willard H. Allen Agrl. Communications Media award, N.J. Agrl. Soc., 1988. Contbr. bus. articles to N.J. Bus. Mag., articles to Ofcl. Dog mag.; appeared on NBC-TV to demonstrate dog tng. Home: Washington Ave Montclair NJ 07042 Office: Star-Ledger Court St Newark NJ 07101

BABBITT, KATHY JEAN, public relations executive, marketing executive; b. Westfield, N.Y., Oct. 9, 1950; d. Clarence Randy and Florence (Porter) Johnson; m. David Clair Babbitt, Feb. 14, 1970; children: Jeannette, Kimberly, Dione. Grad., Lancaster (Pa.) Coll. of Bible, 1969; student, East Tenn. State U., 1975; grad., Moody Bible Inst., Chgo., 1976; postgrad., Ecole de Commerce, Neuchatel, Switzerland, 1977, Ecole de Commerce, 1978. Comml. artist Christian Printing Service, Anaheim, Calif., 1981; newscaster Sta. KABN Radio, Big Lake, Ark., 1983-84; owner Babbitt and Assocs., Palmer, Alaska, 1984-86, Flowery Branch, Fla., 1986—; cons. in field; lectr. on time mgmt. Promotional designer Edna Devries for State Senate, Palmer, 1984; campaign mgr. Al Strawn for Borough Mayor, Palmer, 1984-85; organizer youth employment orgns., 1985. Recipient 1st Place award Pub. Affairs, Speeches, 1985, 1st Place award for Speaking, Toastmasters, Wasilla, Alaska, 1985, Sweepstakes award Alaska Press Women, 1986. Republican. Evangelical. Home: 11908 Elfcroft Dr Austin TX 78758

BABBITT, MICHELLE STAR, lawyer; b. Monticello, N.Y.; d. Alan Gerald and Miriam (Faber) B. BA, Goucher Coll., 1976; JD, St. John's U., 1983. Bar: U.S. Dist. Ct. N.Y. 1984, U.S. Dist. Ct. (so. dist., ea. dist.) N.Y. 1985, U.S. Ct. Claims 1985, U.S. Tax Ct. 1985. Legis. research asst. U.S. Senate, Washington, 1976-78; assoc. Rosenberg & Estis, P.C., N.Y.C., 1983-86, Stroock & Stroock & Lavan, N.Y.C., 1986—; legis. research asst. to Sen. Jacob K. Javits. Elizabeth King Ellicott scholar Goucher Coll., 1976. Mem. ABA, Assn. of Bar of City of N.Y., N.Y. County Lawyers Assn., N.Y. Womens Bar Assn., N.Y. State Bar Assn. Office: Stroock Stroock & Lavan Seven Hanover Sq New York NY 10004

BABCOCK, JANICE BEATRICE, health system specialist; b. Milw., June 2, 1942; d. Delbert Martin and Constance Josephine (Dworschack) B. BS in Med. Tech., Marquette U., 1964; MA in Healthcare Mgmt. and Supervision, Cen. Mich. U., 1975, postgrad. in Edn. in Health Care, 1975—. Registered med. technologist and microbiologist., clin. lab. scientist, Wis.; cert. bioanalytical lab. mgr. Intern St. Luke's Hosp., Milw., 1963-64; microbiologist St. Michael's Hosp., Milw., 1964-65; supr. clin. lab. service VA Regional Office, Milw., 1965-66; hosp. epidemiologist VA Ctr., Milw., 1966-74; supr. anaerobic microbiology and research lab. VA Ctr., Wood, Wis., 1974-78, adminstrv. officer, chief med. tech., 1978-83, quality assurance coordinator, 1983-86, asst. to chief of staff profl. services, 1986—; research assoc. dept. surgery Med. Coll. Wis.; tchr. in field Marquette U., U. Wis., Med. Coll. Wis.; lectr., cons. in field. Contbr. numerous articles to profl. jours. Recipient Wood VA Fed. Woman's award, 1975, Profl. Achievement award Lab. World jour., 1981, Disting. Alumni award Cen. Mich. U., 1986. Fellow Royal Soc. Health, Am. Acad. Med. Adminstrs. (Wis. state dir. 1986—); mem. Inernat. Acad. Healthcare Mgmt., Am. Soc. Microbiology, Am. Coll. Healthcare Execs., Am. Soc. Med. Tech. (Nat. Sci. Creativity award 1974, Nat. Microbiology Sci. (Achievement award 1978, Mem. of Yr. award 1979, Profl. Achievement Lectureship award 1981, French Lectureship award 1983), Assn. Practitioners in Infection Control, Fed. Execs. Assn., Wis. Hosp. Assn., AAUW, Nat. Geog. Soc., Marquette U. Alumni Assn. (Merit award 1979, Profl. Achievement award 1987), Assn. Marquette U. Women (bd. dirs. 1987-91, v.p. 1988-89), Alpha Mu Tau (pres. 1984-85), Alpha Delta Theta, Sigma Iota Epislon, Alpha Delta Pi (Alumni Honor award 1979). Club: Holiday Camera. Home: 6839 Blanchard St Wauwatosa WI 53213 Office: VA Med Center 5000 W National Ave Milwaukee WI 53295

BABCOCK, NELLIE JO, clinical social worker; b. Bozeman, Mont., Mar. 26, 1951; d. Harold C. and Patricia A. (Alexander) B.; m. Christopher J. Krenk, July 3, 1977; 1 child, Hanna Jo. Student, St. Andrews Presbyn. Coll., 1968-70; BA summa cum laude, U. Minn., 1972, MSW, 1974. Registered clin. social worker, Oreg. Psychiat. social worker Lane County Mental Health, Eugene, Oreg., 1974-75, Benton County Mental Health, Corvallis, Oreg., 1975-77, Clackamas County Mental Health, Marylhurst, Oreg., 1978; pvt. psychotherapist and cons. Lake Oswego, Oreg., 1979—; dir. Family Growth Alternatives, Marylhurst, 1980-84; co-founder, dir. Portland Family Inst., 1983—; NIMH trainee, 1972-74. Mem. Nat. Assn. Social Workers, Acad. Cert. Social Workers, Am. Assn. Marriage and Family Therapy. Democrat. Office: 425 SW 2nd St Lake Oswego OR 97034

BABCOCK, PATRICIA ANN, nurse; b. Shelbyville, Ind., Oct. 31, 1934; d. Laurence H. and Reba D. (Conway) Underwood; B.S. in Nursing, Ball State U., Muncie, Ind., 1957, M.A., 1975, 86, Ed.D. (fellow), 1980; m. Robert A. Babcock, Mar. 30, 1958; children—Brett Alan, Richard Scott, Laura Ann. Office nurse, Muncie, 1957-60; staff nurse Porter Meml. Hosp., Valparaiso, Ind., 1961; head nurse St. Joseph Hosp., Logansport, Ind., 1963-65; sch. nurse, Gary, Ind., 1967-76; asst. prof. nursing Purdue U. North Central Campus, Westville, Ind., 1976-82, assoc. prof., 1982—, acting chmn. nursing, 1983-84, chmn. nursing, 1984—; cons. in field. Mem. AAUW (br. pres.), Am. Nurses Assn., Nat. League Nursing, Ind. League Nursing, Ind. Assn. Health Educators, AAUP (chpt. pres.), Nat. Assn. Female Execs., Concern for Dying, Ind. State Nurses Assn. (dist. pres.), Hospice of Porter County, Compassionate Friends, Eta Sigma Gamma, Sigma Theta Tau, Phi Delta Theta, Sigma Kappa. Republican. Methodist. Home: 115 Washington Ave Chesterton IN 46304 Office: Purdue U North Cen Campus Westville IN 46391

BABEY, EVELYN RUTH, college official; b. N.Y.C.; d. Adam and Hedwig (Voigt) Babey; B.A., Queens Coll., 1967; M.S. in Edn. (intern) SUNY, Albany, 1969; Ph.D., N.Y.U., 1981. Asst. registrar N.Y.C. Community Coll., Bklyn., 1968-72, asso. registrar, 1972-74; registrar Kean Coll. of N.J., Union, 1974-82, adj. instr. dept. math., 1981—; dir. records Bklyn. Coll., City U. N.Y., 1982-84; registrar U. Calif.-Davis, 1984—; lectr. in field; mem. steering com. N.J./N.Y. Conf. Registrars and Admissions Officers, 1981-84, treas., 1981-84. Recipient cert. of appreciation N.J./N.Y. Conf. Registrars and Admissions Officers. Mem. Am. Assn. Higher Edn., Am. Assn. Collegiate Registrars and Admissions Officers (institutional studies and research analysis com.), N.J. Coll. and Univ., Registrars, Albany Student Personnel Alumni Assn. (treas. 1975-77, cert. of appreciation 1979), Am. Personnel and Guidance Assn., Am. Coll. Personnel Assn., AAUW, Nat. Assn. for Female Execs., Nat. Micrographics Assn., Pacific Assn. Collegiate Registrars and Officers of Admissions, Crocker Nat. Mus. (patron), Sacramento Opera Assn. (sustaining), Sacramento Symphony Assn. (sustaining), Bravo. Presbyterian. Club: Elizabeth (N.J.) Town and Country, Century. Contbr. articles to profl. jours. Office: U Calif-Davis Registrars Office Davis CA 95616

BACCUS, R. EILEEN TURNER, academic administrator; b. Oxford, N.C., Aug. 8, 1944; d. Nathaniel Benjamin and Gloria Constance (Davis) Turner; B.A., Fisk U., 1964; M.B.A., U. Conn., 1975, Ph.D., 1978; 1 son, Christopher Lloyd. Programmer, systems analyst IBM, N.Y., Mo., 1964-66; substitute tchr., Lakenheath AFB, Eng., 1967-69; asst. dir. fin. aid U. Conn., Storrs, 1970-74, asst. to dean Sch. Edn., 1974-77, dir. personnel services div., 1977-81; adminstr. treasury ops. Aetna Life & Casualty Co., Hartford, Conn., 1981-82, ops. mgr. discretionary asset mgmt., 1982-86; pres. Thames Valley State Tech. Coll., Norwich, Conn., 1986—; cons. Ford Found., 1976, Tchr. Corps, 1977, Meriden (Conn.) Schs., 1979—; dir. Conn. Savs. & Loan Assn. Mem. planning com. Conn. Legis. Black Caucus, 1980; mem. mgmt. team Ujima, Inc., Hartford, 1978-80; co-chmn. bd. Hartford Scholarship Found., 1971-75; treas. bd. Community Council Capitol Region, 1982-86; mem. community adv. bd. Jr. League Hartford, Inc., 1982—. Mem. Am. Ednl. Research Assn., Internat. Platform Assn., Phi Delta Kappa, Pi Lambda Theta, Delta Sigma Theta. Democrat. Episcopalian. Home: 71 Briarwood Dr Windsor CT 06095 Office: 574 New London Turnpike Norwich CT 06360

BACH, MURIEL DUNKLEMAN, author, actress; b. Chgo., May 14, 1918; d. Gabriel and Deborah (Warshauer) Dunkleman; m. Joseph Wolfson, June 16, 1940 (div. Apr. 1962); 1 child, Susan; m. Ira J. Bach, Apr. 14, 1963 (dec. Mar. 6, 1985); stepchildren—Caroline Bach Marandos, John Lawrence; m. Josef Diamond, May 18, 1986. Student Carleton Coll., 1935-37; B.S., Northwestern U., 1939. Researcher original manuscripts for One-Woman Theatre, also costume designer, writer, set designer; actress TV commls., indsl. films, radio commls.; photog. model; tchr. platform speaking techniques to corp. execs. Active sr. citizens groups, youth groups. Recipient Career Achievement award Chgo. Area Profl. Pan Hellenic Assn., 1971. Mem. Screen Actors Guild, AFTRA, Zeta Phi Eta. Clubs: Arts, Tavern (Chgo.). Author: (plays) Two Lives, 1958; ... because of Her!, 1963; Madame, Your Influence is Showing, 1969; MS ... Haven't We Met Before?, 1973; Lady, You're Rocking the Boat!, 1976; Freud Never Said It Was Easy, 1978; Of All the Nerve, 1982; vignettes for theatre.

BACHELER, VIRGINIA MAY, communications educator, reporter; b. Buffalo, Apr. 1, 1951; d. Albert Terry and Barbara Lee (Richardson) B.; m. Carl Francis Battaglia, Oct. 9, 1976; 1 child, Ada. BA in English, Hobart-William Smith Coll., 1973; MS in Broadcasting, Syracuse U., 1974. Feature producer Sta. WCNY-TV, Syracuse, N.Y., 1974; gen. assignment reporter Sta. WSYR-TV, Syracuse, 1975-76; reporter, producer Sta. WXXI-TV, Rochester, N.Y., 1976-78, sr. producer, 1978-79, coordinator ednl. services, 1979-81, exec. producer, 1981-83, freelancer, 1983—; asst. prof. communications SUNY, Brockport, 1983—; on-call advisor Women's Career Ctr., Rochester, 1981—. Frequent host, past exec. producer TV-video series Assignment: The World, 1979—; reported, produced video presentation on the Internat. Summer Spl. Olympics, 1979 (Golden Mic award 1979). Trustee Hobart-William Smith Coll., Geneva, N.Y., 1987—. Mem. Eastern Communication Assn., Broadcast Edn. Assn., Rochester Broadcasting and Journalism Educators Assn., Alpha Epsilon Rho. Office: SUNY Brockport A-10 Edward Hall Brockport NY 14420

BACHER, JUDITH ST. GEORGE, executive search consultant; b. New Rochelle, N.Y., July 14, 1946; d. Thomas A. and Rose-Marie (Martocci) Baiocchi; B.S., Georgetown U., 1968; M.L.S., Columbia U., 1971; m. Albert Bacher, Jan. 2, 1972; 1 son, Alexander Michael. Researcher, Time mag., N.Y.C., 1968-71; librarian Mus. Modern Art, N.Y.C., 1971-72; cons. Informaco Inc., N.Y.C., 1972-74, Booz-Allen & Hamilton, N.Y.C., 1974-79; prin. Nordeman Grimm/MBA Resources, N.Y.C., 1979—; mem. Adv. Com. on Personnel, Exec. Office of Pres., 1979-81; co-founder Research Roundtable, pres. 1981-83. Mem. Phi Beta Kappa. Office: Nordeman Grimm Inc 717 Fifth Ave New York NY 10022

BACHER, RENÉE MARGARET, hotel executive; b. Stamford, Conn., Feb. 4, 1944; d. Romeo and Rose (Killian) Bacher; student public schs. Nat. dir. retail and bus. travel Thomas Cook Travel, N.Y.C., 1975-78; dir. cons. services AAA World Wide Travel, Falls Church, Va., 1978-79; v.p., gen. mgr. Gelco Travel Services, N.Y.C., 1980-82; v.p. corp. travel Liberty Travel, Paramus, N.J., 1982-87; regional sales mgr. Regency Cruises, N.Y.C.; dir. sales and mktg. Inn at Mill River, Stamford, Conn., 1987—.

BACHER, ROSALIE WRIDE, educational administrator; b. Los Angeles, May 25, 1925; d. Homer M. and Reine (Rogers) Wride; AB, Occidental Coll., 1947, MA, 1949; m. Archie O. Bacher, Jr., Mar. 30, 1963. Tchr., English, Latin, history David Starr Jordan High Sch., Long Beach, Calif., 1949-55, counselor, 1955-65, Lakewood (Calif.) Sr. High Sch., 1965-66; research asst., counselor Poly. High Sch., Long Beach, 1966-67; counselor, office occupational preparation, vocational guidance sect. Long Beach Unified School Dist., Long Beach, 1967-68; vice prin. Washington Jr. High Sch., Long Beach, 1968-70; asst. prin. Lakewood Sr. High Sch., Long Beach, spring 1970; vice prin. Jefferson Jr. High Sch., Long Beach, 1970-81, Marshall Jr. High Sch., Long Beach, 1981-87; vice prin. Lindbergh Jr. High Sch., Long Beach, 1987—; counselor Millikan High Sch., 1988—; chmn. vocat. guidance steering com. Long Beach Unified Sch. Dist., 1963—. Mem. Internat. Platform Assn., AAUW, Long Beach Personnel and Guidance Assn. (dir. 1958-60), Long Beach Sch. Counselors Assn. (sec. high sch. segment 1963-64), Phi Beta Kappa, Delta Kappa Gamma (pres. Delta Psi chpt., area dir.; Calif. profl. affairs com. chmn. 1972-74), Phi Delta Gamma (pres. chpt. 1977-78, 87—, nat. chmn. bylaws com. 1980-81, Nat. Conv. Com. 1987-88), Pi Lambda Theta (pres. chpt. 1974-76, v.p. So. Calif. council 1974-76), Phi Delta Kappa (sec. Long Beach chpt. 1977-80). Home: 265 Rocky Point Rd Palos Verdes Estates CA 90274 Home: 17721 Misty Lane Huntington Beach CA 92649 Office: Millikan High Sch 2800 Snowden Ave Long Beach CA 90815

BACHLEDA, KATHLEEN MARGARET, computer manufacturing administrator; b. Trenton, N.J., Dec. 2, 1948; d. John Joseph and Evelyn Marie (Criss) O'Hare; m. Eugene George Most, Nov. 22, 1969 (div. Nov. 1978); 1 child, Michele; m. George Paul Bachleda, Mar. 1, 1987. Grad., Taylor Bus. Inst., Plainfield, N.J., 1967. Sec., IBM Corp., Princeton, N.J., 1967-73, staff asst., 1973-78, adminstrn. mgr., Indpls., 1978-81, adminstrn. ops. mgr., Southfield, Mich., 1981—. Mem. Nat. Assn. Female Execs. Republican. Roman Catholic. Avocations: writing poetry; reading; swimming; traveling. Home: 5101 Fedora St Troy MI 48098 Office: IBM Corp 27800 Northwestern Hwy Southfield MI 48086

BACHMAN, BONNIE JEAN, polymer physicist; b. Mt. Pleasant, Iowa, Sept. 20, 1950; d. Wilbur R. and Josephine (Lyon) Wilson; m. Dennis W. Bachman Feb. 21, 1970 (dec. Mar. 1981); 1 child, Chad M.; m. Lloyd R. Linnell, Nov. 15, 1982. AS, Coll. of DuPage, 1973; BS in Physics, Ill. Benedictine Coll., 1979; MS in Mechanics and Materials Sci., Rutgers U., 1987. Analytical laboratory supr. UOP Inc., Norplex Div., LaCrosse, Wis., 1979-80; mem. tech. staff Bell Labs., Naperville, Ill., 1981-84; mem. tech. staff research AT&T Bell Labs., Murray Hill, N.J., 1984—. Mem. Am. Chem. Soc. (chmn. N.J. Thermal Analysis Topical Group 1988), North Am. Thermal Analysis Soc. (sec. 1985-87, v.p., pres.-elect 1988), Soc. Plastic Engrs. (sr., chmn. plastic analysis div. 1985, chmn. tech. program 1988, exec. appointment to council, 1988, Mem. of Yr. 1985), Am. Physical Soc., Materials Research Soc. Office: AT&T Bell Labs 600 Mountain Ave 2D-225 Murray Hill NJ 07974-2070

BACHMAN, CAROL CHRISTINE, trust company executive; b. Buffalo, Jan. 20, 1959; d. Christian George and Joan Marie (Fincel) B. Student, Grad. Inst. Internat. Study, 1979-80; AB, Smith Coll., 1981; grad., New Eng. Sch. Banking, 1987. Trust asst. BayBank Middlesex, Burlington, Mass., 1984-85, sr. trust asst., 1985-87, trust adminstr., 1987, trust officer, 1987—. Mem. Nat. Assn. Female Execs. Roman Catholic. Home: 10 Marie Dr Wilmington MA 01887 Office: BayBank Middlesex 7 New England Exec Park Burlington MA 01803

BACHMAN, MARGIE KAY, publishing executive; b. Allentown, Pa., Nov. 27, 1953; d. Willard George and Althea Acquilla (Hausman) B.; m. Leslie Wayne Goldstein, May 30, 1982; 1 child, Allison Laurisa Goldstein. AA, Rider Coll., 1973. Adminstrv. asst. Group Travel Assocs., Allentown, Pa., 1972-73; exec. sec. to dir., asst. dir. U. Pitts. Press, 1973-77, promotion asst., 1977-78, promotion and mktg. mgr., 1978-86, spl. adminstrv. projects mgr., subs. rights mgr., 1986—; speaker Northeastern & Mid-Atlantic Regional Presses Meeting, Syracuse, N.Y., 1980. Soloist East Liberty Presbyn. Ch., Pitts., 1983—, deacon, 1985—, sec. of bd. dirs., 1986—; telephone support Parents Helping Parents of High Risk Infants, Pitts., 1986—. Recipient cert. and monetary award Rotary, Allentown, 1971. Mem. Assn. Am. Univ. Presses (mktg. com. nominee 1982, speaker 1983), Performing Arts for Children, Carnegie Inst. Democrat. Club: Western Pa. Conservancy. Home: 345 Barclay Ave Pittsburgh PA 15221-4058 Office: U Pitts Press 127 N Bellefield Ave Pittsburgh PA 15260

BACH-STEWART, GWENDOLYN FAYE, public affairs professional; b. Mamou, La., Jan. 27, 1945; d. Elbert Howard and Elverta (Brunet) Bach; m. Steven Dell Stewart, Sept. 15, 1967 (div. May 1978); 1 child, Jennifer Dell. BA, La. State U., 1966. Reporter State-Times, Baton Rouge, 1966-69; asst. dir. Greater Baton Rouge Safety Council, 1970-71; editor woman's sect.

The Ft. Bend Mirror, Stafford, Tex., 1972-73; coordinator community relations Ft. Bend Ind. Sch. Dist., Stafford, Tex., 1973-77; sr. tech. writer Edelman Systems, Inc., Baton Rouge, 1978-82; dir. pub. affairs La. Dept. Health & Human Resources, Baton Rouge, 1983-87, exec. mgmt. cons., 1987—. fund raiser Arts & Humanities Council, Baton Rouge, 1986—; Community Fund for the Arts, Baton Rouge, 1987. Recipient Addy award Am. Advt. Fedn., 1983. Mem. Pub. Relations Soc. Am. (cert., bd. dirs. local chpt. 1986-87, treas. local chpt. 1988), So. Pub. Relations Fedn. (Lantern award 1986), Pub. Relations Assn. La. (local bd. dirs. 1986, 88—), Baton Rouge Press Club (charter mem.), LWV (mktg. chmn. La. chpt.). Democrat. Roman Catholic. Office: La Dept Health & Human Resources 755 Riverside PO Box 3776 Baton Rouge LA 70821

BACHTEL NASH, ANN ELIZABETH, educational consultant, researcher, educator; b. Winnipeg, Man., Can., Dec. 12, 1928; d. John Wills and Margaret Agnes (Gray) Macleod; m. Richard Earl Bachtel, Dec. 19, 1947; children—Margaret Ann, John Macleod, Bradley Wills; m. 2d, Louis Philip Nash, June 30, 1978. A.B., Occidental Coll., 1947; M.A., Calif. State U.-Los Angeles, 1976. Cert. tchr., adminstr., Calif. Elem. tchr. pub. and pvt. schs. in Calif., 1947-50, 64-77; dir. Emergency Sch. Aid Act program, spl. projects, spl. arts State of Calif., 1977-80; leader, mem. program rev. team Calif. State Dept. Edn., 1981—; cons. Pasadena Unified Sch. Dist., 1981—; teaching asst., adj. prof. U. So. Calif.; cons. sch. dists., state depts. edn.; presenter workshops/seminars; mem. legis. task forces. Chmn. resource allocation com. City of Pasadena, Pasadena-Mishima (Japan) Sister Cities Internat. Com.; mem. Los Angeles World Affairs Council, docent council Pasadena Hist. Soc., Pasadena Philharm. Com., women's com. Pasadena Symphony Assn.; Emergency Sch. Aid Act grantee, 1977-81. Mem. World Council Gifted and Talented Children, Internat. Soc. Edn. Through Art, Council Exceptional Children, Am. Ednl. Research Assn., Assn. Supervision and Curriculum Devel., Nat. Art Educators Assn., Calif. Art Educators Assn., Calif. Humanities Edn. Assn., AAUW, Phi Delta Kappa, Kappa Delta Pi, Phi Lambda Theta, Assistance League of Pasadena. Contbr. articles to publs.; writer/editor: Arts for the Gifted and Talented, 1981; author Nat. Directory of Programs for Artistically Gifted and Talented Students, K-12. Office: 732 Pinehurst Dr Pasadena CA 91106

BACHUS, PATRICIA ANN, rehabilitation organization administrator, consultant; b. San Antonio, Dec. 10, 1950; d. Joseph Sylvester and Edna Mae (Bretzke) McAvey; m. David Charles Bachus, June 26, 1970; children: Charlene Jo, Theresa Lynn, Jeffrey David. Student, Amarillo Coll., 1971-73, 75. Cert. med. asst. Med. sec., transcriptionist Amarillo (Tex.) Hosp. Dist., 1970-76; office supr. Drs. Arvo Neidre, Brad Hall, San Antonio, 1976-85; asst. adminstr. South Tex. Work Assessment and Rehab. Ctr., Inc., San Antonio, 1985—; cons. Joseph A. Ward Behavioral Health Assocs., San Antonio, 1987—. Leader, Girl Scouts; Sunday Sch. tchr. Mem. Am. Assn. Med. Assts., Nat. Assn. Female Execs. Democrat. Lutheran. Office: S Tex Work Assessment and Rehab Ctr Inc 7614 Louis Pasteur Suite 300 San Antonio TX 78229

BACIC, DIANA COPPOLA, business executive; b. Brooklyn Heights, N.Y., Oct. 23, 1946; d. Francis George and Josephine (Manco) Coppola; AS, N.Y.C. Community Coll., 1966; BA, Queens Coll., 1970; m. Peter Raymond Hinkle, Nov. 12, 1982; 1 child, Jason Scott. Media dir. Wesson & Warhaftig Advt., N.Y.C., 1972-77; advt. sales rep. Charles C. Cunningham, Inc. Park Ridge, N.J., 1977-78; dir. media/research MED Communications, Hopelawn, N.J., 1978-82; v.p., media dir. Zip Pac Inc., Highlands, N.J., 1982—; v.p. media Strategic Med. Communications, Cranford, N.J., 1984—; mem. programs and seminars com. Pharm. Advt. Council, 1978—. Vol., Sports for the Handicapped Program, Garden State Rehab. Hosp., 1979—. Mem. Pharm. Advt. Council, Healthcare Bus. Woman Assn., Portland Point Assn. Club: Irish Setter of Long Island. Home: 141 Portland Rd Highlands NJ 07732

BACKE, PAMELA RENEE, auditing administrator; b. Marinette, Wis., Dec. 25, 1955; d. Wilbur Milton and Eulalia Ellen (Johnson) Mandigo; m. Stephen Allen Backe, June 15, 1974. AA, Truckee Meadows Community Coll., 1981, AAS in Data Processing, 1982; BS, U. Nev., 1987. Proof operator Bank of Am., Watsonville, Calif., 1973-76; adminstrv. asst. Truckee Meadows Christian Ctr., Reno, 1976-82; mgr. info. systems Sierra Office Concepts, Reno, 1982-84; auditor EDP Harrah's, Reno, 1984-86, sr. auditor EDP, 1986-87, mgr. internal audit, 1987—. Mem. Data Processing Mgmt. Assn., Inst. Internal Auditors. Republican. Mem. Assemblies of God. Club: Silver State Striders. Home: 12980 Broili Dr Reno NV 89511 Office: Harrah's 300 E 2d St Reno NV 89502

BACKIS, PAMELA CRAYTON, options exchange administrator; b. Newark, Ohio, Nov. 28, 1947; d. Robert Porter and Catherine (Ector) Good; children: Kimberly Meredith Crayton, Alexandra Danielle Backis. B.A., Morris Brown U., 1973, postgrad. Loyola U., Chgo. Cert. police instr., Ga. Pub. safety planner Dept. Pub. Safety, Atlanta, 1975-80; cons. Ga. Peace Officers, Decatur, 1980-81; office mgr. St. Vincent de Paul, Atlanta, 1982; project coordinator Chgo. Bd. Options, Chgo., 1983—; cons. Melear Multimedia, Marietta, Ga., 1981. Author radio script: Slam the Door on Death, 1976 (award); author, editor tng. curriculum: Basic and Advanced Arson Investigation Manual, 1981 (award). Organizer, dir. Commn. for Black Catholic Concerns, Atlanta, 1982; mem. adv. bd. Parents Anonymous of Ga., Atlanta, 1981, bd. dirs., 1982; catechist St. Anthony, St. Ignatius, Atlanta and Chgo., 1982-85. Mem. Nat. Assn. Female Execs., Am. Bus. Women's Assn. (treas. 1977-79). Democrat. Roman Catholic. Avocations: music; acting. Home: 1225 W Chase #E-2 Chicago IL 60626 Office: Chgo Bd Options Exchange 400 S LaSalle Chicago IL 60605

BACKMAN, CARMEN RAE, health science association administrator; b. Yankton, S.D., July 25, 1963; d. Arthur Leo and Sharon Rose (Leise) Wieseler; m. Jude Florian Backman, Feb. 28, 1962; children: Brandan Jackson. BA, A in Bus. Adminstrn., Mt. Marty Coll., 1985. Acct. Burchinal Cooperative, Rockwell, Iowa, 1985-86; acct. Rio Grande Health Maintenance Orgn., El Paso, Tex., 1986-87, controller, 1987—. Mem. Exec. Woman. Republican. Roman Catholic. Home: 415 Redd Rd 13-B El Paso TX 79932

BACKMAN, JEAN ADELE, real estate executive; b. N.Y.C., Mar. 3, 1931; d. Seraphin Michael and Helen Elma (Matthews) Millon; m. Frank F. Backman, Sept. 27, 1954; children: Carl Eric, Adam Andrew. BA, Hunter Coll., 1954; degree in real estate mgmt., Am. U., 1980. Sales assoc. Ted Lingo Realty, Potomac, Md., 1970-73; sales mgr. House and Home Real Estate, Potomac, 1973-74; dist. mgr. Panorama Real Estate, Potomac, 1975-78; v.p., dir. mktg., sales Panorama Real Estate, Tysons Corner, Va., 1978-82; sr. v.p., regional sales mgr. Coldwell Banker Real Estate, Vienna, Va., 1983-88; dir. orgnl. devel. and tng. Coldwell Banker Real Estate, Balt. and Washington, 1988—; cons. Reston Pub. Co., Reston, Va., 1979-82, Panorama Condominiums, Tysons Corner, 1979-82. Mem. Realtors for Pol. Action, Falls Church, Va., 1985. Mem. Am. Mgmt. Assn., Nat. Assn. Realtors, Va. Assn. Realtors, No. Va. Bd. Realtors, Mongomery County Bd. Realtors, Washington Bd. Realtors, Va. C. of C., Potomac C. of C. Republican. Presbyterian. Office: Coldwell Banker Real Estate 465 W Maple St Vienna VA 22180

BACKMAN, MARGARET ESTHER, psychologist; b. Johnstown, Pa.; d. Peter Louis and Helen (McNulty) B. AB, Barnard Coll., 1960; MA, Columbia U., 1961, PhD, 1970; postdoctoral cert. clin. psychology, NYU, 1980-83. Cert. psychologist. Dir. research Internat. Ctr. for Disabled, N.Y.C., 1973-78; dir. program devel. services, exec. dir. personnel devel. Coll. Bd., N.Y.C., 1978-80; clin. instr. psychiatry NYU Med. Ctr., N.Y.C., 1985—; psychologist health services dept. Barnard Coll., N.Y.C., 1985—; pvt. practice clin. psychologist N.Y.C., 1980—; with panel on testing handicapped people Nat. Acad. Scis., Washington, 1979-81, adv. council research and tng. ctr. U. Wis.-Stout, Menomenie, 1976-82. Mem. Am. Psychological Assn., Nat. Rehab. Assn. Office: 30 E 40th St Suite 902 New York NY 10016

BACKUS, ROBERTA, advertising agency executive; b. Miami, Fla., Dec. 15, 1950; d. Louis Alfred and Ann Marie (Downey) Ritchie; m. Lawrence O. Turner, Jr., Dec. 17, 1983; 1 dau., Rene Lynn. Student, U. Miami, 1968; grad. Bank Mktg. Sch., Denver, 1974. Advt. dir. Levitz Furniture, Miami, Fla. and Los Angeles, 1975-76; assoc. media dir. Mike Sloan, Inc., Miami, 1976-78; v.p. advt. service, Ryder & Schild, Miami, 1974-78; pres., chief exec. officer Backus Advt., Miami, 1978—, Backus/SCF, Miami, 1983—. Author: The Sad Merry Go Round, 1984. Chmn. Miami promoting Miami com.; bd.dirs. Zool. Soc. Fla., Karen Carpenter Found., Miami Film Festival, Orange Bowl Com.; Miami Children's Hosp. Telethon; mem. adv. bd. Republican Party, Washington, 1983. Mem. Am. Mktg. Assn., Advt. Fedn. Greater Miami, Nat. Acad. Arts and Scis., Nat. Assn. Advt. Agys., Nat. Assn. for Am. Indians, Bus. Soc. Miami, Greater Miami C. of C. (gov., trustee). Republican. Roman Catholic. Office: Backus & Ptnrs 1441 Brickell Miami FL 33131

BACON, CAROL ANN, nurse; b. Evergreen Park, Ill., Apr.2, 1941; d. Raymond Benjamin and Loretta Carolyn (Diimig) Hanson; RN, St. Mary's Sch. Nursing, 1962; BS, St. Francis Coll., 1978. Cert. safety exec. div. clin. charge nurse U. Ill. Hosp. and Clinics, 1962-71; supr. Oak Park (Ill.) Hosp., 1972-75; adminstr. Addison Med. Ctr., 1976-81; nurse v.p., occupational health program Doctors Emergency Officenter, Mt. Prospect, Ill., 1981-85; owner C.A.B. Cons., occupational health and wellness programs, Hillside, Ill., 1985—. Mem. Am. Assn. Occupational Health Nurses (cert., 1987), Suburban Chgo. Assn. Occupational Health Nurses (v.p. 1981-82, 85-87, pres. 1987—), Emergency Dept. Nurses Assn., Nat. Occupational Nurses Assn., Ill. State C. of C., Am. Soc. Safety Engrs. (chmn. membership com. N.E. Ill. chpt., 1986-87, newsletter editor 87-88), Ill. State Occupational Health Nurses Assn. (fin. dir. 1982-84), World Safety Orgn. (cert. 1986). Roman Catholic.

BACON, JANICE LYNNE, obstetrician-gynecologist; b. Detroit, May 22, 1954; d. Ronald Dennis and Shirley Elaine (Davey) B. BA, Jacksonville (Fla.) U., 1976; MD, U. S. Fla., 1979. Resident Richland Meml. Hosp., Columbia, S.C., 1983-85; asst. prof. U. S.C., Columbia, 1985—; mem. med. adv. bd., trustee Planned Parenthood, Columbia, 1987—. Fellow Am. Coll. Ob-Gyn; mem. AMA, Am. Med. Women's Assn. (pres.), N. Am. Soc. Pediatric and Adolescent Gynecology (budget com.), Am. Fertility Soc. (assoc.), Nat. Bd. Med. Examiners (CBX scoring com.), S.C. Bd. Med. Examiners, Nat. Assn. Female Execs., Delta Delta Delta Alumnae Assn. Home: 103 William and Mary Ct Columbia SC 29205 Office: U SC Sch Medicine Dept Ob-Gyn Two Richland Med Park Suite 302 Columbia SC 29203

BACON, MARGARET KELLER, retired psychological anthropology educator; b. Bourbon, Ind., Nov. 20, 1909; d. Vernon Clay and Jesse Ione (McAlpine) K.; m. Selden Daskam Bacon, May 25, 1946; children: Selden Daskam, Jr., Michael McAlpine. BS, Purdue U., 1931; MA, Brown U., 1933, PhD, 1940. Cert. Am. Bd. Examiners Profl. Psychology. Psychologist Butler Hosp., Providence, 1933-39; fellow Yale U., New Haven, 1939-40; clin. psychologist Yale Med. Sch., New Haven, 1943-45, asst. prof., 1945-47; research grantee Yale/Rutgers U., New Haven/New Brunswick, N.J., 1949-62; prof. Rutgers U., New Brunswick, 1969-80; prof. emeritus Rutgers U. Grad. Sch. Anthropology Dept., New Brunswick, 1971-81; instr. Psychology Dept. Yale U., 1943-45; attending psychologist New Haven Hosp., 1945-47. Contbr. articles to profl. jours. Ford Found. grantee, 1947-58; Rutgers Research Council NIMH grantee, 1950-76, Nat. Office Edn. grantee, 1970-73. Fellow Nat. Am. Psychol. Assn. (life), Am. Anthrop. Assn., Ea. Psychol. Assn.; Mem. Soc. for Cross-Cultural Research (disting. mem.). Club: Old Fields Community (Martha's Vineyard). Home: 16 Renear St RFD 2-41B Vineyard Haven MA 02568 also: West Tisbury MA 02575

BACON, PATRICIA JOY, quality operations supervisor; b. Plainview, Tex., July 7, 1930; d. Henry George and Cora Belle (Land) Robinson; m. Walter Alvin Miller Jr., Oct. 26, 1951 (div. May 1964); children: Walter Munro, Mary Madeline, Jack Lowell, Anne Francene; m. William Bartlett Bacon Jr., Oct. 28, 1971. Student, Mary Hardin-Baylor U., 1947-48, Amarillo Coll., 1977-78, West Tex. State U. & U. Okla., 1987. Bank clk. First Nat. Bank, Panhandle, Tex., 1948-52; cahier, bookkeeper Southwestern Pub. Services Co., Panhandle, 1954-55; chems. clk. Union Carbide Chems. Co., Houston, 1955-60; tech. clk. Mason & Hanger-Silas Mason Co. Inc., Amarillo, Tex., 1960-72, quality inspector, 1972-77, quality supr., 1977—. Contbr. articles to profl. jours. Angel Confederate Air Force, Amarillo, 1975-87, adj., col., 1980—; mem. Va. County Soc., Middleburg, Va., 1987—, Can. War Plane Heritage, Hamilton, Ont., Can., 1985—, Fourth Tex. Mem. Calvary, Lubbock, 1986—. Republican. Episcopalian. Office: Mason & Hanger-Silas Mason Co Inc PO Box 30001 Amarillo TX 79177

BACON, PAULA, educational counselor, instructor; b. Bronx, N.Y, May 14; d. John and Helen (Swensen) Jacobsen; m. George H. Bacon, Apr. 2, 1977; children: Lynn, Randy, Kimberly, Lisa. A in Bus., So. Ill. U., 1967; B in Bus., Pace U., 1980, postgrad., 1985—. Exec. sec. SUNY, Purchase, 1967-74; adminstrv. asst. Pace U., Pleasantville, N.Y., 1974-85; acad. counselor Pace U., Pleasantville, 1985-87, asst. dir. student service ctr., 1987—; instr. Norwalk (Conn.) Community Coll., 1981-83, The Berkeley Bus. Sch., White Plains, N.Y., 1984-87. Vol. Putnam Community Hosp., Carmel, N.Y., 1976-77. Mem. Adminstrv. Council and Pace U. Senate, Nat. Assn. Female Execs., Bus. and Profl. Women's Assn. (sec., treas. 1976-77), Smithsonian Instn. Office: Pace U Bedford Rd Pleasantville NY 10570

BADDOUR, ANNE BRIDGE (MRS. RAYMOND F. BADDOUR), aviatrix; b. Royal Oak, Mich.; d. William George and Esther Rose (Pfiester) Bridge; m. Raymond F. Baddour, Sept. 25, 1954; children—Cynthia Anne, Frederick Raymond, Jean Bridge. Student Detroit Bus. Sch., 1948-50. Stewardess, Eastern Airlines, Boston, 1952-54; instr. aeros. Powers Sch., Boston, 1958; co pilot, flight attendant Raytheon Co., Bedford, Mass., 1958-63; flight dispatcher, ferry Pilot Comerford Flight Sch., Bedford, 1974-76; adminstrv. asst., ferry pilot, Jenney Beechcraft, Bedford, 1976; mgr., pilot Baltimore Airways, Inc., Bedford, 1976-77; pilot, flight facility M.I.T. Lincoln Lab. Flight Test Facility, Lexington, Mass., 1977—; aviation cons., corp. pilot Energy Resources, Inc., Cambridge, Mass., 1974-84. Bd. dirs. Cambridge Opera, 1977-79; mem. campaign council Mus. Transp., Boston; mem. council assos. French Library in Boston; commr. Commonwealth of Mass., Mass. Aero. Commn., 1979-83; chmn. regional adv. council FAA, 1984-88. Winner trophy Phila. Transcontinental Air Race, 1954, New Eng. Air Race, 1957. World Class speed records Boston to Goose Bay, Labrador, 1985, Boston to Reykjavik, Iceland, 1985, Portland, Me. to Goose Bay, 1985, Portland to Reykjavik, 1985, Goose Bay to Reykjavik, 1985. Mem. Fedn. Aeronautique International, Nat. Aero. Assn., Ninety-Nines (winner New Eng. Safety Trophy 1986), Aero Club New England (v.p., dir.), Aircraft Owners Pilots Assn., Nat. Pilots Assn., U.S. Sea Plane Pilots Assn., Assn. Women Transcontinental Air Race, Republican. Episcopalian. Clubs: Bostonian Soc., English Speaking Union, Friends of Switzerland, French Center Library, Belmont Hill, Aero of New Eng. (dir. 1978—), St. Botolph. Home: 96 Fletcher Rd Belmont MA 02178 Office: Draper Flight Test Facility Lincoln Lab MIT PO Box 98 Concord MA 01742

BADER, BETTY JAYNE, medical facility administrator; b. Memphis, Jan. 18, 1947; d. Michael Lewis and Mildred Frederica (Grand) Leskin; m. Charles William Bader, Mar. 1, 1980 (div.); 1 child, Michael Anthony. BS, Bklyn. Coll., 1968. Accounts receivable supr. Hartford Ins. Group, N.Y.C., 1968-71; engr. asst. Mobil Oil Corp., N.Y.C., 1971-76; office mgr. Argano Electric Corp., Ozone Park, N.Y., 1976-80, Harbor Cat Scan, Bklyn., 1980-81; adminstr. Lewis M. Wiener, MD, PC, Bklyn., 1981—; cons. Comprehensive Practice Mgmt., N.Y.C., 1984—; cons. Nat. Neighborhood Counseling Ctrs., Bklyn., 1983-86. Charter mem. Rep. Presdl. Task Force, Washington, 1984; cons. Abbate For Assembly campaign, N.Y., 1986. Recipient Human Relations award L.I. U. Ctr. for Human Devel., N.Y.C., 1984. Mem. N.Y. Acad. Scis., Am. Coll. Utilization Rev. Physicians, Am. Assn. Med. Assts., Am. Med. Record Assn., Am. Med. Peer Rev. Assn., U.S. Senatorial Club. Jewish. Home: 1365 71st St Brooklyn NY 11228 Office: Lewis M Wiener MD PC 5010 Ft Hamilton Pkwy Brooklyn NY 11219

BADGER, ANN STAHL, mental health services adminstrator; b. Rochester, N.Y., Aug. 17, 1942; d. Clement and Edna (Murray) Stahl; children: Maureen, Andrea, Lauren. BA in Sociology, Nazareth Coll., 1965; MSW, Syracuse (N.Y.) U., 1969; M of Profl. Services, New Sch. for Social Research, N.Y.C., 1983. Caseworker Monroe County Dept. Social Services, Rochester, 1965-67; asst. prof. Upstate Med. Ctr., Syracuse, 1969-72; psychiat. social worker Fairmount Children's Ctr., Syracuse, 1973-75, adminstr. outpatient psychiat. program, 1976-78, exec. dir., 1979-88, dep. commr. of mental health, 1988—; asst. prof. child and adolescent psychiatry and pediatrics, SUNY Health Sci. Ctr., Syracuse, 1980—; pvt. practice psychotherapy, Syracuse, 1982—. Bd. dirs. State Task Forces on Home Treatment and Assesment, Albany, N.Y., 1980, Child Abuse Council Onondaga County, Syracuse, 1982—, N.Y. State Office Mental Health, Albany, 1983-84. Mem. Nat. Assn. Social Workers (cert. clin. diplomate), Nat. Assn. Individual Investors. Democrat. Roman Catholic. Home: 121 Iroquois Ln Liverpool NY 13088 Office: Fairmount Children's Ctr PO Box 69 Belle Isle Rd Syracuse NY 13209

BADGER, JULIA MARGUERITE, hospital executive; b. Houston, Feb. 16, 1919; d. John and Julia Bennetta (Amonette) Oliver; m. Newton Augustus Bryson, July 6, 1940 (dec. Mar. 1970); 1 son, Barry Lee Bryson; m. 2d, William Herbert Badger, June 7, 1975. Student Sinclair Coll., 1936-38, U. Houston, 1971, Baylor Coll. Medicine, 1972. Sec.-treas. Houston Concrete Co., 1937-41; v.p. Bryson Lumber Co., Houston, 1948-70; dir. admissions Hermann Hosp., Houston, 1973-76, dir. patient services, 1976-77, coordinator flight ops., 1977-78, dir. flight ops., 1978—; pub. relations dir. Hermann Hosp. and Life Flight, 1976—; chmn. Aircraft Assistance in Disaster, City of Houston, 1982-83. Named Woman of Yr., YWCA, Houston, 1979; Hon., Harris County Sheriff's Dept., Houston, 1979; Marritot/Carlson award for contbns. to hosp. air emergency services, 1985. Mem. Am. Soc. Hosp. Based Emergency Air Med. Services (sec.-treas. 1980-82), Helicopter Assn. Internat. (mem. emergency medicine com.), Am. Helicopter Soc., Helicopter Operators Tex. Republican. Presbyterian. Clubs: Houston Lumberwomen (pres. 1953-54), Am. Osteopathy Aux. Doctor's (Houston). Office: Hermann Hosp 1203 Ross Sterling St Houston TX 77030

BADGER, MARY MARGUERITE, nurse; b. Dallas, Apr. 21, 1941; d. Hannah (Lewis) Williams; m. John Smith, Dec. 9, 1961 (div. 1965); children—Timothy Anthony Williams, Mark Vincent Williams; m. 2d, Napoleon Badger, Dec. 9, 1967. A.A.S., El Centro Coll., 1979. R.N., Tex. Staff nurse St. Paul Hosp., Dallas, 1971-73, VA Med. Ctr., Dallas, 1973—. Instr., Am. Heart Assn., Dallas, 1979—. Recipient Superior Performance award VA Med. Ctr., 1983, Outstanding Participation and Dedicated Service award New Mt. Moriah Bapt. Ch., 1987; named Woman of Yr., New Mt. Moriah Bapt. Ch., 1982.

BADILLA, GLORIA ANN, mechanical engineer; b. Tucson, Ariz., Aug. 28, 1961. BS, Calif. Inst. of Tech., 1983. Tech. staff Rockwell Internat., Downey, Calif., 1983-85; systems engr. SYSCON Corp., Montrose, Calif., 1985-87, sr. systems engr., 1987—. Mem. Soc. Women Engrs. (scholarship chair 1984-86, sec. 1986-87, sect. rep. 1987—), Nat. Assn. Female Execs. Democrat. Roman Catholic. Home: 821 S Cerritos #19 Azusa CA 91702 Office: SYSCON Corp 2550 Honolulu Ave Suite 201 Montrose CA 91020

BADILLO, ANA MARIA, banker; b. Buenos Aires, Aug. 4, 1955; d. Jose Antonio and Carmen Doris (Cainzos) Caldeiro; m. Nelson Badillo, Aug. 29, 1956; 1 child, Sarah Ann. AS in Bus. Adminstrn., Queensboro Community Coll., 1982; BS in Fin., St. John's U., 1986. Internat. officer Banco de La Nación Argentina, N.Y.C., 1974—. Mem. Nat. Assn. for Female Execs., Alpha Beta Gamma, Omicron Delta Epsilon. Roman Catholic. Office: Banco de La Nación Argentina 299 Park Ave New York NY 10171

BADILLO, DIANE, psychologist; b. Aguadilla, P.R., May 14, 1946; d. Daniel and Carmen (Jiménez) B.; m. José Vivaldy Martinez, Sept. 28, 1968; children: Dana, Melissa, José II. MA, U. P.R., 1970; PhD, CUNY, N.Y.C., 1984. Psychologist Pediatric Ctr. for Handicapped Children, Santurce, P.R., 1971-75, Bronx Psychiat. Ctr., 1978-86; pvt. practice psychology Danbury, Conn., 1986—; adj. prof. Western Conn. U., Danbury, 1986—; neuropsychologist DATAHR, Inc., Brookfield, Conn., 1985—; cons. Hartford Mental Health Ctr., 1986—. P.R. Dept Labor scholar, 1970. Mem. Am. Psychol. Assn., Soc. of Neurosci., Am. Pain Soc., Hispanic Psychol. Assn., N.Y. Acad. Scis., Spanish Am. Cultural Assn. (cultural com. 1986—). Baptist. Office: 27 Hospital Ave #303 Danbury CT 06810

BADRAN, LYNDA LEE, engineering company executive; b. Norfolk, Va., Feb. 19, 1947; d. Edward Nicholas and Mildred Belle (Signaigo) Badran; m. Henry John Huelsberg, Jr., Aug. 1, 1970 (div. 1979); children—Henry John, III, Erin Elizabeth. B.A. in Modern Fgn. Langs., Mary Washington Coll., U. Va., 1968. Owner, sec., treas. Heritage Furniture, Norfolk, Va., 1972-78; exec. asst. Systems Engring. Assocs., Virginia Beach, Va., 1978-81; v.p., dir. contracts Am. Systems Engring. Corp., Virginia Beach, 1981—.

BAECHLE, SUSAN JEAN PARKS, insurance company executive; b. Carroll, Iowa, Sept. 19, 1946; d. Neil Clark and Betty Ann (Sebern) P.; m. Thomas Raymond Baechle, Nov. 12, 1943; children: Todd Emil, Clark Alan. BA, U. Nebr., 1968. CLU, charted fin. cons. Corr. policy holder service Bankers Life Nebr., Lincoln, 1968-69; agt. Mass. Mut. Life, Sioux City, Iowa, 1970-77; adminstr. life plans, rep. group mktg. Mammel, Olson, Schropp, Horn and Swartzbaugh, Inc., Omaha, 1977-81; garment salesperson Nat. Strength and Conditioning Assn., Omaha, 1981-87; dir. career devel. Omaha Gen. Agy. Northwestern Mut. Life, 1985—. Mem. Omaha Assn. Life Underwriters, Am. Soc. CLU's and Chartered Fin. Cons., Phi Mu Alumni (pres. 1985-87). Republican. Home: 9125 Dorcas Omaha NE 68124 Office: Northwestern Mut Life 7000 W Center Rd Suite 100 Omaha NE 68106

BAENNINGER, LOUISE POORMAN, psychologist; b. Baton Rouge, Dec. 29, 1938; d. Glenn William and Louise Amanda (Gueno) Poorman; m. Ronald Baenninger, Jan. 1965 (div. 1972); m. Ronald Keith Stoessell, July 1974; 1 child, David Michael. Student, Smith Coll., 1956-59; BA, NYU, 1961; PhD, Johns Hopkins U., 1966; postdoctoral program psychotherapy, La. State U., 1972. Lic. psychologist, La. Research assoc. Temple U., Phila., 1968-71; dir. behavior modification program Baton Rouge Mental Health Ctr., 1971-74; pvt. practice psychology Oakland, Calif., 1974-77, Houston, 1977-78; pvt. practice psychology Baton Rouge, 1978-82, Mandeville, La., 1982—; staff psychologist Southeast La. Hosp., Mandeville, 1982—; chmn. Children's Com. Mental Health Assn. in La., New Orleans, 1985—; presenter numerous seminars, workshops on behavioral psychology. Contbr. articles to profl. jours.; dir. 5 profl. agy. videotapes. Grantee USPHS, Beaver Coll., Glenside, Pa., 1967-68; NIMH fellow Johns Hopkins U., Balt., 1962. Mem. Am. Psychol. Assn., La. Psychol. Assn. (treas. 1979-81, co-chair ins. com., past mem. numerous other coms.), Assn. for Advancement of Behavior Therapy, Assn. for Behavior Analysis, Soc. for Accelerative Learning and Teaching, Psychonomic Soc. Home: 1545 Lakeshore Dr Mandeville LA 70448 Office: Southeast La Hosp PO Box 3850 Mandeville LA 70448

BAER, FRANCES DOROTHEA, real estate executive; b. Belserra, Calif.; m. Benjamin Franklin Baer, Mar. 20, 1942; children: Meridith, Marc Bradley, Bartley B.F. BA, U. So. Calif., 1941, cert. social worker, 1942; cert. social worker, Hastings Coll. of Law, 1959. Social worker Los Angeles County, 1942-46; real estate broker Iowa, Minn., Calif. and Md., 1968—. Past pres. Calif. Council of Coop. Nursery Schs., 1950; founder, chmn. community reorgn. Marin County Citizens Com. Child Guidance Clinic; pres. bd. Marin County PTA; past bd. dirs. LWV, Boy Scouts Am., Camp Fire Girls; pres., founder Nat. Inst. Crime Control; pres. Brooke Press; active, bd. dirs. Dem. and Rep. groups, Calif. Republican. Unitarian. Club: Early Am. Glass. Home: Box 465 Garrett Park MD 20896 Office: Brooke Press Box 526 Garrett Park MD 20896

BAERMANN, DONNA LEE ROTH, insurance analyst; b. Carroll, Iowa, Apr. 28, 1939; d. Omer H. and Awanda Lucille (Mathison) Roth; m. Edwin Ralph Baermann, Jr., July 8, 1961; children—Beth, Bryan, Cynthia. B.S., Mt. Mercy Coll., 1973; student Iowa State U.-Ames, 1957-61. Cert. profl. ins. woman; fellow Life Mgmt. Inst. Ins. agt. Lutheran Mut. Ins. Co., Cedar Rapids, Iowa, 1973; home economist Iowa-Ill. Gas & Electric Co., Cedar Rapids, Iowa, 1973-77; supr. premium collection Life Investors Ins. Co., Cedar Rapids, 1978-83, methods-procedures analyst, 1983—, supr. policy service, 1987—; bd. dirs., v.p. Roth Assoc., Roth Farms, Roth Inc., Roth Apts., 1988-89; mem. telecommunications study group com. 1982-83, mem. productivity task force, 1984—. Mem. Nat. Assn. Ins. Women, Nat. Mgmt. Assn. (bd. dirs. Cedar Rapids chpt.), DAR, Chi Omega. Republican.

Presbyterian. Home: 361 Willshire Ct NE Cedar Rapids IA 52402 Office: Life Investors Ins Co 4333 Edgewood Rd NE Cedar Rapids IA 52499

BAERWALD, SUSAN GRAD, television broadcasting company executive; b. Long Branch, N.J., June 18, 1944; d. Bernard John and Marian (Newfield) Grad; m. Paul Baerwald, July 1, 1969; children—Joshua, Samuel. Degre des Arts and Lettres, Sorbonne, Paris, 1965; B.A., Sarah Lawrence Coll., 1966. Script analyst United Artists, Los Angeles, 1978-80; v.p. devel. Gordon/Eisner Prodns., Los Angeles, 1980-81; mgr. mini-series and novels for TV, NBC, Burbank, Calif., 1981-82, dir. mini-series and novels for TV, 1982, v.p. mini-series and novels for TV, 1982—. Bd. dirs. The Paper Bag Players, N.Y.C., 1974—; vol. Los Angeles Children's Mus., 1978—; mem. awards com. Scott Newman Found., 1982-84. Recipient Vol. Incentive award NBC, 1983. Mem. Am. Film Inst., Acad. TV Arts and Scis. Office: National Broadcasting Co 3000 W Alameda Ave Burbank CA 91523 Other Address: National Broadcasting Co 30 Rockefeller Plaza New York NY 10112 *

BAERWALD, SUSAN MARGERY, librarian; b. Geneva, N.Y., Mar. 1, 1951. BA, Washington U., St. Louis, 1973. Library cataloguer The St. Louis Art Mus., 1973-74; art room asst. St. Louis Pub. Library, 1977-80; research librarian Hellmuth, Obata & Kassabaum, St. Louis, 1980—. Mem. Spl. Libraries Assn., Assn. Archtl. Librarians (chmn. 1988). Office: Hellmuth Obata & Kassabaum 100 N Broadway Saint Louis MO 63102

BAEZ, JOAN CHANDOS, folk singer; b. S.I., N.Y., Jan. 9, 1941; d. Albert V. and Joan (Bridge) B.; m. David Victor Harris, Mar. 1968 (div. 1973); 1 son, Gabriel Earl. Appeared in coffeehouses, Gate of Horn, Chgo., 1958, Ballad Room, Club 47, 1958-68, Newport (R.I.) Folk Festival, 1959-69, extended tour to colls. and concert halls, 1960's, appeared Town Hall and Carnegie Hall, 1962, 67, 68, U.S. tours, 1970—, concert tours, Japan, 1966, 82, Europe, 1970-73, 80, 83, 88; rec. artist for Vanguard Records, 1960-72, A&M, 1973-76, Portrait Records, 1975-80, Gold Castle Records, 1986—, (awarded 8 gold albums, 1 gold single), European record albums, 1981, 83; author: Joan Baez Songbook, 1964, (biography) Daybreak, 1968, (with David Harris) Coming Out, 1971, And A Voice To Sing With, 1987, (songbook) And then I wrote, 1979; extensive TV appearances and speaking tours U.S. and Can. for anti-militarism, 1967-68. Visit to Dem. Republic of Vietnam, 1972; founder, v.p. Inst. for Study Nonviolence (now Resource Ctr. for Nonviolence, Santa Cruz, Calif.), Palo Alto, Calif., 1965; mem. nat. adv. council Amnesty Internat., 1974—; founder, pres. Humanitas/Internat. Human Rights Com., 1979, condr. fact-finding mission to refugee camps, S.E. Asia, Oct. 1979. Office: care Diamonds and Rust Prodns PO Box 1026 Menlo Park CA 94026 also: PO Box 818 Menlo Park CA 94026

BAGARIA, GAIL FRANCES, lawyer; b. Detroit, Oct 6, 1942; d. Vincent Benjamin and Inez Elizabeth (Coffey) Farrell; m. William James Bagaria, Nov. 28, 1964; children—Bridget Ann, William James, Benjamin George. B.A., U. Detroit, 1964; J.D., Catholic U. Am., 1980. Bar: Md. 1980, U.S. Dist. Ct. Md. 1982. Cons. Miller & Webster, Clinton, Md., 1980-82; sole practice, Bowie, Md., 1982—. Mem. Prince George's Women Lawyers Caucus (sec. 1984, pres. 1986), ABA, Md. State Bar Assn., Women's Bar Assn. Md. Democrat. Roman Catholic. Office: Gail Farrell Bagaria PO Box 759 Bowie MD 20715

BAGDAN, GLORIA, interior designer; b. Bronx, N.Y., May 24, 1929; d. Max and Molly (Trufelman) Green; student CCNY, 1947-49, Inst. Interior Design, 1964, Wharton Sch., 1977; m. Kenneth Bagdan, Nov. 25, 1948 (dec. 1974); children—Meryl Bagdan Robins, Scott, Stacy. Founder, 1st pres. Bronx Mcpl. Hosp. Aux., 1955-60; interior designer, Scarsdale, N.Y., 1964—; v.p., treas. Gold Medal Farms, Bronx, 1974-79. Active in fundraising Grasslands Hosp. Heart Assn.; cons. Mental Health Assn., 1967—; bd. dirs. 20 Sutton Pl. S., N.Y.C.; mem. Republican Senatorial Inner Circle, Washington. Mem. Internat. Platform Assn., Mcpl. Art Soc. N.Y., Nat. Trust Hist. Preservation, U.S. Congl. Adv. Bd. Clubs: Atrium (N.Y.C.); Internat. Beaux Arts. Home: 20 Sutton Place S New York NY 10022

BAGLEY, COLLEEN, marketing executive; b. Mountain Home, Ark., Feb. 18, 1954; d. Roy Louis and Dorothy (Fry) B.; m. William A. Haskin, June 28, 1986. BA cum laude, U. South Fla., 1975. Lic. radio broadcaster, FCC 3d class. TV and radio producer Sta. WUSF-TV-FM, Tampa, Fla., 1974-76; TV announcer Sta. WFLA-TV, Tampa, 1974-76, news reporter, 1976-77, news producer, 1977-79; sr. producer Sta. KSTP-TV, Mpls., 1979-80; exec. producer Sta. WPVI-TV, Phila., 1980-82; dir. mktg. Grand Traverse Resort, Traverse City, Mich., 1982—; cons., bd. dirs. Enough Seminars, Phila., 1981-82. Contbg. author Strategic Hotel/Motel Marketing (Am. Hotel and Motel Assn. award), 1985. Mem. Traverse City Ski Council, 1983—, local host com. Nat. Govs.' Assn., 1986-87; chmn. N.Am. Vasa Cross Country Ski Race Mktg. Com., 1987—. Mem. Traverse City Ad Club (awards for advt. excellence 1984-87), Traverse City C. of C. (air service transp. com. 1984-87), Grand Traverse Conv. and Visitors Bur. (mktg. com. 1984—), N.Am. Vasa Cross Country Ski Race Mktg. (chmn. 1987-88), No. Mich. Golf Council (exec. bd. 1986, 88). Republican. Avocations: private pilot, aerobics, weightlifting, yoga, scuba diving. Home: 3471 Blackwood St Traverse City MI 49684 Office: Grand Traverse Resort 6300 US 31 N Grand Traverse Village MI 49610-0404

BAGLEY, CONSTANCE ELIZABETH, lawyer; b. Tucson, Dec. 18, 1952; d. Robert Porter Smith and Joanne Snow-Smith. AB in Polit. Sci. with distinction, with honors, Stanford U., 1974; JD magna cum laude, Harvard U., 1977. Bar: Calif. 1978, N.Y. 1978. Tchg. fellow Harvard U., 1975-77; assoc. Webster & Sheffield, N.Y.C., 1977-78, Heller, Ehrman, White & McAuliffe, San Francisco, 1978-79; assoc. McCutchen, Doyle, Brown & Enersen, San Francisco, 1979-84, ptnr., 1984—; mem. Bur. Nat. Affairs Corp. Practice Series Adv. Bd., 1984—; lectr. bus. law Stanford Grad. Sch. Bus., 1988—; lectr. bus. bd. dirs. exec. program Stanford (Calif.) U. Grad. Sch. of Bus., 1985-87; lectr., mem. planning com. Calif. Continuing Edn. of the Bar, Los Angeles, San Francisco, 1983, 85-87. Author: Mergers, Acquisitions and Tender Offers, 1983, (with others) Proxy Contests, 1983, supplement, 1987; contbg. editor Calif. Bus. Law Reporter, 1983—; also articles. Vestry mem. Trinity Episcopal Ch., San Francisco, 1984-85; vol. Moffit Hosp. U. Calif., San Francisco, 1983-84. Teaching fellow Harvard U., 1975-77. Mem. ABA, San Francisco Bar Assn., Am. Soc. Corp. Secs., Phi Beta Kappa. Republican. Clubs: Golden Gateway Tennis and Swim, Commonwealth (San Francisco). Office: McCutchen Doyle Brown & Enersen 3 Embarcadero Ctr San Francisco CA 94111

BAGLEY, MARY CAROL, educator, writer, broadcaster; b. St. Louis, Mar. 11, 1958; d. Robert Emmet and Harriet Elaine (Hohreiter) B. BA, U. Mo., St. Louis, 1980; MA, U. Mo., 1982. Feature editor Normandy, Mo., 1977-82; mng. editor Watermark Lit. Mag., St. Louis, 1982-85; vis. lectr. So. Ill. U., Edwardsville, 1985—; instr., head. bus. writing St. Louis U., 1985—; news broadcaster Am. Cablevision, Florissant, Ferguson, Mo., 1986—; guest speaker Sta. KMOX-TV, KSDK-TV, St. Louis Writing Festival, St. Louis Community Coll., and others, chancellor's com. Sta. KWMU Radio Adv. Bd., 1980, participant MCKendree Writer's Conf., 1986. Author: The Front Row: Missouri's Grand Theaters', 1984, (with others) The Fabulous Fox Theater, 1985; freelance writer, 1976—; editor: A Guide to St. Louis Theaters, 1984; bd. editors (book), Business Writing Concepts, 1986, Handbood for Professional and Academic Writing, 1988, recipient cert. appreciation, 1986; adv. bd., Business Communications Today, 1986. Campainger, mgr., Young Republicans, St. Louis, 1986; co-chmn, Theater Hist. Soc. Conclave, St. Louis, 1984; pres., Ambassador Theater Trust, 1986. Mem. Writer's Guild, Theater Hist. Soc. (nom. bd. dirs. 1986), Am. Assn. U. Instrs., Nat. Council Tchrs. English, U. Mo. English Alumni Assn. (v.p. 1985, senator rep. 1979), Pi Alpha Delta (hon.). Clubs: St. Louis Numismatic Assn., Mo. Numismatic Assn. Home: 12539 Falling Leaves Ct Saint Louis MO 63141 Office: St Louis Univ 221 N Grand 336 Xavier Hall Saint Louis MO 63141

BAGLIORE, VIRGINIA, poet; b. Bklyn., Mar. 14, 1931; d. James and Josephine (Brunetti) Coglietta; m. James Bagliore, Nov. 8, 1953; children—Rosanne, Lisa. Student NYU, Bklyn. Coll.; student of Kimon Friar. Model, 1952-56; freelance promotional model, 1975-80; poet-tchr. creative poetry workshops, 1975—; condr. workshops Assn. Humanistic Psychology, 1978, 5th Am. Imagery Conf., 1981, Carroll St. Sch., 1981, Public Sch. No. 65, 1981, others; lectr. workshop New Sch., 1982, 85; sponsor, judge High Sch. Poetry Contest, 1977—, pres. Bklyn. Poetry Circle, 1985-87. Editor: Oracles of Light, 1986; co-editor Eve's Legacy Mag., 1980-83, 86; contbr. poems to various poetry mags.; poems represented in anthologies; exhibited 5 poems at Cork Gallery, Loncoln Center, 1981, 84; poems translated into Urdu; essays in The Study and Writing of Poetry; developed communication technique for improving lang. Recipient Cert. of Merit, Alan Foss Leukemia Found., 1975; Bill Burke award, 1976; Louise Bogan Meml. award, 1972; Louise Louis award, 1978. Mem. World Poets' Resource Ctr. (Creative Service award 1979), Nat. League Am. Pen Women (pres. 1986—, v.p. letters 1978-82, pres. 1982—, Disting. Service award 1986), Acad. Am. Poets, N.Y. Poetry Forum, Avalon Soc., Eleanor Gaylee Found., Shelley Soc. N.Y. (hon.), Composers, Authors, and Artists Am., Nat. Assn. Poetry Therapy, Bklyn. Poetry Circle (pres. 1986). Office: PO Box 244 Ryder Street Station Brooklyn NY 11234

BAHCALL, NETA ASSAF, astrophysicist; b. Israel, Dec. 16, 1942; d. Yehezkel Oscar and Gita (Zilberstein) Assaf; m. John Norris Bahcall, Mar. 21, 1966; children—Ron Assaf, Dan Ophir, Orli Gilat. B.S., Hebrew U., Jerusalem, 1963; M.S., Weizmann Inst. Sci., Israel, 1965; Ph.D., Tel Aviv U., 1970. Research fellow Calif. Inst. Tech., 1970-71; mem. staff Princeton U., N.J., 1971-75; research astronomer, 1975-79, sr. research astronomer, 1979-83, now chief gen. observer br., 1983—; now with Space Telescope Sci. Inst., Balt. Contbr. articles to profl. jours. Mem. Am. Astron. Soc. Office: Space Telescope Sci Inst 3700 San Martin Dr Baltimore MD 21218 *

BAHNER, SUE (FLORENCE SUZANNA), radio broadcasting executive; b. Phila.; d. William and Florence (Quinlivan) McElwee; m. David S. Bahner; children—Suzanna Elizabeth, Carol Aileen. Grad. Columbia Bus. Coll., 1950. Various exec. sec. positions, 1954-74; office mgr. Sta. WYRD, Syracuse, N.Y., 1974, gen. mgr., 1974-80; gen. mgr. Sta. WWWG-FM, Rochester, N.Y., 1980—; v.p. Brandon Radio, Rochester, 1985—; pres. The Cornerstone Group, 1986—. Active Eastern Hills Bible Ch. Mem. Greater Rochester Assn. Evangelicals (v.p. 1982—), Nat. Religious Broadcasters (pres. eastern chpt. 1984—, bd. dirs. 1983—). Office: Sta WWWG 1850 S Winton Rd Rochester NY 14618

BAHR, LAUREN S., publishing company executive; b. New Brunswick, N.J., July 3, 1944; d. Simon A. and Rosalind J. (Cabot) B. Student, U. Grenoble, France, 1964; B.A. (Branstrom scholar); M.A., U. Mich., 1966. Asst. editor New Horizons Pubs., Inc., Chgo., 1967, Scholastic Mags., Inc., N.Y.C., 1968-71; supervising editor Houghton Mifflin Co., Boston, 1971; product devel. editor Appleton-Century-Crofts, N.Y.C., 1972-74; sponsoring editor McGraw-Hill, Inc., N.Y.C., 1974-75; editor Today's Sec. mag., 1975-77; sr. editor Media Systems Corp., N.Y.C., 1978; sr. editor coll. dept. CBS Coll. Pub., N.Y.C., 1978-82, mktg. mgr. fgn. langs., dir. mktg. adminstrn., 1982-83; dir. devel. Coll. div. Harper & Row, N.Y.C., 1983-86, dir. mktg. Coll. div., 1986—. Dir. U.S. Patent Model Found., Washington, D.C., 1985—. Democrat. Jewish. Home: 444 E 82d St New York NY 10028 Office: Harper & Row 10 E 53d St New York NY 10022

BAIDEN, DAWN LEE, lawyer; b. Sheboygan, Wis., July 30, 1951; d. Elroy and Betty (Welch) Begalke; m. Kenneth John Freitag, June 2, 1973 (div. Dec. 1982); m. Timothy Francis Baiden, June 6, 1987. BS, U. Wis., 1973, JD, 1976; MBA, U. Wis., Milw., 1985. Staff atty. Wis. Electric Power Co., Milw., 1976-83, Kohler (Wis.) Co., 1983-85; dir. legal services Am. Med. Bldgs., Milw., 1985-87; gen. counsel Donohue & Assocs. Inc., Sheboygan, Wis., 1987—. Mem. ABA, Am. Corp. Counsel Assn., Wis. Bar Assn., Sheboygan Bar Assn. Republican. Home: 5129 Evergreen Dr Sheboygan WI 53081 Office: Donohue & Assocs Inc 4738 N 40th St Sheboygan WI 53083

BAIER, KATHERINE J. (KITTIE), government official; b. Melrose, Mass., Aug. 13, 1953; d. John Leonard and Audrey Eleanor (Sullivan) B. AA in English, Westbrook Coll., 1973; student, Boston U., 1973-74; BFA in Theatre, George Washington U., 1983. Adminstrv. asst. Deaver & Hannaford, Inc., Los Angeles, 1974-77; placement counselor Robert Half, Inc., Mpls., 1978-79; mng. editor Towery Press, Inc., Memphis, Tenn., 1978-79; exec. asst. to assoc. dir. presdl. personnel Office of Pres.-elect, Washington, 1980-81; spl. asst. to sec. U.S. Dept. Interior, Washington, 1981-83, dep. asst. sec. for territorial and internat. affairs, 1984—; mem. Nat. Tourism Policy Council U.S. Dept. Commerce, Washington, 1985, adv. council Virgin Islands Tourism Awareness and Advancement Link, St. Thomas, U.S.V.I., 1986—. Contbr. articles to profl. jours. Active Republican Women's Fed. Forum, Washington, Friends of Kennedy Ctr., Washington, The Am. Film Inst., Washington. Mem. AFTRA. Republican. Episcopalian. Office: Dept of the Interior Territorial & Internat Affairs 18th & C Sts NW Washington DC 20240

BAIER, MARCIE MOWERS, research consulting executive; b. Batavia, N.Y., May 15, 1952; d. Lloyd L. and Jeanette (Brenkus) Mowers; m. Frederick L. Baier, Apr. 26, 1931. BA, Syracuse U., 1974, D of Arts, 1981. Researcher, planner Kanematsu-Gosho USA, Inc., N.Y.C., 1981-83; countertrader Mfrs. Hanover Trust Co., N.Y.C., 1983-84; pres. Frederick L. Baier Assocs., Woodbridge, N.J., 1984—. Mem. Nat. Assn. Female Execs., Soc. for Intercultural Edn., Tng. and Research.

BAILES, BARBARA JEAN, interior decorator, small business owner; b. Sharon, Pa., Apr. 10, 1960; d. Richard Vincent and Helen (Gonder) Davis; m. Benjamin L. Cartwright, Sept. 11, 1982 (div. Nov. 1985); m. Tony Ray Bailes. Student, Evangel Coll., Springfield, Mo., 1978, Clark Tech. Coll., Springfield, Ohio, 1979-83, N.Y. Sch. Interior Design, 1985—. Cashier Red & White Grocery Store, Vandergrift, Pa., 1977-79; part-owner Ben's Bicycle Shop, Urbana, Ohio, 1983-85; cashier Kroger Co., Urbana, 1979-86; decorator World Gift Co., Springfield, Ohio, 1984—; owner Barb Bartholomew's Gift and Decorating Accessories, Dallas and Urbana, Ohio, 1988—; unit star World Gift Co., Springfield, 1985—; sec. bd. Davis Wash on Wheels, 1988—. Mem. Nat. Assn. Female Execs., Nat. Bicycle Shop Owners. Club: Raquet (Springfield).

BAILEY, BERNADETTE WORTMAN, education director; b. Grosse Pointe, Mich., Dec. 26, 1935; d. Albert A. and Elizabeth G. Wortman; m. Thomas Edward Bailey, Aug. 25, 1967; children: Thomas E. Jr., Anne Margaret. BA, Trinity Coll., 1957; MA in Teaching, Johns Hopkins U., 1958. Tchr. Balt. Pub. Schs., 1957-58, South Redford (Mich.) Pub. Schs., 1958-62, Dept. of Def. Schs., overseas, 1962-65, Waltham (Mass.) Pub. Schs., 1965-66, Grosse Pointe Pub. Schs., 1966-68; substitute tchr. Rochester (Mich.) Pub. Schs., 1980-83; instr. Am. Inst. Banking, Detroit, 1980-83, edn. dir., 1983—. Mem. Women's Econs. Club, Am. Soc. of Training and Devel. Roman Catholic. Club: Women's Econs. Office: Am Inst of Banking 1505 Ford Bldg 615 Griswold Detroit MI 48226

BAILEY, BETTE ANN, auto dealer; b. Norman, Okla., Oct. 19, 1932; d. Virgle Lee and Hattie (Talbot) Barnard; m. C. G. Bailey, Dec. 31, 1953 (div. Feb. 1970). Grad., Hill's Bus. Coll., 1952. Office mgr. O'shea's Frozen Food, Oklahoma City, 1950-53; with Bank Am., Arcadia, Calif., 1954-60, Security Pacific Nat. Bank, Covina, Calif., 1960-66; bus. mgr. Bryant Pontiac, Covina, 1966-86; owner, dealer Bryant Honda, Covina, 1986—. Sec., treas. Covina C. of C., 1978-85; bd. dirs. Inter-Community Hosp., Covina, 1987. Recipient Small Bus. award City Covina, 1986-87; named Acct. of Yr. Toyota, 1969-78, Am. Honda, 1978-86, Pontiac Motor Div., 1978-85, Woman of Distinction Citrus Coll., 1987. Lodges: Eastern Star, Kiwanis. Home: 910 E Mountain View Glendora CA 91740

BAILEY, BONNIE, small business owner; b. Birmingham, Ala., July 4, 1940; d. Jack Gates Jr. and Virginia (Oates) Shaw; m. William Charles Bailey, June 8, 1963; children: William Charles Jr., John Faison-Oates, Evans Cecil Cabaniss. BA, Tulane U., 1962; M in Religious Edn., Birmingham Theol. Inst., 1982. Dir., caterer Bonnie Bailey Cooking Classes, Birmingham, 1973-83; dir. cooking classes The Kitchen Shoppe, Birmingham, 1981-83; owner, chef The Highland Gourmet, Inc., Birmingham, 1983—. Mem. Internat. Assn. Cooking Profls., Soc. Foods and Wines, Birmingham C. of C. (creator of food booklets), Kappa Alpha Theta (pres. 1957-58). Republican. Presbyterian. Home: 4212 Caldwell Mill Rd Birmingham AL 35243 Office: The Highland Gourmet 2226 Highland Ave Birmingham AL 35205

BAILEY, CONSTANCE GEORGE, computer executive; b. Erie, Pa., Apr. 4, 1949; d. Philip John George and Eleanor Rose (Dorn) Smith; m. Douglas Charles Bailey, Sept. 12, 1981; children: Reed E. Shupe, Daniel W., Paul D., David J. BS in Math., Edinboro (Pa.) State U., 1967-71; MS in Math., Tufts U., 1971-76. Instr. Middlesex Community Coll., Bedford, Mass., 1975-76, programmer Warner Mgmt. Cons., Champaign, Ill., 1976-77; software engr. MTS Systems Corp., Eden Prairie, Minn., 1977-81; systems analyst Control Data Corp., Bloomington, Minn., 1981-82; mgr. integration and evaluation Star Techs., Mpls., 1982-83; specialist 3M, St. Paul, 1983-86; tech. support exec. Geovision, Inc., Norcross, Ga., 1986—; cons. 3M and Geovision, Inc. 1983-86. Co-author: CD ROM Standards: The Book, 1986; contbr: The New Papyrus: CD ROM, 1986. Membership com. Cub Scouts, Bloomington, 1983-86. Mem. Internat. Interactive Communication Soc., Nat. Assn. Female Execs., Assn Women in Computing, Nat. Info. Scis. Orgn., Assn. Computing Machinery. Clubs: Living Well Lady (Roswell, Ga.). Home: 230 Sheringham Dr Roswell GA 30076 Office: Geovision Inc 270 Scientific Dr Norcross GA 30092

BAILEY, DEBBIE DENISE, educator; b. Atlanta, Sept. 24, 1957; d. Carl Haynes and Sally (Parham) Haynes; m. Robert L. Bailey, Oct. 3, 1975; children—Tamara, Roctavius, Nathan. Student Ga. State U., 1985, St. Leo Coll., 1984-86, Atlanta Jr. Coll., 1975-77; A.A., Ga. State U., 1977. Tchr., Ben Hill Sch., East Point, Ga., 1978-80; Sheltering Arms, Atlanta, 1980-81; youth dir. U.S. Army, Bad Hersfeld, Germany, 1981-84, recreation asst. Fort Stewart, Ga., 1984—. Mem. Nat. Assn. Female Execs. Baptist. Avocations: dance; fitness; travel. Home: B Co 3/8 CAV APO New York NY 09091 Office: Community Recreation Ctr 750 Lindquist Ave Fort Stewart GA 31313

BAILEY, DIANA MARION, educator; b. Ft. Wayne, Ind., Aug. 20, 1951; d. George Henry and Olive (Atwood) B. BS, Ind. U., 1973; MS, Johns Hopkins U., 1976. Cert. tchr., Md.; cert. spl. edn. tchr., Md. With diagnostic/prescriptive dept. Howard County Dept. Edn., Ellicott City, Md., 1975-80, resource person vocat. support service team, 1980-83; liaison vocat. support service team Columbia, Md., 1984-87; coordinator Cen. Regional Ctr. for Vocat. Equity, Md.; diplomat person-to-person Kanagara Internat. Assn., Yokohama, Japan, 1983-84; cons. bias/equity Md. State Dept. Edn., Balt., 1983—, presenter at conf.; facilitator Presdl. Commn. for Employment of the Handicapped, 1985—; trainer Regional Ctr. for Vocat. Equity, Columbia, 1986—. Editor (directory): Non-Traditional Vocational Directory, 1986. Vice chairperson Human Rights Commn., Howard County, Md., 1979-83; chairperson Md. Commn. for Women, Howard County, 1981-83, commr., 1985—. Named one of Outstanding Young Women Am. Mem. Am. Vocat. Assn., Md. Assn. Vocat. Spl. Needs Educators (treas. 1985-86, chairperson equity com. 1986-87). Democrat. Clubs: Bus. and Profl. Womens, Women's Network (Md.). Home: 11510 Little Patuxent Pkwy #402 Columbia MD 21044

BAILEY, ELIZABETH ELLERY, university dean; b. N.Y.C., Nov. 26, 1938; d. Irving Woodworth and Henrietta Dana (Skinner) Raymond; B.A. magna cum laude, Radcliffe Coll., 1960; M.S., Stevens Inst. Tech., 1966; Ph.D. (Bell Labs. grantee), Princeton U., 1972; children—James L., William E. Successively sr. tech. aid, assoc. mem. tech. staff, mem. tech. staff, supr. econ. analysis group, research head econs. research dept. Bell Labs., 1960-77; commr. CAB, 1977-83, v.p., 1981-83; dean Grad. Sch. Indsl. Adminstrn., Carnegie-Mellon U., 1983—; dir. Honeywell, Inc., Kraft, Inc., Coll. Retirement Equities Fund; adj. asst., then assoc. prof. econs. NYU, 1973-77; Founding mem., v.p. bd. trustees Harbor Sch. for Children with Learning Disabilities; trustee Princeton U., 1978-82, Presbyn. U. Hosp., 1984—, Brookings Inst., 1988—; mem. exec. council Fedn. Orgns. for Profl. Women, 1980-82; chmn. Com. on Status of Women in Econs. Profession, 1979-82; mem. corp. vis. com. Sloan Sch. Mgmt., M.I.T., 1982-85; mem. adv. bd. Brookings Inst., 1987—, Center Econ. Policy Research, Stanford U., 1983—. Recipient Program Design Trainee award Bell Labs.; Mem. Am. Econ. Assn. (exec. com. 1981-83, v.p. 1985), Am. Assn. Collegiate Schs. Bus. (v.p. 1987-88). Author: Economic Theory of Regulatory Constraint, 1973; editor: Selected Economics Papers of William J. Baumol, 1976; Deregulating the Airlines, 1985; bd. editors Am. Econ. Rev., 1977-79, Jour. Indsl. Econs., 1977-84. Home: 220 Schenley Rd Pittsburgh PA 15217 Office: Carnegie-Mellon U 5000 Forbes Ave Pittsburgh PA 15213

BAILEY, EMILIE KATHRYN, sales and marketing executive; b. Bloomington, Ind., Oct. 12, 1946; d. Richard Charles and Marjorie (Kirkman) Koontz; m. Gerald Bailey, June 17, 1967 (div. Nov. 1985). Student, Lamar U., 1979, 87-88, Tex. Assn. Realtors Sch., 1985. Lic. real estate agt., Tex. Realtor, sales mgr. Dal Sasso Realty & Constrn., Nederland, Tex., 1979-81; realtor Am. Real Estate, Port Neches, Tex., 1981-82, Nordstrom & Assocs. Realtors, Port Neches, 1982-83; realtor, sales mgr. Mansard Builders, Inc., Beaumont, Tex., 1983-85; realtor Nash Phillips/Copus, Austin, Tex., 1985-86, Easter & Easter Realtors, Austin, 1986-87; nat. dir. sales, mktg. Oak Creek Mfg., Inc., Nederland, 1987—; real estate agt. Don Moss & Assocs., Groves, Tex., 1987—; chmn. Port Neches/Nederland/Port Arthur Bd. Realtors, 1982-83. Mem. Bus. & Profl. Women's Club, Am. Bus. Women's Assn., Nederland C. of C. Republican. Office: Oak Creek Mfg Inc 3612 Nederland Ave Nederland TX 77627 also: Don Moss & Assocs 3747 Charles Ave Groves TX 77619 Mailing: PO Box 7444 Beaumont TX 77706

BAILEY, GRACE ELIZABETH, artist, educator; b. Budapest, Hungary, June 7, 1937; d. Samuel Herbert and Carmen Elizabeth (Stassik) Johnson; m. Philip James Bailey, Aug. 22, 1959; children: Michael Philip, Julia Anne. BA in Sociology, U. Leeds, Eng., 1959; student, Leeds Coll. Fine Arts, 1960. Asst. welfare officer Tootal Co. Ltd., Manchester, Eng., 1958; jr. high sch. tchr. Leeds Edn. Authority, 1959-62; elem. tchr. Bedford (Eng.) Edn. Authority, 1965-68, Westfield (N.J.) Bd. Edn., 1969-72; pottery artist and tchr. Westfield, 1972—; art advisor Girl Scouts U.S., 1972—, Boy Scouts Am., 1972—; demonstrator schs., mus., libraries, company fairs. Participant numerous art shows; featured in numerous mag. articles. Charter mem. bd. dirs. N.J. Theatre Forum, Plainfield, 1974-79; chmn. bd. dirs. Abendmusik, Westfield, 1978-86; head choirmother, bus. mgr. St. Paul's Choir Men and Boys, Westfield, 1973-86; vol. and counselor Spellman Ctr. for HIV disease at St. Clare's Hosp., N.Y., 1987—. Recipient Excellence in Baroque Music award N.J. State Council on Arts, 1980-85, Union County Arts Council, 1980, Merck & Co., 1982, 84, Mobil Oil Co., 1981-85, Morgan Guaranty Bank, 1981-85, Prudential Assurance, 1984, Electro Mktg., 1981-85; named Vol. of Yr., N.J. daily newspaper, 1977, Somerset Messenger Gazette, 1979. Clubs: Advance (sec., v.p.), Couples (Westfield) (v.p.), Raritan Yacht Ladies (skipper). Home and Office: 726 Embree Crescent Westfield NJ 07090

BAILEY, JANICE LARUE, educational counselor; b. Duncan, Okla., Dec. 26, 1939; d. O.H. and Ara D. (Hearn) Jennings; m. A. Lloyd Bailey, July 19, 1963; children—Scott, Elizabeth. A.B. in Biology and Chemistry, Bethany Nazarene Coll., 1962; med. technologist U. Kans., 1963; M.Ed. in Counseling, U. Mo., 1972; EdD in Ednl. Adminstrn. and Counseling U. Mo.-St. Louis, 1988. Research technologist VA Hosp., Oklahoma City, 1964-69; tchr. biology and chemistry Ritenour Sch. Dist., St. Ann, Mo., 1969-73, Hazelwood Sch. Dist., Florrisant, Mo., 1973-80; guidance counselor Frances Howell Sch. Dist., St. Charles, Mo., 1980—; speaker at seminars, workshops and retreats. Author papers in field. Co-chmn. Nazarene Laymen Activities in Mo., 1980—. Mem. Am. Soc. Clin. Pathology, NEA, Assn. Supervision Curriculum Devel., Am. Ednl. Research Assn., Profl. Counselors Assn., Phi Delta Kappa. Home: 23 Spencer Valley Dr Saint Peters MO 63376

BAILEY, JOSELYN ELIZABETH, physician; b. Pine Bluff, Ark.; d. Joseph Alexander and Angeline Elaine (Davis) B.; B.Mus., Manhattanville Coll., 1952; M.Music Edn., Manhattan Sch. Music, 1954; M.D., Howard U., 1971. Straight med. intern Huntington Meml. Hosp., Pasadena, Calif., 1971-72, resident, 1972-74; fell in nephrology Wadsworth VA Hosp., Los Angeles, 1975-77; practice medicine specializing in internal medicine and nephrology, Torrance, Calif.; mem. active staff Torrance Meml., South Bay, Little Company of Mary hosps.; cons. staff Del Amo Hosp.; attending staff Harbor Gen. Hosp.;clin. faculty Dept. Medicine, UCLA; active staff Bay Harbor Hosp., trustee, 1982—; Mem. Renal Physicians Assn., Am. Soc. Internal Medicine, Calif. Soc. Internal Medicine, So. Calif. Pvt. Practice Assn.

BAILEY, JUDITH IRENE, college administrator, consultant; b. Winston-Salem, N.C., Aug. 24, 1946; d. William Edward, Jr. and Julia (Hedrick)

Hege; m. Brendon Stinson Bailey, Jr., June 8, 1968. BA, Coker Coll., 1968; MEd, Va. Tech., 1973, EdD, 1976. Tchr. Chariho Regional high sch., Wood River Junction, R.I., 1969-70, Prince William County Pub. Schs., Woodbridge, Va., 1968-72; asst. prin. Osbourn high sch., Manassas, Va., 1973; secondary sch. coordinator Stafford (Va.) County Schs., 1973-74; middle sch. coordinator Stafford County Schs., 1975-76; human relations coordinator U. Md. Coop. Extension Service, College Park, 1976-79; dep. dir. Univ. D.C. Coop. Extension Service, Washington, 1980-88; asst. v.p. Cooperative Extension Service U. Maine, Orono, 1988—; adj. prof. George Mason U., Fairfax, Va., 1978; Grad. Student advisor, U. Md., 1979-80; speaker in field; cons. in field. Co-Author: Contingency Planning for a Unitary School System; contbr. to profl. jours. Vol. Lake Braddock Secondary Sch., Burke, Va., 1984—. Susan Coker Watson fellow, 1967. Mem. AAUW, Phi Delta Kappa, Phi Kappa Phi, Epsilom Sigma Phi (sec. Mu chpt. 1987, v.p. Mu chpt. 1988, Mid Career award 1987). Mem. United Ch. of Christ. Home: 5422 Aylor Rd Fairfax VA 22032 Office: Coop Extension Service Univ Maine 100 Winslow Hall Orono ME 04469

BAILEY, MARILYNN ANITA, real estate executive; b. Atlanta, June 23; d. Porter and Lula Mae (Tillman) Jackson; m. Jerome Bailey, June 4, 1983. BS in Music Edn., Morris Brown Coll., 1978. Dir. parish services Lutheran Ch. Am., Decatur, Ga., 1979-82; asst. to mgmt. dept. chmn. NYU Grad. Sch. of Bus., 1982-83; real estate assoc. Merrill Lynch, N.Y.C., 1983; rep. Manpower Inc., N.Y.C, 1983—; v.p., computer cons. Bailey & Bailey Assocs., Bklyn., 1986—. field rep. George Dames campaign, Bklyn., 1986; vol. Congressman Owens campaign, 1986, Tenant's Assn. Devel. Corp., Flatbush Community, N.Y., 1984—, corresponding sec.; minister music New Covenant Ch. of Christ(Bapt.). Mem. Am. Guild Organist, Nat. Assn. Female Execs., Profl. Bus. Women's Club, Morris Brown Coll. N.Y. Alumni Assn. (pub. relations chmn.), Omicron Delta Kappa (pres., Pres. award, 1978), Sigma Gamma Rho. Club: President's (Atlanta). Home: 625 Ocean Ave 2-I Brooklyn NY 11226

BAILEY, MARY KAY, mechanical engineer; b. Las Vegas, Jan. 29, 1964; d. Gerald L. and Donna L. (Britz) Logan; m. Larry Alan Bailey, Sept. 5, 1987. BSME, U. Tenn., 1987. Mech. engr. Holston Def. Corp., Kingsport, Tenn., 1988—. Mem. ASME (sec. 1986-87), Soc. Automotive Engrs., Tau Beta Pi, Pi Tau Sigma. Home: 230 Silver Lake Rd #D-8 Church Hill TN 37642

BAILEY, MINNIE LEMON, health educator, nurse consultant; b. Montgomery, Tex., Feb. 8, 1938; d. Redie and Lola (Warren) Lemon; m. Bunard Bailey, June 28, 1958; children—Patricia Ann, Kimberly Elise, Bill. B in Nursing Edn., Prairie View A&M U., (Tex.), 1958; B in Nursing Adminstrn., U. Minn., 1961; MS, Tex. So. U., Houston, 1963, JD, 1988; MS, U. Tex.-Houston, 1972; PhD, U. Houston, 1977. R.N., Tex. Sch. nurse Houston pub. schs., 1962-66; supr. St. Elizabeth Hosp., Houston, 1966-70; indsl. nurse Am. Can Co., Houston, 1970-71; instr. pub. health U. Tex.-Houston, 1972-75; assoc. dir. allied health scis. Tex. So. U., 1977-80; pvt. practice allied health consulting, Houston, 1980—. Mem. ARC, Houston, 1958—, YWCA; active Glenwood Forest Civic Orgn., Houston, 1984. Mem. Allied Health Assn. (pres. 1975-77), U. Minn. Alumni Assn., Prairie View A&M U. Alumni Assn., Booker T. Washington Alumni Assn., Alpha Kappa Alpha (chairperson 1982-84, recipient Cert. of Merit 1983), Chi Eta Phi. Episcopalian. Lodge: Ea. Star (conductress 1978-80). Home: 8438 Gallahad St Houston TX 77078

BAILEY, NANCY MARTIN, university dean; b. Chgo., July 26, 1944; d. Ross J. and Marian Allen (Shepard) M.; m. Richard Ryan Malmgren; 1 child, Ryan Martin; m. Leslie Francis Bailey; 1 child, Stuart Martin. BA, U. Wis., 1967; MA, U. Ill., 1981, PhD, 1985. Specialist, botanist U. Wis.-Madison, 1967-72; English tchr. U. Ill. Univ. High Sch., Urbana, 1977-80; placement dir. Sch. Life Sci. U. Ill., Urbana, 1980-85, asst. dean, 1985-87; assoc. dean Coll. of Vet. Med., U. Ill., 1987—. Contbr. articles to profl. jours. Chmn. Urbana park dist. adv. com. 1982-83; mem. Champaign-Urbana Civic Symphony Bd., 1986—, U. Ill. Student Orgns. Resource Funds Bd., 1986—. Recipient Excellence in Profl. Writing award Midwest Coll. Placement Assn., 1981. Mem. Am. Ednl. Research Assn., Am Orthopsychiatric Assn., Assn. Academic Affairs Adminstrs., Am. Mensa Ltd., Phi Kappa Phi, Kappa Delta Pi, Alpha Chi Omega, Phi Delta Kappa. Club: Thirty (Urbana). Avocation: photography; fishing; flute playing. Office: Univ Ill 2271 Vet Medicine Basic Scis Bldg 2001 S Lincoln Ave Urbana IL 61801

BAILEY, PATRICIA PRICE, government official; m. Douglas L. Bailey; 2 children. BA in History cum laude, Lindenwood Colls.; MA in Internat. Affairs, Tufts U.; JD summa cum laude, Am. U. Bar: U.S. Ct. Appeals (D.C. cir.), U.S. Ct. Appeals (8th cir.), U.S. Supreme Ct. Exec. asst. Bur. for Latin Am., then asst. to dep. coordinator Alliance for Progress, AID, 1961-66; advisor fgn. affairs Rep. F. Bradford Morse, 1967-68; with Office of Counsel to Pres. in White House; spl. asst. to asst. atty. gen. U.S. Dept. Justice, 1977-79; exec. legal asst. to gen. counsel U.S. Merit systems Protection Bd., 1979; commr. FTC, Washington, 1979-87. Office: FTC Office of the Commr 6th St & Pennsylvania Ave NW Washington DC 20580

BAILEY, PATRICIA SUSAN, physician; b. N.Y.C., Dec. 18, 1943; d. Joel and Ethel (Miller) Salzburg; B.S. magna cum laude, Central Mich. U., 1970, M.A., 1972; M.D., Mich. State U., 1977 . Clin. instr. Mich. State U. Coll. Human Medicine, 1976-77; resident Los Angeles County-Harbor Gen. Hosp., UCLA Med. Center, Torrance, 1977-78; partner, physician in emergency medicine Kaiser-Permanente Hosp., Harbor City, Calif., 1978—; instr. Am. Heart Assn.; clin. instr. U. So. Calif. Coll. Medicine. Trustee, Delta Coll., 1972-74. Mem. Am. Coll. Emergency Medicine, Am. Physicians for Human Rights, Am. Physicians for Social Responsibility, Gay Acad. Union, So. Calif. Women for Understanding, NOW. Jewish. Author: (novel) The Summer of the Flea, 1980; contbr. to Echoes from the Heart (poetry anthology), 1982; contbr. articles to various publs. Office: Kaiser Permanente Hosp 1050 W Pacific Coast Hwy Harbor City CA 90710

BAILEY, PEARL, singer; b. Newport News, Va., Mar. 29, 1918; d. Joseph James B.; m. John Randolph Pinkett, Jr., Aug. 31, 1948 (div. Mar. 1952); m. Louis Bellson, Jr., Nov. 19, 1952. Student pub. schs., Phila.; B.A. in theology, Georgetown U., Washington, D.C., 1985, L.H.D. (hon.). Singer, 1933—; vocalist various popular bands; stage debut in St. Louis Woman, N.Y.C., 1946; role in Broadway musical Hello Dolly, 1967-68, Arms and the Girl, House of Flowers, Bless You All, Duey's Tale, Hurry Up America, and Spit; albums include: Bad Old Days, Cole Porter Song Book, Echoes of an Era; motion pictures include: Variety Girl, Carmen Jones, St. Louis Blues, Porgy and Bess, Isn't It Romantic, Norman, Is That You, That Certain Feeling, All the Fine Young Cannibals, The Landlord, Lost Generation; contract artist, Coral Records, Columbia Records, Decca; night club engagements, N.Y.C., Boston, Hollywood, Las Vegas, Chgo., also London, 1950—; star Pearl Bailey Show, ABC-TV, 1970-71; guest artist various TV programs; Spl. Tony award for Hello, Dolly 1967-68; author: Raw Pearl, 1969, Pearlie Mae, Talking to Myself, 1971, Pearl's Kitchen, 1973, Duey's Tale, 1975, Hurry Up, America and Spit, 1976. Spl. rep. U.S. delegation to UN from 1975. Recipient Spl. Tony award for Hello, Dolly, 1967-68; Donaldson award, 1956; Entertainer of the Year Cue Magazine, 1967; March of Dimes award, 1968; U.S.O. Woman of the Year, 1969; citation from Mayor John V. Lindsay of N.Y.C.; Centennial Award, AAUW, 1988. Office: care Tony Santozzi William Morris Agy 151 El Camino Beverly Hills CA 90212 *

BAILEY, RUTH ELIZABETH, financial analyst; b. Boston, Apr. 22, 1955; d. Harwood and Esther Hill) B. BA, Conn. Coll., 1977; MBA, Boston U., 1983. Service rep., patient acts Maine Med. Ctr., Portland, 1977-78; controller Tamarack Mgmt., Pembroke, Mass., 1978-82; staff acct. Price Waterhouse, Boston, 1983-85, sr. acct., 1985; fin. analyst New Eng. Electric System, Westborough, Mass., 1985—. Treas., Edgewood Village Condominium Trust, Marshfield, Mass., 1980-81; mem. fin. com. Appalachian Mountain Club, Boston, 1983-85, treas. Boston chpt., 1985-87. Mem. Am. Soc. Profl. and Exec. Women. Avocations: mountaineering, skiing, tennis, gardening. Home: 88 South St Westborough MA 01581 Office: New Eng Electric System 25 Research Dr Westborough MA 01582

BAILEY, SANDRA ANITA, insurance company executive; b. Los Angeles, May 13, 1949; d. Ernest and Mattie Mae (Nash) Bailey. Student, UCLA, 1967-68, Calif. State U.-Los Angeles, 1977-78; BS in Mgmt., Pepperdine U., 1987. Actuarial clk. Transamerica Occidental Life Ins. Co., Los Angeles, 1968-72, supr., 1972-75, asst. mgr., 1975-79, dept. mgr., 1979-83, asst. sec., 1981-83, asst. v.p., 1983-84, 2d v.p., 1984—, instr., 1980—. Vol. Am. Cancer Soc. Fellow Life Mgmt. Inst. of Life Office Mgmt. Assn. Office: Transamerica Occidental Life Ins Co 1149 S Hill St Los Angeles CA 90015

BAILEY, SARAH TILDEN, marketing professional; b. Washington, May 9, 1960; d. Charles Waldo and Ann Card (Bushnell) B.; m. Robert Harris Gale; 1 child, Angela Eileen Gale. BA in Polit. Sci., U. Vt., 1982. Editor Vermont Cynic, Burlington, 1980-81; mng. editor Valley Voice, Middlebury, Vt., 1983-84; copy editor Burlington Free Press, 1984-85; editor, pub. Winsted (Conn.) Courier, 1985-86; advt. mgr., asst. mktg. dir. Ct. House One, Avon, Conn., 1987-88, dir. mktg., 1988—. Contbr. numerous articles to profl. jours. Pub. relations mgr. Internat. Spl. Olympics, Burlington, 1980. Mem.Internat. Soc. Weekly Newspaper Editors, New Eng. Press Assn., Nat. Assn. Female Execs., Mortar Bd. Soc. Episcopalian. Office: Courthouse One 21 Waterville Rd Avon CT 06001

BAILEY, SUSAN CAROL, savings and loan executive; b. Muskogee, Okla., Apr. 10, 1954; d. William E. and Lula M. (Holloway) Green; m. Wayne M. Bailey, Aug. 6, 1976; 1 child, Nathan W. BS in Fin., So. Ill. U., 1982, MBA in Fin., 1983. Tech. asst. ops. Marsh Stencil Machine Co., Belleville, Ill., 1973-85; loan officer Delmar Fin. Co., Belleville, 1985-86; asst. v.p., asst. br. mgr. Fidelity Fed. Savs. and Loan Assn., Fairview Heights, Ill., 1986; asst. v.p., br. mgr. Fidelity Fed. Savs. and Loan Assn., Belleville, 1986-87, v.p., br. mgr., 1987—; fin. cons., Caseyville, Ill., 1985-86. Mem. Belleville Welcome Wagon (treas.). Mem. St. Louis Fedn. Socs. for Coating Tech. (exec. com. 1980-85, chairperson edn. com. 1983-84), Belleville Bd. Realtors, Edwardsville-Collinsville Bd. Realtors., Women's Council of Realtors, Homebuilders Assn., Belleville Postal Council (bd. dirs.), So. Ill. Network of Women, Fairview Heights C. of C. Home: 710 Belleville Rd Caseyville IL 62232 Office: Fidelity Fed Savs and Loan Assn 5720 North Belt W Belleville IL 62223

BAILEY, VELDA MAY, educational administrator; b. Goodland, Kans., Apr. 29, 1940; d. Vernia L. and Burnetta E. (Day) Peterson; m. Charles Wayne Bailey, June 2, 1962; children: Larissa Lynn, Tiffany Ann. AA, Mesa Coll., 1960; BA, U. No. Colo., 1962, MA, 1966. Tchr. Silt (Colo.) Pub. Schs., 1962-63, Nat. Park Service Mesa Verde, Mancos, Colo., 1963-65, Grand Junction (Colo.) Pub. Schs., 1965-71, Holy Family Sch., Grand Junction, 1972-75; head tchr. Scenic Elem. Sch., Grand Junction, 1975-82; adminstrv. asst. continuing edn. Mesa Coll., Grand Junction, 1982-85, asst. dir. continuing edn., 1985—. Vol. coach Grand Mesa Youth Soccer, Grand Junction, 1982—; bd. dirs. Soccer Booster for Dist. #51, Grand Junction, 1985—, Grand Mesa Youth Soccer Assn., 1986. Office: Mesa Coll PO Box 2647 Grand Junction CO 81502

BAILEY, VELMA NEAL, lawyer; b. Ewing, Ill., Sept. 12, 1938; d. Rolla Blake and Dollie Irena (Akin) Neal; m. Donald E. Bailey, April 21, 1957. BS, So. Ill. U., Carbondale, 1982, JD, 1986. Supr. Horace Mann Ins. Co., Springfield, Ill., 1964-67; determinations specialist State of Ill., Springfield, 1967-69, acct., 1969-74; v.p., adminstr. Lincoln Land Title, Springfield, Lincoln, Ill., 1974-77; ins. broker Allstate Ins. Co., Carbondale, 1977-80; asst. state's atty. Marion County, Salem, Ill., 1986-87, Williamson County, Marion, Ill., 1987—. Named one of Outstanding Young Women of Am., 1973. Mem. ABA, Ill. State Bar Assn., Marion County Bar Assn., Williamson County Bar Assn., Chgo. Bar Assn., The Assn. Trial Lawyers Am., Ill. Trial Lawyers Assn., U.S. Daus. of 1812 (pres. Ill. soc. 1985-87), DAR, Magna Charta Dames, Phi Alpha Delta (alumni advisor 1987—). Home: Rural Rt #1 Neal Hill Ewing IL 62836 Office: Williamson County State's Atty Courthouse Marion IL 62959

BAILEY, ZELDA CHAPMAN, hydrologist; b. Memphis, Aug. 2, 1949; d. John Franklin and Pearl Elizabeth (Skeens) Chapman; m. Charles Millard Bailey, June 3, 1972 (div. Dec. 1983); m. Patrick Tucci, Mar. 23, 1985; 1 child, Cara Nicole. BA in Geology, Ind. U., 1977. Cert. geologist, Ind., Groud Water Profl. Histologist, electron microscopist Ind. U. Med. Ctr., Indpls., 1967-76; hydrologic technician U.S. Geol. Survey, Indpls., 1977-79, hydrologist, 1979-84; hydrologist U.S. Geol. Survey, Nashville, 1984—. Contbr. numerous articles to profl. jours. Mem. Am. Geophys. Union, Internat. Assn. Hydrogeologists, Assn. Women in Sci., Assn. Women Geoscientists. Avocations: photography, silver jewelry fabrication, needlework, gardening. Office: US Geol Survey WRD A413 Fed Bldg US Courthouse Nashville TN 37203

BAILLIE, MARY HELEN, accounting executive; b. Clio, S.C., Aug. 18, 1926; d. Paul Clydus and Laurie (Easterling) Orr; grad. Carolina Bus. Coll., 1946; children—William Sinclair, Carol Anderson. Controller, George I. Clarke, Inc., Atlanta, 1953-57, DuBose Reed Constrn. Co./W. Carroll DuBose, Inc., Ft. Lauderdale, Fla., 1970-74; asst. controller H.B. Fuller Co., Ft. Lauderdale, 1975-76; owner M.H. Baillie & Assocs., Inc., Ft. Lauderdale, 1977—. Mem. Leadership Broward Alumni, 1985—, Ft. Lauderdale Sign Adv. Bd., 1983—, Broward County Commn. on Status of Women, 1985—; bd. dirs., treas. Women in Distress, 1984—. Mem. Nat. Accts. Assn. (dir. 1977-79, dir. spl. activities 1979—), Fla. Accts. Assn. (dir. 1977-79, sec. 1977-79), Ft. Lauderdale C. of C. (dir. 1979—), Internat. Assn. Fin. Planners. Republican. Clubs: Women's Execs. (dir. 1978-80, treas. 1978-80), Ft. Lauderdale Country. Home: 3471 NE 17th Terr Fort Lauderdale FL 33334 Office: MH Baillie & Assocs Inc 746 NE Third Ave Fort Lauderdale FL 33304

BAIMAN, GAIL, real estate broker; b. Bklyn., June 4, 1938; d. Joseph and Anita (Devon) Yalow; m. James F. Becker, Oct. 1970 (div. 1978); children—Steven, Susan, Barbara. Student Bklyn. Coll., 1955-57. Lic. real estate broker, N.Y., Pa., Fla. Personnel-pub. relations dir. I.M.C., Inc., N.Y.C., 1970-72; pres., broker Gayle Baiman Assocs., Inc., N.Y.C., 1972-74; v.p., broker Tuit Mktg. Corp., Mt. Pocono, Pa., 1974-83; pres., broker Ind. Timeshare Sales, Inc., St. Petersburg, Fla. and Mount Pocono, Pa., 1983—; mem. Nat. Timeshare Council. Arbitrator Better Bus. Bur. Mem. Am. Resort and Residential Developers Assn., Nat. Assn. Exec. Women. Avocations: reading, metaphysics, bowling. Office: Independent Timeshare Sales Inc 5680 66th St N Saint Petersburg FL 33709

BAIN, LINDA VALERIE, executive development consultant; b. N.Y.C., Feb. 14, 1947; d. Carlton Louis and Helen V. (Boyd) B.; m. Samuel Green, Mar. 21, 1986. BA, CCNY, 1975. Exec. sec. N.Y.C. Dept. Social Services, 1966-70; program assoc. N.Y. State Dept. Mental Hygiene, N.Y.C., 1970-71, Nat. Council Negro Women, N.Y.C., 1973-79; sr. cons. Donchian Mgmt. Services, N.Y.C., 1980-85; pres., devel. cons. Bain Assocs., Inc., N.Y.C., 1985—; cons. Am. Express Co., Squibb Pharms. Co. Mem. Friends of Alvin Ailey, bd. dirs.; bd. dirs. The Friendly Place, Inc. Recipient Mary McLeod Bethune Recognition award Nat. Council Negro Women, 1974. Mem. Am. Soc. Tng. and Devel., Coalition of 100 Black Women, Council of Concerned Black Execs., Nat. Assn. Female Execs., Nat. and N.Y. Orgn. Devel. Network. Democrat. Office: Bain Assocs Inc PO Box 20789 New York NY 10025-9992

BAIR, DEIRDRE B., English language educator, writer; b. Monongahela, Pa., June 21, 1935; d. Vincent John and Helen (Kruki) Bartolotta; m. Lavon Henry Bair, May 29, 1957; children: Vonn Scott, Katherine Tracy. BA with honors, U. Pa., 1957; MA with honors, Columbia U., 1969, PhD, 1972. Various journalistic positions Calif., Conn. and N.Y., 1957-68; prof. English U. Pa., Phila., 1976-88; instructed part-time at So. Conn. State Coll., 1968-69, Trinity Coll., Hartford, Conn., 1973-74, Cen. Conn. State Coll., New Britain, 1974-75, Yale U., 1975-76. Author: (biography) Samuel Beckett, 1978 (Am. Book award 1981), Simone de Beauvoir, 1988; adv. editor Temple Univ. Jour. Modern Literature, 1987—; contbr. articles to newspapers, profl. jours. including Yale French Studies, N.Y. Times Book Rev. Mem. MLA, Am. Council for Irish Studies (nominating com. 1986—), NOW, Simone de Beauvoir Soc. (nat. v.p. 1984—). Democrat.

BAIR, MYRNA LYNN, state senator; b. Huntington, W.Va., Oct. 26, 1940; d. Charles Thomas and Velma Elvera (Schoenlein) North; B.S. in Chemistry, U. Cin., 1962; Ph.D., U. Wis., 1968; m. Thomas Irvin Bair, Mar. 12, 1966; children—Thomas Irvin, Catherine Lynn. Asst. prof. chemistry Beaver Coll., Glenside, Pa., 1966-70; instr. chemistry U. Del., 1974-76, asst. prof. edn., 1977-79; asst. dir. pub. info. Del. Energy Office, Wilmington, 1978-79; mem. Del. Senate, 1981—. Bd. dirs. Del. Lung Assn.; trustee Wesley Coll.; mem. Nat. Republican Com., Brandywine Region Rep. Women's Club. Recipient Freshman award Chem. Rubber Co., 1959; DuPont Co. Teaching award, 1963; NSF fellow, 1964-66. Mem. AAUW, Delawareans for Energy Conservation, Phi Beta Kappa, Iota Sigma Pi, Alpha Lambda Delta. Author sci. articles. Office: Legislative Hall Dover DE 19901 *

BAIRD, EMILY NADINE BLACKWOOD, marriage and family therapist, educator; b. Collingwood, Tenn., Oct. 18, 1921; d. John Henry and Flora Alice (Goff) Blackwood; B.A. in Journalism, U. Ala., 1946; M.A. in Psychology, U. West Fla., 1972; Ed.D., Nova U., 1976. Marital cons. U. West Fla., Pensacola, 1971-73; clin. counselor Community Mental Health Center, Pensacola, 1973-77; dir. Consultation and Edn., Lakeview Center, Pensacola, Fla., 1977-82; first pres. Favor House, 1979; cons. Rape Crisis Center, Make Today Count, 1978-79; Fla. chmn. cons. and edn. Fla. Council Community Mental Health Ctrs. Chmn. service com. Am. Cancer Soc., 1978-81; chmn. woman's com. YWCA, 1978-80; mem. Gov.'s Commn. on Status of Women, 1982-86; bd. dirs. Mental Health Assn., 1978-85, sec. Fla. div., 1986—; chmn. Reach to Recovery, Am. Cancer Soc., 1976-78, bd. dirs., 1976-80; elder Gulf Breeze Presbyn. Ch., 1980-82; pres. Mental Health Assn. Escambia County, 1983-85. Recipient Citizenship award N.W. Fla. Social Workers, 1980; Woman of Yr. award YWCA, 1983; named Woman of Yr., In-Town Bus. Women, 1985. Mem. Am. Psychol. Assn., Northwest Fla. Psychol. Assn. (pres. 1980-81), Network of Exec. Women (pres.).

BAIRD, KATHERINE LOUISE, investment company executive; b. Walla Walla, Wash., Jan. 28, 1947; d. Gerald Gene and Ruby Louise (Henry) Laufer. BA, U. Wash., 1970; postgrad., U. de Caen, France, 1967-68; PhD, Stanford U., 1981. Tchr. Holy Angels High Sch., Seattle, 1970-72; with Peace Corps Coll. d'Edn. Gen., Lakota, Ivory Coast, 1973-75, U. d'Abidjan, Ivory Coast, 1975-76; trainer Peace Corps, Ivory Coast, 1974-75; supr. tchr. edn. program Stanford U., Calif., 1977-78; adminstr. tchr. edn. program Stanford U., 1978-81; pres., chief exec. officer Criterion Investments Inc., Woodinville, Wash., 1983—. Mem. Nat. Assn. Female Execs., Snohomish County Women Bus. Owners Assn., Woodinville C. of C. Lodge: Rotary. Office: Criterion Investments Inc 14239 NE Woodinville- Duvall Rd Woodinville WA 98072

BAIRD, LISA MORRISON, botany educator; b. Lawrence, Kas., Sept. 16, 1954; d. Irwin Lewis and Irene (Cebula) B.; m. Steven Lowrance Morrison, Nov. 19, 1977. AB, Smith Coll., 1976; MS, U. Calif., Davis, 1978, PhD, 1980. NSF postdoctoral fellow U. Calif., Davis, 1980-81, research agronomist, 1981-83; asst. prof. botany Conn. Coll., New London, 1983—. Grantee NSF 1984-87, 87—. Mem. Bot. Soc. Am., Am. Soc. Plant Physiology, Electron Microscopic Soc. Am., Internat. Soc. Plant Molecular Biology, AAAS. Office: U San Diego Dept Biology San Diego CA 92110

BAIRD, PAMELA JO, banker; b. Blue Earth, Minn., July 18, 1948; d. Dennis and Una Mae (Espeland) Fenske; m. Richard Charles Baird Sr., June 10, 1967; 1 child, Richard. Grad., Winnebago (Minn.) High Sch., 1966. Clk., stenographer Mankato (Minn.) State Coll., 1966-69; legal sec. Krahmer & Krahmer Attys., Fairmont, Minn., 1969-70; buyer, expediter Abex/Aerospace, Oxnard, Calif., 1970-73; sec. Security State Bank, Mankato, 1973-74; sec., supr. Bank of Commerce, Mankato, 1974-77, asst. ops. officer, 1978-85, asst. v.p., 1986—. Vol. United Way, Mankato, 1986—; active Mankato Leadership, 1987—; bd. dirs. YWCA, 1985—, treas., 1987. Mem. Nat. Assn. Bank Women (group pres. 1984-86, chmn. Minn. membership 1986—), Am. Inst. Banking (bd. dirs., pres. Mankato chpt. 1981-86, Minn. bd. dirs. 1986—). Lutheran. Club: Mankato Exchange. Lodge: Zonta. Office: Bank of Commerce 2d and Main Box 820 Mankato MN 56001

BAIRD, PATRICIA ANN, social worker; b. Hot Springs, Mont., Jan. 18, 1932; B.Sociology with highest honors, Ariz. State U., 1968; M.S.W., U. Mich., 1971; children—Darleen, Jeffrey. Adminstr. Maricopa County Dept. Health Services, Div. Public Health, Phoenix, 1971-87; field instr. Ariz. State U., 1972—. Exec. bd. Ariz. Council on Sch.-age Parents, 1977—; mem. exec. bd. adv. council Ariz. Perinatal Program, 1974—; steering com. Teenage Pregnancy Coalition, 1979-87; adv. bd. Planned Parenthood, 1977-79, Phoenix S. Community Mental Health, 1979-87. Mem. Acad. Cert. Social Workers, Nat. Assn. Social Workers, Ariz. Perinatal Social Work Assn., Soc. Govt. Meeting Planners, U. Mich. Alumni Assn., Am. Public Health Assn., Phi Kappa Phi. Democrat. Club: U. Mich. Alumni of Phoenix. Editor Ariz. Perinatal News, 1975-77. Office: 1825 E Roosevelt St Phoenix AZ 85006

BAIRSTOW, FRANCES KANEVSKY, educator, labor relations consultant; b. Racine, Wis., Feb. 19, 1920; d. William and Minnie (DuBow) Kanevsky; student U. Wis., 1937-42; B.S., U. Louisville, 1949; student Oxford U. (Eng.), 1953-54; postgrad. McGill U., Montreal, Que., 1958-59; m. Irving P. Kaufman, Nov. 14, 1942 (div. 1949); m. David Steele Bairstow, Dec. 17, 1954; children—Dale Owen, David Anthony. Research economist U.S. Senate Labor-Mgmt. Subcom., Washington, 1950-51; labor edn. specialist U. P.R., San Juan, 1951-52; chief wage data unit WSB, Washington, 1952-53; labor research economist Canadian Pacific Ry. Co., Montreal, 1956-58; asst. dir. indsl. relations centre McGill U., 1960-66, asso. dir., 1966-71, dir., 1971—, lectr., indsl. relations dept. econs., 1960-72, asst. prof. faculty mgmt., 1972-74, assoc. prof. faculty mgmt., 1974-83, prof., 1983—; spl. master Fla. Pub. Employees Relations Commn., 1985—; dep. commr. essential services Province of Que., 1976—; mediator So. Bell Telephone, 1985; cons. on collective bargaining to OECD, Paris, 1979; cons., Nat. Film Bd. of Can., 1965-69; arbitrator Que. Consultative Council Panel of Arbitrators, 1968—, Ministry Labour and Manpower, 1971—; mediator Canadian Public Service Staff Relations Bd., 1973—; contbg. columnist Montreal Star, 1971—. Chmn. Nat. Inquiry Commn. Wider-Based Collective Bargaining, 1978. Fulbright fellow, 1953-54. Mem. Canadian Indsl. Relations Research Inst. (exec. bd. 1965-68), Indsl. Relations Research Assn. Am. (mem. exec. bd. 1965-68, chmn. nominating com. 1977), Nat. Acad. Arbitrators (bd. govs. 1977-80, program chmn. 1982-83, v.p. 1986—), Soc. Profls. in Dispute Resolution (adv. council). Home and Office: 1430 Gulf Blvd #507 Clearwater FL 34630

BAISDEN, ELEANOR MARGUERITE, airline compensation executive, consultant; b. Bklyn., Nov. 7, 1935; d. Vernon McKee and Ethel Mildred (Cockle) Baisden. B.A., Hofstra U., 1970. Clk., Trans World Airlines, N.Y.C., 1953-55, sec., 1955-64, compensation analyst, 1964-75, compensation mgr., 1975-85, dir. compensation and orgn. planning, 1985—. Mem. Airline Personnel Dirs. Conf. (personnel com. 1984-85), Airline Tariff Pub. Co. (personnel com. 1978—), Nat. Fgn. Trade Council (compensation com. 1980-84), Internat. Personnel Assn. (co. rep. 1980-84), Mensa, Alpha Sigma Lambda (Scholar of Yr. 1965-66). Republican. Methodist. Club: Weatherby Lake Sailing (Mo.). Avocations: boating, swimming, piano, travel. Home: 7818 NW Scenic Dr Weatherby Lake MO 64152 Office: Trans World Airlines 11500 Ambassador Dr Kansas City MO 64153

BAITSELL, WILMA WILLIAMSON, artist, educator, lecturer; b. Palmyra, N.Y., July 5, 1918; d. Glen Hiram and Luetta (Newell) Williamson; m. Victor Harry Baitsell, Oct. 29, 1941; children: Corin Victor, Coby Allan, Corrine Luetta. BSE, SUNY, Oswego, 1957; M.S.E., Western State U., 1958; postgrad. Iowa State Tchrs. Coll., Syracuse U., Ind. State U., Cooper Union, McGill U. (Montreal); HHD, World U., 1982; PhD, U. Cambridge, Eng., 1981. Tchr. rural sch., 1939-41, Phoenix Central Sch., 1957-71, SUNY, Oswego, 1971-77; ret., 1977; cons. area schs., Ford Found., 1965-68; art cons. N.Y. State Dept. Edn., summers 1968-70. Author: Creativity and Intelligence, 1965, Art for Campers, 1972, Crafts for Children, 1976, Christianity, Creativity and Democracy, 1978, Create or Destroy, Love or Hate, Peace or War, 1983; editor Summer Art mag., 1957-71. Chmn. Republican Twp. Com.; pres. Oswego County Women's Rep. Club; chmn. Sch. Bldg. and Orgn. Com., 1954. Ford Found. sci. and math. grantee, 1958-59; recipient 1st prize Mid-States Art Show, 1981, hon. mention for painting, Yamiguchi, Japan, 1981, 1st prize Am. Craftsman's Show, 1973. Mem. N.Y. State Ret. Tchrs. Assn. (life), Internat. Soc. Edn. Through Art, Oswega Art Guild (life), Nat. Ret. Tchrs. Assn., Oswego County and Scriba Hist. Soc. (life), SUNY Oswego Alumni Assn. (life), N.Y. State Grange. Methodist.

Lodge: Order Eastern Star1937-71. Home and Office: Route 4 Box 434 Oswego NY 13126

BAIYOR, BARBARA SUE, engineer; b. Chgo., Oct. 19, 1956; d. Joseph Edward Sr. and Marie (Hoover) B. BSChemE, Northwestern U., 1979; MME, U. Pa., 1986. Engr. Mobil Research & Devel., Paulsboro, N.J., 1979-81; staff engr., 1982; engr. Smith Kline & French Labs., Phila., 1983-84, asst. mgr., 1985-86, sr. project engr., 1986-87; project mgr. McNeil Consumer Products Co. div. Johnson & Johnson, Ft. Wash., Pa., 1988—. Ill. State scholar Evanston, 1974-78, Kiwanis scholar, Elmhurst, Ill., 1974-78. Mem. Am. Soc. Mech. Engring., Am. Inst. Chem. Engrs., Soc. Women Engrs. (student advisor). Clubs: Phila. Girls Rowing, Lombard Swim (Phila.). Home: 308 Gaskill St Philadelphia PA 19147 Office: McNeil Consumer Products Co Camp Hill Rd Fort Washington PA 19034

BAK, SUNNY, public relations executive, photographer; b. N.Y.C., July 25, 1958; d. Chun Suk and Bie Liang (Kwik) B. AB, CCNY, 1976. Staff photographer The Hamptons newspaper mag., Southampton, N.Y., 1978-84; dir. pub. relations H.H. Assocs., N.Y.C., 1985-87; dir. west coast ops. KCG Prodns., N.Y.C., 1987—; prin. Sunny Bak Studio, N.Y.C., 1984—. Photographs include record cover Lic. to Ill, 1987, book Purple, 1988. Mem. Advt. Photographers Am., Assn. Asian Pacific Artists, Women in Photography. Democrat. Buddhist.

BAKALE, KIMBERLY MARIE, bank marketing officer, educator; b. Johnstown, Pa., Mar. 14, 1958; d. Edward George and Patricia Louise (Smith) B. BA in Psychology, Washington & Jefferson Coll., 1980; MA in Communications, Stephen F. Austin State U., 1983. Sales mgr. Sta. WJNL-AM-FM TV, Johnstown, Pa., 1980-81; grad. teaching asst. Stephen F. Austin State U., Nacogdoches, Tex., 1981; social dir. Retirement Inns of Am., Dallas, 1982; grad. adminstrv. asst. Shippensburg (Pa.) U., 1983; caseworker Family Social Services, Johnstown, 1983-84; instr. Am. Inst. Banking, Johnstown, 1984—; asst. v.p. Johnstown Savings Bank, 1984—. Dir. videotape: Women's Shelter, 1981. Mem. AAUW (v.p. membership). Home: 276 Linden Ave Johnstown PA 15902 Office: Johnstown Savings Bank Market at Main Johnstown PA 15901

BAKEMAN, CAROL ANN, administrative services manager, singer; b. San Francisco, Oct. 27, 1934; d. Lars Hartvig and Gwendolyne Beatrice (Zimmer) Bergh; student UCLA, 1954-62; m. Delbert Clifton Bakeman, May 16, 1959; children—Laurie Ann, Deborah Ann. Singer, Roger Wagner Chorale, 1954—, Los Angeles Master Chorale, 1964-86; librarian Hughes Aircraft Co., Culver City, Calif., 1954-61; head econs. library Planning Research Corp., Los Angeles, 1961-63; corporate librarian Econ. Cons., Inc., Los Angeles, 1963-68; head econs. library Daniel, Mann, Johnson & Mendenhall, architects and engrs., Los Angeles, 1969-71, corporate librarian, 1971-77, mgr. info. services, 1978-81, mgr. info. and office services, 1981-83, mgr. adminstrv. services, 1983—. Pres., Creative Library Systems, Los Angeles, 1974-83; library cons. ArchiSystems, div. SUMMA Corp., Los Angeles, 1972-81, Property Rehab. Corp., Bell Gardens, Calif., 1974-75, VTN Corp., Irvine, Calif., 1974, William Pereira & Assos., 1975. Mem. Assistance League, So. Calif., 1956-86, mem. nat. auxilaries com. 1968-72, 75-78, mem. nat. by laws com. 1970-75, mem. asso. bd. dirs., 1966-76. Mem. Am. Guild Musical Artists, AFTRA, Screen Actors Guild, Adminstrv. Mgmt. Soc. (v.p. Los Angeles chpt. 1984-86, pres. 1986-88, internat. conf. chmn. 1988—), Los Angeles Master Chorale Assn. (bd. dirs. 1978-83), Roger Wagner Chorale Planning and Devel. Com., 1988—. Office: Daniel Mann Johnson & Mendenhall 3250 Wilshire Blvd Los Angeles CA 90010-1599

BAKER, ANITA DIANE, lawyer; b. Atlanta, Sept. 4, 1955; d. Byron Garnett and Anita (Swanson) B. BA summa cum laude, Oglethorpe U., 1977; JD with distinction, Emory U., 1980. Bar: Ga. 1980. Assoc. Hansell & Post, Atlanta, 1980—. Mem. ABA (com. on savs. and loan instns.), Atlanta Bar Assn., Ga. Bar Assn., Atlanta Hist. Soc., Order of Coif, Phi Alpha Delta, Phi Alpha Theta, Alpha Chi, Omicron Delta Kappa. Office: Hansell & Post 56 Perimeter Ctr E Suite 500 Atlanta GA 30346

BAKER, AVA JEAN, educator, extension agent; b. Balt., Sept. 7, 1947; d. Raymond Theodore and Anna Virginia (White) Waters; m. Donald Lee Baker, Mar. 28, 1970; 1 child, Jeffrey Sunjata. BS, U. Md. Eastern Shore, Princess Anne, 1969; MS, U. Md., 1979; postgrad., U. Nebr., Omaha, 1973, U. Colo., Colorado Springs, 1982. Cert. profl. tchrs., home economist. Tchr. home econs. Balt. City Pub. Sch., 1969-70, 74-80; tchr. adult edn. Omaha-Nebr. Tech. Schs., 1972-74; tchr. home econs. Dist. #11 El Paso County Sch., Colorado Springs, 1980-83; extension agt. 4-H U. Md. Coop. Extension Service, Cockeyville, 1984-88; extension agt. Home Econs. Md. Coop. Extension Service, Baltimore City, 1988—; mem. vis. com. Mid. States Assn. Colls. and Secondary Schs., Pa., 1977. Co-author curriculum guide Home Economics Course Outlines, 1983. Project leader Big H 4-H Club, Columbia, Md., 1985-87; mem. Nat. Youth Sports Adv. Bd., Essex, Md., 1986-88, PTA, Atholton High Sch., 1985-87. Mem. Nat. Assn. Extension 4-H Agts. (regional contact profl. improvement, Am. Spirit award Md. chpt. 1986), Md. Assn. Extension, 4-H Agts. (pres. elect 1987-88, v.p. 1986-87, editor brochure Balt. County 4-H We're On The Move, 1985, newsletter 4-H Observer 1984-88, Outstanding Md. Youth Worker 1987), Md. Home Econs. Assn., (v.p. program devel. 1988-89, program chmn. 1988—), Howard County Home Econs Adv. Bd., Future Homemakers Am. Adv. Bd., Epsilon Sigma Phi (Rookie of Yr. 1986), Alpha Kappa Alpha (Epsitoleus 1986-87). Office: U Md Coop Extension Service 17 S Gay St Baltimore MD 21202

BAKER, BETTY LOUISE, mathematician, educator; b. Chgo., Oct. 17, 1937; d. Russell James and Lucille Juanita (Timmons) B.; B.E., Chgo. State U., 1961, M.A., 1964; Ph.D., Northwestern U., 1971. Tchr. math. Harper High Sch., Chgo., 1961-70; tchr. math. Hubbard High Sch., Chgo., 1970-85, also chmn. dept.; tchr. Bogan High Sch., 1985—; part-time instr. Moraine Valley Community Coll., 1982-83, 84-86. Cultural arts chmn. Hubbard Parents-Tchrs.-Student Assn., 1974-76, 1st v.p., program chmn., 1977-79, 82-84, pres., 1979-81; organist Hope Lutheran Ch., 1963—. Univ. fellow, 1969-70; cert. tchr. high sch. and elem. grades 3-8 math., Ill. Mem. Nat., Ill. councils tchrs. of math., Math. Assn. Am., Chgo. Tchrs. Union, Nat. Council Parents and Tchrs. (life), Sch. Sci. and Math. Assn., Assn. for Supervision and Curriculum Devel., Am. Guild of Organists, Luth. Collegiate Assn., Kappa Mu Epsilon, Rho Sigma Tau, Mu Alpha Theta (sponsor), Kappa Delta Pi, Pi Lambda Theta, Phi Delta Kappa. Club: Walther League Hiking, Met. Math. Club. of Chgo.. Contbr. articles to profl. jours. Home: 3214 W 85th St Chicago IL 60652 Office: 3939 W 79th St Chicago IL 60652

BAKER, BRIDGET DOWNEY, newspaper executive; b. Eugene, Oreg., Sept. 14, 1955; d. Edwin Moody and Patricia (Petersen) B.; m. Guy Dominique Wood, June 30, 1977 (div. Oct. 1981); m. Rayburn Keith Kincaid, June 27, 1987; stepchildren: Benjamin, Jacob. BA in English, French and Theatre, Lewis and Clark Coll., 1977; MA in Journalism, U. Oreg., 1985. Circulation dist. supr. The Register-Guard, Eugene, 1978-80, pub. relations coordinator, 1980-83, promotion dir., 1983-86, mktg. dir., 1986—; bd. dirs. Guard Pub. Co., Eugene. Bd. dirs. Wilani Council Camp Fire, Eugene, 1982—, pres. bd. dirs., 1986—; bd. dirs. Lane County United Way, 1982—, community info. com. chairperson, 1982-84. Recipient 1st Place Advt. award Editor and Pub. Mag., N.Y.C., 1984, Best Mktg. Idea/Campaign award Oreg. Newspaper Pub. Assn., 1984-85. Mem. Internat. Mktg. Assn. (bd. dirs. Western region 1986—, 4 1st Place Best in the West awards 1983-85), Pub. Relations Soc. Am. (Spotlight award 1986). Republican. Club: Downtown Athletic. Lodge: Zonta Internat. Office: The Register-Guard 975 High St PO Box 10188 Eugene OR 97440

BAKER, CAROLINE FRANCES, librarian; b. Muskegon, Mich., May 4, 1922; d. Frank Anthony and Cora Caroline (Kramer) Schnitzler; m. Joseph Gerard Baker, Aug. 31, 1940 (dec. 1957); children—Thomas Raymond, Joseph Francis, Mary Therese; m. 2d, Francis A. Baker, May 16, 1975. A.B., Aquinas Coll., 1962; A.M. in L.S., U. Mich., 1965; postgrad. Central Mich. U., 1970-74. Instr. English Davenport Coll., Grand Rapids, Mich., 1962-64; asst. librarian Aquinas Coll., Grand Rapids, 1964-67; documents librarian, asst. prof. library sci. Central Mich. U., Mt. Pleasant, 1967-75; reference/periodicals librarian Hackley Pub. Library, Muskegon, 1975—. Mem. Mich. Edn. Assn., ALA, Muskegon City Tchrs. Edn. Assn., Mich. Library Assn., Library Dirs. Adv. Council, Altar Soc., St. Joseph's Women's Guild, Cath. War Vets Am. Dominican Tertiary, Phi Alpha Theta, Beta Phi Mu, Delta Kappa Gamma. Roman Catholic. Club: Faculty Woman's (Mt Pleasant). Asst. editor: Dag Hammarskjold Collection on Developing Nations, 1968-70. Home: 4894 Clearwater Ct Muskegon MI 49441

BAKER, COSETTE MARLYN, religious writer, editor; b. Miami, Fla., Sept. 22, 1933; d. Juel Marlyn and Corene Frances (Emery) Baker; B.B.A., U. Miami, Fla., 1955; M.R.E., So. Bapt. Theol. Sem., 1959. Dir. childhood edn. First Bapt. Ch., Knoxville, Tenn., 1959-63; minister to children South Main Bapt. Ch., Houston, 1964-73; asst. to minister of edn. Central Bapt. Ch., Miami, Fla., 1973-74; cons. in Sunday Sch. Dept., Bapt. Sunday Sch. Bd., Nashville, 1974—, children's program editor, 1974—, cons., children's program editor, 1985—. Recipient YWCA award outstanding woman in religious work U. Miami, 1955. Mem. Tenn. Assn. for Edn. Young Children, Gamma Alpha Chi. Baptist. Author: God's Outdoors, 1967; writer children's teaching tapes for Broadman Press, 1979-81; writer, on-camera person Bapt. Telecommunication Network, 1984—; editor Children's Leadership, 1985—. Home: 100 Longwood Pl Nashville TN 37215 Office: 127 9th Ave N Nashville TN 37234

BAKER, CYNTHIA LOUISE, physical therapist; b. Phila., Nov. 9, 1944; d. Norman Cope and Wilhelmina Louise (Paul) Harvey; m. Daniel Leslie Baker, Aug. 26, 1967; children: Jeffrey Paul, Catherine Louise, Dallas Michael. BS, U. Md., 1966; MS, Towson State U., 1987. Cert. in phys. therapy. Phys. therapist Bryn Mawr (Pa.) Hosp., 1966-67, Suburban Hosp., Bethesda, Md, 1967-69, Group Health Assn., Washington, 1969-70, Union Meml. Hosp., Balt., 1972-75; phys. therapist Burch, Rhoads & Loomis, P.A., Balt., 1976-83, chief phys. therapy, 1983—; clin. educator various colls., 1972—; guest lectr. Towson (Md.) State U., 1984-85. Leader Brownie Troop 925, Lutherville, Md., 1980; leader Girl Scouts U.S., Lutherville, 1986; chair Cub Scout Pack, Timonium, Md., 1986. Mem. Soc. Orthopedic Medicine, Am. Phys. Therapy Assn., Nat. Assn. Female Execs., Arthritis Found. (sec., treas. AHP sect. 1987), Phi Alpha Epsilon. Republican. Episcopalian. Club: Homemakers (sec. Lutherville chpt. 1978-80). Office: Burch Rhoads & Loomis PA 6305 York Rd Suite 203 Baltimore MD 21212

BAKER, DEBORAH WARRINGTON, university administrator; b. Hohenwald, Tenn., Oct. 17, 1949; d. Edward Young and Mattie Nelle (Staggs) W.; divorced; 1 dau., Sarah Elizabeth. B.A., Memphis State U., 1971, postgrad., 1977-78. Asst. editor Holiday Inn Mag. for Travelers, 1971-73, mng. editor, 1973-74; editorial asst. Memphis State U. News Bur., 1975-76; asst. dir. Memphis State U. Office Media Relations, 1976-78; dir. communications and public relations Mid-South Fair, Libertyland, Inc., Memphis, 1978-79; dir. media relations Memphis State U., 1979—. Bd. dirs. Lowenstein House, 1984-85. Mem. Public Relations Soc. Am., Tenn. Coll. Public Relations Assn. (sec. 1982, bd. dirs. 1986-87). Democrat. Office: Memphis State Univ Adminstrn Bldg Rm 303 Memphis TN 38152

BAKER, DEBRA JEANNE, accountant; b. Reno, Feb. 23, 1952; d. Newell Francis and Mildred Helene (Bouverot) Hancock; m. Douglas Allen Baker, May 22, 1976; 1 child, Beau Allen. BS in Secondary Edn., U. Nev., 1974, postgrad., 1975-76. CPA, Nev., Calif. Tchr. Western Australian Sch. System, Perth, 1974-75; staff acct. Pannell Kerr Forster CPAs, Incline Village, Nev., 1976-81; comptroller Incline Village Gen. Improvement Dist., 1981-82; pvt. practice acctg. Incline Village, 1981—. Mem. Nev. Soc. CPAs, Am. Inst. CPAs. Republican. Baptist. Club: Women's (North Tahoe, Nev.) (treas. 1982-84). Lodge: Daus. Nile. Office: PO Box 5653 Incline Village NV 89450

BAKER, EDNA MAE, home economist; b. Guthrie, Okla., May 18, 1922; d. Robert Beecher and Lydia Mae (Guthrie) B.; B.S., Okla. State U., 1950; M.S., U. Wis., 1960. Tchr. elementary sch., Clark County Kans., 1943-48; county extension 4H agt., Okla. State U., El Reno, 1950-53; county extension home demonstration agt Okla. State U., Kingfisher, 1953-60; Northeast, Central and Northwest dist. supr. coop. extension Okla. State U., Stillwater, 1961-84; co-dir. in-service tng. programs for coop. extension, 1967-83, acting dist. dir, coop. extension service, 1973. Kellogg Found. fellow, 1960; Superior Service award Okla. State U. Coop. Extension Service, 1983. Mem. Am. Home Econs. Assn., Okla. Home Econs. Assn. (dist. chmn. 1977-78), Extension Home Economists Assn. (sec. 1957, pres.-elect 1959), Okla. State U. Home Econs. Alumni Assn. (life), Okla. State U. Alumni Assn. (life), Epsilon Sigma Phi (life), Delta Kappa Gamma (sec. 1979, 2d v.p. 1981). Mem. Ch. of Nazarene (youth dir., Sunday sch. tchr., choir mem., chmn. Sunday Sch. bd., ch. bd., ch. bd. sec., dist. ch. bd., dist. ch. bd. nominating com.).

BAKER, EDWARDINE MAE FRANCES, utilities executive; b. Chgo., Aug. 22, 1932; d. James Edward and Vernana Frances (Ward) B. Diploma in profl. acctg., Northwestern U., 1964; BS in Bus. Adminstrn., Roosevelt U., 1979; MS in Acctg., 1984; Cert. in Advanced Mgmt., U. Chgo., 1975. With Peoples Gas, Light & Coke Co., 1950—; supr. customer relations div. Peoples Gas, Light & Coke Co., Chgo., 1980—; discussion leader Baker Fin. Seminars, Chgo., 1984—; cons. in field. Alumni bd. govs. Roosevelt U.; women's bd. Rehab. Inst. Chgo. Mem. League of Black Women, Terra Mus. Am. Art, Am. Mgmt. Assn., Nat. Assn. Female Execs., Nat. Assn. Accts. (mem. controllers council), Ctr. Entrepreneurial Mgmt. Inc., Entrepreneur Inst., Bus. and Profl. Women (treas. Chgo. chpt. 1987-88). Avocation: symphony. Office: The Peoples Gas Light & Coke Co 122 S Michigan Ave Chicago IL 60603

BAKER, ELAINE, social work educator; b. Mound Bayou, Miss., June 30, 1949; d. Joseph and Louise (Slack) B. BA, Tougaloo Coll., 1968; MSW, Atlanta U., 1970; DPA, U. Ga., 1986. Instr. Ft. Valley (Ga.) State Coll., 1970-73; assoc. prof. social work Albany (Ga.) State Coll., 1973—; dir. Human Resources Devel. Ctr., Albany, 1982-83; dir. social services Youth Ednl. Tng. Program, Albany, 1983-84; dir. resource devel. Delta Life Devel. Ctr., Albany, 1982—; cons., liaison Fla. A&M U., Tallahassee, 1971-72; tutor Albany Urban League Inc., 1974; faculty fellow NE Ga. Area Planning and Devel. Commn., Athens, 1980; dir., coordinator Mother-to-Mother Program, Albany, 1986—; cons. Continuum Alliance for Human Devel., Atlanta, 1987—. Author, editor: (directory) Social Services, 1973; contbr. articles to profl. jours. Chmn. Teen Resource Com., Albany, 1987—; bd. dirs. Crimestoppers, Albany, 1987—; adv. com. Project Crossover, Albany, 1986—, Positive Employment and Community Help, Atlanta, 1985—. Recipient Cert. of Appreciation Criminal Justice Club, Albany State Coll., 1987. Mem. Nat. Assn. Social Workers, Ga. Conf. on Social Work, Nat. Assn. Black Social Workers, Pi Alpha Alpha, Alpha Kappa Delta, Delta Sigma Theta (2d v.p. 1983-85, Dedicated Service award 1984). Democrat. Baptist. Office: Albany State Coll 504 College Dr Albany GA 31705

BAKER, ESSIE, editor, communications specialist; b. Columbus, Ga., Apr. 22, 1948; d. Jesse L. Baker and Bessie (Tatum) Holloman. BA in English, Bklyn. Coll., 1972. Asst. editor Random House, N.Y.C., 1969-73; mng. editor Encore Mag., N.Y.C., 1974-75; sr. editor Essence, N.Y.C., 1978; freelance editor Harper and Row, N.Y.C., 1978—, McGraw-Hill, N.Y.C., 1980—, N.Y. Bd. Edn., N.Y.C., 1987—; report supr. communications dept. Peat Marwick Main and Co. (formerly KMA Main Hurdman), N.Y.C., 1984—; ind. contractor, N.Y.C. and Columbus, 1975—. Editor: The Prodigal South Returns to Power, 1978. Mem. Editorial Freelancers Assn. (vol. 1987—), The Exec. Female. Baptist.

BAKER, FRANCES WANETA, elementary educator; b. Barbourville, Ky., Jan. 12, 1936; d. Earl and Emily Edith (Stewart) Messer; m. Arnold Baker, July 7, 1952; 1 child, Donald Earl. BS, Union Coll., Barbourville, 1964, MEd, 1973; cert. rank I, Eastern Ky. U., 1977. Tchr. Knox County Bd. Edn., Barbourville, 1964—. Named to Hon. Order Ky. Col., 1971. Mem. Nat. Edn. Assn., Ky. Edn. Assn., Knox County Tchrs. Assn. Home: HC81 Box 510 Barbourville KY 40906

BAKER, GWENDOLYN CALVERT, association executive; b. Ann Arbor, Mich., Dec. 31, 1931; m. James; children: JoAnn, Claudia, James Jr. BA, U. Mich., 1964, MA, 1968, PhD, 1972. Tchr. Ann Arbor Pub. Schs., 1964-69; lectr. U. Mich., 1969-70, instr., 1970-72, assoc. prof., 1972-76, dir. affirmative action programs, 1976-78; chief minorities and womens' programs Nat. Inst. Edn., Washington, 1978-84; v.p., dean, graduate and children's programs Bank St. Coll. Edn., N.Y.C., 1981-84; exec. dir. YWCA of U.S.A., N.Y.C., 1984—. Office: YWCA of the USA 726 Broadway New York NY 10003

BAKER, HELEN, lawyer; b. Cleve., May 6, 1922; d. Harry and Belle (Speiser) Manheim; m. Marvin Baker, Nov. 10, 1944 (div. 1973); children—Jon, Scott, Lauren. B.S. cum laude, Northwestern U., 1943; J.D. summa cum laude, Cleve. State U., 1977. Bar: Ohio 1979, U.S. Dist. Ct. (no. dist.) Ohio 1979. Staff children's rights project ACLU of Ohio Found., Inc., Cleve., 1977-78; staff counsel ACLU of Greater Cleve. Found., 1979-80, dir. children's rights advocacy project, 1980-81; cons., adv. ACLU, others, 1982—. Contbr. to books, articles to profl. jours. Active politics, civil rights, anti-war movement, nuclear freeze movement, others. Recipient Wall St. Jour. award, 1978; Civil Libertarian award ACLU of Ohio, 1981; Civil Libertarian of Yr. award ACLU of Greater Cleve. Mem. Ohio Bar Assn., ABA, Nat. Lawyers Guild. Home: 27200 Cedar Rd #914 Beechwood OH 44122

BAKER, IRENE JEAN, securities firm administrator; b. Quincy, Mass., Dec. 20, 1960; d. Robert Whitney and Mary Susan (Hughes) George; m. Timothy John Baker; 1 child, Jason Michael. BS in Communications Disorders, No. Ill. U., 1984. Lic. registered rep., registered prin. Nat. Assn. Securities Dealers. Licensing/compliance supr. Dreher & Assocs., Inc., Oakbrook Terrace, Ill., 1985-87, registered rep., 1986—, mktg. coordinator, 1987—. Tchr. religious edn. St. Linus Ch., Natick, Mass., 1983-85, St. James Ch., Glen Ellyn, Ill., 1985—. Mem. Internat. Assn. for Fin. Planners. Roman Catholic. Office: Dreher & Assocs Inc One Oak Brook Terrace Suite 708 Oak Brook Terrace IL 60181

BAKER, JANET NAN, librarian; b. Columbus, Mont., Apr. 16, 1956; d. James Nathan and L. Maxine (Shaw) B. BS in Edn. and Library Sci., Okla. State U., 1978. Library media specialist Lone Star Elem. Sch., Sapulpa, Okla., 1978—, Pretty Water Elem. Sch., Sapulpa, Okla., summer 1985; clerical librarian Eastern State Hosp., Vinita, Okla., 1981 summer; sec., mem. Sequoyah (Okla.) Children's Book Award Program, 1985—. Del. State Rep. Conv., Oklahoma City, 1986. Mem. Okla. Library Assn., Am. Library Assn., Am. Bus. Women's Assn., Lone Star Classroom Tchr's. Assn. (del., officer 1978-86), Tulsa Folk Music Soc., Okla. State U. Alumni Assn., Delta Kappa Gamma (sec. 1984—), Kappa Delta Phi, Phi Kappa Phi. Republican. Club: Indian Territory Dulcimer Celebration. Office: Lone Star Sch PO Box 1170 4000 S Hickory Sapulpa OK 74067

BAKER, JEAN HARVEY, history educator; b. Balt., Feb. 9, 1933; d. F. Barton and Rose (Lindsay) Hopkins Harvey; m. F. Robinson Baker, Sept. 12, 1953; children—Susan Dixon, Robinson Scott, Robert W., Jean Harvey. A.B., Goucher Coll., Towson, Md., 1961; M.A., Johns Hopkins U., Balt., 1965, Ph.D., 1971. Lectr., instr. history Notre Dame Coll., Balt., 1967-69; instr. history Goucher Coll., Balt., 1969, asst. prof. history, 1969-75, assoc. prof. history, 1975-78, prof. history, 1979-82, Elizabeth Todd prof. history, 1981—. Author: The Politics of Continuity, 1973; Ambivalent Americans, 1976; Affairs of Party, 1983 (Berkshire prize in history), Mary Todd Lincoln: A Biography, 1986; editor Md. Hist. Mag., 1979. Fellow Am. Council Learned Socs., 1976, NEH, 1982; recipient Faculty Teaching prize Goucher Coll., 1979. Mem. Orgn. Am. Historians, Am. Hist. Assn., Berkshire Conf. Women Historians, Phi Beta Kappa. Democrat. Home: 8717 McDonough Rd McDonough MD 21208 Office: Goucher Coll Towson MD 21204

BAKER, JOANN G., electronics executive; b. Parsons, Kans., June 16, 1944; d. Earl Raymond and Flora Grace (Swanner) Garrett; m. Steven Lee Martin, Mar. 11, 1966 (div. Aug. 1971); children: Anna Marie, Kristine Elizabeth; m. Donald Eugene Baker, Oct. 9, 1972; children: Raymond Eugene, John Olen. AA in Acctg., Labbette Community Coll., 1976. Adminstn. asst. Sentari Communications Electronics Mfg., Parsons, Kans., 1983-84; v.p. finance Wheatfields Electronics Mfg., Parsons, Kans., 1984-86; v.p. Space Antennas Electronic Wholesaler, Kansas City, Mo., 1986—; cons. J.B. Enterprises, Parsons. Inventor electronic devices. Mem. Title II Parent Adv. Bd., Erie, Kans. 1984, Prairie Schooners 4-H, community leader 1981-86). Mem. Nat. Assn. Female Exec., Computer Users Group (treas. 1982-87). Democrat. Presbyterian. Home: Rt 4 Box 146 Parsons KS 67357 Office: Space Antennas Inc 127 W 10th St Kansas City MO 64152

BAKER, JOANNE EVELYN, government official; b. Crucible, Pa., Dec. 1, 1933; d. George Joseph and Anna Leona (Kagle) Cormack; m. Warren Clair Baker, July 7, 1956 (dec. May 1968); m. James Lewis Wilson, June 2, 1970; (div. Sept. 1984); former stepchildren—James Lloyd, John Thomas, Charles Edward, Debra Ruth, Jeff Lee Wilson. Cert. applied music Waynesburg Coll., 1951. Various clerical positions, 1951-66; supr. U.S. Navy, Washington, 1966-71; pres., treas. Little Round Top Farm, Inc., Gettysburg, Pa., 1971-86; logistician U.S. Navy-U.S. Army, 1974-81; insp. Office of Insp. Gen., U.S. Army, Ft. Ritchie, Md., 1981-84; chief supply and services div. Fort Detrick, Frederick, Md., 1986—. Author: Reflections, 1974. Bd. dirs. Adams County Mental Health Assn., Gettysburg, 1982-87. Recipient Sustained Superior Achievement award Dept. Navy, 1975, Dept. of Army 1986; named an Outstanding Woman of Yr. Ft. Detrick, 1986. Mem. Internat. Graphoanalysis Soc. (Pa. chpt.), Internat. Platform Assn., Adams County Amateur Radio Soc. (sec. 1981-83), World Inst. of Achievement. Roman Catholic. Avocations: handwriting analysis, writing children's stories, ceramics, piano, studying self-improvement and psychology. Home: 5605 Shookstown Rd Frederick MD 21701

BAKER, JOSEPHINE L. REDENIUS (MRS. MILTON G. BAKER), minister, civic leader, retired U.S. Army officer, former public relations company executive; b. Oceanville, N.J., Aug. 31, 1920; d. Jacob and Josephine (Palmer) Redenius; student Columbia U., 1948-49, L.I. U., 1957-58, George Washington U., 1947-48; M.A. in Journalism, Am. U., 1963; L.H.D., Temple U., 1964; M.A. in Religious Studies, St. Charles Sem., 1981; M.Div., Eastern Baptist Theol. Sem., 1984; postgrad., 1987—. Ordained Deacon Episcopal Ch. Enlisted as pvt. WAAC, 1943, advanced through grades to lt. col. U.S. Army, 1963, to col. Pa. N.G., 1967; intelligence officer atomic installations throughout U.S. and Can., 1943-53; asst. in Office Chief of Staff, Army Forces Far East, Japan, 1954-56; public info. officer Office Chief of Info., Washington, 1958-61; chief Women's Army Corps Recruiting, U.S. Army, 1962-66; info. liaison officer U.S. Army, 1966-67, ret., 1967; dir. pub. relations and devel. Valley Forge Mil. Acad. and Jr. Coll., Wayne, Pa., 1967-71, dir., 1970-79; pres. Potential Inc., Ardmore, Pa., 1979-83, Intercounty Trading Co., Inc., Surfside, Fla., 1976-80; deacon All Souls' Episcopal Ch., Miami Beach, Fla. Bd. dirs. Valley Forge Freedom Valley dist. Girl Scouts Am., Republican Women of Pa., Opera Guild of Miami; pres. bd. dirs. St. Cornelius the Centurian Found., 1976—; v.p. Episcopal Ch. Women, Diocese of Pa., 1984-86. Decorated Legion of Merit, Pa. Meritorious Service medal; U.S. Army Commendation medal with oak leaf cluster. Recipient Order Golden Sword Valley Forge Mil. Acad., 1986; named Disting. Alumnus Am. U., 1969; Doctor Ministry fellow Eastern Baptist Theol. Sem., 1985-87. Mem. Pub. Relations Soc. Am., Am. Personnel and Guidance Assn., Am. Coll. Personnel Assn., Nat. Vocat. Guidance Assn., Am. Sch. Counselors Assn., Pa. Med. Missionary Soc. (dir. 1983—), Am. Legion Aux., Ret. Officers Assn., Assn. U.S. Army (Anthony J. Drexel Biddle medal 1968), Army-Navy Union, Assn. Measurement and Evaluation in Guidance, Am. Legion, La Boutique Des Hult Chapeaux et Quarante Femmes, Emergency Aid of Pa., Women in Communications, Order St. Francis, Mil. Order World Wars, Miami Heart Inst. Aux. Episcopalian. Clubs: Surf, Bald Peak Colony (N.H.), Miami Beach (fla.) Women's, St. David's Golf; Acorn. Lodge: Soroptimists. also: 9 Island Ave on Belle Isle Miami Beach FL 33139

BAKER, JOYCE ELAINE, infosystems specialist; b. St. Joseph, Mo., Nov. 17, 1954; d. Earl Leslie and Evelyn Marie (Carlson) Redman; m. Norman Paul Hinrichs, June 22, 1974 (div. Apr. 1984); 1 child, Melissa Kay; m. James Ellsworth Baker, June 22, 1985 (dec. Nov. 1987). Student, Mo. Western State Coll., St. Joseph, 1975-77. Programmer NCR Corp., Kansas City, Mo., 1977-78, Compac Services, Kansas City, 1978-79; programmer cons. Allen Services, Dayton, Ohio, 1979-80; programmer analyst Federated Dept. Stores, Inc., Cin., 1980, McAuto Health Services, St. Louis, 1980-82, Fed. Reserve Bank, St. Louis, 1982—. Democrat. Home: 1800 Bellevue Ave

Saint Louis MO 63143 Office: Fed Reserve Bank PO Box 442 Saint Louis MO 63166

BAKER, JUDITH ANN, educator; b. Auburn, Ind., Apr. 10, 1953; d. Francis Clark and Marvel Irene (Kutzner) Ulm; m. Ronald Eugene Ulm Baker, June 28, 1975; 1 child: Nicholas Matthew. BS in Elem. Edn. magna cum laude, Taylor U., 1975; MS in Reading, Ind. U., 1978. Cert. tchr., Ind., Wis. Tchr. DeKalb Ea. United Schs., Butler, Ind., 1975-77, Tippecanoe Sch. Dist., Lafayette, Ind., 1977-80; dir. Wee Care Day Care, Glendale, Wis., 1980; specialist reading No. Ozaukee Sch. Dist., Fredonia, Wis., 1980—; cons. Purdue Gifted Edn. Doctorate Students, West Lafayette, 1978-80; edn. advisor Purdue U., Concordia Coll., Mequon, Wis., 1977-80, 1988. Cons. (movie) Mainstreaming at Mayflower Mill, McGraw Hill, 1979. Mem. NEA, Wis. St. Reading Assn., Nat. Reading Assn., Chi Alpha Omega. Republican. Methodist. Home: 1492 Horns Corners Rd Cedarburg WI 53012 Office: No Ozaukee Sch Dist 410 Highland St Fredonia WI 53012

BAKER, JUSTINE CLARA, mathematics and physics educator; b. Phila., Oct. 1, 1939; d. Michael Angelo and Justine Catherine (DeFlavia) Boni; m. Harold Jerome Baker, July 23, 1966. A.B., Immaculata Coll., 1963; M.A.T.M., Villanova U., 1970; M.S. in Edn., U. Pa., 1973, Ph.D., 1987. Tchr. math. and sci. pvt. and parochial area schs., Phila. area, 1963-66; tchr. math. Phila. High Schs., 1967-69; tchr. math. and sci. parochial and pvt. and pub. area schs., Phila. and Willingboro, N.J., 1973-80; instr. Goldey Beacom Coll., Wilmington, Del., 1980-84; asst. prof. Del. County Community Coll., Media, Pa., 1984-85; systems engr. RCA Moorestown, N.J., 1985-87; tchr. math. and physics Swarthmore (Pa.) Acad., 1987-88. Author: The Computer in the School, 1975; Computers in the Curriculum, 1976; Microcomputers in the Classroom, 1982. Mem. ACM, Am. Ednl. Research Assn., Math. Assn. Am., Nat. Council Tchrs. Math., Phi Delta Kappa (cert. of recog. 1976, 81, 82, 83, 84, service key 1982). Republican. Roman Catholic. Clubs: Edn. Alumni Assn., U. Pa. Alumnae Assn. Immaculata Coll. Home: 1021 Drexel Ave Drexel Hill PA 19026 Office: Swarthmore Acad 401 Rutgers Ave Swarthmore PA 19081

BAKER, KATHERINE HARVY, biology educator; b. Washington, Apr. 9, 1951; d. Thomas Harvey and Sarah Elizabeth (Held) B.; m. Richard Neal Blutstein, June 17, 1973; 1 child, Benjamin Thomas. BS, Dickinson Coll., 1973; PhD, U. Del., 1980. Postdoctoral fellow U. Va. Dept. Environ. Sci., Charlottesville, 1980-82; asst. prof. biology Western New Eng. Coll., Springfield, Mass., 1982-85, Millersville (Pa.) U., 1985—; bd. dirs. Biodetox Inc., Newark, Del.; prin. investigator cons. Dupont Inc., Newark, 1986—. Contbr. articles to sci. jours. Mem. Am. Inst. Biol. Scis., Ecol. Soc. Am., Am. Soc. for Microbiology. Democrat. Jewish. Office: Millersville U Roddy Sci Ctr Dept Biology Millersville PA 17011

BAKER, KATHERINE JUNE, educator, minister; b. Dallas, Feb. 3, 1932; d. Kirk Moses and Katherine Faye (Turner) Sherrill; m. George William Baker, Jan. 30, 1955; children: Kirk Garner, Kathleen Kay. BS, BA, Tex. Women's U., 1953, MEd, 1979; cert. in religious edn., Meadville Theol. U., 1970; postgrad., North Tex. State U., 1987—; DD (hon.), Am. Fellowship Ch., 1981. Cert. elem., secondary tchr., adminstr., Tex. Mgr. prodn. Woolf Bros., Dallas, 1953-55; display mgr. J.M. Dyer and Co., Corsicana, Tex., 1954; advt. artist Fair Dept. Store, Ft. Worth, 1954-56; artist, instr. Dutch Art Gallery, Dallas, 1960-65; dir. religious edn. 1st Unitarian Ch., Dallas, 1967-69; dir. day care, tchr. Richardson (Tex.) Unitarian Ch., 1971-73; dir. camp Tres Rios YWCA, Glen Rose, Tex., 1975-76; dir. program of extended sch. instrn. Hamilton Park Elem. Sch. Richardson Ind. Sch. Dist., 1975-78, tchr. Dover Elem. Sch., 1978-79, tchr. Jess Harben Elem. Sch., 1979—. Contbr. articles to ch. newspaper, 1967-69; exhibited in group show at Tex. Art Assn., 1966; one-woman show Dutch Art Gallery - Northlake Ctr., Dallas, 1965. Advocate day care Unitarian Universalist Women's Fedn., Boston, 1975-76, mem. nominating com., 1976-77. Mem. NEA, Nat. Council Social Studies, Assn. Supervision and Curriculum Devel., Tex. State Tchrs. Assn. (treas. Richardson chpt. 1984-85), Women's Ctr. Dallas, Sokol Athletic Ctr., Smithsonian Assn., Dallas Mus. Assn., Alpha Chi, Delta Phi Delta (pres. 1952-53), Phi Delta Kappa. Democrat. Club: Toastmistresses. Home: 8835 Larchwood Dallas TX 75238

BAKER, LEE UDEN, educator; b. Seneca, S.C., Apr. 27, 1919; d. Max and Fannie Cecelia (Wickof) Uden; m. Richard M. Baker, Feb. 10, 1946 (div. 1978); children: Leslie Sue, Teri Maxine. AA in Fashion Design, Los Angeles Trade Tech. Coll., 1968, AA in Theatre Arts, 1983; BA of Vocat. EDn., Calif. State U., Los Angeles, 1985, MAin Career Edn., 1987. Designer Sir James Calif., Los Angeles, 1953-54, Exquisite Girl Calif., Los Angeles, 1954-60, Robes of Calif., Los Angeles, 1960-78; tchr. Los Angeles Trade Tech. Coll., 1960—; designer, implementor career edn. proposals for Calif. State U., Los Angeles, Los Angeles Community Colls., 1988. Author: The Third Branch, 1986, Power Play, 1983; co-author (with husband) several musical theatre works, 1967-78. Dir. Citizens Legal Reform, Los Angeles 1986; mem. Sen. Robert Presley's Task Force Legal Reform, Sacramento 1986-87; designer proposal for partnership for Los Angeles Community Coll. and Calif. State U. at Los Angeles, 1987. Mem. Calif. Fashion Designers (pres. 1965-67), Fashion Group Inc. (mem. edn. com. 1970), Beyond War. Democrat. Jewish. Home: 10457 Bloomfield St Toluca Lake CA 91602 Office: Mgmt Employee Tng Assn 10457 Bloomfield St Toluca Lake CA 91602

BAKER, LILLIAN, author, historian, artist, lecturer; b. Yonkers, N.Y., Dec. 12, 1921; student El Camino (Calif.) Coll., 1952, UCLA, 1968, 77; m. Roscoe A. Baker; children: Wanda Georgia, George Riley. Continuity writer Sta. WINS, N.Y.C., 1945-46; columnist, freelance writer, reviewer Gardena (Calif.) Valley News, 1964-76; freelance writer, editor, 1971—; lectr. in field.; founder/editor Internat. Club for Collectors of Hatpins and Hatpin Holders, monthly newsletter Points, ann. Pictorial Jour., 1977—, conv. and seminar coordinator, 1979—; co-founder Ams. for Hist. Accuracy, 1972, Com. for Equality for All Draftees, 1973; chair S. Bay primary campaign S.I. Hayakawa, for U.S. Senator from Calif., 1976; witness U.S. Commn. Wartime Relocation, 1981, U.S. Senate Judiciary Com., 1983, U.S. Ho. Reps. Judiciary Com., 1986. Recipient award Freedoms Found., 1971; Ann. award Conf. Calif. Hist. Socs., 1983; monetary award Hoover Instn. Stanford (Calif.) U., 1985; recipient award Pro-Am. Orgn., 1987. Mem. Nat. League Am. Pen Women, Nat. Writers Club, Soc. Jewelry Historians USA, (charter), Art Students League N.Y. (life), Nat. Historic Soc. (founding), Nat. Trust Historic Preservation (founding), other orgns. Author: Collector's Encyclopedia of Hatpins and Hatpin Holders, 1976, second edit. 1988, 100 Years of Collectible Jewelry 1850-1950, 1978, rev. edit., 1988, Jewelry: Art Nouveau and Art Deco, 1980, rev. edit. 1985, 87, The Concentration Camp Conspiracy: A Second Pearl Harbor, 1981 (Scholarship Category award of Merit, Conf. of Calif. Hist. Socs. 1983), Hatpins and Hatpin Holders: An Illustrated Value Guide, 1983, rev. edit. 1988, Creative and Collectible Miniatures, 1984, Fifty Years of Collectible Fashion Jewelry: 1925-1975, 1986, 2d edit., 1988, Dishonoring America: The Collective Guilt of American Japanese, 1988; also articles; author poetry; editor: Insider; contbg. author Vol. VII Time-Life Encyclopedia of Collectibles, 1979; numerous radio and TV appearances. Home and Office: 15237 Chanera Ave Gardena CA 90249

BAKER, LINDA LESLIE, social services administrator, consultant; b. Eugene, Oregon, Sept. 15, 1948; d. Charles Andrew and Ashley Estelle (Durrett) Marcum; m. Brent Delos Cain, May 28, 1983. Lic. Social Worker. Social worker Dept. Social and Rehab. Services, Topeka, 1972-79; foster care program specialist Kans. Children's Service League, Topeka, 1979-83, dist. dir., 1983—; cons. Nat. Directory Foster Care Program and Ednl. Consultant, 1985—; cons., trainer Permanency Planning Resources for Children, 1983—; field instr. U. Kans., 1986—. Active Kans. Children and Adolescent Service System Programs, Topeka, 1985-86, children's Coalition, Topeka, 1985-86; adv. bd. Family Service and Guidance Ctr., Topeka, 1985-86, Family Preservation Project, 1986—. Mem. Nat. Assn. Social Workers, YWCA, Kans. Assn. Social Workers, Kans. Conf. Social Welfare, Topeka Assn. Human Service Agys. (exec. treas. 1983-86, exec. v.p. 1986-87, pres. 1988), Council on Children and Families (sec. 1979—), Civitan Club, Phi Kappa Phi. Democrat. Home: 2649 SW Ashworth Pl Topeka KS 66614 Office: Kans Children's Service League 2053 Kansas Ave Topeka KS 66605

BAKER, LORRAINE, educational administrator; b. Los Angeles, Aug. 20, 1935; d. Herbert McDowell and Izalia Lewena (Fee) Young; A.A., Los Angeles City Coll., 1955; B.A., Calif. State U., 1972; cert. sch. mgmt. (Rockefeller Found. fellow), Center for Ednl. Leadership, 1975-76; M.Ed., U. LaVerne, 1979; m. Rolland Alvin Baker, Mar. 16, 1955; children—Glenn, Eric. Tchr., La Canada (Calif.) Unified Sch. Dist., 1972-76, prin. Paradise Canyon Sch., 1976-79, bldg. adminstr. Foothill Intermediate Sch., 1979-80, coordinator curriculum K-12, 1980-84, dir. instructional services, 1984-87; dir. tchr. edn. Azusa (Calif.) Pacific U., 1987—. Mem. Assn. Supervision and Curriculum Devel., AAUW, Assn. Calif. Sch. Adminstrs., Women in Bus.

BAKER, MARGIE SPARKMAN, government agency official; b. Leon, Ky., Jan. 28, 1943; d. Frank and Lora Jane (Allen) Sparkman; student No. Va. Community Coll., 1975-77, George Washington U., 1977-79; B.A. in Sociology, Columbia Coll. Arts and Scis., 1979; m. Richard L. Baker, Nov. 21, 1962; 1 dau., Cheri Michelle. Various secretarial and adminstrv. positions U.S. Dept. Def. and U.S. Dept. Agr., Washington area, 1961-69; staff asst. to dep. for programs Am. Revolution Bicentennial Adminstrn., Washington, 1969-75; mgmt. analyst Office of Surface Mining and Reclamation Dept. Interior, Washington, 1978; adminstrv. asst. to legal counsel, Commn. on Accident at Three Mile Island, Washington, 1979; program analyst Mine Safety and Health Adminstrn., U.S. Dept. Labor, Arlington, Va., 1979—. Recipient Sustained Superior Performance award Commn. on Three Mile Island, Outstanding Achievement award and Sustained Superior Performance award Mine Safety and Health Adminstrn. Mem. Nat. Assn. Female Execs., Federally Employed Women, Am. Fedn. Govt. Employees (steward local 12). Home: 6826 Stoneybrooke Ln Alexandria VA 22306

BAKER, MARILYN MILLER, professional association executive; b. Chickasha, Okla., July 13, 1934; d. Basil E. Sr. and Vivian V. (Townsend) Miller; children: Lisa D. Baker, Darryl A. Baker. B in Journalism, U. Tex., 1956. Asst. editor Tex. Press Assn., Austin, 1959-60; asst. editor Tex. Med. Assn., Austin, 1960-62, exec. editor, 1962-83, dir. dept. med. edn., 1979-83, dir. div. med. info., planning, 1987—; pres. Marilyn Baker & Assocs., Austin, 1983-86. Mem. Am. Soc. Assn. Execs. (cert.), Internat. Assn. Bus. Communicators (life, chmn. dist. bd. 1976-78, v.p., bd. dirs. 1978-80, numerous editorial awards). Methodist. Home: 4704 Greystone Dr Austin TX 78731 Office: Tex Med Assn 1801 N Lamar Blvd Austin TX 78701

BAKER, MARY, mechanical engineer; b. Madison, Wis., July 30, 1944; d. John Gordon Baker and Elizabeth Theadora (Nelson) B.; m. Wayne Wallace Pfeiffer, July 4, 1974; children: Elizabeth Ann, Gordon Jay. B.S., U. Wis., 1966; M.S. in Applied Mechanics, Calif. Inst. Tech., Pasadena, 1967, Ph.D. 1972. Registered profl. mech. engr., Calif., 1977. Mem. tech. staff IBM Research Ctr., Yorktown Heights, N.Y., 1972; sr. engr. Rohr Industries, Chula Vista, Calif., 1973-75; mem. sci. staff Systems Science and Software, 1975-77; project mgr., mgr. analytical services, tech. dir. western ops., Structural Dynamics Research Corp., San Diego, 1977—. Mem. ASME, AIAA, Sigma Xi, Phi Kappa Phi, Tau Beta Pi. Contbr. articles to profl. jours. Home: 13864 Boquita Dr Del Mar CA 92014 Office: Structural Dynamics Research Corp 11055 Roselle St San Diego CA 92121

BAKER, MARY JORDAN, educator; b. Chgo. A.B., Stanford U., 1961; M.A., U. Va., 1964; Ph.D. in Romance Lang., Harvard U., 1969. Instr. French, DePauw U., 1964-65; asst. prof. U. Tex.-Austin, 1968-75, assoc. prof. French, 1975-88—; prof. 1988—. Contbr. articles to profl. jours. Recipient Pres. Assocs. Teaching Excellence award 1980, Jean Holloway Excellence in Teaching award, 1987. Mem. MLA, Am. Assn. Tchrs. French, Soc. Study Narrative Literature, Modern Humanities Research Assn. Coauthor: Panaché Littéraire, 1978. Address: French Dept Univ Tex Austin TX 78712

BAKER, MELODY ANN, accountant; b. Los Angeles, Aug. 29, 1959; d. Bill Parke and Sharon Kay (Kyser) Harrison. AS in Acctg., Tulsa Jr. Coll., 1988. Clk. Crown Fin. Co., Tulsa, 1978; credit clk. Lender Service Co., Tulsa, 1978-79, ins. clk., 1979-82, acctg. clk., 1982-84, mgr. data processing, 1984-85, mgr. adminstrv. services, data processing, 1985-86, mgr. ins., 1985-87, sr. acct., 1987—; sec. Versatile Ins. Agy., Tulsa, 1980-82, sec.-treas., 1983-87. Mem. Nat. Assn. Female Execs. Republican. Baptist.

BAKER, RACHELE JEANNE, small business owner; b. Redwood City, Calif., Feb. 15, 1957; d. Alf Torsten and Mildred Jeannette (Gelzinnus) Rylander; m. Paul William Baker, July 17, 1983; 1 child, Lareina Marie. Student, Castleton (Vt.) State Coll., 1980-82. Legal sec. Rodney F. Vieux, Esq., Johnson, Vt., 1973; sec. Raymond Bauer Oil Burner, Rutland, Vt., 1974; legal sec. Sebastian J. Ruggeri, Esq., Greenfield, Mass., 1976; typesetter The Mountain Times, Killington, Vt., 1979-80; legal sec. Griffin and Griffin, Ltd., Rutland, 1980-82; mgr. Edelweiss Motel, Mendon, Vt., 1982-83; owner, operator Lake of the Sky Motor Inn, Tahoe City, Calif., 1984—. Mem. Nat. Assn. Self-Employed, Calif. Lodging Industry Assn., Tahoe North Vis. and Convention Bur. Republican. Office: Lake of the Sky Motor Inn PO Box 227 Tahoe City CA 95730

BAKER, SHIRLEY HODNETT, marketing professional; b. Halifax, Va., Aug. 11, 1951; d. Charlie Thompson and Earlene (Dance) Hodnett; m. Robert H. Baker. Student Cen. Va. Community Coll., 1974-76. Sec. Lynchburg (Va.) Coll., 1969-72; sec. Leggett Dept. Store, Lynchburg, 1972-75, sales mgr., 1975-76; co-owner Decorating Den, Lynchburg, 1976-81; adminstrv. asst. TV Bur. Advt., Atlanta, 1981-82, mktg./sales exec., Dallas, 1982-84; mktg. dir. N.Y. Market Radio Broadcasters Assn., N.Y.C., 1985-87; v.p. sales and mktg. Radio Advt. Bur., N.Y.C., 1987—. Bd. dirs. Mother's Day Council, Father's Day Council. Mem. Am. Women in Radio and TV, Nat. Assn. Female Execs. Baptist. Home: 57 Warren St New York NY 10007 Office: Radio Advt Bur 304 Park Ave S New York NY 10010

BAKER, STEPHANIE CAROL, controller; b. Lawrenceburg, Ind., Jan. 15, 1962; d. David Lawrence and Velma Ruth (Lafary) Green; m. Michael Wayne Baker, June 4, 1983. BS, Ind. U., 1984. Controller Comware, Inc., Cin., 1984—; guest lectr. Purdue U., Versailles, Ind., 1987. Lutheran. Home: 243 Hickory Lawrenceburg IN 47025 Office: 4225 Malsbary Cincinnati OH 45242

BAKER, SUSAN P., public health educator; b. Atlanta, May 31, 1930; d. Charles Laban and Susan (Lowell) Pardee; m. Timothy Danforth Baker, June 23, 1951; children—Timothy D., David C., Susan L. A.B., Cornell U., Ithaca, N.Y., 1951; M.P.H., Johns Hopkins U., Balt., 1968. Research assoc. Office of Chief Med. Examiner, Balt., 1968-81; research assoc. Johns Hopkins Sch. Hygiene and Pub. Health, Balt., 1968-71, asst. prof., 1971-74, assoc. prof., 1974-83, prof. health policy & mgmt., 1983—, joint appointment in environ. health scis., 1975—, joint appointment in pediatrics, 1983—, dir. Injury Prevention Ctr., 1987—; vis. prof. U. Minn. Sch. Pub. Health, 1975—; chmn. nat. rev. panel for nat. accident sampling system Dept. Transp., Washington, 1976-81; vice chmn. com. on trauma research Nat. Research Council, Washington, 1984-85; vis. lectr. in injury prevention Harvard Sch. Pub. Health, 1984—; John T. Law meml. lectr. U. Calgary, Alta., 1984; cons. and lectr. in field. Author: (monograph) Fatally Injured Drivers, 1970 (Prince Bernhard medal 1974); The Injury Fact Book, 1984. Contbr. chpts. to books, articles to profl. jours. Mem. Am. Assn. Automotive Medicine (bd. dirs. 1971-76, pres. 1974-75, Award of Merit 1985), Am. Pub. Health Assn. (governing council 1975-77, jour. bd. 1983—), Am. Trauma Soc. (bd. dirs. 1972—, Disting. Achievement award 1981, Stone Lectureship award 1985), Delta Omega, Phi Beta Kappa. Office: Johns Hopkins U Sch Hygiene & Pub Health 615 N Wolfe St Dept Health Policy & Mgmt Baltimore MD 21205

BAKER, WINDA LOUISE (WENDY), social worker; b. Suwannee County, Fla., July 16, 1952; d. Austin Sidney Baker and Jessie Mae (Williams) Baker Jones; B.A. in Theology, Berkshire Christian Coll., 1974. Clk.-typist State of Fla., Tallahassee, 1974-76; cashier Tallahassee-Eastern Theatres, 1975-76; field rep. Commn. Human Relations, 1976-77; asst. to dir. retirement living, sec., receptionist Advent Christian Village, Dowling Park, Fla., 1977-79, admissions counselor, social worker, after 1979, multi-purpose worker, 1980; geriatric care worker Advent Christian Village, Dowling Park, Fla., 1983-85, med. transcriptionist, 1985, advt. sales staff, 1986-87; legal sec., McAlpin, Fla., 1987—. Vol. ARC and Asso. Charities, 1977—; founder Suwannee County Overeaters Anonymous, Live Oak, Fla., 1982. Mem. Suwannee County Mental Assn., Assn. Informed Travelers, Christian Fin. Planning, Inc., Cheeks Sch. Gymnastics Alumni. Republican. Advent Christian. Home: RR 1 Box 386 McAlpin FL 32062-9785

BAKER, ZELTA LOUISE, insurance company executive; b. Dallas, Dec. 7, 1948; d. Charles Darwin and Maude Zelta (Sanders) B.; m. John Adrian Burden, Oct. 6, 1967 (div. 1969). Grad. high sch., Dallas. Lay-out mgr., printer Calvery Bapt. Ch., Dallas, 1967-68; typist Res. Life Ins. Co., Dallas, 1967, 68-71, sec., 1971-81, statis. analyst, 1981-83, meeting planner, 1983-87, conf. and mktg. adminstr., 1987—. Mem. Nat. Com. to Preserve Social Security and Medicare, Washington, 1987. Mem. Meeting Planners Internat. Baptist. Office: Res Life Ins Co 403 S Akard St Suite 506 Dallas TX 75202

BAKER HOLLIDAY, KAREN, hotel executive; b. Hollywood, Calif., Mar. 21, 1948; d. Frank A. Kelly Jr. and Dee A. (McWhorter) Kelly Archer; m. Kenneth J. Holliday, June 21, 1969 (div. Mar. 1978); 1 child, Tiffany Ann; m. Toby Evans Baker, June 8, 1980 (separated Sept. 1984). Student pub. schs., Woodland Hills, Calif. Mgr., Zane Grey Hotel, Avalon, Calif., 1969—, owner, 1975—. Chairperson Vehicle Rev. Bd., Avalon, 1982—; chairperson accomodations com. Avalon C. of C. Republican. Club: Catalina Racquet (sec. 1972-80, pres. 1985-87) (Avalon). Avocations: tennis; swimming; water skiing; needlework. Home: 199 Chimes Tower Rd Avalon CA 90704 Office: Zane Grey Pueblo Hotel PO Box 216 Avalon CA 90704

BAKER-LIEVANOS, NINA GILLSON, jewelry store executive; b. Boston, Dec. 19, 1950; d. Rev. John Robert and Patricia (Gillson) Baker; m. Jorge Alberto Lievanos, June 6, 1981; children: Jeremy John Baker, Wendy Mara Baker, Raoul Salvador Baker-Lievanos. Student Mills Coll., 1969-70; grad. course in diamond grading Gemology Inst. Am., 1983; student in diamondtology designation Diamond Council Am., 1986—. Artist, tchr., Claremont, Calif., 1973-78; escrow officer Bank of Am., Claremont, 1978-81; retail salesman William Pitt Jewelers, Puente Hills, Montclair, Calif., 1981-83, asst. mgr., Montclair, 1983, mgr., 1983—, corp. sales trainer, 1988—. Artist tapestry hanging Laguna Beach Mus. Art, 1974. Recipient Cert. Merit Art Bank Am., 1968, High Sales award William Pitt Jewelers, 1983, 84, Key award Am. Biographical Inst. for Mgmt. Achievement, 1987. Mem. Nat. Assn. Female Execs., Internat. Platform Assn., C. of C., Compassion Internat. Democrat. Unitarian. Avocations: tapestry weaving, creative writing. Office: William Pitt Jewelers 158 Towne Ctr Santa Maria CA 93454

BALAZS, MARJORIE KARLENE, chemist; b. St. Louis, Nov. 9, 1932; d. Karl John and Marie Antoinette (Hoffman) Balazs; A.B., Washington U., St. Louis, 1954; M.A. (NSF grantee) Stanford U., 1963; M.S., U. San Francisco, 1969. Chemist, chief chem. lab, U.S. Geol. Survey, Denver, 1955-58; tchr. chemistry Jefferson County Schs., Lakewood, Colo., 1958-62; chemist life scis. Stanford (Calif.) Research Inst., 1963-68, chemist analytical physics, 1971-75; chemist semiconductor tech. Applied Materials, Santa Clara, Calif., 1968-71; pres. Balazs Analyt. Lab., Mountain View, Calif., 1975—. Pres. Santa Clara County council Girl Scouts Am., 1988—. Named One of Savvy's Women of Yr., 1984, Calif. Woman Yr., 1986, Outstanding Entrepreneur Am. 1986. Mem. Electrochem. Soc., Filtration Soc., Am. Electronic Assn., ASTM, Peninsula Profl. Women's Network (pres. 1981-82). Contbr. articles to profl. jours. Office: 2284 Old Middlefield Way Suite 10 Mountain View CA 94043

BALCH, CATHY JEAN, sales executive; b. Houston, Nov. 25, 1950; d. Dell Truman and Nelva Joyce (Mansell) B. Student, Stephen F. Austin State U., 1969-70. Payroll adminstrn. FII Corp., Houston, 1973-74; supr. programming, ops. Jagger Assocs., Austin, 1974-76; ops., customer support rep. UCC Houston, 1976-77; data processing mgr. CCI, Austin, 1977-78, Houston Instrument, Austin, 1978-86; product sales mgr. Tymlabs Corp., Austin, 1986—. Treas. Summertree HOA, Austin, 1986, pres., 1987-88. Mem. Nat. Assn. Female Execs., Am. Prodn. and Inventory Control Soc., Hewlett-Packard Internat. and Local Users Group, Basic Special Interest Group. Democrat. Baptist. Office: Tymlabs Corp 811 Barton Springs Rd Suite 511 Austin TX 78704

BALCOM, GLORIA DARLEEN, computer administrative and marketing consultant; b. Porterville, Calif., July 23, 1939; d. Orel A. and Eunice E. Stadtmiller; A.A., El Camino Coll., 1959; student computer sci. Harbor Coll., 1976-77; m. Orville R. Balcom, July 23, 1971; stepchildren—Cynthia Lou, Steven Raymond. Personnel trainee AiResearch div. Garrett Corp., Los Angeles, 1959-60, sales promotion adminstr., 1960-64; sales rep. Volt Temporary Services, El Segundo, Calif., 1965-69, mgr., Tarzana, Calif., 1969-71; co-owner, co-operator Brown Dog Engring., Lomita, Calif., 1972-77; pres., owner, cons. MicroSly Mktg., Lomita, 1977—. Mem. Ind. Computer Cons. Assn., Am. Soc. Profl. and Exec. Women, Nat. Assn. Female Execs. Club: Torrance Athletic. Home and Office: 24521 Walnut St Lomita CA 90717

BALCOM, KAREN SUZANNE, librarian; b. San Antonio, Feb. 15, 1949; d. George Sheldon amd Marian Susannah (Dyer) B.; m. James Louis Garrison. Oct. 8, 1977. AA, San Antonio Coll., 1969; BA, U. Tex., 1971, MLS, 1972. Cataloger San Antonio Coll., 1973-74, systems librarian, 1974—. Mem. Am. Library Assn., Spl. Libraries Assn., Am. Soc. Info. Sci., Tex Library Assn., Am. Assn. U. Profs., Tex. Faculty Assn., LWV. Office: San Antonio Coll Library 1001 Howard San Antonio TX 78284

BALDA, JO, banker; b. Oak Harbor, Wash., Oct. 3, 1922; d. Jake and Jennie (Fakkema) Balda. Student pub. schs., Oak Harbor. With Olympic Bank (now known as First Interstate Bank of Wash.), Oak Harbor, 1942-85, asst. cashier, 1968-79, asst. v.p., ops. officer, 1979-83, asst. v.p., mgr. Midway br., 1983-85, mgr. Midway br., 1985-86; dir. sales and ops. Bank at Oak Harbor, Oak Harbor, 1986—; corp. treas. Island Thrift Shop, 1986—; consumer credit counseling local unit, 1982—, Seattle unit, 1986—. Tchr. Sunday sch. Christian Reformed Ch., Oak Harbor, 1981-82; workshop leader. treas., Am. Cancer Soc., Oak Harbor, 1963, Am. Heart Assn., Island County, Wash., 1971—, Oak Harbor Area council Navy League, 1976—, March of Dimes, Island County, 1978-81, mem. exec. com. Puget Sound chpt., 1984; bd. dirs. Oak Harbor Hist. Soc., 1978, treas., 1979—; pres. Women's Mission Guild, Christian Ref. Ch., Oak Harbor, 1981-82; bd. dirs. Community Concerts, 1982—, treas., 1984; treas. Island County Rep. Cen. Com., 1983—pres. North Whidbey Rep. Women, 1987, 88; mem. personnel adv. bd. City of Oak Harbor, 1984—; treas. Island County Hist. Soc., 1985—; candidate mem. United Way, 1985; adv. com. ARC, 1985-86; bd. dirs. North Whidbey Help House, 1986—, New Leaf, 1987—. Mem. Am. Inst. Banking (instr., workshop leader), Nat. Assn. Bank Women (pres. chpt. 1978-79), Bus. and Profl. Women's Assn. (v.p. 1980-81, pres. 1981-82, 85—, treas. 1984-85, Woman of Achievement 1977), North Whidbey Women's Bowling Assn., North Whidbey C. of C. (trustee 1977-78; Citizen of Year award 1976, Disting. Citizen award 1984). Lodge: Toastmistress (treas. council 1977-78, treas. region 1979-80, v.p. 1984-85), Soroptomists (treas. 1981-83, dir. 1983-84). Home: PO Box 345 Oak Harbor WA 98277 Office: PO Box 769 Oak Harbor WA 98277

BALDASSANO, CORINNE LESLIE, radio executive; b. N.Y.C., May 16, 1950; d. Nicholas and Olga (Phillips) Baldassano. BA cum laude, Queens Coll., CUNY, 1970; MA in Theatre, Hunter Coll., CUNY, 1975; MBA in Fin., NYU, 1986. Program dir., ops. mgr. Sta. KAUM-FM, Houston, 1977-79; dir. programming Sta. WSAI-FM, Cin., 1979-81; dir. programming ABC Contemporary and FM Radio Networks, N.Y.C., 1981-84; regional mgr. affiliate relations United Stations Radio Networks, N.Y.C., 1985-87; dir. ABC Entertainment Radio Network, N.Y.C., 1987—; panelist conf. Am. Women in Radio and TV, Cin., 1981; panelist conv. Nat. Assn. Broadcasters, San Francisco, 1983; guest lectr. Wharton Sch. Bus., Phila., 1983, St. John's U., N.Y.C., 1983-84. Alumni mem. Govs. Com. Scholastic Achievement, N.Y.C., 1984-85. Mem. NYU Bus. Forum, Internat. Radio and TV Soc. (planning com., faculty/industry seminar 1986, 87), Women in Communications, Am. Women in Radio and TV. Democrat. Roman Catholic. Club: Liberty (N.Y.C.). Advocations: travel, theatre, dancing, running. Office: ABC Radio Networks 125 West End Ave 7th floor New York NY 10023

BALDERSTON, BETTYLOU, city manager; b. Salt Lake City, Mar. 22, 1943; d. Albert Thomas Agin and Edith (Nase) Kendall. Student, Wesley Coll., 1960-62. Mfr.'s rep., cons. Representation, Inc., Paoli, Pa., 1965-68; exec. sec. Bucks County Indsl. Devel. Corp., Doylestown, Pa., 1968-70; owner, operator Bettylou's, New Hope, Pa., 1974-76; city mgr. City of New Hope, 1976-87; dir. projects, cons. land devel. Condor Properties, Parsippany, N.J., 1987-88, dir. projects and ops., 1988—. Contbr. articles to profl. jours., 1984—. Bd. dirs. Bucks County Boroughs Assn., Pa., 1984—; mem. adv. council to county commrs., Doylestown, 1985—. Mem. Internat. City Mgmt. Assn., Assn. Pa. Mcpl. Mgrs., Southeastern Pa. Mcpl. Mgrs. Assn., New Hope C. of C. (sec., v.p. 1974-75). Republican. Methodist. Home: 27 Gabriel Dr Montville NJ 07045

BALDERSTON, JEAN MERRILL, psychotherapist, writer; b. Providence, Aug. 29, 1936; d. Frederick Augustus and Helen May (Cleveland) Merrill; m. David Chase Balderston, June 1, 1957. BA, U. Conn., 1957; MA, Columbia U., 1965, EdD, 1968. Pvt. practice psychotherapist N.Y.C., 1968—; adj. faculty Douglas Coll. for Women, New Brunswick, Rutgers U., Montclair State Coll., Upper Montclair, N.J., CUNY, Columbia U., Mt. St. Vincent U., 1965-70; editorial bd. N.Y. Quarterly, N.Y.C., 1971-76. Poems have appeared in various lit. mags., and anthologies. Mem. Am. Assn. Marital and Family Therapy, Am. Psychol. Assn., Poets and Writers, Poetry Soc. Am., Emily Dickinson Soc., Am. Scandinavian Found., Am. Scandinavian Soc. Home and Office: 1225 Park Ave New York NY 10128

BALDI, PATRICIA ANN, public health administrator; b. Muskogee, Okla., Feb. 1, 1943; d. Boxly William and Anne Nell (Smith) Waak; children: Cinira Anne, Rachel Nell. Student Tulane U., 1961-62, U. Houston, 1964-65, George Mason U., 1976-77; diploma Mather Sch. Nursing, 1964. R.N., Va. notary public, N.Y. Peace Corps nurse, Maceio, Alagoas, 1966-68; staff nurse U. Wis. Children's Hosp., Madison, 1968-70; dir. counseling Planned Parenthood, Washington, 1973-75; spl. asst. Devel. Support Bur., U.S. AID, Washington, 1977-78; assoc. dir. Office of Population, AID, Washington, 1978-82; asst. dir. Ctr. for Population and Family Health, Columbia U., N.Y.C., 1982-85; dir. population Nat. Audubon Soc., 1985—; U.S. del. UN Population Commn., 1981-82; cons. Family Planning Internat., 1973, Global Com. of Parliamentarians on Population and Devel., 1984-85; project design team U.S. AID, Zimbabwe, 1985, evaluation team, Kenya, Uganda, Nigeria, 1987; NGO participant UN Mid-Decade Conf. of Women, Copenhagen, 1981; moderator global population anniversary Peace Corps Conf., 1981; lectr. in field. Exec. producer (population videotape) What is the Limit. Mem. McGovern-Shriver Presdl. Campaign Staff, 1972; vice chmn. Arlington Democratic Com., 1974; chmn. Arlington Com. on Status of Women, 1975; dep. campaign mgr. Shriver for Pres. Com., 1976; del. Va. Dem. Conv., 1976, 82; mem. Population Task Force, 1986—, Internat. Union Conservation Nature and Natural Resources, NGO steering com. on Devel., Environment and Population ; del. World Conservation Strategy Conf. Mem. Am. Pub. Health Assn. (population sect. council, com. on women's rights), Nat. Council for Internat. Health (pub. policy com.), Assn. for Women in Devel., Nat. Women's Polit. Caucus, Soc. Internat. Devel., Women in Def. of Environment. Home: 16 N Highland St Arlington VA 22201 Office: National Audubon Soc Nat Capitol Office 801 Pennsylvania Ave SE Washington DC 20003

BALDISSERI, MARIE ROSANNE, physician; b. Providence, R.I., Oct. 31, 1955; d. Aldo Ferrucco and Margaret Teresa (Cavanaugh) B.; m. Srinivas Murali, Oct. 22, 1986. BS with Honors, Boston Coll., 1977; MS, Wagner Coll., 1978; MD, U. Navarra, Pamplona, Spain, 1982. Resident Interfaith Med. Ctr., Bklyn., 1982-85; fellow in critical care medicine Presbyn.-Univ. Hosp., Pitts., 1985-87, mem. ethics and human rights com., 1986—; assoc. dir. adult ICU, assoc. prof. anesthesiology and critical care medicine Magee-Womens Hosp., Pitts., 1987—; lectr. in field. Vol. tchr. Greater Pitts. Literacy Council, Pitts., 1987. Mem. Am. Coll. of Physicians, Pa. Med. Soc., Soc. Critical Care Medicine. Democrat. Roman Catholic. Office: Magee-Womens Hosp Forbes Ave and Halket St Pittsburgh PA 15213

BALDRIGE, LETITIA, public relations consultant; b. Miami Beach, Fla.; d. Howard Malcolm and Regina (Connell) B.; m. Robert Hollensteiner; children: Clare, Malcolm. B.A., Vassar Coll.; postgrad., U. Geneva, Switzerland; D.H.L. (hon.), Creighton U., 1979, Mt. St. Mary's Coll., 1980, Bryant Coll., 1987. Personal-social sec. to ambassador Am. Embassy, Paris, France, 1948-51; intelligence officer Am. Embassy, 1951-53; asst. to ambassador Am. Embassy, Rome, Italy, 1953-56; dir. public relations Tiffany & Co., 1956-61; social sec. to The White House, 1961-63; pres. Letitia Baldrige Enterprises, Chgo., 1964-69; dir. consumer affairs Burlington Industries, 1969-71; pres. Letitia Baldrige Enterprises, Inc., N.Y.C., 1972—; bd. dirs. The Outlet Co., Fed. Home Loan Bank N.Y., Hartmarx Corp. Author: Roman Candle, 1956, Tiffany Table Settings, 1958, Of Diamonds and Diplomats, 1968, Home, 1972, Juggling, 1976, Amy Vanderbilt's Complete Book of Etiquette, 1978, Amy Vanderbilt's Everyday Etiquette, 1979, Entertainers, 1981, Letitia Baldrige's Complete Guide to Executive Manners, 1985, Letitia Baldrige's Complete Guide to A Great Social Life, 1987; columnist: Copley News Syndicate; contbr. to popular mags., also lectr. Bd. dirs. Woodrow Wilson Found., Inst. Internat. Edn.; trustee Kenyon Coll., Gambier, Ohio. Republican. Office: Letitia Baldrige Enterprises Inc 230 Park Ave Room 805 New York NY 10169

BALDWIN, CAROL, small business owner; b. Norfolk, Va., June 20, 1943. BA, George Washington U., 1965; MA, U. Tex., Austin, 1977. Legis. asst. Gov. of Calif., Washington, 1965, U.S. Congressman, Washington, 1967-68; tng. program writer Sterling Inst., Washington, 1968; tchr., researcher Northwestern U., Evanston, Ill., 1968-70; asst. program mgr. Gov. of Ill., Chgo., 1970-71; ind. cons. Washington and Ottawa, Can., 1973-78; legis. analyst small bus. com. U.S. Senate, Washington, 1978-79; pres. Baldwin & Assocs., Washington, 1980—; tchr. Am. U., 1983-85, George Washington U., 1980-85, Montgomery Coll., 1980-86. Appeared on radio and TV news, interview and talk shows; editor booklets and newsletters for clients. Vol. trainer United Way/United Black Fund, 1982—; bd. dirs. employee health program ARC, 1985. Mem. Am. Soc. for Tng. and Devel., Am. Acad. of Mgmt., N.Y. Acad. of Sci.

BALDWIN, CYNTHIA ANN, industrial hygienist; b. Fort Sill, Okla., Sept. 18, 1951; d. Arthur Roy Baldwin and Dolores Mae (Zimdars) Hill; m. Rory Lee Vail, June 6, 1971 (div. Sept. 1978). BS in Biology, Met. State Coll., Denver, 1973; MS in Environ. Health, Colo. State U., 1981. Clk. typist admissions and records Colo. State U., Ft. Collins, 1974-75, student coordinator, office supr. dept. microbiology, 1975-80, grad. research asst. dept. microbiology, 1980-81; indsl. hygienist Consultation div. Iowa Bur. Labor, Des Moines, 1981-84; dir. occupational health Amana (Iowa) Refrigeration, Inc., 1984—; mem. adv. council U. Iowa Inst. Agrl. Medicine and Occupational Health, Iowa City, 1986—. Mem. Am. Indsl. Hygiene Assn. (pres. Iowa-Ill. section 1987-88). Office: Amana Refrigeration Inc Hwy 220 Amana IA 52204

BALDWIN, E. GAYLE, nurse practitioner; b. Stillwater, Okla., Oct. 29, 1950; d. William Fred and Mary Glynn (Munger) Cochran; m. Richard Kent Baldwin, Jan. 28, 1971 (div.); m. Gary Wayne Neely, Jan. 23, 1982 (div. June 1985). Student, Okla. Bapt. U., Shawnee, 1967-71; B.S.N., Central State U., Edmond, Okla., 1973; cert. U. Ariz., 1980. Staff nurse neonatal ICU, U. Okla. Health Scis. Center and Children's Hosp., Oklahoma City, 1973-75; nurse Presbyn. Hosp., Oklahoma City, 1975; pub. health nurse, newborn follow up program Ariz. Dept. Health Services, 1975-77; asst. dir. nursing Westside Community Hosp., Long Beach, Calif., 1977-78; nurse newborn nursery Desert Samaritan Hosp., Mesa, Ariz., 1978-80; neonatal nurse practitioner Good Samaritan Med. Center, Phoenix, 1980-83, neonatal nurse practitioner Air Evac, Phoenix, 1980-85; neonatal nurse practitioner Scottsdale (Ariz.) Meml. Hosp., 1984—; RN auditor Quality, Inc., Dallas, 1987-88; nurse practitioner Good Samaritan Med. Ctr., 1988—; nurse practitioner Mead Johnson & Co. grantee, 1980. Mem. Neonatal Nurse Practitioners Assn. Ariz., Ariz. Perinatal Trust, Parent Care. Office: Scottsdale Meml Hosp 7400 E Osborn Rd Scottsdale AZ 85251 also: PO Box 724 Scottsdale AZ 85252

BALDWIN, EILEEN PAWLIK, nurse, consultant, research organization executive; b. Balt., Jan. 11, 1950; d. Walter Joseph Pawlik and Annamae (Keenan) Russell; m. Ronnie Martin Baldwin, July 10, 1970; 1 child, John Martin. AA in Nursing, Essex Community Coll., 1972; BS in Health Care Adminstrn., St. Joseph's Coll., 1985. RN. Registered nurse Franklin Sq Hosp., Balt., 1972-84; project coordinator, cons. Q.C., Inc., Hunt Valley, Md., 1984—; pres. Clin. Data Review, Inc., Joppa, Md., 1986—; cons. Burn Found., Phila., 1985-87, Johns Hopkins Hosp., Balt., 1986—, Johns Hopkins U., 1986—. Mem. Am. Pub. Health Assn.

BALDWIN, GERALDINE SARAH, librarian; b. Glen Cove, N.Y., Dec. 1, 1950; d. Jeremiah J. and Alice M. (Henry) Mahoney; m. Donald Elliot Baldwin, Mar. 4, 1984. BA, SUNY, New Paltz, 1972; MLS, L.I. U., 1975. Asst. librarian, Mahopac, N.Y., 1972-73, dir., 1973-79; founding dir. Alice and Hamilton Fish Library, Garrison, N.Y., 1980—; advisor Mid-Hudson Library System, Poughkeepsie, N.Y., 1978—; spl. cons. Lexik House Pubs. Active LWV, Putnam Community Hosp. Aux., Carmel, N.Y., Literacy Vols. Putnam County, N.Y. (founding dir. 1977-80); mem. allocations com. local United Way. Grantee Richard Lousnberry Found., 1983, Hudson River Found., 1985-89, Perkins Found., 1987—, NYSCA, 1987-88. Mem. ALA, N.Y. Library Assn., Putnam County (N.Y.) Library Assn. (holder numerous offices). Democrat. Home: Elvins Ln PO Box 208 Garrison NY 10524 Office: Alice and Hamilton Fish Library Rts 403 and 9D Garrison NY 10524

BALDWIN, JANICE MURPHY, lawyer; b. Bridgeport, Conn., July 16, 1926; d. William Henry and Josephine Gertrude (McKenna) Murphy; m. Robert Edward Baldwin, July 31, 1954; children: Jean Margaret, Robert William, Richard Edward, Nancy Josephine. AB, U. Conn., 1948; MA, Mt. Holyoke Coll., 1950; postgrad. U. Manchester, Eng., 1950-51; MA, Fletcher Sch., Tufts U., 1952; JD, U. Wis., 1971. Bar: Wis. 1971, U.S. Dist. Ct. (we. dist.) Wis. 1971. Staff atty. Legis. Council, State of Wis., Madison, 1971-74, 75-78, sr. staff atty., 1979—; atty. adviser HUD, Washington, 1974-75, 78-79. Mem. Dane County Bar Assn. (legis. com. 1980-81), Wis. Bar Assn. (pres. govt. lawyers div. 1985-87, bd. govs. 1985—, treas. 1987—), Wis. Women's Network, AAUW, NOW, LWV, Legal Assn. for Women, Wis. Women's Polit. Caucus, U. Wis. Univ. League, Older Women's League (health, legis., marital property, state and local taxation coms.). Home: 125 Nautilus Dr Madison WI 53705 Office: Legis Council Room 147N State Capitol Madison WI 53702

BALDWIN, JOAN BOLLING (JODY), lobbyist, consultant; b. Norton, Va., Aug. 31, 1930; d. Henry C. and Nelle E. (Mann) Bolling; A.B., Hollins (Va.) Coll., 1953; M.A., U. Va., 1955; m. Donald Winston Baldwin, Nov. 16, 1957; children—Winston Monroe, Elizabeth Bolling, Alan Henry. Sec. to asst. register of copyrights Library of Congress, Washington, 1955-59; mem. profl. staff U.S. Senate Republican Policy Com., 1959-62; press and research asst. to Senator Len B. Jordan of Idaho, 1962-64; research asst. Rep. Nat. Com., 1964; polit. researcher James N. Juliana Assocs., Washington, 1965-69; legis. asst. to Senator James B. Pearson of Kans., 1969-71; spl. asst. to asst. sec. HEW, 1971-73; dep. staff dir. and editor Legis. Notice, Senate Rep. Policy Com., 1973-85, dep. editor 1984 Rep. platform; Washington lobbyist, ptnr. United Internat. Cons. 1985—. del., Va. Rep. Conv., 1973, 80; pres. Alexandria (Va.) Rep. Women's Club, 1965-66; 2d v.p., 1st v.p. Alexandria Jr. Women's Club, 1963-64; treas. The Twig, 1968-69. Mem. Chi Omega. Anglican. Clubs: Capitol Hill; Senate Staff; Belle Haven Country (Alexandria). Office: United Internat Cons 1800 Diagonal Rd Suite 600 Alexandria VA 22314

BALDWIN, MARY LIVINGSTON, advertising and public relations executive; b. New Orleans, Mar. 25, 1954; d. John Hall and Eilyeen (Broyles) Livingston; m. Dan Michael Baldwin, Oct. 25, 1980. B.A. in Journalism, Northeast La. U., Monroe, 1976. Reporter, Alexandria (La.) Daily Town Talk, 1976; editor South Towne Courier, Shreveport, La., 1976-79; editor weekend mag. Shreveport Jour. 1979-81; editor mgr. Shreveport Mag., 1981-85. Task Force mem. Downtown Shreveport Unlimited, 1983—; bd. dirs. La. Assn. Blind, Shreveport, 1979; mem. Holiday In Dixie Diplomats, Shreveport, 1979; participant Leadership Shreveport, 1983-84. Recipient Most Appreciated of News Media award, Shreveport Lions Club, 1977. Mem. Shreveport Advt. Fedn. (bd. dirs. 1983—, 1st v.p. 1984-85, pres. 1985-86), Shreveport Soc. Profl. Journalists (past bd. dirs.). Republican. Presbyterian. Club: Northeast La. U. Alumni (Shreveport) (regional v.p. 1978). Home: 323 Merrick Shreveport LA 71104 Office: Baldwin Enterprises Inc 625 Texas Suite 202 Shreveport LA 71101

BALDWIN, PAMELA, lawyer, consultant; b. Cleve., Apr. 28, 1942; d. Byron Dorland and Jeannette (Martens) Voegelin; children: John, Laura, Graham, Marcus. BA, William and Mary Coll., 1969; JD with honors, U. Md., Balt., 1976. Bar: Md. Lawyer Axley and Crum, P.A., Prince Frederick, Md., 1976-78; legisl. atty. Md. Gen. Assembly, Annapolis, 1978-79; legisl. atty. fed. lands and natural resources Cong. Research Service, Washington, 1979—; revisor Calvert County Code, Prince Frederick, Md., 1982-83, Baltimore City, Md., 1986—. Contbr. articles to profl. jours. Alt. mem. Calvert County Bd. Zoning Appeals, 1986—, mem. Calvert County Commn. Women, 1980-81. Mem. Phi Beta Kappa. Democrat. Episcopalian. Home: Rt 1 Box 161-4 Prince Frederick MD 20678 Office: Library of Congress Rm 230 Madison Bldg Washington DC 20540

BALDWIN, SUSAN OLIN, lawyer; b. Battle Creek, Mich., Sept. 1, 1954; d. Thomas Franklin and Gloria Joan (Skidmore) Olin; m. James Patric Baldwin, Sept. 15, 1979; 1 child, Christopher Mark. BA, Miami U., Ohio, 1976; JD, U. Cin., 1979. Bar: Ohio 1979, Mich. 1984. Assoc. editor Am. Legal Pub. Co., Cin., 1979-80; corp. atty. Hosp. Care Corp., Cin., 1980-84; legal counsel Peak Health Plan, Cin., 1984; assoc. Cook Pringle & Goetz, P.C., Birmingham, Mich., 1984—. Contbr. articles to profl. jours. Pres. Hunter's Green Homeowner's Assn., Independence, Ky., 1982-83; charter mem. Young Reps., Ashland, Ohio, 1972. Mem. ABA, Ohio State Bar Assn., Mich. Bar Assn., Alpha Lambda Delta, Phi Alpha Delta, Am Businesswomen's Assn. (v.p. 1980-81, editor 1980). Club: Birmgingham Evening Newcomers (treas. 1986-87, pres. 1988). Office: 1400 N Woodward Ave Suite 101 Birmingham MI 48011

BALDWIN, VELMA NEVILLE WILSON, personnel consultant; b. Meade, Kans., Aug. 31, 1918; d. Charles Chester and Anna Velma (Neville) Wilson; A.B., U. Kans., 1940; m. Claude David Baldwin, Jan. 31, 1942 (dec. Nov. 1976). Placement working students U. Kans., 1940-41; personnel War Dept., Washington, 1942-45; research asst. Dr. A.C. Kinsey, Ind. U., 1946; with Carter Oil Co., Denver, 1948-50; personnel Bur. Budget, Washington, 1951-55; asst. to dir. personnel Treasury Dept., 1955-59; personnel officer, dir. adminstrn. Office Mgmt. and Budget, 1959-79; cons. in field. Mem. Am. Soc. Pub. Adminstrn. (past exec. bd.), Soc. Personnel Adminstrn. (exec. bd.). Home: 2234 49th St NW Washington DC 20007 Office: Office Mgmt and Budget Washington DC 20503

BALDWIN, WENDY HARMER, social demographer; b. Phila., Aug. 29, 1945; B.A. magna cum laude, Stetson U., DeLand, Fla., 1967; M.A., U. Ky., Lexington, 1970, Ph.D. (NDEA fellow, spl. grantee Population Council), 1973. Research asst. Colombian Assn. Med. Faculties, Bogatá, 1971; research asst. sociology U. Ky., 1971-72; health scientist adminstr. behavioral scis. br. Center Population Research, Nat. Inst. Child Health and Human Devel., NIH, 1972-79, chief demographic and behavioral scis. br., 1979—. Recipient Merit award NIH, 1978; USPHS Superior Service award, 1985; Carl S. Schultz award population amd family planning sec., Am. Pub. Health and Planning Assn. Mem. Population Assn. Am. (dir. 1978-80, 2d v.p. 1984), Am. Sociol. Assn. (sec. population sect. 1977-80, chmn. 1985), So. Sociol. Assn., Phi Beta Kappa. Author articles in field. Office: 7910 Woodmont Ave Room 7C25 Bethesda MD 20892

BALES, JOY DIANE, pharmacist; b. Omaha, Jan. 20, 1958; d. Glenn Leroy and Violet Louise (Cederholm) B. BS, Iowa State U., 1980. Cert. social worker. Youth service worker Orchard Place, Des Moines, 1980-81; social service dir. Omaha Manor, 1981-82; pharmacy technician Neb. Med. Ctr., Omaha, 1982—. Mem. Nat. Women's Pol. Caucus, Washington, 1983—; bd. dirs. Douglas County Citizen's Health Adv. Council, 1983—, Wilderness Soc., Washington. Mem. Nat. Assn. Social Workers, Nat. Assn. Pharmacy Technicians, Nat. Assn. Female Execs., Omaha Long Term Social Workers (officer 1981), DAR (officer 1986-90). Home: 21312 Old Coach Rd Rt 3 Elkhorn NE 68022-1034

BALFE, ELAINE MARIE, information specialist; b. Pitts., Oct. 8, 1960; d. Norman Elmer and Ruth Ann (Mutschler) Goldbach; m. David Royal Balfe, Nov. 29, 1986. BA in Chemistry, Seton Hill Coll., 1982; M in Info. Sci., Drexel U., 1983. Info. chemist Union Carbide Corp., Westlake, Ohio, 1983-85; info. specialist Eveready Battery Co., Inc., Westlake, 1985—. V.p. Lakewest Catholic Young Adults, North Olmsted, Ohio, 1986 (sec. 1985). Mem. Alpha Micro User's Soc., Nat. Assn. Female Execs., Tri Beta. Democrat. Roman Catholic. Office: Eveready Battery Co Inc 25225 Detroit Rd Westlake OH 44145

BALFOUR, LINDA FRIER, statistician, university official; b. Houston, Mar. 29, 1944; d. Robert Henry and Ina Loyce (Riley) Frier; B.B.A., Southwestern U., 1966; postgrad. N.C. State U., 1968, U. N.C., Chapel Hill, 1980; m. Robert F. Hill, Jr., June 7, 1978; 1 son, James Burton. Tchr., Franklin (Tex.) High Sch., 1966-67; sec. N.C. Bd. Higher Edn., Raleigh, 1967-68, statis. analyst, 1968-73; social research asst. gen. adminstrn. U. N.C. System, Chapel Hill, 1973-77, social research asso., 1977-78, dir. data collection and reporting, 1979—; cons. to instnl. researchers on coll. campuses; N.C. Integrated Postsecondary Education Data Systems. Active Nat. Found. Ileitis and Colitis, Nat. Arbor Found. Mem N.C. Assn. Instl. Research (exec. com. 1978—), So. Assn. Instl. Research. Author: Statistical Abstract of Higher Education in North Carolina, 1967—; Higher Educational Opportunities in North Carolina, 1967—. Office: U NC-Gen Adminstrn PO Box 2688 Chapel Hill NC 27514

BALGROSKY, JEAN ANN, health care information systems executive, consultant; b. Berwyn, Ill., Oct. 17, 1952; d. Steven A. and Evelyn Margaret (Cook) B.; m. Parker Hinshaw, June 22, 1985; children—Melissa, Jessica, Sarah, Seth, Wyatt. B.S. magna cum laude, UCLA, 1974, M.P.H., 1980, Ph.D., 1988. Registered med. records adminstr. Research/teaching asst. UCLA Sch. Pub. Health, 1974, 79, 80, 81; adminstrv. analyst Harrington Meml. Hosp., Bremerton, Wash., 1974-75; USPHS Dept. HHS health profls. trainee, 1978-83; office mgr. UCLA Child Care Ctr., 1978-79; info. services mgr. UCLA Hosp. and Clinics, 1979-80; research assoc. Lutheran Hosp. Soc. of So. Calif., Los Angeles, 1980-81; sr. cons. Peat Marwick Mitchell & Co., Los Angeles, 1982-83; dir. info. mgmt. Community Hosp. Indpls., Inc., 1983-86; v.p. info. resources Holy Cross wealth System, South Bend, Ind., 1986—; pres. Health Info Systems Sharing Group, 1987—, bd. dirs., 1983-86; mem. industry adv. com. Computer Tech. Sch. Purdue U., West Lafayette, Ind., 1986—. Contbr. to profl. publs.; author info. systems evaluation methodologies. Mem. parent adv. com. UCLA Child Care Ctr., 1979-80, industry adv. com. Purdue U., West Lafayette, 1986—. Ray Goodman scholar UCLA, 1978-83. Fellow Am. Pub. Health Assn.; mem. Am. Med. Records Assn., Calif. Med. Records Assn., Nat. Assn. Grad. Women, Nat. Assn. Female Execs., NOW. Democrat. Home: 16099 Baywood Ln Granger IN 46530 Office: Holy Cross Health System Corp Office 3606 E Jefferson Blvd South Bend IN 46615

BALICK, HELEN SHAFFER, judge; b. Bloomsburg, Pa.; d. Walter W. and Clarissa K. (Bennett) Shaffer; J.D., Dickinson Sch. Law, 1966; m. Bernard Balick, June 29, 1967; Admitted to Pa. bar, 1967, Del. bar, 1969; probate adminstr. Girard Trust Bank, Phila., 1966-68; pvt. practice law, Wilmington, Del., 1969-74; staff atty. Legal Aid Soc. Del., Wilmington, 1969-71; master Family Ct. Del., New Castle County, 1971-74; U.S. bankruptcy judge Dist. of Del., 1974—; U.S. magistrate, Wilmington, 1974-80; guest lectr. Dickinson Sch. Law, 1981-86, 87; lectr. Dickinson Forum, 1982. Pres. bd. trustees Community Legal Aid Soc., Inc., 1972-74; trustee Dickinson Sch. Law; mem. Citizens Adv. Com. Wilmington, 1973-74, Wilmington Bd. Edn., 1974. Mem. ABA, Del. Bar Assn., Fed. Bar Assn., Nat. Conf. Bankruptcy Judges, Nat. Assn. Women Lawyers, Nat. Conf. Spl. Ct. Judges, Del. Alliance Profl. Women (Trailblazer award 1984), Nat. Lawyers Club, Nat. Assn. Women Judges, Wilmington Women in Bus. (bd. dirs. 1980-83), Dickinson Sch. Law Gen. Alumni Assn. (exec. bd. 1977-80, 87—, v.p. 1981-84, pres. 1984-87), Phi Alpha Delta. Office: US Bankruptcy Ct US Courthouse 6th Floor Wilmington DE 19801

BALICK, LILLIAN ROSEN, music educator, pianist, arts administrator; b. Phila.; d. Joseph and Ida (Rabinowitz) Rosen; m. Jacob Balick; children—Stephanie, Jennifer, Michael, Robert, David, Andrea. BS in Edn., Temple U., 1948; M of Music, West Chester State U., 1978. Social worker Pa. Dept. Pub. Welfare, Phila., 1948-49; tchr. music Bd. Edn., Phila., 1949-52, tchr. music, orch. condr. Cheltenham Twp., Elkins Park, Pa., 1955-56; instr. Coll. Music, Temple U., Phila., 1956-58; arts specialist Del. State Arts Council, Wilmington, 1981—, founder, dir. Contest for Young Musicians, 1972—; organizer, coordinator Grand Opera House Young Artists' Program, Wilmington, 1974; lectr. Del. Humanities Forum, Wilmington, 1978—; founder, pres., artistic dir. Community Showcase Performances, Inc., Wilmington, 1979—; mem. citizens grant rev. panel Del. State Arts Council, Wilmington, 1979-80; talent coordinator Rollins Cablevision, Wilmington, 1980-82; bd. dirs. Del. Chamber Orch., Wilmington, 1980-83, Wilmington Ballet Co., 1981—; state chair Del. Alliance for Arts Edn., 1988-89. Author: The Delaware Symphony, 1984, Reflections on Music, 1985. Recipient Harry Cohen leadership award, 1979, numerous others; Pa Bd. Edn. music scholar, 1944. Mem. Music Tchr. Nat. Conf., Music Tchrs. Nat. Assn., Del. State Music Tchrs. Assn., Astron, Kappa Delta Epsilon, Pi Mu, Pi Kappa Lambda. Democrat. Jewish. Home: 15 Clermont Rd Wilmington DE 19803

BALIN, DONNA FAYE, geologist; b. Hampton, Va., July 5, 1956; d. Henry and Fayrene (Timm) B. BS summa cum laude, U. Tex. at Austin, 1978. Exploration geologist Houston Oil and Minerals Corp., 1978-80; geologist U.S. Geol. Survey, Menlo Park, Calif., 1980-81, Amoco Oil Co., Denver, summer 1983; Amoco found. fellow U. Ariz., Tucson, 1982-83; NSF grad. fellow U. Cambridge, Eng., 1983—. Free-lance interviewer BBC-Radio; contbr. articles to profl. publs. Getty Oil Co. scholar, 1977-78, Grad. Tuition scholar U. Ariz., 1982-83. Fellow Geol. Soc. London, Cambridge Philos. Soc.; mem. Am. Assn. Petroleum Geologists, Phi Beta Kappa, Phi Kappa Phi. Club: Servas, Sierra. Avocations: running, athletics, camping. Home: 127 Claywell San Antonio TX 78209

BALIUNAS, SALLIE LOUISE, astrophysicist; b. N.Y.C., Feb. 23, 1953; d. Joseph Ralph and Eleanor (Druiett) B.; m. Scott Edward Butler, 1977. BS, Villanova U., 1975; PhD, Harvard U., 1980. Astrophysicist Smithsonian Astrophys. Observatory, Cambridge, Mass., 1980—; v.p. mktg. and advt. Keep It Simple Software N.Y., Inc., N.Y.C., 1986—; cons. Hale Observatories, Pasadena, Calif., 1980. Editor: Cool Stars, Stellar Systems and the Sun, 1986; contbr. articles to profl. jours. Recipient Villanova Alumni Medallion award, 1977, Billings award U. Colo., 1979, Newton Lacy Pierce prize, Am. Astron. Soc., 1988, Bok prize, Harvard U., 1988; Hfarvard U. Jewett fellow, 1974, Harvard U. Pickering fellow, 1974, Amelia Earhart fellow, Zonta Internat., 1977-79, Langley-Abbot fellow, Smithsonian Instn., 1980-84. Mem. Am. Astron. Soc., Internat. Astron. Union, Sigma Xi. Office: Smithsonian Astrophys Observatory Ctr for Astrophysics 60 Garden St MS15 Cambridge MA 02138

BALKCOM, CAROL ANN, insurance agent; b. Newport, R.I., June 20, 1952; d. Robert Terrence and Barbara Ruth (Hilton) Hannaway; m. Don E. Phillips, Aug. 26, 1973 (div. 1981); m. Richard Roger Balkcom, Oct. 1981; 1 child, Richard Robert. BA, R.I. Coll., 1974, MA in Teaching, 1981; cert. in fin. counseling, Am. Coll., 1984. CLU, chartered fin. cons. Tchr. Lincoln (R.I.) Jr. High Sch., 1974-78; sales agt. Met. Life Ins. Co., Pawtucket, R.I., 1978-80; mgr., agt. Phoenix Mut., Providence, 1980—; instr. R.I. Lic. Sch., Providence, 1986—. Mem. R.I. Life Underwriters (bd. dirs. 1981-84, 1st v.p. 1983-84). Office: Phoenix Mut 2 Richmond Sq Providence RI 02906-5151

BALL, ANNE H., writer, editor, public relations consultant; b. Dayton, Ohio, June 7, 1939; d. James Leonard and Frieda Engelke Hitch; B.A., Ohio State U., 1961; m. Alan Odendahl, July 21, 1968 (div. May 1985); children—Laura Jean, Cynthia Leonard; m. Robert L. Ball, June 30, 1985 (dec. May 1987). Reporter, Dayton Jour. Herald, 1961-63, Balt. Sunpapers, 1964-66; pub. relations dir. Md. Inst. Coll. Art, 1966, Balt. Mental Health Assn., 1967-68; free lance writer, pub. relations cons., Washington, 1971—; dir. news bur. Cath. U. Am., Washington, 1976-78; co-owner Ad/Ventures, 1986-87; prin. Anne Ball Promotions, 1988—. Mem. Washington Ind. Editors, Zeta Tau Alpha. Democrat. Unitarian. Home: 14828 Fireside Dr Silver Spring MD 20904

BALL, CATHERINE NELSON, computational linguist; b. Leesburg, Va., Aug. 9, 1948; d. Notley Lee Ball and Mary Cleland (Fordney) Diggs. BA, Am. U., 1975; MA, U. Pa., 1979. Programming mgr. Shared Med. Systems, Malvern, Pa., 1979-87; research scientist Unisys Corp., Paoli, Pa., 1987—. Mem. Friends of St. Paul's Cathedral, London. Mem. Linguistic Soc. Am., Assn. for Computational Linguistics, Delaware Valley Assn. for Artificial Intelligence, Nat. Cathedral Assn. Republican. Episcopalian. Club: Faculty. Home: 935 Penn Circle B105 King of Prussia PA 19406 Office: Unisys Corp PO Box 517 Paoli PA 19301

BALL, JEAN GAIL LYONS (MRS. EDWIN LEE BALL), realtor; b. Elizabeth City, N.C., Jan. 17; d. George Cluster and Dorothy Louise (Tillett) Lyons; m. Edwin Lee Ball; 1 child, Diana Lee. Student, Temple U.; diploma, Moore Inst. Design, Kesley Jenney Coll., 1959, Anthony Schs. Real Estate, 1970. Profl. fashion model, singer with various agys. including Neufelt, Phila., Walters, Balt., Powers, San Diego, N.Y.C., Fashionality, San Diego intermittently, 1942-58; owner, broker Ball Realty, El Cajon, Calif., 1970-80; pres. Gail Ball & Assocs., Internat. Real Estate Investment Corp., El Cajon, 1980—; pres., gen. mgr. Gail Ball & Assocs. S.A. de C.V., Baja Calif., Mex., 1980—; broker, gen. ptnr. Internat. Fin. Co., 1980—; pres. Ball/McKinnon, Inc.; owner Dyana's Beauty Salons, El Cajon, 1973-83. Exhibited art in shows at Tivoli Hotel Little Gallery, C.Z. various commns. Mem. Nat. League Am. Pen Women, Inc., El Cajon Valley Bd. Realtors, Calif. Real Estate Assn., Nat. Assn. Real Estate Bds. Home: 1787 Hillsdale Rd El Cajon CA 92020 Office: 772 E Washington Ave El Cajon CA 92020 also: PO Box 2361, Ensenada Baja California Mexico

BALL, JOYCE, retired librarian; b. N.J., Oct. 31, 1932; d. Frank Geza and Elizabeth Martha (Hopper) Csaposs; m. Robert S. Ball, Sept. 10, 1955; children: Stephanie, Valerie, Steven Robert; m. Stefan B. Moses, Mar. 30, 1980. A.B., Douglass Coll., Rutgers U., 1954; M.A., Ind. U., 1959; M.B.A., Golden Gate U., San Francisco, 1979. Fgn. documents librarian Stanford U., 1955-66; head documents librarian, then head reference div. U. Nev., Reno, 1966-75; head public services U. Nev., 1975-80; univ. librarian Calif. State U., Sacramento, 1980-87; mem. Nev. Gov's Adv. Council on Libraries, 1974-78; mem. panel judges Am. Book Awards, 1980; mem. adv. bd. U.S. Dept. Edn. project Libraries and The Learning Soc., 1983-84. Editorial bd.: Coll. and Research Libraries, 1975-80; Contbr. articles to profl. jours. Recipient Louise Maxwell award Sch. Library and Info. Sci. Alumni of Ind. U., 1984. Mem. Assn. Coll. and Research Libraries (dir., pres. 1983-84), ALA. Democrat. Mailing Address: #1186-290 Rt 5 Box 310 Livingston TX 77351

BALL, KAREN LESLIE, advertising executive; b. Martinsville, Ind., Nov. 5, 1961; d. Stanley E. and Judith A. (Pelino) B. Student, Baldwin-Wallace Coll., 1979-80; BA, Taylor U., 1983. Asst. media planner Campbell-Ewald Co., Warren, Mich., 1983-85, specialist local market, 1985-86; media planner Wyse Advt., Cleve., 1986-87, sr. media planner, 1987—. Mem. fund raising com. United Way, Cleve., 1986; vol. Youth for Christ, Internat., Detroit, 1986, Spl. Olympics, Cleve., 1987. Mem. Adcraft Club Detroit. Office: Wyse Advt 24 Public Square Cleveland OH 44113

BALL, KAY EVANS, marketing manager; b. Columbus, Ohio, Nov. 30, 1952; d. T. Quentin and Helen (Brubaker) Evans; m. David Keith Ball, May 12, 1983; children: Jason Keith, Laura Elizabeth. B.S., Manchester Coll., 1975; M.S.W., Western Mich. U., 1979. Social worker Warsaw Community Schs., Ind., 1975-77; exec. dir. Oaklawn Found., Elkhart, Ind., 1979—; mgr. public info. Oaklawn Ctr., Elkhart, 1979-81, dir. community services div., 1981-87, mgr. mktg. and devel., 1987—. Bd. dirs. Planned Parenthood North Central Ind., 1980—; bd. mem. Manchester Coll. Social Work Adv. Council, 1986—; chmn. human services planning and devel. com. United Way Elkhart County. Mem. Nat. Assn. Social Workers, Nat. Ctr. Health Edn. Democrat. Club: Zonta (chmn. scholarship 1985—, bd. dirs.). Office: Oaklawn Hosp 330 Lakeview Dr Goshen IN 46526

BALL, LINDA ANN, educator; b. Des Moines, Aug. 10, 1942; d. Vern Ray and Orletha Ann Carmichael; student Iowa State U., 1960-62; B.S. in Edn., Drake U., 1964; M.S. in Edn., Ill. State U., 1981; m. Robert Ray Ball, Aug. 15, 1964; children—Lindsay, Ryan, Justin. Tchr., Marshalltown, Iowa, 1964-68; TV tchr. Sta. WAND-TV, Decatur, Ill., 1969-71; tchr. Des Moines Public Schs., 1973-79; adv. Ill. State U. Panhellenic, Normal, 1979-80; tchr. Metcalf Lab. Sch., Ill. State U., Normal, 1980—; presenter workshops and confs. Past mem. Jr. Women's Club, Assn. Advocacy and Edn. Disabled Citizens, Mid-Central Planning Commn. for Handicapped, Friends of the Arts; past pres. JayceeEttes, Campfire Girls Council; bd. dirs. United Cerebral Palsy. Co-author: Kaleidoscope, 1987. Cert. reading specialist, early childhood specialist. Mem. Ill. Reading Council, Ill. State Kindergarten Conf. Commn. (chair), Early Childhood Edn. Assn., Ill. Edn. Assn., Ill. Assn. Supervision and Curriculum Devel., Delta Zeta (collegiate province dir.), Delta Kappa Gamma. Democrat. Home: 1603 Budig Dr Normal IL 61761 Office: Ill State U Metcalf Lab Sch Normal IL 61761

BALL, LUCILLE, actress; b. Jamestown, N.Y., Aug. 6, 1911; d. Henry D. and Desiree (Hunt) B.; m. Desi Arnaz, Nov. 30, 1940 (div. 1960); children: Lucie Desiree, Desiderio Alberto IV; m. Gary Morton, Nov. 19, 1961. Ed. high sch., dramatic sch., studied with John Murray Anderson. Pres. Desilu Prodns., Inc., 1962-67, Lucille Ball Prodns., 1967—. Motion picture actress, 1934—; pictures include Broadway thru a Keyhole, 1933, Blood Money, 1933, Moulin Rouge, 1933, Roman Scandals, 1933, Nana, 1934, Bottoms Up, 1934, Hold that Girl, 1934, Bulldog Drummond Stikes Back, 1934, The Affairs of Cellini, 1934, Kid Millions, 1934, Broadway Bill, 1934, Jealousy, 1934, Men of the Night, 1934, Fugitive Lady, 1934, Carnival, 1935, Roberta, 1935, Old Man Rhythm, 1935, Top Hat, 1935, The Three Musketeers, 1935, I Dream Too Much, 1935, Chatterbox, 1936, Follow the Fleet, 1936, The Farmer in the Dell, 1936, Bunker Bean, 1936, That Girl from Paris, 1936, Don't Tell the Wife, 1937, Stage Door, 1937, Joy of Living, 1938, Go Chase Yourself, 1938, Having a Wonderful Time, 1938, The Affairs of Annabel, 1938, Room Service, 1938, The Next Time I Marry, 1938, Annabel Takes a Tour, 1938, Beauty for the Asking, 1939, Twelve Crowded Hours, 1939, Panama Lady, 1939, Five Came Back, 1939, That's Right You're Wrong, 1939, The Marines Fly High, 1940, Too Many Girls, 1940, A Guy, a Girl and Gob, 1940, Look Who's Laughing, 1941, Valley of the Sun, 1942, The Big Street, 1942, Seven Days Leave, 1942, DuBarry Was a Lady, 1943, Best Foot Forward, 1943, Thousands Cheer, 1943, Meet the People, 1944, Without Love, 1945, Abbott and Costello in Hollywood, 1945, Ziegfeld Follies, 1946, The Dark Corner, 1946, Easy to Wed, 1946, Two Smart People, 1946, Lover Come Back, 1946, Lured, 1947, Her Husband's Affairs, 1947, Sorrowful Jones, 1949, Easy Living, 1949, Miss Grant Takes Richmond, 1949, Fuller Brush Girl, 1950, Fancy Pants, 1950, Magic Carpet, 1950, The Long, Long Trailer, 1954, Forever Darling, 1956, The Facts of Life, 1960, Critic's Choice, 1963, A Guide for the Married Man, 1967, Yours, Mine and Ours, 1968, Mame, 1974; star TV shows I Love Lucy, 1951-55, The Lucy Show, 1962-68, Here's Lucy, 1968-73, Life With Lucy, 1986; starred on Broadway in Wildcat; TV movie appearances include Stone Pillow, 1985. Recipient Emmy award for best comedienne, 1952, 55, 67, 68; Golden Apple award, 1973; Ruby award, 1974; Entertainer of Yr. award, 1975; inducted into Television Acad. Hall of Fame, 1984. Presbyterian. Office: Lucille Ball Prodns 9200 Sunset Blvd #916 Los Angeles CA 90069 *

BALL, MARGARET ANN, insurance company executive; b. Lorimor, Iowa, Feb. 23, 1938; d. Edmund Carl and Lola Mary (Edwards) Porter; student Drake U., 1963-70; m. Gary Ernest Ball, June 29, 1954; children—Monte, Marla, Mark. Rater, Farm Bur. Mut., Des Moines, 1957-60; rater Gt. Am. Ins. Co., Des Moines, 1963-66; underwriter The Atlantic Cos., Des Moines, 1966-71; asst. sec. Multiple Line Underwriters, Des Moines, 1971-80; asst. v.p. Employers Mut. Cos., Des Moines, from 1980, now v.p.; mem. faculty Drake U., 1973-78, Simpson Coll., 1974-75. C.P.C.U. Republican. Mem. Christian Ch. (Disciples of Christ). Mem. Order Eastern Star. Home: 579 Lake Panorama Panora IA 50216 Office: 717 Mulberry St Des Moines IA 50309

BALL, OTEKA ANN LITTLE, educator, author; b. Madill, Okla., Feb. 2, 1939; d. Reuel Winfred and Oteka Delores (Wilson) Little; student Okla. U., 1957-59; B.S., So. Methodist U., 1962; postgrad. Rice U., 1962; M.S., Okla. State U., 1976; m. M. Gerald Ball, Sept. 5, 1959; children—Jeremy D., Oteka Lyn. Prin., broker Oteka Ball Real Estate Firm, Shawnee, Okla., 1970-76; instr. Seminole Jr. Coll., 1976-78; asst. prof. home econs. and edn., head home econs. Okla. Baptist U., 1978—; partner Land Oil Co., 1980—. Bd. dirs. Jack Little Found., Madill, 1970—; v.p. bd. dirs. Child's World, Shawnee, 1973-76; bd. dirs. YMCA, Shawnee, Okla., 1978—; mem. Hockaway Alumni Bd., Dallas, 1980-82; mem. Okla. Gov.'s Com. on Children and Youth, 1976-80. Mem. AAUP, Am. Home Econs. Assn., Assn. Couples for Marriage Enrichment, Nat. Council Adminstrs. Home Economists, PEO, Omicron Nu, Phi Kappa Phi. Democrat. Methodist. Home: 1320 N Broadway Shawnee OK 74801 Office: 500 W University Shawnee OK 74801

BALL, PATRICIA ANN, physician; b. Lockport, N.Y., Mar. 30, 1941; d. John Joseph and Katherine Elizabeth (Hoffmaster) B.; m. Robert E. Lee, May 18, 1973; children—Heather, Samantha. B.S., U. Mich., 1963; M.D., Wayne State U., 1969. Diplomate Am. Bd. Internal Medicine, Am. Bd. Hematology, Am. Bd. Med. Oncology. Intern, resident Detroit Gen. Hosp., 1969-71; resident Jackson Meml. Hosp., Miami, Fla., 1971-72; fellow Henry Ford Hosp., Detroit, 1972-74; staff physician VA Hosp., Allen Park, Mich., 1974-77; practice medicine specializing in hematology and oncology, Bloomfield Hills, Mich., 1977—; mem. faculty dept. medicine Wayne State U. Sch. Medicine, Detroit, 1974—. Mem. Founders Soc., Detroit Inst. Arts. Mem. ACP, AMA, Mich. State Med. Soc., Oakland County Med. Soc., Alpha Omega Alpha. Avocations: photography; skiing. Office: 2515 Woodward Suite 290 Bloomfield Hills MI 48013

BALLANFANT, KATHLEEN GAMBER, newspaper executive, public relations company executive; b. Horton, Kans., July 11, 1945; d. Ralph Hayes and Audrey Lavon (Heryford) G.; m. Burt Ballanfant; children: Andrea, Benjamin. BA, Trinity U., 1967; postgrad. NYU, 1976, Am. Mgmt. Inst., 1977, Belhaven Coll., 1985. Pub. info. dir. Tex. Dept. Community Affairs, Austin, 1972-74; pub. affairs mgr. Cameron Iron Works, Houston, 1975-77, Assoc. Builders and Contractors, Houston, 1982-84; pres. Ballanfant & Assoc., Houston, 1977-82, 84—; pres. Village Life Inc., 1985—; pres., chief exec. officer Village Life Publs.; owner Village Life newspaper, Southwest Life newspaper, Houston Observer/Times newspaper, Village Life Printing & Typesetting; mem. adv. council on Construction Edn., Tex. So. U., Houston, 1984—; mem. task force on ednl. excellence Houston Ind. Sch. Dist., 1983—; mem. devel. bd. Inter First Fannin Bank, 1986—. Author: Something Special-You, 1972, Prevailing Wage History in Houston, 1983; editor newspaper Bellaire Texan, 1981-82, Austin Times, 1971. Vice pres. West Univ. Republic Women's Club, Houston, 1984—; fgn. vis. chmn. Internat. Inst. Edn., Houston, 1980—; docent Houston Zoo, 1982. Named Tex. Woman of Achievement Tex. Womans Hosp., 1986; recipient Apollo IX Medal of Honor Gov. Preston Smith, 1970, Child Abuse Prevention award Gov. Dolph Briscoe, 1974, Tex. Community Newspaper Assn. (pres.-elect 1987—, bd. dirs. 1987—). Mem. Bellaire C. of C. (bd. dirs. 1987—). Republican. Presbyterian. Lodge: Rotary. Avocations: traveling, racquetball, reading. Office: Ballanfant & Assoc 2514 Tangley Houston TX 77005

BALLANTINE, MORLEY COWLES (MRS. ARTHUR ATWOOD BALLANTINE), newspaper publisher; b. Des Moines, May 21, 1925; d. John and Elizabeth (Bates) Cowles; m. Arthur Atwood Ballantine, July 26, 1947 (dec. 1975); children—Richard, Elizabeth Ballantine Leavitt, William, Helen Ballantine Healy. A.B., Ft. Lewis Coll., 1975; L.H.D. (hon.), Simpson Coll., Indianola, Iowa, 1980. Pub. Durango (Colo.) Herald, 1952—, editor, pub., 1975-83, editor, chmn. bd., 1983—; dir. 1st Nat. Bank, Durango, 1976—, Des Moines Register & Tribune, 1977-85, Cowles Media Co., 1982-86. Mem. Colo. Land Use Commn., 1975-81, Supreme Ct. Nominating Commn., 1984—; pres. S.W. Colo. Mental Health Center, 1964-65; bd. dirs. Colo. Nat. Hist. Preservation Act, 1968-78; trustee Choate/Rosemary Hall, Wallingford, Conn., 1973-81, Simpson Coll., Indianola, Iowa, 1981—, U. Denver, 1984—, Fountain Valley Sch., Colorado Springs, 1976—; pres. Four Corners Opera Assn., 1983-86, mem. bd. govs. Mill Reef, Antigua, West Indies. Recipient 1st place award for editorial writing Nat. Fedn. Press Women, 1955, Outstanding Alumna award Rosemary Hall, Greenwich, Conn., 1969, Outstanding Journalism award U. Colo. Sch. Journalism, 1967, Distinguished Service award Ft. Lewis Coll., Durango, 1970; named to Colo. Community Journalism Hall of Fame, 1987. Mem. Nat. Soc. Colonial Dames, Colo. Press Assn. (bd. dirs. 1978-79), Colo. AP Assn. (chmn. 1966-67), Federated Women's Club Durango. Episcopalian. Club: Mill Reef (Antigua, W.I.) (bd. govs. 1985—). Address: care Herald PO Drawer A Durango CO 81302

BALLANTYNE, MARGARET MORGAN, speech language pathologist; b. Endicott, N.Y., Nov. 3, 1957; d. Robert James and Lillian (Fteha) Morgan; m. Glenn Ross Ballantyne, July 6, 1985. BS in Edn., SUNY, Fredonia, 1979; MA in Communication Disorders, Bowling Green (Ohio) State U., 1980. Cert. communications counselor, speech pathologist. Speech and lang. pathologist La Junta (Colo.) Med. Ctr., 1980-81; dir. communication disorders dept. Pueblo (Colo.) Regional Ctr., 1981-85; speech and lang. cons. Pueblo Sch. Dist. #60, 1985-87; pvt. practice speech pathology, Pueblo, 1983—. Com. mem. Very Spl. Arts Fair, Pueblo, 1985-87; asst. Spl. Olympics, Pueblo, 1986. Mem. Am. Speech-Lang.-Hearing Assn., Council for Exceptional Children (exec. mem. 1983—), Colo. Speech-Lang.-Hearing Assn. (supervision com. 1982-83), Library of Spl. Edn., Internat. Assn. for Alt. Augmentative Communication. Home: 2416 N Greenwood Pueblo CO 81003 Office: U Colo Dept of Communications Disorders and Speech Sci Boulder CO 80309

BALLARD, BETTY RUTH WESLEY, retired x-ray equipment co. exec.; b. Birmingham, Ala., Nov. 11, 1924; d. Henry Gaston and Ruth Lorine (Whitfield) Wesley; degree Glenn Tech. Inst., 1942-46; m. Douglas Hayden Ballard, Oct. 24, 1941; 1 son, Douglas Hayden. Mgr., Nbc Restaurant, 1960-68; corp. sec. X-Ray Service and Sales, Inc., 1960-68; pres. Ballard X-Ray Co., Birmingham, Ala., 1968—. Exec. com. Democratic Party; election law commr. State of Ala.; hon. dep. sheriff Shelby County, Ala.; mem. adminstrv. bd. 1st United Methodist Ch., Montevallo, Ala. Mem. Ala. Soc. Radiol. Technologists, Ala. Hosp. Assn., Inst. Hosp. Auxilians, Ala. Cattlemen's Assn., LWV, 20th Spl. Forces Group Aux. Methodist (adminstrv. bd., trustee ch.). Club: The Club Inc. Home: Flying-X-Ranch Route 1 Box 29 Montevallo AL 35115

BALLARD, BEVERLY LYNN, management professional; b. Newark, Nov. 11, 1951; d. R.C. and Sarah (Lane) Lynn; m. George W. Ballard Jr., Aug. 31, 1970 (dec. May 1983); 1 child, Amir. BA in Polit. Sci., Rutgers U., 1983. Sec. Youth Dept. United Community Corp., Newark, 1970, Community Program Rutgers 4-H Extension Program, Newark, 1970-71; sec., asst. SPS Employment Agy., Newark, 1971-72; sec., adminstrv. asst. Greater Newark Urban Coalition, 1972-79; mgr. office Gustav Heningburg Assocs. Inc., Newark, 1980—; lobbyist State N.J., Trenton 1983—; freelance writer 1979—. Editor Israel Meml. AME Ch., Newark 1986—; past vol. Am. Cancer Soc., Cerebral Palsy Telethon, Grove St. Sch. PTA, Irvington, United Negro Coll. Fund Telethon, Irvington Tenants Assn., Madison Ave. Sch. PTA, Irvington; pub. relations coordinator local polit. campaigns, 1985—; mem. Irvington Dem. com., sec. 1983-84, 86-87. Mem. N.J. Pub. Policy Research Inst. (v.p. 1984-87), Am. Polit. Sci. Assn., Nat. Assn. Negro Bus. and Profl. Women's Club (chair awards com. 1986). Democrat. Home: 101 21st St #C-5 Irvington NJ 07111 Office: Gustav Heningburg Assocs Inc 40 Clinton St Suite 200 Newark NJ 07102

BALLARD, DOROTHY MAE, labor union representative, consultant; b. Kansas City, Mo., Dec. 8, 1916; d. Frank and Eva (Powell) Cann; widowed; 12 children. Ed. in Labor Edn., Norman Coll. Machinist, N. Am. Aviation, 1942-46; assemblyline worker Gen. Motors Co., Kansas City, Mo., 1953-55, instr. in electronics; labor rep. local 31 United Auto Workers, Kansas City; now cons.; lectr. in labor edn. and prison reform, 1974-85; organizer seminars, Operation PUSH convs., Kansas City, also workshops for women; leader petition drives for women's rights and labor reform. Mem. Black Awareness Program, Lansing, Mo.; co-founder, pres. Greater Kansas City Minority Women's Coalition for Human Rights; co-founder, past pres. Coalition of Labor Union Women, 1974-82; pres. Met. United Citizens for Prison Reform and Assistance; adv. bd. Mid-Am. Regional Council, Jackson County Jail Com., Council on Crimes and Delinquency, Creative Enterprises, New Directions Ctr., Mo. Probation and Parole Bd., Salvation Army Task Force, Job Partnership Tng. Programs; past bd. dirs. Ann Skinner Women's Fellowship, Am. Bapt. Ch.; affirmative action chmn. Greater Kansas City Women's Polit. Caucus; mem. platform com. Mo. Democratic Party, 1978-80; del. Internat. Womens Yr.; mem. Pres. Carters Task Force for Women. Recipient numerous community service awards including Women's award U.S. Sec. Labor, Woman of Yr. award United Auto Workers, Jefferson award. Mem. LWV, Farmaid for Am. Agrl., Nat. Assn. Colored Women, Negro Bus. and Profl. Women (Woman of Yr. Central chpt. 1979), Coalition Labor Union Women (past chpt. pres., nat. exec. bd., chmn. women's history week 1985), Assn. Blacks in Criminal Justice, Nat. Alliance Bus. (task force), Mo. Leadership Assn., Urban League of Greater Kansas City. Address: 13517 Lowell St Grandview MO 64030

BALLARD, GLENDA DAY, health management executive; b. Washington, N.C., Feb. 14, 1943; d. Rion Glen and Mary (Mercer) Day; m. Ronald G. French, Dec. 10, 1967 (dec. Jan. 1973); m. Alan G. Ballard, Oct. 5, 1974. Grad. high sch., Washington, 1961. Copywriter Sta. WITN-TV, Washington, 1961-63; dir. dance Fred Astaire Dance Studio, Norfolk, Va., 1963-67; office mgr. Eugene W. Hodgson, MD, Aurora, N.C., 1970-74; staff photographer Surg. Specialists, Norfolk, 1974-77; credit mgr. ZoneAir, Inc., Johnson City, Tenn., 1978-79; owner, pres. Med. Mgmt. Assocs., Johnson City, Tenn., 1979—; leader seminars, Va. N.C., Tenn., 1985—. Residential chmn. United Way, Johnson City, 1985; bd. dirs. Am. Cancer Soc. Washington County, Johnson City, 1987. Mem. Am. Mgmt. Soc. (bd. dirs. Johnson City chpt. 1981), Johnson City C. of C. (bd. dirs. 1982-85), Health Services Council. Home: 1551 Colony Park Dr Johnson City TN 37601 Office: Med Mgmt Assocs 817 W Walnut St Suites 10 11 12 Johnson City TN 37601

BALLARD, JEANNE STEWART, educator; b. Pitts., Dec. 12, 1925; d. Raymond E. and Mary (Johnson) Stewart; m. Cecil E. Ballard, Sept. 11, 1948; children: Todd, Rick, Jeff. BA, Western Coll., 1948. Tchr. Greenville (S.C.) Pub. Schs., 1968-70, Orange County Pub. Schs., Orlando, Fla., 1970—; ind. interior decorator Orlando, 1972-75; cons. Sarasota (Fla.) Pub. Schs. Author: Bite O' God's Apple, 1968, Teaming, 1978, Leaders Guide, 1979, Brainstorm Is a Verb, 1983. Pres. St. Joseph's Civic Hosp. Aux., Asheville, N.C., 1965, Meml. Mission Aux., 1964; mem. Wekiva Presbyn. Ch. Mem. Orange County League Mid. Schs. (pres. 1983-84), Internat. Tng. in Communication (pres. Seminole Springs chpt. 1984-86), Nat. Beta Club, Delta Kappa Gamma. Republican. Club: Biltmore Forest. Home: 269 Torpoint Gate Longwood FL 32779 Office: Apopka Meml Mid Sch 425 N Park Ave Apopka FL 32703

BALLARD, MARY MELINDA, financial communications, public relations firm executive; b. Sikeston, Mo., Apr. 21, 1951; d. Claude M. and Mary (Birnbach) BBA, NYU, 1976, MBA, 1977; PhD in Communications, Columbia U., 1986. V.p. corp. communications United Brands Co., N.Y.C., 1970-75; v.p. mktg. Oscar de la Renta Ltd., 1975-80; pres., chief exec. officer Ficom Internat., Inc., N.Y.C., 1980—; bd. dirs. Channel Am. TV, Sea Bright Corp., N.J. Aura Enterprises, Chgo.; dir., chief exec. officer Ficom Internat., 1980—. Contbr. articles to profl. jours. Cons. to fgn. govts. and major corps. Mem. Internat. Assn. Bus. Communicators (Golden Quill 1984), Pub. Relations Soc. Am., Urban Land Inst., Nat. Investor Relations Inst. Roman Catholic. Avocations: collecting oriental art, thoroughbred race horses. Home: 40 E 9th St Apt 6F New York NY 10003

BALLARD, SUSAN E., landscape architect; b. Buffalo, June 26, 1956; d. Robert L. and Francis (Henson) B. BA cum laude, Beloit Coll., 1979; cert., Harvard U., 1979; MLA, U. Mass., 1985. Owner Mystic (Conn.) Florist, 1980-84; design cons. Town of Amherst, Mass., 1984-85; tchg., research asst. U. Mass., Amherst, 1983-85; landscape dir. Riverside Park, Agawah, Mass., 1983-85; dept. head McCrone, Inc., Annapolis, Md., 1985-88; sr. project mgr. Greenhorne & O'Mara, Greenbelt, Md., 1988; cons. Pvt. Devel. in Critical Area, Md., 1986-88; pub. speaker numerous schs., and assns., 1985-88. Author: Design Review Board Handbook, 1984, Inventory and Assessment Procedures for Pedestrian Trails, 1985. Recipient FL Olmsted award Harvard Sch. Design, 1979; named Rhodes scholar U. Mass., 1983. Mem. Am. Soc. Landscape Architects, Am. Planning Assn. Young Bus. Women Am. (Women of Yr. 1980), Nat. Park and Conservancy Assn., Waugh Alumni Assn. (conf. chmn. 1985-88). Avocations: raquetball, swimming, theatre, art and antique collecting. Home: 911 Madison Ave Annapolis MD 21403 Office: Greenhorne & O'Mara 9001 Edmonston Rd Greenbelt MD 20770

BALLENTINE, MARTHA ELIZABETH, purchasing administrator; b. St. Louis, Aug. 24, 1939; d. Everett McKinley and Martha Lee (Robinson) Griswold; 1 child, Kevin Juan. BS, Washington U., St. Louis, 1979. Mgr. purchasing Carondelet Foundry Co., St. Louis, 1968—; appraiser JMP Enterprises, St. Louis, 1985-86; sales assoc. Century 21 Classic, St. Louis, 1986—. Contbr. articles to St. Louis Purchaser mag., 1980-82. Recipient Youth Leadership award Christ Pilgrim Rest Ch., 1983. mem. Am. Foundrymen's Soc., Purchasing Mgrs. Assn. (bd. dirs., Pres.'s award 1982). Democrat. Baptist. Home: 16503 Spinnaker Way Lake Chesterfield MO 63040

BALLEW, DORIS EVELYN, controller; b. Knox County, Tenn., Sept. 6, 1938; d. James Elmer and Grace Elizabeth (Wright) Dossett; m. George Thomas Reep, Feb. 4, 1955 (div. June 1969); children: Sherrie Lynn Akins, Kimberley Michelle; m. David Woodward Ballew, Oct. 9, 1969; 1 child, Melissa Marie. Student, U. Tenn., 1975-84, Draughon's Coll., 1982, Knoxville Bus. Coll., 1974. CPA, Tenn. Acct. Shoney's Restaurants, Knoxville, Tenn., 1961-64, Tinsley Tire Co., Knoxville, Tenn., 1964-65; chief acct. Kuhlman-Murphy Co., Knoxville, Tenn., 1965-77; controller, treas. Lawler Wood, Inc. and Wood Properties, Inc., Knoxville, Tenn., 1977—. Mem. Old Smoky Railway Mus. (treas. 1978-83). Mem. Nat. Assn. Accts., Jaycettes, Beta Sigma Phi (pres. 1982, 83). Home: 406 Broadview Dr Knoxville TN 37912 Office: Lawler-Wood Inc 1300 Plaza Tower Knoxville TN 37929

BALLIET, BRENDA O'ROURK, educator; b. Garfield Heights, Ohio, Dec. 28, 1955. BA, Augusta Coll., 1986. Cert. elem. tchr., Ga. Teller Valley Nat. Bank, Phoenix, 1973-79, Trust Co. Bank, Augusta, Ga., 1980-85; tchr. Columbia County Bd. Edn., Appling, Ga., 1985—. Sponsor Evans (Ga.) Middle Sch. Jr. Beta Club, 1986—; pres. United Meth. Women St. Mark Ch., Augusta, 1983-84, chairperson Council Ministries, 1982-83. Mem. Nat. Council Tchrs. Math., Ga. Assn. Educators. Republican. Lodge: Order Eastern Star. Home: 811 Lake Royal Dr Grovetown GA 30813 Office: Evans Middle Sch Evans GA 30809

BALLINGER, JANET LYNN, secondary educator; b. Fresno, Calif., Nov. 23, 1948; d. Michael Thomas and Helen Erika (Kinnunen) Etcheberry; m. Richard Lee Ballinger, June 9, 1979; children: Iley Michael, Richard Daniel. AA, West Hills Coll., Coalinga, Calif., 1968; BA, Calif. State U., Fresno, 1972. Tchr. Houghton-Kearney Elem. Sch., Fresno, 1972-85; coordinator gifted and talented students Cen. Unified Sch. Dist., Fresno, 1985, mentor tchr., 1985-86, coordinator Scholastic Aptitude Test preparation, 1986—. Mem. Calif. Tchrs.' Assn. Democrat. Mem. Pentecostal Ch. Office: Cen Unified Sch Dist 4605 N Polk Fresno CA 93722

BALLMAN, PATRICIA KLING, lawyer; b. Cin., May 1, 1946; d. John Joseph and Margaret Elizabeth (Stacy) Kling; children: Andrew J., Cara E. BS with honors, St. Louis U., 1967; JD with honors, Marquette U., 1977. Computer programmer, systems analyst Gen. Electric Co., Cin., 1967-70; lectr. computer scis. Marquette U., Milw., 1971; ptnr. Quarles & Brady, Milw., 1977—. Mem. fin. div. personnel subcom. United Way, Shorewood Bd. of Rev. Mem. Assn. Trial Lawyers Am., ABA, Wis. Acad. Trial Lawyers, Wis. Bar Assn. (ins. for mems. com.), Milw. Bar Assn. (courts com., legis. com., ct. of appeal bench/bar com.), NOW. Office: Quarles & Brady 411 E Wisconsin Ave Milwaukee WI 53202

BALLOU, KATHY DEANNE TAYLOR, marketing executive; b. Peoria, Ill., Sept. 20, 1951; d. Chas S. and Carol A. (McDonough) Guynn; m. Harold N. Taylor Jr. (dec. Nov. 1982); 1 child, Shawn; m. John A. Ballou, June 5, 1987. AA in Bus., ICC, Peoria; student in mktg. mgmt., Sangamon St., Springfield. Mgr. sales Credit Bur. Accounts, Inc., Peoria, 1986-87; sales exec. Research Inst. of Am., N.Y.C., 1987—. Chmn. bd. Tri-County Heart Assn., Peoria, 1987—, pres., 1986-87; div. and regional mgr. Am. Heart Assn. Ill. affiliate, Springfield, 1985—; active ARC hospice tng., Meth. Med.

Ctr. Vol. Services. Mem. Nat. Assn. Female Execs., Am. Inst. Banking, Peoria Jaycee Women (v.p. 1984), Ill. Jaycee Women (state chaplain, mgr. family life program 1984-85), Morton Jaycettes (pres. 1980). Republican. Home and Office: Northern Oaks Estates Rural Rt 1 Pekin IL 61554

BALL-REED, PATRICE MUNZEL, lawyer; b. Chgo., Sept. 16, 1958; d. Arthur Lee and Portia Mahila (Andrews) Ball; m. Roy Leonard Reed, July 16, 1983; 1 child, Candace Ayanna. BA in Econs., Trinity Coll., 1980; JD, John Marshall Law Sch., 1984. Bar: Ill. 1985. Assoc. Washington, Kennon, Hunter & Samuels, Chgo., 1985—. Trustee Trinity Coll. Scholarships for Ill. Residents. Mem. ABA, Ill. Bar. Assn., Nat. Bar Assn., Women's Bar Assn., Cook County Bar Assn. (newsletter bd. editors, co-chair young lawyers sect.), Chgo. Bar. Assn. (vice chmn. minorities in the profession com., 1986-87, co-chair person minorities in profession com. 1987-88), Black Women Lawyers Assn. Greater Chgo., John Marshall Law Sch. Alumni Assn. (bd. dirs.). Home: 3642 W Douglas Blvd Chicago IL 60623 Office: Washington Kennon Hunter & Samuels 123 W Madison St Suite 2200 Chicago IL 60602

BALLSUN, KATHRYN ANN, lawyer; b. Calif., May 8, 1946; d. Zan and Doris (Pratt) B.; m. Paul L. Stanton, June 1, 1981; 1 child, Brian Paul. BA, U. So. Calif., 1969, MA, 1971; JD, Loyola U., Los Angeles, 1976. Bar: Calif. 1976, U.S. Dist. Ct. (cen. dist.) Calif. 1977. Ptnr. Stanton & Ballsun, Los Angeles; vis. prof. UCLA Law Sch., Loyola U. Law Sch., Los Angeles; adj. prof. U. So. Calif. Law Sch.; lectr. various schs. Editor: How to Live and Die with California Probate; contbr. articles to profl. jours. Mem. graphic arts council Los Angeles County Mus. Art, Children's Council, Westwood Meth. Ch.; co-chmn. for Class of 1976 Greater Loyola Law Sch. Devel. Program, 1983; advisor Am. Cancer Soc. Program; radio vol. sta. KUSC; bd. dirs. Planned Protective Services Inc.; bd. dirs. Los Angeles Philharm. Orch., com. profl. women, treas. 1985-86. Fellow Am. Coll. Probate Counsel; mem. ABA (real property, probate and trust law, taxation sects.), State Bar Calif. (estate planning, trust and probate, bus. law, taxation sects., law revision study team 1983-85), Los Angeles County Bar Assn. (trust and probate, taxation sects.), Beverly Hills Bar Assn. (treas. 1985-86, bd. govs. 1982-84, 84-86, probate and trust com., del. State Bar Conv. 1981-85, v.p. 1987—), Calif. Women Lawyers, Los Angeles Women Lawyers, Women in Business (sec., polit. action com.), Los Angeles County Mus. Art, Los Angeles C. of C., ACLU (Los Angeles chpt.), UCLA Ctr. for Study of Women, ACLU (Los Angeles chpt.), Kappa Alpha Theta. Office: Stanton and Ballsun AVCO Ctr 6th Floor 10850 Wilshire Blvd Los Angeles CA 90024

BALOG, IBOLYA, accountant; b. Subotica, Yugoslavia, July 11, 1953; came to U.S., 1969; d. Balint and Adela (Dohocki) B. B.A., Lehigh U., 1975; M.B.A., Temple U., 1980. Adminstrv. asst. Chain Bike Corp., Allentown, Pa., 1975-77; controller Bicycle Corp. Am., Allentown, 1982-87; acct. Cohen & Rogozinski, CPA's, Allentown, 1987—. Bd. dirs. YWCA, Allentown, 1986—. Mem. AAUW (treas. 1984 85, Outstanding Woman 1985), Nat. Assn. Female Execs., Nat. Assn. Accts. (Lehigh Valley chpt.). Democrat. Avocations: movies; bike riding. Home: 1522 1/2 Chew St Allentown PA 18102 Office: Cohen & Rogozinski CPAs 1427 Chew St Allentown PA 18102

BALSHAW-BIDDLE, KATHERINE, writer, editor; b. Battle Creek, Mich., May 17, 1952; d. Robert Gordon and Ellen Lena (Roos) Balshaw; m. Kevin Thomas Biddle, Apr. 3, 1980; 1 child, Nicholas Roos Biddle. Student Kellogg Community Coll., 1970-72; B.S., Mich. State U., 1974, M.S., 1977; Ph.D., Rice U., 1981. Field engr. Alaskan Resource Scis. Corp., Fairbanks, 1975-76; research asst. Rice U., Houston, 1977-80; writer Houston Woman mag., 1986-87, asst. editor, 1987—; freelance writer, 1984-86; research geologist Exxon Prodn. Research Co., Houston, 1980-83, sr. research geologist, 1983-84; sedimentologist Leg 59 Deep Sea Drilling Project, Philippine Sea, 1978, U.S. Antarctic Program, Ross Sea, 1979, 80. Contbr. articles to profl. jours. Rice U. fellow, 1977-78; Petroleum Research Fund fellow, Houston, 1979.

BALSLEY, IROL WHITMORE, emeritus management educator; b. Venus, Nebr., Aug. 22, 1912; d. Sylvanus Bertrand and Nanna (Carson) Whitmore; m. Howard Lloyd Balsley, Aug. 24, 1947. B.A., Nebr. State Coll., Wayne, 1933; M.S., U. Tenn., 1940; Ed.D., Ind. U., 1952. Tchr. high schs. Osmond and Walthill, Nebr., 1934-37; asst. prof. Ind. U., 1942-49; lectr. U. Utah, 1949-50, Russell Sage Coll., 1953-54; prof. office adminstrn. La. Tech. U., 1954-65, also head dept. office adminstrn., 1963-65; prof. bus. edn. Tex. Tech. U., 1965-72, prof. edn., 1972-75; prof. adminstrv. services U. Ark., Little Rock, 1975-80; prof. emeritus U. Ark., 1980—; adj. prof. Hardin-Simmons U., Abilene, Tex., 1980-81; coordinator USAF clk.-typist tng. program Pa. State U., 1951, instr., head office tng. sect. TVA, 1941-42; editorial asst. South-Western Pub. Co., 1940-41. Author: (with Wanous) Shorthand Transcription Studies, 1968; (with Robinson) Integrated Secretarial Studies, 1963; (with Wood and Whitmore) Homestyle Baking, 1973; Century 21 Shorthand, Vol. I, 1974, (with Robert Hoskinson) Vol. II, 1974; Self-Paced Learning Activities for Century 21 Shorthand, Vol. I, 1977; High Speed Dictation, 1980, Where On Earth?, 1986. Mem. Nat. Bus. Edn. Assn. (past pres. research found.), Adminstrv. Mgmt. Soc., Nat. Collegiate Assn. Secs. (co-founder, past pres., nat. exec. sec. 1976-81), Pi Lambda Theta, Delta Pi Epsilon (past nat. sec.), Beta Gamma Sigma, Phi Delta Kappa, Pi Omega Pi, Sigma Tau Delta, Alpha Psi Omega, Delta Kappa Gamma. Address: 6501 15th Ave W Bradenton FL 34209

BALTER, FRANCES SUNSTEIN, civic worker; b. Pitts.; d. Elias and Gertrude (Kingsbacher) Sunstein; student Sarah Lawrence Coll., 1939-41, New Sch. Social Research, 1941-43, Bennington Coll., summers 1941, 42; cert. Harvard Inst. Arts Adminstrn., 1973; m. James Stone Balter, May 15, 1948 (dec.); children—Katherine (Mrs. Ross Anthony), Julia Frances, Constance (Mrs. Owen Cantor), Daniel Elias; m. 2d, Harry Philip Blum, Mar. 1, 1982. Adminstrv. asst., asso. producer Ednl. Television WQED-TV, Pitts., 1963-67; producer, mng. dir. Freedom Readers, 1964-67; co-founder, incorporator, sec. bd. dirs. Pitts. Council for Arts, 1967-70; cultural cons. Mayor's Office, Dir. of Office of Cultural Affairs, Pitts., 1968; co-founder Three Rivers Arts Festival 1960; co-dir. Ohio and Miss. River Valley Art Festival, 1961-62; mem. Pa. Council on Arts, 1972-78, mem. exec. com., 1975-78; co-founder Pioneer Crafts Council Mill Run Pa., 1972; exec. dir. Poetry On The Buses, 1974—; bd. dirs. Council for Arts MIT, Palm Beach Festival, 1988—. Named Woman of Yr. in Art Post-Gazette, 1969. Mem. Asso. Councils on Arts, Nat. Soc. Arts and Letters. Home: 1021 Devonshire Rd Pittsburgh PA 15213

BALTIKAUSKI, MARY NORBY, county government official; b. Mpls., Nov. 29, 1950; d. Donald Curtis and Joanne (Kohnen) Norby; m. James Anthony Baltikauski, Sept. 2, 1972; 1 child, Anna Marie. Student, Enterprise (Ala.) Jr. Coll., 1969-71; BS, Auburn U., 1973; postgrad., Troy (Ala.) State U., 1975-76. Cert. tchr., Ala., Fla. High sch. sci. tchr. Geneva County Sch. Bd., Hartford, Ala., 1974-77, Holmes County Sch. Bd., Bonifay, Ala., 1978; county agrl. agt. Ala. Coop. Extension Systems, Geneva, 1979—; adv. Wiregrass Feeder Pig Assn., 1979-85, Geneva County Cattlemen's Bd. Dirs., 1979—, Geneva County Purebred Swine Breeders Assn., 1979—, Lower Ala. Cattle Mgmt. Assn., Geneva, 1983—. Contbr. articles to local newspaper. Recognized for outstanding contbn. Ala. Pork Industry, Ala. Farm Bur., 1981, 82, 84. Mem. Ala. Assn. County Agr. Agts., Deep South Dressage Assn. (editor newsletter 1978-80), Epsilon Sigma Phi. Lutheran. Office: Ala Coop Extension Service PO Box 159 Geneva AL 36340

BALVIN, NANCY LOU, nurse; b. Sauk Centre, Minn., June 4, 1937; d. Charles Ernest and Ruth Irene (Hutchinson) B. Diploma, St. John's Sch. Nursing, Huron, S.D., 1958; BS in Nursing, S.D. State U., 1961. Cert. nurse practitioner, S.D. P.m. charge nurse St. John's Hosp., Huron, 1958-59; dormitory nurse S.D. State U., Brookings, 1959-61; asst. clin. instr. St. John's Sch. Nursing, Huron, 1961-62; staff nurse Tschetter & Hohm Clinic, Huron, 1962-74, family nurse practitioner, 1975—; lectr. in field. Treas. Beadle County Women's Dems., Huron, 1986-87; pres. Huron Coll. Bd. Trustees, 1988. Mem. Am. Nurses Assn., S.D. Nurses Assn. (pres. 1975-79). Office: Tschetter & Hohm Clinic 455 Kansas St Huron SD 57350

BALZAC, AUDREY FLOBELLE ADRIAN, psychologist; b. N.Y.C., May 5, 1928; d. Allen Isaac and Mildred Florence (Brown) Adrian; m. Ralph P. Balzac, Jr., May 3, 1961; children: Stephen Rafael, Elena Adrian, Rebecca Lisa. BA in Psychology with honors, Hunter Coll., 1951; MS with honors, Purdue U., 1952; ABD, Columbia U., 1963. Intern in psychology Howard Rusk Inst., NYU and Bellevue Hosp., N.Y.C., 1956-57; clin. psychologist Westchester Community Mental Health Bd., and Children's Ct., White Plains, N.Y., 1957-63; psychol. cons. div. Vocat. Rehab., N.Y.C., 1957—; pvt. practice, 1963—; research psychologist Psychiat. Inst., Columbia Presbyn. Med. Ctr., N.Y.C., 1955-57; cons. Pound Ridge Elem. Sch., 1975-76. Chairwoman Community Relations bd. Pound Ridge Jewish Community Ctr., 1975-79, treas., 1978-79; mem. Westchester Women's Adv. Bd., 1986-87; candidate Bedford Cen. Sch. Bd., 1987, 88. Fellow Rusk Inst., 1956-57; research grantee Columbia U., 1960—. Fellow AAUW; mem. Am. Psychol. Assn., Eastern Psychol. Assn., N.Y. Soc. Clin. Psychologists, Soc. Psychol. Study of Social Issues, Am. Sociol. Assn., Sigma Xi, Psi Chi (treas. 1951-52). Jewish. Home: Route 4 Box 267 Pound Ridge NY 10576

BALZAR, JO ANNE, history educator; b. Saranac Lake, N.Y., Oct. 21, 1946; d. Joseph and Beatrice Anna (LaPlante) Drutz; m. William Edward Balzar, Aug. 1, 1970; children: Beth, Amy. BA, Coll. St. Rose, 1968; MA, SUNY, Albany, 1969. Tchr. Am. history Saranac Lake Middle Sch., 1969-70; tchr. Afro-Asian history H.W. Schroeder High Sch., Webster, N.Y., 1970-73; instr. Larado (Tex.) Jr. Coll., 1984—. Co-chmn. Laredo Sch. Sesquicentennial Com., 1986-87. Mem. Tex. State Hist. Assn., Orgn. Am. Historians, Webb County Hist. Assn. (commr. 1987-88). Democrat. Roman Catholic. Home: 520 Merlin Rd Laredo TX 78041 Office: Laredo Jr Coll West End Washington Laredo TX 78041

BAMFORD, CAROL M., marketing executive; b. Des Moines, May 18, 1948; d. Harry C. and Ellen T. (Andersen) Jensen; m. Bruce S. Nesbit, June 8, 1968 (div. Jan. 1978); m. Paul J. Bamford, June 9, 1979 (div. Dec. 1984). BA, Drake U., 1969, MA, 1972. Lic. tchr., Iowa. Tchr. English Des Moines Pub. Schs., 1969-79; mgr. product and promotional publs. Comshare, Inc., Ann Arbor, Mich., 1979-83; mgr. advt. and sales promotion Univ. Microfilms, Inc. subs. Bell and Howell Co., Ann Arbor, 1983-88, mktg. mgr., 1988—. Recipient awards Soc. for Tech. Communication, 1980-86, Award of Excellence Internat. TV Assn., 1988. Mem. Info. Industry Assn. (1st Pl. award 1986, 87), Info. Industry Assn., Am. Mgmt. Assn., Direct Mktg. Assn., Phi Beta Kappa. Democrat. Lutheran. Office: University Microfilms Internat 300 N Zeeb Rd Ann Arbor MI 48106

BANANTO, DORTHA JANE, nurse anesthetist; b. Horatio, Ark., Feb. 4, 1927; d. Louis Sager and Ressie (Lyon) Everett; m. Norman Joseph Bananto, May 11, 1957; 1 dau., Kerry Ressie. R.N., Tri-State Hosp., Shreveport, La., 1948; grad. in anesthesia Charity Hosp., 1952. R.N., La. Nurse anesthetist St. Anne's Hosp., Raceland, La., 1953-69; chief nurse anesthetist West Jefferson Gen. Hosp., Marrero, La., 1971-84; nurse anesthetist Thibodaux (La.) Gen. Hosp., 1987—. Treas. Meml. United Meth. Ch., Mathews, La., 1984-85. Mem. La. Assn. Nurse Anesthetists, Am. Assn. Nurse Anesthetists (dist. sec. 1977), DAR. Democrat. Clubs: Lioness, Woman's, United Meth. Women (Raceland). Home: PO Box 152 Raceland LA 70394

BANASHEK, MARY-ELLEN, writer, editor; b. Wilkes-Barre, Pa., Dec. 7, 1951; d. Walter Joseph and Irene (Rapchak) B. BA, Emira Coll., 1973. Asst. features editor Mademoiselle mag., N.Y.C., 1973-79; beauty copywriter Harper's Bazaar mag., N.Y.C., 1979-80; beauty and health editor Self mag., N.Y.C., 1980-81; sr. copy writer Avon Products, Inc., N.Y.C., 1982-83; beauty and health editor McCall's mag., N.Y.C., 1983-85; sr. writer Elle mag., N.Y.C., 1986-87; contbg. editor Woman's Day mag., N.Y.C., 1987—; cons. editor In Fashion mag., N.Y.C., 1988. Democrat. Roamn Catholic. Mem. Phi Beta Kappa. Office: Woman's Day 1515 Broadway New York NY 10036

BANCROFT, ANNE (MRS. MEL BROOKS), actress; b. N.Y.C., Sept. 17, 1931; d. Michael and Mildred (DiNapoli) Italiano; m. Mel Brooks, 1964; 1 son. Broadway stage appearances include Two for the Seesaw, 1957 (Tony award 1957), The Miracle Worker, 1959-60 (Tony award 1960), Devils, 1977, Golda, 1977-78, Duet for One, 1981; motion pictures include Treasure of the Golden Condor, 1952, Don't Bother to Knock, 1952, Tonight We Sing, 1953, The Kid from Left Field, 1953, Demetrius and the Gladiators, 1954, Gorilla at Large, 1954, The Raid, 1954, A Life in the Balance, 1954, The Brass Ring, 1954, Naked Street, 1955, New York Confidential, 1955, The Last Frontier, 1955, Girl in the Black Stockings, 1957, Restless Breed, 1957, The Pumpkin Eater, 1964, Seven Women, 1966, Slender Thread, 1966, The Graduate, 1967, Young Winston, 1972, The Prisoner of 2nd Avenue, 1975, The Hindenburg, 1975, Lipstick, 1976, Silent Movie, 1976, The Turning Point, 1977, Fatso, 1979, The Elephant Man, 1980, To Be or Not to Be, 1983, Garbo Talks, 1984, Agnes of God, 1985, 'Night, Mother, 1986, 84 Charing Cross Road, 1987; TV appearances include Kraft Music Hall, Jesus of Nazareth, 1977, Marco Polo, 1982; dir., writer, star: (TV spl.) Annie-The Woman in the Life of Men, 1970 (Emmy award 1970). Recipient Acad. award for performance in The Miracle Worker, 1962. Address: care 20th Century Fox Studios PO Box 900 Beverly Hills CA 90213

BANCROFT, ELIZABETH ABERCROMBIE, publisher, analytical chemist; b. Washington, Mar. 2, 1947; d. John Chandler and Ruth Abercrombie (Robinson) B.; A.B., Harvard U./Radcliffe Coll., 1979; postgrad. in forensic scis. John Jay Coll. Criminal Justice, 1982. Asst. dir. research Bagley Fordyce Research Labs., N.Y.C., 1979-83, dir. research and publs., Washington office, 1984-86; dir. Nat. Intelligence Book Ctr., 1986—; dir. Nat. Intelligence Study Ctr. Mem. Assn. Fgn. Intelligence Officers, Naval Intelligence Profls., Nat. Mil. Intelligence Assn., Nat. Intelligence Study Ctr., Assn. Ofcl. Analytical Chemists, Am. Chem. Soc., Am. Inst. Chemists, N.Y. Acad. Scis., Washington Book Pubs. Assn., Am. Bookseller Assn. Republican. Episcopalian. Clubs: Harvard of N.Y.C., Harvard/Radcliffe of Washington; Chemists of N.Y.; English Speaking Union of N.Y. and Washington. Home: 2737 Devonshire Pl NW Washington DC 20008 Office: Nat Intelligence Book Ctr 1700 K St NW Washington DC 20006

BANCROFT, MARGARET ARMSTRONG, lawyer; b. Mpls., May 9, 1938; d. Wallace David and Mary Elizabeth (Garland) Armstrong; m. Alexander Clerihew Bancroft, Mar. 14, 1964; 1 child, Elizabeth. BA magna cum laude, Radcliffe Coll., 1960; JD cum laude, NYU, 1969. Bar: N.Y. 1971. Reporter Mpls. Star and Tribune, 1960-61, UPI, N.Y. and N.J., 1961-66; assoc. Donovan Leisure Newton & Irvine, Paris, France, 1969-71, N.Y.C., 1971-78, ptnr., 1978-84; ptnr. Finley, Kumble, Wagner, Heine, Underberg, Manley, Myerson & Casey, N.Y.C., 1984-87, Dechert, Price & Rhodes, N.Y.C., 1987—; adj. prof. law NYU. Bd. dirs., exec. com. Vis. Nurse Service N.Y. Mem. ABA (mem. subcom. tender offers and proxy contests), Assn. Bar City N.Y., N.Y. County Lawyers Assn. (com. on securities and exchanges), N.Y. State Bar Assn. (exec. com. banking, bus. law and corps. sect., com. securities regulation). Democrat. Office: Finley Kumble Wagner Underberg Manley Myerson & Casey 425 Park Ave New York NY 10022

BANE, ROSEMARY SULLIVAN, musician, educator; b. Clever, Mo., Jan. 15, 1925; d. Earl Tom and Rosa Ethel (Maples) Sullivan; B.S., S.W. Mo. State U., 1949; M.Ed., U. Mo., 1959; postgrad., U. Cin., Miami U., Oxford, Ohio, 1963-64; m. James Edward Bane, Dec. 22, 1985; 1 son, Tom Donald Chaney; stepchildren—Nancy Bane Schultejans, James William, Ruthmary Bane Brassfield. Tchr. music Clever Consol. Schs. and dir. music First Bapt. Ch., Clever, 1949-53; tchr. Aurora (Mo.) Elem. Schs. and dir. music First Bapt. Ch., Aurora, 1953-57; bass violinist Springfield (Mo.) Symphony Orch., 1949-56; social dir. S.W. Mo. State U., summers 1955-56 and 1957-58; early childhood music specialist Indian Hills Exempted Village Schs., Cin., 1961-80, ret., 1980, on spl. assignment Fine Arts Project, 1980-84; writer curriculum materials for Cin. Symphony Orch. In-Sch. Music Program and dir. tng. docents, 1978-85; speaker at numerous confs., workshops, radio programs. Accompanist numerous concerts, recitals. Chair charities Bennie Clements Guild, 1988—; v.p. Ozarks Genealogical Soc., 1987—, Presbyn. Girls' Regional Shelter Assn., Springfield, Mo., 1988—; dir. bible study First and Calvary Presbyn. Ch., 1988—. Named Tchr. of Yr., Indian Hill Schs., 1979; recipient award of appreciation Cin. Public Schs., 1981. Mem. NEA, Music Educators Nat. Assn., Am. Orff Schulwerk Assn. (bd. govs. Greater Cin. chpt. 1973-77), Mo. State Tchrs. Assn. (pres. 1948-49), Nat. Assn. State Tchrs. Assns.' Pres. (pres. 1949-50), Indian Hill Ret. Tchrs. Assn. (pres. 1982-83), Delta Kappa Gamma, Pi Beta Phi (pres. 1943-44), Sigma Alpha Iota (pres. 1943-44). Clubs: Cin. Woman's (dir. 1982-85), Coll. Cin. (pres. 1979-80), PEO (local pres., dir. Greater Cin. chorus). Compositions include: Clever High Sch. Alma Mater for Band and Chorus, 1949, prepared, presented numerous original children's musicals. Author: Recorder Fun; contbr. articles to profl. jours. Home: 837 S Rogers Springfield MO 65804

BANERJEE, VIRGINIA ELAINE, social worker; b. Youngstown, Ohio, June 29, 1925; d. Claude Alton and Jessie Helen (Miller) Timblin; m. Bani Ranjan Banerjee, Sept. 11, 1948 (dec. Oct. 1985); children: Krishna Elaine, Ravi Roy. BA, Otterbein Coll., 1943; student, U. Chgo., 1947-48; MSW, Rutgers U., 1973. Social worker Luth. Homefinding Soc., Chgo., 1948-50; supr. Lake County Dept. Pub. Welfare, Gary, Ind., 1953-57; field rep. Pa. Dept. Pub. Welfare, Phila., 1968-72; dir. purchase service N.J. Div. Youth & Family Service, Trenton, 1972-76; dir. surveys Child Welfare League of Am., Inc., N.Y.C., 1976-81; pres. Banerjee Assocs., Skillman, N.J., 1981—. Contbr. articles to profl. jour.; author tech. reports. Vol. HiRiders, Allentown, N.J., 1987—. Mem. Nat. Assn. Social Workers (cert.), Am. Pub. Welfare Assn. Democrat. Unitarian. Office: Banerjee Assocs 1 Sycamore Ln Skillman NJ 08558

BANES, SYLVIA JEAN, consumer education coordinator; b. Eldora, Iowa, Aug. 14, 1939; d. Raymond Dysart and Bernice Bessie (Hornung) Andrews; m. Richard Doyle Banes, Mar. 14, 1965; children: Richard II, Shari. BS, Iowa State U., 1961. Cert. home economist. Home service rep. Ill. Power Co., Mt. Vernon, Ill., 1961-62; extension home economist Extension Service State Iowa, Oskaloosa, 1962-66; dir. headstart program So. Iowa Econ. Devel. Assn., Ottumwa, 1967-68; social worker Bethany Home, Moline, Ill., 1978-81; program dir. Voluntary Action Ctr., Moline, 1982-85; instr. Marycrest Coll., Davenport, Iowa, 1984-87; facilitator Consumer Edn. program Ea. Iowa Community Coll. Dist., Davenport, 1985-87; coordinator Consumer Edn. program N.E. Iowa Tech. Inst., Peosta, 1987—. Pres. Quad Cities World Affairs Council, Moline, 1982; chmn. Quad Cities Women's Conf., Davenport, 1986-87. Mem. Am. Home Econs. Assn., Iowa Home Econs. Assn., Nat. Assn. Female Execs., Am. Sewing Guild, AAUW (pres. 1971-73, chair pub. relations com. 1974-76), Dubuque C. of C., Women in Mgmt. Democrat. Methodist. Club: Iowa State U. Alumni. Lodge: PEO (corr. sec. 1978-80, chaplain 1982-83). Home: 2934 Grand Ave Davenport IA 52803 Office: NE Iowa Tech INst 10250 Sundown Rd Peosta IA 52068

BANFIELD, JOANNE, insurance corporation executive; b. Bronxville, N.Y., Feb. 21, 1954; d. George Alfred and Josephine (Bartolotta) B.; m. Thomas Allen Hanlon, Aug. 6, 1978 (div. July 1985). BA, Iona Coll., 1976. Outpatient registrar United Hosp., Port Chester, N.Y., 1976-78; disability benefits specialist Union Mut. Ins. Co., Elmsford, N.Y., 1978-82; staff asst. to exec. administr. Am. Assn. Advt. Agys. Ins. Trust, N.Y.C., 1982-83; sr. claims analyst Gen. Reassurance Corp., Stamford, Conn., 1984—. Mem. Nat. Assn. for Female Execs. Episcopalian. Club: Body Sculptors Fitness Ctr. for Women (Mamaroneck, N.Y.). Office: Gen Reassurance Corp 695 E Main St Stamford CT 06904

BANISTER, JUDITH, demographer, educator; b. Washington, Sept. 10, 1943; d. William Price and Helen Barbara (Myers) B.; m. Dec. 17, 1966; children—Adrian Banard, Dawn Banard. B.A. in History, Swarthmore Coll., 1965; Ph.D. in Demography, Stanford U., 1978. Postdoctoral research fellow East-West Population Inst., Honolulu, 1978-80; statistician/demographer U.S. Bur. of Census, Washington, 1980-82, chief China br. Ctr. for Internat. Research, 1982—; part-time assoc. prof. George Washington U., Washington, 1981—. Author: China's Changing Population, 1987; contbr. articles to profl. jours. Mem. Population Assn. Am., Internat. Union for Sci. Study of Population. Office: Scuderi Bldg Ctr for Internat Research US Bureau Of Census Room 105 Washington DC 20233

BANKARD, LINDA LEE, land development executive, small business owner; b. Cin., Nov. 18, 1942; d. Herbert Stanley and Augustine Clementine (Lavanier) Reitzes; m. Robert George Bankard, Jan. 5, 1964 (div. 1966); children: Robert Joseph, William Jeffrey. Grad. high sch., Cin., 1960. V.p. Headland Properties, Inc., Pacific Palisades, Calif., 1970—; pres. All About Property Mgmt., Inc., Pacific Palisades, 1975—. Dir. Bell Canyon (Calif.) Homeowners Assn., 1980-82. Mem. Nat. Assn. Women in Constrn. Club: Nat. Brussels Griffon (western regional dir. 1977-79). Office: All About Property Mgmt Inc 1515 Palisades Dr Pacific Palisades CA 90272

BANKES, LYN, state legislator; b. Detroit, Aug. 10, 1941; d. Charles and Ruth Childress; m. John R. Bankes, Apr. 28, 1962; children: John R. II, Mark S. AS in Social Sci., Madonna Coll., 1982. Charter commr., treas. Wayne County, Mich., 1980-82, legis. aide to commr., 1983-84; rep. 35th Dist., State of Mich., Livonia. Active LWV, Friends of the Library, Friends of the Rouge, Older Women's League; chmn. legis. com. Child Care Task Force; viec-chmn. Urban Affairs Com.; mem. Livonia Rep. Club, Rep. Women's Task Force, Mich. PTA, chWomen's Adv. Bd. Schoolcraft Coll., Livonia,. Recipient Disting. Service award Delta Kappa Gamma, Mackinac Island, Mich., 1987—, Cert. of Appreciation Boy Scouts Am. Detroit Area Council ; named Legislator of Yr. Mich. Assn. Vol. Adminstrs. Mem. Livonia C. of C. Episcopalian.q. Home: 16834 Bell Creek Ln Livonia MI 48154 Office: Ho Reps. State Capitol Bldg Lansing MI 48913

BANKS, ANNE JOHNSON, art educator; b. New London, Conn., Aug. 10, 1924; d. James Reid and Neva (Palmer) Johnson; m. William Ross Banks, Sept. 13, 1947; children: Ellison Banks Findly, William Ross Jr., Anne Banks Dobson. BA, Wellesley (Mass.) Coll., 1946; MFA, George Washington U., 1968. Lectr. George Mason U., Fairfax, Va., 1968-69, Bapt. Coll. Charleston, S.C., 1969-70; from lectr. to assoc. prof. art No. Va. Community Coll., Alexandria, 1971-80—. One woman shows: Madison Gallery, N.Y.C., 1962, Lyman Allyn Mus., New London, Conn., 1964, Art League, Alexandria, Va., 1973, Foundry Gallery, Washington, 1978, 81, 83, 86; exhibited in group shows: Chrysler Mus., Norfolk, Va., Va. Mus., Richmond, 1971, 83. Mem. Coll. Art Assn. Am., Design Forum, Design History Soc. Club: Wellesley (Washington). Office: No Va Community Coll 3001 N Beauregard St Alexandria VA 22311

BANKS, BETTIE SHEPPARD, psychologist; b. Birmingham, Ala., June 8, 1933; d. Francis Wilkerson and Bettie Pollard (Woodson) Sheppard; B.A., Ga. State U., 1966, M.A., 1968, Ph.D., 1970; m. Frazer Banks, Jr., Mar. 22, 1952; children—Bettie Banks Daley, Lee Frazer III. Clin. asso. Lab. for Psychol. Services, Ga. State U., 1968-70; intern Ga. Mental Health Inst., Atlanta, 1970-71, psychologist, 1971-72, chief psychologist, 1973; pvt. practice, Atlanta, 1972—; assoc. prof. clin. psychology Ga. State U.; mem. peer rev. panel Ga. Med. Care Found., 1980—. Diplomate in clin. psychology Am. Bd. Profl. Psychology. Fellow Ga. Psychol. Assn. (chmn. div. E 1980); mem. Am. Acad. Psychotherapists (exec. com. 1980-82, sec. 1982-86), Am. Psychol. Assn., Am. Group Psychotherapy Assn., Atlanta Group Psychotherapy Soc. (exec. com. 1982), Southeastern Psychol. Assn. Episcopalian. Club: Jr. League. Cons. editor Voices, 1978-84. Office: 595 Wimbledon Rd NE Atlanta GA 30324

BANKS, DEIRDRE MARGARET, church organization administrator; b. Melbourne, Australia, May 9, 1934; came to U.S., 1975; d. Haldane Stewart and Vera Avice (Fisher) B. MA, Simpson Coll., 1980. Missionary nurse Leprosy Mission, Kathmandu, Nepal, 1960-69; dean of women Melbourne Bible Inst., 1970-75; asst. to dir. Bible Study Fellowship, Oakland, Calif., 1975-79; dir. adult ministries First Covenant Ch., Oakland, 1980-87; assoc. pastor for adults, First Covenant Ch., St. Paul, 1987—. Chairperson ch. edn. bd. Pacific S.W. Conf. Evang. Ch., 1985-87, Gilead Group, Oakland, 1985-87; mem. bd. of world mission Evang. Covenant Ch., 1987—. Mem. Bd. of World Mission Evangelists. Mem. Evangel. Covenant Ch. Office: First Covenant Ch 1280 Arcade St Saint Paul MN 55106

BANKS, JONI WHEELER, interior designer, small business executive; b. High Point, N.C., Oct. 18, 1957; d. Johnny Franklin Wheeler and Mary Helen (Dunbar) Penninger; m. Benjamin Thorpe Banks, Mar. 16, 1985; children: Benjamin II, John Robert. BFA in Interior Design, East Carolina U., 1980. Owner, designer Creative Interiors, High Point, 1979-80; interiors coordinator Sea Pines Co., Hilton Head, S.C., 1980; mgr., buyer Fines, Savannah, Ga., 1980-81, Hudson Bay Trading Co., Hilton Head, 1981, Andrew Arnold Clothier, Hilton Head, 1981-83; mgr., head designer The Decorators Unlimited, Hilton Head, 1983-86; owner, designer J. Banks Design Group Inc., Hilton Head, 1986—. Mem. Evening of the Arts preview Island Sch. Council, Hilton Head, 1986, Hliton Head Plantation Comml. and Archtl. Rev. Bd., 1988. Mem. Am. Soc. Interior Designers, Inst. of Arts (party chmn., designers showcase designer 1985). Baptist. Club: Women's of Hilton Head. Home: 8 Myrtle Bank Ln Hilton Head SC 29929 Office: Banks Design Group Main St Hilton Head SC 29938

BANKS, LISA JEAN, government official; b. Chelsea, Mass., Dec. 19, 1956; d. Bruce H. and Jean P. (Como) Banks. B.S. in Bus. Adminstrn., Northeastern U., 1979. Coop trainee IRS, Boston, 1975-79, revenue officer, Reno, 1979-81, spl. agt., Houston, 1981-84, Anchorage, 1984—, fed. womens program mgr., 1980-81. Recipient Superior Performance award IRS, 1981. Mem. Nat. Assn. Treasury Agts., Nat. Assn. Female Execs. Democrat. Roman Catholic Office: PO Box 1500 Anchorage AK 99510

BANKS, MARGARET AMELIA, librarian; b. Quebec City, Que., Can., July 3, 1928; d. Thomas Herbert and Bessey (Collins) B.; B.A., Bishop's U., Lennoxville, Que., 1949; M.A., U. Toronto, 1950, Ph.D., 1953. Archivist Ont. Archives, Toronto, 1953-61; law librarian U. Western Ont., London, 1961—, assoc. prof. faculty law, 1974-86, prof., 1986—. Mem. Am. Assn. Law Libraries, Can. Assn. Law Libraries, Am. Inst. Parliamentarians, Nat. Assn. Parliamentarians, Osgoode Soc. Anglican. Author: Edward Blake, Irish Nationalist, 1957; Using a Law Library, 1st edit., 1971, 4th edit., 1985; Law at Western, 1959-84, 1984. Office: U Western Ont, Faculty Law Library, London, ON Canada N6A 3K7

BANKS, PENELOPE LOUISE, accountant; b. San Francisco, Mar. 17, 1945; d. George Baldwin and Dorothy Elizabeth (Steiner) B. BA, U. Tex., 1967; postgrad., U. Colo., Denver, 1980. CPA, Colo. Ptnr. Gordon, Hughes and Banks, Frisco, 1986—. Mem. Am. Inst. CPA's, Colo. Soc. CPA's. Office: Gordon Hughes & Banks 695 Summit Blvd PO Box 628 Frisco CO 80443

BANKS, STEPHANIE LEIGH, account executive; b. Chgo., Jan. 30, 1946; d. Willie and Mary Louise (Beckley) Jones; m. Michael Edward Banks, Oct. 3, 1965 (div. Mar. 1973); 1 child, Michael Edward II. BS in Bus. Edn., Chgo. State U., 1975; MS in Mktg. Communications, Roosevelt U., 1981. Tchr. Chgo. Bd. Edn., 1975-80; sales rep. Sears Bus. Systems Ctr. div. Sears, Roebuck and Co., Chgo., 1982-86; instr. Chgo. State U., 1985-86; account exec. Sta. WBEE, Chgo., 1986-87, sr. account exec., 1987—. Mem. Black Pub. Relations Soc. (v.p. membership com.), Chgo. Assn. Black Journalists (producer Mayor's Report), League Black Women (bd. dirs., editor newsletter 1985-86), Nat. Assn. for Female Execs., Chgo. Urban League. Office: Sta WBEE 35 E Wacker Suite 2390 Chicago IL 60601

BANNEN, CAROL ANN, librarian; b. St. Paul, Oct. 4, 1951; d. Virgil D. and Patricia A. (Kelly) Swanson; m. John T. Bannen, Aug. 16, 1975; children: Ryan, Kelly. BA, Coll. St. Catherine, St. Paul, 1973. Librarian Peat Marwick and Mitchell, Mpls., 1972-75; head librarian Reinhart, Boerner, Van Dueren, Norris & Rieselbach, Milw., 1975—. Mem. Law Librarians Assn. Wis. (pres. 1987—), Spl. Libraries Assn. (chmn. Ins. and E.B. div., 1986—), Library Council Met. Milw., Am. Assn. Law Libraries. Office: Reinhart Boerner Van Dueren et al 111 E Wisconsin Ave Suite 1800 Milwaukee WI 53202-4884

BANNISTER, CATHERINE ELIZABETH, marketing professional, nurse; b. Oakville, Ontario, Can., July 26, 1954; d. John Douglas Bannister and Elizabeth Anne (Craddock) Hartlaub. BS in Nursing, Columbia U., 1976. RN, Mass., N.J. Staff nurse Children's Hosp. Med. Ctr., Boston, 1976-78, Boston Lying-In Hosp., 1978-80; neonatal/pediatric clin. specialist St. Barnabas Med. Ctr., Livingston, N.J., 1980-81; diabetes edn. cons. Becton Dickinson Consumer Products, Rochelle Park, N.J., 1982-84; product mgr. Becton Dickinson, Rutherford, N.J., 1984-85, Franklin Lakes, N.J., 1985-86; mgr. sales mktg. Becton Dickinson, Fairfield, N.J., 1986—. Contbr. articles to profl. jours. Mem. Am. Heart Assn., Am. Fertility Soc., Am. Assn. Critical Care Nurses, Oncology Nursing Soc. Republican. Presbyterian. Club: Porsche of Am. Home: 55 Bellevue Ave Summit NJ 07901

BANNISTER-PARKS, MARY ALICE, geologist; b. Port Townsend, Wash., Dec. 18, 1953; d. John Joseph and Lisette Kathryn (Barthrop) Bannister; m. Rick L. Parks, June 13, 1987. BS, U. Calif., Santa Cruz, 1976. Cert. profl. geologist, Alaska. Geologist R & M Cons., Anchorage, 1980-83, Quadra Engrs., Anchorage, 1983-84; engring. geologist Peratrovich, Nottingham & Drage Inc., Anchorage, 1985—. Mem. Assn. Inst. Profl. Geologists, Assn. Engring. Geologists (sec., treas. 1986-87), Alaska Geol. Soc. (bd. dirs. 1985-87), Union of Concerned Scientists, ACLU, NOW, Am. Quarter Horse Assn. Office: Peratrovich Nottingham & Drage 1506 W 36th Ave Anchorage AK 99503

BANNON, JOANNE LOUISE, marketing executive; b. Phila., Oct. 12, 1954; d. Thomas James and Jeanne Judith (Jennings) B. BS, Pa. State U., 1975. Tchr. math. Marple Newton Sr. High Sch., Newtown Square, Pa., 1975-76, Chalres Ellis Sch., Newtown Square, 1976-77, Marple Newtown Jr. High Sch., 1977-80; installation dir. Shared Med. Systems, N.Y.C., 1980-83, mktg. rep., 1983-86, mktg. mgr., 1986-87, regional mgr. 1988— . Named Rookie Sales Rep. of Yr., Shared Med. Systems, 1983, Salesperson of Yr., 1984. Mem. Healthcare Fin. Mgmt. Assn. Republican. Roman Catholic. Avocations: gardening, downhill skiing. Home: 1767 Mountain Ave Scotch Plains NJ 07076 Office: Shared Med Systems Burlington Office Park One Wall St Burlington MA 01803

BANONIS, BARBARA ANN CUCCIOLI, nurse, employee health consultant; b. Bklyn., Oct. 6, 1947; d. Robert and Ann (Amalfitano) Cuccioli; m. Edward Joseph Banonis, Nov. 15, 1969; children: Aaron Joseph, Beth Rose. BS in Nursing, Villanova U., 1969; MS in Nursing, W.Va. U., 1988. RN. Coordinator autistic children's research unit Eastern State Sch. & Hosp., Trevose, Pa., 1969-71; pub. health nurse State of Del., Wilmington, 1972; occupational health cons. Div. of Mental Health, New Castle, Del., 1972-75; faculty nursing Del. Tech. and Community Coll., Newark, 1976-78; cons./writer Freelance Contracts, Newark, 1978; dir. Limen House, Inc., Wilmington, 1979-81; pres., chief exec. officer Banonis Assocs., South Charleston, W.Va., 1982—; founder, chmn. peer impaired nurse program Nurse Care Network, W.Va., 1985—. Author (book chpt.) Nursing and Alcohol Related Problems; researcher, contbr. articles to profl. jours. Allocations vol. United Way Kanawha Valley, Charleston, 1984—, allocations panel chmn., 1985, bd. dirs., 1986—; commr. council on family sevices Gov. of Del. Pierre Dupont, Wilmington, 1978; co-founder, bd. dirs. Task Force Women and Chem. Dependency, Wilmington, 1976-83. Mem. Am. Nurses Assn., Assn. Labor Mgmt. Adminstrs. and Cons. on Alcoholism, Inc., Am. Soc. Tng. and Devel., Employee Assistance Resource Network (chmn. pub. relations com. 1984—), Employee Assistance Soc. N. Am., Charleston Women's Forum (pres. 1985-86), Sigma Theta Tau. Home: 2302 Claridge Circle South Charleston WV 25303

BANOUL, ARLENE FRANCES, state agency administrator, consultant; b. Chgo., May 1, 1953; d. Frank and Frances (Kozak) B. BS in Journalism, Northwestern U., 1975; MBA, U. Wis., 1976. Legis. fiscal analyst Legis. Fiscal Bur., Madison, Wis., 1976-78; legis. liaison Office State Pub. Defender, Madison, 1978-83, chief adminstrv. officer, 1983—; cons. Resources, Newport Beach, Calif., 1985, Mott Found., Washington, 1985, Aloha Field Enterprises, Honolulu, 1985—, Madison Wellness Ctr., 1986-87. Feature writer: Decatur Herald and Review, 1974, Lafayette Journal/Herald, 1974. Mem. recreation com. YWCA, Madison, 1979-81; pres. Madison chpt. Lupus Soc. Am., 1983-84. Office: Office State Pub Defender 131 W Wilson St Suite 100 Madison WI 53703

BANTA, CYNTHIA BUSH, nursery school executive, educational consultant; b. Jersey City, Nov. 29, 1946; d. George James and Grace (Culihan) Bush; m. Thomas A. Banta, Feb. 3, 1983; 1 child, Matthew James. BA, Fairleigh Dickinson U., 1969, MA, 1974. Cert. elem. edn. social studies tchr., handicapped tchr., tchr. learning disabilities, tchr. cons., nursery sch. tchr., N.J.; cert. elem. edn., spl. edn. educator, nursery-kindergarten tchr., N.Y. Tchr. Harrington Park (N.J.) Sch., 1969-79, mem. child study team, 1979-83; owner, dir. Stepping Stone Day Nursery, River Edge, N.J., 1983—; tchr. adult edn. Career Devel. Inc., West Orange, N.J., 1973-75; learning cons., 1980—. Chmn. social com. Presentation Ch., Upper Saddle River, N.J., 1983; chmn. edn. com. Village of Chestnut Ridge, N.Y., 1987—. Mem. N.J. Assn. Learning Cons., Childcare Coordinating Council, Rockland County Child Council, Nat. Assn. for Edn. of Young Children. Republican. Roman Catholic. Home: 9 Haller Crescent Chestnut Ridge NY 10877

BANTEL, LINDA MAE, art museum director; b. King City, Calif., May 30, 1943; d. Clifford Burnett and Helen Vernelle (Mallicotte) Bantel; m. David Hollenberg, June 15, 1980; children—Matthew Bantel Hollenberg. M.A., NYU, 1971. Research cons. N.Y. Hist. Soc., N.Y.C., 1975-76; guest cocurator Art Mus. of South Tex., Corpus Christi, Tex., 1977-79; research assoc. Met. Mus. Art, N.Y.C., 1978-80; curator, now dir. of mus. Pa. Acad. Fine Arts, Phila., 1980—. Co-author: (with James Thomas Flexner) The Face of Liberty: Founders of the U.S., 1975; author: The Alice M. Kaplan Collection, 1980; William Rush, American Sculptor, 1982; (with Marcus Burke) Spain and New Spain: Mexican Colonial Arts in Their European Context, 1979; contbr. to American Paintings in the Metropolitan Museum of Art Vol. II: A Catalogue of Works by Artists Born Between 1816-1845, 1985. Mem. Coll. Art Assn., Am. Assn. Mus., Assn. Art Mus. Dirs. Home: 255 S 44th St Philadelphia PA 19104 Office: Pa Acad Fine Arts Broad and Cherry Sts Philadelphia PA 19102

BANTY, CARRIE WALKER, counselor; b. Bessemer, Ala., July 7, 1935; d. John W. and Annie Mamie (Thompson) Walker; m. William Rowles Banty, July 7, 1956; children: Jon Carl, Jennifer Celia. BBA, U. Wis., 1959; MS, U. Wis., Milw., 1970. Lic. bus. tchr. Office worker Gen. Mdse. Co., Milw., 1956-57; tchr. bus. edn. North Div. High Sch., Milw., 1961-68, title I coordinator, counselor, 1969-72; dir. guidance Lincoln High Sch., Milw., 1972-78, Bay View High Sch., Milw., 1978—; scholarship chair St. Mark Scholarship Com., Milw.; adj. admissions counselor U. Wis., Milw. Co-organizer, co-founder Project Helping Adolescents Live Triumphantly, 1986-87; bd. dirs. Greater Milw. Opportunities Industrialization Ctr.; active St. Mark AME Ch., Milw. (Parents of Yr. award 1986). Recipient Outstanding Educator award Bearman Found., 1985-86; named Counselor of Yr. Alpha Phi Alpha, 1973. Mem. Delta Sigma Theta (pres. 1972-73), Phi Delta Kappa. Democrat. Home: 8160 S Woodridge Dr Oak Creek WI 53154 Office: Bay View High Sch 2751 S Lenox St Milwaukee WI 53207

BANZER, CYNTHIA DEANE, state representative; b. Portland, Oreg., Jan. 24, 1947; d. Robert Lewis Banzer and Dorothy (Dennison) Davis; children—McKean Banzer-Lausberg, Eric Banzer-Lausberg. B.S. in Polit. Sci., Oreg. State U., 1969; M.Ed., Ohio U., 1973. Tchr. corps intern Ohio U. Tchr. Corps Program, Parkersburg, W.Va., 1969-70; research assoc. Pres.'s Commn. on Sch. Fin., 1971; legis. asst. Com. on Edn. and Labor, U.S. Ho. of Reps., 1972; adminstrv. asst. Senate Edn. Com., State of Oreg., 1973; citizen participation coordinator Oreg. Land Conservation and Devel. Commn., 1974; community services dir. City of Beaverton, Oreg., 1975-77; presiding officer Met. Service Dist., Portland, Oreg., 1978-85; mem. Oreg. Ho. of Reps., Salem, 1985—; devel. dir. Burnside Community Council, Portland, 1987—. Contbr. articles to profl. jours. Bd. dirs. United of Columbia-Willamette; pres. bd. dirs. Met. Family Services; mem. Assocs. of Good Samaritan Hosp.; bd. dirs. Jr. League of Portland; bd. dirs. Loaves and Fishes; past alt. del. Democratic State Central Com., exec. bd. dirs. Multnomah County Dem. Central Com., other past polit. activities; past mem., chmn. numerous civic groups, assns., cultural orgns. Democrat. Club: Multnomah Athletic (Portland). Office: Burnside Community Council 313 E Burnside Portland OR 97214

BANZHAF, PAULA JEAN, training consultant; b. N.Y.C., Oct. 3, 1944; d. Parker Chamberlain and Jean Erice (Twachtman) B.; m. Horace Hamilton Lowell, Mar. 15, 1986. BA, MacMurray Coll., Jacksonville, Ill., 1967; postgrad., Am. U., Washington. Tchr. Sarasota (Fla.) County Schs., 1967-69; youth devel. counselor dept. pub. welfare State of Pa., Bensalem, 1972-75; tng. specialist dept. pub. welfare, dept. transp. State of Pa., Harrisburg, 1975-80, tng. cons. office adminstrn., 1980-87; tng. staff devel. U. Pa., Millersville, 1987—. Vol. Sta. WITF PBS, Harrisburg, 1984-87, Cerebral Palsy Telethon, Harrisburg, 1986-87. Mem. Am. Soc. Tng. and Devel. (sec. 1984-85, treas. 1986, v.p. for membership 1987, pres elect 1988), Am. Soc. for Pub. Adminstrn., Internat. Personnel Mgmt. Assn., Pa. Women's Network (bd. dirs. Monday Club 1984-85, chmn. 1986). Democrat. Methodist. Club: WISE Investment (Harrisburg) (pres. 1986). Home: 3024 Hoffman St Harrisburg PA 17110 Office: Millersville U Office Human Resources Dilworth Bldg Room 200 Millersville PA 17551

BAPTIST, SYLVIA EVELYN, data service company executive, consultant; b. Chgo., Feb. 15, 1944; d. Clarence Walter and Evelyn Alphild (Fagerberg) Bonin; m. Jeremy Eduard Baptist, July 21, 1962; children: Sarah, Margaret, Catherine. Student Mich. State U., 1961-62; B.S., Roosevelt U., 1965. Instr. IBM, Chgo., 1965-66, systems engr., Topeka, Kans., 1966-67; tchr. computer sci. Lawrence High Sch., Kans., 1968; pres. Multiple Data Services, Leawood, Kans., 1983—; adminstrv. user liaison Kansas City Sch. Dist., 1987—; cons. in field. Alumni Disting. scholar Mich. State U., 1961-62, Internat. Ladies' Garment Workers Union scholar Roosevelt U., 1964-65. V.p. Scandinavian Dancers Kansas City (v.p. 1987—). Lodge: Vasa (master ceremonies 1986-87, vice chmn. 1988—) . Avocations: cooking, writing. Office: Multiple Data Services 3501 W 92d St Leawood KS 66206

BARAD, JILL ELIKANN, toy company executive; b. N.Y.C., May 23, 1951; d. Lawrence Stanley and Corinne (Schuman) Elikann; m. Thomas Kenneth Barad, Jan., 28, 1979; children: Alexander David, Justin Harris. BA English and Psychology, Queens Coll., 1973. Asst. prod. mgr. mktg. Coty Cosmetics, N.Y.C., 1976-77, prod. mgr. mktg., 1977; account exec. Wells Rich Greene Advt. Agy., Los Angeles, 1978-79; product mgr. mktg. Mattel Toys, Inc., Los Angeles, 1981-82, dir. mktg., 1982-83, v.p. mktg., 1983-85, sr. v.p. mktg., 1985-86, sr. v.p. product devel., 1986, exec. v.p. product design, 1986—. Charter mem. Rainbow Guild/Amie Karen Cancer Fund, Los Angeles, 1983, Los Angeles County Mus., 1985. Mem. Am. Film Inst. (charter). Office: Mattel Inc 5150 Rosecrans Ave Hawthorne CA 90250

BARAGER, WENDY AYRIAN, librarian; b. Saranac Lake, N.Y., June 21, 1949; d. Robert Lester and Patricia Margaret (O'Brien) B. Student, Wayne State U., 1967-69; AA in Liberal Arts, Valencia Community Coll., 1969; BA in Edn., Fla. Tech. U. (name now U. Cen. Fla.), 1972; BA in English, U. Cen. Fla., 1976. Clk., typist Orlando Pub. Library, Fla., 1969-70; supr. library Orlando (Fla.) Sentinel Newspaper, 1977-80; display advt. salesperson Thrifty Nickel Want Ads Newspaper, Orlando, 1983; clk., typist State of Fla., div. motor vehicles, Orlando, 1983-84; librarian Fla. Bankers Assn., Orlando, 1984-88, communications asst., 1988—. Contbr. articles to profl. jours. Mem. Friends of the Library, Orlando, 1983. Mem. Spl. Libraries Assn. (Bulletin advt. mgr. 1981-82), Cen. Fla. Libraries Assn. (chmn. 1986-87, chmn. steering com. 1987-88). Republican. Methodist.

BARANOWSKI, CAROLYN AGNES, hospital administrator; b. Somerville, N.J., Apr. 10, 1947; d. Stephen Robert and Agnes (Malinowski) Baranowski. BA, Newark State Coll., 1972; MS, East Stroudsburg State Coll., 1976; postgrad. in respiratory therapy U. Chgo. Hosps. and Clinics, 1976. Registered respiratory therapist. Tchr., coach Bridgewater-Raritan High Sch. W., N.J., 1972-74; respiratory therapist Easton Hosp., Pa., 1975-76, asst. tech. dir. pulmonary medicine dept., 1976-80, tech. dir. pulmonary medicine dept., 1980—; adj. faculty Lehigh County Community Coll., 1976 to present; adv. mem. respiratory therapy program Lehigh County Community Coll., 1980—; cons. respiratory therapy home care, 1984. Mem. Am. Assn. Respiratory Therapy, AAHPER, Nat. Bd. Respiratory Care, Pa. Soc. Respiratory Therapy (dir. Ea. edn. dist. 1987—), Hosp. Assn. Pa. (dist. liaison Ea. dist. 1986—). Roman Catholic. Office: Easton Hosp 21 and Lehigh St Easton PA 18042

BARANSKI, JOAN SULLIVAN, editor; b. Andover, Mass., Apr. 6, 1933; d. Joseph Charles and Ruth G. (McCormack) Sullivan; m. Kenneth E. Baranski, Apr. 20, 1970. B.S., U. Lowell, Mass., 1955. Tchr. Andover Public Schs., 1955-61; asso. editor sci. and reading sch. dept. Holt, Rinehart and Winston, N.Y.C., 1961-65; promotion coordinator sch. dept. Harcourt Brace Jovanovich, N.Y.C., 1965-74; mgr. div. verifiability and testing Harcourt Brace Jovanovich, 1974-75; editor-in-chief Teacher mag., Macmillan Co.; profl. mags. Stamford, Conn., 1975-81; editor-in-chief sch. dept. Harper & Row Pubs., N.Y.C., 1981-84; v.p., editor-in-chief Globe Book Co., Simon and Schuster Edn. Group, 1984—. Contbg. author: Winston Basic Reading Series, 1963, Little Owl Program, 1964. Home: 250 E 87th St New York NY 10128 Office: 50 W 23d St New York NY 10010

BARAQUE, ERNESTINA, tax accountant; b. Cuba, Nov. 9, 1950; came to U.S., 1968; d. Ernesto and Consuelo (Garrido) Perdomo; m. Ivan Baraque, Jan. 6, 1972 (div. 1979). AS in Acctg., Miami Dade Community Coll., Miami, Fla., 1973; BS in Profl. Studies, Barry Coll., Miami, Fla., 1980; MS in Taxation, Pace U., 1986. Tax preparer (part-time) H&R Block, Miami, 1974-78; tax preparer Executax Corp., Miami, 1978-80; tax acct. Lively Arts Tax Service, N.Y.C., 1980-85; owner Elite Tax Service, N.Y.C., 1986—. Mem. Am. Parkinson's Dis. Assn., 1984—. Mem. Nat. Assn. Enrolled Agts., Nat. Assn. Female Execs., Nat. Assn. Accts. Republican. Roman Catholic. Home: 848 43rd St #22 Brooklyn NY 11231 Office: Elite Tax Service 170 W 23d St #5-P New York NY 10011

BARAQUE, TINA, tax accountant; b. Cuba, Nov. 9, 1950; came to U.S., 1968; d. Ernesto Perdoho and Consuelo Carrido; m. Ivan Baraque, Jan. 6, 1972 (div. 1979). BS, Barry Coll.; MS in Taxation, Pace U. Tax accountant Executax, Miami, Fla., 1975-80, Lively Arts, N.Y.C., 1980-85; prin. Elite Tax Service, N.Y.C., 1986—. Active Am. Parkinsons Disease Assn. Mem. Nat. Assn. Female Execs., Nat. Assn. Enrolled Agts., Nat. Soc. Pub. Accts. (assoc.). Home: 848 43rd St 22 Brooklyn NY 11231 Office: 170 W 23rd St S-P New York NY 10011

BARATTI, NANCY JO, marketing professional; b. Louisville, May 16, 1945; d. Richard Schierman and Shirley (Murphy) Crowley; m. John G. Baratti. Cert. in dental hygiene, U. Mich., 1967; BS in Dental Hygiene, Marquette U., 1970; M in Dental Hygiene Edn., U. Mich., 1974. Pvt. practice dental hygiene Flint, Mich., 1967-79; cons. Mary Kay Cosmetics, Milw., 1979-80; sr. sales dir. Mary Kay Cosmetics, Brookfield, Wis., 1982—; instr. dental hygiene Marquette U., Milw., 1974-76. Stand-in for Beverly Sills, Milw. Florentine Opera Co., 1978. Vol. Sojourner Truth House for Battered Women, Milw., 1984-86. Mem. Biznet, Nat. Assn. Female Execs. Republican. Roman Catholic. Club: MacDowell. Home and Office: 3050 Nassau Dr Brookfield WI 53005

BARBA, LINDA LOU, financial analyst; b. Tyler, Tex., Mar. 24, 1952; d. James C. and Katheryne J. (Bowers) Stamps; m. Guy J. Barba III, Jan. 11, 1975 (div. Dec. 1983); 1 child, Lindsey A. AA in Bus., San Jacinto Jr. Coll., Pasadena, Tex., 1972; BBA in Behavior Mgmt., U. Houston, 1974; cert. in real estate, Tyler (Tex.) Jr. Coll., 1984. Account rep. Great So. Life Ins. Co., Houston, 1974-77; portfolio asst. Am. Mgmt. Investment Co., Houston, 1977-84; mgr. statistical and fin. reporting Beall's Dept. Stores, Jacksonville, Tex., 1984—. Instr. First Bapt. Ch., Jacksonville, 1987. Mem. Cherokee Bd. Realtors, Bus. Women and Profl. Club (sec. Jacksonville chpt. 1985-86, treas. 1986-87). Home: 2513 Richland Dr Garland TX 75042 Office: Beall Bros Inc Rusk St Jacksonville TX 75766

BARBEE, MARGARET SOHL, organizational psychologist; b. Bay City, Mich., Oct. 28, 1943; d. William Arthur and Carol Harmony (George) Sohl; m. Joel Ralph Barbee, July 15, 1967. BA, Denison U., 1965; MS, No. Ill. U., 1967; PhD, Colo. State U., 1976. Research asst. Ft. Logan Mental Health Ctr., Denver, 1968-69; research psychologist Denver Gen. Hosp. Psychiatry Service, 1969-72; program evaluator Law Enforcement Assistance Adminstrn., Denver, 1973-75; orgn. devel. cons. Cummins Engine Co., Jamestown, N.Y., 1976-77; orgn. psychologist U. Calif. Lawrence-Livermore (Calif.) Lab., 1977—; adj. faculty U. San Francisco, 1982—; cons. to various cos. and non-profit orgns., San Francisco, 1978—. Contbr. articles to profl. jours. Vol. tng. Community Tng. and Devel. Project, San Francisco, 1980—. Mem. Am. Psychol. Assn., Orgn. Devel. Network (co-chair women in orgnl. devel. 1985), Inst. Noetic Scis., Alpha Kappa Delta, Psi Chi. Office: Lawrence Livermore Lab PO Box L-423 Livermore CA 94550

BARBEE-CUNNINGHAM, ANITA PATRICIA, psychologist, educator; b. Tallahasee, Fla., Mar. 10, 1960; d. Richard Russell and Alices Viola (Miles) Barbee; m. Michael Robert Cunningham, Dec. 28, 1985; 1 child, Robert Michael Richard. BA, Agnes Scott Coll., 1982; MS, U. Ga., 1985, PhD, 1988. Instr. Elmhurst (Ill.) Coll., 1985-86, U. Louisville, 1986—; bd. dirs. Community Coordinated Child Care; tutor Internat. Ctr. U. Louisville, 1986-87. Counselor Shelter for Battered Women, Atlanta, 1982; vol. Cabbage Patch Settlement House Day Care, Louisville, 1987; provisional mem. Jr. League of Louisville, 1987—; mem. Presbyn. CH. Women's Group. Mem. Midwestern Psychol. Assn., Psi Chi (co-chmn. 1984-85, faculty advisor 1987—), Phi Kappa Phi, Agnes Scott Alumnae Club of Ky. (pres. 1987), Soc. for Research in Child Devel., Ia. Network of Interpersonal Relationships, Soc. Southeastern Social Psychologists. Democrat. Office: U Louisville Dept Psychology Louisville KY 40292

BARBER, SHELLEY INEZ, tax service executive; b. Searcy, Ark., Dec. 27, 1949; d. John Pershing and Wava Inez (Skaggs) Fuller; m. Z. James Barber, Aug. 23, 1968. BS, U. Cen. Ark., 1971; postgrad., Miss. State U., 1976. Cert. tchr., Ark. Tchr. Paragould (Ark.) Pub. Schs., 1972, U.S. Army, Ludwigsburg, Fed. Republic Germany, 1973, Elaine (Ark.) Pub. Schs., 1973-76; sewing instr. Singer Corp., Pine Bluff, Ark., 1977-78; tchr. Star City (Ark.) Pub. Schs., 1978-80; customer relations Sears Roebuck & Co., Pine Bluff, 1980-81; franchise owner H&R Block, Inc., Stuttgart, Ark., 1982—. Mem. Stuttgart C. of C., Am. Bus. Womens Assn. (treas. Port O'Cotton chpt., Pine Bluff, 1981-82). Mem. Christian Church (Disciples of Christ). Home: 706 S Grand Ave Stuttgart AR 72160 Office: H&R Block 208 E 3d Stuttgart AR 72160

BARBERA, SHARON GAIL, banker; b. Debry, Conn., Oct. 18, 1947. BA, U. West Fla., 1969; MBA, Ariz. State U., 1979. Cert. sr. escrow officer. Escrow officer First Am. Title, Phoenix, 1979-83, br. mgr., 1983-84; sr. comml. escrow officer Transam. Title, Phoenix, 1984-87, br. mgr., 1987—; mktg. cons. Dance Inst., Scottsdale, Ariz., 1978-79. Mem. Cen. Ariz. Escrow Assn. (pres. 1984-85, chmn. bd. 1985-86), Ariz. State Escrow Assn. (pres. 1986-87), Ariz. Mortgage Bankers Assn., Scottsdale Bd. Realtors.

BARBETTA, MARIA ANN, hospital administrator, consultant; b. Bristol, Pa., Mar. 20, 1956; d. Eugene Charles and Anna (Strozzieri) B. AA, Bucks County Community Coll., 1976; BS, Coll. Allied Health Professions, Temple U., 1978. Dir. med. records Cumberland Regional Health Plan, Vineland, N.J., 1978; dir. med. record dept. St. Mary Hosp., Langhorne, Pa., 1978—; cons. med. records St. Joseph's Home for Aged, Holland, Pa., 1983—; speaker on med. record topics to various orgns., Langhorne, 1983—. Vol. tchr. Jr. High Sunday Sch. Mem. Am. Med. Record Assn., Pa. Med. Record Assn. (edn. com. 1985-87, project mgr. strategic plan 1987-88), Lehigh Valley Med. Record Assn., Southeastern Pa. Med. Record Assn. (chmn. membership com. 1987-88), Nat. Assn. Female Execs., Hosp. Assn. Pa., Pa. Med. Record Assn. (project mgr. 1987-88 strategic plan), Delaware Valley DRG Mgmt. Assn., Southeastern Pa. Assn. of Quality Assurance Profls. Avocations: cross-country skiing, volunteer work, reading, traveling, basket weaving. Home: 4707 Grandview Ave Bensalem PA 19020 Office: St Mary Hosp Langhorne-Newtown Rd Langhorne PA 19047

BARBIERI, CAROLYN MAE, insurance company executive; b. Copiague, N.Y., Dec. 3, 1941; d. Louis A. and Mae E. (Miele) Sisia; m. Gaetano Barbieri, Jan. 20, 1963; children: Joseph Vincent, Maria Lucia, Justine Philomena. BS in Edn., Hofstra U., 1963. Cert. N.Y. state tchr. Tchr. 2d grade Half Hollow Hills Sch. Dist., Huntington, N.Y., 1963; tchr. 1st grade Island Trees Sch. Dist., Levittown, N.Y., 1964-65; 3d grade tchr. Middle Country Sch. Dist., Selden, N.Y., 1965-67; credit adjuster Sears Roebuck and Co., Hicksville, N.Y., 1977-83; adminstr. Grumman Aerospace Corp., Bethpage, N.Y., 1983-86; ins. sales rep. Met. Life Ins. Co., Rego Park, N.Y., 1986—. Community chmn. Girl Scouts U.S.A., Bethpage-Plainview, N.Y., 1983-85; tchr. religion St. Martin of Tours Roman Catholic Ch., Bethpage, 1973-75. Recipient Americanism award Am. Legion Aux., Bethpage, 1959, Sci. award Bausch and Lomb, 1959. Mem. Nat. Assn. Life Underwriters, Nat. Assn. Female Execs., Nat. Assn. Securities Dealers (registered rep.), Life Underwriting Tng. Council (grad.), Leader's Club (award). Republican. Lodge: Order Sons Italy in Am. (corr. sec. Aida club 1984-85). Office: Met Life Ins Co 66 05 Woodhaven Blvd Rego Park NY 11374

BARBOUR, BARBARA GORDON, government strategic planner, consultant; b. Washington, July 1, 1942; d. William Anthony and Goldie (James) G.; m. Nathaniel W. Barbour, Nov. 21, 1964 (Nov. 1972); 1 child, Natalie Renee. BS in Bus. and Mgmt., U. Md., 1976; M in Pub. Adminstrn., U. So. Calif., 1979. Spl. research analyst U.S. Dept. Defense, Ft. Meade, Md., 1970-78; personnel staffing officer U.S. Dept. Def., Ft. Meade, 1978-80, personnel systems officer, 1980-85, career devel. officer, 1985-86, sr. personnel officer, 1986-87, sr. staff planning officer, 1987—; adj. prof. Montgomery Coll., Takoma Park, Md., 1980-86; pres., mgmt. and employment cons. Gordon Cons. & Assocs. Inc., Columbia, Md., 1984—; adj. prof. Bowie (Md.) State U. Grad. Sch. Human Resources Devel. Dept., 1986—. Trainer and supr. Mental Health Assn. Montgomery County, Silver Spring, Md., 1980-82; chmn. hospitality com. Black Caucus of State Legis. Annual Conf., Balt., 1984. Mem. Bus. Profl. Women of Md. (network program chmn. 1987—), Am. Soc. Tng. and Devel., Internat. Personnel Mgmt. Assn., Human Resource Mgmt. Assn., Delta Sigma Theta (Columbia chpt. Saturday Sch. adminstr. 1984-86, Woman of Yr. 1985, Fortitude award 1985). Democrat. Baptist. Home: 9644 Basket Ring Columbia MD 21045 Office: US Dept Def 9800 Savage Rd Fort Meade MD 20755

BARBOUR, BRENDA TOMLIN, social services administrator; b. Charlottesville, Va., Jan. 29, 1949; d. Edgar Thomas and Louise Agnes (Sandridge) Tomlin; m. John Van der Zee Barbour, Mar. 24, 1968 (div. Dec. 1984); children: Thomas Xavier, James Wilson. Grad. high sch., Charlottesville. Tchr.'s aide Brownsville Elem. Sch., Crozet, Va., 1976-80; coordinator Life Support Learning Ctr. U. Va., Charlottesville, 1980-83; dir. Thomas Jefferson Emergency Med. Service Council, Inc., Charlottesville, 1983—; mem. mng. bd. Joint Dispatch Ctr., Charlottesville, 1986—. Author: (handbook) Basic Life Support, 1981, Basic Life Support Administrative Manuel, 1984 (Program award 1984). Mem. basic life support task force Am. Heart Assn., Richmond, Va., 1981—, chmn., 1983-86, affilate faculty, 1983—; mem. Va. Ptnrs. of the Ams., 1984—. Recipient Program Excellence award Nat. Assn. Ptnrs., 1986. Methodist. Lodge: Altrusa (treas. 1985-87). Home: Rt 1 Box 101 Greenwood VA 22943 Office: Thomas Jefferson Emergency Med Service Council Inc 409 D E High St Charlottesville VA 22943

BARBOUR, CAROL GOODWIN, psychologist; b. Morganton, N.C., Sept. 15, 1946; d. Jesse Otho and Edith Adele (Goodwin) B.; m. Sidney Gilman. A.B., Duke U., 1967; Ph.D., U. Mich., 1981. Research analyst State of Ill., Chgo., 1968-69; psychologist Med. Student Mental Health Service U. Mich., Ann Arbor, 1977-80, postdoctoral fellow in clin. psychology, adolescent inpatient psychiatry, 1980-82, supr. Psychol. Clinic, 1982-83, adj. supr. Psychol. Clinic, staff psychologist, 1985-88; pvt. practice psychotherapy, Ann Arbor, 1980—; dir. psychiat. services Lakewood Clinic, Novi, Mich., 1982-85, clin. supr., staff psychologist, 1985—; cons. psychologist Mercywood Hosp., 1986—; adj. lectr. psychiatry U. Mich., Ann Arbor, 1988—. Fulbright grantee, U.S. Ednl. Found. in India, 1967-68. Mem. Am. Psychol. Assn., Mich. Soc. Psychoanalytic Psychology, Assn. for the Advancement of Psychoanalysis, Mich. Psychol. Assn., Assn. Advancement of Psychology, Phi Beta Kappa. Home: 3411 Geddes Rd Ann Arbor MI 48105 Office: 555 E William Suite 23L Ann Arbor MI 48104

BARBOZA, GLORIA, marketing professional; b. Harlingen, Tex., Mar. 24, 1951; d. Sotero and Aurora (Reyna) B. BA in English and Journalism, Tex. Woman's U., 1974. TV editor Houston Chronicle, 1974-79; dir. pub. info. Sta. KUHT-TV, Houston, 1979-81; pvt. practice freelance writer Houston, 1981-82; coordinator mktg. Spaw-Glass Constrn. Inc., Houston, 1982—. Mem. Soc. Mktg. Profl. Services, Houston Advt. Fedn., Am. Mgmt. Assn. Democrat. Roman Catholic. Office: Spaw-Glass Constrn Inc 2727 Kirby Dr Houston TX 77098

BARBOZA-CLARK, FRANCES E., medical technologist; b. Jersey City, June 22, 1938; d. Lawrence and Clementina Frances (Lopes) Barboza; diploma med. tech. Coll. Medicine and Dentistry N.J.-Rutgers U., 1970; div.; children—Donald, Renee, Edward. Chem. lab. technician, 1956-57; histology technician Coll. Medicine and Dentistry N.J.-Rutgers U. Med. Sch., 1969-72, research asst., 1972-75, med. technologist, 1975-81, sr. med. technologist, 1981-86, chief technologist, vivarium supr., 1986—; tchr., trainer students, supr. historology lab. Mem. Am. Soc. Clin. Pathologists (registered affiliate), Am. Soc. Med. Tech., Nat. Soc. Histotech., N.J. Soc. Histotech. (charter), NOW (chpt. coordinator 1979-81, 88—, dir. 1983-86, mem. polit. action com. 1983-86). Office: U Medicine and Dentistry Robert Wood Johnson Med Sch 675 Hoes Ln Piscataway NJ 08854

BARCA, KATHLEEN, marketing executive; b. Burbank, Calif., July 26, 1946; d. Frank Allan and Blanch Irene (Griffith) Barnes; m. Gerald Albino Barca, Dec. 8, 1967; children; Patrick Gerald, Stacia Kathleen. Student, Pierce Coll., 1964, Hancock Coll., 1984. Teller Security Pacific Bank, Pasadena, Calif., 1968-69, Bank Am., Santa Maria, Calif., 1972-74; operator Gen. Telephone Co., Santa Maria, Calif., 1974-83, supr. operator, 1983-84; account exec. Sta. KRQK/KLLB Radio, Lompoc, Calif., 1984-85; owner Advt. Unltd., Orcutt, Calif., 1986-88; regional mgr. A.L. Williams Mktg. Co., Los Alamos, Calif., 1988—. Author: numerous local TV and radio commercials, print advt. Activist Citizens Against Dumps in Residential Environments, Polit. Action Com., Orcutt and Santa Maria; chmn. Community advt. Com., Santa Maria, Workshop Environ. Protection Agy. Tex. Div., Dept. Health Scis. State of Calif. Mem. Nat. Assn. Female Exec., Womens Network-Santa Maria, Cen. Coast Ad (recipient numerous awards), Santa Maria Valley C. of C. Democrat.

BARCH, KAREN MARTIN, publishing executive; b. New Orleans, Jan. 20, 1954; d. Jack John and Katherine (Metzger) Martin; m. David Henoch Barch, July 3, 1977. BS, Mich. State U., 1976; MBA, U. Detroit, 1979. Indsl. engr., mfg. supr. AC Spark Plug div. Gen. Motors, Flint, Mich., 1976-79; indsl. engr. Controls div. Singer Co., Schiller Park, Ill., 1979-80; mgmt. cons. Arthur Young and Co., Chgo., 1980-84; exec. dir. editorial prodn. Encyclopaedia Britannica, Inc., Chgo., 1984—. Leader Girl Scouts U.S., Chgo., 1986—. Mem. Nat. Composition Assn., Chgo. Women in Pub., Chgo. Book Clinic. Club: Chgo. Yacht. Home: 3020 N Sheridan-1S Chicago IL 60657 Office: Encyclopaedia Britannica Inc 310 S Michigan Ave Chicago IL 60604

BARCHERS, NELDA MARIE, retail executive; b. Peoria, Ill., Apr. 1, 1948; d. Charles William and Loretta (Alexander) B.; m. Jeffrey Scot Long, May 30, 1970 (div. Dec. 1975). BFA, R.I. Sch. Design, 1970. Freelance textile designer Leavitt, Watterston Corp., Woodstock, Conn., 1973; owner, mgr., buyer Zosaku Fine Crafts, Berkeley, Calif., 1974—. Artist oil paintings; sculptures displayed in San Francisco Gallery. MacDowell Colony fellow, 1977. Office: Zosaku Fine Crafts 2110 Vine St Berkeley CA 94709

BARCLAY, CARYL ANN MORRIS, data processing consultant; b. Torrance, Calif., Feb. 28, 1945; d. Robert Eugene Sr. and Ruby Lorene (Russell) Morris; m. David Kent Barclay, Sept. 7, 1968; children: Kimberly Jean, David Robert. BA in Psychology, Stanford U., 1967; MBA in Fin., U. Chgo., 1980. Mem. document, tng. staff Tymshare, Palo Alto, Calif., 1967-68; rep. mktg. Gen. Electric Co., Chgo., 1968-71; cons. microcomputer Royal Jersey Inc., El Sobrante, Calif., 1980; cons. ops. Am. Nat. Bank, Chgo., 1980-82, cons. system, 1982-83; cons. Heitman Fin. Services, Chgo., 1983-84; pres. Usable Systems Inc., Lake Forest, Ill., 1984—. Council treas. Moraine Girl Scouts Am., Deerfield, Ill., 1986-88, v.p. Presbyn. Ch. choir, 1987-88; bd. dirs. Lake Forest Jr. High Sch. PTA, Camerata Soc., 1986-88. Mem. Stanford U. Alumni Assn., U. Chgo. Alumni Assn., U. Chgo. Bus. Women. Club: Fortnightly (Chgo.) (social, program coms.). Office: Usable Systems Inc 889 S Greenbay Rd Lake Forest IL 60045

BARD, SUSAN MARTHA, small business owner; b. Trenton, N.J., Apr. 4, 1954; d. Max and Miriam (Marcus) B. BA in Polit. Sci., Douglass Coll. of Rutgers U., 1976; MS in Journalism, Northwestern U., 1977. Reporter, copy editor Commodity News Services, Chgo., 1977-79, asst. bur. chief, 1979; staff writer pub. relations dept. Chgo. Bd. Trade, 1979-80; local trader and broker MidAm. Commodity Exchange, Chgo., 1980-82; mgr. pub. affairs Nat. Futures Assn., Chgo., 1982-83; founder, owner Letters Etcetera, Chgo., 1983—; free-lance writer. Contbr. articles to profl. jours. Mem. Internat. Assn. for Fin. Planning, Futures Industry Assn. (mem. exec. com. Chgo. div. 1986—), Douglass Coll. Alumnae Assn. (sec. Class 1976 chpt. 1981—). Clubs: Plaza (Chgo.) (social com. 1987—); Nat. Writers (Denver). Home: 360 E Randolph St Chicago IL 60601 Office: Letters Etcetera PO Box 811280 Chicago IL 60681-1280

BARDELLI, DONA ALICE, international marketing executive; b. Irvington, N.J., Feb. 27, 1953; d. Alfred and Dona Ellen (Self) B.; m. Harry M. Bainbridge, May 23, 1981. Certificat de Langue, Sorbonne, U. Paris, 1974; BA, U. Ky., 1975; MA in Internat. Studies, Am. U., 1978; MS in Econ. and Social Planning in Developing Countries , U. London, 1979. Research assoc. Woodrow Wilson Internat. Ctr. for Vis. Scholars, Washington, 1976-77, World Bank, Washington, 1977-79; legis. asst. to Congressman Marc Lincoln Marks, Washington, 1979-80; internat. trade analyst Internat. Trade Adminstrn., U.S. Dept. Commerce, Washington, 1980-82; internat. mgmt. cons. Coopers and Lybrand, 1982-86 ; v.p. Bankers Trust Co., Internat. Pvt. Banking, 1986-88; sr. mktg. dir. internat. services Seidman and Seidman/BDO, N.Y.C., 1988—. Chpt. pres. Am. Friends of London Sch. Econs., 1981-83, nat. bd. dirs., 1982-85. Mem. Soc. for Internat. Devel. N.Y. Chpt., Bus. and Profl. Women's Clubs Am. (acad. scholar 1971), Nat. Assn. Female Execs., Am. Platform Assn., Women's Econ. Devel. Corp. Democrat. Lutheran. Office: Seidman and Seidman/BDO 15 Columbus Circle New York NY 10022

BARDEN, JANICE KINDLER, personnel company executive; b. Cleve.; d. Norman Allen and Bessie G. (Black) Kindler; m. Hal Barden, Nov. 12, 1944 (dec. Jan. 1985) 1 child, Sheryl Andrea. BBA, Miami U., Oxford, Ohio, 1947; M in Indsl. Psychology, Kent State U., 1948. Asst. dir. admissions Fairleigh Dickinson U., Teaneck, N.J., 1950-53; gen. mgr. Pilots Employment Assocs., Teterboro, N.J., 1953-71; founder, pres. Aviation Personnel Internat., New Orleans, 1971—; commr. jury U.S. Dist. Ct. (ea. dist.) La., New Orleans, 1965—; lectr. in field. Chmn. History of Aviation Collection U. Tex., Dallas, 1980—. Recipient Disting. Alumnus award Kent State U., 1986. Mem. Nat. Bus. Aircraft Assn. (chmn. conv. 1975, 85, 87), Flight Safety Found. (chmn. corp. seminar), Profl. Aircraft Maintenance Assn., AAUW, Bus. and Profl. Women's Club, Kent State Alumni Assn. (bd. dirs. 1976-82), Psi Chi. Republican. Episcopalian. Lodge: Order of Rainbow (grand coordinator 1973-84). Office: Aviation Personnel Internat PO Box 6846 New Orleans LA 70174

BARDIN, LIVIA, foundation (not-for-profit) executive; b. San Francisco, Dec. 7, 1937; d. Alfred J. and Miriam (Friedman) Goldeen; m. David Jonas Bardin, Mar. 12, 1961; children: Jacob, Matthew, Joseph, Sarah. BA, Smith Coll., 1959. Writer, asst. editor Scholastic Mags., N.Y.C., 1959-61; freelance writer Trenton, N.J., 1974-77, NEA Fair Tax Found., Washington, 1968-69; exec. dir., sec. Fair Tax Found., Washington, 1984—; bd. dirs. Fair Tax Edn. Fund, Washington, sec., 1985—. Bd. dirs. Charles E. Smith Jewish Day Sch., Rockville, Md., 1977—, pres., 1986—; bd. dirs. United Jewish Appeal Fedn., Bethesda, Md., 1986—, Greater Washington Jewish Community Found., Rockville, 1986—. Recipient Community Service award Charles E. Smith Jewish Day Sch., 1983. Democrat. Office: Fair Tax Found 2025 I St NW Suite 813 Washington DC 20006

BARDOS, MARIA ELENA, banker, data processing consultant; b. Canonsburg, Pa., Nov. 6, 1949; d. George Phillip and Victoria (Loutsion) B. B.S. in Math., U. Pitts., 1971, M.B.A., 1976; postgrad. Duquesne U., 1980—. Programmer, analyst Mellon Bank, Pitts., 1971-73; systems cons. Westinghouse Nuclear, Pitts., 1973-75; systems planning analyst Equibank, Pitts., 1975-76; corp. EDP auditor Rockwell Internat., Pitts., 1976-77; pres. Bardos Cons., Pitts., 1977-79; asst. v.p., software devel. mgr. Dollar Bank, Pitts., 1979-82, v.p. electronic banking dept., 1984-85; pres. Dollar Bank Adv. Group, Inc., 1986—; instr. Robert Morris Coll., 1983-84. Bd. dirs. Holy Cross Greek Orthodox Ch., Pitts., 1984—, youth coordinator, 1983-84; youth commr. Greek Orthodox Diocese, 1983-84; vol. Bapt. Ctr., 1982-83; bd. dirs. United Way of Southwestern Pa., 1986-87, Pitts. Bus. Acad., 1986; tech. adviser United Way of Allegheny County. Recipient Thyrsa Amos award U. Pitts., 1970, Helen Garyiannis nat. grantee Greek Orthodox Archdiocese, N.Y.C., 1968. Mem. Data Processing Mgmt. Assn., Assn. Women in Computing, Greek Orthodox Young Adult League (v.p. 1982), Mortar Board. Republican. Home: 14 Pocono Dr Pittsburgh PA 15220 Office: Dollar Savs Bank Oliver Bldg 535 Smithfield St Pittsburgh PA 15222

BARDWELL, REBBECA, psychologist, educator; b. Appleton, Wis., Feb. 4, 1948; d. Roger Willis and Mary (Wells) B.; m. Eugene Fred Braaksma, Aug. 23, 1986. BA, U. Iowa, 1972, MA, 1973, PhD, 1977; postgrad., U. Wis., 1974. Lic. psychologist, Wis. Research scientist U. Iowa, Iowa City, 1976-78; assoc. prof. Marquette U., Milw., 1978-85, dir. tchr. edn., 1979-82; pvt. practice psychology Waukesha, Wis., 1984-86; mem. Wis. Psychology Examining Bd., 1986—. Contbr. articles to profl. jours. Adv. com United Cerebral Palsey, Milw., 1984-86, Wis. Pro Choice, Milw., 1983-86. Mem. Internat. Council Psychologists, Am. Psychol. Assn. (com. chmn. 1980-84), Am. Ednl. Research Assn., Midwest Psychol. Assn., Wis. Psychol. Assn. Office: Marquette U Milwaukee WI 53233

BARDWICK, JUDITH MARCIA, management consultant; b. N.Y.C., Jan. 16, 1933; d. Abraham and Ethel (Krinsky) Hardis; m. John Bardwick, III, Dec. 18, 1954 (div.); children: Jennifer, Peter, Deborah; m. Allen Armstrong, Feb. 10, 1984. B.S., Purdue U., 1954; M.S., Cornell U., 1955; Ph.D., U. Mich., 1964. Lectr. U. Mich., Ann Arbor, 1964-67; asst. prof. psychology U. Mich., 1967-71, asso. prof., 1971-75, prof., 1975-83, assoc. dean, 1977-83; pres. In Transition, Inc., 1983—; mem. population research study group NIH, 1971-75. Author: Psychology of Women, 1971, In Transition, 1979; editor: Readings in the Psychology of Women, 1972; The Plateauing Trap, 1986; mem. editorial bd. Women's Studies, 1973—, Psychology of Women Quar., 1975—; contbr. articles to profl. jours. Mem. social sci. adv. com. Planned Parenthood Am., 1973. Fellow Am. Psychol. Assn.; mem. Midwest Psychol. Assn., N.Y. Acad. Scis., Am. Psychosomatic Soc., Phi Beta Kappa. Office: In Transition Inc 2285 Via Tabara La Jolla CA 92037

BARDYGUINE, PATRICIA WILDE, ballerina, ballet theatre executive; b. Ottawa, Ont., Can., July 16, 1928; came to U.S., 1943; d. John Herbert and Eileen Lucy (Simpson) White; m. George Bardyguine, Dec. 14, 1953; children: Anya, Youri. Student, Profl. Children's Sch., N.Y.C. Dancer Am. Concert Ballet, N.Y.C., 1943-44, Marquis De Queras Ballet Internat., N.Y.C., 1943-45, Ballet Russe De Monte Carlo, tours nationwide, 1945-49; guest artist Roland Petit Ballet De Paris, 1949; prin. ballerina Met. Ballet, touring throughout Europe, 1950, N.Y.C. Ballet, 1950-65; dir. Harkness House, N.Y.C., 1965-67; ballet mistress Am. Ballet Theater, N.Y.C., 1969-82; artistic dir. Pitts. Ballet Theatre, 1982—; bd. dirs. Am. Ballet Theater Sch., 1979-82; dance panelist Nat. Endowment for Arts, N.Y. State Council for the Arts; judge Lausanne Internat. Competition; guest tchr., coach N.Y.C. Ballet, Joffrey Ballet, Dance Theater of Harlem, The Royal Ballet of Harlem, The Royal Ballet of Stockholm, Internat. Summer Seminar, Cologne, Fed. Republic Germany, Heinz Bosl Found., Munich, St. Moritz, Japan, Australia, Republic South Korea. Soloist British Met. Ballet, N.Y. Philharmonic Orch., 1962-65, six European tours, also tour of Orient; numerous TV appearances; commd. by N.Y. Philharm. to choreograph ballets Festival, 1964, At The Ball, 1965, Viennese Evening, 1966, Petite Suite, 1967. Adminstr. scholar fund Sch. Am. Ballet Group; mem. Nat. Bd. Regional Ballet. Fulbright fellow. Mem. Am. Guild Mus. Artists, AFTRA, Dance/USA (bd. dirs.). Office: Pitts Ballet Theatre 2900 Liberty Ave Pittsburgh PA 15201

BAREIS, BEVERLIE ELAINE, nurse; b. Rockland, Maine, July 22, 1925; d. Earle Raymond and Margaret Verrel (Long) Conant; R.N., New Eng. Deaconess Hosp., Boston, 1946; B.S. in Health Sci., Calif. State U., Northridge, 1976; M.A., Calif. State U., Los Angeles, 1981; m. David W. Bareis, Feb. 8, 1947; children—Ellen Ruth Bareis DiGiampaulo, Karl Frederick, Paul Arthur, Kathilynn Bareis Marquette. Inservice supr. Motion Picture Country Hosp., Woodland Hills, Calif., 1960-66; nursing educator Los Angeles City Unified Schs., 1965—; staff devel. coordinator, then dir. community relations Brotman Meml. Hosp., Culver City, Calif., 1970-77; asst. dir. nursing and health programs ARC, 1978-80; asst. prof. Calif. State U., Los Angeles, part-time, 1981—; nursing educator Abram Friedman Occupational Center, Los Angeles 1980—. Recipient Gold medal Los Angeles County Heart Assn., 1966, Clara Barton medal ARC, 1972. Mem. Am. Public Health Assn., Nat. League Nursing, NEA, Am. Assn. Sex Educators, New Eng. Deaconess Hosp. Alumnae Assn., Phi Kappa Phi.

BARFIELD, SHIRLEY ROSALIE, banker; b. Apalachicola, Fla., Sept. 6, 1940; d. Charles Manuel and Loretta Frances (Nasto) Rosalie; m. Wendell W. Barfield, Mar. 2, 1962; children—Wendell W. Barfield, Charles Darrin Barfield. AS, Polk Community Coll., Fla., 1981; postgrad. Standard and Advanced Tng., Am. Inst. Banking, Washington, 1983; postgrad. U. Okla. 1985, 87. Dep. clk. CCC Franklin County, Apalachicola, 1959-61; mgmt. trainee Apalachicola St. Bank, Fla., 1961-66; pub. relations staff Peoples Bank, Lakeland, Fla., 1967; br. mgr. Fla. Nat. Bank, Port St. Joe, 1968; fin. officer Sch. Bd., Franklin County, Apalachicola, 1968-70; compliance officer Barnett Bank of Polk County, Lakeland, 1970—; instr. Polk Community Coll., Winter Haven, Fla., 1981—. Mem. Nat. Assn. Bank Women (com. 1981—), Nat. Assn. Exec. Women, Am. Inst. Banking. Democrat. Roman Catholic. Clubs: Beta (pres. 1956-59), 4-H (Carabelle, Fla., pres. 1953-59). Avocations: piano, reading history, camping. Home: 1125 Lakewood Rd Lakeland FL 33805 Office: Barnett Bank Polk County 331 S Florida Ave Lakeland FL 33802

BARIL, NANCY ANN, gerontological nurse practitioner, consultant; b. Paterson, N.J., May 10, 1952; d. Kenneth Gerald and Jeanette Elenore (Girodet) Keiser; m. Joel Mark Baril, Apr. 15, 1984; 1 child, Jason Kenneth. AA, Gulf Coast Community Coll., 1976; BS in Nursing, Fla. State U., 1978; M in Nursing, UCLA, 1983. Registered pub. health nurse, Calif.; ANA cert. gerontol. nurse practitioner. Charge nurse, nurse preceptor Cedar Sinai Med. Ctr., Los Angeles, 1979-83; RN Nursing Services Incorp., Sherman Oaks, Calif., 1980-83; nurse practitioner Santa Monica Peer Counseling Ctr., Santa Monica, Calif., 1983; nurse cons., gerontol. nurse practioner Summit Health Ltd., Burbank, Calif., 1983-85; nurse cons. Geriatric Assocs., Granada Hills, Calif., 1983-85; nurse cons., gerontol. nurse practitioner Care Enterprises West, Burbank, 1985-86; patient services coordinator, gerontol. nurse practitioner ARA Living Ctrs., Glendale, Calif., 1986-87; dir. nursing, gerontol. nurse practitioner Sing of the Dove, Chatsworth, Calif., 1988—, Topanga Terrace, Conoga Park, 1988—. Mem. PTA, Granada Hills, 1985. Mem. Calif. Coalition of Nurse Practioners, Am. Nursing Assn., Calif. Nursing Assn., Gerontol. Soc., Sigma Theta Tau (rec. sec. 1983-85). Democrat. Episcopalian. Avocations: reading, crossword puzzles, gardening, jet-skiing. Home: 16921 Bircher St Granada Hills CA 91344 Office: ARA Living Ctrs 516 Burchett St Suite 102 Glendale CA 91203

BARILI, ROBERTA JEAN, financial officer; b. West Chester, Pa., Nov. 15, 1942; d. William J. and Jean M. Leary; m. Edward S. Barili, July 18, 1964; children: Christopher T., Kimberly Ann. Student, West Chester State Coll., 1965, Adirondack Community Coll., 1972-73; BS, Empire State Coll. SUNY, Saratoga, 1978; postgrad., Russell Sage Coll., 1980. Sec. West Chester Pub. Schs. Supt.'s Office, 1960-65, Nether Providence Sch. Dist., Wallingford, Pa., 1966; sales clk. Singer Sewing Machines, Glens Falls, N.Y., 1968-69; waitress Howard Johnsons Restaurant, Glens Falls, 1969-74; sec. Edward, Williams et al., CPA's, Glens Falls, 1974-78, staff acct., 1978-81; asst. comptroller Community Workshop, Inc., Glens Falls, 1981-83, fiscal analyst, 1983-86, chief fin. officer, 1986-88, v.p. fin., 1988—. Mem. Jaycees, Adirondack C. of C. (health care cost containment com. 1985-86, adv. com. 1987-88), Am. Mgmt. Assn., Nat. Assn. Accts. (Glen Falls chpt. organizing com. 1986—). Republican. Home: Rural Rt Box 1609 Lake George NY 12845 Office: Community Workshop Inc 36 Everts Ave PO Box 196 Glens Falls NY 12801

BARKAN, VICTORIA LYNN KOEGLE, cable television executive; b. Dayton, Ohio, Dec. 17, 1946; d. Wilbur Robert and Lillian (Lauer) Koegle; m. John Nestor Barkan Jr., July 19, 1971 (div.). B.S.E., Bowling Green State U., 1969. Layout artist Art Staff Studio, Toledo, 1969-71, Higbees, Cleve., 1972-73; freelance artist, 1974-75; account exec. Media 2000, Hudson, Ohio, 1976-77; nat. advt. mgr. Continental Cablevision, Findlay, Ohio, 1977-80; mktg. coordinator United Cable TV Corp., Denver, 1980; dir. mktg. Metrovision, Atlanta, 1980-86; mktg., sales mgr. Cox Cable, Oklahoma City, 1986—. Recipient Bronze Echo, Direct Mail Mktg. Assn., 1979. Mem. Women in Cable (v.p., p. Atlanta chpt. 1982-84, nat. dir. 1984, 87, 88, nat. sec. 1985), Cable TV Adminstrn. Mgmt. Assn. (Tammy award 1982, Award of Distinction 1983, 84, 3d Place award 1984, 3d Place Campaign award 1984, 2 1st Place awards 1985, Case Study Winner 1988). Delta Phi Delta. Club: Atlanta Ski. Office: Cox Cable 2312 NW 10th St Oklahoma City OK 73107

BARKEMEYER, MARCIA JEAN, hospital administrator; b. St. Paul, July 11, 1933; d. Lloyd Wayne and Audrey Emelia (Levine) Barnes; m. Louis Edward Barkemeyer, Dec. 22, 1954; children: Joel Jay, Lorri Sue Alonzo. BA in Sociology, Hamline U., 1954; cert. EEG technician, U. Minn., 1963; postgrad., No. Ariz. U., 1974-77. EEG technician Elizabeth Kenny Inst., Mpls., 1963-66; rep. admitting Flagstaff (Ariz.) Med. Ctr., 1972-74, coordinator admitting, 1977-84; coordinator info. and referral No. Ariz. Council of Govt., Flagstaff, 1974-77; mgr. admitting Flagstaff Med. Ctr., 1984—. Program chmn. PTA, St. Paul, 1962, pres., 1963. Mem. Ariz. Assn. Hosp. Admitting Mgrs. Democrat. Club: Flower Arrangers (Flagstaff) (sec. 1985-86). Office: Flagstaff Med Ctr PO Box 1268 Flagstaff AZ 86002

BARKER, BARBARA ANN, ophthalmologist; b. Paterson, N.J., Nov. 10, 1943; d. Earle Louis and Dorothy Louise (Williamson) Barker; m. Joel Ira Papernik, July 28, 1972. B.A., Connecticut Coll., 1965; B.A., Yale U., 1967; M.A., Rutgers Med. Sch., 1974; M.D., Mt. Sinai Sch. Medicine, 1976. Diplomate Am. Bd. Ophthalmology. Intern, Beth Israel Med. Center, 1977; resident Mt. Sinai Sch. Medicine/Beth Israel Med. Center, 1980, fellow in glaucoma, 1980-81, fellow cornea, refractive surgery, 1981-82, now mem. staff; research technician The Rockefeller U., N.Y.C., 1965-66; tchr. Riverdale Country Sch., N.Y.C., 1967-68; research asst. Sloan Kettering Inst., N.Y.C., 1969-72; clin. instr. Mt. Sinai Sch. Medicine, N.Y.C., 1982—; pvt. practice medicine specializing in ophthalmology, N.Y.C., 1983—; mem. staff N.Y. Eye and Ear Hosp., Cabrini Hosp. Recipient Resident Paper award Beth Israel Med. Center, 1980; Beth Israel Research grantee, 1983; NSF grantee, 1966. Mem. Internat. Soc. Refractive Keratoplasty, AMA, Am. Med. Women's Assn., Women's Med. Soc. N.Y.C., N.Y. County Med. Assn. (mem. com.), Phi Beta Kappa. Home and Office: 11 E 86th St #18B New York NY 10028

BARKER, ELIZABETH ANN, criminal investigator; b. San Francisco, Mar. 7, 1950; d. James Lee Sr. and Evelyn Lois (Mattingly) Williams; m. Chris Harvey Edwards, Mar. 21, 1969 (div. 1979); children: Chris Herbert, Constance Helene; m. Larry Andrew Barker, Nov. 5, 1983. Student, Cochise Jr. Coll., La. State U., 1978, La. State U., 1983. Dispatcher Mandeville (La.) Police Dept., 1975-76; dispatcher, patrolperson Covington (La.) Police Dept., 1977-80, sgt., 1980—, sgt. investigations div., juv. officer, evidence officer, crime prevention, 1984-87; sex crimes investigator St. Tammany Parish Sheriff's Dept., Covington, 1981-83. Recipient Commendation award Mid-Am. Youth Programs, 1985, cert. Achievement Identi-Kit System, 1985. Mem. La. Juvenile Officers Assn. (cert. Achievement 1982, 86, 87), La. Mcpl. Police Officers, La. Peace Officers Assn. Baptist. Office: Covington Police Dept 200 E Kirkland Covington LA 70433

BARKER, KAREN JEAN, real estate broker; b. Boggstown, Ind.; d. James Russell Tillison and Gladys Mae (Lancaster) King; m. Bill Gene Barker, 1961 (dec. 1962); 1 child, Toni Karen Barker; m. Charles Lee Koons, 1971 (dec. 1984). Real estate cert., Fresno City Coll., 1987; student, U. Calif., Davis, 1986; BA, MBA, Western States U., 1985; grad., Realtors Inst. Calif., 1982. Lic. real estate broker, Calif.; cert. internat. appraiser; notary pub., Calif. Telephone operator Ind. Bell Telephone, Indpls., 1954-56; clk., typist Hemphill Noyes & Co., Indpls., 1956-57; tchr. Patricia Stevens Modeling Sch., Indpls., 1957-60; clk., typist RCA, Indpls., 1957-60, City of Fresno, Calif., 1960-61; sr. acctg. clk. Fed. Mktg. Order Grape Crush Adminstrn., Fresno, 1963; clk., typist Calif. Hwy. Patrol, Fresno, 1963-67; radio dispatcher Calif. Dept. Fish and Game, Fresno, 1967-71; real estate agt. various cos., Shaver Lake, Calif., 1974-79; pvt. practice real estate Shaver Lake, 1979—. Mem. Nat. Assn Realtors, Calif. Assn. Realtors, Fresno Bd. Realtors, Internat. Orgn. of Real Estate Appraisers. Democrat. Prebyn. Home: 41617 Tollhouse Rd Shaver Lake CA 93664 Office: PO Box 313 Shaver Lake CA 93664

BARKER, LINDA DARLENE, educator; b. Steubenville, Ohio, Oct. 19, 1947; d. Edward Gregg and Ruth Oreen (Bearden) Donnelly; m. Robert Hal

Barker, Aug. 30, 1969; children: Robert Gregg, Lee Donny. BA, W. Liberty (W.Va.) State U., 1970; MA, U. W.VA., 1979. Tchr. Brooke County Bd. of Edn., Follansbee, W.Va., 1969—. Leader Blue Birds, Hooverson Heights, W.Va., 1972; mem. PTA; asst. cubmaster Boy Scouts Am., Hooverson Heights, 1983; choir dir. Free Meth. Ch., Weirton, W.Va., 1984—, youth dir., 1970-72. Mem. NEA, W.Va. Edn. Assn., Brooke County Edn. Assn., Internat. Reading Assn., 20th Century Woman's Club (sec. 1986—), Alpha Delta Kappa. Democrat. Methodist. Home: 17 Tierra Wheeling WV 26037 Office: Hooverson Heights Elem Sch 200 Rockdale Rd Follansbee WV 26037

BARKER, MICHELLE MARIE, public relations executive; b. Buffalo, Feb. 1, 1955; d. Stanley Andrew and Stella Rosalie (Laskowski) Gull; m. Charles Edward Barker, Feb. 6, 1976 (div. Nov. 1980); 1 child, Kylene Elaine. Student, U. Calif., Santa Barbara, 1973-74, UCLA, 1975-76; BA in Polit. Sci., Calif. State U., Los Angeles, 1980. Asst. to exec. v.p. 1st Gray Line Corp., Los Angeles, 1974-80; asst. pub. relations Calif. Med. Ctr., Los Angeles, 1980-81, asst. dir. pub. relations, 1981-83, dir. pub. relations, 1983-86, sr. v.p. pub. affairs, 1986—. dir. Olympics projects loaned exec. program Cen. City Assn. Los Angeles, 1983-84; bd. dirs. Los Angeles Downtowners, 1983—, Ketchum Downtown YMCA, Los Angeles, 1986—; mem. South Park Task Force Community Redevel. Agy., Los Angeles, 1983—. Recipient Best of the West award Assn. Western Hosps., 1983-84, Touchstone award Am. Hosp. Assn., 1983-84, 86. Mem. Internat. Assn. Bus. Communicators, Women in Communications (bd. dirs. 1987, Clanon award 1985). Democrat. Roman Catholic.

BARKER, SARAH EVANS, judge; b. Mishawaka, Ind., June 10, 1943; d. James McCall and Sarah (Yarbrough) Evans; m. Kenneth R. Barker, Nov. 25, 1972. B.S., Ind. U., 1965; J.D., Am. U., 1969; postgrad. Coll. William and Mary, 1966-67, George Washington U. Bar: Ind., U.S. Dist. Ct. (so. dist.) Ind., U.S. Ct. Appeals (7th cir.), U.S. Supreme Ct. Legal asst. to senator U.S. Senate, 1969-71; spl. counsel to minority govt. ops. com. permanent investigations subcom., 1971-72; dir. research, scheduling and advance Senator Percy Re-election Campaign, 1972; asst. U.S. atty. So. Dist. Ind., 1972-75, 1st asst. U.S. atty., 1976-77, U.S. atty., 1981-84; judge U.S. Dist. Ct. (so. dist.) Ind., 1984—; assoc., then ptnr. Bose, McKinney & Evans, Indpls., 1977-81. Bd. dirs. New Hope of Ind. Mem. Indpls. Bar Assn. (v.p., bd. mgrs.). Republican. Methodist. Office: US Dist Ct 210 US Courthouse 46 E Ohio St Indianapolis IN 46204 *

BARKETT, ROSEMARY, justice; b. Ciudad Victoria, Tamps, Mex., Aug. 29, 1939; came to U.S., 1958; BS summa cum laude, Spring Hill Coll., 1967; JD, U. Fla., 1970. Bar: Fla., U.S. Dist. Ct. (so. dist.) Fla., U.S. Ct. Appeals (5th cir.), U.S. Supreme Ct. Sole practice 1971-79; judge 15th Jud. Cir. Ct., Palm Beach County, Fla., 1979-84, 4th Dist. Ct. Appeal, West Palm Beach, Fla., 1984-85; justice Supreme Ct. Fla., Tallahassee, 1985—; mem. faculty U. Nev., Reno, Fla. Jud. Coll.; former mem. sentencing guidelines commn. State of Fla., Statewide Prosecution Function Commn., Consumer Affairs Hearing Bd., Palm Beach County. Mem. editorial bd. The Florida Judges Manual. Former mem. Mental Health Bd. No. 9, Inc., Palm Beach County, Palm Beach County Adult Corrections Research and Evaluation Steering Com. Recipient Woman of Achievement award Palm Beach County Commn. on Status of Women, 1985. Fellow Acad. Matrimonial Lawyers; mem. Fla. Bar Assn. (family law sect., com. on civil procedure, com. on appellate rules, lectr. on matrimonial media and criminal law continuing legal edn.), Palm Beach County Bar Assn. (com. on needs of children, Hispanic Affairs com.), Assn. Trial Lawyers Am. (Jud. Achievement award 1986), Am. Acad. Matrimonial Lawyers (award 1984), Fla. Assn. Women Lawyers (Palm Beach chpt.), Nat. Assn. Women Judges, Palm Beach Marine Inst. (former chairperson, bd. trustees). Office: Fla Supreme Ct Supreme Ct Bldg Tallahassee FL 32399 *

BARKEY, ANN LAUREN, human resources executive, consultant; b. Rochester, N.Y., Aug. 10, 1949; d. Kenneth Thomas and Virginia Ruth (Nablo) B. BS in English, Ohio U., 1970; MEd, Ariz. State U., 1975, MA in English, 1977. Employment mgr. Hosp. Corp. Am., Atlanta, 1977-78; asst. dir. human resources Fireman's Fund Ins. Co., Atlanta, 1978-80; dir. personnel Marriott Corp., Atlanta, 1980-82; dir. human resources Beefsteak Charlie's, Inc., N.Y.C., 1982-84; dir. tng. The Fur Vault, Inc., N.Y.C., 1984-87; dir. personnel Conran's, N.Y.C., 1987—. Mem. Am. Soc. Personnel Adminstrs., Am. Soc. Tng. and Devel.

BARKLEY, MARILYN JANE, accountant; b. Yakima, Wash., July 9, 1934; d. Philip and Pauline Marie (Coulter) Barkley; m. Frederick Paul Fazi, Nov. 26, 1968 (div. July 1970). Cert. Lawton Sch., 1953. Office nurse W.A. Blampin, M.D., Los Angeles, 1953-55; jr. acct. Markson Bros., Los Angeles, 1955-57; office mgr. Deaf Smith Research Labs., Hereford, Tex., 1958-59; acct. Roy M. Guest, P.A., Dallas, 1960-68; comptroller, gen. mgr. Restaurant Chablis, Dallas, 1970-78; acct. Tannebaum, Bindler & Co., P.C., CPAs, Dallas, 1978—. Mem. Internat. Platform Assn., Humane Soc. U.S. Presbyterian. Office: Tannebaum Bindler & Co PC CPAs 2323 Bryan Suite 700 Dallas TX 75201

BARKLEY, SALLY CAMPBELL, sanitary commission administrator; b. Sapporo, Japan, Oct. 20, 1953. BS, U. Md., 1976; MBA, George Washington U., 1987. Buyer Prince George's County Govt., Upper Marlboro, Md., 1977-80; sr. buyer Washington Suburban Sanitary Commn., Hyattsville, Md., 1981, asst. purchasing agt., 1981-82, supr. procurement, 1982-83, purchasing agt., 1984—. Mem. Nat. Inst. Govtl. Purchasing (cert., sec., treas. met. Washington chpt. 1986-87), Nat. Assn. Purchasing Mgmt. (cert.), Md. Pub. Purchasing Assn., Purchasing Mgmt. Assn. Md. Office: Washington Suburban Sanitary Commn 4101 Lloyd St Hyattsville MD 20781

BARKLEY-WILEN, PAT, legal company executive; b. Los Angeles, Mar. 17, 1951; d. Roy Charleton and Flora Elizabeth (Kennamer) Barkley; m. Daniel Barnett Wilen, Sept. 24, 1981. Degree, Bryan Coll. Ct. Reporting, Los Angeles, 1973; MBA, Pepperdine U., 1985. Cert. shorthand reporter, Calif. Pres., owner Pat Barkley Ct. Reporters, Los Angeles, 1975—; ptnr. Barkley Ct. Reporters, Newport Beach, Calif., 1985—. Mem. Nat. Shorthand Reporters Assn., Calif. Ct. Reporters Assn., Los Angeles Gen. Shorthand Reporters Assn. (treas. 1988), Orange County Ct. Reporters Assn. (bd. dirs. 1986). Republican. Clubs: YWCA, Profl. Women's Breakfast Group, Key Exec. Investment (Los Angeles) (pres.). Office: Pat Barkley Ct Reporters 5850 Canoga Ave 5th Floor Woodland Hills CA 91367 also: 4000 MacArthur Blvd Suite 5500 Newport Beach CA 92660 also: 5850 Canoga Ave Suite 400 Woodland Hills CA 91378

BARKOVICH, BARBARA ROSE, utility consultant; b. Tokyo, Dec. 18, 1950; d. Anthony and Mildred (Donner) B. BA, U. Calif., San Diego, 1972; MS, SUNY, Stony Brook, 1974; PhD, U. Calif., Berkeley, 1987. Asst. energy policy analyst NSF, Washington, 1974-75; research specialist Calif. Pub. Utilities Commn., San Francisco, 1975-78, dir. policy and planning, 1978-83; asst. v.p. 1st Interstate Bancorp, Los Angeles, 1983-84, v.p., 1984-85; cons. Marin County, Calif., 1985-86; ptnr. Barkovich & Yap, San Rafael, Calif., 1987—; mem. Policy Scis. Adv. Bd., 1981-84; mem. com. on electricity in econ. growth Nat. Research Council, 1984-86; chair venture capital com. NASA Joint Enterprise on Aerospace Research and Tech. Transfer, 1987—. Recipient Energy Conservation award Fed. Energy Adminstrn., 1976. Mem. AAAS, Internat. Assn. Energy Economists, Women Energy Assocs. (bd. dirs.).

BARKSDALE, NANCY BURTON, corporate controller; b. Lynchburg, Va., Oct. 22, 1957; d. William Terry and Dorothy Burton (Cardwell) B. BS in Bus., Va. Poly. Inst. and State U., 1979. CPA, Va. Acct. Deloitte, Haskings & Sells, Roanoke, Va., 1979-83; asst. controller Bassett Walker Inc., Martinsville, Va., 1983-87; controller Pluma Inc., Eden, N.C., 1987—. Mem. Am. Inst. CPA's., Va. Soc. CPA's., Beta Alpha Psi, Phi Kappa Phi. Presbyterian. Office: Pluma Inc Fieldcrest Dr Eden NC 27288

BARLAR, REBECCA NANCE, music educator; b. Lawrenceburg, Tenn., Mar. 3, 1950; d. Harold Wilford and Freda Eleanor (Bailey) Nance; m. Douglas Garland Barlar, June 14, 1969; children: Jennifer, Nancy, Jonathan, David. BS, Mid. Tenn. State U., 1972; M in Music, U. South Fla., 1979. Pvt. practice Franklin, Tenn., 1972-76; piano instr. Dept. of Continuing Edn. U. South Fla., Tampa, Fla., 1979-82; prof. of music theory Fla. Coll., Temple Terrace, 1979—, prof. of pian0, 1986—; pvt. piano tchr., Tampa, 1976—. Mem. Friends of Temple Terrace Library, 1978—; fin. com. Fla. Coll. Acad. Tchr.-Parent Assn., Temple Terrace, 1984—, King High Sch. PTSA, Tampa, 1986—, Greco Jr. High PTSA, 1987—; v.p. King High Music Club, 1988—. U. South Fla. Fine Arts fellow, 1977; named One of Outstanding Young Women of Am., 1984. Mem. Music Tchrs. Nat. Assn. (profl. cert. in piano 1987), Mid-State Music Tchrs. Assn. (sec. 1980-82, treas. 1986—), Fla. State Music Tchrs. Assn. (cert. of experience in piano 1986, dist. sec. 1985-87), (life) Delta Omicron Profl. Music Frat., Nat. Piano Found. Mem. Ch. of Christ. Home: 11715 Hoyt St Tampa FL 33617 Office: Fla Coll 119 Glen Arven Ave Temple Terrace FL 33617

BARLEY, BARBARA ANN, accountant; b. Sewickley, Pa., June 19, 1954; d. William Stephen and Maude Adel (Wilt) B. BS in Math., BA in Bus. magna cum laude, Westminster Coll., 1976. CPA, Ohio, Wis. Staff acct. Price Waterhouse & Co., Pitts., 1976-78; internal auditor Federated Dept. Stores, Inc., Cin., 1978-79; gen. ledger mgr. Formica Corp., Cin., 1980-81; staff acct. Bethesda Hosp., Cin., 1981-82; acctg. mgr. Madison Area Assn. for Retarded Citizens Devel. Ctrs. Corp., Madison, Wis., 1982-88; dir. fin. Retardation Facilities Devel. Found., Inc., Madison, 1988—. Treas. Access to Community Services, Inc., 1988—; mem. Environ Def. Fund, 1986—; treas. Peace Project Inc., Madison, 1985—; coms. Wis. Nuclear Weapons Freeze Campaign, Madison, 1985-86, Madison nuclear free zone com., Madison, 1986. Mem. Am. Inst. CPAs, Amnesty Internat., ACLU, Sierra Club, Kappa Mu Epsilon, Omicron Delta Epsilon, Delta Sigma Rho-Tau Kappa Alpha, Omicron Delta Kappa. Unitarian. Home: 186 Dixon St Madison WI 53704 Office: Retardation Facilities Devel Found Inc 2875 Fish Hatchery Rd Madison WI 53713

BARLEY, KATHRYN MYERS, infosystems specialist; b. Miami, Fla., June 3, 1954; d. Ashby Milton and Betty Ruth (Burke) Myers; m. Steven L. Barley, June 25, 1983; 1 child, Bryan Steven. BS in Maths. and Computer Sci., Coll. of William and Mary, 1976. From computer programmer to sr. systems analyst Va. Dept. Social Services, Richmond, 1976-81; data base analyst Best Products Co., Inc., Richmond, 1981-83, supr. data adminstrn., 1983, mgr. data adminstrn., 1983-85, mgr. info. ctr. and data adminstrn., 1985—; mem. adv. bd. ComputerWorld, Framingham, Mass., 1986—; mem. corp. adv. panel for PC Week mag. Mem. Assn. Systems Mgmt., Va. Info. Ctr. Exchange, Delta Omicron. Episcopalian. Office: Best Products Co Inc PO Box 26303 Richmond VA 23260

BARLIN, CAROLE ARLENE, educational administrator; b. Oakland, Calif., Nov. 7, 1935; d. Carl Christian and Leona Lillian (Vielhauer) Barlin; BA, U. Calif., Berkeley, 1958; MS, U. Redlands, 1971; 1 dau., Lizette Leona Swanson. Tchr., San Francisco Unified Sch. Dist., 1966-69, Los Angeles County Supt. Schs., 1971-74, asst. prin., 1974-76, prin., 1976, personnel coordinator, 1976—; lectr.: The Profl. Woman. Mem. Am. Assn. Personnel Adminstrs., Assn. of Calif. Sch. Adminstrs. (officer 1976-86), Assn. of Los Angeles County Sch. Adminstrs. (pres. 1981-82), Women in Ednl. Leadership, Am. Speech and Hearing Assn. Office: 9300 E Imperial Hwy Downey CA 90242

BARLOW, ANNE LOUISE, pediatrician, medical research administrator; b. Skipton-in-Craven, Eng., Jan. 28, 1925; came to U.S., 1951, naturalized, 1954; m. Howard Cadwell, May 19, 1951; children: Barbara Anne, John James Stewart; m. Alastair Ramsay, Dec. 19, 1969. M.B., B.S., London (Royal Free Hosp.) Sch. Medicine for Women, U. London, 1948; diploma in child health, Royal Colls. Eng., 1950; M.P.H. with honors, Yale U., 1952. House physician North Lonsdale Hosp., Barrow-in-Furness, Lancashire, Eng., 1948-49; house surgeon Royal Infirmary (Glasgow), Scotland, 1949; resident to profl. unit of child health Royal Hosp. for Sick Children, Glasgow, 1949-50; jr. hosp. med. officer Knightswood Infectious Diseases Hosp., Glasgow, 1950; Rotary Found. Internat. fellow U. Toronto Med. Sch., Ont., Can., 1950-51; research asst. Yale U. Sch. Pub. Health, New Haven, 1952-53; clinic physician in cancer prevention Arlington, Va., part-time 1953-54; resident, staff physician William H. Maybury Tb Sanatorium, Northville, Mich., 1954-56; research dir. Detroit Feeding Study with the Detroit City Health Dept., 1954-56; research asst., instr. sch. health U. Pitts. Grad. Sch. Pub. Health, 1957-62; pvt. practice medicine, specializing in pediatrics Pitts., 1959-62; mem. courtesy staff St. Margaret Hosp., Pitts., 1959-62; research assoc. Tice Lab for Tb research, Cook County Hosp., Chgo., Ill., 1962; med. writer product info. Abbott Labs., North Chicago, Ill., 1963-66, med. specialist antibiotic medicine, 1966-68; mgr. clin. devel. pharm. products div. Abbott Lab., North Chicago, Ill., 1968-71, asst. med. dir., 1971-72, mgr. parenteral nutrition hosp. products div., 1972-73, med. dir., 1973-80, v.p. med. affairs hosp. products div., 1980-84; pres. Albamed, Inc., 1985—; asst. clin. prof. Med.Coll. Pa., 1988; cons. maternal, child and sch. health, dir. well baby clinic Lake County (Ill.) Health Dept., 1963-76; pres. Tb Sanatorium Bd. Lake County Health Dept., Ill., 1976-79; dir., pres. Lake County Bd. Health, 1979-82; health officer Village of North Barrington, Ill., 1964-67; physician-adviser Head Start Lake County Community Action Project, 1970-84; chmn. profl. adv. com. Lake County Health Dept., 1972-84; preceptor Pediatric Nurse Assoc. Program. Contbr. articles on maternal and infant care, pediatrics and nutrition; patentee high calorie solution of low molecular weight glucose polymer mixtures useful for intravenouse adminstrn. Bd. dirs. Heart Assn. of Lake County, 1979-84, chmn. nutrition com., 1980-82, v.p., 1982-83, pres., 1983-84; mem. sch. bd. Grant Twp. Community High Sch. (Ill. Dist. 124), 1973-79; sec. to governing bd. Spl. Edn. Dist. of Lake County, 1977-79; assoc. Nat. Coll. Edn., Evanston, Ill., 1976-84; chmn. Am. Women's Hosp. Service, 1984—; Charlotte Danstron award for excellence Women in Mgmt., 1984. Recipient award of merit for outstanding contns. to pub. health Ill. Pub. Health Assn., 1975; recipient award of merit for outstanding community service to Lake County Community Action Project, 1976, award for outstanding and dedicated service as pres. Lake County Tb Sanatorium Bd., 1979; TWIN award YWCA, 1983. Mem. Am. Med. Women's Assn. (councilor for orgn. and mgmt. 1977-79, treas. 1980, 1st v.p. 1981, pres. 1983), Med. Women's Internat. Assn. (corr. sec.), Montgomery County Med. Assn., Pa. Med. Soc., AMA, AAAS, NOW, LWV, Sigma Xi. Home and office: 856 Grove Ave Flourtown PA 19031

BARNA, JULIE ANN, dentist, consultant; b. Freeland, Pa., Aug. 23, 1954; d. Edmund Michael and Genevieve Mary (Waskanin) B. BS, Pa. State U., 1976; DMD, U. Pa., 1980. Resident in dentistry U. Pa., Phila., 1981; dentist Dental Health Assocs., Milton, Pa., 1981-83, Century Dental, King of Prussia, Pa., 1983-84; pvt. practice dentistry Lewisburg, Pa., 1984—; cons. dentist Pa. Blue Shield, Camp Hill, 1983—; staff dentist Evangelical Community Hosp., Lewisburg, 1984—. Author, actress ednl. TV program The Haunted Mouth, 1987. Fellow Acad. Gen. Dentistry; mem. Tri County Dental Soc. (chmn. oral cancer screening program 1983, pres. 1985—), Alpha Gamma Delta (award 1976), Psi Omega (award 1980). Republican. ROman Catholic. Home: 314 Market St Lewisburg PA 17837 Office: 222 JPM Rd Lewisburg PA 17837

BARNARD, DOROTHY GASKILL, retired church moderator, religious organization administrator; b. St. Louis, Feb. 28, 1925; d. John Edward and Lucille Anna (Zerweck) Gaskill; m. Eugene R. Barnard, June 10, 1948; children: Susan, Lynn, Cynthia. BS in Edn., Washington U., 1946, AB magna cum laude, 1946; DD (hon.), Westminster Coll., 1982. Ordained elder Presbyn. Ch., 1975. Chairperson Bd. of Women's Work, Presbyn. Ch. U.S., Atlanta, 1969-71; vice-chairperson Gen. Exec. Bd., Presbyn. Ch. U.S., Atlanta, 1972-74; v.p. Ch. Women United, N.Y.C., 1978-81; moderator Gen. Assembly Presbyn. Ch. U.S., Atlanta, 1981-82; trustee Gen. Commn. on Unity and Interreligious Concerns, United Meth. Ch., N.Y., 1985—; co-chmn. Strategy Commn., Consultation on Ch. Unity, Princeton, N.J, 1983; vice-chmn., trustee Presbyn. Sch. of Christian Edn., Richmond, Va., 1983—; chair bd. trustees Presbyn. Children's Services, Farmington, Mo., 1986—. Author: Devotionals for Women, 1966; contbr. articles on ecumenism, women's issues, internat. missions. Trustee St. Luke's Hosp., St. Louis, 1987. Recipient Valiant Woman award Ch. Women United, St. Louis, N.Y.C., 1982. Mem. Phi Beta Kappa, Kappa Delta Pi, Pi Beta Phi (v.p. 1945-46). Home: 2410 Fairoyal Dr Saint Louis MO 63131

BARNARD, ELLEN REBECCA, personnel director, banker; b. Charlotte, N.C., June 4, 1954; d. Irvin Sutherland and Nancy Rives (Butterworth) B. BS, Va. Poly. Inst. and State U., 1976; postgrad., U. Tenn., 1976-77. Employment coordinator Richmond (Va.) Meml. Hosp., 1978-80; employment mgr., personnel officer United Va. Bank, Richmond, 1980-84; v.p., mgr. regional personnel Crestar Fin. Corp. (formerly United Va. Bank), Richmond, 1984—. Bd. dirs. Nat. Tobacco Festival, Richmond, 1979-85. Mem. Am. Soc. Personnel Adminstrs., Richmond Jaycees, Va. Poly Inst. Alumni (bd. dirs. Richmond chpt. 1979-83). Episcopalian. Office: Crestar Fin Corp PO Box 26150 Richmond VA 23235

BARNARD, KATHLEEN RAINWATER, educator; b. Wayne City, Ill., Dec. 28, 1927; d. Roy and Nina (Edmison) Rainwater; B.S., So. Ill. U., 1949, M.S., 1953; postgrad. Ind. U., 1953; Ph.D., U. Tex., 1959; m. Donald L. Barnard, Aug. 17, 1947 (div. Mar. 1973); children—Kimberly, Jill. Tchr. pub. high sch., Wayne City, Ill., 1946-51; faculty asst., lectr. Vocat. Tech. Inst., So. Ill. U., Carbondale, 1951-53; lectr. bus. edn. Northwestern U., Chgo., 1953-55; chmn. dept. bus. adminstrn. San Antonio Coll., 1955-60; chmn. dept. bus. edn. DePaul U., Chgo., 1960-62; chmn. dept. bus. Loop Coll. (noe Harold Washington Coll.), City Colls. Chgo., 1962-67, prof., 1968—, exec. sec., bd. dirs. credit union, 1975-78; cons., evaluator Ill. Program for Gifted Children, State Demonstrator Center, Oak Park (Ill.) Pub. Schs.; cons. First Nat. Bank Chgo., 1974; ednl. cons. Ency. Brit., 1969. Cons. edn. and tng. div. Continental Ill. Nat. Bank & Trust Co., Chgo., 1967, Victor Corp., 1965—; cons. IBM, Inc., summer 1968. Mem. North Central Bus. Edn. Assn., Nat. Bus. Edn. Assn., Chgo. Assn. Commerce and Industry, Delta Kappa Gamma, Pi Omega Pi, Alpha Delta Pi (sponsor), Sigma Phi (sponsor), Delta Pi Epsilon (pres. Alpha Theta chpt. 1958). Contbg. author: College Typewriting, 1960; Business Correspondence, 1962. Home: 920 Courtland Ave Park Ridge IL 60068 Office: 30 E Lake St Chicago IL 60601

BARNARD, KATHRYN ELAINE, nursing educator, researcher; b. Omaha, Apr. 16, 1938; d. Paul and Elsa Elizabeth (Anderson) B. B.S. in Nursing, U. Nebr.-Omaha, 1960; M.S. in Nursing, Boston U., 1962; Ph.D., U. Wash., Seattle, 1972. Acting instr. U. Nebr.-Omaha, 1960-61; acting instr. U. Wash., Seattle, 1963-65, asst. prof., 1965-69, prof. nursing, 1972—; bd. dirs. Nat. Ctr. for Clin. Infant Programs, Washington, 1980—. Chmn. research com. Bur. of Community Health Services, MCH, 1987—. Recipient Lucille Petry award Nat. League for Nursing, 1968, Martha Mae Eliot award Am. Assn. Pub. Health, 1983, Professorship award U. Wash., 1985. Fellow Am. Acad. Nursing (bd. dirs. 1980-82); mem. Inst. Medicine; mem. Am. Nurses Assn. (chmn. com. 1980-82, Jessie Scott award 1982, Nurse of Yr. award 1984), Soc. Research in Child Devel. (bd. dirs. 1981-87), Sigma Theta Tau (founders award in research 1987). Democrat. Presbyterian. Home: 11508 Durland Ave NE Seattle WA 98125 Office: U Wash Mailstop WJ-10 Seattle WA 98195

BARNDT, JANE NILES, educator; b. Elkland, Pa., June 13, 1926; d. Homer Fred and Mamie E. (Spencer) Niles; B.S. in Bus. Edn., Bloomsburg (Pa.) State Coll., 1948; m. E. Ralph Barndt, Aug. 1956; 1 son, Fred S. Tchr. bus. Quakertown Community Sch. Dist. (PA), 1961—, coordinator dept. 1977—, area coordinator, 1980—; operator employment service for bus. students, Quakertown; mem. Pa. Adv. Council Bus. Edn., 1980—. Tchr. nursery sch. United Ch. of Christ, Perkasie, Pa., 8 yrs. Mem. Nat. Fedn. Bus. and Profl. Women's Clubs (pres. Pa. fedn. 1978-80), NEA, Nat. Bus. Edn. Assn., Pa. Ednl. Assn., Eastern Bus. Edn. Assn., Quakertown Community Ednl. Assn., Bucks County Bus. Edn. Assn. (past pres.). Republican. Nat. adv. bd. Today's Sec. mag. Home: 25 Meade St Wellsboro PA 16901

BARNEBEE, ELIZABETH ANN, accountant; b. Flint, Mich., July 25, 1949; d. Irving James and Onalee Delores (Pratt) Soderlund; m. Richard Dale Barnebee, May 23, 1980. Cert. in Secretarial Sci., Northwood Inst., Midland, Mich., 1968, BBA, 1987; AA, Baker Coll., Flint, Mich., 1984; postgrad., Northwood Inst., Flint, Mich. Sr. sec. Consumers Power Co., Flint, Mich., 1968-81, supr. adminstn. services, 1981-85, supr. support services, 1985-86, acctg. supr., 1986-87, gen. acct., 1987; region adminstrv. services supr. Consumers Power Co., Flint, 1987—; mem. Secretarial Word Processing Bd. Baker Coll., Flint, 1986—. Named Boss of Yr. Ad-A-Lite chpt. Am. Bus. Women's Assn. , 1984. Mem. Profl. Secretaries Internat. Presbyterian. Club: Toastmasters (v.p. edn. Flint chpt. 1984-85, pres. 1985-86, sec. 1986—). Office: Consumers Power Co 3201 E Court St Flint MI 48501

BARNES, ANNE LISBETH (BETSY), small business owner; b. Springfield, Ill., May 3, 1946. BA in Spanish Lit., Washington Coll., 1968; MA in Spanish Lit., Case Western Res. U., 1976; MA in Librarianship, U. Denver, 1979. Grad. asst. Case Western Res. U., Cleve., 1968-72, sec., 1972-78; law librarian Schmnidt, Elrod and Wills, Denver, 1981-83; prin. Corp. Library Maintenance Service, Denver, 1983—; v.p. Colo. Consortium Law Libraries, Denver, 1982. One person art exhbn. Foothills Art Ctr., 1986. Mem. Foothills Art Ctr., 1983—. Home and Office: 945 Ogden Apt 401 Denver CO 80218

BARNES, BARBARA JEAN, manufacturing company executive; b. Milw., Jan. 25, 1945; d. Edward August and Gertrude Barbara (Hacker) Treder; m. Michael Alan Barnes, Aug. 19, 1967. B.S. in Edn., Ill. State U., 1968; postgrad. North Hennepin Community Coll., 1976-83. Tchr. pub. high schs., Central Ill., 1968-70; asst. corp. prodn. inventory control supr. Valspar Corp., Mpls., 1972-78; corp. prodn. inventory control mgr. I-Mark Inc., Mpls., 1979; prodn. control mgr. Gage Tool, Mpls., 1980; materials mgr. Delta Systems, Mpls., 1981; purchasing mgr. Resistance Tech. Inc., St. Paul, 1982-84; materials mgr. Despatch Industries, 1985—. Tutor, ESL, Hennepin County, Minn., 1980-87. Mem. Twin Cities Purchasing Mgrs. Assn., Am. Prodn. and Inventory Control. Soc. Club: Wayzata Yacht. Home: 15230 47th Ave N Plymouth MN 55446 Office: Despatch Industries 619 SE 8th St Minneapolis MN 55414

BARNES, CANDACE RAY, retail company executive; b. Kodiak, Alaska, Oct. 23, 1952; d. Marion Carlyle Welch and Virginia (Caldwell) Steineker; m. William L. Barnes, Oct. 8, 1972 (div. July 1979); children—Chadwick W., Kelly C. Student U. Louisville. with Casual Corner, 1972, J. Riggings, Mentor, Ohio, 1972-76; nat. supr. Dan Howard Industries, Chgo., 1979-87; midwest regional mgr. Mondi Internat., Northbrook, Ill., 1987, gen. mgr. Spiegler's Dept. Store 1987—. Avocations: tennis, baseball; needlepoint.

BARNES, CHERYL JO, developer/builder, design consultant; b. Los Angeles, Nov. 12, 1951; d. Joseph Perilli and Edna Mae (Robuck) Fleckenstein; m. Ronald Walter Lindhart, Aug. 14, 1970 (div. 1972); 1 child, Bridget Marie. Grad. high sch., Westminster, Calif. Manual rater Allstate Ins., Santa Ann, Calif., 1972-73; owner Red Barnes Aviation, Carlsbad, Calif., 1974-78; design cons. Sears, Roebuck & Co., San Diego, 1978-84, Design for Living, San Diego, 1984-85; mgr. New Homes Interios, San Diego, 1985-87; owner Southwind Enterprises, Carlsbad, 1987—.

BARNES, CONSTANCE INGALLS (MRS. RUSSELL C. BARNES), retired librarian; b. Atchison, Kans., July 30, 1903; d. Sheffield and Lucy (Van Hoesen) Ingalls; B.A., U. Kans., 1925; M.A., U. Mich., 1950, M.A. in L.S., 1955; postgrad. Ecole du Louvre, France, 1960, Vergilian Soc., Cumae, Italy, summer 1963; m. Russell C. Barnes, Oct. 1, 1927; children—Lucie-Jeanne (Mrs. Todd Seymour), John J.I. Librarian, Cranbrook Acad. Art, Bloomfield Hills, Mich., 1955-74, 80-81. Mem. LWV, AAUW, Internat. Arthurian Soc., Alliance Francaise, Founders Soc. Detroit Inst. Arts, Kappa Alpha Theta. Club: Village Woman's (Bloomfield Hills). Home: 788 Randall Ct Birmingham MI 48009

BARNES, CYNTHIA ALEE, nurse administrator, educator; b. Chgo., July 8, 1952; d. John and Bobbie Jean Barnes. Diploma Wesley Meml. Hosp., Chgo., 1973; B.S. in Nursing, U. Ill., 1975, M.S., 1979, doctoral candidate, 1982—. Mem. nursing staff U. Ill. Hosps., Chgo., 1973-76, head nurse, 1977-78, asst. dir. nursing, 1980—, asst. prof., 1981—; clin. nurse specialist critical care U. Chgo. Hosps., 1978; dir. nursing edn. Neonatal and Pediatric Services, Inc., 1978—. Mem. editorial bd. Neonatal Network. Contbr. articles to profl. jours. Recipient Bronze award Am. Acad. Pediatrics. Mem. Am. Assn. Critical Care Nurses, Soc. Critical Care Medicine, Am. Nurses Assn., Assn. Care Children in Hosps., Sigma Theta Tau. Democrat. Lutheran.

Home: 1411 E 49th St Chicago IL 60615 Office: 1740 W Taylor St Suite 1500 Chicago IL 60620

BARNES, CYNTHIA ANN, academic program director; b. Chgo., July 6, 1949; d. Theadore Thomas and Mary Antoinette (Pulliam) Drew; m. Martin Barnes, Nov. 25, 1972; 1 child, T. Martin II. BA, U. Ill., Chgo., 1970; MAT, Northwestern U., Evanston, Ill., 1971. Cert. tchr., Ill. Tchr. Chgo. Pub. Schs., 1970-73; instr. Predischarge Edn. Program, Kaiserslautern, Fed. Republic of Germany, 1973-74, ednl. advisor, 1974-77; tchr. learning disabilities Morgan Learning Ctr., Denver, 1981-82; adj. faculty English dept. Aurora (Colo.) Community Coll., 1982—, faculty devel. specialist, 1983-84, faculty rep., 1986-87, grant adminstr., 1987—; cons., owner, bus. writer Write On, Denver, 1984—; facilitator adult basic skills Denver Tech. Coll., 1986-87. Editor: Language Arts Newsletter, 1975-77; author bus. column, 1985; contbr. articles to profl. publs. Mem. Montbello Task Force, Denver, 1987. Club: Portfolio West Investment (Denver) (rec. ptnr. 1985—). Office: Write On PO Box 9653 Denver CO 80209

BARNES, DALPHNA RUTH, nurse; b. Lamesa, Tex., May 11, 1933; d. Raymond Vernon and Hazel Blanche (Lemons) Boatright; m. Alvin Burwell Barnes, Jan. 18, 1958; children: David Lynn, Jeanne Michele Barnes O'Neal. AA in Nursing, Texarkana Coll., 1966; BA in Psychology, U. Houston, 1974. Office nurse, 1966; staff nurse Little York Hosp., Houston, 1967-68, Belhaven Psychiat. Hosp., Houston, 1968; intensive care nurse Hermann Hosp., Houston, 1968-69; office nurse, therapist, 1969; from staff nurse to infection control nurse Parkway Hosp., Houston, 1970-77; infection control, employee health coordinator Houston N.W. Med. Ctr., 1977-86, patient advocate, 1986—; adv. bd. Houston Hospice, 1980-82, bd. dirs., 1982-84; meml. chmn. North Harris unit Am. Cancer Soc., 1979, v.p., 1980-81, founder, facilitator Cancer Interaction Group, 1978—, cons. death and dying, dialogue facilitator coach, Tex. div., 1985—. Served with USN, 1957-58. Recipient Sword of Hope award North Harris chpt. Am. Cancer Soc., 1980, 81, 82, 83. Mem. Assn. Practitioners Infection Control (pres. Houston chpt. 1980-81), Tex. Soc. Infection Control Practitioners (William L. Benson Meml. award 1980), Am. Soc. Profl. and Exec. Women, Tex. Soc. Patient Reps., Poets N.W., Poetry Soc. Tex. Club: Toastmasters (pres. Frankly Speaking Chpt. 1986, edn. v.p. 1987). Home: 20319 Belleau Wood Dr Humble TX 77338 Office: 710 FM 1960 West Houston TX 77090

BARNES, HELEN CROSS, banker; b. Portsmouth, Va., Mar. 26, 1945; d. Robert Lee and Frances Phyllis (Motley) Cross; m. L. Gary Barnes, Aug. 10, 1968. BA in Math., Westhampton Coll. of U. Richmond, 1967; spl. courses Am. Inst. Banking, Md. Bankers Sch. of U. Md. Tchr., York County Schs. (Va.), 1967-71; internal cons. Equitable Bank N.A., Balt., 1971-78, project mgr., 1978-82, v.p., dir. bank services, 1982—. Bd. dirs. exec. com., v.p. programs, corp. sec. Jr. Achievement Met. Balt., 1982—; mem. exec. bd., employment steering com., info. processing tng. ctr. steering com., asst. sec. Balt. Urban League, Inc., 1985—. Mem. Assn. Internal Mgmt. Cons., Assn. Info. Systems Profls., Office Tech. Mgmt. Assn., Am. Soc. Performance Improvement. Recipient Bronze Leadership award Nat. Bd. Dirs. Jr. Achievement, Inc. Republican. Methodist. Club: Argyle County (Silver Spring, Md.). Office: Equitable Bank NA 100 S Charles St Baltimore MD 21201

BARNES, IRISH ROSE, medical facility administrator; b. Pt. Norris, N.J., Jan. 3, 1952; d. Ernest Ralph and Nancy Mildred (Smith) B.; 1 child, Kowana Claresse. BA, Rutgers U., 1974; postgrad., Calif. State U., Hayward, 1978-79, U. Calif., Berkeley, 1977-78. Lab. aide W. Oakland (Calif.) Health Ctr., 1978, med. tech. trainee, 1978-79, med. tech., 1979, teaching coordinator, 1981-84, adminstrv. tech., 1985—; sr. tech. Alameda (Calif.) Hosp., 1981-84. Mem. Am. Med. Soc., Calif. Soc. Med. Techs., Adminstrv. Techs. Assn. Democrat. Baptist. Home: 3128 Jo Ann Dr Richmond CA 94806 Office: West Oakland Health Ctr 700 Adeline St Oakland CA 94607

BARNES, ISABEL JANET, microbiology educator, college dean; b. Union City, N.J., Sept. 22, 1936; d. Carl Robert and Isabel Sarah (Cappelletti) B.; m. John D. Bowman, June 15, 1978 (dec. Nov. 1986). BS, Pa. State U., 1958; MS, Cornell U., 1960; PhD, Hahnemann Med. Coll., 1969. Asst. prof. microbiology Hershey Med. Ctr., Pa. State U., 1968-73; asst. prof., then assoc. prof. Sangamon State U., Springfield, Ill., 1973-76; assoc. prof. med. tech. U. Wis., Madison, 1976-85, interim dean Sch. Allied Health Professions, 1981-84; prof. med. tech. Ferris State Univ., Big Rapids, Mich., 1985—, dean Sch. Allied Health, 1985—. Mem. AAAS, AAUP, Am. Soc. Med. Technologists, Am. Soc. Allied Health Profls. Office: Ferris State Univ Sch of Allied Health Big Rapids MI 49307

BARNES, JANE ELLEN, writer, poet; b. Bklyn., Dec. 29, 1943; d. Martin Stephens and Barbara Jane (Krancher) B. Student, Lewis-Clark State Coll., Portland, Oreg., 1961-62, San Francisco State U., 1962-63; BA in Russian and Spanish, Ga. State U., 1966; MA in English, Boston U., 1978. Tech. writer Honeywell Corp. at MIT, Cambridge, 1966-72; poet and novelist Cambridge, 1966—; editor, pub. Dark Horse, Cambridge, 1974-80, Quark Press, Cambridge, 1976—; creative writing tchr., cons. Cambridge, 1977—; editor, pub. Blue Giant Press, Boston, 1981—; tchr., literary mag. advisor The Pilot Sch., Cambridge, 1976; tchr. pub., fiction Boston Ctr. for Adult Edn., 1976, 1988; tchr. writing Somerville (Mass.) Community Schs., 1979, Boston U., 1980; bd. dirs. Boston Book Affair, Cambridge, 1976, First Night Celebration, Boston, 1981. Author: (poetry) Mythologies, 1976, They Say I Talk in My Sleep, 1979, Extremes, 1981; interviewee Sta. WGBH-TV Poet's Corner, 1984; work featured in granite at subway sta., Boston, 1988 (Urban Arts prize); contbr. poetry and fiction to literary mags., articles and revs. to profl. publs. Recipient Syndicated Fiction award PEN, 1988. Home and Office: 24 Concord Ave Apt 308 Cambridge MA 02138

BARNES, JEAN ELEANOR, travel agency manager, consultant; b. Appleton, Wis., June 27, 1960; d. Paul Peter and Donna Mae (Meulemans) Uitenbroek; m. Erik Lee Barnes, May 25, 1984. Grad., McConnell Sch., Inc., Mpls., 1979. Sales clk. H.C. Prange Co., Appleton, Wis., 1977-78, Donaldson's Dept. Stores, Mpls., 1978; clk. Paul Uitenbroek Plastering, Appleton, 1976—; mgr., travel cons. Universal Travel Service, Inc., Appleton, 1979—. Mem. Packerland Travel Agts. Assn. (sec. 1985-88), Northeastern Wis. Women in Travel., Inst. Cert. Travel Agts. (cert. travel cons. 1986). Office: Universal Travel Service Inc 2198 S Memorial Dr Appleton WI 54915

BARNES, JEANNETTE EMILY, nurse anesthetist; b. Scranton, Pa., June 9, 1937; d. Matthew John and Jeannette (Williams) Spott; m. Willis Curtis Barnes, May 8, 1969 (div. Jan. 1980); children: Melissa, Curtis, Rebecca, Jeannette, Willis III. Diploma in nursing, Temple U., 1958; BS in Nursing Edn., Wilkes Coll., 1969; MA in Counseling, Marywood Coll., Scranton, Pa., 1981. RN; cert. registered nurse anesthetist; nat. cert. counselor. Staff nurse Moses Taylor Hosp., Scranton, 1958-60; nurse anesthetist Dr. W. Waterman Clinic, Scranton, 1963-65, Comm. Med. Ctr., Scranton, 1965-69; nurse, counselor Dr. W. Barnes Clinic, Clarks Summit, Pa., 1969-79; nurse anesthetist, counselor Mercy Hosp., Scranton, 1980—; pvt. practice counselor Caring Counseling Services, Scranton, 1980—; v.p., sec., owner M.J. Spott Constrn. Co., Inc., Scranton, 1978—; student counselor Mercy Hosp. Sch. Anesthesia, Scranton, 1980—. Mem. Am. Assn. Nurse Anesthetists (Agatha Hogdins award, 1965), Am. Bd. Cert. Counselors, Pa. Counselors Assn. Home and Office: 526 N Garfield Ave Scranton PA 18504

BARNES, JHANE ELIZABETH, fashion design company executive, designer; b. Balt., Mar. 4, 1954; d. Richard Amos and Muriel Florence (Chase) B.; m. Howard Ralph Feinberg, Dec. 12, 1981. A.S., Fashion Inst. Tech., 1975. Pres., designer Jhane Barnes for ME, N.Y.C., 1976-78, Jhane Barnes Inc., N.Y.C., 1978—. Recipient Menswear award Coty Am. Fashion Critics, 1980, Contract Textile award Am. Soc. Interior Designers, 1983, 84, Product Design award Inst. Bus. Designers and Contract Mag., 1983, 84, 85, 86; named Most Promising Designer Cutty Sark, 1980, Outstanding Designer, 1982; Outstanding Menswear Designer, Council of Fashion Designers Am., 1982. Office: Jhane Barnes Inc 167 Madison Ave New York NY 10016

BARNES, JO ANN, university administrator; b. Marengo, Iowa, June 21, 1935; d. Joseph William and Minnie Ellen (Henderson) B.; m. Dion Morse Markle, Nov. 26, 1954 (div. Mar. 1970). Clerical positions various cities, 1952-67; sec. med. adminstrn. U. Iowa, Iowa City, 1967-74, office coordinator dept. anatomy, 1974-75, editorial assoc., 1975—; Layout designer Capitol News, 1986-87, Iowa City Traditional Song Soc. newsletter, 1987. Mem. Am. Bus. Women's Assn. (sec. 1968-69, v.p. 1969-70, treas. 1979-80, pres. 1980-81, chmn. pub. relations com. 1987, Woman of Yr. 1983). Democrat. Office: The U Iowa Dept of Anatomy BSB Iowa City IA 52242

BARNES, JUDITH TUCKER, corporate communications specialist; b. Evansivlle, Ind., Aug. 24, 1951; d. Thomas Edison and Dorothy (Watson) Tucker; m. David Lester Barnes; 1 stepchild, Shelley D. Student, Hardbarger Coll., 1971-72. Mgr. S&K Famous Foods, Richmond, Va., 1974-78; mktg. rep. Carolina Tel & Tel, Rocky Mount, N.C., 1979-85. Pres. Only In Am. Investment Club, Rocky Mount, 1986-87. Mem. N.C. Telecommunications Assn. (publicity chairperson). Democrat. Methodist. Office: Peoples Bank and Trust Co 130 S Franklin St Rocky Mount NC 27801

BARNES, JULIA O'TEALA, military career officer, healthcare administrator; b. Henderson, N.C., May 13, 1937; d. Bolton Barnes and Annie (Sims) Harris. Diploma, Hahnemann Hosp. Sch. Nursing, 1957; BSN, U. Pa., 1972; MA in Health Resources Mgmt., Pepperdine U., 1978. RN, Pa. Commd. ensign USN, 1958, advanced through grades to capt., 1980; nurse operating room Hahnemann Hosp., Phila., 1957-58; nurse staff operating room Naval Hosp., Oakland Hosp., Calif., 1958-62; supr. operating room Naval Hosp., Guam, Mariana Islands, 1963-64, Great Lakes, 1964-66, Phila., 1966-70; clin. supr. Naval Hosp., 1972-74; chief nurse Naval Hosp., Guam, 1975-76; dir. nursing Naval Hosp., Lemoore, Calif., 1976-85; exec. officer Naval Hosp., Camp LeJeune, Calif., 1985-86; comdg. officer Naval Hosp., Great Lakes, 1986—. Bd. dirs. Urban League, Lake County, Ill., 1980-83, Great Lakes Credit Union, 1986—; mem. Waukegan Symphony Chorus; mem. Great Lakes Credit Union Bd. Dirs. Mem. Nat. Naval Officers Assn. (regional v.p. 1977-79). Democrat. Lodge: Rotary. Home and Office: Naval Hosp Qtrs 202 H Great Lakes IL 60088

BARNES, KATE MILLER, data processing executive; b. Perry, Iowa, Sept. 30, 1953; d. Virgil A. and Cheryl J. (Luellen) Miller; m. Howard A. Barnes, July 21, 1974. BA with honors, U. Iowa, 1975; MBA, U. Phoenix, 1983. Assoc. dir. Dept. Adult Corrections, Cedar Rapids, Iowa, 1973-79; product mgr. DELTAK, Inc., Naperville, Ill., 1979-81; v.p. Barnes Assocs. Systems, Inc., Tucson, 1981-88; pres. Kate Barnes & Assocs Inc., Tempe, Ariz., 1988—; founder, chairperson Dept. Adult Corrections Adv., 1987, Bus. Tech. Expo, Tucson, 1985-86. Author: Using Multimate, 1985 (Best Selling Author award 1986); contbg. editor, columnist PC Week, 1985-86; contbr. articles to profl. jours. Mem. adv. bd. Kirkwood Community Coll., Cedar Rapids, 1977; mem. Citizens Com. on Alcohol, Cedar Rapids, 1978; sec., treas. Houghton Neighborhood Com., Tucson, 1986. Mem. Data Processing Mgrs. Assn. (chairperson edn. 1986-87), Nat. Assn. Women Bus. Owners. Republican. Office: Kate Barnes & Assocs Inc 1414 W Broadway Suite 150 Tempe AZ 85282

BARNES, LILLIAN SIGRID, escrow officer; b. Point Roberts, Wash., Aug. 9, 1930; d. Dui Marino and Elin (Myrdal) Edvalds Andreas; m. Robert Eric Barnes, Nov. 14, 1953 (div. May 1973); children—Elisabeth Darby Britt, Eric Albert, Thomas Arni; m. Claude Joseph Hinds, Dec. 8, 1979. Student Stanford U., 1949-51. Asst. chief stewardess Pacific No. Airlines, Anchorage, 1951-53; legal sec. Richard Nelle Blaine, Wash., 1966-75; escrow officer, pres., Blaine Escrow Inc., 1975—, also bd. dirs. Contbg. author: The Old Fir Tree, 1984. Sec., Blaine Bicentennial Com., 1973-76; mem. N.W. Park and Recreation Dist. Commn., 1980-85. Recipient Disting. Service award Blaine Jaycees, 1974. Mem. Am. Escrow Assn., Escrow Assn. Wash., North Puget Sound Escrow Assn., Blaine C. of C. (sec. 1972-76, Woman of Yr. Westside Record Jour. 1985), PEO. Roman Catholic. Avocations: sailing, painting, antique collecting, gardening, writing. Office: Blaine Escrow Inc 245 Marine Dr Suite B Blaine WA 98230

BARNES, MAGGIE LUE SHIFFLETT (MRS. LAWRENCE BARNES), nurse; b. nr. Spur, Tex., Mar. 29, 1931; d. Howard Eldridge and Sadie Adilene (Dunlap) Shifflett; student Cogdell Sch. Nursing, 1959-60; Western Tex. Coll., 1972-76, grad. Meth. Hosp. Sch. Nursing, Lubbock, Tex., 1975; B.S. in Nursing, W. Tex. State U., 1977; m. T.C. Fagan, Jan. 1950 (dec. Feb. 1952); 1 son, Lawayne L.; m. 2d, Lawrence Barnes, Sept. 2, 1960. Floor nurse D.M. Cogdell Meml. Hosp., Snyder, Tex., 1960-64, medication nurse, 1964-76, asst. evening supr., 1976-78, charge nurse, after 1978, evening nursing supr., until 1980; nursing supr. Scurry, Borden, Mitchel, Fisher, Howard Counties, West Central Home Health Agy., Snyder, 1980-83; emergency room evening supr. Root-Meml. Hosp., 1983, 84—; regional coordinator home health services Beverly Enterprises, 1983. Den mother Cub Scouts Am., Holliday, Tex., 1960-61; mem. PTA, Snyder, Tex., 1960-69; adv. Sr. Citizens Assn.; mem. Tri-Region Health Systems Agency, 1979—; mem. adv. bd. Scurry County Diabetes Assn., 1982—. Mem. Vocat. Nurses Assn. Tex. (mem. bd. 1963-65, div. pres. 1967-69), Emergency Dept. Nursing Assn. Apostolic Faith Ch. (sec., treas. 1956-58). Home: Route 1 Box 9B Hermleigh TX 79526

BARNES, MARGARET ANDERSON, business consultant; b. Johnston County, N.C.; m. Benjamin Barnes, Dec. 26, 1959. BS, N.C. Cen. U., 1958; MA, U. Md., 1975; PhD, Columbia Pacific U., 1986. Math. tchr. Tarboro (N.C.) Sch. System, 1959-61; math. statistician Bur. of Census, Suitland, Md., 1962-67, 69-70, Dist. of Columbia govt., 1967-68; cons. Nat. Insts. of Health, Bethesda, Md., 1970-72, chief of data standards, 1972-73; with exec. clearance office HEW, Rockville, Md., 1973-77; founder, pres. MABarnes Cons. Assoc., Lanham, Md., 1978—; commr. State of Md. Accident Fund, Balt., 1979—; mem. adv. bd. Universal Bank, Lanham, 1980-83, Interstate Gen. Corp., St. Charles, Md., 1981-83. Chairwoman Glenwood Park Civic Assn., Lanham, 1967-80. Democrat. Baptist. Home: PO Box 586 Seabrook MD 20706 Office: MABarnes Con Assocs 9332 Annapolis Rd Lanham MD 20706

BARNES, MARGARET MARIE, physician, radiation oncologist; b. Phoenixville, Pa., June 3, 1954; d. Clifford Gerald and Dorothy (Gindele) B. BS, Indiana U. of Pa., 1976; MD, Tempe U. Sch. Med., 1981. Diplomate Am. Bd. Radiology. Intern Walter Reed Army Med. Ctr., Washington, 1981-82; clin. fellow radiation oncology Nat. Cancer Inst., Bethesda, Md., 1982-85; staff radiation oncologist Walter Reed Army Med. Ctr., Washington, 1985-86; asst. chief radiation oncology Madigan Army Med. Ctr., Tacoma, Wash., 1986—; guest researcher Radiation Oncology Br. Nat. Cancer Inst., Bethesda, 1985—. Contbr. articles to profl. jours. Mem. Am. Soc. Therapeutic Radiology and Oncology, Am. Soc. Clin. Oncologists, Am. Coll. Radiology, AMA, Am. Med. Women's Assn. (Scholastic Achievement award, 1981). Roman Catholic.

BARNES, MARY DILWORTH, state ofcl.; b. Pitts., Oct. 22, 1913; d. John Crossan and Helen (Thompson) Dilworth; A.B., Vassar Coll., 1936; LL.B., U. Pitts., 1939, postgrad., 1959-60; m. Richard Langley Barnes, June 24, 1938; children—Richard D., John C., Mary B. Blair, Helen B. Vantine. Admitted to Pa. bar, 1940; pvt. practice law, Phila., 1941-42, Pitts., 1948—; with Bur. Census, U.S. Dept. Commerce, 1960; commr. Pa. Civil Service Commn., 1963-72, 76-86, chmn., 1981-86; spl. adv. to Commn. Public Opinion, 1970. Bd. dirs. Home for Aged Protestant Women, 1948; women's bd. Western Pa. Hosp., 1950; mem. Pa. Citizens Council, 1960—, Fed. Women's Prison Bd., 1963-71; liaison Nat. Inst. Aging, 1974-75; council mem. Nat. Inst. Child Health and Devel., 1970-75. Mem. Internat. Personnel Mgmt. Assn., Allegheny County Bar Assn. Republican. Presbyterian.

BARNES, MARY WESTERGAARD, chemist; b. Champaign, Ill., May 20, 1927; d. Harald Malcolm and Rachel Harriet (Talbot) Westergaard; m. Hubert Lloyd Barnes; children: Roy Malcolm, Catherine Patricia. BA, Swarthmore (Pa.) Coll., 1948; PhD, Pa. State U., 1966. Research asst. MIT, Cambridge, Mass., 1948-50; tech. asst., tech. staff assoc. Bell Telephone Labs., Murray Hill, N.J., 1952-56; chemist Nat. Bur. Standards, Washington, 1956-60; research assoc. Max Planck Inst. Für Physikalische Chemiç, Göttingen, Fed. Republic of Germany, 1967-68; research assoc. Pa. State U., University Park, Pa., 1977-80, project coordinator, 1980—. Mem. traffic commn. Borough of State College, Pa., 1980-85, chmn., mem. pedestrian commn., 1984-85. Mem. Am. Ceramic Soc., Materials Research Soc., Am. Chem. Soc., Geochem. Soc. Home: 213 E Mitchell Ave State College PA 16803 Office: Pa State U Materials Research Lab University Park PA 16802

BARNES, PHYLLIS MARIE, nurse; b. Ithaca, Mich., July 2, 1935; d. Bernard Gerald and Nilah Adelia (Kennett) Cumming; m. Bartrim James Barnes, Jan. 20, 1957; children: Matthew, Michele, Mark, Michael. RN, Hurley Hosp. Sch. of Nursing, Flint, Mich., 1956. Cert. gerontol. nurse. Staff nurse Gratiot Community Hosp., Alma, Mich., 1956-57; staff nurse, supr. Bixby Hosp., Adrian, Mich., 1957. V.p. Ithaca PTA, 1969-70. Mem. Am. Bus. Women's Assn. (corr. sec. 1979-80, recording sec. 1986-87, woman of yr. 1984-85), Child Study Club. Home: 1225 N Gould St Owosso MI 48867 Office: Shiawassee County Med Care Facility 729 S Norton St Corunna MI 48817

BARNES, TERRY ANN, federal employee; b. Albany, N.Y., Aug. 24, 1951; d. Theresa Agnes (Robitaille) B. BSBA, SUNY, Plattsburgh, 1972; MBA, U. Phoenix, 1988. Sr. aide project dir. City of Schenectady, N.Y., 1977-78; claims rep. N.Y. State Social Security Dept., Schenectady, 1978-80; revenue officer IRS, Phoenix, 1983, clk., 1983-85, teller, 1985-86, office collection, taxpayer rep., 1986—. Democrat. Catholic. Home: 607 S Daley Dr Mesa AZ 85204

BARNES, VERA LEWIS, aerospace engineer; b. Phila., Jan. 27, 1936; d. John and Anna Mae (Smith) Lewis; m. George Henry Barnes, May 4, 1972; stepchildren: George Henry, Margaret Morris. BA in Math., Temple U., 1958, MA, 1961. Logic design engr. Sperry Univac Corp., Blue Bell, Pa., 1960-65; sr. logic design engr. Burroughs Corp., Paoli, Pa., 1965-66, mgr. program systems dept., 1968-79; project mgr. Ultronics Systems Corp., Mount Laurel, N.J., 1966-68; program mgr. space systems div. Gen. Electric Corp., King of Prussia, Pa., 1979—. Patentee in field. Recipient Cert. Achievement for Outstanding Contbns. to Gen. Electric, Phila. YWCA Orgn., 1983. Democrat. Baptist.

BARNES, WINIFRED ANNE, advertising executive; b. Teaneck, N.J., Aug. 26, 1961; d. Warren Whitfield and Maryanne (Germaneso) B. From sec. to account exec. McCaffrey & McCall, Inc., N.Y.C., 1982-85, account supr., 1986, v.p., mng. supr., 1986-87, sr. v.p., 1987—. Mem. Direct Mktg. Assn., Womens' Direct Mktg. Group. Roman Catholic. Office: McCaffrey & McCall Inc 575 Lexington Ave New York NY 10022

BARNESS, CAROL JO, personnel executive; b. Phila., Aug. 18, 1954; d. Lewis Abraham and Elaine (Berger) B.; m. Jon Edward Strange, Sept. 27, 1985; 1 child, Eliot. BA, U. Pa., 1976; MS, NYU, 1980. Research assoc. Equitable Life Assurance Soc., N.Y.C., 1980-84, sr. placement cons., 1984-87; sr. placement cons. Bklyn. Union Gas Co., 1988—. Pres. 15-462 Owners Corp., Bklyn., 1985-88. Mem. Acad. Mgmt., Met. N.Y. Assn. for Applied Psychology (assoc.).

BARNETT, EILEEN HARRIET, nursery school administrator; b. East Orange, N.J., Sept. 20, 1949; d. Samuel Alexander and Sylvia (Neiblum) Klein; m. Mark Philip Barnett, June 26, 1969; children: James Louis, Robert Benjamin. Student, Cedar Crest Coll., 1967-69; BA in English, Psychology, Bloomfield Coll., 1971; cert. media specialist, Kean Coll., 1973. Real estate broker Century 21, Framingham, Mass., 1979-81; tchr. Nursery Sch. at Temple Beth Am, Framingham, 1981-84, dir., 1984—. Mem. Boston Assn. for Edn. of Young Children, Women's American Orgn. Rehab. through Tng. (chair exec. com. 1981-82, regional pres. 1982-83). Office: Nursery Sch at Temple Beth Am 300 Pleasant St Framingham MA 01701

BARNETT, ELIZABETH, foreign service officer; b. San Bernardino, Calif., May 26, 1954; d. John E., Sr., and Joan Olga (Connor) B.; B.A. summa cum laude, U. Mass., 1976; M.A. (fellow), Yale U., 1978. Fgn. service officer Dept. State, Washington, 1979—; civilian observer Multinat. Force and Observers, Sinai, 1984-85. Mem. Am. Fgn. Service Assn., Secs. Open Forum, Consular Officers Assn., Phi Beta Kappa. Clubs: Yale (N.Y.C.); Fgn. Service. Address: care Fgn Service Lounge US Dept State Washington DC 20520

BARNETT, ELIZABETH HALE, management consultant; b. Nashville, Mar. 17, 1940; d. Robert Baker and Dorothy (McCarthy) Hale; m. Crawford F. Barnett Jr., June 6, 1964; children: Crawford F. III, Robert H. BA, Vanderbilt U., 1962. Receptionist, sec. U.S. Atty. Gen. Robert F. Kennedy, Washington, 1962-64; free-lance cons. Atlanta, 1973-76; pres. E.H. Barnett & Assocs., Atlanta, 1976-83; trustee The Ga. Conservancy, Atlanta, 1978—, chmn. bd. trustees, 1986-88, also bd. dirs. Contbg. author: A New Agenda, 1982; contbr. articles to profl. jours. Bd. dirs. Jr. League of Atlanta, 1973-75; mem. Leadership Atlanta, 1976—; chmn., pres. bd. dirs. Vol. Coms. Art Mus. U.S. and Can., 1976-79; bd. dirs. The High Mus. Art, Atlanta, 1977—; chmn. bd. dirs. Met. Atlanta ARC, 1978-80, United Way of Met. Atlanta, 1981-84, mem. community adv. com. N.W. Ga. council Girl Scouts U.S., 1979-83; mem. council USO, Atlanta, 1981—; mem. bd. sponsor Atlanta Women's Network, 1982-86; v.p. Boys Sch., Parents Assn. Westminster Sch., 1985-86. Named one of Ten Outstanding Young Women of Am., 1977; honored by Ga. State Legis., Atlanta, 1978. Mem. LWV. Episcopalian. Office: The Ga Conservancy 8615 Barnwell Rd Alpharetta GA 30201

BARNETT, FLORENCE LLOYD JONES, newspaper executive. V.p. Tulsa Tribune Co. Office: Tulsa Tribune Co PO Box 1770 Tulsa OK 74102

BARNETT, JACALYN F., lawyer; b. Bklyn., Jan. 7, 1952; d. Melvin and Bette (Epstein) Fischer; m. Michael H. Barnett, June 29, 1975 (div. 1982). BA, U. Wis., 1974; JD, Bklyn. Law Sch., 1977. Assoc. Robinson, Silverman, Pearce, Aronsohn, Sand & Berman, N.Y.C., 1977-78; assoc. Hahn, Hessan, Margolis & Ryan, N.Y.C., 1978-79; ptnr. Shea & Gould, N.Y.C., 1979—; lectr. to orgns., women groups. Mem. legal task force NOW; mem. Task Force on Marriage, Divorce, Fedn. Jewish Philanthropies, N.Y.C. Office: Shea & Gould 1251 Avenue of the Americas New York NY 10020-1193

BARNETT, JANE SHELTON, marketing professional; b. Hamilton, Ohio, Sept. 4, 1950; d. Fredrick Robert II and Jewell (Wyatt) Shelton; m. Jeffrey Davis Barnett, Oct. 28, 1979; 1 child, Vanessa Lynn. BA in Communications and English, Bowling Green (Ohio) State U., 1971, MA in Interpersonal and Pub. Communication, 1977. Account exec. Creative Promotions, Cin., 1979-80; dir. market research BCC div. Hillenbrand Industries, Batesville, Ind., 1980-83; dir. mktg. Andrew Jergens Co., Cin., 1983-86; v.p. corp. planning Jergens Co., Cin., 1986—, seminar leader, 1981, chmn. mgmt. info. sci. com., 1986—. Rep. Educators Polit. Action Com., 1974-75; Dem. precinct capt., Chgo., 1978. Mem. Am. Mktg. Assn. (computer software speaker 1985—), Nat. Assn. Female Execs. Unitarian. Home: 45 Orchard Dr Hamilton OH 45013 Office: Jergens Co Spring Grove Ave Cincinnati OH 45013

BARNETT, JOANNE, nurse, health care facility administrator; b. Mineola, N.Y., June 13, 1954; d. John Joseph and Eleanor Joan (Clemens) Samuels; m. Greg John Barnett, Feb. 4, 1979; children: Kelly Lynn, Kristin Leigh. AS in Nursing, Valencia Community Coll., Orlando, Fla., 1976, AA, 1984; BS in Nursing, U. Cen. Fla., 1987. RN, Fla. Lic. practical nurse Cen. Gen. Hosp., Plainview, N.Y., 1972-73, Fla. Hosp., Altamonte Springs, Fla., 1973-76; RN Orlando Regional Med. Ctr., 1976-77, Fish Meml. Hosp., Deland, Fla., 1977—; cons. Orange Belt Pharmacy, Deland, 1985. Mem. Am. Nurses' Assn., Fla. Nurses' Assn (local dist. sec. 1986—), Gold Key Soc., Sigma Theta Tau. Republican. Roman Catholic. Home: PO Box 356 DeBary FL 32713 Office: Fish Meml Hosp PO Box 167 De Land FL 32721-0167

BARNETT, LENA SUE, lawyer; b. Washington, Apr. 23, 1959; d. Edward Martin and Vivian Charlotte (Pear) B. AB cum laude, Muhlenberg Coll., 1981; JD, U. Md., Balt., 1984. Bar: Md. Intern Md. Sixth Jud. Cir. Ct., Rockville, 1983; gen. mgr. Edward M. Barnett, DDS & Assoc., Silver Spring, Md., 1984—, Barnett Enterprises, Silver Spring, 1985—. Vol. coordinator State Sen. Denis Re-election Com., Bethesda, Md., 1986; asst. vol. coordinator Friends of Connie Murella for Congress Com., 1988. Mem. ABA, Md. State Bar Assn., Bar Assn. Montgomery County, Nat. Assn. Female

Execs., Nat. C. of C. for Women, U. Md. Law Sch. Alumni Assn., Phi Alpha Delta, Phi Alpha Theta, Pi Sigma Alpha. Republican. Jewish.

BARNETT, LORI KAREN, marketing executive; b. N.Y.C., Feb. 19, 1960; d. Solomon and Evelyn (Narun) Levine; m. Andrew Jonathan Barnett, May 6, 1984. BS cum laude, SUNY, Albany, 1981. Asst. media planner Neil Faber Media, Inc., N.Y.C., 1981-82; statis. research analyst JC Penney Co., Inc., N.Y.C., 1982-83, media project asst., 1984, market media analyst, 1985, market media specialist, 1986, project mgr. media services, 1987-88. Mem. Nat. Assn. for Female Execs.

BARNETT, LOUANN, medical technologist; b. Birmingham, Ala., Jan. 2, 1945; d. Howard and Myra Lucinda (Mize) Brickner; m. John Edward Barnett, Feb. 3, 1968. BS, Samford U., 1969, U. Ala., Birmingham, 1983. Clk. Birmingham Book and Mag., 1965-67; chief technologist Bibb County Hosp., Centerville, Ala., 1968-69; med. technologist Bapt. Med. Ctr.-Montclair, Birmingham, 1969—. Author computer program, 1984. Mem. bd. stewards Eastwood Ind. Meth. Ch., Irondale, Ala., 1985—. Mem. Am. Soc. Clin. Pathologists (cert.). Home: 533 First St Fultondale AL 35068 Office: Bapt Med Ctr 800 Montclair Rd Birmingham AL 35213

BARNETT, MARGUERITE ROSS, university chancellor; b. Charlottesville, Va., May 22, 1942; d. Dewey Ross and Mary (Douglass) Barnett; m. Stephen A. Barnett, Dec. 18, 1962 (div.); 1 child, Amy Dubois; m. Walter Eugene King, June 30, 1980. A.B. in Polit. Sci., Antioch Coll., 1964; M.A. in Polit. Sci., U. Chgo., 1966, Ph.D. in Polit. Sci., 1972. Asst. prof. Princeton U., N.J., 1970-76; prof., chmn. Howard U., Washington, 1976-80; prof. polit. sci., politics and edn. Tchrs. Coll., Columbia U., N.Y.C., 1980-83; vice chancellor CUNY, 1983-86; chancellor U. Mo., St. Louis, 1986—; bd. dirs. Overseas Devel. Council, Washington, 1977—, Union Electric, Mercantile Bank N.A., Mercantile Corp. Author: The Politics of Cultural Nationalism in South India, 1976. Editor: Education for Disadvantaged Series, 1981—. Trustee spl. contribution fund NAACP, 1979—; bd. dirs. Pub. Edn. Assn., N.Y.C., 1985—. Mem. Am. Polit. Sci. Assn. (mem. exec. council 1977-78), Council on Fgn. Relations. Office: U Mo St Louis 8001 Natural Bridge Rd Saint Louis MO 63121

BARNETT, MARILYN, advertising agency executive; b. Detroit, June 10, 1934; d. Henry and Kate (Boesky) Schiff; B.A., Wayne State U., 1953; children: Rhona, Ken. Supr. broadcast prodn. Northgate Advt. Agy., Detroit, 1968-73; founder, part-owner, pres. Mars Advt. Co., Southfield, Mich., 1973—. Named Advt. Woman of Yr., Women's Club of Detroit, 1986, Outstanding Woman in Agy Mgmt., Am. Women in Radio and TV, Inc., 1987, Outstanding Woman in Broadcast, 1980. Mem. AFTRA (dir. 1959-67), Screen Actors Guild, Adcraft. Women's Adcraft. Creator, producer radio and TV programs, 1956-58; nat. spokesperson on TV, 1960-70. Club: Economic (Ad Woman of Yr. 1986). Office: 24209 Northwestern Hwy Southfield MI 48075 also: Mars Advt Co 7720 Sunset Blvd Los Angeles CA 90046

BARNETT, REBECCA LYNN, telephone company administrator; b. Atlanta, May 7, 1957; d. Robert Joe and Maude (Dickerson) B. BS in Edn., Auburn U., 1980; MBA, Emory U., 1982. Camp dir. NW Ga. Girl Scout Council, Atlanta, 1982; account exec. So. Bell, Atlanta, 1982-83; sales mgr. So. Bell Advanced Systems, Atlanta, 1983-84; asst. product mgr. Bell South Services, Atlanta, 1984-85, product mgr., 1985—; corp. rep. Videotex Industry Assn., Washington, 1985—; dir., sec. Baker Design Group, Atlanta, 1985—; chair Product Team, Atlanta, 1985—. Trainer, instr. NW Ga. council Girl Scouts U.S., Atlanta, 1981—; mem. Nat. Dem. Com., Washington, 1985-87; dir. instrs. outdoor living skills Am. Camping Assn., Bradford Woods, Ill., 1986-87. Mem. NOW, Info. Industry Assn., Am. Mktg. Assn., Sierra Club. Methodist. Home: 884 Derrydown Way Decatur GA 30030 Office: BellSouth Services 675 W Peachtree St Room 34T65 Atlanta GA 30375

BARNETT, SARA MARGARET, educator; b. Sikeston, Mo., Aug. 6, 1941; d. Grady Marvin and Mary Elizabeth (Love) Mills; m. Herman Howard Barnett, Oct. 16, 1959; children: Gregory Lynn, Lori Elizabeth. BS in Med. Tech., U. Tex., Arlington, 1963; MS in Edn., U. Cen. Ark., 1968; PhD, E. Tex. State U., 1984. Intern med. tech. Baylor U. Med. Ctr., 1961-62; asst. supr. lab. Wadley Hosp., Texarkana, Tex., 1963-65, night lab. supr., 1976-77; pub. sch. tchr., Texarkana, 1965-69; med. technologist Collom and Carney Clinic, Texarkana, 1969-72; tchr. biology Liberty-Eylau High Sch., Texarkana, 1972-76; tchr. biology, health occupations coordinator Tex. Sr. High Sch., Texarkana, 1977-87; instr. health occupations edn. Extension Materials Ctr., U. Tex., 1987—; speaker in field. Author: Medical Laboratory Assistant, 1981. Named Tchr. of Yr., Texarkana Ind. Sch. Dist., 1982-83; Martin-Lowrance scholar Delta Kappa Gamma, 1981. Mem. NEA, Am. Soc. Clin. Pathologists, AAUW (chmn. edn. found. Tex. 1972-74), Tex. Tchrs. Assn., Tex. Classroom Tchrs. Assn. (student council advisor N.E. Tex. dist. XIX, 1984-86), Tex. Soc. Med. Tech., Am. Vocat. Assn., Tex. Health Occupations Assn., Ark. Acad. Sci., Tex. PTA (life), Delta Kappa Gamma (pres. chpt. 1984-86), Phi Delta Kappa. Democrat. Methodist. Home: 100 Pioneer St Texarkana TX 75501 Office: 4800 Texas Blvd Texarkana TX 75503

BARNETT, VIVIAN ENDICOTT, curator; b. Putnam, Conn., July 8, 1944; d. George and Vivian (Wood) Endicott; m. Peter Herbert Barnett, July 1, 1967; children: Sarah, Alexander. A.B. magna cum laude, Vassar Coll., 1965; M.A., NYU, 1971; postgrad., CUNY, N.Y.C., 1979-81. Research asst. Solomon R. Guggenheim Museum, N.Y.C., 1973-77, curatorial assoc., 1978-79, assoc. curator, 1980-81, research curator, 1981-82, curator, 1982—. Author: The Guggenheim Museum: Justin K. Thannhauser Collection, 1978, Handbook: The Guggenheim Museum Collection 1900-1980, 1980, Kandinsky Watercolors, 1981, Kandinsky at the Guggenheim, 1983, 100 Works by Modern Masters from the Guggenheim Museum, 1984; "Kandinsky and Science: The Introduction of Biological Images in the Paris Period", Kandinsky in Paris: 1934-44, 1985, Works by Robert Barry, Sol LeWitt, Robert Mangold, Richard Tuttle from the Collection of Dorothy and Herbert Vogel, 1987; also articles. Mem. Am. Assn. Museums (curator com.), Internat. Council Museums, Coll. Art Assn. Am. Office: Solomon R Guggenheim Mus 1071 Fifth Ave New York NY 10128

BARNEY, CAROL ROSS, architect; b. Chgo., Apr. 12, 1949; d. Chester Albert and Dorothy Valeria (Dusiewicz) Ross; m. Alan Fredrick Barney, Mar. 22, 1970; children: Ross Fredrick, Adam Shafer, John Ross. BArch, U. Ill., 1971. Registered architect, Ill. Assoc. architect Holabird & Root, Chgo., 1972-79; prin. architect Orput Assoc., Inc., Wilmette, Ill., 1979-81; prin. architect, pres. Carol Ross Barney Architects, Inc., Chgo., 1981—; asst. prof. U. Ill., Chgo., 1976-78. Plan commr. Village of Wilmette, 1986-88, econ. devel. commn., 1988—; trustee Children's Home and Aid Soc. Ill., Chgo., 1986—; mem. adv. bd. Small Bus. Ctr. for Women, Chgo., 1985—, Loop Coll., Chgo., 1986. Francis J. Plym travelling fellow, 1983. Mem. AIA (bd. dirs. Chgo. chpt. 1978-80, v.p. 1981-82, Disting. Service award Chgo. chpt., 1978, Ill. Council 1978), Nat. Council Archtl. Registration (cert.), Chgo. Women in Architecture (founding, pres. 1978-79), Chgo. Network. Home: 601 Linden Ave Wilmette IL 60091 Office: 11 E Adams Chicago IL 60603

BARNHART, DOROTHY KOHRS, social services adminstrator; b. Des Moines, Apr. 27, 1933; d. Oliver John and Lily Mabel (Smith) Kohrs.; m. 1954 (div. 1977); children—Jacqueline, Dwaine, Jr., Kelly; stepchildren—Billie Jo, Jack, Cindy. Student pub. schs., New Virginia; Internat. Acctg. Soc., Chgo.; Bookkeeper Iowa Credit Union League, 1954-69; Grand Printing Art-O-Type, 1970-72; office mgr. Am. Bus. Forms & Systems, Inc., 1972-76; forms dept. mgr. Action Forms/Action Printers Co., 1976-77; office mgr. Elliott Beechcraft Flying Service, 1977-81; telephone selling rep. Coca Cola Co., 1983-84; adminstrv. asst. Coalition for Family and Children's Service in Iowa, Des Moines, 1985—; developed Wellness Game, 1982-85; pres., owner Wellness Games, Ltd., 1985—; coordinator annual statewide conf. (1987) Chronic Pain Outreach of Central Iowa, Mercy Hosp., 1982-84; Midwest regional dir. Nat. Chronic Pain Outreach, 1985-87 . Mem. Iowa Women's Polit. Caucus; mem. choir Grace United Methodist Ch., disability action com. of Des Moines Area Urban Mission Council. Mem. Nat. Assn. Female Execs., Women's C. of C. of Des Moines. Democrat. Home: 2525 SW 80th Ave Lot 15 Des Moines IA 50321 Office: Coalition Family and Children's Services in Iowa 11 E 5th St Des Moines IA 50309

BARNHART, ELIZABETH ANNE, data processing specialist; b. Daytona Beach, Fla., Oct. 14, 1955; d. David Richards and Elizabeth Frances (Frederick) B. AS in Computer Scis., Daytona Beach Community Coll., 1975. Cert. systems profl. Computer programmer Melweb Signs, Daytona Beach, Fla., 1976; supr. data processing Bunnell (Fla.) Gen. Hosp., 1976-77; computer programmer, operator Daytona Budweiser, Port Orange, Fla., 1977-80; data processing mgr. City of Port Orange, 1980—; cons. Volusia-Lake-Flagler Pvt. Industry Corp., Daytona Beach, 1984-86. Mem. Data Processing Mgmt. Assn. (exec. v.p. Halifax Area chpt. 1983-84, pres. 1985, bylaws dir. 1986, awards dir. 1987, several awards). Democrat. Roman Catholic. Office: City of Port Orange PO Box 290005 Port Orange FL 32029-0005

BARNHART, JO ANNE B., government official; b. Memphis, Aug. 26, 1950; d. Nelson Alexander and Betty Jane (Fitzpatrick) Bryant; m. David Lee Ross, Feb. 14, 1976 (div. June 1983); m. David Ray Barnhart, May 24, 1986. Student U. Tenn., 1968-70; B.A., U. Del., 1975. Space and time buyer deMartin-Marona & Assocs., Wilmington, Del., 1970-73; adminstrv. asst. Mental Health Assn. Wilmington, 1973-75; dir. SERVE nutrition program Wilmington Sr. Ctr., 1975-77; legis. asst. to Senator William V Roth, Jr., Washington, 1977-81; dep. assoc. commr. Office Family Assistance, HHS, Washington, 1981-83, assoc. commr., 1983-86; Rep. staff dir. U.S. Senate Govt. Affairs Com., 1987—. Mem. Nat. Assn. Title VII Nutrition Project Dirs. (v.p. 1976). Republican. Methodist. Office: US Senate Govt Affairs Com Senate Dirksen Bldg Washington DC 20501

BAROCAS, SUSAN HONEY, advertising and public relations agency executive; b. Bronx, N.Y., May 25, 1952; d. David Ralph and Shirley (Fleischman) B. B.S. in Pub. Communication magna cum laude, Boston U., 1974; postgrad. film NYU, 1985. Dir. pub. relations Jewish Community Ctr., Denver, 1974-76; owner, operator SHB Communications, Denver, 1976—; mng. editor Western Wear & Equipment Mag., Denver, 1977-78; dir. pub. relations Loretto Heights Coll., Denver, 1980-81. Asst editor, contbr. articles Am. Horologist & Jeweler, 1977, Beverage Analyst, 1977-78. Adviser, United Synagogue Youth Am., Denver, 1974-75; chairperson publicity Mt. Scopus chpt. Hadassah, Denver, 1977-78; del. Colo. Dem. Conv., 1980; chairperson pub. and community relations com. 1983-87, mem. exec. com., bd. dirs. Am.-Israel Friendship League, Rocky Mountain Region, Denver, 1983—; mem. Assn. Ind. Video and Filmmakers, 1985—. Marsteller scholar, 1973-74; named to Outstanding Young Women Am., U.S. Jaycees, 1981. Office: SHB Communications 1001 Niagara St Denver CO 80220

BARON, ANGELA STASULLI, accountant; b. Paterson, N.J., Oct. 10, 1946; d. Frank V. and Anna M. (Perna) Stasulli; m. Michael R. Baron, Aug. 18, 1974. BS in Acctg., Seton Hall U., 1970. Staff acct. Wiley, Block and White, CPA's, Paterson, 1967-73; fiduciary acct. Patterson Belknap Webb and Tyler, N.Y.C., 1973-78, controller, 1978-81; controller Pitney, Hardin, Kipp and Szuch, Morristown, N.J., 1981-85, adminstr., 1985—. Mem. Am. Inst. CPA's, N.J. State Soc. CPA's, N.Y. Soc. CPA's, Assn Legal Adminstrs. Office: Pitney Hardin Kipp and Szuch 163 Madison Ave Morristown NJ 07960-1945

BARON, CAROL ANN, municipal government official; b. Webster, Mass., Aug. 1, 1950; d. Henry and Jane Alice (Jamrogowicz) Kaczmarek; m. Theodore John Baron Sr., June 15, 1969; children: Jane, Theodore Jr., Mary Rose. Student, Quinsigamond Community Coll., Worchester, Mass., 1968-69, 72-74, Dudley Hall Secretarial Sch., 1969-70, Worcester State Coll., 1984; student treas. cert. program, U. Mass. at Amherst, 1985—. With payroll dept. B-W Footwear, Webster, 1968-69; with billing dept. Cranston Print Works, Webster, 1969-71; matron Dudley (Mass.) Police Dept., 1976-85; clk. to Bd. of Health, Dudley, 1977-85; clk. to town treas. Town of Dudley, 1978-84, asst. treas., 1985, town treas., 1985—. Mem. Dudley Arts Council, 1983-85, Mass. Spina Bifada Assn., 1972—, Mass. Assn. for Retarded Citizens, 1974—, So. Worcester County Assn. for Retarded Citizens, 1974—, Dudley PTA, 1986—, Town Hall Bldg. Com., 1985-87, Town Highway Garage Bldg. Com., 1986—, Police Sta. Bldg. Com., 19876, Computer Study Com., 1986—; mem. St. Anne Sch. Assn., 1978-86, sec., 1983-85; assoc. mem. Dudley Dem. Town Com., 1985—, mem. spl. events com., 1986—, vice-chmn., 1988; booth chmn. Sacred Heart Parish Festival Com., 1982-84, 85-86, mem. steering com., 1984-85; co-chmn. Friends of St. Anne, 1984-86; sec. Dudley Youth Soccer League, 1983-87. Dudley Arts Council grantee, 1984. Mem. Nat. Assn. Female Execs., Mass. Treas. and Collectors Assn., Worcester County Treas. and Collectors Assn., Mass. Govt. Fin. Officers Assn., Mcpl. Treas. Assn. U.S. and Can., Dudley Patrolmen's Wives Assn. (pres. 1981-85)., Dudley Polish Nat. Alliance Group (chmn. children's Christmas party 1974—, recording sec. 1977-79, scholarship chmn. 1980-82, ladies v.p. 1980, pres. 1982-84, treas. 1984—). Roman Catholic. Clubs: Women's Pitch League (capt. 1976-79). Home: 28 Lakeview Ave Dudley MA 01570 Office: Town of Dudley 40 Schofield Ave Box 2 Dudley MA 01570

BARON, HELENA, ballet company administrator, educator, choreographer; b. Prague, Czechoslovakia; came to U.S., 1959; d. Vladimir S. and Ljubow (Bohensky) Slepyan; m. Simon Michael Baron, Aug. 15, 1949; 1 child, Alexander. Student Olga Preobtajenska, Victor and Tatjana Gsovski and Jens Keith. Dancer Deutsche Opera Ballet of Berlin, 1945-59; ballet dir. Ballet Sch., Paramus, N.J., 1961-76, Baron Ballet Co., Waldwick, N.J., 1971—; artistic dir. Petite Ballet Troupe, Paramus, 1971—, Baron Ballet Co., Paramus, 1978—. Choreographer (ballets) Roumanian Rhapsody, 1967, Naiades, 1982, Bolero (Nat. Choreography prize 1985), Vivace, 1984, Andulko, 1986, Visions, 1987, Snowmaiden, 1987. N.J. State Commn. on the Arts fellow, 1987. Mem. NE Regional Ballet Assn. (performing co. regional honor 1984), Nat. Assn. Regional Ballet. Avocations: art, literature. Office: Baron Ballet Co 74 Oak St Ridgewood NJ 07450

BARON, IRENE JO, educator, artist; b. Cleve., Oct. 6, 1938; d. Herbert Herman and Lois Marie (Moore); m. Jacques A. Baron, Feb. 28, 1968 (div. 1981); 1 child, Dominique Michelle. BA, Hiram Coll., 1960; postgrad., Ohio U., 1965-66, 81-82, 86-87, Tex. A&M U., 1964, Coll. of LaVerne, 1980. Cert. tchr., Ohio. Tchr. Los Angeles and Newark, Ohio, 1960-66; info. specialist Battelle Meml. Inst., Bangkok, 1966-70; tchr., dept. chmn. Office Sec. of Def., Kaiserslautern, Fed. Republic Germany, 1970-72; tchr. various pub. schs., Minn., 1979-81, Zanesville, Ohio, 1981—; instr. ARC swimming, canoeing, sailing, first aid, Zanesville and Bangkok, 1955-70, dir. water safety, Muskingum County, 1964-66; mem. Nat. Ski Patrol, 1964-66. Author: Close Proximity of Rainbows, 1987; artist numerous paintings, 1950-87. Trustee West Muskingum Acad. Fund, Zanesville, 1982-87. Recipient Ednl. award Rogge Meml. Found., 1984; named one of Outstanding Young Women of Am., 1971. Mem. Nat. Edn. Assn., Nat. Sci. Tchr's. Assn., Ohio Edn. Assn., West Muskingum Edn. Assn., Sci. Edn. Council of Ohio, Ohio Acad. Sci., Hiram Coll. Alumni Assn. (Outstanding Achievement award 1977). Club: Authors (sec.). Home: 320 E Highland Dr Zanesville OH 43701

BARON, JEAN SZEKERES, lawyer; b. Harrisburg, Pa., June 18, 1943; d. Gaza John and Mary Ann (Gustin) Szekeres; 1 son, Jay. B.S. with high honors, U. Md., 1976; J.D. with honors, U. Balt., 1981. Bar: Md. 1981, U.S. Dist. Ct. Md., 1982. Law clk. Prince George's County Circuit Ct., Upper Marlboro, Md., 1980-81; assoc. firm Ellin & Baker, Balt., 1981-82, Gebhardt & Smith, Balt., 1982-83; asst. atty. gen. State of Md., Balt., 1983—; adj. prof. U. Balt. Sch. Law, 1987—. Mem. ABA, Md. Bar Assn. (chair standing com. on pub. awareness 1987—), Prince George's County Bar Assn., Balt. City Bar Assn., U. Md. Young Alumni Assn. (dir. 1977-79), U. Md. Alumni Assn. (bd. dirs. Prince George's County chpt. 1987—), Mortar Bd., Phi Kappa Phi. Home: 7714 Lakecrest Dr Greenbelt MD 20770 Office: Office Atty Gen 301 W Preston St Room 1502 Baltimore MD 21201

BARON, LAURA ANN, personnel executive; b. Glen Ridge, N.J., Oct. 4, 1962; d. Robert Michael and Joan Katherine (Bollhorst) Baron. BS in Commerce cum laude, Ridge Coll., 1984; postgrad., Pace U., N.Y.C., currently. Intern/compensation analyst Campbell Soup Co., Inc., Camden, N.J., 1984; personnel generalist Vital Signs, Inc., Totowa, N.J., 1984-85; indsl. relations mgr. Crown Cork and Seal Co., Inc., N. Bergen, N.J., 1985-87; dir. personnel Nat. Prescription Adm., Inc., Clifton, N.J., 1987—; conductor seminars in field. Advisor/recruiter Rider Alumni Vols. for Enrollment, Lawrenceville, N.J., 1985—; participant United Labor Agy., Newark, 1986-87; active ARC. Mem. Nat. Assn. Female Execs., Internat. Narcotic Inforcement Officers Assn. Beverage and Brewers Packaging Assn., Nat. Lightning Class Assn., Delta Sigma Pi, Sigma Iota Epsilon, Omicron Delta Epsilon. Roman Catholic. Clubs: Lake Wallenpaupak Yacht, Sunfish Fleet (skipper 1978-87). Office: Nat Prescription Adm Inc 1200 Route 46 Clifton NJ 07013

BARON, LINDA, insurance company executive; b. Blackfoot, Idaho, Jan. 9, 1948; d. Lynn Poole and Mildred Ruth (Tiger) Scott; m. Stanley Lloyd Baron, July 17, 1971; children: Bridget Michele, Eric Jon. BSEd, U. Idaho, 1970; MAT, Lewis and Clark Coll., 1974; student Coll. of Idaho, 1966-67; postgrad. American Coll., 1986. Tchr., Beaverton Sch. Dist. 48, Oreg., 1970-74, 76-81; field underwriter Home Life of N.Y. Ins. Co., Portland, Oreg., 1982; field underwriter, trainer Monarch Life Ins. Co., Portland, 1982-84, field underwriter, Kensington, Md., 1984-86, asst. dir. variable life sales, Springfield, Mass., 1986—. Contbr. poetry The Great American Poetry Anthology, 1987. Sunday sch. choir dir. Meth. Ch., Rockville, Md., 1985-86; active PTA; pres. Farmington West Homeowners Assn., Oreg., 1975; organist Aloha United Meth. Ch., Oreg., 1974-80. Named Agt. of Yr., Monarch Life Ins., Portland, 1983; recipient Golden Poet award, 1987. Mem. Women Life Underwriters, Nat. Assn. Female Execs., Am. Bus. Women's Assn. (corr. sec.), D.C. Life Underwriters. Republican. Avocations: reading, sewing, skiing, tennis, music. Office: Monarch Life Ins Co One Monarch Pl Springfield MA 01133

BARON, LINDA ANN, cosmetic co. exec.; b. Flushing, N.Y., Nov. 9, 1943; d. Leonard Michael Baron and Margaret Mary Cotone. Grad. Gardner Sch. Bus., 1968; student George Washington U., 1970. Adminstrv. asst. U.S. Underseas Cable Corp., Washington, 1968-69; analyst programmer Friden div. Singer Co., Washington, 1969, programming mgr., 1970, systems sales exec., 1971; acct. exec. Clinique Labs., Inc., Washington and Balt., 1972, regional mktg. mgr. Md. and Va. markets, 1973-75, regional mktg. dir. Washington and Mid-Atlantic states, 1976-81, regional v.p. Southeast, 1981-86; v.p. South and Mid-Atlantic, Lancome Inc., 1986—; instr. merchandising, 1976—. Vol., ARC Walter Reed and Bethesda Naval Hosp., Washington, 1969-71. Mem. Washington Fashion Group, Nat. Assn. for Female Execs., U.S. Dressage Fedn., Potomac Valley Dressage Assn., Am. Horse Show Assn. Roman Catholic. Home: 9110 Town Gate Ln Bethesda MD 20817

BARON, NAOMI SUSAN, linguistics educator, computer specialist; b. N.Y.C., Sept. 27, 1946; d. Leonard and Ruth Joan (Josephson) B.; B.A., Brandeis U., 1968; Ph.D., Stanford U., 1972. Asst. prof. linguistics Brown U., Providence, 1972-79, assoc. prof., 1979-85, assoc. dean, 1981-83; vis. instr. R.I. Sch. Design, 1982-83; vis. Nat. Endowment Humanities chair Emory U., 1983-84; Brown vis. chair Southwestern U., 1985-87; assoc. dean, prof. Langs. and Fgn. Studies Am. U., Washington, 1987—; vis. scholar U. Tex., Austin, 1984-85. Bur. Edn. Handicapped grantee, 1975-84; Nat. Endowment for Humanities grantee, 1979-81; Guggenheim fellow, 1984-85. Mem. Linguistic Soc. Am., Semiotic Soc. Am. (pres. 1986-87), Am. Assn. Computing Machinery. Author: Language Acquisition and Historical Change, 1979; Speech, Writing and Sign, 1981; Computer Languages: A Guide for the Perplexed, 1986. Office: Am Univ Dept Langs & Fgn Studies Gray Hall Washington DC 20016

BARONE, ROSE MARIE PACE (MRS. JOHN BARONE), writer, former educator; b. Buffalo, Apr. 26, 1920; d. Dominic and Jennie (Zagara) Pace; B.A., U. Buffalo, 1943; M.S., U. So. Cal., 1950; cert. advanced study Fairfield (Conn.) U., 1963; m. John Barone, Aug. 23, 1947. Tchr., Angola High Sch. (N.Y.), 1943-46, Puente High Sch. (Calif.), 1946-47, Jefferson High Sch., Lafayette, Ind., 1947-50; dir. Warren Inst., Bridgeport, Conn., 1951-53; instr. U. Bridgeport, 1953-54; tchr. bus. subjects Bassick High Sch., Bridgeport, 1954-74, Harding High Sch., Bridgeport, 1974-80; instr. Fairfield U., 1969 freelance writer, 1980—; chair State Poetry Festival, 1987; founder Pet Rescue. Pace-Barone Minority scholar Fairfield U.; recipient Playwriting prize Conn. Federated Women's Clubs, 1955, 1st prize for poetry, 1985, Federated Women Conn. State Short Story award, 1987, 88; Auerbach Found. scholarship, 1956; Citizen award Bridgeport Dental Assn., 1982; State/Town Hero award, 1986. Mem. NEA, AARP (v.p. 1987-88, pres. 1988—), Owl (sec. 1987—), AAUW (treas. 1957-58), Nat. League Am. Pen Women (Bridgeport historian 1966-84, state historian 1983—, treas. br. 1985—, State pres. 1986—, Nat. Historian award 1976), UN Assn. U.S.A. (pres. Bridgeport, 1964-66, 68-70, chmn. area UN Days, 1960—, pres. Conn. 1971—, state chmn. UNICEF to 1984, area UNICEF Ctr., 1984—, state historian 1984—), Conn. Bus. Tchrs., Bridgeport Edn. Assn. (sec. 1966-68), Fairfield Philatelic Soc. (sec. 1971-78, founder advisor Philatelic Jrs. 1972-80), Pi Omega Pi. Clubs: Fairfield University Women's (founder, pres. 1950, 74—, v.p. 1973-74) Southport Woman's (garden dept. sec. 1981-85, chmn. 1985-87) (Fairfield). Home: 1283 Round Hill Rd Fairfield CT 06430

BARONE, SHERRY JOY, test engineer; b. Phila., June 23, 1960; d. Leonard and Linda Gwen (Berger) B. BS, U. Md., 1982; MBA summa cum laude, Nat. U., 1985. Registered profl. engr. Computer programmer Office Instl. Studies, U. Md., College Park, 1982; lead software engr. RCA Astro-Electronics, Princeton, N.J., 1982-83; sr. test engr. ITT Gilfillan, Van Nuys, Calif., 1983-87; sr. project engr. Hughes Aircraft, Los Angeles, 1987—; cons. AMJ Acctg. Firm, Los Angeles, 1984-85, IBM, Los Angeles, 1985—. Author: (with others) Children and Computer, 1982. Mem. Am. Computing Machinery Club, IEEE, Soc. Women Engrs., Soc. Test Engrs., Gilfillan Mgmt. Assn. Republican. Jewish. Club: ITT Ski (Van Nuys). Office: Hughes Aircraft PO Box 92426 Los Angeles CA 90009-2426

BARR, GINGER, state legislator; b. Kansas City, Mo., Dec. 4, 1947; d. W.M. and Ann (Armstrong) Barr; m. Edwin P. Carpenter, Jan. 2, 1984. BS, Baker U., Baldwin, Kans., 1969. Cemetery mgmt. Topeka Cemetery, Kans., 1969-76, Graceland/Fairlawn Cemeteries, Decatur, Ill., 1976—. Rep. Kans. State Legislature, 1983—, vice chmn. fed. and state affairs com., 1987; pres. Crifter Care Co., 1987—; bd. dirs. World Topeka Famous Zoo, 1986—, Humane Soc., Topeka, 1983-87; mem. Jr. League, Topeka, 1985. Mem. Am. Cemetery Assn. (dir. 1980-82), Kans. Cemetery Assn. (pres. 1979-80), Ill. Cemetery Assn. Republican, Humane Soc., Critter Care Co. (pres. 1987). Home and Office: Box 58 Auburn KS 66402

BARR, ROSALINDA, home health care director; b. Marshall, Mo., Feb. 21, 1950; d. Joseph Richard and Margaret Mary (Kopp) B.; m. Robert Francis Rasmussen, Apr. 26, 1984. Student, Avila Coll., 1968-70; registered nurse diploma, Kansas City Gen. Hosp. and Med. Ctr., 1973. RN, Kans., Mo. Staff nurse med./surg. Lakeside Hosp., Kansas City, 1973-74, office nurse, 1974-76; head nurse surg. unit Vets. Hosp., Kansas City, 1976-80; clinician Kansas U. Med. Ctr., Kansas City, 1980-83; dir. A.P.T. Home Health Agy., Shawnee Mission, Kans., 1983—; mem. exec. bd. Kansas City Regional Home Health Assn., 1986—. Co-author: (teaching manual) Hyperalimentation, 1983, Am. Jour. Nursing, 1983. Mem. Am. Bus. Assn. (hospitality chmn. 1985-86), Am. Soc. Opthalology Nurses, Res. Officers Assn. (life, pres. Kansas City chpt. 1986-87, v.p. 1985-86, treas. 1983-84, exec. bd. 1985—, Outstanding Chpt. Pres., 1987), Mo. Res. Officers Assn. (retirement affairs 1985—, jr. v.p. Army Kansas City chpt. 1985-86, Outstanding Jr. Officer). Office: APT Home Health Care Agy 8901 W 74th St Shawnee Mission KS 66204

BARR, VILMA EVELYN, writer, communications executive; b. Phila., Jan. 14, 1936; d. Samuel and Anne (Fink) Leshnoff; divorced; children: Lesley Gale, Glenn Joseph. BS, Drexel U., 1957; SM, MIT, 1973. Asst. buyer Strawbridge & Clothier, Phila., 1957-59; corr. Fairchild Publs., Phila., 1959-64; pres. Vilma Barr Communications and Mktg., Phila. and Boston, 1964-80; mgr. pub. relations ctr. Harza Engrng. Co., Chgo., 1980-85; pres. Bus. Profl. Editorial Services, Inc., N.Y.C., 1986—; lectr. Internat. Forum Mktg. and Merchandising Drexel U., Phila., 1988, Internat. Council Shopping Ctrs., N.Y.C.,1988, Nat. Retail Mchts. Assn., New York, 1988. Author: Ten Years: The Reedy Lectures At RIT, N.Y.C., 1986; co-author: Designing To Sell, 1986 (Excellence award 1986); contbg. editor Mech. Engrng. Mag. Bd. dirs. Friends of Downtown, Chgo., 1983-85. Recipient award Wall Street Jour., 1957; Career Advancement grantee AAUW, 1973. MIT Enterprise Forum N.Y. (bd. dirs. 1986—). Office: Bus Profl Editorial Services Inc 405 W 23rd St #9L New York NY 10011

BARRAGAN, M(ARGARITA) DENISE, tax compliance auditor; b. Napa, Calif., Oct. 20, 1955; d. Raymond Pino and Jennie (Soriano) B. AS with honors, Napa Valley Community Coll., 1979; BBA, Calif. State U., Sacramento, 1985. With mgmt. Napa Valley Bank, 1980-85; revenue agt. IRS, San Francisco, 1985—. Mem. Nat. Assn. Accts., Calif. Soc. Accts., Credit Women Internat., Nat. Assn. Female Execs., Am. Soc. Women Accts. Office: IRS 450 Golden Gate Ave Room 5209 San Francisco CA 94102

BARRATT, CYNTHIA LOUISE, pharmaceutical company executive; b. El Paso, Tex., Feb. 13, 1953; d. John Edward and Louise Joy (Lacy) B.; m. Nat G. Adkins, Jr., Oct. 5, 1980. BJ, U. Tex., 1975. Buyer Joske's of Tex., San Antonio, 1975-80, Craigs of Tex., Houston, 1981-83; v.p. sales ops. Akorn, Inc., Abita Springs, La., 1980-86; chief exec. officer, chmn. bd. dirs. NGLC Corp., Richmond, Tex., 1983—; exec. v.p. OCuSoft Inc., Richmond, 1986—, also bd. dirs.; exec. v.p. CynaCon Inc., Richmond, 1986—, also bd. dirs. Mem. Nat. Assn. Female Execs., Rosenberg/Richmond C. of C., DAR, Ft. Bend County Mus. Assn. Office: OCuSOFT Inc 1305 FM 359 Richmond TX 77469

BARRELLE, ANN MARIE, educator; b. New Orleans, Aug. 5, 1946; d. Eugene Joseph and Claire (Fallon) B. B.S. in Secondary Edn., La. State U., 1970; M.Ed. with honors, U. Nev., 1980. Tchr. English, speech reading, history and govt. Milledon Middle Sch., Violet, La., 1970, Arabi Park Middle Sch., La., 1970-71, Christ the King Internat. Sch., Okinawa, Japan, 1973-74, Kubasaki Adult High Sch., Okinawa, 1974-76; adj. instr. English as 2d lang., Clark County Community Coll., Las Vegas, 1977-87; tchr. William E. Orr Jr. High Sch., Las Vegas, 1978-86, Western High Sch., Las Vegas, 1986—. Mem. NEA, Am. Soc. Tng. Devel., Women in Communications, Nev. State Edn. Assn., Clark County Classroom Tchrs. Assn., Nat. Assn. Female Execs., Nat. Council Tchrs. English, Nev. State Council Tchrs. English, So. Nev. Tchrs. English (recording sec. 1979-80, program v.p. 1980-81, membership v.p. 1981-83). Democrat. Avocations: golf; travel. Office: Western High Sch 4601 W Bonanza Rd Las Vegas NV 89107

BARRES, BERNICE, nurse; b. Phila., Apr. 15, 1927; d. Morris S. and Eleanor (Steinberg) Browndorf; m. Samuel L. Barres, Aug. 31, 1946; children—Rachel Barres Black, Joanne Barres Shaw, Robert Alan. A.S. with high honors, Mt. Ida Jr. Coll., 1978; B.S. in Nursing, Boston U. Sch. Nursing, 1981. Cert. med. asst., R.N. Adminstrv. asst. to registrar Brandeis U., Waltham, Mass., 1965-67; asst. to v.p. Newton Coll. (Mass.), 1971-72; exec. sec. Martin D. Braver Co., Chestnut Hill, Mass., 1972-74; staff nurse Beth Israel Hosp., Boston, 1981-83, Hebrew Rehab. Center for Aged, Boston, 1983—; mem. med. asst. adv. bd. Mt. Ida Jr. Coll., Newton. Vol. reader for blind coll. students; play therapist for multi-handicapped children at Peabody Sch. for Crippled Children; vol. librarian elem. sch. and Temple, Boston Lying-in Hosp., Brookline Hills Nursing Home; mem. nat. women's com. Brandeis U. Mem. Am. Nurses Assn. (cert. gerontological nurse), Mass. Nurses Assn., Hebrew Coll. Women's Assn., Hadassah, Phi Theta Kappa. Democrat. Jewish. Home: 132 Sargent St Newton MA 02158

BARRETT, BEATRICE HELENE, psychologist; b. Cin., Dec. 8, 1928; d. Oscar Slack and Helen (Kaiper) B.; m. Harold Sheffield Van Buren, Oct. 6, 1966 (div. Oct. 1985). BA, U. Ariz., 1950; MA, U. Ky., 1952; PhD, Purdue U., 1957. Lic. psychologist, Mass. Grad. tchg. asst. in psychology U. Ky., Lexington, 1950-52; psychology asst. Longview State Hosp., Cin., 1951, staff psychologist, 1952; staff psychologist Children's Outpatient and Cons. Services, Gary, 1954-57, chief psychologist, 1957-59; instr. psychology Ind. U. Med. Sch., Indpls., 1956-60, research assoc. dept. psychiatry, 1959-60; pvt. practice clin. psychology Indpls., 1957-60; research fellow in psychology Sch. Medicine, Harvard U., Boston, 1960-62; lectr. in spl. edn. Grad. Sch. Edn., Boston U., 1962-63; dir. psychol. research Walter E. Fernald State Sch., Belmont, Mass., 1962-69; dir. behavior prosthesis lab. Walter E. Fernald State Sch., Belmont, 1963—; chief psychologist 1969—; assoc. psychologist Enuice Kennedy Shriver Ctr. for Mental Retardation, Inc., Waltham, Mass., 1982—; instr. Mass. Psychol. Ctr., 1972; lectr. in spl. edn. Lesley Coll. Grad. Sch., 1974-76; adj. assoc. prof. Northeastern U., 1983—; psychology cons. Carter Meml. Hosp., Indpls., 1959-60; mem. exec. com. Boston Behavior Therapy Interest Group, 1973-74. Cons. editor, mem. adv. bds. various profl. jours.; contbr. numerous articles to profl. jours. Mem. Gov.'s Youth Council of Ind., 1959-61; mem. spl. adv. com. on mental retardation Ind. Dept. Pub. Instrn., 1959-61; mem. task force Mass. Mental Retardation Planning Project, 1965-66; mem. adv. bd. Cambridge Ctr. for Behavioral Scis., 1981-87, trustee 1987—; apptd. to com. on dance edn. Spl. Commn. on the Performing Arts, 1976-77; mem. art acquisition com. DeCordova Mus., 1978-80, mem. contemporary arts council, 1985—; trustee Boston Repertory Ballet, 1977-79; trustee Boston Ballet Co., 1970-76, sec. bd., 1974-75, exec. com., 1974-76. Grantee Nat. Assn. for Retarded Citizens, 1963, NIHM, 1963-76. Fellow Am. Psychol. Assn., Mass. Psychol. Assn., Behavior Therapy and Research Soc. (clin.); mem. Assn. for Mentally Ill Children (human rights com. 1979-81), Am. Acad. on Mental Retardation (v.p. 1969-74, at-large exec. com. 1975-77), Eastern Psychol. Assn., Assn. for Advancement of Behavior Therapy, Assn. for Severely Handicapped, Assn. Behavior Analysis (jour. adv. bd. 1983-87, chair task force on right to effective edn. 1986—). Club: Stage Harbor Yacht (Chatham, Mass.) (race com. 1984-86). Home: RFD 7 Box 236A Winter St Lincoln MA 01773 Office: Walter E Fernald State Sch Box 9108 Belmont MA 02178-9108

BARRETT, BETTY ANNE, small business owner, interior designer; b. Antofagasta, Chile, Sept. 4, 1936; came to U.S., 1954; d. Oscar Garvens and Baxter (Gaines) Berger; m. John G. Barrett, Aug. 11, 1956 (div. Dec. 1977); children: John, Mark, Kevin, Jennifer, Gregory. Student, Santiago (Chile) Coll., 1954. Asst. Mario Buatta, Inc., N.Y.C., 1968-78; asst. to pres., office mgr. John F. Saladino, Inc., N.Y.C., 1978-82; pres., owner Betty Barrett Inc., N.Y.C., 1982—. Mem. Interior Design Network, Nat. Assn. Female Execs. Roman Catholic. Club: Vertical (N.Y.C.). Office: 227 E 57th St New York NY 10022

BARRETT, CLAUDETTE ANNE, talent agent; b. Manchester, Eng., Oct. 14, 1952; came to U.S., 1969; d. Gerlad and Iris (Elleston) Barrett; m. Lloyd Dodd, Nov. 19, 1972 (div. Sept. 1985); children: André II, Jon-Carlos. G-rad., Garrett Green Coll., Birmingham, Eng., 1969; postgrad., CCNY, 1974-75. Owner, pres. Baskin-Robbins, N.Y.C., 1972-74; pres. Metamorphosis Modeling Sch., Calif., 1975-78, Hot Gossip Modeling, Calif., 1979-84; head mktg. Internat. Med. Ctr., Miami, Fla., 1985-87; talent agt. Spotlight Prodns., Miami, 1987—. Lectr. Fla. Bd. Edn., Miami, 1982—. Named Outstanding Young Woman Miami Library System of Opalocka, Miami, 1982-83. Adventist. Home: 8412 SW 208th St Miami FL 33189

BARRETT, COLLEEN CROTTY, airline executive; b. Bellows Falls, Vt., Sept. 14, 1944; d. Richard Crotty and Barbara (Hennessey) Blanchard; 1 child, Patrick Allen Barrett. A.A. with highest honors, Becker Jr. Coll., 1964. Legal sec. Oppenheimer Rosenberg Kelleher & Wheatley, San Antonio, 1968-72, adminstrv. asst., paralegal, 1972-78; sec. Southwest Airlines, Dallas, 1978—, exec. asst. to pres. and chmn., 1980—, v.p. adminstrn., corp. sec., 1985—. Mem. Leadership Tex. Democrat. Roman Catholic. Office: SW Airlines Co PO Box 37611 Dallas TX 75235

BARRETT, ELIZABETH ANN MANHART, nursing educator, psychotherapist, consultant; b. Hume, Ill., July 11, 1934; d. Francis J. and Grace C. (Manhart) Fridy; children: Joseph B., Jeffrey F., Paula G. Brown, Pamela M. Shetler Carpino, Scott D. BS in Nursing summa cum laude, U. Evansville, 1970, MA, 1973, MS in Nursing, 1976; grad. Gestalt Assocs. for Psychotherapy, 1982; PhD in Nursing, NYU, 1983. Instr. nursing U. Evansville, Ind., 1970-73, asst. prof., 1973-76; staff nurse Welborn Bapt. Hosp., Evansville, 1975-76; staff nurse Bellevue Psychiat. Hosp., N.Y.C., 1976-79; clin. tchr. CUNY, 1977-82; asst. prof. Adelphi U., 1979-80; group practice Nurse Healers, 1979-82; pvt. practice psychotherapy, 1980—; nurse researcher Mt. Sinai Med. Ctr., N.Y.C., 1982-86, asst. dir. nursing, 1983-86; assoc. prof. Hunter Coll., N.Y.C., 1986—. Mem. com. Regional Health Planning Council, Evansville, 1974-77. Mem. Am. Nurses Assn. (cert. psychiat.-mental health), Nat. League Nursing, Soc. Advancement in Nursing, Soc. Rogerian Scholars (founder, 1st pres. 1988), NOW, Phi Kappa Phi, Sigma Theta Tau (Upsilon chpt. pres. 1986-88), Alpha Tau Delta (founding mem. soc. of Rogerian scholars). Home: 415 E 85th St New York NY 10028 Office: Hunter Coll 425 E 25th St New York NY 10010

BARRETT, GAIL ELIZABETH, computer operations supervisor; b. Pomona, Calif., June 16, 1957; d. Gilbert Earl and Arlette Marie (Zahn) Hamann; m. Mark William Barrett, Oct. 6, 1984; 1 child, Matthew William. Data processing operator, supr. Ed Post Realty, Scottsdale, Ariz., 1974-80; computer ops. supr. Arvin Industries, Inc., Phoenix, 1980—. Archtl. control chairperson Crystal Bay Homeowners Assn., Chandler, Ariz., 1987. Republican. Lutheran. Office: Arvin Industries Inc 500 S 15th St Phoenix AZ 85034

BARRETT, HELEN HUNT, greeting service administrator; b. Paris, Tex., Nov. 2, 1943; d. Leo Charles and Gladys (Stewart) Smith; m. Lawrence B. Hunt, July 29, 1961 (div. 1979); 1 child, Susan; m. Norman Lee Barrett, Sept. 11, 1982; children: Brian, Kevin, Mark. Student, Midwestern State U., Wichita Falls, Tex., 1970-74. Exec. sec. Dept. Def., Wichita Falls, 1969-82; cons. Mary Kay Cosmetics, Wichita Falls, 1977-79; sales dir. Mary Kay Cosmetics, 1979-83; mgr., dir. admissions, cons. Vogue Beauty Coll., Austin and San Antonio, Tex., 1985-86; field mgr. Welcome Wagon, Internat., Austin, 1986—. Solicitor Wichita Falls chpt. Am. Cancer Fund, 1983; fundraiser Lago Vista (Tex.) Women's Club, 1986. Mem. Am. Bus. Women's Assn. (pres. 1973-74), Austin C. of C., Austin Better Bus. Bur. Democrat. Methodist. Clubs: Lago Vista Country, Lago Vista Women's, Retired Officers Wives. Home: 4018 Outpost Trace Lago Vista TX 78645 Office: Welcome Wagon Internat 145 Court Ave Memphis TN 38103

BARRETT, JESSICA (DONNA ANN NIPERT), psychotherapist; b. Paterson, N.J., July 25, 1952; d. Donald Alfred and Gloria Emma (Lustica) Nipert; m. John David Barrett, Sept. 9, 1977 (div. June 1982); 1 child, Ashley Elizabeth. BA, UCLA, 1975; MA, Azusa Pacific U., 1981. Lic. marriage, family, child counselor; cert. hypnosis, Calif. With employee relations Engrs. and Architects Exec. Assn., Los Angeles, 1975-79; practicing psychotherapy Toluca Lake, Calif., 1983—; instr., supr. Calif. Family Study Ctr., Burbank, 1986—; psychotherapist Pasadena Outpatient Eating Disorders Program, Calif., 1987-88; cons. Texaco Employee Assistance Program, Los Angeles, Studio City, 1985-86, NBC Employee Assistance Program, Burbank, 1986-87; lctr. various groups, Burbank, San Fernando Valley, 1983-87. Mem. Assn. Labor-Mgmt. Administrs. and Cons. Alcoholism Inc. (bd. dirs. 1983-86), Am. Assn. Marriage and Family Therapists, Stepfamily Assn. Am., Nat. Assn. Female Exec., Calif. Family Study Ctr. Alumni Assn. (sec.-treas. 1987—). Democrat. Presbyterian. Office: 4444 Riverside Dr Sta 203A Burbank CA 91505

BARRETT, JUDY A., corporate controller; b. Lake Village, Ark., Dec. 26, 1944; d. John Weldon and Edna (Rucker) Hollis; divorced; children: Shawn, Shannon. Student, U. Ark., Monticello, 1968. Corp. controller Specialized Electronics, Greenville, Miss., 1974-78, Trotter Towing Corp., Greenville, 1978-83, CannCo Contractors, Inc., Lake Village, Ark., 1984—. Community collector Am. Cancer Soc., Lake Village, 1985; sec. Jr. Aux., Warren, Ark., 1972, v.p., 1973. Named Best Pub. Speaker, Dale Carnegie, 1978. Mem. S.E. Ark. Bd. Realtors (reporter 1985-86). Baptist. Home: Rt 1 Box 363 Lake Village AR 71653 Office: Cann Co Contractors Inc PO Box 846 Lake Village AR 71653

BARRETT, KAREN MOORE, lawyer; b. Pitts., Jan. 16, 1950; d. James Newton and Grace Naomi (Gigax) Moore; m. Jay Elliott Barrett, June 24, 1972; children: Catherine Grace, Elizabeth Alice. AB, Bryn Mawr Coll., 1972; JD, Harvard U., 1977. Bar: Pa. 1977, U.S. Dist. Ct. (we. dist.) Pa. 1977. Assoc. Buchanan Ingersoll Profl. Corp., Pitts., 1977-84, ptnr., 1984—. Bd. dirs. Planned Parenthood of Pitts. Inc., 1983—. Mem. ABA, Pa. Bar Assn., Allegheny County Bar Assn. Democrat. Presbyterian. Clubs: Harvard-Yale-Princeton of Western Pa. (Pitts.) (bd. dirs. 1986—), Bryn Mawr of Western Pa. (Pitts.) (v.p. 1984-87, pres. 1987—). Office: Buchanan Ingersoll Profl Corp 600 Grant St 58th Floor Pittsburgh PA 15219

BARRETT, MARGARET P. (PEGGY BARRETT), small business owner; b. Miami, Fla., Nov. 13, 1947. BBA, U. Miami, 1981. Asst. personnel mgr. med. campus U. Miami, 1981-84, personel mgr. med. info. systems, 1984-85; personnel mgr. Mack Industries, Inc., Hollywood, Fla., 1985-86; owner Peg's Crafts and Supplies, Inverness, Fla., 1986—. Dist. coordinator Girl Scouts U.S., Inverness, 1986-87, campaign chair, 1986-87, co-leader, 1986-87. Mem. AAUW, LWV. Democrat. Lodge: Women of Moose (treas. 1986-87, sr. regent 1987—). Home: 10236 E Pike Dr Inverness FL 32650

BARRETT, MINNA SARA, psychologist, educator; b. Bklyn., Mar. 13, 1948; d. Leslie Raymond and Rita (Wilner) B.; m. Gretchen Lee Goldfarb, Dec. 21, 1969 (div. May 1984); 1 child, Gretchen Lee. BA in Psychology cum laude, SUNY, Stony Brook, 1969, MA in Psychology, 1972, PhD in Psychology, 1978. Lic. psychologist, N.Y. Clin. cons. psychologist childcare services SUNY, Stony Brook, 1975-80; cons. nat. non-collegiate edn. Albany Ednl. Cultural Ctr. N.Y. Bd. Regents, 1984—; instr. SUNY, Old Westbury, 1975—; asst. clin. asst. adj. prof. social welfare SUNY, Stony Brook, 1980-82; chmn. dept. psychology SUNY, Old Westbury, 1977-79, social work, 1984-86, concentration, 1984—. Author (2 chpts.) China Science Walks on Two Legs, 1974; contbr. articles to profl. jours. Chmn. local chpt. Sci. for the People Coalition, Stony Brook, 1969-75, L.I. Safe Energy Coalition, Port Jefferson, N.Y., 1970-82; mem. Suffolk County Occupational Health SUNY, Stony Brook, 1969-75, Suffolk County Child Care Council, 1970-75. Research fellow Hearst/Avon Publs., 1972, SUNY, 1983, 85. Mem. Am. Psychol. Assn., Assn. Women in Devel., N.Y., Asian, African and Latin Am. Studies, Assn. Improvement of Child Caring. Buddhist. Office: SUNY Coll at Old Westbury Old Westbury NY 11568

BARRETT, NANCY SMITH, economics educator; b. Balt., Sept. 12, 1942; d. James Brady and Katherine (Pollard) Smith; m. Harold C. Barrett, Apr. 16, 1966 (div. 1974); children: Clark, Christopher. BA, Goucher Coll., 1963; MA, Harvard U., 1965. Dep. asst. dir. Congl. Budget Office, Washington, 1975-76; sr. staff Council of Econ. Advisors, Washington, 1977; prin. research assoc. The Urban Inst., Washington, 1977-79; dep. asst. sec. U. S. Dept. Labor, Washington, 1979-81; instr. Am. U., Washington, 1966-67, asst. prof. econs., 1967-70, assoc. prof., 1970-74, prof., 1974—. Author: Theory of Macroeconomic Policy, 1972, 2d rev. edit., 1975, Theory of Microeconomic Policy, 1974, Prices and Wages in U.S., 1974; contbr. articles on econs. of mfg. to profl. jours. Woodrow Wilson fellow, 1963-64; Fulbright scholar, 1973. Mem. Am. Econs. Assn., Phi Beta Kappa. Home: 2034 Hillyer Pl NW Washington DC 20009 Office: Am U Dept Econs Washington DC 20016

BARRETT, PAULETTE SINGER, public relations executive; b. Paris, Dec. 20, 1937; came to U.S., 1947; d. Andrew M. and Agatha (Kinsbrunner) Singer; m. Laurence I. Barrett, Mar. 9, 1957 (div. 1983); children: Paul Meyer, David Allen, Adam Singer. BA, NYU, 1957; MS in Journalism, Columbia U., 1958. News dir. Yardney Electric Corp., N.Y.C., 1958-61; freelance writer newspapers and pub. relations orgns., N.Y.C. and Washington, 1961-73; assoc. dir. pub. info. Columbia U., N.Y.C., 1973-77; from account exec. to v.p., then sr. v.p. Daniel J. Edelman, Inc. of N.Y., N.Y.C., 1977-80, sr. v.p. and gen. mgr., 1980, exec. v.p., gen. mgr., 1986—; exec. v.p. Rowland Co., N.Y.C., 1980-82; exec. dir. communications UJA-Fedn. of N.Y., N.Y.C., 1982-86. Mem. eastern regional com. Israel Tennis Ctrs., N.Y.C., 1986—. Mem. Pub. Relations Soc. Am. (accredited), Counselors Acad., Women Execs. in Pub. Relations, Women in Communications, Inc. Office: Daniel J Edelman Inc 1775 Broadway New York NY 10019

BARRETTA, JOLIE ANN, professional athletics coach, author; b. Phila., Aug. 17, 1954; d. Philip Francis and Norma Roberta (Podoszek) B. Student, U. Calif., Long Beach, 1972-76, U. Florence, Italy, 1974-75. Tchr. gymnastics Los Angeles City Sch. Dist., 1973-77, judge, 1976-82; coach, choregrapher Kips Gymnastic Club, Long Beach, Calif., 1976-78, So. Calif. ACRO Team, Huntington Beach, Calif., 1979-81, UCLA, 1980-82; pres. West Coast Waves Rhythmic Gymnastics, Rolling Hills Estates, Calif., 1980—; tchr., coach Centro Olimpico Nazionale Italia, Rome, 1984-85; lectr. dance phys. edn. Calif. State U. Dominguez Hills, Carson, Calif., 1981-86; French language mistress of ceremonies Rhythmic Gymnastics team, U.S. Olympic Games, 1984; invited observer Inst. Phys. Culture, Bejing, 1985, Bulgarian Gymnastics Fedn., Sophia, 1982, 87; meet dir. State and Regional Championships, Los Angeles County, 1984, 86. Author: Body Alignment, 1985; columnist Internat. Gymnast Mag., 1987. Tour leader Acad. Tours Inc. U.S./Bulgaria Friendship Through Sports Ann. Tour, N.Y. and Bulgaria, 1987. Recipient Recognition Plaque U.S. Womens Sports Awards Banquet, 1984-88. Mem. U.S. Rhythmic Gymnastics Coaches Assn. (pres. 1984—), U.S. Gymnastics Fedn. (bd. dirs. 1985-87, nat. team coach 1984—, delegation mem. and coach internat. competitions in U.S., Mex., Hungary and Bulgaria 1984—, choreographer Children's div. 1987, Olympic Tng. Ctr. staff 1984—), Inst. Noetic Scis., Rhythmic Gymnasts Devel. Program (pres. 1984—). Republican. Office: West Coast Waves 735 Silver Spur Rolling Hills Estates CA 90274

BARRETT-STAFFORD, SUSAN CHRISTINE, accountant; b. Heidelberg, Federal Republic of Germany, Mar. 31, 1960; d. Franklin Eugene and Eleonore (Vöhringer) Barrett; m. Leslie Joel Stafford, Jan. 9, 1982; children: Nathan Edward, Marie Rochelle. BS in Bus. Acctg., Emporia (Kans.) State U., 1982. CPA, Kans. Accountant Arthur Young and Co., Wichita, Kans., 1982-85, F.B. Kubik and Co., Wichita, 1985-88; acct. Rent-a-Ctr., Wichita, Kans., 1988—. Mem. aux. com. bd. dirs. Child Care Assn. Wichita and Sedgwick County, 1986-87; bd. dirs. Planned Parenthood, Wichita, 1987. Mem. Am. Inst. CPA's, Kans. Soc. CPA's, Inst. Internal Auditors, Nat. Assn. Accts., Nat. Assn. Female Execs., Am. Soc. Women Accts., Phi Kappa Phi, Cardinal Key. Lutheran. Office: Rent-a-Ctr 8200 E Rent-a-Center Dr Wichita KS 67226

BARRING, PATRICIA JOYCE, data processing executive; b. Jersey City, Feb. 19, 1956; d. Edward Carol and Joyce Margaret (St. Lawrence) Barring. AA, Ocean County Coll., 1982; BA, Thomas Edison Coll. Hostess, mgr. Restaurant Assocs., Chatham, N.J., 1982-84; computer programmer Beneficial Mgmt. Corp., Peapach, N.J., 1984-85; mktg. rep. Cap Gemini Am., Edison, N.J., 1985-86, Computer Assistance, Edison, 1986-87; account exec. Robinson and Assocs., Clank, N.J., 1987—. Leader Girl Scouts U.S., Morris County, N.J., 1985-86. Served with USN, 1976-81, USNR, 1976—. Mem. Data Processing Mgmt. Assn., Nat. Assn. Female Execs. Republican. Home: 434 Lawrence St #10 Perth Amboy NJ 08861 Office: Robinson and Assocs 100 Walnut Ave Suite 307 Clark NJ 07066

BARRON, BARBARA MARILYN, fibre artist; b. N.Y.C., June 12, 1937; d. Samuel Leo and Anna Laura (Rosenbaum) Weinstein; m. Donald Jerome Barron, June 21, 1959; children: Nancy Ellen, Ruth Allison, Steven Joel. BA, Hunter Coll., 1958; MA, Columbia U., 1965; cert. Oxford U., Eng., 1972, Royal Sch. Needlework, Eng., 1972. Cert. elem. tchr., N.Y., elem. sch. prin., N.Y. Tchr., N.Y.C. Bd. Edn., 1959-61, Deer Park Bd. Edn., N.Y., 1961-65, Suffolk Mus., Dowling Coll., Stony Brook, N.Y., 1971, Old Bethpage Village Restoration, Woodbury Country Club, N.Y., 1975; pres. Knicely Knotted by Barbara Barron, Huntington, N.Y., 1973-79, Interior Design Crafts, Inc., Huntington, 1979-88. Interviews given to Barry Farber, N.Y.C. Radio, Joan May Channel 67, Hauppauge, N.Y. One-woman shows include Pindar Gallery, Soho, N.Y., 1982, Goff Gallery, Orlando, Fla., 1984, Suzanne Brown Gallery, Scottsdale, Ariz., 1984; exhibited in group shows: Art Expo, N.Y., Dallas, Los Angeles, 1982-85, Heckscher Mus., Huntington, 1983; selected commns. A.T. &T., Australian Film Inst., Price Waterhouse, ELFL Hutton, N.Y.C., Shearson, Lehman Hutton, N.Y.C., Premier House, Bklyn., The Madison, Dallas, Penn. Cen., Cin.; commd. artist Kehillath Shalom Synagogue, Cold Spring Harbor, N.Y., 1985; featured artist Posner Gallery, Milw. Bd. dirs. Huntington Arts Council. Democrat. Jewish. Avocations: gourmet cooking, gardening. Home: 5 Larkin St Huntington Station NY 11746 Office: Interior Design Crafts Inc 1943 New York Ave Huntington Station NY 11746

BARRON, DORA JONES, quality engineering supervisor; b. Pinetops, N.C., Sept. 27, 1960; d. Willie James and Fannie (Jenkins) Jones; m. David Norris Barron, May 11, 1985. BS in Materials Engring., N.C. State U., 1982. Sr. quality engr. Black & Decker Corp., Tarboro, N.C., 1983—; instr. Edgecombe Tech. Coll., Tarboro, 1983—, computer programmer, 1984—, geometric tolerancing instr., 1985—. Active Wolfpack Club N.C. State U., Raleigh, 1987—. L.P. Doshi scholar N.C. State U. Sch. Engring., 1981, Scholastic Achievement award N.C. State Dept. Student Affairs, 1981-82. Mem. Soc. Mfg. Engrs., Am. Soc. Metals. Democrat. Baptist. Club: Youth Christian League (Crisp, N.C.) (advisor 1986—). Home: Rt 1 Box 421 Fountain NC 27829 Office: Black & Decker 3301 Main St Tarboro NC 27886

BARRON, ILONA ELEANOR, reading educator, consultant; b. Mass, Mich., Sept. 19, 1929; cert. in elem. teaching No. Mich. U., 1951; B.S. in Elementary Edn., Central Mich. U., Mt. Pleasant, 1961; M.A. in Edn., U. Mich., Ann Arbor, 1966; postgrad. Mich. State U., East Lansing; m. George Barron; 1 son, Fred. Tchr. elem. schs., 1952-67; Title I dir. Saginaw (Mich.) Twp. Community Schs., 1967-68, reading cons., 1971—; elementary intern cons. Mich. State U., 1968-71; elementary reading cons. Saginaw Twp. Public Schs., 1972—. Mem. NEA, Mich., Saginaw Twp. Edn. Assns., Saginaw Area Reading Council. Specialist in reading, methods of teaching developmental reading skills and enrichment. Home: 4891 Hillcrest Dr Saginaw MI 48603 Office: Plainfield Elem Sch 2775 Shattuck Rd Saginaw MI 48601

BARRON, LISBETH RAE, securities executive; b. White Plains, N.Y., July 13, 1962; d. Herman Joseph and Carla (Geminder) B. Student, UCLA, 1979-80; certificat d'etudes, Universite D'Angers, Anjou, France, 1980; BBA, Fla. Atlantic U., Boca Raton, 1982; MBA, Harvard U., 1986. Sales mgr. Cartier, Inc., Palm Beach, Fla., 1980-81; dir bus. affairs High Resolution Sciences, Inc., Los Angeles, 1982-84; v.p., instl. securities analyst Balis Zorn Gerard Inc., N.Y.C., 1986—. U.S. Open Backgammon Champion. Mem. Beta Gamma Sigma. Home: 401 E 34th St Apt 21L S New York NY 10016 Office: Balis Zorn Gerard Inc 80 Broad St New York NY 10004

BARRON, SHIRLEY ANNE, exhibit manager; b. Renfrew, Can., May 31, 1955; d. Gordon Angus and Gertrude Elizabeth (Boyce) Carty; m. Paul Edward Barron, Aug. 17, 1946. Secretarial diploma, Algonquin Coll., Ottawa, Ont., 1974. Sec. I Telesat Can., Ottawa, 1974-77, sec. II, 1974-80, sec. III, 1980-81, sec. to v.p., 1981-83, exhibits and displays coordinator, 1983-85, exhibits and displays officer, 1985-87, sr. advt. and promotionofficer, 1987—. Bd. dirs. United Way of Ottawa Carlton, 1986—, exec. bd. 1987—. Mem. Internat. Exhibits Assn., Assn. Profl. Exhibitors Can. (pres. 1987—), Can. Assn. Exhibit Mgrs., Trade Show Bur., Ottawa Hort. Soc., Ikebana Soc. Mem. United Ch. of Can. Office: Telesat Canada, 333 River Rd, Ottawa, ON Canada K1L 8B9

BARROS, ANNAMARIE, management consultant; b. San Jose, Calif., Mar. 14, 1932; d. Anthony Clarence and Clara Magdalene Pacheco Vierra; B.A., Coll. Holy Names, Oakland, Calif., 1953; M.A., Central Mich. U., 1978; m. Richard L. Barros, June 11, 1960. Intern med. tech. O'Connor Hosp., San Jose, 1953-54; adminstrv. technologist Children's Hosp., San Francisco, 1958-65, Good Samaritan Hosp., San Jose, 1965-74; adminstrv. asst. public relations and mktg. Lab. Services, 1974-76; mgmt. devel. coordinator O'Connor Hosp., 1976-78; mgmt. cons., educator, propr. Health Mgmt. Analysts, Los Gatos, Calif., 1976—; adj. prof. grad. program clin. scis. San Francisco State U., 1976—; lab. ops. advisor Ernst & Whinney, Chgo., 1984—; sec.-treas. Nat. Cert. Agy. Med. Lab. Personnel, 1977-83, v.p., 1983-84; presenter workshops. Bd. dirs. Santa Clara County chpt. ARC, 1980-84; pres. Rinconada Hills Homeowners Assn., 1977-80. Named Med. Technologist of Yr. in Calif., 1969, 77. Mem. Am. Soc. Med. Tech. (pres. 1973-74, chmn. personnel relations com. 1981-84; named Adminstrv. Technologist of Yr. 1973, Mem. of Yr. 1978, recipient Profl. Achievement award 1979), Am. Mgmt. Assn., Calif. Soc. Med. Tech., Clin. Lab. Mgmt. Assn. Republican. Roman Catholic. Author articles, column in field. Address: 129 Callecita St Los Gatos CA 95030

BARROW, GERALDINE, tax accountant; b. St. Clairsville, Ohio, July 12, 1938; d. John B. and Campsie I. (Henry) Washington; m. Albert L. Barrow, Feb. 16, 1958 (div. Mar. 1983). A.A.B., Cuyahoga Community Coll., 1982. Tax dept. clk. Stouffer Corp., Solon, Ohio, 1968-70, tax asst., 1971-72, asst. tax acct., 1972-73, tax acct., 1974-81, state and local tax mgr., 1982—. Mem. Nat. Assn. Female Execs., Tax Club of Cleve. Democrat. Methodist. Home: 4538 Warrensville Ctr Rd North Randall OH 44128 Office: Stouffer Corp 29800 Bainbridge Rd Solon OH 44139

BARROWS, FRANCINE ELEANOR, educator, corporate secretary; b. Bridgeport, Conn., Nov. 16, 1948; d. Joseph John and Eleanor Sylvia (Torok) Csonka; m. Robert Lynn Barrows, Oct. 8, 1983; children: Joshua Lyn, Craig Scott (twins). BA, Sacred Heart U., 1970; postgrad., Fairfield U., 1978. Cert. permanent Tchr., Conn. Sales and office head Howland-Steinbach, Fairfield, Conn., 1967-86; tchr. Garfield Sch., Bridgeport, Conn., 1970—; sec., stockholder RC Hobbies of Conn., Inc., Milford, Conn., 1983—. Mem. NEA, Conn. Edn. Assn., Bridgeport Edn. Assn., Acad. of Model Aero., Milford C. of C., Mother of Twins Club, Pi Sigma Phi. Roman Catholic. Office: RC Hobbies of Conn Inc 374 New Haven Ave Milford CT 06460

BARRY, BEVERLY JEAN, data network executive; b. Boston, May 21, 1951; d. Edgar George and Doris Lillian (Girard) McKenna; m. Arthur J. Barry, Jan. 3, 1981; 1 child, Christin J. BS, U. Mass., 1973; MBA, Babson Coll., 1981. Programmer Linolex div. 3M, Billerica, Mass., 1974-77; software engr. GCA, Andover, Mass., 1977-81; sr. test engr. Honeywell, Billerica, Mass., 1981-83; sr. software specialist Digital Equipment Corp., Burlington, Mass., 1983-86; sr. network specialist Digital Equipment Corp., Littleton, Mass., 1986—. Office: Digital Equipment 550 King St Littleton MA 01460

BARRY, JANE MARY, employee benefits executive, consultant; b. Brockville, Ont., Can., Mar. 21, 1947; came to U.S., 1949; d. James Joseph and Gertrude Frances (Halpin) B.; m. Robert Morgan Epler, Apr. 29, 1978 (dec. 1983). B.A., St. Lawrence U., 1969. Adminstr., New Eng. Life Ins., Boston, 1969-71; cons. Haber & Stoller, Inc., San Francisco, 1971-74; cons., v.p. Robert M. Epler Co., Inc., San Diego, 1974-83; cons., pres. The Epler Co., San Diego, 1983—; bd. mem. Western Pension Conf. ann. meeting, San Diego, 1983. Editor Epler Reports, 1977-85. Mem. Assn. Pvt. Pension and Welfare Plans, Western Pension Conf. (bd. dirs. 1984-86), Women in Bus., Girls Club of East County Found. (pres.). Avocations: reading; swimming; racquetball. Home: 2727 Morena St Suite 105 San Diego CA 92117 Office: 450 B St Suite 750 San Diego CA 92101-8002

BARRY, JANET CECILIA, educator; b. Jersey City, May 12, 1944; d. John Aloysius and Mary Elizabeth (Hart) B.; B.A., Paterson State Coll., 1966; M.A., Georgian Ct. Coll., 1978. Tchr., Paterson (N.J.) Public Sch. No. 12, 1966-68; tchr. Walnut St. Elem. Sch., Toms River (N.J.) Regional Sch. System, 1968—. Recipient N.J. Gov.'s Excellence in Teaching award, 1987. Mem. Nat. Council Tchrs. English, NEA, N.J. Edn. Assn., Ocean County Edn. Assn., Toms River Edn. Assn., Assn. for Supervision and Curriculum Devel., N.J. Reading Assn., N.J. Assn. for Supervision and Curriculum Devel., Internat. Reading Assn., Ocean County Reading Council (rec. sec., 1st v.p., pres.), Georgian Ct. Coll. Grad. Sch. Alumni Assn. (sec.), Delta Kappa Gamma (program chmn.). Address: 219 Wells Mills Rd Waretown NJ 08758

BARRY, JAYNE ANNE, nurse; b. Springfield, Mo., Nov. 30, 1959; d. Charles Leland and Janet Loraine (Wilson) B. BS, SW Baptist U., 1981; BS in Nursing, St. Louis U., 1982. Cert. neurosci. registered nurse. Nurse Cox Med. Ctr., Springfield, Mo., 1982-86, Pub. Health Service, Indian Health Service, Tuba City, Ariz., 1986—; nurse HELP, St. Louis, 1983—, Health Fairs, Springfield, 1983. Camp counselor HMB of So. Bapt. Ch., Idaho, Oreg., Washington, 1978-79, recreation dir., Mo., Idaho, 1976-78. Mem. Nat. Assn. Female Execs., Am. Assn. Neurosurg. Nurses, Sigma Theta Tau. Democrat. Home: 1248 E Harrison Springfield MO 65804

BARRY, JOYCE ALICE, dietitian; b. Chgo., Apr. 27, 1932; d. Walter Stephen and Ethel Myrtle (Paetow) Barry; student Iowa State Coll., 1950-52, Loyala U., 1952-58; B.S., Mundelein Coll., 1955; postgrad. Simmons Coll., 1963-64, U. Ga., 1979, Calif. Western U., 1980—. Prodn. supr. Marshall Field & Co., Chgo., 1955-59; dir. food services Women's Ednl. and Indsl. Union, Boston, 1959-62; dir. food services Wellesley Public Schs., Mass., 1962-70; cons. Stokes Food Services, Newton, Mass., 1960-70; regional dietitian Canteen Corp., Chgo., 1970-83; gen. mgr. bus. devel. Plantation-Sysco, Orlando, Fla., 1983-87; dir. product devel. corp. procurement Mariott Internat. Hdqrs., Washington, 1987—; vis. lectr.; restaurant cons. Mem. Nat. Consumer Panel; research adv. council Restaurant Bus. Mag.; career adv. council, Am. Dietetics Assn.; treas. Dietitians in Bus. Mem. Am. Home Econs. Assn., Internat. Fedn. Home Economists, Home Economists in Bus., Am. Dietetics Assn., Soc. Nutrition Edn., Nat. Assn. Female Execs., Roundtable Women in Food Service, Dieticians in Bus. Intentional Platform Assn. Republican. Roman Catholic. Club: La Chaine des Rotisseurs. Home: 175 Heron Bay Circle Lake Mary FL 32746 Office: Marriott World Hdqrs 1 Marriott Dr Washington DC 20058

BARRY, LEI, medical equipment manufacturing executive; b. Fitchburg, Mass., May 27, 1941; d. Leo Isaacson and Irene Helen (Melanson) Isaacson Godbout; m. Delbert M. Berry (div.); children: David M., Susan L.; m. Frank H. Mahan III, June 25, 1976; stepchildren: Jodi L., Sarah C., Amy S., Frank H. IV. Grad. high sch., Waltham, Mass. Advt. salesperson, broadcaster various radio and TV stas., N.C. and Tex., 1961-67; New Eng. sales rep. Hollister, Inc., Chgo., 1967-71, Northeastern sales mgr., 1971-76; v.p., ptnr. Mahan Assocs., Blue Bell, Pa., 1976—; pres. Blue Bell Bio-Med., Inc., 1982—. Mem. Whitpain Twp. Planning commn.; pres., bd. dirs. Interfaith of Ambler; dir. Elder, United Ch. of Christ, 1978— . Mem. Wissahickon Valley C. of C., Wissahickon Valley Hist. Soc. (past bd. dirs.), Wissahickon Valley Watershed Assn., Nat. Bus. and Profl. Women's Club, Health Associated Reps., Nat. Assn. Female Execs., Bus. Women's Network Phila., NOW. Republican. Avocations: tennis, skiing, gourmet cooking. Office: Blue Bell Bio-Med Inc PO Box 49 Blue Bell PA 19422

BARRY, MARILYN WHITE, educator; b. Weymouth, Mass., Sept. 12, 1936; d. Harland Russell and Alice Louise (Dwyer) White; m. Dennis Edward Barry, July 11, 1959; children—Dennis Edward, Christopher Gerard. BS in Edn. Bridgewater State Coll., 1958; Ed.M. in Spl. Edn., Boston U., 1969, Ed.D. in Spl. Edn., 1974. Tchr. Weymouth pub. schs. (Mass.), 1958-60; spl. edn. instr. Boston U., 1972-74; asst. prof. in spl. edn. Bridgewater State Coll., (Mass.), 1974-79, assoc. prof., 1979-83, prof., 1983—, chmn. spl. edn. dept., 1979-87, coordinator dept. grad. programs, 1979-87, adminstr. bilingual spl. edn. training grant, 1983-86, dean grad. sch., 1987—. Coauthor human service workers curriculum materials. Boston U. fellow, 1967-74; 3 Disting. Service awards, Bridgewater State Coll., 1980, 82, 85; Bilingual Spl. Edn. grantee, 1980, 83. Mem. Council Exceptional Children (Mass. chpt. founder, past pres.), Mass. Assn. Children With Learning Disabilities (past v.p.), Phi Delta Kappa, Pi Lambda Theta. Democrat. Roman Catholic. Home: 138 Bedford St Lakeville MA 02346 Office: Bridgewater State Coll Grad Sch Conant Sci Bldg Bridgewater MA 02324

BARRY, MARY ALICE, financial executive; b. Quincy, Mass., Dec. 31, 1928; d. Lawrence Joseph and Alice Mary (Blaisdell) B. BS, Emmanuel Coll., 1950; postgrad., N.Y. U. With FBI, Boston, 1950-56, Nat. Assn. Investment Cos., N.Y.C., 1958-59, Dreyfus Fund, N.Y.C., 1959-62; corp. sec. The Alliance Fund, Inc., 1965—, Surveyor Fund, Inc., 1966—; asst. v.p. Alliance Capital Mgmt. Corp., N.Y.C., 1985—; corp. sec. Alliance Dividend Shares, Inc., 1986—, Alliance Dividend Shares Inc., 1986—. Home: 520 E 81st St Apt 6A New York NY 10028 Office: Alliance Fund 1345 Ave of Americas New York NY 10105

BARRY, MARY JANE, computer consultant; b. N.Y.C., June 10, 1939; d. William Richard and Marion Rose (Cullen) Connor; m. William Francis Barry, Sept. 21, 1963; children: Denise Margaret, Paul Francis, William Connor. BS in Secondary Edn., Fordham U., 1961; MEd in Adminstrn., U. Mo., St. Louis, 1978. Tchr. N.Y.C. Bd. Edn., 1961-68, Spl. Sch. Dist. St. Louis County, Mo., 1970-77, Archdiocese of St. Louis, 1978-80; instr. St. Louis U., 1980-81; tchr. Villa Duchesne High Sch., St. Louis, 1981-83; prin., pres. MJB Assocs., Inc., St. Louis, 1983—; sub. instr. St. Louis Community Coll., 1984—; panelist U.S. Small Bus. Adminstrn. Entrepreneurship Forum, St. Louis, Kansas City, Mo., 1986. Contbr. articles to local mags. Lay advisor St. Louis Met. Med. Soc., St. Louis, 1985-86. Recipient Gen. Motors scholarship Fordham U., 1957-61. Mem. Ind. Computer Consultants Assn. (v.p. 1984-85, pres. 1985-86, Murray Zuckerman award 1984), Nat. Assn. Women Bus. Owners, Women in Networking, Assn. St. Louis Info. Systems Trainers, Kirkwood (Mo.) C. of C. Republican. Roman Catholic. Club: USCG Wives (sec. N.Y. chpt. 1966, sec. St. Louis chpt. 1969-70); Ladies Sodality (numerous offices St. Louis chpt.). Home and Office: 1447 Breezeridge Dr Saint Louis MO 63131-4210

BARRY, MARYANNE TRUMP, judge; b. 1937; d. Fred C. and Mary Trump. BA, Mt. Holyoke Coll., 1958; MA, Columbia U., 1962; JD, Hofstra U., 1974. Asst. U.S. Atty. 1974-75, dep. chief appeals div., 1976-77, chief appeals div., 1977-82, exec. asst. U.S. Atty., 1981-82, 1st asst., 1981-83; judge U.S. Dist Ct. N.J., 1983—. Office: US Dist Ct PO & Courthouse Bldg PO Box 419 Newark NJ 07101

BARRY, MICHAELA MARIE, data processing company executive; b. Manchester, N.H., Apr. 6, 1960; d. Robert E. and Janet (Smith) B.; m. Douglas Edwards, July 11, 1981 (div. July 1985); m. Kurt D. Baumann, Oct. 31, 1985. AA, U. N.H., 1982; BS, Boston U., 1984. Disc jockey for several entertainment orgns. and radio stas. N.H., Eastbourne, Eng., and Muscat, Oman, 1977-79, 81-82; news dir., reporter Sta. WMUR-TV, Manchester, 1979-81; chief fin. officer Learning Tree Software, Inc., Reston, Va., 1982—; prof. kickboxing instr., judge, 1985—. Author short stories; contbr. articles to profl. jours. Mem. Nat. Assn. Female Execs., Women in Communications, Soc. Profl. Journalists, Afnord Assn. Office: Learning Tree Software Inc PO Box 3567 Reston VA 22090

BARSLY, SALLY JONELLE, manufacturing executive; b. Ephrata, Pa., Sept. 18, 1963; d. Franklin B. and Peggy Lou (Showalter) S. Twinning operator Berk-Tek, Inc., New Holland, Pa., 1983-86, asst. facilitator, tng. coordinator, 1986—; also mem. various coms. Berk-Tek, Inc., New Holland. Author: (newspaper column) Live Wire, 1986-87. Mem. Am. Mgmt. Assn., Mfrs. Assn. Berks County. Office: Berk-Tek Inc RD 1 Box 888 New Holland PA 17557

BARSOOK, BEVERLY JEAN, association executive; b. Detroit, May 4, 1945; d. Burt and Marcella (McNerney) B. BA, U. N.Mex., 1967, M in Community and Regional Planning, 1982. Mgr. Maxwell Mus., Albuquerque, 1968-78; coordinator publs. Mus. Store Assn., Doylestown, Pa., 1983-85, exec. dir., 1985—. Author: Is a Retail Business For You, (with others) 7 Families in Pueblo Pottery, 1974, Fundraising for Nonprofit Institutions, 1987; editor: (book) Financial Analysis for Museum Stores, 1985. Mem. com. Archtl. Rev. Bd., Buckingham Twp., Pa., 1983—, Environ. Study Com., 1983—; active Raptor Edn. Found., Denver. Recipient cert. Minn. Outward Bound, 1982; fellow U. N.Mex., 1978-79; grantee Nat. Endowment for the Arts, 1972. Mem. Am. Soc. Assn. Execs. (cert. in communications 1986). Office: Mus Store Assn 501 S Cherry St Suite 460 Denver CO 80222

BART, MURIEL, library educator; b. N.Y.C., May 9, 1926; d. Harry and Sarah Deborah (Israelite) Singer; m. Leonard Eugene Bart, Feb. 15, 1953; children—Andrew Harrison, Jonathan James. BA U. Conn., 1947, M.A., 1948; M.L.S., Queen's U., SUNY, 1966. Cert. sch. adminstr., N.Y. Tchr. social studies N.Y.C. Bd. Edn., 1949-54, library tchr., 1964-67, librarian-in-charge, 1967-87; dir. N.Y.C. Sch. Library System, 1987—; Mem. editorial adv. bd. High Points, 1970—, asst. to bd. examiners, 1980—; lectr. in field; workshop leader. Contbr. articles, book revs. to profl. jours. NDEA/ESEA grantee, 1972. Mem. ALA (chmn. vocat. tech. panel 1983-85), N.Y.C. Sch. Librarians Assn. (chmn. edn. com. 1974-76), N.Y. Library Club (sec. 1978-80, pres. 1985-86).

BART, POLLY TURNER, realtor; b. Peterborough, N.H., Feb. 28, 1944; d. Benjamin Franklin and Catherine (James) B.; m. Harry Nelson Pharr II, Oct. 27, 1969 (div. May 1972); 1 child, Greta Rose. BA, Radcliffe Coll., 1965; M in City Planning, U. Calif., Berkeley, 1974, PhD, 1979. Cons. city planning Marshall Kaplan, Gans, & Kahn, San Francisco, 1967; city planner County of Napa, Calif., 1968-69; asst. instr. U. Tex., Austin, 1971-72; cons. Dept. HUD, Washington, 1979-81; asst. prof. U. Md., College Park, 1981-84; real estate salesperson Coldwell Banker Comml. Real Estate Services, Balt., 1984-87; pres. Investment Properties Brokerage, Inc., Balt., 1988—; bd. dirs. assoc. Columbia Forum, Md., 1981-85; contbr. Nat Urban Policy Report to Congress, 1980. Co-editor EDRA, 1981; contbr. Nat. Urban Policy Report to Congress; contbr. articles to profl. jours. Mem. Balt. Symphony Chorus. Fellow Radcliffe Coll., 1962-64, Danforth Found., 1975-79, Ford Found., 1981. Mem. Comml. Real Estate Women (founder, treas. 1987), Greater Balt. Bd. Realtors. Home: 629 S Hanover St Baltimore MD 21230 Office: Investment Properties Brokerage Inc 111 S Calvert St Suite 2700 Baltimore MD 21202

BARTA, KELLY LEE, financial analyst; b. Jamestown, N.Y., May 3, 1960; d. Richard Lee and Virginia (Guthrie) Fisher; m. Michael C. Barta, Oct. 20, 1984. A in Applied Sci., Fashion Inst. Tech., N.Y.C., 1980; BS in Mktg., U. Mass., Boston, 1982. Asst. dept. mgr. Bloomingdales, Chestnut Hill, Mass., 1981-83; project fin. officer Mass. Indsl. Fin. Agy., Boston, 1984—; bd. dirs., sec. Mass. Indsl. Fin. Agy., Boston. Active Boston Archtl. Ctr., Boston Mus. Fine Arts. Home: 196 Highland Ave Winchester MA 01890 Office: Mass Indsl Fin Agy 400 Atlantic Ave Boston MA 02210

BARTA, SUE BLAIR, realtor; b. Thorpe, W.Va., Dec. 6, 1938; d. James Joseph and Goldzsie (Chewning) Blair; m. Joseph Arthur Barta, June 18, 1960; children: Mark Blair, Michael Joseph, Amy Sue, Laura. BS, Longwood Coll., 1959; MS, Radford U. Tchr. Morgantown, W.Va., 1960-63, Am. Schs., Aschaffenburg, Fed. Rep. Germany, 1967-68; realtor Jess Realty Inc., Radford, Va., 1983—. Charter mem. Presidential Task Force. Mem. Nat. Assn. Realtors, Va. Assn. Realtors, New River Valley Assn. Realtors. Republican. Roman Catholic. Home: 404 Harvey St Radford VA 24141 Office: Jess Realty Inc Hwy 749 Radford VA 24141

BARTELMAY, JANET LYNN, lawyer; b. Youngstown, Ohio, July 17, 1954; d. Norman Paul and Kathleen Marie (Knight) B.; m. Dennis Paul Koeppel, Oct. 8, 1983; 1 child, Katherine Bartelmay Koeppel. BS in Edn. with honors, U. Mich., 1975; JD with honors, George Washington U., 1983. Bar: D.C. 1983. Atty. Assn. Am. R.R., Washington, 1984—. Bd. dirs. Assn. for Retarded Citizens, 1970-80. Named one of Outstanding Young Women in Am., 1979. Mem. ABA, D.C. Bar Assn. Office: Assn Am RR 50 F St NW Washington DC 20001

BARTELS, ANN-MARIE, public relations company owner; b. Alton, Ill., Dec. 15, 1954; d. Norman William Bartels and Betty L. (Pruessing) Julian. Student, So. Ill. U., 1972-76. Pub. relations dir. Showtime, Inc., St. Louis, 1976-78; pub. relations coordinator Ringling Bros. and Barnum & Bailey Circus, Washington, 1978, pub. relations dir., 1979-81; pub. relations cons., Belleville, Ill., 1981-82; mktg. mgr. Am. Fedn. Info. Processing Socs., Reston, Va., 1982-84, dep. dir. confs., 1984-87; owner The Amber Group, 1987—; dir. pub. relations Mid-Am. Payment Exchange, St. Louis, 1987—. Recipient merit cert. Graphic Arts/Printing Industries Am., 1982, excellence certs. for exhibit promotions Conv. Promotion Assn. Trends, 1983. Mem. Am. Soc. Assn. Execs. Republican. Office: Mid-Am Payment Exchange 330 N 4th St Suite 308 Saint Louis MO 63102

BARTELS WILKINSON, JAMI ELIZABETH, innkeeper, rancher, art consultant, artist; b. Armstrong, Iowa, July 16, 1941; d. Homer Wesley and Dorothy Irene (Bunday) Wilkinson; m. Donald Lee Bartels, June 30, 1974; 1 child by previous marriage, Dina Lyn. Student Drake U., 1959; A.A., Orange Coast Coll., 1971; student Napa Valley Coll., 1980-82. Office mgr., asst. to v.p. Zinsco Elec. Products, Los Angeles, 1963-65; office mgr. Raif Realty Inc., Montebello, Calif., 1965-67; gen. mgr. Chris-Craft West, Inc., Newport Beach, Calif., 1967-69; exec. dir. Orange Coast Coll. Vol. Bur., Costa Mesa, Calif., 1970-72; v.p. Newport Pacific, Inc., Newport Beach, 1972-74; owner Willow House Antiques, El Sobrante, Calif., 1976-80; owner Bartels Ranch & Country Inn, St. Helena, Calif., 1979—; ptnr. Bartels Realtors & Investments, St. Helena, Richmond, Calif., 1974—; dir. Napa Valley Repertory, Calistoga, Calif., 1985—. Chmn. Christian Bookstore Benefit, Grace Episcopal, St. Helena, Calif., 1981; chmn. membership Napa Valley Symphony Assn., St. Helena, 1985; chmn. Hearts for the Arts Benefit, St. Helena, 1986; co-founder, dir., pres. Napa County Arts Council, Yountville, Calif., 1980-84; state/local planner Calif. Arts Council/Napa County Arts Council, Napa, Calif., 1982-83; bd. dirs. Napa Valley Visitors Assn., Napa, 1985—; U.S. Friendship Ambassador to Japan, 1978. Named Saleswoman of Yr., Bayliner Boat Corp., Orcas Island, Wash., 1973-74. Mem. Am. Bed and Breakfast Assn., Wine Country Artists (v.p. 1984), Napa Valley Bed and Breakfast Innkeepers Assn. (v.p. 1984), Bed and Breakfast Innkeepers No. Calif. (dir. 1984-86), Calif. Lodging Industry Assn., Napa County C. of C., St. Helena C. of C. (dir. 1985-86), Epsilon Sigma Alpha. Republican. Lutheran. Club: Orange Coast Coll Law (Costa Mesa, Calif.) (pres. 1969-70). Avocations: art, internat. travel, wine appreciation. Office: 1200 Conn Valley Rd St Helena CA 94574

BARTER, RUBY SUNSHINE, realtor; b. Omaha; d. Harry and Ruth (Gilman) Kolnick; m. Gerson Barter; children: Bruce, Mark, Sharon Sunshine Silverman, Peggy Sunshine Brooks, Jeffrey, Randi Sunshine Simon, JoAnne Sunshine Trombley, Ronald Sunshine. BS in Med. Tech., Creighton U.; postgrad., Clarkson Meml. Hosp. Sch. Med. Tech., U. Colo. Sch. Continuing Edn. Cert. Comml.-Investment Mems. Med. technologist Creighton Meml. St. Joseph Hosp.; realtor Nat. Real Estate and Mgmt. Co., Heller-Mark & Co., Walpin & Co., Denver; Mem. Mayors Adv. Com. on Denver's War on Poverty; project dir. Denver Citywide Headstart Vols.; mem. adv. com. Dialogue Regiis Coll.; mem. exec. com. Anti-Defamation League, Hillel Councils; vol. Nat. Jewish Hosp., Jewish Community Ctr.; mem. exec. bd. Beth Joseph Congregation; active Adult Edn. Council Denver, Internat. House; Dolls for Democracy Lady Dever Pub. Schs. Mem. Nat. Real Estate Commn., Colo. Real Estate Commn., Denver Real Estate Commn. (liaison com.), Bd. Realtors, Real Estate Exchangers, Realtors Nat. Mktg. Inst., Real Estate Securities Syndication Inst. Home: 201 S Dexter St Denver CO 80222 Office: 1550 E 17th Ave Denver CO 80218

BARTHEL, HAZEL PHOEBE, health care executive; b. Young America, Minn., Oct. 13, 1933; d. Clarence William and Phoebe Emilie (Affeldt) Schwich; m. Bruce Owen Barthel, July 14, 1956 (div. Feb. 1985); children: Lisa Ellen, Larry, Scott, Paul. BS in Edn., U. Utah, 1955; MBA, Wayland Bapt. U., 1988. Tchr. Good Shepherd Luth. Sch., Englewood, Calif., 1955-56; coordinator music Grace Luth. Ch., Midland, Tex., 1974-77; edn. coordinator St. Anthony's Hospice, Amarillo, Tex., 1983-85, asst. dir., 1985-86; exec. dir. Hospice of the Plains, Plainview, Tex., 1986—; tchr. Clarendon Jr. Coll., Pampa, Tex., 1987; cons. Hospice of Pampa, 1987. Mem. exec. bd. Rep. Women's Club, Midland, Tex., 1968; vol. coordinator St. Anthony's Hospice, Amarillo, 1982-86; bd. dirs. Tex. Hospice Orgn., 1988—, ethics and standards com., 1987—. Mem. Am. Guild of Organists (Tex. Hospice orgn. dean Midland chpt. 1976-77). Club: Petroleum Engr. Wives' (Amarillo) (pres. 1980-81). Home and Office: Monarch Care Resources 3914 Kileen Amarillo TX 79109

BARTHLOME, RANDIE LEE, law enforcement administrator, consultant; b. Laramie, Wyo., May 4, 1948; d. Ralph Randall and Wilma Lee (Hawk) Benintendi; m. Edward Earl Barthlome, May 5, 1973; children—Sherri Lanee, Lori Lynn, Thomas Arthur, Greg Edward. Student Community Coll. of Denver, 1971-72, Idaho State U. Law Enforcement Acad., 1972-73, Idaho Peace Officer Acad., 1973, Idaho State U., 1977, Duke U., 1985. Advanced law enforcement cert.; cert. law enforcement instr. Advt., pub. relations dir. Consumer Enterprises, Denver, 1969-72; tutor Idaho State U., Pocatello, 1972; officer Blackfoot Police Dept. (Idaho), 1972-73; sec. Idaho Peace Officer Acad., Pocatello, 1973-74; crime prevention officer Pocatello Police Dept., 1974-80, dir., 1980-85; pres. SYNTAX, 1985—; pvt. practice cons., 1983—; circuit rider city mgr. Towns of Fowler, Orduay, and Sugar City, Colo., 1987—. Author weekly newspaper column: Police Watch, 1974-85, also articles. Adv. bd. Salvation Army, Pocatello, 1982-85; com. chmn. Mayor's Com. for Handicapped, Pocatello, 1982—; pres. Pocatello Community Services Council, 1975-76; founder Women's Advocates for Battered Women, Pocatello, 1976—. Named Citizen of Yr., Idaho Pros. Attys. Assn., 1982, Idaho Outstanding Supr., Manpower Consortium, 1981, Disting. Young Woman, Pocatello Jay-C-Ettes, 1979; recipient Nat. Award of Merit, Nat. Crime Prevention Coalition, 1981. Mem. Idaho Crime Prevention Assn. (founding, pres. 1981-82), Idaho Peace Officers Assn., Am. Soc. Tng. and Devel., Internat. City Mgmt. Assn., Idaho Press Club, Am. Bus. Women's Assn., Idaho Assn. for Affirmative Action, Am. Mktg. Assn., Centennial C. of C., Denver C. of C. Baptist. Lodge: Zonta. Home: 1170 E Phillips Dr Littleton CO 80122 Office: Syntax 13111 E Briarwood Ave Suite 250 Englewood CO 80112

BARTHOLD, CLEMENTINE B., judge; b. Odessa, Russia, Jan. 11, 1921; came to U.S., 1925; d. Joseph Anton and Magdalene (Richter) Schwan; m. Edward Brendel Barthold, July 5, 1941 (dec.); children—Judith Anne Barthold DeSimone, John Edward; m. Joel L. Stokes, Jr., Feb. 7, 1981. Student Aberdeen Bus. Coll., 1940; B.G.S., Ind. U. Southeast, 1978; J.D., Ind. U.-Indpls., 1980. Bar: Ind. 1980, U.S. Dist. Ct. (so. dist.) Ind., 1980. Sec. and asst. to mgr. Clark County C. of C. (Ind.), 1959-60; chief probation officer Clark Circuit Ct. and Superior Cts., Jeffersonville, 1960-72; research cons. Pub. Action Correctional Effort, Clark and Floyd Counties, 1972-75; instl. parole officer Ind. Women's Prison, Indpls., 1975-80; atty. State of Ind., 1980-83; judge Clark Superior Ct. No. 1, Jeffersonville, 1983—. Active in developing and implementing juvenile delinquency prevention and alternative programs, group counseling for juvenile delinquents and restitution programs. Treas. Ladies Elks Aux., Jeffersonville. Recipient Good Govt. award Jeffersonville Jaycees, 1966, Good Citizenship award, 1967; Wonder Woman award, 1984, Robert J. Kinsey award, 1986, Sagamore of Wabash award, 1986, Outstanding Community Service award Social Concerns League, Jeffersonville, 1966, Disting. Service award, Outstanding Contbn. to Field of Correction award, Women of Achievement award, Jeff BPW Appreciation award, Juvenile Justice award, Disting. Contemporary Women in History award, Disting. Leadership award. Mem. ABA, Ind. Bar Assn., Clark County Bar Assn., Ind. Correctional Assn. (pres. 1971, Disting. Service award 1967, 85), Nat. Assn. Women Judges, Ind. Judges Assn., Ind. Juvenile and Family Ct. Judges (task force), Jefferson County Women Lawyers Assn., Am. Bus. Women's Assn, NAACP, Jeff Preservation, Inc., Clark County C. of C., Older Women's League, Ind. U. Alumni Assn., Howard Steamboat Mus., LWV, Bus. and Profl. Women's Club. Democrat. Roman Catholic. Home: 948 E 7th St Jeffersonville IN 47130 Office: Clark Superior Ct No 1 500 E Court Ave Jeffersonville IN 47130

BARTHOLOME, PAULA TERESA, marketing consultant; b. Terre Haute, Ind., July 31, 1951; d. Paul Ralph and Lois Virginia (Bilderback) B. B.S. in Bus. with honors, Ind. U., 1973. Mgmt. trainee Irwin Union Bank, Columbus, Ind., 1973-74, systems officer, 1974-76, mktg. officer, 1976-78; asst. v.p. mktg. Pioneer Bank, Chgo., 1979-80, v.p. mktg., 1980; dir. research and product devel. WN Lane Interfin., Northbrook, Ill., 1980-81, dir. mktg. services, 1981-82, v.p. mktg., 1982-86; mktg. cons., 1986; mng. dir. mktg. and communications Bank Adminstrn. Inst., 1986—; dir., past pres., Chgo. Fin. Advertisers. Mem. Publicity Club of Chgo., Bus. Vols. for the Arts (bd. dirs.).

BARTHOLOMEW, ANITA, freelance advertising writer; b. Bay Shore, N.Y., Jan. 14, 1949; d. Guido and Elizabeth (Ornato) Del Giudice m. Frank J. Tomaino, Oct. 5, 1968 (div.); 1 child, Alexander G. Tomaino. Student, SUNY, Purchase, 1981-83, Sch. Visual Arts, N.Y.C., 1984. Copywriter Ventura Assocs., N.Y.C., 1982-83, Equity Advt., N.Y.C., 1983-84, Pace Advt., N.Y.C., 1984-85; prin. Anita Bartholomew Communications, Tarrytown, N.Y., 1985—; freelance copywriter Donnelley Mktg., Holt, Rinehart/CBS Pub., SAS Airlines, The Luce Corp., Westchester Women's News, numerous others. Contbr. articles to profl. jours. Mem. Am. Soc. for Psychical Research, People for the Ethical Treatment of Animals, Mensa.

BARTHOLOMEW, GAIL FRANCES, small business owner, educator; b. La Follette, Tenn., Dec. 10, 1946; d. Ralph and Irene Ida (Hale) Wilson; m. Harold George Prasek, Aug. 15, 1969 (div. July 1979); 1 child, James Harold; m. Donald William Bartholomew, Sept. 15, 1979. AA, Indian Valley Coll., Novato, Calif., 1975, Clark County Community Coll., North Las Vegas, Nev., 1983; B of Mgmt., Golden State U., 1984. Account clk. Drs. Bus. Bur., Long Beach, Calif., 1967-69; library clk. Long Beach Pub. Library, 1970-71; property disposal clk. Def. Property Disposal Office, Hamilton AFB, Calif., 1974-76; payroll clk. USN, Alameda NAS, Calif., 1977-78; adminstr. asst. USAF, Nellis AFB, Calif., 1978-80, Lionel Sawyer and Collins, Las Vegas, Nev., 1981-84; legal asst., owner Legal Links, Las Vegas, Nev., 1985—; instr. Clark County Community Coll., Las Vegas, 1985—, labor relations specialist. Vol. Democratic Party, Las Vegas, 1985-87. Mem. Nat. Assoc. Legal Assts. Democrat. Mormon. Home and Office: 1200 North Lamb #132 Las Vegas NV 89110

BARTHOLOMEW, LYNN MICHELE, marketing executive, optician; b. Louisville, June 10, 1949; d. Richard Deitz and Bette Jean (Beisler) B. BS, Ind. U., 1971, postgrad., 1987—. Lic. optician, Ky. Office mgr. James A. Way, MD, Bloomington, Ind., 1972-76; office mgr., apprentice optician William J. Collis, Pub. Service Co., Lexington, Ky., 1977-78; pvt. practice optician Lexington, 1978-79; owner, optician Bourbon County Optical Co., Paris, Ky., 1980; optician Gates, Stockler, Lenz Opticians, Louisville, 1980-84; buyer Precision Lens Crafters, Cin., 1984, gen. merchandising mgr., 1985-87, dir. product devel. U.S. Shoe-Optical divs., 1987-88; v.p. E.D.B. Holdings, Inc., Milford, Ohio, 1988—. Author, editor: Basic Optics for Precision Lens Crafters Associates, 1984. Mem. Young Dems. of Ky., Louisville, 1978-80. Mem. Ky. Opticians Assn. Roman Catholic. Clubs: Northlake Athletic (Cin.), Scandinavian Health (Cin.). Office: EDB Holdings Inc 400 Techne Ctr Dr Milford OH 45150

BARTLE, ANNETTE GRUBER (MRS. THOMAS R. BARTLE), artist, writer, photographer. came to U.S., 1940; d. Henry and Maria (Harczyk) Gruber; m. Thomas R. Bartle, Dec. 5, 1957; 1 child, Eve Marie. Bacheliere, Sorbonne, Paris, 1940; BA, Elmira Coll., Paris, 1943; student, Ecole des Beaux Arts, Paris, 1940, Art Student League (scholar 1949), 1947-50. One woman shows include: Midtown Galleries, N.Y.C., 1957, 60, 63, 66, Feingarten, Chgo., 1957, Wickersham Gallery, 1970; exhibited in group shows: AAAL, 1963, Detroit Art Inst., 1958, 62, 65, 67, Pa. Acad., 1959, 60, 66, Butler Art Inst., 1960, 64, 65, Cin. Art Mus., 1960, 62, 67; represented in permanent collections: Am. Internat. Underwriters, Union Carbide, Conn. Mut. Life, Mural Port Authority Heliport, N.Y. Worlds Fair; author: African Enchantment, 1980; contbr. articles and photographs to mags., newspapers, jours. including: N.Y. Times, Christian Sci. Monitor, Phila. Inquirer, Los Angeles Times, Palm Beach Life, Travel Weekly, Diverson, American Way, Senior World, numerous others. Active various community drives. Pan Am. Travelling fellow, 1950; recipient citation for outstanding achievements 90th U.S. Congress, 1968. Mem. Am. Fedn. Arts, Artists Equity, Travel Journalists Guild Ltd. Address: 231 E 76th St New York NY 10021

BARTLETT, BONNIE, actress. D. E.E. and Carrie Bartlett; m. William Daniels; 2 children: Michael, Robert. Grad., Northwestern U.; studied with Lee Strasberg, N.Y.C. Appeared in TV series Love of Life, Little House on the Prairie, St. Elsewhere, 1982-88; appeared in TV miniseries Ike, 1979, Celebrity, 1984, The Deliberate Stranger, 1986; appeared in TV films Murder or Mercy, 1974, The Legend of Lizzie Borden, 1975, Killer on Board, 1977, A Death in Canaan, 1978, A Perfect Match, 1980, A Long Way Home, 1981, Dempsey, 1983, Malice in Wonderland, 1985. Recipient Emmy award Acad. TV Arts and Scis., 1986, 87. Office: care Harry Gold & Assocs 12725 Ventura Blvd Suite E Studio City CA 91604 *

BARTLETT, DIANE SUE, mental health counselor; b. Laconia, N.H., Dec. 6, 1947; d. Fred Elmer and Dorothy Pearl (Wakefield) Davis; m. Josiah Henry Bartlett, Aug. 23, 1980; 1 child by previous marriage, Fred Louis Hacker; 1 step child, Juliet. AA, Plymouth State Coll., 1982; B in Gen. Studies summa cum laude, U. N.H. Sch. for Lifelong Learning, 1984; MEd., Plymouth State Coll., 1988. Police communications specialist Div. Motor Vehicles, Concord, N.H., 1970-76, br. office mgr., 1976-83, coordinator motor vehicles registrations, 1983-84; tax collector City of Dover, N.H., 1984; intern Lakes Region Mental Health Div., Laconia, N.H., 1985; counselor Latchkey Pastoral Counseling, Laconia, 1984-87; family therapist, Children's Best Interest, Laconia, 1988—. Mem. Town of Moultonboro Sch. Feasibility Study Commn., 1978; adminstrv. bd. mem., chmn. pastor-parish relations com. United Meth. Ch., Moultonboro, N.H., 1983—, N.H. annual conf., 1986-88, participant N.H. Ann. Conf. on Status and Role of Women, Concord, 1985—. N.H. Charitable Found. grantee, 1985. Avocations: skiing, swimming, reading, writing. Home: PO Box 14 Moultonboro NH 03254

BARTLETT, HEATHER MARY, process engineer; b. Modesto, Calif., Nov. 11, 1957; d. William Randolph and Glenda Loreen (Mollard) Holbrook; m. James Bernard Bartlett, Aug. 29, 1981; 1 child, Stephanie. BS in Engring., Humboldt State U., 1983. Process engr. Simpson Paper Co., Eureka, Calif., 1982—. Mem. Humboldt County Legal Aux. Mem. Eureka Zool. Soc., Humane Soc., Tech. Assn. Pulp and Paper Industry, Water Pollution Control Fedn., Nat. Assn. Female Execs. Republican. Office: Simpson Paper Co PO Box 9600 Eureka CA 95501

BARTLETT, JENNIFER LOSCH, artist; b. Long Beach, Calif., Mar. 14, 1941. B.A., Mills Coll., 1963; B.F.A., Yale U., 1964, M.F.A., 1965; studied with Jack Tworkvov, James Rosenquist, Al Held, Jim Dire. Instr. Sch. Visual Arts, N.Y.C. One-woman shows include Mills Coll., Oakland, Calif., 1963, Reese Paley Gallery, N.Y.C., 1972, Paula Cooper Gallery, N.Y.C., 1974, 76, 77, 79, 81, 82, 83, Saman Gallery, Genoa, Italy, 1974, John Doyle Gallery, Chgo., 1975, Contemporary Art Ctr., Cin., 1976, Dartmouth Coll., 1976, Wadsworth Atheneum, Hartford, Conn., 1977, San Francisco Mus. Modern Art, 1978, U. Calif., Irvine, 1978, Hansen-Fuller Gallery, San Francisco, 1978, Balt. Art Mus., 1978, Margo Leavin Gallery, Los Angeles, 1979, 81, 83, U. Akron, 1979, Carleton Coll., 1979, Heath Gallery, Atlanta, 1979, 83, Galerie Mukai, Tokyo, 1980, Akron Art Inst., 1980, Albright-Knox Art Gallery, Buffalo, 1980, Joslyn Art Mus., Omaha, 1982, Tate Gallery, London, 1982, McIntosh/Drysdale Gallery, Houston, 1982, Gloria Luria Gallery, Bay Harbor Islands, Fla., 1983, Rose Art Mus., Brandeis U., Waltham, Mass., 1984, Long Beach Mus. Art., Calif., 1984, Univ. Art Mus., U. Calif.-Berkeley, 1984, Knight Gallery, Charlotte, N.C., 1985, Cleve. Mus. Art, 1986, Greg Kucera Gallery, Seattle, 1986, Whitechapel Art Gallery, London, 1986; group exbhns. include Mus. Modern Art, N.Y.C., 1971, 81, 83, Whitney Mus. Am. Art, N.Y.C., 1972, 77, 79, 81, 82, 83, Walker Art Ctr., Mpls., 1972, Kunsthaus, Hamburg, Fed. Republic Germany, 1972, Paula Cooper Gallery, N.Y.C., 1973, 74, 76, 77, 78, 81, 83, 84, Corcoran Gallery Art, Washington, 1975, Art Inst. Chgo., 1976, Kunstmuseum, Dusseldorf, Fed. Republic Germany, 1976, Kassel, Fed. Republic Germany, 1977, Contemporary Arts Mus., Houston, 1980, Am. Acad. Arts and Letters, N.Y.C., 1983, Sarah Lawrence Art Gallery, Bronxville, N.Y., 1984, Archer M. Huntington Art Gallery, U. Tex.-Austin, 1984, Hudson River Mus., Yonkers, N.Y., 1984, Tucson Mus. Art, 1984, Leo Castelli Gallery, N.Y.C., 1984, numerous others; represented in permanent collections, Mus. Modern Art, N.Y.C., Met. Mus. Art, N.Y.C., Whitney Mus. Am. Art, N.Y.C., Phila. Mus. Art, Walker Art Ctr., Mpls., Yale U. Art Gallery, New Haven, Art Mus. S.Tex., Corpus Christi, R.I. Sch. Design, Providence, Art Gallery S. Australia, Adelaide, Goucher Coll., Balt., Amerada Hess, Woodbridge, N.J., Dallas Mus. Fine Arts, Richard B. Russell Fed. Bldg. and U.S. Courthouse, Atlanta. Recipient Harris prize Art Inst. Chgo., 1976; recipient Creative Arts award Brandeis U., 1983, award Am. Acad. Arts and Letters, 1983; Creative Artists Public Services fellow, 1974; Lucas vis. lectr. award Carleton Coll., 1979. Office: care Paula Cooper Gallery 155 Wooster St New York NY 10012 *

BARTLETT, SHIRLEY ANNE, accountant; b. Gladwin, Mich., Mar. 28, 1933; d. Dewey J. and Ruth Elizabeth (Wright) Frye; m. Charles Duane Bartlett, Aug. 16, 1952 (div. Sept. 1982); children: Jeanne, Michelle, John, Yvonne. Student, Mich. State U., 1952-53, Rutgers U., 1972-74. Auditor State of Mich., Lansing, 1951-66; cost acct. Templar Co., South River, N.J., 1968-75; staff acct. Franco Mfg. Co., Metuchen, N.J., 1975-78; controller Thomas Creative Apparel, New London, Ohio, 1978-80; mgr. gen. acctg. Ideal Electric Co., Mansfield, Ohio, 1980-85; staff acct. Logangate Homes, Inc., Girard, Ohio, 1985-88; pvt. practice acctg. Youngstown, 1985—; acct. Universal Devel. Enterprises, Liberty Twp., Ohio, 1987—; v.p. Lang Industries, Inc., Youngstown, 1984—. Author: (play) Our Bicentennial-A Celebration, 1976. Soloist various orchestras, Mich., Va.; mem. Human Relations Commn., Franklin Township, 1971-77; treas. Heritage Found., New Brunswick, N.J., 1973-74, New London Proceeds Corp., 1979-83; commr. Huron Park Commn., Ohio, 1979-83; elected Dem. com. mem., N.J., Ohio, 1970-82. Mem. NOW (treas. Youngstown 1986—), Am. Soc. Women Accts. (bd. dirs. 1986-88, v.p. 1988—), Nat. Assn. Female Execs., Bus. and Profl. Women (v.p. 1980—), Am. Soc. Notaries, Women's Jour. Network, Citizen's League of Greater Youngstown, Internat. Platform Assn., 1988—. Democrat. Unitarian. Club: Franklin JFK (treas. 1970-72, v.p. 1973-78), Chataqua Literary, Scientific Circle (pres. 1979—). Home: 4793 Ardmore Ave Youngstown OH 44505-1101 Office: Bartlett Acctg Services 4795 Ardmore Ave Youngstown OH 44505

BARTLETT, VIRGINIA JOYCE, government pension specialist; b. Clarksburg, W.Va., July 20, 1951; d. Thomas Jefferson and Hazel Rae (Smith) B. B.S., W.Va. Wesleyan Coll., 1973. Employee plans/exempt orgn. specialist IRS, Balt., 1973-77; pension investigator Pension and Welfare Benefits Adminstrn., Dept. Labor, Washington, 1977—; acct., mgr. Price Waterhouse & Co., Atlanta. Recipient Meritorious Achievement award Dept. Labor, 1979. Mem. Md. Assn. CPA's, Nat. Assn. Female Execs. Republican. Methodist. Avocations: reading; aerobics. Home: 1934 F Johnson Ferry Rd Atlanta GA 30319 Office: Dept Labor Pension and Welfare Benefits Adminstrn 200 Constitution Ave NW Washington DC 20210

BARTLEY, DIANA ESTHER PELÁEZ RIVERA, educator; b. N.Y.C., May 18, 1940; d. Manuel Peláez Rivera and Lila Esther Camacho; cert. in French, U. Fribourg (Switzerland), 1960; B.A., Rosemont Coll., 1961; cert. in Italian, U. Florence, 1962; M.A., Middlebury Coll., 1963; A.M., Stanford U., 1964, Ph.D., 1970, research scholar U. Leningrad (USSR), Hertzen Pedagogical Inst., Leningrad, 1967-68, U. Moscow and First Moscow State Pedagogical Inst. Fgn. Langs., 1968, U. Helsinki, 1967; 1 son. Tchr., USIA Bi-Nat. Center, Madrid, 1961-62; tchr. French and Spanish, Fairfield (Conn.) Sch. Dist., 1963, Palo Alto (Calif.) Unified Sch. Dist., 1964-66; research asst. Ctr. R&D in Teaching, Stanford U., 1966-69; instr. dept. Spanish and Portuguese, U. Wis.-Milw., 1969-70, asst. prof. dept. curriculum and instrn., 1970-73, asso. prof., 1973-78, 80—, fed. project dir., 1970-78; vis. prof. U. Ala., Tuscaloosa, 1986, dir. summer immersion program, 1986; cons., lectr. in field; mem. nat. rev. panels U.S. Office Edn. and U.S. Dept. Edn., 1975, 77, 80, 81, 82, 83, 84, 85-87, 88; mem. scholar diplomat seminar U.S. Dept. State, 1981. Bd. dirs. Florentine Opera Aux., Milw., 1973-76, Literacy Services of Wis., 1974-76, Centro del Nino, Inc., Milw., 1982-84; con. Mequon-Thiensville Recreation Dept., New World Montessori Sch., Fox Point; past mem. Jr. League, Milw.; past mem. bd. Mequon PTA, 1981-83; other civic activities USIA visitor to Bulgaria, 1979. Fulbright Hays Sr. Fellow U. Warsaw (Poland), 1978-80, Ministry, Edn., Sofia, Bulgaria, 1980. Mem. Am. Assn. Tchrs. French (past), Am. Assn. Tchrs. Spanish and Portuguese, MLA, Nat. Assn. Bilingual Edn., Am. Ednl. Research Assn., AAUW, TESOL, Wis. TESOL Assn., Fulbright Alumni Assn. Author numerous books and monographs, including: The Latin Child Goes Forth, Bilingual Early Education Experience Based Lessons, 1975; The Adult Basic Education TESOL Handbooks, 1979; contbr. numberous articles to profl. jours. Third place Helen H. Heffernan scholar, 1966. Office: Univ Wis Sch Edn Dept Curriculum PO Box 413 Milwaukee WI 53201

BARTLEY, GEORGETTA KATYE, computer systems programmer, behaviorist, stress consultant therapist; b. Jacksonville, N.C., Nov. 14, 1946; d. Talmadge Oliver and Louise Georgetta (Benton) B. A.A. in Data Processing, San Diego City Coll., 1967; B.S. in Info. Systems Mgmt., San Diego State U., 1978; M.S. in Mgmt. Orgn. Devel., U.S. Internat. U., 1981, Ph.D. in Mgmt. Orgn. Devel., 1981. Computer technician Fed. Civil Service, San Diego, 1971-74, computer programmer, 1974-79, computer systems analyst, 1979-84, computer specialist, 1984, computer systems programmer, 1984—, EEO counselor, 1978—; stress cons. therapist Bartley & Bartley, Inc., San Diego, 1981—. Mem. Nat. Urban League, San Diego, 1979—. Mem. Nat. Assn. Female Execs., Sharing Inc. (vol. 1979—). Democrat. Episcopalian. Office: Fleet Combat Directions Systems Support Activity 271 C atalina Blvd San Diego CA 92147

BARTLEY, MELINDA, educational administrator; b. Morgan City, La., Oct. 31, 1947; d. Frank, Jr. and Hazel (Smith) B. BS, So. U., Baton Rouge, 1969, MA, 1973; Degree in Ednl. Specialization, George Washington U., 1975, EdD, 1977. Tchr. St. Mary Parish Schs., Franklin, La., 1969, 76; teenage program dir. YWCA, Balt., 1970-72; counselor Fairfax (Va.) County Schs., 1975; soc. sci. lectr. U. Dist. of Columbia, Washington, 1975-77; coordinator of instrn. Orleans Parish Sch. Bd., New Orleans, 1978-79; dir. developmental studies So. U., New Orleans, 1979-84; v.p. Urban League, New Orleans, 1985-87; assoc. vice chancellor So. U., New Orleans, 1987—; program evaluator Norfolk State U., 1981, Alcorn State U., Lorman, Miss., 1983; cons. in field. V.p. of bd. Dryades YMCA, New Orleans, 1979-83; pres. of bd. Nat. Council of Negro Women, New Orleans, 1982-84; mem. adv. bd. United Way Leadershiop Tng. Ctr., New Orleans, 1985-87; bd. dirs. Family Service Soc. of Greater New Oleans, 1983-84. Office of Edn. fellow, 1972, 73, 74, 75; named Young Woman of the Yr. Dryades YMCA, 1983. Mem. AAUW, (charter) La. Assn. Devel. Edn., New Orleans Alliance of Black Sch. Educators, Phi Delta Kappa, Delta Sigma Theta. Home: 5050 Westlake Dr New Orleans LA 70126

BARTLING, PHYLLIS MCGINNESS, oil company executive; b. Chillicothe, Ohio, Jan. 3, 1927; d. Francis A. McGinness and Gladys A. (Henkelman) Bane; m. Theodore Charles Bartling, Aug. 2, 1946; children—Pamela, Theodore, Eric C. Student, Ohio State U., 1944-47. Bookkeeper, Bartling & Assocs., Bartling Oil Co., Houston 1974-80; sec.-treas., dir. both cos., 1980—. Co-chmn. ticket sales Tulsa Opera, 1956-61; bd. dirs. Tex. Speech and Hearing Ctr., Houston, 1967-70. Republican. Episcopalian. Avocations: tennis; gardening; bicycling; cooking. Home: 11 Inwood Oaks Houston TX 77024 Office: 8550 Katy Freeway Suite 128 Houston TX 77024

BARTOL, CHRISTINE MARTINA, architectural engineer; b. Milw., Sept. 1, 1961; d. Heite Hans Hermann and Evelyn Hedwig (Schmidt) Lattmann; m. Anthony John Bartol, Aug. 22, 1981. BS in Engring., Milw. Sch. Engring., 1983. Registered engr.-in-tng., Wis. Asst. mgr. Pabst Theater, Milw., 1980-83; engring. asst. Wis. Dept. Transp., Milw., 1982; structural engr. Level Valley Dairy, West Bend, Wis., 1983, 85; archtl. engr. Kohler (Wis.) Co., 1983—. Mem. AIA (affiliate), Am. Soc. Heating, Ventilating and Air Conditioning Engrs., NSPE, Kohler Engring. Tech. Orgn.

BARTOL, KATHRYN MARIE, educator; b. Bellevue, Pa.; d. Walter R. and Mary A. (Scherf) Ottinger; B.A., Marygrove Coll., Detroit, 1963; M.A., U. Mich., 1966; Ph.D., Mich. State U., 1972; m. Robert A. Bartol, Sept. 10, 1966. Advt. writer J.L. Hudson Co., 1963-64; systems analyst, project mgr. Mich. Dept. Social Services, 1966-69; asst. prof. U. Mass. Sch. Bus. Adminstrn., Amherst, 1972-74; asso. prof. Syracuse (N.Y.) U. Sch. Mgmt., 1974-77; asso. prof. Coll. Bus. and Mgmt. U. Md., College Park, 1977-80, prof. mgmt., 1980—. chmn. organizational behavior and indsl. relations faculty, 1981-83; mgmt. cons., 1972—. Fellow Acad. Mgmt. (bd. govs. 1980-86, program chmn., 1982-3, pres. 1984-85), Organizational Behavior Teaching Soc., Am. Psychol. Assn. Contbr. numerous articles in field to profl. jours. Office: U Md Coll Bus and Mgmt Dept Organizational Behavior and Indsl Relations College Park MD 20742

BARTOLAMEOLLI, JULIE KAY, computer company executive; b. Iron Mountain, Mich.; d. Ernest Louis and Clarine Marie (Paquin) B.; m. R. Daniel Poeschel. BS, No. Mich. U., 1970, MA, 1972; cert. in adminstrv. supervising, No. Ill. U., 1978; postgrad., U. Colo., 1978. Tchr. English Forest Park Schs., Crystal Falls, Mich., 1970-71; tchr. Marquette (Mich.) Schs., 1971-73; counselor mental health Adams County Sch. Dist. 50, Denver, 1973-78; dir. gifted program Oregon (Wis.) Schs., 1979-82; cons. Madison, Wis., 1982-83; sr. cons. Burroughs Corp., Milw., 1983-87; govt. acct. mgr. Digital Equipment Corp., Brookfield, Wis., 1987—. Home: 6041 N Santa Monica Blvd Whitefish Bay WI 53217

BARTOLDI, ANDREA JANE, environmental engineer; b. Pitts., June 17, 1962; d. Alfred and Jane (Bogacz) B. BS in Chem. Engring., Carnegie-Mellon U., 1984. Instr. U. Pitts., Bradford, Pa., 1985; environ. engring. Witco Corp., Bradford, 1984—, div. liaison, 1986—; cons. Kendall/Amalie Divs., 1986—. Active regional roundtable com., Meadville, Pa., 1986-87. Mem. Nat. Assn. Female Execs. Republican. Roman Catholic. Club: YMCA. Home: 119 N Center St Bradford PA 16701 Office: Witco Corp 77 N Kendall Ave Bradford PA 16701

BARTOLI, DIANE S., social services administrator; b. Plains, Pa., Sept. 21, 1938; d. Anthony J. and Anice (Whiteley) Lupas; m. Bernard J. Bartoli, June 24, 1961; Judith Giovanelli, Eugene, Maria, Shelley. BS in Edn., East Stroudsburg U., 1960. Elem. sch. tchr. Levittown, Pa., 1960-61; owner, bookeeper A.J. Lupas Ins. Agy., Plains, 1977-83; owner, adminstr. Adult Services Unltd., Plains, 1983—; mem. task group Pa. State Com. on Elder Abuse, 1986; pres. NE Pa. Alzheimers Support Group, 1983—. Chair Dem. Com., Laflin, Pa., 1973; chair Laflin Borough Recreation Bd., 1972-80. Recipient Chapel of the Four Chaplains award. Mem. Nat. Adult Day Care Assn., Pa. Adult Day Care (bd. dirs. 1985—), Nat. Assn. Rehab. Facilities (council on aging), Am. Assn. Profl. Cons., Pa. Assn. Rehab. Facilities.,. Democrat. Roman Catholic. Club: Laflin Womens. Office: Adult Services Unltd Inc 220 S River St Plains PA 18705

BARTON, BARBARA A., agriculturist, educator. BS in Animal Sci. with distinction, Pa. State U., 1976; MS in Dairy Sci., U. Wis., 1978, PhD, 1981. Research asst. U. Wis., Madison, 1976-81; asst. prof. U. Maine, Orono, 1981-87; assoc. prof. U. Maine, 1987—; leader agrl. research projects U.S. Dairy Assn., 1982—, Me. Dept. Agriculture, Food and Rural Resources, 1984—, Am. Farm Products, 1983—, Agway, Inc., 1985—, Nat. Assn. Animal Breeders, 1987—, Penobscot County- Soil and Water Conservation Com., 1987—; rep. New Eng. Dairy Coll. Conf., 1982—, chmn. 1987; lectr., conductor seminars in field. Contbr. numerous articles and papers to profl. jours. Recipient Presdl. Pub. Service Achievement award, U. Maine, 1985, Faculty and Instructional Devel., 1986; Carl and Florence B. King scholar, Winrock Internat., 1983; Merck Animal Health Edn. grantee, Merck Co. Found., 1986, teaching grantee, 1987. Mem. Am. Dairy Sci. Assn. (Gold scholar, 1976, jr. faculty advisor 1986, sr. faculty advisor 1987), Am. Soc. Animal Sci. (jr. faculty advisor 1986, sr. faculty advisor 1987, sec./treas. NE chpt. 1986-87, v.p. 1987-88, pres. 1988—, bd. dirs., mem. various coms.), Am. Forage and Grassland Council, Council Agrl. Sci. Tech., dairy Shrine, Alpha Zeta, Phi Kappa Phi, Sigma Delta Epsilon. Sigmi Xi. Home: 11 Gardner Rd Orono ME 04473 Office: U Maine Dept Animal Vet Scis 24A Rogers Hall Orono ME 04469

BARTON, BRIGID ANNE, art history educator; b. Honolulu, June 1, 1943; d. William M. and Ellen (Counsell) Shanahan; m. Douglas H. Barton, Sept. 2, 1968 (div. 1982); children—Gregory, Thomas. B.A., Barnard Coll., Columbia U., 1965; M.A., U. Calif.-Berkeley, 1968, Ph.D., 1976. Instr. Coll. Marin, Kentfield, Calif., 1968-71; asst. prof. art history U. Santa Clara, Calif., 1976-82, assoc. prof. art history, 1982—; chmn. art history dept. U. Santa Clara, 1986-87; dir. De Saisset Mus. U. Santa Clara, Calif., 1979-84. Author: Otto Dix and 'Die neue Sachlichkeit', 1981; German Expressionist Woodcuts: the Rifkind Collection, 1980. NEA grad. fellow, 1967. Mem. Coll. Art Assn., AAUP.

BARTON, CYNTHIA KATHLEEN, architect; b. Houston, Oct. 16, 1958; d. George Randall and Roxanne Inez (Ritter) Hammond; m. Richard Redman Barton, May 28, 1983. BS in Archtl. Studies, U. Ill., 1981, MArch, 1983. Aerospace technician exptl. facilities and equipment NASA Johnson Space Ctr., Houston, 1984-85; architect, project investigator U.S. Army Constrn. Engring. Research Lab., Champaign, Ill., 1985—. Recipient Official Commendation U.S. Army, 1986, 87. Mem. Fed. Women's Program (div. rep. publicity coordinator 1986—), Bldg. Thermal Envelope Coordinating Council, AIA (mem. Champaign sect.), Alpha Xi Delta. Home: 2321 Greenwood Ct Champaign IL 61821-6318 Office: US Army CERL PO Box 4005 Champaign IL 61820-1305

BARTON, DENISE CAROLE, lawyer; b. Charleroi, Pa., Oct. 16, 1953; d. Joseph Leo and Vera Elizabeth (Johnson) B.; m. H. Daniel Mujahid, Sept. 1, 1984. JD, Georgetown U., 1978; BA, Mich. State U., 1985. Bar: Pa. 1978, U.S. Dist. Ct. (we. dist.) Pa. 1979, U.S. Tax Ct. 1985. Law clk. Supreme Ct. Pa., Monessen, 1978-80; jud. atty. Superior Ct. Pa., McKeesport, 1980-88; atty. Dept. Atty. Gen., State of Mich., Lansing, 1988—; instr. Duquesne U., Pitts., 1980; Lyndon Baines Johnson Congl. intern, U.S. Ho. of Reps., Washington, 1975. 1st v.p. NAACP, Mon Valley, Pa., 1982—; legal redress, 1983-87. Mem. ABA, Allegheny County Bar Assn., Pa. Bar Assn. Home: 2394 Twin Lakes Dr Ypsilanti MI 48197

BARTON, GAIL MELINDA, psychiatrist, educator; b. Worcester, Mass., Apr. 20, 1937; d. Walter Earl and Elsa Viola (Benson) B.; m. Duncan John Kretovich, Aug. 31, 1968 (div. 1986); 1 child, Mariah Lynne. AB, Jackson Coll., Medford, Mass., 1959; MD, Women's Med. Coll. Pa., 1966; MPH, U. Mich., 1971. Diplomate Am. Bd. Psychiatry and Neurology. Rotating intern St. Joseph Mercy Hosp., Ann Arbor, Mich., 1966-67; resident in psychiatry U. Mich., Ann Arbor, 1967-70, chief resident dept. psychiatry, 1970-71, asst. prof. psychiatry, dir. continuing care clinic psychiatry dept., 1971-77, assoc. prof., mem. outpatient staff dept. psychiatry, 1979-82; dir. research and devel. dept. mental health State of Mich., East Lansing, 1977-79; assoc. prof. U. Vt., Burlington, 1982-84; med. dir. Howard Mental Health, Burlington, 1982-84; assoc. prof. Dartmouth Coll., Hanover, N.H., 1984-88, prof., 1988—; dir. inpatient psychiatry VA Hosp., White River Junction, Vt., 1984—. Author: Mental Health Administration, 2 vols., 1983, Ethics and Law, 1984; co-editor: Handbook of Emergency Psychiatry, 1986. Incorporator Mt. Ascutrey Hosp., Windsor, Vt., 1987; mem. Search Com. Police Chief, Windsor, 1987; trustee 1st Congregational Ch., Hartland, Vt., 1987—. Fellow Am. Psychiat. Assn. (program com. 1976-82), Am. Coll. Psychiatrists (program com. 1982-84), Am. Coll. Mental Health Adminstrs. (pres. 1987—); mem. Am. Med. Women's Assn. (dir. med. students 1980), Am. Coll. Emergency Physicians (behavioral com.). Office: VA Med Ctr N Hartland Rd White River Junction VT 05001

BARTON, JACQUELINE K., chemistry educator; b. N.Y.C., May 7, 1952; d. William and Claudine (Gutchen) Kapelman; m. Donald John Barton, Nov. 11, 1973 (div.). AB summa cum laude, Barnard Coll., 1974; PhD, Columbia U., 1979; postdoctoral, Yale U., 1979-80. Asst. prof. Hunter Coll, N.Y.C., 1980-82; asst. prof. Columbia U., N.Y.C., 1983-85, assoc. prof., 1985-86, prof. chemistry and biology, 1986—; vis. research assoc. Dept. Biophysics Bell Labs., 1979. NSF Predoctoral fellow, 1975-78, postdoctoral fellow, 1979-80, Alfred P. Sloan fellow Sloan Found., 1984; Camille and Henry Dreyfus tchr.-scholar Dreyfus Found., 1986—; recipient Harold Lamport award N.Y. Acad. Scis., 1984, Alan T. Waterman award, NSF, 1985, Fresenius award, Phi Lambda Upsilon, 1986, Eli Lilly Biochemistry award, 1987, Pure Chemistry award, 1988 Am. Chem. Soc. Mem. Phi Beta Kappa. Office: Columbia Univ Dept of Chemistry New York NY 10027

BARTON, MAXINE BELLE, lawyer; b. Los Angeles, May 11, 1934; d. Norman Nathan and Celia (Rosenthal) Livingston; m. Richard H. Bauman, July 4, 1984; 1 child, Norma Lynn. J.D., Western State U., 1980. Bar: Calif. 1982; lic. realtor. Legal sec., para-legal, mgmt. asst. Indsl. Indemnity Co., San Diego, Sacramento, Los Angeles, 1971—; in-house counsel Indsl. Indemnity, San Diego, 1982-85; sole practice, Hermosa Beach, 1985—. Mem. ABA, Calif. Bar Assn., Los Angeles County Bar Assn. Democrat.

BARTON, PHYLLIS SETTECASE, art historian; b. Dubuque, Iowa, Nov. 5, 1934; d. Joseph T. Settecase and Elizabeth C. (Gaidzik) Neal; m. William Francis Barton, July 10, 1954 (div.); children: Christopher (dec.), Tracy, Shannon. Student, Mt. St. Mary's Coll., 1955-56, U. HI, 1978; BA in Art History, Calif. State U., Long Beach, 1978; MA in Art History, Calif. State U., 1982. Adminstrv. asst. Norton Simon, Inc., 1958-65; art cons. Bangkok, Thailand, 1965-67; art editor Santa Ana (Calif.) Register, 1967-68; art agt., publicist, antiques dealer 1968-76, art writer, lectr., curator, appraiser, 1976—. Author: Sassone-California, 1973, Cecil C. Bell: 1906-1970, 1976, The Art of Alexander Dzigurski, 1979, Sassone-Serigraphs, 1984, William Frederick Foster, A.N.A.: Portrait of a Painter, 1987; contbr. articles to art jours. Recipient Excellence of Book Design award Printing Industries of Am., 1976, 79. Mem. Nat. League of Am. Pen Women (pres. 1984-86). Home and Office: 2601 E Victoria #191 Dominguez Hills CA 90220

BARTON, RENA, professional association administrator, marketing professional; b. Aiken, S.C., May 30, 1940; d. Frederic Jr. and Ruby Lee (Williams) Miller; widowed; 1 child, Shika Darcelle. Grad., Writers Digest Sch., Cin., 1980. Mgr. direct mail solicitations Boys Clubs of Am., N.Y.C., 1970-88; owner Barton Direct Mktg Inc, N.Y.C., 1988—. Author book of poetry, 1978, also short stories. Recipient Bronze Keystone award Boys Clubs of Am., 1986. Mem. Direct Mail Fundraisers Assn., Women Direct Response Group, Nat. Assn. Female Execs.

BARTON, SALLY CAROL, banker; b. Cleve., June 20, 1959; d. Stanley George and Mary Ruth (Nixon) B. BSBA, Bowling Green State U., 1981; grad., Ohio Sch. Banking, 1985; MBA, Cleve. State U., 1986. Mgmt. trainee Soc. Nat. Bank (merger Cen. Nat. Bank and Soc. Bank), Cleve., 1981-83, br. mgr., 1983-84, credit analyst, 1984-85, loan officer, 1985-87, asst. v.p. Bank One Cleve. corp. lending div., 1987—. Mem. Nat. Assn. Female Execs., Am.

Inst. Banking, Ohio Sch. Banking Alumni Assn., Gamma Phi Beta. Home: 7414 S Chestnut Commons Mentor OH 44060 Office: Bank One Cleve 1215 Euclid Ave Cleveland OH 44115

BARTON, SANDRA JANE WHITE, manufacturing executive; b. Knox City, Tex., Feb. 27, 1944; d. Bacyl Weldon and Hazel Margaret (Johnston) Barnett; m. Joe Morris White, Feb. 27, 1962 (div. Nov. 1981); children: Kimberly Jane, Rebecca Lynn; m. Leroy Barton, May 19, 1985. Student, Amarillo Coll., 1965. Supr. data entry 1st Nat. Bank, Roswell, N.Mex., 1965-67; computer operator Chugach Electric Co., Anchorage, 1967-68; systems analyst City of Wichita Falls, Tex., 1969-71; systems analyst Sprague Electric Co., Wichita Falls, 1971-75, mgr. indsl. relations, 1975-79; owner, mgr. White & Assocs., Wichita Falls, 1979-81; mgr. human resources Argon Med. Corp., Athens, Tex., 1981—; mem. adv. bd. Midwestern State U., Wichita Falls, 1975-79, guest lectr., 1976; mem. adv. bd. Trinity Valley Community Coll., Athens, Tex., 1983-87, guest lectr., 1984-87. V.p. Lakeland Community Concerts, Athens, 1986-87; mem. ins. bd. City of Athens, 1986-87; bd. dirs. Athens United Way, 1987. Mem. Athens C. of C. (v.p. 1985-86). Republican. Club: Pilot (Athens). Office: Argon Med Corp PO Box 1970 Athens TX 75751

BARTON, SUSAN MEYER, county recreation administrator, dog breeder; b. Los Angeles, Sept. 4, 1946; d. Edward John and Catherine Dorothy (McInerney) Meyer; m. Richard Emmett Barton, June 29, 1974. B.A., Loyola-Marymount U., Los Angeles, 1972; A.A., Mt. St. Mary's Coll., Los Angeles, 1966. Instr. St. Mary's Acad., Inglewood, Calif., 1972-73; recreation supr. County of Los Angeles, 1973-84, City of Redondo Beach, Calif., 1984—; breeder Old English mastiffs Barton Kennels, Hawthorne, Calif., 1980—; nat. bd. dirs. Learning Resources Network, Thurston, Kans., 1985—. Mem. Nat. Assn. Female Execs., Calif. Parks and Recreation Soc., Mastiff Club Am., Western Mastiff Fanciers, Chi Kappa Rho. Republican. Roman Catholic. Avocation: aerobic dancing. Office: City of Redondo Beach Recreation Dept 1102 Camino Real Redondo Beach CA 90277

BARTONY, KATHLEEN DIANE, pharmacist; b. Ford City, Pa., Nov. 11, 1953; d. Henry Ernest and Mary Catherine (Cacurak) B. BS in Pharmacy, U. Pitts., 1976. Pharmacist Thrift Drug Co., 1976—; asst. mgr. Thrift Drug Co., Steubenville, Ohio, 1977; dist. staff pharmacist Thrift Drug Co., Pitts., 1977-79; mgr. Thrift Drug Co., Greensburg, Pa., 1979-81, Pitts., 1981—. Mem. Pa. Pharm. Assn., Am. Pharm. Assn. Club: Pitts. Ski. Home: 22 W Pine St Delmont PA 15626 Office: Thrift Drug Co 2336 Ardmore Blvd Pittsburgh PA 15221

BARTSCHT, WALTRAUD ERIKA, educator, costume designer; b. Munich, Germany, Oct. 16, 1924; d. Bruno and Edith Frida (Snell) Gutensohn; came to U.S., 1952, naturalized, 1959; diploma Deutsche Meisterschule Für Mode, Munich, 1949; M.A., So. Meth. U., Dallas, 1966; Ph.D., U. Tex.-Dallas, 1986; m. Heri Bert Bartscht, Mar. 31, 1950; 1 son, Martin Donald. Fashion designer, 1949-65, Dallas, 1954-65; instr. German, U. Dallas, Irving, Tex., 1966-69, asst. prof., 1969-80, asso. prof., 1980—, chmn. dept. fgn. langs., 1981—; designer theatrical costumes Knox Street Theater, Dallas, U. Dallas Drama Dept.; textile compositions exhibited Dallas galleries, Purdue U., and elsewhere, 1961—; textile chancel appts. Perkins Chapel So. Meth. U., St. Paul's Luth. Ch., Brenham, Tex. Mem. Tex. Fgn. Lang. Assn., Modern Lang. Assn., South Central Modern Lang. Assn., Assn. Computer in the Humanities, Assn. Lit. and Linguistic Computing, Am. Assn. Tchrs. German (regional chmn. N. Central Tex. 1972-75), Dallas Goethe Center (founding mem.). Lutheran. Transl. and analysis Goethe's Das Maerchen, 1972. Translator poems and articles in Kerygma, 1961, Constantin Review, 1974; Dragonflies, 1980; Dimension, 1980; contbr. articles to Schatzkammer, Rice U. Studies, Procs. of VI Internat. German Tchrs. Congress, Nuernberg, and others. Home: 1125 Canterbury Ct Dallas TX 75208 Office: U Dallas Irving TX 75061

BARTUNEK, HOLLY MARIE, computer teacher; b. Oak Park, Ill., Dec. 17, 1949; d. George John and Helen (Marsick) B. BS, Ill. State U., 1971; MEd, Nat. Coll. Edn., 1986. Elem. tchr. Sch. Dist. 88, Bellwood, Ill., 1971-85, tchr. computers, 1985-87; free-lance computer edn. cons. and trainer Bellwood, 1985—; tchr. Nat. Coll. Edn., Evanston, Ill., 1987—; computer lab. dir. Ctr. for Gifted, Evanston, 1987. Recipient Nat. Vol. award ARC, 1976, Christa McAuliffe scholarship Ill. PTA, 1987. Mem. Ill. Assn. of Tchr. Educators, Nat. Council for the Soc. Studies, Ill. Computing Educators, West Suburban Reading Council, Phi Delta Kappa. Baptist. Club: Big Red Apple. Office: Sch Dist 88 Bellwood IL 60104

BARUCH, MONICA LOBO-FILHO, psychology counselor; b. Rio de Janeiro, Jan. 11, 1954; d. Max and Margot (Hollander) Lobo-Filho; m. Robert Karl Baruch, Dec. 30, 1973 (div. May 1985). BA in Psychology, U. Rochester, 1975; MA in Counseling Edn., U. Mo., Kansas City, 1978. Cert. Nat. Bd. Cert. Counselors. Tchr. curriculum devel. St. Patrick's Sch., Rio de Janeiro, 1974-76; tchr., soccer coach Pembroke Country Day Sch., Kansas City, Mo., 1977-78; tchr., trainer Berlitz Sch. Langs., Kansas City and Washington, 1978-79; counselor, cons. Youth Understanding, Washington, 1979-81; academic faculty counselor Georgetown U., Washington, 1982—. Named one of Outstanding Young Women in Am., 1981. Mem. Am. Assn. Counseling and Devel., Am. Mental Health Counselors Assn., Multiple Personality Study Group. Office: Georgetown U 3800 Reservoir Rd NW Washington DC 20007

BARWIG, ANN FLOODY, senior account executive; b. Rockford, Ill., Mar. 5, 1959; d. Roger Roy and Patricia Ann (Kimler) F. BS, U. Ill., Champaign, 1981. Installation rep. HBO AND CO., Dallas, 1981-83; account exec. Teleci Inc., Dallas, 1983-85; sr. account exec. Universal Communication Systems, Chgo., 1985—. Alumni participant U. Ill. Alumni, Chgo., 1987. Republican. Lutheran. Office: Universal Communication Systems 1530 E Dundee Palatine IL 60067

BARZ, PATRICIA, lawyer; b. Mattoon, Ill., Oct. 18, 1953; d. William E. Barz and Rosemary A. (Easton) Scott; m. Herbert P. Wiedemann, Feb. 12, 1983; 1 child, Sarah Barz Wiedemann. BA, Yale U., 1974; JD, U. Va., 1978. Bar: Va. 1979, Conn. 1982, Ohio 1985. Assoc. Hunton & Williams, Richmond, Va., 1978-81, Davis, Graham & Stubbs, Denver, 1981-82; counsel legal dept. Aetna Life and Casualty Co., Hartford, Conn., 1982-84; assoc. Jones, Day, Reavis & Pogue, Cleve., 1984—. Trustee St. Anthony Trust Assn., New Haven, 1983-86; class agt. Yale Alumni Fund, New Haven, 1985—. Mem. ABA, Ohio Bar Assn., Cleve. Bar Assn., Conn. Bar Assn., Va. Bar Assn., Yale Alumni Assn. Cleve. (v.p. 1986—). Methodist. Home: 3008 Claremont Rd Shaker Heights OH 44122 Office: Jones Day Reavis & Pogue 901 Lakeside Ave Cleveland OH 44114

BASART, ANN PHILLIPS, publisher; b. Denver, Aug. 26, 1931; d. Burrill and Alberta (Mayfield) Phillips; m. Robert David Basart, Jan. 29, 1955; children: Kathryn, Nathaniel. BA in Music, UCLA, 1953; MLS, U. Calif., Berkeley, 1958, MA in Music, 1961. Librarian U. Calif., Berkeley, 1956-60, music librarian, 1960-61, 70—; newsletter editor U. Calif. Music Library, Berkeley, 1976—; editorial asst. U. Calif. Press, Berkeley, 1980-81; instr. music Lone Mountain Coll., San Francisco, 1964-67; owner Fallen Leaf Press, Berkeley, 1984—. Author: Serial Music: A Bibliography, 1961, Perspectives of New Music: An Index, 1984, Sound of the Fortepiano: a Discography, 1986; co-author Listening to Music, 1971. Named Fulbright scholar, 1956-57. Mem. Music Library Assn. (bd. dirs. 1978-80), Internat. Assn. Music Libraries. Office: Univ Calif Music Library 240 Morrison Hall Berkeley CA 94720 also: Fallen Leaf Press PO Box 10034 Berkeley CA 94709

BASCH, LISA SUSAN, financial planner; b. Utica, N.Y., Apr. 12, 1962; d. Michael D. and Diane S. (Schugg) B. BA in Econs. summa cum laude, Cornell U., 1984. Analyst fin. Fed. Express Corp., Memphis, 1982-83; rep. credit and collections Gen. Elec. Co., Bridgeport, Conn., 1984-85; internal auditor Gen. Elec. Credit Corp., Atlanta, 1985; analyst research Gen. Elec. Venture Capital Corp., Fairfield, Conn., 1985-86; acctg. specialist Gen. Elec. Investment Corp., Stamford, Conn., 1986; analyst fin. Gen. Elec. Credit Corp., Stamford, Conn., 1986-87; mgr. portfolio control Gen. Elec. Credit Corp., Englewood, Colo., 1987, mgr. fin. planning and analysis, 1988—; Apple support coordinator Kerr Leasing, Denver 1987-88. mem. Nat. Assn. Female Exec., Phi Beta Kappa, Phi Kappa Phi. Republican. Methodist. Home: 4392 S Hannibal #248 Aurora CO 80015

BASEL, FRANCES RITA, printing company executive; b. Calumet City, Ill., Mar. 8, 1933; d. Henry Adolph and Genevieve Veronica (Novak) Kaminski; m. Raymond John Basel, Feb. 19, 1955; children—Cynthia, Laura, Mark. Grad. Griffith Sch., Ind., 1950. Sec., Aeroquip/Barco, Barrington, Ill., 1955-62; freelance typist, Barrington, 1962-68; bookkeeper, office mgr. R.A.G. Enterprises, Fox Lake, Ill., 1968-78; corp. officer Classic Printery, Inc., Round Lake, 1978—. Republican. Roman Catholic. Office: Classic Printery Inc 316 Main St Round Lake Park IL 60073

BASHEIN, BARBARA JUNE, professional services firm executive; b. Lakewood, N.J., June 3, 1944; d. Hyman and Ann (Kulen) B.; m. David J. Vereeke, June 14, 1965 (div. 1973). BS in Math., Carnegie Mellon U., 1965; MS in Computer Sci., U. So. Calif., 1969. Tchr. high sch. math. Los Angeles City Schs., 1965-67; mathematician The Rand Corp., Santa Monica, Calif., 1967-69; programmer, analyst Quotron Systems, Inc., Los Angeles, 1969-72; project mgr. Citicorp.-Transaction Tech., Inc., Los Angeles, 1972-76; mgr. software devel. Lexar Corp., Los Angeles, 1976-81; ptnr. Arthur Andersen & Co., Los Angeles, 1981—. Contbr. articles to profl. jours. Appointed by Mayor Bradley to Blue Ribbon Com., Los Angeles, 1986-87; bd. dirs. Westside Family YMCA, Los Angeles, 1987. Mem. Soc. Telecommunications Cons., Orgn. Women Execs. (bd. dirs.). Office: Arthur Andersen & Co 911 Wilshire Blvd Los Angeles CA 90017

BASIEWICZ, MARGARET BLACKWELL, retail store manager; b. Hendersonville, N.C., July 3, 1926; d. Ted R. Margaret Elizabeth (Fowler) Blackwell; m. Richard Kirk Henderson, May 7, 1946 (div. July 1955); 1 child, Kathleen; m. William Basiewicz, Aug. 3, 1955; children: Michael, John. Student, Bob Jones Coll., 1942-43; BA in Liberal Arts, U. Md., Berlin, Fed. Republic of Germany. Adminstrv. asst. U.S. Dept. Treasury, Washington, 1943-44; personal asst. to econ. advisor U.S. Govt., Berlin, 1948-49, agt., 1949-52; restaurant owner, mgr. Amarillo, Tex., 1966-68; innkeeper Holiday Inn, Hendersonville, 1974-76; co-owner, pres. Queen Enterprises, Dana, N.C., 1986—; mgr. Sidney's, Hendersonville, 1984—; cons. Queen Enterprises, Dana, 1986-87. Author: Sunshine at Midnight, 1950. Dist. chmn. Girl Scouts U.S., Canal Zone, 1962-64; coordinator Family Services, Canal Zone AFB, 1963-64; pres. Officer's Wives Club, Ft. Carson, Colo., 1954; precinct chmn., Dana, 1982; mem. mall adv. council, Blue Ridge Mall, N.C., 1984-87. Mem. Am. Bus. Women's Assn. (Hendersonville chpt.), Nat. Assn. Female Execs. Democrat. Roman Catholic. Lodge: Lions (charter mem. 4 Seasons chpt.). Home: PO Box 298 Dana NC 28724 Office: Sydney's 1800 Four Seasons Blvd #49 Hendersonville NC 28724

BASILE, ABIGAIL JULIA ELLEN HERRON, employment counselor, state official; b. St. Louis, June 15, 1915; d. Charles Arthur and Abigail (Edwards) Herron; student Kansas City Jr. Coll., 1948-50, U. Kans., 1959; B.S. in Bus. Adminstrn., Rockhurst Coll., 1965; M.Ed., U. Mo., 1967; m. Joseph Basile, Aug. 15, 1939. Employment security dep. Mo. Div. Employment Security, Kansas City, 1945-59, youth coordinator, employment counselor, 1959-65, counselor, supr., 1965-81. Mem. Mo. Assn. Social Welfare. Mem. Am. Personnel and Guidance Assn., Nat. Vocat. Guidance Assn., Am. Vocat. Assn., Internat. Assn. Personnel in Employment Security (pres. Mo. 1966-67, internat. sec. 1968), Nat. Rehab. Assn., Nat. Employment Counselors Assn., Urban League, Am. Legion Aux., Personnel Research Forum, Profl. Counselors Assn. Democrat. Catholic. Home: 5316 Paseo Kansas City MO 64110

BASKETT, ANNE HELEN, travel agy. exec.; b. Kalamazoo, Jan. 22, 1941; d. Robert Elton and Helen Gertrude (Menten) Serfling; B.A., Emory U., 1962. Vol., Peace Corps, Philippines, 1962-64; sales rep., mgr. Smith Bell Travel, Manila, 1964-70; mgr., owner Daly Travel Services, San Francisco, 1970—. Bd. dirs. Friends of Brain Tumor Research. Mem. Am. Soc. Travel Agts., Pacific Area Travel Assn. Pub., editor The Daly News. Office: Daly Travel Service 391 Sutter St San Francisco CA 94108

BASS, CAROL SUE, bank executive; b. Hamilton, Mo., Feb. 27, 1940; d. Leo Hadley and Emma Ruth (Shipley) Mikes; m. Leonard Kenneth Bass; children: Jeff, Michelle, Stacia. Sr. v.p. Standard State Bank, Independence, Mo., 1973—. Mem adv. com. Independence Pub. Schs. Vacat. Guidance and Counseling Program, Community Assn. Arts, Vaile Mansion Soc., Bingham-Waagoner Hist. Soc.; bd. dirs. Community Founds., Independence, 1982, Hope House, Inc., Independence, 1983—, Civic and Cultural Com., Independence, 1984. Mem. Am. Inst. Banking, Am. Bankers Assn., Mo. Bankers Assn. (mktg. com. 1980-83), Bank Mktg. Assn., Independence C. of C. (bd. dirs. 1975—, chmn. elect 1987, chmn. bd. 1988, Centurian award 1980, Disting. Service award 1986). Office: Standard State Bank 10801 E 23rd St Independence MO 64052

BASS, CHRISTY GASTON, management consultant; b. Austin, Tex., Mar. 25, 1959; d. William Dickerson and Eleanor (Grigg) Gaston; m. Russell King Bass. BBA, U. Tex., 1981. Mgr. info. cons. Arthur Andersen & Co., Dallas, 1981—. Active Dallas Jr. League, 1983—, Juvenile Diabetes Found., Dallas, 1984-86, Jr. Achievement, Dallas, 1987; com. chair Am. Heart Assn. Ball, Dallas, 1983—. Mem. Pi Beta Phi Alumni Assn. Episcopalian. Club: Cotillion (Dallas), Slipper. Home: 6005 Northwood Dallas TX 75225 Office: Arthur Andersen & Co 5600 Interfirst Plaza Dallas TX 75225

BASS, JUAREZETTA ELENA, academic program director, educator; b. Los Angeles, Apr. 4, 1943; d. Juarez Charles and Pansy (Culberson) Sudduth; m. Ralph Irving Bass, Aug. 28, 1964; children: Maliaka, Nunu, Ralph Jr. BS, St. Stephens Coll., 1970; MA, George Peabody Coll., 1975, MS, 1977. Asst. adminstr. Meharry Med. Coll., Nashville, 1977-78, adminstr., 1978—, instr., 1979—; cons. children and youth div. Community Mental Health Ctr., Nashville, 1973-75; cons. spl. edn. council Tenn. State U., 1975; cons. Metro Nash Sch. Tchr. Ctr., 1975, Maternal Ch. Health Tng. and Research Ctr., 1977; v.p. Frederick Douglas Research Inst., Nashville, 1986. Treas. Interdenominational Ministers Wives Alliance, Nashville, 1979—; v.p. Am. Bapt. Women First Bapt. Ch., Nashville, 1982-84, pres., 1984-86; vice chair Tri-State Defender, 1981-82; v.p. John Overton High Sch. Band Boosters, 1981-82. Fellow Assn. Social and Behavioral Scis. Republican. Baptist. Office: Meharry Medical Coll Dept Psychiatry Behavioral Scis 1005 D B Todd Blvd Nashville TN 37208

BASS, REBECCA WENDY, electrical company executive; b. Phila., Jan. 27, 1952; d. Herbert Jerome and Lillian E.; m. Franklin G. Vandegrift, Dec. 10, 1977. Diploma, Abington Friends Sch., Jenkintown, Pa., 1969; AB cum laude, Bryn Mawr Coll., 1973; JD, Rutgers U., Camden, N.J., 1976. Bar: N.Y. 1977, Pa. 1977, N.J. 1977. Atty. Mudge Rose Guthrie & Alexander, N.Y.C., 1976-77; asst. gen. counsel E.R. Squibb & Sons, Inc., Princeton, N.J., 1978-79; atty Orloff, Lowenbach, Stifelman & Siegel, Newark, N.J., 1980-81; investment broker Kidder Peabody & Co., N.Y.C., 1981-83; nat. mktg. mgr. E.F. Hutton Credit Corp., Greenwich, Conn., 1983-84; mgr. nat. accounts GE Credit Corp., Stamford, Conn., 1984-85; program mgr. high technology equipment financing GE Credit Corp., Wilton, Conn., 1985-86; mgr., market devel. GE Credit Corp., Wilton, 1986-87; v.p. sales and Ops. GE Healthcare Fin Services, Stamford, Conn., 1987-88; gen. mgr. nat. accounts GE Supply Co., Bridgeport, Conn., 1988—; bd. GE Credit Mktg. Council, Stamford; mem. law review, Rutgers U. Sch. of Law, Camden, N.J., 1976. asst. coordinator, Spl. Olympics, Conn., 1986-87. Mem. Elfun Soc. Office: 10 E Ridge Dr Suite 105 Danbury CT 06810

BASS, RENEE FEIN, lawyer; b. Stuttgart, Ger., Sept. 25, 1946; d. Morris and Helen (Flek) Fein; m. Harvey B. Bass, Dec. 1, 1967; children—Stephanie, Michelle, Bradley. B.S., DePaul U., 1972, J.D., 1976. Bar: Ill. Mem. buyers program staff Marshall Field & Co., Skokie, Ill., 1965-67; ptnr. law firm Bass & Bass & Assocs., Chgo., 1977-80; sole practice law, Chgo., 1980—. Vol., Adlai E. Stevenson Campaign, 1969, Dan Walker Campaign, 1970; mem. Glencoe (Ill.) Village Caucus, 1983. Mem. Am. Immigration Lawyers Assn., Chgo. Bar Assn. (chmn. immigration, naturalization com.). Democrat. Jewish. Home: 90 Harbor St Glencoe IL 60022 Office: 180 N La Salle St Chicago IL 60601

BASS, RUTH, art educator; b. Boston, Oct. 11, 1938; d. Samuel and Beatrice (Wexler) Gilbert; B.A. magna cum laude, Radcliffe Coll., 1960; M.A., N.Y. U., 1962, Ph.D., 1978; m. Harvey Bass, Apr. 15, 1967; 1 child, Michael. Lectr., U. Bridgeport (Conn.), 1963-64; lectr. Queens Coll., N.Y.C., 1965-66; instr. N.Y. U., N.Y.C., 1980-81; faculty Bronx Community Coll., City U. N.Y., 1965-69, asst. prof., 1970-78, assoc. prof., 1978-81, prof. art, 1981—, project dir. NEH ednl. grant, 1984; art critic Art News, 1979—; curator Contemporary Images, Mendik Co., 1986; art writer Arts mag., Art World, Art in Am., McGraw-Hill Dictionary of Art, Dictionary of 20th Century Art, others; correspondent Art-Talk, 1986—. Bd. advisors Artists Choice Mus., 1980; moderator Panel on Realist Art sponsored Bklyn. Mus. and Louis Abrons Arts for Living Center, 1980—; curator, dir. The Bronx Community Gallery, 1987—. Arts and Soc. fellow, 1981; SUNY Research Found. grantee, 1975-76; Bronx Community Coll. fellow, 1979-80, 86-87; CUNY Women's Research and Devel. Fund grantee, 1986-87; recipient Women's Research and Devel. Fund award City U.N.Y., 1986-88. Mem. Coll. Art Assn., Internat. Assn. Art Critics, Art Students League N.Y., AAUP, Women in the Arts, Artists Equity Assn. N.Y., Am. Soc. Aesthetics. Contbr. articles to profl. jours.

BASS, SHIRLEY ANN, lawyer; b. Brockton, Mass., Mar. 1, 1938; d. Ernest Francis and Clarissa May (Atwood) Marcotte; children: Thomas, Robert, John. Cert. Katharine Gibbs Sch., 1958; student San Diego State U., 1963-64; BA, Portland State U., 1975; JD, Lewis and Clark Law Sch., 1979. Bar: Oreg. 1980. With Cyr, Moe & Benner, P.C., 1980-88 . Bd. dirs. Oreg. Fair Plan, 1982-87; vol. lawyer Sr. Law Project, 1985—; mem. planned giving com. Loaves and Fishes, Inc., 1987—, vice chair bd. dirs., chair devel. com., mem. planned giving com. Recipient Estate Planning award Am. Jurisprudence, 1979. Mem. Oreg. Bar (editorial bd., legis. com. estate planning sect.), ABA, Multnomah Bar Assn., Washington County Bar Assn., Estate Planning Council Portland, P.E.O., Phi Alpha Delta. Republican. Episcopalian. Club: Portland City, Altrusa (Portland). Office: Cyr Moe & Benner PC 900 SW 5th Ave Suite 1850 Portland OR 97204

BASSETT, ALICE COOK, state legislator; b. St. Johnsbury, Vt., May 16, 1925; d. Clayton Earlman and Alberta (Campbell) Fisher; m. Clinton Dana Cook, May 21, 1944 (dec. June 1969); children—Dana, Allison, Polly, Timothy, Cynthia; m. Thomas Day Seymour Bassett, May 12, 1979. A.A., Colby Jr. Coll., 1944; B.S., U. Vt., 1971. Bus. mgr. Royall Tyler Theatre, Burlington, Vt., 1977-79; asst. to editor NE Bibliography, Boston, 1979-81; mem. Vt. Ho. of Reps., Montpelier, 1983—. Author (newspaper column) Memo from Montpelier, 1984-86; editor (legis. newsletter) Legis. Alert, 1984-85. Vice pres. LWV, Burlington, 1981-84; bd. dirs. Am. Friends Service Com., Brattleboro, Vt., 1980-85, ACLU, Montpelier, 1983—, Howard Mental Health Services, 1985—, Friends of the Statehouse, 1987—. Democrat. Mem. United Ch. of Christ. Office: State Legis Montpelier VT 05603

BASSETT, BARBARA WIES, editor, publisher; b. Dec. 5, 1939; m. Norman W. Bassett. B.A., U. Conn., 1961; student, New Sch. for Social Research, 1961-62. Product devel. Fearn Soya, Melrose Park, Ill., 1973-75; product devel. Modern Products, Milw., 1973-75; editor, pub. Bestways Mag., Carson City, Nev., 1977—; owner, operator cooking sch. Greensboro N.C. 1969-73. Author: Natural Cooking, 1968, Japanese Home Cooking, 1970; Wok and Tempura, 1969, The Wok, 1971, Super Soy, 1973, The Healthy Gourmet, 1981, International Healthy Gourmet, 1982. Mem. Inst. Food Technologists. Office: Bestways Mag Inc Box 2028 1501 S Surtro Terr Carson City NV 89702

BASSETT, TINA, communication executive; b. Detroit; m. Leland Kinsey Bassett; children: Joshua, Robert. Student, U. Mich., 1974, 76-78, 81, Wayne State U., 1979-80. Advt. and promotion rep. CREEM Mag., Birmingham, Mich., 1971-72; advt. dir. Greenfield's Restaurant, Mich. and Ohio, 1972-73; dir. advt. and pub. relations Kresco, Inc., Detroit, 1973-74; pub's. rep. The Detroiter mag., 1974-75; pub. relations dir. Detroit Bicentennial Commn., 1975-77; prin. Leland K. Bassett & Assocs., Detroit, 1976-86; intermediate job devel. specialist Detroit Council of the Arts, 1977; project dir. Detroit image campaign Dept. Pub. Info., City of Detroit, 1975, spl. events dir., 1978; dep. dir. Dept. Pub. Info. City of Detroit, 1978-83, dir., 1983-86; pres., prin. Bassett & Bassett, Inc., Detroit, 1986—. Publicity chmn. Under the Stars IV, VI, VII and VIII Benefit Balls, Detroit Inst. of Arts Founders Soc., 1983-87, Detroit Inst. of Arts Centennial Ball, 1985; publicity chmn. Mich. Opera Theater, Opera Ball, 1987; program lectr. Wayne County Close-Up Program, 1984; mem. cen. planning com. Am. Assn. Mus.; mem. Founders Soc., Detroit Inst. Arts, North Rosedale Civic Assn., mem. adv. bd. Detroit Jr. League. Mem. Detroit Hist. Soc., Music Hall Assn. Club: Econ. Home: 18644 Gainsborough Rd Detroit MI 48223 Office: 672 Woodbridge St Detroit MI 48226-4302

BASTABLE, DIANE MARIE, manufacuting company administrator; b. Boston, July 7, 1950; d. John Francis and Doris Theresa (Kelly) B. BA in Psychology, U. Mass., Boston, 1981; MEd in Edn., Bridgewater (Mass.) State Coll., 1983. Cert. elem. tchr., Mass. Mgr. bus. exec. Exeter Instruments, Inc., Seabrook, N.H., 1983—. Home: 135 Walnut Ave North Hampton NH 03862 Office: Exeter Instruments Inc 148 Batchelder Rd PO Box 1498 Seabrook NH 03874

BASTEDO, ELEANOR MADAY, real estate executive; b. Passaic, N.J., Feb. 12, 1937; d. Victor Joseph and Helena (Frankovsky) Maday; m. Theodore C. Bastedo, Sept. 2, 1960; children: Laura Helen Naumann, Thea Lyn, Darin J. BA, Montclair Coll., 1960; grad., Realtors Inst., Orlando, Fla., 1976. Tchr. Pompton Lakes (N.J.) Bd. Edn., 1960-61, Fair Lawn (N.J.) Bd. Edn., 1961-63; chemist Fisher Sci., Fair Lawn, 1965, Brit. Chloride, Tampa, Fla., 1972; real estate broker Tharin Agy., Inc., Dunedin, Fla., 1973-78; pres. Bastedo & Cressman, Inc., Dunedin, Fla., 1978—; cons. in field. Participant in establishing local adult congregate living facility, Clearwater, Fla., 1981-82. Fellow NSF, 1959; RCA Corp. scholar, 1960. Mem. Cert. Residential Specialists (cert.), Cert. Real Estate Appraisers (cert.), Greater Clearwater Bd. Realtors, West Pasco Bd. Realtors, AAUW (pres. Clearwater chpt. 1981-82), Head Injury Support, Inc. (founding mem. Tampa Bay chpt.), Dunedin C. of C. Republican. Unitarian. Office: 500 Main St Dunedin FL 34698

BASTIEN, KATHLEEN CHRISTINA CLARK, intelligence analyst; b. Poughkeepsie, N.Y., Jan. 4, 1959; d. Leo John and Jeanne Marie (Wilson) Clark; m. Marc Girard Bastien, Sept. 10, 1983. BS in Chemistry, Marquette U., 1981. Systems analyst Strategic Def. Initiative Teledyne Brown Engring. Corp., Fairfax, Va., 1986; intelligence analyst The Analytic Scis. Corp., Arlington, Va., 1987—. Served to lt. USN, 1981-86. Mem. Am. Chem. Soc., Nat. Assn. Female Execs., Ret. Officer Assn. Roman Catholic. Office: The Analytic Scis Corp 1700 N Moore St Suite 1800 Arlington VA 22209

BASTIN, KATHY LOUISE, investment company executive; b. Kingston, Pa., June 23, 1953; d. Harold Peter and Anne Louise (Hurst) A.; m. Donald Arlie Bastin, Aug. 17, 1974; children: Michael, Matthew, Andrew. BS in Bus., U. Colo., 1975; MBA, U. Colo., Colorado Springs, 1981. V.p. Vaughn Mortgage, Colorado Springs, 1976-80, Preferred Savs. & Loan, High Point, N.C., 1981-83; pres. First Mortgage and Investment, Greensboro, N.C., 1983-87, Comml. Mortgage & Investment Co., Greensboro, 1987—. Vol. Mobile Meals, Greensboro, N.C., 1986—; bd. dirs. Goodwill Industries, Greensboro, 1986—. Am. Inst. Real Estate Appraisers, U. Colo., 1974. Mem. Mortgage Bankers Assn., N.C. Real Estate Commn. (broker). Republican. Roman Catholic. Home: 2339 Brandt Village Greensboro NC 27405 Office: CMI 5509 W Friendly Ave Greensboro NC 27410

BASTOS, EARLA JEAN, marketing executive; b. Cambridge, Mass., Feb. 19, 1956; d. Joseph Norman Jean Phyliss (Porch) B.; m. Peter M. Ricker; 1 child, Melissa Jean. BA in Biology, U. Mass., Boston, 1977. Customer service rep. Genera Bindin Corp., Watham, Mass., 1977-78; research asst. Polaroid Corp., Cambridge, Mass., 1978-82; ptnr. Rickerdata, Burlington, Mass., 1982-84, Maverick Software, Inc., Melrose, Mass., 1984—. Campaign worker Dukakis for Gov., Melrose, 1981; del. State Convention, Mass., 1982; mem. Melrose City com., 1983. Mem. Boston Computer Soc. Democrat. Home: 11 Cass St Melrose MA 02176

BATCHELDER, ALICE M., federal judge; b. 1944; m. William G. Batchelder III; children: William G. IV, Elisabeth. BA, Ohio Wesleyan U., 1964; JD, Akron U., 1971; LLM, U. Va., 1988. Tchr. Plain Local Sch. Dist., Franklin County, Ohio, 1965-66, Jones Jr. High Sch., 1966-67, Buckeye High Sch., Medina County, 1967-68; assoc. Williams & Batchelder, Medina, Ohio, 1971-83; judge U.S. Bankruptcy Ct., Ohio, 1983-85, U.S. Dist. Ct. (no. dist.) Ohio, Cleve., 1985—. Mem. ABA. Office: US Dist Ct 256 US Courthouse 201 Superior Ave NE Cleveland OH 44114

BATCHELOR, GLADYS P., financial planner; b. Plainfield, N.J., Sept. 19, 1932; d. Joseph Frank and Mabel (Kellerman) Purchess; m. Andrew Jackson Batchelor, June 8, 1957; children: Allison Jay, Andrew Jackson Jr. AA in Bus. Mgmt. and Acctg., Rutgers U., 1956; B summa cum laude in Gen. Studies, Ohio U., 1974, MEd, 1978. Adminstr. Pub. Service Electric & Gas Co., Plainfield, 1950-57, Internat. Telephone & Telegraph Corp., Nutley, N.J., 1957-59; coordinator, cons. women's programs Ohio State U., Newark, 1975; counselor, program coordinator Ohio U., Lancaster, 1976-77, asst. to dir. exec. MBA program, 1977-79; sr. fin. cons. Forward Planning Assocs., Columbus, Ohio, 1979-80; pvt. practice fin. planning and cons. specializing in fin. needs of women 1980—. Treas., trustee, mem. organizing com. Ohio Women, Inc., 1977-81; v.p. Ohio Commn. on Status of Women, 1976; v.p., bd. dirs. Lancaster-Fairfield County YWCA; coordinator Internat. Women's Yr., Fairfield County, 1975. Mem. Internat. Assn. for Fin. Planning (pres., dir. Cen. Ohio chpt. 1986-87, chmn. bd. trustees 1988), Inst. Cert. Fin. Planners, Nat. Inst. Fin. (regional assoc.), Lancaster C. of C., World Future Soc., AAUW. Methodist. Home: 1260 Ridgewood Way NE Lancaster OH 43130

BATEMAN, DOTTYE JANE SPENCER, realtor; b. Athens, Tex.; d. Charles Augustus and Lillie (Freeman) Spencer; student Fed. Inst., 1941-42, So. Meth. U., Dallas Coll., 1956-58; m. George Truitt Bateman, 1947 (div. Apr. 1963); children—Kelly Spencer, Bethena; m. 2d, Joseph E. Lindsley, 1968. Sec. to state senator, Tyler, Tex., 1941-42; sec. to pres. Merc. Nat. Bank, Dallas, State Fair of Tex., Dallas, 1942-48; realtor, broker, Garland, Tex., 1956—; co-ptnr. Play-Shade Co.; appraiser Assoc. Soc. Real Estate Appraiser; auctioneer, 1963—; developer Stonewall Cave, 1964—, Guthrie East Estates. Pres., Central Elementary Sch. PTA, 1955-56, Bussey Jr. High PTA, 1956-57; former Rep. Precinct chair, Garland; mem. Rep. Senatorial Inner Circle, 1986—; den mother Cub Scouts Am., 1957-59; chmn. Decent Lit. Com., 1956-58; chmn. PTA's council, 1958; dir. Dallas Heart Assn., 1960, local chmn., 1955-57, county chmn., 1957-60; spl. dir. Henderson County Red Cross, 1945; local chmn. March of Dimes, 1961-63; mem. Dallas Civic Opera Com., 1963-64; mem. homemaker panel Dallas Times Herald, 1955-74, Nat. Rep. Womne and Regents, 1986—. Named Outstanding Tex. Jaycee-Ette Pres., 1953, hon. Garland Jay-Cee-Ette, 1956, hon. Sheriff, Dallas County, 1963; headliner Press Club Awards dinner, 1963-68. Mem. Garland, Dallas (chmn. reception com., past dir., mem. comml.-investment div., mem. make Am. better com. 1973-78, mem. beautify Tex. council 1977-78, by-laws com. 1977-78) bds. realtors, Auctioneers Assn., Internat. Real Estate Fedn., Soc. Prevention Cruelty to Animals, Dallas Women's (project chmn.). Garland (chmn. spl. services com. 1955-56) chambers commerce, Consejo Internacional De Buena Vecindad, Delphian Study Club, Eruditis Study Club, D.A.R. (Daniel McMahan chpt.). Christian Scientist. Clubs: Garland (past v.p., pres.), Tex. (past treas., ofcl. hostess) Jaycee-Ettes, Garland Fedn. Women's (past pres.), Garland Garden, Trinity Dist. Fedn. Women's (past pres.), Pub. Affairs Luncheon, Dallas Press (dir. 1973-74), chmn. house com. 1973-74, chmn. hdqrs. com. 1973-74). Home: 6313 Lyons Rd Garland TX 75043 Office: 5518 Dyer St #1 Dallas TX 75206

BATEMAN, SYLVIA LILAINE, lawyer; b. Chgo., Mar. 5, 1956; d. Russell Clayton and Mamie H. (Johnson) Jones; m. Paul Ehrich Bateman, Aug. 19, 1978; 1 child, Paul Ehrich, Jr. BS with honors, U. Ill.-Chgo., 1976; JD, U. Mich., 1980. Bar: D.C. 1980. Acct. Natural Gas Pipeline Co. Am., Chgo., 1976-77; assoc. firm Hudson, Leftwich & Davenport, Washington, 1980-82; atty. II, Potomac Electric Power Co., Washington, 1982-83, asst. counsel, 1983-84, assoc. counsel, 1984; gen. atty. United Air Lines, Inc., Chgo., 1984—. Mem. ABA, D.C. Bar Assn., Wash. Bar Assn. (panelist law fair 1983), Nat. Bar Assn. Democrat. Episcopalian. Office: United Air Lines Inc PO Box 66100 Chicago IL 60666

BATES, BARBARA J. NEUNER, municipal official; b. Mt. Vernon, N.Y., Apr. 8, 1927; d. John Joseph William and Elsie May (Flint) Neuner; B.A., Barnard Coll., 1947; m. Herman Martin Bates, Jr., Mar. 25, 1950; children—Roberta Jean Bates Jamin, Herman Martin III, Jon Neuner. Confidential clk. to supr. town Ossining (N.Y.), 1960-63; pres. BNB Assocs., Briarcliff Manor, N.Y., 1963-83, Upper Nyack Realty Co., Inc., Briarcliff Manor, 1966-71; receiver of taxes Town of Ossining (N.Y.), 1971—. Vice pres. Ossining (N.Y.) Young Republican Club, 1958; pres. Young Womens Rep. Club Westchester County (N.Y.), 1959-61; regional committeewoman N.Y. State Assn. Young Rep. Clubs, 1960-62; mem. Westchester County Rep. Com., 1963—; mem. Ossining Women's Rep. Club, 1960—, pres., 1984-85; mem. Westchester County Women's Rep. Club, 1957—. Mem. Jr. League Westchester-on-Hudson, DAR, N.Y. State Assn. Tax Receivers and Collectors, Receivers of Taxes Assn. of Westchester County, (legis. liaison, v.p., pres. 1984-85), Hackley Sch. Mothers Assn. (pres. 68), R.I. Hist. Soc., Ossining Hist. Soc., Ossining Bus. and Profl. Women's Club, Am. Soc. Notaries, Westchester County Hist. Soc., Briarcliff-Scarborough Hist. Soc. Congregationalist. Home: 78 Holbrook Ln Briarcliff Manor NY 10510 also: 663 Reynolds Rd Chepachet RI 02814

BATES, BARBARA JEANNE, art reference librarian, writer, lecturer; b. Mpls., May 31; d. Gale Pillsbury and Rhetta Hilyer; m. George Walter Bates, Dec. 12, 1951 (div. 1962); 1 child, Brenda Leigh. Student Beaver Coll., 1947-48; B.A. in Edn., U. Pa., 1950; M.A., Drexel Inst., 1951; Tchrs. Cert., Temple U., 1953. Librarian, Free Library of Phila., 1950-54, reference librarian, 1987—; librarian U.S. Army Overseas Schs., Mannheim, Germany, 1956-61, Lansdown Aldan Sch. Dist., Pa., 1961-71, Kulani Honor Camp, Hilo, Hawaii, 1976; library coordinator Springfield Sch. Dist., Erdenheim, Pa., 1971-82; reference librarian in charge Community Coll. Phila., evenings and weekends 1977-80; pres., producer Betsy Ross Living History Presentations, Valley Forge, Pa., 1982-87 to prepare Am. schs. and communities for celebration of U.S. Constn.; kindergarten tchr. Children's Learning Service, King of Prussia, Pa., 1985-86; co-founder, vice pres., sec. Global Edn. Motivators, Erdenheim, 1980-84. Author, producer, coordinator, actress of video film: Happy Birthday George Washington, 1982 (Freedom Found. award 1982); The Rainbow Experience, 1984. Mem. disaster action team ARC, Phila., 1982—; disaster reservist Fed. Emergency Mgmt. Agy. Eastern Div. , 1984-87; vol. asst. to Archivist Medal of Honor Grove Freedoms Found., Valley Forge, 1980-87, worker for Habitat for Humanity at J. Carter Work Camp, Phila., 1988, cons. to Library and Archival Collection at Valley Forge Hist. Park; literacy tutor for Mayor's Commn. on Literacy for the Prison Literacy Project Project, U.S. div. Books for Youth. Recipient George Washington Honor medal Freedoms Found., 1982; Legion of Merit, Chapel of Four Chaplains, 1982. Mem. NEA (del. conv. 1980, 81), Govs.' Conf. on Libraries and Info. Services (del. 1977), White House Conf. on Libraries and Info. Services, Pa. Library Assn. (Pub. Relations award 1959), World Affairs Council, Japan Study Group II, Valley Forge Hist. Soc., Am. Assn. Mus., U.S. Capitol Hist. Soc., Kappa Delta. Democrat. Mem. and tour guide Washington Meml. Chapel at Valley Forge.

BATES, BETSEY, artist; b. Dobbs Ferry, N.Y., Nov. 29, 1924; d. Homer Morgan and Dorothy (Graef) Smith; B.F.A. magna cum laude, Beaver Coll., 1946; m. Guy C. Bates, Aug. 30, 1947 (div. 1965); children—Carleton Jane, Leslie Collins; m. Joseph M. Gerhart, June 13, 1978. Designer, painter, illustrator, printmaker for advt. agys., corps. and pubs.; works include: Christmas card Easter Seal Soc., 1974, mural for RCA TV Studio, Switzerland, 1977; represented in collections: Washington Hilton Hotel, Houston Marriott, Syracuse Marriott, Chgo. Marriott, Texaco, World Book, Lynell, Grad. Hosp. of Phila, Butler Inst. Am. Art, Danskin, Inc., Episcopal Acad., Hahnemann Hosp., Friends Central Sch., Continental Bank, Fed. Res. Bank, Free Library Phila., Germantown Hosp., Montgomery Hosp. (10), Smith Kline Pharm. Labs., McNeil Pharm. Corp. (2); designer collectible Christmas plates for World Book Publishers, Chgo., 1979—. Recipient cert. of merit Nat. Consumer Fin. Assn., 1963; cert. of excellence Phila. Art Dirs. Club, 1964; award Nat. Community Arts Program, Golden Disc, Beaver Coll., 1975; Best of Show award Norristown Borough (Pa.) Council of Arts, 1980. Mem. Artists Equity Assn., Phila. Art Alliance, Nat. Trust Hist. Preservation, Artists Guild Delaware Valley (Gold awards 1977-84). Home and Studio: 83 Hillside Dr Plymouth MA 02360

BATES, LAURA LYNN, internal auditor, marketing professional; b. Windsor, Ont., Can., May 14, 1962; d. Laverne W. and Lynn J. Bates; m. Jerry L. Sadler, June 28, 1986. BABA, Spring Arbor (Mich.) Coll., 1982; postgrad., Rochester (N.Y.) Inst. Tech., 1986—. Analyst domestic systems Customer Equipment Service div. Eastman Kodak Co., Rochester, 1982-84, analyst internat. systems, 1984-86; internal auditor Eastman Kodak Co., Rochester, 1986-88, mgr. adminstrn. and info. systems, photographic products group, 1988—. Mem. Nat. Assn. Female Execs., Inst. Internal Auditors. Office: Eastman Kodak Co Photographic Products Group Adminstrn and Info Systems 343 State St Rochester NY 14650

BATES, LINDA FAYE, tax specialist; b. San Antonio, Dec. 25, 1939; d. James Fuller Chandler and Linda Stehle Donnelly; m. Richard Curtis Bates, Feb. 8, 1958 (div. 1975); children: Glenda Anne Snider, Roy Glen, Monte Lee. Student, So. Meth. U., 1980-81. Asst. buyer, adminstrv. sec. Esco Mfg. Co., Greenville, Tex., 1969-76; assoc. acctg. Exec. Aircraft Services Inc., Dallas, 1976-78; asst. plant mgr. NL Industries Inc., Dallas, 1978-79; supr. Automatic Data Processing, Dallas, 1979-81, specialist, mgr. unemployment tax, 1984—; dir., adminstrv. sec. Jack Hunter and Assocs., Arlington, Tex., 1981-83; dir., asst. mgr. plant Herbalife Internat., Irving, Tex., 1984-87; automatic data processing mgr. UCM dept. I Tax Specialists, Dallas, 1987—. Playwright: Texas River Ministry, 1965. Dir. Youth Camp So. Bapt. Conv., 9 counties 1960-69, 13 counties 1960-75; chmn. by-laws com. EEO, 1960-69; vol. firefighter, Tye, Tex., 1965-69; active PTA, 1965-69, So. Bapt. Mission Assn., 1965-75; mem. Hendrick Home Children Exec. Assn., 1959—. Mem. Nat. Assn. Female Execs., Tex. Notary Assn. (cert.). Democrat. Home and Office: 5220 Timbercreek Rd Flower Mound TX 75028

BATES, LINDA GILMORE, counselor; b. Homeville, Ga., Aug. 15, 1944; d. Harold LeBruce and MaryJeff (Clements) Gilmore; m. C. Valentine Bates, Jan. 29, 1961 (div. 1981); children: Lisa Bates Hatcher, Jeffrey Charles. BA in Spl. Edn. magna cum laude, U. Fla., 1971; MS in Emotional Disturbance, Nova U., 1985. Cert. spl. edn. tchr., Fla. Counselor USO, 1965-67; therapist Bellevue Nursing Home, Omaha, 1967-68; vocat. edn. specialist Santa Fe High Sch., Gainesville, Fla., 1972-73; tchr. spl. edn. Glen Springs Elem. Sch., Gainesville, 1973-74; tchr. Alachua County Schs., Gainesville, 1972-81, Suwannee County Sch. System, Live Oak, Fla., 1981-87; pvt. counselor Personal Counseling & Ednl. Consultation Ctr., Live Oak, 1987—. Counselor USO, Kadena, Okinawa, Japan, 1967; mem. bd. edn. Sunshine Sch., Gainesville, 1972-81; den mother Boy Scouts Am., Gainesville, 1973; sponsor Jr. Achievement, 1975-80; bd. dirs. Fed. Child Care Alachua County, Gainesville, 1979-80; coordinator Fla. Spl. Olympics, 1980. Recipient Family Services award USAF, 1965-67; named one of Outstanding Young Women Am., 1981. Mem. Am. Assn. for Counseling and Devel., Council for Exceptional Children (bd. dirs. 1980-83, service award), Mental Health Assn., Fla. Assn. Retarded Citizens (pres., bd. dirs. 1973-81). Methodist/Episcopal. Home: 718 Suwannee Ave Live Oak FL 32060 Office: Personal Counseling & Ednl Counsultation 122 N Ohio Ave Live Oak FL 32060

BATES, LURA WHEELER, trade association executive; b. Inboden, Ark., Aug. 28, 1932; d. Carl Clifton and Hester Ray (Pace) Wheeler; B.S. in Bus. Adminstrn., U. Ark., 1954; m. Allen Carl Bates, Sept. 12, 1954; 1 dau., Carla Allene. Sec.-bookkeeper, then officer mgr. Assoc. Gen. Contractors Miss., Inc., Jackson, 1958-77, dir. adminstrv. services, 1977—, asst. exec. dir., 1980—; adminstr. Miss. Constrn. Found., 1977—; sec. AIA-Assoc. Gen. Contractors Liaisonship Coms., 1977—; sec. Carpenters Joint Apprenticeship Coms., Jackson and Vicksburg, 1977—. Sec., Marshall Elem. Sch. PTA, Jackson, 1962-64, v.p., 1965; sec.-treas. Inter-Club Council Jackson, 1963-64; tchr. adult Sunday sch. dept. Hillcrest Bapt. Ch., Jackson, 1975-82; Bapt. Women dir. WMU First Bapt. Ch., Crystal Springs, Miss., 1987—; mem. exec. com. Jackson Christian Bus. and Profl. Women's Council, 1976-80, sec., 1978-79, pres., 1979-80. Named Outstanding Woman in Constrn. Miss., 1962-63; Outstanding Mem. Nat. Assn. Women in Constrn., various times. Fellow Internat. Platform Assn.; mem. Nat. Assn. Women in Constrn. (chpt. pres. 1963-64, 76-77, nat. v.p. 1965-66, 77-78, nat. dir. Region 5, 1967-68, nat. sec. 1970-71, 71-72, pres. 1980-81, coordinator cert. constrn. assoc. program 1973-78, 83-84 guardian-controller Edn. Found. 1981-82, chmn. nat. bylaws com. 1982-83, 85-88, nat. parliamentarian 1983—), Nat. Assn. Parliamentarians, Delta Delta Delta. Editor NAWIC Image, 1968-69, Procedures Manual, 1965-66, Public Relations Handbook, 1967-68, Profl. Edn. Guide, 1972-73, Guidelines & Procedures Handbook, 1987-88; author digests in field. Home: 272 Lee Ave Crystal Springs MS 39059 Office: 2093 Lakeland Dr Jackson MS 39216

BATES, RUBY LEE, corporate administrator; b. Marion, La., July 14, 1940; d. Roy and Wordie B. (Boyette) Shelbon; m. Julius Green, Aug. 18, 1963 (div. 1968); 1 child, Dana; m. Charles Bates, June 30, 1976 (dec.). A.A., Castlemont Coll., Oakland, 1957; S.S.A., Heald Coll., Oakland, 1958. Exec. sec. Golden State Ins., Oakland, 1958-66; adminstrv. office mgr. Simmons & Travis, Oakland, 1966-74; adminstrv. asst. Castle & Cooke, San Francisco, 1975-77, office coordinator, 1977-81, corp. bookkeeper, 1981-85; case adminstr. Kornblum, Kelly & Herlihy, San Francisco, 1986; case adminstr. Kornblum, Kelly & Herlihy, San Francisco, 1986—. Editor: Handbook for Temporary Personnel, 1979. Vol., Gospel Voices, Oakland, 1971-85. Recipient Service award Bible Fellowship Ch., Oakland, 1976. Mem. Nat. Assn. Female Execs., Gamma Phi Delta. Democrat. Baptist. Avocations: Gospel singing, walking, reading. Home: 3822 39th Ave Oakland CA 94619 Office: Kornblum Kelly & Herlihy 445 Bush St 6th Floor San Francisco CA 94108

BATES-NISBET, (CLARA) ELISABETH, piano educator, poet, lawyer; b. Houston, Dec. 4, 1902; d. William David and Kate Broocks (Arnall) Bates. BA, U. Tex., 1938; MA, U. Houston, 1941; LLB, S. Tex. Sch. Law, 1937. Bar: Tex. 1937. Tchr. pub. schs., Houston, 1923-49; prin. Longfellow Elem. Sch., Houston, 1950-52, Mamie Sue Bastian Elem. Sch., Houston, 1952-60, James Arlie Montgomery Elem. Sch., Houston, 1960-73; tchr. piano, Houston, 1928—. Life mem. chancellor's council U. Tex., Tex. Congress Parents and Tchrs.; established John Pelham Border Meml. Fund, San Jacinto Mus. of History Assn.; founder perpetually endowed Presdl. scholarship in law, history, govt. or music, U. Tex. at Austin; founder Kate Broocks Bates award for research in Tex. history, Tex. State Hist. Assn. and DAR, also two Kate Harding Bates Parker Award funds, Jr. Historians Orgns. of Tex. Hist. Assn., and Library of DAR; established Emma Broocks Arnall perpetually endowed Geology Scholarship Fund, U. Okla. at Norman; creator perpetual endowment Fine Arts Ctr., U. Tex. at Austin. Recipient Woman of Achievement award to be honored in the Hereditary Register of the U.S. in celebration of the Bicentennial of the Constn. of the U.S., 1987. Mem. Tex. Bar Assn. (50-year mem. award 1987), Houston Bar Assn., Tex. Tchrs. Assn. (life), Tex. Geneal. Soc., Magna Carta Dames (organizing charter mem. E. Tex. Colony, 3d vice regent courier Round Table Tex. div. 1962-66), Tex. Hist. Assn. (patron, life), Colonial Dames XVII Century (registrar Col. John Alston chpt. 1966-68, mem. nat. com. on Am. history 1966-68), Alston-Willems-Boddie-Hillard Soc. N.C., Colonial Order Crown, San Augustine County Hist. Soc. (charter), San Jacinto Descs., Daus. Republic Tex. (organizing charter mem. Ezekial Cullen chpt. 1953, co-founder perpetual endowment found. for Ezekial Cullen chpt., rec. sec. gen. 1963-65, compiler, editor anns. 1963-65, 2d v.p. gen., chmn. orgn. 1965-67, state chmn. Kate Broocks Bates Award com.), Soc. Descs. Charlemagne, DAR (Texas chpt. regent 1966-68, mem. nat. coms.), Soc. Descs. Knights of Most Noble Order of Garter, Daus. Am. Colonists (organizer charter mem. LaSalle chpt.), UDC Jefferson Davis Chpt., Sovereign Colonial Soc. Ams. Royal Descent, Plantagenet Soc., Dames of Ct. of Honor, Daus. of Founders and Patriots of Am., Freedoms. Found. Valley Forge, Internat. Platform Assn., Smithsonian Instn., Bates Family of Old Va. Assn., Jamestowne Soc. (organizing gov. First Tex. Co. 1982), Nat. Soc. Poets, Ex-Students Assn. U. Tex., Delta Kappa Gamma (life, 1st v.p. Eta Delta chpt. 1966-68). Address: 2305 Woodhead St Houston TX 77019

BATESON, MARY CATHERINE, anthropology educator; b. N.Y.C., Dec. 8, 1939; d. Gregory and Margaret (Mead) B.; m. J. Barkev Kassarjian, June 4, 1960; 1 child, Sevanne Margaret. BA, Radcliffe Coll., 1960; PhD, Harvard U., 1963. Instr. Arabic Harvard U., 1963-66; asso. prof. anthropology Ateneo de Manila U., 1966-68; sr. research fellow psychology and philosophy Brandeis U., 1968-69; assoc. prof. anthropology Northeastern U., Boston, 1969-71; researcher U. Tehran, 1972-74; vis. prof. Northeastern U., 1974-75; prof. anthropology, dean grad. studies Damavand Coll., 1975-77; prof. anthropology, dean social sci. and humanities U. No. Iran, 1977-79; vis. scholar Harvard U., 1979-80; dean faculty, prof. anthropology Amherst Coll., 1980-87; Clarence Robinson prof. anthropology and English George Mason U., 1987—; pres. Inst. Intercultural Studies, from 1979. Author: Structural Continuity in Poetry: A Linguistic Study of Five Early Arabic Odes, 1970, Our Own Metaphor: A Personal Account of a Conference on Consciousness and Human Adaption, 1972, With a Daughter's Eye: A Memoir of Margaret Mead and Gregory Bateson, 1984, (with others) Angels Fear: Towards an Epistemology of the Sacred, 1987, Thinking AIDS, 1988; co-editor: Approaches to Semiotics: Anthropology, Education, Linguistics, Psychiatry and Psychology, 1964. Fellow Ford Found., 1961-63, NSF, 1968-79, Guggenheim Found., 1987-88. Mem. Am. Anthrop. Assn., Soc. Iranian Studies, Lindisfarne Assn., Phi Beta Kappa. Address: 172 Lexington Ave Cambridge MA 02138

BATIN, ADELA GRACE WARD, publisher, graphic designer, photographer; b. Abilene, Tex., May 16, 1953; d. Gunter Eugene and Edna Frieda (Schuster) Johnson; m. Doran Lee Ward, Dec. 23, 1977 (div. Aug. 1981); m. Christopher Michael Batin, Nov. 27, 1982. BA in Advt. Design, Boise State U., 1974. Dir. art Murray, Kraft & Rockey, Anchorage, 1974-75; art specialist U.S. Army Recreational Service, Ft. Richardson, Alaska, 1975-76; Alaska planning team graphic artist U.S. Forest Service, Anchorage, 1976-78; graphic artist U. Alaska, Fairbanks, 1978-79; pres., designer Award Design, Fairbanks, 1979—; dir. art Alaska Outdoors Mag., Anchorage, 1980-84; publisher Alaska Angler Publs., Fairbanks, 1984—. Pub., designer, photographer, illustrator: How to Catch Alaska's Trophy Sportfish, 1984 (Best Fishing Book Produced Cannon S & K Outdoors Writers Assn. Am. 1987, Best of Competition for Writing, Design, Photography Northwest Outdoor Writer's Assn., Cannon/S&K, 1985, First Place Best Publ. NOWA 1985), Hunting in Alaska, 1987. Dancer, singer Fairbanks Light Opera Theater, 1979-82. Mem. Outdoor Writer's Assn. Am. (bd. dirs. 1987—), Am. Bus. Women's Assn. (local chpt. pres. 1985-86, Top Ten Businesswoman award 1986-87). Lutheran. Office: Alaska Angler Publs 520 5th Ave Suite 412 Fairbanks AK 99701

BATORSKI, JUDITH ANN, arts administration executive; b. Eden, N.Y., Oct. 8, 1949; d. John Michael and Ethel (Owens) Batorski; m. Michael J. Rocco (div. Oct. 1980); 1 child, Flora. Student retail mgmt., Colo. Springs Coll. Bus., 1981; AS in Fine Arts, Suffolk Community Coll., 1983; BA, SUNY, Stonybrook, 1985; postgrad., Columbia Coll. Chgo. Film Sch., 1985; MA, SUNY, Stonybrook, 1987. Caretaker, asst. mgr. Farmer's Shared Home, Danbury, N.H., 1979-80; cert. educator Assn. for Childbirth at Home, Internat., Los Angeles, 1980; accts. payable clk. Pikes Peak Community Coll., Colorado Springs, Colo., 1981-82; office mgr. Three Village Meals-on-Wheels, Stonybrook, 1984; grad. sec. art dept. SUNY, Stonybrook, 1986-87, art gallery intern Fine Arts Ctr., 1987; dir. ops., dir. master classes and free concerts Islip Arts Council, East Islip, N.Y., 1987—; participant Arts in Bus. Mgmt. seminar Citibank/ABC, N.Y.C., 1987, community leaders luncheon Fox Channel 5, N.Y.C., 1987. Photographs included in Coll. Photography Annual, 1985. Campaign dir. Food for Poland, Colorado Springs, 1982; organizer Granite State Alliance, Portsmouth, N.H., 1979, Safe 'n' Sound anti-nuclear campaign, Shoreham, N.Y., 1979; grad. rep. Sch. Continuing Edn. SUNY Stonybrook, judicial com. on acad. standing, SUNY Stonybrook, 1986-87; vol. Vietnam Vets. Theatre Ensemble, 1988, New Community Cinema, Huntington, N.Y., 1988. Buddhist. Home: 272 River Ave Patchogue NY 11772

BATT, DONNA ELAINE, assistant principal; b. Nampa, Idaho, Apr. 16, 1946; d. Robert M. and E. Elaine (Doner) B. BA, Coll. Idaho, 1968; MEd, U. Portland, 1970. Cert. secondary prin. and tchr., Idaho, Wash., Alaska, Nev. Tchr. Wilder (Idaho) Sch. Dist., 1971-73; counselor Elko (Nev.) County Sch., 1974-76; dir. student activities Coll. So. Idaho, Twin Falls, 1976-77; with sales div. Links Sch. Bus., Boise, Idaho, 1977-78; counselor Toppenish (Wash.) Sch. Dist., 1978-80, Longview (Wash.) Sch. Dist., 1980-82, Lower Kuskokwin Sch. Dist., Bethel, Alaska, 1982-84; adminstrn. intern Anchorage Sch. Dist., 1984-85, asst. prin., 1985—. Author: The Loneliness, 1976; (contemporary writing) Let's Talk About Dreams, 1978; contbr. articles to profl. jours. Mem. Altrusa, Longview, 1980-82. Mem. Nat. Assn. Secondary Sch. Prins., Anchorage Assn. Sch. Prins., Alaska Assn. Sch. Prins., Nat. Assn. Female Execs., Assn. Supervision and Curriculum and Devel., Alaska Sch. Counselors Assn., Phi Delta Kappa. Republican. Club: Altrusa Women's. Office: Anchorage Sch Dist DeBarr Rd Anchorage AK 99501

BATTAGLIA, BEVERLY ANN, electronics executive, consultant, educator; b. Amsterdam, N.Y.; d. Douglas Bennett and Victoria S. (Tumidajewicz) Greenspan; m. Stephen S. Battaglia; children: David Alan, Richard William. BS in Mgmt., U. Louisville, 1978; MBA, Pepperdine U., 1984. Cert. tchr., Calif. Dir. human resources ARC, Louisville, Ky., 1978-80; assoc. dir. blood ops. recruitment ARC, Los Angeles, 1980-81; dir. human resources Charter Med. Corp. Hosp., Hawaiian Gardens, Calif., 1981; cons. Delta Inst., Los Alamitos, Calif., 1982; pres. Battaglia Ltd. Consulting, Anaheim, Calif., 1985—; instr. Three Community Colls., Orange County, 1982-87, Calif. State U., Long Beach, 1983—, Calif. Poly. U., Pomona, 1987, U. Calif., Irvine, 1986—; adviser Interstate Women's Network, Anaheim, 1985—. Mem. edn. com. AIDS in the Workplace, 1987; mem. program com. YWCA, 1987; program chairperson 1st Ann. Women's Symposium, Orange County, 1986; bd. dirs. Orange County Chamber Orch., 1987. Mem. Am. Soc. Tng. and Devel. (group chairperson industry com. 1983-88, bd. dirs. 1984-86), Orgn. Devel. Network (mem. steering com. 1987-88), AAUW (mem. adv. bd. 1984, 1st chairperson mentor program, 1st Woman of Yr. 1985), Personnel and Indsl. Relations Assn., Prof. Women's Network Orange County (pres., mem. adv. bd.). Office: Interstate Electronics Corp 602 E Vermont Anaheim CA 92803

BATTELLE, BEVERLY KAY, temporary personnel firm executive; b. Louisa, Va., June 11, 1951; d. William Elmer Battelle and Hazel Rebecca (Edenton) Martin; m. George Wayne Weeks, Aug. 18, 1983; 1 child, Wesley Edenton. BS, Va. Commonwealth U., 1973. Dir. social services The Salvation Army, Richmond, Va., 1973-78; br. mgr. Western Temporary Services, Richmond, 1979-82; pres., owner Battelle Temps, Inc., Richmond, 1982—; bus. cons. Project Bus., Richmond, 1985. Vol. Am. Heart Fund Telethon, Richmond, 1984-85; adv. com. Tom Bliley for Senator, Richmond, 1986; other vol. work. Named 1st Place Winner The Met. C. Corp. Challenge, 1984. Mem. Metro C. of C. (chmn.'s club 1982-86, hon. life 1984), Better Bus. Bur., Retail Merchants Assn., Carytown Inc. (mem. com. chairperson 1988), Data Entry Mgmt. Assn. (treas. 1983), Office Automation Assn. of Richmond. Office: Battelle Temps Inc 15 S Belmont Ave Richmond VA 23221

BATTERMAN, PAULA ANNE, designer, merchandiser; b. Norwich, N.Y., Sept. 27, 1953. Student, New Paltz (N.Y.) State U.; AA, Cazenovia (N.Y.) Coll.; BA, Fashion Inst. Tech., N.Y.C.; postgrad., Sch. Visual Arts, N.Y.C. Designer The Goulder Co., N.Y.C., Fairview Noble Co., N.Y.C., Danielle Shepherd/Stein Co., N.Y.C., Leslie Fay Co., N.Y.C., Abvien Import Co., N.Y.C.; designer/merchandiser Perry Mfg. Co., N.Y.C., 1985—. Mem. Nat. Assn. Female Execs., The Fashion Group. Home: 30-94 33 St Astoria NY 11102 Office: Perry Mfg Co 1001 6th Ave New York NY 10018

BATTIN, PATRICIA MEYER, librarian; b. Gettysburg, Pa., June 2, 1929; d. Emanuel Albert and Josephine (Lehman) Meyer; m. William Thomas Battin, June 16, 1951 (div. 1975); children—Laura, Joanna, Thomas. B.A., Swarthmore Coll., 1951; M.S.L.S., Syracuse U., 1967. Asst. librarian SUNY-Binghamton, 1967-69, asst. dir. for reader services, 1969-74; dir. library services Columbia U., N.Y.C., 1974-78, univ. librarian, 1978—, v.p. info. services, univ. librarian, 1978-87; interim pres. Research Libraries Group, Palo Alto, Calif., 1982, also dir.; pres. Common Preservation and Access, Washington, 1987—; trustee Council on Library Resources, Washington, EDUCOM, Princeton, N.J. Contbr. articles to profl. jours. Mem. ALA, Assn. Research Libraries (trustee 1982-85), Phi Beta Kappa, Beta Phi

Mu. Club: Grolier (N.Y.C). Office: Commn on Preservation and Access 1785 Massachusetts Ave NW Suite 313 Washington DC 20036

BATTIN, (ROSABELL HARRIET) RAY, neuropsychologist, audiologist; b. Rock Creek, Ohio; d. Harry Walter and Sophia (Boldt) Ray; A.B., U. Denver, 1948; M.S., U. Mich., 1950; Ph.D., U. Fla., 1959; postgrad. U. Miami (Fla.) Sch. of Medicine, 1957, U. Iowa, 1958; m. Tom C. Battin, Aug. 24, 1949. Instr. in speech pathology U. Denver, 1949-50; audiologist Ann Arbor (Mich.) Sch., 1950-51; audiologist Houston (Tex.) Speech and Hearing Center, 1954-56; dir. speech pathology-psychology Hedgecroft Hosp. and Rehab. Center, Houston, 1956-59; audiologist with Drs. Guilford, Wright and Draper, Houston, 1959-63; pvt. practice in psychology, audiology and psycholinguistics, Houston, 1959—; clin. instr. dept. otolaryngology U. Tex. Sch. Medicine, Galveston, 1964-80; dir. of audiology vestibulography and speech pathology lab. Houston Ear Nose and Throat Hosp. Clinic, 1963-73; adj. clin. instr. U. Houston, 1981—; lectr. The First Word program Sta. KUHT-TV, 1959; guest lectr. to various workshops and schs., 1959—; v.p. Behavioral Perceptual Ctr., 1986—. Bd. dirs. Juvenile Ct. Vols., 1980-83, Children's Resource and Info. Ctr., 1981-85, Dyslexic Adult Support Services, 1986—. Lic. psychologist, Tex. Recipient Gold award for Ednl. Exhibit, Am. Acad. Pediatrics, 1969. Fellow Am. Speech and Hearing Assn. (profl. services bd. 1967-70, com. on pvt. practice 1971-74), World Acad. Inc.; mem. Acad. Pvt. Practice in Speech Pathology and Audiology (pres. 1968-70), Am. Psychol. Assn., Tex. Speech and Hearing Assn. (v.p. 1968), Cleft Palate Assn., Tex., Houston psychol. assns., Harris County Biofeedback Soc. (pres. 1984), Acad. of Aphasia, Internat. Assn. of Logopedics and Phoniatrics, Am. Auditory Soc., Orthopsychiat. Assn., Am. Biofeedback Soc., Tex. Biofeedback Soc., Sigma Alpha Eta. Author: (with C. Olaf Haug) Speech and Language Delay, 1964; Vestibulography, 1974; Private Practice: Guidelines for Speech Pathology and Audiology, 1971; editor (with Donna R. Fox) Private Practice in Audiology and Speech and Language Pathology, 1978; contbr. author: Seminars in Speech, Language, Hearing (Northern); Auditory Disorders in School Children (Roeser and Downs); Current Therapy of Communications Disorder (Perkins); editor Jour. Acad. Pvt. Practice in Speech Pathology and Audiology, 1981-84; contbr. articles in field to profl. jours.; author (with Irvin A. Kraft) The Dysynchronous Child (film), 1971; The Battin Clinic Language Learning Screening Test for Preschool Children, 1985., The Battin Scale of Parent's Attitude Toward Family Experience and Need for Child Cochlear Implant Candidates. Home: 3837 Meadow Lake Ln Houston TX 77027 Office: Battin Clinic 3931 Essex Ln Houston TX 77027

BATTLE, KATHLEEN DEANNA, soprano; b. Portsmouth, Ohio; d. Grady and Ollie (Layne) B. MusB, U. Cin., MusM, D of Performing Arts (hon.), 1983; D of Performing Arts (hon.), Westminster Choir Coll., Ohio U. Appeared with Met. Opera, San Fransisco Opera, Chgo. Opera, Salzburg Festival, N.Y. Philharm., Boston Symphony, Phila. Orch., Chgo. Symphony, Berlin Philharm., Vienna Staatsoper, Paris Opera, Royal Opera/Covent Garden, others; roles include Semele, Cleopatra in Julius Caesar, Pamina in Magic Flute, Rosina in Barber of Seville, Adina in Elixir of Love, Sophie in Der Rosenkavalier, Zerlina in Don Giovanni, Zdenka in Arabella, Zerbinetta in Ariadne Auf Naxos, Susanna in The Marriage of Figaro. Recipient Grammy awards, 1987, 88. Mem. Delta Omicron. Methodist. Office: care Columbia Artist Mgmt Inc 165 W 57th St New York NY 10019

BATTLE, LOIS, writer, actress; b. Subiaco, Australia, Oct. 6, 1941; came to U.S., 1946, naturalized, 1962; d. John Henry and Doreen Mary (White) B.; student Fullerton Jr. Coll., 1956-58; B.A., UCLA, 1962. Author books: Season of Change, 1980, War Brides, 1982, Southern Women, 1984, A Habit of the Blood, 1987; actress. Mem. Writers Guild, Actors Equity Assn., Screen Actors Guild, AFTRA. Office: care St Martin's Press 175 5th Ave New York NY 10010

BATTLE, LUCY TROXELL (MRS. J.A. BATTLE), educator; b. Bridgeport, Ala., June 28, 1916; d. John Price and Emily Florence (Williams) Troxell; student U. Ala., Montevallo, 1934-35; B.S. Fla. So. Coll., 1951; postgrad. U. Fla., 1954, Fla. State U., 1963, Oxford (Eng.) U., 1979, 80, 81; M.A., U. South Fla., 1970; m. Jean Allen Battle, Aug. 25, 1940; 1 dau., Helen Carol. Asst. postmaster, Bridgeport, Ala., 1936-40; asst. dir. personnel office Sebring (Fla.) AFB, 1942-44; tchr. Cleveland Court Sch., Lakeland, Fla., also Forest Hill Sch., Carrollwood Sch., Tampa, Fla., 1949-64; dean of girls Greco Jr. High Sch., Tampa, 1964-68. Bd. dirs. Tampa Oral Sch. for Deaf. Recipient Outstanding Service award Fla. So. Coll. Woman's Club, 1942. Mem. NEA, Am. Childhood Edn. Internat., AAUW, Delta Kappa Gamma, Kappa Delta Pi, Phi Mu. Methodist. Club: Carrollwood Village Golf and Tennis. Author: (with J.A. Battle) The New Idea in Education, 1968. Home and Office: 11011 Carrollwood Dr Tampa FL 33618

BATTLE, MARY VROMAN, English language educator; b. Marshall, Minn., Sept. 8, 1926; d. Alois and Idalie (Vercoutere) Vroman; B.A. in English and French, Coll. of St. Teresa, 1948; M.A. in Speech and Drama, Cath. U., 1954; Ed.D. in Research Methodology and Stats., Memphis State U., 1986; m. Allen Overton Battle, June 14, 1952; 1 son, Allen Overton III. Tchr. English, Albany (Minn.) Sr. High Sch., 1948-49; jr. high sch. tchr. English, Latin and sci., Washington, 1952-56; dean of studies Southwestern High Sch. Scholars Program, Memphis, 1967-71; asst. prof. English. Memphis State U., 1956—. Founder, participant Melrose tutoring project. Mem. NEA, Conf. on Coll. Composition and Communication, Nat. Council Tchrs. of English, Tenn. Edn. Assn., Shelby-Memphis Council Tchrs. of English (co-founder). Roman Catholic. Co-author: The Psychology of Patient Care: A Humanistic Approach; contbr. numerous articles to profl. jours. Home: 2220 Washington Ave Memphis TN 38104 Office: Memphis State U Dept English Memphis TN 38152

BATTLE, STEPHANIE LYNNE, utilities executive; b. Cleve., Nov. 24, 1960; d. James and Hattie Mae (Sanford) B. BS in Bus. Adminstrn., Boston U., 1982; postgrad. in fin., Babson Coll., 1988. Network adminstr. supr. New Eng. Telephone, Worcester, Mass., 1982-83; asst. project mgr. Framingham, 1983, equipment engr., 1984; equipment installation supr. Worcester, 1985; mgr. operator services Roxbury, Mass., 1985-86; staff mgr. operator services Boston, 1986-87, mgr. fin., 1987—. Loaned exec. United Way of Cen. Mass., Worcester, 1983. Named one of Outstanding Young Women Am., 1985, 86. Mem. Assn. Mgmt. Women, Nat. Assn. Female Execs., Minority Mgmt. Assn. Home: 199 Massachusetts Ave Apt 914 Boston MA 02115-3038

BATTY, JANE GRUPPE, hospital safety professional; b. Rochester, N.Y., Dec. 29, 1933; d. Karl William and Statira (Johnson) Gruppe; B.S. in Nursing, Simmons Coll., Boston, 1957; m. Norman Coulston Batty, Jr., Aug. 8, 1959; children—Michael Lawrence, Deborah Johnson. Head nurse Faxton Hosp., Utica, N.Y., 1958-60, instr. edn. and tng. dept., 1969-71, infection control nurse, 1971-75, environ. health and safety coordinator, 1975-80, dir. environ. health and safety, 1980—; public health nurse City of Utica, 1961-62; dir. environ. health and safety Children's Hosp. and Rehab. Center; tchr., cons. area nursing homes and hosps. Cert. health care safety profl., health care safety profl. exec. Mem. Assn. Practitioners in Infection Control, Am. Soc. Hosp. Risk Mgmt., Am. Soc. Safety Engrs. (pres. Mohawk Valley chpt. 1983-85). Republican. Presbyterian. Home: 10 Sherman Circle Utica NY 13501 Office: Faxton Hosp 1676 Sunset Ave Utica NY 13502

BAUDRY, RITA LUCRETIA, real estate executive; b. Biloxi, Miss., Oct. 8, 1925; d. Michael and Marguerite (Misko) Marinovich; m. Clay Frank Baudry, Nov. 14, 1942; children—Clay Frank, Steve M. (dec.), Paul J., Cathy Lynn, Richard D. Student pvt. sch., Biloxi. Apt. owner, mgr. Baudry Apts., Chateaux Elegance Apts., Harrell Sq. Apts., Magnolia Ridge Apts., Biloxi, 1953—, SMB Enterprise, Biloxi, 1979—. Roman Catholic. Home: 2306 Miller Ave Biloxi MS 39530 Office: 2250 W Beach Blvd Biloxi MS 39530

BAUER, CAROLINE FELLER, author; m. Peter A. Bauer; 1 child, Hilary A. BA, Sarah Lawrence Coll., 1957; MLS, Columbia U., 1958; PhD, U. Oreg., 1971. Children's and reference librarian N.Y. Pub. Library, N.Y.C., 1958-62; librarian Hewitt Sch., N.Y.C., 1960-61, Eron Prep. Sch., N.Y.C., 1962-63, Colo. Rocky Mountain Sch., Carbondale, 1963-65; art editor Pacific N.W. Library Assn. Quar., 1967-72; producer, instr. Oreg. Edn. Pub. Broadcasting System, 1973-74; assoc. prof. Sch. Librarianship U. Oreg., 1966-79; cons. Ednl. Cons. Assocs., Denver, 1979-81; vis. storyteller N.Y. Pub. Library, 1962-63; producer/performer Caroline's Corner Sta. KSNO, Aspen, Colo., 1964-66, Caroline: Folktales Around the World, NET affiliate, 1965-66, Caroline's Corner, Oreg. Ednl. Pub. Broadcasting System, 1972-80. Author: Children's Literature, 1973, Storytelling, 1974, Getting It Together With Books, 1974, Caroline's Corner, 1974, What's So Funny? Humor in Children's Literature (cassette), 1977, Handbook for Storytellers, 1977, This Way To Books, 1981, My Mom Travels Alot, 1981, Too Many Books! 1984, Celebrations, 1985, Take a Poetry Break (video cassette) Creative Storytelling (video cassette), 1979, others; contbr. articles to profl. jours. Recipient Ersted award for disting. teaching U. Oreg., 1968, Christopher award Jr. Literary Guild, award of excellence Chgo. Woman in Pub., 1978, Dorothy McKengie award for disting. contbn. to children's lit. So. Calif. Council on Lit. for Young People, 1986. Mem. ALA (notable books com. 1977-79, chmn. 1980, chmn. Laura Ingalls Wilder com. 1973-75, mem. Newbery-Caldecott com. 1972-78, bd. dirs. children's div. 1987—), Pi Lambda Theta, Beta Phi Mu.

BAUER, DEBRA ROSENTHAL, trust company executive; b. Akron, Ohio, Feb. 27, 1952; d. Malcolm G. Rosenthal and Roseanne Rubin Bronstein; m. Daniel Bauer, Dec. 17, 1972; children: Brian David, Bradley Duncan. B in Music Edn., Ohio State U., 1972; cert. in acctg., U. Pitts., 1975. CPA, Hawaii. Asst. auditor Touche Ross and Co., Honolulu, 1975-78; suprvising auditor Peat, Marwick, Mitchell and Co., Honolulu, 1978-81; trust officer Am. Trust Co., Honolulu, 1981-83; v.p., corp. sec. Am. Fin. Services, Inc., Honolulu, 1983—; v.p. and corp. sec. parent co. Am. Trust Co. Pres. Symphony Guild Honolulu, 1982-83; dir. Jewish Community Preschool, 1985-87; treas. Hawaii Children's Museum, 1985—; active Jr. League Honolulu (dir. 1983-84). Mem. Am. Inst. CPA's, Hawaii Soc. CPA's, Am. Soc. Women Accts. (dir. 1979-80), Hawaii Soc. Corp. Planners (dir. 1984-88), Pi Kappa Lambda. Jewish. Club: Plaza (Honolulu). Office: Am Trust Co 841 Bishop St 12th Floor Honolulu HI 96813

BAUER, ELIZABETH HALE WORMAN, legal services agency executive; b. Mpls., Dec. 28, 1937; d. James R. and Virginia H. (Murty) Worman; B.A., Mt. Holyoke Coll., 1959; M.A., Ohio State U., 1975; postgrad. U. Minn., 1959, Wayne State U., 1978, Mich. State U., 1978; m. George Bittner Bauer, Sept. 12, 1959; children—Anna Stuart, Robert Bittner, Virginia Hale, Edward Russell. Tchr. St. Peter's Child Devel. Center, Sewickley, Pa., 1971-72; tchr. cons. spl. edn., Pontiac, Mich., 1975-78; dir. tng. Plymouth Center for Human Devel., Northville, Mich., 1978-80; adminstr. community placement Mich. Dept. Mental Health, Met. Region, 1980-81; exec. dir. Mich. Protection and Advocacy Service , Inc., Lansing, 1981—; cons. devel. disabilities tech. assistance system U. N.C., 1974-75; mem. adv. bd. Georgetown U. Child Devel. Center, 1978—. Founder, Montessori in Arlington, Upper Arlington, Ohio, 1973; bd. dirs. Franklin County (Ohio) Assn. Retarded Citizens, 1973-75, Ohio Assn. Retarded Citizens, 1975; bd. dirs. Southfield Youth Symphony Orch., pres., 1978-79; bd. dirs. Epilepsy Center Mich., Detroit, 1975-80, pres., 1978-80; bd. dirs. Mich. Acad. Dentistry for Handicapped, 1983-86; mem. adv. bd. Mich. Soc. for Autistic Citizens, 1981—, Wayne State Univ. Developmental Disabilities Inst., Detroit, 1984—; trustee St. Mark's Day Sch., Jackson Heights, N.Y., 1962-67; trustee Am. Field Service Internat./Intercultural Programs, Inc., 1971-73, bd. dirs., 1973-84, trustee, 1986—; bd. dirs. Kenny Rehab, Southfield, Mich., 1983-87, 1st v.p., 1986. Named Outstanding Tchr. Sch. Dist. City of Pontiac, 1978. Mem. Council for Exceptional Children, Epilepsy Found. Am., Assn. Persons with Severe Handicaps, Am. Assn. on Mental Deficiency, Nat. Assn. Protection and Advocacy Systems (bd. dirs. 1981-83, sec. bd. dirs. 1985-87, dir Kenny Rehab. 1984-87, 1st v.p. 1986), Nat. Assn. for Retarded Citizens, Mich. Assn. for Retarded Citizens, Nat. Assn. Protection and Adv. Systems (bd. dirs. 1981-83, 85-87, sec. 1985-87), Mt. Holyoke Coll. Alumnae Assn. Episcopalian. Contbr. articles to profl. publs. Home: 1355 Lake Park Birmingham MI 48009 Office: Mich Protection and Advocacy 109 W Michigan Ave Lansing MI 48933

BAUER, ELIZABETH KELLEY (MRS. FREDERICK WILLIAM BAUER), consulting energy economist; b. Berkeley, Calif., Aug. 7, 1920; d. Leslie Constant and Elizabeth Jeanette (Worley) Kelley; A.B., U. Calif. at Berkeley, 1941, M.A., 1943; Ph.D. (fellow), Columbia U., 1947; m. Frederick William Bauer, July 5, 1944; children—Elizabeth Katherine Bauer Berg, Frederick Nicholas. Instr. U.S. history and studies Barnard Coll., N.Y.C., 1944-45; lectr. history U. Calif. at Berkeley, 1949-50, 56-57; research asst. Giannini Found., 1946-49, asst. research agrl. economist, 1957-60; exec. sec. Internat. Conf. on Agrl. and Coop. Credit, U. Calif. at Berkeley, 1952-53, exec. sec. South Asia Project, 1955-56; registrar Holy Names Coll., Oakland, Calif., 1971-72; research asso. Brookings Instn. and Nat. Acad. Public Adminstrn., Washington, 1973; fgn. affairs officer Internat. Energy Affairs, Fed. Energy Adminstrn. Washington, 1974-77; fgn. affairs officer Office of Current Reporting, Internat. Affairs, Dept. Energy, Washington, 1977-81; dir. policy analysis and evaluation Nat. Coal Assn., Washington, 1981-83. Mem. Calif. Com. to Revise the Tchrs. Credential, 1961; trustee Grad. Theol. Union, Berkeley, 1972-74; bd. dirs. St. Paul's Towers and Episcopal Homes Found, Oakland, 1971-72. Recipient Superior Achievement award Dept. Energy, 1980; U. Calif. Alumni citation, 1983. Mem. AAUW (Calif. chmn. for higher edn. 1960-62), Internat. Assn. Energy Economists, Prytanean Honor Soc., AAAS, P.E.O., Mortar Bd., Phi Beta Kappa, Pi Lambda Theta, Sigma Kappa Alpha, Phi Alpha Theta, Pi Sigma Alpha. Democrat. Episcopalian. Author: Commentaries on the Constitution, 1790-1860, 1952; (with Murray R. Benedict) Farm Surpluses: U.S Burden or World Asset?, 1960; (with Florence Noyce Wertz) The Graduate Theological Union, 1970. Co-author, editor: The Role of Foreign Governments in the Energy Industries, 1977. Home: 708 Montclair Dr Santa Rosa CA 95409

BAUER, GRACE MARIE, interior designer, small business owner; b. Nashville, Jan. 2, 1943; married; 4 children. BA in Psychology, U. New Orleans, 1972. Cert. interior designer, La. Pres. Bauer Interior, Inc., New Orleans, 1980—; tchr. interior design Nat. Exec. Houskeepers Assn. Suprs. Edn. Plan, 1984—; guest speaker S.E. Regional Hosp. Conf., 1987. Coordinator Bus. Partnerships in Edn., New Orleans, 1987. Mem. Women Bus. Owners Assn. (bd. dirs. 1985-87), Inst. Bus. Design (bd. dirs. 1987—), Greater New Orleans Exec. Assn. Office: Bauer Interiors inc 914 Jena St New Orleans LA 70115

BAUER, JUDY MARIE, minister; b. South Bend, Ind., Aug. 24, 1947; d. Ernest Camiel and Marjorie Ann (Williams) Derho; m. Gary Dwane Bauer, Apr. 28, 1966; children—Christine Ann, Steven Dwane. Ordained to ministry, 1979. Sec. adminstrv. asst. Bethel Christian Ctr., Riverside, Calif., 1975-79; founder, pres. Kingdom Advancement Ministry, San Diego, 1979—: founder, co-pastor Bernardo Christian Ctr., San Diego, 1981—; evangelism dir. Bethel Christian Ctr., 1978-81, undershepherd minister, 1975-79, adult tchr., 1973-81; condr. leadership tng. clinics, internat. speaker, lectr. in field. Author syllabus, booklet, tng. material packets. Mem. Internat. Conv. Faith Ministries, Inc. (area bd. dirs. 1983-88).

BAUER, KAREN LEE, state mental health administrator; b. Waukegan, Ill., Oct. 16, 1945; d. Milton Herman and Helen LaVerne (Wolf) B. Student, Rock Valley Coll., Rockford, Ill., 1968, 79, U. Ill., Chgo., 1972-73. Nurse Ill. Dept. Mental Health, Rockford, 1966-67, asst. head nurse, 1967-68, incare coordinator, 1968-69, outcare coordinator, 1969-71, community devel. coordinator, 1971-74, legal liaison, 1974-79, asst. to the supt., 1979—, regional forensic coordinator, 1983—; cons. Office Econ. Opportunity, Rockford, 1971-73; mental health liaison Winnebago County Sheriff's Dept., Rockford, 1974—, Ill. Regional Circuit Cts., 1979—. Staff asst. Mayor's Task Force for the Homeless, Rockford, 1987—; chairperson Adult Homeless Subcom., 1987—; mem. Post-Charrette Campaign Com., Rockford, 1972-74. Recipient Appreciation cert. Genesis House Community Ctr., Rockford, 1972. Mem. Rockford Womens' Network. Republican. Congregationalist. Lodge: KC. Home: 1716 Hancock Rockford IL 61103 Office: H Douglas Singer Ctr 4402 N Main St Rockford IL 61105

BAUER, MARION DEEGAN, psychologist. consultant; b. New Haven, Nov. 16, 1942; d. Edward J. and Agnes (Cox) Deegan; children: Elizabeth, Brian J., Timothy. BS, So. Conn. U., 1964; MS, U. Ill., 1967, advanced cert., 1968. Lic. psychologist, Vt. Tchr. Orange, Conn., 1964-66; guidance counselor Tolono, Ill., 1967-68; psychologist Middlebury, Vt., 1971—; sch. cons. therapy with mentally retarded Spl. Edn., Addison County, Vt., 1971—; pvt. practice cons. with youth and families, 1983—. Fellow Am. Orthopsychiat. Assn.; mem. Am. Psychol. Assn., Vt. Psychol. Assn., Am. Assn. Univ. Women, Bus. and Prof. Women's Found. Office: Court Street Marketplace Middlebury VT 05753

BAUER, NANCY ELAINE, marketing executive; b. Alexandria, Va., Sept. 4, 1953; d. Donald Robert and Geraldine (Pisko) B. BA, Glassboro State Coll., 1976, postgrad., 1977-78; postgrad., Rutgers U., 1979. Tchr. Gloucester Twp. Sch. Dist., Blackwood, N.J., 1976-80; group service mgr. Harrah's Holiday Inn Resort, Atlantic City, N.J., 1980-83; tour and travel dir. Resorts Internat. Hotel and Casino, Atlantic City, 1983-84, v.p. bus. devel., 1984-85, sr. v.p., 1987—; v.p. Trump's Castle Hotel and Casino, Atlantic City, 1985-87; ednl. cons. Blackwood Ednl. Improvement Ctr., 1978-80; speaker Futures Unltd. at Camden County Coll., Blackwood, 1986-87. Author: (with others) Global Education, 1980; contbr. articles to profl. jours. Vol. learning disabled tchr., Runnemede, N.J., 1979. Grantee Fulbright Found./N.J. Dept. Edn. for "Project Kenya", 1979. Mem. Am. Mktg. Assn., Am. Mgmt. Assn., Am. Bus. Operators Assn., Promotion Mktg. Assn., Atlantic City C. of C. Home: 591 4th St Absecon NJ 08201 Office: Trump's Castle Huron and Brigantine Blvd Atlantic City NJ 08401

BAUER, SHARON ANN, lawyer; b. Cleve., Mar. 26, 1947; d. John and Gertrude (Dempsey) Bukovac; m. Robert H. Bauer, June 10, 1972. B.A., U. Dayton, 1968; M.S., Wright State U., 1970; J.D., Loyola U., Chgo., 1980. Bar: Ill. 1980. Personnel specialist HEW, Chgo., 1974-77; supervisory mgmt. specialist Social Security Adminstrn., Chgo., 1977-79; supervisory atty. Fed. Labor Relations Authority, Chgo., 1979-86, regional atty., 1986—; instr. Chgo. Kent Coll. Law Ill. Inst. Tech., 1987—. Mem. ABA, Chgo. Bar Assn. Office: Fed Labor Relations Authority 175 W Jackson St Suite A1359 Chicago IL 60604

BAUER, SUSAN CAROL, educator; b. N.Y.C., June 28, 1949; d. Ernest Benjamin and Helene Michalene (Siergiej) Bauer; B.S. in Bus. Edn., Baruch Coll., 1974; M.A. in Secondary Edn.-Bus., Adelphi U., 1976; profl. diploma in sch. adminstrn. C.W. Post Center, L.I.U., 1978; cert. Office Automation Profls., 1987. Exec. sec. Union Carbide Corp., N.Y.C., 1967-72; tchr bus. Sewanhaka High Sch., Floral Park, N.Y., 1974-76; assoc. prof. secretarial sci. and word processing SUNY, Farmingdale, 1976—; condr. word processing seminars. Contbg. author: Webster's New World Secretarial Handbook. Cert. profl. sec. Mem. Assoc. Info. Systems Profls. (pres. L.I. chpt. 1981-83), Profl. Secs. Internat. (chairperson cert. profl. sec. and cdn. com. L.I. chpt. 1980-82, pres. 1983-84, 85-86), Nat. Bus. Edn. Assn., Inst. for Certifying Secs. (edn. sect. 1986—). Office: SUNY Whitman Hall Farmingdale NY 11735

BAUGE, CYNTHIA WISE, distributing company executive; b. Ottumwa, Iowa, Sept. 7, 1943; d. Donald Carlyle and Opal Dorthea (Douglas) W.; m. Harry Grant Bauge, May 1, 1965; 1 child, Melissa Anne. Student Iowa State U., 1962-64, Area XI Community Coll., Ankeny 1974-75. Legal sec. City of Ames, Iowa, 1965-69; acctg. mgr. Vivan Equipment Co., Ames, Iowa, 1969; asst. mgr. Bavarian Motor Lodge, Des Moines, 1969-71; bookkeeper TCP of Iowa, Des Moines, 1971-72, Moffitt Bldg Material co., Des Moines, 1972-73, CS Capital/Mid Am Growth Corp., West Des Moines, 1973-75; v.p. Grant Sales Inc., Plano, Tex., 1976—. Bd. dirs. Power, Allen, Tex., 1985—, chmn. bd. dirs., 1986—; bd. dirs. Cultural Arts Council of Plano, 1985—, treas., 1986-87, v.p. classics, 1985-86; bd. dirs. North Tex. Rehabilitation Services, 1987—. Mem. Nat. Assn. Female Execs., Women's Div. C. of C. Plano (treas. 1981-82), Plano C. of C. (budget and fin. com., Athena/Bus. Woman of Yr. award 1986), Beta Sigma Phi. Republican. Lutheran. Avocations: home decorating, gaming. Office: Grant Sales Inc 1701 Capital Ave Plano TX 75074

BAUGHAN, CAROL COX, accounts professional; b. Copperhill, Tenn., May 15, 1963; d. Kenneth Floyd and Myrtle (Robinson) Cox; m. Phillip Bradley Baughan, Mar. 22, 1986. BBA, Mercer U., 1984. Retail mgr. Levy's, Savannah, Ga., 1984-85, buyer accessories, 1985; adminstrv. asst. Marriott Cor., Savannah, 1985-86; dir. adminstrn. EMC Engring. Services, Inc., Savannah, 1986-87; mgr. accounts receivable Bethea, Jordan and Griffin, Hilton Head Island, S.C., 1987—. Mem. Internat. Mgmt. Council (key mem. 1987—, chairperson 1988). Democrat. Office: Bethea Jordan and Griffin 23 B Shelter Cove Ln PO Box 5666 Hilton Head Island SC 29938

BAUGHER, TARA LOU AUXT, pomologist; b. Hagerstown, Md., Jan. 31, 1953; d. George and Eloise Gordon (Miller) Auxt; m. Phillip Dean Baugher, May 25, 1956; 1 child, Allison Rhea. BA, Western Md. Coll., 1975; MS, W.Va. U., 1979, PhD, 1981. Grad. research asst. W.Va. Univ., Morgantown, 1977-79, extension specialist, assoc. prof. horticulture, 1980—. Presenter lectures to various orgns.; contbr. numerous articles to profl. jours. Chairperson Statewide Impact Com. on Deer Damage and Control, 1984-87; mem. multi-state extension fruit schs. planning com., 1982, 84, forestry forum planning subcom., 1984, statewide direct mktg. com., 1984. Mem. W.Va. Horticultural Soc. (conv. com., program com. 1980-87), Va. Horticultural Soc., W.Va. Peach Council, Nat. Peach Council, Internat. Dwarf Fruit Tree Assn. (mem. nat. fruit tree rootstock com. 1986—), Cumberland-Shenendoah Fruit Workers' Assn., W.Va. County Agts. Assn., Am. Soc. for Horticultural Sci., Am. Pomological Soc., Gamma Sigma Delta, Epsilon Sigma Phi. Republican. Lutheran. Office: W Va Univ Experiment Farm PO Box 303 Kearneysville WV 25430

BAUGHMAN, CHRISTINE MARIE, auditor; b. Iowa City, Jan. 31, 1952; d. Ralph E. and Mary I. (Driscoll) B. BA, Simpson Coll., 1974. CPA, Va.; cert. internal auditor, Va. Auditor EPA, Chgo., 1974-76, Kansas City, Mo., 1976-79, Washington, 1979—. Mem. Assn. Govt. Accts., Va. Soc. CPA's. Roman Catholic.

BAUM, ELAINE JOAN EISELE, historical society administrator; b. Blue Island, Ill., Apr. 12, 1948; d. Herman Adam and Jennie (Miedema) Eisele; m. Kenneth LeRoy Baum Jr., May 15, 1968 (div. 1980); children: Kenneth LeRoy III, David Eisele. AS cum laude, Tidewater Community Coll., 1977; student, Old Dominion U., 1980. Police dispatcher City of Virginia Beach, Va., 1968-70; legal sec. Hofheimer, Nusbaum & McPhaul, Norfolk, Va., 1974; office mgr. N.Am. Lighting Products, Norfolk, 1974-75; credit mgr. Rish Equipment Co., Norfolk, 1978-81; regional credit mgr. Richmond, Va., 1981-83; office adminstr. ARCO-ALSCO, Richmond, Va., 1983; mgr. ops. Vinyl Wholesale Supply, Richmond, 1983-85; v.p. mfg. U.S. Hist. Soc., Richmond, 1985—. Mem. West End Civic Assn., Richmond, 1983—; chmn. pack com. Boy Scouts Am., Richmond, 1983-84; adv. com. Va. House of Dels., 1988—. Served with U.S. Army, 1966-68. Recipient Assocs. award with distinction Nat. Inst. Credit, 1981. Mem. Nat. Assn. Credit Mgmt. (bd. dirs. 1979-82, cert. achievement 1980), Nat. Utility Contractors Assn. (co-chmn. budget com. Tidewater chpt. 1980-81), Nat. Assn. Female Execs. Democrat. Home: 4300 Pine Top Ct Richmond VA 23229

BAUM, SELMA, consumer affairs specialist; b. Bklyn., Jan. 15, 1924; d. Samuel and Tillie (Bayer) Goldman; m. Milton W. Baum, Jan. 19, 1947; children: Victor C., Cynthia Baum-Baicker. Student, NYU New Sch. for Social Research. Communications mgr. Sobel & Goldman, Inc., N.Y.C., 1941-48; public relations cons., 1948-65; comparison shopper Gimbels, Valley Stream, N.Y., 1965-67, mgr. comparison shopping office N.Y. div., N.Y.C., 1967-75, dir. consumer affairs East div., 1975-84; dir. corp. customer relations Saks Fifth Ave., N.Y.C., 1984—; lectr. in field. Writer in field. Arbitrator Met. N.Y. Better Bus. Bur. Mem. Am. Mgmt. Assn. (industry panelist), N.Y. & N.J. Retail Mchts. Council (v.p.), Women in Communication (award N.Y. chpt. 1984), Nat. Retail Mchts. Assn. (consumer affairs com.), Nat. Assn. Female Execs., Fashion Group, Am. Council on Consumer Interests, Soc. Consumer Affairs Profls. in Bus. (chpt. pres. 1981-82, nat. dir. 1983-86, dir. Found. 1985—; nat. treas., fin. chmn., v.p. 1986-87, award N.Y. chpt. 1983), Greater N.Y. WINS (regional affairs com.). Home: 208-07 Estates Dr Bayside NY 11360 Office: Saks Fifth Ave 450 W 15th St New York NY 10011

BAUMANN, JANET ANNE, psychoanalyst, educator; b. Newark, Oct. 1, 1938; d. Clifford Elliott and Gladys (Webber) Lockyer; m. Richard Baumann, Dec. 20, 1962 (div. 1967); 1 child, Roberta. BS in Speech, Northwestern U., 1960; MSW, Jane Addams Grad. Sch. Social Work, 1966;

cert. in psychoanalysis and psychotherapy, Postgrad. Ctr. Mental Health, 1974. Psychotherapist Lakeview Uptown Mental Health Ctr., Chgo., 1966-70; pvt. practice psychoanalys N.Y.C., 1971—; supr. Washington Sq. Inst. for Psychotherapy and Mental Health, N.Y.C., 1979-83; supr., sr. staff mem. Ctr. for Study of Anorexia and Bulimia, N.Y.C., 1983—; cons. Nat. Council Alcoholism, N.Y.C., 1970-81, mem. faculty, supr. Postgrad. Ctr. Mental Health, N.Y.C., 1983—. Mem. Postgrad. Psychoanalytic Soc., Am. Group Psychotherapy Assn., Assn. Psychoanalytic Self Psychology, Urban League. Democrat. Roman Catholic. Office: 27 W 72d St Suite 508 New York NY 10023

BAUMANN, MARY JANE TREMBLE, lawyer; b. Teaneck, N.J., Mar. 19, 1944; d. Roland Smith and Mary Jane (Roberts) Tremble; m. Ulrich A. Baumann, Feb. 4, 1963; children: Kristin, U. Roberts, Jeffrey. BA with honors, Ramapo Coll. of N.J., 1974; M.A. (fellow), Eagleton Inst., Rutgers U., 1978, J.D., 1978; postgrad. Yale U. Legis. asst. to N.J. Assemblyman, 1974-75; chmn. Bergen County (N.J.) Mental Health Bd., 1975-77; dir. consumer affairs Bergen County, 1980; realtor asso., Franklin Lakes, N.J., 1980—; admitted to N.J. bar, 1981; dir. adminstrv. services N.H. Bettigole, Design Engrs., Paramus, N.J., 1981-82; pvt. practice law, Oradell, N.J., 1982—; asst. county counsel, Bergen County, N.J. Mem. Wyckoff Fed. Grants Com., 1976; dir. Friends of Ramapo Coll., 1977-85, Hackensack YWCA, 1983—, Ramapo Coll. Alumni, 1980—; Wyckoff Community Devel. rep., 1979; Dem. candidate N.J. State Assembly, 1979; mem. Bergen County Energy adv. bd., 1980. Recipient Am. Legion award, 1957. Mem. N.J. Realtors Assn., NOW. Episcopalian. Home: 550 Lee Ct Wyckoff NJ 07481 Office: 370 Kinderkamack Rd Oradell NJ 07649

BAUMANN, NANCY RUTH, real estate executive; b. Galveston, Tex., June 6, 1935; d. John Bernard and Lois Elizabeth (Davis) Roubion; m. Donald Gene Baumann, May 29, 1954; children: Susan Lynn Baumann Lab, Donald Gene Jr., Douglas Andrew. Grad. high sch., Galveston. Exec. sec. Am. Gen. Life Ins. Co., Houston, 1955-58; real estate sales mgr. Decker McKim, Realtors, Houston, 1973-77; co-owner, pres. Elegant Realty, Inc., Houston, 1977-79, Baumann & Assocs., Realtors, Houston, 1979—, Baumann Property Mgmt., Inc., Houston, 1980—; adj. instr. Coll. of the Mainland, Texas City, Tex., 1986—;. Founding mem. Trinity Pines Bapt. Assn., 1986. Mem. Gulf Coast Cert. Comml. Investment (chpt. sec. 1985-86), Nasa Property Exchangors (pres. 1986-87), Nat. Assn. of Realtors, Tex. Assn. of Realtors, Houston Bd. of Realtors, Pasadena Bd. of Realtors, Realtors Nat. Mktg. Inst. (Cert. Comml. Investor). Home: 15543 Torry Pines Houston TX 77062 Office: Baumann & Assocs Realtors PO Box 890027 Houston TX 77289

BAUMANN, ROXANNE LEE, industrial products international salesperson; b. St. Paul, Dec. 26, 1953; d. Harold Phillip and Irene Carroll (Rymerson) Kurkowski; m. Robert M. Baumann, Sept. 6, 1986; stepchildren: Dale Robert, David John. BS, U. Wis., Stevens Point, 1975. Linguist Koehring Co. Algerian Project, Milw., 1975-78; internat. parts adminstr. Koehring Internat. Mktg. Co., Milw., 1978-79; internat. sales analyst Waukesha (Wis.) Engine div. Dresser Industries, 1979-84; internat. sales coordinator Artos Engring. Co., New Berlin, Wis., 1984—; speaker Waukesha County Tech. Inst.-Internat. Trade Tech. Ctr., Waukesha, 1987. Mem. Southminster Presbyn., Waukesha, 1986—. Mem. Profl. Dimensions, Milw. World Trade Assn., Alpha Mu Gamma, Alpha Phi. Home: S12 W26421 Chancery Ln Waukesha WI 53188 Office: Artos Engring Co 15600 W Lincoln Ave New Berlin WI 53151

BAUMER, BEVERLY BELLE, journalist; b. Hays, Kans., Sept. 23, 1926; d. Charles Arthur and Mayme Mae (Lord) B.; B.S., William Allen White Sch. Journalism, U. Kans., 1948. Summer intern reporter Hutchinson (Kans.) News, 1946-47; continuity writer, women's program dir. Sta. KWBW, Hutchinson, 1948-49; dist. editor Salina (Kans.) Jours., 1950-57; commd. writer State of Kans. Centennial Year, 1961; contbg. author: Ford Times, Kansas City Star, Wichita (Kans.) Eagle, Ojibway Publs., Billboard, Modern Jeweler, Floor Covering Weekly, other bus. mags., 1962-69; owner and mgr. apts., Hutchinson, 1970—; broadcaster Reading Radio Room, Sta. KHCC-FM, Hutchinson, 1982—; info. officer, maj. Kans. Wing Hdqrs. CAP, 1969-72; participant People to People Citizen Ambassador program, People's Republic of China, summer 1988. Mem. Republican Presdl. Task Force. Recipient Human Interest Photo award Nat. Press Women, 1956; News Photo award AP, 1952, 2d place award Kans. Press Women Contest, 1986. Mem. Fellows Menninger Found., Suffolk County Hist. Soc., Nat. Fedn. Press Women, Kans. Press Women, Am. Soc. Profl. and Exec. Women, Am. Film Inst., Nat. Soc. Magna Charta Dames, Nat. Soc. Daus. Founders and Patriots Am., Nat. Soc. Daus. Am. Colonists, Kans. Soc. Daus. Am. Colonists (organizing regent Dr. Thomas Lord chpt., state chmn. insignia com.), Nat. Soc. Sons and Daus. Pilgrims (elder Kans. br.), D.A.R., Ben Franklin Soc. (nat. adv. bd.), Daus. Colonial Wars, Order Descs. Colonial Physicians and Chirurgiens, Colonial Dames 17th Century (chaplain, charter mem. Henry Woodhouse chpt.), Plantagenet Soc., Internat. Platform Soc., U. Kans. Alumni Assn., Nat. Geneal. Soc. Author book of poems, 1941; editor: A Simple Bedside Book for People Who Are Kinda, Sorta Interested in Genealogy, 1983. Home and Office: 204 Curtis St Hutchinson KS 67502

BAUMER, JOAN LESLIE, marketing researcher, educator; b. Cleve., Oct. 1, 1952; d. Joseph Philip and Helen Saundra (Cohen) Malinas; m. David Lee Baumer, May 23, 1976; children: Erik, Paul. BS in Social Work, Ohio State U., 1974; MBA, U. Miami, 1979. Adminstrv. asst. Am. Psychiat. Assn., Washington, 1975-76; summer intern NOAA, Washington, 1978; lectr. N.C. State U., Raleigh, 1981—; market research cons., 1983-86; pres. Market Solutions, Raleigh, 1987—. Cons. fund raising and publicity Raleigh Presch., 1983-86; fund raising co-chmn. Wiley Elem. Sch., 1985-86; chairperson collegiate relations Triangle. Mem. Am. Mktg. Assn (pres. elect Triangle chpt. 1988). Clubs: N.C. State U. Women's (sec. 1981-82), N.C. State U. Faculty. Home: 1307 College Pl Raleigh NC 27605 Office: Dept Econs and Bus NC State U Rm 311-C Hillsborough Bldg Raleigh NC 27695

BAUMGARDNER, ASTRID REHL, lawyer; b. Montclair, N.J., Mar. 16, 1952; d. W. Richard and Alicia (Stein) Rehl; m. John E. Baumgardner, Jr., Sept. 7, 1974; children—Jeffrey, Julia. B.A. magna cum laude, Mt. Holyoke Coll., 1973; J.D., Rutgers U., 1976. Bar: N.Y. 1977, U.S. Supreme Ct. 1980. Assoc. firm Weil, Gotshal & Manges, N.Y.C., 1976-79, Debevoise & Plimpton, N.Y.C., 1979-80, Edwards & Angell, N.Y.C., 1980-83; ptnr. O'Melveny & Myers, N.Y.C., 1983-85; of counsel Gide, Loyrette & Nouel, N.Y.C., 1985—. Mem. ABA, Assn. Bar City N.Y., Phi Beta Kappa. Home: 140 Riverside Dr Apt 3K New York NY 10024 Office: Gide Loyrette & Nouel 900 Third Ave New York NY 10022

BAUMGARTNER, EILEEN MARY, govt. ofcl.; b. St. Cloud, Minn.; d. Florian H. and Kathleen (Keefe) B.; B.A., Coll. St. Catherine, St. Paul, 1964; M.P.A., U. Minn., Mpls., 1970. Tchr., U.S. Peace Corps, Ethiopia, 1964-66; researcher N.Y. Med. Coll., N.Y.C., 1967-68, Minn. State Planning Agy., St. Paul, 1970-73; legis. analyst tax com. Minn. Ho. of Reps., St. Paul, 1973-78; legis. asst. to Congressman Sabo, U.S. Ho. of Reps., Washington, 1979—. Bd. dirs. Alumni Assn., Hubert H. Humphrey Inst. Public Affairs, U. Minn., 1982—. Mem. Am. Soc. Pub. Adminstrn. Democrat. Roman Catholic. Office: 436 Cannon Office Bldg Washington DC 20515

BAUMGARTNER, JULIE, banker; b. Ft. Huachuca, Ariz., Mar. 12, 1961; d. Lawrence Erickson and Judith Nell (Peebles) Youngdoff; m. William Jay Baumgartner, Dec. 28, 1985. BS in Fin. and Spanish summa cum laude, Kans. State U., 1983; Diploma with dist., Am. Bankers Assn., Norman, Okla., 1987. Comml. lending officer InterFirst Bank Dallas, N.A., Dallas, 1983-85; asst. v.p. First Savs. Bank, Manhattan, Kans., 1985—. Corp. solicitor United Way of Riley County, Manhattan, 1986, pacesetter, 1987. Mem. Credit Profls. (treas. 1986-87, mem. exec. bd. 1987—), Am. Bus. Women's Asssn., Delta Delta Delta (chmn. ways and means com. 1986-87, fin. adv. 1988—). Office: First Savs BAnk 701 Poyntz Ave Manhattan KS 66502

BAUMGARTNER, LEONA, physician; b. Chgo., Aug. 18, 1902; d. William J. and Olga (Leisy) B.; m. Nathaniel M. Elias, 1942 (dec. 1964); m. Alexander D. Langmuir, 1970. A.B., U. Kans., 1923, D.S., 1925; postgrad., Kaiser Wilhelm Inst., Munich, Fed. Republic Germany, 1928-28; Ph.D., Yale U., 1932, M.D., 1934, LL.D. (hon.), 1970; D.Sc. (hon.), Women's Coll., 1950, NYU, 1954, Russell Sage Coll., 1955, Smith Coll., 1956, Western Coll. Women, 1960, U. Mass., 1963, U. Mich., 1967, McMurray Coll., 1967, N.Y. Med. Coll., 1968, Clark Coll., 1969; L.H.D. (hon.), Keuka Coll., 1963; LL.D. (hon.), Skidmore Coll., 1959, Oberlin Coll., 1965. Diplomate Am. Bd. Pediatrics, Am. Bd. Preventive Medicine and Pub. Health. Mem. faculty Colby Community High Sch., Kans., 1923-24; mem. faculty Kans. City Jr. Coll., 1925-26, U. Mont., 1926-28; intern, then asst. resident, asst. in pediatrics N.Y. Hosp. and Cornell Med. Coll., 1934-36; lectr. nursing edn. Columbia U., 1939-42; with N.Y.C. Dept. Health, 1937-62, commdr. health, 1954-62; exec. dir. N.Y. Found., 1953-54; assoc. chief U.S. Children's Bur., Fed. Security Agy., 1949-50, cons., 1950-56; mem. faculty Med. Coll., Cornell U., 1939-66, mem. pediatrics and pub. health faculty, 1957-66; vis. lectr. maternal and child health Med. Sch. Pub. Health, Harvard U., 1948-62; vis. prof. social medicine Harvard Med. Sch., Boston, 1966-76; asst. adminstr. Office Tech. Coop. and Research, AID, Dept. State, 1962-65; exec dir. Med. Care and Edn. Found., Inc., Boston, 1968-72; adviser French Ministry Health, 1945, Indian minister health, 1955; mem. exchange mission to USSR, 1958; lectr. for Tokyo Met. Govt., 1961; mem. nat. adv. council Peace Corps., 1961-63. Contbr. med. and sci. articles to profl. jours. Bd. dirs. N.Y. Fund for Children; trustee council U. Mass., 1973—; trustee New Sch. Social Research, N.Y.C., 1966-74, adv. council, 1964—. Recipient awards, including Elizabeth Blackwell award Hobart and William Smith Colls., 1961, Samuel J. Crumbine award Kans. Pub. Health Assn., 1961, Wilbur Lucius Cross medal Grad. Sch. Assn. of Yale U., 1970, Pub. Welfare Gold medal Nat. Acad. Scis., 1977, others; univ. fellow Yale U. 1930-31; Sterling fellow Yale U., 1931-32. Mem. Harvey Soc., History Sci. Soc., Am. Assn. History Medicine, Am. Pub. Health Assn. (pres. 1958-59, Albert Lasker award 1954), Am. Acad. Pediatrics, Am. Pediatric Soc., Child Welfare League Am. (bd. dirs.), Nat. Social Welfare Assembly (v.p.), Nat. Conf. Social Work (exec. com.), Nat. Health Council (pres. 1956), Am. Acad. Arts and Scis., N.Y. Acad. Medicine, Inst. Medicine of Nat. Acad. Sci., Mortar Bd., Phi Beta Kappa, Sigma Xi, Pi Beta Phi, Phi Sigma. Club: Cosmopolitan. Home: Able's Hill Chilmark MA 02535

BAUMLEIN, MARIANNE, sales representative; b. Fostoria, Ohio, Jan. 24, 1955; d. Arthur Russel and Glenna Ruth (McClain) Wolfarth; m. David Paul Baumlein, Jan. 8, 1977 (div. Apr. 1986); children—Adam Paul, Andrew Ryan. Cosmetician Lane Drug Co., Toledo, 1973, pharmacy technician, 1973-74, store mgr., 1974-85; sales rep. Russ Berrie, Reynoldsburg, Ohio, 1986, regional sales mgr. 1986— ; pres. Findlay Downtown Mchts. Assn., Ohio, 1974-75. Retail rep. Hancock County Alcoholism Council, 1985-86, to Community Devel. Research Found., 1985-86. Recipient Happy Apple award Lane Drug Co., 1974, Faberge award, 1980. Mem. Findlay Area C. of C. (chmn. retail sales booths Community Showcase 1986), Nat. Assn. Female Execs. Roman Catholic. Avocations: photography; cross-stitch; architectural design; interior design. Home: 319 Elm St Findlay OH 45840

BAUNACH, PHYLLIS JO, demographic consultant, lawyer; b. Amityville, N.Y., July 29, 1947; d. Edward Lincoln and Josephine Caroline (Dayton) B.; B.A. (scholar), U. Rochester, 1969; Ph.D., U. Minn., 1974; J.D., George Washington U., 1986; m. July 17, 1976. Bar: Pa., 1987, D.C., 1988. Instr., U. Minn., 1974; vis. asst. prof., 1975; mem. staff Gov.'s Com. on Crime Prevention and Control, 1974-76; asso. professorial lectr. George Washington U., Washington, 1977; instr. Univ. Coll., U. Md., College Park, 1980-82, 1987—, lectr., 1981; correctional research specialist Nat. Inst. Justice, Washington, 1976-82, chief surveys and censuses, 1982-87; cons. Calif. Youth Authority, Murton Found. Criminal Justice. Treas., Evang. Lutheran Mission, 1975; dir. choir, Our Saviors Luth. Ch., 1985-87, mem. worship and music com. Nat. Inst. Justice fellow, 1978-79; AAUW Young scholar, 1982-83; recipient Outstanding Performance award Dept. Justice, 1979, 81, 84, 85. Mem. ABA, Am. Soc. Criminology (chmn. div. women and crime 1982-87, exec. bd. 1987) Am. Correctional Assn., Am. Psychology Assn., Assn. Programs on Female Offenders, Resource Network Female Offenders, Nat. Trust Historic Preservation, Smithsonian Assocs., Womens Bar Assn., Phi Beta Kappa. Author: Mothers in Prison, 1985; contbr. articles to profl. jours. Office: Swidler and Berlin 3000 K St NW Suite 300 Washington DC 20007

BAUSEK, VICTORIA LYNNE, health care consultant; b. Walnut Creek, Calif., Aug. 16, 1955; d. Norman Arthur Karvelis and Marilyn Jean (Derry) Richards; m. Gerald Hubert Bausek, June 10, 1984. Diploma nursing, Samuel Merritt Coll. of Nursing, Oakland, Calif., 1976; BA magna cum laude, Golden Gate U., 987, postgrad., 1988—. RN Calif. RN Herrick Hosp., Berkeley, Calif., 1976-77, John Muir Hosp., Walnut Creek, Calif., 1977-80; mktg. rep. Exxon Office Systems, Florham Park, N.J., 1980-81; sales rep. Parke-Davis Med. Surg., Greenwood, S.C., 1981-83; sr. sales rep. Johnson & Johnson Orthopaedic, New Brunswick, N.J., 1983-84; bus. cons. San Carlos, Calif., 1985-88; mktg. mgr. Advanced Med. Devices, Los Altos, Calif., 1988—; corp. officer Gerald Bausek A Profl. Corp., San Francisco, 1984—; pres., bd. dirs. San Francisco Med. Soc. Aux., Larkin St. Youth Ctr. Found., San Francisco. Med. health care advocate San Francisco Med. Soc. Aux. Legis. Com. Mem. Nat. Assn. Female Execs., Med. Soc. Aux., Calif. Med. Assn. Aux. (media Chmn.). Democrat. Presbyterian. Home and Office: 282 Club Dr San Carlos CA 94070

BAUTISTA-MYERS, LILIAN, writer, editor; b. San Diego; d. Jose Delos Angeles and Juanita (Perez) Bautista; B.A. in English, Calif. State U., Northridge, 1970; M.S. in Edn., SUNY, Albany, 1972; Ed.D. in Ednl. Adminstrn., Okla. State U., 1980; m. Donald Allen Myers, Oct. 28, 1966; 1 son, David Allen; children by previous marriage—Sherri Lynn, Johnny Martin. Adminstrv. officer, writer Capitol Hill Educator, Albany, 1972-73; asst. to dir., tech. editor/writer, coordinator grant and contract activities, contracts and grants mgmt. officer Okla. State U., 1973-79; co-owner/writer The Last Word, writing and graphic arts, Omaha, 1979-81; freelance writer, copywriter, editor, 1972—; coordinator grants mgmt. and devel. Met. Tech. Community Coll., Omaha, 1981-83; devel. officer Cath. Dept. Edn., Archdiocese of Omaha, 1984-85; exec. dir. Cooperating Hampton Rds. Orgns. for Minorities in Engring., Norfolk, Va., 1985—, Chrome, Inc. Democrat. Author, editor in field. Home: 733-056 Willow Lake Circle Virginia Beach VA 23452

BAUTZ, LAURA PATRICIA, astronomer; b. Washington, Sept. 3, 1940; d. Charles Kothe and Laura (Stauverman) B. B.A. in Physics, Vanderbilt U., 1961; Ph.D. in Astronomy, U. Wis., Madison, 1967. From instr. to assoc. prof. astronomy Northwestern U., Evanston, Ill., 1965-75; sr. staff assoc. NSF, Washington, 1975-79, dep. dir. physics div., 1979-81, dir. astronomy div., 1982—. Mem. Am. Astron. Soc., AAAS, Internat. Astron. Union, Phi Beta Kappa. Home: 1325 18th St NW Apt 506 Washington DC 20036 Office: 1800 G St NW Washington DC 20550

BAXENDALE-COOPER, MONICA ANNE, food consultant, educator; b. Preston, Lancashire, Eng., May 12, 1936; came to U.S., 1966; d. Joseph Leo and Elizabeth Gertrude (Dickinson) Baxendale; m. Malcolm Damien Cooper, Feb. 21, 1961 (div. Jan. 1983); children: Sean Michael, Ciaran Mark, Declan James, Brendan Steven. RN, Sharoe Green (Eng.) Hosp., 1957; diploma in neurol. nursing, Western Gen., Scotland, 1961; advanced culinary diploma, London Cordon Bleu, 1982. cert. midwife, Scotland. From student nurse to ward sister various hosps., Eng., Scotland, 1951-63; food cons., writer, stylist MBC Enterprises, Winnetka, Ill., 1979—; lectr., demonstrator; recipe developer. contbr. culinary articles to profl. jours. Mem. Assn. Cooking Profls., Am. Inst. Wine and Food, Chgo. Culinary Guild (publicity chmn. 1985), Nat. Assn. Female Execs. Roman Catholic. Home: 1017 Vine St Winnetka IL 60093

BAXLEY, JUDY G., government affairs representative; b. San Fernando, Calif., Mar. 11, 1946; d. Edmond E. and Ruth E. (Wyrick) Friand; m. Clyde P. Baxley, Feb. 12, 1972 (div. Nov. 1976); children: Patrick E., Jeffrey D. BBA, Calif. State U., Northridge, 1968; cert. in bus. adminstrn., Sawyer Bus. Sch., North Hollywood, Calif. Planner City of San Fernando (Calif.), 1970-78; analyst Roy Raskins & Assocs. Pub. Relations, Los Angeles, 1970-71; spl. services rep. So. Calif. Edison, Rosemead, Calif., 1978—; outside sales rep. Beck Travel Agy, Granada Hills, Calif., 1986-87; mem. women's roundtable So. Calif. Edison, 1983-87. Chmn. United Way campaign, Valencia, Calif., 1979-82, Miss San Fernando Contest, 1978-80; pres. womens' div. San Fernando C. of C., 1979-82; mem. Placerita Jr. High Sch. PTA, Newhall, Calif., 1986-87, Newhall Elem. Sch. PTA, 1986-87. Mem. Pacific Coast Elec. Assn., League of Calif. Cities, So. Calif. Assn. Govts., Santa Clarita Valley Indsl. Assn. Republican. Home: 24837 Quigley Canyon Rd Newhall CA 91341 Office: So Calif Edison 1190 Durfee Ave South El Monte CA 91733

BAXLEY, KATHRYN WISE, social services administrator; b. Little Mountain, S.C., Dec. 15, 1927; d. Burke Miller and Annie (Rast) Wise; m. Daniel Carlyle Baxley, July 18, 1948; children: Carol Lynn Doster, Charles Burke, Ann Baxley Carpenter, Daniel C. Jr. BA, Columbia (S.C.) Coll., 1947. Sec. to chaplain VA Med. Ctr., Columbia, 1947-48; sec. purchasing E.I. duPont Co., Camden, S.C., 1950-51; sec. Baxley Appliance Co., Kershaw, S.C., 1952-54; tchr. Kershaw County Schs., 1954-56; caseworker Dept. Social Services County of Kershaw, Camden, 1961-66, supr., 1966-72, dir., 1972—. Chmn. Camden service unit Salvation Army, 1982-84; pres. dist. S.C. Assn. Conservation Aux., 1979; bd. visitors Columbia Coll., 1988—; mem. adv. council Kershaw County Vocat. Ctr., 1980, Kershaw County Hist. Soc., 1981—. Recipient S.C. Family of Yr. award, 1987, Career Woman of Yr. award Camden Bus. and Profl. Women's Club, 1987. Mem. Am. Pub. Welfare Assn., S.C. Dirs. and Suprs. Assn. (bd. dirs. 1975), Kershaw County Mental Health Assn. (treas. 1972), Kershaw County Interagy. Council (pres. 1975-76), Columbia Coll. Alumnae Club (pres. 1984, 85). Lutheran. Clubs: Camden Dinner (pres. 1987-88), MacDowell Music (pres. 1968). Office: Kershaw County Dept Social Services 816 DeKalb St Camden SC 29020

BAXTER, BETTY, educational administrator; b. Sherman, Tex., 1937; d. Granville E. and Elizabeth (Caston) Carpenter; m. Cash Baxter; children: Stephen Barrington, Catherine Elaine. AA in Music, Christian Coll., Columbia, Mo., 1957; MusB in Voice and Piano, So. Meth. U., Dallas, 1959; MA in Early Childhood Edn., Tchrs. Coll., Columbia, 1972, MEd, 1979, EdD, 1988. Cert. sch. adminstr., N.Y. Tchr. Riverside Ch. Day Sch., N.Y.C., 1966-71; headmistress Episcopal Sch., N.Y.C., 1972-87, headmistress emeritus, 1987—; founding head Presbyn. Sch., Houston, 1988. Author: The Relationship of Early Tested Intelligence on the WPPSI to Later Tested Aptitude on the SAT. Mem. Nat. Assn. Episcopal Schs. (gov. bd., editor Network publ.), Ind. Schs. Assn. Admissions Greater N.Y. (exec. bd.), Nat. Assn. Edn. Young Children, Assn. Tchrs. Ind. Schs., Kappa Delta Pi. Republican. Presbyterian. Club: Cosmopolitan. Home: 5300 Main St Houston TX 77004

BAXTER, CARLA LOUISE CHANEY, insurance underwriter; b. Indpls., Nov. 4, 1955; d. Carlton S. and Jennie B. (Yates) Chaney; m. Andrew Louis Baxter, Sept. 20, 1980; 1 child, Andranise Louise. BA in Mktg., Ball State U., 1979. Lic. realtor, Ind.; CPCU. Zoning technician Dept. Met. Devel., Indpls., 1975; dir. mktg. Urban Tng. and Devel. Systems Inc., Indpls., 1979-80; casualty underwriter Wausau Ins. Cos., Indpls., 1980-84; sr. casualty underwriter CNA Ins. Cos., Indpls., 1984-85; nat. accounts underwriter Nationwide Ins. Cos., Columbus, Ohio, 1985-87; sr. casualty underwriter Home Ins. Co., Indpls., 1987—. Speaker various chs. and civic groups; dir. choir Trinity Ch., Indpls., 1983—. Statonian scholar, 1975-76; N.G. Gilbert scholar Ball State U., 1978. Mem. Indpls. Assn. Ins. Women, Indpls. Underwriters Assn., Ins. Inst. Am. (cert.), Urban League, Alpha Kappa Alpha (Career Day group leader 1984, scholar 1974-75, 75-76). Methodist. Avocations: skating, racquetball, singing, dancing. Office: Home Ins Co 11590 N Meridian St Carmel IN 46032

BAXTER, DOROTHA MAE (DOTTIE), insurance executive; b. Cedar Rapids, Iowa, Aug. 20, 1923; d. Fred Monore and Jennie Ethel (Bradley) Mobley; m. Donald Earl Baxter, Nov. 17, 1942 (div. Mar. 1965); children: Donald, Dennis, Douglas, Dianne Sue Baxter Langan, Dwight Wayne. BS in Bus., Ind. U., 1944; MS in Ednl. Psychology, Butler U., 1974. Meat specialist Am. Meat Commodity Broker, Indpls., 1949-65; broker Chgo. Exchange in Commodities, Indpls., 1964-68; owner gourmet shop, 1968, commodity brokerage, 1968; prof. Ohio State U., Columbus, 1974-82; assoc. prof. Marion Coll., Indpls., 1976; agt., broker Nat. Life of Vt., Indpls., 1976, 81—; broker Norton Ins., Shalimar, Fla., 1987—. Bd. dirs. Meals on Wheels, Marion County, 1969-70; monitor Ind. Humanities Ford/Carter Debates, Marion County, 1975; mem. com. Community Mental Health, Hancock County, Ind., 1972-75, Community Hosp. Mental Health, Marion County, 1972-77. Mem. Life Underwriter's Assn., Female Execs. Assn., Nat. Assn. Humanities, Butler Alumni Assn. Democrat. Roman Catholic. Home: 822 Antique Ct Apt D Indianapolis IN 46260

BAXTER, DUBY YVONNE, personnel management specialist; b. El Campo, Tex., July 21, 1953; d. Ray Eugene and Hazel Evelyn (Roades) Allenson; m. Loran Richard Baxter, April 7, 1979. Student, Alvin Jr. Coll., 1971, Tex. Tech U., 1972; cert. legal sec., Alaska Bus. Coll., 1974; student, Alaska Pacific U., 1981, Anchorage Community Coll., 1981-85, U. Santa Clara, 1982-83; BBA in Mgmt. cum laude, U. Alaska, Anchorage, 1985. Sr. office assoc., legal sec. Municipality of Anchorage, 1975-78; exec. sec. Security Nat. Bank, Anchorage, 1978-80, Alaska Renewable Resources Corp., Anchorage, 1980-82; personnel mgmt. specialist Dept. of Army, Ft. Richardson, Alaska, 1986-87, Civilian Personnel Office, Ft. Drum, N.Y., 1987—; by-laws com. mem. spl. emphasis program Fed. Women's Program, Ft. Richardson, 1986-87; instr. Prevention of Sexual Harassment, Ft. Richardson, 1986—. Contbr. Alaska Repertore Theater, Anchorage, 1982—; leader Awana Christian Youth Orgn., Anchorage, 1985-87. Mem. U. Alaska Alumni Assn., Nat. Assn. Female Execs. Mem. Brethren Ch. Club: Bernese Mountain Dog.

BAXTER, ELAINE, secretary of state; b. Chgo., Jan. 16, 1933; d. Clarence Arthur and Margaret (Clark) Bland; m. Harry Youngs Baxter, Oct. 2, 1954; children: Katherine, Harry, John. BA, U. Ill., 1954; teaching cert., Iowa Wesleyan Coll., 1970; MS, U. Iowa, 1978. History tchr. Burlington (Iowa) High Sch., 1972; mem. Burlington City Council, 1973-75; sr. liaison officer U.S. Dept. HUD, Washington, 1979-81; state rep. Iowa Ho. Reps., Des Moines, 1982-86; sec. state State of Iowa, Des Moines, 1987—; cons. Devel. Research Co., Des Moines, 1982. Sr. advisor Mondale/Ferraro campaign, 1984; del. Dem. Midterm Conv., Kansas City, Mo., 1974; chairperson Steamboat Days, Burlington, 1976; adv. bd. mem. Found. for Iowa Children and Family Services, 1987—; appointed by Pres. Jimmy Carter to 8th Cir. Ct. Appeals nominating panel. Mem. Nat. Assn. Secs. State, Women Execs. in State Govt., Women's Equity Action League (bd. dirs.), Victorian Soc. of Iowa (adv. bd.), Am. Soc. of Pub. Adminstrn. (bd. dirs. Iowa chpt.). Home: 1016 N 4th St Burlington IA 52601 Office: Sec of State Statehouse Des Moines IA 50319

BAXTER, NANCY, medical writer; b. Grand Rapids, Mich., Oct. 3, 1950; d. Robert Emerson and Mary (Knoblauch) Baxter. B.A. in Journalism, Am. U., 1972. Asst. dir. publs. Am. Speech, Lang. and Hearing Assn., Washington, D.C., 1973-77; mng. editor Biomedia, Inc., Princeton, N.J., 1977-79; editor A.M. Best Co., Oldwick, N.J., 1979-81; mng. editor Continuing Profl. Edn. Ctr., Inc., Princeton, N.J., 1981-82; med. writer/editor Biomed. Info. Corp., N.Y.C., 1982-83; pres. Baxter Med. Communications, Co., Berkeley Heights, N.J., 1983—. Mem. Am. Med. Writers Assn., Women in Communications. Home and Office: 459 Emerson Ln Berkeley Heights NJ 07922

BAXTER, PAMELA KATHRYN, cosmetic company marketing executive; b. Pawhuska, Okla., Feb. 14, 1949; d. William Desmond and Gloria Mae (Young) Lohman; m. Barry Richard Baxter, Aug. 17, 1968 (div. July 1971); 1 son, Shannon Richard. Student U. S.D.; cert. LaSalle U. Spl. rep. Charles of the Ritz, N.Y.C., 1973-77; account exec. Princess Marcella Borghese, N.Y.C., 1977-80; regional mktg. dir. Aramis, Inc., N.Y.C., 1980—. Mem. World Affairs Council, Los Angeles, 1981. Mem. Nat. Orgn. Exec. Women, Calif. Cosmetic Assn. Republican. Club: Marina City (Los Angeles).

BAXTER, PATRICIA THERESA, human factors and technology company executive, consultant; b. N.Y.C., July 17, 1950; d. Efrain and Rose Amparo (Serrano) Ronda; m. Kenneth Howard Baxter, July 13, 1974. BS in Edn., CCNY, 1972, MS in Edn., 1977; postgrad., Queens Coll., N.Y., 1980, Columbia U., 1985—. Bilingual tchr. N.Y.C. Bd. Edn., 1972-73, tchr., 1973-76, tchr., trainer Cureton program, 1976-78, dir. Cureton program, 1978-80; mgr. system support unit Chem. Bank, N.Y.C., 1980-84; mgr. office automation Clevepak Corp., Purchase, N.Y., 1984-86; pres. Baxter, Baxter and Assocs., Inc. (formerly The Write Bus.), N.Y.C. and Yorktown Heights, N.Y., 1986—. Contbr. articles to profl. jours. Recipient Bronze award

Advt. Club Westchester, N.Y., 1986. Mem. Am. Soc. Tng. Devel., Nat. Soc. Performance Instrn., Nat. Writers Union, Assn. Documentation Specialists (exec. v.p., bd. dirs. 1986—), Westchester Assn. Women Bus. Owners (editor, bd. dirs. 1985-86, pres. 1987—), Women in Mgmt. (editorial bd. 1986—), Women's Network Putnam/Westchester. Office: Baxter Baxter and Assocs 200 Park Ave Suite 303E New York NY 10166

BAXTER, PRISCILLA JO, loan officer; b. Sapulpa, Okla., July 9, 1957; d. Charles Edward and Leona Mae (Johnson) B.; m. William Carroll Powell, Dec. 4, 1977 (div. Sept. 1983). AA, Northeastern Okla. Agriculture and Mining, 1977; student, Northeastern State U., 1985—. Teller Sooner Fed. Savings & Loan, Tulsa, 1983-84, asst. loan closer, 1984-85, loan processor, 1985-86, loan rep., 1986-88; loan officer Frontier Fed. Savings & Loan, Tulsa, 1986-88, Norwest Mortgage, Tulsa, 1988—; resident agt., life, auto, health Okla. State Ins. Commn., Oklahoma City, 1986-87. Mem. Nat. Assn. Female Execs., Women's Council, Real Estate Sales Assn. Tulsa., Assn. Profl. Mortgage Women. Republican. Roman Catholic. Home: 4707 E 80th #7A Tulsa OK 74136

BAXTER, RITA JO, home economics educator; b. Duncan, Okla., Oct. 4, 1948; d. Bill and Florita (Meadows) Alexander; m. William D. Baxter, June 16, 1979. BS in Home Econs., Southeastern State U., 1971; MS in Home Econs., East Tex. State U., 1976. Vocat. tchr. home econs. Leonard, Tex., 1971-77; home econs. agt. Tex. Agrl. Extension Service of Navarro County, Corsicana, 1977—. Advisor Navarro County Health and Aging Com., 1977—, Adult Basic Edn. program Navarro Coll., 1977—. Mem. Am. Home Econs. Assn., Tex. Home Econs. Assn., Tex. Extension Home Economists (sec. 1978-79), Nat. 4-H Agts. Assn., Texan 4-H Extension Agts. Assn., Epsilon Sigma Phi. Democrat. Methodist. Office: Navarro County Extension Service PO Box 1679 Corsicana TX 75110

BAXTER-BIRNEY, MEREDITH, actress; b. Los Angeles, June 21, 1947; d. Tom and Whitney (Blake) Baxter; m. David Birney, Apr. 10, 1974; children: Ted, Eva, Kate, Peter and Mollie (twins). Student, Interlochen Arts Acad., Mich. Actress (films) including Ben, 1972, Bittersweet Love, 1976, All the President's Men, 1976, (TV movies) The Imposter, 1975, The Night That Panicked America, 1975, Target Risk, 1975, The Stranger Who Looks Like Me, The Rape of Richard Bech, 1985, Kate's Secret, The Long Journey Home, (plays) Guys and Dolls, Talley's Folley, Butterflies are Free, Varieties; star (TV series) Bridget Loves Bernie, 1971-72, Family, 1976-80, Family Ties, 1982—; other TV appearances include The Interns, Police Woman, Medical Story, City of Angels, McMillan and Wife, The Streets of San Francisco. Office: care Gores/Fields Agy 10100 Santa Monica Blvd Suite 700 Los Angeles CA 90067 *

BAYARDI, ELIZABETH AUDREY, health care administrator; b. Valley Stream, N.Y., Sept. 7, 1948; d. James Robert and Audrey (Pierce) Boerckel; m. Armand Bayardi, Oct. 30, 1971; children: Adrian, Julia. BA cum laude, Middlebury Coll., 1970; MBA, Boston U., 1982. Service advisor N.Y. Telephone Co., N.Y.C., 1971-74; mgr. patient access systems Harvard Community Health Plan, Boston, 1974-76; asst. adminstr. Harvard Community Health Plan, Cambridge, Mass., 1976-80; regional health ctr. administr. Harvard Community Health Plan, Wellesley, Mass., 1980-84; exec. v.p. Meml. Health Plan, Worcester, Mass., 1984-86; pres., chief exec. officer Health Ins. Plan of N.J., Medford, 1986—. Singer Chorus pro Musica, Boston, 1974-86, Princeton, N.J., 1986—; trustee Germaine Lawrence Sch., Arlington, Mass., 1984-86, chair devel. com., 1986. Mem. Phi Beta Kappa. Democrat. Quaker. Home: 544 Pineville Rd Upper Makefield PA 18940 Office: HIP of NJ 165 Old Marlton Pike Medford NJ 08055

BAYER, KAREN ELAINE, educator; b. Tulsa, Sept. 24, 1950; d. Kenneth Charles and Vivian (Smith) B. B.S. in Edn. and Psychology, James Madison U., 1975; M.Ed. in Edn., George Mason U., 1985. Cert. tchr. emotional disturbed, mentally retarded and learning disabled, Va. Tchr. mentally retarded Fairfax County Pub. Schs., Va., 1976-81, tchr. learning disabled, 1981—, mem. spl. edn. curriculum team for computer applications, 1985, condr. inservices for classroom mgmt. and new tchr. tng., sch. team leader, sci. fair coordinator, middle sch. sci. fair judge, sci. lead tchr. Fairfax County; mem. adv. council Fairfax County Supts., 1987; co-sponsor Young Astronauts Program, 1986-88, invited guest 2 NASA confs. Decorated U.S. Army Commendation medal; recipient commendation Fairfax County Sch Bd., 1984; named one of Outstanding Young Women Am., 1985. Mem. NEA, Va. Edn. Assn. (del. state convs.), Fairfax Edn. Assn., Council Exceptional Children, Nat. Sci. Tchrs Assn. (presenter paper conv. 1987), Va. Psychol. Assn., Kappa Delta Pi. Avocations: U.S. Army. Office: Crestwood Elementary Sch 6010 Hanover Ave Springfield VA 22150

BAYERS, PATRICIA CAROL, telecommunications company executive; b. Chgo., Sept. 20, 1954; d. Rudolph and Virginia Irene (Makselan) Tilas; m. Robert W. Mielke, Sept. 23, 1972 (div. Mar. 1982); m. Lewis Gary Bayers, May 27, 1984. AAS in Electronics, Coll. of DuPage, Glen Ellyn, Ill., 1976; BS in Mgmt., No. Ill. U., 1979, MS, 1980, EdD, 1985. Telephone operator Illinois Bell Telephone Co., Lisle, Ill., 1972-73; electronics technician AT&T No Ill Works, Lisle, 1973-77, tech. trainer, 1977-79, mfg. supr., 1979-80, buyer, 1980-82; buyer AT&T, Montgomery, Ill., 1982-84; head purchasing dept. Bell Labs., Naperville, Ill., 1984-85, AT&T Teletype Corp., Skokie, Ill., 1985-86; purchasing and transp. mgr. AT&T, Rolling Meadows, Ill., 1986—; instr. Coll. DuPage, 1979—, No. Ill. Univ., DeKalb, 1984—. Author: Vendor Quality, 1987; contbr. articles to profl. jours. Officer Civil Air Patrol, Chgo., 1971—. Recipient Lyle Maxwell award No. Ill. U. Bus. Edn. Dept., 1985. Mem. Delta Pi Epsilon, Sigma Iota Epsilon (chpt. pres. 1978-79). Office: AT&T Corp 3800 Golf Rd Rolling Meadows IL 60008

BAYES, MARJORIE ANDRESS, psychologist; b. Chgo., Dec. 1, 1934; d. Allan Wallace and Mary (Nixon) Andress; m. Andrew H. Bayes, Aug. 25, 1957 (div. 1965); m. Kenneth Purcell, Jan. 17, 1987; children: Stephen Bayes, Christopher Bayes. BA, U. Fla., 1956; MA, U. Ky., 1959; PhD, U. Miami, 1970. Faculty mem. dept. psychiatry Yale Sch. Medicine, New Haven, 1970-80; pvt. practice psychotherapy and consultation Northampton, Mass., 1980-87; freelance writer, cons. Denver, 1987—; cons. staff group relations confs. Yale U. Sch. Medicine, 1970-80. Co-editor: Women and Mental Health, 1981; contbr. articles to profl. jours. Mem. Am. Psychol. Assn., Am. Assn. Univ. Profs., Phi Beta Kappa, Sigma Xi. Democrat. Mem. Unitarian Universalist Ch. Home: 240 S Moncaco Pkwy #507 Denver CO 80224

BAYLES, JANIS RYLO GOLON, oil company executive; b. Cleve., Sept. 18, 1946; d. Francis Andrew and Josephine Elnora (Rylo) Golon; m. William Henry Bayles V, Feb. 16, 1985; children: Andrea Rylo, William Henry VI. BA, Miami U., Oxford, Ohio, 1967; MA, Miami U., 1968; postgrad., Cleve. Inst. Art, 1969, NYU, 1971-72. Producer Station WKYC-TV, Cleve., 1968-69; mgr. promotion Popular Mechanics Mag., N.Y.C., 1970-72; dir. customer service Trans World Airlines, N.Y.C., 1973-75; regional mgr. public relations Trans World Airlines, Phila., 1975-77; mgr. spl. projects corp. communications Trans World Airlines, N.Y.C., 1977-79; sr. specialist media relations Texaco Inc., White Plains, N.Y., 1980-85; regional dir. corp. communications Chevron Corp., N.Y.C., 1985—. Contbr.-photographer to various trade mags., 1975—; photographer profl. jours., 1981-85. Mem. Jr. League City N.Y., 1982-87, Jr. League Fairfield County, Conn., 1987—. Mem. Internat. Assn. Bus. Communicators, Nat. Forensic League (Ohio chpt.), Pub. Relations Soc. Am. (N.Y. chpt. coordinator promotion 1985-86), Assn. Petroleum Writers (assoc.), Young Profls. Group Foreign Policy Assn. Clubs: Nat. Press (assoc.), Sandbar (N.Y.). Office: Chevron Cos 520 Madison Ave New York NY 10022

BAYLESS, KATHRYN REED, lawyer; b. Princeton, W.Va., Feb. 24, 1950; d. Oswald Clifford and Virginia Ruth (Hartsock) Reed; m. Laurence Emory Bayless, Sept. 1972 (div. 1974); 1 child, Michael Shannon. B.S. in Chemistry, Concord Coll., 1972; B.S. in Bus. Adminstrn., W.Va. U., 1976, J.D., 1979. Bar: W.Va. 1979, U.S. Dist. Ct. (so. dist.) W.Va. 1979, U.S. Ct. Appeals (4th cir.) 1980, U.S. Dist Ct. (no. dist.) W.Va. 1982. Tchr., Mercer County Bd. Edn., Princeton, 1972-75; assoc. Garrett, Whittier & Garrett, Webster Springs, W.Va., 1979-80; sr. law clk. to judge U.S. Dist. Ct., Bluefield, W.Va., 1980-82; ptnr. Wiley & Bayless, Princeton, 1982-83, Johnston, Holroyd & Gibson, Princeton, 1984-85; ptnr. Bayless & Wills, 1985—; adj. instr. Bluefield State Coll., 1980—. Bd. dirs. Windy Mountain Learning Ctr., Bluefield, 1980—. Recipient James F. Brown prize W.Va. U. Coll. Law, 1979. Mem. ABA, Mercer County Bar, W.Va. State Bar, Am. Trial Lawyers Assn., Fourth Circuit Jud. Conf., W.Va. Law Rev. Assn. Democrat. Club: Quota (treas. 1984-85, dir. 1982-84) (Princeton). Office: Bayless & Wills 1625 N Walker St Princeton WV 24740

BAYLEY, MOLLY GILBERT, federal agency executive; b. Spokane, Wash., Nov. 19, 1944; d. Frederick Wolcott and Clare Emily (Whitehouse) G.; m. James Burt, June 29, 1968; 1 child, Christopher Whitehouse. B.A. in French, Wellesley Coll., 1967. Sr. analyst market surveillance Nat. Assn. Securities Dealers, Washington, 1972-74, supr. market surveillance, 1974-76, asst. dir. market surveillance, 1976-78, dir. market surveillance, 1978-79, v.p., 1979-84; exec. dir. Commodity Futures Trading Commn., Washington, 1984—. Pres. Jr. League of Washington, Inc., 1982-83; bd. dirs. Assn. Jr. Leagues, Inc., 1985-87; vice chmn. Rec. for the Blind Inc., Washington DC, 1983—. Mem. Exec. Women in Govt. (treas., bd. dirs.). Episcopalian. Home: 3325 Ordway St NW Washington DC 20016 Office: Commodity Futures Trading Commn 2033 K St NW Washington DC 20581

BAYLISS-ALLEN, MADELINE THERESE, marketing executive; b. N.Y.C., Oct. 11, 1954; d. Eugene R. and Madeline D. Bayliss; BA magna cum laude in Human Communications, Colgate U., 1975; MBA, NYU, 1983; m. Jeffrey Thomas Allen, June 20, 1981. Unit dir. United Way N.Y.C., 1976-77, indsl. div. dir., 1977-79; mgr. area communications, United Way Tri-State, N.Y.C., 1979; sr. cons. Urban Bus. Assistance Corp., 1979-80; v.p. corp. mktg. Mfrs. Hanover Leasing Corp., N.Y.C., 1980-85; v.p. mktg., planning and placement, corp. planner CIT Group/Equipment Financing, Livingston, N.J., 1986-88, sr. v.p. nat. accounts and syndication, 1988—. Mem. Am. Mktg. Assn., Phi Beta Kappa.

BAYLOR-REED, CAROLYN L., telephone company executive; b. Cedartown, Ga., Apr. 18, 1950; d. Lewis Cary and Dorothy Ruth (Johnson) Baylor; m. Luther Delano Reed, Feb. 27, 1986; 1 child, Michael Lewis. B.B.A. in Acctg., U. Ga., 1972, M. in Acctg., 1974; cert. real estate Atlanta Area Tech. Coll., 1981. Fiscal coordinator Athens Model Cities (Ga.), 1972-74; internal auditor Nat. Services Industries, Atlanta, 1974-76; staff analyst So. Bell Telephone Co., Atlanta, 1976-78, instr., 1978-81, staff mgr., 1981—. Mem. panel United Way funds allocation, 1983—, loaned exec., 1985, 86; sch. leader Empty Stocking Fund, Archer High Sch., 1982-83; v.p. state at large, bd. mgrs., U. Ga. Alumni Soc., Athens, 1982—; mem. So. Bell Women's Bowling League, 1979-81, Shady Ladies Softball Team, 1977-81; motivator Metro Employment Youth Motivation Day, 1978—; treas. Atlanta Urban Bus. and Profl. Women, 1979-81, pres., 1981-82. Named Young Careerist Atlanta Urban Club-Bus. and Profl. Women, 1979. Mem. Nat. Assn. Female Execs., AAUW, U. Ga.-Athens Black Alumni Assn. (pres. Atlanta 1982-83; treas. 1979-81, Outstanding Alumni Atlanta chpt. 1981), U. Ga.-Athens Alumni Assn. (young alumni council 1979-81), Delta Sigma Theta (treas. Decatur alumnae 1977-70; pres. Athens alumnae 1972-74; pres. chpt. 1971, treas. 1969-70), Zeta Psi. Office: 17F50 So Bell Ctr 675 W Peachtree St Atlanta GA 30375

BAYLY, PATRICIA ANNE, psychologist; b. Troy, N.Y., Dec. 4, 1952; d. Richard Yeilding and Martha (Coffey) Bayly; B.A. cum laude with honors in Psychology (Kellas scholar), Russell Sage Coll., 1974; M.S. in Ednl. Psychology and Statistics, SUNY, Albany, 1975, Ed.S. in Sch. Psychology, 1976, doctoral studies in ednl. psychology, 1978-81, in sch. psychology, 1986—. Psychologist, North Colonic Central Schs., Loudonville, N.Y., 1976-77, Enlarged City Sch. Dist. of Troy, 1977—; adj. instr. psychology Russell Sage Coll., Troy, 1978—. Bd. dirs. Drug Abuse and Prevention Council Troy, 1979-80, sec., 1980-83; bd. dirs., edn. chmn. Jr. League Troy, 1978-79, adv. planning chmn., 1980-81, tng. chmn., 1982-83; bd. dirs. Am. Cancer Soc., 1982-84. Fellow Parson's Child & Family Ctr.; mem. Am. Psychol. Assn., N.Y. State Psychol. Assn., Psychol. Assn. Northeastern N.Y. (sec. 1984-86), Nat. Assn. Sch. Psychologists, N.Y. Assn. Sch. Psychologists, Russell Sage Coll. Alumnae Assn. (exec. bd. 1974-78, sec. 1978-82, 1st v.p. 1982-86, mem. at large 1986—), Athenian Honor Soc., Psi Chi. Roman Catholic. Club: Russell Sage Troy Alumni (pres. 1976-83). Home: 19 Brentwood Ave Troy NY 12180 also: Glass Lake Averill Park NY 12018 Office: 1976 Burdett Ave Troy NY 12180

BAYM, NINA, university official, educator; b. Princeton, N.J., June 14, 1936; d. Leo and Frances (Levinson) Zippin; m. Gordon Baym, June 1, 1958; children—Nancy, Geoffrey; m. Jack Stillinger, May 21, 1971. B.A., Cornell U., 1957; M.A., Harvard U., 1958, Ph.D., 1963. Asst. U. Calif.-Berkeley, 1962-63; instr. U. Ill., Urbana, 1963-67, asst. prof. English, 1967-69, assoc. prof., 1969-72, prof., 1972—, dir. Sch. Humanities, 1976-87. Author: The Shape of Hawthorne's Career, 1976, Woman's Fiction: A Guide to Novels By and About Women in America, 1978, Novels, Readers and Reviewers: Responses to Fiction in Antebellum America, 1984, The Scarlet Letter: A Reading, 1986, Ed Norton Anthology of American Literature; also essays, reviews; mem. editorial bd. Am. Quar., New Eng. Quar., Legacy, A Journal of 19th Century American Women Writers, Jour. Aesthetic Edn., Am. Lit., Tulsa Studies in Women's Lit., Am. Studies. Recipient U. Ill. sr. univ. scholar award, 1985; Guggenheim fellow, 1975-76; AAUW hon. fellow, 1975-76 NEH fellow, 1982-83. Mem. Robert Frost Soc. (adv. bd.), Am. Studies Assn. (exec. council 1982-84), MLA (exec. com. 19th century Am. lit. div., chmn. 1984, adv. council Am. lit. sect., chmn. 1984). Office: U Ill 608 S Wright St Urbana IL 61801

BAYMILLER, LYNDA DOERN, social worker; b. Milw., July 6, 1943; d. Ronald Oliver and Marian Elizabeth (Doern) B. B.A., U. Wis., 1965, MSW, 1969; student U. Hawaii, 1962, Mich. State U., 1965. Peace Corps vol., Chile, 1965-67; social worker Luth. Social Services of Wis. and Upper Mich., Milw., 1969-77, contract social worker, 1978-79; dist. supr. Children's Service Soc. Wis., Kenosha, 1977-78; social work supr. Sauk County Dept. Human Services, Baraboo, Wis., 1979—. Bd. dirs. Zoo Pride, Zool. Soc. Milw. County, 1975-77, Sauk County Mental Health Assn., 1979-84; mem. Harmony chpt. Sweet Adelines, West Allis, Wis., 1970-75, pres. chpt., 1971; pres. bd. dirs. Growing Place Day Care Center, Kenosha, 1977-78; mem. Baraboo (Wis.) Centennial Com., 1982; bd. dirs. Laubach Literary Council, Baraboo, 1986-88. Mem. Nat. Assn. Social Workers, Acad. Cert. Social Workers, Wis. Social Services Assn., AAUW (br. sec. 1982-84), U. Wis. Alumni Assn. (life mem.), Am. Legion Aux., DAR, Mental Health Assn., Nat. Soc. Magna Carta Dames, Eddy Family Assn. (life mem.), Nat. Soc. Ancient and Hon. Arty. Co. of Mass., Morris Pratt Inst., Sauk County Hist. Soc., Internat. Crane Found. (patron), Daus. Colonial Wars, Zool. Soc. Milwaukee County (life), Am. Bus. Women's Assn., Friends of Baraboo Zoo, Alpha Xi Delta. Lodges: Order Eastern Star, Ladies Aux. of Fraternal Order Eagles. Author: (with Clara Amelia Hess) Now-Won, A Collection of Feeling (poetry and prose), 1973. Home: 332 4th Ave Baraboo WI 53913

BAYNE, PATRICIA HARRIS, museum official; b. Houston, July 17, 1948; d. James Gus and Luella Elizabeth (Ross) Harris; m. Harry G. Bayne, Apr. 6, 1985; 1 child, Blake Edward. BFA in Art History, So. Meth. U., 1970. Exec. tng. asst. buying offices Neiman Marcus, Dallas, 1971-74; registrar asst. Dallas Mus. Fine Arts, 1974-75, adminstrv. asst., 1975-78, exec. asst., 1978-80, bus. mgr., 1980-81, supr. accounts, 1981-83, lead computer operator acctg. dept., 1983-84, systems analyst, 1984-86; v.p. HB Enterprises, 1986—. Vol. Channel 13 Pub. Broadcasting System. Mem. Tex. Assn. Mus., Smithsonian Instn., Alpha Delta Pi. Democrat. Methodist. Home: 9511 Mossridge Dr Dallas TX 75238 Office: 1717 N Harwood St Dallas TX 75201

BAYOL, IRENE S., information services specialist; b. Franklin County, N.C., Oct. 11, 1933; d. Walter Ernest and Nonie (Parrish) Sledge; m. Charlie Morton Hamlet, Aug. 23, 1950 (div. Mar. 1956, dec. 1981); 1 child, Marcia Jean; m. Jerome Stollenwerch Bayol, Aug. 9, 1958 (div. May 1972, dec. 1980); children: Jerome Jr., Susan Carol, Keenan Jules. Student, Louisburg (N.C.) Jr. Coll., 1952-53, U. Va., 1970, Northern Va. Community Coll., Alexandria, Va., 1984, Am. U., Washington, 1986—. Computer equipment analyst USAF, Washington, 1970-73; supr. GSA, Washington, 1973-84; computer equipment specialist GSA Inst. for Info. Tech., Washington, 1984-85; policy officer GSA, Washington, 1985-87, program mgr., 1987—; real estate agt., 1973—. Episcopalian. Clubs: Profl. Womens' Club, Toastmistress Club, Travel Club, Investments.

BAZEN, DAPHNE PORTER, nurse; b. Loris, S.C., June 2, 1939; d. Burris Herbert and Naomi Grace (Stevens) Porter; m. Borie Edward Bazen, Mar. 29, 1959; children—Barry Edward, Lesli Maria. A.S. in Nursing, Florence-Darlington Tech. Coll., 1975; B.S. in Nursing, Med. U. S.C., 1984. R.N., S.C. Grad. nurse intern McLeod Meml. Hosp., Florence, S.C., 1975-76, staff nurse, 1976-78; head nurse CCU, McLeod Regional Med. Ctr., Florence, 1978—, instr. basic cardiac life support, 1978-79; mem. nurses' continuing edn. com. for S.C.; vol. S.C. Heart Assn., Columbia, 1979-84; instr. basic electrocardiography course Pee Dee chpt. Area Health Edn. Com., Florence, 1979-80. Named Employee of Yr., Active Med. Staff McLeod Regional Med. Ctr., 1984; McLeod Meml. Med. Aux. scholar Florence-Darlington Tech. Coll., 1975. Mem. Am. Assn. Critical Care Nurses (pres. Pee Dee chpt.), Am. Nurses Assn., S.C. Nurses Assn. (del. 1985), Pee Dee Nurses Assn., Sigma Theta Tau. Republican. Baptist. Lodge: Civitan. Avocations: bicycling; reading; sewing. Office: McLeod Regional Med Ctr 555 E Cheves St Florence SC 29501

BAZIGIAN, ANITA KIZIRIAN, manufacturing company executive, jewelry designer; b. Worcester, Mass.; d. Serop John and Mary (Pilibosian) Kizirian; m. Paul Bazigian, Aug. 25, 1957; children—Lesley Karen, Craig Michael. Student Worcester Art Mus., 1949-53, Sch. Nursing, Cambridge City Hosp., 1953-54; A.S., Becker Coll., 1956. Clerical positions Blackstone Valley News, Northbridge, Mass., 1953-56; med. asst. Bennett I. Fielding, M.D., Worcester, Mass., 1956-58, Agostine Del Signore, M.D., Worcester, 1958-60; freelance artist, Worcester, 1960-64; tchr. Armenian lang. Lang. Sch., Worcester, 1960-64, Worcester Pub. Schs., 1964-70; tchr. Southwest Ednl. Ctr., Walled Lake, Mich., 1970-75; designer fine jewelry Birmingham Jewelers, Mich., 1975—; pres. ANI Designs div. Birmingham Mfg. Corp., Troy, Mich., 1984-88, Burlingame, Calif., 1988—; designer copyrighted jewelry. Exhibited various jewelry trade shows, N.Y.C., San Francisco, Los Angeles, Dallas. Counselor Girl Scouts U.S.A., Farmington Conn., 1952-53. Mem. Jewelers Bd. Trade, Pacific Jewelers Trade Show, Dallas Jewelers Trade Show, Jewelers of Am. Inc., Internat. Jewelry Show. Republican. Armenian Orthodox. Club: Mr. and Mrs. (Southfield, Mich.). Avocations: piano; boating; tennis; surfing; skiing. Office: ANI Designs PO Box 1039 Millbrae CA 94030

BEACH, JOYCE CORNEALIA, educator; b. N.Y.C., Apr. 24, 1936; d. Oscar Frank and Agnes Velma (Wilde) Perry; m. Charles Collver Casson, Dec. 12, 1968 (div. 1968); children: Joseph Wesley, William Michael; m. Charles Edward Beach. BA, So. Conn. State Coll., 1968; MS, U. Bridgeport, 1972; EdD, U. Mass., 1985. Cert. tchr., vocat. sch. supt., Conn. Tchr. math., dept. chmn. Unquowa Sch., Fairfield, Conn., 1966-72, Montachusett Regional Vocat. Sch., Fitchburg, Mass., 1972-79; coordinator vocat. competency testing program, adviser continuing edn. program, program chair grad. occupational edn. Fitchburg State Coll., 1980—; pres. Ednl. Engring., Fitchburg, 1985—. Mem. sch. com. Montachusett Vocat. Sch., 1985—. Mem. Am. Vocat. Edn. Profl. Devel. Assn. (sec.-treas. 1986—, pres-elect 1987-88), Am. Vocat. Assn., NEA, Nat. Council Tchrs. Math. Democrat. Home: 11 Meadowbrook Village Gardner MA 01440 Office: Fitchburg State Coll PO Box 6446 Fitchburg MA 04120

BEACH, MARGARET GASTALDI (MRS. EDWARD WOODBRIDGE BEACH), found. exec., nurse; b. Placerville, Calif., Aug. 10, 1915; d. Giovanni Batista and Josephine (Bisagno) Gastaldi; student Sacramento City Coll., 1934; grad. Mercy Coll. Nursing, 1938; m. Edward Woodbridge Beach, Feb. 15, 1946 (dec. Aug. 1968); children—Laura G. (Mrs. Robert L. Phillips), Edward Woodbridge, Margaret J. In charge urol. dept. Mercy Hosp., Sacramento, 1938-42; tchr. urology to student nurses, 1943-45. Treas., Germana M. Wilson Meml. Scholarship Found., 1967—. Mem. Woman's Aux. AMA, Sacramento County Women Med. Soc., Am. Legion Aux., Italian Cultural Soc. Clubs: Carriage Trade, Women of the Moose, Hon. Guild St. Patrick's Day Mummurs. Home: 6255 14th Ave Sacramento CA 95820

BEACH, NANCY ANN HELEN, English language instructor; b. Kansas City, Kans., Nov. 10, 1944; d. Charles Andrew and Victoria Virginia (Handzel) Nugent; divorced; children: Cathe, Denise, Michelle. AA, East Los Angeles Coll., 1964; BS, Calif. State U., Los Angeles, 1966; postgrad., UCLA, 1966-70. Cert. English teaching credential (life). Tchr. Calif. Pub. Schs., San Gabriel Valley, 1966-77; recreation therapist State of Calif., Pomona, 1966-67; recreation supr. City of Baldwin Park (Calif.), 1967-70; restaurant owner Baldwin Park, 1977; instr. English So. Bay Coll., Baldwin Park, 1984—. Author: Reading Skills, 1971. Bd. dirs. pub. relations com. Civil Air Patrol, El Monte, Calif., 1960-64; mem. U.S.A. Dem. Party, Alhambra, Calif., 1960. Recipient Gold Seal award East Los Angeles Coll., 1964. Democrat.

BEACH, ROSE MARY RANDALL, librarian; b. Waterloo, Iowa, Dec. 11, 1921; d. Charles Warren Milton and Rose Ellen (MacDonald) Randall; m. Thomas C. Beach, Jr., May 5, 1945 (div. 1979); children—Charles Randall, Thomas Christopher, Murray MacDonald. B.A., U. Iowa, 1943; M.S., Drexel U., 1971. News and feature writer Assoc. Press Radio, N.Y.C., 1944-47; faculty Green Mountain Coll., Poultney, Vt., 1950-53, Goldey Beacom Coll., Wilmington, Del., 1956-69, library dir., 1970-87. Mem. ALA, Del. Library Assn., Eastern Bus. Tchrs. Assn., Phi Beta Kappa, Phi Beta Mu. Episcopalian. Home: 5 Deville Ct Newark DE 19711 Office: Goldey Beacom Coll 4701 Limestone Rd Wilmington DE 19808

BEAHLER, ELECTRA CATSONIS, lawyer; b. Washington, Aug. 6, 1933; d. Achilles and Anastasia (Carzis) Catsonis; B.A. with honors, Pa. State U., 1955; J.D. with honors, George Washington U., 1969; m. John Leroy Beahler, Feb. 7, 1973. Bar: D.C. 1970, U.S. Sup. Ct. 1974. Asst. editor Aero Digest, Washington, 1955-56, Fairchild Engine & Airplane Co., Washington, 1956-57; exec. asst. internat. pub. relations dept. Kaiser Industries Corp., Washington, 1957-60; sec. to pres. George Washington U., Washington, 1960-62; legis. asst. to Congressman Donald D. Clancy, Washington, 1962-67; adminstrv. asst. to Congressman John M. Ashbrook, Washington, 1968-73; minority counsel edn. House Com. Edn. and Labor, U.S. Ho. of Reps., Washington, 1981-85; free lance writer; cons. U.S. Dept. State, 1986, U.S. Agy. for Internat. Devel., U.S. Info. Agy., 1988. Recipient Schaeffer award Phi Delta Delta, 1962. Mem. ABA, Internat. Orgn. Women Pilots, Ninety-Nines, Airplane Owners and Pilots Assn., D.C. Bar, Fed. Bar Assn., Women's Bar Assn. D.C., George Washington U. Law Assn., Washington Ind. Writers, Nat. Trust Hist. Preservation.

BEAHN, CAROLE ELIZABETH, senior certified escrow officer; b. Milw., Jan. 9, 1936; d. Frank Anthony and Genevieve Ella (Grueschow) Puhl; m. Don Henri Kragenbrink, Mar. 21, 1953 (div. 1972); children: Robin Dale, Court Lee, Kevin Roy, Ward August, Jenell Marie; m. Glenn Harland Beahn, June 23, 1980. Cert. escrow officer, Nev. Sec. Knudson Real Estate, Brainerd, Minn., 1972-74; office mgr. Knudson Real Estate, Mpls., 1974-79; escrow officer Nev. Title Co., Las Vegas, Nev., 1980-83, Land Title of Nev., Las Vegas, 1986—; bd. mgr.; bd. mgr. Title Ins. of Minn., 1983-84, Nev. Title Co., 1984-86. Mem. Nev. Escrow Assn. (pres. South chpt., 1985-86, pres. 1986-87), Am. Escrow Assn. (bd. dirs. 1988—), Women's Council Realtors. Lodge: Moose (sr. regent). Home: 9457 Las Vegas Blvd S 42 Las Vegas NV 98123 Office: 2800 W Sahara Bldg 3C Las Vegas NV 89102

BEAL, GRETCHEN FRANK, information resources coordinator, researcher; b. Kansas City, Oct. 9, 1937; d. Eugene Maxwell and Wilma Alice (Sedoris) Frank; m. James Harrison Beal, June 17, 1961; children: Elizabeth Harrison, Ellen Wallace, Mary Gretchen. BA in Liberal Arts, DePauw U., 1959; MLS, U. Tenn., 1973. Info. specialist U. Tenn. Bur. Pub. Adminstrn., Knoxville, 1973-75; bibliographer U.S. Dept. Health, Edn. & Welfare, Washington, 1975-77; info. resources coordinator Knox County Met. Planning Commn., Knoxville, 1975—. Author: Knoxville Area Facts and Figures, 1985; author, editor and contbg. editor to profl. jours. Bd. dirs. East Tenn. Children's Hosp., Knoxville, 1974—; vice chmn. bd. Knox County Social Services Adv. Council, 1983—; chmn., founding mem. Greater Knoxville Research Network, 1984—; mem. Children's Hosp. Aux., 1968—, Jr. League of Knoxville, Bijou Limelighters. Mem. Am. Planning Assn., Spl. Libraries Assn., East Tenn. Library Assn., Council Planning Librarians (bd. dirs. 1981-84, nat. pres. 1982-83, editorial bd. 1985—). Office: Met Plannig Commn 400 Main St Cit/County Bldg Knoxville TN 37902

BEALE, BETTY (MRS. GEORGE K. GRAEBER), columnist; b. Washington; d. William Lewis and Edna (Sims) B.; m. George Kenneth Graeber,

Feb. 15, 1969. A.B., Smith Coll. Columnist, Washington Post, 1937-40; reporter and columnist Washington Evening Star, 1945-81; weekly columnist North Am. Syndicate (formerly Field Newspaper Syndicate), 1953—; lectr. in field. Recipient Freedom Found. award, 1969, named Woman of Distinction, 1987. Address: 2926 Garfield St NW Washington DC 20008

BEALE, GEORGIA ROBISON, historian; b. Chgo., Mar. 14, 1905; d. Henry Barton and Dora Belle (Sledd) Robison; m. Howard Kennedy Beale, Jan. 2, 1942; children: Howard Kennedy, Henry Barton Robison, Thomas Wight. AB, U. Chgo., 1926, AM, 1928; PhD, Columbia U., 1938; student Sorbonne and Coll. de France, 1930-34. Reader in history U. Chgo., 1927-29; lectr. Barnard Coll., 1937-38; instr. Bklyn. Coll., 1937-39; asst. prof. Hollins (Va.) Coll., 1939-41, Wellesley Coll., 1941-42, Castleton (Vt.) State Coll., 1968-70; vis. asso. prof. U. Ky., Lexington, 1970-72; professorial lectr. George Washington U., 1983-84. Author: Revelliere-lépeaux, Citizen Director, 1938, 72, Academies to Institut, 1973, Bosc and the Exequatur, 1978; contbg. author Historical Dictionary of the French Revolution, 1985; also articles. Mem. Madison (Wis.) Civic Music Assn. and Madison Symphony Orch. League, 1958—; hon. trustee Culver-Stockton Coll., 1974—. Univ. fellow Columbia U., 1929-30. Mem. AAUW (European fellow 1930-31), Am., So. hist. assns., Soc. French Hist. Studies, Western Soc. French History (hon. mem. exec. council), Am., Brit. socs. 18th century studies, Phi Beta Kappa, Pi Lambda Theta, Phi Alpha Theta, Pi Kappa Delta. Clubs: Reid Hall (Paris); Brit. Univ. Women's (London). Address: The Ridge Orford NH 03777 also: 2816 Columbia Rd Madison WI 53705 also: 110 D St SE Washington DC 20003

BEALE, HELEN RUBY, insurance company brokerage administrator; b. Michigamme, Mich., Mar. 29, 1922; d. Edwin Martin and Katherine Mae (Rahilly) Stensrud; m. Roland Earl Beale, June 19, 1944 (dec.); children—John Robert, Ann Marie Beale Trachtenberg, James Edward. Student Mich. State U., St. Catherine's Coll., U. Wis., Platteville. Cert. adminstrv. mgr. Owner Beale Funeral Home, Michigamme, 1943-60; asst. to pres. Ind. Mgmt. Cons., Madison, Wis., 1966-73; sec. Sch. Dist. Office, Oregon, Wis., 1974-76; adminstrv. asst. Modern Kitchen Supply, Madison, 1976-81; agy. adminstrv. asst. Bankers Life, Madison, 1981—. State advisor U.S. Congl. adv. bd. Am. Security Council Found., Washington, 1983; mem. Sen. Robert Dole Exploratory Com. Mem. Adminstrv. Mgmt. Soc. (pres. 1981-82), Am. Mgmt. Assn., Nat. Tax Limitations Com., Madison Deanery (v.p. 1982-84, regents 1981-85). Roman Catholic. Club: Toastmasters.

BEALL, INGRID LILLEHEI, lawyer; b. Cedar Falls, Iowa, June 18, 1926; d. Ingebrigt Larsen and Olive (Allison) Lillehei; m. George Brooke Beall, Dec. 21, 1951 (div. 1971). A.B., U. Chgo., 1945, M.A., 1948, J.D., 1956. Bar: Ill. 1956. Assoc. firm McDermott, Will & Emery, Chgo., 1956-58, Baker & McKenzie, Chgo., 1958-61; ptnr. Baker & McKenzie, Chgo., Brussels and Paris, 1961—. Mem. ABA, Ill. Bar Assn., Chgo. Bar Assn., Internat. Fiscal Assn. Home: 175 Delaware St Chicago IL 60611 Office: Baker & McKenzie Suite 2800 Prudential Plaza Chicago IL 60601

BEALL, JOANNA MAY, painter; b. Chgo., Aug. 17, 1935; d. Lester Thomas and Dorothy Welles (Miller) B.; student Yale U. Sch. Fine Arts, 1953-57, Art Inst. Chgo., 1957; m. H.C. Westermann, Mar. 31, 1959. One-man shows include: Great Bldg. Crack-Up Gallery, N.Y.C., 1973, James Corcoran Gallery, Los Angeles, 1974, Gallery Rebecca Cooper, Washington, 1975; group shows: Allan Frumkin, Chgo., 1960, 61, Whitney Mus., N.Y.C., 1973, Art Inst. Chgo., 1976, Univ. Galleries, Los Angeles, 1979, Xavier Fourcade, N.Y.C., 1980, 85; vis. artist U. Colo., Boulder, 1979, 84. Mem. Artists Equity Assn., Visual Artists and Galleries Assn. Article The World of Joanna Beall (Melinda Wortz) appeared in Art Week mag., 1974. Home: Box 5028 Brookfield Center CT 06804

BEALL, LAURA SUE, paralegal; b. Bryan, Tex., Oct. 28, 1956; d. Don Martin and Bonnah Belle (Hypes) Brockman; m. Joe Chilton Beall, May 19, 1979; 1 child, Rebecca Tyler. BA in Polit. Sci., Tex. A&M U., 1979, BS in Econs., 1980. Adminstrv. asst. South Cen. Modern Language Assn., Coll. Sta., Tex., 1979-80; account coordinator Western Pacific Servicing Group, Marina Del Ray, Calif., 1980-82; sr. real estate paralegal Ferrari, Alvarez, Olsen & Ottoboni, San Jose, 1982—. Mem. Nat. Notary Assn., Paralegal Assn. Santa Clara County, South Bay Assn. of Women in Comml. Real Estate, San Jose Bus. and Profl. Women (bd. dirs.), Alpha Phi. Republican. Mem. Ch. of Christ. Home: 289 Ellmar Oaks Loop San Jose CA 95136 Office: Ferrari Alvarez Olsen & Ottoboni 333 W Santa Clara St #700 San Jose CA 95115

BEAMAN, JANICE ELLEN, nurse; b. Auburn, N.Y., Sept. 23, 1961; d. Jack Edward and Frances Mary (Kenney) Hole; m. Glenn Peter Beaman, June 6, 1981; 1 child, Nathan James. A.S., Cayuga County Community Coll., 1981. R.N., N.Y. Med.-surg. staff nurse Community Gen. Hosp., Syracuse, N.Y., 1981-84, labor and delivery staff nurse, 1984—. Roman Catholic. Avocations: softball; racquetball; tennis; sewing. Home: 4936 Limehill Dr Syracuse NY 13215-1325 Office: Community Gen Hosp Broad Rd Syracuse NY 13215

BEAN, BECKY SUE, television executive; b. Glenrock, N.J., Apr. 25, 1963; d. James Reiff and Janice Lee (Walton) B. A in Applied Sci., Onondaga Community Coll., 1983; BS, SUNY Coll., Fredonia, 1985. Assoc. producer TV Homefinders Guide, Skaneateles, N.Y., 1986; producer TV Homefinders Prodns., Skaneateles, N.Y., 1986-87; exec. producer TV Homefinders Internat., Inc., Skaneateles, N.Y., 1987—; instr. golf Skaneateles Country Club, 1985. Producer, dir. documentary Rape: Before, During and After, 1985. Mem. Nat. Assn. for Female Execs., Women in Communications, Syracuse Press Club. Club: Syracuse Ad (N.Y.). Home: 38 E Genese St Skaneateles NY 13152 Office: TV Homefinders Internat Inc PO Box 689 Skaneateles NY 13152

BEAN, JOAN NONA, merchant, consultant; b. Chgo., Aug. 9, 1929; d. Joseph John and Otylia Jeanette (Lokanski) Nowicki; m. Alfred E. Brock, Feb., 1950 (div. 1953); m. Harry Raymond Bean, July 22, 1954 (dec. Mar. 1973); children: Harry R. Jr., Elise Josan, James Nathaniel. Student, N.W. Bus. Coll., 1947, Christine Valmy Sch., 1971. Model Patricia Vance Agy., Chgo., 1944-48, Conover Agy., N.Y.C., 1949-50; model, officer mgr. Daisy's Originals, Miami, Fla., 1950-54; owner Judy Bean, Inc., St. Louis, 1966—; sec. Fashion Group St. Louis, 1978—. Contbr. Affairs mag., 1981—. Active Mo. Botanical Gardens, St. Louis, Friends of St. Louis Art Mus., St. Louis Zoo Friends. Home: 4466 W Pine #18C Saint Louis MO 63108

BEAN, NANCY ANN MORGAN, food service broker; b. Williamstown, Ky., Feb. 9, 1936; d. Dora Bell Morgan and Helen (Dunlap) Strother Morgan; m. Philip Lee Crume, Oct. 26, 1960 (div. 1974); children—Ann Morgan Crume Redmon, Lynn Ellis Bean; m. James Ellis Bean, July 26, 1980. B.S., Eastern Ky. U., 1959; M.Pub.Affairs, Ky. State U., 1976. Nutritionist, Ky. Health Dept., Georgetown, 1966-68; dietary cons. Central Ky. Nursing Home, Lexington, 1968-71; dir. food service Ky. Bur. Corrections, Frankfort, 1971-76; sales rep., account exec. A.J. Seibert, Louisville, also Lexington, Ky., 1976-81; owner, pres. Profl. Food Service, Louisville, 1981—. Mem. Louisville Dietetic Assn., Ky. Dietetic Assn., Am. Dietetic Assn., Ky. Restaurant Assn., Nat. Food Brokers Assn., Am. Sch. Food Service Assn. Democrat. Methodist. Lodge: Order Eastern Star. Avocations: gardening, reading. Home: Route 2 Box 266 Cox's Creek KY 40013 Office: Profl Food Service 1006 Phillips Ln Louisville KY 40213

BEARD, ANN VANDERPOORTEN, home economics educator; b. Little Rock, Nov. 25, 1938; d. Gerald Edison and Lucile May (Jacobsen) Vanderpoorten; m. Ronald Lee Beard, July 21, 1984. BS, U. Ark., 1963, BS in Edn. with high honors, 1970; MS, Tex. Tech. U., 1973; PhD, U. Tenn., 1981. Cert. home economist. Research assoc. clin. physiology Health Scis. Ctr. U. Tenn., Memphis, 1963-65; grad. asst. Knoxville, 1978-80; dir. adult and neighborhood programs YWCA, Tulsa, 1965-67; grad. asst. Tex. Tech U., Lubbock, 1972-73; specialist extension clothing Tex. Agrl. Extension Service, College Station, 1973-79, specialist in clothing and textiles, 1981—, chmn. so. region, 1982-84; cons. Learning Seed Co., 1984, Tex. Arts and Crafts Edni. Found., Kerrville, Tex., 1986; chmn. Nat. Extension Workshop, Raleigh, N.C., 1986. Editor Interweave, 1982-84. Mem. com. Bryan (Tex.) Forward, 1985-86. Jewell Taylor scholar, 1979-80. Mem. ASTM (D-13 on textiles com.), Am. Home Econs. Assn., Assn. Coll. Profs. Textiles and Clothing, Tex. Home Econs. Assn., Brazos Valley Home Econs. Assn. (v.p. 1986-87, pres. 1987-88), Epsilon Sigma Phi, Kappa Delta Phi, Omicron Nu, Phi Upsilon Omicron. Baptist. Office: Tex A & M Univ 213 Special Services Bldg College Station TX 77843-2141

BEARD, DORIS MARIE, home economics educator; b. Palestine, Tex., Mar. 20, 1936; d. Henry George and Ola Monteal (Goodin) B. BS, U. Tex., 1958; MS, U. Tenn., 1961; PhD, Ohio State U., 1975. Tchr. Santa Anna (Tex.) High Sch., 1958-60; prof. home econs. Calif. State U., Sacramento, 1961—. Mem. Am. Home Econs. Assn. (chair Family Econs./Home Mgmt. sect. 1987-89), Internat. Fedn. Home Econs., Am. Council Consumer Interests, Coll. Educators Home Equipment, Elec. Women's Round Table, Omicron Nu, Phi Upsilon Omicron. Democrat. Mem. Ch. of Christ. Office: Calif State U Sacramento 6000 J St Sacramento CA 95819

BEARD, DOROTHY REGINA, writer; b. N.Y.C., Jan. 12, 1924; d. Thomas Joseph and Jane Marie (Kearney) McCarthy; m. Bruce Montgomery Beard, Jr., Jan. 22, 1955; children—Jane, Anne, Ellen, Bruce. Fashion publicist Lord & Taylor, N.Y.C., 1942-56; free lance writer, 1956-74, 86—; editor West Windsor-Plainsboro Chronicle, Princeton Junction, N.J., 1974-86.

BEARD, JANET MARIE, health care administrator; b. Olean, N.Y., Feb. 18, 1930; d. Paul Claude and Virginia Maria (Mahaney) B. R.N., St. Catherine's Hosp., 1951; B.S. in Clin. Nursing, St. John's U., 1959, M.S. in Nursing Adminstrn., 1961; M.S. in Adminstrv. Medicine, Columbia U., 1968. Adminstrv. supr. Mary Immaculate Hosp., Jamaica, N.Y., 1957-66; asst. adminstr. Cath. Med. Ctr. Bklyn. and Queens, Jamaica, 1968-70; asst. dir. Yale-New Haven Med. Ctr., 1971-72; asst. dir. St. Barnabas Hosp., Bronx, N.Y., 1972-78, v.p., 1978-83; chief exec. officer Bethel Homes, Ossining, N.Y., 1983—. Contbr. articles to profl. jours. Active Bronx Community Bd., 1977-83; mem. indsl. com. Ossining C. of C., 1983—; active Fedn. Protestant Welfare Agys., N.Y.C., 1978—; planning com. Div. on Aging, N.Y.C., 1978—; adv. com. Aging in Am., Bronx, 1978-87; treas. Ft. Schuyler House, Bronx, 1977-83; pres.-elect Columbia U. Sch. Pub. Health, 1987-88. Fellow Am. Coll. Health Care Execs.; mem. Am. Coll. Health Care Adminstrs., Columbia U. Alumni Assn. (sec. 1976-78, treas. 1978-80). Club: Princeton. Office: The Bethel Homes 19 Narragansett Ave Ossining NY 10562

BEARD, PAULA HELENE, financial planning company official, accountant; b. El Paso, Tex., Jan. 16, 1952; d. Paul and Helen (Brainard) B. BBA in Bus. Accountancy and Quantitative Mgmt., U. Houston, 1975. CPA, Tex., Oreg.; lic. ins. dealer, Calif. Acct. Peat, Marwick, Main & Co., Houston, 1975-80, Portland, Oreg., 1980-81; fin. cons., advisor Beard & Co., San Francisco, 1981—. Mem. Am. Inst. CPA's, Internat. Bd. for Fin. Planners, Bay Area Career Women. Republican. Episcopalian. Home and Office: 28 Marinero Circle Apt 19 Tuburon CA 94920

BEARD, RUTH OLIVIA, retail executive; b. Gettysburg, Pa., Aug. 18, 1942; d. Samuel Clifford and Ruthetta Viola (Utz) Pittinger; m. Charley E. Hager, June 2, 1980 (div. Feb. 1987); children: Laura Jeanne Beard and Timothy Aaron Beard. BS, Towson State U., 1979, MEd, 1983. Tchr. Carroll County Pub. Schs., Westminster, Md., 1961-67, Carroll Christian Sch., Westminster, 1974-77, Odenton (Md.) Christian Sch., 1979-80; gen. mgr. East Wind Imports, Annapolis, Md., 1983-86; owner Dynasty East, Moorestown, N.J., 1987. Mem. Nat. Assn. Female Execs. Office: Olivia's Dynasty East PO Box 575 Moorestown NJ 08057

BEARD, VIRGINIA HARRISON, psychologist; b. St. Louis, Sept. 9, 1941; d. Monroe Colemon and Lula Lucille (Spicer) Harrison; B.A.Ed., Harris Tchrs. Coll., 1964; M.S., So. Ill. U., 1968; Ph.D., St. Louis U., 1976; m. Otis Charles Beard, Aug. 21, 1965; children—Bostic Charles, Bonji Lucille. Counselor, jr. high sch., University City, Mo., 1969-71; psychologist King Fanon Community Mental Health Center, 1973-75; community staff coordinator Med. Sch. St. Louis U., 1976-78, also instr.; exec. dir. Center for Family Mental Health, St. Louis, 1978-80; dir. psychol. services Met. Comprehensive Mental Health Center, 1980-86; dir. student services Clayton (Mo.) Sch. Dist., 1986—; adj. faculty Met. Coll. of St. Louis U. Chmn., Gov.'s Adv. Council on Aging, 1976-78; mem. Regional Adv. Council for Psychiat. Services, 1978-82; 1st v.p. Annie Malone Children's Home, 1975-85; bd. dirs. Conf. on Edn. Ford Found. fellow, 1971-72; Inst. Applied Gerontology fellow, 1973-75; sec. Mid City unit Am. Cancer Soc. Mem. Am. Psychol. Assn., Mo. Psychol. Assn., Nat. Council Negro Women, Coalition 100 Black Women, Nat. Black Child Devel. Assn., Am. Assn. Black Psychologists, Alpha Kappa Alpha. Baptist. Home: 890 Berick Dr Saint Louis MO 63132 Office: 7530 Maryland Clayton MO 63105

BEARDSLEY, BARBARA HOFFMAN, conservator; b. N.Y.C., Mar. 30, 1945; d. Kenneth Landers and Ruth Walker (Brooks) Hoffman; m. Leland Noble Beardsley, June 12, 1971 (div.); children: Laura Anne, Christine Ellen, Elisabeth Marie. BA in Art History and Aesthetic Philosophy, Elmira Coll.; postgrad., U. N.Mex.; M in Conservation of Hist. and Artistic Works, SUNY, Oneonta; postgrad., N.H. Coll. Conservator Intermus. Conservation Assn. Lab., Oberlin, Ohio, 1973-75; founder Art Conservation Lab., Inc.; vis. lectr. U. Del., Winterthur, 1978, 80, 83, New Eng. Conservation Assn., 1980, Cooperstown Grad. Program Hist. and Artistic Works, 1981; lectr. U. N.H., 1983-84, U. Del., Winterthur, 1983, 85, Phillips Exeter Acad., 1984-85, Wellesley Coll., 1987; lectr. conservation Am. Assn. State and Local History, Augusta, Mane, 1973, Am. Assn. Mus., New Eng., 1976, Amherst (N.H.) Hist. Soc.,1979, Raymond (N.H.) Hist. Soc., 1979, 83, art history Wellesley Coll., U. N.H., Plymouth, N.H., 1982; visiting instr. Balsa wood technique for panel paintings Cooperstown Grad. Program of Hist. and Artistic Works, 1975, 76, 78, 79; visiting lectr. Collector's Club, Gallery on the Green, Lexington, Mass., 1982; grant reviewer Nat. Sci Found., 1979-82, 85—, Inter Mus. Services, 1984-87, Mass. Council on the Arts, 1985. Contbr. articles to profl. jours. Bd. dirs. Rockingham Child and Family Services, 1983—, treas. 1984—, chmn. fin. com. 1985—; trustee Dudley Tucker Library, Raymond, 1984—; bd. dirs. Festival of the Arts, Waterville Valley, N.H., 1985—, mem. exec com. 1987—, mem. devel. com. 1987—. Recipient Leadership award Internat. Directory of Disting. Leadership, 1987; named one of Outstanding Young Women of Am., 1977, 80. Fellow Nat. Inst. for the Conservation of Hist. and Artistic Works, Am. Inst. for the Conservation of Hist. and Artistic Works (dir. bulletin subscriptions 1973-75, ethic com. 1977-85, chmn. bylaws com. 1979-80, treas. 1980-81, ins. com. 1981-83, rep. private conservator to bd. of nat. inst. 1982-85, chmn. nat. inst. com. 1982, bd. liason 1982-85, long range planning com. 1983—, chmn. ins. com. 1983-84); mem. Am. Inst. for Conservation (dir. 1976-79), N.H. Hist. Soc. (mus. com. 1979-86), Internat. Council of Mus., Am. Assn. Mus., N.H. Hist. Soc., Nat. Inst. for the Conservation of Hist. and Artistic Works (bylaws com. 1982, chmn. nominating com. 1982). Home and Office: Art Conservation Lab Dudley Homestead Raymond NH 03077

BEARDSLEY, DIANA JEAN, publishing executive; b. Oak Park, Ill., July 22, 1937; d. Colman George and Jean Mytle (Faulkner) Sanford; widowed; children: Lisa Jean, Brooks Frederick. Student, Mich. State U., 1955-56. Pub. Yachting In Chgo., 1970-77; dist. mgr. Young/Conway Pubs., N.Y.C., 1978—. Mem. Nat. Assn. Female Execs., Kansas City Direct Mktg., Chgo. Foodservice Mktg., Women's Advt. Club of Chgo. Episcopalian. Home: 9804 Circle Pkwy Palos Park IL 60464

BEARE, MURIEL ANITA NIKKI, public relations executive, author; b. Detroit, Mar. 7, 1928; d. Elbert Stanley and Dorothy Margaret (Welch) Brink; m. Richard Austin Beare, June 15, 1946; 1 child, Sandra Lee. AA, Miami Dade Community Coll., 1974; BA, Skidmore Coll., 1979. Writer, Key West Citizen (Fla.), 1959, Miami News (Fla.), 1967; field dir. Fla. Project HOPE, 1967-68, southeastern area dir., 1968-69; asst. v.p. pub. relations I/D Assocs., Inc., Miami, 1969-70; pres. Nikki Beare & Assocs., Miami, 1971—; v.p. South Fla. office Cherenson, Carroll & Holzer, Livingston, N.J., 1973; sr. v.p. D.J. Edelman, Inc., 1981-83; moderator, producer Women's Powerline, Sta. WIOD, Miami, 1972-77; co-owner South Miami Travel Service, South Miami, 1976-78; pres. Gov.'s Sq. Travel, Inc., Tallahassee, 1979-85, Travel Is Fun, Miami, 1985—; bd. dirs, corp. sec. Imperial Bank. Author: Pirates, Pineapples and People: Tales and Legends of the Florida Keys, 1961; From Turtle Soup to Coconuts, 1964; Bottle Bonanza, A Handbook for Antique Bottle Collectors, 1965; producer cable TV program Traveler's Digest, 1986—. Chmn. adv. bd. Met. Dade County Library, 1964; active Greater Miami Host Com.; vice chair Met. Dade County Com. Status Women, 1971-76; chair City of Miami Commn. Status Women, 1985—; active Met. Gen. Land Use Master Planning Com., 1973-74; Gov.'s Com. Employment Handicapped, 1970 72; chmn. Met. Dade Fair Housing and Employment Appeals Bd., 1975-78; active Miami YWCA's; chmn. Handicapped and Elderly subcom. Met. Dade Transit Devel. Com.; mem. Fla. Ins. Commn. Task Force, 1975, Dade County Democratic Exec. com., 1972-76, South Fla. Health Planning Council, 1972-74; founding mem. Nat. Women's Polit. Caucus, 1971—; v.p. Herstory, 1971—; candidate Fla. Senate, 1974, Fla. Ho. of Reps., 1976; past pres. adv. bd. Inst. for Women, Fla. Internat. U.; pres. Fla. Feminist Credit Union, 1975-78; bd. dirs. Community Health Inst. South Dade County, 1975-77; mem. Jobs for Miami, 1980-88; chmn. Fla. Gov.'s Small Bus. Adv. Council, 1981-83, Greater Miami Tourism Coalition, 1983-85; co-chmn. FIU Dept. Communication Adv. Bd. Recipient Silver Image award Pub. Relations Assn., 1967-68. Mem. LWV, NOW, Hist. Assn. So. Fla., Friends of Everglades, Women's C. of C. So. Fla., Am. Soc. Travel Agts., Women in Communications, Nat. Assn. Women Bus. Owners, Women's Inst. for Freedom of the Press, Antique Bottle Collectors Assn. Fla. Democrat. Clubs: Tiger Bay, Manatee Bay. Office: Nikki Beare & Assocs Inc 14301 SW 87th Ave Miami FL 33176

BEARMAN, TONI CARBO, information scientist; b. Middletown, Conn., Nov. 14, 1942; d. Anthony Joseph and Theresa (Bauer) Carbo; m. David A. Bearman, Nov. 14, 1970; 1 dau., Amanda Carole. AB, Brown U., 1969; MS, Drexel U., 1973, PhD, 1977. Bibliog. asst. Am. Math. Soc., Math. Revs., 1962-63; coordinator pub. services Brown U. Phys. Scis. Library, Providence, R.I., 1963-66, 67-71; subject specialist U. Wash. Engring. Library, Seattle, 1966-67; teaching and research asst. Drexel U., 1971-74; exec. dir. Nat. Fedn. Abstracting and Indexing Services, Phila., 1974-79; cons. for strategic planning and new product devel. Instn. Elec. Engrs., London, 1979-80; exec. dir. Nat. Commn. on Libraries and Info. Sci., Washington, 1980-86; dean Sch. Library and Info. Sci. U. Pitts., 1986—; mem. adv. com. U.S. Dept. Commerce, Patent and Trademark Office, 1987—; trustee Engring. Index, Inc. Contbr. articles to profl. jours; mem. editorial bds. profl. jours. Bd. dirs. Greater Pitts. Literacy Council; lecturer La. State U., 1988; ASIS Internat. Relations Com.; Spl. Libraries Assn. Task Force. Recipient Disting. Alumni award Drexel U. Coll. Info. Studies, 1984. Fellow AAAS (chmn. sect. T nominating com.), Inst. Info. Scientists; mem. Am. Soc. Info. Sci., Spl. Interest Group on Library Automation and Networks (dir., chmn. networking com., chmn. 50th ann. conf., Watson Davis award 1983), ALA, Spl. Libraries Assn. (Watson Davis award 1983), Soc. Scholarly Pub. Assn., Women's Nat. Book Assn., Nat. Info. Standards Orgn. (bd. dirs.). Home: 5600 Northumberland St Pittsburgh PA 15217 Office: U Pitts Sch Library & Info Sci 135 N Bellefield St Pittsburgh PA 15260

BEARN, MARGARET SLOCUM, lawyer, educator; b. Fanwood, N.J., June 20, 1924; d. Clarence W. and Emma (Elliot) Slocum; B.A. with honors, Swarthmore Coll., 1945; LL.B., Yale U., 1948; m. Alexander G. Bearn, Dec. 20, 1952; children—Helen Bearn Pennoyer, Gordon. Bar: N.Y. 1950. Assoc., Grossman & Grossman, N.Y.C., 1948-50, Lewinson, Lewinson & Fieland, 1950-53, 54-55; dir. admissions Lab. Inst. Mdse., N.Y.C., 1953-54; 55-56, dean, 1956-73; asst. prof. N.Y. Law Sch., 1973-76, asso. prof., 1976-85, asst. dean, 1974-76, asso. dean, 1976-85, acting dean, spring 1980, dir. joint program with U. Bologna (Italy), 1976-85; assoc. prof. law St. John's U. Sch. Law, Jamaica, N.Y., 1985—, asst. dean, 1986—; mem. N.Y.C. Mayor's Com. Judiciary, 1980, 83. Mem. N.Y.C. Community Bd. 1, 1979-85; sec., bd. dirs. Chambers-Canal Civic Assn., 1977-85. Woodrow Wilson fellow, 1979, 80, 83. Mem. ABA (law schs. insp. teams 1978—, com. on jud. edn. and internat. law 1982—), Assn. Am. Law Schs. (chmn. sect. on teaching law outside law sch. 1980-81), N.Y. County Lawyers Assn. (chmn. com. on legal edn. and admission to bar 1980-85), U.S. Supreme Ct. Hist. Soc. (com. student chpts.), Internat. Assn. Jurists (v.p. Am. com. 1981-86, treas. 1986—, chmn. 1983 conf.), Am. Law Inst., Scribes (pres. 1983-84). Presbyterian. Office: St John's U Sch Law Grand Central & Utopia Pkwys Jamaica NY 11439

BEASLEY, DOROTHY TOTH, judge; b. Garfield, N.J.; d. Stephen and Beatrice Elizabeth (Dodd) Toth; m. William H. Beasley Jr. (div.). BA, St. Lawrence U., 1959; LLB, Am. U., 1964; LLM in Judicial Process, U. Va., 1984. Bar: D.C. 1964, Va. 1965, Ga. 1969. Law clk. cir. ct. Arlington County, Va., 1964-66; atty. Shadyac, Berg & Nolan, Arlington County, 1966-67, Fisher & Phillips, Atlanta, 1968-69; asst. atty. gen. State of Ga., Atlanta, 1969-73, asst. U.S. atty, 1973-77; judge Ga. State Ct., Fulton County, 1977-84, Ga. State Ct. Appeals, Fulton County, 1984—; mem. judicial article subcom. Select Com. Constnl. Revision, State of Ga., 1983; mem. Ga. Commn. on Bicentennial of U.S. Constn., 1975, Leadership Atlanta, 1982, Leadership Ga.; mem. adv. bd. Neighborhood Justice Ctr., Atlanta, Atlanta's Table; trustee Ga. Legal History Found.; bd. dirs. Atlanta Community Food Bank; mem. Ga. Commn. on Children and Youth, 1987—. Mem. Am. Judicature Soc., Am. Law Inst., Lawyers Club of Atlanta, Old War Horse Lawyers Club, Ga. Assn. Women Attys., Atlanta Bar Assn., Fulton County Bar Assns., State Bar Ga., ABA (judicial adminstrn. div.), Ga. Bar Found. (charter mem.). Lutheran. Office: Ga Ct Appeals State Judicial Bldg Atlanta GA 30334

BEASLEY, MAURINE HOFFMAN, journalism educator, historian; b. Sedalia, Mo., Jan. 28, 1936; d. Dimmitt Heard and Maurine (Hieronymous) Hoffman; m. William C. McLaughlin, May 20, 1966 (div. 1969); m. 2d, Henry R. Beasley, Dec. 24, 1970; 1 dau., Susan Sook. B.J., B.A. in History, U. Mo., 1958; M.S. in Journalism, Columbia U., 1963; Ph.D. in Am. Civilization, George Washington U., 1974; Cert. in Brit. History, U. Edinburgh, Scotland, 1964. Edn. editor Kansas City (Mo.) Star, 1959-62; staff writer Washington Post, 1963-73; asst. prof. journalism U. Md., College Park, 1975-80, assoc. prof., 1980-86, prof. 1987—. Author: Eleanor Roosevelt and the Media: A Public Quest for Self-Fulfillment, 1987, The New Majority, 1988; author: (with others) Women in Media, 1977; editor: (with others) Voices of Change: Southern Pulitzer Winners, 1978, One Third of a Nation (hon. mention Washington Monthly Book Award 1982), 1981; editor: White House Press Conferences of Eleanor Roosevelt, 1983; mem. adv. bd. Am. Journalism, 1983—; contbr. articles to acad. jours. Violinist, Montgomery Coll. Symphony Orch., 1975—; pres., Little Falls Swimmings Club, Inc. Gannett Teaching Fellowships Program fellow, 1977; Pulitzer traveling fellow Columbia U., 1963; Eleanor Roosevelt studies grantee Eleanor Roosevelt Inst., 1979-80; named one of nation's outstanding tchrs. of writing and editing Modern Media Inst. and Am. Soc. Newspaper Editors, 1981. Mem. Assn. Edn. in Journalism and Mass Communications (standing com. on profl. freedom and responsibility 1985, vice chair 1987-88, sec. history div. 1986-87, vice-head 1987-88), Am. News Women's Club (bd. govs. 1986-87), Women in Communications (bd. dirs. Washington chpt. 1985-87), Nat. Fedn. Press Women, Phi Beta Kappa, Sigma Delta Chi (chair nat. hist. site com. 1986-87, bd. dirs. Washington chpt. 1988—), Omicron Delta Kappa. Democrat. Unitarian. Home: 4920 Flint Dr Bethesda MD 20816 Office: U of Maryland Coll Journalism College Park MD 20742

BEATH, CATHERINE VERONICA, surgical equipment manufacturing executive; b. Phila., Sept. 21, 1949; d. John Jacob and Matilda Ruth (Wolsak) B. BS in Microbiology, Pa. State U., 1970; MBA, Rider Coll., 1984. Sr. microbiologist Stuart Pharms., Wilmington, Del., 1971-77; regulatory analyst McNeil Pharms., Springhouse, Pa., 1977-80; mgr. corp. regulatory affairs C.R. Bard, Inc., Murray Hill, N.J., 1981-85, dir. corp. regulatory affairs, 1985—. Club: Princeton area Penn State (officer 1985—). Office: CR Bard Inc 731 Central Ave Murray Hill NJ 07974

BEATON-SIMMONS, KAREN, fundraiser; b. Providence, Mar. 9, 1944; d. Allan and Arlene Beaton; BA, U. R.I., 1965; MEd, U. Ga., 1974; m. 1965 (div.); children: Laura, Andrew. Speech pathologist, 1965-79; part-time faculty U. R.I., 1978-79; dir. ann. giving Bryant Coll., Smithfield, R.I., 1979-80, dir. devel., 1980-83; v.p. membership services Greater Providence C. of C., 1983-84; dir. pub. relations and devel. Jewish Home for the Aged, 1985-87; dir. devel. and pub. relations St. Anne's Hosp., 1987—; pvt. practice speech pathology, Cranston, R.I., 1979-81. Mem. State Advs. for Gifted Edn., 1980—, pres., 1980-81; mem. nat. adv. council Small Bus. Adminstrn., 1983-85. Mem. Nat. Soc. Fundraising Execs., New Eng. Assn. Hosp. Devel., Nat. Assn. Hosp. Devel., Leadership R.I., Alpha Chi Omega, Kappa Delta

Pi. Baptist (choir, deaconess). Office: St Anne's Hosp 795 Middle St Fall River MA 02721

BEATTIE, BONITA LYNN, physical therapist, military officer; b. N.Y.C., June 28, 1949; d. Joseph Edward and Muriel (Uhl) Heafy; m. John Beattie, July 24, 1974 (div. Dec. 1985). BS in Health and Phys. Edn., East Stroudsburg State Coll., 1971; MS in Phys. Therapy, Baylor U., 1972, MS in Health Care Adminstrn., 1978; postgrad., Tex. A&M U., 1988—; grad., Command and Gen. Staff Coll. Lic. phys. therapist. Commd. 2d lt. U.S. Army, 1971; advanced through grades to lt. col. 1988; phys. therapist Tripler (Hawaii) Army Med. Ctr., 1973-76; health care resident, adminstrv. staff officer Cutler Army Hosp., Ft. Devens, Mass., 1977-78, chief phys. therapy clinic, 1978-80; staff officer Office of the Surgeon Gen., U.S. Army, Washington, 1980-83; staff phys. therapist Walter Reed Army Med. Ctr., Washington, 1983-85; acting dir. U.S. Army-Navy phys. therapy specialist course Acad. Health Scis., Ft. Sam Houston, San Antonio, 1985—, dir. specialists program, 1985—; Contbr. articles to profl. jours. Contbr. articles to newspapers. Named to Outstanding Young Women of Am., 1982. Mem. Am. Phys. Therapy Assn., Cen. Tex. Phys. Therapy Assn. (com. 1986-87), Baylor U. Phys. Therapy U.S. Army Alumni Assn., Kappa Delta Pi. Republican. Club: San Antonio Wheelmen. Office: Acad Health Scis Phys Therapy Br Fort Sam Houston TX 78234-6100

BEATTY, FRANCES FIELDING LEWIS, art dealer; b. N.Y.C., Nov. 23, 1948; d. John Robert Anthony and Anne (Kidder) B.; m. Allen A. Adler; 1 child, Alexander H.L. BA, Vassar Coll., 1970; MA, Columbia U., 1973, PhD, 1980. Instr. Ramapo Coll., Mahwah, N.Y., 1972-74, Columbia U., N.Y.C., 1974-76; editor Art World Mag., N.Y.C., 1976; v.p. Richard L. Feigen & Co., N.Y.C., 1978—. Co-author: Louise Nevelson Catalogue, 1977; contbr. Andre Masson Catalogue, 1977. Mem. contemporary council Mus. Modern Art, N.Y.C., 1978—; bd. dirs. Checkerboard Found., N.Y.C., 1980—. Grantee Columbia U., 1977; Noble Found. fellow Columbia U., 1972, Vassar Coll., 1975. Mem. Nat. Soc. Colonial Dames. Office: Richard L Feigen & Co 113 E 79th St New York NY 10021

BEATY-BATISTE, LYNDA CHRYSTA, nurse educator; b. Oakland, Calif., Mar. 8, 1958; d. Michael W. and Christine H. (Johnson) Morton; m. Larry D. Batiste, July 21, 1985. BS in Nursing, San Francisco State U., 1980; MS in Nursing, U. Calif., San Francisco, 1984. Nurse Herrick Hosp., Berkeley, Calif., 1980—; clin. instr. Merritt Coll., Oakland, Calif., 1984-85, lectr. Calif. State U., Hayward, 1985—; ann. conv. workshop Calif. Student Nurses Assn., Los Angeles, 1986. Camp nurse Oaklanda Parks and Recreation Dept., Quincy, Calif., 1980—; instr. CPR ARC, Berkeley, Calif., 1982. Fellow Am. Lung Assn., 1986. Mem. Black Nurses Assn. (workshop cons. Bay area chpt. 1984—, exec. com. student affairs), Calif. Nurse's Assn. Democrat. Baptist.

BEAUDOIN, CAROL ANN, psychologist; b. Lowell, Mass., Mar. 30, 1949; d. Adrien P. and Rita J. (LeBlanc) B.; B.A. with honors, U. Fla., 1971; M.Ed. in Counseling, Boston U., 1973, Ed.D. in Counseling Psychology, 1979. Psychiat. aide U. Fla.-Shands Teaching Hosp., Gainesville, 1970-71; trainee VA Hosp., Gainesville, 1971-72; attendant Boston State Hosp., 1972, intern, 1973; intern Univ. Hosp., also Counseling Center, Northeastern U., Boston, 1973-74, Dorchester Mental Health Center, also Carney Hosp., 1974-75; staff psychologist Human Resource Inst., Boston, 1974-80, treatment team leader, 1975-80; pvt. practice psychology, Brookline, Mass., 1980—. Mem. Am. Psychol. Assn. Office: 1101 Beacon St Brookline MA 02146

BEAUDRY, DIANNA LEE, real estate developer; b. Rhinelander, Wis., July 25, 1946; d. George Jr. and Shirley Pauline (Coffman) Masten; m. Dale Edward Reid, Aug. 15, 1964 (div. Apr. 1973); m. William A. Beaudry, July 10, 1978. Student, St. Leo Coll., 1974, Draughons Coll., 1980, 81. Med. records clk. Pawating Hosp., Niles, Mich., 1963-64; sec. Sunnymede Furniture Co., Inc., South Bend, Ind., 1964-65; asst. legal sec. Mollison, Hadsell and Carey, Niles, 1965-67; exec. sec. to chief exec. officer Nat. Standard Co., Niles, 1967-73; v.p., adminstr. Ramar Group Co., Inc., Sarasota, Fla., 1973-78; temp. office mgr. Commonwealth Reorgn. Co., Inc., San Antonio, 1978-79; project mgr. Southeastern Devel. Group, Inc., Savannah, 1979—; dir. Fiddler's Cove Beach and Racquet Club, Hilton Head, S.C., 1984-87. Contbr. to American Poetry Anthology, 1986. Dir., sec. Castel Del Mare Homeowners Assn., Sarasota, 1975-78, Village Brooke Homeowners Assn., Sarasota, 1977-78; mem. FM 91 Pub. Radio Sta., Savannah, 1982-87; charter mem. Holistic Health Network, Savannah, 1986-87; chmn. planning com., dir., treas. Unity Ch. of Savannah, 1987—. Mem. Savannah Women's Network (charter mem. 1983—, dir. 1986-87). Mem. Unity Ch. Club: LaVida Health. Office: Southeastern Devel Group 6600 Abercorn Suite 204 Savannah GA 31406

BEAUFAIT, DORIS ELAINE O'DONNELL, reporter; b. Cleve., June 21, 1921; d. John Laurence and Stella Agnes O'Donnell; student Case Western Res. U., 1940-44, John Carroll U., 1944-47, Seton Hall Coll., 1985-88; m. Howard Beaufait, Sept. 1957. With Cleve. News, 1944-58, Cleve. Plain Dealer, 1958-59; with Cleve. Zool. Soc., 1959-62; staff Univ. Hosps., Cleve., 1961-63; reporter Cleve. Plain Dealer, 1963-70; with News-Herald, Willoughby, Ohio, 1970-71, Office of the Mayor, Cleve., 1972-73; investigative reporter/writer Tribune Rev., Greensburg, Pa., 1973—. Mem. Pa. Jud. Merit Selection Commn., Westmoreland County, 1980-81. Mem. Ligonier Valley Hist. Soc., Women in Communications, Pa. Newspaper Women's Assn., Pa. Women's Press Assn., Theta Sigma Phi, Sigma Delta Chi. Roman Catholic. Club: Press. Contbr. articles to profl. jours. Home: 180 Old Forbes Rd Ligonier PA 15658

BEAUMONT, ENID FRANKLIN, public administration executive; b. Los Angeles, Feb. 17, 1930; d. Harry Aron and Barbara Ruth (Grossblatt) Franklin; m. Richard A. Beaumont (div. Nov. 1979). BA, UCLA, 1951; MA, U. Hawaii, 1955; PhD, NYU, 1972. Dir. communications Port Authority of N.Y. and N.J., N.Y.C., 1956-66; sr. assoc. Agy. Internat. Devel., Washington, 1966-68; assoc. adminstr. Human Resources Adminstrn., N.Y.C., 1968-69; assoc. prof. N.J. Institute Tech., Newark, 1969-72; dir. pub. adminstrn. NYU, N.Y.C., 1972-76; asst. dir. Internat. Personnel Mgmt. Assocs., Washington, 1976-78; v.p. Nat. Acad. Pub. Adminstrn., Washington, 1978-82; dir. Acad. State and Local Govt., Washington, 1982—; U. teaching U. So. Calif. and George Washington U., 1976—. Contbr. articles to profl. jours. Mem. Nat. Acad. Pub. Adminstrn. (trustee 1988—), Nat. Assn. Schs. of Pub. Affairs and Adminstrn., Nat. Council Am. Soc. Pub. Adminstrn. Home: 2501 M St NW Suite 715 Washington DC 20037 Office: Acad for State and Local Govt 444 N Capitol St NW Suite 349 Washington DC 20001

BEAUMONT, MONA MAGDELEINE, artist; b. Paris, Jan. 1, 1927; came to U.S., 1942, naturalized, 1945; d. Jacques Hippolyte and Elsie M. (Didisheim) Marx; BA, U. Calif., Berkeley, 1945, M.A., 1946; postgrad. Harvard U., Fogg Mus., Cambridge, postgrad. spl. studies Hans Hoffman Studios, N.Y.C., 1946; m. William G. Beaumont; children—Garrett, Kevin. One-woman shows at Galeria Proteo, Mexico City, Gumps Gallery, San Francisco, Palace of Legion of Honor, San Francisco, L'Armitiere Gallery, Rouen, France, Hoover Gallery, San Francisco, San Francisco Mus. Modern Art, Galeria Van der Voort, San Francisco, William Sawyer Gallery, San Francisco, Palo Alto (Calif.) Cultural Ctr., Galerie Alexandre Monnet, Brussels, Honolulu Acad. Arts, exhibited in group shows at San Francisco Mus. Modern Art, San Francisco Art Inst., DeYoung Meml. Mus., San Francisco, Grey Found. Tour of Asia, Bell Telephone Invitational, Chgo., Richmond Art Ctr., Los Angeles County Mus. Art, Galerie Zodiaque, Geneva, others; represented in permanent collections: Oakland (Calif.) Mus. Art, City and County of San Francisco, Hoover Found., San Francisco, Grey Found., Washington, Bulart Found., San Francisco; also numerous pvt. collections. Recipient Jack London Sq. Ann. Painting award; Purchase award Grey Found.; Ann. awards San Francisco Women Artists (2); Purchase award San Francisco Art Festival; One-Man Show award San Francisco Art Festival; included in Printworld Internat., 1982-88, Internat. Art Diary, N.Y. Art Review, Art in the San Francisco Bay area. Mem. Soc. for Encouragement of Contemporary Art, Bay Area Graphic Arts Council, San Francisco Art Inst., San Francisco Mus. Modern Art, Capp Street Project, Langton Street Ctr., Pro Arts Assn., others. Address: 1087 Upper Happy Valley Rd Lafayette CA 94549

BEAUMONT, ROSALIE MARY, logistics consultant; b. St. Louis, July 30, 1942; d. Ulysses Sylvester and Helen Marie (Hootselle) Simon; ed. Lindenwood Colls., St. Charles, Mo., 1973-76, Harris Tchrs. Coll., St. Louis, 1961, U. Fla., Gainesville, 1964: m. Richard Vaughn, Jan 20, 1968 (dec.); 1 dau., Heather Elizabeth; m. Dennis Jon Beaumont, May 28, 1982. Vol. U.S. Peace Corps, Brazil, 1964-66; tech. analyst, group leader Conductron-Mo., St. Charles, 1966-71; bus. mgr., 1971-77; tech. analyst, maintenance engr. McDonnell Douglas Astronautics, St. Louis, 1977-78; mgr. supply support Northrop Def. Systems Div., Rolling Meadows, Ill., 1978-80; logistics mgmt. cons., Spring Grove, Ill., 1980-85; mgr. logistic and design support Recon/Optical, Inc., Barrington, Ill., 1985—. Adv. council Conductron-Mo. Affirmative Action Program; mem. ch. council, commr. ways and means St. John the Baptist Cath. Ch.; troop leader Sybaquay council Girl Scouts U.S.A. Recipient commendation Conductron-Mo., 1967. Mem. Soc. Logistics Engrs. (Mem. of Yr. award, sr. mem.), Assn. Old Crows, Lindenwood Colls. Assocs. Fine Arts, Nat. Assn. Female Execs., Northside Art Assn. (bus. mgr. News 1968-70). Republican. Home: 2910 Bay View Ln McHenry IL 60050 Office: 550 W Northwest Hwy Barrington IL 60010

BEAUSOLEIL, DORIS MAE, housing specialist, govt. agy. ofcl.; b. Chelmsford, Mass., Jan. 9, 1932; d. Joseph Honorius and Beatrice Pearl (Smith) B.; student State Tchrs. Coll., Lowell, Mass., 1949-51; B.A. in Sociology and Psychology, Goddard Coll., Plainfield, Vt., 1954; M.A. in Human Relations, N.Y. U., 1957. With div. human rights N.Y. State, N.Y.C., 1960-69, housing dir., 1966-68; housing cons. Nat. Com. Against Discrimination in Housing, N.Y.C., 1969-70; housing cons. Edwin Gould Found., N.Y.C., 1970-71; human resources cons. interfaith housing strategy com., housing cons. Fedn. Prot. Welfare Agencies, Inc., N.Y.C., 1971-72; self-employed housing cons., 1972-74; equal opportunity compliance specialist Region II HUD, N.Y.C., 1975—, Fed. women's program coordinator, 1975-79; br. chief Title VI Sect. 109 Compliance div. fair housing and equal opportunity Region II, HUD, N.Y.C., 1979-84; founding mem. N.Y. State HUD Com.; adv. panel Housing Mag., 1979; cons., examiner N.Y. State Civil Service Commn., 1970—. Mem. Nat. Assn. Human Rights Workers (Outstanding Service award 1974), Citizens Housing and Planning Council, Federally Employed Women, Nat. Assn. Housing and Devel. Ofcls. Republican. Unitarian. Clubs: Women's City N.Y., Rep. Bus. Women's (N.Y.C.) (pres. 1985-88). Home: 392 Central Park W New York NY 10025 Office: 26 Federal Plaza Room 3532 New York NY 10278

BEAVIN, MARY JANICE, health care services executive; b. Louisville, Aug. 20, 1962; d. Celestine Borromeo and Jane Carolyn (Jackie) B. Student with high honors, Xavier U., 1982; BA, Mt. Holyoke Coll., 1984; postgrad., U. Louisville, 1985, Sch. Bus. U. Chgo., 1987—. Bus. analyst Scudder, Stevens and Clark, Boston, 1983; intern Citizens Fidelity Bank & Trust, Louisville, 1984; mgmt. intern Humana, Inc., Louisville, 1984-85, treasury ops. analyst, 1985-87. Fin. advisor Jr. Achievement Assn., Louisville, 1985; career advisor Mt. Holyoke Coll. Alumnae, Louisville, 1984-86, coll. recruiter Mt. Holyoke Coll., Louisville, 1984-86. Mem. Nat. Assn. Female Execs., Omicron Delta Epsilon. Democrat. Roman Catholic. Office: 1414 E 59th St Chicago IL 60637

BEBB, JOAN ELLEN, aerospace program manager; b. N.Y.C., Dec. 9, 1938; d. Joseph Jay and Ruth (Weidenbaum) Karp; divorced; children: David Glenn, Susan Ruth. Student, Occidental Coll., Los Angeles, 1956-58; BA, San Diego State U., Los Angeles, 1960; postgrad., UCLA, 1960-61. With Control Data Corp., Los Angeles, 1962-67, System Devel. Corp., Santa Monica, Calif., 1967-74; with TRW, Redondo Beach, Calif., 1974-87, dep. project mgr. security analyst file environ., 1981-82, project mgr. Milstar Satellite Payload, 1982-84, proposal mgr. Space Sta., 1984-85, lab. mgr. info. systems, 1985-86, program mgr. I-S/A Automated Message Processing Exchange program, 1986—; dep. project mgr. Tracking and Data Relay Satellite, Redondo Beach, 1978-81. Editor: (textbook) Fortran IV, 1972. Office: TRW 1 Space Park Redondo Beach CA 90278

BECAN-MCBRIDE, KATHLEEN ELIZABETH, medical and cytogenetic technology educator; b. Houston, Feb. 24, 1949; d. Frank Ernest and Dorothy C. (Sturm) Becan; m. Mark Anerson McBride, July 11, 1970; children: Patrick Becan, Jonathan Aaron. BS in Biology, U. Houston, 1971, MEd in Allied Health, 1973, EdD in Higher Edn. Adminstrn., 1977. Med. technologist St. Luke's Episcopal Hosp., Houston, 1971-73; instr. dept. med. tech. U. Tex., Galveston, 1973-75; instr. med. lab. technician program Houston Community Coll., 1975-77; prof. dept. pathology, dir. program in med. tech. and cytogenetics U. Tex., Houston, 1977—, prof. Grad. Sch. Biomed. Scis., 1986—; instrnl. cons. Pvt. Industry Council, Houston, 1982-85, Peace Corps, Houston, 1984, ITT, Houston, 1985; ednl. research cons. Am. Soc. for Med. Tech., Houston, 1977-79, 83-84; ednl. cons. La. State Bd. Regents, Baton Rouge, 1985, Profl. Seminar Cons., Inc. Author: Textbook of Clinical Lab Sciences, 1982, (with others) Phlebotomy Handbook, 1984, 2d edit. 1988, Essentials for the Small Laboratory and Physician's Office, 1988; contbr. articles and monographs to Med. Lab. Scis. jour., chpts. to books; editor med. jours. Mem. adv. bd. for health occupation, adv. bd. com. for edn. evaluation Houston Ind. Sch. Dist., 1985-87. Grantee U. Tex., Peace Corps, Pvt. Industry Council, Tex. Edn. Agy., ITT. Named one of Outstanding Young Women Am., 1979-82, 84. Mem. Am. Soc. Med. Tech. (coms. chmn.), Tex. Soc. for Med. Tech. (chmn. coms.), Houston Soc. Clin. Pathologists, Tex. Soc. Allied Health Professions (bd. dirs. 1981-82, pres. 1984, 85), Am. Soc. Clin. Pathologists (research and devel. com. 1983—, cert.), Clin. Lab. Mgmt. Assn., Zonta Internat. Exec. Bus. and Profl. Woman's Orgn., Alpha Mu Tau, Omicron Sigma. Democrat. Roman Catholic. Avocations: tennis, jogging, soccer coaching, piano. Home: 3806 Marlowe St Houston TX 77005 Office: U Tex Health Sci Ctr Med Tech/Cytogenetics Dept Houston TX 77225

BECCARI, NANCY JUDITH HALL, educator; b. Marietta, Ohio; d. Robert Earl and Bernice (Underwood) Hall; B.A. cum laude, U. Miami, 1958, M.Ed., 1961, postgrad., 1970—; m. Turner M. Hiers, Oct. 29, 1942; m. Armano A. Beccari, Aug. 31, 1974. Tchr. pub. schs., Ga., Fla.; dir. Reading Center, Nova High Sch., Fort Lauderdale, Fla., 1963-73, Lauderdale Reading Clinic, 1965—. Author: Little Pitchers With Big Ears. Mem. Internat. Reading Assn., Am. Ednl. Research Assn., AAUW, Nat. Soc. for Study Edn., Kappa Delta Pi, Alpha Delta Kappa, Kappa Kappa Iota, Epsilon Tau Lambda, Phi Lambda Pi. Clubs: Le Club Internationale, Rolls Royce Owners. Home: 1224 E Las Olas Blvd Fort Lauderdale FL 33301

BECHER, NANCY ANN KLOPP, educator; b. West Reading, Pa., June 18, 1931; d. Russell William and Alice Elizabeth (Deeds) Klopp; m. William Alfred Becher, Nov. 23, 1957; children: Erica Becher Dye, Mark William. BS in Elem. Edn., Kutztown U., 1953; MS in Reading, Hofstra U., 1975, diploma, 1983, postgrad. Cert. tchr., sch. adminstr., reading tchr. Tchr. Lindenhurst (N.Y.) Pub. Schs., 1953-54, 1957-58, Wyomissing (Pa.) Pub. Schs., 1954-57, West Islip (N.Y.) Pub. Schs., 1963-65, Amityville (N.Y.) Pub. Schs., 1966-73; specialist reading Intermediate School, Bay Shore, N.Y., 1976-83, Jr. Bay Shore Pub. Schs., N.Y., 1983-86; dir. project Summer Sch., Bay Shore, 1979-80; instr. inservice Bay Shore Schs., 1973-80; specialist reading St. Patrick's Sch., Bay Shore, 1986-87; cons. Bay Shore Pub. Schs., 1986—; adj. prof. Coll. New Rochelle, 1986—; cons. Special Edn. Tng. Ctr., Westbury 1986—; instr. Nassau Bd. Coop. Services, Plainview 1980-82; chair adv. bd. NEWSDAY, Melville 1982—. Author nat. curriculum for Newspaper in Edn.; contbr. articles to profl. jours. Trainer Literacy Vols. Am, Hempstead, N.Y. 1987; founder Friends West Islip Library 1968—; leader, cons. Girl Scouts Am. 1966-70. Grantee N.Y. Pub. Found. 1984-86, N.Y. St. Edn. Dept. 1973-74. Mem. N.Y. State Reading Assn. (chair tchrs. special interest group 1986—, speaker st. conf. 1980-86, chair newspaper edn. 1983-85), Internat. Reading Assn. (editor newspaper 1988), Suffolk Reading Specialist Council (pres. 1982-84), Nat. Council Tchrs. English (cons. on commn. for English edn. 1985—), Am. Newspaper Pubs. Assn. Democrat. Home: 472 Everdell Ave West Islip NY 11795 Office: Bay Shore Pub Schs 75 W Perkal St Bay Shore NY 11706

BECHERER, DEBORAH ZORN, banker; b. Youngstown, Ohio, Feb. 9, 1958; d. Robert L. and Joan M. (Wilkos) Zorn; m. William B. Becherer Jr., May 22, 1983. BS in Bus. Edn. magna cum laude, Youngstown State U., 1980; MBA, Coll. of William and Mary, 1983; cert., Grad. Sch. Banking, Madison, Wis., 1987. Trainee advanced mgmt. Bank One of Ea. Ohio, Youngstown, 1983-84, officer comml. loans, 1984-86, asst. v.p., 1986—. Mem. allocation com. United Way Planning, Youngstown, 1984-86; pres. Lake to River Girl Scout Council, Youngstown, 1987—; liaison bd. dirs. Mahoning County Red Cross, Youngstown, Cen. Christian Day Care Ctr., Youngstown. Mem. Am. Inst. Banking, Nat. Assn. Female Execs., Alumni Assn. Coll. of William and Mary, Delta Zeta Alumni Assn. Republican. Methodist. Home: 7099 Oak Dr Poland OH 44514 Office: Bank One of Ea Ohio 6 Federal Plaza W Youngstown OH 44503

BECHT, JANET REGINA, lawyer; b. Springfield, Ohio, May 27, 1950; d. John Anthony and Marjorie Catherine (Conrad) B. BS, U. Dayton, 1972, MS, 1973; JD, Ohio No. U., 1980. Bar: Ohio, 1983. Social worker Clark County Childrens Services, Springfield, 1973-75, Bethany Home, Moline, Ill., 1975-76; office mgr. Catholic Social Services, Sidney, Ohio, 1976-78; atty. Rural Legal Aid, Springfield, 1981-86; dir. Cath. Social Services, Sidney, Ohio, 1986—; Title III coordinator, supervising atty. Rural Legal Aid, Troy, Ohio; instr. Saturday Morning Enrichment Program, Wright State U., Dayton, 1981-83. Grad. asst. U. Dayton, 1972. Mem. ABA, Ohio Bar Assn., Miami County Bar Assn., Assn. Trial Lawyers Am., Phi Alpha Delta (marshall 1979-80). Democrat. Roman Catholic. Home: 1406 Henley Rd Troy OH 45373 Office: 500-A E Court St Sidney OH 45365

BECHT, THERESA ANNE, nursing home management company executive; b. Bklyn., July 26, 1962. BA in Mgmt., U. South Fla., 1984. Controller, treas. Care Mgmt. Inc., Jupiter, Fla., 1984—. Mem. Fin. Mgmt. Assn., Gerontol. Soc. Fla. Roman Catholic. Office: Care Mgmt Inc 18245 US Hwy 1 Jupiter FL 33469

BECK, AUDREY, data management company executive; b. Mpls., July 23, 1954; d. John George and Shirley Hope (Dahley) Neis. Student, Hennepin County Vo-Tech. Coll. Software engr. CPT Corp., Mpls., 1978-85, Datamyte Corp., Minnetonka, Minn., 1985; sr. system support rep. Moore Data Mgmt. Services, Mpls., 1985—; computer contractor, Mpls., 1980—. Avocations: programming, electronics, horses, carpentry. Home: 5601 Judy Ln Brooklyn Center MN 55430 Office: Moore Data Mgmt Services 1660 South Hwy 100 Minneapolis MN 55416

BECK, BRENDA FAYE, communications company executive; b. Grenada, Miss., June 1, 1952; d. Thomas Watson, Jr. and Dorothy Eloise (Clemons) McCaulla; m. Lee Roy Tubbs, Oct. 10, 1971 (div. 1977); m. Charlie Eugene Beck, Apr. 14, 1980; children: Lee Gabriel, Thomas Hugh, Brenda Georgianna. Student, George Meany Ctr. Labor Studies, 1984. Long distance operator South Central Bell Telephone, Grenada, 1969-83; computer operator South Central Bell Telephone, Houston, 1975-76; asst. chief operator South Central Bell Telephone, Grenada, 1977; TSPS operator AT&T Communications, Grenada, 1980, chmn. quality of worklife, 1987—; directory editor Telephone Pioneers Am., Grenada, 1980-81; editor Union First Class, Communications Workers Am., Grenada, 1984—, job steward, 1985—. Asst. coach Grenada Soccer League, 1985—; fund raiser Am. Cancer Soc., Grenada, 1986, St. Jude Children's Hosp., Memphis, 1987. Named Operator of the Year, 1973; recipient first place award Hobby Directory for Telephone Pioneers Am., 1980, first place editorial writing award Communications Workers Am./AFL-CIO, 1984. Republican. Baptist. Home: 815 Mary Ave Grenada MS 38901-4907 Office: AT&T Communications 404 1st St Grenada MS 38901

BECK, CHRISTINE HOEY, social services administrator; b. Balt., Dec. 6, 1955; d. Edmund Frisell and Doris Ann (Thomas) Hoey; m. Karl Wayne Kokinakis, Feb. 21, 1959 (div. Sept. 1984); m. John Nathan Beck, Dec. 1, 1959. BS in Bus. Adminstrn., Elon Coll., 1976. Sales cons. City-County Newspaper, Burlington, 1977; adminstrv. asst. Rare Book Collection, Chapel Hill, 1977-79; sr. flight attendant Eastern Airlines, Inc., Atlanta, 1979-81; mgr., sales coordinator Christy Enterprises, Baldwin, Md., 1981-82; med. asst. Kenneth J. Murray, Md., Towson, Md., 1982-84; ops. dir. Am. Council on Alcoholism, Towson, 1984—; cons., advisor AES, Inc., Towson, 1987—. Youth leader Perry Hall Presbyn. Ch., Balt., 1980-82, tchr. vocat. Bible Sch., 1981-85; v.p. Welcome Wagon, Baldwin, 1982-83. Mem. Md. Soc. Assn. Execs., Nat. Assn. Female Execs., Md. Info. & Referral Providers Council (sec. 1987). Republican. Presbyterian. Office: Am Council on Alcoholism Inc 8501 LaSalle Rd Suite 301 Towson MD 21204

BECK, DOROTHY FAHS, social researcher; b. N.Y.C.; d. Charles Harvey and Sophia (Lyon) Fahs; A.B., U. N.C., 1928; M.A., U. Chgo., 1932; Ph.D. (Gilder fellow), Columbia U., 1944, postdoctoral study, 1955-56; Am.-German Student Exchange fellow, Germany, 1928-29; m. Hubert Park Beck, Aug. 20, 1930; 1 child, Brenda E.F. Dir. econ. research ADA, 1929-32; social worker Emergency Relief Adminstrn. N.J., 1933-34; statistician N.J. State Emergency Relief Adminstrn., 1934-35, U.S. Office Edn., 1935-36; asso. social economist U.S. Central Statis. Bd., 1936-38; research supr., author Am. Coll. Dentists, 1940-42; statistician Am. Heart Assn., 1947-53, Cornell U. Med. Coll., part-time 1951-53; asst. prof. biostats. Am. U. Beirut, part-time 1954: dir. research Family Service Am., N.Y.C., 1956-81, dir. study counselor attitudes and feelings, 1982-87, evaluation research cons., 1982-87. Fellow Am. Sociol. Assn.; mem. Acad. Cert. Social Workers, Am. Assn. Marriage and Family Therapy (affiliate), Nat. Council Family Relations, Groves Conf., Am. Statis. Assn., Nat. Assn. Social Workers, Soc. Study Social Problems, Am. Pub. Health Assn., Phi Beta Kappa. Unitarian-Universalist. Author: Patterns in Use of Family Agency Service, 1962; Marriage and the Family Under Challenge, 1976; New Treatment Modalities, 1978; Counselor Characteristics: How They Affect Outcomes, 1988; co-author: Costs of Dental Care Under Specific Clinical Conditions, 1943; Myocardial Infarction, 1954; Clients' Progress within Five Interviews, 1970; How to Conduct a Client Follow-Up Study, 1974, 2d enlarged edit., 1980; Progress on Family Problems, 1973. Home: 523 W 121 St Apt 63 New York NY 10027

BECK, JANICE MCKLOSKEY, government affairs educator; b. Green Bay, Wis., June 16, 1937; d. Theodore Andrew and Ruth Eleanor (Huybrecht) McKloskey; m. James Donald Beck, Oct. 8, 1971 (dec. 1986); children: Jennifer Jaye. BA in English, Coll. St. Scholastica, 1962; MA in English, U. Wis., 1973. Cert. secondary tchr. Elem. tchr. various schs., Minn., 1959-62; secondary tchr. various schs., Calif., Wis. and Ill., 1962-68; instructional aids specialist Extension Course Inst., Gunter AFB, Ala., 1969-70, edn. specialist, 1970-80; mem. faculty Air War Coll., Maxwell AFB, Ala., 1980-84; mng. editor Air Univ. Rev., Maxwell AFB, 1984-86; mem. faculty dept. nat. security affairs Air War Coll., Maxwell AFB, 1986—. Mem. LWV, Internat. Studies Assn. Latin Am. Studies Assn., Phi Delta Kappa, Lambda Iota Tau. Roman Catholic. Club: Toastmasters.

BECK, JOAN WAGNER, journalist; b. Clinton, Iowa, Sept. 5, 1923; d. Roscoe Charles and Mildred (Noel) Wagner; m. Ernest William Beck, Sept. 9, 1945; children—Christopher, Melinda. B.J. cum laude, Northwestern U., 1945, M.S. in Journalism, 1947. Radio script writer O.W.I. Voice of Am., 1945-46; copy writer Marshall Field & Co., 1947-50; feature writer Chgo. Tribune, 1950—, writer syndicated column about young people, 1956-61, syndicated column about children, 1961-72, editor daily features sect., 1972-75, mem. editorial bd., 1975—; syndicated editorial page columnist, 1974—. Author: How to Raise a Brighter Child, 1967, (with Dr. Virginia Apgar) Is My Baby All Right?, 1973, Effective Parenting, 1976, Best Beginnings, 1983. Hon. chmn. Mother's March of Met. Chgo. chpt. Nat. Found. March of Dimes, 1970-75; trustee Ill. Children's Home and Aid Soc., 1971—; mem. Women's Bd. Northwestern U. Recipient AP award for best newspaper feature series award Ill., 1964; best feature, 1966, best columns, 1983, 84; Alumni Merit award Northwestern U., 1965; Alumnae award, 1977; Nat. award of Achievement Alpha Chi Omega, 1966; 1st place award Penney-U. Mo., 1973; UPI Ill. award for editorial writing, 1984; Woodrow Wilson Found. vis. fellow, 1983—. Mem. Chgo. Network, Chgo. Headline Club, Theta Sigma Phi, Alpha Chi Omega. Methodist. Clubs: Northwestern, Lake Forest. Office: Chgo Tribune 435 N Michigan Ave Chicago IL 60611

BECK, KAREN LYNN, design coordinator, art curator; b. N.Y.C., Dec. 3, 1941; d. Edward and Lillian Marker; student N.Y.C. Community Coll., 1959-61, N.Y.U., 1961-62, New Sch., 1963-64, Ramapo Coll., 1976-77; children: Marni Jill, Julia Dawn. Owner antique bus., Vt. and N.Y., 1965-68; interior designer and antique restorer, 1968-78; ptnr. Interiors Group, Tenafly, N.J., 1978-85; design coordinator, arts curator Robert Martin Co., Elmsford, N.Y., 1985—. Active community art projects, programs to foster arts and emerging artists. Mem. Nat. Assn. Female Execs., Am. Curators Assn., Whitney Mus., Smithsonian Instn., Mus. Modern Art, Women's Mus. Jewish. Home: 40 Dawn Ln Suffern NY 10901

BECK, KATHLEEN GODDARD-LOUISE, educator; b. Columbia, Pa., July 30, 1949; d. Goddard Frederick and Dorothy Marie (Schickling) B. BA in English/Edn., Cabrini Coll., Radnor, Pa., 1971; MS in Edn., Millersville (Pa.) U., 1980. Cert. reading specialist K-12. Tchr. Penn Manor High Sch., Millersville, 1971-75; reading specialist Lancaster-Lebanon Intermediate Unit 13, East Petersburg, Pa., 1975—; reading and edn. cons. to various schs. in south Cen. Pa. and Laurel, Md., 1976—; lectr. in field. Editor:(mag.) Creativity. Founder, dir., coach Conestoga Dolphin Swim Club, 1972-73; tchr. adult scripture study Sacred Heart Ch., also bd. dirs., chair liturgy com.; tchr. High Sch. Religious Studies, Lancaster, 1971—; bd. dirs. Diocesan Pastoral Council, Harrisburg, 1982—; acad. advisors bd. Millersville U., Pa., 1900—. Mem. Internat. Reading Assn., NEA, Nat. Council of Tchrs. of English, Pa. State Edn. Assn., Keystone State Reading Assn., Lancaster-Lebanon Intermediate Unit Edn. Assn., Lancaster-Lebanon Reading Council (scholarship chmn. 1985—). Republican. Home: 838 George St Lancaster PA 17603 Office: Lancaster-Lebanon Intermediate Unit 13 1110 Enterprise Rd East Petersburg PA 17520

BECK, MARGIT, artist; b. Tokay, Hungary; came to U.S., naturalized, 1938; d. Samuel and Johanna (Blau) B.; m. Sidney Schwartz; children: Joan, John. Student, Art Inst. Oradeamare, Rumania, Art Student League, N.Y.C., 1945-46. Theatrical scenic designer 1934-36; formerly mem. art faculty Hofstra U.; now adj. asst. prof. art faculty NYU; faculty Empire State Coll., N.Y. State U. Exhibited works in one man shows, Contemporary Arts, N.Y.C., 1955, 58, 59, San Joquin Mus., Stockton, Calif., 1956, Hofstra Coll., L.I., 1958, Mus. Fine Arts, Greenville, S.C., 1959, Babcock Gallery, N.Y.C., 1962, 64, 66, 68, 71, 72, 75, Phila. Art Alliance, 1968, Mansfield (Pa.) State Coll., 1965, Queens Coll., N.Y.C., 1973, Port Washington (N.Y.) Library, 1978; exhibited in group shows, Whitney Mus. Ann., Corcoran Biennial, Art Inst. Chgo. Ann., Pa. Acad. Ann., Allentown (Pa.) Mus. Fine Arts, Lehigh U., Bethlehem, Pa., Bklyn Mus. Internat. W.C. Biennial, NAD Ann., Butler Inst. Ann., U. Nebr. Ann., Springfield (Mass.) Mus., Akron Art Inst., Am. Acad. Arts and Letters, N.Y.C., Am. Soc. Contemporary Artists, Riverside Mus., N.Y.C., Southeby Parke Bernet, N.Y.C., Art U.S.A., Ringling Mus., Davenport (Iowa) Municipal Gallery, São Paulo Mus., N.Y. World's Fair, Am. Fedn. Arts Internat, travelling exhbns. include State Dept. sponsored exhbns., Am. embassies and museums abroad, Am. embassies in Europe; represented in permanent collections, Peabody Mus., Cambridge, Mass., Speed Mus., Louisville, Morse Mus., Rawlins Coll., Hofstra Coll., Hunter Coll., Herbert Lehman Coll., N.Y.C., Miami U., Oxford, Ohio, Norfolk (Va.) Mus., Sheldon Meml. Mus., Lincoln, Nebr., Glichtenstein Mus., Safaad, Israel, Lyman Allen Mus., New London, Conn., Mansfield (Pa.) State Coll., Whitney Mus., Sofia Mus., Bulgaria, others, also many pvt. collections and pub. bldgs. Recipient Gold medal oil Hofstra Coll., 1954; Purchase prize watercolor, 1955; Silver medal, 1956; Gold medal, 1957; Medal of Honor Nat. Assn. Women Artists, 1956; watercolor award, 1957, 63; oil award, 1958, 64; Winsor and Newton oil award, 1959; others; MacDowell Found. Residence fellow, 1957, 59, 60, 75; Walker award oil Audubon Artists, 1965; Medal Honor, 1968, 71; Henry Ward Ranger Fund Purchase awards (3) N.A.D., 1965, 73; Andrew Carnegie award, 1973; Child Hassam award Am. Acad. Arts and Letters, 1968, 69, 72. Mem. Artists Equity Assn. (past mem. exec. bd.), Audubon Artists (v.p. 1968-71, Stephen Hirsch award 1975, annual exhibit award 1981), NAD (full academician, Edwin Palmer award 1975), Coll. Art Assn. Am., Women in Arts. Address: 35 Nightbridge Rd Great Neck NY 11021

BECK, MARILYN MOHR, columnist; b. Chgo., Dec. 17, 1928; d. Max and Rose (Lieberman) Mohr; m. Roger Beck, Jan. 8, 1949 (div. 1974); children: Mark Elliott, Andrea; m. Arthur Levine, Oct. 12, 1980. AA, U. So. Calif., 1950. Freelance writer nat. mags. and newspapers Hollywood, Calif., 1959-63; Hollywood columnist Valley Times and Citizen News, Hollywood, 1963-65; West Coast editor Sterling Mags., Hollywood, 1963-74; freelance entertainment writer Los Angeles Times, 1965-67; Hollywood columnist Bell-McClure Syndicate, 1967-72; chief Bell-McClure Syndicate (West Coast bur.), 1967-72; Hollywood columnist NANA Syndicate, 1967-72; syndicated Hollywood columnist N.Y. Times Spl. Features, 1972-78, N.Y. Times Spl. Features (United Feature Syndicate), 1978-80, United Press abroad, 1978-80, Editors News and Features, Internat., Chgo. Tribune/N.Y. Daily News Syndicate, 1980—. Creator, host: Marilyn Beck's Hollywood Outtakes spls, NBC, 1977, 78; host: Marilyn Beck's Hollywood Hotline, Sta. KFI, Los Angeles, 1975-77; Hollywood reporter: Eyewitness News, Sta. KABC-TV, Los Angeles, 1981; TV program PM Magazine, 1983-88; Author: Marilyn Beck's Hollywood, 1973, (novel) Only Make Believe, 1988. Recipient Citation of Merit Los Angeles City Council, 1973, Press award Pub. Guild Am., 1974, Bronze Halo award So. Calif. Motion Picture Council, 1982. Office: PO Box 11079 Beverly Hills CA 90213

BECK, MARY VIRGINIA, lawyer, public official; b. Ford City, Pa., Feb. 29, 1908; B.A., U. Pitts., 1929, LL.B., 1932, J.D., 1968. Bar: Mich. 1944. Elected to Common Council City of Detroit, 1950-70; bd. suprs. County of Wayne, Mich., 1950-69; exec. dir. Ukrainian Info. Bur., Detroit. Chmn. Policemen & Retirement Fund Commn., Detroit, 1958-62; chmn. Wayne County Port Commn., 1962-68; mem. Gov.s Commn. on Status of Women, 1962, Gov.'s Commn. on Econ. Devel., 1962. Recipient Cert. of Merit Fashion Group of Detroit, 1955; Ruth Houston Whipple award Plymouth Bus. and Profl. Woman's Club, 1956; Sport Guild award Sprots Guild Detroit, 1956; award Detroit Dental Soc., 1957; citation Detroit Cancer Fighters, 1959; Ukrainian Community Service award Ukrainians of the Free World, 1960; Ukrainian of Yr. award Ukrainian Grad. Club of Detroit and Windsor, 1963; award Amvets of World War II, 1967; Woman of the Yr. award Soroptimist Club, 1968, others. Mem. Mich. State Bar, Detroit Bar Assn., Women Lawyers Assn. Mich., Nat. Assn. Women Lawyers, Detroit Bus. Womans Club, Nat. Fedn. Profl. and Bus. Women, Internat. Platform Assn.

BECK, PAMELA HARDY, educator, consultant; b. Shelbyville, Ill., Mar. 27, 1944; d. Fred Ernest and Alta Jane (Dove) Hardy; m. Gerald Joseph Beck, Nov. 20, 1971. BA, Ohio Wesleyan U., 1966; MEd, Smith Coll., Northampton, Mass., 1967. Tchr. of the deaf elem. schs. Balt., 1967-69; field instr. Cued Speech Gallaudet Coll., Washington, 1969-70; tchr. of deaf elem. schs. Oxon Hill, Md., 1970-72; tchr. of deaf, blind Calif. Sch. Blind, Berkeley, 1972-75; tchr. of deaf Area Cooperative Ednl. Services, New Haven, Conn., 1976-79; adj. prof. So. Conn. State U. Spl. Edn., New Haven, 1980-83; pvt. practice cons. New Haven, 1980-83; dir. N. Coast Cued Speech Services, Cleve., 1985—; Author: (book) Cued Speech and Hearing-Impaired Students, 1987, Discovering Cued Speech, 1986, 2d edit. 1988, also workbook, audio tape; contbr. articles to profl. jours. v.p. LWV, Shaker Heights, Ohio, 1987-88, pres. 1988-89; active Christian Education Comm. Plymouth Ch., Shaker Heights. Mem. Nat. Cued Speech Assn. (dir. 1985—), Council Exceptional Children, Conf. Am. Assn. Instrs. for Deaf.

BECK, PAULA JEAN, communications executive; b. Ironwood, Mich., Apr. 14, 1952; d. Raymond Edward and Barbara Fern (Berbeck) B. BA in Art, U. Wis., Eau Claire, 1974, BA in Journalism, 1984. Asst. mgr. communications Genetic Labs., Inc., St. Paul, 1984-85; mgr. communications ARC, Mpls., 1985—. Mem. Pub. Relations Soc. Am. (co-chair job mart com. 1987). Clubs: Minn. Press, U. Folk Dance (Mpls.), Sons of Desert (Mpls.). Office: ARC Mpls 11 Dell Pl Minneapolis MN 55403

BECK, ROSEMARIE, painter; b. N.Y.C., July 8, 1924; d. Samuel and Margit (Weisz) B.; m. Robert Phelps, Sept. 14, 1945; 1 son, Roger. A.B., Oberlin Coll., 1944; student, Inst. Fine Arts, N.Y.U., 1944-45, Columbia, 1945, Atelier of Robert Motherwell, 1950. tchr. Vassar Coll., 1957-55, 61-62, 63-64, Middlebury (Vt.) Coll., 1958, 60, 63, Queens Coll., 1968—. One-man shows include, Peridot Gallery, N.Y.C., 1953, 55, 56, 59, 60, 63, 65, 66, 68-70, 72, Vassar Coll., 1957, 61, Wesleyan U., Middletown, Conn., 1960, State U. N.Y. at New Paltz, 1962, Zachary Waller Gallery, Los Angeles, 1971, Duke, 1971, Kirkland Coll., 1972, Washburn Gallery, 1972, Poindexter Gallery, 1975, 80, Middlebury (Vt.) Coll., 1979, Ingber Gallery, 1980, 85, Weatherspoon Gallery, 1980, Cornell U., 1980, group shows include, Chgo. Art Inst., 1962, Pa. Acad. Fine Arts, 1954, 66, Whitney Mus., 1955-57, 58, Tate Gallery, London, 1958, Butler Inst., Indpls., 1962, Kootz Gallery, N.Y.C., 1951, Felix Landau Gallery, Los Angeles, 1962, Nat. Inst. Arts and Letters, 1968, 75, 78, 79. Grantee Ingram Merrill Found., 1966, 79, Nat. Endowment Arts, 1986. Address: 6 E 12th St New York NY 10003

BECKER, BETTIE GERALDINE, artist; b. Peoria, Ill., Sept. 22, 1918; d. Harry Seymour and Magdalene Matilda (Hiller) Becker; BFA cum laude, U. Ill., Urbana, 1940; postgrad. Art Inst. Chgo., 1942-45, Art Student's League, 1946, Ill. Inst. tech., 1948; m. Lionel William Wathall, Nov. 10, 1945; children—Heather Lynn (dec.), Jeffrey Lee. Dept. artist Liberty Mut. Ins. Co., Chgo., 1941-43; with Palenskie-Young Studio, 1943-46; free lance illustrator N.Y. Times, Chgo. Tribune, Saturday Rev. Lit., 1948-50; co-owner, operator Pangaea Gallery/Studio, Fish Creek, Wis.; pvt. tutor, tchr. studio classes. Exhibited one-man show Crossroads Gallery, Art Inst. Chgo., 1973; exhibited group shows including Critics' Choice show Art Rental Sales Gallery Art Inst. Chgo., 1972, Evanston North Shore exhbns., 1964, 65, Chgo. Soc. Artists, 1967, 71, Union League, 1967, 72, Women in Art, Appleton (Wis.) Gallery Art, Milw. Art Mus., 1986, Neville Pub. Mus., Green Bay, Wis., 1987; represented in permanent collection Witte Meml. Mus., San Antonio, Miller Art Ctr., Stugeon Bay, Wis.; executed mural (with F. Wiater) Talbot Lab. U. Ill., Urbana, 1940. Active Campfire Girls, Chgo., 1968, 70; art chmn., mem. exec. bd. local PTA, 1959-60; active various art festivals, 1967—. Recipient Newcomb award U. Ill., 1940, awrd U. Ill., 1988. Mem. Chgo. Soc. Artists (rec. sec. 1968-77), Internat. Platform Assn., Accademia d' Europa, Soc. Illustrators, Wis. Arts Council, Northeast Wis. Arts Council (dir.), Alumni Assn. Art Inst. Chgo., Accademia d'Europa, Internat. Platform Assn. Republican. Mem. Unity Ch. Contbr. articles, illustrations to mags. and newspapers. Home: 3992 Juddville Rd Fish Creek WI 54212

BECKER, BLYTHE CHARLIN, systems analyst; b. Port Chester, N.Y., July 10, 1950; d. Charles Anthes and Easter Zoe (Bradner) B.; m. Steven Russell Patrick, Nov. 15, 1986. AB, Ind. U., 1972, MEd, 1975; MBA, U. Indpls., 1986. Tchr. Crawfordsville (Ind.) Sch. Corp., 1972-73; placement counselor Employment div. State of Ind., Crawfordsville, 1976-80; personnel coordinator R.R. Donnelley & Sons Co., Inc., Crawfordsville, 1980-81; personnel adminstr. 1st Nat. Bank and Trust, Crawfordsville, 1981-82; contract instr. State of Ind. Civil Def., Indpls., 1982-84; acct. State of Ind. Pub. Services Commn., Indpls., 1984-85; sr. systems analyst State of Ind. Info. Services Div., Indpls., 1987—; chairperson mktg. Inpls. Tng. Consortium, 1986—, bd. dirs. Vice precinct com. person Crawfrdsville Republicans, 1982-85. Mem. Eta Sigma Phi. Episcopalian. Lodge: Order Eastern Star (star point 1979-80). Home: 440 Newport Ct #C Greenwood IN 46143

BECKER, CAROL ANN, import company executive; b. Bronx, N.Y., Nov. 20, 1954; d. Isidore A. and Adele S. B.; B.S., Syracuse U., 1976. Staff writer public relations Schenley Industries, Inc., N.Y.C., 1976-77, exec. trainee, 1977-78, asst. brand mgr. Schenley Distillers Co. div., 1978-80, product mgr., 1980-84; v.p., dir. mktg. Shaw-Ross Internat. Importers, Inc., 1984—; dir. Lerner Shops, Inc. Jewish. Home: 201 E 62d St New York NY 10021 Office: 126 E 56th St New York NY 10022

BECKER, ELEANOR LOUISE HALEY, real estate executive; b. Attleboro, Mass., Nov. 26, 1929; d. James Robert and Mary Hazel (White) Haley; m. Donald H. Perry (dec. 1964); children: Calvin J., Ronald M.; m. Robert Ivan Becker; stepchildren: Bradford, Don. BE, Boston U., 1964. Lic. tchr. Mass. Tchr. spl. edn. Paxton (Mass.) pub. Schs., 1964-68; tutor in hosps., instns., pvt. homes, Worcester, Mass., 1968-77; real estate assoc. Robert B. Love Co., Paxton, 1985-87; owner, mgr. Paxton Area properties, Ltd., Inc., Paxton, 1987—. Mem. Nat. Assn. Realtors, Mass. Assn. Realtors, Greater Worcester Bd. Realtors, Women's Council Realtors, Women in Sales, Women's Networking, Am. Bus. Women Assn., Sales Execs. Club, Kurlan's Sandler Sales Assn., Paxton Women's Club, Worcester Bus. and Profl. Women, Nat. Assn. Rep. Women., Mass. Assn. Rep. Women, Worcester C. of C., Better Bus. Bur., Boston U. Alumni Assn. Congregationalist. Home and Office: 270 Richards Ave Paxton MA 01612

BECKER, HOPE, securities trader; b. N.Y.C., June 5, 1946; d. Harry Christopher and Lucy (de Villa) B. BA, Coll. of Mt. St. Vincent, 1968; MLS, Pratt Inst., 1972. Reference research librarian Morgan Stanley & Co., Inc., N.Y.C., 1972-75; librarian, research dir. William Sword & Co., Inc., Princeton, N.J., 1976-80, securities trader, 1984—. Adult Advisor Safe Rides, Princeton, N.J., 1985—; bd. dirs. Princeton Nursery Sch., 1985—. Republican. Roman Catholic. Club: Larchmont (N.Y.) Yacht. Office: William Sword & Co Inc 22 Chambers St Princeton NJ 08540

BECKER, JACQUELYN B., information specialist; b. East Chicago, Ind., July 25, 1950; d. Bob S. and Ruth Sarah (Brenman) B. B of Music, Northwestern U., 1972; MS, U. Ill., 1979. Tech. info. specialist Nat. Cancer Inst./NIH, Washington, 1979; corp. librarian Helene Curtis, Chgo., 1980-83, info. ctr. analyst, 1984, mgr. tech. info. services, 1985—; chmn. Info. Ctr. Exchange of Chgo., 1984-86, Chgo. Online User Group, Chgo., 1981-83. Author: The Beauty Industry: An Information Service Book, 1988. Fellow Am. Soc. Info. Sci. (chmn. 1983-84); mem. Associated Info. Mgrs., Soc. Cosmetic Chemists. Home: 1104 Castilian Ct Glenview IL 60025 Office: Helene Curtis 4401 W North Ave Chicago IL 60639

BECKER, JANET ARLENE, medical technologist; b. Wheeling, W.Va., Dec. 1, 1940; d. Ralph Charles and Clara Elizabeth (Bock) B.; B.S. in Med. Tech., West Liberty State Coll., 1963; cert. med. technologist Ohio Valley Med. Ctr., 1963; M.A. in Health Edn., W.Va. U., 1978. Edn. coordinator Ohio Valley Med. Center, Wheeling, W.Va., 1964-65, 1974, med. tech. edn. coordinator, 1965-68, hematology supr., 1968-82; with St. Margaret Meml. Hosp., Pitts., 1982—; ; instr. Wheeling Coll. Clin. Hematology, 1982; instr. Ohio Valley Med. Center, West Liberty State Coll., W.Va. No. Community Coll., Wheeling. Mem. Am. Soc. Clin. Pathologists (cert. med. technologist, specialist in hematology, clin. lab. scientist). Republican. Methodist. Home: RD 2 PO Box 319 W Alexander PA 15376 Office: 815 Freeport Rd Pittsburgh PA 15215

BECKER, JULIE, food products executive; b. Cambridge, Mass., Mar. 21, 1952; d. Stephen David and Mary Elizabeth (Freeburg) B. BA, Harvard U., 1974. Mgr. trainee McDonalds Corp., Boston, 1974, 2d asst. mgr., 1974-76, 1st asst. mgr., 1976-80; store mgr. McDonalds Corp., Norwood, Roslindale, Mass., 1976-80; area supr. McDonalds Corp., suburban Boston, 1980-83; tng. cons. McDonalds Corp., Boston, 1983, field cons., 1984; ops. mgr. McDonalds Corp., R.I., 1985-86; field service mgr. McDonalds Corp., Boston, 1986—. Mem. NOW. Home: 262 Arnold Rd North Attleboro MA 02760 Office: McDonalds Corp 690 Canton St Westwood MA 02090

BECKER, MARGARET WEBB, securities trader; b. Richmond, Va., July 20, 1956; d. E. Lovell and Margaret Webb (Thompson) B. B.A., Marymount Manhattan Coll., 1979; M.B.A., Pace Grad. Sch. Bus., N.Y.C., 1981; Cert., U. Nice, France, 1978. Mktg. specialist Amano Inc., N.Y.C., 1982-83; fin. dir. Interchange Ltd., London, Eng., 1983-85; govt. securities trader Smith Barney Harris Upham & Co., Inc., 1986—. Contbr. to reference book Access New York, 1981-82. Mem. numerous coms. N.Y. Jr. League, 1974—. Recipient Maj. Vol. Action award, Jr. League N.Y. Mem. Colonial Dames. Club: Colony. Home: 133 E 64th St New York NY 10021

BECKER, MARTHA JANE, radio executive; b. Bluefield, W.Va., Aug. 2, 1916; d. Ben H. and Martha Mabel Williams; m. William Pritchard Becker, Aug. 24, 1944; children—Jane Becker Delbridge, Beverly Becker Blvins. AB, W.Va. U., 1937. With Sta. WHIS, Bluefield, 1937-38; with Ziv Advt. Agy., Cin., 1939; tchr. Bramwell Schs. (W.Va.), 1940-44; with Sta. WVOW, Logan, W.Va., 1954—, comml. mgr., 1956—; instr. So. W.Va. Community Coll. Author: Mountain Roots Branching Out, 1976, The Pritchard Tree, 1985, The Diary of a Millionaire Coal Town-Bramwell, 1988. Mem. Logan Bus. and Profl. Women's Club, W.Va. C. of C. (bd. dirs.), Logan C. of C. (dir., past pres., W.Va. Assn. Broadcasters (Mel Burka Distinguished Broadcaster award 1986), DAR. Democrat. Presbyterian. Address: PO Box 1776 Logan WV 25601

BECKER, MARY JULIA, educator, author; b. Akron, Ohio, Aug. 29, 1928; d. Nick and Mary (Krieger) Lengyel; m. Samuel Becker, Dec. 3, 1953 (dec. May 1954); 1 child, Samuella Rebecca. B.S., U. Akron, 1962, M.S., 1965; postgrad. U. London, Cambridge U., Oxford U., U. New Delhi, U. Moscow. Sec. B.F. Goodrich Co., Akron, 1948-50, Goodyear Tire & Rubber Co., Akron, 1954-56; draftswoman Ohio Bell Telephone Co., Akron, 1950-51; tchr. Akron Pub. Schs., 1958—; counselor West Jr. High Sch., Akron, 1964-67. Guest editor Ohio Reading Tchr., Columbus, 1983; writer Ohio Survey Tests 1962-63, adv. editor TV Creative Writing Series Sta. WVIZ; contbr. articles to profl. jours. Vol. Ohio Ballet, 1983; pres. Hadassah, 1985-86. Recipient Martha Holden Jennings Master Tchr. award Kent State U., 1978, Tchr. of Week award Scholastic mag., 1981. Mem. Women in Communications, Akron Assn. Childhood Edn. (pres. 1960-61), Canton Writers Guild, Internat. Reading Assn., Akron Manuscript Club, Ohio Speakers Bur., AAUW, Kappa Delta Gamma. Clubs: Toastmasters, College, Press (Akron). Lodge: B'nai B'rith. Home: 1894 Evergreen Ave Akron OH 44301

BECKER, MARY LOUISE, polit. scientist; b. St. Louis; d. W. R. and Evelyn (Thompson) Becker; B.S., Washington U., St. Louis, 1949, M.A. (Blewett fellow), 1951; Ph.D. (resident fellow 1952-56), Radcliffe Coll., 1957; postgrad. (Fulbright scholar) U. Karachi (Pakistan), 1953-54; div.; children—James, John. Intelligence research analyst Dept. State, Washington, 1957-59; internat. relations officer AID, Washington, 1959-64, community relations officer, 1964-66, sci. research officer, 1966-71, UN relations officer, 1971—; adviser U.S. dels. 19th, 21st, 23d, 25th, 26th, 28th, and 30th Governing Council sessions UN Devel. Program; adv. U.S. del. 3d prep. com. meeting World Conf. UN Decade for Women; lectr. internat. relations civic orgns., student groups, 1954—. Mem. adv. bd., chmn. student placement Washington Citizenship Seminar, Nat. YMCA-YWCA, Washington, 1961-71. Mem. Am. Polit. Sci. Assn., Soc. Internat. Devel., Assn. Asian Studies, Asia Soc., Am. Soc. Public Adminstrn., AAUW, Mo. Soc. Washington (sec. 1959-60), Mortar Bd., Chimes, Alpha Lambda Delta, Beta Gamma Sigma, Eta Mu Phi, Pi Sigma Alpha. Presbyterian. Clubs: International, Harvard (Washington). Author: Muhammed Iqbal, 1965. Contbg. editor: Concise Ency. of Middle East, 1973. Contbr. articles to govt. publs. Office: Agy for Internat Devel Washington DC 20523

BECKER, NANCY CAREN, real estate executive; b. Kenedy, Tex., Jan. 18, 1939; d. Bernard Boone and Cora Belle (Martin) Hinkle; m. Ronald G. Becker, June 8, 1957 (div. 1972); children: Diana Leigh, Ronald G., Guy Allen. Student, SW Tex. State U., 1960-65, Trinity U., San Antonio, 1972-73. Lic. real estate broker. Owner, broker Tri-County Realtors, San Marcos, Tex., 1974-79; pres. The Houston Group, Inc., 1979-82; mktg. dir. Timbertop Condominiums, Houston, 1982-85, Sonterra, San Antonio, 1985-86, The Roanoke, San Antonio, 1986—; v.p. Tex. ops. EN-COM Properties, Ltd., Mission, Kans., 1986—; lectr. tng. cons., San Marcos, Houston, 1971—; mgmt. cons. MPS Cons., Houston, 1980-84. Mem. exec. com. So. Tex. chapter March of Dimes, San Antonio; internat. del. to World's Fair Girl Scouts USA, N.Y.C., 1970. Mem. Bus. and Profl. Women (pres. 1975), League Women Voters, San Antonio C. of C. Republican. Episcopalian. Club: Petroleum. Lodge: Zonta. Home and Office: 7930 Roanoke Run #102 San Antonio TX 78240

BECKER, OLGA AGATHA, law publisher, lawyer; b. St. Louis, Dec. 13, 1909; d. Frank A. and Agatha (Hartmann) B. Student pre-law, Washington U., St. Louis, 1926-28; LLB, Benton Coll. Law, St. Louis, 1933. Bar: Mo., 1931. Sr. tax editor Prentice-Hall, Inc., N.Y.C., 1942-45; opinions atty. U.S. Dept. Justice Mil. Govt. in Korea, 1947-48; adminstrv. asst. to treas. and chmn. bd. Harcourt, Brace & Co., N.Y.C., 1955-56; sole practice St. Louis, 1962—; pres., treas. Index/Citator System, Inc., St. Louis, 1969—. Mem. Mo. Bar Assn., St. Louis Bar Assn., Law Library Assn. St. Louis. Republican.

BECKER, SUSAN ANN, county administrator; b. Chgo., May 23, 1945; d. Marilyn Dubrin. BA, U. Tex., 1967; MA, U. Colo., 1975, Degree Edn. Specialist, 1976. Cert. tchr., counselor, Colo. Vol. VISTA ACTION, U.S. Govt., Houston, 1967-68; tng. specialist Denver, 1972-74; elem. tchr. Dallas Pub. Schs., 1967; secondary sch. tchr. Anchorage (Alaska) Schs., 1970-72; park adminstr. Jefferson County Open Space, Golden, Colo., 1976—. Mem. Colo. Parks and Recreation. Office: Jefferson County Conf Ctr 900 Colorow Rd Golden CO 80401

BECKERMAN, SUSAN JACOB, research chemist; b. Sunbury, Pa., Nov. 12, 1953; d. Robert Gerald and Anna Jean (Bastress) Reichenbauch; m. Jay Harry Beckerman, May, 24, 1986. BS in Chemistry, Bloomsburg State Coll., 1975; MS in Chemistry, Villanova U., 1986. Research chemist Cyprus Splty. Metals/Foote Mineral Co., Exton, Pa., 1975-85, supr. research chemist, 1985—. Patentee in field. Mem. Am. Chem. Soc. Home: 711 Valley Rd Phoenixville PA 19460 Office: Cyprus Splty Metals/Foote Mineral Co Rt 100 Exton PA 19341

BECKETT, GRACE, economics educator emerita; b. Smithfield, Ohio, Oct. 7, 1912; d. Roy Martin and Mary (Hammond) Beckett. AB, Oberlin Coll., 1934, AM, 1935; PhD, Ohio State U., 1939. Music supr. Pub. Schs., Kelleys Island, Ohio, 1935-36; grad asst. econs. Ohio State U., 1936-39; assoc. prof. econs. and music Ind. Central Coll., 1939-41: with U. Ill., Champaign-Urbana, 1941—, asst. prof. econs., 1945-51, assoc. prof. econs., 1951-73, assoc. prof. emerita Coll. Commerce and Bus. Adminstrn., 1973—. Author: Reciprocal Trade Agreements Program, 1941, 72; contbr. profl. pubs. Mem. Am. Econ. Assn., Music Educators Nat. Conf., Ill. Music Educators Assn., Econ. History Assn., Am. Finance Assn., Am. Hist. Assn., AAAS, N.Y. Acad. Scis., Ohio Acad. History, Ohio Hist. Soc., Winchester-Frederick County (Va.) Hist. Soc., Ill. Music Tchrs. Assn., Music Tchrs. Nat Assn., Interlochen Alumni Assn. (life), Friends of Art of the Allen Meml. Art Mus. at Oberlin Coll., Nat. Sch. Orch. Assn., Krannert Art Mus. Assos. (U. Ill.), Ohio State U. Alumni Assn., Nat. Honor Soc., Mary Ball Washington Mus. and Library, Met. Mus. Art (N.Y.C.) (nat. asso.), Oberlin Coll. Alumni Assn., Alpha Lambda Delta (hon.), Phi Beta Kappa, Pi Lambda Theta, Phi Chi Theta (hon.). Methodist. Club: Women's at the University of Ill., Oberlin Coll. Half-Century. Address: PO Box 386 Urbana IL 61801

BECKETT, JANE ELIZABETH, legal assistant; b. Akron, Ohio, Nov. 26, 1935; d. Arzie Lothair and Elizabeth Mary (Roberts) Howell; m. Joseph Karr Beckett, Aug. 26, 1961; 1 child, Linda Christine. BS, U. Akron, 1957; postgrad. U. So. Calif., 1977, UCLA, 1981. Exec. sec. Gen. Tire Co., Akron, 1957-59, legal sec., 1960-61; sec. Japanese polit. affairs U.S. Dept. State, Washington, 1959-60; legal sec. Henry Hardy, Esquire, San Francisco, 1961-68; legal sec. Tenneco West, Inc., Bakersfield, Calif., 1970-75, legal asst., 1976-87. Mem. Pet Pride, Pacific Palisades, Calif., 1974—, Presdl. Task Force Washington, 1984, Kern Children's Service Ctr., Bakersfield, Calif., 1984, Ag Boosters for FFA, Tehachapi, Calif., 1984. Mem. Nat. Assn. Legal Assts. (cert.), UCLA Atty. Asst. Alumni Assn., UCLA Alumni Assn. Republican. Presbyterian. Avocations: traveling, collecting cat figurines, piano, cooking, bicycling. Home: 28711 Gleneagle Ct Star Route 1 Box 2975A Tehachapi CA 93561 Office: Dole Bakersfield Inc 10000 Ming Ave Bakersfield CA 93311

BECKETT, SUSAN KAY, television executive; b. Webster City, Iowa, June 5, 1948; d. Ed Logan and Doris Darlene (Beckett) Oard; children—Gabrielle, Jessica. B.S., Iowa State U., 1969; J.D., U. Iowa, 1974; LL.M., NYU, 1977. Bar: Iowa 1974, N.Y. 1975, D.C. 1978. Assoc., Dewey, Ballantine, Bushby, Palmer & Wood, N.Y.C., 1974-76; trial atty. U.S. Dept. Justice, Washington, 1977-78; sr. atty. law dept. NBC, Inc., N.Y.C., 1978-80, sr. counsel, 1980-81, v.p. bus. affairs enterprises div., 1981—; v.p. NBC Internat. Ltd., Bermuda, 1982—; dir., asst. sec. Living Music, Inc., N.Y.C., 1979, Spectacular Music, Inc., N.Y.C., 1979—; dir., vice chmn. NBC Enterprises, Inc., N.Y.C., 1980—; v.p. NBC Ednl Enterprises Inc., Del., 1982—. Recipient Am. Jurisprudence award Lawyers Coop Pub. Co., 1973. Mem. N.Y. State Bar Assn., Iowa Bar Assn., D.C. Bar Assn., Order of Coif. Office: National Broadcasting Co 30 Rockefeller Plaza Amax Bldg Room 2828 New York NY 10112 •

BECKEY, SYLVIA LOUISE, lawyer; b. Los Angeles, Feb. 8, 1946; d. Andrew Gabriel and Rita Jane (Mayer) B. B.A. with spl. honors, U. Tex.-Austin, 1968, postgrad., 1968-69; J.D., Duke U., 1971; M.A. candidate Johns Hopkins Sch. Advanced Internat. Studies, 1973-74; LL.M., NYU, 1981. Bar: D.C. 1972, N.Y. 1975, U.S. Dist. Ct. (so. and ea. dist.) N.Y. 1975, U.S. Supreme Ct. 1975, U.S. Ct. Appeals (2d cir.) 1980. Legis. atty. Am. law div. Congl. Research Service, Library of Congress, Washington, 1971-74; assoc. Cole & Deitz, N.Y.C., 1975-76, Milberg, Weiss, Bershad & Specthrie,

N.Y.C., 1976-78; law. clk. to judge U.S. Dist. Ct. (so. dist.) N.Y., 1979-80; asst. chief div. comml. litigation Office of Corp. Counsel of City of N.Y., 1980-86; spl. master Supreme Ct. State of N.Y.-N.Y. County, 1984-86; spl. counsel-enforcement U.S. Securities and Exchange Commn., N.Y.C., 1986—; guest speaker U. Witwatersrand Sch. Law, Johannesburg, S. Africa, 1973; guest researcher Ct. Library, Nairobi, Kenya, 1973; pro bono Internat. League Human Rights, N.Y.C., 1974-75, 8th ann. Conf. for World Peace through Law, Abidjan, Ivory Coast, W. Africa, 1973. Co-author Handbook for Drafting Jury Instructions, U.S. Dept. Justice Civil Rights Div., 1970; assoc. editor The Constitution of the United States of America-Analysis and Interpretation, 1972; author legis. reports on Equal Credit Opportunity Act; referee Am. Bus. Law Jour., 1980-81. Bd. dirs. Chalon Cooperative Bldg., Washington, 1972-73; chmn. fine arts com., mem. bd. dirs. St. Bartholomew's Community Club, St. Bartholomew's Episcopal Ch., N.Y.C., 1982-83. Grantee EEO, 1966, Hinds Webbs Fund, 1967. Mem. Women's Bar Assn. City of N.Y., NYU Law Alumni Assn., Duke U. Law Alumni Assn., Fed. Bar Council, Am. Fgn. Law Assn., Consular Law Soc., Dramatists Guild. Protestant Lawyers Guild, English Speaking Union, Met. Mus. Art, Chelsea Block Assn. and Hist. Soc. Democrat. Home: 235 W 22d St New York NY 10011 Office: US SEC NY Regional Office 26 Federal Plaza New York NY 10278

BECKLEIN, CAROL AUDREY MCKINLEY, infosytems business manager; b. N.Y.C., Dec. 30, 1939; d. Carlton Eugene and Gladys Audrey (Gundry) McKinley; m. Charles Becklein, May 12, 1962; 1 child, Alan Charles. AAS, N.Y.C. Community Coll., 1959; student, Inst. Basic Youth Conflicts, N.Y.C., 1975-78, Inst. Biblical Counseling, 1984-87. Dental hygienist R. J. Reilly, DDS, N.Y.C., 1959-64, David Levine, DDS, Smithtown, N.Y., 1972-78, H. Musoff, DDS, Setauket, N.Y., 1975-78; bookkeeper Boca Raton (Fla.) Christian Sch., 1978-81; office mgr. BAC Inc., Boca Raton, 1981-84, bus. mgr., 1984—; sales cons. Lifestyle Software Corp., Boca Raton, 1984-86. Mem. Crimewatch, Boca Raton, 1984-87; mem. firm believers Bibletown Community Ch., 1984-87; christian lay counselor, 1986-87. Republican.

BECKMAN, BRENDA MARSHALL, community college administrator; b. New Malden County, Surrey, Eng., May 8, 1934; came to U.S., 1960; d. Norris Bishop and Edith Rosamund (Clappé) Marshall; m. Erik Beckman, Oct. 23, 1959 (div. 1975); children: Monika Gawne, Kristina Finley, Diana. AA, Macomb County Community Coll., 1972; BA in Polit. Sci., Oakland U., 1973; MA in Polit. Sci., Cen. Mich. U., 1974. Instr. polit. sci. Delta Coll., University Center, Mich., 1974-75, assoc. dean instrn., 1978-83, dean acad. affairs, 1983-85; lectr. polit. sci. Saginaw Valley State Coll., University Center, 1975-77; instr. polit. sci. Oakland U., Rochester, Mich., 1977-78; exec. dean East campus Pima Community Coll., Tucson, 1985-86, v.p. acad. affairs, 1987, exec. dean East campus, 1987—; cons. in field. Contbg. author: (book) Preparing Professional Women for the Future, 1985. Mem. Tucson Tomorrow. U. Mich. Ctr. for Higher Edn. fellow, 1984-85. Mem. Am. Assn. Community and Jr. Colls., Nat. Council Instructional Adminstrs. (Mich. rep. 1983-84). Episcopalian. Office: Pima Community Coll 8202 E Poinciana Dr Tucson AZ 85730

BECKMAN, JUDITH, art educator; b. Amityville, N.Y., Mar. 12, 1951; d. Charles Frederick and Helen Marie (Colville) B. Student, U. Miss., 1969-71, George Washington U., 1971, U. Guadalajara, Mex., 1972, City Coll. City U. N.Y., 1978, Columbia U., 1979; BFA, Colo. U., 1973; MFA, Ohio U., 1975. Teaching assoc. Ohio U., Athens, 1974-75; silkscreen artist Chromacomp, Inc., N.Y.C., 1976; vis. artist Coll. Misericordia, Dallas, Pa., 1977; instr. Spanish Am. Inst., N.Y.C., 1978-79; prodn. coordinator Chromacomp, Inc., N.Y.C., 1978; instr. Coll. Misericordia, Dallas, Pa., 1978, Malcolm-King Coll., N.Y.C., 1979-80; bilingual instr. Lincoln Sch., Orange, N.J., 1979-80; teaching assoc. Ohio State U., Columbus, 1980-88; gallery dir. Kenyon Coll., Gambier, Ohio, 1988—; mem. curriculum com. dept. art history Ohio State U., Columbus, 1984-85; vis. lectr. Ohio State U., Mansfield, 1988; vis. instr. Oberlin (Ohio) Coll., 1988. Exhibited in group shows at Community Gallery, N.Y.C., 1978, The Massillon (Ohio) Mus., 1978, Western Ill. U., Macomb, Ill., 1979, Springfield Art Mus., 1980, Zaner Gallery, Rochester, N.Y., 1981, Frick Art Mus., Wooster, Ohio, 1983, Spark Gallery, 1984, Ohio State U. Gallery, 1985, El Paso Mus. of Art, 1987, Artreach Gallery, Columbus, 1987; presentations include Case Western Res. U., 1982, Ohio State U., 1984, 85, Newcomb Coll./Tulane U., New Orleans, 1985; contbr. articles to profl. jours. Instr. Rape Prevention Program Ohio State U., 1980—; mem. adv. bd. Thompson Recreation Ctr., Columbus, Ohio, 1986—. Ohio State U. grantee, 1986; Com. for the Visual Arts, Inc. Exhbn. grantee, 1978, Bklyn. Arts and Culture Assn. grantee, 1979. Mem. Coll. Art Assn., Women's Caucus for Art (pres., co-founder Ohio chpt.), Nat. Women's Studies Assn., Nat. Mus. Women in Arts, Columbus Art League, Artreach Inc., Ohio State U. Grad. Student Assn. (pres. 1983-84), Zeta Tau Alpha, Alpha Lambda Delta. Home: 5635 Thompson Rd Ashville OH 43103

BECKMAN, JUDITH KALB, financial counselor and planner, lecturer, writer; b. Bklyn., June 27, 1940; d. Harry and Frances (Cohen) Kalb; m. Richard Martin Beckman, Dec. 16, 1961; children: Barry Andrew, David Mark. BA, Hofstra U., 1962; MA, Adelphi U., 1973, cert. fin. planning, 1984. Promotion coordination pub. relations Mandel Sch. for Med. Assts., Hempstead, N.Y., 1973-74; exec. dir. Nassau Easter Seals, Albertson, N.Y., 1974-76; dir. pub. info. Long Beach Meml. Hosp., N.Y., 1976-77; account rep. First Investors, Hicksville, N.Y., N.Y.C., 1977-78; sales asst., then account exec. Josephthal & Co. Inc., Great Neck, N.Y., 1978-81; v.p., cert. fin. planner Arthur Gould Inc., Great Neck, 1981-88; pres. fin. solutions Seco West Ltd. and Goldner Siegfried Assocs. Inc., Westbury, N.Y., 1988—; adj. instr. Adelphi U., Garden City N.Y., 1981-83, Molloy Coll., Rockville Ctr., N.Y., 1982-84; lectr. SUNY-Farmingdale, 1984-85; creater, presenter seminars, workshops on fin., investing, 1981—. Fin. columnist The Women's Record, 1985—; writer quar. newspaper The Reporter, 1987. Recipient citation for leadership Town of Hempstead, N.Y., 1986. Coordinator meat boycott, L.I., 1973; co-founder, chairperson L.I. del. High Profile Men and Women, Colonie Hill, Hauppauque, N.Y., 1985. Recipient Bus. Writer award Press Club, 1987. Mem. Nat. Assn. Women Bus. Owners L.I. (bd. dirs. 1987—), Women's Econ. Developers of L.I. (bd. dirs. 1985—), Internat. Assn. Fin. Planners (L.I. chpt.), Inst. Cert. Fin. Planners, L.I. Ctr. Bus. and Profl. Women (pres. 1984—), C.W. Post Tax Inst., Am. Soc. Women Accts. Republican. Jewish. Avocations: theater, classical music, opera, reading. Home: 2084 Beverly Way Merrick NY 11566 Office: Goldner Siegfried Assocs 400 Post Ave Westbury NY 11590

BECKNER, MARY KATHRYN, accountant; b. Mendota, Ill., Dec. 5, 1904; d. Edward J. and Mary (Hoerner) Cannon; student pub. schs.; m. Lester W. Beckner, Dec. 5, 1931. Pvt. sec., 1922-41; treas. Wayside Press, Inc., 1941—, also dir.; sec.-treas., dir. Kenneth B. Butler & Asso., 1944—; treas. Butler Typo-Design Research Center, 1951—, Surrey Hill Arabians, Inc.; dir., treas. Packaging Digest Inc., 1964-70. Mem. Red Cross Canteen, Mendota Community Hosp. Aux.; bd. dirs. LaSalle County unit Am. Cancer Soc. Mem. Ill., Mendota chambers commerce, Nat. Council Catholic Women, Nat. Secs. Assn. (Sec. of Yr. Aishi chpt., treas. 1977—), Internat. Arabian Horse Assn. Roman Catholic. Elk. Clubs: Woman's (treas. pub. affairs dept.); Antique Automobile of America (sec.-treas. Mendota). Home: 1312 Burlington St Mendota IL 61342 Office: 700 14th Ave Mendota IL 61342

BECKWITH, NANCY ELLEN, quality assurance specialist; b. Worcester, Mass., May 26, 1954; d. Carl Richard and Ann Marie (Ahern) Pedersen; m. Andrew Jackson Beckwith, Aug. 14, 1982; children: George, Tina, Judith. AS, U. New Haven, 1983, BS, 1984; MBA, Rensselaer Poly. Inst., 1986. Sec. Gen. Dynamics/Electric Boat Div., Groton, Conn., 1973-76, quality assurance analyst, 1976-81, quality assurance sr. analyst, 1981-83, quality systems sr. analyst, 1983-86, quality assurance specialist, 1986-88; supr. quality assurance Gen. Dynamics/Electric Boat Div., Groton, 1988—. Mem. Am. Soc. Quality Control (program dir. Groton 1986-87), Nat. Assn. Female Execs., Alpha Sigma Lambda. Democrat. Roman Catholic. Home: 1287 Flanders Rd Mystic CT 06355 Office: Gen Dynamics Electric Boat Div Eastern Point Rd Groton CT 06340

BEDASKE, ANGELA MARGARET, banker; b. Buffalo, N.Y., Jan. 20, 1961; d. Chester Jay and Rose Mary (Carriero) B. BS in Fin., Canisius Coll., 1983. Proof machine operator Metroteller Systems, Inc., Buffalo, 1983-84, mgr. proofing dept., 1984-85, mgr. point of banking dept., 1985-86, asst. v.p. settlement ops. dept., 1986—. Active Ladies aux. Brant (N.Y.) Vol. Fire Co. #1, 1977—, Altar and Rosary Soc. Our Lady of Mt. Carmel Ch., Brant, 1977—, organist, choir dir., 1984—. Mem. Am. Inst. Banking, Nat. Assn. Female Execs. Republican. Home: 10083 Brant Angola Rd Angola NY 14006 Office: Metroteller Systems Inc 237 Main St Suite 1200 Buffalo NY 14203

BEDFORD, DOROTHY LYNN, banker; b. Boonton, N.J., Feb. 10, 1956; d. Nathaniel Forrest and Roberta (Skinner) B.; m. Rush Taggart III, Mar. 29, 1985; 1 child, Natalie Ann. A.B., Princeton U., 1978; M.B.A., Harvard U., 1982. Research asst. Temple, Barker & Sloane, Lexington, Mass., 1978-81; asst. treas. Chem. Bank, N.Y.C., 1982-85, asst. v.p. Banker's Trust, N.Y.C., 1985—. Pres. Princeton U. Class 1978, N.J., 1983-88; mem. exec. com. Alumni Council of Princeton U., 1984—. Republican. Mem. United Ch. of Christ. Clubs: N.Y. Yacht, Princeton of N.Y. (N.Y.C.), Indian Harbor Yacht. Avocation: competitive sailing. Home: 392 Washington Ave Pelham NY 10803 Office: Bankers Trust 280 Park Ave 12-W 10015 Latin Am Mcht Banking New York NY 10015

BEDFORD, MADELEINE ALANN PECKHAM, civic worker; b. Ontario, Calif., Jan. 25, 1910; d. Allen Lewis and Madeleine (Elliott) Peckham; A.B., U. Calif., Berkeley, 1930, M.A., 1937; LL.D. (hon.), Tex. Christian U., 1973; m. Charles Francis Bedford, Dec. 30, 1930; children—Madeleine Alann, Frances Ellen, Charlotte Jean. Supr. tchr. tng. and counseling, in charge testing Univ. High Sch., U. Calif., Berkeley, 1931-38; tchr. English to fgn. born San Leandro (Calif.) Evening Schs., 1931-38; treas. Tarrant County Day Care Assn., 1953-54; pres. Ft. Worth and Tarrant County council Camp Fire Girls, 1961-63, mem. Nat. council, 1968-75, pres. Nat. council, 1965-68, NGO rep. to UN, 1968-69, nat. bd. dirs., 1960-68, bd. dirs. Houston council, 1971-72, mem. congress of Nat. Camp Fire Girls, 1975—; pres. Ft. Worth Lit. Council, 1963-65; v.p. Tarrant County United Fund and Community Council, 1963-66, mem. exec. com. bd. dirs., 1963—; pres. Ft. Worth chpt. Am. Field Service, 1964-66; chmn. budget sub-com. United Fund, 1959-68, chmn. met. div. Tarrant County, 1970; chmn. speakers tours, films div., United Way Tarrant County Campaign, 1973, chmn. planning and research div., 1973-75; v.p. United Way Met. Tarrant County, 1973-75, chmn. community services div., 1985-86; mem. exec. com. United Way Tex., 1979—; sec. Tex. United Community Services, 1968-70, v.p., 1970-73, pres., 1973-75; mem. Mid-Am. Regional Vol. Task group United Way Am., mem. nat. com. agy. support, 1975-80; Tex. state rep. for UNICEF, 1969—, mem. coordinating bd. for U.S. Com. of UN Childrens Fund, 1981—; chmn. Mayor's Council on Youth Opportunity, 1972-73; del. White House Conf. on Children and Youth, 1970; sec. social services adv. com. Tex. Dept. Human Resources, 1975-76, chmn., 1976-77; mem. nat. bd. Nat. Conf. Social Welfare, 1976-80; colleague nat. assembly Nat. Vol. Health and social welfare orgns., 1978-80; bd. dirs. Tarrant County chpt. ARC; bd. dirs. United Cerebral Palsy, pres. Tarrant County Br., 1976-78, mem. nat. corp., 1976—, v.p., Tex., 1977-83, pres., 1983-85; bd. dirs. Tarrant County Community Action Agy., Tarrant County Community Council, Tex. Social Welfare Assn.; trustee Assn. Grad. Edn. and Research, 1971—; trustee Tex. Christian U., also bd. visitors; trustee Tex. Coll. Osteo. Medicine Found., 1980—; mem. adv. council Sch. Social Work, U. Tex., Austin, 1980—; mem. adv. council for fin. assistance Tex. Dept. Human Resources, 1980—; pres. Womens Haven Tarrant County, 1979-81, bd. dirs., 1979-86; mem. exec. com. Community Trust Tarrant County, 1981—; bd. dirs. Family and Individual Services Tarrant County, 1981-87, pres., 1985-87; bd. dirs. Ft. Worth Girls Club, 1979—; mem. nat. bd. dirs. Girls Club Am., 1983-86; bd. dirs. Ft. Worth Acad., 1985—; Fed. Emergency Mgmt. Act, 1985—; pres. bd. dirs. Family Service, 1985—; mem. adv. council for adult basic edn. Ft. Worth Ind. Sch. Dist., 1976—; fellow Forum of Ft. Worth, 1981—; mem. Dallas/Ft. Worth Chaplaincy Bd., 1983—; bd. dirs. Tarrant Area Community of Chs., 1979—, pres., 1984-87. Recipient Gulick award, 1961, Wo-he-lo award, 1968 Camp Fire Girls; award of Excellence for Outstanding Leadership and Service Tarrant County Community Council, 1964, Civic award First Lady Ft. Worth Altrusa, 1966, Hercules award for Outstanding Vol. Leadership in Social Welfare United Way, 1977, award for service to students 1983, Alumni Royal Purple award 1983 (both Tex. Christian U.), award for human service Sertoma, 1983; declared Ecumenist of Yr., Tarrant Area Community of Chs., 1986. Mem. Council World Affairs (pres. 1985-87, v.p. 1987—), Internat. Good Neighbor Council (v.p. 1987-87, pres. 1987—), Ft. Worth Lecture Found., DAR, Mortar Board, Family Service Assn. (bd. dirs.), Phi Beta Kappa (pres. Ft. Worth 1958-59), Alpha Chi Omega, Pi Sigma Alpha. Episcopalian. Clubs: Ft. Worth Woman's (past pres. history sect., Tex. Christian U. Woman's). Home: 7 Westover Rd Fort Worth TX 76107

BEDFORD, MARY RUTH, dietitian, educator, consultant; b. Roswell, N.Mex., May 31, 1923; d. Sidney McHenry and Jennie Pearl (Hutchison) B. B in Dietetics, Inst. Mgmt., James Madison U., 1943; MS, Kans. State U., Manhattan, 1971, PhD, 1975. Registered, lic. dietitian. Intern U. Colo. Med. Ctr., Denver, 1944; dietitian Presbyn. Med. Ctr., Denver, 1944-47, U. Iowa Hosps., Iowa City, 1947-51, Neb. State Tchrs. Coll., Chadron, 1951-52, State Home and Tng. Sch., Wheatridge, Colo., 1952-55; asst. chief dietetic service VA Med. Ctr., Ft. Lyon, Colo., 1955-56; chief dietitian Presbyn. Med. Ctr., Denver, 1956-63; cons. dietition State Bd. Health, N.C., 1963-68; instr. Ind. State U., Terre Haute, 1968-72, Kans. State U., Manhattan, 1972-75; assoc. prof., dir. coordinated undergrad. program in dietetics Va. Poly. Inst. and State U., Blacksburg, 1975-83; prof. grad. program in dietetics Mass. Gen. Hosp.-Inst. Health Professions, Boston, 1983-86; vis. prof. U. So. Miss, Hattiesburg, 1986; lectr. in field; cons. N.C. Bd. Health, Raleigh, 1963-68. Mem. editorial bds., contbr. articles to profl. jours;. Named one of Notable Americans of Bicentennial Era, 1976; recipient of award as designer of one of twenty-five outstanding foodservice facilities in U.S Insts. Mag. for Presbyn. Hosp., 1962; grantee Dept. HEW, 1977-81, VA, 1977-84, Va. Poly. Inst., 1976. Mem. Am. Dietetic Assn. (council edn. 1978-81, review panel accreditation 1986—), Acad. Mgmt., Am. Assn. Adult and Continuing Edn., Am. Sch. Food Service Assn. (cert. and personal devel. com. 1981-83, cert. adv. bd. 1983-84, chmn. coll. personnel sect. 1984-85, task force to develop master plan for edn. 1984, exec. bd. 1984-85, ad hoc nat. breakfast month com. 1984, ad hoc com. to determine sch. food service research needs 1984-85, chmn. coll. personnel sect. 1984-85, nominating com. 1985-86), Am. Soc. Hosp. Food Service Adminstrs. (chmn. spl. com. pubs. rev. 1982-83, research and devel. com. 1984,), Am. Assn. Higher Edn., Am. Ednl. Research Assn., Am. Home Econs. Assn. (co-chmn. instn. mgmt. sect. 1977-79), Am. Mgmt. Assn., Am. Soc. Tng. and Devel., Am. Soc. Allied Health Professions, Food Service Systems Mgmt. Edn. Council (nominating com. 1979-81, com. to study fins. 1981-83, treas. 1981-85, chmn. spl. com. pubs. rev. 1982-83, chmn. com. to develop guidelines for small grants 1983-85, chmn. 1987—), Inst. Food Tech., Soc. Advancement Food Service Research, Soc. Foodservice Systems, Soc. Nutrition Edn., West Cen. Ind. Dietetic Assn. (chmn. edn. and service com., pres.-elect 1971-72), Raleigh Dietetic Assn. (pres.-elect 1964-65, pres. 1965-66), Denver Dietetic Assn. (pres.-elect 1954, pres. 1955), Phi Delta Gamma, Phi Upsilon Omicron, Omicron Nu. Mem. Christian Ch. Home and Office: 110 S Festival Dr Apt A5 El Paso TX 79912

BEDFORD, RUTH ALICE HAEDIKE (MRS. EDWIN GARRARD BEDFORD), librarian; b. Chgo.; d. William Henry and Alice (Lohr) Haedike; student Beloit Coll., 1932-33; B.S., U. Ill., 1936, M.S., 1954, post-grad.; m. Edwin Garrard Bedford, June 6, 1942; children—David Edwin, Ellen Louise. Instr. U. Ill. Library, Urbana, 1954-64; asst. prof. library sci. U. Utah Libraries, Salt Lake City, 1964-68; asso. librarian Butler Library, State U. Coll., Buffalo, 1968-79, mem. personnel com. tech. services div., 1972-75, chmn., 1974-75, mem. faculty advisory council instructional resources, 1971-73. Mem. tech. services com. Western N.Y. Library Resources Council, 1968-73. Mem. State U. N.Y. Librarians' Assn., Am. Assn. U. Profs., ALA, Kenan Center (charter mem.), Delta Phi Alpha. Club: Order Eastern Star. Home: 905 Charlesgate Circle East Amherst NY 14051

BEDIKIAN, RHONDA COLETTE, accountant, financial consultant; b. Jersey City, Jan. 20, 1950; d. Hyman and Marie-Jose Gabrielle (Gerard) Rodetsky; m. Bruce Melvin Miller, Aug. 16, 1969 (div. Aug. 1976); 1 child, Brent Joseph; m. Johnny Nobar Bedikian, Dec. 29, 1985; 1 child, Denise Sarah. AA, Bergen Community Coll., 1976; BS in Acctg. and Fin., U. So. Calif., 1978. Bookkeeper JMRH Inc., Tarzana, Calif., 1977-79; jr. acct. Motown Records Inc., Hollywood, Calif., 1979-80; chief acct. Chrysalis Records Inc., Los Angeles, 1980-83; acctg. mgr. Platt Music Corp., Torrance, Calif., 1983; asst. controller Contempo Casuals Inc. Div. Neiman-Marcus, Los Angeles, 1984-88; dir. acctg. Capitol Records, Inc. Div. Thorn-EMI, Hollywood, Calif., 1988—; cons. in field. Active City of Hope. Office: Capitol Records Inc 1750 N Vine St HV8 Hollywood CA 90028

BEDKE, KATHRYN LYNN, lawyer; b. Kearney, Nebr., Nov. 3, 1951; d. Richard August Tatem and Helen Kathryn (Weitzel) Bedke. B.A. in English and German, Kirkland Coll., 1974; student U. Vienna-Austria, 1972-73; M.T.S. in Religion, Harvard Div. Sch., 1976; J.D., Case Western Res. U., 1979. Bar: N.Y. 1981. Assoc., Demov, Morris, and Hammerling, N.Y.C., 1979-81, White & Case, N.Y.C., 1981—. Pres., Kirkland Coll. Alumnae Assn., 1982—; mem. Hamilton Coll. Alumni Assn., 1981-84. George F. Baker Trust fellow, 1971-72, 73-74; Rockefeller fellow, 1974-75; Soc. Benchers award, 1979. Mem. Case Western Res. Jour. Internat. Law, 1976-77, Case Western Res. Law Rev., 1977-79. Mem. ABA, N.Y. State Bar Assn., (com. on internat. law 1984—), Nebr. Soc. of N.Y., Inc. (pres., legal advisor 1984—). Democrat. Home: 250 W 24th St Apt 1CE New York NY 10011

BEDNAR, BARBARA ANN, executive recruitment specialist; b. Newark, May 6, 1946; d. Charles and Mary (Nagy) B. Student, Newark State Tchr. Coll., 1964-66; AA, Newark Sch. Fine and Indsl. Arts, 1966. Account exec. Keyes, Martin and Co., Springfield, N.J., 1967-82, recruitment dir., 1982-84; sr. account exec. Equity Advt., N.Y.C., 1984-85; v.p. acctg. service Paul D. Weinberg Advt., N.Y.C., 1985-86; mgr. client service Rada Recruitment Communications div. Grey Advt., N.Y.C., 1986-88; dir. recruitment div. Carlino Barish, Princeton, N.J., 1988—. Mem. Nat. Assn. Female Execs., Internat. Assn. Personnel Women, United Luth. Soc., Sokol. Home: 235 Rankin Ave Cranford NJ 07016 Office: Carlino Barish 101 Wall St Princeton NJ 08540

BEDNAR, CAROLYN DIANE, dentist; b. Akron, Ohio, Oct. 7, 1953; d. William Adolph and Marilyn Minns (Hadfield) B.; m. Steven Kent Good, Sept. 25, 1982; 1 child, David Steven Good. BA in Chemistry, De Pauw U., 1975; DDS, Ohio State U., 1978. Gen. practice dentistry Columbus, 1978—; mem. staff Southwest Community Health Ctr., Columbus, Ohio, 1979-82. Vol. pub. oral cancer screenings and dental edn., Am. Cancer Soc., Columbus; vol. speaker dentistry Columbus Pub. Schs., 1982-85, 88; vol. fundraiser Multiple Sclerosis Soc., Columbus, 1986-88. Mem. ADA, Ohio Dental Assn., Columbus Dental Assn., Profl. Women's Forum (sec. 1982-84), Ohio State U. Coll. Dentistry Alumni Assn., Alpha Phi. Republican. Home: 8862 Easton Dr Pickerington OH 43147 Office: 1600 Brice Rd Reynoldsburg OH 43068

BEDNAR, GWEN MICHELLE, service executive, management consultant; b. Cleve., Sept. 19, 1956; d. Edward Joseph and Barbara Ann (Kerley) B. BBA, U. Miami, 1985, MBA, 1987. Flight attendant Am. Internat. Airlines, Pomona, N.J., 1980-81; ops. mgr. Heritage Motor Inn, Cape May, N.J., summers 1978-85, fin. cons., 1985—; mgmt. cons. Contour Piling Corp., Northfield, N.J., 1986—. Mem. Cape May C. of C., Cape May Hotel/Motel Assn., Coconut Grove Jaycees, Internat. Bus. Assn., Assn. MBA Execs. Republican. Roman Catholic. Office: Heritage Motor Inn Beach Dr & Stockton Pl Cape May NJ 08204

BEDNAREK, JANA MARIA, biochemist; b. Bratislava, Czechoslovakia, Mar. 8, 1934; came to U.S., 1966, naturalized, 1971; d. Rudolf and Helena (Lastovickova) Kozdera; m. Milan Kraus, June 23, 1957 (div. 1963); m. Milan B. Bednarek, Nov. 27, 1966; 1 child, Paula Helen. M.S., Charles U., 1959; postgrad. NYU, 1966-67; Ph.D., Med. Sch. Va., 1973. Fellow dept. biochemistry Med. Sch. Va., Charlottesville, 1973-75; research assoc. dept. chemistry U. S.C., Columbia, 1975-79; research assoc. dept. biochemistry, Med. Sch. S.C., Charleston, 1979 80; research chemist hematology and oncology service Walter Reed Army Med Ctr., Washington, 1981—. Contbr. articles to profl. jours. Mem. N.Y. Acad. Scis., Sigma XI. Democrat. Roman Catholic. Avocations: hiking; skiing; volleyball. Office: Walter Reed Army Med Ctr Hematology Oncology Dept Georgia Ave Washington DC 20307

BEDSOLE, ANN SMITH, state senator; b. Selma, Ala., Jan. 7, 1930; d. Malcolm White and Sybil (Huey) Smith; m. Massey Palmer Bedsole, 1958; children: Mary Martin Bedsole Riser, John Henry Martin, Margaret Loraine. Student, U. Ala., 1948, U. Denver, 1955-56; LLD (hon.), Mobile Coll., 1984, Huntingdon Coll., 1985. Mem. Ala. Rep. Exec. Com., 1966-74; del. seconded nomination Nixon for Pres. Rep. Nat. Conv., 1972; Rep. Presdl. Elector, 1972; Ala. state senator, chair com. on agr., conservation and forestry, mem. coms. on edn., health, judiciary, mem. joint interim com. on mcpl. govt., mem. com. arts, tourism and cultural resources; mem. Nat. Conf. State Legislatures. V.p. Mobile Child Care Found.; trustee Huntington Coll., Mobile United, Dauphin Way United Meth. Ch., Hist. Blakeley Authority; active Mobile Hist. Devel. Found., Spring Hill Coll., Hist. Mobile Tours, Inc.; mem. Jr. League of Mobile; bd. dirs. Vol. Mobile, Inc. Recipient M.O. Beale Scroll of Merit award Mobile Press Register, 1971-72, award for outstanding contbn. to forestry in Ala. Soc. Am. Foresters, 1986, Legislative Conservationist of Yr. award Ala. Wildlife Fedn., 1987; named 1st Lady of Mobile, 1972. Mem. Ala. Bus. and Profl. Women's Found. (trustee, inducted into Women's Acad. of Honor 1987). Methodist. Office: PO Box 11642 Mobile AL 36616 *

BEDWAY, MARIANN LOUISE, small business owner; b. Pottsville, Pa., Apr. 29, 1940; d. John Joseph and Mary Ann (Sahadi) B. AA, Pa. State U., Pottsville, 1960. Asst. buyer Woodward and Lothrop, Washington, 1961-67; hostess, guide U.S. Pavilion at Expo '67 U.S. Info. Agy., Montreal, Can., 1967; travel sales rep. Pan Am. Airlines, Washington, 1968-78; pres Internat. Elegance, Washington, 1978—; fashion cons., Washington, 1984—. Mem. Am. Women's Econ. Devel., Japan Am. Soc., Nat. Assn. Female Execs. Roman Catholic. Home and Office: PO Box 19544 Washington DC 20036

BEE, ANNA COWDEN, educator; b. Birmingham, Ala., Feb. 17, 1922; d. Porter Guthrie and Marion Irene (McCurry) Cowden; A.B., Samford U., 1944; student Chalif Sch. Dance, N.Y.C., 1950-54; m. Alon Wilton Bee, Oct. 21, 1942; children—Anna Margaret Bee Foote, Alon Wilton. Mem. faculty Byram High Sch., Jackson, 1945-52; mem. faculty Hinds Jr. Coll., Raymond, Miss., 1952—, dir. Hi-Steppers, girls' precision dance group; chaperone Miss Mississippi to Miss Am. Pageant; condr. charm clinics for teenagers; judge beauty pageants. Bd. dirs. Multiple Sclerosis Soc., Jackson, 1966-72; state chmn. Miss. Easter Seal Soc. campaign, 1966, 79; chmn. women's div. United Way, Jackson, 1973. Named Woman of Achievement, Jackson Bus. and Profl. Women's Club, 1967-78; disting. faculty of the yr. award Hinds Jr. Coll., 1981; Miss. Legislature commendation for contbn. to youth, 1981. Mem. Nat. Faculty Dance Educators Am., Dance Masters Am., Miss. Edn. Assn., Miss. Assn. Health and Phys. Edn., Beta Sigma Omicron. Democrat. Baptist. Producer halftime shows Gator Bowl, 1958, 64, 81, Sugar Bowl, 1960, Hall of Fame Bowl, 1977, 79. Home: 304 Alta Woods Blvd Jackson MS 39154 Office: Hinds Jr Coll Raymond MS 39154

BEEBE, CAROLINE SLOCUM, personnel executive; b. N.Y.C., Apr. 24, 1934; d. Carl Curtis and Charlotte (Slocum) Bryant; m. Richard M. Beebe, Jan. 25, 1958; children: Stacy, Kate. BA in Psychology, Vassar Coll., 1956. Operating v.p. Bloomingdale's Dept. Store, N.Y.C., 1958-87; v.p. personnel Assoc. Mdse. Corp., N.Y.C., 1987—; bd. dirs. Work Place Ctr., Columbia U. Sch. Social Work, 1984—. Bd. dirs., mem. exec. com. YWCA of N.Y.C., 1976—. Recipient Acad. Women Achievers award, YWCA of N.Y.C., 1976, Vol. of Yr. award, Jr. League N.Y.C., 1974. Presbyterian. Clubs: Vassar of N.Y.C.; Larchmont (N.Y.) Yacht. Office: Associated Merchandising Corp 1440 Broadway New York NY 10008

BEEBE, SUSAN KAY, agricultural agent; b. Albany, N.Y., July 6, 1956; d. John Alexander and Evelyn Marie (Tuft) Freer; m. Theodor Joseph Beebe Jr., June 19, 1982; 1 child, Nicholas. AAS, SUNY, Cobleskill, 1976; BS, U. Ga., 1978. Floral designer, sales rep. A. Casagrandi Inc., Albany, 1976-79; agricultur agt. Cooperative Extension, Ballston Spa, N.Y., 1979—. Contbr. articles to profl. jours. Mem. Eastern Dist. Agriculture Agts. Assn. (pres. chmn. 1981), N.Y. State Assn. Agriculture Agts. Republican. Presbyterian. Lodge: Soroptimist. Office: Cooperative Extension Assn 50 W High St Ballston Spa NY 12020

BEER, ALICE STEWART (MRS. JACK ENGEMAN), musician, educator; b. Redwood Falls, Minn., Sept. 29, 1912; d. Robert and Isabel (Montgomery) Stewart; m. Jack Engeman, Dec. 14, 1974; children by previous marriage: W. Robert, Jane K. Beer Mosher, Elizabeth S. Beer-Shilling. MusB, Northwestern U., 1934, MusM, 1952; postgrad., Johns Hopkins U., 1954, 60, Mexico City Coll., 1956, U. Md., 1957. Tchr. pub. schs., Lawton, Mich., 1934-39, Battle Creek, Mich., 1949-51; tchr. Balt. Pub. Schs., 1951-53, supr. music, 1953-77; tchr. summer sessions various colls. and univs., 1957—; adj. faculty Peabody Inst., John's Hopkins U., Balt., 1981-85; cons. Alliance for Arts in Edn., Balt. County Pub. Schs., 1982—, cons. curriculum, 1984—. Author: Teaching Suggestions, Birchard Music Series II and III, 1962, Teaching Music: What, How and Why, 1973, Teaching Music to the Exceptional Child: A Handbook for Mainstreaming, 1980, Teaching Music, 1982, Patriotic Color Sound Filmstrips, 1967-69; contbr. articles to profl. jours. Recipient Director's Recognition award for commitment to music edn. and extraordinary contbn. to art of teaching, 1986. Mem. Md. Hist. Soc., Balt. Mus. Art, Balt. Symphony Assn. Mem. Nat. Fedn. Press Women, Md. Fedn. Press Women, Nat. Conf. Music Educators, Md. Music Educators Assn., Nat. Trust Hist. Preservation, Soc. Preservation Md. Antiquities, Phi Beta. Democrat. Presbyterian. Clubs: Towson Univ., Women's of Johns Hopkins U. Home: 611 Debaugh Ave Towson MD 21204 Office: Johns Hopkins U Peabody Inst Music Edn Dept Baltimore MD 21202

BEER, BETTY LOUISE, lawyer; b. Waco, Tex., July 17, 1943; d. William Lester and Ruth (Parks) B.; m. Sherwood James Franklin, June 16, 1979; 1 son, Jacob Harrison. BA, Oberlin Coll., 1965; JD, St. Louis U., 1974. Bar: Ill. 1974. Assoc. Kavanagh Scully Sudow White & Frederick, Peoria, Ill., 1974-78; owner Betty L. Beer P.C., Aledo, Ill., 1978—; asst. states atty. Mercer County, Aledo, 1979-84. Editor St. Louis U. Law Jour., 1974. Bd. dirs. Mo. Pub. Interest Research Group, 1973-74, Peoria Civic Opera, 1975-78, Prairie State Legal Services, Inc., 1975-77; bd. dirs., pres. Peoria City Beautiful, 1975-78; active Tri County Women Strength, Peoria, 1975-76; founding mem. Mercer County Coalition Against Domestic Violence, 1984-85, Greasepaint Guild Theater (founder), Aledo, 1980-83; mem. Oberlin Planned Giving Council, 1988—. Mem. ABA, Ill. State Bar Assn. (estate planning council 1982, lawyer referral com 1975-82, ins. com., 1987, pres. 1981), Mercer County Bar Assn. (pres. 1985-87). Republican. Baptist. Lodge: PEO. Home: 109 E Main St Aledo IL 61231

BEER, JEANETTE MARY AYRES, foreign language educator; b. Wellington, N.Z.; d. Alexander Samuel and Una Doreen (Castle) Scott; m. Colin Gordon Beer; children: Stephen James Colin, Jeremy Michael Alexander. B.A., Victoria U., N.Z., 1954, M.A. 1st class, 1955; B.A. 1st class, Oxford U., Eng., 1958, M.A., 1962; Ph.D. (fellow), Columbia U., 1967. Asst. lectr. French Victoria U., Wellington, 1956; lectrice French and English U. Montpellier, France, 1958-59; instr. French Otago U., Dunedin, N.Z., 1963-64, Barnard Coll., Columbia U., N.Y.C., 1966-68; asst. prof. French Fordham U., Bronx, N.Y., 1968-69; asso. prof. Fordham U., 1969-76, prof., 1976-80; acting asso. dean Thomas More Coll., 1972-73, dir. medieval studies, 1972-80; prof. French Purdue U., West Lafayette, Ind., 1980—; head dept. fgn. langs. and lits. Purdue U., 1980-83; mem. nat. bd. cons. NEH, 1977—, asst. dir. div. fellowships and seminars, 1983-84. Author: Villehardouin—Epic Historian, 1968, A Medieval Caesar, 1976, Narrative Conventions of Truth in the Middle Ages, 1981, Medieval Fables: Marie de France, 1981; Master Richard's Bestiary of Love and Response, 1985; gen. editor: Teaching Language through Literature, 1971—; contbr. articles to profl. jours. NEH grantee, 1975; research fellow, 1980; summer fellow Ind. Com. for Humanities, 1985; Am. Philos. Soc. grantee, 1986. Mem. MLA, Medieval Acad., Internat. Arthurian Soc., Soc. Rencesvals, Am. Assn. Tchrs. French, Am. Philol. Assn. Anglican. Home: 256 W Hudson Ave Englewood NJ 07631 Office: Purdue U Dept Fgn Langs and Lits West Lafayette IN 47907

BEERBOWER, CYNTHIA GIBSON, lawyer; b. Dayton, Ohio, June 25, 1949; d. Charles Augustus and Sara (Rittenhouse) Gibson; m. John Edwin Beerbower, Aug. 28, 1971; 1 child, John Eliot. BA, Mt. Holyoke Coll., 1971; JD, Boston U., 1974; LLB, Cambridge U., Eng., 1976. Bar: N.Y. 1975. Assoc., Cadwalader, Wickersham & Taft, N.Y.C., 1975-76; assoc. Simpson, Thacher & Bartlett, N.Y.C., 1977-81, ptnr., 1981—. Mem. ABA, Assn. Bar City N.Y., N.Y. State Bar Assn. (com. co-chmn. 1987—). Presbyterian. Home: 720 Park Ave New York NY 10021 Office: Simpson Thacher & Bartlett 1 Battery Park Plaza New York NY 10004

BEERMAN, LIZABETH ROSWELL, commodity service company executive; b. Los Angeles, Dec. 10, 1947; d. Gilbert Francis and Nena (Marquard) Roswell; m. William Elmer Beerman, Jan. 31, 1970 (div.); children: Cade, Vincent. BA, Calif. State U., Los Angeles, 1969; MA, U. No. Colo., 1980. Tchr. various schs., Calif.; coordinator reading programs local schs., Rifle, Colo., 1971-73; dir. admissions CRMS, Carbondale, Colo., 1979-83; dir. ops. CQG, Glenwood, Colo., 1983—; ptnr. Party Perfect, Carbondale, 1986—. Bd. dirs. Mountain Valley Devel., Glenwood, 1974-86; ednl. cons. Coll. Bound, Carbondale, 1986—. Mem. Nat. Assn. for Female Execs., Carbondale C. of C. (pres. 1984-86). Republican. Clubs: Sopris Swim and Dive (bd. dirs. 1984—), Sunlight Ski (bd. dirs. 1984—) (Glenwood). Home: 1609 Defiance Carbondale CO 81623 Office: CQG PO Box 758 Glenwood CO 81602

BEERS, CHARLOTTE L., advertising agency executive; b. Beaumont, Tex., July 26, 1935; d. Glen and Frances (Bolt) Rice; m. Donald C. Beers, 1971; 1 dau., Lisa. B.S. in Math. and Physics, Baylor U., Waco, Tex., 1958. Group product mgr. Uncle Ben's Inc., 1959-69; sr. v.p., dir. client services J. Walter Thompson, 1969-79; chief operating officer Tatham-Laird & Kudner, Chgo., from 1979, now mng. ptnr., chmn. and chief exec officer; dir. Federated Dept. Stores, Chgo. Public TV Channel 11. Named Nat. Advt. Woman of Yr. Am. Advt. Fedn., 1975. Mem. Am. Assn. Advt. Agencies (chmn. from 1987), Women's Advt. Club Chgo., Chgo. Network. Republican. Episcopalian. Office: Tatham-Laird & Kudner 980 N Michigan Ave Chicago IL 60611 *

BEERS, DORIS CREIGHTON, realtor; b. Enfield, N.H., Aug. 6, 1908; d. Harris Edgar and Ada (French) Creighton; grad. public schs.; m. Robert Clayton Beers, Sept. 22, 1934 (dec. Sept. 1965); children—Diane Elaine (Mrs. Edward C. Schmults), Bradford B. Head sec. to chmn. Democratic State Com. N.H., 1929-30; sec. Gen. Motors Acceptance Corp., 1930-32, J.R. Poole, Boston, 1932-36; saleswoman Town & Country Homes, Boston, 1956-58; founder Cedar Realty, Wellesley Hills, Mass., 1958, owner, 1958-81. Sec., Wellesley (Mass.) ARC Fund Drive, 1955; pres. Melrose (Mass.) Jr. High Sch. PTA, 1953; chmn. bus. Wellesley United Fund Drive, 1974. Mem. Greater Boston Real Estate Bd., Nat. Assn. Realtors, West of Boston Realtors (sec. Council 1966), Nat. Assn. Women Realtors, Wellesley C. of C. Congregationalist. (past sec. guild Melrose Highlands). Clubs: Wellesley Republican, Wellesley Women's (rec. sec. 1982-84).

BEESON, MARY RUTH (PETE), personnel mgmt. cons.; b. Glen Rose, Tex., Nov. 15, 1913; d. Quentin Orestes and Maude Elma (Embree) Gaither; student Wright's Law Sch., 1931, U. Tex., 1934, San Antonio Coll., 1937, St. Mary's U., 1937-39, Am. U., 1952-53; m. Charles Edward Beeson, Nov. 15, 1940; children—Peter Gaither Embree, Caroline Jane. Exec. asst. to state dir. of ops., Works Progress Adminstrn., San Antonio, 1935-40; certifying officer, adminstrv. asst. Civilian Personnel Office, Army Air Force, San Antonio Aviation Cadet Center, 1941-46; personnel officer IRS, Washington, 1957-63, employment officer, Austin Service Center, 1963-74, chmn. Fed. Women's Program Planning Com., 1963-68, chmn. Equal Employment Opportunity Planning Com., Austin Service Center, 1963-73, mem. regional commr.'s adv. com. on Fed. Women's Program, IRS, Dallas, Tex., 1972-74; cons. in personnel mgmt., Austin, 1976-77; cons. on curriculum, Camp Gary Job Corps, 1965. Chmn. Parent Edn. Com., Falls Church Schs., 1952-54; mem. exec. com. Community Coordinated Child Care Com., Austin, 1968-72; mem. adv. commn. to Tex. Legis. Council's study on the handicapped, Austin, 1970-73; mem. adv. com. on vocat. office edn. to Austin Ind. Sch. Dist., 1965-69; chmn. mayor's Com. on Devel. Child Care, Austin, 1970-75; chmn. Austin Mayor's Commn. on Status of Women, 1970-75, mem., 1975—; mem. citizens adv. bd. Travis County Juvenile Bd., 1981—. Recipient Outstanding Service to the Deaf award Tex. Edn. Agy., 1967, Fed. Woman's Award Bd. citation, Disting. IRS Worker for the Handicapped award IRS Commr., 1972, Pres.'s Com. on Employment Handicapped award, 1974. Mem. Internat. Personnel Mgmt. Assn., Austin Personnel Assn., Am. Mgmt. Assn. Unitarian. Inventor: Hycab, insulated coaster, car wastebasket. Home and Office: PO Box 160986 Austin TX 78716

BEESON, MONTEL EILEEN, human services administrator, gerontologist; b. El Dorado, Ark., Dec. 22, 1939; d. Waymon Willett and Myrtle May (Roach) B. BS in Recreation, Calif. State U., Hayward, 1963; MA in Edn. and Human Devel., Holy Names Coll., Oakland, Calif., 1979. Lic. nursing home adminstr.; cert. community coll. instr.; cert. gerontologist. Dist. exec. Ariz. Cactus-Pine council Girl Scouts U.S.A., Phoenix, 1963-66; dist. exec. San Francisco Bay council Girl Scouts U.S.A., Oakland, 1966-68, bus. mgr., 1968-71; exec. dir. Shabonee council Girl Scouts U.S.A., Moline, Ill., 1971-73, Tongass-Alaska council, Ketchikan, 1973-74, Muir Trail council, Modesto, Calif., 1974-78, Community Adult Day Health Services, Oakland, 1987—; asst. adminstr. Beulah Home, Inc., Oakland, 1980-86, elder care cons. 1986—; rehab. cons. Career Advancement Ctrs., San Leandro, Calif., 1979-80; preceptor Bd. Examiners Nursing Home Adminstrs., Sacramento, 1985. Mem. Am. Coll. Health Care Adminstrs., Am. Soc. on Aging, Calif. Specialists on Aging. Avocations: cross-country skiing, history, travel, reading, music. Home: 3393 Kiwanis St Oakland CA 94602

BEETS, HUGHLA FAE, educator; b. Eustace, Tex., Aug. 1, 1929; d. Hubert Edgar and Beatrice (Roark) Bonsal; m. Anneel Randolph Beets, Sept. 14, 1946. BA, North Tex. State U., 1958, MA, 1960; postgrad., U. Mass., 1967. Cert. tchr., Tex. Tchr. Seagoville (Tex.) Ind. Sch. Dist., 1958-65, Dallas Ind. Sch. Dist., 1965-70; owner, mgr. Mabank (Tex.) Ins. Agy., 1970-77, Beets Interiors, Mabank, 1970-77; ptnr., mgr. Cedar Creek Title Co., Mabank, 1977-80; tchr. govt. and econs. Athens (Tex.) Ind. Sch. Dist., 1981—; cons. U.S. Office Edn., Washington, 1968-69; mem. devel. com. Edn. Profl. Devel. Act Tex. Edn. Agy., 1969. Cons. edn. com. Goals for Dallas, 1969; vice chairperson Kaufman (Tex.) County Improvement Council, 1975. Recipient Outstanding Ex-Student award Trinity Valley Community Coll., Athens, 1974. Mem. NEA, Athens Edn. Assn. (pres. 1982-83), Tex. State Tchrs. Assn. (pres.-elect Dist. X 1970), Tex. Classroom Tchrs. Assn. (state bd. dirs. 1969-70), Classroom Tchrs. Dallas (pres. 1968-69), Mabank C. of C. (sec. Indsl. Found. 1971-75, bd. dirs. 1978-80, Citizen of Yr. 1977). Democrat. Methodist. Home: 106 Canton St PO Box 318 Mabank TX 75147 Office: Athens High Sch 708 E College Athens TX 75751

BEETZ, MARGARET O'CONNOR, health and beauty business executive, modeling school executive, model; b. Addis Ababa, Ethiopia, Dec. 12, 1955; came to U.S., 1967; d. Kevin Gordon and Mary (Symonds) O'Connor; m. Stephen Paul Beetz, Aug. 19, 1978. Student Aurora Coll., 1974-75; B.S. in Bus. and Fin., U. Ill., 1978. With Paul & Steve, Mendota, Ill., 1978-83; bookkeeper Brookhill Corp., Mendota, 1983—; asst. dir. Montee Modeling Sch., Wheaton, Ill., 1980-83; owner, dir. Elan Sch. Modeling, Peru, Ill., 1983—; pres., owner Total Image, Inc., Peru, 1984—; owner Body Tones, Inc. Collinsville, Ill.; registered model Suzanne Johnson Modeling Agy., Chgo., 1980—; asst. dir. Mrs. Am. Preliminaries, Ill., Iowa, Wis., N.D., S.D., Minn., 1981; asst. dir., scholarship chairperson Miss. Ill. Valley, Peru, 1985; cons. in field. Vice pres. Ill. Assn. Pvt. Colls. and Univs., 1975-76; v.p. Mendota Community Hosp. Aux., 1981, pres., 1982-84. Named to Outstanding Young Women Am., U.S. Jaycees, 1981; recipient Leadership award Ill. Hosp. Assn., 1984. Mem. Chgo. Fashion Exchange, Mendota C. of C. (dir. Nat. Sweet Corn Pageant 1979-81, cons. to pageant 1981-85). Avocations: coin collecting; boating; travel; reading. Office: Total Image Inc 1913 4th St Peru IL 61354

BEFOURE, JEANNINE MARIE, writer, accounting and business consultant; b. N.Y.C., Aug. 6, 1923; d. Thomas James and Frances Marie (Thompson) Nicholson; m. Willard Rockne, Oct., 1940 (div. 1946); children—Rodger Lloyd, Lenore Irene; m. Jean Maure Befoure, Aug. 3, 1974. B.S. in Communications magna cum laude, Woodbury U., 1979, M.B.A., 1981. Audit clk. Sears Roebuck, Seattle, 1946-50; supr. materials U.S. Navy, Guam, 1951-52; self-employed acct., Nev., Calif., Ariz., 1953-68; pres. Yearound Bus. Services, Las Vegas, Nev., 1969-73; writer, cons. The JM People, San Gabriel, Calif., 1982—; TV producer Channel 20, El Monte, Calif., TV access producer Channel 3, El Monte, 1987—; instr. bus. and indsl. mgmt. Calif. Community Colls., 1979-82; mem. IRS/Tax Practioner Bd., Las Vegas, 1972-73; tutor Lauback Literacy Action, Los Angeles, 1981—. Author children's stories and poetry, bus. articles. Trainer Kellogg Found.-United Way, Los Angeles; founding sec. Homeowners of Golden Valley, Ariz., 1961. Mem. World Future Soc., Assn. M.B.A. Execs., Greater Los Angeles Press Club, Phi Gamma Kappa. Republican. Religious Scientist. Avocations: photography; poetry.

BEGELMAN, HEDDA JOAN, psychologist; b. Bronx, N.Y., June 5, 1939; d. Reuben and Edith (Fink) B.; B.S., Adelphi U., 1960; M.S.W., Columbia U., 1965. Diplomate clin. social work. Social worker Sheltering Arms Children's Services, N.Y.C., 1965-67; psychiat. social worker, Girls Town, N.Y.C., 1967-69, Mid-Nassau Guidance Center, Hicksville, N.Y., 1969-76, Hempstead (N.Y.) Consultation Ctr., 1969-74, Mid-Nassau Family Counseling Ctr., Hicksville, 1969-76; pvt. practice psychotherapy, Farmingdale, N.Y., 1975—, social work therapist Cen. Nassau Guidance and Counseling Ctr., Hicksvile, 1988— ; speaker on sexuality various univs. Vol., Am. Cancer Soc. Cert. in psychotherapy Ind. Bronx Consultation Center; cert. in hypnosis, L.I. Soc. Clin. Hypnosis; lic. cert. social worker, N.Y. Mem. Nat. Assn. Social Workers, Acad. Cert. Social Workers. Home and Office: 8 Marlboro Ave Massapequa NY 11758

BEGROWICZ, PATRICIA CROWELL, process engineer; b. Richmond, Va., Apr. 2, 1959; d. Edwin Patrick and Carol Ann (Donahue) C.; m. Alan Nicholas Begrowicz, July 7, 1984. BS in Chem. Engring., U. Notre Dame, 1981; MS in Pulp and Paper Engring., Inst. of Paper Chemistry, Appleton, Wis., 1983. Process engr. Union Camp Corp., Franklin, Va., 1983—. Mem. Soc. Women Engrs. (pres. and founding mem. of sect. 1986-87), Tech. Assn. of the Pulp and Paper Industry. Home: 204 Holly Cove Franklin VA 23851 Office: Union Camp Corp Tech Dept Franklin VA 23851

BEHLING, DOROTHY CLARA, fashion professional; b. Scotia, N.Y., May 25, 1930; d. Paul Carl and Evelyn Elizabeth (Blinsinger) Bazar. m. William Herman Behling, May 21, 1949; children: Gary Paul, Bruce William, Corrine Elizabeth. Student profl. modeling Roemary Bischoff Studios, Milw., 1965. Cert. modeling instr., Wis. Payroll mgr. Sears, Roebuck & Co., Schenectady, N.Y., 1947-49; sec., treas. Maple Grove Oil Co., West Allis, Wis., 1957-70; staff instr. Rosemary Bischoff Studios, 1966-81, profl. model, 1966-85; staff model Boston Stores, Milw., 1967-68, Gimbel Stores, 1968-69; instr. Alyce Stoney Modeling Sch., 1969-70; free-lance fashion profl., Mequon, Wis., 1985—; cons. Max Factor, 1970; fashion model, cons. Alston Stores, Cedarburg, Wis., 1980—. Treas., PTA, Hales Corners, Wis., 1957-58; leader Hales Corners council Boy Scouts Am., 1962-63; chmn. Hales Corners council Girl Scouts Am., 1967-68; mem., coordinator Milw. Soc. Models for United Assn. for Retarded Citizens, 1972-76; mem. Ozaukee (Wis.) Humane Soc. Pet Therapy Program, 1986-87. Mem. Bus. and Profl. Women' Assn., River Oaks Assn. (sec. 1976). Republican. Roman Catholic. Club: Christian Women Orgn. Avocations: tennis; gardening. Home: 10635 N Ivy Ct Mequon WI 53092 also: 154 Palm Dr Naples FL 33962

BEHNER, JANICE ROSE, real estate broker; b. Phoenix, May 20, 1938; d. Jefferson Robert and Oveita (Lawrence) Moore; m. Harvey Lee Acridge, June 8, 1956 (div. Dec. 1968); children—Sharma L., Lainee A., Scott Michael; m. 2d, Richard Leo Behner, Oct. 27, 1973. Student Ariz. State U., 1961-62. Lic. real estate broker; cert. residential specialist. and cert. real estate brokerage mgr. Salesman Goebel Realty, Phoenix, 1969-71, Apollo Enterprises, Glendale, Ariz., 1971-73; pres. Metro Realty, Inc., Phoenix, 1974-78; broker Century 21 Metro, Phoenix, 1973-78; co-founder 50 States Real Estate franchise (doing bus. as Behner and Assocs. Realtors), Phoenix, 1978, broker 1978-83 sec., treas., 1978-87, pres. 1987—, dir., 1978—; co-owner Metro Movers, Phoenix; cons. curriculum com. Glendale (Ariz.) Community Coll., 1978—. Mem. Valley Cathedral, Phoenix, 1969—, Phoenix Bd. Realtors Grievance com., 1985-87. Mem. Women's Council Realtors (pres. 1983-84). Republican. Office: Behner and Assocs Realtors 3504 W Peoria Ave Phoenix AZ 85029-4026

BEHR, UNITA CARMAN, nurse; b. Greenville, Miss., Dec. 10, 1954; d. Jack Baker and Mable Elizabeth (Dowdy) Carman; m. Larry Gene Murphy, June 28, 1975 (div. 1980); m. Christopher Lyell Behr, Mar. 26, 1983. Diploma, Bapt. Hosp. Sch. of Nursing, Memphis, 1975. Staff nurse ICU Bapt. Meml. Hosp., Memphis, 1975-76; clinic RN Physicians Group Practice, Memphis, 1976-77; staff RN St. Francis Emergency Dept., Memphis, 1977-83, Bapt. Hosp. Emergency Trauma Ctr., Pensacola, Fla., 1983, Pleasant Valley Hosp. E.D., Camarillo, Calif., 1984-87. Republican. Mem. Foursquare Gospel Ch. Office: Pleasant Valley Hosp 2309 Antonio Camarillo CA 93010

BEHRENS, BEREL LYN, physician, academic dean; b. New South Wales, Australia, 1940. MB, BS, Sydney (Australia) U., 1964. Cert. pediatrics, allergy and immunology. Intern Roayl Prince Alfred Hosp., Australia, 1964; resident Loma Linda U. Med. Ctr., 1966-68; with Henrietta Egleston Hosp. for Children, 1968-69, T.C. Thompson Children's Hosp., 1969-70, instr. pediatrics Loma Linda U., 1970-72, with dept. pediatrics, 1972—, dean Sch. Medicine, 1986—. Office: Loma Linda U Sch of Medicine Office of the Dean Loma Linda CA 92350

BEHRENS, CRYSTAL MARIE, sales representative; b. N.Y.C., Jan. 11, 1955; d. Dominick Carminati and Margaret (Mazza) Hoffman; m. Carl A. Behrens, Jr., Oct. 14, 1979 (div. Mar. 1984). BS in Nursing, Villanova U., 1977. Staff nurse Columbia Presbyn. Med. Ctr., N.Y.C., 1977-79, nurse epidemiologist, 1979-82; sales rep. Eli Lilly & Co., N.Y.C., 1982-84, Johnson & Johnson Home Health, Dallas, 1984; sales rep., trainer Johnson & Johnson Extended Care, Dallas, 1984-88; div. sales trainer Johnson & Johnson Surgical Products, Mission Viejo, Calif., 1988—. Democrat. Roman Catholic.

BEHRENS, JOSEPHINE STORY, lawyer; b. Atlanta, Aug. 15, 1935; d. King J. and Mollie Aline (Cannady) Story; m. Edward J. Behrens (dec. Jan. 1978); children—Kathy Sharon, Deborah Jean, Gregory R. J.D., U. San Fernando, Los Angeles, 1969. Bar: Calif. 1975. Legal sec. Loeb & Loeb, Los Angeles, 1964-69; tchr., City of Los Angeles, 1967-69; sole practice, Sherman Oaks, Calif., 1975—. Mem. San Fernando Valley Bar Assn., Los Angeles County Bar Assn., San Fernando Valley Women Lawyers Assn. (bd. dirs., officer, charter mem. 1977—). Republican. Baptist. Home: 13630 Addison St Sherman Oaks CA 91423

BEHRMAN, ANNE MARIE, paralegal; b. Bklyn., Apr. 22, 1960; d. Frank Bennett and Anne M. (Mulé) B. BA magna cum laude, Molloy Coll., 1982. Research asst. Research Found. CUNY, N.Y.C., 1982-85, Lexington Ctr., Jackson Heights, N.Y., 1983-86; paralegal Santemma & Murphy P.C., Mineola, N.Y., 1986-87, Certilman, Haff, Balin, Buckley, Kremer & Hyman, East Meadow, N.Y., 1987—. Mem. Delta Epsilon Sigma, Omicron Alpha Zeta. Roman Catholic. Office: Certilman Haff Balin Buckley Kremer & Hyman 90 Merrick Ave East Meadow NY 11554

BEIS, SARA JANE, laboratory executive, pharmacist; b. Akron, Ohio, Aug. 25, 1954; d. George Andrew and Buena Marie (Greer) B. B.S. in Pharmacy, U. Mich., 1977. Registered pharmacist, Ohio. Pharmacy intern Akron Gen. Med. Ctr., 1973-76; staff pharmacist Ohio State U., Columbus, 1977-80; clin. pharmacist VA, Columbus and Columbia, S.C., 1980-82; mgmt. cons. Hosp. Pharmacy, 1982—; sales rep. Smith Kline & French Labs., Phila., 1983-87; pharmacist Barberton (Ohio) Citizens Hosp., 1987—; clin. instr. Coll. Pharmacy, Ohio State U., 1978-81, U. S.C., Columbia, 1981-82. Patentee pill packaging. Vol. Children's Hosp., Columbus, 1983. Recipient dist. achievement award Smith Kline & French Labs., Inc., 1985. Fellow Am. Soc. Cons. Pharmacists; mem. Am. Soc. Hosp. Pharmacists, Akron Area Soc. Hosp. Pharmacists, U. Mich. Alumni Assn. (life), Nat. Assn. Female Execs., Akron alumni (v.p.), Pi Beta Phi (pres. Akron area chpt. 1988—, v.p. Akron area chpt. 1987—). Republican. Roman Catholic. Home: 2556 Durand Rd Akron OH 44313 Office: Barberton Citizens Hosp 155 Fifth St Barberton OH 44203

BEISEIGEL, SHIRLEY-ANN, psychologist; b. Allentown, Pa., May 27, 1927; d. John Calvin and Dorothy Irene (Bear) Shumberger; C.A.G.S. in Psychology and Counseling, Assumption Coll., 1982; A.B. in Biology, Bucknell U., 1949; M.S. in Rehab. Counseling, Va. Commonwealth U., 1969; m. Howard Alan Beiseigel, June 18, 1949; children—Robert Alan, Barry John, John Howard. Supervisory guidance counselor Woodrow Wilson Rehab. Center, Fishersville, Va., 1963-64; spl. edn. tchr. Lansing (Mich.) Public Schs., 1964; asst. home life dir. VFW Nat. Home, Eaton Rapids, Mich., 1964-66; exec. dir. Easter Seal Soc. of Ingham County, Lansing, Mich., 1966; profl. rehab. counselor Woodrow Wilson Rehab. Center, Fishersville, 1966-70, supr. counselors evaluation dept., 1970-71; counselor II, N.H. State Prison, Concord, 1971-72; vocat. evaluation coordinator Vocat. Devel. Center, Manchester, N.H., 1972-77; supr. psychodiagnostic and vocat. evaluation services Good Shepherd Home and Rehab. Hosp., Allentown, Pa., 1977-79, dir. psychol. services, dir. chronic pain mgmt. program, 1979—. Mem. N.H. bd. dirs. Pres.'s Com. on Employment of Handicapped, 1975-76. Cert. psychol. services supr., Pa.; nat. cert.ert. rehab. counselor. Mem. Am. Psychol. Assn., Pa. Psychol. Assn., Assn. Counseling and Devel., Nat. Rehab. Assn., Nat. Rehab. Counseling Assn. (charter), Pa. Rehab. Assn., N.H. Rehab. Assn. (dir. 1973-76), N.H. Rehab. Counseling Assn. (past pres. 1975-76), Va. Rehab. Counseling Assn. (dir. 1967-70), Va. Rehab. Assn. (membership chmn. 1968-69), Phi Mu. Republican. Presbyterian. Club: Order of Eastern Star (matron 1961-62). Home: 438 W Locust Ln Nazareth PA 18064 Office: Fifth and St John Sts Allentown PA 18103

BEISLER, SALLY JEAN, market manager; b. Pitts., Aug. 14, 1945; d. Rexford C. and Susie (Hopta) Arnold; m. Joseph L. Beisler, Feb. 5, 1977; children: Susan Marie, Michael Anthony. BS, U. Pitts., 1971, MBA, 1978. With nuclear fuel mgmt. and sales staff Westinghouse Electric Co., Pitts., 1969-74; internat. mktg. and mgr. mfg. Borg Warner Chem. Co., Parkersburg, W.Va., 1974-78; mem. mktg. staff St. Joe Zinc Co., Pitts., 1978-79; market mgr. Mobay Corp., Pitts., 1980—; bd. dirs. Med. Planning & Cons., Pitts., 1979—. Mem. Exec. Women's Council Pitts., Soc. Plastics Engrs., Flexible Packaging Assn. Home: 947 Valleyview Rd Pittsburgh PA 15243 Office: Mobay Rd Pittsburgh PA 15205

BEKER, GISELA U., artist; b. 1932, Zoppot, Ger.; came to U.S., 1956. Student The Kunst-Institut, Rostock, E.Ger.; pupil of Rudolf Kroll. Solo shows include Bodley Gallery, N.Y., 1973, Women's Bldg., Los Angeles, 1973, Mus. Art, Huntsville, Ala., 1974, Tower Gallery, Southampton, N.Y., 1974, Arts and Sci. Ctr., Baton Rouge, 1975, Wilkes Coll., Pa., 1975, Tower Gallery, 1975, NYU, 1976, Everson Mus., Syracuse, 1976, Tower Gallery, 1976, Wilkes Coll., 1976, G. Sander Fine Art, Daytona Beach, Fla., 1985; represented in permanent collections of Chrysler Mus., Norfolk, Va., New Orleans Mus. Art, Aldrich Mus., Ridgefield, Conn., Fine Art Ctr., Nashville, Okla. Art Ctr., Oklahoma City, Everson Mus., Syracuse, Palm Spring Mus., Calif., Long Beach Mus., Calif., Mus. Art, Huntsville, Ala., Arts and Sci. Ctr., Baton Rouge, Phoenix Art Mus., Mus. Art, Lodz, Poland, others; exhibited in group shows at Jersey City Mus., 1973, Nat. Acad. N.Y., 1973, State Capitol Mus., Olympia, Wash., 1973, Fairleigh Dickenson U., 1973, U. Portland, 1974, Central Wyo. Mus. Art, Casper, Northeastern Okla. A&M Coll., 1974, Rosenberg Library, Galveston, Tex., 1974, Mus. Modern Art, Paris, 1974, 20th Salon de Thouars, France, 1974, Marathon Mus., Warsau, Wis., 1974, Hoyt Inst. Fine Arts, Pa., 1974, Spring Arbor coll., Mich., 1975, LaSalle Coll. Union, Phila., 1975, Pensacola Art Ctr., Fla., 1975, Art Ctr., Richmond, Ind., 1975, Jesse Beser Mus., Alpena, Mich., 1976, Bronx Mus. Art, 1976, Charles and Emma Frye Mus., Seattle, 1976, Watkins Inst., Nashville, 1976, Louisville Sch. Art, 1977, Cayuga Mus. History and Art, Auburn, N.Y., 1977, Tower Gallery, 1977, others. Contbr. articles to profl. jours.

BEKHRAD, FERESHTEH, architect, planner developer; b. Tehran, Iran, Nov. 3, 1946; came to U.S., 1970; d. Mozaffar and Robabeh (Farahani) B. BArch, U. Tehran, 1968, M of Archtl. Engring., 1970; MS of Urban Design and Architecture, Washington U., St. Louis, 1973; postgrad., U. Pa., 1979. Project mgr. AFFA, Tehran, 1964-69, dir. planning and urban design, cons. devel., 1977-79; project mgr., architect Strivers Assocs. Connie Napur, St. Louis, Hartford, Conn. and P.R., 1970-74; prin. land use planner O.D.A. Brideport (Conn.) City Hall, 1974-77; pres., gen. mgr., cons. planning and urban design Dakin Assocs., Tehran, 1976-80; pres. Bekhrad Co., N.Y.C., 1979-81; sr. v.p., gen. mgr. York-Hannover Devel. Inc., N.Y.C., 1981—;

ptnr., prin., cons. downtown revitalization Alexander/Bekhard Cons., N.Y.C., 1984—; cons. devel. Bekhrad Co. Contbr. articles to profl. jours. Bd. dirs., mem. exec. com. Downtown Raleigh (N.C.) Devel. Corp., 1987. Recipient First Place award Am. Land Devel. Assn., St. George's Resort, Bermuda, 1983, Honorable Mention award, 1983, Sir Walter Raleigh award City of Raleigh, 1984. Mem. AIA (assoc.), Am. Inst. Cert. Planners (cert.), Am. Planning Assn., Inst. Urban Design, Internat. Assn. Corp. Real Estate Execs., Iranian Inst. Planners (founder 1968), Urban Land Inst. (assoc.). Clubs: Centurion, Capital City (Raleigh). Home: 145 E 15th St New York NY 10003 Office: York Hanover Devel Inc 488 Madison Ave New York NY 10022

BEKKEN, BARBARA M., educational editor; b. Milwaukee, July 22, 1941; d. Odin Magnus and Marie Elizabeth (Hoecherl) Olson; m. Lawrence Alan Bekken, Sept. 10, 1960; children: Dean, Amy Esme. BS, U. Wis., Milwaukee, 1972. Tchr. Shorewood (Wis.) Pub. Schs., 1972-74; fin. aid adminstr. Ednl. Testing Service, Evanston, Ill., 1974-75; editor Curriculum Innovations, INc., Highland Park, Ill., 1975-81; exec. editor Gen. Learning Corp., Northbrook, Ill., 1981—. cons. Gen. Learning Corp., Northbrook, 1985-87; columnist Sun Features, Inc., Rancho La Costa, Calif., 1979-81; editor: (children's mag.) Writing, 1983-85, journalism exellence, EdPress, 1983, 84, 85, Chgo. Women in Pub. award, 1985, Career World mag., 1975-88. Bd. dirs. Lake County (ILL.) Career Consortium, 1982-84.;. Mem. Ednl. Press. Assn., LWV, Kappa Delta Pi, Phi Kappa Phi. Office: Gen Learning Corp 60 Revere Dr Northbrook IL 60062-1563

BEKSA-SAHAGUN, REGINA, computerized accounting firm executive, translator, consultant; b. Newport Beach, Calif., Aug. 13, 1962; d. Chester Beksa and Blanche Ruth (Hart) Beksa Hart; married; 1 child.. Student Jagiellonian U., Cracow, Poland; A.A., Orange Coast Coll. Adminstr. RMP Mktg., Ensign Corp., MVA Design Group, Costa Mesa, 1983-85; owner, operator Beksa Enterprises, Santa Ana, Calif., 1985—; cons. The Graphic Agy., Costa Mesa, 1985—; translator from Polish lang. Mem. Polish Nat. Alliance (debutante), Nat. Assn. Female Execs., Calif. Scholarship Fedn. Democrat. Roman Catholic.

BELAU, JANE CAROL GULLICKSON, computer products and services company executive; b. Fertile, Minn., Oct. 21, 1934; d. Solon Hubert and Orpha (Love) Gullickson; m. Paul G. Belau, June 22, 1957; children: Steven, Matthew, Nancy Belau Collins. Student, Concordia Coll., Moorhead, Minn., 1952-53; grad., RN, Fairview Hosp. Sch. Nursing, 1956; postgrad., U. Minn. Spl. events dir. Retail Merchants Assn., 1966-71; cons. U.S. HEW, Washington, 1971-77; commr. Minn. State Corrections Authority, Mpls., 1974-75; cons. McKnight Found., Mpls., 1974-78; commr. Minn. State Cable Communications Bd., 1975-78; v.p. state mktg. and govt. affairs Control Data Corp., Mpls., 1978—; cons. in field. Illustrator: Fashion-grams; producer-host cable TV program Community Affairs; contbr. articles to profl. jours. Bd. advisors U. Minn. Grad Sch., 1985—; chmn. nat. adv. council St. John's U., Minn., 1986—; bd. dirs. Minn. Meeting, 1986—, Minn. High Tech Council, 1986—, Minn. Alliance for Sci., 1986—, Minn. Acad. Sci., 1985—; pres. Rochester (Minn.) Area Econ. Devel. Co., 1986—; v.p., bd. dirs. Nat. Luth. Acad., 1985—; founding dir. Vinland Nat. Ctr.; founder Nat. Conf. Developmental Disabilities; chmn. Nat. Developmental Disabilities Adv. Council. Named Bus. and Profl. Woman of Yr., 1974; recipient Outstanding Leadership award Internat. Assn. Women Execs., 1981. Mem. Am. Electronics Assn. (Minn. govtl. chmn.), Women's Econ. Roundtable Minn. (founder, bd. dirs.), U.S. C. of C. (nat. health care com.). Club: Mpls. Decathlon. Home: 433 9th Ave SW Rochester MN 55901 Office: Control Data Corp 8100 34th Ave S Minneapolis MN 55440

BELCHER, DIANA STEINBACH, computer scientist, educator; b. Jersey City, Nov. 28, 1952; d. Edward Sargent and Grace Comstock (Warner) Steinbach; m. Thomas Keith Belcher, June 17, 1978. BA in Math, Miami U., Oxford, Ohio, 1974; MEd, Ohio State U., 1987. Cert. secondary tchr., Ohio. Tchr. Wayne Township Schs., Dayton, Ohio, 1974-78; computer programmer Nationwide Ins., Columbus, Ohio, 1978-79; programmer trainer Nationwide Ins., Columbus, 1981—; tchr. Columbus Pub. Schs., 1979-81; programmer instr. Franklin U., Columbus, 1984—. Prin. clarinetist Upper Arlington (Ohio) Community Orch., 1984—. Methodist. Home: 305 Tappan St Columbus OH 43201 Office: Nationwide Ins One Nationwide Plaza Columbus OH 43216

BELCHER, LA JEUNE, automotive parts company executive; b. Chgo., Nov. 16, 1960; d. Lewis Albert and Dorthy (Brandon) B. BA, Northwestern U., 1982; postgrad., Am. Inst. of Banking, 1983-84. Securities processor Am. Nat. Bank, Chgo., 1983, divisional asst., 1983-84; mgmt. trainee Toyota Motor Distbrs., Carol Stream, Ill., 1984-85, dist. parts mgr., 1985—; rep. to Japan-U.S. Toyota Dealer Meeting, Tokyo, 1985. Mem. NAACP, Nat. Assn. Female Execs., Am. Soc. Profl. and Exec. Women, Am. Mgmt. Assn., Am. Assn. Individual Investors, Delta Sigma Theta. Club: Northwestern of Chgo. Lodge: Toastmasters. Home: 6436 S Green Chicago IL 60621 Office: Toyota Motor Distbrs 500 Kehoe Blvd Carol Stream IL 60187

BELETZ, ELAINE ETHEL, nurse, educator; b. N.Y.C., Jan. 5, 1944; d. Harry and Rose (Friedman) B. RN, Mt. Sinai Hosp., N.Y.C., 1968; BS in Nursing, Fairleigh Dickinson U., 1970; MA, NYU, 1974; MEd, Columbia U., 1978, EdD, 1979. Staff nurse ICU Mt. Sinai Hosp., 1968-70, asst. head nurse, 1970; adminstrv. supervisory relief nurse, 1973-74, 77-78; clin. instr. Roosevelt Hosp. Sch. Nursing, N.Y.C., 1970-73; nurse gerontologist St. Luke's Hosp. Ctr., N.Y.C., 1974; asst. dir. nursing Bklyn. Hosp., N.Y.C., 1975-77; asst. prof. nursing Hunter Coll., CUNY, 1978-81; v.p. nursing Mt. Sinai Hosp., Med. Ctr., Chgo., 1982-83; assoc. prof. nursing Villanova (Pa.) U., 1983—; lectr.; cons. nursing adminstrn., labor relations in health care; mem. task force on block grants. Ill. Dept. Health. Contbr. articles to profl. jours. Fellow Am. Acad. Nursing; mem. Am. Nurses Assn. (bd. dirs. 1982-87, mem. polit. action com. 1982-86), Acad. Polit. Sci., N.Y. State Nurses Assn. (treas. 1977-78, pres.-elect 1978-79, pres. 1979-81, bd. trustees, cert. of appreciation 1981, hon. recognition award 1987), Pa. Nurses Assn., N.Y. Counties Registered Nurses Assn. (nominating com. 1973, dir. 1975-78, Amanda Silvers award 1981), Shershower Benevolent Assn., Sigma Theta Tau, Phi Kappa Phi. Jewish. Office: Villanova U Grad Program Coll Nursing Villanova PA 19085

BELFORT, ANNE ELLEN, computer industry manager; b. N.Y.C., Apr. 6, 1954; d. Alan Michael and Anne Dorothy Belfort. Student, Georgetown U., 1972, U. Pa., 1975; BA, Hollins Coll., 1975; MS in Mgmt., Purdue U., 1976. Mgmt. services industry specialist, Info. Services Bus. div. Gen. Electric Co., Rockville, Md., 1978-79; assoc. mktg. rep., Data Processing div. IBM Corp., Chgo., 1979-80, mktg. rep., Data Processing div., 1980-81, account mktg. rep., Nat. Accounts div., 1982-85; adv. instr., Southwest Mktg. div. IBM Corp., Irving, Tex., 1985—. Editor corp. news mag. The Bottom Line, 1978. Bd. dirs. Vanderbilt U. Model UN Econ. and Social Council, 1974; rep. Hollins (Va.) Coll. Student Govt., 1972-75; sec. gen. Hollins Coll. Model UN, 1975; mem. Purdue U. Pres.'s Council, 1977—, Purdue U./Krannert Sch. Dean's Adv. Council, 1985—, Purdue U./Krannert Grad. Sch. Alumnae Bd., 1980-82. Named One of Outstanding Young Women of Am., 1979; recipient Leadership award YWCA, Chgo., 1980, Voltaire medal Ecole Champlain, Paris, 1970. Mem. Assn. MBA Execs., AAAS. Republican. Club: Alliance Francaise.

BEL GEDDES, BARBARA, actress; b. N.Y.C., Oct. 31, 1922; d. Norman and Helen Belle (Sneider) Bel G.; m. Carl Schreuer, Jan. 24, 1944 (div. 1951); 1 child, Susan; m. Windsor Lewis, Apr. 15, 1951 (dec.); 1 child, Betsy. Student, Buxton Sch., Putney, Andrebrook. Debut on stage in School for Scandal, Clinton (Conn.) Playhouse, 1939, on Broadway in Out of The Frying Pan, 1940; actress: (Broadway plays) Little Darling, 1942, Nine Girls, 1943, Mrs. January and Mr. X, 1944, Deep Are the Roots, 1945 (Clarence Derwent award), The Moon Is Blue, 1952, The Living Room, 1954, Cat on a Hot Tin Roof, 1955, The Sleeping Prince, 1956, Silent Night, Lonely Night, 1959, Mary, Mary, 1961, The Porcelain Year, 1965, Everything in the Garden, 1967, Finishing Touches, 1973, Ah, Wilderness, 1975; films include The Long Night, 1946, I Remember Mama, 1948, Blood on the Moon, 1948, Caught, 1949, Panic in the Streets, 1950, Fourteen Hours, 1951, Vertigo, 1958, The Five Pennies, 1959, Five Branded Women, 1960, By Love Possessed, 1961, The Todd Killings, 1970, Summertree, 1971; appears regularly as Eleanor Southward Ewing on TV show Dallas, 1978-84, 85—; author, illustrator: (children's books) I Like to Be Me, 1963, So Do I, 1972; designer greeting cards for George Caspari Co. Recipient Theatre World award, 1946. Office: Lorimar Productions 3970 Overland Ave Culver City CA 90230 *

BELINA, MARIA, import company administrator; b. Mexico, Jan. 23; came to U.S., 1969; d. Manuel and Rosa (Murua) Garcia; m. July 28, 1979; 1 child, Joseph John. B.A. summa cum laude, Tchr.'s Coll., 1965; M.A., Manhattan Coll., 1974; postgrad. in Japanese lang. and history, Japan Sch. Langs., 1965-68. Cert. tchr., N.Y., N.J. Coll. prof. Aoyama Lakuin U., Tokyo, 1967-69; prof. Technologico de Monterrey U., Mexico City, 1980-81; mgr. adminstrn., corp. sec. Sodick, Inc., Saddle Brook, N.J., 1982-85; import mgr. Eiseman Ludmar, N.Y.C., 1985—; counselor, tchr. St. Catherine of Genoa, N.Y.C., 1970-80. Author: Spanish for Japanese, 1968; The Nobody Bird, 1980; translator: Psychology, 1981. Mem. Multiply Handicapped of N.J. Assn. Republican. Roman Catholic. Office: Eiseman Ludmar Co Inc 56 Bethpage Dr Hicksville NY 11801

BELIVEAU, MARGUERITE ANITA, corporate executive; b. Woonsocket, R.I., May 1, 1944; d. Ephrem Alfred and Jeanne Cecile (Thibodeau) B. BS in Sociology and Social Work, Suffolk U., 1971; MBA, Bentley Coll., 1983. Supr. child care departmental adminstrn. Madonna Hall, Marlboro, Mass., 1966-73; dir. personnel devel. Mt. Florence, Peekskill, N.Y., 1973-77; asst. controller, contract mgr. Univ. Hosp., Solomon Carter Fuller Mental Health Ctr., Boston, 1978-82; dir. material mgmt. Univ. Hosp., Boston, 1982-84, dir. purchasing, 1984-85; assoc. dir. design and constrn. mgmt. Hosp. of U. Pa., Phila., 1985-88; v.p. for material mgmt. West Jersey Health System, Camden, 1988—. Mem. Health Care Fin. Mgmt. Assn., Health Care Materials Mgmt. Assn. Roman Catholic. Home: 130 Ramsey Ave Marlton NJ 08053 Office: West Jersey Health Systems Corp Offices Mt Ephraim & Atlantic Aves Camden NJ 08104

BELKIN, JANET E., lawyer; b. N.Y.C.; d. Irving and Pauline H. Ehrenreich; B.A., Vassar Coll., 1958; Ph.D., St. Johns U., 1975; J.D., Hofstra U.; LL.M., NYU, 1983; m. Myron Belkin, June 29, 1958; children—Lisa, Gary, Kira. Tchr. spl. edn., N.Y.C., 1958-60; adj. faculty St. Johns U., 1970-75, Nassau Community Coll., 1971-75; pvt. counselor, 1971-75; admitted to N.Y. bar, 1979; atty. govt. relations Equitable Life Ins. Co., N.Y.C., 1978—. Chmn. Hudson group Democratic Nat. Com. Task Force, 1981—; mem. legis. com. N.Y.C. Commn. Status Women; bd. dirs. Merrick (N.Y.) Sr. Citizens Center. Mem. ABA (vice chmn. adminstrv. law com.), Assn. Calif. Life Ins. Cos. (dir.), N.Y. State Bar Assn., Fin. Women's Assn., Women in Housing and Fin., Women in Govtl. Relations. Clubs: City (N.Y.C.), B'nai Brith. Home: 3014 Hewlett Ave Merrick NY 11566

BELL, BRITTON, business executive, management consultant; b. Louisville, June 18, 1948; d. Elbert Pinckley and Betsy Ann (Gordon) Watts; B.A. in Bus. Mgmt. and Profl. Communications, Alverno Coll., Milw., 1981; m. James H. Bell, Jr., Mar. 15, 1969 (div. Dec. 1972); 1 son, Scott Elbert. Acct., Am. Mut. Reins. Co., Chgo., 1967-69; office services Shell Oil Co., Detroit, 1969-71; personnel asst. RTE Corp., Waukesha, Wis., 1973-74; law office adminstr. John W. Cusack, S.C., Waukesha, 1974-77; regional rep. Reynolds and Reynolds Co., Milw., 1977-79; dist. rep. Bur. Nat. Affairs, Inc., Washington, 1978-80; founder, owner, pres. Profl. Mgmt. Services, Brookfield, Wis., 1979-84, Britton Bell Co., 1984—, Exec. Environments, Inc., 1983—, speaker, cons., seminar leader in field; instr. continuing legal edn. U. Wis. Law Sch. Author: A Practical Approach to Managing Your Law Practice, 1982; Financial Management—Key to a Successful Practice, 1983. Active local election com., NOW; proj. bus. cons. Jr. Achievement; mem. fund raising com. Florentine Opera, 1983—; vol. ARC Disaster Services and First Aid Corps, 1986—; hospice vol. St. Mary's Hosp., 1986—. Served with USN, 1966-67. Mem. Am. Mgmt. Assn., Internat. Platform Assn., Nat. Assn. Female Execs., Acad. Mgmt., Nat. Assn. Accts., Am. Entrepreneurs Assn., Alverno Coll. Alumnae Profls. Assn. Republican. Roman Catholic. Home: 2310 N 95th St Milwaukee WI 53226

BELL, CAROLYN SHAW, economist, educator; b. Framingham, Mass., June 21, 1920; d. Clarence Edward and Grace (Wellington) Shaw; m. Nelson S. Bell, Aug. 26, 1953; 1 dau. by previous marriage, Tova Maria. AB magna cum laude, Mt. Holyoke Coll., 1941; PhD, London (Eng.) Sch. Econs., 1949; LHD (hon.), Babson Coll., 1983, Denison U., 1988. Economist OPA, 1941-45; research economist London Sch. Econs., 1946-47, Social Sci. Research Council, Harvard, 1950-53; mem. faculty Wellesley Coll., 1950—, prof. econs., 1962—, chmn. dept., 1962-65, 79-82, Katharine Coman prof. econs., 1970—; Pub. mem. Fed. Adv. Council on Unemployment Ins., 1974-77, chairwoman, 1975-77; bd. econ. advisers Pub. Interest Econ. Center; bd. overseers Amos Tuck Grad. Sch. Bus. Adminstrn., Dartmouth, 1973-79; mem. econ. policy council UN Assn., 1976-85; trustee Joint Council Econ. Edn., 1975-83, Tchrs. Ins. and Annuity Assn., 1977-85, UN Assn., 1981—; mem. NRC Assembly Behavioral and Social Scis., 1977-83. Author: (with W.W. Cochrane) Economics of Consumption, 1956, Consumer Choice in the U.S. Economy, 1967, The Economics of the Ghetto, 1970, (with others) Coping in a Troubled Society, 1974; also articles., Radio and television commentator; Mem. bd. editors: Challenge, Jour. Econs. Edn. Mem. Manhattan Inst. (adv. bd), Inst. for Socio-Economic Research, Am. Econs. Assn. (chmn. com. on status of women in econs. profession 1972-74, mem. exec. com. 1975-77), AAUP (pres. Wellesley chpt. 1965-66), AAUW (Shirley Farr fellow 1961-62), ACLU, Assn. Evolutionary Econs. (dir. 1973-75), Eastern Econ. Assn. (exec. bd. 1983-85), Boston Econ. Club, Phi Beta Kappa (pres. Eta of Mass. chpt. 1978-80). Home: 167 Clay Brook Rd Dover MA 02030 Office: Wellesley Coll Wellesley MA 02181

BELL, CONSTANCE CONKLIN, child care association administrator; b. Columbus, Ohio, June 2, 1934; d. John Brevoort and Josephine (Suttles) Conklin; m. Robert Kilbourne Hudnut, Sept. 12, 1957 (div. June 1975); children: Heidi A., Robert K. Jr., Heather E., Matthew C.; m. Gerald Duane Bell, June 25, 1977. BA, Ohio Wesleyan U., 1956; postgrad., Union Theol. Sem., 1956-57. Tchr. Cen. Presbyn. Ch. Nursery Sch., N.Y.C., 1956-59; ctr. coordinator Greater Mpls. Day Care Assn., 1973—, asst. dir., 1977, assoc. dir., 1982; Mem. adv. com. Minn. Licensing Com., 1985—, Minn. Child Care LIcensing Com., 1986-87. Author: How to Start A Child Care Center, 1977, rev. edit., 1983, Sick Child Care, A Problem for Working Parents and Employers, 1983; (with others) Business and Childcare Handbook, 1981. Mem. social ministries com. Greater Mpls. Council of Chs., 1983—; bd. dirs. Mpls. Community Bus. Employment Alliance, 1984-85, Project Self-Sufficiency, Mpls., 1984—; mem. priorities com. United Way Mpls. Area, 1986—. Mem. Minn. Assn. for Edn. of Young Children (area award 1987), Minn. Children's Lobby, Child Care Works Steering Com., Parents in the Workplace (co-dir. 1983—), Kappa Alpha Theta (pres. Delaware, Ohio chpt. 1955-56). Democrat. Home: 6534 Aster Trail Excelsior MN 55331 Office: Greater Mpls Day Care Assn 1006 W Lake St Minneapolis MN 55408

BELL, DARLA DEE, marketing professional; b. Covington, Ky., July 2, 1946; d. Joseph Henry and Ruth Naomi (Kingsbury) Davis; m. Donald R. Bell, July 7, 1979. BS, U. Cin., 1980, MBA, 1983. Adminstrv. asst. Federated Dept. Stores, Cin., 1969-74, David J. Joseph Co., Inc., Cin., 1974-77, Drackett Co., Cin., 1977-80; new products mktg. mgr. Snow Filtration Co., Cin., 1981-83; industry analyst Chem. Mktg. Services, Inc., Cin., 1983-86; lectr. mktg. U. Cin., 1984—; cons. mktg. research projects; project mgr. BMSA Corp., Cin., 1987—. Vol. interpreter Cin. Zoo, 1984—. Mem. Chem. Mktg. Research Assn., Am. Mktg. Assn.

BELL, DOROTHY HAGLER, real estate broker; b. Port Arthur, Tex., Dec. 22, 1935; d. John D. and Amy F. Hagler; m. James D. Bell, June 16, 1956 (div. Mar. 1974); children—Suzanne Clifford, John McLauchlin; m. Thomas R. Serio, June 25, 1983. B.B.A., U. Tex.-Austin, 1956. Real estate broker Duffy & La Roe, Houston, 1973-83, Helena Underwood Realtors, Dallas, 1983—. Finalist Mademoiselle Mag. Coll. Bd., 1953. Active Republican Party, Houston, New Orleans and Dallas; tres. Park Cities Rep. Women; vol. Dallas Mus. Art. Mem. Houston Livestock Show and Rodeo (Sales award), Greater Dallas Bd. Realtors (pub. affairs com., Summit award), Women's Council Realtors (edn. com.), Internat. Platform Assn., Southwestern Watercolor Soc., Million Dollar Club, Alpha Phi. Presbyterian. Club: Houston Panhellenic (sec. 1972-74). Office: Helena Underwood Realtors 5550 Preston Rd Dallas TX 75205

BELL, EILEEN EBERENZ, stockbroker; b. Wellsboro, Pa., Jan. 31, 1936; d. John Gorden and Marion (Reinwald) Eberenz; m. Paul Hayden Bell, Sept. 6, 1935, children: Candace, Christian, Brian. BA, Syracuse U., 1957. Tech. asst. Bell Telephone Labs., Whippany, N.Y., 1956; systems analyst Gen. Electric, Syracuse, 1957-64, Corning (N.Y.) Glass Works, 1966-70; substitute tchr. Corning Painted Post Schs., 1970-76. Chmn. Prof. Women's Network, Corning, 1983—; treas. Chemung County SPCA and Humane Soc., Elmira, 1986—; mem. Women's Ctr., Corning, 1986—. Mem. Soc. Women Engrs. Republican. Methodist. Home: Rural Rt 2 Box 76 Corning NY 14830 Office: First Albany Corp 100 Baldwin St Elmira NY 14901

BELL, HELEN LOUISE, white house staffer; b. Bklyn., Oct. 6, 1959; d. Robert Lloyd and Helen Louise (Matthews) B. BA, Washington and Jefferson Coll., 1980. Mem. White House Staff, Washington, 1981—, corr. analyst, 1981-82, photo office, 1982-85; staff asst. First Lady's office Washington, 1985—; asst. Potrait Project, Washington, 1982-85. Asst. photo editor: People and Power, 1985; show coordinator photography exhbn. Corcoran Gallery Art, Washington, 1985. Mem. admissions bd. Washington and Jefferson Coll., Washington, 1981—, mem. devel. council, 1985—. Recipient Secret Service award, 1984. Mem. Washington and Jefferson Coll. Washington Area Alumni (bd. dirs. 1986—), Washington Jr. League, Art Barn Assn. Republican. Presbyterian. Home: 3246 Que St NW Washington DC 20007 Office: The White House 1600 Pennsylvania Ave NW Washington DC 20500

BELL, JEANNE VINER, public relations counselor; b. Los Angeles, Feb. 27, 1923; d. Herman and Mary (Kaufman) Spitzel; m. Melvin A. Viner, Feb. 1, 1942 (dec.); children—Michael, Karen Viner Fawcett; m. 2d, J. Raymond Bell, Dec. 15, 1974 (dec.). Student UCLA, Am. U., George Washington U. Prin. Jeanne Viner Spl. Services, Washington, 1958-61, Jeanne Viner Assocs., Washington, 1961-82; pub. relations counselor, 1982—; dir. Independence Fed. Bank, Washington, Independence Fed. Service Corp., Washington. Contbr. articles to profl. jours. Presdl. appointee to adv. council SBA, 1983, Pres.'s Com. on Employment of Handicapped, 1982; mem. nat. adv. bd. Fedn. Am. Immigration Reform, Washington, 1984—; bd. dirs., mem. exec. com. Arthritis Found. of Met. D.C., 1982—; mayoral appointee to D.C. Adv. Com. on Resources and Budget, 1981—, D.C. Pvt. Industries Council, 1983—. Recipient Outstanding Leadership and Achievement award State Bus. and Profl. Women's Clubs, Washington, 1981. Mem. Pub. Relations Soc. Am., Capital Press Women (pres. 1980-82, Woman of Achievement 1982), Am. News Women's Club (bd. govs. 1969-70, pres. 1988—). Club: 1969-70), Nat. Press (Washington). Address: 3506 Winfield Ln Washington DC 20007 also: 9460 Hidden Valley Pl Beverly Hills CA 90210

BELL, JOY ANN, librarian; b. Cross Plains, Tenn., June 9, 1944; d. James Ausie and Evelyn Trevenia (Yates) Carpenter; m. George Carter Bell, Sept. 4, 1966. BA cum laude, Western Ky. U., 1964; MS in Library Sci., Simmons Coll., 1972. Asst. catalog librarian U. Tex. Health Sci. Ctr., San Antonio, 1973; cataloger, instr. Trinity U. Library, San Antonio, 1974, special collections cataloger, instr., 1974-75; asst. librarian, asst. prof. Rosenstiel Sch. Marine & Atmospheric Sci., U. Miami, Fla., 1976-79; med. librarian St. Francis Hosp., Miami Beach, Fla., 1979-82; tech. info. specialist US Army Health Care Studies and Clin. Investigation Activity, Ft. Sam Houston, Tex., 1984-86; pvt. practice library cons., researcher San Antonio, 1986—; researcher Blackwell, Walker, Gray, Powers, Flick & Hoehl Law Offices, Miami, 1978-81. Named to Hon. Order Ky. Cols., 1975. Mem. Med. Library Assn., Miami Health Scis. Library Consortium, Nat. Assn. Female Execs. Methodist. Home and Office: 15127 Morning Tree San Antonio TX 78232

BELL, JUDY FRANZ, parks and recreation executive; b. Indiana, Pa., May 1, 1940; d. Robert Casper Franz and Ellen Kathrine (Parks) Pierce; m. Walter Claude Overby, May 11, 1962 (div. 1977); children—Jeffrey Pierce, Lee Turner; m. James Dwight Bell, Dec. 3, 1983. B.A. in Edn., U. Pitts., 1961; M.A. in Documentary Film, UCLA, 1969. Tchr. Roswell (N. Mex.) High Sch., 1964-67, Carmichael (Calif.) High Sch., 1968; adminstrv. aide to chief exec. officer Harris County, Tex., 1976—; bd. dirs. Bayou Preservation Assn., Houston, 1976—, Parks People, Houston, 1980—; adv. Harris County Flood Control Task Force, 1977-80. Named among 84 Most Interesting People in Houston, Houston City Mag., 1984. Mem. Nat. Parks Conservation Assn., Nat. Recreation, Parks Assn., Tex. Recreation, Parks Assn. Republican. Roman Catholic. Home: 1002 Whitestone Ln Houston TX 77073 Office: Harris County 1001 Preston St #911 Houston TX 77002

BELL, LINDA CRAWFORD, magazine editor; b. Harrisburg, Pa., Jan. 13, 1948; d. Elwood F. and Reba J. (Stakley) Crawford; student Pa. State U., 1965-68; m. Daniel Locke Bell II, July 18, 1970 (div.); children: Daniel Locke III, Ian Spencer; m. John W. Wine, Sept. 19, 1986; 1 child, Hannah Virginia. With Soviet Life Mag., Washington, 1969—, sr. editor, 1976—. Bd. dirs., public relations adv. Emerson Gallery Art, McLean, Va., 1976—; cons. polit. campaign, fgn. lit. style editor. Democrat. Episcopalian.

BELL, LINDA R., writer, photographer; b. Columbia, Tenn., Nov. 13, 1949; d. William Fleming Jr. and Dorothy Virginia (Cecil) Rainey; m. Dennis L. Bell, Sept. 11, 1971 (div. Dec. 1980); m. T. Martin Warren, Dec. 17, 1983. BSChemE cum laude, U. Tenn., 1971, MS in Engring. magna cum laude, 1972. Process engr. E.I. du Pont de Nemours, Inc., Chattanooga, 1972-75; design engr. Olin Corp., Charleston, 1975-78; environ. engr. TVA, Knoxville, 1978-85; instr. writing U. Tenn., Knoxville, 1985—; freelance writer and photographer Knoxville, 1982—; speaker Presdl. Mgmt. Interns, Knoxville, 1980; photographer Knoxville Arts Council, 1982—; featured guest poet, Nashville, Tenn., 1982. Author: Environmental Development Plan ACP, 1979, (poems) Love Puzzles, 1982, (poems) January Summers, 1982, (non-fiction book) The Red Butterfly, 1983; contbr. 15 articles to lit. jours. and nat. mags., 117 poems to poetry jours. Vol. Girl Scouts U.S., 1966-69; swim instr. ARC, 1970-71; speaker Bradley County, Tenn., 1977; mem. adv. council Am. Inst. Cancer Research, Washington, 1983—. Named one of Outstanding Young Women of Am., 1985. Mem. Nat. Assn. Female Execs., Nat. Wildlife Fedn. (Backyard Habitat award 1986), Nat. Gardening Assn., Lupus Found. Am. (bd. dirs. East Tenn. chpt. 1985—), Tau Beta Pi (sec. 1970-71). Presbyterian.

BELL, MARSHA LUCILE, electronics administrator; b. Detroit, Oct. 16, 1947; d. Oliver Hyde and Lucile Ruth (Kuhl) B. Student, Mich. Tech. U., 1965-68; BSME, U. Colo., 1970; MBA, Nova U., 1983. Engr. research and devel. design Westinghouse Electric Corp., Churchill, Pa., 1970-73; engr. nuclear design Madison, Pa., 1973-78; mgr. safety analysis Rockwell Hanford Ops., Richland, Wash., 1978-84, mgr. program and constrn., 1984-86, mgr. consolidation, dir. productivity, 1986-87; mgr. plant ops. plutonium metal prodn. Westinghouse Hanford Co., Richland, 1987—; speaker Hanford Speakers Bur., Richland, 1984—. With loaned exec. program United Way, Kennewick, Wash., 1983; adminstr. Hanford Family, Richland, 1987. Mem. ASME, Nat. Mgmt. Assn. (treas. 1985-86, v.p. devel. com. 1986-87, council v.p. 1987—, cert.), Project Mgmt. Inst., Soc. Women Engrs. (section rep. 1983-85), Am. Nuclear Soc., Tau Beta Pi. Club: Desert Ski (Richland) (active ski swap check-in 1985-86). Office: Westinghouse Hanford Co PO Box 1970 Richland WA 99352

BELL, MARY, real estate and investment cons.; b. Bklyn., June 5, 1907; d. Alonzo Chandler and Emily (Cox) B.; student Skidmore Coll., 1924-25; grad. Pratt Inst., 1928; student Hunter Coll., 1926, Berlitz Sch., 1927, U. Fla., 1947; children—Chandler Rogers Dann, Diana Dann Smelser. Photographer, Thomas Cook Co., 1927, Mary Bell Studio, Westfield, N.J., 1928-31, Aero. Art and Advt. Surveys, Ayer, N.Y., 1932; silver designer; advt. work for Timken Detroit Axle Co.; with Bell Electric Motor Co., Garwood, N.J., 1920, mgr. Bell Factory Terminal, Garwood, 1939-41, sec. treas., 1941-45, pres., 1945-52; sec. Bell Haven Inc., Miami, Fla., 1945-51, v.p., 1951-82, also dir.; v.p. Bell Bros. Co., Miami, 1945-82, also dir.; sec. Noren Estates Co., Pt. Reyes, 1975-80, also dir.; founding mem. Central Valley Savs. and Loan (Calif.). Mem. Republican Nat. Com., Rep. Senatorial Com., Rep. Congl. Com.; founding mem. Marin Cultural Center, 1980. Mem. Ariz. State Horsemen, Calif. State Horsemen, Calif. Equestrian Patrol, Pratt Alumni Assn., Fine Arts Mus. Soc. of San Francisco, Smithsonian Assocs. Contbr. articles to New Yorker, N.Y. Herald Tribune, N.Y. Times, Country Life, Popular Aviation, Sportsman Pilot, others. Episcopalian.

BELL, MARY ANNE, graphics artist; b. Cape May, N.J., July 16, 1956; d. Glenn Laross and Margaret Marie (Hinke) Bell. Student Northeast Bergen Tech. Sch., 1971-74, Am. Coll. Paris/Parsons Sch. Design, summers 1987, 88; currently enrolled Parsons Sch. Design, N.Y.C., New Sch. for Social Research. Graphic artist Graphics Workshop, Paramus, N.J., 1974-78; art dir. Filip Assocs., Paramus, 1979-87; free-lance graphics artist and illustrator, 1987—. Mem. Bergenfield Council for Arts, 1985. Mem. Soc. of Children's Book Writers. Roman Catholic. Home: 67 Gordon Ave Dumont NJ 07628

BELL, MARY CATLETT (COCABELL), artist; b. Weleetka, Okla., Sept. 26, 1924; d. Stanley Boulware and Alma Bertha (Cagle) Catlett; BA in Lang., U. Okla., 1946; m. J. Stewart Bell, Sept. 15, 1951; 1 son, William Catlett. One woman shows at R.S. Barnwell Art Center, Shreveport, La., 1980, Exhibit in Gov.'s Gallery, State Capitol, 1981, Okla. Art Center, 1984, Ada Arts & Heritage Ctr., 1986; exhibited in group shows at 61st ann. exhbn. Allied Artists of Am., N.Y.C., 1974, Watercolor U.S.A., Springfield, Mo., 1975, 150th, 153d exhbns. Nat. Acad. Design, N.Y.C., 1975, 78, Okla. Bicentennial Art Exhbn., 1976, White House, Washington, 1988, Smithsonian Inst., Living Women Living Art, Okla. Art Center, Kerr Conf. Center, others; represented in permanent collections at Okla. Heritage Assn., Oklahoma City, Arts Council Oklahoma City, Omniplex Arts and Scis. Mus., Oklahoma City, White House, Washington, 1988, Smithsonian Inst.; numerous commns. Mem. Okla. Art Center, Okla. Watercolor Assn., Okla. Mus. Art, Jr. League of Oklahoma City, Delta Delta Delta. Republican. Methodist. Address: 2 Colony Ln Oklahoma City OK 73116

BELL, M(ARY) KATHLEEN, retired government official, civic leader; b. Washington, July 7, 1922; d. Daniel W. and Sadie (Killeen) B. AB, Smith Coll., 1943, MA (hon.), 1959. With Dept. of State, Washington, 1944-73; fgn. affairs officer Office Internat. Econ. and Social Affairs Bur. Internat. Orgn. Affairs, Washington, 1950-56, officer in charge, 1964-66, chief div. instnl. devel. and coordination, 1966-71; dir. system coordinations staff Office UN, Washington, 1971-73, cons., 1973-75, retired, 1975; asst. to exec. sec. U.S. del. San Francisco Conf. UN, 1945; mem. staff UNESCO, London, 1945-46; asst. to U.S. rep. to 2nd, 3rd, 4th, 5th sessions Econ. and Social Council, Washington, 1946-47; advisor to U.S. rep. Econ. and Social Council, N.Y.C., 1948-70; rep. Econ. and Social Council, Washington, 1948-70, alt. rep., 1971-73, U.S. mem. on com. on non-govt. orgns., 1955-65, U.S. mem. interim com. program meetings, 1950-67, chmn. interim com. program meetings, 1952-54; adviser to U.S. del. prep. commn. Internat. Atomic Energy Agy., Vienna, 1957; advisor to U.S. conf. del. Internat. Atomic Energy Agy., Washington, 1957-61; adviser to U.S. del. 1st Assembly Inter-govtl. Maritime Consultative Orgn., London, 1959; advisor U.S. to Council 1st Assembly Inter-govtl. Maritime Consultative Orgn., Washington, 1959; del. ad hoc com. rules procedures 1st Assembly Inter-govtl. Maritime Consultative Orgn., Washington, 1960; adviser to U.S. del. 16th Gen. Assembly of UN, Washington, 1961, mem. spl. com. on coordination, 1964; advisor to U.S. rep. Tech. Assistance Com., Washington, 1964; advisor U.S. del. 9th, 10th and spl. session governing council UN Devel. Program, Washington, 1970; dep. U.S. rep. to governing council UN Devel. Program, Geneva, 1973; alt. U.S. rep. Joint Meeting Administrv. Com. Coordination and Spl. Com. Coordination, Washington, 1971-72; alt. U.S. rep. 1st session Rev. and Appraisal Com., Washington, 1972; trustee Washington Theol. Consortium, also v.p. bd., chmn. bd. 1972-79; trustee Smith Coll. 1976-82, chmn. bd. 1979-82; mem. Carnege Council Ethic and Internat. Affairs, 1983—; mem. bd. Ctr. Pub. Policy and Ethics, 1985—, v.p. 1987—, Exec. Com. Assn. Theological Schs. 1984-88; bd. dirs. UN Assn. Capitol area div. 1986—. Recipient Outstanding Service award Dept. of Stte, 1959. Lodge: Order of the Holy Sepulchre (dame cmmdr. 1959). Home: 3816 Gramercy St Washington DC 20016

BELL, MARY-KATHERINE, lawyer; b. Los Angeles, July 7, 1910; d. Weldon Branch and Vina (Cowan) Morris; m. Robert Collins Bell, Mar. 22, 1941; children—Robert Collins III, Marianne Bell Reifenheiser. B.A., Stanford U., 1934; J.D., George Washington U., 1943. Bar: D.C. 1943, N.Y. 1952, Conn. 1960. Atty., Cummings & Lockwood, Stamford, Conn., 1944-45, Shearman & Sterling, N.Y.C., 1948-77, Ivey, Barnum & O'Mara, Greenwich, Conn., 1978-83; asst. sec. to Assn. Bar City of N.Y., 1946-47; atty. to Conf. on Personal Fin. Law, N.Y.C., 1947-48; sole practice, New Canaan, Conn., 1983-84; mem. Tax Adv. Com. of Am. Law Inst. Co-editor: U.S. Bankruptcy Guide, 1948. Mem. Democratic Town Com., Conn. Bar Assn., Delta Gamma. Clubs: Cosmopolitan (N.Y.C.), Tokeneke (Darien). Home: 528 Main St New Canaan CT 06840 Office: 16 Forest St New Canaan CT 06840

BELL, MELINDA LEE, writer; b. Wauseon, Ohio, Sept. 16, 1957; d. Herbert Taft and Edith May (Ludwig) Bell; Student Adrian Coll. (Mich.), 1975-77, Bowling Green State U. (Ohio), 1976; B.A. in English, U. Notre Dame, 1980; postgrad. UCLA, 1982-87. Corr., New Day Prodns., Los Angeles, 1980-81; asst. to v.p. communications Vidal Sassoon, Inc., Los Angeles, 1981-83, editor newsletter, 1982-83; internat. film distributor, coordinator MGM/UA, Culver City, Calif., 1983-84, script coordinator, 1984-86; freelance writer 1986—; cons. Ford-Eye Prodns., Venice, Calif., 1981—. Author: Reunion, 1981; (radio play) Ellen and Bobby, 1984, TV scripts two episodes Fame. Democrat. Methodist. Club: Notre Dame Alumni. Office: 3863 Girard Ave Suite 4 Culver City CA 90232

BELL, MIKI ZAK, association executive; b. Tel-Aviv, Jan. 29, 1934; came to U.S., 1964; d. Moshe Tourgeman and Rachel Zak; div.; children: Scott, Julia. Stewardess El-Al, Israeli Airlines, Israel, 1958-62; pres. J&M Internat. Trade Co., Atlanta, 1975-77; agt. Clover Realty, Atlanta, 1977-81; pres. Miki Bell Enterprises, Atlanta, 1981-86, exec. dir., from 1986; pres., founder Internat. Soc. Bus. and Profl. Singles, Inc., 1987—. Contbr. articles to profl. jours. Del. White House Conf. on Small Bus., 1985-86; pres. Ridley Howard House Condominium Assn., 1987-88. Named Outstanding Women Bus. Owner, Ga. Small Bus. Council, 1985. Mem. Nat. Assn. Exposition Mgrs., Meeting Planners Internat., Atlanta Assn. Interpreters and Translators, Nat. Assn. for Female Execs., Ga. Soc. Assn. Execs., Bus. and Profl. Women's Clubs (pres. Atlanta 1987-88), Atlanta Council Internat. Orgns., Inc. Avocations: travel, theater, music, swimming, good conversation.

BELL, MILDRED BAILEY, law educator; b. Sanford, Fla., June 28, 1928; d. William F. and Frances E. (Williford) Bailey; m. J. Thomas Bell, Jr., Sept. 18, 1948 (div.); children—Tom, Elizabeth, Ansley. A.B., U. Ga., 1950, J.D. cum laude, 1969; LL.M. in Taxation, N.Y. U., 1977. Bar: Ga. 1969. Law clk. U.S. Dist. Ct. No. Dist. Ga., 1969-70; prof. law Mercer U., Macon, Ga., 1970—; mem. Ga. Com. Constl. Revision, 1978-79. Mem. ABA, Ga. Bar Assn., Phi Beta Kappa, Phi Kappa Phi. Republican. Episcopalian. Bd. editors Ga. State Bar Jour., 1974-76; contbr. articles to profl. jours., chpts. in books. Home: 516 High Point North Rd Macon GA 31210 Office: Mercer U Law Sch Georgia Ave Macon GA 31207

BELL, PATRICIA LAUDERDALE, government administrator; b. Louisville, July 20, 1930; d. Harry Edward and Mary Theresa (Hayden) Lauderdale; m. Hugh Clay Bell, Jr., Aug. 1, 1953 (dec. Dec. 1974); children—Gordon Edwin, Joanne Marie, Gloria Patricia-Leigh. B.S. in Gen. Edn., Spalding U., Louisville, 1951, postgrad., 1968-69; M.S. in Community Devel., U. Louisville, 1970; postgrad. Fla. State U., Western Ky. State U., 1970-75; Ph.D. in Adult Continuing Extension Edn., Mich. State U., 1979. Continuity writer, announcer, receptionist Sta. WLOU, Louisville, 1952-54; file clk., spl. searcher IRS, Louisville, 1956-65, employment devel. specialist Detroit dist., 1980-83, tng. specialist Data Ctr., 1983—; tchr. St. Bartholomew Sch., Buechel, Ky., 1965-67; tchr. social studies Central High Sch., Louisville Pub. Sch. System, 1967-69; tchr. econs. and sociology Ahrens Nigh Sch., Louisville, 1966-69; supr. social studies Louisville Pub. Sch. System, 1969-70, coordinator Hill Adult Learning Ctr., 1970-73; instr. social sci. Univ. Coll., instr. Office Interdisciplinary Programs, Speed Sci. Sch., asst. dir. profl. devel. U. Louisville, 1973-75, 77-78, dir. Life Planning Ctr., 1978-80; workshop presenter adult and career edn. Chmn. bd. Sacred Heart Model Sch., 1966; mem. Young Artists Promotions, 1969-72; mem. citizens adv. com. Louisville and Jefferson County Air Bd., 1970-72; mem. nominating com. Metro United Way; former mem. adult edn. com. St. Agnes Parish; past mem. bd. dirs. Planned Parenthood, Louisville; former chmn. bd. dirs. Louisville Area Planning Council; mem. women's council Bellarmine Coll.; mem. adv. bd. Creative Employment Project. Recipient Disting. Citizen award Mayor of Louisville, 1980; Black Achiever's award, 1980; Disting. Service award IRS Dist. Office, Detroit, 1981; Service to Edn. award Lewis Coll. Bus., Detroit, 1985. Mem. Am. Soc. for Engring. Edn., Am. Personnel and Guidance Assn., Nat. Assn. Student Personnel Adminstrs., Women in Higher Edn. Adminstrn. (nat. identification program), Ky. Personnel and Guidance Assn., AAUP, Blue Monday Network, Urban League. Democrat. Roman Catholic. Clubs: Friday Niters, Federally Employed Women (Detroit). Avocations: bridge; camping; interior design; promoting unknown artists. Home: 1925 Orleans Detroit MI 48207 Office: IRS Data Center Treasury Dept 1900 John C Lodge Dr Detroit MI 48207

BELL, PEARL THOMAZENA, educator; b. Jamaica, Mar. 25, 1936; came to U.S., 1978; d. Zedekiah Augustus and Clementina (Morris) Morgan; m. Easton Alexander Bell, Apr. 15, 1962; children: Harolde, Easton Jr., Ronald, Omar. BA, U. West Indies, 1973; MS, Adelphi U., 1980; EdM in Psychol. Counseling, Columbia U., 1988. Cert. tchr., N.Y. Prin., tchr. West Indies Union Conf. Sch. Dist., Mandeville, Jamaica, 1959-66; tchr. Wolmers Prep. Sch., Kingston, Jamaica, 1966-72; edn. officer, trainer of tchrs., program developer Jamaica Ministry Edn., Kingston, 1972-78; coordinator communications studies N.Y.C. Bd. Edn., 1978-80; tchr. Northeastern Acad., N.Y.C., 1980-87, dir. student affairs, guidance, counseling services, 1987—; coordinator secondary sch. curriculum Seventh Day Adventists, Lancaster, Mass., 1984—. Mem. AACD, Assn. Supervision and Curriculum Devel., Nat. Council Tchrs. Eng., Phi Beta Kappa. Adventist. Club: Ladies Fellowship (Corona, N.Y.). Home and Office: 23-29 100 St East Elmhurst NY 11369

BELL, REGINA JEAN, business owner; b. Lebanon, Mo.; d. Stephen S. and Ida M. (Reaves) B. B.A., Draughens U., 1958; postgrad., Butler U., 1968, Ind.-Purdue U., Indpls., 1948. Prodn. mgr. Howe Mfg. Co., Inc., Indpls., 1958-64; v.p. budgetary control Howe Engring. Co., Inc., Indpls., 1964-67; mgr. material control Nat. Aluminum Div., Indpls., 1968-84; now owner Brown County Letter Shop, Nashville, Ind. Mem. Indpls. Real Estate Assn.

BELL, SHARON ELAINE, nursing adminstrator; b. Dayton, Ohio, Apr. 25, 1942; d. Jack and Sara (Sabo) Matusoff; B.S. in Nursing, Ohio State U., 1964, M.A. in Edn., 1975; m. George Michael Bell, Jan. 5, 1969; 1 son, Chad Michael. Camp nurse Boston YMCA Camp, N.H., 1964, 65; staff nurse Ohio Tuberculosis Hosp., Columbus, 1964-66, Columbus Public Health Dept., 1966-68; instr. Sch. Practical Nursing Columbus Public Schs., 1968-77, tchr. coordinator, 1977-78, supr. sch., 1978-80, supr. health occupation programs, 1978—; adv. bd. Columbus State Community Coll. Sch. Nursing. Mem. Columbus Adminstrs. Assn., Ohio Orgn. Practical Nurse Educators (v.p. 1987—), Central Office Adminstrs. Assn., Nat. League Nursing, Ohio Assn. for Adult Educators, Am. Vocat. Assn. Jewish. Office: 100 Arcadia Ave Columbus OH 43202

BELL, SHARON KAYE, accountant, consultant; b. Lincoln, Nebr., Sept. 14, 1943; d. Edwin B. and Evelyn F. (Young) Czachurski; m. James P. Kittrell (div. Sept. 1974); children: Nathan James, Nona Kaye; m. Joseph S. Bell, June 5, 1977. Various positions mgmt., bookkeeping 1961-71; bookkeeper Internat. Harvester, Chesapeake, Va., 1971-73, Cheat'AH Engring., Santa Ana, Calif., 1973-74, Fre Del Engring., Santa Ana, Calif., 1974-75; bookkeeper/mgr. Tek Sheet Metal Co., Santa Ana, Calif., 1975-79; owner, bookkeeper Bell's Bookkeeping, Huntington Beach, Calif., 1979-86, Fountain Valley, Calif., 1986—. Mem. Nat. Assn. Accts. (dir. 1985-86, sec. 1986-87, v.p. 1987-88), Nat. Notary Assn., Nat. Assn. Female Execs, Wives of Submarine Vets. World War II (v.p. Los Angeles chpt. 1986-87), Nat. Soc. Pub. Accts. Republican. Office: PO Box 2713 Laguna Hills CA 92654-2713

BELL, VANESSA REGINA, nurse; b. Detroit, Mar. 29, 1955; d. L. J. Harris and Mary Louise (Respress) Kyser; m. Jasper Bell, Nov. 13, 1984 (div.); children: Tanisha Akira, Kevin ReShaun. AS in Nursing, Troy State U., 1983. Cert. chemotherapist, med./surg. nurse. Nursing asst. Harper Grace Hosp., Detroit, 1975-78, St. Margaret's Hosp., Montgomery, Ala., 1978-80; staffing clk., sec. St. Margaret's Hosp., Montgomery, 1981-82, charge nurse pediatrics, nursery, post-partum, 1983-85, charge nurse med.-surg., orthopedics, otolaryngology, 1985-87, head nurse oncology, surg. unit, 1987—; instr. basic cardiac life support ARC, Montgomery, 1987. Active PTA, Montgomery, 1981—; mem. Cardio-Pulminary Resuscitation com., St. Margaret's Hosp., 1986—. Mem. Nat. Assn. Female Execs., Troy State U. Alumni Assn. (ways and means com. 1986—, bd. dirs. 1987), Montgomery Area Mgmt. Assn. (mem. relations com.). Democrat. Baptist. Club: Jazzy Ladies Soc. and Savs. (Montgomery) (pres. 1985-86, sec. 1986-87). Home: 3205 Fredericksburg Dr Montgomery AL 36116

BELL, WINNIE ELIZABETH, librarian; b. Waxahachie, Tex., July 7, 1925; d. John Clifford and Ineeta (Brooks) B.; foster children: Lana, Lynnette, Joann, Gwen. BA, Harding Coll., 1949; MA in Library Sci., Peabody Library Sch., 1961. Sec. Security State Bank, Wewoka, Okla., 1949-59; librarian Harding U. Library, Searcy, Ark., 1959—. Mem. AAUW, Am. Library Assn., Ark. Library Assn. (disting. librarian award 1987), Harding Bus. Women. Mem. Ch. of Christ. Office: Harding U Library Harding U PO Box 928 Searcy AR 72143

BELLA, JEAN, retail proprietor; b. Bklyn., Nov. 11, 1940; d. Philip and Jean (Puleo) Aliamo; m. Peter Bolognese, Sept. 3, 1964 (div. 1980); children—Julie Lynn, Lisa Jean, Peter Philip; m. James Bartolo, Aug. 7, 1982. Diploma, Hollywood High Sch., Propr. Seaport Spas of San Diego, 1981. Mem. NOW, Nat. Assn. Female Execs., Nat. Spa & Pool Inst., Nat. Fedn. Ind. Bus. Democrat. Roman Catholic. Avocations: books; artwork; cooking. Office: Seaport Spas of San Diego 8224 Miramar Rd San Diego CA 92126

BELLAMY, ANGELA ROBINSON, assistant city manager; b. Miami, Fla., Nov. 25, 1952; d. Leon Giddings and Helen (Peavy) Robinson; m. Gregory Derek Bellamy, Dec. 23, 1978; 1 child, Gregory Robinson. BA in Bus. Adminstrn., Econs., Fisk U., 1974; MBA, Vanderbilt U., 1976; postgrad., Harvard U., 1986. Mgr. programs City of Miami, 1976-77, personnel officer, 1977-78, sr. personnel officer, 1978-79, supr. personnel, 1979, asst. to city mgr., 1979-81, asst. dir. human resources, 1981-84, acting dir. human resources, 1984-85, dir. personnel mgmt., 1985-88, asst. city mgr., 1988—; pres. dept. dirs. council City of Miami, 1987. Cons. youth motivation task force Nat. Alliance Bus., 1983. Recipient Outstanding Achievement award Personnel Assn. Greater Miami, 1987. Mem. Internat. Personnel Mgmt. Assn. (sec. south Fla. chpt. 1979, v.p. 1980, resolutions com. so. region 1982, 86, co.-chairperson host com. internat. conf. 1984, chair human rights com. 1985-86, nomination com. 1987, program com. 1987-88, So. region program com. 1987-88), Personnel Assn. Greater Miami (v.p. pub. affairs 1988), Am. Mgmt. Assn., Nat. Forum for Black Pub. Adminstrs., Nat. Assn. Female Execs., Fla. Pub. Personnel Assn. (area coordinator so. Fla. region 1984-86), Fisk Club (v.p. Miami chpt. 1978-84), Delta Sigma Theta (Dade county alumnae chpt. corr. sec. 1985-87, 2d v.p. 1987-89). Office: City Hall 3500 Pan American Dr Miami FL 33131

BELLANTONI, MAUREEN BLANCHFIELD, utility company executive; b. Warren, Pa., Mar. 18, 1949; d. John Joseph and Patricia Anne (Southard) Blanchfield; m. Michael Charles Bellantoni, Aug. 12, 1972; children: Mark Christopher, Melissa Catherine. BS in Fin., U. Bridgeport, 1976; MBA, U. Conn., Stamford, 1979. Fin. analyst Dictaphone Corp., Rye, N.Y., 1970-73, Gen. Telephone & Electronics, Stamford, 1973-74, Smith Kline Ultrasonic Products, now Branson, Danbury, Conn., 1974-77; fin. mgr. Gen. Foods, White Plains, N.Y., 1977-80; v.p. fin. Branson Co. div. Emerson Electric, Danbury, 1980—. Mem. Fin. Execs. Inst. Home: 6 Coach Dr PO Box 5291 Brookfield CT 06804-5291 Office: Branson Ultrasonics Corp Eagle Rd Danbury CT 06810

BELLE, BARBARA, theatrical manager, producer, songwriter, publisher; b. Bklyn., Nov. 22, 1922; d. Joseph and Florence (Deerfield) Einhorn; m. Lee Newman, Feb. 1, 1951 (dec.); children: Joseph, Sari Riva. BA, NYU, 1944. Personal mgr. Louis Prima and Keely Smith, Fran Warren, N.Y.C., 1944-51; author, creator various TV prodns. 1986, 87; pres. House of Melody Madness, Inc., Los Angeles, 1944—. Staff writer CBS-TV show Boing-Boing, 1956-57; creator, developer (with others) TV shows Story Behind The Song, 1987, Reunion, 1987; co-writer TV series Tin Pan Sally; co-author, prod. motion picture Sing Sing Sing; prod. motion picture Hey Boy, Hey Girl; co-author various songs including A Sunday Kind of Love, Early Autumn, You Broke the Only Heart That Ever Loved You. Mem. ASCAP, Women in Film. Office: House of Melody Madness PO Box 480100 Los Angeles CA 90048

BELLES, ANITA LOUISE, health care administrator, advertising and marketing consultant, graphic arts executive; b. San Angelo, Tex., Aug. 30, 1948; d. Curtis Lee and Margaret Louise (Perry) B.; m. John Arvel Willey, July 13, 1969 (div. Aug. 1978); children: Suzan Heather, Kenneth Alan. BA, U. Tex., 1972; MS in Health Care Adminstrn., Trinity U., 1984. Registered emergency med. technician; cert. CPR instr., emergency med. technician tchr., La. Regional emergency med. service tng. coordinator Bur. Emergency Med. Service, Lake Charles, La., 1978-79; exec. dir. Southwest La. Emergency Med. Service Council, Lake Charles, 1979-81; project coordinator Tulane U. Med. Sch., New Orleans, 1982-83; dir. La. Bur. of Emergency Med. Service, Baton Rouge, 1982; pres. Computype, Inc., San Antonio, 1983-86, Emergency Med. and Safety Assocs., La. and Tex., 1982—; dir. family planning Bexar County Hosp. Dist., Tex., 1987; mgmt. engr. Inpatient Support Applications, 1987-88. Editor A.L.E.R.T., 1980-83, San Antonio Executive News, 1987—, Family Living, 1987-88; feature writer Bright Scrawl, 1985-86; contbr. numerous articles on emergency med. services to profl. jours. Bd. dirs. Thousand Oaks Homeowner's Assn., sec., treas., 1985; active Trinity U. Health Care Alumni Assn., Jr. League San Antonio, The Parenting Ctr., Baton Rouge, 1982-83, Jr. League Lake Charles, 1982, Campfire Council Pub. Relations Com., Lake Charles, 1982; newsletter editor Community Food Co-Op, Newsletter Editor, 1979; vol. Lake Charles Mental Health Ctr., 1974. Recipient Outstanding Service award La. Assn Registered Emergency Med. Technicians, 1983, Southwest La. Assn. Emergency Med. Technicians, 1983; named Community Leader KPLC TV, Lake Charles, 1981, regional winner Assn U. Programs in Health Adminstrn., HHS Sec's. Competitions for Innovations in Health, 1982. Mem. Nat. Assn. Emergency Med. Technicians., Tex. Assn. Emergency Med. Technicians, Am. Coll. Health Care Execs., Am. Assn. Automotive Medicine, Southwest La. Assn. Emergency Med. Technicians (founding mem., v.p. 1979-80, CPR com. chmn. 1980-81, pub. relations com. chmn. 1981-82, bd. dirs. 1980-82), Am. Mgmt. Assn., Nat. Soc. Emergency Med. Service Adminstrs., Nat. Coalition Emergency Med. Services, Am. Composition Assn. Methodist. Office: Bexar County Hosp Dist 4502 Medical Dr San Antonio TX 78284

BELLES, MARLENE ANN, financial executive; b. Cleve., Aug. 28, 1943; d. Leo Vincent and Irene Virginia (Hrubo) Bielawski; m. Gerald Duane Holderbaum, Sept. 1, 1962 (div.); m. James Wesley Belles, Dec. 10, 1983 (div.). BBA, Cleve. State U., 1970. Chief acct. Sta. KYW/WKYC-TV, Cleve., 1963-69, bus. dir., 1977-80; acctg. mgr. Sta. WKBF, Cleve., 1969-70; systems mgr. NBC, N.Y.C., 1970-75; mgr. fin. Sta. KNBC-TV, Burbank, Calif., 1975-77; controller Sta. KTVU-TV, Oakland, Calif., 1980—; lectr. broadcasting careers. Adviser Jr. Achievement, Burbank, 1975-77; speaker Explorers div. Boy Scouts Am., Oakland, 1981—; arbitrator Better Bus. Bur., Oakland, 1982—; bd. dirs. Oakland YWCA, 1983—. Named Woman of Distinction, Oakland Soroptimists, 1984; Nat. Geog. scholar, 1960. Mem. Am. Women in Radio and TV (chpt. pres. 1982-83, div., v.p. membership 1984-86, pres.-elect 1986-87, pres. 1987-88), Broadcast Fin. Mgmt. Assn. (bd. dirs. 1985-87), Women's Forum West, Nat. Acad. TV Arts and Scis. Clubs: Highlands Country, Lakeview (Oakland). Office: KTVU-TV 2 Jack London Square Oakland CA 94607

BELLINGER, CHRISTINE BOWMAN, grounds maintenance company executive, nurseryman; b. Kansas City, Mo., Mar. 28, 1955; d. Daniel Benson and Phyllis Joann (Purdy) Bowman; m. Randal Charles Bellinger, Oct. 22, 1977. B.S. in Forestry, Purdue U., 1977. Pub. relations coordinator Sears Lawn & Leaf, Wheeling, Ill., 1977; co-owner, pres. Bellinger's Profl. Grounds Maintenance, Inc., Lafayette, Ind., 1977—. Mem. Ind. Assn. Nurserymen, Am. Assn. Nurserymen, Profl. Grounds Mgmt. Soc., Greater Lafayette C. of C. (Marquis de Lafayette award 1985). Republican. Avocations: skiing; camping; hiking; boating; ice skating; bicycling.

BELLIVEAU, DIANE THERESA, environmental engineer; b. Lowell, Mass., Nov. 12, 1955; d. Harold Joseph and Margaret Inga (Johnson) Robinson; m. Stephen Douglas Belliveau; children: Andrine Denise, Brad Thomas. Student, Northeastern U., 1973-76; BSCE, U. Lowell, 1979, MSCE, 1981. Sanitary engr. waste-water treatment plant City of Lowell, 1979-80; cons. sanitary engr. Dana Perkins & Assocs., Reading, Mass., 1980-82; environ. engr. Commonwealth of Mass. Dept. Environ. Quality Engring., Worcester, 1982—. Roman Catholic. Office: Mass Dept Environ Engring 75 Grove St Worcester MA 01605

BELLM, PEGGY A(NN), public relations executive, civic worker, consultant; b. Highland, Ill.; d. Erwin A. and Margaret J. (Knebel) B. BA in Theatre and Mass Communications, So. Ill. U., 1976. Ptnr. Pig Patch U.S.A., Highland, 1977-83; owner Pegalie's Helvetia Haus, Highland, 1977-83; mng. ptnr. Recollections, St. Louis County, Mo., 1982-86; exec. dir. Highland C. of C., 1987—, bd. dirs., 1979-83, 87—, pres., 1981-82; owner Helvetia Trading Co., Highland, 1988—, Center Stage Promotions, Highland, 1988—; pub. speaker; retail cons. Dir./choreographer numerous local and area theatrical prodns.; emcee/coordinator numerous bridal showcases, fashion shows, beauty pageants and festivals, 1979—. Bd. dirs., founding mem. Friends of Theatre and Dance So. Ill. U., Edwardsville, 1979—, mem. Students in Free Enterprise adv. bd., 1987—; mem. Southwestern Ill. Leadership Council Mktg. Com., 1987—; mem. small bus. adv. bd. U. Ill. Extension Bur., 1987—; mem. Highland Econ. Devel. Research Com., 1986-87; chmn. Highland Interim Econ. Devel. Com., 1987—; producer, dir. Highland Summer Theatre, 1986—, exec. bd., directorial advisor, 1981-86; theatrical pageant author/dir. Highland Bicentennial Commn., 1975-76; mem. post prom com. Highland High Sch., 1987—; coordinator Maifest Festival, 1979-83, 86-88; bd. dirs., theatrical pagent chmn. Highland Sesquicentennial Assn., 1984-87; theatrical pageant producer/dir. Highland Sesquicentennial Commn., 1985-87; bd. dirs. Madison County Arts Council, Ill., 1987—, chmn. fin. com., 1988—; bd. dirs. Helvetia Schweizerfest Assn., Highland, 1988—. Mem. Nat. Assn. Female Execs., So. Ill. U. Alumni Assn., Highland Hist. Soc., Ill. Assn. C. of C. Execs., Metro East C. of C. Assn. Club: Internat. Fedn. Bus. and Profl. Women's (Young Career Woman 1979, Dist. Young Career Woman 1980). Office: PO Box 294 Highland IL 62249

BELLO, SHERE CAPPARELLA, marketing executive, dance studio owner; b. Norristown, Pa., Sept. 4, 1956; d. Anthony Carmen and Patsy Ann (Robbins) Capparella. BA in Langs., Rosemont (Pa.) Coll., 1978; postgrad. in bus., Ursinus Coll., 1986—; postgrad., Rosemont Coll., Gwynedd Mercy Coll., Montgomery County Community Coll. Sales mgr. Spectrum Communications Corp., Norristown, 1977-79, mgr. sales and mktg., 1986-87; asst. sales and adminstrv. asst. Tettex Instruments, Inc., Fairview Village, Pa., 1979-83; owner, instr. Shere's World of Dance and Fine Arts, Jeffersonville, Pa., 1982—; exec. sec. bi-lingual Certainteed Corp., Valley Forge, Pa., 1983-84; exec. sec. internat. dept. Syntex Dental Products, Inc., Valley Forge, 1984-86; v.p. Captrium Devel. Corp., Exton, Pa., 1987—; free-lance tutor languages, Pa. area, 1976-78; free-lance photog. model, Pa. area, 1977-81; v.p. La Bella Modeling Agy., Collegeville, Pa., 1979-82; choreographer La Bella Sch. Performance, Collegeville, 1979-82; free-lance fashion show commentator, 1982—; free-lance lang. translator, 1984—. Judge pageants Miss Am. Scholarship, Jr. Miss, Nat. Teen and Pre-Teen, All-Am. Talent, Ofcl. Little Miss Am., Talent Olympics, Talent Unltd.; producer, choreographer Miss Montgomery County Pageant, Plymouth Meeting, Pa., 1985; co-producer, choreographer Miss Del. Valley Pageant, Horsham, Pa., 1983-84.; Confraternity Christian Doctrine kindergarten tchr. Visitation Parish, 1987-88. Mem. Cen. Pa. Dance Council, Phila. Dance Alliance, Nat. Assn. Female Execs., Christian Children's Fund, Humane Soc. U.S. Republican. Roman Catholic. Office: Captrium Devel Corp 325 W Lincoln Hwy Exton PA 19341

BELLO-REUSS, ELSA NOEMI, physician, educator; b. Buenos Aires, Argentina, May 1, 1939; came to U.S., 1972; d. Jose F. and Julia M. (Hiriart) Bello; B.S., U. Chile, 1957, M.D., 1964; m. Luis Reuss, Apr. 15, 1965; children—Luis F., Alejandro E. Intern J.J. Aguirre Hosp., Chile, 1963-64; resident in internal medicine U. Chile, Santiago, 1964-66; practice medicine specializing in nephrology Santiago, 1967-72; Internat. NIH fellow U. N.C., Chapel Hill, 1972-74; vis. asst. prof. physiology U. N.C., Chapel Hill, 1974-75; Louis Welt fellow U. N.C.-Duke U. Med. Center, 1975-76; mem. faculty Jewish Hosp. St. Louis, 1976-83, asst. prof. medicine, physiology and biophysics Washington U. Sch. Medicine, St. Louis, 1976-86, assoc. prof. physiology dept. cell biology and physiology, 1986; assoc. prof. medicine U. Tex. Med. Br., Galveston, 1986—. Mem. Internat., Am. Socs. Nephrology, Royal Soc. Medicine, Nat. Kidney Found. (med. adv. bd.), Council of Women in Nephronology, Tex. Med. Assn., Am. Fedn. Clin. Research, Am. Physiology Soc., Am. Heart Assn., Kidney Council, Soc. Gen. Physiologists, Math. Assn. Am. Contbr. articles on nephrology and epithelial electrophysiology to med. and physiology jours., chpt. to nephrology text. Office: U Tex Med Br Dept Medicine Nephrology OJS 4 200 Galveston TX 66550

BELLOVICS, DONNA MAE, nurse, educator; b. Rock Island, Ill., June 24, 1932; d. Harry John and Mabel Anna (Krueger) Ohms; R.N. (Annie Yates scholar), Los Angeles County Gen. Hosp., 1954; BSN, Marycrest Coll., 1965; MA, U. Iowa, 1969; Ed.D., Walden U., 1975; m. Stephen M. Bellovics, June 24, 1955; children—Michael, Anne, George. Staff nurse, asst. head nurse Moline (Ill.) Public Hosp., 1956-58; pvt. duty nursing, 1960-64; instr. lic. practical nursing, Davenport, Iowa, 1964-65; instr. Moline Pub. Diploma Nursing, 1965-67; asst. prof. Marycrest Coll., 1969-70; assoc. prof. assoc. degree nursing program, chmn. dept. Black Hawk Coll., 1970-83; chmn. dept. Cameron U., Lawton, Okla., 1983—; co-author CAI Med.-Surg. for med. assocs., 1987. Chmn. nursing scholarship com. Henry County March of Dimes, 1974-83. Mem. Am. Nurses Assn., Okla. Nurses Assn. (pres. Dist. 11 1988—), Nat. League Nursing, Am. Heart Assn., Sigma Theta Tau. Republican. Presbyterian. Home: 1802 NW 80th St DC 8016 4 Lawton OK 73505 Office: Cameron U 2800 W Gore Blvd Lawton OK 73505

BELLOWS, CAROLE KAMIN, judge; b. Chgo., May 24, 1935; d. Alfred and Sara (Liebenson) Kamin; B.A., U. Ill., 1957; J.D., Northwestern U., 1960; m. Jason E. Bellows, June 28, 1958 (dec. June 1980); children—Marcia, Douglas, Daniel. Admitted to Ill. bar, 1960; law clk. Chief Justice Ill. Ct. of Claims, Chgo., 1962-72; partner Bellows & Bellows, Chgo., 1970-79, Reuben & Proctor (now Isham, Lincoln & Beale), Chgo., from 1979; now judge Ill. Cir. Ct. Cook County. Bd. dirs. Uptown Poverty Law Center, 1982—. Recipient Maurice Weigle award for outstanding service to organized bar, 1970, U. Ill. Mothers Assn. medallion of honor, 1975, Northwestern U. Alumnae award, 1978. Fellow Am. Bar Found. (bd. dirs. 1982-85); mem. Am. Bar Assn. (sec. 1967-73, chmn. sect. individual rights and responsibilities 1975—, mem. ho. of dels. 1975—, com. on bar activities and services 1978—), Ill. Bar Assn. (chmn. Bill of Rights com. 1965-67, bd. govs. 1969-79, mem. assembly 1972-79, chmn. budget com. 1976-77, chmn. legis. com. 1978-79, pres. 1977-78), Chgo. Bar Assn. (chmn. constl. revision com. 1973-74), Am. Law Inst., League Women Voters of Ill., Womens Bar Assn. Ill., Decalogue Soc., Nat. Conf. Bar Presidents (exec. council 1977—), Am. Jewish Com. (bd. dirs. 1985—), Northwestern U. Sch. Law Alumni Assn. (pres. 1982-83). Club: Law (Chgo.). Editor: Your Bill of Rights, 1967, 69. Office: 1602 RJ Daley Ctr Chicago IL 60603 *

BELOVANOFF, OLGA, healthcare facility administrator; b. Buchanan, Sask., Can., July 1, 1932; d. Frederick Alexander and Dora (Konkin) B. Grad. high sch., Kamsack, Sask., Can. From clk. to adminstrv. officer Sask. Health Dept. Cancer Clinic, Saskatoon, 1951-78; bus. mgr. Sask. Cancer Found. Saskatoon Clinic, 1979—. Dir. Sask. br. Can. Tenpin Fedn., Inc. Mem. Assn. Adminstrv. Assts. Home: 420 3d Ave N, Saskatoon, SK Canada S7K 2J3 Office: Saskatoon Cancer Clinic, Univ Hosp, Box 37, Saskatoon, SK Canada S7N 0X0

BELOVITCH, JEANNE ANN, public relations writer, editor; b. Cin., June 7, 1945; d. Charles and Mildred Jane (Flinchpaugh) Belovitch; B.S., Boston U., 1967. Asst. v.p. sales promotion Putnam Fund Distbrs., Boston, 1971-74; prin. Jeanne Belovitch & Assocs., Boston, 1974-75; account exec., producer, moderator arts program Sta. WWEL, Medford, Mass., 1975-78; writer public affairs United Way of Mass. Bay, Boston, 1978-82; pub. Boston Firsts poster, 1980; mgr. G&R Publs., Inc., Boston, 1982-86; staff writer South End News, Boston, 1983-85; founder, editor newsletter Remarriage, Boston, 1984-86; editor: Making Remarriage Work, 1987; cons. fund raising Cambridge (Mass.) YWCA, 1979; instr. Fenway Free U., Boston; adv. creative writer's workshop Walpole Prison, 1981-82. Editor: Making Remarriage Work, 1987. Mem. Boston U. Alumni Assn. (dir. Coll. Basic Studies). Contbr. articles to newspapers and mags. Home: 24 Appleton St Boston MA 02116

BELSKY, KATHLEEN MARILYN, telecommunications company executive; b. Phila., Feb. 7, 1949; d. Albert and Mary Ann (McCarey) Masurat; m. Glenn Stuart Belsky, May 26, 1979; 1 child, Steven. BS, Phila. Coll. Textiles and Scis., 1985, MBA, 1987. Ednl. cons. Bell of Pa., Phila., 1975-77, coordinator handicapped services, 1978-83, mgr. direct mktg., 1983-86, staff mktg. mgr., 1986—; dir. Nevil Trust-Girard Bank Telephone Device for the Deaf Project, Phila., 1977-79. Bd. dirs. Pa. Soc. for the Advancement of the Deaf, Phila., 1985-87; mem. Telecommunications for the Deaf. Recipient Outstanding Community Service award Del. Valley region Telecommunications for the Deaf, 1986. Mem. Am. Mgmt. Assn., Nat. Assn. Female Execs. Republican. Club: Lighthouse Point Yacht (Toms River, N.J.). Home: 1220 E Cushmore Rd Upper Southampton PA 18966 Office: Bell of Pa One Parkway 15th Floor Philadelphia PA 19102

BELTON, LINDA WEBER, hospital administrator, nurse; b. Erie, Pa., Jan. 26, 1950; d. James E. and Mildred E. (Dougherty) Weber; R.N., Jameson Sch. Nursing, 1970; student Westminster Coll., 1967-68, Mercyhurst Coll., 1976-77; B.S. in Nursing Adminstrn., Columbia Pacific U., 1981, M.S. in Nursing Adminstrn., 1983; B.S. in Psychology, SUNY, 1982; m. Lawrence Winfield Belton, June 27, 1969; children—Marshall LeMaster, Adrienne Elizabeth. Nursing supr. Chatham (Pa.) Extended Care Facility, 1973-75; clin. coordinator rehab. services St. Vincent Health Center, Erie, Pa., 1975-77; dir. nursing Shady Acres Nursing Home, Madison, Ohio, 1977-79; nurse adminstr. Meml. Hosp. of Carbon County, Rawlins, Wyo., 1979-81, asst. hosp. adminstr., 1981-83; v.p. Mercy Med. Ctr., Oshkosh, Wis., 1983-87; adminstr. div. care and treatment facilities Dept. Health and Social Services, State of Wis., Madison, 1987—; adj. prof. U. Wis.-Oshkosh, 1984-87; cons. Rawlins Health Occupations Center. Mem. Wyo. State Continuing Edn. com., 1981-83; bd. dirs. Am. Cancer Soc., 1980-83; mem. Child Protection Team, Rawlins, 1979-80, Family Life Ministry team, 1981-83. Recipient Am. Cancer Soc. Participation award, 1981. Mem. Nat. League for Nursing, Am. Nurses Assn. (advanced cert. in nursing adminstrn.), Wis. Nurses Assn (Leadership award 1987), Wy. Nurses Assn. (bd. dirs. 1981-83), Wis. Orgn. Nurse Execs., Oshkosh Pregnancy Lifeline (pres.), Sisters of the Sorrowful Mother (assoc.). Club: Bus. and Profl. Women's. Contbr. articles to profl jours. Office: 1 W Wilson St Madison WI 53707

BELTZNER, GAIL ANN, educator; b. Palmerton, Pa., July 20, 1950; d. Conon Nelson and Lorraine Ann (Carey) Beltzner; B.S. in Music Edn. summa cum laude, West Chester State U., 1972; postgrad. Kean State Coll., Temple U., Westminster Choir Coll., Lehigh U. Tchr. music Drexel Hill Jr. High Sch., 1972-73; music specialist Allentown Sch. Dist., Pa., 1973—; tchr. Corps Sch. and Community Developmental Lab., 1978-80, Corps Community Resource Festival, 1979-81, Corps Cultural Fair, 1980, 81. Mem. aux. Allentown Art Museum; mem. womans com. Allentown Symphony; bd. dirs. Allentown Area Ecumenical Food Bank. Mem. Allentown Fedn. Tchrs. (sec., exec. com.), Music Educators Nat. Conf., Pa. Music Educators Assn., Am. Orff-Schulwerk Assn., Soc. Gen. Music, Am. Assn. Music Therapy, Internat. Soc. Music Edn., Assn. Supervision and Curriculum Devel., Choristers Guild, Lenni Lenape Hist. Soc., Allentown Symphony Assn., Allentown 2d Civilian Police Acad., Nat. Sch. Orch. Assn., Lehigh County Hist. Soc., AAUW, Kappa Delta Pi, Phi Delta Kappa, Alpha Lambda. Republican. Lutheran. Home: PO Box 4427 Allentown PA 18105

BEMPORAD, SONYA, child care agency executive; b. Phila., Oct. 31, 1934; d. Sam and Pauline (Nemez) Kaufmann Kasakoff; m. Jack Bemporad, Oct. 10, 1954 (div. Oct. 1976); children—Henry, Raphael. B.A., U. Cin., 1956; M.A., Sarah Lawrence U., 1961. Mem. faculty dept. psychology Sarah Lawrence U., Bronxville, N.Y., 1964-72, dir. Early Learning Ctr., 1970-72; lectr. psychiatry U. Tex. Health Sci. Ctr., 1981-85; exec. dir. Rhoads Terrace Children's Ctr., Dallas, 1974-76; exec. program dir. Child Care Dallas, 1976—; cons. Yonkers Headstart, 1969-71, Dallas County Mental Health-Mental Retardation, 1980-82, Dallas County Child Welfare, 1976—. Pres., Child Care 76, Dallas, 1974-76; mem. at large Women's Council, Dallas, 1974—; co-chmn. Women's Issues Congress, Dallas, 1983-84; chmn. Mayor's Child Care Task Force, Dallas, 1983-84; bd. dirs., chmn. profl. services council, Dallas Child Guidance Clinic, 1986—; bd. dirs. Women's Ctr. Dallas, 1987—. Fellow Am. Orthopsychiat. Assn.; mem. Nat. Assn. Edn. Young Children, Internat. Assn. Infant Mental Health (bd. dirs.), Tex. Assn. Infant Mental Heatlh (pres. 1987—), Phi Beta Kappa. Office: Child Care Dallas 1499 Regal Row Suite 400 Dallas TX 75247

BENACH, SHARON ANN, physician assistant; b. New Orleans, Aug. 28, 1944; d. Wilbur G. and Freda Helen (Klaas) Cherry; m. Richard Benach, Dec. 6, 1969 (div. Oct. 1976); children: Craig, Rachel. Degree, St. Louis U., 1978. Physician asst. VA Hosp., St. Louis, 1982-84, Maricopa County Health Services, Phoenix, 1984—. Served with USPHS, 1978-82. Recipient Outstanding Performance award Dept. Health and Human Services. Mem. Mensa. Jewish. Home: PO Box 1272 Mesa AZ 85221

BENATAR, PAT (PAT ANDREJEWSKI), rock singer; b. Bklyn., 1953; m. Neil Geraldo; 1 child, Haley. Albums include: In the Heat of the Night, 1979, Crimes of Passion, 1980, Precious Time, 1981, Get Nervous, 1982, Live From Earth, 1983, Tropico, 1984, Seven the Hard Way, 1985; popular recs. include Treat Me Right, Hit Me With Your Best Shot, Love is a Battlefield, Hell is for Children. Recipient Grammy award for best female rock vocal performance, 1981, 82, 83, 84. Office: care Barbara Skydel Premier Talent Agy 3 E 54th St New York NY 10022 also: New Star Enterprises Rick Newman 60 W 70th St New York NY 10023

BENBASSETT, JANE SCHUMER, advertising company executive; b. Hempstead, N.Y., Mar. 21, 1961; d. Martin and Sarah (Markowitz) Schumer; m. Lawrence Scott BenBassett, Mar. 8, 1986. BS magna cum laude, U. Md., 1983. Asst. account exec. Abramson Assocs., Washington, 1983-84; asst. account exec. Rosenthal, Greene & Campbell, Bethesda, Md., 1984, account exec., 1984-86, sr. account exec., 1986-87, account supr., 1987—. Office: Rosenthal Greene & Campbell 7910 Woodmont Ave Bethesda MD 20814

BENBOW, CAMILLA PERSSON, psychology educator, researcher; b. Lund, Sweden, Dec. 3, 1956; came to U.S., 1965, naturalized, 1985; m. Robert Michael Benbow, Jan. 5, 1975; children—Wystan R., Bronwen G., Trefor A., Evan M., A. Lovisa, G. Byron, Lena C. BA with honors, Johns Hopkins U., 1977, MA in Psychology, 1978, MS in Edn. of the Gifted, 1980, EdD with distinction in Gifted Edn., 1981. Dir. Study of Mathematically Precocious Youth, Iowa State U., 1986—, Johns Hopkins U., Balt., 1977-79, asst. dir., 1979-81, assoc. dir., 1981-85, co-dir., 1985-86; assoc. research scientist dept. psychology Johns Hopkins U., 1981-86, asst. prof. sociology, part-time 1983-86; assoc. prof. psychology Iowa State U., Ames, 1985—. Contbr. articles to profl. jours.; sr. editor: Academic Precocity: Aspects of Its Development, 1983; editor Intellectually Talented Youth Bull., 1979. Recipient John Curtis Gowan prize Nat. Assn. Gifted Children, 1980, 81; research award Am. Ednl. Research Assn., 1981; Spencer fellow, alt., 1984, 85; research paper award (3) Mensa, 1985; Early Scholar award Nat. Assn. Gifted Children, 1985. Mem. Phi Beta Kappa, Sigma Xi. Office: Iowa State U Dept Psychology Ames IA 50011-3180

BENCINI, SARA HALTIWANGER, concert pianist; b. Winston Salem, N.C., Sept. 2, 1926; d. Robert Sydney and Janie Love (Couch) Haltiwanger; m. Robert Emery Bencini, June 26, 1954; children—Robert Emery, III, Constance Bencini Waller, John McGregor. Mus. B., Salem Coll., 1947; postgrad. grad. Juilliard Sch. Music, 1948-50; M.A., Smith Coll., 1951; postgrad. in piano U. N.C.-Greensboro. Head piano dept. Mary Burnham Sch. for Girls, Northampton, Mass., 1949-51; pianist, composer dance and drama dept. Smith Coll., 1951-52; head music dept. Walnut Hill Sch. for Girls, Natick, Mass., 1952-54; pvt. piano tchr., High Point, N.C., 1954-66; concert pianist appearing in Am. and Europe, 1948—; duo-piano performances with PBS-TV, Columbia, S.C., 1967, Winston Salem Symphony, N.C., 1964-68, Eastern Mus. Festival, Greensboro, N.C., 1969. Democrat. Presbyterian.

BENCZE, EVA IVANYOS, mechanical engineer; b. Budapest, Hungary, Mar. 6, 1932; came to U.S., 1956, naturalized, 1977; d. Jozsef and Katalin (Szabo) Ivanyos; m. Joseph Steven Bencze, Aug. 4, 1956; children: Christina, Ingrid, Caroline, Andrew. MSME, Tech. U. Budapest, 1955. Mech. designer Lockwood Greene, Inc., N.Y.C., 1968-69, Elster's, Inc., Hollywood, Calif., 1972-74; mech. engr. DMJM, Los Angeles, 1974-75; sr. mech. engr. DMJM/KE, Balt., 1975-82, DMJM/HTC, Houston, 1982-83; sr. mech. engr. DMJM/Metro Rail Transit Consultants, Los Angeles, 1983-87, supr. mech. engring., 1985—. Mem. ASHRAE (assoc.). Avocations: reading, listening to music. Home: 5326 Townsend Ave Los Angeles CA 90041 Office: DMJM/Metro Rail Transit 548 S Spring St Los Angeles CA 90013

BENDA, MARILYN VIRGINIA, small business owner; b. Leroy, Ind., Sept. 21, 1935; d. Charles Edward and Bertha Mae (Hoagland) Poisel; m. Augustine A. Benda, May 19, 1956; children: Michelle Bates, Lisa Brickman. Student, Purdue North Cen. U., 1983-84. Exec. sec. McGill Mfg. Co., Valparaiso, Ind., 1965-72, cost estimator, 1972-87; owner, operator Benda's Bridal and Evening, Demotte, Ind., 1985-87, Benda's Heritage House, Valparaiso, 1987—. Mem. Nat. Bridal Services, Nat. Network of Women in Sales (charter mem. Ind. chpt.), Sigma Alpha Chi (pres. 1979). Home: 1806 Alice St Valparaiso IN 46383 Office: 909 N Lafayette St Valparaiso IN 46383

BENDER, BETTY BARBEE, food service professional; b. Lexington, Ky., Apr. 29, 1932; d. Richard Carroll and Sarah Elizabeth (Rodes) Barbee; m. David H. Bender, Dec. 14, 1957; children: Bruce, Carroll. BA in Home Econs., Mont. State U., 1954; MS in Food Service Mgmt., Miami U., Oxford, Ohio, 1980. Adminstrv. dietitan Mass. Gen. Hosp., Boston, 1955-56; asst. chief dietitan Meth. Hosp., Indpls., 1957-61; chief dietitan Community Hosp., Indpls., 1961-63; supervising dietitian Chgo. Area ARA, 1963-67; asst. food service supr. Dayton (Ohio) Bd. Edn., 1969, mgr. food service, 1969—; cons. Nat. Frozen Food Assn., Washington, 1983, Crescent Metal Products Co., Cleve., 1985. Contbr. articles to profl. jours. Recipient 26th Ann. Foodservice Facilities Design award Insts. Mag. for Commissary Design, 1972, Silver and Gold Plate awards Internat. Foodservice Mfrs. Assn.,1985, President's award Ohio Sch. Food Service Assn., 1987; recognized for outstanding contributions to child nutrition programs Ohio Ho. Reps., 1972, 84. Mem. Am. Sch. Food Service Assn. (nat. pres. 1983, chmn. 1978-80 major city sect.), Ohio Sch. Food Service Assn. (pres. 1977), Dayton Sch. Adminstr. Assn., Dayton Sch. Mgmt. Assn., Am. Dietetic Assn. (cert.), Ohio Dietetic Assn., Dayton Dietetic Assn., Soc. Nutrition Edn. (panel 1983). Democrat. Home: 7217 Tarryton Rd Dayton OH 45459 Office: Dayton Bd Edn Food Service Dept 125 Heid Ave Dayton OH 45404

BENDER, BETTY WION, librarian; b. Mt. Ayer, Iowa, Feb. 26, 1925; d. John F. and Sadie A. (Guess) Wion; m. Robert F. Bender, Aug. 24, 1946. B.S., N.Tex. State U., Denton, 1946; M.A., U. Denver, 1957. Asst. cataloger N. Tex. State U. Library, 1946-49; from cataloger to head acquisitions So. Meth. U., Dallas, 1949-56; reference asst. Ind. State Library, Indpls., 1951-52; librarian Ark. State Coll., 1958-59, Eastern Wash. Hist. Soc., Spokane, 1960-67; reference librarian, then head circulation dept. Spokane (Wash.) Public Library, 1968-73, library dir., 1973—; vis. instr. U. Denver, summers 1957-60, 63, fall 1959; instr. Whitworth Coll., Spokane, 1962-64; mem. Gov. Wash. Regional Conf. Libraries, 1968, Wash. Statewide Library Devel. Council, 1970-71. Bd. dirs. N.W. Regional Found., 1973-75, Inland Empire Goodwill Industries, 1975-77, Wash. State Library Commn., 1979-87, Future Spokane, 1983—, vice chmn., 1986-87, pres., 1987—. Recipient YWCA Outstanding Achievement award in Govt., 1985. Mem. ALA (mem. library adminstrn. and mgmt. assn. com. on orgn. 1982-83, chmn. nominating com. 1983-85, v.p./pres.-elect. 1985-86, pres. 1986-87), Pacific N.W. Library Assn. (chmn. circulation div. 1972-75, conv. chmn. 1977), Wash. Library Assn. (v.p./pres.-elect 1975-77, pres. 1977-78), AAUW (pres. Spokane br. 1969-71, rec. sec. Wash. br. 1971-73, fellowship named in honor 1972), Spokane and Inland Empire Librarians (dir. 1967-68), Am. Soc. Pub. Adminstrn. Republican. Lutheran. Club: Zonta (pres. Spokane chpt. 1976-77, dist. conf. treas. 1972). Home: 119 N 6th St Cheney WA 99004 Office: Spokane Public Library Comstock Bldg Library W 906 Main Ave Spokane WA 99201

BENDER, DIANE LOUISE WOLF, lawyer; b. Evansville, Ind, Oct. 21, 1955; d. Thomas Joseph and Margaret Gertrude (Horn) Wolf; m. John Frederick Bender, June 15, 1985. BBA with highest honors, U. Notre Dame, 1977, JD cum laude, 1980. Bar: Ind. 1980. Ptnr. Kahn, Dees, Donovan & Kahn, Evansville, Ind., 1980—. Bd. dirs. Vis. Nurses Assn. of Southwestern Ind., Inc., 1983—, United Way of Southwestern Ind., Inc., 1984—, Health Skills, Inc., Evansville, 1984—, Cath. Press of Evansville, Inc., 1985—. Mem. ABA, Ind. Bar Assn., Evansville Bar Assn., Am. Inst. CPA's, Ill. CPA Soc. Home: PO Box 9164 Evansville IN 47710 Office: Kahn Dees Donovan & Kahn PO Box 3646 Evansville IN 47735-3646

BENDER, ELIZABETH, infosystems specialist; b. Ridgewood, NJ, Feb. 23, 1962; d. Francis and Josephine (Cavalieri) Varrichio; m. Robert Bender, Aug. 3, 1985. BS, St. Peter's Coll., 1984. Programmer AT&T Labs., Short Hills, N.J., 1984-87; sr. analyst Johnson & Johnson Hosp. Services, New Brunswick, N.J., 1987—. Home: Home 543 Winsor St Bound Brook NJ 08805 Office: Johnson & Johnson Hosp Services PO Box 4000 New Brunswick NJ 08903

BENDICK, JEANNE LOUIS, author, illustrator children's science books; b. N.Y.C., Feb. 25, 1919; d. Louis Xerxes and Amelia Marie (Hess) Garfunkel; m. Robert Louis Bendick, Nov. 24, 1940; children—Robert Louis, Jr., Karen Bendick Watson Holton. B.A., Parsons/New Sch., 1939. Author children's sci. books including: Super People; Scare a Ghost, Tame a Monster; Putting the Sun to Work; Egyptian Tombs; How Much and How Many; Mathematics Illustrated Dictionary; The Day the Numbers Disappeared; (with Glenn Blough) Nature Sci. Series; author Sci. Experiences series, The First Books of series (space travel; satellites; automobiles, also others); author, co-author edn. materials: textbooks Ginn Sci. Program, multimedia programs, Starting Points, Learning Experiences, You and Me and Our World; author filmstrips: The Seasons; story editor, writer NBC children's series The First Look for TV. Recipient several Best Sci. Books of Yr. awards. Mem. Nat. Sci. Tchrs. Assn., ALA, Authors League, Authors Guild, Writers Guild of Am. East. Jewish.

BENDIG, JUDITH JOAN, systems consultant, computer company executive; b. Erie, Pa., Oct. 28, 1955; d. Richard W. and Rhea Agnes (Hain) B. B.S. in Music Edn. magna cum laude, Edinboro State Coll., 1977. Tech. cons. Inco, Inc., Washington, 1982; sr. systems analyst Devel. Sci. Services, Inc., Washington, 1982-85; dir. computer systems ADEENA Corp., Arlington, Va., 1985-86; prin. systems cons. WANG Labs., Inc., Bethesda, Md., 1986—; v.p. F&B Computer Assocs., Bethesda, Md., 1985—. Mem. Arlington Community Band, 1986—. Served to lt. comdr. USNR, 1978—, with USN, 1978-82. Mem. Assn. Computing Machinery, IEEE (assoc.), Naval Res. Assn., Nat. Assn. Female Execs. Republican. Roman Catholic. Home: 2783 Stone Hollow Dr Vienna VA 22180

BENDIO, SUSAN MARY, municipal underwriter; b. Buffalo, Dec. 8, 1942; d. Stanley Thaddeus II and Edith Janet (Winkler) Nowak; m. R.V. Lester, Nov. 2, 1961 (Div. 1979); children: Erin Kathleen Kinzel, Jeffrey Forres Lester; m. Ruric H. Bendio, Oct. 24, 1980. Student, U. Ark., Little Rock, 1970-76. Bldg. mgr. Rector Cos., Little Rock; mgr. First Nat. Bldg. Co., Little Rock; project engr. Frank J. Rooney, Inc., Little Rock; multi-family housing coordinator U.S. Dept. Housing and Urban Devel., Little Rock; pres. Lester & Assocs., Boise, Idaho; v.p. Nat. Bank Alaska NA, Anchorage; v.p., credit mgr. Rainier Bank Alaska NA, Anchorage; v.p. pub. fin. capital markets group Bank of Am., San Francisco; v.p. mcpl. underwriter Boettcher & Co., Inc., Anchorage, until 1988; currently dir. Econ. Devel. Div. Fairbanks (Alaska) North Star Borough-Office of the Mayor. Active Pres. Task Force on Developmentally Disabled, Washington, Commonwealth North, Anchorage, 1980—, Gov.'s Task Force Local Govt., Anchorage, 1987; bd. dirs. Alaskan Korean Bus. Council, Anchorage, 1987. Mem. Govt. Fin. Officers Am., Northwest Electric Light Assn., Mcpl. Fin. Officers Alaska, Alaska Mcpl. League. Republican. Home: 570 Hamilton Dr Apt #B Fairbanks AK 99701 Office: City of Fairbanks 520 5th Ave Suite 410 Fairbanks AK 99701

BENDT, NORMA JUNE, procurement professional; b. Hawthorne, Nev., July 25, 1955; d. William Boyd and Sally Lou (Ramsey) Worsham; m. Steven Eric Bendt, July 28, 1973; 1 child, Steven Eric II. Student, Coll. Charleston, S.C., 1983-86. Sec. Med. U. S.C., Charleston, 1974-76, staff asst., 1976-82, ops. mgr., 1982-83; procurement officer Coll. of Charleston, 1983-86; purchasing officer Wildlife and Marine Resources Dept., State of S.C., Charleston, 1986—. Mem. Sea Island Bus. and Profl. Women's Club (Young Career Women award 1983, treas. 1984—), Nat. Assn. Edn. Buyers, Nat. Inst. Govtl. Purchasing Ofcls., S.C. Assn. Govtl. Purchasing Ofcls. (conf. com. 1985, program com. 1985—, chair, 1988, profl. devel. com. 1986-87, chair, 1986-87, bd. dirs. 1986-88, mem. exec. com. 1988, pres. 1988), Purchasing Mgmt. Assn. of Carolinas and Va. (program com. 1985, bd. dirs. local chpt. 1986), Nat. Assn. Female Execs. Republican. Lutheran. Avocations: scuba diving, skiing, racquetball, boating, aerobics. Office: SC Wilflife & Marine Resources PO Box 12559 Charleston SC 29412

BENEDETTO, LORRAINE ANN, computer science professional; b. Newark, Oct. 17, 1949; d. Frank and Hilda May (Holt) Vanna; m. William Robert Benedetto, Sept. 12, 1970; children: Annemarie Lyn, William Francis. BA, Newark State Coll., 1972. Secondary tchr. St. Casimir's Sch., Newark, 1972-73; substitute tchr. various schs., N.J., 1975-86; mgr. Burger King, Hazlet, N.J., 1979-81; computer operator Miller-Wohl Corp., Secaucus, N.J., 1981-83, supr. computer ops., 1983-84, mgr. computer ops., 1984-86; tech. support computer ops. Petrie Stores Corp., Secaucus, 1986—. organizer Local Neighborhood Improvement, Union Beach, N.J., 1977-80. Mem. Nat. Assn. Female Execs. Democrat. Roman Catholic. Home: 100 Beech St North Arlington NJ 07032

BENEDICT, LINDA LOUISE, marketing educator; b. Harrison, Ark., Nov. 28, 1949; d. Ord Wesley and Ruth Leeper (Burns) Larkin; m. Ronald Rollow Benedict, Nov. 14, 1970 (div. Apr. 1979); children: Brian Thomas, Patricia Ruth. BBA, Grand Valley State Coll., 1980, MBA, 1984. Market analyst Stow & Davis Furniture Co., Grand Rapids, Mich., 1980-82; ind. cons. Allendale, Mich., 1982-84; grad. asst. Grand Valley State Coll., Allendale, 1983-84; mktg. researcher Haworth, Inc., Holland, Mich., 1984—; program and curriculum advisor Grand Valley State Facilities Mgmt. Program, Allendale, 1984—. Speaker Am. Soc. Interior Designer's Student Regional Conf. and Career Day, Phoenix, 1987. Recipient scholarship Northwood Inst., 1967. Mem. Am. Mktg. Assn., Bldg. Owners and Mgrs. Assn., Internat. Facilities Mgmt. Assn. Lodge: Eastern Star (worthy matron 1973-74, scholarship 1967). Home: 6440 Henry St Allendale MI 49401 Office: Haworth Inc One Haworth Ctr Holland MI 49423

BENESCH, CONNIE J., editor. BA in English, U. Calif., Berkeley, 1975; postgrad., NYU. Typesetter, paste-up artist Murray Pub. Co., Seattle, 1977; copywriter Jerauld, Douglas & Miller, Seattle, 1977-78; dir. pub. edn., info. specialist Am. Heart Assn., Sacramento, Calif., 1978-79; prodn. asst. intern. Sta. KOCR-TV, Sacramento, 1980; free-lance writer Sacramento, 1980-81; editor, writer Westchester (N.Y.) ArtsNews, 1981-83, mng. editor, 1983—. Mem. Soc. Profl. Journalists, Women in Communications, Internat. Assn. Bus. Communicators. (Excellence award 1985).

BENGOCHEA, JUDITH MCCRACKEN, photographer; b. Terre Haute, Ind., July 8, 1945; d. Leland Conrad and Elizabeth Minerva (Meagher) McC.; m. Joaquin E. Bengochea, July 4, 1965; children: Alicia, Monica. AA, Palm Beach (Fla.) Jr. Coll., 1976. Owner Bengochea Photography, Lake Worth, Fla., 1975—; speaker on copy and restoration old photographs. Producer: (TV show) The Second Fifty Yrs., 1986-87. Mem. Profl. Photographers Am., Am. Photographic Artisan Guild. Roman Catholic.

BENGTSON, ESTHER G., state legislator; b. Froid, Mont., Oct. 30, 1927; d. Goodwin and Elizabeth (Jorgensen) Bergh; m. Lawrence E. Bengtson, 1948; children: Kristianne, Monica, Jennifer. BS, U. Mont. Mem. Mont.

Ho. of Reps., 1975-83, Mont. State Senate, 1985—. Democrat. Lutheran. Office: 8124 Clark Rd Shepherd MT 59079 *

BENHAM, HAZEL LEE, health care executive; b. Lone Grove, Okla., Mar. 20, 1936; d. Lute Washington and Margaret Cattie (McNealy) Wallace; m. Glendon L. Benham, June 29, 1956 (div. 1976); children: Glenn Mark, Alesia Gail. Diploma, Voc. Sch. Nursing, Lubbock, Tex., 1955; AS in Nursing, Mt. San Antonio Coll., Walnut, Calif., 1976; BS in Health Care Adminstrn., L Verne U., 1987. Office nurse Med. Arts Clin., Lubbock, 1956-58; sch. nurse Morton (Tex.) Sch. Dist., 1958-59; office Drs. Fickes, Beller, Smith & Mayfield, LaVerne, Calif., 1959-68; charge nurse Sierra Royale Convalescent Hosp., Azusa, Calif., 1969-72; rev. coordinator, staff nurse Pomona Valley (Calif.) Hosp., 1975-77; rev. coordinator Profl. Standards Rev. Program, Monrovia, Calif., 1977-78; dir. quality assurance and risk mgmt. San Dimas (Calif.) Community Hosp., 1978-83; dir. quality assurance VA Med. Ctr., West Los Angeles, 1983—; instr. Nursing Assn., Covina, Calif., 1983. Contbr. articles to profl. jours. Mem. The Flying Samaritans, Inc. Pico Rivera, Calif., bd. dirs., 1979-85, medicaion coordinator, 1982-85. Recipient Ann. award The Plying Samaritans, 1986. Republican. Methodist. Home: 18828-A Hatteras St TArzana CA 91356 Office: VA Med Ctr Wadsworth Div Wilshire & Sawtelle Blvd Los Angeles CA 90073

BENHAM, LINDA SUE, civil engineer; b. Toledo, Oct. 31, 1954; m. William. H. Benham. BS in Civil Engring., U. Toledo, 1977. Structural engr. Itil and Assocs., Toledo, 1977-78; project engr. Finkbeiner, Pettis and Strout, Ltd., Toledo, 1978—. Mem. ASCE, Am. Water Works Assn., Water Pollution Control Fedn. Republican. Office: Finkbeiner Pettis and Strout Ltd 4405 Talmadge Rd Toledo OH 43623

BENHAM, LIZA ABRAM, journalist; b. Marion, S.C., Feb. 23, 1946; d. Monroe and Doretha (Abram) R.; m. Billy Benham, Dec. 15, 1973 (div.); 1 child, Johari L. BA in English, Bennet Coll., 1968. Tech. editor IBM Corp., Peckskill, Poughkeepsie, N.Y., 1968, 1969-73, Boeblingen, Fed. Republic Germany, 1974; reporter Ledger Newspaper, Columbus, Ga., 1976-81; pub. relations specialist Columbus Coll., 1981-85; features editor Columbus Ledger-Enquirer, 1985-86, columnist, 1986—. Mem. AAUW. Office: Ledger-Enquirer Box 711 Columbus GA 31994

BENITEZ, SHIRLEY ANN, protective services official; b. Lawton, Okla., July 15, 1943; d. William Allen and Zealon Marie (Yarbrough) Sheffield; m. Gary Wallace Brown, Mar. 4, 1966 (div. July 1972); 1 child, Eric Eugene; m. Ramon Bentiez, Nov. 17, 1973; 1 child, Jeremy Daniel. Correction certificate, Lakewood Community Coll., 1981. Sr. fin. worker Hennepin County Welfare, Mpls., 1971-78; rep. service Northwestern Bell Telephone, Mpls., 1979-81; counselor correctional State of Minn. Corrections, Shakopee, 1981-84; correctional officer Bur. Corrections Hennepin County, Shakopee, 1984—; organizer, leader Community Crime Prevention Block Club, 1978-81; vol. Advocate Women Minn. State Prison, 1981—; case mgr. Hennepin County Misdemeanant Probation, 1981—. Co-author: N.E. Resource Directory, 1976. Mem. Food Shelves Hennepin County 1974-78; leader Cub Scouts Am. 1981-83; bd. dirs. Am. Indian Commn. 1973, Am. Indian Haven 1973-75, group leader, facilator Battered Womens Group 1974-78. Recipient Dirs. award for Exceptional Contbns. to Vol. Program Hennepin County Ct. and Field Services, 1988. Mem. Nat. Assn. Female Exec., Am. Correction Assn., Minn. Corrections Assn., Triune Ministries (bd. dirs. 1987—). Democrat. Pentecostal. Home: 440 2nd St NE Minneapolis MN 55413

BENJAMIN, ADELAIDE WISDOM, community volunteer and activist; b. New Orleans, Aug. 23, 1932; d. William Bell and Mary (Freeman) Wisdom; m. Edward Bernard Benjamin Jr., May 11, 1957; children: Edward Wisdom, Mary Dabney, Ann Leith, Stuart Minor. Student, Hollins Coll., 1950-52; BA in English, Newcomb Coll., 1954; JD, Tulane U., 1956; student, Loyola U., New Orleans, 1980-81; grad. Sewanee Theol. Sch., U. South, 1982. Assoc. Wisdom, Stone, Pigman and Benjamin, New Orleans, 1956-58; tchr. ext. courses Sewanee Theol. Seminary, 1984—; speaker, panelist on school issues various local and nat. groups. Active Trinity Episc. Ch., New Orleans, sec. parish council, 1973-75, sec. vestry, 1975-79, mem. numerous coms., 1965—, chairperson several coms., 1977-83, leader Trinity Quartet, 1979-84; bd. dirs. local YWCA, 1967-75, 76-79, sec. bd. dirs., 1967-68, 2d v.p., 1968-69, mem. coms.; mem. bd. trustees Metairie Park Country Day Sch., 1971-79, sec. bd. trustees, 1976-79, pres. PTA, 1975-76, mem. various coms.; mem. Loving Cup selection com. New Orleans Times Picayune, 1985; mem. New Orleans Scoliosis Adv. Bd., 1978; pres. EANDA Charitable Found., New Orleans, 1983—; bd. dirs. Children's Hosp., New Orleans, 1976-79, Kingsley House, New Orleans, 1971-77, RosaMary Charitable Found., New Orleans, 1978—. Recipient Weiss Brotherhood award Nat. Conf. Christians and Jews, 1986, Jr. League Sustainer award, 1987, Disting. Alumna award McGehee Sch., 1987; named Goodwill Ambassador for Louisiana Gov.'s Commn. Internat. Trade, Industry and Tourism, 1987, Sweet Art Contemporary Arts Ctr., 1988. Mem. ABA, La. Bar Assn., New Orleans Bar Assn., New Orleans Symphony, Vol. Am. New Orleans chpt. (bd. dirs. 1984—), Quarante Club (v.p. 1978-79), New Orleans Symphony Chorus, Jr. League New Orleans (mem. exec. com. 1971-72, bd. dirs. 1967-72), LWV, Independent Women's Orgn., Bur. Govl. Research, Com. 21, Am. Symphony Orchestra League. Clubs: Qurante (2d v.p. 1978-79), Sybarites, Debutante, Le Debut des Jeunes Filles. Home and Office: 1837 Palmer Ave New Orleans LA 70118 Office: Place St Charles 201 St Charles Ave New Orleans LA 70170

BENJAMIN, FLEUR KATHLEEN, nurse; b. Vinton, Iowa, Dec. 9, 1934; d. Glenn Ripley and Dorothy Marie (Evans) Healy; m. Roy Glen Ives, June 10, 1956 (div. 1971); children—Mark Alan, John Glenn, Jeanine Renee; m. 2d. David Hinton Benjamin, Oct. 1, 1977. Student Drake U., 1953-54; grad. Broadlawn Sch. of Nursing, Des Moines, 1956. R.N., Iowa; cert. urology nurse. Asst. nurse Broadlawns Hosp., Des Moines, 1956-57; staff nurse Jennie Edmunson Hosp., Council Bluffs, Iowa, 1957-60, Mennonite Hosp., LaJunta, Colo., 1967-70, Flagstaff Community Hosp. (Ariz.), 1972-73; asst. head nurse St. Lukes Hosp., Cedar Rapids, Iowa, 1970-72; asst. unit mgr. Flagstaff Med. Ctr., 1975-86; clin. supr. 1986—.Mem. Am. Nurses Assn., Am. Urol. Assn., Am. Diabetic Assn., VFW Aux. Republican. Mem. Christian Ch. Lodge: Am. Legion Aux. Home: 60 Columbine Mt View Ranchos Flagstaff AZ 86004

BENJAMIN, JOYCE HOLMES, lawyer; b. Winnipeg, Man., Can., Jan. 27, 1931; d. George Andrew and Margaret E. (Wachter) Holmes; m. Jonathan S. Benjamin, July 20, 1951 (div. 1978); children—George Andrew Holmes, Emelia Jane, Elisabeth Ryden. B.A., U. Oreg., 1971, J.D., 1974. Bar: Oreg. 1974. Assoc., Miller, Moulton, Andrews, Eugene, Oreg., 1974-76, Johnson, Harrang, Swanson & Long, Eugene, 1976-81; ptnr. Benjamin, Waggoner, Chapman & Farleigh, Portland, Oreg., 1982-84; assoc. Acad. for State and Local Govt., Washington, 1984, dep. chief counsel State and Local Legal Ctr., 1985—; chmn. Lane County Personnel Rev. Bd., Eugene, 1976-77. Chair, State Oreg. Edn. Reorgn. Commn., Salem, 1967-69; pres. Intermediate Edn. Bd. sect. Oreg. Sch. Bd. Assn., 1965-66; mem., chmn. Lane County Intermediate Edn. Dist. Bd., Eugene, 1964-76; chmn. Gov.'s Commn. on Fgn. Lang. and Internat. Relations Orgn., 1980-82; mem., chmn. Oreg. Bd. Edn., Salem, 1976-84. Named Oreg. Edn. Citizen of Yr., 1970; named Outstanding Oral Advocate, U. Oreg. Law Sch., Eugene, 1972. Mem. Nat. Assn. State Bds. Edn. (dir. 1979-83), Oreg. State Bar (chair govt. law sect. 1980, continuing legal edn. com. 1983-84). Clubs: Multnomah Athletic (Portland); Town (Eugene). Office: Acad State and Local Govt 440 N Capitol St Washington DC 20001

BENJAMIN, MAIRA MERCEDES, software engineer; b. Bklyn., Aug. 27, 1959; d. Reynaldo Mario and Gloria (Moronta) B. BA in Stats., U. Calif., Berkeley, 1983. Reliability engr. Xerox/DiabloSystems, Inc., Fremont, Calif., 1983-84; software engr. Ask Computer Systems, Inc., Los Altos, Calif., 1984—. Vol. Project Literacy, Oakland, 1986, Jesse Jackson for Pres. campaign, Berkeley, 1984. Mem. Nat. Assn. Female Execs., Am. Statis. Assn., Am. Prodn. Inventory and Control Soc., Am. Soc. for Quality Control. Democrat. Clubs: Toastmasters (charter pres. 1985-86) (Los Altos, Calif.); Commonwealth (San Francisco). Home: 250 Grand Ave #18 Oakland CA 94610 Office: Ask Computer Systems Inc 730 Distel Dr Los Altos CA 94022

BENJAMIN, PAMELA SOUTHWORTH, interior designer; b. Hartford, Conn., Oct. 20, 1952; d. James Rollins and Jeanne Marthe (Bouvier) Southworth; B.S., U. Conn., 1975; m. Thomas Gerard Benjamin, July 29, 1972; children: Tyler Ross, Joshua Thomas. Interior designer Continental Ill. Nat. Bank, Chgo., 1979-81; dir. design OFP Total Design Cons., Stamford, Conn., 1981; space planner Midwest Stock Exchange, Chgo., 1981; office planner, interior designer Abbott Labs., North Chicago, Ill., 1982-87; regional sec. Inst. Bus. Designers, 1979-81, v.p., 1981-83, chairperson nat. admissions com., 1985-86. Mem. congressional campaign com., 1972, Midwest Communications Assn., 1981-82. Recipient cert. of recognition for Outstanding Contbn., Inst. Bus. Designers, 1981; First prize Design-A-Toy Contest, Mansfield (Conn.) Tng. Sch., 1975. Mem. Inst. Bus. Designers. Home: 5905 S Fairview Ave Downers Grove IL 60516-2020

BENJAMIN, ROBBA LEE, banker; b. Glendale, Calif., Dec. 1, 1947; d. Gilbert Searle Benjamin and Vivian (Durr) Carpenter; m. Keshaven Nair. AB, Occidental Coll., 1969; MBA, Stanford U., 1978. Treas. Kirk Knight & Co., Inc., Menlo Park, Calif., 1970-74; transaction mgr. Itel Corp., San Francisco, 1975-76, 79-80; mgr. sales adminstrn. Shaklee Corp., San Francisco, 1978; founder, exec. v.p. Benjamin/Nair, Inc., San Francisco, 1981-84; exec. v.p., chief adminstrv. officer MeraBank, Phoenix, from 1984; now with Benjamin/Nair, Inc. Phoenix. Bd. dirs., vice chmn. Jr. Achievement, Ariz., 1985-87; bd. dirs. Ariz. Clean and Beautiful, 1986-87; mem. adv. bd. Ariz. Theatre Co., 1986-87; mem. Phoenix Symphony Steering Com., 1987, Mayor's Commn. on Excellence in Edn., 1987—. Mem. Am. Mgmt. Assn., Nat. Assn. Bank Women, Council Fin. Competition, (adv. bd.), Charter 100, Econ. Club Phoenix (bd. dirs. 1985-87). Office: Benjamin/Nair Inc 3030 E 3rd St Phoenix AZ 85012

BENN, INGRID ILEANA, publishing company executive; b. Arroyo, P.R., May 1, 1953; came to U.S., 1955; d. Roberto and Virginia (Cancel) B.; A.B. magna cum laude, Wilmington (Ohio) Coll., 1975; M.B.A. cum laude, Ohio State U., Columbus, 1977. With Charles E. Merrill Pub. Co., Columbus, 1977—, product mgr., 1979-81, mktg. mgr. trade pub., 1982, now dir. internat. sch. div.; pub. cons. to mayor Columbus, Ohio. Named Power Maker of Month, Bell & Howell Co., 1985. Mem. Assn. M.B.A. Execs., Nat. Assn. Female Execs., ALA, AAUW, Green Key, Beta Gamma Sigma Roman Catholic. Home: 545 Woodingham Pl Columbus OH 43213 Office: 1300 Alum Creek Dr Columbus OH 43216

BENN, PHYLISS ASHMUN, lawyer; b. Washburn, Wis., Aug. 26, 1924; d. Van Sanford and Margaret Fiege Ashmun; B.A., U. Wis.-Madison, 1946; J.D., Valparaiso U., 1975; m. Donald W. Benn, Aug. 30, 1947; children—David W., Martha Ann, Ruth L., Robert Samuel. City editor Niles (Mich.) Daily Star, 1946-47; editorial asst. Towndan Pub. Co., LaPorte, Ind., 1964-71; admitted to Ind. bar, 1975; assoc. firm Smith and Smith, LaPorte, 1975-79; sole practice law, LaPorte, 1979—. Chmn. City of LaPorte Human Rights Commn., 1980-82; precinct committeewoman Democratic County Com., 1974-86; chmn. La Porte County Election Bd. 1986—; del. Dem. Nat. Conv., 1976; vol. Girl Scouts U.S.A., No. Ind. Council, 1948-70, v.p., 1964-67. Mem. ABA, Ind. Bar Assn., LaPorte City Bar Assn. (sec. 1981-82, pres. 1988—), Family Service Assn. (dir. 1979-85), AAUW (LaPorte br. grantee 1973, pres. 1958-59, state dir. 1960-63), Family Mediation Service, Nat. Audubon Soc. (Potawatomi chpt.), Phi Beta Kappa. Home and Office: 1001 Maple Ave La Porte IN 46350

BENNER, ANN WRIGLEY, sales executive; b. Brevard, N.C., Oct. 30, 1943; d. George and Edith Charlotte (Patton) Wrigley; student Converse Coll., 1961-62; children—Arthur, Paige. Store mgr. Heskett's Carpets DBA Gen. Floors, Inc., Oakland, Calif., 1972-76; Pacific Flooring distbr. Burlington House Carpets, Emeryville, Calif., 1976-78; ter. sales mgr. J.P. Stevens & Co., Inc., Gulistan Div., San Francisco, 1978-82; sr. mktg. rep. West Point Pepperell carpet and rug div. Cabin Crafts Carpet, 1982-87; dist. mgr. Salem Carpet Mills Inc., Sante Fe Springs, Calif., 1987—; also condr. various seminars. Patron, Performing Artists Group, San Francisco, 1981—. Recipient Outstanding Sales award Pres.'s Council, Burlington House Carpets, 1977; named to Laurel Soc. and Million Dollar Club, J.P. Stevens & Co. Mem. San Francisco Floor Covering Assn., Internat. Platform Assn., Retail Floor Covering Assn. (Sales Force award 1986). Club: USMC Wives' (pres. 1968). Home: 8061 Peppertree Rd Dublin CA 94568 Office: Salem Carpet Mills Inc 14911 Valley View Sante Fe Springs CA 90640

BENNER, DOROTHY SPURLOCK, educator; b. Greeley, Colo., Dec. 17, 1938; d. Lloyd Elsworth and Helen Rosalee (Pierce) Spurlock; m. Jerry Lee Benner, June 7, 1959; children: Shey Lee, Craig Lloyd. BA, Colo. State Coll., 1962, MA, 1968; EdS, U. No. Colo., 1978. Cert. tchr. elem. and bus. edn., spl. edn. and sch. psychology. Telephone operator Mountain Bell, Greeley, Colo., 1957; sec. Conn. Mut. Life, Greeley, Colo., 1960-61; substitute tchr. Sch. Dist. 6 and Outlying Dists., Greeley, Colo., 1962-67; tchr. Sch. Dist. 6, Greeley, Colo., 1968—; cons. Right to Read, Weld County, Colo., 1980—. Mem. Greeley Tchrs. Assn. (mem. negotiating team 1981—, sec. 1985—), Nat. Edn. Assn. (life), Colo. Edn. Assn., Kappa Delta Pi, Delta Kappa Gamma (pres. 1980-81). Republican. Methodist. Home: 1839 26th St Greeley CO 80631

BENNETT, BARBARA ESTHER, controller; b. Norfolk, Nebr., Nov. 24, 1953. AA, Northeastern Nebr. Community Coll., Norfolk, Nebr., 1973; student, U. Nebr., 1980, U. Colo., Denver, 1985, Harvard U., 1985. Bookkeeper McIntosh, Inc., Norfolk, 1971-77; credit, office mgr. Goodyear Service Stores Inc., Norfolk, 1977-81; pvt. practice acct. Norfolk, 1971-81; base adminstr. Evergreen Helicoptors Inc., Greeley, Colo., 1981-82; pvt. practice acctg. and tax service Denver, 1984—; acctg. supr, asst. controller Saltzgitter Machinery, Inc., Louviers, Colo., Saltzgitter, Fed. Republic Germany., 1982-85; corp. controller Satter, Inc., Denver, 1985—. Phi Theta Kappa, Phi Beta Lambda. Republican. Lutheran. Club: 4H. Home: 963 S Patton Ct PO Box 19070 Denver CO 80219 Office: Satter Distbg Co Inc 4100 Dahlia Denver CO 80207

BENNETT, BETTY BESSE, librarian; b. Omaha, Feb. 18, 1921; d. Gordon Stanley and Besse Harriet (Amos) B.; B.A., Mcpl. U. Omaha, 1942; B.S. in L.S., U. Ill., 1943; M.A., U. Iowa, 1948; M.L.S., Tex. Woman's U., 1960. Asst. documents librarian U. Iowa Library, Iowa City, 1943-50; reference and documents librarian Kans. State Tchrs. Coll. Library, Pittsburg, 1950-57, reference librarian, archivist, 1957-67; reference and research librarian Stephen F. Austin State U. Library, Nacogdoches, Tex., 1967-72, govt. documents librarian, 1972-88; resource cons. Gov.'s Conf. on Libraries, Austin, Tex., 1974. Clk. session Presbyterian Ch., 1967-80, ruling elder, 1975—; exec. dir. Telephone Reassurance Program for Elderly Shut-Ins, 1977-80; mem. ad hoc com. on superseded documents U.S. Govt. Printing Office, 1985-86. Mem. ALA (state document classifcation com. 1974-80, state documents task force) Tex. (chmn. govt. documents round table 1975-76), Southwestern library assns., Tex. Assn. Coll. Tchrs., Nacogdoches Friends of the Library, Alpha Xi Delta. Presbyterian. Office: Stephen F Austin State U Library Nacogdoches TX 75962

BENNETT, BOBBIE JEAN, state official; b. Gwinnett County, Ga., July 13, 1940; d. William Claude and Clara Maude (Nichols) Holcome; B.B.A. magna cum laude, Ga. State U., 1973; 1 dau., Terri Lynne. With Ga. State Merit System, Atlanta, 1960—, sr. acct., 1967, asst. div. dir., 1968-70, fiscal officer, 1970-74, div. dir., 1975-78, asst. dep. commr., 1978—, asst. commr., 1985—. Mem. Ga. Fiscal Mgmt. Council, Ga. Council Personnel Adminstrn., Employers Council Flexible Compensation (dir.), Nat. Assn. Deferred Compensation Adminstrs. (sec.), Ga. Govt. Benefit Assn., Atlanta Govt. Benefit Assn., Beta Gamma Sigma, Phi Kappa Phi, Beta Alpha Psi. Democrat. Home: 2072 Malabar Dr NE Atlanta GA 30345 Office: State Merit System 200 Piedmont Ave Atlanta GA 30334

BENNETT, CAROL ELIZABETH, immunopathologist, researcher; b. Perry, Ga., July 26, 1951; d. William Hearn and Dessie (Rollins) B. BS in Zoology, U. Ga., 1973. Research technician III dept. cell and molecular biology, Med. Coll. Ga., Augusta, 1973-76; research specialist II dept. lab. medicine, Med. U. S.C., Charleston, 1976-81; project coordinator III dept. path. and lab. medicine, Emory U., 1981—; adj. research assoc., Med. U. S.C., 1983—; dir. research adminstrn. and tech. coordination CytRx Corp., Norcross, Ga., 1987—. Contbr. more than 100 articles and abstracts to sci. jours. Chmn. Bloodmobile, Med. U. S.C., 1978-81. Rotary Club scholar, 1969, Regent scholar, 1969-73. Mem. Tissue Culture Assn., Am. Soc. Microbiology, Southeastern Assn. Clin. Microbiologists, Assn. Clin. Scientists (athletic com. 1980-85), AAAS, Ga. Acad. Sci., S.C. Acad. Sci., Sigma Xi (treas. Emory U. chpt. 1984-85). Office: Emory U Dept. Path 760 WMB Atlanta GA 30322

BENNETT, CATHERINE JUNE, data processing manager, educator, consultant; b. Augusta, Ga., June 19, 1950; d. Robert Stogner and Catherine Sue (Jordan) Robinson; m. Danny Marvin Bennett, Sept. 5, 1971; children—Timothy Jordan, Robert Daniel. B.S. in Stats., U. Ga., 1971, M.A. in Bus., 1973. Programmer William M. Shenkel & Assocs., Athens, Ga., 1971-73; systems analyst U. Ga., Athens, 1973-76; product cons. Info. Systems Am., Atlanta, 1976-78, project leader, 1978-80, mngr. product support, 1980-85, hotline mgr., sr. fin. specialist, 1986-88; cons. adv. investment PRISM Model Office, 1988—. Mem. Duluth council Gwinnett County (Ga.) Swim League. Avocations: bridge, swimming, travel. Home: 3458 Larch Pine Dr Duluth GA 30136 Office: Info Systems Am 500 Northridge Rd Atlanta GA 30350

BENNETT, CELESTINE C.T., librarian; b. Winston-Salem, N.C., Nov. 9, 1932; d. Arthur Loveliest and Mamie (Guerrant) Tutt; B.A., Winston-Salem State U., 1952; M.L.S., Columbia U., 1971, D.L.S., 1983; m. Henry McNeal Bennett, Dec. 28, 1977; children—Richard Bennett, Kathryn Bennett. Librarian, Urban Center, Columbia U., N.Y.C., 1971-73, asst. librarian Whitney M. Young Jr. Meml. Library Social Work, 1973-77, librarian, 1978-83; mem. papers adv. com. Whitney M. Young Jr., 1975-78, chmn., 1979-83; mem. adv. com. Whitney M. Young Jr. Disting. Lecture Series, 1983; mem. Oakland's Commn. on Aging, 1986—; adminstrv. analyst Oakland Pub. Library, Calif., 1985. Fellow Brookdale Inst. on Aging and Adult Human Devel., Columbia U., 1983—. Mem. ALA, Calif. Library Assn., Internat. Council Social Welfare, Bay Area Urban League. Home: Lakeside Regency Plaza 1555 Lakeside Dr #22 Oakland CA 94612

BENNETT, CHARLOTTE RUTH, elementary school principal; b. Kankakee, Ill., May 20, 1944; d. Clarence Henry and Ellen Elvina (Danker) Smith; m. Dale Eugene Bennett, June 7, 1980; children: Barry, Chad. BS, Olivet U., 1967; MEd, U. Ill., 1971; PhD, U. Iowa, 1976. Tchr. Kankakee Sch. Dist. 111, 1967-76; asst. prof. edn. Purdue U.-Calumet Campus, Hammond, Ind., 1976-79; basic edn. skills dir. Community Action Program, Evansville, Ind., 1979-81; tchr. Evansville Diocese, 1982-85; prin. Evansville Diocese/St. John Sch., Newburgh, Ind., 1985-87, 87—; adj. prof. U. So. Ind., Evansville, 1985—; cons. Imperial Internat. Learning, Kankakee, 1977-81; U. Iowa teaching assistantship, 1973. Contbr. articles to profl. jours.; author reading program, 1980. Bd. dirs. Evansville Reading Coalition on Adult Literacy, 1986—. Mem. Internat. Reading Assn., Assn. for Supervision and Curriculum Devel., Nat. Council Tchrs. English, NEA, Ind. Non-Pub. Sch. Assn., Ind. Reading Council, Evansville Area Reading Council, Ind. Reading Profs. (sec. 1976-77). Home: 216 Camden Ct Evansville IN 47715 Office: St John Sch 725 Frame Rd Newburgh IN 47630

BENNETT, CONNIE SUE, food product executive; b. Richland Center, Wis., Oct. 4, 1955; d. Robert Eugene And Lillian Theresa (Crusan) Cottrill; m. James A. Bennett III,Oct. 22, 1976. Grad. high sch., Ithaca, Wis. Owner, chef A Taste Of Heaven Restaurant, Anchorage, 1978-80, Saucy Sisters Catering, Anchorage, 1980-86; pres. Good Taste Inc., Anchorage, 1986—. Mem. adv. bd. Hugh O'Brian Found., 1987. Named Small Bus. Person of Yr. State of Alaska, 1987, U.S. Western Region, 1987. Mem. Alaska St. C. of C., Anchorage C. of C., Internat. Assn. Cooking Profl., Am. Inst. Wine and Food, James Beard Found. Office: Good Taste Inc 2000 W Internat Airport #C Anchorage AK 99502

BENNETT, DEBORAH R., employment agency executive; b. Los Angeles, Apr. 8, 1941; d. William H. and Harriet (Hatch) Roome; m. Raymond James Bennett, July 10, 1969; 1 child, Shauna. BS, U. Redlands, 1962. Cert. personnel cons., employment specialist. Exec. sec. Los Angeles Tchrs. Credit Union, 1965-81; sec.-bookkeeper Ronald Sinclair, CLU, Encino, Calif., 1981-83, Gruenfelder's, Canoga Park, Calif., 1984; self-employed, Granada Hills, Calif., 1983-84; owner, mgr. D.R. Bennett and Assocs., Panorama City, Calif., 1984—. Mem. Nat. Alliance of Homebased Women (v.p. 1983-85), Calif. Assn. Personnel Cons. (v.p. Los Angeles chpt.), Nat. Assn. Personnel Cons., Granada Hills C. of C. Republican. Christian Scientist. Avocations: reading, sewing. Home: 17306 Trosa St Granada Hills CA 91344 Office: DR Bennett & Assocs 14600 Roscoe Blvd Suite 207 Panorama City CA 91602

BENNETT, DONNA JEAN, accountant, consultant; b. Warwick, R.I., Oct. 10, 1956; d. William Alexander Bennett and Patricia Mae (Jordon) Walker. Student, Performing and Visual Arts Sch., Houston, 1975, Radcliffe U., 1975-76, U. Houston, 1978. Program dir. Bel-Air Cable, Houston, 1973-75; promoter Concerts West Cobblestone Prodns., Dallas, 1975-78; controller, chief exec. officer VIP Toy Store, Beverly Hills, Calif., 1978-81; pres. VIP Prodns., Beverly Hills, 1980-82; controller Grand Touring Gems, Los Angeles, 1982-84; pres. Jordan, Bennett, Walker & Assocs., Los Angeles, 1984—; model Houston, N.Y., Calif., 1970-82; sec. Dow Jones & Co., Houston, 1977-78. Author: Analytical Analysis: Explained, 1975; co-author musicals including The Joy of Life, 1974, The Faces of Job, 1975. Vol. Rep. Nat. Conv., Kansas City, Mo., 1976, Senate election campaign Barry Goldwater, Jr., Studio City Calif., 1982. presdl. election Ronald Reagan, 1984, St. John's Hosp., Santa Monica, Calif., 1986. Named Miss Mo., 1977. Mem. Nat. Assn. Female Execs., Writers Guild. Roman Catholic. Office: Jordan Bennett Walker & Assocs 3580 Wilshire Blvd Suite 1750 Los Angeles CA 90010-2517

BENNETT, DOROTHY KEMLER, psychologist, educational adminstrator; b. Boston, June 1, 1935; d. Rae Kemler; children: James, Robert. BS, Tufts U., 1956; EdM, Harvard U., 1957, EdD, 1970. Lic. psychologist, Tex., Mass. Sch. psychologist Westwood (Mass.) Pub. Schs., 1969-74; dir. spl. needs Winthrop (Mass.) Pub. Schs., 1974-77; prin. Dallas Ind. Sch. Dist., 1978—. Mem. Am. Psychol. Assn., Council for Exceptional Children, Sigma Xi, Phi Delta Kappa. Home: 3883 Turtle Creek Blvd Dallas TX 75219

BENNETT, ELIZABETH, hypnotherapist; b. Calgary, Alta., Can., Dec. 5, 1950; came to U.S., 1953; d. William Edward and Charlotte Elizabeth (Wilson) Kerr; m. David Morrison Bennett, Dec. 11, 1970 (div. 1983); 1 child, David Edward. Registered hypnotherapist Nat. Hypnotherapy Inst. Food service apprentice Buffums Inc., San Diego, 1973-80, food and beverage mgr., 1980-84; leasing cons. Anza Mgmt. Co., Anaheim, Calif., 1984-87; pvt. practice hypnotherapy Santa Ana, Calif., 1987; instr. The Learning Activity, Anaheim, 1987. Mem. Altrusa Internat., Whittier and La Habra, Calif., 1983. Mem. Am. Hypnotherapy Assn., The Network, Women in Sales. Democrat. Episcopalian. Home: 5601 E Orangethorpe Ave #F-204 Anaheim CA 92807

BENNETT, ELSIE MARGARET, music school administrator; b. Detroit, Mar. 30, 1919; d. Sy and Ida (Carp) Blum; m. Morton Bennett, June 20, 1937 (dec.); children—Ronald, Kenneth. Cert., Ganapal Conservatory Detroit, 1941; B.Mus. in Theory, Wayne State U., 1945; M.A. in Music Edn., Columbia U., 1946; postgrad. Columbia U., Manhattan Sch. Music. Music studio mgr., tchr. Bennett Music Sch., Bklyn., 1946—, dir. 1946—; music arranger, 1946—; tchr. Schiff Sch. Music, 1972-80, owner, 1972—; tchr. Robotti Accordion Acad. and Pkwy. Music Sch., 1945-46; owner Margolies Sch. Music, Acad. of Music Sch.; editor Accordion World Mag., 1945-56; works include: Easy Solos for Accordion, 1946; Bass Solo Primer, 1948; Hebrew and Jewish Songs and Dances for Accordion, 1959, Vol. 1, 1951, Vol. 2, 1953; Hanon for Accordion, 1953; Accordion Music in the Home, 1953; Folk Melodies for Accordion, 1954; Five Finger Melodies for Accordion, 1954; First Steps in Scaleland for Accordion, 1956; First Steps in Chordland for Accordion, Vol. 1, 1961, Vol. II, 1961. Mem. Bklyn. Community Council. Mem. Am. Accordionists Assn. (governing bd., pres. 1973-74, plaque, 1962, service to governing bd. award 1942-60, Silver Cup 1974-75), Bklyn. Music Tchrs. Guild (dir., past sec.),, Accordion Tchrs. Guild, L.I. Music Tchrs. Assn.

BENNETT, F(RANKIE) KATHARINE, rehabilitation consulting executive; b. Flagstaff, Ariz., Feb. 15, 1945; d. Charles Birge and Allie Kathleen (Tanner) Wilson. AA, Stephens Coll., 1965; BA, U. Ariz., 1967, MS, 1969; PhD, Oreg. State U., 1987. Cert. rehab. counselor. Counselor severely disabled

State of Calif., Van Nuys, 1969-77; counselor cons. Innovative Services, Portland, Oreg., 1977-79; co-owner, pres. Germain-Bennett Rehab. Cons., Inc., Lake Oswego, Oreg., 1979-87; counselor, cons. Health Systems Services, Portland, 1987—. Commr., sec. Mossy Brae Water Dist. Clackamas County, Oreg., 1978-81. Mem. Nat. Rehab. Assn., Oreg. Assn. Rehab. Profls. in Pvt. Sector (bd. dirs. 1983—, editor newsletter 1983-84, chmn. legis. com. 1984—), Tng. and Profl. Placement Service (handicapped employment com. 1978-79). Democrat. Avocations: cross-country skiing, boating, bicycling. Office: Health Systems Services 2328 Lloyd Ctr Portland OR 97232

BENNETT, HELEN DONELE, educator; b. Spartanburg, S.C., Feb. 24, 1948; d. Freddie and Julia Beatrice (Rogers) B. BA, U. S.C., 1969; MEd, Converse Coll., 1977. Cert. spl. edn. tchr., psychology, sociology. City planner Model Cities, Inc., Spartanburg, S.C., 1969-70, planning coordinator, 1970-71; tchr., learning disabilities, emotionally handicapped Teszler Learning Adjustment Spartan County Schs., Spartanburg, 1971-87, coordinator Transition Program, 1987—. Active County Bd. Domestic Violence, Spartanburg, 1980-86; exec. committeeman Ward 5 Dems., Spartanburg, 1979—. Mem. Nat. Edn. Assn., Council on Exceptional Children (Spl. Educator of Yr. 1986), S.C. Edn. Assn., County Dem. Women's Club, Sigma Gamma Rho (Basileus-Xi Sigma chpt.). Home: 178 Aden St Spartanburg SC 29303 Office: Spartanburg County Sch Dist #7 Dupree Dr Spartanburg SC 29303

BENNETT, KATHLEEN MCMANUS, forest products company executive; b. S.I., N.Y., May 11, 1948; d. Leo Giblin and Rosemary Katherine (Keenan) McManus; m. Michael Canville Bennett, May 6, 1972; 3 children. BA, Manhattanville Coll., 1970. Adminstrv. asst. Office Congressional Affairs, U.S. Gen. Services Adminstrn., Washington, 1971-72; rep. Pub. Affairs Analysts, Inc., Washington, 1972-74; dir. legis. affairs Am. Paper Inst., Washington, 1974-77; fed. affairs rep. Crown Zellerbach Corp., Washington, 1977-81; presdl. appointee asst. adminstr. air noise radiation EPA, Washington, 1981-83; dir. regulatory affairs Champion Internat. Corp., Stamford, Conn., 1983-86, dir. environ. planning, 1986-87;, mng. dir. corp. environ. affairs dept., James River Corp., Richmond, Va., 1987—; mem. presdl. appointed Nat. Task Force Acid Precipitation, Washington, 1984—; mem. adv. com. to U.S. trade rep. on negotiations implementing Geneva Trade Agreement, 1978-80; head U.S. delegation 1982 Conv. Acidification Environ., Stockholm. Mem. Air Pollution Control Assn., Air Quality Subcom. Prevention Significant Deterioration, Am. Paper Inst. Republican. Roman Catholic. Office: James River Corp PO Box 2218 Richmond VA 23217

BENNETT, LISA GAIL, marketing professional; b. Roanoke, Va., Feb. 19, 1961; d. James Shelton and Stella Lee (Gardner) B. BS, Va. Poly. Inst. and State U., 1983; postgrad., Radford U., 1987—. Sales rep. Appalachian Bus. Concepts, Salem, Va., 1983-84; account exec. Roanoke Times and World News, 1984-85; marketing specialist WSET-TV13, Roanoke, 1985—. Counselor Trust Hotline, Roanoke, 1985-86; chmn. Am. Heart Assn., Roanoke, 1987—. Mem. Am. Mktg. Assn., Nat. Assn. Female Execs., Roanoke Jaycees (project dir. 1986), AD II (v.p. 1985-86), Va. Tech. Alumni Assn., Acctg. Soc. (pres. 1983). Club: Toastmaster (treas. 1985-86). Office: WSET-TV 13 2116 Colonial Ave Roanoke VA 24015

BENNETT, MARGARET ETHEL BOOKER, psychotherapist; b. Spartanburg, S.C., June 15, 1923; d. Paschal and Ovie (Grey) Booker. B.S., N.C. A&T State U., 1944; M.S.W., U. Mich., 1947; Ph.D., Wayne State U., 1980. Caseworker, field instr. Family Services Soc. Met. Detroit, 1947-52; caseworker, field instr., casework supr. Wayne County Cons. Center, 1952-60, Psychiat. Social Service, Wayne County Gen. Hosp., 1960-62; psychotherapist, field instr., asst. dir. Wayne County Mental Health Clinic, 1962-76; asst. dir. psychiat. social service Wayne County Psychiat. Hosp., 1976-77; dir. med. social service Wayne County Gen. Hosp., 1977-78; treatment cons. Project Paradigm; pvt. practice psychotherapy, Detroit, 1965—; psychotherapist, pres. Booker Bennett & Assocs., 1980—; founder Consultation Center of Ecorse, Mich., 1961; instr. Immanuel Luth. Coll., 1944-45; lectr. U. Mich., 1975-76. Bd. dirs. Crossroads, 1980—; exec. council Episcopal Diocese of Mich., 1974-77, 80—, exec. com. 1982—; governing bd. Cathedral Ch. of St. Paul, Detroit, 1971-74, 76-77, 79-82, v.p. governing bd., 1977; bd. dirs. Cathedral Terrace, 1981—, U. Mich. Women, 1982—, Wayne State U. Sch. Social Work Alumni Assn., 1981—. Cert. marriage counselor, cert. social worker, Mich.; cert. Acad. Cert. Social Workers. Fellow Am. Orthopsychiat. Assn.; mem. Mich. Assn. Marriage and Family Therapy, Am. Assn. Marriage and Family Therapy, Mich. Assn. Clin. Social Worker's Nat. Assn. Social Workers, Phi Delta Kappa, Alpha Kappa Alpha. Democrat. Episcopalian. Co-author: The Handbook of Psychodynamic Therapy; contbr. articles to profl. jours. Home and Office: 1971 Glynn Ct Detroit MI 48206

BENNETT, MARIANNE, health coverage company executive, lawyer; b. Bklyn., Oct. 9, 1948; d. Thomas Maurice and Mary Jo (Freese) D.; m. Charles N. Rapson, Sept. 25, 1971; children—Sean Maurice Bennett Rapson, Liam Terrence Bennett Rapson. B.A., Coll. of New Rochelle, 1970; J.D., Bklyn. Law Sch., 1975. Bar: N.Mex., 1976. Dir. Pre-Paid Legal Services, Albuquerque, 1975-76; research asst. prof. Inst. Pub. Law, Albuquerque, 1976-77; dir. Comserv. Ctr. for Legal Rep., Los Lunas, N.Mex., 1977-80, Legal Services-Albuquerque Bar, 1980-81; v.p., gen. counsel N.Mex. Blue Cross and Blue Shield, Albuquerque, 1981-87; v.p., gen. counsel Rocky Mountain Health Care Corp., Denver, 1987—. Contbr. chpt. to book, articles to publs. Pres. bd. dirs. S.W. Maternity Ctr., Albuquerque, 1977-80; bd. dirs. Assn. for Children with Learning Disabilities, 1982-83; mem. Bernalillo County Foster Parents, 1977-78, chair N.Mex. Commn. on Health Care Cost and Access, 1985. Mem. ABA, N.Mex. Bar Assn., Albuquerque Bar Assn. Democrat. Roman Catholic. Office: NMEx Blue Cross & Blue Shield 12800 Indian School NE Albuquerque NM 87110

BENNETT, MARY OLEJARZ, software engineer; b. Homestead, Fla., Nov. 4, 1961; d. Charles Albert and Arlene Emily (Farrell) Olejarz; m. Charles C. Bennet Jr., June 21, 1986. BS in Computer Sci., Northeastern U., 1984. Software engr. Digital Equipment Corp., Nashua, N.H., 1984-87, Infinet Inc., North Andover, Mass., 1987—. Home: 15A Hazel St Manchester NH 03104 Office: Infinet Inc 40 High St North Andover MA 01845

BENNETT, NANCY LOUISE, corporate librarian; b. Detroit, Oct. 23, 1948; d. Frederick Bennett and Lucy Nell (Whittaker) Longtine. BA, Wayne State U., 1981, postgrad., 1987—. Corporate librarian Creative Universal, Inc., Warren, Mich., 1985—. Mem. Spl. Libraries Assn. Office: Creative Universal Inc 12220 E 13 Mile Rd Warren MI 48093

BENNETT, PAMELA MCHARDY, production company executive, actress; b. Chgo., Mar. 4, 1947; d. George and Iris McH.; m. Robert K. Bennett, Mar. 19, 1983; 1 child, Melissa Ashley. B.A., Carroll Coll., 1969. TV and radio spokesperson Allied Van Lines, 1978-80; pres. Square One Prodns. Inc., N.Y.C., 1980—, pres. TV Presence, 1988— . Appeared in various stage and TV shows, radio and TV commls., 1969-80. Mem. Judith Harris Selig Found., N.Y.C., 1979—; sec. Widow to Widowed Internat., Inc., N.Y.C., 1986—. Recipient Wis. Broadcasters award, 1967, 68. Mem. Screen Actors Guild, Actors Equity Assn., AFTRA, Nat. Assn. Female Execs., Internat. Exhibitors Assn., Delta Nu Alpha. Republican. Avocations: singing; piano; guitar; jogging; reading. Office: Square One Prodns Inc PO Box 5122 New York NY 10150

BENNETT, PHYLLIS A., real estate brokerage manager; b. Bonham, Tex., Apr. 14, 1947; d. Joseph Thurman and Anne Alene (Seals) Hamilton; student Draughon's Bus. Sch., 1965; children—Benjamin Dwain, Robert Joseph. Sec., Sheraton-Dallas Hotel, 1965; sec. client service dept. Praetorian Mutual Life Ins. Co., Dallas, 1965-67; mgr. advt. sales aids, editor Compans mag. Life Ins. Co. S.W., Dallas, 1967-69; sales agt. Arlington (Tex.) Real Estate, 1972-73; sec.-treas. Becco, Inc., Arlington, 1973-83; office mgr. Rich Billings Inv., Inc., Arlington, 1983-85; mgr. Synergy Land Investments, Inc., Arlington, 1985—. Mem. Am. Bus. Women's Assn. (Woman of Year 1979), Nat. Assn. Female Execs. Office: Synergy Land Investments Inc 600 Six Flags Dr #616 Arlington TX 76012

BENNETT, PHYLLIS REDMON, human services agency executive; b. Smithville, Tenn., Aug. 1, 1944; d. Henry Clarence and Evelyn Louise (Ours) Redmon; m. Milburn Smith Rodgers, Jr., June 15, 1962 (div. June 1972); 1 child, Milburn Smith III; m. Weyman Herbert Bennett, Dec. 31, 1984; stepchildren: Nancy Lee, Gary Parks, Christian Elliot. Student Tenn. Tech. U., 1963-69. Editorialist Smithville Rev., 1963-65; teller 1st Nat. Bank, Smithville, 1965-68; site mgr. LBJ&C Devel. Corp., Monterey, Tenn., 1969-73; CETA dir. Upper Cumberland Human Resource Agy., Algood, Tenn., 1973-75, transp. dir., 1975-78, exec. dir., 1978—; council mem. Tenn. Dept. Human Services, Cookeville, 1983—. Pres. Cancer Soc., Smithville, 1968-73; hon. staff mem. Tenn. State Senate, 1985; col.-aide de camp Tenn. Gov.'s Staff, Nashville, 1987. Recipient Nat. Rural Transp. award U.S. Dept. Transp., Kansas City, Kans., 1985, Outstanding Service award Tenn. Assn. of HRA's, 1986, Cert. Appreciation Tenn. Commn. on Aging, 1986. Mem. Tenn. Assn. Human Resource Agys. (state pres. 1985—), Tenn. Assn. Spl. Transp. (dir. 1984—), Bus. and Profl. Women's Club (sec.-treas. 1966-72). Democrat. Baptist. Club: Jaycettes (Smithville) (v.p. 1970, Jaycette of Yr. 1972). Home: Route 6 Box 24 Cookeville TN 38501 Office: Upper Cumberland Human Resource Agy 150 W Church St Algood TN 38501

BENNETT, RITA S., rehabilitation organization executive; b. Zanesville, Ohio, Sept. 10, 1944; d. Robert Anthony and Alice Mae (Kirk) B. BS in Edn., Ohio Dominican Coll., 1967; MA in Edn., Ohio State U., 1970, postgrad. in guidance and counseling, 1974-87; PhD, Columbia-Pacific U., 1983. Lic. profl. counselor, adult services dir., rehab. counselor, qualified mental retardation profl. educator, Ohio. Tchr. social studies St. Nicholas Sch., Zanesville, 1964-66; tchr. social studies, counseling asst. Wherle Meml. High Sch., Columbus, Ohio, 1967-71; supr. daily life, coordinator residential staffs Nisonger Ctr. Ohio State U., Columbus, 1972-73, mem. adj. faculty dept. human services edn., 1986—; instr. sociology Franklin U., Columbus, 1972-73; with ARC Industries, Columbus, 1973-75; with Goodwill/Cen. Ohio Rehab. Ctr., Columbus, 1975—, assoc. exec. dir., 1984—; guest lectr. mental health Columbus Tech. Inst., 1976-80; cons.-psychology asst. Ohio Profl. Counseling Services, 1980-83; pvt. practice counseling, 1986—. NDEA grantee Bowling Green State U., 1968. Mem. Am. Assn. Counseling and Devel., Ohio Assn. Counseling and Devel., Am. Mental Health Assn., Ohio Rehab. Adminstrs. Assn., Internat. Assn. Psychosocial Rehab. Services, Internat. Acad. Profl. Counseling Psychotherapy, Nat. Assn. Female Execs. Democrat. Roman Catholic. Office: Goodwill/Cen Ohio Rehab Ctr 1331 Edgehill Rd Columbus OH 43211

BENNETT, ROBIN LEE, paralegal; b. Los Angeles, Dec. 19, 1953; d. Sam and Shirley Adele (Jaffee) Orland; m. Richard Lee Bennett, Aug. 3, 1979; children: Erin Michelle, Samantha Claire. AA, Santa Monica Coll., 1974; BS, Calif. State U., 1976; cert. in real estate law, U. West Los Angeles, 1980, cert. corp. law, probate law, 1982. Consumer law coordinator Bullock's Dept. Stores, Los Angeles, 1976-81; paralegal Cox, Castle & Nicholson, Los Angeles, 1981—; seminar instr. various instns. Mem. Los Angeles Paralegal Assn. (v.p., treas., com. chmn., bd. dirs. 1982—, pres.), U. West Los Angeles Paralegal Alumni Assn. (pres. bd. dirs. 1985), Calif. Alliance Paralegal Assns. (bd. dirs., sec./treas. 1983-86). Home: 12013 Stanwood Dr Los Angeles CA 90066

BENNETT, SARAH ISABEL NEFF (SALLY), author, composer; b. Fountain Springs, Pa.; d. Franklin Daniel and Jennie Catherine (Bright) Neff; student Banks Bus. Coll., 1940-41, Gwen Shock Modeling and Dramatic Sch., 1941-42, U. Pa., 1942; m. Paul H. Bennett, Nov. 1, 1947. Model, John Wanamaker's, Phila., 1942; legal sec. Dept. Justice, Phila., 1945-46; writer, performer, disc jockey Radio and TV Sta. WLWA, Atlanta, 1954-56; playwright, actress Karamu Little Theater and Lakewood Little Theater, Cleve., 1957-59; founder, pres., owner Solar Record Co., Cleve., 1959—; composer Broadcast Music Co., Cleve., 1958—; founder, pres. Composers Showcase, Inc., Cleve., 1965—, Music Pub. Co., Cleve., 1966, First Big Band Hall of Fame, Cleve., 1975—; contbr. to Palm Beach (Fla.) Life, Palm Beacher Daily. Mem. nat. council Met. Opera, N.Y.C., 1967—; mem. John F. Kennedy Center, 1967—; founder, pres. Animal Welfare Vols., Inc., Cleve., 1969—; founding bd. dirs. Great Lakes Shakespeare Festival, Cleve., Cleve. Indian Basebelles. Mem. Nat. League Am. Pen Women (pres. 1962-63, music chmn. Palm Beach chpt., pres. br. 1982-83), Am. Guild Authors and Composers, Am. Women in Radio and TV, Am. Guild Variety Artists, Broadcast Music, Palm Beach Quills, Palm Beach Opera, Preservation Found. Palm Beach, Palm Beach Hist. Soc., Palm Beach C. of C., English Speaking Union (Palm Beach chpt.), DAR. Clubs: Cleve. Yachting, Racquet Internat., Women's City (Cleve.). Author: Sugar and Spice, 1972; composer: Magic Moments.

BENNETT, SHIRLEY LOUISE, travel consultant; b. Ellsworth, Kans., Feb. 5, 1935; d. Cecil Roy and Mary Ann (Houston) Moyer; m. Donald Richard Bennett, Oct. 16, 1953; children: Walter Eugene, Joseph Richard. Grad. high sch., San Fernando, Calif.; student, SST Travel Sch., 1985. Agt. Pro Travel, San Diego, 1986-87; travel cons. Panda Travel, Phoenix, 1987—. Sec. vol. police Half Moon Bay (Calif.) police, 1961-64, police matron, 1963-64; Moon Bay PTA, 1960-64, room mother, 1964-66; mem. San Mateo (Calif.) PTA, pres. Mountain View (Calif.) PTA Council, 1966-67; fund raising chmn. Mountain View Little League, 1964-66; vol. Young Reps., Calif., Ariz., USO; founder Smart Teens in Santa Clara County; mem. Crown Valley Parents Guild, Laguna Niguel, Calif.; narcotic chmn. Santa Clara County PTA Council, 1967-69; vol. ARC, emergency dept. Keno Hosp, Tucson, 1977-78, emergency dept. St. Lukes Hosp., Phoenix, 1979-82, vol. placement chmn. ladies aux.; nurses Aid Emergency Depts. Mem. Am. Soc. Travel Agts. Republican. Home: 1642 W Friess Dr Phoenix AZ 85023 Office: Panda Travel Service 1311 E Northern Ave Phoenix AZ 85023

BENNETT, STEPHANIE MITCHELL, college president; b. Albuquerque, Jan. 19, 1941; d. Claude Stephen and Alma Nelle (Cashion) Mitchell; 1 child, Brendan T. B.A., U. N.Mex., 1963, M.A., 1966; Ph.D., U. Iowa, 1973. Instr. Loretto Heights Coll., Denver, 1967-68; asst. prof. Albion Coll., Mich., 1968-76; dean Westhampton Coll., U. Richmond, Va., 1976-84; pres. Centenary Coll., Hackettstown, N.J., 1984—; pres. So. Assn. Colls. for Women, 1981-82; state coordinator Va. Women Adminstrs. Program, 1983-84; bd. dirs., exec. com. Va. Women's Cultural Hist. Project, Richmond, 1983-84; treas. Ind. Coll. Fund N.J., 1987—. Author filmstrip series Am. Invention and Ingenuity, 1968. Contbr. articles and book revs. to profl. jours. Pres. Maymont Vol. Guild, Richmond, 1980-81. Ford Found. fellow, 1963-65, Earhart Found. fellow, 1974, NEH summer fellow, 1975, program grantee Xerox, IBM, 1978. Mem. Am. Studies Assn., Assn. for Study Higher Edn., Assn. Ind. Colls. and Univs. of N.J. (treas. 1986—), Hackettstown Area C. of C. (bd. dirs. 1986—). Episcopalian. Avocation: hiking. Home: 407 Moore St Hackettstown NJ 07840 Office: Centenary Coll 400 Jefferson St Hackettstown NJ 07840

BENNETT, WANDA MARIE, restaurant owner; b. Simmons, Mo., Jan. 3, 1930; d. Frank and Stella Marie (Coats) Hogan; m. Cecil Paul Bennett, May 22, 1947 (div. 1962); children: William Paul, Elizabeth Kaye Bennett Gomes. Mem. staff Employment Counselor Inc., Springfield, Mo., 1964-66; office mgr. SIC Loan Co., Springfield, 1966-70, Rees Trucking Co., Houston, Mo., 1970-72; mgr. factory outlet Ozark Walnut, Inc., Houston, 1972-78; land developer Hogan's Country Estates, 1977; property mgr. Bob Wright Realty, Springfield, 1978-80; owner, operator Sheraton Inn Gift Shop, Springfield, 1980-82, Garden Patch, Springfield, 1981-87; hostess John A. Hammons Holiday Inn, Springfield, 1987—; owner, operator Entrepeneur, Springfield, 1981—. Mem. Welcome Wagon Alumni, Springfield; vol. United Way Springfield, 1983—, Lester E. Cox Med. Ctr., Springfield, 1983—; circulation coordinator Winners Circle, Springfield, 1983—; active Shealy Self-Help Support Group. Baptist. Home: 2149 E Sunshine Apt #107-C Springfield MO 65804 Office: Entrepeneur PO Box 10136 GS Springfield MO 65808

BENNETT-TALBOT, BETTY MUELLER, educational association administrator; b. Milw.; d. August Joseph and Florence Marie (Schumacher) Mueller; m. John William Bennett, May 24, 1947 (div. Mar. 1981); children: Cynthia, Thomas, Sally, Steven, Nancy, Jane, Mary, Bill, Dan, Amy, Molly; m. John R. Talbot, Jan. 5, 1985. BFA, Mt. Mary Coll., Milw., 1946; postgrad., U. Wis., 1984. Recreation dir. Goodwill Industries Home, Milw., 1949; tchr. Black Earth (Wis.) Schs., 1970-72; owner, dir. Hoofbeat Sch. Horsemanship, Mazomanie, Wis., 1964-84; founder, pres. Horsemanship Safety Assn., Inc., Mazomanie, 1964—. Portrait artist, Wis. and Fla.; contbr. articles to profl. jours. Advisor Lakeshore Equine Coll., Sheboygan, Wis., 1978—; bd. dirs. U.S. Pony Clubs, Inc., West Chester, Pa., 1982-84; religious edn. dir. St. Barnabas Ch., Mazomanie, 1964-70; pres. Madison Diocesan Council Cath. Women, 1986—. Mem. Am. Camping Assn., Am. Horse Council, Wis. State Horse Council, Wis. Dressage Assn. (pres. Madison chpt. 1982-84), Nat. Safety Council (bd. dirs. 1976—, chmn. pub. safety and outdoor recreation sects. 1976—), others. Republican. Roman Catholic. Home: 111 Lakefront Ln NW Lake Placid FL 33852 Office: Horsemanship Safety Assn 5335 Reeve Rd Mazomanie WI 53560

BENNINGTON, BRENDA LEE, videographer; b. Gary, Ind., Nov. 15, 1954; d. Paul Wayland and Shirley Ann (Havard) B.; 1 child, Austin Brooks. Student Principia Coll., Elsah, Ill., 1972-74, Sch. of Art Inst. of Chgo., 1983; B.A. in English with honors, U. Hawaii, 1977. Tchr. English, Peace Corps, Mbuji-Mayi, Zaire, 1977-79, Asahi Cultural Ctr., Osaka, Japan, 1981-82, Osaka Inst. Fgn. Trade, Osaka, 1981-82, Kansai U. of Fgn. Studies, Osaka, 1980-82, Matsushita Electric, Osaka, 1982; pres., owner Video Enterprises, North Palm Beach, Fla., 1983-87. Mem. Palm Beach Opera Chorus, 1984-85. Fred Waring Scholar, 1972. Mem. Exec. Women of Palm Beaches, Fla. Motion Picture and TV Assn., Am. Film Inst., No. Palm Beach County C. of C. (co-chmn. spl. events 1985-86), Better Bus. Bur., Phi Beta Kappa. Republican. Christian Scientist. Avocations: swimming; singing.

BENNINGTON, KRISTEN NOEL, accountant; b. Saginaw, Mich., Apr. 28, 1956; d. Clyde Max and Jenyne Lenore (Ahrens) B. BBA in Acctg., U. Houston, 1983. Staff acct. Daniel L. Whittkopp PC, Bay City, Mich., 1976-77; tax sr. Whiddon & Co., Inc., Houston, 1977-86; tax mgr. Jennings, Hawley, Cederberg & Co., PC, Houston, 1986—. Tchr. 2d grade Cypress Creek Christian Ch., Houston, 1984-86; asst. NW Ministries Food Drives, Houston, 1984—; membership sec. Lincoln Green South Crime Watch Com., Houston, 1986—. Mem. NW Tax Forum, Scuba Divers Anonymous (v.p.), Beta Alpha Psi. Republican. Lutheran. Club: Bammel Breakers (Houston). Office: Jennings Hawley Cederberg & Co 3724 FM 1960 W Suite 300 Houston TX 77068

BENO, CANDICE LYNN, chemical company executive; b. New Brunswick, N.J., Mar. 25, 1951; d. Andrew Jule and Claire May (Blanchard) B. BA magna cum laude, U. Conn., 1973, MS in Biochemistry, 1974. Lab. technician Linde div. Union Carbide Corp., Keasbey, N.J., 1976-78, sr. lab. technician, 1978-79; regional tech. supr. Linde div. Union Carbide Corp., South Plainfield, N.J., 1979; asst. staff engr. Linde div. Union Carbide Corp., Springfield, N.J., 1979-82, staff engr., 1982-84; tech. bus. cons. Linde div. Union Carbide Corp., Danbury, Conn., 1984-85; staff engr. Linde div. Union Carbide Corp., Somerset, N.J., 1985-87; mgr. Linde div. Union Carbide Corp., Springfield, 1987—; supr. Werner Erhard & Assocs., Edison, N.J., 1984-87; guest seminar leader, 1985—, course mgr., 1984-86. Mem. Compressed Gas Assn. (chmn. 1985—, vice chmn. 1983-88), Am. Soc. Quality Control, Semiconductor Equipment and Material Inst. (co-chmn. 1984—, editor jours. 1982-88, Outstanding Service award 1984-88), Mortar Bd., Phi Beta Kappa, Phi Kappa Phi. Democrat. Home: 1000 W 8th St Plainfield NJ 07063 Office: Union Carbide Corp Linde Div 150 Morris Ave PO Box 699 Springfield NJ 07063

BENO, CAROLYN ELIZABETH, pharmacist, marketing professional; b. Council Bluffs, Iowa, Sept. 2, 1953; d. Adolph Frank Jr. and Gertrude Marie Sophie (Spetman) B. BA, U. Nebr., 1975, BS in Pharmacy, 1976; MS, U. Iowa, 1978; postgrad., U. S.C., 1980—. Pharmacy intern Walgreens Gateway, Lincoln, Nebr., 1974-75; pharmacist Hushaw Drug Co., Council Bluffs, Iowa, 1976-77; grad. asst. U. Iowa, Iowa City, 1977-78; asst. prof. pharmacy Temple U., Phila., 1978-80; pharmacist Kroger and Springwood Lake Pharmacies, Columbia, S.C., 1982-84; sr. analyst U.S. pharm. and nutrition group Bristol Myers, Evansville, Ind., 1985—; chmn. drug edn. com. coll. pharmacy U. Nebr., Lincoln, 1973-74; vol. cons. Chem. Dependency Agy. S. W. Iowa, Council Bluffs, 1975-77; vol. pharmacist Iowa City (Iowa) Free Med. Clinic, 1977-78. Contbr. articles to profl. jours. Mem. Am. Pharm. Assn., Alpha Mu Alpha, Kappa Epsilon (co-advisor 1983-84), Phi Lambda Sigma. Republican. Lutheran. Home: 3211 Bellemeade Ave Evansville IN 47715 Office: Bristol Myers US Pharm and Nutrition Group 2404 W Pennsylvania Evansville IN 47721

BENOIT, NANCY L., state legislator, educator; b. New Haven, Conn., Jan. 25, 1944; d. James Michael and Florence Louise (Bray) Wynne; m. Raymond George Benoit, Aug. 8, 1970; children: Michael, Patrick. BA, Albertus Magnus Coll., 1965; MEd, Wayne State U., 1969. Tchr. St. Vincent de Paul High Sch., Detroit, 1965-69; community organizer Social Progress Action Corp., Woonsocket, R.I., 1969-71; dir. Little Shares Day Care Ctr., Woonsocket, 1971-73; edn. coordinator Northwest Head Start, North Providence, R.I., 1978-84; mem. R.I. Ho. of Reps., 1985—, chair joint legis. commn. on child care, 1985—, mem. adult edn. commn., 1985—, mem. health, edn. and welfare com., 1986—, vice chair joint legis. commn. to study affordable housing in R.I., 1987—. Mem. bd. mgrs. Woonsocket Family & Child Care Services, 1973-87; v.p., bd. dirs. Health Services, Inc., Woonsocket, 1974-87; founder Women for Women, 1983—; vol. coordinator Vols. in Action, Providence, 1984-86; bd. dirs. R.I. affiliate Literacy Vols. of Am., 1985—; grant coordinator Community Coll. R.I., Lincoln, 1986-87. Named one of Outstanding Young Women Am., Woonsocket and R.I. Jaycees, 1980; recipient Francesco Cannistra Service award Health Services, Inc., 1986, Outstanding Service award R.I. Day Care Dirs. Assn., 1986. Mem. Common Cause, Sierra Club, Audubon Soc. Democrat. Roman Catholic. Office: RI Gen Assembly Providence RI 02903

BENSEL, CAROLYN KIRKBRIDE, psychologist; b. Orange, N.J., Sept. 21, 1941; d. William Everitt and Margaret Mary (McGlynn) B.; A.B. with honors in Psychology, Chestnut Hill Coll., 1963; M.S., U. Mass., 1964, Ph.D. (Univ. fellow), 1967. Teaching asst. U. Mass., Amherst, 1963-64, research asst., 1964-66; human factors psychologist Grumman Aerospace Corp., Bethpage, N.Y., 1967-71; chief human factors group U.S. Army Natick (Mass.) Research, Devel. and Engring. Ctr., 1971—. Lic. psychologist, Mass. Fellow Human Factors Soc.; mem. Am. Psychol. Assn., Human Factors Soc., Ergonomics Soc., Soc. Engring. Psychologists, Internat. Ergonomics Assn., AAAS, Sigma Xi. Editor: Proc. 23d Ann. Meeting of Human Factors Soc., 1979. Office: Sci & Advanced Tech Directorate Army Natick Research Devel Engring Ctr Kansas St Natick MA 01760

BENSHOFF, DIXIE LEE, psychologist; b. Ravenna, Ohio, Apr. 11, 1950; d. Roy Orrison and Pauline (Gatewood) B. B.A., Hiram Coll., 1972; postgrad. Cambridge (Eng.) U., 1970, 73; M.Ed., Kent State U., 1973, Ph.D., 1977. Counselor, Hiram (Ohio) Coll., 1973; counselor, counseling and group resources center Kent (Ohio) State U., 1973-74, asst. to sch. counseling program for counseling and personnel services edn. dept., 1974-75; asst. dir. Portage County Mental Health Bd., Kent, 1975-78; psychologist, outpatient dir. Kevin Coleman Mental Health Center, Kent, 1978-81; instr. clin. psychology/family medicine Coll. Medicine, Northeastern Ohio U., 1979—; pres. Portage County Council Health and Social Agys., 1980; dir. aftercare and transitional services Western Res. Human Services, Akron, Ohio, 1981—; allied health profl. Akron City Hosp. Diplomate in profl. psychotherapy Internat. Acad. Behavioral Medicine; lic. psychologist, Ohio. Mem. Am. Psychol. Assn., Am. Assn. Marriage and Family Therapists (clin.), Kappa Delta Pi. Contbr. articles in field to profl. jours. Office: 1640 Franklin Ave Suite 200-7 Kent OH 44240

BENSKINA, MARGARITA O. (PRINCESS ORELIA), dancer, singer, musician; b. Colon, Panama, Mar. 16; naturalized U.S. citizen, 1956; d. Jose and Amelia Benskina; student parochial schs., Havana, Cuba, and Colon, Panama, Harren High Sch., N.Y.C.; diploma in modeling instrn., N.Y. Acad. Theatrical Arts, 1962; grad. N.Y. Sch. Floral Designing, 1971; postgrad. Queens Coll., 1982, 1 dau., Pearl A. Quintyne. Has appeared in theatres, night clubs in various cities U.S., including Connie's Inn Broadway Night Club, Broadway Cotton Club, Leon and Eddie's; in Dance with Your Gods, Calling All Stars, Broadway Parade, N.Y.C., after 1935; mem. Afro-Cuban dance team, Orelia and Pete, 1942; toured with Asadata Dofara Dance Opera, Kykunkor, 1947; now appearing with own ensemble; toured Can. with own dance co., Bacanal, 1950; starred in UN program Stars of the West Indies, also TV program Tropical Holiday, CBS; toured with Sam Manning Calypso Concert Co., 1954; personal mgr. for modern jazz group Rouse-Watkins-Les Modes Quintet, 1956, also dance and mus. groups; prod., dir. concerts, N.Y.C., 1959; produced, directed, starred in concert program Princess Orelia's Pot Puree, Town Hall, N.Y.C., 1964; appeared on Ghana radio, 1971-77; owner, mgr. retail religious mdse. store, N.Y.C.; ordained to ministry Internat. Spiritual Healers Fellowship, 1956. Vol., Bellevue Hosp., N.Y.C. Recipient J.F. Kennedy Library for Minorities Heritage award, Am. Honorarium award, 1966. Mem. Broadcast Music, Inc., Synanon, Negro Women's Guild, Washington, Council Negro Am. Women (life), Media Women. Author: (poetry) No Longer Defeated and Other Poems, 1972; The Inflammable Desire to Rebel, 1973; I Have Loved You Already, 1974; I Thank You, Father, 1975; Library To Whom It May Concern, 1978. Contbr. to New Voices in American Poetry, 1972-73. Home: 192-22 100th Ave Hollis NY 11423

BENSMAN, MARCIE ELLEN, employee assistance and health care executive; b. Detroit, July 23, 1956; d. Lawrence Solomon and Barbara Janet (Rose) B. BA cum laude, Mich. State U., 1979; MS, Columbia U., 1983. Cert. social worker, N.Y.; cert. employee assistance profl. Employee assistance intern Columbia-Presbyn. Med. Ctr., N.Y.C., 1982-83; adminstrv., research assoc. Jonah Kleinstein Assocs., N.Y.C., 1982-83; employee assistance counselor Brownlee Dolan Stein Assocs., N.Y.C., 1983-84; sr. account exec. Family Service Am./Nat. Services to Industry, N.Y.C., 1985—; developer employee assistance directory Greater N.Y.C. area, 1983. Vol. Hot Breakfast Project, East Lansing, Mich., 1975-76, Big Bros./Big Sisters, Birmingham, Mich., 1979-80, The Holiday Project, Detroit, 1980-81. Mem. Employee Assistance Soc. N.Am., Nat. Assn. Female Execs., Assn. Labor Mgmt. Adminstrs. and Cons. on Alcoholism, Nat. Assn. Female Execs. Office: Family Service Am Nat Services Industry 254 W 31st St New York NY 10001

BENSON, BETTY JONES, educator; b. Barrow County, Ga., Jan. 11, 1928; d. George C. and Bertha (Mobley) Jones; B.S. in Edn., N. Ga. U., Dahlonega, 1958; M.Ed. in Curriculum and Supervision, U. Ga., Athens, 1968, edn. specialist in Curriculum and Supervision, 1970; m. George T. Benson; children—George Steven, Elizabeth Gayle, James Claud, Robert Benjamin. Tchr. Forsyth County (Ga.) Bd. Edn., Cumming, 1956-66, curriculum dir., 1966—; asst. supt. for instrn. Forsyth County Schs., 1981—. Active Alpine Center for Disturbed Children; chmn. Ga. Lake Lanier Island Authority; mem. N. Ga. Coll. Edn. Adv. Com., Ga. Textbook Com.; adv. Boy Scouts; Sunday sch. tchr. 1st Baptist Ch. Cumming. Mem. NEA, Ga. Assn. Educators (dir.), Nat., Ga. (pres.) assns. supervision and curriculum devel., Assn. Childhood Edn. Internat., Bus. and Profl. Women's Club, Internat. Platform Assn., Ga. Future Tchrs. Adv. Assn. (pres.), HeadStart Dirs. Assn., Forsyth County Hist. Soc. Home: Route 1 Box 12 Cumming GA 30130 Office: 101 School St Cumming GA 30130

BENSON, CAROL SUSAN, programmer, analyst; b. Los Angeles, Dec. 29, 1956; d. Clarence James Jr. and Cecilia Rose (Smith) Chapman; m. Daniel Keith Benson, Aug. 22, 1980. BA in Biology, Calif. State U., 1980; Cert. in computer programming, Control Data Inst., 1982. Programmer Mission Ins. Co., Los Angeles, 1983-85; sr. programmer/analyst Security Pacific Automation Co., Glendale, Calif., 1985—; cons. Mulholland Tennis Club, Los Angeles, 1984. Republican. Lutheran. Office: Security Pacific Automation Co 611 N Brand Blvd G3-01 Glendale CA 91203

BENSON, JANET ELIZABETH, transportation finance executive; b. Ewell, Eng., Apr. 1, 1954; came to U.S., 1981; d. James Gillies and Jean Muriel (Waugh) B. BA with honors, U. London, 1976; MBA, U. Pa., 1983. Econ. cons. Rendel Palmer & Tritton Econ. Studies, London, 1976-81; fin. analyst Morgan Guaranty Trust Co., London, 1982; fin. analyst Am. Airlines, Dallas, 1983-85, controller, 1985; v.p. fin. Am. Airlines Direct Mktg. Corp., Dallas, 1986; dir. reservations ops. Eastern Airlines, Inc., Miami, 1987—. English Speaking Union scholar London, 1981, Teagle scholar Exxon Corp, 1982. Mem. Ch. Eng. Club: Thames Rowing (London). Home: 10540 SW 154 Ct #5 Miami FL 33196 Office: Eastern Airlines Inc Miami Internat Airport Miami FL 33148

BENSON, JANETTE B., developmental psychologist, researcher; b. San Francisco, May 2, 1956; d. Leon Samuel and Lillian S. (Sussman) B. BA, San Francisco State U., 1978; MA, Clark U., 1980, PhD, 1983. Postdoctoral research fellow U. Denver, 1983-86, asst. research prof., 1986-87, asst. prof. psychology, 1987—; cons. statis. computers San Francisco State U., 1977-78, tech. writer, 1978; mem. dissertation com. U. Denver, 1984, asst. research prof. psychology, 1986—. Contbr. numerous articles to med. jours. Del. Dem. Caucus Dist. 1, Denver, 1983, 85. Univ. scholar Clark U., 1978-79, research fellow Clark U., 1979-81; USPHS postdoctoral research fellow U. Denver, 1983-85. Mem. Am. Psychol. Assn., Soc. for Research in Child Devel., Devel. Psychobiology Research Group. Democrat. Office: U Denver Dept Psychology 2040 S York St Denver CO 80208

BENSON, JUDY GAYLE, counselor; b. Tulsa, Sept. 17, 1951; d. Billy Jack and Wilma Dean (Robison) B. BA, Ark. Tech. U., 1973; MS, Okla. State U., 1977. Lic. counselor. Pvt. practice counseling, hypnotherapy Little Rock, 1970—; dep. sheriff Yell County, Dardanelle, Ark., 1969-74; officer parole, transp., riot State Okla., Tulsa, 1973-76; pvt. investigator Pinkerton's Inc., San Francisco, 1976; dep. Alameda County Sheriff's Dept., Oakland, Calif., 1976-77; adminstrv. coordinator Hopeline, Little Rock, 1979-82; dir. Drugline 4, Little Rock, 1982-84; pres. Profl. Extension, Little Rock, 1982-88; rehab. specialist Intracorp, Little Rock, 1987—; cons. prodn. End Line Prodns., Little Rock, 1986; coordinator communications Hands Across Am., Little Rock, 1986; adminstr., coordinator Yell County Juvenile Services, Dardanelle, 1972-74; cons. Ark. Crisis Intervention Ctr. 1983—. Contbr. articles to profl. jours. Photographer Mondale/Ferraro in Ark. campaign and other polit. campaigns. Named Outstanding Young Woman Am., 1983, 85, 87. Mem. Ark. Soc. Clin. Hypnosis, Ark. Assn. Counseling, Guidance and Devel., Am. Mental Health Counselors Assn., Ark. Profl. Mental Health Counselors Assn., AAUW. Democrat. Mem. Christian Ch. Office: Intracorp 11225 Huron Ln Suite #100 Little Rock AR 72211

BENSON, JULIANNE, marketing executive; b. Elmhurst, Ill., May 31, 1953; d. Carl Gustav and Jeanette B. (Freevol) B. Student, Rutgers U., 1983-87. Clk. typist United Labs., Addison, Ill., 1970-72, supr. orders, 1972-76, purchasing mgr., 1977-80, mgr. sales adminstrn., 1980-81; v.p. ops. United Labs., Marlton, N.J., 1981-87, v.p. mktg., 1987—. Mem. Rep. Nat. Com., 1978—; chairperson ways and means com. Camden City Council, 1984-85, recording sec. 1985—. Mem. Soc. for the Advancement Mgmt., Beta Sigma Phi. Mem. Beta Sigma Phi (v.p. 1984-85, pres. 1985-86, Woman of Yr. 1985). Home: 175 E Delaware Pl Chicago IL 60611 Office: United Labs Inc 155 S Rt 53 Addison IL 60101

BENSON, LISA JANE, senior paralegal; b. Omaha, Sept. 24, 1962; d. James M. and Jane (Harris) B. Student, Murray State U., 1980-82, U. South Ala., 1982-84; Diploma in Paralegal Studies, Sullivan Jr. Coll. Bus., 1984; BS in Bus. Mgmt., U. Louisville, 1988. Paralegal Connie E. Cole, Atty. at Law, Louisville, 1985, Gittleman & Barber, Attys. at Law, Louisville, 1985; paralegal Humana Inc., Louisville, 1985-86, sr. paralegal, 1986—; mem. adv. bd. Inst. Paralegal Studies Sullivan Jr. Coll. Bus., 1987-88. Vol. Jefferson County Pub. Law Library, Louisville, 1983, Ky. Ctr. Arts, Louisville, 1985. Mem. Louisville Assn. Paralegals, (bd. dirs. 1988—), Am. Soc. Corp. Secs. (bd. dirs. 1988—), Alpha Omicron Pi, Lambda Chi Alpha. Office: Humana Inc 500 W Main St Louisville KY 40202

BENSON, LUCY PETERS WILSON, political consultant, former under secretary of state; b. N.Y.C., Aug. 25, 1927; d. Willard Oliver and Helen (Peters) Wilson; m. Bruce Buzzell Benson, Mar. 30, 1950. B.A., Smith Coll., 1949, M.A., 1955; L.H.D. (hon.), Wheaton Coll., Norton, Mass., 1965; LL.D. (hon.), U. Mass., 1969; L.H.D. (hon.), Bucknell U., 1972; LL.D. (hon.), U. Md., 1972; L.H.D. (hon.), Carleton Coll., 1973; LL.D. (hon.), Amherst Coll., 1974, Clark U., 1975; H.H.D., Springfield Coll., 1981; L.H.D. (hon.), Bates Coll., 1982. Mem. jr. exec. tng. program Bloomingdale's, N.Y.C., 1949-50; asst. dir. pub. relations Smith Coll., 1950-53; research asst. dept. Am. studies Amherst Coll., 1956-57; pres. Amherst league LWV, Mass., 1957-61; pres. Mass. league LWV, 1961-65; nat. pres. LWV, Mass., 1968-74; mem. Gov.'s cabinet and sec. human services Commonwealth of Mass., 1975; mem. pres.'s spl. commn. 1976-77; mem. spl. commn. on adminstrv. rev. U.S. Ho. of Reps., Washington, 1976-77; under sec. State Security Assistance, Sci. and Tech. U.S. Dept. State, Washington, 1977-80, cons. U.S. Dept. State and SRI Internat., Washington, 1980 81; pres. Benson and Assocs., Amherst and Washington, 1981—; trustee N.E. Utilities, 1971-74, 76-77; dir. Continental Group, Inc., 1974-77, 80-85, Dreyfus Fund, Dreyfus Liquid Assets, Dreyfus Convertible Securities Fund, Dreyfus Long Term Govt. Fund Inc., Dreyfus U.S. Guaranteed Money Fund., Dreyfus Third Century Fund, Inc., Grumman Corp., Sci. Applications Internat. Corp., Combustion Engring., Inc., Communications Satellite Corp. Mem. steering com. Urban Coalition, 1968, exec. com., 1970-75, 80-84, co-chmn., 1973-75; mem. Gov. Mass. Spl. Com. Rev. Sunday Closing Laws, 1961; mem. spl. commn. Mass. Legislature to Study Budgetary Powers of Trustees U. Mass., 1961-62; mem. Gov. Mass. Com. Rev. Salaries State Employees, 1963, Mass. Adv. Bd. Higher Ednl. Policy, 1962-65, Mass. Bd. Edn. Adv. Com. Racial Imbalance and Edn., 1964-65, Mass. adv. com. U.S. Commn. Civil Rights, 1964-73; vice chmn. Mass. Adv. Council Edn., 1965-68; mem. Mass. Com. Children and Youth Com. to Study Report by U.S. Children's Bur., Mass. Youth Service Div., 1967; mem. pub. adv. com. U.S. Trade Policy, 1968; mem. vis. com. John F. Kennedy Sch. Govt.; mem. Trilateral Commn., Council Fgn. Relations. Mem. town meeting, Amherst, 1957-74, finance com., 1960-66; trustee Edn. Devel. Center, Newton, Mass., 1967-72, Nat. Urban League, 1974-77, Smith Coll., 1975-80, Brookings Instn., 1974-77, Alfred P. Sloan Found., 1975-77, 81—, Lafayette Coll., 1985—, Bur. Social Sci. Research, Inc., 1985-87; bd. dirs. Catalyst, 1972—; former bd. govs. Am. Nat. Red Cross, Common Cause, Women's Action Alliance; bd. govs. Internat. Ctr. on Election Law and Adminstrn., 1985-87. Recipient Achievement award Bur. Govt. Research, U. Mass., 1963; Distinguished Service award Boston Coll., 1965; Smith Coll. medal, 1969; Distinguished Civic Leadership award Tufts U., 1965; Distinguished Service award Northfield Mount Hermon Sch., 1976; Radcliffe fellow Radcliffe Inst., 1965-66, 66-67. Mem. Nat. Acad. Pub. Adminstrn., ACLU, UN Assn., Urban League, NAACP, Assn. Am. Indian Affairs, East African Wildlife Soc., Jersey Wildlife Preservation Trust Channel Islands. Home: 46 Sunset Ave Amherst MA 01002 Office: Benson & Assos 1300 19th St NW Suite 700 Washington DC 20036

BENSON, PRISCILLA JENKINS, astronomy educator; b. Newton, Mass., May 6, 1940; d. Benjamin Gilbert and Rebecca (Martin) Jenkins; m. John K. Benson Jr., June 23, 1962; children: Karen Jenkins, John K. III. BA, Smith Coll., 1962; SM, Mass. Inst. Tech., 1979, PhD, 1983. Math, sci. tchr. Tahanto Regional High Sch., Boylston, Mass., 1962-63; acturarial asst. Paul Revere Life Ins. Co., Worcester, Mass., 1963-64; from instr. to asst. prof. Wellesley (Mass.) Coll., 1972—; mem. Council on Undergrad. Research, 1987—. Dudly Obs. grantee, Albany, N.Y., 1984, Research Corp. grantee, 1984-86, NSF grantee, Washington, 1986—. Mem. Am. Astron. Soc. (research grantee 1983), Am. Assn. Variable Star Observers, Internat. Amateur-Profl. Photographic Photometry, Phi Beta Kappa, Sigma Xi (v.p. local chpt. 1985-86, pres. 1986-87). Office: Wellesley Coll Whitin Obs Wellesley MA 02181

BENTALL, SHEILA MARIE, data processing manager; b. Newton, Iowa, Oct. 22, 1952; d. Dean Lee and Stella Rose (Oxford) Bingaman; m. Gregory Robert Bentall, May 25, 1974. BA, U. Iowa, 1970; MBA, Ind. State U., 1979. Grad. asst. Ind. State U., Terre Haute, 1977-79; programmer, analyst Columbia House of CBS, Inc., Terre Haute, Ind., 1979-82; analyst U.S.F. and G., Balt., 1982-83, mgr. data processing, 1983—. Unit leader Hunger and Shelter Program, Balt., 1983—; mem. mission com. First and Franklin St. Presbyn. Ch., Balt., 1983—; trustee Com. of Presbyn. Ch. in City of Balt., 1987. Home: 58 Abbey Bridge Ct Lutherville MD 21093 Office: USF and G PO Box 1138 Baltimore MD 21203

BENTALL, SHIRLEY FRANKLYN, church organization administrator; b. Regina, Sask., Can., July 28, 1926; d. Frank and Viola Louise (Thom) May; m. Charles Howard Bentall, June 15, 1946; children: Edna Louise, Kathleen Margaret, Joan Elizabeth, Barnard Franklin. BA, McMaster U., Hamilton, Ont., 1946. Retreat leader The Bapt. Union Western Can., 1971—; lectr. Bapt. Leadership Tng. Sch., Calgary, Alta., 1975-85; pres. The Bapt. Union of Western Can., 1976-77, Can. Bapt. Fedn., 1985-88; mem. The Bapt. World Alliance Council, 1985-88; mem. The Human Rights Commn. of Bapt. World Alliance, 1985-90. Writer Musings column for The Can. Bapt., 1965—; author: Buckboard to Brotherhood, 1975, Amusings, 1980, The Charles Bentall Story, 1986. Recipient Merit award The Bapt. Union of Western Can., 1982. Home: 500 Eau Claire Ave SW, Apt H 202, Calgary, AB Canada T2P 3R8

BENTEL, MARIA-LUISE RAMONA AZZARONE (MRS. FREDERICK R. BENTEL), architect; b. N.Y.C., June 15, 1928; d. Louis and Maria-Teresa (Massaro) Azzarone; m. Frederick R. Bentel, Aug. 16, 1952; children: Paul Louis, Peter Andreas, Maria Elisabeth. B.Arch., MIT, 1951; Fulbright scholar, Scuola d'Architettura, Venice, Italy, 1952-53. Registered profl. architect, Conn., N.Y., N.J., Va., Vt. registered profl. planner, N.J. Partner Bentel & Bentel (Architects), Locust Valley, N.Y., 1955—; pres. Tesstoria Realty Corp., N.Y.C., 1961—; v.p., sec.-treas. Correlated Designs, Inc., Locust Valley, 1961—; partner Cobblestone Enterprises, 1967; founding mem. Locust Valley Bus. Dist. Planning Commn., 1968—; regional vice-chairperson MIT Ednl. Council; adv. mem. MIT Council for the Arts; asso. prof. architecture N.Y. Inst. Tech.; adv. prof. Queensboro Community Coll., Bayside, N.Y., 1971—; mem. APD panel N.Y. State Council for Arts, 1985—. Archtl. works include C.W. Post Coll. L.I. U (N.Y. State Assn. Architects award 1975, Gold Archi award L.I. Assn. Architects 1974), Hempstead Bank, Nassau Centre Office Bldg, (L.I. Assn. Architects award 1972, N.Y. State Assn. Architects award 1975), North Shore Unitarian Sch, Plandome, N.Y. (L.I. Assn. Architects Silver Archi award 1967, N.Y. State Assn. Architects award 1970), Shelter Rock Library, Searingtown, N.Y. (L.I. Assn. Architects award 1970), St. Anthony's Ch, Nanuet, N.Y. (N.Y. State Assn. Architects award 1972), Kinloch Farm, Va, Steinberg Learning Center-Woodmere (N.Y.) Acad, (N.Y. Library Assn. award 1972, L.I. Assn. Architects award 1975), St. Francis de Sales Ch, Bennington, Vt., Neitlich residence, Oyster Bay Cove, N.Y. (L.I. Assn. Architects Silver Archi award 1971, N.Y. Assn. Architects award 1971), Amityville (N.Y.) Pub. Library, (Silver Archi award L.I. Assn. Architects, N.Y. State Assn. Architects award 1973), Jericho (N.Y.) Pub. Library, (N.Y. State Assn. Architects award, Silver Archi award L.I. Assn. Architects 1974), John B. Gambling residence, Lattingtown, N.Y. (Silver Archi award L.I. Assn. Architects 1974), Glen Cove (N.Y.) Boys' Club at Lincoln House, (Silver Archi award L.I. Assn. Architects 1978), Aquatics Component Mitchel Park, Nassau County, N.Y., Salten Hall, N.Y. Inst. Tech (award N.Y. State Assn. Architects 1977), N.Y. Coll. Osteo. Med. at N.Y. Inst. Tech, Old Westbury, Commack Pub. Library, Commack (N.Y. State Assn. Architects award 1977), St. Mary Star of the Sea Ch, Far Rockaway (Queens C. of C. grand prize 1977), Oberlin Residence (N.Y. State Assn. Architects/L.I. Assn. Architects Archi award 1983); Contbr.: religious architecture chpt. to Time Saver Standards (De Chiara and Callender), 1973. Mem. comml. panel Am. Arbitration Assn.; mem. N.Y. State Council on the Arts Panel; bd. dirs. MIT Alumni Assn., 1984-86; bd. dirs. L.I. Soc. Am. Inst. Architects; chmn. adv. panel on govt. bldg. projects GSA, 1976; chmn. Inst. Internat. Edn.; nat. adv.-selection com. Fulbright-Hays awards, 1976-78, 80, 82; Chairperson Locust Valley Library Adv. Bd., 1973—. Recipient 1st place award for Islip Downtown Urban Renewal Competition, 1976; named Woman Architect of Year Nassau-Suffolk County, 1976. Fellow AIA (corp. mem., chmn. design com., dir. L.I. chpt.); mem. N.Y. State Assn. Architects (chmn. design awards com.), Nat. Council Archtl. Registration Bds., MIT Alumnae Assn., MIT Alumni L.I. (dir., v.p.). Home: 23 Frost Creek Dr Lattingtown NY 11560 Office: 22 Buckram Rd Locust Valley NY 11560

BENTLEY, ANTOINETTE COZELL, insurance executive, lawyer; b. N.Y.C., Oct. 7, 1937; d. Joseph Richard Cozell and Rose (Lafata Cozell) Vila; children: Robert S., Anne W. BA with distinction, U. Mich., 1960; LLB, U. Va., 1961. Bar: N.Y. 1962, N.J. 1971. Assoc. Sage Gray, Todd & Sims, N.Y.C., 1961-65; of counsel Farrell, Curtis, Carlin & Davidson, Morristown, N.J., 1971-73; asst. sec. Crum and Forster, Morristown, 1973, sec., 1973—, v.p., of counsel, 1975-87, sr. v.p., assoc. gen. counsel, 1987—. Mem. policy com. N.J. Future, 1986; trustee Crum and Forster Found., 1979—; vice pres. Mendham Borough (N.J.) Bd. Edn., 1976-79; trustee N.J. Conservation Found., 1981—, pres., 1986—; trustee Morris Mus., 1982, St. Peter's Coll. Mem. ABA, N.J. Bar Assn., Am. Soc. Corp. Secs. (N.Y. regional group, mem. adv. com.), Am. Assn. Corp. Counsel, Women's Econ. Roundtable, LWV, Order of Coif, Chi Omega. Home: Fowler Rd Far Hills NJ 07921 Office: 305 Madison Ave Morristown NJ 07960

BENTLEY, GAIL ELIZABETH, manufacturing company executive; b. San Francisco, Apr. 22, 1954; d. Donald Homer and Margaret Kathryn (Abbett) Outsen; BBA, Tex. Tech. U., 1975; m. David O. Bentley, Aug. 31, 1980; children: Christopher Allen, Jason Thomas, Aileen Elizabeth. Owner, operator The Hayrick, Lubbock, Tex., 1973—, Bookkeeping & Bus. Adv. Service, Lubbock, 1976-82; co-owner C&H Generator Shop, Lubbock, 1983—; treas. bd. dirs., mgr. Johnson Mfg. Fed. Credit Union, 1978-82. Mem. Phi Gamma Nu. Republican. Home and Office: Route 10 Box 5A Lubbock TX 79404

BENTLEY, HELEN DELICH (MRS. WILLIAM ROY BENTLEY), congresswoman; b. Ruth, Nev.; d. Michael and Mary (Kovich) Delich; m. William Roy Bentley, June 7, 1959. Student, U. Nev., 1941-42, George Washington U., 1943; B.J., U. Mo., 1944; LL.D., U. Md., 1970, U. Alaska, 1973, U. Mich., 1974; D.H.L., Bryant Coll., 1971, U. Portland, 1972, L.I. U., 1976, Goucher Coll., 1979. Reporter Ely (Nev.) Record, 1940-42; polit. campaign mgr. for late Senator James G. Scrugham, White Pine County, Nev., 1942; bur. mgr. UP, Fort Wayne, Ind., 1944-45; reporter Balt. Sun, 1945-53, maritime editor, 1953-69; chmn. FMC, Washington, 1969-75, Am. Bicentennial Fleet, Inc., 1973-76; pres. Internat. Resources & Devel. Corp., Washington, 1976-85, HDB Internat., Inc., 1977-85; pub. relations adviser Am. Assn. Port Authorities, 1958-62, 64-67; mem 99th and 100th Congresses from 2d Md. dist. TV and film producer world trade and maritime shows, 1950-64; Editor: Ports of Americas, 1961. Bd. dirs., mem. council Ch. Home and Hosp.; bd. dirs. United Seamen's Service, Oceanic Ednl. Found.; mem. council Md. Hist. Soc., Villa Julie Coll., Stevenson, Md., Montessori Soc. Central Md., Slavic-Am. Nat. Assn.; Republican nominee for Ho. of Reps. from 2d Dist. Md., 1980, 82, 84, 86. Recipient numerous honors including awards from AFL-CIO Maritime Port Council Greater N.Y., 1965, Ironworkers and Shipbuilders Council AFL-CIO, 1966, AOTOS award United Seamen's Service, 1971, Man of Yr. award N.Y. Freight Forwarders and Brokers Assn., 1972, Robert L. Hague Post award Am. Legion, 1973, Robert M. Thompson award Navy League U.S., 1973, Jerry Land medal Soc. Naval Architects and Marine Engrs., 1974, George Washington Honor medal Valley Forge Freedoms Found., 1971, 76, Salute To Congress award Propeller Club of U.S., 1987, Freedom award Alliance Metalworking Industries, 1987, Maritime Industry Salute to Congress award, 1987; named GOP Woman of Year, 1972, Ethnic Woman of Yr., Republican Nat. Heritage Council, 1985. Mem. Greater Balt. Com. (chmn. rail com.). Republican. Greek Orthodox. Home: 408 Chapelwood Ln Lutherville MD 21093 Office: PO Box 10619 Towson MD 21285

BENTLEY, JEANETTE SPRAGUE, public relations executive; b. Escondido, Calif., Apr. 2, 1959; d. Durham Daniel and Jeannette Lalani (Thomas) Sprague, m. Scott Alan Bentley, Oct. 18, 1986. AA, San Diego Mesa Jr. Coll., 19982; BA, San Diego State Coll., 1988. Asst. promotions Sta. KGB-FM Radio, San Diego, 1984-86; dir. program, cons. Say NO to Drugs Inc., San Diego, 1987—; dir. br. Leukemia Soc. Am., San Diego, 1986-88; sole proprietor Sprague-Bentley and Assocs., San Diego, 1987—. Mem. Nat. Assn. Female Execs., Pub. Relations soc., meeting Planners Internat., San Diego Mus. Art, Young Connoisseurs, Arthritis Found., P.S. We Care (founder), San Diego Alumni Assn. (mem. Hall of Champions). Republican. Office: Sprague-Bently and Assocs 701 "B" St #1300 San Diego CA 92101

BENTLEY, KATHI TURNER, advertising company executive; b. Newark, Ohio, Apr. 26, 1951; d. Lloyd Ackley and Joan D. (Van Horn) T.; m. William Gene Bentley, May 19, 1984. B, Marshall U., 1973, Ohio State U., 1976; M, Ohio State U., 1980. Tchr. Columbus (Ohio) Pub. Schs., 1973-76; mem. staff pub. relations State of Ohio, Columbus, 1976-78, Columbia Gas Co., Columbus, 1980-83; pres. Turner Communications, Columbus, 1982-87; account exec. Leff and Squicciarini, Columbus, 1987-88; dir. mktg. Key Oldsmobile/Subaru/Alfa Romeo, Columbus, 1988—; cons. Columbus Pub. Schs., 1984-86, Tandem Group, 1985-87, Kiwani's, 1986. Mem. publicity com. UpdownTowners, 1987; chmn. Capital City Reps., 1980-84, chmn. yr., 1983; resource bd. Spl. Wish Found., 1985-87, speakers' bur., 1987; mem. devel. bd., publicity com. Children's Hosp.; mem. Children's Hosp. Devel. Bd. Mem. Advt. Fedn. Columbus (outstanding young woman yr. region 1985), Pub. Relations Soc. Am., Internat. Assn. Bus. Communicators, Sales Execs. Club, Am. Women in Radio and TV. Methodist. Home: 7568 Lee Rd Westerville OH 43081 Office: Key Oldsmobile 5711 Scarborough Blvd Columbus OH 43232

BENTLEY, LISA JANE, retail executive; b. Lansdale, Pa., Mar. 20, 1936; d. Fred Olin and Beulah Sailor (Flagler) Ricker; m. Ronald F. Pepka, May 20, 1956 (div. 1969); 1 child, Ronald Glenn; m. John Lee Bentley, July 30, 1972. Student, Fresno (Calif.) State U., 1949-51; ordained, Living Bible Ctr., Phoenix, 1987. Mgr., owner Arthur Murray, N.Y.C., Phila. and Key West, Fla., 1956-65; interior designer Lisa's Interiors, Phila., 1965-75; exec. cons. Snelling & Snelling, Phila., 1975-78; pres., treas. Bentley Glass and Mirror, Inc., Las Vegas, Nev., 1979—; also chmn. bd. dirs. Bentley Glass and Mirror, Inc., Las Vegas; pres., treas. Bentley Enterprises, Inc., Las Vegas, 1980—, also chmn. bd. dirs.; pres., treas. Bentley Interiors Worldwide, Las Vegas, 1982—; tchr. Higher New Thought Ctr., Las Vegas, 1987—. Pastor, minister, pres., sec. Worldwide Outreach Awareness Ctr., 1987—; founder, chmn. bd. dirs., pres., sec. metaphysical tchr., healer, counselor Nev. Inst. Applied Metaphysics Inc., 1987—; v.p. Mt. Charleston (Nev.) Home Owners Assn., 1987. Mem. Associated Gen. Contractors, Internat. New Thought Alliance, Glazing Contractors Assn. (legis. chmn. 1985, fin. chmn. 1985, membership chmn. 1985). Office: Bentley Glass and Mirror 3230 Polaris #20 Las Vegas NV 89102

BENTLEY, NANCY WUCINICK, education and career consultant; b. Massillon, Ohio, Dec. 7, 1951; d. Mike Eli and Anna Wucinick; B.A. cum laude, Kent State U. (Ohio), 1973, M.Ed., 1977; postgrad. Ohio U., 1982-83. Residence staff adv. Kent State U. residence halls, 1971-73; social worker Trumbull County Children Services Bd., Warren, Ohio, 1973-75; resident mgr., counselor Trenton (N.J.) State Coll., 1975-76, adv. Coll. Arts and Scis., 1976-77; dir. student services Ohio U., Zanesville, 1977-83; dir. coll. and career devel. services Oakton Community Coll., Des Plaines, Ill., 1983-87; dir. career planning services Midwest Region Am. Coll. Testing Service, Lincolnshire, Ill., 1987—; cons. career/life planning, coll. admissions, computerized advising systems, child abuse. Trustee, Central Presbyterian Ch., 1981-83, mem. worship com., 1980-83, sec., 1982; co-sponsor Zanesville chpt. Parents Anonymous, 1979-81; mem. Big Brother/Big Sister Program Zanesville, 1982-83; bd. dirs. Rolling Meadows United Way, 1985-86, NW Suburban Vol. Ctr. Services Bur., 1987—; mem. Chgo. Area Acad. Advising Network, 1984—; Muskingum County Children Services, 1982-83. Mem. Nat. Assn. Student Personnel Adminstrs., Nat. Assn. Women Deans, Adminstrs., and Counselors, Ill. Assn. Women Deans, Adminstrs. and Counselors, Am. Assn. for Counseling and Devel., Council on Women's Programs (bd. dirs. 1984-86), Am. Coll. Personnel Assn., Ill. Coll. Personnel Assn., Alpha Delta Kappa, Alpha Phi Omega. Club: Pilot (dir. Zanesville 1981-83, dist. compass area leader 1981-82). Author: The Changes of Manpower Utilization in Stark County (Ohio), 1972. Home: 24 Westshore Dr Grayslake IL 60030 Office: 300 Knightsbridge Pkwy Suite 300 Lincolnshire IL 60069

BENTLEY-MCCALL, SHARON RUTH, banker; b. El Paso, Tex., Sept. 17, 1947; d. Ralph Richard and Ruth Garnet (Logue) Wood; m. Ronald Keith Bentley, June 6, 1975 (div. Feb. 1984); children: Deana Lashel, William Warren; m. Harry Mason McCall, June 12, 1985. Student Am. Inst. Banking, 1975-80, Jones Real Estate Coll., 1978, El Paso Community Coll., 1976-78. Lic. real estate salesman, securities dealer. Cashier, Bank of Ysleta, El Paso, 1969-78; real estate salesman Pan Am. Realty, El Paso, 1979-80; with First City Bancorp. Tex., Inc., 1980—, asst. v.p. First City Nat., El Paso, 1980-83, v.p., cashier First City Bank-East, El Paso, 1983-87, sr. v.p., 1987, v.p. First City Nat. Bank El Paso, 1988—. Mem. vocat. adv. com. El Paso Job Corps, 1985-86; vol. fundraiser El Paso Lighthouse for Blind, 1984-85; vol. Amigo Air Show, 1984-85, El Paso Council on Aging, March of Dimes Walkathon, 1988; treas. Eastwood High Class of 1965, El Paso, 1984-86; speaker El Paso Opportunity Ctr. for Handicapped, 1986. Recipient Honor Roll award United Way El Paso County, 1977, Outstanding Achievement awards, 1984, 85; YWCA REACH honoree, El Paso, 1981, 83, 84, named Outstanding Young Woman of America, 1977, 1984. Mem. Nat. Assn. Bank Women (pres. El Paso 1985-86, local scholarship 1985, state awards and scholarship com.), Am. Inst. Banking (bd. govs. 1984-86), El Paso Assn. Personnel Adminstrs., Nat. Assn. for Female Execs., Bank Adminstrn. Inst. (dir. 1984-86).Democrat. Methodist. Club: Vista Hills Exchange (bd. dirs 1988—).Avocations: reading; swimming. Home: 3117 Eads Pl El Paso TX 79935 Office: Fist City Nat Bank El Paso PO Box 1572 320 N Stanton El Paso TX 79948

BENTLEY-SCHECK, GRACE MARY, artist, printmaker, educator; b. Troy, N.Y., Apr. 20, 1937; d. Franklin Paul and Gladys Serena (Sickles) Bentley; m. George Frederick Scheck, July 22, 1967. B.F.A., N.Y. State Coll. Ceramics, Alfred U., 1959, M.F.A., 1960. Cert. tchr., N.Y. Exhbns. include: Gallery on the Green, Lexington, Mass., Bradley Nat. Print and Drawing Exhbn., Boston Printmakers N.Am. Print Exhbn., Am. Artist mag. Golden Ann. Nat. Art Competition (Testrite award), R.I./Australia Exchange Exhbn., Print In? Print Out, Los Angeles Printmaking Soc. Palos Verdes Art Ctr., Town and Gown: Harvard 350, Backyards, Wenniger Graphics, Boston, Ea. U.S. Print and Drawing Exhbn., Charlotte, N.C., Hunterdon Nat. Print and Drawing Exhbn., Rockford Internat. Print Biennale '85, Pratt/Silvermine Internat. Print Exhbn. (Juror's award, Diserio Martin O'Connor and Castiglione Purchase award), Dulin Nat. Works on Paper Competition (Juror's award 1987), 57th Print Club of Phila.; represented in permanent collections; tchr. Mary Warren Sch., Troy, N.Y., 1962-63, Riverhead (N.Y.) Jr. High Sch., 1963-67, North Colonie Central Sch., Latham, N.Y., 1967-72, SUNY-Oswego, 1979-80, Hera Gallery. Recipient Purchase prize Hunterdon Nat., 1982, hon. mention 30th Hunterdon Nat. Print Exhbn., 1986, N.C. Bank Purchase award 9th Annual Ea. U.S. Print and Drawing Exhbn., 1986, Juror's Merit awards 39th Boston Printmakers, Juror's awards 21st and 20th Bradley Nat. Print Exhbn., Juror's awards Works on Paper, Hera Gallery, 1987. Mem. Print Club Phila., Boston Printmakers, World Print Council, Los Angeles Printmaking Soc., Internat. Graphic Arts Found. Democrat. Club: Oswego Art Guild (treas. 1976-77, pres. 1977-78).

BENTON, ELIZABETH LAQUETTA, real estate executive, consultant, educator; b. Ozark, Ala., Apr. 1, 1936; d. Horace and Dovie Lee (Gulledge) Pippin; m. Charles Wayne Benton, Dec. 17, 1954; children: Lisa Ann, Charles W. Jr. Diploma Napier Bus. Coll., 1955; student Minot State Coll., 1963-64, U. Md., 1965, 67; grad. Realtors Inst. Cert. residential broker residential specialist. Sec., Aeronca Aircraft Corp., Ft. Rucker, Ala., 1955, Strachan Shipping, Savannah, Ga., 1956, USAF, Savannah, 1956-58; supr. Internal Revenue, Denver, 1959-60; adminstrv. asst. Chrysler Corp., Izmir, Turkey, 1961-63; substitute tchr. Dept. Edn., Honolulu, 1968-71; agt. Naomi Grout Real Estate, Ewa Beach, Hawaii, 1971-77; v.p., ptnr. Benton & Large Realty, Honolulu, 1977; pres., owner Liz Benton, Inc., Aiea, Hawaii, 1977—; dir. Founders Title & Escrow Co., Honolulu, 1983—; resource person, study on agy. Nat. Assn. Real Estate Lic. Law Ofcls., Salt Lake City, 1984, 85; mem. adv. council Hawaii Real Estate Research and Edn. Ctr., 1985—. Contbr. articles to profl. jours. Mem. Small Bus. Council Am., Honolulu, 1977—; mem. Aloha United Way, Honolulu 1974—; bd. dirs. Big Bros., Big Sisters, Honolulu, 1982—; chmn. Easter Seals VIP Panel, Honolulu, 1981—; mem. Realtors Polit. Action Com., Honolulu, 1980—; bd. dirs. Am. Cancer Soc., 1985-86. Recipient Vol. of Yr. award ARC, 1965, Outstanding Service award Dept. of Air Force, 1966, Top Producer award Naomi Grout Real Estate, 1972, 73, 74, 75, 76, Cert. of Excellence award Nat. Research Co., 1980-87. Mem. Hawaii Assn. Realtors (chmn. convention com. 1984, chmn. edn. com. 1979, dir.-at-large 1979, 80, bd. dirs. 1979, chmn. fin. and audit com. 1980, 81, sec. 1981, judge parade of homes 1982, treas. 1982, v.p. 1983, pres. elect 1986, pres. 1987, mem. strategic planning com. 1984, chmn. strategic planning com. 1986, chmn. nominating com. 1986), Honolulu Bd. Realtors (bd. dirs. 1978, chmn. election com. 1979, sec. 1979, chmn. multiple listing service, 1980, 81, pres.-elect 1982, chmn. realtor of yr. selection com. 1983, pres. 1983, chmn. nominating com. 1984, Realtor of Month award June 1981, Realtor of Yr. award 1981, chair strategic planning com. 1986, chair nominating com. 1986, liaison to real estate commn. 1986), Nat. Assn. Realtors (chmn convention activities subcom 1984, nat bd dirs 1984-86, prof. standards and arbitration com. 1986, 87, state leadership forum, 1986-87), The Investment Group Realtors, Leeward Regional Group, Realtors Nat. Mktg. Inst. (cert., Hawaii chpt., v.p. 1981, pres. 1982, treas. cert. residential brokers chpt. 1985), C. of C. Office: 98-211 Pali Momi St Suite 411 Aiea HI 96701

BENTON, LOUISE WHITE, harpist, educator; b. Henderson, Ky., Aug. 4, 1920; d. George Washington and Mai Elizabeth (Korb) White; m. William A. Benton, June 27, 1942; children—Bruce White, Boyd Allen. A.A., Christian Coll., 1940; B.S., U. Ky., 1942; postgrad. Morehead State U., summer, 1967. Second harpist Evansville Philharmonic Orch. (Ind.), 1963, 64-65; 1st harpist Owensboro Symphony Orch. (Ky.), 1966-77; music librarian Henderson Community Coll., 1968-70; harp instr., Henderson, 1975—, Owensboro Music Camp, Maple Mount, Ky. mem. adj. faculty Brescia Coll., Owensboro, 1975—, U. Evansville, 1975—; accompanist choruses and choirs. Active, Friends of Music, U. Evansville; mem. Philharmonic Guild, Evansville. Mem. Am. Harp Soc. (Outstanding Harpist in So. Region 1977-78), Ky. Fedn. Music Clubs, Phi Beta, Kappa Delta, Pi Kappa Lambda. Methodist. Club: Henderson Music. Home: 4 Philips Ct Henderson KY 42420

BENTON, SUZANNE, sculptor, mask ritualist; b. N.Y.C., Jan. 21, 1936; d. Alex and Florence (Matkoff) Elkins; children—Daniel, Janet. B.A. in Fine Arts, Queens Coll., 1956. Creator Mask Ritual Theatre, over 130 mask ritual performances throughout U.S. and world; performance at Woudschoten, Ziest, Holland, 1982; presentation at Geilsdorfer Gallery, Cologne, Germany, 1982; 3 day workshop, maskmaking, storytelling, London, 1982; artist-in-residence Oberlin Coll., Ohio, 1983; affiliate Image Theatre N.Y.C.; led Art and Mythology tour of Greece, 1985. One woman shows of sculpture include: Wadsworth Atheneum, Hartford, Conn., 1975, Internat. Christian Coll., Toyko, 1976, Chemould Gallery, Bombay, 1977, Hellenic Am. Union, Athens, 1977, Internat. House, New Orleans, 1978, BITEF Internat. Theatre Festival, Belgrade, Yugoslavia, 1978, Condon Gallery, N.Y.C., 1981, Korean Cultural Service Galleries, N.Y.C., 1982, Gallerie Fuchs, Dusseldorf, 1983, Amerika Haus, Koln, Fed. Republic Germany, Wilton Gallery, Conn., 1983, Amendola Gallery, New Haven, 1984, Kent Sch., Conn., 1985, Union Am. Hebrew Congregation Bldg., 1985, Amerika Haus, Stuttgart, Fed. Republic Germany, 1986, Fairfield Library, Conn., 1986, Asia Soc., N.Y.C., 1986, Image Theatre, N.Y.C., 1987, Hudson River Gallery, Ossining, N.Y., 1987, Spectrum Ctr., London, 1987, Silo, New Milford, Conn., 1987; group shows include USIS, Eastern Europe, 1971-75, Stamford Mus., Conn., 1976, Expo '74, Seattle, Nat. Sculpture Conf., Kans. U., 1974, Joods Hist. Mus., Amsterdam, 1986; author: The Art of Welded Sculpture, 1975. Convenor Conn. Feminists in the Arts, 1970-72; nat. coordinator NOW Women in the Arts, 1973-76. Grantee Conn. Commn. on Arts, 1973, 74; United Methodist World and Women's Div., 1976; United Presbyterian Program Agency, 1976; United Ch. Bd. Homeland Ministries, 1976; USIS grantee, Tunisia, 1983, Istanbul, 1986. Mem. Artists Equity N.Y.C., Nat. Korean Women's Sculpture Assn. (hon.), Nat. Assn. Women Artists (Amelia Peabody award 1979). Home and Studio: 22 Donnelly Dr Ridgefield CT 06877

BENTON-BORGHI, BEATRICE HOPE, educational consultant; b. San Antonio, Nov. 7, 1946; d. Donald Francis and Beatrice Hope (Peche) Benton; A.B. in Chemistry, North Adams State Coll., 1968; M.Secondary Edn., Boston U., 1972; m. Peter T. Borghi, Aug. 12, 1980; children—Kathryn Benton Borghi, Sarah Benton Borghi. Tchr. chemistry Cathedral High Sch., Springfield, Mass., 1968-69; tchr. sci. and history Munich (W.Ger.) Am. High Sch., 1969-70; tchr. English, Tokyo, Japan, 1970-71; tchr. chemistry and sci. Marlborough (Mass.) High Sch., 1971-80; project dir., adminstr. ESEA, Marlborough Pub. Schs., 1976-77; project dir., proposal writer Title III, Title IX, U.S. Dept. Edn., 1975-76, 76-77; evaluation team New Eng. Assn. Schs. and Colls., 1974, 78; mem. regional dept. edn. com., 1977-78; ednl. cons., lectr., 1978—. Energy conservation rep. Marlborough's Overall Econ. Devel. Com., 1976; chmn. Marlborough's Energy Conservation Task Force, 1975; dir. Walk for Mankind, 1972; sec. Group Action for Marlborough Environment, 1975-76; bd. dirs. Girls Club, Marlborough, 1979; pres. Sisters, Inc., 1979-83. Mem. Council for Exceptional Children, Nat. Women's Health Network. Home and Office: 2449 Edington Rd Columbus OH 43221

BENVENUTO, ELAINE ELIZABETH, public relations executive; b. Bklyn., Nov. 10, 1943; d. Michael John and Mildred (Di Brienza) De Santis; m. John Anthony Benvenuto, Jr., June 12, 1965 (div.); 1 dau., Kecia. BA, Conn. Coll., 1965. Fashion editor Bride & Home Mag., N.Y.C., 1965-68; reporter, columist Fairchild Pubs., N.Y.C., Washington, 1968-71; consumer specialist Giant Food Inc., Washington, 1971-73; dir. consumer relations Cosmetic, Toiletry and Fragrance Assn., Washington, 1973-76; v.p. Carl Byoir & Assoc., N.Y.C., 1976-85; mgr. pub. relations, 1985-87; dir. corp. pub. relations Avon Products, Inc., N.Y.C., 1987—. Bd. dirs. Medic Alert Found., N.Y.C., 1983-85, Ballet Hispanico, N.Y.C., 1987—. Recipient Silver Anvil, Pub. Relations Soc. Am., 1972. Mem. Soc. Consumer Affairs, Profls. in Bus., Women in Communications. Democrat. Roman Catholic. Office: Avon Products Inc 9 W 57th St New York NY 10019

BERCE, PATRICIA ANN, management consultant; b. Detroit, Jan. 31, 1951; d. Mike and Sarah (Rocco) Berce. BS, Mercy Coll. Detroit, 1973; MBA, Boston U., 1982. Asst. dir. med. record dept. Henry Ford Hosp., Detroit, 1973-74; dir. med. record dept. Nashoba Community Hosp., Ayer, Mass., 1974-77; dir. med. records and quality assurance Lynn (Mass.) Hosp., 1977-79; dir. med. records, quality assurance and risk mgmt. Mt. Auburn Hosp., Cambridge, Mass., 1979-82; owner Mgmt. and Systems Cons., Wakefield, Mass., 1982-85; pres. Hatch Cons. Assocs., Inc., North Reading, Mass., 1985—; bd. dirs. Worth Systems, Inc., West Roxbury, Mass. Mem. Med. Group Mgmt. Assn., Am. Med. Record Assn., Mass. Med. Record Assn., Eastern Middlesex Mental Health Assn. (bd. dirs. 1984—). Home and Office: 51 Brassie Way North Reading MA 01864

BERES, MARY ELIZABETH, management educator, organizational consultant; b. Birmingham, Mich., Jan. 19, 1942; d. John Charles and Ethel (Belenyesi) B. B.S., Siena Heights Coll., Adrian, Mich., 1969; Ph.D, Northwestern U., 1976. Joined Dominican Sisters, 1960; tchr., St. Francis Xavier Sch., Medina, Ohio, 1962-64, St. Edward Sch., Detroit, 1964-67; tchr. Our Lady of Mt. Carmel Sch., Temperance, Mich., 1967-69, asst. prin., 1968-69; tchr. math. St. Ambrose High Sch., Detroit, 1969-70; vis. instr. Cornell U., 1973-74; assoc. prof. orgn. behavior Temple U., Phila., 1974-84; assoc. prof. mgmt. Mercer U. Atlanta, 1984—; cons. in field. Contbr. chpts. to books; organizer of symposia in areas of corp. leadership and cross-cultural communication. Bd. trustees Adrian Dominican Ind. Sch. System (Mich.), 1971-79; bd. dirs. Ctr. for Ethics and Social Policy, Phila., 1980-84. Recipient Legion of Honor membership Chapel of the Four Chaplains, Phila., 1982; Disting. Teaching award Lindback Found., 1982, Cert. for Humanity, Mercer U., 1985; mem. Atlanta Clergy and Laity Concerned, 1986—; chair interdepartmental group in Bus. Adminstrn. U. Ctr. of Ga., 1987—, mem. program planning com., 1987. Mem. Acad. Mgmt., Indsl. Relations Research Assn., Acad. Internat. Bus. (program com. southeast U.S. region 1987, chairperson mgmt. track 1988), The So. Mgmt. Assn., So. Ctr. Internat. Studies, Nat. Assn. Female Execs. Democrat. Roman Catholic. Office: Mercer U Sch Bus and Econs 3001 Mercer University Dr Atlanta GA 30341

BEREST, MYRA, nursing administrator; b. Phila., Dec. 8, 1942; d. Samuel and Dorothy (Hoffman) B. AA, Bucks County Community coll., 1976; BS in Supervision and Mgmt. cum laude, Gwynerd Mercy Coll., 1978, MS in Nursing, 1986. RN; lic. nursing home adminstr., Pa. Dir. nursing Doylestown (Pa.) Manor, 1979-84, asst. adminstr., 1982-84; supr. Arrow Home Healthcare Agy., Phila., 1984-85; dir. nursing Heritage Towers, Doylestown, 1985—. Mem. Nat. Assn. Female Execs., Nat. Gerontol. Nursing Assn., Pa. Assn. Non-Profit Homes for Aging (del. 1985—), Cen. Bucks County Nursing Assn., Long Term Care Nursing Adminstrs. Orgn. (corr. sec. 1984-86), Cen. Bucks County C. of C., Sigma Theta Tau, Phi Theta Kappa, Beta Sigma Phi (corr. sec.). Home: 612 Shady Retreat Rd #58 Doylestown PA 18901

BERG, ANNE POLAND, public relations executive; b. Anniston, Ala.; d. Carter Durwood and Winnie Davis (Mitchell) Poland; m. John G. Berg Jr., Jan. 24, 1970 (dec. Feb. 1977). B, Judson Coll., 1945. V.p., dir. pub. relations Rich's, Atlanta, 1956—; grant cons. Rich Found., Atlanta, 1980—. Bd. dirs. Woodruff Arts Ctr., Atlanta, Atlanta Coll. Arts, English Speaking Union, Trees; state chair 4-H; trustee, exec. com. Ga. Found. for Ind. Colls., Atlanta. Named to U. Ga. Pub. Relations Hall of Fame. Mem. Pub. Relations Soc. of America (former bd. dirs., Phoenix award 1986), Future Homemakers of Am. (hon.). Republican. Episcopalian. Club: Atlanta Press. Home: 2637 Peachtree Rd Atlanta GA 30305 Office: Richs 45 Broad St Atlanta GA 30302

BERG, JEAN HORTON LUTZ, author; b. Clairton, Pa., May 30, 1913; d. Harry Heber and Daisy Belle (Horton) Lutz; m. John Joseph Berg, July 2, 1938; children: Jean Horton, Julie Berg Blickle, John Joel. B.S. in Edn, U. Pa., 1935, A.M. in Latin, 1937. Tchr. creative writing 1968—; speaker in field of creative writing. Author 50 books for children and young people, 1950—, articles, stories, poems for young people, articles for adults. Former mem. Health and Welfare Bd., Phila.; former chmn. Main Line Parents Council. Recipient U. Pa. Alumni award of merit, 1969; Follett award for beginning-to-read book, 1961; medallion City of Phila.; Friends' Central Sch. Distinguished Alumna award, 1978. Mem. Authors Guild, Authors League, ASCAP, Nat. League of Am. Pen Women, Phila. Childrens Reading Round Table, League Women Voters. Home: 207 Walnut Ave Wayne PA 19087

BERG, SISTER MARIE MAJELLA, university president; b. Bklyn., July 7, 1916; d. Peter Gustav and Mary Josephine (McAuliff) B. BA, Marymount Coll., 1938; MA, Fordham U., 1948; DHL (hon.), Georgetown U., 1970, Marymount Manhattan Coll., 1983. Registrar Marymount Sch., N.Y.C., 1943-48; prof. classics, registrar Marymount Coll., N.Y.C., 1949-57; registrar Marymount Coll. of Va., Arlington, 1957-58, Marymount Coll., Tarrytown, N.Y., 1958-60; pres. Marymount U., Arlington, Va., 1960—; pres. Consortium for Continuing Higher Edn. in Va., 1987-88; com. mem. Consortium of Univs. Washington Met. Area, 1987—. Contbr. five biographies to One Hundred Great Thinkers, 1965; editor Otherwords column of N.Va. Sun, Arlington. Bd. dirs. Internat. Hospice, 1984—, HOPE, 1983—, 10th Dist. Congrl. Award Council, No. Va. Recipient commendation Va. Gen. Assembly, Richmond, 1986. Mem. Council of Ind. Colls. (pres. 1986-87), Nat. Assn. Ind. Colls. and Univs., Nat. Assn. of Catholic Colls. and Univs., Arlington C. of C. (bd. dirs. 1978-83). Roman Catholic. Home: 2807 N Glebe Rd Arlington VA 22207 Office: Marymount U Office of Pres 2807 N Glebe Rd Arlington VA 22207-4299

BERG, SANDRA IRENE, screenwriter; b. Santa Monica, Calif., Aug. 8, 1953; d. Theodore W. and Sarah (Gordon) B. BA, UCLA, 1975, MA, 1976. instr. UCLA, 1987. Author: (screenplays) Almost Summer, 1978, Road Games, 1982, Journey to the Center of the Earth, 1987. Mem. Writers Guild Am.

BERG, SYLVIA LOUISE, educator; b. N.Y.C., Dec. 29, 1939; d. Joe and Fay (Streim) Maydeck; B.S., Oswego Coll., 1958; M.S., Hofstra U., 1959; postgrad. N.Y. U., 1960-65; children—Mitchell Ian, Nancy Patricia. Tchr., Public Sch. 158, N.Y.C. Bd. Edn., 1965—; adj. prof. edn. NYU, 1965—; pvt. tutor, 1965—; cons. in field; job presentations; adv. skills in speed reading; condr. sci. seminars Fordham U., Sci. Council; cons. Elaine Goldhill Travel Cons. Bd. dirs. 301 E. 78th St. Corp., N.Y.C., sec., 1979-81; treas. Singles Coordinating Com., N.Y.C. Mem. SUNY Assn., Nat. Assn. Female Execs., Audubon Assn., United Fedn. Tchrs. Home: 301 E 78th St New York NY 10021 Office: Public Sch 158 1458 York Ave New York NY 10021 also: 330 E 33d St Suite 8G New York NY 10016

BERGER, BONNIE G., sport psychologist, educator; b. Champaign, Ill., May 20, 1941; d. Bernard G. and Mildred W. Berger; B.S., Wittenberg U., 1962; M.A., Columbia U., 1965, Ed.D., 1972; 1 son, Stephen Casher. Tchr., George Rogers Clark Jr. High Sch., Springfield, Ohio, 1962-64; supr. phys. edn. Agnes Russell Elem. Sch., N.Y.C., 1964-65; asst. prof. SUNY, Geneseo, 1965-66; asst. prof. Dalhousie U., Halifax, N.S., Can., 1969-71; asst. prof. Bklyn. Coll., 1971-77, assoc. prof., 1978-81, prof., 1982—, also dir. Sport Psychology Lab.; cons. sport psychology. Mem. Am. Psychol. Assn., AAHPERD, Internat. Soc. Sports Psychology, N.Am. Soc. Psychology Sport and Phys. Activity, Can. Soc. Psychomotor Learning and Sport Psychology. Author: Free Weights for Women, 1984; contbr. articles to profl. jours., chpts. to books. Home: 20 Waterside Plaza New York NY 10010 Office: Bklyn Coll Roosevelt Hall Dept Phys Edn Brooklyn NY 11210

BERGER, ELIZABETH ANN, graphic designer; b. Lima, Peru, Sept. 17, 1955; came to U.S., 1959; d. Henry C. and Margaret S. (Benton) B.; m. Howard E. Goldthwaite, Sept. 29, 1978; 1 child, Andrew Thomas. Student, U. N.C., 1973-75; BFA in Advt. Art and Biology, North Tex. State U., 1977; postgrad., SMU, 1987—. Jr. art dir. KCBN Advt., Dallas, 1977-78; art dir., writer Steve Moi & Assocs., Dallas, 1978-79; art dir. Eisenbeig, Inc., Dallas, 1979-81; creative dir., pres. Betsy Berger Assocs., Inc., Dallas, 1981—; vis. lectr. SMU, 1986; adj. prof. North Tex. State U., 1986, Art. Inst. of Dallas, 1986, Brookhaven Community Coll., 1987. Creator, designer Mag. Published work, 1983, 86; creator Print mag., Am. Inst. Graphic Arts Annual, Graphis mag. (Gold Medal N.Y. Art Dirs. Club, 1986), 1986. Communications cons. 500, Inc., Dallas, 1985-86. Mem. Dallas Soc. Visual Communications, Am. Inst. Graphic Arts. Club: Gourmet Soc. Office: 12770 Coit Rd Suite 925 Dallas TX 75230

BERGER, FRANCINE ELLIS, radio executive, educator; b. Albany, N.Y., July 27, 1949; d. David George and Harriet Sylvia (Bookstein) Ellis; m. Jerome Morris Berger, Oct. 9, 1977. BS in Broadcasting and Film, Boston U., 1971; EdM in Adminstrn., Planning and Social Policy, Harvard U., 1981. Traffic mgr. Sta. WCAS Kaiser Globe Broadcasting, Boston, 1971, Sta. WJIB-FM, 1971; continuity supr. WBZ-AM-Westinghouse, Boston, 1971-75; producer, traffic dir. Sta. WMEX/WITS, Boston, 1975-78; newswriter CBS Radio, Sta. WEEI, Boston, 1980; gen. mgr. Sta. WERS-FM, Emerson Coll., Boston, 1980—, asst. prof. radio dept., 1981—, head radio dept., 1983—. Mem. Nat. Acad. TV Arts and Scis., Kappa Gamma Chi, Alpha Epsilon Rho. Avocations: music, cooking. Office: WERS-FM Emerson Coll 126 Beacon St Boston MA 02116

BERGER, JULIE ANN, research analyst, social worker; b. Newark, Sept. 18, 1950; d. Murray M. and Estelle C. (Sperber) Monestersky. Student, U. Wis., 1968-70; BA, Tufts U., 1972; MSW, Rutgers U., 1974. Med. social worker dialysis unit VA Hosp., East Orange, N.J., 1974-76, med. social worker hosp.-based home-care program and outpatient clinic, 1976-77; med. social worker dialysis unit Morristown (N.J.) Meml. Hosp., 1977-81; asst./trainee Donna Aughey Ely and Assocs., Morristown, N.J., 1984; freelance market research, health care and telecommunications cons., 1984-86; telecommunications market researcher, assoc. editor Probe Research, Inc., Morristown, 1986-88; field instr. casework sequence Rutgers U. Grad. Sch. Social Work, 1978; social work rep. to N.J. Renal Network Council, Inc., 1979-81, mem. subcom. on allied health profl. practice, 1978-81, mem. by-laws com., 1978-79, sec. to full council, 1980-81. Social work vol. The Richmond Fellowship, Morristown, 1984. Mem. Acad. Cert. Social Workers, Nat. Assn. Social Workers, Register Clin. Social Workers, Am. Assn. Kidney Patients, Inc., Council Nephrology Social Workers, Nat. Assn. Female Execs., N.J. Dialysis and Transplant Assn. (sec. 1976-78, pres. 1978-80). Home: 7 Hamilton Rd Apt 4B Morristown NJ 07960

BERGER, KAY, public relations executive; b. Pitts., Feb. 18, 1939; d. Alex and Eve (Lando) Singer; m. Ted Stern, Mar. 24, 1984. B.S., UCLA, 1961; M.B.A., Pepperdine U., 1981. Demonstrator Carl Byoir Pub. Relations, Los Angeles, 1960-66; mgr. home econs. Calavo Co., Los Angeles, 1966-69; asst. dir. consumer relations Thermador-Waste King Corp., Los Angeles, 1961-66; exec. v.p. western div. Harshe-Rotman & Druck, Inc. (now Ruder Finn & Rotman), Los Angeles, 1969-80; pres. western region Manning, Selvage & Lee, Inc., Los Angeles, 1980-84; exec. v.p. U.S. regional ops. Manning, Selvage & Lee, Inc., Chgo., 1985-88, exec. v.p. European ops., 1988—, also dir., chmn. long range planning and fin. coms. Mem. com. 1986 Chgo. Internat. Theatre Festival; pub. relations adv. com. grad. sch. U. Chgo.; bd. dirs. New City YMCA. Recipient 1st place award Nat. Council Farm Coops., 1967, Los Angeles Advt. Women, 1967, cert. creative excellence U.S. Indsl. Film Fair, 1974. Mem. Home Economists in Bus. (group chmn. Los Angeles chpt. 1968-69), Internat. Assn. Bus. Communicators, Nat. Investor Relations Inst., Pub. Relations Soc. Am. Home: 875 N Dearborn St Apt 18E Chicago IL 60610 also: 26 Montpelier Pl, London SW7 1HW, England

BERGER, MAUREEN, seminar management executive; b. Leicester, Eng., Mar. 10, 1941; came to U.S., 1962; d. George Frederick and Katherine Irene (Ridgeway) Hill; m. David W. Lucier; children—Deborah, Steven, Donna; m. Richard William Berger, Aug. 10, 1985. Student bus. adminstrn. Leicester U., 1961. Test proctor U.S. Air Force, Phalsbourg, France, 1965-66; asst. adminstr. Oversea Div., Gen. Electric Co., Ramstein, Germany, 1966-67; prodn. mgr. Norman Harwell Assocs., Dallas and Saigon, 1968-7Vietnam, 2; sec. Coopers & Lybrand, Springfield, Mass., 1972-75; owner Latent Image Photography, Springfield, 1975-77; v.p. Tech. Seminars, Inc., Great Neck, N.Y., 1978—. Vol. Jansen Meml. Hospice Program, Tuckahoe, N.Y. Mem. Nat. Assn. Female Execs., NOW, Atomic Indsl. Forum Inc., Assn. Research and Enlightenment. Avocations: golf; racquetball; aerobics; collecting antique bottles and Maxfield Parrish prints. Home: 122 Forest Ave New Rochelle NY 10804 Office: Tech Seminars Inc 425 Northern Blvd Great Neck NY 11021

BERGER, MIRIAM ROSKIN, creative arts therapy director, educator, therapist; b. N.Y.C., Dec. 9, 1934; d. Israel and Florence (Frankel) Roskin; m. Meir Berger, July 16, 1967 (div. June 1981); children: Jonathan Israel. Student, Barnard Coll., 1952-53; BA, Bard Coll., 1956; postgrad., CCNY, 1956-58, NYU, 1981—. Alumni dir. Bard Coll., Annandale-on-Hudson, N.Y., 1958-59; dance therapist Manhattan Psychiatric Ctr., N.Y.C., 1959-60; performer, educator Jean Erdman Theater of Dance, N.Y.C., 1959-62; dir. adult program Hebrew Arts Sch., N.Y.C., 1964-68; faculty Dance Notation Bur., N.Y.C., 1974-75, 77; asst. prof. dance therapy program NYU, 1975—; dir. creative arts therapies Bronx Psychiatric Ctr., N.Y.C., 1970—. producer off-Broadway The Coach with the Six Insides, 1962-63; author, producer Non-Verbal Group Process, 1978; contbr. articles to profl. jours; leader internat. workshops, arts therapy. bd. dirs. Theater Open Eye, 1978-82, v.p., bd. trustees, 1982—. Recipient NYU scholarship, 1981. Mem. Am. Dance Therapy Assn. (founder, bd. dirs. 1967-76, v.p. 1974-76, credential com. 1976-82), Acad. Registered Dance Therapists, Am. Orthopsychiatric Assn.

BERGER, PENNY JOAN, lawyer; b. Danville, Ill., Nov. 28, 1944; d. Sam J. and Pauline S. (Nelson) Lipkin; m. Patrice Marcel Berger, Sept. 18, 1968; children: Gabrielle Nicole, Marc Andre. AB, Barnard Coll., 1966; MA, Columbia U., 1967; JD with distinction, U. Nebr., 1975. Bar: Nebr. 1975. Dir. Neighborhood Youth Corps Lincoln (Nebr.) Action Program, 1971-72; assoc. Wright & Rembolt, Lincoln, 1975-78; ptnr. Rembolt, Ludtke, Parker & Berger, Lincoln, 1979—, mng. ptnr., 1986—. Fundraiser Planned Parenthood of Nebr., Lincoln, 1987; mem. allocations sect. United Way, Lincoln, 1987—; bd. dirs. Lincoln City Libraries, 1980-87, Nebr. Lit. Heritage Assn., Lincoln, 1984—, Lincoln Y-Pals, 1988—; mem. adv. council Nebr. State Library Commn.; trustee, fin. sec. Congregation Bn'ai Jeshurun, 1988—. Recipient Roscoe Pound award Nebr. Assn. Trial Attys., 1974. Mem. ABA, Nebr. State Bar Assn. (lectr. continuing legal edn.), Nat. Assn. Bond Lawyers, U. Nebr. Sch. Law Alumni Assn. (pres., bd. dirs. 1982-84), U. Nebr. Alumni Assn., Order of Coif, Order of Barristers. Democrat. Jewish. Office: Rembolt Ludtke Parker & Berger 1201 Lincoln Mall Suite 102 Lincoln NE 68508

BERGER, SHIRLEY JUNE, graphic arts company executive; b. Washington, June 28, 1932; d. Milton Chapel and Lillian (Pavis) Kurland; m. Kalvin Berger, May 19, 1957 (dec.); children: Andrew Charles, Marilyn. Grad. high sch., Washington. Exec. sec. Mayer & Co., Washington, 1950-56, H.L. Merin Co., N.Y.C., 1957-58; owner, operator Custom Color Lab., Palo Alto, Calif., 1959—, pres., chmn. bd., 1978—; pres. Chutzpah, Inc., 1976-79; seminar leader and pub. speaker in field. Contbr. articles to profl. jours. Bd. dirs. Temple Beth David, Cupertino, Calif., 1973, Louise Salinger Acad. Fashion, San Francisco. Recipient Pub. Service award USO, 1952. Mem. Nat. Fedn. Ind. Bus. (action com.), Assn. Profl. Color Labs. (adv. bd.), Assn. Bay Area Profl. Labs. (past pres.), Photo-Mktg. Assn. Office: 940 Commercial St Palo Alto CA 94303

BERGESON, MARIAN, state legislator; m. Garth Bergeson; children; Nancy, Garth Jr., Julie, James. Student UCLA; BA in Edn. Brigham Young U.; postgrad. UCLA. Pres., regional dir. Calif. Sch. Bds. Assn.; officer, dir. Orange County Sch. Bds. Assn.; mem. Newport Beach City Sch. Dist. Bd. Edn., 1964-65; mem. Newport-Mesa Unified Sch. Dist. Bd. Edn., 1965-77; mem. Calif. Assembly, 1978-82, Calif. Senate, 1984—. Past mem. Orange

County Juvenile Justice Commn., Riles-Younger Task Force for Prevention of Crime and Violence in the Schs., Com. for Revision State Edn. Code, Joint Com. on Revision Penal Code; mem. Calif. YMCA Model Legislature/Ct.; mem. bd. advisors Calif. Elected Women's Assn. Edn. and Research; bd. dirs. Sta. KBIG Adv. Bd.; mem. govt. relations com. Orange County Arts Alliance. Recipient Marian Bergeson Community Services award Orange County Sch. Bds. Assn., 1975; Anchor award Newport Harbor C. of C., women's div., 1967; Community Services award AAUW, 1976; Disting. Women's award Irvine Soroptimists, 1981; Disting. Service award Brigham Young U., 1980-81; Woman of Achievement award Newport Harbor Zonta Club, 1981; Silver Medallion, YWCA, 1983; Pub. Service award Calif. Speech-Lang.-Hearing Assn., 1983; named Outstanding Pub. Ofcl., Orange County chpt. Am. Soc. Pub. Adminstrn., 1983, Woman of Yr., Anti Defamation League B'nai B'rith, 1987, So. Dist. Legislator of Yr., Calif. Assn. for Health., 1987. Office: 140 Newport Ctr Dr Suite 120 Newport Beach CA 92660 also: Office of the State Senate State Capitol Sacramento CA 95814

BERGHERR, DIANA E., investment banker; b. N.Y.C., Dec. 15, 1952; d. William Vincent and Theresa (Tucci) B.; m. Carl Petrie, Dec. 2, 1972 (div. 1985). AA, Queensbrough Community Coll., 1974; BA cum laude Queen's Coll., 1980, MS in Edn., 1981. Vault custodian Home Fed., Little Neck, N.Y., 1972-75, adminstrv. asst., 1975-80; tchr. Great Neck (N.Y.) Sch. Dist., 1981-82; program mgr. E.F. Hutton, Garden City, N.Y., 1983-84, mgr. pvt. placement ops., asst. v.p., 1984—. Queen's Coll. scholar, 1980. Mem. Kappa Delta Pi, Sigma Lambda. Roman Catholic. Avocations: horseback riding, acting, dance, skiing, weightlifting. Office: E F Hutton & Co Inc 1225 Franklin Ave Garden City NY 11530

BERGLIN, LINDA, state senator; b. Oakland, Calif., Oct. 19, 1944; d. Freeman and Norma (Lund) Waterman. B.F.A., Mpls. Coll. Art and Design. Mem. Minn. Ho. of Reps., St. Paul, 1972-80; mem. Minn. Senate, St. Paul, 1980—, chmn. Health and Human Services Com. Mem. Democratic-Farmer-Labor Party. Office: Minn Senate State Capitol Saint Paul MN 55155 also: 2309 Clinton Ave S Minneapolis MN 55404 *

BERGMAN, BETTY LAING, hospital executive; b. Evanston, Ill., May 14, 1923; d. John Crawford and Marion (Buchanan) Laing; m. Richard Joseph Bergman, Oct. 6, 1951. B.A., Lake Forest Coll., 1947; cert. Case Western Res. U., 1977; cert. in teaching No. Ill. U., 1966. Personnel mgr. Wieboldt Stores, Inc., Chgo., 1947-62; tchr. Wooddale (Ill.) Schs., 1962-66; instr. Lorain County Community Coll., Elyria, Ohio, 1975-77; personnel dir. Elyria (Ohio) Home, 1979-81; employment mgr. Lorain (Ohio) Community Hosp., 1981-84, personnel mgr., 1984-85, dir. personnel, 1985—. Chmn. personnel com., sec. bd. trustees ARC, Elyria, 1982—; mem. adv. bd. Lorain City Schs., 1982—, Lorain County Joint Vocat. Sch., 1982—, Lorain County Community Coll., 1986—, Lorain Bus. Coll., 1986—; com. mem. Lorain County Hometown Careers Day, 1982—, chmn., 1984; mem. job service employer com. Ohio Bur. Employment Services, 1985—; div. capt. Heart Assn. Fund Drive, Elyria, 1976; mem., chmn. Lorain County Hist. Soc., 1975—. Named Woman of Achievement, Lorain YWCA, 1983; vol. recognition Elyria Home, 1979, 1st Congl. Ch., 1974; v.p. Elyria Roundtable; trustee 1st Congl. Ch. Mem. AAUW, Am. Soc. Personnel Adminstrs., Greater Cleve. Personnel Council, Greater Lorain County Personnel Adminstrs (sec.-treas.). Republican. Presbyterian. Clubs: Elyria Woman's (pres. 1978-80); Culture (v.p. 1976-77), Roundtable (v.p. 1982-83). Home: 313 Georgia Ave Elyria OH 44035 Office: Lorain Community Hosp 3700 Kolbe Rd Lorain OH 44053

BERGMAN, EMILY ANNE, librarian; b. Tulsa, July 24, 1953; d. Arthur L. and Jean Lucy (Anson) B.; m. Mark Andrew Allen, June 20, 1982; children: Philip Isaac Allen. BA, Goucher Coll., 1975; MLS, U. Tex.-Austin, 1976; student Wroxton Coll., Banbury, Eng., 1974. Research librarian Tracy-Locke Advt., Dallas, 1977-78; cataloger Dallas Pub. Library, 1978-80, head spl. collections, 1980-81; info. specialist, Dallas, 1978-81; asst. library dir. Calif. Sch. Profl. Psychology, Los Angeles, 1981—. Mem. ALA (coms.), Spl. Library Assn., So. Calif. Spl. Library Assn., Calif. Coll. and Research Libraries, Mental Health Librarians (v.p., pres.-elect 1987-88, pres. 1988-89). Democrat. Jewish. Home: 1001 N Geneva Glendale CA 91207 Office: Calif Sch Profl Psychology 2235 Beverly Blvd Los Angeles CA 90057

BERGMAN, JANICE JOAN, nurse; b. Axtell, Kans., Jan. 6, 1938; d. Alban Matthias and Angela Philomena (Karnowski) Haug; R.N., Marymount Coll., 1959; m. Paul Harold Bergman, Nov. 28, 1959; children—Janel, Jolene, Jennifer. Staff nurse Seneca (Kans.) Hosp., 1959; charge nurse St. Mary's Hosp., Kansas City, Mo., 1960-62; asst. dir. nursing services N. Kans. Meml. Hosp., North Kansas City, Mo., 1963-67; dir. health occupations program Kans. Dept Edn., 1976; co-owner, dir. nursing Cresview Manor, Seneca, 1968—; gerontol. nurse cons. Kans. State Dept. Vocat. Edn., 1977; Am. Nurses Assn. rep. Nat. Task Force on Credentialing in Nursing, 1980-83; gerontol. nurse cons. NE Kans. Area Agy. on Aging; ad hoc adv. 1981 White House Conf. on Aging, Nat. Observer. Mem. Am. Nurses Assn. (exec. Com. div. gerontol. nursing practice), ANA Council of Nursing Home Nurses, Kans. Coalition on Aging, Kans. Public Health Assn., Kans. State Nurses Assn., NE Kans. Regional Adv. Com. for Nurses, Bus. & Profl. Women's Club (pres. 1973-75), Nemaha County Mental Health Assn. (pres. 1976-78), Nemaha County Hist. Soc., Dist. 13 Nurses Assn. (pres. 1976-78), Nemaha Valley Community Hosp. Guild, Jaycee Jaynes (pres. 1971), C. of C. Mem. editorial adv. bd. Geriatric Nursing, 1982—; contbr. articles to profl. jours. Home: 1011 Nemaha St Seneca KS 66538 Office: 808 N 8th St Seneca KS 66538

BERGMANN, BARBARA ROSE, economics educator; b. N.Y.C., July 20, 1927; d. Martin and Nellie (Wallenstein) Berman; m. Fred H. Bergmann, July 14, 1965; children: Sarah Nellie, David Martin. B.A., Cornell U., 1948; M.A., Radcliffe Coll.-Harvard U., 1955, Ph.D., 1959. Economist U.S. Bur. Labor Stats., N.Y.C., 1949-53; sr. staff ecomomist, cons. Council Econ. Advisors, Washington, 1961-62; mem. sr. staff Brookings Inst., Washington, 1963-65; sr. econ. advisor AID, Washington, 1966-67; assoc. prof. U. Md., College Park, 1965-71, prof. econs., 1971-87; disting. prof. Am. U., 1987—. Author: (with Chinitz and Hoover) Projection of A Metropolis, 1961, (with George W. Wilson) Impact of Highway Investment on Development, 1966, (with David E. Kaun) Structural Unemployment in the U.S., 1967, (with Robert Bennett) A Microsimulated Transactions Model of the United States Economy, 1985, The Economic Emergence of Women, 1986; mem. bd. editors: Am. Econ. Rev., 1970-73, Challenge, 1978—, Signs, 1978—; columnist econ. affairs, N.Y. Times, 1981-82, Los Angeles Times, 1983—. Mem. Economists for McGovern, 1977; mem. panel econ. advisors Congl. Budget Office, Washington, 1977-87; mem. price adv. com. U.S. council on Wage and Price Stability, 1979-80. Mem. Am. Econ. Assn. (v.p. 1976, adv. com. to U. S. Census Bur. 1977-82), Eastern Econ. Assn. (pres. 1974), AAUP (council mem. 1980-83), Phi Beta Kappa. Democrat. Home: 5430 41 Place NW Washington DC 20015 Office: Am U Dept Econs Washington DC 20016

BERGNER, JANE COHEN, lawyer; b. Schenectady, N.Y., Apr. 6, 1943; d. Louis and Selma (Breslaw) Cohen; m. Alfred P. Bergner, May 30, 1968; children—Lauren, Justin. A.B., Vassar Coll., 1964; LL.B., Columbia U., 1967. Bar: D.C. 1968, U.S. Dist. Ct. D.C. 1968, U.S. Ct. Appeals (D.C. cir.) 1968, U.S. Ct. Claims, 1969, U.S. Ct. Appeals (fed. cir.) 1969, U.S. Tax Ct. 1979. Trial atty. tax div. U.S. Dept. Justice, Washington, 1967-74; assoc. Arnold & Porter, Washington, 1974-76, Rogovin, Huge & Lenzner, Washington, 1976-83; of counsel Arter & Hadden, 1983-86, ptnr. Spriggs & Hollingsworth, 1986—. Bd. dirs. Jewish Social Service Agy., Washington; mem. Nat. Women's Com. Brandeis U. Finalist, Harlan Fiske Stone Honor Moot Ct. Competition, Columbia U. Law Sch.; community adv. bd. WAMU-FM, Washington. Mem. Vassar Coll. Class Alumnae, Bar Assn. D.C. (chair taxation sect.), Fed. Bar Assn., Women's Bar Assn. D.C., Women's Legal Def. Fund, Nat. Assn. Women Lawyers, Tax Litigation Luncheon Group, ABA (sect. taxation, chmn. subcom. Spl. Litigation Issues, ct. procedure com.; vice-liaison mid-Atlantic region, regional liaison meetings com..), Columbia Law Sch. Alumni Assn., Service Guild Washington. Clubs: Vassar (Washington); Hadassah. Home: 5659 Bent Branch Rd Bethesda MD 20816 Office: Spriggs Bode & Hollingsworth 1015 15th St NW Suite 1100 Washington DC 20005-2686

BERGQUIST, KATHLEEN MARIE, government official; b. Coos Bay, Oreg., Apr. 10, 1952; d. Elroy Atlee and Margaret Mary (Connor) B. BA in Social Scis., Oreg. Coll. of Edn., 1976. Personnel asst. U.S. Dept. Transp., Fed. Hwy. Administrn., Portland, Oreg., 1977-78, personnel mgmt. specialist, 1978-81, asst. regional dir. civil rights, 1981-83; exec. dir. Fed. Exec. Bd., Portland, 1983-85; owner Connor Cons., 1987—. Vol. Clackamas County Mental Health, Portland, 1980-83, Paulist Ctr., 1986, Loyola, 1987—; co-founder Womanstory Unltd., Inc.; bd. dirs. Sophia Ctr. Mem. Inst. for Managerial-Profl. Women, Am. Soc. for Pub. Adminstrn., Smithsonian Instutition, Nat. Geog. Soc., Sierra Club. Office: PO Box 19141 Portland OR 97219

BERGQUIST, SANDRA LEE, medical corporation executive, nurse; b. Carlton, Minn., Oct. 13, 1944; d. Arthur Vincent and Avis Lorene Portz; m. David Edward Bergquist, June 11, 1966; children—Rion Eric, Taun Erin. B.S. in Nursing, Barry U., 1966; M.A. in Mgmt., Central Mich. U., 1975; student U. So. Calif., 1980-82. R.N., registered nurse practitioner; cert. physician asst. Commd. 2d lt. U.S. Air Force, 1968, advanced through grades to lt. col., 1985; staff and charge nurse U.S. Air Force, 1968-76, primary care nurse practitioner, McConnell AFB, Kans., 1976-79, officer in charge Wheeler Med. Facility, Wheeler AFB, Hawaii, 1979-83, supr. ambulatory care services, Elgin AFB, Fla., 1983-84; pres. Care Cons. Corp., Niceville, Fla., 1985—, med.-legal cons., 1985—; risk mgr., quality assurance coordinator HCA-Twin Cities Hosp., Niceville, Fla., 1986—. Bd. dirs. Okaloosa County Council on Aging, Fla.; chairperson Niceville/Valparaiso Task Force on Child Abuse Prevention, Fla., 1985—; chmn. home and family life com. Twin Cities Women's Club, Niceville, 1985—; chmn. advancement com. Gulf Coast council Boy Scouts Am., 1985-87; instr. advanced and basic cardiac life support Hawaii Heart Assn. and Tripler Army Med. Ctr., 1981-83. Decorated Commendation medal with 1 oak leaf cluster, USAF Meritorious Service medal, Air Force Commendation medal. Mem. Am. Assn. Critical-Care Nurses, Am. Assn. Physician Assts., Assn. Mil. Surgeons U.S., Soc. Ret. Air Force Nurses, Soc. Air Force Physician Assts., Twin Cities Women's Club. Lutheran. Avocations: computer programming, reading, handicrafts. Office: HCA Twin Cities Hosp Hwy 85 N & Coll Blvd Niceville FL 32578

BERGSCHNEIDER, DIANE KATHLEEN, dental hygienist; b. Milw., Sept. 22, 1947; m. James Leo Bergschneider, July 11, 1970; children: Lisa, Daniel, Jonathan, Kristin. BS in Dental Hygiene, Marquette U., 1969. Adminstr. LaPepiniere Montessori Sch., Milw., 1976-78; with pharm. sales div. Scherer Labs., Dallas, 1984-86; pvt. practice dental hygienist Milw., 1969—; pres. Wis. Dental Connection Ltd., Milw., 1981—; guest lectr. Sch. Dentistry Marquette U., Milw., 1983—; cons. dental in-service programs in nursing homes, Milw., 1981—. Clin. examiner Cen. Regional Dental Testing Service, Topeka, 1983—; bd. dirs. Am. Cancer Soc., Milw., 1986—; v.p. Maple Dale-Indian Hill Parent-Tchr. Orgn., Milw., 1981-83; badge counselor Boy Scouts Am., Milw., 1985—. Named an Outstanding Alumna Dental Hygienist, Marquette U., 1986. Mem. Am. Dental Hygienists Assn. (nat. del. 1980-83, Wis. Dental Hygienists Assn., (pres. 1981-83, editor Wis. Dental Hygiene Bull., 1982-84, Outstanding Service award 1987), Am. Assn. Dental Examiners (past chmn. Wis. Dentistry Examining Bd.), Marquette U. Dental Hygiene Adv. Com. Accreditation, Milw. Regional Dental Hygiene Assn. (pres. 1980-81). Roman Catholic. Home: 9276 N Broadmoor Rd Milwaukee WI 53217 Office: 2011 E Newport Ave Milwaukee WI 53211

BERGSTROM, SUSAN ELAINE, hospital administrator; b. Belleville, Kans., Jan. 30, 1961; d. Charles Ray and Ruth Elaine (Fraser) Wilber; m. Dennis Michael Bergstrom, Aug. 3, 1985. Student, U. Kans., 1980-81; B in Health Scis., Wichita (Kans.) U., 1983. Registered respiratory therapist, Kans. Staff therapist Wesley Med. Ctr., Wichita, 1980-83; dir. respiratory care Republic County Hosp., Belleville, 1983—; cons. Brodstone Meml. Hosp., Superior, Nebr., 1983-86; instr. basic and advanced cardiac life support, Kans., 1983—. Chairperson blood services Republic County chpt. ARC, 1983-86; assoc. Operation Prom Night, Belleville, 1987—; mem. Republic County Recreation Assn. Mem. Am. Assn. Respiratory Care, Am. Heart Assn., Kans Respiratory Care Soc. (bd. dirs. 1985—, cert. of recognition 1986), Nat. Assn. for Female Execs. Lodge: Eagles (aux.). Office: Republic County Hosp 24th and G Prairie View Belleville KS 66935

BERILLA, SUSAN RUTH, sales executive; b. Columbus, Ind., Oct. 3, 1956; d. Louis Elmin and Dorothy (Yunghans) Carr; m. Robert Andrew Williamson, Dec. 13, 1980 (div. 1987); m. James John Berilla, Feb. 14, 1988. BA, Purdue U., 1978. Lic. real estate agt. Adminsrtv. asst. to bd. dirs. Inst. Gas Tech., Chgo., 1978-79; asst. to v.p. ASKO Inc., South Holland, Ill., 1979-80; office mgr. Chrishon Fabricators Inc., Oakmont, Pa., 1980-82; internat. salesperson Custom Materials Inc., Chagrin Falls, Ohio, 1982—. Vol. Campaign Sen. H.J. Heinz II, Pitts., 1985-86; v.p. Aid Assn. Luths., Monroeville, Pa., 1983-85; chmn. Bd. Evangelism Monroeville Trinity Ch., 1983-85, instr., 1982-85, bd. stewardship, 1984. Mem. Nat. Assn. Profl. Saleswomen, Nat. Assn. Female Execs., Purdue U. Alumni Assn., Delta Sigma Phi, Alpha Lambda Delta. Republican. Club: Purdue of Pitts. Home and Office: 1335 Crane Ave Pittsburgh PA 15220

BERK, AMY J., editor; b. Abington, Pa., Jan. 9, 1952; d. Rudolph and Gloria (Kean) B. BA, Oberlin Coll., 1973; MA in Teaching, U. Chgo., 1975. Tchr. Akiba-Schechter Day Sch., Chgo., 1974-76; editorial assoc. U. Chgo. Cancer Research Ctr., Chgo., 1976-79; editor CBE Environ. Rev., Chgo., 1979-82; editorial coordinator Am. Dental Assn., Chgo., 1981-82; devel. editor Am. Soc. Clin. Pathologists, Chgo., 1982, mng. editor, sr. acquisitions editor, 1983-87; instr. U. Chgo. Pub. Program, 1985—; editor sci. Scott Foresman and Co., Glenview, Ill., 1987—; mem. adv. group U. Chgo. Pub. Program, 1987—. Contbr. sci. articles for children and adults to profl. jours. and mags. Mem. Chgo. Book Clinic, Chgo. Women in Pub. (pres. 1986-87, chmn. mgrs. roundtable 1986-87, chmn. long range planning 1985-86, chmn. job placement 1983-85). Home: 535 W Briar Pl Apt 457 Chicago IL 60657-4606 Office: Scott Foresman and Co 1900 E Lake Ave Glenview IL 60025

BERK, CHERYL ANNE, management consultant; b. Miami, Fla., Dec. 16, 1946; d. Billy E. and Millicent Rochelle (Hodges) Teaver; m. Richard B. Berk, Nov. 5, 1967 (div. Sept. 1986); 1 child, Stacey Denise. BS, Barry U., 1980. Rep. M.D. Futch & Assoc., Miami Beach, Fla., 1972-76; asst. to pres. 2d Nat. Banks, North Miami, Fla., 1976-79; systems analyst SE Bank, Miami, 1980-82; sr. auditor Cen. Bancorp, Miami, 1982-84; mgr., cons. Deloitte Haskins & Sells, Miami, 1984—; lectr. in field, various civic and bus. orgns. Mem. Fin. Mgr.'s Soc., Am. Inst. Bankers, Marian Cen. Auxiliary, Bus. Forum, Women's C. of C. of S. Fla. (bd. dirs, sec., exec. com. 1986-87). Republican. Club: Palm Bay. Home: 6335 La Gorce Dr Miami Beach FL 33141 Office: Deloitte Haskins & Sells 1 SE 3rd Ave Miami FL 33131

BERK, PEGGY FAITH, public relations/financial consultant; b. N.Y.C., Feb. 3, 1951; d. Stanley and Naomi Elaine (Herskowitz) B.; divorced; 1 child, Mason Ben-Yair. Student, NYU, 1968-71, New Sch. for Social Research, 1971-73. News editor Herald Newspapers, N.Y.C., 1972-73; mktg. liaison U.S. Dept. Commerce, Tel Aviv, Israel, 1973; mgr. fgn. currency dept. Bank Le'umi BM, Arad, Israel, 1974-75; exec. v.p. Peter Small & Assocs., N.Y.C., 1978-81; prin., pres. Strategic Communications, N.Y.C., 1981—; cons. sr. v.p. The Rowland Co., N.Y.C., 1984-85; prin., pres. BFP Internat. Inc., N.Y.C., 1987—; cons. Council on Fin. Aid to Edn., N.Y., 1979-81, Global Link, Tokyo, 1986—. Contbr. numerous news articles. Bd. dirs. Child Net, Inc., Mass., 1987—. Mem. Citiwomen, Women's Am. ORT.

BERKA, MARIANNE GUTHRIE, fitness and recreation educator; b. Queens, N.Y., Dec. 25, 1944; d. Frank Joseph and Mary (DePaul) Guthrie; B.S., Ithaca (N.Y.) Coll., 1966, M.S. (grad. asst.), 1968; doctoral candidate NYU; m. Jerry George Berka, June 1, 1968; children—Katie, Keri. High sch. tchr. Northport High Sch., 1966-67; full prof. health, phys. edn. and recreation Nassau Community Coll., Garden City, N.Y., 1968—. Mem. Assn. Women Phys. Educators N.Y. State (chpt. chmn. 1973-74, chpt. treas. 1980-84), AAHPER, N.Y. State Assn. Health, Phys. Edn. and Recreation (J.B. Nash scholarship com. 1983—), Am. Assn. Sex Educators, Counselors and Therapists (cert. sex educator). Roman Catholic. Home: 90 Bay Way Ave Brightwaters NY 11718 Office: Nassau Community Coll P226 HPER Garden City NY 11530

BERKBIGLER, MARSHA LEE, gold mining company executive; b. Flint, Mich., May 2, 1950; d. Herbert Ules and Rosy Vernell (Grimes) Cornelison; m. Gary Robert Koontz, June 22, 1968 (div. Nov. 1976); children—Deron Robert, Alicia Michelle; m. James Herbert Berkbigler, Dec. 16, 1977. A. in Bus., Reno Bus. Coll., 1979. Hosp. coordinating sec. LaHabra Community Hosp., Calif., 1973-76; sec., office mgr. Sierra Med. Assocs., Reno, 1976-78, claims rep. Equifax, Reno, 1978-79; legal asst. Freeport Export Co., Reno, 1979-85; pub. and govt. coordinator Freeport-McMoRan Gold Co., Reno, 1985—; cons. Neva. Wilderness Minerals Exploration Coalition, Denver, 1985. Named one of 88 people to watch in 1988, Reno Mag., 1988. Mem. Nev. Republican Woman's Caucus, Reno, 1986; apptd. Reno Commn. Status of Women, 1985. Mem. Nev. Mining Assn., Nev. Landman's Assn., Assn. Exec. Females, Nev. Council Econ. Edn. (exec. com.), Reno Sparks C. of C. (bd. dirs.), Concerned Nevadans for Practical Wilderness. Avocations: skiing; golf; travel. Home: 2090 Allen St Reno NV 89509

BERKE, ANITA DIAMANT, literary agent; b. N.Y.C., Jan. 15; d. Sidney J. and Lea (Lyons) Diamant; m. Harold Berke, Dec. 22, 1945 (dec. 1972); 1 child, Allyson. B.S., NYU. Mem. editorial bd. Forum Mag., N.Y.C., McCalls Mag.; reporter Macy Newspapers; literary agt., pres. Anita Diamant Literary Agy., N.Y.C.; adj. prof. L.I.U. Contbr. articles to profl. jours. Mem. Women in Communications, Inc. (past pres. N.Y. chpt.), Nat. Assn. Newspaper Women, Soc. Author's Reps. Club: Overseas Press (pres. 1981—). Home: 16 Fanton Hill Rd Weston CT 06883 Office: Anita Diamant Lit Agy 310 Madison Ave New York NY 10017

BERKE, JUDIE, publisher, editor; b. Mpls., Apr. 15, 1938; d. Maurice M. and Sue (Supak) Kleyman; student U. Minn., 1956-60, Mpls. Sch. Art, 1945-59. Free lance illustrator and designer, 1959—; pres. Berke-Wood, Inc., N.Y.C., 1971-80, Manhattan Rainbow & Lollipop Co. subs. Berke-Wood, Inc., 1971-80; pres. Get Your Act Together, club act staging, N.Y.C., 1971-80; pres. Coordinator Pubs.,Inc., 1982-87; pres., chief exec. officer, Health Market Communications, 1987—; pres. Pub. and Media Services, Burbank, 1987—; pub., editor Continuing Care Coordinator, Health Watch mags.; pres. Continuing Care Coordinator Convs. and Seminars; cons. to film and ednl. cos.; guest lectr. various colls. and univs. in Calif. and N.Y., 1973—; cons., designer Healthy Lifestyles mag.; writer, illustrator, dir. numerous ednl. filmstrips, 1972—, latest being Focus on Professions, 1974, Focus on the Performing Arts, 1974, Focus on the Creative Arts, 1974, Workstyles, 1976, Wonderworm, 1976, Supernut, 1977; author, illustrator film Fat Black Mack (San Francisco Ednl. Film Festival award, part of permanent collection Mus. Modern Art, N.Y.C.), 1970; designer posters and brochures for various entertainment groups, 1963—; composer numerous songs, latest being Time is Relative, 1976, Love Will Live On in My Mind, 1976, My Blue Walk, 1976, You Make Me a Baby, 1982, Let's Go Around Once More, 1983, Anytime Anyplace Anywhere, 1987, Bittersweet, 1987, Sometimes It Pays, 1987; composer/author off-Broadway musical Street Corner Time, 1978; producer: The Reals Estate TV Shows 1988—; contbr. children's short stories to various publs., also articles. Trustee The Happy Spot Sch., N.Y.C., 1972-75. Mem. Nat. Fedn. Bus. and Profl. Women, Nat. Assn. Female Execs., Am. Acad. Polit. and Social Sci. Home and Office: 958 N Vista St Los Angeles CA 90046

BERKE, SUSAN, interior designer, educator; b. Newburgh, N.Y., Mar. 17, 1946; d. Meyer and Sylvia (Schneider) Zodikoff; m. Jay Samuel Berke; 1 child, Amanda Karen. BS in Housing, Design, Cornell U., 1968, BS in Textiles, Clothing, 1968; student, Harvard U., summer 1965. Cert. interior designer. Textile designer Wamsutta Mills, N.Y.C., 1968-71; fashion coordinator Woodward and Lothrop, Chevy Chase, Md., 1971-73; stylist Stroheim and Romann, N.Y.C., 1973-74; interior designer Susan Berke Interiors, Elkins Park, Pa., 1974—. Home and Office: 1501 Juniper Ave Elkins Park PA 19117

BERKELEY, BETTY LIFE, educator; b. St. Louis, May 25, 1924; d. James Alfred and Anna Laura (Voltmer) Life; m. Marvin Harold Berkeley, Feb. 7, 1947; children—Kathryn Elizabeth, Barbara Ellen, Brian Harrison, Janet Lynn. A.B., Harris Tchrs. Coll., 1947; M.A. in Ednl. Adminstrn., Washington U., St. Louis, 1951; Ph.D., North Tex. State U., 1980. Tchr. St. Louis pub. schs., 1946-48, Clayton pub. schs., Mo., 1948-49, Lamplighter Pvt. Sch., Dallas, 1964-67; program devel. specialist Richland Coll., Dallas, 1980-84, instr., 1981—; adj. prof. North Tex. State U., Denton, 1981—, cons. Sch. Community Services Ctr. for Studies on Aging, 1981—; pres. Retirement Planning Services, Dallas, 1984—. Contbr. articles to profl. jours. Mem. Dallas Commn. on Status of Women, 1975-79; bd. dirs. Dallas Municipal Library, 1979-83; bd. dirs. Council on Adult Ministry Lovers Lane United Meth. Ch., 1982; charter mem. bd. dirs., life mem. Friends of N. Tex. State U. Library; mem. Pres.'s Council N. Tex. State U., mem. vol. mgmt. edn. task force, 1978-82. Mem. AAUW (pres. 1973-75; Outstanding Woman of Tex. 1981). Club: Women's Council of Dallas County (v.p. 1977-79). Avocations: travel, cooking; gardening, needlework. Home: 13958 Hughes Ln Dallas TX 75240 Office: Richland Coll 12800 Abrams Rd Dallas TX 75243

BERKENES, JOYCE MARIE POORE, family counselor; b. Des Moines, Aug. 29, 1953; d. Donald Roy and Thelma Beatrice (Hart) Poore; m. Robert Elliott Berkenes,Jan. 3, 1976; children: Tiffany Noelle, Cory Matthew. BA in Social Work and Biology, Simpson Coll., Indianola, Iowa., 1975. Resident counselor and group home mgr. Chaddock Boys Home, Quincy, Ill., 1976-78; social service dir. N. Adams Nursing Home, Mendon, Ill., 1978; home tchr. Head Start, Camp Point, Ill., 1978-79, home tchr. supr./edn. and parent involvement coordinator, 1979-82; family counselor Iowa Children's and Family Services, Des Moines, 1982-85; family counselor and vol. coordinator Luth. Social Services, Des Moines, 1985—; cons. in field, 1975-76. Mem. Iowa Soc. Autistic Children, Home Based Family Service Assn. (sec. 1984-87), Nat. Assn. Social Workers. Democrat. Methodist. Home: 2901 NE 80th St Altoona IA 50009 Office: Luth Social Services 2525 E Euclid Suite 110 Des Moines IA 50317

BERKEY, BARBARA ANN, management consultant; b. Rochester, Ind., Aug. 1, 1943; d. Arthur Frederick and Edith Mae (Scott) Mohn; children: Debra Ann Berkey Metzger, Terri Lynn. A of Bus. Adminstrn., Internat. Bus. Coll., Ft. Wayne, Ind., 1982. Fin. mgr. Western Rubber Co., Goshen, Ind., 1966-87, Goshen Die Cutting, 1987; prin. Berkey and Assocs., Goshen, 1987—; cons. Western Rubber Co., 1987—. Budget dir. Elkhart (Ind.) United Way, 1984-86; emergency room vol. Goshen Gen. Hosp. Aux., 1984—; fundraising chairperson Greencroft Retirement Group, Goshen and Elkhart, 1985. Mem. Bus. Women's Inst. (charter), Nat. Assn. Female Execs. Republican. Baptist. Office: Berkey and Assocs 62231 County Rd 17 Goshen IN 46526

BERKHEIMER, GERALDINE FAY, educator, librarian; b. York, Pa., Feb. 18, 1934; d. Walter Lewis and Lena Emma (Tresselt) Berkheimer. BS in Edn., Millersville State Coll., 1956; MA in French, Middlebury Coll., 1959; MLS, Syracuse U., 1965. Tchr. French, Penncrest High Sch., Lima, Pa., 1956-58, Westminster High Sch. (Pa.), 1960-61; part-time sec. Sorbonne, Paris, 1961-62; English asst. Jean de la Fontaine Girls' High Sch., Paris, 1962-63; lit. analyst ERIC, Syracuse U. (N.Y.), 1964-65; asst. prof. French, Onondaga Community Coll., Syracuse, 1965-69, 70-71; librarian Reading Area Community Coll. (Pa.), 1971-72; substitute tchr. and librarian pub. schs., Orange County, Calif., 1972-79; library asst. U. Calif.-Irvine, 1979—. Mem. Calif. Library Assn., Alliance francaise, NOW, So. Calif. Women for Understanding, Laguna Outreach, Inst. for Religion and Wholeness, Inst. for Noetic Sci, Nat. Mus. Women in Arts, Abundant Light Found., Older Women's League, So. Calif. Astrologers' Network. Home: 3101 S Fairview St Apt 84 Santa Ana CA 92704

BERKLEY, NANCY MARGOLIS, lawyer, educator; b. St. Paul, Nov. 12, 1940; d. Charles and Dorothy (Wine) Margolis; m. Peter L. Berkley, Aug. 2, 1964; children—James, Alison, John. B.A., U. Minn., 1961; M.A.T., Harvard U., 1962; J.D., Rutgers U., 1985. Bar: N.J. Tchr., Malden, Mass., 1962-63, Newton, Mass., 1963-64, South Orange, N.J., 1964-67; art cons., N.Y. and N.J., 1973-83; law clk. U.S. Dist. Ct. N.J., 1983; law clk. Proskauer, Rose, Goetz & Mendelsohn, N.Y.C., summer 1984; assoc. Sullivan & Cromwell, N.Y.C., 1985—. Editor: Rutgers Law Rev., 1984-85. Trustee Livingston Symphony Orch., N.J., 1981-87, Theresa Grotta Rehab. Ctr., West Orange, N.J., 1967—; active Livingston Recreation Adv. Council, 1981-87; trustee Northwest Essex Suburban Arts Council, 1981-83. Mem.

ABA, N.Y. State Bar Assn., Phi Beta Kappa, Pi Lambda Theta. Home: 16 Fordham Rd Livingston NJ 07039

BERKMAN, CLAIRE FLEET, psychologist; b. New Orleans, Dec. 5, 1942; d. Joel and Margaret Grace (Fishler) Fleet; m. Arnold Stephen Berkman, Apr. 27, 1975; children: Janna Samantha, Micah Seth Siegel. BA, Boston U., 1964; MEd, Harvard U., 1966; EdD, Boston U., 1970. Asst. prof. Counseling Ctr., Mich. State U., East Lansing, 1971-75, assoc. prof., 1975-78, assoc. prof. dept. psychiatry, 1975-82, clin. assoc. prof., 1986-87; pvt. clin. practice, 1975—; cons. Cath. Family Social Service, Lansing, 1979-83; mem. adv. bd. Cir. Ct. Family Counseling Program, 1982—. V.p. Kehillat Israel Synagogue, 1975-76; bd. dirs. Jewish Welfare Fedn., Lansing, 1974-75, 84-87. NDEA fellow, 1968-70. Mem. Am. Psychol. Assn., Mich. Psychol. Assn., Am. Mental Health Assn. of Israel, Mich. Soc. Forensic Psychologists. Office: 4084 Okenos Rd Okemos MI 48864

BERKMAN, SUSAN C. J., educational administrator; b. Los Angeles, Apr. 17, 1953; d. Fred and Alice Hodes Josephs; m. Donald W. Berkman Jr., Aug. 10, 1974; 1 child, Daniel. BA, U. Calif., Irvine, 1974; MA, UCLA, 1977, Calif. State U., Los Angeles, 1988. Cert. adult edn. tchr. Specialist personnel mgmt. U.S. Civil Service Commn., Washington, 1974-75; teaching asst. UCLA, 1976-77; research editor Regensteiner Press, Sherman Oaks, Calif., 1977; dir. music Braille Inst., Los Angeles, 1978-82, asst. dir. student tng., 1982-87, dir. spl. projects, 1987—; Bd. dirs. No. Lights Prodns., Seattle. Author: Teaching Music to the Blind, 1980, Teaching Music to the Visually Handicapped, 1982; (ednl. program) Just Like Me, 1983. Mem. Hermosa Beach (Calif.) Coordinating Council, 1986; bd. dirs. Community Family Guidance Clinic, Cerritos, Calif., 1987—. Travel grantee, UCLA, 1977; Calif. State scholar, 1970-73, William S. Schwartz Meml. scholar, 1974. Mem. AAUW, Assn. for Edn. and Rehab. of the Blind and Visually Impaired (v.p. so. Calif. region 1987—), Calif. Transcribers and Educators of the Blind and Visually Impaired, Kappa Delta Pi, Phi Kappa Phi. Baha'i. Home: 13227 Volunteer Ave Norwalk CA 90650-3123 Office: Braille Inst 741 N Vermont Ave Los Angeles CA 90029

BERKOER, MARILYN ARLENE, purchasing director; b. N.Y.C., Feb. 8, 1944; d. William and Bernice (Goldstein) B. BBA cum laude, Mercy Coll., 1985. Dir. food services New Rochelle (N.Y.) Nursing Home, 1971-73, Riverside Nursing Home, Haverstraw, N.Y., 1973-75; dir. purchasing Kings Harbor Care Ctr., N.Y.C., 1975—. Mem. Hosp. Instl. Food Service Soc. Office: Kings Harbor Care Ctr 2000 E Gun Hill Rd New York NY 10469

BERKOVITS, ANNETTE ROCHELLE, curator, consultant, biologist, educator; b. Kizyl-Kija, Kirgiz Republic, USSR, Sept. 13, 1943; came to U.S., 1959; naturalized, 1964; d. Nachman and Dora (Blaustein) Libeskind; m. David Berkovits; children: Jessica Dawn, Jeremy Haskell. BS in Biology, CUNY, 1965; MS in Adminstrn. and Supervision, Manhattan Coll., 1977. Cert. sch. adminstr., N.Y. Research asst. Sloan Kettering Cancer Research Inst., N.Y.C., 1965-66; sci. tchr. N.Y.C. Bd. Edn., 1966-72; zoology instr. N.Y. Zool. Soc., N.Y.C., 1972-75, coordinator curricula and programs, 1975-77, asst. curator of edn., 1978-80, assoc. curator edn., 1980-82, curator of edn., 1983—; project dir. Wildlife Inquiry through Zoo Edn. program, N.Y. Zool. Soc., 1981—; dir. Animal Kingdom Zoo Camp, N.Y. Zool. Soc., 1977—; project dir., prin. investigator grants program NSF, 1980—; panelist N.Y. State Council on Arts, 1986—; cons., panelist NSF. Contbr. chpt. on zoos to National Science Teacher's Yearbook, 1988; speaker in field. Fellow Am. Assn. Zool. Parks and Aquariums, Consortium of Aquariums, Univs., and Zoos (bd. dirs.), N.Y.C. Mus. Educators Roundtable (chmn. 1982). Office: NY Zool Soc 185th St & Southern Blvd New York NY 10460

BERKOWITZ, JOAN B., chemical company executive; b. Bklyn., Mar. 13, 1931; d. Morris and Rose (Gerber) B.; m. Arthur P. Mattuck, Sept. 7, 1959 (div. 1977); 1 child, Rosemary L. BA, Swarthmore Coll., 1952; PhD, U. Ill., 1955. Research asst. Yale U., New Haven, 1955-57; sr. staff mem. A.D. Little Inc., Cambridge, Mass., 1957-80, v.p., 1980-86; pres., chief exec. officer Risk Sci. Internat., Washington, 1986—; instr. Boston U., 1964-69; mem. sci. adv. bd. EPA, Washington, 1987—; keynote speaker Nat. Solid Waste Mgmt. Assn., Salt Lake City, 1983; bd. dirs. Envirosate Inc., King of Prussia, Pa. Author: (book) Hazardous Waste Plan for New England, 1979; author/editor (books) Treatment of Hazardous Wastes, 1979, Business Opportunities in Hazardous Waste, 1985; contbr. numerous articles to profl. jours. Treas. Children's Ctr. Brooklines, Mass., 1972-74, mem. adv. bd., 1974—. Recipient achievement award Soc. Women Engrs., 1985. Mem. Am. Chem. Soc. (hazardous waste task force), Electrochem. Soc. (pres. 1979-80), Am. Inst. Chemists (councillor 1982-86), Air Pollution Control Assn. (speaker 1986-87), NOW (chpt. treas. 1971-73), Sigma Xi, Phi Beta Kappa. Democrat. Jewish. Office: Risk Sci Internat 1101 30th St NW Washington DC 20007

BERLAGE, GAI INGHAM, sociologist, educator; b. Washington, Feb. 9, 1943; d. Paul Bowen and Grace (Artz) Ingham; m. Jan Coxe Berlage, Aug. 7, 1965; children: Jan Ingham, Cari Coxe. BA, Smith Coll., 1965; MA, So. Meth. U., 1968; PhD, NYU, 1979. Tchr. math. Piner Jr. High Sch., Sherman, Tex., 1968-69; asst. prof. sociology Iona Coll., New Rochelle, N.Y., 1971-83, assoc. prof., 1983-88, prof., 1988—, chmn. dept., 1981—, prof., 1988—; coordinator urban studies program, 1984—, gerontology program, 1985—. Author: Experience with Sociology: Social Issues in American Society, 1983, Understanding Social Issues: Sociological Fact Finding, 1987; contbr. articles to profl. jours. Commr. Wilton Commn. on Aging and Social Services, 1980-88, chmn., 1982-88; co-chmn. Wilton Task Force on Youth council, 1988; chmn. Wilton Task Force Com. for Outreach Program, 1981-82, Wilton Task Force on Day Care, 1983—; mem. Wilton Task Force for Pub. Health Nursing Assn., 1981-82, Wilton Sport Council, 1985—; bd. dirs. Wilton Meals on Wheels, 1983—; fellow North Am. Faculty Network of Northeastern Univs.'s Ctr. for Study of Sport in Soc. NSF trainee, 1967-68. Mem. Am. Sociol. Assn., N.Y. State Sociol. Assn., N.Am. Soc. Sociology of Sport, Inst. Sport and Social Analysis, Internat. Com. Sociology of Sport, Wilton Assn. Gifted Edn. (pres. 1980-81), Internat. Soc. of Sport Psychology. Office: Iona Coll Dept Sociology New Rochelle NY 10801

BERLIN, EMILY, lawyer; b. Bethesda, Md., Apr. 29, 1947; d. Eugene A. and Sylvia W. Berlin; m. John T. Schmidt. BA, Barnard Coll., 1968; MA in Art History, Columbia U., 1970, JD, 1973. Legis. asst. U.S. Senator Joseph Biden, Washington, 1973-74; assoc. Shearman & Sterling, N.Y.C., 1974-81, ptnr., 1981—. Home: 50 Sutton Pl S 19H New York NY 10022 Office: Shearman & Sterling 153 E 53d St New York NY 10022 also: Shearman & Sterling 599 Lexington Ave at 53rd St New York NY 10022

BERLINCOURT, MARJORIE ALKINS, government official; b. Toronto, Ont., Can., June 2, 1928; came to U.S., 1950, naturalized, 1956; d. Herbert John and Ellen Florence (Barker) Alkins; B.A., U. Toronto, 1950; M.A., Yale U., 1951, Ph.D., 1954; m. Ted Gibbs Berlincourt, Feb. 28, 1953; 1 dau., Leslie Ellen Berlincourt Yale. Editorial dir. Tech. Publs., Rocketdyne, 1956-59; lectr. classics U. So. Calif., 1959-61; assoc. prof. classical history Calif. Luth. Coll., 1961-67, Calif. State U., Northridge, 1967-71; prof. Met. State Coll., Denver, 1971-72; program dir. div. fellowships Nat. Endowment Humanities, for summer seminars and fellowships Washington, 1972-78, dep. dir. div. research programs, 1978-84, dir. div. state programs, 1984—; vis. lectr. Georgetown U., 1972. Recipient Calif. Faculty Research award, 1970; Sterling fellow Yale U., 1950-53. Mem. Am. Assn. Ancient Historians. Episcopalian. Author: De Surprise en Surprise, 1953; Entrez Petits Amis, 1954; Victory as a Coin Type, 1973; contbr. articles to profl. jours. Office: 1100 Pennsylvania Ave NW Washington DC 20506

BERLINROOD, WENDY MARCIA, social worker; b. N.Y.C., Feb. 10, 1946; d. Seymour Louis and Beatrice Irene (Planner) Weinberger; m. Martin Berlinrood, Jan. 23, 1966 (div. May 1986); children: Debra Anne, Brian Michael. BS, CCNY, 1966; MSW, U. Tex., 1968; PhD, U. Md., Balt., 1986. Social worker Jewish Family Services, Albany, N.Y., 1968-69; caseworker Rensselaer Dept. Social Services, Troy, N.Y., 1969-70; staff social worker Sheppard Pratt Hosp., Balt., 1971-78; dir. clin. services Hannah More Ctr., Inc., Reisterstown, Md., 1978-81; pvt. practice social work Reisterstown, Md., 1984—; cons. Bent Nursing Home, Reisterstown, 1974-78, Balt. City Dept. Health, 1976, Balt. City Dept. Social Services, 1981, Springfield State Hosp., Eldensburg, Md., 1987; lectr. Balt. Community Coll., 1975, Sch. Social Work U. Md., Balt., 1981; faculty Towson State U. and Sch. Social Work U. Md., 1986—. V.p. Reisterstown-Owings Mills-Glyndon (ROG) (Md.) Coordinating Council, Reisterstown, 1985; mem. Carroll County Children's Council, Westminster, Md., 1986—. U. Md. fellow, 1980, 81, 82. Mem. Nat. Assn. Social Workers, Am. Assn. Marriage and Family Therapists (clin. mem.), Md. Mental Health Assn., Arista, Psi Chi. Office: 606 Main St Reisterstown MD 21136

BERMAN, BARBARA SANDRA, mathematics consultant; b. N.Y.C., Oct. 15, 1938; d. Nathan and Regina (Pasternak) Kopp; m. Murray Berman, June 27, 1959; children: Adrienne, David. BS, Bklyn. Coll., 1959, MS, 1961. Cert. elem. tchr., N.Y., sch. dist. adminstr., N.Y., N.J. Elem. tchr. N.Y.C. Pub. Sch. Dist., 1959-63, 70-76; math. project coordinator grad. sch. edn. Rutgers U., N.J., 1976-80, adj. asst. prof. grad. sch., 1978-80; dir. math. project Edn. Improvement Ctr., West Orange, N.J., 1981-82; adj. asst. prof. Long Island U., Bklyn., 1985-86; pres., dir. Ednl. Support Systems, Inc., Staten Island, N.Y., 1982—; adminstrv. dir. The Foresight Sch., Staten Island, 1985—; sec., treas. B&F Ednl. Cons., Inc., 1987.; lectr. in field.; instr. numerous workshops and seminars in field. Co-author(books): Fractions and Decimals for Junior High School: A Model Integrating Process and Content Skills, 1980, Metric Mini-Course, 1981, Teachers Edition, 1978, Color Tiles, 1986, Mathematics Through Measurement, 1983, Mathematics Institute for the Elementary School Teacher, 1980; revs. for N.Y. State Math. Tchrs. Jour., Sch. Sci, and Math., Curriculum Rev., Arithmetic Tchr.; contbr. articles to profl. jours. Mem. exec. bd., v.p., S.I. Dem. Assn., 1967-74, Susan Wagner High Sch., S.I., 1980-84; mem. exec. bd., Thabo Dance Found., 1984—; bd. dirs., Alzheimers Disease and Related Disorder Assn., Staten Island, 1986—. Mem. N.Y. Acad. Scis., Nat. Staff Devel. Council, Nat. Council Suprs. Math., Nat. Council Tchrs. Math., Assn. Tchrs. of Math. of N.Y., Assn. Tchrs. of Math. of N.Y.C., Am. Nat. Metric Council (mem. bd. dirs., dir. 1983—), Assn. Supervision and Curriculum Devel., Assn. Tchr. Educators, Sch. Sci. and Math. Assn., Early Childhood Edn. Council, Nat. Staff Devel. Council, Mensa, Kappa Delta Pi. Avocations: tennis, reading, travel, theater. Office: Ednl Support Systems Inc 446 Travis Ave Staten Island NY 10314

BERMAN, LINDA FRAN, lawyer; b. Phila., Feb. 26, 1952; d. Martin and Ruth (Krum) B.; m. Paul M. Perlstein, May 25, 1986. A.B., Princeton U., 1973; postgrad. U. Pa., 1973-74, 80; J.D., Villanova U., 1978. Bar: Pa. 1978. Asst. dir. grants Villanova U. (Pa.), 1978; dir. grants Wistar Inst., Phila., 1979; asst. dir. Am. Law Inst., Phila., 1980; exec. editor Pa. Law Jour., 1980-82; mem. firm Schwartzman & Hepps, Phila., 1982-84; assoc. Berger & Montague, P.C., 1984-85; asst. city solicitor, City of Phila., 1985-86; supervising atty. Dessen, Moses & Sheinoff, Jenkintown, Pa., 1986-87; sole practice Phila., 1987—. Bd. dirs. Bus. and Profl. Women's Coalition-Fedn. Jewish Agencies, 1982-84; mem. adv. com. Women's Alliance for Job Equity, 1983—; mem. budget allocation rev. com. United Way, 1982-86; bd. dirs. Women's Resource Ctr., Wayne, Pa., 1986—; bd. dirs. Phila. Vol. Lawyers and the Arts, 1984-87. Mem. Pa. Bar Assn., Phila. Bar Assn. (chmn. lawyers and arts com. 1982-84), Princeton U. Alumni Schs. Com., ABA, LWV (bd. dirs. Lower Merion chpt. 1987—), Sigma Delta Chi. Democrat. Jewish. Clubs: Jr. League, Hadassah. Home: 634 Fariston Dr Wynnewood PA 19096 Office: 538 Church St Norristown PA 19401

BERMAN, LYNNE MOSKOWITZ, marketing professional, newspaper executive; b. Phila., Sept. 17, 1940; d. Morton Paul and Tressa (Silverstein) Moskowitz; m. Peter Henry Berman, Dec. 17, 1961; children: John Kenneth, Elizabeth, Michael Charles. BS in Edn., Simmons Coll., 1962; M in Social Services, Bryn Mawr Coll., 1965. Social worker Traveler's Aid Soc., N.Y.C., 1965-66; social worker, branch dir., asst. dir. Fedn. Day Care Services, Phila., 1973-81; edn. sales mgr. Phila. Newspapers, Inc., 1981—. Founder The Phila. Sch.; bd. dirs. Ctr. Literacy, Phila., Citizens Com. Pub. Edn. Phila.; adv. com. Community Coll. Phila. Home: 2128 Spruce St Philadelphia PA 19103 Office: The Phila Inquirer 400 N Broad St Philadelphia PA 19101

BERMAN, MARLENE OSCAR, neuropsychologist, educator; b. Phila., Nov. 21, 1939; d. Paul Oscar and Evelyn (Hess) (Oscar) Weizenblut; m. Michael Brack Berman, June 23, 1963 (div. Feb. 1980); 1 son, Jesse Michael. B.A., U.Pa., 1961; M.A., Bryn Mawr Coll., 1964; Ph.D., U. Conn., 1968; postgrad., Harvard U., 1968-70. Research assoc. Boston VA Med. Ctr., 1970-72, clin. investigator, 1973-76, research psychologist, 1976—, mem. Com. for Protection Human Participants in Research, 1970-75, chmn., 1983-85, assoc. prof. neurology, 1975-82, prof. neurology and psychiatry, 1982—; dir. lab. neuropsychology, dept. psychiatry Boston U. Sch. Medicine, 1981—; affiliate prof. psychology Clark U., Worcester, Mass., 1975—. Contbr. articles to profl. jours. Coordinator Newton Community Schs. (Mass.), 1978-80. Recipient Research Scientist Devel. award Nat. Inst. Alchol Abuse and Alcholism, 1981-86; Clin. Investigator award VA, 1973-76; USPHS and Dept. Health and Human Services grantee, 1964—. Fellow Mass. Psychol. Assn., Am. Psychol. Assn. (sec.-treas. 1981-83) ; mem. Acad. Aphasia, Soc. Neurosci., Internat. Neuropsychol. Soc., Psychonomic Soc., Huntington's Disease Soc. Am., Internat. Council Psychologists, N.Y. Acad. Scis., Eastern Psychol. Assn. Democrat. Jewish. Office: 150 S Huntington Ave Boston MA 02130

BERMAN, MONA S. (MRS. CARROLL Z. BERMAN), playwright, theatrical director and producer; b. Jersey City; d. Edward and Mary (Auster) Solomon; m. Carroll Z. Berman; children—Marcie S. Berman Ries, Laura Jane. B.A., Beaver Coll., postgrad. Columbia U., M.F.A., Boston U. Tchr. English, drama Jersey City High Schs.; actress Mass. Valley Players, Holyoke; owner, dir. The Theatre Sch. and Producing Co., Maplewood, N.J.; chmn. drama edn. YM-MWHA of Met. N.J. Cons., Clark Ctr. for Performing Arts, N.Y.C., 1965-66; instr. South Orange, Maplewood Adult Sch., 1967; artistic dir. Children's Theatre Co. Inc., Maplewood, 1968-70; cons. The Whole Theater Co., 1974—; dir. pub. relations Co. 3 by 2. Playwright: Hello Joe, 1967; That Ring in the Center, 1968; The Big Show, 1970; Interim, 1974; Who Can Belong?, 1979; Sudden Changes, 1985; Actual Malice, 1987. Producer, dir. A Night of Stars. Guest theatre reviewer El Paso Herald Post, 1980-82. Active Boston United Fund, 1955-59, chmn. Boston residential area, 1957; bd. dirs. Greater Boston Girl Scouts Am., 1956-58, Tufts Med. Faculty Wives, 1956-58. Mem. Am. Theater Assn., Playwrights Unit 42d St. Theater Ctr. N.Y.C., Dramatists Guild. Address: #176 454 Prospect Ave West Orange NJ 07052

BERMAN, OLGA, real estate broker; b. Bklyn., Aug. 10, 1932; d. Percy and Edith (Levy) B. Student, CCNY, 1951-52, Maricopa Tech. Coll., 1967-69, Ariz. State U., 1970, 71, 74. Cert. real estate broker. Broker, owner Aglo Realty, Phoenix, 1984—; instr. A-Mar Sch. Real Estate, Tempe, Ariz., 1987—; designated broker, v.p. David Miller & Assocs. Inc., Phoenix, 1988—. Vol. Hadassah, Reading for the Blind, Phoenix, 1986-87, Nat. Republican party, Phoenix, 1984. Mem. Nat. Assn. Female Execs., Assn. Cert. Profl. Secs. (coordinator nat. conv. 1983-85), Cert. Profl. Secs. Soc. Ariz. (ad hoc chmn. nat. conv.). Jewish. Club: Enterprise Network (Tempe). Home and Office: Aglo Realty 2420 E Clarendon St Phoenix AZ 85016

BERMAN, PATRICIA KARATSIS, visual arts specialist; b. San Francisco, Oct. 2, 1953; d. George Emanuel and Hermoine Linda (Foster) Karatsis; m. William Issachar Berman, May 15, 1979; children: Ian, Melissa, Benjamin. BS, Duke U., 1975; MA, NYU, 1977. Dir. Vorpal Gallery, N.Y.C., 1976-83; visual arts coordinator East End Art and Humanities Council, Riverhead, N.Y., 1983—; cons. N.Y. State Council on Arts, N.Y.C., 1985—, Suffolk Assn. Jewish Schs., Huntington, N.Y., 1985; adj. lectr. dept. anthropology Bklyn. Coll., 1976-77, Drew U., 1977. Contbr. articles to East End Arts News; host cable arts show, 1986-87. Trustee Commack Jewish Ctr., N.Y., 1984-86. Home: 22 Daisy Ln Commack NY 11725 Office: East End Art and Humanities Council 133 E Main St Riverhead NY 11901

BERMAN, SIEGRID VISCONTI, interior designer; b. Bremen, Germany, May 22, 1944; came to U.S., 1951, naturalized, 1956; d. Walter L. and Annegrete M. (Wolf) Knapp; self-educated. Designer, Shepard Martin Assocs., N.Y.C., 1968-76; facilities mgr. Unifert, USA, N.Y.C., 1976-78; owner Siegrid Visconti Berman Interiors, N.Y.C., 1978—; dir. interiors DAT Cons., N.Y.C., 1980-83; dir. design Ralph Mancini Assocs., N.Y.C., 1983-85; sr. designer Karco Davis, Inc., dir. Ten Park Ave Corp., 1979-81. Bd. dirs. Temple Spiritual Research and Learning, 1981-82; reader Lighthouse for Blind. Colo. State Coll. scholar, 1962. Mem. AFTRA, Screen Actors Guild. Composer songs, illustrator book. Office: 52 Duane St New York NY 10007

BERMAN-OLIVO, ROXANNE, health services company executive; b. Durham, N.C., June 22, 1945; d. Morris and Sylvia (Rosenblum) Berman; m. Frank Olivo, Dec. 4, 1965 (div. Apr. 1981); children—Alex, Aaron. B.A., SUNY-N.Y.C., 1983. Asst. dir. pub. relations Assn. Vol. Sterilization, N.Y.C., 1965-69; freelance pub. relations NARAL/ARM, N.Y.C., 1969-80; exec. dir. Nat. Abortion Rights Action League, N.Y.C., 1974-75, Abortion Rights Mobilization, 1977-78; v.p. Comprehensive Profl. Systems, N.Y.C., 1980—; pres. Dynamic Pub. Relations, Inc., 1987—. Lenox Hill Democratic Club, N.Y.C., 1974-76; vice chmn. Community Bd. 6, N.Y.C., 1976-78, chmn. community relations, exec. bd., 1976-80; vice chmn. Beth Israel Methadone Com., N.Y.C., 1976-78; mem. Labor Council, Queens, N.Y., Nassau Civic Club, N.Y.C., 1982—, Nat. Maritime Port Council, N.Y.C., 1983—, Assn. Benefit Adminstrs., N.Y.C., N.Y. Safety Council, March of Dimes, 1985—; bd. dirs. Angel Guardian for Elderly, 1986—. Mem. Nat. Assn. Female Execs., Internat. Found. Pub. Employees Jewish, Dynamic Pub. Relations Inc. (pres. 1986), United Hebrew Trade Assn., N.Y. Labor Council, N.Y. Pub. Sector Coalition. Club: Herut (N.Y.C.) (nat. bd. dirs. 1984-85). Lodge: B'nai B'rith Women's Group. Home: 333 E 23d St New York NY 10010 Office: Comprehensive Profl Systems 144 E 24th St New York NY 10010

BERNABELA, JOSEPHINE E. WALKER, secretarial services executive; b. Boydton, Va., Feb. 8, 1954; d. Joseph Earl and Mattie (Pulliam) Walker; m. McCarthy Lewis II, Apr. 5, 1975 (div.); 1 child, Khaileah Elizabeth; m. Felix Raymond Bernabela, May 4, 1985. BA, Rutgers U., 1977; postgrad., 1980-82. Legal asst. Rutgers U., 1976-80; paralegal Riker, Danzig, Scheerer & Hyland, P.C., Morristown, N.J., 1981, Shanley & Fisher, P.C., Morristown, 1982-83; instr. secretarial sci. Essex County Tech. Career Ctr., Newark, 1984; pres. Courtscribers/Confidential Typing Service, East Orange, N.J., 1975—. Moderator project alert Dept. Child Guidance, Newark, 1981. Grad. and Profl. Edn. grantee, 1981; Legal Edn. Opportunity fellow, 1980. Mem. Nat. Assn. Female Execs. (dir.), Nat. Assn. Secretarial Services, Internat. Profl. Typist Network, Nat. Shorthand Reporters Assn., Rutgers Alumni Assn. (Judge F.J. Bloustein scholar). Office: Courtscribers/Confidential Typing Service PO Box 3276 Brick Church Station East Orange NJ 07019

BERNARD, ANNE ELIZABETH, foreign language educator, academic administrator; b. Lynn, Mass., Mar. 13, 1935; d. Gilbert Edmund and Evelyn Clarissa Brown) B. Asst. credit mgr. patients' accounts Beth Israel Hosp., Brookline, Mass., 1956-57; tchr. Spanish, English and logic Holliston (Mass.) Pub. Schs., 1959-87, dept. chairperson, 1967-81; instrnl. coordinator Holliston High Sch., 1983—; adj. instr. U. Mass., Amherst, 1980-87; cooperating tchr., cons. Framingham (Mass.) State Coll., 1967-87; ptnr. Crystal Assocs., Tewksbury, Mass., 1984—; sec. bd. dirs. Crystal Inc., Tewksbury; cons. Ginn and Co., Boston, 1967-68, Boston Pub. Schs., 1981-84. Author: Role of Senior High School Principals as Instructional Leader, 1984. Dir. Toward Internationalism Program, Holliston, 1979-80; bd. dirs. Boston Internat. Studies and Lang. High Sch., 1981-84; vol. Peace Corps, Bogotá, 1966-67, Framingham Community Ctr., Experiment in Internat. Living, Brattleboro, Vt., Am. Field Service Exchange program, Holliston. Mem. Am. Assn. Teaching Spanish and Portuguese, Am. Council Teaching fgn. Langs., Nat. Assn. Secondary Sch. Prins., Mass. Fgn. Lang. Assn., Phi Delta Kappa. Unitarian. Home: 188 Laurelwood Dr Hopedale MA 01747 Office: Holliston Pub Schs Holliston High Sch Hollis St Holliston MA 01746

BERNARD, CATHY S., management corporation executive; b. Bronx, N.Y., Nov. 13, 1949; d Burton and Norma (Ebb) B. BBA, George Washington U., 1971, M of Pub. Adminstrn., 1978; MA, U. Miami, 1972. Staff asst. HEW, Washington, 1970-74; evaluation specialist OEO, Washington, 1974; tchr. St. Patrick's Acad., Washington, 1975; asst. prof. No. Va. Community Coll., Woodbridge, 1976; staff dir. Dem. Nat. Conv., N.Y.C., 1976; pres., chief exec. officer CSB Assocs. Mgmt. Corp., Hyattsville, Md., 1977—; commr., v.p. Housing Opportunities Commn., Kensington, Md., 1979—, chmn. 1988, vice chair 1980, 87, chair pro tem 1986, chair housing honor roll, 1985-88, MPDU commn.; mem. exec. council Inst. of Real Estate Mgmt., Washington, 1982—, cert. property mgr. Mem. adv. council Suburban Hosp., Bethesda, Md., 1984—; bd. dirs. Jewish Council on Aging, Rockville, Md., 1987, Ivymount Sch. for Handicapped, Potomac, Md., 1986—, Maximun Sav. Bank. Mem. Montgomery County C. of C. (bd. dirs., v.p. housing com. 1981-82), Apt. and Office Bldg. Assn. (bd. dirs.). Office: CSB Assocs Mgmt Corp 5309 38th Ave Hyattsville MD 20781

BERNARD, MARY ELIZABETH, state legislator; b. Dover, N.H.; d. Arthur P. and Margaret (Donnelly) O'Gorman; m. Albert O. Bernard, June 29, 1935. Grad. Carney Hosp. Sch. Nursing, Boston, 1929; student McIntosh Bus. Coll. R.N., Mass. Mem. N.H. Ho. of Reps., 1967-75, 81-87, 5-term mem. regulated revenues com.; historian State of N.H., 1973-74; county clk. County of Strafford (N.H.), 1973-74. Treas. Dem. City Com., Dover, 1965-82; clk. Strafford County Delegation, 1973-74, 81-84. Mem. St. Mary Parish Council, Dover, 1977-80; trustee Cath. Daus. Am., 1977-80.

BERNARDINO, MINERVA, retired ambassador; b. Dominican Republic, May 7, 1907; d. Alvaro and Altagracia (Evangelista) B.; widowed. BS, Santo Domingo U., Dominican Republican. Appointed A. E. and P. of Dominican Republic to Netherlands, 1971, Inspector Embassies and Consulates, 1974; signer of UN Charter, San Francisco, 1945, and OEA Charter; active in equal rights clauses inclusion. Founder Nat. Council for Women, Dominican Republic, 1947; mem. sub-com. on status of women, U.N., 1946; served 14 years Inter-Am. Commn. of Women, OAS, 1945-59; co-founder Commn. on Status of Women, UN, 1948; 1st v.p. ECOSOC, 1957, 1st v.p. exec. bd. UNICEF, 1957; Dominican del. Trusteeship Council UN, 1950-54. Recipient Medal Bolivar and San Martin, 1944, Diploma Nat. Council Negro Women, 1950, Cert. Recognition Nat. Conf. Christians and Jews, 1956, Duarte Decoration Govt. Dominican Republic, 1986, Spl. Gold medal Govt. Dominican Republic; named Woman of Ams. United Women Ams., 1948, Outstanding Dir. Causes of Women in Am. Republics UN, 1949, Most Outstanding Feminist of Yr. United Women Am., 1975; decorated Grand Cross of Order Oranje and Nassau by Queen Juliana Netherlands, 1973. Mem. Am. News Women's Club, United Women Ams., Internat. Platform Assn., Nat. Council Women U.S., LWV, Nat. Assn. Female Execs., Nat. Women's Party, Am. Assn. Internat. Law. Home: 1040 Park Ave 8J New York NY 10028

BERNAS, ELIZABETH ARLENE SNYDER, nurse; b. Mt. Pleasant, Pa., Nov. 25, 1934; d. James H. Snyder and Ruth Catherine (Ferry) Snyder Sprung; m. Albert Earl Bernas, Oct. 1, 1955; children—Debra, Mark, Jeffrey, Brian. R.N., Latrobe Hosp. Sch. Nursing, 1955; postgrad. Lynchburg Coll., 1981. Gen. duty nurse Latrobe Hosp. (Pa.), 1955-57; pvt. duty nurse LaPlata Hosp. (Md.), 1959; vol. nurse ARC, Lynchburg, Va., 1965—; gen. duty nurse Lynchburg Coll., 1969—, coordinator health edn., 1979—, dir. student health services, 1982—. Contbr. articles to profl. jours. Vol., Republican party, Lynchburg, 1968; sec. Blue Ridge Farms Civic Assn., Lynchburg, 1966-67; den mother Boy Scouts Am., Lynchburg, 1966-68; advisor Omni Club, Lynchburg, 1982-87, Sexual Awareness Peer Group, Lynchburg, 1983-86, Alcohol Awareness Group, 1979—; co-coordinator Cen. Va. AIDS Coordinating Counsel, 1987—; vol. nurse Lynchburg Free Clinic, 1987—. Mem. Am. Nurses Assn., Va. Nurses Assn., Am. Coll. Health Assn., Mid-Atlantic Coll. Health Assn. Presbyterian. Clubs: Blumont Garden (historian 1960-63), Order of DeMolay (treas. 1976, 78), Mothers (v.p. 1975-76, pres. 1976). Home: 3025 Cardinal Pl Lynchburg VA 24503 Office: Lynchburg Coll Student Health Services Lynchburg VA 24501

BERNAS, LILIAN HELEN, therapist; b. Winnipeg, Man., Can., July 28, 1948; d. Stanley and Anelia (Walus) B. BPE, U. Man., 1973; MEd, U. Minn., 1980. Cert. therapist in psychogeriatrics. Activity worker Tache Nursing Home, Winnipeg, 1976-78; therapeutic recreation specialist Concordia Hosp., Winnipeg, 1981-88; gerontology educator Red River Community Coll., Winnipeg, 1983—, Tuxedo Villa Personal Care Home, 1988—. Named to Can. Hosps. Honor Roll Concordia Hosp., Winnipeg, 1986. Mem. Nat. Therapeutic Recreation Orgn., Nat. Remotivation Technique Orgn. (instr. 1982—), Assn. Remotivation Therapists Can. (instr. 1982—),

Therapy Dogs Internat. (Pet Therapy Dog of Yr. award 1986), Alzheimer Soc. Can. Mem. New Democratic Party. Roman Catholic. Clubs: Irish Setter Am., Irish Setter Minn. (Mpls.). Home: 852 Talbot Ave, Winnipeg, MB Canada R2L 0S9 Office: Tuxedo Villa Personal Care Home, 2060 Corydon Ave, Winnipeg, MB Canada R2L 0S9

BERNAY, BETTI, artist; b. 1926; d. David Michael and Anna Gaynia (Bernay) Woolin; m. J. Bernard Goldfarb, Apr. 19, 1947; children: Manette Deitsch, Karen Lynn. Grad. costume design, Pratt Inst., 1946; student, Nat. Acad. Design, N.Y.C., 1947-49, Art Students League, N.Y.C., 1950-51. Exhibited one man shows at Galerie Raymond Duncan, Paris, France, Salas Municipales, San Sebastian, Spain, Circulo de Bellas Artes, Madrid, Spain, Bacardi Gallery, Miami, Fla., Columbia (S.C.) Mus., Columbus (Ga.) Mus., Galerie Andre Weil, Paris, Galerie Hermitage, Monte Carlo, Monaco, Casino de San Remo, Italy, Galerie de Arte de la Caja de Ahorros de Ronda, Malaga, Spain, Centro Artistico, Granada, Spain, Circulo de la Amistad, Cordoba, Spain, Studio H Gallery, N.Y.C., Walter Wallace Gallery, Palm Beach, Fla., Mus. Bellas Artes, Malaga, Harbor House Gallery, Crystal House Gallery, Internat. Gallery, Jordan Marsh, Fontainebleau Gallery, Miami Beach, Carriage House Gallery, Galerie 99, Pageant Gallery, Carriage House, Miami Beach, Rosenbaum Galleries, Palm Beach; exhibited group shows at Painters and Sculptors Soc., Jersey City Mus., Salon de Invierno, Mus. Malaga, Salon des Beaux Arts, Cannes, France, Guggenheim Gallery, Nat. Acad. Gallery, Salmagundi Club, Lever House, Lord & Taylor Art Gallery, Nat. Arts Gallery, Knickerbocker Artists, N.Y.C., Salon des Artistes Independants, Salon des Artistes Francais, Salon Populiste, Paris, Salon de Otono, Nat. Assn. Painters and Sculptors Spain, Madrid, Phipps Gallery, Palm Beach, Artists Equity, Hollywood (Fla.) Mus., Gault Gallery Cheltenham, Phila., Springfield (Mass.) Mus., Met. Mus. and Art Center, Miami, Fla., Planet Ocean Mus., Charter Club, Trade Fair Ams., Guggenheim Gallery, N.Y.C.; represented in permanent collections including Jockey Club Art Gallery, Miami, Mus. Malaga, Circulo de la Amistad, I.O.S. Found., Geneva, Switzerland, others. Bd. dirs. Men's Opera Guild; mem. adv. bd. Jackson Meml. Hosp. Project Newborn; mem. women's com. Bascon Palmer Eye Inst.; active Greater Miami Heart Assn., Alzheimer Grand Notable, 2d Generation Miami Heart Inst., Sunrisers Mentally Retarded, Orchid Ball Com. Recipient medal City N.Y., medal Sch. Art Leagues, N.Y.C., Prix de Paris Raymond Duncan, 1958, others. Mem. Nat. Assn. Painters and Sculptors Spain, Nat. Assn. Women Artists, Société des Artistes Français, Société des Artistes Independants, Fedn. Francais des Sociétés d'Art Graphique et Plastique, Artists Equity, Am. Artists Profl. League, Am. Fedn. Art, Nat. Soc. Lit. and Arts, Met. Mus. and Arts Center Miami. Clubs: Palm Bay, Jockey, Turnberry, Club of Clubs Internat. Address: 10155 Collins Ave Apt 1705 Bal Harbour FL 33154

BERNHARDT, LOIS E., graduate counselor; b. Columbia, Pa., Jan. 20, 1939; d. Ralph Emerson and Helen (Garrett) Donley; m. Henry John Bernhardt, Sept. 24, 1940; 1 child, Carole Ann. BS, Lancaster Bible Coll., 1960; postgrad., Western States U. Cert. teaching, Pa. Tchr. bus. Cen. Bapt. Christian High Sch., Hampton, Va., 1974-78; computer operator Black Hawk div. U.S. Army, Ft. Campbell, Ky., 1979-80; acct. U.S. Army Commissary, Ft. Campbell, Ky., 1980-81; tchr. substitute Ft. Campbell High Sch., 1981-83; clinic coordinator USAF Dental Clinic, Reese AFB, Tex., 1984-85; counselor grad. coll. bus. Tex. Tech. U., Lubbock, 1985—; proofreader, asst. editor Southwestern Pub. Co., Cin., 1984-85. Author: Pastor's Operating Office, 1978. Mem. Protestant Women of Chapel (pres. 1980-82). Named Tchr. of Yr. MeLonie Park Bapt. Ch., 1986. Mem. ARC (local chpt. pres. 1962-72, Ten-Yr. award 1976), Girl Scouts Am., Am. Bus. Women Assn., Toastmasters Internat., Nat. Assn. Female Execs., Officer's Wives (nursery coordinator 1969-70, sec. 1970-71). Republican. Home: 5510 First Pl Lubbock TX 79416 Office: Tex Tech U PO Box 4320 Lubbock TX 79406

BERNHEIM, HEATHER STANCHFIELD PETERSON (MRS. CHARLES BERNHEIM), civic worker; b. Houston; d. Weed and Mylla (Stanchfield) Peterson; student U. Tex., 1938-42; m. Charles A. Bernheim, July 18, 1973. Docent chmn. Harris County Heritage Soc., 1969-70, v.p., after 1970; vol. worker Hermann Hosp., 1968-69; team capt. Mus. Fine Arts Ball, Houston, 1969; maintenance fund drive worker Mus. Fine Arts, 1970, trustee, chmn. costume council, 1986-88; docent Costume Inst., Met. Mus. Art, N.Y.C., 1978, co-chmn. Costume Inst., 1980-81, chmn., 1981-82, mus. guide, 1978—; chmn. Costume Inst. Mus. Fine Arts, Houston; trustee Mus. Fine Arts, Houston; auction chmn. Bluebonnet Ball, Harris County Heritage Soc., 1984; bd. dirs. Planned Parenthood N.Y.C. Mem. N.Y. Jr. League, Kappa Alpha Theta Alumni Assn. Club: Houston. Home: 33 E 70th St Apt S-E New York NY 10021 Other: 173 Sage Rd Houston TX 77056

BERNINGER, LORI DOBBS, research executive; b. N.Y.C., Apr. 6, 1961; d. Albert Michael and Veronic (Barrett) Dobbs; m. Daniel Joseph Berninger, Sept. 29, 1984; 1 child, Katherine. BA in Communication Arts, Villanova U., 1983. Research assoc. Johnson, Smith & Knisely, Inc., N.Y.C., 1984, Fulton, Longshore & Assocs., Inc., Haverford, Pa., 1984-85; dir. research MSL Internat., Ltd., Phila., 1985-87; co-owner Classic Homes, Inc., Phila., 1987—; founder, mem Phila. Exec. Search/Research Roundtable, pres. 1986—. Mem. Am. Acad. Health Adminstrn., Phila. Jr. League, Am. Sokol. Orgn. Home: 4612 Chester Ave Philadelphia PA 19143 Office: Classic Homes Inc 4612 Chester Ave Philadelphia PA 19143

BERNINZONI, LAUREL ANN, nurse; b. Bloomington, Ill., Sept. 13, 1939; d. Everett Arnold and Lucille Marcella (Blazina) Boston; m. Ralph Allen Berninzoni, Aug. 25, 1963; children: Jon, Thom, J.R. Diploma in nursing, Mercy Hosp., 1960. RN, Wis., Colo. Mem. nursing staff Ft. Atkinson (Wis.) Hosp., 1960-61; asst. head nurse St. Anthony's Hosp., Denver, 1961-63; tchrs. asst. nurse Jefferson County Schs. for Emotionally Disturbed Children, Denver, 1974-79; nurse Arvada (Colo.) Health Ctr., 1976-80; staff nurse Colo. Luth. Health Care, Arvada, 1980—. Safety coordinator Neighborhood Schs., Arvada; mem. PTA and Room Mother, Arvada, 1969-80; team mother Arvada Football, Soccer and Baseball League, 1973-78. Fellow Colo. Nurses Assn. Republican. Roman Catholic. Home: 6823 Teller Ct Arvada CO 80003

BERNSTEIN, AIMEE SUSAN, psychotherapist, management consultant, educator; b. N.Y.C., Feb. 27, 1949; d. Walter and Sally (Grossman) B. BA, Hunter Coll., 1969; MEd in Counseling Psychology, Boston U., 1975. Cert. marriage family and child counselor, Calif. Counselor New Perspectives, Larkspur, Calif., 1975-78; cons. Marin Juvenile Probation, Larkspur, 1975-78; founder, dir. Living Arts Sch., Marin County, Calif., 1978-80; div. mgr. Lawrence & Assocs., San Rafael and San Francisco, Calif., 1980-83; founder, pres. Women's Devel. Co., Mill Valley and San Francisco, Calif., 1983—; founder and pres. Aimee Bernstein & Assocs., San Francisco and Ft. Lauderdale, Fla., 1986—. Co-writer rock 'n' roll opera (televised on ABC-TV show Tell It Like It Is, 1969). promoter Women Emerging Internat. Inst., Marin County, 1987. Brown belt, aikido 1972. Mem. Calif. Assn. Marriage Family and Child Counselors, NOW, Nat. Assn. Female Execs. Democrat. Jewish. Home: 28 Lower Alcatraz Pl Mill Valley CA 94941

BERNSTEIN, CAROL, molecular biologist; b. Paterson, N.J., Mar. 20, 1941; d. Benjamin and Mina (Regenbogen) Adelberg; m. Harris Bernstein, June 7, 1962; children—Beryl, Golda, Benjamin. B.S. in Physics, U. Chgo., 1961; M.S. in Biophysics, Yale U, 1964; Ph.D. in Genetics, U. Calif.-Davis, 1967. NIH fellow zoology dept. U. Calif.-Davis, 1967-68; research assoc. microbiology dept. U. of Ariz., Tucson, 1968-75, adj. asst. prof., 1975-81, research assoc. prof. microbiology coll. of medicine, 1981—; proposal reviewer NSF, 1978-82, VA, 1983; panel mem grad fellow review NSF, 1984-86. Contbr. articles to prof. jours. Grantee NSF, 1975-77, 77-79, NIH, 1979-81, 82—, Nat. Found., 1975-76. Mem. AAUP (pres. Ariz. state conf. 1983-86, pres. Ariz. chpt. 1983, del. to nat. council 1986—), Am. Soc. Microbiology (invited speaker 1982), Genetics Soc. Am. Democrat. Home: 2639 E 4th St Tucson AZ 85716 Office: U Ariz Coll Med Dept Microbiology & Immunology Tucson AZ 85724

BERNSTEIN, CARYL SALOMON, lawyer; b. N.Y.C., Dec. 22, 1933; d. Gustav and Rosalind (Aron) Salomon; m. William D. Terry, June 12, 1955 (div. 1967); children: Ellen Deborah, Mark David; m. Robert L. Cole, Jr., Oct. 25, 1970 (div. 1975); m. George K. Bernstein, June 17, 1979. B.A. with honors, Cornell U., 1955; J.D., Georgetown U., 1967. Bar: D.C. 1968, U.S. Dist. Ct. D.C. 1968, U.S. Ct. Appeals (D.C. cir.) 1968, U.S. Supreme Ct. 1971. Atty. Covington & Burling, Washington, 1967-73; staff atty. Overseas Pvt. Investment Corp., Washington, 1973-74, asst. gen. counsel, 1974-77, v.p. for ins., 1977-81; sr. v.p., gen. counsel, sec. Fed. Nat. Mortgage Assn., Washington, 1981-82, exec. v.p., gen. counsel, sec., 1982—; dir. Nat. Housing Conf., 1983—. Contbr. articles to profl. jours., chpt. to book; mem. bd. editors Georgetown Law Jour., 1966; mem. editorial adv. bd. Housing and Devel. Reporter, 1986-88. Mem. bd. regents Georgetown U., 1986—; bd. dirs. Council for Ct. Excellence, Washington, 1986—. N.Y. Regents scholar, 1951-55. Mem. ABA, Fed. Bar Assn., D.C. Bar Assn., Phi Beta Kappa, Phi Kappa Phi. Office: Fed Nat Mortgage Assn Office Chmn 3900 Wisconsin Ave NW Washington DC 20016

BERNSTEIN, JOAN EVE, writer, editor, producer; b. N.Y.C.; d. Leo and Hope (North) B. BA summa cum laude, U. Rochester, 1976. Host, interviewer, producer Warner Cable TV, Somerville, Mass., 1977-78; researcher, writer Sta. WBZ-TV, Boston, 1978; newscaster, writer, reporter Sta. WERS-FM, Boston, 1979; news anchor, producer, reporter Sta. WLBZ-TV, Bangor, Maine, 1979, Sta. WCSH-TV, Portland, Maine, 1979; newscaster, producer, editor, reporter Sta. WGSM/WCTO, L.I., N.Y., 1980-83; stringer reporter The Associated Press, N.Y.C., 1981-83; newswriter, editor, producer Am. Broadcasting Co., Inc., N.Y.C., 1983—; actress, singer Springfield St. Dinner Theater, Cambridge, Mass., 1978; narrator, radio commls. , Huntington, N.Y., 1981-82; narrator, actress Vanderbilt Planetarium Centerport, N.Y., 1982-83, Hayden Planetarium, N.Y.C., 1984; tchr. English The Internat. Ctr. N.Y., Inc., 1986-88. Mem. Writers Guild Am., AFTRA, Phi Beta Kappa. Democrat. Office: ABC Radio News 125 West End Ave New York NY 10023

BERNT, CHARLOTTE IRENE, college library administrator; b. Denver, Nov. 9, 1953; d. Harold Eugene Smith and Loretta Marie (Gillham) Schmidt; m. Thomas Joseph Bernt, July 2, 1969; children: Marcus Thomas, Michele Irene. BS in Computer Sci. and Bus. Adminstrn., Kearney (Nebr.) State Coll., 1981, MS in Bus. Adminstrn., 1984. Office mgr. Knapp, Mues, Anderson, et al Law Offices, Kearney, 1981-82; computer programmer Stanal Sound, Ltd., Kearney, 1982; owner, mgr. Computers In Bus., Kearney, 1982-84; instr. Kearney State Coll., 1983—, head access services Calvin T. Ryan Library, 1984—; cons. bus. computers, computer programmer, Kearney, 1987—. Author computer programs. Active Buffalo County Dems., Kearney, 1980—; sec. Kearney Area Baseball Assn., 1986—. Mem. Jr. Mems. Round Table of Nebr. Librarians Assn. (planning com. 1987—), Nebr. Library Assn., Kearney State Coll. Faculty Women, Nat. Assn. for Female Execs. Roman Catholic. Home: 1 Hillcrest Dr Kearney NE 68847 Office: Kearney State Coll Calvin T Ryan Library Kearney NE 68849

BERNTSON, ALICE ROBISON, employee relations administrator; b. Evanston, Ill., Sept. 27, 1952; d. Charles Bennett and Katherine Louise (Parkins) Robison; m. Tom Jack Berntson, Mar. 29, 1975. BA in Psychology, Western Ill. U., 1974; MS in Indsl. Relations, Iowa State U., 1977. Indsl. engring. analyst John Deere Harvester Works, East Moline, Ill., 1978-81, suggestion coordinator, 1981-82; indsl. relations asst. Agripac Inc., Salem, Oreg., 1982-83, employee relations adminstr., 1983—. Loaned exec. United Way, Salem, 1986; chmn. Mid-Willamette Pvt. Industry Council, Salem, 1988—; mem. Youth Coordinating Council, Salem, 1987. Mem. Pacific NW Personnel Mgrs.' Assn. (pres. 1987). Democrat. Club: Phidippides Running. Home: 365 Kevin Ct SE Salem OR 97306 Office: Agripac Inc 325 Patterson NW Salem OR 97304

BERO, MARILYN PROCINO, civic worker, corporate professional; b. Auburn, N.Y., Sept. 12, 1937; d. Jack Anthony and Mary Louise (Cefaratti) Procino; B.A. in Elem. Edn., Marywood Coll., 1959; postgrad. Syracuse U., 1961; m. James Donald Bero, Feb. 10, 1962; children—Mark J., Michael A., Matthew R. Tchr. 3d grade Auburn Sch. System, 1959-61. Sec.-treas. Hampton Rd. Constrn. Corp., Seneca Falls, N.Y. Mem. Seneca Falls (N.Y.) Sch. Dist. Bd., 1976-85, v.p., 1978, pres., 1980-83, dir., 1978—; co-chmn. bldg. fund drive Nat. Women's Hall of Fame, Inc., Seneca Falls, 1978-79, pres., 1980-83; bd. dirs. Seneca County Child Care Ctr., 1975-84, pres., 1976-79; bd. dirs. Alpha Day Sch., Seneca Falls, 1972-75, Happiness House, Geneva, N.Y., 1968-72, CAUSE; adv. commn. Women's Rights Nat. Hist. Park. Named Rotary Citizen of Yr., 1983. Mem. AAUW, Women's League Seneca Falls (pres. 1978-79). Republican. Roman Catholic. Home: Box 670 2934 Route 89 Seneca Falls NY 13148 Office: Hampton Rd Construction Corp 2934 Rt 89 Seneca Falls NY 13148

BERON, GAIL LASKEY, real estate analyst, consultant, appraiser; b. Detroit, Nov. 13, 1943; d. Charles Jack Laskey and Florence B. (Rosenthal) Eisenberg; divorced; children: Monty Charles, Bryan David. Cert. real estate analyst, Mich. Chief/staff appraiser Ft. Wayne Mortgage Co., Birmingham, Mich., 1973-75; pvt. practice fee appraiser S.C., Iowa, Mich., 1976-80; pres. The Beron Co., Southfield, Mich., 1980—; cons. ptnr. Real Estate Counseling Group Conn., Storrs, 1983—, Real Estate Counseling Group Am., prin., 1984—; lectr. real estate confs. Recipient M. William Donnally award Mortgage Bankers Assn. Am., 1975. Mem. Soc. Real Estate Appraisers (bd. dirs. Detroit chpt. 1980-82, nat. faculty mem. 1983—), Am. Inst. Real Estate Appraisers (bd. dirs. Detroit chpt. 1982-86, nat. faculty mem. 1984—), Nat. Assn. Realtors, Detroit Bd. Realtors, Southfield Bd. Realtors, Women Brokers Assn. (treas. Southfield chpt. 1981-83), Young Mortgage Bankers (bd. dirs. 1974-75). Lodge: B'nai Brith. Home: 7008 Bridge Way West Bloomfield MI 48322 Office: Beron Co 17228 W Hampton Rd Southfield MI 48075

BERRA, PAMELA MARIA, marketing professional; b. Coshocton, Ohio, Mar. 10, 1956; d. William Lewis and Marjorie (McCowan) B.; married Clifton Wayne Swafford, Oct. 12, 1985; 1 child, Cody Michelle. BA, Knox Coll., Galesburg, Ill., 1978. Sales rep. Cert. Furniture Leasing Co., Dallas, 1978-80, Standard Register Co., Chgo., 1980-81, R.J. Reynolds Tobacco Co., Lombard, Ill., 1981-85; mgr. merchandising R.J. Reynolds Tobacco Co., Lombard, 1985-86; mgr. devel.,tng. RJR Sales Co., Aurora, Ill., 1986—. Mem. Nat. Assn. Female Execs., Tobacco Action Network, Delta Delta Delta (v.p. Chgo chpt. 1986-87, pres. 1987-89, pledge advisor, 1981-83, corr. sec. 1981-83). Roman Catholic. Home: 97 Newton Ave Glen Ellyn IL 60137

BERRET, BETH ANN, employment manager; b. Endicott, N.Y., Oct. 12, 1956; d. Edward Harvey and Esther Caroline (Webber) Bachman; m. James Joseph Berret, Aug. 27, 1983. B.S., Bloomsburg U., 1978; M.B.A., Phila. Coll. Textiles & Sci., 1984. Asst. to adminstr. Homeland, Harrisburg, Pa., 1978; asst. adminstr. Cameron Manor, Indiana, Pa., 1978-80; employment rep. The Fairmount Inst., Phila., 1980-82; employment mgr. The Reading Hosp. and Med. Ctr., Pa., 1982—. Mem. Hosp. Employment Mgrs. Phila., Internat. Assn. Personnel Women, Am. Soc. Personnel Adminstrn., Nat. Assn. Nurse Recruiters. Home: 1840 Shellbark Dr Sinking Spring PA 19608 Office: The Reading Hosp and Med Ctr Reading PA 19603

BERRIEN, EDITH HEAL, author, educator emeritus; b. Chgo., Aug. 23, 1903; d. Charles Frederick and Eva (Page) Heal; m. Gil Meynier, Oct. 30, 1930 (div. 1944); m. Stephen Berrien, Nov. 22, 1944 (dec. 1982). P.H.B., U. Chgo., 1925; M.A., Columbia U., 1956. Copywriter advt. dept. Marshall Field & Co., Chgo., 1926-28, Sears Roebuck & Co., Chgo., 1930-35, Tucson Daily Citizen, 1935-42; copy chief promotions Conde Nast Publs., N.Y.C., 1944-53, 58-70; prof. Fairleigh Dickinson U., Rutherford N.J., 1953-74. Author: Robin Hood, 1928; The Topaz Seal, 1928; Siegfried, How the World Began, 1930; How the World is Changing, 1931; (as Margaret Powers) World of Insects, 1931; (as Eileen Page) Hound of Culain, 1931; Mr. Pink and the House on the Rook, 1941; (with Louis E. Asher) Send No Money, 1942; Dogie Boy, 1943; This Very Sun, 1944; The Golden Bowl, 1947; Teen-Age Manual, 1948; First Book of America, 1952; Tim Trains his Terrier, 1952; The Shadow Boxers, 1956; (with William Carlos Williams) I Wanted to Write a Poem, 1958; The Young Executive's Wife, 1958; What Happened to Jenny, 1962; (as Edith Heal Berrien) Visual Thinking in Advertising, 1963; Careers, 1966; August Break, 1984; contbr. short stories and articles to jours. in field. Past bd. dirs. Women's Met. Golf Assn. Mem. Soc. Midland Authors.

BERRY, ANN ROPER, diplomat; b. Cleve., Nov. 9, 1934; d. Frank Carson and Doris (Decker) Roper; m. Maxwell K. Berry, Feb. 11, 1959; children: Walter F., Helen D. BA, Ohio Wesleyan U., 1956; MEd, U. Md., 1964. Asst. budget and fiscal officer Am. embassy, Baghdad, Iraq, 1958-59; various teaching positions, Turkey, Zambia and U.S., 1961-75; internat. economist Dept. of State, Washington, 1975-77. asst. chief textiles div., 1977-80; econ. officer Am. embassy, Athens, Greece, 1980-82; dep. chief textile negotiator U.S. Trade Rep., Washington, 1982-84; mem. NATO Def. Coll., Rome, 1984; counselor for econ. affairs Am. embassy, Paris, 1985—. Recipient Superior Honor award Dept. of State, 1980. Mem. Phi Beta Kappa. Office: Am Embassy-Econ APO New York NY 09777

BERRY, AUDREY BERNITA, nurse; b. Bklyn., May 1, 1955; d. Herbert and Helen Caroline (Moore) Screen; B.S. in Nursing, Russell Sage Coll., 1977; cert. in public adminstrn., Dyke Coll., 1982; m. Tommie Berry, Jr., May 12, 1978; children—Lenore Marie, Patrice. Staff nurse Univ. Hosps. Cleve., 1977-78; public health nurse Vis. Nurses Assn., Cleve., 1978-79, Maternity and Infant Care Project, Cleve., 1979-80; nurse, med. team mgr. Kenneth W. Clement Center Family Health Care, Cleve., 1980-84; nurse mgr. Huron Road Hosp., Cleve., 1984-86; pharm. sales rep. Smith Kline & French, 1986—. Registered nurse, Ohio. Mem. Cleve. Council Black Nurses, Assn. for Practitioners in Infection Control, Nat. Pharm. Assn., Nat. Assn. Female Execs., AAUW.

BERRY, CAROLYN, artist; b. Sweet Springs, Mo., June 27, 1930; d. Charles Thomas and Florence Valora (Harrison) B.; m. Robert E. Becker, Oct. 13, 1974; m. Benjamin Bishop, Oct. 12, 1952; children—Deborah Rachael, Rebecca. Student Columbia (Mo.) Coll., 1948-49; B.A., U. Mo., 1953; postgrad. in spl. edn. Humboldt U., 1969-71. One person shows include: Monterey Peninsula Mus. Art, 1966, 75, Marist Coll., Poughkeepsie, N.Y., 1969, Studio Performance, Palo Alto, Calif., 1980, Pacific Grove Art Ctr., UCLA, 1985, Douglass Library, Rutgers U., 1988; group exhbns. include: Franklin Furnance, 1980, Sao Paulo Biennale, Brazil, 1981, Women's Caucus For Art, N.Y.C., 1982, Long Beach Mus. Art, 1983, Otis/Parsons, Pratt U., La. World Expn., 1984, Bookworks Washington Project for the Arts, 1982, 85, Clocktower, N.Y.C., 1985, Tex. Women's U., 1986, Nova Scotia Tech. U., 1986, Am. Cultural Ctrs., New Delhi, Bombay, Ahmedabad, and Madras, India, 1987, King Stephen Mus., Hungary, 1987, Mcpl. Mus., Lyon, France, 1987, Library of Louis Aragon, Choisy le Roi, France, 1987; represented in permanent collection: Monterey Peninsula Mus. Art, Brandeis U., Waltham, Mass., Zone, Springfield, Mass., Tweed Mus., Duluth, Minn., Ind. Press Archive, Rochester, N.Y., Internat. Women's Collection, Copenhagen, Portland (Maine) Sch. Art, Art Inst. Chgo., Marvin Sackner Collection, Judith Hoffberg Collection, UCLA, Spl. Collections Library U. Calif. Santa Cruz; dir. Handicapped Activities Unltd., Pacific Grove, Calif., 1971—. Calif. Arts Council grantee, 1980; recipient Best Small Painting award Pacific Grove Mus. Natural History, 1981. Mem. Womens Caucus for the Arts, Internat. Soc. Copier Arts, Nat. Womens Polit. Caucus. Home: 78 Cuesta Vista Dr Monterey CA 93940 Office: Handicapped Activities Unltd 511 Grand Ave Pacific Grove CA 93950

BERRY, EVE MARIE, executive; b. Austin, Tex., July 21, 1950; d. Jim Smither and Helen (Kirby) B.; m. Anthony Joseph Smokovich, Sept. 16, 1979; children: Erin, Sean. BA, Ind. U., 1972, MA, 1977. Program dir. human resources City Bloomington, Ind., 1973-75, dep. controller, 1975-77; sr. cons., trainer The Grantsmanship Ctr., Los Angeles, 1977-79; pres. Mgmt. Dimensions, Inc., Nashville, 1978—; v.p. EQUICOR-Equitable HCA Corp., N.Y.C., Nashville, 1986-88; cons. Equitable, N.Y.C., 1978-86, Chase Manhattan Bank, N.Y.C., 1983-85, Mfrs. Hanover, N.Y.C., 1985-86. Mem. Planning Forum, Am. Soc. Tng. Devel. Home: 1206 Chickering Rd Nashville TN 37215 Office: 1801 West End Ave Nashville TN 37203

BERRY, MARY ALICE, religious organization administrator; b. Gainesville, Tex., Jan. 8, 1951; d. Travis S. and Bernice Elizabeth (Hayles) B. BA, Baylor U., 1974; MRE, Southwestern Bapt. Theol. Sem., 1982. Prodn. crew Sta. KTVT-TV, Ft. Worth, 1974-76; evangelism coordinator div. student work, Bapt. Gen. Conv. Tex., Dallas, 1976-77; asst. dir. student work Stephen F. Austin State U. Baptist Gen. Conv. Tex., Nacogdoches, 1977-80; min. youth Capital Heights Bapt. Ch., Montgomery, Ala., 1980-83; min. preschool children and youth First Bapt. Ch., Hereford, Tex., 1983-85; dir. media services First Bapt. Ch., Amarillo, Tex., 1985—. Mem. pub. relations adv. com. Bapt. Gen. Conv. Tex. Home: 2832 Mays Amarillo TX 79109 Office: First Bapt Ch Tyler and 13th Amarillo TX 79101

BERRY, NANCY ARLENE, trade association executive; b. Wilson, N.C., Oct. 9, 1946; d. Johnnie Lee and Lillie Louise (Teel) Freeman; m. Patrick Joseph Berry, Aug. 26, 1967; children: Shannon Leigh, Brian Alan. BS in Edn., Fla. State U., 1967; tchr. recertification, St. Petersburg Jr. Coll., 1972; diploma, U. South Fla., 1985; diploma in orgn. mgmt., U. Okla., 1987. Cert. assn. exec. Claims processor Aetna Life and Casualty, Los Angeles, 1968-69; adminstrv. asst. Fla. Bankers Assn., Orlando, 1979-81, registrar, program asst., 1981-84, edn. officer, 1984—. Contbr. articles to profl. jours., mags., newsletters. Vol. Am. Heart Assn., Am. Cancer Soc., March of Dimes; bd. dirs. Homeowners Assn. Mem. Am. Soc. Assn. Execs., Nat. Assn. Female Execs., Fla. Soc. Assn. Execs. (vice chmn. profl. advancement com. 1986—), Cen. Fla. Soc. Assn. Execs. (chmn. newsletter com., dir.-at-large 1987—, scholar 1987). Office: Fla Bankers Assn 341 N Mills Ave Orlando FL 32803

BERRY, PEGGY SUE, public relations executive; b. Chgo., Apr. 11, 1956; d. Charles Vernon and Evelyn Elizabeth (Paus) Berry. Cert., McHenry Community Coll., 1977. Hostess McNeils of McHenry (Ill.) Inc., 1971-73; mgr. restaurant ops. Baron of Beef Inc., Fox Lake, Ill., 1973-76; supr. costume cleaning Marriott Great Am. Park, Gurnee, Ill., 1976-78; supr. plant shipping Owens Nursery-Burgess Seed Co., Bloomington, Ill., 1978-80; audio-visual tech. I Ill. State U., Normal, 1980-84, audio-visual tech. II, 1984-86, mgr. media distbn., 1986—. Mem. Nat. Assn. Female Execs., Internat. Communications Industries Assn., Smithsonian Assocs., U.S. Postal Commemorative Soc., NOW.

BERRY, ROSE BRIGID, social worker; b. McBride Canyon, N.M., Mar. 5, 1926; d. Patrick James and Bertha Cecilia (MacDonald) Berry; B.A., Mount St. Scholastica Coll., 1947; M.S.W., St. Louis U., 1950. Med. social worker Colo. State Hosp., Pueblo, 1948-49; asst. dir. social service VA Hosp., Phoenix, 1951-55; dir., clin. social work cons. social service dept. Phoenix Indian Med. Center, 1956-82; individual practice clin. social worker, 1982—. Mem. Internat. Med. Soc. Paraplegia (asso.), Nat. Assn. Social Workers, Clin. Social Workers Soc., St. Louis U. Alumni Assn. Republican. Roman Catholic. Home: 3894 N 30th St Phoenix AZ 85016

BERRYMAN, KARAN ANN, librarian; b. Cuthbert, Ga., June 26, 1956; d. John Robert and Wilda (Fowler) B.; A.A. cum laude, Andrew Coll., 1975; B.S. with high honors, Auburn U., 1977; M.S.L.S., U. N.C., Chapel Hill, 1979. Dir. library Andrew Coll., Cuthbert, 1980-84; head reference services Louise Wise Lewis Library, Flagler Coll., St. Augustine, Fla., 1984-87; dir. Kinchafoonee Regional Library, Dawson, Ga., 1987-88; hist. researcher, Cuthbert, Ga., 1988—; book reviewer regional publs. Mem. ALA, Southeastern Library Assn., Original Muscogee County Geneal. Soc., Ga. Library Assn., Phi Kappa Phi, Phi Theta Kappa. Club: Pilot (Cuthbert). Home and Office: 111 W Harris St Cuthbert GA 31740

BERRYMAN, MARY, computer systems executive; b. LaGrande, Oreg., Feb. 2, 1947; d. Joseph Leslie and Bonnie Bertha (Osborn) Berryman; 1 child, Barney Justin. B.S. in Secondary Edn./Math. cum laude Eastern Oreg. State Coll., 1969; postgrad. Oreg. State U., 1969-71, Eastern Oreg. State Coll., 1983-85. Programmer, Oreg. State U., Corvallis, 1969-71; sec. Morrow County Extension, Heppner, Oreg., 1972-75; ins. agt. Grange Ins., Union County, Oreg., 1978-81; mgr. regional software E.O.S. Coll., LaGrande, Oreg., 1979-80; systems analyst Computer Ctr., Eastern Oreg. State Coll., 1980-85; system mgr., 1985—, coordinator accad. computing systems, 1985—. Author: OS-3: A User's Manual, 1968, ALGOL: A User's Manual, 1969, OSCAR: A User's Manual, 1969. Den Mother Cub Scouts Den 3, LaGrande, 1984—. Oreg. State U. grad. research assistantship in math., 1969-71. Mem. N.W. Council for Computers in Edn. (treas. 1980-81), Internat. Council for Computers in Edn., Sigma Alpha Chi (treas. 1967-68). Democrat. Methodist. Office: Ea Oreg State Coll Computer Ctr 8th and K LaGrande OR 97850

BERSHAD, KAREN FRANCES, commercial printing company executive; b. Amityville, N.Y., Mar. 29, 1948; d. Wallace Franklin Haskins and Beverly June (Robinson) Rosenthal; m. Barry Gilbert Bershad, Apr. 2, 1978; stepchildren—Ira, Michael, Elissa. Student pub. schs., Amityville. Pres. Plaza Printing Co., Inc. Mem. Sales & Mktg. Execs.-Atlanta, Women Bus. Owners, Nat. Assn. Printers and Lithographers, Ga. Hospitality and Travel Assn., Printing Assn. Ga., Women's C. of C. (bd. dirs.), Atlanta C. of C. Republican. Methodist.

BERSON, JUDITH S., college administrator, automotive executive; b. Bronx, N.Y., Jan. 27, 1945; d. Dudley J. and Beatrice (Mandelberg) B.; m. Thomas Lawrence, July 3, 1967 (div. 1972); m. Zvi Levinson, Dec. 19, 1986. BS, Fairleigh Dickinson U., 1966; MA, Montclair State Coll., 1973. Bookkeeper Creston Industries Inc., Passaic, N.J., 1960-65; jr. acct. Biber & Lawrence CPAs, Fair Lawn, N.J., 1965-67; employment counselor Englewood, N.J., 1967-72; asst. dir. fin. aid Kean Coll. of N.J., Union, N.J., 1972-73; assoc. dir. fin. aid Fairleigh Dickinson U., Teaneck, N.J., 1973-74; dir. fin. aid U. Miami, Coral Gables, Fla., 1974-75, Miami (Fla.)-Dade Community Coll., 1975-81; dir. fin. services Broward Community Coll., Ft. Lauderdale, Fla., 1981—; pres. Equipment Enterprises Inc., Miami, 1983—. Recipient Service to Community award Miami Cuban Lions Club, 1979, Exemplary Practice award Fla. Assn. Community Colls., 1979. Mem. Fla. Assn. Student Fin. Aid Adminstrs. (cert.; bd. dirs. 1983—, editor newsletter 1983—, pres. 1988—), So. Assn. Student Fin. Aid Adminstrs., Nat. Assn. Women Bus. Owners. Jewish. Office: Broward Community Coll 3501 SW Davie Rd Fort Lauderdale FL 33314

BERSON, RONA, pharmaceutical marketing executive; b. Johannesburg, South Africa, Sept. 24, 1937; came to U.S., 1977; d. Theodore and Bettye (Hershel) Grishman; widowed; children: Anthony, Brian, Michele, Martin. Degree in pharmacy, Johannesburg Tech. Coll., 1958. V.p. mktg. Rio Ethicals, (PTY) Ltd., Johannesburg, 1968-77; v.p. sales Springbok Pharms., Houston, 1981-86, Swistex Pharms., Houston, 1986—. Office: Swistex Pharms 7000 Fannin Suite 1810 Houston TX 77030

BERT, CAROL LOIS, educational aide; b. Bakersfield, Calif., Oct. 15, 1938; d. Edwin Vernon and Shirley Helen (Craig) Phelps; m. John Davison Bert, Sept. 26, 1964; children—Mary Ellen, John Edwin, Craig Eric, Douglas Ethan. B.S. in Nursing, U. Colo., 1960. Med. surg. nurse U.S. Army, Washington, 1960-62, Ascom City, Korea, 1962 63, San Antonio, 1963, Albuquerque, 1964-65; tchrs. aide Jefferson County Schs., Arvada, Colo., 1979—. Sec. Parent, Tchr., Student Assn. Arvada West High Sch., 1987-88. Club: Colo. Quilting Council (1st v.p.). Avocations: reading, quilting, camping, fishing, tennis. Home: 5844 Oak St Arvada CO 80004 Office: Allendale Elem Sch 5900 Oak St Arvada CO 80004

BERT, CLARA VIRGINIA, home economics educator, administrator; b. Quincy, Fla., Jan. 29, 1929; d. Harold C. and Ella J. (McDavid) B. B.S., Fla. State U., 1950, M.S., 1963, Ph.D., 1967. Cert. tchr., Fla.; cert. home economist. Tchr. Union County High Sch., Lake Butler, Fla., 1950-53, Havana High Sch., Fla., 1953-65; cons. research and devel. Fla. Dept. Edn., Tallahassee, 1967-75, sect. dir. research and devel., 1975-85, program dir. home econs. edn., 1985—; cons. Nat. Ctr. Research in Vocat. Edn., Ohio State U., 1978; field reader U.S. Dept. Edn., 1974-75. Author/editor booklets. U.S. Office Edn. grantee, 1976, 77, 78. Mem. Am. Home Econs. Assn. (state treas. 1969-71), Am. Vocat. Assn., Fla. Vocat. Assn., Fla. Vocat. Home Econs., Fla. Home Econs., Am. Vocat. Edn. Research Assn. (nat. treas. 1970-71), Nat. Council Family Relations, Nat. Assn. State Suprs. of Vocat. Home Econs., Am. Ednl. Research Assn., Fla. State U. Alumni Assn. (bd. dirs. home econs. sect.), Kappa Delta Pi, Omicron Nu (chpt. pres. 1965-66), Delta Kappa Gamma (pres. 1974-76), Sigma Kappa (pres. corp. bd.), Phi Delta Kappa. Club: Havana Golf and Country. Office: Fla Dept Edn Knott Bldg Tallahassee FL 32399

BERT, ELEANOR LUCILLE, public school system business administrator; b. Fall River, Mass., June 14, 1939; d. Edward Joseph and Eleanor Lucille (Simpkins) Bertolini. BS Marist Coll., 1976; M.B.A., M.H.A., U. Miami, 1977; postgrad. Rider Coll., 1984, SUNY-Albany, 1984, Fordham U. Intergovtl. coordinator Ulster Co., Kingston, N.Y., 1977-78, 86—; bus. mgr. Stuyvesant Inns, Kingston, 1978-79, Morrisville Sch. Dist., Pa., 1979-82; dir. bus. mgmt. service Bensalem Towns Sch. Dist., Pa., 1982-84; bus. adminstr. Catskill Central Schs., N.Y., 1984-86; asst. supt. for bus. Pine Plains Cen. Sch. Dist., 1986—; presenter workshops in field. Bd. dirs. Ulster County council Girl Scouts U.S.A., 1977-78, Ulster County YWCA, 1977-78, Ulster County CAP, Kingston, 1985—. Mem. Delaware Valley Assn. Sch. Bus. Ofcls. (pres. 1981-82), Assn. Sch. Bus. Ofcls., N.Y. Assn. Sch. Bus. Ofcls., Pa. Assn. Sch. Bus. Ofcls. Home: UPO Box 3234 Kingston NY 12401 Office: Pine Plains Cen Sch Dist Box 86 Pine Plains NY 12567

BERTELLE, JEANNE T., publishing company executive, personnel director; b. Bklyn., Oct. 14, 1947; d. John A. and Florence (Bellitti) B.; m. Silvio Rosato. BA in English, Bklyn. Coll., 1968; postgrad. in Drama, Theater Coll., N.Y.C., 1975-77. Personnel adminstr. Chem. Bank, N.Y.C., 1968-70; employment interviewer L.I. Coll. Hosp., Bklyn., 1970-71; sr. job analyst health services mobility study, Research Found. of CUNY, N.Y.C., 1971-76; asst. personnel mgr. Doubleday & Co., N.Y.C., 1976-88; mgr. employee relations McGraw-Hill, N.Y.C., 1988—; com. mem. Direct Mail Assn., N.Y.C., 1984; cons., editor Health Services Mobility Study, N.Y.C., 1976-77. N.Y. State Regents scholar, 1964-68. Mem. Am. Soc. Personnel Adminstrs., Assn. Am. Publishers (chair industry salary survey 1987, 88). Roman Catholic. Club: Scott House (Bklyn.) (v.p.). Home: 1104 Hunters Run Dobbs Ferry NY 10522 Office: McGraw-Hill 1221 Ave of the Americas New York NY 10020

BERTHOLD, BONNIE MADELINE, day care school administrator, consultant; b. Sellersville, Pa., Nov. 23, 1950; d. Willard Miller and Anna Agnes (Dugard) Berthold. B.S. in Elem. Edn. cum laude, Kutztown State U., Pa., 1972; M.S. in Edn. with distng. recognition, Temple U., 1975; Prin.'s cert., U. Pa., 1978. Elem. sch. tchr. Reading Sch. Dist., Pa., 1972-79, summer sch. instr., 1972-79, workshop presenter, 1972-79, curriculum developer, 1974-79, adminstv. inter, 1977-79; owner, adminstr. Wooly Bear Day Care Sch., Lansdale, Pa., 1979—; instr. Montgomery County Community Coll., Blue Bell, Pa., 1985—; cons. in field. Contbr. articles to mags. Recipient Outstanding Tchrs. Am. award Bd. of Advisors, 1975; named Tchr. of Yr. Reading/Berks County C. of C., 1976; George B. Hancher scholar Kutztown State U., 1971. Mem. Montgomery/Bucks Assn. for Edn. of Young Children (pres. 1982-84), Nat. Assn. for Edn. of Young Children, Pa. Assn. for Edn. of Young Children, Pa. Assn. Child Care Adminstrs., Del. Valley Child Care Council, North Penn C. of C. Republican. Lutheran. Club: Newcomers. Avocations: piano, water sports, reading, constructing and designing learning materials. Home: 106 Holly Dr Lansdale PA 19446 Office: Wooly Bear Day Care Sch 128 S Broad St Lansdale PA 19446

BERTHOLD, CAROL ANN, academic administrator; b. Chgo., Sept. 26, 1942; d. Gerard Copeland and Mary Frances (Franta) B. Student, Ill. State U., 1960-62; BA, U. Ill., 1964; MA, Northwestern U., 1965, PhD, 1975. Instr. U. Ill., Chgo., 1966-72; asst. prof. Baylor U., Waco, 1975-76; exec. asst. to Chancellor U. Ill., Chgo., 1976—. Contbr. articles to profl. jours. Mem. Cook County citizens com. Sheriff's Assn. Scholarship Fund, Chgo, 1981-86; vice flotilla comdr. U.S. Coast Guard Aux., Des Plaines, Ill., 1984-85; election judge Cook County, Ill., Chgo., 1966-68. Mem. Cen. States Speech Assn. Home: 709 S Walnut Ave Arlington Heights IL 60005 Office: U Ill at Chgo PO Box 4348 Chicago IL 60680

BERTIGER, KAREN LEE, real estate securities broker; b. Louisville, Ky., Aug. 25, 1954; d. Joseph Henry and Phyllis June (Hupp) Dickhaus; m. Paul Robert Kastensmith, June 3, 1978 (div. June 1980); children: Christine, Jennifer; m. Bary Robert Bertiger, Dec. 28, 1985; stepchildren: Karen, Jeff. Student, Miami U., 1972-73, U. Cin., 1973-75, Am. Open U., 1986—. Pres. Seville Realty and Investment Co., Phoenix, 1983-84; realtor Realty Execs., Phoenix, 1984—; chief exec. officer Rodéo Realty, Ltd., Scottsdale, 1987—, Landvest Securities, Ltd., Scottsdale, 1987—. Leader Ariz. Cactus-Pine Girl Scouts, Phoenix, 1985-86. Mem. Am. Mgmt. Assn., Nat. Assn. Securities Dealers, Nat. Assn. Realtors (grad. Realtor's Inst., 1986, cert.), Scottsdale Bd. Realtors, Phoenix Bd. Realtors (equal housing opportunity com. 1983—, econ. devel. com. 1984—, govt. affairs com. 1984-86). Republican. Office: Landvest Securities Ltd 8655 E Via de Ventura Suite G254 Scottsdale AZ 85258

BERTOLINO, ANGELA MARIA, educational association administrator; b. Phila., Jan. 27, 1944; d. Peter Jude and Mary Louise (Matero) B. BA, Glassboro (N.J.) State Coll., 1967. Negotiator Willingboro (N.J.) Edn. Assn., 1978-84, pres., 1980-84; assembly del. N.J. Edn. Assn., Trenton, 1983—; mem. polit. action com. N.J. Edn. Assn., Willingboro, 1983—; govt. relations specialist Burlington County Edn. Assn., Willingboro, 1983—, pres., 1983—; dir., vice chairperson NEA, Washington, 1988—; vice chmn. Ednl. Info. and Resource Ctr., Sewell, N.J., 1986—; pres. Country Club Ridge Elem. Sch. PTA, Willingboro, 1976-78; mem. Gov.'s Task Force on Child Abuse, 1983. Mem. NEA, N.J. Edn. Assn., Willingboro Edn. Assn., Burlington County Edn. Assn. Roman Catholic. Home: 539 Roosevelt Ave Glendor NJ 08029 Office: Burlington County Edn Assn Beverly Rancocas Rd Willingboro NJ 08046

BERTOLONE, FRANCES JANE, elementary educator; b. Jamestown, N.Y., Apr. 4, 1933; d. James Joseph and Nellie Clara (Bardo) Vitanza; 1 child, Michele Grace. BA, San Jose State U., 1955; postgrad., UCLA, 1955-56, Hartnell Jr. Coll., Salinas, Calif., 1957. Cert. elem. edn. tchr. (life), Calif. Tchr. pub. schs. Greenfield, Calif., 1956-58; tchr. Alum Rock Sch. Dist., San Jose, Calif., 1958-59, Moreland Sch. Dist., San Jose, 1959—. Active dist. caucus work Jimmy Carter Presdl. campaign, 1976, 80, Walter Mondale Presdl. campaign, 1984. Mem. NEA, Calif. Tchrs. Assn., Moreland Dist. Tchrs. Assn. (sec. 1960-61, 75-79, dist. curriculum coms. 1960-87), Calif. Council for Social Studies. Roman Catholic. Office: Rogers Mid Sch 4835 Doyle Rd San Jose CA 95129

BERTRAM, AMY ANN, public relations executive; b. Phoenix, July 19, 1960; d. Richard Justin and Wilma Dorothy (Oetken) B.; m. Steven Israel Celniker, Mar. 27, 1982 (div. July 2, 1987). BS in Telecommunications magna cum laude, Ariz. State U., 1981. Adminstrv. asst., jr. publicist Feltheimer/Knofsky Mgmt. Co., Los Angeles, 1981-82; jr. publicist Rogers & Cowan Pub. Relations, Beverly Hills, Calif., 1982-83, account exec. Lippin & Grant Pub. Relations Co., Los Angeles, 1983-86; account supr. Bozell, Jacobs, Kenyon and Eckhardt Entertainment Group, Los Angeles, 1986; dir. publicity domestic TV div. Paramount Pictures Corp., Los Angeles, 1987—; guest lectr. UCLA; speaker in field. Chevron USA scholar, 1979-81. Mem. Hollywood Radio and TV Soc., Nat. Assn. Female Execs., Women in Communications Inc., Phi Kappa Phi. Avocations: languages, writing, piano, snow skiing, weightlifting.

BERTRAND, DOROTHEA LUCILE MCMASTER, educator; b. LeMars, Iowa, Nov. 30, 1932; d. Albion Paris and Gladys Farne (Kendall) McMaster; m. Willard Gerard Bertrand, Aug. 9, 1952; children: Willard Gerard Jr., Sheryl Lynn Bertrand Fleming. BS in Edn., U. S.C., Spartanburg, 1985. Cert. tchr., S.C. Asst. to traffic mgr. Nat. Foods Inc., Sioux City, Oiwa, 1961-70; adminstrv. asst; dean of girls Heelan High Sch., Spartanburg, 1971-80; parent tchr. trainer U. S.C., Spartanburg, 1982-83; adminstrv. asst. Hines Constrn. Co., Spartanburg, 1983-84; substitute tchr. Dist.7, Dist. 3, Spartanburg, 1983-86; coordinator cherokee 7000/sch. dropout program U. S.C., Spartanburg, 1986—; vice chmn. Infant Mortality Task Force; chair community dropout task force. Vice chmn. Infant Mortality Task Force-Health Planning Commn., 1985-87; vol. Cancer Drive, Heart Fund, 1974-75; pres. Treble Clef Chorus, 1974-75. Mem. LWV (bd. dirs. 1985-87). Republican. Roman Catholic. Club: LanYair Country. Lodge: Sertoma (pres.). Home: 420 Ransdell Dr Spartanburg SC 29302 Office: Cherokee 70001 423 1/2 Garnard St Gaffney SC 29340

BERTRAND, GABRIELLE, Canadian legislator; b. Sweetsburg, Que., Can., May 15, 1923; d. Louis Arthur and Juliette (Bolduc) Giroux; m. Jean-Jacques Bertrand, Oct. 14, 1944; children: Andrée, Jean-François, Suzanne, Pierre, Louise, Philippe, Marie. BSc. Mem. from Brome-Missisquoi Can Ho. of Commons; former parliamentary sec. to Minister of Nat. Health and Welfar, former parliamentary sec. to Minister of Consumer and Corp. Affairs. Pres. Que. div. Red Cross, 1981-83; mem. bd. dirs. Tourist Bur. of Cowansville, Brome-Missisquoi Perkins Hosp., Cie Theatrale des Cantons. Mem. Progressive Conservative Party. Roman Catholic. Address: 769 Principale St, Cowansville, PQ Canada J2K 1J8 *

BERTRAND, WENDY SCOTT, architect; b. Mt. Kisco, N.Y., July 15, 1941; d. Phyllis (Rahlson) Eakin; divorced; 1 child, Shanette Lea Bertrand. BArch with honors, U. Calif., Berkeley, 1971, MArch, 1972. Registered architect, Calif. With Planning Dept. City of Richmond, Calif., 1971; researcher Inst. Urban and Regional Devel. U. Calif., Berkeley, 1972; architect-in-charge Western Div. Engring. Command, Naval Facilities, San Bruno, Calif., 1973-85, supervisory architect, 1985; head archtl. br. Pub. Works Ctr., USN, Oakland, Calif., 1985—; commr. Bd. Archtl. Examiners, Calif., 1987; selectee exec. mgmt. devel. program Naval Facilities Engring. Command, Alexandria, Va., 1988. Panelist Fed. Women's Conf., San Francisco, 1987. Mem. Orgn. Women Architects (founder, mem. steering com. 1973, 77, 82, 87). Club: Bay Area Crochet and Knit Guild (San Francisco) (project leader 1987). Office: Pub Works Ctr USN San Francisco Bay Oakland CA 94623

BERUBE, MARGERY STANWOOD, publishing executive; b. Middleborough, Mass., Nov. 18, 1943; d. John Peter and Dorothy Cole (Stanwood) Wholan; m. Edgar Roger Berube, Sept. 12, 1967. BA in English, Wilkes Coll., 1965. Creative and prodn. mgr., dir. editorial ops. Med. div. Houghton Mifflin Co., Boston, 1978-81, dir. editorial ops. Reference div., 1982-85, v.p., dir. editorial ops. Trade and Reference div., 1986-87, v.p., dir. editorial art prodn. and mfg. services, 1987—. Mem. Bookbuilders (bd. dirs. 1976-80). Office: Houghton Mifflin Co Two Park St Boston MA 02108

BERZINS, ERNA MARIJA, physician; b. Latvia, Nov. 27, 1914; d. Arturs and Anna (Steckenbergs) Meilands; came to U.S., 1951, naturalized, 1956; M.D., Latvian State U., 1940; m. Verners Berzins, Aug. 24, 1935; children—Valdis, Andis. Mem. pediatric faculty Latvian State U., 1940-44; intern Good Samaritan Hosp., Dayton, Ohio, 1951-52; resident in pediatrics Children's Hosp. of Mich., Detroit, 1953-55; practice medicine specialising in pediatrics, Detroit, 1956-60; with ARC, Cleve., 1961-63; physician pediatric outpatient dept. Cleve. Met. Gen. Hosp., 1963-84; asst. prof. emeritus Case-Western Res. U., Cleve., trustee Women's Gen. Hosp., Cleve. Mem. Am., Ohio med. assns., Acad. Medicine, No. Ohio Pediatric Soc., Am. Women's Med. Assn., Am. Med. Polit. Action Com. Lutheran. Address: 5460 Friar Circle Cleveland OH 44126

BERZON, FAYE CLARK, nursing educator; b. New Britain, Conn., Sept. 26, 1926; d. Bernard Francis and Elizabeth Tillie (Gross) Clark; m. Harry Berzon, June 18, 1961. Diploma Beth Israel Hosp., 1947; B.S.N., Boston U., 1957, M.S.N., 1959; cert. advanced grad. studies, U. Mass., 1987. Staff, head nurse, instr. Beth Israel Hosp., Boston, 1948-58; instr. nursing Simmons Coll., Boston, 1958-62, Cath. Labore Sch. Nursing, Dorchester, Mass., 1962-67; asst. prof. nursing Boston U. Sch. Nursing, 1967-70; div. chmn. human services Massasoit Community Coll., Brockton, Mass., 1973-79, prof. nursing, 1970—, chair nursing dept. 1988—; mem. acad. adv. com. to Mass. Bd. Higher Edn., 1975-76. Author: (with Govoni, Berzon, Fall) Drugs and Nursing Implications, 1965. Vol., Milton (Mass.) Meals on Wheels, 1978—. Mem. Am. Nurses Assn., Nat. League Nursing (scholar 1963-79, accreditation visitor 1976—), AAUW (v.p. Milton br. 1981-83), Nursing Archives, Mass. Heart Assn., Nat. Assoc. for Advancement of Assoc. Degree Nursing, Sigma Theta Tau, Delta Kappa Gamma. Democrat. Jewish. Home: 37 Brandon Rd Milton MA 02187

BERZON, JUDITH RAE, human resources executive; b. Passaic, N.J., Apr. 7, 1945; d. Sidney and Mollie Clara (Kanter) Goldberg; m. Norm Berzon, Aug. 23, 1964 (div. Aug. 1985); children: Ian Christopher, Kirsten Jennifer. BA with honors, Rutgers U., 1966; MA, NYU, 1968, PhD, 1974. Social worker N.J. Bur. Children's Services, Somerville, 1966-67; reader Douglass Coll. Rutgers U., New Brunswick, N.J., 1966-67; teaching asst. NYU, N.Y.C., 1968-69; asst. prof. English Iowa State U., Ames, 1971-78, chmn. women's studies com., 1976-77, liberal arts rep. univ. com. on women, 1975-78; lectr. U. San Francisco and Golden Gate U., San Francisco, 1978-79; personnel analyst East Bay Mcpl. Utility Dist., Oakland, Calif., 1979-87, co-chairperson women's employment job fair, 1980; human resources adminstr. Union Sanitary Dist., Fremont, Calif., 1987—; presenter MLA, Chgo., 1975, St. Paul, Minn., 1978; cons., trainer Recreational Equipment, Inc., Berkeley, Calif., 1983. Editor: Promethean jour., 1966; author: Neither Black nor White: The Mulatto Character in American Fiction, 1978. Bd. dirs., Ames Coop. Childcare Ctr., 1972-75, YWCA, Ames, 1975-77; mem. indsl. adv. bd. East Bay Skills Ctr., Oakland, 1981-84, Vallecitos Ctr. for Employment Tng., Hayward, Calif., 1982-83. Recipient Cert. of Appreciation Oakland Mayor's Summer Youth program, 1980, J.F. Kennedy Sch. Mgmt., Orinda, Calif., 1985. Mem. No. Calif. Internat. Personnel Mgmt. Assn. (co-chairperson profl. devel. program com. 1985—, Outstanding Service award 1987), Internat. Personnel Mgmt. Assn., Golden Gate chpt. Am. Soc. Tng. and Devel., Nat. Women's Studies Assn. (Iowa State U. rep. 1977). Jewish. Home: 294 Lee St Oakland CA 94610 Office: Union Sanitary Dist 37532 Dusterberry Way Fremont CA 94536

BESEN, JANE PHYLLIS TRIPTOW, civic worker; b. Chgo., Aug. 6, 1921; d. Richard Herman and Rose (Krips) Triptow; student Northwestern U., 1946-47, East Los Angeles Coll., 1967-68; B.A. in English, Calif. State U., Los Angeles, 1978, postgrad. in English; m. Irving Besen, Mar. 25, 1951 (div. 1978); children—Glenn, Allen. Exec. sec. Chgo. Ordnance Dist., War Dept., 1941-46, Aubrey, Moore & Wallace, Advt. Agy., Chgo., 1946; exec. sec. sales office McGraw-Hill Pub. Co., Chgo., 1947-51; exec. sec. Security Pacific Nat. Bank, Los Angeles, 1978—. Publicity chmn. Am Field Service, 1967-68; sec. Citizens Com for Good Govt., 1961; capt. United Crusade, Monterey Park, Calif., 1967—; publicity chmn. Monterey Park Art Assn., 1966-67, coor. sec., 1968, dir., 1965—, past pres., dir. newsletter, 1970—; chmn. Monterey Park Arts and Culture Com.; dir. in charge Bruggemeyer Library Shows, 1973-74; dep. registrar voters Calif. State U., Los Angeles, 1971-74; 3d v.p. in charge publicity Community Concerts Monterey Park; v.p. United Dem. Club of Monterey Park, 1988—. Recipient Top award Alhambra Open Show, 1972. Mem. Nat. League Am. Pen Women (rec. sec., treas. 1961-65), LWV (sec. Alhambra chpt. 1971-73, pres. chpt. 1973-74, action chmn., publicity chmn. 1977-78, hospitality chmn. 1980—), Residents Assn. Monterey Park. Club: Northwestern U. Alumni So. Calif. (corr. sec. 1979-80). Home: 1540 Arriba Dr Monterey Park CA 91754

BESHAR, CHRISTINE, lawyer; b. Paetzig, Germany, Nov. 6, 1929; came to U.S., 1952, naturalized, 1957; d. Hans and Ruth (vonKleist-Retzow) von Wedemeyer; m. Robert P. Beshar, Dec. 20, 1953; children: Cornelia, Jacqueline, Frederica, Peter. Student, U. Hamburg, 1950-51, U. Tuebingen, 1951-52; B.A., Smith Coll., 1953. Bar: N.Y. 1960, U.S. Supreme Ct. 1971. Assoc. firm Cravath, Swaine & Moore, N.Y.C., 1964-70; partner Cravath, Swaine & Moore, 1971—. Bd. dirs. Catalyst for Women Inc., 1977—; trustee Colgate U., 1978-84, Smith Coll., 1987—. Inst. Internat. Edn. fellow, 1952-53; recipient Disting. Alumnae medal Smith Coll., 1974. Fellow Am. Coll. Probate Counsel, Am. Bar Found.; mem. Assn. Bar City N.Y. (exec. com. 1973-75, v.p. 1985-86), N.Y. State Bar Assn. (ho. of dels. 1971-80, v.p. 1979-80), N.Y. State Bar Found. (bd. dirs. 1977—), UN Assn. (bd. dirs. 1975—), Fgn. Policy Assn. (bd. dirs. 1978-87). Presbyterian. Clubs: Wall St., Downtown Assn., Cosmopolitan, Gipsy Trail. Home: 120 East End Ave New York NY 10028 Office: Cravath Swaine & Moore 1 Chase Manhattan Plaza New York NY 10005 also: Stone House Farm Box 533 Somers NY 10589

BESONEN, JOANNE FRANCES, purchasing consultant; b. Somerville, Mass., July 21, 1946; d. Leo Joseph and Rose Marie (Costa) Fava; m. David Eino Besonen, Apr. 21, 1968; children—David M., Mark R., Amy E., Mara R., Matthew P., Rachel M. Student, Regis Coll. Sales team leader Avon Products Inc., Ayer, Mass., 1975-77; br. office clk. Army and Air Force Exchange Service, Ayer, 1976; asst. to sales/service mgr. John E. Cain Co., Ayer, 1976-77; purchasing agt. Scopus Corp., Lowell, Mass., 1978-81; contract buyer Network Personnel, Billerica, Mass., 1983-84; sr. buyer NETCO Automation, Haverhill, Mass., 1984-86; buyer M/A-COM, Inc., Burlington, Mass., 1986-88; ind. purchasing cons., 1988—. Mem. PTO, South Row Sch., Chelmsford, Mass., 1980—, PTO, Keith Catholic High Sch., Lowell, 1983—. Mem. Nat. Assn. Purchasing Mgmt., Nat. Assn. Female Execs., Purchasing Mgmt. Assn. Boston. Democrat. Roman Catholic. Club: Chelmsford Art Advs. Avocations: cooking, knitting, crocheting, aerobics, biking. Address: 55 Billerica Rd Chelmsford MA 01824

BESS, BARBARA ELLEN, screen printing service owner; b. Buffalo, Jan. 21, 1948; d. Henry A. and Theresa (Szydlowski) B.; 1 child, Chad M. Moretuzzo. Various positions Buffalo, 1965-81; exec. sec. Ad Art Color Process of Buffalo, 1982-85; gen. mgr. Spectra Screen Printing Co., Inc., Buffalo, 1985-87, pres., 1987—. Office: Spectra Screen Printing 36 Mason St Buffalo NY 14213

BESSETTE, CAROL SCHOELLER, defense analyst; b. Passaic, N.J., Aug. 14, 1938; d. Theobald Herman and Evelyn Edna (Lucitt) S.; m. John Francis Bessette, Oct. 3, 1964. AB in Social Studies, Coll. Misericordia, 1960; MA in Internat. Relations, Georgetown U., 1967; MA in Bus. Mgmt., Cent. Mich. U., 1980. Commd. USAF advanced through grades to lt. col., 1960-85; intelligence officer USAF 1964-85; research analyst Anser Corp., Arlington, Va., 1986—. Bd. dirs. Nat. Hist. Intelligence Mus., Washington, 1985—. Mem. Nat. Mil. Intelligence Assn. (bd. dirs. 1983—, nat. pres. 1983-86), Assn. Former Intelligence Officers, Armed Forces Communications and Electronics Assn. Club: Richard III Soc. (chmn. Middle Atlantic chpt.). Home: 8251 Taunton Pl Springfield VA 22152

BEST, (JEAN) KATHLEEN FRANCIS, electrical company executive; b. DeRidder, La., Oct. 20, 1946; d. Billy Gene and Marjorie Kathleen (Frusha) Francis; divorced; children: Eric, Shawn. BA, Tex. Tech U., 1967; MA, Ea. N.Mex. U., 1978. Instr. math. Ector County Ind. Sch. Dist., Odessa, Tex., 1969-70, Schertz Ind. Sch. Dist., San Antonio, 1970-71, Southwest Tex. Jr. Coll., Uvalde, 1975-77; statistician Southwestern Pub. Service Co., Amarillo, Tex., 1979-82, statis. supr., 1982-85, analyst strategic planning, 1985-86, mgr. fuel adminstrn., 1986-87; mgr. forecasting and statis. analysis; chair fed. coal royalties task force Edison Electric Inst., Washington, 1985-87. Bd. dirs. Amarillo Women's Network, Amarillo YMCA, 1987—, chair fin. com., downtown br. bd. dirs. Mem. Am. Statis. Assn., Tex. Assn. Gifted and Talented, Ea. N.Mex. Alumni Assn. (bd. dirs. 1986-88), Phi Mu Epsilon, Gamma Phi Beta. Republican. Lodge: Soroptimists. Office: Southwestern Pub Service 6th at Tyler PO Box 1261 Amarillo TX 79170

BEST, LOYCE MARIE, information systems executive; b. Bklyn., June 1, 1950; d. Beatrice Mae (Crocker) B.; 1 child, Latisha Monique. AA in Computer Mgmt., Prince George's Community Coll., Largo, Md., 1984. Various positions The Washington (D.C.) Post, 1974-84, info. systems mgr., 1984—. Inst. Journalism Edn. fellow, 1986. Mem. Lakeland Civic Assn. (newsletter editor 1986), Nat. Assn. Female Execs., Nat. Council Negro Women, Black Data Processing Assn. (newsletter com. 1984-86). Baptist. Office: The Washington Post 1150 15th St NW Washington DC 20071

BEST, SHARON PECKHAM, college administrator; b. Elmira, N.Y., Aug. 4, 1940; d. Paul Arthur and Beatrice L. (Hunter) Peckham; m. Willard C. Best, Sept. 3, 1961; children: Meryl Elizabeth, Kevin Hunter. BA cum laude, William Smith Coll., 1977. Acting dir. alumnae relations William Smith Coll., Geneva, N.Y., 1976-77; assoc. dir. devel. Hobart & William Smith Colls., Geneva, 1977, dir. devel., 1978-81, exec. dir. devel., 1981-87, v.p. for devel., 1988—; cons. Nazareth Coll., Rochester, N.Y., 1985. Active Ontario County (N.Y.) rep. com., 1968-78, Geneva Hist. Soc., 1975-80; active Geneva Concerts, Inc., 1965—, bd. dirs. 1974-82, pres., 1976-78. Mem. Council for Advancement and Support Edn. (bd. trustees Mid-Atlantic Dist. II 1987—, Gold Medal-Decade Improvement in Fund Raising 1987), Nat. Soc. Fund Raising Execs., League of Women Voters, Phi Beta Kappa, Phi Sigma Iota. Presbyterian. Club: Geneva Country. Home: 859 S Main St Geneva NY 14456 Office: Hobart & William Smith Colls Geneva NY 14456

BESTEHORN, UTE WILTRUD, librarian; b. Cologne, Fed. Rep. of Germany, Nov. 6, 1930; came to U.S., 1930; d. Henry Hugo and Wiltrud Lucie (Vincentz) B. BA, U. Cin., 1954, BEd, 1955, MEd, 1958; MS in Library Sci., Western Res. U. (now Case-Western Res. U.), 1961. Tchr. Cutter Jr. High Sch., Cin., 1955-57; tchr., supr. library Felicity (Ohio) Franklin Sr. High Sch., 1959-60; librarian sci. dept. Pub. Library Cin. and

Hamilton County, 1961-78, librarian info. desk, 1978—; textbook selection com., Felicity-Franklin Sr. High Sch., 1959-60; supr. Health Alcove Sci. Dept. and annual health lectures, Cin. Pub. Library, 1972-77. Book reviewer Library Jour., 1972-77; author and inventor Rainbow 40 marble game, 1971, Condominium game, 1976; mem. violin sect. Cin. Civic Orch., 1987—; patentee indexed packaging and stacking device, 1973, mobile packaging and stacking device, 1974. Mem. Clifton Townb Mtg, 1988—. Recipient Cert. of Merit and Appreciation Pub. Library of Cin., 1986. Mem. Ohio Library Assn., Cin. Chpt. Spl. Libraries Assn. (archivist 1964-64, editor Queen City Gazette bull. 1964-69), Pub. Library Staff Assn. (exec. bd., activities com. 1965, welfare com. 1966, recipient Golden Book 25 yr. service pin, 1986), Friends of the Library, Greater Cin. Calligraphers Guild (reviewer New Letters pub. 1986—), Delta Phi Alpha. Republican. Mem. United Ch. of Christ. Home: 3330 Morrison Ave Cincinnati OH 45220 Office: Pub Library Cin 800 Vine St Cincinnati OH 45202

BEST-HEARN, ANN ELLEN, controller, accountant; b. Lamesa, Tex., Oct. 12, 1943; d. Wesley Moody and Lela (Frances) Neeley; m. Bill J. Hays, Oct. 5, 1960 (div. 1967); children: Thomas R., Gregory Bryan; m. Odis C. Best, Aug. 15, 1969 (dec. 1983); m. O. D. Hearn, May 7, 1988. AS, N.Mex. Jr. Coll., 1975; BBA, Tex. Tech U., 1977. CPA, N.Mex. Mem. acct. staff Peat, Marwick and Mitchell and Co., Midland, Tex., 1977; acct. staff Johnson, Miller and Co. CPA's, Hobbs, N.Mex., 1977-81; controller Barton Oil Producers, Hobbs, 1981—. Treas. United Way Hobbs, 1982-84, 2d v.p., 1987—; bd. dirs. Jr. Achievement, 1985—, Palmer Drug Abuse Program, Hobbs, 1986—. Mem. Am. Inst. CPA's, Petroleum Accts. Soc. (bd. dirs. 1986—), N.Mex. Soc. CPA's (bd. dirs. 1983, chmn. industry 1984-85, outstanding com. chmn. 1985, pres. Oil Patch chpt. 1981-82). Republican. Presbyterian. Club: Altrusa (Hobbs). Lodge: Order Eastern Star. Home: 1903 Helen Dr Brownfield TX 79316

BESTON, ROSE MARIE, college president; b. South Portland, Maine, Sept. 27, 1937; d. George Louis and Edith Mae (Archibald) Beattie; m. John Bernard Beston, Feb. 1, 1970. B.A., St. Joseph's Coll., 1961; M.S., Boston Coll., 1963; Ph.D., U. Pitts., 1967; Cert. of Advanced Study, Harvard U., 1978. Mem. faculty St. Joseph's Coll., Maine, 1967-70; mem. faculty U. Queensland, Australia, 1970-76, Western Australian Inst. Tech., 1970-76, U. Hawaii, Manoa, 1976-77; assoc. acad. dean Worcester State Coll., Maine, 1978-80; dean acad. affairs Castleton State Coll., Vt., 1980-84; pres. Nazareth Coll. of Rochester, N.Y., 1984—; bd. dirs. Council of Ind. Colls., Ind. Coll. Fund of N.Y.; mem. Council Ind. Colls. and Univs. N.Y.; dir. Mfrs. Hanover, N.A., Rochester, 1984. Contbr. articles to profl. jours. Bd. dirs. United Way of Rochester; bd. govs. Genesee Hosp., Rochester; trustee Rochester Mus. and Sci. Ctr., 1985—. Mem. AAUW, Mediaeval Acad. Am., Assn. Commonwealth Lang. and Literature Studies, Rochester C. of C. (trustee 1985—), Phi Delta Kappa. Clubs: Harvard (N.Y.C.); Oak Hill Country (Rochester); Genesee Valley. Office: Nazareth Coll Rochester 4245 East Ave Rochester NY 14610

BETH, MARLENE, federal agency official; b. Fulton, Kans., May 11, 1937; d. Floyd E. and Dora E (Cosens) Beth-Winter; m. R.E. Archer (div. 1961); children: Jeannie, Debbie, Connie, Cindie; m. W.W. Schleiff, Apr. 1961 (div. 1976). Archeology Lab. Tech. (hon.), U. Ark., 1973; BA in Cultural Anthropology, Women Studies, Goddard Coll., Plainfield, Vt., 1985. Food insp. USDA, Springdale, Ark., 1968-75; insp. in charge USDA, Dallas, 1975-79; compliance officer USDA, Los Angeles, 1979-83; compliance specialist USDA, Washington, 1983-86; program review officer USDA, Lawrence, Kans., 1986—. Mem. Exec. Female Assn., Assn. Tech. and Supervisory Profls., Bus. and Profl. Women, (sponsor) Archeol. Soc. of Md., San Luis Obispo County Archeol. Soc., (donor) Kans. Anthrop. Assn. Methodist. Home: PO Box 3748 Lawrence KS 66046

BETHEA-SHIELDS, KAREN, lawyer; b. Raleigh, N.C., Apr. 29, 1949; d. Bryant William and Grace Louise (Parrish) Bethea; m. Kenneth R. Galloway, 1971 (div. 1976); m. Linwood B. Shields, Dec. 1984. AB in Psychology, East Carolina U., 1971; JD, Duke U., 1974. Bar: N.C. 1974. Ptnr. Paul, Keenan, Rowan & Galloway, Durham, N.C., 1974-77, Loflin, Loflin, Galloway, Leary & Acker, Durham, 1977-80; ct. judge 14th Judicial Dist., Durham, N.C., 1980-85; sole practice, Durham, 1986—; mem. faculty Nat. Inst. Trial Advocacy. Recipient Cert. of Recognition, City of Detroit, 1975, Award of Appreciation Delta Sigma Theta, 1977, Cert. of Appreciation N.C. State Assn. Black Social Workers, 1979, Disting. Achievement award NAACP, 1981; named one of Durham's First Black Women in their Chosen Professions Iota Phi Lambda. Mem. ABA, Am. Judicature Soc., Nat. Conf. Black Lawyers (Lawyer of Yr. 1977), Nat. Assn. Women Attys. (Award of Appreciation 1982), Nat. Assn. Black Women Attys., Internat. Platform Assn., N.C. Bar Assn., N.C. Assn. Women Attys. (award of appreciation 1982), N.C. Acad. Trial Lawyers, Nat. Assn. Women Judges, Delta Sigma Theta (contbr. for securing justice for black women), Iota Phi Lambda. Democrat. Baptist. Home and Office: 3525 Mayfair Rd Durham NC 27707

BETHEL, TAMARA ANN, psychiatric nurse, consultant; b. Granville, N.Y., Dec. 5, 1939; d. William Henry and Delphine Ann (McDonough) B. Diploma, Jeanne Mance Sch. Nursing, Burlington, Vt., 1961; BS, Boston Coll., 1968; MEd, Antioch Grad. Ctr., Cambridge, Mass., 1974; PhD, Walden U., Fla., 1981. RN, Mass. Head nurse Dept. Mental Health, Boston, 1961-63, supr., 1963-66; staff nurse VA Hosp., Brockton, Mass., 1966-68; mem. faculty Newton Wellesey Hosp. Sch. Nursing, Mass., 1968-84, chmn. med./surg./psychiat. nursing, 1984-87; exec. dir. Mass. chpt. Lupus Found. of Am., 1987—; cons. in curriculum; mem. adj. faculty in crisis intervention Inst. Open Edn., Cambridge Coll., Bridgewater State Coll.; developer, presenter workshops in mental health and psychiat. nursing, human sexuality ethics. Contbr. psychiat. nursing sect. Little Brown Rev. of Nursing, 1985, articles on lupus to profl. jours., including Lupus News, 1985—; columnist Jour. Nursing Care, 1979-82. Pres. Mass. chpt. Lupus Found. Am., 1985—; bd. dirs. Lupus Found. Am., 1985—. Fellow Am. Orthopsychiat. Assn.; mem. Diploma Nurses Assn. (treas. Mass.), Mass. Mental Health Nurses Assn., Am. Nurses Assn., Am. Med. Writers Assn., others. Home: 54 Mt Pleasant St Westboro MA 01581 Office: 215 California St Newton MA 02158

BETSCH, MADELINE, advertising executive; b. N.Y.C.. Edu. Hunter Coll., N.Y.C., Harvard U. Account exec. Dancer-Fitzgerald-Sample, Inc., N.Y.C., 1963-69; account exec. Knox-Reeves, Mpls., 1970-71; v.p., mktg. dir. Langyn Labs., Potomac, Md., 1971-73; v.p. Campbell Mithun Inc., Mpls., from 1973; now exec. v.p. Campbell-Mithun-Esty (formerly Campbell-Mithun Advertising), Mpls. Chmn. spl. events Mpls. chpt. Am. Diabetes Assn., 1978-80. Office: Campbell-Mithun-Esty 222 S 9th St Minneapolis MN 55402 *

BETTAN, ANITA ESTHER, public relations specialist, writer; b. Cin., Nov. 30, 1928; d. Israel and Ida Judith (Goldstein) B. B.A., U. Cin., 1950; M.A., Columbia U., 1951. Copywriter, Shillito's, Cin., 1953-55; continuity dir. Sta. WSAI, Cin., 1955-57; copywriter, jr. account exec. William F. Holland Agy., Cin., 1957-61; account coordinator Stockton-West-Burkhart, Inc., Cin., 1962-67; asst. to info. officer U. Cin. Coll-Conservatory of Music, 1967-71; info. services writer U. Cin., 1971—, mem. com. on aging, 1981-84. Contbr. articles to mags. Dep. foreman Hamilton County Grand Jury, Cin., 1979, foreman petit jury, 1980; pres. career div. Council Jewish Women, Cin., 1962-64; vol. Jewish Hosp., Cin., 1954-59; mem. Sr. Olympics Com., Cin., 1981-84. Mem. Women in Communications. Home: 2101 Grandin Rd Cincinnati OH 45208 Office: U Cin Mail Location No 65 Cincinnati OH 45221

BETTERIDGE, FRANCES CARPENTER, lawyer, mediator; b. Rutherford, N.J., Aug. 25, 1921; d. James Dunton and Emily (Atkinson) Carpenter; m. Albert Edwin Betteridge, Feb. 5, 1949 (div. 1975); children—Anne, Albert Edwin, James, Peter. A.B., Mt. Holyoke Coll., 1942; J.D., N.Y. Law Sch., 1978. Bar: Conn. 1979, Ariz. 1982. Technician in charge blood banks Roosevelt Hosp., N.Y.C. and Mountainside Hosp., Montclair, N.J., 1943-49; substitute tchr. Greenwich High Sch. (Conn.), 1978-79; intern and asst. to labor contracts office Town of Greenwich, 1979-80; vol. referee Pima County Juvenile Ct.,c Tucson, 1981-85, judge Pro Tempore, 1987; vol. referee Pima County Superior Ct., 1981-85; sole practice immigration law, Tucson, 1982-87; commr. Juvenile Ct., Pima County Superior Ct., Tucson, 1985-87; hearing officer Small Claims Ct., Pima County Justice Cts., Tucson, 1982-85; mediator Family Crisis Service, Tucson, 1982—. Pres. High Sch. PTA, Greenwich, 1970, PTA Council, 1971; mem. Greenwich Bd. Edn., 1971-76, sec., 1973-76; com. chmn. LWV Tucson, 1981; bd. dirs., 1984-85; bd. dirs., sec. Let The Sun Shine Inc., Tucson, 1981—. Mem. ABA, Conn. Bar Assn., Ariz. Bar Assn., Pima County Bar Assn., Nat. Council of Juvenile and Family Ct. Judges, Ariz. Women Lawyers Assn., Am. Immigration Lawyers Assn. Republican. Congregationalist. Club: Point o' Woods (N.Y.). Home and Office: 3442 N Richland Circle Tucson AZ 85719

BETTIN, JANENE EDNA, real estate broker; b. Schaller, Iowa, Nov. 11, 1943; d. Robert A. and Edna (Harris) Bath; m. Thomas L. Bettin, June 20, 1964; 1 son, Christopher. Student U. No. Iowa, 1961; B.S., Tex. A&I U., 1965. Grad. Realtors Inst; cert. residential residential brokerage mgr. Tchr. high sch., Corpus Christi, Tex., 1965-70; tchr. Village Acad., Mt. Lebanon, Pa., 1973-76; broker, assoc. Re/Max Metro Properties, Inc., Denver, 1977-86; broker, br. mgr. Perry & Butler, Littleton, Colo., 1986—. Chmn. Blood Bank, South Suburban Bd. Realtors, 1980, chmn. Schs. Com., 1980; pres. South Suburban Bd. Realtors, 1985-86. Bd. dirs., officer Bristol Cove Homeowners Assn., Littleton, Colo., 1983; officer, treas. Arapahoe Youth League-Warriors, 1981. Mem. Realtors Nat. Mktg. Inst., Womens Council Realtors (pres. 1982-83), Colo. Assn. Realtors (instr. 1981—, dir. 1984, v.p. 1987), Cert. Residential Specialists (pres. Colo. chpt. 1984), Omega Tau Rho (nat. instr. 1985-86), Cert. Residential Brokerage Mgrs. (instr. 1986—). Republican. Methodist. Club: Mt. Lebanon Newcomers (pres. 1973-74). Home: 7540 S Cove Circle Littleton CO 80122 Office: Perry & Butler 8089 S Lincoln St Suite 103 Littleton CO 80122

BETTINGER, JULIE STRAUSS, marketing professional; b. Tallahassee, Apr. 4, 1961; d. Theodore Beroud and June (Fouts) Strauss; m. James Gerard Bettinger, Dec. 10, 1983. B, Fla. State U., 1983. Jr. account exec. Stan Tait and Assocs., Tallahassee, 1982-83; mgr. pub. relations Dixon Ticonderoga Co., Vero Beach, Fla., 1983-85; prin. J. Bettinger Communications, Stuart, Fla., 1985-86; dir. mktg. Linda L. Miles and Assocs., Virginia Beach, Va., 1986-87; free-lance writer Virginia Beach, 1987—. Contbr. articles various mags. Lector Prince of Peach Ch. Lectors, 1987. Mem. Nat. Assn. Female Execs., Am. Mgmt. Assn. Republican. Roman Catholic. Club: Toastmasters. Home and Office: 408 Brougham Ct Chesapeake VA 23320

BETTS, DORIS JUNE WAUGH, author, English language educator; b. Statesville, N.C., June 4, 1932; d. William Elmore and Mary Ellen (Freeze) Waugh; m. Lowry Matthews Betts, July 5, 1952; children: Doris LewEllyn, David Lowry, Erskine Moore II. Student, Woman's Coll., U. N.C., 1950-53, U. N.C., 1954; DLitt (hon.), Greensboro Coll., 1987. Newspaperwoman Statesville Daily Record, 1950-51, Chapel Hill (N.C.) Weekly and News-Leader, 1953-54, Sanford Daily Herald, 1956-57; editorial staff N.C. Democrat, newspaper, 1961-62; editor Sanford (N.C.) News Leader, 1962; lectr. creative writing, English dept. U. N.C., Chapel Hill, 1966—; dir. Freshman-Sophomore English U. N.C., 1972-76, assoc. prof., 1974-78, prof., 1978—, Alumni Disting. prof., 1983—, dir. Fellows program, 1975-76, asst. dean Honors program, 1979-81, chmn. faculty, from 1983; vis. lectr. creative writing Duke U., 1971; staff Ind. U. Summer Writers Conf., 1972, 73; mem. bd. Asso. Writing Programs; mem. lit. panel Nat. Endowment for Arts, 1979-81, chmn., 1981. Author: story collections The Gentle Insurrection, 1954, Beasts of the Southern Wild, 1973; novel Tall Houses in Winter, 1957 (Sir Walter Raleigh award for best fiction by Carolinian 1957), Scarlet Thread (Sir Walter Raleigh award 1965), The Astronomer & Other Stories, 1966, The River to Pickle Beach, 1972, Heading West, 1981; Contbr. stories collections, anthologies.; Editor: Young Writer at Chapel Hill, 1968. Dramatized version of The Ugliest Pilgrim appear as Violet (recipient Acad. Award, Tex. Film Festival award). Mem. N.C. Tercentenary Commn., 1961-62, Sanford City Sch. Bd., 1965-71. Recipient short story prize Mademoiselle mag., booklength fiction prize G. P. Putnam-U. N.C., 1954; N.C. medal for lit., 1975, John Dos Passos award, 1983; Guggenheim fellow, 1958-59. Mem. N.C. Writers Assn. Office: U NC Dept English 230 Greenlaw Hall 066A Chapel Hill NC 27514

BETTS, LINDA BLANEY, real estate broker; b. Bristol, Tenn., Nov. 26, 1946; d. Andrew Thomas and Lillian M. (Nelson) Bentley; m. Robert Blaney, Dec. 5, 1975 (div. 1980); children: Melissa, Robyn; m. Alan Blaine Betts, Mar. 5, 1983. Diploma, Bluff City (Tenn.) High Sch., 1964. Lic. real estate agt. Operator Inter-Mountain Telephone Co., Bristol, Tenn., 1964-66; sec. Md. Casualty Co., Balt., 1966-68; exec. sec. Seaboard Properties, Inc., Balt., 1968-73; asst. ops. mgr., sec. WBAL radio, Balt., 1973-75; realtor Porter & Dennis, Better Homes & Gardens, Salisbury, Md., 1981-83; realtor, dir. edn. and tng. Porter & Dennis, Inc., Salisbury, 1984-85; realtor Ahtes, Hanna Realtors, Salisbury, 1983-84; assoc. broker, office mgr. Roop & Betts Realty, Inc., Salisbury, Md., 1985—; instr. Wor-Wic Tech. Community Coll., Salisbury, Del-Tech., Georgetown, Del. Mem. health planning council, State of Md., 1984-85; publicity chmn. local chpt. March of Dimes, 1982-83; vol. Am. Cancer Soc. Mem. Coastal Bd. of Realtors (pres. 1988, named Realtor of Yr. 1987,), Md. Assn. of Realtors (bd. dirs.). Democrat. Baptist. Home: 908 E Church St Salisbury MD 21801 Office: Roop & Betts Realty Inc 1501-A Edgemore Ave Salisbury MD 21801

BETZ, CECILY LYNN, nursing educator; b. Glendale, Calif., Feb. 26, 1949; d. Cecil Leander and Alda Virginia (Pedersen) B. BS, Calif. State U., Los Angeles, 1976, MS, 1978; PhD, U. So. Calif., 1982. Clin. nurse specialist Children's Hosp., Los Angeles, 1972-77; instr. Pasadena (Calif.) Children'sCtr., 1977-78; asst. clin. prof. nursing UCLA, 1978-85, coordinator nursing tng., assoc. dir., 1985—. Editor Jour. Pediat. Nursing, 1985—; contbr. articles to profl. jours. Mem. Mayfield Alumnae Assn. (pres. 1980-82), Sigma Theta Tau (region I coordinator 1987—).

BEU, MARJORIE JANET, music director; b. Elgin, Ill., Nov. 22, 1921; d. Herman Henry and Hattie Belle (Beverly) B.; MusB, Am. Conservatory Music, 1949; B Musical Ed, 1949, M in Musical Ed., 1953; advanced cert. No. Ill. U., 1969; DEd, U. Sarasota, 1979. Music tchr. Sch. Dist. 21, Wheeling, Ill., 1961-64; music and fine arts coordinator, 1964-68, asst. supt. instrn., 1968-79; minister of music United Meth. Ch., Sun City Center, Fla., 1980—; dir. Sun City Ctr. Kings Point Community Chorus, 1984—; pres. Council Study and Devel. Ednl. Resources, 1971-79. Pres., Wheeling Community Concerts Assn.; dir. Community Chorus; pres. Sun City Center Concert Series. Mem. NEA, Am. Guild Organists and Choir Dirs., Music Educators Nat. Conf., Assn. Supervision and Curriculum Devel., Ill. Edn. Assn., Ill. Council Gifted, No. Ill. Assn. Ednl. Research, Evaluation and Devel. (pres.), Mu Phi Epsilon, Phi Delta Kappa (sec. N.W. Suburban Cook County chpt.), Kappa Delta Pi (pres. also counselor alumni com.). Home: 610 Fort Duquesna Dr Sun City Center FL 33570

BEUERLEIN, SISTER JULIANA, hospital administrator; b. Lawrenceburg, Tenn., June 19, 1921; d. John Adolph and Sophia (Held) B. R.N., St. Joseph's Sch. Nursing, Chgo., 1945; B.S. in Edn, DePaul U., 1947; M.S. in Nursing Edn, Marquette U., 1954; postgrad., St. Louis U. Operating room supr. St. Joseph's Hosp., Alton, Ill., 1945-48; dir. sch. of nursing and nursing service Providence Hosp., Waco, Tex., 1948-56; dir. sch. nursing and nursing service St. Joseph's Hosp., Chgo., 1956-62; asst. adminstr. St. Joseph's Hosp., 1962-63; adminstrv. asst. St. Mary's Hosp., Evansville, Ind., 1963-65; adminstr. St. Mary's Hosp., 1965-73, pres. governing bd., 1965-73; adminstr. St. Joseph Hosp., Chgo., 1973-81; pres. governing bd. St. Joseph Hosp., 1973-75; adminstr. St. Thomas Hosp., Nashville, 1981—; Mem. governing bd. St. Vincent's Hosp., Indpls., 1969-73; mem. governing bd. St. Mary's Hosp., Milw., 1974-75, chmn., 1978-79; mem. governing bd. Providence Hosp., Southfield, Mich., 1975-78, chmn. governing bd., 1977-78; mem. Chgo. Health Systems Agy., 1976-79; mem. governing bd. DePaul Community Health Center, Bridgeton, Mo., 1980—, St. Thomas Hosp., Nashville, Hubbard Hosp., Nashville; pres. governing bd. St Vincent Hosp., Birmingham, Ala.; mem. Am. Hosp. Assn. Commn. on Nursing, 1980—. Fellow Am. Coll. Hosp. Adminstrs. (com. on elections); mem. Cath., Tenn. hosp. assns. Address: St Thomas Hosp Box 380 Nashville TN 37202

BEUGEN, JOAN BETH, communications company executive; b. Chgo., Mar. 9, 1943; d. Leslie and Janet (Glick) Caplan; B.S. in Speech, Northwestern U., 1965; m. Sheldon Howard Beugen, July 16, 1967. Founder, prin., pres. The Creative Establishment, Inc., Chgo., N.Y.C., San Francisco and Los Angeles, 1969-87, founder, pres. Cresta Communications Inc., Chgo. 1988— ; speaker on entrepreneurship for women. Del., White House Conf. on Small Bus., 1979; vice-chmn. Ill. Del. to White House Conf., 1979; trustee Mt. Sinai Hosp. Med. Ctr.; bd. dirs. Chgo. Network; bd. dirs. Chgoland. Enterprise Ctr. Recipient YWCA Leadership award, 1985; named Entrepreneur of Yr., Women in Bus. Mem. Nat. Assn. Women Bus. Owners (pres. Chgo. chpt. 1979), Ill. Women's Agenda, Chgo. Assn. Commerce and Industry, Midwest Soc. Profl. Cons., Chgo. Audio-Visual Producers Assn., Chgo. Film Council, Women in Film, Com. of 200, Nat. Women's Forum, Overseas Edn. Fund Women in Bus. Com. Contbr. articles in field to profl. jours. Office: Cresta Communications Inc 11 W Delaware Pl Chicago IL 60610

BEUTELL, NORMA JEAN, dance educator, administrator; b. St. Louis, Feb. 18, 1934; d. Albert Jacob and Gladene Mildred (Waller) B.; m. William George Van Sickle; children—Denise, Mark. Student pub. schs., Normandy, Mo. Owner, artistic dir. Beutell Sch. of Dance, St. Ann and Manchester, Mo., 1951—; artistic dir. Gateway Ballet of St. Louis, St. Ann, 1974—. Choreographer (ballet) Fugue, 1975, Bras et Jambe, 1981, Amron, 1983. Recipient gold medal ballet, silver medal tap and jazz, Best Choreography cup, Best Costuming cup Nat. Dance Competition, Los Angeles, 1987. Mem. Mo. Bot. Gardens, Friends of St. Louis Art Mus., Tchr., choreographer Miss Dance of Am., 1979, Jr. Miss, 1983. Mem. Dance Masters Am. (1st place 1985), Cecchetti Council Am., Dance Educators Am., West St. Louis County C. of C. Methodist. Avocation: travel. Home: 13570 Amiot Saint Louis MO 63146 Office: Gateway Ballet of Saint Louis 10674 St Charles Rock Rd Saint Ann MO 63074

BEUTLER, LISA, park ranger; b. Oakland, Calif., Sept. 28, 1953; d. Charles Stanley and Beth (Peterson) B.; m. Michael Steven Decker, (div.); 1 child, Emily Decker; m. Ronald Edward Rowan, Dec. 31, 1983; 1 child, Matthew Beutler. Student Coll. San Mateo, Calif., 1976, West Valley Coll., Saratoga, Calif., 1976-77; B.S., U. San Francisco, 1986. Park ranger Calif. Dept. Parks and Recreation, 1974-86; sr. investigator Office of State Controller, Sacramento, 1986—; spl. cons. Office of Lt. Gov., Sacramento, 1982-83; spl. cons. law enforcement and environ. affairs Calif. State Lands Commn., Sacramento, 1983—; mem. Park Mgmt. Adv. Bd., West Valley Coll., 1980—; advisor U.S. Fish and Wildlife Service, Newark, Calif., 1982; legis. coordinator Calif. Union of Safety Employees, Sacramento, 1982-83, legis. dir., 1985-86. Contbr. articles to profl. jours. Recipient Letter of Commendation for Rescue Assistance, Nat. Park Services, 1976; Letter of Commendation for Outstanding Performance Calif. Dept. Parks. Año Nuevo State Res., 1977; Award of Outstanding Achievement, Calif. Union Safety Employees, 1985. Apptd. by Calif. Senate to adv. com. Calif. Dept. Pub. Safety, 1987. Mem. State Park Peace Officers Assn. (bd. dirs. 1981-84, 86), Calif. State Park Rangers Assn., Calif. Peace Officers Assn., Peace Officers Research Assn. Calif., Calif. Boating Safety Officers (legis. com.), NOW, Audubon Soc., Greenpeace, Sierra Club. Democrat. Avocations: performing arts. Office: Calif State Lands Commn 1807 13th St Sacramento CA 95814

BEVELACQUA, DARCY HENDRICKSON, marketing executive, consultant; b. Mt. Kisco, N.Y., Aug. 14, 1949; d. Veryl Philip and Elizabeth S.D. (Ralph) B.; m. George Stanhope Wiedemann, III, Feb. 26, 1978 (div. 1982); m. Antoine Bertram Giaume, Mar. 26, 1983; children—Pearson, Ashton. BA in Psychology, Hood Coll., 1971; MA in Human Resources, New Sch., N.Y.C., 1976. Mktg. ops. cons. Chem. Bank, N.Y.C., 1974-77; systems cons. Revlon, N.Y.C., 1977-78; personnel mgr. Pfizer, N.Y.C., 1978-80; dir. bus. devel. Am. Express Co., N.Y.C., 1980-85; mgr. fin. services and mktg. Trintex, White Plains, N.Y., 1985—; mktg. cons., 1975—. Cons., lectr. Counseling Women program, N.Y.C., 1980—, Women in Bus. program YMCA, N.Y.C., 1984—; Recipient Percy Johnson award Chem. Bank, 1976, Isadore Lubin award New Sch., 1976. Mem. Direct Mktg. Idea Exchange, Direct Mktg. Assn. (pres. salary com. 1980-81), NOW. Republican. Episcopalian. Club: Amateur Comedy. Avocations: sailing, tennis, swimming, motor cycling. Home: 118 Cross Hwy Westport CT 06880 Office: Trintex 445 Hamilton White Plains NY 10601

BEVERIDGE, LOUISE WATSON, nursing educator; b. Chatham, Va., Jan. 22, 1934; d. John Eddie and Emma Pearl (Robinson) Watson; m. Louis Edward Beveridge, Nov. 5, 1954; children: Sheila, Louis Jr. Diploma in nursing, Provident Hosp., 1956; BS in Nursing, Hampton U., 1976, postgrad., 1977; postgrad., Christopher Newport Coll., 1980-82. Lic. nurse. Staff nurse Riverside Hosp., Newport News, Va., 1956, health nurse, 1957-58; pvt. duty nurse Hampton and Newport News Registry, Hampton, Va., 1958-61; head nurse Mary Immaculate Hosp., Newport News, 1958-60; supr. head nurse Ea. State Hosp., Williamsburg, Va., 1968-82; nurse coordinator Stop Orgn., Norfolk, Va., 1982-84; instr. nursing Career Devel. Ctr., Newport News, 1984-86, Bel and Bel Assn., Newport News, 1987—. Mem. Community Relations Com., Newport News, 1984—; treas. Newport News Chpt. NAACP, 1982-86. Mem. Am. Nurses Assn., (reference com. 1984-86), Va. Nurses Assn., (human rights commr. 1984-86), Dist. X Nurses Assn. (pres. 1986-87), fNat. Ass. Negro. Bus. Profl. Women (chairperson govtl. relations com 1982—), Chi Eta Phi. Democratic. Baptist. Home: 93 Scufflefield Rd Newport News VA 23602

BEVERSDORF, ANNE ELIZABETH, educational marketing consultant; b. Houston, Tex., Aug. 14, 1949; d. S. Thomas and Norma (Beeson) B. BA, U. Tex., 1972; MLS, Ind. U., 1974. Founding librarian Social Studies Devel. Ctr. Ind. U., Bloomington, 1975-79, info. specialist Vocat. Edn. Services, 1982-83, info. dissemination specialist Devel. Tng. Ctr., 1983; librarian Agy. for Instructional TV, Bloomington, 1980-82; info. specialist Ind. Clearinghouse for Computer Edn., Indpls., 1983-86; Calif. mktg. rep. Minn. Ednl. Computing Corp., San Marcos, Calif., 1986-88; cons. Ednl. Tech. and Change, San Marcos, 1988—; conf. planner Ind. Council for the Social Studies, Bloomington, 1976-79; cons. Procter & Gamble Ednl. Services, Cin., 1981-85, Brazil Office of Tech. Edn., Rio de Janeiro, Porto Alegre, 1986; instr. Ind. U., Indpls., 1986. Editor computer newsletter; contbr. over 25 articles to profl. jours. Mem. Computer Using Educators, Computers and Social Edn. Home: 1119 Anza Ave Vista CA 92084 Office: Ednl Tech and Change 1635 Lake San Marcos Dr San Marcos CA 92069

BEVIS, PATRICIA ANN, finance and marketing executive; b. Florence, Ala., May 9, 1955; d. G. Joe and Billie (Grisham) B. Ed., U. Ala., 1977, Smith Coll.; cert., U. Paris Sorbonne, summer 1977. Buyer R.H. Macy's, N.Y.C., 1981-82; bank officer dept. mktg. Citibank, N.Y.C., 1982-83; fin. and mktg. analyst, asst. v.p. Shearson Lehman Hutton Co. (formerly E.F. Hutton Co., Inc.), N.Y.C., 1983—. Bd. dirs. Mary Anthony/Phoenix Dance Co.; mem. vol. council N.Y. Philharm. Symphony; vol. Bellevue Childlife Hosp. Recipient Outstanding Young Alumnae award U. Ala., 1982; named one of Outstanding Young Women Am., 1985. Mem. Panhellenic (rec. sec. 1980), U. Ala. Alumni Assn. (v.p. student affairs, v.p. alumni), N.Y. Jr. League, Fin. Women's Assn., Partnership Analyst Soc. N.Y. (founder), Am. Mktg. Assn., Mu Phi Epsilon, Alpha Delta Pi (holder various offices, Outstanding Alumna). Presbyterian. Club: Smith (N.Y.C.).

BEXTERMILLER, THERESA MARIE, architect; b. St. Charles, Mo., Feb. 9, 1960; d. Charles Frederick and Loretta Joan (Unterreiner) B. BArch, Kans. State U., 1978-83; postgrad., Wash. U., St. louis, 1985, Pratt Inst., 1988—. Grad. architect Fleming Corp., St. Louis, 1984-85; project architect, prototype mgr. Casco Corp., St. Louis, 1985-87; architect HBE Corp., St. Louis, 1987-88, Hal A. Dorfman, N.Y.C., 1988—. Mem. AIA. Roman Catholic. Home: Pratt Inst 215 Willoughby Ave #1415 Brooklyn NY 11205 Office: Hal A Dorfman Architects 145 W 45th St Suite 1111 New York NY 10036

BEY, EILEEN KRANTZ, construction executive; b. Mpls., Apr. 18, 1950; d. Gordon Christian and Bernice Marie (Madsen) Krantz; m. Sheldon MacDonald Bey, June 13, 1970; children: Matthew Oskar, Lindsey Ellen. Student, Macalester Coll., 1968-70; BA, U. Minn., Morris, 1972. Head bookkeeper Orville E. Madsen & Son, Inc., Mpls., 1972-73, project mgr., 1976-80; sec. Val Michelson & Assoc., St. Paul, 1974-76; with mktg. and pub. relations dept./ Madsen Corp., Madison, Wisc., 1980-81, 82-83, constrn. mgr., 1981-82, asst. to pres., 1983—; planning com. U. Wis. Extension Specifications and Contracts, Madison, 1982; speaker Madison Sch. Dist., 1982, Portage (Wisc.) Dist., 1985, 86; steering com. Bldg. Research and Info.

Ctr., 1986—. Contbr. articles to profl. jours. Loaned exec. United Way, Madison, 1984; bus. cons. Access to Independence, Madison, 1985; bd. dirs. Friends of Civic Ctr., Madison, 1985; ruling elder Caledonia Presbyn. Ch., Portage, 1985. Mem. Constrn. Specifications Inst. (chpt. sec. 1978-82, pres. 1982-86, mem. long range planning com. 1986). Club: Caledonia Community (Portage) (sec. 1982-83, pres. 1987—). Office: Madsen Corp PO Box 7760 Madison WI 53707

BEYER, CHARLOTTE BISHOP, investment management marketing executive; b. N.Y.C., Oct. 16, 1947; d. Edward Morton and Charlotte Reid (Handy) Beyer; B.A., Hunter Coll., 1969; m. Warren P. Weitman, Jr., July 28, 1967; children—Catherine Scott, Michael Benjamin. With Bankers Trust Co., N.Y.C., 1970-81, v.p. trust services and securities ops., 1979-81; dir. Can. mktg. Technimetrics, 1981-83; new bus./mktg. trust officer Fidelity Union Bank, Morristown, N.J., 1983-85; v.p. dir. client service and mktg. Wood Struthers and Winthrop Mgmt. Corp. subs. Donaldson Lufkin and Jenrette, N.Y.C., 1985-87, sr. v.p., 1987—. Trustee Westover Sch., Middlebury, Conn., 1987—. Episcopalian.n., 1987—. Episcopalian. Office: Wood Struthers and Winthrop 140 Broadway New York NY 10005

BEYER, KAREN ANN, social worker; b. Cleve.; d. William and Evelyn Haynes; B.A., Ohio State U., 1965; M.S.W., Loyola U., Chgo., 1969; postgrad. Family Inst., Northwestern U., 1979; 1 dau., Jennifer. Diplomate clin. social work. With Cuyahoga County Div. Child Welfare, Cleve., 1965, Dallas County Child Welfare Unit, Dallas, 1966; with Lutheran Welfare Services Ill., Chgo., 1967-73; pvt. practice psychotherapy, family mediation, Schaumburg, Ill., 1975—; therapist Family Service Assn. Greater Elgin (Ill.), 1973-77, dir. profl. services, 1977-83; dir. HHS Village of Hoffman Estates, Ill., 1983—; fieldwork social work instr. for Loyola U., U. Ill., 1977-80. Bd. dirs. Talkline, 1982-85; mem. mental health adv. bd. Elgin Community Coll. Mem. Nat. Assn. Social Workers, Acad. Cert. Social Workers (clin. and approved supr.), Am. Assn. Marriage and Family Therapy, Am. Orthopsychiat. Assn. Unitarian. Home: 824 Brendon Dr Schaumburg IL 60194

BEYER, MARIE ELENA O'NEILL, association executive; b. Newark, N.J., Oct. 3, 1945; d. Eugene and Anne O'Neill; m. Raymond M. Beyer, Apr. 8, 1972; children: Sean Christopher, Michelle Lisa. BA in Psychology, Rutgers U., 1967. Dir. pub. relations and communications Raritan Valley Regional C. of C., New Brunswick, N.J., 1970-73; adminstr. New Brunswick C. of C., 1973; v.p. ops. Willow Run Recreation Assn., Lewisville, N.C., 1983; exec. dir. Franklin Township C. of C., Somerset, N.J., 1986 . Editor: Commerce Magazine, 1970-73; Dialogue Newsletter, 1986—. Founder Neighborhood Assn., Lewisville, N.C., 1983; mem. Somerset Valley Office Ctr., 1986—. Mem. Douglass Coll. Alumnae Assn. (chair student events 1986-87). Home: 8 Lorraine Ct East Brunswick NJ 08816 Office: 1320 Hamilton St PO Box 1 Somerset NJ 08873

BEYER, MARILYN JEANNE, funeral services executive; b. Williamsburg, Pa., Jan. 28, 1949; d. Adolph Edward Jr. and Alice Esther (Adams) Primm; m. Harry William Beyer, Sept. 16, 1972 (dec.); children: Aaron Christopher, Brett Alan, Curt Andrew, Damon Joseph. AS, Miami-Dade Jr. Coll., 1978. Funeral dir. Beyer Funeral Home, Key Largo, Fla., 1979-84; pres., owner H.W. Beyer Funeral Home, Inc., Key Largo, 1984—. Den mother Cub Scouts Am., Key Largo, 1982-84; bd. dirs. Grove Park Facilities, Miami, 1984. Mem. Nat. Funeral Dirs. Assn., Internat. Order of Golden Rule, Fla. Funeral Dirs. Assn., Upper Keys Athletic Assn. (coach 1980-85, sec. 1982-85, v.p. 1987), Bus. and Profl. Women Assn. Lodges: Lioness, Moose, Keycombers. Office: HW Beyer Funeral Home Inc PO Box #15 Key Largo FL 33037

BEYER, MARY IRENE, controller; b. Milw., Jan. 12, 1962; d. Gail A. and Catherine (Patrinos) B.; m. Ivan M. Sarich, Aug. 20, 1982 (div. Sept. 1984). Student, Carroll Coll., 1980-82, U. Fla., 1983; BA, U. South Fla., 1983. Legal asst. Finn Janowiak & Maloney, Milw., 1979; ins. specialist New York Life Ins. Co., Milw., 1979; adminstrv. asst. Wis. Gas Co., Milw., 1981-82; bookkeeper Gail A. Beyer, Acctg., Milw., 1976-82; controller ISE, Inc., Chgo., 1983—. Mem. Annunciation Greek Orthodox Ch., Milw.; treas. Neighborhood Watch Crime Prevention, Ft. Myers, Fla., 1983. Mem. Nat. Assn. Accts., Am. Mgmt. Assn., Nat. Assn. Female Execs. Home: 535 N Michigan Ave Chicago IL 60611 Office: ISE Inc 401 S LaSalle Suite 500 Chicago IL 60605

BEYER, SUZANNE, advertising agency executive; b. N.Y.C., Dec. 28, 1928; d. Harry and Jennie Hillman; student Nassau Community Coll., 1963-65; grad. Conservatory of Musical Art, N.Y.C., 1947; m. Isadore Beyer, Oct. 19, 1947; children—Pamela Claire, Hillary Jay. Singer, tchr. piano, N.Y.C., 1947-66; asst. to v.p. media dir. Robert E. Wilson, Advt., N.Y.C., 1967-72; media planner, media buyer Frank J. Corbett div. BBDO Internat., N.Y.C., 1972-77; media planner, media buyer Lavey/Wolff/Swift div. BBDO Advt., N.Y.C., 1977-80, sr. media planner, 1980-83, media supr., 1983—; soprano Opera Assn. Nassau, 1976—; soprano United Choral Soc., Woodmere, L.I., 1970—, Armand Sodero Chorale, Baldwin, L.I., 1980-86, Rockville Centre Choral Soc, 1986—. Mem. Pharm. Advt. Council, L.I. Advt. Club, Healthcare Bus. Women's Assn. Home: 66 Fonda Rd Rockville Centre NY 11570 Office: 488 Madison Ave New York NY 10022

BEYER-MEARS, ANNETTE, physiologist; b. Madison, Wis., May 26, 1941; d. Karl and Annette (Weiss) Beyer. B.A., Vassar Coll., 1963; M.S., Fairleigh Dickinson U., 1973; Ph.D., Coll. Medicine and Dentistry N.J., 1977. NIH fellow Cornell U. Med. Sch., 1963-65; instr. physiology Springside Inc., Phila., 1967-71; teaching asst. dept. physiology Coll. Medicine and Dentistry N.J., N.J. Med. Sch., 1974-77, NIH fellow dept. ophthalmology, 1978-80; asst. prof. dept. ophthalmology U. Medicine and Dentistry N.J., N.J. Med. Sch., Newark, 1979—, asst. prof. dept. physiology, 1980-85, assoc. prof. dept. physiology, 1986—, assoc. prof. dept. ophthalmology, 1986—; cons. Alcon Labs. Chmn. admissions No. N.J., Vassar Coll., 1974-79; mem. minister search com. St. Bartholomew Episcopal Ch., N.J., 1978, fundraising chmn., 1978, 79; del. Episc. Diocesan Conv., 1977, 78; long range planning com. Christ Ch., Newark, 1985-87. Recipient NIH Nat. Research Service award, 1978—, Found. CMDNJ Research award, 1980; grantee Juvenile Diabetes Found., 1985-87, Pfizer, Inc., 1985-87. Mem. Am. Physiol. Soc., N.Y. Acad. Scis., Soc. for Neurosci., Am. Soc. Pharmacology and Exptl. Therapeutics, Assn. for Research in Vision and Ophthalmology, Internat. Soc. for Eye Research, AAAS, The Royal Soc. Medicine, Internat. Diabetes Found., Am. Diabetes Assn., Aircraft Owners and Pilots Assn., Civil Air Patrol, Sigma Xi. Contbr. articles in field of diabetic lens and kidney therapy to profl. jours. Office: NJ Med Sch Dept Physiology 185 S Orange Ave Newark NJ 07103

BEYNON, SANDRA ANTOINETTE, college administrator; b. Scranton, Pa., Dec. 6, 1949; d. Daniel William and Sophie Theresa (Krahel) B. BBA, U. Scranton, 1978; MBA, Wilkes Coll., 1985. Adminstrv. asst. Dept. Community Affairs, Scranton, 1969-76; community, bd. liaison Anthra-Penn Community Devel. Corp., Hazleton, Pa., 1976-77; dir. devel. Crystal Devel. Corp., Bloomsburg, Pa., 1977-78; dir. small bus. devel. ctr. Wilkes Coll., Wilkes Barre, Pa., 1978-85, dir. office of founds. and grants mgmt., 1985—; Mem. adv. bd. northeast tier Ben Franklin Partnership, 1981—. Mem. Wilkes Barre Ballet Theater, 1984—; bd. dirs. Pa. Energy Devel. Authority, Harrisburg, 1984-86, Drug Alcohol Adv. Bd., Wilkes Barre, 1987—. Mem. Council for Advancement and Support of Edn., Nat. Council of Univ. Research Adminstrs., Soc. Research Adminstrs., Pa. Assn. for Women Deans, Adminstrs., COunselors, Am. Bus. Women's Assn. (past pres.). Office: Wilkes Coll 170 S Franklin St Wilkes Barre PA 18766

BEYRER, MARY KATHERINE, health education educator; b. South Bend, Ind., Mar. 3, 1922; d. Charles H. and L. Marie (Brickell) B.; B.A., Macalester Coll., 1944; M.S., MacMurray Coll., 1950; Ph.D., Ohio State U., 1959. Tchr. health and phys. edn. Buffalo (Minn.) High Sch., 1944-47, Harrisonburg (Va.) High Sch., 1948-51; teaching asst. MacMurray Coll., 1947-48; asst. prof. health and phys. edn. Madison Coll., Harrisonburg, 1951-56; teaching assoc. Ohio State U., Columbus, 1956-57, instr. health edn., 1957-59, asst. prof., 1959-61, assoc. prof., 1961-64, prof., 1964—, dir. Sch. Health, Phys. Edn., and Recreation, 1977-81. Recipient Alumni citation Macalester Coll. 1964, Luther Halsey Gulick medal, 1988; AAHPERD scholar, 1978-79. Mem. AAHPERD. (Honor Fellow award 1969, exec. com. 1981-84, nat. pres. 1982-83; health edn. award Midwest dist. 1984), Am. Acad. Phys. Edn., Am. Pub. Health Assn., Am. Sch. Health Assn., Assn. Supervision and Curriculum Devel., Ohio Assn. Health, Phys. Edn., Recreation and Dance (cert. of merit 1967), Assn. Advancement Health Edn. (Profl. Service to Health Edn. award 1976, Scholar award 1978), Eta Sigma Gamma(Nat. Honor award), Phi Delta Kappa. Republican. Presbyterian. Author: (with D. Oberteuffer) School Health Education, 1966; (with M.K. Solleder) Directory of Selected References and Resources for Health Education, 1969, 2d edit., 1981; editor: Health Education Completed Research, 1974, 2d edit., 1979. Home: 4012 Lyon Dr Columbus OH 43220 Office: 1760 Neil Ave Columbus OH 43210

BHATT, SMITA BHARAT, physician, pathologist; b. Ahmedabad, India, Mar. 11, 1945; came to U.S., 1969, naturalized, 1978; d. Ramanlal Narotamdas and Bhanumati Ramanlal (Mahadevia) Magiawala; M.B., B.S., B.J. Med. Coll., 1975. Resident in pathology Mt. Carmel Mercy Hosp., Detroit, 1971-75; assoc. pathologist Samaritan Health Ctr., Detroit, 1976—, med. dir. Med. Lab. Technology Scho. Craft Coll. Diplomate Am. Bd. Pathology. Mem. Coll. Am. Pathologists, Am. Soc. Clin. Pathologists, Mich. Soc. Pathologists, Mich. Soc. Cytology, South Central Soc. Microbiology, Am. Soc. Cytology, Internat. Soc. Pathologists. Office: Samaritan Health Ctr 5555 Connor Ave Detroit MI 48213

BIAFORA, ROSANNE, marketing executive; b. Morgantown, W.Va., Apr. 2, 1962; d. Frank A. and Phyllis Sue (Robinson) B. BS in Pub. Relations, U. Fla., 1984; MBA, Nova U., 1988. Pub. relations asst. Shands Hosp., Gainesville, Fla., 1985, pub. relations specialist, 1985-87, coordinator mktg., communications, 1987-88; dir. mktg. Winter Park (Fla.) Pavilion, 1988—. Co-chmn. Am. Heart Assn., Gainesville, 1986, bd. dirs. 1986-88. recipient Best in East award Va. Soc. PRMC, Addy award, Gainesville Advt. Soc., 1986. Mem. Am. Hosp. Assn., Fla. Hosp. Assn., Nat. Assn. Female Execs., Fla. Pub. Relations Exec. Republican. Baptist. Office: Winter Park Pavilion 1600 Dodd Rd Winter Park FL 32792

BIAGGI, CRISTINA SHELLEY, sculptor; b. Lausanne, Switzerland, July 24, 1937; came to U.S., 1948; d. Leo Luciano Biaggi and Virginia Musser (Howard) Redmond; m. Clark Anderson (div. 1964); children: Diana Athena Green, John Clark. Student, Vassar Coll., 1955-57, U. Mexico City, Mexico, 1956, Harvard, 1957; BA in Classics, U. Utah, 1969; MA in Art Edn., NYU, 1975, PhD in Art and Philosophy, 1983. Dir. Spectrum Gallery, Rome, 1961-64; actress various cos., N.Y. and N.J., 1965-69; instr., gallery dir. Rockland Community Coll., Suffern, N.Y., 1972-80; costume and set designer Youth Shakespeare Theater, Palisades, N.Y., 1974-78; instr. art Dominican Coll., Sparkill, N.Y., 1977-80; sculptor Cristina Studios, Palisades, N.Y., 1980—; lectr. Female Imagery in the Works of 20th Century Women Sculptors, Hopper House, Nyack, N.Y., 1977, The Great Goddess, U. Besançon, France, 1986; presenter papers Malta Archaeology and Fertility Cult Conf., 1985, World Archaeol. Conf., Eng., 1986. One-woman shows include Spectrum Gallery, Rome, 1962, Palisades Presbyn. Ch., 1968, Rockland Community Coll., 1980, Rising Phoenix Gallery, Cambridge, Mass., 1984, Soho 20 Art Gallery, N.Y.C.; exhibited in group shows at Ctr. Internat. d'Art Contemporain, Paris, 1984, Metropolis Gallerie Internat. D'Art, Geneva, 1985, Pleiades Gallery, N.Y.C., 1985-86, La Mandragore Galerie, Paris, 1986, Rockland Ctr. for the Arts, 1987, Soho "20", 1988; contbr. articles to archeol. books; producer videos The Web, Mildred. Mem. Women's Ancient Studies Group, Edn. Assocs. NYU, Martial Arts Inst. Am. (black belt 1st dan), People for the Ethical Treatment of Animals, Animal Agenda, Soc. Women Geographers, Seneca Falls Peace Encampment, Nuclear Freeze, Sierra Club. Democrat. Home: 1 Ludlow Ln Palisades NY 10964 Office: Cristina Studios PO Box 208 Palisades NY 10964

BIALCZAK, BARBARA, computer consultant; b. Hartford, Conn., July 24, 1959; d. Edwards Gibson and Barbara (Stengle) Atwood; m. Dean David Bardenheuerm May 19, 1979 (div. 1983); m. Anthony Craig Bialczak, Aug. 6, 1983. Student, Simmons Coll., Boston, 1978. Mgr. network control Advest, Inc., Hartford, Conn., 1978-87; cons. Securities Software & Consulting, Bloomfield, Conn., 1987—; mem. security com. Advest, Inc., Hartford, 1983-87, standards & procedures com., 1985-87. Sunday sch. tchr., First Congregational Ch., East Hartford, Conn., 1980-84, 86—. Mem. Nat. Assn. Female Execs. Republican. Home: 116 Cider Brook Dr Wethersfield CT 06109 Office: Securities Software & Consulting 695 Bloomfield Ave Bloomfield CT 06002

BIANCHI, DOREEN ELIZABETH, asbestos technology professional; b. Syracuse, N.Y., May 4, 1947; d. Pelleno John and Mary Elizabeth (Miller) B.; m. David M. Rood, May 28, 1966 (div. Apr. 1969). BA in English, Fredonia State, 1971; MEd, Fla. Atlantic U., 1977; MS in Telecommunications, Syracuse U., 1979. cert. tchr., N.Y. Reading specialist Palm Beach County Schs., W.Palm Beach and Pahokee, Fla., 1974-78; pres. Bianchi-Trison Corp., E.Syracuse, N.Y., 1980-83; dir. Environtl. Safety and Control Corp., E.Syracuse, 1983-85; pres., exec. dir. Inst. of Asbestos Tech. Corp., E.Syracuse, 1985—; adj. instr. Le Moyne Coll., Syracuse, 1979-80; keynote spkr. Women's Day, N.Y. State Fair, Syracuse, 1983. Producer, writer, moderator (TV program), Insight, 1980-82; author Syracuse mag., 1981. Candidate N.Y. State Senate, 1986; mem. congressman George Wortly bus. and indsl. council, Syracuse, N.Y. State Gov.'s Task Force on Asbestos, 1987—. Recipient Women of Achievement award, Post-Standard Newspaper, 1984. Mem. Nat. Assn. Women Bus. Owners, AAUW, Am. Insdl. Hygiene Assn., Syracuse Fedn. Womens Clubs (Women of Achievement award 1984), Mensa, Cen. N.Y. Assn. Bus. and Profl. Women in Constrn. (founder, pres.), Greater Syracuse C. of C., Am. Soc. Safety Engrs., Profl. Women in Constrn. Republican. Roman Catholic. Office: Inst of Asbestos Tech Corp 5900 Butternut Dr East Syracuse NY 13057

BIANCO, NICOLE ANN, data processing executive; b. Allentown, Pa., Sept. 30, 1949; d. Welch Collerige and Ruth Ellen (Sacher) Everman; m. William Joseph Bianco, Aug. 19, 1971. Cert., Pa. State U., 1967. Programmer RCA, Moorestown, N.J., 1967-69, Trenton (N.J.) Trust Co, 1969-71, Food Fair, Inc., Phila., 1971-73; data processing officer Provident Nat. Bank, Phila., 1973-77; grant coordinator Burlington County Coll., Pemberton, N.J., 1977-79; asst. v.p. Valley Nat. Bank, Phoenix, 1979-85; cons. in field Phoenix, 1985-87; dir. tech. services Trak-Tech, Inc., Phoenix, 1987—; educator/tchr. Computer Systems Devel., Phoenix, 1985-87; adv. editor John Wiley & Sons, Inc., 1986-87. Author: (textbooks) Introduction to Data Base, 1985, Data Communications, 1985, Advanced Project Management, 1986; author and devel.: (software) Parolee Tracking System, 1987. Mem. Profl. Software Programmers Assn. Home: 9209 N 63d Dr Glendale AZ 85302 Office: Trak-Tech Inc 7310 N 16 St Phoenix AZ 85020

BIANUCCI, KATHERINE PETTAS, real estate broker; b. Chgo., Sept. 15, 1937; d. John and Celia (Dragonas) Pettas; m. Donald Bianucci, Nov. 4, 1956; children—Denise Bianucci Spetter, Angela. Student pub. schs. Installment loan staff Cicero State Bank (Ill.), 1963-70; broker Pav/Hanson Realty, Berwyn, Ill., 1974-75; broker owner Village Ctr. Realty, Berwyn, 1975; with Century 21 K-Rich Realty, Berwyn, Ill., 1976—, now co-owner, dir.; dir. West Town Bd. Realtors, Cicero, 1980-82, dir., 1984-86. Mem. Women's Council Realtors. Greek Orthodox. Office: Century 21 K-Rich Realty Inc 6508 W Cermak Rd Berwyn IL 60402

BIAZAR-NOORANI, CYNTHIA LYNN, business executive; b. Denver, Feb. 11, 1960; d. Loujuan S. and Pauline Ann (Jones) Green; m. Esfandiar Biazar, Dec. 12, 1981 (dec. Aug. 1984); 1 child, Chad Arash; m. Nosratollah Noorani, Apr. 1987, 1 child, Bejan Michael. BS in Bus. Adminstrn., Chapman Coll., Orange, Calif., 1982. Student asst. Chapman Coll. Student Store, 1979, sec., 1979-80, asst. mgr., 1980-82; mgr. United Art Co. div. Follett Corp., Chapman Coll. Bookstore, Orange, 1982-84; controller Fed. Am. Fin. Corp., Newport Beach, Calif., 1984-87; sr. acct. World Citrus West, Inc., Fullerton, Calif., 1987—. Recipient Internat. Youth in Achievement award Internat. Biog. Ctr., 1981. Mem. Nat. Assn. Female Execs., Beta Chi (sec., treas. 1979-81; Orange). Home: 2807 E Roberta Dr Orange CA 92669 Office: World Citrus West Inc 130 E Santa Fe Fullerton CA 92631

BIBLE, FRANCES LILLIAN, mezzo soprano, educator; b. Sackets Harbor, N.Y.; d. Arthur and Lillian (Cooke) B. Student, Juilliard Sch. Music, 1939-47. Artist-in-residence Shepherd Sch. of Music Rice U., Houston, 1975—. Appeared throughout, U.S., Australia, Europe including, Vienna Staatsoper, Karlsruhe Staatsoper, Dublin Opera Co., N.Y.C. Opera, NBC-TV Opera, San Francisco Opera, Glyndebourne Opera, San Antonio Opera Festival, New Orleans Opera, Houston Grand Opera, Miami Opera, Dallas Opera; appeared in concert with major symphonies. Mem. Am. Guild Mus. Artists (past 3d v.p.), Sigma Alpha Iota (hon.), Beta Sigma Phi (hon.). Republican. Episcopalian. Home: 2225 Bolsover Houston TX 77005

BIBLER, CAROL JEAN, geologist; b. Calgary, Alta., Can., July 16, 1958; d. Louis Allen and Eleanor Jean (Fritzen) B. BS in Geology, U. Puget Sound, 1981; MS in Geology, Montana State U., 1986. Research asst. U. Puget Sound, Tacoma, 1979-80; wellsite geologist Teague Geol. Inc., Shelby, Mont., 1981-82; petroleum geol. Harrington, Bibler and Stewart, Billings, Mont., 1986-87, consulting petroleum geologist, 1988—. Contbr. articles to profl. jours. Mem. Am. Assn. Petroleum Geol., Geol. Soc. Am., Mont. Geol. Soc. (sec. 1986-87). Home: 409 W Harrison Bozeman MT 59715 Office: 14 S Wilson Suite 4 Bozeman MT 59715

BICK, KATHERINE LIVINGSTONE, scientist, government official; b. Charlottetown, Can., May 3, 1932; came to U.S., 1954; d. Spurgeon Arthur and Flora Hazel (Murray) Livingstone; m. James Harry Bick, Aug. 20, 1955 (div.); children: James A., Charles L.; m. Ernst Freese, 1986. BS with honors, Acadia U., Can., 1951, MS, 1952; PhD, Brown U., 1957. Research pathologist UCLA Med. Sch., 1959-61; asst. prof. Calif. State U., Northridge, 1961-66; lab. instr. Georgetown U., Washington, 1970-72, asst. prof., 1972-76; dep. dir. neurol. disorder program Nat. Inst. Neurol. and Communicative Disorders and Stroke, NIH, Bethesda, Md., 1976-81, acting dep. dir., 1981-83, dep. dir., 1983-87, dep. dir. extramural research, 1987—. Editor: Alzheimer's Disease: Senile Dementia and Related Disorders, 1978, Neurosecretion and Brain Peptides, Implications for Brain Functions and Neurol. Disease, 1981, The Early Story of Alzheimer's Disease, 1987; contbr. articles to profl. jours. Pres. Woman's Club, McLean, Va., 1968-69; bd. dirs. Fairfax County YWCA (Va.), 1969-70; pres. Emerson Unitarian Ch., 1964-66, Bethesda Place Homeowner's Assn., 1982. Recipient Can. NRC award Acadia U., 1951-52, fellow, 1951-52; Universal Match Found. fellow Brown U., 1956-57; NIH Dir.'s award, 1978; Fed. Exec. Inst. Leadership fellow, 1980; Spl. Achievement award NIH, 1981, 83; Superior Service award USPHS, 1986. Mem. Am. Neurol. Assn., Am. Acad. Neurology, AAAS, Am. Soc. Zoologists, Western Soc. Naturalists, Assn. for Research in Nervous and Mental Disease, Internat. Brain Research Orgn., World Fedn. Neurology Research Group on Dementias (exec. sec. Am. region 1984-86, chmn. 1986—). Office: Nat Inst Health Dept of Health & Human Services Office of the Director 9000 Rockville Pike Bethesda MD 20892

BICKERS, CONSTANCE RADCLIFFE, insurance company executive, health care consultant; b. Lorain, Ohio, Aug. 11, 1933; d. Howard Hugh and Harriet Alice (Lipple) Radcliffe; student LaSalle U., Lorain Community Coll.; BS, Radwate Dyke Coll., 1986. m. Herbert Bennett Bickers, Nov. 24, 1955. Bookkeeper, McGeachie Plumbing and Heating Co., Lorain, 1950-51, Penn Rubber Co., Lorain, 1951-52, office mgr. Packard Motor Co., Lorain, 1952-54, Bay View Hosp., Bay Village, Ohio, 1954-57, acct., 1957-65, asst. adminstr., 1965-76; dir. provider affairs Blue Cross N.E. Ohio, Cleve., 1976-81, v.p. benefits adminstrn., 1981-84. Recipient Lorain County Women of Achievement award, 1986. Fellow Am. Coll. Healthcare Execs., Am. Coll. Osteopathic Hosp. Execs.; mem. Hosp. Fin. Mgmt. Assn. (recipient Frederick T. Muncie award 1973, Dale L. Reed award 1969, 70, 71, 73, William G. Follmer award; nat. dir. 1973-74), Am. Coll. Osteo. Hosp. Adminstrs. (bd. examiners), Am. Soc. Women Accts., Am. Coll. Hosp. Adminstrs., Ohio Hosp. Assn., Health Care Adminstrs. N.E. Ohio, Fedn. Community Planning, Citizens League Greater Cleve., Am. Coll. Nursing Home Adminstrs., Am. Hosp. Assn., Nat. Council for Prescription Drug Program, Am. Med. Record Assn., Med. Group Mgmt. Assn. Club: Women's City (Cleve.). Contbr. articles to profl. jours. Home: 315 Harris Rd Sheffield Lake OH 44054 Office: 2066 9th St E Cleveland OH 44115

BICKERSTAFF, LORETTA LOIS, security personnel executive; b. Brownfield, Tex., Dec. 7, 1937; d. Joseph Alburtus and Opal Lucy (Anderson) B. Ptnr. Vinson Guard Service, Inc., New Orleans, 1963—; owner Northshore Cons., Inc., Lacombe, La., 1987—. Mem. Nat. Assn. Accts., World Assn. Detectives (historian 1979—). Republican. Baptist. Lodge: Eastern Star. Home: PO Box 1250 Dogwood Dr Lacombe LA 70445 Office: Vinson Guard Service Inc Vinson Detective Agy Inc 955 Howard Ave New Orleans LA 70113-1179

BICKLER, JAN MARIE, television production specialist; b. Chgo., Nov. 10, 1949; d. William Clifford and Juliette M. (Brosius) B. BA in Journalism, Creighton U., 1971. Asst. talent agt. The Jim Halsey Co., Los Angeles, 1981-84; bus. mgr. Argus Mgmt. Co., Santa Monica, Calif., 1984-86; TV prodn. coordinator Tall Pony Prodns., Los Angeles, 1983-86, Fox Square Prodns., Los Angeles, 1986—; TV prodn. acct., 1983—. Roman Catholic. Home: 220 Via del Caballo Agoura CA 91301

BICKNESE, EVELYN HOLLISTER, advertising agency executive; b. Gary, Ind., Nov. 14, 1934; d. Ross R. and Leona Colburn (Metzker) Hollister; B.S., Clayton U., St. Louis, 1980; m. Donald Dale Bicknese, June 29, 1952; children: Ross, Leona, Ralph, Kent, Eileen, Susan. Owner, mgr. Bick Outdoor Advt. Co., Gary, Ind., 1957-80, Valparaiso, Ind., 1963-73, La Porte, Ind., 1963—, St. Louis, 1981—; advt. exec. D'Arcy, Masius, Benton & Bowles, Inc., St. Louis. Leader Singing Sands council Girl Scouts U.S.A., 1972-75, Potawattomi council Boy Scouts Am., 1963-72; pres. Principia Patrons of Northwestern Ind., 1977-79; treas., exec. bd. Principia Mothers Club, 1981-82; 4-H vol. worker; co-founder Kent Hollister Bicknese Found. to prevent crime, 1983. Mem. Eight Sheet Outdoor Advt. Assn. (dir. 1975—, pres. 1982—), Ind. Sign and Display Assn. (editor newsletter 1979, dir. 1978-80), Michiana Advt. Exec. Club, C. of C., Advt. Fedn. St. Louis (speakers' bur., edn. com.). Republican. Christian Scientist. Clubs: Ambassadors, Greater Advt. St. Louis. Author: Mostly Manners and Survival Manners for Teenagers. Office: 0353 E 900 N La Porte IN 46350

BIDDICK, DIANE KAY, health care management; b. Madison, Wis., Nov. 8, 1954; d. Scott Hathaway and Betty Darline (Womack) B. BS in Nursing, Wash. State U., Pullman, 1976; M of Mgmt. Info. Systems, West Coast U., 1986. Charge nurse Del Amo Hosp., Torrance, Calif., 1976-78; supr. Kaiser Found. Hosp., Los Angeles, 1978-81; asst. dept adminstr. So. Calif. Permanente Med. Group, Los Angeles, 1981-84, dept. adminstr., 1984—. Sec., bd. dirs. Fair Oaks Homeowners Assn. Mem. Am. Nurse Assn. Republican. Congregationalist. Office: So Calif Permanente Med Group 4900 Sunset Blvd Los Angeles CA 90027

BIDDIX, JOAN SELL, mobile home company owner; b. Johnson City, Tenn., May 5, 1936; d. Earl Walter and Jeanne Mason (Lyle) Sell; m. Dale L. Moss, Jan. 15, 1956 (div. Nov. 1977); children: Carol Anne, John D.; m. Edward Eugene Biddix, Nov. 2, 1978. BS, East Tenn. State U., Johnson City, 1961. Cert. tchr., Tenn., Ga. Tchr. Asbury Sch., Johnson City, 1961-62, Richard Arnold High Sch., Savannah, Ga., 1964-66, Windsor Forest High Sch., Savannah, 1966-67, Boones Creek High Sch., Jonesborough, Tenn., 1967-68; co-owner Moss-Sell Mobile Homes, Johnson City, 1968-77; co-owner Biddix Budget Homes, Inc. (formerly Budget Mobile Homes), Johnson City, 1978-87, v.p., sec., 1987—. Mem. Tenn. Manufactured Housing Assn., Upper East Tenn. Manufactured Housing Assn., DAR. Republican. Presbyterian. Club: Eastern Star. Home: Rt 3 PO Box 9 Knob Creek Rd Johnson City TN 37604 Office: Budget Mobile Homes 3301 N Roan St Johnson City TN 37601

BIDDLE, MARY GERALDINE STATON, nurse; b. Camden, N.J., May 16, 1943; d. Maurice Glen and Mary Dolores (McNamara) Staton; diploma in nursing, Pa. Hosp., Phila., 1964; m. Theodore Long Biddle, June 6, 1970; children—Katherine Mary and Margaret Ann (twins), Theodore Richard. Staff nurse hosps. in Phila. and Denver, 1964-70; mem. adminstrv. staff nephrology U. Rochester (N.Y.) Med. Center, 1970-84, nephrology nurse cons.; faculty mem. Sch. Nursing, U. Rochester, 1975-84; mem. N.J. Spl. Task Force on Organ Retrival, 1987; program chairperson 3d Internat. Nephrology Nursing Conf., N.Y.C., 1987, Brit. Am. Nephrology Nursing Seminar, London, 1987. Mem. editorial bd. several profl. publs. Named Profl. Person of Yr., Genessee Valley Kidney Found., 1976. Cert. hemodialysis nurse Bd. Nephrology Examiners. Mem. Am. Nephrology Nurses Assn. (dir. 1976-81, nat. pres. 1985-86; outstanding contbn. award 1985), Nat. Kidney Found. (nat. program chmn., nursing 1982, exec. com. nursing council, v.p. region I 1987), Am. Heart Assn., End Stage Renal Disease Network Coordinating Council (exec. com. 1979-84). Author papers in field. Home: 10 Pepper Ln Loudonville NY 12211 Office: ANNA North Woodbury Rd/56 Pitman NJ 08071

BIEBER, KAREN RUTH, lawyer; b. San Francisco, Dec. 12, 1949; d. Leo Anthony and Evelyn (O'Brien) Gambone; m. Clifford Ralph Pohl, Sept. 6, 1969 (div. 1978); m. 2d Scott Alan Bieber; Mar. 13, 1983. B.S. with honors, Wright State U., Dayton, Ohio, 1970; cert. grad. Inst. Paralegal Studies, Phila., 1973; J.D., U. Chgo., 1979. Bar: N.Y. 1980, Ill. 1982, U.S. Dist. Ct. (ea. and so. dists.) N.Y. 1980, U.S. Dist. Ct. (no. dist.) Ill. 1982. Tchr. Dayton City Schs., 1970-72; lawyer's asst. Harter, Secrest & Emery, Rochester, N.Y., 1973-76; assoc. Davis Polk & Wardwell, N.Y.C., 1979-81; assoc. Levy and Erens, Chgo., 1981-83, ptnr., 1984; counsel Goldberg, Kohn, Bell, Black, Rosenbloom & Moritz, Ltd., Chgo., 1984-85, ptnr., 1985—. Founder Chgo. chpt. Israel Cancer Research Fund, 1983; bd. trustees Congregation Rodfei Zedek, Chgo., 1984. Decalogue Soc. of Chgo. scholar, 1978. Mem. ABA, Chgo. Bar Assn., Chgo. Council Lawyers. Democrat. Home: 3012 Wilmette Ave Wilmette IL 60091 Office: Goldberg Kohn Bell Black Rosenbloom & Moritz Ltd 55 E Monroe St Suite 3900 Chicago IL 60603

BIEDERMAN, MARY ANN, service professional; b. Birmingham, Ala., Apr. 3, 1933; d. Frank Curtis and Julia Vernon (Vaughn) Wall; m. E. Charles Biederman, Jan. 22, 1954; children: James Charles, Frank Kelly. Student, Howard Coll., 1952-53. Cashier So. Bell Tel. and Tel., Nashville, 1953-54; sec. Nat. Life and Accident Co., Nashville, 1956-59; adminstrv. asst. Baird Ward, Nashville, 1959-61, customer service rep., 1961-70, acct. mgr., 1971-83, mgr. customer service, 1983-87, mem. pres. staff, 1984-87, group mgr. customer service, 1987—; speaker Folio, 1986. Fellow Printing Assn. Am., Web Offset (speaker 1987). Office: Arcata Graphics/Baird Ward PO Box 539 Thompson Lane & Powell Ave Nashville TN 37202

BIEGEL, EILEEN MAE, hospital executive; b. Eau Claire, Wis., Nov. 13, 1937; d. Ewald Frederic and Emma Antonia (Conrad) Weggen; student Dist. One Tech. Inst., 1974, also part time, corr. student U. Wis., Madison; grad. mgmt. seminars; student Upper Iowa U., 1984—; m. James O. Biegel, Oct. 6, 1956; children—Jeffrey Alan, John William. Exec. sec. to pres. Broadcaster Services, Inc., Eau Claire, Wis., 1969-74; exec. sec. to exec. v.p. Am. Nat. Bank, Eau Claire, 1975-77; exec. asst. to pres. Luther Hosp., Eau Claire, 1977—, asst. corporate sec., 1984—; mem. exec. staff, 1985—; asst. corp. sec. Luther Health Care Corp., 1984—; mem. secretarial adv. council Dist. One Tech. Sch. 1975—. State pres. Future Homemakers Am., 1955. Cert. profl. sec., 1980. Mem. Eau Claire Womens Network (founder, mem. steering com.), Profl. Secs. Internat. (chmn. goals and priorities com., pres. Eau Claire chpt. 1982-83), Chippewa Valley Hist. Mus. Lutheran. Home: 4707 Tower Dr Eau Claire WI 54701 Office: 310 Chestnut St Eau Claire WI 54701

BIEL, PATRICIA KATHLEEN, comptroller; b. East Chicago, Ind., Mar. 27, 1946; d. Robert Louis and Dorothy Kathleen (Watters) Hargis; m. Robert ARthur Biel, Aug. 27, 1966 (div. 1981); children: Michael Anthony, Martin Andrew, Matthew Aaron. BSBA, Ind. U., 1981. Sole owner tax service Ft. Wayne, Ind., 1981-85; adminstrv. asst. Dr. R.L. Hargis, Ft. Wayne, 1981-83; controller Myers & McCarty, Ft. Wayne, 1983-84; asst. controller Weingart, Inc., Ft. Wayne, 1984-85; comptroller B&H Industries of SW Fla., Inc., Ft. Myers, 1985—. Mem. Nat. Assn. Accts., Am. Mgmt. Assn., Nat. Acctg. Assn. (bd. dirs. local chpt.), NAFE (local chpt.). Home: 8366 Charter Club Circle #2104 Fort Myers FL 33919 Office: B&H Industries of SW Fla Inc 15851 Chief Ct Fort Myers FL 33912

BIELAWSKI, ELIZABETH ANNE, purchasing group executive; b. Fall River, Mass., Jan. 27, 1950; d. Joseph Paul and Frances Sophie (Wojcik) Czerwonka. Research assoc. R.I. Hosp., Providence, 1972-74; planner, evaluator Bristol County Home Care, Fall River, Mass., 1974-75, exec. dir., 1975-86; v.p. long term care PACE Shared Services, Sioux Falls, S.D., 1986-88; exec. dir. Nebr. Assn. Pvt. Resources, Lincoln, 1988—; instr. Bristol Community Coll., Fall River, 1985-86; adj. prof. bus. and engring. div. Augustana Coll., 1987—. Host (talk show) The Best Times, 1986. Chair chpt. ARC, Fall River, 1978-86, bd. dirs. Sioux Falls chpt., 1986; zone chair United Way, Fall River, 1983-86. Mem. Am. Soc. on Aging, Mass. Assn. Home Care Programs, Inc. (treas. 1975, v.p. 1985), Nat. Council on Aging, Nat. Council of Sr. Citizens. Democrat. Roman Catholic. Home: 1226 S 166th St Omaha NE 68130 Office: Nebr Assn Private Resources 608 S 14th St Suite 403 Lincoln NE 68508

BIELEFELDT, CATHERINE C., sales executive; b. Bellwood, Ill.; d. William Anton and Linda (Buchert) B. B.Music in Piano Performance, Chgo. Conservatory Coll.; student El Conservatorio de Mex., Mexico City; postgrad. Northwestern U., CBS Sch. Mgmt., 1980. Dept. mgr. Fair Store, Oak Park, Ill., 1950-62; piano sales cons. Lyon & Healy Co., Oak Park and Oak Brook, Ill., 1963-77; dir. Steinway Hall, dir. nat. sales tng. Steinway & Sons, Long Island City, N.Y., 1978-82; v.p. sales, pub. relations and advt. Hendricks Music Co., Downers Grove, Ill., 1983—; sales seminar instr. Jordan-Kitt's Music, Wells Music, Washington and Denver, 1983-85. Author: The Wonders of the Piano, The Anatomy of the Instrument, 1984; contbg. author The Keynote Newsletter; contbr. articles to profl. jours. Mem. Women in Communications, Inc., Evanston Music Club, Sigma Alpha Iota (past pres. alumnae chpt., recipient numerous awards). Republican. Lutheran. Home: 190 S Wood Dale Rd Apt 1101 Wood Dale IL 60191 Office: Hendricks Music 421 Maple Ave Downers Grove IL 60515

BIELINSKI, SHARON MARIE, hospital administrator; b. Decatur, Ill., May 12, 1950; d. Herbert Jerry and Ruth Marie (Kaufman) Younger; m. Stephen Peter Bielinski, June 2, 1973; children: Melanie Ann, Michelle Marie. BA, So. Ill. U., 1976; Cert. in respiratory therapy, U. Chgo., 1978. Respiratory therapist Copley Meml. Hosp., Aurora, Ill., 1974-78, therapeutic coordinator, 1978-79, shift supr., 1979-82, dir. heart ctr., respiratory care, 1982—. Vol. Am. Heart Assn., Aurora, 1985-86, chair com. 1986-87; troop leader Girl Scouts of U.S., Aurora, 1986-87. Mem. Am. Assn. Respiratory Care, Women in Mgmt. Home: 2433 Cambridge Aurora IL 60506 Office: Copley Meml Hosp Lincoln and Weston Aves Aurora IL 60505

BIENENSTEIN, KATHLEEN LINDA, engineering company executive; b. Detroit, June 20, 1951; d. Charles August and Emily Linda (Tomolillo) B.; m. Alfred Reginal Trainer, III, Sept. 11, 1970 (div. 1972). BA Oakland U., Mich., 1973; AA in Bus., Kellogg Community Coll., Battle Creek, 1980. Owner retail store, Livonia, Mich., 1973-75; designer Criterion Design, Royal Oak, Mich., 1975-77; designer Eaton Corp., Galesburg, Mich., 1977-81; v.p. engring. services Charles S. Davis & Assoc. Inc., Pontiac, Mich., 1981-87, gen. mgr., 1984-85; engring. group mgr. Ruecker Engring Ltd., 1987-88; chief exec. officer, pres. Celtech Inc., 1988— . Patentee camshaft bushing. Sponsor, Star Theatre, Flint, Mich., 1983-86. Mem. Soc. Automotive Engrs., Soc. Body Engrs., NOW, Nat. Assn. Female Execs. Democrat. Office: Celtech Inc 400 Monroe #400 Detroit MI 48226

BIERBOWER, ANN SHAFER, food products manufacturing executive; b. Lewistown, Pa., Apr. 13, 1948; d. Ira Roy and Helen Elizabeth (Brant) S.; m. William Walter Topper, Aug. 22, 1966 (div. Apr. 1970); children: Jonathan Michael, Faye Elizabeth; m. Park Pershing Bierbower, Mar. 5, 1975 (div. Aug. 1985). AS, Pa. State U., 1970, BS, 1972. Registered profl. engr., Pa. Process engr. Charmin Paper Products, Mehoopany, Pa., 1972-74; staff engr. Susquehanna River Basin Com., Mechanicsburg, Pa., 1974, Gannett, Fleming, Corddry and Carpenter, Camp Hill, Pa., 1974-78, Ralston Purina Co., Mechanicsburg, Pa., 1978-81; plant engr. San Giorgio Macaroni, div. of Hershey Foods, Lebanon, Pa., 1981-84, mgr. plant ops., 1984-85; mgr. mfg. Am. Beauty Macaroni div. Hershey Foods, Fresno, Calif., 1985-88, plant mgr., 1988—. Mem. YMCA Indian Princesses (asst. nation chief Fresno chpt. 1987—), Fresno Zoo Soc. Republican. Office: Am Beauty Macaroni PO Box 12416 Fresno CA 93776

BIERCE, CAROL ANNE HOOVER, computer software specialist, city official; b. Pensacola, Fla., Jan. 30, 1954; d. Ralph Alwin Hoover Jr. and Hazel Floyce (Warren) Roberts; m. Daniel Ambrose Bierce, Oct. 17, 1975; children: Adam Anthony, Joseph Alexander. BA in Math. with highest distinction, U. North Fla., 1975, BAE with highest distinction, 1976, MBA, 1979. Programmer Sav-A-Stop, Inc., Orange Park, Fla., 1975-76; with City of Jacksonville, Fla., 1976—, sr. application analyst, 1980-82, asst. computer systems officer, dep. tech. dir., 1982-88, tech. dir., 1988—; project leader water and electric computer services, tech. support; cons. for Jacksonville Software Devel. Corp. Active Riverside-Avondale Preservation Soc., Fla. Epilepsy Found., Jacksonville Zool. Soc., Jacksonville Mus. Arts and Scis., St. Mark's Women of Ch. Mem. Assn. MBA Execs., Nat. Assn. Female Execs., Phi Theta Kappa, Pi Mu Epsilon. Democrat. Episcopalian. Home: 1624 Cherry St Jacksonville FL 32205 Office: City Hall 220 E Bay St Jacksonville FL 32202

BIERGAUM, GRETCHEN, artist. instr. Cuyahoga Valley Art Ctr., Ohio, 1983—. One woman show: Akron (Ohio) Women's City Club, 1983. Mem. North Coast Collage Soc. (founder). Home: 254 W Streetsboro St Hudson OH 44236

BIERLEIN, MARCILEE ANN WILSON, state agency administrator, personnel specialist; b. Winfield, Kans., Sept. 23, 1942; d. Kenneth Ivan and Audrey Eleanor (Watkins) Menzie; m. John David Bierlein, May 30, 1964; children: Christopher David, Julie Melissa. BA in Psychology and Sociology, U. Kans., 1964, MA in Child Devel., 1968; M of Pub. Admnstrn., U. Del., 1978; postgrad., Harvard U., 1983. Adminstrv. asst. to council pres. New Castle County Council, Wilmington, Del., 1978-79; exec. asst. to sec. of Dept. Labor State of Del., Wilmington, 1979-84, dir. employment services, 1984, dir. employment and tng., 1984-85, acting Sec. of Labor, 1984-85; state personnel dir. Dover, 1985—; mem. State Del. Bd. Pension Trustees, Dover, 1985—, Deferred Compensation Council, Dover, 1981—, Del. Pvt. Industry Council, Wilmington, 1984—; co-chairperson Del. Statewide Labor Mgmt. Com., Wilmington, 1984—. Mem. Gov.'s Council on Labor, Wilmington, 1978-79; personnel com. United Way of Del., 1986—; trustee Peninsula United Meth. Homes, Inc., 1988—. Named one of 6 Women to Watch Del. Today mag., 1973, Person to Watch Del. Today mag., 1986. Mem. Women Execs. in State Govt., Wilmington Women in Bus., Nat. Assn. State Personnel Execs., Del. Assn. for Pub. Adminstrn. (pres. 1983-84, Outstanding Woman Mem. 1983, 85), Internat. Personnel Mgmt. Assn., Nat. Pub. Employers Labor Relations Assn., LWV (state pres. 1975-76, local pres. 1973-75). Republican. Unitarian. Home: 5 Wellington Rd Wilmington DE 19803 Office: State of Del Office of Personnel PO Box 1401 Dover DE 19901

BIES, SUSAN SCHMIDT, financial company executive; b. Buffalo, May 5, 1947; d. Louis Howard and Gladys May (Metke) Schmidt; m. John David Bies, Aug. 29, 1970; children: John Matthew, Scott Louis. BS, State U. Coll.-Buffalo, 1967; MA, Northwestern U., 1968, PhD, 1972. Banking structure economist FRS, St. Louis, 1970-72; asst. prof. econs. Wayne State U., Detroit, 1972-77; assoc. prof. Rhodes Coll., Memphis, 1977-80; tactical planning mgr. First Tenn. Nat. Corp., Memphis, 1980-81, dir. corp. devel., 1982-83, treas., 1983-84, sr. v.p., chief fin. officer, 1984-85, exec. v.p., chief fin. officer, 1985—; mem. fin. adv. com. City of Germantown, Tenn., 1978-86; mem. investment adv. com. Tenn. Consol. Retirement System, Nashville, 1981-86; instr. MidSouth Sch. Banking, 1985-86; exec. in residence Memphis State U.; bd. dirs. Memphis Ptnrs. Pres., bd. dirs. North Germantown Homeowners Assn., 1978-83; treas. Germantown Area Soccer Assn., 1985-86; mem. task force Com. on the 21st Century, Rhodes Coll., Memphis, 1986-87. Fellow Ctr. for Urban Affairs, 1968-69, Fed. Res. Bank Chgo., 1970. Mem. ABA (exec. com., 1986-88), Nat. Assn. Bus. Economists, Am. Econ. Assn., Planning Execs. Inst., Fin. Execs. Inst., Planning Forum (Managerial Excellence award Memphis chpt. 1986), Memphis Area C. of C. (bd. dirs. 1988—), Omicron Delta Epsilon, Lambda Alpha. Episcopalian. Office: First Tenn Nat Corp 165 Madison Ave Memphis TN 38103

BIESEL, DIANE J., librarian; b. N.Y.C., Feb. 15, 1934; d. Douglas and Runa (Patterson) Stevens; m. Donald W. de Cordova, June 24, 1956 (div. July 1971); m. David Barrie Biesel, Sept. 25, 1982. BS, Trenton State Coll., 1956; MLS, Rutgers U., 1969; MA in Edn., Seton Hall U., 1974, cert. in supervision, 1976. Tchr., librarian Arlington (Va.)) Bd. Edn., 1956-58; media specialist elem. schs., libraries River Edge (N.J.) Bd. Edn., 1958—; lectr., instr. children's lit. Alphonsus Coll., Woodcliff Lake, N.J., 1969-72; field service cons. N.J. Dept. Edn., 1969-71; cons. New Books Preview Baker and Taylor Co., 1972-76; adj. prof. Seton Hall U., 1978-79; mem. awards com. Rutgers U. Grad. Sch. Library Service, 1978-79. Sec. Lay Readers Guild, Episcopal Diocese Newark, 1975-76, v.p., 1977-78, pres., 1979-80, chmn. com. resolutions, 1978-79, adminstr. Bishop's Bunch, 1979-80, mem. com. rules of order, 1980-81; moderator Forum on J.P. Stevens boycott, 1978; mem. Com. of 100, 1979; co-chmn. East Bergen Convocation ACTS campaign, 1979; active Girl Scouts Am. 1941-71; mem. com. academically gifted River Edge Bd. Edn., 1977-83, choir All Saint's Ch., Bergenfield, 1971—, vestrywoman, 1980-83, del. to Diocesan Conv., 1978—. Mem. ALA, Am. Assn. Sch. Librarians (mem. com. instrnl. media 1971-76, affiliate assembly by-laws com. 1977-78, Ednl. Media Assn. N.J. (state chmn. recruitment 1968-69, state chmn. hospitality 1972-73, state chmn. county liaison 1973-74, co-pres. 1977-78), Bergen County Sch. Libraries Assn. (pres. 1966-68), River Edge Tchrs. Assn. (pres. 1964-66), Assn. Ednl. Communications Tech. (nat. nominating com. 1978-79, council 1978-79, steering com. 1979-80, evaluation com. 1979, co-chmn. liaison com. with Am. Assn. Sch. Librarians 1979-83, nat. nominating com. 1980-82, awards com. 1981—), Sch. Media Specialists (program com. 1982-84, bd. dirs. region II 1983-84, pres. 1986, mem. task force on libraries and info. sci., White House, writing com., co-author: Information Power, 1988.). Home: 315 Schraalenburgh Rd Haworth NJ 07641-1203 Office: 410 Bogert Rd River Edge NJ 07661

BIESEL, DUANE MACDONALD, manufacturing company executive; b. Chgo., June 9, 1931; d. Lorne Evan and Marie Eileen (Lyness) MacDonald; m. Garnett Biesel, May 1, 1954 (div. June 1970). B.S., Monmouth Coll., 1952; postgrad. Northwestern U., 1956-57. Chemist, Underwriters Lab., Inc., Chgo., 1952-56; Toni Co. div. Gillette Co., Chgo., 1956-61; chemist Gillette Co., Chgo., 1964-74; product devel. mgr., Boston, 1974-87; research and devel. dir. Frank Fuhrer Internat., Pitts., 1987—. Patentee in hosiery field. Mem. Soc. Cosmetic Chemists. Avocations: reading; classical music; travel; golf. Office: Frank Fuhrer Internat Inc 400 Chess St Coraopolis PA 15108

BIESELE, SUSAN CLEGG, county official; b. Elko, Nev., Aug. 5, 1953; d. Daris Rae and Betty Ida (Beal) Clegg; m. Calvin Paul Goff, May 20, 1973 (div.); m. 2d William Henry Biesele, Apr. 12, 1979; 1 stepson, William Michael. Clerk steno cert. Utah Tech. Coll., 1972, B in Polit. Sci. U. Utah, 1988. Adminstrv. sec. Model Cities, Salt Lake City, 1972-73; clk. stenographer Salt Lake County Office Personnel Mgmt., Salt Lake City, 1973-74, personnel specialist, 1974-78, personnel analyst, 1978, supervising analyst, 1978-80, mgr. classification and selection, 1980-87; research and devel. mgr., 1987—; developer employment examinations and systems. Author personnel and tng. manuals. Active Utah Commn. on Employment and Careers for Women, 1981-82. Recipient Miss Annex award Utah Tech. Coll., 1971; outstanding performance awards Salt Lake County Govt., 1973, 74, 83, 84, 85, 87, extra-meritorious performance awards, 1977, 81, 15 yrs. county service award, 1988. Mem. Internat. Personnel Mgmt. Assn. (Utah chpt. pres. 1981, treas. 1987-88), Internat. Personnel Mgmt. Assn. (acting membership chair assessment council 1978—, acting membership chmn. 1978), Am. Compensation Assn., (cert. compensation profl.), Am. Soc. Pub. Adminstrs., Salt Lake Area Compensation Group (chmn. elect 1988, co-founder), Utah Personnel Assn. Lodge: Zonta. Home: 3303 E Oakcliff Dr Salt Lake City UT 84124 Office: Human Resources Div 2001 S State St N4600 Salt Lake City UT 84190-3150

BIEVER, ANGELA MARY, financial company executive; b. Lloydminster, Sask., Can., Aug. 19, 1953; came to U.S., 1977; d. Vernon Adam and Lila Mae (Enzenauer) B. B Commerce with honors, Queen's U., Kingston, Ont., Can., 1975; MBA, Harvard U., 1979. Chartered acct. Auditor Peat, Marwick, Mitchell & Co., Toronto and Ottawa, Ont., Can., 1975-77; cons. McKinsey & Co., N.Y.C., 1979-82; gen. mgr. ofcl. Olympic souvenir program Sports Illustrated subs. Time Inc., N.Y.C., 1983-84; dir. fin. and planning Books Group div. Time Inc., N.Y.C., 1984-87; v.p. mktg. Time-Life Home Video div. Time Inc., N.Y.C., 1986-87; v.p. corp. strategic planning Am. Express Co., N.Y.C., 1987—; bd. advisors Search Alternatives Inc., Princeton, N.J., 1987—. Mem. Harvard Club Harvard Bus. Sch., 1978. Home: 333 E 66th St Apt 9J New York NY 10021 Office: Am Express Co World Financial Ctr Am Express Tower - 50th Floor New York NY 10285

BIGAOUETTE, LAURA ANN, telephone company administrator; b. Bklyn., May 26, 1960; d. Eugene C. and Yvonne Marie (Koteff) B. BA in History, Russian Lang., U. Rochester, N.Y., 1982; cert., Pushkin Inst., Moscow, 1981. Staff mgr. N.Y. Telephone Co., N.Y.C., 1983—; exec. v.p. N.Y. Women's Network, N.Y.C., 1986—. Mentor N.Y.C. Bd. Edn., 1984, N.Y. Mentoring Program, 1986. Mem. Am. Council Tchrs. Russian, Nat. Assn. Female Execs., Phi Sigma Sigma (div. pres. 1984-86). Republican. Roman Catholic. Home: 354 93d St Brooklyn NY 11209

BIGELOW, MARTHA MITCHELL, historian; b. Talladega Springs, Ala., Sept. 19, 1921; divorced; children—Martha Frances, Carolyn. B.A., Ala. Coll., Montevallo, 1943; M.A. (tuition fellow, Julius Rosenwald scholar 1943-44, Cleo Hearson scholar, summer 1944, Ency. Brit. fellow 1944-45), U. Chgo., 1944, Ph.D., 1946. Assoc. prof. history Miss. Coll., Clinton, 1946-48, Memphis State U., 1948-49, U. Miss., 1949-50; assoc. curator manuscripts Mich. Hist. Collections, U. Mich., Ann Arbor, 1954-57; prof. history Miss. Coll., 1957-71, chmn. dept. history and polit. sci., 1964-71, dir. Bur. History, Mich. Dept. State; sec. Mich. Hist. Commn., Mich. Dept. State, also state historic preservation officer, 1971—; coordinator for Mich., Nat. Hist. Publs. and Recs. Commn., 1974—. Contbr. articles profl. publns. Mem. Am. Assn. State and Local History (pres. 1979-81, fellow summers 1958, 59), Orgn. Am. Historians, Nat. Assn. State Archives and Recs. Assn., So. Hist Assn., Mich. Hist. Soc., Miss. Hist. Soc. Home: 223 Cowley St East Lansing MI 48823 Office: Bur History Mich Dept State 208 N Capitol St Lansing MI 48918

BIGELOW, PAGE ELIZABETH, public policy professional; b. Louisville, Feb. 9, 1948; d. William Simpson and Page Elizabeth (Smith) B. BA, Wells Coll., 1970; postgrad., NYU, 1971-72, Gen. Theol. Sem., 1971-72. Research asst., librarian Nat. Mcpl. League, N.Y.C., 1970-75, research dir. ethics in govt. project, 1975-80, dir. representation project, 1981-84; sr. assoc. Nat. Civic League (formerly Nat. Mcpl. League), N.Y.C., 1983-87; mem. sr. staff Inst. Pub. Adminstrn., N.Y.C., 1987—; staff cons. state-city commn. on integrity in govt. N.Y., N.Y.C., 1986-87. Author: Lobbying Laws In The States: A Comparative Study, 1980; editor: Forms of Local Representation, 1982. Mem. citizens adv. panel to joint legis. com. on revision and simplification of tax code, N.Y., 1982-86; del. Ednl. Priorities Panel, N.Y.C., 1984—; mem. Citywide Sch. Bd. Elections Com., N.Y.C., 1985—. Mem. Council on Govtl. Ethics Laws, Nat. Assn. for Female Execs. Episcopalian. Club: Jr. League (N.Y.C.) (corp. sec. 1986—). Office: Inst Pub Adminstrn 55 W 44th St New York NY 10036

BIGGERSTAFF, MARILYN ANNE, social work educator; b. Coffeyville, Kans., Dec. 23, 1946; d. Ellis and Mary Anne (Boren) B. BA, Baker U., 1967; MSW, U. Kans., 1969; D Social Work, U. So. Calif., 1976. Social worker City and County of Denver Dept. Welfare, 1969-70; clin. social worker Community Mental Health Ctr., Denver Gen. Hosp., 1970-73; lectr. Sch. Social Work U. So. Calif., Los Angeles, 1975-77, dir. adminstrn. curriculum devel. project, 1976-77; asst. prof. Sch. Social Work Va. Commonwealth U., Richmond, 1977-82, assoc. prof., 1982—. Author: Study Guide—Am. Assn. of State Social Work Boards, 1987; also articles. Bd. dirs. Emergency Shelters, Inc., Richmond, 1981-84. Mem. Nat. Assn. Social Workers (bd. dirs. Va. chpt. 1977-84), Assn. for Women in Social Work (nat. steering com. 1986—), Am. Assn. State Social Work Bds. (chairperson exam. com. 1987—), Council on Social Work Edn. (commn. on role and status of women 1983-86). Office: Va Commonwealth Univ Sch Social Work 1001 W Franklin St Richmond VA 23284

BIGGS, MARGARET KEY, educator, author; b. Troy, Ala., Oct. 26, 1933; d. Samuel Elbert and Maggie Lee (Jackson) Key; m. Wayne Saunders Biggs, Apr. 1, 1956. B.S. in English Edn., Troy State U., 1954; M.A. in Humanities, Calif. State U.-Dominquez Hills, 1979. Instr. Port St. Joe Jr./Sr. High Sch., Fla., 1954-86; adj. prof. Gulf Coast Community Coll., Port St. Joe, 1984-86; freelance writer, 1986—. Author poetry: Swampfire, 1980; Sister to the Sun, 1981; Magnolias and Such, 1982; Petals from the Womanflower, 1983; Plumage of the Sun, 1986; contbg. editor Earthwise, Tempest, Negative Capability; contbr. articles to profl. jours., poems to anthologies. Recipient Pulitzer Prize nominee, 1986, Gulf County Star Tchr. award, 1965; Port St. Joe Jr.-Sr. High Sch. Tchr. of Yr. award, 1973; Fla. Speech award, 1980; Insight Press award for teaching creative writing exceptionally, 1981, 83; Rusel Leavit Meml. award, 1980; Poetry Monthly First Poem award, 1981; award for Advancing the Growth and Devel. of Edn. in State of Fla., 1982; Nat. Fedn. State Poetry Socs. award, 1983; Ind. Hist. award, 1983; Katherine F. Gordy award, 1983; others. Mem. Panhandle Writers Guild (life), Nat. League Am. Pen Women, Ala. State Poetry Soc., Fla. League Am. Pen Women, Fla. State Poets Assn. Inc., Nat. Fedn. State Poetry Socs., Nat. League Am. Pen Women (award 1983), Panhandle Writers Guild, DAR, Delta Kappa Gamma, Alpha Omega. Democrat. Methodist. Office: Port St Joe Jr-Sr High Sch 800 Niles Rd Port Saint Joe FL 32456

BIGGS, RITTIE JEAN, county official; b. Martin County, N.C., Jan. 16, 1942; d. Dennis Robert and Marie (Wynn) B. B.S., East Carolina U., 1964, M.S., 1974. Tchr., Edenton City Schs., N.C., 1964-67, Martin County Schs., Williamston, N.C., 1967-68; social worker Martin County Dept. Social Services, Williamston, 1968-72, dir., 1972—. Named Outstanding Dir. Social Services in N.C., N.C. Assn. County Commrs., 1979-80. Mem. N.C. Assn. County Dirs. Social Services (pres. 1979-80), N.C. Social Services Assn. Democrat. Baptist. Club: Williamston Bus. and Profl. Women (pres. 1977-78). Avocations: reading, quilting, crocheting, gardening, church work. Office: Martin County Dept of Social Services PO Box 809 Williamston NC 27892

BIGGS, ROBERTA ELIZABETH, educational administrator; b. Chgo., Oct. 3, 1929; d. Thomas Jesse and Claytie Agnes (Day) Allen; m. Horace S. Biggs, May 29, 1949; 1 child, Helena Elizabeth. B.S., Ariz. State U., 1947. Tchr. Navajo children Bur. Indian Affairs, Navajo Reservations, Ariz. and N.Mex., 1947-49; owner, dir. LaFloresta Childrens Ctr., Albuquerque, 1969—; chmn. bd. Learning Tech. Ctr., Albuquerque, 1984—, originator, 1982—; cons. St. Francis Nursing Home, Albuquerque, 1982; coordinator child care workshops N.Mex. Polit. Women, 1974-77. Contbr. articles to profl. jours. Bd. dirs. All Faiths Receiving Home, Albuquerque, 1972-84, Assn. Commerce and Industry, Albuquerque, 1981-84; chmn. Com. on Women's Issues 1983—; com. mem. Small Bus. Com., N.Mex., 1985—. Mem. Nat. Assn. Child Care Mgmt. (dir.), N.Mex. Lic. Child Care Assn. (pres. 1974-77). Avocations: collecting and recording Navajo folklore; storytelling; collecting out-of-print children's books. Office: Learning Tech Ctr 2801 California NE Albuquerque NM 87110

BIGGY, MARY VIRGINIA, college dean; b. Boston, Oct. 15, 1924; d. John J. and Mary C. (Dwyer) B. B.S., Boston U., 1945, Ed.M., 1946, Ed.D., 1953. Tchr. bus. edn. Needham (Mass.) High Sch., 1944-45; reading cons. Plainville (Conn.) Public Schs., 1946-47; coordinator elem. edn. Concord (Mass.) Public Schs., 1947-62; dir. N.E. instrnl. TV project, dir. instrnl. TV Eastern Ednl. Network, Boston, 1962-67; asst. supt., supr. Concord Public Schs. and Concord Carlisle Regional Sch. Dist., 1967-69; prof. edn. U. Lowell, Mass., 1969—; dean U. Lowell (Coll. Edn.), 1979—; pres. (Designs for Edn.), 1969—; cons. Corp. Pub. Broadcasting; mem. Acton Boxborough (Mass.) Regional High Sch. Dist. Sch. Com., 1963-66; chmn. Mass. Bd. Library Commrs., 1973-78; project dir. criteria for funding major initiatives Corp. Pub. Broadcasting, 1981-85. Author: Independence in Spelling, 1966, (with others) Spell Correctly, 1965-86, 5th edit., 1986. Recipient Ida M. Johnston award Boston U., 1981. Mem. NEA, Am. Assn. Sch. Adminstrs., Am. Ednl. Research Assn., Assn. Supervision and Curriculum Devel., AAUP, Internat. Reading Assn., New Eng. Reading Assn., Pi Lambda Theta (nat. pres. 1961-65, 83 Disting. Pi Lambda Thetan award), others. Democrat. Roman Catholic. Home: 162 Park Ln Concord MA 01742 Office: U Lowell Coll Edn Lowell MA 01854

BIGHAM, WANDA DURRETT, academic administrator. m. William Bigham; children: Jan, Bill, Julie. B of Music Edn., Murray State U., 1956; MusM, Morehead State U., 1971, M of Higher Edn., 1973; EdD, U. Ky., 1978. Tchr. music, English pub. schs., Ky.; dir. Trio Programs Morehead (Ky.) State U., dir. instructional systems, assoc. dean acad. affairs, acting dean grad. and spl. acad. programs; exec. asst. to pres. Emerson Coll., Boston; v.p. devel. and coll. relations Emerson Coll.; pres. Marycrest Coll., Davenport, Iowa, 1986—; Ky. state coordinator Am. Council on Edn.'s Nat.

Identification Program for Women in Higher Edn., 1981-84; 1st treas. Nat. Council of Ednl. Opportunity Assns., 1981-83, bd. dirs., 1983-85, chairperson task force on constitution, 1980-82, membership and credentials com., 1981-83, mem. fin. affairs com., 1981-82. Contbr. articles to ednl. jours. Bd. dirs. Frinedly House, Jr. Achievement. Title III grantee, Morehead State U.; Program of the Am. Council on Edn. fellow. Mem. So. Assn. Ednl. Opportunity Program Personnel (v.p. 1979-81, pres. 1983-85), Ky. Assn. of Ednl. Opportunity Program Personnel (pres. 1973-74, 77-78), Sigma Alpha Iota, Kappa Delta Pi, Phi Kappa Phi, Phi Delta Kappa. Office: Marycrest Coll Office of the President Davenport IA 52804

BIHLER, NANCY ELAINE, personnel manager; b. Chgo., Feb. 5, 1948; d. Harlow Duane and Ethel Irene (Peterson) Woodruff; m. Frederick H. Bihler Jr., Feb. 22, 1975; children: Barbara, Douglas, Carol, Susan. BS, U. Ill., 1972. Office mgr. Fujitsu Am. Inc., Lake Bluff, Ill., 1976-83; mgr. personnel Advantest Am. Inc., Lincolnshire, Ill., 1983—; cons. Takeda-Riken Am. Inc., Lake Forest, Ill., 1983. Mem. Am. Mgmt. Assn., Am. Soc. Personnel Adminstrn., No. Ill. Assn. Personnel Adminstrs., No. Ill. Indsl. Assn. Home: 435 E Illinois Rd Lake Forest IL 60045 Office: Advantest Am Inc 300 Knightsbridge Pkwy Lincolnshire IL 60069

BIKOFF, MARY BETSY, business executive; b. Glendale, Calif., Nov. 25, 1944; d. James and Margaret (Stewart) Bone; m. David Bikoff, Aug. 28, 1965. BS in Bus., Ind. U., 1966. Claims clerk Rees-Staly Med. Clinic, San Diego, 1967-68; claims asst. United Bonding Ins. Co., Indpls., 1968-69; from office mgr. to v.p. Allied Fidelity Ins. Co., Indpls., 1969-80; mgr. personnel services Walker Research, Inc., Indpls., 1980-81, group mgr., 1981-83, v.p. corp. services, 1983-86, v.p. adminstrn. and human resources, 1987—. Account exec. United Way Campaign, Indpls., 1986, sect. chmn., 1987; mem. A. Burkhart Bd. Leadership Program. Mem. Am. Soc. Personnel Assn., Advt. Club Indpls., Council Am. Survey Research Orgns. (co. rep. 1983—, bd. dirs. 1987—), Marion County Mental Health Assn. (bd. dirs. 1986—), Kappa Kappa Gamma. Club: Keystone Crossing. Lodge: Kiwanis. Office: Walker Research Inc 3939 Priority Way S Dr Indianapolis IN 46240

BILES, MARILYN MARTA, painter; b. Wilmington, Del., Oct. 3, 1935; d. Albert Humbert and Anne Marie (DeRogatis) Marta; m. George Ronald Bower, June 30, 1956 (div. May 1970); children—Michele Bower Alvarado, Nancy Bower Guthrie, Randall William. Student Moore Coll. Art, 1953-54, St. Mary's Coll., 1959-61, Mus. Fine Arts, Houston, 1972-74. Art tchr. Contemporary Arts Mus., Houston, 1969-73, 80-81; head art dept. preprimary div. Duchesne Acad., Houston, 1970-72; project coordinator Nan Fisher, Inc., Houston, 1983-84; one-woman shows: 1st Nat. City Bank, Houston, 1980, Christ Ch. Cathedral, 1981-82, Toni Jones Gallery, 1981, U. Houston, 1982, Station Gallery, Greenville, Del., 1984, Boyar Norton & Blair, 1986, Martha Turner Properties, 1986; group shows include: U. Houston, 1977, 79, Nat. Cape Coral Exhbn., Fla., 1979, Toni Jones Gallery, 1979, Assistance League of Houston, 1979, 80, Golden Crescent Gallery, Houston, 1984; coordinator, designer art programs Spring Branch Schs., Houston, 1968-70. Bd. dirs. Spring Branch YWCA, Houston, 1973-74; docent Harris County Heritage Soc., Houston, 1970-72; mem. bd., v.p. Arcs Found., Inc., Houston, 1983; bd. dirs., gala chmn. Houston Grand Opera Guild, 1983-84, governing bd. assn., 1984-85, co-chmn. gala, 1985; founder, pres. Mus. Med. Sci. Assn., Houston, 1986-87; mem. com. Can-Do-It Charity Fundraiser. Mem. Artists Equity (dir. Houston chpt. 1980), Art League Houston, Tex. Fine Arts Assn. Republican. Episcopalian. Clubs: Racquet, World Trade (v.p. women's assn. 1974-75) (Houston), Westlake. Home: 148 Litchfield St Houston TX 77024

BILHARDT, DIANE MARIE, marketing manager; b. Phila., Aug. 14, 1952; d. William Durkin and Elaine Claire (Rosato) B. BA, Douglass Coll., 1974; MBA, Rutgers U., 1980. Asst. mktg. dir. Franklin State Bank, Somerset, N.J., 1975-79; staff mgr. AT&T, Basking Ridge, N.J., 1980-82, staff mgr. AT&T Info Systems, Morristown, N.J., 1983, dist. mktg. mgr., 1984-87, Bridgewater, N.J., 1987—. Mem. Am. Mktg. Assn. (award No. N.J. chpt. 1980), Beta Gamma Sigma. Republican. Episcopalian. Office: AT&T 295 N Maple Ave Room C17-5341C2 Basking Ridge NJ 07920

BILKEY, BEVERLY YVONNE, medical technologist, social services official; b. Madison, Wis., Oct. 14, 1926; d. Rush Hillary and Amalie (Christen) Watson; m. Frederick Williams Bilkey, June 29, 1950 (dec. Dec. 1974); children—Barry W., Frederick D., Lorelei. B.S. in Med. Technology, U. Wis.-Madison, 1948. Lic. medical technologist. Chief technician Levin-Delavan Clinic, Delavan, Wis., 1948-49; asst. supr. Meml. Hosp., Wausau, Wis., 1949-50; supr. Gen. Hosp., Dodgeville, Wis., 1950-74; staff technologist Meml. Hosp. of Iowa County, Wis., 1974-76; supr. Dodgeville Clinic Lab., Wis., 1976-84. Mem. Health Planning Council, Dodgeville, 1978-84; chmn. Iowa County Social Services, Dodgeville, 1980-84, Iowa County Pub. Health Agy., Dodgeville, 1979-84; Iowa County bd. suprs. Fin. Personnel Community Action Agy.; gov.'s appointee Regional Planning Commn., 1980-82; chmn. bd. trustees Dodgeville United Ch. of Christ; candidate for State for Rep., 1980. Mem. Registry Am. Soc. Clin. Pathologists. Republican. Lodges: Rainbow Girls (mother adviser 1960), Order of Eastern Star (worthy matron 1964). Avocations: politics, crafts. Home: 4929 Whitcomb Dr Madison WI 53711

BILLER, PATRICIA LOUISE, nurse practitioner; b. Harrisonburg, Va., Oct. 4, 1958; d. Donald Welton and Nellie Rose (Woerner) Biller; BSN cum laude, W.Va. Wesleyan Coll., 1980; MS in Nursing, U. Colo., 1983. Cert. family nurse practitioner. Staff nurse charge relief Denver VA Med. Ctr., 1980-83; family nurse practitioner Cedar Ridge Family Physicians, Strasburg, Va., 1983-85; family nurse practitioner emergency dept. Johns Hopkins Hosp., Balt., 1985-86; family nurse practitioner, clin. dir. E. A. Hawse Health Ctr., Baker, W.Va., 1986—. Author Palliative Treatment Program-A Ray of Sunshine booklet, 1982 (outstanding work with hospice). Author vol. 1 and 2 newsletters Cedar Ridge Health Notes, 1984; contbr. articles to profl. jours. Active mem. Am. Guild of Organists, Buckhannon, W.Va., 1980. Named W.Va. 4-H All Star, 1976; recipient Outstanding Sci. and Math Achievement award Baush-Lomb, 1976; Robert C. Byrd scholar, 1976. Mem. W.Va. Nurses Assn., Am. Nurses Assn., Phi Kappa Phi. Epsilon Delta chpt. Sigma Theta Tau, Beta Beta Beta. Democrat. United Methodist. Club: Lost River Extension (W.Va.) (v.p. 1984-85, pres. 1987-88). Home: General Delivery Lost River WV 26811 Office: EA Hawse Health Ctr PO Box 97 Baker WV 26801

BILLHARZ, CONSTANCE ELLEN CLARK, speech and language pathologist, educational diagnostician; b. Golden City, Mo., July 29, 1921; d. Harley B. and Flossie J. (Mitchell) Clark; m. Roger William Billharz, Jan. 12, 1946; 1 child, Roger Clark. BA, Pace U., 1971; MA, NYU, 1975; MPS, Manhattanville Coll., 1978. Cert. tchr. N.Y. Speech pathologist St. Joseph's Mental Health Clinic, Peekskill, N.Y., 1978-79; speech and lang. pathologist Rye (N.Y.) City Sch. Dist., 1980-82; speech therapist, spl. edn. tchr. Hartsdale Sch., Elmsford, N.Y., 1985—; pvt. practice ednl. diagnostician North Tarrytown, N.Y., 1979—. Mem. Am. Speech, Lang., and Hearing Assn. (cert.), N.Y. State Speech, Lang., and Hearing Assn., Westchester Assn. for Children with Learning Disabilities, Am. Arbitration Assn. Republican. Address: 467 Munroe Ave North Tarrytown NY 10591

BILLIA, DARLENE A(NGELA), advertising executive; b. N.Y.C., Nov. 3, 1948; d. Peter and Dorothy (Ziomek) B. AAS in Retail Mktg., N.Y.C. Community Coll., 1968; BBA in Mktg., Pace U., 1971. Research asst. Kendall Co., N.Y.C., 1971-72; research project dir. Needham Harper & Steers (now DDB Needham), N.Y.C., 1972-74; assoc. research dir. Batten, Barton, Durstine & Osborne, N.Y.C., 1974-76; sr. v.p., group dir. D'Arcy Masius Benton & Bowles, N.Y.C., 1976—; loaned exec. Am. Assn. Advt. Agys., Washington, 1979-80. Contbr. article to Nursing World Jour., 1986. Mem. Am. Mktg. Assn. (asst. treas. 1979, asst. sec. 1982-83, bd. dirs. N.Y. chpt. 1983-84, 86—). Office: D'Arcy Masius Benton & Bowles 909 Third Ave New York NY 10022

BILLIG, ETEL JEWEL, theater director, actress; b. N.Y.C., Dec. 16, 1932; d. Anthony and Martha Rebecca (Klebansky) Papa; m. Steven S. Billig, Dec. 23, 1956; children: Curt Adam, Jonathan Roark. BS, NYU, 1955, MA; student, Herbert Berghof Studio, N.Y.C., 1955-56. Cert. elem. and high sch. tchr. Actress Washington Square Players, N.Y.C., 1950-55, Dukes Oak Theatre, Cooperstown, N.Y., 1955, Triple Cities Playhouse, Binghampton, N.Y., 1956, Candlelight Dinner Playhouse, Summit, Ill., 1970, 73, 76, 78; mng. dir. Theatre 31, Park Forest, Ill., 1971-73; asst. mgr. Westroads Dinner Theatre, Omaha, 1973-76; mng. dir., actress Ill. Theatre Ctr., Park Forest, 1976—, Goodman Theatre, Chgo., 1987; dir. drama Rich Cen. High Sch., Olympia Fields, Ill., 1978-86; cons. and lectr. in field. Appeared in films including The Dollmaker, Running Scared. V.p. Nat. Council Jewish Women, Park Forest, 1968-70; sec. Community Arts Council, Park Forest, 1984-86, pres., 1986—. Recipient Risk Taking award NOW, 1982; grantee Nebr. Arts Council, 1975, Ill. Arts Council, 1984-86. Mem. Am. Fedn. TV and Radio Artists, Actors' Equity Assn., Screen Actors Guild, League Chgo. Theatres. Office: Ill Theatre Ctr 400A Lakewood Blvd Park Forest IL 60466

BILLINGS, CHRISTINE D., government office administrator; b. Laurinburg, N.C., May 1, 1942; d. William and Evelyn (Pate) D. BS, N.C. Cen. U., 1963; MS, Columbia U., 1976; PhD, Fla. State U., 1976. Dept. chmn., assoc. prof. Fla. A&M U., Tallahassee, 1971-76, Fayetteville (N.C.) State U., 1976-77; ednl. cons. Dept. Edn. State of Fla., Tallahassee, 1978-79; asst. dir. adm. services Dept. Labor State of Fla., Tallahassee, 1979-80; dep. dir. office policy and planning D.C. Govt., Washington, 1986—; part-time cons. U.S. Dept. Edn., Washington, 1983—, Nat. Inst. Human Relations, Washington, 1985—. Contbr. articles to profl. jours. Named one of Outstanding Young Women Am., 1976, 77. Democrat. Lodge: Zonta. Home: PO Box 21462 Washington DC 20009 Office: DC Govt Office of Policy 801 N Capitol St Washington DC 20002

BILLS, PATRICIA LEE, convention bureau director; b. Salem, Oreg., June 22, 1937; d. Eddie Ahrens and Erna Pauline (Batterman) Kilpatrick; m. J. Robert Bills, June 22, 1958; children: Bradley, Betsy, Brenda. BA, Pacific Luth. Univ., 1959. Exec. dir. Medford (Oreg.) Vis. and Conv. Bur., 1980—. Bd. dirs. Britt Festival Assn., Medford, 1984—, Medford Boy Scouts Am., 1983-84; exec. dir. Rogue Council Camp Fire Girls, Medford, 1969-79; chmn. Jackson County Fair Bd., 1984—; pres. Medford Ch. Council, 1984. Mem. Southern Oreg. Visitors Assn. (pres. 1983-87), Oreg. Assn. Conv. Visitors Burs. (pres. 1985-86), Oreg. Travel Industry Council (sec. 1986—), Women Entrepreneurs Orgn. Republican. Lutheran. Lodge: Rotary. Office: Visitors-Conv Bur 304 S Central Ave Medford OR 97501

BILLS, SHERYL JEAN, newspaper editor; b. Rushville, Ind., Aug. 4, 1945; d. Robert Jackson and Mary Elizabeth (Kehl) B.; m. John M. Heckler, Nov. 30, 1985. B.A., Ind. U., 1968. Mem. staff Cin. Enquirer, 1967-82, asst. mng. editor features, 1979-80, mng. editor, 1980-82; planning editor USA Today, Gannett Newspapers, 1982-83, mng. editor life sect., 1983-85, sr. editor, 1985-86, cons. editor, 1986—. Recipient writing award Ohio Newspaper Women's Assn., 1971, 74; recipient Ohio AP award for enterprise in journalism, 1974, award mag. covers-Outdoor Writers Ohio Ohio Press Photographers Assn., 1976, Penney-Mo. award for newspaper lifestyle sect., 1978, Outstanding Career Woman award Cin. YWCA, 1981, Disting. Alumni award Rushville High Sch., 1983. Mem. Piedmont Foxhounds, Old Dominion Hounds, Middleburg Hunt Club. Office: Kelvedon Box 1772 Middleburg VA 22117

BILSEL, ZELIHA, pediatrician; b. Kirklarel, Turkey, Apr. 24, 1924; d. Ismet and Emine (Tanriover) M.D., Med. Sch., 1947; m. Yilmaz C. Bilsel, Oct. 29, 1960; children—Deniz, Kurt. Dir. orphanage in Turkey, 1947-49; resident in pediatrics, Turkey, 1949-52; dir. orphanage, practice medicine specializing in pediatrics, Kirklarel, 1952-57; resident in pediatrics Homer Phillips Hosp., St. Louis, 1957-61, chief resident newborn premature nursery, 1959-61; fellow in cardiology, Augusta, Ga., 1961-63; practice medicine specializing in pediatrics, Kirklarel, 1963-66, Fairview Heights, Ill., 1970—; pediatrician outpatient clinic St. Louis Children's Hosp., 1966-70; pediatrics cons. for Pediatrics Clinic; cons. staff mem.; mem. staff Cardinal Glennon, St. Louis, Meml. Hosp., Belleville, Ill.; former attending physician to high risk newborns and premature for So. Ill. Christian Welfare Hosp., East St. Louis, Ill. Mem. AMA, St. Clair Med. Soc., So. Ill. Med. Soc.

BINCER, WANDA LAWENDEL, psychiatrist; b. Warsaw, Poland, Oct. 4, 1930; came to U.S., 1950, naturalized, 1961; d. Leonard and Evelyn (Glocer) Lawendel; M.D., Royal Coll. Surgeons, Ireland, 1956; m. Adam M. Bincer, Apr. 2, 1972; children—Yvonne, Brian, Michael. Rotating intern St. Mary's Hosp., Rochester, N.Y., 1957-58; resident in psychiatry City Hosp., Elmhurst, N.Y., 1958-59, 61-63; house officer Princess Margaret Hosp., Nassau, Bahamas, 1959-60; staff psychiatrist Pontiac (Mich.) State Hosp., 1965-66; cons. psychiatrist Bur. Social Services, Grand Forks, N.D., 1966-68, Community Mental Health Center, Grand Forks, 1966-68; staff psychiatrist VA Hosp., Atlanta, 1968-70, Center for Interpersonal Study, Smyrna, Ga. and Brawner Hosp., 1970-72; practice medicine specializing in psychiatry, Madison, Wis., 1972—; med. cons. Office of Social Security Disability, 1983—. Mem. City-County Com. on Sexual Assault, Madison, 1978-80; cons. Parental Stress Center, 1978—; chpt. co-leader, bd. dirs. Parents of Murdered Children. Served with Polish Underground, 1944. Decorated Bronze Cross of Merit. Mem. Am. Psychiat. Assn. (task force on victimization), Wis. Psychiat. Assn. (com. on women), Am. Acad. Psychotherapists. Cons. editor Voices, 1978-80; contbr. to Problem Solver (ed. Zastro et al), 1976, Voices, 1983.

BINDER, AMY FINN, public relations company executive; b. N.Y.C., June 13, 1955; d. David and Laura (Zeisler) Finn; m. Ralph Edward Binder, Aug. 15, 1976; children: Ethan Max, Adam Finn, Rebecca Eve. BA with honors, Brown U., 1977. Freelance photographer, N.Y.C., 1977-78; account exec. Newton & Nicolazza, Boston, 1978-79, Agnew, Carter, McCarthy, Boston, 1979-80; dir. pub. relations City of New Rochelle, N.Y., 1980-82; dir. urban communications Ruder Finn & Rotman, N.Y.C., 1982-85, v.p., 1985-86, exec. v.p., 1986-87, pres., 1987—; bd. dirs. Castle Art Gallery, New Rochelle. Photographer: Museum without Walls, 1975, The Spirit of Man: Sculpture of Kaare Nygaard, 1975, Knife Life and Bronzes, 1977. Mem. Madrid com. Sister City program, N.Y.C.; bd. dirs. New Rochelle Community Fund. Democrat. Jewish. Office: Ruder Finn & Rotman Inc 301 E 57th St New York NY 10022

BINDER, MILDRED KATHERINE, retired county public welfare agency executive; b. York, Pa., Jan. 5, 1918; d. Jemie Irving and Emma Jane (Billet) Binder; B.A. magna cum laude in Sociology, Hood Coll., 1940. Sec., mgr. Stock's Appliances, York, 1940-42; caseworker York County Bd. Assistance, Pa. Dept. Public Welfare, 1942-49, 1953-58, supr., 1949-53, 1958-59, exec. dir., 1959-83. Past mem. exec. com. York County Employment and Tng. Com.; past mem. dept. task forces Social Service Delivery to Client Info. System, also mem. ops. rev. bd.; past mem. bd. York County Council Alcoholism, 1959-62, Community Progress Council, 1965-67; co-chmn. Community Dialogue Com., 1968-69; mem. bd. Pre-Paid Health York, Inc., 1979; mem. human services planning coalition United Way, 1978-83, chmn. council agy. execs., 1967-71, 1976-78; past mem. consumer adv. councils Gen. Telephone, Met. Edison; bd. dirs. Literacy Council of York County, 1985-86; mem. York County Human Services Adv. Com., 1983-87. Named Boss of Yr., Am. Bus. Women, 1973; named in commendations Pa. gov., Pa. Ho. of Reps. Mem. Am. Public Welfare Assn., Exec. Dirs. Assn. Pa. (exec. com. 1979-83, sec. 1980-83), AAUW (bd. dirs. York br. 1984—), York County Hist. Soc. Clubs: Coll. of York, Hood Coll. (York). Home: 1611 W Market St York PA 17404

BINDRIM, PATRICIA MASTERILLI, marketing communications director, consultant; b. Phila., Mar. 9, 1954; d. Frank Anthony and Kathryn Susan (Crawford) Masterilli; m. Mark William Bindrim, June 7, 1975; 1 child, Kira Lee. B.S., Pa. State U., 1975; M.Ed., U. Md., 1979. Md. High sch. English tchr. Prince George County (Md.) Schs., 1975; account adminstr. U. Md., College Park, 1977-79; communications specialist Internat. Bank, Washington, 1979-82; communications dir. Heritage div. Beverly Enterprises, Rockville, Md., 1982-83; dir. corp. communications TU Internat., Inc., Falls Church, Va., 1984-86; mktg. communications mgr. Entre Computer Ctrs., Inc., McLean, Va., 1986—; promotions cons. 1983, Hannover Healthcare, 1986. Mem. Pa. State U. Alumni Assn., Kappa Kappa Gamma. Methodist. Home: 8312 Cottage Hill Ct Gaithersburg MD 20877 Office: 1430 Spring Hill Rd McLean VA 22102

BINER, MARGARET LAVIN, communications company executive; b. Worcester, Mass., May 1, 1952; d. Walter Douglas and Ellen M. (Gilligan) Lavin; m. Stanley Biner, Sept. 4, 1983; 1 child, W.J. B.A., Assumption Coll., 1974; M.B.A., Clark U., 1976, postgrad., 1976-77. Asst. mgr. New Eng. Telephone and Telegraph, Boston, 1978-80; sr. rate analyst Am. Electric Power, Columbus, Ohio, 1980-81; mkt. supr. GTE Satellite Co., Stamford, Conn., 1981-83; staff mgr. AT&T Communications, Basking Ridge, N.J., 1983—. Solicitor AT&T Polit. Action Com., Basking Ridge, 1985; new membership com., ritual com. Temple Emanu-El, Westfield, N.J., sec., 1982. Mem. Am. Statis. Assn., Nat. Assn. Bus. Economists, Am. Mktg. Assn. (v.p. programs for N.J. 1985-86). Jewish. Office: AT&T Communications 295 N Maple Ave Basking Ridge NJ 07920

BINGHAM, JINSIE SCOTT, broadcast company executive; b. Greencastle, Ind., Dec. 28, 1935; d. Roscoe Gibson and Alpha Edith (Robinson) Scott; m. Frank William Wokoun, Jr. (dec.); children: Douglas Scott, Richard Frank; m. Richard Innes Bingham, June 24, 1964. Student, DePauw U., Greencastle, 1952-53, Northwestern U., 1953, Coe Coll., 1953-54. Exec. sec. Ind. Young Dems., 1958-60; receptionist Ind. House of Reps., Indpls., 1959; saleslady Avon Products, Greencastle, 1961-64; sales mgr. Sta. WJNZ (formerly WXTA), Greencastle, 1969-77, owner, pres., gen. mgr., 1977—; former ptnr. Sta. WVTL, Monticello, Ill., Sta. KBIB, Monette, Ark.; speaker DePauw U. Communications Seminar, 1981, 85; vis. lectr., 1986-87. Com. chair Legis. Awareness Seminar, 1978-86; co-chair Greencastle Gaelic Festival, 1983-84; charter mem. Greencastle 2001, 1985—, Greencastle Civic League, 1984—, Greencastle Merchant's Assn., 1983—, Community Resources Council, 1982—; charter mem., corp. sec. Main St., Greencastle, 1983—, v.p., 1987-88, pres., 1988-89; bd. dirs. Greencastle Vol. Fire Dept., 1986, Greencastle Community Child Care Ctr., 1983—; mem. Greencastle Zoning Bd. Appeals, 1984—, v.p., 1985-88, pres., 1988; announcer Putnam County Fair Parade, 1977—; community host Hoosier Hospitality Days, 1981-84; active Putnam County Com. for Econ. Strength, 1979-83. Named Outstanding Citizen, Greencastle Jaycees, 1981. Mem. Am. Women in Radio and TV (pres. Ind. chpt. 1979-82), Indpls. Network Women in Bus. (charter), Women in Communications, Inc. (bd. dirs. 1983-84, MATRIX cochair 1984), Am. Legion Aux., Nat. Assn. Broadcasters, Ind. Broadcasters Assn. (v.p. FM 1982), Greencastle Bus. and Profl. Women's Club (pres. 1976-77, 79-80), Indpls. Ad Club, Women's Press Club Ind., Indpls. Press Club, Nat. Fedn. Press Women, Ind. Dem. Editorial Assn., Ind. C. of C., Greencastle C. of C. (bd. dirs. 1979-83, pres. 1982), VFW (pres. ladies aux. 1966-68), Milestone Car Soc., Packard Club Ind., Ind. Soc. Pioneers, Daus. of 1812 (pres. Tippecanoe chpt. 1981, state v.p. 1982), DAR, Delta Theta Tau, Sigma Delta Chi. Mem. Christian Ch. (Disciples of Christ). Club: Windy Hill Country. Lodges: Order Eastern Star, Internat. Order Job's Daus. (life), Women of Moose. Office: Sta WJNZ PO Box 494 Greencastle IN 46135

BINGHAM, JOYCE BARBARA WINGFIELD, music educator; b. Appomattox, Va., May 28, 1930; d. James Julian and Zelia Page (Jones) Wingfield; m. Floyd Everett Bingham, July 3, 1959; 1 child, Susan Page. BA in Music Edn., Va. Poly. Inst., 1951; MusM Edn., Columbia U., 1955, U. Va., 1964. Tchr. vocal music William Campbell High Sch., Campbell County, Va., 1951-53; music band and vocal dir. Jr. High Sch., Danville, Va., 1953-55; band dir. Appomattox High Sch., 1955-64; tchr. music Seven Hills Sch., Lynchburg, Va., 1972-73; tchr. sci. lang. arts Elem. Sch., Amherst, Va., 1978—; counselor Va. Music Camp, Massenetta Springs, 1958-59. Census taker U.S. Govt., Appomattox, 1970; judge parade Appomattox R.R. Festival, 1984. Mem. Lynchburg Hist. Found., Inc., Nat. Assn. Female Execs., U. Va. Alumni Assn., Radford U. Alumni Assn. Republican. Baptist. Clubs: Pan Am. (Radford, Va.)(life), Jr. Women's (Danville, Va.)(2d v.p. 1954-55). Home: PO Box 335 Appomattox VA 24522

BINGO-DUGGINS, KAREN LEIKO, personnel specialist; b. Honolulu, Dec. 15, 1942; d. Warren Tsutomu and Shizue (Shiroma) Bingo; m. Michael Oniel Bingo-Duggins, Aug. 18, 1976. Student, Chaminade Coll., 1963-64; BA, U. Hawaii, 1965. Classification trainee Pacific region U.S. Army, Okinawa, Japan, 1967-71, personnel staffing specialist Pacific region, 1971-72; position classification specialist U.S. Army, San Francisco, 1972-74; personnel mgmt. specialist material command U.S. Army, Washington, 1974, mgmt. employee specialist material command, 1974-76, personnel evaluation specialist material command, 1976-78, classification specialist, 1978-80; personnel mgmt. specialist USAF, Washington, 1980-84, chief sr. exec. service mgmt., 1984—. Mem. Internat. Personnel Adminstrn., Minority Women in Govt., Fed. Exec. Inst. alumni Assn. Home: 4327 Stream Bed Way Alexandria VA 22306 Office: Headquarters USAF/DPCZ Pentagon Room 4E232 Washington DC 20330-5060

BINION, LINDA DIANE, systems technologies researcher; b. Birmingham, Ala., Apr. 21, 1948; d. James Marvin and Sara Meredith (Moore) Binion; m. Norman Willard Holman, June 20, 1981 (div. 1983); m. Paul Anthony DeLorenzo, Aug. 16, 1986. Student, U. Ala.-Tuscaloosa, 1966-67, U. Ala.-Birmingham. Data base adminstr. Carraway Methodist Med. Ctr., Birmingham, Ala., 1970-78; mgr. systems and program Brookwood Health Services Inc., Birmingham, 1979-80; sr. v.p. Innovative Systems Inc., Birmingham, 1980-83; pres. Amitec Inc., Birmingham, 1983-85; dir. research-info. systems technologies Ala. Metal Industries Corp., Birmingham, 1986; pres. AMICO Research Corp., 1986— ; cons. in field. Designer: (software system) Innovative Healthcare Support System, 1980. Guest speaker U. Ala. Sch. Community Allied Health Services, 1986, numerous others. Mem. C. of C. (Birmingham), Mensa, Assn. Systems Mgmt. (past pres.), Internat. Platform Assn. Democrat. Am. Baptist. Office: AMICO Research Corp 1075 S 13th St Suite 250 Birmingham AL 35205

BINSFELD, CONNIE BERUBE, state senator; b. Munising, Mich., Apr. 18, 1924; d. Omer J. and Elsie (Constance) Berube; B.S., Siena Heights Coll., 1945, D.H.L. (hon.), 1977; postgrad. Wayne State U., 1966-67; m. John E. Binsfeld, July 19, 1947; children—John T., Gregory, Susan, Paul, Michael. County commr., Leelanau County, Mich., 1970-74; mem. Mich. Ho. of Reps., 1974-82; mem. Mich. Senate, 1982—, asst. majority leader. Del., Republican Nat. Conv., 1980. Named Mich. Mother of Year, Mich. Mothers Com., 1977; Northwestern Mich. Coll. fellow. Mem. Nat. Council State Legislators, LWV, Siena Heights Coll. Alumnae Assn. Republican. Roman Catholic. Home: 8944 County Rd 675 Maple City MI 49664 Office: Mich Senate State Capitol Lansing MI 48909 *

BIONDOLILLO, DEBORAH LYNN, human resources director; b. Raleigh, N.C., Feb. 26, 1952; d. Thomas and Frances (Pardue) Blackmon; m. Joseph C. Biondolillo, Apr. 28, 1979; 1 child, Stephen M. BA, U. N.C., 1974. Office mgr. Greyhound Temporary, Santa Clara, Calif., 1975-76; human resource specialist Electronic Arrays, Mountain View, Calif., 1976-77; human resources specialist Intel, Santa Clara, 1977-79; ind. cons. Manila, Philippines, 1979-81; dir. human resources Apple Computer Inc., Cupertino, Calif., 1982—. Office: Apple Computer Inc 20525 Mariani Ave Cupertino CA 95014

BIRCH, DANA FEASTER, personnel executive; b. Miami, Fla., Mar. 28, 1929; d. Jerome Twichell and Maude (Mason) Feaster; m. N.R. Frame Jr., July 28, 1951 (div. Aug. 1967); children: Dorothy Livingston Frame, N. Renville Frame III; m. John A. Birch Jr., June 1968. BA, Duke U., 1951. Cert. tchr., real estate broker. Pvt. practice real estate Miami, 1969-75; sales rep. Gundaker Realtors, St. Louis, 1975-79; pres. Your Personal Palette, St. Louis, 1980—; pres., founder Fresh! Fresh Fashions, Inc., St. Louis, 1985—; exec. search cons. Michael Latas and Assocs., St. Louis, 1987—. Active Welcome Wagon, New Canaan, Conn., 1960-62; pres. New Neighbors League. Mem. AAUW, St. Louis Bd. Realtors, Jr. League of St. Louis, Vol. Service Council, United Daughters of Confederacy (pres. 1983-85), DAR (sec. 1983-85), Pi Beta Phi. Republican. Christain Scientist. Home: 937 Forestlac Dr Creve Coeur MO 63141 Office: Michael Latas and Assocs 1311 Lindbergh Plaza Ct Saint Louis MO 63132

BIRCH, GRACE MORGAN, library administrator, educator; b. N.Y.C., June 3, 1925; d. Milton Melville and Adeline Ellsdale (Springer) Morgan; m. Kenneth Francis Birch, Oct. 26, 1947; children—Shari R., Timothy F. B.A., U. Bridgeport, 1963; M.L.S., Pratt Inst., 1968. With Bridgeport Pub. Library, Conn., 1949-66; asst. town librarian Fairfield Pub. Library, Conn., 1966-69; dir. Trumbull Library System, Conn., 1969—; lectr. Housatonic Community Coll., Bridgeport, 1970—. Judge, Barnum Festival Soc. Bridgeport, 1971-73. Mem. ALA, New Eng. Library Assn., Conn. Library

Assn. (pres. 1972), Southwestern Conn. Library Council (pres. 1975-77), Fairfield Library Adminstrs. Group (pres. 1976-77), Nat. Assn. Female Execs. Democrat. Episcopalian. Avocations: sketching; dancing; traveling. Home: 175 Brooklawn Ave Bridgeport CT 06604 Office: The Trumbull Library 33 Quality St Trumbull CT 06611

BIRCH, MARY LYNN, engineer; b. Sparta, Wis., Aug. 10, 1945; d. Rex Lawrence and Lavern Gertrude (Perry) Snippen; m. John O. Birch, Sept. 2, 1967 (div. Jan. 1970). BS, U. Wis., 1968, MS, 1974. registered profl. engr., N.C.; cert. health physicist. Chemist State of Wis., Madison, 1968-72; asst. health physicist Duke Power Co., Charlotte, N.C., 1972-74, health physicist, 1974-82, system engr., 1982—; cons. low-level waste program EG & G Idaho, Idaho Falls, 1983—. Mem. Health Physics Soc., Soc. Women Engrs., Am. Nuclear Soc., Women Execs. (v.p. Charlotte chpt.), Charlotte Bus. and Profl. Women (pres. 1985-87). Office: Duke Power Co PO Box 33189 Charlotte NC 28242

BIRCH, TOBEYLYNN, librarian; b. Los Angeles, Nov. 26, 1949; d. George Walter and Phyllis Jacqueline (Barnes) B.; m. Michael Frederick Cowan, May 17, 1975; children—Stephanie Gayle, Natalie Claire. B.A. in Psychology, U. Calif.-Santa Cruz, 1972; M.A. in Librarianship, U. Denver, 1976. Acquisitions asst. UCLA, 1976-79; asst. librarian Calif. Sch. Profl. Psychology, Los Angeles, 1980-81, dir. library, 1981—. Mem. ALA (sec. Library Instrn. Round Table 1985-86, v.p. 1987-88), Spl. Libraries Assn., Calif. Library Assn., Beta Phi Mu. Democrat. Home: 4510 W 231st St Torrance CA 90505 Office: Calif Sch Profl Psychology 2235 Beverly Blvd Los Angeles CA 90057

BIRCHETT, JO ANN, government official; b. Emporia, Kans., Feb. 19, 1944; d. Clarence Othel and Wilma Jane (Young) Birchett; B.S., Tex. A&I U., Kingsville, 1967. Cooperative edn. student NASA-Johnson Space Center, Houston, 1963-67, computer programmer, data analyst, 1967—. Mem. Fed. Women's Program com., 1979-81. Mem. Nat. Mgmt. Assn., Am. Fedn. Govt. Employees (women's coordinator 1980-81, treas. 1981—). Democrat. Mem. Christian Ch. Home: Route 2 Box 2222 7510 Sunflower St Pearland TX 77584 Office: NASA Johnson Space Ctr Houston TX 77058

BIRD, DONNA, home economics educator; b. Vernal, Utah, July 30, 1926; d. Jasper LaMar and Josephine Marie (Hacking) B. BS, Brigham Young U., 1959; MA, Calif. State Coll., Long Beach, 1966. Various positions Bank of Am., Santa Monica, Calif., 1944-59; tchr. Venice (Calif.) High Sch., 1959-60, Hollywood (Calif.) High Sch., 1960-66; home econs. instr. Brigham Young U., Provo, Utah, 1966-72; home economist, 4-H youth agt. extension services Utah State U., Provo, 1972—; asst. advisor Omicron Nu, Provo, 1967-71; various positions Elec. Women's Round Table, Utah, 1975-78. various offices Utah Valley Family Life Conf., Utah County, 1972—; mem. exec. bd. and bd. dirs. Utah County Fair Bd, 1976—. Mem. AAUW (asst. treas, treas.), Nat. Assn. Extension 4-H Agts, Nat. Assn. Extension Home Economists (nat. com. 1972—), State Extension 4-H (chmn. policy/resolutions bd.), State Extension Home Economists (pres., v.p., sec. 1972—, treas. 1979-82), Utah Assn. Home Economists. Mormon. Office: Utah County Extension Service 100 E Center Provo UT 84601-2808

BIRD, MARY LYNNE MILLER, association executive; b. Buffalo, Feb. 25, 1934; d. Joseph William and Mildred Dorothy (Wallette) Miller; m. Thomas Edward Bird, Aug. 23, 1958; children: Matthew David, Lisa Bronwen. AB magna cum laude, Syracuse U., 1956; postgrad., Columbia U., 1956-58. Mem. research staff Ctr. for Research in Personality, Harvard U., Cambridge, Mass., 1959-62, Ctr. Internat. Studies, Princeton (N.J.) U., 1962-66, Inst. Internat. Social Research, Princeton U., 1965, Sch. Internat. Affairs, Columbia U., N.Y.C., 1966-67, Council Fgn. Relations, N.Y.C., 1967-69, Twentieth Century Fund, N.Y.C., 1969-72; asst. to pres. World Policy Inst., N.Y.C., 1972-74; dir. devel. Fund for Peace, N.Y.C., 1974-78; dir. fellows program Exec. Council Fgn. Diplomats, N.Y.C., 1978-79; dir. devel. Assn. Vol. Sterilization, N.Y.C., 1979-83; exec. dir. Am. Geog. Soc., N.Y.C., 1983—; cons. Fedn. Am. Scientists, Washington, 1974-75. Trustee Bel Canto Opera Co., N.Y.C., 1975—. Maxwell Citizenship scholar Syracuse U., 1952-56. Mem. Assn. Am. Geographers, Soc. Woman Geographers, Nat. Council Geographic Edn., Internat. Geography Union (liason mem. U.S. nat. com.), Conf. Latin Americanist Geographers, St. David's Soc., English Speaking Union, Phi Beta Kappa, Phi Kappa Phi, Eta Pi Upsilon. Office: Am Geog Soc 156 Fifth Ave Suite 600 New York NY 10010-7002

BIRD, ROSE ELIZABETH, former chief justice; b. Tucson, Nov. 2, 1936. B.A. magna cum laude, L.I. U., 1958; J.D., U. Calif., Berkeley, 1965. Bar: Calif. 1966. Clk. to chief justice Nev. Supreme Ct., 1965-66; successively dep. public defender, sr. trial dep., chief appellate div. Santa Clara County (Calif.) Pub. Defenders Office, 1966-74; tchr. Stanford U. Law Sch., 1972-74; sec. Calif. Agr. and Services Agy., also mem. governor's cabinet, 1975-77; chief justice Calif. Supreme Ct., 1977-86; chairperson Calif. Jud. Council, Commn. Jud. Appointments; pres. bd. dirs. Hastings Coll. Law, U. Calif.; bd. councilors U. So. Calif. Law Center, 1975-77; past mem. Western regional selection panel President's Commn. White House Fellowships; bd. assos. San Fernando Valley Youth Found; TV commentator, 1988. Named Most Outstanding Sr. L.I. U., 1958; Ford Found. fellow, 1960. Democrat. Address: PO Box 51376 Palo Alto CA 94306

BIRD-PORTO, PATRICIA A., personnel director; b. N.Y.C., June 16, 1952; d. Jacques Robert and Muriel (Cooper) B.; m. Joseph Porto, May 5, 1984; 1 child, Jennifer Ashley. BA, U. So. Calif., 1975; cert. in legal assistanceship, U. Calif., Irvine, 1987. Mgr. Bullock's Westwood, West Los Angeles, 1976-78; mgr. ops. Lane Bryant, Los Angeles, 1978-79; supr. employment, dir. personnel May Co. Dept. Stores, 1979-81; adminstr. personnel, dir. benefits Zoetrope Studios, Hollywood, Calif., 1981-82; personnel and ops. analyst Auntie Barbara's, Beverly Hills, Calif., 1982-86; dir. personnel Baylyop, Santa Ana, Calif., 1986-88; pres. Creative Personnel Assocs., 1986—. Mem. Personnel Indsl. Relations Assn. Home: 7 Stardust Irvine CA 92715

BIRDSALL, JANE ELAINE, financial executive; b. Buffalo, Aug. 26, 1947; d. Roy George and Geraldine J. (Steffan) Fink; m. Arthur Anthony Birdsall, Jan. 28, 1967; children—Robert James, Thomas Michael, William Mathew. B.B.A., Saginaw Valley State Coll., 1982. Cert. Fin. Planner, Mich. Acct. exec. Thomson McKinnon Securities, Inc., Midland, 1982-88, fin. cons., 1988—. Mem. Tri City Task Force for Econ. Devel. of Women, Midland, Bay City, Saginaw, Mich., 1984—; bd. dirs. Bay County YWCA. Mem. Am. Bus. Women's Assn. (pres. 1985-86, Woman of Yr. award 1986-87), Bus. & Profl. Women's Assn. (v.p. 1984-86, pres. 1986-87), Inst. Cert. Fin. Planners, Internat. Assn. Fin. Planning, Women's Bus. Alliance Mid. Mich. (v.p. 1986-87, pres. 1988—), AAUW (women's chmn. 1987—), Diocese of Saginaw Fin. Council, 1987—. Office: Thomson McKinnon Securities Inc 121 1/2 E Main St Midland MI 48640

BIRDWELL, GAYLE KAYE, management and sales executive, entrepreneur; b. Brookfield, Mo., Oct. 24, 1952; d. Joseph Isaac and Dorothy Rosella (Butterfield) Kaye; m. Jack Ken Birdwell, June 25, 1977; 1 child, Natalie Kaye. BBA, U. Mo., 1974. Sales rep. Procter & Gamble, Dallas, 1974-77, Wallace Bus. Forms, Dallas, 1977-81; gen. mgr. Birdwell & Assocs., Garland, Tex., 1981—, GKB Enterprises, Garland, 1987—; owner Scholastic Aid Services, Garland, 1987—. Mem. PTA. Mem. Dallas Microcomputer Users Group (membership dir., v.p.), Dallas Computer Council (founding bd. dirs.), U. Mo. Alumni Assn. Methodist. Office: Birdwell & Assocs 2332 Gus Thomasson Suite 128 Dallas TX 75228

BIRKEL, BONNIE STANLEY, nurse, consultant; b. White Plains, N.Y., Dec. 12, 1947; d. William J. and Catherine (Bonnyman) Stanley; m. J. Wayne Birkel, June 10, 1972. BS in Nursing, Duke U., 1969; MPH, Johns Hopkins U., 1985. RN, cert. ob-gyn nurse practitioner. Pub. health nurse Prince George's County Health Dept., Cheverly, Md., 1969-72, charge nurse, nurse clinician, 1974-77; free-lance tchr. Saigon, Vietnam, 1972-74; teletypist U.S. Embassy, Saigon, 1972-74; sch. nurse Morrison Christian Acad., Taichung, Taiwan, 1977-78; research asst. U.S. Consulate Gen., Hong Kong, 1979-81; nurse, epidemiologist Dept. Health and Hosps., City of Boston, 1981-84; cons. Washington, 1985; nurse cons. Dept. Health and Mental Hygiene, State of Md., Balt., 1985—. Vol. LWV, Hong Kong Council Women, Hong Kong Family Planning Assn., 1978-81, commn. Prince George's County Commn. for Women, 1977. Mem. Am. Pub. Health Assn. (Frances Etchberger award Md. chpt. 1987), Nurses Assn. Am. Coll. Ob-gyn. (cert.), Nat. Assn. Nurse Practitioners in Family Planning, Met. Washington Pub. Health Assn. Democrat. Home: 611 Elliott St NE Washington DC 20002

BIRKHOFF, DEBORAH LORRAINE, legal secretary; b. Roanoke, Va., Feb. 12, 1959; d. Cornelius F. and Anna S.M. (Anderson) B. B.S. in Econs., Radford U., 1981; cert. paralegal George Washington U., 1982. Sec., Radford U., Va., 1980-81; congl. asst. Congressman Robinson, Washington, 1981-83; police officer U.S. Capitol Police, 1983-86, research analyst, 1985-86; legal sec. Woods, Rogers & Hazlegrove, Roanoke, 1986—. Active congl. campaigns. Mem. Fraternal Order of Police, Internat. Narcotic Enforcement Officers Assn., Am. Fedn. Police, Sigma Sigma Sigma. Republican. Baptist. Office: Woods Rogers & Hazlegrove 105 Franklin Rd SW Roanoke VA 24014

BIRKHOLZ, GABRIELLA SONJA, communication agency executive; b. Chgo., Apr. 11, 1938; d. Ladislav E. and Sonja (Kosner) Becvar. BA in Communications and Bus. Mgmt., Alverno Coll., 1983. Editor, owner Fox Lake (Wis.) Rep., 1962-65, McFarland (Wis.) Community Life and Monona Community Herald, 1966-69; bur. reporter Waukesha (Wis.) Daily Freeman, 1969-71; community relations staff Waukesha County Tech. Inst., Pewaukee, Wis., 1971-73; pub. relations specialist JI Case Co., Racine, Wis., 1973-75, corp. publs. editor, 1975-80; v.p., bd. dirs. publs. Image Mgmt., Valley View Ctr., Milw., 1980-82; pres. Communication Concepts, Unltd., Racine, 1983—; guest lectr. Alverno Coll., U. Wis.; adj. faculty U. Wis.-Parkside. Contbr. articles to profl. jours. Bd. dirs. Big Bros./Big Sisters Racine County, Girl Scouts Racine County; mem. Downtown Racine Devel. Corp., Downtown Racine Assn.; mem. community adv. bd. Sta. WGTD-FM. Recipient awards Wis. Press Assn., Nat. Fedn. Press Women; named Wis. Woman Entrepreneur of Yr., 1985. Mem. Internat. Assn. Bus. Communicators (accredited mem.; bd. dirs. 1982-85, various awards), Wis. Women Entrepreneurs, Nat. Assn. Female Execs., Alverno Alumnae Assn. (governing bd.), Ad Club of Racine (bd. dirs.), Sigma Delta Chi. Home: 901 Kingston Ave Racine WI 53402 Office: 927 Main St Racine WI 53403

BIRKITT, LINDA ANN AYLMER, physical therapist; b. Oakland, Calif., Feb. 8, 1946; d. William Stanley and Phyllis Jane (King) Aylmer; student U. Md. at Munich, W.Ger., 1967-68; B.S., Calif. State Poly. U., 1963-69; M.A. (HEW scholar), U. So. Calif., 1973; m. John C. Birkitt, Sept. 13, 1980; children: Andra, Robert, Lowell, Daniélle, William. Staff phys. therapist Valley Presbyn. Hosp., Van Nuys, Calif., 1973-75; chief therapist Ingleside Mental Health Center, Rosemead, Calif., 1975-79; mem. Speakers Bur., 1976-79; lectr. Santa Monica City Coll., 1976-79; asst. chief phys. therapist Alhambra (Calif.) Community Hosp., 1979-81; pvt. practice phys. therapy, San Juan Capistrano, Calif., 1981—; dir. ops. Healthtech Rehab., Inc., Irvine, Calif., 1985-88; adminstr. Mariners Rehab. Inc., Santa Ana, Calif., 1988—. Vol. fire fighter, El Cariso Village, Calif., 1979—; mem. sch. improvement council San Juan Elem. Sch.; mem. guild Capistrano Ballet. Contbr. articles to profl. jour. Mem. AAUW, Nat. Assn. Female Execs., Nat. Mgmt. Assn. Episcopalian. Research in motivation as a factor in performance of phys. skill, verticality perception distortion in hemiplegic patients. Home: 32536 Ortega Hwy El Cariso Village Lake Elsinore CA 92330

BIRMAN, CAROLINE (CARINA), lawyer; b. Graz, Styria, Austria, June 1; came to U.S., 1941, naturalized, 1946; d. Armin and Anna (Fischer) B. J.D., U. Vienna, 1924; Licenciée en droit, U. Paris, 1929; LL.B., Bklyn. Law Sch., 1946, J.D., 1967. Bar: N.Y. 1947, U.S. Supreme Ct. 1960. Exec. sec. Commn. for Distbn. of Rolling Stock of former Austro-Hungarian Monarchy, Vienna, 1923-26; legal advisor Austrian legation and Austrian consulate, Paris, 1930-38; French legal counsellor, Paris, 1930-40; pvt. practice law, N.Y.C., 1947—; specialist in French Austrian and German law. Mem. editorial staff Revue Internationale des Societes, Paris, 1933-38. Decorated knight's cross Austrian Order of Merit. Mem. ABA, N.Y. Women's Bar Assn., New York County Lawyers Assn. Mem. Liberal Party. Home: 104-60 Queens Blvd Suite 9B Forest Hills NY 11375

BIRNBAUM, JOAN WELKER, religious foundation executive; b. Oil City, Pa., Apr. 26, 1923; d. George Ernest and Josephine Wilson (Powell) Welker; m. Theodore Birnbaum, Jan. 8, 1949 (div. 1977); children—Lyuba, Margaret Jane (Meg), L. Crispin. B.A. in Econs., Wellesley Coll., 1945; postgrad. Northwestern U. Grad. Sch. Bus. Adminstrn., summer 1945, Nat. Planned Giving Inst., 1979, Philanthropy Tax Inst. Jr. acct. Price, Waterhouse and Co., N.Y.C., 1945-50; sec. to asst. treas. Rockefeller Found., N.Y.C., 1950; acct. Rye Youth Council, N.Y., 1976-84; exec. dir. Mamaroneck/Larchmont LIFE Ctr., N.Y., 1973; assoc. dir. vols. United Hosp., Port Chester, N.Y., 1974; bus. mgr. Burke Rehab. Ctr. Day Hosp., White Plains, N.Y., 1974-78; planned giving officer Save the Children Fedn., Inc., Westport, Conn., 1979-82; exec. dir. N.Y.-Conn. Found. of United Meth. Ch., White Plains, 1982—. Bd. dirs. Rye United Fund, sec., mem. nominating com.; elder, deacon pres. Women's Assn. Rye Presbyterian Ch.; chmn. maj. reunion fund campaign Wellesley Coll. Class, 1980-85, chmn. reunion, 1975, class historian, 1965—, admissions chmn. for Wellesley in Westchester Club; bd. dirs., pres. Planned Parenthood of Eastern Westchester; pres. Rye Family Service; telephone listener and source of referral Rye/Larchmont/Mamaroneck Hot Line; treas., exec. com. Rye Youth Council; sec., treas., v.p., pres. 15th Twig of United Hosp., also bd. dirs.; past pres. Rye High Sch. Mothers' Guild, chmn. 1st direct solicitation fund drive; bd. dirs. Woman's Club of Rye, pres. jr. sect.; membership chmn., bd. dirs. Midland Sch. of Rye (voted Parent of Yr.). Mem. Nat. Assn. United Meth. Founds. (treas. 1983—), Planned Giving Group of Greater N.Y. (v.p. 1983-84, pres. 1984-85), Internat. Assn. Fin. Planners, Devel. Assn. of So. Conn. (chmn. program com. 1983-84), Nat. Soc. Fund Raising Execs., Assn. Westchester Devel. Officers. Republican. Presbyterian. Club: Wellesley (so. Conn.). Avocations: silversmithing; handweaving; piano; guitar; Great Books.

BIRNBAUM, SHEILA L., lawyer, educator; b. 1940. B.A., Hunter Coll., 1960, M.A., 1962; LL.B. NYU, 1965. Bar: N.Y. 1965. Legal asst. Superior Ct., N.Y.C., 1965; assoc. Berman & Frost, N.Y.C., 1965-70, ptnr., 1970-72; prof. Fordham U., N.Y.C., 1972-78; prof. NYU, N.Y.C., 1978-86; ptnr. Skadden, Arps, Meagher, Slate & Flom, 1984—; assoc. dean NYU, 1982-84. N.Y.C Bar Assn. (mem. exec. com. 1978—, jud. com. 1977), ABA (chmn. product gen. liability, consumer land coms.), Assn. of Bar of City of N.Y. (exec. com. 1978—, 2d century com. 1984-86), Phi Beta Kappa, Phi Alpha Theta, Alpha Chi Alpha. Author: (with Rheingold) Products Liability, Law, Practice Science, 1974. Office: Skadden Arps Slate Meagher & Flom 919 3d Ave New York NY 10022

BIRNEY, SANDRA ANN, medical distribution executive; b. Torrington, Conn., Apr. 18, 1939; d. Clarence Joseph and Amelia Emily (Couerchesgne) Ruwet; m. Thomas Henry Birney, Nov. 9, 1932 (div. Apr. 1977); children: Lauren Beth, Cristin Valli, Kathleen Kyle. RN, St. Francis Hosp., 1960; postgrad. in Nursing, U. Phoenix. Mgr. Staff Builders, Orange, Calif., 1976-78; nat. sales mgr. Itrex Corp, Santa Ana, Calif., 1978-79; prin. Birney Med. Systems, Santa Ana, 1979—. Home and Office: 1907 E Fruit St Santa Ana CA 92701

BIRNHAK, SANDRA JEAN, film company executive; b. Los Angeles, Apr. 27, 1945; d. Charles William and Edna Mae (Cante) Reynolds; m. Bruce I. Birnhak, Feb. 4, 1964 (div. 1970); 1 child, Scott Alan; m. David R. Ames, Dec. 22, 1984. Degree in Advanced Film Studies, MIT, 1981-82, Am. Film Inst., 1983. Pres., dir. Subtle-T, Inc., Boston, 1974-77; dir. mktg. RKO Gen. Broadcasting, Boston, 1978-80; vis. lectr. pub. relations Boston Coll., 1980-81; line producer, auditor Cannon Films Internat., N.Y.C., 1983; exec. v.p., chief fin. officer Hartwest, Inc., N.Y.C., 1983-85; pres., chief exec. officer Showcase Prodns. Internat., N.Y.C., 1985—; dir. Women's Perspective Prodns., Boston, 1981; cons. Smith/Richmond Films, Los Angeles, 1985—, Films Around the World, N.Y.C., 1986—. Producer, dir. Corporate Women, 1980, Balloons, 1981; assoc. producer Mr. North, 1987. Vol. Kennedy Meml. Hosp. for Children, Boston, 1980, St. Vincent's Hosp., N.Y.C. Recipient Nat. Disting. Service award March of Dimes, Boston, 1980, Govs. award, Boston, 1979. Mem. NOW, N.Y. Women in Film, Ind. Filmmakers Assoc., Nat. Assn. Broadcasters, Am. Fedn. TV and Radio Artists. Democrat. Unitarian.

BIRNKRANT, JEANNE ANN, artist, actress, social worker; b. N.Y.C.; d. William Benjamen and Dorothy Leona (Solow) B. BA, Barnard Coll.; MSW, Columbia U.; postgrad., New Sch. Social Research, 1968-70, Arts Students League, 1970-75, Berghoff Acting Studios, 1975-80. Chief psychiat. social worker N.Y. Psychoanalytic Inst., 1970-76; children's psychotherapist Bellevue Hosp., N.Y.C., 1976-78; psychotherapist, dir. social work Met. Hosp., N.Y.C., 1978-84; actress various cos. Prin. sculpture works include (bronze) Strident Man (1st prize South Park Artist Group, N.Y.C. 1984), Winged Bird Fantasy (1st prize Nantucket Contemporary Gallery, Mass., 1985); appeared in movies Turk 182, Cotton Club, Nuts, Radio Days, Ghostbusters, Round Midnight, Prizzi's Honor, Fatal Attraction; appeared in TV show Superman Anniversary Spl., 1988. County Com. woman Village Ind. Dems., N.Y.C.; patron Mus. Modern Art. Nat. Mental Health fellow, Jewish Guild for Blind fellow. Mem. Screen Actors Guild, Actors Equity Assn., Nat. Assn Social Workers (cert.), AFTRA. Home and office: 240 Central Park S New York NY 10019

BIROS, LORRAINE, mental health counselor; b. Cleve., June 8, 1946; d. John A. and Ann L. (Ferrara) Biros; B.S., Ohio State U., 1967; M.A., Goddard Coll., 1979. Nat. cert. counselor, 1986. Tech. editor Am. Psychol. Assn., Washington, 1968-72; prodn. coordinator, sr. staff editor John F. Holman & Co., Inc., Washington, 1974-79; mem. core faculty Goddard Coll., 1980-81, cons., 1981-82; feminist counselor in pvt. practice, Silver Spring, Md., 1979—; mem., bd. dirs. Whitman-Walker Clinic, Inc., Washington, 1979-80; co-founder/coordinator Lesbian Resource and Counseling Center, Washington, 1978-80, mem. core staff, 1985—, cons., 1980—; charter mem. D.C. Area Feminist Alliance, 1976-78; mem. core staff Washington Area Women's Center, 1976-78. Mem. editorial bd. Women and Therapy: A Feminist Quar., 1986—. Recipient Gene Frey award Whitman-Walker Clinic, 1987. Mem. Am. Assn. Counseling and Devel., Nat. Assn. for Children of Alcoholics, Assn. for Women in Psychology, Himalayan Internat. Inst. Yoga Sci. and Philosophy, Nat. Assn. Lesbian and Gay Alcoholism Profls., Nat. Gay and Lesbian Task Force, NOW, Women's Nat. Health Network, Women Strike for Peace, Women's Internat. League Peace and Freedom. Democrat. Home: 806 Malcolm Dr Silver Spring MD 20901

BIRSCHTEIN, BARBARA ANN, county official; b. Atlantic, N.J., Apr. 22; d. Morris and Helen (Rellis) B. BEd, U. Toledo, 1976. Cert. tchr. Ohio, N.J. Income maintenance technician Atlantic County Div. Welfare, Atlantic City, 1977-78, income maintenance specialist, 1978-80, income maintenance supr. non-pub. assistance food stamps, 1980-85, income maintenance supr. match overissuance/overpayment unit, 1985—. Mem. Am. Pub. Welfare Assn., United Council Welfare Fraud, Welfare Assn. So. N.J., AAUW. Home: 4A N Providence Ave Atlantic City NJ 08401 Office: Atlantic County Div Welfare 1333 Atlantic Ave Atlantic NJ 08401

BIRTCHER, WENDY CATHARINE, real estate executive; b. Newport Beach, Calif., Sept. 6, 1962; d. Arthur Belt and Shirley Rae (Garibaldi) B. BA magna cum laude, Sweet Briar (Va.) Coll., 1984. V.p. aquisitions Birtcher Investments, Laguna Niguel, Calif., 1984—. Bd. dirs. S. County Community Clinic, San Juan Capistrano, Calif., 1985—; bd. overseers Sweet Briar Coll., 1984-87. Sweet Briar scholar 1984. Mem. Nat. Assn. Indsl. and Office Parks, Urban Land Inst., Young Execs. Am., C. of C. (bd. dirs. San Juan Capistrano 1987—), Phi Beta Kappa, Pi Gamma Mu. Republican. Roman Catholic. Office: Birtcher Investments 27611 La Paz Rd Laguna Niguel CA 92677

BISCHAK, CYNTHIA D., technical publishing administrator; b. Columbus, Ohio, Apr. 1, 1956; d. Donald Rex, Jr., and Nancy May (Dawson) Barnes; m. Frank William Bischak, Mar. 16, 1977. BS in Botany and Marine Sci., U. Wash., 1981, MPA, 1985. Water quality technician Ohio EPA, Columbus, 1978; exec. sec. Dan A. Carmichael, AIA, Columbus, 1978-79; supr. publs. Vitro Corp., Silverdale, Wash., 1982-85; sr. tech. writer water pollution control dept. Municipality Met. Seattle (Metro), 1985—; bd. dirs. Hood Canal Environ. Council, Seabeck, Wash., 1985-88; chmn. conservation com. Kitsap Audubon, Poulsbo, Wash., 1982-84. Author: Citizen's Guide to Municipal Incorporation in the State of Washington, 1985. Tech. advisor and publicity co-chmn. Silverdale Inc. Com., 1983-85. Mem. Am. Soc. Pub. Adminstrn. (student rep. Evergreen chpt. Council 1984-85, council mem. Evergreen chpt. 1986-88), Soc. for Tech. Communication, Council Biology Editors, Western Govtl. Research Assn. Club; Cityclub (Seattle). Avocations: backpacking, canoeing, scuba diving, gardening, stained glass. Home: PO Box 187 Seabeck WA 98380-0187 Office: Metro 821 Second Ave MS-82 Seattle WA 98104

BISGYER, BARBARA GINETTE, sculptor; b. N.Y.C., June 7, 1933; d. Edgar S. Peierls and Betsy (Vogel) Peierls Evans; m. Melvin Bisgyer, Sept. 4, 1952 (div. 1961); children—Marcia, Ann, Susan; m. Eric M. Cohn, May 19, 1965; stepchildren—Andrew E., Lee Cameron. Student Sarah Lawrence Coll., 1955, Bennington Coll.; student indsl. design Kostellow, N.Y.C. Free lance exhbn. designer. One woman shows include: Environment Gallery, N.Y.C., 1966, 68, 72, 75; exhibited in group shows: Aldrich Mus., 1974, Audubon Ann., N.Y.C., 1967, 68, 69, 70, 71, 73, 77, Jersey City Mus., 1969, Lever House, 1970, 71, 72, 76, 77; represented in permanent collections Smithsonian Instn., Washington, Aldrich Mus. Contemporary Art, Ridgefield, Conn. Recipient award Westchester Art Soc., 1967, 68, Mamaroneck Artists Guild, 1967, 72; Today's Art medal Audubon Artists, 1971, Pres.'s award Audubon Artists, 1977. Mem. Abraxas, Am. Crafts Council, Am. Soc. Contemporary Artists (bd. dirs. 1985—), Artists Craftsmen of N.Y. (bd. govs. 1964-69, design and craftsmanship award 1971), Artists Equity.

BISHOP, C. DIANE, state agency administrator, educator; b. Elmhurst, Ill., Nov. 23, 1943; d. Louis William and Constance Oleta (Mears) B.; m. Richard Lee Morse, Oct. 20, 1984. BS in Maths., U. Ariz., 1965, MS in Maths., MEd in Secondary Edn., 1972. Lic. secondary educator. Tchr. math. Tucson Unified Sch. Dist., 1966-86, mem. curriculum council, 1985-86, mem. maths. curriculum task teams, 1983-86; state supt. of pub. instrn. State of Ariz., 1987—; assoc. faculty Pima Community Coll., Tucson, 1974-84; adj. lectr. U. Ariz., 1983, 85. Mem. Ariz. State Bd. Edn., 1984—, chmn. quality edn. commn., 1986-87, chmn. tchr. cert. subcom. 1984—, outcomes based edn. adv. com. 1986-87, liaison bd. dirs. essential skills subcom. 1985-87, gifted edn. com. liaison 1985—; mem. high sch. task force Ariz. Bd. Regents, 1984-85, com. on preparing for U. Ariz., 1983; mem. Ariz. Stat Bd. Regents, 1987—, Ariz. State Community Coll. Bd., 1987—. Woodrow Wilson fellow Princeton U., summer 1984; recipient Presdl. Award for Excellence in Teaching of Maths., 1983, Ariz. Citation of Merit, 1984, Maths. Teaching award Nat. Sci. Research Soc., 1984, Distinction in Edn. award Flinn Found., 1986; named Maths. Tchr. of Yr. Ariz. Council of Engring. and Sci. Assns., 1984. Mem. Nat. Council of Tchrs. of Maths. Council of Chief State Sch. Officers, NEA, Ariz. Edn. Assn., Tucson Edn. Assn., Ariz. Assn. Tchrs. of Maths., Women in Maths. Edn., Math. Assn. of Am., NRC (math. scis. edn. bd. 1987—), Ednl. Commn. of the States, Nat. Forum on Excellence in Edn., Nat. Honors Workshop, Pi Mu Epsilon, Pi Lambda Theta. Democrat. Episcopalian. Office: Ariz State Dept Edn 1535 W Jefferson Phoenix AZ 85007

BISHOP, FLORENCE H., state agency administrator; b. Trenton, N.J., Nov. 16, 1929; d. Hosie and Ella V. (Watts) Holliday; m. Robert G. Bishop, Mar. 19, 1950 (div. 1964); children: Brent L., Robert Jr., Steven, Sandra E., Ramona L., Curtis. AA, Mercer County Community Coll., Trenton, 1969; BA, Ramapo Coll., Mahwah, N.J., 1977; MA, Rider Coll., 1981. Field rep. N.J. Pub. Advocate, Trenton, 1975-78, supervising field rep., 1978—. Recording sec. Carver Youth and Family Ctr., Trenton, 1984—; bd. dirs. Trenton Theater Guild, 1987—. Mem. N.J. Black Adminstrs. Network (corresponding sec. 1987—, v.p. 1984-87, Unsung Adminstr. award 1969), Zeta Phi Beta (v.p. Epsilon Xi Zeta chpt. 1984—). Democrat. Methodist. Home: 124 Robbins Ave Trenton NJ 08638 Office: NJ Dept Pub Advocate 25 Market St Trenton NJ 08625

BISHOP, FRANCES BLACKBURN, civic worker; b. West Palm Beach, Fla., Mar. 3, 1925; d. Julius Magath and Adele Eleanor (Berg) Blackburn; B.Mus.Ed., Fla. State U., 1945; postgrad. Columbia, 1959-62; M.A. in Musicology, U. Mo., 1958; M.A. Teaching English as 2d Lang., Hunter Coll., 1986; m. Ben Bishop, May 20, 1946 (div. 1952); 1 dau., Jewel. Music tchr., Joiner, Ark., 1946-47, Franklin Square, N.Y., 1957-69; asst. placement dir. of internat. counselor exchange program. Assn. for World Travel Exchange, N.Y.C., 1970-74; exec. sec. Army Relief Soc., N.Y.C., 1975-76; adminstrv. sec. Am. Music Center, 1977-78; editorial asst. Sci. Digest, 1978-86; violinist Bloomingdale Chamber Orch.; tchr. English adult evening classes, N.Y.C., 1972-75; mem. Met. Greek Chorale. Vol. Internat. Center. Author reading textbook for English; collaborator on Japanese English dictionary of new words. Home: 36 W 84 St New York NY 10024

BISHOP, HELEN HUMPHRIES, finance executive; b. St. Louis, Jan. 14, 1943; d. Malcolm B. and Mary Lee (Alderson) Epstein; children: John M., Karen E. BA in Zoology, U. Mo., 1964; MA in Early Music, San Diego State U., 1984, MEd in Tech., 1987. Vol. U.S. Peace Corps, Ethiopia, 1964-67; dir. research John & E. Sturge Ltd., Birmingham, Eng., 1968-70; music tchr. Lossiemouth, Scotland, 1972-78, San Diego, 1978—; trainer Mission Bay Mortgage, San Diego, 1981-84; dir. tng. WestWind Mortgage Co., San Diego, 1984-86; tng. specialist Guild Mortgage Co., San Diego, 1986—. Contbr. articles to profl. jours. Dir. religious edn. Unitarian Universalist Fellowship San Dieguito, Solano Beach, Calif., 1980-85; curriculum designer Unitarian Universalist Assn., Boston, 1985—; chair Dist. Religious Edn. Com., Los Angeles, 1986—. Recipient Service award PTA, 1983; Soroptimists scholar, 1985. Mem. Nat. Assn. Female Execs., Nat. Soc. for Performance and Instrn., San Diego Early Music Soc., Mortgage Bankers Assn. (tng. subcom. 1986—), Polio Survivors Network, Phi Beta Kappa, Phi Kappa Phi. Democrat. Home: 14247 Kendra Ct Poway CA 92064 Office: Guild Mortgage Co 4180 Ruffin Rd San Diego CA 92123

BISHOP, JOYCE ANN, financial planner; b. West Mansfield, Ohio, June 16, 1935; d. Frederic J. and Marjorie Vere (Stephens) Armentrout; m. Belinda Lee, Thomas James. AB, Albion Coll., 1956; MA, Western Mich. U., 1969, postgrad., 1972-87. Cert. social worker. Tchr. phys. edn., health and cheerleading Walled Lake (Mich.) Jr. High Sch., 1956-58; instr. slimnastics adult edn. Milw. Pub. Schs., 1959-65; demonstrator, co. rep. Polaroid Corp., Cambridge, Mass., 1960-81; research asst. fetal electrocardiography Marquette U., Milw., 1962-64; tchr. phys. edn., health and cheerleading Brown Deer (Wis.) High Sch., 1963-65; instr. slimnastics adult edn., instr. volleyball Lakeview High Sch., Battle Creek, Mich., 1966—; dir. student activities, counselor, asst. prof. Kellogg Community Coll., Battle Creek, 1971-87, transfer counselor; asst. prof. Olivet (Mich.) Coll., 1969-71. Sec. adult bd. Teens, Inc., 1965-68; bd. dirs. Battle Creek Day Care Ctrs., sec., 1984, pres., 1984-86; team capt. United Way Awareness Week, 1984, United Arts Fund Dr., 1985, chmn., 1986; mem. Battle Creek Leadership Acad. Recipient Master Teaching award Lakeview Schs., 1969, 87. Mem. Mich. Assn. Collegiate Registrars and Admissions Officers (pres. 1979-80, historian 1984-87), Am. Assn. Collegiate Registrars and Admissions Officers (mem. com. 1984-87), Am. Personnel and Guidance Assn., Am. Coll. Personnel Assn., Mich. Personnel and Guidance Assn., Mich. Coll. Personnel Assn., Mich. Assn. Women Deans, Adminstrs. and Counselors, Mich. Assn. Coll. Admissions Counselors, AAUW, Alpha Chi Omega, Beta Beta Beta. Clubs: Battle Creek Road Runners (v.p. 1983-85), Battle Creek Altrusa. Home: 721 Eastfield Dr Battle Creek MI 49015 Office: Richard M Groff Assocs Inc 5320 Holiday Terr Kalamazoo MI 49009

BISHOP, KAREN CHRISTINE, finance company administrator; b. Ft. Wayne, Ind., Jan. 13, 1959; d. Emery Franklin and Betty Lou (Streets) Thurston; m. Matthew Wayne Bishop, June 19, 1981. B. Ind. U., 1981. Br. mgr. Firefighters Credit Union, Ft. Wayne, 1981-84; mgr. Slater Credit Union, Ft. Wayne, 1984—; bd. dirs. Northeastern Ind. Credit Union, Ft. Wayne. Home: 1311 Dundee New Haven IN 46774 Office: Slater Ft Wayne Fed Credit Union 2400 Taylor St W Fort Wayne IN 46802

BISHOP, KATHRYN ELIZABETH, film company executive, writer; b. Seattle, July 7, 1945; d. Wesley Thomas Bishop and Muriel (Robert) Leisher; m. Randolph Stiles, May 22, 1985; 1 child, Zachary. BA, Wartburg Coll., 1966. Voice over talent Chgo. Bd. Edn. Radio Network, 1960-62; prodn. asst. Sta. CBS-TV, WBBM-TV, Chgo., 1961-63; disk jockey, engr., writer Sta. KWAR-FM, Waverly, Iowa, 1964-65; assoc. producer Bing Crosby Prodns. Inc., Chgo., 1966-69; producer Sedelmaier Films, Chgo., 1969-73; v.p., head prodn. Wakeford/Orloff Inc., Los Angeles, 1977-78; producer Katy Bishop Prodns. Inc., Los Angeles, 1973—; exec. producer The Colman Group Inc., Los Angeles, 1982-87; co-founder, co-owner Rapport Films, Inc., Hollywood, Calif., 1987—. Co-author: (screenplay) Millionaire's Club; screenwriter: Cinnamon Bear. Mem. TV Acad. Arts and Scis., Dirs. Guild Am. Office: Rapport Films Inc 1645 N Vine Suite #532 Los Angeles CA 90028

BISHOP, MARGARET, retired educator, writer; b. Urbana, Ill., July 4, 1920; d. Charles Maxwell and Prudence Emily (Pratt) McConn; m. Edwin Samuel Bishop, Aug. 22, 1942; children—Peter Boehler, Margaret. B.A., Barnard Coll., N.Y.C., 1943. Reporter, wire editor York Gazette and Daily, York, Pa., 1942-45; remedial reading tutor, Queens, N.Y., 1958-68; in-house writer Appleton-Century-Crofts, N.Y.C., 1964-70, McGraw-Hill, N.Y.C., 1971-74; reading specialist Fortune Soc., N.Y.C., 1976-85. Author: The ABC's and All Their Tricks, 1986, Ode on Reason and Faith, 1981, (workbooks) Phonics with Write and See, 1968, also articles. Exec. sec. NAACP, York, 1943-48; mem. LWV, York, 1946-50, Reading Reform Found., N.Y.C., 1958—; pres. N.Y. met. chpt., 1981-85. Mem. Mayor's Profl. Exchange, Adult Basic Edn. Providers. Democrat. Humanist. Avocations: hiking; camping; backpacking.

BISHOP, MARGARET ANN, coal company executive; b. Owensboro, Ky., Mar. 2, 1949; d. Vernon Lee and Emma Frances (Smith) Frashure; m. Allen Ray Bishop, Nov. 11, 1972 (dec. Feb. 1987); m. Paul David Anderson, Apr. 4, 1969 (div. May 1971). Student Victor Bus. Coll., 1970, U. Ky., 1983. Fingerprint technician FBI, Washington, 1968-69; supr. Thomas Industries, Beaver Dam, Ky., 1971-74; lab. mgr. Island Creek Coal Co., Madisonville, Ky., 1974—. Named Ky. Col., 1978. Mem. ASTM, Am. Mgmt. Assn., LWV. Democrat. Presbyterian. Club: Bus. and Profl. Women's (Madisonville) (Woman of Yr. award 1978, pres. 1980-81). Lodge: Order Eastern Star (assoc. conductress 1983-84). Home: Route 1 Box 156 Sacramento KY 42372 Office: Island Creek Coal Co 407 Brown Rd Madisonville KY 42431

BISHOP, MARY ROBINSON, educator, administrator; b. Chikasha, Okla., July 9, 1922; d. Scott Vernon and Mary Eugenia (Peery) Robinson; m. Ray Phillip Kawal, Sept. 17, 1944 (div. 1960); children: Ray, Ronald; m. George Bishop (div. 1980). BA, Okla. Coll. for Women, 1943; spl. cert. engring., U. Tex., 1944; cert. in adminstrn., Calif. State U., 1959, MA, 1968. Aero. engr. Curtiss-Wright Aircraft Corp., St. Louis, 1944-45, North Am. Aviation, Inglewood, Calif., 1945-46; tchr. Los Angeles Unified Sch. Dist., 1959-67, tchr. of gifted children, 1968-74, curriculum cons., 1974-76, advisor gifted program, 1976-77, with staff-devel. div., 1977-78; with adminstrn. staff Victoria Ave. Sch., Southgate, Calif., 1978-81, Chatsworth, Calif., 1982-86; with adminstrn. staff Germain St. Sch., Chatsworth; Author and editor: Critical Thinking, 1978. Hon. life mem. PTA, 1986—; chmn. 43d Ch. of Christ Scientist, Woodland Hills, Calif., 1972-85. Mem. Delta Kappa Gamma (pres. 1976-78, internat. rep. 1976). Republican. Home: 17260 Signature Dr Granada Hills CA 91344

BISHOP, SUSAN KATHARINE, search company executive; b. Palm Beach, Fla., Apr. 3, 1946; d. Warner Bader Bishop and Katharine Sue (White) McLennan; m. Robert Uchitel, Dec. 27, 1973 (div. 1979); 1 child, Rachel. B.A., Briarcliff Coll., 1968; M.B.A., Fordham U., 1985. Actress, N.Y.C., 1968-72; producer, hostess Sta. KIMO-TV, Anchorage, 1972-74; dir. programming Visions Pay TV, 1974-79; recruiter Joe Sullivan & Assocs., N.Y.C., 1980-82; prin. Johnson, Smith & Knisely, 1982-87, ptnr., 1988—. Mem. Cable TV Adminstrn. and Mktg. Soc., Women in Cable. Office: Johnson Smith & Knisely 475 Fifth Ave New York NY 10017

BISHOP, VIRGINIA WAKEMAN, librarian, humanities educator; b. Portland, Oreg., Dec. 28, 1927; d. Andrew Virgil and Letha Evangeline (Ward) Wakeman; m. Clarence Edmund Bishop, Aug. 23, 1953; children: Jean Marie Bishop Johnson, Marilyn Joyce. BA, Bapt. Missionary Tng. Sch., Chgo., 1949; BA, Linfield Coll., McMinnville, Oreg., 1952, MEd, 1953; MA in Librarianship, U. Wash., 1968. Ch. worker Univ. Bapt. Ch., Seattle, 1954-56, 59-61; pre-sch. tchr. parent coop presch., Seattle, 1965-66; librarian Northwest Coll., Kirkland, Wash., 1968-69, U. Wash. undergrad. library, Seattle, 1970; librarian, instr. Seattle Central Community Coll., 1970—. Leader Totem council Girl Scouts U.S., 1962-65; pres. Wedgwood Sch. PTA, Seattle, 1964-65; chairperson 46th Dist. Democratic Orgn., Seattle, 1972-73; candidate Wash. State Legislature, Seattle, 1974, 80. Recipient Golden Acorn award Wedgwood Elem. Sch., 1966. Mem. Wash. Commn. for Humanities (Humanist scholar 1979-80), Wash. Library Assn. (legis. rep. 1972), U. Wash. Grad. Sch. Library and Info. Sci. Alumni Assn. (1st v.p. 1986-87, pres. 1987—), Community Coll. Librarians and Media Specialists, Seattle Community Coll. Fedn. Tchrs., LWV. Unitarian. Avocations: swimming, hiking, reading. Home: 3032 NE 87th St Seattle WA 98115 Office: Seattle Cen Community Coll 1701 Broadway Seattle WA 98122

BISHOPP, THELMA JEAN, academic administrator, former educator; b. Lafayette, Colo., Nov. 4, 1939; d. John Joseph and Vauna Cora (Sherratt) Hartnagle; m. Frank John Bishopp, Jan. 25, 1964; 1 child, Errin Lea. BA, U. Colo., 1962, MA, 1966, PhD, 1982. Cert. acad. adminstr., supr. Tchr. German Boulder (Colo.) Valley Sch. Dist., 1962-63; coordinator fgn. lang. programs Weld County Sch. Dist. #6, Greeley, Colo., 1968-69; head dept. fgn. langs. John Evans Jr. High Sch., Greeley, 1970-75, tchr. German, 1965-75; adminstrv. intern Niwot (Colo.) High Sch., 1976; asst. prin. Northeast Jr. High Sch., Longmont, Colo., 1977, Longmont High Sch., 1977-81; prin. Longs Peak Jr. High Sch., Longmont, 1981-88, Niwot High Sch., 1988—. Contbr. articles to profl. jours. Mem. U. Colo. Assn. Edn. Alumni and Friends, Nat. Assn. Secondary Sch. Prins., Colo. Assn. Sch. Execs., St. Vrain Valley Sch. Adminstrn. Assn. (pres. 1985-86), Phi Delta Kappa, Delta Phi Alpha. Democrat. Lutheran. Office: St Vrain Valley Sch Dist 395 S Pratt Pkwy Longmont CO 80501

BISS, CHRISTINE HELEN, management professional; b. Passaic, N.J., May 31, 1940; d. John and Rose (Sondej) Miskowicz; m. Ronald M. Biss, June 2, 1962 (div. Nov. 1984). BS cum laude, Montclair State Coll., 1986. Jr. sec. Fairleigh-Dickinson U., Rutherford, N.J., 1958-59; sec. Kearfott Div. Gen. Precision Inc., Clifton, N.J., 1959-74; exec. sec. Singer Kearfott Div., Little Falls, N.J., 1974-81; administr. engring. Singer Kearfott Div., Wayne, N.J., 1981-85; sr. administr. engring. Singer Electronic Systems Div., Wayne, 1985—. Coordinator U.S. Savs. Bond Campaign, C3I Systems directorate Singer Electronic Systems, 1982—, also United Way (tri-state) Campaign, 1982—. Mem. Oak Ridge Civic Assn., Nat. Assn. Female Execs., Singer Kearfott Chess Club (co-dir. 1983—), 2nd Careers. Office: Singer Electronic Systems Div 164 Totowa Rd Wayne NJ 07474

BISSEL, SUSAN JANE, public relations educator; b. Owatonna, Minn., Dec. 29, 1946; d. Alfred William and Benita Helen (Wilker) Kruckeberg; m. Dean Alfred Bissel, Apr. 20, 1968; children: Stephanie, Jeremy. BA in English, Wartburg Coll., 1969; MA in Journalism, No. Ill. U., 1974; PhD in Mass Communications, U. Iowa, 1985. With pub. relations dept. Luth. Gen. Hosp., Park Ridge, Ill., 1969-73; extension information specialist U. Minn., St. Paul, 1973-76; instr. journalism U. Iowa, Iowa City, 1976-79; asst. professor mass communications Northwest Mo. State U., Maryville, 1979-83; coordinator pub. relations degree program SUNY, Albany, 1983—. Vol. ARC, Waterloo, Iowa, 1976-79. Mem. Pub. Relations Soc. Am., Assn. for Edn. in Journalism and Mass Communication. Lutheran. Home: Werik Apts 21 North Gate Dr Albany NY 12203

BISSELL, BETTY DICKSON, stockbroker; b. Salina, Kans., Sept. 9, 1932; d. Henry Shields and Alta May Dickson; student U. Kans., 1949-52; cert. fin. planner, Coll. Fin. Planning, 1976; m. Buford Lyle Bissell, Jr., Nov. 1, 1952; 1 son, Bradford Dickson. With Dean Witter Reynolds Inc., Menlo Park, Calif., 1975—, asst. br. mgr., 1978-82, asso. v.p. investments, 1980-82, 1st v.p. investments, 1982-86, sr. v.p. investments, 1986—. Pres. Jr. League San Jose (Calif.), 1963-64. Mem. Internat. Assn. Fin. Planners, Peninsula Stock and Bond Club, Pi Beta Phi. Republican. Episcopalian. Clubs: Commonwealth Calif., Summit League (Saratoga-Los Gatos), Jr. League (San Jose, Calif.); Menlopolitans (Menlo Park, Calif.). Office: 720 Santa Cruz Ave Menlo Park CA 94025

BISSELL, JEAN GALLOWAY, circuit judge; b. Due West, S.C., June 9, 1936; d. Robert Stone and Clara Elizabeth (Agnew) G.; m. Gregg Claude Bissell, June 11, 1969. Student, Erskine Coll., 1952-54; B.S. magna cum laude, U. S.C., 1956, LL.B., 1958; LL.D. (hon.), Converse Coll., 1976, Furman U., 1987. Bar: S.C. 1958. With Haynsworth, Perry, Bryant, Marion and Johnston, Greenville, S.C., 1958-71; ptnr. McKay, Sherrill, Walker & Townsend, Columbia, S.C., 1971-76; sr. v.p., gen. counsel S.C. Nat. Bank, Columbia, 1976-80, exec. v.p., gen. counsel, 1980-81, vice chmn., chief adminstrv. officer, gen. counsel, 1981-84; sr. v.p., gen. counsel S.C. Nat. Corp., Columbia, 1976-80, exec. v.p., gen. counsel, 1980-81, vice chmn., chief adminstrv. officer, gen. counsel, 1981-84, dir., 1982-84; circuit judge U.S. Ct. Appeals Fed. Circuit, Washington, 1984—; lectr. Sch. Law U.S.C., 1971-78, 80-84. Mem. adv. council S.C. State Library, 1971-76, Erskine Coll., 1971-74, Columbia Coll., 1974-78, Furman U., 1972-84; mem. pres.'s nat. adv. council U. S.C., 1981-84; mem. bd. Columbia Philharm. Orch., 1975-78, Greater Columbia Community Relations Council, 1976-79; regent Leadership S.C., 1979-81; mem. merit selection panel S.C. Pub. Service Commn., 1980-84; chmn. Richland County Pub. Library, 1975-78; mem. S.C. Library Bd., 1982-84; mem. bd. S.C. Council Econ. Edn., 1984. Recipient Disting. Service award S.C. Library Assn., 1973, 1st ann. Friend of Libraries award, 1976, Algernon Sydney Sullivan award. Mem. ABA, S.C. Bar Assn. Clubs: City Tavern (Washington). Office: US Ct Appeals 717 Madison Pl NW Washington DC 20439

BISSETT, BARBARA ANNE, steel distribution company executive; b. Cleve., Sept. 27, 1950; d. George Jr. and Helen (Kirkwood) B.; m. Kerry Mark Kitchen, Oct. 6, 1979; m. Mark Jeffrey, Lauren Brooke. BFA, U. Denver, 1974. Inside sales rep. Bissett Steel Co., Cleve., 1977-78, inside sales mgr., 1978-80, v.p., 1980-88, pres., 1988—; mentor strategic planning course Greater Cleve. Growth Assn., 1987—. Mem. Am. Soc. Metals, Steel Service Ctr. Inst. (com. mem. Young Execs. Forum 1987—), Council Smaller Enterprises, Assn. Women in Metals Industries. Republican. Presbyterian. Club: Cleve. Yacht. Home: 1994 Coe's Post Run Westlake OH 44145 Office: The Bissett Steel Co 9005 Bank St Valley View OH 44125

BISSETT, CATHERINE, accountant; b. Plainfield, N.J., Feb. 8, 1961; d. Robert C. and RoseAnn (McAnerney) B. BS, Seton Hall U., 1983. CPA, N.J. Acct. Mayfair Super Mkts. Inc., Elizabeth, N.J., 1983—. Roman Catholic. Home: 269 Metape Circle S Bound Brook NJ 08805 Office: Mayfair Super Mkts Inc 681 Newark Ave Elizabeth NJ 07208

BISSLAND, MARY LOU, chiropractic assistant, radiological technologist; b. Angels, Pa., Oct. 20, 1935; d. Charles Scott and Emma Grace (Burrus) Weitzel; m. James Ronald Bissland, Dec. 28, 1957; children: James Scott, Deborah Elaine, Robin ONallie, David MArtin, Ronald Paul. Cert. in nursing, James Martin Sch. of Nursing, Phila., 1956. Lic. practical nurse; cert. acupuncture asst., chiropractic physician's asst., X-ray technologist. Nurse Overbrook Sch. for Blind, Phila., 1956-57, Lankanau Hosp., Phila., 1957, Drs. Hosp., Bethlehem, Pa., 1958-59; chiropractic asst. Chiropractic Intensive Care Ctr., Tulsa, 1972-77; chiropractic asst. Bissland Chiropractic, Eldridge, Iowa, 1963-65, Kalona, Iowa, 1965-72, Titusville, Fla., 1977—. Republican. Baptist. Lodge: Order Ea. Star. Office: Bissland Chiropractic 1410 S Washington Ave Titusville FL 32780

BISSON, MARY ALDWIN, educator; b. Fairfield, Calif., Oct. 24, 1948; d. Francis Joseph and Anne Frances (Tutak) Aldwin; m. Terrence Paul Bisson, Aug. 24, 1968. B.A., U. Chgo., 1970; Ph.D., Duke U., 1976. Postdoctoral trainee U. N.C., Chapel Hill, 1976-77; research fellow U. Sydney, Australia 1978-80; asst. prof. biol. scis. SUNY-Buffalo, 1980-86; assoc. prof. biol. scis. 1986—. Contbr. articles to profl. jours., chpts. in books. Australian Research Grants Com. grantee, 1979; NSF grantee, 1982—. Mem. AAAS, Assn. Women in Sci. (chpt. pres.), N.Y. Acad. Sci., Am. Soc. Plant Physiologists, Sigma Xi. Democrat. Avocations: music. Home: 372 Voorhees Ave Buffalo NY 14216 Office: SUNY Buffalo Dept Biol Sci Buffalo NY 14260

BITA, LILI, author, actress; b. Zante, Greece, Dec. 23, 1935; came to U.S., 1959, naturalized, 1969; d. George and Eleni (Makri) Bitas; fine arts degree in music, Greek Conservatory of Music, 1954, in drama, Athens Sch. Drama, 1956; M.A. in Drama, U. Miami, 1978; m. Robert Zaller, Jan. 19, 1968; children—Philip, Kimon. Performer in Greek repertory Art Theatre, Civic Theatre and Royal Palace Garden Theatre, 1955-57; instr. Emporia (Kans.) Coll., 1960-62, U. Toledo, 1963-65, Bklyn. Conservatory of Music, 1967-68; guest lectr., condr. master classes, performer classic theatre various univs., U.S. and Europe, 1970—; artist in residence, Drexel U., Phila.; actress radio, TV and stage; writer; books include: Steps on the Earth, 1955; Lightning in the Flesh, 1968; Furies, 1969; Zero Hour, 1971; Blood Sketches, 1973; Sacrifice, Exile, Night, 1976; Fleshfire: New and Selected Love Poems, 1980, 2d edit., 1984; translator: Anais Nin, A Spy in the House of Love, 1974, 2d edit., 1983, Firewalkers, 1985, Bacchic Odes, 1986; anthologies include: City Lights Anthology, 1974; Contemporary Greek Women Poets, 1979; guest dir. Fla. Internat. U., Aegean Inst. Women's Studies; cons. Dade County Poetry in the Schs. Program; charitable performances include ACLU, Ethical Culture Soc., Nat. Women's Week, Poetry Therapy Program, Odyssey House, Jackson Meml. Hosp. Italian Inst. Study fellow, 1956-57; Circle in the Sq. Theatre fellow, 1967-68; recipient group performance award Austin Theatre, 1978. Mem. Southeastern Theatre Conf., Alpha Psi Omega. Greek Orthodox. Club: Order of Knights of St. Dennis of Zante. Home and Office: 326 Bryn Mawr Ave Bala Cynwyd PA 19004

BITKER, MARJORIE MARKS (MRS. BRUNO VOLTAIRE BITKER), writer, editor; b. N.Y.C., Feb. 9, 1901; d. Cecil Alexander and Rachel (Fox) Marks; A.B. magna cum laude (Caroline Duror Meml. fellow), Barnard Coll., 1921; M.A., Columbia U., 1922; m. James C. Jacobson, 1922 (div. 1942); children—Emilie J. Jacobi, Margaret J. Strange, Elizabeth J. Reiss; m. 2d, John C. Mayer, Oct. 24, 1942 (dec. June 1945); m. 3d, Bruno Voltaire Bitker, Oct. 10, 1957 (dec. 1984). Free lance writer, 1922—; editor Farrar Straus, N.Y.C., 1946-47, G.P. Putnam's Sons, N.Y.C., 1947-53, David McKay Co., N.Y.C., 1953-55; now editorial cons., book reviewer, feature writer. Lectr., Hunter Coll., Coll. City N.Y., 1949-53; Women's Chair for Humanistic Studies, Marquette U., 1972-73. Mem. pres.'s council Alverno Coll., 1975-77; bd. visitors U. Wis., 1962-68; alumnae trustee Barnard Coll., 1964-68, Barnard-in-Milw.; co-founder, past pres., hon. bd. dirs. in perpetuity Bookfellows: Friends Wis. Libraries. Recipient Barnard Alumnae Recognition award, 1978. Mem. AAUW, Women's Nat. Book Assn., Bookfellows Milw. (pres. 1971-73, dir.), Phi Beta Kappa. Author: (novels) Gold of Evening, 1975, A Different Flame, 1976; contbr. articles, and book revs. to mags. and newspapers. Address: 2330 E Back Bay Milwaukee WI 53202

BITLER, CATHY FITZPATRICK, utility company technician; b. Ft. Benning, Ga., Apr. 24, 1958; d. Benjamin Elbert and Barbara (Hayman) Fitzpatrick; m. David Levi Bitler, Sept. 11, 1982; 1 child, Sarah Kathryn. BS in Communications, Ohio U., 1980. Reporter Sta. WHOK Inc., Lancaster, Ohio, 1980-83; dir. news Sta. WHOK Inc., Lancaster, 1983—, dir. promotions, 1985-88; staff asst. South Cen. Power, Lancaster, 1988—. Author: Fairfield Monthly, 1984. Pres. United Cerebral Palsy Lancaster, 1986—; mem. adv. com. Southeastern Correctional Inst., 1983—; mem. adv. bd. Fairfield County Youth, 1985—, Special Wish Found., 1986—. Mem. Ohio Assoc. Press (bd. dirs. 1984-85) (best regularly scheduled news award, 1986), Unity Singers, Ohio U. Aumni Assn. Republican. Home: 566 Lynnwood Ln Lancaster OH 43130 Office: South Cen Power 2780 Coonpath Rd Lancaster OH 43130

BITTEL, MURIEL HELENE, managing editor; b. N.Y.C., Mar. 22; d. Ernest Henry and Helen Minnie (Seibel) Albers; m. Robert Gifford Walcutt, June 15, 1946; children—Lynn Lowell Walcutt, Mark James Walcutt, Judith Anne Walcutt; m. Lester Robert Bittel, May 8, 1973. B.A., Douglass Coll. Feature writer Daily Home News, New Brunswick, N.J.; editor Fawcett Pubs., N.Y.C., 1940-46; pub. relations dir. Electrovox/Walco Inc., East Orange, N.J., 1946-62; mng. editor Acad. Hall Pubs., Bridgewater, Va., 1974—. Mng. editor: Ency. Profl. Mgmt., 1978; Handbook Profl. Mgrs., 1985. Home: 106 Breezewood Terrace Bridgewater VA 22812

BITTERMAN, JOAN ASELTINE, research associate; b. Evanston, Ill., Mar. 25, 1954; d. James Merrill and Lorraine Elizabeth (Hinks) A.; B.A., Aurora U., 1976; M.S.Ed., No. Ill. U., 1982, now postgrad. Asst. to registrar Ill. Benedictine Coll., Lisle, Ill., 1976-77; asst. registrar George Williams Coll., Downers Grove, Ill., 1977-79; dir. acad. advisement Aurora (Ill.) U., 1979-85, registrar, 1985-86; research assoc. No. Ill. U., 1986—. Mem. Nat. Acad. Advisement Assn., Ill. Adult and Continuing Educators Assn., Adult Edn. Assn. Home: 1849 Kerrybrook Ct Sycamore IL 60178 Office: No Ill U Coll Continuing Edn DeKalb IL 60115

BITTINGER, MARY BOUDREAU, business owner; b. Washington, Oct. 17, 1949; d. Richard James and Catherine Mary (Bitting) Boudreau; m. Edmund Stuart Bittinger, Jan. 8, 1983. BS in Secondary Edn., English, Pa. State U., 1970. cert. tchr., Pa. English tchr. Gen. Wayne Jr. High Sch., Malvern, Pa., 1970; mgr., exec. mgr., dir. tng. Barbara Ellen Enterprises, inc., Lanham, Md., 1972-79; v.p. Fairfield (Iowa) Potpourri, 1979-80; residence course dir. Internat. Meditation Soc., Washington, 1980-81; exec. asst. to pres., project mgr. World Computer Graphics Assn., Washington, 1981-85; pres. Portrait Representatives, Inc., Washington, Balt., 1985—. Contbr. poetry to Scholastic Mag. (2d Nat. prize 1966, 3d Nat. prize 1967). Mem. Chevy Chase Citizens Assn. Mem. Nat. Assn. Female Execs. Republican.

BITTMANN, SUSAN WILKINS, social studies educator; b. Lumberton, N.C., Nov. 10, 1946; d. William Earl and Leslie Daniel (McNeill) Wilkins; m. Christopher Jacob Bittmann, Jr., Apr. 20, 1973. Student, Meredith Coll., 1964-66; AB in Edn., U. N.C., 1968, MA in History, 1971; postgrad., U. South Fla., 1979-80. Cert. social studies tchr. Tchr. social studies Gt. Bridge High Sch., Chesapeake, Va., 1968-69, J. P. Moore Jr. High Sch., Lumberton, 1971-72, Chamberlain High Sch., Tampa, Fla., 1972—; mem. social studies textbook selection com. Fla. Dept. Edn., Hillsborough County, 1985-86, mem. revision com. for social studies, 1988; reader Ednl. Testing Service, Princeton, 1986-88, test developer, 1987-89; mem. Fla. Content Area Exam. Devel. Com. on History and Humanities, 1987-88. Co-editor: Limited English Proficient Manual, 1986. Sec. Carrollwood Service League, Tampa, 1974-76, mem. ways and means com., 1978-79; mem. pres. council U. South Fla., Tampa, 1983—. Named Social Studies Tchr. of Yr., Hillsborough County, 1986, Tchr. of Yr. Chamberlain High Sch., 1987; Fla. Humanities grantee, 1985-86; recipient Master Tchr. award, 1986. Mem. NEA (Fla. teaching profession), Nat. Council for Social Studies, Fla. Council for Social Studies, Phi Delta Kappa, Alpha Delta Kappa, Phi Sigma Kappa, Phi Mu (sec. alumna Tampa 1975-77), Hillsborough Classroom Tchrs. Assn. Democrat. Methodist. Office: Chamberlain High Sch 9401 North Blvd Tampa FL 33612

BITTNER, BARBARA NEWMAN, educational administrator; b. Pitts., May 4, 1931; d. Daniel Stephen and Hallie Harper (Wager) Newman; B.A., U. Pitts., 1953; M.Ed., Fla. Atlantic U., 1966; 1 son, Benjamin J. Lectr. dept. speech U. Pitts., 1953-55; sec. to v.p. Farmers Bank of Pompano, Pompano Beach, Fla., 1956-57; tchr. Hillsboro Country Day Sch., Pompano Beach, 1957-68; tchr., div. chmn. A.D. Henderson U. Sch., 1968-73, dir., 1973—. Mem. Am. Assn. Sch. Adminstrs., Assn. Supervision and Curriculum Devel., Nat. Assn. Lab. Schs. (dir. 1983-84, rec. sec. 1984-85, pres. 1987-88), Fla. Assn. for Gifted, Fla. Assn. Supervision and Curriculum Devel., Phi Delta Kappa. Clubs: Pilot (Ft. Lauderdale, Fla.); Torch (Boca Raton, Fla.). Home: 4420 W Tradewinds Ave Lauderdale by the Sea FL 33308 Office: 500 NW 20th St Boca Raton FL 33431

BITTNER, MARY ELLEN, judge; b. Lake Forest, Ill., May 15, 1947; d. Ralph H. and Mary Elizabeth (Ewing) Rockwood; m. David J. Benard, Aug. 17, 1968 (div.); 1 child, Mary Elizabeth; m. Herbert E. Bittner, Feb. 20, 1987. B.S. in Math., U. Ill., 1969, J.D., 1972. Bar: Ill. 1972, D.C. 1975. Counsel NLRB, Washington, 1972-76, asst. chief counsel, 1976-80, adminstrv. law judge, 1980-87; adminstrv. law judge Drug Enforcement Adminstrn., Washington, 1987—. Mem. outreach com. St. John's Ch., Lafayette Sq., Washington, 1976—; bd. dirs. Coop. Urban Ministry Ctr. Inc., Washington, 1983-85. Recipient cert. of commendation NLRB, 1980. Mem. ABA (com. devel. law under Nat. Labor Relations Act 1979—), Nat. Assn. Women Judges, NLRB Profl. Assn. (pres. 1975-76), Forum of U.S. Adminstrv. Law Judges (pres. 1985-87). Democrat. Episcopalian. Club: Zonta of Washington (bd. dirs. 1983—, chmn. fin. com. 1983-85, chmn. pub. affairs com. 1985-88, chmn. mem. com. 1988, 2d v.p. 1987-88, 1st v.p. 1988—). Home: 4819 Morgan Dr Chevy Chase MD 20815 Office: Drug Enforcement Adminstrn 1405 I St NW Washington DC 20537

BIVENS, JOYCE FEIDLER, postmaster; b. Denver, May 13, 1943; d. Norman Paul Chambers and Marguerite Clyde (Osborne) Vasilka; m. George Edward Feidler, June 2, 1962 (div.); children—Darcus Ann, Julie Deenette; m. Roger Adrian Bivens, Feb. 4, 1984. B.A., Metropolitan State, 1973. Postmaster, U.S. Postal Service, Dumont, Colo., 1973-80, Kremmling, Colo., 1980-84, Placida, Fla., 1985—. Mem. steering com. Clear Creek Sanitation Dist., Dumont, Colo., 1973, bd. dirs., 1974-79, W. Grand County Mental Health, Kremmling, Colo., 1984; capt. Dumont Vol. Fire Dept. Woman's Hose Cart Team, 1974; v.p. Have A Heart Handicapped Fishing Tournament, Placida, 1986, 87; chair Rotunda Am. Cancer Soc. Drive, 1987. Mem. Nat. Assn. Postmasters (2d v.p. 1979-80, Fla. service rep. 1986—), Woman's Program U.S. Postal Service (bd. dirs. 1984—). Republican. Episcopalian. Avocations: back packing; snow skiing; sewing; leaded glass windows. Home: PO Box 1 Placida FL 33946 Office: US Postal Service Placida FL 33946

BIX, HELEN HELMAN, manufacturing company executive; b. Celle, Fed. Republic Germany, May 6, 1935; came to U.S., 1948; d. Heinrich and Berta (Nass) Hellmann; m. Harold Charles Bix, Dec. 19, 1954; children: Cindy J., Barbara C., Brian S. B in Bus., U. Minn., 1954. Trainee buyer's program Dayton-Hudson Corp., Mpls., 1952-54; pres. Beco-Helman Co., Inc., Mpls., 1954—. Bd. dirs. Washington U., St. Louis, 1982-84; mem. planning com. Shanghai Re-Union, Los Angeles; chmn. Beth El Synagogue, Mpls., 1979-85; chmn. scholarship com. Sch. of Adult Jewish Studies, Mpls., 1980. Recipient Humanitarian award Jewish Nat. Fund, 1974, Golden Book award. Mem. Nat. Assn. Female Execs., League of Women Voters, Walker Art Ctr., Solomon Guggenheim Mus., Mus. Modern Art of N.Y.C., Jewish Mus. N.Y.C., Council of Jewish Women, U. Minn. Alumni Assn. Jewish. Club: Northwest Tennis. Lodge: B'nai B'rith, Hadassah. Office: Beco-Helman Inc 801 Washington Ave N Minneapolis MN 55401

BIXBY, YVONNE BERNARDINE, travel agency executive; b. Leishout, Noord Brabant, Netherlands, Oct. 17, 1936; d. Anton A. and Yolanthe Eline (Poel) Kessels; m. Franklin L. Beck, Dec. 12, 1956 (div. 1961); children: Marilyn Yolanthe, Gwendolyn Joyce; m. Roy Franklin Bixby, Nov. 7, 1974. Student, Bath (Eng.) Tech. Sch., 1954-55, Alliance Francaise, Paris, 1955-56. Cert. travel agt. Travel agt. Atlas Travel, Denver, 1961-63, Air Sea Travel, Denver, 1963-66; mgr. Bomatco Travel, Melbourne, Fla., 1967-75; pres., chief exec. officer Yvonne's Travel, Inc., Melbourne, 1975—; chmn. bd. dirs. Fla. Travel Careers Sch., Melbourne; cons. in field. Mem. Am. Cancer Soc., South Brevard County chmn. 1976-77, pres. 1981; pres. South Brevard County C. of C., 1982; mem. Fla. Inst. Tech. Adv. Bd., 1983—. pres. Community Found. Brevard County, 1984. Named Outstanding Businesswoman Brevard County South Brevard Women's Ctr., 1982. Recipient Am. Cancer Soc. Sword of Hope award, 1983. Mem. Am. Cancer Soc. (South Brevard County chmn. 1976-77, pres. 1981, Sword of Hope award 1983), Melbourne Area C. of C. (bd. dirs. 1976-83, named one of top twenty salespersons, 1983), South Brevard C. of C. (pres. 1982), Honor Am. (pres. elect), Profl. Women's Network. Republican. Club: Tiger Bay (Brevard County). Lodge: Soroptomist (bd. dirs. Melbourne chpt. 1977-81). Home: 9500 S Tropical Trail Merritt Island FL 32952 Office: Yvonne's Travel Inc 1520 S Babcock Melbourne FL 32901

BIZUB, JOHANNA CATHERINE, law librarian; b. Denville, N.J., Apr. 13, 1957; d. Stephen Bernard and Elizabeth Mary (Grizzle) B. BS in Criminal Justice, U. Dayton, 1979; MLS, Rutgers U., 1984. Law librarian Morris County Law Library, 1981-83, Clapp & Eisenberg, Newark, 1984-86; dir. library Sills Cummis, 1986—. Mem. Assn. Legal Adminstrs., N.J. Law Librarians Assn. (treas. 1987—), Am. Assn. Law Libraries, N.J. Library Assn., Spl. Libraries Assn., Law Library Assn. Greater N.Y., Am. Legion Aux. (treas. Rockden unit 175 1983—). Democrat. Roman Catholic. Home: 11 Elm St Rockaway NJ 07866 Office: Sills Cummis 33 Washington St Newark NJ 07102

BIZZOTTO, ANITA JEAN, postal service executive; b. Blue Island, Ill., Sept. 29, 1952; d. George and Virginia (Little) B. BA, Knox Coll., 1974. With U.S. Postal Service, 1975—; supt. postal ops. U.S. Postal Service, Steger, Ill., 1979-81; profl. specialist U.S. Postal Service, Chgo., 1981-83, revenue protection specialist, 1983-86, classification support specialist, 1986—. Bd. dirs. Cen. Region Postal Credit Union, Chgo., 1985—. Democrat. Home: 4820 N Seeley Ave Chicago IL 60625-1422

BJORKMAN, ARLENE DORIS, social service administrator; b. Fosston, Minn., Apr. 8, 1947; d. Fred John and Lucille Lenora (Weigand) Becker; m. Terry Lee Stone, Feb. 1, 1970 (div. June 1973); m. Thomas Raymond Bjorkman, June 11, 1974; children: Jal Thomas, Toby Thomas. BA, U. Minn., Duluth, 1972, MSW, 1973. Vol. VISTA, Del Rio, Tex., 1968-69; asst. dir. project mainstream Concentrated Employment Program, Duluth, 1969; group leader Northwood Children's Home, Duluth, 1968-73; instr. Bemidji (Minn.) State U., 1973-74; social worker St. Louis County Social Service Dept., Duluth, 1974-78, adminstrv. asst. I, 1978-83, dir. fin assistance, 1986-87, adminstrv. asst. II, 1983-86, 87—; planning and evaluation staff Victims Witness Program, St. Louis County Atty.'s Office, Duluth, 1975-76, Minn. Victims of Sexual Assault Program, 1975, bd. dirs. 1975-76. Mem. Duluth Downtown Housing Commn., 1986—; active United Way, panel com., 1986—, vice chair Panel H, 1987-88, Cen. Agy. Relations com., 1987—; vol. Victims Sexual Assault Program, recognition award, 1987, Duluth Coalition for Homeless, 1987—; bd. dirs. YMCA, 1985—, mem. program com. 1987—; bd. dirs. Displaced Homemaker Program, 1981-82, Duluth Food Shelf, 1985—, Duluth Downtown Housing Commn., 1986—. Mem. Minn. Social Service Assn. (statewide conf. coordinator 1977-78, pres. 1980-81, bd. dirs. 1982-83, Appreciation for Service award 1981, 82), Am. Pub. Welfare Assn. Home: 626 W Second St Duluth MN 55806 Office: St Louis County Social Service Dept 320 W 2 St Duluth MN 55802

BJORSETH, LILLIAN, public relations manager; b. Uniontown, Mo., Oct. 22, 1942; d. Charles John and Ella Amanda (Vogel) Bingenheimer; children: Scott, Troy. B in Journalism, U. Mo., 1964. Copywriter Schoonmaker & Haskell, Inc., Kalamazoo, Mich., 1965; dir., pub. relations Goodwill Industries of Southwestern Mich., Kalamazoo, 1966-68; copy editor, writer Graphic Herald, Downers Grove, Ill., 1970-71; mgr. pub. relations Graphicom, Inc., Hinsdale, Ill., 1972; dir. pub. relations Evang. Hosp. Assn., Oak Brook, Ill., 1973-75; owner, mgr. Byline Pub. Relations, Downers Grove, 1975-76; rep. communications NICOR, Naperville, Ill., 1977-79; pub. relations rep. AT&T Bell Labs, Naperville, 1979-83; staff mgr. pub. relations AT&T, Lisle, Ill., 1983-87, mgr. data cons. programs, 1988—; exec. on loan Nat. Alliance Bus., Chgo., 1978. Chair communications workshop United Way, Chgo., 1981-82; co-founder Parties Unltd. and Seminars Unltd., Downers Grove, 1987. Mem. Nat. Assn. Female Execs., Suburban Press Club Chgo. (Best Pub. 1979), Downers Grove C. of C., Nat. Assn. Future Women (speaker Naperville chpt. 1983). Lutheran. Office: AT&T 4513 Western Ave Lisle IL 60532

BLACK, ANITA MARGARET, health care administrator; b. Lacombe, Alta., Can., July 4, 1960; d. Gosta Bertil and Kaija Kaarina (Kuivisto) Richt; m. Colin Black, Dec. 20, 1980. AN, Camosun Coll., Victoria, B.C., Can., 1982. Registered nurse Sidney Personal Care Home, Sidney, B.C., Can., 1982-83, dir. care, 1983—; registered nurse Victoria (B.C.) Gen. Hosp., 1982-87. Mem. Dirs. of Care Group, Victoria area, 1984—. Mem. Registered Nurses Assn. B.C. Liberal. Seventh Day Adventist. Club: Sidney Fitness. Home: 1744 Wain Rd, Rte 4, Sidney Can V8L4R4 Office: Sidney Personal Care Home, 9888 Fifth St, Sidney Can V8L2X3

BLACK, BONNIE LEE, food writer, editor, caterer; b. Jersey City, May 18, 1945; d. Kenneth W. and Emily R. (Stanzlaus) B.; m. James Jason, 1964 (div. 1966); 1 child, Whitney Lee. B.A. in Lit. and Writing, Columbia U., 1979. Editorial asst. Rhodesian Farmer, Salisbury, Rhodesia, 1969-72; editor Inside Midlantic mag. Midlantic Banks, Inc., Newark, 1972-75, Thirteen mag., Sta. WNET TV, N.Y.C., 1975-76; copywriter John Wiley & Sons, Inc., N.Y.C., part time 1977-79; freelance writer, editor, N.Y.C., 1979-82; writer, editor Coopers & Lybrand, N.Y.C., 1982-85; owner Bonnie Fare Catering, 1986—. Author: Somewhere Child, 1981. Mem. Am. Woman's Econ. Devel. Corp., Roundtable for Women in Food Service, James Beard Found. Home and Office: 310 Riverside Dr New York NY 10025

BLACK, CATHLEEN PRUNTY, newspaper company executive; b. Chgo., Apr. 26, 1944; d. James Hamilton and Margaret (Harrington) B. B.A., Trinity Coll., 1966. Advt. sales rep. Holiday mag., N.Y.C., 1966-69, Travel & Leisure mag., N.Y.C., 1969-70; advt. sales rep. New York mag., 1970-72, assoc. pub., 1977-79, pub., 1979-83; pres. USA Today, from 1983, now publisher; advt. dir. Ms. mag., 1972-75, assoc. pub., 1975-77. Home: 325 E 72d St New York NY 10021 Office: USA Today PO Box 500 Washington DC 20044 *

BLACK, DORIS ANN, nurse; b. Bedford, Va., Apr. 15, 1941; d. William Louis and Cora Mae (Farley) Rakes; R.N., Grace Hosp., Richmond, Va., 1962; m. Henry Peter Black, II, May 15, 1976; children—Roger, Robin, Henry. Dir. nursing Eastview Lodge, Richmond, Va., 1974; cert. officer Va. Dept. Health, 1974-78; adminstr., preceptor for adminstr.-in-tng. Richmond City, 1980; spl. projects, nursing home adminstr. Eastern div. Beverly Enterprises, 1980-83; pres. D&H, Ltd., Richmond, Va., 1983—; cons. in field. Mem. Va. Health Care Assn., Assn. Practitioners in Infection Control. Republican. Episcopalian. Author manuals. Home: 8400 Chelmford Rd Richmond VA 23235 Office: D&H Ltd 200 Turner Rd Richmond VA 23335

BLACK, ESTELLE MARY, librarian; b. Rockford, Ill., Jan. 27, 1932; d. Thomas and Esther Naomi (Parker) Elmore; m. Charles Robert Black, June 14, 1952; children—DeVonne Marie, Charles Thomas, Jeffrey Clinton, Lisa Lyn. B.S., Rockford Coll., 1977; M.A., U. Wis., 1979. Asst. librarian Rockford Pub. Schs., 1960-65; asst. librarian Rock Valley Coll., Rockford, 1965-66; spl. librarian Ipsen Industries, Rockford, 1966-67; assoc. dir. Social, Ednl., Research & Devel., Inc., Rockford, 1971-72; br. mgr. Rockford Pub. Library, 1972-79, reference librarian, 1979-80, asst. dir., 1980—; exec. bd. dirs. Met. Libraries Sect. ALA/Pub. Library Assn.; mem. adv. bd. Ednl. Resource Ctr., Rock Valley Coll., 1980-82. Pres., Nat. Council Negro Women, Rockford, 1970, Woman of Yr. award, 1975; bd. dirs. Crime Stoppers, 1981-87 ; bd. dirs. Gannett News Agy. Lend-A-Hand, 1979-82, City-County Planning Commn., 1977-79, Winnebago County Energy Adv. Council, 1980-81; bd. dirs. YWCA, 1967-68, chmn. steering com. Leader Luncheon, 1988; community adv. council Womanspace, 1986—; exec. bd. dirs. Rockford Council Arts and Scis., 1975-80, S.W. Bus. Assn., 1973-77; mem. land utilitzation com. Rockford Pub. Schs., 1983-84; bd. dirs. bldg. better bds. com. Rock Valley Coll., 1983-84; panelist WROK Viewpoint, Rockford, 1980-82; co-chmn. Beattie Is Com.-Music and Dance, 1980-82; mem. community adv. council Jr. League of Rockford, Inc., 1985-87 . Recipient Rockford Coll. Alumnae of Distinction award, 1981; Alta Hewlett award for professions Rockford YWCA, 1984; Ill. State Library scholar, 1978. Mem. ALA (chmn. planning process discussion group 1982-84, com. library edn., spl. com. long range planning, chpt. relations com.), Ill. Library Assn. (councilor to ALA 1984-88), Pub. Library Assn., Library Adminstrs. Conf. of No. Ill. (v.p., pres. 1988—), Taus Service Club, Delta Kappa Gamma (hon.). Democrat. African Methodist Episcopalian. Office: Rockford Public Library 215 N Wyman St Rockford IL 61101

BLACK, JAN KNIPPERS, political scientist; b. Lawrenceburg, Tenn., Mar. 10, 1940; d. Ottis J. and Opal (Moody) Knippers; B.A. in Art and Spanish, U. Tenn., 1962; M.A. in Latin Am. Studies, Am. U., 1967, Ph.D. in Internat. Relations, 1975; m. John D. Black, 1967 (dec. 1974); m. Martin C. Needler, 1976; stepchildren—John D., II, Marc Black, Steve Needler, Dan Needler; 1 foster dau., Mary Marfise. Singer, pianist, 1954-58; comml. artist Sta. WSM-TV, Nashville, 1960; vol. Peace Corps, Chile, 1962-64, mem. staff, 1965; research polit. scientist div. fgn. area studies Am. U., 1968-75, chmn. Latin Am. research team, editor area handbooks for Latin Am., 1975-76; program coordinator State Dept. funded study Latin Am. petroleum policies U. N.Mex., 1976-78, sr. research assoc. div. inter-Am. affairs, 1976—, coordinator interdisciplinary courses Latin Am. Inst., research assoc. prof. Div. Public Adminstrn., 1979-85; research prof. 1986— ; mem. faculty World Campus Afloat, 1966, Dag Hammarskjold Coll., 1974, George Mason U., 1975-76; cons. in field; TV appearances include MacNeil-Lehrer Report, 1976. Del., Nat. Young Democrats Conv., 1965, N.Mex. Dem. Conv., 1978, 80, 82, 84; v.p. N.Mem. Dem. Council, 1983-87; exec. com. N.Mex. Progressive Polit. Action Com., 1984-87, pres., 1987—; mem. fgn. policy adv. team Dem. Presdl. Campaign., 1972; mem. Mayoral Transition Team, City of Albuquerque, 1977; mgr. various polit. campaigns. Recipient Outstanding Dissertation award Am. U., 1967. Mem. Latin Am. Studies Assn. (chmn. subcom. ethical guidelines 1976-78), Inter-Am. Council Washington (v.p. 1975-76), Am. Polit. Sci. Assn., Internat. Studies Assn., Phi Kappa Phi. Contbg. author books on Latin Am. and Caribbean, including: The Restless Caribbean, 1979; co-author 17 books in Area Handbook series, 1969-75; author: United States Penetration of Brazil, 1977; The Dominican Republic: Politics and Development in an Unsovereign State, 1986; Sentinels of Empire; The United States and Latin American Militarism, 1986; editor books on Latin Am. and Caribbean, including: Area Handbook for Cuba, 1976; Area Handbook for Trinidad and Tubago, 1976; Latin America: Its Problems and Its Promise, 1984. contbr. numerous articles to profl. jours., popular publs. Home: 421 Solano Dr SE Albuquerque NM 87108 Office: U NMex Dept Polit Sci Albuquerque NM 87131

BLACK, JOANNE MARTENA REINHARD, air force officer, nurse; b. Fish Creek, Wis., Apr. 5, 1939; m. Joe A. Black. Diploma Chgo. Wesley Meml. Hosp. Sch. Nursing, 1960; B.S. in Nursing, Columbia U., 1972; M.S. in Med.-Surg. Nursing, U. Calif.-San Francisco, 1974; Ph.D. in Clin. Nursing Research, U. Tex., 1983. Staff nurse med./surg. ICU, Chgo. Wesley Meml. Hosp., 1960-62, 63-64; staff nurse cardiothoracic unit Univ. Hosps., Madison, Wis., 1962-63; courier nurse Santa Fe Ry., Chgo., 1964-66; head nurse trauma unit Cook County Hosp., Chgo., 1966-68; nurse research asst. Hektoen Inst., Chgo., 1968-69; nurse research asst. dept. surg. metabolism Mt. Sinai Hosp., N.Y.C., 1969-70, staff nurse surg. ICU, 1970-72, clin. nurse, hemodialysis, renal transplant and cardiothoracic units, 1972-73; commd. capt. Nurses Corps, U.S. Air Force, 1973, advanced through grades to lt. col., 1986; staff nurse dept. surg. nursing Wilford Hall USAF Med. Ctr., Lackland AFB, Tex., 1974-76, clin. instr. dept. nursing edn., 1976-78, clin. nurse investigator div. nursing, 1983-86, nurse researcher Office of USAF Surgeon Gen., Andrews AFB, Md., 1986—; surg. nurse clin. specialist USAF Regional Hosp., Lakenheath, Eng., 1978-80; nurse research cons., Office of USAF Chief Nurse, Bolling Rock AFB, D.C., 1986— Contbr. chpt., articles to profl. publs. Office: Office of USAF Surgeon Gen 1118-1 Columbus Circle Andrews AFB MD 20335

BLACK, LISA, artist; b. Lansing, Mich., June 19, 1934; d. W. Eugene and Eugenia (Anikeeff) Hunter; m. Thomas Howard Black, June 6, 1959; children—Kelly Hunter, Leslie Cheney. Diplome d'etudes de civilisation Francaise, Paris, 1955; B.A., U. Mich., 1956. One woman shows include Wildwood Studios, Lake Orion, Mich., Conn. Bank & Trust Co., New Canaan, Noroton Gallery, Darien, Conn., Gates Gallery, New Canaan, Conn., Easter Seal Rehab. Ctr., Stamford, Conn., Landmark Lobby Gallery, Stamford; exhibited in group shows at Terrain Gallery, N.Y.C., 1970, Stamford Mus., 1972, Williams Gallery, Darien, Conn., 1974, Greenwich Art Barn, Conn., 1976, New Haven Paint and Clay Annual Juried Exhbn., Conn., 1983, Darien Sport Shop, Gallery Group, White Plains, N.Y., Landmark Tower, Stamford, Conn. Hospice of Branford, 1987, Eagle Tower, Stamford, 1987, Invited Artists of Westport Ctr., Bridgeport (Conn.) Hilton, 1988; represented in permanent collection Conn. Bank & Trust Co. Recipient numerous art show and art society awards. Mem. Greenwich Art Soc., Old Greenwich Art Soc., Stamford Art Assn., New Haven Paint and Clay Club. Republican. Avocations: handicrafts, family life, dogs, antique shows. Home: 17 Brushy Hill Rd Darien CT 06820

BLACK, MARTHA SUSAN LOWE, lawyer; b. Maryville, Tenn., Sept. 18, 1945; d. Ernest Broyles and Esther Charlotte (Carlson) Lowe; B.A. with honors, Mount Holyoke Coll., 1967; postgrad. (NDEA fellow), Rice U., 1967-69; J.D. (Green scholar), U. Tenn., 1973; m. David T. Black, June 7, 1975; children—Charlotte Carlson, Elizabeth Cannon. Admitted to Tenn. bar, 1974; asst., then asso. prof. U. Tenn. Coll. Law, Knoxville, 1973-81; mem. firm Kizer & Black, P.C., Maryville, Tenn., 1981—; chmn. U. Tenn. Commn. Women, 1979-80. Chmn., Blount County Foster Care Review Bd., 1976-83; bd. dirs., chmn. Blount County Children's Home; mem. community adv. council Maryville Coll.; mem. Blount County Hist. Trust. Recipient Am. Jurisprudence and Corpus Juris Secundum awards, 1972; named Grad. of Yr., U. Tenn., 1973. Mem. Am. Bar Assn., Tenn. Bar Assn., Blount County Bar Assn. (pres. 1987), Order Coif. Home: Hollybrook Rd Rockford TN 37853 Office: 329 Cates St Maryville TN 37801

BLACK, MAUREEN, realty company executive; b. Manchester, Eng., Feb. 4, 1937; came to U.S., 1957, naturalized, 1962; d. William Henry and Kathleen Mary (Cleaver) Jackson; grad. Felt and Tarrant Comptometer Sch., Eng., 1953; student Alamogordo br. N.Mex. State U., 1959-60, 62-63; m. Charles J. Dugan, Nov. 1979; 1 dau., Karen Elizabeth Black. Office mgr., personnel dir. J.C. Penney Co., Alamogordo, 1958-66; exec. sec. to project mgr. Re-entry System div. Gen. Electric Co., Holloman AFB, 1967-68; soc. editor, columnist Alamogordo Daily News, 1968-73; regional corr. El Paso (Tex.) Times, 1968-75; free lance writer and photographer; script writer Film Unit 505, Alamogordo, 1971; realtor asso. Shyne Realty, Alamogordo, 1975-77, West Source Realtors, 1977-80; owner, broker Hyde Park West Realty Co., 1980—. Pres., Alamogordo Music Theatre, 1971-72. Mem. planning com. tourism, recreation, convs. Gov. of N.Mex., 1965; mem. N.Mex. State Film Commn., 1973-74; life mem. Aux. of Zia Sch. for Handicapped Children, pres. Aux., 1975-76, 80-82, mem. sch. bd., 1982-83; pres. Zia Found., 1984-85. Recipient service award Nat. Found., March of Dimes, 1971; Americanism medal DAR, 1972; named Career Woman of Yr., Alamogordo chpt. Am. Bus. Women's Assn., 1971. Mem. Alamogordo C. of C. (chmn. convs. and motion picture com. 1965—), Nat. Assn. Realtors, Realtors Assn. N.Mex., Internat. Realtors Assn. Alamogordo Bd. Realtors (chmn. public relations com., v.p. 1981-82, pres. 1983-84), N.Mex. Opera Guild. Home: 1206 Desert Eve Dr Alamogordo NM 88310 Office: PO Box 2021 Alamogordo NM 88310

BLACK, NAOMI RUTH, writer, editor; b. Springfield, Mass., Oct. 19, 1957; d. Henry Arnold and Zelda Edith (Hodosh) B. BA in Anthropology, Beloit Coll., 1979. Project coordinator, editor Woodward-Clyde Cons., San Francisco, 1978-80; asst. editor, travel editor William Morrow Co., N.Y.C., 1980-83; mng. editor Quarto Mktg. Ltd., N.Y.C., 1983-85; freelance writer N.Y.C., 1985—. Author: (with others) The American Mail-Order Gourmet, 1986, (with others) East Coast Bed and Breakfast Guide, 1986, Seashore Entertaining, 1987, Dude Ranches of the American West, 1988; contbr. articles to periodicals. Bd. dirs. Writers and Pubs. Alliance for Nuclear Disarmament, N.Y.C., 1987-88.

BLACK, PAGE MORTON, civic worker; b. Chgo.; d. Alexander and Rose Morton; m. William Black, Mar. 27, 1962. Student, Chgo. Mus. Coll. Singer, pianist, Pierre Hotel, N.Y.C., Warwick Hotel, One Fifth Ave. Sherry Netherland Hotel; singer radio show and comml. Chock Full o' Nuts Corp., now hon. chmn.; rec. artist Atlantic Records; co-founder Page and William Black Post-Grad. Sch. Medicine, Mt. Sinai Med. Sch., 1965—; chmn., mem. exec. bd. Parkinsons' Disease Found., Columbia U. Med. Ctr. Recipient Ann. award Parkinsons' Disease Found., 1987. Home: Premium Point New Rochelle NY 10801

BLACK, PATTI CARR, museum administrator; b. Sumner, Miss., May 18, 1934; d. Samuel Bismarck and Velma Lewis (Carnathan) Carr; m. D. Carl Black, Feb. 10, 1957 (div. 1968); 1 child, Elizabeth. B.A., Miss. U. for Women, 1955; M.A., Emory U., 1968. Research librarian Miss. Dept. Archives and History, Jackson, 1957-63; research librarian Met. Mus. Art, N.Y.C., 1968-69, Time Inc., N.Y.C., 1969-70; curator of exhibits Miss. State Hist. Mus., Jackson, 1976—, dir., 1976—; mem. nat. adv. bd. Ctr. for Study So. Culture, 1978—, Smithsonian Nat. Mus. Act, 1984—. Editor: Mules and Mississippi, 1978, 81, Made by Hand: Mississippi Folk Art, 1980, Documentary Portrait of Mississippi: The Thirties, 1982, Eudora, 1984. Founder New Stage Theatre, Jackson, 1965, bd. dirs., 1965—; bd. dirs. Miss. Inst. Arts and Letters, 1984—; mem. devel. panel So. Arts Fedn.; bd. dirs. Southeastern Mus.' Council. NEA fellow, 1975. Mem. Miss. Hist. Soc. (merit award 1980), Am. Assn. Mus. for State and Local History (awards com. 1976-80, exec. council 1983-85), Miss. Mus. Assn. (pres. 1979-80). Democrat. Episcopalian. Home: 1157 Quinn St Jackson MS 39202 Office: Miss State Hist Mus Box 571 Jackson MS 39205

BLACK, ROSALIE JEAN, human resources manager, university official; b. Dunsmuir, Calif., Dec. 29, 1938; d. Allen B. Henry and Margaret R. Albonico Luther Lea (stepfather); m. James H. Black, June 12, 1956 (div. 1965); 1 dau., Kimberly Elaine. A.A. equivalent, Foothill and Ohlone, 1964-74. Contracts adminstr. U.S. Air Force, Los Angeles and Shelby, Ohio, 1956-58; ops. planner/adminstr. Lockheed Missiles & Space Co., Inc., Sunnyvale, Calif., 1958-81; mgr. human resources Dialog Info. Services, Inc., Palo Alto, Calif., 1981—; instr. Supervisory program, 1982-84; mem. Lockheed Univ. Relations and Mgmt. Adv. Councils, Calabassas, Calif., 1982—; lectr., guest panel mem. Contbr. articles to profl. jours. Recipient Cert., Human Resources Inst., 1982; Achievement award in English, Bank of Am., 1956. Mem. Am. Soc. Personnel Adminstrn., No. Calif. Human Resources Council, Calif. Scholarship Fedn. (life), Henry and Worthington Descendent Assn., Siskiyou County Hist. Soc. Democrat. Lutheran. Home: 1400 Fallen Leaf Ln Los Altos CA 94022 Office: Dialog Info Services Inc 3460 Hillview Ave Palo Alto CA 95014

BLACK, SANDRA, public relations consultant; b. N.Y.C., Apr. 5, 1951; d. David Eastern and Norma (Springer) B.; B.A., Cornell U., 1975; student NYU Sch. Law, 1977-78. Paralegal Queens Legal Services Corp., Jamaica, N.Y., 1978-79; legal asst. Corbin, Silverman, Sanseverino & Taylor, N.Y.C., 1980-82; adminstrv. cons. N.Y. Cons. Group Ltd., N.Y.C., 1982-83; prin., cons. Imago Pub. Relations, N.Y.C., 1983—. Resource person Cornell Alumni Career Resource File, 1978—, class corr. alumni news mag.; mem. Cornell Council, 1982-83; v.p. pub. relations Network of Black Career Women, 1982—; sec. bd. dirs. Found. Vital Arts, Inc., 1986-88. N.Y. State Regents scholar, 1969-74; Cornell U. grantee, 1969-74. Mem. Pub. Relations Soc. Am. (former mem. coms.), Cornell Black Alumni Assn., Cornell Alumni Assn. N.Y.C. (council 1982-83), NAACP. Democrat. Episcopalian. Office: PO Box 195 New York NY 10027

BLACK, SUSAN HARRELL, judge; b. Valdosta, Ga., Oct. 20, 1943; d. William H. and Ruth Elizabeth (Phillips) Harrell; m. Louis Eckert Black, Dec. 28, 1966. B.A., Fla. State U., 1964; J.D., U. Fla., 1967. Bar: Fla. 1967. Asst. state atty. 4th Jud. Circuit Fla.; asst. gen. counsel City of Jacksonville, Fla.; judge County Ct. of Duval County, Fla.; judge 4th Jud. Circuit Ct. of Fla.; U.S. dist. judge Middle Dist. Fla., Jacksonville, 1979—; faculty Fed. Jud. Ctr.; mem. U.S. Judicial Conf. Com. on Judicial Improvements; bd. trustees Am. Inns Ct. Found. Trustee Law Sch. U. Fla., Am. Inns Ct. Found.; pres. Chester Bedell Inn of Ct. Mem. Am. Bar Assn., Fla. Bar Assn., Jacksonville Bar Assn., Conf. Circuit Judges (former chmn. edn. com., dean New Judges Coll.). Episcopalian. Office: US Dist Ct PO Box 53135 Jacksonville FL 32201-3135

BLACKBURN, CATHERINE ELAINE, lawyer, pharmacist; b. Columbus, Ohio, Nov. 5, 1953; d. Robert Jerome and Patricia Ann (Buchman) B. BS in Pharmacy with high distinction U. Ky., 1978; JD with honors, Ohio State U., 1982. Bars: Ohio 1982, U.S. Dist. Ct. (so. dist.) Ohio 1983. Chief pharmacist Louisa Community Hosp., Ky., 1978; pharmacist Riverside Meth. Hosp., Columbus, Ohio, 1978-82; law clk. Michael F. Colley Co., L.P.A., Columbus, 1980-82, assoc., 1982-87; asst. prof. law U. Louisville Sch. Law, 1987—; workshop leader Ohio Drug Studies Inst., Columbus, 1982, 83, 14th Nat. Conf. on Women and the Law, Washington, D.C., 1983, 15th Nat. Conf., 1985; lectr./speaker Iowa Trial Lawyers Assn., Iowa City, 1984; speaker Nat. Assn. for Rights Protection and Advocacy, Nat. Conf., Boston, 1986; lectr. legal writing Coll. Law Ohio State U., 1986; mem. aids edn. task force, subcom. on legal ethical issues U. Louisville, 1988—; speaker nat. conf. Nat. Assn. Protection and Advocacy Systems, Washington, 1988; cons. Ohio Legal Rights Service, 1985—, Mich. Protection and Advocacy Service, 1988—. Contbr. article to profl. jour. Staff writer, editor Ohio State U. Law Jour., 1980-82. Trustee Women's Outreach for Women, Columbus, 1982-85, Amethyst, Inc., 1985-87; incorporator Columbus Career Women Inc., 1986-87, treas., 1986-87. Fellow Am. Soc. Pharmacy Law; mem. ABA, Assn. Trial Lawyers Am. (lectr./speaker 1982—), Ohio Acad. Trial Lawyers, Columbus Bar Assn., Ohio Bar Assn., Order of Coif, Phi Beta Kappa, Rho Chi Soc. Democrat.

BLACKBURN, MARTHA GRACE, corporate executive, publisher; b. London, Ont., Can., Oct. 9, 1944; d. Walter Juxon and Marjorie Ludwell (Dampier) Blackburn; children—Richard Antony Frederick, Sarah Dampier,

Annabelle Grace. B.A. in French, U. Western Ont., London, 1969. Chmn. bd., pres. Blackburn Group Inc, London, Ont., 1984, also dir.; pub. London Free Press Printing Co. Ltd., 1984, also dir.; dir. CFPL Broadcasting Ltd., London, Netmar Inc. (formerly Pennysaver Publs.), CKNX Broadcasting Ltd., Compusearch Market and Social Research Ltd.; pres. Kilbyrne Investments Inc. Mem. adminstrn. and fin. com. Diocese of Huron; mem. adv. bd. Performing Arts Ctr.; mem. adv. council Orch. London; bd. dirs. World Wildlife, 1985—. Mem. Can. Press. Anglican. Club: London Hunt and Country. Office: Blackburn Group Inc, PO Box 2280, London, ON Canada N6A 4G1

BLACKBURN, MARY KATHERINE (KATHIE), business executive; b. Honolulu, Apr. 19, 1949; d. Joseph Gibson and Mary Louise (Anton) B.; m. Ron Bailey, 1968 (div. 1969); m. 2d, John David Howard, June 26, 1971 (div. Mar. 1976). Student Marjorie Webster Jr. Coll., 1967-68, U. Mo.-Kansas City, 1969; lic. real estate Stapleton Sch. Real Estate, Honolulu, 1976; cert. of completion U. So. Calif., Honolulu, 1976; cert. in CPR. Notary pub., Hawaii. Dir. mail order div. Am. Rental & Sales, Kansas City, Mo., 1974-76; media rep. Hawaii Tourist News, Honolulu, 1976-77; sales exec., sales mgr. Inflight Mktg., Honolulu, 1977-79; owner Kakalina o Maui, Kahului, Hawaii, 1979-81; membership dir. Maui C. of C., Kahului, 1981-83; dir. advt. HBH Publication Services, Kaanapali, Hawaii, 1983-85; prodn., sales dir. Uniquely Maui Catalog, 1985; pres. Maui Gift Baskets, Inc. 1985—; cons. various firms. Photographer: Latitude 20, 1977-81; publisher, editor: (conv. bull.) Nat. Assn. Life Underwriters, 1980. Bd. dirs., sec. Big Bros./Big Sisters of Maui, 1980-86; mem. Maui Community Coll. Adv. Com. on Coop. Edn., 1982-83; media chmn. Kemper Open Golf Tournament; mem. Maui Visitors Bur., 1983-84; vol. Hospice Maui, 1983-84; various coms. Aloha Week, 1985-86; chmn. aloha week com. Monarchy Ball 1986; mem. Made in Maui Trade Council. Recipient Cert. of Appreciation Kiwani's Club Maui, 1982; Gov.'s cert. media Chair King Kamehameha Commn., 1984. Mem. Maui Hotel Assn., Maui Portuguse C. of C. (sec. 1987-88, bd. dirs. 1987—), Maui C. of C. Office: Maui Gift Baskets PO Box 1263 Wailuku HI 96793

BLACK CARTER, WANDA, real estate broker; b. Wichita Falls, Tex., May 25, 1928; d. Orbie and LaVonia (Davis) Collum; deceased; children: Sharon Ann McKay, Paula Lorene Riddle, Jay Emerson Black. Student, East Cen. Okla. State U., 1960-61, Cen. State U., Okla., 1977-78. Sales assoc. ERA Kay's Real Estate, Duncan, Okla., 1981-83; broker Wanda's Real Estate, Waurika, OK, 1983—. Mem. Nat. Assn. Realtors, Okla. Assn. Realtors (cert. Grad. Realtors Inst.), Nat. Notary Assn., Nat. Assn. Master Appraisers (master sr. appraiser 1984), Bus. and Profl. Women (state membership chmn. 1979-80, pres. Waurika chpt. 1987—), Duncan Bd. Realtors (bd. dirs. 1983), Waurika C. of C. (bd dirs 1985-86, pres. 1987—). Democrat. Methodist. Club: Gen. Fedn. Women's (Waurika). Lodge: Rebekah (noble grand 1972-73). Home: 612 Monroe Waurika OK 73573 Office: Wanda's Real Estate Agy 117 N Main Waurika OK 73573

BLACKER, HARRIET, public relations executive; b. N.Y.C., July 23, 1940; d. Louis and Rebecca (Siegel) B.; m. Roland Algrant, Aug. 6, 1970 (div. Jan. 1981); m. Matthew E. Harlib, Aug. 25, 1988. B.A., U. Mich., 1962. Exec. asst. Nat. Book com., N.Y.C., 1965-67; dir. publicity Hawthorn Books, N.Y.C., 1967-69, Coward-McCann & Geoghegan, N.Y.C., 1969-74; exec. dir. publicity Random House, N.Y.C., 1974-79; East Coast v.p. Pickwick Maslancky Koenigsberg, N.Y.C., 1980-81; v.p. pub. relations Putnam Pub. Group, N.Y.C., 1981-85; pres. Harriet Blacker, Inc., N.Y.C., 1986—. Mem. Publishers Publicity Assn. (sec. 1973-75, treas. 1982-83, pres. 1983-85), Women's Media Group. Home: 310 E 75th St New York NY 10021 Office: Harriet Blacker Inc 381 Park Ave S New York NY 10016

BLACKER, HELEN VIRGINIA, business manager, engineer; b. Boulder, Colo., Aug. 4, 1925; d. John Decatur and Anna Frost (Gloyd) Means; m. Leo Merrill Blacker, Nov. 11, 1954. BS in Aero. Engring., U. Colo., 1950. Engr. Bur. of Reclamation, Yuma, Ariz., 1950-52, Geol. Survey, Denver, 1952-60; phys. scientist Nat. Bur. of Standards, Nat. Oceanic and Atmposphere Adminstrn., Boulder, 1960-80; mgr. Means Rentals, Boulder, 1966—. Active Boulder Forum of Rep. Women 1982—, bd. dirs. 1983-87, pres. 1984-85; active Blue Ribbon Com., Erie, Colo., 1986. Mem. Erie C. of C.

BLACKERT, VIRGINIA ROSE, publisher, editor; b. Teaneck, N.J., Aug. 4, 1948; d. Charles Maynard and Rose Marie (Ferraro) B.; m. Matthew R. Englert, Mar. 10, 1968 (div. 1971); 1 child, Hilary Jane Englert. Grad., pub. schs., Bogota, N.J., 1966. Staff artist Rutland (Vt.) Daily Herald, 1974-75; advt. dir. Entertainment Enterprises, Inc., Rutland, 1975-79; writer Phillip C. Camp Assocs., Inc., Woodstock, Vt., 1979-81; freelance writer 1980-82; writer Vt. Ski Areas Assn., Woodstock, 1981-82; pub., editor Prosper Pub., Inc., Barnard, Vt., 1982—, also pres., 1987—. Editor, pub.: (magazines) Essence of Stowe, 1979-80, Woodstock Common, 1982, Stowe Country, 1984, Rutland Seasons, 1986. Bd. dirs. Woodstock Learning Clinic, 1986—; tutor Woodstock Elem. Sch. Excellence Program., 1987; advisor Woodstock Union High Sch. Endowment Assn., 1988—. Mem. Stowe Area Assn., Woodstock C. of C., Woodstock Sister City Coalition. Home: PO Box 206 Barnard VT 05031 Office: Prosper Pub Inc Rt 12 Barnard VT 05031

BLACKHAM, ANN ROSEMARY (MRS. JAMES W. BLACKHAM), realtor; b. N.Y.C., June 16, 1927; d. Frederick Alfred and Letitia L. (Stolfe) DeCain; m. James W. Blackham Jr., Aug. 18, 1951; children: Ann C., James W. III. AB, Ohio Dominican Coll., 1949; postgrad., Ohio State U., 1950. Mgr. br. store Filene & Sons, Winchester, 1950-52; broker Porter Co. Real Estate, Winchester, 1961-66; sales mgr. James T. Trefrey, Inc., Winchester, 1966-68; pres., founder Ann Blackham & Co. Inc., Realtors, Winchester, Mass., 1969—. Mem. bd. econ. advisors to Gov., 1969-74; participant White House Conf. on Internat. Cooperation, 1965; mem. Presdl. Task Force on Women's Rights and Responsibilities, 1969; mem. exec. council Mass. Civil Def., 1965-69; chmn. Gov.'s Commn. on Status of Women, 1971-75; regional dir. Interstate Assn. Commn. on Status of Women, 1971-74; mem. Gov. Task Force on Mass. Economy, 1972; mem. Gov.'s Judicial Selection Com., 1972, Mass. Emergency Fin. Bd., 1974-75; corporator, trustee Charlestown Savs. Bank, 1974-84; corporator Winchester Hosp., 1983—; mem. design rev. commn. Town of Winchester; bd. dirs. Phoenix Found., Bay State Health Care, Mass. Taxpayers Found., Speech and Hearing Found.; mem. regional selection panel White House Fellows, 1973-74; mem. com. on women in service U.S. Dept. Def., 1977-80; 2d v.p. Doric Dames, 1971-74, bd. dirs., 1974—; pres. Mass. Fedn. Rep. Women, 1964-69; sec. Nat. Fedn. Rep. Women, 1967-71, 2d v.p., 1972-78; New Eng. regional dir., 1967-78; pres. Women's Rep. Club Winchester, 1960-62, 83-84; dep. chmn. Mass. Rep. State Com., 1965-66; sec. Mass. Rep. State Conv., 1970, del., 1960, 62, 64, 66, 70, 72, 74, 78; state vice chmn. Mass. Rep. Fin. Com., 1970; alt. del.-at-large Rep. Nat. Conv., 1968, 72, del., 1984; v.p. Rep. Club Mass., 1980—; pres. Scholarship Found., 1976-78, Mass. Fedn. Women's Clubs; mem. Winchester 350th Aniversary Commn. Recipient Pub. Service award Commonwealth of Mass., 1978, Merit award Rep. Party, 1969, Pub. Affairs award Mass. Fedn. Women's Clubs, 1975; named Civic Leader of Yr., Mass. Broadcasters, 1962. Mem. Greater Boston Real Estate Bd. (bd. dirs.), Mass. Assn. Real Estate Bds. (bd. dirs.), Nat. Assn. Real Estate Bd. (women's council). Brokers Inst., Council Realtors (pres. 1983-84), Winchester C. of C. (bd. dirs.), Greater Boston C. of C., Nat. Assn. Women Bus. Owners, Million Dollar Club (life). Republican. Clubs: Capitol Hill (Washington); Ponte Vedra, Winchester Boat, Winchester Country, Wychemere Harbor, Womens City Boston. Home: 60 Swan Rd Winchester MA 01890 Office: 11 Thompson St Winchester MA 01890

BLACK-KEEFER, SHARON KAY, telecommunications executive; b. Denver, Jan. 23, 1949; d. Benoni Franklin and Loretta Marie (Meals) B.; m. Stephin Malone Keefer, Aug. 3, 1974. Student, U. Costa Rica, 1969; BA in Internat. Affairs magna cum laude, U. Colo., 1971, MS in Telecommunications, 1972. Research positions U. Colo., Boulder, 1968-71; analyst telecommunications policy Office Telecommunications U.S. Dept. Commerce, Boulder, Colo., 1971-76; sr. systems analyst Norwest Info. Services Inc., Mpls., 1976-84, cons. data ops., 1984-85; mgr. voice communications Northwestern Nat. Life Ins., Mpls., 1985—; adj. faculty mem. U. Minn. Sch. Mgmt., St. Mary's Coll. Grad. Ctr., and telecommunications adv. bd., mem. adv. bd. U. Colo. Telecommunications Program. Chair Community Action Com., Stillwater, Minn. 1984-86; mem. communications adv. com. Met. Council Twin Cities, St. Paul 1977-78; co-chair Cub Scout Pack, Stillwater 1987; elder First Presbyterian Ch., Stillwater 1984-86. Mem. Internat. Communications Assn. (academic devel. com.), Nat. Rolm Users Group (chair Maintenance com.), Minn. Telecommunications Assn. Office: Northwestern Nat Life Ins 20 Washington Ave S Minneapolis MN 55440

BLACKLER, SHARON RENDA, hospital program director; b. Coventry, Eng., Dec. 11, 1947; d. Gerald William and Renda Winifred (Robson) B.; m. Stanford Bingham Jr., Mar. 16, 1974 (div. Oct. 1979); 1 child, Jason A. Registered diagnostic X ray technician, Stanford U. Med. Ctr., 1968, registered therapy technician, 1969; BS in Health Services Adminstrn. cum laude, U. Phoenix, 1982. Staff technologist Santa Clara Valley Med. Ctr., San Jose, Calif., 1969-70, 1972; jr. radiographer Manchester (Eng.) Royal Infirmary, 1971; staff technologist Peninsula Hosp., Burlingame, Calif., 1972-76; sr. technologist Sequoia Hosp., Redwood City, Calif., 1976-81, tech. dir. Radiation Oncology sect., 1981—. Mem. Am. Assn. Med. Dosimetrists (recording sec. 1987-90), Soc. Radiographers, Radiologists Bus. Mgrs. Assn., Soc. Radiation Oncology Adminstrs., Am. Soc. Radiologic Technologists. Republican. Episcopalian. Home: 4454 Junipero Serra Ln San Jose CA 95129 Office: Sequoia Hosp Dept Radiation Oncology Whipple and Alameda Redwood City CA 94062

BLACKMAN, BETTY LOU, hospital social services administrator; b. Sarasota, Fla., Oct. 2, 1930; d. Jim and Ola Vastiah (Coker) Fowler; m. Frank Ogilvie Blackman, Aug. 26, 1951 (dec. 1964); children: Katherine Lynn, Brenda Sue; m. John Quincy Woosley, Dec. 4, 1970 (div. 1978). Student Columbia Bible Coll., S.C., 1948-51, So. Bapt. Theol. Sem., 1964-65; BA in Sociology and Psychology, Ky. So. Coll./U. Louisville, 1968; MS in Social Work, Kent Sch. Social Work, U. Louisville, 1970. Lic. clin. social worker, lic. marriage and family therapist Fla. Dept. Profl. Regulations, 1982—. Bank teller, Tex., Ky., Ga., 1951-66; child care nursery dir. Fowler's Toddler's Inn, Sarasota, Fla., 1968; social worker Ky. Dept. Child Welfare, Louisville, 1969, Family Relations Ctr., Louisville, 1970-72; sr. social worker River Region Mental Health-Mental Retardation, Louisville, 1972-78; clin. social worker, psychotherapist W. Central Fla. Human Resources Ctr., Ocala, 1978; treatment team Sarasota Palms Psychiat. Hosp., Fla., 1978-79; dir. social services Venice Hosp., Fla., 1979-81, Morton F. Plant Hosp., Clearwater, Fla., 1981-88; pres. Betty Blackman Enterprises, 1988—, pvt. practice counseling, 1988—; sec. to dir. Louisville and Jefferson County Children's Home, 1956-57; recreational dir. Perrine Bapt. Ch., Miami, Fla., 1965; condr. workshops, speaker chs., schs. Greater Louisville area; field instr. grad. sch. students U. Louisville. Chmn. Agys. United Appeal, 1974, 75; mem. Greater Louisville Area Mental Retardation Com.; act. ch. activities, tchr., counselor, condr. workshops; sec. Venice Area Community Council, 1980, pres., 1981; bd. dirs., dir. edn. Widow to Widow Program; adv. com. Ctr. for Counseling and Human Devel; mem. resource com. NRC, Clearwater; mem. adv. council Independent Home Health Agy. Named one of Sarasota County's 10 Most Eligible Bachelorettes, 1980-81. Mem. Nat. Assn. Social Workers (county coordinator 1982-83, chairperson-elect Tampa Bay Unit 1982-83, chairperson 1983-85, named Social Worker of Yr. Tampa Bay Unit 1984, nat. registry clin. social workers 1985—), Am. Assn. Marriage and Family Therapists, Pinellas Assn. Marriage and Family Therapists, Acad. Cert. Social Workers (cert.), Nat. Assn. Hosp. Social Work Dirs., Fla. Assn. Hosp. Social Work Dirs. (treas. 1982-84, pres. elect 1984-85, pres. 1985-86), Fla. Chpt. Assn. Social Workers. Baptist. Home: 181 Garland Circle Palm Harbor FL 34683 Office: Exec Ctr Office Plaza 2280 US Hwy 19N Suite 132 Clearwater FL 34623

BLACKMAN, GHITA WAUCHETA, residential energy consultant; b. Chgo., Feb. 19, 1932; d. William Harveston Joseph and Zelda (Booth) Harris; m. David Edward Blackman, June 7, 1953 (div. Oct. 1976); children—Anasa, Anthony, Cynthia, Tracy. Student NYU, 1949-50, U. Dayton, 1952-53. Various secretarial positions U.S. Air Force, Dayton, Ohio, then Am. Humanist Assn., Yellow Springs, Ohio, 1950-64; sec. Antioch Coll., Yellow Springs, 1964-66, Fels Research Inst., Yellow Springs, 1966-70; cons. direct sales Fashion Two Twenty, Dayton, 1966-72; mem. sales staff Prophet & Friends Inc., New Britain, Conn., 1972-76; customer relations clk. Conn. Natural Gas Corp., Hartford, 1976-80, natural energy cons., 1980—. Mem. Dayton Jr. Philharm. Orch., 1947-53, second violin Springfield Symphony, Ohio, 1956-64; v.p. Conn. Capitol Area chpt. Older Women's League, Hartford, 1985-87; sec. Spiritual Assembly of the Baha'is of West Hartford, Conn., 1977-78; corr. sec. Spiritual Assembly of the Baha'is of Hartford, 1982—. Mem. Nat. Assn. Female Execs., Nat. Assn. Profl. Saleswomen. Avocation: music. Home: 31 Woodland St Hartford CT 06105 Office: Conn Natural Gas Corp 100 Columbus Blvd Hartford CT 06103

BLACKMAN, JEANNE A., consumer advocate; b. Decatur, Ill., Sept. 23, 1943; d. Robert Russell and Elizabeth Irene (DeWolfe) Shulke; m. Gary L. Blackman, Apr. 16, 1963 (div. Aug. 1983); children: Jeffrey Lynn, Stephanie Sue. BS Elem. Edn., Ind. U., 1965; MS in Edn. Adminstrn., Eastern Ill. U., 1979. Cert. tchr. and administr.; lic. real estate salesperson. Elem. tchr. Taylorville (Ill.) Community Sch. Dist., 1965-86; real estate salesperson Craggs-Adams Realtors, Taylorville, 1985-87; adminstrv. asst. to chief of staff Ill. Dept. of Aging, Springfield, 1986-87, consumer advocate, 1987—; pres. Taylorville Edn. Assn., 1983-85; mem. adv. council Gov.'s Rehab., Springfield, 1987—. Co-founder, treas. Ill. Vol. Optometry Services to Humanity, Taylorville, 1976—; v.p. Capitol City Rep. Women's Club, 1988—; candidate Christian County Bd. Seat, Taylorville, 1984—; fundraiser, chairperson Ill. Women's Polit. Caucus, Springfield, 1985—; pres. Am. Field Service Student Exchange Program, Taylorville, 1985-87. Mem. AAUW (edn. chairperson Taylorville chpt. 1985—), Older Women's League (legis. liaison 1987—), Ill. Women in Govt. Pub. Relations (bd. dirs. 1988—), Ill. Gerontology Consortium, Mid-Am. Council on Aging, Network, Ill. Fedn. Rep. Women (bd. dirs. 1988—, ways and means com. 1987—). Presbyterian. Home: #19 Washington Pl Springfield IL 62702 Office: Ill Dept on Aging 421 E Capitol Springfield IL 62702

BLACKMAN, JESSICA LYNN, lawyer; b. Bklyn., June 1, 1954; d. Norman Sidney and Sylvia (Bader) B.; B.A., Syracuse U., 1975; J.D., Western New Eng. Coll., 1978; m. Bruce Gary Freedman, July 14, 1985. Admitted to Mass. bar, 1978; legis. asst. Senator John Tower, 1978-79, D.C. Mayor's Office, 1979-80, Congressman Alvin Baldus, Washington, 1980-81, Congressman Gus Savage, Washington, 1981-83; legis. dir. Congressman Edward F. Feighan, 1983-84; owner Resumes for Success, 1984—; teaching fellow Northfield/Mt. Hermon Sch., 1974. Reginald Heber Smith fellow, 1978. Mem. ABA, Mass. Bar Assn., Mass. Women's Bar Assn., D.C. Women's Bar Assn., Phi Alpha Delta, Delta Delta Delta. Democrat.

BLACKMAN, LEANN HARDEN, educator; b. Birmingham, Ala.; d. Joseph Lee Jr. and Patricia Ruth (Gafford) Harden; m. James Henry Belcher, June 26, 1971 (div. June 1982); children: Jonathan Marcus Belcher, Tyler Austin Belcher; m. Gregory Dean Blackman, July 11, 1987. BS, U. Ala., Birmingham, 1975, MA, 1977, Edn. Specialist, 1987. Cert. tchr., Ala. Sr. recreation leader City of Fultondale, Ala., 1975-77, City of Gardendale, Ala., 1977-79; tchr. Jefferson County Bd. Edn., Birmingham, 1981-84, Birmingham City Bd. Edn., 1984—; mem. State Fgn. Lang. Textbook Com., Birmingham, 1985-86; chmn. Curriculum Com. Ten-Yr. Accreditation Evaluation, Birmingham, 1986. Contbr. articles to profl. jours. Coach dance team Banks High Sch., Birmingham, 1986-87, track team, 1986-87; vol. Muscular Dystrophy Telethon, Birmingham, 1986, St. Jude's Hosp., Birmingham, 1986, Am. Heart Assocs., Birmingham, 1987. Mem. Kappa Delta Epsilon, Phi Kappa Phi. Club: S.E. Lake Computer (Birmingham) (sponsor 1986-87). Office: SE Lake Middle Magnet Sch 720 S 86th St Birmingham AL 35216

BLACKMAN, MONTIE ROSE, fundraising specialist; b. Jackson, Miss., Oct. 4, 1950; d. Willie C. and Jessie (Myles) (stepmother) Davis; 1 child, Etta Kemyata Davis; m. Jerry L. Blackman (div. Sept. 1976). BA, Jackson State U., 1972; MA, U. So. Miss., 1974. Cert. paralegal generalist. Announcer radio Sta. WORV, Hattiesburg, Miss., 1974-75; coordinator spl. events Chgo. Urban League, 1976-78; press asst. Ill. State Comptroller, Chgo., 1978-80; publicist Sta. WLS (ABC), Chgo., 1978-80; mgr. regional project United Negro Coll. Fund Inc., Chgo., 1980-85; owner Monkem Corp, Chgo., 1988—; cons. People United to Save Humanity Excel NBA Probasketball Tournament, 1987—, Mrs. Chgo. Pageant Inc, 1987—, "Lena" The Lady and Her Music, 1985; assoc. producer Lou Rawls TV Spl., 1985. Cons. Citizens Elect Joe Gardner Commr., 1988; mem. Women Elect Harold Washington, 1984. Nominated Outstanding Woman Chgo., Chgo. Jaycees, 1976. Mem. Ill. Paralegal Assn., Nat. Assn. Media Women, Bus. and Profl. Womens Clubs, Congl. Awards Counsel (fundraiser 1985), Delta Sigma Thetha (pres. 1971-72). Baptist. Home: 416 W Barry Chicago IL 60657 Office: Monkem Corp 416 W Barry Chicago IL 60657

BLACKSTEN-PLANTZ, ANNA MARIE, public safety officer, investigator; b. Fargo, N.D., Dec. 23, 1948; d. Ove Harold and Florence Mildred (Holsinger) Anderson; m. Ralph H. Plantz; children: David, Angela, Brooke. Student Lane Community Coll., 1972-74; criminology cert. of competancy Inst. Applied Sci., 1978; grad. Oregon Police Acad., 1984. Cert. radiol. monitoring, 1982; cert. State of Oregon first responder, 1984-87, gen. level law enforcement data system operator, 1987. Crime prevention officer, lab. technician Eugene (Oreg.) Police Dept., 1974-79; fire prevention technician, investigator Seaside Fire Dept., Seaside, Oreg., 1980-83; pub. safety lt., Oreg. Health Scis. U., 1985—. Bus. and Profl. Women's Club scholar, 1976-77. Mem. Oreg. Fire Marshal's, Bus. and Profl. Women, Internat. Assn. Arson Investigators, Exec. Females, Inc., Oreg. Fire Edn. Assn., Oreg. Peace Officers Assn. Home: 237 NW Merle Dr Hillsboro OR 97124 Office: Oreg Health Scis U 3181 SW Sam Jackson Park Rd Portland OR 97201

BLACKSTOCK, VIRGINIA LEE LOWMAN (MRS. LEROY BLACKSTOCK), civic worker; b. Bixby, Okla., July 2, 1917; d. Joseph Arthur and Winifred (Lundy) Lowman; student Tulsa Coll. Bus., 1935-37; m. Leroy Blackstock, Dec. 29, 1939; children—Vincent Craig, Priscilla Gay (Mrs. Richard S. Kurz), Birch Lee, Lore Anne (Mrs. Dwight Mitchell), Trena Jan (Mrs. Frank Dale). Legal sec. law firm, Tulsa, 1937-41. Chmn. program Internat. Students in Tulsa, 1955-65; mem. Tulsa Council Camp Fire Girls, 1963-66; mem. youth com. Tulsa Philharmonic Soc., 1969-70; now mem. women's assn.; pres. Eliot Elementary P.T.A., 1961-62, Edison High Sch. P.T.A., 1971-72; mem. Tulsa Opera Guild. Co-chmn. Democratic precinct No. 132, 1960-67. Mem. Tulsa County Bar Aux. (pres. 1954-55, sec. 1962-63, chaplain 1966-67). Baptist. Clubs: Summit, Petroleum. Home: 7213 S Atlanta St Tulsa OK 74136

BLACKSTONE, SANDRA LEE, lawyer, educator, former government official; b. Washington; d. Fred J. and Madeline S. Blackstone; B.A., U. Vt., 1969; J.D., U. Denver, 1977; Ph.D., Colo. Sch. Mines, 1979. Systems analyst Martin Marietta Aerospace, Denver, 1969-74; cons. legal, econ. and regulatory matters W.R. Grace & Co., Colo. Energy Research Inst., Colo. Sch. Mines, Sherman & Howard, Denver, 1976-79; mgr. bus. devel. for synthetic fuels Rocky Mountain Energy subs. Union Pacific Corp., Denver, 1979-81; dep. dir. energy and mineral resources Bur. Land Mgmt., Dept. Interior, Washington, 1981-83; prof. Denver Coll. Law, 1983—; mem. Colo. Adv. Council on Energy and Energy-Related Mineral Research, 1980-82; mem. Bd. on Mineral and Energy Resources, Nat. Acad. Scis., 1983—; mem. Nat. Coal Council, 1984—; mem. Colo. Women's Forum, 1976—. Republican precinct committeewoman, 1970-74; del. Denver County Rep. Conv., 1971, 74, Colo. State Rep. Conv., 1972. Colo. Energy Research Inst. fellow, 1974-76; Mobil Oil Co. natural resources fellow, 1975-76; Kennecott Corp. fellow, 1976-77. Mem. Am. Bar Assn., Colo. Bar Assn., Denver Bar Assn., Nat. Coal COuncil, Colo. Women's Forum. Republican. Contbr. articles to profl. jours. Office: U Denver Coll Law 1900 Olive St Denver CO 80220

BLACKWAY, MADELINE ENDERS, librarian; b. Halifax, Pa., June 8, 1934; d. A. Marlin and Bertha Ellen (Straub) Enders; m. William Henry Blackway, Jr., Nov. 25, 1960; children—Julie Anne Blackway Kotkiewicz, William Enders. B.A., Pa. State U., 1956; M.S.L.S., Shippensburg U., 1980, M.Ed., 1982, EdD, Temple U., 1987. Tchr. Susquehanna Twp. Sch. Dist., Harrisburg, Pa., 1956-61. Millersburg-Upper Paxton Sch. Dist. (Pa.), 1962-64; tchr. Halifax (Pa.) Area Sch. Dist., 1967-68, elem. librarian, 1968—. Active Harrisburg Community Theatre, 1970's; active Twin Valley Players, Halifax, 1970—, bd. dirs., 1983-84, 86—, Halifax Area Hist. Soc. 1987—. Mem. Am. Bus. Women's Assn., ALA, Pa. Sch. Librarian Assn., Pa. Edn. Assn., Soc. Sch. Librarians INternat., Halifax Edn. Assn. (pres. 1970-72, 78-80), Delta Kappa Gamma, Phi Delta Gamma. Republican. Lodge: Order Eastern Star (Esther 1956-57). Home: Mountain View Dr PO Box 168 Halifax PA 17032 Office: Halifax Elem Sch RD 3 PO Box 7 Halifax PA 17032

BLACKWELL, ANTOINETTE LYNN, systems analyst, consultant; b. Anderson, Ind., Apr. 14, 1960; d. Donald Hugh and Janet Louise (Slaughter) B. Student in Computer Sci., Purdue U., 1978-79, Anderson Coll., 1980. Programmer/analyst Community Hosp., Anderson, Ind., 1979-81, Dynamic Control, Boston, 1981-82, project leader, Winter Park, Fla., 1982-84, mgr. implementations, Longwood, Fla., 1984-85, sr. tech. cons., Longwood, 1985—; developer spl. project internat. services Baxter Systems Div., 1986-88, sr. analyst tech. cons.,1988—. Recipient Vocat. Edn. award, Anderson Rotary Club, 1978. Mem. Office Edn. Assn. (parliamentarian 1977-78, awards 1977-78), Electronic Computing Health Oriented, Common-IBM Users Group, Nat. Assn. Female Execs. Avocations: photography, writing, reading, volleyball, racquetball. Office: Baxter Systems Div 587 E Sanlando Springs Dr Longwood FL 32750

BLACKWELL, DORIS CLAIRE, social services administrator; b. Winston-Salem, N.C., Nov. 1, 1950; d. Crist Watts and Doris (Bugden) B. BA, U. N.C., 1972; MRE, Duke U., 1974; M Div. cum laude, Emory U., 1976. Chaplain intern Grady Meml. Hosp., Atlanta, 1975-76; grant coordinator HEW Grady Hosp. Psychiatry, Atlanta, 1976-77; dir. social services Ashton Woods Conv. Ctr., Atlanta, 1977-82; dir. resident services Campbell-Stone No. Apts., Atlanta, 1982-83, adminstr., 1983—; sem. leader in field. Mem. Sandy Springs C. of C. (past sec.), Ga. Assn. Social Workers Long Term Care (pres. 1980), Ga. Gerontol. Soc., Ga. Assn. Homes for Aging (sec., bd. dirs. 1988), Am. Assn. Homes for Aging, Nat. Leased Housing Assn. Office: Campbell-Stone No Apts 350 Carpenter Dr Atlanta GA 30328

BLACKWELL, LUCY WHITE, retired state official; b. Jackson, Tenn., Apr. 22, 1912; d. William Francis and Ethel (White) Blackwell; A.B., Lambuth Coll., 1933; postgrad. West Tenn. Bus. Coll., 1934-35. Stenographer, Tenn. Emergency Relief Adminstrn., Jackson, 1935; accounting clk. FSA, Jackson, Brownsville, Tenn., 1936-39; stenographer Tenn. Dept. Pub. Welfare, Jackson, 1939-40; clk., interviewer, local office mgr. Tenn. Dept. Employment Security, Jackson, 1940-73. Comdr. Am. Cancer Soc., Madison County, Tenn., 1943-54, dist. comdr. W. Tenn., 1947-48, rec. sec. Tenn. div., 1954-56, bd. dirs., 1945—, organizer Madison County unit, 1954, pres., 1954-55; bd. dirs. Jackson Community Chest, 1955-57; pres. League Women Voters, 1951. Treas., chmn. bd. trustees Jackson Free Library, 1948-57. Recipient R.E. Womack Alumni Achievement award Lambuth Coll. Alumni Assn., 1956; named Jackson-Madison Woman of Year, 1955. Mem. Internat. Assn. Personnel Employment Security (pres. Jackson chpt. 1956), Lambuth Coll. Alumni Assn. (pres. 1962-63). Presbyterian. Clubs: Pilot Internat. (past pres. Jackson, dist. gov. Tenn., internat. dir. exec. com.). Altrusa Internat. (chmn.). Home: 45 Belle Haven Dr Jackson IN 38305

BLACKWELL, PENNY LEE, lawyer; b. Coco Solo, C.Z., Sept. 24, 1948; d. Frank Charles and Norma Madeline (Bryant) B.; m. John Kenneth Sanstead, Apr. 15, 1978; 1 dau., Rebecca Randolph. B.S., Portland State U., 1971; J.D., Am. U., 1974. Bar: Md., Pa. Atty., Wapora, Bethesda, Md., 1975-76, U.S. EPA, Phila., 1976-78; ptnr. Wolfson & Blackwell, York, Pa., 1980—. Bd. dirs. Displaced Homemakers, York, 1983-86, housing council, 1986—, Jr. League of York, 1984-85; mem. steering com. Martin Meml. Library, York, 1984, bd. dirs. York County Literacy Council, 1985—. Mem. ABA, Pa. Bar Assn., Md. Bar Assn., York County Bar Assn. (chmn. profl. responsibilities 1984), Nat. Assn. Women Lawyers. Democrat. Unitarian. Club: Young Women's (bd. dirs. 1983-84) (York). Office: Wolfson & Blackwell 29 E Princess St York PA 17401

BLACKWELL, SAUNDRA COCHRAN, franchising company executive; b. Gainesville, Fla., Mar. 28, 1946; d. Will Harrell and Nancy Lucielle (Best) Cochran; m. Ronald Blackwell; 1 child, Kimberly Anne Brewer. Student, Columbus Coll., 1960, U. Hawaii, 1974-77, Fayetteville Tech. Inst., 1978. Sales rep. Peters, Griffin and Woodward, Inc., N.Y.C., 1972, Telerep, Inc., N.Y.C., 1973; media dir. Smith and Allen Advt., Fayetteville, N.C., 1978-79, Mathes Co., Athens, Tex., 1979-80, ColorTyme, Inc., Athens, Tex., 1980-82;

franchise compliance ColorTyme, Inc., Athens, 1982—. Mem. Am. Women in Radio and TV, Advt./Pub. Relations of East Tex., Meeting Planners Internat., Bus. and Profl. Women's Club (pres.). Republican. Lutheran. Home: Rural Rt 6 Box 6713 Athens TX 75751 Office: ColorTyme Inc 501 Dallas Hwy Athens TX 75751

BLADE, MELINDA KIM, educator, researcher, archaeologist; b. San Diego, Jan. 12, 1952; d. George A. and Arline A. M. (MacLeod) B. BA, U. San Diego, 1974, MA in Teaching, 1975, MA, 1975, EdD, 1986. Cert. secondary tchr., Calif.; cert. community coll. instr., Calif.; registered profl. historian, Calif. Instr. Coronado Unified Sch. Dist., Calif., 1975-76; head coach women's basketball U. San Diego, 1976-78; instr. Acad. of Our Lady of Peace, San Diego, 1976—, chmn. social studies dept., 1983—, counselor, 1984—, co-dir. student activities, 1984-87, coordinator advanced placement program, 1986—; mem. archaeol. excavation team U. San Diego, 1975—, hist. researcher, 1975—; lectr., 1981—. Author hist. reports and research papers. Editor U. San Diego pubs. Vol. Am. Diabetes Assn., San Diego, 1975—; coordinator McDonald's Diabetes Bike-a-thon, San Diego, 1977, 78. Mem. Nat. Council Social Studies, Calif. Council Social Studies, Soc. Bibl. Archeology, Assn. Supervision and Curriculum Devel., Assn. Scientists and Scholars Internat. for Shroud of Turin, Medieval Acad. Am., Medieval Assn. Pacific, Am. Hist. Assn., Western Assn. Women Historians, Renaissance Soc. Am., San Diego Hist. Soc., Phi Alpha Theta (sec.-treas. 1975-77), Phi Delta Kappa. Office: Acad Our Lady of Peace 4860 Oregon St San Diego CA 92116

BLADES, JANE M., technical writer; b. Jersey City, Dec. 1, 1953; d. Nunzio Thomas and Evelyn Rose (Spizzirro) Savino; m. Brian Hilton Blades, Sept. 20, 1980; children: Adam Hilton, Erik Thomas. BA, Kean Coll., 1983. Cert. handicapped tchr., N.J. Staff asst. Am. Telephone and Telegraph Co., Parsippany, N.J., 1979-81; spl. edn. tchr Perth Amboy Pub. Schs., N.J., 1984; mgmt. cons. J. Anthony and Assocs., Inc., Hillsborough, N.J., 1986-87, project mgr., 1987-88; cons. Datanomics, Inc., Piscataway, N.J., 1988—; cons. in field. Mem. Nat. Assn. Female Execs., Soc. for Tech. Communication, Kappa Delta Pi, Phi Kappa Phi. Republican. Presbyterian. Home: 27 Hill Ave Somerset NJ 08873

BLAGDEN, CAROLYN MARGARET, editorial executive, writer; b. Summit, N.J., Apr. 19, 1944; d. Raymond and Margaret Ida (Noll) Hunt; m. Robert B. Blagden, June 25, 1966 (div. Jan. 1984); children: Kathryn E., Michael G. BA in German, English, Grove City (Pa.) Coll., 1966; MS in Communicative Disorders, San Francisco State U., 1981. lic. speech pathologist, Calif., Iowa. Speech, lang. clinician Scottish Rite Clinic, San Francisco, 1980-83, Alameda Unified Sch. Dist., 1983-84; editorial mgr. LinguiSystems, Inc., Moline, Ill., 1984—. Author: (with others) (books) UnTherapy for Thinking Skills, 1985, RAPP: Resource of Activities for Peer Pragmatics, 1986; (test) Interpersonal Language Skills Assessment, 1983, 84, Teaching Vocabulary Worksheets, 1987, Good Thinking!, 1987, Thinking to Go, 1987; (pictures) PPICS: Picture Program for Interpersonal Communicative Skills, 1986, Blooming Recipes, 1987, Blooming Language Arts, 1988, Ready, Set, Grammar!, 1988. Mem. Am. Speech., Lang. and Hearing Assn. (cert. clin. competence), Iowa State Speech. Lang. and Hearing Assn., Quad Cities Speech, Lang. and Hearing Assn. (pub. awareness chairperson, 1986-87). Republican. Home: 4545 Aspen Hills Circle Bettendorf IA 52722 Office: LinguiSystems Inc 716 17th St Moline IL 61265

BLAICH, VICKI, data processing executive; b. Montgomery, Ala., Aug. 28, 1952; d. John Etysl and Edna Lucille (Miller) Stephenson; m. Thomas Blaich, Jan. 25, 1977. Student, U. Ala., 1986—. Cert. Pub. Mgr., Ala. Data entry operator II State of Ala. Dept. Revenue, Montgomery, 1976-77; data entry operator II Lurleen Wallace Developmental Ctr. State of Ala. Dept. Mental Health, Decatur, Ala., 1977-78, computer operator, 1978-81, systems mgmt. technician, 1981-83, systems mgmt. specialist, 1983-86, ops. ctr. mgr., 1986—. Mem. Nar. Assn. Female Execs., Inc., Assn. Retareded Citizens, Friends of Wallace Ctr. Office: State of Ala Dept Mental Health L B Wallace Devel Ctr PO Box 2224 Decatur AL 35602

BLAIN, JACQUELYN ALICE NASH GRIPPIN, cosmetologist; b. Springfield, Mass., Sept. 21, 1928; d. Roger Warren and Kathleen Alice (Proctor) Nash; student Springfield Conservatory Music, 1944-47, Hartford Conservatory Music, 1971-72, with concertmaster Bill Dalton, 1963-78; grad. Cosmetic Acad., 1978, Mansfield Beauty Acad., 1980. Children—Diana Grippin, Lea Grippin, Lyn Grippin. With Watkins Bros., Inc., Hartford, Conn., 1964-79, asst. to owner, 1974-79; cosmetologist, Longmeadow, Mass., 1982—; mem. Zotos Creative Design Group, 1982; skin technician rep. Princess Nyla Skin Care Products, 1959—; make-up technician for various stage companies. Recipient Merit award Redkin Labs., 1977. Mem. Hammond Organ Assn., Mass. State Cosmetology Assn. (dir., Pres. of Yr. award 1985), Internat. Platform Assn., Springfield Cosmetology Assn. (pres. 1984-85). Home: 80 Kenmore Dr Longmeadow MA 01106

BLAINE, DOROTHEA CONSTANCE RAGETTÉ, lawyer, b. N.Y.C., Sept. 23, 1930; d. Robert Raymond and Dorothea Ottilie Ragetté; B.A., Barnard Coll., 1952; M.A., Calif. State U., 1968; Ed.D., UCLA, 1978; J.D., Western State U., 1981; postgrad. in taxation Golden Gate U. Bar: U.S. Dist. Ct. (ea., so. and cen. dists.) Calif., 1986—. Mem. tech. staff Planning Research Corp., Los Angeles, 1964-67; asso. scientist Holy Cross Hosp., Mission Hills, Calif., 1967-70; career devel. officer and affirmative action officer County of Orange, Santa Ana, Calif., 1970-74, sr. adminstrv. analyst, budget and program coordination, 1974-78; spl. projects asst. CAO/Spl. Programs Office, 1978-80, sr. adminstrv. analyst, 1980-83; admitted to Calif. bar, 1982; sole practice, 1982—; instr. Am. Coll. Law, Brea, Calif., 1987. Bd. dirs. Deerfield Community Assn., 1975-78, Orange YMCA, 1975-77. Mem. Assn. Trial Lawyers Am., Calif. Trial Lawyers Assn., Orange County Trial Lawyers Assn., Calif. Women Lawyers, Nat. Women's Polit. Caucus, ABA, Calif. Bar Assn., Orange County Bar Assn., Orange County Women Lawyers Assn. ACLU, Delta Theta Phi, Phi Delta Kappa. Office: 17541 17th St Suite 201 Tustin CA 92680

BLAIR, BETTY STEPP, marketing consultant; b. Odessa, Tex., July 2, 1947; d. William Fleming and Barbara Jane (Thompson) Stepp; m. Stephen Randolph Blair, Mar. 25, 1968 (div. 1978); children: Stacy Rae, Brian Randolph. BBA, SW Tex. State U., 1970. Sales rep. stas. KYXY and XETV, San Diego, 1975-77; owner, mgr. Royal Suite, San Diego, 1977-79; internat. design cons. T. Goodrich & Assocs., Del Mar, Calif., 1979-80; acct. Sickels O'Brien Co., San Diego and La Jolla, Calif., 1980-81; property mgr. Total Office/Koll, San Diego, 1981-83; asst. devel. dir. Am. Cancer Soc., San Diego, 1983-86, also bd. dirs.; assoc. D'Agostino, Underwood & Assocs., 1986-87; dir. devel. Combined Arts and Edn. Council of San Diego County, 1987, spl. event prodn. and mktg., Blair Rubin & Assocs., 1987—; cons. Poway Firewood Co., Calif., 1980-84, Starflight Prodns., San Diego, 1985-86. Mem. Republican Central Com., San Diego, 1977, steering com. Young Connoisseurs, San Diego Mus. of Art, 1982-84, San Diego Rep. Businesswomen, 1984-86; bd. dirs. Rep. Bus. and Profl. Club, San Diego, 1986, The Soc. Club, Am. Cancer Soc., Single Profl. Soc. for Arts; vol. charitable orgns. and theaters. Recipient State award Am. Cancer Soc., 1985. Mem. Nat. Soc. Fund Raising Execs., Chi Omega. Avocation: sailing. Home: 3435 Lebon Dr #1134 San Diego CA 92122 Office: Blair Rubin & Assocs PO Box 174 La Jolla CA 92038

BLAIR, CERISE CAMERON, computer adminstrator; b. Lamesa, Tex.; d. Harold E. and Lucille (Howell) Cameron; m. Thomas R. Blair, Mar. 28, 1956; children: Steven Cameron, Paul Calvin. BJ, U. Tex., 1956. Account exec. Bevel Assocs., Ft. Worth, 1956-57; sales promoter Sta. KFJZ-TV, Ft. Worth, 1957; legal adminstr. Tex. Crude Oil Co., Ft. Worth, 1957-61; adminstrv. asst. C. B. Smith Sr. (Philanthropist), Austin, Tex., 1969-72; office mgr. East Tex. Area Council Camp Fire, Longview, 1976-79; adminstrv. assoc. Intel Corp., Austin, 1979-81; adminstrv. supr. Execucom Systems Corp., Austin, 1981-83; program adminstr. advanced computer architecture Microelectronics & Computer Tech. Corp., Austin, 1983—; pres., bd. dirs. Harrison St. Day Care Ctr., Longview, 1976-79. Pub. relations rep. Laguna Gloria Arts Mus., Austin, 1973-74. Mem. Am. Mgmt. Assn., Alpha Gamma Delta (internat. officer 1966-75). Republican. Presbyterian. Office: MCC 3500 Balcones Ctr Dr W Austin TX 78759

BLAIR, ELIZABETH TYREE, banker; b. Richmond, Va., Oct. 11, 1947; d. Walter Hines Page and Elizabeth Ann (Mudd) Young; m. Michael Joseph Lyons, Dec. 31, 1965 (div. 1971); 1 child, Anthony Page Lyons; m. Richard Stuart Blair, Sept. 19, 1973. A, Tidewater Community Coll., 1971. Br. mgr. Gen. Electric Mortgage, Tampa, Fla., 1981-83; secondary mktg. adminstr. PSFS Credit Corp., Tampa, 1983-85; br. mgr. mortgage div., corp. officer Carteret Mortgage Co. div. Carteret Savs. Bank, Tampa, 1985—. Mem. Fla. Mortgage Brokers Assn., Mortgage Bankers Assn., Tampa C. of C. Democrat. Home: 6212 S Church Ave Tampa FL 33616

BLAIR, JANE COLEMAN, retired educator; b. N.Y.C., Apr. 7, 1928; d. Leighton Hammond and Jane (Fraser) Coleman; m. William Draper Blair, Jr., June 25, 1949; children: Jane Blair Gelston, Elizabeth Blair Jones. Student, Bryn Mawr Coll., 1946-49; BA, Am. U., 1974, MEd, 1976. Cert. secondary tchr., Md. Tchr., dir. admissions Stone Ridge Country Day Sch. of the Sacred Heart, Bethesda, Md., 1976-86. Pres., bd. dirs. Jr. League of Washington; bd. dirs. Columbia Hist. Soc., Meridian House Internat., Hillcrest Children's Ctr.; mem. Am. Hist. Soc. Mem. Visiting Nurse Assn. Democrat. Episcopalian. Club: F St. (bd. dirs. 1986—). Home: 118 E Melrose St Chevy Chase MD 20815

BLAIR, JEAN MARIE, actress; b. Winston-Salem, N.C., Nov. 15, 1947; d. James Thomas and Margaret Helen (Christman) B.; m. Robert William Christianson, June 22, 1985. BFA, U. N.C., 1969. V.p., treas. Great Immediately Prodns., N.Y.C., 1982—. Appeared with various stock cos., N.Y., Pa. and N.C., 1969-73; appeared in Broadway plays Godspell, 1976-77, Grease, 1978, with mime cos. Orkidstra, 1977—, Mime Field, 1980—. Pres. Residential Co-op Bldg., N.Y.C. Mem. NOW, People for the Am. Way. Democrat. Roman Catholic. Home and Office: 423 W 22d St New York NY 10011

BLAIR, KATHIE LYNN, social services worker; b. Oakland, Calif., Sept. 29, 1951; d. Robert Leon Webb and Patricia Jean (Taylor) Peterson; m. Terry Wayne Blair, Dec. 29, 1970 (div. 1972); 1 child, Anthony Wayne. Eligibility worker Dept. Social Services, San Jose, Calif., 1974-76; adult and family services worker State of Oreg., Portland, 1977—; guest speaker welfare advocacy groups, Portland, 1987. Contbr. articles to mags. Mem. Nat. Geographic Soc., Nat. Assn. Female Execs. Democrat. Office: Adult and Family Services 4531 SE Belmont Portland OR 97215

BLAIR, MARIE LENORE, educator; b. Maramec, Okla., Jan. 9, 1931; d. Virgil Clement and Ella Catherine (Leen) Strode; m. Freeman Joe Blair, Aug. 26, 1950; children: Elizabeth Ann Blair Crump, Roger Joe. BS, Okla. A. and M. Coll., 1956; MS, Okla. State U., 1961, postgrad., 1965-68. Reading specialist Pub. Schs. Stillwater (Okla.), 1966—. Past bd. dirs. Okla. Reading Council. Mem. Internat., Okla., Cimarron (past pres.) reading assns., NEA, Okla. Edn. Assn., Stillwater Edn. Assn., Kappa Kappa Iota. Democrat. Mem. Disciples of Christ. Lodges: Demoley Mothers, Rainbow Mothers, Lahoma, White Shrine Jerusalem (past worthy high priestess). Order White Shrine Jerusalem (past supreme queen's attendant), Internat. Order of Rainbow for Girls (Okla. exec. com.), Order Eastern Star (past grand Martha, past grand rep. of Nebr. in Okla.). Home: Route 1 Maramec OK 74045

BLAIR, MARY PATRICIA, educator; b. Belton, Tex., Oct. 16, 1931; d. Ballard Andrew and Cleo (Miller) Guest; m. Major Elliot Blair; children: Major Elliot Jr., Randall Scott, Kellie Ann. BS, Baylor U., 1952. Sec. First Nat. Bank, Kelleen, Tex., 1952-54, Dothan (Ala.) Nat. Bank, 1954-55; tchr. Barton Acad., Mobile, Ala., 1955-56, Killeen (Tex.) Ind. Sch. Dist., 1960-68, 80—; sec. First Nat. Bank, Killeen. Pres. Modern Study Club, Killeen, 1972-74, chmn. ladies com.; v.p., bd. dirs. Viveles Arts Soc., Killeen, 1976-87; sec. United Meth. Women, Killeen, 1978-79. Mem. Gemological Iinst. Am. Cert. Diamond Appraisers, Greater Killeen C. of C. Democrat. Methodist. Home: 2000 Stone Ave Killeen TX 76541 Office: Harker Heights Elem Sch Harley Dr Harker Heights TX 76543

BLAIR, MATTIE D., city official, consultant; b. Chgo., Nov. 26; d. James and Geraldine (Oliver) Cannon; div.; 1 child, Lisa Marie. B.S. in Bus. Adminstrn. in Acctg., Roosevelt U., 1979; M.B.A. in Fin., DePaul U., 1985. Pub. auditor Arthur Andersen & Co., Chgo., 1978-81; controller Johnson Products & Co., Chgo., 1981-82; mgr. fiscal policies United Way of Chgo., 1982-86; dir. devel. fin. City of Chgo., 1986—; cons. on fin. and mgmt. to small non-profit orgns. Developer network to assist black profls. in fin. and acctg. Mem. League of Black Women (v.p. 1983—). Democrat. Mem. United Ch. of Christ. Avocations: Tennis; jogging; sports. Office: City of Chgo Dept Revenue 121 N LaSalle Chicago IL 60606

BLAIR, PATRICIA JEAN, corporate personnel executive; b. Fairhaven, Minn., Mar. 17, 1939; d. Earl Philip and Doris Elizabeth (Seeley) B. BS in Mgmt., U. San Francisco, 1978; MBA in Human Resources, Golden Gate U., 1982. Jr. escrow officer Transam. Title Co., Phoenix, 1965-68; adminstr. Transam. Info. Services, Los Angeles, 1968-72; mgr. adminstrn. Syner-Graphics, Inc., San Francisco, 1972-80; dir. adminstrv. services Transam. Corp., San Francisco, 1980—, dir. corp. personnel, 1985—. Night unit leader LWV, Alameda, Calif., 1980-82; advisor Dance Action, Inc., San Francisco, 1983—; bd. dirs. Philharmonia Baroque, San Francisco, 1985—; bus. vol. for the arts San Francisco C. of C., 1983—. Mem. Am. Compensation Assn., Am. Soc. Personnel Adminstrs., No. Calif. Human Resources Conf., Bay Areas Human Resource Profls. Republican. Lutheran. Office: Transamerica Corp 600 Montgomery St San Francisco CA 94111

BLAIR, PRUDENCE LEWIS, business owner; b. Boston, Mar. 9, 1946; d. Wolfram L. and Elsie (Cole) Lewis; student U. Madrid (Spain), 1966; m. J. Kent Blair, Jr., Jan. 26, 1986. Corr., John P. Maguire Co., N.Y.C., 1968-71; asst. to pres. Cromwell Corp., N.Y.C., 1971-72, also corp. sec.; adminstrv. asst. to the exec. v.p. Rinfret Assocs., N.Y.C., 1973-76; asst to chmn. Friedlich, Fearon & Strohmeier, N.Y.C., 1976-77; v.p. mgmt., sec.-treas. Morgan Newman Assocs., Inc., Washington, 1977-84; v.p. mgmt. Balloon-Age, Short Hills, N.J., 1984—; pres. Products for the Filthy Rich, 1985—. Cert. CPR. Mem. Smithsonian Assocs., Nat. Assn. Female Execs. Republican. Episcopalian. Club: Jr. League of Summit, N.J. Office: PO Box 334 Short Hills NJ 07078

BLAIR, PRUDENCE WADDOCK, public relations executive, editor; b. St. Louis, Oct. 23, 1925; d. Joseph Patrick and Annie Laurie (Page) Waddock; B.J., U. Mo., Columbia, 1947; postgrad. Northwestern U., Chgo. campus, 1953-54; m. Giles Allen Blair, Jr., June 6, 1959; children—Annie-Laurie, Giles Allen, Rebecca Ralls. With news dept. KXOK Radio, St. Louis, 1947-48; agrl. editor Pet, Inc., St. Louis, 1949-52; asst. dir. public relations Am. Angus Assn., Chgo., 1953-56, St. Joseph, Mo., 1956-57; editor Bank-Trust News, Centerre Bank, Inc., St. Louis, 1957-62; substitute tchr./tchr. aide Webster Groves (Mo.) Sch. Dist., 1971-78; dir. public relations Edgewood Children's Center, Webster Groves, 1979-83; community relations and devel. dir. Care & Counseling, Inc., Creve Coeur, Mo., 1983—; notary public, 1978-82. Active Chgo. Young Democrats, 1953-56; asst. Brownie leader Girl Scouts U.S.A., 1965-66, 69-70, asst. scout leader St. Louis council, 1970-71, troop cookie chmn., 1974-78; active PTA, 1965-82; active United Fund campaigns, 1958-62, 78—, loaned exec. United Way, 1981, recipient Grand award to indsl. publs. editor, 1959, certs. of excellence, 1960, 61; mem. planning com. local history project Community Sch., Webster Groves, 1978. Mem. Nat. Assn. Mental Health Info. Officers (1st Place newsletters and spl. projects communications contest 1982), Nat. Soc. Fund Raising Execs., Community Service Public Relations Council Greater St. Louis (dir. 1980-83; pres. 1983), Webster Groves Hist. Soc. (dir. 1983-84), Alpha Chi Omega. Episcopalian. Contbr. articles to nat. press. Home: 44 Sylvester Ave Webster Groves MO 63119 Office: Care and Counseling Inc 12145 Ladue Rd Creve Coeur MO 63141

BLAIR, RUTH VIRGINIA VAN NESS, writer; b. St. Michael, Alaska, June 9, 1912; d. Elmer Eugene and Eula Willie (McIntosh) Van Ness; m. Glenn Myers Blair, June 27, 1934; children: Glenn Myers, Sally Virginia Coleman. Diploma, Seattle Pacific Coll., 1932; voice studies, Seattle, 1930-34, N.Y.C., 1937-38. Tchr. Everett (Wash.) Pub. Schs., 1932-34, Champaign, Ill., 1952-61; presenter Writing for Children workshops U. S. Fla. at St. Petersburg, Fla. So. Coll., writers' confs. Author: (children's books) Piddle Duck, 1966, A Bear Hibernates; Why Can't I?, 1972, Willa Willa, The Wishful Witch, 1972, Mary's Monster (Jr. Lit. Guild Selection), 1975; contbr. poetry to Voices Internat., Lyric, Classical Outlook, The Pen Women; contbr. stories, articles to Athene Mag., Mus. Jour., Christian Living, Amelia, Cricket, Young World, Ranger Rick; contbr. Ency. Britannica, 1974, chpt. poetry textbook, 1983; editor Symphony Guild Tchrs. Guide, 1974. Soloist Champaign-Urbana (Ill.) chs., 1938-61; edn. chmn. Symphony Guild, Champaign-Urbna, 1970-74. Mem. Nat. League Am. Pen Women (pres. Clearwater chpt. 1980—), Chgo. Children's Reading Round Table, Clearwater (Fla.) Friends Library, Fla. State Poetry Assn., Nat. Soc. Children's Book Writers. Club: Univ. (Urbana). Home and Office: 51 Island Way Clearwater FL 33515

BLAIR, SONIA MARIE, real estate broker; b. Bklyn., May 21, 1941; d. Nicholas Salim and Mary Frances (Risk) Kateb; m. Bruce Douglas Blair, Jan. 22, 1966 (div. 1979). BA in Mktg., U. Miami; internat. student, Am. U. Beirut; student, Burt Rodgers Sch. Real Estate. Registered real estate broker. Adminstrv. asst. States Attorney's Office, Miami, 1957-63; court reporter Grand Jury Dade County, Miami, 1957-63; with Walters, Moore, Costanzo, Miami, 1965-66; saleswoman Howard Johnson Co., Miami and N.Y.C., 1966-69; with William B. Russell Realtor, Miami, 1969-74, Atty.'s Gen.'s Office, Miami, 1963-65; realtor Sonia M. Blair Inc., Miami, 1974—. Mem. Humane Soc. Greater Miami, Big Bros.-Big Sisters, Sunrisers Home Mentally Retarded Children, Angel Villa Maria Nursing Home, Presl. Task Force; Realtor's Lawyers Com., Leg. Com.; chmn. Realtors Polit. Action Com. rep. 1985, Met. Art Mus., Lowe Art Mus. Named Broker to the Stars. Mem. Coral Gables Bd. Realtors (dir. 1985-86). Home: 4017 SW 10th St Miami FL 33134 Office: Sonia M Blair Inc Realtor 265 Sevilla Ave Coral Gables FL 33134

BLAIR, THERESA LUCILLE, records manager, electrical contractor; b. Hernandez, N.Mex., June 27, 1943; d. Ben and Lucy (Roybal) Lovato; m. Roger Charles Blair, Feb. 23, 1963; children—Darrell, Yvette, Sean, DeVonne. B.S. in Bus. Adminstrn., U. Albuquerque, 1979; M.B.A., Highlands U., Las Vegas, 1982. Office sec. Sandia Nat. Labs., Albuquerque, 1964-79, mem. lab. staff, records mgr., 1980—, dir.'s rep. employee contbr. program, 1981—; elec. contractor, owner, operator T.L. Blair Electric Co. Mem. planning and allocations panel United Way Greater Albuquerque, 1984. Mem. Assn. Records Mgrs. and Adminstrs. Democrat. Roman Catholic. Home: 2126 Matthew Ave NW Albuquerque NM 87104 Office: Sandia Nat Labs PO Box 5800 Albuquerque NM 87185

BLAIR, VIRGINIA ANN, public relations executive; b. Kansas City, Mo., Dec. 20, 1925; d. Paul Lowe and Lou Etta (Cooley) Smith; m. James Leon Grant, Sept. 3, 1943 (dec. July 1944); m. 2d, Warden Tannahill Blair, Jr., Nov. 7, 1947; children—Janet, Warden Tannahill, III. B.S. in Speech, Northwestern U., 1948. Free-lance writer, Chgo., 1959-69; writer, editor Smith, Bucklin & Assocs., Inc., Chgo., 1969-72, account mgr., 1972-79, account supr., 1979-80, dir. pub. relations, 1980-85; pres. GB Pub. Relations, 1985—; judge U.S. Indsl. Film Festival, 1974, 75; instr. Writer's Workshop, Evanston, Ill., 1978; dir. Northwestern U. Library Council, 1978—. Emmy nominee Nat. Acad. TV Arts & Scis., 1963; recipient Service award Northwestern U., 1978, Creative Excellence award U.S. Indsl. Film Festival, 1976, Gold Leaf merit cert. Family Circle mag. and Food Council Am., 1977. Mem. Pub. Relations Soc. Am. (counselors acad.), Women's Advt. Club Chgo. (pres.), Publicity Club Chgo., Nat. Acad. TV Arts & Scis., Zeta Phi Eta (Service award 1978), Alpha Gamma Delta. Author dramas (produced on CBS): Jeanne D'Arc: The Trial, 1961; Cordon of Fear, 1961; Reflection, 1961; If I Should Die, 1963; 3-act children's play: Children of Courage, 1967. Home and Office: 463 Highcrest Dr Wilmette IL 60091

BLAIS-GRENIER, SUZANNE, Canadian legislator. married; 2 children. Student econs., U. Paris; degree in sociology and social work, Laval U., McGill U. Dir.. Social Services div. Health and Welfare Can., 1975-78; dir. Can. Human Rights Commn., 1978-81; exec. dir. Assn. paritaire de prevention pour la sante et la securite au travail du Quebec, Can., to 1984; M.P. from Rosemont dist. Ho. of Commons, Ottawa, Ont., Can., 1984—; minister of environ. 1984-85, minister of state for transport, 1985. Office: House of Commons, 485 Confederation Bldg, Ottawa, ON Canada 21A 0A6

BLAKE, CAROL T., county social service administrator; b. Buffalo, Sept. 17, 1950; d. Robert Wilson and Constance Jane (Milburn) Temple; m. Charles Grierson Signor Blake, Nov. 3, 1973; children: Andrea Lynn, Kevin McFarland. Student Hobart and William Smith Coll., 1968-70; BA in Liberal Arts, SUNY, Geneseo, 1972. Outreach worker Orleans Community Action, Albion, N.Y., 1973; dir. resident services Orchard Manor Nursing Home, Medina, N.Y., 1973-75; dir. Orleans County Office for the Aging, Albion, 1975—; field instr. social work dept. SUNY, Brockport, 1985-86, 87-88, SUNY, Buffalo, 1986—; bd. dirs. Western N.Y. Network on Aging; cons. Genesee County Office for Aging, N.Y., 1983-84. Treas. Orleans Coop. Extension, Albion, 1977-80, Orleans Community Counseling Ctr., Albion, 1979; asst. campaign mgr., bd. dirs. Orleans United Way, Albion, 1983-88. Mem. N.Y. State Assn. of Area Agys. on Aging (chmn. rural affairs 1985 statewide conf.), Western N.Y. Network on Aging (presenter edn. conf. 1983), State Assn. Gerontological Educators. Democrat. Episcopalian. Avocations: classical music, dance, gardening, reading, vocal music. Home: 13579 Waterport-Carlton Rd Waterport NY 14571 Office: Orleans County Office For Aging 14016 Route 31 Albion NY 14411

BLAKE, CECILE CARTEE, investor relations company executive; b. Paducah, Ky., Mar. 26, 1938; d. Walter Edward and Charlene (Peck) Cartee; m. Glenn A. Blake, Feb. 20, 1965; children—Glynnis, Mitchell, Kyle, Amy. B.A. in Math., U. St. Thomas, 1980; M.S. in Biometry, U. Tex., 1982, Ph.D. in Biometry, 1985. Clin. chemist M.D. Anderson Hosp., Houston, 1959-60; dir. research and devel. Hycel Inc., Houston, 1960-65; prin. Frequency Forecasting, Houston, 1985-87; v.p. McCormick & Pryor, N.Y.C., 1985-87; pres. Statwatch, Inc., Houston 1987—; v.p. research and devel. Centre D'Observation Prospective Sociales, N. Am., Paris, Richmond, Va., 1987—; statis. cons. AID, Washington, 1984—, Pan-Am. World Health Orgn., 1984—. Mem. Am. Statis. Soc., Nat. Inst. Investor Relations., Simulation Soc.; Republican; Club: Glenbrook Valley Investment (pres. 1966-67) (Houston). Avocations: bicycling, sewing, reading. Home: 7510 Del Monte Houston TX 77063 Office: Statwatch Inc Three Riverway Suite 620 Houston TX 77056

BLAKE, DARLENE EVELYN, political worker, consultant, educator; b. Rockford, Iowa, Feb. 26, 1947; d. Forest Kenneth and Violet Evelyn (Fisher) Kuhlemeier, m. Joel Franklin Blake, May 1, 1975; 1 child, Alexander Joel. AA, N. Iowa Area Community Coll., Mason City, 1967; BS, Mankato (Minn.) State Coll., 1969; MS, Mankato (Minn.) State U., 1975. Cert. profl. tchr., Iowa; registered art therapist. Tchr. Bishop Whipple Sch., Faribault, Minn., 1970-72; art therapist C.B. Wilson Ctr., Faribault, 1972-76, Sedgwick County Dept. Mental Health, Wichita, Kans., 1976-79; cons. Batten, Batten, Hudson & Swab, Des Moines, 1979-81; pres. Blake Seminars, Des Moines, 1984—; polit. cons. to Alexander Haig for Pres., 1987-88. Exhibited in one-woman show at local library, 1970. Chmn. U.S. Selective Service Bd. #27, Polk County, Iowa, 1981—; sustaining mem. Rep. Nat. Com.; Rep. candidate Polk County Treas., Des Moines, 1982; chmn. Polk County Rep. Party, 1985-88; commr. Des Moines Commn. Human Rights and Job Discrimination, 1984—; mem. Martin Luther King Scholarship Com., 1986—; mem. Iowa State Bd. Psychology Examiners, 1983—. Mem. Am. Art Therapy Assn., (cert., standards com. 1986—), Am. Soc. Tng. Devel., Iowa Art Therapy Assn. (pres. elect. 1984-85, founder), Iowa Assn. Counseling and Devel. Lutheran. Clubs: Des Moines Garden (pres. 1984-85), Saylorville Yacht (Des Moines) (social chair 1983), Polk County Rep. Women (pres. elect 1983-85). Home: 2802 SW Caulder Des Moines IA 50321

BLAKE, ILENE MILLS, county official; b. Kegley, W.Va., Aug. 31, 1932; d. Ile Sheron and Okley Fay (Reid) Mills; student Concord Coll., 1950-51; B.B.A., George Washington U., 1967; m. Warren Porter Blake, May 24, 1951; children—Ile Wayne, Edward Dean. Adminstrv. asst. Arlington County, Arlington, Va., 1959-67; adminstrv. asst. Fairfax County, Fairfax, Va., 1967-71, budget analyst, 1971-72, budget officer, 1972-73, dir. Office Mgmt. and Budget, 1973—; treas. Blake-Mills Ltd. Founder, bd. dirs. Blake Pvt. Sch., Amigos Taco Hut Inc., MBL Assocs. Mem. Municipal Fin. Officers Assn. Home: 125 Evergreen St Sterling VA 22170

BLAKE, LAURA, architectural designer; b. Berkeley, Calif., Dec. 26, 1959; d. Igor Robert and Elizabeth (Denton) B. BA in Art History, Brown U., 1982; MArch, UCLA, 1985. Cons. Willis & Assocs., San Francisco, 1984-85, IDG Architects, Oakland, Calif., 1985-86; archtl. designer, draftsperson The Ratcliff Architects, Berkeley, 1986—. Organizer charity ball The Spinsters of San Francisco, 1988. Mem. Alpha Rho Chi (Bronze medal 1985). Republican. Episcopalian. Office: The Ratcliff Architects PO Box 1022 Berkeley CA 94701

BLAKE, MARCIA, magazine publisher; b. Chicago, Oct. 10, 1944. Student, Oreg. State U., 1962-63. Freelance writer Tracy, Calif., 1970-77; editor, pub. On the Deck Mag., Sacramento, 1977-82; owner, dir. Blake & Assocs. Advt. and Pub. Relations, Paradise, Calif., 1982-87; managing editor Turbo Technix Mag. div. Borland Internat., Inc., Scotts Valley, Calif., 1987; pub. Turbo Technix Mag. div. Burland Internat., Inc., Scotts Valley, Calif., 1987—; cons. pub. speaking, 1977-82. Pub. relations liaison Theatre in the Ridge, Paradise, 1985-86, Community Auditorium Bldg. Campaign, Paradise, 1985. Mem. Mag. Publishers Assn., Ridge Mchts. and Bus. Assn. (co-founder, bd. dirs. 1984-86). Republican. Episcopalian. Office: Borland Internat 4585 Scotts Valley Dr Scotts Valley CA 95066

BLAKE, MARY HUMPHREY, banker; b. Greensboro, N.C., Sept. 9, 1951; d. Harold Gilmer Humphrey and Julia Ann (Moyer) Humphrey Pace; m. Kenneth Marshall Blake, June 18, 1973 (div.). B.S., U. N.C.-Greensboro, 1973. Exec. sec. Odell Assocs., Inc., Greensboro, N.C., 1973, Am. Bank & Trust Co., Charlotte, N.C., 1973-74, Community Bank of Carolina, Greensboro, 1974-75, W.H. Weaver Constrn., Greensboro, 1975-76, asst. cash mgr. Ashland Exploration, Houston, 1977-80; corp. cash mgr. APS, Inc., Houston, 1980-87; product mgmt. officer First City Nat. Bank, Houston, 1987—. Mem. Nat. Corp. Cash Mgmt. Assn., Houston Corp. Cash Mgmt. Assn., AAUW, LWV. Methodist. Home: 13734 Chancery Rd Houston TX 77034 Office: First City Nat Bank 1001 Main St Houston TX 77002

BLAKE, MARY SUSAN, clinical psychologist; b. Louisville, Ky., Mar. 21, 1951; d. Richard Lee and Martha Helen (Renfro) B. BA magna cum laude, St. Louis U., 1973, MS, 1976, PhD in Clin. Psychology, 1979. Lic. psychologist, Ky., Ohio. Clin. psychologist No. Ky. Comprehensive Care Ctr., Covington, 1980-84; clin. psychologist U. Cin. Psychol. Services Ctr., 1984-88, dir. tng., 1986-88; cons. Women Helping Women, Cin., Ohio, 1986-88. Dancer Flying Cloud Acad. of Vintage Dance, 1982-88. Mem., prison coordinator Amnesty Internat. Group 86, Cin., 1980-88. Mem. Am. Psychol. Assn., Ohio Psychol. Assn., Assn. for Women in Psychology, Phi Beta Kappa, Psi Chi Nat. Honor Soc. Office: U Cin 316 Dyer Hall M L 34 Cincinnati OH 45221

BLAKE, PEGGY ANN, real estate broker; b. Newark, May 18, 1947; d. William Halstead and Mildred (Wallace) Hahn; m. David W. Connors, Dec. 12, 1970 (div. Apr. 1980); children: David W. Jr., Shannon E.; m. Raymond A. Blake, Apr. 11, 1980. Legal sec. Howard and Clancy, Boston, 1966-70, Rabinowitz, Rafel and Swartz, Norfolk, Va., 1971-72; real estate sales rep. Century 21 Executive Realty, Virginia Beach, Va., 1976-77, Blake-Veeder Realty, Glens Falls, N.Y., 1977-81; broker, owner Dyer Blake Real Estate, Glens Falls, Corinth and Saratoga Springs, N.Y., 1981—. Chmn. Am. Heart Assn., Hudson Falls, N.Y., 1985, Washington County, N.Y., 1986, Greenwich, N.Y., 1987. Named Realtor of Yr., Glens Falls Bd. of Realtors, 1987. Mem. Glen Falls Bd. Realtors (pres. 1986-87, Realtor of Yr. 1987), Adirondack Regional C. of C.(chairperson membership com.). Republican. Roman Catholic. Home: 26 School St Hudson Falls NY 12839 Office: Dyer Blake Real Estate 300 Bay Rd Glens Falls NY 12801

BLAKE, ROBERTA SHARON SAVAGE, nurse; b. Scott County, Ill., Jan. 14, 1941; d. Carl Alvin Wesley and Helen Margaret (Price) Savage; R.N., Passavant Meml. Area Hosp., Jacksonville, Ill., 1961; m. Daniel H. Blake, Dec. 27, 1960; children—Heather Anne, Amber Noelle. Staff nurse White Hall (Ill.) Hosp., 1961-75, utilization rev. coordinator, 1976-79, inservice dir., 1979-83, acting dir. nurses, 1979-80, dir. nurses, 1980—, interim adminstr., 1987, asst. adminstr., 1988—. Mem. North Greene Adv. Council, 1976-82; bd. dirs. Two Rivers council Girl Scouts U.S.A., 1978-83, troop leader, 1976-83; mem. nominating com. Two Rivers Council Girl Scouts U.S., 1985-87; mem. Greene County Bd. Health, 1985—; Greene County bd. dirs. Am. Cancer Soc., 1985—. Mem. Ill. Soc. Nurse Adminstrs. Republican. Methodist. Club: Royal Neighbors Lodge. Home: 217 S Carrollton St White Hall IL 62092 Office: 407 N Main St White Hall IL 62092

BLAKELY, CARRELL RAE, metal products company executive; b. Hemingford, Nebr., July 27, 1936; d. Ray Willard and Marjorie Darlene (Carrell) Stull; A.A. in Bus. Adminstrn. and Acctg., Trinidad State Coll., 1974; m. Herbert S. Blakely, Aug. 31, 1972; children by previous marriage—Mickey F. Pugh, Rickey K. Pugh. Various secretarial and bookkeeping positions, 1953-65; legal sec. Wright & Kastler, Raton, N.Mex., 1965-68; pres. Elco Metal Products Corp., Clayton, N.Mex. and Burns Flat, Okla., 1970—. Mem. Nat. Assn. Archtl. Mfrs. Republican. Roman Catholic. Author: True Marriage Vows, 1974. Home: 1005 Jenkins Rd Clayton NM 88415 Office: Elco Metal Products Corp Box 100 Burns Flat OK 73624

BLAKEY, SHERRY LYNN, social psychologist; b. Pontiac, Mich., Oct. 20, 1954; d. David Austin and N. Susan (Skrobeck) B. BS, So. Meth. U., 1976; MA, U. Mo., 1978; postgrad., U. Conn., 1979-81; PhD, Wayne State U., 1988. Research lab. technician Ctr. for Research in Social Behavior, U. Mo., Columbia, 1978-79; spl. research technician Inst. for Social Inquiry/The Roper Ctr., U. Conn., Storrs, 1979-81; instr. psychology Wayne State U., Detroit, 1981-86; instr. tng. courses Chrysler Corp., Highland Park, Mich., 1986-87; needs assessment coordinator community planning and problem solving dept. United Community Services, Detroit, 1986—; research cons. Mich. Bell Telephone Co., Detroit, 1984, Dept. Personnel and Human Resources Wayne County, Mich., 1985, Wayne State U., 1986, Sandy Corp., 1986. Contbr. articles to profl. jours.; speaker in field. Mem. Nat. Assn. Female Execs., Am. Psychol. Assn. (student affiliate), Midwestern Psychol. Assn., Soc. Personality and Social Psychology, Wayne State Grad. Social Psychology Club (pres.), U. Mo. Grad. Sch. and Grad. Student Assn., Psi Chi (pres.), Zelta Tau Alpha (activities and politics chair.). Methodist. Clubs: Motor City Striders, Met. Detroit Downtown Running Group, GM Truck and Bus Racquetball Assn. Office: United Community Services 1212 Griswald at State Detroit MI 48226-1899

BLANCHARD, CATHERINE LEE, insurance executive; b. Rochester, Pa., Nov. 29, 1951; d. Louis Carl and Constance Cecelia (Todd) Braun. BBA, Geneva Coll., 1974; MLS, U. Pitts., 1976. Asst. mgr. CIGNA, Pitts., 1973—. Mem. Am. Mgmt. Assn., Health Ins. Assn. of Am. (sec. Pa. western chpt. 1985—). Presbyterian. Office: Conn Gen Life Ins Co 600 Grant St Suite 1200 Pittsburgh PA 15219

BLANCHARD, HELEN MAE, government official; b. Pender, Nebr., May 17, 1926; d. Frank and Anna Florence (Rihanek) Pallas; m. John J. Blanchard, June 25, 1946; (dec. June 1974); children—Bruce Alan, Cheryl Ann Sonnenwald. Phys. sci. technologist Navy Electronics Lab., San Diego, 1960-75; supervisory sci. technologist Naval Ocean Systems Ctr., San Diego, 1975-83, communications specialist, 1983-84, head visitors info. and presentations br., 1984-85, head tech. info. dir., 1985—. Author numerous tech. reports on fleet tests. Named Woman of Yr., Navy Electronics Lab., 1971. Mem. Nat. Speakers Assn., San Diego Navy League, Profl. Speakers Assn., Save Our Heritage Assn., Toastmasters Internat. (dist. gov. 1976-77, internat. dir. 1978-80, 3d v.p. 1982-83, 2d v.p. 1983-84, sr. v.p. 1984-85, pres. 1985-86). Office: Naval Ocean Systems Ctr San Diego CA 92152

BLANCHARD, LINDA LEA, import and export company executive; b. Wessington Springs, S.D., Oct. 18, 1948; d. Lee Miles and Irene Ruth (Tschetter) Scott; m. Charles Hadley Blanchard; children: Charles Hadley Jr., Joseph Miles. BA in Religion, U. Minn., 1974. Hatha Yoga teaching staff, sec. Himalayan Internat. Inst. Yoga, Sci. and Philosophy, Honesdale, Pa., 1971—; bd. dirs. East-West Books, Inc., N.Y.C., 1979-87; trustee Himalayan Inst. Edn., Honesdale, 1986—; ptnr. India Imports, Honesdale, 1979—. Author: Hatha Yoga Manual 1, 1977, Hatha Yoga Manual 2, 1978. Home: Rural Rt 1 Box 400 Honesdale PA 18431 Office: Himalayan Internat Inst Rural Rt 1 Box 400 Honesdale PA 18431

BLANCHARD, NORMA JEAN, service company manager; b. Hickory, N.C., Sept. 26, 1940; d. Ray Brittian and Ethel Pauline (Miller) Cooke; m. Robert Brent Drum, June 22, 1958 (div. 1970); children: Kathy Jean, Michael Robert, Martha Rae; m. Calvin L. Blanchard, 1973 (div. 1979). Student, Catawba Valley Tech. Coll., 1968. Br. exec. dir. Am. Cancer Soc., Hickory, 1969-70; cons., treas. Personnel Registry, Hickory, 1970-78; br. mgr. Manpower Temporary Services, Hickory, 1980—. Active Am. Cancer Soc., 1967—; organizer Compassionate Friends Group, 1979; mem. Hickory Rep. Women's Club, 1975—. Mem. Catawba County C. of C. (numerous offices), Women's Resource Exchange. Republican. Lutheran. Home: 1743 39th St NE Hickory NC 28601 Office: Manpower Temporary Services Hickory NC 28602

BLANCHARD WILDMAN, SUZANNE, composer, educator; b. Boston, Jan. 4, 1940; d. Wells and Helen Lane Blanchard; grad. San Francisco Conservatory Music, Vocal major, 1957; A.B., Classics, Stanford U., 1958; m. Ben. H. Wildman, July 28, 1952 (div. 1958); children—Helen LeRoy, Benjamin Henry, Ludwig Altmann. Concert pianist, performing at Palace of Legion of Honor, San Francisco, 1961, Temple Emmanuel, San Francisco, 1961, Meml. Ch., Stanford U., 1962; tchr. elem. piano San Francisco Conservatory, 1963-64. Foster parent Operation Happy Child, Taiwan; active Met. Opera Raffle, UNICEF; mem. Republican Town Com., Manchester, Mass. Mem. Am. Security Council, Manchester Hist. Soc., Stanford U. Alumni Assn. Republican. Christian Scientist. Clubs: Pebble Beach (Carmel, Calif.); Singing Beach Beach (Manchester); Revolutionary Ridge Book (Concord, Mass.). Composer: The Governor Proposes, 1962, additional scenes, 1985; Five Christmas Duets for Teacher and Beginner, Preludes 1-3, Fugue, 1962, Prelude 4, 1984, Julia Song Cycle for Robert Herrick North Shore Community Coll. Sch. of Music, 1984, ballet suite The Leonardo, 1987, (background music for TV prodn.) Preview of Shakespeare in Camelot, 1988. Home: 27 Pine St Manchester-by-the Sea MA 01944 Office: University Ln Manchester MA 01944

BLANCHET, JEANNE E. MAXANT, artist, educator, performer; b. Chgo., Sept. 25, 1944; d. William H. and L. Barbara (Martin) Maxant; m. Yasuo Shimizu, Apr. 28, 1969 (div. 1973); m. William B. Blanchet, Aug. 21, 1981. BA summa cum laude, Northwestern U., 1966; MFA, Tokyo Fine Arts U., 1971; MA, Ariz. State U., 1978; postgrad., Ill. State U., 1979-80. Instr. Tsuda U., Kodaira, Japan, 1970-71; free-lance visual, performing artist various cities, U.S., 1973—; artist in residence YMCA of the Rockies, Estes Park, Colo., 1976-81 summers; prof. fine arts Rio Salado Coll., Sun City, Ariz., 1976—; lectr. Ariz. State U. (West), Sun City, 1985—. Author: Original Songs and Verse of the Old (and New) West, 1987, A Song in My Heart, 1988; contbr. articles to newspapers, jours., 1975—; writer/artist The Wester, Sun City West, 1987—; featured entertainer Seafare Atlantic, Phoenix, 1975-78. Founding mem. Del Webb Hosp. Woodrow Wilson fellow, 1966; recipient numerous art, music awards including 2d in Show Tokyo Budokan Exhbn., 1970. Mem. Nat. League Am. Pen Women (sec. chpt. 1987—, v.p. 1988—), Nat. Art Edn. Assn., Nat. Rifle Assn. (disting. expert 1983), Ariz. Press Women (4 awards in original graphics and writing 1988), Nat. Fedn. Press Women, Northwestern U.'s John Evans Club, Henry W. Rogers Soc. Phi Beta Kappa. Roman Catholic. Office: Rio Salado Coll Area West 10451 Palmeras Dr Sun City AZ 85373

BLANCK, BARBARA ANNE, financial services analyst; b. N.Y.C., Dec. 14, 1951; d. Arthur and Rhoda (Shapiro) B. BA in History, SUNY Albany, 1973; MA in History, U. Mass., 1974; paralegal cert., Adelphi U., 1976. Law librarian, paralegal G & W Industries Inc., N.Y.C., 1974-79; paralegal, legis. asst. MasterCard Internat. Inc., N.Y.C., 1979-84; sr. analyst fin. services Stroock & Stroock & Lavan, Washington, 1984—. Contbr. articles to profl. jours. Mem. Women in Housing and Fin. (chmn. pub. relations com. 1987—). Democrat. Jewish. Office: Stroock & Stroock & Lavan 1150 17th St NW Washington DC 20036

BLANCO, AMANDA, photographer; b. San Salvador, El Salvador, Oct. 23, 1933; d. Felix and Julia Isabel (Raimundo) Blanco; M.F.A., Calif. Inst. Arts, 1981; B. Profl. Arts, Inst. Photography, Santa Barbara, Calif., 1971; m. Mario Escobar (div. 1966); children—Maurice, César-E., Rosa Eugenia, and Rocio E. Blanco. Instr., Calif. State U., Northridge, 1977-79; asst. course organizer Calif. Inst. Arts, Valencia, 1980-81; faculty Idyllwild Sch. Music and Arts, 1980-82; exhibits: U. Calif., Northridge, Getty Mus., Los Angeles Mus. Sci. and Industry, other galleries and mus.; free lance photographer, Los Angeles, 1981—. Ahmanson Found. scholar, 1980; Lew and Eddie Wasserman scholar, 1979. Mem. Calif. Women Higher Edn. (exec. bd. 1975-78), AAUW, Profl. Photographers Am. Club: Rounce and Coffin. Author: The Many Faces of Jake Zeitlin, 1978; About Norman Corwin, 1980; Richard Hoffman at Seventy, 1982; Isomata: The Place and Its People, 1983, Ward Ritchie, 1987. Home and Office: 10551 Yarmouth Ave Granada Hills CA 91344

BLANCO, ANNA, publishing company executive; b. Havana, Cuba, June 14, 1955; came to U.S., 1961; d. Jose and Aracelia (Beltran) B. BA in English, CUNY, 1979; MBA in Mktg., Pace U., 1987. Asst. editor Us Mag., N.Y.C., 1981-83; publicity dir. US Mag., N.Y.C., 1985-86; dir. spl. projects Macfadden Holdings, Inc., N.Y.C., 1986—. Mem. Am. Mktg. Assn. Democrat. Office: Macfadden Holdings Inc 215 Lexington Ave New York NY 10016

BLAND, BARBARA VANCE, nurse; b. Hardinsburg, Ky., Aug. 17, 1940; d. Fred and Eula (Blair) Vance. Diploma, Ky. Bapt. Hosp. Sch. Nursing, 1961; BS in Nursing, Bellarmine Coll., 1982. Staff nurse Ky. Bapt. Hosp./Bapt. Hosp. East, Louisville, 1962-76, advanced level staff nurse, 1976-80, nursing quality assurance coordinator, 1980—; mem. adv. panel quality assurance task force Am. Coll. Ob-gyn., 1985. Mem. Nurses Assn. of Am. Coll. Obstetricians nd Gynecologists (pres. 1976, chairperson Ky. sect. 1971-72), Nat. Assn. Quality Assurance Profls., Ky. Assn. Quality Assurance Profls. (v.p. 1986-87), Assn. Operating Room Nurses (bd. dirs. 1978-79), Kappa Gamma Pi. Office: Bapt Hosp East 4000 Kresge Way Louisville KY 40207

BLAND, EVELINE MAE, real estate corporation officer; b. Hughsville, Pa., Aug. 24, 1939; d. Burton Anthony and Mary Margaret (Mack) Morgan; m. Theodore D. Bland; 1 child, Susanna Elisabeth. BA, Mansfield (Pa.) U., 1961; Orff Schulwerk cert., Royal Conservatory, Toronto, Can., 1976. Tchr. Newburgh (N.Y.) Jr. High Sch., 1961-62, Cedar Grove (N.J.) Bd. Edn., 1962-66, West Caldwell (N.J.) Bd. Edn., 1973-76, Covenant Christian Sch., N. Plainfield, N.J., 1976-77; salesperson Janett Realtors, Verona, N.J., 1977-79; sales mgr. Degnan Boyle Realtors, Caldwell, 1979-88, Schlott Realtors, Montclair, 1988—; prin. Camp Shawnee, Waymart, Pa., 1961-71. Organist, choir dir. 1st Conglist. Ch., Verona, 1978—; bd. trustees Montclair Hist. Soc., 1970. Mem. Nat. Realtors Assn. (cert.), N.J. Assn. Realtors (profl. standards and edn. coms.1987), West Essex Bd. Realtors (v.p., sec. 1985-86, pres. 1987, career trainer 1987, Realtor of Yr. 1987), West Essex C. of C., Lambda Mu. Republican. Baptist. Lodge: Gideons Aux. (various offices 1982-87).

BLAND, HELEN FAY, retired manufacturing executive; b. Eldorado Springs, Mo., Aug. 21, 1921; d. Walter Fred and Bertha Fern (Fowler) Davis; m. Len W. Bland, July 4, 1942. Student, S.W. Mo. State U. Tchr. Country Rural Sch., Eldorado Springs, 1938-42; with Hallmark Cards Inc., Kansas City, Mo., 1942—, sec., 1943-63, asst. fleet mgr., 1963-69, fleet mgr., 1969—. Mem. Nat. Assn. Fleet Adminstrs. (vice chairperson Mid-Am. chpt. 1973-74, 75-76, sec. 1977-78, 3d v.p. 1979-80, 2d v.p. 1981-82, 1st v.p. 1983-84, pres. 1985-86, Disting. Service award 1981), Jackson County Rose Soc., Johnson County Rose Soc. Republican. Mem. Ch. of God. Home: 10111 E 69th Terr Raytown MO 64133

BLANDIN, NANETTE MARIE, political scientist; b. Seattle, May 10, 1948; d. J. Julien and Evelyn B. Baget; m. Don Michael Blandin, Sept. 2, 1972. Diplome, Institut d'Etudes Politques Universite de Bordeaux (France), 1969; BA in Polit. Sci. and French with honors, U. Calif., Davis, 1970; MPA, Washington Pub. Affairs Ctr. U. So. Calif., 1976. Hdqrs. personnel officer Dept. Mental Hygiene, Sacramento, 1970-72; program dir. Calif. Adv. Coordinating Council Pub. Personnel Mgmt., Sacramento, 1972; budget examiner, mgmt. analystExec. Office Pres. Office Mgmt. Budget, Washington, 1973-79; spl. asst. to insp. gen. Dept. Labor, Washington, 1979-80; chief div. assessment and tech. dir. div. program and policy assessment Office of Insp. Gen., Washington, 1980-84; sr. staff mem. Ctr. Pub. Policy Edn. The Brookings Instn., Washington, 1984—; founder, co-chmn. Washington Young Profls Forum, 1974-76; bd. dirs. Nat. Ctr. Pub. Services Internship Programs, 1972-73; prof. adv. bd. George Mason U., 1978-79. Contbr. articles in field; bd. editors Pub. Adminstr. Rev.; bd. dirs., series editor The Bureaucrat. Mem. Am. Soc. Pub. Adminstrn. (chmn. fin. and adminstrn. com. 1979-80, nat. council 1978-81, v.p. Nat. Capital Area chpt., Leadership award Nat. Capital Area 1978), World Future Soc., Pi Sigma Alpha (life). Home: 1913 Shepherd St NW Washington DC 20011 Office: 1775 Massachusetts Ave NW Washington DC 20036

BLANDING, CAROL YOUNG, accountant; b. Burlington, N.C., June 10, 1954; d. Alan Nelson and Olga Marion (Harcovitz) Young; m. Donald Sly Blanding, Feb. 25, 1978; children: Trevor Alan, Kendall Jackson. BS in Acctg., Va. Polytech. Inst. and State U., 1976. CPA, Va. Fin. analyst ITT Electro Optical Products, Roanoke, Va., 1976-78; acct. Ernst & Whinney, Roanoke, 1978-81; mgr. fin. rev., analysis Dominion Bankshares Corp., Roanoke, 1981-86, regulatory reporting for mergers, 1986—. Treas. Women of St. Elizabeth's Ch., Roanoke, 1985-86. Fellow Am. Inst. CPA's, Va. Soc. CPA's, Nat. Assn. Accts. Episcopal. Club: Brambleton Jr. Women's. Office: Dominion Bankshares Corp 213 S Jefferson St Roanoke VA 24040

BLANE, BRENDA JO, social services organization executive; b. Louisville, Sept. 3, 1945; d. Rozelle F. and Johneva (Owsley) Poignard; m. Doye E. Blane, June 10, 1967; children: Doye Anton, Crystal Shaton. BS, Ky. State U., 1967; MEd, Miami U., Oxford, Ohio, 1976. Cert. tchr., Ohio. Computer specialist Wright Patterson AFB (Ohio), 1967-70; tchr. Dayton pub. schs. (Ohio), 1971-79; spl. services coordinator Atlanta U., 1979-80; project dir. Urban League, Dayton, 1980-81, v.p. adminstrn., 1980-84, interim pres., 1984-85; community relations and youth adv. Dayton Pub. Schs., 1985-87; cons. Bd. dirs. Montgomery County Devel. Corp., Miami Valley Regional Planning Commn. (Ohio), Agy. of United Way Execs., Annie E. Casey Planning Com., Leadership Dayton.; exec. dir. YWCA of Dayton, 1987—. Grantee Ednl. Policy Fellows Program, George Washington U., 1981; recipient Leadership Dayton 83 award, 1983. Mem. Miami Valley Personnel Com., Alpha Kappa Alpha. Lodge: Kiwanis. Home: 3564 Cornell Dr Dayton OH 45406

BLANEY, CAROL ANN, mortgage banking company executive; b. Cheltenham, Eng., Mar. 15, 1946; came to U.S., 1952; d. Matthew Francis and Noan (Barker) B.; m. James Lenners, Jan. 16, 1965 (div. Oct. 1980); children: Gregory M., Kathryn M. Lenners McCabe. Student, Anchorage Community Coll., 1974-82; mortgage banker's cert., Northwestern U., 1979; comml. banking cert., U. Wash., 1982. Mgr. mortgage servicing, v.p. Nat. Bank Alaska, Anchorage, 1973-84; mgr. mortgage lending, v.p. United Bank Alaska, Anchorage, 1984-88; owner, pres. Mgmt. Solutions, Alamogordo, N.Mex., 1988—; cons. on mortgage system devel. M&I Software Devel., Milw. Mem. Nat. Assn. Bank Women, Nat. Assn. Female Execs. Republican. Office: Mgmt Solutions PO Box 1310 Alamogordo MN 88310

BLANKE, GAIL ANN, communications executive; b. Cleve., Jan. 20, 1941; d. Warren J. and Isabelle (Voigt) B.; m. Franklin James Cusick, Feb. 22, 1969; children—Katharine Jennings, Abigail Jennings. A.B., Sweet Briar Coll., 1963. Mgr., Lifetime Sports Found., Washington, 1965-66, CBS, N.Y.C., 1966-69; v.p. Allen & Dorwood Advt., N.Y.C., 1969-72; v.p. communications Avon Products, Inc., N.Y.C., 1972—. Mem. Am. Women in Radio and TV (bd. dirs. 1971), Internat. Assn. Bus. Communicators, Soc. of Mayflower Desendants. Clubs: Metropolitan (N.Y.C.); Lawrence Beach (L.I., N.Y.); Rockaway Hunt (Cedarhurst, N.Y). Office: Avon Products Inc 9 W 57th St New York NY 10019

BLANKENBAKER, VIRGINIA MURPHY, state legislator; b. Indpls., Mar. 29, 1933; d. Charles J. and Francis June (Hesler) Murphy; m. Richard Blankenbaker, 1959; children: Susan, Sharon, David, Betty, James. BS, Purdue U., 1955; MS, Butler U., 1979. Tchr. Pensacola, 1955-56, Indpls., 1976-81; in pub. relations Colonial Food Store, 1957-59; sec., treas. Richards Market Baskets, Inc., 1961—; mem. Ind. State Senate, 1981—. Republican. Methodist. Office: 5019 N Meridian St Indianapolis IN 46208 •

BLANKENHEIMER, SUSAN LESLIE, lawyer; b. Washington, Aug. 25, 1952; d. Bernard and Rosalind (Drescher) B.; m. Joseph J. Geraci, Jan. 9, 1982. Student Johannesburg, South Africa, 1968-70, London Polytech. 1973; B.A. with honors, Syracuse U., 1974; J.D., Vanderbilt U., 1977. Bar: Pa. 1979, U.S. Ct. Appeals (D.C. cir.) 1980, U.S. Ct. Appeals (fed. cir.) 1982, D.C. 1984, N.Y. 1984, U.S. Supreme Ct. 1984. Law clk. Presdl. Clemency Bd., White House, Washington, summer 1975, FCC, Washington, summer 1976, Office Opinions and Rev., FCC, Washington, 1977-78; atty. CAB, Washington, 1979-84; atty. Law Dept. Comptroller of the Currency, Washington, 1985—. Assoc. editor Vanderbilt Jour. Transnat. Law, 1975-76, contbr. articles to law jour. Mem. Fed. Bar Assn., D.C. Bar Assn., Eta Pi Upsilon, Pi Sigma Alpha, Alpha Chi Omega. Club: Internat. Aviation (Washington). Home: 5413 Duvall Dr Bethesda MD 20816 Office: Comptroller of the Currency Law Dept 490 L'Enfant Plaza E SW Washington DC 20219

BLANKENSHIP, CHERYL KAY, health care administrator, educator; b. Fargo, N.D., July 12, 1946; d. Carl Albert and Ruth Pauline (Pribbernow) Freeberg; m. Charles P. Berry, Dec. 18, 1965 (div. 1973); 1 child, Craig; m. Dennis Michael Blankenship, May 14, 1977; children: Michael, Ross. BA, Gustavus Adolphus Coll., 1966; BS in Med. Record Adminstrn., Coll. St. Mary, 1974; MS in Health Care Adminstrn., U. Nebr., 1977. Tchr. Fargo Pub. Sch. System, 1966-70; asst. prof. U. Nebr. Med. Ctr., Omaha, 1974-77; instr. Metro Community Coll., Omaha, 1975-77; adminstr. Baylor Med. Ctr., Dallas, 1977-81; instr. Tex. Women's U., Dallas and Denton, 1980-81; adminstr. Texarkana (Ark.) Kidney Disease and Hypertension Ctr., Inc., 1984—, also bd. dirs.; instr., advisor Texarkana Community Coll., 1986—; cons. Omaha Home for Girls, 1974-76. Participant panel TV program Youth Wants to Know, 1987; dir., author instructional film A Medical Secretary, 1976; contbr. articles to profl. jours. Chpt. sec. Am. Diabetes Assn., Texarkana, 1986—, pres., 1987&; mem. exec. bd. Bowie-Miller County Med. Aux., Texarkana, 1986—; chpt. exec. com. Nat. Kidney Found., 1985—; mem. Women for Arts., 1985—, Mother-to-Mother Group, 1983. Recipient Fishel Askanase award Askanase Family, 1962. Mem. Nat. Renal Adminstrs Assn. (govt. affairs com. 1988), Am. Med. Record Assn., NEA (faculty del. 1969), Nat. Dialysis Assn. (bd. dirs. Washington hdqtrs. 1986—). Roman Catholic. Home: 6205 Stoneridge Dr Texarkana TX 75503 Office: Texarkana Kidney Disease Hypertension 422 Beech St Texarkana AR 75502

BLANKENSHIP, JENNY MARY, marketing company executive, fund raiser; b. Mpls., Nov. 15, 1955. AA, Weatherford Coll., Tex., 1984; BBA, U. Tex.-Arlington, 1986. List acquisition coordinator Fingerhut, Minnetonka, Minn., 1978-80; pub. relations Family Service, Ft. Worth, 1983-85; dir. pub. relations Hope, Inc., Mineral Wells, Tex., 1985-86; pres. Gloss Mgmt., Arlington, Tex., 1986—. Author: Are We Having Fun Yet?, Poetry of the Old Testament; copy editor Crossroads newspaper; contbr. articles to profl. jours. bd. dirs. Social Service Bd., Weatherford, 1985-86. Mem. Nat. Assn. Female Execs., Women In Communication Inc., Network for Exec. Women, Mensa, Phi Theta Kappa, Jaycees. Clubs: UMW (pres. 1984-88), Civic (officer 1985-86) (Weatherford). Avocations: painting, singing.

BLANKENSHIP, LINDA MANLEY, safety engineer; b. Knoxville, Tenn., Mar. 1, 1939; s. Hal Clinton and Katherine (Lee) Manley; children from previous marriage: D. Lynn Spruill, Frank C. Spruill III; m. John Guy Blankenship, June 6, 1978. BA, U. Tenn., 1976; MPH in Environ., Occupational Health and Safety, 1983. Cert. accident investigator. Safety analyst Martin Marietta Energy Systems, Inc., Oak Ridge, 1978-84, safety engr., 1984—; chmn. off-the-job safety standing com. Nat. Safety Council, Chgo., 1985—, mem. programming/communications com., 1984—, indsl. div. mem.-at-large, 1985—, chem. sect., 1986—; conv. speaker on off-the-job injury econs. Nat. Safety Congress, Chgo., 1984, San Francisco, 1988, Western N.Y. Safety Conf., Buffalo, 1985, on accident investigation techniques Tenn. Safety Congress, Nashville, 1987. Mem. Am. Soc. Safety Engrs. (sec. East Tenn. chpt. 1983-84, chmn. tech. session 1984, v.p. 1984-85, pres. 1985-86, Safety Profl. of Yr. award 1985, Region VII Safety Profl. of Yr. award

1986), Am. Nat. Standards Inst. (Z16.3 standards revision com. ad hoc mem. 1987-88) Club: Martin Marietta Energy Systems Toastmasters (Oak Ridge). Avocations: reading, travel, bridge, photography. Home: 101 Umbria Ln Oak Ridge TN 37830 Office: Martin Marietta Energy Systems I Y-12 Plant Bldg 9116 MS 8098 PO Box 2009 Oak Ridge TN 37831

BLANKINSHIP, KATHLEEN FLO, personal and professional development company executive, cleaning service executive, cosmetologist; b. Loma Linda, Calif., Nov. 5, 1947; d. Boyde Jefferson and Nell (Miller) Henderson; m. Floyd Jerome Smith, Oct. 25, 1969 (div. 1972); m. 2d Edwin Allen Blankinship, Oct. 15, 1977; 1 child, Robert Allen Smith. Cert. bookkeeping/acctg. Calif. Bus. Sch., San Bernardino, 1966; AA, San Bernardino Valley Coll., 1975; student Riverside (Calif.) City Coll., 1985. Lic. Cosmetologist. Bookkeeper Laurentide Fin. Co., San Bernardino, 1969-70; loan officer Avco Thrift, San Bernardino, 1972-74; waitress Agro Land & Cattle, [illegible] 1976-80; stylist, mgr. Mane St. Hair Design, Loma Linda, Calif., 1980-83; owner, profl. speaker, cons. U.&I Enterprises, Grand Terrace, Calif., 1983—; organizational analyst Pomona Valley Praise Temple, Calif., 1985—; rep. Equitable Life Assurance Soc. U.S., 1986—; mentor Positive Force, Highland, Calif., 1985—; owner Higher Image Hair, Riverside, 1988—; fin. cons. BancVest Fin. Services Inc., 1986; stylist Ann & Friends, 1987. Author: Seasons of My Times, 1980, Winning Isn't For Everyone, 1986; contbr. monthly make-over column to mag., 1980-83. Mem. Vols. in Child Abuse and Neglect, 1978; campaign worker McCartney for Judge, 1969-70; Trainer Choices Program Riverside County Sch. Dist., 1987. Mem. Nat. Assn. Female Execs., Equitable Life Assurance Soc. U.S. (registered rep.), Women in Networking, Greater Riverside C. of C. (bd. dirs. 1986—, chmn. Bus. in Action, chmn. edn. com. 1987—), Redlands C. of C. (ambassador). Republican. Club: S.B. Pro-Club (bd. dirs.). Lodge: Toastmasters. Avocations: skiing, reading, personal development. Home: 12168 Mt Vernon St #51 Grand Terrace CA 92324 Office: U & I Enterprises PO Box 1737 Colton CA 92324

BLANKS, ARLENE LYNNETTE, lawyer; b. Washington, June 6, 1950; d. Isaac Renell and Elouise (Curry) Blanks; m. Donald W. Robinson, Aug. 1, 1980 (div. 1986). B.A., Wayne State U., 1977, J.D., 1980. Bar: Mich. 1981; Ill. 1982; Tex. 1983. Assoc., Baxter & Hammond, Grand Rapids, Mich., 1980-81; law clerk to presiding justice U.S. Dist. Ct., Houston, 1982-83; staff trial atty CNA Ins. Co., Houston, 1983-85; assoc. McLain, Cage, Hill & Niehaus, Houston, 1986—; adj. prof. law U. Houston, 1984—. Active Democratic Party, Detroit, 1982. Recipient Bd. Gov.'s scholarship Wayne State U., 1979. Mem. State Bar Assn. Tex., State Bar Assn. Mich., Ill. State Bar Assn., ABA, Am. Judicature Soc. Congregationalist. Office: McLain Cage Hill & Niehaus Suite 800 6363 Woodway Houston TX 77057

BLANKSTEIN, MARY FREEMAN, violinist; b. Rutherfordton, N.C., Oct. 26; d. Spurgeon Lee and Dexter (Forney) Freeman; diploma (Scholar) Juilliard Sch. Music, 1955, BS, 1958; student (Fulbright fellow) Brussels Conservatoire, 1958-59; MusM, U. Maine, 1975; student Emmett Gore, Christine and Edouard Dethier, Arthur Grumiaux, Joseph Fuchs, Erica Morini, others; m. Joseph Blankstein, Mar. 6, 1958; children: Margot, Philip. Violin soloist Little Orch. Soc. in Town Hall, 1955; asst. concertmaster Am. Symphony, N.Y.C., 1965-68, concertmaster, 1968-72; tchr. violin, prep. div. Juilliard Sch. Music, N.Y.C., 1968-69; tchr. violin Manhattan Sch. Music, 1969-85; pvt. tchr. violin and chamber music, 1970—; head instrumental dept. Chapin Sch., N.Y.C., 1973-88; co-founder, mem. N.Y. Lyric Arts Trio, 1974-84; solo recitals, U.S. and Europe; co-founder Downeast Chamber Music Center, Castine, Maine, 1977; faculty Downeast Chamber Music Ctr.; rec. artist Musical Heritage Soc. Rec., also recs. with Am. Symphony under Leopold Stokowski. Mem. Am. String Tchrs. Assn., Music Tchrs. Nat. Assn. Club: Bohemians. Home: 55 East End Ave Apt 5L New York NY 10028

BLANSFIELD, CATHERINE GOSS, sales executive; b. Danbury, Conn., Dec. 13, 1954; d. Henry Nelson and Lorraine (Lombardi) Blansfield. BSN, U. Vt., 1976. Staff nurse Beth Israel Hosp., Boston, 1976-77, charge nurse intensive care unit, 1977-78, nurse clinician, 1978-81; profl. sales rep. Bristol Labs., Warwick, R.I., 1983-84; territory mgr., mgr. sales devel. and tele-sales critical care div. Baxter-Edwards, Irvine, Calif., 1984—. Mem. Humane Soc., Sierra Club, Nature Conservancy, NOW. Democrat. Roman Catholic. Home: 1 Evening Shadow Irvine CA 92715 Office: Baxter-Edwards 17221 Red Hill Ave Irvine CA 92711-1150

BLANTON, JUDITH ANN, insurance company executive; b. Charleston, W.Va., May 28, 1943; d. Sheldon Ellsworth and Hilda Jean (Stone) Stanley; m. Blaine Blanton, Jr., May 13, 1966; 1 child, Kimberly Ann. AB in Math., Ind. U., 1965; cert. CPCU, Am. Inst. for Property and Liability Underwriters, Malvern, Pa., 1983; cert. CLU, Am. Coll., 1987. Tchr. math. Med. Sch. Dist. Wayne Twp., Indpls., 1965-66, Met. Sch. Dist. Lawrence Twp., Indpls., 1966-67, Lebanon (Ind.) Community Sch. Corp., 1972-76; with systems/programming Am. States Ins. Co., Indpls., 1976—. Mem. Soc. CPCU's. Office: Am States Ins 500 N Meridian ST Indianapolis IN 46207

BLANTON, SHIRLEY ANN, manufacturing official; b. Connersville, Ind., Nov. 6, 1949; d. Lawrence Michael and Catherine Ann (Pflum) Risch; B.S. in Prodn. Mgmt. (Hoosier scholar), Ball State U., Muncie, Ind., 1982; m. Randell Blanton, Apr. 20, 1968; children—James Randell, Angela Marie. Sec. purchasing Stant Mfg., Connersville, 1968-72; sec. customer service H.H. Robertson, Connersville, 1974-77, prodn. control coordinator, supr., 1977-81, mgr. prodn. control, 1981-84, mgr. material control, 1984-86; supr. straight sales, scheduling, 1986-87; adminstr., Connersville Engring. Services, Inc., 1987—. Supr. Fayette County Girls Club; com. Fayette County blood drives, Fayette County Investment Club. Mem. Golden Key, Beta Gamma Sigma. Roman Catholic. Club: K.C. Aux. Home: Route 1 Box 108 Connersville IN 47331 Office: 800 W 18th St Connersville IN 47331

BLASKO, JANICE MARIE, marketing professional; b. Homestead, Pa., Jan. 30, 1958; d. Julius James and Irene Marie (Chorba) B. Lic. pvt. pilot. Coordinator constrn. Catalina Homes, Orlando, Fla., 1982-84; regional mgr. Avian Corp., Orlando, 1984-86; mgr. sales, mktg. Hangar One Inc., Orlando, 1986—. Vol. Goals 2000 Arts Task Force, Orlando, 1987—; scouting coordinator Boy Scouts Am. Mem. Greater Orlando C. of C., Tampa C. of C., Fla. Bus. Travel Assn. Roman Catholic. Club: Aviation Council (Orlando) (sec. 1986-87). Home: 421 Poplar Ct Maitland FL 32751 Office: Hangar One Inc 600 Herndon Ave Orlando FL 32803

BLASSINGAME, SANDRA LOU, nurse, educator, university dean; b. Dallas, Nov. 8, 1937; d. James and Jessie (Leonard) Sears; B.S.N., Baylor U., 1960; M.S., Tex. Women's U., 1970; Ed.D., Nova U., 1980; m. Kenneth E. Blassingame, Sept. 27, 1963. Instr., Meth. Hosp. Sch. Nursing, Dallas, 1960-70; asst. prof. Dallas Bapt. U. Sch. Nursing, 1970-74, assoc. prof., 1974-81, prof., 1981—, dean Sch. Nursing, 1970—, assoc. dean acad. programs, 1981-82, dean acad. affairs, 1982—, acting v.p./dean of coll., 1984-85. Mem. Dist. 4 Tex. Nurses Assn. (dir. 1980-84), Tex. Nurses Assn. (dir., sec. 1982-84), Am. Nurses Assn., Nat. League for Nursing, Sigma Theta Tau. Democrat. Baptist. Club: Altrusa. Home: 6227 Highgate Ln Dallas TX 75214

BLATT, GENEVIEVE, state judge; b. East Brady, Pa., June 19, 1913; d. George F. and Clara (Laurent) B. AB, U. Pitts., 1933, MA, 1934, JD, 1937; LLD (hon.), St. Francis Coll., 1959, Villanova U., 1960, St. Joseph's U., 1964, Barry Coll., 1966, Seton Hill Coll., 1968, LaSalle U., 1970, Elizabethtown Coll., 1974, Dickinson Coll. Law, 1974, York (Pa.) Coll., 1975, St. Charles Sem., 1975, Cedarcrest Coll., 1976, Allentown Coll. of St. Francis de Sales, 1976, Shippensburg U., 1987, Wilson Coll., 1987. Bar: Pa. 1938. Mem. faculty U. Pitts., 1934-38; sec., chief examiner Pitts. CSC, 1938-42; asst. solicitor City of Pitts., 1942-45; dep. treas. State of Pa., 1945, exec. dir. treasury dept., 1945-49, sec. internal affairs, 1955-67; asst. dir. Pres.'s Office Econ. Opportunity, Washington, 1967-68; spl. counsel Shared Services Assn., Daus. of Charity, 1968-71; dir. departmental audits Pa. Auditor Gen.'s Office, 1969; counsel to Morgan, Lewis & Bockius, Attys., 1970-72; judge Commonwealth Ct. Pa., 1972-83, sr. judge, 1983—; founder, exec. dir. Pa. Intercollegiate Conf. on Govt., 1934-72; mem. Pa. Bd. Pardons, 1955-67; sec. Pa. Indsl. Devel. Authority Bd. and Gen. State Authority Bd., 1956-67; Pa. del. to Interstate Oil Compact Commn., 1955-67, vice chmn., 1959-60; mem. weights and measures adv. com. Nat. Bur. Standards, 1960-67; mem. adv. com. women in armed services Def. Dept., 1964-67; mem. Pres.'s Consumer Adv. Council, 1964-66, Pres.'s Commn. on Law Enforcement and Adminstrn. Justice, 1965-67. Bd. dirs. Center for Research in Apostolate, 1972-75, 80-85, vice chmn., 1972-75; mem. adv. council Nat. Conf. Catholic Bishops, 1972-75; mem. Nat. Bishops Bicentennial Com., 1974-76; chmn. Harrisburg Diocesan Bicentennial Com., 1974-76; Sec. Pa. Democratic Com., 1948-70; Dem. nominee for auditor gen. Pa., 1952; pres. Young Dem. Clubs Pa., 1942-50; exec. bd. Pa. Fedn. Dem. Women, 1940-72; del. Dem. Nat. Convs., 1936-68; Dem. nominee for U.S. Senate, 1964; Dem. nat. committeewoman Pa., 1970-72; fellow Harry S Truman Library, Lyndon B. Johnson Library; founder, v.p. James A. Finnegan Fellowship Found., 1960—; bd. mgrs. 41st Internat. Eucharistic Congress, 1975-76. Recipient Disting. Dau. of Pa. award, 1956, Mother Gerard Phelan Gold medal Marymount Coll., 1965, Elizabeth Seton medal Seton Hill Coll., 1960, Pro Ecclesia et Pontifice medal Pope Paul VI, 1966, Louise de Marillac medal St. Joseph's Coll., 1966, Dubois medal Mt. St. Mary Coll., 1970, St. Thomas More Legal award City of Pitts., 1974, FAME award Greater Phila. Women's Clubs, 1978, Elizabeth Ann Seton medal St. John's U., 1978—, Benemerenti Gold medal Pope John Paul II, 1979, Govtl. Service citation Pa. Elected Women's Assn., 1983, Service to Women award Pa. Commn. for Women, 1987, Bicentennial medal of distinction U. Pitts., 1987; named Woman of Yr. in Govt., City of Pitts., 1959, Woman of Yr. in Nat. Govt., 1963, Woman of Yr., Pa. Fedn. Bus. and Profl. Women's Clubs, 1972, one of Foremost Women of 20th Century, City of Cambridge, Eng., 1987, Woman of Yr., Monday Club of Harrisburg, 1988, Outstanding Service award Pa. Bar Assn., 1988; featured in TV film documentary: An Uncommon Woman, 1988. Mem. Am. Bar Found., ABA, Pa. Bar Assn., Dauphin County Bar Assn., Am. Judicature Soc., Nat. Assn. Women Judges, Nat. Assn. Women Lawyers, LWV (award 1964), Bus. and Profl. Women, Cath. War Vets. Aux., Nat. Council Cath. Women, Nat. Cath. Women's Union, Mortar Bd., Phi Beta Kappa, Delta Sigma Rho, Pi Tau Phi, Pi Sigma Alpha, Beta Sigma Phi, Delta Kappa Sigma. Lodges: Eagles (hon., Liberty Under Law award 1980), Soroptimists (hon.), Equestrian Order of Knights and Ladies of Holy Sepulchre Vatican (comdr. 1978). Office: 517 South Office Bldg Harrisburg PA 17120

BLATT, MELANIE JUDITH, commercial food equipment sales professional; b. Phila., Sept. 29, 1946; d. Jack and Rose (Ginsburg) Weinberger; children: Marnie, Keath, Lindsay. BA, Antioch U., 1980; postgrad., U. Phoenix, 1988—. Cert. human service worker. Social worker Dept. Pub. Welfare Pa., Doylestown, 1977-80; mgr. customer service Qualidine Inc., Lansdale, Pa., 1980-81; sales rep. Sharp Products, Tempe, Ariz., 1982-83, Hobart Corp., Tempe, 1984—. Bd. dirs. Bucks County Jewish Family Service, Bucks City, 1982. Mem. Retail Grocers Assn. Ariz. Home: 14637 N Winston Ln Fountain Hills AZ 85268 Office: Hobart Corp 929A Hobokam Dr Tempe AZ 85281

BLATTNER, MEERA MCCUAIG, educator; b. Chgo., Aug. 14, 1930; d. William D. McCuaig and Nina (Spertus) Klevs; m. Minao Kamegai, June 22 1985; children: Douglas, Robert, William. B.A., U. Chgo., 1952; M.S., U. So. Calif., 1966; Ph.D., UCLA, 1973 . Research fellow in computer sci. Harvard U., 1973-74; asst. prof. Rice U., 1974-80; assoc. prof. applied sci. U. Calif. at Davis, Livermore, 1980—; adj. prof. U. Tex., Houston, 1977—; vis. prof. U. Paris, 1980; program dir. theoretical computer sci. NSF, Washington, 1979-80. NSF grantee, 1977-81. Mem. Soc. Women Engrs., Assn. Computing Machinery, IEEE Computer Soc. Contbr. articles to profl. jours. Office: U Calif Davis/Livermore Dept Applied Sci Livermore CA 94550

BLATZ, LINDA JEANNE, market manager; b. N.Y.C., Dec. 8, 1950; d. William Edmund and Jeanne Grace (Hyman) B. BS, U. Md., 1972. Mgr. sales Milliken & Co., N.Y.C., 1972-81; retail mkt. mgr. Greenwood Mills Mktg. Co., N.Y.C., 1981—. Contbr. articles to profl. jours. Mem. N.Y.C. Ballet guild; PEO; tng. mgr. N.Y. Jr. League, 1985—. Mem. Nat. Assn. Uniform Mfrs. and Distbrs., U. Md. Alumni Assn., Am. Woman's Econ. Devel. Corp., Alpha Gamma Delta. Congregationalist. Club: Sandbar Beach (membership bd.).

BLAU, FLORENCE HARRIETT, public relations and editorial cons.; b. Bklyn., July 19, 1928; d. Henry Morris and Elsie Rebecca (Weiss) Berman; B.A., N.Y. U., 1948; m. Edmund J. Blau, Apr. 7, 1946 (div. Dec. 1967); children—Barbara, Richard, Henry. Retail account exec. Berry & Price Advt., Washington, 1971; editorial asst. U.S. C. of C., Washington, 1971-73; public relations and community relations specialist, dir. vol. services Greater S.E. Community Hosp., Washington, 1973-78; public relations cons., copy editor Smithsonian Expn. Books, 1979-81; public relations and editorial cons., Washington, 1981—; communications prodn. editor Nat. Assn. Mfrs., 1984—. Active Explorer program Boy Scouts Am., 1974-78; 2d v.p., spl. events chmn. S.E. unit Am. Cancer Soc., 1974-80, trustee D.C. div., 1976—, Community Service award, 1981, 87; public relations chmn. D.C. Congress PTAs, 1978-79; bd. dirs. Potomac River Jazz Club, 1983. Recipient cert. of appreciation Nat. Press Club, 1985, 86, 87. Mem. Nat. Press Club, Public Relations Soc. Am., Capital Press Club, Lit. Group No. Va. Club: Potomac River Jazz. Copy editor: The American Land, 1979; Every Four Years: The American Presidency, 1980; Fire of Life: The Smithsonian Book of the Sun, 1981. Address: 720 Beall Ave Rockville MD 20850

BLAU, FRANCINE DEE, economics educator; b. N.Y.C., Aug. 29, 1946; d. Harold Raymond and Sylvia (Goldberg) B.; m. Richard Weisskoff, Aug. 1969; m. Lawrence Max Kahn, Jan. 1, 1979; children—Daniel Blau Kahn, Lisa Blau Kahn. B.S., Cornell U., 1966; A.M., Harvard U., 1969, Ph.D., 1975. Vis. lectr. Yale U., New Haven, 1971; instr. econs. Trinity Coll., Hartford, Conn., 1971-74; research assoc. Ctr. for Human Resource Research, Ohio State U., Columbus, 1974-75; asst. prof. econs. and labor and indsl. relations U. Ill., Urbana, 1975-78; assoc. prof. U. Ill., 1978-83, prof., 1983—; cons. law firms, 1979, 81-83, EEOC, 1981-85, U.S. Commn. on Civil Rights, 1976, 20th Century Fund Task Force on Working Women, 1970-71; mem. Nat. Acad. Scis. Panel on Technology and Women's Employment, 1984-86; mem. Nat. Acad. Scis. Panel on Pay Equity Research, 1985—. Author: Equal Pay in the Office, 1977; The Economics of Women, Men and Work, 1986 (with Marianne Ferber); mem. editorial bd. Social Sci. Quar., 1978—, Signs: Jour. Women in Culture and Society, 1979—, Women and Work, 1984—; contbr. articles to profl. jours. Harvard U. fellow, 1966-68; U.S. Dept. Labor grantee, 1977-80. Mem. Am. Econ. Assn., Indsl. Relations Research Assn. (exec. bd. 1987-89), Midwest Econ. Assn. (v.p. 1983-84). Office: Inst Labor and Indsl Relations U Ill 504 E Armory Ave Champaign IL 61820

BLAYLOCK, JUDITH RAMONA, real estate and finance executive; b. Roanoke Rapids, N.C., Jan. 9, 1956; d. Clarence Waddell and Marion Doretha (Scott) Gatling; m. Ronald Edward Blaylock, Sept. 3, 1983; 1 child, Garret R. BA, U. N.C., 1977; MA with honors, U. Md., 1982. Research, legis. asst. U.S. Congress, Washington, 1979-83; asst. v.p. State N.Y. Mortgage Agency, N.Y.C., 1983-84; asst. dir. devel. N.Y.C. Housing Devel. Corp., N.Y.C., 1984—. Contbr. articles to profl. jours. Mem. Nat. Assn. Female Execs., Women in Housing and Fin., Omni Women Inc. (founding mem. 1987). Democrat. Baptist. Home: 487 Berkeley Ave South Orange NJ 07079

BLAYLOCK, NANCY ANNE, literary agent; b. Boston, Oct. 10, 1951; d. Alvin Lester and Margaret Anne (Mahoney) Nigrosh; m. William Warren Blaylock, Nov. 5, 1944. BFA, NYU, 1973; MFA, UCLA, 1976. Free-lance film editor Los Angeles, 1974-79; story editor Sandy Howard Prodns., Los Angeles, 1979-80; head literary dept. Gersh Agy., Los Angeles, 1981—. Mem. Women in Film. Office: Gersh Agy 222 N Canon Dr Beverly Hills CA 90210

BLAYTON, DORIS, lawyer, educator, accountant; b. Atlanta; d. Jesse Bee and Willa May Blayton; A.B., Spelman Coll.; postgrad. U. Chgo., 1943-44; J.D., John Marshall Law Sch., 1949; M.B.A., Atlanta U., 1962, M.Ed., 1977. Mem. staff Jesse B. Blayton, C.P.A., Atlanta, 1943-77; admitted to Ill. bar, 1950, Ga. bar, 1951; mem. firm Daugherty & Combs, Atlanta, W.M. Mathews and D.A. Blayton, Atlanta; mem. faculty Ga. State Indsl. Coll., 1944-45, Ark. A.M.&N. Coll., 1966-67; supply tchr., Atlanta, 1974—. Mem. Nat. Bar Assn. (commercial law sect.), State Bar Ga., Atlanta Bar Assn., Gate City Bar Assn., Ga. Assn. Black Women Attorneys, Cosmopolitan Sr. Ctr., Black Women's Coalition of Atlanta, Nat. Council Negro Women, NEA, Ga. Edn. Assn., Atlanta Consumers Clubs, Delta Sigma Theta. Home and Office: 1235 Martin Luther King Jr Dr SW Atlanta GA 30314

BLEAM, DONNA LEES, real estate executive; b. Quakertown, Pa., June 17, 1944; d. Harry Lawrence and Dorothy (Clark) Lees; m. Howard John Bleam, June 23, 1962; children: Karl David, Kurt Tyler. Student, James Madison U. With sales dept. Home Land Realty Co., Inc., Harrisonburg, Va., 1978-82, assoc. broker, 1982-84; broker, owner Buyers Brokerage, Harrisonburg, 1985—; lectr. in field; chmn. Real Estate Resources, Harrisonburg, 1985-87. Author various mag. articles on hist. Va. country property, 1981-82. Bd. dirs. Welcome Wagon, Harrisonburg, 1977-79. Mem. Am. Assn. Real Estate Appraisers (cert.), Va. Assn. Realtors (membership com. 1986-87, profl. standards com. 1987, cert. ethics instr. 1987-88,), Harrisonburg-Rockingham Bd. Realtors (bd. dirs. 1985—, Realtor of Yr. 1987), Working Women's Forum (founding mem.), DAR. Office: Buyers Brokerage 420 E Market St Harrisonburg VA 22801

BLECK, PHYLLIS CLAIRE, surgeon, musician; b. Oak Park, Ill., Mar. 10, 1936; d. William Fred and Mildred A. (Jones) B. BS, U. Ill., 1958; MM, Northwestern U., 1968; DMA, U. So. Calif., 1970; postgrad., Autonoma U., Guadalajara, Mex., 1973-76; MD, Rush Med. Coll., 1979; MS in Surgery, U. Ill., 1983. Prin. trumpet Fla. Symphony Orch., 1960-66, Orch. Sinfonica Nat. de Peru, 1965; instr. Thornton Jr. Coll., 1966-68; lectr. U. So. Calif., 1969-73; asst. prof. Whittier Coll., 1973; asst. in gen. surgery Rush Presbyn. St. Luke's Med. Ctr., Chgo., 1979-82, instr. gen. surgery, 1982-84; resident in cardiothoracic surgery U. Medicine and Dentistry N.J., 1984-87; practice medicine specializing in cardiothoracic surgery, Aurora, Ill., 1987—. Editor: Mozart Divertimento for Winds; research on vascular ischemia. Mem. Kappa Delta Pi, Pi Kappa Lambda, Sigma Alpha Iota.

BLECK, VIRGINIA ELEANORE, illustrator; b. Waukegan, Ill., Dec. 22, 1929; d. George William and Eugenia (Van Honder) Pavlik; m. Thomas Frank Bleck, June 16, 1951; children: Thomas G., James H., Catherine Bleck-Muschler, Marilynn Bleck-Cobbs, Robert F., Susan M., Linda M., John W., Charles D. Student, U. Ill., 1947-48, Art Inst. Chgo., 1948-50. Free lance artist Waukegan, Ill., 1950-86; artist Merrill-Chase Galleries, Chgo., 1972-77, Hallmark Cards Inc., Kansas City, Mo., 1977—; owner, operator Bleck Tree Farms, Waukegan, Green Oaks, Grayslake, Ill., 1972—. Republican. Roman Catholic. Home and Office: 10330 W Yorkhouse Rd Waukegan IL 60087

BLECKER, NAOMI PERLE, credit manager; b. N.Y.C., Mar. 3, 1956; d. Sidney and Zelda (Pologe) B. Student, CUNY, 1973-77. Credit mgr. new accounts Gimbel's Dept. Store, N.Y.C., 1975-78; credit mgr. Eue/Screen Gems div. Columbia Pictures Corp., N.Y.C., 1977-82, JSL Video Services, Inc. subs. AME, Inc., N.Y.C., 1982—. Mem. Nat. Assn. Credit Mgmt. (chmn. motion picture and t.v. group 1982—), Nat. Assn. Female Execs., Am. Jewish Congress. Democrat. Home: 141-30 Pershing Crescent Briarwood New York NY 11435

BLEED, ANN LEA, engineer, researcher, educator; b. N.Y.C., Mar. 16, 1942; d. Edward M. and Marguerite (Rost) Salomon; m. Peter A. Bleed, Mar. 19, 1966; children: James Grey, Jacob David. AB, Earlham Coll., 1964; MS, Pa. State U., State College, 1966; PhD, U. Wis., 1974; MS, U. Nebr., 1982. Registered profl. engr., Nebr. Instr. sch. life sci. U. Nebr., Lincoln, 1976-78, vis. asst. prof. indsl. engring., 1981-82, asst. prof. water resource ctr., 1982-84, asst. prof. conservation and survey div., 1984-88, asst. prof. forestry fisheries and wildlife, 1985-88; state hydrologist Nebr. Dept. Water Resources, 1988—. Contbr. articles to profl. jours. Founding bd. dirs. Asian Arts and Culture Guild, Lincoln, 1984—; mem. Landfill Monitoring Com., Lincoln, 1987—; vice chair Mayors Landfill Siting Com., Lincoln, 1985-86; chair Mayors Solid Waste Alt. Task Force, Lincoln, 1986; sec. Lincoln-Lancaster County Bd. Health, 1987—. Recipient YWCA Tribute To Woman award Lincoln Young Womens Christian Assn., 1986. Mem. Water Resources Assn., Soc. Inst. Indsl. Engrs., Lincoln-Lancaster League of Women Voters (pres. 1978-80), Alpha Pi Mu (pres. student chpt. 1980-81), Sigma Xi. Office: U Nebr Conservation and Survey Div 113 Nebraska Hall Lincoln NE 68588-0517

BLEEKER, MERRY LYNN, principal; b. Hanson County, S.D., Apr. 10, 1943; d. Englebert Ervin and Verona Valeta (Weber) Terveen; m. Lin L. Bleeker, Dec. 22, 1964; 1 child, Karl. BS, Sioux Falls Coll., 1965; MA, U. S.D., 1979. Cert. elem. tchr., prin., S.D. Tchr. Crooks (S.D.) Sch. Dist., 1964-65, Sioux Falls (S.D.) Sch. Dist., 1965-68, Vermillion (S.D.) Sch. Dist., 1968-69; counselor Ft. Morgan (Colo.) Sch. Dist., 1973-74; tchr. Jefferson (S.D.) Sch. Dist., 1977-79; prin. Lennox (S.D.) Sch. Dist., 1979-80, Hanson Sch. Dist., Alexandria, S.D., 1981-87, Mitchell (prin.) Sch. Dist., 1987—. Mem. Nat. Assn. Elem. Sch. Prins., S.D. Assn. Elem. Sch. Prins., Sch. Adminstrs. S.D., Phi Delta Kappa, Delta Kappa Gamma. Republican. Baptist. Home: PO Box 85 Alexandria SD 57311 Office: Mitchell Sch Dist 117 E 4th Ave Mitchell SD 57301

BLEEZARDE, JUDITH BACON, language educator; b. Troy, N.Y., Sept. 23, 1939; d. Joseph Alfred and Dorothy Everest (Barrett) Bacon; m. Thomas Warren Bleezarde, July 15, 1961; children: Philip Michael, Stephen Thomas. BA, SUNY, Albany, 1961; MEd, North Adams (Mass.) State Coll., 1976. Cert. tchr. Vt., Mass. Tchr. Lee (Mass.) Cen. Sch., 1961-62; reading specialist Williamstown (Mass.) Pub. Schs., 1970-77; editor alumni dir. Williams Coll., Williamstown, Mass., 1977-78; tchr. English North Adams (Mass.) Mid. Sch., 1978-79; lang. arts tchr. Stamford (Vt.) Cen. Sch., 1979—; tchr. Developing Capable Young People, Stamford, Vt., 1984-85. Mem. PTA, Eqqus Handicapped Program. Grantee U. Vt., 1981, New Eng. Sch. Drug and Alcohol, 1984. Mem. Nat. Council Tchrs. English, New Eng. Council Tchrs. English, NEA, Vt. Edn. Assn. (chmn. negotiating com. 1984-85) , Kappa Delta. Congregationalist. Home: 187 Sand Springs Rd Williamstown MA 01267 Office: Stamford Sch 718 Main Rd Stamford VT 05352

BLEICH, ANNA LORETTA, nurse; b. Mineville, N.Y., Feb. 18, 1924; d. John Francis and Louise Marie (Fields) McKown; R.N., Champlain Valley Hosp., Plattsburg, N.Y., 1944; B.S. in Nursing, Northwestern State U., Shreveport, 1970; M.Ed., Northwestern State U., Natchitoches, La., 1971; M.S. in Nursing U. Tex., 1973; m. LaMoyne Charles Bleich, May 6, 1946 (dec. 1985); children: Edward Joseph, John Francis, Anne Marie, Rebecca. Pvt. duty nurse, Washington, 1944; instr. Washington Vis. Nurse Soc., 1946-47; mem. nursing staff Park Ave. Hosp., Rochester, N.Y., 1947-48; vol. ARC, 1955-65; regional dir. continuing edn. in nursing Northwestern State U., 1971-72; instr. med.-surg. nursing Northeastern La. U., Monroe, 1972-73, asst. prof., then assoc. prof., 1973-74; asso. prof. Northwestern State U., Shreveport, 1975-76; pvt. practice psychotherapy, Ruston, 1976—; dir. religious edn. St. Thomas Ch. Pres. Mental Health Assn. Lincoln Parish, 1978-79, chmn. edn. program, 1979—; bd. dirs. Ruston Emergency Pregnancy Service, Ruston Alcohol and Substance Abuse Clinic; past pres., disaster chmn. ARC, Lincoln Parish. Served to 1st lt. Army Nurse Corps. 1945-46. Mem. Am. Nurses Assn., Nat. League Nursing, Council Advanced Practitioners in Psychiat.-Mental Health Nursing. Am. Personnel and Guidance Assn., Am. Orthopsychiat. Assn., La. Nurses Assn., Nurses Coalition for Action in Politics, Ruston Dist. Nurses Assn., LWV, Ruston Bus. and Profl. Women, Phi Kappa Phi, Sigma Theta Tau. Republican. Roman Catholic. Home and Office: 1004 D'Arbonne St Ruston LA 71270

BLEVINS, ANNE HELEN, microbiologist; b. Kankakee, Ill.; d. George and Mary Anne (Hoffman) B.; R.N., Wausau Meml. Hosp. Sch. Nursing, 1927; student Columbia U., 1929-36, Marquette U., 1941, N.Y. U., postgrad. Med. Sch., Columbia U., 1936. Research asso. Post Grad. Hosp., Columbia U., N.Y.C., 1940-47; chief bacteriologist Univ. Hosp., N.Y.U. Bellevue Med. Center, 1948-53; chief supervising bacteriologist Meml. Hosp., Meml. Sloan-Kettering Cancer Center, N.Y.C., 1953-68, asst. to dir., 1968-85; cons. hosp. epidemiology, 1985—. Fellow Am. Acad. Microbiology; mem. Am. Soc. Microbiology (hon. mem. southeastern br., 40 Yr. Club, recipient life achievement award N.Y.C. br., 1987, Elizabeth O. King award in clin. microbiology, 1970) Am. Pub. Health Assn. (life), N.Y. Acad. Scis. (life). Club: Soroptimist International of New York. Home: 501 W 123d St New York NY 10027 Office: Memorial Hosp 1275 York Ave New York NY 10021

BLEVINS, KATHLEEN SUESSDORF, microbiologist, educator; b. Houston, Nov. 2, 1945; d. Frank and Ruth (Stotlemeyer) Suessdorf; m. Wendell Lee Blevins, Sept. 4, 1976; 1 child, Aimee Lynn. BA in Zoology,

Washington U., St. Louis, 1967; MS in Microbiology, U. Mo., 1977; post-grad., U. Okla., 1981—. Blood bank technologist St. Luke's Hosp., Kansas City, Mo., 1968-69; research technologist Washington U., 1969-72, Gentofte County Hosp., Copenhagen, Denmark, 1972-73, Washington U. Med. Sch., 1973-74; microbiology technologist U. Mo. Med. Ctr., Columbia, 1976-79; asst. prof. U. Okla. Coll. Allied Health, Oklahoma City, 1980—. Vol. Leukemia Soc., Edmond, Okla., 1985, Am. Cancer Soc., Oklahoma City, 1987—. Mem. Am. Soc. Med. Tech., Southwestern Assn. Clin. Microbiology, Am. Soc. Allied Health Professions, Phi Mu Alumnae. Republican. Methodist. Office: U Okla Coll Allied Health PO Box 26901 Oklahoma City OK 73190

BLIESATH, LISSA SPENCER, itinerant public health nurse; b. Neenah, Wis., Feb. 16, 1955; d. Selden Palmer and Ruth Geraldine (Kuehmsted) Spencer III; m. Robert Douglas Bliesath Jr., Sept. 22, 1979. BA in Native Am. Studies summa cum laude, U. Minn., 1976; BS in Nursing, U. Wis., 1978. Cert. pub. health, Wis. Staff RN Theda Clark Meml. Hosp., Neenah, Wis., 1979-80; Neenah pub. health nurse 1980-81; home care nurse Visiting Nurse Assn., Oshkosh, Wis., 1981-83; surg. staff nurse, home care nurse Albany (Oreg.) Gen. Hosp., 1983-84; itinerant pub. health nurse State of Alaska, Ft. Yukon, 1985—. Vol. Ft. Yukon Rescue Squad, 1986—. Mem. Alaska Pub. Health Assn. Office: Ft Yukon Itinerant Nursing Office Box 316 Fort Yukon AK 99740

BLIGAN, MARTHA ELIZABETH, recruiter; b. Akron, Ohio, July 17, 1959; d. Archbishop Trevor Wyatt and Marcena May (Idle) Moore; m. Kevin C. Bligan, July 18, 1981. BA in Sci., Pa. State U., 1981. Personnel specialist Family Health Council of Western Pa., Pitts., 1981-83; asst. v.p. Eastman Borne & Assocs., Chgo., 1983-85; sr. assoc., dir. research Howard Fischer Assocs., Phila., 1985—. Mem. dir. Phila Exec. Search/Research Roundtable, 1986-87. Mem. Nat. Assn. Female Execs., Am. Mgmt. Assn. Democrat. Eastern Orthodox. Office: Howard Fischer Assocs Inc 1530 Chestnut St Suite 808 Philadelphia PA 19102

BLISS, ANNA CAMPBELL, artist, architect, color consultant; b. Morristown, N.J., July 10, 1925; d. Leo Manning Campbell and Agnes (McManus) Campbell; m. Robert Lewis Bliss, Apr. 2, 1949. BA, Wellesley Coll., 1946; MArch, Harvard U., 1950; postgrad., MIT, 1950, U. Mpls. Sch. of Art, 1954-63, U. Utah. Registered architect, Minn. Ptnr. Bliss & Campbell, Salt Lake City, 1956—; lectr. Utah State U., 1975, U. Md., 1976, Syracuse U., 1976, UCLA, 1977, Yale U., 1979, U. Va., 1982, also various profl. groups and mus.; cons. Peerless Lighting Co., Berkeley, Calif., 1979—, Conoco Oil Co., Ponca City and Wilmington, Del., 1983; pres. Contemporary Arts Group, Salt Lake City, 1984-85. One woman shows include Lowe Art Gallery, Syracuse, N.Y., 1976, Utah Mus. of Fine Arts Traveling Exhibit, 1979-81, Yale U., New Haven, 1979, Ohio State U. Gallery of Fine Art, Columbus, 1980, Focus Gallery, San Diego Mus. of Art, 1981, Salt Lake Art Ctr., 1983; exhibited in group shows at Utah Mus. of Fine Arts, 1985, Finch Lane Gallery of SLC Arts Council, 1980-86, SW Mus. Sci. and Tech., Dallas, 1986-87, Reynolds Gallery, U. Pacific, 1987, Calif. Coll. Arts and Crafts, 1987, Salt Lake Art Ctr. Invitational, 1988, Western States Print Comp, Eules Art Ctr., Ogden, 1988, Ten Utah Artists, Utah Mus. Fine Arts, 1987, Stuttgart Design Ctr., Germany, 1987, 81, Hearst Art Gallery, Moraga, Calif., 1988; represented in permanent collections Met. Mus. N.Y.C., Art Inst. of Chgo., Minami Gallery, First Nat. Bank, Research Park Assocs., Salt Lake City, Springville Mus. Art, Utah Bank and Trust, Salt Lake City Complex, U. Pacific, Stockton, Ga., Cliff Lodge, Snowbird, Utah, represented in numerous corp. and pvt. collections. Adv. bd. Repertory Dance Theatre, Salt Lake City, 1965-70; Utah Mus. Fine Arts, Salt Lake City, 1972—, Utah Arts Festival, Salt Lake City, 1979-81; mem. Chamber Music Soc., Salt Lake City, 1970—; sec. Salt Lake City Design Bd., 1979-84. Fellow Am. Acad. in Rome, 1984; grantee Graham Found., 1980. Mem. Am. Soc. Interior Designers (presdl. citation 1981, del. chmn. mem. Color Mktg. Group (lectr.), Inter Soc. Color Council (bd. dirs. 1983-86), Color Mktg. Group (lectr.), Artist's Equity. Clubs: New Yorker, Salt Lake Swim and Tennis (Salt Lake City). Office: Bliss & Campbell Architects 27 University St Salt Lake City UT 84102

BLISSITT, PATRICIA ANN, nurse; b. Knoxville, Tenn., Sept. 23, 1953; d. Dewitt Talmadge and Imogene (Bailey) B. BS in Nursing with high honors, U. Tenn., 1976, MS in Nursing, 1985. RN, cert. critical care nurse, cert. neurosci. nurse. Staff nurse neurosci. unit City of Memphis Hosp., 1976-78, head nurse neurosci. dept., 1978-79; physician's asst. Dr. John D. Wilson, Columbus, Miss., 1979-81; staff nurse med. and surg. trauma intensive care unit U. Tenn. Meml. Hosp., Knoxville, 1982-83; staff nurse neurosci. intensive care unit Bapt. Meml. Hosp., Memphis, 1985-86, clin. nurse specialist neurosci., 1986—; mem. Health Edn. Consortium, Memphis, 1985-87; nurse cons. neurosci. VA Hosp., Memphis, 1986. Mem. Am. Assn. Neurosci. Nurses (treas. local chpt. 1987—), Am. Assn. Critical Care Nurses (lectr.), Am. Nurses Assn. (council med. and surg. nurses, council clin. nurse specialists), Tenn. Nurses Assn., Nat. Head Injury Found., Tenn. Head Injury Found., Nat. Assn. Female Execs., Sigma Theta Tau, Alpha Lambda Delta, Gamma Phi Beta. Methodist. Avocation: music. Home: Embassy House 475 Perkins Rd S Apt 314 Memphis TN 38117 Office: Bapt Meml Hosp 899 Madison Ave Memphis TN 38146

BLITZ, PEGGY SANDERFUR, corporate travel management company official; b. Pitts., Apr. 12, 1940; d. Charles I. and Rebecca Polk (McBride) Wallace; m. Clark L. Blitz, Aug. 25, 1962 (div. Apr. 1976); children: Danette L., Jonathan D. BS, Ball State U., 1962; postgrad., No. Ill. U., 1976-77. Cert. speech therapist, spl. edn. tchr. Tchr. mentally retarded Anderson (Ind.) Pub. Schs., 1962-64; speech therapist Elgin (Ill.) Pub. Schs., 1964-66; pvt. practice speech therapy Elgin, 1966-68; tchr. mentally retarded Easter Seal Rehab. Ctr., Elgin, 1968-77; account exec. Whitehall Hotel, Chgo., 1977-79; regional mgr. IVI Travel Inc., Milw., 1979-85; sr. v.p. IVI Travel Inc., Dallas, 1985-88; sr. corp. analyst Travelmasters, Inc., Chgo., 1988—; mem. pres.'s council Braniff Airlines, Dallas, 1977-78. Presbyterian. Home: 505 N Lake Shore Dr #3207 Chicago IL 60611 Office: Travelmasters Inc 450 W Algonquin Rd Arlington Heights IL 60005

BLITZER, PATTY VOLK, advertising executive; b. N.Y.C., July 16, 1943. Office: DDB Needham New York 437 Madison Ave New York NY 10022

BLITZ-WEISZ, SALLY, speech pathologist; b. Buffalo, Nov. 9, 1954; d. Isaac and Paula (Goldstein) Blitz; m. Andrew Weisz, Dec. 16, 1984. BA in Speech Pathology, Audiology, SUNY, Buffalo, 1976, MA in Speech Pathology, 1978. Lic. speech/lang. pathologist, Calif. Speech, lang. pathologist Lang. Devel. Program, Tonawanda, N.Y., 1978-82, Bailey and Drown Assocs., La Habra, Calif., 1982-83; speech, lang. specialist, cons. Pasadena (Calif.) Unified Schs., 1983—. Active Anti-Defamation League, San Fernando Valley, 1985-86; mem. 2d Generation Holocaust Survivors, Los Angeles, 1986—. Recipient Excellence in Studies award Temple Shaarey Zedek, Buffalo, 1968. Mem. Am. Speech-Lang.-Hearing Assn. Democrat. Club: Jewish Young Adults. Lodge: B'nai Brith. Home: 11671 Amigo Ave Northridge CA 91326 Office: Pasadena Unified Sch Dist 351 S Hudson Ave Pasadena CA 91101

BLIZNAKOV, MILKA TCHERNEVA, architect; b. Varna, Bulgaria, Sept. 20, 1927; came to U.S., 1961, naturalized, 1966; d. Ivan Dimitrov and Maria Kesarova (Khorozova) Tchernev; m. Emile G. Bliznakov, Oct. 23, 1954 (div. Apr., 1974). Architect-engr. diploma, State Tech. U., Sofia, 1951; Ph.D., Engrng.-Structural Inst., Sofia, 1959; Ph.D. in Architecture, Columbia U., 1971. Sr. researcher Ministry Heavy Industry, Sofia, 1950-53; pvt. practice architecture Sofia, 1954-59; assoc. architect Noel Combrisson, Paris, 1959-61; designer Perkins & Will Partnership, White Plains, N.Y., 1963-67; project architect Lathrop Douglass, N.Y.C., 1967-71; assoc. prof. architecture and planning Sch. Architecture, U. Tex., Austin, 1972-74; prof. Coll. Architecture, Va. Poly. Inst. and State U., Blacksburg, 1974—; prin. Blacksburg, 1975—; bd. dirs., founder Internat. Archives Women in Architecture, Va. Poly. Inst. and State U. Prin. works include Speedwell Ave. Urban Renewal, Morristown, N.J., 1967-69, Wilmington (Del.) Urban Renewal, 1968-70, Springfield (Ill.) Central Area Devel, 1969-71, Arlington County (Va.) Redevel, 1975-77. William Kinne scholar, summer 1970; NEA grantee, 1973-74; Am. Beautiful Found. grantee, 1973; Fulbright Hays research fellow, 1983-84; Internat. Research and Exchange Bd. grantee, 1984. Mem. Internat. Archive Women in Architecture (founder, chair bd. dirs.), Am. Assn. Tchrs. Slavic and East European Langs., Soc. Archtl. Historians, Nat. Trust Hist. Preservation, Am. Assn. Advancement of Slavic Studies, Assn. Collegiate Schs. of Planning, Inst. Modern Russian Culture (chairperson architecture, co-founder, dir.), Assn. Collegiate Schs. of Architecture. Home: 2813 Tall Oaks Dr Blacksburg VA 24060 Office: Va Poly Inst and State U Coll Architecture Blacksburg VA 24061

BLOCH, BARBARA JOYCE, author, editor; b. N.Y.C., May 26, 1925; d. Emil William and Dorothy (Lowengrund) Bloch; m. Joseph B. Sanders, Aug. 3, 1944 (div. 1961); children—Elizabeth Sanders-Hines, Ellen Janice Benjamin; m. 2d, Theodore S. Benjamin, Sept. 20, 1964. Student NYU, 1943-45, New Sch. Social Research, 1966. Office mgr. Writers War Bd., N.Y.C., 1943-45, Westchester Democratic Com., White Plains, N.Y., 1955-56; mgr. Westchester Symphony Orch., 1957-62; mng. editor Cooking Ency., Rutledge Books, N.Y.C., 1970-71; pres. Internat. Cookbook Services, White Plains, 1978—; columnist House Beautiful, 1984-87; cons. in field; tchr. cooking classes White Plains, 1975-80; lectr. in field. Author: Anyone Can Quilt, 1975; Meat Board Meat Book, 1977; If It Doesn't Pan Out, 1981; Garnishing Made Easy, 1983; editor/author: All Beef Cookbook, 1973; In Glass Naturally, 1974; Fresh Ideas with Mushrooms, 1977; Holly Farms Complete Chicken Cookbook, 1984; Gulden's Cookbook, 1985, A Centennial Celebration-Recipes from Solo, 1988; Am. adapter The Cuisine of Olympe, 1983, Baking Easy and Elegant, 1984, Best of Cold Foods, 1985, Cakes and Pastries, 1985, series of 12 Creative Cuisine books, 1985, The Art of Cooking, 1986, The Art of Baking, 1987, A Century of Recipies from Solo, 1988; editor contbr. various books; contbr. articles to profl. jours. Nat. bd. dirs. Emcampment for Citizenship, N.Y.C., 1966-72; bd. dirs. YWCA Central Westchester, 1965-71, Westchester Ethical Humanist Soc., 1968-70; exec. com., pres. Internat. Student Exchange of White Plains, 1955-70; bd. dirs. Westchester Chamber Music Soc., 1986—. Jewish. Home: 21 Dupont Ave White Plains NY 10605 Office: Internat Cookbook Services 21 Dupont Ave White Plains NY 10605

BLOCH, BARBARA MARIE, public relations executive; b. Bridgeport, Conn., Apr. 9, 1933; d. Harry and Ida (Ashley) Mielke; m. Lawrence J. Bloch, Oct. 26, 1953; children: Curtis J., Adrienne D. Bloch Greenberg. RN, Plattsburgh State Coll. (now SUNY), 1951; student, Columbia (S.C.) Bus. Sch., 1954; AA, Cypress (Calif.) Coll., 1977, Calif. Inst. for Applied Design, Newport Beach, 1980. Med. asst. Columbia Med. Group, 1953-55; office mgr. Quality Constrn. Co., Miami, Fla., 1955-61; rep. Home Interiors, Cypress, 1975-81; exec. Bloch Enterprises, Anahcim, Calif., 1982—. Mem. adv. bd. Cypress Coll. Re-Entry Program, 1982-83; chairperson Cypress Traffic Commn., 1984—; co-chairperson 2d Supervisorial Dist. Leadership Adv. Group, Orange County, Calif., 1986—. Recipient Americana award Cypress Coll., 1985. Mem. Am. Assn. of Cost Engrs. (pub. relations com. 1982), Internat. Home Interiors Assn., Calif. Fedn. Women's Clubs (chairperson 1985-86, Golden Bear award 1981), Nat. Assn. Female Execs., Cypress C. of C. (ambassador 1980, bd. dirs. 1984, named Ambassador of Yr. 1980). Republican. Jewish. Clubs: Soroptomists Internat. (Cypress), Woman's (Cypress) (pres. 1984-85.

BLOCH, JULIA CHANG, government official; b. Chefoo, Peoples Republic of China, Mar. 2, 1942; came to U.S., 1951, naturalized, 1962; d. Fu-yun and Eva (Yeh) Chang; m. Stuart Marshall Bloch, Dec. 21, 1968. BA, U. Calif., Berkeley, 1964; MA, Harvard U., 1967, postgrad. in mgmt., 1987; DHL (hon.), Northeastern U., Boston, 1986. Vol. Peace Corps, Sabah, Malaysia, 1964-66, tng. officer East Asia and Pacific region, Washington, 1967-68, evaluation officer, 1968-70; mem. minority staff U.S. Senate Select Com. on Nutrition and Human Needs, Washington, 1971-76, chief minority counsel, 1976-77; dep. dir. Office of African Affairs, U.S. Internat. Communications Agy., Washington, 1977-80; fellow Inst. Politics, Harvard U., Cambridge, Mass., 1980-81; asst. adminstr. Bur. for Food for Peace and Voluntary Assistance, AID, Washington, 1981-87, asst. administr. Bur. for Asia and Near East, 1987—; U.S. Senate rep. World Conf. on Internat. Women's Yr., Mex., 1975; advisor U.S. Del. to Food and Agr. Orgn. Conf., Rome, 1975; rep. Am. Council Young Polit. Leaders, Peoples Republic China, 1977; charter mem. Sr. Exec. Service, 1979; head U.S. del. Biennial Session World Food Programme, Rome, 1981-86, Devel. Assistance Com. Meeting on Non-Govtl. Orgns., Paris, 1985, Intergovtl. Group on Indonesia, The Hague, The Netherlands, 1987, World Bank Consultative Group Meeting, Paris, 1987; mem. U.S. Nat. Com. for Pacific Econ. Cooperation, 1984—; mem. adv. bd. Women's Campaign Fund, 1976-78; exec. bd. mem. Internat. Ctr. for Research on Women, 1974-81; bd. dirs. Minority Legis. Edn. Prgoram, 1976-78. Co-author: Chinese Home Cooking, 1986. Mem. exec. bd. Internat. Ctr. for Research on Women, 1974-81; mem. adv. bd. Women's Campaign Fund, 1976-78, Nat. Women's Polit. Caucus, 1978-84, Nat. Presdl. Debate Forum, 1987—; mem. nat. adv. council Experiment in Internat. Living, 1981—; bd. dirs. Minority Legis. Edn. Program, 1976-78. Recipient Hubert Humphrey award for internat. service, 1979, Humanitarian Service award AID, 1987, Leader for Peace award Peace Corps, 1987; named Outstanding Woman of Color, Nat. Inst. for Women of Color, 1982, Woman of Distinction, Nat. Conf. for Coll. Women Student Leaders and Women of Achievement, 1987, Woman of Yr. Orgn. Chinese Am. Women, 1987; Ford Found. Study fellow for internat. devel. Harvard U., 1966; Shriver Peace Worker program fellow . Mem. Exec. Women in Govt., Orgn. Chinese Am. Women (founder, chair 1977—, bd. dirs., Woman of Yr. 1987), Prytannean Honor Soc., Mortar Bd. Republican. Avocations: ceramics, gourmet cooking, collecting art. Office: US Dept State Agy Internat Devel Bur Asia and Near East Room 6724 NS Washington DC 20523 also: Internat Dev Coop Agy 1400 Wilson Blvd Arlington VA 22209

BLOCH, SUSAN LOW, law educator; b. N.Y.C., Sept. 15, 1944; d. Ernest and Ruth (Frankel) Low; m. Richard I. Bloch, July 10, 1966; children—Rebecca, Michael. B.A. in Math., Smith Coll., 1966; M.A. in Math., U. Mich., 1968, M.A. in Computer Sci., Ph.C., 1972, J.D., 1975. Bar: D.C. 1975. Law clk. to chief judge U.S. Ct. Appeals, Washington, 1975-76; law clk. to assoc. justice Marshall, U.S. Supreme Ct., Washington, 1976-77; assoc. Wilmer, Cutler & Pickering, Washington, 1978-82; assoc. prof. Georgetown U. Law Ctr., Washington, 1983—; contbr. Mich. Law Rev., Wis. Law Rev., Georgetown Law Rev., Supreme Ct Preview, 1984, Voice of Am., 1983. Active Common Cause, ACLU, Women's Legal Def. Fund. Mem. ABA, D.C. Bar (Bicentennial of Constn.)Assn., Soc. Am. Law Tchrs., Inst. Pub. Representation (bd. dirs.), Order of Coif, Phi Beta Kappa, Sigma Xi. Home: 4335 Cathedral Ave NW Washington DC 20016 Office: Georgetown U Law Ctr 600 New Jersey Ave NW Washington DC 20001

BLOCK, JANET LEVEN (MRS. JOSEPH E. ROSEN), public relations consultant; b. Chgo.; d. Benjamin J. and Rosebud (Goldsmith) Leven; student Brenau Coll. for Women, Gainesville, Ga., Northwestern U.; m. Albert William Block, Sept. 27, 1947 (div.); m. Joseph E. Rosen, Dec. 5, 1985; children: Mitchell, Stephanie Block McEwen. Reporter, Chgo. Am. Newspaper, 1939-40; catalog advt. Alden's Chgo. Mail Order Co., N.Y.C., Chgo., 1940-42; stylist and public relations dir. Fashion Advt. Co., N.Y.C., 1942-44; asst. account exec., stylist Buchanan & Co., Advt. Agy., N.Y.C., 1944-46; advt. agy account exec. Abbott Kimball Co., Chgo., 1946-47; freelance merchandising and public relations rep., Cin., 1960-64; v.p. public relations Lazarus spl. events (previously Shillito's), Cin., 1964-87; cons. pub. relations & advt. Cin.; Bd. dirs. Children's Heart Assn., 1975—; bd. dirs. Friends of Hamilton County Parks, 1979-80, treas., 1982; vice chair adv. bd. Hoxworth Blood Ctr., 1986-87, chair 1988; bd. dirs. ARC, 1984-86, Salvation Army, 1983-85; Great Rivers council Girl Scouts U.S.A., 1980-83, Family Service, 1985-88; Cin. Commn. on the Arts, Cin. Ballet 1985-88; mem. licensing com. Cin. Bicentennial Com., 1985-87. Recipient Silver Medal award Advertisers' Club Cin., 1976; named YWCA Career Woman of Achievement, 1982. Mem. Fashion Group Cin. (past regional dir.), Downtown Council (promotion chmn. 1975-76, 80-81), Public Relations Soc. Am. (dir. 1974-75, sec. 1976, treas. 1977), TV Soc. Am., Bus. and Profl. Women's Club, Advt. Club. Cin. (dir. 1967—, v.p. 1972, Advt. Woman of Yr. 1972, mem. Speakers Bur. 1973—, pres. 1973-74, AAF Silver medal 1976), Women in Communications. Home: 2502 Washington Circle Cincinnati OH 45215

BLOCK, LYNNE WOOD, accountant; b. New Orleans, July 13, 1943; d. John Sorber and Emilie Douglas (Poe) Wood: m. Lawrence Richard Block, Oct. 2, 1983. Student, Ursuline Acad., 1957-61, Hunter Coll., 1968-69, Pace U., 1978-79. Clk. Dunn & Bradstreet, New Orleans, 1961-64; fashion model Stewart Model's, N.Y.C., 1965-70; prin. The Real Tinsel Antiques, N.Y.C., 1970-75, Other World Furniture Imports, W. Hampton, N.Y., 1976; pvt. practice acctg. The Lynne Wood Co., N.Y.C., Ft. Myers Beach, Fla., 1976—; seminar leader, Ft. Myers Beach, 1983—; cons. Cross and Desire Corp., N.Y.C., 1980—. Author: Evelyn the Raccoon, 1984. Named Model of the Yr., Photograph Annual, 1968. Mem. Pilot Internat., Am. Bus. Women's Assn. (sec. 1986—).

BLOCK, PAMELA JO, vocational administrator; b. Freeport, Ill., May 25, 1947; d. Carl and Leona Mae (Stukenberg) B. BS, Iowa State U., 1969; MEd, U. Ill., 1973. Tchr. Palatine (Ill.) High Sch., 1969-85, dept. chairperson, 1973-85; mgr. N.W. Suburban Career Coop., Palatine, 1985—; cons. Household Internat., Prospect Heights, Ill., 1982-83; evaluator Ill. State Bd. Edn., 1976—. Contbr. articles to profl. jours. Bd. dirs. Ill. Women's Agenda, Chgo., 1986-87; mem. Suburban Adv. Council United Way, 1984-87. Named an Outstanding Young Woman of Ill., 1982. Mem. AAUW (pres. Wheeling-Buffalo Grove, Ill. br. 1982-84, chair Ill. div. found. 1985-87, program com., cons. nat. found. 1987—), Am. Vocat. Assn. Lutheran. Lodge: Rotary (vocat. service com. chair Buffalo Grove club 1987-88). Home: 190 Woodstone Dr Buffalo Grove IL 60089 Office: Northwest Suburban Career Coop 1750 S Roselle Rd Palatine IL 60067

BLOCK, RUTH, retired insurance company executive; b. N.Y.C., Nov. 7, 1930; d. Albert and Celia (Shapiro) Smolensky; B.A., Adelphi U., 1952; m. Norman Block, April 5, 1952. With Equitable Life Assurance Soc. of U.S., 1952-87, v.p., planning officer, 1973-77, sr. v.p. in charge individual life ins. bus., 1977-80, exec. v.p. individual ins. businesses, 1980-87, duties expanded to include all individual and small group lines of bus., group life and health businesses, chief ins. officer, 1984-87; bd. dirs. Amoco Corp., Avon, Ecolab Inc., Tandem Fin. Group, Donaldson, Lufkin & Jenrette, ACM Govt. Income Securities and Spectrum Funds, Alliance Balanced Shares and Dividend Shares Mut. Funds, Alliance Bond, Alliance Tax Free Income, Alliance Mortgage Income Funds; trustee Life Underwriter Tng. Council, 1983-85; chmn., chief exec. officer Equitable Variable Life Ins. Co., 1981-84; vis. exec. Mobil Co. U. Iowa, 1978. Bd. dirs. Stamford (Conn.) YWCA, 1977-80. Recipient Disting. Alumni award Adelphi U. Sch. of Bus., 1979, Catalyst award 1983, WEAL award, 1983, N.Y.C. YMCA award; nat. chmn. Equitable United Way, 1978. Mem. Nat. Assn. Securities Dealers (gov. at large 1982-84), Data Processing Mgmt. Assn., Com. of 200. Office: PO Box 4653 Stamford CT 06906

BLOCKSON, RITA VERLENE HAYNES, special education educator; b. Decatur, Ill., Sept. 13, 1952; d. Verne Floyd Haynes and Lura Emily (Wiley) Brockett; m. Richard Brian Day, June 21, 1970 (div. Apr. 1976); m. Bruce Willard Blocksom, Nov. 22, 1978; children: Jason Matthew, Jaimee Erickа. BS, Eastern Ill. U., 1984; MA, Wright State U., 1988. Cert. elem., spl., and gifted edn. tchr., Ill., Ohio. Dir. Engine City Sta., Olney, Ill., 1980-84; author, cons. Pinâroo Pub., Bend, Oreg., 1987-88; author, editor D.O.K. Publs., East Aurora, N.Y., 1986-88; ednl. cons. Sch. Profl. Psychology Wright State U., Dayton, Ohio, 1986-87; dir., cons. Children's program, Wright State U., Dayton, Ohio, 1987—. Author: Nurturing Early Promise, 1988; (with others) Gifted Education, 1988; co-editor: Pre-primary/Primary Center, 1988; (ednl. series) Create-A-Kid Series, 1986-88. Recipient Cert. of Merit Ohio Assn. Gifted Children, 1986-88. Mem. Assn. Supervision and Curriculum Devel., Nat. Assn. Gifted Children, Phi Delta Kappa. Home: 19196 Glynwood Rd Saint Marys OH 45885

BLOEMER, MICHELE PAUL, day care executive; b. Ft. Wayne, Ind., Mar. 27, 1960; d. Dean Eldon Paul and Peggy Joyce (Jones) West; m. Bernard William Bloemer, Dec. 12, 1960. BA, Ea. Ky. U., 1982; MA, U. Tenn., 1983. Account rep. Quaker Oats Co., Nashville, 1984-86; sales rep. Sunshine Biscuit Co., Nashville, 1985-86, account mgr., 1986; sales rep. Aratex Services, Nashville, 1986-87; owner TLC for Kids, Inc., Nashville, 1987—. Vol. Dunn for Gov., Nashville, 1986; area dir. Steve Hewlett PSC Campaign, Nashville, 1986; promotions chmn. Vanderbilt Children's Hosp., Nashville, 1986-87. Mem. Nashville Assn. Women Entrepreneurs, Tenn. Assn. for Prevention of Child Abuse (fund raising com. 1987, bd. dirs. 1987—), Internat. Nanny Assn. (founding mem., contbg. editor nat. newsletter), Nashville Jr. League, Nashville C. of C., Kappa Delta Alumnae Assn. (pres. 1986-87, membership com. 1987—). Republican. Home: 4805 Magnolia Place Nashville TN 37211 Office: TLC for Kids Inc PO Box 50637 Nashville TN 37205

BLOMQUIST, SUSAN GAIL, graphic artist; b. Chgo., Dec. 25, 1953; d. Howard Joseph and Evelyn Gene (Reynolds) B. A.A., Am. Acad. Art, 1973. Apprentice prodn. artist Am. Graphics, Chgo., 1973-74; prodn. mgr. Graphic Services, Chgo., 1974-77; gen. mgr. Graphic Connections, Chgo., 1977-80; freelance prodn. artist Source/Inc., Chgo., 1980-82, Perception, Chgo., 1982-84; prodn. art dir. Robert Case & Assoc., Chgo., 1984-86; freelance prodn. artist, 1986—. Illustrations pub. in Talk to Yourself, Why Not, 1976. Recipient of Robert Allerton Art Scholar., U. of Il., 1969, auto crossing first place award, 1979, 80, 81. Mem. Nat. Assn. Female Execs. Club: Porsche of Am. (sec. 1981-82) (Chgo.). Avocations: auto racing; skiing; community theater. Home: 401 Fullerton Pkwy Apt 603 E Chicago IL 60614

BLONSKY, LORENA M'LISS LEWISON, personnel consultant; b. Miami Beach, Fla., June 6, 1961; d. Robert Jay and Rita (Kirschner) Lewison; m. Adam Robert Blonsky, June 18, 1983. BA in Econs., Cornell U., 1983; MBA in Fin. and Mktg., U. Chgo., 1985. Banking assoc. Continental Ill. Nat. Bank, Chgo., 1985; sr. assoc. cons. Korn/Ferry Internat., Chgo., 1986—. Mem. Nat. Assn. Female Execs., U. Chgo. Women's Bus. Group (v.p. programs 1986—). Democrat. Club: Execs. (Chgo.). Office: Korn/Ferry Internat 120 S Riverside Plaza Suite 918 Chicago IL 60606

BLOOM, CAROLYN, career planning administrator; b. Bklyn., Feb. 17, 1939; d. Nathan and Sally (Hodes) Romanoff; m. David Stephen Bloom, June 21, 1958; children: Michael Scott, Rhonda Susan. Student, Bklyn. Coll., 1956-58, Fairfield (Conn.) U., 1979. Exec. sec. Columbia Pictures Inc., N.Y.C., 1956-58, Fairchild Publs., N.Y.C., 1958-60; mktg. asst. Kaiser Communications Inc., Northbrook, Ill., 1974-76; v.p. sales and mktg. August West Systems Inc., Westport, Conn., 1976-79; personnel counselor Employment Agy., Fairfield, 1979-83, Westport, 1982-83; owner, ptnr. Success Unlimited Inc., Westport, 1983—. Pres. Women's Am. Out Reach Team, Merrick, N.Y., 1970. Mem. Internat. Assn. Personnel Women. Club: Hadassah (Conn.). Office: Success Unlimited Inc 225 Main St Westport CT 06880

BLOOM, KATHRYN RUTH, public relations executive. d. Morris and Frances Sondra (Siegel) B. BA, Douglass Coll.; MA, U. Toronto, Can. Dir. spl. projects United Jewish Appeal, N.Y.C., 1973-78; mgr. pub. affairs Bristol-Myers Co., N.Y.C., 1978-86, mgr. pub. relations pharm. and nutritional div., 1986—. Mem. com. Women's Campaign Fund, N.Y.C., 1984—; v.p. bd. dirs. N.Am. Conf. on Ethiopian Jewry, N.Y.C., 1985—. Mem. Women Execs. in Pub. Relations, Phi Beta Kappa. Office: Bristol-Myers Co 345 Park Ave New York NY 10003

BLOOM, SALLY ANN FOX, health science administrator; b. Buffalo, Feb. 11, 1926; d. Harry Zackery and Anna (Fox) Rosenberg; m. Arthur Bloom, Dec. 14, 1947; children: Eric Arthur, Robin Andrew, Peter Donal. BFA in Drama, Carnegie-Mellon U., 1947. Speech tchr. Buffalo Pub. Schs., 1947-48; actress Armstrong Circle Theatre, N.Y.C., 1949; speech tchr. Stella Niagara Acad., Buffalo, 1950-52, Sch. for Retarded Children, Buffalo, 1955-56; project coordinator biochem. genetics div. SUNY Sch. Medicine, Buffalo, 1957-69, adminstrv. assoc., 1969-75, asst. dir., 1975—; art instr. Adult Sch. Amherst, N.Y., 1977-83; cons. genetics div. Cabral Hosp., Dominican Republic, 1986—. Contbr. articles to profl. jours. Mem. Amherst Artists. Democrat. Jewish. Home: 48 Hancock Terr Snyder NY 14226 Office: SUNY Buffalo Dept Biochem Genetics 352 Acheson Hall Buffalo NY 14214

BLOOM, SUSAN, computer executive; b. Dorchester, Mass., Jan. 24, 1951; d. Stephen and M. Elaine (Doran) Vlachos; m. William D. Doyle, Sept. 21, 1974 (div. 1979); m. J. Robert Bloom, July 22, 1982. B in Econs., Smith Coll., 1976. Merchandiser Zayer Corp., Framingham, Mass., 1976-79; mgr. agy. automation Comml. Union, Boston, 1979-82; lead analyst Southeast

Bank, Miami, Fla., 1982-85, mgr. bus. design Am. Express, Great Neck, N.Y., 1985-86; officer, system devel. TIAA-CREF, N.Y.C., 1986—; v.p. Cambridge Bus. Services, Miami, Fla. and N.Y.C., 1983—. Contbr. articles to profl. jours.; editor: Handbook of Business Strategies, 1986. Tchr. SETA-Women Off Welfare, Boston, 1981, tutor, 1987. Mem. Nat. Assn. Female Execs., Nat. System Design Analysts (co-founder, dir.), Nat. Assn. Ins. Women. Roman Catholic.

BLOOMGARDEN, KATHY F., public relations executive; b. N.Y.C., June 9, 1949; d. David and Laura (Zeisler) Finn; m. Zachary Bloomgarden; children: Rachel, Keith, Matthew. BA, Brown U., 1970; MA, Columbia U., PhD. Pres. Research & Forecasts, N.Y.C., Ruder, Finn & Rotman, N.Y.C. Bd. dirs. N.Y. Arthritis Found. Mem. Pub. Relations Soc. Am., Nat. Investor Relations Inst., Pharm. Advt. Council, Swedish-Am. C. of C. Jewish. Office: Ruder Finn & Rotman Inc 301 E 57th St New York NY 10022

BLOS, JOAN W., author, critic, lecturer; b. N.Y.C., Dec. 9, 1928; m. Peter Blos, Jr., 1953; 2 children, 1 deceased. B.A., Vassar Coll., 1950; M.A., CCNY, 1956. Asso. publs. div., mem. tchr. edn. faculty Bank St. Coll. Edn., N.Y.C., 1958-70; lectr. Sch. Edn., U. Mich., Ann Arbor, 1972-80; U.S. editor Children's Literature in Education, 1976-81. Author: "It's Spring!" She Said, 1968, (with Betty Miles) Just Think!, 1971, A Gathering of Days: A New England Girl's Journal, 1830-32, 1979 (Newbery medal ALA, Am. Book award 1980), Martin's Hats, 1984, Brothers of the Heart: A Story of the Old Northwest, 1837-1838, 1985, Old Henry, 1987. Office: care Curtis Brown Ltd Ten Astor Pl New York NY 10003

BLOUIN, ANNE, canadian legislator; b. Ste. Anne de Beaupré, Que., Can., Sept. 14, 1946; d. Aimé and Marguerite (Thibault) Fortin; m. Roch Blouin, Dec. 20, 1969. Student, École des Arts and Métiers, Que. Mem. Can. Ho. Commons, 1984—; mem. Can.-Europe Parliamentary Group, Can. Group Inter-Parliamentary Union. Mem. Internat. Assn. French Lang. Speakers. Mem. Progressive Conservative Party. Roman Catholic. Office: House of Commons, Parliament Bldgs, Ottawa, ON Canada K1A 0A6 *

BLOUNT-RAINEY, GLORIA NADINE, data processing executive; b. Ft. Bragg, N.C., Mar. 22, 1956; d. James Clinton and Ruebell (Moore) B.; m. Eugene Rainey, Mar. 22, 1986; 1 child, James Edmund. Cert. computer technician, N.C. State U., 1977; BA, St. Augustine Coll., 1978; Master of Human Services, Lincoln U., 1987. Asst. coordinator Commerce Coll. of Balt., 1981; data processing instr., mgr. Computer Commerce Inst., Balt., 1979-83; bus. instr. Watterson Skill Ctr., Balt., 1982-83; instr., supr. Cantonsville (Md.) Community Coll., 1985; data process instr., mgr. Balt. Urban League-IPTC, 1983-85; coordinator electronic info. services Edison Electric Inst., Washington, 1985-87; pres. GEJ & Assocs., Balt., 1982—; project mgr. adult basic edn. Community Coll. Balt., 1987—. Active Faith Tabernacle United Holy Ch., Washington, 1987, Julia West Hamilton League, Inc., 1987; chairlady stewardess bd. Faith Tabernacle, Washington, 1987; coordinator Young Peoples Holy Assn.-Faith, Washington, 1987. Recipient State of Md. Citizens award Govs. Office, Annapolis, 1984. Mem. NAACP, Nat. Assn. Female Execs., Nat. Urban League (Balt. chpt., Mgmt. Team of Quarter 1983-85, Spl. Recognition award), Data Proceesing Mgmt. Assn. (v.p. 1983-85). Democrat. Pentacostal. Home: 198 Easton S Suite 102 Laurel MD 20707 Office: GEJ & Assocs 4629 Colehorne Rd Baltimore MD 21229

BLOZIS, JOLENE MCCOY, social index editor; b. Washington, Sept. 17, 1941; d. Wilbur Milton and Bernys Dovie (Adee) McCoy; m. Raymond LeRoy Blozis, Dec. 28, 1974. B.A., Roberts Wesleyan Coll., Rochester, N.Y., 1963; legal advocacy cert., George Washington U., 1981; M.L.S., Cath. U. Am., 1975. Abstracter, Lawyers Title Ins. Corp., Washington, 1962; indexer Nat. Geog. Soc., Washington, 1963-75, index editor, mgr. indexing div., 1975—. Legal adv. Emmaus Services to Aging, Washington, 1979-84. Mem. ALA, Am. Soc. Indexers, Am. Soc. Info. Sci., D.C. Library Assn., Bibl. Archaeol. Soc., Am. Sch. Oriental Research, Nat. Press Club, Austrian Soc. Republican. Methodist. Home: 2555 Pennsylvania Ave NW Washington DC 20037 Office: Nat Geog Soc 1600 M St NW Washington DC 20036

BLUE, CATHERINE ANNE, lawyer; b. Boston, Feb. 17, 1957; d. James Daniel and Angela Devina (Savini) Mahoney; m. Donald Sherwood Blue, Oct. 4, 1980; children: Mairead Catherine, Edward Pierce. BA, Stonehill Coll., North Easton, Mass., 1977; JD, Coll. William and Mary, 1980. Bar: Pa. 1980. Atty., Aluminum Co. Am., Pitts., 1980-83, Pa. Dept. Revenue, Harrisburg, 1983-85, State Workmen's Ins. Fund, Pitts., 1985-87, Met. Pitts. Pub. Broadcasting, 1987—. Mem. Pa. Bar Assn., Allegheny County Bar Assn. Republican. Home: 7414 Richland Pl Pittsburgh PA 15208 Office: Met Pitts Pub Broadcasting Inc 4802 Fifth Ave Pittsburgh PA 15213

BLUE, EDNA JENKINS GOSSAGE, civic worker; b. Emory Gap, Tenn., Aug. 7, 1909; d. Arthur A. and Lennie Belle (Bailey) Jenkins; m. Roy Lee Gossage, Jan. 17, 1927; children—Dorothy, Daniel Arthur; stepchildren—Roy Lee, Margaret; 1 foster child, Helen Kendall; m. William F. Blue, Sept. 20, 1978. Student Tenn. Poly. U., 1926, U. Tenn., 1940-48, Tenn. Tech. U., 1950-60, Mars Hill Coll., 1965, Roane State Community Coll., 1977. With Tenn. Dept. Human Services, Clinton and Crossville, 1949-77, sr. counselor, 1970-77. Pres. Anderson County Parents Council Cerebral Palsy, Tenn., 1949-51; founder Daniel Arthur Ctr. Cerebral Palsy, 1950, Daniel Arthur Rehab. Ctr., Oak Ridge, Tenn., 1951—; chmn. New Eyes for Needy program, Cumberland County, Tenn., 1960-77; pres., bd. dirs., co-founder Cumberland County Girls Club, 1976-77; mem. steering com., founder Hilltoppers, Inc., Cumberland, 1975, bd. dirs., 1975—, sec. bd., 1976-79; pres. Cumberland County Assn. Retarded Citizens, 1978-79; pres. Janet Clark Meml. Group Home, Ind., 1977—; bd. dirs. United Fund, Cumberland, 1978-80, Four C's Cultural Found., 1978; vol. Local Group Homes for Developmentally Disabled, 1976-78; chmn. Santa for All Yr. Fund for Needy Children in Foster Care, 1975-78; ch. treas. Homesteads United Methodist Ch., 1964-78, ch. historian, 1978—. Author: Cumberland Homestead, 1933-1955, 2d edit., 56, A Church Is Born, 1961, A People Dared, God Cared, 1984; also articles, poems; columnist Cumberland Homesteader, 1935-39. Named Anderson County's Mother of Yr., 1951, Cumberland County's Woman of Achievement, 1963, Bicentennial Woman of History, 1976; named to ABI Hall of Fame, 1987; recipient Silver plaque Cumberland County chpt. ARC, 1985, Golden Poet award, 1985, 86, 87, medal of honor ABI, 1987, others. Mem. Cumberland County Bus. and Profl. Women's Club (pres. 1960-62, 69-70, 76-77), Tenn. Fedn. Bus. and Profl. Women (dist. dirs. East II 1967), Costeau Soc. (founding), Women in Arts (founding), World Inst. of Achievement (1st prize poetry contest, 1987). Clubs: Homesteads United Meth. Women (pres. 1960-78, 83-85). Address: 12 Grassy Cove Rd Route 3 PO Box 202 Crossville TN 38555

BLUE, LEE, editor; b. N.Y.C., May 6, 1942; d. Alexander Lymon Abbott and Florence Elizabeth (Bragdon) Hellum; m. James L. Blue, June 11, 1966; children: Jennifer Marie, Alexander James. AB, Smith Coll., 1964; MA, NYU, 1967; cert. pub. specialist, George Washington U., 1984. Adminstrv. asst., newsletter editor The Washington Ctr., Washington, 1979-80; copy editor, writer Prospect Assocs., Rockville, Md., 1981-82; prodn. editor Computer Sci. Press, Rockville, 1982-84; prodn. editor Computer Soc. Press of IEEE, Washington, 1984-88, mng. editor, 1988—; freelance editor, 1981-84. Editor: Paradigms and Programming with Pascal, 1983, Elements of Digital Satellite Communication, 1984. Mem. Cultural Arts Commn., Rockville, 1980-83; trustee Unitarian Ch. of Rockville, 1980-82, search com. for minister, 1985-86, chair music com. 1986-88. Mem. Washington Edn. Press Assn. (steering com. 1987), Women's Nat. Book Assn., Soc. for Scholarly Pub., Profl. Communication Soc. Home: 1386 Kersey Lane Rockville MD 20854 Office: Computer Soc Press of IEEE 1730 Massachussetts Ave NW Washington DC 20036-1903

BLUE, NANCY ANN, home economics educator; b. Huron, S.D., Aug. 18, 1934; d. Edward Martin and Gladys (Erickson) Rudloff; m. Vernon Wilford Blue, June 3, 1954; children: Debra, David, Diana, Paul, Mark, Ruth. Student, Augustana Coll., Sioux Falls, S.D., 1952-53, Huron Coll., 1953-54, U. Ill., Chgo., 1966-67; BA in Home Econ. Edn., Western Wash. U., 1970. Cert. vocat. home economist. Home econs. tchr. Mt. Vernon (Wash.) High Sch., 1970—. Docent Valley Mus. Art, La Conner, Wash., 1984-85; bd. dirs. Youth Encouragment Service, 1985; sec. to council Immaculate Conception Ch., 1980-83. Mem. AAUW (2d v.p. 1984-86), NEA, Am. Vocat. Assn., Wash Vocat Assn., Am Home Econs. Assn., Wash. Home Econs. Assn. (mktg. chmn. 1984-85, recognition chmn. 1986-87), Wash. Assn. Edn. Young Child. Roman Catholic. Home: 521 Shoshone Dr Mount Vernon WA 98273 Office: Mt Vernon High Sch 314 N Ninth Mount Vernon WA 98273

BLUE, ROSE, author, educator; b. N.Y.C.; d. Irving and Frieda (Rosenberg) Bluestone. B.A., Bklyn. Coll.; postgrad. Bank St. Coll. Edn., 1967. Tchr., N.Y.C. Public Schs., 1967—; writing cons. Bklyn. Coll. Sch. Edn., 1981-83. Author: A Quiet Place, 1969; Black, Black Beautiful Black, 1969; How Many Blocks Is The World, 1970; Bed-Stuy Beat, 1970; I Am Here (Yo Estoy Aqui), 1971; A Month of Sundays, 1972; Grandma Didn't Wave Back, 1972 (teleplay 1983); Nikki 108, 1973; We are Chicano, 1973; The Preacher's Kid, 1975; Seven Years from Home, 1976; The Yo Yo Kid, 1976; The Thirteenth Year, 1977; Cold Rain on the Water, 1979; My Mother The Witch, 1981 (teleplay 1984); Everybody's Evy, 1985; Heart to Heart, 1986, Goodbye Forever Tree, 1987. Lyricist: Drama of Love, 1964, Let's Face It, 1961, Give Me a Break, 1962, My Heartstrings Keep Me Tied To You, 1963, Homecoming Party, 1966. Contbg. editor: Teacher mag., Day Care mag. Mem. Authors Guild Am., Authors League Am., PEN, Mensa, Profl. Women's Caucus, Broadcast Music, Inc. Home and Office: 1320 51st St Brooklyn NY 11219

BLUESTEIN, JUDITH ANN, rabbi, educator diversified industry executive; b. Cin., Apr. 2, 1948; d. Paul Harold and Joan Ruth (Straus) Bluestein; BA, U. Pa., 1969; postgrad. Am. Sch. Classical Studies, Athens, Greece, 1968, Vergilian Soc., 1970, 76, 77, 78, Hebrew Union Coll., Jewish Inst. Religion, Jerusalem, 1971, 1979-80, Am. Acad. in Rome, 1975; MA in Religion, Case Western Res. U., 1973, MA in Latin, 1973; MEd, Xavier U., 1984; MAHL, Hebrew Union Coll.-Jewish Inst. Religion, Cin., 1983. Ordained rabbi, 1984. Sec., Paul H. Bluestein & Co., Cin., 1964—; v.p. Panel Machine Co., 1966—, Blujay Corp., 1966—, Ermet Products Corp., 1966—; ptnr. Companhia Engenheiros Indsl. Bluestein do Brasil, Cin., 1971—; tchr. Latin, Cin. Public Schs., 1973-79; rabbi Temple Israel, Marion, Ohio, 1980-84, Temple Sholom, Galesburg, Ill., 1985-86; co-chmn. Interfaith Plea for Soviet Jews, 1986; lectr. Hebrew Union Coll.-Jewish Inst. Religion, 1986—; vis. lectr./Jewish chaplain Denison U., 1987-88; bd. dirs. Cin. Council for Soviet Jews, 1982-84, 85—, sec. 1985-87. Fellow Case Western Reserve U., 1970-73, Hebrew Union Coll.-Jewish Inst. Religion, 1985—; Revson fellow Jewish Theol Sem. Am., 1984-85; Hausmon Meml. fellow Hebrew Union Coll. Jewish Inst. Religion, 1985-86; Isadore and Goldie Millstone fellow Hebrew Union Coll., 1986-87. Mem. Archeol. Inst. Am., Assn. Jewish Studies, Am. Acad. Religion, Classical Assn. Middle West and South (v.p. Ohio 1976-79), Central Conf. Am. Rabbis, Am. Classical League, Ohio Classical Conf. (council 1976-79), Vergilian Soc., Soc. Bibl. Lit., Cin. Assn. Tchrs. Classics (pres. 1976-78), Am. Philol. Assn. Address: 3420 Section Rd Cincinnati OH 45237

BLUESTEIN, VENUS WELLER, psychologist, educator; b. Milw., July 16, 1933; d. Richard T. and Hazel (Beard) Weller; m. Marvin Bluestein, Mar. 7, 1954. B.S., U. Cin., 1956, M.Ed., 1959, Ed.D., 1966. Diplomate Am. Bd. Examiners in Profl. Psychology. Psychologist-in-tng. Longview State Hosp., Cin., 1956-58; sch. psychologist Cin. Public Schs., 1958-65; asst. prof. psychology U. Cin., 1965-70, asso. prof., 1970-79, prof., 1979—, dir. undergrad. studies, 1976—, dir. sch. psychology program, 1965-70, co-dir. sch. psychology program, 1970-75; cons. child psychologist. Sec., U.S. exec. com. research Children's Internat. Summer Villages, 1964-68; chmn. Ohio Interuniv. Council Sch. Psychology, 1967-68. Editor Ohio Psychologist, 1961-68, co-editor, 1972-79; contbr. articles to profl. publs. Recipient George B. Barbour award, 1985. Mem. Am. Psychol. Assn., Cin. Psychol. Assn. (sec. 1961-62), Ohio Psychol. Assn. (citation 1972, Disting. Service award 1968), Sch. Psychologists Ohio, AAUP, Forum for Death Edn. and Counseling, Kappa Delta Pi, Sigma Delta Pi, Psi Chi (award for outstanding mentor 1985). Office: U Cin Dept Psychology Cincinnati OH 45221

BLUHM, SHARYL KAY, insurance company executive; b. Worthington, Minn., Feb. 27, 1945; d. Harold Joseph and Evelyn Marie (Skyberg) Erickson; children: Dennis Dean, Shari Lee. Grad. high sch., Waseca, Minn. Registered psychiat. tech., Minn.; lic. ins. Psychiat. tech. St. Minn., Fairbault, 1966-67; counselor special schs. St. Minn., Owatonna, 1967-72; office mgr. Pepsi-Cola, Taylorville, Ill., 1975-79; sales assoc. Am. Family Life Assurance Co., Columbus, Ga., 1979-80, mgr. dist., 1980-82, mgr. regional, 1982-85, mgr. St. Ill., 1985—; speaker Women's Expo '87, Ea. Ill. U., 1987. Treas. Sr. Baseball League, Taylorville, 1980-82; pres. PTA, Taylorville, 1981-82. Named one of Outstanding Young Women Am., Minn. Jaycees, 1975. Mem. Nat. Assn. Female Exec., Research Inst. Am. Inc Personal Report, Nat. Women's Econs. Alliance. Republican. Lutheran. Club: Jaycee, Owatonna. Office: Am Family Life Assurance Co PO Box 1327 Effingham IL 62401

BLUM, BARBARA DAVIS, banker; b. Hutchinson, Kans., July 6, 1939; d. Roy C. and Jo (McKinnon) Davis; children—Davis, Devin, Hunter, Ragan. Student, U. Kans., 1955-56, B.A., Fla. State U., 1958, M.S.W., 1959. Mem. faculty Pediatric Psychiatry Clinic, U. Kans. Med. Center, Lawrence, 1960-62; acting adminstr. Suffolk County (N.Y.) Mental Health Clinic, Huntington, L.I., 1963-64; founder, partner Mid-Suffolk Center for Psychotherapy, Hauppage, L.I., N.Y., 1964-66; v.p. Restaurant Associates of Ga., Inc., Atlanta, 1966-74; dep. adminstr. U.S. EPA, Washington, 1977-81; mem. Pres.'s Interag. Coordinating Counci; pres., chief exec. officer Adams Nat. Bank; adv. U.S. Del. to UN Environment Program Governing Council, Nairobi, Kenya, 1978, 79; chairperson U.S. Del., U.S./Japan Environ. Agreement, Tokyo, Japan, 1977-79; head 1st. U.S. Environ. Del. to Peoples' Republic of China, 1979; chmn. Environ. Policy Inst., 1981-86; dir., sr. adviser UN Environment Program; bd. dirs. Washington Bd. Trade. Chmn. D.C. Econ. Devel. Fin. Corp.; bd. dirs., exec. com. Environ-Law Inst.; pres. Save America's Vital Environment, Atlanta, 1972-76, Friends of the River, Inc., 1972-75; vice chairperson Fulton County (Ga.) Planning Commn., 1973-76; dep. polit. dir. Carter-Mondale Presdl. Campaign, 1976; nat. dep. dir. Carter-Mondale presdl. campaign, 1976; dir. ops. Carter/Mondale Transition Team, Washington, 1976-77; chmn. Nat. Adv. Commn. for Resource Conservation and Recovery; del. UN Mid Decade Conf. on Women, 1980, 1981; bd. dirs. Nat. Water Alliance, Global Waters; bd. dirs., pres. UN U. for Peace Found.; adv. bd. UN Audio Visual Trust. Decorated comdr.'s cross Order of Merit W. Ger.; recipient Disting. Service award Federally Employed Women, 1978, Spl. Conservation award Nat. Wildlife Fedn., 1976, Orgn. of Yr. award Ga. Wildlife Fedn., 1974, Disting. Service award Americans for Indian Opportunity, 1978. Mem. Washington Women's Network (dir., founder). Democrat.

BLUM, BARBARA MEDDOCK, association executive; b. Oil City, Pa., Nov. 8, 1938; d. Marvin Lee and Hazel Genevieve (Jackson) Meddock; B.A. in Psychology, Allegheny Coll., 1960; m. Stuart Hollander Blum, Sept. 21, 1963. Psychometrist, researcher Hofstra U., Hempstead, N.Y., 1960-62; adminstrv. asst., editor The Asia Soc., N.Y.C., 1962-66, exec. asst., 1966-72, adminstrv. officer, 1972-85, dir. adminstrn., 1985—. Mem. Am. Mgmt. Assn. Office: The Asia Soc 725 Park Ave New York NY 10021

BLUM, ELEANOR GOODFRIEND, educator; b. Detroit, July 16, 1940; d. William Henry and Dorothy Elaine (Oslander) Goodfriend; B.S. in Edn., Wayne State U., 1962, M.Ed., 1983; children—Beth Goodfriend, Sara Caroline. Kindergarten tchr. Livonia, Mich., 1962-63, Montgomery County, Md., 1963-64; tchr. Detroit Public Schs., 1977—, also reading coordinator King High Sch.; mem. edn. com. New Detroit Inc., 1981—. Vol. Detroit office of Senator Robert Griffin, 1972-74, asst. to appointments sec. to Pres. Nixon, Washington, 1972-74; chmn. March of Dimes Drive, Farmington, Mich., 1975; pres. Potomac Village Homeowners Assn., 1975; mem. 19th dist. Republican Com., 1975—, precinct del. 20th precinct, West Bloomfield, Mich.; alt. del. to Nat. Rep. conv., 1976; mem. exec. com. Oakland County Rep. Com., 1977-78; mem. Bloomfield Women's Rep. Club, West Bloomfield Rep. Women's Club; chmn. health com. Doherty Elem. Sch., 1975—; social studies tchr. Longfellow Middle Sch., 1983—. mem. library com. Temple Beth El, Birmingham, Mich., 1976, mem. library and arts coms., 1977-78; mem. urban affairs com. Jewish Community Council, 1977-78, community relations com., 1978-80, chmn. met. concerns com., 1979; mem. adv. bd. Oakland County March of Dimes, 1977-78, mem. bd., 1979; bd. dirs. Oakland Citizens League, 1983—; mem. Friends of West Bloomfield Library, 1975—, NAACP, 1979—; mem. com. on sheltered workshops, dept. mgmt and budget State of Mich., 1978-80; community relations com. Jewish Community Council, 1986—. Address: 31755 Ridgeside Dr Apt 21 Farmington Hills MI 48018

BLUM, JOAN KURLEY, fund raising exec.; b. Palm Beach, Fla., July 27, 1926; d. Nehad Daniel and Eva (Milos) Kurley; BA, U. Wash., 1948; m. Robert C. Blum, Apr. 15, 1967; children: Christopher Alexander, Martha Jane, Louisa Joan, Sherifa Carolyn, Paul Helmuth. Cert. fund raising exec. U.S. dir. Inst. Mediterranean Studies, Berkeley, Calif., 1962-65; devel. officer U. Calif. at Berkeley Alumni Assn., 1965-67; pres. Blum Assocs., Fund-Raising Cons., San Anselmo, Calif., 1967—; mem. faculty U. Calif. Extension, Inst. Fund Raising, SW Inst. Fund-Raising U. Tex., U. San Francisco, U.K. Vol. Movement Group, London, Australasian Inst. Fund Raising. Recipient Golden Addy award Am. Advt. Fedn.; Silver Mailbox award Direct Mail Mktg. Assn., Best Ann. Giving Time-Life award, others. Mem. Nat. Soc. Fund-Raising Execs. (dir.), Nat. Assn. of Hosp. Devel., Women Emerging. Club: Tamalpa Running. Lodge: Rotary. Contbr. numerous articles to profl. jours. Home: Kentfield CA 94904 Office: 292 Red Hill San Anselmo CA 94960

BLUM, MELANIE RAE, lawyer; b. N.Y.C., Aug. 6, 1949; d. Theodore and Gertrude (Brawer) Sands; m. Michael Phillip Blum (div. Oct. 1986); 1 child, Megan Alyse; m. Mark E. Roseman, Apr. 12, 1987. BA, Calif. State, Northridge, 1971; MBA, Calif. State U., Long Beach, 1978; JD, Loyola U., Los Angeles, 1981. Bar: Calif. 1981. Acct. Shain & Cohen, Los Angeles, Calif., 1969-71, INA, Los Angeles, 1971-72, Louis Kelso, San Francisco, 1972-75, O Asian, Inglewood, Calif., 1975-78; assoc. Law Offices of Richard Dickson, Newport Beach, Calif., 1982-83; sole practice Newport Beach, 1983—. Mem. ABA, Calif. Bar Assn., Orange County Bar Assn., Assn. Trial Lawyers Am., Calif. Trial Lawyers Assn., Phi Kappa Phi, Beta Gamma Sigma. Office: 4041 MacArthur Blvd Suite 250 Newport Beach CA 92660

BLUMBERG, ALYSE NEIBURG, financial planner; b. Phila., Dec. 17, 1946; d. Sidney Aaron and Deborah Pearl (Burstein) Neiburg; m. Peter S. Blumberg; children: F. Scott, Sarah Beth. BS, Pa. State U., 1968; MEd, Temple U., 1971. Tchr. North Pa. Sch. Dist., Lansdale, 1969-75; owner The Enchanted Closet, Spring House, Pa., 1980-82; pres. Soft Power, North Wales, Pa., 1984—; brokerage mgr. Transam. Occidental Life Cos., Lansdale, 1986—; registered rep. Transam. Fin. Resources, Lansdale, 1987—; ins. com. North Pa. Sch. Dist., Lansdale, 1969-72. Mem. mother's com. Germantown Acad., Ft. Washington, Pa., 1975—, 10K race dir., 1979-84, computer com., 1984-86. Mem. Nat. Assn. Female Execs., Montgomery County Women's Network, AAUW (bd. dirs. 1972-78), Montgomery County Estate Planning Council, Montgomery County Assn. Life Underwriters, Nat. Assn. Life Underwriters, Jaycettes (com. 1969-74), Phi Sigma Sigma. Republican. Jewish. Home: PO Box 1487 North Wales PA 19454 Office: Transam Occidental 121 Crestwood Dr Lansdale PA 19446

BLUMBERG, BARBARA MARILYN, history educator, writer; b. Bronx, N.Y., Oct. 27, 1936; d. Albert A. and Yvette (Beneck) Schneck; m. Paul Marvin Blumberg, Aug. 25, 1955 (div. 1973); 1 child, Ira Joseph; m. Alan L. Krumholz, Apr. 12, 1974; 1 child, Mark Reuben. A.B. in History, U. Calif.-Berkeley, 1968, M.A. in History, 1962; Ph.D. in History, Columbia U., 1974. Prof. history Adelphi U., Garden City, N.Y., 1967-68, Queens Coll., Flushing, N.Y., 1968-75, Pace U., N.Y.C., 1971—. Author: The New Deal and the Unemployed: The View from NYC, 1979; Celebrating the Immigrant: An Administrative History of the Statue of Liberty National Monument, 1952-82, 1985; editor NYC: Readings in History, Literature, and Culture, 1982. Mem. Inst. Research in History (dir. 1983-84, mem. exec. com., sec. 1985-86, editor The Memorandum), Women in the Hist. Profession (co-chmn. coordinating com. N.Y. 1983-84), Am. Hist. Assn., Orgn. Am. Historians, Phi Beta Kappa. Office: Pace Univ Pace Plaza New York NY 10570

BLUMBERG, BARBARA SALMANSON (MRS. ARNOLD G. BLUMBERG), state housing official; b. Bklyn., Oct. 2, 1927; d. Sam and Mollie (Greenberg) Salmanson; B.A., De Pauw U., 1948; postgrad. New Sch. for Social Research, N.Y.C.; m. Arnold G. Blumberg, June 19, 1949; children—Florence Ellen Schwartz, Martin Jay, Emily Anne. Pub. relations Nate Fein & Co., N.Y.C., 1948-51; free lance, 1960—; councilwoman, North Hempstead, 1975-82; adviser to energy com. N.Y. State Assembly, 1982-84; dir. spl. needs housing Div. Housing and Community Renewal, State of N.Y. Pres., UN Assn. Great Neck, N.Y., 1967-69, chmn. China Study Workshop, 1966-67; pres. Shalom chpt. Hadassah, 1955-57; exec. v.p. Lakeville P.T.A., Great Neck, 1963-65; exec. v.p. Great Neck S. Jr. High Sch., 1965-66; co-chmn. Great Neck UNICEF, 1968-70, mem. speakers bur., 1971—; v.p. Herricks Community Life Center, 1976-77, B'nai B'rith, Lake Success, N.Y.; coordinator, 6th Congl. Dist., N.Y. McGovern for Pres.; bd. dirs. New Democratic Coalition of Nassau, Am. Jewish Congress, Am. Jewish Com., Day Care Council of Nassau County; v.p. Reform Dem. Assn. Great Neck; bd. dirs. Citizen's Sch. Com., Great Neck; mem. platform com. Nassau Dem. Com.; mem. adv. com. to speaker N.Y. State Assembly. Recipient award Anti-Defamation League, New Hyde Park, N.Y., 1975, Alumni award DePauw U., 1977, Hadassah New Life award, 1980. Mem. N.Y. Alumni Club DePauw U. (trustee), North Shore Archeol. Assn. (chmn. study group), Women in Communication, Internat. Platform Assn., L.I. Women's Network (co-convenor), Alpha Lambda Delta. Home: 12 Birch Hill Rd Great Neck NY 11020 Office: HFA 3 Park Ave New York NY 10016

BLUMBERG, JULIA BAUM, community leader, educator; b. Hazleton, Pa.; d. Benjamin and Ida Ruth (Lurie) Baum; Ph.B. summa cum laude, Muhlenberg Coll., Allentown, Pa.; postgrad. NYU, Columbia U.; m. Dr. Leo Blumberg, Aug. 9, 1938. Mem. faculty Bethlehem (Pa.) Sr. High Sch., dir. placement comml. grads., 1938-46. Life mem. B'nai B'rith Women, organized Bethlehem group, 1938, pres. Bethlehem, 1938-39, pres. Dist. 3, 1945-46, mem. nat. exec. bd., 1957-59, rep. nat. orgn., 1957-59, chmn. nat. vocat. guidance, 1957-59, chmn. dist. 3 Klutznick scholarship award, 1966-69, mem. bd. B'nai B'rith Women of Wilmington, pres. vocational service bd., 1962-64; life mem. Temple Beth Emeth Sisterhood, mem. bd., 1949-59, 70-88; treas. Dist 8, Nat. Fedn. Temple Sisterhoods, 1952-56; mem. nat. exec. bd. nat. fedn., 1953-57; gen. chmn. Dist. 8 conv., Wilmington, 1957; pres. community adv. bd. Hillel Counselorship, U. Del., 1979-88; mem. bd. Wilmington City Fedn. Women's Clubs and Allied Orgns., 1951—, 1st v.p., 1961-63, pres., 1963-65; mem. bd. mgrs. Florence Crittendon Home of Del., 1955-61; mem. Women's div. Brandeis U.; life life mem. Aux. Kutz Home for Aged, also bd. dirs. aux., 1972-88, named Hon. Life Chmn. Bd., 1983; mem. Nat. Commn. Vocational Service, 1957-59, Mayor's Com. for Christmas, Mayor's Com. for UN; mem. bd. UNICEF, 1972-82; mem. steering com. CARE, Inc., 1971-82; mem. Del. Nature Edn. Soc., Inc., 1963-88, Del. Council on Crime and Justice; chmn. bldg. and furniture com., dedication com. Hillel Found. at U. Del., 1963-64, hon. life chmn. community adv. bd. B'nai B'rith Hillel Counselorship, U. Del.; mem. women's div. Jewish Fedn. Del.; mem. bldg. fund com. St. Francis Hosp., 1973; v.p. bd. dirs. Kutz Home Aux. Appointed chmn. survey com. for accreditation Bethlehem (Pa.) Sr. High Sch. Author accrediting guide: The Philosophy and Aims & Objectives of Secondary Education. Mem. Nat. Council Jewish Women (life), Greater Wilmington Fedn. Women's Orgns. (dir. 1965-69, 69-73, 73-77, 77-86, pres. Past Officers Club 1965-67, historian 1973-75, dir. 1975—), Del. Mental Health Assn., Crippled Children and Adults Soc. Del., Hadassah (life), B'nai B'rith Women (life), Phi Sigma Iota. Jewish (life mem., pres. Sisterhood 1952-53, mem. bd. 1970-88, dir. temple 1952-55). Clubs: Widener U. Faculty Wives (hon. life), Wilmington New Century (internat. relations com. 1978-88, edn. com. 1978-86). Home: 1401 Pennsylvania Ave Apt 406 Wilmington DE 19806

BLUMBERG, NANCY FERN, accountant; b. Bronx, N.Y., July 19, 1946; d. Samuel and Sabina (Sauer) Kowlowitz; m. Jay A. Blumberg; children: Richard, Marc. BS in Acctg., Queens Coll., 1967; MS in Taxation, Widener U., 1982; postgrad., Coll. of Fin. Planning, 1986—. CPA, Del. Revenue agt. IRS, Richmond and Wilmington, Va. and Del., 1967-71; tax supr. Krieger, Dwares and Stein, CPA's, Wilmington, 1972-80; dir. tax dept. Simon, Master and Sidlow, P.A., Wilmington, 1980—; planning com. Del. Tax Inst., Wilmington, 1986—; speaker Del. Women's Conf., 1987, Del. Tax Inst., 1986. Contbr. articles to profl. jours. Asst. treas. Cong. Beth Shalom, 1986—, treas., 1986—. Mem. Wilmington Women in Bus., Wilmington Tax

Group, Am. Inst. CPA's (Elijah Watt Sells award 1983), Am. Soc. Women Accts., Delaware Soc. CPA's. Jewish. Lodge: B'nai B'rith Women (v.p. 1974-77, treas. 1972-74). Office: Simon Master and Sidlow PA 2002 W 14th St Wilmington DE 19806

BLUME, ELIZABETH RENEE, office manager, clinical research coordinator; b. Warren, Pa., Aug. 29, 1953; d. William Wesley and Betty Josephine (Anderson) B. Grad. Little Valley Central Sch. Motor vehicle acct. Cattaraugus County, Little Valley, N.Y., 1971-76; asst. office mgr. Dr. Widger and Dr. Gutierrez, Salamanca, N.Y., 1976-80; adminstrv. sec. The U. Tex. Med. Sch., Houston, 1980; exec. sec. Stanley J. Dudrick, M.D., Houston, 1980-87; office mgr. Joseph J. O'Donnell MD, Livingston, Tex., 1988—. Co-author Annals of Surgery, 1983, Transactions of the So. Surg. Assn., The Yearbook of Surgery and Gastroenterology. Co-chmn. United Way Campaign dept. surgery The U. Tex. Med. Sch., Houston, 1980. Recipient Sorosis Literary Guild award for English N.Y. State Fed. Women's Clubs, 1971, Eastern Star award, 1971. Mem. Stanley J. Dudrick Found. and Soc., Am. Soc. for Nutritional Support Services (exec. sec., bd. dirs. 1983-87, co-author Sci. poster session 1982, 84, 85, Exceptional Contbrn. award 1986), Am. Soc. for Parenteral and Enteral Nutrition (co-author sci. poster session 1982, 84), Eur. Soc. Parenteral and Enteral Nutrition (co-author sci. poster session 1985), Theta Rho (pres. 1969-70). Home: PO Box 971 Livingston TX 77351 Office: 205 N Houston Livingston TX 77351

BLUME, GINGER (ELAINE), psychologist; b. Lock Haven, Pa., Apr. 8, 1948; d. Martin Luther and Virginia Ruth (Rudy) B.; B.A., U. Fla., 1970, M.A., 1975, Ph.D., 1979. Predoctoral intern in psychology VA Hosp., West Haven, Conn., 1976-77; postdoctoral intern in psychology Elmcrest Psychiat. Inst., Portland, Conn., 1977-78; pvt. practice clin. psychology, Middletown, Conn., 1978—; corp. cons., 1983—; assoc. Harrison Assocs., Inc., Cons., Berkeley, Calif.; co-owner, program dir. PMT Assocs. Inc.; affiliated faculty New Eng. Type Inst. mem. adj. psychology faculty Middlesex Community Coll., Antioch Grad. Sch., Keene, N.H.; bd. dirs. Gilead House halfway facility, SAFE sexual assault clinic, Family Resource Center; cons. in field. Mem. Am. Psychol. Assn., Conn. Psychol. Assn., Orthopsychiatry Assn., Internat. Imagery Assn., Am. Soc. Tng. and Devel., Orgnl. Devel. Network, AAUW (chairperson edn. found. program), Phi Kappa Phi, Kappa Delta. Club: Soroptimists, Exchange. Home: 77 Oak Ridge Dr Haddam CT 06438 Office: 11 S Main St Middletown CT 06457

BLUME, JUDY SUSSMAN, author; b. Elizabeth, N.J., Feb. 12, 1938; d. Rudolph and Esther (Rosenfeld) Sussman; m. John M. Blume, Aug. 15, 1959 (div. Jan. 1975); children: Randy Lee, Lawrence Andrew; m. George Cooper, June 6, 1987; 1 stepchild, Amanda. B.A. in Edn, N.Y. U., 1960; LHD (hon.), Kean Coll., 1987. Author: fiction books including Are You There God, It's Me Margaret (selected as outstanding children's book 1970), Then Again, Maybe I Won't, 1971, It's Not the End of the World, 1972, Tales of a 4th Grade Nothing, 1972, Otherwise Known as Sheila the Great, 1972, Deenie, 1973, Blubber, 1974, Forever, 1976, Superfudge, 1980, Tiger Eyes, 1981, Just As Long As We're Together, 1987, others; adult novels Wifey, 1978, Smart Women, 1984; Letters to Judy: What Your Kids Wish They Could Tell You, 1986. Bd. dirs. Sex. Info. and Edn. Council of the U.S., Planned Parenthood Advocates. Recipient Carl Sandburg Freedom to Read award Chgo. Pub. Library, 1984, the Civil Liberties award ACLU, 1986, John Rock award Ctr. for Population Options, 1986; numerous Children's Choice awards, U.S.A., Europe, Australia. Mem. Authors League and Guild, Soc. Children's Book Writers, PEN, Nat. Coalition Against Censorship (council of advisers). Office: care Harold Ober Assos 40 E 49th St New York NY 10017

BLUME, SHEILA BIERMAN, psychiatrist; b. Bklyn., June 21, 1934; d. Benjamin and Rose (Lazar) Bierman; student Cornell U., 1951-54; M.D. cum laude, Harvard U., 1958; m. Martin Blume, June 12, 1955; children—Frederick, Janet. Intern, Children's Hosp. Med. Center, Boston, 1958-59; Fulbright fellow to Tokyo U., 1959-60; resident in psychiatry Central Islip Psychiat. Center, 1962-65; dir. Charles K. Post Alcoholism Rehab. Center, Central Islip Psychiat. Center, 1964-79; dir. N.Y. State Div. Alcoholism and Alcohol Abuse, 1979-83; med. dir. Nat. Council on Alcoholism, 1984; med. dir. Alcoholism, Compulsive Gambling and Chem. Dependency Programs, South Oaks Hosp., 1984—; clin. assoc. prof. psychiatry Albany Med. Center, 1979-82; clin. prof. psychiatry SUNY-Stony Brook, 1984—; apptd. to Nat. Commn. Alcoholism and Other Alcohol Related Problems, 1980; mem. Nat. Commn. Confidentiality of Health Records, 1976-80, Nat. Council on Compulsive Gambling, adv. bd., 1972—; bd. dirs. Children of Alcoholics Found., 1983—. Recipient Dr. Milton Helpern Disting. Physicians award for contbn. field of alcoholism, 1980, Harold Riegelman award for contbn. to field of alcohol policy, 1983. Mem. L.I. Council Alcoholism (dir. 1972-79), Am. Med. Soc. Alcoholism (dir., pres. 1979-80), Nat. Council Alcoholism, (dir.). Editor: (with S. Zimberg and J. Wallace) Practical Approaches to Alcoholism Psychotherapy, 1978; editor Bull. Suffolk County Med. Soc., 1969-76; contbr. articles profl. jours., chpts. in books. Home and Office: 284 Greene Ave Sayville NY 11782 also: South Oaks Hosp Amityville NY 11701

BLUSHI, CATHERINE MANGANELLO, finance company executive; b. Weymouth, Mass., Jan. 23, 1961; d. Lucius and Ruth Frances (Johnson) Manganello; m. Joseph Thomas Blushi Jr., Nov. 3, 1984. AS, Aquinas Jr. Coll., Milton, Mass., 1981; BS, Lesley Coll., 1984, MS, 1987. Sec. John Hancock Mut. Life Ins. Co., Boston, 1982-83; asst. to treas. John Hancock Advisers, Inc., Boston, 1983-84, asst. mgr. mut. funds, 1984-86, mgr. mut. funds, 1986—. Mem. Mass. Paralegal Assn. Office: John Hancock Advisers Inc 101 Huntington Ave Boston MA 02199

BLUST, JEANNE ELIZABETH, nurse; b. N.J., Jan. 10, 1943; d. Vincent Maurice and Ellen Kennedy (Adams) B.; A.A., Union Jr. Coll., 1963; R.N., Elizabeth Gen. Hosp. Sch. Nursing, 1964; B.A., Marymount Manhattan Coll., 1978; M.A. in Bus. Mgmt. and Human Relations, Webster U., St. Louis, 1983. Supr. nursing Elizabeth Gen. Hosp., 1970-71; asst. and head nurse Mt. Sinai Hosp., N.Y.C., 1967-70, clin. nursing coordinator intravenous and transfusion therapy, 1971-78, coordinator IV therapy cert. course Sch. Continuing Edn. in Nursing, 1978-80; clin. supr. cardiothoracic surgery Mt. Sinai Med. Center, N.Y.C., 1978-80; cons., lectr. IV and transfusion therapy, 1978—; ednl. coordinator blood services ARC, Louisville, 1981-83, asst. to mgr. program devel. and evaluation, 1981-85; adminstr. Medicare for Quality Care Nursing Service, Louisville, 1985-87; house supr. Jefferson Hosp., Jeffersonville, Ind., 1987—; pres. Chelsea Health Care Cons., Jeffersonville, 1987—; instr. St. Johns Coll. Pharmacy, 1977-80, Ind. Vocat. Tech. Coll., Sellersburg, 1987—. Allentown Paint Co. scholar, 1961-64. Mem. Nat. Intravenous Therapy Assn., IV Therapist Assn. Greater N.Y. (past pres.), Hosp. Alumni Assn., Am. Assn. Blood Banks, Am. Nurses Assn. Nurse rep. nat. coordinating com. on large volume parenterals U.S. Pharmacopia, 1977. Mem. editorial bd. Am. Jour. IV Therapy, 1975—. Home: 208 Hopkins Ln Jeffersonville IN 47130

BLUTTER, JOAN WERNICK, interior designer; b. London, July 6, 1929; naturalized, 1948; d. Samuel and Bertha (Cohn) Wernick; m. Melvyn Blutter, Oct. 29, 1948; 1 child, Janet Lesley. Student, Northwestern U., 1944. Pres. Blutter Shiff Design Group, Chgo., 1955—; ptnr. Mel Blutter Co., Chgo.; partner Designers Collaborative, San Francisco, 1975—; design cons. Reed, Ltd., Toronto, Can., Exec. House Ltd., Chgo.; bd. dirs. Fashion Group. Contbr.: articles to Interior Design; others. bd. dirs. United Cerebral Palsy. Fellow Am. Soc. Interior Designers (past pres. Ill. chpt., past nat. sec., nat. chmn. industry 1978-79, nat. chmn. Design Interest program 1981-82, recipient Gold Key award, design award, Presdl. citation, Designer of Year 1979); mem. Nat. Soc. Interior Design (past chpt. pres., sec., bd. chmn.), LWV, Nat. Home Fashions League, Mchts. and Mfrs. Club, Art Inst. Chgo., Mus. Contemporary Art. Home: 2801 N Sheridan Rd Chicago IL 60657 Office: 1648 Merchandise Mart Chicago IL 60654 also: 85 Blvd Berthier, Paris 17 France

BLYTH, MYRNA GREENSTEIN, magazine publisher, editor, author; b. N.Y.C., Mar. 22, 1939; d. Benjamin and Betty (Austin) Greenstein; m. Jeffrey Blyth, Nov. 25, 1962; children: Jonathan, Graham. B.A., Bennington (Vt.) Coll., 1960. Sr. editor Datebook mag., N.Y.C., 1960-62, Ingenue mag., N.Y.C., 1963-68; book editor Family Health mag., 1968-71; book and fiction editor, then assoc. editor Family Circle mag., N.Y.C., 1972-81; exec. editor Family Circle mag., 1978-81; editor-in-chief Ladies' Home Jour., 1981—, pub. dir., 1987—; freelance writer, contbr. mags. Author: novels Cousin Suzanne, 1975, For Better and For Worse, 1978; contbr. articles to New Yorker mag., New York mag., Redbook mag., Cosmopolitan mag., Reader's Digest. Bd. dirs. Child Care Action campaign, N.Y.C., 1987-88. Mem. Am. Soc. Mag. Editors (exec. com. 1987-88), Women's Media Group, Authors League. Office: Ladies' Home Journal 100 Park Ave New York NY 10017

BO, KRISTIE LEE, graphic designer; b. Chgo., Dec. 20, 1954; d. Jack Edward and Bernice Dell (Hagen) Falls; m. Steven Knute Bo, Apr. 8, 1982 (div. Sept. 1986). AA, Lake County Coll., 1975; BFA in Graphic Design, Ariz. State U., 1978. Operator Ill. Bell Telephone Co., Libertyville, 1971-76; sec. activities dept. Lake County Coll., Grayslake, Ill., 1973-76; designer Clark Pub. Co., Phoenix, 1977; tng. cons., asst. Spectra Cons., Tempe, Ariz., 1977-78; designer Habitat, Tempe, 1978-79, Henry Schmidt Design, Boulder, Colo., 1979-80; mgr. graphics dept. Willdan Assocs., Phoenix, 1980-82; owner, pres. The Cricket Contrast, Phoenix, 1982—. Mem. Nat. Assn. Female Execs., Arizonans for Cultural Devel., Phoenix Soc. Communicating Artists, Graphic Artists Guild. Office: The Cricket Contrast 2301 N 16th St Phoenix AZ 85006

BOAMAN, MARY ANN ELIZABETH, systems consultant; b. Darby, Pa., Dec. 17, 1957; d. John James and Mary Ann (Timlin) Murphy; m. Stephen Carlin, July 23, 1976 (div. Oct. 1983); 1 child, Stephen Matthew; m. James Peter Boaman, Oct. 13, 1984. Cert. in life, property and casualty ins., Profl. Sch. Bus., 1980; student, U. Pa., 1982-83, Widener U., 1983—. Lic. property and casualty broker. Caterer Murphy's Delicatessen/Catering, Drexel Hill, Pa., 1972-77; gen. supr. Lee Fin. Services, Upper Darby, Pa., 1977-78; mgr. All. Am. Ins. Agy., Trenton, N.J., 1978-81; supr. CIGNA, Phila., 1981-82; acctg. asst. mgr. CIGNA, Wilmington, Del., 1982-83; ops. mgr. CIGNA, Phila., 1983-85; methods cons. CIGNA, Voorhees, N.J., 1985-87, systems cons., 1987—. Mem. Alpha Sigma Lambda. Republican. Roman Catholic. Club: Christian Youth Orgn. (Drexel Hill) (adult vol. 1986—). Lodge: Soroptomists (v.p., del. Phila. chpt. 1985-86). Home: 326 Clearbrook Ave Lansdowne PA 19050 Office: CIGNA 401 White Horse Rd Voorhees Township NJ 08043

BOARDMAN, ROSANNE VIRGINIA, military science executive; b. Twin Falls, Idaho, Oct. 4, 1946; d. Gordon Ross and Garnet Othalia (Peterson) Tobin; m. Lowell Jay Boardman, May 12, 1973. BA cum laude, Occidental Coll., 1968; MA with honors, Columbia U., 1969, postgrad., U. Calif., Irvine, 1971-72, U. Calif., Santa Barbara, 1973-74. Cert. jr. coll. tchr., Calif., cert. secondary tchg., Calif. Instr. U. Calif., Irvine, 1971-72, Ventura (Calif.) Community Coll., 1973-77; engring. analyst John J. McMullen Co., Ventura, 1978-80; sr. logistics specialist Raytheon Co., Ventura, 1977-78, 80-83; civilian tech. writer, editor USN, Port Hueneme, Calif., 1983-84, civilian logistics mgr., 1984—. Author numerous manuals and logistics guides. Internat. fellow Occidental Coll., 1967; recipient Outstanding Performance award Naval Ship Weapon Systems Engring. Sta., 1985, 86. Mem. Soc. Logistics Engrs., Phi Beta Kappa.

BOARDO, ELIZABETH ANNE, entertainer; b. Dorchester, Mass., Oct. 22, 1961; d. James O. and Jeanette (Parrella) B. Grad. high sch., Holliston, Mass. Appeared in TV's 21st Ann. Acad. Music Awards, Acad. Country Music's Hat Awards, 1986; records include First Time I Saw You, You're Making it Easy, Still Enough of Us, Need to Be Loved Again, Help Yourself to My Heart. Religious class tchr. St. Mary's Ch., Holliston, 1983-84; fund raiser entertainer Charles River Assn. for Retarded Citizens, Boston, 1986. Recipient Most Promising Female award Mass. Country Music Awards Assn., 1982, Peoples Choice award Mass. Country Music Awards Assn., 1984, 85, Top Female Vocalist award Mass. Country Music Awards Assn., 1986, Achievement award Country Music Festival Nebr., 1986; named #1 Female Artist Cash Box Ind., 1987. Office: PO Box 412 Holliston MA 01746

BOATMAN, SARA ADAMS, college administrator; b. Nebraska City, Nebr., July 3, 1943; d. Ellis Wilse and Corinne Faye (Whitfield) Adams; m. Thomas Max Boatman, June 27, 1965; 1 child, Elizabeth C. BA, Nebr. Wesleyan U., 1965; MA, U. Nebr., 1973, PhD, 1985. Tchr. Dorchester (Nebr.) Pub Schs., 1965-67, Lincoln (Nebr.) S.E. High Sch., 1967-70; grad. teaching asst. U. Nebr., Lincoln, 1971-73, program mgr. Nebr. Union,, 1974-78, dir. campus activites and programs, 1978—, instr. speech communication, 1981—; instr. communications Doane Coll., Crete, Nebr., 1973-74; instr. Am. Inst. Banking, Lincoln, 1970-71; cons. colls. and univs., 1984—. Contbr. articles to profl. jours.; presenter numerous workshops at nat. and regional seminars and confs. Pres. community adv. council Lincoln East Jr.-Sr. High Sch., 1985—; panelist communication and common sense project, Planned Parenthood, Lincoln, 1985—; commr. Chancellors' Commn. on Status of Women, U. Nebr., 1986—; chair com. Nebr. Wesleyan Centennial Celebration Com., Lincoln, 1986—. Recipient Outstanding Alumni award Nebr. Wesleyan U., 1987. Mem. Internat. Communication Assn., Nat. Assn. for Campus Activites (chair 1983-84, Founders' award 1987, Sara Boatman award established in her honor 1984), Nat. Assn. Student Personnel Adminstrs., Speech Communication Assn., Am. Coll. Personnel Assn., Assn. Voluntary Action Scholars, Am. Assn. Counseling and Devel., Cen. States Speech Communication Assn., Nebr. Speech Communication Assn. Democrat. Methodist. Office: U Nebr 200 Nebr Union Lincoln NE 68588-0453

BOATRIGHT, ANN LONG, dancer, music educator, choreographer; b. Louisville, Jan. 11, 1947; d. William Frazier and Mary Madolin (Hagan) Long; m. Ned Collins Boatright Jr., June 15, 1968; 1 child, Elizabeth. Student, Jordan Coll. Music, 1960-65, Butler U., 1965-68; BA, SUNY, Plattsburgh, 1970; MusM, Ithaca Coll., 1974. Cert. tchr. N.Y., Ohio. Music tchr. pub. schs., Plattsburgh, Ithaca, and Rochester, N.Y., 1970-76; head dance program Columbus (Ohio) Sch. for Girls, 1977-82; instr. Suzuki piano Capital U., 1982-85, instr. eurythmics, 1982—, developer tchr. tng. for music and movement, 1985-88; past tchr. eurythmics, music, movement Lake Forest Coll., Capital U., Wittenberg U., Ohio State U., Eastern Mich. U., Denison U., Utah State U.; tchr. Suzuki and traditional piano, Columbus, 1985—; ballet soloist with Jordan Coll. Music Co., Butler U., Ithaca Ballet Co.; dancer with Indpls. Civic Ballet Co., Columbus Theatre Ballet Co.; pianist with Butler U. String Trio. Choreographer: (ballets, mus. comedies) Odds 'n Ends, 1980, Little Match Girl, 1979, Crusades, 1982, Ballet of Unhatched Chicks, 1982, Wheels, 1979, Marathon, 1981. Mem. Arts For Peace-Unify Ohio, 1986, women's service bd. Grant Med. Ctr., Franklin Park Conservatory, St. Mark's Episcopal Ch., jr. council Columbus Mus. Art, Zephyrus League. Mem. Music Tchrs. Nat. Assn. (nat. cert.), Ohio Music Tchrs. Assn. (condr. various workshops, clinician 1986-87, summer camp 1988), Nat. Guild Piano Tchrs., Am. Coll. Musicians (faculty), Suzuki Assn. Ams., Suzuki Assn. Ohio, Alpha Chi Omega, Sigma Alpha Iota. Republican. Home: 4000 Newhall Rd Columbus OH 43220

BOATWRIGHT, MARY HOWARD, mem. Republican Nat. Com.; b. Houston, Apr. 8, 1920; d. Arch Franklin and Dorothy (Bennett) Howard; A.B., Trinity Coll., Washington, 1941; m. Victor Taliaferro Boatwright, Aug. 29, 1945; children—Mary Dorsey, John Lord, William Howard, Mary Taliaferro. Mem. Bd. Wardens and Burgesses Stonington (Conn.) Borough, 1960-64; mem. Conn. Ho. of Reps. from 43d Dist., 1962-66; mem. Rep. Nat. Com. for Conn., 1972—. Roman Catholic. Address: 16 Denison Ave Stonington CT 06378

BOAZ, DONALEE, psychotherapist, consultant; b. Grand Junction, Colo., Apr. 8, 1934; d. Leon T. and Marian (Fonder) Hutton; m. Richard Boas, Apr. 7, 1956 (div. 1983); children: Roxanne, Annika, Becca. Cert. pastoral ministry Seattle U., 1978; cert. clin. pastoral edn. Va. Mason Hosp., 1979; BA, Antioch West, 1980; postgrad. Lan Ting Inst., Fujian Province, China, 1986, C.G. Jung Inst., Zurich, 1986, 87. Cert. neuro-linguistic programmer, 1982. Owner Donalee's Studio of Dance, Kirkland, Wash., 1952-63; adminstrv. asst. Ch. of Redeemer, Kenmore, Wash., 1974-76; counselor Eastside Mental Health, Bothell, Wash., 1976-79; psychotherapist, Seattle, 1979—; owner, cons. Optimum Options, Seattle, 1979—; mem. adj. faculty Seattle U. Northwest Coll. Holistic Studies and Huston Sch. Theology, 1980-87; cons. various non-profit orgns., Phoenix, Los Angeles, Seattle. Vice pres. Episcopal Ch. standing com. on stewardship, 1979-81; active in local politics, 1968-80. Assoc. mem. Clin. Pastoral Edn., Pacific N.W. Speakers Assn., Wash. Assn. Counseling and Devel. Avocations: philosophy; carpentry; bridge; entertaining; travel. Office: Optimum Options Grosvenor House 500 Wall St Suite 322 Seattle WA 98121

BOB, SHARON HELENE, college management and financial consultant; b. Buffalo, Apr. 4, 1949; d. Ruth (Gitlin) B. Student, SUNY, Cortland, 1967-68; BA in Psychology summa cum laude, SUNY, Buffalo, 1971; MEd, U. Md., 1974, cert. advanced grad. specialist, 1984, PhD, 1976. Asst. admissions U. Md., College Park, 1971-74; officer fin. aid Montgomery Coll., Rockville, Md., 1974; dir. fin. aid Takoma Park, Md., 1974-76; coordinator fin. aid programs State Council Higher Edn. for Va., Richmond, 1976-79; fellow in edn. policy Inst. for Ednl. Leadership George Washington U., Washington, 1979-80; exec. asst. to pres. Strayer Coll., Washington, 1980-82, v.p. for external affairs, 1983-84; v.p., dir. Arlington (Va.) campus Strayer Coll., 1984-86; exec. dir. Nat. Coll. Services, Ltd., Gaithersburg, Md., 1987-88; govt. affairs specialist Clohan, Adams & Dean, Washington, 1988—. Author: (with others) (fin. aid booklet) The College Financial Aid Emergency Kit, 1982-88; editor Va. Assn. Student Fin. Aid Adminstr.'s Jour.; contbr. articles to profl. jours. Mem. Columbia Pike Revitalization Task Force Arlington Econ. Devel. Div. Recipient cert. of appreciation Va. Assn Student Fin. Aid Adminstrs., 1978; State of N.Y. grantee, 1971. Mem. Assn. Ind. Colls. and Schs. (student fin. aid adminstrs. com., evaluation teams, faculty mid-level mgmt. seminars), Arlington C. of C. (chmn. edn. com.), Phi Beta Kappa, Kappa Delta Pi. Home: 1900 Lyttonsville Rd #1105 Silver Spring MD 20910

BOBINSKI, BARBARA LYNN, health company director; b. Edinburgh, Scotland, Nov. 1, 1960; d. Konrad John and Wilma Nadine (Glass) B. BS in Mktg., Fla. State U., 1983. Fitness instr. Westwood Fitness, Tallahassee, 1982-83; service and tng. cons. Physicians Weight Loss Ctr., Akron, Ohio, 1984-86; area dir. Physicians Weight Loss Ctr., Tampa, Fla., 1986—. Pres. high sch. DECA program Wm. R. Boone Sr. High Sch., Orlando, Fla. Mem. Nat. Assn. Female Execs., Fla. State U. Alumni Assn. Republican. Roman Catholic. Home: 7585 E Peakview Ave #922 Englewood CA 80111 Office: PWLC 11210 N Dale Mabry Tampa FL 33618

BOBITT, CARLENE SHINN, advertising executive; b. Blue Ridge, Tex., Jan. 25, 1929; d. John Ross and Ethelene (Patterson) Shinn; m. Thomas William Bobitt, June 27, 1947; 1 child Robyn Elise. Grad. high sch., Farmersville, Tex. Collector Gen. Electric Credit Corp., Dallas, 1947-50; supr. printing ops. systems and procedures dept. Republic Gas Co., Dallas, 1950-61; co-owner Bobitt's Printery, Austin, Tex., 1974-78, Bobitt's Advt., Paris, Tex., 1978—. Cellist Paris Community Orchestra, 1984-86. Republican. Methodist. Clubs: Altrusa (v.p., treas., Altrusan of Yr. 1987-88); Tempo Music (pres. 1985-87).

BOCHENKO, CAROLE ANNE, personnel manager; b. Phila., Nov. 27, 1945; d. Walter Francis and Margaret Jane (Hindman) Thompson; m. Robert Bochenko, Nov. 22, 1980 (div. May 1983). B.A., Temple U., Phila., 1978. Cert. occupational health and safety, Temple U., Villanova U. Asst. safety supr. Phila. Coke Co. Inc., Phila., 1969-71, safety supr., 1971-73, dir. personnel and safety, 1973-78; div. mgr. safety and security Kelsey Hayes Co., Phila., 1978-86, corp. mgr. personnel, Heintz Corp., 1986-88, exec. v.p., dir. Powell Envirn., Inc., 1988—; pres., chmn. Data Research, Inc., Phila., 1983—; dir. Affiliated Med., Phila., 1983—; lectr. Drexel U., 1983-84; cons in field Contbr. articles to profl. jours. Chmn. first aid and safety programs ARC, Phila., 1974-76. Recipient safety achievement awards Phila. Safety Council. Mem. Am. Soc. Safety Engrs. (treas. Phila. chpt. 1978-79, 80), Nat. Safety Mgmt. Soc., AAUW, Nat. Assn. Female Execs., Am. Soc. Personnel Adminstrs., Nat. Fire Protection Assn., Ind. Relations Assn. Phila., Am. Mgmt. Assn. Republican. Home: 206 Berkeley Trace Bensalem PA 19020 Office: Heintz Corp 11000 Roosevelt Blvd Philadelphia PA 19116

BOCHICCHIO-AUSURA, JILL ARDEN, photographer; b. Indpls., Jan. 22, 1951; d. Anthony Joseph and Claire Gilbert (Parkin) Bochicchio; m. Robert Vincent Ausura Apr. 21, 1979; 1 child, Bret Anthony Bochicchio-Ausura. AA, Montgomery Coll., 1971; BS, Ind. State U., 1974, MS, 1976. Cert. master photographer, profl. photographer. Instr. photography Montgomery Coll., Rockville, Md., 1976-79; prin. Bochicchio Photography, Gaithersburg, Md., 1983—; lectr. in field. Contbr. photographs to So. Exposure. Recipient Kodak Crystal award Eastman Kodak Co., 1987, Kodak Gallery award Eastman Kodak Co., 1987, 88. Mem. Profl. Photographers Am. (master photographer 1987), Southeastern Profl. Photographers Assn. (1st pl. creative photograph 1985, 1st pl. wedding photograph 1985), Md. Profl. Photographers Assn. (fellow 1985, bd. dirs. 1984—, Photographer of Yr. 1984, Creative Photographer of Yr., 1984, 85, 86, 87, Hartig Meml. award, 1985, 86, 87,88), Upper Montgomery County C. of C. Home and Office: Bochicchio Photography 808-101 Quince Orchard Blvd Gaithersburg MD 20878

BOCHOW, SHAR LYNN, realtor; b. Lynwood, Calif., Oct. 10, 1947; d. Milton Lee and Emogene (Robertson) Anderson; m. Tarry Lee Cluff, Jan. 17, 1964 (div. Sept. 1976); children: Tarron Reneé, Todd L., Tarek Benjamin. Student, UCLA, 1966-68. Finished goods coordinator Teledyne Water Pik Internat., Ft. Collins, Colo., 1977-79; trainer, documentation coordinator Del Webb Corp., Las Vegas, Nev., 1979-81; dir. pub. relations Nev. Airlines, Las Vegas, 1981-83; dir. pub. relations, promotion Sunworld Internat. Airways, Las Vegas, 1983-86; realtor Coldwell Banker, Las Vegas, 1986—. Bd. dirs. Nat. Kidney Found., Las Vegas, 1983-86, March of Dimes, Make A Wish Found., others; vol. Wednesday's Children, Big Bros./Big Sisters Inc. Republican. Office: Coldwell Banker 3690 E Tropicana Ave Suite 7 Las Vegas NV 89120

BOCK, CAROLYN ANN, education materials company consultant, writer; b. New Bavaria, Ohio, Jan. 25, 1942; d. Wilfred Ignatius and Marcella Mary (Birkemeier) Gerschutz; m. Donald Charles Bock, Sept. 7, 1974; 1 son, Jonathon Edward. Student Notre Dame Coll., 1960-62, 87, John Carroll U., 1962-66. With sales and promotions dept. Schaffer Diversified Corp. and other cos., Cleve., 1962-74; columnist, writer West Life Newspaper, Westlake, Ohio, 1980-83, Westlaker Times, Lorain, Ohio, 1983-84; cert. coordinator Personal Dynamics Inst., Mpls., 1985; owner Dynamic Living Assocs., Westlake, 1986—. Feature writer, bus., arts, families. Author: Authors, Artists and Auras, 1988, Gerschutz family history, 1988. Cofounder, trustee Community Action Team, Westlake, 1980-85, Westlake Arts Council, 1984—, co-founder, 1983-84, pres., 1984-85; chmn. Morning Seminar, Rocky River, Ohio, 1981-85; pres. Westlake PTA Council, 1980-82, Parkside Jr. High PTA, Westlake, 1983-84; active Boy Scouts, Cub Scouts, Westlake, 1977-82; mem. Clague Playhouse, Westlake, 1983—, Westlake Hist. Soc., 1985—, Nuclear Freeze Campaign, Cleve., 1984—. Recipient Outstanding Service award Westlake Cub Scouts, 1980; hon. life mem. Ohio PTA, 1982; Ohio Arts Council grantee, 1984, 85; Notre Dame Coll. scholarship, 1960. Mem. Nat. Assn. Female Execs., Am. Entrepreneurs Assn., N.E. Ohio Speakers Assn., Sigma Delta Chi. Republican. Unitarian Universalist. Avocations: traveling; reading; sewing; cooking. Home and Office: 23553 Belmont Dr Westlake OH 44145

BOCKHOFF, ESTHER IDA, curator; b. Cleve., July 16, 1929; d. Frank Paul and Celia (Balzano) Camperchioli; m. Frank James Bockhoff, Jan. 27, 1951; children: Frank Matthew, Susan Virginia, Celia B. Flateman, James Paul. Student, Flora Stone Mather Coll., 1948-50; BA, Case Western Res. U., 1969, postgrad., 1970-73. Research asst. Cleve. Mus. Natural History, 1972-74, staff anthropologist, 1974-76, co-dir. materials conservation lab., 1975-78, assoc. curator, head dept. cultural anthropology, 1976—, dir. materials conservation lab., 1978—; cons. Cleve. Am. Indian Ctr., 1976; vis. lectr. Cleve. Inst. Art, 1980; dir. replication program Ohio Acad. Scis., Columbus, 1987. Author exhibition catalogs, 5 pamphlet series, articles, brochures and book revs. Active PTA, Mayfield Heights, Cleveland Heights, Ohio, 1956-72; active Cub Scouts Am., Mayfield Heights, 1959-60; troop leader, mem. exec. com. Girl Scouts Am., Mayfield Heights, Cleveland Heights, 1960-65; bd. dirs. Native Am. Arts and Crafts Guild, Cleve., 1977. Adopted mem. Blue Heron clan Seneca Nation of Indians, 1977; recipient Award of Achievement No. Ohio Live mag., 1984-85, 21 grants, 1975-85. Mem. Council for Mus. Anthropology, Am. Anthropol. Assn., Am. Assn. of Mus., Internat. Inst. for Conservation, Native Am. Art Studies Assn. Home: 3015 Scarborough Rd Cleveland Heights OH 44118 Office: Cleve Museum Natural History University Circle Wade Oval Cleveland OH 44106

BOCKIAN, DONNA MARIE, computer systems manager; b. N.Y.C., June 4, 1946; d. Forrest Mager and Mary C. (Lovelace) Hastings; m. James Bernard Bockian, Sept. 16, 1984; children: Vivian Shifra, Adrian Adena, Lillian Tova. BA in Psychology, Vassar Coll., 1968; diploma in systems analysis NYU, 1978. Computer programmer RCA, N.Y.C., 1968-71; systems analyst United Artists Corp., N.Y.C., 1971-78; project leader Bradford Nat. Corp., N.Y.C., 1978-81; project mgr. Mfrs. Hanover Trust, N.Y.C., 1981-83; project mgr. Chem. Bank, N.Y.C., 1983-86; project mgr. fin. systems Salomon Bros., N.Y.C., 1986—. Mem. Assn. Women in Computing (exec. com. 1982-83). Club: Vassar (N.Y.C.). Avocation: photography. Home: 26 Farmhouse Ln Morristown NJ 07960

BODA, VERONICA CONSTANCE, lawyer; b. Phila., Oct. 8, 1952; d. Louis Paul and Helen Ann (Zwigaitis) B. AB, Wilson Coll., 1974; JD, Vermont Law Sch., 1978. Staff atty. Cape-Atlantic Legal Services, Atlantic City, 1978-79, sole practice Phila., 1980—; tchr. Am. Inst. for Paralegal Studies, Phila., 1982-86; tchr. paralegal program Pa. State U., King of Prussia, Pa., 1987—; ins. agt. Prudential Ins. Co., Wayne, Pa., 1985-86; ins. broker V C Boda & Co., Phila., 1986—; aide admissions Wilson Coll., Chambersburg, Pa., 1981—; title ins. atty. Neshaminy Abstract Co., Doylestown, Pa., 1987—; coordinator planned giving Wilson Coll., Chambersburg, 1985—. Author: (with others) Newberg on Class Actions, 1985; contbr. articles to profl. jours. Bd. dirs. Colonial Phila. Hist. Soc., 1983, 87—, pres. 1984-86. Mem. Nat. Assn. Women Lawyers, Phila. Bar Assn. (com. chair real estate section 1984-86). Democrat. Roman Catholic. Club: Down Town. Office: 225 Church St Philadelphia PA 19106

BODDEN, JANE ELLEN, airline reservations manager; b. George Town, Grand Cayman, British West Indies, Dec. 7, 1948; came to U.S., 1969; d. Clarence Vernon and Dorothy (Gressman) Thompson; m. Ashby A. Bodden, Sept. 10, 1969. Student Miami Dade Community Coll., 1984-85, Embry Riddle Aero. U., 1985—. Receptionist Coral Caymanian Hotel, Seven Mile Beach, Grand Cayman, 1965-66; teller Royal Bank Can., Georgetown, 1966-69; teller Pan Am. Bank, N. Miami Beach, Fla., 1970-73; reservations Mackey Internat. Airlines, Ft. Lauderdale, Fla., 1973-78; reservations mgr. Cayman Airways Ltd., Coral Gables, Fla., 1978—; mem. South by Southeast, Miami, 1983—. Elder Faith Presbyterian Ch., Pembroke Pines, Fla., 1984, chmn. Women of Ch. Ruth Circle, 1982-84. Mem. Fla. Airlines Reservations Mgrs. Assn. (pres. 1983-84). Office: Cayman Airways Ltd 250 Catalonia Ave Suite 602 Coral Gables FL 33134

BODE, BARBARA, foundation executive; b. Evanston, Ill., Aug. 4, 1940; d. Carl and Margaret Emilie (Lutze) B. B.A. magna cum laude, U. Md., 1962, M.A. Woodrow Wilson Nat. Found. fellow 1963-64, 1966; scholar, Ludwig-Maximillians-Universitat, Munich, W. Ger., 1960-61; English Speaking Union scholar, U. London, summer 1964; Bundesrepublik scholar, Goethe Institut, Lubeck, W. Ger., summer 1965; postgrad. NDEA fellow, UCLA, 1966-67. Woodrow Wilson teaching fellow N.C. Central U., Durham, 1965-66; community developer Community Devel. Dept. Prince George's County, Md., 1967-68; field dir. Nat. Council Hunger and Malnutrition in U.S., Washington, 1968-70; pres. Children's Found., Washington, 1970-86; dir. Nat. Agenda for Community Founds. Council on Founds., 1986-88, sr. cons. to pres., 1988—; sr. cons. Pettus-Crowe Found., 1988—; mem. food industry adv. commn. Fed. Energy Adminstrn., 1975-76. Author: School Lunch Bag, 1971, Barriers to School Breakfast, 1979; contbr. numerous articles to profl. jours. Mem. Citizens Bd. of Inquiry into Brookside Miners Strike, Harlan, Ky., 1974; mem. nat. adv. com. Food Day, 1975, 76, 77, Rural Am. Women, 1978-80, Project VOTE, 1981-86; dir., mem. exec. com. Human Services Inst. for Children and Families, 1973-75; bd. dirs., v.p. Am. Freedom from Hunger Found., 1973-78, U.S. Com. on Refugees, 1976-78; dir. RAINBOW TV Works, 1976—, Nat. Council Women, Works and Welfare, 1976-77, Nat. Com. Responsive Philanthropy, 1975—; bd. dirs. Am. Parents Com., 1974-78, Rural America, Inc., 1975-79, Coalition for Children and Youth, 1975-79, FWR Found., 1982—, Human SERVE Found., 1983—, Women's Campaign Fund, 1984-88, Child Care Action Campaign, 1984-86; cons., mem. steering and adv. coms. commns. and organs in field; convenor Nat. Women's Polit. Caucus, 1971; mem. nat. adv. bd. Women's Campaign Fund, 1975-77, Washington Area Women's Fund, 1985-87; active in press bur. Poor People's Campaign, 1968; mem. planning com. Women's Leadership Conf. Dem. Nat. Com., 1972, vice chmn. com. on regional conf. planning and strategy, 1969-70; active voting and civil rights campaigns, 1961—. Named one of Ten Outstanding Young Women of Am. various women's orgns., 1977. Mem. Women and Founds. Corp. Philanthropy. Episcopalian. Home: 1661 Crescent Pl NW Washington DC 20009 Office: Council on Founds 1828 L St NW Washington DC 20036

BODE, LURA JEAN, social worker; b. Enid, Okla., Jan. 16, 1962; d. Charles R. Dahlem and E. Jean (Whitworth) Millard; m. J.W. Bode, Nov. 8, 1986. BS in Orgn. Adminstrn., Okla. State U., 1984. Social worker Dept. Human Services State Okla., Kingfisher, 1985-87, Garfield County Dept. Human Services, Enid, Okla., 1987—. Mem. Nat. Assn. Female Execs., NW Okla. Country and Western Dance Assn., Okla. Pub. Employees Assn., Okla. Health Welfare Assn. Office: State Okla Dept Human Services PO Box 3628 Enid OK 73702

BODENBERG, DAWN LOUISE, personnel coordinator; b. Gettysburg, Pa., Dec. 2, 1952; d. Adam F. and Ruth E. (Golden) Lobaugh; m. Frank F. Bodenberg, June 14, 1975; children: Andrea Dawn, Katherine Elizabeth. AA, Goldey Beacom Coll., Wilmington, Del., 1972. Clk. St. Francis Hosp., Wilmington, 1971-72; sec. Adams County Coop Extension Service, Gettysburg, 1972-73; sec. Adams Electric Cooperative, Inc., Gettysburg, 1973—, supr., 1981—, personnel coordinator, 1985—. Mem. bus. edn. advisory com. Biglerville (Pa.) and Gettysburg High Schs., 1981—; publicity chmn. Nat. Apple Harvest Festivals, Arendtsville, Pa, 1986, 87. Mem. Bus. and Profl. Women's, Gettysburg (edn. com. 1986, first runner-up Young Career Woman of Pa., 1981), Upper Adams Jaycees, Biglerville (individual v.p. 1986, Pa. Jaycee of the year award, 1986). Republican. Lutheran. Lodge: Elks (women's aux. 1987). Home: 55 Fidler Rd Gettysburg PA 17325 Office: Adams Electric Coop Inc 153 N Stratton St PO Box 130 Gettysburg PA 17325

BODI, CHERYL ANDEE, communications executive; b. Uniontown, Pa., Apr. 25, 1957; d. Andy and Gertrude (Hrivnak) B. BS in Indsl. Mgmt., U. Cin., 1979; MBA, Xavier U., 1985. Sales rep. Hilton Davis div. Sterling Drug, Chgo., 1979-81; account exec., industry cons. mktg. br. AT&T, Columbus, Ohio, 1981-86; instr., staff mgr. Nat. Sales Sch. AT&T, Cin., 1986—. Mem. JR Arts Council, Alpha Chi Omega. Republican. Roman Catholic. Home: 9882 Timbers Dr Cincinnati OH 45242 Office: 15 W 6th St Cincinnati OH 45202

BODIFORD, CHARLENE, educator; b. Saginaw, Mich., Sept. 26, 1953; d. Ralph and Olean (McGhee) B.; 1 child, Charlotte. BA, Saginaw Valley Coll., 1974, MA, 1976. Tchr. pre-kindergarten Buena Vista Schs., Saginaw, 1974-80; dispatcher Saginaw County Govt., 1980-81; day care dir. Mid-Mich. Kinder-Kare, Saginaw, 1981-82; tchr. Saginaw City Schs., 1982—. Author: (with others) Ready or Not, 1986. Stewardess St. Luke Christain Meth.-Episcopal Ch. Mem. NEA, Saginaw Edn. Assn., Mich. Edn. Assn., NAACP (life). Democrat. Methodist. Home: 3341 Livingston Dr Saginaw MI 48601 Office: 3025 Davenport Saginaw MI 48601

BODINE, DELLA L., nursing administrator; b. Trenton, Oct. 16, 1951; d. Richard Stauffer and Jessie Mae (Beck) White; m. Wayne H. Bodine, July 2, 1972; 1 child, Jessica Leigh. Diploma Helene Fuld Sch. Nursing, Trenton, 1972; B.S.N., Trenton State Coll., 1980; M.S.N., U. Pa., 1983. Lic. nursing home adminstr. N.J. Dir. nursing Lakewood House, Burlington, N.J., 1972-73, Moorestown Nursing Home, N.J., 1973-78; staff nurse Burlington County Meml. Hosp., N.J., 1978-80, head nurse, 1980-81; dir. nursing Mt. Holly Ctr., N.J., 1981-82; assoc. dir. nursing Hamilton Hosp., Trenton, 1983-85 ; nursing supr. Hickory House Nursing Home, Honeybrook, Pa., 1986-87, asst. dir., 1986-87; owner, mgr. Marsh Creek Campground, Lyndell, Pa., 1984—. Home: PO Box 257 Lyndell PA 19354 Office: Hickory Hoose Nursing Home Rd 4 Rt 322 Honeybrook PA 19344

BODKIN, RUBY PATE, corporate executive, real estate broker, educator; b. Frostproof, Fla., Mar. 11, 1926; d. James Henry and Lucy Beatrice (Latham) P.; m. Lawrence Edward Bodkin Sr., Jan. 15, 1949; children: Karen Bodkin Snead, Cinda, Lawrence Jr. BA, Fla. State U., 1948; MA, U. Fla., 1972. Lic. real estate broker. Banker Lewis State Bank, Tallahassee, 1944-49; ins. underwriter Hunt Ins. Agy., Tallahassee, 1949-51; tchr. Duval County Sch. Bd., Jacksonville, Fla., 1952-76; pvt. practice realty Jacksonville, 1976—; tchr. Nassau County Sch. Bd., Jacksonville, 1978-83; sec., treas., v.p. Bodkin Corp., R&D/Inventions, Jacksonville, 1983—; pvt. practice tutoring, Jacksonville; substitute tchr. Duval County Sch. Bd., 1980—. Mem. Jacksonville Symphony Guild, 1985—, Mus. Sci. And History Guild, Jacksonville, 1959—, Southside Woman's Club, Jacksonville, 1957—, Garden Club Jacksonville, 1976—. Recipient 25 Yr. Service award Duval County Sch. Bd., 1976, Tchr. of Yr. award Bryceville Sch., 1981. Democrat. Baptist. Clubs: San Jose Country; Ponte Vedra Oceanfront Resort. Home: 1149 Molokai Rd Jacksonville FL 32216 Office: Bodkin Jewelers and Appraisers PO Box 16482 Jacksonville FL 32216

BODMAN, HELENE DUNN, musicologist; b. N.Y.C., Nov. 22, 1936; d. Kempton and Susan Barret (Gill) Dunn; m. Richard S. Bodman, Jan. 28, 1961; children—Taylor, James Martyn. Ed. New Eng. Conservatory, 1957-60; B.Mus., San Francisco Conservatory of Music, 1968; M.A. in Music, Am. U., 1982. Dir. Opera and Symphony Previews, San Francisco, 1966-67; instr. piano, music theory, San Francisco, 1969-71, Wilmington, Del., 1973-76; case dir. Congressman William S. Mailliard, Washington, 1973; arts coordinator Del. State Arts Council, 1977-78; music librarian Am. U., Washington, 1981-84; pres. Music Info. Specialists, 1984—, dir. Discovering Musical, 1984—; cons. Boys Clubs of Am. Young Artists Program. Author: Chinese Musical Iconography: A History of Musical Instruments Depicted in Chinese Art, 1987, program annotator Dumbarton Concert Series; Handel Festival Orch. Bd. dirs. Spring Opera of San Francisco, 1967-71, Wilmington Music Sch., 1973-78, Washington Performing Arts Soc., 1980—; bd. dirs. Nat. Symphony Orch., Washington, 1979-82, record archivist, discographer; trustee San Francisco Conservatory of Music, 1967-71; bd. overseers New Eng. Conservatory, 1985—. Mem. Am. Musicol. Soc., Smithsonian Instn. (bd. dirs.). Home: 3211 R St NW Washington DC 20007 Office: 1690 36th St NW Rm 410 Washington DC 20007

BOE, LORI MARIE, computer analyst; b. Logansport, Ind., Mar. 21, 1961; d. James Kenneth and Alma Jane (Turner) B. BS, Ind. State U., 1983. Data resource analyst Riggs Nat. Bank, Washington, 1984-85; systems analyst Texaco, Inc., Houston, 1985-86; tech. specialist Fed. Res. Bank, Atlanta, 1986—; cons. Adopt-A-Student Program, 1986—. Mem. inaugural dinner and ball com. Ind. Soc. Washington, 1985; actuality vol. Reagan-Bush, Washington, 1984; mem. Houston Ballet Guild, 1985-86, Soc. League Against Molestation, Houston, 1984-86, Young Reps., Houston, 1985-86, Adopt-A-Student Program, 1986-87, Atlanta Ballet Assocs., 1987—; mem. spl. events com. Atlanta Hist. Soc. Lutheran. Mem. Women in Info. Processing. Club: Toastmasters (Washington) (sgt.-at-arms 1985). Avocations: theater, reading, skiing, volunteer work. Home: 2060 Brian Way Decatur GA 30033 Office: Fed Res Bank 104 Marietta St Atlanta GA 30303

BOECKMAN, ANN SOFIOS, bank administrator; b. Indpls., Nov. 30, 1957; d. Peter Thomas and Patricia Ann (Speropoulos) Sofios; m. Ronald Paul Boeckman, June 13, 1987. B.S. in Speech, Northwestern U., Evanston, Ill., 1980. Asst. state (Ind.) dir. Howard Baker (Rep.) for U.S. Pres., Indpls., 1980; aide constituent service U.S. Senator (Ind.) R.G. Lugar, Indpls., 1980-81; dep. campaign mgr. Friends of Dick Lugar, Indpls., 1981; fin. dir., 1981-82; personal asst. U.S. Senator Lugar, Washington, 1982-84, dep. adminstrv. asst., 1985-87; comml. loan officer State Savs. Bank, Columbus, Ohio, 1987—; participant Nat. Rep. Campaign Workshop, Indpls., 1981; pub. relations dir. Indpls. Scoliosis Assn., 1980-82. Writer Sen. Lugar campaign newsletters, 1981-82; co-editor campaign manual, 1981. Mem. Assn. Jr. Leagues, Inc., (Columbus, Washington, Indpls., 1981—); docent Corcoran Gallery Art, Washington, 1983-87, Nat. Mus. Women in Arts, 1985-87; mem. Cathedral Arts, Inc., Indpls., 1980-82; coordinator Chgo. Hellenic Ind. Day, 1978; chmn. Washington Twp. (Ind.) Bicentennial Celebration, 1975-76. Named Sagamore of Wabash, Gov. Indiana, 1982; Hoosier scholar State of Ind., 1976; Order AHEPA, Daus. Penelope scholar, 1976-79; recipient Citizenship award Soroptimist Club, Indpls. 1976. Mem. Women in Communications, Northwestern U. Alumni Assn., Mortar Bd., Kappa Kappa Gamma Alumni Assn. Greek Orthodox. Clubs: Rivera (Indpls.). Lodges: Jr. Pan Hellenic (pub. relations chmn. 1976-77), Maids of Athena, Daus. of Penelope. Home: 2488 Powell Ave Bexley OH 43209 Office: State Savs Bank 20 E Broad St Columbus OH 43215

BOECKMANN-ROSS, LAVERNE, publishing executive, foundation executive; b. Glendale, Calif., Oct. 14, 1949; d. Herbert F. and Jane Boeckmann; m. Steven A. Ross, Apr. 14, 1984. A.A., Glendale Jr. Coll., 1969; B.A., San Diego State U., 1971; teaching credential, U. So. Calif., 1975. Elem. tchr. Los Angeles Sch. Dist., 1974-78; account exec. Valley Mag., Granada Hills, Calif., 1978-86; v.p. Tara Labs., Panorama City, Calif., 1982—; account exec. KABC Let's Talk Mag., Granada Hills, Calif., 1985-86; co founder World Research Found., Sherman Oaks, Calif., 1983—. Coordinator Beauty Contest, Northridge, Calif., 1983. Mem. San Fernando Valley Exec. Assn. (bd. dirs. 1982-83), Nat. Female Execs. Assn., Women's Network Assn. Republican. Avocations: painting, danicng, skiing, travel, singing. Office: World Research Found 15300 Ventura Blvd #405 Sherman Oaks CA 91403

BOEHM, JOANNE ROSE, medical service administrator, educator; b. Cleve., Sept. 7, 1949; d. Joseph John and Martha Emily (Lebar) Bukovec; m. Randall Bruce Boehm, Sept. 4, 1971; children: Andrea Lee, Paula Lynn. P-rogram dir. Sch. of Radiol. Tech. Lake County Meml. Hosps., Willoughby, Ohio, 1971-85; mgr. med. imaging Mednet Clinics, Euclid, Ohio, 1985—; educator radiol. tech. Lakeland Community Coll., Mentor, Ohio, 1976—; cons. radiol. edn. Davis and Assocs., Troy, N.Y., 1987—. Mem. Am. Healthcare Radiology Adminstrs., Assn. Educators in Radiol. Tech. of State of N.Y., Am. Slovenian Cath. Union of U.S.A. Lodge: St. Vitus'. Office: Mednet Clinics 18599 Lakeshore Blvd Euclid OH 44119

BOEHM, MARY MAGDALENE, interior designer, space planning consultant; b. Bluffton, Ohio, June 23, 1944; d. Marvin George and Martha Leoda (von Stein) B. B.S. in Interior Design, U. Cin., 1967. Designer, Taylor Designs, Cin., 1967-68, Space Design/Interior Architecture, Cin., 1968-74, Caudill, Rowlett, Scott, Houston, 1974-76; dept. head interior design, The Klein Partnership, Houston, 1977-80; propr. Boehm Design Assocs., Houston, 1980—; expert witness Tex. Health Facilities Comm.; tchr. interior design Jewish Community Ctr., Cin., 1968. Contbr. articles on interior design to profl. jours., newspapers. Recipient Hexter award, 1969, 76, Nat. award Inst. Bus. Designers, 1974, Burlington House award Burlington House Corp., 1974. Mem. Neartown Civic Assn., Preservation Alliance, Tex. Soc. Architects, Houston chpt. AIA; assoc. mem. AIA.

BOEHMER, RAQUEL DAVENPORT, television producer, newsletter editor; b. Bklyn., Feb. 24, 1938; d. John Joralemon Davenport and Fanny (Barberis) Allison; m. Peter Joseph Boehmer; children: Kristian Ludwig, Louisa, Timothy Joralemon. BA, Wells Coll., 1959. Radio producer Maine Pub. Broadcasting Network, Bangor, 1977—; developer, editor consumer newsletter Seafood Soundings, Monhegan, Maine, 1986—; speaker Seafare, 1986, Los Angeles; keynote speaker Beyond Wells Day, Wells Coll., Aurora, N.Y., 1988. Writer, producer (weekly radio spot) Whole Foods for All People, 1977—; producer, host (TV cooking program) Different Kettle of Fish, 1984; author: A Foraging Vacation, 1982, Raquel's Main Guide to New England Seafoods, 1988. Writer legislation, Maine legis., 1985, 87; treas. Monhegan Plantation, 1970-72, chair bicentennial com., 1976; chair Monhegan Sch. Bd., 1973-74; co-chair Monhegan Solid Waste Com., 1988-89. Recipient Pub. Service award Maine Nutrition Assn.; named Gt. New Eng. Cook Yankee mag., 1986. Mem. Nat. Newsletter Assn., Women's Fisheries Network, Colonial Dames Am., Women's Strike for Peace. Home and Office: Lobster Cove Rd Monhegan Island ME 04852

BOEHRINGER, MONICA EMMA, fashion forecaster; b. Yonkers, N.Y., June 9, 1963; d. William and Ernesta (Castelli) B. Student Emerson Coll., 1981-82; Assoc. Occupational Studies, Tobe Coburn Sch., N.Y.C., 1985. Owner, contractor Blade Williams Fashion Coordination, Jackson, N.J., 1982-86; account exec. Wendi Winters Public Relations, N.Y.C., 1984-85; dept. mgr. Abraham & Straus, Eatontown, N.J., 1985-86; ter. mgr. Tobe Coburn Sch., N.Y.C., 1985-87; fashion forecaster Fashionworks, 1987—. Fashion show coordinator DECA, N.Y.C., 1983-84; promotional model DeLeigh Agy., Lakewood, N.J., 1983—, career cons. Mgr. Donovan High Sch., Toms River, N.J., 1985—. Fellow nat. Asn. Female Execs., Toba Coburn Alumni Assn., Fashion Group, Cousteau Soc., Nat. Geog. Soc., Nat. Wildlife Fedn. Republican. Roman Catholic. Avocations: horseback riding; theatre; Egyptology; creative writing; costume design. Office: Fashionworks 39 W 38th St New York NY 10018

BOEMI, PAMELA LYNNE BOGAN, marketing executive; b. Evanston, Ill., Jan. 11, 1953; d. Ralph A.L. and Margaret (Wickman) Bogan; m. Andrew A. Boemi, Nov. 4, 1978. B.A. in Journalism and English, Butler U., 1975; cert. bus. adminstrn. Keller Grad. Sch. Mgmt., Chgo., 1977. Mgr. client and industry planning Peat Marwick, Chgo., 1977-82; dir. mktg. Kupferberg, Goldberg & Neimark, Chgo., 1982-87; pres. Bogan-Goem Mktg. Services, Inc., Chgo, 1987—. Contbr. articles to profl. jours. Bd. dirs. Chgo. chpt. Nat. Com. Prevention of Child Abuse, 1983—; bd. dirs., residential fundraising chmn. Northfield United Way, 1981—; v.p. pub. relations 1985-86; chmn. membership com. Chgo. Council Volunteerism, 1983-87. Mem. Am. Mktg. Assn., Women in Communications, Soc. Profl. Journalists. Clubs: Lake Geneva Country (fin. com. 1982—) (Wis.); Woman's Athletic (Chgo.). Office: PO Box 8319 Northfield IL 60093

BOERNER, JO M., real estate broker; b. Wayne, Okla., Apr. 17, 1944; d. James Olman and Virgie M. (Jones) Whitaker; m. Buddy Dennis Boerner, July 3, 1964; children: Christopher Alexander, James Dennis, Edward Floyd. Student, U. Okla., 1983-85. Assoc. Abide Realtors, Oklahoma City, 1976-83; managing broker Merrill Lynch Realtors, Oklahoma City, 1983-86; owner J&B Investments, Oklahoma City, 1980—; dir. career devel. Marolyn Pryor & Assocs., Oklahoma City, 1986-87, Long & Foster, Realtors, Fairfax, Va., 1987—; regional v.p. Women's Council of Realtors, Chgo., 1987; dir. Oklahoma City Bd. Realtors, 1984-85; instr. Realtors Inst. Okla. State U., 1987. Contbr. articles to profl. jours. Bd. govs. Wednesday's Child Found., Oklahoma City, 1987; mem. Allied Arts Council, Oklahoma City, 1985, Realtors Polit. Action Com., Oklahoma, 1984—. Recipient State of Excellance award Okla. State Gov., 1987, Omega Tau Rho medal. Mem. Nat. Women's Council of Realtors (gov. bd. 1985-87), Nat. Assn. Realtors, Women's Council of Realtors (pres. 1985, gov. 1986), Okla. Assn. Realtors, Siga Internat. (trustee 1982-83). Republican. Club: Toastmasters. Office: Long & Foster, Realtors 11351 Random Hills Rd Fairfax VA 22030

BOESHAAR, PATRICIA CHIKOTAS, astronomer, educator; b. Butler Township, Pa., Sept. 25, 1947; d. Joseph Stanley and Anna (Geritis) Chikotas; m. J. Anthony Tyson, Jan. 23, 1981; 1 child, Kristopher Tyson. Student, Duqesne U., 1965-67; BS in Physics, Northwestern State U., La., 1969; PhD in Astronomy, Ohio State U., 1976. Instr. U. Washington, Seattle, 1975-77; asst. prof. physics U. Oregon, Eugene, 1977-80; research assoc. U. Ariz., Tucson, 1980-81; asst. prof. Rider Coll., Lawrenceville, N.J., 1981-84, assoc. prof., 1984-87, prof. physics, 1987-88; assoc. prof. Drew U., Madison, N.J., 1988—; cons. AT&T Bell Labs., Murray Hill, N.J., 1981—; peer reviewer Kitt Peak Nat. Obs., 1985, Astron. Jour, Astrphysics Jour. Contbr. articles to profl. jours. NSF grantee 1977-78, 84-85, 86-88. Mem. Am. Rhododeudron Soc., Am. Astron. Soc., Astron. Soc. Pacific, Sigma Xi, Sigma Pi Sigma, Phi Kappi Phi. Office: Drew U Dept Physics Madison NJ 07940

BOGAD, ALICE ROSE, beverage company executive; b. Waterbury, Conn., July 26, 1922; d. Edward A. and Catherine A. (Wood) Rose; m. Alfred J. Bogad, Sept. 30, 1971; children by previous marriage: Nancy, Karen, Eric. Student CUNY Coll., 1943, U. Okla., 1944, Am. U., 1945. Propr., dir. Mid-Hudson Floor & Wall Co., Poughkeepsie, N.Y., 1948-51, Hudson Valley Welding and Supply, Poughkeepsie, 1951-55; propr. Colonial Knolls Devel. Co., 1955-65; asst. mgr. Dutchess County (N.Y.) Airport, 1965-68; propr. and mgr. Queen's Ransom Gallery, Poughkeepsie, 1967-71; sec., treas., dir. G.H. Ford Tea Co., Inc., Poughkeepsie, 1974—; guest lectr. on tea various schs. and community orgns., 1974—. Pres., Arlington High Sch. PTA, 1963-64; chmn. scholarship com. Arlington Sch. Dist., 1960-64; sec. to zoning bd. Town of Poughkeepsie, 1955-60, dep. zoning adminstr., 1971-73, chmn. Zoning Bd. Appeals, 1976-78; trustee Vassar Temple, 1979-87, chmn. membership, 1978-84; bd. dirs. Dutchess County (N.Y.) Arts Council, 1979-81, chmn. public funding com., 1979-80; mem. citizens' adv. com. Dutchess Community Coll. Served with WAVES, 1942-45. Recipient Life Member award PTA, N.Y. State, 1964, Outstanding Citizen award Dutchess County Bd. Legislators, 1981; named Woman of Yr., NYU Ctr. Food and Hotel Mgmt., 1987. Mem. Tea Assn. U.S. (assoc. bd. dirs. 1977-78, chmn. 1979). Culinary Inst. Am. (cons. 1975—, mem. corp. 1980—, chmn. fellows com.) Bus. and Profl. Women's Assn. Republican. Club: Zonta (sec. 1978-79). Contbr. articles on tea industry to bus. and trade jours. Home: 7 Wilbur Ct PO Box 3506 Poughkeepsie NY 12603 Office: 110 Dutchess Turnpike PO Box 3407 Poughkeepsie NY 12603

BOGAN, MARY FLAIR, stock broker, former actress; b. Providence, July 9, 1948; d. Ralph A.L. and Mary (Dyer) B.; B.A., Vassar Coll., 1969. Actress, Trinity Sq. Repertory Co., R.I., Gretna Playhouse, Pa., Skylight Comic Opera, Milw., Cin. Playhouse, Playmakers' Repertory, Va.; mem. nat. co. No Sex, Please, We're British; also TV commls., 1970-77; account exec. E.F. Hutton & Co., Inc., Providence, 1977-86; account v.p. Paine Webber, 1986—; econ. reporter Sta. WPRI-TV, 1982-85, Sta. WJAR-TV, 1987—. Treas. Red Bridge Council Rep. Women; chmn. new mems. com. R.I. Fedn. Rep. Women. Recipient Century Club award, 1980, 81, 82, 83, 85; Blue Chip Sales award, 1983, 85, Pacesetter Sales Award, 1986, 87. Mem. Internat. Platform Assn., Newport Preservation Soc., Providence Preservation Soc. Clubs: Providence Art, Turks Head, Brown Faculty. Home: 18 Cooke St Providence RI 02906 Office: 1520 Hospital Trust Tower Providence RI 02903

BOGARD, JACQUELINE ALONSA, industry association administrator; b. Saginaw, Mich., Apr. 8, 1951; d. John Edwin and Alice Noreen (Hoke) B. BS in Wildlife Ecology, U. Wis., 1973; MBA, U. Calif., Berkeley, 1984. Cons. environment Woodward-Clyde Cons., San Francisco, 1976-82; engr. mktg. Intel Corp., Santa Clara, Calif., 1984-85, Hillsboro, Oreg., 1985-86; dir. environ. programs Santa Clara County Mfg. Group, 1986—. Recipient Tribute to Women and Industry award, 1988. Office: Santa Clara County Mfg Group 5201 Great America Pkwy Suite #426 Santa Clara CA 95054

BOGART, GRACE ELIZABETH, information scientist; b. Bolton, Mass., June 10, 1923; d. Francis Gould and Grace Effie (Smith) Mentzer; B.S., U. Mass., 1945; M.S., Simmons Coll., 1975; m. Lindsay Boyd, Aug. 6, 1944 (dec.); children—David Gordon, Bethanne, Sandra Lindsay; m. 2d, Victor Brociner, Nov. 13, 1971 (dec.); m. 3d, Stanley C. Bogart, Aug. 7, 1977. Librarian, Lincoln Lab. Library, MIT, Lexington, 1959-77; dir. info. services Roberts Info. Service, Inc., Fairfax, Va., 1977-78; pres. Bogart-Brociner Assocs., Bolton, Mass., 1978—; rep. to adv. bd. Nat. Transls. Center, John Crerar Library, Chgo., 1975-86. Mem. Spl. Libraries Assn. (chmn. spl. com. translation problems 1973-76), Am. Soc. Info. Sci. (local arrangements chmn. nat. conf. Boston 1975, publicity chmn. nat. conf. 1980, mem. nat. conf. com. 1983, chmn. Nat. Conf. Boston arrangements 1987), Compiler, A Guide to Scientific and Technical Journals in Translation, 1972; How to Obtain a Translation, 1976. Home and Office: 295 Main St Bolton MA 01740

BOGGS, ANGELA ROSALIE, occupational health and safety administrator; b. Phila., Dec. 27, 1947; d. Nicholas Concetta and Benedetta (Graci) Muni; m. Roger Alan Boggs, Nov. 1, 1970; children: Derek Ethan, Jared Christian. BA magna cum laude, The Cath. U. Am., 1969; MS, Harvard U., 1983. Jr. chemist Smith, Kline & French Labs., Phila., 1969; analytical chemist WARF Inst., Madison, Wis., 1970-72; environ. analyst IEP, Inc., Northboro, Mass., 1982-83; research asst. Harvard U., Boston, 1983-84; environ. chemist, pub. health specialist Geotech. Engrs., Inc., Winchester, Mass., 1984; engr. hazardous materials Shipley Co., Newton, Mass., 1984-85, supr. environ. health and safety, 1985, mgr. safety health and security, 1986-88; mgr. indsl. and environ. health Adams-Russell Electronics Co. Inc., Waltham, 1988—; mem. program com. Am. Conf. on Chem. Labeling, 1986—. Mem. Am. Chem. Soc., Semiconductor Safety Assn., Risk and Ins. Mgmt. Soc., Sigma Xi. Roman Catholic. Home: 305 Concord Rd Wayland MA 01778 Office: Adams-Russell Electronics Co Inc 1370 Main Stt Waltham MA 02154

BOGGS, CORINNE CLAIBORNE (LINDY BOGGS), congresswoman; b. Brunswick Plantation, La., Mar. 13, 1916; d. Roland Philoman and Martha Corinne (Morrison) Claiborne; m. Thomas Hale Boggs, Jan. 22, 1938 (dec.); children—Barbara (Mrs. Paul F. Sigmund, Jr.), Thomas Hale Jr., Corinne (Mrs. Steven V. Roberts), William Robertson (dec.). B.A., Sophie Newcomb Coll., Tulane U., 1935; L.L.D. (hon.); Litt.D., U. St. Thomas; D.Pub. Service (hon.), Trinity Coll., Washington, 1975; hon. degree St. Mary of Woods; LL.D., Loyola U. Tchr. history and English, St. James Parish, La., 1936-37; elected to 93d Congress to fill vacancy caused by death of husband, 1973; re-elected to 93d-100th Congresses from 2d La. Dist., 1973—, mem. appropriations com. majority mem. from Ho. of Reps., Am. Revolution Bicentennial Adminstrn. Bd., chmn. Commn. Ho. of Reps. Bicentenary; mem. campaign com. Democratic Nat. Com., 1974; chairwoman Dem. Nat. Conv., 1976; mem. Com. on Bicentennial of U.S. Constn. Pres., Dem. Congl. Wives Forum, 1954, Womans Nat. Democratic Club, 1958-59, Congl. Club, 1971-72; co-chmn. Inaugural Balls for Presidents John F. Kennedy, 1961, Lyndon Johnson, 1965; mem. Nat. Hist. Publs. and Records Com. Bd. dirs. La. Council for Music and Performing Arts; hon. bd. dirs. Met. New Orleans chpt. Nat. Found. March of Dimes; bd. advisers. CLOSE-UP and Presdl. Classroom; regent emeritus Smithsonian Instn.; mem. president's council Tulane U. Recipient Weiss Meml. award NCCJ, 1974; Nat. Oak award La. Assn. Ind. Colls. and Univs., Disting. Service medal Saint Mary's Dominican Coll., 1976, Humanitarian award AMVETS Nat. Aux., Torch of Liberty award B'nai B'rith, 1976, Gala IV award Birmingham So. U., 1976, Eleanor Roosevelt Humanitarian award, 1977, E. Roosevelt Centennial award, 1984, 1st woman recipient Disting. Alumna award Tulane U., 1986; 1st woman recipient VFW Congl. award, 1986. Mem. Nat. Soc. Colonial Dames, LWV, Internat. Fedn. Catholic Alumni. Avocations: flower arranging, dancing. Office: Rayburn Ho Office Bldg Room 2353 Washington DC 20515

BOGGS, DEBBIE-SUE, office administrator; b. Phila., May 7, 1956; d. Jack D. and Janet (Conston) Miller; m. Jerry A. Boggs, Dec. 26, 1982. BA, BS in Social Welfare and Spanish, Pa. State U., 1977. VISTA paralegal So. Ariz. Legal Aide, Tucson, 1978-79; youth counselor VisionQuest, Tucson, 1979; gen. edn. instr. Tucson Job Corps Ctr., 1979-81; legal sec. Molloy, Jones & Donahue, Tucson, 1981-85, paralegal, 1985-86; office adminstr. Murphy, Clausen & Goering P.C., Tucson, 1986—. Mem. ABA, Nat. Assn. Legal Adminstrs., Nat. Assn. Legal Assts., Tucson Assn. Legal Adminstrs., Pa. State Club Greater Tucson (pres. 1987—). Democrat. Jewish. Home: 3000 W Treeline Dr Tucson AZ 85741 Office: Murphy Clausen & Goering PC 1840 E River Rd Suite 302 Tucson AZ 85718

BOGGS, ELLEN ELIZABETH, actress; b. Palo Alto, Calif., Mar. 23, 1956; d. Stephen Taylor and JoAn (Whitehorn) B. BA in Drama and Theatre, U. Hawaii, 1978. Actress Theco, Inc., N.Y.C., 1982-83, 84-85, Chicken Lips Comedy Improvisation Troupe, N.Y.C., 1982-84, Pan Asian Repertory Co., N.Y.C., 1986, R.A.P.P. Arts Ctr., N.Y.C., 1986—. Appeared in numerous plays including Pygmalion, Romeo and Juliet, The Glass Managerie, The Maids. Recording sec. Riverview Neighborhood Assn., Jersey City, 1986. Recipient Georgie best supporting actress award Honolulu Mag., 1977. Mem. Actors' Equity Assn., AFTRA. Home: 4417 Windom Pl NW Washington DC 20016

BOGGS, NANCY LEA, nurse; b. Morrison, Ill., Nov. 4, 1948; d. Albert L. and Arlene E. (Montgomery) Benedict; B.S. Nursing, Ill. Wesleyan U., 1970; M.A., Central Mich. U., 1984; m. Harold C. Piepenbrink, Aug. 4, 1972 (dec. Dec. 1976); 1 dau., Alison Lea; m. Wesley K. Boggs, June 13, 1987. Cert. mental health adminstr. Nurse, Ill. Dept. Med. Health, Chgo., 1970-73; head nurse VA Research Hosp., Chgo., 1973-75, VA Hosp., Bklyn., 1975-76, Ohio State Univ. Hosp., Columbus, 1976-77; nurse cons. on accrediation Ohio Dept. Mental Health, Columbus, 1977-78; dir. nursing Pauline Warfield Lewis Ctr., Cin., 1978—. Mem. Am. Nurses Assn. (cert. nurse adminstr.), Ohio Nurses Assn., Dirs. of Nursing of Ohio Mental Health, Dirs. of Nursing of Greater Cin. Area, Assn. Mental Health Adminstrs. (cert. mental health adminstr.). Home: 9499 Mapleknoll Cincinnati OH 45239

BOGIGIAN, CATHY JOAN, artist, educator; b. Evergreen Park, Ill., Dec. 2, 1951; d. Harold A. and Lucille (Enochian) B. Student, Butler U., Indpls., 1969-70; BS in Edn., No. Ill. U., 1973, MA in Art, 1979. Dir. creative services Nat. Electric Sign Assn., Oak Brook, Ill., 1975-76; art instr. Lyons Twp. High Sch., LaGrange, Ill., 1976—. Exhibited at Mazur Mazur Gallery, Deerfield, Ill., 1983, Facet Fine Art Ctr., Taos, N.Mex., 1984, Mus. Contemporary Art Shop, Chgo., 1985; one-woman show at Hartford Bldg., Chgo., 1974. Mem. NEA, Nat. Art Edn. Assn. Office: Lyons Twp High Sch 100 S Brainard LaGrange IL 60525

BOGNER, MARGARET ANN, health service executive; b. Joliet, Ill., Apr. 19, 1947; d. Harold R. and Dolores R. (Telfer) B. BA, No. Ill. U., 1972; M in Mgmt., Northwestern U., 1983. Adminstrv. asst. Northwestern Meml. Hosp., Chgo., 1972-79; bus. mgr. The Thresholds, Chgo., 1981—. Mem. Lincoln Park Conservation Assn., Chgo., Art Inst., Chgo., Chgo. Arch. Found., Chgo., Lincoln Park Zool. Soc., Chgo., Mus. of Sci. and Industry, Chgo.; mem. Shakespearan Festival, Stratford, Ont. Mem. Nat. Alliance for Mentally Ill. Club: Chgo. Met. Ski Council (regional v.p. 1984-85, 87—, credential chmn. 1985-86), Pine Point Ski (midwest chmn. 1987—). Office: The Thresholds 2700 N Lakeview Chicago IL 60614

BOGORYA-BUCZKOWSKI, YVONNE, university dean, educator, consultant; b. Warsaw, Poland, July 27, 1942; citizen of Can.; married, 2 children. M.Phil., U. Warsaw, 1966; M.A., York U., Toronto, Can., 1971, Ph.D., 1979; PhD, Union Grad. Sch., Cin. Instr. dept. humanities Atkingson Coll. York U., 1971-72; lectr. bus. communication dept. and mgmt. devel. inst. Ryerson Poly. Inst., Toronto, 1972-77; editor, pub. relations officer New Canadian Publs., 1977-78; dir. acad. affairs, prof. Canadian Sch. Mgmt. and Northland Open U., 1978-81, dean acad. affairs, 1981—, sec.-treas. bd. govs. 1977—, also v.p.; pres. Bogorya Cons., 1979—; chmn. acad. standards com. Univ. Without Walls Internat. Council, 1980—; vis. internat. prof. Internat. Mgmt. Centre from Buckingham, U.K., 1983—, bd. dirs. N.Am. Acad. Advs., 1983—; editorial dir. Mgmt. Decision Jour., Innovative Higher Edn., 1984—; mem. editorial adv. bd. Mgmt. Research News, 1984—; cons. Inst. Profl. Secretaries; adj. prof. Union Grad. Sch; bd. dirs. Multiheritage Community Alliance, Toronto. Author (with G. Korey): University Without Walls, 1980. Contbr. articles to profl. jours. Fellow Royal Soc. for Encouragement of Arts, Manufactures and Commerce; mem. Assn. Women Execs., Acad. Mgmt., Am. Bus. Communication Assn., Am. Mgmt. Assn./Canadian Mgmt. Centre, Internat. Council on Distance Edn., Council for Advancement of Experiential Learning, Am. Assembly of Collegiate Schs. Bus., Acad. Internat. Bus., Can. Soc. for Comparative Study of Civilizations (pres. 1983—). Office: Canadian Sch Mgmt, 150 Bloor St, Suite 715, West Toronto, ON Canada M5S 2X9

BOGSTAHL, DEBORAH MARCELLE, medical publishing company executive; b. Irvington, N.J., June 5, 1950; d. Marcel and Helena Christina (de Jaroszynsky) Bogstahl; m. Richard Neil Press, Mar. 20, 1976; 1 child, Alexandra Boman. B.A. in English Edn., Trenton State Coll., 1972. Cert. tchr., N.J. Project dir. U.S. Testing Co., Hoboken, N.J., 1973-75; project dir. J. Walter Thompson Co., N.Y.C., 1975-77; research account exec. Dancer Fitzgerald Sample, N.Y.C., 1977-80; group research mgr. Bristol-Myers Co., N.Y.C., 1980-87; dir. research Med. Econs. Co., Oradell, N.J., 1987—. Contbr. poetry to anthology. Mem. Am. Mktg. Assn., Pharm. Adv. Council, Healthcare Bus. Women's Assn. Democrat. Roman Catholic. Avocations: sailing, reading, writing, horticulture, guitar. Office: Med Econs Co Inc 690 Kinderkamack Rd Oradell NJ 07649

BOHANNON, SHARI ANN, business executive; b. Bakersfield, Calif., July 27, 1946; d. Vernon David and Jacqueline Sharon (Kramer) Hobbs; A.A., West Valley Jr. Coll., 1968; B.S., San Jose State U., 1972; children by previous marriage—Michelle, Richard, Garld. Asst. dir. core area devel. San Jose C. of C., 1969-71; asst. dir. health occupations Modesto Jr. Coll., 1971-75; mgr. Microwave Assocs. Communications Co., Sunnyvale, Calif., 1978-81; field engring. supr. Four Phase Systems, Inc., Cupertino, Calif., 1981-83; mgr. Rayne Plumbing & Sewer Service Inc., 1983-84; mgr. M/A COM MAC, Inc., 1984—. Mem. Nat. Assn. Female Execs. (network dir.). Home: 6571 American Ct San Jose CA 95120 Office: 1494 Hamilton Ave Suite 204 San Jose CA 95125

BOHLE, SUE, public relations executive; b. Austin, Minn., June 23, 1943; d. Harold Raymond and Mary Theresa (Swanson) Hastings; m. John Bernard Bohle, June 22, 1974; children: Jason John, Katie Christine. BS in Journalism, Northwestern U., 1965, MS in Journalism, 1969. Tchr. pub. high schs Englewood, Colo., 1965-68; account exec. Burson-Marsteller Pub. Relations, Los Angeles, 1969-73; v.p., mgr. pub. relations J. Walter Thompson Co., Los Angeles, 1973-79; founder, pres. The Bohle Co., Los Angeles and San Francisco, 1979—; former exec. v.p. Ketchum/Bohle Pub. Relations, Los Angeles; free-lance writer, instr. communications Calif. State U. at Fullerton, 1972-73; instr. writing Los Angeles City Coll., 1975-76; lectr. U. So. Calif., 1979—. Contbr. articles to profl. jours. Dir. pub. relations Los Angeles Jr. Ballet, 1971-72; pres. Panhellenic Advisers Council, UCLA, 1972-73; mem. adv. bd. Los Angeles Valley Coll., 1974-75, Coll. Communications Pepperdine U., 1981—; bd. visitors Medill Sch. Journalism, Northwestern U., 1984—. Univ. scholar, 1961-64, Panhellenic scholar, 1964-65. Mem. Pub. Relations Soc. Am. (bd. dirs. Los Angeles chpt. 1981-82, v.p. Los Angeles chpt. 1983, del. to nat assembly 1984, officer Counselors Acad. 1984—), Women in Communications, Shi-ai, Delta Zeta (editor The Lamp 1966-68), Kappa Alpha Tau. Office: The Bohle Co 1901 Ave of the Stars Suite 450 Los Angeles CA 90067 *

BOHLKEN, DEBORAH KAY, data processing executive; b. Anchorage, Nov. 16, 1952; d. Darrell Richard and Gertrude Ann (Merkle) B. BA, U. Ark., 1975, MSW, 1977. Specialist community devel. State of Ark., Little Rock, 1976-77, supr. community area, 1977-78, mgr. evaluation and data processing, 1978-80; corp. analyst Systematics, Inc., Little Rock, 1980-83, mgr. corp. planning and research, 1983-85, group mgr., 1985—. Contbr. articles and papers to profl. publs. Bd. dirs. Cen. Ark. Radiation Therapy Inst. Hotline, Little Rock, 1980-82, Cancer Soc., Little Rock, 1986—; state chair Cansurmount, Little Rock, 1985—. Nat. Juvenile Justice Law Enforcement Adminstrn. explimary data processing grantee, 1976-78. Mem. Nat. Assn. Bank Services, Cash Mgrs. Assn., Fin. Mgrs. Assn., Mortgage Bankers Assn., U.S. Savs. and Loan Assn., Am. Mgmt. Assn. Democrat. Methodist. Office: Systematics Inc 4001 Rodney Parham Rd Little Rock AR 72212

BOHN, CAROLYN CELIA, hydrologist; b. Detroit, Oct. 23, 1950; d. Gerald B. and Ruth (Fryman) B. BA in Zoology, Ecology, U. Washington, 1975; MS in Rangeland Mgmt., Oreg. State U., 1984. Biol. technician Bur. of Land Mgmt., Vale, Oreg., 1978-79; grad. research asst. Oregon State U., Corvalus, 1980-83; hydrology technician U.S. Forest Service, John Day, Oreg., 1983-85; hydrology lab research assoc. U. Nev. at Reno, Elko, 1985-88; hydrologist U.S. Forest Service Intermountain Research Sta., Boise, Idaho, 1988—. Contbr. articles to profl. jours. Vol. Recycling, John Day, Oreg., 1983-85; organizer Ruby Mt. Recycling Network, Elko, 1987. Mem. Am. Water Resources Assn., Soc. for Range Mgmt., Sigma Xi, Gamma Sigma Delta. Office: 316 E Myrtle Boise ID 83705

BOHNING, ELIZABETH EDROP, educator; b. Bklyn., June 26, 1915; d. Percy Tom and Marion Lothrop (Stafford) Edrop; m. William H. Bohning, Aug. 18, 1943; children: Barbara Bohning Young, Margaret Bohning Anderson. BA, Wellesley Coll., 1936; MA, Bryn Mawr Coll., 1938, PhD, 1943; postgrad., Middlebury Coll., 1936, U. Cologne, 1936-37, U. Munich, 1955. Mem. faculty Bryn Mawr (Pa.) Coll., 1938-39, Stanford (Calif.) U., 1939-40, Grinnell (Iowa) Coll., 1940-41; prof. German U. Del., Newark, 1967-85, prof. emeritus, 1985—, chairperson dept. langs. and lit., 1971-78; mem. faculty Middlebury Coll., summers 1956, 58. Author: The Concept "Sage" in Nibelungen Criticism, 1944; contbr. articles on lit. to profl. jours. Vice-chairperson Del. Humanities Council, 1981-82; pres. Del. Council Internat. Visitors, 1982-85. Recipient Lindback award for excellence in teaching, 1962. Mem. Soc. German-Am. Studies, Am. Assn. Tchrs. German (cert. of merit 1982), Am. Soc. 18th Century Studies, Am. Council Study of Austrian Lit., Middle State Assn. Colls. and Schs. (trustee 1974-80), Phi Beta Kappa, Delta Phi Alpha, Phi Kappa Phi, Alpha Chi Omega. Episcopalian. Clubs: Wellesley Alumnae, Bryn Mawr Alumnae. Home: Box 574 Newark DE 19715

BOIMAN, DONNA RAE, art academy executive; b. Columbus, Ohio, Jan. 13, 1946; d. George Brandle and Donna Rae (Rockwell) Hall; m. David Charles Boiman, Dec. 8, 1973. BS in Pharmacy, Ohio State U., 1969; student, Columbus Coll. Art & Design, 1979-83. Registered pharmacist, Ohio. Pharmacist, mgr. various retail stores, Cleve., 1970-73, Columbus, 1973-77; owner L'Artiste, Reynoldsburg, Ohio, 1977-81; pres. Cen. Ohio Art Acad., Reynoldsburg, 1981—; cons. to Mayor City of Reynoldsburg, 1986-87. Represented in permanent collections including Collector's Gallery Columbus Mus. Art, Gallery 200, Columbus, Art Exchange, Columbus, The Huntington Collection, Dean Witter Reynolds Collection, Zanesville Art Ctr. Author: Anatomy and Structure: A Guide for Young Artists, 1988; represented in permanent collections Mt. Carmel East Hosp., Columbus, Corp. 2005, Radisson Motels, Mich. and Ohio, Fifth 3d Bank, Bexley, On Line Computer Library, Dublin, Cintas Corp. Recipient John Lennon Meml. award for the Arts award Internat. Art Challenge com., 1987. Mem. Pa. Soc. Watercolorists, Nat. Soc. Layerists in Multimedia, Columbus Art League, Cen. Ohio Watercolor Soc. (pres. 1983-84), Am. Quarter Horse Assn., Ohio Quarter Horse Assn., Allied Artists of Am. (assoc.), Licking County Art Assn., Nat. Wildlife Fedn., Ohio State U. Alumni Assn., Ohio State U. Pharmacy Alumni Assn. (charter). Office: Cen Ohio Art Acad 7297 E Main St Reynoldsburg OH 43068

BOISE, OLA IRENE, music educator; b. Parkersburg, W. Va., Dec. 1, 1946; d. Manford and Ollie Irene (Arthur) B. BA in Fine Arts, Ohio U., 1968, MA in Mus. Edn., 1974. Cert. music edn. elem. through high sch., Ohio. Tchr. music Warren Local Schs., Vincent, Ohio, 1968-69; tchr. elem., music Wood County Schs., Parkersburg, W.Va, 1969-73; tchr. music Amherst (Ohio) Exempted Village Schs., 1974-76, W. Muskingum Local Schs., Zanesville, Ohio, 1976-83, Belpre (Ohio) City Schs., 1983—. Chmn. bike-a-thon St. Jude's Children's Research Hosp., 1987; mem. exec. bd. Belpre area bi-centennial commn., 1987—. Mem. Belpre Edn. Assn. (exec. council 1986-87), Ohio Music Edn. Assn. (dist. 9 various positions), Belpre Area C. of C. (bd. dirs. 1988—). Republican. Baptist. Home: 821 Main St Belpre OH 45714 Office: Belpre City Schs 2014 Washington Blvd Belpre OH 45714

BOJARSKI, JEANNE FRANCES, technical writer; b. N.Y.C., Dec. 20, 1951; d. Frank J. and Theodosia H. (Trzcinski) B.; 1 child, Jessica James (dec.). BA in Philosophy, New Coll., Sarasota, Fla., 1974; postgrad. in econs., U. Chgo., 1979-81. Adminstrv. asst. Nat. Bus. Lists, Inc., N.Y.C., 1974-76; freelance writer, N.Y.C., 1976-77; asst. to pres. Tribal Arts Gallery, N.Y.C., 1977-78; instr. econs. Roosevelt U., Chgo., 1980-83; sr. cons. Cooley/Baker, Inc., Chgo., 1981-85; dir. tech. writing and proposal coordination Control Systems Internat., Overland Park, Kans., 1986—. Editor: The Grackle (jazz criticism), 1976. Bd. dirs. Studio Infinity Ltd., N.Y.C., 1976-77; hon. parent Gillis Home for Children, Kansas City, 1985. Mem. Soc. for Tech. Communication. Republican. Clubs: Nat. Rifle Assn., Mutual Musician's Found. (Kansas City). Avocations: hunting, photography, bicycling, jazz, trap shooting.

BOK, SISSELA, writer, philosopher; b. Stockholm, Dec. 2, 1934; d. Gunnar and Alva (Reimer) Myrdal; m. Derek Bok, May 7, 1955; children—Hilary, Victoria, Tomas. BA, George Washington U., 1957, MA, 1958, LHD (hon.), 1986; PhD, Harvard U., 1970; LLD (hon.), Mt. Holyoke Coll., 1985, Clark U., 1988. Lectr. Simmons Coll., Boston, 1971-72; lectr. Harvard-MIT Div. Health Scis. and Tech., Cambridge, 1975-82, Harvard U., Cambridge, 1982-84; assoc. prof. philosophy Brandeis U., Waltham, Mass., 1985—; mem. ethics adv. bd. HEW, 1977-80; bd. dirs. Population Council, 1971-77, Hastings Inst., 1976-84. Author: Lying: Moral Choice in Public and Private Life, 1978 (Melcher award, George Orwell award), Secrets: On the Ethics of Concealment and Revelation, 1982, Alva: Ett kvinnoliv, 1987; mem. editorial bd. Ethics, 1980-85, Criminal Justice Ethics, 1980—. Mem. adv. bd. Cultural Survival, 1986—; bd. dirs. Inst. for Philosophy and Religion, Boston U. Recipient Abram L. Sachar Silver medallion Brandeis U., 1985. Fellow Hastings Ctr. (dir. 1976-84); mem. Am. Philos. Assn. Office: Brandeis U Dept Philosophy Waltham MA 02254

BOKROSS, AGNES HELEN, educator documentalist; b. Budapest, Hungary, Jan. 9, 1922; came to Can., 1957, naturalized, 1962; d. Lajos Ferenc and Andrea (Tömöry) Szakonyi; B.A. with honors in English, Sir George Williams U., Montreal, Que., Can., 1970; Ph.D. in Comparative Lit. (Woodrow Wilson fellow 1970-71, Ford fellow 1970-71, Can. Council doctoral awards 1972-74), McGill U., Montreal, 1974; m. Béla E. Bokross, 1943 (div. 1945); 1 dau., Apollonia Elizabeth Bokross Schofield. Indexer and archivist Internat. Civil Aviation Orgn., Montreal, 1957-72; lectr. in English lit. Concordia U., Montreal, 1974-80; multilingual annotator Nat. Library Can., Ottawa, Ont., 1975-81; documentalist Public Service Commn. Can., Ottawa, 1981—; tchr., cons. in field. Recipient Gold medal Gov. Gen. Can., 1970; McGill U. travel research grantee, 1973. Mem. MLA, Can. Soc. Comparative Study Civilizations, Nat. Geog. Soc. Roman Catholic. Author Nat. Library of Can. Annotations Manual, 1979; contbr. essays to lit. jours.; papers to confs. Office: Public Service Commn L'Esplanade Laurier West Tower, B1123 300 Laurier W, Ottawa, ON Canada K1A 0M7

BOLAND, ELLEN CLARK, social service administrator; b. Scranton, Pa., Jan. 7, 1955; d. John Thomas and Alice Frances (McDonald) Clark; m. John Francis Boland, June 29, 1973; children: Colleen, Thomas. BS in Human Services, U. Scranton, 1981. Homemaking supr. Allied Services for the Handicapped, Scranton, 1981-82, program coordinator, 1982-85, homemaker program dir., 1985-87, dir. in-home services, 1987—, chmn. employee task force, 1986—; mem. Allied Services Speakers Bur. Loaned exec. Scranton C. of C., 1987; vice chmn. Lackawanna County Coalition for Aging Services, 1986—, chair 1988; mem. Hill Neighborhood Assn., Lackawanna County Resource Rev. Com. Mem. Nat. Assn. Home Care, Pa. Assn. Home Care. Democrat. Roman Catholic. Home: 1025 Monroe Ave Scranton PA 18510 Office: Allied Services for the Handicapped Inc 119 Mulberry St Scranton PA 18503

BOLAND, JANET LANG, judge; b. Kitchener, Ont., Can., Dec. 6, 1924; d. George William and Miriam Janet (Geraghty) Lang; m. John Brown Boland, Oct. 1, 1949; children: Michael, Christopher, Nicholas. B.A., Waterloo Coll., 1946; law degree, Osgoode Hall, 1950; hon. doctorate of law, Sir Wilfred Laurier U. Bar: Ont. 1950, named Queen's counsel 1965. Mem. firm White, Bristol, Beck & Phipps, Toronto, Ont., 1959-69; partner firm Lang Michener, Toronto, 1969-72; county ct. judge Toronto, 1972-76; judge Supreme Ct. of Ont., Toronto, 1976—; co-chmn. Penal Reform for Women Joint Com., 1956-58. Mem. Jr. League Toronto. Roman Catholic. Office: Osgoode Hall, Queen St, Toronto, ON Canada M5H 2N7

BOLDEN, ROSAMOND, state official; b. Beggs, Okla., May 5, 1938; d. Benjamin James and Mary Crosby; m. James Alan Bolden, Jan. 27, 1963 (dec. Dec. 1973); 1 child, Stacie Lenore. B.S., U. Calif.-Berkeley, 1961, MA 1971. Employment counselor to office mgr. Calif. Dept. Employment, Sacramento, 1965-75; asst. civil rights officer Calif. Dept. Health, Sacramento, 1976-77; chief Office Bldg. and Grounds, Calif. Dept. Gen. Services, Sacramento, 1977—; chmn. merit award bd. dept. personnel adminstrn., State of Calif. Sacramento, 1979-84; mem. women's adv. bd. Calif. Personnel Bd., Sacramento, 1980-84. Bd. dirs. Tierra Del Oro council Girl Scouts U.S.A., Sacramento, 1984, Sacramento Urban League, 1986-89; mem. citizen rev. bd., chmn. admission/allocation subcom. United Way, Sacramento, 1984; founding mem. Sacramento Black Women's Network, 1981. Recipient award of appreciation United Calif. State Employee Campaign, 1980; cert. of appreciation Nat. Assn. Retarded Citizens, 1981 United Way, 1984. Mem. Bldg. Owners and Mgrs. Assn. (co-founder Calif. chpt. 1986, mem. govt. bldg. com.), NAACP, Black Advocates in State Service, Alpha Kappa Alpha. Home: PO Box 22457 Sacramento CA 95831 Office: State of Calif 915 Capital Mall Room 106 Sacramento CA 95831

BOLDREY, BRENDA MARIE, family therapist; b. Phoenix, May 14, 1957; d. Melvin C. Boldrey and Helen M. (Ploghoft) McPherson; 1 child, Lyndsay M. Rowell. AA, Maple Woods Community Coll., 1978; BA, U. Mo. Kansas City, 1980; MA, 1981. Lic. profl. counselor, Mo. Family counselor Turning Point, Leawood, Kans., 1983-85; owner, dir., counselor Potentials Counseling Ctr., Kansas City, Mo., 1985—; bd. dirs. Potentials, Kansas City, 1985—. Mem. Better Bus. Bur., Kans. City, 1986—. Mem. Am. Acad. Counseling and Devel., Nat. Assn. Female Execs., Am. Assn. Bus. Women, Mo. Assn. Counseling and Devel., U. Mo. Kans. City Alumni Assn., Phi Theta Kappa, Psi Chi. Presbyterian. Home: 1121 W 77th St Kansas City MO 64114 Office: Potentials 7920 Ward Pkwy #209 Kansas City MO 64114

BOLE-BECKER, LUANNE CHRISTINE, information systems consultant, free-lance writer, instructional designer; b. Cleve., Apr. 8, 1957; d. Victor John Bole and Anne Marie (Gradizar) Chansky; m. Robert Roy Becker, Sept. 9, 1978; 1 child, Christopher William. BBA in Acctg. summa cum laude, Cleve. State U., 1978. Bus. mgr. Sta. WCSB Cleve. State U., 1976-78; fin. analyst Cardinal Fed. Savs. & Loan, Cleve., 1978-79; EDP auditor Fed. Res. Bank, Cleve., 1979-81, project mgr., 1981-84; cons. Ernst & Whinney, Cleve., 1984-86; pvt. practice cons. Cleve., 1987—; writer Cleve. Waterfront Coalition, 1985-86. Co-author E&W Structured Analysis and Design Standards, 1985; contbr. articles to profl. jours. Bd. trustees New Orgn. Visual Arts, Cleve., 1984-86; vol. NASA, Cleve., 1987. Democrat. Lutheran.

BOLEN, LANORA LUKE, educator; b. Oklahoma City, Mar. 12, 1934; d. Elmer Werthon and Nellie Lois (Owensby) Luke; student Okla. Bapt. U., 1952-55, Baylor U., 1953, Okla. Central State U., 1957, S.W. Mo. State U., 1960-61, St. Louis Inst. Music, 1964, So. Ill. U., 1968-70; B.Mus. Edn., So. Ill. U., 1970; postgrad. N. Tex. State U., 1975, Tex. Christian U., 1977, Northwestern U., 1986, Cambridge (Eng.) U., 1987, MEd North Tex. State U., 1987; children by previous marriage—Paul Anthony DeOgny, Frederick Ronald DeOgny, Terri Sue DeOgny. Pvt. piano tchr., 1956-68; elem. music tchr. Clayton (Mo.) Sch. Dist., 1969-74; profl. musician TV comml. artist, 1967-75; exec. dir. Youth Orch. of Greater Ft. Worth, 1979-80; dir. founder Kinderplatz of Fine Arts, Inc., Ft. Worth, 1979—. Fin. chmn. LWV, St. Louis, 1966, pres. Republican Women's Club, Lewisville, Tex., 1976; vice chmn. Rep. Party, Tarrant County, Tex., 1977; bd. dirs. Youth Orch. Greater Ft. Worth, 1976-81, pres., 1979-81, Schola Cantorum Tex., 1983; chmn. Oktoberfest Symphony League, Ft. Worth, 1978; bd. dirs. Ft. Worth Symphony, 1980—; mem. exec. com. Youth Orch. div. Am. Symphony Orch. League, 1980—. Mem. Am. Orff-Schulwerk Assn., Nat. Music Educators Conf., Nat. Assn. for Edn. Young Children, Nat. Assn. for Gifted and Talented Edn., AAUW (bd. dirs. Tarrant County), Youth Orch. Assn., Nat. Fedn. Rep. Women, Am. Symphony Orch. League, Delta Kappa Gamma, Sigma Alpha Iota. Presbyterian. Clubs: Women's. Contbr. articles to profl. jours. Office: 3320 W Cantey Fort Worth TX 76109

BOLENE, MARGARET ROSALIE STEELE, bacteriologist, civic worker; b. Kingfisher, Okla., July 11, 1923; d. Clarence R. and Harriet (White) Steele; student Oreg. State U., 1943-44; B.S., U. Okla., 1946; m. Robert V. Bolene, Feb. 6, 1948; children—Judith Kay, John Eric, Sally Sue, Janice Lynn, Daniel William. Technician bacteriology dept. Okla. Dept. Health, Oklahoma City, 1946-48; asst. bacteriologist Henry Ford Hosp., Detroit, 1948-49; bacteriol. cons., also asst. bus. mgr. Ponce Gynecology and Obstetrics, Inc., 1956—. Organizing dir. Bi-Racial Council, 1963; lay adviser Home Nursing Service, 1967-68; mem. exec. bd. PTA, 1956-71; active various community drives; sponsor Am. Field Service; patron Ponce Playhouse; bloodmobile vol. ARC; vol. Helpline. Republican precinct organizer, 1960. Mem. AAUW (treas. 1964-66), DAR (sec.-treas. 1961-67, 1st vice regent 1972-73, chpt. treas. 1974-84), Kay-Noble County Med. Aux. (treas. 1957-58, 66-67), Ponca City Art Assn., Pioneer Hist. Soc., Okla. Heritage Assn., Daus. Founders and Patriots (state pres. 1980-84), Nat. Huguenot Soc., Hereditary Order First Families Mass. Daus. Am. Colonists (chpt. pres. 1982-84), Magna Charta Dames (treas. Okla. chpt. 1984), Order Colonial Physicians and Chirurgiens (life), Ancient and Honorable Arty. Co. Women Descs. Okla. Ct. (treas. 1983-84, registrar 1986—), Dames of Ct. of Honor, Colonial Dames of 17th Century, Hereditary Order of First Families of Mass., U. Okla. Assn. (life), Lambda Tau, Phi Sigma, Alpha Lambda Delta. Presbyterian (elder 1983-86). Clubs: Ponca City Country, Ponca City Music, Red Rose Garden (pres. 1983-84), Twentieth Century. Home: 2116 Juanito Ave Ponca City OK 74604

BOLEY BOLAFFIO, RITA, artist; b. Trieste, Italy; d. Angelo Luzzatto and Olga Senigaglia; came to U.S., 1939, naturalized, 1944; studied with Joseph Hoffmann, Kunstgewerbe Schule, Vienna, Austria; diploma violin Music

Conservatory, Vienna; student of F. Ondricek; m. Orville F. Boley; children—Lucius R., Bruno A. Fashion and textile and interior designer Wiener Werkstatte, Vienna and Milan, Italy; murals and displays throughout U.S., maj. exhns. collage and assemblage include Mus. of Art, Columbia, S.C., Am. House, N.Y.C., J.L. Hudson Gallery, Detroit, Pen and Brush Club, N.Y.C., Richard Kollmar's Gallery, N.Y.C., Guild Hall Mus., East Hampton, N.Y., James Pendleton Gallery, N.Y.C. Washington Art Assn. Conn., Galerie St. Etienne, N.Y.C. Mem. arts group ARC, 1942-44. Mem. Composer, Author and Artists Am. Studio: 310 W 106th St New York NY 10025

BOLI, SARAH COLLINS, property manager; b. Warren, Pa., July 18, 1958; d. Hugh C. and Elizabeth (Harper) Wood; m. Robert McPherson Boli, Dec. 22, 1982; 1 child Jonathan William. AA in Liberal Arts, Jamestown Community coll., N.Y., 1978; BA in Environ. Science, Alfred U., N.Y., 1980. Lab. asst. Jamestown Community Coll., Jamestown, N.Y., 1976-78; dir. commercial ops. Tech and Turf Inc., Madison, N.J., 1980-81; mgr. King's Motel Pacific Land Assoc., Enumclaw, Wash., 1985—; owner Plan'dscape; mem. design rev. bd. City of Enumclaw. Author: Jamestown Community College Preserve, 1978. Tourism com. C. of C., Enumclaw, Wash., 1985—. Served as sgt. U.S. Army, 1981-85. Mem. Bus. and Profl. Women (Young Career Woman award Wash. state dist. 4 1986). Republican. Methodist. Home and Office: 1334 Roosevelt Way East Enumclaw WA 98022

BOLIN, TERESA MATTHEWS, real estate corporation officer; b. Houston, Dec. 31, 1946; d. Robert Arlyn and Maxine (Steen) Matthews; m. George Rodney Bolin. Exec. dir. Pres. First Lady's Spa, Houston, 1966-70; owner, operator Spring Of Youth Of Am. Spas, Jackson, Miss., 1970-74; with real estate dept., Mitchell Energy and Devel., Houston, 1974-76, Nat. Western Life Ins. Co., Houston, 1976-78; pres. Bolin Realty, Inc., Houston, 1978—; apptd. mem. Harris County Appraisal Rev. Bd., Houston, 1986—. Bd. dirs. Theatre Under the Stars, Houston, 1980-82; mem. exec. com. Houston Internat. Festival Found., Houston, 1986—; legis. advisor State of Miss., Jackson, 1971, senate advisor, 1972. Mem. Nat. Assn. Women Comml. Real Estate (founding mem., 1st v.p. 1979-84, Appreciation award 1980), Houston Bd. Realtors, Houston C. of C. Democrat. Roman Catholic. Home: 4944 Post Oak Timber Houston TX 77056

BOLINE, DOLORES MARJORIE, elementary educator; b. Chico, Calif., Oct. 30, 1927; d. Jewell Ulysses and Alli Julia (Lampi) Friend; m. Norman Edward Boline, Aug. 20, 1952; children: Richard, Janis E., Ronald. AB in Gen. Elem. Edn., Calif. State U., Chico, 1949. Tchr., prin. Brown's Valley Sch., Napa, Calif., 1949-53; tchr. Riverside Sch., Sacramento, 1953-54, Pueblo Sch., Napa, 1955-56, Fremont Sch., Fresno, Calif., 1958-61, Teilman Sch., Fresno Unified Sch. Dist., Fresno, 1960-67, Thomas Sch., Fresno, 1967-88. Mem. NEA, Calif. Tchrs. Assn., Fresno Tchrs. Assn., Calif. Native Daus. Democrat. Baptist. Home: 3831 E Garland Fresno CA 93726

BOLING, JEWELL, retired government official; b. Randleman, N.C., Sept. 26, 1907; d. John Emmitt and Carrie (Ballard) Boling; student Women's Coll., U. N.C., 1926, Am. U., 1942, 51-52. Interviewer, N.C. Employment Service, Winston-Salem, Asheboro, 1937-41; occupational analyst U.S. Dept. Labor, Washington, 1943-57, placement officer, 1957-58, employment service adviser, 1959-61, occupational analyst, 1962, employment service specialist counseling and testing, 1963-69, manpower devel. specialist, from 1969. Recipient Meritorious Achievement award U.S. Dept. Labor, 1972. Mem. AAAS, N.Y. Acad. Scis., Am. Assn. Counseling and Devel., Nat. Career Devel. Assn., Am. Rehab. Counseling Assn. (archivist 1964-68), Assn. Measurement in Counseling and Devel., Assn. Humanistic Psychology, Planetary Soc., Smithsonians, Sierra Club, Nature Conservancy, Internat. Platform Assn., Audubon Naturalist Soc., Nat. Capital Astronomers (editor Star Dust 1949-58). Author: Counselor's Handbook, 1967; Counselor's Desk Aid, Eighteen Basic Vocational Directions, 1967; Handbook for New Careerists in Employment Security, 1971; contbr. articles to profl. publs. Address: Route 2 Box 176 Randleman NC 27317

BOLING, JUDY ATWOOD, civic worker; b. Madras, India, June 19, 1921 (parents Am. citizens); d. Carroll Eugene and Marion Frances (Ayrer) Atwood; A.A., San Antonio Jr. Coll., 1940; student Rogue Community Coll., Grants Pass, Oreg., 1978-79, So. Oreg. State Coll., Ashland, 1982—; m. Jack Leroy Boling, Apr. 8, 1941; children—Joseph Edward, Jean Ann, James Michael, John Charles. First aid instr. ARC, various locations, 1940-65, chmn. vols., Calif., 1961-62, Eng., 1964-65; den mother cub scouts Boy Scouts Am., Monterey, Calif., 1951-52; active Girl Scouts U.S.A., 1953—, council pres., Winema (Oreg.) Council, 1971-73, 79-82, del. to nat. council, 1966, 72, 81, cons. for nat. pubs., 1971, 79; Sunday sch. tchr. Base Chapel, Pyote, Tex., 1949-51, choir dir., 1951; Sunday sch. adminstr. Base Chapel, Morocco, 1954-55; Sunday sch. tchr. Hermon Free Meth. Ch., Los Angeles, 1956-57; active United Way campaign, 1967-84, Childrens Festival, 1974—; former liaison with local people in Japanese-Am., Franco-Am., Anglo-Am. orgns.; mem., patron Rogue Craftsmen Bd., Grants Pass, 1972-85, sec., 1972-78, v.p., 1978-85; bd. dirs. Rogue Valley Opera Assn., 1978-85, Community Concert, 1979—; historian Josephine County Republican Women, 1982-86, treas., 1986—; frequent public speaker. Recipient Thanks badge Girl Scouts U.S.A., 1957, 60, 73, Girl Scouts Japan, 1959, United Kingdom Girl Guides, 1982; others; cert. of appreciation USAF, 1959, City of Hagi, City of Fukuoka (Japan), Gov. of Fukuoka Prefecture; 2 citations Internat. Book Project; Oreg. Vol. award Sen. Packwood, 1983; Community Woman of Year award Bus. and Profl. Women, 1984. Mem. Josephine County Hist. Soc., So. Oreg. Resources Alliance, Am. Host Found., Friends of Library, Women's Investment Group (pres.), Grants Pass Art Mus. Republican. Club: Knife and Fork. Contbr. articles to profl. jours. Address: 3016 Jumpoff Joe Creek Rd Grants Pass OR 97526

BOLING, PATTI ZIMMERMAN, accountant; b. Hartford, Conn., Nov. 14, 1958; d. Earl Kenneth and Elsie Joy (Dees) Zimmerman; m. Timothy Ray Boling, July 19, 1986. BS in Bus. Adminstrn., U. S.C., 1981. CPA, S.C. Bookkeeper James K. Davis, CPA, Lancaster, S.C., 1977-81; staff acct. Peat, Marwick, Mitchell & Co., Greenville, S.C., 1981-83; mgr. Thompson & Davis, CPA's, Lancaster, 1983-85; ptnr. Thompson, Davis, Cauthen & Co., Lancaster, 1986—. Mem. fin. com. Reformation Luth. Ch., Lancaster, 1985; adv. youth group, 1987. Mem. AIA (Catawba chpt.), S.C. Assn. CPA's, Am. Inst. CPA's. Republican. Home: 714A Rugby Rd Lancaster SC 29720 Office: Thompson Davis Cauthen & Co 100 S Catawba St Lancaster SC 29720

BOLITHO, LOUISE GREER, educational administrator, consultant; b. Wenatchee, Wash., Aug. 13, 1927; d. Lon Glenn and Edna Gertrude (Dunlap) Greer; m. Douglas Stuart, June 17, 1950 (div. Dec. 1975); children: Rebecca Louise, Brian Douglas. BA, Wash. State U., 1949. With Stanford (Calif.) U., 1967-86, adminstrv. asst. physics labs., 1974-77, mgr. ctr. for research in internat. studies, 1977-84, law sch. fin. and adminstrv. services dir., 1984-86; computer cons., Palo Alto, Calif., 1984—; acting mgr. Inst. for Internat. Studies, 1987-88, fin. analyst, 1988—. Mem. Peninsula vols., Menlo Park, Calif., 1986—; budget com. chmn., bd. dirs. Mid-Peninsula Support Network, Mountain View, Calif., 1984-86. Mem. AAUW (bd. dirs. 1987-88), Stanford/Palo Alto IBM Personal Computer User's Group, Palo Alto C. of C. Home and Office: 410 Sheridan Ave #445 Palo Alto CA 94306

BOLLER, MARGARET MARY, cable television executive; b. N.Y.C., Mar. 23, 1956; d. Raymond Jerome and Winifred Mary (Zamow) B.; m. Paul Steven Erstein, May 29, 1983; 1 child, Kali Beth. BA in Psychology, Coll. Holy Cross, 1977. Adminstrv. asst. Showtime Entertainment Inc., N.Y.C., 1978-79, nat. tng. coordinator, 1980-81, mgr. nat. promotions, 1981-83; mgr. trade advt. Showtime/The Movie Channel, N.Y.C., 1984, dir. direct response mktg., 1985-88, v.p. mktg. adminstrn., 1988—. Mem. Nat. Acad. Cable Programming, Cable TV Adminstrn. and Mktg. Soc., Direct Mktg. Assn. Democrat. Jewish. Office: Showtime/The Movie Channel Inc 1633 Broadway New York NY 10019

BOLLHEIMER, (CECILIA) DENISE, marketing professional, finance executive; b. Memphis, Sept. 8, 1950; d. Parker Cecil Jr. and Kathleen Alice (Reinhart) Henderson; m. Philip Anthony Bollheimer Jr., June 10, 1972. Student, Rhodes Coll., 1968-69; BBA in Mktg., Memphis State U., 1972, MBA in Fin., 1979; cert. in Banking, Rutgers U., 1983; cert. in Trust Ops., So. Trust Sch., 1984. Research analyst, mgr. Union Planters Corp., Memphis, 1973-75, asst. to mktg. dir., 1975-76, asst. v.p., 1976-77, v.p. mktg. div., 1977-83, sr. v.p. fin. mgmt. group, 1984-86; sr. v.p. trust group Union Planters Nat. Bank, Memphis, 1983-84; dir. advt., promotions, mktg. communications Meth. Health Systems, Memphis, 1986-87, dir. mktg., 1987-88; v.p. mktg. and planning Univ. Physicians Found., Memphis, 1988—. Mem. planned giving council Rhodes Coll., Memphis, 1985-86, alumni fund-raising com. 1987; mem., class rep. Leadership Memphis, 1985-88; chmn. world championship barbecue cooking contest Memphis in May Internat. Festival, 1986-88; chmn. gala com. Am. Heart Assn., Memphis, 1986, 87; pres. bd. dirs. Commitment Memphis, 1984-87; bd. dirs. Memphis Literacy Council, 1986—, Lupus Found. Am., Memphis, 1987—. Mem. Med. Group Mgmt. Assn., Memphis Advt. Fedn., Am. Inst. Banking (Banker of Yr. Memphis region 1981), Beta Gamma Sigma, Alpha Omicron Pi. Lodge: Kiwanis (sec. bd. dirs. Kiwanis Charities, Inc. 1988—). Home: 628 N Trezevant Memphis TN 38112 Office: Univ Physicians Found 66 N Pauline Memphis TN 38105

BOLLING, CHERIE ROSEMARIE, communications executive; b. Southgate, Calif., Dec. 13, 1939; d. Russell Alonzo and Violet Drucilla (Van Cleave) Drake; m. William Edward Bolling, July 1, 1960; children: Richard Lee, William Edward II, Dennis Keith. AA, Santa Monica Coll., 1959; BS, UCLA, 1963; postgrad., Calif. State U., Northridge. Entertainer TV and stage Los Angeles, 1952-60, musician, tchr., 1954-60; designer clothing Athens, 1963-65; dir. sch. U.S. Military, Athens, 1962-63; consumer advocate Consumers United Palo Alto, Calif., 1972-76; head TV production Teleprompter Cable TV, Santa Clara, Calif., 1974-76; pres. C & R Productions, Palo Alto, Los Angeles, 1976-83; v.p. Renaissance, San Marcos, Calif., 1981—; pres. Mine, Yours & Ours, San Marcos, 1982—. Mem. Santa Clara County Adv. Commn. Consumer Affairs, 1974-76. Mem. Nat. Assn. Female Exec., Nat. Alliance Homebased Bus. (treas. 1986-88), Am. Film Inst., Am. Women Radio and TV, Beta Sigma Phi.

BOLLINGER, DEBRA MARIE, lawyer, state government official; b. Huron, S.D., May 2, 1956; d. Gerald Edmund and Mary Jean (Dunn) B. B.S. in Bus. Adminstrn., U. S.D., 1978, M.B.A., 1981, J.D., 1981. Bar: S.D. 1981. Franchise adminstr. State of S.D., Pierre, 1981-83, dep. dir. div. securities Dept. Commerce, 1983-86, dir., 1986—. Dir. Oahe Fed. Credit Union, 1982-86; party worker S.D. Republican Party and Rep. Women, 1981—; campaign treas. for S.D. U.S. Ho. Reps., 1988; pres. Blue Ribbon panel on pub. relations U. S.D., 1987-88; actress, asst. dir. Pierre Players, 1981-83. Mem. ABA, S.D. Bar Assn., N.Am. Securities Adminstrs. Assn. (bd. dirs., treas. 1986-88). Roman Catholic. Club: Cen-Kota (pres. 1985-87) (Pierre). Home: 319 E Church St Pierre SD 57501 Office: Div of Securities 910 E Sioux Ave Pierre SD 57501

BOLLYKY ISTOK, MARGIT, psychotherapist; b. St. Marton, Czechoslovakia; came to U.S., 1951; d. Kalmán and Margaret (Kleiber) Istok; m. L.L. Bollyky; children: Andrea, Paul, Thomas. AB, Coll. New Rochelle, 1962; MSW, Columbia U., 1964. Cert. clin. social worker. Psychiat. social worker Manhattan VA Hosp., N.Y.C., 1964-70; cons. Child and Adolescent Psychology Assocs., 1981—; exec. dir. Pan Am. com. Internat. Ozone Assn., Norwalk, Conn., 1983—. bd. dirs. Holy Spirit Sch., Stanford, 1972-77. Mem. Nat. Assn. Social Workers (cert.). Roman Catholic. Home: 1332 Riverbank Rd Stamford CT 06903 Office: Internat Ozone Assn 83 Oakwood Ave Norwalk CT 06850

BOLOGNA, JOANNE DENISE, systems development supervisor; b. Albany, N.Y., Mar. 22, 1961; d. Matthew Joseph and Viola Theresa (Audi) B. BA in Computer Sci., LeMoyne Coll., 1983; postgrad. Rensselear Poly. Inst., 1983, Russel Sage Coll., 1984, 1986—. Documentation specialist McAuto Systems Group, Inc., Menands, N.Y., 1983-84, sr. programmer/analyst, 1984-85; systems analyst Empire Blue Cross & Blue Shield, Albany, N.Y., 1985-86; lead systems analyst Computer Scis. Corp., Menands, 1986-88, supr. systems devel., 1988—. Mem. Nat. Assn. Female Execs. Roman Catholic. Avocations: jogging, skiing, reading, computers, tax consulting. Home: 4066 Albany St Schenectady NY 12304 Office: Computer Scis Corp 800 N Pearl St Menands NY 12204

BOLSEN, BARBARA ANN, association newspaper editor; b. Cin., Aug. 27, 1950; d. William Dornette and Ida Louise (Krueck) B.; m. Roy Austin Petty, May 19, 1979. BS, Northwestern U., 1971. Reporter Aroostook County Times, Presque Isle, Maine, 1972; copy editor, reporter Lerner Newspapers, Chgo., 1972-73; assoc. editor Am. Med. News., Chgo., 1973-75, sr. editor, 1975-77, 78-81, sr. editor Washington, 1981-82, exec. editor, 1982—; editorial dir. Book Developers, Inc., Chgo., 1977-78; assoc. editor med. news. sect. Jour. AMA Washington, 1981-82. Recipient Gold Circle award Am. Soc. Assn. Execs., 1984. Office: Am Med News 535 N Dearborn St Chicago IL 60610

BOLSTER, JACQUELINE NEBEN (MRS. JOHN A. BOLSTER), cosmetic company executive; b. Woodhaven, N.Y.; d. Ernest William Benedict and Emily Claire (Guck) Neben; student Pratt Inst., Columbia U.; m. John A. Bolster, May 8, 1954. Promotion mgr. Photoplay mag., 1949-53; merchandising mgr. McCall's, N.Y.C., 1953-64; dir. promotion and merchandising Harper's Bazaar, N.Y.C., 1964-71; dir. advt. and promotion Elizabeth Arden Salons, N.Y.C., 1971—; dir. creative services Elizabeth Arden, Inc., 1976-78, dir. communications Elizabeth Arden Salons, 1978—. Recipient Art Director's award 1961, 66. Mem. Fashion Group, Fashion Execs. Roundtable, Inner Circle, Advt. Women N.Y. (life), Mag. Promotion Assn. Home: 8531 88th St Woodhaven NY 11421 Office: Elizabeth Arden Inc 55 E 52d St New York NY 10022 also: Halsey Neck Ln Southampton NY 11968

BOLTE, CANDICE REGINA, communications administrator; b. Jersey City, Oct. 18, 1948; d. George John and Frances Margaret (Hawkridge) B. BA in Math. Edn., Jersey City State Coll., 1970, MA in Math. Edn., 1972. Cert. systems profl. Tchr. high sch. math. Belleville (N.J.) Bd. Edn., 1970-79; developer system devel. tng. AT&T Long Lines, Piscataway, N.J., 1979-84; system planner AT&T Communications, Piscataway, 1984-87; system mgr. AT&T, Basking Ridge, N.J., 1987—. Head usher Marble Collegiate Ch., N.Y.C., 1986—. Mem. Assn. for Systems Mgmt. (pres. N.Y. chpt. 1983-86, div. dir. 1987-88, adv. com. internat. edn. 1984-86, internat. com. chair 1986-87, internat. dir. 1988—, Outstanding Service 1981, 87, 88, Disting. Service award 1988). Mem. Dutch Reformed Ch. Office: AT&T 295 N Maple Ave Basking Ridge NJ 07920

BOLTON, DEBORAH PARHAM, television news editor; b. Homerville, Ga., Sept. 29, 1957; d. Paul Henry II and Molly Frances (Chaney) Parham; m. John Mark Bolton, June 27, 1981. BA in Communications, Auburn U., 1981. Lic. FCC. Exercise instr. Figure Magic Spa, Jackson, Ala., 1973-75; disk jockey, news and program dir. Sta. WHOD-AM/FM-Radio, Jackson, 1977-78; news reporter, anchor Sta. WJHO-Radio, Opelika, Ala., 1978-81; asst. news dir., anchor Stas. WSGF/WKBX-Radio, Savannah, Ga., 1982; news dir., anchor Sta. WQCN-Radio, Savannah, 1983, Stas. WWSA/WCHY-Radio, Savannah, 1983-87; assignment editor Sta. WSAV-TV, Savannah, 1987—. Vice chmn. bd. Silent Witness, Savannah, 1983-87, chmn. 1988—; mem. speaker's bur. Safe Shelter(for abused women), Savannah, 1986—; media com. United Way of Coastal Empire, Savannah, 1987. Recipient 16 1st pl. awards since 1980, Pacemaker award, 1985, 86, awards for best investigative reporting, best regularly scheduled newscast, for news series Drugs: High Road to Nowhere, 1986, all from AP, Sch. Bell award, Ga. State Dept. Edn. 1988; named Best Radio News Anchor in Ga., 1985 and Radio News Dir. of Achievement, 1987 Atlanta chpt. Am. Women in Radio-TV. Mem. Ga. Assn. Newscasters (bd. dirs. 1983-87, 1st woman pres. 1985-86, Mem. of Yr. award 1986), Ga. AP Broadcasters Assn. (bd. dirs. 1984-87, 1st woman pres. 1985-86), Radio-TV News Dirs. Assn. (bd. dirs. 1984-87, dir.-at-large 1987—, state coordinator 1985-87), Oglethorpe Bus. and Profl. Women (exec. com. 1985—, com. chmn. 1986-87, Young Careerist award 1986), Am. Women in Radio-TV (organizer), Auburn Alumni Assn. (sec. Savannah chpt. 1982-87), Alpha Epsilon Rho, Chi Omega Alumni Assn. Methodist. Home: 4 Port Dr Richmond Hill GA 31324 Office: Sta WSAV-TV PO Box 2429 Savannah GA 31404

BOLTON, PAULA TAYLOR, director of education; b. Decatur, Ala., May 17, 1955; d. Carman Allen and Marguerite (Bonds) Taylor; m. John Clark Bolton, Mar. 4, 1978; 1 child, Ashley Summer. Student, Calhoun Coll., 1978. Office supr. Security Mut. Fin. Corp., Decatur, Ala., 1973-76; acctg. clk. Amalgamaize Co., Decatur, 1976-78; legal sec. Cauthen and Haddock, Attys., Decatur, 1978-79; office mgr. Aldridge and Haddock, Attys., Decatur, 1979-84; admissions rep. Nat. Career Coll., Decatur, 1985, dir., 1985—. Mem. Downtown Area Revitalization Effort, Parents and Children Together; active Jr. League of Morgan County. Mem. Ala. Assn. Pvt. Colls. and Schs. (sec. 1986—), Decatur C. of C., Women's C. of C., Nat. Assn. Female Execs. Democrat. Baptist. Club: Decatur Cotillion. Office: Nat Career Coll 224 2d Ave SE Decatur AL 35601

BOLZ, SARAH DAVIS, local government administrator; b. Saginaw, Mich., Mar. 14, 1945; s. Siegel Bloore and Kathleen (McGarvey) Davis; m. Charles R. Bolz, Sept. 7, 1968 (div. 1973). B.A., Albion Coll., 1967, M.A., Mich. State U., 1970. Curator, O. Henry Mus., Austin, Tex., 1973-78, Elisabet Ney Mus., Austin, 1978-83; spl. event coordinator Park and Recreation Dept., Austin, 1983-86, grants, ptnrships. mgr., 1986—. Vice commodore city land events Austin Aqua Festival, 1985. Mem. Austin Soc. for Pub. Adminstrn., Smithsonian Instn. Office: City of Austin Parks and Recreation Dept PO Box 1088 Austin TX 78767

BOLZ, SARAH JANE, mathematics educator; b. Milw., June 6, 1955; d. Robert Arthur and Carol Esther (Gruetzmacher) B. BS, U. Wis., Milw., 1977, MS, 1983. Cert. secondary tchr., Wis. Math. tchr. Hamilton High Sch., Milw., 1978, Washington High Sch., Milw., 1978-80; math., computer tchr., head math. dept. Milw. Luth. High Sch., 1980—. Volleyball ofcl. Wis. Ind. Athletic Assn., 1975—; asst. basketball coach Milw. Luth. High Sch., 1980-87, asst. softball coach, 1981—. Mem. Nat. Council Tchrs. of Math., Wis. Math Council, Wis. Baseball Coaches Assn., Nat. Fedn. Interscholastic Coaches, Nat. Fedn. Interscholastic Ofcls. Lutheran. Office: Milw Luth High Sch 9700 W Grantosa Dr Milwaukee WI 53222

BOMAR, PORTIA HAMILTON, psychoanalyst, clinical psychologist; b. Cleve., July 19; d. Charles Brooks and Marion (Clements) Goulder; m. William P. Bomar, July 1, 1966. B.A., U. Mich., 1923; postgrad. Oxford U. (Eng.), 1923-25; M.A., Columbia U., 1932, Ph.D., 1940. Pvt. practice psychoanalysis and psychotherapy, N.Y.C., 1930-58; dir. teaching clinic Columbia Presbyn. Med. Ctr., N.Y.C., 1942-50; assoc. prof. psychology U. Richmond, Va., 1964-66; lectr. psychology U. Tex.-Austin, 1968-71; mem. faculty Southwestern Grad. Sch. Banking, So. Meth. U., Dallas, 1975-78. Author: When 'Mid This Glory I Was Young, 1980; contbr. articles to profl. jours. Vice-chmn. Human Relations Commn., Ft. Worth, 1968-71; bd. dirs. Tarrant County Hist. Soc. (Tex.), 1968—, Child Study Ctr., Ft. Worth, 1972-78, Tarrant County Mental Health Assn., 1974-76, Casa Manana, Ft. Worth, 1974-76; mem. corp. Eye Research Inst. of Retina Found., Boston. Fellow Am. Psychol. Assn.; mem. Psychical Research Found., Parapsychology Assn., Chi Omega, AAUW. Clubs: Rivercrest Country (Ft. Worth); University, Womans' (Sarasota, Fla.). Address: 700 John Ringling Blvd Sarasota FL 34236

BOMBA, MARGARET ANN, lawyer; b. Bklyn., July 1, 1947; d. Fred S. and Mary (Alban) Bomba; B.S., St. Francis Coll., 1975; postgrad. Columbia U., 1977; J.D., Bklyn. Law Sch., 1982; m. John N. Pizzuto, May 27, 1978. Sec., adminstrv. asst. Fieldcrest Mills, Inc., N.Y.C., 1966-71, product mgr. textiles for the home 1973-84; sole practice, N.Y.C., 1984—; sales and product mgmt. Wamsutta Mills Inc., N.Y.C., 1972-73; prof. law Parsons Sch. Design, 1985—; arbitrator N.Y. Stock Exchange, 1987—; sole practice, N.Y.C., Newark, 1984—. Mem. N.Y. County Lawyers Assn. (trade regulation com. 1985, real property com. 1986), ABA, Assn. Bar City of N.Y., Assn. Trial Lawyers Am., N.Y. State Bar Assn. Office: 14 Wall St New York NY 10005 also: 99 Chapel St Newark NJ 07105

BOMBARDIERI, MERLE ANN, psychotherapist; b. Atlanta, Mar. 16, 1949; d. Sol and Sadie (Drucker) Malkoff; m. Rocco Anthony Bombardieri, Jr., Aug. 22, 1971; children—Marcella, Vanessa. B.A. in Psychology, Mich. State U., 1971; M.S.W., San Diego State U., 1976. Cert. nat. register clin. social workers, Mass.; diplomate Nat. Assn. Social Workers. Crisis intervention worker and trainer Listening Ear, East Lansing, Mich., 1969-71; tchr. English as 2d lang. Instituto Brasil Estados Unidos, Rio de Janeiro, 1971-73; supr. infant unit Married Student Day Care Ctr., Mich. State U., East Lansing, 1973-74; psychotherapist/family life educator Family Service Assocs., San Diego, 1975-77; psychotherapist Dade Wallace Mental Health Ctr., Nashville, 1977-78; psychotherapist/workshop leader Met. Beaverbrook Mental Health Ctr., Waltham, Mass., 1980-81; pvt. practice psychotherapy, Acton-Belmont, Mass., 1982—; clin. dir. Resolve, Inc., infertility orgn., Belmont, 1982-84; clin. cons., 1984—; cons. HealthData Internat., Westport, Conn., 1983—, Open Door Soc., Newton, Mass., 1983—, First Day Film Corp., 1985—, Mass. Dept. Social Services, 1987, others; psychology seminar leader; radio and TV appearances. Author: The Baby Decision, 1981; founder, editor, pub. Wellspring newsletter; contbr. articles to profl. and med. jours. N.Y. State Regents scholar, 1967; NIMH trainee, 1970. Mem. Acad. Cert. Social Workers, Phi Beta Kappa, Phi Kappa Phi. Home: 4 Broadview Rd Acton MA 01720 Office: 26 Trapelo Rd Belmont MA 02178

BOMBECK, ERMA LOUISE (MRS. WILLIAM BOMBECK), author, columnist; b. Dayton, Ohio, Feb. 21, 1927; d. Cassius Edwin and Erma (Harris) Fiste; m. William Lawrence Bombeck, Aug. 13, 1949; children: Betsy, Andrew, Matthew. BA, U. Dayton, 1949; holder 14 hon. degrees. Columnist Newsday Syndicate, 1965-70, Pubs.-Hall Syndicate (now N.Am. Syndicate), 1970-85, Los Angeles Times Syndicate, 1985-88, Universal Press Syndicate, Kansas City, Mo., 1988—; contbg. editor: Good Housekeeping mag., 1969-74. Author: At Wit's End, 1967, Just Wait Till You Have Children of Your Own, 1971, I Lost Everything In The Post-Natal Depression, 1974, The Grass Is Always Greener Over The Septic Tank, 1976, If Life is a Bowl of Cherries, What Am I Doing in the Pits?, 1978, Aunt Erma's Cope Book, 1979, Motherhood: The Second Oldest Profession, 1983, Family: The Ties That Bind... and Gag!, 1987. Mem. Am. Acad. Humor Columnists, Theta Sigma Phi (Headliner award 1969). Office: Universal Press Syndicate 4900 Main St Kansas City MO 64112

BOMGAARS, MONA RUTH, physician, educator; b. Orange City, Iowa, Feb. 15, 1939; d. Arie John and Artha H. (Korver) B. B.A., Westmar Coll., 1959; M.D., U. Nebr.-Omaha, 1963; M.P.H., U. Calif.-Berkeley, 1972. Diplomate Am. Bd. Family Practice. Intern, Wayne County Gen. Hosp., Eloise, Mich., 1963-64; resident U. Nebr. Hosp., Omaha, 1964-66; fraternal worker United Presbyn. Ch., N.Y.C., 1967-76, staff physician Francis Newton Hosp., Ferozepore, Punjab, India, 1968-69, chief med. officer Bhagwant Meml. Hosp., Christian Med. Coll., Ludhiana, Punjab, India, 1969-71, dir. Lalitpur Community Health Services, Kathmandu, Nepal, 1972-75; exec. officer for devel. health mgmt. devel. staff U. Hawaii Sch. Medicine, Honolulu, 1976-81; chief communicable disease div. Hawaii Dept. of Health, Honolulu, 1981-84, acting med. dep. dir., 1983-84. asst. prof. dept. family practice and community medicine U. Hawaii Sch. Medicine, 1976-79, assoc. prof., 1979-81, clin. prof., 1982-84; assoc. prof. dept. family medicine, coordinator U. Medicine and Dentistry N.J.-Rutgers, 1984-86; chairperson Dept. Family Practice Cook County Hosp., Chgo., 1986—. Contbr. articles to med. jours., chpts. to books. Bd. dirs. Ch. World Servic, 1988—; trustee Westmar Coll., 1986. Recipient Disting. Alumna award Westmar Coll., 1975. Fellow Am. Acad. Family Physicians (sec. Hawaii chpt. 1983, pres.-elect 1984; trustee N.J. chpt. 1986); mem. Am. Pub. Health Assn., AMA, Soc. Tchrs. Family Medicine.

BOMIÁ, GOLDIE ROSE, lyricist, songwriter, poet; b. Monroe, Mich., June 7, 1949; d. Carl Arthur and Frances Rose (Bomia) Rose; m. George Eugene Heath, Nov.23, 1968 (div.); children: George Eugene Heath Jr., Kimberly Dawn Heath. Student, Stautzenberger Bus. Coll., 1967-68, Ohio State Barber Styling Coll., 1977-78. Asst. staff coordinator Profl., Inc., Toledo, 1975-77; barber stylist, shop mgr. Deutch's Barber Styling Shop, Indpls., 1978-83; co-owner, pres., treas., chmn. Bomiá & Carman Enterprises, Inc., Indpls., 1984—. Author 11 poetry anthologies, 1982-88; composer 30 songs, 1984-88. Recipient Golden Poet award World of Poetry Press, Sacramento, 1985, 86, 13 Merit awards, 1982-88. Mem. ASCAP (assoc.), Ariz. Songwriters Assn., Indpls. Songwriters Assn., Am. Astrology Assn., Musicians

Contact Service. Mem. Unity Ch. Home and Office: Bomiá & Carman Enterprises Inc 11322 Allens Cove Beach Luna Pier MI 48157

BONASKIEWICH, SHARON JANE, data processing executive; b. Darby, Pa., June 8, 1956; d. Louis Francis and Dorothy Jane (Kline) Murray; m. Michael J. Bonaskiewich, Oct. 20, 1979; 1 child, Kaitlin Michelle. AS, Montgomery County Community Coll., 1978; BS cum laude, Gwynedd-Mercy Coll., 1983. Programming aid Sperry Corp., Blue Bell, Pa., 1977-79, sr. programming aid, 1979-81, assoc. programmer, 1981-83, systems programmer, 1983-85; project leader UNISYS, Blue Bell, 1985—. Mem. Am. Prodn. Inventory Control Soc. (chairperson programs 1985-86, v.p. 1986-87). Democrat. Roman Catholic. Home: 60 Church Rd Norristown PA 19401 Office: UNISYS Township Line & Jolly Rds. Blue Bell PA 19424

BONCHER, MARY, talent agent; b. Green Bay, Wis., Jan. 19, 1946; d. Anthony Peter and Bernice Mary (Lannoye) Williams; m. Joseph Phillip Boncher, Jan. 7, 1967; children—Yvette, Noelle. Diploma, Rosemary Bischoff Sch. Modeling, Milw., 1965. Dir. Mary Boncher Model Agy. & Sch. Ltd., Bloomington and St. Charles, Ill., 1970-80, Mary Boncher Model Agy. Ltd., St. Charles, 1980-84, Mary Boncher Model Mgmt. Ltd., Chgo., 1985—; fashion reporter TV and radio Men's Fashion Assn., N.Y.C., 1975-80; Eleanor Lambert's Am. Designer, N.Y. Fashion Press, N.Y.C., 1975-80; fashion corr. Green Bay Daily News, 1975-76. Lector Cath. mass, 1983—. Mem. Ill. Women in Film, Advt. Photographers Assn. Republican. Roman Catholic. Office: Mary Boncher Model Mgmt Ltd Presidential Towers Suite 802 575 W Madison St Chicago IL 60606

BONCYK, ELAINE MARIE, chemical engineer; b. Youngstown, Ohio, Apr. 12, 1960; d. Carl S. and Jennie L. (Ostrowski) B. B of Engring., Youngstown State U., 1982; MS, U. So. Calif., 1986. Head cashier, supr. Hills Dept. Store, Youngstown, 1979-83; chem. engr. Belvoir Research, Devel. and Engring. Ctr., Ft. Belvoir, Va., 1983—. Mem. NSPE, Ohio Soc. Profl. Engrs., Am. Inst. Chem. Engrs., Youngstown State U. Alumni Assn. Democrat. Roman Catholic. Home: 12166 Springwoods Dr Woodbridge VA 22192 Office: Belvoir Research Devel Engring Ctr Attention STRBE-JMn Fort Belvoir VA 22060-5606

BOND, A(MANDA) ODESSA, educator; b. Phila., Dec. 4, 1942; s. Noah and Elizabeth (Watlington) B. BA, Morgan State U., Balt., 1965; MA, Villanova U., 1979; postgrad., U. Pa., 1986—. Cert. tchr. Pa. Tchr. Bd. Edn., Phila., 1969—; pres. Watlington O Bond Edn. Corp., Wilmington, Del., 1979—. Author: The Double Tragedy, 1970; contbr. articles to newspapers, mags. and profl. jours. Active Rep. Presdl. Task Force, 1982—, World Affairs Council, 1976—, Goodwill Industries, life mem., 1981. Club: Peale.

BOND, BEVERLY JEAN, communications specialist; b. Chgo., Aug. 29, 1952; d. E. Monte and Betty Jane (McCollister) B.; B.A., Tex. Tech U., 1974. Exec. mgmt. trainee Sears Roebuck & Co., Lubbock, Tex., 1973-75; chief assigner Southwestern Bell Telephone Co., Houston, 1976, chief deskman, 1976-77, repair foreman, 1977-78, installation foreman, 1978, chief deskman, 1978-79, PBX foreman, 1979-80; staff specialist bus. transition task force AT&T, Basking Ridge, N.J., 1981-82, staff mgr., 1982—. Fin. dir. Jr. Achievement, 1977-78. Mem. Nat. Assn. Female Execs., AT&T Achievers Club. Republican. Roman Catholic. Home: 8D Dorado Dr Morristown NJ 07960 Office: 99 Jefferson Rd Room 2039 Parsippany NJ 07954

BOND, JANICE SACHIKO, English educator; b. Lihue, Hawaii, Aug. 4, 1941; d. Tooru and Yukiko (Miura) Yamane; m. David Edward Stem, June 25, 1962 (div. Jan. 1977); children: John David, Lawrence Edward; m. Jerry Don Bond, Feb. 3, 1978 (dec. June 1987). BEdn, Kansas State Tchrs. Coll., 1963; postgrad., Brigham Young U., Laie, Hawaii, 1967, 68, U. Hawaii Manoa, 1976, Kauai Community Coll., Lihue, 1976. Cert. tchr. English and speech, Hawaii. Receptionist Coll. Info. Office, Emporia, Kans., 1960-67; distbr. Tupperware, Kapaa, Hawaii, 1966-69, Amway, Kapaa, 1974—; disc jockey Sta. KTOH, Lihue, 1960, 67; tchr. English Kauai High and Intermediate Schs., Lihue, 1967-68, 70-71, 88—, Kapaa High and Intermediate Schs., 1971-74, 75-87; salesperson The Westin Kauai, Lihue, 1987—; advisor Nat. Honor Soc., Kapaa, 1984-87. Dir. publicity, mother's march March of Dimes, Kauai, 1980—, coordinator bid for bachelors, 1988, rep. telethon, Honolulu, 1984; foster family mother, Dept. Human Services, 1981-87; program chmn. Girl Scouts U.S., Kauai, 1972-74, advisor Girl Scouts Srs., Kapaa, 1966-69, career cons., N.Y.C., 1972, del. Dallas, 1972, Honolulu, 1972, 73, 74; vol. Kapaa Missionary Ch. Vacation Bible Sch., mem. prayer line, 1984-85, choir, 1978, tchr. 2-yr. olds, dir. cradle roll., 1980-82; den mother Boy Scouts Am., 1977-79, mem. troop com., 1980-88; facilitator Am. Cancer FreshStart Clins., 1981-87, vol. neighborhood canvass; participant Big Sisters/Big Bros., Kauai, 1968-74, bd. dirs. nominating com. 1970-72; mem. Kapaa High Band Boosters, 1973-88, pres. 1986-88; active Children's Home Steering Com., 1988—. Mem. Nat. Council of Tchrs. English, Hawaii Council of Tchrs. English, Hawaii State Tchrs. Assn., Delta Kappa Gamma (state conv. com. 1988-89). Home: PO Box 574 Kapaa HI 96746

BOND, MARY LOU, title company executive; b. Enid, Okla., Nov. 29, 1936; d. Harold Earnest and Nellie Maude (Cowles) Taft; m. Charles D. Bond, July 25, 1956; children: Michael Lowell, Bryan Timothy, Mark Stephen. Student, Okla. State U., 1954-56. Exec. sec. Shell Oil Co., Midland, Tex., 1960-63, Gordon Knox & Assocs., Midland, 1963-64; escrow sec. Tarrant Title Co., Ft. Worth, 1978-83, mgr. Airport Freeway br., 1988—; escrow officer Safeco Land Title Co., Hurst, Tex., 1983-88. Mem. Tex. Land Title Assn. (assoc.), N.E. Tarrant County Bd. Realtors (assoc.; mem. women's council 1983-87), Pi Beta Phi Alumni Assn. Republican. Mem. Christian Ch. (Disciples of Christ). Home: 2806 Shady Grove Bedford TX 76021 Office: Tarrant Title Co 1851 Central Dr Suite 300 Bedford TX 76021

BOND, VICTORIA, conductor, composer; b. Los Angeles, May 6, 1945; d. Philip and Jane (Courtl) B.; m. Stephan Peskin, Jan. 27, 1974. B Mus. Arts, U. So. Calif., Los Angeles, 1968; M Mus. Arts, Juilliard Sch. Music, 1975, D Mus. Arts, 1977. Composer, condr. 1974—. Guest condr. Cabrillo Music Festival, Calif., 1974, White Mountains Music Festival, N.H., 1975, Aspen (Colo.) Music Festival, 1976, Shenandoah Music Festival, W.Va., 1977, Colo. Philharm., 1978, Houston Symphony, 1979, 86, Buffalo Philharm., 1979, Pitts. Symphony, 1980, Anchorage Symphony, 1980, N.W. Chamber Orch., Seattle, 1980, Ark. Symphony, 1981, Hudson Valley Philharm., N.Y., 1981, Newton Symphony, Boston, 1982, Hartford Symphony, 1982, RTE Symphony, Dublin, Ireland, 1983; music dir. New Amsterdam Symphony Orch., N.Y.C., 1978-80, Pitts. Youth Symphony Orch., 1978-80, Empire State Youth Orch., 1982-86, Southeastern Music Ctr., 1983-84, Bel Canto Opera Co., 1983, Roanoke (Va.) Symphony Orch., 1986-88; Exxon/Arts Endowment condr., Pitts. Symphony, 1978-80; recs. include Twentieth Century Cello (Recipient Victor Herbert Conducting award Juilliard Sch. 1977), Two American Contemporaries; commd. by Pa. Ballet, 1978, Jacob's Pillow Dance Festival, 1979, Am. Ballet Theater, 1981, Empire State Inst. Performing Arts, 1983, 84, Stage One, Louisville, 1986, Ga. State U.; artistic dir. Bel Canto Opera Co., 1986-88. Recipient Victor Herbert award 1977. Mem. ASCAP (awards 1975-86), Am. Symphony Orch. League, Am. Fedn. Musicians, Mu Phi Epsilon.

BONDINELL, STEPHANIE, educational administrator; b. Passaic, N.J., Nov. 22, 1948; d. Peter Jr. and Gloria Lucille (Burden) Honcharuk; m. Paul Swanstrom Bondinell, July 31, 1971; 1 child, Paul Emil. B.A., William Paterson Coll., 1970; M.Ed., Stetson U., 1983. Cert. elem. educator, Fla.; guidance counselor, grades K-12, Fla. Tchr. Bloomingdale Bd. Edn., N.J., 1971-80; edn. dir. Fla. United Methodist Children's Home, Enterprise, 1982—. Sec. adv. com. Deltona Jr. High Sch., Fla., 1984—; sec. Deltona Jr. PTA, 1982; mem. secondary sch. task force Volusia County Sch. Bd., 1986—. Academic scholar Becton, Dickinson & Co., N.J., 1966; N.J. State scholar, 1966-70; named girls state rep. Am. Legion, N.J., 1966; recipient Vol. Service award Volusia County Sch. Bd., Deland, 1985. Mem. Am. Assn. for Counseling and Devel., Assn. for Curriculum Devel., Council for Exceptional Children, Div. for Learning Disabilities, Fla. Personnel and Guidance Assn., N.J. Edn. Assn., Internat. Platform Assn., Deltona Civic Assn. Republican. Avocations: painting, creative writing, dancing. Home: 1810 W Cooper Dr Deltona FL 32725 Office: Fla United Meth Children's Home Enterprise FL 32725

BONDS, MARLENE KRIEWALD, lawyer; b. Robstown, Tex., June 15, 1935; d. Bruno Louis and Alvina Alma (Loep) Kriewald; m. Billy Ivas Bonds, Jan. 11, 1958; children—Douglas Blaine, Lawrence Ivas. BS, Tex. Luth. Coll., 1957; JD, La. State U., 1979. Bar: La. 1979. Lab. technician U. Tex. Med. Sch., Galveston, 1957-58; high sch. sci. tchr. Robstown Ind. Sch. Dist., 1959-62; substitute tchr. Spring Branch Ind. Sch. Dist., Houston, 1968-70; sole practice law, Baton Rouge, 1979—. Chmn. Commn. for Mission in Tex.-La., Evang. Luth. Ch. in Am., (bd. of pensions 1987—), mem. mgmt. com. Div. for Mission in N.Am., 1982—, chmn. sub-com. on ch. in mission, 1982—, mem. study commn. on war and peace, 1983—. Mem. ABA, La. Bar Assn., Baton Rouge Bar Assn. (various coms. 1979—, chair family law section), Baton Rouge Assn. Women Attys., Alumni Assn. Tex. Luth. Coll. (pres. 1986-88), Phi Delta Phi. Democrat. Club: Bal Masque (Baton Rouge). Office: Marlene K Bonds Atty at Law 1346 Main St Baton Rouge LA 70802

BONDURANT, SARAH DICKERSON, newspaper editor; b. Collierville, Tenn., Dec. 10, 1955; d. Harvey Eugene and Betty (Downs) Tyler; m. Danny Michael Dickerson, May 25, 1974 (div. Feb. 1984); 1 child, Michael Eugene; m. Robert Francis Bondurant, Apr. 19, 1985. Student, NW Miss. jr. Coll., 1983. Reporter Tate County Democrats, Senatobia, Miss., 1973-77, 80-81; news editor Tate County Democrat, Senatobia, Miss., 1981-83; editor Tate County Democrat, Senatobia, Miss., 1983—. Mem. adv. council Tate County 4-H, Senatobia, 1986—, Tate County Heart Assn. (publicity chmn. 1986—). Mem. Nat. press Women, Nat. Newspaper Assn., Miss. Press Women (sec. 1986, chair 1987, 2d v.p. 1987—, Woman of Achievement 1987). Mem. Assembly of God Ch. Home: 8892 Thunderbird Hernando MS 38632 Office: Tate County Democrat 219 E Main Senatobia MS 38668

BONE, JANET WITMEYER (JAN), author; b. Shamokin, Pa., Dec. 19, 1930; d. Paul Eugene and Kathryn (Bender) Witmeyer; B.A., Cornell U., 1951; MBA, Roosevelt U., 1987; m. David P. Bone, Oct. 27, 1951; children—Jonathan, Christopher, Robert, Daniel. Newspaper and trade mag. writer, freelance writer, 1962—; sr. writer spl. advt. sects. Chgo. Tribune, 1986—; co-author: Understanding the Film, rev. edit., 1985; author: Opportunities in Film Production, 1983; Opportunities in Cable Television, 1983; Opportunities in Telecommunications, 1984; Opportunities in Computer-Aided Design and Computer-Aided Manufacturing (CAD/CAM), 1986; Opportunities in Robotics, 1987; Opportunities in Laser Technology, 1988; tchr. creative writing adult edn. Sch. Dist. 211, Palatine, Ill., 1974—. Trustee William Rainey Harper Community Coll., Palatine, 1977-85, sec. bd. trustees, 1979-85. Recipient Chgo. Working Newsman's award, 1968, Sch. Bell award Ill. Edn. Assn., 1968, Am. Polit. Sci. Assn. award disting. reporting public affairs, 1970. Mem. Phi Theta Kappa, Alpha Omicron Pi. Address: 353 N Morris Dr Palatine IL 60067

BONELLI, NORMA LEE, graphic design company executive; b. Robinson, Ill., Nov. 6, 1945; d. Raleigh John and Minnie Edith (Milam) Garrard; m. Richard F. Bonelli Jr., Aug. 26, 1967 (div. Aug. 1980); 1 child, Buffi Lee. Grad. high sch., Robinson, 1963. Personal sec. Marathon Oil Co., Robinson, 1963-70; owner Yahama/H-D Bike Shop, Robinson, 1972-80, TTFN Specialities, Urbana, Ill., 1979—; typographer Precision Graphics, Champaign, Ill., 1983-85; owner Typesetting Plus, Urbana, 1985—; typographer Champaign County Humane Soc., 1987, Ill. Children's Choir, Champaign, 1987; designer, typographer Illini Christian Children's Home, St. Joseph, Ill., 1986-87. Named Small Bus. Person of Yr., Urbana-Champaign C. of C. and Parkland Coll., 1987; recipient 5 Nat. Titles, WERA Roadracing Assn., 1978, 80-81. Mem. Women's Bus. Council (chairperson directory 1985—, newsletter com. mem. 1985—, exec. bd. dirs. 1985—), Urbana-Champaign C. of C., Am. Motocycle Assn. (life mem.). Home: 81 Toni Ln Urbana IL 61801

BONGIORNO, MARGARET ROHDE, psychologist; b. Chgo., Apr. 23, 1954; d. Raymond Richard and Patricia Catherine (Curry) Rohde; m. Joseph Salvatore Bongiorno, Nov. 13, 1953. BS in Psychology, Loyola U., Chgo., 1976, MA in Clin. Psychology, 1979, PhD in Clin. Psychology, 1981. Lic. psychologist, Ill. Clin. psychologist Assocs. in Adolescent Psychiatry, Skokie, Ill., 1981—, program dir., 1985—, dir. tng., 1982-85, asst. program dir., 1985; sec. DuPage Consortium, Inc., Glen Ellyn, Ill., 1985—; mem. allied staff HCA Riveredge Hosp. Mem. Am. Psychol. Assn., Ill. Psychol. Assn., Nat. Register Health Service Providers. Roman Catholic. Office: Assocs in Adolescent Psychiatry 8311 W Roosevelt Rd Forest Park IL 60130

BONGIORNO, SANDRA L., health counselor; b. Worcester, Mass.; d. Gerald Michael and Janet (Gentile) Turturo; m. Frank P. Bongiorno; children: Justin Leigh, Brooke Yuka. BA in Edn., Anna Maria Coll., 1967; MS in Counseling, SUNY, Albany, 1968; MA in Psychology, Rosebridge Inst., 1982. Cert. counselor Nat. Bd. Cert. Counselors. Dir. counseling Elizabeth Seton Coll., Yonkers, N.Y., 1968-70; adminstr. asst. U. Hawaii Sch. Med., Honolulu, 1971-73; adminstr. officer U. Hawaii Sch. Medicine, Honolulu, 1973-75; drug and alcohol counselor U.S. Army Hosp., Nuremburg, Fed. Republic Germany, 1975-76; counseling instr. Solano Community Coll., Susuin City, Calif., 1980-82; dir. family support specialist Family Support Ctr. Yokota AFB, Tokyo, 1983-85, dir., 1983-85; Optifast program dir., Wellness Program specialist Humana Hosp., Neuman, Ga., 1987—. Mem. Am. Bus. Women's Assn., Internat. Soc. (co-chmn. soc. service com.). Lutheran. Club: Pilot. Office: Humana Hosp 60 Hosp Rd Newnan GA 30263

BONHAM, JEANNE CECIL, writer, editor; b. Uhrichsville, Ohio, Jan. 19, 1928; d. Jesse W. and Zola P. (McConnell) Cecil; m. Roger D. Bonham, May 17, 1952; 1 sons, Christopher Dean. B.A., Ohio State U., 1945-48. Editorial asst. Am. Ceramic Soc. Columbus, Ohio, 1949-52, tech. indexer, 1967-77, tech. editor, 1986—; editor publs. Med. Bur., Columbus, 1952-56; reviewer Columbus Dispatch, 1952-77; exec. dir. for Ohio, Am. Acad. Pediatrics, Columbus, 1970-78, Ohio Council Home Health Agys., Columbus, 1974-84; exec. dir. Ohio Continuum Care Council, 1986—; mem. adv. bd. Med. Personnel Pool, 1987—; columnist, book page editor Columbus Dispatch, 1977-84; co-editer, co-pub. Columba: The Midwest Review of Books; contbr. book rev. segment Sta. WCOL; cons., lectr. Recipient Disting. Service award Worthington Friends of the Library, 1982, Dorothy Royce award Ohio Council Home Health Agys., 1984. Mem. Nat. Book Critics Circle. Coauthor: Some People Would Rather Read than Eat, 1981; contbr. numerous articles to popular and profl. jours. Home and Office: 101 E Wilson Bridge Rd Worthington OH 43085

BONHAM, REBECCA JUNE, business association executive, educator; b. Goshen, Ind., Sept. 11, 1945; d. Max. M. and Margaret (Girten) Bickel; m. James R. Bonham, June 17, 1967; children: Michael James, Geoffrey Scott. BS, Ind. U., 1967, MS, 1976. Spl. edn. tchr. South Bend (Ind.) Community Sch. Corp., 1967-71; edni. resource cons. Council for the Retarded, South Bend, 1975-76; due process hearing officer State Ind. Dept. Pub. Instrn., Indpls., 1978-80; supr. mental health/social services Project Head Start, South Bend, 1975-82, adminstrv. asst. to dir., 1982-83; conv. and tourism coordinator SBMACC, South Bend, 1983-84; v.p. Conv. and Tourism div. SBMACC, South Bend, 1984—; adj. lectr. Ind. U., South Bend, 1975-81; mem. U.S. Chamber Inst. for Organizational Mgmt., 1984-87, C. of C. Leadership Tng., 1982-83. Mem. Charitable Solicitation Commn., South Bend, 1985—, Jr. Leagues. Recipient Disting. Edn. Alumnus award Ind. U., 1980. Mem. East Race Devel. Corp., Am. Soc. Assn. Execs., Internat. Assn. C&V Burs., (Jr. League), YMCA, Mental Health Assn., Boy's Club South Bend, Phi Delta Kappa. Democrat. Mem. Brethren Ch. Club: CANCO. Office: C of C 401 E Colfax South Bend IN 46617

BONHAM-YEAMAN, DORIA, law educator; b. Los Angeles, June 10, 1932; d. Carl Herschel and Edna Mae (Jones) Bonham; widowed; children—Carl Q., Doria Valerie-Constance. B.A., U. Tenn., 1953, J.D., 1957, M.A., 1958; Ed.S. in Computer Edn., Barry U., 1984. Instr. bus. law Palm Beach Jr. Coll., Lake Worth, Fla., 1960-69; instr. legal environment Fla. Atlantic U., Boca Raton, 1969-73; lectr. bus. law Fla. Internat. U., North Miami, 1973-83, assoc. prof. bus. law, 1983—. Editor: Anglo-Am. Law Conf., 1980; Developing Global Corporate Strategies, 1981; editorial bd. Attys. Computer Report, 1984-85, Jour. Legal Studies Edn., 1985—. Contbr. articles to profl. jours. Bd. dirs. Palm Beach County Assn. for Deaf Children, 1960-63; mem. Fla. Commn. on Status of Women, Tallahassee, 1969-70; mem. Broward County Democratic Exec. Com., 1982—; pres. Dem. Women's Club Broward County, 1981; mem. Marine Council of Greater Miami, 1978—, Service award, 1979. Recipient Faculty Devel. award Fla. Internat. U., Miami, 1980; grantee Notre Dame Law Sch., London, summer 1980. Mem. Am. Bus. Law Assn., No. Dade C. of C., Am. Acctg. Assn., AAUW (pres. Palm Beach County 1965-66), Alpha Chi Omega (alumnae club pres. 1968-71), Tau Kappa Alpha. Episcopalian. Office: Fla Internat Univ North Miami FL 33181

BONHOMME, DENISE, law firm administrator; b. Paris, Jan. 20, 1926; came to U.S., 1947, naturalized, 1951; d. René Louis and Jeanne Anna (Giroud) B.; children—Claire Helen Quebedeau-Schreiner, Norman Quebedeau. Baccalauréat, Acad. de Lille, 1943; student Sorbonne, U. Paris, 1943-45; M.A., U. Oreg., 1969. French-English translator and interpreter U.S. Forces in Europe, 1945-47; legal and adminstrv. sec., Austin, Tex., 1954-64; instr., asst. prof. French lang. and lit. Mount Angel Coll., Oreg., 1964-72; office worker, Monterey, Calif., 1973-74; part-time tchr. French lang. and lit. Acad. Arts and Humanities, Seaside, Calif., 1975-76, Monterey Inst. Fgn. Studies, 1976; program sec. Electric Power Research Inst., Palo Alto, Calif., 1977-80; word processor, sec. Nat. Semiconductor, Santa Clara, Calif., 1981-83; tchr. night class French lang. and lit. Mission Community Coll., Santa Clara, 1982; with law firm Pillsbury, Madison & Sutro, San Jose, Calif., 1983—. Author: Le Collier Symbolique d'Alfred de Vigny, 1968; The Esoteric Substance of Voltairian Thought, 1975. Vol. lectr. esoteric lit. Soledad State Prison, Calif., 1973-74.

BONI, MIKI, artist; b. Bklyn., Nov. 10, 1938; B.A., U. Guanajuato, 1974; m. Lawrence Boni, Nov. 16, 1956; children—Andrew, Viki. Dir. advt. and pub. relations Kebo, Inc., Natick, Mass., 1965-74; tchr. painting and drawing U. Guanajuato (Mex.), 1974-76; exec. dir. Kreativ Assos., Watertown, Mass., 1976-82; prin. Miki Boni Assocs., 1982-86; mem. staff Interface Found., Watertown, 1987—. Recipient spl. painting award Lincoln Center, 1978. Mem. Nat. Assn. Neurolinguistic Programming (master practitioner), Women Art Profls. (founder, v.p.). Editor, designer Interface Catalog.

BONIFANTI, ALISANN MARIE, educator; b. Scranton, Pa., Nov. 15, 1946; d. George John and Alice (Altier) B. BA, Marywood Coll., 1972, MS in Edn., 1978; postgrad., U. Pa., 1985—. Cert. elem. edn./spl. edn. tchr., secondary/elem. prin., Pa. Tchr. spl. edn. Pocono Mountain Sch. Dist., Swiftwater, Pa., 1972-78; med. lab. specialist U.S. Army, Landstuhl, Fed. Republic of Germany, 1978-81; intelligence analyst USAR, Washington, Ft. Meade, Md. and Wilmington, Del., 1981—; tchr. spl. edn. Pocono Mountain Sch. Dist., Swiftwater, 1982-86; prin. Overbrook Sch. for Blind, Phila., 1986-87; spl. edn. tchr. Phila. Sch. Dist., 1988—; edn. cons. Spl. Olympics, Pa., Fed. Republic of Germany, 1969—; adminstrv. asst.West Phila. High Sch., 1985-86; mem. mgmt. team Spl. Olympics, Phila., 1986—, adminstrv. coordinator for leadership confs., Dec. 187-Sept. 1988. Author: Animals Have Feelings Just Like Me, 1978. Recipient acad. scholarship U. Pa., 1986, commendation medal U.S. Army. 1986, Army Reserve Achievement medal, 1987. Mem. Women in Edn. (exec. bd., program dir. 1985-86), Phila. Area English Lang. Arts Soc. (charter mem.), Council for Exceptional Children (membership chmn. 1969-70), Council for Exceptional Children of Council Adminstrs. Spl. Edn., Am. Bd. Master Educators, Pi Lambda Theta, Phi Delta Kappa. Democrat. Clubs: Big Pocono Ski (Stroudsburg) (pres., founder 1973-75). Home: 362 1/2 N Rebecca Ave Scrantron PA 18504

BONIFAS, BARBARA J., human resources executive; b. Delphos, Ohio, Apr. 2, 1947; d. Robert Eugene and Alice (Hoelderle) B. BS in Social Welfare, Ohio State U., 1971; postgrad., Harvard Bus. Coll., 1980-85. Field dir. Appleseed Ridge Girl Scout Council, Lima, Ohio, 1971-73; program dir. Heart of Ohio Girl Scout Council, Zanesville, Ohio, 1973-75; exec. dir. Pennyroyal Girl Scout Council, Owensboro, Ky., 1975-76; asst. exec. dir. Kentuckiana Girl Scout Council, Louisville, 1976-80; chief exec. officer Girl Scout Council St. Croix Valley, St. Paul, 1980—; Instr. Jr. High Religious Edn., 1983-85. Agy. champaign chair United Way, St. Paul, 1987, mem. cabinet, 1985; pres., v.p. treas. Council Agency Dirs., St. Paul, 1981-85; mem. fin. com. local Ch., 1983-84; mem. fin. com. Home Owners' Assn., 1987. Mem. Assn. Girl Scout Exec. Staff, Am. Mgmt. Assn., Exec. Dirs. Refugee Orgns., St. Paul C. of C. Roman Catholic. Lodge: Rotary. Office: Girl Scout Council St Croix Valley 400 S Robert St Saint Paul MN 55107

BONIUK, VIVIEN, ophthalmologist, lawyer; b. Glace Bay, N.S., Can., Nov. 25, 1940; d. Hyman and Rachel (Luchtiker) B. M.D., Dalhousie U., 1964; J.D., N.Y. Law Sch., 1979. Bar: N.Y. 1980; diplomate Am. Bd. Ophthalmology. Intern, Victoria Gen. Hosp., Halifax, N.S., Can., 1963-64; resident MacMillan Hosp., Washington U. Sch. Medicine, St. Louis, 1964-67; fellow Rosales Hosp., San Salvador, El Salvador, 1967; fellow in ophthalmic pathology, Coll. Medicine, Baylor U., Houston, 1967-68; teaching fellow in ophthalmology Sch. Medicine, Yale U., New Haven, 1968-69; staff ophthalmologist Toronto Gen. Hosp. (Ont., Can.), 1969-72; staff surgeon Hosp. for Sick Children, Toronto, 1969-72; cons. in ophthalmology Ont. Crippled Children's Ctr., Toronto, 1970-72; asst. attending ophthalmologist Flower & Fifth Ave. Hosp., N.Y.C., 1972-75, assoc. attending, 1976-78; asst. vis. ophthalmologist Met. Hosp., N.Y.C., 1972-75, assoc. attending, 1976-79; attending L.I. Jewish Hosp., New Hyde Park, N.Y., 1979—; dir. ophthalmology Queens Hosp. Ctr., Jamaica, N.Y., 1979—; clin. instr. dept. ophthalmology U. Toronto, 1969-72, teaching fellow in ophthalmology, 1969-70; asst. prof. ophthalmology N.Y. Med. Coll., N.Y.C., 1972-75, assoc. prof., 1976; assoc. prof. SUNY-Stony Brook, 1980. Contbr. articles to profl. publs. Entrance scholar Dalhousie U., 1957; Math. Congress scholar, 1957, 58; Univ. scholar, 1958; entrance scholar Dalhousie U. Med. Sch., 1959; Fogarty Internat. Found. fellow, USSR, 1977. Fellow Royal Coll. Surgeons Can.; mem. AMA, Assn. Research in Vision and Ophthalmology, Can. Ophthalmol. Soc., Am. Acad. Ophthalmology and Otolaryngology, Am. Med. Women's Assn., Am. Soc. Law and Medicine, ABA, N.Y. State Bar Assn., Alpha Omega Alpha. Office: LI Jewish/Queens Hosp Affiliation 82-68 164th St Jamaica NY 11432

BONNELL, VICTORIA EILEEN, sociologist; b. N.Y.C., June 15, 1942; d. Samuel S. and Frances (Nassau) B.; m. Gregory Freidin, May 4, 1971. B.A. Brandeis U., 1964; M.A., Harvard U., 1966, Ph.D., 1975. Lectr. politics U. Calif.-Santa Cruz, 1972-73, 74-76; asst. prof. sociology U. Calif.-Berkeley, 1976-82, assoc. prof., 1982—. AAUW fellow, 1979; Regents faculty fellow, 1978; Fulbright Hays faculty fellow, 1977; Internat. Research and Exchanges Bd. fellow, 1977, 88; Stanford U. Hoover Instn. nat. fellow, 1973-74; Guggenheim fellow, 1985; fellow Ctr. for Advanced Study in Behavioral Scis., 1986-87; grantee Am. Philos. Soc., 1979, Am. Council Learned Socs., 1976. Mem. Am. Sociol. Assn., Am. Assn. Advancement Slavic Studies. Author: Roots of Rebellion: Workers' Politics and Organizations in St. Petersburg and Moscow, 1900-1914, 1983; editor: The Russian Worker: Life and Labor under the Tsarist Regime, 1983; contbr. articles to profl. jours. Office: U Calif Dept Sociology Berkeley CA 94720

BONNER, BESTER DAVIS, educator; b. Mobile, Ala., June 9, 1938; d. Samuel Matthew and Alma (Davis) Davis; m. Wardell Bonner, Nov. 28, 1964; children: Shawn Patrick, Matthew Wardell. BS, Ala. State Coll., 1959; MS in Library Sci., Syracuse U., 1966; PhD, U. Ala., 1982. Cert. tchr. Librarian Westside High Sch., Talladega, Ala., 1959-64; librarian, tchr. lit. Lane Elem. Sch., Birmingham, Ala., 1964-65; head librarian Jacksonville (Ala.) Elem. Lab. Sch., 1965-70; asst. prof. library media Ala. A&M U., Huntsville, 1970-74; adminstv. asst. to pres. Miles Coll., Birmingham, 1974-78, chmn. div. edn., 1978-85; specialist media Montgomery County Pub. Schs., Ala., 1987-88; dir. library & media services div. of ednl. technology Dist. of Columbia Pub. Schs., 1988—; forum leader Nat. Issues Forum, Domestic Policy Assn. U. Ala., Birmingham 1983-84. Contbr. writer The Developing Black Family, 1975. Chmn. ethics commn. St. Ala., Montgomery 1977-81; radiothon site coordinator United Negro Coll. Fund, Birmingham 1981. Mem. Ala. Instructional Media Assn. (pres. dist. II, 1971-72), Am. Library Assn., Assn. Women Deans and Adminstrs., Montgomery County Edn. Assn., Montgomery County Media Specialists Assn., Com. 100, Alpha Kappa Alpha, Ala. St. Alumni Assn. (sec. Talladega Chpt. 1964-65). Democrat. Methodist. Home: 9703 Woodland Dr Silver Spring MD 20910

BONNER, PATRICIA ANNE, science writer, government official; b. N.Y.C., Sept. 19, 1944; d. Cornelius John Bonner and Mary Catherine (Donovan) Moakler. BA in English, Carnegie Inst. Tech., 1966; MS in Tech. Writing and Communication, Rensselaer Poly. Inst., 1968; postgrad. in mktg. UCLA, 1970-71. Cert. tchr. English and history, Pa., Calif. Writer, program control mgr. AiResearch Corp., Anaheim, Calif., 1968-69; sr. mktg. writer Beckman Instruments, Fullerton, Calif., 1969; copy contact Barnes Chase Advt., San Diego, 1970-71; info. dir. Integrated Environ. Mgmt. Project, San Diego, also communications advisor Environ. Devel. Agy., San Diego County, 1971-73; writer Gen. Analysis Corp., San Diego, 1973-74; head info. services U.S. Dept. State, Internat. Joint Commn. U.S. and Can., Windsor, Ont., Can., 1974-84; head program mgmt. and communications EPA Chesapeake Bay Program, 1984—; speaker in field. Author, editor publs. Internat. Joint Commn.; contbr. writings to publs., papers to confs. Mem. steering com. Gt. Lakes Info. Referral Ctr. (Sea Grant/Gt. Lakes Basin Commn.), 1979-81, Chmn. Windsor br. Can. Inst. Internat. Affairs, 1984-85; trainer United Way Campaign, Windsor, 1982; mem. steering com. Hazardous Waste Siting Project LWV Mich., 1979-82; trustee, chmn. communications com., publicity chmn. spl. fundraising Mich. chpt. Nat. Multiple Sclerosis Soc., 1983-84. Recipient tech. publs. awards, Nat. Assn. Counties, 1975, Tech. Communications Soc., 1983; Carnegie-Mellon U. scholar, 1962-66; teaching fellow, Rensselaer Poly. Inst., 1966-68. Mem. Women in Communication, Internat. Assn. Environ. Coordinators (charter mem., governing council N.Am. chpt.), AAUW, Soc. for Tech. Communications, Air Pollution Control Assn. (publicity chmn. confs.), Carnegie Alumni Assn., Rensselaer Alumni Assn., Kappa Kappa Gamma. Office: EPA Chesapeake Bay Program 410 Severn Ave Annapolis MD 21403

BONNEY, NANCY MAE, computer scientist; b. Bridgeport, Conn., Apr. 6, 1943; d. Russell Norwood and Catharine Homiller (Yerkes) B.; B.A. in Math., U. Del., 1964; M.S. in Mgmt. Sci., Johns Hopkins U., 1968. Tech. asst. gen. engring. dept. Chesapeake & Potomac Telephone Co., Balt., 1964-66; cons., Benefacts Inc., 1966-68; programmer analyst Aries Corp., McLean, Va., 1968-71; analyst EG&G Wolf Research & Devel. Corp., Riverdale, Md., 1971-74; analyst EG&G Mason Research Inst., Rockville, Md., 1974-79, mgr. biomed. info. scis. dept., 1979-81; program mgr. Dynamac Corp., Rockville, 1982—. Cert. data processor, cert. systems profl. Mem. Assn. Women in Computing (founder 1978, rec. sec. 1978-84, treas. 1985-86, mem. at large bd. dirs., 1986—), Assn. Computing Machinery, Am. Women in Sci., NOW (convenor No. Prince Georges County chpt. 1971), Nat. Women's Polit. Caucus, Am. Arbitration Assn., Laurel (Md.) Oratorio Soc. Office: 11140 Rockville Pike Rockville MD 20852

BONNY, HELEN LINDQUIST, music therapist; b. Rockford, Ill., Mar. 31, 1921; d. Gustavus Elmer Emmanuel and Ethel Mae (Geer) Lindquist; m. Oscar E. Bonny, Aug. 17, 1943 (div. 1980); children: Beatrice Starrett, Erich Lind, Francis Albert. B in Music, Oberlin Conservatory, 1943; B in Music Edn., Kans. U., 1961-64, M in Music Edn., 1968; PhD in Music and Psychology, Union Grad. Sch., 1976. Instr. string dept. Anthony (Kans.) Pub. Schs., 1948-50; instr. violin St. Mary Coll., Xavier, Kans., 1958-60; music therapist Parsons (Kans.) State Hosp., 1965; research investigator VA Hosp., Topeka, Kans., 1966-69; coordinating sec. Nat. Assn. Music Therapy, Lawrence, Kans., 1967-69; research asst. Md. Psychol. Research Ctr., Balt., 1969-73, research fellow, 1973-75; dir. music therapy Cath. U. Am., Washington, 1975-80; founder, dir. Inst. for Cons. & Music, Port Townsend, Wash., 1973-86; owner Music Rx, Port Townsend, 1985—; lectr. U. Md., Balt., 1974-75; research advisor Walden U., Mpls., 1982—; field advisor Antioch Coll., Seattle, 1983; external examiner The Fielding Inst., Santa Barbara, Calif., 1986-87. Co-author: Music and Your Mind, 1973; contbr. articles to profl. jours. Founder Council Grove Conf., Topeka, 1968; mem. edn. com. Peninsula Coll., Port Townsend, 1985—. NIMH grantee, 1964. mem. Am. Assn. Musical Therapy, Nat. Assn. Music Therapy (pres. 1976-77). Lutheran. Office: Music Rx 5515 Hendricks Port Townsend WA 98368

BONOMI, FERNE GATER, public relations executive; b. Council Bluffs, Iowa, July 27, 1923; d. Roy Winfield and Leona Hazel (Bays) Gater; m. Robert Foch Bonomi, Sept. 3, 1949 (div. 1974); children: Robert Duff, David Scott. BA magna cum laude, U. Iowa, 1948. Editor Silver City (Iowa) Times, 1940-41; reporter, photographer, Sunday editor Cedar Rapids (Iowa) Gazette, 1943-47; mem. pub. info. staff Iowa Devel. Commission, Des Moines, 1950-51, Gov. William S. Beardsley, Des Moines, 1951-53; v.p. Bonomi Assocs. Inc., Des Moines, 1954-72; adminstr. Mid-Iowa Drug Abuse Council, Des Moines, 1972-74; cons. Plain Talk Pub. Co., Des Moines, 1974-75; communications dir. Iowa Assn. Sch. Bds., Des Moines, 1975-86; owner, operator Bonomi & Co., Des Moines, 1986—; chmn. pubs. evaluation Am. C. of C. Execs., Washington, 1977-81; workshop presenter various nat. and state confs., 1976—; Iowa reporter Edn. USA and Ed-Line, Arlington, Va., 1983—. Author: Show Me A Man, 1969; editor Iowa Sch. Bd. Dialogue, 1975-86; assoc. editor Leader's Mag., 1964-72. Chmn. communications Des Moines Area Religious Council, 1980-82; mem. Gov.'s Com. on Employment Handicapped, 1968-74. Mem. Pub. Relations Soc. Am. (pres. Iowa chpt. 1980-82, chmn. accreditation, outstanding contbr. 1983), Nat. Sch. Pub. Relations Assn. (cert., gold medallion award 1987), Am. Assn. Sch. Adminstrs., Phi Beta Kappa, Alpha Delta Pi (nat. editor 1959-62, outstanding alumna 1977). Republican. Mem. United Ch. Christ. Office: Bonomi and Co 3845 51st St Des Moines IA 50310-1812

BONTEZ, MARIA, nurse; b. Boston, Mar. 28, 1933; d. Robert Bontez and Carmel (Brannon) Lopes. AAS, Brooklyn Coll., 1960; BS, Pace U., 1979; MS, New Rochelle Coll., 1981; postgrad., Columbia U., 1988—; D (hon.), U. Fla., 1973. RN, cert. gerontologist, nursing home adminstr. Dir. nursing Gramercy Park Nursing Home, N.Y.C., 1963-71, Morris Park Nursing Home, Bronx, N.Y., 1971-76; adminstr. Throgs Neck Nursing Home, Bronx, 1976; asst. adminstr. Park Cresant Nursing Home, N.Y.C., 1980-81; dir. nursing St. John's Episcopal Home for the Aged, Bklyn., 1982-84; pres., cons. Colly-Bon Assn. Inc., Mt. Vernon, N.Y., 1984—; agt. N.Y. State Ins. Dept., 1976—; patient assessor N.Y. State, 1986. Served with U.S. Army, 1952-54. Mem. Am. Pub. Health Assn., Veterans Assn. Democrat. Club: New Eng. (N.Y.C.). Lodge: Rosicrucians (chairperson bd.). Office: Colly-Bon Assocs Inc 10 Fiske Pl Mount Vernon NY 10550

BOOCKS NEFF, NANCY LOUISE, marketing coordinator; b. Columbus, Ohio, May 27, 1952; d. Charles Jackson and Thelma Irene (Mowery) Boocks; m. John Neff; children: Bryan Christopher, Kenneth John. Student, Ohio State U., 1975-76, Colo. Women's Coll., 1977-78. Program asst. Western State Arts Found., Santa Fe, 1976-77; dir. mktg. and promotions Baney, Gutzmer, Inc., Kahului, Hawaii, 1979-81; media buyer Margo Wood Advt. Co., Honolulu, 1981-82; mktg. coordinator Ema Office Machines, Honolulu, 1982-83; media coordinator, advt. copywriter, account exec., media buyer Sellers Advt. Inc., Honolulu, 1983-86; cons. pvt. enterprises 1987-88; security cons. Alert Alarm Inc., 1988—. Mem. Am. Mktg.Assn. (chmn.). Home and Office: PO Box 548 Puunene HI 96784

BOOHER, ALICE ANN, lawyer; b. Indpls., Oct. 6, 1941; d. Norman Rogers and Olga (Bonke) B. BA in Polit. Sci., Butler U., 1963; LLB, Ind. U., 1966, JD, 1967. Bar: Ind. 1966, U.S. Dist. Ct. (so. dist.) Ind. 1966, U.S. Tax Ct. 1970, U.S. Ct. Customs and Patent Appeals 1969, U.S. Ct. Mil. Appeals 1969, U.S. Ct. Appeals (D.C. cir.) 1969, U.S. Supreme Ct. 1969; cert. tchr., Ind. Research asst., law clk. Supreme and Appellate Cts. Ind., Indpls., 1966; legal intern, atty., staff legal advisor Dept. State, Washington, 1966-69; staff legal adviser Bd. Vets. Appeals, Washington, 1969-78; sr. atty. 1978—; former counselor D.C. Penal Facilities and Shelters. Author: The Nuclear Test Ban Treaty and the Third Party Non-Nuclear States, also children's books; contbr. articles to various publs., chpts. to Whiteman Digest of International Law; exhibited crafts, needlepoint in juried artisan fairs. Bd. dirs. numerous community groups, including D.C. Women's Commn. for Crime Prevention, 1980-81. Recipient various awards; named Ky. Col., 1988. Mem. ABA, Womens Bar Assn. D.C., D.C. Sexual Assault Coalition (chmn. legal com.), Butler U. Alumnae Assn., LWV, Nat. Mus. Women in Arts, Bus. and Profl. Womens Club U.S.A. (pres. D.C. 1980-81, nat. UN fellow 1974, nat. bd. dirs. 1980-82, 87—, Woman of Yr. award D.C. 1975, Marguerite Rawalt award D.C. 1986), Alpha Chi Omega, numerous other orgns. Clubs: Women's Democratic, Nat. Lawyers, Army-Navy (Washington). Home: Crystal Plaza 316 S 2111 Jefferson Davis Hwy Arlington VA 22202 Office: Vets Appeals 810 Vermont Ave NW Washington DC 20420

BOOHER, JANE ANDERSON, rehabilitation program coordinator; b. Kingsport, Tenn., Jan. 21, 1955; d. Samuel Harold Jr. and DeLois (Hicks) Anderson; m. Michael Bruce Booher, May 28, 1983; 1 child, Samuel Michael; five stepchildren. BA in Psychology, U. Tenn., 1977, MS in Vocat. Rehab. Counseling, 1981. Employment counselor Snelling and Snelling, Knoxville, Tenn., 1977-78; gen. mgr., vocat. evaluator Inst. Human Resources, Knoxville, 1978-81; asst. dir. Daniel Arthur Rehab. Ctr., Oak Ridge, Tenn., 1981-87; vocat. services coordinator Helen Ross McNabb Ctr., Knoxville, 1987—. Mem. Nat. Rehab. Assn., Nat. Rehab. Adminstrs. Assn., Nat. Rehab. Counseling Assn., Vocat. Evaluation and Work Adjustment Assn. Lutheran. Home: 6633 Ridgerock Ln Knoxville TN 37909 Office: Helen Ross McNabb Ctr 1520 Cherokee Trail Knoxville TN 37920

BOOKER, BETTY MAE, writer; b. Allentown, Pa., Nov. 26, 1948; d. Harold George and Bessie (Bealer-Miller) Bartholomew; m. Samuel Efford Booker III, June 27, 1970; children, Liesel Tamarah, Dacey Justin. BA in English, Millersville State Coll., 1970. Contbr. poetry to jours. and lit. mags. including Plainsong, America, The Christian Century, Poetry Now. Home: 3511 Valley View Ave NW Roanoke VA 24012

BOOKER, CHERYL ELAINE, educator; b. Lincoln, Nebr., Mar. 30, 1962; d. Robert Langston and Audrey Elaine (Fordham) B. BS in Edn., Oakwood Coll., 1984. Tchr. Bethel Elem. Sch., Bklyn., 1984-86, Green Valley Elem. Sch., Temple Hills, Md., 1986—. Named one of Outstanding Women Am., 1983. Mem. NEA, Md. State Tchrs. Assn., Assn. for Childhood Edn. Internat., Nat. Assn. Female Execs., Smithsonian Assocs., Assn. Supervision and Curriculum Devel.

BOON, JANICE CAROL, psychologist, consultant; b. Charleston, W.Va., Oct. 6, 1951; d. Joseph Gilman and Hazel Jane (McGraw) B.; m. Walter Dale McCollam, May 31, 1975 (div. Oct. 1979); m. Paul Stewart Buck, Mar. 21, 1981; children: Donovan Paul, Briana Leigh. BA, Duke U., 1973; MA, Vanderbilt U., 1977, PhD, 1982. Lic. psychologist, Okla. Clin. internship U. Okla., Oklahoma City, 1979-80; asst. project coordinator treatment of depression collaborative research program NIMH, Oklahoma City, 1980-82; psychol. cons. Rehab. Inst. of Okla., Oklahoma City, 1982-83; dir. adult services Willow View Hosp., Spencer, Okla., 1983-85; clin. instr. health sci. ctrs. U. Okla., Oklahoma City, 1983—; owner Behavioral Medicine Assocs., Oklahoma City, 1985—; clin. dir. High Pointe, Oklahoma City, 1987—; mem. affiliate staff St. Anthony Hosp., Oklahoma City, 1985—, Bapt. Med. Ctr., Oklahoma City, 1985—, Shawnee (Okla.) Med. Ctr., 1986—; cons. psychology staff Willow View Hosp., Spencer, 1985—. Grantee VA, 1978-79, Nat. Inst. Alcohol Abuse/Alcoholism, 1976-78. Mem. Okla. Psychol. Assn. (sec. 1987—), Am. Psychol. Assn., Mental Health Assn. of Oklahoma County, Phi Beta Kappa. Democrat. Mem. Christian Ch. Clubs: Christian Womens Fellowship (Midwest City, Okla.) (pres. 1987—); Regency (Oklahoma City) (v.p. 1988—). Office: Behavioral Medicine Assocs 3330 NW 56th St Suite 604 Oklahoma City OK 73112 Office: High Pointe 6501 NE 50th St Oklahoma City OK 73141

BOONE, ANNA LEE, service executive; b. Manning, S.C., Oct. 1, 1944; d. Ammon and Mattie (Clark) Miller; m. George Boone, May 11, 1968 (div. 1982); children: Georgielle and Gerrilynne (twins), Aaron and Ammon (twins), Jermain. AS, Fshion Inst. Tech., 1966; BBA, Baruch Coll., 1986. Claims adjuster Met. Life Ins. Co., N.Y.C., 1963-66; designer Lady Ann's Boutique, N.Y.C., 1966-78; data processing mgr. N.Y.C. Health and Hosp. Corp., 1978-82, assoc. dir. patient accts., cons., 1983—; speaker N.E. Decision Scis. Inst., Atlantic City, 1987. Mem. United Meth. Women; asst. leader angelic club Salen United Meth. Ch., N.Y.C., 1986-87. Scholar Baruch Coll., 1983. Mem. Am. Mgmt. Assn., Am. Hosp. Assn., N.Y. Assn. Ambulatory Care. Democrat. Office: Queens Hosp Ctr NYC Health & Hosp Corp 82-86 164th St Jamaica NY 11432

BOONE, BEVERLY SHARON, telecommunications executive; b. Columbia, Mo., July 2, 1952; d. Ernest Oscar III and Lorraine Mildred (Frost) B. BA, Ind. U., 1972; M in Social Work, Atlanta U., 1974. Customer service rep. So. Bell, Atlanta, 1975-77, communications cons. bus. mktg., 1977-79, sales supr. mktg. and customer service, 1979-81, mgr. sales tng., 1981-84, mgr. sales ops., 1984-86, program mgr. direct mktg., 1986—; sales cons. AIM Co., 1975—; assoc. Intelligent Heart Prodns., 1974—. Contbr. articles to profl. jours. Fundraiser United Negro Coll. Fund, Atlanta, 1983—, High Mus. Art, Atlanta, 1983—, Atlanta Symphony, 1984-85, Woodruff Arts Ctr., Atlanta, 1984—, Council on Battered Women, Atlanta, 1985—, United Way, Atlanta, 1983—, co-chair telemktg., vol. NAACP, Atlanta, 1981-84, Martin Luther King Ctr. for Social Change, Atlanta, 1981-83, Jr. Achievement, Atlanta, 1985-86, Lit. Action, Atlanta, 1987—. Recipient Vol. Merit award Nat. Assn. Educators, 1984-86, Gov's. Merit award Jr. Achievement, Ga., 1985, Recognition award United Negro Coll. Fund, Atlanta, 1985; named one of Outstanding Young Women Am., 1981. Mem. Am. Bus. Women's Assn., Direct Mktg. Assn. Pacific Inst. Alumni Assn., Delta Sigma Theta. Democrat. Roman Catholic. Office: So Bell 27D55 So Bell Ctr 675 W Peachtree St NE Atlanta GA 30375

BOONE, DEBORAH ANN (DEBBY BOONE), singer; b. Hackensack, N.J., Sept. 22, 1956; d. Charles (Pat) Eugene and Shirley (Foley) B.; m. Gabriel Ferrer, 1979; children: Jordan Alexander, Gabrielle Monserrate and Dustin Boone (twins), Tessa Rose. Student Calif. schs. Singer with father, Pat Boone, and family group, 1970—, profl. rec. artist, 1977—; numerous appearances on TV talk and variety programs; appeared in ABC-TV Movie of the Week, Sins of the Past, 1984; author: Debby Boone--So Far; starred in Seven Brides for Seven Brothers nat. tour and Broadway, 1981-82. Recipient Am. Music award (Song of Year), Grammy award (Best New Artist), 1977, Grammy award for best inspirational performance, 1980, Grammy award for best Gospel performance for Keep the Flame Burning, 1984, Nat. Assn. Theatre Owners award (Best New Personality), Dove award, 1980, Dove award for album Surrender, 1984, Country Music award for Best New Country Artist, 1977; named Singing Star of Yr. AGVA, 1978, Working Mother of Yr., 1982. Mem. Ch. on the Way. Address: 12001 Ventura Pl Suite 201 Studio City CA 91604

BOONE, KAY LANIER, public relations consultant; b. Ft. Worth, Sept. 3, 1941; d. John David and Reba Louise (Smith) Lanier; m. William T. Boone, July 22, 1967; children: Katherine, Lisa, Suaznne. Student, Abilene (Tex.) Christian U., 1959-60; BA in Journalism, North Tex. State U., 1964. Reporter Daily Oklahoman/Oklahoma City Times, 1964-66; feature writer Houston Post, 1967; info. rep. Okla. Dept. Inst., Social and Rehab. Services, Oklahoma City, 1967-73; dir. pub. info. United Way Mecklenburg-Union, Charlotte, N.C., 1974-76; account mgr., sr. writer Epley Assocs./Pub. Relations, Charlotte, 1977-78; account mgr. Yarbrough Co./Advt., Pub. Relations, Dallas, 1979-82; owner Boone & Assoc./Pub. Relations and Advt., Richardson, Tex., 1982—. Author, editor History of Child Welfare In Oklahoma, 1976. Mem. Pub. Relations Soc. of America, Assn. Women Entrepreneurs of Dallas (pres. 1987—), Richardson C. of C. (editor newsletter 1986-87). Unitarian. Office: Boone & Assocs/Pub Relations 777 S Central Expressway #1Q Richardson TX 75080

BOONE, LESLIE SPEARMAN, educator; b. W. Palm Beach, Fla., July 18, 1930; d. Robert Ewell and Zonise (Wood) Spearman; B.A., U.S. Fla., Tampa, 1975, M.Ed., 1981; m. Floyd E. Boone, June 3, 1950; children—Zonise Jeanette Boone Swanson, Robert Edward, William Gordon. Head Start tchr. Manatee County (Fla.), 1967-75, head tchr. Bradenton (Fla.) Center, 1973-75; kindergarten tchr. Orange Ridge Elementary Sch., Bradenton, 1975—. Sunday sch. tchr. Trinity United Methodist Ch., Bradenton, 1958-78; instr. swimming, social worker ARC; active local PTA, Girl Scouts, Heart Fund. Mem. UDC, DAR, Nat. Soc. Colonial Dames XVII Century, Alpha Delta Kappa (pres. 1984-86). Democrat. Club: Sons of Norway. Home: 2611 26th Ave Dr W Bradenton FL 34205 Office: 400 30th Ave W Bradenton FL 33505

BOONE, MELISSA JANE, residential design company executive; b. Elwood, Ind., Sept. 24, 1950; d. John William and Rosenelle (McIntosh) P.; m. Albert Derrell Boone, Aug. 7, 1971 (div. 1977); 1 child, Kevin Derrell. Student, Ind. U., 1968-69; BFA, Stetson U., 1972. Cert. art tchr., residential contractor, Fla. Art instr. Adult Edn. D.B.C.C., Daytona, Fla., 1972-73; residential drafting Welnec and Assoc., Ormond Beach, Fla., 1980-81; residential designer R.V.H. Developer, Port Orange, Fla., 1980-84; v.p., project mgr. Summer Trees Devel. Corp., Port Orange, Fla., 1983—; pvt. practice residential contractor Port Orange, Fla., 1985—; cons. Summer Trees Homes, Port Orange, 1985—, Fla. Land Market Inc., Port Orange, 1985—; instr. Casements Cultural Ctr., Ormond Beach, Fla., 1983, 85. Recipient 1st place award Deland Art Festival, 1972, Shrimp Boat Art Festival, 1973, Daytona Beach Art League, 1981. Mem Daytona Beach Home Builders Assn. (rep. Summer Trees Homes), Daytona Beach Art League. Office: Summer Trees Devl Corp 1649 Taylor Rd Port Orange FL 32014

BOONE, REBECCA A., university administrator; b. Springfield, Ohio, Mar. 7, 1946; d. Roger S. and Elizabeth Lupton (Walker) Boone; m. Dennis David Ash, Aug. 7, 1967 (div. 1975); m. Frederick Kellogg, July 11, 1979 (div. 1988). Student, Earlham Coll., 1964-67; BA, Case Western Res. U., 1968; MLS, U. N.C., 1970. Asst. reference librarian Princeton (N.J) U., 1970-76; head cen. reference dept. U. Ariz., Tucson, 1976-84, assoc. dean Coll. Arts and Scis., 1984—; adminstrv. staff Ariz. Bd. Regents, 1988-89. Mem. ALA (div. pres. 1985-86), Nat. Assn. for Female Execs., Exec. Women's Council So. Ariz. Mem. Soc. of Friends. Home: 1018 E Greenlee Pl Tucson AZ 85719 Office: Ariz Bd Regents 3030 N Central Suite 1400 Phoenix AZ 85012

BOONSHAFT-LEWIS, HOPE JUDITH, public relations executive; b. Phila., May 3, 1949; d. Barry and Lorelei Gail (Rienzi) B. B.A., Pa. State U., 1972; postgrad. Del. Law Sch., Kellogg Inst. Mgmt. Tng. Program writer Youth Edn., N.Y.C., 1972; legal aide to judge, Phila., 1973; dir. spl. projects Guiffre Med. Center, Phila., 1975; Arlen Specter senatorial campaign fin. dir., Phila., 1975; fin. dir. Jimmy Carter Presdl. Campaign, Atlanta, 1976; nat. fin. dir. Democratic Nat. Com., 1977-78; dir. devel. World Jewish Congress, N.Y.C., 1978; dir. devel. Yeshiva U., Los Angeles, 1979; dir. communications Nat. Easter Seal Soc., Chgo., 1979-83; chief exec. officer Boonshaft-Lewis & Savitch Pub. Relations and Govt. Affairs, Los Angeles, 1983—; spl. adv. community relations The White House, 1977-80; guest lectr. U. Ill., 1982, May Co.'s Calif. Women in Bus. Bd. dirs. Los Angeles Arts Council, Hollywood Heritage Council. Named 1 of 6 Non Stop Achievers, GermaineMonteil. Mem. Nat. Soc. Fundraisers, Am. Inst. food and Wine, Women's Nat. Dem. Club, Alpha Chi Omega. Home: 1234 N Wetherly Dr Los Angeles CA 90069 Office: 1888 Century Park E Suite 330 Los Angeles CA 90067

BOOSVELD, BETTY SUE, histologist; b. Cin., Mar. 6, 1935; d. Christopher Ulysses and Evelyn (Graves) B. AS, U. Cin., 1953. Endocrinology technician William S. Merrell Co., Cin., 1955-60; cancer research technologist Henry Ford Hosp., Detroit, 1960-65; supr. cancer research Oreg. Regional Primate Research Ctr., Beaverton, 1966-69; biochemistry technologist U. Cin. Med. Sch., 1969-72; histology supr. Providence Hosp., Cin., 1974—; cons. Dept. Health and Rehab. Services, Jacksonville, Fla. Author numerous research papers in field. Active John F. Kennedy Presdl. Campaign, 1960, Luth. Women's Missionary League, Cin., 1969—; vol. with Cin. Symphony Orch., 1986-87. Grantee NIH, 1960-72. Mem. Nat. Soc. Histology, Assn. Clin. Pathologists, Ohio Soc. Histotech., S.W. Ohio Soc. Histotech. Democrat. Lutheran. Club: Sub Deb (Cin.). Office: Providence Hosp 2446 Kipling Ave Cincinnati OH 45239

BOOTH, BARBARA R., civic worker; b. N.Y.C., May 2, 1928; d. Benjamin C. and Ceclia (Lowe) Ribman; A.A., Centenary Jr. Coll., Hackettstown, N.Y., 1948; B.A., Barnard Coll., 1950; m. Mitchell B. Booth, July 13, 1952; 1 son, Brian S. Pres. women's alliance, chmn., Christmas fair 1st Congl. Ch. of City of N.Y., 1959-63; mem. vol. com. Sheltering Arms Children's Service, N.Y.C.; vol., coordinator high sch. visits, 1st v.p. aux. N.Y. Hosp.; trustee Florence K. Griswold Meml. Fund. Com., All Souls Unitarian Ch., N.Y.C.; dir. women's div. Jefferson Dem. Club. N.Y.C.; committeewoman N.Y. County Dem. Com.; bd. govs., v.p. N.Y. Fruit and Flower Mission, Inc.; del. city conv., chmn. East Manhattan br. LWV. Home: 75 East End Ave New York NY 10028

BOOTH, BEATRICE CROSBY, biological oceanographer; b. Mpls., Aug. 29, 1938; d. George Christrian and Beatrice (Goodrich) Crosby; m. Theordore William Booth, Dec. 23, 1960; children: Marguerite Morse, Kristina Wells, George Crosby. B.A., Radcliffe Coll., 1960; M.A.T., Harvard U., 1962; M.S., U. Wash., 1969. Teaching asst. U. Wash., Seattle, 1974, instr., 1975-78, research oceanographer, 1975-80, sr. oceanographer, 1980-83, prin. oceanographer, 1983—; oceanographer NOAA, Seattle, 1978-79. Contbr. articles to profl. jours. NSF grantee, 1978-80, 80-82, 82-84, 84-86, 86—. Mem. Am. Soc. Limnology and Oceanography, AAAS, Phycological Soc. Am. Democrat. Home: 5521 17th St Ave NE Seattle WA 98105 Office: Sch Oceanography Univ of Wash Seattle WA 98195

BOOTH, RACHEL ZONELLE, nursing educator; b. Seneca, S.C., Feb. 10, 1936; m. Richard B. Booth, Feb. 13, 1957; 1 child, Kevin M. Student, Furman U., 1953-54; diploma in nursing, Greenville (S.C.) Gen. Hosp., 1956; student, U. Alaska, 1966-68; BS in Nursing, U. Md., Balt., 1968; MS in Nursing, U. Md., 1970, PhD in Adminstrn. Higher Edn., 1978. RN. Staff nurse VA Hosp., Murfreesboro, Tenn., 1957-58, U. Colo. Med. Ctr., Denver, 1957-58; nurse psychiatry dept. Patton State Hosp., Calif., 1958-59; staff nurse USAF Dispensary, Iraklion, Greece, 1959-60; charge nurse psychiatry Santa Rose Med. Ctr., San Antonio, 1961; staff nurse Shannon S.W. Tex. Meml. Hosp., San Angelo, 1962; supervisory clin. nurse, head nurse U.S. Dept. Health, Edn., and Welfare/USPHS/Indian Health Service, Anchorage, 1962-66; staff nurse U.S. Dept. Health, Edn., and Welfare/USPHS, Balt., 1966, 68; assoc. dir. dept. nursing U. Md. Hosp., College Park, 1970-76, dir. primary care nursing service, 1976-81; asst. prof. Sch. Nursing U. Md., College Park, 1972-76, asst. prof. Sch. Pharmacy, 1972-80, acting assoc. dean Sch. Nursing, 1979-81, assoc. prof. Sch. Nursing, 1979, assoc. prof. clin. pharmacy, 1980-83, assoc. dean for undergrad. studies Sch. Nursing, 1981-83, co-dir. nurse practitioner program Sch. Nursing, 1972-76, chairperson grad. program dept. primary care, 1976-79; asst. v.p. health affairs, dean nursing dept., prof. Duke U. Med. Ctr., Durham, N.C., 1984-87; dean Sch. of Nursing U. Ala. at Birmingham, University Station, 1987—; instr. Sch. Medicine U. Md., 1972-83, program dir. primary care nurse practitioner program continuing edn., 1976-82, project dir. Robert Wood Johnson Nurse Faculty Fellowship program, 1977-82; mem. joint practice com. Med. and Chirurg. Faculty Md., 1974-77, mem. tech. adv. com. for physician's assts. Bd. Med. Examiners Md., 1975-80; mem. adv. com. nursing program Community Coll. Balt., 1976-79; mem. Joint Commn. on Accreditation of Hosps., pres. Md. Council Dirs. of Assoc. Degree, Diploma, and Baccalaureate Programs, 1982-83; mem. adv. bd. nursing Essex Community Coll., 1983; mem. peer rev. panel advanced nurse edn. nursing div. U.S. Dept. Health and Human Services, 1987—. Editor (with others): Hospital Pharmacy, 1971-72; asst. editor Jour. Profl. Nursing, 1984—; contbr. articles on nursing to prof. jours. Bd. dirs. Health and Welfare Council Cen. Md., Inc., 1974-78, v.p., 1975-78; mem. health adv. com. to Pres. of Pakistan, 1983. Recipient numerous grants for nursing adminstrn., 1972—. Mem. Internat. Council Nurses (observer conf. 1981), Am. Nurse's Assn. (mem. nat. rev. com. 1975-78, v.p. 1977, chair 1978), Nat. Acad. Practice for Nursing (vice-chairperson 1984—), Nat. Orgn. for Nurse Execs., Nat. League for Nursing, Council Nat. Acad. Practice, Am. Assn. Colls. in Nursing (dean's summer seminar com., 1984-85, edn. and credentialing com. 1985-86, nominating com. 1986—), N.C. Orgn. Nurse Execs. (bd. dirs. 1986—), Sigma Theta Tau (chairperson nominating com. 1974, mem. 1975, recording sec. 1980—). Home: 3112 Bradford Pl Birmingham AL 35242

BOOTHE, SABRINA ANNE, federal government official; b. Bklyn., Mar. 26, 1958; d. Robert Stanley and Matilda Sulla (Edwards) B. BA in Econs., Fordham U., 1983; postgrad., Pace U., 1984—. Bus. mgr. Fay & Allen's Foodhalls, N.Y.C., 1979-80, Ctr. for Study of Presidency, N.Y.C., 1980-84, Am. Friends of Chung-Ang U., 1982-84, Flatbush Devel. Corp., Bklyn., 1985-87; asst. nat. bank examiner Office Comptroller of Currency, U.S. Treasury Dept., 1987—; cons. mgmt. Maverick Ctr. for Self Devel., Bronx, N.Y., 1980—. Staff asst. The Ethnic Woman, 1980—; mgr. bus. Presdl. Studies Quar., 1982-84. Exec. dir. Global Women of African Heritage, N.Y.C., 1981—. Named one of Outstanding Young Women of Am., 1984. Mem. Nat. Assn. Female Execs., UN Assn. of US. Republican. Home: 2620 Beverley Rd #11B Brooklyn NY 11226

BOOTS, LINDA MARIE, nurse; b. Mitchell, S.D., Feb. 26, 1951; d. Paul Spencer and Carla Jean (Norgren) Schonher; m. Donald Dale Boots, Jan. 1,

1979 (div.). BS in Nursing, Marycrest Coll., 1973; MS in Nursing, U. Tex., 1977. RN, Iowa, N.Y., Minn., S.D., Okla. Staff nurse N.Y. Hosp., 1973-74, St. Mary's Hosp., Rocheste, Minn., 1975; instr. Marycrest Coll., Davenport, Iowa, 1975-77; specialist critical care clin. McKennan Hosp., Sioux Falls, S.D., 1977-79; dir. nursing St. Anthony Hosp., Oklahoma City, 1979—; mem. profl. adv. group Amcare Ambulance Trust, Oklahoma City, 1979—. Mem. Am. Assn. Critical Care Nurses, Am. Orgn. Nurse Execs., Okla. Orgn. Nurse Execs., Internat. Soc. Heart Transplantation. Republican. Roman Catholic. Home: PO Box 60922 Oklahoma City OK 73146 Office: St Anthony Hosp 1000 N Lee Oklahoma City OK 73162

BOOZ, CINDY BRENIZE, library media specialist; b. Shippensburg, Pa., Oct. 12, 1951; d. Sharpe Adam and Thelma May (Cover) Brenize; m. Donald Ray Booz; children: Amanda Rhea, Colleen Renee. BS in Edn., Shippensburg U., 1972, MS in Library Sci., 1974; postgrad., Bethany Theol. Sem., 1978-83. Library media specialist Shippensburg Area Sch. Dist., 1973-77; asst. catalog librarian Bethany Theol. Sem., Oak Brook, Ill., 1977-80, catalog librarian, 1980-82; asst. cataloger Maitland (Fla.) Pub. Library, 1982-83; library media specialist Orange County Sch. Dist., Orlando, Fla., 1983—. Bd. dirs. Fla. and P.R. dist. Ch. of Brethren, 1983-86, chairperson Child Devel. Ctr. Com., Winter Park, Fla., 1983-86, mem. study com. for Christian edn., 1987—. Mem. NEA, Orange County Classroom Tchr.'s Assn., Fla. Assn. Media in Edn., Orange County Assn. Ednl. Media. Democrat. Office: Ocoee Elem Sch 400 S Lakewood Ave Ocoee FL 32761

BOOZ, GRETCHEN ARLENE, marketing executive; b. Boone, Iowa, Nov. 24, 1933; d. David Gerald and Katherine Bevridge (Hardie) Berg; m. Donald Rollett Booz, Sept. 3, 1960; children: Kendra Sue (dec.), Joseph David, Katherine Sue. AA, Graceland Coll., 1955. Mktg. services mgr. Herald Pub. House, Independence, Mo., 1975—. Author: (book) Kendra, 1979. Mem. Citizens Adv. Bd., Blue Springs, Mo., 1979—; bd. dirs. Child Placement Services, Independence, Mo., 1987—, Hope House, Inc., Independence, Mo., 1987—; trustee Graceland Coll., Lamoni, Iowa, 1984—. Mem. Independence C. of C. (diplomat). Republican. Mem. Reorganized Ch. Jesus Christ Latter Day Saints. Home: 1200 Crestview Dr Blue Springs MO 64015 Office: Herald Pub House 3225 S Noland Rd Independence MO 64055

BORAH, MARIA LENA, computer systems technologist; b. Watervliet, Mich., June 8, 1957; d. Peter Joseph and Mary Louise (Bradley) Fohs; m. Lawrence Kevin Borah, June 27, 1975 (div. May 1982). A in Tech., BA in Math., Cameron U., 1981; MS in Computer Sci., Midwestern State U., Witchita Falls, Tex., 1986. Research systems analyst Field Artillery Sch., Ft. Sill, Okla., 1978-82; weapons systems analyst Boeing Mil. Airplane Co., Witchita, Kans., 1982-83; coordinator for acad. support systems Cameron U., Lawton, Okla., 1983-87; systems developer SAS Inst., Austin, Tex., 1987—. Mem. Mensa, Phi Kappa Phi. Roman Catholic.

BORCHELT, SHERYL LYNN, sales and marketing consultant; b. Carrollton, Ky., Oct. 17, 1949; d. Ruben Carl and Jessie D. (Bartlett) Johnson; m. James Caldwell Borchelt, Feb. 25, 1967; children—Kristi Ann, Jennifer Lynn. Cert. hosp. mgmt. Xavier U., 1982; student Coll. Mount St. Joseph. Cardiovascular technician Christ Hosp., Cin., 1976-78, mgr. cardiac cath lab., 1978-84; profl. model Familiar Faces, Cin., 1980—; mgr. Optimum Services, Inc., div. Bethesda Hosp., Cin., 1984-87; dir. profl. relations, Tristate Biotherapeutics, 1988—. Recipient Human Relations and Achievement award Dale Carnegie Inst., Cin., 1985. Mem. Assn. Fitness in Bus., Am. Mgmt. Assn. Republican. Club: TCH Drama (Cin.) (v.p. 1981-82). Avocations: dancing; acting; white water rafting; gardening. Office: Tri-State Biotherapeutics 2800 Winslow Ave Suite 211 Cincinnati OH 45206

BORDELEAU, NANCY VIVIAN, state agency administrator; b. Boston, Aug. 30, 1934; d. Edmund and Dorothy (Goldstein) McIntosh; m. Roland John Bordeleau, June 18, 1955; children: John Michael, Lisa Marie, Michele Denise. EdB, R.I. Coll., 1955; MBA, Bryant Coll., 1985. Tchr. Hugh B. Bain Jr. High Sch., Cranston, R.I., 1955-57; social caseworker R.I. Dept. Social Welfare, Cranston, Johnston, Scituate and Foster, 1957-60; dir. Dept. Pub. Welfare, Cranston, 1966-85, R.I. Dept. Human Services, Cranston, 1985—; mem. Ea. Regional Conf. Council of State Govts. Resolutions Com., Nat. Gov.'s Assn. Com. on Health and Human Services, 1987—; mem. Gov.'s Task Force Long Term Care for Elderly, 1987. Trustee Butler Hosp., Providence, 1968-84; chairperson State Employees Combined Charitable Campaign, R.I., 1987; past mem. social action com. Am. Bapt. Chs. R.I.; founder Eastman House, Inc., Cranston. Recipient Charles B. Willard Achievement award Alumni Assn. R.I. Coll., Providence, 1978, Exemplary Program award Council for Community Service, 1982, Outstanding Woman award YWCA Greater R.I., 1985, 87; Henry Toll fellow Council State Govts., Lexington, Ky., 1986. Mem. Nat. Council State Human Services Adminstrs. (council 1985-87, chair housing task force 1987), Am. Pub. Welfare Assn., R.I. Conf. Social Services (v.p., bd. dirs. 1968-82), Gov.'s Council on Mental Health, Gov.'s Human Services Adv. Council, Mental Health Services of Cranston, Johnston and Northwest R.I. Republican. Baptist. Home: 70 Poppy Dr Cranston RI 02920 Office: RI Dept Human Services 600 New London Ave Cranston RI 02920

BORDEN, BRENDA JANE, technical writer; b. Newark, Feb. 2, 1958; d. Irving and Sonya (Spade) Gertzog; m. Craig Scott Borden, Sept. 10, 1961. BS in Bus/Mktg., Fairleigh Dickinson U., 1980. Mktg. asst. AgfaGevaert, Teterboro, N.J., 1980-81; product support specialist CompuScan, Fairfield, N.J., 1982-83; tech. writer Ambi Corp., Stamford, Conn., 1984-86, Dictaphone Corp., Stratford, Conn., 1986-88, ChannelNet, Shelton, Conn., 1988—. Treas. Circle K. Spl. Olympics, Madison, N.J., 1978-80. Mem. Soc. for Tech. Communication, Nat. Assn. for Female Execs. Home: 178 Austin River Ln Brandford CT 06405 Office: ChannelNet 230 Long Hill Cross Rd Shelton CT 06484

BORDEN, SANDRA MCCLISTER, day care center administrator, dancer; b. Trenton, Oct. 18, 1946; d. Harry Arthur and Ruth West McClister; m. Robert Stetson Borden, Mar. 23, 1968; children: Robert Freeman, Randolph McClister, David Buckley, Christian Delano. BA, Eastern Nazarene Coll., Quincy, Mass., 1968; MA, Nova U., 1986. Tchr. kindergarten Doves Nest Day Care Ctr., Rockland, Mass., 1979-84, owner, adminstr., 1979—; owner, adminstr. Dove's Nest Day Care Ctr., Weymouth, Mass., 1980-82, Abington, Mass., 1980-83; owner, editor Barter & Trade Jour., Rockland, 1980-83; owner Dove's Nest Family Day Care System, Rockland, 1984—; co-owner Carriage House Day Care Ctr., Brockton, Mass., 1986—, Commonwealth Child Care Cons., 1987—, Bevell Assocs., Stoughton, Mass., 1987—, Beginning Roots Day Care Ctr., Stoughton, 1987—. Dancer Foggs Dancers, Boston, 1980—; dir. Country Dance Soc., Boston, 1982—, v.p. 1986—, dancer, 1984-85, pres. 1988; co-founder, dancer Rapscallion Rapper Sword Team, 1985—. Bd. dirs. LWV, Rockland, 1972-73. Mem. Nat. Assn. Young Children, Royal Scottish Dance Soc., Country Dance Soc. (pres. elect 1987), Nat. Assn. Female Execs., Assn. for Childhood Edn. Internat. Baptist. Clubs: Women Aglow (sec., bd. dirs.) (Brockton); New Eng. Folk Festival Assn. (Boston). Home: 1040 Plymouth St Abington MA 02351 Office: The Dove's Nest Day Care Ctr 1040 Plymouth St Abington MA 02351

BORGERS, BEVERLY KAY, educator; b. Cumberland, Md., Dec. 19, 1943; d. George William and Nel Hazil (Morris) Mefford; m. Edgar Lee Borgers, Nov. 13, 1968. BA, Anderson (Ind.) Coll., 1966; MA, U. Mo., Kansas City, 1979. Elementary tchr. Met. Sch. Dist., Anderson, Ind., 1966-69, Ft. Osage Sch. Dist., Independance, Mo., 1970—; coordinator North Cen. Accreditation, Independance, 1986-87, vis. team mem., 1987; bldg. rep. Ft. Osage Computers, 1986-87. State coordinator Women of the Ch. of God, Mo., 1984—; chair Mission and Outreach Bd., Kansas City, 1985—; presenter Mid-West Historical Conference, Springfield, Mo., 1980. Mem. Orgn. Am. Historians, Community Educators Assn. (chair welfare 1981-83, 2d v.p. 1988), Mo. Assn. Community and Jr. Colls., Assn. for Supr. and Curriculum Devel., Phi Delta Kappa, Delta Kappa Gamma. Republican. Home: 2400 London Dr Blue Springs MO 64015 Office: Blue Hills Elementary Sch 24 Highway and Blue Hills Rd Independence MO 64058

BORGES, WANDA, lawyer; b. Bronx, N.Y., Aug. 29, 1950; d. Jaime Nemesio Borges and Ada C. (Pujadas) Borges Mady. Bar: N.Y. 1979, U.S. Dist. Ct. N.Y. 1979, U.S. Supreme Ct. 1984. Legal sec. firm Jules Teitelbaum, N.Y.C., 1972, law clk., 1972-79, assoc., 1979-82; assoc. Teitelbaum & Gamberg P.C., N.Y.C., 1982-84; ptnr. Jules Teitelbaum P.C., N.Y.C., 1985—; lectr. Am. Mgmt. Assn., 1982—, Nat. Assn. Credit Mgmt., N.J., 1983—; adj. prof. Seton Coll., Yonkers, N.Y., 1986—. Recipient Human Valor award, 1985. Mem. ABA, Fed. Bar Council, N.Y. State Bar Assn., Bankruptcy Lawyers Bar Assn., Mercy Coll. Alumni Assn. (v.p., dir.). Roman Catholic. Club: Fairfield County Chorale; U.S. Power Squadron. Home: 1096 Main St Stamford CT 06902 Office: 121 E 18th St New York NY 10003

BORGESE, ELISABETH MANN, author, political science educator; b. Munich, Germany, Apr. 24, 1918; emigrated to U.S., 1938, naturalized, 1941, became Can. citizen, 1983; d. Thomas and Katia (Pringheim) Mann; m. Giuseppe Antonio Borgese, Nov. 23, 1939; children: Angelica, Dominica. Diploma, Conservatory of Music, Zurich, 1937; Ph.D. (h.c.), Mt. St. Vincent U., 1986. Research assoc., editor Common Cause, U. Chgo., 1945-51; editor Perspective USA; Diogenes (Intercultural Publs.), 1952-57; exec. sec. bd. editors Ency. Brit., Chgo., 1964-66; sr. fellow, assoc. Center for Study Democratic Instns., Santa Barbara, Calif., 1965—; Killam sr. fellow Dalhousie U., Halifax, N.S., Can., 1978-79; prof. dept. polit. sci. Dalhousie U., 1980—; assoc. dir. Lester Pearson Inst. Internat. Devel., 1985-87; chmn. planning council Internat. Ocean Inst., 1971—; chmn. Internat. Ctr. for Ocean Devel.; advisor Austrian del. 3d UN Conf. on Law of Sea, 1976-82; Prep. Commn. Jamaica, 1983-86. Author: To Whom It May Concern, 1962, Ascent of Woman, 1963, The Language Barrier, 1965, The Ocean Regime, 1968, The Drama of the Oceans, 1976, Seafarm: The Story of Aquaculture, 1980, The Mines of Neptune, 1985, The Future of the Oceans: A Report to the Club of Rome, 1986; (plays) Only the Pyre, 1987; contbr. short stories, essays to mags. Decorated medal of High Merit (Austria); recipient Sasakawa Internat. Environ. prize UN, 1987. Mem. Acad. Polit. Sci., AAAS, Am. Soc. Internat. Law, World Acad. Arts and Scis., Third-World Acad. Sci. Order of Can. Home: Sambro Head, Halifax, NS Canada Office: Dahlousie U, Dept Polit Sci, Halifax, NS Canada B3H 4H6

BORGMAN, JANET JEAN, accountant; b. Temple, Tex., July 20, 1962; d. Eugene Emil and Betty Jane (Vanicek) Engbrock; m. Jeffrey Scott Borgman, July 13, 1985. BBA in Acctg., U. Tex., 1984. CPA. Staff acct. KMG Main Hurdman, San Antonio, 1984-85; controller La. Capital Corp., San Antonio, 1985-86; acct. D. Meadows Bookkeeping and Tax Services, San Antonio, 1986-87; sr. acct. Clifton Gunderson & Co. CPAs, Denver, 1987—. Mem. Am. Inst. CPAs, Colo. Soc. CPAs, Tex. Soc. CPAs. Roman Catholic. Office: Clifton Gunderson & Co CPAs 11990 Grant St Suite 304 Denver CO 80233

BORICHEVSKY, JOAN FRAPPIER, hospital administrator; b. Proctor, Vt., June 8, 1936; d. Cornelius Waldorf Frappier and Josephine Louise (Decicco) L'Herault; m. Donald John Borichevsky, May 25, 1957; children: John Frappier, Steven Carl. BS, Vt. Coll., 1980, MA, 1987. Personnel adminstr. Norton Co., Granville, N.Y., 1971-82; personnel mgr. Whitney Blake, Inc., Bellows Falls, Vt., 1982; adminstrv. mgr. Sta. EMCO-TV, Manchester, Vt., 1983-84; dir. human resources Bellevue Maternity Hosp., Schenectady, N.Y., 1984-87; pres., mgmt. cons. Joan F. Borichevsky & Assocs., Baldwinsville, N.Y., 1987—. Past chair PTA. Mem. Am. Soc. Personnel Adminstrs., Mohawk Regional Human Capabilities Assn. (bd. dirs. 1984—), Tri-Cities Personnel Assn., Capital Dist. Personnel Assn. (bd. dirs.), Indsl. Relations Research Assn. Republican. Episcopalian. Lodges: Order Eastern Star (Grand Chaplain local orgn. 1979), Shriners. Home: 141 Grouse Rd Lysander NY 13094 Office: PO Box 161 Baldwinsville NY 13027

BORIS, SYLVIA, psychologist; b. Havana, Cuba, May 3, 1956; d. Charles Andrew and Emily Jeannette (Danino) Breitenbach; m. Alan Carey Boris, May 26, 1974. BA, N.Y.U., 1977; MA, Yeshiva U., 1981, PhD, 1984. Lic. psychologist, N.Y. Psychologist Manhattan Psychiat. Ctr., N.Y.C., 1981-85; sr. psychologist, clin. coordinator Lincoln Med./Mental Health Ctr., Bronx, N.Y., 1985-87; sr. psychologist Bellevue Hosp. Ctr., N.Y.C., 1987—; pvt. practice psychologist N.Y.C., 1986—. Mem. NOW, Am. Psychol. Assn., N.Y. Soc. Clin. Psychiatrists, Ea. Psychol. Assn., Coalition of Hosp. and Instl. Psychologists. Office: Bellevue Hosp Ctr 27th St at 1st Ave 20S9 New York NY 10016

BORLAND, BARBARA DODGE (MRS. HAL BORLAND), author; b. Waterbury, Conn.; d. Harry G. and Grace (Cross) Dodge; student Oberlin U., 1922-23, Columbia U. Sch. Journalism, 1923; m. 2d, Hal Borland, Aug. 10, 1945 (dec. Feb. 1978); 1 dau., Diana (Mrs. James C. Thomson, Jr.). Editorial cons. various pubs., 1923-35; condr. Writers Workshop, N.Y.C., 1934-38; writer, also collaborator with husband, fiction for Colliers, McCalls, Good Housekeeping, Cosmopolitan, Redbook, others, 1946-56; garden columnist Berkshire Eagle, Pittsfield, Mass., 1960. Recipient Distinguished Alumna award St. Margaret's Sch., 1972. Congregationalist. Mem. Authors League Am. Author: The Greater Hunger, 1962 (chosen Ambassador Book, English Speaking Union 1963); This is the Way My Garden Grows ... and This is the Way My Garden Cooks, 1986; contbr.: New England: The Four Seasons, 1980; editor: Twelve Moons of the Year (by Hal Borland), 1979. Address: Weatogue Rd Salisbury CT 06068

BORLAND, FREDRICKA MONTAGUE, surgeon; b. Houston, Oct. 11, 1950; d. Thomas Cooper and Willimina (Montague) B. BA, Vanderbilt U., 1972; MD, Baylor Coll. Medicine, 1976. Cert. Am. Bd. Surgeons. Resident in gen. surgery Vanderbilt U. Hosps., Nashville, 1976-79, Med. U. of S.C., Charleston, 1979-81; dir. emergency room Charleston County Hosp., 1981-82; fellow in vascular surgery U. Miss. Med. Ctr., Jackson, 1982-83; practice medicine specializing in gen., vascular surgery McAllen, Tex., 1983—; asst. instr. surgery Med. Univ. S.C., Charleston, 1981-82; vascular, gen. surgeon Rio Grande Regional Hosp., Mission Hosp., McAllen Med. Ctr., 1983—. Fellow ACS; mem. AMA, Tex. Med. Assn., Hidalgo-Starr County Med. Assn. Office: 222 East Ridge Rd Suite 203 McAllen TX 78503

BORN, BROOKSLEY ELIZABETH, lawyer; b. San Francisco, Aug. 27, 1940; d. Ronald Henry and Mary Ellen (Bortner) B.; m. Alexander Elliot Bennett, Oct. 9, 1982; children: Nicholas Jacob Landau, Ariel Elizabeth Landau. A.B., Stanford U., 1961, J.D., 1964. Bar: Calif. 1965, D.C. 1966. Law clk. U.S. Ct. Appeals, Washington, 1964-65; legal researcher Harvard Law Sch., 1967-68; asso. firm Arnold and Porter, Washington, 1965-67, 68-73; partner Arnold and Porter, 1974—; lectr. law Columbus Sch. Law, Cath. U. Am., 1972-74; adj. prof. Georgetown U. Law Center, Washington, 1972-73. Pres. Stanford Law Rev, 1963-64. Chairperson bd. visitors Stanford Law Sch., 1987; bd. dirs. Nat. Legal Aid and Defenders Assn., 1972-79; chairperson bd. dirs. Nat. Women's Law Ctr., 1981—; trustee Center for Law and Social Policy, Washington, 1977—, Women's Bar Found., 1981-86. Mem. Am. Bar Assn. (chairperson sect. individual rights and responsibilities 1977-78, chairperson fed. judiciary com. 1980-83, chairperson consortium on legal services and the pub. 1987—), D.C. Bar (sec. 1975-76, bd. govs. 1976-79), Am. Law Inst., Lawyers' Com. for Civil Rights Under Law (trustee 1978—), Am. Judicature Soc. (bd. dirs. 1984—), Order of Coif. Office: Arnold & Porter 1200 New Hampshire Ave NW Washington DC 20036

BORNHOLDT, LAURA ANNA, university administrator; b. Peoria, Ill., Feb. 11, 1919; d. John and Barbara (Kohl) B. A.B., Smith Coll., 1940, M.A., 1942; Ph.D., Yale U., 1945. Asst. prof. history Smith Coll., Northampton, Mass., 1945-52; internat. relations asso. AAUW, Washington, 1952-57; dean Sarah Lawrence Coll., Bronxville, N.Y., 1957-59; dean women, adj. prof. history U. Pa., Phila., 1959-61; dean coll., prof. history Wellesley (Mass.) Coll., 1961-64; v.p. Danforth Found., St. Louis, 1964-73; sr. program officer Lilly Endowment Inc., Indpls., 1973-76; v.p. for edn. Lilly Endowment Inc., 1976-84; spl. asst. to pres. U. Chgo., 1984—; Nat. adv. com. on black higher edn. and black colls. and univs. Dept. Edn., 1977-82; mem. Yale U. Council, 1977-82; emerita life trustee Coll. of Wooster, Ohio, 1977—; trustee St. Louis U., 1971-75; mem. bd. Nat. Council on Library Resources, 1983—. Contbg. editor Change Mag., 1980—. Recipient Yale U. Wilbur Cross medal, 1976, Smith Coll. Alumnae medal, 1987. Mem. Am. Assn. Higher Edn., Phi Beta Kappa. Home: 5000 S East End Ave Apt 25A Chicago IL 60615 Office: U Chgo 5801 S Ellis Ave Chicago IL 60637

BORNSTEIN, SARAH BARBARA, personnel manager; b. Phila., Nov. 3, 1947; d. Nathan and Frances (Goldberg) Bornstein; m. Alexander Cockrell O'Reilly, Aug. 27, 1975 (div.); 1 child, Kevin Bernard. B.A., Chatham Coll., 1969; M.A., Rutgers U., 1970; M.S.I.R., Loyola U., Chgo., 1985. Adminstrv. asst. Temple Sholom, Chgo., 1972-76; exec. sec. Borg-Warner Corp., Chgo., 1976-79, communications assoc., 1979-81, grants coordinator Borg-Warner Found., Chgo., 1980-81; sr. communications specialist Dart & Kraft, Inc., Northbrook, Ill., 1981-85, personnel specialist, 1985-86; mgr. personnel services Premark Internat., Inc., Deerfield, Ill., 1986—; dir. Health Evaluation & Referral Services, Chgo., 1980—; mem. Jr. League of Chgo., 1983—. Trustee, Chatham Coll., 1984-87. Recipient YWCA Leadership award Metropolitan Chgo., 1980; Woodrow Wilson fellow, 1969. Mem. Internat. Assn. Bus. Communicators (Gold Quill 1982, Spectra, Silver Quill 1983) (dir. Chgo. 1982-83), Phi Beta Kappa. Democrat. Jewish. Office: Premark Internat Inc 1717 Deerfield Rd Deerfield IL 60015

BORNT, DOROTHY ELLEN, information specialist; b. Bklyn, Aug. 7, 1961; d. George and Carol Ann (Kramer) DeNoto; m. Scott J. Bornt, June 26, 1987. BA, SUNY, Stonybrook, 1983; MLS, SUNY, Albany, 1984. Info. specialist Urbach, Kahn & Werlin PC, Albany, 1984—. Mem. Spl. Libraries Assn., Am. Soc. Info. Sci. Republican. Roman Catholic. Home: 91A Kennsington Ct Guilderland NY 12084 Office: Urbach Kahn & Werlin PC 66 State St Albany NY 12207

BOROCHOFF, IDA SLOAN, real estate executive, artist; b. July 29, 1922; d. Louis and Eva (Bistrick) Sloan; ed. U. Ga., 1939-40, Ga. State U., 1940, Chgo. Sch. Interior Decorating, 1966, Allegro Sch. Ballet, Chgo., Atlanta Ballet, 1948-54, Emory U., 1971-72; m. Charles Zachary Borochoff, Jan. 11, 1942; children—Lynn Borochoff Gould, Jean Sue Borochoff Shapiro, Toby Ann Borochoff Bernstein, Lance Mark. Investor and owner real estate, 1941—; v.p. Designs Unltd., Inc., Atlanta, 1964—; pres. Sloan Borochoff Gallery, Atlanta, 1970—; art lectr. Met. Ednl. Service; tchr. Ga. Inst. Tech.-Free U.; producer live talk health show on cable TV, Atlanta, 1983—; exhibited several one-woman shows, 1961-71, including Lovett Sch., 1972, 75, Ga. Inst. Tech., 1972, 75, Atlanta Mdse. Mart; art rev. columnist Northside Neighbor Newspapers. Bd. dirs. Atlanta Ballet, 1950-57; bd. dirs. Atlanta Music Club, also co-editor Newsletter; hostess Atlanta Arts Festival; capt. Heart Fund, 1968-76, area chmn. dr.; active various multi-media groups; artistic dir. Atlanta Playhouse Theatre, Little Miss Ga. Pageant, Little Mr. Dogwood Festival Pageant; active Dogwood Festival; chmn., trustee Atlanta Playhouse Theatre; mem. U.S. Congl. adv. bd. Am. Security Council, 1983—. Recipient several art awards; Caber award, 1984; named hon. alumnus Atlanta Art Inst., 1968, One of Ten Leading Ladies of Atlanta, J.C. Singles, 1976; City grantee, 1985. Mem. Atlanta Press Club, Atlanta Writers Club (membership com.), Atlanta Artists Club, Atlanta Women's C. of C. (chmn. fine arts 1977-78), LWV, High Mus. Art, Ga. Writers Assn., Arts High Mus. (patron), Corcoran Gallery (patron), Nat. Mus. Women in Arts (charter mem.), Internat. Platform Assn. Mem. B'nai B'rith Women (pres. chpt. 1975, mem. SE regional bd.). Clubs: Jockey, Progressive. Home: 3450 Old Plantation Rd NW Atlanta GA 30327 Office: 733 Glendale Rd Scottdale GA 30079

BOROWSKI, JENNIFER LUCILE, corporate administrator; b. Jersey City, Oct. 23, 1934; d. Peter Anthony and Lucy (Zapolska) B. BS, St. Peter's Coll., 1968; postgrad., Pace Coll., 1976-77. Mgr. benefits Amerada Petroleum Corp., N.Y.C., 1951-66, Mt. Sinai Hosp., N.Y.C., 1966-67; mgr. payroll Haskins & Sells, N.Y.C., 1967-74; mgr. payroll and payroll tax Cushman & Wakefield, Inc., N.Y.C., 1975—. Mem. Am. Payroll Assn. (bd. dirs. 1979-81, cert.), Am. Mgmt. Assn. Republican. Roman Catholic. Home: 36 Front St North Arlington NJ 07032 Office: Cushman & Wakefield Inc 1180 Ave of the Americas New York NY 10036

BOROWY, SANDRA ANN, accountant; b. Cleve., Dec. 29, 1955; d. Michael Borowy and Evelyn Alice (Auten) Yusko. AA, Saddleback Community Coll., Mission Viejo, Calif., 1984; BA, Calif. State U., Fullerton, 1987. Controller Donald B. Black, Inc., Laguna Beach, Calif., 1981-87; acct. Lesley, Thomas, Schwarz & Postma, Inc., Newport Beach, Calif., 1987—. Mem. Nat. Assn. Accts., Am. Soc. Women Accts., Fullerton Acctg. Soc. (sec., chair 1986), Nat. Assn. Female Execs., Alpha Gamma Sigma. Democrat. Methodist. Home: 18832 Florida Ave #40 Huntington Beach CA 92646

BORST-MANNING, DIANE GAIL, management consultant; b. Rochester, N.Y., Nov. 5, 1937; d. Howard Louis and Emily Kathleen (Crew) Borst; m. Steven Manning, Sept. 11, 1979. B.A. cum laude, Wagner Coll., 1959; M.B.A., N.Y.U., 1966. Planner N.Y.U. Med. Ctr., N.Y.C., 1962-76, assoc. dir. planning, 1976-78, dir. mgmt. services, 1978-80; dir. human resources Mt. Sinai Med. Ctr., N.Y.C., 1980-85, dir. planning, 1985-86; sr. v.p. The Manning Orgn., Inc., 1986—; pres. Diane Borst Manning Assocs., Inc., 1986—; inst. dept. health care mgmt. Mt. Sinai Sch. Medicine, CUNY, 1982—; adj. faculty Orange County Community Coll., Sarah lawrence Coll., New Sch. Social Research, 1986— . Editor: Managing Non-Profit Organizations, 1979. Author: (cassette) Managers and Secretaries - How to Achieve Teamwork, 1980. Chairperson grants Port Jervis Council for Arts; mem. Health Systems Agy. Bd., N.Y.C., 1976-79. Fullbright fellow, 1959. Mem. N.Y. Personnel Mgmt. Assn. (bd. dirs. 1974-76), Greater N.Y. Hosp. Assn., Am. Compensation Assn., Bur. Nat. Affairs (personnel policy forum 1983-84), Am. Assn. Hosp. Planners, Assn. Am. Med. Colls. Group on Instrl. Planning. Club: City (N.Y.) Avocations: gardening; auto mechanics; carpentry, real estate. Office: 40 W 55 St Suite 9D New York NY 10019

BORTOLETTO, DANIELA, physicist; b. Domodossola, Italy, Nov. 24, 1958; came to U.S., 1986; d. Adelino and Liliana (Rondolini) B. Laurea in Fisica, U. Pravia, Italy, 1972; MS in Physics, Syracuse U., 1987. Research asst. Syracuse (N.Y.) U., 1975—. Contbr. articles to profl. jours. Fellow Lombardy Region Pavia, 1982-83, U. Geneva, Switzerland, 1983-84. Mem. Am. Phys. Soc. Roman Catholic. Home: 8441/2 Sumner Ave Syracuse NY 13210 Office: Syracuse U 201 Physics Bldg Syracuse NY 13244

BORTON, MARILYN MILLER, recreation therapist; b. Paterson, N.J., Oct. 3, 1930; d. Calvin Henry and Lillian (Bennett) Miller; B.A. in Recreation, Syracuse (N.Y.) U., 1951; B.S. in Edn., Paterson State Tchrs. Coll., 1953; postgrad. Fairleigh Dickinson U.; m. Lee John Borton, June 9, 1951; children—Lee John, Nancy Lee, James Christopher, Susan Elizabeth. Dir., Village Sch. Retarded Children, Ridgewood, N.J., 1951-53; elementary sch. tchr., Wyckoff, N.J., 1953-56; tchr. Abbott Nursery Sch., Prospect Park, N.J., 1956-59; dir. Robin's Nest Nursery Sch., Bernardsville, N.J., 1964-66; dir. recreation Birchwood Convalescent Center, Edison, N.J., 1975—; sec.-treas. Borton Bus. Forms, Inc., 1968—. Bd. dirs. St. David's Kindergarten, Peters Twp., Pa., 1961-62, Passaic Twp. Youth Center, 1971-74, Watchung Hills Pop Warner Football, 1972-74; chmn. Helping Hand program Passaic Twp. Jaycees Wives, 1970-72; mem. Millington First Aid Squad, 1966—; charter mem., bd. dirs. Passaic Twp. First Aid Squad, 1974—, pres., 1976-77, 83, capt., 1984-87; instr. CPR and 1st aid ARC, 1974—; sec. Bicentennial Commn. Passaic Twp., 1974-76. Named Chmn. of Year, Passaic Twp. Jaycee Wives, 1970-71. Mem. Nat. Therapeutic Recreation Assn. Republican. Episcopalian. Home: 151 Division Ave PO Box 406 Millington NJ 07946 Office: 1350 Inman Ave Edison NJ 08820

BORUCH, YVONNE CLEMENCE, accountant; b. Shirley, Mass., Nov. 2, 1952; d. Don Loper and Marie Claire (Brien) Randolph; m. Christopher Philip Boruch, Sept. 6, 1980. AS, No. Va. Community Coll., 1981; BS in Bus., SUNY, Albany, 1986; MS in Acctg., L.I. U., 1987. Personnel asst. Lawrence (Mass.) Maid div. W.R. Grace, 1972-74; adminstrv. mgr. Paragon Industries, Inc., Lawrence, 1974-80; cons. Office Connection Inc., Arlington, Va., 1981; staff acct. Edward Lee Curtis, CPA, Alexandria, Va., 1982-83; supervisory acct. U.S. Mil. Acad., West Point, N.Y., 1986-87; bd. dirs., treas. Abetment Specialists, Inc. and Asbestos Aid Specialists, Inc., Lawrence, Mass., 1988—. Religion tchr. Sacred Heart Ch., Lawrence, 1979-80, St. David's Ch., Newburgh, N.Y., 1985; Red Cross vol. Bon Secours hosp., Methuen, Mass., 1978; mem. Nat. Multiple Sclerosis Soc., 1987—. Mem. Nat. Assn. Female Execs., Beta Epsilon Phi, Delta Mu Delta. Republican. Roman Catholic. Office: Abatement Specialists Inc Asbestos Aid Specialists Inc Andover MA 01810

BORUM, ELIZABETH ANN, psychologist; b. Newman, Calif., May 4, 1930. BA with honors, U. Calif., Berkeley, 1951, MA in Psychology, 1953. Licensed Psychologist, Calif. Staff/ pvt. practice Walnut Creek (Calif.) Hosp., 1978—; supr. psychologist Contra Costa County Probation, Concord, Calif., 1986—; staff East Bay Hosp., San Francisco, 1986—. Mem. People-to-People (pres. East Bay chpt. 1976—), Berkeley Bus. and Profl. Women's Club, 1960— (pres. 1967-68, Meritorious Service award for UNICEF 1973, Woman of Achievement award 1980-81), Bay Area Ethical Culture Council (pres. fellowship com. 1960-63, 66-69), com. Non-Govtl. Orgns. Adv. to Mayor's com. for UN 20th Anniversary Celebration in San Francisco, Bicentennial Com. of the Mayor of city of Berkeley, Am. Conservatory Theatre, Oakland Mus. Assn., Mus. Soc. San Francisco, Oakland Symphony Assn., Friends of the Oakland Ballet; chmn. West Coast Council for Ethical Culture, 1965-67; chmn. pro-tem San Francisco Ethical Forum, 1967; Trustee Menninger Found., 1985—. Recipient Fremont Poetry award, 1947, Anchor Poetry award, 1969. Mem. Am. Assn. Correctional Psychologist, Am. Psychol. Assn., Soc. for Psychol. Study Social Issues, Western Psychol. Assn., Am. Assn. Advancement Sci., Am. Acad. Polit. and Social Sci., Calif. State Psychol. Assn., (life) Internat. Humanist and Ethical Union, Internat. Platform Assn., People for the Am. Way, World Federalist Assn., Planetary Citizens, AAUN-USA (treas. East Bay Chpt. 1975-85), (life) Calif. Alumni Assn. Office: Psychol Clinic 2525 Stanwell Dr Concord CA 94520

BORUM, REGINA ANN, university program director; b. Dayton, Ohio, July 28, 1938; d. Robert Cortner and Vivien (Hayes) Prear; m. Butler Borum, Oct. 14, 1956; children: Joy Louise, Mark Randall, Michael Rodney. BA in Communications, Capital U., 1984. Exec. asst. Good Samaritan Hosp., Dayton, 1970-73; asst. to the dean Wright State U., Dayton, 1975-79, asst. to v.p., 1979-81, interim dir. Bolinga Ctr., 1982-85, dir. univ. and community events, 1981—. Mem. allocation com. United Way, Dayton, Dayton Urban League. Mem. AAUW, Meeting Planners Internat. (bd. dirs. Dayton chpt.), Am. Soc. Tng. and Devel., Nat. Coalition of Black Meeting Planners (leader workshops), Soc. Pub. Relations Officers, Nat. Council of Negro Women, Delta Sigma Theta. Democrat. Methodist. Home: 8189 Forney Rd New Lebanon OH 45345 Office: Wright State U 3640 Colonel Glenn Hwy Dayton OH 45435

BORUM, SHERRY LYNN, nurse; b. St. Louis, Aug. 13, 1956; d. Mary Lou (Heinrich) Perkins; m. Michael Dean Casper, June 1, 1974 (div. Mar. 1981); 1 child, Rachael Kaye Casper; m. Art Borum, Oct. 3, 1984. AAS, Kaskaskia Jr. Coll., Centralia, Ill., 1972-74; student, So. Ill. U., 1987—. Nurses' aide Carlyle (Ill.) Healthcare Ctr., 1973-75; staff nurse Jefferson Meml. Hosp., Mt. Vernon, Ill., 1976; office nurse Basch Med. Clinic, Patoka, Ill., 1976, 1979-85; staff nurse Centralia Care Ctr., 1976-77; home health nurse Vis. Nurse Assn., Centralia, 1977-79; staff nurse Pub. Hosp. of Salem, Ill., 1982-83; nurse coordinator Total Health Care, Centralia, 1985—; vol. emergency med. technician Patoka Ambulance Service, 1983-85; instr. Am. Heart Assn., 1983-87. Mem. Nat. League for Nursing, Nat. Assn. Female Execs., Group Health Assn. Am. Republican. Home: 614 W Broadway Centralia IL 62801 Office: Total Health Care Inc 650 W Noleman Centralia IL 62801

BORUP, DODIE TRUMAN, government official; b. Sept. 12, 1938; d. Gordon MacKintosh and Josephine (Kleinhans) Truman; children—David Charles, John William; m. Jerry H. Borup. Student, San Jose State U. Investigative reporter Oakland Tribune, Calif., 1960-68; communications specialist Calif. State Dept. Fin., Sacramento, 1971-74; writer, researcher Deaver & Hannaford, Los Angeles, 1978-79; dir. corr. dept. Reagan-Bush Campaign, Los Angeles, 1979-80; spl. asst. to pres. U.S., The White House,, Washington,, 1981-84; commr. HHS, Washington, 1984—; mem. Nat. Adv. Bd. on Child Abuse and Neglect, 1984—; chmn. prevention and intervention work group Youth Suicide Task Force, HHS; chmn. Fed. Interagy. Task Force of Internat. Youth Yr., 1985; mem., rep. Office of Juvenile Justice and Delinquency Prevention Adv. Com., 1984—; mem. Pres.'s Working Group on th Family; mem. interagy. planning com. Pres.'s Child Safety Partnership and Pres.'s Interagy. Task Force on Adoption; chair communications com. Intra-Deptartmental Council on Indian Affairs; mem. Adv. Com. on Foster Care and Adoption Info.; mem. Nat. Interagy. Steering Com. on Transition into Elem. Sch. Writer Reagan for Pres. campaign, Los Angeles, 1976; sec. Fremont Place Homeowners, Los Angeles, 1980; mem. 43d Assembly Dist. Adv. Com., Los Angeles, 1977-78. Mem. Nat. Fedn. Republican Women, Phi Mu. Mem. Ch. of Jesus Christ of Latter-Day Saints. Office: Dept of Health & Human Services Children Youth & Families 400 6th St SW Washington DC 20201

BORUP, SHIRLEY ANN, risk manager; b. Alvin, Tex., Dec. 17, 1949; d. Claude Chestine and Alice Ruth (Dalbosco) Morris; m. Wilburn Douglas Miller, Oct. 8, 1966 (div. Aug. 1978); children: Wilburn Douglas Jr., Lori Ann; m. James Robert Borup, July 13, 1985. A, Alvin Community Coll., 1979. Med. lab. technologist Lifemark, Alvin, 1979-81; quality assurance and risk mgr. AMI/LMK, Alvin, 1981-84; quality assurance amanager, risk mgr. SCH, Houston, 1984—. Mem. Nat. Assn. of Female Execs., Houston Med.-Legal Soc. Republican. Baptist. Home: 3302 Lazy Lane La Marque TX 77560

BORUT, JOSEPHINE, insurance executive; b. Bridgeport, Conn., Aug. 3, 1942; d. Frank and Catherine (Russo) Occhipinti; m. Arthur Lee Borut, Nov. 22, 1963; 1 child, Adam Seth. BS in Art, Hofstra U., 1964, MA in Humanities, 1971; cert. in mgmt., Adelphi U., 1984. Cert. art tchr., N.Y.S. Art tchr. Cen. Islip (N.Y.) Elementary, 1964-65; coordinator art dept. Mineola (N.Y.) Jr. High, 1965-70; art tchr., coordinator Brandeis Sch., Lawrence, N.Y., 1979-81; mgr. community relations Empire Blue Cross Blue Shield, N.Y.C., 1984-85, mgr. conf. planning, 1985—; freelance artist, East Meadow, 1978-79. Recipient hon. mention L.I. Art Tchrs. Assn. Art Show, 1966, 3d Place art show Hofstra U., 1966, 2d Place East Meadow Pub. Library Juried Art Show, 1979. Mem. Nat. Assn. Female Execs., Am. Soc. of Assn. Execs., Meeting Planners Internat. (bd. dirs. Greater N.Y. chpt., com. chmn.), Am. Soc. Profl and Exec. Women, Ins. Conf. Planners. Home: 1823 Kent St Westbury NY 11590 Office: Empire Blue Cross Blue Shield 622 3d Ave New York NY 10017

BORYSEWICZ, MARY LOUISE, editor; b. Chgo.; d. Thomas J. and Mabel E. (Zeien) O'Farrell; B.A., Mundelein Coll., 1970; postgrad. in English lit. U. Ill, 1970-71; grad. exec. program U. Chgo., 1982; m. Daniel S. Borysewicz, June 11, 1955; children—Mary Adele, Stephen Francis, Paul Barnabas. Editor sci. publs. AMA, Chgo., 1971-73; exec. mng. editor Am. Jour. Ophthalmology, Chgo., 1973—; asst. sec., treas Ophthalmic Pub. Co., 1985—; guest lectr. U. Chgo. Med. Sch., 1979, Harvard U. Med. Sch., 1978, Northwestern U. Med. Sch., 1979, Am. Acad. Ophthalmology, 1976, 81. Mem. Am. Soc. Profl. and Exec. Women, Council Biology Editors (fin. com. 1985—, bd. dirs. 1988—), Bus. Vols. for the Arts (1988—), Internat. Fedn. Sci. Editors Assns. Contbr. articles to sci. publs.; editor: Ophthalmology Principles and Concepts, 6th edit., 1986. Home: 4415 N California Ave Chicago IL 60625 Office: 435 N Michigan Ave Chicago IL 60611

BOS, CAROLE DIANNE, lawyer; b. Grand Rapids, Mich., May 31, 1949; d. James and Alberdean (Kooiker) Berkenpas; m. James Edwin Bos, Apr. 3, 1969; B.A. with high honors, Grand Valley State Coll., 1977; J.D. cum laude, T.M. Cooley Law Sch., Lansing, Mich., 1981. Bar: Mich. 1981. Asst. mgr. Army & Air Force Base Exchange, Soesterberg, Netherlands, 1969-73; mgmt. asst. Selfridge Air Nat. Guard Base, Mt. Clemens, Mich., 1973-74; legal asst. John Boyles, Grand Rapids, 1974-77; law clk. Cholette, Perkins & Buchanan, Grand Rapids, 1977-82; trial atty. Hecht, Buchanan & Cheney, Grand Rapids, 1982-84; ptnr. Buchanan & Bos, Grand Rapids, 1984—; mem. adv. bd. Grand Valley State Coll., 1981—. Co-author: Video Techniques in Trial and Pretrial, 1983, Video Technology: Its Use and Application in Law, 1984, How to Use Video in Litigation, 1986; (co-author) Women Trial Lawyers: How They Succeed in Practice and in the Courtroom, 1986; contbr. articles to profl. jours. Bd. dirs. Jellema Ho., Grand Rapids; trustee Grand Valley State Coll. Found. Breen scholar, 1977. Mem. Grand Rapids Bar Assn. (library com. 1983—), Mich. State Bar Assn. (communications com. 1983—), ABA, Fed. Bar Assn. (regional dir. 1984—), Am. Trial Lawyers Assn. Office: Buchanan & Bos 6th Floor Frey Bldg Grand Rapids MI 49503

BOS, JOCELYN SUSAN, health facility administrator; b. Buffalo, Nov. 21, 1952; d. William Johan and Jocelyn Jeanie (Woodward) B.; m. Keith Alan Fisher, Aug. 15, 1982; children: Hadley Keith, Jocelyn Lauren. BA, U. N.C., 1974; MEd, U. Mass., 1982. Cert. tchr. Mass., Colo. Tchr., coordinator elem./exceptional unit Sch. Dist. 6, Greeley, Colo., 1974-78; asst. dir. basic skills program Riverside Industries, Easthampton, Mass., 1979-80; coordinator community services Dept. Mental Health/Mental Retardation Franklin/Hamphire Area Office, Northampton, Mass., 1980-82; supr. adult residential services N.Y. State Assn. Retarded Children Inc. Erie County Chpt., Buffalo, 1983-84; adminstr. intermediate care facility Geneva B. Scruggs Community Health Care Ctr., Buffalo, 1984-87; dir. Health Related Services People Inc., Buffalo, 1987—; cons. St. Coletta Sch., Jefferson, Wis., 1983—, Children's Hosp., Buffalo, 1984—, DD Long Range Planning Subcom., Buffalo, 1983—, Western N.Y. Community Residential Tng. Consortium, Buffalo, 1983—; mem. infant care rev. com. Buffalo Children's Hosp. Mem. residential subcom. Erie County Long Range Planning Com., day program subcom. Erie County Long Range Planning Com. Mem. AAUW, Am. Assn. Mental Deficiency, Nat. Assn. Female Execs., N.Y. State Community Residential Adminstrs. Home: 9664 Knoll Rd Eden NY 14057 Office: People Inc 320 Central Park Pl Buffalo NY 14214

BOSCHAN, ROBERTA (BOBBIE), retail executive; b. Pasadena, Calif., Jan. 16, 1937; d. Samuel and Sadie (Ganulin) Rice; m. Robert H. Boschan, Dec. 18, 1960; children: Paul, Howard. Student, U. Calif., Berkeley, 1954-56; BA in Edn., UCLA, 1958. Tchr. Beverly Hills (Calif.) Unified Sch. Dist., 1958-60, Culver City (Calif.) Unified Sch. Dist., 1961-66; free-lance designer, writer Los Angeles, 1970-73; direct mail coordinator Instl. Objectives Exchange, Los Angeles, 1973-76, Citizens for John Tunney, Los Angeles, 1976; founder Aprons Only, Los Angeles, 1977; pres. Aprons Only, Inc., Los Angeles, 1979—. Pres. Los Angeles Pub. Utilities & Trans. Commn., 1973-79. Office: Aprons Only Etc 265 Santa Monica Pl Santa Monica CA 90401

BOSKEY, ADELE LUDIN, biochemistry educator, researcher; b. N.Y.C., Aug. 30, 1943; d. Benjamin and Anne (Monoson) Ludin; m. James Bernard Boskey, June 30, 1970; 1 child, Elizabeth Rona. BA, Barnard Coll., N.Y.C., 1964; PhD, Boston U., 1970. Editor Cambridge Data File, England, 1970-71; research fellow The Hosp Spl. Surgery, N.Y.C., 1971-73, asst. scientist, 1973-75; asst. prof. Cornell U. Med. Coll., Ithaca, N.Y., 1973-75, assoc. scientist, 1975-81, assoc. prof. biochemistry, 1977-81, sr. scientist, 1981—, prof. biochemistry, 1986—. Contbr. articles to profl. jours. Recipient NIH merit award Nat. Inst. Dental Research, 1987. Fellow Am. Inst. Chemists; Mem. Orthopaedic Research Soc. (mem. at-large), Internat. Assn. Dental Research (chair constrn. com.), Am. Crystallographic Assn., Sigma Xi. Office: The Hosp Spl Surgery 535 E 70th St New York NY 10021

BOSS, CAROLYNN JOANNE, computer company executive; b. Chgo., Jan. 29, 1955; d. John and Nellie (Brink) B.; 1 child, James Eric. BBA, Elmhurst Coll., 1986. Designer IBM-Rolm Systems, Chgo., 1979-80; from CSR mgr. to dir. installation Rolm Ill., Schaumburg, 1980-86, area mgr., 1986—. Republican. Mem. Christian Reformed Ch. Office: Rolm Ill 1100 Woodfield Rd Schaumburg IL 60195

BOSTED, DOROTHY STACK, public relations executive; b. Newark, Apr. 6, 1953; d. Richard Joseph and Dorothy Marie (Irvin) S.; m. Kenneth James Bosted, Aug. 22, 1976; 1 child, Danielle Whitney. Student, Lyndon State Coll., 1971-73; BA, NYU, 1975. Reporter The Daily Advance, Succasunna, N.J., 1974-75; producer, tech. intern Manhattan Cable TV, N.Y.C., 1975; editorial asst. Calif. Sch. Employees Assn., San Jose, 1975-76; news dir., anchor UA-Columbia Cablevision, Oakland, N.J., 1977-79; dir. pub. relations Overlook Hosp., Summit, N.J., 1981-84; pres. Dorothy Bosted Pub. Relations, Harding Twp., N.J., 1984-86; dir. pub. relations, communications Middlesex County Coll., Edison, N.J., 1986-88; mgr. corp. communications Hoechst Celanese Corp., Bridgewater, N.J., 1988—; ptnr. Bosted-Burton Assocs., Dover, N.J., 1986—; cons. Middletown, N.J., 1986—. Co-author: Writing with Impact, 1986; contbr. articles to N.Y. Times, various mags. Seminar leader Kinnelon (N.J.) Enrichment Program, 1978; trustee Middlesex County Coll. Found., Edison, 1986-88; bd. dirs. Middlesex County Coll. Alumni, 1986-88. Recipient scholarships The Mennen Co., 1971, The Neighborhood House, 1971, Knights of Pythias, 1971, (Tribute to Woman and Industry award Ridgewood N.J. YWCA, 1979), News Program Excellence award Nat. Cable TV Assn., 1979, Percy award N.J. Hosp. Mktg. and Pub. Relations Assn., 1982, 84. Mem. Tribute to Women and Industry Mgmt. Forum (v.p. pub. relations 1986-87), Pub. Relations Soc. Am. (editor NJ chpt. newsletter 1987—), Internat. Assn. Bus. Communicators (Spectrum of Talent Merit award 1982), Council for Advancement Secondary Edn. Republican. Methodist. Home: 225 Clubhouse Dr Middletown NJ 07748 Office: Hoechst Celanese Corp Rt 202-206 N Somerville NJ 08876

BOSTER, JOLYNN BARRY, lawyer, state legislator; b. Maricopa County, Ariz., Aug. 21, 1951; d. Jack and M. Jackie (Hamilton) Barry. B.S., Ohio State U., 1973, J.D., 1976. Bar: Ohio 1976. U.S. Tax Ct. 1976, U.S. Dist. Ct. (so. dist.) Ohio 1977, U.S. Supreme Ct. 1981. Assoc. Emens, Hurd, Kegler & Ritter, Columbus, Ohio, 1976-78; asst. city solicitor City of Gallipolis, Ohio, 1978-81; ptnr. Eachus & Boster, Gallipolis, 1978-81, Cowles & Boster, Gallipolis, 1981—; mem. Ohio Ho. of Reps., Columbus, 1983—. Mem. adv. council Ohio U. Sch. Nursing, Athens, mem. adv. bd. Inst. for Local Govt. Adminstrn. and Rural Devel.; mem. exec. com. Ohio's N.W. Ordinance and U.S. Constn. Bicentennial Commn.; trustee Big Bros./Big Sisters, Gallipolis. Named Woman of Yr., Gallipolis Bus. and Profl. Women, 1983, Mental Health Adv., Athens Hocking Vinton Mental Health Bd., 1984. Mem. Ohio State Bar Assn., ABA, Gallia County Bar Assn., Ohio Assn. Trial Attys. Democrat. Presbyterian. Avocations: jogging; tennis; snow skiing; bicycling. Office: Cowles & Boster Co 26 Locust St Gallipolis OH 45631

BOSTIC, STEPHANIE EVON, public relations executive; b. Jamaica, N.Y., Mar. 22, 1953; d. Joseph Edward and Maud Gertrude (Wilson) B.; 1 child, Charly Evon Simpson. BS in Pub. Communications, Boston U., 1975. Pub. relations asst. U.S. Tennis Assn., N.Y.C., 1975-77, asst. dir. pub. relations, 1977-80, pub. relations coordinator women's circuit, 1983-85; media relations mgr. ASME, 1985-86; pres. Bostic & Small Cons., Inc., 1985-86; editor, writer and pub. info. specialist Stone & Webster Engring. Corp., 1986-87, Doremus Porter Novelli, Garden City, 1987-88, Bostic & Small Cons., Inc., Garden City, 1985—; editorial asst. U.S. Tennis Assn. Player Records, 1975, 76, stats. coordinator U.S. Tennis Assn. Tennis Yearbook, 1976, project editor U.S. Tennis Assn. Player Records, 1977, 78, 79, U.S. Open Tennis Championships Media Guides, 1976, 77, 78, 79; dir. pub. relations Women's Tennis Assn., 1980, D. Parke Gibson Assocs., Inc., N.Y.C., 1981-82; feature writer Queens Tribune, 1981; press-publicity coordinator Mercedes Tournament Champions, World Championship Tennis, 1984. Chmn. pub. relations com., gen. vol. com. 4th Ann. United Negro Coll. Fund/Arthur Ashe Tennis Benefit, 1978; pub. relations-publicity co-coordinator Forest Hills/Pro-Celebrity Tennis Tournament-Juvenile Diabetes Found., 1984; com. mem. Harlem Jr. Tennis Tournament, 1984. Mem. Nat. Assn. Media Women (dir. publicity Met. N.Y. chpt. 1979), Nat. Coalition 100 Black Women, Pub. Relations Soc. Am. (com. on minorities), Boston U. Sch. Pub. Relations Alumni Assn., (CEBA awards judge), Delta Sigma Theta. Home: 412 Old Country Rd Garden City NY 11530

BOSTON, LEONA, organization executive; b. Joliet, Ill., Aug. 4, 1914; d. Dorie Philip and Margaret (Mitchell) B. Student LaSalle Extension U., 1936-37, 1946, U. Chgo., 1944-45. Tchr., Nat. Stenotype Sch., Chgo., 1937; stenotypist Rotary Internat., Evanston, Ill., 1937-44, sec. to comptroller, 1944-50, head personnel dept., 1950-65, exec. asst. to gen. sec., 1965-77, mem. exec. com. North Shore Festival of Faith, Northfield, Ill., 1978. Bd. dirs. YWCA, Evanston, 1961-63. Mem. Bus. Profl. Women's Club Evanston (chmn. fin. com. 1977-78). Evangelical (fin. sec. Bible Ch., Winnetka 1965-68, treas. 1979-80). Club: Zonta (Evanston)(v.p., chmn. program com. 1969-70, pres. 1970-71, chmn. membership com. 1976-78, historian 1979-84, mem. past pres.' com. 1972—, mem. fin. com. 1985—, chmn. fin. com. 1987—). Home and Office: 350 W Schaumburg Rd Schaumburg IL 60194

BOSWELL, WINTHROP PALMER, writer; b. Bklyn., Dec. 17, 1922; d. Carleton Humphries and Winthrop (Bushnell) Palmer; B.A., Smith Coll., 1943; postgrad. U. S.C., 1956-58; M.A., San Francisco State Coll., 1969; m. James Orr Boswell, Oct. 26, 1946; children—James Lowell, Rosalind Palmer, John Winthrop. Research asst. G-2 Spl. Br., U.S. Army, 1943-46; research asst. Hoover Instn., Stanford, Calif., 1976; docent Filoli, 1979-80; books include The Roots of Irish Monasticism, 1970; Irish Wizards in the Woods of Ethiopia, 1971; The Snake in the Grove, 1972; The Killing of the Snake King in Abyssinia, 1973; Hisperica Famina or The Garden of God, 1974; Bruce and the Question of Geomancy at Axum: The Evidence from the Norman Bayeux Tapestry, 1986. Mem. Soc. History of Discoveries, Medieval Assn. of Pacific, Societe Francaise pour les Etudes Ethiopiennes. Club: Peninsula Country (San Mateo, Calif.), Francisca (San Francisco).

BOTHELLO, PAMELA KAY, engineering administrator; b. Auburn, Calif., Sept. 21, 1959. BS, San Diego State U., 1981. Employee relations specialist San Diego Employers Assn., 1981-83; programmer Jack D. Eberl, CPA, San Diego, 1983; programer Q.S.A., San Diego, 1984; sales support mgr. Parron Hall Office Interiors, San Diego, 1986-87; analyst engring. documentation Gen. Dynamics, San Diego, 1984-86, sr. engring adminstr., 1987—. Mem. Nat. Assn. Female Execs.

BOTTARI, HELEN CAROL, marketing professional; b. N.Y.C., Jan. 6, 1959; d. Andrea Paul and Helen Bottari. BS, St. Thomas Aquinas Coll., 1981. Dental cons. Healthco Dental Internat., N.Y.C., 1981-83; equipment cons. Saslow Dental Corp., South Hackensack, N.J., 1983; dental sales rep. Xerox Med. Systems, Paramus, N.J., 1983-84; terrtory mktg. rep. US Mktg. Group, Xerox Corp., Oradell, N.J., 1984—; dir. St. Thomas Aquinas Coll. Alumni Network, Sparkill, N.Y., 1985—. Mem. Nat. Assn. Female Execs., St. Thomas Aquinas Coll. Alumni Assn. (treas. 1982—).

BOTTARI, MARIANNA TERESA, public relations executive, fund raiser, editor; b. Phila., Nov. 17, 1941; d. Guido Albert and Malvina Rose (Seccia) B. Student U. Pa., 1962-64, Charles Morris Price Sch. Journalism and Advt., 1964-66. News relations asst. Smith Kline & French Labs., Phila., 1962-64; pub. relations asst. St. Luke's and Children's Med. Ctr., Phila., 1964-66, Thomas Jefferson U. Hosp., Phila., 1969-71; pub. relations dir. Albert Einstein Med. Ctr., Phila., 1971-74, John Muir Meml. Hosp., Walnut Creek, Calif., 1974-77, Peralta Hosp., Oakland, Calif., 1977-80; community relations and devel. dir. Sequoia Hosp., Redwood City, Calif., 1980-82; community relations and mktg. dir. Valley Meml. Hosp., Livermore, Calif., 1982-84; owner PR Woman & Co. Bd. dirs. Coop. Center Council, 1976-77; v.p. Sun Country Homeowners Assn., 1977-79. bd. dirs. Yqnacio Terr. Homeowners Assn., 1986—. Served with USNR, 1979-81. Recipient MacEachern nat. citation, 1973, MacEachern cert. of merit, 1976. Mem. Acad. Hosp. Pub. Relations, Hosp. Pub. Relations Assn. No. Calif., Internat. Assn. Bus. Communicators, Nat. Assn. Hosp. Devel., Nat. Assn. Female Execs. Office: 101 Kinross Dr #4 Walnut Creek CA 94598

BOTTENBERG, JOYCE HARVEY, social services executive; b. Melrose, Mass., June 29, 1945; d. Robert Willis and Amy Sheppard (Wood) Harvey; 1 child, Joanne Harvey; m. Norman G. Bottenberg, 1985. BA, U. Mass., 1967, diploma grad. journalism program, 1969; diploma, Simmons Coll. Grad. Sch. Mgmt., 1984. Cert. social worker, Mass. Sr. tech. writer Itek Corp., Lexington, Mass., 1967-70; dir. pub. info. Walla Walla (Wash.) Community Coll., 1970; profl. interviewer McGraw Hill Research, N.Y.C., 1971-73; coordinator pub. relations James B. Rendle Assocs., Malden, Mass., 1973-76; exec. dir. ARC, Melrose, Mass., 1976-80, regional mgr., 1980-84; regional mgr. ARC, Lynn, Mass., 1984-85; tech. writer Municipality of Met. Seattle, 1985-86; exec. dir. Epilepsy Assn. Western Wash., Seattle, 1986-87; dir. devel. ARC, Seattle, 1988—. Chmn. adv. bd. Mass. Dept. Pub. Welfare Community Service Area; mem. Melrose Mayor's Energy Commn.; civic adv. bd. Met. Bank and Trust; instr. 1st aid, CPR, ARC; merit badge counselor Boy Scouts Am. New Eng. Newspaper fellow, 1969; Cert. of merit ARC, 1981. Mem. AAUW, DAR, Nat. Conf. Social Welfare, Soc. Mayflower Descendents, Nat. Assn. Female Execs., Soc. Tech. Communications, Nat. Ski Patrol System (sr. patroller), Alpha Phi Gamma. Episcopalian. Lodge: Zonta. Home: 2205 197th Ave SE Issaquah WA 98027 Office: 1900 25th Ave S PO Box 24286 Seattle WA 98124

BOTTGE, PEGGY ANN, gas company administrator; b. Mount Kisco, N.Y., Sept. 7, 1956; d. Otto William and Anna Marie (Mazza) B. Service mgr. Suburban Propane Gas, Millerton, N.Y., 1981-82, office-service mgr., 1982-83, dist. mgr., 1983-86; dist. mgr. Suburban Propane Gas, Saratoga Springs, N.Y., 1986—. Mem. N.Y. Gas Assn., Saratoga C. of C. Republican. Baptist. Office: Suburban Propane Gas 610 Maple Ave PO Box 364 Saratoga Springs NY 12866

BOTTICELLE, MARIE JOHNSON, infosystems specialist; b. DeKalb County, Ind., July 29, 1940; d. Edward R. Johnson and Emogene Emrick Sowle; m. James T. Botticelli, Jan. 30, 1971 (div. 1976); 1 child, Stanley E. Alger. BS, Manchester Coll., N. Manchester, Ind., 1962; MS, U. Wisc., Milw., 1976. Tchr. pub. schs. Ind., Wisc., 1962-67; programmer Blue Cross and Blue Sheild, Milw., 1967-68, trng. coordinator, 1969-71; sytems rep. Burroughs Corp., Milw., 1976-79, sytems specialist, 1979-81, dist. mktg. supt. mgr., 1982-84; mgr. tech. services Milw. Pub. Schs., 1984—. Active Women's Polit. Caucus, Women's Coalition. Mem. NOW, Am. Mgmt. Assn., Data Processing Mgmt Assn., Assn. Profl. Women, Telecommunications Profls. Wis., Wis. Telecom Assn. Office: Milw Pub Schls Drawer 10K Milwaukee WI 47587

BOTTOM, DORIS ALLENE, educator; b. Weatherford, Okla., Aug. 4, 1936; d. Aubrey Daniel and Buena Vista (Wilson) Shewmaker; m. George Grayson Bottom, Oct. 9, 1955; children: Earl Grayson, Paula Allene, Allen Elwood, Jo Ann. BS in Elem. Edn., Southwestern Okla. State U., 1969, BS in Bus. Edn., 1986, MEd, 1987; postgrad., U. Fla., 1973-75. Cert. tchr. Fla., Okla. Tchr. Duvall Pub. Sch., Jacksonville, Fla., 1969, Baker County Pub. Sch., Macclenny, Fla., 1969-81; prin. Sew-N-Nook, Macclenny, Fla., 1977-79; tchr. Hammon (Okla.) Pub. Sch., 1981—. Mem. Okla. Edn. Assn., Fla. Edn. Assn. (bd. dirs. 1977), NEA, Okla. Edn. Microcomputer Assn., Nat. Bus. Edn. Assn., Assn. Classroom Tchrs., Okla. Bus. Edn. Assn., Delta Kappa Gamma. Democrat. Mem. Ch. Christ. Home: Rte 1 Box 146A Hammon OK 73650 Office: Hammon Pub School 8th & Common St Box 279 Hammon OK 73650

BOUCHARD, MAY BLANCHETTE, elementary educator; b. Eagle Lake, Maine, May 15, 1947; d. Odeo and Bertha (Gallant) Blanchette; m. Ellery W. Bouchard, June 15, 1968; children: Michael Ellery, Lori Anne. BS, U. Maine, 1968; M, U. Maine, Orono, 1973, cert. advanced study, 1976; EdD, Nova U., 1986—. Cert. elem. tchr., Maine. Tchr. 2d grade Maine sch. Adminstrv. Unit #33, Frenchville, 1968-76, Maine Sch. Adminstrv. Unit #31, Howland, 1976-83; media specialist Maine Sch. Adminstrv. Unit #24, Van Buren, 1983-87; tchr. for tchrs. aide course U. Maine, Presque Isle, 1987—. Editor: Odds n' Ends Read em and Like em, 1984-88. Dir. Reading is Fundamental, Van Buren, 1984—. Mem. Maine Reading Assn. (bd. dirs. region 1 1983-87), Van Buren Tchrs. Assn., Maine Sch. Adminstrv. Unit #33 Tchr. Assn. (pres. 1974-75), Delta Kappa Gamma (v.p. Pi chpt. 1982-83, v.p. Rho chpt. 1974-76, 84-86, pres. 1986—), Aroostook Right to Read (bd. dirs. 1983-87). Democrat. Roman Catholic. Home: 26 Poplar St Van Buren ME 04785 Office: Gateway Elem Sch Wright St Van Buren ME 04785

BOUCHER, ANNE CAREY, public relations consultant; b. Balt., Feb. 1, 1938; d. James III and Mary Lewis (Hall) Carey; m. William Boucher III, May 26, 1962. Student, Sarah Lawrence Coll., 1955-56, Md. Inst. Art,

1956-58. Asst. fashion stylist Hutzler Bros., Balt., 1956-57; mgr. Doroty Lamour Cosmetics, Balt., 1960-61; pres. Jolie Maison Inc., Balt., 1963-66, Anne Boucher & Assocs., Balt., 1983-85, Boucher & Assocs., Balt., 1986—; ptnr. Barry, Boucher & Yuhanick, Balt., 1988—; cons. communications RTKL Inc., Balt., 1966-67; advt. dir./owner Balt. Scene mag., 1980-83; sec./treas. Westfalls Devel. Corp., Balt., 1986—. Bd. dirs. Med. Eye Bank Md. Inc., 1967-85, chmn. 1970-75; bd. dirs. Commerce and Industry Combined Health Appeal, 1968, Balt. Forward Trust Inc., 1972-74, Balt. Assn. for Visually Handicapped, 1976, Balt. chpt. ARC, 1983—, S.T.E.P. Inc., 1987—, Renewal Inc.; chmn. Md. Commn. on Status Women, 1970-75; chmn./co-chmn. CARE Com. Greater Balt., 1975-84, hon. chmn., 1986—; treas. Friends of Govt. House, 1979-87; trustee Balt. Mus. Art, 1982-85; active other civic orgns. Named One of Outstanding Women Balt. County, AAUW, 1976. Mem. Delta Kappa Gamma (life hon.). Democrat. Home: 1900 Western Run Rd Cockeysville MD 21030 Office: Boucher & Assocs 15 Charles Plaza Suite 203 Baltimore MD 21201

BOUCHER, CELESTE SUZETTE, human resources executive; b. Great Lakes, Ill., Mar. 23, 1956; d. Thomas Louis Sr. and Mary Helen (Marr) B. Cert. in Profl. Mgmt., Lake Forest Coll., 1988. Human resources asst. MCC Powers, Northbrook, Ill., 1980-82, supr. human resources adminstrn., 1982-84, mgr. human resources, 1984-86, mgr. dept. benefits and compensation, 1986-87; mgr. dept. benefits and compensation Dynascan Corp., Chgo., 1987-88, dir. human resources, 1988—. Mem. Am. Soc. for Personnel Adminstrn., Soc. Human Resources Profl., Am. Compensation Assn. (cert.), Midwest Personnel Mgmt. Assn., Nat. Assn. Female Execs. Republican. Roman Catholic. Office: Dynascan Corp 6460 W Cortland St Chicago IL 60635

BOUDREAU, NANCY ANNA, banker; b. Portola, Calif., Oct. 29, 1947; d. William Ellis and Hazel Harriett (Sanders) Bennett; m. James Louis Boudreau, Apr. 2, 1966; children: Rene' Christine, Jamie Danielle. Student, U. Wis., River Falls, 1966, U. Wis., Stevens Point, 1965-67; BA, Winona State U., 1975. Instr. evening sch. Western Wis. Tech. Inst., La Crosse, 1972-75; youth placement specialist Job Service Wis., La Crosse, 1975-82; human resource officer First Bank La Crosse, 1982-83, asst. v.p. ops. and human resources, 1983-84, asst. v.p., 1984-86; v.p. ops. First Bank of Platteville (Wis.), 1986-87, exec. v.p., 1987—, also bd. dirs.; instr. Am. Inst. Bankers, Madison, Wis., 1985—; corp. sec. First Nat. Bank of Platteville, 1988—; bd. dirs. Platteville Area Indsl. Devel. Corp. Contbr. articles to profl. jours. Pres. YMCA, La Crosse, 1985; co-chmn. YM-YW Joint Exec. Com., La Crosse, 1985; div. chmn. United Way, La Crosse, 1980-86; bd. dirs. Luth. Hosp. Corp., La Crosse, 1986. Grantee Coop. Ednl. Services Agy., 1974-75. Mem. Am. Soc. Personnel Adminstrs., Wis. Bankers Assn. (bd. dirs., treas. bank mktg. sect. 1988), La Crosse Area Personnel Assn. (pres. elect 1986), Greater L Crosse C. of C., Platteville C. of C. (bd. dirs., pres. elect). Republican. Methodist. Club: AVANT Women in Bus. Leadership (La Crosse). Lodges: Rotary (Platteville), Rotary Internat. Office: First Nat Bank of Platteville 170 W Main St Platteville WI 53818

BOUDREAUX, GLORIA MARIE, nurse; b. Lafayette, La., May 2, 1935; d. Simon Zepherin and Orta Marie (Pierret) B. Diploma in nursing, Charity Hosp. Sch., 1962; BA, St. Edward's U., 1974; MS, Tex. Women's U., 1976. Head surg., med. nurse Lafayette (La.) Charity Hosp., 1962-65; psychiat. staff nurse VA Hosp., New Orleans, 1968-72; psychiatric nurse U.S. Army Nurse Corp., San Francisco and Augusta, Ga., 1966-67; instr. Tex. Woman's Univ. Sch. of Nursing, Houston, 1976-80; clin. specialist VA Med. Ctr., Houston, 1980-87; psychiatric nursing coordinator Spring Shadows Glen, Houston, 1987—. Served to col. with U.S. Army, 1966—. Mem. Reserve Officers Assn. (chpt. pres. 1981-83), Assn. Mil. Surgeons of U.S., Am. Nurses Assn. (cert. in psychiatric mental health nursing), Sigma Theta Tau. Home: 509 Brand Ln #104 Stafford TX 77477

BOUDRIS, JANET LYNN, marketing professional; b. Balt., July 22, 1954; d. Adam Danielevicz and Loretta Regina (Wooden) B.; m. Thomas Edward Goodrich, Aug. 23, 1986. BA, U. Md., Balt., 1976; cert., Goethe Inst., Munich, 1977; MA, Johns Hopkins U., 1978. Asst. dean of students U. Md., Balt., 1976; editorial asst. Am. Soc. Internat. Law, Washington, 1976-78; sec. We. Union Co., Washington, 1978-79; bus. analyst We. Union Co., Upper Saddle River, N.J., 1978-80, mgr. carrier relations, 1980, mgr. product info., 1980-82, mgr. product internat. TLX, 1982-84, sr. product mktg. mgr., 1983-84, asst. V.P., product line mgr., 1984, v.p., product line mgr., 1984-86, v.p. industry mktg., 1986—. Contbr. articles to profl. jours. Mem. NOW, Nat. Assn. Female Execs., Phi Kappa Phi. Democrat. Office: Western Union 1 Lake St Upper Saddle River NJ 07458

BOULANGER, DEBRA ANN, marketing executive, information technology specialist; b. Pawtucket, R.I., Oct. 9, 1956; d. Robert N. and Joyce P. (DeFontes) B.; m. Paul Thomas Miner, July 7, 1979 (div. Nov. 1984); m. Neal Marshall Goldsmith, Sept. 21, 1986. BS in Edn. and Clin. Psychology, Lesley Coll., 1978. Master tchr. Coop. Ednl. Services, Wilton, Conn., 1978-82; adminstrv. asst. N. Dean Meyer & Assocs., Ridgefield, Conn., 1983-84, mktg. mgr., 1984-86; account rep. Western region Gartner Group, Inc., Stamford, Conn., 1986-87, account exec. So. New England, 1987—; cons. advanced office automation, Stamford. Home: 79 Harbor Dr Stamford CT 06902 Office: Gartner Group Inc 56 Top Gallant Rd Stamford CT 06902

BOULANGER, LOUISE S., legal services professional; b. Aberdeen, Miss., Feb. 14, 1931; d. Roy Edward and Clarene (Guin) Smith; m. Richard Stuard, July 27, 1953 (div. 1976); children: Barbara, Richard; m. Eugene P. Boulanger (dec.). Student, Office Tng. Sch., 1950; BBA, Memphis State U., 1982. Legal sec. Poore, Cox, Baker & McCauley, Knoxville, Tenn., 1952-55, Moses, McClellan, Arnold, Owen & McDermott, Little Rock, 1955-61, Whitten, Harrell & Wilcox, Abilene, Tex., 1961-67, Murray, Scott, McGavick & Graves, Tacoma, 1966-67; legal sec. McDonald, Kuhn, Smith, Miller & Tait, Memphis, 1967-70, legal adminstr., 1970-87. Pres. Recreation Services for the Handicapped, Memphis, 1986-87. Mem. Memphis Assn. Legal Adminstrs. (past sec.). Democrat. Baptist. Club: Pilot (Memphis). Home: 5618 Clarke Address Memphis TN 38115 Office: McDonald Kuhn Smith Miller & Tait 81 Monroe 2d floor PO Box 3160 Memphis TN 38173-0160

BOULANGER, MARY JANET, accountant; b. Martin, S.D., Sept. 7, 1950; d. James Mike and Claradel (Tellifero) Pich; m. Floyd Terkildsen, Mar., 1967 (div. 1969); 1 child, Larry Paul; m. Loren Lee Boulanger, Aug. 11, 1972; 1 child, Jon Christian. BS in Math., Natural Sci., U. Wyo., 1986. Dental asst. Jerome L. Behounek, DDS, Casper, 1973-74; teller Hilltop Nat. Bank, Casper, 1974-75; accts. maintenance clk. Soil Conservation Service, Casper, 1975-76; acctg. clk. U.S. Geol. Survey, Casper, 1976-79; acctg. technician U.S. Dept. of Energy, Casper, 1979-85, staff acct., 1985—; Dept. of Energy rep. Women's Exec. Leadership Program, 1988. Active vol. Big Bros./Big Sisters, Casper, 1977-78, Home Sch. Assn. Cresthill Elem. various programs, Casper, 1983—, Casper Jr. Baseball league, 1986—, Casper Amateur Hockey Assn., 1986—; instr. Presidential Classroom for Young Ams., Alexandria, Va., 1987. Recipient Outstanding Performance award Naval Petroleum and Oil Shale Res., Washington, 1983, 84; named Outstanding Tech. Employee, Fed. Exec. Council, 1985, Female Civil Servant of the Yr., Fed. Exec. Council, 1986. Mem. Nat. Assn. Female Execs., Am. Legion Aux. (Martin). Republican. Baptist. Office: US Dept of Energy 800 Werner Ct Suite 342 Casper WY 82601

BOULDES, RUTH IRVING, public relations executive; b. N.Y.C., Nov. 22, 1946; d. Charles Ullman Bouldes and Fannye (Irving) Gibbs. BBA, Bernard Baruch Coll., 1975; MBA, Fordham U., 1977. Various mktg. positions Overseas div. Gen. Motors, N.Y.C., 1965-78; dist. mgr. Denmark div. Gen. Motors, Copenhagen, 1978-79; mgr. dealer devel. US Cars div. Gen. Motors, Antwerp, Belgium, 1979-81; mgr. new bus. devel. Adam Opel div. Gen. Motors Corp., Fed. Republic Germany, 1981-82; asst. zone mgr. Chevrolet Motor div. Gen. Motors Corp., Detroit, 1983-84, Mpls., 1984-86; northeast pub. relations mgr. Chevrolet Motor div. Gen. Motors Corp., Purchase, N.Y., 1986—. bd. dirs., chairperson pub. relations com. Campfire, Inc., Danbury, Conn., 1986—. Mem. Internat. Motor Press Assn., Washington Automotive Press Assn., Nat. Coalition of 100 Black Women. Office: Gen Motors Corp Chevrolet Motor Div 2500 Westchester Ave Purchase NY 10577

BOULDING, ELISE MARIE, sociologist, educator; b. Oslo, Norway, July 6, 1920; came to U.S., 1923, naturalized, 1929; d. Joseph and Birgit (Johnsen) Biorn-Hansen; m. Kenneth Boulding; Aug. 31, 1941; children: John Russell, Mark David, Christine Ann, Philip Daniel, William Frederic. B.A., Douglass Coll., 1940; M.S., Iowa State Coll., 1949; Ph.D., U. Mich., 1969. Research asso. Survey Research Inst., U. Mich., 1957-58, Mental Health Research Inst., 1959-60; research devel. sec. Center for Research on Conflict Resolution, 1960-63; prof. sociology, project dir. Inst. Behavioral Sci., U. Colo., Boulder, 1967-78; Montgomery vis. prof. Dartmouth Coll., 1978-79, chmn. dept. sociology, 1979-85, prof. emerita, 1985—; mem. program adv. council Human and Social Devel. Program, UN Univ., 1977-80; mem. governing council, 1980-86. Translator: Polak Image of the Future, 1961; author: From a Monastery Kitchen, 1976, (with Nuss, Carson and Greenstein) Handbook of International Data on Women, 1976, The Underside of History: A View of Women Through Time, 1976, Women in Twentieth Century World, 1977, (with Passmore and Gassler) Bibliography on World Conflict and Peace, 1979, (with Burgess and K. Boulding) Social System of Planet Earth, 1980, Children's Rights and the Wheel of Life, 1980, (with Moen, Lilleydahl and Palm) Women and the Social Costs of Economic Development, 1981, Building a Global Civic Culture: Education for an Interdependent World, 1988. Internat. chairperson Womens Internat. League for Peace and Freedom, 1967-70; mem. Internat. Com. for a Just World Peace, 1984—; mem. Exploratory Project on Conditions for Peace, 1984—; mem. U.S. Commn. for UNESCO, 1978-84, mem. UNESCO Peace Prize jury, 1980-87. Recipient Disting. Achievement award Douglass Coll., 1973, Ted Lentz Peace prize, 1977, Nat. Woman of Conscience award, 1980; Danforth fellow, 1965-67. Mem. AAAS, AAUP, Am. Sociol. Assn. (Jessie Bernard award 1982), Internat. Sociol. Assn., Internat. Peace Research Assn. (newsletter editor 1983-87), World Future Studies Fedn., World Future Soc., Colo. Women's Forum. Quaker. Home: 624 Pearl St Apt 206 Boulder CO 80302

BOUNDS, NANCY, modeling and talent company executive; b. Rodney, Ark.; d. William Thomas and Mary Jane (Fields) Southard; m. Robert S. Bounds, 1960 (div. 1965); 1 child, Ronnie Jean; m. Mark Curtis Sconce, Nov. 28, 1972. Student Northwestern U., 1950. Exec. dir. Internat. Fashion/Modeling Assn., N.Y.C., 1978; founding pres. Internat. Talent and Model Schs. Assn., N.Y.C., 1979-80; pres. Nancy Bounds Internat., Omaha, 1959—. Contbr. articles to profl. jours. Producer TV Heart Fund Auction, 1965; chairperson Douglas/Sarpy County Heart Assn., Omaha, 1966, 73-74. Recipient Nat. Tchr.'s award MiLady Pub. Co., 1965, Outstanding Service award Mayor of Omaha, 1984, Uta Halee Girls Village, 1983-87, March of Dimes service award, 1977, 84, Toys for Tots service award, 1986, Muscular Dystrophy citation of merit, 1982. Mem. Internat. Models and Talent Assn. Unitarian. Avocations: reading, painting, travel, golf, tournament bridge. Home and Office: 4803 Davenport Omaha NE 68132

BOUNDS, SARAH ETHELINE, historian; b. Huntsville, Ala., Nov. 5, 1942; d. Leo Deltis and Alice Etheline (Boone) Bounds; A.B., Birmingham-So. Coll., 1963; M.A., U. Ala., Tuscaloosa, 1965, Ed.S. in History, 1971, Ph.D., 1977. Tchr. social studies Huntsville City Schs., 1963, 65-66, 71-74; residence hall adv., dir. univ. housing U. Ala., Tuscaloosa, 1963-65, 68-71; instr. history N.E. State Jr. Coll., Rainsville, Ala., 1966-68; instr. history U. Ala., Huntsville, 1975, 78-80, 85—, dir. Weeden House Mus., 1981-83; asst. prof. edn., supr. student tchrs. U. North Ala., Florence, 1978. Mem. AAUW, Assn. Tchrs. Educators, Nat. Council Tchrs. Social Studies, NEA, Ala. Hist. Assn., Ala. Assn. Historians, Ala. Assn. Tchrs. Educators, Huntsville Hist. Soc., Historic Huntsville Found., Alpha Delta Kappa, Kappa Delta Pi, Phi Alpha Theta. Methodist. Club: Huntsville Pilot. Home: 1100 Bob Wallace Ave SE Huntsville AL 35801

BOURDEAU, MARGARET M., city clerk; b. Albany, N.Y., May 29, 1964; d. Joseph Peter and Mary Jane (Vail) M.; m. David M. Bourdeau, May 30, 1987. Student, Bay Path Jr. Coll., Long Meadow, Mass., 1984. Asst. mgr. Brooks Fashions, Schenectady, N.Y., 1984; dep. city clk. City of Rensselaer (N.Y.), 1984-86, city clk., 1986—. Mem. Internat. Inst. of Mcpl. Clks., N.Y. State Assn. Women Officeholders. Democrat. Roman Catholic. Home: 201 Washington Ave Rensselaer NY 12144

BOURGAULT, LISE, Canadian legislator; b. St. Pamphile, Que., Can., June 5, 1950. Student, U. Laval, École Nat. d'Adminstrn. Pub. Mem. Can. Ho. of Commons, 1984—. Contbr. articles to profl. publs. Mem. Homeowners Assn. Que. (dir. gen.), Assn. des Proprietaires de Logements Locatifs du Que. (founding pres.). Mem. Progressive Conservative Party. Address: 230 Mary St, Lachute, PQ Canada J8H 2C6 *

BOURGELAIS, DONNA CHAMBERLAIN, medical research company executive; b. Battle Creek, Mich., May 20, 1948. BS, MIT, 1970. Sr. research scientist Avco-Everett Research Lab., Everett, Mass., 1970-82; dir. research Laakmann Electro-Optics, San Juan Capistrano, Calif., 1982-83; pres. Med. Laser Research & Devel., Malden, Mass., 1983—. Contbr. more than 30 articles on laser physics and medical uses of lasers to profl. jours. Mem. AAAS, Optical Soc. Am., Am. Soc. for Laser Medicine and Surgery, Soc. Photo Optical Instrumentation Engrs. Office: Med Laser Research & Devel Corp PO Box 539 Malden MA 02148-0005

BOURGEOIS, LOUISE, sculptor; b. Paris, Dec. 25, 1911; came to U.S., 1938, naturalized, 1953; d. Louis and Josephine (Fauriaux) B.; m. Robert Goldwater, Sept. 12, 1938; children: Michel, Jean-Louis, Alain. Baccalaureat Ecole des Beaux Arts, U. Paris, 1934; postgrad., École du Louvre, 1936, 37, 38, Academie Ranson (Atelier Bissiere), 1936-37, Academie de la Grand Chaumiere (Atelier Vlerick), 1937-38, Academie Julian; also with, Fernand Legar, 1938; D.F.A. (hon.), Yale U., 1977. Docent Louvre, 1937-38; teaching asst. Atelier Yves Brayer, Grande Chaumiere, 1937, 38; tchr. Great Neck (NY) Schs., program, 1960, Bklyn. Coll., 1963-68; tchr. Pratt Inst., 1965-67, Goddard Coll., 1970. One-woman shows include, Norlyst Gallers, 1947, Peridot Gallery, 1949, 50, 53, Allan Frumkin Gallery, Chgo., 1953, White Art Mus., Cornell U., Ithaca, N.Y., 1959, Stable Gallery, 1964, Rose Fried Gallery, 1964, Mus. Modern Art, N.Y.C., 1982, Akron Art Mus., 1983, Contemporary Art Mus., Houston, 1983, Daniel Weinberg Gallery, Los Angeles, 1984, Robert Miller Gallery, 1984, Serpentine Gallery, London, 1985, Naeght-Lelong, Zurich, 1985, Paris, 1985; exhibited in numerous group shows, U.S., Europe, including 64th Whitney Biennial, 1987; represented in permanent collections Mus. Modern Art, N.Y.C., Whitney Mus., R.I. Sch. Design, NYU, also pvt. collections; works reproduced in Contemporary Sculpture (Giedion Welker), 1955, Sculpture of This Century (Michel Seuphor), 1959, Form and Space (Trier), 1961, A Concise History of Modern Sculpture, (Herbert Read), 1964, Modern American Sculpture (Dore Ashton), 1968, History of Modern Art (H.H. Arnason), 1968, What is Modern Sculpture, 1969, Sculpture in Wood (J.C. Rich), 1970, numerous others, also various mags. Recipient Pres.'s Fellow award R.I. Sch. Design, 1984. Mem. Sculptors Guild, Am. Abstract Artists, Coll. Art Assn., Women's Caucus (Outstanding Achievement award 1980), La Jeune Sculpture, Paris. Address: care Robert Miller Gallery 41 E 57th St New York NY 10022-1908

BOURNE, MARY BONNIE MURRAY (MRS. SAUL HAMILTON BOURNE), music publishing company executive; b. Salix, Iowa, Sept. 13, 1903; d. Thomas William and Kathryn (McDermott) Murray; student Morningside Normal Coll., 1922-23; student Am. Banking Inst., N.Y.C.; m. Saul Hamilton Bourne, Apr. 12, 1928; 1 dau., Mary Elizabeth. Appeared with George White Scandals, Ramblers, Cocoanuts, Ziegfield Follies, 1925-28; owner, mgr. Bourne Co., N.Y.C., 1960—. Mem. social work recruiting com. United Hosp. Fund. Trustee S.H. Bourne Found., Coll. New Rochelle; trustee N.Y. Infirmary, 1945—, chmn. social service youth bd., 1947—, bd. visitors Sch. Music, Catholic U. Am., Washington. Mem. A.S.C.A.P. (dir., pubs. adv. com.). Home: 14 E 75th St New York NY 10021 Office: 5 W 37th St New York NY 10016

BOURNE, VICTORIA TYSON, speech pathologist; b. Bluefield, W.Va., Aug. 2, 1952; d. John Calvin and Mildred Norita (Gallien) Tyson; m. G. Steve Bourne Jr., July 12, 1975; children: Ryan S., Hillary K. BS, W.Va. U., 1974; MS, Vanderbilt U., 1975. Speech/language pathologist Mercer County Bd. Edn., Princeton, W.Va., 1975-83; pvt. practice speech/language pathologist Bluefield, 1981—; speech/language pathologist Contemporary Care, Inc., Bluefield, 1981—, Glenwood Nursing Home, Princeton, 1981—, Mercer County Health Ctr., Bluefield, 1985—, St. Lukes Hosp., Bluefield, 1987—. Vol. Am. Cancer Soc., Bluefield, 1984-87. Mem. DAR, Am. Speech and Hearing Assn. (cert. clin. competence). Republican. Presbyterian. Office: 308 North St Bluefield WV 24701

BOURQUE, LINDA ANNE BROOKOVER, public health educator; b. Indpls., Aug. 25, 1941; d. Wilbur Bone and Edna Mae (Eberhart) Brookover; m. Don Philippe Bourque, June 3, 1966 (div. Nov. 1974). BA, Ind. U., 1963; MA, Duke U., 1964, PhD, 1968. Postdoctoral researcher Duke U., Durham, N.C., 1968-69; asst. prof. sociology Calif. State U., Los Angeles, 1969-72; asst. prof. to assoc. prof. pub. health UCLA, 1972-86, prof. pub. health, 1986—, acting assoc. dir. Inst. for Social Sci. Research, 1981-82. Contbr. articles to profl. jours. Violoncellist with Santa Monica (Calif.) Symphony Orch., 1978—, Los Angeles Doctors' Symphony, 1981—. Mem. Am. Sociol. Assn. (mem. med. sociology sect. council 1975-78, co-chmn. com. freedom research and teaching, 1975-78, cert. recognition 1980), Pacific Sociol. Assn. (co-chmn. program com. 1982, v.p. 1983), Am. Pub. Health Assn. (mem. standing com. on status of women 1974-76), Sociologists for Women in Society, Am. Assn. Pub. Opinion Research, Assn. Research in Vision and Ophthalmology, Delta Omega, Phi Alpha Theta. Home: 817 Venezia Ave Venice CA 90291 Office: UCLA Sch Pub Health Los Angeles CA 90024

BOUSLEY, GLORIA DIANE PARRISH, educator; b. Evansville, Ind., Dec. 3, 1932; d. Thomas Clifford Parrish and Cecelia Elizabeth (Graul) Parrish Armstrong; B.A. in Bus. Edn., Evansville Coll., 19S3; M.S. in Bus. Edn., Ind. U., 1958; Ph.D. in Occupational Edn., So. Ill. U., 1977; m. Donald R. Bousley, Aug. 2, 1958 (dec.). Guidance counselor, bus. tchr. Bridgeport (Ill.) Twp. High Sch., 1953-71; bus. tchr., chmn. bus. and human devel. div. Olney (Ill.) Central Coll., 1971—; adj. asst. prof. vocat. studies So. Ill. U., Carbondale, 1979—; mem. Ill. State Adv. Panel for Coop. Edn. at Post Secondary Level, 1979; mem. U. Ill./Ill. State Bd. of Edn. Staff Devel. adv. com., 1977-79; active in Ill. State Competency Based Edn. project, 1977—. Sec., 1st v.p. N.W. Ter. Art Guild, 1968-71; chmn. found. com. Bus. and Profl. Women's Orgn., 1978, 79, chmn. dist. young careerist program; 1st v.p. Olney Bus. and Profl. Women, 1983, 84, pres. 1985, 86; active Ill. Bus. and Profl. WOmen (mem. state young careerist com. 1986-87); vol. counselor Ill. State Dept. Vocat. Rehab., 1972—, Southeastern Ill. Mental Health Center, 1976-77. Recipient Nat. Office Mgmt. award, 1953, State Ill. grantee, 1979. Mem. Ill. Bus. Edn. Assn. (1st v.p. 1980, pres. 1981), Ill. Vocat. Assn. (dir. 1980), Am. Vocat. Assn. (state membership chmn. 1979), Nat. Bus. Edn. Assn. (state membership chmn. 1979), Nat. Secs. Assn., Internat. Soc., Eastern Ill. Bus. Edn. Assn., So. Ill. Bus. Edn. Assn., Phi Kappa Phi, Delta Kappa Gamma, Delta Pi Epsilon, Iota Lambda Sigma, Phi Mu (life). Contbr. articles to profl. publs.; co-author chpt. Business Education into the Eighties, 1979. Home: 13 Brian Dr Olney IL 62450 Office: Olney Central Coll Route 3 Olney IL 62450

BOUTELLE, JANE CRONIN, fitness consultant; b. Arlington, Mass., Nov. 3, 1926; s. William Francis and Sara (Gillis) Cronin; m. G. William Boutelle, 1953 (dec. 1973); children—Jeanne E., William R., James G. B.S., Boston U., 1948; M.A., Columbia U., 1953. Cert. tchr., Mass. Tchr. dance and health edn. Newton High Sch., Mass., 1948-51, Scarsdale High Sch., N.Y., 1951-55, Marymount Coll., Tarrytown, N.Y., 1955-58, Manhattanville Coll., Purchase, N.Y., 1958-59; pres., fitness cons. The Boutelle Method, Inc., Greenwich, Conn., 1973—. Author: Lifetime Fitness for Women, 1978. Contbr. articles to mags. Pres Westchester Dance Council, Westchester County, N.Y., 1956-57; mem. Nat. Alumni Bd. Boston U., 1981— (chmn. 40th reunion); mem. woman's com. Lighthouse, Westchester County, N.Y., 1983. Recipient Bravo award Greenwich YWCA, 1978. Mem. AAUW (chmn. edn. 1963-68), Soroptimists Internat. (chmn. scholarship com.) , Greenwich Woman's Club Gardeners (chmn. scholarship com.) Assn. Women in Phys. Edn. (chmn. 1954-55), Greenwich Assn. Pub. Schs. (chmn. 1968-73). Home: Huckleberry Ln Greenwich CT 06831 Office: The Boutelle Method Inc Huckleberry Ln Greenwich CT 06831

BOVARD, FAITH JEAN, economist; b. N.Y.C. Dec. 13, 1938; d. Martin and Grace vom Lehn; student CCNY, 1956-60; B.A., Hofstra U., 1969; M.B.A., U. Houston, 1980, C.M.A., 1985; children—Victoria, Jacqueline, Tracy. Staff mgr. Rayburn Country, Houston, 1973; exec. sec. Gulf Oil Corp., Houston, 1974-76, fin. analyst, 1976-80, sr. fin. analyst, 1980-83, sr. econ. analyst, 1984-85; economist Chevron Corp., San Francisco, 1985—. Mem. jr. bd. Kent County Hosp., Dover, Del., 1973; bd. dirs. Dover Newcomers Club, 1973; econ. advisor Jr. Achievement, 1984. Mem. Inst. Mgmt. Acctg., Nat. Acctg. Assn., Beta Gamma Sigma. Republican. Club: Forum (Houston). Office: 6001 Bollinger Canyon San Ramon CA 94583

BOVENZI, MARY LOUISE, banking personnel executive; b. Worcester, Mass., Sept. 17, 1957; d. Louis Ralph and Ann Elizabeth (Sullivan) B. BA, Clark U., 1979. Personnel clk. Sweet Life Foods, Northboro, Mass., 1980-82; customer service rep. Consol. Group Trust, Natick, Mass., 1982-83; personnel asst. Multibank Computer Corp., Auburn, Mass., 1983-84; adminstr. then supr. personnel Multibank Service Ctr., Dedham, Mass., 1984-86; mgr. personnel Multibank Service Ctr., Dedham, 1986—. Mem. Auburn Good Citizen Search com. Mem. Cen. Mass. Employers Assn., Personnel Mgmt. Assn. of Cen. Mass. Office: Multibank Fin Corp 100 Rustcraft Rd Dedham MA 02026

BOWATER, MARIAN LARSON, retired art gallery director; b. Emmons, Minn., Sept. 5, 1924; d. James Melvin and Hannah Elvira (Olson) Larson; student Gustavus Adolphus Coll., 1941-42; m. John J. Bowater, Jan. 22, 1945; children—Christine, Julianna, John James. Owner, dir. Bowater Gallery of Fine Art, Los Angeles, 1975-86; active mus. shows; lectr. art clubs. Mem. Art Dealers Assn. So. Calif. Home: 1168 Wales Pl Cardiff-by-the-Sea CA 92007

BOWDEN, ANN, bibliographer, educator; b. East Orange, N.J., Feb. 7, 1924; d. William and Anna Elisabeth (Herrstrom) Haddon; m. Edwin Turner Bowden, June 12, 1948; children—Elisabeth Bowden Ward, Susan Turner, Edwin Eric; m. 2d, William Burton Todd, Nov. 23, 1969. B.A., Radcliffe Coll., 1948; M.S. in Library Services, Columbia U., 1951; Ph.D., U. Tex., 1975. Cataloger, reference asst. Yale U., 1948-53; manuscript cataloger, rare book librarian, librarian Humanities Research Ctr., librarian Acad. Ctr., U. Tex., Austin, 1958-63, lectr., sr. lectr. Grad. Sch. Library and Info. Sci., 1964-85, 88—; coordinator adult services Austin Pub. Library, 1963-67, asst. dir., 1967-71, dep. dir., 1971-77, assoc. dir., 1977-86; bd. dirs. Tex. Info. Exchange, Houston, 1977-78; bd. dirs. AMIGOS Bibliog. Council, Dallas, 1978-82, chmn. bd., 1980-81, trustee emeritus, 1986—; chmn. AMIGOS '85 Plan, 1984-86; scholar in residence Rockefeller Found. Villa Serbelloni, Bellagio, Italy, 1986. Author (with W.B. Todd) Tauchnitz International Editions in English, 1988; editor: T.E. Lawrence Fifty Letters: 1921-1935, 1962; Maps and Atlases, 1978; assoc. editor Papers of the Bibliographical Soc. Am., 1967-82; contbr. articles to profl. jours. Served as cpl. USMC Women's Res., 1944-46. Mem. ALA (council 1975-79), Assn. Coll. and Research Libraries (chmn. rare book and manuscript sect. 1975-76), Tex. Library Assn. (chmn. publs. com. 1965-71), Bibliog. Soc. Am., Phi Kappa Phi, Kappa Tau Alpha. Club: Grolier (N.Y.C.).

BOWDEN, DOROTHY JEAN WELBORN, librarian; b. Moulton, Ala., May 18, 1935; d. E.S. and Shirley Jane (Green) Welborn; m. Leonard J. Bowden, Aug. 17, 1963; 1 child, Kevin Andrew. BA in English, Tenn. Temple Coll., 1957, George Peabody Coll. for Tchrs., 1959; MLS, George Peabody Coll. for Tchrs., 1960. Asst. librarian Tenn. Temple Coll., Chattanooga, 1960-64, 65-69; reference librarian Lake County Pub. Library, Merrillville, Ind., 1973-76; tchr., librarian Berachah Christian Acad., Huntsville, Ala., 1976-84; librarian So. Inst. Jr. Coll., Huntsville, 1984—. Mem. Tenn. Library Assn. (sec. 1961-63), Ala. Library Assn. Baptist. Office: So Jr Coll 1001 Airport Rd Huntsville AL 35810

BOWDEN, SUSAN HOLLY, home economics educator; b. Glen Cove, N.Y., Dec. 20, 1957; d. Philip Julian and Joan (Baron) B. BS in Edn., Home Econs., Keene State Coll., 1980. Tchr. child devel. Stamford (Conn.) High Sch., 1980-81; tchr. home econs. Kingswood High Sch., Woleboro, N.H., 1982-84; tchr. textiles Parker Middle Sch., Reading, Mass., 1984-85; tchr. foods/nutrition Sanborn Reg. High Sch., Kingston, N.H., 1985—; product demonstrator N.E. Group, Bedford, Mass. 1982—; product rep. Ganile State

Nktg., Londonderry, N.H. 1983—. Mem. N.H. Home Econs. Assn. (regional chair 1985-87, newsletter editor 1987—). Office: Sanborn Reg High Sch Main St Kingston NH 83848

BOWEN, ANNE SHAFFER, healthcare administrator; b. Odessa, Tex., May 24, 1952; d. Paul D. and Thelma M. S.; m. Peter N. Bowen. B.S. in Biology, Tex. Christian U., 1974; B.S. in Nursing, U. Pa., 1975; M.H.A., Ga. State U., 1981. Staff nurse Pa. Hosp., Phila., 1976-77, Hosp. Med. Coll. Pa., 1977-79, Shallowford Community Hosp., Chamblee, Ga., 1980-81; adminstrv. resident, asst. to adminstr. Goddard Meml. Hosp., Stoughton, Mass., 1981-82; v.p. ancillary services Meml. Hosp., York, Pa., 1982—. Bd. dirs. South Central York County Sr. Ctr. Mem. Am. Hosp. Assn., Am. Coll. Hosp. Adminstrs., Sigma Theta Tau. Home: PO Box 9 Glen Rock PA 17327 Office: 325 S Belmont St York PA 17403

BOWEN, BARBARA LYNN, computer company executive; b. Toledo, May 19, 1945; d. John Thomas and Grace Elizabeth (Spaulding) B. A.B., Oberlin Coll., 1967; M.S., So. Conn. U., 1968; Ph.D., Cornell U., 1972. Asst. prof. Queens Coll., Flushing, N.Y., 1979-81; mgr. mktg. support-tng. Logo Computer Systems, Inc., N.Y.C., 1981-83; dir. Apple Edn. Found., Apple Computer, Inc., Cupertino, Calif., 1983-84; program dir. edn. affairs Apple Computer, Inc., Cupertino, 1984-86, mgr. external research , 1986—; mem. Nat. Task Force on Ednl. Tech., 1984-86; bd. advisers N.E. Regional Exchange Teleconference Project, Bolton, N.H., 1984-85, Nat. Ctr. on Computer Equity, N.Y.C., 1985—. Author: Apple Logo Training Manual, 1983. Mem. editorial bd. Nat. Rural Spl. Edn. quar., 1986—. Bd. dirs. Ctr. for Econ. Conversion, Mountain View, Calif., 1985, 86, pres. bd. dirs., 1986; trustee Saybrook Inst., 1986—. Mem. Am. Assn. Artificial Intelligence, Am. Ednl. Research Assn., Bus. Execs. for Nat. Security. Home: 749 Ramona Ave Sunnyvale CA 94087 Office: Apple Computer Inc 20525 Mariani Ave Cupertino CA 95014

BOWEN, CHRISTINE LYN, computerized health-care billing company executive; b. Troy, N.Y., July 23, 1952; d. Joseph William and Evelyn Ann (Webster) Sneden; m. Alan Leslie Deyo, May 20, 1974 (div. Dec. 1977); 1 child, Jason Alan Deyo; m. Robert Charles Bowen, Sept. 12, 1981. B in Applied Social Sci., SUNY-Binghamton, 1979. Office mgr. Maine Med. Group, N.Y., 1977-78; med. edn. coordinator Binghamton Gen. Hosp., 1978-82; systems operation mgr. Med. Office Systems of So. Tier, Inc., Binghamton, 1983-85, chief operating officer, systems ops. mgr., med. edn. coordinator, med. office mgr., 1985—; past owner, operator tanning company; owner, pres. CSB Assocs., 1986-88; cons. N.Y. and Pa. Editor Erudition Digest newsletter, 1982. Mentor B-R-I-D-G-E, Binghamton, 1981-84; active Port Dickinson Community Assn., Binghamton, 1984—; co-chairperson disaster service, bd. dirs. Broome County chpt. ARC, 1984—; bd. dirs., chairperson evangelism Ogden Hillcrest United Methodist Ch., Binghamton, 1985—. Served to 1st lt. U.S. Army, 1970-73. Mem. Women's Network, MOSST User Group (bd. dirs. 1983—), Altrusa (local treas. 1982-83). Democrat. Avocations: cross-country skiing, antique hunting, camping, swimming, golfing. Home and Office: MR 90 Krager Rd Binghamton NY 13904

BOWEN, GWEN LORRAYNE, dance educator, choreographer, dance company artistic director; b. Denver, May 9; d. Walter Lee and Estermae (Brandfas) B. BA, U. Denver, 1951, postgrad., 1951-52. tchr. dance Lillian Cushing Sch., Denver, 1945-49; tchr. Denver Pub. Schs., 1951-53; tchr. dance, owner Gwen Bowen Sch. Dance Arts, Denver, 1953—; artistic dir. Premiere Dance Arts Co., 1959—, hon. life artistic dir., 1963—; mem. theatre faculty Metro State Coll., Denver, 1973; tchr., various orgns., including Arts IV Celebration, 1975. Author graded system for ballet, tap dance; choreographer numerous ballets, operas, musicals, 1953—. Grantee Colo. Council Arts and Humanities, 1975. Mem. Colo. Dance Tchrs. (v.p. 1963-64), Dance Educators Am. (life, area chmn. 1974-86), Dance Masters Am. (life), South Cen. Improvement Assn., Washington Park Community Ctr., dance Educators Am., Metro Denver Arts Alliance, Colo. Dance Alliance, Kappa Delta. Lodge: Soroptimists. Home and Office: Gwen Bowen Sch of Dance Arts 714 S Pearl St Denver CO 80209

BOWEN, MARCIA KAY, customs house broker; b. Bradford, Pa., July 20, 1957; d. George W. Allen Jr. and Katherine (Jema) Allen; m. Glenn Edward Rollins, June 26, 1975 (div. 1979); m. Michael James Bowen, Dec. 27, 1983; 1 child, James Derek. Student Houston Community Coll., 1978-81; student Am. Mgmt. Assn., 1984-85. Lic. customs house broker. Asst. mgr. W.R. Zanes & Co. of La., Inc., Houston, 1975-76; sec. Westchester Corp., Houston, 1973-75; import br. mgr. Schenkers Internat., Inc., Houston, 1976-85; br. mgr. F.W. Myers & Co., Inc., El Paso, 1985—. Mem. Houston Customs House Brokers Assn. (sec. 1977-79, mem. U.S. customs com. 1979-83), El Paso Customs House Brokers Assn., Houston Freight Forwarders Assn., El Paso Fgn. Trade Zone Assn., Nat. Assn. Female Execs., Soc. Global Trade Execs., El Paso/Juarez Transp. and Distbn. Assn., Inc. Roman Catholic. Office: FW Myers & Co Inc 9801 Carnegie St El Paso TX 79925

BOWEN, MARY H., agricultural equipment leasing company executive; b. Olean, N.Y., May 15, 1951; d. William F. and Mary (Sherwood) Hogan; m. John E. Bowen, Dec. 10, 1977; children: Joseph W., Michael F. BBA cum laude, St. Bonaventure U., 1973; cert. in lease and fin., PREP Inst. of Am., 1983; cert. in leasing for profit, Am. Mgmt. Assoc., 1987. With mgmt. devel. program Chase Manhattan Bank, N.A., N.Y.C., 1973-74, asst. mgr., 1975-77, asst. treas., 1977-80; asst. treas. Agway Inc., DeWitt, N.Y., 1980-82; mgr. leasing and collection Telmark Inc., DeWitt, 1983—; 1st v.p. Agway Credit Union, DeWitt, 1986, pres., 1987—. Coordinator Jr. Achievement, Syracuse, 1982; capt. United Way of Cen. N.Y., Syracuse, 1983-85; den leader Boy Scouts Am., Fayetteville, N.Y., 1986-87. Mem. Am. Assn. of Equipment Lessors, Syracuse Profl. and Managerial Womens Group. Home: 5103 Duguid Rd Manlius NY 13104 Office: Telmark Inc PO Box 4943 Syracuse NY 13221

BOWEN, SANDRA DIXON, state official; b. South Boston, Va., Apr. 13, 1941; d. Royster Bratcher and Ruth Josephine (Deese) Dixon; m. E.J. Bowen, Aug. 17, 1963; children: Sydney McKenna, Charles Neville, Anne Lindsay. AB, Coll. William and Mary, 1963; MA, U. Richmond, 1981. Spl. asst. to Gov. Charles Robb Commonwealth of Va., Richmond, 1983-85; Sec. of Commonwealth 1986—; dir. Baliles for Gov. Campaign, Richmond, 1985, Gubernatorial Transition, 1985-86. Del. Nat. Dem. Conv., N.Y., 1980; mem. cen. com. Dem. Party Va., 1981—; chmn. Richmond City Dem. Com., 1980-81, 3d Dem. Dist. Com., 1987—; bd. dirs. Richmond Urban League, 1980-82. Named one of Outstanding Young Women Am., 1974. Mem. Nat. Assn. Secs. of State, Women Execs. in State Govt. Baptist. Home: 206 Grande Dr Richmond VA 23229 Office: Sec of the Commonwealth 114 9th St Ofc Bldg Richmond VA 23201

BOWEN, SHEILA KATHLEEN, registered insurance representative, broker; b. North Attleboro, Mass., July 29, 1944; d. Francis Joseph and Shirley Eileen (Bowen) Hopkins; m. Thomas Joseph Condon, May 29, 1965 (div. Sept. 1979); children: Sheila Kathleen, Michael Frank. Student, U. Detroit, 1962-63; BA magna cum laude, Wayne State U., 1987. Legal sec. James Fowler, Atty., Redford, Mich., 1976-80; adminstrv. asst. Tex. Instruments, Southfield, Mich., 1979-80, Ctr. for Policy Alternatives, MIT, Cambridge, Mass., 1981-82; sales rep. Data Industrial, Pocasset, Mass., 1982-85; registered rep. Equitable Fin. Services, Sagamore, Mass., 1985-88; ind. ins. broker Bowen Ins. Co., Harwich, Mass., 1988—; sec. Harwich Bd. Appeals, Mass., 1986. Sunday sch. tchr. Our Lady Loretto Parish, 1973-78; player agent Redford Little League Baseball, 1978-79; vol. various state and nat. polit. campaigns, 1960—; delegate Mass. Dem. State Conv., 1985-87; active Dem. Town Com., Harwich, 1986— (chmn. 1988). Mem. Nat. Assn. Life Underwriters (chmn. state legis. com., bd. dirs. 1987), Cape Cod Women's Orgn. (pres. 1986—, v.p. 1985, sec. 1982-84, Woman of Yr. 1985), Phi Beta Kappa.

BOWEN, SHIRLEY E., physical education educator; b. Moravia, N.Y., Nov. 27, 1942; d. Howard Harry Bowen and Eva Lucille (Jennings) Coon. BS, SUNY, Cortland, 1964; MS, SUNY, Brockport, 1966. Tchr. phys. edn., coach Churchville (N.Y.)-Chili High Sch., 1964-69; tchr. phys. edn. Fairbanks Rd. Elem. Sch., Churchville, 1969-75; dir. phys. edn. and athletics E. Irondequoit Cen. Sch., Rochester, N.Y., 1976-80, Brighton Cen. Sch., Rochester, 1980—. Mem. N.Y. State Coaches Assn. (honor award 1979), N.Y. State Assn. for Health, Phys. Edn., Recreation, and Dance (Semper Fidelis award 1987). Club: Rochester Press-Radio (Giambrone award 1985). Office: Brighton High Sch 1150 Winton Rd S Rochester NY 14618

BOWER, BARBARA JEAN, nurse; b. Akron, Ohio, Aug. 25, 1942; d. William Howard and Maxine (Goodykoontz) Sturm; m. Howard Bower, Aug. 25, 1961 (div. 1973); children: Nancy, Janet. BA, Elmhurst Coll., 1974, postgrad., 1987—; diploma, Evang. Sch. Nursing, 1970. RN. Supr. nursing Med. Ctr.; nurse critical care Loyola U., Maywood, Ill., 1970-78, Med. Staffing Services, Oak Park, Ill., 1978-84; pres. Heart Care Unltd., Bridgeview, Ill., 1982—. Creator ednl. programs for cardiac patients, families, 1971—. Mem. AAUW, Am. Nurses Assn., Am. Assn. Critical Care Nurses, Am. Heart Assn., Elmhurst Coll. Alumni Assn. Mem. Christ Ch. Home: 8022 W 93d St Hickory Hills IL 60457 Office: Heart Care Unltd PC PO Box 2027 Bridgeview IL 60454

BOWER, FAY LOUISE, nurse; b. San Francisco, Sept. 10, 1929; d. James Joseph and Emily Clare (Andrews) Saitta; B.S. with honors, San Jose State Coll., 1965; M.S.N., U. Calif., 1966, D.N.Sc., 1978; children—R. David, Carol Bower Tomei, Dennis James, Thomas John. Office nurse Dr. William Grannis, Palo Alto, Calif., 1950-55; staff nurse Stanford Hosp., 1964-72; asst. prof. San Jose State U., 1966-70, asso. prof., 1970-74, prof., 1974-82, coordinator grad. program in nursing, 1977-78, chairperson dept. nursing, 1978-82; dean U. San Francisco, 1982—; v.p. acad. affairs, speaker; cons. univs.; vis. prof. Harding Coll., 1977, U. Miss., 1976; lectr. U. Calif., San Francisco, 1975. Cert. public health nurse, sch. nurse, Calif. Fellow Am. Acad. Nursing; mem. Calif. Nurses Assn., Nurses Assn. Coll. Ob-Gyn, Calif. Tchrs. Assn., AAUP, Public Health Assn. Calif., Nat. League Nursing (bd. dirs.), Calif. League for Nursing (pres.), Western Gerontol. Assn., Sigma Theta Tau (pres. Beta Gamma chpt.), Jesuit Deans in Nursing (chair). Democrat. Roman Catholic. Club: Commonwealth (San Francisco). Author: (with Em O. Bevis) Fundamentals of Nursing Practice: Concepts, Roles and Functions, 1978; (with Margaret Jacobson) Community Health Nursing, 1978; The Process of Planning Nursing Care, 3d edit., 1982; Theoretical Foundations of Nursing I, II, and III, 1972; editor: Normal Development of Body Image, 1977; Distortions in Body Image in Illness and Disability, 1977; Foundations of Pharmacologic Therapy, 1977; Nursing Assessment, 1977. Home: 1820 Portola Rd Woodside CA 94062 Office: U San Francisco Sch Nursing San Francisco CA

BOWER, JEAN RAMSAY, court administrator, lawyer; b. N.Y.C., Nov. 25, 1935; d. Claude Barnett and Myrtle Marie (Scott) Ramsay; m. Ward Swift Just, Jan. 31, 1957 (div. 1966); children: Jennifer Ramsay, Julia Barnett; m. Robert Turrell Bower, June 12, 1971. A.B., Vassar Coll., 1957; J.D., Georgetown U., 1970. Bar: D.C. 1970. Exec. dir. D.C. Dem. Central Com., Washington, 1969-71; sole practice, Washington, 1971-78; dir. Counsel for Child Abuse and Neglect Office, D.C. Superior Ct., 1978—. Mem. Mayor's Com. on Child Abuse and Neglect, 1973—, vice chmn., 1975-79; mem. Family Div. Rules Adv. Com., 1977—; pres., bd. dirs. C.B. Ramsay Found., 1984—. Mem. mgmt. bd. Child Advocacy Ctr., 1980— . Mem. Women's Bar Assn. (found. 1986—), D.C. Bar Assn., Women's Bar Assn. Found (bd. dirs. 1986). Named Washingtonian of the Yr., Washingtonian Mag., 1979, Woman Lawyer of the Yr., Women's Bar Assn., D.C., 1985. Office: DC Superior Ct Room 4235 500 Indiana Ave NW Washington DC 20007

BOWER, MARGE EMILY, educator; b. Chgo., June 8, 1941; d. Elmore Arthur and Elsie Ruth (Sauer) B.; B.A., U. Mich., 1963; M.A., Loyola U., Chgo., 1967; postgrad. Loyola U., DePaul U., Bradley U., Western Mich. U., U. Mich. Tchr. English, sch. newspaper advisor South Shore High Sch., Chgo., 1963-67; guidance counselor, tchr. Elmwood Park (Ill.) High Sch., 1967-84; dir. guidance Immaculate Conception High Sch., Elmhurst, Ill., 1985—. Chmn. com. out-of-state admissions and scholarships U. Mich. Nat. Alumnae Council, 1972-75, governing bd., 1972-75. Wall St. Jour. Newspaper Fund fellow, 1967. Mem. Nat. Assn. Women Deans, Adminstrs. and Counselors (exec. bd. 1979-81), Ill. Assn. for Counseling and Devel., Ill. Sch. Counselors Assn., U. Mich. Alumni Assn. (dist. sec. 1986—). Club: North Shore U. Mich. Alumni (scholarship chmn. 1976—). Editorial bd. Ill. Guidance and Personnel Assn. Quar., 1981-85, NAWDAC Jour., 1981-83. Home: 555 W Cornelia Ave Apt 707 Chicago IL 60657

BOWERS, LEE AILES, psychotherapist, management consultant; b. Erie, Pa., Sept. 1, 1950; d. Burr Freer and Phyllis Esther (Varner) Ailes; m. James Robert Bowers, Dec. 2, 1977. BS in Psychology, U. Pitts., 1971; MA in Counseling Psychology, Norwich U., 1984. Cert. employee assistance profl.; nat. cert. counselor. Personnel researcher Panhandle Ea. Corp., Houston, 1979-83; pres. The Productivity Group, Houston, 1984-86, Downingtown, Pa., 1986—; personnel mgr. Lord & Taylor, Washington, 1977; personnel exec. Woodward & Lothrop, Washington, 1977-79; cons. Internat. Oil and Gas Co., Houston, 1985-87, Comprehensive Psychol. Services, Bala Cynwyd, Pa., 1986, Suburban Psychol. Services, Lansdowne, Pa., 1986—, State of Pa. Employee Assistance Program, 1986—; instr. Houston Community Coll., 1987. Pres. Amigos de Ser, Houston, 1982, 85; mem., vol. Chester County Soc. Prevention Cruelty to Animals, West Chester, Pa., 1986—; mem. Humane Soc. U.S., Washington, 1980—, People for Am. Way, Washington, 1985—. Served to 1st lt. USAF, 1976. Recipient Amigo of Yr. award SER Jobs for Progress, Houston, 1981, Citizen of Yr. award Am. Legion, North East, Pa., 1968; named one of Outstanding Young Women of Am., 1982. Mem. Am. Assn. Counseling and Devel., Am. Assn. Marriage and Family Therapy (assoc.), Pa. Assn. Marriage and Family Therapy, Assn. Labor and Mgmt. Adminstrs and Cons. on Alcoholism (1st v.p. 1987—), Indsl. Human Services Council, Downingtown C. of C. (bd. dirs. 1987), Delta Soc. Episcopalian. Office: 11 Quail Hill Ln Downington PA 19335

BOWERS, LEOLA DELEAN, educator, nurse; b. Birmingham, Ala., May 5, 1919; d. Jasper Wiley and Lonie (Dunsford) B. Diploma Carraway Methodist Hosp. Sch. Nursing, Birmingham, 1946, Brook Army Med. Ctr. Sch. Anesthesia, Ft. Sam Houston, Tex., 1953; student U. Ga., 1954, U. Md., 1955; B.S.N., U. Ala.-Tuscaloosa, 1959; class B cert. in secondary edn. Jacksonville State U., 1960, M.S. in Edn., 1961; postgrad. Spring Hill Coll., 1962, U. Ala.-Mobile, 1963; cert. Nat. Respiratory Disease Course for Nurses, New Orleans, 1969; postgrad. Pepperdine U., 1971-74; cert. health occupation edn. U. Ala., Birmingham, 1975. R.N., Ala.; cert. secondary tchr., Ala. Hosp. supr. Citizens Hosp., Talladega, Ala., 1946-47, surg. nurse, 1949-50; gen. duty nurse Sylacauga Hosp. (Ala.), 1948; instr. med.-surg. nursing Sylacauga Sch. Nursing, 1963-71; tchr. health occupations Talladega City Vocat. Ctr., 1971—, coordinator Health Occupation Edn. Student Clin. Citizens Hosp. and Nursing Home, 1971—. Instr. ARC, Talladega, 1975—; CPR instr. Am. Heart Assn., Talladega, 1979—, adv. projects, 1978-83; mem. telephone com. for election legislators, Talladega, 1982. Served as capt. Nurses Corps, U.S. Army, 1950-58; ETO. Recipient CD cert. State Ala., 1980, cert. service City of Talladega, 1983; named Tchr. of Yr., Talladega City Vocat. Ctr. and Health Occupation Edn., 1979, 83, 84, Outstanding Ala. Tchr., Ala. Vocat. Dept., 1983, 84. Mem. Am. Nurses' Assn., Ala. Nurses' Assn., Bus. and Profl. Women's Club, Talladega Nurses' Assn., Health Occupation Students Am. (adviser local club 1976—, adviser Dist. III Ala. 1981-85). Methodist. Lodge: Order Eastern Star. Home: Route 4 Box 239 Talladega AL 35160 Office: Talladega City Vocat Ctr 110 Picadilly Circle Talladega AL 35160

BOWERS, MARIANNE, clergywoman; b. Lafayette, Ind., Feb. 5, 1919; d. Gilbert Melville and Mary Frances (Montgomery) Wilson; m. Carl Eugene Bowers, June 19, 1964 (dec.); children by previous marriage—Frederic Kelly, Deborah Kelly Kivisels, Karen Kelly Wootton. B.S., Purdue U., 1940; grad. Unity Ministerial Sch., 1980. Ordained to ministry Unity Ch., 1980. Exec. sec. Tex. Lic. Vocat. Nurses Assn., Austin, Tex., 1964-66; employment counselor Tarrant Employment Agy., Austin, 1966-68; owner, mgr. Horizons Unlimited (book stores), Austin and San Antonio, 1968-72; with devel., mktg., pub. relations depts. First Nat. Bank, Harlingen, Tex., 1973-76; exec. officer Rio Grande Valley Apt. Assn., 1976-78; minister Unity Ch. of San Angelo (Tex.), 1980—. Mem. Assn. Unity Chs., Internat. New Thought Alliance, AAUW, Scriveners, Alpha Lambda Delta, Delta Rho Kappa, Chi Omega, Nat. Assn. Female Execs., Internat. Platform Assn. Address: PO Box 1221 San Angelo TX 76902

BOWERS, MARY ELLEN KATHRYN, quality control executive, chemist; b. Cleve., Nov. 3, 1949; d. Arthur L. and Dorothy Virginia (DeLuia) Jakllc; 1 child, Matthew Anthony. A.A. with honors Lakeland Community Coll., 1985. Lab technician W.S. Tyler, Inc., Cleve., 1969-71, C-E Tyler, Cleve., 1974-76; quality control mgr. Morton Salt, Painesville, Ohio, 1977—. Treas., com. mem. Boy Scouts Am., 1986, 87, sr. mem. explorer scouts marksmanship post, 1987, sec. local com., 1987; mem. Lake County Indsl. Commlunity Awareness Emergency Response Adv. Panel, 1987. Mem. Nat. Assn. Female Execs., AAAS. Republican. Roman Catholic. Avocations: traveling; photography; tutoring math. Home: 1651 Mentor Ave Bldg 6 Unit 604 Painseville OH 44077 Office: Morton Salt Div Morton Thiokol Inc PO Box 428 Grand River OH 44045-0428

BOWERS, PATRICIA ELEANOR FRITZ, economist; b. N.Y.C., Mar. 21, 1928; d. Eduard and Eleanor (Ring) Fritz. Student scholar, Goucher Coll., 1946-48; B.A., Cornell U., 1950; M.A., NYU, 1953, Ph.D., 1965. Statis. asst. Fed. Res. Bank N.Y., N.Y.C., 1950-53; lectr. Upsala Coll., East Orange, N.J., 1953-59; researcher Fortune mag., N.Y.C., 1959-60; teaching fellow NYU, N.Y.C., 1960-62, instr., 1962-64; mem. faculty Bklyn. Coll., CUNY, 1964—, prof. econs., 1974—. Author: Private Choice and Public Welfare, 1974. Mem. Am. Econ. Assn., Econometric Soc., N.Y. Acad. Scis., Fgn. Policy Assn., Met. Econ. Assn. (sec. 1963-68, pres. 1974-75), Am. Statis. Assn. (univs. chmn. ann. forecasting confs. 1970-71, 71-72). Club: Talbot Country (Easton, Md.). Home: 145 E 16th St New York NY 10003 Office: CUNY Bklyn Coll Dept Econs Brooklyn NY 11210

BOWERS, PATRICIA NEWSOME, public relations executive; b. Baton Rouge, June 21, 1944; d. Carl Allen and Sue Mayre (Powell) Newsome; m. Robert Lloyd Bowers Jr., Aug. 19, 1967 (div. Nov. 1979); children: Paige Ivy, Katherine Elizabeth. BJ, La. State U., 1967. Sr. writer, editor Litton Industries, Pascagoula, Miss., 1978-80; sr. presentations supr. Martin Marietta Aerospace, Orlando, Fla., 1980-81; mgr. presentations Martin Marietta Aerospace, Balt., 1981-85, mgr. pub. relations, 1985—. Coach Parkville Recreation Council, Balt., 1985-87. Mem. Pub. Relations Soc. Am. (bd. dirs. Chesapeake chpt. 1987), Navy League (bd. dirs. Balt. council 1986-87), Balt. County C. of C. (leadership program 1986-87). Republican. Episcopalian. Office: Martin Marietta Aero & Naval Systems MP E-105 103 Chesapeake Park Pl Baltimore MD 21220

BOWERS, SUSAN MARIE, educator; b. Monongahela, Pa., May 4, 1950; d. Louis and Mary Gilda (Albero) Corbelli; m. Roy Paul Bowers, May 30, 1981; 1 child, Ashley Lauren. BS in Elem. Edn., Calif. U. of Pa., 1972, MA in Elem. Edn., 1976; grad., Inst. Children's Lit., Conn., 1983. Cert. elem. tchr., Pa. Tchr. elem. Ringgold Sch. Dist., Monongahela, 1972—; writing cons. Pa. Dept. Edn., Harrisburg, 1982—, Ringgold Sch. Dist., Monongahela, 1984—. Mem. PTA, Monongahela, Monongahela Hist. Soc., Nat. Trust for Hist. Preservation, Washington. Mem. Pa. State Edn. Assn., Ringgold Edn. Assn. Democrat. Roman Catholic. Home: 900 Lawrence St Monongahela PA 15063 Office: 1200 Chess St Monongahela PA 15063

BOWERS, ZELLA ZANE, real estate broker; b. Liberal, Kans., May 24, 1929; d. Rex and Esther (Neff) Powelson; m. James Clarence Bowers, Aug. 12, 1949; (div. 1977); 1 child: Dara Zane. B.A., Colo. Coll., 1951. Cert. real estate brokerage mgr. Sec. Bowers Ins. Agy., Colorado Springs, Colo., 1955-59, Cen. Colo. Claims Service, Colorado Springs, 1959-63; pres. Premium Budgeting Co., Colorado Springs, 1962-67; pres., owner Monument Valley Realty, Inc., Colorado Springs, 1981—. Hon. trustee The Palmer Found., Colorado Springs, 1980—, pres., 1983-84; trustee Pikes Peak United Way, 1988-91; pres. Vis. Nurse Assn., Colorado Springs, 1966-67, 74; dir. Colo. League Nurses, Denver, 1968; advisor Found. of the Robin, Colorado Springs, 1985—; sec. Care & Share, Colorado Springs, 1984; chmn. McAllister House Mus., Colorado Springs, 1973-74; docent chmn. Colorado Springs Fine Arts Ctr., 1969-70; pres. Friends of the Library, 1971-72; pres. Woman's Ednl. Soc. Colo. Coll., 1974-77; civil adminstrv. staff asst. Air Def. Filter Ctr., 1956-57, ground observer, 1956, others. Named State Regent for Life, Daus. of Am. Colonists, 1973. Recipient Women's Trade Fair Recognition award, 1987. Mem. Nat. Assn. Realtors, Colo. Assn. Realtors, Colorado Springs Bd. Realtors (dir., v.p., pres.-elect), Children of the Am. Revolution (pres. 1956-57. 1988—), Daus. of Am. Colonists (state regent 1970-73), DAR, Gamma Phi Beta. Avocations: geneaology, travel. Home: 11 W Caramillo St Colorado Springs CO 80907 Office: Monument Valley Realty Inc PO Box 7894 Colorado Springs CO 80933

BOWES, FLORENCE (MRS. WILLIAM DAVID BOWES), writer; b. Salt Lake City, Nov. 19, 1925; d. John Albreckt Elias and Alma Wilhelmina (Jonasson) Norborg; student U. Utah, 1941-42, Columbia, 1945-46, N.Y. U., 1954-55; grad. N.Y. TV Workshop, 1950; m. Samuel Ellis Levine, July 15, 1944 (dec. July 1953); m. 2d, William David Bowes, Mar. 15, 1958 (dec. 1976); 1 son, Alan Richard. Actress, writer Hearst Radio Network, WINS, N.Y.C., 1944-45; personnel and adminstrv. exec. Mut. Broadcasting System, N.Y.C., 1946-49, free-lance editor, writer, 1948-49; freelance writer NBC and ABC, 1949-53; script editor, writer Robert A. Monroe Prodns., N.Y.C., Hollywood, Calif., 1953-56; script and comml. dir. KUTV-TV, Salt Lake City, 1956-58; spl. editor, writer pub. relations dept. U. Utah, Salt Lake City, 1966-68, editor, writer U. Utah Rev., 1968-75; author: Web of Solitude, 1979; The MacOrvan Curse, 1980; Interlude in Venice, 1981; Beauchamp, 1983. Mem. Beta Sigma Phi. Home: 338-K St Salt Lake City UT 84103

BOWLES, BARBARA LANDERS, food company executive; b. Nashville, Sept. 17, 1947; d. Corris Raemone Landers and Rebecca Aima (Bonham) Jennings; m. Earl Stanley Bowles, Nov. 27, 1971; 1 son, Terrence Earl. B.A., Fisk U., 1968; M.B.A., U. Chgo., 1971. Chartered fin. analyst, 1977. Banker to v.p. First Nat. Bank of Chgo., 1968-81; asst. v.p. Beatrice Cos., Chgo., 1981-84; v.p. investor relations Kraft Inc., Chgo., 1984—. Recipient Salute to Am.'s Top 100 Black Bus. and Profl. Women award Delta Sigma Theta and Dollars & Sense Mag., 1985. Mem. Fin. Analysts Fedn., Nat. Assn. Investment Clubs, Nat. Investor Relations Inst., Chicago Fisk Alumni Assn. (pres. 1983-85). Mem. United Ch. of Christ. Club: University (Chgo.). Avocations: tennis, bridge. Office: Kraft Inc Kraft Ct Glenview IL 60025

BOWLES, BETSY ELLIS, graphic design consultant; b. Richmond, Va., Sept. 13, 1942; d. Joseph Ellis and Bertha Mae (Cropper) Lipscombe. Student, Milligan (Tenn.) Coll., 1970-73, Va. Commonwealth U., 1973. Artist Lake Area Advertiser, Antioch, Ill., 1966-75; dir. art Fox Pub. Co., Des Moines, 1974-75; rep. sales Ad Color Press Co., Des Moines, 1975-76; pres. Penguin Studio, Inc., Des Moines, 1976—; mem. faculty Drake U., Des Moines, 1985-87; del. White House Conf. on Small Bus., Washington, 1986. Mem. gov.'s adv. bd. Polk County Retarded Citizens, Des Moines, 1977-84; bd. dirs. Mitchellville (Iowa) Reformatory, 1984-85, YWCA, Des Moines, 1985-87. Mem. Nat. Assn. Women Bus. Owners (charter, v.p. publicity Iowa chpt. 1986-87), NEXUS-Exec. Women's Alliance (charter, pres. 1979-80), Advt. Profls. Des Moines (bd. dirs. 1976-81), Des Moines C. of C. (mem. Met. 2000 Com. 1980-81). Democrat. Mem. Ch. of Christ. Home: 706 38th St Des Moines IA 50312 Office: Penguin Studio Inc 108 3d St Suite 300 Des Moines IA 50309

BOWLES, MARTHA THOMAS, utility company executive; b. Greensboro, N.C., Dec. 29, 1952; d. Hargrove Jr. and Jessamine Woodward (Boyce) B.; m. Geoffrey McKewen Curme, Dec. 31, 1977; 1 child, Jonathan Woodward Bowles Curme. B.A., U. N.C., 1975; M.B.A., Harvard U., 1979. Asst. treas. Chem. Bank, N.Y.C., 1975-77; mgr. spl. projects Belk Stores Services, Charlotte, N.C., 1979; sr. fin. analyst Duke Power Co., Charlotte, 1980-84, sr. fin. analyst long term fin., 1984-85, sr. fin. analyst cash mgmt., 1985-87, dir. cash ops., 1986-87, vice chmn. Mecklenburg Co. Indsl. Facilities Pollution Control Fin. Authority, Charlotte, 1983-87, adminstr. spl. projects, 1987—. Mem. Charlotte Community Concert Assn., 1981-84; trustee Sacred Heart Coll., Belmont, N.C., 1983-84; mem. community adv. bd. Sta. WTVI, 1986—; bd. dirs. Planned Parenthood Greater Charlotte, 1987—. Mem. Women Execs., Women for Peace, Phi Beta Kappa. Democrat. Episcopalian. Office: Duke Power Co 422 S Church St Charlotte NC 28242

BOWLES, NIKY OSBORNE, travel company executive; b. Iraklion, Crete, Greece, Aug. 21, 1946; came to U.S., 1965; d. Evaggelos Charalambou and Zafirena (Chereti) Xilourie; m. Robert A. Osborne, June 6, 1965 (div. 1979); children: Michael R., Nicole Deana; m. Thomas Joseph Bowles, Nov. 21,

1981. Owner, pres. Exec. Travel, Inc., Davenport, Iowa, 1972—. Mem. bd. govs. Better Bus. Bur., Bettendorf, Iowa, 1983—. Recipient award Quad Cities Advt. Fedn., 1987. Mem. Pres. Club C. of C. (chmn. 1985—, Beautification award 1985, Com. Service award 1985, named Outstanding Chmn. 1985). Republican. Greek Orthodox. Office: Exec Travel Inc 327 Brady St Davenport IA 52801

BOWLIN, BRENDA SUE, publishing administrator; b. Berea, Ky., Feb. 19, 1952; d. William Croucher and Nannie Marie (Kidwell) Davidson; m. Marvin Ray Bowlin, Sept. 19, 1970 (div. Mar. 1975); 1 child, Kristina Marie. Cert., H. Sparks Vocat. Sch., 1970. Office mgr. State Farm Ins., Richmond, Ky., 1979-81; office mgr. Berea Coll. Press, 1981-85, mgr., 1985—. Named to Hon. Order Ky. Cols., 1983. Mem. Internat. Assn. Quality Circles (sec. 1982-83), Inplant Printers Mgmt. Assn., Nat. Assn. Printers and Lithographers, Am. Mgmt. Soc., Nat. Assn. Female Execs. Lodge: Lioness (Berea). Home: 212 Jackson St Berea KY 40403 Office: Berea Coll Press CPO 2272 Berea KY 40404

BOWLING, JOY CHERRYLYN, telecommunications specialist; b. Chgo., Feb. 4, 1947; d. Coral and Etta Lee (Williams) Miller; m. Clarence Bowling, Aug. 9, 1969; children: Joslyn P., Jasmin. AA, Waubonsee Coll., 1979; BA, Nat. Coll. Edn., 1988. Sec., dept. head World Book Ency., Chgo., 1964-68; sec. to pres. Three Worlds, Inc., Chgo., 1969-70; with pub. relations dept. Barber-Greene Co., Aurora, Ill., 1970-76; affirmative action asst. AT&T Bell Labs., Naperville, Ill., 1976-86, telephone adminstr., 1987—. Bd. dirs. Cen. Bapt. Childrens Home ; co-founder Tomorrow's Scientists, Technicians and Mgrs., 1984. Mem. Am. Soc. Profl. and Exec. Women, League Black Profl. Women, Hope Fair Housing, NAACP, Chgo. Urban League, Aurora Urban League (bd. dirs., chmn. membershipdrive 1985, Outstanding Leadership award 1986), Aurora Women's Networking Group. Baptist. Club: Jack and Jill Am., Inc. (Naperville) (chmn. teen group). Home: PO Box 983 Aurora IL 60506 Office: AT&T Bell Labs 2000 Naperville Rd Naperville IL 60566

BOWLING, PATRICIA HENDY, artist, publisher; b. Cin., Apr. 4, 1955; d. Harry Leo and Margaret (Kelsh) Hendy; m. David Louis Bowling, May 28, 1977; children: David Patrick, Patricia Pearl. Art student, Coll. Mt. St. Joseph, 1974; BA/BS in Edn., U. Cin., 1978. Tchr. Cin. Pub. Schs., 1979-82; artist, publisher Inka Dinka Ink/HeBo, Inc., Cin., 1978—, pres., 1984—. Illustrator (children's books) Dirty Dingy Daryl, 1981, DDD for President, 1983; designer (dolls) The Dingies, 1986. Roman Catholic. Home: 4741 Guerley Rd Cincinnati OH 45238

BOWLING, RITA JOAN, nurse; b. Martins Ferry, Ohio, Feb. 20, 1949; d. Edgar Lee and Pauline Winifred (Bernard) Wilson; m. Chester John Bowling, Jr., Dec. 23, 1978; 1 child, Melissa Ann. BS in Nursing, Wayne State U., 1972, MS in Nursing, 1978; postgrad., Baldwin-Wallace Coll., 1986—. Med. surg. clin. nurse specialist, Am. Nursing Assn. Staff nurse Grace Hosp., NW, Detroit, 1972-73, Providence Hosp., Southfield, Mich., 1973-76; staffing supr. Health Care I, Inc., Southfield, 1976-78; cardiac clin. nurse specialist St. Joseph Mercy Hosp., Pontiac, Mich., 1978-81, Aultman Hosp., Canton, Ohio, 1982—; review bd. Clin. Nurse Specialist Jour., 1986—. Mem. Am. Heart Assn. (bd. dirs. E. Cen. Ohio affiliate), Am. Assn. of Critical Care Nurses, Medina County Nurses Assn. (pres. 1983-86), Sigma Theta Tau, Delta Zeta. Episcopalian. Home: 7161 River Styx Rd Medina OH 44256 Office: Aultman Hosp 2600 6th St SW Canton OH 44710

BOWMAN, ARLEEN DRIMMER, fashion designer; b. Bklyn., July 14, 1945; d. Nathan and Minnie (Goldhor) Drimmer; m. Darko Velcek, Nov. 22, 1987. student N.Y.C. Community Coll., 1962-63. Prodn. coordinator M.P.O., music and film TV commls., N.Y.C., 1966-67; prodn. mgr. Richard Druz and Victor Lukens Assocs., music and film TV commls., N.Y.C., 1967-68; producer Flickers Inc., TV commls., N.Y.C., 1969-72; owner, buyer Family Boutique, Amsterdam, Netherlands, 1972-74; owner, designer, pub. relations dir. Bowman Trading Co., Inc., N.Y.C., 1974-84; mgr. Arleen Bowman Boutique, N.Y.C., 1987—; owner, designer, pub. relations dir. Arleen Bowman Industries, Inc.; cons. China Trade; speaker in field. Recipient Clio award for TV comml. campaign, 1970; Effie award for TV comml., 1970. Guest editor Fashion mag., 1978. Patentee compact for cosmetics, 1975. Profiled on ABC World News Tonight, 1978. Office: 209 W 38th St New York NY 10018

BOWMAN, BARBARA SHERYL, banker; b. Cleve., Sept. 2, 1953; d. Bert and Shirley Marie (Regan) B. BS magna cum laude, Calif. State U., Fresno, 1976; MS, Am. Grad. Sch. Internat. Mgmt., 1976; MBA magna cum laude, Loyola-Marymount U., 1980. Asst. to pres. Aerol Co., Los Angeles, 1976-77; mgmt. trainee 1st Interstate Bank of Calif., Los Angeles, 1977-78; mgr. consumer credit Brentwood, Calif., 1978-79; asst. v.p. Beverly Hills, Calif., 1979-82, v.p., 1982-84, v.p., sales mgr., 1985—; v.p. Mercantile Nat. Bank, Los Angeles, 1982; v.p., asst. mgr. Real Estate div. Fical, San Diego, 1986-87; sr. v.p. Fimsa West Los Angeles, 1988—; speaker San Diego Mortgage Bankers Assn., 1986. Mem. Nat. Assn. Female Execs., Am. Bus. Women's Assn., Nat. Assn. Bank Women (v.p. Los Angeles chpt. 1984-86), Loyola-Marymount Alumni Assn., Bldg. Industry Assn., St. Mary's Acad. Alumni Assn., Phi Kappa Phi. Republican. Roman Catholic. Office: 1st Interstate Bank 707 Wilshire Blvd Los Angeles CA 90017

BOWMAN, BEVERLY ANN HATFIELD, educator; b. Kenova, W. Va., July 11, 1946; d. Roy Edward and Joyce Mae (Adkins) Hatfield; m. Max N. Bowman, Aug. 16, 1969; children: Kimberli, Bryce. BA, Houghton Coll., 1968; MS, U. Bridgeport, 1979; postgrad., So. Ill. U. Cert. tchr., N.Y., Ill. Tchr. English N.Y. St. Pub. Schs., New City, 1968-73; instr. Lees McRae Coll., Banner Elk, N.C., 1979-80; lctr. Boston Coll., 1980, Kent (Ohio) State U., 1981-82; cons. pub. relations El Paso Community Coll., 1982-83; lctr. English U. Tex., El Paso, 1983-85; chair El Paso Assn. Gifted, 1985-86; tchr. English Bond Community Schs., Greenville, Ill., 1986—. Pianist Coronado Ch., El Paso 1983-86, Greenville Meth. Ch., 1987; vol. Cancer Assn., El Paso 1984. Fellow Mid Ill. Edn., 1987. Mem. Nat. Assn. Tchrs. English, Tchrs. Union, El Paso Assn. Gifted and Talented (chmn. dirs. 1984-87), Christian Womens. Republican. Methodist.

BOWMAN, DEBORAH ANNE, sales executive; b. Lansing, Mich., Dec. 20, 1957; d. Norman James and Christine Ruth (Levring) B. B.S. in Bus. Adminstrn., U. Fla., 1980. Sales rep. D. Van Nostrand Co., Gainesville, Fla., 1980-81, Benjamin-Cummings Pubs., Dallas, 1981-84, Mc-Graw Hill Book Co., Dallas, 1984-85, sales mgr., Los Angeles, 1985-86; ter. mgr. Norrell Services, Dallas, 1986— . Active mem. United Way. Named to Outstanding Young Women in Am., 1983, Young Career Woman Yr., 1987. Mem. Assn. for Computing Machinery (assoc.), Nat. Assn. for Female Execs., Las Colunas Bus. and Profl. Women (pres.), Irving C. of C. (women's div., diplomat), Irving Women's Career Network, Phi Kappa Phi, Alpha Lambda Delta, Alpha Omicron Pi. Roman Catholic. Club: Dallas Gator (sec.). Office: Norrell Services Inc 800 W Airport Freeway #115 Irving TX 75062

BOWMAN, GEORGIANA HOOD, state public utilities executive; b. Middletown, Ohio, Jan. 19, 1937; d. George Simpson and Corinne Lula (Hunter) Hood; B.S. in Edn., Wilberforce U., 1965; M.A. in Adult Edn., Ohio State U., 1973, Ph.D. in Humanities Edn., 1976; m. Harris C. Bowman, Sept. 10, 1961. Tchr., Columbus (Ohio) Public Schs., 1965-72, ethnic studies planner, 1972-73, research planning and auditing specialist Title III project, 1973-74; coordinator black student programs and devel. Ohio State U., 1974-80; pres. G.H. Bowman Co., Mgmt. Cons., Columbus, 1980-85; edn. cons. Div. Equal Ednl. Opportunity urban programs sect. Ohio Dept. Edn., 1983-84; chief EEO sect. Pub. Utilities Commn. Ohio, 1984—, dep. dir., 1986—, asst. to chmn., 1987—, exec. asst. to chmn., 1988—; human relations cons. Columbus Public Schs. Sec., bd. dirs. YWCA; bd. dirs. Columbus Urban League; 2d v.p., sec., bd. dirs. North Cen. Mental Health Ctr.; bd. dirs., exec. bd. South Side Settlement House; 2d v.p. Columbus chpt. NAACP; charter mem. Columbus Assn. Performing Arts Colleagues; mem. adv. bd. Ohio State U. Black Studies Extension Ctr. Recipient cert. of appreciation Ohio Ho. of Reps., 1980, public service awards Delta Sigma Theta, Sertoma Club, Alpha Kappa Alpha, Big Bros./Big Sisters Assn. Mem. Youth Service Guild, Nat. Council Negro Women (Columbus pres., Pub. Service award), Ohio State Univ. Hosps. Aux., Phi Delta Kappa (chpt. pres.), Pi Lambda Theta, Eta Phi Beta. Home and Office: 2671 Cleveland Ave Columbus OH 43211

BOWMAN, HAZEL LOIS, educator; b. Plant City, Fla., Feb. 18, 1917; d. Joseph Monroe and Annie (Thoman) B.; A.B., Fla. State Coll. for Women, 1937; M.A., U. Fla., 1948; postgrad. U. Md., 1961-65. Tchr., Lakeview High Sch., Winter Garden, Fla., 1939-40, Eagle Lake Sch., Fla., 1940-41; welfare visitor Fla. Welfare Bd., 1941-42; specialist U.S. Army Signal Corps, Arlington Hall, Va., 1942-43; recreation worker, asst. procurement officer ARC, CBI Theater, 1943-46; lab. technician Am. Cyanamid Corp., Brewster, Fla., 1946-47; instr., asst. prof. gen. extension div. U. Fla., Fla. State U., 1948-51; free-lance writer, editor, indexer, N.Y., Fla., 1951-55; staff writer Tampa (Fla.) Morning Tribune, 1956; staff writer, telegraph editor Winter Haven (Fla.) News-Chief, 1956-57; registrar/admissions officer U. Tampa, 1957-59; coll. counselor, Atlantic states, 1959-60; registrar/freshman adviser Towson State Tchrs. Coll., Balt., 1960-62; dir. student personnel, guidance, admissions Harford Jr. Coll., Bel Air, Md., 1962-64; instr. York (Pa.) Coll., 1965-66, asst. prof. English, journalism, 1966-69; tchr. S.W. Jr. High Sch., Lakeland, Fla., 1969-70; tchr. learning disabled Vanguard Sch., Lake Wales, Fla., 1970-82; docent, hist. calendar editor Polk County Hist. and Geneal. Library, Bartow, Fla., 1984—. Mem. AAUW, Nat. Geneal. Soc., Mortar Bd., NOW, Alpha Chi Alpha, Chi Delta Phi. Editor: Tampa Altrusan, 1958-60. Home: 511 NE 9th Ave Mulberry FL 33860

BOWMAN, MARIAN LOUISE, auditor; b. Louisville, Apr. 20, 1921; d. Arthur George and Sadie Louise (Frost) Bodemann; m. Francis Mason Miles, Nov. 27, 1942 (dec. Mar. 1986); 1 child, Joseph Arthur; m. John Russell Bowman, July 3, 1947 (dec. Nov. 1979); 1 child Tracy Leigh. A in Acctg., Clark Coll., 1939-41. Bookkeeper Cissell Mfg. Co., Louisville, 1941-54; office mgr. Apex Wrecking Co., Louisville, 1964-66; bus. mgr. The Lincoln Sch., Simpsonville, Ky., 1966-69; adminstrv. asst. Dept. of Fin./State Govt., Frankfort, Ky., 1970-71; controller Whitney Young Job Corps Ctr., Simpsonville, 1971-80; asst. corp. controller Res-Care, Inc., Louisville, 1980-84, corp. controller, 1984-86; corp. auditor Res-Care Devel. Co., Inc., Louisville, 1986—. Recipient City of Louisville Effort medal, The Louisville Times, 1936; Louisville Collegiate scholar, 1936. Mem. Exec. Women's Internat., Leukemia Soc. (trustee Louisville chpt.), Am. Legion Aux. Lodge: Order Eastern Star. Office: Res-Care Devel Co Inc 1300 Embassy Square Office Park Louisville KY 40299

BOWMAN, MARTHA ALEXANDER, librarian; b. Washington, June 8, 1945; d. Lyle Thomas and Helen (Goodwin) Alexander; m. David Henry Bowman, June 11, 1965 (div. 1982); 1 child, Elaine. B.A., U. Md., 1967; M.S. in Library Sci., Cath. U. Am., 1969. Librarian U. Md., College Park, 1969-72, head acquisitions, 1973-75; asst. univ. librarian George Washington U., Washington, 1975-78, assoc. univ. librarian, 1978-82; univ. librarian U. Louisville, 1983—; chmn. bd. dirs. SOLINET (Southeastern Library Network). Coordinator U. Louisville United Way, 1987. Mem. ALA (chmn. poster sessions 1983-85, co-chmn. nat. conf. in Cin. 1989), Am. Assn. Higher Edn., Athletic Assn. U. Louisville (chmn. personnel), D.C. Library Assn. (pres. 1981-82), Women Acad. Library Dirs. Exchange Network. Episcopalian. Home: 1830 Woodfill Way Louisville KY 40205 Office: Univ of Louisville Libraries Louisville KY 40292

BOWMAN, MARVIS, cost analyst; b. Phenix City, Ala., Dec. 19, 1936; d. Willie Lee and Lillie Mae (Fleming) Pugh; m. Raymond Bowman, Nov. 17, 1960; children: Darell Alan, Pamela Kay, Tracy Dafina. Assoc's., Sinclair Coll., 1980; BS in Bus., Wright State U., 1981; postgrad., U. Dayton, 1983, Cen. Mich. U., 1988. With USAF, Wright-Patterson AFB, Ohio, 1957—, mgmt. analyst, 1974-76, fin. specialist, 1976-84, cost performance analyst, 1984—. Mem. Am. Mgmt. Assn., Nat. Assn. Female Execs., Am. Soc. Mil. Comptrollers, Blacks in Govt. (chmn. publicity com.). Baptist. Home: 5301 Pinnacle Rd Dayton OH 45418

BOWMAN, MARY BETH, state agency administrator; b. Berkeley, Calif., Jan. 1, 1948; d. Ben and Geneva (Morrison) B. BA, Henderson State U., 1970, MS, 1977. Social services worker State of Ark., Malvern, 1971-72; social worker Ouachita Regional Counseling and Mental Health Ctr., Hot Springs, Ark., 1972-75; dir. Community Devel. Dept., Malvern, 1976-80; assoc. Clayton Comml. Devel., Malvern, 1981; pvt. practice cons. Malvern, 1981-82; dir. Ark. Manufactured Home Commn., Little Rock, 1982—; pres., co-owner Bow-Mill Enterprises, Inc., Little Rock, 1986-87; apptd. Ark. voting del. Nat. Conf. States on Bldg. Codes and Standards, Herndon, Va., 1983—, 1st v.p., 1986-87, pres. 1987—; apptd. mem. Nat. Manufactured Home Adv. Council, Washington, 1984-85, 87—, exec. com. 1987—; apptd. mem. Ark. Dist. Export Council, Little Rock, 1984—; chmn. states' task force Fed. Manufactured Home Program, Washington, 1985—. Bd. dirs. Advs. for Battered Women, Little Rock, 1986—, sec. 1987—. Mem. Downtown Little Rock Bus. and Profl. Women's Orgn. (mem. women in workplace com. 1984-86, pres. Little Rock chpt. 1986-87, Woman of Yr. 1985). Home: 12810 Saint Charles Blvd Little Rock AR 72211 Office: Ark Manufactured Home Commn Suite 440 1st Federal Plaza 401 W Capitol Ave Little Rock AR 72201

BOWMAN, NANCY MOFFETT, counselor; b. Harrisonburg, Va., Feb. 20, 1942; d. John Guthrie and Florence Ellen (Reese) Moffett; m. Wayne St. Clair, Aug. 17, 1965; children: John Moffett Stuart, George Holland Dudley. BA, High Point Coll., 1963; MS, Va. Commonwealth U., 1965. lic. profl. counselor. Dean women Vardell Hall, Red Springs, N.C., 1964-65; asst. dir. St. Andrews Presbyn. Coll., Laurinburg, N.C., 1965; counselor Bon Air Sch. for Girls, Richmond, Va., 1966-69; vocat. evaluator Bon Air Sch. for Girls, Richmond, 1969-70; disability sepcialist State Dept. Vocat. Rehab., Richmond, 1970-72; counselor Union Theol. Sem., Richmond, 1983—, Next Step, Inc., Richmond, 1984-85; owner, counselor Bowman Counseling Assocs., Richmond, 1985—; vol. counselor St. John's Vianny Ctr., Richmond, 1980; vol. counselor Project Jump St., Richmond, 1977-79; bd. dirs. Brookfield, Inc., Richmond. Author: Mental Deficiency, 1969, Psychological Testing, 1969, Assertiveness Training, 1984, Children of Alcoholics, 1988. Bd. dirs. Historic Richmond Found., 1978—; pres. West End Community Ctr., Richmond, 1973-74; ofcl. electoral bd. City of Richmond, 1976—; deacon 1st Presbyn. Ch., Richmond, 1986—; cons. Big Bros./Big Sisters of Richmond, 1988—. Mem. Am. Assn. Counseling and Devel., Va. Counselors Assn., Va. Assn. Drug and Alcohol Problems, Richmond Area Women Bus. Owners, Richmond Area Mental Health Counselors Assn. Club: Stonewall Court. Office: Bowmand Counseling Assocs 3108 Parham Rd Suite 5023 Richmond VA 23229

BOWMAN, PATRICIA ANN, real estate executive; b. Potsdam, N.Y., Oct. 20, 1949; d. Wilton and Shirley Ann (Hay) B. BS in Bus. Adminstrn., Susquehanna U., 1971; cert. in real estate, Inst. for Paralegal Tng., Phila., 1972. Legal asst. Weinberg & Green, Balt., 1972-74; real estate closing officer Callahan, Caldwell & Laudeman, Balt., 1974-77; asst. dir. mortgage financing Monumental Properties Trust, Balt., 1977-79; sr. real estate analyst The Equitable Live Assurance Soc., N.Y.C., 1979-82; project mgr. real estate Chem. Bank, N.Y.C., 1982—. Mem. Young Mortgage Bankers Assn., Bldg. Owners and Mgrs. Inst. (candidate registered pub. acct. designation). Republican. Episcopalian. Home: 5425 Valles Ave Apt 5G Riverdale NY 10471 Office: Chem Bank NY 633 3d Ave 8th Floor New York NY 10022

BOWMAN-DALTON, BURDENE KATHRYN, educator, computer consultant; b. Magnolia, Ohio, July 13, 1937; d. Ernest Mowles and Mary Kathryn (Long) Bowman; B.M.E., Capital U., 1959; MA in Edn., Akron U., 1967, postgrad. 1976—; m. Louis W. Dalton, Mar. 13, 1979. Profl. vocalist, various clubs in the East, 1959-60; music tchr. East Liverpool (Ohio) City Schs., 1959-62; music tchr. Revere Local Schs., Akron, Ohio, 1962-75, elem. tchr., 1975-80, elem. team leader/computer cons., 1979-85, tchr. middle sch. math., gift-talented, computer literacy, 1981—, dist. computer specialist, 1987—; local and regional dir., Olympics of the Mind, also World Problem Captain for computer problem, 1984-86; cons., workshop presenter State of Ohio, 1987—. Mem. Citizen Com., Akron, 1975-76; profl. rep. Bath Assn. to Help, 1978-80; mem. Revere Levy Com. 1986; audit com. BATH, 1977-79; volunteer chmn. Antique Car Show, Akron, 1972-81; dist. advisor MidWest Talent Search, 1987—; dist. statistician of standardized test results. Martha Holden Jennings Found. grantee, 1977-78; Title IV ESEA grantee, 1977-81. Mem. Assn. for Devel. of Computer-Based Instructional Systems, Assn. Supervision and Curriculum Devel., Ohio Assn. for Gifted Children, Phi Beta. Republican. Lutheran. Home: 353 Retreat Dr Akron OH 44313 Office: 3195 Spring Valley Rd Bath OH 44210

BOWREN, FAY FRANCES, education educator; b. Oklahoma City, Sept. 15, 1924; d. Frank and Fay (Horton) Herrmann; m. Russell A. Bowren; children: Joy Elene, Linda Ruth, Timothy Lee, Diana Gayle. BA, Bob Jones U., 1945, MA, 1946; postgrad., U. Chgo., 1967; EdD, U. N.Mex., 1969. Missionary So. Bapt. Conv., Puertocato, N.Mex., 1946-60; cons. reading Grants (N.Mex.) Community Schs., 1960-64, Los Lunas (N.Mex.) Schs., 1964-68; dir. reading clinic Manzanita Ctr. U. N.Mex., Albuquerque, 1968-69; prof. edn. Ill. State U., Normal, 1969—; ednl. cons., Ill., 1969—; cons. computer edn., Ill., 1980—. Author: Teaching Reading in Adult Basic Education, 1977; contbr. articles to profl. jours. Trustee Judson Coll., Elgin, Ill., 1978—; violinist Bloomington (Ill.) Symphony, 1980-84, Cen. Ill. Chamber Orch., Bloomington, 1982—, Wesleyan Civic Symphony, Bloomington, 1984—; bd. dirs. Ill. State Bapt. Assn., 1972—;. Mem. Internat. Reading Assn., Ill. Reading Council, DAR, Pi Delta Kappa, Pi Lambda Theta, Sigma Alpha Iota. Club: Amateur Music (Bloomington). Office: Ill State U DeGarmo 5 Normal IL 61761

BOWRON, PATRY-IRENE DAMON MACGREGOR MATHEWETZ (MRS. JAMES EDGAR BOWRON), retired association executive; b. N.Y.C., Feb. 17, 1908; d. Ralph Waldo Emerson MacGregor and Daisy Agnes Damon; m. Raymond Joseph Mathewetz, June 17, 1938 (dec.); m. Frederick Lorimer Patry, May 8, 1958 (dec.); m. James Edgar Bowron, Apr. 14, 1971 (dec.). AB, Adelphi U. Mem. DAC, DAR (life, past 2d vice regent Manatee chpt.), Ancient and Honorable Welles Family, Descendant Col. Gov., Northeast Women and Aux. Manatee Meml. Hosp., Magna Charta Dames, Descendant Col. Clergy (life), Women Descendant Ancient and Honorable Artillery Co., Col. Dames XVII Century (orgn. auditor William Bassett chpt.), Order of Washington (life), Welles Fam. Assn., Here. Order Descendant Col. Govs., Here. Ord. 1st Family of Mass. (founder), Nat. Soc. Old Plymouth Colony Descendants, Manasota Geneal. Soc., Scottish Heritage USA, Inc., North South Northeast Women (orgn. colony pres.), Ohio Geneal. Soc., Retired Officers Club Bradenton, Nat. Assn. Parliamentarians (past pres. Bradenton unit, past parliamentarian, past bd. dirs.), Am. Assn. Univ. Women, Manatee River Garden Club (past parliamentarian, pub. chmn.), Manatee County Mental Health Assn. (past treas., bd. dirs.), Aux. Manatee Meml. Hosp., English Speaking Union, Manatee Bus. and Profl. Women's Club, League Women Voters, Bradenton Women's Club (past devotionals), Manatee County Panhellenic Assn. (charter), Woman's Aux. to Med. Assns., Soc. Descendants of Founders of Hartford, Sigma Kappa. Lodge: Ladies Oriental Shrine (past bd. dirs. charter orgn., parliamentarian SAR-I Ct.). Home: 5912 Riverview Blvd W Bradenton FL 33529

BOWSER, ANITA OLGA, educator; b. Canton, Ohio, Aug. 18, 1920; d. Nicholas B. Alby and Emile Stobbe. AB, Kent State U., 1945, LLB, William McKinley U., 1949; MS, Purdue U., 1967; MA, U. Notre Dame, 1972, PhD, 1976. Instr. Kent (Ohio) State U., 1945-46; prof. Purdue U. North Cen. Campus, Michigan City, Ind., 1950—. State Rep. Ind. Gen. Assembly, Indpls., 1980—. Mem. Delta Kappa Gamma. Home: 1912 E Coolspring Michigan City IN 46360

BOWSER, EMILIE LOUISE, nurse, educator, dress designer; b. Newark, Ohio, July 16, 1941; d. James Elbert and Geraldine Mae (Utts) Drumm; m. Gary L. Bowser, June 6, 1964 (div. July 1980); children—Deborah, Diana, David. B.S.N. in Nursing, Ohio State U., 1964; M.S. in Nursing, Wayne State U., 1984. R.N., Ohio. Charge nurse West Paces Ferry Hosp., Atlanta, 1972-73; clin. instr. St. Vincent's Hosp., Toledo, Ohio, 1976; staff nurse Toledo Hosp., parttime 1976—; staff nurse Flower Hosp., Toledo, 1978-79; clin. instr. U. Toledo, 1979; assoc. prof. nursing Owens Tech. Coll., Toledo, 1979—, cons. continuing edn., 1981-87; owner Emilie's Original Bridal Creations ; advisor Nat. Student Nurses Assn., Toledo, 1981—. Cub scout com. chmn. Wolverine council Boy Scouts Am., 1983—; mem. youth com. Trinity Episcopal Ch. Mem. Ohio Nurses Assn. (publicity com. 1980-82), Bedford Band Boosters, Alpha Delta Pi. Republican. Club: Tamaron Country (Toledo). Office: Owens Tech Coll Oregon Rd Toledo OH 43699

BOWYER, JOAN ELIZABETH, medical technologist, realtor; b. Ellensburg, Wash., July 11, 1944; d. Chester Joseph and Rita Geneva (Newell) Howarth; 1 child, Suzanne Elise. BA, Ft. Wright Coll. of Holy Names, 1966; grad., Real Estate Sch. Oreg., 1982. Lic. med. technologist. Med. technologist Lab. of Clin. Medicine, Seattle, 1967-69, Sacred Heart Gen. Hosp., Eugene, Oreg., 1969-73, 74-76, McKenzie Willamette Hosp., Springfield, Oreg., 1976-77, Mid-Columbia Hosp., The Dalles, Oreg., 1977-82; realtor Red Carpet/Rich Hall Realty, Hillsboro, Oreg., 1982-85, Century 21 Columbia Realty, Portland, 1985—; med. technologist ARC, Portland, 1982—. Co-editor: The Dalles Gen. Hosp. Newspaper, 1980-82. Pres. Wasco County Edn. Service Dist. Parents Group, The Dalles, 1978-82; founder, pres. Mid-Columbia Parents of Deaf, 1978-82; parental spokesperson Spl. Edn. Adv. Com., Salem, Oreg., 1980-82; activist parent for deaf/hearing impaired, 1977—. Mem. Med. Technologists of Am. Soc. Pathologists, Nat. Assn. Realtors, Nat. Assn. Female Execs., Century 21 Investment Soc. Democrat. Mem. Ch. of Jesus Christ of Latter Day Saints. Avocations: photography, dancing, hiking, travel. Home: 704 SE 38th St Portland OR 97214 Office: Century 21 Columbia 202 SE 181st St Portland OR 97233

BOXELL, KAREN ANN, social researcher; b. Amesbury, Mass., July 21, 1944; d. Walter Leo Boxell and Ethel Laura (Berry) Hillidge; m. Frank N. Kelley, Apr. 28, 1963 (div. July 1986); children: Kathrine, Frank N. III, Keith. BA in Communication, Northeastern U., Boston, 1982. Field interviewer Ctr. for Survey Research, Boston, 1982—; cons. OmniCom, Newbury, Mass.; tchr. communication-pub. speaking Town of Andover, Mass., 1986. Author: (tchr. manual) Communication Skills, 1986, (booklet) Byfield Parish Ch., 1972. Basic Skills sub.-com., Assn. of Sch. Coms., Boston, 1985-86, basic skills adv. com. Mass. Bd. of Edn., Boston, 1986-88, sch. com. Newbury (Mass.) Pub. Sch., 1974—, Haverhill (Mass.) Vocat. Sch., 1976—; vol. Girl Scouts of Am. Mem. Nat. Speech Communication Assn., Nat. Assn. Female Execs., Mass. Tchrs. Assn. Episcopalian. Home: 31 Downfall Rd Byfield MA 01922

BOXER, BARBARA, congresswoman; b. Bklyn., Nov. 11, 1940; d. Ira and Sophie (Silvershein) Levy; m. Stewart Boxer, 1962; children: Doug, Nicole. B.A., Bklyn. Coll., 1962. Stockbroker Merrill Lynch, N.Y.C., 1962-65; journalist, assoc. editor Pacific Sun, 1972-74; congl. aide to rep. 5th Congl. Dist. San Francisco, 1974-76; mem. Marin County Bd. Suprs., San Rafael, Calif., 1976-82; mem. 98th-100th Congresses from 6th dist. Calif., 1983—, mem. budget com., armed services com., select com. children, youth and families, chairwoman budget com. task force on AIDS, majority whip at large. Pres. Marin County Bd. Suprs., 1980-81; mem. Bay Area Air Quality Mgmt. Bd., San Francisco, 1977-82, pres., 1979-81; bd. dirs. Golden Gate Bridge Hwy. and Transport Dist., San Francisco, 1978-82; founding mem. Marin Nat. Women's Polit. Caucus, Marin Community Video; pres. Dem. New Mems. Caucus, 1983. Recipient Open Govt. award Common Cause, 1980. Jewish. Office: 307 Cannon House Office Bldg Washington DC 20515

BOXX, RITA MCCORD, banker; b. Greenwood, S.C., Aug. 10, 1930; d. John Thomas Logan and Dempsie (Dixon) McCord; student public schs.; m. John Douglas Boxx, Apr. 17, 1949; children—John Stephen, Eric Wesley, Merry Christine. Asst. mgr. Greenwood Ins. Agy., 1951-65, mgr., 1967-80; with Bankers Trust S.C., Greenwood, 1951—, asst. v.p. charge ins. dept., 1980—; tchr. ins. seminars. Mem. Nat. Assn. Ins. Women, Ind. Ins. Agts. Greenwood, Ind. Ins. Agts. S.C., Ind. Ins. Agts. Am., Greenwood Assn. Ins. Women, Greenwood C. of C. (dir. 1974-76, chmn. environ., energy and conservation com. 1974, chmn. edn. com. 1977). Baptist. Club: Greenwood Country. Home: 434 Dogwood Dr Greenwood SC 29646 Office: PO Box 1058 Greenwood SC 29648

BOXX, VERONICA RAE, telemarketing manager, consultant; b. St. Louis, Feb. 13, 1947; d. Martin Anthony and Anna Laura (Unger) Mueller; m. Jerry Lynn Boxx. BA in Psychology, U. Mo., 1970. Med. asst. Northland Clin. Lab, St. Louis, 1965-73; sales asst. Gregg div. McGraw-Hill Book Co., St. Louis, 1973-77, mktg. rep., 1978-81, telemarketing rep., 1978-81, telemarketing mgr., 1981-84; telemarketing mgr. Coll. div. McGraw-Hill Book Co., St. Louis, 1984—; cons. McGraw-Hill Inc., various locations, 1983—; speaker McGraw-Hill Inc., 1983, Nat. Soc. Sales Tng. Execs., Ft. Lauderdale, Fla., 1985, Sales & Mktg. Execs Greater Met. St. Louis, 1987, Bus. Profl. Advt. Assn., 1988; lectr. St. Louis Community Coll., 1988; tchr.

Pattonville Schs. Adult Edn., Bridgeton, Mo., 1967. Contbr. articles to profl. jours. Donor ARC, St. Louis, 1972. Recipient scholarship Lions Club, 1965, PTA scholarship Hazelwood Sch. Dist., 1965. Mem. Bus. and Profl. Advt. Assn. Club: St. Louis Connection. Office: McGraw-Hill Book Co Coll Div 13955 Manchester Rd Manchester MO 63011

BOYARSKY, ROSE EISMAN, psychologist; b. Jersey City, Mar. 16, 1924; d. Isadore and Clara (Klingenstein) Eisman; m. Saul Boyarsky, June 17, 1946; children: Myer William, Terry Linda, Hannah Gail. BS in Chemistry, U. Vt., 1944; MA, Columbia U., 1946; PhD, Duke U., 1969. Psychologist Durham (N.C.) County Mental Health Clinic, 1969-70; counselor U. Mo. Counseling Center, St. Louis, 1971-72; research assoc. Masters and Johnson Inst., St. Louis, 1972-75; pvt. practice psychology, Boyhill Center, St. Louis, 1975—; research assoc. depts. surgery and urology Washington U. Med. Ctr., St. Louis, 1977—; mem. assoc. staff Jewish Hosp. of St. Louis, 1971—; dir. Archway Community for Drug Rehab., 1973—; mem. Ea. Mo. Regional Adv. Council for Psychiat. Services, 1975-81; apptd. mem. Mo. State Com. Psychologists, 1983—, chmn., 1986-88. Contbr. articles in field to profl. jours.; mem. editorial bd. Profl. Psychology, 1979—, Psychology and Pvt. Practice, 1983—, Young Couples Internat., 1983—; editor SCOP Newsletter, 1984-87. Trustee Judea Reform Congregation of Durham-Chapel Hill, N.C., 1967-69, Portland Place Assn., 1980-83; mem. adv. bd. Victim Service Council, 1985—. Mem. Psychologists in Pvt. Practice, Mo. Psychol. Assn. (pres. 1977-78), Am. Psychol. Assn., AAAS, Am. Women in Psychology, Soc. of Columbia Chemists, Phi Beta Kappa, Iota Sigma Pi. Home: 45 Portland Pl Saint Louis MO 63108 Office: 4625 Lindell Blvd Saint Louis MO 63108

BOYCE, DOREEN ELIZABETH, educational foundation executive; b. Antofagasta, Chile, Apr. 20, 1934; d. George Edgar and Elsie Winifred Vaughan; B.A. with honors, Oxford (Eng.) U., 1956, M.A. with honors, 1960; Ph.D., U. Pitts., 1983, D. in Hum. Lit., Westminster Coll., 1986; m. Alfred Warne Boyce, Aug. 11, 1956; children—Caroline Elizabeth, John Trevor Warne. Lectr. and tutor in econs. U. Witwatersrand, South Africa, 1960-62; provost and dean of faculty, prof. econs. Chatham Coll., Pitts., 1963-79; prof. econs., chmn. dept. econs. and mgmt. Hood Coll., Frederick, Md., 1979-82; exec. dir. Buhl Found., Pitts., 1982—; dir. Duquesne Light Co., Dollar Bank, FSB, Microbac Labs., Inc. Del. White House Conf. on Small Bus., 1980; mem. Gov.'s Conf. Small Bus., 1979-82; trustee Franklin and Marshall Coll., 1982—, Frick Edn. Commn., 1980—, Buhl Sci. Ctr., 1982—; mem. citizens sponsoring com. Allegheny Conf. Community Devel., 1982—; mem. Fed. Jud. Nominating Commn., 1977-79, Pa. Gov.'s Commn. on Financing of Higher Edn., 1983-85 bd. dirs. World Affairs Council, 1984—. Mem. Am. Econs. Assn., Exec. Women's Council, Am. Assn. Higher Edn. (mem. com. prof. devel. Council Founds.), Grantmakers of Western Pa. (pres.). Office: 4 Gateway Ctr Room 1522 Pittsburgh PA 15222

BOYCE, EMILY STEWART, library and information science educator; b. Raleigh, N.C., Aug. 18, 1933; d. Harry and May (Fallon) B. BS, East Carolina U., 1955, MA, 1961; MS in Library Sci., U. N.C., 1968; postgrad., Cath. U. Am., 1977. Librarian Tileston Jr. High Sch., Wilmington, N.C., 1955-57; children's librarian Wilmington Pub. Library, 1957-58; asst. librarian Joyner Library East Carolina U., Greenville, N.C., 1959-61, librarian III, 1962-63; ednl. supr. II ednl. media div. N.C. State Dept. Pub. Instrn., Raleigh, 1961-62; assoc. prof. dept. library and info. scis. East Carolina U., Raleigh, 1964-76, prof., 1976—, chmn. dept., 1982—; cons. So. Assn. Colls. and Schs., Raleigh, 1975—. Mem. Pitt County Hist. Preservation Soc., Greenville, Pitt County Mental Health Assn. Mem. ALA, AAUW, N.C. Library Assn., Southeastern Library Assn., Assn. Library and Info. Sci. Educators, Spl. Libraries Assn., LWV, NOW. Democrat. Home: 1406 Rondo Dr Greenville NC 27858 Office: East Carolina U Dept Library and Info Scis Greenville NC 27878-4353

BOYD, CATHERINE E. (KATY), communications executive, writer; b. Dixon, Ill., Jan. 24, 1918; d. Carl Albert and Regina Barbara (Haas) Buchner; m. Allen James Boyd, Oct. 12, 1940 (div. 1964); children: James Allen, Barbara Mae Fane. BA, MacMurray Coll., 1939; postgrad., No. Ill. U., 1964, Ohio State U., 1982—. Cert. airline transport pilot, flight instr. Office mgr., charter pilot Ill. Aircraft, Chgo., 1965-66; instr. Aviation Tng. Enterprises, Chgo., 1967; dir. ground tng. Aviation Tng. Enterprises Calif., Santa Monica; dir. tnr. Ross Aviation, Tulsa; dir. edn. Accel. Grad. Sch., Atlanta; dir. course devel. Traveling Aviation Seminars, Columbus, Ohio, 1983; adminstrv. asst. Olentangy Assocs., Columbus, 1983—; Cons. aerospace Govt. People's Republic of China, Summer, 1987. Author: ATP-Airline Transport Pilot, 1969, 3d edit., 1987, Weather Or Not, 1975 (Citation of Merit 1976), ATP-FAR 135, 1983. Leader Cub Scout Troop, Girl Scout Troop; bd. dirs. ARC; braille transcriber, Dixon, Ill., 1940-64. Named Pilot of Yr. Chgo. 99's, 1969. Mem. Aviation Space Writers Assn., Nat. League Am. Pen Women (treas. 1986-88), Planetary Soc., Rock and Mineral Soc. Republican. Methodist. Home: 1301 Old Henderson Rd Columbus OH 43220

BOYD, CATHERINE ROBERTSON, home economist; b. Shawnee, Okla., June 10, 1938; d. James Marvin and Cleo Rebecca (Snyder) Robertson; B.S., U. Ky., 1959, M.S., 1962; Ph.D., U. Ala., 1982; m. Leroy H. Boyd, Jan. 28, 1958; children—Susanne, Diane. Tchr. jr. and sr. high sch., Versailles, Ky., 1959-62; med. research asst. U. Ky. Med. Center, Lexington, 1962-63; prof. home econs. Miss. State U., 1969—; dir. for Miss., Make it Yourself with Wool Contest, 1972—. Mem. adv. council Oktibbeha County 4-H; vol. 4-H leader. Recipient Teaching award Miss. State U. Coll. Agr., 1981, 83, 86. Mem. Am. Home Econs. Assn., Assn. Coll. Profs. Textiles and Clothing, Mid-South Ednl. Research Assn., Miss. Home Econs. Assn., Phi Upsilon Omicron, Omicron Nu, Kappa Delta Pi, Gamma Sigma Delta, Kappa Omicron Phi, Phi Delta Kappa. Baptist. Club: Miss. State U. Women's. Author 4-H bulletins. Home: 9 Oriole Dr Starkville MS 39759 Office: Miss State U Drawer HE Mississippi State MS 39762

BOYD, CHARLENE GAYE, bookstore administrator; b. Paintsville, Ky., Oct. 9, 1948; d. Russell and Marvel (Brown) Boyd; m. Danny Gale Bailey, Aug. 26, 1972 (div.). B.S., Morehead State U., 1972, M.A. in Edn., 1977, M.B.A., 1985. Tchr. math. Anderson County Bd. Edn., Lawrenceburg, Ky., 1972, Franklin County Bd. Edn., Frankfort, Ky., 1972-73; bookstore mgr. Ashland Community Coll., Ky., 1973—. Mem. Nat. Assn. Coll. Stores (regional steering com. 1978, 82), Ky. Assn. Coll. Stores (bd. dirs. 1985-90, pres. 1983). Republican. Methodist. Avocation: tennis, scuba diver. Office: Ashland Community Coll 1400 College Dr Ashland KY 41101

BOYD, CINDY L., association executive; b. Dallas, June 5, 1959; d. John L. and Mildred P. (Rollinson) B. B of Acctg., U. Houston, 1984. Asst. credit mgr. La. Pacific Railways, Conroe, Tex., 1977-79; credit mgr. High Strength Steel Corp., Houston, 1979-81, Fisk Electric Co., Houston, 1981-84; membership dir. Houston Assn. Credit Mgmt., 1984—. Mem. Houston Women's Credit Group, Nat. Assn. Female Execs. Republican. Methodist. Home: 5400 Memorial Dr #802 Houston TX 77007 Office: Houston Assn Credit Mgmt 5325 Kirby Dr Houston TX 77005

BOYD, GWENDOLYN VIOLA, police officer; b. Sneads, Fla., June 4, 1954; d. Willie Charles and Vera Mae (McClendon) Mathis; m. Harold James Boyd, Feb. 20, 1976; children: Sherhonda, Lakeesha. Cert. in police sci., BA, St. Thomas Villanova, 1980; AA, Miami-Dade Jr. Coll., 1974; MPA, Fla. Internat. U., 1982; cert., U. La., 1985. Instr.'s certification, Fla. Pub. Service Aide Miami (Fla.) Police Dept., 1974, officer, 1974-81, sgt., 1981-85, maj., 1985—; instr. Miami Police Acad., 1981—; assessor, Assessment Designs, Inc., Miami, 1983—. Mem. atty. gen.'s crime task force, Miami, 1983; active Big Bros./Big Sis. of Am., Miami, 1986; mem. Alternatives to Incarceration, Miami, 1987; mem. Overtown Adv. Bd., Miami, 1987; mem. Dade Coutny Coalition for Homeless, Miami, 1987. Recipient Outstanding Physical Fitness award South Fla. Police Olympics, 1975-86, Outstanding Performance award South Fla. Corps., 1985, 86, Outstanding Service award Miami-Community Police Benevolent Assn., 1979, 86, Outstanding Achievement award Nat. Orgn. of Black Law Enforcement Exec., 1986, Outstanding Achievement Nat. Assn. of Negro Bus. and Profl. Women, 1986. Mem. Fraternal Order of Police, Family Christian Assn., Miami Assn. Women Police, Urban League of Greater Miami. Democrat. Pentacostal. Home: 16905 NW 52 Pl Miami FL 33055 Office: Miami Police Dept 400 NW 2 Ave Miami FL 33128

BOYD, JANIE BARNES, elementary educator; b. Hopkinsville, Ky., Dec. 7, 1924; d. Oscar Lafayette and Ivyl Pearl (Rogers) Barnes; m. James Edward Boyd, Aug. 30, 1945; children: Laura Boyd Kort, Jane Boyd Thomas, James Edward Jr. Student, Georgetown (Ky.) Coll., 1944-45; AA, Palm Beach Jr. Coll., 1968; BS, Fla. Atlantic U., 1971; MS, Nova U., Ft. Lauderdale, Fla., 1978. Tchr. Palm Beach County Schs., West Palm Beach, Fla., 1960-66, asst. librarian, 1967-68, profl. instr., 1970—; clk. Palm Lake Bapt. Assn., Palm Beach County, 1968-70. Contbr. articles to profl. jours. Mem. AAUW, Classroom Tchrs. Assn., Phi Delta Kappa. Democrat. Home: 7100 Clarke Rd West Palm Beach FL 33406

BOYD, JEAN K., psychiatrist; b. Wellesley, Mass., Sept. 7, 1944; d. James G. and Marie K. (Pfeifer) B. BA, Boston U., 1966; MD, Med. Coll. Pa., 1971. Intern. resident in psychiatry Hahnemann Med. Coll., Phila., 1971-74; staff psychiatrist Med. Ctr. Western Mass., Springfield, 1974-75; practice medicine specializing in psychiatry Milford, Mass., 1975—; mem. faculty U. Mass., Tufts U., 1974-78; mem. courtesy staff Milford-Whitinsville Regional Hosp.; mem. courtesy staff (Mass.) Hosp.; cons. Mass. Rehab. Com., 1976-81. Mem. Mass. Med. Soc., Am. Psychiat. Soc., Mass. Psychiat. Soc., Am. Med. Women's Assn. Office: PO Box 2537 Providence RI 02906-0537

BOYD, LEONA JOHNSTON POTTER, former county welfare administrator; b, Creekside, Pa., Aug. 31, 1907; d. Joseph M. and Belle (McHenry) Johnston; grad. Ind. Normal Sch., 1927; student Las Vegas Normal U., summer 1933; courses Carnegie Inst. Tech. Sch. Social Work, summer 1945, U. Pitts. Grad. Sch. Social Work, 1956-57; m. Edgar D. Potter, July 16, 1932 (div.); m. 2d, Harold L. Boyd, Oct. 9, 1972. Tchr., Creekside Pub. Schs., 1927-30, Papago Indian Reservation, Sells, Ariz., 1931-33; caseworker, supr. Indiana County (Pa.) Bd. Assistance, 1934-54, exec. dir., 1954-68; ret., 1968; cons. assoc. Community Research Assocs., St. Paul; mem. bd. Lake Havasu Counseling Center Aux. Former mem. bd. dirs. Indiana County United Fund, Salvation Army, Indiana County Guidance Ctr., Armstrong-Indiana Mental Health Assn. Recipient award for community services Indiana County Bus. and Profl. Women's Club, 1965, Ind. Jaycees award for Disting. Service, 1966. Mem. Daus. Am. Colonists, Indiana County Tourist Promotion Bur. (hon. life), Am. Assn. Ret. Persons (chpt. historian Lake Havasu City), Sierra County (N.Mex.) Hist. Soc., Internat. Platform Assn., Sierra Vista Hosp. Aux. Lutheran. Club: Hot Springs Women's. Home: 507 N Foch St Truth or Consequences NM 87901

BOYD, LINDA CAPPS, writer; b. Mangum, Okla., Feb. 29, 1940; d. Travis B. and Virginia (Dorrill) Capps; m. William C. Boyd, June 15, 1963; children—William C. and Stanford Scott. B.S. in English and Edn., Tex. Tech. U., 1962; B.A. in Journalism, U. Houston, 1978. Cert. tchr., Tex. Tchr. pub. schs., Amarillo, Tex., 1962-63, Pasadena, Houston and Spring Branch, Tex. 1965-80; writer-trainee Houston Chronicle, 1981-82; freelance writer, contbr. numerous articles to popular mags., 1982—. Active Houston Symphony, Alley Guild Houston Theater, Rep. Women, Nat. Fedn. Rep. Women. Mem. Tex. State Tchrs. Assn., Women in Communications. Presbyterian. Home and Office: 3632 Ella Lee Ln Houston TX 77027

BOYD, LINDA JOYCE (HICKS), academic administrator; b. Annapolis, Md., Dec. 10, 1946; d. James Melcar and Evelyn (Johnson) Hicks; m. Gerald Bernard Boyd, Jan. 2, 1969; 1 child, Kimberly Elaine. BS, Morgan State U., 1968; MEd, Bowie (Md.) State Coll., 1978; EdD, Nova U., 1986. With Anne Arundel County Pub. Schs., Annapolis, 1968-69, 71-87, asst. prin., 1980-81, prin., 1981-87; counselor, test proctor Edn. Devel. Agy., Worms, Fed. Republic of Germany, 1969-71; supr. elem. schs. Carroll County (Md.) Pub. Schs., 1987—; participant Madeline Hunter Tchr. Effectiveness Tng., Anne Arundel County, 1981-85; bd. dirs., co-chairperson New Wave of Entertainment, Annapolis, 1986—. Registrar St. Philip's Episc. Ch. Vestry, Annapolis, 1985—. Recipient award George Cromwell faculty, 1983, Tyler Heights faculty, 1986. Mem. NEA, Assn. for Ednl. Leadership (sec. 1985-86), Nat. Assn. Elem. Sch. Prins., Nat. Assn. Secondary Schs. (assessor 1982—), Md. Assn. Elem. Sch. Prins. (com. on profl. devel. 1986-87), Med. State Tchrs.' Assn., Nat. Assn. Female Execs., Delta Sigma Theta. Democrat. Club: Episc. Women's (Annapolis) (sec. 1977—). Home: 613 Marti Ln Annapolis MD 21401

BOYD, M. JUDITH, fundraising consultant; b. Garden City, N.J., Apr. 8, 1940; d. Bert Crawford and Ruth (McCarthy) Goss; m. John Dalzell Boyd, Oct. 13, 1965; childre: Andrew Goss, Sarah McCarthy. BA, Skidmore Coll., 1962; MA, Hunter Coll., 1965. Editorial asst. Pub. Relations Soc. of Am. Jour., N.Y.C., 1964-67; prodn. editor House and Gardens Guides, N.Y.C., 1967-70; mgr, mktg. dir. Lubric Import Co., Mt. Lakes, N.J., 1975-78; dir. publicity The Morris Mus., Morristown, N.J., 1978-84; devel. officer The Morris Mus., Morristown, 1984-87. Bd. dirs. Mt. Lakes (N.J.) Home and Sch. Assn., 1974. Mem. NJSFRE (bd. dirs., bd. trustees Deaf Contact Ctr.), AAUW, LWV (editor newsletter 1972). Episcopalian. Club: Jr. Women's (chair benefits 1973). Home: PO Box 32 35 Howell Rd Mount Lakes NJ 07046 Office: Robert F Semple Assocs One Edgewood Ave Nutley NJ 07110

BOYD, MARY DEXTER, newspaper editor; b. Columbus, Ga., Feb. 5, 1913; d. Charles Amory and Lydia Cook (Folwell) Dexter; m. Francis William Boyd, Jr., Sept. 1, 1934 (dec. July 1972); children—Robert Alexander, Richard Dexter, Mary Frances Boyd Logback, Elizabeth Folwell Boyd James. Student Agnes Scott Coll., 1930-31; B.S., Kans. State U., 1934. Cert. tchr., Kans. Tchr., Kensington High Sch., Kans., 1934-35; asst. editor Jewell County Record, Mankato, Kans., 1940-72, editor, 1972—. Mem. Comml. Devel. Assn., Mankato, 1972—, Mankato Endowment Assn., 1972—, Housing Authority City of Mankato, 1975—, Jewell County Fair Bd., 1980—. Mem. Kans. Press Assn., Kans. Press Women, Omicron Nu, Kappa Alpha, Xo Chi Omega (v.p. 1932-33). Clubs: Modern Minerva (pres. 1939-40), Desire Tobey Sears, DAR, P.E.O.. Home: 405 S Center St Mankato KS 66956 Office: Jewell County Record 111 Main St Mankato KS 66956

BOYD, MARY H. (MERRILL), assn. exec.; b. Winnetka, Ill., Sept. 11, 1929; d. Harold Gatton and Martha Emily (Lawson) Heberling; student Long Beach City Coll., 1956, UCLA, 1973; cert. in human services U. Calif.-Riverside, 1973-74; B.S. with honors, LaVerne U., 1982; children—Constance Anne Boyd, Richard Parker Boyd Jr. Exec. sec. Ontario-Pomona Assn. for Retarded Citizens, Montclair, Calif., 1962-65, exec. dir., 1965—; instr. Chaffey Coll., Alta Loma, Calif., 1972-76, coordinator classes for disabled, 1972-76; instr. weekend series LaVerne U., 1974, vis. lectr., 1969-74; vis. lectr. Mt. San Antonio Coll., 1976, U. Calif. at Riverside, 1972, UCLA, 1981-82; trainer various subjects Kellogg Found., OPARC Aux. Found., 1969; lectr. in field. Founder, Mental Retardation Service Council of San Gabriel Valley, 1965; mem. Calif. Developmental Disabilities Area planning bd., Area 12, Inyo, Mono, Riverside, San Bernardino counties, 1970-76, chmn. profl. adv. counsel, 1977-80; mem. steering com. for development of Regional Ctrs. Inland Counties, 1969-70, San Gabriel Valley, 1973; active Girl Scouts U.S.A., 1960-68; leader, advisor Tri-Hi-Y, 1968-71; bd. dirs. PTA, 1958-62; chmn. Mt. Baldy United Way Conf. Execs., 1983, 86-87; adv. bd. Mt. San Antonio Coll. Allied Health Adv. Bd., 1975-80, Los Angeles United Way, 1966—, Calif. Inst. for Men, 1968-72, San Bernardino County Child Health and Disability Prevention, 1975-78, chmn., 1977-78; adv. bd. Chaffey Coll., 1972-78. Recipient Award of Merit, San Bernardino County Council of Community Services, 1966; Hon. Service award Ontario Montclair Sch. Dist., 1971: Humanitarian award, San Bernardino County, 1976; Chaffey Community Rep. Women Federated Recognition award, 1977; Community Service, Lioness award U. LaVerne, 1982, Service award ARC, 1983, Calif. CCE Leadership award ARC, 1983, 85, Outstanding Leadership award United Way, 1987-88; HEW grantee, 1968, 69, 70, 72, 73, 74, 75, 76, 79; Calif. Community Found. grantee, 1968; Price Found. grantee, 1969, 72; Calif. Dept. Rehab. grantee, 1972, 73, 74, 75, 79, 81; Calif. Dept. Health grantee, 1976, 77. Mem. Assn. for Retarded-U.S. (pres. SW chpt. 1987), Assn. for Retarded-Calif. (v.p. 1979-81, pres. 1981-82), Conf. of Execs. of Assns. for Retarded U.S. (charter), Conf. Execs.-Calif. (chmn. 1982-83), Council Agy. Execs. Republican. Baptist. Author: (with J.Cook, J. Travers) Parents as Natural Helpers to Physicians at Time of Diagnosis of Developmental Disability, 1979. Home: 940 W 5th St Ontario CA 91762 Office: 5405 Arrow Hwy Suite 102 Montclair CA 91763

BOYD, MARY MICHELE, health care facility administrator; b. Elizabeth Twp., Pa., Sept. 16, 1953; d. Michael John Gogoel and Helen Barbara Korona; m. Thomas Edward Boyd, Oct. 27, 1978; children: Marshall Thomas, Natalie Helen. BS in Nursing, Pa. State U., 1981; M of Pub. Mgmt., Carnegie Mellon U., 1986. Staff nurse critical care unit West Penn Hosp., Pitts., 1974-77; dir. staff edn. Pitts., 1987—; staff nurse critical care unit South Hills Health System, Pitts., 1977-80, health educator, 1980-83, corp. mgr. tng. and devel., 1983-85; clin. asst. Pa. State U., University Park, 1981. Mem. Am. Heart Assn., Am. Soc. Tng. and Devel. Roman Catholic. Club: Twentieth Century. Home: 1001 Golfview Dr Elizabeth Township PA 15135 Office: West Penn Hosp 4800 Friendship Ave Pittsburgh PA 15224

BOYD, PATSY JEAN, accountant; b. Houston, Nov. 2, 1940; d. William Andrew and Stella Agnes (Nichols) Scott; m. Charles J. Boyd Jr., Aug. 27, 1960; children: Blair Vali Boyd Upchurch, Eric Austin. BBA, U. Tex., Tyler, 1981. CPA, Tex. Payment clk. United Mercantile Security Life, Dallas, 1960-63; sec. T.C. Wilson, PA, Jacksonville, Tex., 1965-67; sec. legal Norman, Hassell, Spiers, Jacksonville, 1967-79; controller, analyst Allied Tex. Bank, Jacksonville, 1980-83; controller Pizza Systems, Inc., Tyler, 1983—, sec./treas., controller, 1987—. Organist First Bapt. Ch., Jacksonville, 1985—. Mem. Tex. Soc. CPA's. Office: Pizza Systems Inc 3808 Old Jacksonville Rd Tyler TX 75701

BOYER, LAURA MERCEDES, librarian; b. Madison, Ind., Aug. 3, 1934; d. Clyde C. and Dorcas H. (Willyard) Boyer. A.B., George Washington U., 1956; A.M., U. Denver, 1959; M.L.S., George Peabody U., 1961. Pub. sch. tchr., Kankakee, Ill., 1957-58; asst. circulation librarian U. Kans., Lawrence, 1961-63; asst. reference librarian U. of Pacific Library, Stockton, Calif., 1963-65, head reference dept., 1965-84, coordinator reference services, 1984-86; reference librarian Calif. State U.-Stanislaus, Turlock, 1987—. Compiler of Play Anthologies Union List, 1976. Author article in profl. jour. Mem. Am. Soc. Info. Sci., ALA, Calif. Library Assn., AAUP, Nat. Assn. Female Execs., Nat. Assn. Vietnamese Am. Educators, DAR, Daughters of the Am. Colonists, Phi Beta Kappa, Kappa Delta Pi, Beta Phi Mu. Republican. Episcopalian. Home: 825 Muir Rd Modesto CA 95350

BOYER, LILLIAN BUCKLEY, artist, educator; b. Paterson, N.J., Mar. 1, 1916; d. George and Adele (Roomy) Buckley; B.A. in Art Edn., U. Ky., 1975; m. Floyd E. Boyer, Jr., Sept. 7, 1935; children—Karen Boyer Lloyd. Field interviewer Survey Research Center, U. Mich., 1963-68; 20 regional one-woman shows; instr. art U. Ky., Lexington; Ky. reporter for Sunshine Artists mag., 1976-85. Crusade chmn. Am. Cancer Soc., Anaheim, Calif., 1958, Orange County, Calif., 1959; active PTA, 1950-62, hon. life mem. Recipient 56 awards for print-making, painting and sculpture. Mem. AAUW, Lexington Arts Council, Ky. Citizens for the Arts, Lexington Art League (pres. 1976-80, 82-83, 84-86, dir., life mem.), Ky. Guild Artists and Craftsmen, U. Ky. Alumni Assn., Living Arts and Sci. Ctr., Friends of U.K. Art Mus., Nat. Mus. Women in Arts, JB. Speed Art Mus., Headley Whitney Mus., Ky. Women's Heritage Mus., Friends Ky. Ednl. TV. Methodist. Address: 969 Holly Springs Dr Lexington KY 40504

BOYER, MILDRED VINSON, educator; b. Newport, Tenn., June 1, 1926; d. Creed McNabb and Mildred Lucile (Vinson) B. BA, Baylor U., 1947, MA, 1949; PhD in Romance Langs., U. Tex., 1956. Asst. in Spanish Baylor U., Waco, Tex., 1947-49; instr. Baylor U., Waco, 1950-51; teaching fellow in Spanish U. Tex., 1949-50, 1951-53, instr., 1953-54, asst. prof. Spanish, Italian, 1958-59, assoc. prof. Spanish, 1962-66, prof. Spanish, Edn., 1966-86, prof. emeritus, 1986—; instr. English U. P.R., summer 1950, Spanish, Italian, U. Ill. 1955-58; asst. prof. Spanish, Italian, U. Ark. 1958-59; assoc. dir. Foggy Bottom Conf. Washington 1960; cons. schs., sorps, pubs., Edn. Testing Service, profl. jours. Author: (with Theodore Andersson) Bilingual Schooling in the United States, 2 vols., 1970, The Texas Colllection of Comedias Sueltas: A Descriptive Bibliography, 1978; translator: (with Harold Morland) (Dreantigers Jorge Luis Borges), 1964; contbr. articles to profl. jours. Inst. Internat. Edn. scholar Cuba, 1947; Fulbright scholar Italy, 1954-55; recipient research grants. Mem. Am. Assn. Tchrs. Spanish and Portuguese (nat. exec. council 1968-70), Tex. Fgn. Lang. Assn. (hon.), S. Cen. Modern Lang. Assn., MLA (ERIC nat. adv. bd. 1971-73). Home: 902 Lund St Austin TX 78704 Office: U Tex Dept Spanish and Portuguese Austin TX 78712

BOYKIN, FRANCES LEWIS, retired social worker; b. Boston; d. Joel Randolph and Frances Virginia (Kenney) Lewis; m. Herbert Charles Boykin Jr., Dec. 23, 1951 (div. 1958). BS, Simmons Coll., 1945, MS, 1946. Cert. social worker, N.Y. Caseworker Family Service of Orange County, Maplewood, N.J., 1946-47; child welfare worker Riverdale Children's Assn., N.Y.C., 1946-51; supr., casework coordinator Assoc. Day Care Services of Greater Boston, 1952-53; caseworker, advancing to sr. caseworker Salvation Army-Family Service, N.Y.C., 1955-74; psychiat. researcher, 1957-62; student supr. NYU Sch. Edn., 1969-74, field supr. student unit, 1976-79; field supr. for student unit Salvation Army Corps and Community Ctrs., N.Y.C., 1974-79, adv. orgn. mem. Salvation Army N.Y. State, 1979-86 (meritorious service award); adj. asst. prof. NYU Sch. Social Work, 1977-79. Bd. dirs. Assn. Bronx Community Orgns., 1964-73, v.p., 1968-69, treas., 1970-73; bd. dirs. N.Y.C. region NCCJ, 1976—, mem. exec. com., 1977—; mem. Bronx adv. com. Urban League, 1966-69. Recipient Service plaque for 30 yrs. with Salvation Army N.Y.C., 1986; pres. 12th Ch. Christ Scientist, N.Y.C., 1988—. Mem. Nat. Assn. Social Workers, Acad. Cert. Social Workers, Internat. Conf. Social Work (del. 1964-84). Home: 2235 Fifth Ave New York NY 10037

BOYKIN, MARY JONES, nursing administrator; b. Columbia, S.C., Mar. 9, 1948; d. Jim Bob and Jessie Bell (Watts) Jones; m. Eddie Boykin, Jr., May 1, 1971; children—Ginger Renee, Darrell Timothy. A. in Nursing, U. S.C., 1975; B.S.N., N.C. Central U., 1983. Nurses' asst. Richland Meml. Hosp., Columbia, S.C., 1966-67, lic. practical nurse, 1968-75; staff nurse Duke U. Med. Ctr., Durham, N.C., 1975-80, nursing supr., 1980-85, asst. dir. nursing, 1985-87, orthopaedic head nurse 1987—, career counselor intern, 1985. Selected Outstanding Woman of Achievement, YWCA, 1984. Mem. Am. Assn. Critical Care Nurses, Am. Mental Health Counselors Assn., Nat. Employment Counselors Assn., Nat. Vocat. Guidance Assn., Am. Assn. Counseling and Devel. Club: Durham Adoptable Family Support Group (v.p. 1983-85). Avocations: camping; reading; traveling; interior decorating. Home: 5802 Sandstone Dr Durham NC 27713

BOYLAN, VIRGINIA WALKER, lawyer; b. Washington, Dec. 29, 1941; d. Robert D. and Dorothy Elizabeth (Compton) Walker; B.A., Am. U., 1964; J.D., Cath. U. Am., 1979; 1 dau., Kaithlin Janine. Admitted to Va. bar, 1979; resource specialist LWV of U.S., 1968-71; legis. asst. to Rep. John Melcher, 1971-76; spl. counsel Select Com. on Indian Affairs, U.S. Senate, Washington, 1979—. Trustee, Nat. Reyes Syndrome Found., 1980-85. Democrat. Office: 838 Hart Senate Office Bldg Washington DC 20510

BOYLE, BARBARA DORMAN, motion picture company executive; b. N.Y.C., Aug. 11, 1935; d. William and Edith (Kleiman) Dorman; m. Kevin Boyle, Nov. 26, 1960; children: David Eric, Paul Coleman. B.A., U. Calif., Berkeley, 1957; J.D., UCLA, 1960. Bar: Calif. 1961, N.Y. 1964, U.S. Supreme Ct. bar 1964. Atty. bus. affairs dept, corp. asst. sec. Am. Internat. Pictures, Los Angeles, 1960-65; partner firm Cohen & Boyle, Los Angeles, 1967-74; exec. v.p., gen. counsel, chief operating officer New World Pictures, Los Angeles, 1974-82; sr. v.p. prodn. Orion Pictures Corp., Los Angeles, 1982-85; exec. v.p. prodn. RKO Pictures, 1986—; co-chmn. entertainment law symposium adv. com. UCLA Law Sch., 1979-80. Author articles in field. Mem. adv. bd. Am. Film Inst., Womens Directing Workshop. Mem. Acad. Motion Picture Arts and Scis., Women in Film (pres. 1977-78), Hollywood Women's Polit. Com., Women Entertainment Lawyers Assn., Calif. Bar Assn., N.Y. State Bar Assn., Hollywood Women's Polit. Com., Am. Film. Inst. (bd. dirs. Women dir.'s workshop). Office: RKO Pictures 1900 Ave of the Stars Suite 1562 Los Angeles CA 90067

BOYLE, BARBARA TERESA, foundation (not-for-profit) administrator; b. N.Y.C., Feb. 14, 1939; d. Michael Joseph and Mary Catherine (Buchanan) Ducey; m. James Francis Boyle, July 9, 1936; children: Geraldine, Lauren, James. BA, Hunter Coll., N.Y.C., 1960; MSE, Queens Coll., N.Y.C., 1967. Field dir. Girl Scout Council N.Y., N.Y.C., 1973-75, county dir., 1975-77; community devel. dir. Spanish Trails Girl Scout Council, Pomona, Calif., 1977-78; exec. dir. Cystic Fibrosis Found., Los Angeles, 1978-85; nat. fundraising dir. Juvenile Diabetes Found., N.Y.C., 1985-87; nat. exec. dir. Nat. Found. Ileitis and Colitis, N.Y.C., 1987—; chmn. Nat. Health Agys., Orange

City, Calif., 1978-80, Cystic Fibrosis Nat. Staff Conf., Denver, 1985; cons. in field. Mem. AAUW, Am. Assn. Profl. Women, Nat. Health Planning Council, Council Nat. Vol. Health Agys., Am. Soc. Assn. Execs., Nat. Soc. Fund Raising Execs., ASEA. Avocations: reading, painting. Home: 18 Hawthorne Rd Short Hills NJ 07078 Office: Nat Found Ileitis and Colitis 444 Park Ave S New York NY 10016

BOYLE, CAROLYN MOORE, public relations practitioner, marketing communications manager; b. Los Angeles, Jan. 29, 1937; d. Cory Orlando Moore and Violet (Brennan) Baldock; m. Robert J. Ruppelt, Oct. 8, 1954 (div. Aug. 1964); children: Cory Robert, Traci Lynn; m. Jerry Ray Boyle, June 1, 1970 (div. 1975). AA, Orange Coast Coll., 1966; BA, Calif. State U., Fullerton, 1970; student, U. Calif., Irvine, 1970-71. Program coordinator Newport Beach (Calif.) Cablevision, 1968-70; dir. pub. relations Fish Communications Co., Newport Beach, 1970-74; mktg. rep. Dow Pharm. div. Dow Chem. Co., Orange County, Calif., 1974-77, Las Vegas, Nev., 1980-81; mgr. product publicity Dow Agrl. Products div. Dow Chem. Co., Midland, Mich., 1977-80; mgr. mktg. communications Dowell Fluid Services Region div. Dow Chem. Co. Houston, 1981-84; adminstr. mktg. communications Swedlow, Inc., Garden Grove, Calif., 1984-85; cons. mktg. communications, 1985-86; mgr. mktg. communications Am. Convertors div. Am. Hosp. Supply, 1986-87; mgr. sales support Surgidev Corp., Santa Barbara, Calif., 1987-88; Western mktg. dir. Neufield Swiss Am., 1988—; guest lectr. Calif. State U., Long Beach, 1970; seminar coordinator U. Calif., Irvine, 1972; mem. Western White House Press Corps, 1972; pub. relations cons. BASF Wyandotte, Phila., 1981-82. Author: Agricultural Public Relations/Publicity, 1981; editor Big Mean AG Machine (internal mag.), 1977; contbr. numerous articles to trade publs.; contbg. editor Dowell Mktg. Newsletter, 1983; creator, designer Novahistine DMX Trial Size nat. mktg. program, 1977. Com. mem. Dow Employees for Polit. Action, Midland, 1978-80; bd. dirs. Dowell Employees for Polit. Action Com., Houston, 1983-84. World Campus Afloat scholar, U. Seven Seas, 1966-67; recipient PROTOS award, 1985. Mem. Pub. Relations Soc. Am. (cert.), Soc. Petroleum Engrs., Internat. Assn. Bus. Communicators. Episcopalian. Recipient first rights to televise President Nixon in Western White House. Address: 16488 Cabrillo Dr Victorville CA 92392

BOYLE, KAY, writer; b. St. Paul, Feb. 19, 1902; d. Howard Peterson and Katherine (Evans) B.; m. Richard Brault, June 24, 1923 (div.); m. Laurence Vail, Apr. 2, 1931 (div.); children—Sharon Walsh, Apple-Joan, Kathe, Clover, Faith Carson, Ian Savin; m. Baron Joseph von Franckenstein (dec. 1963). Student, Ohio Mechanics Inst., 1917-19; Litt.D. (hon.), Columbia, 1971; L.H.D. (hon.), Skidmore Coll., 1977, So. Ill. U., 1978, Bowling Green State U., 1986, Ohio State U. Lectr. in writing San Francisco State U., 1963-79. Author: poems A Glad Day, 1930, Wedding Day; short stories, 1930, Plagued by the Nightingale; novel, 1931, Year Before Last; novel, 1932, Gentlemen, I Address You Privately; novel, 1933, My Next Bride; novel, 1934, Death of a Man; novel, 1936, The White Horses of Vienna; short stories, 1937, Monday Night; novel, 1938, His Human Majesty: novel, 1939, The Crazy Hunter; short novels, 1940, Primer for Combat; novel, 1942, Avalanche, 1943, A French Man Must Die; novel, 1945, American Citizen; poems, 1944, Thirty Stories, 1946; 1939, novel, 1947, His Human Majesty, 1949, The Smoking Mountain; essays, 1951, The Seagull on the Step; novel, 1955, Three Short Novels, 1958, children's book The Youngest Camel, 1959, novel, Generation Without Farewell, 1960, Collected Poems, 1962, essay, Breaking the Silence, 1962, novel, Nothing Ever Breaks Except the Heart; short stories, 1966, Pinky, the Cat Who Likes to Sleep, 1966, editor: The Autobiography of Emanuel Carnevali, 1967, Being Geniuses Together; memoir, 1968, children's book Pinky in Persia, 1968, Testament For My Students; poems, 1970, The Long Walk at San Francisco State; essays, 1970, The Underground Woman; novel, 1975, Fifty Stories, 1980, Words That Must Somehow Be Said: The Selected Essays of Kay Boyle 1927-1984, This is Not a Letter; poems, 1985; contbr. short stories to mags. Recipient O. Henry Meml. prize, 1936, 1941; San Francisco Art Commn. award, 1978, Columbus Found. Am. Book award 1983, The Los Angeles Times Robert Kirsch award, 1986; Guggenheim fellow, 1934, 61; sr. citizen grantee Nat. Endowment for Arts, 1980. Mem. Am. Acad. Arts and Letters. Address: care Watkins/Loomis Agy 150 E 35th St New York NY 10016

BOYLE, MARY LOU, business executive; b. Youngstown, Ohio, May 24, 1935; d. Harold G. and Mary Helen (Shook) Morris; m. Bryan Joseph Boyle, May 4, 1957; children: Bryan Jr., J. Thomas, Jamie L. Student Youngstown Coll., 1954, Miami U., Oxford, Ohio, 1953-54, Rollins Coll., 1964, U. Cen. Fla., 1981, 84. Account exec. Sta. WLOF, Orlando, Fla., 1978-80, Sta. WESH-TV, Winter Park, Fla., 1980-82; pres. Boyle Advt., Inc., Orlando, 1982-87; pres., chief exec. officer WCN Prodns., Winter Park, 1988—; pres., chief exec. officer We're Cooking Now, Inc., Winter Park 1984—. Creator, exec. producer TV series, We're Cooking Now, 1984, 85; exec. producer, writer TV series The Flower Shop, 1987—; Author: We're Cooking Now, Vol. 1, 1984, The Flower Shop Vol. 1, 1987, The Melody of Floral Design, 1988. Mem. Acad. TV Arts and Scis., Fla. Motion Picture and TV Assn., Orlando Area Ad Fedn. Republican. Episcopalian. Avocations: writing, walking. Office: PO Box 307 Winter Park FL 32790

BOYLE, PATRICIA JEAN, judge. Student, U. Mich., 1955-57; B.A., Wayne State U., 1963, J.D., 1963. Bar: Mich. Practice law with Kenneth Davies, Detroit, 1963; law clk. to U.S. Dist. judge, 1963-64; asst. U.S. atty., Detroit, 1964-68; asst. pros. atty. Wayne County; dir. research, tng. and appeals Wayne County, Detroit, 1969-74; Recorders Ct. judge City of Detroit, 1976-78; U.S. dist. judge Eastern Dist. Mich., Detroit, 1978-83; justice Mich. Supreme Ct., Detroit, 1983—. Active Women's Rape Crisis Task Force, Vols. of Am. Named Feminist of Year Detroit chpt. NOW, 1978; recipient Outstanding Achievement award Pros. Attys. Assn. Mich., 1978; Spirit of Detroit award Detroit City Council, 1978. Mem. Women Lawyers Assn. Mich., Fed. Bar Assn., Mich. Bar Assn., Detroit Bar Assn., Wayne State U. Law Alumni Assn. (Disting. Alumni award 1979). Office: Mich Supreme Ct PO Box 30052 Lansing MI 48909 *

BOYLE, RENÉE KENT, cultural organization executive, translator; b. Cairo, Egypt, July 4, 1926; came to U.S., 1946; d. Maurice Colin and Victoria Smith; m. John E. Whiteford Boyle, Feb. 2, 1950; children: Vanessa Whiteford Wayne, Christopher, Andrea Heller, Mara Whiteford. Diploma, St. Clare's Coll., Heliopolis, Egypt, 1944; postgrad., Rice U., 1947-48, Santa Monica Coll., 1950-51. Dep. dir. Am. Friends of Mid. East, Tehran, Iran, 1959-62, Les Amis Americains du Maghreb, Tunis, Tunisia, 1962-64; v.p. Fgn. Services Research Inst., Washington, 1964—; v.p. Whiteford Internat. Enterprise, Villars sur Ollon, Switzerland, 1967-74. Editor: Primers for the Age of Inner Space series, Beyond the Present Prospect, 1978, The Indra Web, 1982, Graffiti on the Wall of Time, 1982, Of the Same Root: Heaven, Earth & T. Mem. Dem. Nat. Com., Washington, 1982—. Mem. Internat. Acad. Ind. Scholars (exec. officer), Ams. for Dem. Action, People for Ethical Treatment of Animals, Sierra Club. Unitarian. Avocation: cordon bleu cooking. Home: 2718 Unicorn Ln NW Washington DC 20015-2234 Office: Fgn Services Research Inst Box 6317 Washington DC 20015

BOYLE, SUSAN JEANNE, medical sales professional; b. Evanston, Ill., Dec. 31, 1952; d. John E. and Annette (Kleinman) B.; m. Jack Richard Henry, Oct. 11, 1986. BS, Colby-Sawyer Coll., 1974, Southeastern Okla. State U., 1978. Med. technologist Northwestern Meml. Hosp., Chgo., 1974-75, Assocs. Internal Medicine, Chgo., 1975-81; mgr. dist. sales Am. Diagnostics, Newport Beach, Calif., 1981-83; specialist tech. sales Coulter Electronics Inc., Hialeah, Fla., 1983—. Mem. Am. Assn. Clin. Pathologists (cert.), Phi Theta Kappa. Republican. Roman Catholic. Home: 198 Spruce Dr Shrewsbury NJ 07702 Office: 98 Mayfield Ave Edison NJ 08818

BOYLES, MATTIE LEE, manufacturing executive; b. Blair, Okla., Feb. 15, 1928; d. Earl E. Mattie V. (Walker) Hasty; divorced; children: Mark E., Melodye D. Grad. high sch., Altus, Okla., 1946. Asst. to CPA Scott Quigley, CPA, Altus, 1946; bookkeeper Hammond Concrete, Altus, 1947-48, mgr., 1948-67; pres. Empire Asphalt, Inc., Lawton, Okla., 1959; ptnr. Lawton Transit Mix, Inc., 1964; pres. Boyles & Assocs., Inc., Lawton, 1976—; owner Empire Asphalt, Inc., Lawton, 1964—, Hammond Concrete Co., Altus, 1959—, Lawton Transit Mix, Inc., 1964—, Southwestern State Sand Corp., Snyder, Okla., 1967—; bd. dirs. Cache Rd Nat. Bank, Lawton. Bd. dirs. Goodwill Industries, Lawton, 1974-86, Vo-Tech Action Task Force, Lawton, 1982—, Lawton Chamber & Industry, 1982—; trustee, mem. adminstrv. bd. 1st United Meth. Ch., Lawton, 1981-84, mem. pastor parish bd., fin. bd. 1981—. Mem. Alpha Gamma Delta. Democrat. Home: 7605 NW Stonegate Dr Lawton OK 73505 Office: Lawton Transit Mix Inc 2208 F Ave Lawton OK 73501

BOYNTON, EDALENIA JOAN DALMATA, educator; b. Gloversville, N.Y., Sept. 15, 1943; d. John Edward and Helen Jennie (Selufsky) Dalmata; m. Walter James Boynton, June 6, 1964; children: Walter R., Craig L. BS, SUNY Coll., Plattsburgh, 1964. Cert. tchr., N.Y., Fla. Tchr. home econs. Johnstown (N.Y.) City Schs., 1964-67; home economist Fulton County Coop., Gloversville, 1966-71; tchr. Mayfield (N.Y.) Cen. Sch., 1971-87; agt. Fulmont Travel World, Gloversville, 1984-87; tchr. home econs. DeSoto Mid. Sch., Arcadia, Fla., 1987-88, Venice Area Middle Sch., Sarasota County, Fla., 1988—; with curriculum team Fulton-Montgomery County Bds. Coop. Ednl. Services, Johnstown, 1985-86. Educator, counselor Planned Parenthood of S.W. Fla., 1987. Mem. Am. Fedn. Tchrs., N.Y. State Union Tchrs., Fulton County Home Econs. Assn. (sec.), Mayfield Tchrs. Assn. (sec. 1983—). Club: Mayfield Yacht. Home: 572 Whippoorwill Dr Venice FL 34293

BOYSEN, MELICENT PEARL, finance company executive; b. Houston, Dec. 1, 1943; d. William Thomas and Mildred Pearl (Walker) Richardson; m. Stephen M. Boysen, Sept. 10, 1961 (dec. 1973); children: Marshella, Stephanie, Stephen. Student, Cen. Mo. State, 1973-75. Owner, pres. Boysen Enterprises, Kansas City, Mo., 1973—, Boysen Agri-Services, Kansas City, 1984—; fin. cons., underwriter New Eng. Life Ins. Co., Kansas City, 1978-81; cons. San Luis Rey (Calif.) Tribal Water Authority, Wind River (Wyo.) Reservation, Cheyenne River (S.D.) Sioux, Iroquois Nations (N.Y.) 1983—; bd. dirs. Visible Horizons 1987—. Founding bd. dirs. Rose Brooks Ctr. battered women, Kansas City, 1979—, treas., 1979-81. Mem. Internat. Fin. Planners Assn., Internat. Agri-Bus. Assn., Nat. Assn. Securities Dealers, DAR, Kans. C. of C. and Industry, Kansas City C. of C. Republican. Methodist. Office: Boysen Enterprises PO Box 9104 Shawnee Mission KS 66201

BOZA, CLARA BRIZEIDA, marketing professional, arts management consultant; b. Havana, Cuba, Apr. 18, 1952; came to U.S., 1957; d. Eduardo Otmaro and Hubedia Marta (Garcia) B. BA in English summa cum laude, Barry Coll., 1973. Legal asst. supr. Steel Hector & Davis, Miami, Fla., 1978-80; program adminstr. Dade County Council Arts & Scis., Miami, 1980-82; dir. program devel. Nat. Found. for Advancement in Arts, Miami, 1982-85; exec. dir. Bus. Vols. for Arts, Miami, 1985-86; dir. communications Steel Hector & Davis, Miami, 1986—; S.E. regional cons. Arts & Bus. Council, N.Y.C., 1986—; bd. advisors Mary Luft and Co./Tigertail Prodns., Miami, 1987—; panelist So. Arts Fedn., Atlanta, 1983-84, Fla. Arts Council, 1983-84, 86-87; panelist and speaker various local, state and nat. orgns. and assns. Recipient ednl. scholarship Barry Coll., Miami, 1969-73, Fla. Bd. Regents, 1969-73. Mem. Women in Communications Inc., Greater Miami C. of C., Nat. Assn. Law Firm Mktg. Adminstrs., Am. Mktg. Assn. Office: Steel Hector & Davis 4000 Southeast Financial Ctr 200 S Biscayne Blvd Miami FL 33131-2398

BOZE, BARBARA CHESLENE, agricultural company executive; b. Union City, Ind., May 23, 1953; d. Chelsey Owen and Anne Marie (Snyder) B. AA, U. Dayton, 1973. Lab. technician Cargill, Inc., Dayton, Ohio, 1974-75, lab. supr., 1975-76, finishing supr., 1976-81; lab. mgr. Cargill, Inc., Memphis, 1981-85; refinery supt. Cargill, Inc., Cedar Rapids, Iowa, 1985-87; terminal mgr. Cargill, Inc., Elizabeth, N.J., 1987—; chmn. IFT, Memphis, 1983. Mem. Nat. Woman's Network, Elizabeth C. of C. (com. mem. 1987—). Office: Cargill Inc 132 Corbin St Elizabeth NJ 07201

BOZEMAN, DOROTHY WOODARD, day care center administrator and owner; b. Bamberg, S.C., Dec. 22, 1923; d. Willie Leon and Maude Agnes (Kinsey) Woodard; m. Larence Rigdon Bozeman, Apr. 2, 1942; 1 child, Larence Rigdon Jr. Student Tampa Bus. Coll., Fla., 1952-53. Acct., Lindsay, Squire & Everett, Greensboro, N.C., 1958-60; bookkeeper United Fund, Greensboro, 1961-62; unit buying control office, sportswear dept. Sears, Roebuck & Co., Greensboro and Concord, N.C., 1962-72; pres. Dorothy W. Bozeman Inc., doing bus. as Wonderworld Day Sch., Salisbury, N.C., 1973—. Republican. Baptist. Office: Wonderworld Day Sch 305 Link Ave Salisbury NC 28144

BOZONE, BILLIE RAE, librarian; b. Norphlet, Ark., Oct. 7, 1935; d. Guy Samuel and Vera (Jones) B. B.S. in Library Sci, Miss. State Coll. for Women, 1957; M.A., George Peabody Coll. for Tchrs., 1958. Asst. ref. librarian Miss. State U., State College, 1958-61, serials librarian, 1961-63; asst. ref. librarian U. Ill. at Urbana, 1963-65; asst. librarian New Eng. Mut. Life Ins. Co., Boston, 1965-67; sr. ref. librarian U. Mass., Amherst, 1967-68; head circulation dept. Smith Coll., Northampton, Mass., 1968-69; asst. librarian Smith Coll., 1969-71, coll. librarian, 1971—; Bd. dirs. Hampshire Inter-library Center, Amherst, 1971—; mem. exec. com. NELINET, 1977-79; chmn. Five Coll. Librarians Council, 1980-82. Mem. ALA, Assn. Coll. and Research Libraries, Alpha Beta Alpha, Alpha Psi Omega. Home: 20 S Whitney St Amherst MA 01002 Office: Smith Coll Library Northampton MA 01063

BRAATEN, BRENDA LEE, nutrition educator; b. Oroville, Calif., Aug. 15, 1951; d. Alfred Joe and Ruth LaVerne (Smith) McCoy; m. Laurie Jay Braaten, Aug. 25, 1973; children: Sara Charis, Rebecca Elise. BA, Pt. Loma Nazarene Coll., San Diego, 1973; MA, U. Kans., 1976; PhD, Tufts U., 1987. Instr. Biology Cleve. Chiropractic Coll., Kansas City, Mo., 1976-78, Ea. Nazarene Coll., Quincy, Mass., 1979—; pre-nursing advisor Ea. Nazarene Coll., 1980-87. Chmn. library com. Muraco Pub. Sch., Winchester, Mass., 1985-87; mem. missionary soc. Malden (Mass.) Ch. Nazarene, 1986-87; assoc. guide Winchester Trails, 1987; bd. dirs. Hunger Attack, Boston. USDA research fellow, Boston, 1982-86. Mem. Phi Delta Lambda.

BRABANT, SARAH CALLAWAY, sociologist, educator; b. LaGrange, Ga., Nov. 18, 1932; d. Enoch and Jennie Louisa (Crowell) Callaway; m. Wilmer Everett Mac Nair, Aug. 14, 1973; children by previous marriage—Jennie Crowell, Enoch Callaway, Anne Delebart. Student Newcomb Coll., 1950-52, Auburn U., 1952-53; BS, Memphis State U., 1967, MA, 1968; PhD, U. Ga., 1973. Instr. sociology Memphis State U., 1968-70; vis. asst. prof. anthropology La. State U., summers 1973, 74; asst. prof. sociology U. Southwestern La., Lafayette, 1973-77, assoc. prof., 1977-83, prof., 1983—. Pres. Lafayette Mayor's Commn. on Needs of Women, 1977-79; bd. dirs. United Christian Outreach; pres. Faith House, 1982-83. Recipient Am. Personnel and Guidance Assn. Research award, 1977; Martin Luther King Humanitarian Service award Lafayette Council on Human Relations, 1978; Disting. Prof. award U. Southwestern La. Found., 1980, vol. activist award Acadiana, 1985; Blue Key Alumni Faculty Excellence award, 1986, Outstanding Alumna for Community Service award Phi Mu, 1986. Mem. Mid-South Sociol. Assn. (v.p. 1976-77), So. Sociol. Soc., Southwestern Sociol. Assn., Am. Sociol. Assn., AAUP. Democrat. Episcopalian (vestry 1984-87). Club: Jr. League of Lafayette. Co-editor Sociological Spectrum. Contbr. articles to profl. jours. Home: 149 Memory Ln Lafayette LA 70506 Office: U Southwestern La PO Box 40198 Lafayette LA 70504

BRABEC, BARBARA ANN, writer, publisher; b. Buckley, Ill., Mar. 5, 1937; d. William Jonas and Marcella Eliza (Williams) Schaumburg; m. Harry Joseph Brabec, Aug. 26, 1961. Student pub. schs., Buckley. Adminstrv. asst. Investment Guide Advt., Inc., Chgo., 1962-65; pub. Artisan Crafts mag., Reeds Spring, Mo., 1971-76; pub., gen. mgr. Countryside Books, Barrington, Ill., 1979-81; owner Artisan Crafts, Springfield, Mo., 1981-84, Barbara Brabec Prodns., Naperville, Ill., 1984—. Author: Creative Cash, 1979, 81, 86; Homemade Money, 1984, rev. 1988; pub. newsletter Nat. Home Bus. Report, 1981—. Mem. Am. Soc. Journalists and Authors, Nat. Writers' Club. Home and Office: PO Box 2137 Naperville IL 60566

BRABSTON, MARY ELIZABETH, university program director; b. Birmingham, Ala., July 2, 1948; d. Donald C. Sr. and Mary Jane (Coolman) B. BA, Vanderbilt U., 1969; cert., Ala. Trust Sch., 1976. From mgmt. trainee to asst. trust officer 1st Ala. Bank, Birmingham, 1970-77; asst. campaign mgr. for George McMillan Birmingham, 1978, 82-86; exec. asst. to lt. gov. State of Ala., Birmingham, 1979-83; dir. prospect research Capital campaign office U. Ala., Birmingham, 1987-88, coordinator adminstrv. systems Devel. Officer, 1988—. commr. Ala. Film Commn., Montgomery, 1976-83; mem. Nat. Conf. State Legislatures Arts and States Com., Denver, 1979-83, vice chairperson, 1982-83; treas. Birmingham Internat. Ednl. Film Festival, 1976-81, Birmingham Festival Theatre, 1979-80, sec. bd. dirs. 1988—; bd. dirs. Ala. Epilepsy Council, Birmingham, 1975-77, Ala. Sch. Fine Arts, 1982-87, Found. for Pastoral Counseling, Birmingham, 1985-86; campaign treas. for George McMillan, 1973-86, for David Herring, 1974-83; deacon Ind. Presbyn. Ch. Named Outstanding Young Career Woman, Met. Bus. and Profl. Women, 1976. Mem. Profl. Women's Network, Birmingham Jaycees (hon. 1976, one of Outstanding Young Women in Am. 1978-83). Democrat. Club: Birmingham Vanderbilt (pres. 1979). Home: 4216 Groover Dr Birmingham AL 35213 Office: U Ala Station MJH 229 Birmingham AL 35294

BRACHMANN, CLAIRE RUTH, computer specialist; b. Windsor Locks, Conn., Oct. 14, 1955; d. Ira John and Ruth Muriel (Gardner) B. Student, U. Conn., 1973-75. Machinist Stanadyne Diesel Systems, Windsor, Conn., 1976-83, Kennametal Inc., Windsor Locks, 1983-85; rep. customer service telescope div. Bausch & Lomb, East Hartford, Conn., 1985-86; computer technician Great Am., Windsor, 1986—. Home: PO Box 604 Windsor Locks CT 06096

BRACIALE, VIVIAN LAM, immunologist; b. N.Y.C., June 5, 1948; d. Wing Ching and Wai Ching (Li) Lam; m. Thomas J. Braciale Jr., Aug. 5, 1972; children—Kara, Michael Stephen, Laura. A.B., Cornell U., 1969; Ph.D., U. Pa., 1973. Postdoctoral fellow U. Pa., Phila., 1974-75, Washington U. Med. Sch., St. Louis, 1975-76, research instr. immunology, 1978-83, research asst. prof. pathology, 1983—; mem. clin. scis. study sect. NIH, 1985—. Contbr. articles in immunology to profl. jours. N.Y. State Regent scholar; NIH Research Service awardee; vis. fellow Australian Nat. U., Canberra, 1976-78. Mem. Am. Assn. Immunologists, NIH (clin. scis. study sect. 1985—), Am. Diabetes Assn. Lutheran. Office: Washington Univ Med Sch Dept Pathology 660 S Euclid Saint Louis MO 63110

BRACK, RITA MACDONALD, state legislator, educator, counselor; b. Roxbury, Mass., May 15, 1918; d. Daniel Joseph and Mary Ellen (O'Brien) MacDonald; B.S. in Edn., Boston State Coll., 1939; M.Ed., Rivier Coll., Nashua, N.H., 1966; Ed.D., Nova U., 1978; m. John Joseph Brack, Oct. 4, 1942; children—Joan R. Brack Asbury, Lynda M., Susan T., John J., Judith A. (dec.), Lisa Brack Zoller, Anne M., Martha, Maura. Assoc. prof. N.H. Coll. Acctg. and Commerce, Manchester, 1963-68; prof. edn., dir. counseling and placement Notre Dame Coll., Manchester, 1968—; mem. N.H. Ho. of Reps., 1976—; chmn. N.H. Coll. and Univ. Council Placement Dirs. Com., 1973-75; v.p. New Eng. Assn. Sch., Coll. and Univ. Staffing; vice chmn. New Eng. Bd. Higher Edn., 1980—; mem. profl. standards bd. N.H. Dept. Edn.; mem. 50th ann. com. Eastern Coll. Personnel Officers. N.H. coordinator Women in Community Service; organizer, adviser Manchester Hot Line; rep. to N.H. Gen. Ct.; mem. Stop and Shop Consumer Bd.; bd. Incorporators, trustee Cath. Med. Center, Manchester, Mental Health Center; pres. Sacred Heart Hosp. Assocs., 1972-75; vice-chmn. bd. trustees Community Correctional Center, Manchester; mem. Gov. N.H. Commn. Pub. Edn.; del. N.H. Dem. Com., 1972, gen. chmn. conv., 1974; mem. Manchester Sch. Bd., 1976-88; mem. Manchester Charter Revision Commn., 1981. Recipient various certificates of recognition; Woman of Achievement award Manchester chpt. Bus. and Profl. Women, 1979. Mem. Am. Personnel and Guidance Assn., AAUP, Women in Community Service. Address: 60 Hubbard St Manchester NH 03104 Office: 2321 Elm St Manchester NH 03104

BRACKEN, DARCIA DAINES, government policy analyst; b. Logan, Utah, Aug. 20, 1946; d. Dwyth Merrill and Constance (Blair) Daines; m. Charles Franklin, Dec. 27, 1967 (div. 1975); 1 child, ConiSue Faythe Bracken. B.A., Utah State U., 1967, M.A., 1972; M.A. in Urban and Regional Planning, Auburn U., 1973; Ph.D. in Pub. Adminstrn. George Washington U., 1985. Water resources policy analyst Nat. Commn. on Water Quality, Washington, 1974-75; sci. cons. Sci. and Tech. Com., U.S. Ho. of Reps., Washington, 1975-79; prin. assoc. U.S. Conf. Mayors, Washington, 1979-82, tech. transfer analyst detail to NASA, 1979-81, state and local govt. liaison detail to HUD, 1981-82; tech. mgmt. specialist Dept. Commerce, Nat. Tech. Info. Service, Washington, 1983—; student membership chmn. Am. Water Resources Assn., Washington, 1973-75; mem. planning com. Fed. Lab. Consortium, Washington, 1983-85; mem. Pub. Employees Roundtable, Washington, 1985. Author: Trends in Environmental Law Related to Water Resources Management, 1973; Author, editor: (with others) Domestic Technology Transfer, 1979. Contbr. articles to profl. jours. Head debate coach Annandale High Sch., Va., 1984—; Dept. Interior grantee, 1971-73; NDEA fellow, 1967-68. Mem. Tech. Transfer Soc., Am. Soc. Pub. Adminstrn., George Washington U. Alumni Assn., Pi Alpha Alpha (v.p. 1979-81). Office: Nat Tech Info Service 5285 Port Royal Rd Springfield VA 22161

BRACKEN, KATHLEEN ANN, nurse; b. Chgo., Mar. 14, 1947; d. Thomas James and Catherine Anastasia (Cowal) B.; RN, CCRN, Little Company of Mary Hosp., Evergreen Park, Ill., 1968; BSN, Lewis U., 1984. Mem. staff Little Company of Mary Hosp., Evergreen Park, 1968-69, 71—, supr. ICUs, 1976-79, dir. ICUs, 1979—; staff nurse coronary care unit Little Co. of Mary Hosp., Torrence, Calif., 1969-70; staff nurse Chgo. Lying-In Clinic, U. Chgo., 1970-71; instr.-trainer cardiopulmonary resuscitation; bd. dirs., mem. CPR tng. com., chmn. nursing cardiovascular com. South Cook Heart Assn., 1977-83, recipient Meritorious Service award, 1979, 81, 82, 83, 84, 85, 86. Mem. Am. Nurses Assn., Council on Nursing Adminstrn., Chgo. Heart Assn., Assn. for Advancement Med. Instrumentation, Am. Assn. Critical Care Nurses (pres. Southside Chgo. Area chpt. 1983-84, rec. sec. 1984-85), Am. Heart Assn. (cardiovascular nursing council), Ill. Orgn. Nursing Execs., Nat. Assn. Female Execs., Delta Epsilon Sigma, Sigma Theta Tau. Home: 10321 S Campbell Ave Chicago IL 60655 Office: Little Co of Mary Hosp 2800 W 95th St Evergreen Park IL 60642

BRACKEN, PEG, author; b. Filer, Idaho, Feb. 25, 1918; d. John Lewis and Ruth (McQuesten) B.; m. Parker Edwards, Mar. 17, 1966; 1 dau., Johanna Kathleen. A.B., Antioch Coll., 1940. Author: The I Hate to Cook Book, 1960, The I Hate to Housekeep Book, 1962, I Try to Behave Myself, 1963, Peg Bracken's Appendix to The I Hate to Cook Book, 1966, I Didn't Come Here to Argue, 1969, But I Wouldn't Have Missed It for the World, 1973, The I Hate to Cook Almanack - A Book of Days, 1976, A Window Over the Sink, 1981. Mem. AFTRA, Screen Actors Guild, Authors Guild, PEN.

BRACKENRIDGE, ELOISE WILSON, industrial communications consultant specializing in technology transfer; b. Taylor, Tex., Oct. 22, 1939; d. John Adams III and Eloise (Wilson) B. BFA in Communications, U. Tex., 1961, MA in Communications, 1969. Fgn. service staff officer U.S. Dept. State, Washington, 1961-66; campaign aide Rep. George Bush, Houston, 1970; communications cons. Austin (Tex.), Houston, and Washington, 1970-73; pub. relations mgr. Tex. Internat. Airlines, Houston, 1973-75; communications mgr. Dresser Industries Inc., Houston, 1975-83; v.p. corp. communications CRS Sirrine Inc., Houston, 1983-86; indsl. communications cons. Houston, 1986—; mng. ptnr. Brackenridge and Eilert, Houston and Austin, 1972—; bd. dirs. Hobby Community Bank, Houston. Author: Mota Bonita, 1979; editor: Anthology of Communication Theory, 1967; prod. and dir. ednl. and indsl. film series, 1970-73; contbr. articles to profl. jours. Mem. selection bd. USIA, Washington, 1971; active Houston Council Performing Arts, Houston Econ. Devel. Forum; patron Houston Jr. League, 1974—. Recipient Meritorious Honor award U.S. Dept. State, 1964, Best Nat. Trade Show Exhibit award U.S. Trade Show Assn., 1982, Nat. Excellence award Soc. Mktg. Profl. Services, 1985, numerous awards for advt. and speaking. Mem. Internat. Platform Assn., Phi Kappa Phi, Alpha Epsilon Rho. Republican. Episcopalian. Club: Houston Forum. Home: 3524 Greystone Dr #199 Austin TX 78731

BRACKETT, BARBARA HELEN, accountant; b. Knoxville, Tenn., Mar. 17, 1955; d. James Frederick and Helen Louise (Dehart) Wheeler; m. Joseph L. Griffy, Dec. 30, 1977 (div. Jan. 1980); 1 child, Jacob F. Griffy; m. Deke W. Brackett, Apr. 8, 1980 (div. Aug. 1985); children: Russell, David. BS, U. Tenn., 1979, M of Accountancy, 1984. CPA. Staff acct. McGladrey, Hendrickson & Pullen, Knoxville, Tenn., 1984-85; mgr. Elkins & Roy, P.C., Knoxville, 1985—. Sunday sch. tchr. St. John Neumann Ch., Knoxville, 1986—. Fellow Tenn. Soc. CPAs (sec. 1987-88, v.p. 1988-89), Am. Inst.

CPAs, Knoxville Estate Planning Council, Nat. Assn. Female Execs. Democrat. Roman Catholic. Club: Kiwanis (Knoxville). Office: Elkins & Roy P.C. 531 S Gay St Suite 1112 Knoxville TN 37902

BRACKETT, DEBORAH EVELYN, marketing executive; b. Lakeland, Fla., Sept. 5, 1950; d. Charles Joseph and Hazel (Whitten) B.; m. J. Russell Hornsey (div.). Student, U. Cen. Fla., 1979-83. Model Screen Actors Guild/AFTRA, N.Y.C., 1969-84; mktg. rep. Gen. Devel. Corp., Fla., 1983—; mem. polit. action com. Mem. Screen Actors Guild. Republican. Roman Catholic. Office: Gen Devel 2500 Port Macabar Blvd Palm Bay FL 32905

BRACKETT, GAIL BURGER, budget administrator, political science educator; b. Bloomington, Ind., June 25, 1950; d. Clifford Robert and Opal June (McKinnon) Burger; m. Denis C. Brackett, July 14, 1973. BS, So. Ill. U., 1971, MS, 1972, PhD, 1984. Project coordinator instnl. research and studies So. Ill. U., Carbondale, 1972-80, budget analyst, 1980-81, adminstrv. asst. budget office, 1981-87, adj. asst. prof. polit. sci., 1987; sr. budget analyst Commonwealth of Va., Richmond, 1987—; adj. asst. prof. polit. sci., So. Ill. U., 1987; mem. adminstrv. profl. staff council, 1978-80; speaker Coll. and U. Machine Records Conf., 1979, 84, 87; jour. referee Assn. for Computing Machinery Jour., 1978. Active Friends Sallie Logan Library, 1986-87, sta. Friends WSIU pub. radio, 1985-87, pres. Lydia Unit United Meth. Ch., 1987. Fellow Post-doctoral Acad. Higher Edn. (bd. dirs. 1986-87); mem. Bus. and Profl. Women, Nat. Assn. Female Execs., Assn. Instl. Research, Ill. Assn. for Instl. Research (panel 1983), Pi Omega Pi, Phi Kappa Phi, Phi Delta Kappa. Home: 21 Chase Gayton Circle #518 Richmond VA 23233 Office: Commonwealth of Va Dept Planning and Budget PO Box 1422 Richmond VA 23211

BRADBURY, DIANNA, sales executive; b. Elmer, N.J., Feb. 11, 1963; d. James Joseph and Angeline (Appoloney) B. Grad. high sch., Glassboro, N.J. Clk., salesperson Eckerd Drugs, Glassboro, 1979; clk., cashier Burger King, Glassboro, 1980-81; salesperson Bamburgers, Ford, N.J., 1981-82; clk., salesperson The Southland Corp., Turnersville, N.J., 1982-83; asst. mgr. Runnemede, N.J., 1983-84; store mgr. Deptford and Paulsboro, N.J., 1984-85, Moorestown, N.J., 1985-86; mgmt. trainee Marlton, N.J., 1986; mgr. personnel, chair charity com. Mays Landing, N.J., 1986, field counsellor, 1986—. Gannet Corp. scholar, 1980. Mem. Nat. Assn. Female Execs. Democrat. Roman Catholic. Home: 413 University Blvd Glassboro NJ 08028

BRADBURY, LORRE JO, sales professional; b. Ridgewood, N.J., Apr. 17, 1957; d. Joseph and Doris (Simmons) Distasio; m. W. David Bradbury, May. 7, 1983. BS, Drexel U., 1982; grad., Chevrolet Dealership Mgmt. Acad., 1987. Mktg. asst. Video Systems Corp., Pennsauken, N.J., 1977-80; mgr. leasing and sales Distasio Chevrolet, Marlton, N.J., 1980—. Office: Distasio Chevrolet 444 Rt 73 S Marlton NJ 08053

BRADDOM, CAROLYN LENTZ, trade association director; b. Dayton, Ohio; m. L. Braddom; 3 children. BS in Elem. Edn., Manchester Coll., 1964; MA in Psychology, Ohio State U., 1966, postgrad., 1966-67, 85; EdD, U. Cin., 1988. Cert. ednl. adminstrv. specialist, elem. prin., elem. tchr., sch. psychologist, Ohio; lic. psychologist, Ohio. Elem. tchr. Worthington Exempted Schs., Columbus, Ohio, 1964-66; sch. psychologist Southwestern City Schs., Columbus, 1966-69, Forest Hills Sch. Dist., Cin., 1974-76, Cin. Pub. Schs., 1976-79; pvt. practice ednl. and behavioral services 1979-84; exec. dir. Assn. Acad. Psychiatrists, 1982—; grad. asst. dept. edn. Adminstrn. U. Cin., 1985—; instr., psychologist Ohio State U., 1972, adj. asst. prof. Burlington County Coll., 1972-74. Cons. early learning ctr. Mountview Bapt. Ch., Upper Arlington, Ohio, 1969-71; children's coordinator Anderson Hills United Meth. Ch., Cin., 1976-78, trustee, pres. nursery sch., 1978-81, chmn. commn. on edn., 1981-84; mem. bd. edn. Forest Hills Sch. Dist., pres., 1986—. Mem. Am. Soc. Assn Execs., Assn. for Supervision and Curriculum Dirs., Nat. Sch. Bds. Assn., Am. Congress Rehab. Medicine, Ohio Sch. Bds. Assn, Ohio Psychological Assn., Southwestern Ohio Sch. Psychologists Assn., Nat. Assn. Ch. Psychologists, Ohio Sch. Psychologists Assn. Home: 2722 Montchateau Dr Cincinnati OH 45244 Office: Assn Acad Psychiatrists 8000 Five Mile Rd Suite 340 Cincinnati OH 45230

BRADEN, BETTY JANE, legal association administrator; b. Sheboygan, Wis., Feb. 5, 1943; d. Otto Frank and Betty Donna (Beers) Huettner; children: Jennifer Tindall, Rebecca Leigh; m. Berwyn Bartow Braden, Nov. 5, 1983. BS, U. Wis., 1965. Cert. elem. tchr., Wis. Tchr. Madison (Wis.) Met. Sch. Dist., 1965-70, 71-72, sub. tchr., 1972-75; adminstrv. asst. ATS-CLE State Bar of Wis., Madison, 1978, ATS-CLE program coordinator, 1979, coordinator, 1980, adminstr. coordinator, 1980-84, adminstrv. dir., 1984-87, dir. adminstrn., bar services, 1987—. Mem. Meeting Planners Internat. (sec. Wis. chpt. 1981-82, pres. 1982-83); Adminstrv. Mgmt. Soc., Am. Mgmt. Assn., Am. Soc. for Personnel Adminstrn., Am. Soc. of Assn. Execs., Wis. Soc. of Assn. Execs., LWV, Nat. Assn. Bar Execs. Home: 52 Golf Course Rd Madison WI 53704 Office: State Bar of Wis 402 W Wilson St Madison WI 53703

BRADEN, DANA DANIELLE, lawyer; b. Detroit, June 8, 1951; d. William A. and Majorie L. (Badertscher) B. BA, Mich. State U., 1973; JD, Detroit Coll. Law, 1977; postgrad. U. Miami, 1979-81. Bar: Mich. 1977, Fla. 1978. Asst. bank mgr. Community Nat. Bank, Pontiac, Mich., 1973-76; asst. trust officer Genesee Bank, Flint, Mich., 1976-78; trust officer Sun Banks of Fla., Orlando, 1978-79; assoc. Storms Krasny et al, Melbourne, Fla., 1979, Lake Worth, Fla., 1986—; sole practice, West Palm Beach, 1981-85, Lake Worth, Fla., 1987—. Contbr. articles on estate planning and planned giving to profl. jours. Rep. precinct del., 1972; 2d vice chmn. Oakland County Reps., Mich., 1972; bd. dirs. Big Bros./Big Sisters Brevard County, Fla., 1978. Joseph S. Burak scholar, 1977. Mem. ABA, Mich. Bar Assn., Fla. Bar Assn., Martin County Estate Planning Council (co-founder), Planned Giving Council Palm Beach County (co-founder, pres. 1982—), Nat. Assn. Planned Giving Council (co-founder). Congregationalist. Home: 4000 Shelley Rd S West Palm Beach FL 33407 Office: 2290 10th Ave N Penthouse Suite 600 Lake Worth FL 33461-3208

BRADFORD, BARBARA TAYLOR, author, journalist, novelist; b. Leeds, Eng., May 10, 1933; came to U.S., 1964; d. Winston and Freda (Walker) Taylor; m. Robert Bradford, Dec. 24, 1963. Student pvt. schs., Eng. Women's editor Yorkshire (Eng.) Evening Post, 1951-53, reporter, 1949-51; editor Woman's Own, 1953-54; columnist London Evening News, 1955-57; exec. editor London Am., 1959-62; editor Nat. Design Center Mag., 1965-69; syndicated columnist Newsday Spls., L.I., 1968-70; nat. syndicated columnist Chgo. Tribune-N.Y (News Syndicate), N.Y.C., 1970-75, Los Angeles Times Syndicate, 1975-81. Author: Complete Ency. Homemaking Ideas, 1968, A Garland of Children's Verse, 1968, How to be the Perfect Wife, 1969, Easy Steps to Successful Decorating, 1971, Decorating Ideas for Casual Living, 1977, How to Solve Your Decorating Problems, 1976, Making Space Grow, 1979; novel A Woman of Substance, 1979; Luxury Designs for Apartment Living, 1981; novel Voice of the Heart, 1983, Hold the Dream, 1985, screen adaptation, 1986, novel Act of Will, 1986, To Be the Best, 1988. Recipient Dorothy Dawe award Am. Furniture Mart, 1970, 71, Matrix award N.Y. Women in Communications, 1985. Mem. Authors Guild, Nat. Soc. Interior Designers (Distinguished Editorial award 1969, Nat. Press award 1971), Am. Soc. Interior Designers. Office: 450 Park Ave New York NY 10022

BRADFORD, CHRISTINA, newspaper editor; b. Dec. 23, 1942; d. J. Robert and Lesley (Jones) Merrill; m. Alan Bradford, Sept. 24, 1966 (div. 1973). A.A., Stephens Coll., Columbia, Mo., 1962; B.Journalism, U. Mo.-Columbia, 1964. Asst. city editor Detroit Free Press, 1975-80; asst. mng. editor Democrat and Chronicle, Rochester, N.Y., 1980-82, mng. editor, 1982-86; mng. editor/news Detroit News, 1986—. Mem. AP Mng. Editors, Am. Soc. Newspaper Editors. Club: Detroit Athletic. Home: 208 Main Sail Ct Detroit MI 48207 Office: Detroit News 615 W Lafayette Detroit MI 48231

BRADFORD, LOUISE MATHILDE, social worker; b. Alexandria, La., Aug. 3, 1925; d. Henry Aaron and Ruby (Pearson) Bradford; B.S., La. Poly. Inst., 1945; cert. in social work La. State U., 1949; M.S., Columbia U., 1953; postgrad. Tulane U., 1962, 64, La. State U., 1967; cert. U. Pa., 1966. With La. Dept. Public Welfare, Alexandria, 1945-78, welfare caseworker, 1950-53, children's caseworker, 1957-59, child welfare cons., 1959-73, social services cons., 1973-78, state cons. day care, 1963-66; dir. social services St. Mary's Tng. Sch., Alexandria, La., 1978—; del. Nat. Day Care Conf., Washington, 1964; mem. early childhood edn. com. So. States Work Conf., Daytona Beach, Fla., 1968; mem. La. adv. com. 1970 White House Conf. on Children, also del.; mem. So. region planning com. Child Welfare League Am., 1970-73; mem. profl. adv. com. Cenla chpt. Parents Without Partners, 1970; adj. asst. prof. sociology La. Coll., Pineville, 1969-85, lectr. Kindergarten workshop, 1970-72; mem. La. 4-C Day Care Licensing Rev. Com., Central La. 4-C Steering Com.; social services cons. La. Spl. Edn. Ctr., Alexandria, 1980-86; del. Internat. Conf. on Social Welfare, Nairobi, 1974, Jerusalem, 1978, Hong Kong, 1980, Brighton, 1982, Montreal, 1984. Pres., Les Soignees, Alexandria, 1947-48. Bd. dirs. Cenla Community Action Com., Alexandria, 1966-68. Mem. Acad. Cert. Social Workers, Nat. Assn. Social Workers, La. Bd. Cert. Social Worker; diplomate in clin. social work; So. La. Assns. Children under Ssix, La. Conf. Social Welfare, Internat. Council on Social Welfare, Am. Pub. Welfare Assn. (S.W. region planning com. 1965), Am. Assn. on Mental Deficiency, DAR, Central La. Pre-Sch. Assn. (dir. 1967-70), Marquis Biog. Library Assn. (adv.). Methodist (kindergarten bd. 1967-87), ofcl. bd. 1974-75, 77-81, 83-85). Clubs: Rapides Golf and Country, Pilot (Alexandria). Home: 5807 Joyce St Alexandria LA 71302 Office: PO Box 7768 Alexandria LA 71306

BRADFORD, ORCELIA SYLVIA, infosystems specialist; b. Kansas City, Mo., Apr. 28, 1953; d. Thomas Wayne and Sylvia (Fueston)Ryan; m. Stanley Lynn, Sept. 26, 1975; children: Richard Lee, April Orcelia. Grad., Belleville Area Coll., 1979. Operator Fin. Data Systems, St. Louis, 1979-81; operator Community Fed. Savs. and Loan, St. Louis, 1981-82, scheduler, 1982-84; prodn. control scheduler Citicorp Person-to-Person, Inc., St. Louis, 1984-87; tech. cons. Cap Gemini Am., Overland Park, Kans., 1987; data analyst Source Cede, Overland Park, 1987—. Republican. Baptist. Home: 9303 Alden Rd Lenexa KS 66215 Office: AT&T 2121 E 63d St C100 Kansas City MO 64130

BRADFORD, SHARON MARIA, legal assistant; b. Ft. Worth, Aug. 20, 1956; d. John Nicholas and Norma Fern (Zigler) Kratochvil; m. Timothy Lee Bradford, Feb. 6, 1981; children: Jeremy, Julie, Kristy, Mark. AS, Amarillo Coll., 1976; cert. paralegal studies, West Tex. State U., 1981. Legal sec. Stokes, Carnahan & Fields, Amarillo, Tex., 1976-78; legal sec., then legal asst. Law Offices of Ben L. Sturgeon, Amarillo, 1978-79; legal asst. Chambers & Sturgeon, Amarillo, 1979-84, Houston & Klein, Inc., Tulsa, 1984—. Treas. Parents' Com. First Bapt. Ch. Learning Ctr., Tulsa, 1986—. Mem. State Bar Tex. (dir. Dist. 7 Legal Assistants 1981-83), Okla. Paralegal Assn. (v.p. 1985-87), Tulsa Assn. Legal Assistants (bar liaison chmn. 1987). Republican. Roman Catholic. Office: Houston & Klein Inc 320 S Boston Suite 700 Tulsa OK 74103

BRADFUTE, JILL CAROLYN, foundation administrator; b. Bronxeville, N.Y., July 29, 1958; d. Jack White and Jacqueline Lorraine (Fisher) B.; m. Francis Sabatino Mancini, July 23, 1983. BS, Roger Williams Coll., 1981. Asst. dir. R.I. Rape Crisis Ctr., Providence, 1977-79; exec. dir. Newport (R.I.) County Women's Resource Ctr., 1979-81; div. dir. United Way Southeastern New Eng., Providence, 1981-86; v.p. United Way Southeastern New Eng., 1987—. Chmn. R.I. Women's Polit. Caucus, 1980; bd. dirs. R.I. Council on Domestic Violence, 1979-81. Named Vol. of the Yr., YWCA of Greater R.I., 1977.

BRADLEY, BONNIE, mezzo soprano; b. Wilmington, Del., 1951; d. Archie Merill and Blanche Ruth Bradley; Certs. in Oratorio, Song, Opera, Britten-Pears Sch. Advanced Musical Studies, Snape-on-Maltings, Eng.; cert. in Opera, Inst. Musical Studies, Graz, Austria, Mozarteum Sommerakadamie, Salzburg, Austria; B.Mus. in Voice, Westminster Choir Coll.; M.Mus. in Opera Performance, Manhattan Sch. Music, N.Y.C., 1975; m. Nicholas Nicosia, June 28, 1975; children: Francesca Maria Aida, Jonathan Gregory. Operatic and concert artist performing with opera cos. and maj. symphony orchs., recitalist U.S., Eng., Germany, Austria, the Caribbean, 1975—; instr. master classes colls. and univs.; adjudicator maj. vocal competitions. Helene Rubenstein Found. grantee; winner Artists Internat. Competition, Liederkranz Found. competition, Oratorio solo competition; recipient Minna Kauffman Ruud Found. competition award. Mem. Am. Guild Musical Artists, Nat. Assn. Tchrs. of Singing, Coll. Music Soc., Washington Arts Group. Office: care Metropolitan Musical Artists 2836 Flagmaker Dr Falls Church VA 22042

BRADLEY, FLORENE JORDAN, librarian; b. Magnolia, Ark., Aug. 18, 1917; d. Thomas Scott and Nellie (Nipper) Jordan; student So. State Coll., Ark., 1935-37; B.A., Henderson State Tchrs. Coll., 1939; B.S. in L.S., Peabody Coll., 1947; m. Steve Bradley, Nov. 23, 1966. Librarian, tchr. Burdette High Sch., 1939-42, Calhoun High Sch., 1942-43, Magnolia High Sch., 1943-51; regional librarian Columbia-Lafayette-Ouachita-Calhoun Regional Library, Magnolia, 1951—. Pres., United Way Columbia County, 1979; sec. City Planning Commn., Columbia County Fair Bd. Named Magnolia Woman of Year service and civic clubs, 1963; Citizen of Yr., 1968. Mem. Magnolia Bus. and Profl. Women's Club (Woman of Year 1979), AAUW, Magnolia LWV, Ark. (past pres.), Southwestern (past chmn. pub. library div.) library assns., ALA (mem. notable books council adult services div. 1962-64), C. of C. (dir.), Delta Kappa Gamma. Methodist. Club: Quota. Home: 405 W Calhoun St Magnolia AR 71753 Office: 220 E Main St Magnolia AR 71753

BRADLEY, GWENDOLYN, opera singer, soprano; b. N.Y.C.; degree N.C. Sch. Arts, Curtis Inst., Acad. Vocal Arts. Debut with Lake George Opera as Nanette in Falstaff, 1976; debut with Met. Opera as Le Rossignol in Ravel's L'Enfant et les Sortileges, 1981; Met. Opera performances include Ariadne auf Naxos, Rigoletto, Porgy and Bess, Tales of Hoffmann, Le Rossignol, Siegfried, Abduction from the Seraglio, Arabella, L'Enfant et les Sortilégès, Die Frau ohne Schatten, 1980-88 seasons; internat. operatic debut Corfu Festival, Greece, summer 1981; other European engagements include Netherlands Opera, Paris Radio, Hamburg Staatsoper, Glyndebourne Festival, Berlin Deutsch Opera, Monte Carlo Opera, Nice Opera; has appeared with Phila., Cleve., Central City Operas, Mich. Opera Theater; recitalist, concert performer; soloist Phila. Orch., Nat., Seattle, Denver, Honolulu, St. Louis Symphonies, Kansas City Philharm., Aspen Festival Chamber Orch.; recitals include Carnegie Recital Hall, Phillips Gallery, Dumbarton Oaks, Washington, community concerts. Nat. finalist Met. Opera Guild auditions; winner 26 competitions and awards. Office: care Columbia Artists Mgmt Inc 165 W 57th St New York NY 10019

BRADLEY, JANET LITZ, state official, civil rights advocate; b. Balt., May 9, 1935; d. Francis Joseph and Ella Doris (Manning) Litz; m. Richard Alan Bradley, Dec. 27, 1958; children—Anne Marie, M. Katheryn, Alana, Richard Alan. B.A. magna cum laude, Dunbarton Coll., 1957; postgrad. U. Paris, 1957, U. Dijon, Cours Etrangers, France, 1957-58, U. Alaska, 1975-77; M.A. in French, U. Wash., 1973. Lectr. French, U. Alaska, Juneau, 1970-73; exec. sec. Arts and Humanities Council, Juneau, 1973; asst. dir. Alaska Commn. for Human Rights, Juneau, 1974-82, exec. dir., Anchorage, 1982—. Coordinator, Southeastern Alaska McGovern for Pres. campaign, 1972; v.p. U. Alaska Policy Adv. Council, Juneau, 1980, pres., 1982. Fulbright scholar, 1957-58. Mem. Nat. Assn. Civil Rights Workers, NAACP, NOW, Bus. and Profl. Women's Club, Alaska Women's Lobby, Nat. Women's Polit. Caucus, Internat. Assn. Ofcl. Human Rights Agys. (sec. to bd.). Democrat. Roman Catholic. Lodge: Soroptimists. Office: Ala State Commn Human Rights 800 A St Suite 202 Anchorage AK 99501

BRADLEY, JANICE ELAINE, home economist; b. St. Bernice, Ind., Oct. 8, 1935; d. Kenneth and Lucille (Hollingsworth) Jones; m. Loren William Bradley, Aug. 9, 1935; children: William Gregory, Gretchen Ann, Grant Edward. BS, Ind. State U., 1957, MS, 1962. Tchr. Vermillion County (Ind.) Schs., 1957-62; ext. home econ. Purdue U., Terre Haute, Ind., 1964-72, Terre Haute, 1983—. Mem. Am. Home Econ. Assn., Nat. Home Econs. Assn., Ind. Home Econs. Assn., Ind. Extension Agents Assn., Home Econs. in Homemaking, Delta Kappa Gamma, Epsilon Sigma Phi. Home: Rural Rt 1 Box 926 Clinton IN 47842 Office: Vigo County Extension Service 275 Ohio Terre Haute IN 47808

BRADLEY, JOSEPHINE D., social worker, educator; b. Greensboro, N.C., Mar. 7, 1949; d. Robert L. and Cora Lee (Dungee) Boyd; m. Hayworth Lee Bradley, Aug. 10, 1963; children: Paulette Yvonne , Teresa Michelle. BA, N.C. Cen. U., 1963; MSW, Mich. State U., 1966. Exec. sec. Redevel. Commn., Durham, N.C., 1963-66; clin. social worker St. Lawrence Hosp., Lansing, Mich., 1966-67, dir. social services, 1967-68; coordinator tng.-alcoholism tng. program So. U., Baton Rouge, 1970-77; social work tchr. Tusculum Coll., Greeneville, Tenn., 1977—; cons. Morristown Coll., 1982—, Morris Coll., Sumter, 1983. Chair person bd. dirs. George Clem Meml. Scholarship Found., Citizens for Children's Day Care, Greensboro, 1982—; bd. dirs. Vocat. Rehab., Greeneville, 1982-84. Fellow Emory U., Atlanta, 1987. Mem. Nat. Assn. Social Workers, (chmn. 1979-82) (named Social Worker Yr. 1983), Greeneville/Greene County Interagy. Council, Alpha Kappa Alpha. Methodist. Club: Negro Women's Civic (pres. 1982-84). Home: 200 Mayor Ave Greeneville TN 37743

BRADLEY, KITTY, organization administrator, writer; b. N.Y.C., July 23, 1922; m. Omar N. Buhler, 1966; 1 child, Elizabeth Dorsey. Grad., Washington Manhattan Coll., 1942; postgrad., Kans. Wesleyan U., U. So. Calif., U. Calif., Los Angeles, LaVerne Coll.; LLD, Park U. Kans., U. Beverly Hills. lectr. TV script writer (episodes) including programs The Untouchables, My THree Sons, Dragnet, The GE Hour, others; screenwriter China Doll; research editor A General's Life, 1982; contbr. articles to mags. including Look. Founder Omar N. Bradley Found., Carlisle Barracks, Pa.; hon. presidential appointee Am. Battle Monuments Commn.; rep. State Calif. for French Am. ScholarshiFound.; with Omar N. Bradley Library, West Point, N.Y., Omar N. Bradley Spirit of Independence event, Shreveport, La., USO; bd. dirs. Normandie Mus., France. Mem. Voice of Am., Exec. Women in Govt., Writers Guild Am., Women in Film, Nat. League Pen Women. Club: Women's Nat. Republican (chairperson Los Angeles chpt.).

BRADLEY, LISA KAY, agriculturalist; b. Cambridge, Ohio, Jan. 5, 1960; d. John Glen and Eva Mae (St. Clair) Holmes; m. Benjamin David Bradley, Aug. 31, 1985. BSA, Ohio State U., 1982, MS in Agrl.Edn., 1983. With Ohio Coop. Extension Service, 1982—; adminstrv. asst. Columbus, 1982-83; 4-H program asst. Eaton, 1983-84, instr. 4-H, 1984-88; instr. 4-H Greenville, 1988—; 4-H horse judge Ohio Coop. Extension Service, Columbus, 1982—. Author:(leaflet) 4-H Horse Project Planning Guides, 1987; co-author, editor:(tabloid) Special 4-H Editon of Register Herald, 1984, 85, 86, 87, 88. Mem. Nat. Assn. Extension 4-H Agts., Ohio Coop. Extension Agts. Assn. (program com.1984-87) Ohio Quarter Horse Assn., Sigma Alpha Agrl. Sorority Nat. Bd. (pres. 1985-87. Democrat. Presbyterian. Office: Darke County Coop Extension Service 700 Wayne St Greenville OH 45331

BRADLEY, RAMONA KAISER, curator; b. Hamilton County, Ohio, Aug. 9, 1909; d. Oliver Barnard and Grace Lytle (Edwards) Kaiser; student Oakhurst Coll., Cin., 1926-28, Schuster-Martin Sch. Drama, 1931-33; m. Judson M. Bradley, Sept. 4, 1954. Sec. to patent atty., Cin., 1939-54; curator Sherman Indian Mus., Riverside, Calif., 1970—; cons. Title IV Project, Indian edn. Riverside Sch. Dist. Bd. dirs. Riverside Library, 1966-74, Riverside Cultural Heritage, 1974-80. Recipient Appreciation award Sherman Indian High Sch., 1977, honored for civic service City and County Riverside, 1980, honor award D.A.R., 1981. Mem. Nat. League Am. Pen Women, D.A.R., Daus. Am. Colonists, Printing House Craftsmen, Inland Empire Mus. Consortium. Republican. Methodist. Club: Citrus Belt (hon.). Author: Glimpses Into the Past, 1940, Weavers of Tales, 1965. Home: 9130 Andrew St Riverside CA 92503 Office: 9010 Magnolia Ave Riverside CA 92503

BRADLEY, REBECCA LYNN, insurance company executive; b. Kansas City, Mo., Nov. 11, 1956; d. Frank Joseph and Joanne (Peak) B. BBA, So. Meth. U., 1979; MBA, North Tex. State U., 1983. Acct. Dallas Power & Light Co., 1979-81; fin. planner John Hancock Ins., Dallas, 1983; registerd rep. Fidelity Investments, Irving, Tex., 1983-85; supr. retirement dept. Bright Banc, Dallas, 1985-86; sr. v.p. Advantage Life Ins. Co., Dallas, 1986—; pvt. practice tax cons., Dallas, 1983—. Deacon Highland Park Presbyn. Ch., Dallas, coordinating com., 1982-85; big sister PALS, Dallas, 1987—; vol. numerous charity orgns., Dallas, 1985—. Named on of Outstanding Young Women Am., 1984. Mem. Nat. Assn. Female Execs. republican. Presbyterian. Home: 8668 Thackery Dallas TX 75225 Office: Advantage Life Ins. Co 8333 Douglas Dallas TX 75225

BRADLEY, ROSALEE, psychologist, horse breeder and trainer; b. Calhoun, Mo., Sept. 20, 1939; d. Wayne Beecher and Alice Maureen (Shrout) B. B.S., U. Kansas City, 1961; M.A., Hollins Coll., 1963; Ph.D., Wash. State U., 1969. Lic. psychologist, Calif., Wash. Staff psychologist No. State Hosp., Sedro-Woolley, Wash., 1968-74; staff psychologist Calif. Correctional Ctr., Susanville, Calif., 1974-78, adminstrv. asst. to supt., 1975-78, EEO officer, 1975-78, women's liaison rep., 1975-78; pvt. practice clin. psychology, Susanville, 1978—; cons. Right Way Homes, boy's ranch; tchr. in field; horse breeder, trainer, 19—. Mem. Lassen County Women Democrats. Recipient numerous awards in horse show circuit, 1981, 82. Mem. Am. Psychol. Assn., Mortar Bd., Psi Chi. Democrat. Clubs: Appaloosa Horse (Bronze Medallion award 1975), Honey Lake Valley Riders. Exhibited photography: Lassen Community Coll. (Merit award), 1982, Lassen County Fair (2 First place awards and 2d place award), 1981. Avocation: cribbage (numerous tournament awards). Home: PO Box 88 Janesville CA 96114 Office: 617 Main Suite 204 Susanville CA 96130

BRADLEY, VELMA JEAN, insurance company executive; b. Ft. Wayne, Ind., Dec. 22, 1951; d. Vincent Joseph Lijewski and Vera Caroline (Strange) Reardon; m. Alan D. Bradley, Jan. 26, 1974; children: Jacob, Jared. Student, Indiana U., Ft. Wayne, 1971, Davenport Coll., Grand Rapids, Mich., 1975. Office mgr. Ash Brokerage Co., Ft. Wayne, Ind., 1971-74; asst. supr. collection dept. Old Kent Bank, Grand Rapids, Mich., 1975-79; mgr. sub-standard dept. Ash Brokerage Co., Ft. Wayne, 1982-86; dir. spl. markets Mutual Security Life, Ft. Wayne, 1986—. Cons. Jr. Achievement Project Bus., Ft. Wayne, 1987. Mem. Nat. Assn. Life Underwriters, Ft. Wayne chpt. Nat. Assn. Life Underwriters (bd. dirs. 1988—). Roman Catholic. Home: Mut Security Life 3000 Coliseum Blvd North Fort Wayne IN 46805

BRADSHAW, CONSTANCE MATILDA, insurance executive; b. Rochester, N.Y., Mar. 24, 1934; d. Geo B. Richards and Constance (Schickler) Sawdey; m. Robert L. Bradshaw, June 6, 1953 (div. Nov. 1985); children: Sharon L. Deming, Cynthia L. James; m. R. Peter Barker, Dec. 29, 1985. BS in Bus. Adminstrn., Empire State Coll., 1984. Ins. assoc. Ithaca (N.Y.) Agy., 1965-70; inside sales assoc. Kendall Agy., Rochester, 1970-73; agy. mgr., sales Barker Agy., Rochester, 1973-81; agy. chief ops. officer, ptnr. Barker, Heslip, Bradshaw Agy., Rochester, 1981—; pres. Monroe Co. Agts. Assn., Rochester, 1983-84. Bd. dirs. Camp Fire Girls and Boys, Rochester, 1986—; mem. council Greece Vocat., Rochester, 1986, 87; sec. I.A.P.W., Rochester, 1983. Mem. Adminstrv. Mgmt. Soc. (v.p. 1987). Republican. Episcopalian. Office: Barker Heslip Bradshaw Agy 2450 Ridge Rd W Rochester NY 14626

BRADSHAW, CYNTHIA HELENE, educator; b. S.I., N.Y., May 9, 1954; d. Frederick Thomas and Audrey Helene (Stetter) B. B.S. in Elem. Edn., Wagner Coll., 1975; M.S. in Edn., U. Miami, 1979. Cert. elem. tchr., adminstr., and supr. Tchr. Young Scholars Montessori Sch., S.I., 1975-76, Lutheran Schs., Mo. Synod, S.I., 1976, Hialeah and N. Miami, Fla., 1976-80, Dade County pub. schs., Miami, 1980-88, Rahway (N.J.) pub. schs., 1988—; reliability study subject Fla. Dept. Edn., Tallahassee, 1984—. Sch. chairperson United Way, Miami, 1983—. Recipient Cert. of Recognition Dade County Pub. Schs., 1984. Mem. United Tchrs. Dade, United Tchrs. Dade Polit. Orgn., U. Miami Sch. Edn. Allied Professions Alumni Assn. (mem. alumni telephone funding campaign 1984), Alpha Delta Kappa. Republican. Lutheran. Lodge: Order Eastern Star. Avocation: Music. Home: 34 Douglas Ave Staten Island NY 10310 Office: Roosevelt Elem Sch 811 Saint Georges Ave Rahway NJ 07065

BRADSHAW, GLENDA MARIE, management executive; b. Amarillo, Tex., Oct. 6, 1946; d. John Carson and Frances (McWhorter) McP.; m. Roger Dale Bradshaw, June 10, 1965 (div. May 1986); children: Andrea Lea, Kara Lyn. Student, Amarillo Jr. Coll., 1966. Teller, loan processor First Fed. Savs. and Loan, Amarillo, 1964-66; govt. document specialist Tex. A&M U., College Station, 1966-69; income tax preparer Precell Tax Preparer

Service, Prentiss, Miss., 1971; with auto rental dept. Tom McClellan Ford, Amarillo, 1977-78; adminstrv. asst. Lynden Airfreight Forwarding, Anchorage, 1978-79; personnel dir. N.W. Tech. Services, Inc., Anchorage, 1982, mgr. adminstrv. services, 1982-83, dir. contracts, 1984-85, gen. mgr., 1986-87; franchise div. dist. mgr. Todays Temporary, Dallas, 1987—. Mem. Alliance Oilfield Support Service Orgn., Anchorage, 1985-87. Mem. Nat. Assn. for Female Execs., Nat. Assn. Temporary Services, Anchorage Personnel Assn., Anchorage Better Bus. Bur., Anchorage C. of C., Bus. and Profl. Women Orgn. Republican. Baptist. Home: 1515 Rio Grande #1113 Plano TX 75075

BRADSHAW, LILLIAN MOORE, retired librarian; b. Hagerstown, Md., Jan. 10, 1915; d. Harry M. and Mabel E. (Kretzer) Moore; m. William Theodore Bradshaw, May 19, 1946. B.A., Western Md. Coll., 1937, DLitt (hon.), 1987; B.L.S., Drexel U., 1938, Litt.D. (hon.), 1978. Asst. adult circulation dept. Utica (N.Y.) Pub. Library, 1938-41, asst. head, 1941-43; adult librarian Enoch Pratt Free Library, Balt., 1943-44; asst. coordinator work with young adults Enoch Pratt Free Library, 1944-46; br. librarian Dallas Pub. Library, 1946-47, readers adviser, 1947-52, head dept. circulation, 1952- 55, coordinator work with adults, 1955-58, asst. dir., 1958-62, dir., 1962-84; asst. mgr. City of Dallas, 1984-85; mem. adv. group on libraries Library of Congress, 1976-77. Mem. bd. publs. So. Meth. U., 1970-78; mem. curriculum com. Leadership Dallas, 1978-79, mem. adv. com., 1978-82; mem. Tex. Gov.'s Commn. on Status of Women, 1970-72, Tex. Com. for Humanities, 1980-84, Nat. Reading Council, Washington, 1970-73; pres. Tex. Humanities Alliance, 1986—; conferee and asst. task force leader Goals for Dallas, 1966-69, vice chmn. achievement com. for continuing edn., 1971, chmn., 1972, chmn. citizen info. and participation com., 1976-77, trustee, 1977-88 , sec., 1977, treas., 1979-83, exec. com., 1977-84; hon. chair Literacy Vols. Am., Dallas, 1987—; mem. Com. to Plan the Future Goals for Dallas, 1973-74, Dallas County Hist. Found., 1987—; mem. adv. bd. Tex. Library Systems Act, 1974-77; del. White House Conf. on Library and Info. Services, 1979; Tex. del. Nat. Commn. on Libraries and Info. Services; mem. ad hoc com. for planning and monitoring White House Conf. follow-up activities, 1980; bd. dirs. Hoblitzelle Found., 1971—, Univ. Med. Ctr., 1984-87; trustee Lamplighter Sch., 1974-81, Friends of Dallas Pub. Library, 1984—, Dallas Ballet, 1986—, Dallas Arboretum and Bot. Garden, 1986—; pres. Tex. Humanities Alliance, 1986—. Named Tex. Librarian of Year, 1961; recipient Disting. Alumnus award Drexel U. Library Sch., 1970; Titche's Arete award for epitome of excellence in chosen field, 1970; Public Adminstr. of Yr. award, 1981; Excellence in Community Service award Dallas Hist. Soc., 1981; citation of honor Dallas chpt. AIA, 1982; Lillian Moore Bradshaw chair in library and info. studies established in her honor Tex. Woman's U. Mem. ALA (v.p. adult services div. 1966-67, pres. adult services div. 1967-68, council 1968-69, pres. 1970-71, endowment trustee 1984-88), Tex. Library Assn. (pres. 1964-65, chmn. pub. libraries div. 1955-56, chmn. awards com. 1973-74, 79-80, Disting. Service award 1975), Tex. Soc. Architects (hon. 1982), Dallas Hist. Soc. (trustee 1984-87), Dallas County Hist. Found. Club: Zonta (pres. Dallas I 1976-77, Service award 1981). Home: 6318 E Lovers Ln Dallas TX 75214

BRADSHAW, NANCI MARIE, business executive; b. Schenectady, Aug. 21, 1940; d. Leo Arthur and Angela Bertha (Bonk) Bradshaw; m. William Clayton Hoehn, Oct. 12, 1963 (div. 1979); children: Sharon Ann, Theresa Lynn; stepchildren: Eugene Augustine Jr., Patricia Ann, William Francis, Mary Teresa, Martin Joseph. BS, Skidmore Coll., 1977. Asst. to pres. Schenectady Indsl. Drafting, 1978-79; bus. exec. math dept. SUNY, Albany, 1979-86, sec. council on acad. freedom and ethics, 1983-85; Evangelist Newspaper, Albany, 1986—; cons., lectr. trustee, v.p., sec. Help Ctr., Inc., Troy, N.Y., 1982—; lectr., cons. Organizational Mgmt., Albany, Schenectady and Troy, 1984—. Coordinator, originator Pre-Kindergarten PTO, Schenectady, 1976-78, Sunday sch. program Immaculate Conception Ch., Schenectady, 1970-79; mem. Pruyn Cultural Ctr., N.Y. Mem. Nat. Assn. Female Execs., N.Y. Acad. Scis., Math. Assn. Am., Albany Cath. Press Assn., Am. Mgmt. Assn. Republican. Roman Catholic. Lodge: Soroptimist Internat. Avocations: refinishing antiques, reading, music, fitness. Home: 157 Maple Ave Troy NY 12180 Office: Albany Cath Press Inc 39 Philip St Albany NY 12207

BRADSHAW, REBECCA PARKS, academic administrator; b. Chattanooga, Tenn., Dec. 10, 1928; d. Cleve and Rebecca (Brittian) Parks; m. Horace Lee Bradshaw Sr., June 22, 1951; children: Horace Lee Jr., Ronald Cleve, Rebecca Christina, Reneé Sara. BA in Math., Clark Coll., 1949; BS in Edn., D.C. Tchr.'s Coll., 1957; MA in Edn. and Psychology, Howard U., 1968; PhD, Walden U., 1981. Cert. tchr., Washington. Census supr. U.S. Govt., Suitland, Md., 1949-59; educator Montgomery County Sch. System, Boyds, Md., 1959-63; educator, adminstr. Dist. Columbia Sch. System, Washington, 1964—; Dean of Students Washington Saturday Coll., 1975-77, dir. student tchrs. Dist. Schs., 1965-80, demonstration tchr. Dir., prin., tchr. Shiloh Bapt. Ch. Sch., Washington, 1952-85, mem. usher bd., 1970-85, mem. Shiloh Child Devel. Ctr., Choir, co-dir. Drama Club, speaker Youth Day, leader Martha Missionary Group, leader Sunshine Circle, sec. Circle Leader's Council; bd. mem. Garden Resources of Washington, 1985-86; contact person, N.W. Civic Assn., Washington, 1969-75, staff cons., Watkins Sch. PTA, 1965-75, life mem.; contact person, den mother Shiloh Boy Scouts Am., Washington, 1955-60; mem., dir., trainer Cultural and Acad. Programs com. of D.C. Cong. of Tchrs. and Parents. Named Tchr. of Yr. Dist. Columbia, 1975, Prin. of Yr. Dist. Columbia, 1976; recipient Gold Dust in Shiloh award Shiloh Bapt. Ch., 1974, cert. award Washington Saturday Coll., 1975, cert. D.C. Tchrs. Conv., 1986; fellow Waldon U., 1980, Outstanding and Dedicated Service award Watkins Sch. PTA, 1981. Mem. Bus. and Profl. Women (life), Phi Delta Kappa. Home: 7515 16th St NW Washington DC 20012

BRADSTOCK, GLENDA WOODARD, doctor of chiropractic medicine; b. Dallas, Mar. 10, 1947; d. Gay Tilman and Beola (Parr) Woodard; m. Phillip Lewis Bradstock, June 15, 1968 (div. June 1971). BA in Philosophy, Mills Coll., 1969; student, Scripps Coll., 1966, Harvey Mudd Coll., 1967; postgrad., So. Meth. U., 1968; D of Chiropractic medicine, Tex. Chiropractic Coll., 1982; med. technologist cert., Internat. Health Inst., 1985-86. Lic. chiropractor, Tex., Okla.; diplomate Los Angeles Coll. Chiropractic Orthopedics.; cert. metabolic tech. Service rep. Bank Am., No. Calif., 1969-70; data processing supr. Mentor Corp., Menlo Park, Calif., 1970-71; acctg. supr. Intel Internat., San Francisco, 1971-72; free-lance film producer Europe, Middle East, 1972-74; free-lance pictorial essayist Calif., N.M., Tex., 1973-76; edn. photographer Tex. Chiropractic Coll., Pasedena, 1978-80; pvt. practice chiropractic medicine Century Chiropractic Ctr., Plano, Tex., 1982—, N.Y. Ave. Chiropractic Clinic, Arlington, Tex., 1984—; mem. adv. bd. Tex. Dept. Pub. Health, 1985—; speaker-lecturer U. Tex., 1985, Century Chiropractic Ctr. Tng. Extension., Plano, 1985—. Photographer: Native Life in Middle East exhbn., 1973; contbr. articles and photographs to profl. jours. Active City Planning, Plano, 1983-84. Mem. Internat. Acad. Neurovascular Disease, Nat. Health Fedn. (v.p. 1984—), Parker Chiropractic Research Found., Tex. Chiropractic Assn. (regional dir. 1987), Plano C. of C. , Arlington C. of C., Tex. Chiropractic Coll. Alumni Assn. Republican. Methodist. Office: Century Chiropractic Ctr 906 18th St Plano TX 75074

BRADT, DONA MARY SONTAG, corporate information center manager; b. Hastings, Minn., Oct. 17, 1930; d. Edwin Gervase and Maude Marie (Hatten) S.; student Mt. St. Marys Coll., 1948, Library Sch. U. Minn., 1968-70; B.A., Met. State U., 1975; Mt. m. Arnold L. Bradt (div.); children—Michael Edwin, Robert Dana, Jeffrey Arnold, Peter Matthew, Andrew Hatten. librarian Ecolab., Inc., St. Paul, 1965—, head librarian, 1979-80, mgr. corp. info. center, 1980—. Mem. Am. Soc. Info. Sci., Spl. Libraries Assn., ALA. Republican. Roman Catholic. Home: 7981 115th St S Cottage Grove MN 55016 Office: Ecolab Inc Corp Info Ctr 840 Sibley Meml Hwy Saint Paul MN 55118

BRADT, PATRICIA THORNTON, aquatic biologist; b. Phila.; d. George Hilyard and Elizabeth Watson (Boynton) Thornton; m. Lynn Jack Bradt, Sept. 6, 1952; children: James. T., Julia E., George H. BA, Cornell U., 1952; MS, Lehigh U., 1970, PhD, 1974. Asst. prof. biology Lehigh U., Bethlehem, Pa., 1974-78; lectr. biology Lafayette Coll., Easton, Pa., 1975-79, Kutztown (Pa.) U., 1984, Allentown Coll. of St. Frances de Sales, Center Valley, Pa., 1985; research scientist Lehigh U., Bethlehem, 1984—; adj. assoc. prof. biology Lehigh U., Bethlehem, 1978-84; v.p., bd. dirs. Hawk Mt. Sanctuary, Kempton, Pa., 1978-86; cons. biologist Environ. Resource Mgmt., Inc., West Chester, Pa., 1980, Easton Sewer Authority, 1986-87; mem. air and water tech. adv. com. PADER, Harrisburg, Pa., 1978—. Author: Biology of Nonvascular Plants, 1984; contbr. articles to profl. jours. Council pres. St. Johns Luth. Ch., Easton, 1984-85. Fellow AAAS (environ. sci.); mem. Am. Soc. Limnology and Oceanography, Ecol. Soc. Am., Am. Inst. Biol. Scis., N.Am. Benthological Soc. Office: Lehigh U Environ Studies Ctr Chandler-Ullman #17 Bethlehem PA 18015

BRADY, ADELA MARIE, biochemist; b. Flint, Mich., Feb. 26, 1951; d. Loren Dean and Rita Ann (Zyber) Crandell; divorced; children: Chip, Seth, Cecily, Coral. BS, Saginaw (Mich.) Valley State U., 1982. Lab. technician Nutra Sweet Co. div. G.D. Searle, Harbor Beach, Mich., 1982, microbiologist, 1983, biochemist, 1986-88, microbiologist, 1988—. Mgr. food coop., Bad Axe, Mich., 1980-83; tchr. Cath. religious edn., Bad Axe, 1973-85; leader Girl Scouts Am., Boy Scouts Am. Roman Catholic. Office: NutraSweet Co 30 Buell St Harbor Beach MI 48441

BRADY, ADELAIDE BURKS, public relations agency executive, giftware catalog executive; b. N.Y.C., June 27, 1926; d. Earl Victor and Audrey (Calvert) Burks; B.S., Boston U., 1946; m. James Francis Brady, Jr., June 22, 1946 (div. 1953); 1 son, James Francis. Exec. v.p. Media Enterprises, 1952-55; dir. group relations Save the Children Fedn., N.Y.C., 1955-59; dir. pub. affairs div. Girl Scouts U.S.A., N.Y.C., 1959-69; pres. Communication Internat., Inc., Washington, 1969-73, Burks Brady Communications, N.Y.C., 1972—, Adelaide's Angel Shopper Catalog Inc., Wilton, Conn., 1976—; exec. v.p. Arts in the Parks Inc., Washington, 1971—; bd. dirs. Lenox Hill Hosp., N.Y.C.; past bd. dirs. Achievement Rewards for Coll. Scientists Found.; pres. Animal Lovers Inc. Mem. Nat. Womens Rep. Club., N.Y.C. Recipient Silver Reel award for film The Children of Now, Save the Children Fedn.; decorated comndr. Order St. John of Jerusalem (Eng.), 1974. Mem. Nat. Assn. Women Bus. Owners, Public Relations Soc. Am., AAUW, NEA, Am. Women in Radio and TV, Nat. Ednl. Broadcasters Assn., Am. Soc. Profl. and Exec. Women, Women Execs. in Public Relations, N.Y. Press Women, Nat. Fedn. Press Women (state pres.), Women's Econ. Roundtable, Nat. Assn. Profl. Women, Nat. Assn. Female Execs., DAR. Episcopalian. Club: Capitol Hill (Washington), Officers (Wash.). Home: 267 Westport Rd Wilton CT 06897 Office: 785 Park Ave New York NY 10021 Other: Box 647 Wilton CT 06897

BRADY, BENNETT MANNING, mathematician, government official; b. Orangeburg, S.C., Apr. 11, 1943; d. William Ellis and Elizabeth (Mays) Manning; m. Roscoe Owen Brady, June 10, 1972; children: Roscoe Owen, Randolph Owen. Student, Agnes Scott Coll., 1961-62; A.B., Vassar Coll., 1965; Fulbright fellow, Cambridge U., 1965-66; M.A. NSF fellow, U. Calif.-Berkeley, 1968; DSc, George Washington U., 1987. Sr. mgmt. cons. Ernst & Ernst, Washington, 1968-70; research assoc. Pres.'s Commn. Fed. Stats., Washington, 1970-71; U.S. internat. statis. liaison OMB, Washington, 1971-78; spl. asst. to commr. labor stats. Bur. Labor Stats., Washington, 1978-79, dir. Office Program Coordination and Evaluation, 1979-86; program mgr. Nuclear Regulatory Commn., Washington, 1986—; cons. ops. research USAF, 1967-68; mem. faculty U. Calif.-Berkeley, 1968; mem. U.S. delegation UN Statis. Commn., 1972. Author: (with J.S. Duncan) Statistical Services in Ten Years' Time, 1978, (with E. Robins and K.S. Tippet) Going Places with Children in Washington, 9th edit., 1979; editor: OSD Statis. Notes, 1980—; contbr. articles on statis. devels. and research to profl. jours. NASA fellow, 1964. Mem. Am. Math. Soc., Am. Statis. Assn., Inst. Mgmt. Sci., Ops. Research Soc. Am., Washington Ops. Research Mgmt. Sci. Council, Washington Statis. Soc., Phi Beta Kappa, Omega Rho, Sigma Xi. Presbyterian. Club: Vassar (Washington); Metro Toastmistress (pres.). Home: 6026 Valerian Ln Rockville MD 20852

BRADY, DEBRA PATRICIA, nurse, educator; b. Pitts., Jan. 15, 1953; d. Frank and Winifred Patricia (Griffin) Rizzo; m. Martin John Brady, Sept. 11, 1976. B.S.N. cum laude, U. Pitts., 1974, M.N.ed., 1981. Staff nurse Presbyn. Hosp., Pitts., 1974-76, Westmorland Hosp., Greensburg, Pa., 1976-79; instr., cons. U. N.Mex., Albuquerque, 1981-84; staff nurse, cons. Presbyn. Hosp., Albuquerque, 1981-84; nursing edn. cons. N.Mex. Bd. Nursing, 1984—; instr. ARC, Albuquerque, 1981-84. Author: Psychosocial Assessment Across the Lifespan; contbr. articles to publs. Bd. dirs. Nurses Polit. Action Com., 1982-84, vice chmn., chmn. polit. edn. com. Mem. Am. Nurses Assn., Sigma Theta Tau. Democrat. Roman Catholic.

BRADY, DONNA LAURA, sales professional; b. Baytown, Tex., Jan. 20, 1948; d. Hubbard G. and B. Vernice (Chambers) Campbell; m. Mark W. Brady, June 1, 1968 (div.); children: Anne, D. Laura, Mark C., Paul D. Student, Stephen F. Austin U., 1967, U. Houston, 1968, Pan Am. U., 1980. Bookkeeper Moore Paper Forms Co., Harlingen, Tex., 1978-79; sales rep. Litton Office Products, Brownsville, Tex., 1980-82; sales rep. Dick Office Supply Co., Harlingen, Tex., 1982-83, sales mgr., 1984—; sales rep. Bairs Office Products Co., Austin, Tex., 1983-84. Chmn. Austin Travis Country Livestock Show, 1987—. Mem. Met. Bus. Exchange (sec.), Exec. Women Internat., Cedar Park C. of C. Roman Catholic. Home: 1401 Piney Creek Cedar Park TX 78613 Office: Dick Office Supply Co 13096 Research Blvd Austin TX 78750

BRADY, GAIL PAMELA, controller; b. Montclair, N.J., Oct. 19, 1945; d. Paul Manda Handel and Alice Reid (Lawson) Lightner; m. Walter J. Brady. BA, Upsala Coll., 1967; MBA, Seton Hall U., 1974. CPA, N.J. Auditor Deloitte, Haskins & Sells, Newark, 1967-71; asst. controller Elizabethtown Water Co., Elizabeth, N.J., 1971-83, controller, 1983—; lectr. U. Utah, 1978—. Treas., bd. dirs. Occupational Ctr. of Union County, Roselle, N.J., 1977—. Recipient Twin Corp. award YMCA, 1986—. Mem. Am. Inst. CPA's, Am. Soc. Women CPA's, Nat. Assn. Utility Regulatory Commrs., Nat. Assn. Water Cos. (past chmn., bd. dirs. N.J. chpt. 1975—), N.J. Soc. CPA's, Exec. Women of N.J. Office: Elizabethtown Water Co One Elizabethtown Plaza Elizabeth NJ 07207

BRADY, JEAN MARIE, scientific writer; b. Lockport, N.Y., Mar. 3, 1933; d. William Aloysius and Agnes Alice (Perkins) B. BS, Siena Heights Coll., Adrian, Mich., 1953; MS, L.I. U., 1967; PhD, NYU, 1974. Med. technologist Lockport Meml. Hosp., 1953-64, Niagara Falls (N.Y.) Meml. Hosp., 1964-65; research assoc. St. Luke's, also St. Vincent's hosps., N.Y.C., 1965-75; assoc. prof. biology Alphonsus Coll., Woodcliffe Lake, N.J., 1970-74, Felician Coll., Lodi, N.J., 1974-83; sr. microbiologist Becton-Dickinson Co., East Rutherford, N.J., 1979-83; dir. sterilization and tech. services Nat. Contract Sterilizing Corp., West Paterson, N.J., 1983-84; sr. staff sci. writer Lederle Labs., Pearl River, N.Y., 1984—. Author articles in field. Mem. N.Y. Acad. Scis., Am. Handwriting Analysis Found. Roman Catholic. Home: 401 Country Club Ln Pomona NY 10970 Office: Middletown Rd Pearl River NY 10965

BRADY, JEANNE MARIE, mechanical engineer; b. Boston, Oct. 1, 1956; d. David Joseph and M. Lorraine (Chartrand) B. BSME, BS in Humanities and Sci., MIT, 1979, postgrad., 1980-86. Engr. Northrop Corp, PPD, Norwood, Mass., 1979-81; sr. engr. Northrop Corp, PPD, Norwood, 1981-85; mem. tech. staff Draper Lab., Cambridge, Mass., 1985—. Sponsor Christian Children's Fund, Richmond, Va., 1974—; vol. Diabetes Control & Complications Trial Joslin Clin., Boston, 1986—. Named one of Outstanding Young Women Am., U.S. Jaycees, 1982. Mem. So. Poverty Law Ctr., Am. Diabetes Assn., Joslin Diabetes Ctr., Juvenile Diabetes Found., Mass. Soc. for Med. Research, Medic Alert Found., Smithsonian Inst. (assoc.), People For Am. Way, Girls Latin Sch./ Latin Acad. Assn. Club: The Judas Goats. Office: Charles Stark Draper Lab 555 Technology Square Cambridge MA 02139

BRADY, KATHLEEN MARIE, rehabilitation consultant; b. Los Angeles, Dec. 19, 1952; d. Emmett Michael and Mary Alice (Pearce) B. BS, U. Minn., Duluth, 1974; MS, Mankato State U., 1981; Cert., Mpls. Sch. Massage, 1983. Cert. rehab. counselor. Human services specialist Div. Vocat. Rehab., St. Paul, 1974-75, Mpls., 1976-80; tng. officer Div. Vocat. Rehab., St. Paul, 1980-81; pvt. practice rehab. cons. Mpls., 1981—; assoc. Lee, Hecht, Harrison, N.Y.C., 1986—; prin. Kathleen Brady: Training for a Positive Life, Mpls., 1986—; workers compensation rehab. cons. Gen. Casualty Co., Mpls., 1984—, Reliance Ins. Co., 1981-84; outplacement cons., counselor Roth/Young, Mpls., 1987—. Contbr. articles to profl. jours. Chairperson transitional vol. program Mpls. United Way, 1978-80; bd. dirs. Values Realization Inst., Hadley, Mass., 1984—. Mem. Minn. Assn. Rehab. Providers (bd. dirs. 1982-83), Minn. Rehab. Assn. (bd. dirs. 1982-83), Assn. Humanistic Edn. Home and Office: 5104 41st Ave South Minneapolis MN 55417

BRADY, LINDA CAROL, architect; b. N.Y.C., May 18, 1949; d. John Joseph and Irene H. (Olawska) B.; B.Arch., Pratt Inst., 1971. Staff technician, draftsperson Gruzen & Partners, 1970-72; staff designer Warner, Burns, Toan, Lunde, 1973-75; archtl. cons. Citibank N.A., N.Y.C., 1976-77, staff architect, 1977—, asst. v.p., 1981-86, v.p., sr. project mgr. corp. facilities, 1986—; corp. sec. Citidel, Inc., 1982-86. Registered architect, N.Y. Mem. Am. Legion Aux., Pratt Alumni Assn., Nat. Classical Soc., Internat. Facilities Mgmt. Assn. (charter mem. N.Y. chpt.). Office: One Citicorp Center New York NY 10043

BRADY, PAMELA JO, elementary school adminstrator; b. Schenectady, N.Y., Mar. 27, 1958; d. Joseph Brady and June (Avalon) Mugits. BE, Potsdam State U., 1980; MA in Theology, Gordon-Conwell Theol. Sem., South Hamilton, Mass., 1985. Cert. elem. tchr. Tchr. Loudonville (N.Y.) Christian Sch., 1980-83; prin. Essex North Christian Sch., West Newbury, Mass., 1985—. Composer duet for clarinet Duo-Antics, 1979. Recipient Crane cert. of Merit Crane Sch. Music, 1980, Pres.'s scholarship in Christian Edn., 1984-85; named Internat. Youth in Achievement, 1980. Mem. Assn. Christian Schs. Internat. (New Eng. program com. 1985—, Adminstrn. cert. 1985, workshop leader 1986), Assn. Supervision and Curriculum Devel., Byington Fellowship in Christian Edn., Div. Ministry in Christian Edn., Phi Alpha Chi. Congregationalist. Office: Essex North Christian Sch 381 Main St West Newbury MA 01985-3087

BRAGA, LINDA JEAN, lawyer; b. Nottinghamshire, Eng., Dec. 15, 1953; came to U.S., 1955; naturalized, 1961; d. Douglas Colin and Jean (Sampson) B. B.A. summa cum laude, SUNY-Buffalo, 1974, J.D., 1978. Bar: Tex. 1978. Title atty. S.W. Land Title Co., Dallas, 1977-78; assoc. firm Green, Gilmore & Rothpletz, Dallas, 1979-82, ptnr., 1983-86; ptnr. Linda J. Braga, Profl. Legal Corp., Dallas, 1986—; commr. City of Garland Plan Commn., 1987—. N.Y. State Regents scholar; SUNY-Buffalo undergrad. research asst., and grad. teaching asst. grantee. Mem. ABA, State Bar Tex., Dallas Bar Assn., Garland Bar Assn., Am. Immigration Lawyers Assn., Dallas Assn. Young Lawyers, Dallas Estate Planning Council, SUNY-Buffalo Alumni Assn., SUNY-Buffalo Law Alumni Assn., Phi Beta Kappa, Noon Garland Exchange Club, Garland Bus. Profl. Women's Club. Office: 12820 Hillcrest Rd Suite 116 Dallas TX 75230 also: 3960 Broadway Blvd Suite 105 Garland TX 75043

BRAGG, ANNA LOU SPENCER, real estate broker; b. Denton, Tex., May 25, 1943; d. Thomas Morris and Betty Lou Rachel (Bradham) Spencer; m. Bobby J. Bragg, Sept. 5, 1964; children—Robert Morris, Jennifer Suzanne. A.A., San Jacinto Coll., 1962; B.S., U. Houston, 1964. Aerospace engr. NASA Johnson Space Center, Houston, 1964-66, reliability and quality assurance engr., 1966-69; instr. adult edn. Coll. Mainland, Texas City, Tex., 1974-76, Alvin Community Coll. (Tex.), 1975-76; agt. Jim Baker Realtors, Dickinson, Tex., 1976-80; pres. Bayou Realtors, Inc., Dickinson, Tex., 1980—. Mem. Tex. Assn. Realtors, Gulf Coast Bd. Realtors (dir. 1983-86), Dickinson C. of C. (bd. dirs. 1983-87, pres. 1986-87), Nat. Assn. Realtors, AAUW (v.p.), Mortar Bd., Tex. Garden Clubs (bd. dirs. 1979-84, treas. 1981-83, dist. vice dir. 1983-85; master flower show judge). Home: 2706 Mt Vernon Dr Dickinson TX 77539 Office: Bayou Realtors Inc 1613 Pine Dr Dickinson TX 77539

BRAGG, PAMELA KAY, health facility administrator; b. Fresno, Calif., June 19, 1951; d. Richard Lewis and Delynn (Eaken) Seyller; m. Ronald E. Bragg, Feb. 2, 1974 (div. Mar. 1983); children: Leslie, Laura. BA in Home Econs., Calif. State U., Fresno, 1974; BS in Edn., Memphis State U., 1978. Mgr. Fashion Fabrics, Kennewick, Wash., 1974-75; univ. teaching asst., secondary tchr. Memphis City Schs., 1977-79; co-owner Spraywest, Fresno, 1980-82; dir. wellness St. Agnes Med. Ctr., Fresno, 1982-83, asst. dir. pub. relations, 1983-84; adminstr. dir. Calif. Eye Inst., St. Agnes Med. Ctr., Fresno, 1984—; coordinator med. skills courses, Calif., 1985—. Calif. Heart Symposium, Yosemite, Calif., 1985. Fund raiser St. Agnes Assocs., Fresno. Mem. Am. Acad. Ophthalmic Adminstrs., Am. Acad. Ophthalmology, Womens Health Care Execs., Fresno Womens Network. Republican. Presbyterian. Home: 6557 N San Pablo Fresno CA 93704 Office: Calif Eye Inst 1360 E Herndon Suite 240 Fresno CA 93710

BRAGMAN, RUTH SUSAN, educator; b. Bklyn., Dec. 9, 1947; d. Benjamin and Miriam (Brown) Bragman; B.S., U. Wis., 1969; M.Ed., U. Tex., 1973; Ph.D., U. Md., 1980. Tchr./vol. Sherut La'Am, Tel Aviv, Israel, summer 1969-71; recreational therapist Austin (Tex.) State Sch., 1972; acad. asst. in phys. edn. for handicapped U. Tex., Austin, 1971-73, intern in adaptive phys. edn., 1972-73; head motility tchr. Diagnostic Edn. Sch., Tidewater Rehab. Inst., Norfolk, Va., 1973-76; water safety instr. for handicapped, ARC, Norfolk, 1975-76; grad. asst. in recreation U. Md., College Park, 1976; adaptive phys. edn. tchr. Alternative Sch., Washington, 1977; grad. asst. spl. edn. U. Md., 1977-79, intern in arts for handicapped, 1979-80; project coordinator Nat. Com. Arts for Handicapped, Washington, summer 1980; asst. prof. dept. spl. edn. and rehab. Memphis State U., 1980-83; program asst. coordinator South Atlantic Regional Resource Ctr., 1983—; cons. in field; condr. workshops in field. Asst. in cardiac prevention and rehab. program Jewish Community Center, Norfolk, 1974-75; founder, leader handicapped Girls Scouts U.S.A., Norfolk, 1974-75; com. mem. exec. com. Spl. Olympics, Norfolk, 1974-76; com. mem. ad hoc com. on arts for handicapped children State of Tenn., 1981; mem. state monitoring team spl. edn. Dept. Edn., State of Tenn., 1981; steering com. spl. edn. alliance Memphis, 1982-83. Memphis State U. faculty research grantee, 1982; U. Md. fellow, 1979-80, grad. assistantship in spl. edn., 1977-78, 78-79, in recreation, 1976-77; U. Tex. grad. study grantee, 1971-72, 72-73. Mem. Am. Ednl. Research Assn., Am. Psychol. Assn., Council for Exceptional Children, Evaluation Network, Nat. Council on Measurement in Edn., Phi Kappa Phi, Phi Lambda Theta. Contbr. articles to profl. jours. Home: 7804 Lakeside Blvd Apt G404 Boca Raton FL 33434 Office: South Atlantic Regional Resource Ctr 1236 University Dr N Plantation FL 33322

BRAHAM, DELPHINE DORIS, government accountant; b. L'Anse, Mich., Mar. 16, 1946; d. Richard Andrew and Viola Mary (Niemi) Aho; m. John Emerson Braham, Sept. 23, 1967 (div. Dec. 1987); children: Tammy, Debra, John Jr. BS summa cum laude, Drury Coll., 1983; M in Mgmt., Webster U., St. Louis, 1986. Bookkeeper, Community Mental Health Ctr., Marquette, Mich., 1966-68; credit clk. Remington Rand, Marietta, Ohio, 1971-72; acctg. technician St. Joseph's Hosp., Parkersburg, W.Va., 1972-74; material mgr. U.S. Army, Ft. Leonard Wood, Mo., 1982-86, accountant, 1986—;instr., adjunct faculty Columbia Coll., 1987—; Park Coll., 1988—. Leader Girls Scouts U.S.A., Williamstown, W.Va., 1972-74, Hanau, W.Ger., 1977-79. Mem. AAUW (treas. Waynesville br. 1986—), Nat. Assn. Female Execs., Assn. Govt. Accts., Am. Soc. Mil. Comptrollers. Home: RT 2 Box 248L #28 Waynesville MO 65583

BRAINARD, JAYNE DAWSON, civic worker; b. Amarillo, Tex., Nov. 1; d. Bill Cross and Evelyn (McLane) Dawson; m. Ernest Scott Brainard, Nov. 26, 1950; children: Sydney Jane, Bill Dawson. AB, Oklahoma City U., 1950. Sec.-treas. E.S. Brainard Inc., from 1980, now v.p. personnel and mktg.; v.p. J. Thornton Cattle Co., 1981—. Guardian Camp Fire Assn., 1960-65; vol. N.W. Tex. Hosp. Aux., 1960-63; state chmn. Am. Heritage, DAR, 1963-67, regent chpt., 1966-67, parliamentarian chpt., 1975-79, state historian, state chmn. marshalls, 1967-70, 73-76, mem. state organizing com., 1967-70, nat. vice chmn. marshalls, 1969-79, state rec. sec., 1970-73, editor cookbook, 1972, nat. vice chmn. motion picture com., 1971-73, mem. nat. bd. mgmt., nat. chmn. state regent's dinner, 1980-81, mem. Nat. Officers Club, 1979—, Nat. Chmn.'s Assn., 1981—, mem. Tex. speakers staff, 1972-76, 76-79, Tex. vice-regent, 1976-79, pres. nat. vice-regents club 1977-78, vice chmn. state fin. com., 1976-79, Tex. DAR Gen. Conf. chmn., 1975, 78, state chmn. state regents project, 1973-76, area rep. nat. speakers staff, 1977-80, 82-83, editor Tex. Roster, 1976, mem. state by law com., 1973-76, pres. chpt. regents Club, 1973-74, pres. vice-regents club, 1977-78, Tex. state regent, 1979-82, pres. Tex. DAR State Officers Club, 1980-81, state parliamentarian, 1982-85; organizing pres. Children Am. Revolution, 1963-65, state chmn. mag. sustaining fund; organizing regent Daus. Am. Colonies, 1972, chmn., 1974-76; bd. dirs. Tamassee DAR Sch., Kate Duncan Smith Sch.; pub. relations Amarillo Little Theater, 1965-69, pres., 1968-69, dir., 1966-69; bd. mem., program com. chmn. Amarillo Camp Fire Council, 1965-67, 75—, vice chmn. council, 1976—, pres., 1977-78; chmn. Camp Fire Leaders Assn., 1964-65, bd. dirs., 1974-79, pres. Amarillo council, 1977-78; br. pres. AAUW, 1963-65, pub. relations, 1965-67, world affairs rep., 1965-67; sec.-treas. group League Democratic Women, 1964; pres. Panhandle Geol. Soc. Aux., 1959, Starlighters Dance Club, 1963-64; pres. Speaking of Living Study Club, 1962-63, sec., 1973-74, parliamentarian, 1976-77, pres., 1977-78; pres. Republican Woman's Club, 1968, 73, v.p., 1972; steering com. Nat. Library Week, 1966, 67, 68, Amarillo Chischom Trail Centennial, 1967; vol. St. Anthony's Hosp. Aux.; mem. Revitalize Amarillo Com., 1972, Amarillo Heart Bd., 1972-73, Historic Markers Task Force. Recipient Martha Washington award and medal of appreciation SAR. Mem. Internat. Platform Assn., U.D.C. (rep. to Amarillo Geneal. Adv. Bd. 1973-74, 75-76, 76-77, pres. Amarillo Geneal. Adv. Bd. 1982-84), Nat. Assn. Parliamentarians (profl., registered parliamentarian; pres. Hazel Crowley unit 1980-81, unit v.p. 1986-87, Yearbook 1987-88, Parlimentarian of Yr. 1987), Tex. Assn. Parliamentarians (recording sec. 1988—), United Daus. 1812 (organizing regent, state chmn. 1984-86), Daus. Colonial Wars, Nat. Soc. So. Dames (nat. protocol chmn. 1984-85). Mem. Christian Ch. (bd. parliament 1965-66). Club: Jr. Trail Study. Home: 2119 S Lipscomb St Amarillo TX 79109 Office: 2920 Dunivan Circle Suite 10 Box 1101 Amarillo TX 79105

BRAINARD, JAYNE DAWSON (MRS. ERNEST SCOTT BRAINARD), civic worker; b. Amarillo, Tex., Nov. 1; d. Bill Cross and Evelyn (McLane) Dawson; A.B., Oklahoma City U., 1950; m. Ernest Scott Brainard, Nov. 26, 1950; children—Sydney Jane, Bill Dawson. Sec.-treas. E.S. Brainard Inc., 1980-84, v.p., 1984-88; v.p. J. Thornton Cattle Co., 1981—. Guardian, Camp Fire Assn., 1960-65; vol. N.W. Tex. Hosp. Aux., 1960-63; state chmn. Am. Heritage, DAR, 1963-67, regent chpt., 1966-67, parliamentarian chpt., 1975-79, state historian, state chmn. marshalls, 1967-70, 73-76, mem. state organizing com., 1967-70, nat. vice chmn. marshalls, 1969-79, state rec. sec., 1970-73, editor cookbook, 1972, nat. vice chmn. motion picture com., 1971-73, mem. nat. bd. mgmt., nat. chmn. state regent's dinner, 1980-81, mem. Nat. Officers Club, 1979—, Nat. Chmn.'s Assn., 1981—, mem. Tex. speakers staff, 1972-76, 76-79, Tex. vice-regent, 1976-79, pres. nat. vice-regents club 1977-78, vice chmn. state fin. com., 1976-79, Tex. DAR Gen. Conf. chmn., 1975, 78, state chmn. state regents project, 1973-76, area rep. nat. speakers staff, 1977-80, 82-83, editor Tex. Roster, 1976, mem. state by law com., 1973-76, pres. chpt. regents Club, 1973-74, pres. vice-regents club, 1977-78, Tex. state regent, 1979-82, pres. Tex. DAR State Officers Club, 1980-81, state parliamentarian, 1982-85; organizing pres. Children Am. Revolution, 1963-65, state chmn. mag. sustaining fund; organizing regent Daus. Am. Colonies, 1972, chmn., 1974-76; bd. dirs. Tamassee DAR Sch., 1979-85; bd. dirs. Kate Duncan Smith Sch., mem. fin. com., 1979-82; pub. relations Amarillo Little Theater, 1965-69, pres., 1968-69, dir., 1966-69; bd. mem., program com. chmn. Amarillo Camp Fire Council, 1965-67, 75—, vice chmn. council, 1976—, pres., 1977-78; chmn. Camp Fire Leaders Assn., 1964-65, bd. dirs., 1974-79, pres. Amarillo council, 1977-78; br. pres. AAUW, 1963-65, pub. relations, 1965-67, world affairs rep., 1965-67; sec.-treas. group League Democratic Women, 1964; pres. Panhandle Geol. Soc. Aux., 1959, Starlighters Dance Club, 1963-64; pres. Speaking of Living Study Club, 1962-63, sec., 1973-74, parliamentarian, 1976-77, 87, pres., 1977-78; pres. Republican Woman's Club, 1968, 73, v.p., 1972; parliamentarian Rep. Party Potter County, 1986-88; steering com. Nat. Library Week, 1966, 67, 68, Amarillo Chischom Trail Centennial, 1967; mem. Revitalize Amarillo Com., 1972, Amarillo Heart Bd., 1972-73, Historic Markers Task Force; vol. St. Anthony's Hosp. Mem. Internat. Platform Assn., U.D.C. (rep. to Amarillo Geneal. Adv. Bd. 1973-74, 75-76, 76-77, pres. Amarillo Geneal. Adv. Bd. 1982-84), Nat. Assn. Parliamentarians (profl. registered, pres. Hazel Crowley unit 1980-81, v.p. 1985-86, instr. parliamentarian law, 1986—, recording sec. Tex. 1988—), Amarillo Women's Network, United Daus. 1812 (organizing regent, state chmn. lineage and hist. records 1984-86), Daus. Colonial Wars, Nat. Soc. So. Dames (nat. chmn. protocol, 1985-87), Jr. Travel Study Club. Mem. Christian Ch. (bd. parliament 1965-66). Home: 2119 S Lipscomb St Amarillo TX 79109 Office: Box 1101 Amarillo TX 79105

BRAINERD, MARY KEITH, health insurance executive; b. St. Paul, Minn., Sept. 28, 1953; d. Keith K. and Mary F. (Fitzgibbon) Knopp; m. Richard Charles Brainerd, Mar. 31, 1984; children: Andrew D., Mary Angela. BA, U. Minn., 1975; MBA, St. Thomas Coll., St. Paul, 1979. Health educator Teenage Med. Service, Mpls., 1976-78; tng. devel. St. Mary's Hosp., Mpls., 1978-79; research analyst Blue Cross & Blue Shield, Eagan, Minn., 1979-81; mgr. mkt. research Blue Cross & Blue Shield, Eagan, 1981-84; v.p. Health Maintenance Orgn. Minn., Eagan, 1984-85, chief operating officer, 1985—; instr. faculty Metro State U. St. Paul, 1984-86. mem. sch. bd. Mounds Park Acad., St. Paul, 1986—. Mem. Women's Health Leadership Trust, Minn. Council Health Maintenance Orgns., Audobon Soc., Nature Conservancy. Club: Nature Conservancy.

BRAISTED, MADELINE CHARLOTTE, military officer, personnel administrator; b. Jamaica, N.Y., Nov. 23, 1936; d. Melvin Vincent and Charlotte Marie (Klos) B. A.A.S., Nassau Community Coll., 1968; B.A., Hofstra U., 1973, M.A., 1975. Enlisted woman U.S. Marine Corps., Cherry Point, N.C., 1954-57; reservations agt. Airline Industry, N.Y.C., 1957-64; reservations controller Auto Lease Industry, N.Y.C., 1964-66; nuclear medicine technician Queens Gen. Hosp., Jamaica, N.Y., 1969-70; lab. mgr. CUNY, 1970-80; commd. capt. U.S. Army Reserve, 1980, advanced through enlisted grades to major, 1984; cons. Energy Etcetera, Flushing, N.Y., 1979-85; capt. U.S. Army Res., Fort Totten, N.Y., 1977-80; major AMEDD Profl. Support Agy., U.S. Army, Washington, 1980—. Author, pub. Energy Etcetera catalog, 1981-85; artist On Shore painting (hon. mention 1974). Merit badge counselor Boy Scouts Am., Queens County, N.Y., 1980-83; active mem. PTA, Jamaica, 1980-84. Decorated Army Commendation medal with one oak leaf, Army Achievement medal with one oak leaf cluster; named Community Leader and Noteworthy Am., Hist. Preservation of Am., 1976. Mem. Assn. Mil. Surgeons of U.S., Res. Officers Assn., Nat. Assn. Female Execs., Am. Pub. Health Assn., Soc. Nuclear Medicine. Roman Catholic. Avocations: painting; sculpture. Office: US Army Med Dept Officer Procurement PO Box 4649 Bay Terrace NY 11360

BRAITINGER-GOEHRING, MARLIESE URSULA, business executive; b. Stuttgart, Ger., Jan. 27, 1938; d. Raymond and Anna (Weber) Braitinger; B.A.; Thiel Coll., 1960; M.A., Syracuse U., 1962; m. Walter G. Goehring II, June 16, 1962; children—Heidi U., Marliese O. Test adminstr. Thiel Coll., 1959-60; staff dean of women Syracuse U., 1960-62; prof. German and Spanish, Endicott Coll., Beverly, Mass., 1962-83, also acting acad. dean, asso. dean women, dir. advanced studies, supervisory dept. head dept. fgn. langs.; v.p., founder, dir. Investment Soc., Inc., 1983—; Bd. dirs Danvers YMCA, 1980-83; mem. Am. Security Council, 1979—, Republican Nat. Com., 1979—. Named Most Disting. Sponsor, Phi Theta Kappa, 1976, 79, Most Disting. Advisor Phi Theta Kappa, 1982; recipient German Govt. Outstanding Studies in Lang. and Lit. award, 1962, Nat. Alumni award Thiel Coll., 1987. Mem. Women for Constl. Govt. Congregationalist Home: 5 Puritan Rd Wenham MA 01984 Office: 8 Essex Center Dr Beverly MA 01960

BRAM, ISABELLE MARY RICKEY MCDONOUGH (MRS. JOHN BRAM), clubwoman; b. Oskaloosa, Ia., Apr. 4; d. Lindsey Vinton and Heddy (Lundee) Rickey; B.A. in Govt., George Washington U., 1947, postgrad., 1947-49; m. Dayle C. McDonough, Jan. 20, 1949; m. 2d, John G. Bram, Nov. 24, 1980. Dep. tax assessor and collector Aransas Pass Ind. Sch. Dist., 1939-41; sec. to city atty., Aransas Pass, Tex., 1939-41; info. specialist U.S. Dept. State, Washington, 1942-48. Treas. Mo. Fedn. Women's Clubs, Inc., 1964-66, 2d v.p., 1966-68, 1st v.p., 1968-70, pres., 1970-72; bd. dirs. Gen. Fedn. Women's Clubs. Mem. steering com. Citizens Com. for Conservation; mem. exec. com. Missourians for Clean Water. Pres., DeKalb County Women's Democratic Club, 1964. Bd. dirs. DeKalb County Pub. Library, pres., 1966; bd. dirs. Mo. Girls Town Found. Mem. AAUW, Nat. League Am. Pen Women, DeKalb County Hist. Soc., Internat. Platform Assn., Law Soc. U. Mo., Jefferson Club of U. Mo., Zeta Tau Alpha, Phi Delta Delta, Phi Delta Gamma. Democrat. Episcopalian. Mem. Order Eastern Star. Clubs: Tri Arts, Shakespeare, Wimodausis, Gavel, Ledgers, Jefferson. Editor: Mo. Clubwoman mag. Home: Sloan and Cherry Sts Box 156 Maysville MO 64469

BRAMAN, HEATHER RUTH, technical writer; b. Wilmington, Ohio, Apr. 27, 1934; d. William Barnett and Violet Ruth (Davis) Hansford; m. Barr Oliver Braman, June 29, 1957 (div.); children: Sean Robert, Heather Paige. BA, Hiram Coll., 1956; postgrad., Sinclair Community Coll., Dayton, Ohio, 1977-85, Wright State U., Dayton, 1986. Personnel clk. USAF, Wright-Patterson AFB, Ohio, 1956, specification editor, 1956-57, publs. editor, writer, 1957-63, asst. mgr., acctg. mgr. tennis club, 1977-81; homemaker, vol. children's med. ctr. Dayton Pub. Schs., 1963-73; tchr. Gloria Dei Montessori Sch., Dayton, 1973-77; tech. writer Miclin, Inc., Alpha, Ohio, 1982, Indsl. Design Concepts, Dayton, 1982-83; tech. writer, cons. Belcan Corp., Cin., 1984—. Founder, bd. dirs. Trotwood (Ohio) Women's Open Tennis Tournament, 1976-81; pres. Dayton Tennis Commn., 1978-80; mem. parents exec. com. Hiram (Ohio) Coll., 1985—; ct.-appointed Spl. Advocate/Guardian Ad Litem (CASA GAL), 1988—. Mem. NOW, NAACP, Dayton Pub. Schs. Orgns., Dayton Tennis Umpires Assn., Sigil of Phi Sigma. Democrat. Quaker. Home: 320 Elm Hill Dr Dayton OH 45415 Office: Belcan Corp 10200 Anderson Way Cincinnati OH 45242

BRAME, CAROLE LYNN, public relations executive; b. Miami, Fla., June 1, 1960; d. Charles Lowell and Barbara Ann (Speer) B. BA, Emory U., 1982. Legis. sec. Fla. Ho. of Reps., Sarasota, 1982; legis. aide Fla. Ho. of Reps., Pompano Beach, 1982-87; bd. dirs. Am. Cancer Soc. Vol. Emory Alumni Admissions Program, Atlanta, 1982—, Am. Cancer Soc., North Broward, Fla., 1985—, Friends of Stranahan, Ft Lauderdale, 1986—; active Jr. League of Ft. Lauderdale, 1983-87, Rep. Exec. Com., Broward County, 1987; trustee Pompano Beach Bd. Trade, 1987, trustee, 1987-88, chmn., 1987-88. Named one of Outstanding Young Women In Am., 1986. Mem. Pompano Beach Bus. and Profl. Women, Greater Pompano Beach/North Broward C. of C. (bd. dirs. 1986—). Baptist. Office: 1620 S Federal Hwy #771 Pompano Beach FL 33062

BRAMEL, TAMARA ANN, accountant; b. Terre Haute, Ind., Mar. 17, 1961; d. Jack Rae and JoAnn Elizabeth (Harlow) Taylor; m. Stanley Russell Bramel, July 7, 1984. BBA in Acctg., U. Okla., Norman, 1983. CPA, Okla. Audit intern Stover, Fisher, Gray & Moore, Norman, 1982-83; acct. Leadership Properties, Inc., Oklahoma City, 1983-85; controller Midwest Cellular Telephone Co., Oklahoma City, 1985—; fin. advisor Delta Gamma Sorority, Norman, 1987—. Mem. Am. Inst. CPA's, Okla. Soc. CPA's, Am. Women's Soc. Cert. Accts., Nat. Assn. Female Execs. Democrat. Methodist. Home: 11105 Markwell Ct Oklahoma City OK 73132 Office: Cellular One 5509 N Pennsylvania Ave Oklahoma City OK 73118

BRAMNICK, LEA SHAPIRO, educational materials company executive; b. phila., Aug. 23, 1938; d. Irving Benjamin and Sylvia (Bloom) Shapiro; B.S. in Edn., Temple U., 1959, M.S. in Edn., 1962; children—Michael Richard, Gary David. Tchr. elem. schs., Phila. Bd. Edn., 1959-65; project mgr., designer ednl. materials Instructo, McGraw Hill, Paoli, Pa., 1971-74; dir. home products unit Research for Better Schs., Phila., 1974—; pres. The Lobster Factory, Inc., designers ednl. materials, Merion Station, Pa., 1976—; dir. corp. communications AJ Wood, corp. dir. Direct Mail div., 1985, customer service div., 1986. Creator Cooking for Kids program. Author: The Great Cook's Guide to Children's Cookery, 1976; The Kids Kitchen Encyclopedia, 1979; The Parents Solution Book, 1983.

BRAMSON, RUTH NANCY, human resources executive; b. N.Y.C., May 17, 1943; d. Max H. Bohrer and Frances (Rosenfeld) Sadolsky; children: Marjorie, Amy, Deborah; m. Sheldon H. Bramson, Nov. 24, 1984. BA cum laude, Barnard Coll., 1961; postgrad. Cornell U. Personnel coordinator Estee Lauder Internat., N.Y.C., 1973-75; asst. dir. personnel Brandeis U., Waltham, Mass., 1975-79; dir. corp. personnel Zayre Corp., Framingham, Mass., 1979-83; v.p. human resources Scandinavian Design, Natick, Mass., 1983-86, Mast Industries, The Limited, Inc., Andover, Mass., 1986-87, sr. v.p. J. Bildner & Sons, Inc., Boston, 1987, v.p. human resources Cone Communications, Boston, 1988—, sr. v.p. Framingham State Coll., 1983-84; bd. dirs. N.E. Human Resources Assn., 1988; adviser MBA students Babson Coll., Wellesley, Mass., 1985. Mem. secondary sch. com. Cornell U., 1980-84. Recipient cert. of appreciation Waltham Job Placement Program, 1979, U.S. Dept. Labor, 1983. Mem. Am. Soc. Tng. and Devel., Am. Soc. Personnel Adminstrs., Womens Network, Assn. Affirmative Action Profls., New Eng. Soc. Personnel Mgmt., LWV (dir. Wellesley chpt. 1969-72). Democrat. Jewish. Club: Cornell (Boston) (bd. dirs., program chair). Avocation: tennis.

BRAMWELL, MARVEL LYNNETTE, nurse; b. Durango, Colo., Aug. 13, 1947; d. Floyd Lewis and Virginia Jenny (Amyx) B. Diploma in lic. practical nursing, Durango Sch. Practical Nursing, 1968; AD in Nursing, Mt. Hood Community Coll., 1972; BS in Nursing, BS in Gen. Studies cum laude, So. Oreg. State Coll., 1980; cert. edn. grad. sch. social work, U. Utah, 1987. RN, LPN, cert. counselor alcohol, drug abuse. Staff nurse Monument Valley (Utah) Seventh Day Adventist Mission Hosp., 1973-74, La Plata Community Hosp., 1974-75; health coordinator Tri County Head Start Program, 1974-75; nurse therapist, team leader Portland Adventist Med. Ctr., 1975-78; staff nurse Indian Health Service Hosp., 1980-81; coordinator village health services North Slope Borough Health and Social Service Agy., 1981-83; nurse, supr. aides Bonneville Health Care Agy., 1984-85; staff nurse Latter Day Saints Adolescent Psychiat. Unit, 1985—; coordinator adolescent nursing CPC Olympus View Hosp., 1986—; charge and staff nurse adult psychiatry U. Utah, 1987—; assisted with design and constrn. 6 high tech. health clinics in Ala. Arctic, 1982-83; creator after care program Greatest Love, 1986-87. Contbr. articles to profl. jours. Active Mothers Against Drunk Driving; mem. acad. rev. com. Community Health Assn. Program U. Alaska Rural Edn., 1981-83. Recipient Cert. Appreciation Barrow (Alaska) Lion's Club, 1983, U.S. Census Bur., Colo., 1970. Mem. Nat. League Nurses, Assn. Women Sci., Nat. Assn. Female Execs., Am. Soc. Circumpolar Health, NOW, Casandra. Home: PO Box 511282 Salt Lake City UT 84151

BRANAN, CAROLYN BENNER, accountant, lawyer; b. Wiesbaden, Fed. Republic Germany, Mar. 7, 1953; came to U.S., 1958; d. Huebert Harrison and Kathryn Wilfreda (Diggs) Benner; m. Robert Edwin Branan, Oct. 3, 1981; 1 child, Lynn. BA in Philosophy, U. S.C., 1973, JD, 1976. Bar: S.C. 1977, U.S. Dist. Ct. S.C. 1977, U.S. Ct. Appeals (4th cir.) 1977; C.P.A., N.C. Sole practice law, Columbia, S.C., 1977-79; sr. mgr. Deloitte Haskins & Sells, Charlotte, N.C., 1979—; cons. Gov.'s Bus. Council Task Force on Infrastructure Financing, 1983. Contbr. articles to profl. jours. Mem. exec. com., former treas., v.p., chmn. budget com. Charlotte Opera Assn., 1981—; v.p. Opera Carolina 1985-87; exec. com., chmn. 1st and 2d ann. funding campaigns N.C. Opera, 1982—; exec. com. mayor's study com. Performing Arts Ctr., Charlotte, 1983—; former mem. adv. council, bd. dirs., chmn. performing arts Springfest, Charlotte, 1982-86; fin. chmn. Opening of New Charlotte Transit Mall, 1984-85; bus. adv. council Queens Coll., Charlotte, 1984—. Mem. ABA (chmn. important devels., gen. acctg. matters, regulated pub. utilities tax sect. 1984—), N.C. Bar Assn., S.C. Bar Assn., Charlotte Estate Planning Council, Nat. Assn. Accts. (bd. dirs., dir. profl. devel., dir. community affairs 1979-84), N.C. Assn. C.P.A.s, Founders Soc. of Charlotte Opera Assn. (life). Episcopalian. Club: Charlotte City. Home: 530-A N Poplar St Charlotte NC 28202 Office: Deloitte Haskins & Sells 2000 First Citizens Plaza Charlotte NC 28202

BRANCAFORTE, CHARLOTTE LANG, language educator; b. Munich, Fed. Republic Germany, July 26, 1934; came to U.S., 1958; d. Christoph and Marieloise (Unglert) Lang; m. Benito Brancaforte, Nov. 11, 1961; children—Elio Christoph, Daniela Beatrix, Stephanie Andrea. D. in Teaching, Landshut Coll., Germany, 1954; B.A. in Edn., Denver U., 1958; Ph.D. in German and Polit. Sci., U. Ill., 1967. Asst. prof. German, U. Wis., Madison, 1966-73, assoc. prof., 1973-78, prof., 1978—, chair Dept. of German, 1980-84, dir. Max Kade Inst. German-Am. Studies, 1984—. Author: Venus, critical study, 1974; Partial Latin Translation of Lazarillo De Tormes, 1983; coauthor: Lazarillo De Tormes, 1977. Chmn., Western European Area Studies Program, U. Wis., 1980-86. Mem. Modern Lang. Assn., Soc. Renaissance and Baroque Studies, Nat. Assn. Dept. Fgn. Langs. (pres. 1984). Home: 1727 Summit Ave Madison WI 53705 Office: U Wis Dept German 1220 Linden Dr Madison WI 53706 also: U Wis Max Kade Inst German-Am Studies 901 University Bay Dr Madison WI 53705

BRANCHAW, BERNADINE PATRICIA, English language educator; b. Joliet, Ill., Jan. 23, 1933; d. Louis and Catherine (Svircek) B. AB, Coll. St. Francis, 1964; MS in Edn., No. Ill. U., 1970, EdD, 1972. Prof. bus. communication Western Mich. U., Kalamazoo, 1971—; cons. in field; mem. adv. bd. Ctr. for Women's Services Western Mich. U. Co-author: Business Report Writing, 1984, SRA Reference Manual, 1986, Business Communication, 1987; author: English Made Easy, 2d edit., 1986. Recipient Governing Bds. award Mich. Assn. Governing Bds., 1987, ABC Disting. Mem. award, 1987. Mem. Assn. for Bus. Communication (bd. dirs. 1986, Francis Week's award 1982). Republican. Roman Catholic. Lodge: Zonta (past pres. Kalamazoo chpt. 1976). Home: 809 Weaver Ave Kalamazoo MI 49007 Office: Western Mich U Kalamazoo MI 49008

BRAND, CONNIE SUE RENTZ, accountant; b. Paola, Kans., June 15, 1959; d. Arnold Fredrick and Leona Jeanett (Lohaus) Rentz; m. Paul Eric Brand, Sept. 22, 1984. BSBA, Pitts. State U., 1981. CPA, Kans., Mo. Audit sr. Laventhol & Horwath, Kansas City, Mo., 1981-84; sr. supr. Arthur Young & Co., Kansas City, 1984-87; fin. analyst Shawnee Mission (Kans.) Sch. Dist., 1987—. Dir. youth edn., bd. dirs. youth ministry Bethany Luth. Ch., Overland, Kans.; vol. Spl. Olympics. Mem. Am. Mgmt. Assn., Kans. Soc. CPAs, Healthcare Fin. Mgmt. Assn., Govt. Fin. Officers Assn. Home: 7013 Cottonwood Shawnee KS 66216

BRANDES-BOWEN, ILA ANN, merchandising executive; b. Charlotte, Apr. 3, 1954; d. Roddy Arthur and Marguerite (Johnson) Brandes; m. Timothy Ray Bowen, July 1, 1984. B.A., U. N.C., Greensboro, 1977. Asst. supr. quality control Ball Corp., Asheville, N.C., 1977-79, indsl. engr., Muncie, Ind., 1979-80, methods and standards engr., 1980-82, materials handling engr., 1982-85, customer service engr., 1983-85; cons. Porsche Market Group, Rockaway, N.J., 1985-86; owner, pres. IAM, Asheville, N.C., 1985-87; owner PIP, Statesville, N.C., 1986— ; addressed 1984 Internat. Exposition Food Processors (speech pub.). Counselor Young Life, Greensboro, 1972-77, Jr. Achievement, Muncie, 1979-81; bd. dirs. Muncie Symphony Membership Dr., 1981, Corp. Challenge, Muncie, 1981-83, United Way Fund Dr., Muncie, 1982-83. Mem. Nat. Assn. Female Execs. Republican. Presbyterian.

BRANDIN, JILL FELDMANN, finance executive, consultant; b. Angola, Ind., Mar. 16, 1951; d. Howard E. and Mary A. (Hunt) Feldmann; m. Mark S. Brandin, May 16, 1976 (div. 1981). BA, Mt. Holyoke Coll., 1973; MBA, U. Chgo., 1977. Loan officer First Chgo. Bank, 1973-77; v.p. Bank of Am., San Francisco, 1977-82; mng. dir. Argent Group Ltd., San Francisco, 1982—. Chief Fin. Officer Sonoma Meadows (Calif.) Homeowners Assn., 1985—. Office: Argent Group Ltd 3 Embarcadero Ctr Suite 1680 San Francisco CA 94111

BRANDOW, JUDY MICHAEL, journalist; b. Hamilton, Ont., Can.; d. Clare Lorne and Ora Maude (Johnson) B. Grad. high sch., St. Catharines, Ont. Reporter St. Catharines Standard, 1964-68; editor women's sect. Toronto Telegram, 1968-71, Hamilton Spectator, 1971-73; instr. Ryerson Poly. Inst., Toronto, 1973-74; editor family sect. Toronto Star, 1974-77; editor-in-chief Canadian Living mag., Toronto, 1977—. Club: Toastmasters. Office: Telemedia Publishing Co, 50 Holly St, Toronto, ON Canada M4S 3B3

BRANDSDORFER, TRUDY, computer consultant; b. N.Y.C., Aug. 20, 1951; d. Samuel and Ethel (Cymerman) B. BA in Computer Sci., U. Del., 1973, BS in Elem. Edn., 1973; MBA in Mgmt., Temple U., 1981. Programmer Pa. Mut. Life Ins., Phila., 1973-76; programmer, analyst Fed. Res. Bank, Phila., 1976-78; sr. systems desginer CIGNA Corp., Phila., 1978-85; sr. programmer, analyst Evaluation Research Corp, Fairfax, Va., 1985-87; cons. Info. Tectonics, Marlton, N.J., 1987—; pres. Trucomp Consulting and Tng. Services, Stratford, N.J., 1987—; instr. Drexel U., Phila., 1985; cons. Camden County Coll., Blackwood, N.J., 1987. Mem. Nat. Assn. Women Bus. Owners, Tech. Assn. of Personal Computer Cons., Phila. Area Computer Soc. Office: TruComp Consulting and Tng Services 2 Elinor Ave Stratford NJ 08084

BRANDT, AVRENE LAURA, clin. psychologist; b. N.Y.C., July 3, 1942; d. Max Bernard and Pauline (Slatin) Brandt; B.A., Hunter Coll., 1964; M.S. (NIMH fellow), U. Mass., 1968, Ph.D., 1971; m. William Hall, June 24, 1973; children—Wiley, Gabhriel, Elissa. Staff psychologist Ashbourne Sch., Elkins Park, Pa., 1969-71; chief psychologist Pottstown (Pa.) Area Mental Health Clinic, 1971-74; clin. service dir. Devereux Found., Devon, Pa., 1975—; cert. instr. Assertive Relations with Children, Phila. Bd. dirs. Resources for Human Devel., pres. Albert Einstein Acad. Mem. Phila. Clin. Neuropsychol. Group, Am. Psychol. Assn. Office: Devereux Found 19 S Waterloo Rd Devon PA 19333

BRANDT, BARBARA KAY, nurse, childbirth educator; b. Montgomery, Ala., Jan. 17, 1939; d. Woodrow W. Busby and Hazel B. Weber; m. Kenneth L. Brandt, Dec. 9, 1959 (div. 1985). BA, Stockton State Coll., Pomona, N.J., 1977; MA, Fairleigh Dickinson U., 1986. RN, N.J.; cert. childbirth educator, N.J. Research analyst Merrill, Lynch, Pierce, Fenner & Smith, N.Y.C., 1960-63; traffic coordinator Doyle Dane Bernbach, Inc., N.Y.C., 1963-67; adminstrv. asst. Carl Ally Inc., N.Y.C., 1967-70; RN Freehold (N.J.) Hosp., 1979-80, Med. Ctr. at Princeton, N.J., 1980-82, Hertzel Hosp., Detroit, 1982-83, Med. Ctr. at Princeton, N.J., 1983-87, UMDNJ Community Mental Health Ctr., Piscataway, N.J., 1987—. Mem. Nurses Assn. of Am. Coll. of Obstetricians and Gynecologists.

BRANDT, TERESA MAE, accountant; b. Sacramento, Feb. 1, 1957; d. Paul Joseph and Rose Marie (Jereczek) B. AA in Acctg., Am. River Coll., Sacramento, 1976; BS in Acctg., Calif. State U., Sacramento, 1979; MBA in Internat. Mgmt., Loyola Marymount U., Los Angeles, 1983. CPA, Calif. Mgr. audit Arthur Young & Co., Palo Alto, Calif., 1979-86, Advanced Micro Devices, Sunnyvale, Calif., 1986—; mem. program adv. bd. Resource Ctr. for Women, Palo Alto, 1986-87; seminar instr. Inst. Internal Auditors, San Jose, Calif., 1987. Contbr. articles to Mt. View Newspapers. Treas. Monte Loma Neighborhood Assn., Mountain View, Calif., 1987-88. Mem. Am. Inst. CPA's, Calif. Soc. CPA's. Republican. Roman Catholic. Office: Advanced Micro Devices 901 Thompson Pl PO Box 3453 M/S 68 Sunnyvale CA 94088

BRANIGAN, HELEN M., educator; b. Albany, N.Y., Sept. 24, 1944; d. James J. and Helen (Weaver) B. BS in Bus. Edn., Coll. St. Rose, Albany, 1967, MA in English, 1972; postgrad., SUNY, Albany, 1973-81. Tchr. dept. bus. edn. S. Colonie Sch. Dist., Albany, 1968-81; assoc. Bur. Bus. Edn. N.Y. State Edn. Dept., Albany, 1981-87, assoc. Bur. Occupational Edn. Program Devel., 1987—; mem. adv. council SUNY-Cobbleskill, 1985—; lectr. in field. Editor McGraw-Hill Book Co., N.Y.C., 1986-88; contbr. articles to profl. jours. Lay vol. Archdiocese of Anchorage, 1967-68. Mem. Nat. Assn. State Suprs. Bus. Edn., Bus. Tchrs. Assn. N.Y. State, Ea. Bus. Edn. Assn., Nat. Bus. Edn. Assn., Nat. Assn. for Supervision and Curriculum Devel., Delta Pi Epsilon. Democrat. Roman Catholic. Home: 540 New Scotland Ave Albany NY 12208 Office: NY State Edn Dept Bur Occupational Edn Program 1 Commerce Plaza Rm 1623 Albany NY 12234

BRANNOCK, BETTY BOYD, sales executive; b. Waynesboro, Va., June 8, 1952; d. Boyd James and Opal (Smith) B.; m. Melvin Lee Milton, June 15, 1974 (div. 1981). BA, Elon (N.C.) Coll., 1974. Employment counselor Snelling & Snelling, Durham, N.C., 1974-77; dist. supr., ops. mgr. Easco Photo, Richmond, Va., 1977-81; area mgr. Colorcraft Corp., Durham, 1981-85; sales account exec. Eastman Kodak Co., Rochester, N.Y., 1985—; speaker in field. Vol. Cape Fear Food Bank., Wilmington, N.C., 1987. Republican. Baptist. Home: 4482 William Louis Dr Wilmington NC 28405 Office: Eastman Kodak Co PO Box 5587 Sta 1 Wilmington NC 28403

BRANNON, EMMA COLLINS, writer, essayist, poet, speaker; b. Elbert County, Ga.; d. Oscar L. and Hannah M. (Bell) Collins; grad. Sam Houston Normal Inst., 1913, student Washington Sch. Art, 1922; B.S., Stephen F. Austin U., 1957, M.A., 1959; m. Jameston R. Brannon, Nov. 25, 1915 (dec. 1965); 1 foster son, James; 1 son, Jameston R. Jr. Tchr. public schs., Panola County, Tex., 1911-12, 15-16, 33-35, Gary, Tex., 1913-15, 16-24; bus. mgr. Brannon's Farms and Grocery Store, Carthage, 1929-40; postmaster U.S.

Post Office, Carthage, 1940-55; religious, patriotic, inspirational, humorous and historic poems, ch. and prison ministry tracts writer, 1913—. Active Blue Bird council Girl Scouts U.S.A., 1957-59; sponsor Camp Fire Girls, 1959-68; Sunday Sch. tchr. 1st Bapt. Ch., Gary, 1913-34, Carthage, 1936-70, Rose Park Bapt. Ch., Shreveport, La., 1970-78; mem. U.S. Congl. Adv. Bd.; presdl. guest White House staff briefing, 1984. Recipient Silver Tray award Carthage Postal Service Rural/City Carrier-Clk. group, 1955, plaque U.S. Postal Service; Silver medal Congl. Bd. Mem. Acad. Am. Poets, Poetry Soc. Tex., Panola Hist. Soc., Panola C. of C., Tex. Geneal. Soc., La. Geneal. Soc., DAR, Internat. Platform Assn., Am. Security Council, Nat. Fedn. Republican Women, Nat. Alliance Sr. Citizens, Sam Houston Alumni Assn., Stephen F. Austin State U. Alumni Assn. Baptist. Clubs: Altrua (dir. 1950-52), Carthage Garden (pres. 1967-69). Author: These Passed Our Way, 1972; Wayside Blossoms (collection of poems), 1979. Home: Carthage TX 75633

BRANSCOMB, ANNE WELLS (MRS. LEWIS MCADORY BRANSCOMB), lawyer, communications consultant; b. Statesboro, Ga., Nov. 22, 1928; d. Guy Herbert and Ruby Mae (Hammond) Wells; m. Lewis McAdory Branscomb, Oct. 13, 1951; children: Harvie Hammond, Katharine Capers. B.A., Ga. State Coll. Women, 1949; BA, U. N.C., 1949; postgrad., London Sch. Econs., 1950; MA, Harvard U., 1951; JD with honors, George Washington, 1962. Bar: D.C. 1962, Colo. 1963, N.Y. 1973, U.S. Supreme Ct. 1972. Research assoc. Pierson, Ball and Dowd, Washington, 1962; law clk. to presiding judge U.S. Dist. Ct., Denver, 1962-63; assoc. Williams & Zook, 1963-66; sole practice Boulder, 1963-69; assoc. Arnold and Porter, Washington, 1969-72; communications counsel Teleprompter Corp., N.Y.C., 1973; v.p. Kalba-Bowen Assocs. Inc., communication cons., Cambridge, Mass., 1974-77, chmn. bd., 1977-80, sr. assoc. dir., 1980-82; pres. The Raven Group, Concord, Mass., 1986—; trustee Pacific Telecommunications Council, 1981-83, 86—; Inaugural fellow Gannett Ctr. Media Studies, Columbia U., 1985; mem. tech. adv. bd. Dept. Commerce, 1977-81; WARC adv. com. Dept. State, 1978-79; mem. Carnegie Corp. Task Force on Pub. Broadcasting, 1976-77; mem. overseers, vis. com. Harvard U. Office of Info. Tech., 1977-83; vis. scholar Yale U. Law, 1981-82; mem. program on information resources and pub. policy Harvard U., 1986—; chmn. program com. Legal Symposium Telecom '87, Internat. Telecommunications Union, 1986-87; bd. dirs. Pub. Interest Radio, 1986—; adj. prof. internat. law Tufts U., 1988—; mem. adv. bd. Atwater Inst., Ottawa, Can. Contbr. articles to profl. jours.; mem. editorial bd.: Info. Soc.; editor: Toward a Law of Global Communications Networks; contbg. editor: Jour. Communications, 1980—. Housing comm. Boulder Pub. Housing Authority, 1969-70; bd. dirs. Nat. Pub. Radio, 1975-78; trustee EDUCOM, Interuniv. Communications Council Inc., 1975-78; vice chmn. Colo. Dem. State Central Com., 1967-69; del., mem. permanent orgn. com. Dem. Nat. Conv., 1968; trustee, exec. com. Rensselaer Poly. Inst., 1980—. Recipient Alumni Achievement award Ga. Coll., 1980; recipient Rotary Found. fellowship, 1950-51; inaugural fellow Gannett Ctr. for Media Studies Columbia U., 1985. Mem. ABA (Nat. Conf. Lawyers and Scientists ABA/AAAS 1985—, chmn. communications com. sci. and tech. sect. 1980-82, chmn. communications law div. 1982-84, mem. council sci. and tech. sect. 1981-85), Am. Polit. Sci. Assn., Internat. Communications Assn., Internat. Inst. Communications, Soc. Preservation of First Wives and First Husbands (nat. pres. 1981—), Order of Coif, Valkyries, Phi Beta Kappa, Alpha Psi Omega, Chi Delta Phi, Pi Gamma Mu. Home: 5 Hidden Oak Ln Armonk NY 10504

BRANSON, MARY LOU, military administrator; b. Tulsa, June 11, 1932; d. Clarence Leo and Peg (McDonald) Jester; m. Robert K. Branson, Sept, 8, 1956 (div. Dec. 1976); children: Malinda, Scott, Craig. BA, Okla. State U., 1956; MS, Tex. Woman's U., 1981, PhD, 1984. Cert. drug and alcohol counselor, marriage and family therapist. Claims rep. Social Security Adminstrn., Ohio, La., N.Mex., 1957-63; reconsideration specialist State of Fla. Disability Determinations, Tallahassee, 1975-79; intern Office Families, Washington, 1982; sr. regional employee assistance program counselor Control Data Corp., Dallas, 1983-85; dir. Family Service Ctr. Naval Air Sta., Dallas, 1985-87; dep. dir. Family Service Ctr. Naval Support Activity, Holy Loch, Scotland, 1987—; mem. com. single parent families Nat. Council Family Relations, Mpls., 1984-85, co-op edn. bd. Tex. Woman's U., Denton, 1985-86. Author, editor: (book) Tallahassee Coloring Book, 1972. Dir. Cerebral Palsy Nursery Sch., Baton Rouge, 1961; bd. dirs. Diablo Valley Montessori Sch., Lafayette, Calif., 1966; pres. La. State U. Faculty Wives, Baton Rouge, 1962. U. Tulsa scholar, 1950, Texas Woman's U. scholar, 1980-85. Mem. Am. Assn. Marriage and Family Therapy (clin.), Nat. Council on Family Relations, Assn. Labor-Mgmt. Adminstrs. and Cons. on Alcoholism, Internat. Family Therapy Assn., Employee Assistance Soc. N.Am., Kappa Alpha Theta Alumni Club (v.p. 1973). Home: Gowanbank House, Dunoon Scotland Office: Family Service Ctr Naval Support Activity FPO New York NY 09514-1008

BRANTLEY, ASTRA PAULLETTE WILLIAMS, psychologist; b. St. Louis, Nov. 8, 1947; d. Andrew Robert and Ruby Stene (Randolph) Williams; m. Robert Louis Brantley, Jan. 30, 1967; 1 child, Damon. BA, DePaul U., 1970; MSEd, Chgo. State U., 1973; D in Psychology, Cen. Mich. U., 1983. Lic. psychologist, Md., D.C.; cert. nat. counselor. Various positions Garfield Park Comprehensive Community Mental Health Ctr., Inc., Chgo., 1971-74, psychologist II, 1974-77; clin. dir. Afro Youth Community, Inc., Chgo., 1977-79; asst. prof. psychology Towson (Md.) State U., 1982-83; psychology instr. Coppin State U., Balt., 1983; psychologist Spring Grove Hosp. Ctr., Catonsville, Md., 1984-86, coordinator psychol. services and spl. care level, 1986—; lectr. psychology Anne Arundel Community Coll., Arnold, Md., 1986—; cons. Dept. Health and Human Services, Balt., 1986-87. Co-chmn. adv. com. Assoc. Dean of Minority Affairs, Towson State U., 1983-84; chmn. Baltimoreans United In Leadership Devel. com. Zion Baptist Ch., Balt., 1987. Doctoral Research Support grant Cen. Mich. U., 1980; receipient 1st Black Doctorate Cen. Black Student Union, 1981, scholarship AKA Sorority, 1965. Mem. NAACP, LWV, Am. Psychol. Assn., Nat. Register of Health Service Providers in Psychology, Am. Assn. for Counseling and Devel., Assn. Black Psychologist, Md. Psychol. Assn., Black Mental Health Alliance. Home: 7673 Ridge Rd Hanover MD 21076 Office: The Brantley Group 2901 Druid Park Dr Baltimore MD 21215

BRANTLEY, HELEN THOMAS, clinical psychologist; b. Palmerton, Pa., Jan. 29, 1942; d. Francis Clyde and Elizabeth (Jennings) Thomas; B.A., Duke U., 1963, Ph.D., 1973; m. John Croft Brantley, June 15, 1963; children—Elizabeth Ann, John Thomas. Psychologist pub. schs., Boothwyn, Pa., 1967; pvt. practice psychol. cons., Chapel Hill, N.C., 1971-77, 81—; research asso. Duke U., Durham, N.C., 1975-78; postdoctoral fellow in child psychology U. N.C. Sch. Medicine, Chapel Hill, 1977-78, research asst. prof., 1978-79, asst. prof. psychology, 1979-81. NIMH fellow, 1980-81. Mem. Am. Psychol. Assn., N.C. Psychol. Assn. Contbr. articles to profl. publs. Home: 635 Totten Pl Chapel Hill NC 27514 Office: 109 Conner Dr Suite 204 Chapel Hill NC 27514

BRANTLEY, PHOEBE FRANCES, ballet director, choreographer; b. Hastings, Nebr., Mar. 2, 1926; d. Louis Damron Kinney and Helen Cook Batham; m. Joseph Patton Brantley III, June 15, 1944 (dec. Aug. 6, 1964); children—Joseph Patton IV, John Bretton, David Wightman. Student George Washington U. With Washington Ballet, 1940-44; artistic dir. La. Ballet, Baton Rouge, 1976—, also choreographer. Mem. Southwest Regional Ballet Assn. (pres. 1981-82). Republican. Episcopalian. Home: 5845 Glenwood Dr Baton Rouge LA 70806 Office: Louisiana Ballet 1765 Dallas Dr Baton Rouge LA 70806

BRASBERGER, JOANNE MARIE, controller; b. Phila., Mar. 3, 1957; d. John Frances and Anne Marie (Quinn) Higgins; m. Thomas G. Brasberger, May 27, 1978 (div.); 1 child, Thomas Michael. BS in Acctg., Villanova U., 1979. Jr. staff acct. Safeguard Bus. System, Inc., Ft. Washington, Pa., 1979-80; staff acct. Safeguard Bus. System, Inc., Ft. Washington, 1980-81, mgr. fin. reporting, 1981-82, mgr. corp. acctg., 1982-83, asst. corp. controller, 1983—. Mem. Nat. Assn. Accts., Nat. Assn. Female Execs. Roman Catholic. Home: 100 Coventry Circle Lansdale PA 19446 Office: Safeguard Bus Systems Inc 455 Maryland Dr Fort Washington PA 19034

BRASSEAUX, LORNA MARIE, lawyer; b. Crowley, La., Apr. 28, 1957; d. Ervin and Mary Irene (Meche) Brasseaux. B.A. in English, U. Southwest La., 1979; J.D., La. State U., 1982. Bar: La. 1983. Law clk. 1st Cir. Ct. Appeals, La. State Cts., Baton Rouge, 1983—. Mem. ABA, La. State Bar Assn., Assn. Trial Lawyers Am., Am. Judicature Soc., Phi Delta Phi, Phi Kappa Phi. Democrat. Roman Catholic.

BRASSEAUX, MARY THERESE, hospital administrator; b. Utica, N.Y., Oct. 5, 1951; d. James Robert and Winifred Pearl (Donahue) Meneilly; m. Earl Cooper Brasseaux, Nov. 5, 1983. BA in Sociology, Hartwick Coll., 1973; MA in Health Care Adminstrn., Trinity U., 1979. Asst. adminstr. Pasadena (Tex.) Bayshore Hosp., 1979-81; adminstr. Gen. Hosp. Lakewood, Dallas, 1982-83; mktg. dir. Hosp. Corp. Am., Arlington, Tex., 1983-84; adminstr. St. Mary's Hosp., Enid, Okla., 1984—. Bd. dirs. Enid United Way, 1984-87, Community Speech and Hearing Ctr., Enid, 1985-87; com. mem. Community AIDS Task Force, 1987. Served with USAF, 1974-77. Recipient Foster G. McGaw award Am. Hosp. Supply Corp., 1978. Mem. Greater Enid C. of C. (bd. dirs.), Community Devel. Support Assn, Enid, 1985-86. Roman Catholic. Office: St Marys Hosp 305 S Fifth St Enid OK 73701

BRASSELL, ROSELYN STRAUSS, lawyer; b. Shreveport, La., Feb. 19, 1930; d. Herman Carl and Etelka (McMullan) Strauss. BA, La. State U., 1949; JD, UCLA, 1962. Bar: Calif. 1963. Legal sec. Welton P. Mouton, Lafayette, La., 1949-50; office sec. Leake, Henry, Golden & Burrow, Dallas, 1950-57; atty. CBS, Los Angeles, 1962-68, sr. atty., 1968-76, asst. gen. atty., 1976-83, broadcast counsel, 1983—. Co-writer: Life After Death for the California Celebrity, 1985; bd. editors U. Calif. Law Rev., 1960-62. Named Angel of Distinction Los Angeles Cen. City Assn., 1975. Mem. Calif. Bar Assn., Los Angeles County Bar Assn. (exec. com. 1970—, sect. chmn. 1980-81), Beverly Hills Bar Assn., Los Angeles Copyright Soc. (treas. 1977-78, sec. 1978-79, pres. 1981-82), Am. Women in Radio and TV (nat. dir.-at-large 1971-73, nat. pub. affairs chmn. 1977-78), Nat. Acad. TV Arts and Scis., Women in Film, Los Angeles World Affairs Council, U. Calif. Law Alumni Assn. (dir. 1971-74), Order of Coif, Alpha Xi Delta, Phi Alpha Delta. Republican. Home: 631 N Wilcox Ave Los Angeles CA 90004 Office: 7800 Beverly Blvd Los Angeles CA 90036

BRATAAS, NANCY, state senator; b. Mpls., Jan. 19, 1928; d. John Draper and Flora (Warner) Osborn; m. Mark Gerard Brataas, 1948; children—Mark, Anne. Ed. U. Minn. First elected to Minn. legislature, 1975; now mem. Minn. Senate; pres. Brataas Systems. Minn. Republican state chairwoman, 1963-69; state chairwoman Minn. Rep. Fin. Com., 1969-71. Mem. League Women Voters, AAUW, Zonta Internat. Episcopalian. Office: Minn Senate State Capitol Saint Paul MN 55155 Address: 839 10-1/2 St SW Rochester MN 55902

BRATCHER, TWILA LANGDON, conchologist, malacologist; b. Smoot, Wyo.; d. Willis G. and Pearl (Graham) Langdon; m. Ford F. Bratcher, Sept. 10, 1942. Research assoc. Los Angeles Mus. Natural History, 1965—; mem. Ameripages Sci. Expedition to Galapagos Islands, 1971; author stories for blind children about skin diving, sea shells, creatures of the sea pub. Braille Inst., 1964-72; work with schs. for blind. Mem. Conchological Club So. Calif. (pres. 1966, 88; life hon. mem.), Am. Malacological Union (councilor at large 1971), Western Soc. Malacologists (pres. 1973), Hawaiian Malacological Soc., Conchologists Am. (exec. bd. 1985—), San Diego Shell Club, Pacific Shell Club (life hon. mem.). Club: So. Calif. Woman's Press (pres. 1977-79). Author: Living Terebras of the World; contbr. articles to sci. jours. Home: 8121 Mulholland Terr Hollywood CA 90046

BRATHWAITE, HARRIET LOUISA, nursing educator; b. Rye, N.Y., Aug. 28, 1931; d. James Pierce and Mattie (Collins) Bowling; m. Leroy L. Brathwwaite, Feb. 18, 1950; 1 child, Helene Ann Brathwaite Ward. AAS in Nursing, Bklyn. Coll., 1959; BSN, L.I. U., 1965; postgrad., Tchrs. Coll. of Columbia U., 1965-68; MSN, Adelphia U., 1973. Staff nurse Kings County Hosp., Bklyn., 1959; head nurse City Hosp. at Elmhurst, Queens, N.Y., 1959-62; instr. Kings County Hosp. Sch. Nursing, 1963-65, Downstate Med. Ctr. Sch. Nursing, 1965-69; nurse community mental health South Beach Psychiat. Ctr., 1969-73; cons. psychiat. nursing service HEW and N.Y. State Health Dept., Albany, 1973-74; chief of service Creedmoor Psychiat. Ctr., Queens Village, N.Y., 1974-87; asst. prof. nursing L.I. U., Queens, 1987—. Co-leader Allied Dems., Jamaica, N.Y., 1959-62; bd. dirs. South Queens Dems., Howard Beach, N.Y.; mem. adv. bd. Transitional Services, Queens, 1983-85. Mem. Nat. Black Nurses Assn. (chmn. 1981-88, legis. com. Queens chpt.), Am. Nurses Assn., N.Y. State Nurses Assn. (Dist. 14 25 Yr. Membership award 1986), Orthopsychiatry Assn., AAUW, NAACP. Club: Knickerbocker (chmn. fin. and scholarship com.). Home: Cuffee Dr PO Box 1841 Sag Harbor NY 11963 Office: Long Island U Dept Nursing 144-01 133d Ave Queens NY 11436

BRATKO, ALICE LILLIAN, educator; b. Chgo., Nov. 24, 1953; d. Edward Joseph and Florence Josephine (Brzezinski) B. BA in Sociology and Edn., Northeastern Ill. U., 1975; BFA, Sch. Art Inst., 1986. Asst. research Alliance to End Repression, Chgo., 1971-74, Sociol. Dept. Northeastern Ill. U., Chgo., 1973-75; leader adaptive phys. edn. recreation Chgo. Park Dist., 1975-76; tchr. Chgo. Assn. Retarded Children, 1976-78; tchr. learning disabilities and emotionally handicapped Chgo. Bd. Edn., 1978—; staff photographer Chgo. Breeze Major League Volleyball Team, 1988, ToDay's Chgo. Woman Mag, 1986-88, Chgo. Area Women Sports Assn. Newspaper, 1983—, DuSable Dial Newspaper, 1984—, yearbook DuSable High Sch., Chgo., 1984-85; varsity head volleyball coach, 1980—; women's track coach, 1979-81. Founder, pres. Greyshirts Softball/Baseball Umpires Assn., Chgo., 1983—; Chgo. liaison Women's Sports Found. New Agenda Conf., Washington, 1983. Mem. Women's Sports Found., World Wildlife Fund Inc., Amateur Softball Assn. (ofcl.), Am. Film Inst., Nat. Assn. Female Execs., Alliance Phys. Edn. Recreation and Dance (coach), Nat. Fedn. Ofcls. and Coaches Assn., Smithsonian Instn., Soc. Photographic Edn., Ill. High Sch. Assn. (ofcl., coach), Ill. Coaches Assn., Chgo. Area Women's Sports Assn. (treas. 1984). Democrat. Roman Catholic. Clubs: U.S. Recreational Ski Assn. (N.Y.C.), Pine Point Ski (Chgo.), U.S. Volleyball Assn., DuSable Photography and Video (dir., founder 1979—). Home: 4950 W Nelson St Chicago IL 60641 Office: DuSable High Sch 4934 S Wabash Ave Chicago IL 60615

BRATTON, IDA FRANK, educator; b. Glasgow, Ky., Aug. 31, 1933; d. Edmund Bates and Robbie Davis (Hume) Button; m. Robert Franklin Bratton, June 20, 1954; 1 son, Timothy Andrew. B.A., Western Ky. U., 1959, M.A., 1962. Cert. secondary tchr., Ky. Tchr. math. and sci. Gottschalk Jr. High Sch., Louisville, 1959-65; tchr. math. Iroquois High Sch., Louisville, 1965-79, Waggener High Sch., Louisville, 1979—. Mem. NEA, Ky. Edn. Assn., Jefferson County Tchrs. Assn., AAUW. Democrat. Methodist. Avocations: travel; needle crafts. Home: 304 Paddington Ct Louisville KY 40222 Office: Waggener High Sch 330 S Hubbards Ln Louisville KY 40207

BRATTON, KATHLEEN WILSON, mutual fund executive, lawyer; b. Wilmington, Del., Oct. 29, 1949; d. William Wilson and Julie Clare (Hallahan) B.; m. Brian F. Wruble, Apr. 20, 1985. A.B., Radcliffe Coll., 1971; J.D., U. Chgo., 1974. Bar: N.Y. 1975, Md. 1979, U.S. Dist. Ct. (so. dist.) N.Y. 1975, U.S. Ct. Appeals (2d cir.) 1975, U.S. Supreme Ct. 1978. Assoc. firm Reid & Priest, N.Y.C., 1974-78, William Wilson Bratton, Elkton, Md., 1979-80; asst. counsel Equitable Life Assurance Soc. U.S., N.Y.C., 1980, assoc. counsel, 1980-81, asst. gen. counsel, 1981-84, v.p. counsel, 1984-87, sector head mut. fund product devel., 1987—; pres. The Equitable Funds, N.Y.C., 1987—; exec. v.p. Equico Securities, 1987—; mem. 1933 and 1934 Act Subcom. Am. Council Life Ins., Washington, 1982-87. Mem. ABA, N.Y. State Bar Assn., DAR (head Elk chpt., Elkton, Md.). Democrat. Home: 411 West End Ave Apt 14B New York NY 10024 Office: Equitable Life Assurance Soc US 1755 Broadway 3d floor New York NY 10019

BRATYANSKI, DORIS MADELINE (DORI BRYANT), advertising manager; b. Perth Amboy, N.J., Oct. 8, 1952; d. Adolph Joseph and Frances Mae (Griffin) B. B.A., Douglass Coll., 1974. Tchr. Perth Amboy Bd. Edn., 1974-75; dist. sales mgr. Hertz Corp., N.Y.C., 1975-80; adv. acct. exec. N.Y. Daily News, N.Y.C., 1980-81, Omni Mag., Penthouse, N.Y.C., 1981-82; travel advt. mgr. USA Today/Gannett, N.Y.C., 1981-85; advt. mgr. Hanover Pub., N.Y.C., 1985-86 , N.Y. advt. mgr. So. Mag., dir. Ark. Writer's Project, 1985-87; northeastern advt. mgr. Southern Mag., 1987—. Morris Goldfarb scholar, 1970. Mem. Nat. Assn. Female Execs., Am. Soc. Travel Agts., Caribbean Tourism Assn., Travel and Tourism Research Assn., Travel Industry Assn. Can. Republican. Roman Catholic. Avocations: languages; writing plays and musical scores.

BRAUER, JACQUELINE SUE, account services executive; b. Saginaw, Mich., July 20, 1948; d. Russell Lewis and Flora Ann (Andreotti) Murphy; m. Max T. Brauer, Nov. 29, 1975 (div. Sept. 1983). B.A., Mich. State U., 1971. Editorial asst. Mich. State U., East Lansing, 1973-74; account exec. Tom O'Brien & Assocs., Lansing, Mich., 1974-77; info. coordinator Mich. State U. Info. Services, East Lansing, 1977-81; account exec. Anthony M. Franco, Inc., Detroit, 1981-82; purchasing mgr. Beurmann-Marshall Corp., Lansing, 1982-87, account services mgr., Beurman-Marshall Corp., 1987— . Mem. Women in Communications, Inc. (publicity chmn. 1979-81), Internat. Assn. Bus. Communicators. Home: 322 Kipling Blvd Lansing MI 48912 Office: Beurmann-Marshall Corp 5840 Enterprise Dr Lansing MI 48910

BRAUER, JANE ZION, language educator; b. Allentown, Pa., Aug. 26, 1952; d. David Meyer and Harriet Gertrude (Lubow) Sinberg; m. Jon E. Zion, June 2, 1973 (Jan. 1985); 1 child, Jennifer Vera Zion; m. Martin Walter Brauer, Oct. 26, 1986. BS in Edn. cum laude, Boston U., 1974, MEd, 1981. Cert. tchr. elem. edn., bilingual edn. Tchr. bilingual elem. Framingham (Mass.) Pub. Schs., 1974-77, ESL elem. tchr., 1977-82; tchr. trainer Boston, 1983—; ESL lectr. CELOP at Boston U., 1986-87; trainer consulting and sales Attanasio and Assocs., 1986—; ednl. cons., Mass., N.H., Conn., 1987—. Author: (textbook series) Open Sesame for English as a Second Language, 1986. Mgr. state rep. campaign, Mass., 1976, other state campaigns, 1977-82. Fellow Tchrs. of Speakers of Other Langs., Mass. Assn. Tchrs. of Speakers of Other Langs. (elem. rep. 1983-85), Phi Sigma Iota, Pi Lambda Theta. Democrat. Jewish. Home and Office: 13 Johnson Ave Hudson MA 01749

BRAUGHTON, LORRAINE ESTELLE, health care facility administrator, nurse; b. Sibu, Sarawak, Indonesia, Mar. 24, 1954; d. Vernon Kenworth and Yvonne Una (Stoddard) Fewkes; m. Robert Leonard Waldrum, May 27, 1982 (div. Aug. 19, 1984); m. John Mark Braughton, Dec. 23, 1985; 1 child, Trevor George. BS in Nursing, U. Manchester, Eng., 1976. RN, Ark. Staff, charge nurse U. Ark. Med. Ctr., Little Rock, 1977-80, nutritional cons., 1982-84; supr. ICU Doctor's Hosp., Little Rock, 1980-81; supr. cardiovascular ICU Bapt. Med. Ctr., Little Rock, 1981-82; nursing adminstr. Caremark Inc., Little Rock, 1984-86; clin. cons. Travenol Labs., Fayetteville, Ark., 1986-87; br. mgr. Nat. Med. Ctr., Wichita, Kans., 1987—; nutritional cons. Vis. Nurse Assn., Little Rock, 1984—. Tchr. Literacy Vols. Am., Wichita, 1987. Grantee Royal Acad. Balley, London, 1970. Am. Soc. Parenteral and Enteral Nutrition, Nat. Intraveneous Therapy Assn., Royal Acad. Ballet, Nat. Assn. Female Execs. (dir. Wichita chpt. 1987). Baptist. Home and Office: 2314 S Lulu Wichita KS 67211-5222

BRAUN, ANNE EILEEN, nurse, educator; b. Wilmington, Del., Aug. 16, 1948; d. William Eber and Madeleine (Off) Frame; 1 child, Kelly Eileen. BS in Nursing, U. Del., 1970; MS in Nursing, Widener U., 1982. Staff nurse Med. Ctr. of Del., Wilmington, 1973-77, 82-84; clin. asst. U. Del., Newark, 1978-81; staff nurse Riverside Hosp., Wilmington, Del., 1978-81; instr. critical care nursing Crozer-Chester (Pa.) Med. Ctr., 1984—; adj. prof. Widener U. Coll. Nursing, Chester, Pa., 1985—; cons. Burn Found.-Nurse Adv. Council, Phila., 1984—; lectr. Millcreek Community Hosp., Erie, Pa., 1986, Trends in Critical Care, Phila., 1986, Nat. Teaching Inst., AACN, 1987—. Contbr. articles to profl. jours. Cons. Girl Scouts U.S., Wilmington, 1970. Named Woman of Yr. Bus. and Profl. Women, 1987; recipient scholarship Nat. Teaching Inst., 1987. Mem. Nat. Assn. Female Execs., Am. Assn. Critical Care Nurses (Southeastern Pa. chpt., library chairperson 1984—), Am. Burn Assn., Am. Nurses Assn., Del. Nurses Assn., Mothers Against Drunk Driving, Sigma Theta Tau. Home: 104 Griffith Dr New Castle DE 19720 Office: Crozer-Chester Med Ctr 15th St and Upland Ave Chester PA 19013

BRAUN, BONNIE SUE, program director; b. Warrensburg, Mo., Sept. 27, 1947; d. Cleo Francis and Kathlyn Louise (Hudson) Fitterling; m. William Joel Braun, Dec. 17, 1967; children: Joel Douglas, Jennifer Grace. BS, Cen. Mo. State U., 1969, MS, 1971; PhD, U. Mo., 1979. Cert. home econs. educator, Mo. Instr. home econs. Cen. Mo. State U., Warrensburg, 1972-75; assoc. prof. Okla. State U., Stillwater, 1977-83; assoc. dean human resources Va. State U., Blacksburg, 1983—; assoc. dir. programs Va. Co-op Extension Service, Blacksburg, 1983—; interim dep. adminstr. Extension Service USDA, 1988—; cons. in field. Contbr. over 30 articles to profl. jours. Pres. Stillwater PTA, 1981-83; chairperson Long Range Planning-Hillcrest Bapt., 1981-82; co-dir. mid. sch. Blacksburg Bapt. Ch., 1984-87; bd. dirs. No. Va. 4H Ctr., Front Royal. W.K. Kellogg Found. fellow, 1985-88, U.S. Adminstrn. on Aging fellow, 1976. Mem. Am. Home Econs. Assn. (pre-conf. 1983-85), Adminstrs. Home Econs. Assn. (pub. policy chair 1986-87, bd. dirs. 1988—), Home Econs. Pub. Policy Council (welfare reform chair 1986-87). Office: Va Coop Ext Services 336 Burruss Hall Blacksburg VA 24061

BRAUN, EUNICE HOCKSPEIER, author, religious order executive, lecturer; b. Alta Vista, Iowa; d. George Phillip and Lydia (Reinhart) Hockspeier; student Gates Coll., 1932-34, Coe Coll., 1937-39, Northwestern U., 1944-47; m. Leonard James Braun, May 29, 1937. Freelance writer for mags., newspapers, 1947-52; bus. mgr. Baha'i Publishing Trust, Wilmette, Ill., 1952-55, mng. dir., 1955-71; internat. news editor Baha'i News, 1952-70; tchr. Baha'i schs., Alaska, Can., Europe and U.S., 1958—; lectr. Baha'i Faith in U.S., Central Am., Europe, Africa, Asia, 1953 ; cons. Baha'i Pub. Trust, New Delhi, India, 1972; mem. aux. bd. Continental Bd. Counselors, Baha'i Faith in the Ams., 1972—. Mem. Nat. League Am. Pen Women, Baha'i Faith, Iota Sigma Epsilon. Author: Know Your Baha'i Literature, 1959; The Dawn of World Peace, 1963; Baha'u'llah: His Call to the Nations, 1967; From Strength to Strength, Half Century of the Formative Age of the Baha'i Faith, 1978; A Crown of Beauty, 1982; The March of the Institutions, 1984; A Reader's Guide: The Development of Baha'i Literature in English, 1986; contbr. essays to Baha'i World, Internat. Record. Home: 1025 Forestview Ln Glenview IL 60025

BRAUN, LENORE MARIE (MUSIELSKI), psychotherapist, educator, consultant, researcher, writer; b. Bridgeport, Conn., Mar. 12, 1955; d. Joseph Stanislaus and Dolores Marie (Palumbo) Musielski; m. John Richard Braun, Mar. 9, 1979; 1 stepchild, John Richard. BS in Psychology, U. Bridgeport, 1979, MS in Psychology, 1979; postgrad., Harvard U., N.Y. Med. Coll.; postgrad. in psychology, Saybrook Inst. Lic. broker-dealer in securities and ins., N.Y., Conn; cert. supr. of mediators. Interviewer for unemployment compensation claims security div. State of Conn., New Haven, 1976; fin. cons., rep. Investors Diversified Services, Fairfield, Conn., 1976-77; asst. supr. dept. customer service Bank Americard, Fairfield, 1977; mental health therapist Hall-Brooke Psychiat. Hosp./Found., Westport, Conn., 1977-79; exec. dir. Psychotherapeutic Cons. and Research Service, Westport, 1980—; adj. faculty/guest lectr. in psychology U. Bridgeport, 1980—, Albertus Magnus Coll., 1980—, Western Conn. State U., 1982-86, Norwalk Community Coll., 1985; psychotherapist/cons. in behavioral medicine; free-lance writer in psychology, 1980—; cons., researcher AFL-CIO/OPEIU; vol. psychotherapist St. Andrew Sch., 1980-86. Co-author: (appendix) Personal Orientation Inventory Handbook for Publisher: Educational Industrial Testing Service, 1987. Grantee Mellon Found., Silverstone Co. Mem. Am. Psychol. Assn. (assoc.), Eastern Psychol. Assn., (assoc., presenter conv. 1987), New Eng. Psychol. Assn., Soc. Behavioral Medicine, Am. Soc. Profl. Exec. Women, Am. Assn. Univ. Profs., AAAS, Am. Arbitration Assn., N.Y. Acad. Scis., World Fedn. Mental Health, Nat. Writers Union, Inst. Advancement Health, Assn. Humanistic Psychology, Am. Mgmt. Assn., Internat. Women's Writing Guild (cons., educator 1986—), Am. Assn. Family Counselors and Mediators (cert. supr. mediators, registered community mediator, family mediator), Am. Mental Health Counselors Assn., Am. Assn. for Counseling and Devel., Biofeedback Soc. Am., Assn. for Specialists in Group Work, Assn. for Measurement and Evaluation in Counseling and Devel., Indsl. Relations Research Assn., Nat. Writers Club, Assn. for Multicultural Counseling and Devel. Democrat. Roman Catholic. Research on creativity, health psychology, wellness and optimal human functioning. Office: Psychotherapeutic Cons and Research Service Box 3359 Westport CT 06880-9991

BRAUN, MARY JO, artist tour manager; b. Dayton, Ohio, June 1, 1961; d. Robert Leo Braun and Billie Sue (Bustle) Bayman. BS in Journalism, Ohio

U., 1985. Rep. mktg. NRB Engrng., Dayton, 1986-87; campaigner Ohio Pub. Interest, Dayton, 1987—; musician tour mgr. Hunter Davis, San Francisco, 1987—; reporter Athens (Ohio) Messenger, 1984; co-producer Canal St. Tavern, Dayton, 1987; vol. disc jockey Sta. WYSO, Yellow Springs, Ohio, 1987—. With pub. relations dept. campaign of Dean Kahler, Athens, 1985. Mem. Nat. Assn. for Female Execs., Assn. for Female Execs., Aircraft Owners and Pilots Assn.

BRAUN, PATRICIA, art workshops sponsor; b. Phila., Feb. 5, 1926; d. John F. and Mary K. (Sweeney) Heilmann; m. George A. Braun, Apr. 19, 1952; children—George, Jr., Mary E., Mark C., Janet M. Student Temple U. Art Sch., 1967-71, Du Cret Sch. Arts, 1979. Owner, founder Pocono Pines Gallery and Workshops, Pa., 1980—; painter; serveral oil paintings in pvt. collections. Mem. Hazelton Art League, Wyoming Valley Art League, Monroe County Arts Council, Artist League of Central N.J., Oreland Art Ctr. Republican. Roman Catholic. Avocations: swimming, sailing, skiing. Home: PO Box 676 Pocono Pines PA 18350 Office: Pocono Pines Gallery & Workshops Old Route 940 Pocono Pines PA 18350

BRAUN, SUSIE JANE, cytologist; b. Beaver Dam, Wis., Nov. 19, 1962; d. Dwayne Arther and Carol Ann (Rosemeier) B. Student, U. Wis., LaCrosse, 1981-83; cert. cytology, Milw. Sch. Medicine, 1984. Cytologist Cytology Pathology Services Inc., Indpls., 1984—. Mem. Am. Soc. Clin. Pathologists, Cytology Soc. Ind., Nat. Assn. Female Execs., Am. Soc. Cytotechnology. Roman Catholic. Home: 8006 Stonehinge Circle #134 Indianapolis IN 46260 Office: Cytology Pathology Services Inc 5865 N Michigan Rd Indianapolis IN 46208

BRAUNSCHWEIG, AUDREY A., nurse; b. White Plains, N.Y., Sept. 2, 1930; d. George Burr and Frances (Wells) Askew; children: Carol L., Laurie Braunschweig Corbacho, Ann L. BS in Nursing, Keuka Coll., 1951; postgrad., Nazareth Coll., 1970, U. Rochester, 1972. RN. Staff nurse Rochester (N.Y.) Gen. Hosp., 1951-52; field nurse Health Assn. Rochester and Monroe County, Rochester, 1952-53; pub. health nurse Monroe County, Rochester, 1964; sub. sch. nurse Fairport Sch. System, Rochester, 1969-72; sch. nurse St. Louis Sch., Pittsford, N.Y., 1972-73; staff nurse Weight Loss Clinic, Pittsford, 1977; coordinator Weight Control Clinic for Children and Adolescents, Rochester Med. Ctr., 1979-87; adv. bd. Dairy Council, Rochester, N.Y., 1985-87; coordinator Summer Camp for Overweight Girls, 1982-86. Contbr. articles to profl. jours.

BRAVERMAN, DONNA CARYN, fiber artist; b. Chgo., Apr. 4, 1947; d. Samuel and Pearl (Leen) B. Student, U. Mo., 1965-68; BFA in Interior Design, Chgo. Acad. Fine Arts, 1970. Interior designer Ascher Dental Supply-Healthco., Chgo., 1970-72, Clarence Krusinski & Assocs. Ltd., Chgo., 1972-74, Perkins & Will Architects, Chgo., 1974-77; fiber artist Fiber Co-op Fibrecations, Chgo., 1977, Scottsdale, Ariz., 1977—. Exhibited in group shows at Mus. Contemporary Crafts, N.Y.C., 1977, James Prendergast Library Art Gallery, Jamestown, N.Y., 1981, Grover M. Herman Fine Arts Ctr., Marietta, Ohio, 1982, Okla. Art Ctr., 1982, Middle Tenn. State U., Murfreesboro, 1982, Redding (Calif.) Mus., 1983, Tucson Mus. Art, 1984, 86, The Arts Ctr., Iowa City, 1985, The Wichita Nat., 1986; in traveling exhibitions Ariz. Archtl. Crafts, 1983, Clouds, Mountains, Fibers, 1983; represented in permanent collections Phillips Petroleum, Houston, Metro. Life, Tulsa, Directory Hotel, Tulsa, Keys Estate Ariz. Biltmore Estates, Phoenix, Sohio Petroleum, Dallas, Reichold Chem., White Plains, N.Y., Rolm Telecommunications, Colorado Springs, Mesirow & Co., Chgo., Exec. House Hotel, Chgo., Cambell Estate, Ariz.; contbr. articles to profl. jours. Home and Office: 7920 E Camelback Rd #511 Scottsdale AZ 85251

BRAVERMAN, LOUISE M., architect; b. N.Y.C., Nov. 23, 1948; d. Don S. and Madlyn (Barotz) B.; m. Steven Z. Glickel, July 1, 1984; 1 child, Jennifer Liberty. BA, U. Mich., 1970; MArch, Yale U., 1977. Registered architect, N.Y. Ptnr., architect Austin Braverman Patterson, Architects, N.Y.C. and Southport, Conn., 1982—; guest design critic Yale U., Columbia U., U. Pa., Cooper Union U., Syracuse U., Bryn Mawr Coll., Ohio State U. Mem. Am. Inst. Architects, Archtl. League, Assn. Real Estate Women, Nat. Women's Mus. (charter). Club: Yale (N.Y.C.). Office: Austin Braverman Patterson Architects 39 E 31 St New York NY 10016

BRAVMANN, CAROL RUTH, psychologist; b. N.Y.C., Apr. 30, 1956; d. Ludwig and Lotte (Simon) B.; m. Stewart David Lipner, Aug. 7, 1977 (div. Feb. 1987). BA, CCNY, 1977; MS, Yeshiva U., N.Y.C., 1981, PhD, 1982; cert. in child and adolescent psychotherapy, Adelphi U., Garden City, N.Y., 1987. Sch. psychologist The Alternative Sch., Bklyn., 1981-84; pvt. practice psychology Port Washington, 1983—; sch. psychologist Farmingdale (N.Y.) Pub. Schs., 1984—; adj. clin. supr. Psychology Ferkauf Grad. Sch. Psychology, 1987—; adj. prof. Ferkauf Grad. Sch. Psychology, 1988—. Mem. Am. Psychol. Assn., Nassau County Psychol. Assn., Adelphi Soc. for Psychoanalysis and Psychotherapy (mem. exec. bd. 1986-87), N.Y. Soc. Clin. Psychologists , Phi Beta Kappa. Home: 86 Summit Rd Port Washington NY 11050 Office: 2 Haven Ave Port Washington NY 11052

BRAVO, LEONORE MCCRYSTLE, biologist, psychologist, conservationist; b. Vallejo, Calif., July 14, 1914; d. Arthur Bernard and Geraldine Marie (Winslow) McCrystle; B.A., San Francisco State U., 1934; M.A., U. Calif., Berkeley, 1947; m. Ignacio Bravo-Caro, Aug. 2, 1939; children—Nacho E., Michael A. Tchr. Indian schs. in Nev. and Calif., 1937-40; tchr., adminstr. schs. in Calif., 1940-47; head psychologist Sacramento County schs., 1948-51; tchr. San Francisco secondary schs., 1953-62; asst. prin. Indio (Calif.) High Sch., 1962-63; psychologist Oakland (Calif.) pub. schs., 1963-72, cons., 1972—; lectr. San Francisco Community Coll. Dist., 1975-87; exec. sec. Tamalpais Conservation Club, 1974-77, bd. dirs., 1974-88; pub. mem. Calif. Cling Peach Processors Adv. Bd., 1975-79; mgr. honeybee exhibit San Francisco Flower Show, 1979—. NSF fellow, 1957, 59-62; scholar intergroup relations Stanford U. NCCJ, 1959; fellow OAS, 1970. Mem. Am., Interam., Calif. psychol. assns., Calif. Tchrs. Assn., Calif. Acad. Scis., Calif. Sch. Psychologists Assn., Western Apicultural Soc. (charter), People for Preservation of the Natural and Wild in Bay Area Open Space (founder, pres. 1977), San Francisco Beekeepers Assn. (founder 1976, pres. 1978, exec. sec. 1977-79), Women's Internat. League Peace and Freedom, Common Cause, Amnesty Internat., Calif. Wilderness Coalition, Am. Beekeeping Fedn., Calif. State Beekeepers Assn., San Francisco Democratic Women's Forum (dir. 1978-81, v.p. 1979), San Francisco Women for Peace, ACLU, Tamalpais Conservation Club (v.p. 1984, pres. 1986), Am. Friends Service Com., Friends of Earth, UN Assn., Wilderness Soc., Calif. Native Plant Soc., Save the Redwoods League (life), U. Calif. Alumni Assn. (life), Consumers Coop. Berkeley. Author articles. Address: 47 Levant St San Francisco CA 94114

BRAVO, ROSE MARIE, retail executive; b. N.Y.C., Jan. 13, 1951; d. Biagio and Anna (Bazzano) LaPila; m. Charles Emil Bravo, June 13, 1971 (div. 1977); m. William Selkirk Jackey, Oct. 9, 1983. B.A. in English, Fordham U., 1971. Exec. trainee, dept. mgr. A&S, Bklyn., 1971-74; assoc. buyer Macy's, N.Y.C., 1974-75, buyer, 1975-79, councillor, 1979-80, adminstr., 1980-84, group v.p., from 1984; chmn., chief exec. officer, I. Magnin, San Francisco, 1988—. Chmn. retail com. March of Dimes Birth Defects Found., 1980-81. Home: 201 E 21st St New York NY 10010 Office: I Magnin & Co 135 Stockton St San Francisco CA 94108 *

BRAWER, PATRICIA ELAINE, securities brokerage exec.; b. N.Y.C., July 3, 1945; d. Oscar I. and Iris (Pashman) Brawer; student U. Edinburgh (Scotland), 1965; BA, Smith Coll., 1966; postgrad. N.Y. Inst. Fin., 1968. Prodn. asst. Merrill Lynch, N.Y.C., 1967-69; asst. to br. mgr. Shearson Hammill, N.Y.C., 1969-71; with Thomson McKinnon Securities, N.Y.C., 1971—, now asst. v.p. mktg. Bd. dirs. Village Light Opera Group Ltd., N.Y.C.; trustee Pop Warner Little Scholars; program dir. Regional Emergency Med. Services Council of N.Y.C. Mem. English Speaking Union, Mensa.Club: N.Y. Smith Coll. Address: 250 E 73d St New York NY 10021

BRAWN, LINDA CURTIS, state legislator; b. Rockland, Maine, June 16, 1947; d. Charles Samuel and Alice (Jenkins) Curtis; m. William Preston Brawn, Aug. 19, 1969; children: Charles, Michael. A in Liberal Studies, U. Maine, Augusta, 1978; BS in Edn., U. Maine, Orono, 1981. Tchr. Mother Goose Nursery Sch., Camden, Maine, 1973-82; kindergarten tchr. Rockland, Maine, 1983-85; mem. Maine State Senate, Augusta, 1986—. Author: Festival Memories, 1987. Mem. Camden Conservation com., 1984—; bd. dirs., chmn. pub. issues Am. Cancer Soc., 1986—; chmn. Knox County Rep. Com., 1985-86. Mem. Maine Fedn. Women's Clubs (1st v.p. 1986—). Baptist. Lodge: Order Eastern Star (1st conductress). Home: 59 Park St Camden ME 04843 Office: State House Augusta ME 04333

BRAY, CAROLYN SCOTT, educational administrator; b. Childress, Tex., May 19, 1938; d. Alonzo Lee and Frankie Lucille (Wood) Scott; m. John Graham Bray, Jr., Aug. 24, 1957 (div. May 1980); children—Caron Lynn, Kimberly Anne, David William. B.S., Baylor U., 1960; M.Ed., Hardin-Simmons U., 1981; Ph.D., N. Tex. State U., 1985. Registered med. technologist. Research asst. Fairleigh-Dickinson Research Ctr., Hardin-Simmons U., Abilene, Tex., 1979; adj. prof. bus. communication Hardin-Simmons U., 1981-84; dir. career placement, 1979-82, assoc. dean students, 1982-85; assoc. dir. career planning and placement U. North Tex., Denton, 1985—, adj. prof. higher edn. adminstrn., mem. Mentor program; cons. univs. Interim youth dir. 1st Baptist Ch., Abilene, 1972-73; coordinator single adult ministry 1st Baptist Ch., Denton, 1985—; organizer, mem. Abilene Women's Network, 1982-85; mem. Abilene Art Mus., 1975-86, Abilene Philharm. Assn., 1969-79; mem. scholarship com. U. North Tex. League for Profl. Women, v.p. 1988-89. Mem. Assn. Sch., Coll. and Univ. Staffing, S.W. Placement Assn. (profl. devel. and adv. com. liberal arts network), Tex. Assn. Sch., Coll. and Univ. Staffing (v.p. 1986-87, pres. 1987-88), Coll. Placement Council, North Cen. Assn. Sch. Personnel Adminstrs. and Univ. Placement Personnel (pres. 1987-88), Internat. Platform Assn., Denton C. of C. (pub. relations com.), Dallas Personnel Assn., Nat. Assn. Female Execs., Leadership Denton (co-dir. curriculum 1988—), Denton Cultural Arts Assn., Abilene Jr. League, Pi Lambda Theta. Republican. C-lub: Abilene Country. Avocations: skiing; water skiing; tennis; golf; reading. Office: PO Box 13378 Denton TX 76203

BRAY, JANET BALTUCH, association executive; b. Bklyn., Dec. 28, 1950; d. Robert and Adrienne (Kassin) Baltuch; m. Joel S. Goldhammer, June 27, 1971 (div. 1979); m. Richard Allan Bray, Nov. 2, 1980. BA in Edn., U. Md., 1973; MA in Adult Edn., George Washington U., 1979. Dir. communications Nat. Environ. Systems Contractors Assn., Arlington, Va., 1973-75; mgr. continuing edn. Am. Soc. Microbiology, Washington, 1976-79; dir. tng. and edn. Community Assn. Inst., Arlington, 1979-82; v.p. tng. and meetings Internat. Communications Industries Assn., Fairfax, Va., 1982-87; v.p., mems. program Printing Industries Am., Arlington, 1987—; trainer Nat. Alliance Bus., Washington, 1973-74; speaker in field. Contbr. articles to profl. jours. Mem. Greater Washington Soc. Execs. (chair edn. com. 1987-88), Am. Soc. Assn. Execs. (mem. edn. council 1985-87), Nat. Assn. Exposition Mgrs., Am. Soc. Tng. and Devel., Nat. Soc. Performance and Instrn., World Future Soc. Office: Printing Industries Am 1730 N Lynn St Arlington VA 22209

BRAY, PENNY NELSON, music educator; b. Fargo, N.D., Feb. 6, 1952; d. Arthur Warren and Betty Dale (Carlson) Nelson; m. James Waldo Speirs, Dec. 28, 1974 (div. Aug. 1981); 1 child, James Arthur; m. David Charles Bray, Mar. 18, 1982; 1 child, Geoffrey David. MusB, Black Hills State Coll., 1974. Vocal instr. Milbank (S.D.) High Sch., 1974-76; substitute tchr. Mt. Pleasant (Iowa) Pub. Schs., 1978-81; music instr. Meade 46-1 Sch. Dist., Sturgis, S.D., 1981-86, Douglas Sch. Dist., Ellsworth AFB, S.D., 1986—. Mem. P.E.O. Chpt. N, Spearfish, S.D., 1974, 81-86, Chpt. Original A, Mt. Pleasant, Iowa, 1977-81, Chpt. BR, Rapid City, S.D., 1987—. Named One of Outstanding Young Women Am., 1981. Mem. Assn. Supervision and Curriculum Devel., Music Educators Nat. Conf. Democrat. Methodist. Home: 3701 Westridge Rd Rapid City SD 57702 Office: Francis Case School Patriot Dr Ellsworth AFB SD 57706

BRAZEAL, DONNA SMITH, psychologist; b. Greenville, S.C., Feb. 10, 1947; d. G.W. Hovey and Ollie Occena (Crane) Smith; m. Charles Lee Brazeal, June 27, 1970 (div. May 1980). BA, Clemson U., 1971, MEd, 1975; postgrad., Western Carolina U., 1974, Furman U., Greenville, 1977. Lic. sch. psychologist, S.C., N.C. Instr., head med. record dept. Greenville Tech. Coll., 1971-73; chief psychologist Greenville County Schs., 1975-80, Union County Schs., Monroe, N.C., 1980—; pvt. practice psychology Monroe and Charlotte, N.C., 1986—; mem. learning disabilities com. Greenville County Schs., 1978-79; co-founder, bd. dirs. Ctr. for Spiritual Awareness of N.C., Monroe, 1982—. Co-author, co-editor: Exceptional Children, 1980. Child find program coordinator Union County, 1980-85; mem. various coms. Assn. for Retarded Citizens, Monroe; mem. interagy. council Piedmont Mental Health, Monroe, 1983—. Catawba Bus. Women scholar, 1965; N.C. Dept. Pub. Instrn. Pre-Sch. Incentive grantee, 1984. Mem. Nat. Assn. Sch. Psychologists, N.C. Assn. Sch. Psychologist (mem. pub. relations com. 1984-85), Animal Protection Inst. Am., Greenpeace, Union County Humane Soc., River Hills Community Ch. (mem. adult edn. com. 1985-86), Delta. Libertarian. Unitarian. Home: PO Box 240173 Charlotte NC 28224

BRAZEE, LOUISE ANN, communications company marketing executive; b. Milford, Conn., Nov. 23, 1956; d. John Ashley and Eleanor Arlyle (Wood) B. BS in Home Econs., U. N.C., Greensboro, 1978; postgrad., Kennesaw Coll., 1979-82; MBA in Mktg., U. Ga., 1984. Quality control technician RJR Foods, Inc., Atlanta, 1979-80; quality assurance technician Federated Foods, Inc., Norcross, Ga., 1980-82; trade cons. Internat. Trade Devel. Ctr., Athens, Ga., 1982-83; new products mgr. Scovill Apparel Fasteners Inc., Watertown, Conn., 1984-87; product mgr. Holt Lloyd Corp., Tucker, Ga., 1987-88, OKI Telecom, Norcross, Ga., 1988—; speaker in field. Loaned exec. Waterbury (Conn.) United Way, 1984, group chairperson, 1985, mem. speaker's bur., 1985-86; adv. Jr. Achievement of Waterbury, 1984-85, ctr. mgr., 1985-86; mem. Cambodian Refugee Relocation com., Naugatuck, Conn., 1985-86, mem. Northside Hosp. Aux., Atlanta, 1987—. Mem. Inst. Food Technologists, Am. Mktg. Assn., U. N.C. Alumni Assn., U. Ga. Alumni Assn., Grad. Bus. Alumni Assn., Norcross-Peachtree Corners Jaycees (pres. 1988—). Republican. Presbyterian. Home: 3343-E Peachtree Corners Circle Norcross GA 30092 Office: OKI Telecom 4317 Park Dr Norcross GA 30071

BRAZELTON, JEAN MARY, educator; b. St. Paul, Jan. 24, 1931; d. George M. and Florence (MacIntyre) Sausen; m. Robert Sage Brazelton; children: Robert, Michael, Anne, Kevin, Steven, Kathryn. BA, Coll. of St. Catherine, 1952. Cert. secondary tchr., Minn., Calif. Tchr. Fairfax (Minn.) High Sch., 1952-53, Arrowview Jr. High Sch., San Bernardino, Calif., 1953-55, Calif. High Sch., Whittier, 1955-60, St. Joseph High Sch., Lakewood, Calif., 1985—; Leader Jr. Great Books, Downey, Calif., 1967-85. Bd. dirs. Downey YMCA, 1976-82, Sir Thomas More Marriage Counseling Ctr., 1987-89; basketball coach Downey Pony Tail, 1978-82, Catholic Youth Orgn., 1982-83; sec. exec. bd. dirs. Downey YMCA 1982-83; commr. community services City of Downey, 1983-87; mem. commn. Friends of the Library, Downey, 1985-87; bd. dirs., chmn. St. Joseph High Sch. Found., 1987-89. Mem. Downey Symphony Assn., Cath. Women's Guild, Phi Beta Kappa, Kappa Gamma Pi. Republican. Roman Catholic.

BRAZIER, SHARLENE, association executive; b. Palo Alto, Calif., Nov. 18, 1959; d. Rollie Dean and Corinne (Rogers) B. Student El Centro Coll., 1976-78; B.A., So. Meth. U., 1982. Edn. dir. Dallas Urban League, 1982—; com. mem. Dallas Ind. Sch. Dist., 1982—, com. mem. Orgn. Task Force, 1982—. Vol., Rape Crisis Prevention, Dallas, 1980; mem. adv. com. NCCJ, 1982—; mem. adv. com. Charles Rice Elem. Sch. Mem. Delta Sigma Theta. Democrat. Baptist.

BRDLIK, CAROLA EMILIE, accountant; b. Wuerzburg, Fed. Republic Germany, Mar. 11, 1930; came to U.S., 1952; d. Ludwig Leonard and Hildegard Maria (Leipold) Baumeister; m. Joseph A. Brdlik; children: Margaret Louise, Charles Joseph. BA, Oberrealschule Bamberg, Fed. Republic Germany, 1948; MA, Bavarian Interpreter Coll., Fed. Republic Germany, 1949; postgrad. Interpreter, exec. sec. NCWC Amberg, Schweinfurt, Ludwigsburg and Munich, Fed. Republic Germany, 1949-52; exec. sec. Red Ball Van Lines, Jamaica, N.Y., 1952; interpreter Griffin Rutgers Inc., N.Y.C., 1952-53; office mgr., exec. sec. Rehab. Ctr. Summit Co., Inc., Akron, 1953-56; pvt. practice acctg. Cuyahoga Falls, Ohio, 1956-61, Uniontown, Ohio, 1961-82; fin. and tax cons. Omaca, Inc., Uniontown and Deerfield Beach (Fla.), 1982—; sec.-treas. Shipe Landscaping, Inc., Greensburg, Ohio, 1968—, Sattler Machine products, Copley, Ohio, 1981-87; asst. treas. Mar-Lynn Lake Park, Inc., Streetsboro, Ohio, 1969. Bd. dirs., trustee Czechoslovak Refugees, Cleve. and Cin., 1968. Mem. Nat. Soc. Tax Profls., Pub. Accts. Soc. Ohio, Ohio Soc. Enrolled Agts./Auditors, Nat. Soc. Pub. Accts., Nat. Assn. Tax Preparers, Ohio Soc. Pub. Accts., Nat. Assn. Enrolled Agts. Roman Catholic. Home: 2026 SW 17th Dr Deerfield Beach FL 33442

BREAKEY, LISA KATHERINE, speech pathologist; b. Los Angeles, Oct. 21, 1945; d. Melvin Harvey and Inez (Rey) Smith. BA in Speech Pathology and Audiology, U. Calif., Santa Barbara, 1967; MA in Speech Pathology, San Jose State U., 1975. Cert. community coll. spl. edn. tchr., Calif. Speech pathologist Manitoba (Can.) Rehab. Hosp., 1968-69; speech pathologist Kingston (Ont.) Health Unit, Can., 1969-70, dir. speech therapy, 1970-73; pvt. practice San Jose, Calif., 1975—; cons. Atari Inc., Sunnyvale, Calif., 1977-79, Evergreen Valley Community Coll., San Jose, 1977-80, Los Gatos (Calif.) Rehab. Hosp., 1977—, VA Med. Ctr., Livermore, Calif., 1979-83, Irwin Lehrhoff and Assocs., Beverly Hills, Calif., 1985-86; profl. staff priviledges Santa Teresa Hosp., San Jose, 1981—, Mission Oaks Hosp., San Jose, 1982—, Good Samaritan Hosp., San Jose, 1983—; presenter numerous seminars, workshops in adult communication disorders, 1979—; guest lectr. San Jose State U., 1975-88. Contbr. articles to profl. jours. Mem. Am. Speech Lang. and Hearing Assn. (legis. counselor 1986—, congl. action contact 1985, cert. appreciation 1983, 84), Calif. Speech Lang. Hearing Assn. (chmn. printing com. 1977, mem. conf. commn. 1982-84, task force on occupational therapy, 1983-84, hospitality com. 1984, legis. handbook com. 1985, state nominating com. 1986-88, editor newsletter 1985, dist. dir. elect 1988—, Outstanding Achievement award 1986), Calif. Speech Pathologists and Audiologists in Pvt. Practice (v.p. 1979-81, pres. 1983-85, chmn. speakers bur. 1981, 82, current trends workshop 1980, pvt. practice workship 1978-80, rev. course in preparation com. 1978-81, 83, 85-86, govt. affairs com. 1983—, nomination com. 1985—, cert. appreciation 1982), Santa Clara County Speech-Lang.-Hearing Assn. (bd. dirs. 1987—), Calif. Assn. Post Seconary Educators of Disabled, Profl. Group for Adult Communication Disorders (1st pres. 1977), Bay Area Group for Non-Oral, Bay Area Neurolinguistic Group, Bay Area Pvt. Practitioners Speech Pathology and Audiology (1st pres. 1977), Washington Sq. Soc.-San Jose State U., Phi Kappa Phi. Democrat. Roman Catholic. Office: 2444 Moorpark Ave Suite 300 San Jose CA 95128

BREAKSTONE, KAY LOUISE, public relations executive; b. Allentown, Pa., Sept. 9, 1936; d. Morris H. and Mabel (Gruber) Senderowitz; B.S., N.Y. U., 1967; m. Jules L. Breakstone, Dec. 3, 1960; children—Enid, Jessica. With N.Y. Conf. Bd., 1967-69, Bache, Halsey Stuart, N.Y.C., 1969-70; securities analyst Dean Witter, N.Y.C., 1970-71; vice-pres. Burson Marsteller, Inc., N.Y.C., 1971-79; dir. investor relations Kennecott Corp., Stamford, Conn., 1979-81; sr. v.p. Burson-Marsteller, 1981-87, exec. v.p., 1987—; dir. First Women's Bank. Mem. Nat. Investor Relations Inst. (pres. 1980-81). Office: 230 Park Ave S New York NY 10003

BRECHBILL, SUSAN REYNOLDS, government official; b. Washington, Aug. 22, 1943; d. Irving and Isabell Doyle (Reynolds) Levine; B.A., Coll. William and Mary, 1965; J.D., Marshall-Wythe Sch. Law, 1968; m. Raymond A. Brechbill, June 29, 1973; children—Jennifer Rae, Heather Lea. Admitted to Va. bar, 1969, Fed. bar, 1970; atty. AEC, Berkeley, Calif., 1968-73, indsl. relations specialist AEC, Las Vegas, 1974-75; atty. ERDA, Oakland, Calif., 1976-77; atty. Dept. Energy, Oakland, 1977-78, dir. procurement div. San Francisco Ops. Office, 1978-85, asst. chief counsel, 1985—; mem. faculty U. Calif. Extension; speaker Nat. Contract Mgmt. Assn. Ann. Symposiums, 1980, 81, 83, 84; speaker on doing bus. with govt. Leader Girl Scouts U.S.A., San Francisco area. Named Outstanding Young Woman Nev., 1974. Mem. Va. State Bar Assn., Fed. Bar Assn., Nat. Contract Mgmt. Assn. (pres. Golden Gate chpt. 1983-84, N.W. regional v.p. 1984-86), Nat. Assn. Female Execs. Republican. Contbr. articles to profl. jours. Home: 67 Scenic Dr Orinda CA 94563

BRECHEISEN, VIRGINIA H., human resource executive; b. Houston, Jan. 10, 1930; d. William Edgar and Mytle Altus (Pickens) Hull; m. Karl William Brecheisen, June 4, 1955; 1 child, Kurt William. BA, So. Meth. U., 1951, MRE, 1953; postgrad., Montclair (N.J.) State U., 1957-58, Rutgers U., 1959-61, Kean Coll., 1963-64. Dir. edn. Lovers Lane Meth. Ch., Dallas, 1952-56; instr. art Harding Twp. Sch., New Vernon, N.J., 1957-68; instr. Centenary Coll., Hackettstown, N.J., 1981-82; chief exec. officer Effectiveness Unlmtd., Chester, N.J., 1984—; dir. Paradigm Assocs. NW, Chester, N.J., 1986—; program chmn. Nat. Alliance Homebased Bus., Morris County, N.J., 1986-87. Mem. steering com. for Thorough and Efficient Edn., Chester, N.J., 1979-80; bd. dirs. League Woman Voters, 1969-75, current mem. Mem. Am. Soc. Tng. and Devel., Nat. Alliance Home Based Bus., Nat. Assn. Female Execs. Republican. Unitarian. Home and Office: 25 Cherry Tree Ln Chester NJ 07930

BRECHT, SALLY ANN, computer standards and security manager; b. Trenton, N.J., Aug. 5, 1951; d. Charles L. and Helen (Orfeo) B. BBA, Coll. William & Mary in Va., 1973; MBA, Rider Coll., 1981. Electronic data processing auditor McGraw Hill, Inc., Hightstown, N.J., 1976-79, State of N.J., Mercerville, 1979-80, NL Industries, Hightstown, 1980-84; systems tech. planning specialist Ednl. Testing Service, Princeton, N.J., 1984-85, acting div. dir. application devel., 1985-87, mgr. computer standards and security, 1987—. Office: Ednl Testing Service Rosedale Rd Princeton NJ 08520

BRECKENRIDGE, BETTY GAYLE, industrial psychologist consultant; b. Austin, Tex., Dec. 8, 1945; d. Glen Floyd and Mary Margaret (Stone) B. BA, Baylor U., 1966; postgrad., U. Houston, 1981-82; MA, So. Meth. U, 1984. Commodities specialist Merrill Lynch, Pierce, Fenner & Smith, Houston, 1976-78; owner Fun Ctr. U.S.A., Inc., Houston, 1978-80; counselor Gen. Homes, Inc., Houston, 1980-81; cons., N.Y.C., 1983-85, Devel. Dimensions Internat., Pitts., 1985—. Mem. Soc. for Indsl. Orgnl. Psychology. Home and Office: 332 W Fairmount State College PA 16801

BREDAEL, DEBRA JEAN, economist; b. Chgo., May 12, 1959; d. Donald Edward and Dorothy Mae (Aufmann) Ryckaert; children: Kristi Diane, Michael Brian. BS in Stats., Econs., No. Ill. U., 1981; postgrad., DePaul U., 1982—. Economist Harris Trust and Savs. Bank, Chgo., 1981—. Mem. Am. Statis. Assn., Nat. Assn. Bus. Economists, Nat. Economists Club, Nat. Assn. Female Execs. Home: 1859 Pebble Beach Circle Elk Grove IL 60007 Office: Harris Trust and Savs Bank 111 W Monroe 6E Chicago IL 60690

BREDAHL, JANICE ANN, automotive corporation executive; b. Mpls., Sept. 4, 1957; d. George Franklin and Loraine May (Graham) Lunger; m. John Patrick Bredahl, Mar. 9, 1980 (div. Jan. 31, 1985). BA in Phys. Edn., Point Loma Coll., 1979. Clk. typist San Diego Econ. Devel. Corp., 1978-79; data entry operator, customer relations sec. BMW of N.Am., Inc., Los Angeles, 1979-82, sec. regional service, regional parts mgr., 1982-84; tchr. computers The Berkley Sch., White Plains, N.Y., 1986; substitute tchr. The Berkley Sch., White Plains, 1987; info. ctr. trainer BMW of N.Am., Inc., Montvale, N.J., 1984—, info. ctr. analyst, 1987—. Sec. bd. mgrs. Mountainview Condominium Assn., Valley Cottage, N.Y., 1988—; mem. Statue of Liberty-Ellis Island Found., 1984-88. Republican. Lutheran. Clubs: Bergen County Geneal. Soc. (Bergen, N.J.); Rockland Lake Runners' Assn. (N.Y.). Office: BMW of NAm Inc BMW Plaza S Montvale NJ 07645

BREEDEN-CSESZKO, REBECCA SUE, property manager; b. Terre Haute, Ind., July 10, 1943; d. Rex Earl and Joy Rosalie (Conley) Breeden; m. M. Thomas Hopkins, June 30, 1962 (div. 1967); children: Jeffery Thomas, Kimberly Allyson; m. Robert James Cseszko, Nov. 23, 1974; children: Christian Robert, Emily Rebecca, Rachel Elisabeth. Student, Ind. U., 1961, 62; cert., Johnson Inst., Mpls., 1982, Tri-County Alcoholism Ctr., Columbus, Ohio, 1982. Copywriter Virginian Pilot/Ledger Star, Norfolk, 1962-64; v.p. Custom-Brushed, Inc., Columbus, Ind., 1975—; ptnr. Imagination II Advt., Columbus, 1977-81; owner Trilogy Mgmt. Co., Columbus, 1983—; counselor Pleasant Grove Hosp., Louisville, 1982, Bartholomew Consol. Sch. Corp., Columbus, 1986-87, Columbus Parks and Recreation Bd., 1987—; bd. dirs., sec. Brex Corp. 1966-83. Mem. Bartholomew County Hosp. Auxiliary, Columbus, 1968-73, Columbus Arts Guild, 1970-74, Columbus Area Alcohol and Drugs Council, 1982—, Bartholomew Assn. Gifted Edn., Columbus, 1986—, Driftwood Valley Arts

Council, Columbus Art League; mem. Columbus Jayshees, 1968-74, bd. dirs. 1969-73; bd. dirs., treas. Columbus Gymnastics Ctr., 1986—; publicity chmn. United Way Fund Drive, Columbus, 1980, 82; chmn. Spl. Olympics, Columbus, 1972; facilitator Family Hope Recovery Program, Columbus, 1981-85; mem. Columbus Peace Fellowship. Recipient Nat. Art Dirs. award, 1963. Profl. mem. U.S. Gymnastics Fedn. Home: 1621 Franklin St Columbus IN 47201

BREEDING, ANN WARREN, lawyer; b. Atlanta, Aug. 18, 1942; d. Julian Benjamin and Martha Elizabeth (Malone) Warren; m. Earle Griffith Breeding, Aug. 16, 1980; 1 dau., Martha Malone. B.A., Tulane U., 1964, M.A., 1965; J.D., George Washington U., 1980. Bar: D.C. 1980. Instr. English, U. Hawaii, 1965-67; tchr., librarian Piedmont Acad., Monticello, Ga., 1970-71; librarian Jasper County Library, Monticello, Ga., 1968-70; tchr. Willingham High Sch., Macon, Ga., 1971-72; tchr., librarian Mt. De Sales High Sch., Macon, 1972-73; aide Congressman John J. Flynt, Jr., Washington, 1973-79; sole practice, Washington, 1980—. Bd. dirs. Capitol Hill Restoration Soc., Washington, 1984. Mem. ABA, D.C. Bar Assn., Fed. Bar Assn., Assn. Trial Lawyers Am., Nat. Cathedral Assn., Phi Beta Kappa, Phi Delta Phi. Home: 529 14th St SE Washington DC 20003

BREEN, FAITH FEI-MEI LEE, economist, management consultant; b. Burbank, Calif., Feb. 3, 1951; d. John Quong and Eleanor S.G. (Choy) Lee; m. George Edward Breen, Jr., Nov. 30, 1974; children—Erika Lee, George Edward III. B.A., U. Md., 1972; M.A., U. Pitts., 1975. Asst. dir. Ctr. for Health Policy Research, Am. Enterprise Inst. Pub. Policy, Washington, 1975-77; economist U.S. Dept. Labor, Bur. Internat. Labor Affairs, Washington, 1978; Nat. Gov.'s Assn., Ctr. Pub. Policy Research, Washington, 1978-79; expert cons., economist Pres.'s Adv. Com. Women, Washington, 1979-81; polit. econ. cons. Nat. Assn. State and Territorial Solid Waste Mgmt. Ofcls., Washington, 1981-82; expert cons., economist to dep. under sec. mgmt. U.S. Dept. Edn., Washington, 1980-83; adj. faculty dept. econs. Central Mich. U., Washington, 1978—; asst. prof. sch. bus. and dept. econs. Prince Georges Community Coll., Largo, Md., 1985—; lectr. in field. Contbr. articles to profl. jours.; exec. producer TV program: Saccharin and the Public Interest, 1978. past pres. Inner Wheel of College Park, 1986-87, nat. v.p. programs Orgn. Chinese Am. Women, 1987, del. Women-to-Women Exchange program, 1987; chair fin. com. University Park Rep. Women's Club, 1985; controller Nat. Rep. Com.'s Nat. Rep. Heritage Group Council, 1985—. Recipient Nat. Def. Lang. fellow, 1973-75; cert. of appreciation Sec. U.S. Dept. Edn., 1983; Fulbright-Hays Seminar Abroad, 1986. Mem. Am. Econ. Assn. Roman Catholic. Club: Univ. Hills Swim. Avocations: tennis, swimming, bridge. Home: 3915 Commander Dr College Heights Estates MD 20782 Office: Prince Georges Community Coll 301 Largo Rd Largo MD 20772

BREEN, JOANELL CATHERINE, systems librarian, consultant, researcher; b. Chgo., Feb. 7, 1939; d. Joseph Edward and Ann Genevieve (Moriarty) B. BA, Rosary Coll., 1959, MLS, 1960; MBA, Roosevelt U., 1970. Supr. pub. relations research World Book Encyclopedia, Chgo., 1960-70; archtl. librarian Art Inst., Chgo., 1970-72; head librarian Bank Mktg. Assn., Chgo., 1972-73; head tech. librarian Met. San. Dist., Chgo., 1973-79; programmer Continental Bank, Chgo., 1979-81; programmer, analyst FMC Corp., Chgo., 1981-83; systems librarian, infr. scis. cons. Midwest Stock Exchange, Chgo., 1985—; advt. researcher J. Walter Thompson, Tatham Laird Kudner, Olgolvie & Mather, Chgo., 1983-85; documentation evaluator Digital Equipment Corp., Chgo., 1987—. Author thesaurus MSE Library Systems, 1986; editor numerous manuals. Vol. Kennedy for Pres., Chgo., 1960, Thompson for Gov., 1978, Hart for Pres., 1984. Named one of Outstanding Young Women Am., 1976. Mem. Am. Soc. Info. Sci., Am. Mktg. Assn. (indexer 1985). Clubs: Lakeshore, Ski (Chgo.). Office: Midwest Stock Exchange 440 S LaSalle Chicago IL 60605

BREEN, KATHERINE FRANCES LAROCHELLE, educator; b. Atlanta, July 12, 1950; d. Florence Lightfoot and Katherine Frances (Hinson) B.; m. Mark Bryan Bell, May 20, 1972 (div. 1977). BA, Emory U., 1972; MEd, Ga. State U., 1984. Gen. asst. Sawyer Advt. Agy., Gainesville, Ga., 1972-73; teller Gainesville Nat. Bank, 1973-77; account exec. Poultry & Egg Mktg. Pubs., Gainesville, 1977-78; shelter supr. Hall County Humane Soc., Gainesville, 1978-79; account exec. Visual Persuaion Advt. Agy., Atlanta, 1979-80; adminstrv. asst. Vintage Enterprises, Atlanta, 1980-81; dir. edn., pub. relations Atlanta Humane Soc., 1981—; educator Columbus (Ga.) Coll., 1986—. Editor Humane Edn., 1984-87. Educator Grace Episc. Ch., Gainesville, 1972-77; bd. dirs. Hall County Humane Soc., Gainesville, 1977-82, Total Living Commmn. (for deaf), Atlanta, 1985—; vol. Egleston Hosp. for Children, Atlanta, 1987—. Mem. Am. Humane Assn., Ga. Animal Adv. Com., S.E. Animal Control Assn., N.W. Atlanta Bus. Assn., DAR (sec., chmn. pub. relations com. Gainesville chpt. 1973-77). Democrat. Office: Atlanta Humane Soc 981 Howell Mill Rd NW Atlanta GA 30318

BREEN, PATRICIA CARLA, transportation company executive; b. Wenatchee, Wash., June 23, 1930; d. Carlyon Durrand and Marion Carter (Cameron) Whitener; m. Orville Clyde Breen, Aug. 1, 1948 (div. Aug. 1975); children—Steven C., Jay N., Janet C. Breen Hovik, Scott T. (dec.); m. John Damien Malloy, Oct. 23, 1976. Student Wash. State U., 1947-51. Electronics trouble shooter and coordinator Boeing Airplane Co., Renton, Wash., 1957-59; asst. regional cargo mgr. Pacific North Airline, Seattle, 1959-70; owner, mgr. Valley Produce Inc., Kent, Wash., 1968-73; owner, pres. Associated Couriers Inc., Renton, 1979—. Mem. Seattle C. of C. (transp. com. 1974 75), Air Cargo Assn. (v.p. Seattle chpt. 1966, 69, 74, 75), World Trade Club (sec. Seattle chpt. 1976-77, pres. chpt. 1978-79). Republican. Presbyterian. Office: Associated Couriers Inc PO Box 98870 Seattle WA 98188

BREEN, PATRICIA HELEN HALL, financial consultant; b. Detroit, Sept. 15, 1926; d. John William and Ethel Viola (Mardian) Hall. B.B.A., U. Mich., 1949; postgrad. U. Mich.-Detroit, 1953-54. Policy and procedure sec. Gen. Motors Central, Detroit, 1949-50; trust investment analyst Nat. Bank of Detroit, 1950-51; investment analyst Baxter & Co., Cleve., 1952; sr. fin. cons. Merrill Lynch, Farmington Hills, Mich., 1957—; founder, chmn., pres., chief exec. officer Good Food Co., Livonia, Mich.; radio and TV lectr. Mem. Nat. Assn. Female Execs. (pres. Oakland County 1985-87), U. Mich. Alumnae Assn. (bd. dirs. 1973-74). Republican. Roman Catholic. Club: Detroit Boat (Belle Isle, Mich.). Avocations: silversmithing; oil painting; writing; water and snow skiing; golf. Home: 17959 University Park Dr Livonia MI 48152 Office: Merrill Lynch Pierce Fenner & Smith Inc 32255 Northwestern Hwy Farmington Hills MI 48018

BREGMAN, LORRAINE ROSE, distillers company executive; b. Bronx, N.Y., June 19, 1946; d. Louis Richard and Felicia (Pascente) Tancredi; m. Robert William Bregman, Aug. 1, 1970; 1 child, Laura Felicia. Sec. Degree, Drake Bus. Sch., Bronx, 1966. From clk. typist to mgr. Joseph E. Seagram Adminstrn., N.Y.C., 1964-86; mgr. House of Seagram, N.Y.C., 1987—. Mem. polit. action com. J.E. Seagram & Sons, Washington, 1984—; active Ringwood Council Girl Scouts U.S. Mem. Nat. Assn. Beverage Importers (chmn. imports com. 1987—), Womens Assn. Allied Beverages Industries, N.Y. Traffic Assn., N.Y. Assn. Female Execs., Bus. Women's Tng. Inst. (cert. stress mgmt. 1985). Democrat. Office: House of Seagram 375 Park Ave New York NY 10152-0192

BREHM, DEBORAH LEE, theatre company executive; b. Lincoln, Nebr., Jan. 26, 1950; d. Russell Dwayne and Ellen Josephine (Mares) B. BS in Edn., U. Nebr., 1972. Spl. edn. tchr. Dallas Pub. Schs., 1972-74, Lincoln Pub. Schs., 1974-78; advt. dir. Douglas Theatre Co., Lincoln, 1978-85, v.p., 1980—; bd. dirs. Ctr. Assocs. organizer Children's Free Christmas Party, Douglas Theatre Co., 1982—; county chmn. Kay Orr for Gov. campaign, Lincoln, 1986; vol. Nebr. Rep. Party, Lancaster Rep. Party; dist. chmn. U.S. Constitutional Bi-Centennial Commn. of Nebr., 1987—; bd. dirs. mgmt. com. YMCA, 1985—. Named Outstanding Vol. Nebr. Rep. Party, 1986, Lancaster County Rep. Party, 1984, 86. Mem. Quarter Horse Assn. Nebr. (futurity com. 1986—), MENSA. Republican. Lutheran. Office: Douglas Theatre Co 1300 P Lincoln NE 68508

BREHM, JUANITA R(OSE), entrepreneur; b. Pulaski Twp., Wis., Oct. 10, 1947; d. Arnold and Mary Gertrude (Neff) Richter; m. Michael Robert Brehm, May 5, 1946; children: Eric Michael, Kevin Michael. AA, Madison (Wis.) Bus. Coll., 1969. Legal sec. Lawrence Hall, Atty., Madison, 1969-70; computer operator Interstate Electric, Racine, Wis., 1978-79, system adminstr., 1979-85; owner, pres. Software City, Racine, 1985—. Mem. Data Processing Mgmt. Assn. (bd. dirs. 1983-84). Roman Catholic. Home: 2818 Orchard St Racine WI 53406 Office: Software City 4700 Washington Ave Racine WI 53406

BREHMER, MARCIA LYNNE, lawyer; b. Circleville, Ohio, July 31, 1949; d. Robert Louis, Jr., and Marilyn Elizabeth (Lutz) B. B.A., Miami U., Oxford, Ohio, 1971; J.D., Boston U., 1976. Bar: Ohio. Law Library clk. Supreme Ct. Ohio, Columbus, 1974; law clk. Leist & Kitchen, Circleville, Ohio, 1975; staff atty. Legal Aid Soc. Columbus, 1976-78, supervising atty., 1978-82, exec. dir., 1982—; commn. mem. Franklin County Pub. Defender, Columbus, 1983-88; bd. dirs. St. Mark's Health Ctr., 1988—. Vol. Am. Cancer Soc., Columbus, 1983-84, United Way, 1984-85. Mem. ABA, Ohio Bar Assn., Columbus Bar Assn., Ohio State Legal Services Assn. (bd. dirs.), Women Lawyers Franklin County. Episcopalian.

BREIDENBACH, CHERIE ELIZABETH, lawyer; b. Aberdeen, S.D., Aug. 20, 1952; d. Neil Allen and Portia Elizabeth (Bradner) Johnson; m. Steven Theodore Breidenbach, Aug. 9, 1975. BS, U. S.D., 1975, JD, 1979. Bar: S.D. 1979, Calif. 1981; CPA, Calif. Sole practice La Jolla, Calif., 1982-84; assoc., acct. Law Offices of Larry Siegel, San Diego, 1984-86; ptnr. Fout, Breidenbach & Chin, San Diego, 1986-88, Rose, Munns & Fout, Coronado, Calif., 1988—. Mem. ABA, Calif. Bar Assn., S.D. Bar Assn., Phi Delta Phi. Republican. Methodist.

BREMER, KENDA POWELL, health care executive; b. Versailles, Mo., Sept. 27, 1942; d. Kenneth Lee and Mildred Marie (Rasa) Spalding; R.N., Mo. Baptist Sch. Nursing, St. Louis, 1963; grad. in health systems mgmt. U. Mo., 1984; neuro nurse specialist Methodist Hosp., Houston, 1970; student social gerontology Central Mo. State U.; m. William Darrell Bremer, Aug. 5, 1972; 1 son, John Sanford Powell III. Infirmary dir. U. Corpus Christi (Tex.), 1964; staff nurse Thomas Spann Clinic, Corpus Christi, 1964-65, Meth. Hosp., 1965-70; unit coordinator Tex. Inst. Rehab. and Research, 1970-71; dir. nursing Westwood Nursing Center, Clinton, Mo., 1972; exec. v.p. ops. new projects and planning Brooking Park Geriatrics Inc., Sedalia, Mo., 1972-87; chief operating officer, Brooking Park, Inc. Mem. Am. Nurses Assn., Mo. Nurses Assn., Am. Coll. Nursing Home Adminstrs., Am. Health Care Assn., Mo. League Nursing Home Adminstrs., Sigma Phi. Republican. Lutheran. Club: Sedalia Altrusa (dir., treas. 1978-82). Home: Route 6 Box 148 A Sedalia MO 65301 Office: PO Box 1667 Sedalia MO 65301

BRENCHLEY, JEAN ELNORA, microbiologist, researcher, biotechnology director; b. Towanda, Pa., Mar. 6, 1944; d. John Edward and Elizabeth (Jefferson) B. BS, Mansfield U., 1965; MS, U. Calif., San Diego, 1967; PhD, U. Calif., Davis, 1970. Research assoc., Biology Dept. MIT, Cambridge, 1970-71; from asst. prof. to assoc. prof. microbiology Pa. State U., Univ. Pk., 1971-77, head. Dept. Molecular and Cell Biology, dir. Biotech. Inst., 1984-87; assoc. prof. then prof. biology Purdue U., West Lafayette, Ind., 1977-81; research dir. Genex Corp., Gaithersburg, Md., 1981-84; mem. bioprocess com. Nat. Acad. Sci.; bd. trustees Biosis, 1983—. Recipient Waksman award Theobald Smith Soc., 1985. Mem. AAAS (biol. scis. nominating com. 1987—), Am. Soc. Microbiology (pres. 1986-87), Assn. Women in Sci., Am. Soc. Biol. Chemists, Am. Chem. Soc. (com. Toxic Substances Control Act), Sigma Delta Epsilon (hon.). Office: Pa State Univ 519 Wartik Lab University Park PA 16802

BRENDEN, RITA ANN, microbiologist; b. Hannibal, Mo., Feb. 26, 1953; d. Ray Gustave and Rosemarie Virginia (Bopp) Wagner; m. Daniel Raymond Brenden, Aug. 28, 1977. AA, Mo. Bapt. Coll., 1973; BS cum laude, U. Mo., 1977; MS, Ill. State U., 1980, PhD, 1984. Med. technologist Pekin (Ill.) Meml. Hosp., 1977-83; postdoctoral scientist Mt. Sinai Hosp., N.Y.C., 1983-85; research assoc. U. Ill. Coll. Medicine, Peoria, 1986; chief microbiology Bronx (N.Y.) VA Hosp., 1986-88; research microbiologist Calgon Westal Labs., St. Louis, 1988—. Contbr. articles to profl. jours. Mem. Am. Soc. Clin. Pathologists (cert.), Am. Soc. for Microbiology, Nat. Assn. for Female Execs., Phi Sigma (treas. Beta Lambda chpt. 1981-82).

BRENNAN, ANCI ERZSEBET, small business owner; b. Szekszard, Hungary, June 15, 1954; came to U.S., 1968; d. Mihaly and Anci (Schneringer) Abel; m. Clifford Charles Brennan, June 15, 1985; 1 child, Esti. BA in Psychology, Cleve. State U., 1975. Salesperson Holiday Inns, Inc., Cleve., 1975-77; mgr. Today's Headlines, Inc., Rocky River, Ohio, 1978-83; pres., owner, mgr. Tomorrows, Rocky River, 1983—. Republican. Roman Catholic. Office: Tomorrows 19300 Detroit Rd Rocky River OH 44116

BRENNAN, EILEEN HUGHES, nurse; b. Atlanta, Sept. 26, 1951; m. David Lee Altizer, May 11, 1974 (div. Dec. 1978); m. Scott Curtis Brennan, Feb. 6, 1982. Student, North Ga. Coll., 1969-70; diploma, Ga. Bapt. Sch. Nursing, 1973; student, Tift Coll., 1970-73, Ga. State U., 1980-85, SUNY-Albany, 1986-88. Cert. nurse operating room, registered nurse. Orthopedic charge nurse Grady Meml. Hosp., Atlanta, 1974; operating room pvt. circulator DePaul Hosp., Norfolk, Va., 1974-76; nurse orthopedics Cabell Huntington (W.Va.) Hosp., 1976; surg. charge nurse VA Hosp., Huntington, 1976-77; mem. operating room open heart team VA Hosp., 1986—; orthopedic nurse specialist Peachtree Orthopedic Clinic, Atlanta, 1982; operating room charge nurse Doctors Meml. Hosp., Atlanta, 1982-85, chmn. operating room policy and procedures, 1982 84. Editor: Urology Pamphlet, 1986, Open Heart Instrumentation, 1987. Vol. ARC, Atlanta, 1970-88, Am. Heart Assn., Atlanta, 1987-88, Atlanta Lung Assn., 1985-88, Am. Lung Assn., Atlanta, 1988. Recipient Cert., United Fund Campaign, Atlanta, 1981, Spl. Incentive award VA Med. Ctr., Decatur, Ga., 1981, Performance award Nurse Profl. Standards Bd., Decatur, 1987, Achievementaward, 1987. Mem. Assn. Operating Room Nurses (co-chmn. Project Alpha 1986-87), Nurses Orgn. of Va. Episcopalian. Club: East Lake Country (Atlanta). Home: 2044 2d Ave Decatur GA 30032 Office: VA Med Ctr 1670 Clairmont Ave Decatur GA 30033

BRENNAN, EILEEN REGINA, actress; b. Los Angeles, Sept. 3, 1935; d. John Gerald and Jeanne (Menehan) B.; m. David John Lampson, Dec. 28, 1969 (div. 1975); children: Samuel John, Patrick Oliver. Student, Am. Acad. Dramatic Arts, 1955-56. Appeared off-Broadway in Little Mary Sunshine (Theatre World award 1960, Obie award 1960, Newspaper Guild award 1960); appeared on Broadway in Hello, Dolly, 1964-66, appeared in nat. co. The Miracle Worker, 1961-62; films include Divorce American Style, 1967, The Last Picture Show, 1971, The Sting, 1974, Murder By Death, 1976, The Cheap Detective, 1978, FM, 1978, Private Benjamin, 1980 (Acad. award nomination for best supporting actress 1981, Golden Globe award 1981, Clue, 1985; in TV series Private Benjamin, 1980-81 (Emmy award as best supporting actress 1981); TV appearance in Off the Rack. Mem. Actors Equity, Screen Actors Guild, AFTRA. Roman Catholic. Office: STE Representation Ltd 211 S Beverly Blvd Beverly Hills CA 90212 *

BRENNAN, MAUREEN THERESE M.T., newspaper editor; b. Newark, Apr. 29, 1951; d. John Francis and Mary Angela (McDonald) B.; m. Richard Siebert Gralert, July 11. AA, Bergen Community Coll., 1971. Vet. technician Ridgewood (N.J.) Animal Hosp., 1966-72, Midland Park (N.J.) Animal Hosp., 1972-82; copy editor, writer Suburban News, Franklin Lakes, N.J., 1982-83, asst. mng. editor, 1983-84, mng. editor, 1984-86, columnist, 1984—; exec. editor Paramus, N.J., 1986—; rep. pub. relations for Tommy John, N.Y.C., 1980—; with pub. relations dept., sec. Ctr. for Life Enrichment and Renewal, Wyckoff, N.J., 1982-85. Contbr. articles to N.Y. Yankees mag., 1980-82. Clubs: North Jersey Press (awards), PICA (sec. 1984-85, v.p. 1985-86, pres. 1987—, awards). Home: 47 Van Riper Elmwood Park NJ 07407 Office: Suburban News 50 Eisenhower Dr Paramus NJ 07652

BRENNEMAN, MARY L., psychiatrist, consultant; b. Sewickley, Pa., Oct. 14, 1923; d. George Edward and Laura Marjory (Dryden) Black; m. Richard Henry Brenneman (div. 1971); children: Gayne Slay, James, Donna, Heidi. MD, U. Toronto, Ont., Can., 1947; MA in Pub. Health, U. Pitts., 1958; student, C.G. Jung Inst., 1975-78. Rotating intern Western Pa. Hosp., Pitts., 1947-48, resident I in pediatrics, 1948-49; resident II in pediatrics Children's Hosp., Pitts., 1949-50; pediatrician Pitts. Pub. Health Dept. and B.C.G. Vaccine Program, 1950-57, Kaiser Hosp., Hollywood, Calif., 1957-58, Santa Monica (Calif.) Hosp., 1961-62; resident I, 2, 3 in psychiatry Camarillo (Calif.) State Hosp., 1968-71, psychiatrist, 1968-73; day-care psychiatrist St. John's Hosp., Santa Monica, 1973-75; psychiatric cons. St. John of God Nursing Hosp., 1975—; staff psychiat. Met. St. Hosp., Norwalk, 1987—; clin. instr. U. Pitts. Pediatrics, 1950-57, UCLA, 1957-68; cons. staff Rancho Los Amigos Hosp., 1963-65; founder Prolixin Clinic St. John's Hosp., 1974-75; sch. physician L.A. Bd. Edn., 1962-68; psychiatric dir. Penny Ln. Inst. for Teenage Emotionally Handicapped, Sepulveda, Calif., 1975-80. Mem. Am. Psychiatric Assn., So. Calif. Psychiatric Soc., Los Angeles Soc. for Adolescent Psychiatry, West Soc. for Scientific Study of Sex, YMCA, Am. Med. Womens Assn., Sierra Club. Club: Sierra. Office: 10477 Santa Monica Blvd Westwood CA 90025

BRENNER, ANNE MANON, pediatrician, allergist; b. Jacksonville, Fla., Oct. 21, 1944; d. William Lambert and Aileen (Clark) B. BA, Tex. Tech. U., 1966; MD, U. Tex., 1971. Diplomate Am. Bd. Allergy and Immunology, Am. Bd. Pediatrics. Intern in family practice John Sealy Hosp. U. Tex., Galveston, 1971-72, resident in pediatrics, 1972-74; practice medicine specializing in pediatrics Galveston, 1974-77; fellow in immunology and respiratory medicine Nat. Jewish Ctr., Denver, 1977-80, sr. staff physician, 1981—; sr. staff physician Nat. Asthma Ctr., Denver, 1980-81; assoc. clin. prof. pediatrics U. Tex., Galveston, 1974-77; asst prof. pediatrics U. Colo. Health Scis. Ctr., Denver, 1981—. Contbr. articles to profl. jours. Mem. Am. Acad. Pediatrics, Am. Acad. Allergy and Immunology. Roman Catholic. Office: Nat Jewish Ctr Immunology and Respiratory Medicine Denver CO 80206

BRENNER, ARLEEN PASVANIS, nurse; b. Youngstown, Ohio, Oct. 8, 1947; d. Peter Alexander and Kathleen (Kefalos) Pasvanis; diploma Sch. Nursing Ohio Valley Hosp., 1968; m. Gary Rogers Brenner, June 19, 1976; children: Ashley Kate, Derek Gordon. Staff nurse Presbyn. U. Hosp., Pitts., 1968-69; asst. head nurse Ohio State U. Hosp., Columbus, 1969-72, staff nurse Dameron Hosp., Stockton, Calif., 1972-73; asst. clin. nursing coordinator, staff nurse Stanford (Calif.) U. Hosp., 1974—. Mem. Assn. Operating Rm. Nurses, Am. Women's Vol. Soc., Friends of Nursing Stanford U. Med Center. Greek Orthodox. Avocation: jazz exercise. Home: 1523 Altura Way Belmont CA 94002

BRENNER, ESTHER LERNER, fundraiser; b. Washington, July 27, 1931; d. Mayer and Ethel Sarah (Kawarsky) Lerner; children: Mayer Alan, Saul Daniel, Matthew H. BA with distinction, George Washington U., 1953; MBA, U. Judaism, Los Angeles, 1987. Speech therapist Alexandria area schs. for handicapped, Va., 1952-54; speech therapist, pvt. practice Los Angeles, 1954-62; tchr. Los Angeles area pvt. schs., 1962-72; exec. dir., lobbyist Mfrs. Assn., Los Angeles, 1980-82; exec. dir. Citizens for Constl. Rights, Beverly Hills, Calif., 1982-86; regional coordinator U.S. Holocaust Meml. Council, Washington, 1986-88; pres. Los Angeles Hebrew High Sch., 1987—. Mem. Beverly-Angeles Homeowners Assn. (pres. 1978-87), Westside Civic Fedn. (sec., bd. dirs. 1978—), Los Angeles; bd. dirs. Meals On Wheels, Beverly Hills, Friends of the Beverly Hills Library; v.p. Los Angeles Hebrew High Sch. Endowment Fund. Mem. Nat. Soc. Fund Raising Execs., Soc. of Calligraphers, So. Calif. Council of Jewish Communal Service, Phi Beta Kappa. Home: 1264 Beverly Green Dr Beverly Hills CA 90212 Office: 1875 Century Park E Suite 950 Los Angeles CA 90067

BRENT, LINDA RAE, producer, workshop leader; b. Coldwater, Mich., Feb. 18, 1945; d. Arthur C. Kellogg and Mary Ingrid (Rutzebeck) Cress; m. Thomas Baron Lief, Sept. 9, 1972 (div.); children: Shannon Marie, Barbara Anne; m. Charles Brent, Mar. 19, 1988. Grad., Burklyn Bus. Sch. for Entrepreneurs, East Burke, Vt., 1978. Ordained minister Ch. by the Bay, 1983. With advt. dept. First Travel Corp., Encino, Calif., 1973-77; ptnr. The Great Life, Inc., San Diego, 1978-84, Channel Light Prodns., Los Angeles, 1985—; workshop leader Inner Balance/Outer Expression; speaker on radio and TV in field. Contbr. articles to profl. jours. Mem. The Inside Edge. Office: Channel Light Prodns PO Box 3579 Santa Monica CA 90403

BRESALIER-KOODIN, JUDITH ABBY, college official; b. Bklyn., Apr. 29, 1947; d. Alexander and Ruth Dorothy (Daneloff) Shapiro; B.A., SUNY, Stony Brook, 1967, M.S., 1968; m. William Stephen Bresalier, Dec. 18, 1971 (div. 1983); 1 son, Alexander; m. Jeffrey F. Koodin, Aug. 18, 1985. Asst. dean for residence SUNY, Delhi, 1968-69; counselor Suffolk County Community Coll., Selden, N.Y., 1969-78, dir. acad. advisement programs, 1978-80, dir. student activities, 1980-85, counselor, 1985—. Bd dirs. Suffolk County chpt. ARC. Mem. Nat. Assn. Women Deans, Adminstrs. and Counselors, N.E. Assn. Pre-law Advisors, Nat. Acad. Advising Assn., NOW, Alpha Beta Gamma (hon.), Phi Theta Kappa (hon.). Jewish. Contbr. article to profl. publ. Home: 136 E Woodside Ave Patchogue NY 11772 Office: Spenk-Riverhead Rd Riverhead NY 11901

BRESCIA, BARBARA M., antique shop executive, artist, art researcher; b. N.Y.C., Mar. 6, 1923; d. Andreas and Lyna (Russell) Randel; m. Victor J. Brescia, Apr. 8, 1953; children—Valerie, Vance. Student Pratt Inst., 1941-44; B.S., Columbia U., 1945, M.A., 1946. Cert. art cons., N.Y. Tchr. art Union Free Sch. Dist., Elmont, N.Y., 1950-64, Unified Free Sch. Dist. I, Smithtown, N.Y., 1965-80, ret., 1980; pres. The Little Red Sled antiques, Port Jefferson, N.Y., 1981—. Mem. Smithtown Twp. Arts Council. Life mem. N.Y. Acad. Scis., AAUW, Am. Soc. Psychical Research. Republican. Methodist. Home: 190 Asharoken Ave Northport NY 11768 Office: The Little Red Sled Antiques 218 E Main St Port Jefferson NY 11777

BRESLAUER, ELLEN GIRDLER, financial executive; b. Santa Monica, Calif., Nov. 13, 1947; d. Lew and Lorena E. (Stripp) Girdler; m. Russell Lynn Breslauer, Aug. 27, 1967. BA, U. Calif., Berkeley, 1968, MBA, 1975. CPA, Calif. Statis. clk. Bank of Am., San Francisco, 1968-71, salary survey analyst, 1971; asst. to treas. BankAm. Realty Services, Inc., San Francisco, 1971-73, asst. treas., 1973-80, treas., 1980—; cons. Project Bus., San Francisco, 1983-87; sec., treas. BRE properties, Inc. (name formerly BankAm. Realty Service), 1987—, San Francisco, 1987—. Mem. fund council U. Calif.-Berkeley, 1982-83. Winner regional speaking contest Am. Inst. Banking, 1977. Mem. Am. Inst. CPAs, Calif. Soc. CPAs, Calif. Bus. Alumni (v.p. 1977-79), Phi Beta Kappa. Office: BRE Properties Inc Telesis Tower One Montgomery St Suite 2500 San Francisco CA 94104

BRESLIN, LORRETTA C. LYNDE, human resources director; b. Billings, Mont., Feb. 4, 1947; d. Myron Wayne and Eleanor Della (Graf) Lynde; m. Charles A. Breslin, Dec. 28, 1967. BA in Journalism, U. Mont., 1967, MA in Journalism, 1979. Sales rep. The Missoulian, Missoula, Mont., 1972-76; advt. dir. T&W Chevrolet, Missoula, 1976-78; sales mgr. The Messenger, Missoula, 1978-81; v.p. Sage Advt., Billings, Mont., 1981-83; sales mgr. Neighbors sect. Billings Gazette, 1983-84, dir. human resources, 1984—. Mem. Am. Mgmt. Assn., Am. Soc. for Tng. and Devel., Newspaper Personnel Relations Assn., Yellowstone Valley Personnel Assn., Mont. Assn. for Female Execs.,. Office: Billings Gazette 401 N Broadway Billings MT 59101

BRESLIN, MARY, college president; b. Chgo., Sept. 27, 1936; d. William J. and Margaret D. (Hession) B. B.A., Mundelein Coll., Chgo., 1958; M.A., Marquette U., 1961; J.D., Loyola U., Chgo., 1977. Bar: Ill., Fed. Ct.; joined Sisters of Charity of Blessed Virgin Mary, Roman Cath. Ch., 1961. Internal auditor Fed. Res. Bank, Chgo., 1958-59; asst. bus. mgr. Mundelein Coll., Chgo., 1964-67, bus. mgr., treas., 1967-75, v.p. bus. affairs, treas., 1975-85, pres., 1985—; cons., evaluator North Central Accreditation Assn., Chgo., 1978—, Middle State Accreditation Assn., Phila., 1981—. Home and Office: Mundelein Coll 6363 N Sheridan Rd Chicago IL 60660

BRESLOW, TINA, public relations executive; b. Phila., Feb. 18, 1946; d. Harry and Doris (Stein) Horowitz; m. Alan Breslow, Aug. 28, 1965 (div. 1970); children: Peter, Jennifer, Brett. Office mgr. Temple U. Ctr. City, Phila., 1976-79; publicist Temple U. Theater, Phila., 1979-81; pub. relations mgr. Hershey Phila. Hotel, 1981-83; dir. pub. relations Franklin Plaza Hotel, Phila., 1983-84; account mgr. Sommers Rosen, Inc., Phila., 1984-85; prin. Tina Breslow Pub. Relations, Phila., 1985—; pub. relations cons. Dock St. Beer, Phila., 1986-87, Sheraton Soc. Hill Hotel, Phila., 1985-86. chmn. pub. relations com. Phila. Convention and Vis. Bur., 1985. Recipient Super Communicator award Women in Communication, 1984, Best New Bus. Intro. award Phila. Better Bus. Bur., 1986. Mem. Phila. Pub. Relations Assn.,

Pub. Relations Soc. Am., Greater Phila. C. of C. (chmn. Image com. 1986). Jewish. Office: Tina Breslow Pub Relations 1718 Locust St Philadelphia PA 19103

BRESSANT, MICHELE RENÉE, government official; b. Perth Amboy, N.J., Aug. 7, 1956; d. Ronald and Evelyn Pauline (Hall) Bressant. BS in Psychology, U. Pitts., 1978. Undergrad. teaching fellow U. Pitts., 1978; info. operator Greyhound Buslines, Pitts., 1978; med. clk. typist VA Hosp., Houston, 1979-81, patient services asst., 1981-82, psychology technician, 1982; revenue officer IRS, Houston, 1982—. Vol. Rape Crisis Ctr., Houston, 1980, Income Tax Assistance Program, Houston, 1984. Recipient Golden Panther award U. Pitts., 1978, Suggestion award VA Hosp., Houston, 1981; named Employee-of-the Month group 1400 IRS, Oct., Nov., Dec. 1985, June 1986. Mem. Nat. Assn. Female Execs., Fed. Bus. Assn. Democrat. Baptist. Office: IRS 8876 Gulf Fwy Stop 5435 GF Houston TX 77017

BRETON, TRACY A., journalist; b. N.Y.C., July 16, 1951. BA in Journalism, Polit. Sci., Syracuse U., 1973. Reporter Danbury (Conn.) News-Times, summer 1972; reporter in legal affairs Providence Jour.-Bulletin, 1973—; vis. prof. Univ. R.I., Kingston. Past contbg. editor Auto Week mag.; contbr. articles to New Woman Mag. and otherprofl. and popular mags. mem. R.I. Supreme Ct. Com. on Cameras in Courtroom, Providence, 1980—, Italian Food and Wine Commn., N.Y., 1985—; fundraiser Internat. House of R.I., Providence, 1986—. Recipient Best Feature Story for large met. newspaper award UPI, 1976, Service to Women in R.I. award Gov.'s Permanent Adv. Commn. on Women, 1977. Mem. Providence Newspaper Guild (mem. Grievance Com.), Kappa Kappa Gamma Alumni Group (past pres. social dir.), Phi Kappa Phi Honor Soc. Democrat. Home: 335 Angell St Providence RI 02906 Office: Providence Journal-Bulletin 75 Fountain St Providence RI 02902

BRETSCHNEIDER, ANN MARGERY, histotechnologist; b. Newton, Mass., May 11, 1934; d. Herman Frederick and Elizabeth Louise (Brady) B.; B.S., Northeastern U., Boston, 1957; M.S., Rutgers U., 1979. Histopathologic technician NIH, Bethesda, Md., 1957-58; chief histologic technician U. Ala. Med. Center, Birmingham, 1958-61; chief med. technologist in histology, instr. Muhlenberg Hosp., Plainfield, N.J., 1961-67; instr. anatomy Northeastern U., 1967-68; research-teaching specialist U. Medicine and Dentistry-Rutgers U. Med. Sch., 1968—; workshop leader, cons. in field. Mem. Am. Soc. Clin. Pathologists (affiliate), Nat. Soc. Histotech., Electron Microscopy Soc. Am., N.J. Soc. Histotech. Co-author: Thin Is In: Plastic Embedding of Tissue for Light Microscopy, 1981. Home: 96 Lennox Ct Piscataway NJ 08854 Office: Teaching Labs UMDNJ R W Johnson Med Sch Piscataway NJ 08854

BRETT, ANNABELLE, educational administrator; b. Chelmsford, Essex, Eng., Dec. 23, 1947; came to U.S., 1950; d. George Fairburn and Josephine (Carlton) B. AB, Swarthmore Coll., 1969; doctoral candidate, Harvard U. V.p. Work Options, Unltd., Boston, 1978-87; tchr. Borough of Haringey, London, 1971-72, Newark (Del.) Pub. Schs., 1972-74; asst. dir. career services Radcliffe Coll., Cambridge, Mass., 1976-83; dir. career planning and placement, Grad. Sch. Edn. Harvard U., Cambridge, 1983—; v.p. Work Options Unltd., Boston, 1978-87. Mem. Assn. Sch. Coll. and Univ. Staffing, Am. Soc. Tng. and Devel., Am. Ednl. Researchers Assn., Am. Assn. Sch. Adminstrs., Mass. Assn. Women Deans, Adminstrs. and Counselors. Office: Harvard Grad Sch Edn Longfellow Hall Appian Way Cambridge MA 02138

BRETT, MAUVICE WINSLOW, educational administrator, consultant; b. Xenia, Ohio, May 24, 1924; d. Perle Alonzo and Lurena Belle (Hamilton) W.; m. John Woodrow Brett, Sept. 20, 1943; children—Diane, John, Anthony, Loretta. B.S. in Psychology, Howard U., 1944, M.S. in Psychology, 1946; Ph.D. in English, Union Grad. Sch., Cin., 1978. Tchr. English, Hertford County Schs., Winton, N.C., 1959-76, ednl. supr., 1977-80, dir. personnel, 1981—; cons. N.C. Council English Tchrs., Charlotte, 1979; com. mem. quality assurance program N.C. State Dept. Pub. Instn., Raleigh, 1980-81. Sec. Hertford County Arts Council, 1977; mem. Hertford County 400th Anniversary Com., 1982-83; trustee Elizabeth City State U., 1983—. Mem. N.C. Assn. Sch. Adminstrs. (dist. rep.), Am. Assn. Sch. Adminstrs., N.C. Assn. Supervision and Curriculum Devel., Bus. and Profl. Women's Club, Delta Sigma Theta. Home: Route 2 Box 260A Ahoskie NC 27910 Office: Hertford County Schs PO Box 158 Winton NC 27986

BRETT-MAJOR, LIN, lawyer; b. N.Y.C., Sept. 21, 1943; d. B.L. and Edith H. Brett; children from previous marriage: Dania S., David M. BA, U. Mich., 1965; JD cum laude, Nova Law Ctr., 1978. Bar: Fla. 1978, U.S. Dist. Ct. (so. dist.) Fla. 1978, U.S. Ct. Appeals (5th and 11th cirs.) 1981, U.S. Tax Ct. 1981, U.S. Dist. Ct. (middle and no. dists.) Fla. 1982, U.S. Supreme Ct. 1984, U.S. Dist. Ct. (mid., no. dists.). Internat. communications asst. Mitsui and Co., Ltd., N.Y.C., 1962; with dept. pub. relations and devel. St. Rita's Hosp., Lima, Ohio, 1965-66; reporter The Lima News, 1969-70; intern U.S. Atty.'s Office, Miami, 1977; sole practice Ft. Lauderdale, Fla., 1980—; participant Gov.'s Conf. on World Trade, Mia and Jacksonville, Fla., 1984—; speaker Bus. Owners Conf., Hollywood, Fla., 1986, Nova U. Law Ctr. 1988. Mem. Ft. Lauderdale Opera Soc., 1985—, Ft. Lauderdale Mus. of Art, 1985—. Recipient Silver Key award ABA, 1977. Mem. Assn. Trial Lawyers Am., Fed. Bar Assn., Fla. Bar Assn., Broward County Bar Assn., Univ. Mich. Alumni Assn., U. Mich. Gold Coast Alumni Assn. (pres. 1988—). Club: Propeller of U.S. (Port Everglades, Fla.) (nat. del. 1981—). Office: Galleria Profl Bldg 915 Middle River Dr Fort Lauderdale FL 33304

BRETZ, (ALMA) LINDA, library adminstrator; b. Far Rockaway, N.Y., Sept. 22, 1934; d. Rocco Joseph and Linda Alma (Ley) Mazza; B.S. in L.S., SUNY, Geneseo, 1956; M.F.A. in Dramatic Arts, Columbia U., 1959; m. Robert Lawrence Bretz, June 10, 1961; children—Erika Katharine, John Michael, David Reinhard. Librarian, N.Y.C. Public Library, 1956-59; asst. prof. library edn. SUNY Coll., Geneseo, 1959-66; librarian Lincoln br. Rochester (N.Y.) Public Library, 1966-67, head br., 1967-72; inservice tng. cons. Monroe County (N.Y.) Library System, Rochester, 1972-73, children's services cons., 1973-75, asst. dir. system, 1976-78, dir. Rochester Public Library and Monroe County Library System, 1978—; adv. com. Community Savs. Bank, 1981-84; del. N.Y. Gov.'s Conf. Libraries, 1978, White House Conf. on Library and Info. Scis., 1979; trustee Reynolds Library; mem. N.Y. State Profl. Librarians Cert. Exam. Com., 1973-78, chmn. 1977; mem. N.Y. State Edn. Commr.'s Adv. Com. Equal Opportunity for Women, 1985—. Registrar, Rochester Bach Festival, 1975—; bd. dirs. Opera Theatre of Rochester, 1981-85, Rochester Health Network, 1982-88, Genesee Health Service, 1986—, Rochester Area Health Maintenance Orgn., 1987—. Mem. N.Y. Library Assn. (councilor-at-large 1976-80, pres. 1982), ALA, Am. Soc. Pub. Adminstrn. (pres. Rochester-Monroe County chpt. 1979-80), Rochester Area Ednl. TV Assn. (nominating com. 1987—). Office: 115 South Ave Rochester NY 14604

BRETZFELDER, DEBORAH MAY, museum exhibit designer; b. Hazelton, Pa., Sept. 21, 1932; d. Joseph and Rose (Smulyan) Hirsh; m. Robert Bretzfelder, Dec. 24, 1955; children: Karl, Marc. Student, Syracuse U., 1950-53. Textile colorist, designer Cohn-Hall-Marx, N.Y.C., 1954-55; fashion coordinator Hecht's Dept. Store, Washington, 1956; free lance artist Washington, 1956-58; exhibits technician Smithsonian Instn., Washington, 1958-59, supr. exhibits prodn., 1959-63, exhibits specialist Nat. Mus. Am. History, 1963-75, visual info. specialist, project mgmt. officer, 1975-83, acting chief of design, 1983; chief of design Smithsonian Instn., 1983-87, assoc. asst. dir. exhibits and pub. spaces, 1987—; cons. various firms, orgns., mus. personnel, instr. mus. programs. Mem. violin sect. George Washington U. Orch. Mem. Am. Assn. Mus., Internat. Com. Mus., Nat. Soc. Hist. Preservation, Tau Sigma Delta. Jewish. Club: Potomac Appalachian Trail. Home: 2748 Woodley Pl NW Washington DC 20008 Office: Smithsonian Nat Mus Am History 14th and Constitution NW Room 5212 Washington DC 20560

BREUNIG, SUSAN BROCK, information systems specialist; b. Atlanta, Mar. 16, 1955; d. John Robert and Florence Lanell (Grainger) Brock; m. Edward Andrew Breunig, Mar. 21, 1981. AS in Math., Emory U., 1975; BS in Math., Ga. State U., 1980. Mortgage loan processor Churchill Mortgage, Atlanta, 1979-80; systems engr. Electronic Data Systems, Atlanta, 1980-84; systems analyst, infosystems officer Citizens & So. Nat. Bank, Atlanta, 1984-87, asst. v.p., mgr. internat. banking systems, 1987—. Democrat. Episcopalian. Home: 1986 Ellwyn Dr Chamblee GA 30341

BREVOORT, SHARON LYNN, data processing executive; b. Charleston, W.Va., Dec. 14, 1946; d. Frank Leroy Jr. and Mary Louise (Pierce) B. Diploma de Estudios Hispanicos, Universidad de Barcelona, Spain, 1968; BA, U. Del., 1969; MA, Ea. Mich. U., 1986. Computer programmer I E.I. duPont de Nemours & Co., Inc., Wilmington, Del., 1968-69, Ind. U., Bloomington, 1969-72; computer programmer II St. Joseph Mercy Hosp., Ann Arbor, Mich., 1974-75; programmer, analyst U. Mich., Ann Arbor, 1975-80; mem. tech. staff Comshare, Inc., Ann Arbor, 1980-82; sr. systems analyst U. Mich., Ann Arbor, 1982; sr. systems programmer, analyst ADP, Collision Estimating Services, Ann Arbor, 1983-84; product engring. group leader ISDOS, Inc., Ann Arbor, 1984-85; data processing systems mgr. Merit Systems, Inc., Troy, Mich., 1985—; sec., treas. Ω Mu Nications Corp., Ann Arbor, 1983-84. Author (with others): OHDS: An Introduction to Osiris Hierarchical Data Structures. Elder Calvary Presbyn. Ch., Ann Arbor, 1987—; elder commr. Presbytery of Detroit, 1987—; bd. dirs. Interfaith Christian Counseling, Ann Arbor, 1987—. Mem. Nat. Assn. Female Execs., Interex, Southeast Mich. User's Group (Hewlett-Packard), Phi Kappa Phi. Home: PO Box 2742 Ann Arbor MI 48106

BREWER, JANICE KAY, state legislator, property and investment firm executive; b. Hollywood, Calif., Sept. 26, 1944; d. Perry Wilford and Edna Clarice (Bakken) Drinkwine; m. John Leon Brewer, Jan. 1, 1963; children—Ronald Richard, John Samuel, Michael Wilford. Med. asst. cert. Valley Coll., Burbank, Calif., 1963, practical radiol. technician cert., 1963; D. Humanties, (hon.), Los Angeles Chiropratic Coll., 1970. Pres., Brewer Property & Investments, Glendale, Ariz., 1970—; mem. Ariz. Ho. of Reps., Phoenix, 1983-86, Ariz. Senate, 1987—. Committeeman, Republican Party, Phoenix, 1970, 1983; legis. liaison Ponderosa Rep. Women, Phoenix, 1980; bd. dirs. Westside Mental Healty Agy., Phoenix, 1983—. Named Woman of Yr., Chiropractic Assn. Ariz., 1983. Mem. Nat. Fedn. Rep. Women, Am. Legis. Exchange Council. Lutheran. Home: 6835 W Union Hills Dr Peoria AZ 85345 Office: Office of the State Senate State Capitol Phoenix AZ 85007 *

BREWSTER, ELIZABETH WINIFRED, English language educator, poet, novelist; b. Chipman, N.B., Can., Aug. 26, 1922; d. Frederick John and Ethel May (Day) Brewster. B.A., U. N.B., 1946; M.A., Radcliffe U., 1947; B.L.S., U. Toronto, Ont., Can., 1953; Ph.D., Ind. U., 1962; D.Litt., U. N.B., 1982. Cataloger Carleton U., Ottawa, Ont., 1953-57; cataloger Ind. U. Library, Bloomington, 1957-58, N.B. Legis. Library, 1965-68, U. Alta. Library, Edmonton, Can., 1968-70; mem. English dept. Victoria U., B.C., 1960-61; reference librarian Mt. Allison U. Library, Sackville, N.B., 1961-65; vis. asst. prof. English U. Alta., 1970-71; mem. faculty U. Sask., Saskatoon, Can., 1972—, asst. prof. English, 1972-75, assoc. prof., 1975-80, prof., 1980—. Author: East Coast, 1951, Lilloot, 1954, Roads, 1957, Passage of Summer, 1969, Sunrise North, 1972, In Search of Eros, 1974, Sometimes I Think of Moving, 1977, The Way Home, 1982, The Sisters, 1974, It's Easy to Fall on the Ice, 1977, Digging In, 1982, Junction, 1982, A House Full of Women, 1983, Selected Poems (2 vols.), 1944-84, 1985, Visitations, 1987, Entertaining Angels, 1988. Recipient E.J. Pratt award for poetry U. Toronto, 1953, Pres.' medal for poetry U. Western Ont., 1980. Mem. League Can. Poets, Writers' Union Can., Assn. Can. Univ. Tchrs. English. Office: Dept English, U Saskatchewan, Saskatoon, SK Canada S7N 0W0

BREWSTER, OLIVE NESBITT, librarian; b. San Antonio, July 19, 1924; d. Charles Henry and Olive Agatha (Nesbitt) B.; B.A., Our Lady of Lake Coll., 1945, B.S. in L.S., 1946. Asst. librarian aeromed. library U.S. Air Force Sch. Aviation Medicine, Randolph AFB, Tex., 1946-60, chief cataloger aeromed. library Sch. Aerospace Medicine, Brooks AFB, Tex., 1960-83, chief tech. processing, 1983—. Mem. ALA, Am. Soc. Indexers, Mensa. Anglican. Home: 1906 Schley Ave San Antonio TX 78210 Office: Aeromed Library USAF Sch Aerospace Medicine Brooks AFB TX 78235

BREWSTER, ROBERTA KAY, accountant, educator; b. Grand Island, Nebr., June 4, 1941; d. Robert S. Fox and Dorothy Mae (Deeds) Brown; m. Robert E. Brewster, Sept. 9, 1972 (dec. Dec. 1981); children: Tnita Dutro, Todd Pearson, Robert Pearson, Hank Pearson. BBA in Acctg., Nat. U., San Diego, 1980, MBA in Fin. Mgmt., 1981; postgrad., U.S. Internat. U., San Diego, 1987, Coll for Fin. Planning, Denver, 1988—. Asst. controller H.M. Electronics, San Diego, 1978-80; mgr. acctg. services Oak Industries, Inc., San Diego, 1984-87; registered securities rep. Am. Pacific Securities, San Diego, 1988; controller Robbins Research Internat., Inc., La Jolla, Calif., 1988—; adj. prof. Nat. U., San Diego, 1982—. Mem. Nat. Assn. Enrolled Agts. (lic.), Calif. Soc. Enrolled Agts., Nat. Assn. Accts. (faculty adv.), Nat. U. Alumni Assn. Republican. Office: Robbins Research Internat Inc 3366 N Torrey Pines Ct Suite 100 La Jolla CA 92037

BREYMAIER, ANN MEREDITH (MEREDITH CHENEY), writer, poet, educator; b. Elyria, Ohio, June 17, 1925; d. Harvey Chapman and Ethel Josephine (Steffen) Cheney; m. Robert William Breymaier, May 24, 1952; 1 foster child, Christina Lipe Torres; 1 adopted child, Walter William II. BA, Ohio State U., 1947; MA, Eastern Mich. U., 1972, MA in Lang. and Lit., 1986. Provisional secondary teaching cert., Mich. Asst. to editor Clintonville Booster, Columbus, Ohio, 1947-48; copywriter, performer continuity Sta.-WLEC, Sandusky, Ohio, 1948-49; typist Sta.-WERE, Cleve., 1950; record librarian, music shows producer Sta.-WDOK, Cleve., 1950-51, traffic mgr., 1951-52, also performer, writer, producer children's show, 1951-52; writer pub. info. Sta.-WEMU, Eastern Mich. U., Ypsilanti, 1977-80, also on-air work, 1978-80; substitute tchr. Ypsilanti Pub. schs., 1981—; coordinator newsletter writer Ypsilanti Food Coop., 1981-85; Latin tutor. Contbr. poems to lit. jours. and anthologies. Recipient 4th prize Seven Mag. Jesse Stuart Internat. poetry contest, 1975, 2d Place award Terre Haute Poetry Soc. Winter Contest, 1975, 2d prize Seven Mag. Jesse Stuart Internat. poetry contest, 1978, 4th prize Mich. Poetry Soc., 1974, 1st prize Mich. Poetry Soc., 1974, 2d prize Mich. Poetry Soc., 1975, spl. mention certs. World of Poetry contests, 1984—, Golden Merit award World of Poetry Conv., 1985-87. Mem. Women in Communications, Inc., Chimes, Mich. Reading Assn., Washtenaw Reading Council, Poetry Soc. of Mich., Alpha Epsilon Rho, Phi Mu. Club: Ypsilanti Area Garden (pres. 1981). Presbyterian. Avocations: reading, radio, television, writing for newsletters, gardening. Home and Office: 1376 Skyway Dr Ypsilanti MI 48197

BRIAN, SHARON LYNN, information systems technician; b. El Dorado, Ark., Nov. 23, 1946; d. Raymond Elbert and Beulah Lynn (Cook) Smith; m. Alfred Thomas Brian, Aug. 10, 1968; children: Christopher Aron, Kelly Lynn. BS in Math., So. Ark. U., 1968; postgrad., U. Houston, 1971-73, So. Meth. U., 1974-75. Tchr. math. El Dorado Pub. Schs., 1968-69; computer programmer, systems analyst, systems mgr. Tex. Instruments, Dallas, 1969-85, sr. mem. tech. staff, 1985-86; cons. dental offices, Tex., 1985—. Publicity chmn. PTA, Allen, Tex., 1985-86, pres., 1986-88; treas. United Meth. Women, Allen, 1976. Mem. Am. Mgmt. Assn., Guide Internat. (group mgr. 1984-86). Club: Plano Maple (Tex.) (pres. 1985-86). Avocations: reading, needlework, water skiing. Home and Office: Box 1137 Allen TX 75002

BRIASSOULIS, HELEN, educator; b. Rethymnon, Crete, Greece, Oct. 8, 1953; came to U.S., 1980; d. Michael and Anastasia Kapetanakis; m. Demetres Briassoulis; July 6, 1975; children: Alexia, Paraskevi. Diploma in Architecture, Nat. Tech. U., Athens, Greece, 1975; M in Urban Planning, U. Ill., 1984, PhD in Regional Planning, 1985. Registered archtl. engr., urban regional planner. Teaching asst. U. Ill., Urbana, 1983, research asst., 1983-85; instr. summer planning program in Greece U. Ill., Kavala, 1984; visiting asst. prof. U. Cin., 1986—; mem. team for planning projects Nat. Mortgage Bank of Greece, Urbana, 1983. Contbr. articles to profl. jours. Mem. Regional Sci. Assn. Office: U Cin Sch of Planning DAAP Cincinnati OH 45221-0016

BRICE, BARBARA ANN, educator; b. Hanover, Va., Feb. 13, 1947; d. Wallace Albert and Ada Marie (Lewis) Green; m. Thomas Cellous Brice, Dec. 17, 1968 (div. 1986); children: Thomas Cellous, Derrick Lamar. BA, Va. Union U., 1968. Thcr. Richmond (Va.) Pub. Schs., 1968—; instrnl. coordinator Westhampton Sch., Richmond, 1981—. Recipient cert. Gov. Chuck Robb, State of Va., 1984. Democrat. Baptist. Home: Route 1 Box 450 Rockville VA 23146

BRICKER, VICTORIA REIFLER, anthropology educator; b. Hong Kong, June 15, 1940; came to U.S., 1947, naturalized, 1953; d. Erwin and Henrietta (Brown) Reifler; m. Harvey Miller Bricker, Dec. 27, 1964. A.B., Stanford U., 1962; A.M., Harvard U., 1963, Ph.D., 1968. Vis. lectr. anthropology Tulane U., 1969-70, asst. prof., 1970-73, assoc. prof., 1973-78, prof., 1978—. Author: Ritual Humor in Highland Chiapas, 1973, The Indian Christ, The Indian King: The Historical Substrate of Maya Myth and Ritual, 1981 (Howard Francis Cline meml. prize Conf. Latin Am. History), A Grammar of Mayan Hieroglyphs, 1986; book rev. editor: Am. Anthropologist, 1971-73; editor: Am. Ethnologist, 1973-76; gen. editor: Supplement to Handbook of Middle American Indians, 1977—. Guggenheim fellow, 1982; Wenner-Gren Found. Anthropol. Research grantee, 1971; Social Sci. Research Council grantee, 1972. Fellow Am. Anthrop. Assn. (exec. bd. 1980-83); mem. Am. Soc. Ethnohistory (exec. bd. 1977-79), Linguistic Soc. Am., Seminario de Cultura Maya, Societe des Americanistes. Office: Tulane Univ Dept Anthropology New Orleans LA 70118

BRIDGE, PATSY ANN, nursing home administrator; b. Rushville, Nebr., July 9, 1942; d. James A. and Hazel L. (Watson) Johnson; m. Richard L. Bridge, July 31, 1960; children: Morgan, Terry, Kirby, Wendy. Student, Chadron State Coll. Exec. dir. Housing Authority, Hay Springs, Nebr., 1968-73; city clk. City of Hay Springs, 1973; adminstr. Pioneer Nursing Home, Hay Springs, 1973—. Editor: Hay Springs: 100 Years, 1985. Chmn. Hay Springs Centennial Com., 1983-85; mem. adv. council Chadron (Nebr.) State Coll., 1986—. Mem. Nebr. Health Care Assn. (bd. dirs. 1982-87, pres. we. dist.), Am. Assn. Health Care Adminstrs., Hay Springs C. of C. Mem. Soc. Friends. Lodge: Job's Daughters. Office: Pioneer Manor Nursing Home Box 310 Hay Springs NE 69347

BRIDGES, BERYL CLARKE, marketing executive; b. N.Y.C., Oct. 27, 1941; d. David and Edith (Foster) Clarke; m. R. Shaw Bridges, Sept. 2, 1962 (div. May 1985); children: Robert Shaw Jr., Margaret Clarke, John Morrison. BA in English, Philosophy, Wheaton Coll., 1963. Acct. exec. McMoran-Redington Pub. Relations, Greenwich, Conn., 1975-77; mgr. sales promotion Lindenmeyr Graphic Resource Ctr., Greenwich, 1977-79; corp. mgr. promotions Lindenmeyr Paper Corp., Greenwich, 1979-81; mgr. southeastern region Paper Sources Internat. (div. Cen. Nat. Gottesman), Hobe Sound, Fla., 1981-83; v.p. mktg. Paper Sources Internat. (div. Cen. Nat. Gottesman), L.I., N.Y., 1983-84; pres., dir. Rutherford, N.J., 1984—; cons. and lectr. in field. V.p. Greenwich Hist. Soc., 1974-77; mem. Jr. League, Greenwich, 1971-78. Mem. Am. Inst. Graphic Arts. Republican. Episcopalian. Clubs: Jupiter Island, Hobe Sound Yacht. Home: 214 S Beach Rd Hobe Sound FL 33455

BRIDGES, ELEUTHERIA (ELTRIA), artist, sculptor, interior designer; b. Adrianople, Turkey, Nov. 28, 1905; came to U.S., 1917, naturalized, 1943; d. Constantine Nicolaides and Aikaterine (Constantinou) Bezas; A.A., Cooper Union, 1926; student Art Students League, N.Y.C., 1925-26, Indsl. Sch. Art, N.Y.C., 1926-28, Grand Central Sch. Art, N.Y.C., 1928-29, William O. Forrest Summer Art Sch., Brooklin, Maine, 1932; m. Robert Wallace Bridges, June 22, 1933; children—Constance Louise (Mrs. Phillip Bodley), Rosalind Ellen. Stylist, Dennison Mfg. Co., N.Y.C., 1922; artist W.W. Brown, Engravers, N.Y.C., 1922-24; interior designer Darling Studios, N.Y.C., 1924-27; asst. to credit mgr. Mallinkrot Chems., N.Y.C., 1927; specialist for subscriber services dept. Moody's Investors Service, N.Y.C., 1928; asst. to sales devel. mgr. Fred F. French Investing Co., N.Y.C., 1928-29; free-lance artist, sculptor, interior designer, poet, author, 1947—; exhibited one-woman show, Blue Hill, Maine, 1968; mem. traveling art exhibit, Proctor & Gamble, 1932-34; exhibited group shows: Indsl. Sch.-Art, N.Y.C., 1927, Art League, Huntington, N.Y., 1963, 64, 65, Artists Group, East Meadow, N.Y., 1967, Solon Soc., Hempstead, N.Y., 1968, 69, 70. Mem. Solon Soc., Carman Ave. Artists Group, Huntington Twp. Art League, Sedgwick Hist. Soc., Daus. Penelope. Club: The Maine. Author: What Now, Iphigenia, 1971. Address: 2825 NE 21st Ave Fort Lauderdale FL 33306 also: Fairhill Sedgwick ME 04676

BRIDGES, EMMA LOU, cytotechnologist; b. Indpls., Mar. 25, 1924; d. James Alverson and Helen Carolyn (Baldock) B.; student DePauw U., Ind. U., Cornell U. Med. Coll. Research asst., instr. Papanicolaou Research Lab., Cornell U. Med. Coll., 1956-60; chief cytotechnologist Papanicolaou Cancer Research Inst., Miami, Fla., 1961-66; chief cytotechnologist, instr., research asst., teaching coordinator Hahnemann Med. Coll. and Hosp., Phila., 1966-70; chief cytotechnologist, instr. Temple U. Med. Coll. and Hosp., Phila., 1970-73; owner, supr. Mary G. Papanicolaou Lab. Diagnostic Cytology, Plainfield, Ind., 1979—; past chmn. tech. adv. com. Dade County (Fla.) Community Cervical Cytology Program; cons. in field. Mem. Am. Soc. Clin. Pathologists, Inter-Soc. Cytology Council, Am. Soc. Cytology (1st sec. cytotechnologists adv. com. 1957-59), Am. Soc. Cytotech., AAAS, N.Y. Acad. Scis., Delta Alpha Gamma. Author research papers in field. Address: 1407 Miami Ct N Plainfield IN 46168

BRIDGES, JOYCELYN YVETTE, naval officer; b. Hattiesburg, Miss., July 30, 1955; d. Olon Bridges and Eleanor (Maury) Wright; m. Ezekiel Bell, Apr. 11, 1973 (div. May 1980); children: Eleanor Elizabeth Bell. BA, U. So. Miss., 1978. Sec. U. So. Miss., Hattiesburg, 1975-76; counselor Vocat. Rehab., Hattiesburg, 1978-80; commd. ensign USN, 1981, advanced through grades to lt., br. officer computer ops. Fleet Combat Tng. Ctr. of Atlantic, 1981-84; personnel exchange officer Navy to AF, AF Manpower and Personnel Ctr., San Antonio, 1984-85; project liaison officer Navy Civilian Personnel Data System Ctr., San Antonio, 1985; asst. for mgmt. info. support Enlisted Programs Implementation Br., Washington, 1985-87, asst. for human immunodeficiency virus policy, 1987—. Vol. social services Community Outreach Program St. Augustine's Cath. Ch., Washington, 1987—. Fellow Women Officers' Profl. Assn.; mem. Nat. Naval Officers Assn. (program coordinator 1986-87), Nat. Assn. Female Execs. Republican. Roman Catholic. Home: 803 S Ode St Arlington VA 22204 Office: Mil Personnel Policy Command OP-135DII/OPNAVSUPPACT Washington DC 20356-2000

BRIDGETT-CHISOLM, KAREN, data processing executive; b. Jamaica, N.Y., Mar. 25, 1956; d. Leonard Lewis and Barbara Louise (Dennis) Bridgett; m. Darryl A. Chisolm, Sept. 15, 1984. BBA, Pace U., 1979. Programmer EBASCO Services, Inc., N.Y.C., 1978-80; mktg. specialist Computer Scis. Corp., Lyndhurst, N.J., 1980-83; mgr. project tng. Info. Sci., Inc., Montvale, N.J., 1983-84; project leader Sony Corp. of Am., Park Ridge, N.J., 1984-87; cons. The Hunter Group Inc., Balt., Md., 1987—; instr. LaGuardia Community Coll., Long Island City, N.Y., 1986—. Mem. The EDGES Group, Inc., Human Resources Systems Profls., Inc., Zeta Phi Beta Sorority, Inc. Office: The Hunter Group Inc 11 E Chase St Baltimore MD 21202

BRIDWELL, CHARMAINE CLAUDETTE, financial officer; b. Chula Vista, Calif., June 25, 1953; d. Charles Mike and Louise Julia (Flegal) Erreca; m. Dennis Wayne Bridwell, July 7, 1971 (div. 1976); 1 child, Joshua Wayne. Student, Southwestern Coll., Chula Vista, 1971. Bookkeeper Erreca's, Inc., Spring Valley, Calif., 1973-81, chief fin. officer, 1981—. Home: 1507 Sunrise Shadow Ct El Cajon CA 92019 Office: Erreca's Inc 8555 Paradise Valley Rd Spring Valley CA 92077

BRIEN, LOIS ANN, psychologist, educator; b. Cleve., Sept. 24, 1928; d. Alexander and Anne Lois (Katz) B.; m. Melvin Lintz, June 1961 (div. June 1964). BFA, Ohio U., 1950; MA, U. Ala., 1953; PhD, U. Iowa, 1959. Instr. Auburn (Ala.) U., 1953-55; clin. instr. Baylor Coll. Medicine, Houston, 1959-64; diagnostician Houston Speech and Hearing Ctr., 1959-64; faculty, speech com. Case Western Reserve U., Cleve., 1965-69; faculty, psychology San Francisco State U., 1970-72; pvt. practice San Francisco, 1969-79; faculty Calif. Sch. Profl. Psychology, Berkeley, 1971-79; pvt. practice Palm Springs, 1981-82; faculty, women's studies San Diego State U., 1983-86; pvt. practice Encinitas, Calif., 1982—; prof. psychology Nat. U., San Diego, 1984-87; dean Sch. of Psych. and Human Behavior Nat. U., 1987—. Contbr. articles to profl. jours. and textbooks. Commr. Marin County on the status of women, 1974-77. U.S. Office Edn. grantee, 1970-71. Mem. Am. Psychol. Assn., Calif. Assn. Marriage, Family Therapy, Am. Assn. Marriage, Family Therapy, Am. Acad. Psychotherapists NOW. Democrat. Jewish. Office: 1012 Second St Suite 200 Encinitas CA 92024

BRIER, HARRIET, theatre school director; b. Phila., Aug. 29, 1922; d. Ben and Gertrude (Lerner) Brier; m. Bernard Fine, May 23, 1942 (div. Mar. 1971); children—Diane Davids, Kenneth; m. Milton Glick, Mar. 19, 1971. Grad. Phila. Sch. Drama Art, 1940; student U. Pa., 1940-42, St. Joseph Coll., 1965, Barnes Found., 1969-76; postgrad. theater arts Villanova U., 1975. Practice tchr. creative dramatics Phila. Sch. System, 1962; dir. children's theater New Hope, Bucks County, 1963; dir. high sch. theater Cornelia Otis Skinner Playhouse, Lower Merion Sch. System, 1967; instr. improvisational theater Harcum Jr. Coll., 1967, Main Line Sch., 1971; tchr. Lower Merion Sch. Dist., 1971-74; dir. children Bala Cynwyd Library, Narberth, Pa., 1964-74, Belmont Hills Sch., Narberth, Pa., 1972—, Childrens Theatre Workshop, Main Line Ctr. of Arts, Haverford, Pa., 1975-79, ednl. activites Walnut St. Theater, Phila., 1979, children's theater Royal Palm Theater, Boca Raton, Fla., 1979-87, childrens theater workshop Palm Beach (Fla.) Recreational Ctr., 1987—; instr. creative dramatics Merion Elem. Sch., 1971, guides Bicentennial hist. tours Walnut St. Theater, Phila., 1975-76, children's theater Palm Beach (Fla.) Recreational Ctr., 1987—. Author: What Makes An Actor and Artist and Not Just a Performer, 1969. Mem. Am. Ednl. Theater Assn. Home: 605 Conshohocken State Rd Penn Valley Narberth PA 19072 also: 3400 Ocean Blvd Apt 1-1D Palm Beach FL 33480 also: PO Box 491 Palm Beach FL 33480

BRIERTON, CHERYL L. WOOTTON BLACK, lawyer; b. Hartford, Conn., Nov. 11, 1947; d. Charles Greenwood and Elizabeth (Grechko) Wootton; m. David Martin Black, Oct.12, 1968 (div. 1978); m. John Thomas Brierton, Sept. 6, 1982; 1 child, John Greenwood. BA, Wellesley Coll., 1969; JD, U. San Diego, 1982. Bar: Calif. 1983. Tchr., librarian Anglican High Sch., Grenada, West Indies, 1972-74; dep. dir. Transalpino Student Travel, Paris, 1975-76; asst. dir. adminstn. Project OZ, YMCA, San Diego, 1976-78; asst. coordinator policy and advocacy Community Congress San Diego, 1978-81; field dir. Calif. Child, Youth and Family Coalition, San Diego, 1981-83; asst. exec. dir. Community Congress San Diego, 1984-85; exec. dir. Calif. Child, Youth and Family Coalition, Sacramento, 1985-86; lawyer Defense Logistics Agency, Defense Depot Tracy, Calif., 1986-88, Dept. of the Navy, Mare Island Naval shipyard, Vallejo, 1988—; faculty Nat. Juvenile Judges Conf. Dispositional Alternatives Serious Offenders, 1982, 6th and 7th Nat. Conf. Juvenile Justice 1979-80; cons. San Diego Youth Involvement Project 1983-84, San Diego Youth and Community Services 1983-84, S. Bay Community Services, Chula Vista 1983. Scholar U. San Diego 1979. Mem. Juvenile Justice Commn., Golden Hill Neighborhood Justice Cen. Planning Bd, Regional Criminal Justice Planning Bd. Com. Judicial Process, MENSA. Home: 1329 Bancroft St San Diego CA 92102 Office: Defense Logistics Agy Defense Depot Tracy Tracy CA 95376

BRIGGS, HEATHER, lawyer; b. Bronxville, N.Y., Sept. 30, 1953; d. Philip and Jean (Sloan) B.; m. Peter Stephen Erly, Sept. 8, 1983. A.B., Middlebury Coll., 1975; J.D., U. Akron, 1978; LL.M., Georgetown U., 1982. Bar: D.C. 1979, Ga. 1983. Atty., Fed. Labor Relations Authority, Washington, 1979-82; assoc. Jackson, Lewis, Schnitzler & Krupman, Atlanta, 1982, Mack, Eason & Briggs, Atlanta, 1983-87, Downs, Rachlin & Martin, Burlington, Vt., 1987—. Editor Law Rev., Akron, 1977-78. Mem. ABA, Bar Assn. D.C., Ga. Bar Assn. Republican. Office: Downs Rachlin & Martin 199 Main St Burlington VT 05402

BRIGHT, BETTY SUIDA, air pollution control official; b. Harbor Beach, Mich.; d. David Frank and Suzanne (Olshove) Suida. A.A. in Bus., Eastern Mich. Coll. Commerce; A.A. in Liberal Arts, Macomb Coll.; B.A. in Polit. Sci., Wayne State U., later postgrad.; postgrad. U. Detroit, Cranbrook U.; grad. Congl. Sch., Washington, 1980; M.B.A., Central Mich. U. With product design office Chrysler Corp.; commr. Mich. Air Pollution Control Commn., 1982—; speaker to women's groups. Congl. candidate 18th Congl. Dist., 1980; mem. Mich. State budget com., 1982, state issues com., 1972; mem. Oakland County Exec. Com., 17th Congl. exec. com.; bd. dirs. Lincoln Republican Club; nat. del., Kansas City, 1976; nat. hon. sgt.-at-arms, Miami Beach, Fla., 1972; Rep. precinct delt.; mem. Oakland County campaign com.; mem. Mich. State com., 1980—; past v.p. Royal Oak Area Rep. Com. (Mich.); sponsor Mich. Opera Theatre; bd. dirs. women's com. Am. Lung Assn.; mem. Project Hope, Founders' Soc., Detroit Art Inst.; mem. women's assn. Detroit Symphony Orchestra. Recipient Women to Watch award Cobo Hall, 1980. Mem. Bus. Women's and Profl. Assn. (legis. liaison), Women of Wayne, Jr. League (past pres.), Internat. Platform Assn., Rep. Women's Bus. and Profl. Forum, Gold Key, Beta Sigma Phi, Pi Sigma Alpha, Sigma Iota Epsilon. Clubs: Detroit Yacht, Women's Econ. (publicity com.), Economic, Chrysler Mgmt. (Detroit). Address: 32608 Inkster Rd Franklin MI 48024

BRIGHT, DEBRA ANN, environmental consultant; b. Los Angeles, Sept. 17, 1957; d. Donald Bolton and Patricia Jean (McLaughlin) B. BS in Biology, U. So. Calif., 1979; MPH in Epidemiology, UCLA, 1982. Research asst. Alpha Therapeutics, Pasadena, Calif., 1979; environ. specialist Bright & Assocs., Placentia, Calif., 1980-83, v.p., 1983—; guest lectr. U. Calif., Irvine, 1986—. Pub. Health Service grantee, 1981-82. Mem. Am. Pub. Health Assn., Air Pollution Control Assn., Harbor Assn. of Industry and Commerce. Republican. Methodist. Office: Bright & Assocs 1000 Ortega Way Suite A Placentia CA 92670-7125

BRIGHT, LINDA JEAN, accountant, university official; b. Pittsfield, Ill., Nov. 9, 1945; d. Homer and Beverly D. (Turnbaugh) Ator; m. Talmadge C. Bright, Mar. 19, 1982; 1 dau., Kelle. BSBA, U. Albuquerque, 1979; postgrad. N.Mex. Highlands U., 1979-80; MBA, U. Houston. CPA. Acctg. supr. Lovelace Bataan Med. Ctr., Albuquerque, 1971-77; v.p., controller Empire Clarklift Inc., Albuquerque, 1977-81; asst. controller U. Houston, 1981-83, asst. v.p., 1983-84, treas., 1984—. Mem. Nat. Assn. Corp. Treasurers, Nat. Assn. Coll. and Univ. Bus. Officers, Nat. Corp. Cash Mgrs. Assn., So. Assn. Coll. and Univ. Bus. Officers, Tex. Assn. Coll. and Univ. Bus. Officers, U. Houston Exec. MBA Alumni Assn. (pres. 1988). Republican. Mem. Soc. of Friends. Home: 1042 Wakefield St Houston TX 77018 Office: Univ Houston 4600 Gulf Freeway Suite 603 Houston TX 77023

BRIGHT, S. EILEEN, manufacturing company executive; b. N.Y.C.; d. Harry G. and Bridie (Fegan) McNeill; m. Don K. Bright; children: Conor S., Erin Rose. BS in Food Sci. and Bus. Mgmt., Calif. Poly. Inst., 1978; postgrad., Tex. A&I, 1983. Quality control mgr. Del Monte Foods, Emeryville, Calif., 1978-80; contract specialist USAF, Kelly AFB, Tex., 1984-86; contract negotiator USAF, Sunnyvale, Calif., 1986-87; ops. mgr. Freshpack, Salinas, Calif., 1987—. Recipient Sustained Superior Perfromance award USAF, 1987. Mem. Inst. Food Technologists, Calif. Poly Inst. Alumni Assn. Republican. Methodist. Office: Freshpack 126 Sun St Salinas CA 93901

BRIGHT, SHERRY L., marketing professional; b. Kansas City, Mo., May 8, 1952; d. Joe Leonard and Marjory (Hentschel) B. BSEd, U. Mo., 1974, MSPH, 1975. Cert. tchr. Claims authorizer Social Security Dept., HHS, Kansas City, 1976-79, planning analyst Pub. Health Service,, 1979-82; mgr. mktg. analysis Am. Med. Internat., Houston, 1982-84, dir. mktg. support, 1984-85, asst. v.p. prodn. devel., 1985-86; v.p. mktg. Baystate Health Systems, Springfield, Mass., 1986—. Mem. Soc. Hosp. Pub. Relations and Mktg., Am. Health PLanning Assn., Am. Mktg. Assn., Health Service Acad. Club: Young Patrons of Art. Office: Baystate Health Systems 759 Chestnut Springfield MA 01199

BRIGNET, HELEN PAULETTE, human resources professional; b. Jasper, Ala., Mar. 18, 1947; d. Paul Joffre and Helen (Hall) B.; m. George W. Thompson III; children: Elizabeth, Adrienne Ann. BA, Birmingham-So. U., 1967; MA, U. Ala., 1971, PhD, 1980. Tchr. disadvantged children Huntsville (Ala.) City Schs., 1967-68; vocat. counselor Ala. State Employment Service, 1968-71; psychologist II, ward dir. Bryce Hosp., Tuscaloosa, Ala., 1971-74; tng. coordinator Ala. Dept. Mental Health, Montgomery, 1974-78, asst. dir. planning, 1978-83, chief, human resource devel., 1983—. Vice chmn. Ala. Task Force Mental Health and Deafness, Montgomery, 1981-86; chmn. cuuriculum com. Ala. Cert. Publ. Mgr. Program, 1985—; pres. Hospice of Montgomery, 1981-83; bd. dirs. Montgomery Community Action, 1981-83, Jr. League of Montgomery, 1982-87, also vol. Recipient Disting. Service award Ala. Council Mental Health and Mental Retardation, 1982. Mem. Am. Soc. Tng. and Devel. (bd. dirs. 1983-84, chmn. chpt. achievement 1983), So. Orgn. Human Service Educators (bd. dirs. 1981-86), NIMH (grant revewier 1987). Office: Ala Dept Mental Health & Mental Retardation 200 Interstate Park Dr Montgomery AL 36193-5001

BRILES, JUDITH, writer, consultant; b. Pasadena, Calif., Feb. 20, 1946; d. James and Mary Tuthill; M.B.A., Pepperdine U., 1980; children—Shelley, Sheryl. Brokers asst. Bateman, Eichler, Hill, Richards, Torrance, Calif., 1969-72; account exec. E. F. Hutton, Palo Alto, Calif., 1972-78; pres. Judith Briles & Co., Palo Alto, 1978-85, Briles & Assocs., Palo Alto, 1980—; instr. Menlo Coll., 1978-85, Skyline Coll., 1981-86; instr. U. Calif.-Berkeley Sch. Continuing Edn., U. Calif.-Santa Cruz Sch. Continuing Edn., U. Hawaii; mem. Woman to Woman: From Sabotage to Support. Pres., v.p., sec., bd. dirs. Foothill-DeAnza Coll. Found., Los Altos Hills, Calif., 1979-81; mem. adv. bd. Flint Ctr., Cupertino, Calif. Mem. Nat. Assn. Female Execs. (adv. bd. buswoman's. mag. 1981—), Peninsula Profl. Women's Network, Nat. Speaker's Assn. Republican. Club: Commonwealth. Author: The Woman's Guide to Financial Savvy, 1981; Money Phases, 1984, Woman to Woman: From Sabotage to Support, 1987, Dollars and Sense of Divorce, 1988, Faith and Savvy Too!, 1988. Home and Office: 558 Cambridge Ave Palo Alto CA 94306

BRILEY, MARTHA CLARK, insurance company executive; b. Glen Ridge, N.J., May 31, 1949; d. David Ormiston and Marion Jane (Drury) Clark; m. Richard Keith Dentel, Dec. 29, 1972 (dec. Feb. 1974); m. Joseph Coyle Briley, Mar. 25, 1978; children: Christopher, Alexis. AB, Brown U., 1971; MBA, Harvard U., 1978. CLU, 1986, ChFC 1987. Asst. treas., trainee Chase Manhattan Bank, N.Y.C., 1971-74, 2d v.p. corp. fin., 1974-76, v.p., team leader corp. lending, 1978-81; v.p. corp. fin. Prudential Ins. Co., Newark, 1981-83, v.p., treas., 1983—. Trustee Brown U., 1987—. Recipient Alumni Service award Brown U., Providence, R.I., 1984. Mem. Fin. Womens Assn. (bd. dirs.), Treas.'s Group N.Y., Assn. Alumni Brown U. (bd. dirs., mem. exec. com. 1982-87, treas. 1982-84). Republican. Presbyterian. Office: The Prudential Ins Co Am 745 Broad St Newark NJ 07101

BRILL, BONNIE, physical therapist; b. Charleston, S.C., Nov. 2, 1948; d. Harry Harris II and Virginia (Stern) B. Lic. phys. therapist. Pediatric phys. therapist Ga. State Health Agys., Atlanta, 1973-73; staff phys. therapist Peachtree Orthopedic Clinic, Atlanta, 1974; contractor Ga. Health Care Orgns., Atlanta, 1975-79; engr., cons. Medicas Systems Corp., Houston, 1979-81, Bay Area Hosps., San Francisco, 1981-82; chief phys. therapist San Francisco Gen. Hosp., 1982-83; dir. phys. therapy Ralph K. Davies Med. Ctr., San Francisco, 1983-84; contractor Calif. Health Care Orgns., San Francisco area, 1984-86; founder Pacific Phys. Therapy, San Francisco, 1986—; cons. in field. Mem. Am. Phys. Therapy Assn. (Calif. chpt., pvt. practice sect.), Eckankar.

BRILL, NORA KENDALL, public relations and marketing executive; b. Worcestershire, Eng., Jan. 28, 1931; d. Kenneth William and Sibyl Winnifred (Brown) Kendall; B.A., Queens U., Kingston, Ont., 1971; m. Lawrence Brill Mar. 8, 1957 (dec.); children—Dianne, Jonathan, Troy, Michael. Tchr., Arthur Murray Studios, Toronto and Havana, 1950-52; reservation agt. United Airlines, Chgo., 1953-54; society columnist Tampa Times, 1975-82; dir. pub. relations HFI Medinorm Div., Houston, 1983-85; mktg. dir. River's Edge Club, Tampa, 1985-86; freelance writer, 1986—; mem. Arts Watch Task Force, 1981; pres. Las Damas De Arte, 1972; bd. dirs. Tampa Symphony Guild, Guilders of Tampa Bay Art Center, Easter Seal Guild. Named Outstanding Vol., Tampa Bay Art Center, 1975; named Woman of the Year in the Arts, 1975, recipient Diana award NOW, 1979. Mem. Athena Soc. (dir.), PEN, Tampa Bay Press Club, Women in Communications. Democrat. Home: 10604 Ilex St Tampa FL 33618 Office: 2780 Riverside Dr Tampa FL 33602

BRILLIANT, BARBARA, television host, producer; b. Montreal, Que., Can., Sept. 24, 1935; d. Saul and Esther (Saltzman) Lecker; m. Erwin Brilliant, June 29, 1958; children: Bradley, Todd, Michelle. Student, McGill Tchrs. Coll., 1953, McGill Conservatory of Music; AA, Sir George Williams U., Montreal, 1955; BA in Psychology summa cum laude, Boston Coll., 1975. Tchr. Protestant Sch. Bd., Montreal, 1953-58, dir. drama sch., 1957-58; artist-in-residence City of Boston, 1978-83; TV host, producer Sta. WBZ-TV, Boston, 1979—; freelance writer, composer, lyricist; advisor Radcliffe Coll., Cambridge, Mass., 1985—. Actress Montreal area, 1957-58, Boston area, 1985—; artistic dir. City of Boston, 1985—; vocalist, mus. dir. Two on the Aisle, Newton, Mass., 1985—; speaker in field. Advisor Cultural Affairs Commn., Newton, Mass., 1980-82, Nat. Com. to Study and Resolve Problems of Older Ams., Boston, 1984—; mem. adv. bd. Radcliffe Coll. Women; spokesperson Alzheimers Disease and Related Disorders Assn., Boston, 1985—; mem. White House Conf. on Aging, Washington, 1981; mem. Time Capsule Harvard Schlessinger Library, Cambridge, Mass., 1980. Recipient Cert. of Recognition City of Boston, 1979, Media award Am. Assn. Retired Persons, 1980, Lifestyle Achievement award WW Group Internat., Boston, 1987; Nat. Press Found. fellow, Washington, 1987; named to Hon. Order Ky. Cols., 1987, One of Boston's 100 Most Interesting Women, Boston Woman Mag., 1988. Mem. Screen Actors Guild, Am. Fedn. TV and Radio Artists. Office: Sta WBZ-TV 1170 Soldiers Field Rd Newton MA 02134

BRINCKMAN, MICHELLE LYNN, legal assistant; b. Alexandria, Va., Aug. 10, 1968; d. Johnathon Joseph Squires and Donna Lee (Timberlake) Testerman; m. Kevin Terry Brinckman, Feb. 28, 1987; 1 child, Heather Ashley. Grad., NRI Paralegal Inst., 1987. Seminar coordinator Padgett-Thompson, Leawood, Kans., 1985-87; sales cons. Mary Kay Cosmetics, Dallas, 1987—; pvt. practice leagl asst. Lenexa, Kans., 1988—. Mem. Nat. Assn. Female Execs. (bd. dirs. 1988—). Democrat. Baptist. Home and Office: 8704 Pflumm Ct Lenexa KS 66215

BRINKER, MARLENE ANN, health care executive; b. Greene, Iowa, Apr. 12, 1934; d. Bernard Charles and Marian Bertha (Crimmings) Dailey; R.N., St. Mary's Hosp., Rochester, Minn., 1955; B.A. in Geology, Rutgers U., 1975; m. Ray Brinker, Jan. 12, 1957; children—Sally Jean, Marc Henry, Sheri Louise, Sara Jane, Lisa Ann, Wendy Renee. Staff med.-surg. nurse VA Hosp., Iowa City, Iowa, 1955-57; nurse radiology dept. Mason Clinic, Seattle, 1957-58; staff nurse USPHS Hosp., Staten Island, N.Y., 1958; instr. nursing Holy Name Hosp., Teaneck, N.J., 1963-64, St. Luke's Hosp., St. Louis, 1967-69; supr. Kelly Services, Ann Arbor, Mich., 1979-80; service dir. Kelly Health Care, Ann Arbor, 1980-81, dist. mgr. for Mich. and Ind., 1981-83; pres. Brinker Cons., Inc., 1983—; bd. dirs. Vis. Nurse Huron Valley, chmn. community relations, 1985-86; mem. program and sub area coms. Comprehensive Health Planning, 1980-83. Mem. Pres.'s community relations bd. Rutgers U., 1975. Mem. N.Y. Acad. Scis, Nat. Assn. Home Care, Mich. Home Health Assembly, Fed. Legis. Com., Am. Assn. Continuity of Care. Democrat. Roman Catholic. Home and Office: 1622 Saddlebrook Ct Toledo OH 43615

BRINKLEY, BETSY ANNE, purchasing administrator; b. Richmond, Va., May 11, 1959; d. Martha Lou (Caplinger) B. BBA, James Madison U., 1981, MBA, 1983. Procurement analyst Calculon Corp., Germantown, Md., 1983-85; agt. purchasing, subcontracts ORI/Calculon Corp., Rockville, Md., 1986-87; adminstr. contracts ORI/Calculon Corp., Rockville, 1987—. Mem. beautification com. Watkins Mill Homeowner's Assn., Gaithersburg, Md., 1986—. Mem. Nat. Contract Mgmt. Assn. Democrat. Presbyterian. Home: 10232 Millstream Dr Gaithersburg MD 20879 Office: ORI/Calculon Corp 1350 Piccard Dr Rockville MD 20850

BRINKLEY, ELISE HOFFMAN, nurse, educator, biofeedback counselor; b. Barry, Tex., Mar. 10, 1922; d. James Edward and Laura Jack (Foster) Gay; R.N., Hermann Hosp., Houston, 1966; B.A. in Psychology, U. Houston, 1971; M.Ed., Prairie View U., Tex., 1973; postgrad. U. Tex., Austin, 1975-76; Ed.D. in Coll. Adminstrn., Nova U., Ft. Lauderdale, Fla., 1976; B.S. in Nursing, Tex. Womans U., Houston, 1982; postgrad. U. Tex., Galveston, 1978—; m. Billy Clarence Hoffman, June 20, 1941 (div. Nov. 1980); children—Rosilyn Gay, Billy May; m. Roger M. Brinkley, Nov. 26, 1981. Staff nurse labor, delivery and emergency room, supr. operating room Polly Ryon Meml. Hosp., Richmond, Tex., 1960-63, dir. Sch. Vocat. Nursing, 1966-71; campus nurse supr. Tex. Dept. Mental Health and Mental Retardation, Richmond State Sch., 1971-72; dir. asso. degree nursing program Alvin (Tex.) Community Coll., 1972-79, chmn. Bicentennial Show Case, 1976, also mem. pres.'s merit award com. for faculty, fin. and scholarship com., fin. affairs com.; instr. San Jacinto Coll., Pasadena, Tex., 1981-83, Midland Coll., 1983-85, Lee Coll.,Baytown, Tex., 1985—; biofeedback, counselor, 1984—; mem. Red Cross Nursing and Health Programs Adv. Com., 1974—; mem. Council Deans and Dirs. Nursing Schs. in Tex., 1975—; instr. cardio-pulmonary resuscitation Am. Heart Assn., 1976—; mem., conv. speaker Statewide Com. on Competencies, 1977—. Pres., Rosenberg PTA, 1953-55, Ft. Bend County PTA, 1956-57, Band Boosters, 1957-59; Rosenberg city chmn. Mothers March on Polio, 1954-58; mem. Gov.'s Com. on Drug Use and Drug Abuse, 1971-72; leader 4-H Club, 1952-54, Girl Scouts U.S.A., 1953-56; sponsor Alvin Nursing Students Assn., 1974-76; parliamentarian Democratic Party Ft. Bend County, 1970-71; bd. dirs. Salvation Army, 1958-60. Life mem. Nat. PTA, Tex. PTA; mem. AAUP, Tex. Jr. Coll., Alvin Community Coll. tchrs. assns., Am., Tex. nurses assns., Nat., Houston Area leagues for nursing, R.N.s of Ft. Bend County. Methodist. Club: Rosenberg Rebekah Lodge (past dist. dep. pres.). Author: Neurological Conditions of the Newborn, 1975; works listed in ERIC Clearinghouse for Jr. Colls., 1975, 76, 78. Home: 5114 Hwy 3 Dickinson TX 77539 Office: U Houston Clearlake 2700 Bay Area Blvd Houston TX 77058-1098 also: Peschel Psychosocial Services 1601 Main St Suite 302 Richmond TX 77469

BRINKLEY, PHYLLIS, speaker, program artist, stained glass artisan; b. Madison, Wis., May 28, 1926; d. Reynale R. and Florence (Jarvis) Crosby; B.A. in Speech and English, U. Wis., 1948, postgrad. in speech and oral interpretation of lit., 1949; m. William Malry, Jr., Aug. 5, 1949. Speaker, program artist, 1956—, current programs include First Ladies of our Land, Women of Worth, Portrait of the Lincolns, Mary and Abraham, Stained Glass: Gift of Light; radio artist Focus on Books, Sta. WHA, 1967-72; tchr. speech, 1951-56; interpretative reader, 1950-58. Vol. hosp. aux.; public affairs chmn. Madison Civics Club; pres. Madison Women's Mcpl. Golf League, 1959; chmn. Little Sisters of Sisters of St. Benedict, 1968-69. Recipient award of excellence Wis. Fedn. Women's Clubs; named hon. cannoneer St. Louis Civil War Roundtable. Mem. Internat. Platform Assn., Nat. League Am. Pen Women, Phi Beta. Author: Abraham Lincoln and His Wife, Mary: Two Human Beings, 1975; The Lincolns: Targets for Controversy, 1986. Home: 6115 Imperial Dr Route 2 Waunakee WI 53597

BRINSON, CHRISTINE LITZSINGER (TINA), university program director; b. St. Louis, Jan 29, 1951; d. Herbert Stuart and Alma Georgia (Dunford) Litzsinger; m. Ed Lane Brinson Jr., Dec. 27, 1972; 1 child, Ed Lane. BA in History and Secondary Edn., U. Wash., 1972; MEd in Student Personnel Work, Loyola U., 1977. From employment adminstr. to job analyst The Quaker Oats Co., Chgo., 1974-78; career counselor Western Wash. U., Bellingham, 1978-82, coordinator career planning services and programs, 1982-87, assoc. dir. career planning and placement, 1987—. Mem. personnel com. Mt. Baker Planned Parenthood, Bellingham, 1986-87; mem. steering com. YWCA Speakers program, 1986-87; mem. New Whatcom Choral Soc., Bellingham, 1977-87, bd. v.p.; trustee Gov.'s Mansion Found., Wash. Mem. Western Coll. Placement Assn., Kappa Kappa Gamma (co-chairperson area membership com. 1978-87). Office: Western Wash U Office Career Planning and Placement Bellingham WA 98225

BRINSON, ELAINE KOGER, real estate and securtiies broker; b. Charleston, S.C., Nov. 21, 1936; d. James Edgar and Hazel Elizabeth (Martin) Koger; m. Thomas Woodrow Brinson, Apr. 6, 1958 (div. 1979); children—Thomas Benjamin, Alise Michele; m. David Morris Wiggs, Mar. 27, 1983. B.A., Furman U., 1957; M.A.T., The Citadel, Charleston, S.C., 1978. Cert. secondary sch. tchr., S.C.; lic. real estate, securities , and ins. broker. Tchr., instr. jr. and sr. high sch. and tech. coll., 1972-83; ind. contractor comml. and investment real estate, 1981-84; assoc. realtor/broker Charleston Comml., Inc., 1984-86, Spectrum Properties, Charleston, 1986-87; owner, broker-in-charge Excel Properties, Inc., 1987—. Founder, pres. Meml. Soc. of Charleston, 1969—, Givens Found. (local investment group), 1983-84; model Citadel Mall Trend Bd., 1987—; bd. dirs. My Sister's House; active various community activities, programs committee chairmanships; bd. dirs., transp. coordinator HELP, 1969-71; rep. Lutheran Service Ctr., 1967-69; Luther League advisor, nursery chmn., adult Sunday sch. tchr., pres. and v.p. Churchwomen, Faith Luth. Ch., 1962-70. Named Mrs. South Carolina, 1969. Mem. Nat. Assn. Realtors, Trident Bd. Realtors, Comml. and Investment Properties Council of Charleston, Cert. Comml. Investment, Realtors Nat. Mktg. Inst., Nat. Assn. Female Execs., Am. Congress Real Estate Investors, Am. Soc. Prevention Cruelty to Animals, NEA (del. 1983), S.C. Edn. Assn. (rep. 1982-83), Charleston County Edn. Assn. (rep. 1982-83), Charleston Women's Network, Trident C. of C. (mem. leadership council 1986-87, legis. task force, mem. Transpn. com. 1987—, chmn. scholarship com. 1987—), Beta Sigma Phi (pres. Alpha Tau chpt. 1965-66, pres. city-wide 1966-67). Avocations: rare coin collecting, gardening, gourmet cooking, sailing, swimming. Lodge: Kiwanis (bd. dirs. North Charleston club). Home: 16 Edenwood Ct Charleston SC 29407 Office: Excel Properties Inc 2231 Technical Pkwy Suite A Charleston SC 29418

BRINTON, JANE, record promotions and management company executive; b. England, Aug. 8, 1950; came to U.S., 1970; d. Leslie Aisne and Dorothy May (Crumpton) B. Student, Castle Coll., Dudley, England, 1966. Sec. Joseph Lucas Auto Parts, Los Angeles, 1970-72; v.p., co-founder Aristocrat Discotheques, Inc., Los Angeles, 1972-76; v.p. David Wallace Pub. Relations & Advt., Los Angeles, 1973-76; dir. publicity internat. promotion Salsoul Records, N.Y.C., 1977-78; chart co-ordinator Billboard Publs., Los Angeles, 1978; v.p. Tom Hayden Record Promotions, Los Angeles, 1978-79; pres., founder Brinton & Co., Los Angeles, 1979-80; v.p., gen. mgr. Pavillion Records div. CBS, N.Y.C., 1980-83; pres., founder This Beats Workin', N.Y.C., 1983—. Named Promotion Person Big Apple Urban Cont. Music Awards, N.Y.C., 1980; recipient Gold Records, 1980-84. Anglican. Home and Office: This Beats Workin' Mgmt 330 W 56th St 7M New York NY 10019

BRISCOE, ANNE M., scientist, educator; b. N.Y.C., Dec. 1, 1918; M.A., Vassar Coll., 1945; Ph.D. (Sterling jr. fellow, USPHS fellow), Yale U., 1949; m. William A. Briscoe, Aug. 20, 1955. From research asso. to asst. prof. Cornell U. Med. Coll., 1950-56; faculty Columbia U. Coll. Physicians and Surgeons, N.Y.C., 1956—, prof. emeritus, 1987, spl. lectr., 1987—; lectr. Harlem Hosp. Center Sch. Nursing, 1968-77; adj. asst. prof. Hunter Coll., 1951-64, 73-75. Mem. N.Y.C. Commn. on Status of Women, 1979—, vice chairperson, 1982—; non-govtl. orgn. del. to UN; mem. adv. council Inst. Nuclear Power Ops., 1979-84. Fellow Am. Inst. Chemists (sec. N.Y. chpt. 1981-83). Recipient Yale medal, 1986 N.Y. Acad. Scis. (chairperson women in sci. com. 1978—, bd. govs. 1981); mem. AAAS (mem. council 1982-85), Am. Chem. Soc., Am. Soc. Clin. Nutrition, Am. Fedn. Clin. Research, Harvey Soc., Fedn. Orgns. for Profl. Women (treas. 1978-80), Assn. Women in Sci. Ednl. Founds. (pres. 1978-82), Assn. Women in Sci. (editor newsletter 1971-74, nat. pres. 1974-76), Assn. Yale Alumni (assembly rep. 1978—, bd. govs. 1982-85), Yale Grad. Sch. Alumni Assn. (pres. 1981-82). Contbr. articles to profl. jours.). Contbr. articles to profl. jours. Home: 2 Peter Cooper Rd New York NY 10010 Office: Harlem Hosp Ctr Dept Medicine New York NY 10037

BRISCOE, CATHERINE GRAY, investment firm executive; b. Roanoke, Va., May 15, 1920; d. Wilfred Wysor and Virginia Lucille Gray; m. Dan Edward Briscoe, Jr., Nov. 22, 1939; children—Dana Briscoe Robinette, Cary Gray, David Edward. Student, East Tenn. State U., 1971, Va. Intermont Coll., 1982, King Coll., 1984. Ptnr., Briscoe Investment Co., Bristol, Tenn., 1950—; cons. interior design, Bristol, 1950—. Bd. dirs. Bristol YWCA, 1965-71, treas., 1969-71. Republican. Presbyterian. Avocations: collecting antique furniture and paintings; swimming; travel. Home: 221 Mapletree Dr Bristol TN 37620 Office: Briscoe's Motor Inn 2412 W State St Bristol TN 37620

BRISCOE, JOYCE ELIZABETH, accountant; b. Pampa, Tex., Aug. 28, 1950; d. Joseph Frank and Martha Enna (Cox) Fischer; m. Barry Bernard Briscoe, July 2, 1971; 1 child, Brian. B of Bus. Adminstrn., Tex. Tech. U., 1972, postgrad., 1973. CPA. Acct. Tenneco Chems., Houston, 1974-75; acct. metals div. Duval Corp. subs. Pennzoil Co., Houston, 1976-78, staff acct., 1978, sr. staff acct., 1978-81, mgr. staff acctg., 1981-82, mgr. corp. acctg., 1982-85; mgr. corp. acctg. Pennzoil Sulphur Co., Houston, 1985, mgr. acctg., 1985-86; mgr. oil revenue and royalty Pennzoil Co., Houston, 1986—.

Mem. Am. Inst. CPA's, Tex. Soc. CPA's (and Houston chpt.). Office: Pennzoil Co 700 Milam PO Box 2967 Houston TX 77252-2967

BRISKIN, JACQUELINE ELIZABETH, author; b. London; came to U.S., 1938, naturalized, 1944; d. Spencer and Marjorie Orgell; m. Bert Briskin, May 9, 1948; children—Ralph, Elizabeth, Richard. Author: (novels) California Generation, 1970; Afterlove, 1974; Rich Friends, 1976; Paloverde, 1978; The Onyx, 1982; Everything and More, 1983; Too Much Too Soon, 1985, Dreams Are Not Enough, 1987. Recipient LMV Peer award, 1985. Mem. Authors Guild, PEN.

BRISTOL, LINDA JANE, medical technologist; b. Houston, June 5, 1947; d. Carl Robert and Hattie (McKinney) Carlson; B.S., Lewis and Clark Coll., 1969; m. Thomas L. Bristol, Dec. 27, 1968; children—Robert, John, Elizabeth. Intern, Good Samaritan Hosp., Portland, Oreg., 1968-69; researcher U. Oreg. Med. Sch., 1969-70; staff microbiologist Kaiser Hosp., Portland, Oreg., 1971; staff med. technologist ARC Lab., Portland, 1971-72. Vol. coordinator Gubser Sch., Salem-Keizer Sch. Dist., 1987-88. Mem. Am. Soc. Clin. Pathologists, Alpha Gamma. Republican. Mem. Ch. of Christ.

BRISTON, LOUISE FITZGERALD, nurse; b. Moorestown, N.J., Mar. 24, 1935; d. Edward William and Katherine (D'Arcy) Fitzgerald; children: John Edward, Eric Charles. RN, W. Jersey Hosp., 1956; BS in Nursing, U. Pa., 1975; MS, U. Del., 1985. RN, N.J. Nurse W. Jersey Hosp., Camden, N.J., 1956-57, Mount Holly (N.J.) Hosp., 1957-59, Good Samaratin Hosp., Syracuse, N.Y., 1959-61, Syracuse Vet. Admininstn. Med. Ctr., 1961-64; med. staff nurse Phila. Vet. Administn. Med. Ctr., 1967-80, staff nurse ICU, 1969-70, surg. staff nurse ICU, 1970-73, night coordinator, 1973-78; nurse Wilmington (Del.) Vet. Administn. Med. Ctr., 1980-86; headnurse/supr. Coatesville (PA.) Vet. Adminstn. Med. Ctr., 1986—. Mem. Nurses Vet. Administn. (v.p. Coatsville chpt., nat. membership com.), Geromtology Council Am. Nurses Assn., Kansas City, Am. Nurses Assn. Roman Catholic. Club: Brandywine Valley Assn. Office: Coatesville Vet Adminstn Med Ctr Coatesville PA 19320

BRITT, GEORGETTA LEE CULTON, corporate executive; b. Junction City, Ky., Feb. 21, 1932; d. James Thomas and Anabel (Nevius) Culton; m. William Edward Britt, Dec. 25, 1955; children: James Edward, Susan Lee, Laura Anne. Degree in acctg., Spencerian Comml. Coll., Louisville, 1952. Acct. George C. Baird & Co., Augusta, Ga., 1963-65, E.H. Bridger, Raleigh, N.C., 1970-72; acct., asst. sec. Saleeby, Inc., Raleigh, 1972-74; corp. sec.-treas. Saieed Constrn. Co., Inc., Raleigh, 1974-77; sec.-treas., office mgr. Associated Fire Protection, Inc., Raleigh, 1977—. Co-chair Precinct for Rep. Party, Raleigh, 1970-73. Mem. Nat. Assn. Accts., Am. Soc. Women Accts. (charter), Nat. Assn. Women in Constrn. (bd. dirs. Raleigh chpt. 1976-77, 84-85, treas. 1977-78). Presbyterian. Avocations: swimming, dance, bicycling, bridge. Home: 425 Millbrook Rd Raleigh NC 27609 Office: Associated Fire Protection Inc PO Box 28022 Raleigh NC 27611

BRITT, RUTH EVANGELINE BURGIN, civic worker; b. Fayette, Mo., Mar. 15, 1907; d. Samuel Herschel and Lora (Miller) Burgin; student Wesleyan Woman's Coll., 1926-27; A.B., Tallahassee Woman's Coll., 1928; m. James T. Britt, Sept. 18, 1930; children—Thomas Burgin, Robert McCammon. Bd. dirs. Spofford Home for Children, 1937-38, Della Lamb Neighborhood House, 1937-38, YMCA, 1938-39; mem. Woman's City Club, Kansas City, Mo., 1931-73, chmn. hosp. com., 1931-35; mem. Guild Friends Art at William Rockhill Nelson Gallery, 1961-75; mem. fireside com. Kansas City Art Inst., 1948-49; mem. women's div. Kansas City Philharmonic Assn., 1966-78, Kansas City Mus. Assn., 1966-71; bd. mgrs. George H. Nettleton Home for Aged Women, 1968-73. Chmn. Christian-social relations Women's Soc. Christian Service, 1946-48, pres., 1937-38, chmn. missions, 1961-63; chmn. St. Francis Aux. of St. Francis Home for Boys, Salina and Ellsworth, Kan., 1946-48, supplies com. Community Chest Dr., 1951; vol. visitor for aged Mattie Rhodes Settlement House, 1948; Hosp. Gray Lady, 1948-50. Mem. UDC, D.A.R. (regent 1942-43). Methodist (mem. adminstrv. bd.). Address: 409 W 58th Terr Kansas City MO 64113

BRITTAIN, LAURA READING, dancer, educator; b. Longmont, Colo., July 25, 1945; d. David R. and Jeanne (McKibbin) Reading; AA in Theatre, Bakersfield Jr. Coll., 1965; BA in Theatre Arts, UCLA, 1968, MA in Dance, 1971; m. Darryl A. Brittain, June 28, 1969 (div.). Dancer, Gus Solomons Dance Co., N.Y.C., 1971-73; asso. prof. dance and dance edn., artist-in-residence N.Y.U., 1973—, dir. N.Y. U. Washington Sq. Repertory Dance Co.; performer Michelle Berne Dance Co., Marjorie Gamso & Dancers, Linda Diamond Dance Co.; choreographer; regional co-dir. Am. Coll. Dance Festival, N.Y.C., 1980; guest lectr. Jerusalem Rubin Acad. Music and Dance, 1982, 83. Recipient Prof. of Yr. award N.Y.U. Sch. of Edn., 1984; Mem. Nat. Dance Assn., N.Y. State Dance Assn., Am. Assn. Univ. Profs. Presbyterian. Democrat. Office: NYU 35 W 4th St New York NY 10003

BRITTON, DOROTHEA SPRAGUE, health organization administrator; b. Cleve., Oct. 30, 1922; d. Paul Epworth and Ruth Emily (Horrocks) Sprague; m. Alan B. Britton, Sept. 27, 1952; children: Dana Sprague Chabina, Deborah Beckwith Tracy Tuttle. AB, U. Mich., 1948, MA, 1949; postgrad., Columbia U., 1975. Mgr. personnel George Worthington Co., Cleve., 1951-52; pres. Tacydot Products, Scarsdale, N.Y., 1964-70; adminstr. program devel. Nellie J. Crocker Health Ctr., Ossining, N.Y., 1971-72; adminstrv. dir. vol. services Roosevelt Hosp., N.Y.C., 1973-77; dir. community and pub. relations Peoples Bank for Savs., New Rochelle, N.Y., 1977-80; dir. pub. relations St. John's Riverside Hosp., Yonkers, N.Y., 1980-85; coordinator Blood Services ARC Greater New York City, 1987—; lectr. on women and mgmt., handicrafts, community banking. Author: An Op-Art Easter Bazaar, 1959, Dot Britton's 1969 Bazaar Book, Dot Britton's 1970 Christmas Bazaar Book, The Complete Book of Bazaars, 1973, The New Volunteer, 1976, The Legends of Christmas, 1978, 30 Years of Christmas Nonsense, 1981, Christmas in Hudson River Valley, 1984, Four Centuries of Christmas, 1988. Mem. Am. Assn. Vol. Services Coordinators (cert.), N.Y. Assn. Dirs. Vols., Am. Soc. Hosp. Pub. Relations, Am. Soc. Dirs. Vol. Services, Am. Hosp. Assn., Savs. Bank Women N.Y., Pi Beta Phi. Clubs: Scarsdale Golf, Scarsdale Woman's. Home: 4 Rock Hill Ln Scarsdale NY 10583

BRITZ, DIANE EDWARD, investment company executive, chemical trader; b. York, Pa., June 15, 1952; d. Everett Frank and Billie Jacqueline (Sherrill) B.; m. Marcello Lotti, Sept. 9, 1978; children: Ariane Elizabeth, Samantha Alexis. BA, Duke U., 1974; MBA, Columbia U., 1982. Asst. mgr. Columbia Artists, N.Y.C., 1974-76; gen. mgr. Eastern Music Festival, Greensboro, N.C., 1977-78; v.p. Britz Cobin, N.Y.C., 1979-82; pres. Pan Oceanic Mgmt., N.Y.C., 1983, also bd. dirs.; pres. Pan Oceanic Advisors, Ltd., 1988—, also bd. dirs. Mem. Bus. Vols. For Arts; active Duke U. Ann. Fund Drive. Mem. NOW, Fin. Women's Assn., Internat. Platform Assn., Columbia Bus. Sch. Clubs: Quaker (N.Y.C.), Doubles, Wings Office: Pan Oceanic Mgmt Ltd 122 E 42d St Suite 205 New York NY 10168

BRIZUELA, BARBARA SUE, librarian; b. Chgo., Sept. 17, 1944; d. Thomas Patrick and Edith Barbara (Dorn) Moran; m. Hernan R. Brizuela, Aug. 9, 1969 (div. 1983); children: Benjamin G., Karen Moran. BA in Chemistry, Clarke Coll., 1966; MS in Info. Studies, Drexel U., 1984. Lab. technician Balt. City Hosps., 1966-68; research technician Loma Linda (Calif.) U., 1968-70; research technologist Sinai Hosp., Balt., 1973-76; research asst. Temple U., Phila., 1977-82; temp. reference librarian Phila. Coll. Pharmacy and Sci., 1983-84, reference librarian, 1985-88, head of pub. services, 1988—. Mem. Spl. Libraries Assn., Med. Library Assn., Phila. Regional Interlibrary Loan Group (steering com. 1982—), Beta Phi Mu (bd. Sigma chpt. 1986—). Office: Phila Coll Pharmacy and Sci 42d St at Woodland Ave Philadelphia PA 19104

BRIZZOLARA, AMY L., sales administrator; b. Chgo., Jan. 23, 1957; d. Robert John and Mary Jane (Arburn) B. Mgr. gen. merchandise Dominick's Finer Foods, Chgo., 1974-81; rep. sales McCormick & Co., Inc., Rosemont, Ill., 1981-84; mgr. dist. sales Chgo., 1984-87; mgr. sales Active Services, Inc., Chgo., 1987—. Democrat. Office: Active Services Inc 2590 E Devon #110 Des Plaines IL 60018

BRKLACICH, LYNN LOUISE, automobile dealership manager; b. Grand Rapids, Mich., Feb. 13, 1944; d. William Kaye and Rosemary Fay (Schmuck) McElwain; m. Michael George Brklacich, Nov. 19, 1971; 1 child, Scott. Student, U. Minn., 1968-69, LaSalle Extension U., 1973. With Savage Motors, Inc., Monrovia, Calif., 1970-87; bus. mgr. Savage Motors, Inc., Monrovia, 1980-87, Savage Hyundai, Monrovia, 1986-87; sec.-treas. Savage Hyundai/Savage Motors, Inc., Monrovia, 1986-87; owner Lynn Brklacich Acctg., Monrovia, Calif., 1988—. Mem. Automobile Dealers Mgrs. Assn. (bd. dirs. Los Angeles chpt. 1980—), Quota Internat., Monrovia Hist. Mus. also: Savage Hyundai/Savage Motors Inc 1451 S Mountain St Monrovia CA 91016

BROADBENT, AMALIA SAYO CASTILLO, advertising executive, graphic arts designer; b. Manila, May 28, 1956; came to U.S., 1980, naturalized, 1986; d. Conrado Camilo and Eugenia de Guzman (Sayo) Castillo; m. Darrie Noel Broadbent, Mar. 14, 1981; children: Charles Noel Castillo, Chandra Noel Castillo. BFA, U. Santo Tomas, 1978; postgrad. Acad. Art Coll., San Francisco, Alliance Francaise, Manila, Karilagan Finishing Sch., Manila, Manila Computer Ctr.; BA, Maryknoll Coll., 1972. Designer market research Unicorp Export Inc., Makati, Manila, 1975-77; asst. advt. mgr. Dale Trading Corp., Makati, 1977-78; artist, designer, pub. relations Resort Hotels Corp., Makati, 1978-81; prodn. artist CYB/Young & Rubicam, San Francisco, 1981-82; freelance art dir. Ogilvy & Mather Direct, San Francisco, 1986; artist, designer, owner A.C. Broadbent Graphics, San Francisco, 1982—. Works include: Daing na Isda, 1975, (Christmas coloring) Pepsi-Cola, 1964 (Distinctive Merit cert.), (children's books) UNESCO, 1973 (cert.). Pres. Pax Romana, Coll. of Architecture and Fine Arts, U. Santo Tomas, 1976-78, chmn. cultural sect., 1975; v.p. Atelier Cultural Soc., U. Santo Tomas, 1975-76; mem. Makati Dance Troupe, 1973-74. Recipient Merit cert., Inst. Religion, 1977. Mem. Alliance Francaise de San Francisco, Nat. Assn. Female Execs. Roman Catholic. Office: A C Broadbent Graphics 402 Jackson St San Francisco CA 94111

BROADHURST, RACHEL BARBER, real estate executive; b. Gastonia-Kings Mt., N.C., May 11, 1941; d. Robert Lee and Addie (Hall) Barber; m. James L. Broadhurst, Nov. 9, 1962; children: James L. Jr., Jeffrey L. Grad. high sch., Charlotte, N.C. Lic. real estate broker, S.C., N.C. Co-owner Real Estate Mart, Myrtle Beach, S.C., 1970-74; owner, broker McAlpine Marsh Broadhurst/Century 21, Myrtle Beach, 1974—; owner Barefoot Vacations, Myrtle Beach, 1980—; co-owner Century 21 Seacoast, Surfside Beach, S.C., 1984-87; S.C. rep. Nat. Brokers Council, 1984-85. Pres., chmn. Horry County Cancer Soc., Myrtle Beach, 1974-80; bd. dirs. Horry County United Way, 1978-80; mem. bd. adjustments City of Myrtle Beach, 1978-83, mem. planning/zoning bd., 1987—. Named Career Woman of Yr., Bus. Woman's Assn. Myrtle Beach, 1973, 87, Outstanding Young Woman Am., 1976; Realtor Yr. State of S.C., 1974. Mem. Nat. Assn. Realtors (Omega Tau Rho medal 1978), S.C. Assn. Realtors (Realtor of Yr. 1974), Myrtle Beach Bd. Realtors (pres. 1973-75, mem. honor bd. 1974-75, Realtor of Yr. 1974), Realtors Multiple Listing Service (pres. 1972-73), Bus. and Profl. Womens Orgn. (pres. 1978), Horry County Bd. Realtors. (pres. 1973-74), Realtors Inst. (cert. residential specialist, cert. broker mgr.). Republican. Baptist. Club: Pilot (Myrtle Beach). Lodge: Rotary. Home: 4706 Camellia Dr Myrtle Beach SC 29577 Office: Century 21 McAlpine Marsh Broadhurst Myrtle Beach SC 29577

BROADHURST, VIRGINIA MARY, real estate broker; b. Lawrence, Mass., Oct. 9, 1943; d. James Thomas and Mary Veronica (Gardener) Burgess; m. Arthur J. Broadhurst, Nov. 9, 1963; children: Arthur J., David J., Kathleen M. Broker, owner Classic Homes Va. Realty, Methuen, Mass., 1977—. Sec. Greater Lawrence Bd. Realtors, Methuen, 1984-86, bd. dirs., mediator 1988; bd. dirs. Mass. Bd. Realtors, Boston, 1987; pres. Metheun Rangers Athletic Assn., 1982. Mem. Merrimack Valley C. of C., Greater Salem Bd. Realtors. Roman Catholic. Home: 8 Weybosset St Methuen MA 01844 Office: Classic Homes Va Realty 147 Lowell St Methuen MA 01844

BROADWAY, ANGELA SHARON, lawyer; b. Charleston, S.C., Sept. 22, 1957; d. Reid Archie and Althea (Sineath) Broadway. BS, Med. U. S.C., 1980; JD, U. S.C., 1983. Bar: S.C. 1983. Law clk. Law Office Donald Rothwell, Columbia, part-time, 1981-82; assoc. Law Office Wheeler M. Tillman, Charleston, S.C., 1983-86, Tillman & McConnell, 1987—. Mem. ABA, S.C. Bar Assn., Charleston County Bar Assn., Assn. Trial lawyers of Am., S.C. Hist. Soc., S.C. Trial Lawyer's Assn., Phi Delta Phi. Club: Pilot (Charleston). Avocations: photography, sailing. Home: 1082 Meader Ln PO Box 935 Mount Pleasant SC 29464 Office: 6296 Rivers Ave Post-Courier Bldg Suite 202 North Charleston SC 29418

BROADWAY, NANCY RUTH, landscape design and construction company executive; b. Memphis, Tenn., Dec. 20, 1946; d. Charlie Sidney and Patsy Ruth (Meadows) Adkins. B.S. in Biology and Sociology cum laude, Memphis State U., 1969; postgrad. Tulane U., 1969-70; M.S. in Horticulture, U. Calif.-Davis, 1976. Lic. landscape contractor, Calif. Claims adjuster Mass. Mut. Ins., San Francisco, 1972-73; community garden coordinator City of Davis, Calif., 1976; supr. seed propagation Bordier's Wholesale Nursery, Santa Ana, Calif., 1976-78; owner, contractor Calif. Landscape Co., Stockton, Calif., 1978—, Design and Mgmt. Cons., Wallace, Calif.; NDEA fellow Tulane U., 1969-70. Mem. Am. Hort. Soc., Net. Assn. Gen. Contractors, Calif. Native Plant Soc., Stockton C. of C. Democrat. Office: Calif Landscape Co/Design & Mgmt Cons PO Box 122 Wallace CA 95254

BROCHIN, LEONA NELKIN, real estate management executive; b. Boston, Apr. 28, 1932; d. Samuel and Mary (Birnbach) Nelkin; m. Murry David Brochin, Sept. 20, 1959; children—James Lewis, Nathaniel Edward, Esther Elizabeth. B.A., Mt. Holyoke Coll., 1953; M.A., Columbia U., 1955, M. Philosophy, 1978. Pres. Ruxton Mgmt. Corp., Millburn, N.J., 1979—. Nat. chmn. steering com. for establishment of chair of Jewish studies Mt. Holyoke Coll., South Hadley, Mass., 1983—; bd. dirs. women's div. Jewish Community Fedn. of MetroWest, East Orange, N.J., 1984-85; bd. dirs., B/Nai Keshet, Montclair, N.J.; bd. dirs. Jewish Vocat. Services, East Orange, co-chairperson scholarship com.; bd. govs., Reconstructionist Rabbinical Coll. Mem. Internat. Council of Shopping Ctrs., Exec. Women of N.J., Bus. and Profl. Women (steering com). Democrat. Avocations: art collecting, reading, singing, walking, raising labrador retrievers. Office: Ruxton Mgmt Corp 225 Millburn Ave Millburn NJ 07041

BROCK, BARBARA HANAUER, accounting educator; b. Milw., Oct. 3, 1933; d. Erwin R. and Alice M. (Lehmann) Hanauer; m. F.W. Lander, June 9, 1955 (div. 1968); 1 child, Martha J. Lander Schwegler; m. Douglas H. Brock, Mar. 21, 1970. BS, SUNY, Buffalo, 1971, MBA, 1973, PhD, 1979. Cert. internal auditor, mgmt. acct. Assoc. prof. acctg. Canisius Coll., Buffalo, 1974—. Author: The Development of Public Utility Accounting in New York State, 1981. Mem. mgmt. assistance com. United Way, Buffalo, 1982—; treas. Erie County Com. on Rape and Sexual Abuse Inc. Mem. Nat. Assn. Parliamentarians, Am. Inst. Parliamentarians, Inst. Internal Auditors (gov. Western N.Y. chpt. 1983-85), Am. Soc. Women Accts. (nat. pres. 1985-86), Beta Gamma Sigma. Republican. Home: 135 Meadow Rd Buffalo NY 14216 Office: Canisius Col 2001 Main St Buffalo NY 14208

BROCK, CHARLOTTE ELAINE SALIBA, sales professional; b. Dothan, Ala., Nov. 29, 1956; d. Arthur Haleem and Hester Elaine (Tierce) S. BS, Auburn U., 1978. Chief vocat. evaluator Goodwill Industires South Fla., Miami, 1979-80; asst. adminstr. Jackson Meml. Hosp., Miami, 1980-83; sales rep. DePuy Orthopedics, Atlanta, 1983-85; occupational med. rep. Humana, Inc., Atlanta, 1985-86; account mktg. exec. Dental One, Atlanta, 1986-87; sr. sales rep. GTE/Chesapeake Directories Sales Corp., Atlanta, 1987—. Coauthor: Occupational Medical Representative Training Manual, 1985, Occupational Evaluator Manual, 1980, Patient Unit Assistant Manual, 1981. Pres. Turnberry Homeowners Assn., Marietta, Ga., 1986-87; active Am. Cancer Soc. Mem. Am. Soc. Exec. Women, Nat. Assn. Female Execs. Republican. Episcopalian. Club: Toastmasters. Office: CDSE 4 North Park Dr Suite 500 Cockeysville MD 21030

BROCK, JOYCE LAWTON, lawyer; b. N.Y.C., Sept. 7, 1948; d. Vasco Lawton and Rita (Castagna) B.; m. Robin L. Hitchcock, Dec. 30, 1981. BA, Cornell U., 1965; JD, U. S.C., 1978. Bar: S.C. 1978, U.S. Dist. Ct. S.C. 1981, U.S. Ct. Appeals (4th cir.) 1982. Law clk. to presiding judge S.C. Cir. Ct., 1978; asst. atty. gen. S.C. Atty. Gen., Charleston, 1978-81; ptnr. Durban & Brock, Charleston, 1981-82, Brock & Settlemyer, Charleston, 1982-83; sole practice, Charleston, 1983-84; ptnr. Brock & Hitchcock, Charleston, 1984—. Chmn. Cornell U. Alumni Assn. Secondary Sch. Com., 1978-80; head Cornell Club of Hilton, S.C. Recipient Outstanding Work award Am. Jurisprudence Soc., 1976. Mem. S.C. Bar Assn. (mem. ethics adv. com. 1981—), Charleston County Bar Assn., Dorchester County Bar Assn., Trident C. of C., Summerville C. of C., Am. Trial Lawyers Assn., ABA, S.C. Trial Lawyers Assn., S.C. Hist. Soc., Carolina Arts Assn., Order Wig and Robe. Home: 12 Wentworth St Charleston SC 29401 Office: Brock and Hitchcock 31 Broad St Sumnerville SC 29401 also: Brock & Hitchcock 107 W 5th N St Sumnerville SC 29483

BROCK, JUDITH ANNE, publisher, magazine editor, marketing consultant; b. McAlester, Okla., July 8, 1950; d. Eddie W. and Irene Laverne (Hicks) Lee; m. James Lavern Hodge, Jan. 30, 1970 (div. Dec. 1977); 1 child, Joshua Lee; m. Paul Edward Brock, May 31, 1980. AA in Bus., Crowder Coll., 1972. Pres. J.L.L., Neosho, Mo., 1981—, v.p., mktg. The Brock Corp., Neosho, 1982—; founder, editor In..Joplin (Mo.) Met. Mag., 1984—; founding pres. The Apricotery, Neosho, 1987—; dir. mktg. TechMark, Ltd.; entrepreneur, mktg. cons. Neosho, 1980—. inventor card games Josh, 1982, E.W. Lee, 1988. Pres. Neosho PTA, 1982-84. Named Woman of Yr., Beta Sigma Phi, Neosho, 1983-84; recipient Bringing Out Your Best award Budweiser Light, 1983. Mem. Am. Mktg. Assn. (exec.), Neosho C. of C. (retail dir. 1983-84), Gifted Assn. (pres. 1985—), Mensa. Lodge: Soroptimist (treas. 1984-85). Office: The Brock Corp 317 Fairground Rd Neosho MO 64850

BROCK, KATHY THOMAS, librarian, coordinator media services; b. Atlanta, Feb. 2, 1945; d. Charles Allen Sr. and Bessie Virginia (Friddell) Thomas; m. William Hiram Brock, June 9, 1968; 1 child, Kevin William. BA, West Ga. Coll., 1967, MEd, 1975; EdS, Ga. State U., 1985, postgrad., 1986—. Tchr. English various high schs. 1967-73; librarian Oak Mountain Acad., Carrollton, Ga., 1973-75; sch. media specialist Douglas County Bd. Edn., Douglasville, Ga., 1975—. Mem. Ga. Library Media Assn. (chmn. 1987-88), Am. Library Assn., Ga. Library Assn. (chmn. sch. div. 1980-82, parliamentarian 1982-86), Am. Assn. Sch. Librarians, Profl. Assn. Ga. Educators, Carroll County Geneal. Soc. (pres. 1986). Democrat. Methodist. Home: PO Box 833 Temple GA 30179 Office: Douglas county Pub Sch PO Box 1077 Douglasville GA 30133

BROCK, LUCY RAY BRANNEN, science educator; b. Atlanta, July 23, 1950; d. Rupert Guy and Madge Rabena (Williams) Brannen; m. Michael Levin Brock, May 1, 1983; stepchildren: Eric James, Jason Leon. BS, U. Ga., 1972; MS, N.C. State U., 1975, PhD, 1981. Lab. dir., research assoc. Ctr. Reproductive Research and Testing, Raleigh, N.C., 1981-85; head sci. dept. Wake Christian Acad., Raleigh, 1985—. Contbr. articles to profl. jours. Mem. N.Y. Acad. of Scis., Nat. Wildlife Fedn. (affiliate), World Wildlife Fund (affiliate), N.C. Zool. Soc., N.C. Wildlife Fedn. (affiliate), Nat. Assn. Female Execs., Sigma Xi. Republican. Baptist. Office: Wake Christian Acad 5500 Acad Dr Raleigh NC 27603

BROCK, MARILYN AMY, engineer; b. Kittanning, Pa., Sept. 30, 1957; d. Wilbur Larue and Fumie (Ohtsuka) Mathieson; m. Christopher W. Brock, May 19, 1984. B in Mech. Engring., Stevens Inst. Tech, 1979; postgrad., Rutgers U., 1980-85; M in Engring., cert. in mech. design, Stevens Inst. Tech, 1987. Registered profl. engr., N.J. Assoc. engr. Lockheed Electronics Co., Plainfield, N.J., 1979-81; sr. design engr. Ohaus Scale Corp., Florham Park, N.J., 1981-84, project engr., 1984-87, sr. project engr., 1987—. Inventor in field. Mem. NSPE, Am. Soc. Testing and Materials. Office: Ohaus Scale Corp 29 Hanover Rd Florham Park NJ 07932

BROCK, THERESA JEAN, educator; b. Ft. Worth, Aug. 30, 1929; d. Theodore Roosevelt and Naomi (Jones) Roberson; B.A., San Francisco State Coll., 1951; M.A., Mills Coll., Oakland, Calif., 1981; m. Buddy LeRoy Brock, Apr. 6, 1952; children—Angela Lynn, Richard LeRoy. Classroom tchr. Oakland Public Schs., 1969—, tchr. Crocker Highlands Elem. Sch., 1974-86, Elizabeth Sherman Elem. Sch., 1986-87; master tchr. San Francisco State U. and Mills Coll., 1970—; prin. Charles P. Howard Elem. Sch., Oakland, 1987—; presenter tchr. workshops; cons. Piaget Conf., Stanford U., 1977; tchr. cons. Bay Area Writing Project, U. Calif.-Berkeley; facilitator Project Learning Tree, 1981-82; writer social sci. curriculum Calif. Dept. Edn., 1981; mem. policy bd. Alameda/Contra Costa County Tchr. Edn. and Computer Center. Active Crocker Highlands Parent-Tchr.-Student Assn. Teaching activities filmed by Fuji Telecasting Co., Ltd., Tokyo, 1978; recipient Service award Calif. Congress Parents and Tchrs., 1978; Oakland Tchr. of Yr. award, 1981; Alameda County Tchr. of Yr. award, 1981; Marcus A. Foster Distinguished Educator award, 1987. Mem. Assn. Childhood Edn. Internat., Calif. Council Social Studies, East Bay Council Social Studies, Nat. Council Tchrs. of English, Assn. Supervision and Curriculum Devel., Nat. Council Tchrs. of Math., Calif. Math. Council, Alameda-Contra Costa Counties Math. Educators, NEA, Calif. Tchrs. Assn., Oakland Edn. Assn., NAACP, Nat. Council Negro Women, LWV (adminstrv. v.p. Oakland 1967-69), Delta Sigma Theta, Phi Delta Upsilon. Methodist. Home: 38 Drake Ln Oakland CA 94611 Office: 525 Midcrest Rd Oakland CA 94610

BROCKWAY, LAURIE SUE, journalist; b. N.Y.C., Dec. 18, 1956; d. Lee L. and Shirley Ruth B. A.A., Laguardia Community Coll., 1978; student Hunter Coll., 1978-81. Features editor The Bklyn. Paper, 1978-81; editor-in-chief The Iniator, N.Y.C., 1982-83; pub., editor The Transformer, N.Y.C., 1983-84; co-producer, writer The Brockway Good News Report, N.Y.C., 1984-85; N.Y. bur. chief Women's News, N.Y.C., 1983—, Manhattan corr., 1985—; account supr., Brockway Assocs., Inc., N.Y.C., 1985; co-producer, writer, host, news anchor/writer, moderator This Is the New Age, The One Show, Whole Life Expo. Contbr. articles to mags., newspapers. Recipient LaGuardia Meml. award, 1978; Laguardia Student Council scholar, 1978; Expository Writing award, LaGuardia English Dept., 1978. Mem. Transformedia (founding), Pub. Relations Soc. Am., Acad. TV Arts and Scis., Am. Woman's Econ. Devel. Corp., Am. Women in Radio TV, Nat. Acad. TV Arts and Scis., Women in Communications.

BROCZKOWSKI, DIANE CAROL, accountant; b. Bronx, N.Y., Feb. 28, 1958; d. Rino Lodovico and Dolores Estelle (Pagano) Godino; m. Daniel Louis Broczkowski, Sept. 22, 1984. BA, Moravian Coll., 1980. CPA, CMA, N.J. Supr. Coopers & Lybrand, Newark, N.J., 1980-85; sr. mgr. Beneficial Mgmt. Corp., Peapack, N.J., 1985—. Mem. Am. Inst. CPA's, N.J. Soc. CPA's, Inst. Cert. Mgmt. Accts., Nat. Assn. Female Execs. Republican. Home: 3310 Highfield Cir Bethlehem PA 18017 Office: Beneficial Mgmt Corp 400 Beneficial Ctr Peapack NJ 07977

BRODER, PATRICIA JANIS, art historian, author, lecturer; b. N.Y.C., Nov. 22, 1935; d. Milton W. and Rheba (Mantell) Janis; m. Stanley H. Broder, Jan. 22, 1959; children: Clifford James, Peter Howard, Helen Anna. Student, Smith Coll., 1953-54; B.A., Barnard Coll., Columbia U., 1957; postgrad., Rutgers U., 1962-64. Stock brokerage trainee A.M. Kidder & Co., N.Y.C., 1958; registered rep. Thomson & McKinnon, N.Y.C., 1959-61; ind. registered investment advisor 1962-64. Art cons., art investment advisor; writer on art history: books include Bronzes of the American West (Hebert Adam Meml. medal Nat. Sculpture Soc. 1975), 1974 (Gold medal Nat. Acad. Western Art 1975), Great Paintings of the Old American West, American Indian Painting and Sculpture, Taos: A Painter's Dream (Western Heritage Wrangler award, Border Regional Library Assn. award 1980), Hopi Painting: The World of the Hopis, Dean Cornwell: Dean of Illustrators, The American West: The Modern Vision (new award 1984, Trustees award Nat. Cowboy Hall of Fame 1984). Recipient Western Heritage Wranglers award for best article on Am. West, 1975; Gold medal Nat. Acad. Western Art. Mem. Western History Assn., AAUW. Home: 488 Long Hill Dr Short Hills NJ 07078

BRODEUR, MARIANNE, valve and instrument company executive; b. Springfield, Mass., May 1, 1951; d. Victor Louis and Miriam Alice (Malcolm) Bissonnette; m. Frederic Alcide Brodeur, III, Sept. 1, 1973; children—Frederic A. IV, Jaime Lynn, JoniBeth, Ashley Marie. Student Western New Eng. Coll., Springfield, 1980—. Salesperson, with customer relations dept. Atlantic Valve Corp., Westfield, Mass., 1976-82, sales mgr., 1979-82; founder, pres. Internat. Valve & Instrument, Springfield, Mass., 1982—, IVI

Rebuilders, Inc., Springfield, 1983—. Mem. Nat. Assn. Power Engrs., Instrument Soc. Am. Republican. Roman Catholic. Avocations: sailing; tennis; aerobics. Home: 75 Joanne Circle Feeding Hills MA 01030

BRODIE, DIANA MARY, manufacturing executive, musician; b. Washington, Dec. 17, 1947; d. James Cruden and Urania Mary (Stephens) B. Student, Elmira Coll., 1965-67, Pima Coll., 1976, Twin Lakes Vo-Tech., 1984. Designer jewelry Designs in Metal, Sperryville, Va., 1973-75; designer jewelry Tucson, 1975-76, Leslie, Ark., 1977—; prin. Brodie & Assocs.: Dist. for Success Motivation Inst., Leslie, Ark, 1986—; mem. standards com. Ozark Foothills Craft Guild, Mt. View, Ark., 1987; bd. dirs. Cove Creek Natural Foods Store, Leslie, 1981-84. Band leader Lunatic Fringe, Mason-Dixon Lyne, 1967-73, Rivershoes, 1986—. Mem. Nat. Assn. Female Execs., Searcy County C. of C. (bd. dirs. 1986), Leslie Mcht. Assn. Home: 211 Oak St Leslie AR 72645 Office: Designs in Metal 211 Oak St Box 161 Leslie AR 72645

BRODKIN, ADELE MEYER RUTH, psychologist; b. N.Y.C., July 8, 1934; d. Abraham J. and Helen (Honig) Meyer; m. Roger Harrison Brodkin, Jan. 26, 1957; children: Elizabeth Anne, Edward Stuart. BA, Sarah Lawrence Coll., 1956; MA, Columbia U., 1959; PhD, Rutgers U., 1977. Lic. psychologist, N.J. Research cons. Horace-Mann-Lincoln Inst., N.Y.C., 1959-61; sch. psychologist River Edge and Norwood Schs., N.J., 1961-66, Morristown (N.J.) Schs., 1967-69, Chatham (N.J.) Schs., 1969-73; cons. psychologist United Hosps. of Newark, 1973; assoc. dir. Infant Child Devel. Ctr. St. Barnabas Med. Ctr., Livingston, N.J., 1977-79; postdoctoral fellow Yale U., New Haven, 1978-79, Rutgers-Princeton Program for Mental Health Research, New Brunswick, N.J., 1981-83; clin. asst. prof. dept. psychiatry Med. Sch. U. Medicine and Dentistry of N.J., Newark, 1979—; vis. scholar Hastings (N.Y.) Ctr. for Life Scis., 1979; mem. Essex County Mental Health Adv. Bd., Essex City, N.J., 1985-87. Co-author: The Meaning of Psychotherapy, 1962; author, producer: (videotape documentary) Competing Commitments, 1984 (Best Ednl. Videotape award 1984), co-authoer, producer: Passage to Physicianhood, 1985, The Insidious Epidemic, 1986. Columbia U. Adelaide M. Ayer scholar, 1961. Mem. Am. Psychol. Assn., N.J. Psychol. Assn. (Psychol. Recognition 1982, 86), Am. Sociol. Assn., Am. Orthopsychiat. Assn., N.Y. Acad. Scis. Jewish. Home: 520 White Oak Ridge Rd Short Hills NJ 07078 Office: U Medicine and Dentistry NJ 100 Bergen St Newark NJ 08903

BRODMAN, ESTELLE, educator, librarian; b. N.Y.C., June 1, 1914; d. Henry and Nettie (Sameth) B. A.B., Cornell U., 1935; B.S., Columbia U., 1936, M.S., 1943, Ph.D., 1954; post-doctoral study, UCLA, 1959, U. N.Mex., 1960; D.Sc. (hon.), U. Ill., 1975. Asst. librarian Cornell U. Sch. Nursing Library, N.Y.C., 1936-37; asst. med. librarian Columbia Libraries, N.Y.C., 1937-49; asst. librarian for reference services Nat. Library Medicine, Washington, 1949-61; librarian, assoc. prof. med. history Washington U. Sch. Medicine, St. Louis, 1961-64; librarian, prof. med. history Washington U. Sch. Medicine, 1964-81, librarian, prof. med history emerita, 1981—; documentation expert UN Tech. Assistance program UN, Central Family Planning Inst., New Delhi, 1967-68; documentation expert WHO, New Delhi, 1970, Manila, 1983; documentation expert ECAFE, Bangkok, 1973, AID, 1975, UNFPA, 1976; Mem. Pres.'s Commn. Libraries, 1968-70, Mo. Gov.'s Adv. Commn. Libraries, 1977-78; study sect. NIH, 1971-75, chmn., 1973-75; instr. Columbia U., 1946-52, 84, Cath. U. Am., 1957; vis. prof. Keio U., Tokyo, 1962, U. Mo., 1971, 73, Washington U. Med. Sch., 1964-81. Author: Development of Medical Bibliography, 1954, Bibliographical Lists for Medical Libraries, 1950; Editor: Bull. Med. Library Assn, 1947-57; guest editor N.J. Medicine, 1988. Mem. ALA, Med. Library Assn. (spl. award 1957, Noyes award 1971, Gottlieb award 1977, Frank B. Rogers info. advancement award 1985; pres. 1964-65), Spl. Libraries Assn. (dir. 1949-52, John Cotton Dana award 1981), Am. Assn. History Medicine, N.J. Med. History Soc. (treas. 1985-88, v.p. 1988—). Home: 19-09 Meadow Lake Hightstown NJ 08520

BRODNAX-WATSON, SHIRLEY JEAN, microbiologist; b. Norfolk, Va.; d. John B. and Louise (Booker) Holloway; m. Jack Leon Brodnax, July 31, 1976; children: Melodie, Tracey, Maisha. AA, Contra Costa Coll., 1978; BS in Cell and Molecular Biology, San Francisco State U., 1985. Jr. accountant Philco Corp., Phila.; sec., supr. U.S. Govt., Phila. and San Francisco, 1968-76; research asst., microbiologist Kelly Tech. Services, Oakland, Calif., 1986; microbiologist Nabisco Brands, Inc., Oakland, 1986—. Kennedy King scholar Contra Costa Coll., 1978-80. Mem. Internat. Platform Assn. Roman Catholic. Home: 1537 Hellings Ave Richmond CA 94801 Office: Nabisco Brands Inc 98th Ave Oakland CA 94630

BRODOWSKI, JUDITH ANN, educator; b. Milw., Jan. 3, 1939; d. Norbert Anthony and Louise Angeline (Sowinski) B. BS, Alverno Coll., 1960; MS, U. Wis., Milw., 1972. Cert. elem. educator; cert. reading specialist; cert. coll. instr., Wis. Elem. tchr. Archdiocese of Milw., 1960-62; tchr. English Good Counsel High Sch., Chgo., 1962-63; tchr. jr. high schs. Archdiocese of Chgo., 1964-66; elem. tchr. Milw. Pub. Schs., 1966-76, reading diagnostician city-wide reading clinic, 1976-82, pod coordinator, 1982—; instr. Alverno Coll., Milw., 1985—. Dir. TV segment on reading disorders, Milw., 1985. Vol. food distbr. Marquette U. High Sch., Milw., 1986—; active Young Astronauts Club 21st St Sch, Milw., 1987; mem. Intergroup Council for Women. Mem. Internat. Reading Assn. (membership com. 1972-78), Delta Kappa Gamma (sec. local chpt. 1978-80, del. 1979, 1st v.p. 1980-82), Phi Delta Kappa (scholarship com. 1986-87), Pi Lamda Theta. Democrat. Roman Catholic. Office: Milw Pub Schs 2121 W Hadley Milwaukee WI 53221

BRODRICK, LOIS HUNTER, real estate broker; b. Altoona, Pa., Aug. 31, 1920; d. Frank Mathew and Faye (McKague) Hunter; m. Richard Boyd Brodrick, Apr. 20, 1946 (dec.); children—Victoria, Barrie Bea. BA, Pa. State U.-State College, 1942; postgrad. U. Calif.-Berkeley, extensions, 1978. Lic. real estate broker. Prin., Brodrick Real Estate and Devel., Shingle Springs, Calif., 1980-82; Brodrick Real Estate Co., Shingle Springs, 1982-84; rep. Titan Capital Corp., Sacramento, 1983—. Pres. Calif. Rep. Assembly, Lamorinda unit, Orinda, Calif., 1978; v.p. Orinda Rep. Women, 1977; bd. dirs. Hacienda Del Orinda Homeowners, 1978-79. Mem. Internat. Fin. Planners, Nat. Assn. Security Dealers (registered rep.), Kappa Kappa Gamma (past pres. Bay Area). Club: Cameron Park Country (Calif.). Home: 3490 Fairway Dr Shingle Springs CA 95682

BRODY, ANITA BLUMSTEIN, judge; b. N.Y.C., May 25, 1935; d. David Theodore and Rita (Sondheim) Blumstein; m. Jerome I. Brody, Oct. 25, 1959; children—Lisa, Marion, Timothy. A.B., Wellesley Coll., 1955; J.D., Columbia U., 1958. Bar: N.Y. 1958, Fla. 1960, Pa. 1972. Asst. atty. gen. State N.Y., 1958-60; sole practice, Ardmore, Pa., 1972-79; ptnr. Brody, Brown & Hepburn, Ardmore, 1979-81; judge Pa. Ct. Common Pleas 38th Jud. Dist., Norristown, 1981—. Mem. Montgomery Bar Assn. (dir.). Republican. Jewish. Office: Court House Swede St & Airy St Norristown PA 19404

BRODY, NANCY LOUISE, lawyer; b. Chgo., Nov. 17, 1954; d. Mitchell and Grace Yaden (Williams) Block; m. Daniel Matthew Brody, Oct. 28, 1979. BA, U. Mich., 1975; JD, Loyola U., Chgo., 1979. Bar: Ill. 1979, Pa. 1980, Ariz. 1981. Sec., gen. counsel Block & Co., Inc., Indiana, 1981—, also bd. dirs. Bd. dirs. Ind. YMCA, 1986-87. Named one of Outstanding Young Women Am., 1983. Fellow Am. Bar Found. (life), Pa. Bar Found (bd. dirs. 1984—, life); mem. ABA (ho. dels. 1987—, state membership chmn. Pa. 1986—), Ill. State Bar Assn., Pa. Bar Assn. (bd. govs. 1984-87, chairperson 1985-86 treas. young lawyers div. 1983-84), Internat. Platform Assn., Zonta (parliamentarian Ind. chpt. 1985-86, 87—), Pi Beta Phi. Republican. Office: 39 N 7th St Indiana PA 15701

BROER, EILEEN DENNERY, management consultant; b. Phila., Sept. 7, 1946; d. Vincent Paul and Jane Dorothy (Knight) Dennery; m. Paul Alan Broer, Nov. 26, 1970 (div. 1980); m. Charles Kenneth ReCorr, Sept. 10, 1981; 1 child, Matthew Vincent; stepchildren: Kenneth, Christopher. BA, Coll. Mt. St. Vincent, 1969. Media dir., control mgr. Merrill Anderson Co., N.Y.C., 1970-72; adminstrv. asst. fin. McCall Pattern Co., N.Y.C., 1972-74, personnel specialist, 1974-77, mgr. employee relations, 1978; dir. personnel Notions Mktg. Inc., N.Y.C., 1978-79; 2nd v.p. personnel Manhattan Life Ins. Co., N.Y.C., 1979, v.p. human resources, 1980-82; v.p. human resources McM Corp., Raleigh, N.C., 1982-85; pres. The Human Dimension, 1985—; bd. dirs. Ctr. For Health Edn. Inc.; lectr. bus. writing NYU, 1975-78. Mem. Human Resource Planning Soc., Orgn. Devel. Network, Nat. Assn. Women Bus. Owners (pres. N.C. chpt. 1988-89),Am. Soc. for Tng. and Devel., Raleigh C. of C., Gestalt Inst. Cleve. Office: The Human Dimension 975 Walnut St Suite 354 Cary NC 27511

BROGAN, AMY GENTHER, lawyer; b. Tarentum, Pa., Aug. 4, 1956; d. Richard and Patricia Joan (Gardner) Genthner; m. John J. Brogan, Aug. 17, 1985. BA, Dickinson Coll., 1978; JD, N.Y. Law Sch., 1985. Bar: N.J. 1985, N.Y. 1986. Atty. Warren, Goldberg, Berman, Lubitz, Princeton, N.J., 1985-87, Curry, Stein and Bennardo, Toms River, N.J., 1987—. Mem. ABA, N.J. State Bar Assn., N.Y. State Bar Assn., Ocean and Monmouth County Bar Assns. Home: 33 Sickles Pl Shrewsbury NJ 07701 Office: Curry Stein & Bennardo 505 Main St Toms River NJ 08753

BROGAN-WERNTZ, BONNIE B., police officer, municipal agency administrator; b. Pine Grove Mills, Pa., Mar. 28, 1941; d. Gilbert Chester and Rosalie Evelyn (Reed) Bailey; m. Donald M. Brogan, Aug. 12, 1960 (div. Oct. 1971); children: Donna Lynn Gregory, Rodney Marshall Brogan; m. Robert R. Werntz, Aug. 28, 1982. A in Criminal Justice, Ind. U., 1976, BS, 1981. Cert. instr. law enforcement tng., Ind. Stenographer South Bend (Ind.) Police Dept., 1970-73, police officer, 1973-75, police officer, cpl. accident investigation, 1975-80, detective sgt., investigator sex crimes, 1980-85, field tng. officer administr., shift comdr. lt., 1985—; bd. dirs. Women's Com. on Sex Offenses, South Bend; vol., trainer rape crisis Sex Offense Services, South Bend, 1980-87; recorder, treas. Child Sexual Abuse Consortium, South Bend, 1982-85; mem. Giarretto Task Force/Family and Children Ctr., Mishawaka, Inc., 1985. Iniator ordinance St. Joseph County Funds for Examinations and Victims of Sex Crimes, 1983. Bd. dirs. Parents Anonymous, South Bend, 1982, Women's Shelter for Battered Women, South Bend, 1985, South Bend Credit Union Supervisory Commn., 1983; mem. Children and Adolescent Adv. Council, South Bend, 1984. Recipient Joseph J. Newman award Protective Bd./Council for Retarded St. Joseph County, 1982, Child Abuse Investigator award The Breakfast Exchange Club, 1982, award for Exceptional Quality in Investigative Child Abuse/Neglect, Child Protective Services of St. Joseph County Dept. Pub. Welfare, 1983, Outstanding Service award Women's Com. on Sex Offenses, 1983, Outstanding Officer of Yr. award, St. Joseph County Council of Clubs, 1985, Police Officer of Yr. award, Ind. Council Fraternal Vets. and Social Scis., 1985, Outstanding Achievement award YWCA Tribute to Women, 1986. Mem. Internat. Assn. of Women Police (Hon. Mention Officer of Yr. 1985), Fraternal Order of Police. Democrat. Home: 1709 E Altgeld St South Bend IN 46614 Office: South Bend Police Dept 701 W Sample St South Bend IN 46625

BROGLA, MARTHA LEONE, insurance agent; b. Taylorville, Ill., Oct. 31, 1955; d. Richard Wayne and Susan Bernadine (Adermann) Lamb; m. Vernon Gerard Brogla, May 20, 1978; children: Lucinda, Cynthia, Garrett. B in Acctg., Ill. State U., 1981. CPA, Ill.; CLU. Tax acct. State Farm Ins., Bloomington, Ill., 1982-88; agt. State Farm Ins., Blooomington-Normal, Ill., 1988—. Fellow Life Office Mgmt. Assn.; mem. Am. Inst. CPA's, Ill. CPA Soc., Soc. Chartered Life Underwriters, Inst. Mgmt. Accts. Roman Catholic. Club: Toastmasters (competent Toastmaster). Home: 2002 Woodfield Rd Bloomington IL 61704 Office: State Farm Ins 301 W Beaufort St Normal IL 61761

BROGLEY, ANN, personnel executive; b. Phila., May 23, 1950; d. Elwood Kenneth and Anna (Neugebauer) Wharton; m. William Joseph Brogley; Dec. 20, 1969. Student, Phil. Community Coll., 1973. Adminstrv. asst. to pres. Henry Mann, Inc., Huntingdon Valley, Pa., 1974-78; account rep. RCA Global Communications, N.Y.C., 1978-82, Cylix Communications, Memphis, 1982-83; v.p. CRT Personnel Services, Phila., 1983—; ptnr. Most Products Co., Phila., 1987—. Active various political orgns. Mem. Mid-Atlantic Assn. Temp. Services (pres. 1987-88), Am. Legion. Republican. Methodist. Home: 3317 S Keswick Ter Philadephia PA 19914 Office: CRT Personnel Services Inc 1101 Market St Suite 1210 Philadelphia PA 19107

BROGLIATTI, BARBARA SPENCER, television and motion picture executive; b. Los Angeles, Jan. 8, 1946; d. Robert and Lottie (Goldstein) Spencer; m. Raymond Haley Brogliatti, Sept. 19, 1970. B.A. in Social Scis. and English, UCLA, 1968. Asst. press. info. dept. CBS TV, Los Angeles, 1968-69, sr. publicist, 1969-74; dir. publicity Tandem Prodns. and T.A.T. Communications (now Embassy Communications), Los Angeles, 1974-77, corp. v.p., 1977-82, sr. v.p. worldwide publicity, promotion and advt. Embassy Communications, Los Angeles, 1982-85; sr. v.p. worldwide corp. communications Lorimar Telepictures Corp., Culver City, Calif., 1985—; bd. govs. TV Acad., Los Angeles, 1984-86. Bd. dirs. KIDSNET, Washington, 1987. Recipient Gold medallion Broadcast Promotion and Mktg. Execs., 1984. Mem. Dirs. Guild Am., Publicists Guild, Acad. TV Arts and Scis. Office: Lorimar Studios 10202 W Washington Blvd Culver City CA 90232

BROGLIN, JOYCE LYNN, data processing executive; b. Indpls., Feb. 13, 1945; d. Lowell Harris and DeLois Elizabeth (Doerr) DitzenBerger; m. John H. Broglin, Dec. 15, 1966. Cert. in bus., Ind. U.-Purdue U., Indpls., 1963; cert. in real estate, Ind. U.-Purdue U., 1972. Proof operator, teller Merchants Nat. Bank, Indpls., 1962-73; systems analyst NCR Corp., Indpls., 1973-81; v.p. item processing re:Member Data Services, Inc., Indpls., 1981—. Office: Member Data Services Inc 12220 N Meridian St Carmel IN 46032

BROGNA, LUANNE ELIZABETH, nurse; b. S.I., N.Y., Oct. 5, 1957; d. Louis Joseph and Carol Anne (Beyer) B.; m. Michael A. Kowalski, Nov. 28, 1986. BSN, Hunter Coll.-Bellevue Sch. Nursing, 1979, MSN, 1985. Cert. enterostomal therapist, med.-surg. nurse. Lic. practical nurse Hosp. for Spl. Surgery, N.Y.C., 1978-79; staff RN Mt. Sinai Hosp., N.Y.C., 1979-81, sr. clin. nurse, 1981-83, enterostomal therapy RN, 1985-87; enterostomal therapy RN Columbia-Presbyn. Med. Ctr., N.Y.C., 1983-85, Hackensack (N.J.) Med. Ctr., 1987—; pvt. practice clin. nursing, N.Y. and N.J., 1986-87; med. advisor N.Y. Ileal Pullthrough Group, N.Y.C., 1986—. Contbr. articles to profl. jours. Mem. Am. Nurses Assn., Internat. Assn. Enterostomal Therapy, Metro-N.Y. Enterostomal Therapists (treas. 1986-87), North Jersey Enterostomal Therapy Nurses (sec. 1986—), Ileostomy Assn. N.Y., Colostomy Soc. N.Y., Bergen County Ostomy Assn., Nat. Found. Ileitis and Colitis, Sigma Theta Tau. Roman Catholic. Office: Hackensack Med Ctr Hackensack Home Health Agy 30 Prospect Ave Hackensack NJ 07601

BROIDO, LUCY, art gallery director; b. N.Y.C., Jan. 19, 1924; d. David and Ruth Tarshes; m. Arnold Peace Broido; children: Jeffrey, Lawrence, Thomas. Student, Cornell U., 1941-44; BS, Columbia U., 1945; postgrad., Adelphi Coll., 1950-52. Cert. elem. tchr. Tchr. Union Tree Sch. Dist. #21, Rockville Centre, N.Y., 1959-69; pres. Lucy Broido Graphics, Ltd., Bryn Mawr, Pa., 1972—. Author: French Opera Posters 1868-1930, 1976, The Posters of Jules Chéret, 1980. Mem. Appraisers Assn. Am., Art Alliance. Home and Office: 908 Wootton Rd Bryn Mawr PA 19010

BROMBERG, BETSY DOROTHY, communications company executive, consultant; b. San Francisco, Nov. 11, 1953; d. Jerrold Leland Bromberg and Beverly (Rosenthal) Frendo Randon. Diplome d'etudes politiques, Institut d'Etudes Politiques, Paris, 1974; BA in Polit. Sci., U. Calif., Berkeley, 1977. Cons. in field San Francisco, 1979-80; creative dir. Hemming & Gilman, N.Y.C., 1980-83; dir. communications Am. Hotel and Motel Assn., N.Y.C., 1983-87; pres. Betsy Bromberg & Assocs., Denver, 1987—. Author: U.S. Trivia Trip Game, 1984. Recipient Presdl. Citation, U.S. White House, 1987. Mem. Travel Industry Assn. (press and pub. relations com. 1984—, Mktg. award 1984, 85). Club: Club de Cadence (Malta) (pres. 1986—). Office: Am Hotel and Motel Assn 888 7th Ave New York NY 10106 Office: 18 E 65th St New York NY 10021

BROMBERG, JANICE MAYER, civic activist; b. Chgo., Dec. 26, 1912; d. Harry Adolph and Natalie (Deiches) Mayer; m. Henri Louis Bromberg Jr., Apr. 12, 1936, Henri L. III. Student, Tulane U. Mem. bd. exec. com., v.p. Women's Council of Dallas County, Tex., Inc., 1974-78; mem. exec. com. United Way of Met. Dallas, 1975-81, mem. exec. com., 1977-81; mem. bd. edn. Dallas Ind. Sch. Dist.; active numerous other social civic and vol. orgns. in the Dallas area. Recipient Nat. Brotherhood awardof Nat. Conf.of Christians and Jews, 1979, Human Relations award Dallaschpt. Am. Jewish Com., 1970. Club: Dallas Womans'. Home: 4842 Brookview Dr Dallas TX 75220

BROMLEY, JOANNE, banker; b. Chgo., Apr. 15, 1935; d. Walter David and Alva Estelle (Hickman) Jones; divorced; children: Janet Bromley Mandraes, John. Student, Mesa Coll., 1972-78. Sec. comml. loans Valley Nat. Bank, Scottsdale, Ariz., 1969-75, loan officer, 1975-84, mgr. br., 1984—. Bd. dirs. Scottsdale Symphony Soc., 1986—. Mem. Nat. Assn. Bank Women (bd. dirs. 1986—), Scottsdale C. of C. (prospectors com. 1985—). Republican. Lodge: Sertoma. Home: 134 Madrid Plaza Mesa AZ 85201 Office: Valley Nat Bank PO Box 1117 Scottsdale AZ 85201

BRONN, LESLIE JOAN BOYLE, radiologist, medical administrator; b. White Plains, N.Y., Aug. 23, 1948; d. Myles Joseph and Harriet Geib (Warburton) Boyle; m. Donald George Bronn, Aug. 21, 1973; children: Jacob Alexander, Natasha Nisa. BS, Ohio State U., 1970, MD, 1976. Diplomate Am. Bd. Radiology. Intern internal medicine Ohio State U. Hosp., Columbus, 1976-77, resident internal medicine, 1977-78, resident diagnostic radiology, 1978-81; chief radiology service VA Outpatient Clinic, Columbus, 1981-86; chief diagnostic radiology service Allen Park (Mich.) VA Hosp. Med. Ctr., 1986-87, chief nuclear medicine and diagnostic radiology services, 1987—; clin. asst. prof. radiology Ohio State U. Coll. Medicine, 1981-86, Wayne State U. Sch. Medicine, 1986—. mem. Am. Coll. Radiology, Radiol. Soc. N.Am., Assn. VA Chiefs of Radiology, Am. Assn. Women Radiologists, Am. Inst. Ultrasound in Medicine, Phi Beta Kappa, Alpha Lambda Delta. Office: VA Med Ctr Chief Radiology Service Outer Dr and Southfield Rd Allen Park MI 48101

BRONNENKANT, ANNA COLLIS, lawyer; b. Syracuse, N.Y., Aug. 13, 1949; d. Nicholas and Helen P. (Panarites) Collis; m. Rex P. Bronnenkant, Sept. 20, 1975; children—Tyler N. and Adam P. (twins), Andrew Rex, Tess Heléne. B.A., Skidmore Coll., 1971; J.D., Syracuse U., 1975. Bar: Ariz., U.S. Dist. Ct. Ariz. Atty. Community Legal Services, Phoenix, 1975-78; assoc. counsel 1st Fed. Savs. and Loan Assn. Ariz., Phoenix, 1978-85; counsel S.W. Savs. and Loan Assn., Phoenix, 1985—. Admissions corr. Skidmore Coll., Phoenix, 1980—. Mem. ABA, Ariz. Bar Assn., Maricopa County Bar Assn. (corp. counsel sect.), Assn. Women Lawyers (pres. 1983), Exec. Bus. and Profl. Women (com. chmn. 1983-84, v.p. 1984-85), Phi Delta Phi (v.p. 1974-75, J. Mark McCarthy award 1975). Republican. Greek Orthodox. Office: SW Savs and Loan Assn Ariz 3101 N Central Ave 3d Floor Phoenix AZ 85012

BRONOCCO, TERRI LYNN, telecommunications company executive; b. San Antonio, Jan. 7, 1953; d. Lawrence and Jimmie Doris (Mears) B.; m. Martin L. Lowy, July 5, 1975 (div. Jan. 1979). Student in communications U. Tex.-Austin, 1970-73. Pub. relations mgr. Assocs. Corp., Dallas, 1976-79; editor-in-chief Nat. Tax Shelter Digest, Dallas, 1979; fin. editor Dallas/Ft. Worth Bus., Dallas, 1979-80; pub. affairs dir. Gen. Telephone Co., Lewisville, Tex., 1980-82; pub. info. mgr. GTE Corp., Stamford, Conn., 1982-83, media communications mgr., 1983-84, media relations and communications mgr., 1984-86; v.p. external affairs U.S. Sprint Communications Co., Dallas, 1986—. Fundraiser, pub. relations counsel Am. Shakespeare Theatre, Stratford, Conn., 1984-86; bd. dirs. Music Found. for the Handicapped, Bridgeport, Conn., 1984-86; precinct chmn. Dallas County Dem. Party, 1982; bd. dirs. Far Mill River Assn., Stratford, 1983-86; mem. adv. commn. State Tex. Emergency Communications, 1987—. Recipient award for Newspaper Series Dept. Transp., 1980. Mem. Internat. Assn. Bus. Communicators (Best Photograph award 1977), Women in Communications (Matrix award 1985), Women in Mgmt., Am. Mgmt. Assn., Dallas C. of C. (telecommunications com. 1987, Spl. Recognition award 1978). Roman Catholic. Home: 1600 N Oak St Arlington VA 22201 Office: US Sprint Communications Co 2002 Edmund Halley Dr Reston VA 22091

BRONSON, CLAIRE SEKULSKI, finance educator; b. Memphis, Oct. 14, 1947; d. Julian Bernard and Opal Geneva (Scruggs) Sekulski; m. George D. Bronson, May 28, 1968; children—Christopher, Kevin, Meredith. B.A., Conn. Coll. for Women, 1969; M.A., U. Conn., 1971, Ph.D., 1982. Substitute tchr. Enfield pub. schs., Conn., 1979-82; part-time instr. econs. Manchester Community Coll., Conn., 1974-76, Asnuntuck Community Coll., Enfield, 1975-79; asst. prof. econs. Western New Eng. Coll., Springfield, Mass., 1983, vis. asst. prof. fin., 1983-84, asst. prof. fin., 1984—, mem. investment inst. adv. com., 1983-84; mem. adv. bd. Suffield Bank; book editor for various pubs.; mem. adv. bd. Suffield Bank; cons. small bus. Contbr. articles to profl. jours. Mem. Enfield Cultural Arts Commn., 1983-86; mem. adv. com. Enfield Bd. Edn., 1981-83; pres. Nathan Hale PTO, Enfield, 1980-81. Mem. Am. Fin. Assn., Am. Econ. Assn., Eastern Fin. Assn., Fin. Mgmt. Assn., Fin. Mgmt. Assn. Republican. Roman Catholic. Club: Twin Mothers (Hartford, Conn.). Avocations: collecting antique jewelry, tennis, golf, reading. Home: 21 S Meadow Ln Enfield CT 06082 Office: Western New Eng Coll Wilbraham Rd Springfield MA 01119

BRONSTHER, ELLYN LEE, design company executive, foundation administrator; b. N.Y.C., Jan. 12, 1929; d. Oscar Leonard Kaiser and Carrie (Goldfarb) Erwich; m. Burton Bronsther, June 17, 1951; children: Fredrika, Oscar Leonard, Judith Alison. BA in Psychology, Adelphi U., 1949; BS in Edn., Bklyn. Coll., 1950; postgrad., Hofstra U., 1968-69. Cert. tchr., N.Y. Tchr. N.Y.C. Sch. System, 1951-65; v.p. Money Talks, Hewlett, N.Y., 1978-81, Flowers by Rika, Hewlett, 1978—, Rika Art and Design Ltd., Hewlett, 1985—. Mayor Village Hewlett Bay Park, N.Y., 1980-86; trustee Schneider Children's Hosp., New Hyde Park, N.Y., 1970—; v.p. Surg. Aid to Children of the World, Rockville Centre, N.Y., 1980—; bd. dirs. N.Y. Statewide Health Coordinating Council, Albany, 1980—, Five Town Music and Art Found., Hewlett, 1968—, Greater Five Towns YMCA, YWCA, Cedarhurst, N.Y., 1985—; bd. govs. Legal Aid Soc., Mineola, N.Y., 1980-85. Hon. tchr. Med. Coll., Beijing, 1988. Mem. Elected Women Ofcls. of State N.Y. Home: 114 Cedar Ave Hewlett Bay Park NY 11557

BRONTE, D. LYDIA, foundation executive; b. Memphis, Dec. 27, 1938; d. Paul and Dorothy Vivian (Hamilton) B. BA with high honors, Hendrix Coll., Conway, Ark., 1960; postgrad. U. d'Aix-Marseille, Aix-en-Provence, France, 1960-61; PhD, U. N.C., 1969. Instr. then asst. prof. French, George Washington U., 1965-70, asst. prof. English, 1969-71; spl. asst. to dir. Folger Shakespeare Library, Washington, 1970-71; dir. research and publ. Nat. Humanities Series, Princeton, N.J., 1971-73; cons. in humanities Rockefeller Found., N.Y.C., 1973-74, asst. dir. humanities, 1974-77, assoc. dir., 1977-79, program officer central adminstrn., 1979-80; cons. to program policy com. MacArthur Found., Chgo., 1980-82; cons. Carnegie Corp. N.Y., 1982—, cons., staff dir. The Aging Soc. project, 1983—; cons., dir. Third Quarter of Life project Acad. for Ednl. Devel., 1987—. Co-editor (with Alan Pifer) Our Aging Society: Paradox and Promise, 1986; contbr. in field. Bd. dirs. Am. Assn. Gifted Children, 1983—. Recipient cert. of appreciation Am. Inst. Character Edn., 1980; Nat. Merit scholar, 1956-60; Fulbright fellow, 1960-61, Woodrow Wilson fellow, 1961-62, 62-63. Mem. MLA, Women and Founds./Corp. Philanthropy. Democrat. Clubs: Princeton, Cosmoplitan, Coffee House, Women's City (N.Y.C.).

BROOK, GESELL SAVANNAH, administrative analyst, manufacturing company executive; b. Seattle, Nov. 28, 1946; d. Lloyd Edward and Shirley Jean (Karl) Anderson; m. Bradford Whiting; children—Rob, Chris. B.S. in Speech Pathology and Audiology with honors, U. Oreg., 1970; M.S. in Interdisciplinary Studies with honors, Oreg. State U., 1979. Linn-Benton speech and lang. specialist Edn. Service Dist., Albany, Oreg., 1970-81; speech cons. Monroe, Oreg., 1981-83; exec. dir. Benton County Jr. Achievement, Corvallis, Oreg., 1981-83; v.p. Oregon Electro-MEC, Corvallis, 1970—, vice chmn. bd., 1970-83; program adminstrv. budget analyst State Oreg., Salem, 1983-85. Author: What Do You Think, Lunch, The Shack, Checkers, Make a Rug, Can You Make a Ship?, On Mount Shasta, numerous others. Mem. City Corvallis Budget Commn., 1979-81; Oreg. del. White House Conf. Families, 1980; chmn. Corvallis Sch. Dist., 1980—; bd. dirs. Corvallis Arts Center, 1981-82; pres. Symphony Soc., 1987—. Named First Citizne of Corvallis, 1986-87. Mem. Womens Networking Alliance (v.p. program 1983, pres. 1987-88), Oreg. Speech and Hearing Assn. (assoc. editor), AAUW (pres. 1979-81), Corvallis C. of C. (edn. com.).

BROOKER, PATRICIA LEE, accountant, financial consultant, directro; b. Helena, Mont., Sept. 28, 1956; d. Clifford and Phyllis Ruth (Wolf) Madsen; m. Edwin Dale Brooker, Dec. 25, 1975; 1 child, Stephanie Lee. Student, Gustavus Adolphus Coll., 1974-75, U. Mont., 1975; diploma in acctg., McGraw Hill Coll., 1988. Teller Am. Fed. Savs. & Loan, Helena, Mont., 1976-77; from office asst. to asst. mgr. fin. ITT, Orlando, Fla., 1977-86; acctg. supr. Plantscape House Inc., Orlando, Fla.., 1986-87; exec. dir. acctg. Mars Inc., Missoula, 1987—; acct. B&B Enterprises, Missoula, 1985—. Dir. adminstrn. and leadership courses CAP , Orlando, 1980-87. Recipient membership ribbons and unit citations CAP, 1980-87. Mem. Nat. Assn. Female Execs. Republican. Home: 245 W North Ave Missoula MT 59801 Office: Mars Inc 2791 N Reserve Missoula MT 59803

BROOKER, SUSAN GAY, personnel executive; b. Washington, Sept. 4, 1949; d. Robert Morris and Mildred Ruby (Parler) B. BA, St. Mary's Coll., St. Mary's City, Md., 1971. News editor WPGC Radio, Lanham, Md., 1971; mgr. trainee Household Fin. Corp., Silver Spring, Md., 1972; career counselor Place-All, Bethesda, Md., 1972-73; exec. v.p. New Places, Inc./Get-A-Job, Washington, 1973—, also bd. dirs.; mem. Emploibank, Washington, 1978-79. Recipient Cert. Appreciation U.S. Fish and Wildlife Assn., 1985. Mem. Pell-Capital Personnel Services Assn. (cert.), NOW, St. Mary's Coll. Alumni Assn. (bd. dirs. 1987—). Democrat. Home: 9902 Sidney Rd Silver Spring MD 20901 Office: New Places Inc 1925 K St Suite 407 Washington DC 20006

BROOKINS, CAROL ELAINE, purchasing administrator; b. Elsie, Mich., Dec. 17, 1933; d. Russell Allen and Vaudrey Leoma (Curtis) Barnard; m. M. Kenneth Leavitt, Dec. 30, 1950 (div. 1956); stepchildren: Marilyn Leavitt, Gregory Leavitt, Joseph Leavitt; m. Myron Charles Ostrander, Mar. 24, 1964 (div. 1979); 1 child, Penny Elaine; m. Dale Alvah Brookins, July 9, 1983. Grad. high sch., White Pine, Mich. Mgr. soft lines receiving Topps Inc., Lansing, Mich., 1962-65; head bookkeeper Painters Supplies, Lansing, 1965-68, The Fig Leaf, White Pine, 1974-78; dir. purchasing Ontonagon (Mich.) Meml. Hosp., 1978—. Facility graphic artist Ontonagon Meml. Hosp. Mem. Nat. Assn. for Female Execs., Smithsonian Instn., Health Care Material Mgmt. Soc. Home: 134 Cherry Ln Ontonagon MI 49953

BROOKS, ANDREE NICOLE, journalist, journalism educator, author; b. London, Feb. 2, 1937; d. Leon Luis and Lillian (Abrahamson) Aelion; m. Ronald J. Brooks, Aug. 16, 1959 (div. Aug. 1986); children—Allyson, James. Journalism cert., N.W. London Poly., 1958. Reporter Hampstead News, London, 1954-58; story editor Photoplay mag., N.Y.C., 1958-60; N.Y. corr. Australian Broadcasting Co., N.Y.C., 1961-68; elected rep. Elstree, Eng., 1973-74; columnist N.Y. Times, N.Y.C., 1978—; free-lance journalist 1978—; adj. prof. journalism Fairfield U., Conn., 1983—. Recipient numerous awards including 1st place for news writing Conn. Press Women, 1980, 83, 85, 86, Outstanding Achievement award Nat. Fedn. Press Women, 1981, 1st place award Fairfield County chpt. Women in Communications, 1982, 83, 86, 87, 2d place award in mag. writing Nat. Assn. Home Builders, 1983, Spl. Service award Conn. chpt. Am. Planning Assn., 1983, 1st place award for mag. writing Nat. Fedn. Press Women, 1983. Mem. Conn. Press Women (chmn. nominating com. 1983-86), Women in Communications (contest co-chmn. 1983-84). Home: 15 Hitchcock Rd Westport CT 06880 Office: care NY Times 229 W 43d St New York NY 10036

BROOKS, ANN, public administrator; b. Dallas, Apr. 19, 1956; d. Kenneth Ardell and Martha Ellen (Blalack) B.; m. Lorin S. Evans, Dec. 11, 1981 (separated 1984); 1 child, Emilie. BA in Polit. Sci., Trinity U., San Antonio, 1977; postgrad., Lyndon B. Johnson Sch. Pub. Affairs, 1979; MPA, U. So. Calif., 1987. Campaign mgr. Tex. State Legis. Race, Houston, 1978; restaurant mgr. Rainbow Lodge Restaurant, Houston, 1978-79; project mgr., specialist intergovtl. affairs Dept. Def. Office Sec., Washington, 1980—; def. rep. Security Planning Commn. Los Angeles Olympics, 1983-84, Pan Am. Games Law Enforcement Council, Indpls., 1985-87, Nat. Assn. Federally Impacted Schs., 1981-87; mem. def. liaison High Impact Mil. Sch. Dist. Supts., 1987—. Mem. Nat. Women's Polit. Caucus, Washington, 1981-87;, Dem. Nat. Com., 1982-87; bd dirs. Montrose Dems., Houston, 1978-79. Mem. Am. Soc. Pub. Adminstrn., Office Sec. Def. Sr. Profl. Women, Sierra Club. Club: Speculum Medieval Acad. (Cambridge, Mass.). Office: Office Sec of Def Pentagon 4C767 Washington DC 20301

BROOKS, ANNMARIE MANZI, electrical contracting executive; b. Methuen, Mass., Sept. 13, 1953; d. Albert Peter and Anna Louise (Mikolajczyk) Manzi; m. Wayne Clinton Brooks. AA, Bradford (Mass.) Coll., 1973; BA, U. N.H., 1975; MS, Georgetown U., 1977. Cert. fluency in Italian Lang. Sr. researcher, translator Nat. Geographic Soc., Washington, 1977-84; asst. treas. Manzi Elec. Corp., Lawrence, Mass., 1984—; v.p., treas. Windjammer Constrn. Co. and Windjammer Properties, Seabrook, N.H., 1984—; media cons., Washington, 1980-84. Photographer for book: Mills, Mansions, Mergers, 1982. Democrat. Roman Catholic. Home: 123 Atlantic Ave Seabrook NH 03874 Office: Manzi Elec Corp PO Box 69 Lawrence MA 01842

BROOKS, ANTOINETTE MARIE, real estate executive; b. Worcester, Mass., Dec. 3, 1940; d. Philip F. and Madeline (Rondinone) Inangelo; m. Richard E. Brooks, Dec. 27, 1958; children: Richard E. Jr., Marlo L., Jeffrey Paul. A in Bus., Cen. NE Coll., 1958; student, Thomas Edison Sch., 1959, Am. Inst. Banking, 1973, Lee Inst. Real Estate, 1965. Credit clk. Pub. Finance Co., Worcester, Mass., 1958-61; asst. treas. Trans Ea. Corp., Worcester, Mass., 1961-65; pres. Antoinette M. Brooks Real Estate Assocs., Worcester, 1965-79; sales rep. Dennison's Mfg. Co., Framingham, Mass., 1979-81; mgr. N.E. Indsl. Park, Holliston, Mass., 1982-83, Coldwell Banker, Resdl., Northborough, Mass., 1983—. Justice of the Peace, Mass., 1983—. Mem. Women's Council Realtors, Greater Worcester Bd. Realtors (coms. 1977—), Nat. Assn. Female Execs. (bd. dirs. local chpt. 1987), Nat. Assn. Realtors, Mass. Assn. Realtors, Worcester Bd. Realtors (profl. standards com. 1987—, speaker 1987), Worcester Order Son's of Italy. Democrat. Roman Catholic. Home: 293 Davis St Northborough MA 01532 Office: Re-Max Real Estate Assocs Pendalton Sq Main St Northborough MA 01532

BROOKS, CLAUDIA A., software company administrator; b. Atlanta, Jan. 18, 1957; d. John William and Annette (Thompson) B.; m. Robert A. Davis, Mar. 22, 1974 (div. Aug. 1978); 1 child, Robert. Student, Coastal Carolina Community Coll., Jacksonville, N.C., 1977-78; AA in Computer Sci., Clayton Jr. Coll., Morrow, Ga., 1980; BBA in Info. Systems, Ga. State U., 1984. Cert. in Info. Systems, Bus. Adminstrn. Data processing, fin. coordinator UFCW Union and Employers Trust Fund, Atlanta, 1981; programmer, analyst, asst. data ctr. mgr. Davidson Mineral Properties, Inc., Atlanta, 1981-82; product specialist, programmer Info. Systems Am., Inc., Atlanta, 1982-83; programmer, analyst Software Shop Systems, Inc., Atlanta, Farmingdale, N.J., 1983-85; mgr. product devel. Software Shop Systems, Inc., Farmingdale, 1985-88. Vol. op. new life USN, Guam, 1975, ARC, Guam, 1975. Mem. Nat. Assn. Female Execs., Mensa, Cousteau Soc., Audubon Soc., Phi Theta Kappa, Alpha Beta Pi. Presbyterian.

BROOKS, CLAUDIA MARIE, lawyer; b. Oakland, Calif., Aug. 2, 1952; d. Rex E. and Colleen M. (Walker) Brooks; m. James A. Smith. A.B., U. Calif.-Berkeley, 1974; J.D., U. Calif. Hastings Coll. of Law San Francisco, 1979; postgrad. Monterey Inst. Fgn. Studies (Calif.), 1974, Institut de Francais, Villefranche-sur-Mer, France, 1979, 84, Oxford U. (Eng.), 1973, Hague Acad. Internat. Law (Netherlands), 1980. Bar: Calif. 1979, U.S. Dist. Ct. (no. dist.) Calif. 1979, U.S. Ct. Appeals (9th cir.) 1979. Extern for justice William P. Clark Calif. Supreme Ct., San Francisco, 1978; assoc. Smith & Brooks, Attys. at Law, Redlands, Calif., 1979-82, ptnr., 1982—. Editor-in-chief Hastings Internat. and Comparative Law Rev., 1978-79; contbr. article to law rev. Pub. mem. Fgn. Service selection bds. U.S. Dept. State, Washington, 1983; del. U.S./China Joint Session on Trade, Investment, Econ. Law, Beijing, 1987; bd. dirs. Redlands Community Music Assn. Mem. State Bar Calif., San Bernardino County Bar Assn. (mem. jud. selection com. 1982-83). Clubs: San Francisco Press. Office: Smith & Brooks 130 W Vine St PO Box 672 Redlands CA 92373

BROOKS, DEBORAH CLEMMONS, association executive; b. Rock Hill, S.C., Aug. 11, 1959; d. Harold Everett and Jean (Suggs) C. BA in Polit. Sci., Clemson U., 1980. Research specialist Houston C. of C., 1981-83, adminstrv. asst. in research and ops., 1983-84, adminstrv. assoc., 1984-85; exec. v.p. Conway (S.C.) Area C. of C., 1985—; chairperson Project Free Enterprise, Conway, 1985-86, Better Water Week Com., Conway, 1986—. Editor various commerce publs. Mem. Conway Lioness Club, 1986. Mem. Tex. Econ. and Demographic Assn. (Houston chpt.), Jaycees, So. Assn. Am. C. of C. Execs., Assn. Membership Execs. Methodist. Club: Toastmasters (Conway). Office: Conway Area C of C 203 Main St Conway SC 29526

BROOKS, DEBORAH DEE, infosytems engr. b. Kingman, Kans., Jan. 18, 1951; d. Delbert Dexter and Ella Mae (Linscheid) B.; m. John S. Waterman, June 11, 1983. B.A. in Computer Sci., Kans. State U., 1973; M.L., Emporia (Kans.) State U., 1974. Asst. librarian Northwestern U., 1974-77; programmer, analyst Mgmt. Systems Tech., Inc., Chgo., 1977-78; tech. dir., systems analyst CALS project Elgin (Ill.) Community Coll., 1978-80; product mgr. Advanced Systems Inc., Elk Grove Village, Ill., 1980-81; data base adminstr. Wilson Jones Co., Chgo., 1981-86; sr. sytems software engr. Kraft, Inc., 1987—, pres. Sys-Soft, dir. CALS Services Group Ltd.; cons. in field. Mem. Assn. Computing Machinery, ALA, Am. Soc. Info. Sci. (chmn. Chgo. chpt. 1979). Presbyterian. Home: PO Box 8496 Northfield IL 60093 Office: Kraft Inc 1 Kraft Ct Glenview IL 60025

BROOKS, DIANA D., auction house executive; b. Glen Cove, N.Y., 1950. Grad. Yale U. Formerly exec. v.p. Sotheby's North America, N.Y.C., now pres., dir. Office: Sotheby's N Am 1334 York Ave New York NY 10021 *

BROOKS, GWENDOLYN, author; b. Topeka, June 7, 1917; d. David Anderson and Keziah Corinne (Wims) B.; m. Henry L. Blakely, Sept. 17, 1939; children: Henry L., Nora. Grad., Wilson Jr. Coll., Chgo., 1936; L.H.D., Columbia Coll., 1964. Instr. poetry Columbia Coll., Chgo., Northeastern Ill. State Coll., Chgo.; mem. Ill. Arts Council; cons. in poetry Library of Congress, 1985-86. Author: poetry A Street in Bronzeville, 1945, Annie Allen, 1949, Maud Martha; novel, 1953, Bronzeville Boys and Girls; for children, 1956, The Bean Eaters; poetry, 1960, Selected Poems, 1963, In the Mecca, 1968, Riot, 1969, Family Pictures, 1970, Aloneness, 1971, To Disembark, 1981; autobiography Report From Part One, 1972, The Tiger Who Wore White Gloves, 1974, Beckonings, 1975, Primer for Blacks, 1980, Young Poets' Primer, 1981, Very Young Poets, 1983, The Near-Johannesburg Boy, 1986, Blacks, 1987. Named One of 10 Women of Year Mademoiselle mag., 1945; recipient award for creative writing Am. Acad. Arts and Letters, 1946; Guggenheim fellow for creative writing, 1946, 47; Pulitzer prize for poetry, 1950; Anisfield-Wolf award, 1969; named Poet Laureate of Ill., 1968. Mem. Soc. Midland Authors. Home: 7428 S Evans Ave Chicago IL 60619

BROOKS, HELENE MARGARET, editor-in-chief; b. Jersey City, Apr. 1, 1942; d. Sinclair Duncan and Helen Margaret (McDermott) B. BA, C.W. Post Coll., 1977. Asst. editor McCall's Mag., N.Y.C., 1969-72, assoc. editor, 1972-75, editor features and travel, 1975-83; managing editor 50 Plus Mag. Whitney Comm., N.Y.C., 1983, exec. editor, 1983-87; editor in chief Network Mag./Internat. Airlines Travel Agt. Network, N.Y.C., 1987—; editorial cons. Am. Hairdressing Industry , N.Y.C. 1983. Mem. Am. Soc. Mag. Editors, Am. Assn. Travel Editors. Democrat. Presbyterian. Home: 84 Trellis Ln Wantagh NY 11793 Office: Internat Airlines Travel Agt Network 300 Garden City Plaza Suite 418 Garden City NY 11530

BROOKS, JUDITH (ANN MARIE), foundation administrator; b. Portland, Maine, July 14, 1940; d. Ralph D. and Jacqueline (Lucas) B. BBA, U. Maine-Orono, 1962; cert. teaching English as a fgn. lang. U. Mich., 1964. Profl. cert. Armed Forces Recreation Soc., 1980. Vol. Peace Corps, 1964-66; sr. counsel, resident leader Poland Spring (Maine) Job Corps Center, 1966-67; with USO, 1967—, exec. dir., Thailand, 1967-75; dir. Airport USO Lounge, San Francisco Internat. Airport, 1975-76, exec. dir., Wiesbaden, Fed. Republic Germany, 1977-78, exec. dir., Naples, Italy, 1978-79, Pacific Area exec., 1979-85, So. Europe Area exec., Naples, 1985-86, dir. personnel/hqrs. services USO World Hqrs., Washington, 1986-87, coordinator spl. projects, 1987—. Recipient civilian patriotic citation U.S. Army, 1978, placques of recognition USAF, Thailand, 1972, 75. Mem. Nat. Assn. Female Execs., Nat. Parks and Recreation Assn. Democrat. Episcopalian. Office: USO World Hqrs 601 Indiana Ave NW Washington DC 20004

BROOKS, JULIE AGNES, psychiatrist; b. Grand Rapids, Mich., Apr. 16, 1941; d. Wesley Clyde and Janet Niven (Nicol) B. BA in Bacteriology, Fla. State U., 1963; Degree in Med. Tech., Mercy Hosp., San Diego, 1968; MD, U. Autonoma, Guadalajara, 1980. Cert. med. tech. Am. Soc. Clin. Pathologists. Intern U. Iowa, Iowa City, 1980; resident U. Iowa, 1980-81, Cherokee (Iowa) Mental Health Inst., 1982-83; practice medicine specializing in psychiatry Aberdeen, S.D., 1984-86, Ft. Myers, Fla., 1987—; mem. staff Ga. State Mental Hosp., Savannah, 1986-87, G. Pierce Wood Meml. Hosp., Arcadia, Fla., 1987—; vol. physician Mexican Govt., 1979; cons. psychiatrist Sioux reservations, Eagle Butte, Sisseton, 1984-86; med. dir. Columbus (Ga.) Mental Health, Mental Retardation, Substance Abuse Program, 1987. Mem. Am. Psychiat. Assn., Nat. Assn. Female Execs., U. Autonoma Guadalajara Alumni Assn. Home: PO Box 30280 Fort Myers FL 33905 Office: G Pierce Wood Meml Hosp Arcadia FL 33821 also: 2149 McGregor Blvd Fort Myers FL 33905

BROOKS, KAREN HARLEY, construction executive; b. Macon, Ga., Dec. 7, 1943; d. William I. and Beryl (Hightower) Harley; m. James Donald Brooks; children: Clint, Thumper, Jessica. Student, Women's Coll. Ga., DeKalb Coll., Southern Tech. Sec. corp. Homeland Communities Inc., Atlanta, 1975-81; owner Brooks Interiors, Atlanta, 1976-86; pres. Justin Berry Inc., Atlanta, 1983—; owner Magnum Builders, Atlanta. Mem. Nat. Homebuilders Assn., Nat. Remodelers Assn., Better Bus. Bur., Inst. Residential Mktg., Homeowners Warranty. Democrat. Presbyterian. Clubs: Porsche, Sports Car Am. Home: 215 La Chaize Circle Atlanta GA 30327 Office: Justin Berry Inc 90 West Wieuca Suite 105 Atlanta GA 30342

BROOKS, LINDA PATRICIA, electrical supply company manager; b. OxFord, England, Aug. 24, 1955; d. Lewis and Iris Ellonwy (Davis) Allen; m. Don Lee Brooks, June 26, 1977; children: Don II, Allen. Student, Calif. State U., Sacto. Personnel adminstr. Amfac Industry Plumbing, Folsom, Calif., 1984-85; personnel specialist Amfac Supply Co., Folsom, 1985, mgr. human resources, 1985-86; mgr. personnel adminstrn. Amfac Distbn., Folsom, 1986-87; mgr. human resources Amfac Electric Supply, Folsom, 1987—. Office: Amfac Electric Supply 81 Blue Ravine Rd Folsom CA 95630

BROOKS, LORRAINE ELIZABETH, educator; b. Port Chester, N.Y., Mar. 10, 1936; d. William Henry Sr. and Marion Elizabeth (Harrell) B. BS in Music Edn., SUNY, Potsdam, 1958; M of Performance, Manhattan Sch. Music, 1970. Dir. Camp Spruce-Mountain Lakes, North Salem, N.Y., 1964-73; youth adviser St. Peter's Episcopal Ch., Port Chester, N.Y., 1964-65, St. Andrew's-St. Peter's Ch., Yonkers, N.Y., 1970-73; v.p. South Yonkers Youth Council, 1970-76; assoc. Sisters of Charity of N.Y., Scarsdale, 1978—; eucharistic minister, lector Our Lady of Victory Ch., Roman Cath., Mt. Vernon, N.Y., 1981—; Roman Cath. chaplain White Plains (N.Y.) Med. Ctr., 1981—; cons. Quincy Tenants Assn., Mt. Vernon, 1986—. vestrywoman St. Andrew's Episc. Ch., Yonkers, 1971-75; contralto soloist St. Peter's Episc. Ch., Port Chester, N.Y., 1959-69; mem. Collegiate Chorale, N.Y.C., 1958-68;. service team mem. Charismatic Community, Scarsdale, N.Y., 1975—; v.p. Willwood Tenant Assn., Mt. Vernon, 1981-82, pres., 1982-84. Selected as master tchr. Middle and Jr. High Sch. Music Tchrs. N.Y. State program, Albany, 1988. Mem. Westchester County Sch. Music Assn. (exec. bd.), Scarsdale Tchrs. Assn. (exec. bd.). Democrat. Roman Catholic. Office: Scarsdale Pub Schs Post Rd Scarsdale NY 10583

BROOKS, MARY JEANETTE TIDWELL, lobbyist; b. Dallas, July 14, 1951; d. Earl Carl Edwin and Leta Virginia (McDonald) Tidwell; m. Eldon Lloyd Brooks, Mar. 18, 1972 (div.); children: Kari Rene, Chad Ryan. BA in History cum laude, U. Tex., Arlington, 1973; MA in Social Sci., U. Okla., 1978. Tchr., Hurst (Tex.) Pub. Schs., 1975, Lawton (Okla.) Pub. Schs., 1976; research analyst Okla. Legis. Council, Oklahoma City, 1979; legis. rep. state govt. affairs Texaco USA, Houston, 1980-83; sr. rep. state govt. affairs Panhandle Eastern Corp., Houston, 1983-84, mgr. state govt. affairs, 1984—. Author: (with others) Agencies, Boards and Commissions of Oklahoma, 1979. Mem. Internat. Platform Assn., Ohio Gas Assn. (legis. com., regulator com.), Ill. C. of C. (energy com.), Ill. Mfrs. Assn. (energy com.), Ohio C. of C. (pub. affairs com.), Ohio Mfrs. Assn. (govt. affairs com.), Arlington Alumni Assn., U. Okla. Alumni Assn., Alpha Chi, Phi Alpha Theta, Sigma Delta Pi. Methodist. Club: Third House (Ill.). Home: 5107 Westerham Houston TX 77069 Office: Panhandle Eastern Pipe Line Co 3000 Bissonnet Houston TX 77005

BROOKSHIER, PEGGY ANN, mechanical engineer; b. Idaho Falls, Idaho, Mar. 14, 1955; d. Yutaka and Miyoko (Konishi) Morishita; B.S., Calif. State U., 1977; m. Alan L. Brookshier, Nov. 18, 1978. Mech. engr., project mgr. U.S. Dept. Energy, Idaho Falls, 1977—. Mem. ASME. Office: 785 DOE Pl Idaho Falls ID 83402

BROOKSHIRE, SHIRLEY ANN, health company executive; b. Tryon, N.C., June 20, 1950; d. Julius Earle and Mary Evelyn (Hooker) Brock; m. Richard Gwyn Brookshire, July 25, 1970; 1 child, Richard Anthony. Diploma in nursing, N.C. Bapt. Hosp. Sch. Nursing, Winston-Salem, 1971; student, Miami U., 1976, Xavier U., Cin., 1979-80. Staff nurse Hampton (Va.) Gen. Hosp., 1971-72; staff, charge nurse Riverside Hosp., Newport News, Va., 1972-74; coordinator utilization rev. Hillhaven Convalescent Ctr., Marietta, Ga., 1976-78, Midwest Found. for Med. Care, Cin., 1978-79; dir. med. services OhioCare, Cin., 1979-80; analyst med. claims Physicians Health Services, Trumbull, Conn., 1980-81, coordinator inpatient rev., 1981-82, adminstr. inpatient rev., 1982-84, v.p. health services, 1984—; cons. Office Prepaid Health Care, Rockville, Md., 1985—. Mem. Am. Med. Care and Rev. Assn., Bridgeport (Conn.) C. of C. Home: 362 South Ave New Canaan CT 06840 Office: Physicians Health Services 120 Hawley Ln Trumbull CT 06611

BROPHY, NANCY ANTIONETTE, education facility executive; b. Peekskill, N.Y., June 14, 1937; d. Anthony and Jean Marie (Arcadipane) Montibello; m. Dennis Matthew Brophy; children: Thomas, Shawn. BS, SUNY, Potsdam, 1960. Cert. tchr. Tchr. Cerro de Pasco (Peru) Mining Corp., 1960-61; tchr. history and English Brewster (N.Y.) High Sch., 1961-63; tchr. U.S. Army Sch., Chinon, France, 1963-65; tchr. history and English Ashland (Mass.) Pub. Schs., 1965-67, Copper Beech Mid. Sch., Shrub Oak, N.Y., 1967-68; owner, dir. Tom Thumb Presch., Inc., Mohegan, N.Y., 1968—. Mem. Assn. for Improvement Mohegan Lake, 1982-87, Mohegan Lake Improvement Corp., 1987. Mem. Nat. Assn. Female Execs., N.Y. State Supervision and Curriculum Devel., Westchester Assn. for Edn. Young Children. Republican. Roman Catholic. Office: Tom Thumb Presch Inc 1949 E Main St R-3 Box 2 Mohegan NY 10547

BROSIN, DIANE LOUISE, sales executive; b. Sacramento, Calif., Dec. 18, 1952; d. Isadore G. and Rosalyn Naomi (Kaufman) B.; m. Timothy R. Machold, May 13, 1982. BS in Biology, Calif. State U., 1975. Mgr. quality control Fillmore Foods, Hayward, Calif., 1977-78; tech. sales rep. Whatman, Inc., Clifton, N.J., 1978-80; product specialist Varian Instruments, Palo Alto, Calif., 1980-81; mktg. mgr. Hitachi Instruments, Inc., Santa Clara, Calif., 1980-84; regional sales mgr. U.S. Analytical Instruments, San Carlos, Calif., 1984—. Mem. ACS, Union Concerned Scientists, Nat. Assn. Female Execs. Home: 65 Bernal Ave Moss Beach CA 94038 Office: US Analytical Instruments 1511 Industrial Rd San Carlos CA 94070

BROSIOUS, MARY ANNE, municipal official; b. Chgo., Mar. 29, 1951; d. Donald W. and Virginia M. (Catanzaro) B. BS, U. Ill., 1973; postgrad., Roosevelt U., 1978-80. Recreation ctr. dir. Zion (Ill.) Park Dist., 1973-80; mgr. Fitness Ctr., Champaign, Ill., 1980-82; dir. North Berywn Park Dist., Ill., 1982-84; supr. recreation Franklin Park (Ill.) Park Dist., 1984—. Bd. dirs. ARC, Lake County, Ill., 1978-80.; pres. North Suburban Park and Recreation Assn., NE Ill. Spl. Recreation Assn. Bd., 1979-80. Named Boss of Yr. Profl. Secs. Internat., 1987. Mem. Nat. Recreation and Park Assn., Suburban Park and Recreation Assn., Ill. Park and Recreation Assn. (cert., bd. dirs. 1979-80). Office: Franklin Park Park Dist 9560 Franklin Ave Franklin Park IL 60131

BROSNAN, CAROL RAPHAEL SARAH, musician, arts reports specialist; b. Paterson, N.J., July 19, 1931; d. Basil Roger Warnock and Mary Ellen Carroll (McDonald) Brosnan; student George Washington U., Washington, 1956-61, U. Va., 1975, U. Oxford (Eng.), 1975; B.A. in History, George Washington U., 1981, postgrad., 1983-87; pupil Iris Brussels, Helen Yakobson. Adminstrv. clk. Dept. of Army, Def., Pentagon, Office of asst. chief of staff intelligence, Washington, 1955-58; clk. fgn. sci. info. program NSF, Washington, 1958-60, adminstrv. clk., 1960-65, adminstrv. fellowship clk. grad. fellowship program, 1965-72; reports specialist Nat. Found. Arts and Humanities, Nat. Endowment for Arts, Washington, 1972—; music tchr. piano, Paterson, N.J., 1945-53; piano recitalist U.S., Heidelberg, W. Ger. Served with WAC, 1953-55. Recipient Young People's Concerts award, 1945. Hon. fellow Harry S. Truman Library Inst. Nat. and Internat. Affairs, 1975. Fellow Intercontinental Biog. Assn.; mem. Am. Assn. for Advancement Slavic Studies, Am. Hist. Assn., Am. Philol. Assn., Acad. Polit. Sci. (contbg.), Am. Classical League, Friends of Bodleian Library (Oxford U.), Luther Rice Soc. of George Washington U. (life), Phi Alpha Theta. Home: 4338 Carmelo Dr Apt #202 Annandale VA 22003 Office: NEH 1100 Pennsylvania Ave NW Washington DC 20506

BROSSEAU, IRMA FINN, business executive; b. Boston, Sept. 4, 1930; d. Harry Miller and Alfreda (Zimmerman) Dyer; m. George Brosseau, Jan. 14, 1977; children by previous marriage—Hester, Jonathan, Sarah. B.S., Simmons Coll., 1952; hon. doctorate, Hawthorne Coll., 1984. Cert. assn. exec. Asst. to prodn. mgr. Houghton Mifflin Pub. Co., Boston, 1952-56; desk editor, women's editor Quincy (Mass.) Patriot Ledger, 1956-58; desk editor, reporter, feature writer, women's editor Anchorage Times, 1958-60, 66-71; desk editor Anchorage News, 1965-66; program dir. Nat. Fedn. Bus. and Profl. Women's Clubs, Inc., Washington, 1972-77; exec. dir. Nat. Fedn. Bus. and Profl. Women's Clubs, Inc., 1977-84; chief exec. officer Fedn Bus. and Profl. Women and Bus. and Profl. Women Found., Washington, 1984-87; pres. The Brosseau Group, Reston, Va., 1987—; founder Women's Exec. Groups, 1987, Double Track Mgmt. System; dir. Nat. Council on Future of Women in Workplace; cons. vol. leadership devel., mgmt., writer and workshop leader; speaker, trainer in mgmt. and strategic planning. mem. Reston Bd. Commerce; bd. of 10 Outstanding Young Women of Am. Recipient Alumnae Achievement award Simmons Coll., 1987. Mem. Am. Soc. Assn. Execs. (trustee found.), Greater Washington Soc. Assn. Execs., Potomac Bus. and Profl. Women's Club, AAUW, Nat. Platform Assn., Bus. Execs. Nat. Security, Network Entrepreneurial Women. Office: 11345 Sunset Hills Rd Reston VA 22090

BROTHERS, ANITA UHL, physician, psychiatrist; b. Alameda, Calif., Dec. 19, 1913; d. Joseph J. Uhl and Augusta Kelm; m. Ridgway Brothers, Mar. 21, 1953 (dec. Nov. 1961). BA, San Francisco State Coll., 1934; MA, Stanford U., 1942; MD, Women's Med. Coll. of Pa., 1949. Diplomate Am. Bd. Psychiatry and Neurology. Intern Herrick Meml. Hosp., Berkeley, Calif., 1949-50, resident, 1952-53; resident Warren (Pa.) State Hosp., 1950-52; mem. staff Herrick Hosp. and Health Ctr., 1955—; gen. practice medicine Berkeley, 1955—; staff mem. Everett A. Gladman Meml. Hosp., Oakland, Calif., 1979—, Highland Gen. Hosp., Oakland, 1957—; clin. asst. prof. psychiatry Stanford (Calif.) U., 1965-74; clin. cons. psychiat. residency tng. Herrick Meml. Hosp., 1957-77. Contbr. articles to profl. jours. Ambassador Dwight Shattuck Assn. Fellow Am. Psychiat. Assn., Royal Soc. Health; mem. Alameda Contra Costa Med. Assn. (councilor 1970—), Calif. Med. Assn., AMA, Berkeley C. of C. Presbyterian. Clubs: Berkeley City Commons, Commonwealth (San Francisco). Office: 2486 Shattuck Ave #305 Berkeley CA 94704

BROTHERS, JOYCE DIANE, psychologist; b. N.Y.C.; d. Morris K. and Estelle (Rapoport) Bauer; m. Milton Brothers, July 4, 1949; 1 child, Lisa Robin. BS, Cornell U., 1947; MA, Columbia U., 1950, PhD, 1953; LHD (hon.), Franklin Pierce Coll., Gettysburg Coll. Asst. psychology Columbia U., N.Y.C., 1948-52; instr. psychology Hunter Coll., N.Y.C., 1948-52; ind. psychologist, writer 1952—. Co-host: TV program Sports Showcase, 1956; appearances: TV program Dr. Joyce Brothers, 1958-63, Consult Dr. Brothers, 1960-66, Ask Dr. Brothers, 1965-75; hostess (TV syndication) Living Easy with Dr. Joyce Brothers, 1972-75; columnist TV syndication, N.Am. Newspaper Alliance, 1961-71, Bell-McClure Syndicate, 1963-71, King Features Syndicate, 1972—, Good Housekeeping mag., 1962—; appearances

Sta. WNBC, 1966-70; radio program Emphasis, 1966-75, Monitor, 1967-75, WMCA, 1970-73, ABC Reports, 1966-67, NBC Radio Network Newsline, 1975—; news analyst radio program, Metro Media-TV, 1975-76, news corr., TVN, Inc., 1975-76, Sta. KABC-TV, 1977-82, Sta. WABC-TV, 1980-82, , 86—, Sta. WLS-TV, 1980-82, NIWS Syndicated News Service, 1982-86, The Dr. Joyce Brothers Program, The Disney Channel, 1985, Sta. WABC-TV, 1987—; spl. feature writer Hearst papers, UPI; author: Ten Days to a Successful Memory, 1959, Woman, 1961, The Brothers System for Liberated Love and Marriage, 1975, How to Get Whatever You Want Out of Life, What Every Woman Should Know About Men, 1982, What Every Woman Ought to Know About Love and Marriage, 1984. Co-chmn. sports com. Lighthouse for Blind; door-to-door chmn. Fedn. Jewish Philanthropies, N.Y.C.; mem. fund raising com. Olympic Fund; mem. People-to-People Program. Recipient Mennen Baby Found. award, 1959, Newhouse Newspaper award, 1959, Am. Acad. Achievement award, Am. Parkinson Disease Assn. award, 1971, Sigma Delta Chi Deadline award, 1971, Pres.'s Cabinet award U. Detroit, 1975, Woman of Achievement award Women's City Club Cleve., 1981, award Calif. Home Econs. Assn., 1981, award Distributive Edn. Clubs Am., 1981, Pub. Service award Ridgewood Women's Club, 1987. Mem. Sigma Xi. Office: NBC 30 Rockefeller Plaza New York NY 10020

BROTHERS, KATHRYN ANN, lawyer, banker; b. Endicott, N.Y., June 26, 1955; d. Robert Douglas and Evelyn Juanita (Coffey) Brothers. BA in Polit. Sci., U. Ky., 1977, JD, 1981, MA in Diplomacy and Internat. Commerce, 1983. Bar: Ky. 1982. Sole practice law and legal research, Lexington, Ky., 1982-84; internat. credit analyst Sovran Bank/Cen. South, Nashville, 1984-86, internat. banking officer, 1986—. Active adoption group Amnesty Internat., Lexington, 1982-84, YWCA, Lexington, 1982—; campaign worker Harvey Sloane for Gov. Ky., 1979. Mem. ABA, Ky. Bar Assn., Phi Beta Kappa, Phi Delta Phi. Democrat. Episcopalian. Office: Sovran Bank/Cen South Internat Banking Dept One Commercer Pl Nashville TN 37219

BROTHERS, M(URIEL) ELIZABETH, college official; b. Bklyn.; d. Sydney Inman and Marguerite Olley (Taylor-Lindsay) B.; AB with distinction in Spanish, Vassar Coll., 1950; postgrad. Latin Am. Inst., N.Y. Sch. Employing Printers, Philanthropy Tax Inst. Various editorial positions McCall Corp., 1951-62; devel. officer Mt. Holyoke Coll., South Hadley, Mass., 1962-67, 71-73; dir. publs. and dir. pub. info., 1967-71, dir. devel., 1973-80; assoc. v.p. devel Rollins Coll., Winter Park, Fla., 1980—; dir. Mass. Congl. Fund, 1979-80; lectr., cons. fin. planning for women. Author articles, handbooks in field. Moderator 1st Congl. Ch., Winter Park, 1986—; v.p. Christopher D. Smithers Found.; bd. govs. Crosby Found.; bd. dirs. English Speaking Union. Recipient Outstanding Profl. Fund Raiser award, 1985. Mem. AAUW, Mt. Holyoke Alumni Assn. (hon.). Republican. Clubs: Cosmopolitan (N.Y.C.); University (Winter Park); Vassar of Cen. Fla.; Fla. Exec. Women (dir.) (Orlando); Mt. Holyoke of Del. (hon.). Office: Rollins College Winter Park FL 32789

BROUCH, VIRGINIA M., educational consulting company executive; b. Aurora, Ill., Feb. 17, 1939; d. John Edward and Louise Barbara (Brummel) B. AB, Coll. St. Francis, 1961; MA in Art Edn., Ariz. State U., 1965, EdD, 1970; postdoctoral, Phoenix Coll., 1971-72, 85-86. Cert. tchr., Ariz. Tchr. OLPH Elem. Sch., Glendale, Ariz., 1962-63; from instr. to assoc. prof. art edn. Ariz. State U. Coll. Fine Arts, Tempe, 1965-74; from assoc. prof. to prof., chmn. dept. art edn./craft design Fla. State U. Sch. Visual Arts, Tallahassee, 1974-81; gen. ptnr. Desert World, 1981—; pres. Palo Verde Research Assocs., 1981—; pres. Playful Goat Prodns., 1984—; vis. faculty art dept. Phoenix Coll. Evening Div., 1981—; adj. grad. prof. U. Houston Coll. Edn., 1977-84; vis. prof. U. Tex. Lubbock, summer program at Junction, 1979; summer vis. faculty U. Ariz. Art Dept., Tucson, 1966; art tchr., cons. Alhambra Elem. Dist., Phoenix, 1964-65; lectr. in field; art edn. cons. SeaWorld, Orlando, Fla., 1981; cons. Ind. State Dept. Pub. Instrn., 1974; project dir. Evaluating Sandy Hook Artist-Tchr. Inst. for NEA and N.J. State Arts Council, 1978-79. Author one book; contbr. articles to profl. jours.

BROUDE, JOSEPHINE RACHEL, university administrator; b. N.Y.C., May 25, 1927; d. Emanuel and Eva (Lieberson) Rosen; A.B., Antioch Coll., 1949; m. Henry W. Broude, June 29, 1947. With Shepley, Bulfinch, Richardson & Abbott, Boston, 1950-54; interior designer, adminstrv. asst. Douglas Orr, AIA, New Haven, 1954-65; exec. asst. to provost, cons. for interior planning Yale U., New Haven, 1965—, fellow Silliman Coll. Bd. govs. Mory's Assn., 1974—. Guest editor Mademoiselle mag., 1948. Club: Elizabethan. Office: Yale U Provost's Office New Haven CT 06520

BROUGHTON, BEVERLY JANE, construction executive; b. Detroit, Oct. 8, 1927; d. Donald John and Ida Mae (Coller) Garpow; m. Howard Millar Trerice, Jan. 3, 1953 (div. Mar. 1974); children: Howard Owen, Bruce Whitney. BA, Wayne U., 1949, cert. in teaching, 1951. Free-lance lectr. 1951-54; ins. agt. Donald Garpow Agy., Detroit, 1954-64; ptnr. Mobile Office Equipment Co., Detroit, 1979-85; owner, pres. Best Mobile Office/Modulars, Pontiac, Mich., 1985—. Acrylic art represented in pvt. collections. Alt. del. Mich. Reps., Grand Rapids, 1984. Mem. Nat. Assn. for Self-Employed, Nat. Assn. for Female Execs., Constrn. Assn. Mich. Christian Scientist. Office: Best Mobile Office Modulars 4080 Dixie Hwy Drayton Plains MI 48020

BROUGHTON, SHARON KAY, social services administrator; b. Mt. Clemens, Mich., Sept. 25, 1953; d. Frederick Ray and Helen May (Tower) Ridge; m. Robert Lee Broughton, Aug. 19, 1972; children: Kimberly Dana, Paul Robert. BS, Ind. State U., 1974; MS, Ind. U. Southeast, New Albany, 1977. Cert. tchr., time study analyst, Ind. Tchr. home econs. and biology Crawford County Community Schs., Marengo, Ind., 1974-76; mgmt. trainee John C. Groub, Co., Corydon, Ind., 1976-77; mgr. med. office Dr. Fred Ridge, Corydon, 1978-79; time study analyst Dept. Commerce, Jeffersonville, Ind., 1979-81; extension agt. Purdue U. Coop. Extension Service, English, Ind., 1981—; bd. dirs. Maternal Health and Well-Child Bd., English. Bd. dirs. comml. foods adv. bd. South Cen. Area Vocat. Sch., Rego, Ind., 1983-87. Mem. Nat. Assn. Extension Home Economists, Ind. Extension Agts. Assn. (chmn. com. 1986-87, Team Work award 1986, Bob Amick Youth Agt. award 1986), Nat. Assn. 4-H Agts., Crawford County C. of C. (chmn. com. 1983-84), Crawford County Social Services Assn. (sec. 1982-87). Presbyterian. Club: English Civic (bd. dirs. county fair 1981-87). Lodge: Order Eastern Star (asst. conductress 1978-81, conductress 1981-82, worthy matron 1982-85, marshall 1986-87). Home: Rt 1 Box 237 Marengo IN 47140 Office: Coop Extension Service 110 N Main St English IN 47118

BROUSE, ANN GUSTINA, librarian, storyteller; b. Hornell, N.Y., July 22, 1948; d. Edward Daniel and Wanda Mary (Wenderlich) Gustina; m. Gary Eugene Brouse, Apr. 22, 1978. B.S. in Edn., SUNY-Cortland, 1970; M.L.S., George Peabody Coll. for Tchrs., 1971. Cert. pub. librarian, sch. library media specialist, N.Y. Librarian, Steele Meml. Library, Elmira, N.Y., 1971—, br. head Elmira Heights Br. Library, 1977-80, Southside Br. Library, Elmira, 1980-83, head tech. services dept., parent library, 1983—; storyteller, various local and regional events, Ithaca and Elmira, 1979—; speaker various regional library workshops, 1982—. Scriptwriter, announcer Library News Spots, Cable-TV, 1976-77; book reviewer Sch. Library Jour., N.Y.C., 1979—. Mem. Chemung County LWV, Elmira, 1981—, historian, 1983-85, v.p., 1985-86, pres., 1986-87. Mem. ALA, N.Y. Library Assn., Internat. Reading Assn., N.Y. State Reading Assn., Nat. Assn. for Preservation and Perpetuation of Story Telling, Beta Phi Mu. Democrat. Roman Catholic. Home: 3261 Easterbrook Dr Horseheads NY 14845 Office: Steele Meml Library 1 Library Plaza Elmira NY 14901

BROUSSARD, CAROL MADELINE, writer, photographer; b. Albany, Calif., Apr. 24, 1942; d. Roy E. and Adele (Belfils) Avila; m. Marvin E. Broussard; children: Valerie Madeline, Sean Hunter. Student, West Hill Coll., Coalinga, Calif., Coll. Sequoias, Visalia, Calif., Inst. Metaphysics, La Brea, Calif. Pub. TV Watch, Tyler, Tex., 1969-74; resource sec. John C. Fremont Sch., Corcoran, Calif., 1974-77; editor Coalinga (Calif.) Record, 1978-81; pub. Kern Valley Chronicle, Lake Isabella, Calif., 1981-84; free-lance journalist Selma, Calif., 1987—. Recipient Best Feature Photo award Calif. Justice System, 1984, World of Child Photo award Fresno City and County Offices, 1980. Republican. Home and Office: 1451 Mill St #105 Selma CA 93662

BROUSSARD, MARGARET FAYE, office manager; b. Lafayette, La., Nov. 26, 1952; d. Chester Joseph and Mary Broussard; m. Steven Edmond, June 2, 1973 (div.). Student, U. Southwestern La., 1970-73; cert., San Jacinto Jr. Coll., Houston, 1975; BS, Tex. So. U., 1978. CRT operator, sr. terminal operator 1st City Nat. Bank, Houston, 1974-75; sec., librarian Tex. So. U. Banking Ctr., Houston, 1975-78; part-time sec. Tex. So. U. Day Care Ctr. and Temporaries Inc., Houston, 1978-79; adminstrv. sec., accounts payable clk. Temporaries Inc., Houston, 1979-80; accounts payable clk., in-house temp. Met. Transit Authority, Houston, 1980-81; office asst., word processing specialist Houston Oil & Minerals, Houston, 1981-82, Tenneco Oil Corp. (acquired Houston Oil & Minerals 1982), Houston, 1982-83; adminstrv. asst. Hoover Keith & Bruce Inc., Houston, 1983-87; office mgr. Collaboration in Sci. and Tech. Inc., Houston, 1987—. Vol. Sheltering Arms, Houston, 1981-83, March of Dimes 12 Mile Walk, Houston, 1985, Head Start & Food Pantries, Houston, 1985—. Recipient Nat. Def. grantee U. Southwestern La., 1970-73. Mem. Nat. Assn. Female Execs. Office: Collaboration in Sci and Tech Inc 15835 Park Ten Place Suite 105 Houston TX 77084-5131

BROWER, ANN M., retired newspaper executive; b. Stowe, Pa., Nov. 26, 1924; d. Ralph J. and Mary A. (St. Cross) Capaldi; student Pottstown Sch. Bus., 1942-43; m. Francis T. Brower, Oct. 22, 1949; children—Patricia A., Karen L., Richard A. Bookkeeper, sec. Levin's Dept. Store, 1943-48; payroll clk., bookkeeper Pottstown (Pa.) Mercury, 1948-52, 66-73, office mgr., 1974-79, comptroller, 1979-83; teller 1st Fed. Savs. and Loan, 1952-53. Active fundraiser Cub Scouts Am., Boy Scouts Am., 1969-79. Mem. Nat. Assn. Female Execs., North Coventry Fire Co. Aux. Home: 103 W Cedarville Rd Pottstown PA 19464

BROWER, VERA ANN, banker, consultant; b. Nutley, N.J., Aug. 10, 1932; d. Stanley Joseph and Vera Edith (Gray) Newitts; m. Charles William Brower, July 17, 1950 (dec. 1973); children: Gayle Ann Feld, Jeffrey Charles. Student, Montclair State Coll., 1949-50, Stonier Grad. Sch. Banking, New Brunswick, N.J., 1976-78, Am. Inst. Banking, Morris County, N.J. Teller Bank of Nutley, N.J., 1950-51, Nat. Newark & Essex Bank, Caldwell, N.J., 1961-66; platform asst., asst. br. mgr., comml. loan officer Am. Nat. Bank, Morristown, N.J., 1966-76; bus. devel. officer, br. mgr., tng. dir. United Jersey Banks, Hackensack, N.J.; dir. retail tng. United Jersey Banks, Princeton, N.J., 1986-88; cons. Vera Brower, Holland, Pa., 1984—; instr. Am. Inst. Banking, Bloomfield, N.J., 1982—; adj. instr. Morris County Coll., Randolphe, N.J., 1985-86; lectr. in field. Bd. dirs., sec.-treas., com. chmn. Women Bus. Owners Ednl. Coalition, Lawrenceville, N.J., 1986-88; bd. dirs., sec. N.J. Network Bus. and Profl. Women, Kearney, N.J., 1982-87; bd. dirs. Pvt. Industry Council, Bergen County, 1982-85; pres. East Hanover Library Assn., 1956-60. Recipient Nat. Pub. Speaking award Am. Inst. Banking, Mpls., 1975. Mem. Am. Inst. Banking (chpt. pres. 1972), Nat. Soc. for Performance and Instrn., Am. Bank Trainers and Cons., Am. Soc. for Tng. and Devel.

BROWES, PAULINE, Canadian legislator; b. Harwood, Ont., Can., May 7, 1938; d. Robert Earle and Clara (Sandercock) Drope; m. George Harold Browes, Sept. 12, 1961; children: Tammy, Janet, Jeffrey. Student, Toronto Tchrs. Coll., York U., McLaughlin Coll. Mem. for Scarborough Can. Ho. of Commons. Mem. Progressive Conservative Party. Anglican. Club: Albany of Toronto, U. Women's Club, Scarborough Golf and Country Club. Office: 251 Confederation Bldg, Ottawa, ON Canada K1A 0A6 *

BROWN, ALICE ROBERTA, customer service manager; b. Pottsville, Pa., July 5, 1952; d. Emmett Franklin and Ruth Minnie (Nagle) Miller; m. Edward Martin Brown, Dec. 7, 1974; children—Jeremy Scott, Travis Edward. B.S. in Psychology, Millersville U., 1973; M.S. in Human Resource Mgmt., U. Utah, Stuttgart, W.Ger., 1978. Lab. technician, Bio-Med. Labs., Friedensburg, Pa., 1969-71; mgr. Sico, Lancaster, Pa., 1971-73; quality control mgr. Berkley Products Co., Akron, Pa., 1974-75, order dept. clk., 1978-79, customer service mgr., 1979—, safety and health officer, 1979—, personnel employment counselor, 1980—, gen. mgr. chmn. mgmt. div., 1988—; switchboard operator U.S. Army, Stuttgart, 1975-77. Mem. Nat. Assn. Female Execs. Republican. Avocations: camping; gardening; motorcycling; reading. Office: Berkely Products Co PO Box E Akron PA 17501

BROWN, ANN CARLSON, psychiatrist; b. Lorain, Ohio, June 19, 1930; d. Benjamin and Edna (Dellinger) Carlson; B.S., Otterbein Coll., Westerville, Ohio, 1948; M.D., Case-Western Res. U., 1956; children—Catherine, Elizabeth, Robert, Andrew. Intern, St. Luke's Hosp., Cleve., 1956-57, resident in pediatrics, 1957-58; resident in psychiatry Hall Inst., Columbia, S.C., 1976-80; practice medicine specializing in psychiatry, Charlotte, N.C., 1980—. Recipient Ohio Gov.'s award for community action, 1974, Service to Mankind award Sertoma, Zanesville, Ohio, 1976. Office: 1900 Randolph Rd Charlotte NC 28207

BROWN, ANN LOUISE, corporate account executive; b. Portsmouth, Ohio; d. Ernest Joseph and Imogene Elizabeth (Shay) Redoutey; m. LeRoy Chester (L.C.) Brown, Apr. 14, 1967; children: Anthony, Tina Marie. Student, Sears Sch. Modeling, 1972. Mgr., buyer JoAnn's Boutique, New Carlisle, Ohio, 1960-73; free-lance model Ohio and Ga., 1972-79; mem. staff pub. relations Valdosta (Ga.) Sheraton Inn, 1974-75; free-lance vocalist Valdosta, 1974-76; tchr. Eileen's Sch. Modeling, Valdosta, 1975-76; rep. mktg., pub. relations Cadillac Fairview, Atlanta, 1977-81; corp. acct. exec. Sunshine Furniture, Atlanta, 1983-84, Aaron Rents and Sells Office Furniture, Atlanta, 1984—. State finalist Mrs. Georgia pageant, 1985, 86. Fellow Nat. Network Women in Sales; mem. Nat. Assn. Female Execs., Female Execs. of N. Atlanta, Atlanta C. of C. Roman Catholic. Home: 3149 N Woods Trail Douglasville GA 30135 Office: Aaron Rents & Sells Office Furniture 4194A NE Expressway Atlanta GA 30340

BROWN, ANNE BARBARA, financial executive; b. Bronxville, N.Y., Sept. 22, 1949; d. Paul Robert and Anne (Brady) B.; m. William Lawrence Farrell, Sept. 28, 1975; 1 dau. B.A., Trinity Coll., Washington, 1971; M.B.A., U. Pa., 1973. Fixed income salesperson Goldman, Sachs & Co., N.Y.C., 1973-78, v.p., 1978-83, v.p., fin. futures specialist, Dallas, 1983-87; v.p. fixed income div., N.Y.C., 1987—. Mem. women's com. Girl Scouts of N.Y., N.Y.C., 1982-83. Heubner fellow Wharton Grad. Sch., U. Pa., 1972. Mem. Trinity Coll. Alumni Assn. N.Y., Wharton Grad. Alumni Assn., Phi Beta Kappa. Roman Catholic. Club: Wharton (N.Y.C.) (officer 1975-79). Office: Goldman Sachs & Co 85 Broadway St New York City NY 10004

BROWN, ARLENE ANN, data communications company executive; b. Cleve., Feb. 21, 1951; d. Lawrence Francis and Irene Marie (Kandzer) Tamasovich; m. William David Brown, June 25, 1977; children—Raymond Noel, Lawrence Joseph. B.S., Notre Dame Coll., Cleve., 1971; postgrad. Baldwin-Wallace Coll., 1974-76. System analyst Ohio Bell Telephone Co., Cleve., 1971-76; mktg. specialist So. Bell Telephone Co., Atlanta, 1977-78; acct. exec. Teletype Corp., Skokie, Ill., 1978-79, sales mgr., 1979-80, regional sales mgr., 1980-82; v.p. sales David Brown Assoc., Atlanta, 1982; computer cons. Notre Dame Coll., 1972-73. Sec. Stonehaven Homeowners Assn., Ga., 1986. NSF grantee, 1970; recipient Digilog Sales award Digilog, Inc., 1984-85. Mem. Am. Mgmt. Assn., Ga. Telecommunications Assn., Nat. Assn. Female Execs. Roman Catholic. Avocations: golfing, tennis, sailing, traveling. Office: David Brown Assos Inc PO Box 1048 Stone Mountain GA 30086

BROWN, ARLENE PATRICIA THERESA, artist; b. Elizabeth, N.J., Jan. 3, 1953; d. William J. and Adelaide Elizabeth (Von Krasa) B.; student Union Coll., 1971; B.A., Kean Coll., 1980. Owner, pres. Reni Co., Roselle, N.J., 1979—; pvt. tchr. art, Roselle, 1979—; owner Twinks Trademark and Associated Characters. Exhibited in The Children's Mus., Ind.; patentee in field. Recipient 3d Place award Custom Car and Van Show, Meadowlands, N.J., 1981, 2d place award Custom Car and Van Show, Asbury Park, N.J., 1982. Mem. Graphic Artists Guild, Artists' Equity Assn., Summit Art Assn., Princeton Art Assn., Am. Women's Econ. Devel. Assn., Found. Christian Living, Positive Thinkers Club, N.J. Art Dirs. Club, Westfield Art Assn., Alumni Assn. Kean Coll. Mailing Address: PO Box 186 Roselle Park NJ 07204

BROWN, BARBARA JEAN, gift shop owner; b. Houston, Mar. 9, 1941; d. Ralph Barrett and Martha Jeanette (Burress) Lee; m. Sam J. Brown, III, Aug. 15, 1964 (div. July 1978); children—Sheryl Jean, Samuel Jones IV. B.B.A., Baylor U., 1963. Co-owner, Butterflies Cards & Gifts, Houston, 1978—; co-owner Namesakes Personalized Gifts, Houston, 1984—; ptnr. A Better Idea, Houston, 1980—; dir. Spur Land Co., Houston. Third v.p., then 4th v.p. Houston Jr. Forum, 1973-76, treas., 1976-78. Mem. Nat. Assn. Female Execs. Gift Assn. Am., Nat. Assn. Women Bus. Owners. Republican. Baptist. Home: 11707 Wickhollow Houston TX 77043 Office: Butterflies Cards & Gifts 2423 Post Oak Blvd Houston TX 77056

BROWN, BARBARA JEANERAUD, nurse; b. Detroit, Oct. 7, 1944; d. Henry and Agnes (Godwin) Watkins; married; children: Henry, Oliver, Clifford, Joy, Shyamala. BS, Fla. A&M U., 1964, Fla. A&M U., 1965; RN, Coll. of the Desert, 1984. Cardiac nurse Desert Hosp., Palm Springs, Calif., 1984—. Active Desert Mus., 1980—, Nat. Charity League, Tiempo De La Ninos. Democrat. Mem. Pentacostal Ch. Home: 940 Avenida Olivos Palm Springs CA 92262

BROWN, BARBARA LYNN, nurse; b. Tuscaloosa, Ala., Sept. 12, 1950; d. John Thomas and Kathryn Irene (Clifton) Jones; m. Randy Lee Brown, Mar. 26, 1971 (div. Feb. 1979); 1 child, Randy Lee II. BS in Nursing, U. Ala., 1978; MS in Nursing, U. Fla., 1984. Staff nurse VA Med. Ctr., Tuscaloosa, Ala., 1978-81, Murfreesboro, Tenn., 1981-82; clin. nurse specialist HCA Grant Ctr. Hosp., Citra, Fla., 1984-85, nurse coordinator, 1985-86, asst. dir. nursing, 1986-87, mem. speakers bur., 1985-87; dir. nursing HCA Harbour Shores Hosp., Ft. Pierce, Fla., 1987-88, HCA Sonora Desert Hosp., Tucson, 1988—; mem. speakers bur. HCA Harbour Shores Hosp., Ft. Pierce, Fla., 1987. Bd. dirs. Dist. III. Mental Health Bd., Inc., Gainesville, 1982-84. Mem. Am. Nurses Assn., Fla. Orgn. of Nurse Execs., Nat. Assn. Female Execs., Sigma Theta Tau. Democrat. Baptist. Office: HCA Sonora Desert Hosp 1920 W Rudasill Rd Tucson AZ 85704

BROWN, BEATRICE, symphony conductor; b. Leeds, Eng., May 17, 1917; came to U.S., 1921, naturalized, 1927; d. Abraham and Sarah (Levinson) B.; m. Morris Rothenberg, Jan. 29, 1961. BA, Hunter Coll., 1937; MA, N.Y.U., 1939; Berkshire Music Center scholar, 1948-49; Condr. Chamber Music Assocs., N.Y.C., 1950-53; music dir., condr. Scranton (Pa.) Philharm. Orch., 1963-72, Ridgefield (Conn.) Orch., 1969—, Western Conn. Symphony Orch., Danbury, 1981—, Housatonic Chamber Orch., 1982—; condr. N.Y., N.J., Conn. opera cos.; TV appearances; lectr.; violist symphony orchs., 1944—, Chamber Music Group, Musique Vivante, Am. Symphony Orch., N.Y. Pops Orch., 1979—; instr. music Hunter Coll., 1937-43; tchr. music N.Y.C. Pub. Schs., 1944-61; adj. asst. prof. Lehman Coll., 1972-74; tchr. music Bronx High Sch. Sci., N.Y.C., 1970-79. Fulbright grantee, 1953-55, Martha Baird Rockefeller grantee, 1957-59, Peace award UN, 1980, Wellington award, 1981; named to Hunter Coll. Hall of Fame, 1972; named One of 100 Disting. Women in Conn., 1976, One of 5 outstanding Women in Ridgefield, Conn., 1979. Mem. Am. Symphony Orch. League (bd. dirs.), Condrs. Guild Am. (bd. dirs. 1985—), Phi Beta Kappa. Home and Office: 3 Seir Hill Rd Apt C2 Norwalk CT 06850-1328

BROWN, BEATRICE SANDRA, musicologist, educator, performing arts director; b. Louisville, July 14, 1950. B.M.Ed., U. Louisville, 1972; M.A., Ph.D., Columbia Pacific U., 1987. Music and choral dir. Holy Temple Ch., 1978—; music dir. AC-BAW Ctr. for Arts, 1982-84; dir., music tchr. Holmes elem. Sch., Mt. Vernon, N.Y., 1983-84; performing arts cons. N.Y. State Council for Arts, 1984—; founder, dir. Mt. Vernon African-Am. Music Arts Festival; dir., music dir. Musical Arts of Creative Expression, 1972—; founder, dir. Mus. Arts Inst. Creative Expression for Children, 1986—; choral dir., tchr. music U. Louisville, 1969-75; cons. N.Y. State Council for Arts, 1984—. Recipient letter of award U. Louisville, 1970; Songwriter award Sta. WLOU Radio, Louisville, 1971; cert. U. Louisville, 1974, Appreciation award African-Am. Music Arts Festival Commn., 1984. Mem. Sigma Gamma Rho (hon.). Office: PO Box 203 New York NY 10460

BROWN, BERNICE LEONA BAYNES, foundation consultant, educator, consultant; b. Pitts., June 19, 1935; d. Howard Leon and Henrietta Lydia (Hodges) Baynes; m. James Brown, May 4, 1964; 1 child, Kiyeseni Anu. BFA, Carnegie Mellon U., 1957; MEd, U. Pitts., 1966. Tchr. Pitts. Pub. Schs., 1957-65; lectr. Carlow Coll., Pitts., 1964-67; edn. specialist Bay Area Urban League, San Francisco, 1967-68; asst. prof. San Francisco Coll. for Women, 1968-72; dean students Lone Mountain Coll., San Francisco, 1972-76; dir. San Francisco Pub. Schs. Commn., 1976; program exec. San Francisco Found., 1977-86; ednl. cons. San Francisco, 1987—; vis. scholar Stanford (Calif.) U., 1987-88. Mem. Bd. of Govs., Calif. Community Colls., 1975-81, Calif. Post Secondary Edn. Commn., Sacramento, 1978-80, State Supt's Adv. Com. on Black Affairs, Calif., 1985—; chair Found. Community Service Cable T.V., San Francisco, 1982-84; trustee Schs. of the Sacred Heart, San Francisco, 1982-87. Mem. Women and Founds. Corp. (bd. dirs. 1985-87), Assn. Black Found. Execs. (bd. dirs. 1978-82). Club: Commonwealth of Calif. (bd. govs. 1988—). Home and Office: 1271 23d Ave San Francisco CA 94122

BROWN, BETTY JO, state services administrator; b. Nacogdoches, Tex., Nov. 21, 1949; d. Clinton C. and Sarah (Washington) Upshaw; m. Clifford Allen Brown Sr., Dec. 19, 1970; children: Clifford Allen Jr., Courtney Allison. BS magna cum laude, Stephen F. Austin State U., 1971, postgrad., 1978—. Purchasing agt. Internat. Paper Co., Nacodoches, 1971-73; counselor Adult Basic Edn. Corp., Rusk, Tex., 1973-76; counselor Deep East Tex. Council of Govts., Lufkin, 1976-78, counselor coordinator, 1978-80, computer dir., 1979-80, program dir., 1980-83, job tng. program dir., 1983, program dir., 1984-87. Mem. Nat. Council Negro Women, Inc., Washington, 1985-87. Mem. Nat. Assn. Female Execs., Assn. Employment and Tng. Profls., Job Tng. Program Dirs. Assn. (treas. Austin 1985—), Tex. Assn. Pvt. Counselors, Delta Sigma Theta. Democrat. Methodist. Home: Rt 14 Box 7430 Nacogdoches TX 75961

BROWN, BEVERLY JEAN, educator; b. Pensacola, Fla., Jan. 24, 1943; d. Elisha and Melanie Alfreda (Creal) Jones; m. Ozie Marion Portis, May 1, 1963 (div. Apr. 1976); 1 child, Diedra LaShalle; m. Ernest Arnell Brown, Oct. 13, 1978. BS, Fla. A&M U., 1966; M of Edn., U. North Fla., 1986. Tchr. Meriwether County Sch. Dist., Greenville, Ga., 1966-67, Hamilton County Sch. Dist., Jasper, Fla., 1968-69; tchr. Duval County Sch. Dist., Jacksonville, Fla., 1969-82, primary resource tchr., 1982—. Mem. Am. Fedn. Tchrs., Fla. Edn. Assn. (sec. minority affairs), Duval County Reading Assn., Duval Tchrs. United (chmn. minority affairs), Phi Delta Kappa. Democrat. African Methodist Episcopalian. Lodge: Order Ea. Star. Home: 5135 Chivalry Dr Jacksonville FL 32208

BROWN, BEVERLY KAY, educator; b. Bloomington, Ind., Dec. 31, 1946; d. Fredrick Blaine and Wanda Ellen (Frye) Deckard; m. Stephen Lloyd Brown, June 21, 1969; 1 child, Sean Lane. BE, Ind. U., 1969; MEd, Mich. State U., 1978. Long distance operator Indiana Bell, Bloomington, 1965-69; elem. tchr. Livonia (Mich.) Pub. Schs., 1969-78, tchr. gifted students (Alternate Classroom for the Academically Talented program), 1978—. Mem. Mich. Assn. Computer Users Learning (speaker), Mich. Apple Club. Office: Alternate Classroom 34633 Munger Livonia MI 48154

BROWN, BILLIE AUGUSTINE, educator, artist; b. Pangburn, Ark., Aug. 1, 1924; d. Prince Colombus and Icy May Wood; m. James A. Brown, Nov. 26, 1969; children by previous marriage—Terry Wood, Dawn Elizabeth, Benjamin McLove, Laura Delphine. BS in Edn., Harding Coll., Searcy, Ark., 1962, MS, 1966; MA in Guidance and Counseling, U. Central Ark., 1974. Librarian, White County, Ark. 1947-52; U.S. postal clk., 1954; pub. sch. tchr., 1959—; art specialist Pulaski County (Ark.) Spl. Sch. Dist., 1978-79, instructional coordinator art, 1979-87 ; sculptor, Little Rock, 1987—; lectr. art edn. U. Ark., Little Rock, 1987—; co-founder, bd. advisers Ark. Young Artists Assn.; mem. Very Spl. Arts Bd., 1986—, treas., 1987—, U.S.A. Art Mentor Handicapped in Art. Recipient 1st place award in pastel White County Art Show, 1957, 1st place in illus. poetry Ark. Festival Arts, 1973, Patron of Arts award Ark. Young Artists Assn., 1985, Spl. Achievement award Phi Delta Kappa, 1985. Mem. Nat. Art Edn. Assn., Ark. Art Educators, Mid-So. Watercolorists (chair profl. growth com.), Ark. for Arts, Delta Kappa Gamma. Democrat. Baptist. Home and Office: 5302 Dreher Ln Little Rock AR 72209

BROWN, BONITA BOGER, state agency administrator, accountant; b. Akron, Ohio, Apr. 1, 1947; d. Vernon Glenn Boger and Nancy Anne (Kalaj) Corbett; m. Gregory George Bozin, Sept. 13, 1969 (div.); m. Ben R. Brown, Sept. 8, 1973; children: Ben R. Jr., George A., Gena Lee. BS, Ohio State U., 1969, MS, 1970; MS, La. State U., 1971. CPA, La. Librarian La. State Library, Baton Rouge, 1972-73; assoc. librarian La. State U., Baton Rouge, 1973-80; acct. Postlethwaite & Netterville, CPA's, Baton Rouge, 1981-82; contract administr. State of La., Baton Rouge, 1982—. Mem. Am. Inst. CPA's, La. Soc. CPA's, Am. Soc. Women Accts. (pres. Baton Rouge chpt. 1987—), Phi Beta Kappa. Office: State of La Contract Rev Div Adminstrn PO Box 94095 Baton Rouge LA 70804

BROWN, BONITA STARLIPER, nursing home administrator; b. Winchester, Va., May 26, 1942; d. Howard P. and Margaret E. Starliper; R.N., Winchester Meml. Hosp., 1963; BBA, Mary Baldwin Coll., 1988; m. Richard F. Brown, Mar. 10, 1962; children—Elizabeth, Christopher. Office nurse, 1963-66; mem. staff Shawnee Springs Nursing Home, Winchester, 1973-87, orientation coordinator, shift supr., 1978-81, dir. nursing, asst. adminstr., 1978-81, nursing home adminstr., 1981-87; dir. tng. Beverly Enterprises Ea. Div., 1987—, mem. adv. com., 1984-87; mem. nursing craft adv. com. health occupations Dowell J. Howard Vocat. Sch., Winchester, 1977-79; adj. faculty nursing program Shenandoah Coll., 1980-82; adv. craft com. James Rumsey nursing asst. program Martinsburg (W.Va.) Vocat. Sch., 1978-81; mem. edn. and tng. com. Va. Health Care Assn., 1980-81, membership chmn., 1984-86; employee adv. com. Va. Employment Commn., 1980-82; mem. health tech. curriculum adv. com. Lord Fairfax Community Coll., 1984-86; preceptor bd. examiners for nursing home adminstrs. State of Va., 1984-87; mem. Joint Subcom. to Study Supply and Demand for Nurses in Va., 1988—. Mem. Am. Coll. Nursing Home Adminstrs., Am. Coll. Health Care Adminstrs., Va. Health Care Assn. (chairperson state edn. and tng. com. 1986-87, chairperson conv. com. 1985, sec. cen. dist. 1986). Winchester Bus. and Profl. Women's Club (chmn. Nat. Bus. Women's Week). Baptist. Address: 928 Baja Ct Virginia Beach VA 23456

BROWN, BONNIE LOUISE, state legislator; b. San Francisco, Oct. 5, 1942; d. Wilbert Lauren and Thelma (Asbury) Wonderley; m. Gary Leigh Brown, June 13, 1965; children—Mollie Shannon, Joel Alexander. Student, Oreg. State U., 1962-65, U. Idaho, 1965-69; B.A. in English, Morris Harvey Coll., 1971. Tchr. theatre Morris Harvey Coll., Charleston, W.Va., 1973; legis. coordinator W. Va. Citizen Action Group, Charleston, 1975-76; project dir. Com. for Humanities and Public Policy, Charleston, 1976-77; cons. Appalachian Ednl. Lab., Charleston, 1980; state legislator 23d Dist. Charleston, W.Va., 1982—; lobbyist W.Va. NOW, 1976-82; ERA field organizer, 1978-82. Contbr. articles to profl. jours. Chmn., South Charleston Human Rights Commn., 1976; advisor W.Va. Women's Commn., 1977—. Recipient 1st ann. Susan B. Anthony award, 1980; named Bus. and Profl. Women's Woman of Yr., 1987. Mem. Order Women Legislators. Democrat. Home: 2328 Woodland Ave South Charleston WV 25303

BROWN, BRENDA LEE, military officer; b. Ft. Bragg, N.C., Feb. 5, 1963; d. Fletcher C. and Octavia (Grace) B. BS in Computer Sci., Winston-Salem State U., 1985. Cmmd. 2nd lt. U.S. Army, advanced through grades to 1st lt., 1985. Democrat. Methodist. Home: 3608-A Hereford Ln Killeen TX 76541 Office: 54th Signal Battalion B Co Fort Hood TX 76544

BROWN, CAROL ANNE, manufacturers' representative; b. Detroit, Feb. 26, 1947; d. Bruno Walter and Irene Sabina (Derengowski) Siedlarz; student Los Angeles City Coll., 1971, DeAnza Community Coll., 1973; m. Leonard Brown, Apr. 24, 1976; 1 son, David. Sec., Fairchild Semicondrs., Detroit, 1965-69, inside sales rep., Mountain View, Calif., 1969-74; sales rep. Calif. Circuit Engring., Sunnyvale, 1974-76; owner, operator Brown Sales Co., Mission Viejo, Calif., 1976-79; pres., gen. mgr. S.W. Contemporary Sales, Inc., Scottsdale, Ariz., 1979—. Mem. Bus. and Profl. Women Am., Network Female Execs. Republican. Roman Catholic. Home and Office: 12580 N 84th Pl Scottsdale AZ 85260

BROWN, CAROLYN MARGUERITE HUTCHINSON, computer systems manager; b. Hampton, Va., Dec. 6, 1936; d. Mark Edwin and Myrtle Rowena (Wood) Hutchinson; m. Ronald Lee Taylor, Sept. 28, 1957 (div. Mar. 1961); m. Sidney James Brown, Feb. 15, 1969; adopted children: Debra Kathleen Brown Peters, Stephen Paul, Gregory Lawrence, Tracy Lynn Brown Bullock. Student, Va. Poly. Inst., 1956-57, Fla. Tech. Coll., 1964-65. Cost acct. Beoing Aerospace Co., Cape Canaveral, Fla., 1967-69; acct. Bechtel Power Corp., Morgantown, Md., 1969-70; engring. aide Bechtel Power Corp., Gaithersburg, Md., 1970-72; planning engr. Bechtel Power Corp., Grand Gulf, Miss., 1975-77; systems analyst Pacific Internat. Corp., Gaithersburg, 1972-74; field engr. Canadian Bechtel Ltd., Ft. McMurray, Alta., Can., 1974; systems analyst Bechtel Corp., San Francisco, 1979-80; project scheduler TERA Corp., Berkeley, Calif., 1980-81; sr. staff cons. customer base Systonetics, Inc., Fullerton, Calif., 1981-87; mgr. automated systems, program planning, and control Electro-Mech. div. Northrop Corp., Anaheim, Calif., 1987—; cons. Systonetics Customer Base, 1981—; speaker in field. Author: The Dictionary of Power Plant, 1973, Project Management Techniques, 1984, VISION Planning and Schedule Guide, 1985, VISION Resource and Cost Guide, 1986. Mem. Project Mgmt. Inst., New Eng. Geneal. Historic Soc., Gen. Soc. of Mayflower Descendents, Nat. Geneal. Soc., Soc. Genealogists. Republican. Home: 1956 Brookhaven Ave Placentia CA 92670 Office: Northrop Corp Electro-Mech div 500 E Orangethorpe Ave Anaheim CA 92801

BROWN, CAROLYN MARIE, automobile manufacturing company administrator; b. Seattle, Oct. 12, 1948; d. Clifton Matthewus and Mary Ethel (Holliday) Morgan; m. Jerome Brown, Feb. 13, 1951 (div. 1985) children: Cesha, Channelle, Clifton. BA, Anderson (Ind.) Coll., 1970; postgrad., U. Calif., Berkeley, 1970; MA, Ball State U., 1976. Tchr. Indpls. Pub. Sch., 1970-71; clk. Delco Remy div. Gen. Motors Corp., Anderson, 1971, sec., 1971-72, supr., 1972-75, buyer, 1975-83, sr. buyer, 1983-86, gen. supr., 1986—. Chairperson Equal Opportunity Day Urban League, Anderson, 1977-85; sec. mayor's Blue Ribbon Edn. com., Anderson, 1982-84; mem. Ind. Regional Minority Purchasing Council, Indpls., 1983-86, Madison County Fine Arts Commn., Anderson, 1984-86, Women of Ch. of God club, 1979-86. Mem. Nat. Minority Supplier Devel. Council, Urban League (sec. 1976-77, pres. 1977-78, William B. Harper award 1984, Pres. award 1985), NAACP. Republican.

BROWN, CAROLYN SMITH, communications educator, consultant; b. Salt Lake City, Aug. 12, 1946; d. Andrew Delbert and Olive (Crane) Smith; m. David Scott Brown, Sept. 10, 1982. BA magna cum laude, U. Utah, 1968, MA, 1972, PhD, 1974. Instr. Salt Lake Ctr., Brigham Young U., Salt Lake City, 1976-78; vis. asst. prof. Brigham Young U., Provo, 1978; asst. prof. Am. Inst. Banking, Salt Lake City, 1977—; prof., chmn. English, communication and gen. edn. depts. Latter Day Saints Bus. Coll., Salt Lake City, 1973—, acad. dean, 1986—; founder, pres. Career Devel. Tng., Salt Lake City, 1979—; field mktg. dir. Personal Dynamics/Performax Inc., Mpls., 1978—; cons. inhouse seminars First Security Realty Services, USDA Soil Conservation Service, Utah Power & Light, Utah State Social Services, Utah State Dept. Corrections, Intermountain Health Care, Continental Bank; chmn. centennial coordination com. Latter Day Saints Bus. Coll., 1986-87, N.W. accreditation self-study com. 1980-82, 87, Title IX self-evaluation com., 1977, 79, grievance com., 1979—. Author: Writing Letters & Reports That Communicate, 6 ed., 1985; contbr. articles to profl. jours. Demi-soloist Utah Civic Ballet (now Ballet West), Salt Lake City, 1964-68; active Mormon Ch. Named Tchr. of Month, Salt Lake City Kiwanis, 1981; NDEA fellow, U. Utah, 1972. Mem. Am. Bus. Communications Assn. (lectr. West/N.W. regional chpt. 1987), Delta Kappa Gamma (2d v.p. 1977-79), Lambda Delta Sigma (Outstanding Woman of Yr. 1983), Kappa Kappa Gamma (Outstanding Alumnus in Lit. 1974). Republican. Clubs: Alice Louise Reynolds Literary (Salt Lake City) (v.p. 1978-79, sec. 1985-86). Office: LDS Bus Coll 411 E South Temple Salt Lake City UT 84111

BROWN, CHARLENE B., publisher, songwriter; b. Sheridan, Wyo., Aug. 27, 1953; d. Almer George and Alice (McCurdy) B. BA, Western N.Mex. U., 1974. With Macmillan Pub. Co., 1975-77, Kabaret Pub., 1977-79, United Resource Service, Irvine, Calif., 1979—; cons. Dept. Energy, 1978-79. Pub. Polit. Woman mag., 1986—; author Insider's Guide to Clearing Your Credit; composer songs, winner 4 Am. Song Festival awards, 1982-83, Grand Prize World Song Festival, 1984. Dir. Child Abuse Fund, Irvine, 1983 . Office: United Resource Services 4521 Campus Dr #388 Irvine CA 92115

BROWN, CHERRIL LYNN, investment broker; b. Little Rock, July 17, 1942; d. F. Lyn and Gretchen (Schulz) Gladstone; m. M. James Brekhus, Sept. 1, 1961 (div. May 1983); 1 child, Michael J.; m. Donald W. Brown, Feb. 19, 1988. BFA, U. S.D., 1964; postgrad., Coll. Fin. Planning, Denver, 1983—. Technician Calif. Test Bur., Monterey, 1964-65; tchr. Sturgis (S.D.) Pub. Schs., 1965-66, Rapid City (S.D.) Pub. Schs., 1966-67; pvt. instr. piano Rapid City, 1967-80; investment broker A.G. Edwards and Sons, Inc., Rapid City, 1981—, instr. investments and fin. planning, 1982—; instr. investments and fin. planning adult edn. program Rapid City Pub. Schs., 1982—. Bd. dirs. Rapid City chpt. Am. Cancer Soc., 1978—. Mem. Inst. Cert. Fin. Planners, Women's Bus. Network. Republican. Lutheran. Club: Arrowhead County (Rapid City) (chair Ladies Golf Assn. 1978-80). Lodge: Zonta Internat. (fin. chair Black Hills chpt. 1978-80). Home: 3823 Ridgemoor Dr Rapid City SD 57702 Office: A G Edwards and Sons Inc 440 Mount Rushmore Rd Rapid City SD 57701

BROWN, CINDY ARMSTRONG, advertising administrator; b. Lubbock, Tex., Dec. 7, 1960; d. H. S. and Nelda (Ellison) A.; m. Jerry Lee Brown, Apr. 18, 1980. Student, Angelo State U., 1979, Am. Comml. Coll., 1980. Sec. Furr's Planning & Engring., Lubbock, 1980-84; mgr. ops. N. Armstrong Advt. Agy., Lubbock, 1984—. Mem. Lubbock Advt. Fedn. (bd. dirs.). Republican. Presbyterian. Office: N Armstrong Advt Agy 8200 "C" Nashville Suite 103A Lubbock TX 79423

BROWN, CYNTHIA VREELAND, nurse, consultant; b. Chgo., Apr. 20, 1945; d. Royel Emmons and Carol Elnore (Ahlberg) Vreeland; m. Edward Charles Sporleder, June 5, 1976; children: Christopher Allen, James Matthew. Cert. in nursing, Crawford Long Hosp. Sch. of Nursing, 1967. Lic. nurse, Ga. Staff nurse emergency and operating rooms Crawford Long Hosp., Atlanta, 1967-72, in-service dir. operating room, 1973-77, clin. nurse coordinator emergency dept., 1977—; nurse clinician West Paces Ferry Hosp., Atlanta, 1972-73; mem. editorial bd. Current Concepts in Wound Care, Chgo., 1986, Jour. of Emergency Nursing, Florham Park, N.J., 1987—. Mem. Emergency Nurses Assn. (pres. 1984-85). Office: Crawford Long Hosp 550 Peachtree St Atlanta GA 30365

BROWN, DALE SUSAN, government administrator, writer; b. N.Y.C., May 27, 1954; d. Bertram S. and Beatrice Joy (Gilman) B. B.A., Antioch Coll., 1976. Research asst. Am. Occupational Therapy Assn., Rockville, Md., 1976-79; writer Pres.' Com. on Employment of Handicapped, Washington, 1979-82, program mgr., 1982—; writer Am. Rehab. Mag., Washington, 1982—; cons. in field; instr. Open U., Washington, 1978; gen. assembly speaker nat. conv. Gen. Fedn. Women's Clubs, 1981; mem. Rehab. Services Adminstrn. Task Force on Learning Disabilities, 1981—. Author: Steps to Independence for People with Learning Disabilities, 1980; writer film: They Could Have Saved Their Homes, 1982; editorial bd. Perceptions, 1981-83. Pres. Assn. Learning Disabled Adults, Washington, 1979-80; bd. dirs. Closer Look Nat. Info. Ctr., Washington, 1980—, Am. Coalition of Citizens with Disabilities, 1985-86. Found. for Children with Learning Disabilities grantee, 1982. Mem. Nat. Network of Learning Disabled Adults (founder, pres. 1980-81), Nat. Assn. Govt. Communicators (Blue Pencil award 1986), Assn. for Children and Adults with Learning Disabilities (bd. dirs. 1986-88), ALA. Democrat. Jewish. Office: Pres' Com on Employment Handicapped 1111 20th St NW Room 600 Washington DC 20036

BROWN, DARMAE JUDD, librarian; b. Jefferson City, Mo., Sept. 14, 1952; d. William Robert and Dorothy Judd (Curtis) B. BA, W.Va. Wesleyan Coll., 1974; MA, U. Denver, 1975; postgrad. Odessa Coll., 1982-84, U. No. Ia., 1984—. Searching assoc. Bibliog. Ctr. for Research, Denver, 1975-76; librarian N.E. Colo. Regional Library, Wray, 1976-81; head tech. services Ector County Library, Odessa, Tex., 1981-84, Waterloo (Iowa) Pub. Library, 1984—. Organist numerous chs. in Md., W.Va., Colo., Tex., 1969-84, St. Barnabas Episc. Chapel, Odessa, 1981-84. Mem. ALA, Iowa OCLC Users Group (pres. 1986-87), Iowa Library Assn., Library and Info. Tech. Assn., Beta Phi Mu, Sigma Alpha Iota. Home: 1143 Lantern Sq #12 Waterloo IA 50701

BROWN, DEBORAH ANN, economist, small business consultant; b. Falfurrias, Tex., Oct. 28, 1957; d. Paul Douglas and R. Gale (O'Keefe) B.; m. Henry T. Sanchez Jr. B.S. in Econs., Tex. Woman's U., 1979, M.B.A., 1986. Economist Bur. Labor Stats., Dallas, 1978—. Mem. fin. com. Lakewood United Methodist Ch., 1985—, co-treas., 1986. Mem. Bus. and Profl. Women-Dallas (chairperson individual devel. program 1982, young career woman program 1986-87, 2d v.p.-chair issues mgmt. 1987-88, Young Career Woman award 1986), Federally Employed Women (agy. rep.), Nat. Assn. Female Execs., Dallas Hispanic C. of C., Internat. Assn. Personnel in Employment Security, Thorstein Veblen Soc., Tex. Econ. Devel. Assn. Office: Bur Labor Stats Fed Bldg 525 Griffin Room 221 Dallas TX 75202

BROWN, DEBORAH SHARON, oil company official; b. Shamokia, Pa., Feb. 6, 1955; d. John M. and Gloria Ann (Leshinski) Miller. A.A. in Bus., Brandywine Coll., 1975; B.S. in Bus. Mgmt., U. Md., 1978; M.S. in Bus. Communication, Am. U., 1978. Adminstr., Pentagon, Arlington, Va., 1975-77; press officer FDA, Washington, 1977-79; sr. bus. analyst Shell Oil Co., Houston, 1979-83, supr., 1983—; dir., sec. Tex. Ozonator, Houston, 1982-84. Mem. Assn. Info. Processors, Elec. Woman's Roundtable, Nat. Assn. for Female Execs. Office: Shell Oil Co 777 Walker PO Box 4302 Houston TX 77210-4302

BROWN, DEBRA AZER, human resource manager, health promotion consultant; b. Hackensack, N.J., Oct. 2, 1951; d. Irving and Faye (Prensky) Azer; m. Robert E. Brown, Oct. 12, 1975. BA, SUNY, Cortland, 1973; MSW, U. Mich., 1978. Cert. employee assistance professional. Tchr. Branchburg (N.J.) Cen. Sch., 1973-74; program asst. West Bergen Mental Health Ctr., Ridgewood, N.J., 1975; probation officer Bergen County Probation Dept., Hackensack, 1975-77; asst. adminstr. employee assistance program Oldsmobile div. Gen. Motors Corp., Lansing, Mich., 1978; owner, cons. Debbie Brown Assocs., East Windsor, N.J., 1979-85; clinician Community Mental Health Ctr. Rutgers Med. Sch., Piscataway, N.J., 1982-85; v.p. Motivational Programs & Tng., Inc., East Windsor, N.J., 1982-85; adminstr. employee assistance program Am. Express Co., N.Y., 1985—; spl. health services coordinator Continental Ins. Cos., Livingston and Neptune, N.J., 1980-81; assoc. Orgnl. Systems, Inc., Princeton, N.J., 1980; health promotion cons. Live for Life program Johnson & Johnson Corp., New Brunswick, N.J.1980-85; cons. Health Edn. and Communications Corp., Moorestown, N.J., 1985. Contbr. articles to profl. jours. Bd. trustees Middlesex (N.J.) Council on Alcoholism, 1977-80. Mem. Assn. Labor and Mgmt. Adminstrs. and Cons. on Alcoholism (chpt. v.p. 1981-82). Jewish. Home: 45 Brooktree Rd East Windsor NJ 08520

BROWN, DEBRALEE SANDRA, hotel chain executive; b. Kitchener, Can., July 26, 1952; d. Patrick Gerard and May Cavell (Koehler) B. Student in hospitality and tourism mgmt., U. Calgary, 1986-87. Bartender Jasper (Alb.) Park Lodge, 1977-78, mgr. Henry Steakhouse, 1979-82, mgr. sales, 1982-84; sales mgr. convs. Calgary Tourism and Conv. Bur., 1984-85; asst. mgr. Sheraton-Cavalier, Calgary, 1985—. Mem. Calgary C. of C. (mem. com., tourism com., Ambassador club). Club: Les Compagnons Des Vins de France (Calgary) (v.p. 1985-86). Home: 234 Edgedale Gardens NW, Calgary CAN T3A 4M8 Office: Sheraton-Cavalier, 2620-32 Ave NE, Calgary CAN T1Y 6B8

BROWN, DELOIS MARIE, nurse, psychologist; b. Shreveport, La., Feb. 12, 1942; d. James Metcalf and Kate Bertha (Robinson) Hulett; m. Taff Brown, Aug. 13, 1966 (div. 1979); children: Cherise Marie, Theresa M. BS, Prairie View U., 1965; MS, U. Md., 1967; MA in Pub. Adminstrn., Bernard Baruch Coll., 1984. Supr. nurse Child Study and Treatment Ctr., Tacoma, 1967-70; instr. sch. nursing U. Wash., Seattle, 1970-72, project dir. sch. medicine, 1972-73; sch. nurse Tacoma Sch. Dist. 10, 1974—; cons. mental health expeditor program Model Cities, Tacoma, 1971-72, Tacoma Community Coll., 1978; on-call nurse therapist Peare St. Ctr., Tacoma, 1987. Bd. dirs. Tacoma Human Rights Commn., 1985—, Tacoma Urban League, 1978-84. Mem. Sigma Theta Tau. Democrat. Pentecostal. Home: 3414 38th Ave Ct W Tacoma WA 98467

BROWN, DENISE SCOTT, architect, urban planner; b. Nkana, Zambia, Oct. 3, 1931; came to U.S., 1958; d. Simon and Phyllis (Hepker) Lakofski; m. Robert Scott Brown, July 21, 1955 (dec. 1959); m. Robert Charles Venturi, July 23, 1967; 1 child, James C. Student, U. Witwatersrand, South Africa, 1948-51; diploma, Archtl. Assn., London, 1955; M of City Planning, U. Pa., 1960, MArch, 1965; DFA (hon.), Oberlin Coll., 1977, Phila. Coll. Art, 1985, Parsons Sch. Design, 1985; LHD (hon.), N.J. Inst. Tech., 1984. Registered architect, U.K. Asst. prof. U. Pa., Phila., 1960-65; assoc. prof., head urban design program UCLA, 1965-68; with Venturi, Rauch and Scott Brown, Phila., 1967—, ptnr., 1969—; vis. prof. architecture U. Calif., Berkeley, 1965, U. Pa., 1982-83; vis. prof. architecture Yale U., 1967-70, 87; mem. vis. com. MIT, 1973-83; mem. adv. com. Temple U. Dept. Architecture, 1980—; policy panelist design arts program Nat. Endowment for Arts, 1981-83. Coauthor: Learning from Las Vegas, 1972, rev. edit., 1977, A View from the Campidoglio: Selected Essays, 1953-84, 1985; contbr. numerous articles to profl. jours. Mem. curriculum and adult edn. com. Phila. Jewish Children's Folkshul, 1980-86; mem. bd. advisors Architects, Designers and Planners for Social Responsibility, 1982—; mem. capitol preservation com. Commonwealth of Pa., Harrisburg, 1983-87; bd. dirs. Cen. Phila. Devel. Corp., 1985—, Urban Affairs Ptnrship., Phila., 1987—; trustee Chestnut Hill Acad., Phila., 1985—. Recipient numerous awards, citations, commendations for design, urban planning, Chgo. Architecture award, 1987, order of merit Republic of Italy, 1987. Mem. Am. Planning Assn., Archtl. Assn. London, Alliance Women in Architecture N.Y., Soc. Archtl. Historians (bd. dirs. 1981-84), Royal Inst. Brit. Architects. Democrat. Jewish. Office: Venturi Rauch and Scott Brown 4236 Main St Philadelphia PA 19127

BROWN, DIANE LOUISE, pharmaceutical company administrator; b. South Bend, Ind., Aug. 31, 1954; d. Richard Thomas and Iola (Keller) B. BS, Purdue U., 1974; MA, Johns Hopkins U., 1978; MBA, U. Mich., 1980. Asst. to v.p. comml. devel. Genex Corp., Gaithersburg, Md., 1980-81, mgr. mktg., 1981-82, dir. tech. mktg., 1982-84, dir. corp. devel., 1984-85, dir. comml. devel., 1985; officer indsl. devel. UN Indsl. Devel. Orgn., Vienna, Austria, 1986; mgr. assoc., product mgr. Schering-Plough Corp., Kenilworth, N.J., 1986—; bd. dirs. Morse Rubber Products, Keokuk, Iowa. Mem. Phi Beta Kappa. Methodist.

BROWN, DOREEN LEAH HURWITZ, development company executive; b. Marseille, France, June 11, 1927; came to U.S., 1939, naturalized, 1941; d. Nathan and Anne (Silverstone) Hurwitz; m. Donald L. Brown, Dec. 30, 1951 (dec.); children: Claudia Geraldine, Nicole Deborah. BA cum laude, Bryn Mawr Coll., 1947. Adminstrv. asst., interpreter, translator FAO, Washington, 1949-51; with Aldon Constrn. & Mgmt. Corp., Washington, 1951—, v.p., exec. officer, 1977—; consumer liaison Nat. Acad. Scis., 1973. Author: Window on Washington: the Trade Deficit. Nat. chmn. nat. affairs Nat. Council Jewish Women, N.Y.C., 1971-75; pres. Consumer Edn. Council on World Trade, 1973-78, Consumers for World Trade, Washington, 1977—; mem. Women's Nat. Dem. Club, 1960—; mem. Internat. Trade Importers and Retailers Textile Adv. Com., Dept. Commerce. Mem. Bryn Mawr Coll. Alumnae Assn., World Trade Forum. Club: Woodmont Country. Office: 1001 Connecticut Ave NW Suite 800 Washington DC 20036

BROWN, DOROTHY MCKENNA, academic administrator; b. July 19, 1938; m. James Earl Brown Jr.; children: Mary Marguerite, Sheila Ann. BS in Biology, Coll. Misericordia, Dallas, Pa., 1960; MS in Biology, Villanova U., 1962; EdD in Sci. Edn., U. Pa., 1973. From instr. to prof. biology Cabrini Coll., Radnor, Pa., 1962-79, chairperson, 1964-72, v.p. acad. affairs, 1972-79; pres. Rosmemont (Pa.) Coll., 1979—; treas. Commn. for Ind. Colls. and Univs., 1980-82, 1st vice-chmn. 1982-83, chmn. of commn., 1983-84, past chmn., 1984-85; mem. com. on personal affairs, commn. on higher edn. study com. on off-campus programs Pa. Assn. of Colls. and Univs., 1979; chmn. acad. policies task group Pa. region 1, continuing edn. project Compact for Life Long Ednl. Opportunities, 1977-79; chmn. Pa. Dept. Edn. Program Approval, 1972-80, Md. Dept. Edn., 1979; trustee, chmn. exec. com., mem. nominating com., mem. acad. affairs com. Hahnemann U., 1979—; bd. dirs. Mut. Life Ins. Co., Inst. Planning Com., St. Charles Seminary, Phila., Pa. Bd. dirs. Mayor's Commn. for Women, Phila., 1981-83; acad. bd. advisors Armenian Sisters' Acad., Radnor, 1974-82. Mem. Assn. Cath. Colls. and Univs. (bd. dirs. 1985—), Mid. States Assn. of Colls. and Schs. (chmn. 4 accrediting teams, mem. 2 accrediting teams). Office: Rosemont Coll Office of the Pres Rosemont PA 19010

BROWN, DOROTHY NICHOLSON, real estate consultant, appraiser; b. Lilesville, N.C., Oct. 26, 1938; d. Grady James Nicholson and Mary (Tillman) Beatty; children: Randy, Joseph, Candace. Cert. real estate, NYU, 1972; BA, Coll. New Rochelle, 1977. Real estate asst. U.S. Postal Service, N.Y.C., 1967-70, transaction specialist, 1970-71; realty specialist U.S. Army CE, N.Y.C., 1971-73; specialist U.S. Postal Service, N.Y.C., 1973-86; prin. Dorothy N. Brown & Assocs., Hastings-on-Hudson, N.Y., 1986—; cons. Ronald Kern & Assocs., White Plains, N.Y., 1986—. V.p. Nat. Council Negro Women, Inc., Bronx, N.Y., 1970-77; councilwoman Co-op City Council, Bronx, 1970-72; vol. St. John's Feed the Homeless, N.Y.C., 1985—, Ferry Sloops Environ., Hastings-on-Hudson, 1986—. Mem. AAUW, Am. Soc. Appraisers (v.p. 1987-88), Assn. Real Estate Women, Nat. Assn. Ind. Fee Appraisers (pres. 1981-83), Ebon Postal Assn. (founder, interim pres.). Club: Just Friends. Home: Box 214 Hastings-on-Hudson NY 10706

BROWN, DRENDA KAY, psychologist; b. Carrollton, Mo., Jan. 15, 1952; d. Ethan Lyle Pracht and Wilma Estelene (Henderson) Lucas; m. David Kent Brown, June 23, 1973; 1 child, Matthew Kent. BA in Psychology, William Jewell Coll., 1974; MS in Clinical Psychology, Cen. Mo. State U., 1976; postgrad. in clin. psychology, Fielding Inst., Santa Barbara, Calif., 1987—. Lic. psychologist, Minn. Therapist Briscoe Carr Cons., Kansas City, Mo., 1978-79; psychologist Crittenton Ctr., Kansas City, 1979-81, Cen. Minn. Mental Health Ctr., St. Cloud, 1981-85, St. Cloud Hosp., 1985-87; gen. practice psychology St. Cloud, 1985—; cons. St. Benedicts Ctr., St. Cloud, 1984—, St. Cloud Manor, 1986—. Mem. Cen. Minn. Child Abuse Team, St. Cloud, 1981-85; bd. dirs. Cen. Minn. Child Care Assn., St. Cloud, 1982-83. Mem. Cen. Minn. Psychological Assn. (pres. 1984-85), Minn. Licensed Psychologists, Minn. Psychol. Assn., Mo. Psych. Assn., Alpha Delta Pi Alumni Assn. Presbyterian. Office: 2025 Stearns Way Suite 113 Saint Cloud MN 56303

BROWN, EDITH, community development agency administrator; b. Milw., Nov. 25, 1935; d. Anton J. and Elizabeth K. (Kribitsch) Volk; m. Edward S. Brown. B.S., U. Wis., 1958, M.S. in Social Work, 1964; M.S. in Mgmt., Cardinal Stritch Coll., Milw., 1985. Hosp. admissions worker, 1958-60; welfare worker, 1960-62; with Kiwanis Children's Ctr. and Children's Hosp. Psychiat. Clinic, Milw., 1962-64; social worker Lutheran Social Services, Milw., 1964-67; foster care supr. Milwaukee County Dept. Social Services, 1967-71, social services adminstr. child protection and parent services, comprehensive emergency services and a coordinated community edn. and support services, 1971-79; assoc. dir. Community Devel. Agy., City of Milw., 1979—; tech. advisor for child abuse, neglect, woman abuse, domestic violence; grantswriter, tchr., cons. in field. Mem. Summerfest Adv. Council, Mayor's Beautification Com.; chmn. Summerfest Planting, 1972—; chmn. Milwaukee County Child Abuse and Neglect Task force, 1976-78; chmn. adv. council Milw. Boy's Club, 1981-84; vice chmn. Internat. Yr. for Disabled Persons, 1982; liaison Nat. Yr. for Disabled Persons, City of Milw., 1982-83; asst. chairperson City of Milw. United Way Campaign, 1983; mem. Mayor's Youth Initiatives Task Force, 1984-85; mem. adv. panel M.P.A. degree program U. Wis., 1984—. Office of Vocat. Rehab. scholar, 1962-64; Successful Women in Mgmt. award J. Wis., 1977; award Community Tchrs. Corps, 1977; Changemaker award Wis. Fed. Jr. Women's Clubs, 1978; Outstanding Community Services award Milwaukee County, 1979, Outstanding Services award, 1979, Exemplary Service award, 1982; Woman of Yr. award Mcpl. Women's Assn., 1981. Mem. Acad. Cert. Social Workers, Nat. Assn. Social Workers, Internat. Council on Social Welfare, Internat. Fedn. Social Welfare, Am. Soc. for Pub. Adminstrn. (pres. Milw. chpt., Outstanding Service and Dedication award 1984-85), Research Clearinghouse, Am. Bus. Women's Assn. (Woman of Yr. award 1975), Internat. Graphoanalysis Soc. (pres. Wis. chpt.). Club: Variety of Wis. Tech. contbr. to profl., community, resource documents, 1971—; author print and broadcast programs. Office: Community Devel Agy 200 E Wells St Milwaukee WI 53202

BROWN, EILEEN MARIE, social service administrator; b. Eden, N.Y., Jan. 24, 1935; d. Samuel Walter and Marian Lenore (McIntyre) Whetzle; m. Thomas Joseph Brown, Nov. 12, 1955; children: Michelle Marie Brown Acevedo, Dianne Marie Brown Long, Brian Thomas. Student, Barry Coll., Miami, Fla., 1953-55, U. Houston, 1967-68; cert. vol. mgmt., U. Colo., 1985-86. Trainer Juvenile Ct. Vols. of Harris County, Houston, 1978-87, assoc. dir., 1979-87, recruiter, cons. for devel. vol. programs criminal justice div., 1985-87. Contbr. articles to profl. jours. Active Nat. Runaway Hotline, Houston/Austin, 1975-78; com. co-chmn. Mayor's Conf. on Children and Youth, Houston, 1986-87. Mem. Nat. Assn. Female Execs., Nat. Assn. Vols. in Criminal Justice, Nat. Juvenile Detention Assn. (wksp. dir 1980-87), Am. Vol. Assn., Tex. Juvenile Detention Assn. (wksp. dir. 1980-87), Tex. Corrections Inst., Houston Area Vol. Assn., Nat. Inst. for Advanced Study of Volunteerism (charter mem., research assoc., bd. dirs.). Home: 13905 Skyview Dr Sugarland TX 77478 Office: Juvenile Ct Vols of Harris County 3540 W Dallas PO Box 13258 Houston TX 77219

BROWN, ELIZABETH BELLE, software engineer; b. Battle Creek, Mich., Feb. 11, 1957; d. George Alexander and Daisy Eliza (Wassenaar) Lamberton; m. Danny Edward Brown, June 22, 1985. BS, U. Evansville, 1981. Computer programmer Naval Weapons Support, Crane, Ind., 1981-86; software engr. Goodyear Aerospace Corp., Akron, Ohio, 1986—. Mem. Assn. Computing Machinery, IEEE. Home: 534 Northeast Ave Tallmadge OH 44278

BROWN, ELLEN RUTH, theoretical physicist; b. N.Y.C., June 15, 1947; d. Aaron Joseph and Grace (Presser) B. B.S., Mary Washington Coll., 1969; M.S., Pa. State U., 1971; Ph.D. (Govs. fellow), U.Va., 1981. Physicist, Naval Weapons Lab., Dahlgren, Va., 1969; instr. physics Lord Fairfax Community Coll., Middletown, Va., 1971-74; summer faculty fellow NASA, Langley, Va., 1974-75; engr. EG&G Washington Analytical Services Center, Dahlgren, Va., 1979—, head dept. analysis and evaluation, 1982-86; v.p. Windy Knoll Enterprises, Inc., Magnolia, Tex., 1981—. First violinist Coll. and Community Orch., Fredericksburg, Va., 1981— . NSF Summer Sci. Faculty fellow, 1973; IEEE Summer Sci. Faculty fellow NASA, 1974-75. Mem. Am. Phys. Soc., Sierra Club, Sigma Xi. Club: Barry Lee Bressler Science (pres.). Home: PO Box 1397 Fredericksburg VA 22402 Office: EG&G PO Box 552 Dahlgren VA 22448

BROWN, FRANCES ANNE, therapist; b. Newport News, Va., Feb. 13, 1946; d. Quincy and Frances (Williams) B. AA in Nursing, Chowan Coll., 1968; BS in Profl. Arts, St. Joseph's Coll., North Windham, Ma., 1980. Staff nurse in psychiatry Duke U. Med. Cen., Durham, N.C., 1968-71; head nurse in psychiatry Duke U. Med. Cen., Durham, 1971-76; pvt. practice counseling Chapel Hill, N.C., 1976—; trainer assertiveness Durham (N.C.) Tech. Inst., Duke U. Med. Ctr., Piedmont Tech. U., 1980-83; cons. Ctr. Wellbeing, CArrboro, 1987; photographer Alderman's Galleries, Durham, House of Frames, Durham. Co-chair Orange County Domicilliary Home Adv. Com., 1985-87; bd. dirs. Orange County Rape Crisis Cen. (chair 1986-87). Mem. Hillsborough Historical Soc., NOW (publicity/photography com. 1981—), Nat. Assn. Women Bus. Owners (cons. 1987, sec. 1987—), Am. Psychol. Assn. (assoc.), Chapel Hill/Carrboro C. of C. (mem. speakers bur., cons. 1981-87), N.C. Soc. Clin. Hyponosis Soc. Baptist. Lodge: Women Moose. Home: 29 Bluff Trail Chapel Hill NC 27516 Office: 104 S Estes Dr Suite 304 Chapel Hill NC 27514

BROWN, GERALDINE REED, lawyer; b. Los Angeles, Feb. 18, 1947; d. William Penn and Alberta Vernice (Coleman) Reed; m. Ronald Wellington Brown, Aug. 20, 1972; children—Kimberly Diana, Michael David. B.A. summa cum laude, Fisk U., 1968; J.D., Harvard U., 1971, M.B.A., 1973. Bar: N.Y. 1974, U.S. Dist. Ct. (so. and ea. dists.) N.Y. 1974, U.S. Ct. Appeals (2d cir.) 1974, U.S. Supreme Ct. 1977. Assoc. firm White & Case, N.Y.C., 1973-78; atty. J.C. Penney Co., Inc., N.Y.C., 1978—. Bd. dirs. Council Concerned Black Execs., N.Y.C., 1977—, Studio Mus. in Harlem, N.Y.C., 1980-81; mem. Montclair Devel. Bd., ad hoc com. on Montclair Econ. Devel. Corp. Mem. Women's Econ. Roundtable, Harvard Bus. Sch. Club, Harvard Law Sch. Assn., Coalition 100 Black Women, ABA (several coms. sect. corp., banking and bus. law, sect. internat. law and practice), Assn. Bar City N.Y. (corp. law com. 1978-81), N.Y. County Lawyers Assn. (corp. law com.), N.Y. State Bar Assn. (vice chmn., exec. com. of corp. counsel sect., chmn. com. on SEC, fin., corp. law and governance), Harvard Bus. Sch. Black Alumni Assn., Harvard Law Sch. Black Alumni Assn., Phi Beta Kappa, Delta Sigma Theta (chair social action com. Montclair alumnae chpt., chair bylaw com., parlimentarian). Club: Harvard (N.Y.C.). Home: 180 Union St Montclair NJ 07042 Office: JC Penney Co Inc 1301 Ave of Americas New York NY 10019

BROWN, GLENDA CAROL, insurance executive, small business owner; b. Jackson, Miss., June 30, 1949; d. Troy Snow and Bonnie Glenn (Gill) Brown Jr., A.A. in Radio and TV, Marjorie Webster Jr. Coll., 1969; B.A. in Radio and TV, U. Md., 1974; M.A. in Bus. Mgmt. and Supervision, Central Mich. U., 1975. Adminstrv. asst. Dept. Navy (NTDA), Washington, 1970-78; tech. writer, editor VSE Engring., Alexandria, Va., 1979; agt. Aetna Life Ins. Co., McLean, Va., 1979-84; gen. agt. Western Fidelity Ins. Co., Washington, 1985—; real estate agt. Hyde Co. Realtors, Fairfax, Va. Mem. Nat. Assn. Female Execs., D.C. Assn. Life Underwriters, Profl. Ins. Agts., Arlington C. of C., No. Va. Bd. Realtors. Avocations: reading, piano, tennis, ice skating, phys. fitness. Home and Office: 9321 Lancelot Rd Fort Washington MD 20744

BROWN, GLENDA SHARON, data processing executive; b. Hollywood, Fla., Jan. 5, 1947; d. Earl Isaac and Helen Sarah (Segal) B. BA in Math., U. Fla., 1968. Project mgr. J.C. Penny's, N.Y.C., 1969-77; systems mgr. S.D. Leidesdorf/Ernst & Whinney, N.Y.C., 1977-78; sr. cons. Lambda Tech., N.Y.C., 1978-81; dir. Sterling Software, N.Y.C., 1981—. Mem. Exec. Females. Republican. Jewish. Home: 353 72nd St Apt 5D New York NY 10021 Office: Sterling Software 401 Park Ave S New York NY 10016

BROWN, HEATHER, microcomputer analyst; b. Scituate, Mass., Sept. 12, 1950; d. Thomas Edward and Jeanne Louise (Eisenhauer) B. AS in Bus. Adminstrn. with highest honors, Massasoit Community Coll., 1979; BS in Acctg., Bentley Coll., 1981, MBA, 1987. Claims clk. CNA Ins., Boston, 1970-71; export clk. Cabot Corp., Boston, 1971-76, fin. sec., 1977, acct., 1978-81; fin. analyst Cabot Corp., Waltham, Mass., 1981-86, microcomputer analyst, 1987—, dir. credit union, 1978—; geology lab asst. Bentley Coll., Waltham, 1980-83. Contbr. articles to Bentley Newspaper, 1980-82, Cabot Corp. Newspaper, 1979-80; editor Cabot Corp. PC Network Newsletter, 1987—. Mem. Nat. Assn. Female Execs. Roman Catholic. Office: Cabot Corp 950 Winter St Waltham MA 02254

BROWN, HELEN DAVIS, biology educator; b. Charlotte, N.C., Mar. 23, 1934; d. William Herbert Sr. and Helen (Davis) B. AA, Mars Hill Coll., 1954, Mars Hill (N.C.) Jr. Coll., 1954; BS magna cum laude, Appalachian State Coll., 1956, MA, 1959; PhD, U. Fla., 1972. Tchr. Arlington Jr. High Sch., Gastonia, N.C., 1956-62; math and sci. tchr. USAF Schs., Woodbridge, Eng., 1962-64; biology tchr. Satellite Beach (Fla.) Jr. High Sch., 1964-66; asst. prof. biology Augusta (Ga.) Coll., 1969-71; asst. prof. biology Clayton Jr. Coll., Morrow, Ga., 1972-80, assoc. prof., 1980-86; assoc. prof. Clayton State Coll., Morrow, 1986—; environ. cons. Claude Terry & Assocs., Atlanta, 1978; participated Alt. Energy Sources Workshop Argonne (Ill.) Nat. Labs., 1977. Past contbr. articles to sci. jours. Trustee Reynolds Nature Preserve, Morrow, 1980—. Grantee NSF, U. Minn., 1966. Mem. Phycological Soc. Am., Assn. Southeastern Biologists, Ga. Acad. Sci. (sec. biology sect. 1978-79, chmn. biology sect. 1979-80), Ga. Bot. Soc. (1st v.p. 1976-79, pres. 1979-81, exec. com. 1975-83), Ga. Conservancy, Ga. Genetics Soc., Beta Beta Beta, Delta Kappa Gamma. Home: 1612 Dellwood Circle Morrow GA 30260 Office: Clayton State Coll Lee St PO Box 285 Morrow GA 30260

BROWN, HELEN GURLEY, author, editor; b. Green Forest, Ark., Feb. 18, 1922; d. Ira M. and Cleo (Sisco) Gurley; m. David Brown, Sept. 25, 1959. Student, Tex. State Coll. for Women, 1939-41, Woodbury Coll., 1942. Exec. sec. Music Corp. Am., 1942-45, William Morris Agy., 1945-47; copywriter Foote, Cone & Belding (advt. agy.), Los Angeles, 1948-58; advt. writer, account exec. Kenyon & Eckhardt (advt. agy.), Hollywood, Calif., 1958-62; editor-in-chief Cosmopolitan mag., 1965—; editorial dir. Cosmopolitan internat. edits., 1972—. Author: Sex and the Single Girl, 1962, Sex and the Office, 1965, Outrageous Opinions, 1966, Helen Gurley Brown's Single Girl's Cook Book, 1969, Sex and the New Single Girl, 1970, Cosmopolitan's Love Book: A Guide to Ecstacy in Bed, 1978, Having It All, 1982. Recipient Francis Holmes Achievement award for outstanding work in advt., 1956-59; Distinguished Achievement award U. So. Calif. Sch. Journalism, 1971; Spl. award for editorial leadership Am. Newspaper Woman's Club, Washington, 1972; Disting. Achievement award in Journalism Stanford U., 1977; named 1 of 25 most influential women in U.S. World Almanac, 1976-81. Mem. Authors League Am., Am. Soc. Mag. Editors, AFTRA, Eta Upsilon Gamma. Office: Cosmopolitan The Hearst Corp 224 W 57th St New York NY 10019

BROWN, IONA, violinist, orchestra director; b. Salisbury, Wiltshire, England, Jan. 7, 1941. Studied w. Hugh Maguire, London, Remy Principe, Rome, Henryk Szeryng, France. Violinist Nat. Youth Orch. of Gt. Britain, 1955-60, Philharmonia Orch. of London, 1963-66; violinist Acad. of St. Martin-in-the-fields, 1964—, concertmaster, dir., 1974—; artistic dir. Norwegian Chamber Orch., Oslo; prin. guest dir. City of Birmingham Symphony Orch., Birmingham, England; music dir. Los Angeles Chamber Orch., Los Angeles, 1987—. Office: Los Angeles Chamber Orch 315 W 9th St Suite 300 Los Angeles CA 90015

BROWN, IRIS LAVERNE, educator; b. Sayre, Okla., Feb. 14, 1943; d. Laddie Leroy Brown and Reta Elizabeth (Turbyfill) Thompson; m. James Woodrow Elliff, May 30, 1959 (div. 1971); children: James Clark Elliff, Timothy Mark Elliff, Pamela Cleo Elliff. BS, Cameron U., Lawton, Okla., 1973; MEd, U. Okla., 1976. Tchr. learning resource ctr. Jackson Elem. Sch., Lawton, 1973-74; tchr. elem. Douglass Learning Ctr., Lawton, 1974—, primary team coordinator, 1975-87, tchr. adult edn. math, 1975-80, 86—; tchr. summer sch. Carriage Hills Elem. Sch., Lawton, 1973-79, Almor West Elem. Sch., 1981, Cen. Jr. High Sch., 1985, Tomlinson Jr. High Sch., Lawton, 1986; tchr. calligraphy Community Edn., 1984—. Mem. NEA, Okla. Edn. Assn., Profl. Educators of Lawton, Internat. Reading Assn., Okla. Reading Council, Phi Kappa Phi, Kappa Kappa Iota. Democrat. Methodist. Home: 6603 NW Ferris Lawton OK 73505 Office: Douglass Learning Ctr 102 E Gore Blvd Lawton OK 73501

BROWN, JACQUELINE ELAINE, obstetrician-gynecologist; b. Houston, Sept. 20, 1948; d. Issac Cleve Brown and Hazel Eva (Mullen) Hill; m. Felton Watkins, Dec. 31, 1971 (div. Jan. 1974); 1 child, Alan Christopher Watkins; m. Ronald Hayes, Nov. 9, 1985. BA, North Tex. State U., 1970; postgrad., Tex. So. U., 1971-72; MD, U. Tex., Dallas, 1980; MPH, Johns Hopkins U., 1985. Intern in ob-gyn Pa. Hosp., Phila., 1980-84, resident in ob-gyn, 1980-84; ob-gyn physician Johns Hopkins Health Plan, Balt., 1984-85, Kaiser Permanente Health Plan, Washington, 1985-87; asst. med. dir. ob-gyn Johns Hopkins Health Plan, Balt., 1987—; advisor Black Women's Health Project, Phila., 1983-84; cons. Women's Resource and Devel. Ctr., Balt., 1984—, Teen Parenting Prevention Program, Balt., 1985—, Straight Talk, Washington, 1987. Mem. bd. trustees Bethel African Meth. Episcopal Ch., Balt., 1985. Southwestern Found. scholar, Dallas, 1976. Fellow Am. Coll. Ob-Gyn (jr.); mem. Am. Med. Women's Assn., Alpha Kappa Alpha. Home: 11 Senta Ct Baltimore MD 21207 Office: Johns Hopkins Health Plan 1000 E Eager Baltimore MD 21202

BROWN, JACQUELINE LEY WHITE, computer software executive; b. Blue Island, Ill., Apr. 14, 1948; d. William Raymond and June Irene (Cowing) L.; m. Arthur Lee White, May 2, 1970 (div. Mar. 1982); m. William John Brown, May 7, 1988. BA, U. Fla., 1969; MA, Rider Coll., 1977. From supr. to dir. social services Steuben County (N.Y.) Dept. Social Services, Bath, N.Y., 1970-75; from sr. to prin. N.J. Dept. Pub. Welfare, Trenton, N.J., 1975-78; mgmt. cons., nat. seminar leader sales and mktg. Nathaniel Hills & Assocs., Raleigh, N.C., 1978-79; from dir. mktg. to v.p. Concord Mgmt. Systems, Tampa, Fla., 1979—; cons. Action Planning Assocs., Trenton, 1976-78; bd. dirs. Tex. Instruments Users Group, 1983-84; speaker in field, 1984—. Dir., pres. Data Bus. , St. Petersburg, 1985—. Democrat. Methodist. Club: YMCA Masters (Silver Spring). Home: 1486 72d NE Saint Petersburg FL 33702 Office: Concord Mgmt Systems 5301 W Cypress St Tampa FL 33607

BROWN, JANE MARTIN, health science center administrator; b. Elberton, Ga., Mar. 6, 1951; d. Laurie William and Mary Frances (Martin) Thornton; m. Donald McCarty Brown Jr., June 14, 1980; children Laurie Elizabeth, Judson McCarty. Student, U. Ala., 1969-70, Georgetown Coll., 1970-71; BS, Minot State Coll., 1973, MS, 1974. Speech-lang. pathologist Duval County Sch. System, Jacksonville, Fla., 1974-77, Newberry (S.C.) County Schs., 1977-78, Tri-County Spl. Edn. Coop., Murphysboro, Ill., 1978-79; speech-lang. pathologist Ga. Retardation Ctr., Atlanta, 1980-82, dir. speech-lang. pathology, 1982-87, coordinator of quality circles, 1983-86, coordinator of interdisciplinary habilitation, 1986-87, dir. programs, evaluation, research and tng., 1987—; chairperson Ga. Mental Retardation, Developmentally Disabled Network, Atlanta, 1987—; expert panel mem. Speech Pathology Assessment Instrument Team, Athens, 1986-87, Ga. Dept. Edn., Atlanta, 1987. Presentor: (paper) Developmental Disabilities: Where do we go from Here?. Pres. Citizen's Adv. Com., Atlanta, 1985—; mem. Gainsbor. Civic Assn., Atlanta, 1985—, Gov's. Edn. com., N.D., 1972-74, Com. for Networking Conf., Atlanta, 1985—. Grantee Minot State Coll., 1973-74. Mem. Ga. Speech-Lang.-Hearing Assn., Retarded Citizens of Atlanta (Vital Service award 1987), Am. Assn. of Mental Deficiency, Council for Exceptional Children, Mental Retardation Inst.. Democrat. Methodist. Office: Ga Retardation Ctr 4770 N Peachtree Rd D201 Atlanta GA 30338

BROWN, JANET MACKEY, architectural programmer, educator; b. Louisiana, Mo., Feb. 21, 1943; d. Frances Marion and Helen (Prewitt) Mackey; m. Charles T. Brown (div. 1971); children: Margaret Courtney, Charles Andrew. BS, U. Mo., 1974; MS, U. Ky., 1975; PhD, Pa. State U., 1983. V.p. Hellmuth, Obata & Kassabaum, St. Louis, 1983—; asst. prof. Washington U., St. Louis, 1987—. Mem. Environ. Design Research Assn. Office: Hellmuth Obata & Kassabaum Inc 100 N Broadway Saint Louis MO 63102

BROWN, JOAN MAZZAFERRO, telephone company executive; b. Greenport, N.Y., Jan. 1, 1956; d. Joseph Anthony and Sophia (Kroleski) M.; m. Joan Mazzafero Brown, May 15, 1988. BS, SUNY-Brockport, 1978; MS, Purdue U., 1980. Sr. tech. assoc. Bell. Tel. Labs., Whippany, N.J., 1978-79, mem. tech. staff, 1979-83; staff analyst Pacific Bell Co., San Francisco, 1983-84, staff mgr., 1984-85, dist. staff mgr., San Ramon, Calif., 1985—. Kodak scholar, 1978. Mem. Nat. Assn. Female Execs. Roman Catholic. Club: Young Adults (San Ramon). Avocations: skiing, sailing, aerobics, theatre, dance. Office: Pacific Bell 221 W Winton Ave Room C318 Ramon CA 94544

BROWN, JOAN PHILLIPS (ABENA), foundation administrator; b. Chgo.; d. Lueola Reed; divorced. BA, Roosevelt U., 1954; MA, U. Chgo., 1963. Dir. West Side YWCA, Chgo., 1963-65; cons. human relations YWCA of Met. Chgo., 1965-72, dir. program services, 1972-82; pres. ETA Creative Arts Found., Chgo., 1982—. Pres. Midwest African Am. Theater Alliance, 1980—; sec. Dept. Cultural Affairs Bd., Chgo., 1983—; vice chairperson Muntu Dance Theatre, Chgo., 1985—; pres. emeritus African Am. Arts Alliance, Chgo.; mem. Woman's Bd. Chgo. Urban League; mem. League Chgo. Theaters. Home: 7637 S Bennett St Chicago IL 60649 Office: ETA Creative Arts Found 7558 S South Chicago Ave Chicago IL 60619

BROWN, JOANNE CARLSON, religion educator; b. Pitts., Sept. 19, 1953; d. James Walker and Ruthe Eleanor (Carlson) B. AB, Mt. Holyoke Coll., 1975; M of Div., Garrett-Evang. Theol. Sem., 1978; PhD, Boston U., 1983. Lectr. Sch. Theology Boston U., 1980-82, asst. dean of chapel, 1981-82; dir. restoration program Washington Sq. Ch., N.Y.C., 1982-83; asst. prof. Pacific Luth. U., Tacoma, 1983-88, St. Andrews Coll., Saskatoom, Sask., Can., 1988—; lectr., speaker in field. Contbr. (book): Something More Than Human, 1986; contbr. articles to profl. jours. Elder United Meth. Ch., 1982—; v.p., bd. dirs. Pacific Peaks council Girl Scouts U.S., Olympia, Wash., 1984-87; del. nat. council Girl Scouts U.S., 1987—. United Meth. Sem. scholar, 1976-77; fellow Boston U., 1978-79. Mem. Am. Acad. Religion (regional exec. sec. 1983—), Am. Soc. Ch. History. Democrat. Office: St Andrews Coll, 1121 College Dr, Saskatoon, SK Canada S7N OW3

BROWN, JOY MAUREEN, obstetrician-gynecologist; b. Coral Gables, Fla., Dec. 21, 1957; d. Edward Thomas and Loretta Patricia (Urbanski) B.; m. Anthony Casciano III. BS, Biscayne Coll., 1978; MD, U. South Fla., 1981. Resident ob-gyn. Allentown (Pa.) Hosp., 1981-85, pvt. practice ob-gyn., 1985-86; pvt. practice ob-gyn. Stroudsburg (Pa.) Pocono Hosp., 1986—; bd. dirs. Crisis Pregnancy Ctr., Stroudsburg. Bd. dirs. People Who Care, Stroudsburg. Mem. Pa. Med. Soc., Am. Coll. Ob-Gyn. (jr. fellow). Democrat. Roman Catholic.

BROWN, JUANITA ORA LUCKETT, financial manager; b. Chgo., July 31, 1948; d. Clifford Homer and Irma Jean (Maxwell) Luckett; m. Oddie Lee Brown, July 17, 1971; children: Odili Njoli, Chapelle Beth. BS in Math., U. Chgo., 1969; MBA, Columbia U., 1971. Cons. Union Carbide, N.Y.C., 1971-74, sr. cons., 1974-77, supr. client service, 1977-79, sr. fin. analyst, 1979-80; mgr. ops. analysis Am. Can Co., Greenwich, Conn., 1980-81, Mgr. corp. analysis standards and measurements, 1981-82, dir. fin., 1983-84, dir. asset mgmt., 1984-85, dir. resource analysis, 1985-86; mgr. fin. analysis Bristol-Myers Co., N.Y.C., 1987—; seminar leader Assn. for Integration Mgmt., N.Y.C. and Washington, 1976-79. Active Twp. of Teaneck (N.J.) Facilities Com., 1986—, Friends of the Teaneck Library, 1986—; treas. Working Parents Assn., 1985-87, Lowell Sch. PTO, 1981-83; fundraiser U. Chgo., Newark, 1986; pianist Varick Meml. AMEZ Ch., Hackensack, N.J., 1979—. Recipient Black Achiever award Harlem YMCA, 1978. Mem. Nat. Assn. Female Execs., Nat. Black MBA Assn. (nat. pres. 1977-78), Alumni Assn. Columbia U. (dir. 1976-77). Methodist. Club: Toastmasters (treas. N.Y.C. chpt. 1973-75). Office: Bristol-Myers Co 345 Park Ave New York NY 10154

BROWN, JUDITH ANN, sales professional; b. Brunswick, Md., Aug. 8, 1945; d. Harvey Copeland and Ruth Ann (Thompson) Waldron; m. Hugh Michael Crawford, June 26, 1964 (div. Nov. 1970); 1 child, Jonathan Michael; m. Roland William Brown, July 23, 1972 (dec. Aug. 1977). Grad. high sch., Frederick, Md., 1963. Clk. typist Balt. Life Ins. Co., 1963-64; sr. stenographer Equitable Trust Co., Balt., 1964; office mgr., sec. Anne Arundel County Govt., Annapolis, Md., 1969-75; office mgr. Md. Gen. Assembly, Annapolis, 1975-80; mktg. rep. Exxon Office Systems, Balt., 1980-82; govt. accounts mgr. CPT Corp., Balt., 1982-85; regional sales mgr. Computer-Link Corp., Wilmington, Mass., 1985-86; SE regional mgr. Sentinel Office Products, Hyannis, Mass., 1986; mgr. sales devel. Salesquest, Frederick, 1987-88; sr. sales assoc. Info. Mgmt. Assocs., Leesburg, Va., 1988—. Sec., mem. adminstrv. bd. Mt. Vernon Place United Meth. Ch., Balt., 1985-87, staff-parish relations com., 1988—. Recipient awards for photography, sewing. Mem. Nat. Assn. Female Execs. Republican. Home: 10102 Putnam Rd Frederick MD 21701 Office: Info Mgmt Assocs Inc 26A W Market St Leesburg VA 22075

BROWN, JUDITH GWYN, illustrator; b. N.Y.C., Oct. 15, 1933; d. Philip S. and Freida C. (Robinson) B. Student, Cooper Union for Advancement of Arts and Scis., 1951-52; BA, NYU, 1956; postgrad., Parsons Sch. Design, 1956-57. Illustrator, instr. N.Y.C., 1958—. illustrator numerous children's books, including The Cry of Victory (Padriac Colum), Mandy (Julie Andrews Edwards), The Best Christmas Pageant Ever, King of the Dollhouse, The Happy Voyage, Alphabet Dreams; works featured in permanent collections Boston Pub. Library, Met. Mus. Art, Hutington (Calif.) Library, numerous univs. Active various animal welfare groups, N.Y.C., Mass. Home and Studio: 522 E 85th St New York NY 10028

BROWN, JUDITH LEE, language educator, editor; b. Washington, Mar. 13, 1937; d. Charles Richard and Mildred (LeDuc) Potter; m. Jared A. Brown; children: Lauren Anne, Edward John. BS, Ithaca (N.Y.) Coll., 1959; MS, Western Ill. U., 1974. Specialist communications Lansing Cen. Sch., Ludlowville, N.Y., 1959-60; editorial asst. Burgess Pub. Co., Mpls., 1962-65; tchr. English Roosevelt High Sch., Mpls., 1963-65; instr. English Western Ill. U., Macomb, 1974-78, 80—, coordinator Writing Ctr., 1987—, dir. writing exam., 1987-88; prodn. asst. Lake Argyle Hist. Project, Argyle, Ill., 1981; coordinator writing workshop Elms Nursing Home, Macomb, 1982; cons. script devel. Rushville (Ill.) Hist. Project, 1982, Good Hope (Ill.) Meth. Ch. Hist. Project, 1982. Editor: The Fabulous Lunts, 1980-86; editor, research asst.: Biography of Zero Mostel, 1987—; dir., actress: (play) Memories from the Prairie, 1982-86; actress plays for Lake Argyle Hist. Project, 1985, Univ. Theatre, Macomb Community Theatre, Vocal Minority Concert Readers, cabarets and coffeehouses; newsletter editor various portfolios. Founding mem. LWV, Macomb, 1965-72. Named Best Featured Actress, Macomb Community Theatre, 1976, 78; recipient Merit award Western Ill. U., 1977; Ill. Arts Council grantee, 1984. Mem. Nat. Council Tchrs. English, Am. Fedn. Tchrs. (del. 1985—), Ill. Tchrs. English, Phi Kappa Phi. Office: Western Ill U Dept English West Adams Rd Macomb IL 61455

BROWN, JUDY STEINBACH, editor; b. N.Y.C., June 2, 1952; d. Irving Henry and Dorothy (Buchsbaum) Steinbach; m. Joseph Alec Brown, Feb. 4, 1984; 1 child, Jason Andrew. BA, Union Coll., 1974. Editor Hart Pub. Co., N.Y.C., 1975-78; sr. editor Am. Way, N.Y.C., 1978-79; mng. editor Am. Way, Dallas Ft. Worth Airport, Tex., 1979-87; sr. corr. exec. office Am. Airlines, Dallas Ft. Worth Airport, 1987—. Mag. of Yr. award Am. Soc. Journalists and Authors, 1985, Bronze Quill award of Excellence Internat. Assn. Bus. Communicators, Ft. Worth, 1986. Democrat. Jewish. Office: Am Airlines Dallas-Fort Worth Airport 5E12 Dallas TX 75261-9616

BROWN, JULIE ANN, actress, singer; b. Aug. 31, 1958; d. Leonard Francis Brown and Celia Jane (McCann) Arden; m. Terrence E. McNally, June 11, 1983 (div. Aug. 1988). AA in Theater, Valley Coll., Van Nuys, Calif., 1977; hon. degree, Am. Conservatory Theatre, San Francisco, 1978. Performed as lead singer on albums including Goddess in Progress, 1984, Trapped in a Body of a White Girl, 1987; co-writer, appeared in movie Earth Girls Are Easy, 1987. Mem. Writer's Guild Am., Screen Actors Guild, AFTRA. Democrat.

BROWN, JUNE GIBBS, government agency official; b. Cleve., Oct. 5, 1933; d. Thomas D. and Lorna M. Gibbs; children: Ellen Rosenthal, Linda Gibbs, Victor Janezic, Carol Janezic. B.B.A. summa cum laude, Cleve. State U., 1971, M.B.A., 1972; postgrad., Cleve. Marshall Law Sch., 1973-74; J.D., U. Denver, 1978; postgrad. Advanced Mgmt. Program, Harvard U., 1983. Real estate broker, officer mgr. N.E. Realty, Cleve., 1963-68; staff acct. Frank T. Cicirelli, C.P.A., Cleve., 1970-71; asst. to comptroller S.M. Hexter Co., Cleve., 1971; grad. teaching fellow Cleve. State U., 1971-72; dir. internal audit Navy Fin. Ctr., Cleve., 1972-75; dir. fin. systems design Bureau of Land Mgmt., Denver, 1975-76; project mgr. Bureau of Reclamation, 1976-79; insp. gen. Dept. Interior, Washington, 1979-81, NASA, Washington, 1981-85; v.p. fin. and adminstrn. Systems Devel. Corp., a Burroughs Co., 1985-86; assoc. adminstr. for mgmt. NASA, 1986-87; insp. gen. U.S. Dept. Def., Arlington, Va., 1987—; bd. dirs. Fed. Law Enforcement Tng. Ctr., 1984-85, Interagy. Auditor Tng. program Dept. Agrl. Grad. Sch., 1983-85; chmn. interagy. com. on Ifon. Resource Mgmt., 1984-85; mem. bd. advs. Nat. Contract Mgmt. Assn., 1987—;. Mem. bd. advisors Howard U. Sch. Bus., 1987—. Recipient award Am. Soc. Women Accts., 1969, 70, 71, Raulston award Cleve. State U., 1971, Pres.'s award Cleve. State U., 1971, Outstanding Achievement award U.S. Navy, 1973, Career Service award Chgo. region Fed. Exec. Bd., 1974, Outstanding Contbn. to Fin. Mgmt. award Denver region Fed. Exec. Bd., 1977, Fin. Mgmt. Improvement award Joint Fin. Mgmt. Improvement Program, 1980, Outstanding Service award Nat. Assn. Minority CPA Firms, 1980, NASA exceptional service medal, 1985, Outstanding Achievement in Aerospace award, 1987, Woman of Yr. award Bur. Land Mgmt., Dept. Interior, 1975. Mem. Assn. Govt. Accts. (nat. pres. 1985-86, nat. exec. com. 1977-87, vice chmn. nat. ethics com. 1978-80, chmn. fin. mgmt. standards bd. 1981-82, service award 1973, 76, outstanding achievement award 1979, Robert W. King Meml. award 1988), Am. Inst. CPAs, Am. Accts. Assn., Assn. Fed. Investigators, Nat. Contract Mgmt. Assn. (bd. advisors), NASA Alumni Assn., Women in Aerospace, Am. Soc. for Pub. Adminstrn., Exec. Women in Govt., Beta Alpha Psi. Office: Office of Inspector Gen Dept of Defense 400 Army Navy Dr Arlington VA 22202-2884

BROWN, JUNE WILCOXON, writer; b. W. Lafayette, Ohio, Aug. 14, 1914; d. Ralph Foster and Pearl Almeda (Marx) Wilcoxon; B.A., U. Md., 1935; m. Albert W. Brown, Nov. 3, 1938; 1 son, Peter Wilcoxon. Freelance writer, 1945-60, 81—; editor Select mag., Madison, Wis., 1959-65; radio script writer Beverly Stark Radio Show, 1963-68, John Doremus Show, 1971-72; sit-in hostess Mary Brooks Jackson radio show, St. Thomas, V.I., 1966-75, Louise Noble Radio Show, St. Thomas, 1975-81; author monthly column Caribbean Corner, 1977-78; author fiction and articles in nat. magazines. Mem. Nat. League Am. Pen Women (pres. Madison 1954), St. Thomas Community Music Assn. (v.p. 1970-71), Women in Communications (Writers cup Madison 1951), Kappa Kappa Gamma. Republican. Address: Box 7396 Saint Thomas VI 00801

BROWN, KAREN LEE, educator; b. Des Moines, Feb. 7, 1943; d. Frederick Robert and Evelyn Marie (Jeffress) Brannen; m. Dennis Leon Brown, Oct. 29, 1940; children: Janice, Audrey. BS, Kans. Wesleyan U., 1971; MS, Mankato (Minn.) State U., 1986. Cert. elem. tchr., Minn. Tchr. Salina (Kans.) Pub. Schs., 1971-73, Edina (Minn.) Pub. Schs., 1974-78; tchr. Ind. Sch. Dist. 191, Burnsville, Minn., 1978—, mem. curriculum council, 1985—; co-chmn. conv. Childhood Edn. Internat., Salina, 1973. Tchr. Christ Presbyn. Ch., Edina, 1975—; coach soccer Edina Soccer Assn., 1979-81. Named honor tchr., Burnsville Edn. Assn., 1983-84.

BROWN, KAREN LYNN, energy company executive; b. San Antonio, Jan. 9, 1957; d. James Roscoe and Margaret Mary (Dauwe) B. B.B.A. magna cum laude, St. Mary's U., San Antonio, 1979. CPA, Tex. Assoc. acct. Valero Energy Corp., San Antonio, 1979-80, acct., 1980-81, div. supply and distbn. coordinator, acct., 1981-82, div. supr. natural gas liquids supply and distbn., acct., 1982—. Mem. campaign com. City Council Elections, San Antonio, 1979. Recipient Free Enterprise Scholar award Travis Savs. and Loan Assn., 1979. Mem. Gas Liquids Distbn. Assn. (dir. 1982—), St. Mary's U. Alumni Assn., Delta Epsilon Sigma. Democrat. Roman Catholic. Club: Belgian Am. (San Antonio). Home: 3225 Timmons Ln #40 Houston TX 77027 Office: Valero Mktg Co Two Allen Ctr Suite 900 1200 Smith St Houston TX 77002 also: 2203 W Travis St San Antonio TX 78207

BROWN, KAY (MARY KATHRYN), state official; b. Ft. Worth, Tex., Dec. 19, 1950; d. H.C., Jr. and Dorothy Ruth (Ware) B.; m. William P. Dougherty, Dec. 15, 1978 (div. 1984). B.A., Baylor U., 1973. Reporter, UPI, Atlanta, 1973-76; reporter, feature writer Anchorage Daily Times (Alaska), 1976-77; reporter, co-owner Alaska Advocate, Anchorage, 1977; aide, researcher Alaska State Legislature, Juneau, 1979-80; dep. dir. div. of oil and gas (formerly div. minerals and energy mgmt.) Alaska Dept. Natural Resources, Anchorage, 1980-82, dir., 1982-86. Chmn. ways and means com. Alaska Woman's Polit. Caucus, 1982-84, mem. steering com., 1982-86; bd. dirs. Blood Bank Alaska, 1984-86 ; del. Alaska Democratic Conv., 1984; elected Alaska Ho. of Reps., 1986.

BROWN, LARITA EARLY DAWN, childrens/parents guide book publisher, computer/educational products manufacturer; b. Santa Monica, Calif., Dec. 21, 1937; d. Robert Walter and Lela Shirley (Sims) B. AA, Santa Monica City Coll., 1956; BA, Los Angeles State Univ., 1973; D (hon.), Boston U., 1977. Tchr. parochial sch. Gardena, Calif., 1968-70; supr. Early Childhood programs/tchr. Los Angeles City Schs.-Headstart Program, 1970-72; project asst. Mayor's Office Employment and Job Devel., Los Angeles, 1972-76; community services specialist U.S. Dept. Commerce, Washington, 1976-81; owner, founder N and Out Publishing Co., Richardson, Tex., 1984—; dir. tutorial programs resource ctrs.; cons. human resources, Dallas area, 1985—; contractor Reading Is Fundamental assn., 1984; robot programmer; computer scis. specialist, cons.; founder, dir. Skooter Sam Ednl. Software Co., Dallas; founder Electronics Tech. Consortium; founder (pvt. sch.) Skooter Sam New Age Space Sch. Author: Ginalyn's Surprise, 1984, Skooter Sam in Texas, 1985, Skooter Sam Series, Queens/Kings of African Heritage, African American Inventors, Skooter Sam: Key to the Future, others; patentee numerous childrens' computer products. Active Dallas PTA Council; supr. various polit. campaigns, Calif. and Tex., 1970—; advisor youth and coll. student div. NAACP, 1981-82; media cons. Nat. Womens Polit. Caucus, Hollywood, Calif., 1976. Recipient trophy from Los Angeles County Community Colls., 1980, Service award U. So. Calif., 1970, Dallas Kiwanis Clubs, 1984, Silver Poet award, 1986, Sesquicentennial Tex. Logo award, 1986. Mem. Anthropol. Assn. Am., Phi Beta Alpha Gamma. Methodist. Office: N and Out Pub-Mfg PO Box 2712 Richardson TX 75083

BROWN, LAURA LEE, accountant; b. Chgo., Aug. 12, 1962; d. Gary Wayne and Mary Ann (Grudzien) B. BS, So. Ill. U., 1985. CPA, Ill. Auditor corp. staff Wash. Nat. Corp., Evanston, Ill., 1985-88; tax acct., corp. staff A.C. Nielsen, Northbrook, Ill., 1988—. Mem. Ill. CPA Soc., Am. Inst. CPA's. Roman Catholic. Home: 8213 Knox Ave Skokie IL 60076

BROWN, LAURIE LIZBETH, educator; b. Nyack, N.Y., July 26, 1946; d. Bruce McClave and Helen Frances (Brown) B.; m. Christopher Dana Condit, June 13, 1985; 1 child, Ian McClave. AB, Middlebury Coll., 1968; MS, U. Wyoming, 1972; PhD, Oreg. State U., 1974. Asst. prof. U. Mass., Amherst, Mass., 1974-80, assoc. prof., 1980—; visiting prof. U. Wyoming, Laramie, 1980-81, N.Mex. Inst. Mining and Tech., Socorro, 1983-84; visiting scientist Jet Propulsion Lab. Caltech. U., Pasadena, Calif., 1986, 87. Contbr. articles to profl. jours. Recipient Scientific Research award Nat. Sci. Found., 1976, 78, 80, Visiting Professorship for Women award Nat. Sci. Found, 1983-84. Mem. Am. Geol. Inst. (chmn. com. women geoscientist 1979-82), Am. Geophys. Union (sec. Paleomagnetism sect. 1986-88), Geol. Soc. of Am., Soc. of Exploration Geophysicists, Assn. Women Geoscientists. Office: U Mass Dept of Geol Amherst MA 01003

BROWN, LEANNA, state senator; b. Providence, 1935; d. Harold and Esther Young; B.A. with honors, Smith Coll., 1956; m. W. Stanley Brown; children—William, Stephen. Mem. profl. staff govt. dept. Ednl. Testing Service, Princeton, N.J., 1956-60; councilwoman, Chatham Borough, 1969-72; mem. taxation and fin. com. Nat. Assn. Counties, 1976-79; dir. Morris County Bd. Chosen Freeholders, 1976, mem., 1972-81; bd. dirs. Chatham Trust Co., dir. 1982—; pres. N.J. Assn. Counties, 1978; chmn. N.E. N.J. Transp. Coordinating Com., 1979-80; mem. N.J. Assembly, 1980-83, N.J. Senate, 1984—; mem. Casino Revenue Fund Study Commn., 1984-86, Madison YMCA Capitol Campaign Com., 1986—, chmn., Primary Gifts com., 1987—; devel. council, NJ Sci./Tech. Ctr., Liberty State Park, 1986—; trustee, Ctr. for Nonprofit Corps., 1985—; mem. Gov.'s Commn. on Internat. Trade, 1986—; vice chmn., Congressman Dean Gallo's Small Bus. Export Opportunity task force, 1987—; N.J. Hist. Commn., 1986—; coordinator, Kean for Gov., Morris County 1985; trustee Morris Mus. Arts and Sci., 1975—; trustee Arts Council of Morris Area, 1973—; del. White Ho. Conf. on Children, 1970; devel. council N.J. Sci. and Tech. Ctr., Liberty State Park, 1986—. Mem. N.J. Assn. Elected Women (pres. 1982, 83). Home: 7 Dellwood Ave Chatham NJ 07928 Office: Cory Commons 123 Columbia Turnpike Florham Park NJ 07932

BROWN, LINDA COCKERHAM, quality assurance scientist; b. Durham, N.C., Dec. 4, 1946; d. Harry Lee and Amanda Emmaline (Parks) Cockerham; divorced; children: Eva Angelique, Benjamin James Jr. BS, Agrl. and Tech. U. of N.C., 1970. Lab. technician Burlington Industries, Greensboro, N.C., 1969; tchr. Wayne Community Coll., Goldsboro, N.C., 1976-77; lab. technician ICI Americas Inc., Goldsboro, 1978-80, sr. lab. technician, 1980-82, quality assurance scientist, 1982—; mem. Council Agrl. Sci. and Tech., 1983—. Sec., pres. Protestant Women of Chapel, Goldsboro, 1972, 75; mem. City Planning Com., Goldsboro, 1987; sec./treas. Goldsboro Wayne Youth Bowling Assn.; bd. dirs. Community Concert Council, Goldsboro, 1987, bd. dirs. admissions and budget com. United Way, Goldsboro, 1987. Recipient research stipend NSF, 1966, Saslow award, 1970. Mem. Soc. Quality Assurance, Nat. Assn. Female Execs., Agrl. and Tech. U. N.C. Alumni Assn. (sec. 1982—). Baptist. Club: Officers' Wives (newspaper editor 1973). Office: ICI Americas Inc PO Box 208 Goldsboro NC 27530

BROWN, LINDA CURRENE, small business executive; b. Clovis, N.Mex., Oct. 28, 1942; d. Currie Oscar and Minnie Irene (Rodgers) Bell; m. Harvey Robert Brown, June 11, 1961; 1 child, Christopher Robert. Youth dir. Sandia Bapt. Ch., Clovis, 1969-76; v.p. Linda's, Clovis, 1974—; portrait cons. Triangle Home Ctr., Clovis, 1977-81, dept. supr., 1979-81, customer relations rep., 1981-82, advt. dir., 1982-83; merchandising mktg. dir., advt. dir., customer relations rep. Hollands Office Equipment, Clovis, 1983-85; office mgr. Poka Lambro Telecommunications, Clovis, 1985. Patentee decorative designs. Active Clovis High Plains Hosp. Aux., 1983. Democrat. Baptist. Home and Office: 1940 Cameo Clovis NM 88101

BROWN, LINDA GAY, city market executive; b. Delta, Colo., Jan. 14, 1949; d. Lester Allen and Ruth LaVern (Thomas) Doyle; m. B. Terry Brown, Dec. 21, 1967; children: Shannon, Evan, Kimberly, Misty. Student pub. schs., Cedaredge, Colo. Lab. foreman Holly Sugar Co., Delta, 1974-77; mgr. gen. mdse. dept. City Market Corp., Delta, 1979—. Coordinator Delta County Crisis Teams; mem. Delta Sch. Bd., 1985—, vo-tech bd. Delta Montrose Area, 1985—; mem. Inter-Govt. Affairs Com. Delta County. Republican. Mormon. Avocation: herb gardening. Home: 1374 D Dr Delta CO 81416 Office: City Market 625 Meeker Delta CO 81416

BROWN, LINDA JOYCE, school food service administrator, nutrition consultant; b. Jacksonville, Fla., Jan. 8, 1954; d. Willie James and Katie Lee (Taylor) Lockett; m. Thomas Lee Brown, Dec. 18, 1982; children: Ashanti, William, Timothy. BS in Agr., U. Fla., 1975, M of Agr., 1981. Chemist/microbiologist Green Giant Co., Alachua, Fla., 1975-77; lab. technologist II U. Fla., Gainesville, 1977-81, extension agt. I, Ft. Myers, 1981-85, extension agt. II, 1985-87, West Palm Beach, 1987-88; supr. Palm Beach County Sch. Food Service Area, 1988—; nutrition cons. Congregate Meals, Ft. Myers, 1984-87, Serenity House, Ft. Myers, 1985-87; food service adminstr., instr. Palm Beach County Sch. Food Service, Riviera Beach, Fla., 1987—. Contbr. articles to profl. jours. Mem. exec. bd. Community Coordinating Council, Ft. Myers, 1985; co-founder Friends of Hearing Impaired Youth, Gainesville, 1976; tutor-coordinator Sampson, Gainesville, 1973; mem. Jr. League, Ft. Myers, 1987, Palm Beach, Fla., 1987. State U. System Bd. Regents grantee, 1980. Mem. Soc. Nutrition Edn. (legis. network chmn.), Am. Dietetic Assn. (network of blacks in nutrition, chair legis. com. 1988—), Fla. Dietetic Assn. (chair minority issues com., chair membership 1987-88, chair edn. and registration 1988-89), Caloosa Dietetic Assn. (sec.), Nat. Assn. Female Execs., Nat. Assn. Extension Home Econs. Agts., Internat. Platform Assn., Nutrition Today Soc., Urban League, Alpha Zeta, Epsilon Sigma Phi. Club: Greater Palm Beaches Bus. and Profl. Women (minority student mentor, role model mentor). Avocations: singing, violin. Office: Palm Beach County Sch Food Service 7061 Garden Rd Riviera Beach FL 33406

BROWN, LINDA LEE, technical writer, graphic designer; b. Raton, N.Mex., Oct. 29, 1955. AS, Amarillo Coll., 1975; student West Tex. State U., 1975-77, BBA, Century U., Beverly Hills, Calif., 1984, MBA, 1987; student Newport U. Sch. Law, 1988—. Teaching asst. Amarillo (Tex.) Coll., 1974-75; drafter natural gas div. Pioneer Corp., Amarillo, 1975-76, sr. drafter exploration div. Amarillo Oil Co. 1976-77; drafting supr., engring. services supr., dir. speakers' bur. Thunder Basin Coal Co., Atlantic Richfield Co., Wright, Wyo., 1977-86; ptnr., tech. and adminstrv. cons. Rose Enterprises, 1986—; tech. writer Eaton Corp., Riverton, Wyo., 1986—; cons. State Wyo. Office on Family Violence and Sexual Assault, Cheyenne, 1986—, Diamond L Industries, Inc., Gillette, Wyo., 1986—; tech. writer, pubs. cons. Morton Thiokol, Inc., Brigham City, Utah, 1987—. Bd. dirs. Campbell County Drafting Adv. Council, 1984-85; mem. Nat. Assn. Female Exec., 1979—; sec. bd. dir. exec. com. Am. Inst. Design and Drafting, 1984-85, tech. pub. chairperson, 1984-85. Named Most Outstanding Woman, Beta Sigma Phi, 1980, 81; recipient Woman in the Industry recognition Internat. Reprographics Assn., 1980; grand prize winner Wyo. Art Show with painting titled Energy, 1976. Mem. Am. Legion Aux., mem. Ocean Research Edn. Soc., Gloucester, Mass. (grant proposal writer, 1984). Clubs: Wright Writers, 4-H. Author (poetry): God was Here, but He Left Early, 1976, Gift of Wings, 1980; Solo, 1987; columnist, Wytech Digest; contbr. numerous articles to profl. jours. Home: PO Box 114 Wright WY 82732

BROWN, LINDA M., sales executive; b. Robesonia, Pa., Jan. 8, 1950; d. Clarence Daniel and Esther Lavina (Forry) Gelsinger; m. Richard A. Brown, Aug. 12, 1973. AA, Pa. Jr. Coll. Med. Arts, 1969; BA, St. Joseph's U., 1975. Supr. Ergocardiography Dept. Lankenau Hosp., Phila., 1970-76; sales rep. Medical Monitors, Wyncote, Pa., 1976-77, Data Med., Inc., Wynnewood, Pa., 1977-81; systems specialist Cardiac Data Corp., Bloomfield, Conn., 1980-81; mktg. rep. Cardio Data Systems, Haddonfield, N.J., 1981-83; nat. sales mgr. Cardio Data Systems, Haddonfield, 1983—. Grantee HEW, 1971. Mem. Soc. Profl. and Exec. Women, Nat. Assn. Female Execs., Am. Mgmt. Assn., Am. Mktg. Assn. Republican. Home: 613 Nantucket Circle King of Prussia PA 19406 Office: Cardio Data Systems 56 Haddon Ave Haddonfield PA 08033

BROWN, LORRAINE ANN, sales executive, designer; b. Providence, Mar. 15, 1947; d. Leonard Francis and Elaine Frances (Pettis) Millen; m. Jeffrey Schofield Brown, May 22, 1976 (div. 1983); 1 child, Kaneeta Sage; m. Dieter Paul Wuennenberg, July 14, 1965; 1 child, Desiree Jacqueline Wuennenberg. Student, Manhattan Sch. Printing, 1972, Los Angeles Trade Tech Coll., 1981-83. Communications rep. TransAmerica Occidental, Los Angeles, 1973-77; owner, designer The Lorraine Brown Co., El Segundo, Calif., 1979-83; mgr. Silk Lingerie Outlet, Sherman Oaks, Calif., 1982-83; office mgr. Am. Silk Label, Los Angeles, 1984; asst. prodn. coordinator Pacific Coast Mills, Los Angeles, 1984-85; asst. design, interior designer Judy Knapp Inc., Los Angeles, 1986—. Designer jewelry. Asst. leader Girl Scouts U.S., El Segundo, 1985-87. Mem. Young Exec. Singles. Home: 133 1/2 Virginia St El Segundo CA 90245

BROWN, LOUISE DONA, marketing professional; b. Inglewood, Calif., Sept. 19, 1959; d. Robert Edward Fleischman and Donna May (Paris) Woods; m. Steven Ross Brown; children: Kimberlee, Geoffrey. AA, Antelope Valley Coll., 1986. Sales and service rep. Lyle Parido Ins. Agy., Inc., Palmdale, Calif., 1982—, promotion coordinator, 1985—; art cons. Collectors Corner of Calif.; pub. speaker Antelope Valley Hosp. Eating Disorders Unit, Lancaster, Calif., 1985—. Founding editor (monthly jour.) E.D.E.N. News, 1985—; founding pres. Network, columnist; author (short story) Success, 1985. Affiliate mem. Palmdale Bd. Realtors; founder, pres. Antelope Valley Bus. Breakfast Club. Democrat. Lodge: Optimists (program chmn. Palmdale club, sec./treas.). Home: 16844 Valeport Ave Lancaster CA 93535 Office: Lyle E Parido Ins Agy Inc 640 West Ave Q-12 Palmdale CA 93551

BROWN, LUCIE, computer programmer, analyst; b. Paris, Feb. 15, 1930; d. Leon A. and Lola (Prager) Bader; m. Albert Brown, Dec. 1, 1962. BA in Math. magna cum laude, NYU, 1960, postgrad., 1960-61. Programmer Univac Service Bur., N.Y.C., 1961-62, U. Pa. Biology Research Lab., Phila., 1962-65, NYU Sch. Engring., N.Y.C., 1965-71, NYU Bellevue Med. Ctr., N.Y.C., 1971-75; tchr. meditation Internat. Meditation Soc., N.Y.C., 1975-79; programmer/analyst Cunard Lines Ltd., N.Y.C., 1979-82; sr. programmer/analyst Pitney Bowes, Stamford, Conn., 1982—. Mem. Phi Beta Kappa. Office: Pitney Bowes 25 Washington Blvd Stamford CT 06902

BROWN, MABEL ETHEL, tax accountant; b. Norwich, N.D., Dec. 2, 1910; d. Edward and Augusta (Schwab) Simmons; student Fosters Tax Sch., San Leandro, Calif., 1952-53, Del Mar Coll., 1954, Bancroft Adult Sch., 1955-56, Alameda Adult Sch., 1955-62, U. Calif., 1961-62, Chabot Coll., 1963, Sunset Hi Adult Sch., 1967-68, Tech. Adult Sch., Oakland, Calif., 1965-73; m. George Victor Brown, Feb. 25, 1954; children—Arthur Ralph, Edward James (dec.), Jerry Lee Larsen. Prin., Mabel's Tax Service, Oakland, 1943-54; owner Gilroy Motel (Calif.), 1945-47; owner, operator Chatterbox, Avoca, Iowa, 1947-49; owner, mgr. Brown's Bus. Service, Flour Bluff, Tex., 1954-55, Hayward, Calif., 1954-84; owner Rocks Rough & Ready, jewelry shop, Browns Bus. Service. Mem. VFW Aux. Democrat. Lutheran. Address: 28105 Mission Blvd Hayward CA 94544

BROWN, MARCIA, author, artist, photographer; b. Rochester, N.Y., July 13, 1918; d. Clarence Edward and Adelaide Elizabeth (Zimber) B. Student, Woodstock Sch. Painting, summers 1938, 39; student painting, New Sch. Social Research, Art Students League; B.A., N.Y. State Coll. Tchrs., 1940; student Chinese calligraphy, painting, Zhejiang Acad. Fine Arts, Hangzhou, Peoples Republic China, 1985, 87. Tchr. English, dramatics Cornwall (N.Y.) High Sch., 1940-43; library asst. N.Y. Pub. Library, 1943-49; tchr. puppetry extra-mural dept. U. Coll. West Indies, Jamaica, B.W.I., 1953; tchr. workshop on picture book U. Minn.-Split Rock Arts Program, Duluth, 1986, workshop on Chinese brush painting Brush Artists Guild, 1988. Illustrator: The Trail of Courage (Virginia Watson), 1948, The Steadfast Tin Soldier (Hans Christian Andersen), 1953, Anansi (Philip Sherlock), 1954, The Three Billy Goats Gruff (Asbjornsen and Moe), 1957, Peter Piper's Alphabet, 1959, The Wild Swans (Hans Christian Andersen), 1963, Giselle, 1970, The Snow Queen (Hans Christian Andersen), 1972, Shadow (Blaise Cendrars), 1982 (Caldecott award 1983); author, illustrator: The Little Carousel, 1946, Stone Soup, 1947, Henry Fisherman, 1949, Dick Whittington and His Cat (retold), 1950, Skipper John's Cook, 1951, The Flying Carpet (retold), 1956, Felice, 1958, Tamarindo, 1960, Once a Mouse (retold), 1961 (Caldecott award), Backbone of the King, 1966, The Neighbors, 1967, The Bun (retold), 1972, All Butterflies, 1974 (Boston Globe Honor Book, Horn Book), The Blue Jackal (retold), 1977, Walk Through Your Eyes, 1979, (with photographs) Touch Will Tell, 1979, (with photographs) Listen to a Shape, 1979, Lotus Seeds; Children, Pictures and Books, 1985; translator. illustrator: Puss in Boots, 1952, Cinderella (Charles Perrault), 1954 (Caldecott award), How, Hippo!, 1969 (honor book Book World Spring Book Festival); author, photographer: film strip The Crystal Cavern, 1974; woodcut prints exhibited, Bklyn. Mus., Peridot Gallery, Hacker Gallery, Library Congress, Carnegie Inst., Phila. Print Club; Chinese brush pntg and calligraphy exhibited at Hammond Mus., North Salem, N.Y., 1988; prints in permanent collection, Library of Congress, N.Y. Pub. Library, pvt. collections; writer, illustrator picture books for children. Recipient Disting. Service to Children's Lit. award U. So. Miss., 1972; Regina medal Cath. Library Assn., 1977; Disting. Alumnus medal SUNY, 1969; U.S. nominee Andersen award illustration, 1966, 75; Life fellow Internat. Inst. Arts and Letters, 1961. Mem. Authors Guild, Print Council of Am., Art Students League, Oriental Brush Artists Guild, Sumi-e Soc. Am.

BROWN, MAREL, writer; b. Carroll County, Ga., Dec. 17, 1899; d. George Britt and Olive (Summers) Snow; student Atlanta pub. schs.; m. Alex B. Brown, Oct. 8, 1919 (dec. Dec. 1975). Sec., asst. to editor Christian Index, Atlanta, 1924-30; sec., asst. to Bapt. pastor, 1930-37; freelance writer, 1938—; books include: Red Hills, 1941; Hearth-Fire, 1943; Fence Corners, 1952; The Shape of a Song (Writer of Yr. award Atlanta Writers Club 1968-69, Poet of Yr. for Ga. award Dixie Council 1968), 1968; Lily May and Dan, 1946; The Greshams of Greenway, 1950; The Cherry Children, 1956; Three Wise Women of the East, 1970; Presenting Georgia Poets, 1979; instr. writing workshops; chmn. Ga. Poetry Day, 1957-59; participant World Congress Poets, Fla., 1985. Ga. chmn. Books for Russia, World War II; pub. relations coms. Atlanta Bond Drive, High Mus. Art; mem. Ga. Hist. Soc., Atlanta Hist. Soc., DeKalb County Hist. Soc., Druid Hills Bapt. Ch.; bd. dirs. Warren Boys Club, 1984-85, also mem. edn. com., funder Poetry Reading and Writing Program, 1984—. Recipient Ann. Spl. award Dixie Council Authors and Journalists, 1980. Mem. Nat. League Am. Pen Women, Poetry Soc. Am., Poetry Soc. Ga., Ga. State Poetry Soc., Internat. Acad. Poets, World Congress Poets, Am. Acad. Poets. Ladies Burns Club Atlanta, Dixie Council Authors and Journalists, Rader Poetry Group Miami. Home: Regency House 341 Winn Way Apt 101 Decatur GA 30030

BROWN, MARGARET DEBEERS, lawyer; b. Washington, Sept. 24, 1943; d. John Sterling and Marianna Hurd (Hill) deBeers; m. Timothy Nils, Aug. 28, 1965; children—Emeline Susan, Eric Franklin. B.A. magna cum laude, Radcliffe Coll., 1965; postgrad. Harvard U. Law Sch., 1965-67; J.D., U. Calif.-Berkeley, 1968. Bar: Calif. 1969, U.S. Ct. Appeals (9th cir.) 1971, U.S. Supreme Ct. 1972, U.S. Ct. Appeals (D.C. cir.) 1986, U.S. Ct. Appeals (2d cir.) 1987. Assoc. White, Hamilton, Wyche, Shell & Pollard, Petersburg, Va., 1968-70, Heller, Ehrman, White & McAuliffe, San Francisco, 1970-73; sole practice, San Francisco, 1973-77; atty. Pacific Telephone (name changed to Pacific Bell 1984), San Francisco, 1977-83, sr. atty., 1983-85; sr. atty. Pacific Telesis Group, 1985—; speaker McGeorge Law Sch., Sacramento, 1983. Mem. ABA, San Francisco Bar Assn., Phi Beta Kappa. Office: Pacific Telesis Group 130 Kearny St Rm 3659 San Francisco CA 94108

BROWN, MARGARET REE, nurse; b. Sandersville, Ga., Mar. 1, 1949; d. Roger Lee Brown and Gladys Olee (Lawson) Arp; m. Bruce Edward Brown. BS, Northeastern U., 1975. RN, Mass. Asst. team leader Mass. Rehab. Hosp., Boston, 1975-77; head nurse Jewish Meml. Hosp., Boston, 1977-81; med. nurse coordinator Roxbury (Mass.) Comprehensive Community Health Ctr., 1981-83; clin. nurse coordinator Mattapan (Mass.) Community Health Ctr., 1983-86; asst. dir. nursing Fuller Men. Health Ctr., Boston, 1985—; nursing educator Concord Bapt. Ch. Nurses Unit, Boston, 1977—. Site coordinator Nat. Health for Vol. Orgns., Dorchester, Mass., 1981-84; bd. dirs. Am. Cancer Soc., Mattapan, 1981, Hawthorne Youth and Community Ctr., Roxbury, 1986. Mem. NAACP, Mass. Nurses Found., Mass. Nurses Assn., New Eng. Regional Black Nurses Assn. (sec. 1984—, bd. dirs.). Democrat. Baptist. Home: 103 Homestead St Dorchester MA 02121 Office: Fuller Mental Health Ctr 85 E Newton St Boston MA 02118

BROWN, MARGARET RUTH ANDERSON, state legislator; b. Scottsbluff, Nebr., Oct. 11, 1944; d. Everett Howard and Ruth (Nichols) Anderson; m. Kermit Campbell Brown, 1966. BA, U. Wyo., 1966, postgrad. 1971-73; postgrad. Pepperdine Coll., 1967-68. Mem. Legis. Exec. Commn. on Reorgn. of State Govt., 1974-78; mem. Wheatland (Wyo.) Town Council, 1974-75, Carbon County Council of Govts., 1976—, chmn., 1980-83; mem. adv. council for Div. of Community Programs, 1979-85, chmn., 1983-85, adv. council Dept. Health and Social Services, 1982-85; mem. bd. dirs. Nat. Assn. Regional Councils, 1982-86; mem. Wyo. Ho. of Reps., 1983-87. Mem. AAUW, Soroptomists. Republican.

BROWN, MARILYN BRANCH, social service executive; b. Richmond, Va., Apr. 11, 1944; d. Elbert LeRoy and Edna Harriett (Eley) Branch; m. Winfred Wayland Brown, Jr., June 19, 1982; 1 dau., Lesli Antoinette; 1 dau. by previous marriage, Kara Rachelle Lancaster. B.S., Va. State U., 1966; M.S., U. Nebr., 1968. Nat. Tchr. Corps intern U. Nebr. at Omaha and Omaha Pub. Schs., 1966-68; tchr. McKlenburg County Pub. Schs., Boydton, Va., 1968-71; community organizer model cities health planning Capital Area Comprehensive Health Planning Council, Richmond, Va., 1971-72; asst. dir. com. mental health mental retardation services bd. Va. Dept. Mental Health & Mental Retardation, Richmond, 1972-75, spl. edn. dir., 1975-76; civil rights coordinator Va. Dept. Social Services, Richmond, 1976—, chmn. EEO adv. com., 1984—; chmn. adv. com. on Black adoption Va. Dept. Social Services. Program coordinator Swansboro Bapt. Ch., Richmond, 1979—; mem. Swansboro Ensemble, 1974—. Recipient Youth Motivation Commendation, Nat. Alliance of Bus., 1983. Fellow Am. Orthopsychiat. Assn.; mem. Am. Assn. Affirmative Action, Black Adminstrs. in Child Welfare, Alliance for Black Social Welfare, Psi Chi, Alpha Kappa Alpha. Baptist. Home: 5500 Larrymore Rd Richmond VA 23225 Office: Va Dept Social Services 8007 Discovery Dr Richmond VA 23288

BROWN, MARILYN VOLKER, securities research executive; b. Somerville, N.J., Aug. 8, 1937; d. Harry Charles and Evelyn (Wilson) Volker. BA cum laude, Mt. Holyoke Coll., 1958; postgrad., Duke U., 1958-59. Cert. C.F.A. Securities analyst DeVerg & Co., N.Y.C., 1961-62; sr. analyst Investors Diversified Services, Mpls., 1962-63, Dain Bosworth, Mpls., 1963-69; asst. research dir. Equity Research Assocs., N.Y.C., 1969-70; v.p. Drexel Burnham Inc., N.Y.C., 1970-75; pres. Marilyn V. Brown & Assocs., N.Y.C., 1975-80; v.p. Becton Dickinson, Paramus, N.J., 1980-83; free-lance cons. Paramus, 1983-86; pres. Lyon Research Corp., Paramus, 1986—. Contbr. articles to profl. jours. Mem. ERISA adv. council U.S. Dept. Labor, Washington, 1978-81. Recipient Woman Achiever Greater N.Y. YWCA, 1983; named Outstanding Woman in Internat. Industry YWCA, 1983. Mem. Inst. Chartered Fin. Analysts, Fin. Analysts Fedn. (program chair 1971-73), Nat. Assn. Bus. Economists, Nat. Investor Relations Inst., Fin. Womens Assn. N.Y. Club: Econ. N.Y. Office: Lyon Research Corp 145 E 16th St New York NY 10003

BROWN, MARLENE, association administrator; b. Chgo., June 9, 1938; d. Archie and Herta Elizabeth (Erlenbach) Molay; m. Michael M. Brown, June 21, 1959 (div. Sept. 1981); children: Diane Estelle, Sharon Ann. Student, U. Ill., Urbana, 1956-57, U. Ill., Chgo., 1957-59; BA, Northeastern Ill. State U., 1975. Substitute tchr. Chgo. Pub. Schs., 1975-82; exec. dir. Norwood Park C. of C., Chgo., 1986—; pvt. piano tchr., Chgo., 1975—; pres. The Link Corp., Chgo., 1986—. Bd. dirs. John. M. Palmer PTA, 1968-82; chairperson missions, social concerns Mayfair United Meth. Ch., Chgo., 1970's; vol. chorus tchr. Palmer Sch.; edn. chair N. River Commn., 1979-81, pres. 1983-84; co-chair Involved Citizens Against Crosstown, Chgo., 1972; sec., founder

NW Citizens League; ch. sch. tchr., 1986—. Mem. Common Cause, Amnesty Internat., Greenpeace, Clergy and Laity Concerned, Nat. Wildlife Fed., Sane/Freeze, Audubon Soc. Office: 6044 N Avondale Chicago IL 60631

BROWN, MARY ELEANOR, physical therapist, educator; b. Williamsport, Pa., Jan. 1, 1906; d. Sumner Locher and Mary Kate (Eagles) Brown. Student U. Wis.-Madison, 1927-28; B.A., Barnard Coll., 1931; M.A., NYU, 1941, postgrad., 1942-45, Western Reserve U., 1960-61; postgrad. U. Miami, Miami-Dade Jr. Coll., 1971-72, Cuesta Community Coll., 1977-79. Supervising phys. therapist, research asst. Inst. for Crippled and Disabled, N.Y.C., 1941-46; instr. edn. N.Y.U., 1942-46; phys. therapist Childrens Rehab. Inst., Cockeysville, Md., 1946; organizing dir. phys. edn. State Rehab. Hosp., West Haverstraw, N.Y., 1946-47; phys. therapy cons. Nat. Soc. for Crippled Children and Adults, Chgo., 1947-49; physical therapy cons., dir. prof. services, dir. cerebral palsy sch. N.Y. State Dept. Health, Albany, N.Y. and Eastern N.Y. Orthopedic Hosp. Sch., Schenectady, N.Y., 1949-53; chief phys. therapist Bird S. Coler Hosp. for Chronic Diseases, N.Y.C., 1953-54; chief phys. therapist, instr. edn. St. Vincents Hosp. and N.Y.U., 1954-58; chief research asso. hand research Highland View Hosp., Cleve., 1958-64, cons. on kinesiology, hand research, 1964-65; supr. continuing edn. for phys. therapists, asst. prof. phys. therapy Case Western Res. U., Cleve., 1964-68; dir. phys. therapy Margaret Wagner House of Benjamin Rose Inst., Cleve., 1968-70; free lance writer, 1970—; 1st Mary Eleanor Brown lectr. clin. phys. therapy research Inst. Rehab. and Research, Tex. Med. Center, Houston, 1979; Adv. bd. Community Services Dept. Cuesta Community Coll., San Luis Obispo, Calif., 1977—; vol. UN and Univ. for Peace, Costa Rica, 1982—. Recipient Award of Merit, Case-Western Res. U., 1970; award for clin. research Inst. Rehab. and Research, Tex. Med. Center, Houston, 1979; Lucy Blair Service award Am. Phys. Therapy Assn., 1984, Disting. Alumna award Lancaster Country Day Sch., 1987. Mem. Inst. Gen. Semantics, Internat. Soc. Gen. Semantics, Am. Phys. Therapy Assn., Planetary Citizens, Better World Soc., Morro Bay Art Assn. Contbr. articles in field to profl. jours. Home: 659 Bernardo Ave Morro Bay CA 93442

BROWN, MARY OLIVER, opera singer, musician, writer; b. Cleve., Mar. 7, 1953; d. James Beaty and Jeannette (Glover) Oliver; m. Otis William Brown Jr., Sept. 4, 1974 (div. 1979); 1 child, Otis W. III; m. David Preston, May 8, 1987; 1 stepchild, Maria Helena Muriel. AB in Philosophy and Music, Bryn Mawr Coll., 1976; MFA, Goddard Coll., 1981; PhD in Comparative Lit., U. Pa., 1982, PhD in Music, 1987; EdD, Temple U., 1985. Cert. secondary sch. tchr., Pa. Editorial sec. dept. sociology U. Pa., Phila., 1979-80; English tchr. Temple Univ. High Sch., Phila., 1979—; opera singer Opera Ebony, Phila., 1986—, Opera Co. Phila., 1986—. Author: (poetry) Lightyears: 1973-76, 1982 (Pulitzer Prize nominee 1982), Blue Cyclone, 1982 (CBS Writing Fellowship Honor 1982). Pianist Marlboro (Vt.) Festival, 1986—; mem. Met. Opera Guild, 1987—; nominating com. Pulitzer Prize in Poetry, Phila., 1986; active Mayor's Commn. on Neighborhoods, Phila. Served with Pa. N.G., 1971. Grantee Pa. Council on the Arts, 1979. Mem. Poetry Soc. Am., Acad. Am. Poets (awards 1981, 82), Nat. Info. Soc., The Word Guild, Inc. Democrat. Nichiren Shoshu Buddhist. Home and Office: 4238 Chestnut St #4 Philadelphia PA 19104

BROWN, MONA WRIGHT, research and development company administrator; b. Washington, Feb. 18, 1958; d. Robert Albert Sylvester and Margaretha (Frank) B. Student U. Nev., 1977—. Receptionist, br. mgr. sect. Wells Fargo Mortgage Co., Las Vegas, 1980-81; resident installation control clk. Cen. Telephone Co., Las Vegas, 1981-82; sec. customer service asst. mgr., 1982-84; tour guide Grayline Tours of Nev., Las Vegas, 1985-86; model various agy., Las Vegas, 1984—; adminstrv. coordinator Sci. Applications Internat. Corp., Las Vegas, 1984—. Bd. dirs. Nev. affiliate Am. Diabetes Assn., Las Vegas, 1985—, chmn. fund raising, 1985-86, ann. meeting chmn., 1985—; vol. Las Vegas C. of C. membership com., 1982; registration coordinator Youth 2000 Nat. Conv. Recipient Appreciation award Cen. Telephone Co. for United Way campaign, 1982. Mem. Am. Bus. Women's Assn. (pres. Gambleier's chpt. 1984-85, chmn. assoc. night banquet 1983-84), Am. Diabetes Assn. (nat. task force on gen. membership 1986-87, Most Outstanding Mem. award Nev. affiliate 1985-86). Clubs: Toastmasters (sec. 1984), I'll Drink to That (Las Vegas) (bull. editor 1983-84). Office: Sci Applications Internat Corp 3349 S Highland Dr Suite 403 Las Vegas NV 89109

BROWN, MURIEL JEAN, savings and loan executive; b. Goffstown, N.H., Apr. 4, 1946; d. Walter Scott Wheeler and Marion Aida (Plante) Thompson. Grad. high sch., Manchester, N.H. Lic. real estate saleswoman. Consumer loan trainee, sec. to v.p. lending Bank of N.H. (formerly Manchester Nat. Bank), 1967-72; supr. consumer loan ops. Daniel Webster br. Mchts. Savs. Bank (now Numerica Savs. Bank), Manchester, 1972-74, consumer loan officer, 1974-75, mgr. trainee, 1975, mgr. Daniel Webster br., 1975-78, asst. treas, 1976-78, asst. v.p., security officer, 1978-84; br. mgr. Trails Office asst. v.p. for security First Fed. Savs. & Loan, Ormond Beach, Fla., 1984-86; br. mgr. Palm Coast (Fla.) office First Fed. Savs. & Loan, Ormond Beach, 1986—, v.p., 1987—; owner, ptnr. Ms. Wheeler Secretarial Services, Orlando, Fla., 1988—; product installation mgr. Modular Info. Systems, Inc., Orlando, 1986. Co-chmn. pub. and pvt. schs. United Way Manchester, 1980-81; treas. N.H. Heart Assn., Manchester, 1981, state bd. dirs., 1982-83; com. mem. March of Dimes Walkathon, 1986; fin. chmn. for banks United Way Flagler County, 1987. Recipient Campaign award United Way Flagler County, 1987. Mem. Flagler C. of C., LWV. Home: 2494 Oak Pkwy Orlando FL 32822 Office: Security First Fed Savs and Loan Assn 300 Palm Coast Hwy Palm Beach FL 32037

BROWN, MURIEL WINDHAM, librarian, writer; b. Dallas, Nov. 19, 1926; d. Charles Wyatt and Gladys Mae (Patman) Windham; m. George W. Brown, II, Jan. 28, 1951; children—Laurence Windham, David Mitchum, Leslie Ann. B.A., So. Meth. U., 1949, M.A., 1950; M.L.S., North Tex. State U., 1974, postgrad., 1974—. Library assoc. Dallas Pub. Library, 1964-66, librarian lit. and history, 1966-66 children's librarian, 1966-72, head children's dept., 1967-69, children's selection new brs., 1972-77, children's lit. specialist, 1977—; cons. in field. Author: Books for You, 1981; co-author: Notable Children's Books 1976-1980, 1986; compiler bibliographies for Behind the Covers, 1984, Behind the Covers II, 1988; contbr. chpt. to School Library Media Annual, 1987. Mem. presch. edn. com. Am. Heart Assn., Dallas, 1982-83. Jesse Jones fellow, 1949. Mem. ALA (children's Notable books re-evaluation com. 1983—, Newberry award com. 1984-85), Tex. Library Assn. (chmn. children's round table, Siddie Joe Johnson Children's Librarian award 1988), So. Meth. U. Alumni Assn. (sec. 1972-73), Alpha Theta Phi, Beta Phi Mu, Alpha Lambda Sigma. Democrat. Unitarian. Home: 10415 Church Rd Dallas TX 75238 Office: Dallas Pub Library 1515 Young St Dallas TX 75201

BROWN, NANCY ALICE, human resources management executive, association executive; b. Chgo., Feb. 14, 1934; d. Daniel Webster and Mary Ella (Earls) Hampton; m. James D. Brown (div.); children: Robert Anthony Hebert, Donna Marie Hebert-Parker, Lawrence A. Brown. BA, DePaul U., MA. Personnel mgr. Martin Luther King Health Ctr., Chgo., 1974-81; staff specialist Am. Hosp. Assn., Chgo., 1981-85; employee relations mgr. Chem. Bank, Chgo., 1985-87; dir. Am. Hosp. Assn., Chgo., 1987—. Bd. dirs. Chgo. met. chpt. So. Christian Leadership Conf., 1979-84, Community Leadership Orgn., Chgo., 1984-85. Mem. Am. Soc. Personnel Adminstrn., Human Resources Mgmt. Assn. of Chgo. (com. mem.), NAACP, Operation People United to Save Humanity, Am. Soc. Dirs. of Vol. Services, Am. Soc. Assn. Execs., Chgo. Soc. Assn. Execs., League of Black Women. Democrat. Baptist. Home: 756 E 167 Pl South Holland IL 60473

BROWN, NANCY J., state representative; b. Chgo., Sept. 3, 1942; d. Herman Hugo Becker (dec.) and Katherine Evelyn (Gralund) Johnson; m. Myron Douglass Brown, June 7, 1968; children: Derek Douglass, Jason Alan. BS, Barat Coll., 1978; postgrad., U. Mo., 1982—. Treas. Village of Riverwoods (Ill.), 1975-76, trustee, 1976-78, 79-80, plan commr., 1978; twp. trustee, mem. zoning bd. Oxford (Kans.) Twp. Johnson Co., 1981-84; mem. Kans. Ho. of Reps., 1984—; cons. TRW Credit Data, Chgo., 1978-80; extension asst. U. Kans., Lawrence, 1980-81, office mgr. Gubernatorial Campaign, Kans., 1981-82. Mem. Nat. Hazardous Mat. Transp. Adv. Council, 1985-87, State Task Force on Autism, Kans., State Emergency Response Commn., Kans.; chmn. Community Devel. Block Task Force, Kans.; former bd. dirs. LWV. Recipient Excellence in Edn. award Blue Valley Sch. Dist., 1984. Mem. Nat. Assn. Towns and Twps., Kans. Assn. of Twps. (exec. dir. 1983—), Blue Valley Community Council (chmn.), Blue Valley Hist. Soc., Am. Soc. Pub. Adminstrn. Republican. Address: 1549 Overbrook Ln PO Box 23314 Stanley KS 66224

BROWN, NANCY JONES, social worker; b. Pitts., Jan. 27, 1943; d. Oliver Woodford and Alma (Wesley) Jones; BA, Mt. Holyoke Coll., 1965; MSW, Smith Coll., 1967; m. George Dixon Brown, May 20, 1972; children: George Oliver Robinson, Janice Marileine. Caseworker 1, Child and Family Service, Norfolk, Va., 1967-68; sch. social worker, spl. services project Middletown (R.I.) Sch. System, 1969; sr. psychiat. social worker Newport County Mental Health Clinic, Newport, R.I., 1969-72; sch. social worker Wayne (Mich.)-Westland Community Schs., 1972-73; staff social worker Child Evaluation and Treatment Center, Barnert Hosp., Paterson, N.J., 1973-74; sr. social worker Community Center for Mental Health, Dumont, N.J., 1974-75; unit supr. Catholic Children's Aid Soc. Met. Toronto (Ont., Can.), 1975-76; exec. dir. Halton (Ont.) Family Services, 1976—. Mem. Nat. Assn. Social Workers, Acad. Cert. Social Workers, Ont. Assn. Profl. Social Workers, Ont. Coll. Cert. Social Workers, Family Mediation Can. Republican. Methodist. Home: 129 All Saints Crescent, Oakville, ON Canada L6J 5Y6 Office: 235 Lakeshore Rd E, Oakville, ON Canada L6J 5C1

BROWN, NANCY LYNN, design consultant; b. Newark, Ohio, Apr. 28, 1948; d. Thomas Aloysius and Ruth Esther (Hardbarger) B. BS in Indsl. Design, Ohio State U., 1980; MBA, Calif. State U., 1986. Various positions Nationwide Ins. Cos., Columbus, Ohio, 1967-76; test analyst A.M. Jacquard Systems, Manhattan Beach, Calif., 1980-82; program controls adminstrn. Hughes Aircraft Co., El Segundo, Calif., 1982-84; systems support cons. Metier Mgmt. Systems, Irvine, Calif., 1984-86; sr. staff analyst McDonnell Douglas Astronautics, Huntington Beach, Calif., 1986-87; independent cons. Brownline Design and Cons., Long Beach, Calif., 1987-88. Counselor Hugh O'Brian Youth Found., Los Angeles, 1986, dir. judging, 1987. Mem. Nat. Assn. for Female Execs., Women in Design (chair membership 1983), Ohio State U. Alumni Assn. Office: United Technologies Corp PO Box 49028 San Jose CA 95161-9028

BROWN, NANCY TURNER, nurse; b. Savannah, Ga., July 16, 1957; d. DeLamar Jr. and Catherine (Lankenau) Turner; m. James Younger Brown Jr., Nov. 21, 1981; 1 child, James Younger III. A in nursing, Armstrong State Coll., 1977, BS in Nursing, 1980. RN, Ga. Surg. nurse Meml. Med. Ctr., Savannah, 1977-79, ICU nurse, 1979-81; ICU nurse Glynn Brunswick (Ga.) Meml. Hosp., 1981-82, head nurse Progressive Coronary Care Unit and Coronary Care Unit, 1982—. Mem. Am. Assn. Critical Care Nurses. Methodist. Office: Glynn Brunswick Meml Hosp 3100 Kemble Ave Brunswick GA 31520

BROWN, NATALIA TAYLOR, former contract specialist; b. St. Louis, Mar. 3, 1928; d. Gentry and Olivia (Webb) Taylor; diploma with honors, Hubbard Bus. Coll., St. Louis, 1949; B.S., St. Louis U., 1983; m. Edward Brown, Sept. 30, 1951. Civilian with U.S. Army, St. Louis, 1964-86, contract specialist Aviation Systems Command, 1973-86; substitute tchr. St. Louis Pub. Schs., 1986—. Mem. Coalition 100 Black Women, John N. Doggett Scholarship Found., St. Englebert Sch. Bd. Recipient Sustained Superior Performance award U.S. Army, 1970. Mem. NAACP, Knights of St. Peter Claver, Ladies Aux., Internat. Tng. in Communication, Women's Assn. of St. Louis Symphony Soc., Internat. Tng. Communication, Gamma Phi Delta (Elizabeth Garner Meml. award 1966). Roman Catholic.

BROWN, NORA E., chef; b. Indpls., Mar. 19, 1947; d. Walter Emmett and Pearl Marie (Henzmann) Ellis; m. Jerry L. Brown, Apr. 18, 1981; children: Elliot, Valerie. Apprentice Columbia Club, Indpls., 1972-73; chef Puerta Verde Restaurant, St. Augustine, Fla., 1973-75, Garden on the Green Restaurant, Indpls., 1975-76; pvt. chef Allen W. Clowes, Indpls., 1976-83; research chef Steak N Shake, Indpls., 1984-88; chef Kroger Co., Indpls., 1988—; pvt. cooking lessons; guest lectr. Purdue U. Mem. Chef DeCuisine Assn. (sec. 1985-87). Mem. Disciple of Christ Ch. Home: 4260 Rookwood Indianapolis IN 46208

BROWN, NORMA JEAN, commerce chief; b. Liberty, Miss., Aug. 1, 1947; d. Lethaniel Sr. and Queen Esther (Winding) Chandler; m. Charlie Brown Jr., Dec. 26, 1968; 1 child, Keith Charleton. BA, Tougaloo Coll., 1969; M of Pub. Adminstrn., Fla. Internat. U., 1982. Sec., fin. aide clk. Tougaloo (Miss.) Coll., 1969; employment interviewer, guidance specialist Miami Work Incentive Program, Fla., 1970-72, adjudicator, 1972-74; selective placement specialist Hollywood (Fla.) Job Services, 1974-79, employer services rep., 1979-81; pub. info. officer Metro-Dade Procurement Mgmt. Div., Miami, 1982; personnel clk., analyst Lynwood (Calf.) Unified Sch. Dist., 1983-84; dir. procurement N.J. Small Bus. Devel. Ctr., Rutgers Grad. Sch. Mgmt., Newark, 1984-87; chief, office of women bus. enterprise N.J. Dept. commerce, Energy and Econ. Devel., Trenton, 1987—; project dir., trainer Office Small Bus. Assistance, Trenton, 1984-87; host Jobline, Sta. WABC-TV, Miami, 1979-82. Author profl. brochures. Div. leader Econ. Forum for Pres. Reagan's visit to Somerset County, N.J., 1988. Named Woman to Watch in 1988 Jersey Woman mag. Mem. Nat. Assn. Female Execs., Women Bus. Ownership Ednl. Coalition, Inc. (govt. rep. 1987-88), Am. Govt. Mktg. Asst. Specialists, Am. Contract Compliance Assn., Nat. Contract Mgmt. Assn. Home: 2406 Trafalgar Sq Somerville NJ 08876 Office: Office Women Bus Enterprise 20 W State St Trenton NJ 08625

BROWN, OLLIE DAWKINS, scientific researcher, author; b. Martin County, Tex., May 30, 1941; d. Wilma Loree (Turner) Dawkins; m. Robert Jerry Brown, Sept. 28, 1958 (div.); children: Mark Allen, James Russell. BS, Tex. Tech U., 1965; MEd, North Tex. State U., 1973; MS, East Tex. State U., 1983. Cert. tchr., Tex. Tchr. Eastfield Community Coll., Dallas, 1966-72; diagnostician Lillian Solomon, Ph.D., Dallas, 1972-82; exec. sec. Environ. Health Ctr., Dallas, 1982-83, author, researcher, 1983—; psychotherapist Counseling and Edn. Ctr., Dallas, 1985—. Contbr. articles to profl. jours., chpts. to med. textbooks. Mem. Prestwood Bapt. Ch., Dallas, 1985-87. Mem. Am. Psychol. Assn., Tex. Psychol. Assn. Republican. Clubs: Toastmasters, Townnorth Trendsetters (treas. 1984-85). Home: 634 Williams Way Richardson TX 75080 Office: Pastoral Counseling and Edn Ctr 4525 Lemmon Ave Dallas TX 75219

BROWN, PATRICIA COCHRAN, artist, educator; b. Pitts., Nov. 16, 1955; d. Paul Edmund and Patricia Wilson (Cochran) B. BS, Purdue U., 1979; MS, East Tenn. State U., 1983. State park naturalist State of Ind., Indpls., 1975; botanist Carnegie Mus. Natural HIstory, Pitts., 1977-79; isntr. chemistry East Tenn. State U., Johnson City, 1981-83; isntr. biology U. Pitts., 1984-87; instr. art South Arts, Bethel Park, Pa., 1987—; botany artist Bayberry Studio, Upper St. Clair, Pa., 1987—; instr. art Lincoln Community Ctr., West Lafayette, Ind., 1974. Exhibited in group shows Pitts. Soc. Artists, 1987, Am. Artists Profl. League, N.Y.C., 1987 Salmagundi Club, N.Y.C., 1987. Mem. Soc. Econ. Botany, Ft. PItt. Soc., DAR, Beta Beta Beta. Republican. Episcopalian. Home and Office: Bayberry Studio 1531 Redfern Dr Upper Saint Clair PA 15241

BROWN, PATRICIA MURRAY, accountant, financial manager, educator; b. Erie, Pa., Aug. 15, 1935; d. John Glenn and Ruth Agnes (Heinlein) Murray; m. Charles Lloyd Brown, Oct. 25, 1957; children: Julie, Elaine, Suzanne, Elizabeth, Colleen, Charles III. BS, Villa Maria Coll., Erie, 1957; MBA, Gannon U., 1984. Tchr. Wesleyville (Pa.) High Sch., 1957-58; acct. McKnight Ins. Claims, Erie, 1969-70, House Communications, Erie, 1970-72; bus. mgr. McCormick Materials, Erie, 1974-78; fin. mgr. Am. Sterilizer Co., Erie, 1979—. Mem. Villa Maria Coll. Alumnae Bd., Erie, 1975-76; planner Long Range Planning Com. Milkreek Sch. Dist., Erie, 1976. Mem. Nat. Assn. Accts., Assn. MBA Execs. Democrat. Roman Catholic. Office: Am Sterilizer Co 2425 W 23 St Erie PA 16514

BROWN, PATRICIA WHITE, medical technologist; b. Houston, Nov. 30, 1951; d. Albert Carr and Willie Mae (Sneed) White; m. Herbert Charles Pete, May 24, 1980 (div.); 1 dau., Sheatri Denise; m. 2d, Arthur Lee Brown, Sept. 25, 1982 (div.). BS Tex. Christian U., 1974. Med. technologist, edn. coordinator Riverside Gen. Hosp., Houston, 1974-76; chief lab. technologist Almeda Med. Lab., Houston, 1976-80; med. technologist Jefferson Davis Hosp., Harris County Hosp. Dist., Houston, 1980—. Founder Coalition of Pre-Sch. Dirs., 1982—; dir. Parents Calling Parents, Houston, 1980—; and 3d v.p. Vols. in Pub. Sch. Adv. Bd., Houston, 1981, 2d v.p., 1983, pres. 1986—; mem. Tex. State Bd. for Vols. in Pub. Sch., 1982—, 1st v.p., 1985, pres., 1986, sec. 1987—; chairperson Bucks for Belts Coalition for Sch. Bus Seat Belts, 1985; mem. Mayor's Task Force on Edn., Houston, Mayor's Com. on Child Abuse Prevention; mem. adv. bd. Blueridge Health Dept., Attucks Community Coll.; pres. Reynolds Elem. Parent Tchr. Orgn., 1982, treas., 1984; sec. Pershing Middle Sch., PTO, 1985; pres. Kings Row Child Care Parent Tchrs. Orgn., 1978; mem. Nat. Sch. Vol. Program 1982—, Mo. City Space; panelist Houston Area Black Sch. Educators, 1987; bd. dirs. Women in Action, 1984-85; mediator Dispute Resolution Ctr., 1984—; chair Salute to Sch. Vols., 1984-86. Recipient Vols. in Pub. Sch. Spl. Service cert., 1984; recipient numerous certs. of appreciation. Mem. NAACP, Delta Sigma Theta. Recipient Cert. of Appreciation, Vols. Am., 1980, Vols. in Pub. Schs., 1986, 87, Houston Ind. Sch. Dist., 1981, 82, 83, pres.' award Vols. in Pub. Schs., 1986; Outstanding Service award Reynolds Sch., 1982, cert. recognition Training Tchrs. and Adminstrs. for Parent Involvment, 1986, Kay On-going Edn. Ctr., Pershing Mid. Schs., 1987. Democrat. Baptist. Club: Top Ladies of Distinction. Home: 3134 Sunbeam St Houston TX 77051

BROWN, PAULA KINNEY, heating and air conditioning contractor; b. Portsmith, Va., June 19, 1953; d. Curtis Wade and Joan (Glascoe) Kinney; m. Wayne Howard Brown, Feb. 12, 1983; 1 child, Rebecca Jo. A.S., Lake Sumter Community Coll., 1973, 77; student Lake County Area Vocat. Ctr., 1979, 80. Pres. Kinney's Air Conditioning and Heating, Leesburg, Fla., 1981—; head computer system operator, 1986—;, mem. adv. com. for Area Lake Air Conditioning and Heating Vo-Tech. Sch., Eustis, Fla., 1981-82. Mem. Ch. of Christ. Home: Route 1 Box 719B Fruitland Park FL 32731 Office: Kinney's Air Conditioning and Heating 409 N 13th St Leesburg FL 32748

BROWN, QUINCALEE, association executive; b. Wichita, Kans., Nov. 9, 1939; d. Quincy Lee and Lorene (York) B.; m. James Parson Simsarian, June 24, 1978. B.A., Wichita State U., 1961; M.A., U. Pitts., 1963; Ph.D., U. Kans., 1975. Asst. prof. speech communications, dir. debate Wichita State U., 1963-69, Ottawa U., 1970-73; adminstrv. asst. Montgomery County (Md.) Commn. for Women, 1973-74, exec. dir., 1975-80; mgr. fed. women's program Govt. Printing Office, Washington, 1974-75; exec. dir. AAUW, Washington, 1980 85, Gen. Fedn. of Women's Clubs, 1986, Water Pollution Control Fedn., 1986—. Contbr. articles to profl. jours. Recipient award for contbn. to public service Women for Equality, award for contbn. to public service Montgomery County Govt., 1975, Outstanding Contbn. to Sex Equity, 1979, Career Achievement award Profl. Fraternity Assn., 1981. Mem. Am. Soc. Assn. Execs. (bd. dirs. 1985-88, cert. assn. exec.), Greater Washington Soc. Assn. Execs., Speech Communications Assn., AAUW, Kappa & Delta Epsilon (hon.), Zeta Phi Eta (Outstanding Service award 1975). Office: 601 Wythe St Alexandria VA 22314-1994

BROWN, RITA LEE, educator; b. Giessen, Fed. Republic of Germany, Mar. 12, 1948; came to U.S., 1949; d. Walter Smith Jr. and Annette Authea (Ballard) Lee; m. George Joseph Brown, May 1, 1970 (div. July 1977); children: George Walter, Joseph Reuben, Lisa Carolyn. BS, Hampton U., 1970; postgrad., U. Colo., Denver, 1974-75, Western Carolina U., 1985—. Cert. tchr., N.C., Va., Mass. Educator Weston (Mass.) Pub. Schs., 1970-71, Asheville (N.C.) City Schs., 1977-81, 85—; personal banker Wachovia Bank & Trust Co., Asheville, 1981-82; dep. register deeds Buncombe County Register Deeds, Asheville, 1982-83; fed. case worker Congressman James McClure Clarke, Asheville, 1983; cons. children's program N.C. Dept. Human Resources, Asheville, 1984-85. Mem. Buncombe County Dem. Women, 1981-84; bd. dirs. N.C. Council on Status of Women, 1983-85, N.C. Task Force on Domestic Violence, 1984-85; chmn. bd. Asheville-Buncombe Commn. Status Women, West Asheville, N.C., 1985-87; faculty rep. Asheville Jr. High Sch. PTO, 1986—. Mary Dolciani scholar, 1987. Mem. Nat. Council Tchrs. Math., N.C. Assn. Educators. Methodist. Home: 74 Tacoma Circle Asheville NC 28801 Office: Asheville Jr High Sch 197 S French Broad Ave Asheville NC 28801

BROWN, ROSALIE LEDBETTER, agriculture company executive; b. Sinton, Tex., Dec. 4, 1937; d. Leander Madison and Dora Eva (Moses) Ledbetter; m. Lawrence Ray Brown, Dec. 4, 1947; children: Patricia Brown Kelly, Jerry Ray, Carol Brown Moore. Student, Port Arthur (Tex.) Bus. Coll., 1937. Legal sec., then bookkeeper Sinton, 1937, ind. bookkeeper, 1953-75; adminstrv. asst. to exec. dir. San Patricio County Community Action Agy., Sinton, 1977—; freelance reporter San Patricio County News, Sinton, 1969—. Mem. Urban Renewal Sinton Commn., 1971-72, Sinton Community Action Agy., 1972-73; exec. com. Sinton Community Concerns, 1964—, chmn., 1968; del. Tex. Dem. Conv., 1978-80, 82; mem. Sinton City Council, 1975-86, mayor, 1980-85; foreman San Patricio County Grand Jury, 1979, commr., 1980; mem. Tex. Adv. Commn. on Intergovernmental Relations, 1983-86, Coastal Bend Regional Rev. Commn.; mem. adv. bd. San Patricio County Mental Health Ctr., 1987—. Mem. Sinton C. of C. (dir. 1967-70), Women in Communication, Am. Assn. Small Cities (dir.-at-large), Tex. Assn. Elected Women (dir.), Tex. Mcpl. League (pres. region II 1982-83), Coastal Bend Council Govts. (treas.), Tex. PTA (life). Home: 802 E Main St Sinton TX 78387 Office: 125 W Sinton St Sinton TX 78387

BROWN, ROSE MARIE, personnel administrator; b. Washington; d. William B. and Thelma Meyer Dunnigan; divorced; children: Ronald Christopher, Michael Jonathan Dunnigan Brown. Student, Howard U., 1957-59, W. F. Bolger Mgmt. Acad., 1985-86. Clk. typist U.S. Postal Service, Washington, 1964-69, clk. personnel, 1969, personnel asst., 1969-71, specialist personnel mgmt., 1971-85, counselor Office of EEO, 1981—, mgr. nat. exhibits, coordinator spl. emphasis programs Office of EEO, 1986, specialist affirmative action programs, 1986-87, asst. automatic data processing resources, 1987—, also coordinator retirement seminar. Tutor, advisor Anacostia High Sch., Washington, 1985-86; aide councilman, Washington, 1986. Mem. NAACP, Federally Employed Women, U.S. Postal Service Internat. Tng. and Communication (hon.).

BROWN, RUTH PRICE, association administrator; b. Stoneville, N.C., Sept. 27, 1933; d. C.L. Price and Mary O. (Roland) Price; m. G.C. Triplett, Mar. 16, 1956 (div. Jan. 1974); 1 child, David; m. Russell G. Brown Sr., Aug. 29, 1975. Grad. high sch., Stoneville. Office mgr. Assocs. Discount Corp., Winston Salem and Greensboro, N.C., 1953-64; broker Triplett Realty, Kernersville, N.C., 1965-71; exec. dir. Kernersville C. of C., 1973—; treas. Our Town, Kernersville, 1976. Vice-chmn. Kernersville Precinct, 1972—; del. to county, dist. and state convs. Rep. Party, 1974—; mem. Friends of the Library, 1980—. Mem. Bus. and Profls. Woman's Club (pres. 1976-77, Club Woman of Yr. 1976), Arts and Crafts Guild (hon. 1983-84). Republican. Methodist. Home: 210 Beaucrest Rd Kernersville NC 27284 Office: Kernersville C of C 100 S Main St Kernersville NC 27284

BROWN, SALLY JEAN, specialty food products executive; b. Seattle, Feb. 12, 1940; d. Paul S. and Myrtle E. (Sherblom) Ford; m. Larry R. Brown; children: Carrie K. York, Brice S. York. BA in Editorial Journalism, U. Wash., 1962. Asst. editor Mercer Island (Wash.) Reporter, 1962-64, columnist, sect. editor, 1969-80, advt. sales, 1980; centrex demonstator N.Y. World's Fair, Flushing, 1964; columnist East Side Jour., Kirkland, Wash., 1967-69; mktg. dir. Bulk Commodities Exchange, Seattle, 1981; food broker Sally J. Brown Specialty Foods, Mercer Island, 1981—, cons., 1985—; columnist Northwest Gourmet, Seattle, 1985-86. Editor mag. sect., 1976-80; feature writer various articles. Vol., mem. advanced learning com. Mercer Island Schs.; chpt. pres. N.W. Gifted Childrens Assn., Mercer Island; leader, troop del. to nat. conf. Totem Girl Scout Council, Seattle, 1976; bd. dirs. Jr. League of Seattle. Recipient Bicentennial award Mercer Island City Council, 1976; named Outstanding Parent, West Mercer Island Sch., 1977. Mem. Nat. Assn. Specialty Food and Confection Brokers, N.W. Culinary Alliance (bd. dirs. 1985-87), Gamma Phi Beta Alumni Assn. (pres. 1980-85). Episcopalian. Office: PO Box 849 Mercer Island WA 98040

BROWN, SANDRA JANE, pharmaceutical research company executive; b. N.Y.C., July 7, 1945; d. Walter Joseph and Ina Buckley (McClurg) B. A.S., Dean Jr. Coll., 1965. Med. sec. Bergen Pines County Hosp., Paramus, N.J., 1965-66; adminstrv. asst. Info. Handling Services, Englewood Cliffs, N.J.,

1966-70; clin. research assoc. Biometric Testing, Inc., Englewood Cliffs, 1970-79; corp. sec., dir. Pharma Control Corp., Englewood Cliffs, 1979—; sec./treas. TDI Pharm. Systems, Englewood Cliffs, 1980-83; v.p. Chateau Condo Assn., Cliffside Park, N.J., 1982—. Office: Pharma Control Corp 661 Palisade Ave Englewood Cliffs NJ 07632

BROWN, SANDRA MARIE, dog breeder, consultant; b. LaFollette, Tenn., July 10, 1958; d. Gene and Beaulah M. (Letner) Hale; m. Thomas Garrett Brown, Dec. 12, 1981. Student, Lincoln Meml. U., 1973-76. Asst. restaurant and catering mgr. Holiday Inns. Inc., Knoxville, 1975-80; singer and TV personality Knoxville, 1976-80; dog breeder and designer of pet clothes Paw Pals Inc., Knoxville, 1987—; cons. Humane Soc., Knoxville, 1986, K-9 Acad., Knoxville, 1986, Little Bits Creations, LaFollette, 1985—. Author: Life in Applachia, 1973. Mem. Nat. Republican Com., 1987; spokesperson Crestwood Mills Orgn., 1982-87, Knox County Homeowners Assn. , 1986—. Mem. Knox County Humane Soc. (top breeder poodles 1984), Northshore Animal League. Baptist. Clubs: DeaneHill Country, Young Women's Auxiliary (pres. 1970-73), Sweet Adelines. Home: 308 Bridgewater Rd Knoxville TN 37923

BROWN, SARA LOU, accounting firm executive; b. Houston, Oct. 11, 1942; d. William Hale and Ruth Elizabeth (Hearon) Rutherford; m. Joseph Kurth Brown, Dec. 21, 1965 (div. Mar. 1979); 1 child, Derek Kurth. B.A., Rice U., 1964; M.B.A., U. Tex., 1966. C.P.A., Tex. Mem. staff Peat, Marwick, Mitchell & Co., Houston, 1966-69, mgr., 1969-73, ptnr., 1973—; asst. treas. Zool. Soc. of Houston, 1986, 87. Treas. Houston Grand Opera, 1973-74, Parks and Recreation Bd., City of West University Place, Tex., 1983, 84. Mem. Am. Inst. C.P.A.s, Tex. Soc. C.P.A.s. Home: 2404 Stanmore Houston TX 77019 Office: Peat Marwick Main & Co 3000 Republic Bank Ctr Houston TX 77210

BROWN, SARAH E., lawyer; b. Topeka, Kans., Aug. 9, 1936; d. Paul Shannon and Alice (Rafter) B.; A.B., Vassar Coll., 1958; JD, Georgetown U., 1963; m. Ralph J. Temple, July 17, 1960; children—Katherine Esme, John Anthony. Admitted to D.C. bar, 1964; staff mem. U.S. Senator Estes Kefauver, Washington, 1958; legis. aide U.S. Senator Vance Hartke, Washington, 1959-60; staff asst. John F. Kennedy Presdl. Campaign, Washington, 1960; asst. to dir. compliance surveys and research Pres.'s Com. on EEO, Washington, 1961-65; cons. Migrant div. Office Econ. Opportunity, Washington, 1965-66; practiced in Washington, 1968-71; staff atty. Pub. Defender Service, Washington, 1971—; adj. prof. criminal law George Washington U. Grad Sch., Washington, 1974-76; faculty Nat. Inst. Trial Advocacy Georgetown U. Law Center, 1980-81; mem. D.C. Bar Com. on D.C. Cts.; treas., dir. N.W. Investment Co., Washington, 1964-66; vol. atty. ACLU, Washington, 1969-71; bd. dirs. Women's Legal Def. Fund, 1976-77; past mem. criminal justice com. D.C. Commn. on Status of Women; bd. dirs. Washington Halfway House for Women; bd. dirs., Law Students in Ct., 1979-82, dir., 1979—. Mem. Criminal Practice Inst. Com., Women's Bar Assn., Judicial Conf. for D.C. Cts., Nat. Assn. Criminal Def. Attys., Washington Council Lawyers (dir. 1979-82), Women's Legal Def. Fund, Lawyers Com. of Washington Opera. Home: 8132 Inverness Ridge Rd Potomac MD 20854 also: Dillons Run Rd Capon Bridge WV 26711 Office: 451 Indiana Ave NW Washington DC 20001

BROWN, SARAH RUTH, accountant, educator; b. Chattanooga, July 3, 1956; d. Elmon Huey Sr. and Janie Margaret (Stevens) B. BS, Athens State Coll., 1977; MBA, U. North Ala., 1981; postgrad., Miss. State U., 1984—. CPA, Ala. Staff acct. Garrard, Humphries, and Snow CPAs, Muscle Shoals, Ala., 1978-80; div. acct. State of Ala. Hwy. Dept., Tuscumbia, 1980-84; grad. asst. Miss. State U., Starkville, 1984-85; acctg. instr. U. North Ala., Florence, 1985—. Recipient research grant U. North Ala., 1987. Mem. Nat. Assn. Accts. (dir. ednl. projects 1986-87, dir. community responsibilities 1987—), Pi Tau Chi. Methodist. Lodge: Optimists. Home: Rt 1 Box 499 Florence AL 35630 Office: Univ North Ala Box 5206 Florence AL 35632

BROWN, SHARON CAROLYN, psychotherapist, educator; b. Chgo., Mar. 11, 1944; d. Wallace Edward and Bernice Beatrice (Wurglitz) B. RN, Columbus Hosp. Sch. Nursing, 1965; BA, Mundelein Coll., 1972; MS, George Williams Coll., 1981. RN. Supr. nursing staff devel. Columbus Hosp., Chgo., 1976-78, supr. neurol. sci., 1978-79; counselor 1st Ch. Community Counseling Ctr., Lombard, Ill., 1981-82; tchr. Coll. of DuPage, Glen Ellyn, Ill., 1982—; pvt. practice psychotherapy Wheaton, Ill., 1982—; co-founder Phoenix Rising, Wheaton, 1984—. Co-author: Living On Purpose, 1988. Office: Phoenix Rising PO Box 3088 Glen Ellyn IL 60138

BROWN, SHARON ELIZABETH, computer science administrator; b. Lynn, Mass., Nov. 23, 1960; d. Leland James Brown and Vail (Wilkinson) Bartelson. BSChemE, U. Mass., 1982. Software engr. K&L Automation div. Daniel Industry, Tucson, 1983-86, sr. software engr., 1986-87, asst. mgr. software systems, 1987; software mgr. Daniel Automation, Houston, 1987-, mgr, software dept., 1987—. Mem. NSPE, Am. Inst. Chem. Engrs. Republican. Home: 2851 Wallingford Dr Apt 1222 Houston TX 77042 Office: Daniel Automation 9753 Pine Lake Dr Houston TX 77255

BROWN, SHARON GAIL, data processing executive; b. Chgo., Dec. 25, 1941; d. Otto and Pauline (Lauer) Schumacher; B.G.S., Roosevelt U.; m. Robert B. Ringo, Aug. 2, 1984; 1 dau. by previous marriage, Susan Ann. Info. analyst Internat. Minerals & Chems., Northbrook, Ill., 1966-71, programmer analyst, 1971-74; programmer analyst Procon Internat. Inc. subs. UOP Inc., Des Plaines, Ill., 1974-76, systems analyst, 1976-77, project leader, 1977-78; mgr. adminstrv. services, 1978-82; spl. cons. to pres. IPS Internat., Ltd., 1982-83; spl. cons. to pres. CFI Supply Co. div. Sigma-Chapman, Inc., 1984-87, ptnr. and co-founder Brown, Ringo & Assocs., 1987—; data processing cons. Mem. Buffalo Grove (Ill.) Youth Commn., 1978-82; mem. adv. com. UOP Polit. Action Com., 1979-82; Mem. Rep. Senatorial Com. Inner Circle. Mem. Am. Mgmt. Assn., Chgo. Council on Fgn. Relations, Lake Forest-Lake Bluff Hist. Soc. Home: 550 E Deerpath Lake Forest IL 60045

BROWN, SHARON HENDRICKSON, broadcasting company executive; b. Malta, Mont., Mar. 27, 1944; d. Elmer Theodore and Dorothy Harriet (Flom) Hendrickson; m. Monty Charles Brown, Oct. 24, 1962; children—Michael Charles, Misty Dawn. Cert. med. lab. technologist, Profl. Bus. Inst., 1962; student Alaska Meth. U., Meth. Coll. Lic. 3d class broadcaster, FCC. On-air, traffic, copywriter various radio stas., Alaska, Tex., Mont., 1967-73; asst. news dir., prodn. mgr. Sta. KIXS-Radio, Killeen, Tex., 1973-74; prodn. mgr., continuity dir. Cape Fear Broadcasting, Fayetteville, N.C., 1978-81, account exec., 1981-85; gen. mgr. Ad Channel (television), Fayetteville, 1985-86, market cons., 1986; sales mgr. Sta. WFAI-Radio (Beasley Broadcasting Group), Fayetteville, 1986-87; prin. Two-ShA Art Gallery, Columbus, N.Mex. 1988—. Judge Miss Ft. Bragg Pageant, N.C., 1983; mem. parade com. Dogwood Festival, Fayetteville, 1983, mem. publicity com., 1984-85, mem. Deming (N.Mex.) Arts Council, 1988-89. Painting included in The Gov.'s Show, Santa Fe, 1988. Mem. Tex. Press Women (pres. Dist. 10 1973-74, 1st place award 1973), Fayetteville Area Advt. Fedn. (Gold ADDY award 1984, Silver ADDY award 1984), Nat. Assn. Female Execs., Assn. U.S. Army, Fayetteville Area Bd. Realtors, Fayetteville C. of C. Lutheran. Avocations: painting, writing, photography. Home: PO Box 506 Columbus NM 88029

BROWN, SHERRIE LYNN, journalist; b. Ponca City, Okla., Dec. 13, 1961; d. Frank Clark and Glenda Kay (McClaskey) B. AA, No. Okla. Coll., 1982; BA, Cen. State U., 1984. Co-producer, anchor Sta. 2CSU-TV, Edmond, Okla., 1984; editor, assoc. producer Sta. KOCO-TV, Oklahoma City, 1984-85; reporter Sta. KSWO-TV, Lawton, Okla., 1985—. Recipient Valuable Service award Handicaps Unltd., 1986. Mem. Alpha Epsilon Rho. Office: Sta KSWO-TV Lawton OK 73501

BROWN, SHIRLEY ANTOINETT MCGEE, legal administrator; b. Savannah, Ga., Nov. 24, 1948; d. Henry and Wilhelmina (Cutter) McGee; m. Sage Brown; children—Lavanda, Sagdrina, Sage W. B.S., Savannah State Coll., 1971; M.S., Central Mich. U., 1983. Tchr. Richmond County Sch., Augusta, Ga., 1971-73; owner, mgr. Southeastern Service System, Ltd., Savannah, Ga., 1975-80; legal adminstr., 1978—. Bd. dirs. Girl Scouts U.S.A., Savannah, 1980—; v.p. bd. dirs. Greenbriar Children's Ctr.; chmn. Mt. Olive Holiness Ch. Women's Assn., 1981—; pres. bd. dirs. Mt. Olive Holiness Ch., 1984—. Recipient Scroll of Thanks, Savannah Girl Scout Council, 1979. Mem. Hostess City Bus. and Profl. Women's Club, Sigma Iota Epsilon, Alpha Kappa Alpha. Club: Jack and Jill Inc. (Savannah, Ga.); Zonta Internat. Avocations: swimming; tennis; reading.

BROWN, STELLA CHANEY, advt. agy. exec.; b. East St. Louis, Ill., Apr. 1, 1924; d. James Oscar and Lela Elizabeth (Hartill) Chaney; student Northwestern U., 1941-42, Jefferson Coll., 1942-45; m. A. Harvey Brown, Nov. 1, 1946 (div. Nov. 1960); children—Wendy Alexandra Brown Kennedy, Deborah Elisabeth Brown Garrity. Advt. mgr. Sonnenfelds, St. Louis, 1943; dir. men's wear advt. Stix, Baer & Fuller, St. Louis, 1944; account exec., copy writer Hillman Shane Breyer Agy., Los Angeles, 1945; copy dir. Harry Serwer Agy., N.Y.C., 1945-46; advt. mgr. Libson Shops, St. Louis, 1946-47; asst. advt. dir. Edison Bros. Stores, Inc., 1947-53; copy dir., account exec, Hirsch-Tamm & Ullman Agy., 1957-58; pres. Stella Chaney Brown Advt., Inc., Clayton, Mo., 1959—, dir. St. Louis Broadcasting Co., Inc.; fashion editor Prom Mag., 1946—. Mem. Am. Fedn. Astrologers. Editor: Wheelspin, 1953-58. Address: 9180 Ladue Rd Saint Louis MO 63124

BROWN, STEPHANIE B., insurance company executive; b. Bangor, Maine, Apr. 4, 1943; d. Stephen A. and Marvia P. Barry. BA in Math. magna cum laude, U. Maine, 1965. EDP tng. coordinator Eastman Kodak, Rochester, N.Y., 1965-67; data processing cons. Arthur D. Little, Cambridge, Mass., 1967-73; with New Eng. Life Ins. Co., Boston, 1974—, asst. v.p., 1978-79, 2d v.p. corp. planning and research, 1979-82, v.p. corp. planning and research, 1982-84, v.p. fin. planning, 1984—; pres. New Eng. Fin. Advisors, Inc.; mem. adv. bd. Ins. and Fin. Services Inst., Northeastern U., 1987—. Mem. Commonwealth of Mass. Gov.'s Mgmt. Task Force, 1975. Mem. Internat. Assn. for Fin. Planning (pres. Greater Boston chpt., mem. SRO com., mem. corp. program adv. task force). Office: 501 Boylston St Boston MA 02117

BROWN, SUSAN ANNE, data processing executive; b. Malone, N.Y., Dec. 16, 1961; d. Richard C. and Joyce Marie (Jeror) B. BA in Maths. magna cum laude, Keuka Coll., 1983. Data processing mgr. A.L. Lee Meml. Hosp., Fulton, N.Y., 1984—. Chairperson Lee Hosp. United Way campaign, 1985-86. Mem. Nat. Assn. Female Execs., Data Processing Mgmt. Assn. Democrat. Roman Catholic. Home: 217 Elizabeth St Syracuse NY 13205 Office: AL Lee Meml Hosp 510 S 4th St Fulton NY 13069

BROWN, SUSAN KAY, educator; b. Des Moines; d. E.J. and L. Marvelle (King) Stichter; 1 child, Sean David Brown; m. Thomas Douglas Gaffney, Sept. 26, 1986. AA in Mass Communications, Scottsdale Community Coll., 1981; BA in Edn., Ariz. State U., 1983. Cert. tchr., Ariz. Tchr. pre-sch. Scottsdale (Ariz.) Sch., 1983-85; head tchr. Alphabet Tree, Reno, Ariz., 1985-86; tchr. pre-sch. S.A.G.E., Phoenix, 1986-87; coordinator Play and Learn Schs., Scottsdale, 1986—. Mem. Women in Communications, Phi Theta Kappa. Roman Catholic. Home: 7845 E Keim Dr Scottsdale AZ 85253

BROWN, SUZANNE WILEY, musuem executive; b. Cheyenne, Wyo., Aug. 28, 1938; d. Robert James and Catharine Helen (Schroeder) Wiley; B.S. with honors, U. Wyo., 1960, M.S., 1964; postgrad. U. Cin. Med. Sch., 1965-66, U. Ill., 1969-72; m. Ralph E. Brown, July 19, 1968; 1 dau., Nina M. Research asst. Harvard Med. Sch., 1962-63; research asst. U. Cin. Med. Sch., 1964-65; sr. lab. asst. U. Chgo., 1966-67; research assoc. U. Colo. Med. Sch., 1968; teaching asst. U. Ill., 1971-73; exec. asst. Chgo. Acad. Scis., 1974-82, asst. dir., 1982-84, assoc. dir., 1984—. NDEA fellow, 1960-62. Mem. Mus. Educators of Greater Chgo., Am. Assn. Museums, Internat. Council Museums, Brookfield Zool. Soc. (bd. govs.), Pub. Relations in Service to Musuems, Midwest Mus. Conf., Phi Beta Kappa, Sigma Xi, Phi Kappa Phi. Office: 2001 N Clark St Chicago IL 60614

BROWN, TERRANCE SUZETTE, child care center administrator; b. Corpus Christi, Tex., Feb. 17, 1955; d. Earl Edward and Nora Ann (Rossow) Moore; m. Philip Lee Brown, Nov. 14, 1973; children—Tiffany Ann, Patrick Edward. A. English, San Antonio Jr. Coll., 1972-73; B.B.A., U. Tex.-Austin, 1977-79. Cert. tchr., Tex.; child care lic., 1981. Instr./model Ben Shaw Modeling Studios, San Antonio, 1972-74; distbr. Ideal Incorp., San Antonio, 1976; accounts clk. Scobey Moving Storage, San Antonio, 1974-76; CRT operator The Woman's Shop, San Antonio, 1976-77; resident asst. U. Tex., Austin, 1978-79; distributive edn. tchr. Austin Ind. Sch. Dist., 1979-80; owner/operator Terri's Tender Care, Dallas, 1981—, ednl. coordinator, nutritional cons., phys. activities dir., 1981—; managerial cons. P.L. Brown Service Contracting, Dallas, 1983—. Sustaining sponsor Living Bibles Internat., 1981—; mem. Nat. Republican Senatorial Club, 1984; sustaining mem. Republican Nat. Com., 1983-84; charter mem. Rep. Presdl. Task Force, Washington, 1982—; vol. nat. election, Dallas, 1980, gubernatorial election, 1982. Mem. Tex. Tchrs. Assn., Distributive Edn. Clubs Am., NEA, Austin Voc. Assn., Tex. Vocat. Tchrs. Assn., Tex. Assn. Distributive Edn. Tchrs., Pi Omega Pi. Roman Catholic. Clubs: Altar Soc. (v.p.), St. Elizabeth's Cir., Pre Sch. Moms. Address: 11308 Gatewood Pl Dallas TX 75218

BROWN, TINA, magazine editor; b. Maidenhead, Eng., Nov. 21, 1953; d. George Hambley and Bettina Iris Mary (Kohr) B.; m. Harold Evans, Aug. 20, 1981; 1 child, George Frederick. M.A., Oxford U. Columnist Punch Mag., London, 1978; editor in chief Tatler Mag., London, 1979-83, Vanity Fair Mag., N.Y.C., 1984—. Author: (play) Under the Bamboo Tree, 1973 (Sunday Times Drama award), (play) Happy Yellow, 1977, (book) Loose Talk, 1979, (book) Life As A Party, 1983. Named Most Promising Female Journalist, recipient Kathrine Pakenham prize Sunday London Times, 1973; named Young Journalist of Yr., 1978. Office: Vanity Fair Mag 350 Madison Ave New York NY 10017

BROWN, VALERIE ANNE, psychiatric social worker, educator; b. Elizabeth, N.J., Feb. 28, 1951; d. William John and Adelaide Elizabeth (Krasa) B.; B.A. summa cum laude (fellow), C.W. Post Coll., 1972; M.S.W. (Silberman scholar), Hunter Coll., 1975. Social work intern Greenwich House Counseling Center, N.Y.C., 1973-74, Metro Cons. Center, N.Y.C., 1974-75; sr. psychiat. social worker, co-adminstr. Saturday Clinic, Essex County Guidance Center, East Orange, N.J., 1975-80; pvt. practice psychiat. social work, psychotherapy, 1979—; sr. psychiat social worker John E. Runnells Hosp., Berkeley Heights, N.J., 1980-86; dir. social work Northfield Manor, West Orange, N.J., 1987; clin. coordinator Project Portals East Orange Gen. Hosp., 1987—; co-founder Women's Growth Ctr., Cedar Grove, N.J., 1979; counselor Passaic Drug Clinic, 1978-80; field instr. Fairleigh Dickinson U., Madison, N.J., 1981-86; field supr. Union Coll., Cranford, N.J., 1986; instr. Sch. Social Work, NYU, N.Y.C., 1980-83, asst. prof., 1983-85; evaluator Intoxicated Driver Resource Ctr., Essex County, N.J., 1987—. Fund raiser Am. Heart Assn. Mem. Nat. Assn. Social Workers (diplomate in clin. social work, listed in nat. register of clin. social workers), N.J. Assn. Clin. Social Workers, Nat. Assn. Social Workers, N.J. Assn. Women Therapists, Am. Soc. Tng. and Devel., Psi Chi, Pi Gamma Mu, Sigma Tau Delta. Office: 250 N 19th St Kenilworth NJ 07033

BROWN, VALERIE G., computer executive; b. Evanston, Ill., Apr. 4, 1948; d. L. Sheldon and Beatrice (Orr) B.; m. Wilford Alexander Phelps (div.). BFA, Ariz. State U., 1971. Adminstr. asst. Cir. Ct. of Cook County, Chgo., 1979-83; adminstrv. mgr. Computer Ptnrs., Inc. subs. Computer Scis. Corp., Oakbrook, Ill., 1983—. Mem. Chgo. Orgn. of Data Processing Educators, Assn. of Bank Trainers and Cons., AAUW. Episcopalian. Office: Computer Ptnrs Inc 122 W 22d St Suite One Oak Brook IL 60521

BROWN, VALERIE MARY, nurse, program administrator; b. Meriden, Conn., Jan. 6, 1950; d. Lawrence Lester and Marian Gertrude (Hartin) Tompkins; m. Edward Francis Brown, Oct. 27, 1979; children: Jonathan Edward, Matthew Michael. Diploma in Nursing, Mass. Gen. Hosp., 1971; BA, Emmanuel Coll., Boston, 1977; MS, Marion Coll., 1988. R.N., Mass., Ind. Unit tchr. Mass. Gen. Hosp., Boston, 1973-76; staff nurse coronary care unit Cooley Dickinson Hosp., Northampton, Mass., 1977-79; patient care mgr. Methodist Hosp. Ind., Indpls., 1979-81, project coordinator, 1981-84, cancer data system coordinator, 1984-86, assoc. dir. cancer ctr., 1986-87; dir. info. resource mgmt. Ind. Univ. Hosp., Indpls., 1987—. Mem. Ind. Cancer Registrars Assn. (pres. 1986-87), Assn. Community Cancer Ctr. Spl. Adminstrs., Am. Mgmt. Assn., Symposium for Computer Applications in Med. Care Spl. Interest Group for Nurses (regional coordinator for Ind. 1985-88). Avocations: flower gardening; interior decorating. Home: 11336 Fieldstone Ct Carmel IN 46032 Office: Ind U Hosp 926 W Michigan St UH A-111 Indianapolis IN 46223

BROWN, VERLIA MONICA, registered nurse; b. Kingston, Jamaica, July 16, 1947; d. Arthur and Sylvia (Bennett) B. BS, Bklyn. Coll., 1977, MA, 1982. RN, N.Y. Staff nurse Kings County Hosp., Bklyn., 1974-77, asst. head nurse, 1977-82, head nurse, 1982—; staff nurse per diam Beth Israel Med. Ctr., N.Y.C., 1983—; lectr. career day Bklyn. Pub. Sch., 1988—. Mem. N.Y.C. Emergency Service Systems, Am. Nurses Assn. (del 1986—), N.Y. State Nurses Assn., Nurses Assn. County Long Island Inc., Kings County Hosp. Ctr Scho. Nursing Alumni Assn., Bklyn. coll. Alumni Assn. Democrat. Roman Catholic. Home: 250 E 29th St #4G Brooklyn NY 11226 Office: Kings County Hosp 451 Clarkson Ave Brooklyn NY 11203

BROWN, VICKIE ADAMS, gift items manufacturer, designer; b. Lubbock, Tex., Jan. 1, 1951; d. Weldon Travis and Dorothy Faye (Gardner) Adams; m. John Michael Brown, July 28, 1978. B.F.A., Tex. Tech. U., 1974. Advt. mgr. J.C. Penney Co., Lubbock, 1979-81; advt. sales rep. Lubbock Avalanche Jour., 1981-83; owner, mgr. Vickie B's, Inc., Lubbock, 1979—. Author: Florals Gift Shop Wreaths, 1986, Wreaths to Grace Your Christmas Season, 1987. Mem. Woodmere Art Gallery, Soc. Craft Engrs., Soc. Craft Designers. Baptist. Avocations: cooking; painting. Home: 719 Marietta Dr Ambler PA 19002

BROWN, VIRGINIA RUTH, physicist; b. Wollaston, Mass., Mar. 11, 1934; d. George William Brown and Ruth Young (Doane) Brewer. BS, Northeastern U., 1957; PhD, McGill U., Montreal, Can., 1963. Post doctoral research appointee Yale U., New Haven, 1963-64; post doctoral fellowship Lawrence Livermore Nat. Lab., Calif., 1965-67; sr. staff scientist Lawrence (Calif.) Livermore Nat. Lab., 1964—; Guest researcher IKP, Jülich, Fed. Republic Germany, 1980—; adj. prof. U. Calif., Davis. Fellow Am. Phys. Soc. (Div. Nuclear Physics econ. concerns com. 1973-77, exec. com. 1980-82, sec.-treas. 1986—). Office: Livermore Nat Lab Box 808 Livermore CA 94550

BROWN, VIVIAN MARIA, mortgage loan executive; b. Decatur, Ala., May 10, 1957; d. Frank wilson and Lillie Marie (Couch) B.; m. Rand Calloway Hayes, Aug. 30, 1975 (div. Feb. 1980). Assoc. Bus. Adminstrn., Jefferson State Jr. Coll., 1985; postgrad., U. Ala., Birmingham, 1986. Loan sec. Guaranty Fed. Savs. & Loan, Decatur, 1975-82; loan processor 1st Fed. Savs. & Loan, Decatur, 1982-83; br. mgr. SouthTrust Mortgage Corp., Birmingham, 1983—. Mem. Nat. Assn. for Female Execs., Mortgage Bankers Assn. Birmingham (pres. elect), Network Birmingham, Birmingham Area Bd. Realtors, Greater Birmingham Assn. Homebuilders, Women's Council Realtors. Republican. Roman Catholic. Home: 3216 Cahaba Brook Circle Birmingham AL 35243 Office: SouthTrust Mortgage Corp 100 Office Park Dr Birmingham AL 35223

BROWN, WENDY ELAINE, systems programmer; b. Los Alamos, N.Mex., Apr. 28, 1956; d. Leon J. and Dorothy (Stern) B. B.A., Northwestern U., 1978. Software engr. Prime Computer Inc., Natick, Mass., 1978-80; systems programmer Dialcom, Silver Spring, Md., 1980-85; systems programmer, analyst APA, Falls Church, Va., 1985-86; mem. tech. staff Corp. for Open Systems, McLean, Va., 1986—. Mem. Prime User's Group, (sec. treas. 1986), Electronic Networking Assn. Democrat. Jewish. Avocations: swing dancing; theatre/stage crew, electronic networking. Home: 2248 Washington Ave #203 Silver Spring MD 20910 Office: COS 1750 Old Meadow Rd McLean VA 22102-4306

BROWN-BUCHANAN, DEBORAH ANN, banker, paralegal; b. Camden, N.J., Dec. 26, 1956; d. Robert James and Audrey Ann (Deso) Brown; m. Stephen Timothy Buchanan, April 25, 1987. AA, Gloucester County Community Coll., 1980; cert., Am. Inst. Paralegal Studies, Mahwah, N.J., 1983. Skip tracer W.T. Grants, Woodbury Heights, N.J., 1975-78; recovery supr. Princeton Bank (formerly Bank of N.J.), Moorestown, N.J., 1978, Bank of Princeton, Moorestown, 1979-82; asst. sec. 1st People's Bank of N.J., Westmont, 1982-85; asst. v.p. Equibank, Pitts., 1985-86; asst. sec. Continental Bank of N.J., Haddonfield, 1986—. Asst. to author/editor: Compliance Book on Banking Regulations, 1986. Mem. South Jersey C. of C., St. Margaret Mary Catholic Ch. (sec. fin. com. 1985—). Home: 123 E Chestnut St Merchantville NJ 08109 Office: Continental Bank of NJ 1 Walnut St Haddonfield NJ 08033

BROWN-DUGGAN, GLORIA LORENE, health care administrator; b. Alpine, Utah, July 22, 1927; d. George Alfred and Alice Cleora (Adams) Brown; BS with honors, San Diego State U., 1957, postgrad., 1964-74; m. George F. Duggan Jr., Aug. 25, 1972; 1 son, Gregory P. Maynard. Sch. nurse, tchr. Sweetwater Union High Sch., National City, Calif., 1966-68; resident head nurse Mary C. Wheeler Sch., Providence, 1968-70; sub-regional trainer Calif. State Drug program Calif. Dept. Edn., 1970-71; hearing conservation program San Francisco Schs., San Francisco Dept. Pub. Health, maternal and child welfare, 1974; clin. lab. instr. community health R.I. Coll., Providence, 1975-76; exec. dir. Pawtucket (R.I.) Neighborhood Health Centers Inc., 1976—; lectr. in field. Publicity dir. LaJolla aux. San Diego Symphony Orch., 1966-68, chmn. symphony summer music festivals, 1967—; past chmn. health adv. com. Dept. Human Services, State of R.I.; exec. com. R.I. Health Ctr. Mem. Nat. Assn. Community Health Centers, Inc. (past treas. region 1, program planning com. 1978-88), R.I. Health Center Assn. (exec. com., publicity dir. 1978, bd. dirs., legis. com., data evaluation com.), New Eng. Community Health Center Assn., AAUW (publicity dir. chpt. 1966), Am. Pub. Health Assn., New Eng. Pub. Health Assn., Phi Kappa Phi. Mem. Ch. Jesus Christ Latter-day Saints. Home: 7 Gilbert St Warwick RI 02886 Office: 401 Mineral Spring Ave Pawtucket RI 02860

BROWNE, ANN APRIL, purchasing manager; b. Washington, Apr. 9, 1945; d. Benjamin and Sarah (Barr) Mudrick. BA in Bus. Mgmt., Eckerd Coll., 1987. Purchasing mgr. Gen. Kinetics, Rockville, Md., 1972-73; assoc. buyer Control Data Corp., Rockville, 1973-74; outside sales rep. Mid Atlantic Industries, Bladensburg, Md., 1974, U.S. C. of C., San Antonio, 1975; inside sales coordinator Frabimore Equipment & Controls, Inc., Elk Grove Village, Ill., 1976-77; customer service rep. Viracon, Inc., Bensenville, Ill., 1977; purchasing mgr. vectrol div. Westinghouse Elec. Corp., Oldsmar, Fla., 1978-83; purchasing agt. Tarpon Springs (Fla.) Gen. Hosp., 1987—. Mem. Material Mgmt. Assn., Nat. Assn. Purchasing Mgmt. (cert.), Phi Theta Kappa.

BROWNE, JANE JORDAN, literary agent; b. Los Angeles, Apr. 14, 1931; d. Francis Emmett and Margaret Eleanor (Gray) B.; m. William O. Petersen, Nov. 25, 1978. B.A., Smith Coll., 1952; Diplome de la Langue Francaise, U. Neuchatel, Switzerland, 1953; M.A., UCLA, 1962. Mng. editor Hawthorn Books, N.Y.C., 1963-65; editor Thomas Y. Crowell, N.Y.C., 1965-67; freelance writer, Beverly Hills, Calif., 1967-68; gen. editorial and prodn. mgr. Macmillan Ednl. Services Inc., Beverly Hills, 1968-70; lit. agt. Multimedia Product Devel. Inc., Beverly Hills and Chgo., 1970—. Ghostwriter: When Towns Had Walls, 1970; writer, editor: Architectural Digest Book of Celebrity Homes, 1976. Contbr. articles to consumer mags., profl. jours. Bd. dirs. Ill. Ctr. for the Book, Chgo., 1985. Mem. Modern Poetry Assn. (v.p. 1983—), Midwest Writers Assn. (bd. dirs. 1983—), Ind. Lit. Agts. Assn. Republican. Roman Catholic. Clubs: Fortnightly, Friday (Chgo.). Avocations: gardening; cooking; travel. Office: Multimedia Product Devel Inc 410 S Michigan Ave Chicago IL 60605

BROWNE, JOY, psychologist; b. New Orleans, Oct. 24, 1950; d. Nelson and Ruth (Strauss) B.; Carter Thweatt, June 9, 1966 (div. 1979); 1 child, Patience. BA, Rice U.; PhD, Northeastern U.; postgrad., Tufts U. Registered psychologist, Mass. With research/optics dept. Sperry Rand, Boston, 1966-68; engr. space program Itek, Boston, 1968-70; head social services dept. Boston Redevel. Authority, 1970-71; staff psychologist South Shore Counselling Assocs., Boston, 1971-82; on-the-air psychologist Sta. WITS, Boston, 1978-82, Sta. KGO, San Francisco, 1982-84; host, news Sta. KCBS, San Francisco, 1984-85; on-the-air psychologist Sta. WABC, N.Y.C., 1985-

87, ABC Talkradio, N.Y.C., 1987—; dir. Town of Hull Adolescent Outreach Program. Author: The Used Car Game, 1971, The Research Experience, 1976, Nobody's Perfect, 1988. Mem. Am. Psychol. Assn., Phi Kappa Phi (Communicator of Yr.). Office: ABC Talkradio 125 W End Ave New York NY 10023

BROWNE, LESLIE, dancer, actress; b. N.Y.C., June 29, 1957; d. Kelly and Isabel (Mirrow) B. Grad., Profl. Children's Sch., N.Y.C. Mem. corps de ballet N.Y.C. Ballet, 1974-76; soloist Am. Ballet Theatre, 1976-86, Prin., 1986—; appearances in films Turning Point, 1977, Nijinsky, 1980. Recipient Dance Edn. of Am. award. Mem. Acad. Motion Picture Arts and Scis. Address: Am Ballet Theatre 890 Broadway New York NY 10003 *

BROWNE, RENNI, communications executive; b. Charlotte, N.C., May 29, 1939; d. Edwin Spotswood Dillard and Jean Dillard (Twitty) Hutcheson; m. Aldis Jerome Browne III (div. 1970); 1 child, Ross Spotswood. Student, Agnes Scott Coll., 1957-60; BA, U. Tenn., 1961. Editor Charles Schribner's Sons, N.Y.C., 1965-68; sr. editor Stein and Day Publ., Scarborough, N.Y., 1968-76, William Marrow and Co., N.Y.C., 1977-78; pres. The Editorial Dept., Grandview, N.Y., 1978—. Episcopalian. Office: The Editorial Dept 541 Rt 9-W Grandview NY 10960

BROWNELL, EILEEN OLIVIA, community services administrator; b. Chico, Calif., Aug. 16, 1945; d. Kenneth Leventon and Jessie Eileen (Aitken) B.; m. Thomas Lee Balentine, Sept. 6, 1969 (div. Apr. 1971). AA, Shasta Coll., 1966; BA, Chico State U., 1968; MS, Calif. State U., Long Beach, 1973. Cert. park and recreation supervision, Calif.; registered recreator. Recreation leader III Long Beach (Calif.) Recreation Dept., 1968-71, sr. recreation leader, 1971-73; supr. community services Westminster (Calif.) Community Services Dept., 1973-79; mgr. community services Fullerton (Calif.) Community Services Dept., 1979-87; mgr. Fountain Valley (Calif.) Community Services Dept., 1987—; bd. dirs. Calif. Park and Recreation Soc., instr. Calif. State U., Long Beach, Calif., 1974-79, Coastline Community Coll., Fountain Valley, Calif., 1978; cons., owner Brownell Leisure Services, Costa Mesa, Calif., 1982—. Author: (book) Low Income Individuals Recreation Needs, 1976 (research award 1975); contbr. articles to profl. jours. Adv. Crippled Childrens Guild, Long Beach, 1971-73, ARC, Westminster Calif., 1977-79, N. Orange County Human Services Agy., Anaheim, Calif., 1980-82, N. Orange County Regional Occupational Program, Brea, Calif., 1982-87, Family Services Agy., Fullerton, 1986-87; Boys Participation chmn., Longfellow PTA, Long Beach, 1971-73, Recreation chair, Barton Sch. PTA, Long Beach, 1972-73; den leader, games chmn., photo counselor, Boy Scouts Am., Long Beach Chpt., 1971-79; vol. State Spl. Olympics, floor hockey, UCLA, 1980-81, Vols. in Parole, Orange County, Calif., 1983-85. Mem. Calif. Park and Recreation Soc., (offices state sec., treas., so. rep., exec. council, pres. recreation suprs. sect. 1980-83) (mem. various coms.). Democrat. Home: 1710 Missouri St Costa Mesa CA 92626 Office: Fountain Valley Community Services 10200 Slater Ave Fountain Valley CA 92708

BROWNELL, JUDI LEE, management communication educator; b. Ithaca, N.Y., 1949; d. Herbert E. and Dorothy M. (Spaulding) Broadwell; m. Gary D. Brownell; children: Conor Eric, Cody Joel. BS, Ithaca Coll., 1971; MS, SUNY, Cortland, 1973; PhD, Syracuse U., 1978. Cert. tchr., English, Speech, N.Y. Tchr. English, speech Homer (N.Y.) Cen. High Sch., 1971-72; asst. prof. SUNY, Cortland, 1973-79, Binghamton, 1980-86; asst. prof. sch. hotel adminstrn. Cornell U., Ithaca, 1986—. Author: Building Active Listening Skills, 1986; contbr. articles to profl. jours. Syracuse U. fellow, 1977; Improvement of Undergrad. Instrn. grantee, SUNY Binghampton, 1986. Mem. Internat. Listening Assn. (sec. 1987-88), Am. Soc. for Tng. and Devel. (pres. so. Tier chpt. 1985-86), Acad. Mgmt., Am. Mgmt. Assn., Speech Communications Soc., N.Y. State Communications Assn. (v.p. regional activities 1975-77, v.p. elect 1978). Office: Cornell U Sch Hotel Adminstrn Ithaca NY 14853

BROWNE-MILLER, ANGELA CHRISTINE, social research association executive; b. Whittier, Calif., June 26, 1952; d. Lee Winston and Louisa Francesca (de Angelis) Browne; m. Richard Louis Miller, Feb. 22, 1986; 1 child, Evacheska. BA in Biology and Lit. with honors, U. Calif., Santa Cruz, 1976; postgrad. in spl. edn., Sonoma State U., 1976-77; MSW, U. Calif., Berkeley, 1981, MPH, 1983, Dr. Social Welfare, 1983. Lic. real estate agt., Calif.; lic. clin. social worker, Calif. Child and family counselor Clearwater Ranch Children's Home, Mendocino County, Calif., 1976-77; conselor, spl. edn. tchr. Bachman Hill Sch., Mendocino County, Calif., 1977-78; substitute tchr. Marin County (Calif.) Sch. Dist., 1978-79; founder Metatech Corp. Services, 1982—, also bd. dirs.; research dir. Cokenders Alcohol and Drug Problem, Emeryville, Calif., 1983—; policy and program analyst White House Conf. on Families, Washington, summer 1980 to spring 1981; research analyst Office for Families, Adminstrn. for Children Youth and Families HHS, 1981, grant reader, 1982, 84, 85, 86; day care program evaluator, budget cons. care programs, San Francisco Bay area, summer 1983; field cons., lectr. Sch. Social Welfare U. Calif., Berkeley, 1984, lectr., 1984-87; program cons. Wilbur Hot Springs Health Sanctuary, 1984-87; pres. Cokenders Alcohol and Drug Inst., Emeryville, 1986—; lectr. Sch. Pub. Policy U. Calif., Berkeley, 1986—; guest White House Conf. for a Drug-Free Am., 1987-88; lectr. in field. Contbr. numerous articles to profl. jours; panelist numerous nat. radio and TV appearances. Pub. dir. Californians for Drug Free Youth Conf., 1986; mem. Nat. Task Force on Drug Abuse, 1984. Recipient Presdl. Mgmt. Internship award, 1982; grantee Adminstrn. for Children Youth and Family Welfare, 1980; NIMH postdoctoral fellow, 1988—. Mem. Am. Pub. Health Assn., Nat. Assn. Social Workers, Assn. Labor and Mgmt. Alcoholism Counselors and Adminstrs., Am. Acad. Psychotherapists, Mensa. Office: Cokenders Alcohol and Drug Program 1240 Powell St 2d floor Emeryville CA 94608

BROWNER, FRANCINE, clothing manufacturer; b. N.Y.C., Sept. 10, 1945; d. Arnold and Chickie (Ulrich) Lehrer; divorced; children—Stacy Lyn, Jacqueline Beth. Student Syracuse U., 1963-64, Parsons Sch. Design, 1964-66, Queens Coll., 1973-76. Designer Organically Grown, Los Angeles, 1978-79; designer, merchandiser Bronson of Calif., Gardena, Calif., 1979; designer Robyn's Nest, Los Angeles, 1979-80, Calif. Class, Los Angeles, 1982-83; dir. merchandising and design Spare Parts, Los Angeles, 1983-84; owner, pres. Rue de Reves, Los Angeles, 1984—. Founder Los Angeles Mus. Contemporary Art. Democrat. Jewish. Avocations: sailing, cars, films, tennis. Office: Rue de Rêves 1936 Mateo Los Angeles CA 90015

BROWNETT, THELMA DENYER, artist, educator; b. Jacksonville, Fla., Oct. 26, 1924; d. Harry and Olivia May (Hook) B. BFA in Painting and Art History, Wesleyan Conservatory, 1946; postgrad., Columbia U., 1948; MFA in Painting and Art History, U. Ga., 1952; postgrad., U. Fla. Dir. Gertrude Herbert Inst. Art, Augusta, Ga., 1951-55; head dept. art Duval County High Schs., Jacksonville, 1955-65; chmn. dept. fine art Fla. Jr. Coll., Jacksonville, 1965-69; prof. art Fla. Community Coll., Jacksonville, 1965-85; owner, operator Oxford Gallery, Jacksonville, 1956-86, Oxford Stained Glass Studio, Jacksonville, 1986—; head dept. art Augusta Coll., 1952-55; instr. art U. Ga., Athens, 1952-55; chmn. art dept. Jacksonville U., 1956-58; juror numerous art exhbns. throughout Fla. and Ga. Author: Painting, 1976, Painting, Studio Handbook, 1982; represented in permanent collections at Ga. Mus. Art, Atlanta Art Mus., Gertrude Herbert Mus.; represented in numerous pvt. collections; exhibited in many art shows, mus., galleries and colls. throughout U.S. State art commr. State of Ga., Atlanta, 1954-57; bd. dirs. Jacksonville Arts Council, 1969-72; chmn. visual arts Jacksonville Arts Festival, 1968-69. Recipient Academi Braszera De Ciencias Humanus award, 1975, Gold medal Accademia Italia, 1980. Mem. Fla. Artists Group (sec.-treas. 1959-61), Assn. Ga. Artists (state pres. 1952-53), Fla. Fedn. Art (state bd. dirs. 1962-63), Alpha Mu Omega. Episcopalian. Home: 4774 Apache Ave Jacksonville FL 32210

BROWNING, JUDY ANN, military officer; b. Hazelhurst, Ga., Dec. 22, 1956; d. Truman Redding and Lollie Clara (Coleman) B.; m. Arthur John Pue, Jr., Mar. 15, 1982. BBA, U. So. Miss., 1985. Commd. U.S. Army, 1985, advanced through grades to 1st lt., 1986; fin. officer Soldier Support Ctr. U.S. Army, Indpls., 1985, master fitness trainer course soldier support ctr., 1985; disbursing officer 105th Fin. Support Unit U.S. Army, Augsburg, Fed. Republic Germany, 1985—. Fin. advisor Transatlantic council Boy Scouts Am., southwestern Bavarian Dist., Augsburg, Fed. Republic Germany, 1986—. Mem. Nat. Assoc. Female Execs., Outstanding Young Women Am., Assn. of U.S. Army, Phi Kappa Phi, Beta Gamma Sigma, Omicron Delta Kappa, Phi Delta Rho. Republican. Baptist. Club: Am. Wandering (Augsburg), Augsburg Toastmasters (charter mem., pres.), Toastmasters Internat. Home: 96 Ravenwood Way Warner Robins GA 31093

BROWNING, LISA KAY, marketing executive; b. Dayton, Ohio, Sept. 30, 1962; d. John R. Jr. and Louise (Hall) B.; m. James R. Walker, Aug. 10, 1984 (div. Oct. 1985). Student, W.Va. State Coll., 1980-83; student in acctg., Tenn. State Acctg., 1987—. Prodn. technologist Sterling Drilling, Charleston, W.Va., 1980; asst. to v.p. Registry Drilling, Charleston, 1981-83; v.p. fin. Parrish Drilling, Nashville, 1984; account exec. McDonough Caperton, Charleston, 1984; v.p. Exec. Planning Group, Hurricane, W.Va., 1985; exec. v.p. Mil. Assistance Corp., Elizabethtown, Ky., 1986; customer support cons. UNISYS Corp., Nashville, 1987; dist. sales acct. BFI, Nashville, 1987-88; dir. mktg. ExecuTrain of Tenn., Brentwood, 1988—. Membership chmn. Davidson County Young Reps.; mem. Bravo Nashville. Named one of Outstanding Young Women Am. Mem. Nat. Assn. Female Execs., Nat. Assn. Profl. Saleswomen, Soc. Computer Profls., Inc. (v.p.). Republican. Nazarene. Office: ExecuTrain 200 Powell Pl Suite 100 Brentwood TN 37027

BROWNING, RACHEL BRIGGS, banker; b. Springfield, Tenn., Sept. 13, 1941; d. James Carney and Pauline (Durham) Briggs; m. Billy Ray Browning, Nov. 17, 1961; children: William Kent, Edward Brent. Student, Vol. State Community Coll., Tenn. Sch. Banking. Sec. Robertson County Register Deeds, Springfield, 1959-61; bookkeeper 1st Nat. Bank, 1963-69, teller, 1969-70, note teller, sec., 1970-75, asst. cashier, supr. dept., 1975-78, asst. v.p., supr. dept., 1978-85, v.p., 1985—. Mem. Bus. and Profl. Women's Club (pres. 1987-88, Bus. Woman Yr. 1985). Republican. Office: Dominion Bank Mid Tenn 2127 Meml Blvd Springfield TN 37172

BROWNING, REBA SMITH, bus contractor; b. Jacksonville, Fla., Dec. 5, 1926; d. Reuben F. and Emmie Ruth (Hopkins) Smith; m. Richard McGuire, July 26, 1945 (div. July 1949); children—Michael Vernon, Patricia Gail; m. Elwood Likens Browning, Aug. 17, 1957; 1 child, Bruce Morgan. Ed. pub. schs., Jacksonville. Bus owner, contractor Duval County Schs., Jacksonville, 1969-75; owner, pres. Browning Transp., Inc., Jacksonville, 1975—; driver tng. instr. Mem., sec. Fla. Vol. Chaplain Cert. Com., Jacksonville, 1984-85. Recipient Outstanding Christian of Yr. award Hogan Baptist Brotherhood, Jacksonville, 1971; Nat. Safety Slogan of Yr. award Gateway Transp., 1972. Mem. Nat. Fedn. Ind. Bus., U.S. C. of C., Duval County Sch. Bus Contractor's Assn. (pres. 1970-73, 81-83, bd. dirs.), Nat. Save-the-Children Club, Jacksonville Be-a-Friend Club. Republican. Baptist. Avocations: public speaking; poetry; furniture refinishing. Office: Browning Transportation Inc 8655 Phillips Hwy Jacksonville FL 32216

BROWNING, RENONA CAROL, lawyer; b. Franklin, Ky., June 29, 1950; d. Fred Carol and Frances Pauline (Stuart) B.; m. Kenneth Cecil Rueff, Nov. 23, 1973 (div. Dec. 1979). BA, Western Ky. U., 1978; JD, U. Louisville, 1981. Bar: Ky. 1981, U.S. Dist. Ct. (we. dist.) Ky. 1982. Assoc. Rueff and Assocs. Attys., Morgantown, Ky., 1982-83; gen. ptnr. Deye and Browning, Attys., Morgantown, 1983—; bd. dirs. Cumberland Trace Legal Services, Inc., Bowling Green, Ky. Treas. Butler County Hist. Soc., Morgantown, Ky., 1986—. Mem. Ky. Bar Assn., Warren County Bar Assn., Butler County Bar Assn., Ky. Acad. Trial Attys., Jaycees (legal officer 1984-86). Office: Deye and Browning PO Box 340 112 W Ohio St Morgantown KY 42261

BROWNING, RUTH ANNA, home economics educator; b. Indpls., July 7, 1932; d. Charles Perry and Mary Margaret (Miller) Wright; m. Scott David Browning, June 8, 1953; children: Donald, Douglas. BA, Earlham Coll., 1953; MEd, Indiana (Pa.) U., 1971; PhD, U. Pitts., 1981. Dietitian Northwestern U., Evanston, Ill., 1953-54; bookkeeper Wright Coal and Oil Co., Indpls., 1954-56; tchr. Bishop Carroll High Sch., Ebensburg, Pa., 1966-70; prof. Indiana (Pa.) U., 1970—. Contbr. articles to profl. jours. Mem. Am. Vocat. Assn., Pa. Vocat. Assn., Assn. for Supervision and Curriculum Devel., Am. Home Econs. Assn., Pa. Home Econs. Assn., Pa. Assn. for Vocat. Spl. Needs (pres. 1985-86), Phi Delta Kappa. Republican. Methodist. Office: Indiana U of Pa Home Econs Edn Dept Indiana PA 15705

BROWNING-SLETTEN, MELISSA ANN, mechanical engineer; b. Steubenville, Ohio, Aug. 31, 1947; d. Milton M. and Mabel (Steele) Trudix; m. Darwin N. Sletten; 1 child, Erik Darby. B.S. in M.E., U. Colo., Boulder, 1977. Purchasing agt. Eastman Kodak, Windsor, Colo., 1971-73; mech. engr. Public Service Co. of Colo., Denver, 1978-85, supr. prodn. standards, 1985-87; maintenance services mgr., 1987—. cons. Hvar Service, Inc. Mem. ASME, CSE. Episcopalian. Home: 11023 Tennyson Pl Westminster CO 80030 Office: 5900 E 39th Ave Denver CO 80201

BROWNLEE, PAULA PIMLOTT, college president, chemistry educator; b. London, June 23, 1934; came to U.S., 1959; d. John Richard and Alice A. (Ajamian) Pimlott; m. Thomas H. Brownlee, Feb. 10, 1961; children: Kenneth Gainsford, Elizabeth Ann, Clare Louise. B.A. with honors, Somerville Coll., Oxford (Eng.) U., 1957; D.Phil. in Organic Chemistry, Oxford (Eng.) U., 1959; Postdoctoral fellow, U. Rochester, N.Y., 1959-61. Research chemist Am. Cyanamid Co., Stamford, Conn., 1961-62; lectr. U. Bridgeport, Conn., 1968-70; asst. prof. Rutgers U., New Brunswick, N.J., 1970-73; assoc. dean, then acting dean Douglass Coll. Rutgers U., 1972-76; assoc. prof. chemistry Rutgers U., Newark, 1973-76; dean faculty, prof. chemistry Union Coll., Schenectady, N.Y., 1976-81; pres., prof. chemistry Hollins (Va.) Coll., 1981—; bd. dirs. Colonial Am. Bank. Author articles, lab. manual. Bd. dirs. Roanoke Symphony, Sci. Mus. of Va. Fellow Chem. Soc. London; mem. Am. Chem. Soc., Nat. Assn. Ind. Colls. and Univs. (bd. dirs.), Am. Assn. Higher Edn. (chair), Soc. Values in Higher Edn., Sigma Xi. Episcopalian. Office: Hollins Coll Office of Pres Hollins College VA 24020

BROWN-MOHR, KAREN LEE, paper company executive, former state legislator; b. Rumford, Maine, Apr. 14, 1953; d. Leland Richard and Barbara May (Dougherty) B.; B.A. in Psychology, U. Mass., 1975. Mem. Maine Ho. of Reps., 1976-84; public relations cons. Boise Cascade Corp., Portland, Maine, 1981-84, mgr. govtl. affairs for Maine, 1984—; mem. Oxford County Republican Com., 1975-80; vice chmn. 2d Congressional Dist. Conv., 1978-80, chmn., 1986—; chmn. Sen. William Cohen's U.S. Mil. Acad. selection com. Home: 37 Kenwood St Portland ME 04102 Office: Boise Cascade Corp One Portland Sq Portland ME 04101

BROWN-OLMSTEAD, AMANDA, public relations agency executive; b. Jackson, Miss., Oct. 7, 1943; d. J.A. and Iris (Williams) Brown; m. George T. Olmstead; children: Vanessa, Blake. Student in Liberal Arts, U. Miss., 1965. In pub. relations, fashion direction and coordination Rich's, J.P. Allen, and Saks Fifth Ave., 1965-71; founder, pres., owner A. Brown-Olmstead Assocs., Atlanta, 1972—; v.p. Pinnacle Group; instr. courses Emory U. and SBA. Bd. dirs. Atlanta chpt. Muscular Dystrophy, 1968-73, pres., 1972-73; adv. bd. YMCA Women of Achievement, 1983; founder Young Careers div. High Mus. Art, 1970; mem. annual ball com. Bot. Gardens, 1981-82, Piedmont Ball Com., 1975, 78; mem. Atlanta Clean City Commn., 1978-81, Leadership Atlanta, 1978, Central Atlanta Progress, 1983; active Atlanta Ballet, 1969-76. Recipient Gold Medal N.Y. Film and TV Festival, 1968; named one of Ten Outstanding Young People of Atlanta, 1976; featured as one of six young tycoons in fashion in U.S., Mademoiselle mag., 1970. Mem. Pub. Relations Soc. Am., Fashion Group, Atlanta C. of C. (Phoenix House award adv. bd. 1983). Democrat. Episcopalian. Clubs: Atlanta City, World Trade. Writer, dir. TV spl.: The Land of Cotton, 1968. Home: 36 Wakefield Dr Atlanta GA 30309 *

BROWNRIGG, JOAN ESTELLE, federal agency administrator; b. Ottawa, Ont., Can., Apr. 12, 1930; d. Rowland George and Jane Ann (Sloan) Ford; m. Stephen Joseph (dec. Nov. 1979); children: Jane, Dennis, Helen, Joseph. Student in polit. sci., Carleton U., Ottawa. Researcher Gloucester Hist. Soc., Ottawa, 1970-71; chmn. ministerial service Pub. Works Can., Ottawa, 1972-86, chmn. exec. support, word processing, 1984-85, chief bus. planning and resources, 1986—; historian, researcher Gatineau Hist. Soc., Manotick, Ont., 1980—, Gloucester Hist. Soc., Manotick, 1980—. Co-author, editor: (book) As Long As Love and Laughter Last, 1985. Area adminstr. Fed., Provincial, Mcpl. Polit. Orgn., Gloucester, Ont., 1956-71; sec. St. Leonard's Parish Ch., Manotick, 1982-85, bookkeeper, 1985-86, historian, 1981-88, chairperson ladies aux., 1979-82, mem. exec. com., 1986-88. Mem. Adminstrn. Assn., Writer and TV Artists Assn., Hist. Soc., Royal Can. Legion (treas., historian 1985—, Sec.'s medal 1985, Treas.'s medal 1986, Jubilee medal 1986). Roman Catholic. Home: 2765 Flannery Dr, Ottawa, ON Canada K10 9S9

BRTICEVICH, DIANA JULIA, trucking company executive; b. Chgo., May 21, 1933; d. Frank and Julia (Naccarato) Cosentino; m. Michael George Brticevich, Sept. 5, 1953; 1 child, Mark. Grad. Kelly High Sch. Clk., Little Company of Mary Hosp., Evergreen Park, Ill., 1958-61; inventory control supr. All-Bright & Nell, Chgo., 1961-66; pres. Fast Motor Services, Inc., Brookfield, Ill., 1966—; pres. U.S. Internat. Inc., Brookfield, 1984—, also dir. Treas. Citizens Com. of Jerry Cosentino, Brookfield, 1974—. Mem. Ill. Trucking Assns., Inc. (bd. dirs.). Democrat. Roman Catholic. Avocations: reading, ceramics. Office: Fast Motor Services Inc 9100 W Plainfield Rd Brookfield IL 60513

BRUBAKER, GWENDOLYN LEE, choral conductor, educator; b. Leadville, Colo., Feb. 28, 1944; d. Harold Harry and Frances Helen (Frey) B. B.M., Hastings Coll., 1966; M.M.E., Drake U., 1968; Ph.D., Northwestern U., 1982. Tchr. vocal music kindergarten through 12th grades Central Dallas Sch., Minburn, Iowa, 1967-69; tchr. vocal music Lane Jr. High Sch., West Allis, Wis., 1969-78; vis. lectr. in music edn. Roosevelt U., 1979-80; vis. lectr. in jr. high sch. music Northwestern U., 1980; instr. choral music edn. U. Wis., LaCrosse, 1980-85; asst. prof. choral music edn. Wright State U., Dayton, Ohio, 1985—; dir. grad. studies in music Wright State U., 1986—, dir. music Trinity Lutheran Ch., LaCrosse; dir. music, Grace United Meth. Ch., Dayton, Ohio, 1986—, musical dir. community theaters, Milw., LaCrosse. Mem. Am. Choral Dirs. Assn., Music Educators Nat. Conf., Ohio Music Educators Conf., Phi Delta Kappa, Pi Kappa Lambda. Choral compositions: Love Is Come Again, 1972; Sing Praise, 1972; The Lone Wild Bird, 1978; Orientale, 1982; The Proud Mysterious Cat, 1983. Home: 4316 Grayson St Kettering OH 45129 Office: Wright State U Creative Arts Ctr Dayton OH 45435

BRUBAKER, KAREN SUE, tire manufacturing company executive; b. Ashland, Ohio, Feb. 5, 1953; d. Robert Eugene and Dora Louise (Camp) B. BSBA, Ashland Coll., 1975; MBA, Bowling Green State U., 1976. Supr. tire ctr. ops. B.F. Goodrich Co., Akron, Ohio, 1976-77, supr. tire acctg., 1977-79, asst. product mgr. radial passenger tires, 1979-80, product mgr. broadline passenger tires, 1980-81, group product mgr. broadline passenger and light truck tires, 1981-83, mktg. mgr. T/A high tech radials, 1983-86; product mgr. B.F. Goodrich T/A radials, The Uniroyal Goodrich Tire Co., Akron, 1986—. Sect. chmn. indsl. div. United Way, Akron, 1983-86. Recipient Alumni Disting. Service award Ashland Coll., 1986; Alpha Phi Clara Bradley Burdette scholar, 1975. Mem. Am. Mktg. Assn. (pres. Akron/Canton chpt. 1982-83, Highest Honors award 1983, v.p.-elect bus. mktg., elected to nat. bd. dirs. 1984-86, v.p. profl. chpts., 1987—), Susan B. Anthony Soc. of Akron Women's Network, Nat. Assn. Female Execs., Beta Gamma Sigma, Omicron Delta Epsilon. Lodge: Zonta. Home: 1862 Indian Hills Trail Akron OH 44313 Office: The Uniroyal Goodrich Tire Co 600 S Main St Akron OH 44397-0001

BRUBAKER, MELANIE ANN, marketing professional; b. Ashland, Ohio, Jan. 29, 1955; d. Larry Dean Brubaker and Virginia Beth Keiser. Student, Miami U., 1975-76, Rutgers U., 1981-82; BA in Mktg., U. Pa., 1988. Med. bookkeeper C.L. Kresge and E. Helfman, M.D., Middletown, Ohio, 1976-77; br. chem. buyer McKesson Chem. Co., Phila., 1978-83; materials supr. Colorcon Inc., West Point, Pa., 1983—; editorial staff Colorcon employee publ. The Spectrum, West Point, 1985—. Mem. Am. Prodn. and Inventory Control Soc., Purchasing Mgmt. Assn. Club: The Wharton Bus. Sch. Home: 4717 Cedar Ave Philadelphia PA 19143

BRUBECK, ANNE ELIZABETH DENTON, artist; b. Beardstown, Ill., Mar. 5, 1918; d. Harry B. and Helen Jean (Gibbs) Denton; student Christian Coll., 1935-36; B.Design, Newcomb Coll., Tulane U., 1939; postgrad. Art Inst. Chgo., 1939-40; A.A. (hon.), Wabash Valley Coll., 1981; m. William E. Brubeck, Dec. 14, 1940; children—Jean Brubeck Stayman, William E. Instr. painting Wabash Valley Coll., Mt. Carmel, Ill., 1962-67; painter; one-man shows include N.Y.C., 1961, 63-67, Evansville, Ind., 1963-69; retrospective, Wabash Valley Coll., 1980; juried exhbns. include: Evansville Mus., 1963, 64, 65, Swopes Gallery, Terre Haute, Ind., 1964, 68, Nashville, 1967. Trustee, Mt. Carmel Pub. Library, 1954—, chmn., 1975-6; mem. cultural events com. Wabash Valley Coll., 1976-80. Brubeck Art Center named in her and her husband's honor, 1976; named to Mt. Carmel High Sch. Centennial Hall of Fame, 1982. Mem. Ill. Library Assn., Nat. League Am. Penwomen, PEO. Methodist. Club: Reviewers Matinee. Home and Office: 729 Cherry St Mount Carmel IL 62863

BRUCE, ELIZABETH (BETSEY) ALICE, broadcast journalist; b. Gary, Ind., Dec. 27, 1948; d. Kenneth Ashel Barnette and Mary Elizabeth (Lasher) Myers; m. Robert S. Bruce, Dec. 11, 1971; 1 child, Whitney Elizabeth Anne. B.J., U. Mo., 1970. Writer, editor Sta. KMOV-TV (formerly Sta. KMOX-TV), St. Louis, 1970-71, staff reporter, 1971—, 5 P.M. News co-anchor, 1973, 74-76, host Newsmakers program, 1976—, pollt. editor, 1978—, weekend news anchor woman, 1978—; pub. speaker; seminar instr. Jr. League, St. Louis, 1980, 82, 86; journalism advisor St. Louis Med. Soc., 1983. Trustee Cystic Fibrosis Found., 1979—, treas., sec., v.p.; pres. adv. council Girl Scouts U.S.A., St. Louis, 1979—; trustee, pres. Carrswold Subdiv., Clayton, Mo., 1979-87. Recipient honor cert. for broadcast reporting Valley Forge Freedom Found., 1982, Media award Mental Health Patient Advocacy Group, 1982, Emmy award, St. Louis chpt. Nat. Acad. TV Arts and Scis., 1981, 84, cert. of leadership St. Louis YWCA, 1983, Spl. Leadership award for communications, 1984. Mem. Soc. Profl. Journalists (2d v.p. 1982-84), Women in Communications (Philpott-Collins award 1978), Investigative Reporters and Editors, AFTRA, Women's Polit. Caucus, U. Mo. Alumni Assn. (publs. com.), Kappa Alpha Theta. Office: Sta KMOV-TV 1 Memorial Dr Saint Louis MO 63102

BRUCE, JEAN MADIE, author, political activist; b. Eclectic, Ala., June 15, 1944; d. James William Kendrick and Madie Claudia (Buce) Newman; m. William Curtis Bruce, May 6, 1961; children: Kimalynn Ann, Micheal Gilchrist. Field worker Carter for Pres., Maine and N. H., 1976; field coordinator Charles Ravenel for Senate, Spartanburg, S.C., 1978-79; cons. Life Long Learning Multi-Cultural Coop., Pine Mountain, Ga., 1976; freelance novelist, writer Spartanburg, 1977—. Author short stories, poetry; contbr. articles to mags. Precinct coordinator Spartanburg County Dems., 1982; founder Vol. Edn. Work, Harris County, Ga., 1975, S.C. Women's Pol. Caucus, Spartanburg, 1980; vol. VISTA. Named Woman of Year Spartanburg C. of C. 1980. Episcopalian. Home: 12 Brookline Ln Spartanburg SC 29303

BRUCE, JUDITH WINSOR, nursing home administrator; b. Paterson, N.J., May 21, 1948; d. Lawrence Hunt and Margaret Ruth (Ruppe) B.; m. Stephen James Smith, June 2, 1972 (div. 1976). BS in Secondary Edn. cum laude, U. Vermont, 1970; MPH, NYU, 1977. Adminstrv. asst. Hanover (N.H.) Terr. Healthcare, 1972-74; med. care evaluation asst. Cabrini Med. Ctr., N.Y.C., 1974-76, supr. utilization rev., 1976-77, asst. adminstr., 1977-78, v.p. long term care, 1978-82; assoc. exec. dir. Met. Jewish Geriatric Ctr., Bkln., 1982-87, sr. v.p., chief operating officer, 1987—; cons. Akin, Gump, Hauer, Strauss, Feld, Washington, 1983. Chair liaison Blue Cross Blue Shield Gt. N.Y., N.Y.C., 1981-82; mem. adv. bd. Elizabeth Seton Coll., Yonkers, N.Y., 1981-82; trustee First Unitarian Ch., Bkln., 1986—. Mem. Am. Coll. Health Care Adminstrs., Am. Soc. Profl. and Exec. Women, Hosp. Fin. Mgmt. Assn., N.Y. Assn. Homes and Services on Aging (bd. dirs. 1980-82, chair program com. 1982), Phi Beta Kappa. Republican. Unitarian. Home: 305 Hicks St Brooklyn Heights NY 11201 Office: Met Jewish Geriatric Ctr 4915 Tenth Ave Brooklyn NY 11219

BRUCK, EVA DOMAN, business director; b. Budapest, Hungary, Apr. 29, 1950; d. Zoltan and Clara (Biro) Doman; m. Stuart A. Bruck, May 4, 1980; 1 child, Spencer B. Doman. BA with honors, Northeastern U., 1972; postgrad., Boston U., 1973-75; BS in Urban Landscape Architecture, CCNY, 1978. Adminstrv. asst. Sargent Coll. Boston U., 1972-75; asst. to chmn. Internat. Design Conf. in Aspen, N.Y., 1975-76; asst. to pres. Milton Glaser, Inc., N.Y.C., 1977-83, bus. mgr., 1983—; tchr. Sch. of Visual Arts, N.Y.C., 1983—; design mgmt. cons. N.Y.C., 1985—; speaker in field. Contbr. articles to profl. jours. Mem. Internat. Council Graphic Design Assns. (mem. design com.), Graphic Arts Guild, Am. Inst. Graphic Arts, Am. Notary Assn., Am. Inst. Landscape Architecture. Office: Milton Glaser Inc 207 E 32d St New York NY 10016

BRUCK, PHOEBE ANN MASON, landscape architect; b. Highland Park, Ill., Nov. 26, 1928; d. George Allen and Louise Townsend (Barnard) Mason; m. F. Frederick Bruck, June 30, 1956. Student Bard Coll., 1946-49; B.S., Ill. Inst. Tech., 1954; M.L.A., Harvard U., 1963. Trainee, Nat. Gallery of Art, Washington, 1947, Mus. Modern Art, N.Y.C., 1948; head design dept. Design Research Inc., Cambridge, Mass., 1955-60; assoc. The Architects Collaborative & Sert, Jackson Assocs., Inc., 1960-63; v.p. F. Frederick Bruck, Architect & Assoc., Inc., Cambridge; vis. design critic dept. landscape architecture Harvard U. Grad. Sch. Design, 1971-79. Contbr. to New Landscapes for Living, 1980. Judge, New Eng. Flower Show, Mass. Hort. Soc., 1971-79, Thoreau Awards, Assn. Landscape Contractors, 1980; mem. Sci. Adv. Group for Edn., Cambridge Pub. Schs., 1981-82; chair Harvard Sq. Adv. Commn., 1987—. Mem. Mass. Bd. Registration of Landscape Architects (vice chmn.), Am. Arbitration Assn., Am. Soc. Landscape Architects, Boston Soc. Landscape Architects (pres. 1973-75, examining bd. 1978-81), Mass. Soc. Mayflower Descendants, Harvard Sq. Def. Fund (chmn. adv. ocm. 1987, bd. dirs. 1984-85, pres. 1985-86), Harvard U. Grad. Sch. Design Alumni Assn. (officer 1972-78), Soc. for Protection of New Eng. Antiquities (design adv. com). Episcopalian. Home: 148 Coolidge Hill Cambridge MA 02138

BRUCKER, CONNIE, police officer, consultant; b. Detroit, June 29, 1946; d. Joseph Schwenk and Errawanna Coates; 1 child, Debra June Huegel. Student San Jose State Coll., 1980, East Los Angeles Coll., 1978. Legal sec. Lapin & Chester, West Los Angeles, Calif., 1972-75; police officer Santa Monica Police Dept., Calif., 1977—, mem. "K9 bite" rev. bd., mem. various award coms.; instr. Santa Monica Jr. Coll.; speaker, lectr. Lady Beware Programs, Los Angeles Area; cons. Safety Products, Calgary, Can., Calif. Council Hosps., Los Angeles, TV movies and spls. and interviews, Los Angeles. Author writings in field. Bd. dirs. ARC, Santa Monica, 1984—. Recipient Medal of Courage, City of Santa Monica, 1979, Mayor's Commendation, 1982. Mem. Internat. Police Assn., Women Peace Officers Assn., Los Angeles Peace Officers Assn., Santa Monica Police Officers Assn., Sexual Assault Investigators Assn., Calif. Sexual Assault Investigators Assn. (pres. 1987). Office: Santa Monica Police Dept 1685 Main St Santa Monica CA 90401

BRUCKER, ROBIN RAE, educator; b. Cleve., Oct. 13, 1956; d. Robert Ray and Dorothy Jean (Gross) Switzer; m. James Merrill Brucker, July 30, 1983; 1 child, Robert Merrill. BA, Mt. Union Coll., 1978; MA, Coll. Mt. St. Joseph, 1988. Instr. art 7-12th grades Northmor Local Schs., Galion, Ohio, 1978-80; instr. art 7th, 9-12th grades Mt. Gilead (Ohio) Exempted Village Schs., 1980—; tchr. counselor Am. Leadership Study Group, Europe, 1979; advisor Mt. Gilead High Sch. Art Club, 1980—, jr. class, 1986—; mem. Inservice Com., Mt. Gilead, 1985—, Prin.'s Adv., 1986—. Instr. Hobby Horse Craft Shop, Mt. Gilead, 1980-86; juror Morrow County, Marion County community activities and art shows, 1980—; pres. Morrow County Fine Arts Guild, Mt. Gilead, 1984-86, 87—; mem. Mt. Gilead Citizens for Zoning Campaign, 1986. Recipient 1st place award Morrow County Fine Arts Fine Craft Show, Mt. Gilead, 1985, 2d place award, 1986; named one of Outstanding Young Women of Am., 1985. Mem. NEA, Ohio Edn. Assn., Ohio Art Edn. Assn. (rep. publicity 1985-86, North Cen. Outstanding Art Tchr. award 1986). Republican. Methodist. Office: Mt Gilead High Sch Park Ave Mount Gilead OH 43338

BRUCK-LIEB, LILLY, consumer advisor, broadcaster, columnist; b. Vienna, Austria, May 13, 1918; came to U.S., 1941, naturalized, 1944; d. Max and Sophie M. Hahn; Ph.D. in Econs., U. Vienna; postgrad. Sorbonne, Paris, Sch. of Econs., London, Sch. of Bus., Columbia U., 1941-42, Sch. of Social Work, N.Y. U., 1964-66; m. Sandor Bruck, Mar. 7, 1943; 1 child, Sandra Lee (Mrs. John David Evans III); m. David L. Lieb, Dec. 7, 1985. Dir. consumer edn. Dept. Consumer Affairs, City of N.Y., 1969-78; project dir. Am. Coalition of Citizens with Disabilities, 1977-78; consumer advisor, broadcaster In Touch Networks, N.Y.C., 1978—; consumer affairs commentator Nat. Public Radio, 1980-82. Chmn. Westchester County, Bonds for Israel, 1960-64. V.p. Jewish Community Ctr., White Plains, N.Y. Recipient Eleanor Roosevelt award Bonds for Israel, 1963; Woman of Yr. award Anti Defamation League, 1972; Community Service award local council Girl Scouts U.S.A., 1974. Mem. Soc. of Consumer Affairs Profls. Democrat. Author: Access, The Guide to a Better Life for Disabled Americans, 1978; contbr. articles on disability and rehab. to books, ency., and mags. Home: 25 Murray Hill Rd Scarsdale NY 10583 Office: In Touch Networks 32 W 48th St New York NY 10036

BRUCKNER, LOIS MARIE, marketing executive; b. Providence, Dec. 16, 1954; d. Louis Robert and Martha E. (Horton) B. BA, U. R.I., 1976; M in Mgmt., Northwestern U., 1986. Housing div. coordinator Diocese of Providence, 1977; project coordinator Providence Bus. Devel., 1978; econ. planner City of Providence, 1979-84; bus. devel. analyst Consolidated Rail Corp., Phila., 1986—; distributor Multipure Water Systems, 1987. mgmt. cons. leadership program United Way, Providence, 1984; mktg. cons. Ecology Co-op, Phila., 1986—. Mem. Am. Mktg. Assn. Democrat. Home: 501 S 13th St 2F Philadelphia PA 19147

BRUCKNER, WILLA COHEN, lawyer; b. Paterson, N.J., Apr. 27, 1954; d. Seymour and Anita (Sax) Cohen. BS, U. Mich., 1975; MA, Yale U., 1976; JD, U. Pa., 1981. Bar: N.Y. 1982, N.J. 1983. Asst. analyst Congressional Budget Office, Washington, 1976-78; asst. counsel/atty. Mfrs. Hanover Trust Co., N.Y.C., 1981-85; dep. counsel/assoc. atty. Bank of Tokyo Trust Co., N.Y.C., 1985—. Mem. ABA, NOW, Women's Bar Assn. N.Y., Phi Beta Kappa. Home: 87 Oakview Ave Maplewood NJ 07040 Office: Bank of Tokyo Trust Co Legal Dept 100 Broadway New York NY 10005

BRUDNAK, PEGGY HELENE, fast-food chain executive; b. Chgo., Jan. 8, 1923; d. Michael and Theresa (Hricisin) Kundrat; m. George Andrew Brudnak, June 16, 1946; children—Teresa M. Brudnak Luddy, George A. II, Catherine A. R.N., Englewood Hosp. Sch. Nursing, Chgo., 1944; B.A. with distinction, U. Redlands, Calif., 1977, MA, 1988; cert. occupational health nurse, U. Calif.-Riverside, 1977-79. Occupational health nurse Kaiser Cement Co., Lucerne Valley, Calif., 1971-73, City of San Bernardino, Calif., 1974-79; instr. trainer CPR, San Bernardino County Am. Heart Assn., 1973-78; franchisee, dir. ops. Burger King Restaurant, Hesperia, Calif., 1979—; cons., Victorville Burger King Restaurant, 1974—. Choir mem. Holy Family Ch., Hesperia, 1970-72, Sunday sch. tchr., 1971-72. Served as 2d lt. Nurses' Corps, U.S. Army, 1944-45, PTO. Recipient Key to City, San Bernardino, 1977; Service award Am. Heart Assn., 1977. Mem. Inland Ctr. Assn. Occupational Health Nurses (treas. 1974-75), Burger King Franchisee Orgn. Republican. Roman Catholic. Club: Shoreline Yacht (Long Beach, Calif.). Avocations: boating; scuba diving; swimming; hiking; golf. Home: 17433 Aspen St Box 104 Hesperia CA 92345

BRUDNER, HELEN GROSS, social sciences educator; b. N.Y.C.; d. Nathan and Mae (Grichtman) Gross; m. Harvey Jerome Brudner, Dec. 18, 1963; children: Mae Ann, Terry Joseph, Jay Scott. B.S., NYU, 1959, M.A., 1960, Ph.D., 1973. Tchr. N.Y.C. Bd. Edn., 1959-60; instr. Pratt Inst., Bklyn., 1959-61; asst. prof. history N.Y. Inst. Tech., N.Y.C., 1961-63, dir. guidance, 1962-63; assoc. prof. Fairleigh Dickinson U., Rutherford, N.J., 1963-73, prof. history and polit. sci., 1974—, dir. Honors Coll., 1972—, chmn. dept. social sci., 1980—, pres. univ. senate, 1975-78, asst. provost, 1983—, asst. dean, 1984; v.p. HJB Enterprises, Highland Park, N.J., 1970—; vice chmn. bd. WLC Inc., Highland Park, 1976—; cons. auto ednl. systems, 1971—. Contbr. articles to profl. jours. on constl. law, transfer of tech., futurism. Active. NSF Women in Politics project, 1981, NEH and Woodrow Wilson Found. Consortium project Women in Am. History, Princeton, N.J., 1980, Consortium on Global Interdependence, Princeton, 1984; vice chmn. bd. dirs. Fairleigh Dickinson U. Fed. Credit Union. Recipient Woman of Yr. award Am. Businesswomen's Assn., 1980. Mem. Am. Judicature Soc., Am. Hist. Soc., Acad. Polit. Sci., Phi Alpha Theta. Office: Fairleigh Dickenson U Dept History and Polit Sci Rutherford NJ 07070 also: HJB Enterprises Inc 812 Abbott St Highland Park NJ 08904

BRUEHL, MARGARET ELLEN, human relations consultant; b. Phila., Nov. 22, 1935; d. George Martin and Virginia (Fowler) Gauger; m. William Justice Bruehl, Aug. 4, 1956; children—Amelia Susan, Alexandra Anne. B.S., West Chester U., 1956. Elem. tchr., pub. schs., Lindenhurst, N.Y., 1956-58, 59-60, Ridley Park, Pa., 1958-59; trainer Margaret Bruehl Assocs., N.J., N.Y., Pa., 1976-80; ptnr. Pneuman/Bruehl/Assocs., Ohio, N.Y., 1981-87; coordinator, leader of human-relations programs Princeton Theol. Sem.'s Ctr. for Continuing Edn., N.J., 1980—; sr. cons. conflict dept. The Alban Inst., Washington. Co-author: Managing Conflict, 1982. Mem. Assn. Creative Change (profl.), Soc. for Profls. in Dispute Resolution, SUNY-Stony Brook Univ. Assn., People and People Dispute Resolution Del. to the People's Republic of China. Democrat. Avocations: cooking, film and video, jazz, classical music, gardening. Home and Office: 107 Main St PO Box 2826 Setauket NY 11733

BRUEMMER, LORRAINE VENSKUNAS, funeral director, real estate broker, nurse; b. Waterbury, Conn., Jan. 25; d. Anthony George and Mary Agnes (Kritchman) Venskunas; m. Jay Porter Bruemmer, Oct. 28, 1973; 1 child by previous marriage: Linda L. Rocco Sovak. R.N., St. Francis Hosp. Sch. Nursing, 1950; B.S., Columbia U., 1958; M.Ed., U. Hartford, 1961. Head nurse pediatrics Cook Hosp., Hartford, Conn., 1953-56; instr. pediatrics Bellevue Hosp., N.Y.C., 1958-59; instr. med. surg. nursing New Britain Gen. Hosp., 1959-62; hosp. supr. New Britain Gen. Hosp., 1962-63; owner Venskunas Funeral Home, New Britain, 1962—; owner Bruemmer Venskunas Real Estate, New Britain, 1974—; commr. New Britain Health Dept., 1965-74; nurse blood bank ARC, N.Y.C., 1957-59, New Britain, 1960-69. Vol. Republican Party, New Britain. Mem. New Britain Funeral Dis. Assn. (pres. 1975-78), Conn. Funeral Dirs., Nat. Funeral Dirs., New Britain Bd. Realtors, Hartford Bd. Realtors, Nat. Bd. Realtors, Multiple Listing Service Greater Hartford. Roman Catholic. Clubs: Ladies Guild (pres. 1969), Shuttle Meadow Country. Avocations: antiques; golf; tennis; swimming; bicycling; gardening. Home: 36 Roslyn Dr New Britain CT 06052 Office: Venskunas Funeral Home 665 Stanley St PO Box 1612 New Britain CT 06051

BRUER, JACQUELYN JEAN, production planning executive; b. Indpls., May 13, 1957; d. Ralph Arthur Bruer and Arlou (Scott) Schmidt; m. Lawrence Hughbanks Jr., May 13, 1978 (div. Nov. 1984). AA, Purdue U., 1981, BS, 1981; postgrad., Ind. U., Ft. Wayne, 1983. With Manpower Temp. Services, Terre Haute, Ind., 1978, Ft. Wayne, Ind., 1981-83; procurement analyst Gen. Foods Co., Lafayette, Ind., 1983-86, sr. procurement analyst, 1986; prodn. scheduler Chesebrough-Pond's Inc., Jefferson City, Mo., 1988—. Advisor Jr. Achievement, Lafayette, 1984-87, (exec. advisor 1986-87); dir. Brandonwood Community Assn., Ft. Wayne, 1982-83. Mem. Am. Production Inventory Control Soc. (v.p. adminstn. 1986-87, dir. 1985-86, cert.), Jefferson City Jaycees, Nat. Assn. for Female Execs. Lutheran. Lodge: Am. Legion, (historian 1982-83). Office: Chesebrough-Pond's Inc 8900 Truman Blvd Jefferson City MO 65109

BRUESEKE, DERONDA JEAN, accountant; b. Poplar Bluff, Mo., June 22, 1954; d. Marion Edward and Emma Jean (Kenley) O.; m. Dean Brueseke, June 8, 1973 (div. 1983); 1 child, Michael. A in Applied Sci., E. Cen. Coll., 1987. Acctg. clk. D&E Acctg. & Tax Service, Inc., Sullivan, Mo., 1976-83, pres., owner, 1983—; speaker Sullivan Kiwanis Club; acct. Victory Christian Ctr., St. Clair, Mo., 1985-87. mem. parent adv. bd. Little Friends Pre-Sch., Sullivan, 1985-86. Mem. Bus. & Profl. Women (speaker), Nat. Soc. Pub. Accts., Indep. Accts. Soc. Mo., Nat. Assn. Tax Preparers, Sullivan C. of C. Republican. Office: D&E Acctg & Tax Service 311 W Springfield Sullivan MO 63080

BRUESEWITZ, LYNN JOY, computer executive; b. Milw., July 6, 1952; d. Frank Alexander and Wanda Marie (Behmke) Bonczkiewicz; m. Ralph James Cheske, July 19, 1972 (div. July 1975); m. Stephen Roland Bruesewitz, May 19, 1979; children: Wendy Sue, Jessica Rose. Student, Milw. Area Tech. Coll., 1969-71. Mgr. loan service Wauwatosa (Wis.) Savs. & Loan, 1969-71; mgr. ops. McCreedy Art Studio, Milw., 1971-72; office mgr. Schellgell Food Service, Milw., 1974-80; office and systems mgr. Wiviott's, Milw., 1980-82; cons. software support systems St. Charles, Ill., 1982-84; dir. computer services, systems analyst midwest regional office Real Estate, Glendale Heights, Ill., 1984-87; pres. FSN Computer Services, Naperville, Ill., 1986-87; owner, pres. Software Support Systems, St. Charles, 1987—; mgr. system conversion DATA Intelligence Systems, Boston, 1976, Montalbano Builders, Westmont, Ill., 1983, Ptnrs. Midwest, 1984-86; mgr. system design ADC, Milw., 1978-80; advisor 1st Computers, Chgo., 1984-86. Mem. Greater O'Hare Assn. (pres.), Nat. Assn. for Female Execs. Roman Catholic. Office: Software Support Systems Saint Charles IL 10174

BRUETT, KAREN DIESL, sales and marketing consultant; b. N.Y.C., May 15, 1945; d. Francis J. and Dorothy (Peterson) Diesl; m. William H. Bruett, Jr., Mar. 18, 1967; 1 child, Lindsey Diesl. BA in English, St. Lawrence U., 1966; MA, Hunter Coll., 1971. Tchr. English Freeport (N.Y.) pub. schs., 1966-70; exec. interviewer, researcher Louis Harris & Assocs., N.Y.C., 1970-72; dir. adult edn. West Side YMCA, 1972-76, mem. bd. mgrs., 1978-83; v.p. new bus. devel. Gaylord Adams & Assocs., Inc., N.Y.C., 1976-81; account exec. John Blair Mktg., N.Y.C., 1981-83, v.p. sales, 1983-84, sr. v.p., gen. sales mgr., 1984-86; ind. sales and mktg. cons.; bd. dirs. Resolution, Inc., Winsooki, Vt. Trustee St. Lawrence U., 1978—, chmn. alumni fund, 1983-84, chmn. annual giving, 1984—, chmn. planning com., mem. exec. com., 1987—; trustee Vt. Council on Arts, 1986—; del. Am.-Soviet Youth Forum, Baku, USSR, 1974. Home and Office: RR 1 Box 1740 Hinesburg VT 05461

BRUFF, BEVERLY OLIVE, public relations consultant; b. San Antonio, Dec. 15, 1926; d. Albert Griffith and Hazel Olive (Smith) Bruff; B.A., Tulane U., 1948; postgrad. Our Lady of Lake Coll., 1956, Okla. Center for Continuing Edn., 1960-70. Asst. dir. New Orleans Theatre Guild, 1948-50; dist. dir. San Antonio Area council Girl Scouts U.S.A., 1958-70, public relations dir., 1970-83; free-lance pub. relations, 1983—; mem. Council of Pres., v.p., 1981-82, 84—; mem. Council of Internat. Relations. Zoning commr. Hill Country Village, Tex., 1973-76, 83-85, 88-90; councilwoman Hill Country Village, 1985-88; bd. dirs. Camp Fire, Inc. Mem. Pub. Relations Soc. Am., Tex. Pub. Relations Assn. (Silver Spur award), Women in Communications (historian 1969-70, v.p. 1970-71, treas. 1971-73), Tex. Press Women (recipient state writing contest awards 1971, 72, 73, 74, mem. exec. bd. dirs. 1970-71, 73-74, dist. treas. 1972-73, dist. v.p. 1973), Nat. Fedn. Press Women, Internat. Assn. Bus. Communicators, Speech Arts of San Antonio (pres. 1964-66, 70-72, 84—, dir. 1964-72, chmn. bd. dirs. 1966-69), Am. Women in Radio and TV (dir. chpt. 1974, sec. 1975, pres. 1979-80), San Antonio Soc. Fund Raising Execs., Assn. Girl Scout Exec. Staff. Home: 508 Tomahawk Trail San Antonio TX 78232

BRUHNKE, JOAN MURPHY, sales executive; b. Aurora, Ill., June 21, 1949; d. John Anthony and Florence M. (Rieser) Murphy; m. Paul Edward Bruhnke, Aug. 29, 1970. BS in Mktg., U. Ill., 1973. Sales rep. Mich. Bell, Grand Rapids, 1973-76; account exec. Mich. Bell., Grand Rapids, 1976-79, account exec. II, 1979-81; mgr. telecommunications Steelcase Inc., Grand Rapids, 1981-87, mgr. bus. info.-access line, 1987—. V.p. Manhattan Neighborhood Assn., East Grand Rapids, Mich., 1985—; mem. com. ARC Kent County, Grand Rapids, 1986—, bd. dirs., 1987. Mem. Internat. Communications Assn., West Mich. Telecommunications Assn. (pres. 1981-83). Roman Catholic. Home: 210 Lakewood SE East Grand Rapids MI 49506 Office: Steelcase Inc 901 44th St SE Grand Rapids MI 49506

BRUIN, LINDA LOU, lawyer; b. Grandville, Mich., June 7, 1938; d. John and Tena (Groeneveld) B. A.A., Grand Rapids Jr. Coll., 1958; A.B., Hope Coll., 1961; postgrad. U. Stockholm, Sweden, 1963-64; A.M., U. Mich., 1967; J.D., Wayne State U., 1973. Bar: Mich. 1973, U.S. Dist. Ct. (we. dist.) Mich. 1980, U.S. Ct. Appeals (6th cir.) 1984. Tchr. Georgetown Pub. Sch., Jenison, Mich., 1959-63, Bullock Creek Area Sch., Midland, Mich., 1964-70; legal supr. Legis. Service Bur., Mich. State Legis., Lansing, 1973-79; legal counsel Mich. Assn. Sch. Bds., Lansing, 1979—. Monthly columnist Mich. Sch. Bd. Jour., 1981—. Mem. Citizen's Commn. to Improve Mich. Courts, 1986. Fellow Inst. Ednl. Leadership, 1982. Mem. ABA (com. mem. 1983—), Women Lawyers Assn. Mich. (pres. 1984-85), Mich. State Bar Assn. (com. chmn. 1987-87, State Bar Rep. Assembly 1986—), LWV. Democrat. Office: Mich Assn Sch Bds 421 W Kalamazoo Lansing MI 48933

BRUKOFF, JOYCE MARSHALL, advertising and public relations executive; b. Oak Park, Ill., Jan. 3, 1927; d. Aubrey Leroy and Ruth Cecelia (Johnson) Marshall; m. Barry Brukoff, May 17, 1959 (div. Sept. 1966); 1 child, Christopher David. Student, Chgo. Musical Coll., 1954-57; MusB, U. Chgo., 1954; postgrad., Northwestern U., 1958-59. Dir. sales promotions and pub. relations Air France, Chgo., 1957-63; v.p. Fred Joyce & Co., Chgo., 1969-75; owner, pres. Joyce M. Brukoff & Assocs., Evanston, Ill., 1975—. Contbg. editor Chgo. Assn. Commerce and Industry mag., 1975—; contbr. articles to profl. jours., 1974—. Mem. exec. bd. womens' bd. Lincoln Park Zoo, Chgo., 1978-79; mem. exec. bd., sec. womens' bd. Glen Ellyn (Ill.) Children's Chorus, 1984—. Recipient service award Lincoln Park Zool. Soc., Chgo., 1984, The Nature Conservancy, 1977.

BRULÉ, A. LORRAINE, commercial property manager; b. Yakima, Wash., Aug. 16, 1925; d. Arthur E. and Helen (Auvé) Brulé; student Seattle U., 1943-44, Dominican Coll. San Rafael, 1944-45; B.S. in Sociology, Seattle U., 1947; m. Nolan D. Roach, Oct. 24, 1959 (div. Jan. 1978); children—Dusty Dean, Susan Marie, and Dean Patrick Roach, Gaylen Leigh Brulé. Bookkeeper, Harper Meggee, Inc., Seattle, 1947-48; sec. bookkeeper Griffin Envelope Co., Seattle, 1948-50; with Yukon Investment Co., Inc., Seattle, 1950-59, 75-85, treas., 1977-85, mgr. comml. properties, 1975-85, asst. sec., 1975-85; cons. property mgmt., 1985—. Mem. Seattle U. Alumni Assn., Bldg. Owners and Mgrs. Assn. Seattle, Bldg. Owners and Mgrs. Assn. Internat., Seattle Downtown Assn., AAUW, Nat. Assn. Female Execs. Roman Catholic. Club: Wash. Athletic. Home and Office: Seven Highland Dr Unit 703 Seattle WA 98109

BRUMBAUGH, DARLA JEAN, travel agency executive; b. Troy, Ohio, Oct. 23, 1961; d. Calvin Maywood and Betty Lou (Smith) B. AA, Sinclair Community Coll., Dayton, Ohio, 1982; cert. in travel, Global Career Acad., Silver Spring, Md., 1983. Tchr.'s asst. Sinclair Community Coll. Early Childhood Learning Ctr., Dayton, 1982; dir., tchr. Quaker Vols., Wilmington, Ohio, 1982-83; travel agt. Robustelli Corp. Services, Ltd., Vandalia, Ohio, 1984-86, travel agy. mgr., 1986—. Fin. sec. West Milton (Ohio) Friends Ch., 1986—, Sunday sch. tchr., 1982—, youth advisor, 1978—; judge Miami County County Fair for Camp Fire Girls, Troy, 1981—, judge Ohio State Fair, Columbus, 1981—; Quaker vol. Friends United Meeting, Wilmington, 1982-83; Bible sch. tchr. Christian Service Internat., Muncie, Ind., 1982, Jamaica; camp counselor Friends Ch., Wilmington, 1983, Syracuse, Ind., 1981-85. Mem. Future Homemakers of Am./Home Economics Related Occupations (pres. Clayton 1979-80, sec. 1978-79, regional rally judge 1983), Phi Theta Kappa. Home: 117 N Poplar St West Milton OH 45383 Office: Robustelli Corp Services Ltd Nat Ticket Distbn Suite 103 Dayton Airport Hotel Vandalia OH 45377

BRUMFIELD, GAYLA DIANNE, real estate executive; b. Olton, Tex., July 25, 1953; d. Marvin Creston and Mary Hope (Crist) Huguley; m. Don Wayne Brumfield, June 24, 1972; children: Cristi Deonne, Derek Wayne. Student, West Tex. State, 1971, East N. Mex. U., 1972—; lic. broker, Norris Real Estate Sch., 1986. Sec. Huguley & Co., Clovis, N.Mex., 1970-74, sales agt., 1974-78; sales agt. Century 21, Clovis, 1978-79; sales agt. Colonial Real Estate, Clovis, 1979—, owner, mgr., 1985—. Mem. Clovis Sch. Bd. Adv. Com., 1985; bd. dirs. Play, Inc., Clovis, 1986—, YMCA, Clovis, 1986—; tchr. First Baptist Ch., Clovis. Mem. Nat. Assn. Realtors, Realtors Assn. N.Mex. (bd. dirs. 1985—, strategic planning com. 1986—, chmn. state edn. com.), Clovis Bd. Realtors (chair coms., 1979—, v.p. 1983-84, pres. 1984-86, chair pub. relations 1983, 1st Place State of N.Mex., 1983, Realtor of the Yr., 1985, Top 5 Producers 1983, 84, 85), Grad. Realtors Inst., Women's Golf Assn. Democrat. Club: Pilots (Clovis). Home: 4 Box 225 Clovis NM 88101

BRUMMENES, BILLIE CHERYL, health consultant; b. Los Angeles, May 31, 1948; d. William Daniel and Eleanor Mary (Harvey) Barry; m. Harold Brummenes, July 10, 1971; 1 child, Cheri Gail. B magna cum laude, San Diego State U., 1970; postgrad., U. LaVerne. Tchr. Cajon Valley Sch. Dist., El Cajon, Calif., 1970-86; mfr.'s rep. Jem Mktg., Los Angeles, 1987—; physician's cons. Total Lifestyles, Newport Beach, Calif., 1987. Rep. exec. bd. Cajon Valley Ednl. Assn., 1980-83, rep.-at-large, 1984-85; mem. profl. adv. council Cajon Valley Union Sch. Dist., 1981-83, mem. supt. legis. subcom., 1985-86; pres. Tierrasanita Jr. Women's Club. Mem. Nat. Assn. Tchrs. (pres. 1986—), San Diego Jr. Women's Club (Rookie of Yr. 1984). Home: 10930 Viacha Ct San Diego CA 92124

BRUMMUND, FRANCINE ANN, public relations specialist; b. Tacoma, Apr. 7, 1960; d. Arnold Raymond Brummund and Georgia Lenore (Fischer) Holmstrom. B in Univ. Studies, N.D. State U., 1985. Seminar coordinator YMCA of N.D. State U., Fargo, 1980-83; coordinator Knorr for U.S. Senate campaign, Fargo, N.D., 1982; intern U.S. Senator Mark Andrews, Washington, 1983; interviewer Job Service of N.D., Fargo, 1983-84; pub. relations vol. coordinator Altenburg for Cong., Fargo, 1984; with pub. relations GTE-Sylvania Corp., Orange, Calif., 1985—. Youth mem. Gov.'s Employment and Tng. Forum, Bismarck, N.D., 1980-82. Republican. Roman Catholic. Home: 2307 E Ball Rd Anaheim CA 92806 Office: GTE Sylvania Cons Services 1483 N Main Orange CA 92667

BRUNDAGE, MARJORIE UNDERWOOD, computer executive; b. Bellefontaine, Ohio, Feb. 5, 1940; d. James Madison and Mary Louise (Mustaine) Underwood; m. Richard Keith Brundage, Dec. 20, 1967; children: Jennie Lee, Judith Lynn. BS, Bowling Green State U., 1962. Systems trainee IBM, Toledo, 1962-63; systems analyst Kaiser Jeep Corp., Toledo, 1963-64, Lazarus Dept. Store, Columbus, Ohio, 1964-66; research assoc. Ohio State U., Columbus, 1966-67, supr. computer dept., 1967-79, dir. computer dept., 1979—; cons. U.S. Post Office, Columbus, 1972, labor reseach service, Columbus, 1971-79, local bank, Columbus, 1978-79. Contbr. articles to profl. jours. Trustee and violinist Met. Chamber Orch., Columbus, 1979—; elder and tchr. Cen. Presbyn. Ch., Columbus, 1966—; com. mem. Scioto Valley Presbytery, Columbus, 1985—; mem. Columbus Landmarks Nat. Trust, 1980—. Mem. Assn. Computer Machinery, Assn. Female Execs, The Execs. Club, Ohio Hist. Soc. Republican. Home: 328 Glenmont Ave Columbus OH 43214 Office: Ohio State U Coll Bus 1775 College Rd Columbus OH 43210

BRUNDAGE, PATRICIA LOUNSBURY, art gallery director; b. Orange, N.J., Sept. 11, 1953; d. John Denton and Ann (Lounsbury) Brundage; m. William Bryant Copley, Nov. 12, 1983; children: Bryant, Caroline Ann. Student Washington & Jefferson Coll., 1971-73; B.F.A., U. Ga., 1975. Asst. to dir. Castelli-Sonnabend Tapes and Films, Inc., N.Y.C., 1976-77, dir., 1977—; dir. Leo Castelli Gallery N.Y.C., 1984—. Episcopalian. Club: Jr. League (N.Y.C.). Home: 38 W 9th St New York NY 10011 Office: Leo Castelli Gallery 420 W Broadway New York NY 10012

BRUNEAUX, DEBRA LOUISE, costume designer; b. Orange, Calif., Oct. 19, 1953; d. James Fredricksen and Carol Gwen (Cashner) B. BA in Exptl. Psychology, U. Calif., Santa Barbara, 1975. Residents women's cutter/draper Ctr. Theatre Group, Los Angeles, 1978-79; asst. to resident costume designer Oreg. Shakespearean Festival Assn., Ashland, 1980-82; costume shop supr. Sacramento Theatre Co., Calif., 1982-83; resident costume designer Sacramento Theatre Co., 1983—; costume shop mgr., cons. Berkeley Repertory Theatre, Calif., 1979. Home: 2526 G St #7 Sacramento CA 95816 Office: Sacramento Theatre Co 1419 H St Sacramento CA 95814

BRUNER, DARLENE HILDAGARDE, retired industrial company official; b. Creston, Nebr., Oct. 8, 1928; d. Otto Frederick and Hildegard Eleanor (Dasenbrock) Feye; B.A. in Bus. Adminstrn., Midland Luth. Coll., 1949; m. James L. Paulin, Oct. 23, 1949 (div., 1963); children—James D., Jamie L., Kathryn D. Paulin Lackey; m. 2d Robert T. Bruner, Dec. 23, 1970. Acctg. clk. Kavich's Furniture, Fremont, Nebr., 1948-50; asst. acct. Gamble-Skogmo, Fremont, 1950-51; acctg. clk., plant acct. Hydro-Conduit Corp., Fremont, 1962-65; acctg. clk., plant acct., mgr. services CF Industries, Inc., Fremont, 1965-84, ret., 1984; tax preparer H&R Block. Elected to Nebr.

Ednl. Service Unit Bd., 1987—. Mem. Mensa. Democrat. Presbyterian. Home: 2139 William Fremont NE 68025

BRUNER, PATRICIA LATTIMORE, state agency administrator; b. Forrest City, Ark., Apr. 22, 1949; d. Robert Holmes and Betty (Dorsey) Lattimore; m. Roy D. Bruner, Feb. 26, 1972; children: Trevor, Daniel. Diploma, Colegio Internat. de Carabobo, Valencia, Venezuela, 1967; BA in Modern Lang., Ind. U., 1971. Sales assoc. Cecil Woods Real Estate, Norman, Okla., 1972-75; administrv. coordinator Office of Okla. Atty. Gen., Oklahoma City, 1983—; tchr. Spanish Mexico City, 1971; consumer mediator Atty. Gen., Oklahoma City, 1985-86; conf. planner So. Conf. of Atty.'s Gen., Oklahoma City, 1986. Chmn. Heritage Hills Hist. House Tour, Oklahoma City, 1983; founder Condr.'s Circle, Okla. Symphony Orch., 1983, assoc. bd. 1982—; co-developer Child Care Info. and Referral Service, Oklahoma City, 1982. Mem. Jr. League of Oklahoma City. Republican. Home: 3732 Summer Cloud Dr Edmond OK 74013 Office: Atty Gen of Okla 112 State Capitol Oklahoma City OK 73105

BRUNGARDT, HELEN RUTH, minister; b. Littlefield, Tex., Sept. 2, 1931; d. Isaac Henry and Helen Irene (Hanna) P.; m. Guido Milton Brungardt, July 22, 1950 (div.); children: Karla Kay, Linda Gail, Mark Douglas, Celeste Dawn. Student, Tex. Christian U., 1948-49, U. N.Mex., 1969, Divine Sci. Ednl. Ctr., 1976-80. Tchr. Napoleon Hill Acad., Albuquerque, 1964-66; practitioner First Ch. Religious Sci., Albuquerque, 1969-72, tchr., 1971-72; founder, minister Symphony of Life Ch., Albuquerque, 1972-81; founder, dir., pres. Inst. for the Emerging Self, Albuquerque, 1981—; cons. ministers, individuals, 1977—; lectr. various orgns., radio, tv, 1975—; instr. Profl. Leadership Tng., Albuquerque, 1965-82; bd. dirs., founder Grand Teton Retreat. Author: Contemplation, 1975, Mystical Meaning of Jesus, 1980, Beyond Liberation, 1985; contbr. articles to profl. jours. Mem. Divine Sci. Fedn., Internat. New Thought Alliance. Republican. Mem. Ch. Divine Sci. Home: PO Box 567 Columbus NM 88029 Office: Inst for Emerging Self PO Box 75159 Sta 14 Albuquerque NM 87194

BRUNI, KIMBERLY ANN, pharmaceutical company representative; b. Warwick, R.I., Oct. 11, 1963; d. John Joseph Bruni and Patricia Johnett Collins. Student, Simmons Coll., Boston; BS in Chemistry, Indiana U., Bloomington, 1985; 2-83. Pharm. rep. Merck Sharp and Dohme, Hartford, Conn., 1985—. Mem. Nat. Assn. Female Execs. Home: 196 Woodland Dr Cromwell CT 06416

BRUNK, BRENDA MOORE, cable television and radio executive; b. Winston-Salem, N.C., Nov. 18, 1942; d. Garland Edward and Eusebia Mae (Watkins) Moore; m. Rollis Gene Brunk, May 22, 1963; children—Jeffrey Wayne, Kelly Lynn. Programming cert. Automation Inst., Charlotte, N.C., 1962. Personnel clk. R. J. Reynolds Industries, Winston-Salem, 1962-63; with Summit Communications, Inc., Winston-Salem, 1971—, system mgr., 1975-81, gen. mgr., 1981-82, v.p., 1982—; officer Summit Cable Services of Thom-A-Lex, Inc., Lexington, N.C., 1982—. bd. dirs. Lexington Area United Way, 1988. Mem. Internat. Mgmt. Council (chpt. program chmn. 1982—, 2d v.p. 1987, 1st v.p. 1988), Bus. and Profl. Women's Club (local treas. 1984-85, v.p. 1987), Women in Cable (charter; pres. N.C. chpt., bd. dirs. 1987-88) Soc. Cable TV Engrs., Cable TV Adminstrn. and Mktg., N.C. Cable TV Assn. (customer service adv. com.), Am. Bus. Women's Assn., Davidson County Art Guild, Thomasville Community Gen. Hosp. Guild. Democrat. Methodist. Avocations: photography; backpacking; fishing; reading; charcoal landscapes. Home: 204 Ridgecrest Dr Lexington NC 27292 Office: Summit Cable Services of Thom-A-Lex Ins PO Box 667 Lexington NC 27293

BRUNKE, JUDY ELIZABETH, university administrator; b. Dayton, Ohio, May 17, 1950; d. William Howard and Ruth Carolyn (Stephens) Dunn; m. William D. West (div. Nov. 1985); 1 child, Jason; m. John W. Brunke, Feb. 1, 1986. BS in Edn., U. Louisville, 1978, MS in Edn., 1984. Tchr. Hardin County Schs., Elizabethtown, Ky., 1978-80, Ft. Knox (Ky.) Community Schs., 1980-85; account exec. Retterer & Assocs., Elmhurst, Ill., 1985-86; personnel counselor Whizz Office Service, Chgo., 1986; counselor admissions Embry-Riddle Aero. U., Chgo., 1986—. Mem. Nat. Assn. Coll. Admissions Counselors, Soc. Human Resource Profls., Ill. Assn. Coll. Admissions Counselors, Ill. Tng. and Devel. Assn. Office: Embry-Riddle Aero U Box 8622 Rolling Meadows IL 60008

BRUNNER, LILLIAN SHOLTIS, nurse, author; b. Freeland, Pa., Mar. 29; d. Andrew J. and Anna (Tomasko) Sholtis; m. Mathias J. Brunner, Sept. 8, 1951; children—Janet Brunner Hoch, Carol Anne, Douglas Mathias. Diploma, Sch. Nursing Hosp., U. Pa., 1940; B.S., U. Pa., 1945, Litt.D (hon.), 1985; M.S.N. in Nursing, Case-Western Res. U., 1947; Sc.D. (hon.), Cedar Crest Coll., 1978. Registered nurse. Operating room supr. U. Pa. Hosp., Phila., 1942-45; head, fundamentals of nursing dept. U. Pa., 1945-46; asst. prof. surgical nursing Yale U. Sch. Nursing, New Haven, Conn., 1947-51; surgical supr. Yale-New Haven Hosp., 1947-51; research project dir. Sch. Nursing Bryn Mawr Hosp., Pa., 1973-77; co-founder History of Nursing Mus., Pa. Hosp., Phila., 1974; mem. bd. overseers Sch. Nursing, U. Pa., 1982—; chmn. nursing adv. Presbyn.-U. Pa. Med. Ctr., Phila., 1970—, trustee, 1976—, vice chmn., bd. trustees, 1985—;. Author: Manual of Operating room Technology, 1966; (with others) Lippincott Manual of Nursing Practice, 1974, 4th edit., 1986, Textbook of Medical and Surgical Nursing, 1964, 6th edit., 1988; mem. editorial bds. jours. Nursing and Health Care, Topics in Clin. Nursing, Nursing '88, Nursing Life, Nursing Photobook Series, 1978—. Recipient Disting. Alumnus award Frances Payne Bolton Sch. Nursing, Case Western Res. U., 1980. Fellow Am. Acad. Nursing; mem. Am. Nurses Assn., Nat. League for Nursing (judge nat. writing contest 1982-84, Disting. Service award 1979), Nat. League Am. Pen Women (sec. Phila. chpt. 1972-76, nat. sec. 1984-86), Am. Med. Writers Assn., Assn. Operating Room Nurses, Nurses Alumni Assn. U. Pa. Hosp., Ben Franklin Soc., Internat. Old Lacers Soc., Sigma Theta Tau. Home and Office: 1247 Berwyn-Paoli Rd Berwyn PA 19312

BRUNNER, NANCY R., human resource development manager, educator; b. Williamsport, Pa., Apr. 18, 1930; d. Carl H. Hall and Marian E. (Dilks) Hall; m. Richard B. Brunner, June 27, 1953; (div. 1966); 1 son, Curtis Evan. A.B. magna cum laude, Lycoming Coll., Williamsport, Pa., 1952; M.A. cum laude, NYU, 1975; postgrad. Columbia U. Sch. Bus., 1977-78. Dir. publs. Rider Coll., Trenton, N.J., 1966-69; pub. relations specialist Hoffman-LaRoche Inc., Nutley, N.J., 1969-71, career devel. assoc., 1971-75, mgr. orgn. devel., 1975-81; mgr. tng., devel. Lehn & Fink Products Co., Montvale, N.J., 1981-87; adj. prof. Fairleigh Dickinson U. Sch. Bus., 1977—, pres. New Directions, Montclair, N.J. Writer, composer, dir. 2 musical theatre shows, Williamsport; author film For Life's Sake, 1973; editor: The New School Architecture, 1969; contbr. article to profl. jour. Bd. dirs. Jr. League, Williamsport, 1966; mem. allocations com. United Fund, Lycoming County, Pa., 1965, 66. Recipient Time-Life publs. award for Distinction in Coll. Publs., 1965, 66, 68; Tribute to Women in Industry, N.J. Industries, 1977. Mem. Human Resource Planning Soc., Acad. Mgmt., Am. Mgmt. Assn., Phi Kappa Phi.

BRUNNER, SULTRA ELAINE, lawyer, county official; b. Meridian, Miss., July 20, 1950; d. Moses and Hazel Juanita (Davis) B.; B.A. in Psychology, UCLA, 1973; M.A., Calif. State U., Los Angeles, 1976; J.D., Southwestern U., Los Angeles, 1982. Bar: Calif. 1983. Resource cons. Los Angeles County Dept. Mental Health, 1970-74; with Los Angeles County Dept. Health Services, 1974-87, program mgr., 1975-77, legis. analyst, 1977-82, budget analyst, 1982-85, program adminstr., 1985-87, legal dir., 1987—; with Maxicare Health Plans Inc, 1987—. Office: 5200 W Century Blvd Los Angeles CA 90045

BRUNO, AUDREI ANN, nurse; b. Pitts., Oct. 31, 1946; d. Vincent Joseph and Julia Elizabeth (Karaffa) Mataya; m. Edward Orlando Bruno, Apr. 30, 1966; children: Brent Edward, Bradley Edward. AA, Community Coll. Allegheny County, 1976; B, Pa. State U., 1984; MSN, U. Pitts., 1988. Psychiat. nursing supr. Western Psychiat. Clinic and Inst., Pitts., 1976-81; staff charge nurse Magee Women's Hosp., Pitts., 1981-82; charge team leader Central Med. Pavillion, Pitts., 1982-84; clin. specialist Vis. Nurse Assn. of Allegheny County, Pitts., 1984—; instr., mem. speakers bur. Community Coll. Allegheny County, West Mifflin, Pa., 1986—; project devel. WPIC Adolescent Module, Pitts., 1980-81. Chair Suicide Awareness and Prevention Com., N. Huntingdon, Pa., 1986—; fieldworker Project Star, Pitts., 1986—; mem. Pa. Task Force on Elder Abuse, Nurses Interested in the Cure of the Elderly, Geriatric Ednl. Network. Mem. Nat. Nursing Orgn., Grad. Student Orgn., Nursing Quality Assurance (cons. 1985—), Sigma Theta Tau. Home: 14071 Ridge Rd North Huntingdon PA 15642 Office: Vis Nurse Assn Alleghany County 6655 Frankstown Ave 6th fl Pittsburgh PA 15206

BRUNO, GRACE ANGELIA, accountant, educator; b. St. Louis, Oct. 11, 1935; d. John E. and Rose (Goodwin) B. BA, Notre Dame Coll., 1966; MEd, So. Ill. U., 1972; MAS, Johns Hopkins U., 1983; PhD, Walden U., 1985. CPA, Mo., Md., N.J. Tchr. Sisters of Notre Dame, St. Louis, 1962-80; pres. Bruno-Potter, Inc., Avon-By-The-Sea, N.J., 1981—; asst. treas., instr. acctg. Coll. of Notre Dame of Md., Balt., 1978-79, treas., 1979-80; asst. prof. acctg. Georgian Ct. Coll., Lakewood, N.J., 1985—; fin. advisor James Harry Potter Gold Medal Award, N.Y.C., 1980—. Elected to Internat. Platform Assn., 1987. Mem. Am. Inst. CPA's (tax div.), N.J. Soc. CPA's, N.J. Bus. Educators, St. Louis Bus. Educators (treas. 1972-73). Democrat. Roman Catholic. Home and Office: 419 Third Ave Avon By The Sea NJ 07717

BRUNS, LINDA MARIE, management consultant; b. Herrin, Ill., Apr. 22, 1946; d. Bernard Richard and Cora Marie (Blythe) B.; m. Ralph N. Smithson. BA, So. Ill. U., 1967; MLS, U. Ill., 1968; MBA, No. Ill. U., 1977. Supr. info. Standard Oil of Ind., Naperville, Ill., 1968-78; mgr. info. services Cetus Corp., Berkeley, Calif., 1978-79; program mgr. SRI Internat., Menlo Park, Calif., 1979-84, sr. cons., 1984—. Mem. Am. Fedn. Info. Processing, Nat. Assn. Bus. Economists. Republican. Roman Catholic. Office: SRI Internat 333 Ravenswood Menlo Park CA 94025

BRUNSMANN-HUGHES, SANDRA MARY, business owner, speaker, consultant; b. St. Louis, Mar. 30, 1937; d. Albert Henry and Ruth Josephine (Byrne) Spaeth; m. Kenneth George Brunsmann, Nov. 28, 1957 (div. 1968); children: Kathleen, Karen Marie, Steven Allen, Keith Andres, Kurt Joseph; m. Thomas Michael Hughes, Dec. 31, 1985. Student, St. Louis Community Coll., 1974-75. Rev. analyst Mo. Pacific R.R., St. Louis, 1968-86; bus. agt. Brotherhood R.R. and Airline Clks., St. Louis, 1979-81; owner, speaker, cons. S.M. Brunsmann Assn., St. Louis, 1983—. Canvasser Harriet Woods, St. Louis, 1980-86. Mem. Nat. Speakers Assn. (v.p., dir. St. Louis chpt. 1987-88), Bus. and Profl. Women's Orgn. (program dir. Hill chpt. 1987—). Democrat. Roman Catholic. Home and Office: S M Brunsmann Assn 6808 Wise Ave Saint Louis MO 63139

BRUNSON, DOROTHY E., broadcasting executive; b. Glensville, Ga., Mar. 13, 1938; d. Wadis and Naomi (Ross) Edwards; children: Edward, Daniel. BS, Empire State Coll. Entered print communications industry 1960-62; asst. gen. mgr. radio sta. WWRL, N.Y.C., 1964-68, corp. coordinator, liason dir., 1968-72; v.p. Howard Sanders Advt., Inc., N.Y.C., 1972-79; corp. v.p. Inner City Broadcasting Corp., N.Y.C., 1973-79, corp. gen. mgr., 1979; pres. Sta. WEBB, Balt., 1979, Sta. WIGO, Atlanta, 1979, Sta. WBMS, Wilmington, N.C., 1979—; lectr., speaker bus., econ. devel., affirmative action, communications, women rights, religious and human issues throughout country; panelist bus. and communications White House, 1977. Contbr. articles to Vogue, Black Enterprise, Newsweek. Recipient awards including citation NCCJ. Methodist. Office: Brunson Broadcasting Co 3000 Druid Park Dr Baltimore MD 21215 also: WIGO AM 1526 Howell Mill Rd Atlanta GA 30318

BRUNS-WILLIAMS, BARBARA LEE, small business owner, consultant, architect; b. Elmhurst, Ill., May 17, 1959; d. Robert Lee and Phyllis Marie (Overholt) Bruns; m. Ethan Robert Williams, Aug. 6, 1983. BS in Agr., So. Ill. U., 1981. Conservationist Lake County Forest Preserve Dist., Libertyville, Ill., 1974-77; design and sales mgr. Anna (Ill.) Nursery and Garden Ct., 1977-78, Maintain, Inc., Oklahoma City, 1978-82; landscape architect Amlings Co., Melrose Park, Ill., 1982-85; owner Bruns-Williams Landscape Co., Matteson, Ill., 1985—; cons. Wildflower Works-Chgo., 1985—. Editor: Flora and Fauna Study of Des Plaines River, 1977. Mem. Ill. Landscape Contractors Assn., Nat. Assn. Nurserymen, Am. Soc. Landscape Architects, Nat. Hort. Soc., Nat. Assn. Female Execs., Audubon Soc., Sierra. Office: Bruns-Williams Landscape RR 1 2 Dewey Ln Matteson IL 60443

BRUSH, PENELOPE, corporate executive, real estate broker; b. San Antonio, Feb. 10, 1946; d. Paul F. and Doris (Robison) Rhodes; m. Barry Brush, Dec. 24, 1970; children: Jennifer, Joanna. BA in Mgmt., Trinity U. Exec. asst. CIM, Dallas, 1975-76; facilities mgr. Insyte Corp., Dallas, 1976-77; regional mktg. mgr. Applied Data Research, Dallas, 1977-79; prin. real estate broker, Dallas, 1979—; pres. Profl. Secretatial Services, Dallas, 1979-83; producer, TV program moderator for LWV of Dallas, 1982-84. Pub. relations dir. Dallas Music Tchrs., 1982—; appointed mem. Community Access Cable Bd., Dallas, 1985-86. Named Cable Producer of Yr. City of Dallas, 1982; Edn. Vol. Dallas Ind. Schs., 1980. Mem. Tex. Real Estate Brokers, Nat. Music Tchrs. Assn., Am. Coll. Musicians, LWV (chmn. TV prodns. 1981-85, mem. League Internat.). Presbyterian.

BRUST, SHARRON PITTS, clinical social worker; b. Ft. Lauderdale, Fla., Feb. 11, 1943; d. Alburnie A. and Alma E. (Groom) Pitts; m. Bruce Allen Brust, Apr. 3, 1943; children: Michelle S., Bryan A. AA, Morris County Coll., Randolph, N.J., 1974; BA summa cum laude, Paterson Coll., Wayne, N.J., 1976; MSSW, Columbia U., 1980. Cert. clin. social worker Nat. Registry Health Care Providers; cert. sch. social worker. Social worker Greystone Park Psychiat. Hosp., Morris Plains, N.J., 1976-78; clin. cons. Lakeview Learning Ctr., Dover, N.J., 1982-86; pvt. practice psychotherapy Morristown and Rockaway, N.J., 1980—; bd. dirs. Jersey Battered Women's Service, Morris County, 1975-78, Mental Health Assn. Morris County, Madison, 1980-84. Community liaison to Office of Mayor, Rockaway, 1974; county committeewoman Democratic Party, Rockaway, 1974-76. Mem. Nat. Assn. Social Workers, N.J. Assn. Clin. Social Workers. Home and Office: Lenox Rd Rockaway NJ 07866

BRUST, SUSAN MELINDA, telecommunications executive; b. N.Y.C., Sept. 27, 1951; d. Stanley Milton and Preva Joan (Simons) B.; m. William S. Boorstein. BA in Geology, Hunter Coll., 1973; postgrad., Bernard Baruch Coll., 1988—, Tel Aviv U., 1971, U. Colo., 1973. Sales rep. Burroughs Corp., N.Y.C., 1976-81; pvt. network specialist Tymnet, Inc., N.Y.C., 1981-85; regional sales mgr. Dama Telecommunications, N.Y.C., 1985-87; account exec. Network Equipment Technologies, N.Y.C., 1987—; ind. telecommunications cons. Brust & Associates, N.Y.C., 1983—. Mem. NOW, N.Y.C., 1979—; exec. bd. mem. Jewish Guild for the Blind, N.Y.C., 1975; assoc. Spl. Olympics, N.Y.C., 1984—. Mem. Nat. Assn. Female Execs., Assn. Women in Computing, Empire Women in Telecommunications. Democrat. Home: 101 W 79 St New York NY 10024 Office: Network Equipment Techs 33 Whitehall St New York NY 10017

BRUSTEIN, CAROLE NIVASCH, lawyer; b. N.Y.C., May 7, 1944; d. Henry and Esther (Miaskoff) Nivasch; m. Joel M. Brustein, Jan. 30, 1965; children—Hope, Marshall, Samuel. A.A., Fullerton Jr. Coll. (Calif.), 1976; B.A. in Religious Studies, Calif. State U.-Fullerton, 1979; J.D., Loyola U., Los Angeles, 1982. Bar: Calif. 1982, U.S. Dist. Ct. (central dist.) Calif. 1983. Ptnr. firm Brustein & Barnes, Orange, Calif., 1982-85. Mem. staff Internat. and Comparative Law Jour., 1981-82; editor: Bus. Law and Litigation Jour., 1982. Mem. ABA, Orange County Bar Assn., Orange County Barristers (mem. com. Bridging the Gap program 1983), Calif. Women Lawyers. Democrat.

BRYAN, BILLIE MARIE (MRS. JAMES A. MACKEY), biologist; b. Norfolk, Va., Dec. 30, 1932; d. William B. and Marie (Fortescue) Bryan; B.A. in Biology, U. Richmond, 1954; M.Ed., Am. U., 1966; m. James A. Mackey. Bacteriologist, Arlington County Health Dept., Arlington, Va., 1954-58; med. bacteriologist Walter Reed Army Inst. Research, Walter Reed Army Med. Center, Washington, 1959-62; tchr. Fairfax (Va.) High Sch., 1962-66; biologist NIH, Washington, 1966—. Mem. Am. Pub. Health Assn., Am. Soc. Info. Sci., Am. Med. Writers Assn., DAR. Contbr. articles to profl. jours. Home: 201 Quaint Acres Dr Silver Spring MD 20904 Office: NIH-NIDDK Westwood Bldg Room 637 Bethesda MD 20852

BRYAN, CHRISTINA HELEN, labor relations specialist; b. Jamaica, N.Y., Dec. 29, 1948; d. Albert James and Margaret Mary (Jones) Bowers; m. John Warren Bryan, Oct. 17, 1970. BA, Hofstra U., 1976. Adjustment's coordinator Hecht/May Co., Laurel, Md., 1971-73; aast. dir. continuing edn. Hofstra U., Hempstead, N.Y., 1976-78; asst. cataloguer Hofstra U., Hempstead, 1978-82; grad. intern personnel Blue Cross/Blue Shield, N.Y.C., 1983-84; personnel rep. The Bank of N.Y., Valley Stream, 1984-85; human resource devel. cons. The Port Authority of N.Y. and N.J., N.Y.C., 1985-87, labor relations specialist, 1987—; cons. L.I. Railroad, Hollis, N.Y., 1987—, Chase Manhattan Bank, N.Y.C., 1987—. Calligrapher posters, 1978—; seminar lectr. Mem. Am. Soc. Personnel Adminstrs. (bd. dirs. N.Y. 1987—, chairperson pub. relations 1987—), Am. Mgmt. Soc., Nat. Assn. Female Execs., N.Y. State Banker's Assn. (mem. personnel relations com.). Roman Catholic. Home: 157 Sherman Ave Merrick NY 11566 Office: The Port Authority NY-NJ Labor Relations One World Trade Center 61S New York NY 10048

BRYAN, CLARICE ADINA, lawyer; b. St. Thomas, V.I., Apr. 30, 1923; d. C. Arthur and Iza Anita (Lanclos) B.; A.B., Howard U., 1943; LL.B., Columbia U. and Howard U., 1949; 1 dau., Charlene Smith. Admitted to V.I. bar, 1950; tax assessor Govt. of V.I., 1950-60, asst. atty. gen., 1961-65, asst. commr. of labor, 1965-68, dir. consumer affairs, 1968-73; individual practice law, St. Thomas, 1950—; dir. People's Bank, 1971-75; trustee V.I. Retirement System. Vice pres. V.I. Constl. Conv., 1977, del., 1964, 81; mem. UN Status of Women Commn. Mem. ABA, Internat. Women Lawyers Assn., V.I. Bus. and Profl. Women (state pres. 1964-65). Roman Catholic. Home: 245A Bourne Field Saint Thomas VI 00801 Office: Room B2 Professional Bldg Saint Thomas VI 00801

BRYAN, EDNA EUGENIE, nursing administrator; b. Two River Bridge, W.I., Feb. 21, 1936; came to U.S., 1967; d. Samuel Uriala and Brenda (Wellington) Distant; m. Everton Wesley Bryan, Mar. 25, 1961; children: Sheila, Angus. BS, Mercy Coll., 1978; MS in Health Care Mgmt., Biscayne Coll., 1983. RN N.Y. Charge nurse Southwestern Hosp., London, 1962-63, Purley Hosp., Surrey, Eng., 1963, Wilson Hosp., Mitchum, Eng., 1963-64; supr. St. Heliers Hosp., Surrey, 1964-65; vis. nurse Croydon Dist. Nursing Assn., Surrey, 1965-67; charge nurse Mt. Sinai Hosp., N.Y.C., 1967-68, Bronx Lebanon Hosp., N.Y.C., 1968-69; asst. head nurse Westchester Square Hosp., N.Y.C., 1970-71; supr. No. Med. Group, N.Y.C., 1971-73; asst. dir. nursing Waring Nursing Home, N.Y.C., 1973-85; head nurse Miami (Fla.) VA Hosp., 1985—; supr. nursing Miami Jewish Home and Hosp. for Aged, 1985—; cons., inservice instr., N.Y.C., 1974-75. Mem. pub. edn. com. Cancer Soc., 1982—. Mem. Nat. Assn. Female Execs. Republican. Mem. Assembly of God Ch. Home: 19445 NW 19th Ct Miami FL 33056 Office: Miami Jewish Home & Hosp for Aged 151 NE 52d St Miami FL 33137

BRYAN, ELIZABETH PATRICIA, accountant; b. Jacksonville, N.C., Apr. 21, 1960; d. Robert Preston Sr. and Elizabeth Woodson (Scott) B. BA in Acctg. magna cum laude, N.C. State U., 1982. CPA. Staff acct. Deloitte Haskins & Sells, Raleigh, N.C., 1982-85; v.p. acctg. Investors Title Co., Chapel Hill, N.C., 1985—. Lloyd Weeks Endowed scholar, 1979. Fellow N.C. Assn. CPA's; mem. Nat. Assn. Accts. (bd. dirs.). Avocations: jogging, golf, biking, tennis, reading. Home: 7201 Canaan Ln #216 Raleigh NC 27615 Office: Investors Title Co 137 E Rosemary St Chapel Hill NC 27514

BRYAN, MARIE ELIZABETH, library administrator; b. Oakland, Calif., Jan. 21, 1952; d. Joseph Wheatley and Martha Marie (Stirling) B.; m. William Allen Krause, Apr. 19, 1980. B.A. in French, Holy Names Coll., 1972; M.L.S., U. Calif.-Berkeley, 1973. Library student asst. Contra Costa County Library, El Cerrito, Calif., 1969-73, children's librarian, Antioch, Calif., 1973-75, Walnut Creek, Calif., 1975-77; children's project dir. North State Coop. Library System, Willows, Calif., 1977-79, editor children's services corr. course, 1987; library dir. Willows Pub. Library, 1979-88, Woodlands (Calif.) Library, 1988— ; asst. librarian, Calif. State U., Chico, 1985—; chmn. Gladys English Collection Com., Sacramento, 1983-84. Chmn. Math. Sci. Conf. Young Women, Willows, 1983, 84. Mem. Calif. Library Assn. (councilor 1980), ALA (membership task force 1983-88), League of Women Voters, Bus. and Profl. Women, AAUW. Democrat. Roman Catholic. Club: Book Collectors (sec. 1984-85). Home: 2 Glacier Peak Ln Chico CA 95926 Office: Woodland Pub Library 250 1st Sten St Woodland CA 95695

BRYAN, MARY ANN, interior designer; b. Dallas, Nov. 16, 1929; d. William C. and Harriet E. (Carter) Green; m. Frank Wingfield Bryan, Aug. 31, 1957; children: Frank Wingfield, Elizabeth F. BS in Interior Design U. Tex., 1950. Head of stock Foleys Dept. Store, Houston, 1952-53, asst. buyer, 1953-54, buyer, 1955-60, exec. tng. dir., 1960-61; owner, pres. Mary Ann Bryan Design Assocs., Inc., Houston, 1961—; mem. adv. bd. Houston Art Inst. Active Bluebird Circle, Houston, 1967-84; del. Friendship Among Women, 1983. Mem. Am. Soc. Interior Designers (nat. bd., 1984—, pres. Gulf Coast chpt. 1975), Chi Omega. Republican. Home: 10023 Locke Ln Houston TX 77042 Office: Mary Ann Bryan Design Assocs Inc 1502 Augusta St 100 Houston TX 77057

BRYAN, NANCY LEE CRAVENS, operations manager, management consultant, financial planner; b. Los Angeles, May 2, 1936; d. Mark Clarence and Susan Louise (Fernsil) Cravens; children—April Lynn Bryan, Robert Lee Bryan. B.S. in Bus. Adminstrn., Pepperdine U., 1978, M.B.A., 1980, Ph.D. (hon.), 1986. Lic. real estate salesperson, Calif. Dir. procurement Aircraft Govs., Burbank, Calif., 1966-71; bus. mgr. Motown Record Corp., Hollywood, Calif., 1971-76; controller Pepperdine U., Malibu, Calif., 1976-79; mgr. contracts Gen. Electric, Sunnyvale, Calif., 1979-82; pres. Redwood Corp., Sunnyvale, 1982—; cons. Apple/Macintosh, Freemont, Calif., Intel Corp., Santa Clara, Calif., Micro Systems, Sunnyvale; pres. Redwood Corp. Painter oils; editor various TV plays; author: Manufacturing Manual for Installation CIM, 1983. Vol. Suicide Prevention Ctr., Fish; ch. ambassador. Recipient service awards Los Angeles City Schs. Mem. Artists in Industry, Nat. Soc. Women Accts., Am. Prodn. and Inventory Control Soc., Nat. Assn. Female Execs., Pepperdine Alumni Assn. Clubs: Photography (pres.) (North Hollywood); Swim (Soquel, Calif.); Ski (Sunnyvale); Personal Computer. Avocations: swimming; photography; painting; stained glass; cloisonne; computers; volleyball; skiing; racquetball. Home: PO Box 61833 Sunnyvale CA 94088 Office: Redwood Corp PO Box 61833 Sunnyvale CA 94088

BRYAN, SHARON ANN, medical writer, editor; b. Kansas City, Mo., Dec. 18, 1941; d. George William and Dorothy Joan (Henn) Goll; children: Lisa Ann, Holly Renee. BJ, U. Mo., 1963; diploma Stanford Radio and TV Inst., 1961; postgrad. NYU Sch. Arts and Sci., 1963-64; Personal Fin. Planning profl. designation UCLA, 1986; student U. So. Calif. Law Ctr., 1986—. Proofreader, copy editor Cadwalader, Wickersham, and Taft, N.Y.C., 1963-64; manuscript editor, writer nonsci. sects. N.Y. State Jour. Medicine, Med. Soc. State of N.Y., N.Y.C., also mng. editor Staffoscope, 1965-66; manuscript editor Transactions, also editor Perceiver, Am. Acad. Ophthalmology and Otolaryngology, Rochester, Minn., 1969-72, hist. writer, 1972-82; writer publicity articles Ft. Lee (Va.) Community Theatre. Mem. vol. honor roll Soc. of Meml. Sloan-Kettering Cancer Center; active N.Y. Hosp. Women's League, 1965-67 ; docent Los Angeles County Mus. Natural History. Mem. Am. Med. Writers Assn. (editor conv. bull. 1966), AAAS, Internat. Platform Assn., N.Y. Acad. Scis., NOW, Women's Lawyers Assn. of Los Angeles, Kappa Tau Alpha, Kappa Alpha Theta (chmn. membership com. N.Y. chpt. 1966). Club: Stanford. Author: Pioneering Specialists: History of the American Academy of Ophthalmology and Otolaryngology. Home: 533 Via del Monte Palos Verdes Estates CA 90274

BRYAN, VIRGINIA ANN, lawyer; b. Wolf Point, Mont., May 18, 1953; d. Harvey W. and Lily Eldora (Stensland) Bryan. B.A., Rocky Mountain Coll., 1975; J.D. with honors, U. Mont., 1979. Dir. deferred prosecution program Yellowstone County Attys. Office, Billings, Mont., 1975-76; assoc. firm Hibbs, Sweeney & Colberg, Billings, 1979-83; atty., owner Virginia A. Bryan, atty. at law, Billings, 1983—; lectr. family law Rocky Mountain Coll. Paralegal Inst., Billings, 1983. Founding mem. Billings Rape Task Force, 1975, Yellowstone Valley NOW, Billings, 1979. Mem. ABA, State Bar Mont., Yellowstone County Bar Assn., Am. Judicature Soc., Mont. Assn. Female Execs. Democrat. Office: 344 Hart-Albin Bldg PO Box 3093 Billings MT 59103

BRYAN-BROWN, DARLENE ALETA, pharmaceutical company sales representative, educator; b. N.Y.C., Aug. 28, 1954; d. Hugh Leslie and Geraldine Marie (Prillerman) B. B.A., Hampton Inst., 1976. Retail salesperson, asst. stock mgr. Hempstead China, N.Y.C., 1977-79; profl. cons. Petro Internat., N.Y.C., 1979-80; account exec. Reuben H. Donnelley, N.Y.C., 1980-86; profl. med. rep. Ciba-Geigy, Cherry Hill, N.J., 1986—; tchr. dance, choreographer Trenton Bd. Edn., 1976—; profl. dancer, theatrical and film prodns., 1976—. Choreographer Hamilton High West, 1976-87, Hamilton Theatre II Summer Stock, Trenton, 1980, Lawrence High Sch., N.J., 1983, 84, 85, 87, 88. Named one of Outstanding Young Women of Am., U.S. Jaycees, 1983. Mem. Nat. Assn. Female Execs., North Hudson Exec. Profl. Assn., Repnet, Alpha Psi Omega. Avocations: dancing; tennis; jazzobics; travel.

BRYANT, ANN ALEACE, recreation therapist; b. Roanoke, Va., Apr. 13, 1961; d. John Junior Bryant and Alice Margaret (Davis) Rice. BS, Longwood Coll., 1983; M of Pub. Adminstrn., Auburn U., 1988. Cert. therapeutic recreation specialist. Recreation therapist VA Med. Ctr., Tuskegee, Ala., 1983—; therapeutic recreation cons. VA Med. Ctr., Montgomery, Ala., 1984—. Recipient Superior Performance award VA Med. Ctr. Recreation Service, Tuskegee, 1983, Outstanding Performance award, 1984, 86, 87; Spl. Recognition cert. U.S. Congress, 1985. Mem. Nat. Therapeutic Recreation Soc., Nat. Recreation and Parks Assn., AAUW, Alpha Sigma Phi, Delta Psi Kappa, Phi Kappa Phi. Avocations: reading; cooking; crossword puzzles; walking. Home: Box 47 VA Med Ctr Tuskegee AL 36083 Office: VA Med Ctr Recreation Service (11K) Tuskegee AL 36083

BRYANT, ANNE LINCOLN, association executive; b. Jamaica Plain, Mass., Nov. 26, 1949; d. John Winslow and Anne (Phillips) B.; m. Peter Harned Ross, June 15, 1986; stepchildren: Charlotte Ross, George Ross. BA in English, Secondary Edn., Simmons Coll., 1971; EdD in Higher Edn., U. Mass., 1978. Intern U. Mass., Amherst, 1972; asst. to dean Springfield Tech. Community Coll., 1972-74; dir. Nat. Assn. Bank Women Ednl. Found., Chgo., 1974-86; v.p. P.M. Haeger, Chgo., 1978-86; exec. dir. AAUW, Washington, 1986—. Contbr. articles to profl. jours. Mem. exec. com. Simmons Coll., Boston, 1971—; adv. commr. Edn. Commn. States, 1986—; chmn. bd. trustees Council for Adult and Experiential Learning, 1985-86, mem., 1980-87; bd. dirs. Washington Ctr. for Learning Alternatives, 1986—. Recipient William H. Cosby Jr. award U. Mass., 1983; named Woman of Yr. for Edn., YWCA, 1976. Fellow Am. Soc. Assn. Execs. (bd. dirs. 1985-88); mem. Am. Assn. for Higher Edn. (bd. dirs. 1980-87), Bus. Execs. for Nat. Security. Episcopalian. Office: AAUW 2401 Virginia Ave NW Washington DC 20037

BRYANT, BARBARA ANN, retail executive; b. Mpls., July 9, 1957; d. Richard Leroy and Darlene Helen (Slauf) Nallick. Asst. mgr. Ole', Inc., Hampton, Va., 1981-82; cashier K & K Toys, Inc., Hampton, Va., 1981, mgr., 1982-85; mdse. distbn. coordinator K & K Toys, Inc., Norfolk, Va., 1985—. Mem. Nat. Assn. Female Execs. Republican. Roman Catholic. Home: 5745 Bartee St Norfolk VA 23502 Office: K & K Toys Inc 2555 Ellsmere Ave Norfolk VA 23502

BRYANT, BARBARA EVERITT, market research company executive; b. Ann Arbor, Mich., Apr. 5, 1926; d. William Littell and Dorothy (Wallace) Everitt; m. John H. Bryant, Aug. 14, 1948; children—Linda Bryant Valentine, Randal E., Lois B. A.B., Cornell U., 1947; M.A., Mich. State U., 1967, Ph.D., 1970. Editor art Chem. Engring. magazine McGraw-Hill Pub. Co., N.Y.C., 1947-48; editorial research asst. Univ. Ill., Urbana, 1948-49; freelance editor, writer, 1950-61; with continuing edn. adminstrn. dept. Oakland Univ., Rochester, Mich., 1961-66; grad. research asst. Mich. State Univ., East Lansing, 1966-70; from sr. analyst to v.p. Market Opinion Research, Detroit, 1970-77, sr. vp., 1977—. Author: High School Students Look at Their World, 1970, American Women Today & Tomorrow, 1977. Contbr. articles to profl. jours. Mem. U.S. Census Adv. Com., Washington, 1980-86, Mich. Job Devel. Authority, Lansing, Mich., 1980-85; state editor LWV of Mich., 1959-61. Mem. Detroit Chpt. of Women in Communications, Inc. (pres. 1974-75, Nat. Headliner award 1980), Detroit Chpt. of Am. Mktg. Assn. (pres. 1976-77), Am. Mktg. Assn. (midwestern v.p. 1978-80, v.p. mktg. research 1982-84). Republican. Presbyterian. Club: Renaissance. Avocation: swimming. Home: 1505 Sheridan Dr Ann Arbor MI 48104 Office: Market Opinion Research 243 Congress St Detroit MI 48226

BRYANT, BETTY JANE, shopping center exec.; b. Camden, Ind., June 19, 1926; d. Claude Raymond and Louise (Eckert) Wickard; B.S., Purdue U., 1947; m. Harry R. Bryant, Aug. 21, 1949; children—Susan, Patricia. Retail mgmt. and advt. L.S. Ayres, Indpls., 1947-49, Burdine's, Miami, Fla., 1950-51, Joske's, San Antonio, 1968, Dillard's, San Antonio, 1968-70; with Sterling Advt. Agy., N.Y.C., 1949; mktg. dir. Mary Ann Fabrics and Designer's Fabrics By Mail, Evanston, Ill., 1971-75; instr. Ray-Vogue Sch., Chgo., 1976; mktg. dir. Woodfield Shopping Center, Schaumburg, Ill., 1977—. Mem. council Fashion Group of Chgo. Bd. dirs. Northwest Area council Girl Scouts Am., 1982-83, Greater Woodfield Conv. and Visitors Bur., 1984-85, sec., 1986—. Mem. N.W. Suburban Assn. (dir.), Commerce and Industry (v.p. 1981-82), Chgo. Area Shopping Center Mktg. Dirs.'s Assn., Women in Mgmt., Mortar Board, Kappa Kappa Gamma. Home: 2008 Bayberry Ln Hoffman Estates IL 60195 Office: Woodfield Merchants Assn 5 Woodfield Mall Schaumburg IL 60195

BRYANT, BRENDA JOYCE, university administrator; b. Greenville, Ala., Dec. 24, 1950; d. Maudest L. and Sarah Mae (Kelly) Lowery; m. LaZarus B. Bryant, Sept. 3, 1972 (div. Oct. 1986); children: LaZarus II, Mario. BS, Ala. State U., 1973, MEd, 1974. Clerk-typist, then registration asst. Ala. State U., Montgomery, 1973-76, asst. dir. instnl. research, 1976-80, dir. instnl. research, 1980—. Mem. Queen of Hearts Womens' Club, Montgomery. Mem. Assn. for Instnl. Research, Southern Assn. Instnl. Research, Traditionally Black Colls. and Univs. Democrat. Baptist. Office: Ala State U 915 S Jackson St Montgomery AL 36195

BRYANT, DEBRA SUZANNE, telecommunications executive, systems consultant; b. Warrensburg, Mo., Mar. 28, 1953; d. William Ricks and Juanita Maria (Gago); m. Billy Michael Nix, June 2, 1949 (div. July 1978); children: Joshua Bryant, Chelsea Suzanne. BBA with honors, U. Tex., 1983. Owner Secret Garden, Dallas, 1976-78; asst. buyer Calco Lumber Co., Austin, 1978-79; dir. software devel. Politechs, Inc., Austin, 1983-84; programmer Austin Ind. Sch. Dist., 1984; programmer analyst City of Austin, 1984-85; account exec. Southwestern Bell Telephone Co., Austin, 1985—. Judge Tex. Sci. and Engring. Fair, Austin, 1987; facilitator Austin Plan Steering Com., 1987, City of Austin Cultural Affairs Task Force, 1987-88; active Austin Lyric Opera Found., Paramount Theatre Guild, Laguna Gloria Art Mus. Recipient Presdl. Endowed scholarship U. Tex., 1982-83. Mem. Am. Mktg. Assn., Am. Mgmt. Assn., Nat. Assn. Female Execs., Tex. Computer Industry Council, Data Processing Mgmt. Assn., Am. Inst. for Fgn. Study, U. Tex. Ex-Students Assn., Planned Parenthood Found., Phi Kappa Phi, Beta Gamma Sigma. Club: Met. Breakfast. Home: 1608 Kimmerling Austin TX 78758 Office: Southwestern Bell Telephone Co 712 E Huntland Dr Room 229 Austin TX 78752

BRYANT, DENISE DELISLE, university administrator; b. Fitchburg, Mass., June 6, 1946; d. Norman and Anita (Leblanc) Delisle; m. Larry Bryant, May, 1974. BS in English, Fitchburg State Coll., 1968; MA, Eastern Ky. U., 1971; MS in Systems Sci., U. Louisville, 1983. Tchr. Knoxville Sch. System, 1968-69, Estill County Schs., Irvine, Ky., 1969-70; grad. asst. Eastern Ky. U., Richmond, 1970-71; supr. Mountain Comprehensive Care, Pikeville, Ky., 1971-75; cons. tchr. Fayette County Sch. System, Lexington, Ky.; unit dir. Ky. Dept. Edn., Frankfort; coordinator Green River Coop., Owensboro, Ky.; asst. dean adminstrn. Coll. Urban and Pub. Affairs U. Louisville, 1983—. Contbr. articles to profl. jours. Mem. Soc. Gen. Systems Research, Bus. and Profl. Women. Office: U Louisville Coll Urban and Pub Affairs Louisville KY 40292

BRYANT, ERNA BALLANTINE, management consultant, civic worker; b. Boston, Aug. 29, 1939; d. John Edward and Clementina (Redman) Adamson; m. Bernard E. Bryant; children: J. Kurtis, Erna Celeste, Valarie, Bernard Jr. EdM, Harvard U., 1970, cert. in adnvanced studies, 1971, cert. in mgmt. devel., 1973, EdD, 1974. Exec. dir. Black Ecumenical Commn., Boston, 1974-80; dir. Ctr. for Racial Justice, YWCA, N.Y.C., 1980-82; cons. dir. YWCA, Atlanta, 1982-83; asst. dean Atlanta U., 1983-85; fin. planner Phoenix, Atlanta, 1987—. Nat. pres. Women in Community Service, 1987—; pres. United Black Christians United Ch. of Christ, Southeast, 1987—; bd. dirs. The So. Africa Edn. Fund, Inc. Recipient Crispus Attucks Day Care Ctr. award, 1975, Ba'Hai of Boston, 1979, Boston YWCA award, 1981, award Ga./S.C. Assn. United Ch. of Christ, 1987. Republican.

BRYANT, EVA LOU, brokerage manager; b. Orrick, Mo., Aug. 15, 1941; d. William Maurice and Lena Mae (Gooch) Hall; m. David Lynn Bryant, Aug. 20, 1960; children—Alan, Karen, James, Diane, Jason, Zane. A.A., Purdue U., Ft. Wayne, 1982; A.A., Ind. U., 1982, B.S., 1983. Owner Day Nursery, Colorado Springs, Colo., 1973-76; asst. mdse. coordinator House of Fabrics, Hastings, Nebr., 1978-79; with GTE Directories Corp., Ft. Wayne, 1980-81, service rep., 1981-83, telephone sales rep., 1983-85, dist. sales mgr., 1985-86; telemktg. mgr. Stas. WMEE/WQHK, 1986-87; discount brokerage mgr. Lincoln Nat. Bank and Trust Co., Ft. Wayne, 1987—. Vestry chmn. St. Alban's Episcopal Ch., Ft. Wayne, 1986—, (lic. layreader and chalice-bearer of Episcopal diocese), active PTA, Episcopal Ch. Women, Girl Scouts U.S.A., Boy Scouts Am., 4-H, Little League, Am. Arthritis Found., Am. Cancer Soc., Am. Heart Assn. Recipient Pres.'s award, GTE, 1984, Top Gen. Sales award, 1984, Top Sales Travel Incentive, 1985, 86. Mem. Am. Bus. Women's Assn., AAUW, Nat. Assn. Female Execs., Delta Zeta. Republican. Episcopalian. Club: Lake Forest Swimming and Tennis. Avocations: needlework; reading; sports.

BRYANT, FRANCES JANE, newspaper editor; b. Cushing, Okla., Dec. 10, 1933; d. Edward Glahn and Dorothy Evelyn (McLean) B. AA, Christian Coll., Columbia, Mo., 1953; BJ, U. Mo., 1955. Reporter The Norman (Okla.) Transcript, 1955-57, wire editor, 1957-59, city editor, 1959-67, mng. editor, 1967—. Bd. dirs. Juvenile Services, Inc., Cleveland County, Okla., 1981-87, pres., 1984-85; bd. dirs. Cleveland County chpt. ARC, 1987—. Named Oustanding Bus. Woman Bus. and Profl. Women, Norman, 1971, State Woman of Year Theta Sigma Phi, U. Okla., 1968; recipient Disting. Alumni award Columbia Coll. (formerly Christian Coll.), 1980. Mem. AP/Okla. News Execs. (pres. 1970-71), Soc. Profl. Journalists, Altrusa Internat. (pres. Norman chpt. 1969-71). Democrat. Epsicopalian. Home: 606 Sherwood Dr Norman OK 73071 Office: The Norman Transcript 215 E Comanche Norman OK 73069

BRYANT, GAY, magazine editor, writer; b. Newcastle, Eng., Oct. 5, 1945; came to U.S., 1970; d. Richard King and Catherine (Shiel) B.; m. Charles Childs, Apr. 10, 1982. Student, St. Clare's Coll., Oxford, Eng., 1961-63. Sr. editor Penthouse Mag., N.Y.C., 1968-74; assoc. editor Oui mag., N.Y.C., 1974-75; founding editor New Dawn mag., N.Y.C., 1975-79; exec. editor Working Woman mag., N.Y.C., 1979-81, editor, 1981-84; editor, v.p. Family Circle mag., N.Y.C., 1984-86; adj. prof. Sch. Journalism, NYU, 1982-87. Author: The Underground Travel Guide, 1973, How I Learned To Like Myself, 1975, The Working Woman Report, 1984. Recipient award Acad. Women Achievers, YMCA, N.Y.C., 1982. Mem. Women's Media Group, Am. Soc. Mag. Editors. Home: 34 Horatio St New York NY 10014

BRYANT, JANET HOUGH, actress, voice teacher, performing artist; b. Rockford, Ill.; d. Roy Arthur and Ida Elissa Bertha (Bergman) Hough; m. Charles Herbert Bryant Jr., Dec. 28, 1938 (dec. 1942); 1 child, Janna Lee Wright. Student, U. Iowa, 1931; AM, Stephens Coll., 1934; BE, Drake U., 1937; student, Vassar Experimental Theatre, 1935, Am. Conservatory Music, Chgo., 1942; MS in Music Edn., U. So. Calif., 1961; cert., Ecole d'Art Am., Fontainebleau, France, 1965; student, Am. Inst. Musical Studies, Graz, Austria, 1979. Tchr. music Los Angeles Schs., 1955-76; pvt. voice tchr. Newport Beach, Calif., 1955—. Appeared in plays Born Yesterday, Rumpelstiltskin, Stage Door, The Heiress, Darling Delinquent, You Can't Take It With You, So You Want To Be A Mother; appeared in operas Dance of Death, La Boheme, Faust, Rape of Lucretia, La Traviata, Stabat Mater; performed as guest artist throughout Orange County, Calif.; exhibited in art shows at Lido Village, Bullock's Dept. Store, Jewel Court, City Hall of Newport, Orange County, Calif., Orange Coast Plaza. Pres. Musical Arts Orange County, 1980-82, chmn. program, 1978-80, rec. sec., 1977-78; chmn. program Orange County Philharm. Soc., 1984-86, 88-89, chmn. ways means, 1986-88, chmn. publicity, 1980-82; chmn. program Musical Theatre Guild Orange County, 1978-80; founder Opera Pacific; charter mem. Rep. Nat. Task Force, Nat. Mus. of Women in Arts, 1988—. Mem. Nat. Assn. Tchrs. Singing, Music Tchrs. Assn., Music Tchrs. Assn. Calif., Costa Mesa Art League, South Coast Repertory Theatre Guild, Camelot Chpt. Performing Arts Ctr., Delta Gamma. Home and Studio: 2022 Barranca Newport Beach CA 92660

BRYANT, (LOIS) JEAN, editor; b. South Bend, Ind., Dec. 31, 1925; d. Ford Happa and Iva May (White) Bunch; m. Harland Hiram Bryant, Feb. 14, 1944; children: Daniel Eugene, Janet Alyce, Clayton Max, Elizabeth Ann, Adam Lee. Exec. secretarial diploma South Bend Coll. Commerce, 1943; grad. Pacific Coast Bapt. Bible Coll., 1970; student Bapt. Coll., Springfield, Mo., 1957-59; D of Sacred Laws and Letters, (hon.), Clarksville Sch. Theology, 1981. Editor, pub. LOIS mag., Rialto, Calif., 1978-81; asst. editor Here's Life Pubs., San Bernardino, Calif., 1981-83, assoc. editor, 1983-84, mng. editor, 1984—. Dir. publicity Calvary Bapt. Ch., Redlands, Calif., 1985-86; instr. quality editing seminars, 1986—. Mem. Nat. Assn. Female Execs. Republican. Avocations: art, music. Home: 2700 Little Mountain Dr Colton CA 92324 Office: Here's Life Publs Inc 795 S Allen St San Bernardino CA 92402

BRYANT, JOYCE ERICKSON, finance company executive; b. Portland, Oreg., Mar. 19, 1937; d. Harold W. and Sarah (Ledin) Erickson; m. Thomas E. Bryant, May 26, 1973. BS, U. Minn., 1960. Home economist Pillsbury Co., Mpls., 1960-61; tchr. 8th grade St. Louis Park (Minn.) Jr. High Sch., 1961-62; menu planner dept. Army and Air Force U.S. Army, Giessen, Fed. Republic of Germany, 1962-64; dir. home econs. Overseas Service Corp., San Francisco, 1965-73; dir. money mgmt. inst. Household Fin. Corp., Prospect Heights, Ill., 1973-77, v.p. consumer affairs, 1977—; mem. consumer edn. com. Credit Research Council, 1978; mem. credit publ. com. U.S. Dept. Commerce, 1980; mem. adv. com. on bus. and humanities Northeastern Ill. U., 1983-84. Mem. adv. council Better Bus. Bur. Chgo., 1977—; mem. career adv. council Wheeling (Ill.) High Sch., 1979-85; mem. bd. trustees, exec. com. Ill. Council Econ. Edn., Chgo., 1985—. Recipient Gabriel award Nat. Consumer Fin. Assn., 1982, Consumer Edn. award Better Bus. Bur., Chgo., 1983, Louis M. Linxwiler award Nat. Found. Consumer Credit, 1983. Mem. Am. Fin. Services Assn. (ednl. relations com. 1973-76, spokesperson 1977-84, pub. relations task force 1978-79, consumer credit edn. task force 1982-84), Nat. Assn. Industry/Edn. Cooperation (editorial bd., nominating com. 1976—), Soc. Consumer Affairs Profls. (profl. devel. com. 1980, nat. consumer edn. com. 1980, treas. Chgo. chpt. 1980, program com. 1982, chairman sponsorship com. 1983, consumer edn. com. 1984, chmn. 1985, Mobius editorial com. 1984, nat. bd. dirs. 1985—, sec. to bd. dirs. 1986—, program adv. com. 1986—), Nat. Home Economists In Bus. (western regional adv. 1968-70, nominating com. 1974, long range planning com. 1974-76, internat. chmn. 1980, profl. devel. com. 1982, internat. relations com. 1984), Chgo. Home Economists In Bus. (chmn. publicity for bus. workshop 1976, chmn. ways and means 1976, nominating chmn. 1977, program com. 1979, sec. 1983-84, nominating com. 1985, Home Economist in Bus. of Yr. 1982), Am. Home Econs. Assn., Am. Council Consumer Interests, Ill. Consumer Edn. Assn., Ill. State C. of C. (edn. com. 1974—, chmn. higher edn. subcom. 1978-79, future of edn. task force 1984—). Republican. Presbyterian. Home: 730 Ingleside Pl Evanston IL 60201 Office: Household Fin Services 2700 Sanders Rd Prospect Heights IL 60070

BRYANT, JUDITH WILDER, librarian; b. Jersey City, Sept. 28, 1940; d. Robert Dennison and Eloise (Hulphers) Wilder; m. Carter Harrison Bryant, II; 1 son, Sean. B.A., U. Del.-Newark, 1962; M.L.S., U. Tex.-Austin, 1974; certs. Pratt Inst., 1977, 80; Braille cert. ARC, 1978. Library clk. U. Tex., Austin, 1973-75; circulation librarian Collier County Library, Naples, Fla., 1975; nat. cons. Inst. for Intellectual Devel. of Children and Young Adults, Tehran, Iran, 1975-76; outreach librarian Ridgewood Pub. Library (N.J.), 1977-78; children's librarian Jersey City Pub. Library, 1978-79, br. head/children's librarian, 1979-87, children's dept. head, 1987-88, asst. children's librarian Paramus (N.J.) Pub. Library, 1988—; co-chmn. Hudson-Essex Summer Committee. Contbr. articles Jour. Childrens Pub. Libraries; author (with others) Children's Manual; author Library Skills Manual; co-author Crafts Manual; researcher, article, 1973. Friends of Tex. Libraries spl. scholar 1973. Mem. ALA, PLA, N.J. Library Assn., Am. Mus. Natural History, Nat. Wildlife Fedn. Democrat. Office: Jersey City Pub Library 472 Jersey Ave Jersey City NJ 07302

BRYANT, KAREN ANN, nurse; b. St. Louis, Aug. 6, 1955; d. Albert Lee and Loretta (Hadley) B. Diploma, Ga. Bapt. Hosp. Sch. Nursing, 1978; BS in Nursing, Med. Coll. Ga., 1982; MS in Nursing, U. Ala., Birmingham, 1984. RN; cert. emergency nurse, critical-care nurse. Staff nurse intensive care unit Houston County Hosp., Warner Robins, Ga., 1978-79, charge nurse intensive care unit, 1979-81; staff nurse neuro intensive care unit Univ. Hosp., Augusta, Ga., 1981-82; staff nurse emergency dept. Med. Ctr. Cen. Ga., Macon, 1981-82, clin. nurse emergency ctr., 1986-87, clin. specialist critical care, 1987—; staff nurse intensive care Med. Ctr. Houston County, 1982-84; clin. supr. intensive care unit and critical care unit Charter Northside Hosp., Macon, 1984-86; instr. advanced cardiac life support Am. Heart Assn., Ga., 1982—. Mem. Am. Nurses Assn., Ga. Nurses Assn., Am. Assn. Critical Care Nurses (pres. Ga. chpt. 1986-87), Emergency Nurses Assn., Sigma Theta Tau. Baptist. Home: 214 Randy Circle Warner Robins GA 31088 Office: Med Ctr Cen Ga 777 Hemlock St Macon GA 31208

BRYANT, KAREN WORSTELL, marketing executive; b. Cadillac, Mich., Sept. 7, 1942; d. Harley Orville and Rose Edith (Bell) Worstell; children: Lynda Jean, Tracey Jo, Cynthia Jill, Troy Thomas; m. Robert Melvin Bryant, Nov. 29, 1968. Student, Cen. Mich. U., 1963-67, Mich. State U., 1966, Johns Hopkins U., 1982-83. Sales rep. Xerox Corp., Southfield, Mich., 1972-74; cons. employment contracts Joint Policy Study Group, Johnson & Johnson, IBM World Trade Asia and others, Tokyo, 1974-79; area sales mgr. Universal Plastics, McLean, Va., 1979-81; exec. product mgr. The Western Union Telegraph Co., Upper Saddle River, N.J., 1981-86; dir. mktg. and sales support The Nat. Guardian Corp., Greenwich, Conn., 1986-88; fin. cons. Shearson Lehman Hutton, Pearl River, N.Y., 1988—. Mem. Direct Mktg. Assn., Nat. Assn. Female Execs. Republican. Home: 19 Sky Meadow Rd Suffern NY 10901 Office: Shearson Lehman Hutton One Blue Hill Plaza Pearl River NJ 10965

BRYANT, LYNN ANDREA, senior software engineer; b. Lock Haven, Pa., May 1, 1952; d. George Arthur and Ethel June (Fritz) Smith; m. Jerry King Musser, June 11, 1970 (div. Oct. 1977); m. Gregory Alan Bryant, July 17, 1978; children: Griffin Richard, Tiffany Michelle. Student, Harrisburg Area Community Coll., 1970-71, Temple U., 1971-73; BS in Math. and Computer Sci. with highest distinction, Pa. State U., 1974; MS in Computer Sci., Boston U., 1986. From assoc. to sr. software engr. Raytheon Co., Sudbury, Mass., 1975-83; sr. software engr. Sequoia Systems, Inc., Marlborough, Mass., 1983—. Recipient Group Achievement award NASA, 1984. Republican. Office: Sequoia Systems Inc. 3 Metropolitan Corp Ctr Marlborough MA 01752

BRYANT, MARGERY DAVIS(DEE), newspaper editor; b. Fairhope, Ala., Mar. 26, 1942; d. John Henry Jr. and Margery Eunice (Davis) Wienand; children: Paul William, Kellie Cronin. BA, U. Ala., 1964. Reporter The Ala. Jour., Montgomery, 1964-66; editor Fuller and Dees Mktg. Group, Montgomery, 1966-68; freelance writer Montgomery, 1968-69; reporter, features editor Marietta (Ga.) Daily Jour., 1969-75; asst. city editor The Columbus (Ga.) Ledger, 1975-76, city editor, 1976-80; editor The News-Examiner, Gallatin, Tenn., 1976-80, The Leaf-Chronicle, Clarksville, Tenn., 1983—; pres. Tenn. Associated Press Mng. Editors Assn., 1985-86, Credit Bur. Clarksville, 1986-87; chmn. Tenn. Press Inst., 1986. Co-founder, bd. dirs. Clarksville-Montgomery Hist. Mus. Guild, 1984-86; charter mem. Clarksville-Montgomery County Edn. Found., 1985—, mem. steering com., blue ribbon goals and objectives com., 1985-86; v.p., co-founder, mem. exec. com. Leadership Clarksville, 1986—; mem. pastoral council Immaculate Conception Cath. Ch., 1985—. Mem. Am. Soc. Newspaper Editors (human resources com. 1984-88, nominations com. 1988—), Mid-Am. Press Inst. (bd. dirs. 1985—), Tenn. Press Assn. (mem. freedom of info. com. 1984—), Clarksville C. of C. (mem. mil. affairs com. 1983—). Office: The Leaf-Chronicle 200 Commerce St Box 829 Clarksville TN 37040

BRYANT, MARILYNNE REGAN, lawyer; b. Norwood, Mass., Nov. 21, 1954; d. David H. Jr. and Elizabeth (Barnes) Regan; m. Suzanne Bryant. Cert. in alcohol counseling, Stonehill Coll., 1980, BA in Psychology magna cum laude, 1981; JD, New Eng. Sch. of Law, 1986. Bar: Mass. 1986, U.S. Dist. Ct. Mass., 1987; cert. in family mediation. Paralegal, adminstr. Hoffman Law Offices, Walpole, Mass., 1972-86; ptnr. Bryant & Burt, Walpole, 1986—. Contbr. articles to profl. jours. Mem. adv. bd. Harry H. Clinton and Edith K. Clinton Charitable Found., 1983-86. Mem. ABA (law practice sect., family law sect.), Boston Bar Assn. (family law sect., young lawyers sect. 1986-87), Mass. Bar Assn. (jud. adminstrn. sect. council 1984-86, long range planning task force 1984-85, law practice sect., family law sect. 1983—), Mass. Acad. of Trial Attys., Mass. Council on Family Mediation, Inc.

BRYANT, MARY SNELL, pilot educator; b. Mexico, Mo., Feb. 27, 1949; d. William Ernest and Marie Louise (Austin) Snell; m. Timothy Clark Bryant, Jan. 17, 1981. BA Northwestern U., 1971; MBA U. Ill., 1973. CPA, Ill., Tex. Dir. eval. and projects G.D. Searle & Co., Skokie, Ill., 1977-78, spl. asst. to exec. v.p. fin., 1979; dir. planning Searle Med. Products, Dallas, 1980, controller ventures, 1981; dir. planning Pearle Health Services, Inc., Dallas, 1981-83, v.p. internat., 1983-85; mgr. mgmt. cons. services Alexander Grant & Co. (now known as Grant Thornton), Tampa, Fla., 1985-87; gen. mgr. R&B Aviation, Clearwater, Fla., 1987-88; instr. pilot Piper Aircraft Corp., Vero Beach, Fla., 1988—. Trustee Am. Stage Co. Treas., bd. dirs. St. Petersburg YWCA, 1986—. Winner Great So. Air Race, 1988. Mem. Am. Inst. CPA's, Tex. Soc. CPA's, Ill. Soc. CPA's, Fla. Race Pilots Assn., Air Race Classic Ltd., Aircraft Owners and Pilots Assn. Clubs: The 500 Inc. (Dallas); Chandler's Yacht; The 99s (membership chmn. Suncoast chpt. 1987—). Home: 307 Brightwaters Blvd NE Saint Petersburg FL 33704 Office: Piper Aircraft Corp 2926 Piper Dr Vero Beach FL 32960

BRYANT, PAMELA KAYE, registered nurse; b. Cullman, Ala., Aug. 19, 1953; d. James Franklin and Dorothy Marie (McAfee) Hancock; m. Patrick Dwight Bryant, Oct. 22, 1971; children: Joshua Patrick, Jody Lee. AAS in Nursing cum laude, Wallace State Community Coll., 1978; BS in Nursing with honors, U. Ala., Birmingham, 1982. Registered nurse, Ala. Nursing asst. Cullman Med. Ctr., 1975-76; RN Ensor, Baccus, Williamson OB/GYN, Cullman, 1978-80, Carraway Meth. Med. Ctr., Birmingham, 1982-85, ARC, Birmingham, Ala., 1983, Cullman Internal Medicine, 1985—. Recipient various awards Ala. State Fair, local county fairs for pen, ink and pencil drawings. Mem. Sigma Theta Tau. Democrat. Baptist. Home: 1400 E Hanceville Rd SE Cullman AL 35055 Office: Cullman Internal Medicine 402 Arnold St Suite 108 Cullman AL 35055

BRYANT, RUTH ALYNE, banker; b. Memphis, Jan. 12, 1924; d. James Walter and Leola (Edgar) B. Student, Rhodes Coll. (formerly Southwestern Coll.), Memphis, 1941-43. Clk. Fed. Res. Bank of St. Louis (Memphis Br.), 1943-47, exec. sec., 1947-68, asst. cashier, 1968-69, asst. v.p., 1969-73, v.p., 1973—. Mem. Chancellor's Council U. Mo., St. Louis, 1979—, chmn., 1985-88; mem. adv. bd. Salvation Army, St. Louis, 1983—, DePaul Health Ctr., St. Louis, 1984—; bd. dirs. Assocs. of St. Louis U. Libraries, 1977—, pres., 1983-85; bd. dirs. The Vanderschmidt's Sch., 1980-86. Mem. Am. Inst. Banking (nat. women's com. 1962-63, pres. Memphis chpt. 1968-69), Mo. Bankers Assn. (mktg. and pub. relations com. 1974-76), Nat. Assn. Bank Women (editor Woman Banker 1959-62, v.p. so. region 1967-68, v.p. 1969-70, pres. 1970-71, trustee ednl. found. 1974-75), English Speaking Union, Bank Mktg. Assn. (dir. Mo.-Ill. chpt. 1976-79). Home: 4466 W Pine Blvd Apt 15E Saint Louis MO 63108 Office: Fed Res Bank of St Louis 411 Locust St Saint Louis MO 63102

BRYANT, SANDRA RENEE, municipal administrative executive; b. Norfolk, Va., July 29, 1959; d. James Thomas and Wincie (Jackson) B. BA in Polit. Sci, Old Dominion U., 1981, MA in Urban Studies, 1988. Credit leader Gen. Electric Co., Chesapeake, Va., 1981-84; adminstrv. analyst City of Suffolk, Va., 1984-86, sr. adminstrv. analyst, 1986; asst. city mgr. City of Emporia, Va., 1986—. Treas. Emporia-Greensville affiliate Am. Heart Assn., 1987-88; vice chmn. Chesterfield-Emporia Community Diversion Program, 1986; fiscal agt. Emporia Greensville Recreation Adv. Commn.,

Airport Commn.; coordinator Community Improvement Council; adv. bd. Southampton Community; bd. dirs. Southeastern Tidewater Opportunity Project, Inc., 1984-86, South Cen. Pvt. Industry Council, 1986—, Community Diversion Incentive Program, 1986—; coordinator Emporia-Greensville-Jarratt Community Improvement Council. Old Dominion U. grantee, 1984-85. Mem. Nat. Recreation and Parks Soc., Am. Parks and Recreation Soc., Nat. Assn. Female Execs. (bd. dirs. 1986, Am. Soc. Pub. Adminstrs. (affiliate, planning com.), Internat. City Mgmt. Assn. (assoc., award 1985), Va. Local Govt. Mgrs. Assn., Va. Analyst Network, Va. Parks and Recreation Soc., Emporia-Greensville C. of C. Roman Catholic. Home: 502B Broad St Emporia VA 23847 Office: City of Emporia 201 S Main St PO Box 511 Emporia VA 23847

BRYANT, TANYA (MRS. GLENDELL W. DOBBS), real estate executive; b. Sliema, Island of Malta, May 15, 1920; d. Jose Louis and Vera (Jarmonkine) Mifsud; student pvt. schs.; m. Arthur J. W. Pitt, Nov. 17, 1937 (div. Feb. 1952); children—Natasha, Valerie Pitt Deeds, F. David, Micheline Pitt Magdaleno; m. 2d, William Cullen Bryant, Dec. 29, 1959 (div. June 1960); m. 3d, Jack F. Cutler, May 4, 1963 (div. Oct. 1968); m. 4th, Glendell W. Dobbs, Mar. 1969. Came to U.S., 1949, naturalized, 1957. Imported model Jacques Heim, Paris, France, 1949-50; Conover model all major fashion shows and TV shows U.S., 1950-52; sportswear buyer, exec. trainee Neiman Marcus, Dallas, 1952-54; mgr. ladies wear Broadway Dept. Store, Panorama City, Calif., 1954-56; owner, buyer Brides and Besides shops, Los Angeles, Bakersfield, Westwood, Calif., 1956-60; owner Tanya Bryant, Realtor, Lodi, Calif., 1957—; pres. San Joaquin Software Systems, Inc. Originator, dir. Pamper House, Rockefeller Center, 1952. Staff asst. ARC, London, 1942-45; gray lady, Los Angeles, 1957-60. Bd. dirs. Better Bus. Bur., 1976—; mem. San Jose City Tenant/Landlord Com., 1975-79. Mem. Women's Council Nat. Assn. Real Estate Bds. (chpt. pres. 1966, 69), San Fernando Valley Bd. Realtors (dir. 1966), Stockton Bd. Realtors (chmn. investment div. Dist. 7), Lodi Bd. Realtors (bd. dirs. 1983—), Calif. Real Estate Assn. (dir. 1966-72, chmn. public relations 1969, 70, polit. affairs com. 1972-74, legis. com. 1973), San Jose Real Estate Bd. (dir. 1970, sec. 1970), Internat. Inst. Valuers (sr. cert. valuer), Internat. Platform Assn., C. of C. (dir. 1966), Internat. Traders Club. Contbr. articles to profl. jours. Home: 11421 Fortyniner Circle Gold River CA 95670 Office: 107 W Lockeford St Lodi CA 95240

BRYANT, TARA ANN, computer consultant; b. Smithtown, N.Y., Nov. 3, 1963; d. Thomas Nelson and Kathleen Mary (Repetto) B. BA, SUNY, Stony Brook, 1985, MS in Tech. Systems Mgmt., 1986; postgrad., NYU, 1988. Cert. secondary sch. social studies tchr., N.Y. Substitute tchr. Three Village Central Sch. Dist., Stony Brook, N.Y., 1984-86; grad. teaching asst. SUNY, Stony Brook, 1985-86; exec. asst. to dir. mgmt. info. systems unit City of N.Y., dept. of parks and recreation, N.Y.C., 1986-87, fiscal auditor, 1987; computer trainer, support analyst Price Waterhouse & Co., N.Y.C., 1987—. Vol. Spl. Olympics, Hauppauge, N.Y., 1984, Three Village Democratic Club, Stony Brook, 1986; campaign worker, Hochbrueckner for Congress, Stony Brook, 1986. Mem. Nat. Assn. Exec. Women, MASS-11 User's Group, Digital Equipment Computer User Group. Roman Catholic. Office: Price Waterhouse & Co 153 E 53d St New York NY 10022

BRYANT-REID, JOHANNE, investment company executive; b. Farmington, W.Va., Mar. 11, 1949; d. Leslie David and Jessie Lee (Scruggs) Bryant. B.A. in Psychology, W.Va. U., 1971. Placement counselor, mgr. Ran Assocs., Cleve., 1971-78; exec. recruiter Merrill Lynch, N.Y.C., 1978-80, corp. employment mgr., 1980—, v.p., 1982-88, dir. corp. human resources, 1988—. Mem. adv. bd. Nat. Council Negro Women, Black World Championship Rodeo, Nat. Assn. for Equal Opportunity in Higher Edn., Mnhattan Community Coll.; exec. bd. James Robert Braxton Scholarship Fund. Recipient Black Achiever award YMCA of Greater N.Y.C., 1981. Mem. Employment Mgrs. Assn., Am. Soc. Personnel Adminstrs., Edges Group, Inc. Democrat. Baptist. Home: 788 Columbus Apt #17-R New York NY 10025 Office: WFC South Tower New York NY 10080-1108

BRYAN-YALE, DIANE MARIE, television station official; b. Johnson City, N.Y., Aug. 10, 1959; d. William Robert and Phyllis Christine (Rudenauer) B. BA, Calif. State U., Fullerton, 1982. Writer, reporter Century Cable, Brea, Calif., 1980-81, Sta. KEZY-AM-FM and Sta. KIKF-FM, Anaheim, Calif., 1981; TV reporter, news writer cameraperson Sta. KOLO-TV, ABC affiliate, Reno, 1981; talk show host Storer & Group Cable TV, Anaheim, 1980-82; intern Donrey Media, Sta. KOLO-TV, Reno, 1982; TV prodn. asst., talk show host Community Cablevision, Newport Beach, Calif., 1982-84, producer, 1987—; tele-mktg. rep. Yale Video, Anaheim, 1987, account exec., 1987—; community cablevision programming coordinator Channel 3, Irvine, Tustin and Newport Beach, Calif., 1984-87. Mem. adv. com. coop. TV acad. Coastline Community Coll. Mem. Women in Communications, Radio, TV and Film Soc. (v.p. 1981-82), Internat. TV Assn., Nat. Fedn. Local Cable Programmers, Orange County Cable Assn. (bd. dirs.). Office: Yale Video 2796 Miraloma Ave Anaheim CA 92806

BRYDON, PATRICIA CAROL, nurse, educator; b. McLeansboro, Ill., Aug. 21, 1947; d. William Albert and Melba Lee (Adams) Moorman; m. James Collins Brydon, May 10, 1973. Diploma in nursing Jewish Hosp. Sch. Nursing, St. Louis, 1968; AA, Saddleback Community Coll., 1976; BSN, Calif. State U.-Fullerton, 1977; MSN, Calif. State U.-Los Angeles, 1980; JD, Western State U., 1988. Cert. critical care nurse, advanced cardiac, pediatric home health care nurse. Surg. nurse Northwestern Meml. Hosp., Chgo., 1968-69; nursing supr. Kingstown Manor, North Kingstown, R.I., 1969-70; pediatric intensive care nurse U. Calif. Med. Center, Orange, 1970-72; critical care Victory Meml. Hosp., Waukegan, Ill., 1972-74; critical care unit nursing supr. Tustin Community Hosp. (Calif.), 1974-79; nursing instr. Golden West Coll., Huntington Beach, Calif., 1980-83, 84—; nurse educator VA Med. Center, Long Beach, Calif., 1983-84; ednl. cons. ACCESS, Corona Del Mar, Calif., 1983-84; pediatric nursing tutor. Author slide-tape program, Swan-Ganz Catheters, 1978; co-author simulated learning on pediatric nursing, 1982. Fundraiser, bd. dirs., vol. Seaside Child Devel. Center, Long Beach, 1983; vol. ARC, Santa Ana, 1979, Orange County Health Planning Council, Tustin, 1977, Make-A-Wish Found., 1983—. Mem. Calif. Assn., Calif. Nurses Assn. Am. Assn. Critical Care Nurses, Nat. Critical Care Inst., Am. Fedn. Tchrs. Democrat. Contbr articles to profl. jours. Home: 307 21st St Huntington Beach CA 92648 Office: Golden West Coll 15744 Golden West St Huntington Beach CA 92640

BRYSON, JO-ANN KNIGHT, health care administrator; b. Newport, R.I., Mar. 25, 1943; d. George K. and Josephine E. (DeRosier) Knight; m. Neil F. Bryson, 1967 (div. 1975); 1 son, Neil Kerry. B.S.Nursing, Boston Coll., 1965; M.S.Nursing, U. R.I., 1974; Ed.D., Internat. Grad. Sch., 1985. Lic. nurse, Ohio, 1977. Staff nurse, supr. U.S. Navy, Newport, 1965-68; instr. Youville Hosp., Cambridge, Mass., 1969-73, U. R.I., Kingston, 1973-75; asst. dir. Decatur Meml. Hosp. (Ill.), 1975-77; dir. sch. nursing Bethesda Hosp., Cin., 1977-85; asst. v.p. profl. services Bethesda Hosps., Inc., Cin., 1986—; cons. in field; mem. ad hoc com. nursing edn. Ohio Bd. Nursing, 1980-83. Bd. dirs. Project Literacy Council of Clermont County, Ohio, 1987—. Author: Cost-Effective Management in Schools of Nursing, 1982; contbr. articles to profl. jours. Mem. Ohio Council Diploma Nurse Educators (chmn. 1980), Assembly of Hosp. Schs. Nursing (mem. governing council 1980-83), Am. Hosp. Assn., Ohio League for Nursing (v.p. 1981-83, mem. steering com. Ohio River Valley council 1981-83), Nat. League for Nursing (mem. bd. 1983-87, chmn. council diploma programs), Phi Kappa Phi. Roman Catholic. Clubs: Boston Coll. Alumni, Moeller High Sch. Mother's (Cin.). Home: 1878 Stockton Dr Loveland OH 45140 Office: Bethesda Hosp Inc 619 Oak St Cincinnati OH 45140

BUAAS, SHARON SHAPIRO, marketing professional; b. Chgo., Jan. 15, 1950; d. Harry H. and Miriam (Gitlin) Shapiro; m. Robert Andrew Buaas, June 22, 1985. BS in Bus. Adminstn., Mktg., So. Ill. U., 1972; certificate in Hyperalimentation, U. Tex., 1979; MBA, Roosevelt U., 1982. Rep. pharm. sales Eli Lilly and Co., Chgo., 1973-76; rep. therapeutic systems Alza Corp., Chgo., 1976-78; mgr. nutrition ter. Am. McGaw, Chgo., 1978-82; account exec. Vicom Assocs., San Francisco, 1982-83; sr. account exec. V. Montegrande and Co., Irvine, Calif., 1983-85; pres. Buaas Corp., Huntington Beach, Calif., 1985—; account supr. Forsythe Marcelli Johnson, Newport Beach, Calif., 1987—. Mem. Med. Mktg. Assn. (San Diego officer 1986), Women in Bus., Bus./Profl. Advt. Assn. (com. chair 1986). Home: 20271 Bancroft Cir Huntington Beach CA 92646 Office: Forsythe Marcelli Johnson 4 Civic Plaza Newport Beach CA 92660

BUBENIK, PATRICIA JEAN HADLE, assistant superintendent; b. Denver, Jan. 12, 1947; d. H. Paul and Allie Hadle; B.A., Colo. State U., 1969; M.A., U. Calif., Santa Cruz, 1970; Ed.D., U. San Francisco, 1981; m. David M. Bubenik, June 21, 1969. Tchr. Madrone Sch., Sunnyvale Sch. Dist. (Calif.), 1970-77; tchr. Demonstration Sch. for Gifted, San Jose State U., 1977; lang. arts specialist Sunnyvale Sch. Dist., 1977-78, vice prin., Madrone Sch., 1978-79, prin. summer sch., 1979, prin. Lakewood Sch., 1979-82; prin. Columbia Community Sch., Sunnyvale, 1982-85; asst. supt. Mountain View Sch. Dist., 1985—; ednl. cons., Calif., 1977—; established Kids Can Write Project; founder Jr. Scribe, dist. wide student mag. Bd. dirs. Calif. Young People's Theatre, Umbrella House; founder Mayor's Youth Council, 1964. Fellow, Bay Area Writing Project, U. Calif., Berkeley, 1978; Boettcher Found. scholar, 1965. Recipient Vol. award Calif. Parks and Recreation Assn., 1983. Mem. Assn. Calif. Sch. Adminstrs. (exec. bd.), Assn. Curriculum and Supervision Devel., Santa Clara Reading Council (exec. bd.), Calif. Reading Assn., Nat. Council Tchrs. English, Calif. Assn. Gifted, Calif. Assn. Tchrs. English, Internat. Reading Assn., Am. Assn. Sch. Adminstrs., Phi Delta Kappa, Phi Beta Kappa, Phi Kappa Phi, Phi Sigma Iota. Club: Women Leaders in Edn. Author: A New Direction: Focusing on the Whole Person Through the Affective Domain, 1977; Effects of Principal-Delivered Written Positive Reinforcement on Teacher and Class Behavior, 1981. Office: 220 View St Mountain View CA 94041

BUBNIC, ANNE MARIE, university adminstrator; b. Springfield, Mass., Jan. 17, 1949; d. Stephen Borowiec and Marcelle (Denis) Weitzel; m. Brian J. Bubnic, May 23, 1979. BS in Biology and Chemistry, Coll. of Our Lady of the Elms, Chicopee, Mass., 1970; MPA, U. San Francisco, 1987. Cert. fund raising exec. Med. tech. Monson State Hosp., Palmer, Mass., 1970; biochemist Purdue U., W. Lafayette, Ind., 1970-73; indsl. microbiologist Hazleton Labs., Vienna, Va., 1974-75; med. tech. No. Va. Tng. Ctr., Fairfax, 1975-76; research physiologist Cutter Labs., Berkeley, Calif., 1977-82; exec. dir. Nat. Found. Ileitis and Colitis, San Francisco, 1982-87; dir. sustaining gifts U. San Francisco, 1987—. Contbr. articles to profl. jours. Pres. Nat. Found. for Ileitis and Colitis, 1982; bd. dirs. Self-Help Clearing House of the Bay Area, San Francisco, 1982-86. Recipient Grad. Student Research award 1988. Mem. AAUW, Nat. Soc. Fund Raising Execs. (bd. dirs. 1987—, Abel Hanson award 1986, 87, Pres.'s award 1988, Founder's award 1988), Am. Soc. Assn. Execs., Nat. Assn. Female Execs., Soc. Nonprofit Orgns., Women in Computing, Community Entrepreneurs Orgn., Nat. Assn. Desk Top Pubs. Democrat. Lodge: Zonta. Home: 3 Oak Forest Rd Novato CA 94949 Office: U San Francisco Office Devel Cowell Hall #400 San Francisco CA 94117

BUCHANAN, BRENDA J., computer manufacturing executive; b. San Diego; d. Fred and Annie M. (Winston) B. BS in Math., Physics and Chemistry, U. Denver; MA in Math., Washington U., 1973; postgrad. McGill U., 1973-75, U. Cologne, Fed. Republic Germany. Math. instr. Washington U., St. Louis, 1969-71; programmer/analyst United Aircraft of Can., Longueil, Que., 1971-73; ops. research analyst Consol. Bathurst Ltd., Montreal, Que., 1973-76; corp. new product planning mgr. Digital Equipment Corp., Maynard, Mass., 1976-80, new product program mgr., Springfield, Mass., 1980-84, tapes bus. mgr., 1984-88, corp. purchasing program office mgr., dist. mfg. ops., Northboro, Mass., 1988—; mem. Digital Equipment Women's Adv. Com., 1986—. Leader, Can. Girl Guides, Montreal, 1972-74; mem. mayor's blue ribbon com. Dept. Pub. Works, Springfield, 1983. Fulbright fellow, Fed. Rep. Germany; recipient Experiment in Internat. Living award Fed. Republic Germany, 19. Mem. Can. Ops. Research Soc., League of Women Voters (treas. 1984-86), Alpha Kappa Alpha (Basileus, Ivy of Yr., Denver chpt.). Democrat. Baptist. Club: Links, Inc. (Springfield) (treas. 1984-86). Home: 4E Strathmore Shire PO Box 49 North Uxbridge MA 01538 Office: Digital Equipment Corp 3 Results Way Marlboro MA 01752-9103

BUCHANAN, CAROLYN SUSAN, advertising and marketing account executive; b. Maryville, Mo., May 14, 1957; d. Lawrence Vincent and Margaret Marie (Lawrence) Barmann; m. Richard Neal Buchanan, July 2, 1983; 1 child, Neal Lawrence. BS in Edn., NW Mo. State U., 1978; MS in Mass Communication, U. S.C., 1982. Media planner, buyer Brewer Advt., Kansas City, Mo., 1979-81; grad. asst. Coll. Journalism U. S.C., Columbia, 1981-82; media planner Henderson Advt., Greenville, S.C., 1983-84; account exec. Newman Saylor & Gregory, Columbia, S.C., 1984—. Mem. Columbia Advt. Club. Office: Newman Saylor & Gregory 2817 Millwood Ave Columbia SC 29205

BUCHANAN, DIANNE JEAN JOHNSON, human resources executive; b. Harvey, Ill., Sept. 12, 1948; d. Virgil Albert and Jean (Armstrong) J; m. Dennis Michael Buchanan, May 7, 1988. BBA in Mktg., U. Tex., 1970. Mktg. research asst. Belden Assocs., Dallas, 1970-72; personnel staff Meisel Photochrome Co., Dallas, 1972-75; personnel staff Geosource, Inc., Houston, 1975-77, corp. compensation specialist, 1977-78; personnel officer, compensation and benefits mgr. Capital Bank, Houston, 1978-79; compensation specialist Anderson Clayton & Co., Houston, 1979-81, dir. human resources Ranger Ins. subs., 1981-84, corp. compensation dir., 1984-87; v.p. human resources NBC Bank, Houston, 1987—. Mem. assoc. vestry Saint John the Divine Ch., Houston, 1983; bd. dirs. Meadowbriar Home for Girls, Houston, 1978-79. Mem. Houston Compensation Assn. (dir. 1983-87, pres. 1985-86, v.p. 1984-85), Houston Personnel Assn. (com. 1982-84), Am. Soc. Personnel Adminstrs., Am. Compensation Assn. (com. 1983, 85-87). Club: River Oaks Breakfast (Houston) (v.p. membership sect. 1988). Office: NBC Bank-Houston 3800 N Washington Ave Houston TX 77007

BUCHANAN, EDNA, journalist; b. Paterson, N.J.. Journalist Miami Beach (Fla.) Daily Sun, 1965-70, The Miami (Fla.) Herald, 1970—. Author: Carr: Five Years of Rape and Murder, 1979, The Corpse Had a Familiar Face: Covering America's Hottest Beat, 1987; contbr. articles to Family Circle mag., Cosmopolitan mag., Rolling Stone mag. Recipient Green Eye Shade award Soc. Profl. Journalists, 1982, Pulitzer prize for gen. reporting, 1986. Mem. United Ch. of Christ. Office: The Miami Herald One Herald Plaza Miami FL 33101

BUCHANAN, SUSAN SHAVER, publishing company executive; b. Tuscaloosa, Ala., Mar. 24, 1954; d. Frederick Thomas Shaver and Gussie Parker (Wingard) Gibbons; m. Roger N. Buchanan, Apr. 11, 1981; children: Sarah Anne, Ryan Frederick. BS, Auburn U., 1976. Programmer analyst So. Ry., Atlanta, 1976-80; database cons. Applied Data Research, Atlanta, 1980-81; data adminstr. McGraw-Hill, Hightstown, N.J., 1981—, dir. data adminstrn., sr. dir. corp. systems devel., sr. dir. customer service, v.p. info. tech. resources, 1987—; cons. data adminstr. Pvt. Sector Council, Washington, 1986—.

BUCHANAN, VIRGINIA LOUISE, purchases and contracts agent; b. Winfield, Kans., Nov. 17, 1945; d. Harley Bruce and Barbara Louise (Briscoe) Parsons; m. Enrique Escobar, May 20, 1968 (div. Dec. 1972); m. John Edward Buchanan, Mar. 15, 1980; stepchildren—Teresa C., David M. B.A. cum laude, Southwestern Coll., 1967; M.S., Emporia State U., 1969. Prof., U. Industrial de Santander, Bucaramanga, Colombia, 1968-70; tchr. English, Bi-Nat. Ctr., Bogotá, Colombia, 1970-72; campaign sec. Putnam Community Hosp., Carmel, N.Y., 1972-73; legal sec. Arent, Fox, et al, Washington, 1973-75; contract mgr. Devel. Alternatives, Washington, 1975-81; contracts and purchases agt. Bechtel Petroleum, Houston, 1981-86; sr. technical aide gas contracts Stone & Webster Mgmt. Cons., Houston, 1988—. Emporia State U. fellow, 1967-69. Mem. Nat. Contract Mgmt. Assn. (chpt. sec. 1983-86, chpt. pres. 1987—), Am. Rose Soc., Phi Beta Tau. Methodist. Home: 14203 Stokesmount Dr Houston TX 77077

BUCHBINDER, SHARON BELL, professional association executive assistant, health researcher; b. Washington, Nov. 27, 1951; d. James Wright and Effie Naomi (Rhodes) Bell; m. Dale Buchbinder, May 9, 1976; 1 child, Joshua. BA in Psychology, U. Conn., 1973; MA in Psychology, U. Hartford, 1976; AAS in Nursing, SUNY, Albany, 1981; postgrad., U. Ill., Chgo., 1986—. RN. Intravenous technician Harford (Conn.) Hosp., 1974-76; supr. Albany Med. Ctr. Hosp., 1976-80; asst. research scientist N.Y. Dept. Mental Hygiene, Albany, 1980-81; staff specialist Nat. Commn. on Nursing, Chgo., 1982-83, Am. Hosp. Assn., Chgo., 1983-84; sr. research assoc. AMA, Chgo., 1984-86, exec. asst., 1986—. Contbr. articles to profl. jours. Recipient research grant Mut. Life Ins. Co. of N.Y., 1986. Mem. N.Y. Acad. of Scis., Nat. Assn. for Female Execs., Am. Pub. Health Assn., The Cat Fanciers Assn. Inc. (breed council sec. 1984-86). Democrat. Jewish. Office: AMA 535 N Dearborn St Chicago IL 60610

BUCHENHORNER, MARIANNE, psychotherapist, psychoanalyst; b. Budapest, Hungary, Sept. 15; d. Tibor and Agnes Aczel (Marks) de Nagy; B.A., Vassar Coll.; M.S.W., Columbia U., 1966; cert. in psychotherapy and psychoanalysis Postgrad. Center for Mental Health, 1975, cert. mental health cons., 1976, cert. in supervision, 1977; m. Walter Buchenhorner, Aug. 16, 1965. Research asst., librarian Psychoanalytic Inst., Columbia U., N.Y.C., 1960-61; asst. to dir. of social sci. and humanities textbooks McGraw Hill Co., N.Y.C., 1961-63; case aide Youth House, N.Y.C., 1963-64; social worker Community Service Service Soc. N.Y.C., 1966-69; supr. State U. Hosp., Bklyn., 1969-71; dir. Multiple Service Center, Big Bros. Inc., N.Y.C., 1971-72; dir. counseling services Postgrad. Center for Mental Health, N.Y.C., 1976-81, tchr., 1974—, supr., pvt. practice psychotherapy, N.Y.C. Mem. Nat. Assn. Social Workers, Soc. Clin. Social Work Psychotherapists, Postgrad. Psychoanalytic Soc. Office: 200 E 33rd St New York NY 10016

BUCHERRE, VERONIQUE, development company executive, international cultural consultant; b. Casablanca, Morocco, Nov. 20, 1951; came to U.S., 1967; d. Maurice Daniel Bucherre and Lucette Jaqueline Piani; m. Douglas Lee Frazier. Diploma Para Profesores, Gregorio Maranon, Madrid, 1972; MA, San Francisco State U., 1974; PhD, U. Paris, 1980; diploma in conf. interpreting, London Sch. of Poly., 1983. Instr. French Peace Corps, Baker, La., 1968; editorial asst. Newsweek mag., San Francisco, 1970-72; mem. faculty San Francisco State U., 1972-74, 77; conf. interpreter-translator, France and U.S., 1974-85; rural developer, France and U.S., 1976-86; pres. Bucherre & Assocs., Washington, 1985-88, inventor The Rainbank Group, 1988—; bd. dirs. Rainbank Project; pres. Rainbank Group Ltd.; bd. dirs. Rainbank Group Ltd.; mem. bd. mgmt. Institut des Hautes Etudes de L'Amerique Latine, Paris, 1975-76; mem. Lab III, Centre National de Recherche Scientifique, Paris, 1975-77; mem. Interamerican Def. Inst. Civilian Personnel Assn. (pres. 1988—). Author: Florence, 1979, Uruguay, 1980. Club: Droit Humain, G.I.T.E. (Paris).

BUCHHOLZ, CAROLYN LEIGH, lawyer; b. Boulder, Colo., Dec. 10, 1955, d. Glen Elvis and Alice Joy (McIntosh); m. Roger Alan Buchholz, Oct. 4, 1980; B.A. cum laude, Middlebury Coll., 1978; J.D., U. Colo., 1981. Bar: Colo. 1981, U.S. Dist. Ct. Colo. 1981, Mont. 1988. Research asst. Rocky Mountain Mineral Law Found., Boulder, Colo., 1979-80; assoc. firm Sisk, Foley, Hultin, & Driver, Denver, 1981-83, Hultin, Driver & Spaanstra, Denver, 1983-85, Hultin & Spaanstra, Denver, 1985-86; asst. atty. gen. Colo. Dept. of Law, Denver, 1986-88; assoc. Cogswell & Wehrli, Denver, 1988—; mem., atty. program to provide legal services to indigent, Denver, 1982-86. Mem. procedural rules subcom. Colo. Air Quality Control Commn., 1983-84; mem. Lafayette (Colo.) City Council, 1987—. Mem. ABA, Colo. Bar Assn., Denver Bar Assn. (legal fees arbitration com. 1983-84), Am. Bus. Women's Assn, Lafayette Planning Commission, Lafayette Louisville Downtown Revitalization, Inc. (pres. 1986—), Boulder County Long Range Planning Commn. Alliance Profl. Women (bd. dirs. 1986—). Democrat. Methodist.

BUCHHOLZ-SHAW, DONNA MARIE, immunologist; b. Chgo., May 27, 1950; d. Arthur George and Doris Hedwig (Lewis) B. BS in Biol. Sci., Quincy Coll., 1972; Assoc. in Law (hon.), Loyola U., Chgo., 1974; MS in Microbiology and Immunology, U. Ill. Med. Ctr., 1975, PhD in Microbiology and Immunology, 1978. Post-doctoral researcher Argonne (Ill.) Nat. Labs., 1978-80; research info. scientist Abbott Labs., Abbott Park, Ill., 1980-82, project mgr., 1982-85, sr. project mgr., 1985-87, ops. mgr. thrombolytics venture, 1987—; faculty Northeastern Ill. U., Chgo., 1984—. Editor: Developments in Industrial Microbiology, 1983, 84; contbr. articles to profl. jours. Mem. nat. sci. and engring. com. Exploring Div. Boy Scouts Am., 1983— (mem. exec. bd. northeast Ill. council 1988—), Citizens Adv. Com. Du Page Airport, West Chicago, Ill., 1984—, West Chicago Energy Commn., 1985. Recipient award Am. Assn. Immunology, 1980—, Woman of Achievement award YWCA, 1987, Abbott Labs. Presdl. awards, 1984, 88. Fellow Am. Acad. Microbiology; mem. Am. Soc. Microbiology, Soc. for Indsl. Microbiology, Ill. Soc. for Microbiology (council), Sigma Xi (pres. 1984, mem. program initiatives com. 1985—, mem. regional nominating com. 1985—, mem. nat. nominating com. 1985—, head centennial planning com. 1986, mem. membership at large com., research award 1975). Home: 1329 E Canton Ct Deerfield IL 60015 Office: Thrombolytics Venture D48N AP9 Abbott Labs Abbott Park IL 60064

BUCHIN, JEAN, psychologist; b. N.Y.C., Aug. 15, 1920; d. Mac and Celia Jacobs; B.A., City U. N.Y., 1941; M.A., Tchrs. Coll. Columbia U., 1948; Ph.D., NYU, 1965; m. May 18, 1941; children—Peter J., John D. Tchr., N.Y.C. Pub. Schs., 1946-59, part time 1959-62; counselor, asst. prof. CUNY, 1962—; asst. prof. coordinator Which Way With Women program Baruch Coll., 1980-82; vis. asst. prof. N.Y.U., 1969-72; cons. N.Y.C. Tchrs. Consortium, 1981-85; tng. cons. Met. Life Ins. Co., N.Y.C., 1985—; tng. cons. Met. Life , Fordham; lectr., cons., leader workshops. NYU, Queens Coll., Marymount Manhattan Coll., A.W.E.D., Washington Sq. Coll. fellow, 1961-62. Mem. Am. Psychol. Assn. (pres. Tri State chpt. Div. 35, 1977—), Am. Assn. Counseling and Devel., Met. N.Y Assn. for Applied Psychology, Bus. and Profl. Women, AAUP. Club: Muttontown Golf and Country. Author: Singular Parent, 1982.

BUCHMAN, MARION, poet, educator; b. Balt.; d. Jacob Solomon and Mildred (Valinski) Friedmond. Poetry reader Rider Coll., Trenton, N.J., 1963; instr. prosody Community Coll. Balt., 1970, Am. U., Washington, 1976, Johns Hopkins U., Balt., 1976-82, Balt. Free U., 1976-82. Author: A Voice in Ramah, 1960, America, 1976, In His Pavilion, 1986; contbr. numerous poems to mags., newspapers, anthologies, jours. including The N.Y. Times, Md. Eng. Jour., Ariz. Quar., Poet Lore, Stanza, Cats, Poetry View, Redbook. Recipient Cheltenham prize Arts Council Gt. Britain, John Masefield award, Al Di La prize Franklin Coll. Switzerland, Golden Poet award. Mem. Poetry Soc. Am. (awards 1978—), London Poetry Secretariat, Poetry Soc. G.B., N.Y. Poetry Forum, Nat. Fedn. State Poetry Socs., Md. Council English Tchrs. (hon.), Nat. Council Tchrs. English (affiliate), Author's Guild Am., Author's League Am. Home: 5955 D Pimlico Rd Baltimore MD 21209 Office: Haskell House Pubs Ltd 1533 60th St Brooklyn NY 11219

BUCHMANN, MOLLY O'BANION, choreographer, ballet educator; b. Baton Rouge, Nov. 22, 1949; d. James Dennis and Annie Laurie (Joffrion) O'Banion; m. Fred J. Buchmann, Aug. 23, 1969; children: F. Jason, Dennis Andrew. BS in Secondary Edn., La. State U., 1971, MS in Dance, 1973. Artistic dir. Baton Rouge Ballet Theatre, 1976—; choreographer Baton Rouge Little Theatre, 1983—; instr. dance Baton Rouge Magnet High Sch., 1979-85; owner, mgr. The Dancers' Workshop, Baton Rouge, 1973—; dir. dance Scotlandville Magnet High Sch., 1986—; vis. artist Arts and Humanities Council of Greater Baton Rouge, 1976; choreographer Aubin Lane Dinner Theatre, Baton Rouge, 1980-82; mem. cultural caucus steering com. La. State Div. of Arts, cons., 1986; spokesperson Friends of La. Broadcasting. Editor La. Dance News, 1976-77. Choreographer numerous ballets. State of La. Div. Arts Choreographic grant, 1982; Baton Rouge Alumni Fedn. scholar, 1967. Mem. Southwest Regional Ballet Assn. (bd. dirs., sec. 1984—). Democrat. Roman Catholic. Avocations: performing, resting, reading. Office: Dancers' Workshop 3875 Government St Baton Rouge LA 70806

BUCHS, PATRICIA ELLEN, social worker; b. Hicksville, N.Y., Nov. 30, 1954; d. Charles George and Viola Ella (Krass) B. AA, Grand Rapids (Mich.) Jr. Coll., 1976; BS in Edn., Cen. Mich. U., 1978. Lab technician Davis Dental Labs., Grand Rapids, 1973-74; intern Grand Rapids Police Dept., 1975-76; mgr. concessions Grand Rapids Pub. Schs., 1974-82; juvenile group worker Kent County Child Haven, Grand Rapids, 1981-87, supr. juvenile group workers, 1987—. Umpire Mich. High Sch. Athletic Assn., Lansing, 1974—; coach Grand Rapids Pub. Schs., 1978—; playground supr. Grand Rapids Recreation Dept., 1974-81; CPR and first aid instr. Kent County Red Cross, Grand Rapids, 1986—; motorcycle instr., 1987—. Mem.

Kent County Employees Union (asst. steward 1984—, del. 1984-87), Mich. Assn. Children's Alliances. Republican. Methodist. Home: 3161 Taft SW Wyoming MI 49509

BUCHWALD, NAOMI REICE, federal magistrate; b. Kingston, N.Y., Feb. 14, 1944; BA cum laude, Brandeis U., 1965; LLB, cum laude, Columbia U., 1968. Bar: N.Y. 1968, U.S. Ct. Appeals (2d cir.) 1969, U.S. Dist. Ct. (so. and ea. dists.) N.Y. 1970, U.S. Supreme Ct. 1978. Litigation assoc. Marshall, Bratter, Greene, Allison & Tucker, N.Y.C., 1968-73; asst. U.S. atty. So. Dist. N.Y., 1973-80, dep. chief civil div., 1976-79, chief civil div., 1979-80; U.S. magistrate U.S. Dist. Ct. (so. dist.) N.Y., N.Y.C., 1980—. Recipient spl. citation FDA Commrs., 1978. Mem. ABA, Fed. Bar Council (v.p. 1982-84), Assn. of Bar of City of N.Y., N.Y. State Bar Assn., Phi Beta Kappa, Omicron Delta Epsilon. Editor, Columbia Jour. Law and Social Problems, 1967-68. Office: US Courthouse Foley Sq New York NY 10007

BUCK, ALISON JENNIFER, writer, marketing professional; b. Bangor, Maine, Dec. 11, 1952; d. George Hill and Anna (Komisaruk) B. BS, U. Maine, Orono, 1974; MA, Brigham Young U., 1978. Cert. tchr., Maine, Mass. Vol. program coordinator Head Start/Hampshire Community Action Commn., Northampton, Mass., 1980; career edn. specialist, job developer Hampshire Ednl. Collaborative, Northampton, 1981; documentation specialist Amherst (Mass.) Assocs., 1981-84; sr. tech. writer Visual Intelligence Corp., Amherst, 1984-85; tech. documentation specialist Video Communications Inc., Feeding Hills, Mass., 1986-87; contract tech. writer Digital Equipment Corp., Westfield, Mass., 1987; mktg. coordinator, tech. publs. mgr. Millitech Corp., South Deerfield, Mass., 1988. Co-author: The Coffee Maker Cookbook, 1988. Mem. Soc. for Tech. Communication. Democrat.

BUCK, BARBARA JAMISON, chemical company executive; b. Pitts., Sept. 21, 1951; d. George Gale and Mary Jane (Butler) Jamison; BSChemE, Carnegie-Mellon U., 1973; m. John Ashley Buck, May 19, 1973; Process design engr. Union Carbide Corp., Tarrytown, N.Y., 1973-75, sales engr., Tarrytown, 1975-77, asst. region sales mgr., 1977-79, asst. to v.p., bus. analyst, N.Y.C., 1979-81, product mgr. custom catalysts, Danbury, Conn., 1981-82, mgr. fin. analysis and planning, 1982-84, product mgr. engring. polymers, 1985-88, mgr. product mgmt. and ops. planning Amoco Performance Products Inc. div. Amoco Chems. (formerly Union Carbide Corp.), Ridgefield, Conn. 1986—. Mem. Soc. Women Engrs. (chmn. nat. conv. 1980, mem. adv. com. nat. conv. 1980, 81, 82, exec. com. 1982-83, nat. conv. treas. 1986), Delta Delta Delta. Office: Amoco Performance Products Inc Ridgefield CT 06877

BUCK, BETH MARIE, accountant; b. Pitts., Mar. 6, 1955; d. Attlee Gay and Rebecca Elizabeth (Mewha) Shinaberry; m. William Richard Buck, June 25, 1977. BSBA summa cum laude, Robert Morris Coll., 1977; MS in Fin., Carnegie Mellon U., 1987. CPA, Pa. Sr. auditor Coopers & Lybrand, Pitts., 1977-81; mgr. spl. project H.J. Heinz Co., Pitts., 1981-86; dir. fin. Physicians Health Plan, Pitts., 1987—; cons. Mellon Bank, 1987. Mem. fin. com. Muryo Dance Group, Pitts. Mem. Am. Inst. CPA's, Nat. Assn. Accts. Club: Toastmasters. Office: Physicians Health Plan 5700 Corporate Dr Pittsburgh PA 15237

BUCK, KATHLEEN ANN, lawyer; b. South Bend, Ind., Nov. 14, 1948; d. Betty Jo and Cecil and Betty Jo (Parfitt) B.; m. Raymond Donald Battocchi, Aug. 20, 1975; 1 son, Adam. B.A. cum laude, St. Mary's Coll., Notre Dame, Ind., 1970; J.D., Ind. U., 1973; student U. Iberoamericana, Mexico City, 1968. Bar: D.C., Fla. Trial atty. F.R.L.S., Delray Beach, Fla., 1973-75; atty. Swift & Co., Washington, 1975-77; atty., asst. dir. govt. relations Esmark, Inc., Washington, 1977-81; asst. gen. counsel U.S. Dept. Def., Washington, 1981-86; gen. counsel USAF, Washington, 1986-87, Dept. Defense, Washington, 1987—. mem. Def. Privacy Bd., 1981—. Bd. dirs. Va. Fedn. Republican Women, 1979-81; mem. Fairfax County Rep. Com., 1978-81; Republican precinct capt., Great Falls, Va., 1978-81; mem. Great Falls Citizens Assn. Mem. ABA, D.C. Bar, Fla. Bar, Women in Govt. Relations (Most Disting. Mem. 1979), Pi Sigma Alpha. Clubs: Capitol Hill Equestrian Soc. Home: 10120 Forest Brook Ln Great Falls VA 22066 Office: Dept of Defense Gen Counsel The Pentagon Washington DC 20330

BUCK, LINDA DEE, executive recruiting company executive; b. San Francisco, Nov. 8, 1946; d. Sol and Shirley D. (Setterberg) Press; student Coll. San Mateo (Calif.), 1969-70; divorced. Head hearing and appeals br. Dept. Navy Employee Relations Service, Philippines, 1974-75; dir. personnel Homestead Savs. & Loan Assn., Burlingame, Calif., 1976-77; mgr. fin. placement VIP Agy., Inc., Palo Alto, Calif., 1977-78; exec. v.p., dir. Sequent Personnel Services, Inc., Mountain View, Calif., 1978-83; Founder, pres. Buck & Co., San Mateo, 1983—. Publicity mgr. for No. Calif., Osteogenesis Imperfecta Found. Inc., 1970-72; cons. Am. Brittle Bone Soc., 1979-88. Mem. Nat. Assn. Personnel Cons., Calif. Assn. Personnel Cons. Jewish. Office: Buck and Co 100 S Ellsworth Ave 9th Floor San Mateo CA 94401

BUCK, NANCY MARGARET TIMMA, accountant, bank executive; b. Seattle, June 16, 1945; d. Guy Church and Nancy L. (Fraser) B.; m. George L. Wittenburg (div. May 1972); 1 child, Guy Charles. Student, Stephens Coll., 1963-64. Legal adminstr. Mullen, McCaughey & Henzell, Santa Barbara, Calif., 1965-67; trust adminstr. First Interstate Bank of Calif., Santa Barbara, 1974-84; pres., owner, acct. N.T.B. Exec. Service, Santa Barbara, 1984-87; chief fin. officer Montecito Pump Protection Systems, Santa Barbara, 1987—; chief fin. officer Specialty Crane Corp., Santa Barbara, 1985—; trustee pvt. trusts, 1984—; mem. Continuing Edn. Bar. Mem. Hospice of Santa Barbara, 1987—. Mem. Am. Inst. Banking, Nat. Assn. Female Execs. Republican. Episcopalian. Club: Santa Barbara Assocs., University (Santa Barbara).

BUCK, NATALIE SMITH, former state ofcl.; b. Carlsbad, N.Mex., Jan. 10, 1923; d. Milton R. and Rosa Adele (Binford) Smith; student Coll. William and Mary, 1940-41; B.B.S., U. Colo., 1943; postgrad. U. Tex., 1945-46; m. C. B. Buck, Sept. 12, 1948; children—Warren Z., Barbara Anne. Chief clk., State Senate, N.Mex., 1951-53; sec. of state, N.Mex., 1955-59; chief personnel adminstr. N.Mex. Health and Social Services Dept., 1959-73. Democrat. Home: 108 W Alicante Rd Santa Fe NM 87501

BUCKARDT, CINDY SUE, purchaser; b. Valentine, Nebr., Nov. 14, 1962; d. Harry Walter and Alice Marie (Prang) Hayward; m. David Lee Buckardt, Aug. 20, 1983. BS, U. Wyo., 1984. Dir. purchasing Colo. Precast Concrete, Inc., Loveland, 1980—. Mem. Nat. Assn. Women in Constrn., Nat. Assn. Female Execs., Nat. Precast Concrete Assn., Colo. Precast Concrete Assn. (sec. 1985—), Kappa Delta. Republican. Methodist. Home: 127 Ranae Dr Loveland CO 80537 Office: Colo Precast Concrete Inc 1820 SE 14th St Loveland CO 80537

BUCKINGHAM, KAREN WEBSTER, marketing executive; b. Balt., Nov. 10, 1956; d. Milton Worthington and Marguerite (Sweeney) Webster; m. William Andrew Buckingham Jr., June 26, 1981. BS cum laude, U. Balt., 1985. Cert. Fin. Planner. Administrv. asst. Md. Nat. Corp., Balt., 1977-79, exec. asst. to chmn., 1979-85; v.p., dir. of mktg. The Plan First Co., Cockeysville, Md., 1985-87; dir. mktg. PSA Fin. Ctr., Lutherville, Md., 1988—. Contbr. articles to profl. jours. Bd. dirs. Balt. Chamber Opera, 1986-87. Mem. Internat. Assn. for Fin. Planning (bd. dirs. Balt. chpt. 1984—), U. Balt. Alumni Found., Inst. Cert. Fin. Planners. Democrat. Episcopalian. Club: Center (Balt.). Office: PSA Fin Ctr 1304 Bellona Ave Lutherville MD 21093

BUCKLES-DEANS, DELORA ELIZABETH, educational diagnostician, consultant; b. Houston, Apr. 19, 1940; d. Joseph Bernhardt and Helen Elizabeth (Phillips) Blazek; m. Richard George Buckles, June 26, 1962 (div. Oct. 1969); children—Gregory, Deborah; m. 2d, Harry Alexander Deans, Jan. 1, 1975; 1 dau., Catherine; stepchildren—Laurie, Daniel, Melissa, Andrew. B.A., U. Tex., 1962; postgrad. Cornell U., 1962; M.Ed., Boston U., 1966, cert. advanced grad. study, 1966; Ed.D., U. Houston, 1981. Instr., Boston U., 1964-66; coordinator Harris County Dept. Edn., Houston, 1969-72; dir. resource services Klein Ind. Sch. Dist., Spring, Tex., 1972-75; coordinator, ednl. diagnostician area 6 Houston Ind. Sch. Dist., 1975-78; inservice coordinator Coll. Edn. U. Houston, 1979-81; ednl. diagnostician Vocat. Evaluation Ctr. for Handicapped, Houston, 1981-84; coordinator ednl./vocat. evaluation Houston Ind. Sch. Dist., 1984-86; cons. Aldine Ind. Sch. Dist., Houston, 1981-82, Harlingen Ind. Sch. Dist. (Tex.), 1982-83, Humble Ind. Sch. Dist., 1986—, ednl. diagnostician, 1986—; adj. prof. U. Houston at Clearlake, 1984—. Contbr. articles to profl. jours.; patentee in field. Campaign worker Democratic Party Tex., Houston, 1979-86. Named Outstanding Student, U. Tex., Austin, 1962. Mem. Council Ednl. Diagnostics Services (sec. 1981-83), Tex. Council Exceptional Children (chmn. 1980-82), Tex. Ednl. Diagnostics Assn. (pres. 1981-82), Tex. Div. for Career Devel. (pres. 1986—), Phi Delta Kappa, Zeta Tau Alpha. Democrat. Episcopalian. Home: 1931 Wroxton St Houston TX 77005

BUCKLEY, ANNA PATRICIA, state legislator; b. Brockton, Mass., Mar. 21, 1924; d. Michael and Ann (Fitzmaurice) Hernan; m. Daniel J. Buckley, 1946; children—Kevin Michael, Daniel J., Paul, Patrice, Nancy J. Grad. Williams Sch. Bus., 1943. Telephone operator New Eng. Telephone Co., 1945-56, sec., 1956-57; broker Fitzgerald Ins. Agy., Brockton, 1957-63; adminstrv. asst. to lt. gov. Mass., 1963-65, to Mass. auditor, 1965-72; councilperson-at-large Brockton City Council, Mass., 1971-72; mem. Mass. Senate, Boston, 1973—. Active Plymouth County Democratic League, Mass., 1956—; mem. Mass. Dem. State Com., 1960—; mem. Dem. Nat. Com.; del. Dem. Nat. Conv., 1980. Served with WAC, 1943-45. Recipient Legislator of Yr. award Mass. Mcpl. Assn., 1982. Roman Catholic. Office: Mass Senate State Capitol Boston MA 02133 Address: 213 W Harvard St Brockton MA 02401 *

BUCKLEY, HILDA MAYER, textiles and apparel educator; b. Gondelsheim, Federal Republic of Germany, Nov. 16, 1948; arrived in U.S., 1951; d. John and Mary (Zugay) Mayer; 1 child, Aaron John; m. Edward William Lakner, July 9, 1983. BS, Mt. Mary Coll., 1970; MS, U. Wis., Madison, 1972, PhD, 1979. Asst. personnel mgr. Evans-Singer Women's Apparel, Milw., 1967-70; librarian psychology library U. Wis., Madison, 1971-72; instr. U. Ill. at Urbana-Champaign, 1975-79, asst. prof., 1979-85, assoc. prof., 1985—; seminar leader, 1984—. mem. editorial bd. Home Econs. Research Jour., 1982-84, 86—, Clothing and Textiles Research Jour., 1983-87; contbr. articles to profl. jours. USDA grantee 1976—, U. Ill. Research Bd. grantee, 1980-81, USIA grantee, 1986—. Mem. AAAS, Assn. Coll. Profs. of Textiles and Clothing (mem. various coms. 1977—, pres. cen. region 1984-85, counselor, 1985, nat. sec. 1986—), Am. Home Econs. Assn. (mem. various coms. 1984—), Am. Psychol. Assn., Assn. for Consumer Research, The Costume Soc. of America, Acad. Mktg. Sci., Midwest Psychol. Assn., Omicron Nu, Sigma Delta Upsilon, Sigma Xi. Roman Catholic. Office: U Ill 905 S Goodwin Ave Urbana IL 61801

BUCKLEY, LORRAINE MADSEN, biology educator; b. Memphis, Feb. 22, 1953; d. Grant Chesley and Doris Virginia (Christenbury) Madsen; m. Jay Benedict Buckley, June 27, 1980; 1 child, Crystal Dawn. BS, U. Tenn., 1976; MS, La. State U., 1979. Instr. lab. Biology Dept. U. Tenn., Martin, 1975-76, Zoology and Physiology Dept. La. State U., Baton Rouge, 1976-79; asst. research Mus. Natural History La. State U., Baton Rouge, 1978-79; curatorial technician Bernice P. Bishop Mus., Honolulu, 1979-81; research and adminstrv. asst. Hawaiian Shrimp Co., Honolulu, 1980-81; instr. Chapman Coll., Pearl Harbor, Hawaii, 1980-81; instr., marine coordinator Windward Community Coll., Kaneohe, Hawaii, 1980-84; marine sci. specialist Blue Water Marine Lab. U. Hawaii, Honolulu, 1982; instr. biology Jackson (Tenn.) State Community Coll., 1984—; assoc. investigator Hawaiian Backyard Aquaculture Program, Kaneohe, 1983-84; staff mem. Maui Underwater Transect Workshop U. Hawaii, 1983, 84; capt. dive team Data Acquisition Project, Puako, Hawaii, 1983. Contbr. articles on aquaculture, botany, ichthyology and behavioral ecology to profl. jours. Judge Hawaii Sci. Fair, 1980-84, county/city sci. fairs, Jackson, 1985—; mem. membership com. YMCA, Jackson, 1986—. Marine edn. grantee Sea Grant Agy., 1982-84; recipient cert. appreciation marine and aquaculture edn. Marine Option Program U. Hawaii, 1984. Mem. Am. Soc. Ichthyologists and Herpetologists, Animal Behavior Soc., Assn. Southeastern Biologists, Audubon Soc., Tenn. Acad. Sci. Office: Jackson State Community Coll 2046 North Pkwy Jackson TN 38301

BUCKLEY, PRISCILLA LANGFORD, magazine editor; b. N.Y.C., Oct. 17, 1921; d. William Frank and Aloise (Steiner) B. B.A., Smith Coll., 1943. Copy girl, sports writer U.P., N.Y.C., 1944; radio rewrite U.P., 1944-47; corr. U.P., Paris, France, 1953-56; news editor Sta. WACA, Camden, S.C., 1947-48; reports officer CIA, Washington, 1951-53; with Nat. Review mag., N.Y.C., 1956—; mng. editor Nat. Review mag., 1959-86, sr. editor, 1986—; Mem. U.S. Adv. Commn. Pub. Diplomacy, 1984—. Columnist: One Woman's Voice Syndicate, 1976-80. Club: Sharon (Conn.) Country (sec. 1973-77, pres. 1978-80). Home: Great Elm Sharon CT 06069 Office: Nat Review 150 E 35th St New York NY 10016

BUCKNELL, SARAH J., nurse; b. Belleville, Ill., Sept. 23, 1960; d. Roger W. and Betty Ann (Krummerich) Bucknell. BS in Nursing, Ill. Wesleyan U., 1982; MS, No. Ill. U., 1986. Staff nurse Swedish Am. Hosp., Rockford, Ill., 1982-86; clin. specialist perinatal Rockford Meml. Hosp., 1986—. Mem. Ch. Choir, Rockford. Mem. Am. Nurses Assn., Ill. Nurses Assn. (bd. dirs. 1986—, pub. chmn. 1986—), Nurses' Assn. Am. Coll. Obstetricians/Gynecologists, Sigma Theta Tau. Presbyterian. Home: 4438 Blackberry Knoll Loves Park IL 61111 Office: Rockford Meml Hosp 2400 N Rockton Ave Rockford IL 61103

BUCKNER, LINDA IVERSON, insurance, software, and marketing consultant, author; b. Lincoln, Nebr., July 14, 1950; d. Joseph Thomas and Henrietta Mae (McClure) Fisher; m. David Lynn Iverson, Dec. 29, 1967 (div. May 1980); children: Rachelle, Meggan, Elyssa; m. John David Buckner, Apr. 17, 1981. BS in Bus., U.S.D., 1974; student in Direct Mktg., Northwestern U., 1986-87. Lic. life, accident and health ins. agt., 1980, property and casualty agt., 1985. Mktg. rep. ESCO, Northfield, Ill., 1975-76; sales mgr. Safecom, Inc., Schaumburg, Ill., 1976-79; account exec. CNA, Inc., Chgo., 1979-81; mktg. mgr. Computer Sci. Corp., Chgo., 1981-83; ptnr., v.p. mktg. Buckner & Assocs., Wheaton, Ill., 1981—; account exec., mgr. nat. accounts devel. Marsh-McLennan Group, 1984-87; pres. Buckner & Assocs., 1987—; cons. Ins. Agy. Automation, 1979-81, CARA Corp., Lombard, Ill., 1983-84. Dem. election judge, DuPage County, Ill., 1977—; mem. DuPage County Citizens Adv. Com., 1978-80; mem. Hoffman Hallmark Choir, 1978-80, fundraiser Acad. Performing Arts, Chgo., 1981—. Mem. Nat. Assn. Female Execs., Nat. Assn. Ins. Women, Soc. Mgmt. Info. Systems (assoc.), Data Processing Mgmt. Assn., Am. Mgmt. Assn., Am. Soc. Assn. Execs., Chgo. Soc. Assn. Execs. Home and Office: Buckner & Assocs 505 W Union St Wheaton IL 60187 Office: 222 S Riverside Plaza Chicago IL 60606

BUDACH, VALERIE JEAN, licensing and sports marketing professional; b. Chgo., Oct. 7, 1953; d. Rudolph and Janet (Melin) B. BA cum laude, Augustana Coll., 1975; legal assistance tng., Lewis U., Glen Ellyn, Ill., 1975. Adminstrv. asst. Am. Sch. Dressage, Fairfield, Maine, 1976-77; paralegal Anesi, Ozmon, Lewin & Assocs., Ltd., Chgo., 1977-79; legal asst. McDonald's Corp., Oak Brook, Ill., 1979—, corp. legal supr., 1979—, trademark adminstr., 1979-83, supr. legal services, 1983-86; pub. relations, media coordinator for equestrian events St. James Farm, Warrenville, Ill. Home: 5157 Washington Hillside IL 60162 Office: McDonald's Corp McDonald's Plaza Oak Brook IL 60521

BUDLER, MELITTA M(ARY), media executive; b. Elgin, Ill., Jan. 26, 1952; d. Joseph Anton and Rose (Horehled) Charvat; divorced; 1 child, Robert Joseph. BA in communication Arts and Scis. magna cum laude, Rosary Coll., 1974. Communications coordinator Rosary Coll., River Forest, Ill., 1974-77; writer, editor Luth. Gen. Hosp., Park Ridge, Ill., 1977-78; asst. editor employee communications, news bur. rep. United Airlines Corp. Communications, Chgo., 1978-80, corp. communications rep., 1986-87, media producer, 1987-88, media relations mgr., 1988—; free-lance writer, publicist Algonquin, Ill., 1980-83; owner The Writer's Bloc, Mundelein, Ill., 1983-86. Program and publicity dir., fundraiser Summit Sch. for Exceptional Children, Dundee, Ill., 1985. Recipient Disting. Service award Publicity Club Chgo., 1978, Golden Trumpet Award, 1980, 87, Gold Quill Award of Excellence Internat. Assn. Bus. Communicators, 1987, 88, Best Newspaper Award of Excellence Chgo. Assn. Bus. Communicators, 1980, Spl. Achievement award United Airlines Corp. Communications Div., 1987, Golden Trumpet Award of Merit. Mem. Internat. TV Assn., Nat. Assn. Female Execs. Democrat. Roman Catholic. Office: United Airlines Corp Communications PO Box 66100 Chicago IL 60666

BUDNEY, LINDA MCDONALD, computer analyst; b. Stamford, Conn., Nov. 26, 1946; d. Harold Thomas and Dorothy (Nungesser) McDonald; B.A. in Econs., Cath. U., 1969; postgrad. in tech. of mgmt., Am. U., 1972-75; m. Thomas J. Budney, Mar. 4, 1978. Computer specialist HEW, Washington, 1969-73; area mgr. computer measurement and evaluation Data Mgmt. Center, HEW, 1973-77, chief systems programming br., 1977-79; EDP project coordinator Pension Benefit Guaranty Corp., Washington, 1979-84, asst. dir. project computers, 1984; group dir. IMTEC, U.S. Gen. Acct. Office, 1984—. Mem. Reston (Va.) Chorale, 1976-78, treas., 1977; mem. Rockville (Md.) Community Chorus, 1978-79; mem. Parish Council, Our Lady of Mercy Ch., Potomac, Md. Mem. Assn. Computing Machinery, Computer Measurement Group, Ops. Research Soc. Am., Pi Gamma Mu. Home: 9908 Newhall Rd Potomac MD 20854 Office: 2020 K St NW Washington DC 20006

BUDOFF, PENNY WISE, physician, researcher; b. Albany, N.Y., July 7, 1939; d. Louis and Goldene Wise; m. Seymour L. Budoff, June 24, 1962; children—Jeff, Cynthia. Student U. Wis.; B.A., Syracuse U., 1959; M.D., SUNY-Upstate Med. Sch., 1963. Intern, St. Luke's Meml. Hosp., Utica, N.Y., 1963-64; practice medicine specializing in family practice and women's health, Woodbury, N.Y., 1964-85, 85—; founder Penny Wise Budoff Women's Med. Ctr., Bethpage, N.Y.; lectr., TV guest on women's medicine; mem. Nat. Com. on Women in Family Medicine; clin. research on menstrual pain and women's health problems. Contbr. articles to profl. jours. Named Women of Yr., C.W. Post Coll., L.I., 1981; recipient Nat. Consumers League award, 1983, Max Cheplove award Erie chpt. N.Y. State Acad. Family Physicians, 1983. Fellow Nassau County Med. Soc., Am. Acad. Family Physicians (nat. com. on pub. relations); mem. AMA, NOW, Am. Med. Women's Assn. (co-chmn. nat. women's health com.), Nassau Acad. Family Physicians (past pres.). Author: No More Menstrual Cramps and Other Good News, 1980; No More Hot Flashes and Other Good News, 1983. Home: 11 Fairbanks Blvd Woodbury NY 11797 Office: Women's Med Ctr 4300 Hempstead Turnpeak Bethpage NY 11714

BUECHE, KRISTINE LOUISE, director of human resources; b. Ithaca, N.Y., June 16, 1947; d. Arthur Maynard and Margaret Louisa (Bassler) B. B.A., U. Dayton, 1970; M.S., Wright State U., 1974. Pres., Behavior Mgmt. Inc., Dayton, 1972-74; specialist employee relations Gen. Electric, Cin., 1977-78, mgr. compliance mgmt., Utica, N.Y., 1978-79; mgr. Lord Lindsay, Knoxville, Tenn., 1979-80; mgr. salaried employee relations Gen. Electric, Wilmington, N.C., 1980-83, mgr. orgn. and staffing, Milw., 1983-85; dir. human resources Quantum Med. Systems, Issaquah, Wash., 1985—. Mem. Bus. Vols. for the Arts. Mem. Human Resource Planning Soc., Am. Electronics Assn., Am. Mgmt. Assn. Republican. Roman Catholic. Club: Jr. League (Seattle). Avocations: swimming; sailing. Office: Quantum Med Systems 1040 12th Ave NW Issaquah WA 98027

BUEHL, OLIVIA IRENE, editor; b. N.Y.C., July 24, 1943; d. Oliver Sidney and Eleanor Sylvia (Weinstein) Bell; m. Ronald E. Buehl, Nov. 19, 1965; children: Jeffrey, Suzanna. BA, Smith Coll., 1965. Photo editor Am. Heritage, N.Y.C., 1976-77; assoc. editor Horizon Mag., N.Y.C., 1977-78; project editor Chanticleer Press, N.Y.C., 1978-80; features editor Home Mag., N.Y.C., 1980-81, exec. editor, 1981, editor, 1981-86, v.p., 1984-86; editor Working Mother mag., N.Y.C., 1986—. Mem. Am. Soc. Mag. Editors, Nat. Home Fashions League, NOW, Women in Communications, Child Care Action Campaign, Nat. Assn. Female Execs. Democrat. Home: 60 Ludlow Dr Chappaqua NY 10514 Office: Working Mother Mag 230 Park Ave New York NY 10314

BUEHLER, MICHELLE MARGUERITE, editor; b. Phila., Oct. 27, 1957; d. John Miller and Arlene Lucille (Cararo) B. BJ, U. Mo., 1979. Editorial specialist Service Employees Internat. Union, Seattle, 1979-81; editor Los Angeles City Employees Union, 1981—. Mem. Los Angeles City Task Force Family Diversity, 1986—, mem. Women in Workforce Commn. Los Angeles County Fedn. Labor, 1986—, grass roots orgn. Californian's Quality Govt., 1986-88, campaign to restore Cal OSHA, 1987—; precinct walker Cecil Green Campaign Calif. State Assembly, Norwalk, Calif., 1987, Homer Broome Council Campaign, Los Angeles, 1987. Mem. Nat. Assn. Female Execs., Am. Soc. Newspaper Editors, Western Labor Press Assn., Sigma Delta Chi. Roman Catholic. Office: Los Angeles City Employees Union 548 S Spring St Los Angeles CA 93013

BUELL, EVANGELINE CANONIZADO, consumer coop. ofcl.; b. San Pedro, Calif., Aug. 28, 1932; d. Estanislao C. and Felicia (Stokes) Canonizado; student San Jose State Coll., 1952-53; grad. U. San Francisco, 1978; m. Ralph D. Vilas, 1952 (dec.); m. Robert Alexander Elkins, July 1, 1961 (dec.); children—Nikki Isaacs, Stacey Vilas, Danni Vilas Plump; m. William David Buell, Feb. 21, 1987. With Consumers Coop. of Berkeley (Calif.) Inc., 1958—, edn. asst. for community relations, 1964-73, supr. edn. dept., 1973-76, asst. to edn. dir., 1976-78, program coordinator edn. dept., 1980-81, personnel tng. coordinator, 1981—; events coordinator Internat. House, U. Calif., Berkeley, 1984; also guitar tchr. Mem. Community Adv. Com., Bonita House, Berkeley, 1974; mem. steering com. for cultural and ethnic affairs Guild of Oakland Mus., 1973-74; dir. various activities YMCA, YWCA, Oakland City Recreation Dept., 1959-73; pres. Berkeley Community Chorus and Orch. Recipient Honor award U. Calif. Student Coop., 1965, other awards. Mem. Coop. Educators Network Calif. Democrat. Unitarian. Columnist Coop. News, 1964—. Home: 516 Santa Barbara Rd Berkeley CA 94707 Office: 2299 Piedmont Berkeley CA 94720

BUFFKIN, BEVERLY EDITH, government agency administrator; b. Sonoma, Calif., Nov. 3, 1961; d. Lawrence Robert and Anna Olivia (Anderson) J.; m. Mark D. Buffkin, Dec. 12, 1987. BS in Fin., Marist Coll., 1983. Fin. mgmt. trainee Navy Fin. Ctr., Long Beach, Calif. and Cleve., Ohio, 1984-86; budget dir. USN, Long Beach, 1986—; counselor EEO, Dept. of the Navy, Long Beach, 1987—. Mem. Am. Soc. Mil. Comptrollers (sec. 1986—, v.p. 1984-86, pres. 1987—), Fed. Mgrs. Assn., Nat. Assn. Female Execs., Delta Zeta (v.p. 1982). Club: Long Beach Rowing. Lodge: Circle K (lt. gov. 1983-84). Office: Dept Navy Naval Sta Code 22 Long Beach CA 90822

BUFFUM, NANCY KAY, interior designer; b. Portland, Oreg., Aug. 10, 1941; d. William Cheely and Wanda (Camblin) Whitman; student Shasta Coll., 1959-60, U. Calif.-Berkeley, 1960-63; m. Jack Erwin Buffum, Mar. 24, 1961 (div. 1981); children—Andrew Lewis, Airenne. Exec. sec. Pacific Mut. Life Ins. Co., San Francisco, 1961-63; gen. cashier N.Am. Brokers, San Francisco, 1963-64; mgr. So. area office Lindsey & Co., Sacramento, 1964-65; escrow office, sales rep. Kennicott Constrn. Co., Redding, Calif., 1967-69; office mgr., gen. ptnr. Buffum & Assocs., Redding, 1969-72; asst. designer Penthouse Interiors, Redding, 1973-75; owner, designer The Design Works, Redding, 1975—; lectr. on design and antiques to community groups. Pres., Shasta County Easter Seal Soc., 1971-73; pres. Redding Elem. Sch. PTA, 1973-77, trustee, adv. com., sch. bd., 1975-78; bd. dirs. Redding Mus. League; adviser KIXE Pub. TV Sta.; mem. Redding Planning Commn., 1981—; mem. adv. bd. Council; vol. Riverfront Playhouse. Recipient award for pub. service Rotary Internat., 1976, named Business Woman of Yr., 1982. Mem. Nat. Home Furnishing Assn., Am. Soc. Interior Designers (assoc.), Inst. Bldg. Designers, DAR (hon. pub. service award), Redding C. of C. (v.p. 1984-85; Bus. Woman of Year 1982). Republican. Club: Soroptimist. Office: 1600 California St #100 Redding CA 96001

BUFORD, DELORES PHIFE, researcher, educator; b. Dallas, Dec. 18, 1933; d. George Jefferson and Louisa May (Daniel) Phife; m. Thomas Oliver Buford, Dec. 27, 1954; children—Russell Warren, Robert Carl, Anna Louise. B.A., North Tex. State U., 1954; postgrad. Boston U., 1958-60; M.A., Furman U., 1974; Ed.D., Nova U., 1982. Tchr. Dallas Pub. Sch. Dist., 1954-55; tchr. high sch. Ft. Worth Pub. Sch. Dist., 1955-58; mem. steering com. Jr. Great Books Program, Greenville County (S.C.) Pub. Schs., 1968-72; research assoc. Office Instnl. Planning and Research, Furman U., Greenville, S.C., 1974—, instr. ednl. research and learning process grad. div., 1977—. Mem. Greenville Fine Arts Festival Com., 1975; pres. Eastside High Sch. PTA, 1976; mem. edn. com. Mental Health Assn. of Greenville County, 1986—. Mem. AAUW (bd. dirs. Great Branch area 1969—), Assn. Instnl.

Research, So. Assn. Instl. Research, S.C. Assn. Instl. Research (sec. 1987-88, pres.-elect 1988-89), N.C. Assn. Instnl. Research, PEO (state exec. bd. 1980-86, pres. 1985-86, past pres. club 1987-88, nominating com., Internat. chpt. 1987-89). Democrat. Baptist. Scholarship to Edn. Fund Program named in her honor by Greenville br. AAUW, 1979. Avocations: needlwork, reading, entertaining. Home: 75 Regent Dr Greenville SC 29609 Office: Furman U Office Instnl Planning Poinsett Hwy Greenville SC 29613

BUFORD, EVELYN CLAUDENE SHILLING, printing company executive; b. Fort Worth, Sept. 21, 1940; d. Claude and Winnie Evelyn (Mote) Hodges; student Hill Jr. Coll., 1975-76; m. William J. Buford, Mar. 1982; children by previous marriage—Vincent Shilling, Kathryn Lynn Shilling Vassar. With Imperial Printing Co., Inc., Fort Worth, 1964-70, 77—, gen. sales mgr. comml. div., 1982—, corp. sec., 1977—; with Tarrant County Hosp. Dist., Fort Worth, 1973-77, asst. to asst. adminstr., 1981-84. Mem. Exec. Women Internat. (dir., publs. chmn., v.p. 1984, pres. 1985, chmn. adv. com. 1986, 87, scholarship dir. 1988—, corp. publ. com. 1988,), Nat. Assn. Female Execs., Presidents Club Tex. Republican. Methodist. Home: 1025 Kenneth Ln Burleson TX 76028 Office: Imperial Printing Co Inc 1429 Hemphill Fort Worth TX 76104

BUGBEE-JACKSON, JOAN, sculptor; b. Oakland, Calif., Dec. 17, 1941; d. Henry Greenwood and Jeanie Ogden (Abbot) B.; B.A. in Art, San Jose (Calif.) State Coll., 1964, M.A., 1966; student Nat. Acad. Sch. Fine Arts, N.Y.C., 1968-72, Art Students League, N.Y.C., 1968-70; m. John Michael Jackson, June 21, 1973; 1 dau., Brook Bond. Apprentice to Joseph Kiselewski, 1970-72; Instr. art Foothill (Calif.) Jr. Coll., 1966-67; instr. design De Anza Jr. Coll., Cupertino, Calif., 1967-68; instr. pottery Greenwich House Pottery, N.Y.C., 1969-71, Craft Inst. Am., N.Y.C., 1970-72, Cordova (Alaska) Extension Center, U. Alaska, 1972-79, Prince William Sound Community Coll., 1979—; one-woman exhbns. in Maine, N.Y.C., Alaska and Calif.; group exhbns. include Allied Artists Am., 1970-72, Nat. Acad. Design, 1971, 74; pres. Cordova Arts and Pageants Ltd., 1975-76; commns. include Marie K. Smith Commemorative plaque, 1973, Bob Korn Pool Commemorative Plaque, 1975, Eyak Native Monument, 1978, Anchorage Pioneer's Home Ceramic Mural, 1979, Alaska Wildlife Series Bronze Medal, 1980, sculpture murals and portraits Alaska State Capitol, 1981, Pierre De Ville Portrait commn., 1983, Robert B. & Evangeline Atwood, 1985, Armin F. Koernig Hatchery Plaque, 1985, Cordova Fishermen's Meml. Sculpture, 1985, Alaska's Five Govs., bronze relief, Anchorage, 1986, Reluctant Fisherman's Mermaid, bronze, 1987, Charles E. Bunnell, bronze portrait statue, Fairbanks, 1988, also other portraits. Scholarship student Nat. Acad. Sch. Fine Arts, 1969-72; recipient J.A. Suydam Bronze medal, 1969; Dr. Ralph Weiler prize, 1971; Helen Foster Barnet award, 1971; Daniel Chester French award, 1972; Frishmuth award, 1971; Allied Artists Am. award, 1972; C. Percival Dietsch prize, 1973; citation Alaska Legislature, 1981, 82. Fellow Nat. Sculpture Soc. Address: Box 374 Cordova AK 99574

BUGG, JUNE MOORE, state legislator; b. Altoona, Ala., Oct. 7, 1919; d. Sims Smith and Bertie Edith (Powell) Moore; m. Bill Knight Bugg (dec. Dec. 1987); children: Barbara Bugg Zack, Bill Jr. BA in Edn., U. Ala., 1940, postgrad., 1970; MS in Edn., Jacksonville (Ala.) State U., 1970. Librarian Gadsden (Ala.) High Sch., 1941-46, tchr. English, 1952-65; librarian Ala. Tech. Coll., Gadsden, 1949-51; mem. Ala. Ho. of Reps., Montgomery, 1983—; librarian Gadsden Ctr., U. Ala.; student-tchr. supr., U. Ala., Birmingham, 1975-80. Chair Project Our Town, Gadsden; mem. Ala. Dem. Exec. Com., 1982—. Recipient Pres.'s award Downtown Action Council, 1976-77, award AAUW, 1981. Mem. Alpha Xi Delta (Order of Rose 1987). Methodist. Office: Ala Ho of Reps Union St Montgomery AL 36130

BUIE, ELISSA PAULINE, financial planning officer; b. Anderson, S.C., Sept. 16, 1960; d. Richard Emerson and Eileen Elizabeth (Stanley) B.; m. Wayne Ludwig Grove, July 20, 1985. BS in Commerce, U. Va., 1982; MBA in Fin. Planning, U. Md., 1987. Lic. securities dealer, Va.; registered fin. planner. Due diligence officer Heritage Fin. Group Inc., Falls Church, Va., 1982 ; v.p., dir. Heritage Fin. Advisers; exec. v.p., dir. Heritage Fin. Ins. Agy. Author case study in textbook, 1986. Mem. Internat. Assn. Fin. Planning, Inst. Cert. Fin. Planners. Office: Heritage Fin Advisers 5113 Leesburg Pike 511 Falls Church VA 22041

BUIST, JEAN MORFORD, hospital administrator; b. Newton, N.J., Oct. 5, 1951; d. Richardson and Jean (Mackerly) B. AB, Cornell U., 1973; MEd, Coll. William and Mary, 1974; MBA, U. Pa., 1987. Mgr. The Korman Corp., Jenkintown, Pa., 1975-77; v.p. ops. Community Assn. Mgmt. Co., Havertown, Pa., 1977-78; adminstrv. asst. Albert Einstein Med. Ctr., Phila., 1978-83; assoc. adminstr. Meml. Hosp. Burlington County, Mt. Holly, N.J., 1983-87; v.p. Overlook Hosp., Summit, N.J., 1987—. Mem. Am. Coll. Healthcare Execs., Am. Hosp. Assn., Cornell Club (Phila. chpt.), Wharton Alumni. Home: 54 Mount Airy Rd Bernardsville NJ 07924 Office: Overlook Hosp Summit NJ 07901

BUKAR, MARGARET WITTY, administrator, civic leader; b. Evanston, Ill., June 21, 1950; d. LeRoy and Catherine Ann (Conrad) Witty; m. Gregory Bryce Bukar, June 5, 1971; children—Michael Bryce, Caroline Nicole. BS, DePaul U., 1972, MBA, 1981. Staff med. technologist The Evanston (Ill.) Hosp., 1972-75, immunopathology lab. supr., 1975-77, lab. mgr., 1977-84, dir. lab. adminstrn., 1984-85; bookkeeper Ronald Knox Montessori Sch., Wilmette, Ill., 1986-87. Den leader Cub Scouts, Boy Scouts Am., Wilmette, 1985-87, den leader coach, 1987-88; active PTA of St. Francis Xavier Sch., 1985—, chair rummage sale, 1987-88; mem. sch. bd. St. Francis Xavier Sch., 1986-87, sec. 1988—. Recipient Emily Withrow Stebbins award Evanston Hosp., 1985. Mem. Nat. Assn. Female Execs., Am. Soc. Clin. Pathologists, Wilmette Hist. Soc. Avocations: knitting, restoring old homes, interior design. Home: 1611 Greenwood Ave Wilmette IL 60091

BUKER, BARBARA H. HOEMEYER, nursing adminstrator; b. Pine Bluff, Ark., Apr. 4, 1942; d. Waldon Robert and Luella (Helm) Hoemeyer; m. David C. Warner, Apr. 18, 1964 (div. June 1977); m. William Scott Buker, May 23, 1987. BS in Nursing, U. Mo., 1974; MS in Nursing, Boston U., 1975; postgrad., U. Mo., 1975—. Staff nurse Barnes Hosp., St. Louis, 1963-64; staff nurse U. Mo. Hosps., Columbia, 1964-65, supr., 1965-75, follow-up coordinator, 1978-81, instr. Coll. of Nursing,, 1975-85, coordinator edn., 1981-85, asst. dir. nursing, 1983-85; asst. exec. dir. The Ohio State U. Hosps., Columbus, 1985, adminstr. nursing services, 1985—; mem. nat. task force Am. Spinal Injury Nursing, 1980-85. Contbr. articles to profl. jours. mem. Am. Orgn. Nurse Execs., Assn. Rehab. Nursing (editorial bd. jour.), Am. Congress Rehab. Medicine, Am. Nurses Assn. Unitarian Universalist. Lodge: PEO. Office: The Ohio State U Hosps 410 W 10th Ave 104 Doan Hall Columbus OH 43210

BUKOWSKI, ELAINE LOUISE, physical therapist; b. Phila., Feb. 18, 1949; d. Edward Eugene and Melanja Josephine (Przyborowski) B. BS in Phys. Therapy, St. Louis U., 1972; MS, U. Nebr., 1977. Licensed phys. therapist, N.J., Mo., Pa. Clk. City of Phila., 1967; staff phys. therapist St. Louis Chronic Hosp., 1973, Cardinal Ritter Inst., St. Louis, 1973-74; dir. campus ministry musicals Creighton U., Omaha, 1974-75; teaching asst. U. Nebr. Med. Ctr., Omaha, 1975-76; lectr. in anatomy U. Sci. and Technology, Kumasi, Ghana, 1977-78; chief physical therapist Holy Family Hosp., Berekum, Ghana, 1978-79; coordinator info. & guidance The Am. Cancer Soc., Phila., 1979-81; staff phys. therapist Holy Redeemer VNA, Phila., 1981-83; rehab. supr. Holy Redeemer VNA, Swainton, N.J., 1983-87; asst. prof. phys. therapy Stockton State Coll., Pomona, N.J., 1987—; bd. dirs. The Bridge, Phila., 1979-80; mem. profl. adv. council Holy Redeemer VNA, Swainton, N.J., 1982—, mem. personnel com., cons. hospice program, 1985—, rehab. cons. 1987—. Co-author slide study program, 1976, (video) Going My Way? The Low Back Syndrome, 1976; contbr. articles to profl. jours. Vol. Am. Cancer Soc., Phila., 1979-82, Walk-a-Day-in-My Shoes program Girl Scouts Am., Cape May County, N.J. 1983—; task force phys. therapy program Stockton State Coll., Pomona, N.J., 1985—. U.S. Govt. trainee, 1971, 72; Physical Therapy Fund grantee, 1975, 76; recipient Vol. Achievement award Am. Cancer Soc., 1981. Mem. Am. Phys. Therapy Assn. (community health, edn. traineeship, geriatric sects.), Smithsonian Assn., Phys. Therapy Club (sec. 1971-72). Office: Stockton State Coll Phys Therapy Program Pomona NJ 08240

BUKSBAZEN, DARLENE, medical technologist; b. N.Y.C., July 8, 1946; d. Morris and Mina Antonia (Colon) Brender; m. Victor Buksbazen, Sept. 25, 1971 (div. Dec. 1980); children: Paul Victor, Victoria Elizabeth. AAS, N.Y.C. Community Coll., 1966; BS, St. John's U., 1969. Staff technologist Shiel Lab., Queens Village, N.Y., 1969-70; technologist, supr. Jefferson Meml. Hosp., Alexandria, Va., 1971-72; chief technician Mobile Med. Care Montgomery County, Rockville, Md., 1976-79; tchr. music Hicksville (N.Y.) Nursery Sch., 1980; pianist First Love Presbyn. Ch., Babylon, N.Y., 1982-85; lab. mgr. L.I. Med. Care Services, North Babylon, 1983-86, technician, 1986—; microfilm converter Town of Babylon, Lindenhurst, N.Y., 1987—. Town rep. Neighborhoods Uniting Project, Mt. Ranier, Md., 1978-79, conv. del., 1974-79;mem. 8th Precinct Civic Assn., Chillum, Md., 1974-78; v.p. Rollingcrest Recreation Council, Chillum, 1975-77. Mem. Christian Bus. and Profl. Women's Club. Republican. Mem. Evangelical Ch. Home: 69 Beverly Rd Babylon NY 11702

BULKELEY, CHRISTY CLAIRE, foundation executive; b. Galesburg, Ill., Feb. 10, 1942; d. Gerald Clough and Patricia Ann (Pettingell) Bulkeley; m. Perry David Finks, Sept. 6, 1975. B.J., U. Mo., 1964. Reporter, The Times-Union, Rochester, N.Y., 1964-72, editorial page editor, 1973-74; pres., pub., editor Saratogian, Saratoga Springs, N.Y., 1974-76, 84; pres., pub., editor Comml. News, Danville, Ill., 1976-84; v.p. central region newspaper div. Gannett Co. Inc., 1981-84, v.p. spl. corp. projects, 1984; v.p. Gannett Found., 1985—; dir. WRI Inc., Albany and N.Y.C. Contbg. author: New Guardians of the Press, 1983. Bd. dirs. Danville Area Econ. Devel. Corp., 1981-84, Community Coll. Found., Danville, 1979-84, Vermilion County OIC, Danville, 1978-82, Travers Com., Saratoga, N.Y., 1984; leadership giving capt., nominating com. Greater Rochester United Way, 1986—; adv. bd. U. Mo. Sch. Journalism, 1986—; v.p. Rochester Grantmakers Forum, 1986—; mem. steering com. Rochester Womens Fund. Recipient awards Gannett Co. Inc., 1984; Outstanding Contbns. Ill. Mcpl. Human Relations Assn., 1981; Young Achiever Nat. Council Women, 1976. Mem. Women in Communications Inc. (pres. 1975-76, headliner 1978), Am. Soc. Newspaper Editors (bd. dirs. 1983-84), Inland Daily Press Assn. (bd. dirs. 1983-84), AP (nominating com. 1979-84), Women and Found/Corp. Philanthropy (mem. com. 1987—), Soc. Profl. Journalists., Danville Area C. of C. (bd. dirs. 1980-84). Clubs: Brooklea (Rochester, N.Y.); Carolina Trace (Sanford, N.C.). Home: 1501 Highland Ave Rochester NY 14618 Office: Gannett Found Lincoln Tower Rochester NY 14604

BULL, ELINOR BORENSTEIN, psychotherapist; b. Boston, June 1, 1943; d. Fred Eugene and L. Sophie (Mazer) Borenstein; m. Thomas Albert Bull, Dec. 18, 1966; children: Jonathan, Ian. BS, Boston U., 1965, MS, 1970. Staff nurse Harvard Med. Sch.-Boston City Hosp., 1965-67; head nurse Boston U.-Boston State Hosp. Psychiat. Home Treatment Service, Dorchester, Mass., 1967-69; psychotherapist Dr. Thomas Bull, Inc., Duxbury, Mass., 1970—; cons. Berrybrook Nursery Sch., Duxbury, 1981-85. Chmn., founder Duxbury Creative Arts Council, 1977-84; mem., co-chmn. art adv. com. Helen Bumpus Gallery, Duxbury, 1982—. Mem. Am. Nurses Assn. (cert., mem. council clin. specialists in psychiat. mental health nursing). Democrat. Unitarian-Jewish. Office: Dr Thomas Bull Inc PO Box 1682 Duxbury MA 02331

BULLARD, HELEN (MRS. JOSEPH MARSHALL KRECHNIAK), sculptor; b. Elgin, Ill., Aug. 15, 1902; d. Charles Wickliffe and Minnie (Cook) Bullard; student U. Chgo., 1921-29; m. Lloyd Ernst Rohrke, June 11, 1924 (div. Feb. 1931); children—Ann Louise (Mrs. Ross DeWitt Netherton), Barbara Jane (Mrs. Valtyr Emil Gudmundson); m. 2d, Joseph Marshall Krechniak, Jan. 30, 1932 (dec. Feb. 1964); 1 dau., Mariana (Mrs. Wilfred Martin). With research dept. L.V. Estes, Inc., Chgo., 1920-22; operator Square D Co., Detroit, 1922-24; researcher Commerce and Adminstrn. library U. Chgo., Detroit, 1924-25, dir. Crossville (Tenn.) Play Ctr., 1949-50. Creator hand-carved dolls, 1949—, wood sculpture, 1959—; exhibited with Nat. Inst. Am. Doll Artists Exhbns., Los Angeles, 1963, Cin., 1964, Washington, 1965, Chgo., 1966, Boston, 1967, New Orleans, 1969, Detroit, 1970, Los Angeles, 1971, Omaha, 1972, Louisville, 1973, Miami, Fla., 1974, Milw., 1975, Watts Bar Dam, Tenn., 1976, Chgo., 1977, N.Y.C., 1979, others until 1987, also craftsmen's fairs, 1954-65, The Club, Birmingham, Ala., 1963, Oak Ridge Art Ctr., 1965, Children's Mus., Nashville, 1967, McClung Mus., Knoxville, 1969; one woman show Tenn. State Mus., 1972, Nashville, Knoxville, Asheville, N.C.; author: Dr. Woman of the Cumberlands, 1953, The American Doll Artist, 1965, Vol. II, 1974, A Bullard Family, 1966, Dorothy Heizer, the Artist and Her Dolls, 1972; Crafts and Craftsmen of the Tennesee Mountains, 1976, (monograph) My People in Wood, 1984, Faith Wick: Doll Artist Extraordinaire, 1986, Cumberland County, 1956-86, Vol. II, 1987, (with husband) Cumberland County's First Hundred Years, 1956. Campaign chmn. Cumberland County unit Am. Cancer Soc., 1947-52. Mem. So. Highland Handicraft Guild (dir. 1957-59), Highland Handicraft Guild, Nat. Inst. Am. Doll Artists (founder, pres. 1963-67, 69-71, chmn. bd. 1977—), United Fedn. Doll Clubs (2d v.p. 1977-79), Am. Craftsmen's Council, Tenn. Folklore Soc., Mensa. Democrat. Unitarian.

BULLARD, JUDITH EVE, psychologist, systems engineer; b. Oneonta, N.Y., Oct. 5, 1945; d. Kurt and Herta (Deutsch) Leeds; divorced; children: Nicholas A., Elizabeth A. BA in Polit. Sci., Spanish U., Oreg., 1966, MA in Psychology, 1973. Supr. residential program Skipworth Juvenile Home, Eugene, Oreg., 1966-68; research asst. Oreg. Research Inst., Eugene, 1968-69, 83-85; supr. residential program Ky. Correctional Facility, Lexington, 1969-70; research asst. U. Oreg., Eugene, 1970-73; asst. dir. Regional Mental Health Clinic, Frankfort, Ind., 1974-76, dir. mental health Lane County Mental Health, Eugene, 1977-80; cons. Managerial Communications, Eugene, 1980-83; systems engr. AT&T Bell Labs., Holmdel, N.J., 1985—; instr. mental health subjects, various ednl. instns. Bd. dirs. Asbury Park 10K, Jersey Shore 1/2 Marathon, 1985—, Women's Resource and Survival Ctr., Keyport, N.J., 1986—. Mem. Women's Profl. Network (trustee Holmdel br. 1987—), Partnership in Edn. and Bus., Corrections in Mental Health, Human Factors Soc. Office: AT&T 1K505 Crawfords Corner Rd Holmdel NJ 07733

BULLARD, SHARON WELCH, librarian; b. San Diego, Nov. 4, 1943; d. Dale L. and Myrtle (Sampson) Welch; m. Donald H. Bullard, Aug. 1, 1969. B.S.Ed., U. Central Ark., 1965; M.A., U. Denver, 1967. Media specialist Adams County Sch. Dist. 12, Denver, 1967-69; tchr., librarian Humphrey pub. schs., Ark., 1965-66, librarian, 1969-70; catalog librarian Ark. State U., Jonesboro, 1970-75; head documents cataloging Wash. State U., Pullman, 1979-83; head serials cataloging U. Calif.-Santa Barbara, 1984—; cons. Center for Robotic Systems Microelectronics Research Library, Santa Barbara, 1986, Ombudsman's Office U. Calif., Santa Barbara, 1988 ; distributor Amway, 1985—. Canvasser, Citizens for Goleta Valley, 1985-86. Mem. ALA, Library Assn. U. Calif. (tech. services chpt., Santa Barbara subcom. on advancement and promotion 1987), Nat. Assn. Female Execs., So. Calif. Tech. Processer Group (membership com. 1987). Avocations: t'ai chi chih, walking, swimming, reading.

BULLER, SUSAN MARIE, petroleum engineer; b. Denver, Sept. 30, 1961; d. Harold Louis and Carol Marie (Krieger) Blaser.; m. Daniel Scott Buller, May 30, 1987. BSc, Colo. Sch. Mines, 1983; MSc, U. So. Calif., 1986. Petroleum engr. UNOCAL, Santa Paula, Calif., 1983—. Mem. Soc. Petroleum Engrs. (chmn. spl. programs 1986-87), Am. Petroleum Inst. Office: UNOCAL 1003 E Main St Santa Paula CA 93060

BULLOCK, ANN MYERS, home health administrator; b. Feb. 12, 1953; d. Ephriam Lee Myers and Dorothy Marie (Johnson) Weeks; children: Daniel David II, Jennifer Lynn. Physician asst. cert. med., U. S.C., 1980; BS cum laude in Nursing, Clemson U., 1976. Asst. dir. nursing Greenwood (S.C.) Meth. Home, 1976; nursing cons. Dept. Mental Retardation, Greenwood, S.C., 1977; office nurse, mgr. James W. Gilbert, M.D., McCormick, S.C., 1977-78; physician asst. Megals Rural Health Assn., McCormick, 1980-82; staff nurse Vis. Nurses Assn., Self Meml. Hosp., Greenwood, S.C., 1980-82, nursing supr., 1982-84, patient care adminstr., 1984—; mem. adv. bd. practical nurse program Greenwood Vocat. Facility, 1983-87, chmn., 1983-84, 85-86; adv. bd. allied health program, 1987—; mem. Community Edn. Council, 1984—, pres., 1988—; instr. Am. Heart Assn. Mem. Nat. Assn. Female Exec., United Ostomy Soc. (adv. bd. 1984—, pres. 1987—), Honor Soc. Coll. Allied Health Med. U. S.C., Sigma Theta Tau. Republican. Baptist. Home: 307 Orchard Dr Greenwood SC 29646 Office: Self Meml Hosp Vis Nurse Assn 1029A Edgefield St Greenwood SC 29646

BULLOCK, BARBARA LEE, nursing educator; b. Los Angeles, Aug. 2, 1941; d. Harry Benjamin and Lois Maxine (Farr) Radford; m. Talmadge Glen Bullock, Apr. 13, 1968; children—Sheila Anne, Brian Glen, Douglas Allen. B.S.N., U. Colo., 1963; M.S.N., U. Tex.-San Antonio, 1977. Staff nurse Framingham Union (Mass.), 1963-65; asst. supr., instr. Meth. Hosp., Houston, 1965-68; supr. relief Good Shepherd Hosp., Longview, Tex., 1975; instr. Kilgore Coll. (Tex.), 1975-76; asst. prof. Samford U., Birmingham, Ala., 1977-85, asst. prof. U. Ala.-Birmingham, 1985-86; cardiac rehab. nurse St. Vincent's Hosp., Birmingham, 1986—. Author: Cardiovascular Nursing, 1971; researcher Comparative Study Registered Nurses, 1980; editor: Pathophysiology, 1984, 2d edit., 1988. Mem. PTA, Vestavia Hills, Ala., 1983. Mem. Critical Care Nurses Assn., Sigma Theta Tau, Alpha Omicron Pi. Republican. Methodist.

BULLOCK, FRANCETTE LEE H., health resource educator; b. Long Beach, Calif., June 9, 1949; d. Edward G. Hatchell and Huguette M. (Seror) Dudley; m. Joseph Edward Bullock, July 8, 1972; 1 child, Brian Edward. AA, St. Petersburgh Jr. Coll., Clearwater, Fla., 1969; BS, Fla. State U., 1971; MEd, U. West Fla., 1974; postgrad., Fla. State U., 1987—. Cert. tchr., adminstr., Fla. Tchr. Bay Dist. Schs., Panama City, Fla., 1971-86, health resources tchr., coordinator, 1986—; cons. Growing Healthy program, S.C., Tenn., Fla. 1980—; instr. Gulf Coast Community Coll., Panama City, 1985. Bd. dirs. Panama City chpt. Am. Heart Assn., 1985-87; adv. bd. Bay Med. Ctr., Panama City, 1986-87; adminstrv. bd. St. Andrews United Meth. Ch., Panama City, 1987—; mem. Bay Arts Alliance, Panama City, 1985—. Mem. Fla. Sch. Health Assn., Assn. for Supervision and Curriculum Devel., Phi Delta Kappa. Democrat. Methodist. Club: Cloverleaf Clogging (pres. 1981-87). Home: 341 Floyd Dr Lynn Haven FL 32444 Office: Bay Dist Schs 5205 West Highway 98 Panama City FL 32401

BULLOCK, GWENDOLYN CATRINA, financial analyst; b. Mullins, S.C., July 24, 1956; d. Edward Willie Sr. and Hattie Mae (Edge) B. BA in Math., U.N.C., 1978; MS in Mktg. Mgmt., Purdue U., 1980. Bus. opportunity program counselor sch. mgmt. Purdue U., W. Lafayette, 1979-80; asst. mktg. mgr. Southern Bell, Atlanta, 1980-81; WATS interviewer MARC Opinion Research, Atlanta, 1982-83; sub. tchr. Richmond County Bd. Edn., Augusta, Ga., 1984; mktg. specialist Augusta (Ga.) Minority Bus. Devel. Ctr., 1984-85, fin. analyst, 1985—. Tutor Upward Bound, Chapel Hill, N.C., 1975-78; vol. Big Sister/Little Sister Program, Chapel Hill, 1977-78; active Mt. Calvary Baptist Ch., Augusta, 1984—, Black Youth and Entrpreneurship Program, Athens, Ga., 1985—; invited to participate in People to People Tour Citizen Ambassador program, Peoples Republic of China, 1987. Recipient cert. Appreciation Black Youth Entrepreneurship Porgram, 1986. Mem. Nat. Assn. Female Execs., Am. Soc. of Profl. and Exec. Women, Nat. Bus. LEague, Greater Augusta C. of C., Ga. Assn. of Minority Entrepreneurs, Purdue Alumni Assn., U. N.C.-Chapel Hill Alumni Assn., Alpha Kappa Alpha (v.p. Chapel Hill 1977). Democrat. Home: 3425 Chadbourne St Augusta GA 30906 Office: Augusta Minority Bus Devel Ctr 1208 Laney Walker Blvd Augusta GA 30901

BULLOCK, MARIE, real estate investment executive, educator; b. Washington, Aug. 18, 1941; d. Jerry John and Anna Marie (Horstkamp) McCarthy; m. Patrick Ettien, May 31, 1965 (div. Sept. 1969); m. 2d, Charles Edward Bullock, Mar. 3, 1973; children—Ryan, Bennett. BA in Spl. Edn., Marymount Coll., 1984, MA in Counseling, Trinity Coll., 1987. Cert. in spl. edn., Va. Sec., treas. McCarthy Mfg. Co. Inc., Alexandria, Va., 1969-82; v.p. EduTrainer, Inc., Alexandria, 1979-83; mng. ptnr. C&E Partnership, Alexandria, 1971—. Pres. St. Andrew's Episcopal PTA, Bethesda, 1981. Mem. Montgomery County Assn. for Children with Learning Disabilities, Council Exceptional Children (v.p. 1984), Psi Chi. Democrat. Christian. Clubs: Kenwood Country (Bethesda, Md.); Zonta Internat. Avocations: reading; theater; cooking; biking; skiing. Home: 5118 Dalecarlia Dr Bethesda MD 20816

BULMAHN, LYNN, journalist, free-lance writer; b. Waco, Tex., Feb. 18, 1955; d. Franklin Harrold and Louise (Stolte) B. BA, SW Tex. State U., 1977. Gen. assignment reporter Waco Tribune Herald, 1977—, city desk rewrite person, 1977-78, editor/reporter religion page, 1978-81, human services reporter, 1978-83, med. reporter, 1978—, Help-Line columnist, 1981-86 ; free-lance writer, 1975-77; gen. assignment reporter, 1977-88, med./health features writer, Waco Tribune-Herald, 1988—. Voter registration chmn. Waco area LWV, 1977-80; vol. Family Abuse Ctr., Waco, 1982—; asst. instr. Mary Barkley Aerobic Dance. Recipient Anson Jones citation of Merit, Tex. Med. Assn., 1978; Outstanding Contbn. award Nat. Found. March of Dimes, 1980; Pub. Health award for media excellence Tex. Pub. Health Assn., 1980, 85, 88; First Place award Readers Digest Mag. Workshop Tex. Competition, 1981; award for feature writing North and East Tex. Press Assn., 1983; Media Appreciation award McLennan County Med. Assn., 1985. Mem. Central Tex. Journalists, Waco Jaycees (Outstanding New Mem. of Month 1985), Sigma Delta Chi. Office: Waco Tribune-Herald 900 Franklin Ave Waco TX 76702

BULOW, KATHERINE, government official; b. Kansas City, Mo., Oct. 4, 1943; 1 child, Dick. Grad., Acad. Notre Dame, 1961. With Fed. Res. System, 1962-67; with Office Congressional Affairs, The White House, Washington, 1969-73; adminstrn. Petrochem. Energy group, 1973-75; dir. bldg. mgmt. div. Republican Nat. Com., 1977-81; spl. asst. Asst. Sec. for Adminstrn., 1981-83; dep. asst. sec. adminstrn. U.S. Dept. Commerce, Washington, 1983-84, asst. sec. adminstrn., 1984—. Office: Office of Sec Dept Commerce 15th & Constitution Ave NW Washington DC 20230

BULTEMEIER, JOYCE ELAINE, accountant; b. Princeton, Ill., July 25, 1948; d. Edgar Merle and Rose Ann (Harrison) LaRue; m. Bruce Charles Markworth, May 27, 1966 (div. July 1973); children: Tammara Adora Cornelius, Bryce Conrad; m. Gary Wayne Bultemeier, Feb. 12, 1977. Student, Longview Community Coll., 1981-82. Accounting clk. Apprill's Oak Barn, Higginsville, Mo., 1968-73; customer service rep. Unitog Co., Warrensburg, Mo., 1973-77; appraiser Cass County Assessor's Office, Harrisonville, Mo., 1977-83; owner Archie (Mo.) Tax Service, 1982—; assemblyline worker Gen. Motors, Kansas City, Kans., 1983-87. Mem. Cass County Zoning Bd., 1980-84. Mem. Nat. Assn. Tax Preparers. Democrat. Club: Sports Booster. Home: Rt 1 Box 236 Archie MO 64725 Office: Archie Tax Service D-Li-My Shopping Ctr Bus Hwy 71 Archie MO 64725

BUMGARDNER, RENA JEWELL, psychotherapist; b. Athens, Tex., Nov. 28, 1940; d. Willie and Eula Ellen (Bass) Jewell; m. Thomas Arthur Bumgardner, Aug. 25, 1962; children—Melody, Susan, Judy. Student Tex. Woman's U., 1959-62; B.S. with honors, U. Minn., 1964, M.S.W., 1966. Cert. social worker. Instr. sociology, social work U. Wis.-Superior, 1966-67; family therapist Duluth (Minn.) Family Services, 1967-68; clin. social worker Human Resource Center of Douglas County, Superior, 1970-82, exec. dir., 1982-87, psychotherapist Dept. Psychiatry Duluth (Minn.) Clinic, 1987—. Chmn. bd. dirs. Children's Corner Day Care, Superior, 1975-77; bd. dirs. Spectra, Inc., Duluth, 1983-85; mem. Superior Community Housing Resource Bd., 1985-87. Mem. Nat. Assn. Social Workers, Acad. Cert. Social Workers, Am. Bus. Women's Assn. (charter chpt. woman of yr. 1984), Nat. Assn. Female Execs., Mental Health Assn. (dir. 1982-87). Democrat. Photography.

BUMGARNER, ELIZABETH ALICE, audio visual company executive, consultant; b. Aurora, Ill., Dec. 9, 1945; d. John William and Shirley Mae (Housholder) B. BS, No. Ill. U., 1967. Cert. technologies specialist. Tchr. Lena/Winslow High Sch., Lena, Ill., 1967-69, Argo Community High Sch., Summit, Ill., 1969-70; curriculum writer Waubonsee Community Coll., Sugar Grove, Ill., 1970-71; test specialist Houghton Mifflin Co., Geneva, Ill., 1971-73; editor, writer Laidlaw Brothers, Inc., River Forest, Ill., 1973-74; pres., chmn. bd. GMA Audio/Visual, Inc., Lombard, Ill., 1975—; speaker, cons. various local chambers and clubs, St. Charles, Batavia, Geneva, Ill., 1975—. Phone vol. Am. Cancer Soc. Radio-thon, Chgo., 1976-77, Easter Seal Soc. Telethons, 1987-88; campaign worker Republican Party, Lena, 1968; time vol. United Way, Aurora. Mem. Internat. Communications Industries Assn. (cert. techs. specialist), Phi Alpha Theta. Republican. Methodist. Avocations: reading, cooking, entertaining, knitting. Office: GMA Audio/Visual Inc 30 N Park Lombard IL 60148

BUNCE, TAMMY JOAN, protective services official; b. Niagara Falls, N.Y., Apr. 21, 1958; d. Theodore Marquis and Thelma JoAnne (Mauk) Bunce. Student, Niagara County Community Coll., 1977-79, Tarrant County Jr. Coll., 1979, Buffalo State U., 1981-83; student in criminal justice, Dallas/Ft. Worth Police Acad., 1980—. Service worker Mt. St. Mary's Hosp., Lewiston, N.Y., 1976-79; police officer Dallas/Ft. Worth Dept. Pub. Safety, 1979-81; security officer N.Y. State Power Authority, Lewiston, 1981—. Mem. Nat. Photographers Assn., Nat. Police Assn. Republican. Home: 4430 Miller Rd Niagara Falls NY 14304 Office: NY State Power Authority PO Box 277 Niagara Falls NY 14302

BUNCH, DONNA MARIE, accountant; b. Little Rock, May 14, 1963; d. James and Freddie Mae (Shepherd) B. BS in Acctg., Purdue U., 1984. CPA. Rates assoc. Pub. Service Ind., Plainfield, 1984-85, payroll acct., 1985-86, staff acct., 1986-87; assoc. payroll dept. Ameritech Services, Arlington Heights, Ill., 1987-88, asst. mgr. taxes, 1988—; vol. in income tax assistance IRS, Indpls., 1987—. Escort Untied Way, Plainfield, 1986; chair youth Christ Missionary Baptist Ch., Indpls., 1987; active Big Sisters of Indpls., 1987. Mem. Nat. Assn. Black Accts (chair com. 1986-87). Democrat. Baptist. Club: Toastmasters. Office: Ameritech Services 3040 Salt Creek Ln Payroll Dept Arlington Heights IL 60005

BUNDY, BARBARA KORPAN, former college president; b. Chgo., May 13, 1943; husband dec.; 1 child. B.A., U. Ill., 1964; Ph.D. in Comparative Lit., Ind. U., 1970. Asst. prof. Slavic and comparative lit., U. Calif., Berkeley, 1966-69; lectr. Russian and German, U. Calif., Santa Cruz, 1969-71; with Dominican Coll. of San Rafael, Calif., 1971-87, prof., pres., 1980-87. Contbr. articles to profl. jours. Address: 96 Elizabeth Way San Rafael CA 94901

BUNDY, ELIZABETH CAMPBELL, electronics consulting company executive; b. N.Y.C., May 15, 1960; d. Clifford Blaine and Jeanne (Maher) Campbell; m. Christopher Bruce Bundy, Aug. 30, 1980; children: Christopher Douglass, Patricia Elizabeth, Victoria Frances. BSBA, Calif. State U., Chico, 1981. Research mgr. The Bradbury Mgmt. Group, San Jose, Calif., 1981-84, dir., 1985-86; dir. research MSL Internat., Ltd., San Francisco, 1985-86; cons. Holland Rusk & Assocs., San Francisco, 1986; pres. Connect Worldwide, Palo Alto, Calif., 1986—; bd. dirs. DC Systems, Pleasanton, Calif. Mem. Nat. Assn. Female Execs. Republican. Episcopalian.

BUNN, DOROTHY IRONS, court reporter; b. Trinidad, Colo., Apr. 30, 1948; d. Russell and Pauline Anna (Langowski) Irons; m. Peter Lynn Bunn; children—Kristy Lynn, Wade Allen, Russell Ahearn. Student No. Va. Community Coll., 1970-71, U. Va., Fairfax, 1971-72. Registered profl. reporter; cert. shorthand reporter. Pres., chief exec. officer Ahearn Ltd., Springfield, Va., 1970-81, Bunn & Assocs., Glenrock, Wyo., 1981—. Cons., Bixby Hereford Co., Glenrock, 1981—. Del., White House Conf. on Small Bus., Washington, 1986. Mem. Nat. Shorthand Reporters Assn., Wyo. Shorthand Reporters Assn. (chmn. com. 1984—), Nat. Assn. Female Execs., Nat. Fedn. Ind. Businesses, Nat. Assn. Legal Secs., Nat. Fedn. Bus. and Profl. Women, Nat. Assn. Legal Secs. Internat., Am. Indian Soc. Avocations: art, music. Home: PO Box 1602 Bixby Hereford Co Glenrock WY 82637 Office: Bunn & Assocs 506 W Birch St Glenrock WY 82637

BUNNER, PATRICIA ANDREA, lawyer; b. Fairmont, W.Va., Sept. 16, 1953; d. Scott Randolph and Virginia Lenore (Keck) B. AB in History and English, W.Va. U., 1975, JD, 1978. Bar: W.Va. 1978, U.S. Dist. Ct. (so. dist.) W.Va. 1978, U.S. Dist. Ct. (no. dist.) W.Va. 1985, U.S. Supreme Ct. 1988. Mem. staff Dem. Nat. Com., Washington, 1978-79; assoc. Gailer, Elias & Matz, Washington, 1979-81, N.Y. State Bankers Assn., N.Y.C., 1981-83; ptnr. Bunner & Bunner, Fairview, W.Va., 1984—; exec. dir. N.Y. State Consumer Mortgage Rev. Bd.; chmn. dist. VIII Consumer Mortgage Rev. Com., N.Y.C., 1982-83; cons. atty. Energy Cons. Assocs., Spring Harbor, N.Y., 1981; of counsel Monongahela (W.Va.) Soil Conservation Dist., 1985. Author: N.Y. State Bankers Assn. Legis. Directory, 1983. Pres. Monongalia County Dem. Women, 1987—; sec. Monongalia County Devel. Authority, 1984—; pres. United Taxpayers Assn., Inc., W.Va., 1985-88; bd. dirs. W.Va. U., Morgantown, 1974-75. Rilla Moran Woods fellow Nat. Fedn. Dem. Women, Washington, 1978. Mem. ABA (vice chmn. legal econs. and new lawyers coms. 1986—, litigation sect., 1st amendment rights and media law com., gen. practice com., corps. and banking com.), W.Va. Bar Assn. (com. econs. of law practice 1987—), Assn. Trial Lawyers Am., N.Y. State Bar Assn., Monongalia County Bar Assn., Marion County Bar Assn., Women's Info. Ctr. (founding), LWV, Nat. Assn. Female Execs., W.Va. Alliance for Women's Studies (founding), Bus. and Profl. Women, Climates, Inc., Monongalia County Hist. Soc., Clay-Battelle Alumni Assn., W.Va. Coll. Law Alumni Assn., Nat. Rifle Assn. (life), Nature Conservancy, Nat. Arbor Day Found., World Wildlife Fund, AAUW, Sierra Club, Audobon Soc., Young Dems. Club W.Va. (sec. 1976), Phi Alpha Theta (chpt. pres. 1974-75), Phi Beta Kappa, Zeta Phi Eta, Alpha Rho (chpt. pres. 1974). Mem. Ch. of Christ. Club: Woman's (bd. dirs. Morgantown chpt. 1986—). Home: Rt 2 Box 341 Fairview WV 26570 Office: 818 Monongahela Bldg 235 High St Morgantown WV 26505

BUNT, LYNNE JOY, insurance broker; b. Corning, N.Y., Sept. 25, 1948; d. William Henry and Cleo Ann (Williams) Prentice. A.A., Foothill Coll., 1969; ins. studies IIAAC, IEA, WAIB; C.P.C.U. Vice-pres., account exec. Jardine Emmett & Chandler, Inc., San Francisco, 1979—; tchr. ins. seminars. Mem. Western Assn. Ins. Brokers, Underwriters Forum, Ins. Forum (program chair). Congregationalist. Republican. Office: 333 Bush St San Francisco CA 94120

BUNTING, JANE DISHAROON, civic leader; b. Salisbury, Md., Feb. 26, 1937; d. Ernest Preston and Mabel Cora (Powell) Disharoon; m. William Gardner Bunting, Jan. 25, 1958; children: Beth Marie, William Gardner Jr., Barbara Ann. Legal sec. Marcus J. Williams, Atty., Berlin, Md., 1956-57; payroll clk. Atlas Poultry Co., Berlin, 1957; legal sec. Staton, Whaley & Price, Snow Hill, Md., 1957-58; pvt. sec. Buntings' Nurseries, Selbyville, Del., 1958-60. Appointed mem. Worcester County Bd.Edn., Newark, 1980—; mem. Showell (Md.) Sch. Adv. Bd., 1976-77; asst. leader Berlin Girl Souts U.S., 1972; treas. Peninsula Hosp. Aux., Berlin, 1975; regent DAR Gen. Levin Winder chpt., Pocomoke, Md., 1983-86. Mem. Nat. Assn. Bds. Edn., Md. Assn. Bds. Edn. (com. mem. 1982, 86), Worcester County Bd. Edn. (v.p.), Delta Kappa Gamma. Democrat. Methodist. Club: Worcester County Garden. Home: Rte 3 Box 130 Berlin MD 21811 Office: Worcester County Bd Edn Rte 1 Box 110 A Newark MD 21841

BUNTING, SHEILA MCGUIRE, nursing educator; b. Chgo., Jan. 6, 1936; d. Thomas J. and Pauline (Wilson) McGuire; m. Roger K. Bunting, June 7, 1958; children: Bryan, Rachel, Laura, Stephen. Cert. RN, St. Ambrose Coll., 1957; BS, U. Ill., 1978; MS, No. Ill. U., 1980. Staff nurse Mennonite Hosp., Bloomington, Ill., 1968-74, staff devel. instr., 1978-82, staff devel. coordinator, 1982-85; staff nurse Edgware Gen. Hosp., London, 1974-75; instr. Mennonite Coll. Nursing, Bloomington, 1985-87; research asst. Ctr. for Health Research, Detroit, 1988—. Contbr. articles to profl. jours. Bd. dirs. Am. Cancer Soc., McLean County, Ill., 1980—. Mem. Am. Nurses Assn., Ill. Nurses Assn. (bd. dirs. 1983-85), Cassandra Feminist Nurses Network (convening coordinator 1985—), Sigma Theta Tau. Office: Ctr for Health Research 5557 Cass Ave Detroit MI 48202

BUNTING, SUSAN ETHEL, auditor; b. Chgo., Aug. 29, 1956; d. Roy R. Breitenbach Sr. and Cecilia J. (Cunha) Cass; m. Russell R. Dworzack, Nov. 3, 1973 (div. Aug. 1978); 1 child, Neil Eric; m. Thomas Garnet Bunting, Feb. 1979; children: Roy Garnet, Jordan Arthur. BS, Calif. State U., Hayward, 1982, MBA, 1988. CPA, Tex. Acctg. clk. Pacific Stereo, Emeryville, Calif., 1975-80; fin. auditor Safeway Stores, Inc., Oakland, Calif., 1982-85; electronic data processing auditor Safeway Stores, Inc., Oakland, 1985-87; internal auditor Pacific Gas and Electric, San Francisco, 1987—. Mem. Inst. Internal Auditors, EDP Auditors Assn., Am. Inst. CPA's. Office: Pacific Gas and Electric 4 Embarcadero Ctr #200 San Francisco CA 94106

BURAS, BRENDA ALLYNN, public affairs executive; b. New Orleans, May 1, 1954; d. Allen Anthony and Gloria Violet (Short) B. BA in Commerce, Loyola U., New Orleans, 1976, MBA, 1984. Stenographer Texaco Inc., New Orleans, 1974-76, engr.'s asst., 1976-78, natural gas contracts analyst, 1978-80, pub. affairs asst., 1980-83, pub. and govt. affairs coordinator S.E. region, 1983—; owner Achievements Unltd.; cert. lectr. Silva Method Mind Devel. and Stress Control. Loaned exec. United Way Greater New Orleans, 1978-79, mem. speakers bur., 1979-83; cons. Jr. Achievement Project Bus., 1979-80; voting commr. St. Bernard Parish, 1976-80; mem. Friends of Audubon Zoo, Sta. WYES-(PBS) TV, New Orleans Mus. Art; mem. membership and pub. relations coms. Emergency Food Bank New Orleans, Vol Leadership Devel. Program United Way, 1987; chmn. subcom. United Way Corp. Recognition/Thank-You, 1988—; speaker Boy Scouts Explorers program. 1984—; active media com. Rep. Convention, 1988. Mem. Pub. Relations Soc. Am., Women in Communications, Inc., Press Club New Orleans, Inst. Noetic Scis., Assn. for Humanistic Psychology, People to People Internat. Inc., Ark. and Ala. Petroleum Councils (state working groups), La. Mid-Continental Oil and Gas Assn. (mem. pub. relations com.). Republican. Clubs: U.S. Figure Skating Assn., Dixieland Figure Skating, Heritage Plaza Health. Office: Texaco Inc 400 Poydras St New Orleans LA 70160

BURBANK, GLADYS VERENA, labor union educational administrator; b. Titusville, Pa., Oct. 2, 1947; d. Stephen Farnsworth and Frances Pauline (Baney) Antill. BS in Secondary Edn., Clarion (Pa.) State Coll., 1971. Tchr. Redbank Valley High Sch., New Bethlehem, Pa., 1971; caseworker State of Pa., Phila., 1971-74; social worker State of Fla., Daytona Beach, 1974-77; organizer Am. Fedn. State, County and Mcpl. Employees, Olympia, Wash., 1978-79; dir. edn. and organizing Wash. Fedn. State Employees div. Am. Fedn. State, County and Mcpl. Employees, Olympia, 1979—; mem. Gov.'s affirmative action policy com. State of Wash., Olympia, 1983—; mem. adv. com. labor ctr. The Evergreen State Coll., 1987—. Mem. Coalition of Labor Union Women. Democrat. Office: Washington Fedn State Employees 1212 Jefferson St SE Suite 300 Olympia WA 98501

BURBEY, THERESA ROSE STADTMUELLER, accounting company executive, accountant; b. Oshkosh, Wis., Sept. 17, 1942; d. John Andrew and Anna Marie (Binder) Stadtmueller; m. Paul Michael Burbey, June 6, 1962 (div. May 1980); children: Mark Paul and Michael Robert (twins). BBA, Silver Lake Coll., 1983. Tax cons. H & R Block Inc., Manitowoc, Wis., 1970-83; acct., pres. T. R. Burbey Acctg. & Tax Assocs., Manitowoc, 1983—, Milw., 1984—; instr. Silver Lake Coll., Manitowoc, 1984—; advisor Circle K Internat. Coll. Level Kiwanis, Silver Lake Coll., 1986—; seminar presenter Manitowoc C. of C., 1986—. Contbr. articles Small Business Counselor, 1986-87. Pres., bd. dirs. Big Brothers/Big Sisters, Manitowoc, 1986—; v.p. Manitowoc County Hist. Soc., 1986. Mem. Nat. Soc. Pub. Accts., Wis. Assn. Accts., Wisconsin Women Entrepreneurs, Small Bus. Adminstn. (active corp execs. vol.), Manitowoc/Two Rivers C. of C. (v.p. 1987), Silver Lake Coll. Alumni Assn. (pres. 1984-86). Republican. Roman Catholic. Lodge: Kiwanianne (pres. 1984). Office: T R Burbey Acctg & Tax Assocs 1701 Washington St Manitowoc WI 54220

BURBIDGE, ELEANOR MARGARET PEACHEY, astronomer, educator; b. Davenport, Eng.; d. Stanley John and Marjorie (Stott) Peachey; m. Geoffrey Burbidge, Apr. 2, 1948; 1 child, Sarah. B.S., Ph.D., U. London; Sc.D. hon., Smith Coll., 1963, U. Sussex, 1970, U. Bristol, 1972, U. Leicester, 1972, City U., 1973, U. Mich., 1978, U. Mass., 1978, Williams Coll., 1979, SUNY-Stony Brook, 1985, Rensselaer Poly. Inst., 1986, U. Notre Dame, 1986. Mem. staff U. London Obs., 1948-51; research fellow Yerkes Obs., U. Chgo., 1951-53, Calif. Inst. Tech., Pasadena, 1955-57; Shirley Farr fellow Yerkes Obs., 1957-59, assoc. prof., 1959-62; mem. Enrico Fermi Inst. for Nuclear Studies, 1957-62; prof. astronomy dept. physics U. Calif.-San Diego, 1964—, univ. prof., 1984—; dir. Royal Greenwich Obs. (Herstmonceaux Castle), Hailsham, Sussex, Eng., 1972-73; Lindsay Meml. lectr. Goddard Space Flight Ctr., NASA, 1985; Abby Rockefeller Mauze prof. MIT, 1968; David Elder lectr. U. Strathclyde, 1972; V. Gildersleeve lectr. Barnard Coll., 1974; Jansky lectr. Nat. Radio Astronomy Observatory, 1977; Brode lectr. Whitman Coll., 1986. Author: (with G. Burbidge) Quasi-Stellar Objects, 1967; editor: Observatory mag., 1948-51; mem. editorial bd.: Astronomy and Astrophysics, 1969—, SUNY-Stonybrook 1985. Recipient (with husband) Warner prize in Astronomy, 1959, Bruce Gold medal Astronomy Soc. Pacific, 1982; hon. fellow Univ. Coll., London, Girton Coll., Lucy Cavendish Coll., Cambridge; U.S. Nat. medal of sci., 1984; Sesquicentennial medal Mt. Holyoke Coll., 1987. Fellow Royal Soc., Nat. Acad. Scis. (chmn. sect. 12 astronomy 1986), Am. Acad. Arts and Scis., Royal Astron. Soc.; mem. Am. Astron. Soc. (v.p. 1972-74, pres. 1976-78; Henry Norris Russell lectr. 1984), Internat. Astron. Union (pres. commn. 28 1970-73), Grad. Women Sci. (nat. hon. mem.). Office: U Calif-San Diego Ctr for Astrophysics and Space Scis Mail Code C-011 La Jolla CA 92093

BURBRIDGE, KATHERINE ANN, economist, researcher; b. Peoria, Ill., June 18, 1953; d. Lloyd Hubert and Genevieve Ann (Vaster) B. BS in Environ. Biology, Eastern Ill. U., 1974; MA in Math., Ops. Research, 1984; M in Pub. Adminstrn., Sangamon State U., 1984. Vol. U.S. Peace Corps, Philippines, 1974-77; technician biology Northern Regional Research Ctr. USDA, Peoria, 1977-78; intern mgmt. ops. analysis Dept. Adminstrv. Services State of Ill., Springfield, 1979-81; asst. chief Commerce Commn. State of Ill., Springfield, 1981-86; rate cons. Tampa (Fla.) Electric Co., 1986—; cons. Jr. Achievement Project, Tampa, 1988. Vol. Planned Parenthood, Springfield, 1985-86; marshal math. program com. Sangamon State U., 1981. Mem. AUW, Beta Beta Beta. Roman Catholic. Office: Tampa Electric Co PO Box 111 Tampa FL 33601

BURCH, MARCIA ANN, publishing company executive; b. Washington, May 14, 1947; d. Sidney M. and Rhoda Lea (Goldstein) B.; m. James Lawrence Greig; children: Deborah Burch Greig, Caroline Burgh Greig. BA, Syracuse U., 1969. Asst. Penguin Books, N.Y.C., 1969-70, publicity dir., 1970-75; publicity dir. Viking Penguin, N.Y.C., 1975-80, dir. publicity and spl. promotion, 1980—. Mem. Pubs. Publicity Assn. (bd. dirs. 1983—, sec. 1982-83, treas. 1981-82). Office: Viking Penguins 40 W 23d St New York NY 10010

BURCH, NANCY LEA THORNALL, public relations executive, writer; b. Houston, June 6, 1940; d. Clarence Eugene and Marian Weston (Hearne) Thornall; children: Duncan Kyle, Andrew Wesley, Bonnie Lea. BA, Rice U., 1961. Flight attendant Pan Am. Airways, Miami, Fla., 1962-64; Spanish tchr. Houston I.S.D., 1964-65; librarian Rice U., Houston, 1965-66, sports info. dir., 1977-83; advt./pub. relations dir. Wilson's Bus. Products, Houston, 1984-85; pub. relations/spl. events dir. Tex. Children's Hosp., Houston, 1985-86; acct. exec. Ogilvy & Mather Pub. Relations, Houston, 1987—; media relations dir. Houston-Tenneco Marathon, 1985—; cons. San Jacinto Mus. History, Houston, 1985—. Author: Introduction to Physical Education: A Contemporary Careers Approach, 1984. V. chair Richmond State Sch. Vol. Council, 1970-74; mem. Houston Ballet Guild, 1975—, mem. Greater Houston Sesquicentennial Commn.; communications chair St. Paul's Meth. Ch., Houston, 1987—. Mem. Pub. Relations Soc. Am., Soc. Rice U. Women (pres. 1982-83), Rice U. Bus. and Profl. Women (v.p. 1985-87), World Wings Internat. (sec. 1984-85), Rice U. Alumni Assn. (pub. relations com. chair 1985-86), Clipt Wings (pres. 1969-70). Home: 3311 Stoney Brook Houston TX 77063 Office: Oglivy & Mather Pub Relations 1415 Louisiana Suite 2600 Houston TX 77002

BURCH, SUSAN WELLER, economist; b. Ashville, N.C., Jan. 30, 1933; d. John Maurice Weller and Eunice Estelle (Mattson) Robinson; children: Melissa, Elena, William. AB, Smith Coll., 1955; BA, Somerville Coll., Oxford (Eng.) U., 1958, MA, 1961. Stock analyst Dean Witter, San Francisco, 1959-61; economist U.S. Bur. Labor Stats., Washington, 1963-66, U.S. Fed. Res. Bd., Washington, 1966—; Contbr. numerous articles to profl. jours. Referee Rev. Econs. and Stats., 1975-80. Marshall Aid Commemoration scholar Oxford U., 1956-58. Mem. Am. Econs. Assn., Phi Beta Kappa. Home: 2853 Ontario Rd NW #107 Washington DC 20009 Office: Fed Res Bd 20th and Constn Ave NW Washington DC 20551

BURCHAM, JILL M., marketing executive; b. Phila., Feb. 20, 1952; d. William A. and Jean Carol (Dungan) McAllister; m. Danial R. Burcham, Dec. 28, 1984; children: Sean, Cara, Brian, P.J. Student, Meth. Coll., Fayettville, N.C., 1973. Sales rep. D.A.R. Indsl. Products, Phila., 1969-79; v.p. mktg. DARCO So., Inc., Independence, Va., 1981—; bd. dirs. extension div. Internat. Trade Linkage Unit. Mem. Nat. Assn. Female Execs. (regional dir. 1986—), Nat. Insulating Contractors, Fluid Sealing Assn., World Trade Assn. S.W. Va. (v.p. 1987—), Whytheville Econ. Devel. Ctr. Methodist. Home: Rt 2 Box 191 Galax VA 24333 Office: DARCO So Inc 253 Darco Dr PO Box 454 Independence VA 24348

BURCHAM, TERI MADISON, advertising agency executive; b. Passiac, N.J., Nov. 20, 1953; d. Benjamin Pawlowski and Charlotte (Brylczyk) Rydzewski. Student pub. schs. Advt. clk. community newspapers, Glen Cove, N.Y., 1970-72; advt. coordinator Newsday, Garden City, N.Y., 1972-76; account exec. Bernard Hode Advt., N.Y.C., 1976-80; br. mgr. Jon Rob Advt., Los Angeles, N.Y.C., 1980-81 ptnr. Transworld Mktg., Los Angeles, 1981-82; pres. Transworld Advt. Mktg., Inc., Dallas, 1982—. First v.p., membership chmn. Am. Women Owned Businesses Dallas, 1982—. Mem. Dallas C. of C. Office: 12820 Hillcrest Rd Suite 209 Transworld Advt Mktg Inc Dallas TX 75230

BURDEN, JEAN (PRUSSING), poet, author, editor; b. Waukegan, Ill., Sept. 1, 1914; d. Harry Frederick and Miriam (Biddlecom) Prussing; m. David Charles Burden, 1940 (div. 1949). B.A., U. Chgo., 1936. Sec. John Hancock Mutual Life Ins. Co., Chgo., 1937-39, Young & Rubicam, Inc., Chgo., 1939-41; editor, copywriter Domestic Industries, Inc., Chgo., 1941-45; office mgr. O'Brion Russell & Co., Los Angeles, 1948-55; adminstr. pub. relations Meals for Millions Found., Los Angeles, 1955-65; editor Stanford Research Inst., South Pasadena, Calif., 1965-66; propr. Jean Burden & Assocs., Altadena, Calif., 1966-82; lectr. poetry to numerous colls. and univs., U.S., 1963—; supr. poetry workshop Pasadena City Coll., Calif., 1961-62, 66, U. Calif. at Irvine, 1975; also pvt. poetry workshops. Author: Naked as the Glass, 1963, Journey Toward Poetry, 1966, The Cat You Care For, 1968, The Dog You Care For, 1968, The Bird You Care For, 1970, The Fish You Care For, 1971, A Celebration of Cats, 1974, The Classic Cats, 1975, The Woman's Day Book of Hints for Cat Owners, 1980, 84; Poetry editor: Yankee Mag, 1955—; pet editor: Woman's Day Mag, 1973-82; Contbr. numerous articles to various jours. and mags. MacDowell Colony fellow, 1973, 74, 76; Recipient Silver Anvil award Pub. Relations Soc. of Am., 1969, 1st prize Borestone Mountain Poetry award, 1963. Mem. Poetry Soc. Am., Acad. Am. Poets, Authors Guild. Address: 1129 Beverly Way Altadena CA 91001

BURDETTE, JANE ELIZABETH, association executive; b. Huntington, W.Va., Aug. 17, 1955; d. C. Richard and Jewel Kathryn (Wagner) B. A.A.S., Parkersburg Community Coll., W.Va., 1976; B.S., Glenville State Coll., W.Va., 1978; M.A., W.Va. U., 1984. Fund raiser, recruiter Muscular Dystrophy Assn., Charleston, W.Va., 1973, 74, 75; sec., bookkeeper Nationwide Ins. Co., Parkersburg, 1975; v.p. Burdette Funeral Home, Parkersburg, 1976—; intake and referral specialist Wood Sheltered Workshop, Parkersburg, 1984-85; exec. dir. YWCA, Parkersburg, 1985—. Bd. dirs. Sheltered Workshop, Parkersburg, 1982—, Western Dist. Guidance Ctr., Parkersburg, 1984—; bd. advisors Parkersburg Community Coll., 1980—, Domestic Violence Interdisciplinary adv. com., 1987, Just Say No, 1987—; mem. Wood County Commn. on Crime, Delinquency and Corrections, Parkersburg; chmn. Mid Ohio Valley United Fund Agy. Heads, Community Service Council, 1985; liaison Gov. Commn. on Disabled Persons, Charleston, W.Va.; mem. Career Adv. Network, 1987—; treas. W.Va. Women's Conf., 1987; exec. com. W.Va. chpt. Muscular Dystrophy Assn., 1987—; mem. We've Been There Parent Support Group, 1987—; mem. A Spl. Wish Found., 1988; mem. Parkersburg Consumer Adv. Group, founding com. Banquet of Wealth, 1988—; past transition plan team leader Wood County Bd. Edn.; past liason Internat. Yr. Disabled Persons; past treas. and program chmn. Gov.'s Conf.; former pres. Y Teen Club, YWCA; former adv. com. Mountwood Pk. White Oak Village. Named Miss Wheelchair W.Va., 1981, Outstanding Young Woman of Yr. for W.Va., 1981, Outstanding Young Woman of the Yr, 1986; recipient Kenneth Hieges award Muscular Dystrophy Assn., 1982, Outstanding Citizen award Frat. Order of Police, 1984, Community Service award Moose Lodge, 1987, Cert. Appreciation State W.Va., Gov. Jay Rockefeller, Cert. Appreciation Am. Legion Aux., Trail of New Beginning award. Mem. Nat. Assn. Female Execs., World Communication Assn., W.Va. Women in Higher Edn., W.Va. Funeral Dirs. Assn., AAUW. Democrat. Roman Catholic. Avocation: designing. Home: 2500 Brooklyn Dr Parkersburg WV 26101 Office: Young Women's Christian Assn 2501 Dudley Ave Parkersburg WV 26101

BURDICK, ANDREE MARIE, real estate broker, property manager; b. Waterbury, Conn., Apr. 7, 1949; d. William Robert Pothier and Anna Teresa (Dritsas) Tough; m. Michael O. Kehrlein (div. 1970); children: Jennifer Therese, Mosely (Ace) Astin; m. R. Kip Burdick (div. 1986); 1 child, Kelly Ray. Student, San Francisco State U., 1968. Salesperson, mgr. The Great Put On, Mendocino, Calif., 1973-79; sales rep. Radio KMFB, Mendocino, 1977-78; property mgr. ERA Bob Carlile Real Estate, Eugene, Oreg., 1979-81; real estate owner, property mgr. Andree & Assocs., Inc., Springfield, Oreg., 1981—; owner, mgr. Associated Contractors, Inc., Springfield, 1985—. Mem. Springfield Exec. Assn. (sec., treas. 1986-87, bd. dirs.), Springfield Bd. Realtors (civic affairs dir. 1986—), Springfield C. of C. Home: 6534 Thurston Rd Springfield OR 97478 Office: Andree & Assocs Inc 1810 N 15th St Suite A Springfield OR 97477

BURDICK, CAROLYN JANE, physiologist; b. Westerly, R.I., Jan. 10, 1938; d. Thomas John and Amy (Eaton) B.; B.A., Smith Coll., 1959; Ph.D., Harvard U., 1965. NIH fellow Harvard U., Cambridge, Mass., 1962-64, dept. cell biology Rockefeller U., N.Y.C., 1964-66; lectr. physiology Hunter Coll., N.Y.C., 1966; asso. prof. biology Bklyn. Coll., 1966—; mem. corp. Marine Biol. Lab, Woods Hole, Mass., 1972—. Mem. Am. Soc. Zoologists, Phi Beta Kappa, Sigma Xi. Author: Laboratory Manual for General Physiology, 1978; contbr. numerous articles in field to profl. jours. Office: Bklyn Coll Dept Biology Brooklyn NY 11210

BURDICK, MARY LUELLA, hospital executive; b. Olean, N.Y., Sept. 22, 1929; d. Leone Leslie and Ida Florence (Tompkins) Sturtevant; student public schs.; m. Kenneth Gerald Burdick, Aug. 31, 1946; children—Ronald Leone, Anna Marie, Gerald Ralph. Bookkeeper, cashier Things Shoe Store, Lockport, N.Y., 1954-55; mgr. trainee Joanlee Dress Shop, Lockport, 1958; supr. Syncro Corp., Hicksville, Ohio, 1960-67; various positions Tribune Printing Co., Hicksville, 1969-77; seamstress, Hicksville, 1976-79; mgr. forms, mgmt. Parkview Meml. Hosp., Fort Wayne, Ind., 1979—. Treas., Hicksville Missionary Ch., 1970-80, 82—, past dir. children's group; mem. Nat. Assn. FemalE Execs., Am. Business Women's Assn. Home: 04512 State Route 18 Hicksville OH 43526 Office: Parkview Meml Hosp 2200 Randallia Dr Fort Wayne IN 46805

BURDINE, LINDA SHARON, educator, author; b. Milw., July 23, 1950; d. Carl and Ruby (Dirk) Wiedmann; m. Stephen Michael Burdine, May 16, 1975; children—Scott, Kristine. B.S., Ball State U., 1973; M.S., Ind. U., 1979. Tchr. bus. edn. Washington High Sch., Indpls., 1974-76; tchr. bus. edn. Perry Meridian High Sch., Indpls., 1976—; chairperson textbook adoption State of Ind., 1976. Author: Typing Bulletin Board Projects, 1985; Awards, Rewards Coupons, 1985; Learning General Business, 1985; Learning Shorthand Learning Typing, 1985; Creations, Inc., A Typewritng Simulation, 1986. Mem. Ind. State Tchrs. Assn., Indpls. Bus. Edn. Assn., Perry Edn. Assn. (mem. negotiation team 1977, bldg. rep. 1985—), Phi Delta Kappa. Avocations: reading; writing; swimming. Office: Perry Meridian High Sch 401 W Meridian Sch Rd Indianapolis IN 46217

BURENGA, JANIS MARIE, radio network executive; b. Somerset, N.J., Mar. 15, 1951; d. Nicholas and Louanna Gertrude (Chamberlin) B. BJ, Lock Haven U., 1973. Sr. dir. field ops. Am. Freedom Train Found., Alexandria, Va., 1973-77; cons. Balt., 1977-78; pub. relations dir. Electrolert Inc., Troy, Ohio, 1978; pres. The Burenga Agy. Inc., N.Y.C., 1978-85; v.p. creative services United Stas. Radio Networks, N.Y.C., 1985—; bd. dirs. Black River and Western Pub. Relations, Ringoes, N.J., 1985—. Pub., editor On Radio, N.Y.C., 1985—. Mem. Broadcast Promotion and Mktg. Execs. Office: United Stations Radio Networks 1440 Broadway New York NY 10018

BURFORD, ANNE MCGILL, lawyer; b. Casper, Wyo., Apr. 21, 1942; d. Joseph John and Dorothy Jean (O'Grady) McGill; m. David Gorsuch, June 4, 1964 (div. 1982); children: Neil, Stephanie, J.J.; m. Robert Fitzpatrick Burford, Feb. 20, 1983. Student, Nat. U. Mex., summers 1955-56, 58, Regis Coll., Denver, summer 1959; BA, U. Colo., 1961, LLB, 1964. Bar: Colo. 1964, D.C., 1985. Fulbright scholar, Jaipur, India, 1964-65; asst. trust adminstr. 1st Nat. Bank of Denver, 1966-67; instr. Metro State Coll., 1966-67; asst. dist. atty., Jefferson County, 1968-71; dep. dist. atty., Denver, 1971-73; hearing officer Real Estate Commn., State Bds. Cosmetology, Optometric Examiners, Profl. Nursing and Vet. Medicine, 1974-75; corp. counsel Mountain Bell Telephone Co., Denver, 1975-81; mem. Colo. Ho. of Reps., 1977-81, chmn. state affairs com., 1979-80, chmn. legal services com., 1980; del. Nat. Conf. State Legislators; mem. Nat. Conf. Commrs. on Uniform State Law, 1979, 80; presdl. del. to Kenya's Independence, 1983; loaned exec. mgmt. and efficiency task force Colo. Dept. Regulatory Agys., 1976; adminstr. EPA, Washington, 1981-83; now lectr. Author: Are You Tough Enough, 1986. Former bd. dirs. YMCA. Mem. D.C. Bar Assn., Mortar Bd., Phi Alpha Delta, Delta Delta Delta. Republican. Roman Catholic. Home and Office: 5505 Seminary Rd #105N Falls Church VA 22041

BURFORD, MARY ANNE, medical technologist; b. Paris, Ark., Aug. 24, 1939; d. Anthony John and Julia Elizabeth (Hoffman) Elsken; B.S. in Biology, Benedictine Coll., 1961; grad. in med. tech. St. Mary's Sch. Med. Tech., 1962; m. Joseph Paul Burford, May 11, 1968 (div. Feb. 1983); children—Sarah Elizabeth, Shawn Anthony, Joseph Paul, Daniel Aaron. Evening supr. St. Vincent's Infirmary, Little Rock, 1962-65; med. technologist Holt-Krock Clinic, Ft. Smith, Ark., 1966-68, Ball Meml. Hosp., Muncie, Ind., 1971-72, Pathologist Assoc., Muncie, 1972-73; chief technologist Ob-Gyn Inc., Muncie, 1975—; instr. microbiology St. Vincent's Infirmary, 1962-65, Sparks Med. Ctr., Ft. Smith, 1966-68. Chmn. liturgical life, St. Mary's Catholic Ch., 1979-86; treas Met. Football League, 1983-85. Mem. Am. Soc. Clin. Pathologists (affiliate mem., registered med. technologist), Am. Assn. Clin. Chemists, Am. Soc. for Microbiology. Club: Muncie Altrusa (chmn. materials and records com., constn. and by-laws com. 1985-86, chmn. community service 1984-85, recording sec. 1986-87, chmn. budget com. 1986-87, bd. liaison to youth services, bylaws, materials and records 1986-87, 2d v.p. 1987-88, bd. liaison to pub. relations/flowers, gifts and memls. 1987-88, bd. liaison to ways and means 1987-88, 1st v.p. 1988-89, bd. liasion pub. relations 1988-89, program coordinator 1988-89). Home: 1509 W Buckingham Dr Muncie IN 47302 Office: 2501 W Jackson St Muncie IN 47302

BURG, RUTH (THELMA) COOPER, administrative judge; b. Phila., Mar. 29, 1926; d. Philip and Rose Anna (Applebaum) C.; m. Max Gunter Breslauer, Dec. 21, 1946 (dec. Aug. 1964); m. Maurice Benjamin Burg, Dec. 30, 1967; children—Elizabeth, Lawrence, Joan, Robert. B.S. in Chemistry, George Washington U., 1945; postgrad., George Washington U. Sch. Medicine, 1945-46; J.D. cum laude, George Washington U., 1950. Bar: D.C. 1950, Md. 1954, U.S. Supreme Ct. 1968. Report Analyst Naval Research Lab., Washington, 1946-48; clk. U.S. Tax Ct., Washington, 1950-53; sole practice Washington, 1953-65; asst. to chairman Bd. Contract Appeals, Energy Commn., Bethesda, Md., 1965-72; adminstrv. judge Armed Services Bd. Contract Appeals, Falls Church, Va., 1972—; lectr. in field. Taxation editor George Washington Law Rev., 1949-50. Contbr. articles to legal jours. Vice chmn. Harriet B. Burg Found., Washington, 1983—; recipient John Bell Larner medal George Washington U., 1950. Fellow Am. Bar Found.; mem. ABA (chmn. pub. contract law sect. 1984-85), Phi Sigma Sigma (internat. pres. 1954-56). Democrat. Jewish. Lodge: B'nai B'rith (dist. 5 pres.-elect 1968, founding pres. Kroloff chpt. 1960). Home: 3106 Que St NW Washington DC 20007 Office: Armed Service Bd Contract Appeals 5109 Leesburg Pike Skyline 6 Suite 700 Falls Church VA 22041

BURGDORFF, JEAN T., real estate executive; m. Douglas Burgdorff (dec. 1968); children—Charles, Peter. B.A. in Edn., Columbia U.; postgrad. New Eng. Conservatory Music. Mem. piano faculty Douglass Coll., Rutgers U.; sales rep. Burgdorff, Realtors, 1958-68, pres., 1968—; dir. Country Living Assocs. Recipient Summit Community Service award, 1964; Mem. Intercommunity Relocation (nat. pres.), N.J. Cert. Resdl. Brokers (pres.), N.J. Assn. Realtors (state dir.). Office: Burgdorff Realtors 560 Central Ave Murray Hill NJ 07904

BURGE, VICKIE LOU, dentist, teacher; b. Indpls., Mar. 1, 1947; d. Rex Banton and Margaret Jean (Sinn) B.; m. Dean Alan Burton, Nov. 6, 1982; children: Dena Rae, Evan William. BA, Ind. Cen. U., 1969; cert. of honors, U. Edinburgh, Scotland, 1969; MS in Edn., Ind. U., 1971; DDS, Ind. Sch. Dentistry, 1982. Tchr. So. Hancock County High Sch., New Palestine, Ind., 1969-72; reading specialist DeKalb County High Sch., Atlanta, 1972-75, Warren Twp. High Sch., Indpls., 1979-83; med. technician blood bank Wishard Hosp., Indpls., 1979-83; dentist Family Dental, Indpls., 1982—. Speaker Say No to Drugs, Indpls., 1986-87; nursery sch. sponsor, Indpls. Mem. ADA, Ind. Dental Assn., Indpls. Dental Assn., Ky. Dental Assn., So. Regional Dental Assn., Women in Dentistry. Republican. Lutheran. Home: 3306 N Richardt Indianapolis IN 46226

BURGESS, CAROLYN JANE, counselor, musician; b. Columbus, Ohio, Sept. 26, 1933; d. John Anderson and Mabel (McCullough) Twitty; m. Braxton V. Burgess, Dec. 17, 1966; 1 son, John. Student Ohio State U., 1951-52; B.A. cum laude, Wilberforce, U., 1972; postgrad. Wayne State U., 1971-72. Pvt. music tchr., various cities, Ohio, W.Va. and Mich., 1948-80; counselor Greater Flint Opportunities Industrialization Ctr. (Mich.), 1982-88; counselor Met. C. of C., Flint, Mich., 1988—; organist, choir dir., accompanist various chs. and musical groups; minister music Allen Temple African Methodist Episcopal Ch., Detroit, 1968-73, Freeman Ave United Ch. Christ, Cin., 1973-75, Allen Chapel A.M.E. Ch., Kalamazoo, 1975-80. 2d v.p. Women's Missionary Soc. A.M.E. Ch., 1960—, pres. Mich. conf. br., 1980—, organizer, ex-officio mem. bd. Mich. conf. br. Quality of Life Ctr., Detroit, 1980—; mem. new dimensions workshop com. Ch. Women United Greater Flint, 1982—, pres., 1988—); mem. dialysis unit fund raising com. Hurley Med. Ctr., Flint, 1984—; mem. exec. bd. Kalamazoo br. NAACP, 1978-80, del. nat. conv., 1980; former mem. laity leadership dept., Southwestern Ohio assn. United Ch. Christ, task force on instl. racism Ohio conf. United Ch. Christ; bd. dirs. Flint YWCA, 1981—; bd. dirs. Family Services Agy. Genesee County, 1984-85. Mem. Nat. Council Negro Women, World Fedn. Meth. Women, Nat. Assn. Negro Musicians, Am. Guild Organists, Ch. Women United, Alpha Kappa Mu, Sigma Omega, Delta Sigma Theta. Democrat. Office: Met C of C 1204 Harrison St Flint MI 48502

BURGESS, EILEEN KILEY, personnel consultant; b. Cin., July 14, 1960; d. Roger Lee and Geraldine Isabel (Fay) Kiley; m. Alan Ray Burgess, June 13, 1981; 1child, Renee Michelle. BS in Indsl. Mgmt. with honors, Ga. Inst. Tech., 1981. Customer service rep. Hercules Inc., Wilmington, Del., 1981-84; personnel coordinator Uniforce Temporary Services, Atlanta, 1984-86; account exec. OM-5, Atlanta, 1986—. Home: 1720 Branch Valley Dr Roswell GA 30076 Office: OM-5 229 Peachtree St Suite 601 Atlanta GA 30303

BURGESS, EUNICE LESTER, psychologist; b. Madison, Fla., Dec. 17, 1935; d. Thomas and Rebecca (Royal) Lester; m. Miller Burgess, Jr., Aug. 18, 1958; children—Brenda, Joyce, Wanda Renee, Kenneth Bernard. B.S. in Elem. Edn., Tuskegee Inst., 1958, M.Ed. in Psychology and Guidance, 1963; postgrad. U. N.C., 1967-68, U. South Fla., 1980-83. Coordinator student affairs Tuskegee Inst., Ala., 1960-64; vocat. counselor Job Corps Ctr. for Women, St. Petersburg, Fla., 1964-66; vocat. rehab. counselor State Dept. Edn., St. Petersburg, 1966-68; elem. counselor Pinellas County Sch. System, Clearwater, Fla., 1968-77; guidance coordinator St. Petersburg Vocat.-Tech. Inst., 1977-80, coordinator outreach recruitment, 1980-86; coordinator Evening Vocat. Guidance, 1986—; cons. in career edn.; staff devel. tchr. in humanistic edn. Bd. dirs. NAACP, 1975-85; v.p. Pinellas County Black Polit. Caucus, 1976-77; co-chmn. St. Petersburg Community Alliance, 1974-75; mem. Guidance Adv. Bd. Pinellas County, 1975-76; sec., treas. St. Petersburg Fair Housing Bd., 1976-78; mem. Pinellas Profl. Dem. Women's Club, 1976—; v.p. Pinellas County Biracial Adv. Com., 1980-82; v.p. region IV Fla. Spl. Needs Assn., 1983-85, pres., 1986-87. Recipient Service Award Elem. div. of Fla. Sch. Counselor Assn., 1975, Service and Leadership award St. Petersburg C. of C., 1975, Outstanding Performance award City of St. Petersburg, 1973, Community Service awards Bethune Cookman Alumni Assn., 1976, St. Petersburg C. of C., 1977, Disting. Educator award Fla. Grand Lodge of Free and Accepted Masons, 1983, Outstanding Contbn. to Vocat. Edn. award Fla. Spl. Needs Assn., 1986, Outstanding Service to Vocat. Edn. plaque Am. Vocat. Assn./Spl. Needs div., 1986, Resolution of Dedication, State Dept. Edn. Fla. div. Spl. Needs, 1987; named Outstanding Educator of Yr., Pinellas County Sch. Bd., 1983, Nat. Parent, Tuskegee Inst., 1983; Fla. Sch. Counselor Human Rights award named in her honor, 1984. Mem. Am. Personnel and Guidance Assn., Fla. Personnel and Guidance Assn., Suncoast Personnel and Guidance Assn. (sec. 1981-82), Am. Sch. Counselor Assn. (human rights coordinator 1977-82), Fla. Sch. Counselor Assn. (v.p. post-secondary 1980-82), Suncoast Sch. Counselor Assn., NEA, Am. Vocat. Guidance Assn., Fla. Vocat. Assn. (v.p., bd. dirs. 1986-87), Assn. Non White Concerns, Sickle Cell Found. Pinellas County, Tuskegee U. Alumni Assn. (state dir. 1986—), Zeta Phi Beta (Woman of Yr. 1976, treas. 1980-82). Democrat. Baptist. Home: 3012 DeSoto Way S Saint Petersburg FL 33712 Office: St Petersburg Vocat Tech Inst 901 34th St S Saint Petersburg FL 33712

BURGESS, GLORIA JEAN, communication consultant; b. Oxford, Miss., May 23, 1953; d. Earnest Jr. and Mildred (Blackmon) McEwen; m. John Everett Burgess, July 25, 1975; 1 child, Quinn Meredith. B in Gen. Studies, U. Mich., 1975, MA, 1977; MBA, U. So. Calif., 1986, PhD, 1980. Prodn. specialist Univ. Microfilms div. Xerox, Ann Arbor, Mich., 1971-75; faculty U. Mich., Ann Arbor, 1975-77, U. So. Calif., Los Angeles, 1977-80; sr. tech. writer Honeywell Info. Systems, Los Angeles, 1979-81; editor Trade Service Publs., Los Angeles, 1980; sr. tech. staff Citicorp/TTI, Santa Monica, Calif., 1981, mgr. tech. info. services, 1981-87; pres. Infoman, Edmonds, Wash., 1987—; freelance cons., Los Angeles, 1983—; faculty UCLA, 1985-87. Mem. Speech Communication Assn. Lutheran.

BURGESS, HEATHER HAYDEN, non-profit executive; b. Sheridan, Wyoming, Dec. 21, 1951; d. Henry Amos and Mary Ralston (Hayden) B. BFA, U. Oreg., 1976; student, Art Student League, 1978, 80, 81. Founder Northern Rockies Regional Exhibition, Sheridan, 1982; dir. residency program Ucross (Wyo.) Found., 1983-86, v.p., 1986, exec. dir., 1987—; Dir. Wyo. Futures Project, Casper, 1985—. Home: 21 Apache Rd Clearmont WY 82835

BURGESS, JANET HELEN, interior designer; b. Moline, Ill., Jan. 22, 1933; d. John Joseph and Helen Elizabeth (Johnson) B.; student Augustana Coll., Rock Island, Ill., 1950-51, U. Utah, Logan, 1951-52, Marycrest Coll., 1959-60; m. Richard Everett Guth, Aug. 25, 1951; children—John Joseph, Marshall Claude, Linnea Ann Guth Layman Sinclair; m. Milan Andrew Vodick, Feb. 16, 1980. One-person shows: El Pao, Bolivar, Venezuela, 1952-62; represented in pvt. collections, U.S., Europe, S.Am.; producer, designer Playcrafters Barn Theatre, Moline, Ill., 1963-65; designer, gen. mgr. Grilk Interiors, Davenport, Iowa, 1963-87; dir. Fine Arts Gallery, Davenport, 1978-84; chmn. bd. Product Handling, Inc., Davenport, 1981-88; owner mail order bus. Amazon Vinegar & Pickling Works Drygoods, Davenport. Contbr. articles to profl. jours.; design work featured in Gift & Decorative Accessories mag., 1969, 80, Decor mag., 1979. Bd. dirs. Rock Island Art Guild, 1974—, Quad Cities Arts Council, 1980-84 ; bd. dirs. Village of East Davenport (Iowa) Assn., 1973-84 , pres., 1981; bd. dirs. Neighborhood Housing Services, Davenport, Davenport Area Conv. and Tourism Bur., 1981; mem. adv. bd. interior design dept. Scott Community Coll., 1975-80; mem. Mayor's Com. Historic Preservation, Davenport, Iowa, 1976-77, 85—; bd. dirs. retail com. Operation Clean Davenport, 1981; mem. 16th Iowa Civil War Re-enactment Union. Mem. Gift and Decorative Accessories Assn. (nat. merit award 1969), Am. Soc. Interior Designers (assoc.), Davenport C. of C., Nat. Trust Hist. Preservation, Preservation Group, State Iowa Hist. Soc. Home: 2801 34th Ave Ct Rock Island IL 61201 Office: 2218 E 11th St Davenport IA 52803

BURGESS, JEANNE LLEWELLYN, professional foundation institute executive, publishing executive; b. New Albany, Ind., Aug. 6, 1923; d. Jesse Joel and Lydia Ann (Young) Llewellyn; m. Quentin F. Burgess, Dec. 24, 1941 (dec. Nov. 1984). Student, Ind. U., 1948-49, Ind. U. SE, New Albany, 1979. Supr. policy dept. Wabash Life Ins. Co., Indpls., 1952-53, claim examiner Acacia Mut. Life Ins. Co., Washington, 1954-61; exec. sec. System Devel. Corp., Falls Church, Va., 1962-64; mgr. stockholder relations Brown-Forman Corp., Louisville, 1965—; sec., treas. Airline Mushroom Producers, New Albany, 1977-84; exec. dir. Sylvan Forest Inst., Louisville, 1984—. Co-editor Corporate Fact Book, 1987; mgr. Brown-Forman Ann. Report, 1970-87; contbr. numerous poems and articles for mags. and newspapers. Active arts council, Floyd and Orange Counties, Ind. and met. Louisville 1977—; mem. adv. bd. Gov.'s Task Force on Forest Mgmt., Indpls., 1980; cons. Jr. Achievement, Floyd County, 1981-82, judge nat. essay contest, 1983; bd. dirs. Flyd City Histl. Soc., Fairview Historic Cemetery, New Albany; mem. Dodrasquicentennial of New Albany, 1988; del. citizens ambassador program People to People Internat., 1988. Recipient Clarion Merit award Women In Communications, 1982, Cert. of Accomplishment Four Seasons Wine Symposium, N.Y.C., 1970. Mem. Nat. Investor Relations Ins., Corp. Transfer Agts. Assn., Am. Forestry Assn., Nat. Assn. Investors (corp. adv. bd. 1981-83), So. Ind. Poets and Writers Assn. Republican. Methodist. Home: 4000 Persimmon Ln New Albany IN 47150 Office: Brown-Forman Corp 850 Dixie Hwy Louisville KY 40210

BURGESS, MEREDITH NANCY STRANG, advertising agency executive; b. Rockland, Maine, Apr. 27, 1956; d. Walter P. and Charlene M. (Perkins) Strang; BS, U. Maine-Orono, 1978; m. James L. Burgess, June 24, 1978; children: Christopher James, Matthew Strang. Store activities rep. McDonald's Corp., Boston, 1978-79; account exec. Arnold & Co., Inc., Portland, Maine, 1979-80, field account supr., 1980-81, account supr. for McDonald's advt. in Maine, 1981-83, account service mgr., 1984, v.p., 1985-86; pres., owner Burgess, Brewer, Stanyon & Payne Inc., Portland, 1986—. Mem. Camden (Maine) Republican Town Com., 1974-80, Cumberland (Maine) Rep. Town Com., 1980—; del. Rep. Conv. Maine, 1974, 76, 78, 80, 88; 1st alt. to Rep. Nat. Conv., 1976; com. woman from Knox County, Maine Rep. Com.; bd. dirs. Ronald McDonald House, U. Maine Alumni Council. Mem. Greater Portland Advt. Club (bd. dirs.), Soil Conservation Soc. Am., Natural Resource Council Maine, Alpha Phi. Home: 12 Country Charm Rd Cumberland ME 04021 Office: Thomas Block 100 Commercial St Suite 300 Portland ME 04101

BURGESS, MYRTLE MARIE, lawyer; b. Brainerd, Minn., May 3, 1921; d. Charles Dana and Mary Elzaida (Thayer) Burgess. B.A., San Francisco State U., 1947; J.D., Hastings Coll. Law, 1950. Bar: Calif. 1951. Pvt. practice law, San Francisco, 1951-52, Reedley, Calif., 1952—; judge pro tem Fresno County Superior Ct., 1974-77; now owner/operator Hotel Burgess. Bd. dirs. Reedley Indsl. Site Devel. Found., 1970-81; dir., 2d v.p. Kings Canyon unit Calif. Republican Assembly, 1973-75; pres., bd. dirs. Sierra Community Concert Assn., Reedley council Girl Scouts U.S.A., 1955-56; commr. Fresno City-County Commn. Status of Women; bd. dirs., treas. Reedley Downtown Assn., 1983—; bd. dirs. Kinship Program, 1988; bd. dirs., sec. Kings View Found. Recipient award for remodeling and preservation of old bldg. Fresno Hist. Soc., 1975, others. Mem. ABA, Calif. Bar Assn., Fresno County Bar Assn., World Peace Through Law Internat., Am. Trial Lawyers, Reedley C. of C. (bd. dirs. 1958-63, 87—, Woman of Yr. 1971, Athenian award 1988). Republican. Presbyterian. Clubs: Bus. and Profl. Women's (pres.). Lodge: Order Eastern Star. Home: 1076 N Kady Ave Reedley CA 93654 Office: 1107 G St Reedley CA 93654

BURGESS, PATRICIA ANN, nurse, educator; b. Carson City, Nev., Oct. 20, 1938; d. Joseph Cecil and Victorine Virginia (Sciarini) Morrison; children—Heather, Michael. Diploma, Mary's Help Coll. Nursing, 1959; B.S.N. (Profl. Nurse trainee), U. Nev., 1974, M.S., 1981. Cert. rural nurse practitioner, child and adolescent nurse. Staff nurse Marin Gen. Hosp., San Rafael, Calif., 1959; staff nurse Washoe Med. Ctr., Reno, 1959, head nurse emergency room, 1960, staff nurse ICU, 1961-64, head nurse ICU, 1965-66, staff nurse pediatrics, 1978, 82—; lectr. U. Nev., 1974-81, asst. prof. pediatrics, 1982—; Contbr. articles in profl. jours. Mem. Nev. Task Force on Child Abuse and Neglect. Mem. Am. Nurses' Assn., Nev. Nurses' Assn., Orvis Sch. Nursing Hon. Roman Catholic. Home: 1479 Coronet Circle Reno NV 89509 Office: U Nev Orvis Sch Nursing Reno NV 89557

BURGETT, FERN MARIE, writer; b. Japan, Oct. 28, 1956; d. Ralph Judson and Tomoe (Kobayashi) B. Student, Ohio State U., 1975-77; BS in Social Sci., U. Houston, 1980. Lic. radiotelephone operator's. Disc jockey, bus. sta. mgr. WOSL Radio, Lima, Ohio, 1976-77; free-lance video producer Houston, 1977-88; video producer Taylor Entertainment, Houston, 1977-85, convention co-chair, 1980-83; screenwriter Taylor Entertainment Group, Houston, 1982-84; freelance writer Alvin, Tex.; housekeeping mgr. U. Houston. Mem. U. Houston Staff Council, 1987-88. Recipient Service award Residence Halls, Mental Health, Mental Retardation Authority, Harris County, 1985, Service and Support award Council Ethnic Orgns., Houston, 1985-88, Esteemed Service Student Program Bd., Houston, 1986. Mem. Nat. Assn. Exec. Housekeepers (affiliate), Assn. Coll. Unions Internat. (profl. 1986—). Democrat. Baptist. Home: PO Box 1330 Friendswood TX 77546-1330 Office: U Houston UC Bldg Service 4800 UC Bldg Calhoun UC Room N-12 Houston TX 77004

BURGIO, JANE, state government official; b. Nutley, N.J.; m. John Burgio; children: John E., James. Student, Newark Sch. Fine and Indsl. Arts. Mem. N.J. State Assembly, Trenton, 1973-81; sec. of state State of N.J., Trenton, 1982—; chief election officer State of N.J.; chmn. N.J. Bd. Canvassers; alt. del. Rep. Nat. Conv., 1972, 88, del. and mem. platform com., 1984; past mem. arts, tourism, and cultural resources com. Nat. Conf. State Legis. Bd. dirs. Trustees for the Support of Free Pub. Schs.; trustee Caldwell Coll., Rider Coll., Planned Parenthood of Essex County, North Essex Devel. Council; MBA adv. bd. Seton Hall Coll.; past trustee Arts Council Essex area, Julie Maloney Dance Co.; former mem. St. Barnabas Hosp. Devel. Com.; past pres. James Caldwell High Sch. PTA.; participant Rotary Internat. Exchange Student Program. Recipient Alumni Recognition award Univ. Coll., Rutgers U., Newark, Hist. award N.J. League Hist. Socs., Cert. N.J. Humane Soc., Newark. Mem. Nat. Assn. Secs. of State (chmn. by-laws and constitution com.), Nat. Conf. State Legislature, Millburn-Short Hills Bus. and Profl. Women, Women's Polit. Caucus N.J., West Essex LVW (trustee). Home: North Caldwell NJ 07006 Office: New Jersey Dept State State House CN 300 Trenton NJ 08625

BURGMAN, DIERDRE ANN, lawyer; b. Logansport, Ind., Mar. 25, 1948; d. Ferdinand William Jr. and Doreen Yvonne (Walsh) B. BA, Valparaiso U., 1970, JD, 1979; LLM, Yale U., 1985. Bar: Ind. 1979, D.C., 1988, U.S. Dist. Ct. (so. dist.) Ind. 1979, N.Y. 1982, U.S. Dist. Ct. (so. dist.) N.Y. 1982, U.S. Ct. Appeals (7th cir.) 1982, U.S. Ct. Appeals (D.C. cir.) 1984, U.S. Ct. Appeals (2d cir.) 1984, U.S. Supreme Ct. 1985, D.C. 1988. Law clk. to chief judge Ind. Ct. Appeals, Indpls., 1979-80; prof. law Valparaiso (Ind.) U., 1980-81; assoc. Dewey, Ballantine, Bushby, Palmer & Wood, N.Y.C., 1981-84, Cahill Gordon & Reindel, N.Y.C., 1985—. Note editor Valparaiso U. law rev., 1978-79; contbr. articles to law jours. Mem. bd. visitors Valparaiso U. Sch. Law, 1986—. Ind. Bar Found. scholar, 1978. Mem. ABA (trial evidence com., profl. liability com.), Assn. Bar N.Y.C., N.Y. County Lawyers Assn. (asst. chmn. com. Supreme Ct. 1987—, Outstanding Service award 1988). Home: 164 E 61st St New York NY 10021 Office: Cahill Gordon & Reindel 80 Pine St Suite 1700 New York NY 10005

BURGOON, MARCIA SIBLEY, marketing and public relations professional, consultant; b. Balt., Aug. 30, 1944; d. Jonathan Ogden and Marcia Elma (Wilcox) Sibley; m. Norman Richard Burgoon, Apr. 9, 1966; children: Sherrie, Danielle, Michelle. BS, U. Md., College Park, 1966; postgrad., U. Md., Balt., Orange County Community Coll., Middletown. Tchr. Balt. County Bd. Edn., Towson, Md., 1966-70; editor newsletter Nu-Dy-Per Baby Products, Inc., Balt., 1970-73; dir. mktg. Hall of Fame of Trotter, Goshen, N.Y., 1979-81; exec. dir. ops. Goshen C. of C., 1981-82; dir. corp. communications Highland Telephone and Sylvan Lake (N.Y.)Telephone, 1982-84, Cartelco, Inc., Annapolis, Md., 1984-85; pvt. practice cons. Md., 1985—; exec. dir., charter mem. Orange County Tourism Promotion Corp., Goshen, 1980-81; mktg. and pub. relations cons. for various firms. Mem. pub. relations team campaign United Way Orange County, Middletown, N.Y., 1982-83; bd. dirs. Queen Anne's County C. of C., Chester, Md., 1986—; coordinator, founder Chesapeake Women's Network, Eastern Shore, Md., 1986-87; coordinator adult ministries Kent Island Meth. Ch., Md. Republican. Methodist. Home: 209 Drovers Way Stevensville MD 21666 Office: Marcia Burgoon Assocs Little Village Plaza Chester MD 21619

BURGOYNE, PATRICIA HAWKINS, freelance writer; b. Chgo., May 22, 1953; d. William Emery and Lorraine (Udall) Hawkins; B.A. cum laude, U. So. Calif., 1975; m. David Burgoyne II, June 23, 1973; children—Michael Lundy, Megan Louise. Staff mem. KUSC-FM Radio, Los Angeles, 1971-73; dir. public relations Tucson Mus. Art, 1975-76; contbg. editor Tucson Mag., 1976-78, Scottsdale (Ariz.) Progress Saturday Mag., 1980-82; freelance writer, 1975—. Chmn. pub. relations Maricopa County Med. Soc. Aux., 1979-80; bd. dirs. Planned Parenthood Cen. and No. Ariz., 1981-82, 82-83; pres. Planned Parenthood Aux., 1981-83; chmn. publicity Kachina County Day Sch. Aux., 1979-80; docent Phoenix Art Mus., 1984—; chmn. Scottsdale Meml. Hosp. Honor Ball, 1988; bd. trustees Scottsdale Meml. Health Found., 1988; bd. dirs. Contemporary Forum Phoenix Art Mus., 1987-88. Mem. Women in Communications, Inc., Maricopa County Med. Soc. Aux., Scottsdale Med. Wives, Kappa Kappa Gamma.

BURGOYNE, SHIRLEY JEAN, lawyer; b. Saginaw, Mich., Oct. 25, 1932; d. Marshall Albert and Beatrice Viola (Clements) Cox; A.B., J.D., U. Mich., 1956; m. Bert Burgoyne, Apr. 22, 1955 (div.); children—Deborah Jeanne, David Edward, Douglas Jeffrey. Law clk. Oreg. Supreme Ct., Salem, 1956-57; admitted to Oreg. bar, 1957, Mich. bar, 1959; practiced in Roseburg, Oreg., 1957-58, Lansing, Mich., 1959-63, Ann Arbor, Mich., 1963—; mem. firm Burgoyne & Burgoyne, Roseburg, 1957-58, Thomas C. Walsh, Lansing, 1959-63, Burgoyne & Morris, Ann Arbor, 1968-69, Burgoyne & Pratt, Ann Arbor, 1977—; legal counsel Mich. Abortion Referendum Com., 1969-73. Mem. Mich. Women's Commn., 1971-72; bd. dirs. Mich. Council for Study of Abortion, 1971-73. Mem. Am. (family law sect., chair codification com.), Mich. (council family law sect.), Oreg. bar assns., Am. Trial Lawyers Assn., Am. Judicature Soc., AAUW, Kappa Beta Pi. Presbyn. Home and Office: 206 Miller St Ann Arbor MI 48104

BURIK, TERRY OTTILLA, learning consultant; b. Auerbach, Fed. Republic Germany, Dec. 13, 1944; came to U.S., 1949; d. Richard Henry and Olga Josephine (Polniak) Stankowski; m. Paul Henry Burik, Sept. 19, 1972 (div. 1981); children: Brett, Brooke. BA in Psychology, Rutgers U., 1968, MEd, 1969, EdD, 1986. Cert. tchr., N.J. Tchr. New Brunswick (N.J.) Parochial Schs., 1964-68; tchr. spl. edn. East Brunswick (N.J.) Schs., 1968-72, Red Bank (N.J.) Child Study Services, 1972—; assoc. mem. Pace Clin. Services, Princeton, 1985—; dir. Psycho Ednl. Services, Millstone Twp., N.J., 1986—; speaker Inst. Research on Women, Rutgers U., New Brunswick, 1987—. Mem. NEA, N.J. Assn. Learning Cons., Assn. Supervision and Curriculum Devel., Council Learning Disability, N.J. Edn. Assn., Nat. Assn. Female Execs., Millstone Soccer Assn., Kappa Delta Pi. Democrat. Roman Catholic. Club: Millstone Womens. Home: 103 Valley Dr Millstone Township NJ 07726 Office: Red Bank Child Study Services 101 Harding Rd Red Bank NJ 07701

BURK, MARGUERITE CATHERINE, educator; b. Ottawa, Kans., July 12, 1915; d. Ralph G. and Clara A. (Eberhart) Burk; A.B., U. Kans., 1937, M.A., 1938; Ph.D. (fellow), U. Minn., 1948; postgrad. Am. U., 1938-40, U. Wis., 1940, Cambridge (Eng.) U., 1955-56. Statis. clk., economist U.S. Dept. Agr., Washington, 1939-45; head consumption sec. Bur. Agr. Econs., Washington, 1945-60; agrl. economist Econ. Research Service, Washington, 1960-61; prof. agrl. econs. and home econs. U. Minn., 1961-69; leader food consumption research group Dept. Agr., Washington, 1969-75; prof. program internat. studies in human ecology Howard U., Washington, 1975-80; cons. FAO program, Rome, 1961, Philippine Food and Nutrition Research Inst., Manila, 1977, 79; cons. U.S. Dept. Agr., 1980—, AID, 1983; cons. in field. Recipient Superior Service award U.S. Dept. Agr., 1954; USOE grantee internat. studies in human ecology, 1975-77. Mem. Am. Econ. Assn., Am. Home Econs. Assn.; fellow Am. Council Consumer Interests (pres. 1961-62). Author handbooks. Contbr. articles to profl. jours. Editor: The Nat. Food Situation, 1945-60.

BURK, SYLVIA JOAN, petroleum landman, free-lance writer; b. Dallas, Oct. 16, 1928; d. Guy Thomas and Sylvia (Herrin) Ricketts; m. R. B. Murray, Jr., Sept. 7, 1951 (div. Jan. 1961); children—Jeffery Randolph, Brian BeVaughn; m. Bryan Burk, Apr. 26, 1973. B.A., So. Meth. U., Dallas, 1950, M.L.A., 1974; postgrad. U. So. Calif., 1973-74. Landman, E. B. Germany & Sons, Dallas, 1970-73; asst. mgr. real estate Atlantic Richfield

Co., Los Angeles, 1973-74; landman Goldking Prodn. Co., Houston, 1974-76; oil and gas cons./landman, co-owner Burk Properties, Burk Ednl. Properties, Houston, 1976—. Author: Petroleum Lands and Leasing, 1983 ; contbr. articles to jours. and photographs. Mem. The Author's Guild, Inc., Foremost Women 20th Century, Am. Assn. Petroleum Landmen (dir. 1980-82, 2d v.p. 1982-83), Houston Assn. Petroleum Landmen (dir. 1978-79), The Authors Guild, Inc., Nat. Writer's Club, Women's Inst. Houston. Republican. Presbyterian. Clubs: Dallas Woman's, Sugar Creek Country. Office: Burk Ednl Properties 1605 Parkway Blvd Title USA Bldg Sugar Land TX 77478

BURKE, ANTONIA SCOTTO, educator; b. Pensacola, Fla., May 18, 1954; d. Anthony Pasquel and Janet Alberta (Treadway-Stoddard) Scotto; m. John Michael Burke; children: Laurie, Patrick. BS in Home Econs. and Edn., Miss. U. Women, 1975. Welfare worker Office Family Services, New Orleans, 1976-77; adoption worker div. children and family services New Orleans Region State of Louisiana, 1977-78; dir., tchr. My Tree House Day Care-PreSch., Lindenhurst, Ill., 1983—; substitute tchr. E. Jefferson High Sch., New Orleans, 1975-76. Sec. Prince of Peace Parish Sch. Bd., Lake Villa, Ill., 1985—; advisor Prince of Peace Youth Group, Lake Villa, 1980—; adv. com. care and guidance children Lake County Area Vocat. Ctr., Coll. Lake County. Mem. Chgo. Assn. for the Edn. Young Children, Am. Assn. Univ. Women. Roman Catholic. Home: 1038 Gracewood Dr Libertyville IL 60048 Office: My Tree House 309 Granada Lindenhurst IL 60046

BURKE, ARLENE LOUISE, physician, army officer; b. Long Beach, Calif., Jan. 20, 1947; d. Lester Blair and Margaret Ethelyn (Rives) Larch; children—: David, Christiene, Sandra. Vocat. nurse lic. Biola Sch. Missionary Medicine, Los Angeles, 1965; B.A. in Biol. Scis. with honors, Loma Linda U., 1976; D.O., U. Health Scis. of Osteo. Medicine, Kansas City, Mo., 1981; MPH Johns Hopkins U., 1987. Clk. Biola Book Room, Los Angeles, 1965; bank teller, bookkeeper, Garden Grove, Calif., 1966-67; PBX operator, bookkeeper Tamarisk Country Club, Palm Springs, Calif., 1970-71; nurse Eisenhower Med. Ctr., Palm Desert, Calif., 1972, Desert Hosp., Palm Springs, Calif., 1974-76; commd. 2d lt., M.C., U.S. Army, 1978, advanced through grades to maj., 1987; intern Silas B. Hayes Army Community Hosp., Ft. Ord, Calif., 1981-82, resident, 1982-83; family practitioner U.S. Army, Ft. Irwin, Calif., 1983-85, preventive medicine med. officer, 1983, sr. med. officer Camp Casey, S. Korea, 1985-86, preventive medicine resident, Madigan Army Med. Ctr. Tacoma, Wash., 1987—. Youth dir. Univ. Baptist Ch., Palm Desert, 1969, Seventh Day Adventist Ch., Palm Desert, 1983; foster parent Riverside county Health Dept., Palm Desert, 1970-77. United Spanish War Vets. Aux. nursing grantee, 1965; Loma Linda U. worthy student grantee, 1973-75; Mayr Found. scholar, 1974-75. Mem. Am. Osteo. Assn., Assn. Mil. Osteo. Physicians, Am. Med. Woman's Assn., Am. Coll. Gen. Practitioners, Am. Pub. Health Assn., Alpha Phi Omega, Delta Omega. Republican. Adventist. Office: Preventive Medicine Service (HSHJ-PV) Madigan Army Med Ctr Tacoma WA 98431-5062

BURKE, BARBARA JEAN, fundraising executive; b. Hartford, Ala., Oct. 24, 1948; d. Clarence Lee and Syble (Simmons) Peters; m. Michael Wayne Foster, 1966 (div. 1976); children: Michaelle, Jonathan; m. Robert Edmund Burke, June 11, 1977; children: Mark, Kathleen, Colleen, Sean, Alan. AA, Enterprise State Jr. Coll., 1970; BA, U. South Fla., 1974; MA, Trinity U., San Antonio, 1975; postgrad. Universidad Nacional Autonoma de Mexico, 1982. Instr., San Antonio Coll., 1975; planner Econ. Opportunities Devel. Corp., San Antonio, 1976, Alamo Area Council Govts., San Antonio, 1977-82; devel. officer Oblate Missions, San Antonio, 1982—; cons. Bob Burke & Assocs., San Antonio, 1982—. Author: Paratransit Provider Handbook, 1978. Contbg. author: Human Responses to Aging, 1976; Transportation for Elderly Handicapped Programs and Problems, 1978. Contbr. articles to profl. publs. Named one of Outstanding Young Women of Am., 1985. Mem. Nat. Soc. Fund Raising Execs. (pres. San Antonio chpt.), Council Advancement and Support Edn. Democrat. Roman Catholic. Office: Oblate Missions PO Box 96 San Antonio TX 78291

BURKE, BEVERLY ANN, psychologist; b. Pulaski, Va., Jan. 31, 1943; d. Jack E. and Mary (Brewer) B. BS cum laude, David Lipscombe Coll., 1965; MEd summa cum laude, Cen. State U., 1969; PhD cum laude, U. Okla., Norman, 1977. Lic. psychologist Wash., Okla. Tchr. Demonstration Sch. David Lipscombe Coll., Nashville, 1964-65, Met. Nashville Pub. Sch., 1965-66; instr. Dept. Edn. and Psychol. Cen. State U., Edmond, Okla., 1969-71; psychologist S.W. Guidance Ctr., Wheatland, Okla., 1974-78; psychologist, dir. Canadian County Guidance Ctr., El Reno, Okla., 1978-80; psychologist Seattle Indian Health Bd., 1981-84; private practice psychology Seattle, 1983—; cons. Jones Acad., Hautshorne, Okla., 1976, Nat. Inst. Drug Abuse, Rockville, Md., 1976-81. Mem. Am. Psychol. Assn., Washington State Psychol. Assn., Okla. Psychol. Assn., Okla. Indian Edn. Assn. (bd. dirs. 1970-80), Okla. City Cherokee Community Orgn. Office: 150 Nickelson Suite 203 Seattle WA 98109

BURKE, DENISE WILLIAMSON, broadcasting executive; b. Bridgeport, Conn., Mar. 24, 1947; d. Philip Edmund and Ingrid (Williamson) Burke. A.S., Vt. Coll., 1967. Exec. sec. ABC, N.Y.C., 1967-73, 76-78; exec. sec. Pepsico, Purchase, N.Y., 1973-74, Am. Can Co., Greenwich, Conn., 1974-76; mgr. awards ABC, Inc., N.Y.C., 1978-81, dir. awards and spl. projects, 1981—. Mem. Nat. Acad. TV Arts and Scis., Am. Women in Radio and TV, Acad. TV Arts and Scis., Internat. Radio and TV Soc., Women in Communication. Home: 1196 The Strand Teaneck NJ 07666 Office: ABC 1330 Ave of Americas New York NY 10019

BURKE, ELLEN SMITH, health science facility human resources director; b. Mt. Kisco, N.Y., Apr. 23, 1952; d. Eugene Andrew and Florence Johanna (Tirkot) Smith; 1 child, Allison Ambler. BA in Writing Arts and English cum laude, Oswego State U., 1974; MBA in Indsl. Relations, Pace U., 1979. Service rep. N.Y. Telephone Co., White Plains, 1974-76; wage and salary asst. Albert Einstein Coll. Med., Bronx, N.Y., 1977-78; asst. dir. personnel Beth Abraham Hosp., Bronx, 1978-84, dir. human resources, 1984—. Scholar U.S. Nat. Merit Soc., N.Y., 1970, N.Y. State Bd. of Regents, 1970=74; grantee Mellon Found. Soc., 1976-79. Mem. Internat. Found. Employee Benefits Plan, Assn. Hosp. Humam Resources Adminstrs. (chairperson spl. projects com. Bronx chpt. 1987-88), Human Resources Info. Mgmt. Soc., Am. Soc. Hosp. Human Resources Adminstrs., Am. Soc. Personnel Adminstrs., DAR, Mensa. Republican. Presbyterian. Home: Raymond Rd North Salem NY 10560 Office: Beth Abraham Hosp 612 Allerton Ave Bronx NY 10467

BURKE, LINDA BEERBOWER, lawyer; b. Huntington, W.Va., June 19, 1948; d. William Bert and Betty Jane (Weddle) Beerbower; m. Timothy Francis Burke, Jr., Aug. 26, 1972; children—Ryan Timothy, Hannah Elizabeth. B.A., Coll. William and Mary, 1970; J.D., U. Pitts., 1973; postgrad. acctg. U. Pitts., 1976. Bar: Pa. 1973, U.S. Claims Ct. 1982. Tax atty. ALCOA, Pitts., 1973-77, gen. tax atty., 1977-80, mgr. legal and planning taxes, 1980-86, tax counsel, 1987—. Industry coordinator Allegheny Conf. Partnerships in Edn., Pitts. pub. schs., 1981—; mem. United Way adv. com. for Vol. Action Ctr., Pitts.; trustee St. Edmund's Acad.; bd. dirs. YWCA Greater Pitts. Recipient salute Triangle Corner, Pitts., 1983. Mem. Tax Execs. Inst. (pres., bd. dirs., inst. dir.), Pitts. Internat. Taxation Soc., Pitts. Tax Club, ABA, Pa. Bar Assn., Allegheny County Bar Assn. Clubs: Pitts. Athletic Assn., Longue Vue, Rivers. Office: Aluminum Co Am 1501 Alcoa Bldg Pittsburgh PA 15219

BURKE, LUCILLE PENNUCCI, systems analyst, programmer; b. Morristown, N.J., Jan. 31, 1938; d. Bernard and Pauline Lucy (Corea) Pennucci. Student parochial schs., Morristown and Madison, N.J. Sr. console operator Beneficial Mgmt. Co., Morristown, 1955-66; asst. keypunch supr. Cessna, Inc., Morristown, 1966-68, control supr., keypunch supr. Keuffel & Esser, Morristown, 1968-71; encoding (data entry) mgr. Newsweek mag., Livingston, N.J., 1971-73; mgr. data entry, Litton Publs., Oradell, N.J., 1973-75; sr. systems analyst, trainer Gen. Computer Systems, N.Y.C., 1975-76; regional tng. coordinator, sr. system engr., customer rep. No. Telecom Systems Corp., Houston, 1976-79; contract programmer Houston Ind. Sch. Dist., 1979; contract programmer Bechtel Corp., Houston, 1979, data entry supr., 1979-81, sr. system analyst, 1981—. Vol., The Sheltering Arms, Houston, 1978—. Democrat. Roman Catholic. Home: 2660 MariLee #A59 Houston TX 77057 Office: Bechtel Inc 5400 Westheimer Houston TX 77056

BURKE, MARGARET ANN, computer and communications company specialist; b. N.Y.C., Feb. 25, 1961; d. David Joseph and Eileen Theresa (Falvey) B. BS in Computer Sci., St. John's U., Jamaica, N.Y., 1982. Software specialist C&P Telephone Co., Washington, 1983—. Commr. C&P Telephone Softball League, 1986-87. Mem. Nat. Assn. Female Execs., Alliance Francaise, Nat. Fedn. Rep. Women, League Rep. Women D.C. Roman Catholic. Home: 4422 42d St NW Washington DC 20016 Office: C&P Telephone Co 13101 Clumbia Pike Silver Spring MD 20904

BURKE, MARJORIE ANN, volunteer; b. Waltham, Mass., Nov. 26, 1935; d. Joseph Paul nad M. Alice (Ward) Mogan; m. Donald Edmund Burke, Oct. 17, 1959; children: Lloyd Andrew, Ward Edmund. BS in Pharmacy, Mass. Coll. Pharmacy, 1957; postgrad., Boston U., 1957. Registered pharmacist. Staff pharmacist Children's Hosp. Med. Ctr., Boston, 1957-61, 62; relief hosp. pharmacist various hosps., Boston, 1962-75; ch. sch. supt. Ch. of Our Redeemer, Lexington, Mass., 1971-75; pres. Episcopal Ch. Women, Diocese of Mass., Boston, 1980-86; rep. province I Nat. Episcopal Ch. Women's Bd., N.Y.C., 1985—; cons. leader workshops for church women, Mass., 1980-86; pres., trainer Episcopal Ch. Women, Ch. Ctr., 1987. Editor: ECW Communiqué. Sec. Lexington pre-Sch. PTA, 1965. Mem. Episcopal Communicator's Network, Weaver's Guild Boston, Alumni Mass. Coll. Pharmacy. Club: Rainbow Girls. Home: 120 Simonds Rd Lexington MA 02173

BURKE, MARY JOAN THOMPSON, psychiatric social worker; b. Louisville, Apr. 1, 1933; d. Thomas Earl and Imelda C. (Mattingly) Thompson; B.S., Nazareth Coll., 1955; M.S.W., U. Pitts., 1969; m. Joseph Charles Burke, Sept. 1, 1956; children—Anne Maura, Colleen Elizabeth. Psychiat. social worker Homestead Community Mental Health Center, Pitts., 1969-70, Mental Hygiene Instr., Montreal, Que., Can., 1971-73, Champlain Valley Physicians Hosp., Plattsburgh, N.Y., 1973-79; also pvt. practice psychol. counseling; instr. Empire State Coll., 1988—. Bd. dirs. Assn. Retarded Children, Center Emotionally Disturbed, 1974-76, Clinton County Community Services, 1974—; mem. profl. adv. com. Clinton County Health Dept.; co-chmn. Conf. on Psychiatry and Medicine, 1974-82; mem. Lake Champlain Com. Bd. Mem. Nat. Assn. Social Workers, Am. Assn. Marriage and Family Counselors, Am. Acad. Certified Social Workers, LWV, Internat. Coll. Psychomatic Medicine, N.Y. State Assn. Community Service Bds. (1st v.p.). Roman Catholic. Home: 385 State St Albany NY 12210-1201

BURKE, M(ARY) MADELINE, service executive, small business owner; b. Houston, Nov. 8, 1938; d. William L. Burke and Mary M. (Flint) Heard. Student, Tex. Tech. Coll., 1957-59, Tex. Woman's U., 1959-60, U. Houston, 1962, Mus. of Fine Arts Sch., Houston, 1964-66. Property underwriter Security Ins. Group, Houston, 1961-64, Gulf Ins. Co., Houston, 1968-70; owner Madeline's Lawn and Garden Service, Mt. Ida, Ark., 1979—; handler Montgomery County Livestock Auction, Mt. Ida, 1979-86, River Valley Livestock Market, Ola, Ark., 1986—. Mem. Nat. Assn. Female Execs. Republican. Home and Office: State Rt 1 Box 185A Mount Ida AR 71957

BURKE, PATRICIA ANNE, corrosion engineer, consultant, researcher; b. Norwich, Conn., Aug. 13, 1955; d. Edward Martin and Shirley Mae (Siedel) B.; m. Robert Mark Shammas, Nov. 12, 1977 (div. 1980); m. Peter Elliott, Apr. 17, 1987. BSCE, U. R.I., 1977; MS in Corrosion Sci. and Engring., U. Manchester, Eng., 1985. Constrn. engr. Chevron USA, Denver, 1977-79, chem./corrosion engr., Midland, Tex., 1980-81; sr. corrosion engr. Mitchell Energy Corp., Woodlands, Tex., 1981-84; staff engr. Cortest Labs., Cypress, Tex., 1986-87; sr. engr. Westvaco Corp., Laurel, Md., 1987-88; supr. materials and metallurgical testing lab., Ciba-Geigy, Toms River, N.J., 1988—; lectr. Ctr. for Profl. Advancement, 1987—. Editor: Advances in CO2 Corrosion II, 1985; contbr. articles on CO2 corrosion, acid corrosion to profl. jours., 1984—. Mem. Nat. Assn. Corrosion Engrs. (com. mem., sec. and chmn.), Inst. Corrosion Sci. and Tech., Soc. Petroleum Engrs. (jr.), ASM, Soc. Am. Bus. Women. Republican. Roman Catholic.

BURKE, RANDEE LYNN, exercise physiologist, educator, consultant; b. Chgo., July 12, 1952; d. Anderson Walter and Gladys Emma (Shaver) Burke. BS, U. Wis., 1976; MS, Ft. Hays State U., 1977; grad. with honors Columbus Regional Police Acad., 1976 Head athletic trainer U. Redlands (Calif.), 1977-79; cardiac rehab. staff U. Wis., Madison, 1979-82; therapist Richard Bachrach, D.O., N.Y.C., 1982-83; exercise physiologist Park E. Chiropractic, N.Y.C., 1983; fitness instr. Biofitness Inst., N.Y.C., 1983-84; health cons., therapist, N.Y.C., 1982-85; health cons. to Liza Minnelli, N.Y.C., 1982-85; police officer Columbus, Ga., 1986—. Served with U.S. Army as airborne med. specialist, 1985-86. Recipient Outstanding Female Athlete award Wis. Interscholastic Athletic Assn., 1970, All-Am. Track award U.S. Track and Field Assn., 1975, 76, Honor Grad. award Columbus Coll. Regional Police Acad., 1986. Mem. Am. Coll. Sports Medicine, Nat. Athletic Trainers Assn., U. Wis. Alumni Ass. Republican. Presbyterian. Club: Nat. W. Lodge: Fraternal Order of Police. Home: 2616 Avalon Rd Columbus GA 31903

BURKE, REBECCA LEE, clothing shop owner; b. East Liverpool, Ohio, Oct. 27, 1951; d. Robert Lee and Lenora Van Fossen; m. Keith Hal Burke, Aug. 16, 1969; children: Keith Robert, Kevin Charles. Diploma Cosmetology, A&H Sch. of Cosmetology, East Liverpool, Ohio, 1969. Lic. cosmetology instr., mgr. Salesman advt. Evening Review, East Liverpool, 1983-84, Buckeye Pub., Lisbon, Ohio, 1984-85; owner Little Bit More, East Liverpool, 1985—, Salem, Ohio, 1986—, Steubenville, Ohio, 1986—. Speaker Salem YWCA, 1987; cons., speaker, Obesity Counciling Group, Salem, 1987; pres. East Liverpool Bus. Assn.; mem. Steubenville Bus. Assn., East Liverpool High Sch. band booster. Mem. Salem C. of C., East Liverpool C. of C. (bd. dirs.), Nat. Assn. Female Execs., Bus. and Profl. Women of Am., East Liverpool High Sch. Alumni Assn., Quota Club. Republican. Home: 775 Center St East Liverpool OH 43920 Office: Little Bit More 16761 St Clair Ave East Liverpool OH 43920

BURKE, YVETTE MARIE, data processing official, computer programmer, consultant; b. Independence, Mo., Aug. 14, 1965; d. Ralph Lawrence and Jeanetta Faye (Drury) B. Student, Electronic Computer Programming Inst., Kansas City, Mo., 1985, AS in Computer Sci./Bus. Adminstrn., 1988. Quality control computer clk. DST Systems, Inc., Kansas City, 1983-84; computer operator/programmer Kimberly Services Inc., Overland Park, Kans., 1985-86; computer programmer Lawrence Photog. Inc., Kansas City, Kans., 1986-88; mgr. data processing Vasos, Kugler and Kickerson Law Office, Kansas City, Kans., 1986—. Mem. Nat. Assn. Female Execs. Democrat. Baptist. Home: 1927 Ewing Ave Kansas City MO 64126 Office: Vasos Kugler and Dickerson 707 Minnesota Ave Suite 512 Kansas City KS 66101

BURKE, YVONNE WATSON BRATHWAITE (MRS. WILLIAM A. BURKE), lawyer; b. Los Angeles, Oct. 5, 1932; d. James A. and Lola (Moore) Watson; m. William A. Burke, June 14, 1972; 1 dau., Autumn Roxanne. A.A., U. Calif., 1951; B.A., UCLA, 1953; J.D., U. So. Calif., 1956. Bar: Calif. bar 1956. Mem. Calif. Assembly, 1966-72, chmn. urban devel. and housing com., 1971, 72; mem. 93d Congress from 37th Dist. Calif., 94th-95th Congresses from 28th Dist. Calif., House Appropriations Com.; chmn. Congl. Black Caucus, 1976; ptnr. Jones, Day, Reavis & Pogue, Los Angeles; dep. corp. commr., hearing officer Police Commn., 1964-66; atty., staff McCone Commn. (investigation Watts riot), 1965; bd. dirs. Ednl. Testing Service, 2A br. Fed. Res. Bank. Vice chmn. 1984 U.S. Olympics Organizing Com.; bd. dirs. or bd. advisers numerous orgns.; regent U. Calif., Bd. Ednl. Testing Service, Amateur Athletic Found.; bd. dirs. Ford Found. Recipient Profl. Achievement award UCLA, 1974, 84; named one of 200 Future Leaders Time mag., 1974; recipient Achievement awards C.M.E. Chs.; numerous other awards, citations.; fellow Inst. Politics John F. Kennedy Sch. Govt. Harvard, 1971-72; Chubb fellow Yale, 1972. Office: Jones Day Reavis & Pogue 355 S Grand Ave Suite 3000 Los Angeles CA 90071 also: Jones Day Reavis & Pogue 901 Lakeside Ave Cleveland OH 44114

BURKES, SARAH BEATRICE, educator, insurance agent; b. Clarksdale, Miss., Feb. 28, 1948; d. Henry and Eldora (Abshaw) Burkes; student Jackson State U., 1966-68; B.S., Tex. Coll., 1970; M.A., East Tex. State U. With Progressive Community Center, Chgo., 1970-72; tchr. Chgo. Bd. Edn., 1972—; with Blue Cross-Blue Shield, Chgo., 1972-75; communications counselor Malcolm X Coll., Chgo., 1975-77; instr. reading and English, Accounter Community Center, Chgo., 1977-80; agt. Equitable Life Ins., Chgo., 1980—; rep. World Book-Childcraft Encyclopedia, 1981—. Mem. Internat. Reading Assn., Nat. Council Tchrs. English, MLA, Chgo. Reading Assn., Nat. Life Underwriters Assn., United Ednl. Employees Assn., Alpha Kappa Alpha. Home: 1109 S Troy St Chicago IL 60612 Mailing Address: PO Box 12051 Chicago IL 60612

BURKET, GAIL BROOK, author; b. Stronghurst, Ill., Nov. 1, 1905; d. John Cecil and Maud (Simonson) Brook; A.B., U. Ill., 1926; M.A. in English Lit., Northwestern U., 1929; m. Walter Cleveland Burket, June 22, 1929; children—Elaine (Mrs. William L. Harwood), Anne, Margaret (Mrs. James Boyce). Pres. woman's aux. Internat. Coll. Surgeons, 1950-54, now bd. dirs. Mus.; nat. vice chmn. Am. Heritage of DAR, 1971-74; pres. Northwestern U. Guild, 1976-78; sec. Evanston women's bd. Northwestern U. Settlement, 1979-81, pres., 1984-86; mem. cen. com., 1986—. Recipient Robert Ferguson Meml. award Friends of Lit., 1973. Mem. Nat. League Am. Pen Women (Ill. state pres. 1952-54, nat. v.p. 1958-60), Soc. Midland Authors, Poetry Soc. Am., Women in Communications, AAUW (pres. N. Shore br. 1961-63), Ill. Opera Guild (bd. dirs. 1982—, 1st v.p. 1986—), Daus. Am. Colonists (state v.p. 1973-76), Colonial Dames Am. (chpt. regent 1974-80), Phi Beta Kappa, Delta Zeta. Author: Courage Beloved, 1949; Manners Please, 1949; Blueprint for Peace, 1951; Let's Be Popular, 1951; You Can Write a Poem, 1954; Far Meadows, 1955; This is My Country, 1960; From the Prairies, 1968. Contbr. articles, poems to lit. publs. Address: 1020 Lake Shore Dr Evanston IL 60202

BURKETT, MYRL HODGSON, advertising agency executive; b. Kansas City, Kans., Dec. 4, 1944; d. John Thomas, Jr. and Myrl O'Neill (Hodgson) B.; m. Dickinson Hale McGuire, Nov. 10, 1965 (div. Aug. 1974); children—Samuel D., John T.; m. 2d, John William Borecky, Mar. 25, 1977 (div. Oct. 1985). A.A., Stratford Coll., 1964. Prodn. control mgr. L. Honold Mfg. Co., Folcroft, Pa., 1974-76; media dir. Arnold Advt. Corp., Reading, Pa., 1977—. Pub. relations dir., bd. dirs. YWCA, Reading, 1981-87; fin. developer Wallingford Fine Arts Ctr. (Pa.), 1970-73, bd. dirs., 1970-73; officer St. James Episcopal Ch. Women, Aston, Pa., 1969-75. Mem. Sales and Mktg. Execs. Reading, Am. Women in Radio and TV, Bus. and Profl. Advt. Assn. (CBC cert., chmn. various coms.), Berks County C. of C. (com. chmn. 1986-88), Phila. Club. Advt. Women (bd. dirs., officer 1985—), Berks Women's Network (bd. dirs., officer). Home: 53 Muirfield Dr Reading PA 19607 Office: Arnold Advt Corp 3608 St Lawrence Ave Reading PA 19606

BURKHALTER, HARRIETTE HAELIG, volunteer; b. Chgo., Apr. 12, 1936; d. Arthur Frank and Elizabeth (Thornhill) H.; m. John Phillip Burkhalter, June 29, 1957; children: Carl, Kristine. BS, U. Wis., 1957. Pres. LWV, Sioux City, 1960-62, Hopkins, Minn., 1974-76, Minn., 1980-82; chairperson council LWV, Twin Cities, Minn., 1976-78; v.p. LWV, Minn., 1978-79, 1986—. Recipient Hope Washburn award LWV-Minn., 1985. Episcopalian. Home: 5 W St Albans Hopkins MN 55343

BURKHARDT, DOLORES ANN, library consultant; b. Meriden, Conn., July 28, 1932; d. Frederick Christian and Emily (Detels) Burkhardt; B.A., U. Conn., 1955; M.S., So. Conn. State Coll., 1960; postgrad. Central Wash. State Coll., 1962, Columbia, 1964—; 6th yr. diploma U. Conn., 1972. Asst. librarian So. Conn. State Coll. Library, summers 1960, 62; sch. library tchr. Farmington High Sch., Unionville, Conn., 1955-65; library cons.; media specialist East Farms Sch., Farmington, Conn., 1967-70; sch. library coordinator K-12, Durham-Middlefield, Conn., 1970-72; media specialist regional dist. 10, Burlington-Harwinton, Conn., 1972-78; ednl. media cons., 1978—. Instr. Boston U. Media Inst. Spl. cons. Conn. Dept. Edn., 1965—. Mem. AAUW (sec. 1956-58), NEA, Conn. Edn. Assn., New Eng. (pres. 1969-70), Conn. (2d v.p. 1965—, chmn. sch. library devel.; chmn. standards com. 1970-72, chmn. instructional materials selection policy com. Region 10) sch. library assns., Am. Assn. Sch. Librarians, New Eng. Sch. Devel. Council, Phi Delta Kappa. Lutheran. Home and Office: 812 Savage St Southington CT 06489

BURKHARDT, MARY CATHERINE, real estate broker, real estate developer; b. St. Stephens, S.C., Feb. 13, 1927; d. Mack Daniel Britt and Mary Helen (Funk) Hoyle; m. Graham, June 6, 1945 (div. 1957); children: Wayne W., Thomas Kim; married; children: Ralph William, Ann Patrice, Mary Susan. Student, Winthrop Coll., 1942-43. Salesman Mt. Comfort Cemetery, Alexander, Va., 1960-63; resident mgr. Webster Real Estate, Oxen Hill, Md., 1963-64; salesman real estate Klein Devel. Land Sales, Miami, Fla., 1964-70; gen. real estate Marvin Smith, West Palm Beach, Fla., 1970-76; salesman condominiums Harte-Biltmore Ltd., Palm Beach, 1977-81; broker, owner B&B Projects, Inc., West Palm Beach, 1981—. Club: Palm Beach County Real Estate Exchange. Home: 1660 S Blvd West Palm Beach FL 33415 Office: B&B Projects Inc 4758 Sunny Palm Circle West Palm Beach FL 33415

BURKHART-COBB, EVELYN LAVERNE, geologist, businesswoman; b. Lenoir City, Tenn., June 6, 1945; d. Walter Leo and Edith Almira (Snodderly) Burkhart; m. Cornelius Quincy Cobb, Oct. 26, 1962; children—Andrea, Aaron Schadwicke. B.S., U. Tenn., 1965, M.S., 1974, student South Tex. Coll. Law, 1986—. Teaching asst. U. Tenn., Knoxville, 1965-66, 73-74; geologist Texaco Bellaire Research Labs., Houston, 1974-76; geologist/project mgr. Office Nuclear Waste Isolation, Oak Ridge (Tenn.) Nat. Lab., 1976-78; mgr. geology Gruy Petroleum Tech., Inc., Houston, 1978-84; pres. L.B. Cobb & Assocs., Geologists and Engrs., Houston, 1984—; pres. Cobb and Co., Realtors, 1986—. 1st v.p. LWV, Greeneville, Tenn., 1969-70. NSF student fellow, Knoxville, Oak Ridge, 1959, 60, 61; Grand Champion award, So. Appalachian Sci. Fair, 1962. Mem. Am. Assn. Petroleum Geologists, Am. Inst. Profl. Geologists (cert.) Soc. Econ. Paleontologists and Mineralogists, Houston Geol. Soc. (asst. editor bull. 1983-84), Houston Bd. Realtors. Office: PO Box 980894 Houston TX 77007

BURKLUND, PATRICIA HELEN, marketing professional; b. Chgo., Mar. 12, 1944; d. John Lawrence and Virginia Mae (Brader) Stackpool; m. Sidney Andrew Burklund. Student, Shoreline Community Coll., 1972-76; BA, U. Puget Sound, 1981. Lic. refrigeration operating engr. Mgr. service Genesee Fuel Co., Seattle, 1976-79; asst. service mgr. MacDonald Miller Co., Seattle, 1979-81, mgr. constrn. project, 1981-83; mgr. service Hill Refrigeration, Tukwila, Wash., 1983-84; gen. mgr. Care Co., Bellevue, Wash., 1984-85; pres. P. Burklund and Assocs., Bothell, Wash., 1985—. Mem. Wash. State Refrigeration Contractors Assn. (sec. 1983-84), Nat. Assn. Female Execs., Am. Assn. Profl. Cons., Womens Network. Roman Catholic. Club: W.S. Yacht. Office: P Burklund and Assocs Inc 23525 3rd SE Bothell WA 98021

BURKS, ELIZABETH JERNIGAN, former county goverment offical; b. Beech Grove, Tenn., June 19, 1922; d. Luke E and Mary (Robinson) Jernigan; m. Willie Ray Burks; children: Ann Brawner, Beverly Sandlin. Student, Mid. Tenn. State U., 1939-42, Motlow Community Coll., 1978. Commr. Coffee County Legis. Body, Manchester, Tenn., 1978-86; chmn. bd. trustees Coffee Med. Ctr., 1984-86. Mem. council on hosp. governance Tenn. Hosp. Assn., Nashville, 1984-86. Democrat. Presbyterian. Home: Box 28 Beech Grove TN 37018

BURKS, GLADYS PEEPLES, school system administrator; b. Ft. Lauderdale, Fla., Dec. 29, 1928; d. Robert James and Pauline (White) Peeples; 1 child, Beverly Kim. BA in Social Sci., Western Mich. U., 1970, MA in Elem. Edn., 1972; MEd, Mich. State U., 1977, PhD, 1986. Service observer Mich. Bell Telephone, Benton Harbor, Mich., 1952-70; head start dir. Tri-County Action Agy., Benton Harbor, 1969-70; tchr. Benton Harbor Area Schs., 1970-73, elem. prin., 1973-74, coordinator compensatory program, 1974-80, dir. state fed. program, 1980—; creator ednl. program Project Help, U.S. Dept. Edn., 1976; trainer Willow Run Sch. Dist., Mich., 1976, Mich. Dept. Edn., Lansing, 1977—; adj. instr. Mich. State U., East Lansing, 1980—. Pres. SW Mich. Women Polit. Coalition, Berrien County, 1987. Named Today's Woman, Herald Palladium, Mich., 1985, Upton Vol., Blossomland United Way, 1987. Mem. AAUW, Bus. and Profl. Women (Women of Yr. 1980), Mich. Assn. Supervision and Curriculum Devel. (sec. bd.), Western Minority Assn. (disting. alumni 1982), Coll. Edn. Alumni Assn. (bd. dirs.), Squaws Inc., Phi Delta Kappa, Delta Kappa Gamma. Republican. Baptist. Home: 169 Orchard Ln Benton Harbor MI 49022 Office: Benton Harbor Area Schs 711 E Britain Benton Harbor MI 49022

BURKS, JOAN CONSTANCE TRAVERS, insurance company executive; b. Balt.; d. Edwin H. and Florence M. (Leonard) T.; m. Waylon D. Burks, Dec. 29, 1986; children: Janet, Terrence. BS, Columbus Coll., 1974, MBA, 1978. CPA, Ga., cert. internal auditor. Internal auditor Blue Cross/Blue Shield Ga., Columbus, 1974-79, internal audit mgr., 1979-83, v.p. actuarial, underwriter, 1983-85, sr. v.p., 1985—. Mem. Leadership Columbus, 1985; mem. nominating com. Columbus Profl. Women's Network, 1983, 85; mem. alumni council Columbus Coll., 1984-86; bd. dirs. ARC, Columbus, 1987—. Mem. Am. Inst. CPA's, Ga. Soc. CPA's, Inst. Internal Auditors (charter pres. 1977-78), Mensa (testing coordinator 1985—). Office: Blue Cross & Blue Shield Ga PO Box 7368 Columbus GA 31908

BURLAND, BARBARA LEE, real estate professional; b. Pitts., Oct. 12, 1937; d. Norman I. and Madeline H. Robertson; divorced; children: Elizabeth Hill, Norman Hill, David Hill. Grad. high sch., Mars, Pa. Lic. real estate broker. Sales assoc. A.R. Nicklas Realtor, Valencia, Pa., 1974-84; sales mgr. Comprehensive Safety Compliance, Gibsonia, Pa., 1984-86; mgr. Bernhard Realty, Pitts., 1986—. Mem. Nat. Realtors Assn. Office: Bernhard Realty 4840 McKnight Rd Pittsburgh PA 15237

BURLEIGH, CORINNE, service company executive; b. Morden, Man., Can., Mar. 31, 1947; d. Clive Kenelm Rampton and Joyce (Barker) Gardner; m. Winston Ralph Burleigh, Sept. 18, 1965; children: Sharlene Roselle, Brenton Myles. Ed. pub. schs., Winnipeg. Edit supr. Comcheq, Winnipeg, Man., 1970-78; br. mgr. Winnipeg div., Comcheq, 1978-80; mgr. ops. Comcheq, Winnipeg, Man., 1980-83; v.p. ops. Comcheq Services, Ltd., Winnipeg, Man., 1983—. Active French Immersion Parents, Assn., Winnipeg, 1983—. Mem. Can. Payroll Assn. (voting mem. 1980—), Can. Mgmt. Assn. Office: Comcheq Services Ltd, 296 Garry St, Winnipeg, MB Canada R3C 1H3

BURLEIGH, RITA JEAN, educator, librarian; b. Santa Monica, Calif., Mar. 19, 1943; d. Charles Patrick and Jeanne (DeWitt) Loftus; m. Thomas William Scott, June 12, 1965 (div. 1975); children—Graham Robert, Shelly Amber; m. Edward William Burleigh, Oct. 23, 1980; children—Edward William, Rebecca Dawn. B.A., U. Redlands, 1965, M.A., 1967; M.L.S., Immaculate Heart Coll., Los Angeles, 1969. Librarian, Pomona Pub. Library, Calif., 1967-69, U. La Verne, Calif., 1970-72, Rio Hondo Coll., Whittier, Calif., 1973-79; learning resources dir. Citrus Coll., Azusa, Calif., 1979-86, assoc. dean instrn., 1986—; pres. San Gabriel Community Colls. Library Coop., 1982-86. Corr. sec. Pomona Valley Art Assn., 1979; draft bd. mem. U.S. Selective Service, 1981—; sr. warden St. Paul's Episcopal Ch., Pomona, 1984. Fellow Claremont Grad. Sch., 1984-87. Mem. Assn. Calif. Community Coll. Adminstrs., Calif. Community Coll. Librarians (sec.-treas. 1985), Mortarboard, Citrus Coll. Faculty Assn. (sec. 1981-82). Democrat. Office: Citrus Community Coll Dist 1000 W Foothill Glendora CA 91740

BURLESON, CAROLYN ODOM, educator, minister, consultant; b. Phila., Aug. 1, 1942; d. Frederick and Cornelia Alice (Veney) Odom; m. Richenel Johan Burleson, May 16, 1981; 1 child, Cornell Douglas Williams. BS in Edn., Cheyney State Coll., 1965; postgrad., Temple U., 1971; PhD, Columbia Pacific U., 1986. Cert. English tchr., Pa.; cert. psychotherapist, Pa. Instr. English Audenried Jr. High Sch., Phila., 1965-72; instr. English University City High Sch., Phila., 1972-87, dir. intercultural learning project, 1983-87; pres., cons., seminar leader COB Assocs., Inc., Phila., 1985—. Author: Lifestream-Your Flow of Creative Living, 1985, From The Eye of The Hurricane, 1985. Recipient citation Phila. Commn. on Human Relations, 1986; Phila. Alliance for Teaching Humanities in the Schs. grantee, 1984. Mem. Nat. Council Tchrs. English, Nat. Assn. Supervision and Curriculum Devel., Am. Assn. Religious Counselors, Internat. New Thought Alliance, Nat. Assn. for Female Execs., Clergy Women United, Alpha Kappa Alpha. Democrat. Mem. Unity Ch. Lodge: Rosicrucian (sec. bd. 1976-78, lectr. mid. Atlantic region 1978—, master 1980-81, regional monitor Pa. and Del. 1985-87). Home: 400 S Harvard Blvd Apt #115 Los Angeles CA 90020 Office: COB Assocs PO Box 76383 Los Angeles CA 90076

BURLESON, KAREN TRIPP, lawyer; b. Rocky Mount, N.C., Sept. 2, 1955; d. Bryant and Katherine Rebecca (Watkins) Tripp; m. Robert Mark Burleson, June 25, 1977. BA, U. N.C., 1976; JD, U. Ala., 1981. Bar: Tex. 1981, U.S. Dist. Ct. (so. dist.) Tex. 1982, U.S. Ct. Appeals (fed. cir.) 1983. Law clerk Tucker, Gray & Espy, Tuscaloosa, Ala., 1978-81, to presiding justice Ala. Supreme Ct., Montgomery, summer 1980; atty. Exxon Prodn. Research Co., Houston, 1981-86, coordinator tech. transfer, 1986-87; assoc. Arnold, White and Durkee, Attys. at Law, Houston, 1988—. Contbr. articles to profl. jours. Recipient Am. Jurisprudence award U. Ala., 1980, Dean's award, 1981. Mem. Houston Bar Assn. (internat. transfer tech. com. 1983-84), Houston Intellectual Property Lawyers Assn. (outstanding inventor com. 1982-84, chmn. student edn. com. 1986, sec. 1987-88, bd. govs., chmn. awards com. 1988-89), Tex. Bar Assn. (antitrust law com. 1984-85, chmn. Internat. Law com. of Intellectual Property Law Sect.), ABA, Am. Intellectual Property Lawyers Assn. (sec. 1987-88), Phi Alpha Delta (clerk 1980). Republican. Methodist. Office: Arnold White & Durkee 750 Bering Dr Houston TX 77057

BURLEW, CANDACE LOUISE, lawyer, accountant; b. Greenville, S.C., July 5, 1946; d. Conover Herbert and Evelyn Louise (Galbraith) Burlew; children—Amy, Robyn, Jeffrey. B.S. summa cum laude Lander Coll., 1979; J.D., U. S.C., 1982. Bar: S.C. 1982, U.S. Dist. Ct. S.C., U.S. Ct. Appeals (4th cir.). acctg. lab. asst. Lander Coll., Greenwood, S.C., 1978-79; legal research asst. Sherrill & Townsend, Columbia, S.C., 1980-82; acct. Summersett & Babinec, Columbia, 1982; contracts atty. S.C. Dept. Social Services, Columbia, 1982-84; atty. adminstr. legal services S.C. Health and Human Services Fin. Com., 1984—. Vol. S.C. Reps., Columbia, 1980-88, Town Theatre, Columbia. Recipient Scholastic awards Lander Coll., 1978, 79. Mem. ABA (coms.), S.C. Bar Assn., S.C. Bus. & Profl. Women, S.C. Trial Lawyers Assn., Am. Pub. Welfare Attys., Blue Key, Alpha Chi, Alpha Kappa Psi, Phi Delta Phi. Episcopalian. Home: 1340 Longcreek Dr Columbia SC 29210 Office: SC Health and Human Services Fin Commn Adminstrv Legal Services PO Box 8206 Columbia SC 29202

BURLEY, DEBORAH KAY, utility executive; b. Zanesville, Ohio, Aug. 6, 1947; d. Robert Winfield Burley and Virginia Rose (Summers) Quinn. BS in Home Econs. and Bus., Kent State U., 1969. Home service advisor Columbia Gas. of Ohio, Inc., Elyria, 1969-71; dist. home service dir. Norwalk, 1971-74; gas utilization rep. Sandusky, 1974-79; area mgr. Port Clinton, 1979-80, Bucyrus, 1980-85; div. mgr. Chillicothe, 1985—. v.p. pub. relations Ross County United Way, Chillicothe, 1987. Named one of Outstanding Young Women of Am., 1978, 80. Mem. Ohio Bus. and Profl. Women (recording sec. 1985-87, chair ind. devel. 1982-84, Outstanding Mem. award 1987), Bucyrus Bus. and Profl. Women (pres. 1984-85, leadership trainer 1984, Woman of Yr. 1984), Nat. Home Econs. in Bus. (regional advisor 1978-80), NE Ohio Home Econs. in Bus. (pres. 1979-80), Chillicothe-Ross C. of C. (pres. 1987-88). Clubs: Sandusky Ski (pres. 1978-79), Rotary (Chillicothe chpt.). Office: Columbia Gas of Ohio Inc 843 Piatt Ave Chillicothe OH 45601

BURLEY, KATHLEEN MARY, instructional systems designer; b. Minot, Md., Jan. 17, 1942; d. Harry Jerome and Cathern (Doyle) Brickner; m. Henry Richard Burley, Dec. 27, 1966. BS in Music and Edn., Minot State U., 1963; MA in Edn., Ariz. State U., 1966; cert., Inst. of Children's Lit., 1981; MBA, U. Phoenix, 1984. Tchr. pub. and pvt. sch. systems, various locations, 1963-81; instructional systems designer Northrop Corp., Hawthorne, Calif., 1984—; pres. BCD Enterprises, Torrance, Calif., 1986—. Author: Who You Are, Where You Are, 1986, Looking Back, Book One, 1987. Named one of Best New Poets Am. Poetry Assn., 1986. Mem. Am. Soc. Tng. and Devel. (designer, trainer 1986—), Nat. Soc. for Performance and Instruction, Nat. Assn. Female Execs. Office: BCD Enterprises 1251 W Sepulveda Blvd #170 Torrance CA 90502

BURMAN, DIANE BERGER, organization development consultant, educator; b. Pitts., Dec. 7, 1936; d. Morris Milton and Dorothy June (Barkin) Berger; m. Sheldon Oscar Burman, Dec. 15, 1926; children: Allison Beth, Jocelyn Holly, Harrison Emory Guy. BA, Vassar Coll., 1958; MA, Middlebury Coll., 1961. Tchr. of French Allderdice High Sch., Pitts., 1960-61, Mamaroneck (N.Y.) High Sch., 1961-64; personnel specialist G.D. Searle & Co., Skokie, Ill., 1972-77, orgn. devel. tng. cons., 1977-78; personnel and orgn. devel. cons. Abbott Labs., North Chgo., 1978-82; orgn. devel. cons., asst. v.p. Harris Bank, Chgo., 1982—. Mem. editorial bd. Orgn. Devel. Jour., 1987. Mem. Am. Soc. Tng. and Devel. (bd. dirs. Chgo. career devel. profl. practice area 1987—), Orgn. Devel. Network (exec. dir. Chgo. chpt. 1986—), Assn. Psychol. Type Bd.-Nat. Conf., Orgn. Devel. Inst. (adv. bd. 1987—), Nat. Assn. Bank Women. Jewish. Club: Vassar (Chgo.) (bd. dirs. 1975-80). Home: 247 Prospect Ave Highland Park IL 60035 Office: Harris Bank 111 West Monroe Chicago IL 60690

BURMAN, MARSHA LINKWALD, lighting manufacture executive, marketing and management development trainer; b. Balt., Jan. 9, 1949; d. William and Lena (Ronin) Linkwald; m. Robert Schlosser, July 2, 1972 (div. 1980); m. John R. Burman, June, 1986; children—Melanie, David, Heather, Richard. B.S. cum laude in Edn., Kent State U., 1970, M.A. summa cum laude in Sociology, 1971. Cert. secondary edn., Ohio. Spl. project dir. Tng. and Research Ctr., Planned Parenthood, Chgo., 1978; with mgmt. edn. ctr. Gould, Inc., Chgo., 1979, program adminstr., 1979-80; systems trainer Lithonia Lighting, 1981, mgr. tng. and edn., 1981-86, dir. mktg., tng. and devel., 1986—. Author: (booklet) Putting Your Best Foot Forward (award Am Soc. Tng. and Devel.), 1982. Facilitator single parenting interaction group, Atlanta, 1984-85. U.S. Office Edn. grantee, 1971. Mem. Lithonia Lighting Mgmt. Club (v.p. 1982-83), Am. Soc. of Tng. and Devel. (bd. dirs. 1982, spl. projects. dir. Atlanta chpt. 1982, Vol. of Yr., Community Leader Am. 1987). Avocation: reading. Office: Lithonia Lighting Div of Nat Service Industries 1400 Lester Rd Conyers GA 30207

BURMEISTER, DOROTHY MARY, real estate broker; b. LaCrosse, Wis., June 3, 1919; d. Ernest A. and Ida (Steppe) Leaser; m. Clifford M. Peterson, May 9, 1941 (div. 1960); 1 child, Thomas E.; m. Robert E. Burmeister, Dec. 26, 1968. Grad., T.C. Bus. Coll., St. Paul, 1939. Billing machine operator Northwest Bell Telephone, Mpls., 1939-42; warehouse and office mgr. SKF Industries, Inc., Mpls., 1946-60; office mgr., treas. Burmeister Electric Co., Mpls., 1960-73; rental mgr., owner Dot's Island Rentals, LaPointe, Wis., 1976—; real estate broker Dot's Island Rentals, LaPointe, 1982—. Town chmn. LaPointe, 1983. Mem. Chequamegon Bd. Realtors (sec.-treas. 1984-87), Madeline Island C. of C. (sec.-treas. 1985-87). Home and Office: PO Box 160 LaPointe WI 54850

BURMEISTER, KRISTEN SCHNELLE, trade association administrator; b. Lamar, Mo., Aug. 25, 1960; d. Wayne Howard and Shirley Ann (Head) Schnelle; m. David John Burmeister, June 30, 1984. BS in Bus. and Indsl. Communication, Southwest Mo. State U., 1981; MA in Mgmt., Webster U., 1986. Sales mgr. Tulsa Excelsior Hotel, 1981-83; asst. v.p. Farm Equipment Mfrs. Assn., St. Louis, 1983—; speaker, instr. in field. Contestant Miss Mo. Pageant, 1979, counselor, 1980. Mem. Am. Soc. Assn. Execs., Nat. Agri-Mktg. Assn. (program com. 1987—), Phi Kappa Phi. Republican. Lutheran. Home: 12551 Round Robin Ct Creve Coeur MO 63146 Office: Farm Equipment Mfrs Assn 243 N Lindbergh Blvd Saint Louis MO 63141

BURN, LOIS ANN, speech pathologist; b. Glen Cove, N.Y., Aug. 3, 1952; d. Edward Alfred and Rose Mary (Perrone) Murphy; m. Robert Edward Burn, Aug. 8, 1976; 1 child, Kelly Ann. BS, SUNY, Geneseo, 1974; MA, Hofstra U., 1978; postgrad., C.W. Post Coll., 1982, 83, Gallaudet Coll., 1985, 86. Speech pathologist Mill Neck (N.Y.) Manor Sch. for the Deaf, 1975-85, 86 , supr. student tchrs., 1978-82; tchr. sign lang. Bethpage (N.Y.) High Sch., 1981-82; sign lang. interpreter Nassau Community Coll., Garden City, N.Y., 1985-86; freelance interpreter L.I. Soc. for the Deaf, Herricks, N.Y., 1985—. Co-author: Developmental Elicited Language Sample (DELS) Test, 1984. Mem. negotiation com. Mill Neck Manor Ednl. Assn., 1978-79; local pres. N.Y. State United Tchrs., 1979-81, 84-85, v.p. 1981-82, parliamentarian 1986-87. Mem. N.Y. State Assn of Educators of the Deaf, L.I. Registry of Interpreters for the Deaf, Am. Speech-Hearing-Lang. Assn. (cert. 1987), Mill Neck Manor Ednl. Assn. (negotiation com. 1978-79, local pres. 1979-81, 84-85, v.p. 1981-82, parliamentarian 1986-87), N.Y. State United Tchrs., Mich. Championship Auto Racing Team. Democrat. Roman Catholic. Home: 29 Ellen St Bethpage NY 11714

BURNE, RAE M., small business owner; b. Stamford, Conn., Sept. 17, 1947; d. John Joseph and Josephine (Costa) Mercede; children: Sandra, Kara. Owner contract space planning design firm Mercede Assocs., Mount Freedom, NJ. Republican. Office: Mercede Assocs Millbrook Plaza Mount Freedom NJ 07970

BURNETT, BRENDA BULLOCK, government agency official; b. Red Mountain, Calif., Apr. 12, 1941; d. Miles Wallace and Harriet Jane (Wittmeyer) Bullock; student U. Redlands, 1959-60, 61-62; B.A., U. Md., 1967; m. Daniel George Burnett, Oct. 3, 1970. With U.S. Navy, various locations, 1969—, asso. head budget div. Naval Weapons Center Office Fin. and Mgmt., China Lake, Calif., 1975-77, head reports and analysis br., 1977-78, head fin. mgmt. Br. A, 1978-81, mem. staff Hdqrs. Dept. Def. Schs. Ger., 1982-84, head plans and programs br., 1984—. Mem. Ridgecrest City Council, 1980-81; instr. Stop Smoking Clinic, Am. Cancer Soc.; founding mem. Maturango Mus., Ridgecrest, ins. treas. and trustee 1987. Mem. Am. Soc. Public Adminstrn., Am. Soc. Mil. Comptrollers (ins. pres., China Lake chpt., 1987), NAACP. Democrat. Home: 735 Sonja Ave Ridgecrest CA 93555 Office: Naval Weapons Ctr Code 0835 China Lake CA 93555

BURNETT, CAROL, actress, comedienne, singer; b. San Antonio, Apr. 26, 1936; d. Jody and Louise (Creighton) B.; m. Joseph Hamilton, 1963 (div.); children: Carrie Louise, Jody Ann, Erin Kate. Student, UCLA, 1953-55. Introduced comedy song I Made a Fool of Myself Over John Foster Dulles, 1957; Broadway debut in Once Upon a Mattress, 1959; regular performer in Garry Moore TV show, 1959-62; appeared several CBS-TV spls., 1962-63; star Carol Burnett Show, CBS-TV, 1966-77; appeared on Broadway, play Fade Out-Fade In, 1964, play Plaza Suite, 1970, musical play I Do, I Do, 1973, Same Time Next Year, 1977; films include Pete 'n' Tillie, 1972, Front Page, 1974, A Wedding, 1977, Health, 1979, Four Seasons, 1981, Chu Chu and the Philly, 1981, Annie, 1982; TV movies Friendly Fire, 1978, The Grass is Always Greener Over the Septic Tank, 1979, The Tenth Month, 1979, Life of the Party, 1982, Between Friends, 1983, Hostage, 1988; club engagements, Harrah's Club, The Sands, Caesar's Palace, MGM Grand. Recipient outstanding comedienne award Am. Guild Variety Artists, 5 times; Emmy award for outstanding variety performance Acad. TV Arts and Scis., 5 times; TV Guide award for outstanding female performer, 1961, 62, 63; Peabody award, 1963; Golden Globe award for outstanding comedienne of year Fgn. Press Assn., 8 times; Woman of Year award Acad. TV Arts and Scis.; People's Choice award favorite all-around female entertainer, 1975, 76, 77; 1st ann. Nat. TV Critics Circle award for outstanding performance, 1977; San Sebastian Film Festival award for best actress for A Wedding, 1978; Horatio Alger award Horatio Alger Assn. Disting. Ams., 1988; named One of 20 Most Admired Women Gallup Poll, 1977. Address: ICM 8899 Beverly Blvd Los Angeles CA 90048 *

BURNETT, DONNA SUE, lawyer; b. Houston, Apr. 6, 1948; d. Travis E. and Yvonne (Thompson) B.; m. Gary B. Conine, Sept. 2, 1983. BBA with highest honors, U. Tex., Austin, 1975; JD magna cum laude, U. Houston, 1980. Bar: Tex. 1980. Ptnr. firm Liddell, Sapp Zivley, Hill & LaBoon, Houston, 1980—. Editor-in-chief Houston Law Rev., 1979-80. Mem. ABA, Houston Bar Assn., Nat. Assn. Bond Lawyers, Houston Law Rev. Alumni Assn., Order of Barons, Beta Gamma Sigma. Republican. Mem. Disciples of Christ Ch. Club: Jr. League (Houston). Home: 3422 Gannett Houston TX 77025 Office: Liddell Sapp Zivley et al 3500 Texas Commerce Tower Houston TX 77002

BURNETT, JANET FLORA, educator; b. Cin., Mar. 26, 1936; d. Louis William and Flora Bertha (von Kaenel) Wiedenbein; m. Lonnie Avril Burnett, June 15, 1957; children: Robert Edward, Laurie Ann. BS in Elem. Edn., U. Cin., 1957, M in Spl. Edn., 1975; PhD, Miami U., Oxford, Ohio, 1987. Cert. elem. tchr., prin., spl. edn. tchr., supr. Spl. edn. cons. Tri-City Elem. Schs., Fairfield, Ohio, 1976-77; grad. asst. Cin. Ctr. for Devel. Disorders, 1977-78; teaching asst. Clermont Tech. Coll., Batavia, Ohio, 1978-79; spl. edn. cons. Kenwood Psychol. Service, Cin., 1979-80; dir. lunch time learning Miami U., Oxford, Ohio, 1980-82; asst. dir. McGuffey Lab Sch., Oxford, 1982-83; edn. coordinator CareUnit Hosp. Cin., 1985—; newsletter editor, Ohio Mid. Schs., Columbus, Ohio, 1984-85; trans. chair Nat. Mid. Sch. Conv., Columbus, 1984. Soprano May Festival Chorus, Cin., 1982—. Mem. Ohio Edn. Assn., Nat. Mid. Sch. Assn., Council for Exceptional Children, Assn. Supervision and Curriculum Devel., Ednl. Computer Consortium Ohio, Phi Delta Kappa. Home: 7216 Quail Hollow Cincinnati OH 45243 Office: CareUnit Hosp Cin 3156 Glenmore Ave Cincinnati OH 45243

BURNETT, SUSAN WALK, personnel service company owner; b. Galveston, Tex., Aug. 21, 1946; d. Joe Decker and Ruth Corinne (Lowe) Walk; m. Rusty Burnett, Dec. 27, 1973; stepchildren—Barbara, Sara. B.A. in Journalism, U. Ark.-Fayetteville, 1968. Asst. pub. relations mgr. sta. KATV, Little Rock, 1968-69; speech writer Assoc. Milk Producers, Inc., Little Rock, 1969-70; mgr. Allied Personnel, Houston, 1970-74; owner Burnett Cos. Consol., Inc., Houston, 1974—. Speaker Job Search Seminars, Houston, 1984; worker Easter Seals Telethon. Recipient Appreciation awards Lyndon Johnson Space Ctr., NASA, 1983, State of Tex., 1984. Mem. Tex. Assn. Personnel Cons. (v.p. 1985), Houston Assn. Personnel Cons. (pres. 1986, v.p. 1985), Nat. Assn. Personnel Cons., Houston C. of C., Chi Omega Alumnae. Republican. Methodist. Avocations: Reading; golf; flying; sailing. Office: Burnett Cos Consol Inc 9800 Richmond Suite 800 Houston TX 77042

BURNETTE, JEAN HUDSON, municipal executive; b. Unadilla, Ga., June 24, 1935; d. James Hollis and Ola (Peavey) Hudson; m. John L. Burnette; children: Russell Craig, Richard Douglas, Linda Burnette Geoghagan, John Steven. Student, U. Ga., Ga. Tech., Brewton Parker Coll. Various sec. positions Cordele, Ga., 1952-53; with personnel and acctg. dept. Cordele Casualwear Corp., 1953-59; clk. Lee. M. Paul. Ins., Perry, Ga., 1959; sec. acctg. City of Cordele, 1959-64, adminstrv. asst., 1964-69, dir. urban renewal, 1969-74, dir. community devel., 1974—. Sec. Bd. Zoning Appeals, Cordele, 1972—, Cordele Office Bldg. Authority, 1974—, Elec. Bd. Appeals, Cordelle, 1982—, Plumbing Bd., 1982—, Downtown Improvement Com., 1987; mem. Cordele Crisp Planning Commn., Cordele, 1976—, planning com. dept. community affairs State of Ga., Atlanta, 1981, rural devel. ctr. U. Ga., Tifton, 1983-85. Mem. Ga. Assn. of Zoning Adminstrs., So. Bldg. Code Congress, Internat. Assn. of Elec. Inspectors, Am. Planning Assn., Ga. Planning Assn., Nat. Assn. of Rev. Appraisers and Mortgage Underwriters (sr.), Bldg. Officials Assn. of Ga. Home: 1009 Schley Ave Cordele GA 31015 Office: City of Cordele 501 N 7th St PO Box 569 Cordele GA 31015

BURNETTE, PATRICIA BAUER, social services administrator; b. Evansville, Ind., June 11, 1937; d. John L. and Jessie (Whitaker) Bauer; m. Rand Burnette, June 14, 1958; children: Patrick Rand, Catherine Mary, Mark William. BA, MacMurray Coll., 1958; MA, Ind. U., 1962, PhD, 1972. From instr. to asst. prof. Carthage Coll., Kenosha, Wis., 1962-68; asst. prof. MacMurray Coll., Jacksonville, Ill., 1969, 71-72; project dir., exec. dir. Prairie Council on Aging, Jacksonville, 1974—; chmn. Ill. Synod Task Force on Aging, 1986-87. Democrat. Lutheran. Home: 234 Webster Jacksonville IL 62650 Office: Prairie Council on Aging 200 W Douglas Jacksonville IL 62650

BURNHAM, DOLORES FRANCINE, electrical sales executive; b. Phila., Nov. 10, 1944; d. John Albert Burnham and Frances Rose (Peake) Riggione; m. Michael J. Moffa, Jan. 17, 1963 (div. Feb. 1971); children: Michael John, William Thomas. BS in Mgmt. with honors, Phila Coll. Textile & Sci., 1979. Outside salesman Penn Electric, Phila., 1978-83; field sales rep. Searle Pharms., Pa., 1983, Bryant Electric Wiring Device div. Westinghouse Corp., N.J. & Dela., 1983-86; outside salesman Tab Electric, Trenton, N.J., 1986—. Mem. Nat. Assn. Profl. Saleswomen, Alpha Sigma Lambda. Republican. Roman Catholic. Home: 34-K Village of Stoney Run Maple Shade NJ 08052 Office: Tab Electric 1601 Greenwood Ave Trenton NJ 08609

BURNHAM, HELEN ANDERSON, librarian; b. Seattle; d. Andrew and Fredrika (Johnson) Anderson; m. Wesley Burnham, Oct. 23, 1948; children—Barbara, Laurie, Ray. BSLS, U. Wash., 1932, postgrad., 1932-33. Children's librarian Seattle Pub. Library, 1933-41, Bklyn. Pub. Library, 1941-49; dir. Croton Free Library, Croton-on-Hudson, N.Y., 1968-84, trustee, 1985—; v.p. Croton Library Bd., 1988—; , mem. exec. com., chmn. library expansion campaign, 1985-87. Testified before Nuclear Regulatory Commn., Concerned Parents about Indian Point, 1983; adv. bd. United Fund, 1981, 83, 85; mem. Adult Edn. Adv. Bd., 1981—. Recipient Recognition award for personal achievements and contbns. to community Croton Cortlandt Women's Ctr., 1980, Cert. of Merit, Town of Cortlandt and Village of Croton, 1985. Mem. Pub. Library Dirs. Assn. (exec. bd.), ALA, Westchester Library Assn., N.Y. State Library Assn., Common Cause. Home: Rt 1 Box 133 Thetford Center VT 05075 Office: Croton Free Library 171 Cleveland Dr Croton-on-Hudson NY 10520

BURNHAM, PATRICIA WHITE, banker; b. Omaha, July 30, 1933; d. William Max and Berniece Irene (Shockey) Orr; m. William L. White, June 18, 1955 (div. Nov. 1979); children: Lucinda, Christopher, Duncan; m. Robert A. Burnham, Feb. 23, 1980. BA in English, DePauw U., Greencastle, Ind., 1955; MA in English, Ill. State U., 1966, PhD in Adminstrn., 1977. Tchr. Morton Grove (Ill.) and Evansville (Ind.) pub. schs., 1955-60; instr. Ill. State U., Normal, 1963-71, dir. Nat. Student Exchange, 1971-74, dir. continuing edn., 1974-76, asst. dean, 1976-79; assoc. dir. Ill. Bd. Higher Edn., Springfield, 1979-80; assoc. vice provost Ohio State U., Columbus, 1980-81; specialist bus. ins. Nationwide Ins. Co., Columbus, 1981-83; v.p. pvt. banking Chase Manhattan Bank, N.A., N.Y.C., 1983—; cons. profl. devel. Ill. area community colls., 1977-79; cons. retirement and fin. planning various univs., N.Y. and Ill., 1986—. Contbr. articles to profl. jours. Bd. dirs. Mennonite Hosp., Bloomington, Ill. Mem. Internat. Assn. Fin. Mgrs., Am. Mktg. Assn., Fairfield County Exec. Women (bd. dirs. 1987—), Phi Beta Kappa, Phi Delta Kappa. Presbyterian. Clubs: PEO (pres. Evansville chpt. 1959-61); Women's City of N.Y. (Manhattan). Office: Chase Manhattan Bank NA 350 Park Ave New York NY 10018

BURNHAM, SHEILA KAY, accountant; b. Alliance, Ohio, May 7, 1955; d. Donald Everald and Marilyn Arlene (Datz) B. AS, Cen. Ohio Tech. Coll., 1977. CPA, Ohio. Staff acct. E.A. Guelde & Assocs., Newark, Ohio, 1973; staff acct., sr. acct. Wells & Snyder, Newark, 1973-78; mgr. Wells, Snyder, Digman & Co., Newark, 1978-83; acctg. instr. Cen. Ohio Tech. Coll., Newark, 1982-83; prin. Digman, Burnham & Co., Newark, 1983-84, Sheila K. Burnham, CPA, Newark, 1984—; panelist Tax Facts Radio and TV program, Columbus, Ohio, 1983—. Bd. dirs., treas. The Easter Seal Soc. of Licking County, Newark, 1983—, Ohio, 1987—, The Ctr. for Alternative Resources, Newark, 1986—; bd. dirs. YWCA, 1988—, treas., 1988—; Big Sister, Newark, 1984—; mem. adv. com. for acctg. tech. Cen. Ohio Tech. Coll., Newark, 1984—; instr. Vol. Income Tax Assistance Program, Newark, 1985—; trustee, mem. adminstrv. bd., chairperson fin., choir mem., Sunday Sch. tchr. Christ United Meth. Ch., Newark, 1969—; bd. dirs., treas. Ohio Easter Seal Soc., 1987—. Recipient Outstanding Alumni award Cen. Ohio Tech. Coll., 1983. Mem. Ohio Soc. CPA's, Am. Womens Soc. CPA's, Am. Soc. Women Accts., Newark Area C. of C., Mental Health Assn., Easter Seal Soc. of Licking County, Zonta Internat. Republican. Methodist. Lodge: Zonta. Home: 345 Central Ave Newark OH 43055 Office: 85 N Third St Newark OH 43055

BURNISTON, KAREN SUE, nurse; b. Hammond, Ind., May 20, 1939; d. George Hubbard and Bette Ruth (Ambler) B.; R.N., Parkview Methodist Hosp., Ft. Wayne, Ind., 1961; B.S. in Nursing, Purdue U., 1974; M.S., No. Ill. U., DeKalb, 1976. Staff nurse Parkview Meml. Hosp., 1961-63, 71-73; physician office and operating room nurse, 1963-67; nurse N.W. Ind. Home Health Services, 1974; mem. faculty Michael Reese Hosp. Sch. Nursing, Chgo., 1977-79; asst. dir. nursing Mt. Sinai Hosp. Med. Center, Chgo., 1977-79; asst. adminstr. patient services St. Margaret Hosp., Hammond, 1980-85; asst. adminstr. patient services St. Catherine Hosp., East Chgo., Ind., 1985-86, chief operating officer, 1986— ; vis. assoc. prof. Purdue U. Sch. Nursing; adj. faculty Ind. U. Sch. Nursing. Bd. dirs. South Lake Ctr. Mental Health, Ancilla Home Health, Inc., Chgo., 1987—, Hospice of N.W.Ind., 1987—. Served with Nurse Corps, USAF, 1967-71. Mem. Am. Nurses Assn., Am. Orgn. Nurse Execs., Ind. Orgn. Nurse Executives (pres. 1984), No. Ind. Orgn. Nurse Execs., East Chgo. C. of C. (bd. dirs. 1988), Sigma Theta Tau. Mem. Christian Ch. (Disciples of Christ). Home: 824 Kenmare Pkwy Crown Point IN 46307 Office: St Catherine Hosp 4321 Fir St East Chicago IN 46312

BURNS, ANNE MARIE, educator; b. Providence, Apr. 13, 1921; d. James B. and Annie (Hagan) B.; Ph.B., Providence Coll., 1964; M.A., U. Conn., 1965. Tchr., Providence Sch. Dept., 1961—, also nursing asst. R.I. Hosp., Providence, 1972—. Sec. del. to Democratic Nat. Conv., 1980; appeared in BBC TV film on Dem. Nat. Conv., 1980. Mem. Providence Tchrs. Union, R.I. Hist. Soc. Roman Catholic. Club: Cath. Women's. Home: 1 Sheila Ln Smithfield RI 02917 Office: 195 Nelson St Providence RI 02908

BURNS, BARBARA BELTON, service executive, investment company executive; b. Fredericktown, Mo., Dec. 10, 1944; d. Clyde Monroe and Mary Celestial (Anderson) Belton; m. Larry J. Bohannon; Mar. 27, 1963 (div.); 1 child, Timothy Joseph; m. Donald Edward Burns, Nov. 1, 1980; stepchildren: Brian Edward, David Keone. Student, Ohio State U., 1970-75. Dir. nat. sales Am. Way, Chgo., 1976-77; recruiter Bell & Howell Schs., Columbus, Ohio, 1978-80; pres., founder Bardon Investment Corp., Naples, Fla., 1980—; founder Cambridge Mgmt. Co., Columbus, 1983-86; pres., chairperson The Cleaners, Inc., Columbus, 1984—; cons. in field. Treas. Vicace/Columbus Symphany, 1981-82; fund raiser Grant Hosp., Columbus, 1986; chairperson Impresarios/Opera Columbus, 1986-87; founding mem. Columbus Women's Bd. 1986-87. Mem. Internat. Drycleaners Congress, Internat. Fabricare Inst., Am. Hotel & Motel Assn., U.S. Trotting Assn. Republican. Office: The Cleaners Inc 200 Bradenton Ave Dublin OH 43017

BURNS, CAROL J(ANE), architect, educator; b. Cedar Rapids, Iowa, Nov. 24, 1954; d. Robert Joseph and Alice T. (Neuhaus) B. Student, Bryn Mawr Coll., 1973-75; BA, Yale Coll., 1980, MArch, 1983. Designer Osborne and Stewart, San Francisco, 1975-77; project architect Hunter Smith and Assocs., New Haven, 1983-85; project designer A.M. Kinney and Assocs., Cin., 1985-86; asst. prof. U. Cin., 1984-86; adj. prof. R.I. Sch. Design, Providence, 1986-87; asst. prof. Harvard U., Cambridge, Mass., 1987—; prin. C. Burns, Architect, Guilford, Conn., 1986—. Editor jour. Yale Sch. Architecture Perspecta 21, 1984; designer bank br. (Soc. Am. Reg. Architects award 1988); group shows include Erector Sq. Gallery, New Haven, 1987, Tangeman Gallery, Cin., 1986, Canessa Gallery, San Francisco, 1985, Norfolk 4 Plus 4: Architects and Sculptors, Norfolk, Conn., 1983. Mem. Guilford Land Trust, 1987—, Women's Nat. Art Mus., Washington, 1988—. Grantee U. Cin. Research Council, 1985, 86, Graham Found., 1983; Eero Saarinen fellow, 1983. Mem. Shoreline Alliance Arts. Club: Yale (New Haven). Office: Harvard U 48 Quincy St Cambridge MA 02148

BURNS, CATHERINE ELIZABETH, art dealer; b. Winnipeg, Man., Can., June 21, 1955; came to U.S., 1955; d. Robert Franklin and Claire Margaret (Lillington) B. BA, U. Calif., Davis, 1975; MA in Museology, U. Minn., 1978. Adj. prof., curator univ. gallery U. Mass., Amherst, 1978-80; curator Washington U. Gallery of Art, St. Louis, 1981-82; dealer in 19th and early 29th century prints and drawings Catherine E. Burns Fine Prints, Oakland, Calif., 1982—, also appraiser. Author catalogs. Organizer San Francisco Fine Print Fair. Nat. Endowment for Arts grantee, 1981-82. Mem. Nat. Trust for Hist. Preservation, Oakland Heritage Alliance, Graphic Arts Council, Art Deco Soc. Calif. Office: PO Box 11201 Oakland CA 94611

BURNS, CHARLOTTE MARY, legal administrator; b. Orange, N.J., Sept. 26, 1947; d. Thomas L. and Mary J. (Virtue) B. BS, Rutgers U., Newark, 1981; MBA, Fairleigh Dickinson U., 1987. Exec. sec. RCA Corp., Harrison, N.J., 1967-75; adminstr. Melvin J. Wallerstein, P.A., West Orange, N.J., 1975-86; legal adminstr. Wallerstein, Hauptman & Richmond, West Orange, N.J., 1986—; speaker Passaic County Bar Assn., Paterson, N.J., 1985; lectr. Assn. Legal Adminstrs., New Brunswick, N.J., 1986. Contbr. articles to The Adv., 1987—. Mem. Internat. Assn. Legal Adminstrs., N.J. State Bar Assn. (exec. com. sect. econs. 1985-86, speaker 1986), N.J. Assn. Legal Adminstrs. (treas. 1983-84, pres. 1984-85, founder, editor newsletter 1984—), Cert. Office Automation Profls. (cert.). Office: Wallerstein Hauptman & Richmond 200 Executive Dr Suite 100 West Orange NJ 07052

BURNS, DEBORAH DENISE, financial planner, broker; b. Houston, Mar. 15, 1953; d. Allie (Burns) Sneed; divorced; 1 child, James E. Beard. BS in Psychology, U. Houston, 1983. Collection clk. Foley's Dept. Store, Houston, 1973-76; clk. U.S. P.O., Houston, 1976-81; office mgr. LFA, Inc., Houston, 1981-83; ind. sales agt. First Continental Ins. Co., Houston, 1983-86; unit mgr. Summit Mktg. Group, Houston, 1985—, broker, 1985—. counselor Julia C. Hester House United Way Agy., Houston, 1984. Roman Catholic. Office: First Continental Ins Co 2303 Smith Houston TX 77006

BURNS, DOTT, talent agency executive; b. Louisville, Aug. 9; d. Homer Lee and Katharine (Van Seggren) Moss; children: Kimberli. Student, Ringling Sch. Art, Sarasota, Fla., 1954, Caldwell Theatrical Sch., Tampa, 1956, Meyer Theatrical Sch., Tampa, 1955, Art Inst. of Pitts., 1955. Freelance artist Fla. and N.Y., 1950-70, fashion model, 1950-70; lead model Fashions for You, Channel 13, 1955; art coordinator Gasparika Arts Festival WEDU-TV; owner, founder Dott Burns Talent Agy., Tampa, Fla., 1970—; lectr. in field; numerous appearances on TV talk shows. permanent work (watercolor) in Capital Bldg., Tallahassee. Recipient Jonas Salk award; named Mother of the Yr., 1962, many others. Mem. Screen Actors Guild, Greater Tampa C. of C., Actors Equity Assn., Am. Fedn. Radio and TV, Tampa Ad Fedn., Agts. Talent Assn., Am. Artists Profl. League (arts coordinator), Fla. Gulf Coast Symphony Guild (arts coordinator), Country Music Assn., Fla. Assn. Talent and Modeling (founder), Tampa Conv. Bur. Republican. Episcopalian. Office: 478 Severn Tampa FL 33606

BURNS, ELLEN BREE, judge; b. New Haven, Conn., Dec. 13, 1923; d. Vincent Thomas and Mildred Bridget (Bannon) Bree; m. Joseph Patrick Burns, Oct. 8, 1955 (dec.); children: Mary Ellen, Joseph Bree, Kevin James. BA, Albertus Magnus Coll., 1944, LLD (hon.), 1974; LLB, Yale U., 1947; LLD (hon.), U. New Haven, 1981, Sacred Heart U., 1986. Bar: Conn. 1947. Dir. legis. legal services State of Conn., 1949-73; judge Conn. Circuit Ct., 1973-74, Conn. Ct. of Common Pleas, 1974-76, Conn. Superior Ct., 1976-78, U.S. Dist. Ct. Conn., New Haven, 1978—. Trustee Fairfield U., 1978-87, Albertus Magnus Coll., 1985—. Recipient John Carroll of Carrollton award John Barry Council K.C., 1973, Judiciary award Conn. Trial Lawyers Assn., 1978, Cross Pro Ecclesia et Pontifice, 1981, Law Rev. award U. Conn. Law Rev., 1987. Mem. ABA, Am. Bar Found., Conn. Bar Assn. (Judiciary award 1987, trustee), New Haven County Bar Assn. Roman Catholic. Office: US Dist Ct 141 Church St New Haven CT 06510

BURNS, GLADYS KING, political scientist, author; b. Gadsden, Ala., Feb. 7, 1927; d. Leslie Cooper and Gladys (Angle) King; B.A., Huntingdon Coll., Montgomery, Ala., 1963; M.A., Auburn (Ala.) U., 1965; Ph.D., U. Ala., 1977; m. J.A. Burns, 1946 (div. 1963); 1 child, Elizabeth King. Mem. faculty N.E. State Jr. Coll., Rainesville, Ala., 1965-66; prof. polit. sci. Jefferson State Coll., Birmingham, Ala., 1966—, dir. Women's Center, 1980, dir. sex. discriminaton Ala. Gen. Assistance Center, U. Ala., 1975-77. Mem. Ala. Hist. Assn., Internat. Platform Assn., DAR, Phi Alpha Theta, Kappa Delta Pi. Home: 1163 Montclair Rd Birmingham AL 35213 Office: Jefferson State Jr Coll 2601 Carson Rd Birmingham AL 35215

BURNS, HEATHER L., management consultant; b. Worcester, Mass., Jan. 11, 1951; d. Harry Warren and Priscilla (Howard) B. BA with distinction, magna cum laude, Colby Coll., 1973; M in Community Planning, U. R.I., 1975. Jr. planner then sr. planner Met. Area Planning Council, Boston, 1975-77; from cons. to prin. Booz, Allen and Hamilton, Bethesda, 1977—. Contbr. articles to profl. jours.

BURNS, HELENE B., accountant; b. Bronx, N.Y., Oct. 16, 1953; d. Joseph and May (Klapp) Burstein; m. Dennis M. Burns, July 1, 1979. BS in Acctg. cum laude, Bklyn. Coll., 1975; MBA in Fin. with hons., St. John's U., 1986. Staff acct. Price Waterhouse & Co., N.Y.C., 1975-76; acctg. supr. Joseph E. Seagram & Sons, Inc., 1976-78; asst. to controller Petroleum div. St. Joe Minerals Corp., 1978-82; cons. The Oved Group, S.I., N.Y., 1985-87; owner, pres. Temporary Solutions, S.I., 1987—. Mem. Nat. Assn. Female Execs., Omicron Delta Epsilon, Beta Gamma Sigma. Republican. Jewish. Home and Office: 46 Purdue St Staten Island NY 10314

BURNS, KATHRYN KAY, accounting administrator; b. Beaumont, Tex., Jan. 14, 1960; d. Reuben Stuart and Nancy Louelda (Jordan) Richardson; m. Kerry Michael Eckert, Feb. 27, 1983 (div. 1985); m. Brian Kelly Burns, Nov. 10, 1986; 1 child, Jason Tyler. Acctg. clk. Sweet & Treats, Inc., Houston, 1978, Coca-Cola Bottling Co., Houston, 1978-79; acct. Exlog Inc., Houston, 1979-86; acctg. adminstr. Paciolan Systems, Long Beach, Calif., 1987—. Office: Paciolan Systems 2875 Temple Ave Long Beach CA 90806

BURNS, MARGARET COLLINS, electrical engineer; b. Pitts., July 31, 1956; d. Thomas Dennis and Virginia Ann (Collins) Burns. BSEE, Drexel U., 1979; postgrad., George Washington U., 1982-84. With Air Force Data Services Ctr., Washington, 1975-77, Westinghouse Elec. Corp., Pitts., 1978; cons. Hittman Med. Systems, Columbia, Md., 1978-79; tech. staff BETAC Corp., Rosslyn, Va., 1980-82; instr. Montgomery Coll., Takoma Park, Md., 1980-86; mgr., sr. systems engr. IBM Corp., Gaithersburg, Md., 1982—. Mem. IEEE (computer soc.), Assn. Computing Machinery. Democrat. Roman Catholic. Home: 5519 N 9th Rd Arlington VA 22205

BURNS, MARIAN LAW, administrative law professional; b. Drexel Hill, Pa., Jan. 10, 1954; d. Vincent Charles and Agatha M. (Paoletti) Law; m. Lawrence Joseph Burns, Sept. 29, 1979; children: Peter Andrew, Rita Marie. Paralegal, legal sec. Tuso and Gruccio, Vineland, N.J., 1972-74; legal sec. Swartz, Campbell and Detweiler, Phila., 1974-80; adminstrv. mgr. Drinker Biddle and Reath (formerly Smith, Lambert, Hicks and Beidler, P.C.), Princeton, N.J., 1980-88; legal adminstr. Sherr & Zuckerman, Norristown, Pa., 1988—. Mem. ABA (assoc., sect. economics of law practice), N.J. Assn. Legal Adminstrs. Office: Sherr & Zuckerman 601 DeKalb St PO Box 1180 Norristown PA 19404

BURNS, MARY ELIZABETH, lawyer; b. Vermillion, S.D., July 30, 1946; d. Phillips Barton and Mary Elizabeth (Beasom) Crew; m. Damon Russell Jorgensen, Sept. 21, 1968 (div. 1976); 1 child, Amy Jennifer; m. William Mason Burns, May 12, 1978 (div. 1986). BA in English, Mills Coll., 1968; MA in History, U. S.D., 1977, JD, 1980. Bar: S.D. 1980, Idaho 1981, U.S. Dist. Ct. Idaho 1981. Assoc. atty. Dial, Looze & May, Pocatello, Id., 1981-83; clk. Niels Pearson P.C., Las Vegas, 1984-85; ptnr. Crew Law Offices, Vermillion, 1985—. Troop leader Girl Scouts U.S., Vermillion, Pocatello, Idaho, 1978-83; bd. dirs. Vermillion Day Care Ctr., Vermillion, 1978-80, Girl Scouts U.S. Silver Sage council, 1983, Frontier council, 1984-85, chmn. personnel com., 1984-85. Mem. VHS Music Boosters (bd. dirs., sec., 1987—). Democrat. Methodist. Office: Crew Law Offices 11 E Main St Vermillion SD 57069

BURNS, NORMA DECAMP, architect; b. N.Y.C., Dec. 14, 1940; d. Cyrus and Stella (Werner) DeCamp; m. Robert Paschal Burns, Dec. 4, 1973; 1 child, Linda Paige. BS, Fla. State U., 1962; MArch, N.C. State U., 1976. Registered architect, N.C. Tchr. high schs., Fla., Md., 1962-73; pres., owner Burnstudio Architects P.A., Raleigh, N.C., 1977—, WorkSpace, Inc., Raleigh, 1981—. Past chmn. City of Raleigh Appearance Commn.; mem. land use com Triangle J Council Govts.; mem. Downtown Adv. Com., Raleigh; bd. advisers Preservation Found. N.C., Raleigh, 1985—; mem. bus. adv. council Peace Coll., Raleigh, 1985—; councilman-at-large Raleigh City Council, 1985-87, —, mem. law and fin. com., 1987—, chmn. comprehensive planning com., 1988—, downtown com., 1988—, univ. liaison. Recipient numerous awards including Owens-Corning Energy award, 1984; Adaptive Reuse award Durham Preservation Soc., 1983, 84; cited in Ten Best Designs of 1984, TIME mag. Loeb fellow, Harvard U. 1986-87. Mem. AIA (nat. interiors com. 1981-84, nat. design com. 1985-88, nat. housing com. 1988, chmn. N.C. historic resources com. 1983-85, selected exhibitor 1988 exhbn. by Women in Architecture), Nat. Trust Historic Preservation. Office: Burnstudio Architects PA PO Box 25688 Raleigh NC 27611

BURNS, RUTH ANN M., television executive; b. New Brunswick, N.J., Nov. 7, 1944; d. Chester Patrick and Mary Francis (Norko) Shea; m. Carl William Burns, Sept. 6, 1965; children: Christopher Carl, Heather Shea. BA, Douglass Coll., 1967; MA, Rutgers U., 1976. War corr. AP, N.Am. Newspaper Alliance, Vietnam, 1967; editor News Tribune, Woodbridge, N.J., 1967-70; writer, cons. Star Ledger, N.Y. Times, Parade mag., 1970-76; sr. research and program assoc. Eagleton Inst. of Politics, New Brunswick, 1976-81; project dir. Ctr. for Am. Woman & Politics, New Brunswick, 1978-81; v.p. Sta. WNET, N.Y.C., 1982-84, sr. v.p., 1984—. Author: Women in Municipal Management, Choice, Challenge, Change, 1980 (HUD award); contbg. author: Women and the American City, 1981; also articles. V.p. Edison (N.J.) Bd. Edn., 1975-82; advisor Sch. Communications Rutgers U., 1985-87; trustee Rutgers U., 1987—. Recipient Nat. Writing award William Randolph Hearst Found., 1967, Achievement award Am. Soc. Pub. Adminstrn., 1981, Woman of Yr. award Raritan Valley Regional C. of C., 1982. Mem. Nat. Assn. TV Arts and Scis., Am. Soc. Women in Radio and TV, Eastern Ednl. Network, Douglass Soc. Democrat. Roman Catholic. Home: 6 Longview Rd Edison NJ 08820 Office: Sta WNET 356 W 58th St New York NY 10019

BURNS, SHELLEY DIBBLE, clinical engineer; b. Painesville, Ohio, Sept. 24, 1960; d. Roderick Alfred and Barbara Jane (Hobby) Dibble; m. Douglas Lester Burns, Sept. 15, 1984. BS in Biology, Chemistry, Heidelberg Coll., Tiffin, Ohio, 1982; MS in Clin. Engring., Case Western Res. U., 1984. Clin. engr. Ind. U. Hosps., Indpls., 1985-87, dir. clin. engring., 1987—. Mem. Am. Soc. for Hosp. Engrs., Am. Bus. Women's Assn., Nat. Assn. Female Execs., Assn. for the Advancement of Med. Instrumentation. Republican. Methodist. Office: Ind U Hosps 1100 W Michigan St Indianapolis IN 46223

BURNS, VICTORIA LEE, data processing consultant; b. Tulsa, July 18, 1954; d. Robert Otis and Virginia Lovina (White) Martin; m. William Michael Burns, Dec. 18, 1982. Student U. Tulsa, 1971-75. Assoc. systems analyst Sperry Co., Tulsa, 1975-77, sr. systems analyst, 1979-83; computer analyst City of Tulsa, 1978-79; systems specialist AES, Houston, 1983-84; owner Nat. Postal Ctr., Houston, 1984-88; pvt. practice data processing cons., Houston, 1988—. Sec. Bus. and Profl. Women, Tulsa, 1978-79; pres. West Airport Homeowners Assn., Houston, 1983-86. Mem. Data Processing Mgmt. Assn., Am. Prodn. and Inventory Control Soc., Houston Mothers of Multiples (bd. dirs. 1988-89, editor newsletter), Kappa Delta. Republican. Roman Catholic. Home and Office: 12003 Ripple Glen Houston TX 77071

BURNS, VIRGINIA LAW, educator, newspaper publisher; b. Redford, Mich., May 23, 1925; d. Alvin John and Leola Miriam (Wadley) Law; divorced; children: James Ritchie, Duncan Ritchie, Margaret Ritchie. Student, Cranbrook Acad. Art, Bloomfield Hills, Mich., 1943, U. Mich., 1943-47; BA, Mich. State U., 1956. Cert. tchr., Mich. Tchr. elem. schs. State of Mich., 1969-87; editor, publisher Enterprise Press, Laingsburg, Mich., 1987—; vis. author, writer Mich. Council for Humanities. Contbr. articles to newspapers, mags.; author (juvenile biographies) Frontier Doctor, 1978, Frontier Soldier, 1980, First Frontiers, 1985, Tall Annie, 1987. Leader Boy Scouts Am., DeWitt, Mich., Girl Scouts U.S., East Lansing, Mich., 4-H Club, Onaway, Mich. Mem. Soc. Children's Book Writers, Detroit Women Writers Assn., Greater Lansing Writers Assn. Home: 9600 Fenner Rd Laingsburg MI 48848 Office: Enterprise Press 8600 Fenner Rd Laingsburg MI 48848

BURNS-BLAGMON, DJUANA PHAE, public health analyst; b. Little Rock, Oct. 4, 1944; d. James Venice and Cleopatra (Diamond) Burns; m. Lowell E. Balgmon, Aug. 29, 1981; 1 child, Vache Nieri. Student, Little Rock U., 1964; BS in Zoology, Howard U., 1966; postgrad., USDA Grad. Sch., 1970-71, Am. Soc. Clin. Pathologists, Hawaii, Paris and Montreal, Que., Can. Cert. hemotologist. Histotechnologist Georgetown U. Med. Sch., Washington, 1966-68; research technologist Washington Hosp. Ctr. Research Found., 1968-69; cardiopulmonary research technologist Hosp. for Sick Children, Washington, 1969; med. technologist, supr. hematology Bur. of Lab., D.C. Dept. Pub. Health, 1969-77; Medicaid program specialist in lab. sci., pub. health analyst D.C. Commn. Pub. Health, Washington, 1978—; leader surveillance/utilization rev. team for nat. cert. of D.C. Medicaid Mgmt. Info. System, 1982; cons./adviser to various orgns. and agys. Contbr. articles to profl. jours. Dancer D.C. Recreation Dept. Showmobile, 1967; mem. community modeling group for charitable orgns., 1971-73; mem. commn. on membership and evangelism, class leader local Meth. Ch. Recipient Longevity Service award D.C. Govt., 1980, Sustained Excellence in Job Performance award, D.C. Govt., 1983-87, Outstanding Job Performance award, D.C. Govt., 1984. Mem. Am. Soc. Clin. Pathologist (assoc., cert. in histology), Am. Pub. Health Assn., Am. Inst. Biol. Scis., AAUW, D.C. Neighborhood Health Ctr. Technologists (rec./corr. sec. 1970-74). Club: Bridge. Home: 9801 Justina Ct Lanham MD 20706 Office: 1331 H St NW Suite 601 Washington DC 20005

BURNS-HOWARD, ROBERTA JEANNE, editor, writer; b. Jacksonville, Fla., Nov. 19, 1946; d. J.H.D. and Roberta (Fitzhugh) Burns; m. G. Bradley Burns-Howard, June 1, 1968; children: Meagan, Kathryn. BA, Belhaven Coll., 1970. Food editor Jackson (Miss.) Daily News, 1966-67, asst. state editor, 1969-70; reporter, photographer Kosciugko (Miss.) Star Herald, 1967-68; tchr. English Lanier High Sch., Jackson, 1970-71; freelance reporter, editor Farmington Valley Herald, Simsbury, Conn., 1976-79; editor Farmington Valley Herald, 1983-86; exec. dir. Housing Coalition Inc., Hartford, Conn., 1979-83; mng. editor Farmington News, Avon News, W. Hartford, Conn., 1983; editor Hartford Woman, Conn., 1987; editorial page editor Bristol (Conn.) Press, 1987—. Author, editor: Housing Supporters Primer, 1983; contbr. articles to various jours. Vice chmn. Farmington Library Blg. Com., 1979-83; founder Unionville History Mus., 1983-84. Mem. Women Communications, Hartford Women's Network, LWV (pres. local un. 1977-79, dir. urban crisis 1978-79), NOW.

BURNSIDE, BETH, biology educator; b. San Antonio, Apr. 23, 1943; d. Neil Delmont and Luella Nixon (Kenley) B. BA, U. Tex., 1965, MA, 1967, PhD in Zoology, 1968. Instr. med. sch. Harvard U., Boston, 1970-73; asst. prof. U. Pa., Phila., 1973-76; asst. prof. U. Calif., Berkeley, 1976-77, assoc. prof., 1977-82, prof., 1982—, dean biol. scis., 1984—. Contbr. numerous articles to profl. jours. Scientific adv. bd. Mills Coll., Oakland, Calif., 1986—; trustee Bermuda Biol. Sta., St. George's, 1978-83. Research grantee NSF. Mem. Am. Soc. for Cell Biology (council 1980-84), NIH (research grantee 1972—), Bay Area Career Women (community relations com. 1984—). Office: U Calif Coll Letters & Sci 201 Campbell Hall Berkeley CA 94720

BURNSIDE, DELORES, education facility director; b. Pelican Rapids, Minn., June 29, 1933; d. Adolph and Emma Schattschneider; m. Orvin Burnside; children: Bruce, Kristi. BS with high distinction, U. Nebr., 1972. Cert. tchr., Nebr., Minn. Tchr. Adrian, N.D., 1952-55; tchr. reading Lincoln, Nebr., 1972-85; dir., tchr. Jehovah Luth. Presch., St. Paul, 1985—. Pres. PTA, Lincoln, 1972, weight clinic, Lincoln, 1979-82; v.p. Ladies Guild Messiah Luth. Ch. Mem. Alpha Delta Kappa (treas. local chpt. 1982—). Lutheran. Home: 1545 McClung Dr Arden Hills MN 55112 Office: Jehovah Luth Presch 1566 Thomas Saint Paul MN 55104

BURNSIDE, MARY ARDIS, psychologist; b. Milw., May 14, 1950; d. Glenn Grover and Edna Mae Chrystine (Mueller) B.; B.A., Rice U., 1972; M.A., U. Houston, 1976, Ph.D., 1980; m. Bruce Edward Anderson, July 17, 1973; children—Aaron Hunter Anderson-Burnside, Andrew Chase Anderson-Burnside. Clin. asst. prof. dept. psychiatry Baylor Coll. Medicine, Houston, 1980—; adj. faculty psychology dept. U. Houston, 1984—, Rice U., 1986—. Lic. psychologist, Tex. Mem. Am. Psychol. Assn., Tex. Psychol. Assn., Houston Psychol. Assn., Phi Kappa Phi. Office: 4710 Bellaire Blvd Suite 160 Bellaire TX 77401

BURNS-LARSON, MARY WARD, systems analyst; b. Oxnard, Calif., Dec. 23, 1952; d. John Philip and Pansy Jo (Jasper) Ward; m. Thomas B. Burns (div. May 1977); 1 child, Lynda; m. Richard A.N. Larson, May 9, 1981; stepchildren: Richard Jr., Todd. AA, Moorpark (Calif.) Community Coll, 1973; BA, Calif. Luth. Coll., 1974; grad. cert. in info. systems, George Washington U., 1985. Eligibility interviewer County of Ventura, Oxnard, 1973-74; CETA contract monitor County of Ventura, Calif., 1977-79; mgmt. analyst Setac, Inc., Falls Church, Va. and Camarillo, Calif., 1979-82; sr. staff Veda, Inc., Arlington, Va., 1982-83, 84—; systems analyst Delex Systems, Arlington, 1983-84; adj. instr. George Washington U., 1985; cons. in field, 1984—. Treas. Vince Turner for Trustee, Camarillo, 1979, Greentree Homeowners Assn.; vol. United Way, Ventura, 1980-81; tchr. United Meth. Ch. Sunday Sch., Springfield, Va., 1985. Mem. Nat. Assn. Female Execs. Democrat. Office: Veda Inc 1755 S Jefferson Davis Hwy #200 Arlington VA 22202

BURNSTEIN, FRANCES, commercial association administrator; b. N.Y.C., Oct. 13, 1935; d. Benny and Yetta Kirshenbaum; m. Barry Burnstein, Oct. 16, 1955; children: Steven, Barbara, Lori. Student, CCNY, 1953-55; grad., Insts. Orgn. Mgmt., 1983. Dep. mayor Twp. of Cherry Hill, N.J., 1975-77; exec. dir. Cherry Hill C. of C., 1977—; commr. Camden County Parks, 1986—. Trustee Cooper Found. Med. Ctr., Camden, N.J., 1982-84; v.p. United Way, 1981-84, pres.'s cabinet 1982-84; dir. ARC, Camden County, 1981—, Guidance Ctr., 1982-84; trustee House of Kinds, Inc. Ronald McDonald House; co-chair Del. River Region Tourism Council, 1983. Named Newsmaker of Yr., Cherry Hill C. of C., 1984; Frances Burnstein Little League Softball Field dedicated to her, 1980; selected for cover of N.J. Woman Mag. and named one of seven Women to Watch in 1986, State of N.J. Mem. N.J. Assn. C. of C. (v.p.), N.J. Assn. C. of C. Execs. (bd. dirs. 1979-80), Am. Assn. C. of C., Am. Assn. C. of C. Communications Council, Nat. Assn. Membership Dirs. Republican. Jewish. Lodge: Garden State Rotary (person of yr. 1980). Office: Cherry Hill C of C 1040 Kings Hwy N Cherry Hill NJ 08034

BURPULIS, EUGENIA G., telephone company executive; b. Salem, N.J., Nov. 21, 1942; s. George S. and Thelma (Pirovolos) B.; student Kent State U., 1961-62, Cuyahoga Community Coll., 1977, Capital U., 1987—. With Ohio Bell Tel. Co., Cleve., 1961—, Supr., 1964-71, asst. mgr. multi-media, 1971-75, asst. mgr. course devel., 1975-78, mgr. course devel., 1978—. Mem. women's com., task force Great Lakes Theatre Festival, 1986-87; trustee, exec. bd. St. Demetrios Greek Orthodox Ch., 1986-88. Mem. Am. Soc. Tng. and Devel., Nat. Soc. Performance and Instrn., Am. Bus. Woman's Assn. (editor bull., newsletter editor 1982-84, edn. chmn. 1982; Woman of Year), Ohio Bell Pioneers (editor newsletter 1980-81), St. Demetrios Philoptochos Soc., Nat. Chios Soc. (cmv. sec.). Club: Women's City (Cleve.). Greek Orthodox (mem. choir, past pres., treas.). Home: 35270 Drake Rd North Ridgeville OH 44039 Office: Ohio Bell Telephone Co 45 Erieview Pl Rm 704 Cleveland OH 44114

BURR, CYNTHIA M., insurance company executive; A.A., Hartford Coll. for Women, 1953; B.A., Conn. Coll., 1955. With Conn. Gen. Life Ins. Co., Hartford, 1955—, supr. fin. reporting cont. dept., 1972, asst. sec., 1973-74, asst. sec., 1974-78, asst. dir. corp. devel. mgmt. services, 1974-76, dir. mgmt. services, 1976-77, 2d v.p. mgmt. services dept., 1977-78, 2d v.p. corp. personnel ops., 1978-80, v.p. personnel ops., 1980-83, sr. v.p. group pension, 1983—. Office: Conn Gen Life Ins Co PO Box 2975 Hartford CT 06104

BURRELL, EUGENIA BREEN, chemical company executive; b. Tucson, Apr. 11, 1958; d. Alan Roger and Katherine Ann (Breen) Burrell; m. Karl B. Ulrich, Apr. 19, 1986. BA in Econ., BS in Chem. Engring., U. Notre Dame, 1980. Product quality engr. E. I. Dupont, Brevard, N.C., 1980-82; process engr. E. I. Dupont, Front Royal, Va., 1982-85; research engr. E. I. Dupont, Wilmington, Del., 1985-86; systems resource prodn. supr. Front Royal, 1986—. Mem. Am. Inst. Chem. Engrs., Washington Women in Bus. (community relations com. 1986). Roman Catholic. Home: Rt 2 Box 2985 Front Royal VA 22630 Office: E I Dupont de Nemours PO Box 4000 Front Royal VA 22630

BURRIDGE, JUDITH ANN STEELE, home economist; b. Astoria, Oregon, Sept. 9, 1938; d. John Henderson Steele and Agnes Marie (Lillenas) Jeppesen; m. Henry Charles Burridge, Aug. 18, 1962; children: John Charles, Julie Ann. BS, Oreg. State U., 1960, MS, 1971; PhD, U. Oreg., 1985. Extension agt. Washington County Extension Service Oreg. State U., Hillsboro, 1960-62; extension agt. at large Extension Service Oreg. State U., Corvallis, 1970-71, extension home economist Benton County Extension Service, 1971-80; extension home economist Yamhill County Extension Service Oreg. State U., McMinnville, 1985—, staff chair, 1983-85. Fellow Nat. Farm Found., 1981. Mem. Nat. Assn. Extension Home Economists, Am. Home Economists Assn. (pres. Oreg. chpt. 1976-77, chair pub. affairs., 1983-87, bd. dirs.), Oreg. State U. Extension Assn., Yamhill County Farm Bur., McMinnville C. of C., Omicron Nu. Republican. Episcopalian. Lodge: Zonta Internat. Home: 1059 NW Fucshia Way Corvallis OR 97330 Office: Oreg State U Yamhill County Extension Service 2050 Lafayette Ave McMinnville OR 97128

BURRIS, FRANCES WHITE, personnel director; b. Cuero, Tex., Oct. 18, 1933; d. Marian Cecil and Dorothy Christine (Pruetz) White; m. Berlie Burris Jr, Mar. 8, 1958 (div. 1982); children: William Alan, Joel Maurice. BA, Mary Hardin Baylor Coll., Belton, Tex., 1955; M in Eng., Trinity U., San Antonio, 1959. Cert. tchr., Tex. Elem. tchr. East and Mt. Houston Independent Sch. Dist., 1956, Edgewood Ind. Sch. Dist., San Antonio, 1956-57, 58-59; tchr. Edna (Tex.) Ind. Sch. Dist., 1957-58; elem. tchr. Northside Ind. Sch. Dist., San Antonio, 1960-62, Southside Schs., San Antonio, 1962-63; mgr. Michael's Dept. Store, Houston, 1980-81; eligibility worker Tex. Dept. Human Resources, Houston, 1981—. Mem. Meridith Manor Civic Club, Houston, 1966-78, Settlers Valley Civic Club, Katy, Tex., 1979-81. Mem. Tex. State Employees Union (exec. bd. 1984—, del. gen. assembly 1984-86, lobbyist 1985-87). Democrat. Baptist. Club: Bridge (Houston).

BURROUGHS, BONNIE LEIGH, commercial artist, advertising executive; b. Appleton, Wis., July 4, 1950; d. Robert J. and Charlotte (Clausen) B.; children—John Burroughs Zacherl, Paul Burroughs Zacherl. Student Marian Coll., Fond du Lac, Wis. Media dir., artist understudy James Spallas & Assocs., Fond du Lac, 1969-75; artist, art dept. Mercy Marine, Fond du Lac, 1970-73; pres. Burroughs & Assocs., Fond du Lac, 1980—. Mem. County Bd. Suprs., Fond du Lac, 1979-81; bd. dirs., pres. Fond du Lac County Legal Aux.; bd. dirs. Fond du Lac County Hist. Soc., 1980—, Wau Bon Council Girl Scouts U.S.A. Mem. Fond du Lac C. of C., Fond du Lac Home Builders. Avocations: tennis, reading, swimming, golf. Home: 86 Martin Pl Fond du Lac WI 54935 Office: Burroughs & Assocs 76 S Macy St Fond du Lac WI 54935

BURROUGHS, CANDICE JACKSON, corporate meeting planner, consultant; b. Kansas City, Mo., May 10, 1947; d. Archie G. and Priscilla (Brigden) Jackson; children: Hollie Ann, Richard Brigden. BS, Calif. State U., Long Beach, 1969. Prin. Just Kiddin', Laguna Niguel, Calif., 1979-82, The Finished Look, Newport Beach, Calif., 1980-86; account exec. N. U. Enterprises, Laguna Niguel, 1986; prin. Kustom Incentive Concepts, Laguna Niguel, 1986—. Mem.-at-large Laguna Niguel Community Council, 1983—; mem. Orange County Rep. Cen. Com., Santa Ana, Calif., 1984-86; pres. Parents Who Care, Capistrano Valley, Calif., 1985-86; v.p. Laguna Niguel Rep. Women's Club, 1985-86. Named Citizen of Month, Laguna Niguel Community Council, 1985. Mem. Meeting Planners Internat. (pub. relations com. 1986), Soc. Incentive Travel Execs., Children's Home Soc. (v.p. Laguna Niguel chpt. 1984-85).

BURROUGHS, MARGARET TAYLOR GOSS, artist, former museum director; b. St. Rose, La., Nov. 1, 1917; d. Alexander and Octavia (Pierre) Taylor; m. Bernard Goss, 1937; 1 dau., Gayle; m. Charles Burroughs, 1949; 1 adopted son, Paul. B.A. in Edn, Art Inst. Chgo., 1946, M.A., 1948; L.H.D. (hon.), Lewis U., 1972; D.H.L. (hon.), Chgo. State U., 1983. Tchr. art Chgo. Public Schs., 1944-68; prof. humanities Kennedy King Coll., Chgo., 1969-79; exec. dir. DuSable Mus. African Am. History, Chgo., 1961-84, dir. emeritus, 1984—; group shows include: Los Angeles County Mus., 1976, Corcoran Gallery, 1980; mem. Chgo. Council Fine Arts, 1976-80, Nat. Commn. Negro History and Culture, 1981—; founder Nat. Conf. Artists, 1959. Fellow Nat. Endowment Humanities, 1968. Office: DuSable Museum 740 E 56th Pl Chicago IL 60657 *

BURROW, DONNA GALE, business systems analyst; b. Chgo., Sept. 21, 1952; d. Robert William and Lois Muriel (Eich) B.; m. Richard. BS, Western Ill. U., 1974; MBA, Ball State U., 1981. Cert. systems profl. Phys. (program) dir. YMCA, Anderson, Ind., 1976-79; mgr. internal systems Mktg. Decisions, Inc., Woodland Hills, Calif. and Mpls., 1981-83; sr. bus. systems analyst RCA Direct Mktg., Indpls., 1983—. Mem. Assn. Systems Mgmt. (facilities chmn. 1985-86, chmn. pub. relations com. Indpls. chpt. 1986—), Mktg. Research Assn. Office: RCA Direct Mktg 6500 E 30th St Indianapolis IN 46219

BURROWS, ELIZABETH MACDONALD, religious organization executive; b. Portland, Oreg., Jan. 30, 1930; d. Leland R. and Ruth M. (Frew) MacDonald. Certificate, Chinmaya Trust Sandeepany, Bombay; PhD (hon.), Internat. U. Philosophy and Sci., 1975. Ordained to ministry First Christian Ch., 1976. Mgr. credit Home Utilities, Seattle, 1958, Montgomery Ward, Crescent City, Calif., 1963; supr. Oreg. Dist. Tng. West Coast Telephone, Beaverton, 1965; pres. Christian Ch. Universal Philosophy, Seattle, 1971—, Archives Internat., St. Louis, 1971—; v.p. James Tyler Kent Inst., 1984—, Internat. Inst. Complimentary Psychology, 1986—. Author: Crystal Planet, 1979, Pathway of the Immortal, 1980, Glory of Revelation, 1981, Maya Sangh, 1981, Harp of Destiny, 1984, Commentary for Gospel of Peace of Jesus Christ according to John, 1986. Mem. Internat. Speakers Platform, Internat. New Thought Alliance. Home: 10529 Ashworth Ave N Seattle WA 98133 Office: Christian Ch Universal Philosophy 10529 Ashworth Ave N Seattle WA 98133

BURSTEIN, KAREN SUE, auditor general, lawyer, city official; b. Bklyn., July 20, 1942; d. Herbert and Beatrice (Sobel) B. B.A., Bryn Mawr Coll., 1964; postgrad. Fisk U., 1964-65; New Sch. Social Research, 1965; J.D., Fordham U., 1970. Bar: N.Y. 1971, U.S. Dist. Ct. (ea. and so. dists.) N.Y. 1971. Instr. Fisk U., Nashville, 1965; film editor Colorvision, Inc., N.Y.C., 1966; staff atty. Nassau County Law Service, N.Y., 1970-72; mem. N.Y. Senate, 1973-78; spl. prof. law Hofstra U., N.Y.C., 1976-78; commr. Pub. Service Commn., Albany, N.Y., 1978-80; exec. dir., chmn. Consumer Protection Bd., Albany, 1981-83; pres. CSC, Albany, 1983-87; auditor gen. N.Y.C., 1987—; co-chmn. N.Y. Gov.'s Commn. on Domestic Violence, 1979—; co-leader N.Y. State study group to Japan, 1984; chmn. Temp. Commn. on Workers' Compensation, Albany, 1984-86, Gov.'s Blue Ribbon Panel on Pub. Power, 1986. Contbr. articles to profl. publs., chpts. to books. Del. Democratic Nat. Conv., 1976, Am. Council Young Polit. Leaders' del. to USSR, 1979, Nat. Women's Conv., Houston, 1977; mem. exec. bd. Coalition to Free Soviet Jews; mem. governing council Am. Jewish Congress. Recipient Outstanding Service award South Shore div. Am. Jewish Congress, Personal Devel. award Bus. and Profl. Women's Club, Humanitarian award L.I. Rehab. Assn., Myrtle Wreath Achievement award Nassau region Hadassah, Women of Action award B'nai B'rith Women, Benjamin Potokin award N.Y. State Employees Brotherhood Com. Mem. Hadassah (life), ACLU, Nassau County Bar Assn., NAACP, Nat. Council Jewish Women, Wilderness Soc., Ctr. Women in Govt., NCCJ, Democrat. Office: Auditor Gen 217 Broadway Suite 206 New York NY 10007

BURSTEIN, ROSE ANNE KORNBLUM, librarian; b. N.Y.C., May 3, 1922; d. M.J.C. and Myrille (Soloman) Kornblum; m. Lucien Burstein, Nov. 15, 1943; children—Barton M., Emily M., Daniel. A.B. with honors, Olivet Coll., 1943; M.A., Yale U., 1949; M.S. with honors, Sch. Library Sci., Columbia U., 1965. Econ. analyst U.S. Dept. State, Washington, 1944-45; reference librarian New Haven Pub. Library, 1947-48; research librarian Benton Bowles advt. agy., N.Y.C., 1949-50, William Weintraub & Co., Inc. (advt. agy.), N.Y.C., 1950-52; library staff Sarah Lawrence Coll., Bronxville, N.Y., 1956-74, library dir., 1974—; mem. N.Y. State Librarians' Task Force on Statewide Serials Database, 1979. Editor: Westchester Union List of Serials, 3d edit., 1979; co-editor: Library and Information Sources on Women. Bd. vistors Pratt Grad. Sch. Library and Info. Sci., Bklyn., 1981-87; trustee METRO: N.Y. Met. Reference and Research Library Agy., 1982—. Mem. ALA, N.Y. Library Assn., Westchester Library Assn., Assn. Acad. and Research Libraries (exec. bd. dirs. N.Y. chpt.). Office: Sarah Lawrence Coll Esther Raushenbush Library 1 Meadway Bronxville NY 10708

BURSTYN, ELLEN (EDNA RAE GILLOOLY), actress; b. Detroit, Dec. 7, 1932; m. Paul Roberts; m. Neil Burstyn; 1 son, Jefferson. LHD, Dowling Coll.; DFA, Sch. Visual Arts. Artistic dir. The Actor's Studio, N.Y.C., 1982—. Appeared regularly on Jackie Gleason TV show, 1956-57; made Broadway debut in Fair Game, 1957-58; other play appearances include summer stock John Loves Mary, 1960, Broadway prodns. of Same Time, Next Year, 1975 (Tony award as best actress), 84 Charing Cross Road, 1982, (off-Broadway) Park Your Car in Harvard Yard with Burgess Meredith, Driving Miss Daisy, 1988; film appearances include: Goodbye Charlie (under name Ellen McRae), 1964, Tropic of Cancer, Alex in Wonderland, 1971 (named Best Supporting Actress N.Y. Film Critics, Nat. Soc. Film Critics, Acad. Award nominee for Best Supporting Actress), The King of Marvin Gardens, 1972, The Exorcist, 1973 (Acad. Award nominee for Best Actress), Harry and Tonto, Alice Doesn't Live Here Anymore, 1974 (Acad. Award as Best Actress, Golden Globe award, Brit. Acad. award), Providence, 1977, A Dream of Passion, 1978, Same Time Next Year (Tony award for Best Actress 1975), 1978 (Acad. award nominee, Golden Globe award), Resurrection, Silence of the North, 1980, Twice in a Lifetime, 1985, Hannah's War, 1987; TV movies include Thursday's Game, 1974, The People vs. Jean Harris, 1981 (Emmy nomination), Act of Vengeance, Into Thin Air, Surviving, Something in Common, 1986, Pack of Lies, 1987 (Emmy nomination); dir. off-Broadway play Judgement, 1981, Into Thin Air, 1985; star TV series The Ellen Burstyn Show, 1986. Mem. individual artists grants and policy overview panels Nat. Endowment for the Arts, Theater Adv. Council City of New York. Mem. Actors Equity Assn. (pres. 1982-85). Office: The Actors Studio Inc 432 W 44th St New York NY 10036

BURT, CYNTHIA MARIE MAULTSBY, health science facility administrator; b. Geneva, N.Y., Sept. 18, 1951; d. Alvin Renus and Dorothy (Marciano) Maultsby; m. Raymond Lee Burt, Aug. 19, 1979 (div. Sept. 1984). BA, East Carolina U., 1973, MS, 1977; MS, U. N.C., 1981. Registered occupational therapist. With Northridge (Calif.) Hosp. Med. Ctr., 1980—, staff therapist, 1980-81, sr. therapist, 1981-83, clin. supr., 1983-85, dir. rehab., 1985-87; coordinator occupational therapy UCLA Med. Ctr., 1987—; advisor tech. 20th Century Fox Prodns., Los Angeles, 1985-87; cons. Valley Village, Northridge, 1986—. Contbr. articles to profl. jours. Mem. Nat. Rehab. Assn., Am. Occupational Therapy Assn., World Fedn. Occupational Therapy, Am. Congress Rehab. Medicine, Occupational Therapy Assn. Calif. (pres. 1986-88). Home: 1042 17th St Santa Monica CA 90403 Office: UCLA Rehab Ctr 1000 Veteran Ave Los Angeles CA 90024-1788

BURT-EDWARDS, BARBARA, English language educator, lawyer; b. Paterson, N.J., Jan. 13, 1945; d. Edward Lee and Jane (Kennedy) Knopf; m. Richard Allen Burt, June 1, 1968 (div. 1978); children—Jennifer Ashley, Richard Allen; m. 2d, William Green Edwards, Nov. 26, 1980. Student Syracuse U., 1962-63; B.A., Kenne Coll., 1966; M.A., U. Miami, 1968, J.D., 1982. Tchr., Newark Bd. Edn., 1966-67, Dade County Bd. Edn., Miami, Fla., 1968-72; asst. project dir. Ministerial Alliance, Miami, 1976-77; assoc. prof. English, Miami-Dade Community Coll., 1977—, assoc. dean, 1985-86. Mem. Nat. Testing Network in Writing, Coll. English Assn., Fla. Assn. Community Colls., ABA, Assn. Trial Lawyers Am., Am. Judicure Soc., LWV. Home: 6045 SW 106 St Miami FL 33156 Office: Miami-Dade Community Coll 11011 SW 104th St Miami FL 33158

BURTNER, SUSAN BURNS, govt. ofcl.; b. Chgo., Nov. 30, 1942; d. William Grady and Margaret (MC Donald) Burns; B.A., Purdue U., 1964; M.S.L.S., U. Ill., 1967; M.A., George Washington U., 1979; m. Carrol E. Burtner, June 7, 1980. Catalog librarian HEW, Washington, 1967; librarian U.S. Air Force, Japan, 1968-70, Dept. Commerce, Washington, 1970-73; chief readers services Gen. Acctg. Office Library, Washington, 1973-75, library dir., 1975-80, dir. Office Info. Systems and Services, 1980-81, dep. dir. gen. services and controller div., 1981—. Mem. Spl. Library Assn., ALA. Roman Catholic. Home: 4013 N Tazewell St Arlington VA 22207 Office: GAO Gen Services and Controller Gen Washington DC 20548

BURTON, ANNA MARJORIE, nurse; b. Pontiac, Mich., May 1, 1931; d. Harold Vale and Sophia (Eaton) Kelly; m. Alexander Frank Burton (dec.); children—Julie A. Burton Stone, William A., Rory R., Kenneth G. Student Mich. State U., 1949-51; A.A., Fla. Keys Community Coll., 1976, A.S. in Nursing, 1983; R.N., Fla., Calif., N.Y. Orthodontic technician Birmingham, Mich., 1960-67; claims rep. Social Security Adminstrn., Lexington, Ky., 1967-71, Key West, Fla., 1972-79; pvt. duty nurse, 1979—. Recipient Appreciation award Vets. Council, 1974; hon. Conch and Key, City of Key West, 1974. Mem. U.S. Coast Guard Aux. (permanent) (comdr. 1976), U.S. Power Squadron, Key West Power Squadron (sec. 1984-85), Am. Nurses Assn., Fla. Nurses Assn., Dist. 25 Nurses Assn., Bus. and Profl. Women, Handicapped Boaters Assn., Boat Owners Assn. of U.S., U.S. Yacht Racing Union, Key West Art and Hist. Soc., Am. Cancer Soc., Am. Diabetes Assn., Juvenile Diabetes Assn., Am. Heart Assn. Club: Key West Yacht (hon.). Home: 1420 Von Phister St Key West FL 33040

BURTON, CHARLOTTE LYETH, development and fundraising executive, consultant; b. Bethesda, Md., Dec. 20, 1943; d. John Mortimer Richardson Lyeth and Patricia (Dobson) Lyeth Webb; m. Michael Augustus Dively, June 17, 1978 (div. 1981); m. Bruce Robert Burton, Oct. 30, 1985. B.A., Principia Coll., 1965; cert. N.Y. Sch. Interior Design, 1966. Asst. to treas. fin. com. to re-elect Pres., Washington, 1972-73; congl. liaison Adv. Council on Hist. Preservation, Washington, 1973-74; exec. asst. Capital Fund Campaign, N.Y. Bot. Gardens, 1976-78; regional chmn. Americans for an Effective Presidency, N.Y.C., 1980; pres. Mich. Assn. Community Arts Agys., Lansing, Mich., 1981-82; dir. area devel. U. Mich., Ann Arbor, 1983-85; dir. devel. N.Y. Bot. Garden, 1985—; cons. Capital Campaign Albion Coll., Mich., 1978-82; cons. Pathfinder Sch., Traverse City, Mich., 1978-79; dir. Longyear Realty Corp., Marquette, Mich., 1975—; gen. ptnr. Longyear Heirs, Inc., Marquette, 1980-86; gen. ptnr. J.M. Longyear Heirs, 1987—. Past pres. Human Relations Commn., Albion; former dir. Impressions V Mus., Lansing, Neighborhood Playhouse Repertory Theatre, N.Y.C., Richard Morse Mime Theatre, N.Y.C., Women's Nat. Republican Club, N.Y.C.; various positions numerous Jr. Leagues; mem. Marquette Hist. Soc., Albion Hist. Soc., Nat. Trust Hist. Preservation, Washington; bd. dirs., v.p. Hist. Soc. Mich., 1984-86; bd. dirs. Artrain, Inc., Detroit, 1984-86. Mem. Christian Sci. Ch. Avocations: sailing; skiing. Home: 21 Indian Spring Rd Rowayton CT 06853 Office: NY Botanical Garden Dir Devel New York NY 10458

BURTON, ELLEN IRWIN, county extension service educator; b. Muscatine, Iowa, Dec. 25, 1946; d. Paul Joseph and Elsie Irene (Laeser) Irwin; m. Bryan Ledru Braucht, Sept. 1, 1968 (dec. Jan. 1974); m. Paul David Burton, June 21, 1975; 1 child, Paul William. BS in Home Econs., U. Ill., 1969; MS, Ill. State U., 1975. Youth extension advisor Coop. Extension Service, Bloomington, Ill., 1969-70; home econs. advisor Coop. Extension Service, Eureka, Ill., 1970—; mem. curriculum devel. com. Ill. Cen. Coll., East Peoria, 1973-75. Vice chairperson Eureka Community Nursery Sch., 1983-87; dir. Cen. Ill. Agy. on Aging, Peoria, 1978-84, 86—, Cen. Ill. Health Systems Agy., Peoria, 1978-82; mem. council Eureka Community Hosp., 1979-83, 88—. Mem. Nat. Assn. Extension Home Economists (chairperson membership com. 1986, Florence Hall award 1974, Disting. Service award 1980, Pub. Affairs award 1984), Ill. Assn. Extension Home Economists (pres. 1985, regional chairperson 1976-78, 82-83, Peer award 1981, 84), Am. Home Econ. Assn., Ill. Home Econs. Assn. (chairperson pub. policy com. 1977-78, 80-82), Woodford Area Home Econs. Assn. (sec. 1975), Epsilon Sigma Phi (Alpha Nu award 1975), Omicron Nu, Phi Upsilon Omicron, Gamma Sigma Delta. Mem. Christian Ch. Lodge: Order of Eastern Star. Office: Coop Extension Service 117 W Center Box 137 Eureka IL 61530

BURTON, JANIS ELAINE (JAN), sports publications director; b. Waitsburg, Wash., May 25, 1933; d. Carroll Everett and Hope Olive (Bolender) Fairbanks; m. Armond Sidney Burton Jr., June 14, 1953; children: Charity Ann Burton Jones, Armond Fairbanks. B, Phillips U., 1958; postgrad., U. Okla., 1973. Cert. tchr., Okla. Tchr. home econs. Madison Jr. High Sch., Bartlesville, Okla., 1960-67; proofreader The Norman (Okla.) Transcript, 1968-69, reporter, 1969-71, asst. wire editor, 1972-75; assoc. writer Media Info. U. Okla., Norman, 1975-77, writer Media Info., 1977-78, sr. writer Media Info., 1978-79, assoc. Sports Info., 1980-84, dir. Sports Publs., 1984—, cons. Athletic Novelties, 1985—. Editor football programs (Best in Dist. 1982, 1984), sports brochures. Mem. Football Writers Am., Coll. Sports Info. Dirs. Am. (awards publicity com., recipient numerous awards), Okla. Coaches' Wives Assn., U. Okla. Pres.'s Ptnrs., U. Okla. Profl. Staff Assn. Democrat. Mem. Christian Ch. Office: U Okla Sports Publs 180 W Brooks #220C Norman OK 73019

BURTON, JENNIFER, educator; b. Bklyn., Oct. 10, 1961; d. Orlando and Everlena Burton. BA, Howard U., 1982; MA, NYU, 1984, NYU, 1987. Cert. tchr. Tchr. United Bus. Inst., Rego Park, N.Y., 1983, Comml. Programming Unltd., N.Y.C., 1983-84, Crown Bus. Inst., Jamaica, N.Y., 1984-85, Tilden High Sch. Bklyn. Bd. Edn., 1985—; Pres. founder Eloquence Designer Greeting Card Co., N.Y.C., 1986—. Mem. Women's Caucus for Congressman Edolphus Towns, Bklyn., 1985. Mem. N.Y. Assn. Black Journalists, Bus. Edn. Assn., Delta Pi Epsilon. Home: 361 Wortman Ave #5E Brooklyn NY 11207

BURTON, KATHRYN CURRAN, public relations executive; b. N.Y.C., Oct. 7, 1941; d. George A. and Dorothy A. (Stillwell) McKeon; B.A., N.Y.U., 1961; postgrad. Russian Inst., Fordham U.; m. James L. Burton, Dec. 17, 1986. Account exec., pub. relations B.B.D.O., 1969-71; v.p. pub. relations Wisser & Sanchez, Inc., N.Y.C., 1971-75; v.p. BritAm Promotions, N.Y.C., 1975-78; exec. v.p. Inter Americas Advt., N.Y.C., 1978—; pres. Curran Assocs Advt./Pub. Relations, N.Y.C., 1980-86; pres. Burton, Curran & Assocs., 1987—; cons. in field. Mem. Am. Women in Radio and TV, N.Y. Women in Communications, Am. Platform Assn. Republican. Club: Publicity (N.Y.C.). Home: 8514 Waverly Ave Oklahoma City OK 73120 Office: 237 Park Ave New York NY 10016

BURTON, PEGGY, advertising executive; b. N.Y.C.; B.S.B.A., NYU. Freelance TV producer, N.Y.C., 1964-67; TV producer Young & Rubicam, N.Y.C., 1967-69; sr. acct. exec. Daniel & Charles, N.Y.C., 1969-74; ptnr., v.p. Bruderer Hartnett Advt. Agy., N.Y.C., 1974-76; dir. Communications Am. Express Co., N.Y.C., 1976-83; v.p. advt. Dreyfus Corp., N.Y.C., 1983— Mem. Internat. Advt. Assn., Advt. Women of N.Y. Office: Dreyfus Corp 767 Fifth Ave New York NY 10153

BURTON, VIRGINIA UNDERWOOD, state agency administrator; b. Monroe, La., Oct. 27, 1950; d. Robert Ray and Elise (Abernathy) Underwood; m. William S. Burton III, Feb. 20, 1971; children: Heather Michelle, William Bowman, Neal Douglas. BBA, N.E. La. U., 1971. CPA, La. Revenue auditor Office Legis. Auditor State of La., Baton Rouge, 1971-72, auditor-in-charge, 1972-85; quality assurance mgr. div. audit services Dept. Health and Human Resources, Baton Rouge, 1985-86, asst. dir. div. audit services, 1986—. Mem. Shenandoah Civic Assn., Baton Rouge, 1976—; mem. Greater Baton Rouge Edna Gladney Aux., Baton Rouge, 1981—, rec. sec., 1982-83. Mem. Am. Inst. CPA's, Soc. La. CPA's, Assn. Govt. Accts. Republican. Roman Catholic. Club: YMCA (Baton Rouge). Home: 5503 Stonewall Dr Baton Rouge LA 70817 Office: Dept Health and Human Resources Div Audit Services 1771 Wooddale Blvd Baton Rouge LA 70806

BURTT, ELIZABETH ALLENE, retired public health nurse; b. Exeter, N.H., July 31, 1926; d. William Abbot and Elizabeth Pride (Cole) Burtt; diploma in Nursing, Hillsborough County Gen. Hosp., 1947; B.S., Johns Hopkins U., 1961, M.P.H., 1977; M.S. in Public Health Nursing, Boston U., 1965. Staff nurse Mass. Gen. Hosp., Boston, 1948-49; head nurse, supr. emergency dept. Johns Hopkins Hosp., Balt., 1950-55; resident sch. nurse Oldfields Sch., Glencoe, Md., 1955-60; sr. public health nurse Balt. City Health Dept., 1961-63; instr. public health nursing U. R.I., Kingston, 1965-68; asst. prof. public health nursing U. N.H., Durham, 1968-72; public health nurse epidemiologist N.H. Div. Public Health Services, Concord, 1972-73, ednl. cons., 1973-75, chief Bur. Public Health Nursing, 1975-84, coordinator Tb Program and Refugee Health Program, 1984-88; N.H. State Tb control officer, 1981-88; summer camp nurse Vt., 1955-59, N.Y., 1965, Mass., 1966, R.I., 1968; public health nurse cons. Exeter Vis. Nurse Assn., 1967; adv. N.H. Student Nurse Assn., 1979-81. Chmn. Epping (N.H.) Health Com., 1969-70, N.H. Immunization Task Force, 1977-79. Mem. Am. Nurses Assn., N.H. Nurses Assn. (dir. 1979-81, chmn. legis. com. 1978-80). Am. Public Health Assn., Nat. League Nursing, N.H. League Nursing (dir. 1977-78, pres. 1981-83), Sigma Theta Tau. Contbr. to Nursing Clinics of North America, 1972. Home: Route 1 Exeter NH 03833 Office: Hazen Dr Concord NH 03301

BURWELL, JEAN LOUISE, principal, educator; b. Newark, Aug. 25, 1932; d. Milton Sr. and Emily Louise (Rollins) Miles; m. William Alfred Burwell, July 29, 1960; children: Milton, Tracey. BS, NYU, 1955; cert., William Paterson Coll., 1965, Harvard U., 1966; MA, Seton Hall U., 1969. Cert. tchr., N.J. Head tchr. Passaic (N.J.) Pub. Schs., 1968-70, asst. prin., 1970-72, prin., 1972—; guest lectr. Nat. Assn. Elem. Sch. Prins., Alexandria, Va., 1987—. Bd. dirs. Essex County Youth House, 1968, 69. Recipient Outstanding Achievement award Belle Mead Sch., 1968-72, Loyal and Devoted Support award Passaic Boys Club, 1971, Disting. and Devoted Service award Miss Pro Classic, 1972, Outstanding Chairperson Messiah Bapt. Ch., 1982, 83, Cert. Appreciation, Messiah Bapt. Ch., 1985, Proclomation City of Passaic, 1987. Mem. Alpha Kappa Alpha. Home: 803 S 10th St Newark NJ 07108 Office: Passaic Adminstrs and Suprs 101 Passaic Ave Passaic NJ 07055

BURY, MARY JO ELEANOR, stockbroker; b. New York, July 14, 1951; d. Joseph Michael and Mary Mildred (Esposito) Cassano; m. Thomas S. Bury, Aug. 24, 1980. BS cum laude, St. John's U., 1972, MBA, 1986. Lic. registered rep. and gen. prin. Nat. Assn. Securities Dealers, London Stock Stock Exchange. Exec. asst. The Ford Found., N.Y.C., 1972-74; paralegal asst. Miller & Seeger, N.Y.C., 1974-77; bus. mgr. W. Greenwell Assocs., N.Y.C., 1977-83; fin. mgr. W. Greenwell Inc., N.Y.C., 1983-85; v.p., gen. prin. Midland Montagu Capital Mkts., N.Y.C., 1985-87; v.p. Kleinwort Grieveson Securities, Inc., N.Y.C., 1987—. Mem. Women Investment Brokers, Fin. Women's Assn. N.Y., N.Y. Assn. Internat. Investments, St. John's U. Alumni Assn. Office: Kleinwort Greiveson Securities 200 Park Ave New York NY 10166

BUSBY, BRENDA VLK, program analysis officer; b. Washington, Feb. 3, 1947; d. Wesley Jr. and Virginia (Sloper) Vlk; m. Edwin I. Busby, Oct. 26, 1968 (div. Feb. 1980). Student in bus. mgmt., U. Va., 1969-70, Richard Bland Coll., 1975-79, Chapman Coll., 1975-79; student in arts and sci., Ga. State U., 1982—. Budget clerk typist program and budget div. comptroller's office U.S. Army, Ft. Lee, Va., 1966-73, accounts maintenance clerk, 1973-74, budget analyst, 1974-80; budget analyst program and budget div. comptroller's office U.S. Army, Ft. McPherson, Ga., 1980-83; program analyst resource mgmt. div. Dir. of Chief of Staff for Logistics U.S. Army, Ft. McPherson, 1983-84; program analysis officer, dep. chief of staff logistics resource mgmt. div. U.S. Army, Ft. McPherson, 1985—; mgmt. analyst mgmt. div. comptroller's office U.S. Army, Ft. Gillem, Ga., 1984-85. Editor Seven Speaks Newsletter, 1979. Treas. Atlanta Crisis Aid, 1980-81, vice chmn., 1981-82; mem. Atlanta Friendship Force, 1982-87; sponsor High Mus. Art., Atlanta, 1987. Named Fed. Woman Yr. Civilian Personnel Office Ft. McPherson, 1982, one of Outstanding Young Women Yr., 1982. Mem. Internat. Tng. in Communication, Am. Soc. Mil. Comptrollers (charter), Assn. U.S. Army, Sunshine Region (pres. 1986-87). Republican. Methodist. Home: 2799 Clairmont Rd Apt A Atlanta GA 30329

BUSBY, SHANNON NIXON, teacher; b. Gainesville, Tex., Nov. 30, 1955; d. James H. and Helen M. (Ross) Nixon; m. Larry W. Busby, Apr. 3, 1982; 1 child, James Ross. BS in Home Econs. Edn., Tex. Tech U., 1977; MEd, Sul Ross State U., Alpine, Tex., 1982. Cert. profl. ednl. diagnostian, tchr. of lang. and/or learning disabilities, tchr. of vocat. homemaking. Home econ. tchr. Pecos (Tex.)-Barstow-Toyah Ind. Sch. Dist., 1978-83, ednl. diagnostian spl. edn. dept., 1983—; bd. dirs. Dept. Mental Health and Mental Retardation, Pecos, 1980-83. Chairperson Tex. War on Drugs, Pecos, 1980-83.

Mem. AAUW (local pres. 1982-86, local v.p. 1978-81, Tex. state bd. dirs. 1982-83), Tex. Ednl. Diagnosticians Assn. Home: 1519 Mary St Pecos TX 79772

BUSCH, MARGARET SNYDER, professional baseball team executive; b. 1916; m. August A. Busch, Jr. Student, Washington U., St. Louis. With Anheuser Busch, Inc., St. Louis, 1942-79, sec. indsl. products, adminstrv. asst., v.p. corp. promotions; v.p. corp. promotions Anheuser-Busch Cos., Inc., St. Louis, from 1979; now v.p., dir. St. Louis Cardinals. Office: St Louis Cardinals Busch Stadium Saint Louis MO 63102 *

BUSCH, MARIANNA ANDERSON, chemistry educator; b. Pitts., Oct. 28, 1943; d. John Ray and Anna (White) Anderson; m. Kenneth Walter Busch, Dec. 15, 1968. BA, Randolph-Macon Woman's Coll., 1965; cert., U. Heidelberg, Fed. Republic of Germany, 1965; PhD, Fla. State U., 1972. Postdoctoral assoc. Cornell U., Ithaca, N.Y., 1972-74, Robert A. Welch fellow Baylor U., Waco, Tex., 1974-75, NSF fellow, 1976, asst. prof., 1977-84, assoc. prof. chemistry, 1984—; lectr. Cornell U., 1972; vis. scientist Calif. Inst. Tech., Pasadena, 1983, E.I. DuPont & Nemours, Wilmington, Del., 1986; cons. Nat. Bur. Standards, Gaithersburg, Md., 1984—. Contbr. numerous articles to profl. jours. Fulbright scholar Victoria U., Wellington, New Zealand, 1966; grantee Robert A. Welch Found., 1979-83, Standard Oil Co., 1983, Am. Petroleum Inst., 1984-85. Fellow Am. Inst. Chemists; mem. AAUW (corp. rep. Waco br. 1980—, pres. 1985-86), Am. Chem. Soc. (chmn. Heart O' Tex. sect. 1978-79, grantee 1978-80, James Lewis Howe award 1965), Am. Water Works Assn., Sigma Xi, Phi Lambda Upsilon, Phi Beta Kappa. Office: Baylor U Chemisty Dept Waco TX 76798

BUSCH, NANCY ELIZABETH, marketing/communications consulting firm executive; b. Manitowac, Wis. Sept. 7, 1944; d. Edgar Wilhelm and Dorothy Janette (Blust) Putz; m. Charles Nels Busch, Aug. 21, 1965; 1 son, Alexander. B.A. in Journalism, U. Mich., 1966. Sales rep. Grosse Pointe News (Mich.), 1966-68; pres. Nels Advt. Co., Birmingham, Mich., 1968-75, Busch & Morris, Birmingham, 1975-80, Busch & Assocs., Birmingham, 1980—; cons. U. Mich. Devel. Bd., Ann Arbor, 1973-80. Mem. Econs. Club of Detroit, Adcraft Club of Detroit, Am. Mktg. Assn., Southeastern Mich. Hosp. Assn. (awards for concept and creative devel. in reports, brochures and other collateral materials 1975-80), Am. Hosp. Assn., Mich. Hosp. Assn. (awards for reports, brochures and other materials 1975-80), U. of Mich. Alumni Assn. Office: Busch & Assocs PO Box 1024 Birmingham MI 48012

BUSCHING, MARCIA JOAN, lawyer; b. Chgo., May 10, 1950; d. Dean Lavern and Betty Jean (Phillips) B.; m. Nathan Robert Niemuth, Aug. 20, 1976; 1 child, Toffler Ann. BBA, U. Wis., 1972, MBA, JD, 1977. Bar: Ariz. 1977, U.S. Dist. Ct. Ariz. 1977, U.S. Ct. Appeals (9th cir.) 1982. Bank examiner State Wis., Madison, 1972-74; assoc. Snell and Wilmer, Phoenix, 1977085, Sacks, Tierney, Kasen & Kerrick, Phoenix, 1985—. Mem. Ariz. Women United (pres. 1982-83), ABA (real property com. 1981—), Ariz. Bar Assn. (vice-chmn. corp. bus. banking sect. 1986-87, chmn. 1987-88, mem. continuing legal edn. com. 1983—, outstanding contbr. continuing legal edn. award 1986), Maricopa County Bar Assn., German Wine Soc. (activities coordinator Phoenix 1977-78). Office: Sacks Tierney Kasen & Kerrick 3300 N Central Ave 20th Floor Phoenix AZ 85012

BUSH, BARBARA PIERCE, wife of United States Vice President; b. Rye, N.Y., June 8, 1925; d. Marvin and Pauline (Robinson) Pierce; m. George Herbert Walker Bush, Jan. 6, 1945; children: George Walker, John Ellis, Neil Mallon, Marvin Pierce, Dorothy Walker. Student, Smith Coll., 1943-44; hon. degrees, Stritch Coll., Milw., 1981, Mt. Vernon Coll., Washington, 1981, Hood Coll., Frederick, Md., 1983, Howard U., Washington, 1987. Bd. dirs. Reading is Fundamental, Bus. Council for Effective Literacy; mem. adv. council Soc. of Meml. Sloan-Kettering Cancer Ctr.; hon. mem. bd. dirs. Children's Oncology Services of Met. Washington, The Washington Home, The Kingsbury Ctr.; hon. chmn. nat. adv. council Literacy Vols. of Am., Nat. Sch. Vols. Program; sponsor Laubach Literacy Internat.; nat. hon. chmn. Leukemia Soc. of Am.; trustee Morehouse Sch. of Medicine; hon. nat. chmn. Nat. Organ Donor Awareness Week, 1982-86; pres. Ladies of the Senate, 1981; mem. women's com. Smithsonian Assocs., Tex. Fedn. of Rep. Women, life mem. Recipient Nat. Outstanding Mother of Yr. award, 1984, Woman of Yr. award USO 1986, Disting. Leadership award United Negro Coll. Fund 1986, Disting. Am. Woman award Coll. Mt. St. Joseph, 1987. Mem. Tex. Fedn. Republican Women (life). Episcopalian. Club: Internat. II (Washington); Magic Circle Republican Women's (Houston). Address: The VP's House Washington DC 20501

BUSH, BRENDALEE, communications executive; b. Lebanon, Ind., July 12, 1949; d. John Jr. and Wilma (Owen) B. BS, Ind. State U., 1972. With pub. relations Ea. Express Trucking Co., Terre Haute, Ind., 1972-76; with employee services Blue Cross/Blue Shield of Ind., Indpls., 1976-77; mem. energy group Ind. Dept. Commerce State of Ind., Indpls., 1977-79; dir. pub. affairs White River Park Devel. Commn., Indpls., 1980-84; mgr. market and community devel. Meth. Hosp. Ind., Indpls., 1984—. Vice chmn. precinct Indpls. Reps., 1980; mem. dinner com. AAU James E. Sullivan award, Indpls., 1981-86; founder White River Park State Games, 1980, mem. steering com., 1982—; bd. dirs. Near North Devel. Corp., Indpls., 1984-86, InterFaith Housing, Indpls., 1986—. Named one of Outstanding Young Women of Am., 1983. Mem. Pub. Relations Soc. Am., Am. Mktg. Assn., Advt. Club Indpls., Stanley K. Lacy Alumni, Soc. Hosp. Planning and Mktg. Mem. Soc. of Friends. Office: Meth Hosp Ind 1701 N Senate Blvd Indianapolis IN 46202

BUSH, CAROL STEINBERG, accounting manager; b. Sioux Falls, S.D., Nov. 4, 1938; d. Tony T. and Estelle (Greenhut) Steinberg; m. Mel B. Bush, Mar. 20, 1960 (div. Aug. 1976); children: Steven B., David H., Richard E. BA, Met. State U., St. Paul, 1978; M in Mgmt. and Adminstrn., Met. State U., 1986. Mgr. office Premier Plasters, Mpls., 1968-74; acct. Henkel Swanson Pub. Acct., Mpls., 1975-76; mgr. office Twin City Chromium Plating, Mpls., 1976-81; acct., mgr. acctg. Ault, Inc., Mpls., 1981—. Com. officer PTA, Mpls., 1971-74; active Cubs Scouts, Mpls., 1971-77; dir. Parents Without Ptnrs., Mpls., 1977-80. Mem. Minn. Women's Network, Profl. and Exec. Women, Nat. Assn. Accts. (bd. dirs. 1986—). Republican. Jewish. Clubs: Matched Singles Tennis, Ullr Ski. Office: Ault Inc 1600 Freeway Blvd Minneapolis MN 55430

BUSH, DEBBIE JO, accountant; b. Wichita, Kans, Mar. 30, 1961; d. Larry J. and Veda J. (Pike) B. BBA, U. Okla., 1982. CPA, Okla. Staff acct. Johnson & Grigbsy, Inc. CPA's, Chickasha, Okla., 1982-84; v.p. Universal Savs. Assn. FSLA, Chickasha, 1984—. Mem. Jr. Social Workers, Chickasha, 1984—; treas., bd. dirs. Miss Chickasha Scholarship Pageant, 1984—; treas. ARC, Chickasha, 1985—. Mem. Am. INst. CPA's, Okla. Soc. CPA's, Fin. Mgrs. Assn., Chickasha C. of C. Republican. Methodist. Clubs: PEO, Panhellenic (Chickasha) (treas. 1984—).

BUSH, DOROTHY ELENORA WRIGHT, tool and die company executive, retired teacher; b. New Holland, Ohio, Apr. 21, 1921; d. Ercell J. and Gaylle Marie (Steinhauser) Wright; m. Lloyd Eugene Bush, June 18, 1939; children: Ronald Eugene, Diana E. Bush Eycke. Grad., Columbus (Ohio) Bus. U., 1940; BS magna cum laude, Ohio U., 1959. Cert. elem. and high sch. tchr., Ohio. Bookkeeper Beneficial Fin., Columbus, 1940-43; precision insp. Curtiss-Wright, Columbus, 1943-44; owner, operator Bush Locker, Williamsport, Ohio, 1947-55, Castle Theater, Williamsport, 1950-54; tchr. Chillicothe (Ohio) Schs., 1956-61, Westfall and Williamsport (Ohio) Schs., 1961-86; ptnr. Bush Tool and Die, Williamsport, 1981-86, pres., treas., 1987—; income tax form preparer, New Holland and Williamsport, 1940-65; part time postal clk., 1958-84. Mem. 4-H Club Congress, Pickaway County, 1938. Republican. Methodist. Lodge: Order Eastern Star (worthy matron, dist. pres., page grand chpt. 1979). Home: 111 S Water St PO Box 44 Williamsport OH 43164 Office: Bush Tool and Die 108 Mill St Williamsport OH 43164

BUSH, GERALDINE TERESA, electronics company executive; b. Phila., Apr. 14, 1946; d. Charles William and Marie Frances (Barnes) B. B.A., Temple U., 1968. Chemist, Union Camp Corp. Research and Devel., Princeton, N.J., 1968-71; asst. scientist N.L. Industries Corp., Hightstown, N.J., 1971-73; sales engr. UPA Tech., Syosset, N.Y., 1973-74, dist. mgr., 1974-75, field sales mgr., 1975-77, dir. sales and mktg., after 1977; now owner, pres. Voss Electronic, Inc., Santa Ana, Calif.; lectr. in field. Recipient Salesman of Yr. award, 1973, 74, 75; Recognition award Dept. Commerce, 1978. Mem. ASTM, Am. Electroplaters Soc., Am. Soc. Quality Control, Am. Mgmt. Assn. Club: Internat. Bus. Roundtable (Adelphi U., Garden City, N.Y.). Contbr. articles to profl. jours. Office: Voss Electronics Inc 1848 E Carnegie Ave Santa Ana CA 92705

BUSH, JILL GERSEWITZ, food importer/broker; b. Bklyn., May 11, 1950; d. Jack and Esther Barbara (Tennenbaum) Gersewitz; 1 child, Lafe C. BS, SUNY, New Paltz, 1971; MBA, Bernard Baruch Coll., N.Y.C., 1987. Benefits adminstr. Nathan's Famous, N.Y.C., 1974-76; book importer Anthroposophic Press, Spring Valley, N.Y., 1977-79; food importer, broker Orlando Food Corp., Maywood, N.J., 1979—. Mem. Nat. Assn. Female Execs. Jewish. Home: 224 Kearsing Pkwy Monsey NY 10952

BUSH, MARGERY PECK, clinical social worker; b. Bristol, Conn., Mar. 22, 1934; d. Seymour Roe and Margery (Earl) Peck; B.A. in Psychology, Wells Coll., Aurora, N.Y., 1956; M.S.W., U. Conn., 1975; m. Edward Wallace Bush, Jr., Feb. 28, 1958; children—Kimberly, Barbara, David. Lic. social worker, Conn. Intern, Family Service Soc., Hartford, Conn., 1973-74, Inst. Living, Adult Outpatient Clinic, Hartford, 1974-75; cons., sch. social worker East Hartford Bd. Edn., 1976; family counselor Family Service, Inc., New Britain, Conn., 1976-79; family Therapist Youth and Family Resource Center, Glastonbury, Conn., 1980-82. pvt. practice individual, marital, and family counseling, West Hartford, 1979-86; pvt. practice counseling, Noank, 1987—; instr. program Living in Fuller Effectiveness (LIFE), 1979—. Corporator, Oak Hill Sch. Blind, 1968—; trustee Larrabee Fund Assn., 1970-73, chmn. Hartford con., 1970-72; bd. dirs. Hartford Interval House, 1977-78. Mem. Nat. Assn. Social Workers, Acad. Cert. Social Workers, Conn. Soc. Clin. Social Workers, Hartford Audubon Soc., Internat. Platform Assn. Congregationalist. Club: Hartford Ski. Address: 28 Church St Noank CT 06340

BUSH, MARJORIE EVELYNN TOWER-TOOKER, educator, media specialist, librarian; b. Atkinson, Nebr., Mar. 12, 1925; d. Albert Ralph and Vera Marie (Rickover) Tower-Tooker; student U. Nebr., 1951, Wayne State Coll., 1942-47; B.A., Colo. State Coll., 1966, U. No. Colo., 1970; postgrad. Doane Coll., 1967-68, U. Utah, 1973-74, Ph.D. (hon.), 1973; m. Louis T. Genung, Feb. 2, 1944 (dec. Jan. 1982); 1 son, Louis Thompson; m. Laurence Scott Bush, Sept. 22, 1984; 1 stepson, Roger A. Bush. Elem. tchr. Atkinson Public Schs., 1958-69; adminstr. libraries and audiovisual communications Clay County Dist. I-C, Fairfield, Nebr., 1972-81; media specialist Albion (Nebr.) City Schs., 1981—; mem. Neb. Gov.'s White House Conf. on Libraries. Chmn. edn. adminstrv. bd. Park Hill United Meth. Ch., Denver; sec. Denver Symphony Guild. Mem. NEA (life), Nebr., Colo. edn. assns., Assn. Childhood Edn. Internat., ALA, Nebr., Mountain Plains library assns., Nat. Council Tchrs. English, AAUW, Nebr. Ednl. Media Assn., Assn. Supervision and Curriculum Devel., Assn. Ednl. Communications and Tech., Internat. Visual Literacy Assn., Nat. Council Exceptional Children, Alumni Assn. U. No. Colo. (life charter), Women Educators Nebr., United Meth. Women (pres.), Am. Legion Aux., Nebr. Lay Citizens Edn. Assn. (exec.), Am. Nat. Cowbelles, Nebr. Cowbelles, DAR (regent 1971, dist. treas. 1968-71), Internat. Platform Assn., LWV, Women's Soc. Christian Service, Ak-Sar-Ben. Club: Windsor Gardens (Denver). Lodges: Opti-Mrs. (pres.), Optimists Internat., Columbine Optimists (pres. 1987-88), Eastern Star. Home: 9655 E Center Ave Denver CO 80231

BUSH, VIRGINIA CARNITA, educator; b. Pima, Ariz., Dec. 17, 1933; d. John Gabriel and Elizabeth Harriet (Britkrite) Becht; m. Abraham L. Pennington, June 12, 1954 (div. Dec. 1968); children—Kay Pennington, Steven Pennington; m. John Augustus Bush, Aug. 2, 1969 (div. Apr. 1976). B.S., N.Mex. Western Coll., 1954; M.A., Western N.Mex. U., 1964. Cert. elem., secondary and community coll. tchr., Calif. High sch. Spanish and elem. tchr. Cliff Consol. Schs., N.Mex., 1956-57, 58-62; inst. Western N.Mex. U., Silver City, 1962-64; tchr. Spanish, Lincoln Jr. High Sch., Taft, Calif., 1964-72, tchr. fgn. langs., 1979—; tchr. Spanish, Singapore Am. Sch., Singapore, 1973-75; tchr. English, Roosevelt Sch., Taft, 1975-79. NEH stipendee U. Wyo. seminar on French metaphys. novel, 1984. Mem. Taft Elem. Tchrs. Assn. (pres. 1976-77), Calif. Tchrs. Assn., NEA, Bus. and Profl. Women (v.p. chpt. 1985-86, pres. 1986-87). Republican. Mem. Ch. of Religious Science. Avocations: graphology; photography; gourmet cooking; travel.

BUSHMAN, LANNA RAE, nutritionist; b. New London, N.H., Dec. 15, 1950; d. Raymond Eugene and Raylene Carole (Griswold) Twombly; m. David Norman Bushman, Aug. 12, 1972; children: Ashley Rae, Lindsay Gilbert. BS, U. N.H., 1972, MA, 1975. Lic. dietitian, Ga. Cons. Dept. Edn. State of N.H., Concord, 1972-75, dir., 1975-76; nutritionist USDA, Burlington, Mass., 1976-77; specialist food programs USDA, Atlanta, 1977-86; dir. food services Marietta (Ga.) City Schs., 1986—; coordinator s.e. region nutrition edn., tng. USDA, Atlanta, 1979-81. Patron Bartlett Jr. Grange, past master, 1958-65. Mem. Am. Sch. Food Service Assn. (cert. dir.), Exec. Profl. Women's Assn., So. Assn. Sch. Bus. Officials. Club: White Oak Country (Newman, Ga.). Home: 93 Clubview Dr Newnan GA 30263

BUSHNELL, CATHARINE, marketing consultant, licensing, marketing representation, consultation and production company executive; b. Pullman, Wash, July 2, 1950; d. David and Catharine Howe (Goodfellow) B.; m. H. Michael Sisson, Oct. 31, 1975. B.S. in Speech, Northwestern U., 1972. Prodn. mgr. Mike White Advt., Chgo., 1972; stage actress, Chgo., 1972-73; ptnr., dir. photography Mome, Raths & Outgrabe, Chgo., 1973-75; exec. v.p. Sisson Assocs., N.Y.C., 1975—; pres. Illusion Gallery, Creative Resource Co., N.Y.C., 1981—, The Sisson Group Inc., 1986—; faculty New Sch.-Parsons Sch. of Design, 1985-86. Photographer motion picture stills for various films, N.Y.C., 1975—; author: Raggedy Ann and Andy in the Tunnel of Lost Toys, 1980; Raggedy Ann and Andy and the Pirates of Outgo Inlet, 1981; Linda's Magic Window, 1981; Frannie's Magic Kazoo, 1982. Judge ann. student photog. portfolio rev. High Sch. of Art and Design, N.Y.C., 1979-83. Mem. Licensing Industry Assn., Internat. Photographers of Motion Picture Industry, Internat. Soc. Photography (charter), Actors Equity Assn., Northwestern U. Alumnae Assn., Delta Zeta. Office: The Sisson Group Inc 300 E 40th St New York NY 10016

BUSKELL, ELIZABETH ROOSS, office administrator; b. Bridgeport, Conn., Dec. 30, 1944; d. Philip Anthony and Josephine (Carlson) Rooss.; m. Richard Paul Buskell, Aug. 27, 1966 (div. Mar. 1984); children: David Anthony, Melissa Gade. AS, Cazenovia Coll., 1964; student, Nat. Inst. Real Estate, Vienna, Va., 1983. Sec. IRS, Washington, 1964-65; adminstrv. asst. Barnes, Richardson, & Colburn, Washington, 1965-67; office mgr. Nat. Real Estate Co., Fairfax, Va., 1973-75; real estate agt. Long & Foster, Vienna, 1983-84; office mgr., adminstrv. asst. Karl E. Kohler Assocs., Vienna, 1984—. Com. mem. Jr. League No. Va., Arlington, 1978-83; tuitor Fairfax Social Service Orgn., 1983-85; listener Hotline No. Va., Arlington, 1986-87; chairperson Mid-Atlantic Parent Group of DeSisto Sch., No. Va., 1983—. Republican. Club: Westwood Country (team capt. tennis com. 1978-80). Home: 8528 Raglan Rd Vienna VA 22180 Office: karl E Kohler Assocs 301 Maple Ave W Vienna VA 22180

BUSSELL, BETTY ROSE, insurance executive; b. Chgo., Aug. 4, 1933; d. Howard and Laura (Rose) Denton; m. Charles William Bussell Jr., Dec. 23, 1962; children: Julia Renee Bussell Barnes, Charles William III. Grad. high sch., Chgo. From supr. to personnel analyst U.S. Army, Chgo., 1962-69; personnel coordinator Chgo. Urban League, 1969-71; orgn. analyst Blue Cross-Blue Shield, Chgo., 1971-73, mgr. compensation, 1973—. Leaguer of Urban League, Chgo., pres., 1965-68. Mem. Am. Compensation Assn., Conf. Bd. Democrat. Baptist. Office: Blue Cross-Blue Shield 676 N St Clair Ave Chicago IL 60611

BUSSEY, HOLLY JEAN, information and advertising executive; b. Takoma Park, Md., Dec. 9, 1954; d. Alfred Gordon and Dorothy Ann (McElvenny) B.; m. James B. Sanders. AA, Bucks County Community Coll., Newtown, Pa., 1975; AB magnum cum laude, Wheaton Coll., Norton, Mass., 1978; M in Library and Info. Mgmt., Rutgers U., 1981. Info. documentalist N.W. Ayer ABH Internat., N.Y.C., 1978-80; info. specialist N.W. Ayer, Inc., N.Y.C., 1980-81, computer info. specialist, 1981-82, mgr. info. services, 1982—. Asst. to sec. bd. N.Y. Choral Soc. Mem. Am. Mgmt. Assn., Am. Mktg. Assn., Spl. Libraries Assn., Assn. Info. Mgrs., Demographic Inst., N.Y. Choral Soc. (asst. to sec. bd.), Phi Beta Kappa. Unitarian. Office: N W Ayer Inc 1345 Avenue of the Americas New York NY 10105

BUSSIE, DELORES LAVERN, chiropractor; b. Pompano Beach, Fla., June 26, 1955; d. Theodore and Mamie Ruth (Dowdell) B. BS, Bennett Coll., 1977; Dr. Chropractic, Life Chiropractic Coll., Marietta, Ga., 1984. Diplomate Am. Bd. Chiropractic Medicine. Adminstrv. asst. Deerfield Beach (Fla.) Housing Authority, 1979-80; intern. then assoc. dir. Walker's Life Chiropractic Clin., Atlanta, 1982-85; med. claims rev. AccuMed, Ft. Lauderdale, Fla., 1985-86; assoc. dir. Aronoff Chiropractic Ctr., Cooper City, Fla., 1986-87; proprieter, prin. Bussie Chiropractic Ctr., West Palm Beach, Fla., 1987—. Bd. dirs. Community Partnership: United Way, Ft. Lauderdale, 1979-80. Named Outstanding Young Woman Am., 1983. Mem. Fla. Chiropractic Assn., Palm Beach County Chiropractic Assn., Internat. Chiropractic Assn. Democrat. Baptist. Club: Bethlehem Grand Chpt. Lodge: Masons. Office: Bussie Chiropractic Ctr 5900 Broadway Suite 3 West Palm Beach FL 33407

BUSSY, GILLIAN ELIZABETH, transportation executive; b. San Diego, June 10, 1958; d. Richard Fulmer Bussy and Jean (Ballin) Knofler. BS, No. Ariz. U., 1980. Ski patroller Mt. Holly ski area Northland Recreation, Beaver, Utah, 1980-82; rep. customer service Skywest Airlines, Page, Ariz., 1982-83; station mgr. Skywest Airlines, Twin Falls, Idaho, 1983-84; dir. tng. Skywest Airlines, St. George, Utah, 1984—. Editor: Skywest Customer Service Department Manual, 1983—, Skywest (FAA) Security Manual, 1984—. Republican. Episcopalian. Home: 400 E Riverside #1104 Saint George UT 84770 Office: Skywest Airlines 50E 100 South Suite 202 Saint George UT 84770

BUSTER, LISA B., athlete representative, sports promoter; b. Phila., June 26, 1959; d. Leonard David and Arlene Linda (Segal) B. Student Georgetown U., 1977-79; BA in Spanish, U. N.C., 1981. Asst. to sports dept. WDVM-TV, Washington, 1978-79; sports reporter WCHL Radio, Chapel Hill, N.C., 1980; sports reporter, anchor WDCG-WDNC Radio, Durham, N.C., 1980-81; anchor, reporter KTVG-TV, Helena, Mont., 1982-83; dir. celebrity promotions, Starpower, Feasterville, Pa., 1984; pres., owner Promotion in Motion Internat., Ltd., Jenkintown, Pa., 1984—. Mem. Phila. Jaycees; vol. Phila. Conv. and Vis's. Bur., Girl Scouts U.S., Phila. Mem. The Athletics Congress, U. N.C. Alumni Assn., Acad. Natural Scis. (dinosaur docent). Avocations: horseback riding, travel, languages, music. Address: Promotion in Motion Internat Ltd PO Box 181 Jenkintown PA 19046

BUSTIN, BEVERLY MINER, state senator; b. Morrisville, Vt., Feb. 14, 1936; d. Donald Haze and Della Mae (Kenfield) Miner; children: Catherine Margaret, David Wayne. BS, Thomas Coll. Maine state senator, 1979—, chair joint select com. on alcoholism services, 1982-84, chair instl. services com., 1983-84, chair bus. and commerce commn., 1985—. Mem. Kennebec County (Maine) Dem. Com.; treas. Uplift, Inc., 1980—; vice chair Kennebec County Regional Health Agy., 1984-88, chair audit program rev., 1987—, mem. banking and ins. com., 1987—, chair joint select com. on corrections, 1987—, chair Commn. on Overcrowding at AMHI-BMAI, 1987—. Office: State House State Senate Augusta ME 04330

BUSWELL, DEBRA S., small business owner, programmer/analyst; b. Salt Lake City, Apr. 8, 1957; d. John Edward Ross and Marilyn Sue (Patterson) Potter; m. Randy James Buswell, Aug. 17, 1985. BA, U. Colo., Denver, 1978. Programmer, analyst Trail Blazer Systems, Palo Alto, Calif., 1980-83; data processing mgr. Innovative Concepts, Inc., San Jose, Calif., 1983-86; owner Egret Software, Milpitas, Calif., 1986—. Mem. No. Calif. Pick Users, Commonwealth Club of Calif. Home and Office: 807 Folsom Circle Milpitas CA 95035

BUSWELL, SUSAN ROWE, state legislator; b. Denver, Sept. 13, 1935; d. Kenneth Wyer and Leone (Krumling) Rowe; children—Janice, Scott. B.A., Carleton Coll., 1957; postgrad. U. Copenhagen, 1958. Analyst, Dept. Def., Washington, 1959-62; officer mgr. Green Street Coalition, Annapolis, Md., 1980-81; exec. dir. Md. Assn. Elem. Sch. Adminstrs., College Park, 1981-83; del. Md. Gen. Assembly, Annapolis, 1983—; exec. dir. Md. Assn. Nonpub. Spl. Edn. Facilities, 1985—. Mem. Howard County Bd. Edn. (Md.), 1973-83, Howard County Recreation and Parks Bd., 1975-79; bd. dirs. Howard County Commn. on Arts, 1975-80. Recipient Mortar Board award Carleton Coll., Northfield, Minn., 1957. Mem. LWV, Delta Kappa Gamma. Democrat. Mem. United Ch. of Christ. Club: Soroptimists. Office: Md Gen Assembly Lowe Office Bldg Room 219 Annapolis MD 21401

BUTCHER, AMANDA KAY, university administrator; b. Lansing, Mich., Oct. 25, 1936; d. Foster Eli and Mayme Lenore (Taft) Stuart; m. Claude J. Butcher, Aug. 24, 1957; 1 child, Mary Beth. BS in Bus., Cen. Mich. U., 1981. Office asst. Dept. Dairy Sci., East Lansing, Mich., 1966-76; bus. mgr dept. Dept. Pathology, Mich. State U., East Lansing, 1976—. Mem. Adminstrv. Profl. Suprs. Assn. (v.p. 1982—), Adminstrv. Profl. Assn. East Lansing (pres. 1976-80). Democrat. Home: 610 Emily Lansing MI 48910 Office: Mich State U Dept Pathology 622 E Fee East Lansing MI 48824-1316

BUTCHER, JUANITA M., school system coordinator; b. N.Y.C., June 3, 1943; d. William Edward and Margaret (Harvey) James; children: Joelle, Jamal. BBA, Pace U., 1979; MS, Hofstra U., 1986, cert. advanced study, 1987. Cert. secondary sch. tchr., dist. adminstr., sch. adminstr. and supr., N.Y. Tchr. Beach Channel High Sch. N.Y.C. Bd. Edn., Rockaway Park, 1980—, coordinator pre coop program, 1984—, coordinator bus. edn., 1986—; adj. prof. bus. Kingsborough Community Coll., N.Y., Queensborough Community Coll., N.Y. Mem. Rockaway Dem. Club, 1986—. Mem. NEA, Nat. Assn. Negro Bus. and Profl. Women (corresponding sec. 1987—), Nat. Alliance Black Sch. Educators, Bus. Assn. Edn., Assn. Supervision and Curriculum Devel., Delta Pi Epsilon, Phi Delta Kappa. Democrat. Office: Beach Channel High Sch 100-00 Beach Channel Dr Rockaway Park NY 11694

BUTCHER, SUSAN H., dog kennel owner, sled dog racer; b. Boston, Dec. 26, 1954; d. Charles and Agnes (Young) B.; m. David Lee Monson. Driver 1st dog team to summit Mt. KcKinley, Alaska 1979; winner among top 10 finishers Long Distance Sled Dog Races, Alaska and Minn., 1978-87; 5th pl. Iditarod Race, Anchorage and Nome, Alaska, 1980, 81, 2d pl., 1982, 84, champion, winner 1st pl., 1986, 87, world record holder, 1986-87; champion, winner 1st pl. Coldfoot Classic Race, Brooks Range, Alaska, 1985; bd. dirs. Iditarod Trail Com., Wasilla, Alaska, 1980-86, ambassador of good will Iditarod Sport of Sled Dog Racing, 1982—; mem. nutrition adv. panel Purina Pro Plan, St. Louis, 1986—; tech. advisor Allied Fibers, N.Y.C., 1985—. Contbr. articles to profl. jours. Hon. chmn. March of Dimes, Anchorage, 1986, Spl. Olympics, Anchorage, 1987. Named Musher of Yr. Team and Trail, N.H., 1987, one of Profl. Sports Women of Yr. Womens Sports Found., N.Y.C., 1987; recipient Victor award, Las Vegas, Nev., 1987, legis. commendation States of Alaska and Mass., 1986-87. Mem. Iditarod Trail Com., Iditarod Trail Blazers (life), Beargrease Race Com., Kuskokwim 300 Race Com. Club: Interior Dog Mushers (Manley, Alaska); Nome Kennel; Norton Sound Sled Dog. Home and Office: Trail Breaker Kennel 1 Eureka Eureka AK 99756

BUTCHER-JOHNSON, SHARON JEAN, public relations professional; b. Augsburg, Fed. Republic of Germany, Aug. 15, 1962; d. Arthur Jackson and Jean Francis (Rickett) B.; m. Kevin Lenard Johnson. BS in Pub. Relations, N. Tex. State U., 1984. Reporter North Tex. Daily Newspaper, Denton, 1982-83, editor, 1983; media asst. Vance-Mathews Advt., Inc., Beaumont, Tex., 1985; traffic asst., news writer Pyle Communications Media Group, Beaumont, 1985; film dir., dir. pub. service Sta. KFDM-TV, Beaumont, 1985-87; coordinator pub. edn. Del. Council on Crime and Justice, Wilmington, 1987—. Contbr. articles to profl. pubs. Mem. Nat. Assn. Female Execs. Democrat. Baptist. Club: Brandywine Valley Press. Home: 16 Blyth Ct New Castle DE 19720

BUTEAU, MICHELLE DIANE, energy company executive; b. Oakland, Calif., Mar. 6, 1952; d. Bernard Lamonthe and June (Dowler) B.; m. Barry Crawford Anderson, Nov. 1974 (div. 1982); 1 child, Damon Buteau-Anderson. BA in Liberal Arts, Cath. U. Am., 1974, postgrad. Loyola/Notre Dame Coll. Dir. U.S. Summer Sch. Inst., U.S. Dept. State/USIA, Posnan, Poland, 1975-76; bookkeeper Internat. Energy Assocs. Ltd., Washington, 1980-83, research assoc., 1983-84, research assoc., 1984-85, project mgr., 1984—, sr. cons., 1987—. Actress and dir. dinner theatres, 1974—. Intern Senator E. Dirksen, Washington, 1968; pres. Catholic Youth Orgn., Bethesda, Md., 1968-70. Mem. Am. Mgmt. Assn., Nat. Assn. Female Execs. Roman Catholic. Avocations: acting, dancing, singing, writing. Office: ERC Internat 3211 Jermantown Rd Fairfax VA 22030

BUTERA, ANN MICHELE, consulting company executive; b. Bayside, N.Y., Apr. 27, 1958; d. Gaetano Thomas and Josephine (Inserro) B. BA, L.I. U., 1979; MBA, Adelphi U., 1982. Dept. mgr. Abraham & Straus Stores, Huntington, N.Y., 1978-80; mgmt. cons. Chase Manhattan Bank N.A., Lake Success, N.Y., 1980-83, Nat. Bankcard Corp., Melville, N.Y., 1983-84; owner, mgr. Whole Person Project, Elmont, N.Y., 1984—. Bd. dirs. Nassau County council Girl Scouts U.S.A., 1985—. Mem. Nat. Assn. Female Execs., L.I. Networking Entrepreneurs (pres. 1984—), North Shore Bus. Forum, L.I. Ctr. for Bus. and Profl. Women. Republican. Roman Catholic. Home and Office: Whole Person Project 2085 Belmont Ave Elmont NY 11003

BUTERO, LAURA LEE, education association professional; b. Berkeley, Calif., Nov. 25, 1946; d. Percy Dorval and Gertrude (Brown) Barchard. BS in Journalism, U. Oreg., 1984. Sr. tester quality control Owens Corning Fiberglas, Santa Clara, Calif., 1965-67, 70-72; serviceperson Pacific Gas & Electric Co., San Jose, Calif., 1975-77; pipeperson, gas serviceperson N.W. Natural Gas Co., Eugene, Oreg., 1979-81; field rep. Oreg. Edn. Assn. Choice Trust, Tigard, 1985—. Served with USN, 1967-70. Democrat. Home: 980 Randall Eugene OR 97401 Office: Oreg Edn Assn Choice Trust 6900 SW Haines Tigard OR 97223

BUTLER, ALMA, marketing professional; b. Evansville, Ind., Aug. 29, 1951; d. Herbert and Rhoda (Outlaw) Edwards; m. Floyd L. Butler, Oct. 25, 1975; children: Latoia, Arthur. BS in Mgmt., U. So. Ind., 1977. Various clerical positions Social Security Adminstrn., Evansville, 1967-72; sec. Babcock & Wilcox, Evansville, 1969-73; salesperson Sears, Evansville, 1969-73; sec. Gen. Foods, Evansville, 1973-75; clerical adminstr. IBM, Evansville, 1975-76, systems engr., 1976-77, acct. mktg. rep., 1976—; pres. Min-Bus, Evansville, 1973—. Chmn. Ebony Fashion Fair, 1986-87, Minority in Bus., 1986-87; bd. dirs. Girl Scouts USA, 1986—; lector, Eucharistic Minister St. Mary's Cath. Ch. Mem. Delta Sisma Theta. Democrat. Roman Catholic. Office: IBM 301 SE 6th St Evansville IN 47708

BUTLER, ANNE HAWARD, information management director, consultant; b. Charleston, W.Va., July 3, 1947; d. Harry Lee and Christine (Walker) B. BA in English, U. N.C., Greensboro, 1969; MLS, Emory U., 1971. Librarian Alston & Bird, Atlanta, 1971-82, mgr. info. services, 1982-86, dir. info. mgmt., 1986—; lectr. Emory U., Atlanta, 1974-80; advisor Westlaw-West Pub. Co., St. Paul, 1987—; Bowker Legal Reference Pub. Adv. Bd, R.R. Bowker, N.Y., 1987—. Author: Opening a Law Office; co-author Manual of Procedures for Private Law Libraries, 1984 supplement, article in book The Art of Managing Your Support Staff. Mem. Exec. Women Internat., Atlanta Law Libraries Assn. (charter, pres. 1974), Am. Assn. Law Libraries (pres. Southeastern chpt. 1979-80). Episcopalian. Home: 31 Muscogee Ave NW #4 Atlanta GA 30305 Office: Alston & Bird 35 Broad St NW Suite 1200 Atlanta GA 30335

BUTLER, BERNADETTE, nursing educator; b. Howell, Mich., May 28, 1937; d. Felix V. and Sophia (Kuffel) Knetchel; m. Robert F. Butler, Oct. 11, 1974; 1 child, Kristen. Diploma in Nursing, Mercy Sch. Nursing, 1958; BS in Nursing, Mary Manse Coll., 1960; MS in Nursing, Ind. U., 1967; EdD, U. Toledo, 1985. RN, Ohio. Instr. Mercy Sch. Nursing, Toledo, 1960-77; instr. Med. Coll. Ohio Sch. Nursing, Toledo, 1977-81, asst. prof. Med. Coll., 1981-87, assoc. prof., 1988—. Mem. Am. Nurses Assn., Nat. League Nurses, Nurses Assn. Am. Coll. Ob-Gyn (local chairperson 1980-84), Midwest Nursing Research Soc., Ohio Perinatal Assn., Sigma Theta Tau (sec. Zeta Theta chpt. 1986-88). Office: Med Coll Ohio Sch Nursing CS 10008 Toledo OH 43699

BUTLER, CANDACE LYN, consumer marketing representative; b. Woodbury, N.J., Dec. 27, 1952; d. Walter Hildebrand and Gladys (Gardiner) B. BS, W.Va. Wesleyan Coll., 1975; MEd, U. N.C., Greensboro, 1980. Supr. food prodn. Stouffer's Mgmt. Food Service, Haverford and Broomall, Pa., 1977-78; asst. dir. dietary Louise Obici Hosp. subs. Marriott Mgmt. Food Service, Suffolk, Va., 1980-81; extension home economist Rutgers Coop. Extension Atlantic County, New Brunswick, N.J., 1981-86; rep. consumer mktg. South Jersey Gas Co., Folsom, N.J., 1986—; mem. adv. council home econs. dept. Glassboro (N.J.) State Coll., 1986—; mem. adv. bd. Atlantic Food Bank, Inc., Atlantic City, 1986—. Author: (radio program) Consumer Update, 1982-86, (brochure) Pick-A-Peach, 1984; co-author: (slide program) Selecting Reliable Nutrition Resources, 1985; author, editor: (newsletter) Home Economics Educator, 1981-86; developer (teaching guide) Seafood, Nothing Goes to Waist, 1988. Mem. Am. Home Econs. Assn., N.J. Home Econs. Assn. (trustee 1986—), So. Counties Home Econs. Assn. (chmn. 1986—), So. N.J. Nutrition Council (chmn. nutrition month 1984-87), Nat. Assn. Extension Home Economists (pub. relations com. 1985-86), N.J. Assn. Extension Home Economists (Elizabeth T. Roth award 1983), Alpha Gamma Delta (fin. advisor Zeta Mu chpt. 1985—). Home: 626 First Ave Absecon NJ 08201 Office: South Jersey Gas Co #2 Heathercroft Sq Northfield NJ 08232

BUTLER, CARMEN DELORES, educator; b. Oklahoma City, Nov. 26, 1949; d. Nathaniel and Blonzine (Henderson) B. BA, Langston U., 1971; MA, Cen. (Okla.) State U., 1977; postgrad., Rose State Coll., Midwest City, Okla., 1985. Cert. tchr., Okla. Tchr. Okla. Bd. Edn., Oklahoma City, 1971-73, 1977—; tape librarian Hertz Reservation Ctr., Oklahoma City, 1973-77. Campaign worker Archibal Hill for Senate, Oklahoma City, 1980, Kevin Cox for Representative, Oklahoma City, 1980, Visano Johnson for Senate, Oklahoma City, 1982, Robert S. Kerr for U.S. Senate, Oklahoma, 1983, Vicki Miles-LaGrange for Senate, Oklahoma City, 1986, Jesse Jackson for pres., 1988; youth counselor St. Joseph's Children Home, Oklahoma City, 1981-82. Mem. Nat. Council Negro Women, Urban League Guild Oklahoma City, Urban League of Oklahoma City, Oklahoma County Assn. for Mental Health, (Ding mem.), Eta Phi Beta (v.p. 1984-86, mem. nat. parliamentarian 1986—, Outstanding mem. 1981), Alpha Kappa Alpha (grad. advisor 1980-85), Phi Delta Kappa. Home: 1708 NE 48 Oklahoma City OK 73111

BUTLER, CAROL DENTON, government official; b. York, Nebr., Apr. 8, 1931; d. Robert Ralph and Fern V. (Mann) Denton; BA summa cum laude, York Coll., 1952; m. Charles Farrell Butler, Jan. 17, 1959; children: Robert Charles, Julie Ann. Reporter, staff asst. York (Nebr.) Daily News Times, 1952-54; claims rep. Social Security Adminstrn., Lincoln, Nebr., 1955-57, disability examiner, cons., policy specialist, staff assoc., Balt., 1957-69, sect. chief disability operations, 1970, chief med. policy, 1971-74, chief rehab. div., 1974-76, dep. asst. bur. dir. fed./state programs, 1976-78, dep. asst., bur. dir. systems and methods, 1978-79, dir. office pub. concerns, 1979-85; ret., 1985; disability examiner Div. Vocat. Rehab., State of Md., 1985—. Counselor, Howard County Sexual Assault Center, 1976-79, bd. dirs., 1979-85, pres. bd., 1981-83; mem. Md. Gov's. Adv. Bd. on Rape and Sexual Offenses, 1982-84; bd. dirs. Baltimore County Sexual Assault and Domestic Violence Ctr., 1986-87, v.p. bd., 1987-88. Recipient Commrs. citations Social Security Adminstrn., 1968, 78; citation Assoc. Commr. for Disability, 1985, 86. Mem. ACLU, Women's Alliance Md., NOW, Nat. Assn. Disability Examiners (v.p. Md. chpt. 1988), Am. Assn. Ret. Persons. Alpha Chi.

BUTLER, CAROL KING, radio advertising sales executive; b. Charlotte, N.C., May 29, 1952; d. Charles Snowden Watts and Marion (Thomas) King; m. James Rodney Butler, Aug. 12, 1972 (div. 1975). Student U. N.C., Greensboro, 1970-72. Sales rep. Sta.-WKIX, Raleigh, N.C., 1978-82, N.C. Box, Inc., Raleigh, 1982-84; radio sales account exec. WRAL-FM, Raleigh, 1984-88, team sales mgr., 1988—. Mem. Nat. Assn. Female Execs. Republican. Episcopalian. Avocations: water skiing, snow skiing, tennis, boating, bicycling. Home: 11917 Shooting Club Rd Raleigh NC 27612 Office: WRAL-FM 711 Hillsborough St Raleigh NC 27605

BUTLER, GRACE CAROLINE, medical administrator; b. Lima, Peru, Dec. 19, 1937; (parents Am. citizens); d. Everett Lyle and Mary Isabella (Sloatman) Gage; m. William Langdon Butler, Dec. 28, 1961; children: Mary Dyer, William Langdon Jr. AA, Stephens Coll., 1957; BS in Nursing, Columbia U., 1960; postgrad., Union County Coll., 1984. Head nurse N.Y. State Psychiat. Inst., N.Y.C., 1960-61; clin. instr. Columbia U., N.Y.C., 1960-61; staff nurse, educator Vis. Nurse Service, Summit, N.J., 1962-63; health adminstr. Eagle Island Girl Scout Camp, Tupper Lake, N.Y., 1964; evening supr. Ashbrook Nursing Home, Scotch Plains, N.J., 1968-72; teaching asst. Scotch Plains-Fanwood (N.J.) Sch. System, 1975-78; staff nurse Westfield (N.J.) Med. Group, 1980-82, head nurse, 1982-83, supr., 1983-84; office adminstr. Harris S. Vernick, MD, PA, Westfield, 1984-86, corp. v.p., office adminstr., 1986-88; corp. v.p., office adminstr. Assocs. in Medicine, Westfield, 1988—; diabetes educator Boehringer Manneheim Diagnostics, 1984-87, Eli Lilly and Co., Indpls., 1984—; microbiologist tester Med. Technol. Corp., Somerset, N.J., 1984-88; computer advisor Cordis Corp., Miami, 1985-88. Asst. leader Girl Scouts of America, Fanwood, N.J., 1970-73; religious educator All Saints Episcopal Ch., Scotch Plains, 1967-82; bd. dirs. PTA, Scotch Plains, Fanwood, 1973-79; social dir. Highland Swim Club, Scotch Plains, 1973-78. Mem. League For Ednl. Advancement for Registered Nurses, Am. Soc. of Notaries, Columbia U./Presbyn. Hosp. Sch. of Nursing Alumni Assn. Republican. Episcopalian. Home: 125 Russell Rd Fanwood NJ 07023 Office: Assocs in Medicine 128 S Euclid Ave Westfield NJ 07090

BUTLER, H. JO, real estate developer, consultant; b. La Dalles, Oreg., Mar. 16, 1948; d. Phillip William and Sara Ruth (Dolph) Foraker. Student, Washburn U., 1969-72, Austin (Tex.) Community Coll., 1983-84, Am. Coll., Austin, 1984. V.p. advt. Green Brier BH & G, Topeka, 1978; real estate broker Residential Cos., Topeka, 1979-81, Austin, 1981-82; comml. broker Conti Fin. Corp., Austin, 1982-84; pvt. practice real estate developer Austin, 1984—; cons. Oriens Park and Internat. Plaza, Austin, 1987—; mktg. cons. Valley Devel., Inc., Napa, Calif. Producer: (TV comml.) Big is Best, 1978 (Creativity award 1978); author: (manuel) Be All You Can Be, 1984. Sec. Topeka Advertisers, 1976-81, Austin Exchange Group, 1987; dir. Neighborhood Dir. Lone Star Girl Scouts U.S., Austin, 1983-87; pres. Springhollow Assocs., Austin, 1985—; mem. com. Austin Econ. Devel., 1987. Mem. Austin Real Estate Exchange (sec. 1987), Austin C. of C. (coms. 1987). Republican. Home: PO Box 160772 Austin TX 78716

BUTLER, LESLIE ANN, advertising agency owner; b. Salem, Oreg., Nov. 19, 1945; d. Marlow Dole and Lala Ann (Erlandson) Butler. Student Lewis and Clark Coll., 1963-64; B.S., U. Oreg., 1969; postgrad. Portland State U. 1972-73. Creative trainee Ketchum Advt., San Francisco, 1970-71; asst. advt. dir. Mktg. Systems, Inc., Portland, Oreg., 1971-74; prodn. mgr., art dir., copywriter Finzer-Smith, Portland, 1974-76; copywriter Gerber Advt., Portland, 1976-78; freelance copywriter, Portland, 1978-80, 83-85; copywriter McCann-Erickson, Portland, 1980-81; copy chief Brookstone Co., Peterborough, N.H., 1981-83; creative dir. Whitman Advt., Portland, 1984-87. Co-founder, v.p., newsletter editor Animal Rescue and Care Fund, 1972-81. Recipient Internat. Film and TV Festival N.Y. Finalist award, 1985, 86, Internat. Radio Festival of N.Y. award, 1984, 85, Hollywood Radio and TV Soc. Internat. Broadcasting award, 1981, TV Comml. Festival Silver Telly award, 1985, TV Comml. Festival Bronze Telly, 1986, AVC Silver Cindy, 1986, Los Angeles Advt. Women LULU, 1986, 87, Ad Week What's New Portfolio, 1986, N.W. Addy award Seattle Advt. Fedn., 1985, Best of N.W. award N.W. Seminar Film and Video, 1985, numerous others. Mem. Portland Advt. Fedn. (Rosey Finalist award 1986), Portland Art Assn., Assn. Research and Enlightenment, Nat. Wildlife Fedn., ASPCA, People for Ethical Treatment of Animals. Address: 6005 SE 21st Ave Portland OR 97202

BUTLER, MARY FRANCES, nurse; b. Elrode, Ala., Sept. 10, 1931; d. Leon and Beatrice (Nixon) Mosely; m. Harry M. Butler; children from previous marriage—Keith Wheeler, Pat Wheeler Clark. A.D. in Nursing, Kansas City Jr. Coll., 1974. R.N. Lic. practical nurse St. John's Hosp., Leavenworth, Kans., 1956-64, surg. technician, 1962-63; lic. practical nurse Cushing Meml. Hosp., 1963-65; lic. practical nurse VA Med. Ctr., Leavenworth, Kans., 1965-75, charge nurse, 1975—. Recipient Quality Increase award Leavenworth VA Hosp., 1971, 79, Advanced Proformance award, 1981. Ch. sch. tchr., 1976—. Baptist. Home: 104 Fern Cliff Lansing KS 66043

BUTLER, OCTAVIA ESTELLE, free-lance writer; b. Pasadena, Calif., June 22, 1947; d. Laurice and Octavia Margaret (Guy) B. AA, Pasadena City Coll., 1968; student, Calif. State U., Los Angeles, 1969—. Free-lance writer Los Angeles, 1975—. Author: Patternmaster, 1976, Mind of my Mind, 1977, Survivor, 1978, Kindred, 1979, Wild Seed, 1980, Clay's Ark, 1984, Dawn, 1987, Adulthood Rites, 1988; also sci. fiction short stories. Recipient fifth prize Writer's Digest Short Story Contest, 1967, Creative Arts Achievement award Los Angeles YWCA, 1980, Sci. Fiction (Hugo) Best Novelette award World Sci. Fiction Conv., 1985, Best Short Story award World Sci. Fiction Conv., 1984, Nebula Best Novelette award Sci. Fiction Writers Am., 1985, Locus Best Novelette award, 1985, Best Novelette award Sci. Fiction Chronicle Reader, 1985. Mem. Sci. Fiction Writers Am. Address: PO Box 6604 Los Angeles CA 90055

BUTLER, RUTH ELAINE, nurse, educator; b. New Martinsville, W.Va., Oct. 4, 1950; d. Hobert Eugene and Lola Louise (Wilson) Davis; m. Dolen Martin Butler, June 27, 1970; 1 child, Ryan David. Diploma in Nursing, St. Anthony Hosp., Oklahoma City, Okla., 1972; BS in Nursing, Avila Coll., 1985—; postgrad., U. Mo., Kansas City, 1985—. Med. surg. staff nurse St. Anthony Hosp., 1972-73; head nurse oncology St. Luke's Hosp., Kansas City, 1973-75; med. surg. staff nurse St. Elizabeth's Hosp., Youngstown, Ohio, 1975-76; med. surgical staff nurse Sts. Mary & Elizabeth's Hosp., Louisville, 1976-78; staff nurse intensive care unit Research Med. Ctr., Kansas City, 1978-80, asst. head nurse intensive care unit, 1980-84; coordinator critical care edn. Research Med. Ctr., Kansas City, Mo., 1984—; instr. advanced cardiac life support Am. Heart Assn., Kansas City, 1983—, basic life support, 1985—; mem. faculty ACLS Affiliate. Mem. Am. Assn. Critical Care Nurses (cert. 1981, local chpt. prog. com. 1987—), Sigma Theta Tau. Mem. Ch. of the Nazarene. Home: 12725 Oakland Grandview MO 64030 Office: Research Med Ctr 2316 E Meyer Blvd Kansas City MO 64132

BUTLER-EAVES, GLORIA DEAN, promotion director; b. Vicksburg, Miss., Jan. 29, 1958; d. Buel and Dean (Clark) Butler. BS in Social Rehab., U. So. Miss., 1979; postgrad., Reformed Theol. Sem., 1988—. Program devel. specialist Miss. Vocat. Rehab. for the Blind, Jackson, 1980; profl. employment counselor Snelling & Snelling, Jackson, 1980-81; sales asst. ITT Telecommunication, Corinth, Miss., 1982-83; creative services producer Sta. WTOK-TV, Meridian, Miss., 1983-86; exec. coordinator Keep Am. Beautiful, City of Meridian, 1986-88; promotion dir. Sta. WDBD-TV, Jackson, 1988—. Contbr. articles to newspapers; contbr. poetry to So. Poetry Rev., 1987— (Blue Ribbon award 1988). Grad. asst. Dale Carnegie Tng., Meridian, 1987 (Human Relations award). Recipient 1st Place State Distributive Edn. Clubs Am., 1976, Human Relations award, 1987, Commendation award City of Meridian, 1986-88. Mem. Jackson Advt. Club, Nat. Assn. Female Execs., Meridian C. of C. (area appearance com., 1986—). Republican. Baptist. Club: Pilot (Jackson).

BUTNER, BONNIE JEAN, nurse, educator; b. Starkville, Miss., Sept. 12, 1952; d. Otis Len and Opal (Adams) Malone; m. Philip Charles Butner, June 11, 1976; children: Bridgette Ann-Marie, Brittany Lynn. Student, Miss. State U, 1971; BSN, Miss. Coll., 1977. Registered nurse. Nurse tech. Hinds Gen. Hosp., Jackson, Miss., 1972-76; nurse St. Dominic's Hosp., Jackson, 1976-78; nurse supr. Forrest Gen. Hosp., Hattiesburg, Miss., 1978-82; edn. dir. Southeast Miss. Air Ambulance, Hattiesburg, 1982-85; adminstrv. supr. Meth. Hosp., Hattiesburg, 1985-87; clin. dir. for dialysis Hattiesburg Clinic, 1987—. chmn. blood pressure Am. Heart Assn., Hattiesburg, 1982—. Served to capt. U.S. Army N.G., 1975—. Mem. Pinebelt Assn. Critical Care Nurses, Southeast Miss. Emergency Nurses Assn. Republican. Baptist. Home: Rt 3 Box 300-P Purvis MS 39475

BUTON, JENNIFER LYNNE, insurance company executive; b. Tiffin, Ohio, July 15, 1953; d. Earl Cutting Jr. and Esther Rose (Winters) B.; m. James Francis Walsh IV, Aug. 8, 1981 (div. May 1985). BA in Spanish and Math., SUNY, Cortland, 1976; MBA in Internat. Bus., Pace U., 1979; cert., U. Salamanca, Spain, 1983. Cert. math., Spanish, early secondary tchr., N.Y. Research analyst office of edn. HEW, N.Y.C., 1975-77; mkt. devel. specialist World Trade Inst., N.Y.C., 1977-80; mgmt. cons. Brooks Internat. Corp., Montvale, N.J., 1980-83; internat. methods cons. CIGNA Corp., Phila., 1983-85; planning and field services mgr. CIGNA Corp., Coral Gables, Fla., 1985-86, asst. dir., 1986—; mgmt. cons., v.p. ops. Creative Dimensions in Mgmt., Phila., 1985—. Mem. World Affairs Council, Phila., 1983-85; vol. Big Sisters, Phila., 1984-85, Spl. Olympics, Phila., 1984. Mellon Found. scholar, 1976-78, Regents scholar N.Y. State U., 1971-75; named one of Outstanding Young Women of Yr., 1978. Democrat. Methodist.

BUTTERFIELD, DIANE MARIE, financial executive, accountant, consultant; b. Albert Lea, Minn., Aug. 24, 1950; d. William Roland and Genevieve Elaine (Mahowald) B. BA in Acctg., S.W. Minn. State U., 1972. CPA, Minn. Various Peat Marwick Mitchell and Co., Mpls., 1972-80; sr. mgr. N.Y.C., 1980-83; cons. Edmond, Okla., 1983-84; dir. acctg. Policy and Research Household Internat., Prospect Heights, Ill., 1984—; alternate FASB emerging issues task force, 1984-87, fin. instruments, 1986—; alt. mem. com. corp. reporting Fin. Execs. Inst. Mem. Am. Inst. CPA's, Minn. Soc. CPA's. Home: 510C Woodview Rd Barrington IL 60010 Office: Household Internat 2700 Sanders Rd Prospect Heights IL 60070

BUTTERMAN, ELIZABETH B(IERMANN), legal assistant; b. N.Y.C., Feb. 27, 1944; d. Carl O. and Lucille (Lacey) Biermann; m. John A. McTaggart, Dec. 19, 1965 (div. 1970); 1 dau., Elan Lacey; m. Donald J. Butterman, Apr. 7, 1976. B.A., Mt. Holyoke Coll., 1965; cert. Litigation Asst., Adelphi U., 1986. Asst. buyer J.C. Penney Co., N.Y.C., 1966-70; buyer Woolco, Secaucus, N.J., 1970-74, K-Mart, North Bergen, N.J., 1974-76; personnel dir. Korvettes, N.Y.C., 1976-79, AMC/Federated Dept. Stores, N.Y.C., 1979-82; v.p. merchandising Empire Shield Co. Inc., Bklyn., 1983-85; sales and mktg. exec. Elkay Industries, N.Y.C., 1986; litigation lawyer's asst. Internat. Paper Co., 1986—; Mem. Am. Women's Econ. Devel. Orgn. Republican. Episcopalian. Office: Internat Paper Co 2 Manhattanville Rd Purchase NY 10577

BUTTERWECK, KAREN ANN, data processing executive; b. Allentown, Pa., Oct. 11, 1951; d. Ralph J. and Ruth M. (Bealer) Mack; m. Richard John Butterweck, Dec. 26, 1970; children: Denise, Kyle. A in Computer Sci., Montco U., 1971; A in Mgmt., Ins. Inst. Am., 1986; postgrad., Ursinus U., 1987—. Clerical Harleysville (Pa.) Ins. Co., 1972-75, programmer, 1975-77, program analyst, 1977-81, sr. program analyst, 1981-83, mgr., 1983—. Home: 1025 Lake Ln Pennsburg PA 18073 Office: Harleysville Ins Co 355 Maple Ave Harleysville PA 19438

BUTTERWORTH, JANE ROGERS FITCH, physician; b. Louisville, Aug. 3, 1937; d. Howard Mercer and Jane Rogers (McCaw) Fitch; m. William Butterworth, Sept. 5, 1958 (div. Feb. 1968); children: Jane Rogers, William Stoddard, Robert Mercer, Benjamin Richard Mallory, Anne Lewis. BS, U. Louisville, 1971, MD, 1974. Rotating intern Humana Hosp. Audubon (formerly St. Joseph's Hosp.), Louisville, 1974-75, resident in radiology, 1975-76; resident in phys. medicine and rehab. Frasier Rehab. (formerly Inst. of Phys. Medicine and Rehab.), Louisville, 1976-80; staff physiatrist Rockford (Ill.) Meml. Hosp., 1980-83; clin. instr. Rockford Sch. Medicine, 1980-83; med. dir. phys. medicine and rehab. Western Res. Care System, Youngstown, Ohio, 1983—, mem. teaching staff residency program, 1983—; clin. instr. Northeastern Ohio U. Coll. of Medicine, Rootstown, 1983—, chairperson phys. medicine subcouncil, mem. acad. rev. and promotions com., 1985—; adj. faculty Youngstown State U., 1984—; regional med. advisor Rehab. div. Ohio Indsl. Commn., Youngstown, 1985—. Mem. choir St. John's Epis. Ch., Youngstown, 1985—; bd. dirs. Goodwill Industries, Youngstown, 1985—, rehab. div. advisor, 1986—; mem. med. rev. staff Hospice, Youngstown, 1984—; dir. med. services Easter Seals Soc., Youngstown, 1987—; mem. med. bd. pub. TV, Youngstown, 1986—; violinist Youngstown State U. Orch, 1985. Mem. AMA, Ohio State Med. Assn., Mahoning County Med. Soc., Jefferson County Med. Soc., Ky. Med. Assn., Am. Congress of Rehab. Medicine, Colonial Dames Soc. in Am., Phi Beta, Chi Delta Phi, Kappa Alpha Theta. Republican. Home: 186 Rockland Dr Boardman OH 44512 Office: Western Res Care System Southside Hosp 345 Oakhill Youngstown OH 44501

BUTTERWORTH, NONA ANGEL, artist; b. Spartanburg, S.C., Jan. 28, 1929; d. James Oscar and Joyce (Beatty) Angel; student Randolph Macon's Womans Coll., 1947-49, Ringling Sch. Art, 1949-50, Art Students League, N.Y.C., 1950-51; m. James Ebert Butterworth, Jr., Dec. 18, 1954; children—James Ebert III, Alison Angel, Joy Evans. Jr. curator art Pack Meml. Library, Asheville, N.C., 1951-52; artist. advt. dept. Ivey's Dept. Store, Asheville, 1952-53; comml. artist Ayer & Gillette advt. agy., Charlotte, N.C. 1953-55; one woman show Charlotte Country Club, 1972, Charlotte Country Day Sch., 1977, Copeland House Art Gallery, 1982, Christ Episcopal Ch., 1982; 2-woman show Charlotte Meml. Hosp., 1985, Ivey's Dept. Store, 1985; exhibited in group shows First Union Bank, Charlotte, 1973, 74, 75, 76, 77, 85, Wachovia Bank, 1975, WSOC-TV, 1975-78; Lincolnton (N.C.) City Hall, 1974, 75, N.C. Nat. Bank, 1971, 72, 76-77, 84, 85, Charlotte Festival in the Park, 1972-86, Spl. Bicentennial Invitational Exhibit Queens Coll., 1976, N.C. State Art Mus. Juried Shows, 1977, 78, N.C. Watercolor Show, High Point, 1976, Greenville, 1977, Fayetteville, 1986, Lexington, 1987, Davidson Coll., 1979, Shelby Nat. Juried Show, 1983-84, 85, N.C. Nat. Bank, 1984, N.C. Watercolor Soc., 1985, Elon Coll., 1986; represented in permanent collections, Phila., Charlotte, Asheville, Gastonia; tchr. art, children Mint Museum, Charlotte, 1973-76, Charlotte Country Day Sch., 1975-76, 77; watercolor tchr. Central Piedmont Community Coll., 1981—; pvt. tchr. art; free-lance writer Charlotte Mag., 1981-84. Pres. Friends of Mint Museum, 1972-73; v.p. Artists Guild, 1973-74, 2d v.p. Women's Aux. Mint Mus., 1975-76, chmn. overseas tours, 1975—; chmn. Christ Episcopal Ch. Fair, 1968; bd. dirs. Women's Assn. Charlotte Symphony, also co-chmn. Symphony Designerhouse, 1975; mem. artists' adv. bd. Mint Mus., 1977—; bd. dirs. Arts and Sci. Council, 1978-81, Guild Charlotte Artists, 1984-85, Charlotte Writers Club, 1984-85; mem. co. Charlotte Little Theater, 1981, 84, 85, 87, Piedmont Community Coll. Summer Theater, 1983. Recipient Merit award Pa. State Hort. Soc., 1966; Purchase award Mint Mus., 1977; 1st prize WSOC-TV Invitational, 1978; honorable mention Guild Charlotte Artists, 1983, 3d prize, 1983; Best Actress in a Supporting Role Charlotte Little Theatre, 1987. Mem. Guild Charlotte Artists (dir. 1983-84, pres. 1976-77), Affiliates Arts and Sci. Council (sec. exec. com. 1977—), N.C. Watercolor Soc. (sec., dir. 1978-79), Jr. League, Charlotte Writer's Club (pres. 1982-84, 1st prize children's story contest 1981). Republican. Episcopalian. Club: Charlotte Country. Home: 1438 Queens Rd W Charlotte NC 28207

BUTTERY, JANET LOUISE, movie theatre company executive; b. Columbus, Ohio, May 19, 1953; d. Thomas William and Pauline Adelaide (Burgess) B.; B.A., U. Kans., 1975, M.B.A., 1978; Troisième Degré, Université de Bordeaux (France), 1975. Real estate devel. Am. Multi Cinema, Kansas City, Mo., 1978—. Mem. Assn. MBA Execs., Internat. Council Shopping Ctrs. Avocations: cooking, music, theatre, reading, jogging. Home: 5409 Foxridge Dr Apt 203 Mission KS 66202 Office: Am Multi Cinema Inc 106 W 14th St Suite 1700 Kansas City MO 64105

BUTTI, MARY MADELINE, school principal; b. N.Y.C., Nov. 20, 1921; d. Ernest Charles and Anna (Mazzoni) Fusi; m. Lewis Charles Butti, Apr. 6, 1947; children: Claire Butti Myers, Lawrence Richard. BA, Hunter Coll., 1943; MA, Columbia U., 1945. Tchr. English N.Y.C. Sch. System, 1947-67; asst. prin. N.Y.C. Sch. System, Bklyn., 1967-76; prin. Jr. High Sch. 223, Bklyn., 1976—; v.p. Council Suprs. and Adminstrs., Bklyn., 1978—, trustee/sec. welfare fund, 1980—, retirees welfare fund, 1983—ž. V.p. New Hyde Park (New Hyde Park) Health Ins. Plan Consumer Council, 1976—; pres. Commonwealth Civic Assn., Douglaston, N.Y., 1981—; mem. Community Bd. 11, Bayside, N.Y., 1983—; bd. dirs. Highpoint Condominion, Douglaston, 1985—. Mem. Nat. Assn. Secondary Sch. Prins., Jr. High Sch. Prins. Assn. (exec. bd. 1981-83), Delta Kappa Gamma (Elizabeth Turbin Pi award 1981), Phi Delta Kappa (St. John's U. chpt.). Roman Catholic. Home: 244-16 73d Ave Douglaston NY 11362

BUTTLER, JEWELL ANN, public relations executive; b. Detroit, July 10, 1937; d. John Martin and Grace Katherine (Gibes) Moranda; m. Francis Anthony Buttler, July 28, 1973. BA in Journalism, BS in Econs., Oakland U., 1983. Asst. mgr. communications dept. Greater Detroit C. of C., 1966-73; dir. pub. relations and devel. Ctr. for Creative Studies Coll. of Art and Design, Detroit, 1974-79; dir. pub. relations Detroit Inst. for Children, 1983—. Mem. Nat. Assn. Female Execs., Mensa. Home: 5048 Buckingham Pl Troy MI 48098

BUTTNER, ANN DANIELLE MECKLENBORG, nurse; b. Phila., July 29, 1952; d. Robert Henry and Helen Gail (Gallagher) Mecklenborg; m. Edward George Buttner, Jan. 7, 1978; 1 dau., Rachel Caroline. Assoc. Nursing, Gwynedd-Mercy Coll., 1972; B.S., 1974; M.A., U. No. Colo., 1980; M.A. in pub. adminstrn. Troy State U., 1987. Staff nurse Chestnut Hill Hosp., Phila., 1972-74; profl. pub. health nurse N. Pa. Vis. Nurse Assn., Ambler, 1974-75; nursing instr. community health U. Wyo., Laramie, 1978-81; staff pub. health nurse Health Cons. Services, Alamogordo, N.Mex., 1982, coordinator nursing program N.Mex. State U., Alamogordo, 1983-84; sch. nurse Sembach Elem. Sch., Fed. Republic Germany, 1984-87, Dept. Def. Dependents Schs., 1987—; sch. nurse Hahn AFB Elem. Sch., 1987—; mem. child advocacy multi-disciplinary team Sembach AFB, 1984-87; patient edn. cons./instr. Am. Lung Assn., Albuquerque, 1983; adv. bd. mem., cons. Alamogordo Home Care, 1983. Pub. edn. chmn. Am. Cancer Soc., Dist. V Otero County Unit, Alamogordo, 1982-83; CPR instr. ARC, Phila., 1972-76; health careers cons. C. of C., Inc., Alamogordo, 1983. Served to 1st lt., Nurses Corps, USAF, 1976-78. Recipient awards Am. Cancer Soc., 1981—. Mem. Am. Nurses Assn. Council of Nursing Adminstrn., N.Mex. Nurses Assn. (nursing edn. planning com. 1983). Democrat. Roman Catholic. Club: Hahn AFB Wives (Fed. Rep. Germany). Home: PO Box 1246 APO New York NY 09109

BUTTNER, ELEANOR HOLLINGSWORTH, educator; b. Balt., Apr. 30, 1953; d. Walter Douglas and Sarah Alexander (Russell) B.; B.A., Hollins (Va.) Coll., 1975; M.B.A., U. Pa., 1977 Ph.D., U. N.C., 1986. Asst. prof. mgmt. U. N.C.-Greensboro, 1985—. Recipient Elizabeth Kennedy Chance award Hollins Coll., 1975. Mem. Acad. Mgmt., Durham-Triangle Personnel Assn. Contbr. articles to profl. publs. Home: 8010 Pate Dr Oak ridge NC 27310 Office: Dept Mgmt U NC Greensboro NC 27412

BUTTS, VIRGINIA, corporate public relations executive; b. Chgo.. B.A., U. Chgo. Writer, producer Dave Garroway radio show NBC, N.Y.C., 1953; writer, producer, talent Sta. WBBM-TV, Chgo.; midwest dir. pub. relations for mags. Time, Fortune, Life and Sports Illustrated, Time Inc., 1956-63; dir. pub. relations Chgo. Sun-Times and Chgo. Daily News, 1963-74; v.p. pub. relations Field Enterprises Inc., Chgo., 1974-84, The Field Corp., 1984—. Contbr.: Lesly's Public Relations Handbook, 1978, 83. Recipient Clarion award Women in Communications Inc., 1975, 76; recipient Businesswoman of the Yr. award Lewis U., 1976. Mem. Pub. Relations Soc. Am. (nat. bd. ethics 1987—), Publicity Club Chgo. (recipient Golden Trumpet award 1968, 69, 75, 76, 80), Nat. Acad. TV Arts and Scis., The Chgo. Network. Club: Mid-Am. (Chgo.). Office: The Field Corp 333 W Wacker Dr Chicago IL 60606

BUXTON, CHANDRA DAWN, travel agency executive; b. Balt., Aug. 24, 1948; d. Arthur Brent and Ruth Alverta (Whitcomb) Hall; m. James C. Pochron, Feb. 14, 1974 (div. 1980); 1 child, Douglas Stanley; m. Roger Basil Buxton, Jan. 24, 1981; children—Dustin Brown, Dallas Ramee. Cert. travel counselor. Travel agt. Aladdin Travel, Glen Burnie, Md., 1966-67; internat. travel agt. Travel Guide, Balt., 1967-70; mgr. Tobys Travels, Reistertown, Md., 1970-72; owner, mgr. Welcome-Aboard Travel, Frederick, Md., 1972-80; mgr. Pardee Travel, Frederick, 1980-82; owner, mgr. Buxtons World of Travel, Damascus, Md., 1982—. Mem. Am. Soc. Travel Agts., Assn. Retail Travel Agts., Inst. Cert. Travel Agts. Democrat. Methodist. Avocations: swimming; redecorating. Office: Buxton's World of Travel 26217 Ridge Rd Damascus Sq Damascus MD 20872

BUXTON, MARILYN PHILBRICK, logistician, consultant; b. Springfield, Mass., Feb. 15, 1947; d. Harold Frank and Mary F. (Farquhar) Philbrick; m. John Howard Buxton, June 13, 1970. BS in Bus., Russell Sage Coll., 1969; MA in Mgmt., Cen. Mich. U., 1975. Commd. 2d lt. USAF, 1973, advanced through grades to maj.; mgr. computer systems USAF, Udorn Royal Thai AFB, Thailand, 1975-76; acad. counselor USAF Acad., Colorado Springs, Colo., 1976-82; logistics officer USAF, Hanscom AFB, Bedford, Mass., 1982-85; retired USAF, 1985; logistics analyst Raytheon Co., Bedford, 1985-86. Advisor Boy Scouts Am., Ft. Walton Beach, Fla., 1986-88. Mem. Soc. Logistics Engrs. AAUW. Home and Office: 5354 Anvil Ct Fairfax VA 22030

BUZZELLI, CHARLOTTE GRACE, educator; b. Akron, Ohio, Mar. 21, 1947; d. Edmund Albert and Sarah Agnes (Russo) Buzzelli. B.S., U. Akron, 1969, M.S. in Edn., 1976. Tchr. St. Anthony Sch., Akron, 1969-76; program coordinator, tchr. Akron Montessori Sch. Continuing Edn. Program, Eastwood Ctr., Akron, 1976-77, dir. edn. Fallsview Psychiat Hosp., Cuyahoga Falls, Ohio, 1977—, developer job tng. partnership grant program and spl. needs handicapped grant program; cons. in field pioneered first spl. edn. program in Ohio for adult state psychiat. hosp.; developed 1st community-based adult basic edn. program in state instn. in Ohio. Named Ohio Tchr. of Yr., 1979; recipient A Key award U. Akron. Mem. Council Exceptional Children (chpt. pres.), Assn. Supervision and Curriculum Devel., Assn. Children with Learning Disabilities, Internat. Reading Assn., U. Akron Alumni Assn., Pi Lambda Theta (pres.), Phi Delta Kappa, Delta Kappa Gamma, Gamma Beta (pres.). Clubs: Univ., Akron Women's City. Home: 662 Dayton St Akron OH 44310 Office: Fallsview Psychiat Hosp 330 Broadway East St Cuyahoga Falls OH 44221

BYAM, MARIE ELIZABETH, data processing management consultant; b. Cooperstown, N.Y., Oct. 31, 1949; d. Harmon Leigh and Elizabeth Virginia (Baldo) B. BA, Ga. State U., 1972; postgrad., Columbia So. Sch. Law, 1976-78. Programmer Coastal States Life Ins. Co., Atlanta, 1973-75; programmer, analyst So. Airways, Atlanta, 1975-76; cons. computer programming Atlanta, 1978-82; sr. cons., field mgr. Computer Dynamics, Woodland Hills, Calif., 1983-84; owner, cons. MEB Assocs., Canoga Park, Calif., 1984—; frequent speaker on career planning schs., profl. confs. and meetings. Guest co-host Ms. Biz radio show, 1987. Bd. dirs. Opera Guild So. Calif., Los Angeles, 1984—. Mem. Data Processing Mgmt. Assn. (publications dir. 1988), Assn. Women in Computing (pres. Los Angeles chpt. 1985-87, nat. conf. chmn. 1986), Sierra Club. Republican. Home and Office: MEB Assocs 6846D Hatillo Canoga Park CA 91306

BYARS, ILA PEARL, organization executive, civic worker; b. Travis, Tex., June 25, 1908; d. William Lafayette and Sibyl Allen (Massey) B.; student public schs. With Mid-west States Telephone Co., Blanco, 1924-53; with Bigden Ins. and Real Estate, Tex., 1953-55; pvt. kindergarten tchr., Blanco, 1955-56; waitress various restaurants, 1956-62, 63-65; with Wall Furniture, also Wall Funeral Home, Bianco, 1952-53, 65-66; staff food dept. Blanco Mill Nursing Home, 1966—. County chmn. Am. Heart Assn., 1957-72, meml. and campaign mgr., 1957-72; bd. dirs. Blanco County unit Am. Cancer Soc., 1959-72, unit sec., 1971-74, 86—, pres., 1974-76; trustee Blanco Library, 1950-53, librarian, 1952-53; bd. dirs. Blanco County Tb Assn., 1951-53; sec. Council on Ministries, United Meth Ch., 1986—, sec. chancel choir, 1985-86, mem. nominating com., 1982—, parish com., 1986, Sunday Sch. tchr., 1949—, dir. Vacation Bible Sch., from 1968, asst. dir., 1986, chmn. children's dept., 1986—. Recipient Achievement citations Am. Heart Assn., 1970, 71, 73; citation Am. Cancer Soc., 1971, 25-yr. pin., 1985. Mem. Blanco C. of C. (sec. 1967-72, dir. 1967-71), Daus. of Nile, Wesleyan Service Guild (co-founder 1952, pres. 1968—), Nat. Trust Hist. Preservation, Tex. Hist. Found., The Smithsonian Assocs. United Meth. Women (reporter 1986). Lodges: Daus. of Nile, Order Eastern Star (past matron; organist, sec. 1986, 87). Home: PO Box 246 Blanco TX 78606

BYBEE, KATHLEEN MARGARET, investment banker; b. Logan, Utah, Apr. 28, 1956; d. Sirren Florenz and Barbara Nelsa (Neilson) B. BA, Harvard U., 1978; M in Mgmt., Yale U., 1982. Asst. editor Deseret Book Co., Salt Lake City, 1978-79; reporter Sta. KWMS-AM, Salt Lake City, 1979-80; pvt. practice cons. Boston and Washington, 1981-83; fin. asst. U.S. Dept. Commerce, Washington, 1983, small bus. tech. analyst, 1983-85; asst. treas. strategic planning Bankers Trust Co., N.Y.C., 1985-87, assoc. in investment banking and pub. fin., 1987—. Author: (govt. publ.) Guide to Innovation Resources for Smaller Businesses, 1985. Vol. Cancer Care, N.Y.C., 1986-87; womens' auxiliary sec. Mormon Ch. Greater N.Y.C., 1986—. Mem. Harvard Alumni Assn. (com. mem. 1983-88). Club: Radcliffe of Washington (sec. 1985) and of N.Y.C. Home: 333 W 86th St Apt #1104 New York NY 10024

BYBEE, SHARON LEE, association administrator; b. Loogootee, Ind., Mar. 18, 1940; d. William Arnold and mary Eloise (Mc Guire) Greene; m. Gary D. Patterson, Nov. 30, 1958 (div. 1963); children: Clark Alan, Christina Rene Patterson-Wonder; m. Joe ByBee, Jan. 4, 1986. Student, Vincennes U., 1978—. Project dir. YMCA dba Sr. Services Project, Washington, Ind., 1975—. Civic mem. City Task Force, Washington, 1987. Named to Royal Order Ky. Cols., 1987; nominee Jesse Dickenson award, J.P. Hagel award, 1987. Mem. Ind. Assn. Home Service Agy., Fellows and Sponsors, Aging Service Provider Assn. (treas. 1984—), Nat. Assn. Female Execs. Democrat. Roman Catholic. Home: 503 Meredith St Washington IN 47501 Office: Sr Services Project 101 NE 6th St Washington IN 47501

BYE, ROSEANNE MARIE, marketing professional; b. Chgo., Nov. 27, 1946; d. Paul David and Gwendalynn Luciell (Hipp) Forrester; BS in Foods and Nutrition, Western Ill. U., 1969; m. Richard Wayne Bye, June 14, 1969. Banquet mgr. Western Ill. U., 1967-69; new product home economist Hunt/Wesson Foods, Fullerton, Calif., 1969-73; retail and restaurant home economist Lawry's Foods, Los Angeles, 1973-74; mgr. product devel. Carl Karcher Enterprises, Anaheim, Calif., 1974-81; v.p. research and devel. Denny's Restaurants, La Mirada, Calif., 1981-88; owner Bye & Assocs., Anaheim, 1988—; mem. speakers bur. mktg. fast food Industry/Edn. Council. Mem. food service adv. com., Calif. State U., Long Beach, Chapman Coll., adv. com. Santa Ana Jr. Coll., Garden Grove Sch. Dist. Recipient Nat. Mktg. award for devel. of Charbroiler Steak Sandwich, 1975-76, serve-yourself salad bar, 1978-79. Mem. Am. Home Econs. Assn., Calif. Home Econs. Assn. (Outstanding Economist in Bus. 1977, 79, 86, pres. 1977-79), Home Economists in Bus. (award of excellence, Western regional adv. 1976-78, nat. pub. relations chmn. 1983-85), Women in Mgmt., Nat. Restaurant Assn. (chmn. mktg. research div., nat. conf. speaker), NOW, Anaheim C. of C. (publicity chmn. 1977-78), Soc. Advancement Food Service Research (bd. dirs. 1986-88, co-chair regional meetings 1988—, Fellowship award 1987), Internat. Food Service Editorial Council, MUFSO, COEX, Internat. Platform Assn. Republican. Presbyterian. Clubs: Tennis and Swim; Gourmet/Wine; Teddy Bear; Literary Guild; Newport Harbor Art Mus.; Bower's Art Mus.; Gem Theatre Guild. Office: 3943 E La Palma Ave Anaheim CA 92807

BYER EISENBERG, KAREN SUE, nurse; b. Bklyn., Mar. 11, 1954; d. Marvin and Florence (Beck) Byer; 1 child, Carly Beth; diploma nursing L.I. Coll. Hosp. Sch. Nursing, 1973; B.S. in Nursing, L.I. U., 1976, M.Profl. Studies, 1977; m. Howard Eisenberg, May 11, 1974. Nurse recovery room and surg. intensive care unit Downstate Med. Center, Bklyn., 1973-75; utilization rev. analyst Bezallel Health Related Facility, Far Rockaway, N.Y., 1975-76; utilization rev. analyst, R.N. supr. Seagirt Health Related Facility, Far Rockaway, 1976; staff nurse neurosurg. and rehab. nursing Downstate Med. Center, Bklyn., 1978, nurse intensive care unit, 1978-79, asst. nursing dir. pathology, clin. research asso. Research Found., 1979—. Mem. Oncology Nursing Soc., Am. Nurses Assn., N.Y. State Nurses Assn., N.Y. Acad. Scis., L.I. Coll. Hosp. Alumnae Assn. Contbr. articles to profl. jours. Office: 450 Clarkson Ave Box 25 Brooklyn NY 11203

BYERLY, KATHLEEN MAE, military officer; b. Newport News, Va., Feb. 5, 1944; d. Joseph Paul and Lucille (Alessandroni) Donahue. BA, Chestnut Hill Coll., 1966; postgrad., Pepperdine U., 1975-77; grad., Naval War Coll., 1978. Commd. ensign U.S. Navy, 1966, advanced through grades to capt., 1986; comdg. officer Personnel Support Activity U.S. Navy, HI, 1986-88; spl. asst. to dep. chief Naval ops. U.S. Navy, Washington, 1988—. Mem. NOW, Women's Equity Action League, U.S. Naval Inst. Roman Catholic. Home: 4360 Greenberry Ln Annandale VA 22003 Office: Office of Chief Naval Ops Washington DC 20350-2000

BYERS, CAROL ANN, personnel director; b. Albany, Oreg., Sept. 27, 1933; d. Edward B. and Anna Schrock Roth; m. Dean R. Byers, Oct. 28, 1951; children: LaVelle, Lonnie, Randall. BS in Fin. Law, Portland State U., 1986. Office mgr. pathology dept. Salem (Oreg.) Gen. Hosp., 1971-78; personnel adminstrv. coordinator Port of Portland, Oregon, 1979; human resources information ctr. technician Port of Portland, Oreg., 1980-82, human resources information ctr. supr., 1982-86, human resources information ctr. mgr., 1986—; pres. info. bd. Info. Sci. Inc., Montvale, N.J., 1987—. Mem. Am. Soc. Personnel Adminstrs., Am. Payroll Assn., Human Resource System Profls. Republican. Club: Royal Reserves Investment (Portland) (chmn. 1987—). Office: Port of Portland PO Box 3529 Portland OR 97208

BYERS, DEBRA JANE, real estate executive; b. Butler, Pa., Oct. 9, 1956; d. John A. and Edith Belle (Byers) Daugherty. AA, Butler (Pa.) Community Coll., 1976. Lic. real estate agt. Mgr. security K-Mart Corp., Butler, 1975-78; mgr. beverages Seven Springs Mountain Resort, Champion, Pa., 1978-81; mgr. food and beverages Aunt Teaks and Uncle Junks, Strongsville, Ohio, 1981-85; mgr. property Specialty Restaurant Corp., Clearwater, Fla., 1985-87; agt. comml. leasing Tourtelot Bros., St. Petersburg, Fla., 1987—; mem. Pinellas Office Devel. Council. Mem. Pinellas County Schs. Exec. Internship Program. Mem. Nat. Assn. Female Execs., St. Petersburg Bd. Realtors, St. Petersburg C. of C., Hospitality Industry Assn. Democrat. Home: 11401 9th St N Apt 913 Saint Petersburg FL 33702 Office: Tourtelot Bros 414 4th St N Saint Petersburg FL 33701

BYERS, FLEUR, artist; b. Washington, June 5, 1928; d. Roy Danby and Jeanne Cecile (Nordstrom) Bateman; m. Howard Franklin Byers, May 14, 1955 (div. 1972); children: Diane Linda, David Michael, Brett Douglas. BA, U. Pa., 1949; MS, U. Tenn., 1951; postgrad., Corcoran Gallery Sch. Art, 1951-52, Eliot O'Hara Sch. Art, 1952, Pa. Acad. Fine Arts, 1959. Art tchr. Manhasset (N.Y.) Continuing Edn., 1986—, Oyster Bay (N.Y.) Adult Edn., 1986—, Levittown (N.Y.) Adult Edn., 1986—; lectr., demonstrations in field for various orgns. Visual artist, over 250 exhibitions include galleries in N.Y., Boston, Washington, Conn., R.I., Pa., Md., N.J., current exhibitions include Veerhoff Galleries, Washington, William Ris Galleries, Camp Hill, Pa., Sales Gallery, Art Assn. Harrisburg, Pa.; works include: Dawn (recipient Mann Meml. prize, 1979, Knockerbocker award, 1979, plaque Pastel Soc., 1980, award Pastel Soc., 1981), City Shadows (second prize 1981, hon. mention, 1983). Mem. social responsibility com., Unitarian Ch., Garden City, N.Y., 1983—, liason Service com., pub. relations. Recipient First Prize Belmont ARts and Crafts Assn., 1976, Samuel Mann Meml. Prize Nat. Assn. Women Artists, 1979, Winsor and Newton award nat. League of Am. Pen Women, 1981, Pastel Soc. Am. award Am. Artists Profl. League, 1981, Town of Oyster Bay award Suburban Art League, 1983, Catherine Lorillard Wolfe Cas award, 1983, Palmer Art award Mamaroneck Artists Guild, 1985, Holbein award Arts Council of E. Islip 4th Annual Juried Art Exhibit, 1986, OPA Internat. award, 1987, numerous others. Mem. Nat. Assn. Women Artists, Catharine Lorillard Wolfe Art Club (C.L. Wolfe award 1983), Am. Artists Profl. League (Pastel Soc. award 1981), Nat. Drawing Assn., The Pen and Brush, Oil Pastel Assn., Foud. for the Community of Artists, Art Assn. of Harrisburg, Pastel Soc. Am., Phi Beta Kappa, Sigma Xi. Democrat.

BYNUM, BARBARA STEWART, health scientist administrator; b. Washington, June 13, 1936; d. Oliver Walton and Mabel (Easton) Stewart; m. Elward Bynum, Apr. 4, 1959; 1 son, Christian. B.A. in Chemistry, U. Pa., 1957; postgrad. in biochemistry, Georgetown U., 1958-60. Chemist Nat. Cancer Inst.-NIH, Bethesda, Md., 1958-71; adminstrv. asst., office assoc. dir. for adminstrn. NIH, Bethesda, 1971-72, sci. grants program specialist div. research grants, 1972-75, health scientist adminstr. div. research grants, 1975-78, asst. chief for spl. programs, sci. rev. br. div. research grants, 1978-81; dir. div. extramural activities Nat. Cancer Inst., Bethesda, 1981—; reviewer, cons. AAAS, Washington, 1974—. Contbr. articles to profl. jours. Recipient Dirs. award NIH, 1980; recipient Sr. Exec. Service Superior Performance award HHS, 1982, 1987. Mem. Am. Assn. Cancer Research, Am. Assn. Pathologists, AAAS, Biophys. Soc. Democrat. Roman Catholic. Office: Nat Cancer Inst Div of Extramural Activities Bldg 31 Room 10A03 9000 Rockville Pike Bethesda MD 20892

BYNUM, ELIZABETH ANN, interior designer; b. Sevierville, Tenn., July 20, 1950; d. Samuel Dawson and Ruby (Redmond) Easterly; m. John H. Bynum. BS, U. Tenn., 1974. Interior designer McQuiddy Office Design Knoxville, Tenn., 1976-78, sr. designer, 1979-81, mgr., 1982—. Mem. Inst. Bus. Designers (membership v.p. 1985-87), Am. Soc. Interior Designers (sec. 1982-85), Knoxville C. of C. (econ. devel. council 1986). Office: McQuiddy Office Designers Inc 255 N Peters Rd Knoxville TN 37923

BYNUM, JULIA REBECCA BRANYON, elementary educator; b. Fayette, Ala., Jan. 21, 1948; d. Thomas Aaron Sr. and Edna Josephine (Madden) Branyon; m. William Michael Hopkins, Apr. 3, 1971 (dec. Aug. 1972); stepchildren: Lena Faye, Othelia Marie, William Carl; 1 child, Julia Michele; m. Thomas Homer Bynum, July 18, 1975; stepchildren: Thomas Tyrone, Michael Daren; 1 child, Amanda Paige. BA, Samford U., 1970; MA, U. Ala., 1974, AA cert., 1977. Cert. elem. sch. tchr., Ala. Elem. tchr. Muscogee County Bd. Edn., Columbus, Ga., 1970-71, Fayette (Ala.) County Bd. Edn., 1974—. Mem. UDC, Fayette, 1973—, Fayette Music Study Club, 1986—, reporter, 1987-88. Mem. NEA, Ala. Edn. Assn., Fayette County Edn. Assn., Alpha Delta Kappa (pres. Rho chpt. 1984-86, altruistic chmn. Ala. chpt. 1987-88, cen. dist. chmn. 1988—). Baptist. Home: PO Box 3 Fayette AL 35555 Office: Fayette Elem Sch 509 2d St NE Fayette AL 35555

BYRD, DONNA SUE, entrepreneur; b. Macon, Ga., Aug. 1, 1949; d. Walter Duett and Mary (Knight) Woodard; m. Jay Sumner Philpott, June 22, 1969 (div. Jan. 1979); children: David, Dena; m. Jim Thomas Byrd, Feb. 22, 1983; stepchildren: Mark, Chris. BA in Edn., U. Cen. Fla., 1970; MBA, Fla. Inst. Tech., 1981. Cert. tchr. V.p., bd. dirs. JAI, Inc., Melbourne, Fla., 1980-82; investor Real Estate Mgmt., Cocoa Beach, Fla., 1983-84; pres., bd. dirs. Tri-Care, Inc., Palm Bay, Fla., 1985—. Founder Learn and Play, Orange Park, Fla., 1976. Mem. Nat. Assn. Female Execs., Palm Bay C. of C. Republican. Office: Tri-Care Inc PO Box 060102 Palm Bay FL 32906-0102

BYRD, JOAN COUNTS, rehabilitation nurse, consultant; b. Lynch, Ky., June 19, 1931; d. Arthur Richard and Erma Anne (Colley) Counts; m. Ben K. Byrd, Oct. 24, 1951; children: Rick, Kathy, Emmett. Grad., E. Tenn. Bapt. Hosp. Sch. Nursing, Knoxville, 1951. Cert. ins. rehab. specialist, profl. counselor. Office nurse Penn Clinic, 1951-52; pvt. duty nurse 1953; office nurse Acuff Clinic, 1959-62; staff nurse E. Tenn. Bapt. Hosp., Knoxville, 1962-68, U. Tenn. Hosp., Knoxville, 1968-76; rev. coordinator Tenn. Found. Med. Care, Nashville, 1976-78; rehab. specialist Internat. Rehab. Assn., Louisville, 1978-82; rehab. cons. Rehab. Opportunities, Richmond, Va., 1981-82; pvt. practice rehab. cons. Rehab. Resources, Knoxville, 1982—. Vol. ARC, Knoxville; dir. Epilepsy Found., Knoxville. Mem. Assn. Rehab. Nurses (charter pres. Tenn. chpt. 1980-82), Nat. Assn. Rehab. Providers Pvt. Sector. Republican. Baptist. Office: 2017 Kemper Ln Knoxville TN 37920

BYRD, JOANN KATHLEEN, newspaper editor; b. Baker, Oreg., Jan. 5, 1943; d. Joe Bryant and Anne Bradford (Dickson) Green; m. James Douglas Byrd, Mar. 11, 1978; 1 child by previous marriage—Drew Joseph Gibbs. BS in Journalism, U. Oreg., 1964. Student reporter East Oregonian, Pendleton, 1956-64; reporter Spokane Daily Chronicle, 1964-69, 72-74, asst. city editor, 1974-78; city editor The Herald, Everett, Wash., 1978-81, mng. editor, 1981, exec. editor, 1981—; bd. dirs. New Directions for News, 1987—; juror 1988 Pulitzer prizes. Bd. visitors John S. Knight Fellowships, Stanford U., 1983-84, program com., 1984—; continuing studies chmn. Wash. AP News Execs., 1984-85, v.p. 1986-87, pres. 1987-88; judge Ernie Pyle awards, 1984. Mem. Am. Soc. Newspaper Editors, Am. Press Inst., Women in Communications, Soc. of Profl. Journalists, Sigma Delta Chi. Home: 7930 53d Ave W #203 Mukilteo WA 98275 Office: The Herald Grand and California Sts Everett WA 98206

BYRD, KATHLEEN MARY, state archeologist; b. Stamford, Conn., Feb. 2, 1949; s. Daniel Lester and Catherine Ruth (Byrne) Byrd; m. Robert Walter Neuman, May 4, 1980. B.A., Marquette U., 1971; M.A., La. State U., 1974; Ph.D., U. Fla., 1976. Archaeol. and zooarchaeol. cons. Baton Rouge, 1976-78; archaeologist II, State of La., Baton Rouge, 1978-79, state archaeologist, 1979—. Contbr. articles to profl. jours. Mem. La. Archaeol. Survey & Antiquities Commn., 1979—. Mem. Soc. Am. Archaeology, Soc. for Hist. Archaeology, La. Archaeol. Soc., Sigma Xi.

BYRD, MARTHA JEAN, educational administrator; b. Heathman, Miss., Mar. 10, 1928; d. Gabe Edward and Lela Elizabeth (Ponder) Lee; m. William Earl Byrd, June 3, 1952; children—Beth, David, Neil. B.A. in Elem. Edn. and Music, Millsaps Coll., 1950; M.A. in Elem. Edn. and Sch. Adminstrn., Miss. Coll., 1970, specialist in elem. edn. and adminstrn., 1974. Cert. adminstr. elem. edn., Miss. Tchr. Indianola Sch., Miss., 1950-52, Yazoo City pub. schs., Miss., 1953-55, 64-69, Benton Sch., Miss., 1955-62, Bentonia Sch., Miss., 1962-64; tchr. Manchester Acad., Yazoo City, 1969-72, prin., 1972—; Bd. dirs. Yazoo Arts Council, 1978-84; founder, pres. Mozart Music Club, 1957—; organist First Baptist Ch., Indianola, 1946-52, Yazoo City, 1954-74. Mem. Miss. Pvt. Sch. Educators Assn. (officer 1969—), Miss. Pvt. Sch. Assn. (bd. dirs. 1985), Miss. Educators Assn. (state choral dir. 1963-64), Miss. Educators Assn., Yazoo City C. of C. Republican. Baptist. Avocations: traveling; music; sewing. Home: 2046 Fenwood Terr Yazoo City MS 39194 Office: Manchester Ednl Found PO Box 155 Yazoo City MS 39194

BYRD, MICHAELE ABNER, computer software company executive; b. Bklyn., June 22, 1949; d. Philip Russell and Yvonne Edythe (Dixon) Abner; student U. Pa., 1966-68, Marymount Coll., 1968-69; B.A., U. Pa., 1971; m. David Caulbert Byrd, III, July 24, 1976. Mktg. support rep. IBM, Washington, 1971-74, mktg. support rep. staff instr., Dallas, 1974-78, mktg. support mgr., McLean, Va., 1978-79, adminstrv. systems ops. mgr., Gaithersburg, Md., 1979-81, mktg. support rep. sch. tng. mgr., Dallas, 1981-82, office systems edn. specialist, 1982-84; info. systems mktg. cons., Bethesda, Md., 1984-85; nat. tng. mgr. Temporaries, Inc., Washington, 1985-88; owner, pres. Software Edn., Inc., Rockville, Md., 1988—. Mem. Nat. Assn. Female Execs., Nat. Assn. Profl. Saleswomen, Nat. Assn. Women Bus. Owners. Home and Office: 5523 Englishman Pl Rockville MD 20852

BYRD, SANDRA JUDITH, communications company executive; b. Detroit, July 14, 1960; d. Brian Kenneth and Ruth (Jocius) Paukstys; m. Michael Keith Byrd, Nov. 23, 1985; 1 child, Kristin Michelle. Student, So. Ill. U., 1979-84. Asst. mgr. Colony West Swim Club, 1979, mgr., summers, 1980-82; aquatic supr. So. Ill. U., Carbondale, 1982; asst. mgr. Body Shop, Vero Beach, Fla., 1984; office mgr. Insta-Med Clinics, Inc., Vero Beach, 1984; receptionist Redgate Communications Corp., Vero Beach, 1985, circulation asst., 1985-87, circulation mgr., 1987—. Ill. State scholar, 1979-82. Mem. Nat. Assn. Female Execs. Home: 425 Seagrass Ave Sebastian FL 32958

BYRNE, CATHERINE (THERESE), management consulting company executive; b. N.Y.C., July 8, 1933; d. Timothy and Catherine Therese (O'Shea) B. BA, Hunter Coll., 1954. Broadcast mgr. Compton Advt. Agy., N.Y.C., 1958-69, Doremus & Co., N.Y.C., 1969-72; owner, mgr. Honey House Gourmet Foods Ltd., Higganum, Conn., 1972-81; adminstrv. asst. Archbishop of Hartford, Conn., 1981—; v.p., dir. Ross Research Inc., 1983—, T.J. Byrne Mgmt. Cons. Inc., 1985—; mem. parish council St. Peter's Cath. Ch., Higganum. Home: 691 Saybrook Rd Haddam CT 06438

BYRNE, EDITH TERESA, federal agency administrator; b. San Tome, Venezuela, Oct. 16, 1945; m. J. Hunter Williams Jr., May 27, 1978. BA, Vassar Coll., 1968. Acting dir. Gov.'s office Affirmative Action Council, Harrisburg, Pa., 1972; program assoc. Pa. Dept. of Edn., Harrisburg, 1972-75; asst. dir. Ill. Office of Edn., Chgo., 1976-78; staff asst. U.S. Drug Enforcement Adminstrn., Washington, 1979-84; chief Office of Program Support U.S. Dept. of Interior, Washington, 1984-86; special asst., dep. asst. atty. gen. U.S. Dept. of Justice, Washington, 1986—; chairperson Dept. of Justice Hispanic Employees Assn., Washington, 1987—. Mem. Assn. of Hispanic Execs., Nat. Assn. Female Execs. Office: US Dept of Justice JMD/IAS 10th St and Constitution Ave NW Washington DC 20530

BYRNE, MARY BERNADETTE, television-film packaging company executive, communications consultant; b. N.Y.C.; d. Thomas Gorman and Maurica (Lloyd) B. Student Manhattanville Coll., U. Florence; B.A., U.

Wash.; M.A., Middlebury Coll.; postgrad. Tchrs. Coll., Columbia U., Editor house organ Olivetti Corp. Am., N.Y.C., advt. specialist; publicity assoc. Time-Life Films, N.Y.C.; mgr. programming Visualscope TV div. Reeves Communications Corp., N.Y.C., dir. internat. div., v.p. parent co. in charge of Visualscope TV div., N.Y.C., officer parent co.; pres. Mary Byrne Assocs., N.Y.C., 1982—; media panelist N.Y. State Council on Arts, 1980-83. Mem. Nat. Acad. TV Arts and Scis., N.Y. Women in Film. Office: 30 W 60th St New York NY 10023

BYRON, BEVERLY BUTCHER, congresswoman; b. Balt., July 27, 1932; d. Harry C. and Ruth Butcher; m. Goodloe E. Byron, 1952 (dec.); children: Goodloe E. Jr., Barton Kimball, Mary McComas; m. B. Kirk Walsh, 1986. Student, Hood Coll., 1962-64. Mem. 96th-100th Congresses from 6th Md. Dist., 1979—; mem. armed services com., chmn. subcom. on military personnel and compensation. State treas. Md. Young Democrats, 1962, 65; bd. assocs. Hood Coll.; bd. visitors U.S. Air Force Acad.; trustee. St. Mary's Coll.; bd. dirs. Frederick County chpt. ARC; sec. Frederick Heart Assn., 1974-79; mem. Frederick Phys. Fitness Commn.; chmn. Md. Phys. Fitness Commn.; mem. Frederick County Landmarks Found.; bd. dirs. Am. Hiking Soc. Episcopalian. Home: 306 Grove Blvd Frederick MD 21701 Office: 2430 Rayburn House Office Bldg Washington DC 20515

BYRON, DANIELLE ANNE, systems analyst; b. Woodstock, Ill., Jan. 23, 1960; d. Spence D. and Barbara (Kunzer) B. BA, Northwestern U., 1982. Mktg. systems analyst Quaker Oats Co., Chgo., 1982—. Home: 6255 N Sheridan Rd 30 Chicago IL 60660 Office: Quaker Oats Co PO Box 9001 Chicago IL 60604-9001

BYRON, MARIA ELENA, corporate security professional, consultant; b. Albuquerque, Jan. 20, 1943; d. Juan Antonio and Mary Emerenciana (Otero) Candelaria; m. David John Byron, Feb. 2, 1963; children: Juan David, Michael John. BA in Comparative Lit., U. N.Mex., 1964; postgrad., Calif. State U., Hayward, 1981-85. Police officer U. Calif. Police, Berkeley, 1972-76, San Leandro (Calif.) Police Dept., 1976-77; substitute tchr. Unified Sch. Dists., So. Alameda County, Calif., 1977-78; police officer, sgt. U. Calif. Police, Berkeley and San Francisco, 1978-83; staff corp. security Pacific Bell, San Francisco, 1983-86; cons. security, pvt. investigator Hayward, Calif., 1988—. Mem. Alameda County Commn. on the Status Women, Calif., 1985-86, Leadership Devel. Program. Mex.-Am. Legal Def. and Edn. Fund, Alameda County, 1984. Mem. Calif. Women Peace Officers Assn., Latino Peace Officers Assn. Democrat. Roman Catholic.

BYRON, SISTER MICHAEA, college president; b. Waseca, Minn., Aug. 7, 1927; d. Arthur and Marion (Burns) B. BS, Coll. St. Teresa, 1954; MS, Iowa State U., 1955; PhD, U. Minn., 1974. Tchr. St. Peter Sch., St. Paul, 1948-52; mem. faculty, chairperson dept. family life Coll. St. Teresa, Winona, Minn., 1955-85, pres., 1985—; mem. accreditation team for secondary schs., Minn. Mem. LWV, Tri-Coll./Tri-County Poverty Program, Winona Area Hospice Coalition, Community Meml. Hosp. Pastoral Team, Winona Sr. Citizens Advocacy Bd.; mem. exec. council Sisters of St. Francis; chmn. bd. St. Anne's Hospice. Mem. Nat. Council Aging, Am. Gerontol. Soc., Nat. Council Family Relations, Am. Home Econ. Assn., Nat. Cath. Council Home Econs., Acad. Polit. and Social Scis., Minn. Home Econ. Assn., Minn. Home Econs. Tchr. Educators, Minn. Council on Family Relations, Winona County Home Economists, AAUW, Winona C. of C. (mem. higher edn. task force), Pi Gamma Mu, Omicron Mu, Phi Kappa Beta, Phi Lambda Theta. Roman Catholic. Office: Coll of St Teresa Office of the Pres Winona MN 55987

BYRON, RITA ELLEN COONEY, travel executive, publisher, real estate agent; b. Cleve.; d. Harry James and Marie (Hakey) Cooney; m. Carl James Byron Jr., Nov. 27, 1954 (dec.); children: Carey Lewis, Carl James, Bradford William. Student Cleve. Coll., 1954, Western Res. U., 1955, John Carroll U., 1956; PhD (hon.), Colo. State Christian Coll., 1972. Mgr. European Immigration dept. U.S. Steamship Lines, Cleve., 1956; real estate agt. W.I. White Realtor Inc., Shaker Heights, Ohio, 1965-67, J.P. Malone Realtors Inc., Shaker Heights, 1967-70, Thomas Murray & Assocs., 1971-76, Mary Anderson Realty, Shaker Heights, 1978-79, Barth Brad & Andrews Realtors Inc., Shaker Heights, 1979—, Heights Realty, 1986—; v.p., co-owner Your Connection To Travel, Kent, Ohio, 1980—; v.p., gen. mgr. World Class Travel Agy., 1985—; dir. Travel One div. Quaker Sq., Akron, Travel Trends for Singles, 1985, Playhouse Sq. Travel, 1986, World Class Internat., 1986. Mem. U.S. Figure Skating Assn., 1960—, Wightman Cup Women's Com., 1965—; mem. women's com. Cleve. Mus. of Art, 1969—, Friendship Force Ohio, 1986 ; co-chmn. Cleve. Invitational Figure Skating Competition, 1972—; chmn. Gold Rush Rush, U.S. Ski Team, 1982, Cleve. benefit U.S. Olympic Teams, Midas Touch, 1983, Gran Apres-Ski Prix, 1981, blue ribbon ball Hunt Club for Handicapped; patron Cleve. 500, 1983; originator Benefits Unltd., Exceptional Single Person's, Connections Unltd., 1983; founder, coordinator Singled Out Club, 1983; co-ptnr., adv. bd. The Service Service, 1984; benefit chmn., patroness various balls and fund-raising events; vol. Foster Parents Inc., 1983; vol. Council on World Affairs, 1983, Bellefaire Home for Spl. Children, 1983, Big Sisters Greater Cleve., 1983, Camp Cheerful, 1983, Chisholm Ctr., 1983, Children's Diabetic Camp Ho Mita Koda, 1984, Young Audiences, 1985; adv. trustee Friends of Fairmount Theatre of the Deaf, 1983; mem. Greater Cleve. Growth Assn., 1983. Mem. Western Res. Hist. Soc., Garden Ctr. Greater Cleve., Friends Cleve. Pub. Library, UN Assn. of U.S., Cleve. Council World Affairs, U.S. Ski Ednl. Fund (chmn. benefits), English Speaking Union (jr. bd.), Travel Age Exchange, Globetrotters Internat. Fedn. Women's Travel Orgns., North Coast Exec. Women's Network, Growth Assn., Council on Small Enterprises. Cleve. Real Estate Bd. Clubs: Cleve. Skating, Broadmoor World Arena Figure Skating, Colony Beach and Racquet, Suburban Ski, Cleve. Advertising, Communicator's, Towne Hall, Women's City, Gilmour Acad. Women's, Mid-Day, Cleve. Wellesley, Arctic Circle, Intrepid Traveler, Tibet, Mongolia and China Explorers', Himalaya Yeti (1987 Nepal Expdn.). Co-pub., exec. editor The Single Register, other publs.; featured in numerous publs. Home: 18126 Lomond Blvd Shaker Heights OH 44122 Office: World Class Travel 3520 Ingleside Rd Shaker Heights OH 44122 Also Office: Es Turo Edificio, Kontiki, Majorica Balearic Islands Spain

BYRUM, MARNI ELAINE, lawyer; b. Warrenton, N.C., Apr. 16, 1955; d. Charles Curtis and Maxine (George) Byrum. BA, Va. Poly. Inst. and State U., 1976; JD, Pepperdine U., 1979. Bar: Va. 1979, U.S. Supreme Ct. 1983, D.C. 1987. Atty.-advisor Fed. Labor Relations Authority, Washington, 1979-82, exec. asst. to mem. authority, 1982-83, asst. to chmn., 1983-84; pvt. practice, 1984—; arbitrator Better Bus. Bur., Washington, 1980-87. advisor Va. State Task Force on Missing and Abused Children. Recipient Spl. Achievement cert. Fed. Labor Relations Authority, 1983-84; named Outstanding Young Woman Am., 1980, 81, 83, 84-87. Mem. ABA (law student div. liaison 1978-79, Silver Key award 1978-79), Va. State Bar, Va. Women's Attys. Assn. (bd. dirs. 1986-88, pres.-elect 1988—), Women's Bar Assn., Phi Alpha Delta (internat. assoc. tribune 1986—, dist. justice 1979-86), Legal Svcs. North Va. (bd. dirs. 1986—). Office: Fed Labor Relations Authority 2009 N 14th St Suite 412 Arlington VA 22201

BYRUM-ELLERMAN, KAY FRANCES, financial planning executive; b. Dover, Ohio, Jan. 29, 1942; d. Charles Woodrow Stahl and Marjorie Augusta (Knight) Simonson; m. Ron Eugene Byrum, Mar. 12, 1968 (div. 1976); children: Karen Kay, Robert Allen; m. James Howard Ellerman, Oct. 13, 1984. Student, Cerritos Jr. Coll., 1959-61, Coll. for Fin. Planning, Denver, 1987—. Asst. to chmn., chief exec. officer Denny's, Inc., La Mirada, Calif., 1973-79; career agt. N.Y. Life Ins. Co., Fullerton, Calif., 1979-81; exec. v.p. Fin. Services Unltd., Inc., Newport Beach, Calif., 1981—, seminar speaker, 1982—. Bd. dirs. YWCA, Santa Ana, Calif., 1986—. Named Orange County Woman of Excellence Woman's World Internat., 1985. Mem. Internat. Assn. Fin. Planners. Republican. Clubs: WeCan (pres. 1987—); Women in Bus. (bd. dirs. 1984-86). Home: 2175 Via Teca San Clemente CA 92672 Office: Fin Services Unltd Inc 24411 Ridge Rt Suite 220 Laguna Hills CA 92653

BYSIEWICZ, SHIRLEY RAISSI, lawyer, educator; b. Enfield, Conn.; d. Kyriakos and Anna (Gavala) Raissi; m. Stanley J. Bysiewicz, July 18, 1959; children: Susan, Walter John, Karen, Gail. B.A., J.D., M.S. in L.S, U. Conn. Bar: Conn. 1954. Mem. firm Raissi & Raissi, Enfield, 1954—; faculty U. Conn., West Hartford, 1956—; prof. law U. Conn., law librarian., 1956-83; Mem. Permanent Commn. on Status Women for Conn., 1976-80, pres., 1978-79; mem. Conn. Law Library Adv. Com., 1976—; mem. Conn. Law Revision Commn., 1980—, co-pres., 1987—; Superior Ct. referee; mem. Conn. Law Revision Commn., 1980—; founder Conn. Women's Edn. and Legal Fund. Author: (with Max White) Forms of Town Government in Connecticut, 1954, Survey of County Law Libraries in Connecticut, 1967, Dictionary of Legal Terms, 1983, Selected Annotated Bibliography on Education for Professional Responsibility, 1968, (with Weckstein) Effective Legal Research, 1979; bus. mgr.: Law Library Jour, 1968-72; editor: Connecticut Juvenile Law Handbook, 1985, Sources of Conneticut Law, 1987; co-editor: (with Whitman) Materials on Estate Planning, 1969. Contbr. law articles to profl. jours. Mem. Bar Assn. Conn. (treas. 1975-78), Nat. Assn. Women Lawyers, ABA, Hartford County Bar Assn. (exec. com.), Conn. Bar Assn. (presider juvenile justice coms. 1982-85, women lawyers sect.), Am. Assn. Law Schs. (co-presider sect. on status of women, sect. legal research 1974), Am. Assn. Law Librarians (law library jour. com., sec. 1980-83), U. Conn. Law Sch. Alumni Assn. (exec. sec. 1958-68), New Eng. Law Librarians (pres. 1970), Women's Equity Action League, Delta Zeta. Greek Orthodox. Home: S Plumb Rd Middletown CT 06457 Office: 65 Elizabeth St Hartford CT 06105

CABANAS, ELIZABETH ANN, food service administration executive; b. Port Arthur, Tex., Oct. 27, 1948; d. William Rosser and Frances Merle (Block) Thornton. BS, U. Tex., 1971; MPH, U. Hawaii, 1973. Registered dietitian. Clin. nutritionist Family Planning Inst., Honolulu, 1972-74; dietitian Kauikeolani Hosp., Honolulu, 1974-75; dietitian San Antonio Ind. Schs., 1975-84, asst. food service adminstr., 1984—; lectr. nutrition U. Hawaii, Honolulu, 1974-75; lectr. St. Mary's U., San Antonio Coll., 1984—; cons. in field. Contbr. articles to profl. jours. Mem. Allegro San Antonio Symphony Orch., 1984—, Texans for Barberra, San Antonio, 1986. Mem. Am. Dietetic Assn., Am. Sch. Food Service Assn., Tex. Sch. Food Service Assn. (dist. bd. dirs. 1977-78), San Antonio Sch. Food Service Assn. (com. chmn. 1975—), Tex. Assn. Sch. Bus. Ofcls., Tex. Restaurant Assn., San Antonio Adminstrs. Assn., San Antonio Mus. Assn., Randolph C. of C. Republican. Methodist. Clubs: Hawaii (chmn. entertainment com. 1983), Los Amigos Ski (San Antonio). Home: 13643 Oak Meadows Universal City TX 78148 Office: San Antonio Ind Sch Dist 806 N Salado San Antonio TX 78207

CABATIT-SEGAL, BETSY ROZELLS, educational administrator; b. Penang, Brit. Malaysia, Feb. 27, 1932; came to U.S., 1957, naturalized, 1969; d. Fructoso Ramos and Mathilda (Rozells) Cabatit; m. Marvin Segal, Dec. 17, 1974. B.S. in Nursing, U. Philippines, 1955; M.A. in Edn., U. Chgo., 1960. Instr. U. Philippines, Quezon City, 1955-56; chmn. med./surg. nursing U. Nueva Caceres, Philippines, 1956-57, Philippine Women's U., Manila, 1961-64; USA exchange vis. staff nurse Cook County Hosp., Chgo., 1957-60, instr., 1960-61, 64-65; instr. U. Ill., Chgo., 1965-68; dir. staff devel. Rush-Presbyterian St. Luke's Hosp., Chgo., 1968-69; instr. Coll. of DuPage, Glen Ellyn, Ill., 1970-74, asst. dean, 1970-78, assoc. dean, assoc. prof. health and public services, 1978—; mem. task force Coalition for Preservation Ill. Nurse Practice Act, 1986—; mem. health occupations adv. council Ill. State Bd. Edn, 1984—. Mem. bd. dirs. Edn. Network for Older Adults, Chgo., 1980—, DuPage County Heart Assn., Ill., 1980—; cons. Excellence in Edn., Ohio Bd. Regents, 1986; mem. Ill. Community Coll. Coalition for Advancement of Assoc. Degree Nursing; trustee DuPage Med. Soc. Found. Public Adminstrn. scholar, 1961. Mem. Am. Nurses' Assn., Ill. Nurses' Assn. (del. to Internat. Nurses Assn. conv. Chgo. 1978, 83, 85), Nat. League Nursing, Ill. League Nursing, Am. Soc. Allied Health Professions', Ill. Assn. Allied Health Professions' (treas. 1981-82), Health Edn. Resources Council for No. Ill. (pres. 1980-81), Philippine Nurses Assn. Chgo. (pres. 1967-68, 75-76), Am. Assn. Community and Jr. Colls. Women Adminstrs., Ill. Vocat. Assn. (mem. council of local adminstrs. 1980—), Ill. Health Occupations Assn., Nat. Orgn. for Advancement of Assoc. Degree Nursing. Democrat. Roman Catholic. Office: Coll DuPage Main Campus Adminstrn 22d St and Lamber Glen Ellyn IL 60137

CABRINETY, PATRICIA BUTLER, software company executive; b. Earlville, N.Y., Sept. 4, 1932; d. Eugene Thomas and Helen Sylvester (Fulmer) Butler; m. Lawrence Paul Cabrinety, Aug. 20, 1955; children: Linda Anne, Margaret Marie, Stephen Michael. BS in Elem. Edn. and Music, SUNY, Potsdam, 1954. Cert. tchr. N.Y., Pa., Minn., Mass. Asst. tchr. music Hamilton (N.Y.) Cen. Sch., 1948-50; tchr. Cherry Lane Sch., Suffern, N.Y., 1954-56; instr. music, Towanda, Pa., 1960-63, Sayre, Pa., 1963-79; pres. Superior Software Inc., Mpls., 1981—; poet and illustrator, Edina, Minn., 1981—; cons. in field. Composer, artist numerous compositions; inventor: Musical for Computer, 1981; author monthly column on Boy Scouts, 1975-78, also more than 70 pub. poems and 35 pub. illustrations. Recipient Golden Poet award World of Poetry, 1985-87, Poet of Month award All Season's Poetry, 1986, Vantage Press Invitational award, 1985-88, Poet of Month award Editor's Desk, 1986, Internat. Poet award, 1986. Mem. Nat. Assn. Female Execs., Am. Soc. Profl. and Exec. Women, Nat. Assn. Bus. and Profl. Women, Nat. Writers Assn., Am. Mgmt. Assn., DAR, AAUW, Pioneers, Legion of Mary, Third Order Carmelite, Mpls. Music Tchrs. Forum, Edina C. of C., Worcester County Music Assn., Worcester County Poetry Assn. Avocations: philately, art, needlecraft, photography, outdoor activities. Home: 925 Pearl Hill Rd Fitchburg MA 01420 Office: Superior Software Inc PO Box 113 7074 Amundson Ave Minneapolis MN 55435

CACCAMISE, GENEVRA LOUISE BALL (MRS. ALFRED E. CACCAMISE), retired librarian; b. Mayville, N.Y., July 22, 1934; d. Herbert Oscar and Genevra (Green) Ball; B.A., Stetson U., DeLand, Fla., 1956; M.S. in L.S., Syracuse U., 1967; m. Alfred E. Caccamise, July 7, 1974. Tchr. grammar sch., Sanford, Fla., 1956-57, elem. sch., Longwood, Fla., 1957-58; tchr., librarian Enterprise (Fla.) Sch., 1958-63; librarian, media specialist Boston Ave. Sch., DeLand, 1963-82; head media specialist Blue Lake Sch., DeLand, 1982-87; ret., 1987. Charter mem. West Volusia Meml. Hosp. aux., DeLand, 1962—; Girl Scout leader, 1955-56; area dir. Fla. Edn. Assn., Volusia county, 1963-65; bd. dirs. Alhambra Villas Home Owners Assn., 1972-75; trustee, pres., DeLand Pub. Library, v.p. Friends of DeLand Pub. Library, 1987. Mem. AAUW (2d v.p. chpt. 1965-67, rec. sec. 1961-65, 78-80, pres. 1980-82, parliamentarian 1982-84), Assn. Childhood Edn. (1st v.p. 1965-66, corr. sec. 1963-65), DAR (chpt. registrar 1969—; asst. chief page Continental Congress, Washington 1962-65), Bus. and Profl. Women's Club (corr. sec. DeLand 1968-71, 2d v.p. 1969-70), Stetson U. Alumni Assn. (class chmn. for ann. fund drive 1968), Volusia County Assn. Media in Edn. (treas.), Volusia County Retired Educators Assn., Unit II, 1988, Soc. of Mayflower Descendants (pres. Francis Cook Colony, 1988), Pilgrim John Howland Soc., Colonial Dames XVII Century, Magna Charta Dames, Delta Kappa Gamma (pres. Beta Psi chpt.). Democrat. Episcopalian. An author Volusia County manual Instructing the Library Assistant, 1965. Address: PO Box 241 De Land FL 32721

CACIOPPO, LISA JANE, public relations executive; b. Passaic, N.J., Mar. 9, 1960; d. Peter John Cacioppo and Doris (Mowen) Senack. BA in English and Journalism, U. Mass., 1982; MS in Corp. and Internat. Pub. Affairs., Boston U., 1988. Features editor Setonian, South Orange, N.J., 1979; staff reporter Today, Wayne, N.J., 1980, Times-Observer, Toms River, N.J., 1981; v.p. Sales Presentation Aids Co., Manahawkin, N.J., 1982-85; pres. ASC/PR & Advt., Newton, Mass., 1985—; cons. Rational Systems, Natick, Mass., 1987, Binary Engring., Waltham, Mass., 1987, Adra Systems, Lowell, Mass., 1987, MathWorks, Sherborn, Mass., 1987, Epoch Systems, Marlborough, Mass., 1988, Wellfleet, Bedford, Mass., 1988, ICAD, Cambridge, Mass., 1988, EventTechs., Waltham, 1988, Digital, Maynard, Mass., 1988, Natural MicroSystems, Natick, 1988, ReflectionTech., Cambridge, 1988, Senack Industries, Franklin Lakes, N.J., 1985-86, Lanen Co., Wellesley, Mass., 1986, UN, Boston, 1986, Dudley, Anderson & Yutzy, N.Y.C., 1985. Mem. Nat. Orgn. Female Execs., Women in Communication. Home and Office: 75 Norwood Ave Newton MA 02159

CACKOWSKI, IRENE KATHLEEN, librarian; b. Englewood, N.J., Sept. 9, 1946; d. Richard Jerome and Kathleen Elyse (Andrews) Dunphy; m. Leonard Francis Cackowski, July 11, 1970; children—Kathleen, Beth and Celia (twins). B.A., Coll. New Rochelle (N.Y.), 1968; M.L.S., L.I. U., Greenvale, N.Y., 1969. Cert. pub. librarian, ednl. media specialist, N.J. Library asst. New Rochelle Pub. Library, 1968-69, children's librarian, 1969; children's librarian Johnson Pub. Library, Hackensack, N.J., 1969-70; librarian South River High Sch. (N.J.), 1970-72; dir. South River Pub. Library, 1972-88 ; regional supt. librarian Ocean County Library, 1988—. Bd. dirs. Woodbridge Devel. Ctr., 1983-88; pres. bd. Literacy Vols. Middlesex County, N.J., 1981-86; sec. exec. bd. Regional Library Coop. Mem. ALA, N.J. Library Assn., Library Pub. Relations Council, Libraries of Middlesex (pres. 1983-84). Home: 15 Henry St East Brunswick NJ 08816 Office: Ocean County Library 101 Washington St Toms River NJ 08753

CADWELL, KAREN LYNN DELANEY, corporate executive; b. DuBois, Pa., Apr. 9, 1957; d. Michael Jerome Delaney and Mary Constance (Guth) Stuyvesant; m. Robert Morris Cadwell, Sept. 11, 1982. Student, Duquesne U., 1976-78, George Washington U., 1982. Clk. admissions DuBois Hosp., 1973-77; mgr. adminstrv. services Vector Group Inc., Pitts., 1976-80; supr. UFCW, Washington, 1980-84; mgr. office InterBank, Washington, 1985-86; v.p. adminstrv. services Med. Care Mgmt. Systems, Bradenton, Fla., 1986—. Vol. Mondale-Ferraro campaign, Washington, 1984; instr. CPR Red Cross, 1979-81, 87—. Mem. Nat. Assn. Female Execs., Am. Soc. Personnel Adminstrn., United Food Community Workers Union, NAACP, Am. Com. Sane Nuclear Policy. Democrat. Roman Catholic. Home: 6632 Schooner Bay Circle Sarasota FL 34231

CADY, JANET ARLENE, association executive; b. Atlanta, Mich., Aug. 19, 1949; d. Arthur F. and Jean M. (Maanika) C.; m. Jeffrey M. Davidson. Student Oakland U., 1967-69; B.A. with high honors, Mich. State U., 1971; postgrad. Taiwan Normal U., 1972-74; M.A., U. Mich., 1975. Pub. relations officer Chinese Acupuncture Sci. Research Found., Taipei, Taiwan, 1972-74; project asst. Chinese econ. studies program U. Mich., 1975-77; program dir. internat. Asian studies program Yale-China Assn., New Haven, 1977-78; program dir. Nat. Com. U.S.-China Relations, N.Y.C., 1978-86; dir. Tufts-China Exec. Devel. Program Tufts U., 1986—. Mem. Assn. Asian Studies, Nat. Assn. Fgn. Student Affairs, Yale-China Assn., Fgn. Policy Assn., World Affairs Council, Nat. Com. US-China Relations, Nat. Council for the Social Studies, Phi Beta Kappa, Phi Kappa Phi. Editor: Understanding China newsletter, 1974-75; (with E.A. Winckler) Urban Planning in China: Report of the U.S. Urban Planners Delegation to the People's Republic of China, 1980; Economic Reform in the People's Republic of China, 1985; author: Historic Preservation in the People's Republic of China, 1984; contbg. author: Urban Innovation Abroad: Problem Cities in Search of Solutions, 1984.

CADY, JANET LYNN, systems analyst; b. Merkel, Tex., Apr. 10, 1960; d. Royce Marion and Dolores Dale (Bullock) Shoemate; m. Louis Byron Cady, May 13, 1984. BS, Howard Payne U., 1984. Programmer, analyst Am. Nat. Ins. Co., Galveston, Tex., 1984-85; cons. Houston Met. Ministries, 1985-86; systems analyst Unisys, Houston, 1986-87; programmer, analyst III System One Corp., Houston, 1987—; cons. Harry Rice, Inc., Galveston, 1986; owner Apex Computer Cons., 1986—. Mem. Nat. Assn. For Female Execs., U.S. Chess Fedn. Baptist. Club: Galveston Gun. Home: 510 Ninth St Galveston TX 77550 Office: System One CorpOps 8451-A Houston TX 77006

CADY, NELL GOODHUE, investment banker; b. Boston, May 10, 1961; d. Kendall Bingham Cady and Carol Helen (Conrad) Keyser. B.S. with honors, Cornell U., 1984, M.B.A., 1985. Intern trade fin. Continental Ill. Nat. Bank, Chgo., summer 1982; Intern Gt. Lakes dist. Mfrs. Hanover Trust, N.Y.C., summer 1984; trainee Bankers Trust Co., N.Y.C., 1985-86, assoc. leveraged buyouts, 1986-87, v.p. leveraged buyouts, 1988—. Republican. Episcopalian. Avocations: sailing; scuba diving, skiing. Office: Bankers Trust Co 280 Park Ave New York NY 10017

CAFFERATA, PATRICIA ANN, advertising executive; b. Smithville, Mo., Sept. 6, 1944; d. Jack and E. Agnes (Sims) Shepherd; m. D. Michael Cafferata, Mar. 27, 1976; 1 child, Diane L. BS in Home Econs. cum laude, N.W. Mo. State U., 1969. Research assoc. Barickman Advt., Kansas City, Mo., 1969-73; research assoc. Needham, Harper and Steers, Chgo., 1973-74, assoc. research dir., 1974-82, sr. v.p., research dir., 1982-87; pres., chief exec. officer Young and Rubicam, Chgo., 1987—. Mem. The Adv. Council J.L. Kellogg Grad. Sch. Mgmt. Northwestern U., Evanston, Ill., 1987, pres. council Museum Sci. and Industry, Chgo., 1987; bd. dirs. James Webb Young Fund U. Ill., 1987, Chgo. Area Council Boy Scouts Am., 1987, Mus. Broadcast Communicatins, Chgo., 1987. Mem. Am. Psychol. Assn., Am. Mktg. Assn., The Chgo. Network. Clubs: Chgo. Advt. (bd. dirs. 1986-87), Women's Advt., Econ. of Chgo. Office: Young & Rubicam Chgo 111 E Wacker Dr Chicago IL 60601

CAFFEY-FLEMING, DOLORES EMILY, child development specialist; b. Providence, R.I., May 5, 1947; d. Walter Floyd and Jacqueline (Holland) Caffey; m. Arthur W. Fleming, Apr. 8, 1978; 1 child, Erik S. BS, Howard U., 1968, MS, 1969. Pre-kindergarten tchr. D.C. Pub. Schs., Washington, 1968-83; counselor Women's Med. Ctr., Washington, 1972-83; instr. Dept. of Leisure Services, Rancho Palos Verdes, Calif., 1987—; staff Rolling Hills Country Day Sch., Rolling Hills Estates, Calif., 1987—. vol. King-Drew Med. Ctr., Los Angeles, 1983—; active Friends of Drew, Los Angeles, 1983—; den leader Cub Scouts Am. Mem. Am. Fedn. of Tchrs., Nat. Med. Assn. (aux.), Golden State Med. Assn. (aux.), Charles R. Drew Med. Soc. (aux.), Black Heritage Assn. of Palos Verdes, Inc., Art at Your Fingertips (docent), Omicron Nu. Club: UCLA Med. Faculty Wives. Home: 6671 Crest Rd Rancho Palos Verdes CA 90274 Office: Rolling Hills Country Day Sch 26444 Crenshaw Blvd Rolling Hills Estates CA 90274

CAGGINE, CAROLYN CASSANDRA, publishing executive; b. Bklyn., Nov. 12, 1932; d. Charles Cosmo and Rose Louise (Daversa) C. BA cum laude, St. John's U., Jamaica, N.Y., 1954. Reprint editor Prentice-Hall, Inc., Englewood Cliffs, N.J., 1954-58; asst. editor Dun & Bradstreet, Inc., N.Y.C., 1958-59; mng. editor Promenade Mags., Inc., N.Y.C., 1959-70; dir. publs. Girl Scouts U.S.A., N.Y.C., 1970—, mng. editor Girl Scout of the U.S.A. Leader mag., 1984—. Republican. Roman Catholic. Office: Girl Scouts USA 830 Third Ave New York NY 10022

CAGGINS, RUTH PORTER, nurse, educator; b. Natchez, Miss., July 11, 1945; d. Henry Chappelle and Corinne Sadie (Baines) Porter; m. Don Randolph Caggins, July 1, 1978; children—Elva Rene, Don Randolph, Myles Thomas Chapelle. B.A., Dillard U., New Orleans, 1967; M.A., N.Y.U., 1973; doctoral candidate Tex. Woman's U., 1987—. Staff nurse Montefiore Hosp., Bronx, 1968-70, head nurse, 1970-72; nurse clinician Met. Hosp., N.Y.C., 1973-74, clin. supr., 1974-76; asst. prof. U. S.W. La., Lafayette, 1976-78, Prairie View A&M U. Coll. Nursing, Houston, 1978—. Mem., The Links Inc., Houston, 1982-86, Cultural Arts Council, Houston. Mem. Am. Nurses Assn., Am. Group Psychology Assn., A.K. Rice Inst., Houston Group Psychotherapy Soc., Sigma Theta Tau, Delta Sigma Theta. Democrat. Baptist. Avocations: Singing; sewing; traveling; aerobics; writing; teaching. Home: 5602 Goettee Circle Houston TX 77091 Office: Prairie View A&M U Coll Nursing 6436 Fannin Houston TX 77030

CAGLE, DIANE DAY, county official; b. Greenville, S.C., Jan. 29, 1946; d. Ivey Edward and Carrie (Gossett) Day; m. Allan Bill Cagle, Apr. 17, 1971; 1 child, Allan Ivey. Student, Draughon's Bus. Coll., Greenville, 1966. Sec. Indian Head Yarn Co., Greenville, 1964-69; v.p., sec. Dixie Iron & Metal Co., Greenville, 1969-84; magistrate Greenville County, 1984—. Mem. S.C. Magistrtaes Assn., Westcliff Community Club, Greenville Profl. Women, S.C. Numismatic Assn. Baptist. Club: Greenville Coin. Home: 521 Westcliffe Way Greenville SC 29611 Office: Greenville County Magistrate's Office 6247 White Horse Rd Greenville SC 29611

CAHILL, LISA SOWLE, educator, author, lecturer; b. Phila., Mar. 27, 1948; d. Donald Edgar and Gretchen Elizabeth (MacRae) Sowle; m. Lawrence R. Cahill, Mar. 25, 1972; children—Charlotte Mary, James Donald. B.A., U. Santa Clara, 1970; M.A., U. Chgo., 1973, Ph.D., 1976. Instr., Concordia Coll., Moorhead, Minn., 1976; asst. prof. theology Boston Coll., Chestnut Hill, 1976-82, assoc. prof. theology, 1982—; vis. scholar Kennedy Inst. Ethics Georgetown U., fall 1986. Author: Between the Sexes: Toward a Christian Ethics of Sexuality, 1985. Contbr. articles to profl. jours.; assoc. editor Religious Studies Rev., 1981—, Jour. Religious Ethics, 1981—; adv. bd. Logos: Philos. Issues in Christian Perspective, Jour. of Law and Religion, 1983—; assoc. editor Horizons: A Publ. of the Coll. Theology Soc., 1983—. Active Instnl. Rev. Bd. Harvard Community Health Plan,

1979-85; mem. bioethics com. March of Dimes, 1985—; mem. theology and ethics com. Cath. Hosp. Assn., 1985—. Boston Coll. Summer Research grantee, 1977; Faculty fellow, 1986. Mem. Am. Acad. Religion (program com. 1979-82), Soc. Christian Ethics (dir. 1983-86). Cath. Theol. Soc. Am. (moral theology steering com. 1984-87), Coll. Theology Soc. Democrat. Office: Boston Coll Dept Theology Chestnut Hill MA 02167

CAHILL, PAMELA LEE, state legislator; b. Belfast, Maine; d. B.D. and Catherine (Snow) Sanborn; m. Bradley W. Cahill; children: Veronica Lynn, Brandon. Student, U. Maine. Former mem. Maine Ho. of Reps.; mem. Maine State Senate. Exec. dir. Reagan-Busch campaign, Maine, 1984. Republican. Address: Office of the State Senate Augusta ME 04333 *

CAHILL, PHYLLIS HENDERSON, marketing executive, educator; b. Phila., Nov. 5, 1954; d. Phyllis Henderson Garofalo; m. Peter Joseph Cahill, Mar. 26, 1977 (div. June 1982). B.S. in Food Mktg., St. Joseph's Coll., Phila., 1976; student Carnegie Inst., 1982-83. Cert. instr. numerous Dale Carnegie courses. Account rep. Quaker Oats Co., Cranford, N.Y., 1976-77; mktg. mgr. Lumex, Inc., Bayshore, N.Y., 1978, Foodmaker, Inc., Hauppauge, N.Y., 1979, Yorkshire Food Sales, New Hyde Park, N.Y., 1980-84, CutCo Industries, Jericho, N.Y., 1984-86; mgr. advt. and sales promotion Nutri/System, Willow Grove, Pa., 1986—. Home: 350 Hilltop #104 King of Prussia PA 19406 Office: Nutri/System 3901 Commerce Ave Willow Grove PA 19090

CAHILL, TERI MARIE, electrical engineer; b. Corona, Calif., Dec. 26, 1956; d. Ambrose Brian and Margaret (Huber) C. B in Math, Harvey Mudd Coll., 1978; MSEE, Loyola Marymount U., Los Angeles, 1983. Tech. staff Aerojet Electrosystems, Azusa, Calif., 1978-82, Hughes Aircraft, El Segundo, Calif., 1982; research scientist Teledyne Systems, Northridge, Calif., 1982—. V.p. Etiwanda Townhomes Condominium Assn., Reseda, Calif., 1987—. Mem. Soc. Women Engrs. (sr. mem.), Tau Beta Pi, Alpha Sigma Nu. Libertarian. Home: 7115 Etiwanda #13 Reseda CA 91335 Office: Teledyne Systems 19601 Nordhoff/MS53 Northridge CA 91324

CAHILL-TRYON, JANE ANN, public relations executive; b. Portage, Wis., Sept. 13, 1950; d. Kenneth John and Norene Alta (Carney) Solheim; m. Lee A. Tryon, Nov. 3, 1979 (div. 1986); 1 child, Sarah Jane Scultz. Degree, Maraine Park Tech. Sch., 1970; student, U. Wis., Oshkosh, 1972. Planning coordinator Advocap, Inc., Fond du Lac, Wis., 1972-74, dir. community services, 1974-79; exec. dir. Skilled Jobs for Women, Madison, Wis., 1980-83; ptnr. Cahill, Wolfgram & Assocs., Madison, 1983—. Chair Odyssey, Inc., Madison, 1984-87. Republican. Office: Cahill Wolfgram & Assocs 30 W Mifflin #502 Madison WI 53703

CAILLIEZ, LINDA JOYCE, educator; b. Detroit, Dec. 5, 1943; d. George William and Agnes Anita (Stoffer) Munro; m. Donald Craig Cailliez, Sept. 3, 1970 (div. 1987); children: Jason, Margeaux. BA in Edn., Theater and English, Hope Coll., 1965; MA in Edn., Lang. Arts, Mich. State U., 1968. Cert. elem., secondary tchr., Mich. Secondary educator Springlake (Mich.) Pub. Schs., 1965-66, Kalamazoo Pub. Schs., 1966-67; elem. educator St. John's (Mich.) Pub. Schs., 1968-69, Lansing (Mich.) Pub. Schs., 1969-71; dir. youth devel. Mpls. YWCA, 1972-76; dir. body shop Meth. Hosp., Mpls., 1977-82, dir. body shop U.S.A., 1983—; Dir. story theater players YWCA, Mpls., 1974-76; counselor youth devel. YMCA, Mpls., 1976-77; cons. program devel. health orgns., nationwide, 1982—; nat. speaker in field, 1980—. Author: (program package) The Body Shop. Den leader Boy Scouts of Am., Mpls., 1984; liason legis. action Minnetonka (Minn.) Pub. Schs., 1987—. Mem. Assn. for the Care of Child Health, Nat. Wellness Inst., Am.Soc. for Hosp. Pub. Relations (MacEachern award 1984), Internat. Assn. Bus. Communicators (Gold Quill award 1984), Ctr. for Adolescent Obesity, Am. Pub. Health Assn., Pi Kappa Delta (award of Excellence 1963), Pi Epsilon Delta. Office: Nat Youth Wellness Ctr PO Box 565 Excelsior MN 55331

CAILLOUETTE, JOY MELINDA, communications executive; b. Chattanooga, Tenn., Dec. 13, 1952; d. Harry Henderson and Julia Marie (Graves) C. Graphic designer The Printery, Harriman, Tenn., 1980-82, Graffix Inc., Knoxville, Tenn., 1982-83; graphics equipment coordinator Whittle Communications, Knoxville, 1983—. Judge Student Photography Competition, U. Tenn., 1987. Mem. Am. Mgmt. Assn., Nat. Assn. for Female Execs., Cousteau Soc., Profl. Assn. Diving Instrs. Democrat. Methodist. Office: Whittle Communications 505 Market St Knoxville TN 37902

CAIN, CARLEN YVONNE, nurse; b. Hahn, Fed. Republic Germany, Sept. 30, 1956 (parents Am. citizens); d. James Richard, Jr. and Georgia (Yelverton) Cain. Assoc. Nursing, Jones County Jr. Coll., 1976; B.S. in Nursing, U. Miss., 1984; advanced cardiac life support tng., 1984. R.N., Miss.; cert. CPR instr. Surg. nurse Miss. Bapt. Med. Ctr., Jackson, 1976; med.-surg. nurse Smith County Hospital Raleigh, Miss., 1977-80; emergency room nurse, ambulance supr. Covington County Hosp., Collins, Miss., 1980-83; staff nurse, adult emergency room, mem. flight team Lifestar I. U. Miss. Med. Ctr., Jackson, 1983-84; staff nurse ICU/CCU, River Oaks Hosp., Flowood, Miss., 1984-86; nursing edn. instr. dept. hosp. edn. St. Dominic Jackson Meml. Hosp., 1986—; mem. health care team The Care-A-Van. Mem. Am. Nurses Assn., Miss. Nurses Assn., H.A.R.E. Educators Assn., Jones County Jr. Coll. Alumni Assn., SHARE (south cen. health and related educators assn.), Committee for the Share Assn. U. Miss. Sch. Nursing Alumni Assn., Am. Heart Assn., Miss. Heart Assn. Baptist. Home: 2945 Layfair Dr #315 Jackson MS 39208 Office: St Dominic Jackson Meml Hosp Lakeland Dr Jackson MS 39208

CAIN, DEBORAH ANNE, insurance company executive, researcher; b. Glen Ridge, N.J., Apr. 26, 1947; d. Donald and Sarah Elizabeth (Youngs) Crosby; m. Russel Byron Cain, Feb. 21, 1970 (div. Oct. 1972); 1 child, Sarah. Student, U. Vt., 1965-67; BFA, Bowling Green (Ohio) State U., 1969. Systems analyst The Hartford (Conn.) Ins. Group, 1978-83, applications supr., 1983-86, assoc. knowledge engr., 1986—. Presbyterian. Office: Hartford Ins Group Hartford Plaza Hartford CT 06115

CAIN, FLORINE KLATT, engineer; b. Joliet, Ill., June 1, 1928; d. Fred George and Mildred Carletta (Schmuhl) Klatt; m. A. Chaney Bender, Mar. 3 1951 (dec. Dec. 1953); m. Richard Alton Cain, Nov. 24, 1954. BS in Aero. Engring., Purdue U., 1951. Design/test eng. Armour Research Found., Ill. Inst. Tech., Chgo., 1951-54; sr. missile test engr., coordinator satellite ground support equipment Lockheed Missile Div., Van Nuys, Calif., 1954-62; proj. engr. nuclear hardness surveillance Minuteman Missile Program Autonetics Strategic Systems div. Rockwell Internat., Anaheim, Calif., 1962—. Recipient Commendation award NASA, 1961. Mem. Nat. Mgmt. Club. Republican. Club: Watercolor West. Home: 14 Lago Norte Irvine CA 92715 Office: Rockwell Internat 3370 Miraloma Anaheim CA 92303

CAIN, JOANNA MARY, gynecologist, oncologist, educator; b. Yakima, Wash., July 11, 1950; d. Estill Virgil and Marguerite E. (Bottker) Cain; m. C. Norman Turrill, May 18, 1974. B.S., U. Wash., Seattle, 1973; M.D., Creighton U., Omaha, 1977. Diplomate Am. Bd. Ob-gyn. Resident in ob-gyn U. Washington, 1977-81; fellow in gyn.-oncology Meml. Sloan Kettering Cancer Ctr., N.Y.C., 1981-83; asst. attending physician, 1983-85; asst. prof. U. Wash., Seattle, 1985—. Contbr. articles to med. publs. Am. Cancer Soc. jr. clin. fellow, 1981-83; Am. Cancer Soc. faculty fellow, 1984-86. Fellow Am. Coll. Ob-Gyn (jr.); mem. N.Y. Acad. Sci., Soc. Gynecol. Oncologists. Office: U Wash RH-20 Div Gynecol Oncology Seattle WA 98195

CAIN, JULIE ANNE, former art gallery administrator; b. Houston, Sept. 21, 1956; d. Thomas Edward and Therese Catherine (Arnold) C. BA, Vanderbilt U., 1978. Salesperson, Meinhard Galleries, Houston, 1978-81, dir. gallery, 1982-84; asst. dir. Office Spl. Projects, U. Houston, 1986. Mem. Coll. Cabinet, Vanderbilt U., 1983. Mem. Phi Beta Kappa. Republican. Methodist.

CAIN, LINDA CHARLOTTE, communications company executive, educator; b. Boston, Oct. 5, 1941; d. Charles Cummings Cain and Edna Augusta Cain Clark. BA in History and Govt., Boston U., 1963; MEd, Northeastern U., 1967. Admissions officer Children's Hosp. Med. Ctr., Boston, 1964-65; exec. asst. to mgr. Mass. Rep. State Com., 1965-67; tchr. Dover (Mass.) Pub. Schs., 1967-81; owner, mgr. Cain and Clark, Medfield, Mass., 1971—; pres. Beehive Communications, Inc., Medfield, 1982—; corp. clk., dir. Bay Shores Homeowners Assn., Inc., North Falmouth, Mass., 1978-82; chair pub. TV auction com. Sta. WGBH-TV, 1973-76. Author: Blast-Off, 1973; author, developer mktg. and pub. service booklets. Mem. Mass. Tchrs. Assn., Dover Sherborn Edn. Assn. (past pres.). Republican. Home: 11 Pleasant St Medfield MA 02052-2603

CAIN, LINDA JOANNE, librarian; b. Oakland, Calif., Aug. 5, 1943; d. John Gunnar and Virginia Helen (Johnson) Lyle; A.B. in History, U. Calif., Berkeley, 1965; A.M.L.S., U. Mich., 1967; m. Mark E. Cain, Mar. 15, 1985. Supr. microform reading room, periodicals reading room, interlibrary loan unit at grad. library U. Mich., 1967-69; mem. library staff U. Calif., Berkeley, 1969-78, reference, coll. devel. librarian Moffitt Undergrad. Library, 1969-72, coordinator public services Moffitt Undergrad. Library, 1972-75, adminstrv. asst. to assoc. univ. librarian for public services, 1977-78, instr. bibliography I, 1971, 74-75; head librarian reference services dept. gen. libraries, then acting asst. dir. public services U. Tex., Austin, 1978-80, assoc. dir. public services, 1980-84, assoc. dir., 1984-87; dean, univ. librarian, U. Cin., 1987—. Council Library Resources acad. library mgmt. intern, 1975-76. UCLA sr. fellow, 1985. Mem. ALA. Author articles in field. Editorial bd. Jour. Acad. Librarianship, 1980-83. Office: U Cin Langsam Library Mail Location 33 Cincinnati OH 45221

CAIN, MARCENA JEAN BEESLEY, retail store executive; b. Kingman, Kans., May 1, 1935; d. Albert Eugene and Stella Wanda (Ruthowski) Beesley; m. Kenneth B. Cain, Aug. 4, 1951; children—Kenneth Thomas, David Raymond. With AMVETS Thrift Stores, D.C., 1971—, asst. dir., 1971—, asst. dir. Amvets Value Village Thrift Stores, Balt.; ptnr. Bank St. Joint Venture Realty, Del-Mar Realty; pres. Family Thrift Ctr., Inc.; v.p. 4 corps. Mem. Bus. and Profl. Women's Club, Highlandtown Businessmen Assn., DAV Aux. (past nat. historian), PTA Valley Forge Mil. Acad. (D.C. area rep.), Highlandtown Mchts. Assn. (pres. 1983-84), Govanstown Mchts. Assn. (rec. sec.), Affiliated Mchts. Assn. Balt. (pres.). Republican. Christian Scientist. Office: 3424 Eastern Ave Baltimore MD 21224

CAIN, MAY LYDIA, lawyer; b. Chgo., Feb. 13, 1956; d. William A. and Audrey (Rosin) C. Student, U. Ill., 1973-74; BA, Northwestern U., 1977; postgrad., U. Miami, Coral Gables, Fla., 1979-80; JD, DePaul U., 1980. Bar: Fla. 1980, U.S. Dist. Ct. (so. dist.) Fla. 1980, U.S. Ct. Appeals (5th and 11th cirs.) 1981, U.S. Supreme Ct. 1986. Ptnr. Cain and Cain, North Miami, Fla., 1980—; adj. prof. Barry U., Miami Shores, Fla., 1986; atty. Pub. Interest Law Bank, Miami, 1982-83. Editor The Fla. Bar Gen. Practice Sect. newsletter, 1984-86, vice chmn. editorial bd. Fla. Bar Jour. and News, 1986, 87-88; guest editor The Fla. Bar Jour. Appellate Practice: Setting the Record Straight, 1988; contbr. articles to profl. jours. Mem. ABA, Dade County Bar Assn., North Dade Bar Assn., Fla. Bar Gen. Practice Sect. (exec. council 1984—), Fla. Assn. Women Lawyers (v.p. 1982-83, pub. relations dir. 1984-85, sec. 1984-86, pres. Dade County chpt. 1983-84, bd. dirs. 1986—). Office: 11755 Biscayne Blvd 401 North Miami FL 33181

CAIN, PATRICIA JEAN, financial executive, accountant; b. Decatur, Ill., Sept. 28, 1931; d. Paul George and Jean Margaret (Horne) Jacka; m. Dan Louis Cain, July 12, 1952; children: Mary Ann, Timothy George, Paul Louis. Student, U. Mich., 1949-52, Pasadena (Calif.) City Coll., 1975-76; BS in Acctg., Calif. State U., Los Angeles, 1977, MBA in Acctg., 1978; M in Taxation, Golden Gate U., Los Angeles, 1988. CPA, Calif. Tax supr. Stonefield & Josephson, Los Angeles, 1979-87; chief fin. officer Loubella Extendables, Inc., Los Angeles, 1987—; participant program in bus. ethics U. So. Calif., Los Angeles, 1986. Bd. dirs. Sierra Madre Girl Scout Council, Pasadena, 1968-73, treas., 1973-75, elected nat. del., 1975; mem. Town Hall, Los Angeles, 1987—. Mem. Am. Inst. CPA's, Am. Women's Soc. CPA's (bd. dirs. 1986-87, v.p. 1987—), Calif. Soc. CPA's (chairperson free tax assistance program 1983-85, high rd. com. 1985-86, chairperson pub. relations com. 1985-87, microcomputer users discussion group, taxation com., fin. com./speaker computer show and conf. 1987-88), Internat. Arabian Horse Assn., Beta Alpha Psi. Democrat. Episcopalian. Club: Wrightwood Country (Calif.). Home: 3715 Fairmeade Rd Pasadena CA 91107 Office: Loubella Extendables Inc 2222 S Figueroa St Los Angeles CA 90007

CAIN, SHARON LEE, real estate executive; b. Houston, Aug. 5, 1944; d. Cary Bennett and Ellen Marguerite (Covington) Moss; m. Herbert R. Littleton, Apr. 10, 1961 (div. 1969); 1 child, Herbert Lee. Student, U. Houston, 1961-63, U. Ark., Little Rock, 1986—. Clk. Prudential Ins. Co., Houston, 1963-66; clk. River Ridge Devel., Inc., Little Rock, 1966-67, property mgr., 1967-70; v.p. River Ridge Devel. and Cedar Hill Corp., Little Rock, 1970-79, Fausett & Co., Little Rock, 1979-86; pres. The Property Mgmt. Co., Little Rock, 1986—. Bd. dirs. The Parent Ctr., Little Rock, 1983—; vol. Youth Home, Little Rock, 1984—. Mem. Inst. Real Estate Mgmt. Ark. chtp. (officer, Gold award 1985), Bldg. Owners & Mgrs. Assn., Nat. Assn. Homebuilders. Republican. Methodist. Clubs: Little Rock Yacht, Power Squadron. Office: The Property Mgmt Co 650 S Shackleford Suite #400 Little Rock AR 72211

CAIRNES, MARY JO, actuary; b. Milw., Mar. 13, 1965; d. Joseph Francis Cairnes and Molly (O'Connor) Holland. BA in Actuarial Sci., Ohio St., 1987. Actuarial analyst Mercer-Meidinger-Hansen, Inc., Columbus, 1985—.

CAIRNS, LORRAINE JOYCE, insurance company executive; b. Winnipeg, Man., Can., Jan. 14, 1939; d. Alfred Carl and Isny Ida (Harrison) Johnson; m. Gerald Stuart Cairns, Oct. 12, 1957. Student, U. Winnipeg, 1982-84. Adminstr. Winnipeg Free Press, 1955-64; exec. asst. Great-West Life Ins. Co., Winnipeg, 1964-71, adminstr., 1971-76, tng. asst., 1976-79, asst. tng. and devel. mgr., 1979—; com. mem. Life Office Mgmt. Assn., Atlanta, 1984—. Mem. Man. Soc. Tng. and Devel. (pres. 1986-87), Human Resources Devel. Can. (pres. 1987-89). Office: Great-West Life Assurance Co, 100 Osborne St N, Winnipeg, MB Canada R3C 3A5

CAIRNS, MARION G., state legislator; b. Sparta, Ill., June 8, 1928; d. Frank McClellan and Pertie (Boyington) Huey; m. Donald F. Cairns, Sept. 2, 1950; 1 child, Douglas Scott. BA, Monmouth Coll., 1950. Prin. Ellis Grove (Ill.) Elem. Sch., 1951-52; tchr. Nebr. High Sch., Falls City, 1952-54; layout designer Hallmark Corp., Kansas City, Mo., 1954-55; instr. evening sch. Washington U., St. Louis, 1959; substitute tchr. Webster Groves (Mo.) High Sch., 1960-66; instr. Hickey Bus. Sch., St. Louis, 1966-70; state legislator State of Mo., Webster Groves, 1977—; adj. prof. Webster U., Webster Groves, 1978—; mem. Children's Services Commn., State of Mo., Jefferson City, 1980—; bd. dirs. Edgewood Children's Ctr., Webster Groves, UN Assn., St. Louis. Advocate crime victims Mo. Victim Assistance Network. Named Citizen of Yr., Webster Groves C. of C., 1984, Child Advocate of Yr. Mo. Child Care Assn., 1985, St. Louis Council Child Abuse and Neglect, 1987. Mem. Nat. Conf. State Legislators, Nat. Order Women Legislators (regional chmn.), Nat. Fedn. Rep. Women. Presbyterian. Home: 17 E Swan Ave Webster Groves MO 63119 Office: State Capitol Bldg House Post Office Webster Groves MO 65101

CAIRNS, ROBERTA A. E., librarian; b. Waltham, Mass., Feb. 1, 1945; d. Robert H. and Elizabeth F. (Peck) C. B.A., Stonehill Coll., 1966; M.S., U. R.I., 1969. Librarian, Fiske Pub. Library, Wrentham, Mass., 1966-71; dir. Barrington Pub. Library (R.I.), 1971-79; dir. library services East Providence Pub. Library (R.I.), 1979—; adv. com. U. R.I. Grad. Library Sch., Kingston, 1983. Author: History of St. Mary's Church, 1978. Bd. dirs. Am Cancer Soc., East Providence, 1983, Bradley Hosp. ; chairperson Citizens Adv. Commn. Cable TV, East Providence, 1983—; Coordinator pub. relations City of East Providence, 1985—; mem. Cable TV Statewide Adv. Council, 1984—. Named East Providence Woman of Yr., 1985. Mem. ALA, East Providence C. of C. (bd. dirs. 1983—, v.p. 1983-85), East Providence Profl. Managerial and Tech. Employees Assn. (v.p. 1983-86), New Eng. Library Assn., R.I. Library Assn. (pres. 1986), Pub. Library Assn. Roman Catholic. Home: 1355 Wampanoag Trail East Providence RI 02915 Office: East Providence Pub Library 41 Grove Ave East Providence RI 02914

CALABIA, DAWN T., legislative staff consultant; b. Bklyn., May 22, 1941; d. Thomas Michael and Alice Brady (Diver) Tennant; B.A., St. John's U.; M.S.W., Fordham U., 1969; m. Florentine Calabia; children—Florentine Christopher, Theodore Rizal, Alison Maria Clara. Local area analyst N.Y.C. Planning Commn., 1967-68; urban planner Manoussoff Assos., 1969-72; fundraiser, cons. N.Y. State ADA, 1973-74; legis. asst. to Rep. Solarz (N.Y.), Washington 1978-84; staff cons. House Fgn. Affairs Com., 1984—. Mem. Nat. Assn. Social Workers, Ams. for Democratic Action (nat. bd. dirs.), St. John's U. Alumni Assn. (v.p.), Democratic Women Capitol Hill, NOW, Lambda Kappa Phi. Office: 707 House Annex I Washington DC 20515

CALABRETTA, MARTI ANN, senator; b. Sandusky, Ohio, Dec. 14, 1940; d. Wilfred and Ida (Gerding) Beutler; m. Joseph Miller, Feb. 2, 1963 (div. Mar. 1976); m. Bennie G. Calabretta, Dec. 18, 1976; children: Joseph, Patrick, Rebecca, Debora, John, Ben, Lisa. Student, Case Western Res. U., 1961-63; BA, U. Utah, 1963, MSW, 1966; cert. mental health mgmt., U. Wash., 1981. Mental health specialist 4 Corners Mental Health Services, Moab, Utah, 1972-75, Idaho Mental Health Services, Coeur d'Alene, Idaho, 1975-81; sch. social worker Wallace (Idaho) Sch. Dist., 1981-85; state senator Boise, Idaho, 1984—. Pres. Valley Coordinating Corp., Kellogg, Idaho, 1982-86; mem. Pvt. Industry Council, Coeur d'Alene, 1984—, Idaho State Council on Developmental Disabilities, 1986—; vice chmn. Silver Valley Human Resources task force, Kellogg, 1982—. Mem. Idaho Edn. Assn. (del. 1983-84), Nat. Conf. State Legis. (health and welfare com.). Democrat. Episcopalian. Home: Nuchols Gulch Box 784 Osburn ID 83849 Office: Wallace Sch Dist 393 Wallace ID 83849

CALARCO, MARGARET MARIE, nurse; b. Cleve., June 20, 1956; d. Carl Joseph and Margaret Marie (Potenza) C. BS in Nursing, U. Cin., 1978; MS in Nursing, Case Reserve U., 1982; postgrad., U. Mich., 1986—. RN. Nurse U. Cin. Med. Ctr., 1978-79, U. Hosps. Cleve, 1979-80, Huron Rd. Hosps., Cleve., 1980-82; clin. nurse specialist Cleve. VA Med. Ctr., 1982-84; head nurse Ctr. for Stress Recovery div. Cleve. VA Med. Ctr., Cleve., 1984-85; clin. nurse specialist Cleve VA Med. Ctr., 1985-86; nurse specialist clin. studies unit U. Mich. Hosps., Ann Arbor, Mich., 1986—. Mem. Am. Nursing Assn., Midwest Nursing Research Soc., Mich. Nurses Assn., Sigma Theta Tau. Home: 1320 Wisteria Ann Arbor MI 48104 Office: U Mich Hosps D9605 Box 0118 Ann Arbor MI 48109

CALAWAY, CYNTHIA KATHLEEN, management professional; b. Cambridge, Ohio, Jan. 18, 1958; d. Gordon Lyle and Constance L. (Hayes) C. BBA, Bowling Green State U., 1980. Buyer Diamond Shamrock Corp., Houston, 1980-81, project purchasing agt., 1981-83; sales rep. Am. Hosp. Supply, Denver, 1983-84; account mgr. Am Hosp. Supply, Des Moines, 1984-85; account exec. Donnelley Mktg. div. Dunn and Bradstreet, Oak Brook, Ill., 1985-86, account mgr. Official Airlines Guide div., 1986—. Mem. Rep. Nat. Com., 1981—. Mem. Nat. Assn. Female Execs. Presbyterian.

CALDAREA, GAIL LAURIE, marketing professional; b. Detroit, May 10, 1953; d. Nicholas George Caldarea and Norma Mae (Logan) Dewey; m. Michael Ghiaciuc, Sept. 24, 1983(div. Jan. 1984). Assoc. in Bus. Adminstrn., Oakland Community Coll., Royal Oak, Mich., 1983; BBA, U. Detroit, 1987. Technician, typist Mich. Dept. of State, Highland Park, 1972-78; sec. Mich. Dept. of State, Oak Park, Mich., 1978-81; adminstrv. support staff Mich. Dept. of Military Affairs, Oak Park, 1981-84, facilities mgr., 1984-88, personal mgmt. analyst, 1988—. Mem. AAUW, Nat. Assn. Female Execs., Mktg. Club, Alpha Sigma Lambda, Beta Gamma Sigma. Presbyterian. Club: SkiWi Ski (Sterling Heights, Mich.). Home: 425 W LaSalle Royal Oak MI 48073 Office: Mich Dept of Mil Affairs 2500 S Washington Lansing MI 48913-5101

CALDER, JOAN MILLER, social worker; b. Syracuse, N.Y., Oct. 30, 1939; d. John Robert and Marjorie (Reid) Foreman Miller; m. George Donald Calder, June 24, 1961; children—Jeanette, George Donald. Student Russell Sage Coll., 1957-60; B.A., Bloomfield Coll., 1962; M.S.W., Fordham U., 1980. Cert. social worker, N.Y. Teenage program dir. YWCA, Elizabeth, N.J., 1962-65; adoption specialist, social worker Children's Aid and Adoption, Bogota, N.J., 1980-85; v.p. Family and Children's Service, Montclair, N.J., 1978-85; exec. dir. League for Family Service Bloomfield and Glen Ridge, N.J., 1985—. Task force chmn. state pub. affairs Jr. League N.J., 1976-77; community v.p. Montclair-Newark Jr. League, 1977-78; leader Girl Scouts U.S.A., 1970-82; trustee Bloomfield Coll. Mem. Nat. Assn. Social Workers, Acad. Cert. Social Workers, Morris County Human Resource Assn., Bloomfield Coll. Alumni Fedn. (pres.). Home: 87 Douglas Rd Glen Ridge NJ 07028 Office: 29 Park St Bloomfield NJ 07003

CALDERON, LINDA CARON, nurse; b. N.J., Nov. 22, 1951; d. Arthur Donovan and Lillian Thomas; B.S.N., Calif. State U., Los Angeles, 1974, M.A., 1982; grad. nurse midwifery program, 1982; m. Rudy J. Calderon, May 3, 1975; children—Mikel Louis, John Matthew, Natalie Caron. Nurse, Huntington Meml. Hosp., Pasadena, Calif., 1975, nurse clinician, 1980, labor/delivery asst. head nurse, 1981-83; pvt. practice nurse midwife, 1983—. Mem. ACLU Found. Reproductive Project, 1981—. Mem. Calif. Perinatal Assn., Am. Coll. Nurse Midwives (assoc., chpt. treas.), Consortium for Nurse Midwives. Democrat. Roman Catholic. Home: 1145 Leonard St Pasadena CA 91107 Office: 620 S Pasadena Ave Pasadena CA 91105

CALDERONE, MARY STEICHEN, physician; b. N.Y.C., July 1, 1904; d. Edward J. and Clara (Smith) Steichen; m. Frank A. Calderone, Nov. 1941 (dec. 1987); children: Linda Steichen Hodes, Francesca Calderone-Steichen, Maria S. B.A., Vassar Coll., 1925; M.D., U. Rochester, 1939; M.P.H., Columbia U., 1942; D.Med. Sci. (hon.), Women's Med. Coll., 1967; L.H.D. (hon.), Newark State Coll., 1971, Dickinson Coll., 1981, Jersey City State Coll., 1982; Sc.D. (hon.), Adelphi U., 1971, Worcester Found. Exptl. Biology, 1974, Brandeis U., 1975, Haverford Coll., 1978, Columbia U., 1985; LL.D., Kenyon Coll., 1972; Ped.D. (hon.), Hofstra U., 1978; D. Hum. (hon.), Bucknell U., 1982. Intern Bellevue Hosp., N.Y.C., 1939-40; med. dir. Planned Parenthood-World Population, 1953-64; co-founder, dir., pres. Sex Info. Edn. Council U.S., N.Y.C., 1964-82; adj. prof. program in human sexuality NYU, N.Y.C., 1982—; lectr. human sexuality; 33d Lower lectr. Acad. Medicine and Cleve. Clinic, 1970; Rufus Jones lectr. Friends Gen. Conf., 1973; Hundley lectr. gynecology, Balt., 1973; president's disting. visitor Vassar Coll., 1983; 7th ann. Bronfman lectr. Am. Pub. Health Assn., 1968. Author: Release From Sexual Tensions, 1960; co-author: Family Book about Sexuality, 1981 (pub. Japan and Germany); co-author: Talking with Your Child about Sex, 1982 (pub. Japan, Germany and Brazil); editor: Abortion in U.S, 1958, Manual of Family Planning and Contraceptive Practice, 1964, rev. edit., 1970, Sexuality and Human Values, 1974. Contbr. articles to profl. jours., mags., textbooks, encys. Recipient 4th Ann. award for distinguished service to humanity Women's Aux. Albert Einstein Med. Center, Phila., 1966; Woman of Conscience award Nat. Council Women, 1968; citation Merrill-Palmer Inst. Human Devel. and Family Life, Detroit, 1969; Woman of Achievement award Greater N.Y. chpt. women's div. Albert Einstein Coll. Medicine, Yeshiva U., 1969; Haven Emerson award N.Y.C. Public Health Assn., 1970; Ann. award Soc. Sci. Study of Sex, 1976; Elizabeth Blackwell award for disting. service to humanity Hobart and Wm. Smith Coll., 1977; Margaret Sanger award Planned Parenthood Fedn. Am., 1980; recipient Abram Sachar silver medal Brandeis U. Nat. Women's Com., 1983, Mcdonald House award Univ. Hosps. Women's Com., Cleve., 1983, Human Service award Mental Health Assn. New York and Bronx Counties, 1983, Lifetime Achievement award Schlesinger Library Radcliffe Coll., 1983, Disting. Alumni award Columbia U., 1984, Jake Gimbel hon. lectr. award U. Calif. Sch. Medicine, 1984, cert. of commendation Am. Acad. Pediatrics, 1985; named one of America's 75 Most Important Women Ladies Home Jour., 1971; one of 50 most influential women in U.S. Newspaper Enterprises Assn., 1975. Fellow Am. Public Health Assn. (Edward W. Browning award for prevention of disease 1980), Soc. Sci. Study Sex (hon. life mem.); mem. Am. Coll. Sexologists, Am. Assn. Marriage and Family Counselors (hon. life mem.), Am. Assn. World Health, AMA (hon. life), Soc. Sex Therapy and Research, Alpha Omega Alpha. Quaker. Office: NYU Dept Health Edn Program in Human Sexuality 239 Greene St 6th Fl New York NY 10003

CALDICOTT, HELEN, physician; b. Melbourne, Australia, Aug. 7, 1938; d. Philip and Mona (Coffey) Broinowski; m. William Caldicott; 3 children. MBBS, U. South Australia, 1962. Intern Royal Adelaide (Australia) Hosp., 1962-63; fellow in nutrition Children's Hosp. Med. Ctr., Boston, 1967-68; researcher Adelaide Children's Hosp., 1973-75; mem. faculty Harvard Med. Sch., 1975-80; pres. Physicians for Social Responsibility, 1978-

83. Author: Nuclear Madness: What You Can Do!, 1979, Missile Envy: The Arms Race and Nuclear War, 1984. Fellow Royal Australian Coll. Physicians; mem. Women's Action for Nuclear Disarmament (founder). Address: 245 Highland Ave West Newton MA 02165 *

CALDWELL, CAROL GRAY, lawyer; b. Gadsden, Ala., Mar. 23, 1954; d. Jack E. and Jean Carol (Gillespie) Gray; m. Harry E. Caldwell Jr., Jan. 7, 1984. AB, U. Ala., 1976; JD with distinction, Duke U., 1979. Bar: N.Y. 1980, Ala. 1984. Assoc. Dewey, Ballantine, Bushby, Palmer & Wood, N.Y.C., 1979-83; ptnr. Sirote, Permutt, McDermott, Slepian, Friend, Friedman, Held & Apolinsky, P.C., Birmingham, Ala., 1983-87; mem. dean's adv. council Duke U. Sch. Law, Durham, N.C., 1985. Editor Duke U. Law Jour., 1978. Mem. ABA, Ala. Bar Assn., Birmingham Bar Assn., Nat. Assn. Bond Lawyers, Phi Beta Kappa. Home: Rt 1 Box 306B Helena AL 35080

CALDWELL, CHERYL NORMAN, marketing representative; b. Buffalo, Oct. 28, 1954; d. Franklin Leonard and Ruth Faverman (Norman) C. B.A. in Art, SUNY-Geneseo, 1977; M.B.A, N.C. Central U., 1981. Tchr., Durham City Schs. (N.C.), 1979-81; application programmer mktg. rep. IBM, N.Y.C., 1981—. Active Nat Alliance Bus.-Youth Motivation Task Force, Durham, 1981—, Tech. Literacy Corp., N.Y.C., 1984—. Mem. Women in Sales, Coalition 100 Black Women. Lutheran. Office: IBM 590 Madison Ave New York NY 10022

CALDWELL, ELEANOR, artist; b. Kansas City, Mo., May 1, 1927; d. Earl Kendrick and Etta (Clark) C.; B.S. magna cum laude, in Edn., Southwest Mo. State U., 1948; M.A., Columbia U. Tchrs. Coll., 1953, Ed.D. (Alumni fellow, Dow scholar 1958-59), 1959. Tchr. art high schs. in Mo. and Iowa, 1948-52; instr. art Southwest Mo. State U., 1953-54; asst. prof. Ft. Hays (Kans.) State U., 1954-57; instr. Columbia U. Tchrs. Coll., lectr. art edn. Queen's Coll., also supr. children's art carnival Mus. Modern Art, N.Y.C., 1957-59; prof., chmn. dept. art NW Mo. State Coll., Maryville, 1959-60; assoc. prof. Edinboro (Pa.) State Coll., 1960-62, Pa. State U., 1962-63; assoc. prof. No. Ill. U., DeKalb, 1963-64, prof. art, 1967-83; prof. emeritus, 1983—; assoc. prof. Ft. Hays State U., 1964-67; dir. Oakbrook (Ill.) Invitational Crafts Exhbn., 1968-84; cons., tchr. Arrowmont Sch. Arts and Crafts, Gatlinburg, Tenn., 1974-85; represented in permanent collections Denver Public Schs., Colo. Women's Coll., Denver, Ft. Hays State Coll., No. Ill. U., Sheldon Meml. Art Mus., Lincoln, Nebr., Arrowmont Sch. Arts and Crafts. Recipient Public Service award Ill. Sesquicentennial Commn., 1968; grantee No. Ill. U., 1968, 70, 74-80. Mem. Soc. N.Am. Goldsmiths, Am. Crafts Council, Ariz. Designer Craftsmen, Delta Kappa Gamma, Pi Lambda Theta, Kappa Delta Pi. Editor: Contemporary Jewelry, 1970.

CALDWELL, HOLLY ROBNETT, healthcare facility executive; b. Brownsville, Tenn., Aug. 27, 1954; d. Everett B. and Jean (Hopkins) Robnett; m. G. Scott Gieszl Jr., Dec. 31, 1984; 1 child, Katherine G. Gieszl. BA in Econs., Vanderbilt U., 1975, MA in Econs., 1976; postgrad., Harvard U., 1978. Asst. dir. program planning Vanderbilt U. Med. Ctr., Nashville, 1976-78; mgr. strategic planning Hosp. Corp. of Am., Nashville, 1978-80; spl. asst. to asst. sec. HHS, Washington, 1981-83; v.p. planning and mktg. Samaritan Health Service, Phoenix, 1983-85; v.p., exec. dir. Samaritan Med. Found./Samaritan Research Inst., Phoenix, 1985—; bd. dirs. New Times, Inc., Phoenix. Contbr. 12 articles to profl. jours. Panelist Presdl. Classroom for Young Ams., Washington, 1982; leader Jr. Achievement, Phoenix, 1983-84. Mem. Soc. for Hosp. Planning and Mktg., Ariz. Hosp. Assn., Planning Forum, Phi Beta Kappa, Omicron Delta Kappa. Episcopalian. Clubs: Plaza (Phoenix); Harbor Island Yacht (Nashville). Home: 1065 E Calle Monte Vista Tempe AZ 85254 Office: Samaritan Med Found 2700 N 3d St Suite 2015 Phoenix AZ 85004

CALDWELL, JUDY CAROL, advertising executive, public relations executive; b. Nashville, Dec. 28, 1946; d. Thomas and Sarah Elizabeth Carter; m. Eddie Herschel Oates, Aug. 12, 1967 (div. Sept. 1975); 1 child, Jessica; m. John Cope Jr, June 24, 1984. BS, Wayne State U., 1969. Tchr. Bailey Mid. Sch., West Haven, Conn., 1969-72; editorial asst. Vanderbilt U., Nashville, 1973-74; editor, graphics designer, field researcher Urban Observatory of Met. Nashville, 1974-77; account exec. Holden and Co., Nashville, 1977-79; bus. tchr. Federated States of Micronesia, 1979-80; dir. advt. Am. Assn. for State and Local History, Nashville, 1980-81; dir. prodn. Mktg. Communications Co., Nashville, 1981-83; owner, pres. Ridge Hill Corp., Nashville, 1983—. Office: Ridge Hill Corp 1717 West End Ave Suite 216 Nashville TN 37203

CALDWELL, MARY PERI, educator, counseling psychologist; b. Cleve., Aug. 21, 1935; d. Francesco and Gerlanda (Gagliano) Peri; m. Robert Joseph Caldwell, 1956 (div. 1962); children: Deborah Ann, Thomas Robert. BS in Edn., Kent State U., Ohio, 1961; MA in Counseling Psychology, Alfred Adler Inst., Chgo., 1981. Cert. clin. mental health counselor; lic. mental health counselor, Fla. Tchr. various sch. systems in Cleve. area, 1957-85; pvt. practice as counseling psychologist, Brunswick, Ohio, 1980-87; mem. faculty, dir. Cleve. Inst. Adlerian Studies, 1983—, exec. sec., 1978-82, pres., 1982-84; pvt. practice psychology, Coral Springs, Fla., 1987—; mem. med. staff Care Unit, Coral Springs; lectr. U.S. and Can. Author: Stress/Distress/Burnout: Resolving the Puzzle of Stress, 1983; editor: Adlerian Psychology Bull., 1983-86; contbr. articles to profl. jours. Leader various parent edn. groups, 1981—. Jennings Found. grantee, 1979; recipient Disting. Service award N.E. Ohio Tchrs. Assn., 1983. Mem. N.Am. Soc. Adlerian Psychology (clin. mem., assembly del., Outstanding Woman award 1980), Am. Assn. Counseling and Devel., Am. Mental Health Counselors Assn., Fla. Assn. Counseling and Devel., Broward County Mental Health Assn., Exec. Women Coral Springs, Am. Bus. Women's Assn., Gamma Phi Beta (pres. 1967-70). Avocations: tennis, travel, piano, watercolor painting. Home: 8208 NW 100th Way Tamarac FL 33321 Office: 3300 University Dr Suite 615 Coral Springs FL 33321

CALDWELL, NAOMI ROSALIND, banker; b. Nashville, May 1, 1939; d. James Walter and Mabel Rosalind (Travis) Walker; m. Gary Keith Ackers, Sept. 8, 1959 (div. May 1983); children: Lisa Ellen, Sandra Lauren, Keith James; m. Colin Spencer Caldwell, Aug. 15, 1987. Student, Harding Coll., 1957-60; BA with highest honors, U. Va., 1977; cert. mgmt. studies, U. Balt., 1979, MBA, 1982. Mgmt. trainee, asst. mgr. First Nat. Bank of Md., Balt., 1979-81, br. mgr., br. officer, 1981-83, pvt. banking officer, pvt. banking exec., 1984-85; bus. devel. officer CentraBank, Balt., 1985-86, mgr. bus. devel., jr. bd. dirs., 1986—, asst. v.p., 1987-88, chmn., 1988—. Vol. Recording for the Blind, Charlottesville, Va., 1967-72, Girl Scouts, Charlottesville, 1968-70; bd. dirs. PTO, Charlottesville, 1973; hosp. visitation Towson Presbyn. Ch., Balt., 1985—, bd. elders 1987—. Mem. Exec. Women's Network, Nat. Assn. Bank Women (membership chair 1986-87, chmn. pub. affairs 1987-88), Nat. Assn. Female Execs., Alpha Chi, Phi Alpha Theta, Delta Mu Delta. Democrat. Club: Univ. Va., Vested Interest Investment. Home: 6507 Darnall Rd Baltimore MD 21204 Office: NCNB Bank Md 201 N Charles St Baltimore MD 21201

CALDWELL, PAULA DAY, telecommunications executive; b. Colorado Springs, Colo., Nov. 11, 1954; d. Taylor Arnold and Constance Theo (Jenkins) Day Pearson; m. Michael Anthony Caldwell, Feb. 21, 1981. BS, Lindenwood Coll., 1981; MBA, Dallas Bapt. U., 1986. Exec. sec. Minority Econ. Devel. Agy., St. Louis, 1974-76; adminstrv. asst. New Age Fed. Savs. and Loan, St. Louis, 1976-78; bookkeeper Family Planning Council, 1978-81; account exec., cons. AT&T Corp., Dallas, 1981—; co-owner Jewelry Connection. Mem. Nat. Assn. Female Execs. Dallas Women's Found. Democrat. Baptist. Home: PO Box 763845 Dallas TX 75376 Office: AT&T Corp 5525 LBJ Freeway 3d Floor Dallas TX 75240

CALDWELL, SANDRA MARIE, accountant; b. Lexington, Ky., Apr. 11, 1959; d. Francis Mark and Frances Jane (Thomas) C. B.S. in Acctg., U. Ky., 1983; M.B.A., Xavier U., Cin., 1987. Record clk. Good Samaritan Hosp., Lexington, 1976-85; acctg. clk. Semicon Assocs., Lexington, 1985-86, acctg. analyst, 1986-87, fin. planner Cox Fin. Corp., Cin., 1987—, partnership analyst Pizza Huts Cin., 1987—. Mem. Nat. Assn. Accts., Nat. Soc. MBA's, Nat. Assn. Female Execs. Office: Pizza Huts of Cin 800 compton Rd Unit 37 Cincinnati OH 45231

CALDWELL, SARAH, opera producer, conductor, stage director and administrator; b. Maryville, Mo., Mar. 6, 1924. Student, U. Ark., Hendrix Coll., New Eng. Conservatory, Berkshire Music Ctr., Tanglewood, Mass.; D. Mus. (hon.), Harvard U., Simmons Coll., Bates Coll., Bowdoin U. Mem. faculty Berkshire Music Center; dir. Boston U. Opera Workshop, 1953-57; created dept. music theater Boston U.; founded Boston Opera Group (later became Opera Co. of Boston), 1957, sinced served as artistic dir. and condr. Asst. to Boris Goldovsky in direction of New Eng. Opera Co.; operatic directorial debut with Rake's Progress, Opera Workshop, 1953; operatic debut as condr. with Opera Group of Boston, 1957, Carnegie Hall debut with Am. Symphony Orch., 1974; condr. and/or dir. maj. opera cos. in U.S., including N.Y. Met. Opera, Dallas Civic Opera, Houston Grand Opera, N.Y.C. Opera; condr. with maj. orchs. including: Indpls. Symphony, Milw. Symphony, Am. Symphony, N.Y. Philharmonic; condr. at Ravinia Festival, 1976. Recipient Rogers and Hammerstein award. Office: Opera Co Boston PO Box 50 Boston MA 02112

CALDWELL, SUSAN ELAINE, virologist; b. Knoxville, Feb. 4, 1952; d. Calvin Harold and Hope (Owen) C.; m. Michael Charles Cerrone, Nov. 27, 1981. BA in Biology, U. Tenn., 1978; PhD in Virology, Wake Forest U., 1985. Research assoc. Bowman Gray Sch. Medicine, Wake Forest U., Winston-Salem, N.C., 1983-87; assoc. scientist Genelabs, Inc., Redwood City, Calif., 1987-88, scientist, 1988—; speaker in field. Contbr. articles to profl. jours. Mem. Nat. Assn. Female Execs. Democrat. Home: 762 Bounty Dr Apt 6203 Foster City CA 94404

CALDWELL, TONI MARIE, tobacco company administrator; b. Winston-Salem, N.C., Aug. 19, 1951; d. Sammie Lee Sr. and Mary (Caldwell) Bivins; 1 child, Christopher Bradley Bowman. Student, U. Tenn.; BS in Commerce, Knoxville Coll., 1979. Adminstr. Eastman Kodak Co., Kingsport, Tenn., 1973, R.J. Reynolds Tobacco Co., Winston-Salem, 1974—. Served with U.S. Army, 1981. Mem. NAACP, Nat. Assn. Female Execs., Smithsonian Assocs., Piedmont Flight Dirs. Program. Democrat. Baptist. Office: RJ Reynolds Tobacco Co 11th Floor Plaza Bldg Winston-Salem NC 27107

CALDWELL, ZOE, actress, director; b. Hawthorn, Victoria, Australia, Sept. 14, 1933. Attended Methodist Ladies Coll., Melbourne, Australia; m. Robert Whitehead. Theater debut as mem. of Union Theatre Repertory Co., Melbourne, 1953; other appearances in "Colette", N.Y.C., 1970, "A. Bequest to the Nation", London, 1970, "The Creation of the World and Other Business", N.Y.C., 1972, "Love and Master Will", Washington, 1973, "The Dance of Death", N.Y.C., 1974, "Long Day's Journey Into Night", N.Y.C., Washington, 1976, "Medea", N.Y.C., 1982 (Tony award for best actress); plays directed include: An Almost Perfect Person, N.Y.C., 1977, "Richard II", Stratford, Ont., 1979, "These Men", N.Y. off-Broadway, 1980, "The Taming of the Shrew", Hamlet, Am. Shakespeare Theatre, 1985; appeared in The Madwoman of Chaillot, Goodman Theater, Chgo., 1964, repertory theater Stratford-on-Avon, 2 seasons, The Way of the World and The Caucasian Chalk Circle, Mpls., Slapstick Tragedy (Tony award for best supporting actress), N.Y.C., 1966; appeared in Antony and Cleopatra, Richard III and The Merry Wives of Windsor at Stratford, Ont. Shakespeare Festival, 1967; appeared in The Prime of Miss Jean Brodie (Tony award for best actress 1968), appeared in one-woman play Lillian. Decorated Order Brit. Empire; recipient Word award, 1966. Address: care Whitehead-Stevens 1501 Broadway New York NY 10036

CALESTINO, KAREN JOAN, construction company executive; b. Providence, R.I., Sept. 18, 1952; d. Astillodore and Maria (Micheletti) Diodati; m. Peter George Calestino, Apr. 11, 1976; children: Maria, Peter A. Student, R.I. Jr. Coll., Warwick, 1972. Notary Public. Exec. sec. A&D Constrn. Co., Inc., Cranston, R.I., 1974-87, asst. treas., 1980-87, also bd. dirs. Recipient Honor award Hist. Preservation Soc., Providence, 1983. Mem. Women in Constrn, Bldg. Trades Assn. Roman Catholic. Office: A&D Constr Co Inc 116 Preston Dr Cranston RI 02910

CALHOUN, ANN BRASINGTON, social services administrator; b. Bennettsville, S.C., Apr. 18, 1932; d. Charles Norman and Gladys Barron (Carlisle) Brasington; m. Wade Hampton Calhoun, 1954 (div. June 1973); 1 child, Doris Ann Calhoun Breeden. BA, Limestone Coll., 1954; ThM, Luther Rice Sem., 1978. Cert. in child protective services, S.C.; cert. in adult protective services, S.C.: cert. permanency planning, S.C.; cert. in foster parent tng. and adult services, S.C. Caseworker Marlboro County Dept. Social Services, Bennettsville, 1959-67, 70-80, supr. econ. service, 1967-70, supr. human service, 1980-83, dir. county social service, 1983—. Author: To You I Give, 1960. Bd. dirs. Tb Assn., Bennettsville, 1959, S.C. Social Welfare Forum, Columbia, S.C., 1980; coordinator Marlboro County Civil Def., Bennettsville, 1962—. Named Woman of Yr., Bennettsville Jr. Charity League, 1984-85. Mem. Am. Pub. Welfare Assn., S.C. State Employees' Assn. (v.p. Marlboro County chpt. 1982-83), County Dirs. and Suprs. Assn., County Human Service Adminstrs. Home: 120 Townsend St Bennettsville SC 29512 Office: Marlboro County Dept Social Services Parsonage St Extension Bennettsville SC 29512

CALHOUN, EVELYN WILLIAMS, social worker; b. Tyler, Tex., Sept. 12, 1921; d. James Stanley and Norma (Skelton) Williams; B.A., Baylor U., 1941; M.S.W., Worden Sch. Social Work, 1960; postgrad. U. Chgo., 1955-56; m. William Benjamin Calhoun, Jr., Mar. 15, 1942 (div. Mar. 1949); children—William Benjamin III, Anne Stanley (Mrs. Donald Elliot Loyd). Field worker Tex. Dept. Pub. Welfare, Tyler, 1953-55; field placement Salvation Army Family Service, Chgo., 1955-56; child welfare worker Tyler-Smith County Child Welfare Unit, 1957-59; field placement Tex. Inst. Rehab. and Research, Baylor U., Houston, 1959-60, med. social worker, 1960-64; research social worker pre-natal research project dept. obstetrics and gynecology U. Tex. Med. Br. at Galveston, 1964-66, supr. social service dept. obstetrics and gynecology, 1966-74, cons. satellite clinics, 1967-74, cons. family planning project, 1969-74, cons., supr. head and neck cancer service, ear, nose and throat, chest surgery and neurosurgery, 1974-78, cons., supr. plastic surgery and oral surgery service, 1975-78, supr. internal medicine services, otolaryngology, ophthalmology and dermatology, 1978-81; field instr. U. Houston Grad. Sch. Social Work, 1968-81. Bd. dirs. Galveston County Community Action Council, 1966-68, Galveston chpt. Am. Cancer Soc., 1974-81; trustee Houston Intergroup Assn., 1974-76. Lic. social psychotherapist, Tex.; cert. social worker, advanced clin. practitioner, Tex. Mem. Nat. Assn. Social Workers (chmn. research council San Jacinto chpt. 1963-64, dir. chpt. 1964-67, chmn. Galveston br. 1964-67, sec. 1967-68; group leader so. regional inst. 1966, alt. Tex. del. 1969-71, Tex. del. 1971-73, dir. 1969-73; alt. del. Tex. state council 1967), Acad. Cert. Social Workers, Galveston County Soc. Social Service Dirs. (sec. 1979-80), AAUW, Baylor Alumnae Assn., Daus. King (pres. 1976-78), Order De Moley, Delta Alpha Pi. Episcopalian. Toastmistress. Home: PO Box 893 Galveston TX 77550

CALHOUN, GLORIA LYNN, experimental psychologist; b. Mpls., Nov. 12, 1951; d. Robert Willard and Wilma Marie (Schmoock) Alrutz; B.A., Coll. Wooster, 1974; M.A., Wright State U., 1984; m. Kevin Paul Calhoun, Apr. 20, 1974 (div.); children—Mark Allan, Brian Patrick. Document research analyst Bunker Ramo Corp., Dayton, Ohio, 1974-75; human factors engr., Dayton, Ohio, 1975-81; research psychologist Systems Research Lab., Dayton, 1981-82; engring. research psychologist Armstrong Aerospace Med. Research Lab., Dayton, 1982—. Wright State U. scholar, 1980; NSF grantee, 1973. Recipient Leach Meml. prize in psychology Coll. Wooster, 1974. Mem. Human Factors Soc., Soc. Info. Display, Sigma Xi (asso.). Contbr. numerous articles to profl. publs. Home: 2814 Bahns Dr Beavercreek OH 45385 Office: AMRL/HEA Wright-Patterson AFB Dayton OH 45433

CALHOUN, SALLY HANSON, clinical psychologist, educator; b. Wauwatosa, Wis., July 7, 1939; d. Lee Delbert and Olive Elizabeth (Congdon) Hanson; B.A. with distinction in English, U. Mich., 1961, M.A. in English, 1963; M.A. (USPHS fellow), Northwestern U., 1967, Ph.D. in Clin. Psychology, 1970; m. David Redfearn Calhoun, Sept. 5, 1964; children—Douglas David, Julie Katherine. Clin. clk. Hines VA Hosp., 1964; psychologist Ill. State Psychiat. Inst., 1965-69; cons. Nelson Hall Pub. Co., 1972-78, also lectr. Northeastern Ill. U., 1972-77; with Assoc. Psychotherapists of Chgo., 1973-74; pvt. practice clin. psychology, Glenview, Ill., 1978—; assoc. prof., core faculty Forest Inst. Profl. Psychology, 1979-85, assoc. prof. 1985—; editor-in-chief Journal of Training and Practice in Profl. Psychology, 1988. Recipient awards for fiction Scholastic Mag., 1954, 56, Avery Hopwood writing award U. Mich., 1958. Mem. Am. Psychol. Assn., Ill. Psychol. Assn., Nat. Council Health Service Providers Psychology, Nat. Soc. Arts and Letters, Mortar Bd., Nat. Soc. DAR (21st Star chpt., nat. defense chairperson), Pi Beta Phi, Psi Chi. Office: 1717 Glenview Rd Suite 200 Glenview IL 60025

CALKINS, JOANN RUBY, nursing administrator; b. Mich., June 28, 1934; d. William Russell and Imajean (Dunkle) Armentrout; A.S., Delta Coll., 1964; B.S., Central Mich. U., 1972, M.A., 1977; m. James W. Calkins, 1952; children—Russell, Jill, Cindy; m. W. Arthur Brindle, May 7, 1983. Staff nurse, L.P.N. clin. instr., asst. dir. Sch. Nursing, Midland (Mich.) Hosp., 1964-71; dir. nursing, dir. substance abuse unit Gladwin (Mich.) Hosp., 1972-76; prin. Calkins Profl. Counseling & Cons., Harrison, Mich., 1976-78, part-time, 1978-83; dir. nursing service Central Mich. Community Hosp., Mt. Pleasant, 1978-83; dir. nursing Oaklawn Hosp., Marshall, Mich., 1983-87; dir. nursing Betsy Johnson Meml. Hosp., Dunn, N.C., 1987—; part-time prin. W. Arthur and Assocs. Cons.; conducted workshops Mich. Dept. Public Health; Mich. Hosp. Assn.; exec. dir. Holistic Health Agy., 1977-82. Trustee, Mid-Mich. Community Coll. Recipient Murial A. Grimmason Nursing Scholarship award, 1962; Cert. nursing adminstr. Mem. Mich. Soc. Hosp. Nursing Adminstrs. (mem. steering com. 1979-80, dir., 14 county rep. 1980-83, pres. 1983-84, chmn. devel. com.), Mich. Nurses Assn., Am. Nurses Assn., Am. Orgn. Nurse Execs., Nat. Assn. Female Execs. Methodist. Lodge: Lioness Internat. (3d v.p. 1985). Home: 513 Argyll Dr Sanford NC 27330 Office: 800 Tilghman Dr Dunn NC 28334

CALLAHAM, BETTY ELGIN, librarian; b. Honea Path, S.C., Oct. 8, 1929; d. John Winfred and Alice (Dodson) C. B.A., Duke U., 1950; M.A., Emory U., 1954, Master Librarianship, 1961. Tchr. public schs. in N.C., Ga. and S.C., 1951-60; field services librarian S.C. State Library, 1961-64, adult cons., 1964-65, dir. field services, 1965-74, dep. librarian, 1974-79, dir., 1979—; Conf. coordinator Gov.'s Conf. on Public Libraries, 1965, S.C. White House Conf. Library and Info. Services, 1978-79; del. White House Conf. Library and Info. Services, 1979; mem. OCLC Users Council, 1982-84, 86-87; chair del. SOLINET, 1983-84; bd. dirs. Southeastern Library Network, 1984-88, vice chmn., 1985-86, chmn. bd. 1986-87. Mem. ALA (council 1977-80), S.C. Library Assn. (fed. relations coordinator 1976-80, chmn. pub. library sect. 1965, mem. legis. com. 1984—, Intellectual Freedom award 1986, v.p., pres. elect 1987—, Educator of Yr. award 1987), Southeastern Library Assn., S.C. Assn. Pub. Library Dirs., S.C. Women in Govt., South Caroliniana Soc., Hist. Columbia Found., Chief Officers State Library Agys., Friends of S.C. State Mus. Home: 733 Poinsettia Pl Columbia SC 29205 Office: SC State Library PO Box 11469 1500 Senate St Columbia SC 29211

CALLAHAN, BEVERLY JEAN, marketing professional; b. East Liverpool, Ohio, Aug. 13, 1949; d. Clarence Eugene and Lena Elizabeth (Battalio) C. BS in Med. Tech., Miami U., 1971; postgrad., Case Western Reserve U. Med. technologist U. Hosp. Cleve., 1970-78, supr. clin. chem. lab., 1978-82; instr. clinical Sch. Med. Tech. Case Western Reserve U., Cleve., 1978-82; rep. tech. sales Fisher Scientific Co., Pitts., 1982-85, specialist clin. chem., 1985-86, mgr. accounts, 1986—. Mem. Clin. Lab. Mgmt. Assn., Am. Soc. Med. Tech. (chmn. 1981-84). Lutheran. Office: Fisher Med Div 585 Alpha Dr Pittsburgh PA 15238

CALLAHAN, BOBBIE YOLANDA, lawyer; b. London, England, June 24, 1949; d. Wladyslaw and Halina (Winter) Stodolski; m. James Patrick Callahan IV, Aug. 23, 1969 (div. 1983); children: Tracey Lynn, K.C. BA in English, Purdue U., 1971; MA in Psychology, Ball State U., 1978; JD, U. Tulsa, 1981. Bar: Okla. 1981. Tchr. Warren Township High Sch., Indpls., 1971-75; training dir. Blue Cross/Blue Shield, Tulsa, 1977-78; assoc. Ungerman, Corner & Little, Tulsa, 1981-84, atty., United Energy Resources, 1984-86; atty. Coulter & Rayll, 1986—; presenter in field. Named to Outstanding Young Women of Am., 1978. Mem. ABA, Okla. Bar Assn., Tulsa County Bar Assn. (pro bono 1985—, speaker's bur. 1986—), Am. Trial Lawyers Assn., Okla. Trial Lawyers Assn., Phi Alpha Delta. Republican. Roman Catholic. Office: Coulter & Rayll 1602 S Main Tulsa OK 74119

CALLAHAN, CHRISTINE MARIE, author, artist; b. Milw., June 29, 1943; d. Viril Herbert and Ruth Ann (Gohde) Schultz; m. Arthur Anthony Callahan, June 29, 1963; children: Bonnie Kay, Richard Jay, Kevin Ray. Grad., Famous Artists Sch., Westport, Conn., 1967; student, Waukesha County Tech. Coll., Pewaukee, 1980-81. Free-lance artist Milw. and Sussex, Wis., 1960—; free-lance author Sussex, 1983—; tchr. and speaker in field. Author: Two Score and Growing Up, 1986. Home and Office: N69 W23930 Michele Ln Sussex WI 53089

CALLAHAN, ELAINE SHAW, retail jeweler; b. Gilmer, Tex., July 14, 1926; d. Ellie Hugh and Emily Ethel (Campbell) Shaw; B.S. in Business, East Tex. Bapt. U., 1983; m. J. Carroll Callahan, Mar. 19, 1949; children—J. Kim, J. Elaine. Founder, 1953, since owner Carolane Co., jewelers, Longview, Tex.; owner Carolane Investment Co., 1953—, Carolane Fin. Co., 1953—. Active Piney Woods chpt. ARC. Mem. Longview Lawyers Wives, Longview Woman's Forum, Longview Fedn. Women's Clubs, Christian Women's Fellowship, Longview Symphony Guild, Henderson Woman's Forum, Longview Womans Forum, Christian Womens' Fellopship (pres.), Phi Sigma Alpha (sec. Tex. Delta Mu). Mem. Christian Ch. (Disciples of Christ). Club: Order Eastern Star. Office: 1200 E Cotton St Longview TX 75602

CALLAHAN, JEAN MARIE, furniture manufacturing and distribution company director; b. Weymouth, Mass., Jan. 15, 1956; d. William Francis and Mildred Anne (Robertson) C.; m. Stuart Baker, Nov. 14, 1987. BA, Franklin Pierce Coll., 1978. Sec. to pres. mgr. Shimazaki Corp., N.Y.C., 1980-82; asst. to v.p. mktg. Bing & Grondahl Inc., Elmsford, N.Y., 1982-83; mgr. A&B Am., Yonkers, N.Y., 1983-86; mng. dir. U.S. ops. A&B Sweden Inc., Plymouth, Mass., 1986—. Actress Mt. Vernon (N.Y.) Scholar Program, 1980-83, St. Peter and Paul PLayers, Mt. Vernon, 1985; asst. Andy Spano Campaign, White Plains, N.Y., 1985. Mem. Plymouth C. of C. Democrat. Roman Catholic. Clubs: Irish Am. of Westchester, Ferry Sloop. Office: A&B Sweden Inc 29 North St Plymouth MS 02360

CALLAHAN, MARGUERITE POYNOR, academic adviser; b. Waco, Tex., July 6, 1947; d. Phelps and Norma Louise (Luther) Smith; divorced; children: David A., Alan (dec. 1987), Pamela; m. 2nd Michael Thomas Callahan; stepchildren: Aaron, Mary, Nathan. BA, So. Meth. U., 1969; MEd, N. Tex. State U., 1984, postgrad., 1985. Tchr. Park Cities Acad., Dallas, 1981-84; pre medicine, presci. adviser So. Meth. U., Dallas, 1985—, med. bd. reviewer, 1985; cons. testing CETA, Dallas, 1982, N. Dallas High Sch., 1983. PTA room mother McCulloch Middle Sch., Dallas, 1982-84; den mother Council 10, Boy Scouts Am., Dallas, 1979-80; group coordinator Dallas Charity Dog Show, 1975-77. Mem. Am. Assn. Counseling and Devel., Tex. Assn. Counseling and Devel., Tex. Sch. Counselors Assn., Nat. Assn. Advisors to Health Professions, Tex. Assn. Advisors to Health Professions, Kappa Delta Pi, Psi Chi, Phi Delta Kappa, Beta Beta Beta. Republican. Presbyterian. Clubs: Skye Terrier of Am.; Scottish Country Dancers, Scottish Soc. (Dallas). Avocations: Scottish dancing and history, gardening, traveling. Home: 2921 Westminster St Dallas TX 75205 Office: So Meth U Dedman Coll Dallas TX 75275

CALLAHAN, MARILYN JOY, social worker; b. Portland, Oreg., Oct. 11, 1934; d. Douglas Quinlin and Anona Helen (Bergemann) Maynard; m. Lynn James Callahan, Feb. 27, 1960 (dec. June 1979); children: Barbara Erin, Susan Dana and Jeffrey Lynn (twins). BA, Mills Coll., 1955; degree secondary teaching, Portland State U., 1963, MSW, 1971. Cert. secondary tchr., Oreg.; registered clin. social worker, Oreg. Child welfare counselor Clackamas County Pub. Welfare, Oregon City, Oreg., 1955-58; med. social worker U. Oreg. Med. Sch., Portland, 1958-59; counselor Multnomah County Juvenile Ct., Portland, 1959-62, Marion County Juvenile Ct., Salem, Oreg., 1965-69; devel., adminstrn. 1st ednl. program Oreg. Women's Correctional Ctr., Salem, 1966-67; mental health counselor Benton County Mental Health Clinic, Corvallis, Oreg., 1970-71; tchr. inst. Hillcrest Sch., Salem, 1975-81; social worker Mid Will Valley Sr. Service Agy., Salem, 1981—; bd. dirs. Vols. for Srs., Tri County Area Conservator-Guardian Program, Statewide Seminar on Age Discrimination, 1985. Mem. exec. bd. South Salem Neighborhood Assn., 1982—, sch. bd. Sacred Heart Acad., 1977-81, Boys and Girls Aid Soc., past dist. v.p.; bd. dirs. Camp Fire Girls, 1971-81. Mem.

Nat. Assn. Social Workers (cert. clin. social worker, acad. cert. social worker, diplomate), Acad. Cert. Social Workers, AAUW (past v.p., past bd. dirs., directed study on family ct. bill 1967), Salem City Club (directed and published research study), U.S. Power Squadron, Catalina 22 Nat. Sailing Assn. Republican. Methodist. Club: Eugene Yacht (Oreg.). Home: 2880 Mountain View Dr S Salem OR 97302 Office: Mid Willamette Valley Sr Services Agy 410 Senator Bldg 220 High St NE Salem OR 97301

CALLAHAN, MARY CULLIPHER, insurance agency executive; b. Reydell, Ark., Jan. 27, 1932; d. John Edward and Pearl Terresa (Wood) Cullipher; m. Robert Leon Callahan, Dec. 4, 1949 (dec. Mar. 1982); children—C. Douglas, R. Dean. Office mgr., Ron Lusby Service Co., Pine Bluff, Ark., 1978-82; field rep. Fed. Crop Ins., Jackson, Miss., 1982-84; owner, mgr. Callahan Ins. Agy., Pine Bluff, 1984—; pub. acct.; income tax preparer. Justice of the Peace Jefferson County Quorum Ct., Pine Bluff, 1978-79; chmn. Jefferson County ARC, 1982. Mem. Am. Bus. Women's Assn. (pres. Bluff City chpt. 1981-83), Ark. Am. Bus. Womens Conv. (sec. treas. 1982), Ins. Women of S. Ark. (employee relations 1985-86). Democrat. Baptist. Home: Route 1 Box 139 Sherrill AR 72152 Office: Callahan Ins Agy 100 E 8th St 2301 Federal Bldg Pine Bluff AR 71611

CALLAHAN, PIA LAASTER, research virologist; b. Chapell-lez-Herlaimont, Belgium, Sept. 21, 1955; came to U.S., 1956; d. Heino and Helga (Sepp) Laaster; m. Lynn T. Callahan III, June 26, 1981. BS in Microbiology, Cornell U., 1977; M in Clin. Microbiology, Hahnemann U., 1979. Registered microbiologist. Research asst. Temple U. Med. Coll., Phila., 1979-80; microbiologist Thomas Jefferson Hosp., Phila., 1980-81; staff virologist Merck Sharp and Dohme Research Labs., West Point, Pa., 1981-84, research virologist, 1984—. Contbr. articles to profl. jours. Mem. Am. Soc. Microbiology. Republican. Lutheran. Home: 907A Stockton Ct Lansdale PA 19446 Office: Merck Sharp and Dohme Research Labs Sumneytown Pike West Point PA 19486

CALLAN, CLAIR MARIE, physician, laboratory director, educator; b. Sleaford, Lincolnshire, Eng., May 18, 1940; d. Joseph Edward and Margaret Mary (Hart) Mills; m. John Patrick Callan, Apr. 4, 1964; children—Eoin, Grainne, Colm, Maeve. M.B., B.Surgery, B. in Art of Obstetrics, Univ. Coll., Dublin, Ireland, 1963. Intern Mater Hosp., Dublin, 1963-64, resident in anesthesia, 1964-65; staff physician State of Conn., Middletown, 1966-68; anesthesiologist St. Francis Hosp., Hartford, Conn., 1972-76; med. dir. Dept. of Income Maintenance, State of Conn., Hartford, 1978-84; dir. med. affairs Abbott Labs., Abbott Park, Ill., 1985—; clin. asst. prof. med., Chgo. Med. Sch./U. Health Scis., 1987—. Contbr. articles to profl. jours. Pres. PTA, Wethersfield, Conn., 1974, Capitol Region Assn. of Pvt. Swim Clubs, Hartford, 1978. Mem. Am. Med. Women's Assn. (pres. 1984-85, councillor 1981-83), AMA (pres. Conn. aux. 1979-81), Am. Acad. Med. Dirs. Republican. Roman Catholic. Avocations: tennis; golf; needlework. Home: 816 Paddock Ln Libertyville IL 60048 Office: Abbott Labs D970 Abbott Park IL 60061

CALLAN, T. EARLENE, advertising executive; b. Carpenter, Okla., Nov. 6, 1938; d. Aubrey D. and Buena V. (Wilson) Shewmaker; m. Jay Bailey, Sept. 1961 (div. 1967); 1 child, P. Diane; m. James Ruskin Callan, Aug. 17, 1973; stepchildren: Jamie, Kelly, Kristy. BA in Math., Harding U., 1961; postgrad., Okla. U., 1962; student, IBM, Okla. City, 1969. Time and motion analyst Western Electric, Oklahoma City, 1961-62; programmer, analyst State Okla. Mental Health Dept., Norman, 1968-69; systems analyst State of Okla. Welfare Dept., Oklahoma City, 1970-73; pres. C Systems, Ltd., Ridgefield, Conn., 1975—. Leader Campfire Girls, Ridgefield, 1976-78; fundraiser various charities, 1975-80. Mem. Bus. Profl. Advt. Assn., Data Processing Mgmt. Assn. (dir. Oklahoma City chpt. 1971-73, treas. 1972-73). Club: Ridgefield Tennis. Home: 332 N Salem Rd Ridgefield CT 06877 Office: C Systems Ltd 590 Danbury Rd Ridgefield CT 06877

CALLANAN, KATHLEEN JOAN, electrical engineer, airplane company executive; b. Detroit, Feb. 10, 1940; d. John Michael and Grace Marie (Kleehammer) C. BSE in Physics, U. Mich., 1963; postgrad. in physics Northeastern U., 1963-65; MSEE, U. Hawaii, 1971; diploma in Japanese lang. St. Joseph Inst. Japanese Studies, Tokyo, 1973; cert. in mgmt. Boeing Mil. Airplane Co. Employee Devel., 1985. Vis. scholar Sophia U., Tokyo, 1976-79; elec.-electronic components engr. Boeing Mil. Airplane Co., Wichita, Kans., 1979-83, instrumentation design engr., 1983-85, strategic planner for tech., 1985-86, research and engring. tech. supr., 1986-87 ; electromagnetic effects Avionics mgr., 1987—. Contbr. articles to profl. jours. Mem. Rose Hill Planning Commn., Kans., 1982-85; coordinator Boeing Employees Amateur Radio Soc., Wichita, 1982-83. Mem. Soc. Women Engrs. (sr. mem., sect. rep. 1981-83, sec. treas. 1985-86, regional bd. dirs. 1983-85, sect. pres. 1987-88), AIAA, Bus. and Profl. Women, Quarter Century Wireless Assn. (communications com. 1985-86). Lodge: Toastmasters (local pres. 1985-86, competent toastmaster 1985). Avocations: amateur radio, singing, bowling. Home: 1201 N West St Rose Hill KS 67133 Office: PO Box 7730 Wichita KS 67277-7730

CALLANDER, KAY EILEEN PAISLEY, educator; b. Coshocton, Ohio, Oct. 15, 1938; d. Dale Olas and Dorothy Pauline (Davis) Paisley; m. Don Larry Callander, Nov. 18, 1977. BSE, Muskingum Coll., 1960; MA in Speech Edn., Ohio State U., 1964, postgrad., 1964-84. Cert. elem., gifted, drama, theater tchr., Ohio. Tchr. Columbus (Ohio) Pub. Schs., 1960-70, 80-88, drama specialist, 1970-80, classroom, gifted/talented tchr., 1986—; coordinator Artists-in-the-Schs., 1977-88; cons., presenter numerous ednl. confs. and sems., 1971—. Producer-dir., Shady Lane Music Festival, 1980-88; dir., tchr. (nat. distbr. video) The Trial of Gold E. Locks, 1983-84; rep., media pub. relations liason Sch. News., 1983-88. Benefactor, Columbus Jazz Arts Group; v.p., bd. dirs. Neoteric Dance and Theater Co., Columbus, 1985-87; tchr., participant Future Stars sculpture exhibt, Ft. Hayes Ctr., Columbus Pub. Schs., 1988; tchr. advisor Columbus Council PTA's, 1983-86, ch-chmn. reflections com., 1984-87; mem. Humane Soc. of U.S., Statue of Liberty-Ellis Island Found., Inc., Columbus Mus. Art; mem. call and worship coms. Old Trinity Luth. Ch., Columbus; supt.'s adv. council, Columbus Pub. Schs., 1967-68; presenter Young Author Sem., Ohio Dept. Edn., 1988; cons. and workshop leader for sem./workshop Teaching about the Constitution in Elem. Schs., Franklin County Ednl. Council, 1988; presenter for Illustrating Methods for Young Authors' Books, 1986-87; mem. Call and Worship Com. Trinity Luth. Ch., Columbus. Named Educator of Yr., Shady Lane PT, 1982; Sch. Excellence grantee Columbus Pub. Schs.; Commendation Columbus Bd. Edn. for Child Assault Prevention project, 1986-87. Mem. NEA, Ohio Edn. Assn., Ohio PTA, Columbus Edn. Assn., Capital Area Humane Soc., Cen. Ohio Tchrs. Assn., Ohio State U. Alumni Assn., Friends of We. Ohio State U., NOW, Nat. Trust for Hist. Preservation, U.S. Army Officers' Club (def. constr. supply ctr., Columbus), The Navy League, Liturgical Art Guild Ohio, Columbus Jazz Arts Group, Columbus Mus. of Art, Humane Soc. of U.S., Internat. Platform Assn. Republican. Home: 570 Conestoga Dr Columbus OH 43213 Office: Columbus Pub Schs Shady Lane Elem Sch 1488 Shady Ln Rd Columbus OH 43227

CALLAWAY, MARY MCDOWELL, lawyer, educator, accountant; b. Tallahassee, June 26, 1929; d. Charles G. and Mary M. (Hogan) McDowell; children: Sara, Julia, Mark. AA, Pensacola Jr. Coll., 1972; BA, U. West Fla., 1972; JD, Fla. State U., 1974; LLM, Emory U., 1981. Bar: Fla. 1975. Asst. states atty. Fla. First Jud. Dist., Pensacola, 1975-76, chief asst. states atty., 1977-78; individual practice law, Pensacola, Fla., 1978—; asst. prof. dept. fin. and acctg. U. West Fla., Pensacola, 1978—; arbitrator Community Juvenile Arbitration Program for Escambia County. Mem. N.W. Fla. Creek Indian Council, 1981—, sec., 1983-88; bd. dirs. Pensacola Mental Health Assn., 1985—, Family Outreach Vols. Inc., 1987-88, Creek Indian Mus., Blountstown, Fla., 1986—. Mem. Am. Inst. CPAs, Fla. Inst. CPAs (dir. West. Fla. chpt. 1985-87, bd. govs. 1985-87, pres. 1985-86), ABA, Fla. Bar Assn., Escambia-Santa Rosa Bar Assn., Estate Planning Council N.W. Fla. (dir. 1985-86), Fla. Women's Network (dir. 1986—), Network of Exec. Women (pres. 1983-84), Phi Delta Phi. Democrat. Methodist. Clubs: UWF Women's, Panhandle Tiger Bay. Office: PO Box 3697 Pensacola FL 32506

CALLAWAY, RISA SHIMODA, marketing consultant, brand management specialist; b. Englewood, N.J., Sept. 4, 1955; d. Midori Arthur and June (Yamashita) Shimoda; m. Forrest Kevin Callaway, Aug. 23, 1986. BS, Stanford U., 1977. Design engr. Procter and Gamble Co., Cin., 1978-79, mktg. brand asst., 1979-81; assoc. brand mgr. M&M/Mars Co., Hackettstown, N.J., 1981-82, brand mgr., 1983-84; brand mgr. Coca Cola Co., Atlanta, 1984-86, assoc. brand dir., 1986-87; prin. cons., owner Risa and Co., Denver, NC, 1987—. Olympic project coordinator M&M/Mars, Hackettstown, N.J., 1982-83. Named one of 10 Best Whitewater Paddlers in U.S. Canoe Mag., 1987, Outstanding Young Women of Am., 1984. Mem. Charlotte Women Bus. Owners Assn., Am. Whitewater Affiliation (bd. dirs. 1986, exec. dir. 1987—), Stanford Alumni Assn. (past pres.). Home and Office: PO Box 375 Denver NC 28037

CALLENDER, NORMA ANNE, educator; b. Huntsville, Tex., May 10, 1933; d. Cleburn William Carswell and Nell Ruth (Collard) Hughes Bost; m. Billy Gene Callender, July 13, 1951 (div. Mar. 1964); children: Teresa Elizabeth, Leslie Gemey, Shannah Hughes, Kelly Mari. BS in Edn., U. Houston, 1969; MA, U. Houston at Clear Lake, 1977; postgrad. Lamar U., 1972-73, Tex. So. U., 1971, St. Thomas U., 1985, 86, U. Houston-Clear Lake, 1979, 87, 88, San Jacinto Coll., 1988. Aerospace Inst., NASA, Johnson Space Ctr., 1986. Cert. reading specialist, Tex. Tchr., Houston Ind. Schs., 1969-70; co-counselor and instr. Ellington AFB, Houston, 1971; tchr. Clear Creek Schs., Seabrook, Tex., 1970-75; part-time instr. San Jacinto Coll., Pasadena, Tex., 1980-81; tchr. Clear Creek Schs., Webster, Tex., 1975-86; adj. instr., 1986, supr. student tchrs., 1986—, U. Houston, Clear Lake, Tex., 1986; supr. student tchrs.1986—; owner, dir. Bay Area Tutoring and Reading Clinic, Clear Lake City, Tex., 1970—; owner Bay Area Tng. Assocs., Houston, 1981—; mem. adv. bd. Clear Creek Ednl. Resource Ctr. Publ., League City, 1976-77; mem. Prin's Council of Excellence, 1985-86; owner Bay Area Tng. Assocs., Webster, 1981-87. Editor: A Prism of Prose and Poetry, 1983. Mem. Bay Area Rep. Women's Fedn., 1987-88, Republican Presdl. Task Force (charter), 1982; state advisor U.S. Congl. Adv. Bd., 1985-87; charter mem. Clear Creek Assn. Retarded Citizens, Houston, 1982; mem. Assn. Children with Learning Disabilities, Novato, Calif., 1973; bd. dirs. Ballet San Jacinto, 1985-87. Recipient Franklin award U. Houston, 1965-67; Delta Kappa Gamma/Beta Omicron scholar, 1967-68; PTA scholar, 1973; Berwin scholar, 1976; Mary Gibbs Jones scholar, 1976-77; Found. Econ. Edn. scholar, 1976; Insts. Achievement Human Potential scholar, Phila., 1987-88. Mem. Clear Creek Educators Assn. (honorarium 1976, 77, 85), Internat. Reading Assn. (research com. chpt. 1976-77), U. Houston at Clear Lake Alumni Assn. (charter), Gulf Coast Council Fgn. Affairs, Leadership Clear Lake Alumni Assn. (charter, program and projects com mem. 1986-87, edn. com. 1985), Tex. Soc. Coll. Tchrs. Edn., Kappa Delta Pi, Phi Delta Kappa, Phi Kappa Phi. Mem. Life Tabernacle Ch. Club: Toastmasters. Home: 963 Seagate Ln Houston TX 77062 Office: PO Box 890932 Houston TX 77289-0932

CALLIHAN, HARRIET K., medical society executive; b. Chgo., Feb. 8, 1930; d. Harry Louis and Josephine (Olstad) Kohlman; m. Clair Clifton Callihan, Dec. 17, 1955; 1 child, Barbara Clair Callihan. BA, U. Chgo., 1951, MBA, 1953. Personnel dir. Leo Burnett Co., Chgo., 1953-57, John Plain & Co., 1957-62, Follett Pub. Co., 1962-64, Needham, Harper & Steers, N.Y.C., 1966-68, Bell, Boyd, Lloyd, Haddad & Burns, 1964-66, Hume, Clement, Hume & Lee, 1968-70; owner, operator PersD, 1970-75; exec. dir. Inst. Medicine Chgo., 1975—, mng. editor ofcl. med. publ. Proceedings, 1975—. Sec./treas. Interagy. Council on Smoking and Disease. Mem. Chgo. Soc. Assn. Execs., Conf. Med. Soc. Execs. Greater Chgo. (pres.), Am. Med. Writers Assn. (pres., v.p. publicity club), Nat. Sci. Writer's Assn., Lincoln Park Zool. Soc., Field Mus. Soc. Natural History, Nat. Soc. Fund Raising Exec. Profl. Conv. Mgrs. Assn., Chgo. Council Fgn. Relations, Chgo. Connection, Met. Chgo. Coalition Aging, Midwest Pharm. Advt. Club. Clubs: Westmoreland Country, Michigan Shores, Cliffdwellers. Office: Inst Medicine of Chgo 332 S Michigan Ave Chicago IL 60604

CALLOWAY, DIONNE CLICHÉ, federal agency administrator; b. N.Y.C., Mar. 10, 1956; d. Alfred Clifford and Joan (Locklear) C. AB, Vassar Coll., 1978; postgrad., Hofstra U., 1978-79; cert., U. Strasbourg, France, 1979, diploma in French studies, 1980; MA, Johns Hopkins U., Bologna, Italy and Washington, 1982. Legislative analyst Legi-Slate, Inc., Washington, 1983-84; desk officer U.S. Peace Corps., Washington, 1984-86; internat. trade analyst U.S. Dept. Commerce, Washington, 1986—. Mem. Nat. Assn. Female Execs., Women Internat. Trade Assn. Office: US Dept Commerce ITA 14th St and Constitution Ave NW Washington DC 20230

CALLOWAY, DORIS HOWES, university provost; b. Canton, Ohio, Feb. 14, 1923; d. Earl John and Lillian Ann (Roberts) Howes; m. Nathaniel O. Calloway, Feb. 14, 1946 (div. 1956); children: David Karl, Candace; m. Robert O. Nesheim, July 4, 1981. B.S., Ohio State U., 1943; Ph.D., U. Chgo., 1947. Head metabolism lab., nutritionist, chief div. QM Food and Container Inst., Chgo., 1951-61; chmn. dept. food sci. and nutrition Stanford Research Inst., Menlo Park, Calif., 1961-63; prof. U. Calif., Berkeley, 1963—, provost profl. schs. and colls., 1981-87; mem. expert adv. panel nutrition WHO, Geneva, 1972—; trustee Internat. Maize and Wheat Improvement Ctr., 1983—; trustee, bd. dirs. Winrock Internat. Inst., 1986—; cons. FAO, UN, Rome, 1971,74-75,81-83; adv. council NIH, Nat. Inst. Arthritis, Metabolic and Digestive Diseases, Nat. Inst. Aging, Bethesda, Md., 1974-77, 78-82. Author: Nutrition and Health, 1981, Nutrition and Physical Fitness 11th edit., 1984. Recipient Meritorious Civilian Service Dept. Army, 1959; named Disting. Alumna Ohio State U., 1974, Wellcome vis. prof. Fedn. Am. Soc. Exptl. Biol., U. Mo., 1980. Mem. Am. Inst. Nutrition (pres. 1982-83, sec. 1969-72, editorial bd. 1967-72; Conrad A. Elvehjem award 1986), Am. Dietetic Assn. (editorial bd. 1974-77, Cooper Meml. lectr. 1983), Inst. Medicine Nat. Acad. Scis., Sigma Xi. Office: U Calif Morgan Hall Berkeley CA 94720

CALMESE, LINDA, computer training center executive, consultant; b. East St. Louis, Ill., June 3, 1947; d. Lonnie Daniel and Louise (Anderson) C. BS, So. Ill. U., 1969, MS, 1972, specialist degree counselor edn., 1978. Tchr. bus. edn. St. Teresa Acad., East St. Louis, 1969-73, DODDS, Madrid, Spain, 1973-84; computer cons. Scott AFB, Ill., 1984-87, Norton AFB, Calif., 1986, Navy Fin. Ctr., Cleve., 1987, Billy Mitchell Air Field, Milw., 1987, Richards Gebaur AFB, Kansas City, Mo., 1988, NASA, Cleve., 1988, Army Corps Engrs., St. Louis, 1988, Nat. U. San Diego, 1988; pres. Bits and Bytes Computer Tng. Ctr., Belleville, Ill., 1985—; instr. State Community Coll., East St. Louis, 1986-87, Office Personnel Mgmt. San Diego, San Francisco, Los Angeles; computer cons. Army Aviation Systems Command, St. Louis, 1986-87, Navy Fin. Ctr., Cleve., 1987—, Billy Mitchell Air Field, Milw., 1987—, Ohio Army N.G., Worthington, Ohio, 1986, 88, Mil. Personnel Records Ctr., St. Louis, 1986, Richards-Gebaur AFB, Kansas City, Mo., 1988, City of San Francisco, 1988, City of San Diego, 1988. Contbr. chpt. to book: Business Education for the 70's, 1969. Clk. Mt. Zion Baptist Mission East Ch., East St. Louis, 1987—. Mem. Nat. Assn. Female Execs., Delta Pi Epsilon, Pi Omega Pi. Baptist. Avocations: travel, computing, reading, aerobics. Office: Bits and Bytes Computer Tng Ctr 56 S 65th St Suite 1 Belleville IL 62223

CALMIA, KATHY MALINA, human resource consultant; b. Houston, Nov. 5, 1948; d. Robert Benno and Mildred Elizabeth (Lane) Malina; m. Gary Howard Calmia, Jan. 10, 1981; children: Malina Lane Pearson, Richard B. Pearson III. BA, U. Houston, 1973. Personnel asst. Bechtel Power Corp., Houston, 1973-78; personnel adminstr. Drilling Equipment div. Geosource Inc., Houston, 1978-81; employment mgr. Dallas Morning News, 1981-83; human resource cons. Control Data Benefit Services, Dallas, 1983-87; regional mgr. human resources Businessland, 1987—. Coordinator Dallas Morning News United Way Fund Drive, 1981-82, Parkland Hosp. Blood Drive, Dallas, 1986, 87; mem. Mayor's Council to Hire Handicapped, Dallas, 1982, 83. Mem. Am. Soc. Personnel Adminstrn. Republican. Lutheran.

CALO, NERISSA BETH SMITH, publishing company representative; b. Arlington, Mass., May 12, 1961; d. Robert Harry and Betty Lou (Adams) Smith; m. Ron J. Calo, Feb. 15, 1986. BA, Mt. Holyoke Coll., 1983. cert. tchr., Mass. Exec. sec. Millipore Corp., Bedford, Mass., 1983-84; office mgr. A-Temps, Tewksbury, Mass., 1984; customer service rep. D.C. Heath & Co., Lexington, Mass., 1984-85, mktg. asst., 1985, sales rep., 1985—. Mem. Nat. Assn. Female Execs., Mass. Council Tchrs. of English. Mem. Ch. of Christ. Home: 3 Norfolk St 125 Spring St Nashua NH 03060

CALPOTURA, (MARIA) MINERVA O. (DDOO), sociologist, fund organizer; b. Manila, Apr. 21, 1952; came to U.S. Sept., 1984; d. Venancio Concepcion and Lorenza (Caluag) C. BS in Social Work cum laude, U. Philippines, 1974, MA in Sociology, 1981. Registered social worker, Philippines. Population edn. tng. officer Asian Labor Edn. Ctr. U. of the Philippines, Quezon City, 1974-76; community work trainer Agy. for Community Edn. Services, Quezon City, 1977-78; researcher Agy. for Community Ednl. Services, Quezon City, 1978, head research dept., 1978-81, also bd. dirs.; mem. teaching staff Asian Social Inst., Manila, 1979-80; cons. community orgn. IROTECH/U. Philippines, Quezon City, 1979-80; head dept. research and evaluation Devel. Acad. of the Philippines, Pasig, Philippines, 1981-84; conventional and govt. funder Homestead Savs., Millbrae, Calif., 1985—. Contbr. articles to profl. jours. Mem. Phi Kappa Phi. Home: 220 Linden Ave San Bruno CA 94066

CALVERT, BARBARA JEAN, energy executive; b. Washington, Feb. 6, 1954; d. Charles M. and Jean D. (Bowman) C. BA in French summa cum laude, U. Md., 1976; cert. in Polish studies, Jagiellonian U., Krakow, Poland, 1978; MA in Internat. Relations, Johns Hopkins U., 1979. Economist Dept. Labor, Washington, 1976-77; intern Commn. of European Communities, Brussels, 1977-78; fgn. sales rep. Industrializzione Brevetti e Marchi, Bologna, Italy, 1978-79; internat. economist Dept. Treasury, Washington, 1979-81; sr. analyst pub. affairs Royal Dutch/Shell Corp., N.Y.C., 1981-84, mgr. internat. pub. affairs, 1984-86; pres. USA Copeland, Wickersham, Wiley Cons., Inc., N.Y.C., 1987; alt. adv. bd. mem. Council of the Ams., N.Y.C., 1981-86. Republican.

CALVERT, LOIS WILSON, civic worker; b. Hartford, Conn., Sept. 12, 1924; d. Royal Wouldhave and Evelyn Charlotte (Danielson) Wilson; m. Wallace Erdix Calvert, Mar. 29, 1947; children: Pamela, Gary, Craig and David (twins). Grad., Bryant Coll., 1943. Registrar of voters Town of Simsbury, Conn., 1982—. Hist. columnist Imprint Publs., West Hartford, Conn., 1986-87. Bd. dirs. Simsbury Hist. Soc., 1978—; mem. Simsbury Com. on Aging, 1980—, Dem. Town Com., Simsbury, 1982—, also archivist, Conn. Hist. Soc., Hartford, 1984—, Simsbury Cemetery Assn., 1987—, Friends of Simsbury Library; del. 6th dist. Dem. Conv., Bristol, Conn., 1984, 86; trustee Simsbury Land Trust, 1984—; justice of the peace Town of Simsbury, 1985—, mem. constitutional conv. bicentennial commn., Hometown Hero, 1986.; alt. Conn. Dem. Conv. for Gov., Hartford, 1986—; mng. dir. Simsbury Hist. Soc. Named a Simsbury Woman Hartford Woman Mag., 1987. Mem. Registrar of Voters Assn. Conn. Congregationalist. Home: 28 Riverside Rd Simsbury CT 06070

CALVIN, DOROTHY VER STRATE, computer company executive; b. Grand Rapids, Mich., Dec. 22, 1929; d. Herman and Christina (Plakmyer) Ver Strate; m. Allen D. Calvin, Oct. 5, 1953; children—Jamie, Kris, Bufo, Scott. BS magna cum laude, Mich. State U., 1951; MA, U. San Francisco, 1988. Mgr. data processing. Behavioral Research Labs., Menlo Park, Calif., 1972-75; dir. Mgmt. Info. Systems Inst. for Prof. Devel., San Jose, Calif. 1975-76; systems analyst, programmer Pacific Bell Info. Systems, San Francisco, 1976-81; staff mgr., 1981-84; mgr. applications devel. Data Architects Inc., San Francisco, 1984-86; pres. Ver Strate Press, San Francisco, 1986—. Instr., Downtown Community Coll., San Francisco, 1980-84, Cañada Community Coll., 1986—; mem. computer curriculum adv. council San Francisco City Coll., 1982-84. Vice pres. LWV, Roanoke, Va., 1956-58; pres. Bulliss Purissima Parents Group, Los Altos, Calif., 1962-64; bd. dirs. Vols. for Israel, 1986-87. Mem. Nat. Assn. Female Execs., Assn. Systems Mgmt., Assn. Women in Computing. Democrat. Avocations: computing; gardening; jogging; reading. Office: Ver Strate Press 1645 15th Ave San Francisco CA 94122

CALZONE, ANGELA SUE, truck company manager; b. Newark, N.J., June 12, 1962; d. Anthony Ralph and Beatrice (Fania) C. BA, Upsala Coll., 1984. Lic. N.J. real estate sales. Pub. service dir. Sta. WFMU Radio, East Orange, N.J., 1978-83; technician radio stas., N.J., 1982-84; program asst. Sta. WMTR, Morristown, N.J., 1984-85; office mgr. Am. Advt. Dist., Montville, N.J., 1985; asst. v.p. Archie Schwartz Co. Realtors, East Orange, 1985-86; term leasing mgr. Resources Trailer Leasing, East Orange, 1986—. Editor lit. mag. Foci, 1981-84; contbr. poetry to mags. Mem. William Carlos Williams Ctr. for Performing Arts, Rutherford, N.J.; vol. animal rights groups. Mem. Am. Mktg. Assn., Ind./Comml. Real Estate Women. Office: Resources Trailer Leasing 112 Washington St East Orange NJ 07017

CAMACHO, BLANCA ESTER, actress; b. N.Y.C., Nov. 19, 1956; d. Gilberto and Blanca Erlinda (Peña) C.; m. Anthony Ruiz, Oct. 6, 1984. BS in Ednl. Theatre, NYU, 1978. Actress Lamb's Theatre Co., N.Y.C., 1986, Pub. Theatre, N.Y.C., 1986, East Lynne Co., N.Y.C., 1986, Duo Theatre, N.Y.C., 1986—; founding mem. Latin Am. Theatre Experiment Associated, N.Y.C., 1983-87; mem. Ubu Repertory Theater, 1988, N.Y. Internat. Festival of the Arts. Appeared in Guiding Light, 1979-80, All My Children, 1986, various commls. Recipient Citizenship award Am. Legion, 1970. Mem. Screen Actors Guild (ethnic employment opportunities com.), Nat. Assn. Female Execs., Hispanic Orgn. of Latin Actors

CAMASSO, JO ANN MARIA, nurse; b. Abington, Pa., Oct. 4, 1950; d. Ralph and Lucy (Rose) C. Diploma in nursing, Abington (Pa.) Hosp., 1971; BS in Nursing, U. Pa., 1975. Cert. nursing adminstr. Pub. health nurse City Phila., 1972-73, 75-78; rehab. nurse Internat. Rehab. Assn., Hallendale, Fla., 1978-79; mem. admissions staff Associated Home Health, Ft. Lauderdale, Fla., 1979-80; supr. Ctr. for Living, Ft. Lauderdale, 1980-81; dir. nursing Resthaven, Phila., 1981-83; dir. profl. service Helping Hand, Jenkintown, Pa., 1983-84; dir. nursing Unicare, Dresher, Pa., 1984-86, Miami, Fla., 1986; div. nurse Unicare, Ft. Lauderdale, 1986-87; dir. nursing Palm Garden North Miami Beach, Fla., 1987—. Contbr. articles to profl. jours., 1985-86. Mem. Am. Nursing Assn., Fla. Nursing Assn. Democrat. Roman Catholic. Home: 2520 N Andrews Ave Wilton Manors FL 33305

CAMBRIA, CATHY A., television producer; b. Rockville Center, N.Y., Oct. 26, 1955; d. Francis Martin and Dorothy Frances (McCormack) C. AA, Westbrook Coll., 1975; MFA magna cum laude, L.I. U., 1977. Mem. prodn. staff CBS, N.Y.C., 1977-81, 82—, NBC, N.Y.C., 1981-82; prodn. exec. CTV-USA Network, N.Y.C., 1985; mem. prodn. staff ABC, N.Y.C., 1986; pres. No Regrets Prodns. Inc., N.Y.C., 1988—. Major TV credits include: assoc. producer As the World Turns, CBS, The Drs., NBC, 1981-82, A Fine Romance, CBS, 1982, Kate & Allie, CBS, 1982-86, Robert Klein Show, ABC, 1986; Stiller and Meara Show, NBC, 1986, co-producer Kate & Allie, 1986—; producer Salute to Thames TV, WNET, Baby on Board, CBS, 1987-88; line producer Ragu Commercials. Vol. Conn. Spl. Olympics, Greenwich, 1985—. Mem. Producers Guild Am., Dirs. Guild Am., Acad. TV Arts and Scis. Home: 350 W 57th St New York NY 10019 Office: Kate & Allie 1697 Broadway Suite 307 New York NY 10019

CAMELI, SANDRA ANN, accountant; b. Scranton, Pa., Jan. 21, 1961; d. George E. and Elaine S. (Sofranko) C. BS in Acctg., U. Scranton, 1982. CPA, Pa. Staff asst. to sr. acct. Parente, Randolph, Orlando, Carey & Assocs., Wilkes-Barre, Pa., 1982-86; sr. acct. RJR Nabisco, Inc., Wilkes-Barre, 1987—. Mem. Nat. Assn. Female Execs., Am. Inst. CPA's, Pa. Inst. CPA's. Home: 620 E Warren St Dunmore PA 18512

CAMERA, JOAN ANN, hospital administrator; b. N.Y.C., Nov. 19, 1955; d. Louis Anthony and Anna C. (Cinque) C. BS, Fordham U., 1977; MPH, Columbia U., 1980. Admissions officer Our Lady of Mercy Med. Ctr., N.Y.C., 1974-81; adminstrv. resident Montefiore Hosp., N.Y.C., 1979-80; asst. dir. North Cen. Bronx Hosp., N.Y.C., 1980-84; asst. adminstr. Hillside div. Long Island Jewish Med. Ctr., New Hyde Park, N.Y., 1984—. Mem. Hosp. Execs. Club (bd. dirs., sec. 1986—), Met. Health Adminstrs. Assn., Am. Coll. Healthcare Execs. Office: LI Jewish Med Ctr 75 59 263 St Glen Oaks NY 11004

CAMERON, COLLEEN IRENE, alcoholism counselor; b. Stillwater, Minn., Nov. 3, 1952; d. Lyle James and Mary Rose (Jesse) C.; 1 child, Natalie Irene. Grad. high sch., Lindstrom, Minn. Cert. alcoholism counselor, Wis. Counseling supr. St. Croix Health Ctr., New Richmond, Wis., 1977-83; dir. Out Lady's Inn, St. Louis, 1984; dir. ops. Carpenter Health Care Systems, St. Louis, 1984-86; supr. Edgewood Program St. John's Mercy

Med. Ctr., St. Louis, 1986—, St. Elizabeth Med. Ctr., Granite City, Ill., 1986—. Roman Catholic. Office: Edgewood Program 1121 University Dr Edwardsville IL 62025

CAMERON, ELSA SUE, curator, consultant; b. San Francisco, Nov. 19, 1939; d. L. Don and Betty (Jelinsky) C.; m. Michael Lerner, Dec. 24, 1979 (div. 1981). BA, San Francisco State U., 1961, MA, 1965; teaching credential, 1962. Curator Randall Jr. Mus., San Francisco, 1963-65, Fine Arts Mus. Downtown Ctr., San Francisco, 1976-80, San Francisco Airport Galleries, 1980—; exec. dir. Community Arts, Inc., San Francisco; reporter Council on Mus., N.Y.C., 1973-80; asst. prof. art edn. U. So. Calif., Los Angeles, 1982-83; cons. U. Art Mus., Berkeley, 1980-82, instr. 1981, 101 California Venture, San Francisco, 1986—; cons. Art in Pub. Pls., Miami, Fla., 1988. Reporter: (book) The Art Museum as Educator, 1977, (exhibit catalogue) Airport Cafe, 1986. Fellow NEA, 1973, 77. Mem. Western Regional Conf. (v.p. 1974-75), Am. Assn. Museums. Office: San Francisco Internat Airport Exhibition Box 8097 San Francisco CA 94128

CAMERON, IDA JANE, state government official; b. St. Paul, June 2, 1937; d. Bernis James and Elizabeth Mae Arcand; B.S., Eastern Mich. U., 1962; m. Don R. Cameron, Aug. 16, 1958; children—Amanda Marie, Benjamin David. Tchr., Mich. schs., 1962-76; exec. Fla. chpts. NOW, 1977-79; adminstrv. asst. State of Fla., 1979-80; exec. staff dir. Fla. Dept. Profl. Regulation, Tallahassee, 1978-81, div. dir. adminstrv. services, 1981-83; pres. I.J. Cameron, Mgmt. Consultants, Washington, 1984—. Chmn. Tallahassee Area ERA fundraising, 1978; mem. founding bd. Tallahassee Center Victims Spouse Abuse, 1979-80. Mem. NOW (chmn. Tallahassee chpt. 1977-79), Nat. Assn. Female Execs., AAUW. Home: 4322 Westover Pl NW Washington DC 20016

CAMERON, IRMA KYLLIKKI, food products executive; b. Rovaniemi, Finland, Dec. 25, 1948; came to U.S., 1967; d. Antti Antero Napankangas and Laura Vappu (Karvonen) Makkyla; m. Matt Kullervo Kosola, Dec. 24, 1964 (div. July 1972); 1 child, Jari; m. Jerry Lee Massmann, Aug. 25, 1984. BA in Mid Mgmt., Hennepin County Community Coll., 1982; postgrad. in bus. mgmt., Coll. of St. Thomas, 1983-85. Supr. sales Gen. Mills, Inc., Mpls., 1970-75; mgr. sales office Tampa, Fla., 1975-77; mgr. customer service Mpls., 1977-80, mgr. consumer relations, 1980—. Contbg. author: Business Communication Today, 1986. Arbitrator Better Bus. Bur. Minn., Mpls., 1981—; mem. exec. com. Community Action Team Gen. Mills, Mpls., 1985—, chmn. Adopt-A-Highrise Project, 1986—. Recipient Leadership award Mpls. YWCA, 1981. Mem. Grocery Mfrs. Am., Soc. Consumer Affairs Profls., Nat. Assn. Female Execs. Republican. Office: Gen Mills Inc PO Box 1113 Minneapolis MN 55440

CAMERON, JUDITH ELAINE MOELLERING, marketing and public relations company executive; b. Eagle Grove, Iowa, May 26, 1943; d. Albert Edwin and Marion (Trask) Moellering; m. William Ewen Cameron, Aug. 13, 1966 (div. 1970). BA, Drake U., 1965. Intern, Washington; model Younkers, Des Moines, 1962-65, asst. to columnist Harlan Miller, 1962-65, asst. buyer, copywriter, 1965-66; dir. personnel 4th Northwestern Nat. Bank, Mpls., 1966; head copywriter SPF Advt., Mpls., 1966-68; dir. spl. projects program U. Minn., Mpls., 1968-70; cons. pub. relations Fed. Republic of Germany, Italy, Spain, 1970-71; mgr. Jetset Sportswear, Footville, Wis., 1971-72; artist Almunecar, Spain, 1972-74; dir. pub. relations Topspin, Totalplan Sports Internat., A.G., Madrid, 1974-76, mng. dir., Madrid and London, 1976-80; European mgr. Siam Internat. Amalgamated Mfrs. Ltd., London, 1977-80; European rep. Siam Cement Trading Co., London, 1979-80; European mgr. Third Wave Electronics Co., Inc., London, 1980-82; exec. v.p., dir. Electronic Specialty Products, Inc., N.Y.C., 1983-84; pres. Comml. Brain, Inc., N.Y.C. and N.Mex., 1984—, Rennert and Cameron, Inc., N.Y.C., 1984-86. Six one-woman shows, Spain; 4 group exhbns., Europe. Mem. Republicans Abroad, Women Bus. Owners of N.Y., Nat. Assn. Female Execs., Iowa Soc. N.Y. (founding mem., pres.), Council on Internat. Relations, bd. dirs. N.Mex. Repertory Theater, Spotlighters, N.Mex. 1st Task Force, Alpha Phi.

CAMERON, JUDITH LYNNE, educator, hypnotherapist; b. Oakland, Calif., Apr. 29, 1945; d. Alfred Joseph and June Estelle (Faul) Moe; m. Richard Irwin Cameron, Dec. 17, 1967; 1 child, Kevin Dale. AA in Psychol., Sacramento City Coll., 1965; BA in Psychol., German, Calif. State U., 1967; MA in Reading Specialization, San Francisco State U., 1972; postgrad., Chapman Coll.; PhD, Am. Inst. Hypnotherapy, 1987. cert. tchr. Calif. Tchr. St. Vincent's Catholic Sch., San Jose, Calif., 1969-70, Fremont (Calif.) Elem. Sch., 1970-72, LeRoy Boys Home, LaVerne, Calif., 1972-73; tchr. Grace Miller Elem. Sch., LaVerne, Calif., 1973-80, resource specialist, 1980-84; owner, mgr. Pioneer Take-out Franchises, Alhambra, San Gabriel, Calif., 1979-85; resource specialist, dept. chmn. Bonita High Sch., LaVerne, Calif., 1984—; mentor tchr. in space sci. Bonita Unified Sch. Dist., 1988—; bd. dirs., recommending tchr., asst. dir. Project Turnabout, Claremont, Calif.; Teacher-in-Space cons. Bonita Unified Sch. Dist., LaVerne, 1987—; advisor Peer Counseling Program, Bonita High Sch., 1987—; advisor Air Explorers/Edwards Test Pilot SCh., LaVerne, 1987—. Vol. advisor Children's Home Soc., Santa Ana, 1980-81. Mem. Council Exceptional Children, Calif. Assn. Resource Specialists, Calif. Elem. Edn. Assn., Nat. Edn. Assn., Calif. Teacher's Assn., Calif. Assn. Marriage and Family Therapist, Planetary Soc., Com. Scientific Investigation L5 Soc. Republican. Clubs: Chinese Shar-Pei Am., Concord, Rare Breed Dog, Los Angeles. Home: 3257 La Travesia Dr Fullerton CA 92635 Office: Bonita High Sch 115 W Allen Ave San Dimas CA 91773

CAMERON, MARION A., metals company financial executive; b. Cork, Ireland, Nov. 8, 1950; came to U.S., 1970, naturalized, 1980, d. Sean S. and Siobhan P. (Foley) O'Leary; m. Michael J. Cameron, July 11, 1970; 1 child, Donald. Student Trinity Coll., Dublin, Ireland, 1968-70; B.B.A., Pace U., 1980, M.B.A., 1980. Treas., Amalgamet, Inc., N.Y.C., 1970-75, Bruxelles Lambert Group, N.Y.C., 1975-80; v.p. fin., treas. Sipi Metals Corp., Chgo., 1982—. Mem. The Copper Club, Mensa. Avocations: opera; theatre. Home: 301 Sheridan Rd Wilmette IL 60091 Office: Sipi Metals Corp 1720 Elston Ave Chicago IL 60622

CAMERON, ROSEMARY OLIVIA, library assistant; b. Orosi, Calif., Apr. 30, 1926; d. Peter D. and Madeline B. (Pavicic) Pavicich; m. William H. Swanson, Nov. 16, 1945 (dec. 1958); children: William H. II, Olivia Marie Faries; m. Max B. Cameron, 1961 (dec. Mar. 1984). Student, Bakersfield Jr. Coll., 1944-45. Acct. Cardswell Acctg., CPA, Delano, Calif., 1952-58; head bookkeeping and gen. ledger div. Manchester Mortgage Co., Fresno, Calif., 1959-61; co-owner, buyer Cameron Men's Store, Delano, 1961-64; account clk. Calif. Poly. U., San Luis Obispo, 1964-68; library asst. I documents sect. Calif. Poly. U. Library, San Luis Obispo, 1968-70, library asst. I cataloging, 1970-72, library asst. II spl. collections, 1972-74, library asst. II govt. documents, 1974-77, library asst. III res. room supervision, 1977—; fashion show coordinator, seminars Cameron Men's Store, Delano, 1961-64. Active mem. Missionary Assn. of Mary Immaculate, Belleville, Ill., 1987—; hon. citizen Boys Town, Nebr., 1987—. Mem. Nat. Assn. Female Execs., Inc., Calif. Poly. Univ. Club (bd. dirs. 1986—), Nat. Geographic Soc. Republican. Roman Catholic. Club: Aero-Crats (Delano) (v.p. 1946-48).

CAMERON, SUZANNE HAYDEN, land developer, market analyst, securities and real estate broker; b. Newark, Ohio, Sept. 28, 1949; d. George Allen and Virginia (Scott) Hayden; B.A., (U. Rehab. scholar), Ohio State U., 1972, postgrad., 1976-78; postgrad. U. Chgo., 1973-78; 1 son, Allen. With Plikerd & Assos., Newark, 1973-77; market research product design, sales/mktg. Sea Pines Plantation, Hilton Head Island, S.C., 1978-80, market research, developer coordination mktg., sales program Daufuskie Island, 1980; mktg. and land devel. cons., 1980-85; v.p. mktg., land devel. Arvida/Disney, Arvida/JWB, Miami, Fla., 1985-88, Mobil Land Devel. Corp., Miami, 1988 —. Mem. Urban Land Inst. (community devel. council), Nat. Assn. Homebuilders, Am. Mktg. Assn., Am. Resort and Recreation Assn., Builders Assn. South Fla., Nat. Assn. Securities Dealers, S.C. Bd. Realtors, Nat. Assn. Bds. of Realtors, Nat. Council Barrier-Free Devel., Ohio State U. Alumni Assn., Fla. Real Estate Adv. Council, Kappa Kappa Gamma. Office: Am Resort Recreation Devel Aassn 2790 SW 23rd Ave Coconut Grove FL 33133

CAMIN, MARGARET BRUCE, electrical manufacturing company executive; b. New Orleans, Mar. 29, 1950; d. John Markey and Irma Druscilla (Weisdorffer) B.; m. Lynden Carl Camin, May 25, 1974. BEE, La. State U., 1972; M in Computer Sci., Union Coll., 1976. Engr. Gen. Electric Co., Pittsfield, Mass., 1973-80; lead engr. Gen. Electric Co., 1980-81, mgr. tng., computer engr., 1981-86, mgr. tng. software engring., 1986-87, mgr. tng. program engr., 1987—. Advisor Boy Scout Exployers, Pittsfield, 1980-85. Mem. Tau Beta Pi. Roman Catholic. Club: Coll. (Pittsfield) (pres. 1981-83). Home: Cheshire Rd Lanesboro MA 01237 Office: Gen Electric Ordnance Systems 100 Plastics Ave Pittsfield MA 01201

CAMM, GERTRUDE ELIZABETH, physician, writer; b. Enid, Okla., Aug. 21, 1930; d. John Palmer and Gertrude (Hollis) C. AB, Duke U., 1951, postgrad., 1951-53; postgrad., Sarah Lawrence Coll., 1962-63, Columbia U., 1963-64, U. Okla, 1964-66; MD, U. Pa., 1968. Researcher in biochem. and biophys. Duke U. Sch. Medicine, Durham, N.C., 1953-55; intern and resident in internal medicine Royal Victoria Hosp., Montreal, Que., Can., 1968-70; resident in pediatrics U. Ill. Hosp., Chgo., 1970-71, Emory U. Affiliated Hosps., Atlanta, 1971-72; practice medicine specializing in pediatrics and family medicine Cen. Fla., 1973-75, Ala., 1975-76; practice medicine specializing in emergency medicine Chgo., 1976-84, Cen. Fla., Ala., Ga., 1984—; instr. pediatrics U. Ill., Chgo., 1970-71, Advanced Cardiac Life Support, 1982—; lectr. med. topics for community groups, 1974—; dir. hosp. emergency depts., 1984-87, community emergency med. system, 1984-86. Author: In the Deep Blue Sea, 1961; contbr. articles to profl. jours. and mags. Musician amateur community symphony orchs., 1953—; sec. Fla. Symphony Orch. affiliate bd. Lake County; mem. Environ. Groups, Orlando and Ormond Beach, Fla., 1982—, John F. Lindsey Campaign for Mayor, N.Y.C., 1960. Served as vol. physician M.C. U.S. Army, 1972, Vietnam. AMA grantee, 1972. Mem. AAAS, AAUW (pres. Ormond Beach chpt. 1974-75), So. Med. Assn., Flying Physicians Assn., Aircraft Owners and Pilots Assn., Phi Beta Kappa. Presbyterian. Club: Fox Meadow Tennis, Marina Point Yacht.

CAMP, ALETHEA TAYLOR, state agency administrator; b. Wingo, Ky., Nov. 12, 1938; d. Wayne Thomas and Ethel Virginia (Austin) Taylor; children: Donna Paul, Sean Richard. BA, Murray State U., 1961; MA, So. Ill. U., 1975. Tchr. McClean and Hopkins (Ky.) County Schs., 1961-64; instr. homebound Harrisburg (Ill.) Community Sch. Dist., 1971-73; counselor evaluation Coleman Rehab. Ctr., Shawneetown, Ill., 1974-75; counselor corrections and parole Dept. Corrections, State Ill., Springfield, 1975-77, supr. casework, 1977, supr. parole, 1977-80; asst. warden programs Dept. Corrections, State Ill., Hillsboro, 1980-84, warden, 1984—. Mem. Am. Correctional Assn., Ill. Correctional Assn., N. Am. Wardens Assn. Office: Ill Dept Corrections Graham Correctional Cen Hillsboro IL 62049

CAMP, BARBARA ANN, municipal government official; b. Lancaster, Pa., Feb. 13, 1943; d. Linton Ferguson and Anna (Wills) Mennig; m. Nils Victor Anderson, Nov. 25, 1961 (div. 1972); children—Barbara Jean, Susan Michelle, Jennifer Eileen; m. Robert Tomlin Camp, Dec. 29, 1973. Registered mcpl. clk., N.J. Sec., Sun Oil Corp., Phila., 1960-61; sales clk. Thomas Jewelers, Ocean City, N.J., 1969-71; composite typist Avalon Herald, N.J., 1971-72; exec. sec. Publs. Press., Pleasantville, N.J., 1972-74; clk.-typist Twp. of Upper Tuckahoe, N.J., 1977-78, mcpl. clk., 1978—. Editor twp. calendar, 1984-86. Mem. Mcpl. Clks. Assn. of N.J. (asst. treas. 1985-87, treas. 1987, asst. sec. 1988), Internat. Inst. Mcpl. Clks., Cape May County Clks. Assn. (past sec., past v.p., past pres.), Assn. Twps. (sec.). Avocations: snow skiing; boating. Home: 223 Laurel Dr Marmora NJ 08223

CAMP, HAZEL LEE BURT, artist; b. Gainesville, Ga., Nov. 28, 1922; d. William Ernest and Annie Mae (Ramsey) Burt; student Md. Inst. Art, 1957-58, 62-63; m. William Oliver Camp, Jan. 24, 1942; children—William Oliver, David Byron. One-woman shows at Ga. Mus. Art, Rockville Art Mus., Coll. Notre Dame (Balt.), U. Md., Balt. Vertical Gallery, Cleveland Meml. Gallery (Balt.), Unicorn Gallery, 1982, Hampton Ctr. for Arts and Humanities (Va.), 1985, others; exhibited in juried shows at Peale Mus., Balt., Wilmington (Del.) Fine Arts Center, Smithsonian Instn., Turner Gallery, Balt., City Hall Balt., Bendann Art Gallery, Balt., 1980, City Hall Gallery, Balt., 1982, Balt. Watercolor Soc., 1983, others; represented in permanent collections: Ga. Mus. Art, Peabody Inst. (Balt.), Rehoboth Art League, numerous pvt. collections. Recipient 1st prize Md. chpt. Artists' Equity, 1967; St. Marys County Art Assn., 1964, 67, 1st prize still life Cape May, N.J., 1969, Catonsville (Md.) Community Coll., 1969, St. John's Coll., 1969, Best in Show York (Pa.) Art Assn. Gallery, 1972, 2d award Md. Inst. Alumni Founding Chpt., Balt., 1976, Best in Show Three Arts Club, 1978, Watercolor award State Art Exhbt., Nat. League Am. Pen Women, 1979, also 3d prize oil, Tulsa biennial, 1966, Honorable Mention, Rehoboth Art League, 1983; Purchase award Old Point Nat. Bank, Hampton, Va., 1985, Merit award Hampton (Va.) City Hall, 1986, Juror's Choice award Twentieth Century Gallery, Williamsburg, Va., 1987. Mem. Nat. League Am. Pen Women (pres. Carroll br. 1968-70, editor The Quill 1975-76, editor for Carroll br. 1982-83; rec. sec. nat. exec. bd. 1979-80; nat. nominating com. 1982; Md. art chmn. 1982), Artists' Equity, Rehoboth Art League, Va. Watercolor Soc., Md. Fedn. Art, Md. Inst. Alumni Assn., Balt. Watercolor Soc. (hon. mention 1982, sec. 1978-80), Peninsula Fine Arts Ctr. Democrat. Methodist. Contbr. illustrations to mags., booklets. Home: 2 Bayberry Dr Newport News VA 23601

CAMP, LAURIE SMITH, lawyer; b. Omaha, Nov. 28, 1953; d. Edson and Virginia Elizabeth (Abbott) Smith; m. Jon Allan Camp, May 12, 1975; children: Jonathan Scott, Abigail Anne. B.A. with honors, Stanford U., 1974; J.D., U. Nebr., 1977. Bar: Nebr. 1977, Kans. 1979. In-house counsel 1st Nat. Bank, Lincoln, Nebr., 1977-78; assoc. Turner & Boisseau, Great Bend, Kans., 1978-80; gen. counsel Nebr. Dept. Correctional Services, Lincoln, 1980—; gen. ptnr., counsel Haymarket Historic Real Estate Rehab., Lincoln, 1982—. Editor-in-chief Nebr. Law Rev., 1976-77; contbr. articles to profl. jours. Mem. Nebr. Bar Assn., Kans. Bar Assn., Nebr. Correctional Assn. (pres. 1982-83). Office: Nebr Dept Correctional Services PO Box 96441 Lincoln NE 68509

CAMP, LINDA JOYCE, communications executive; b. Plattsburgh, N.Y.; d. Maurice B. and Katherine E. (Trombley) C. BS, Cornell U., 1973, M of Pub. Sci., 1977. Media specialist N.Y. Sea Grant Program, Ithaca, 1973-76; mgr. communications, cable communications officer City of St. Paul, 1980—; mem. met. council telecommunicaions task force, St. Paul, 1982-85; mem. Minn. Telecommunications Council, St. Paul, 1984-85. Vol. Big Sister Program, St. Paul, 1980-83. Bush fellow, 1987. Mem. Nat. Assn. Telecommunications Officers (pres. 1983, Pres.'s award 1985), Am. Mgmt. Assn., St. Paul Women in City Mgmt. Club: Cornell U. (Minn.). Office: City of St Paul 233 City Hall Saint Paul MN 55102

CAMPAGNA, KAREN RAE ZILE, digital systems project manager; b. Dayton, Ohio, Jan. 19, 1958; d. William and Sharon Rae (Ferrigan) Z. A.A. in Gen. Edn., Fla. Jr. Coll., Jacksonville, 1978; B.S. summa cum laude in Bus. Adminstrn., U. Fla.-Gainesville, 1981; M.B.A. with high honors, U. Central Fla., 1986. Programmer, Riverside Hosp., Jacksonville, Fla., 1974-77; salesperson Body Shop Sportwear, Jacksonville, 1977-78; asst. buyer Tee-To-Green Sportswear, Gainesville, 1980-81; dir. advt. Fla. Software, Orlando, Fla., 1981-82, product mgr. fiber optics Stromberg-Carlson, 1983-85; fiber optic nat. account mgr. Stromberg-Carlson, Lake Mary, Fla., 1982-87; project mgr. digital systems, 1987—; cons. U. Central Fla., Orlando, 1983. Mem. Am. Mktg. Assn., Am. Mgmt. Assn., U. Fla. Alumni Assn., Phi Kappa Phi, Beta Gamma Sigma. Democrat. Club: Gator (Orlando). Office: Stromberg-Carlson Corp 400 Rinehart Rd Lake Mary FL 32746

CAMPANA, ANA ISABEL, architect; b. Banes, Oriente, Cuba, Jan. 16, 1934; came to U.S., 1967, naturalized, 1974; d. Abelardo Joaquin and Amparo (Cabrera) C. B.S., Instituto del Vedado, Havana, 1953; postgrad., Havana U., 1962, Albany (N.Y.) Inst. History and Art, 1970. Architect, Havana U., 1962, Ministry of Pub. Works, Havana, 1962-67; architect designer various firms, N.Y., 1967-74; sr. architect Gen. Electric Co., Schenectady, 1974—. Recipient 1st nat. award Nat. Mus. Com., Havana, 1948, 1st Province award, 1948, several international archtl. performance awards. Mem. AIA (assoc.). Roman Catholic. Home: 10 Mill Ln Apt 109 Schenectady NY 12305 Office: Gen Electric Co 1 River Rd Bldg 23 Room 384-B Schenectady NY 12345

CAMPBELL, BONNIE JEAN, lawyer; b. Norwich, N.Y., Apr. 9, 1948; d. Thomas Glenn and Helen Henrietta (Slater) Pierce; m. Edward Leo Campbell, Dec. 24, 1974. BA summa cum laude, Drake U., 1982, JD, 1984. Bar: Iowa 1985, U.S. Dist. (no. and so. dist.) Iowa 1985. Clk. U.S. Dept. Housing and Urban Devel., Washington, 1965-67, U.S. Senate Subcom. on Inter Govtl. Relations, Washington, 1967-69; case worker Hon. Harold E. Hughes, Washington, 1969-74; field rep. U.S. Senator John C. Culver, Des Moines, 1974-80; assoc. Wimer, Hudson, Flynn & Neugent, P.C., Des Moines, 1984—. Mem. awareness com. Powell III, Iowa Meth. Hosp., Des Moines, 1984; mem. adv. com. Des Moines Community Coll., Ankeny, Iowa, 1985; mem. adv. bd. The Assistance Ctr., Des Moines, 1985; bd. dirs. Meth. Hill Children's Ctr., Des Moines, 1986—; state chmn. Iowa Dems., Des Moines, 1987—. Mem. Iowa Bar Assn. (lawyers helping lawyers 1985—), Phi Beta Kappa. Home: 300 Walnut #187 Des Moines IA 50309 Office: Wimer Hudson Flynn & Neugent PC 222 Equitable Bldg Des Moines IA 50309

CAMPBELL, BONNIE MARIE, real estate professional; b. Belle Fourche, S.D., Mar. 2, 1944; d. James Julius and Anita Marie (Nelsen) Wiessner; m. Scott Harrison Campbell, Sept. 17, 1977; children: Keith Edward, Kimberly Denise, Tyson Scott; 1 stepchild, Shad Harrison Campbell. Student, Portland (Oreg.) State U., 1966. Lic. real estate agt., Oreg., Wash. Asst. to dir. Dept. Vocat. Rehab., Portland, 1966-69; asst. to pres. Reddaway Truck Lines, Portland, 1973-75; mgr. procurement Notestine Enterprises, Portland, 1976-80; salesman real estate Realty World, West Linn, Oreg., 1980-83, Profls. 100, Inc., Portland, 1983—. Mem. Nat. Assn. Realtors, Nat. Council Exchangers (Gold Card mem.), Comml.-Investment Real Estate Council, Clackamas County Bd. Realtors (Million Dollar Club), Portland Bd. Realtors, Nat. Assn. Female Execs. Hist. Preservation. Roman Catholic. Club: Toastmasters (Portland). Office: Profls 100 Inc Realtors 5285 SW Meadows Dr #161 Lake Oswego OR 97035

CAMPBELL, CAROL CANDY, accountant; b. Vermillion, S.D., Mar. 12, 1948; d. Wyatt T. and Ruby G. (Drafhal) C.; grad. Barnes Sch. Commerce, Denver, 1971. Pub. acct., 1971—; pvt. practice acctg., Denver, 1979—. Mem. Nat. Soc. Enrolled Agts., Colo. Soc. Enrolled Agts. (sec. 1978-79), Nat. Soc. Pub. Accts., Colo. Soc. Pub. Accts., Nat. Assn. Female Execs. Episcopalian. Clubs: Women of St. John's, Pilot Internat. (dir. Denver 1980-81, corr. sec. 1984—, builder S.W. dist. club 1987), Pilot of Denver (pres. 1986-87), Pilot Bridge Marathon (S.W. dist. pilot coordinator for outreach div. 1983-84). Home: 2621 S Green Ct Denver CO 80219 Office: 4800 Happy Canyon Rd Suite 290 Denver CO 80237

CAMPBELL, CAROL NOWELL, lawyer; b. Phoenix, Dec. 16, 1944; d. Richard Converse Nowell and Nancy (Newcomb) Olson; m. Robert Norman Campbell, Jan. 2, 1965 (div. 1968); 1 child, Kelly Christine; m. Harding Briggs Cure, June 28, 1984. B.A., Ariz. State U.-Tempe, 1972, J.D., 1978. Bar: Ariz. 1979, Calif. 1979, U.S. Dist. Ct. Ariz. 1979, U.S. Dist. Ct. (cen. dist.) Calif. 1984, U.S. Ct. Apls. (9th cir.) 1981. Ptnr. O'Connor, Cavanagh, Anderson, Westover, Killingsworth & Beshears, Phoenix, 1978—; faculty mem. Pacific regional chpt. Nat. Inst. Trial Advocacy, 1985-86. Bd. dirs. Ariz. Council of the Blind, Social Services and Rehab. Inc., 1980-85, sec., 1980-82, v.p. ops. 1983-84; bd. dirs. Phoenix Childrens Theatre, 1981-83, v.p. ops., 1982-83; bd. dirs. Ariz. Cen. Credit Union, 1985-87; judge pro tem Ariz. Ct. Appeals. 1985. Mem. ABA (vice-chmn. rules and procedures com. 1983-87, chair-elect, 1987, co-chmn. long range planning subcom. 1984-85, chmn. ann. mtg. arrangements TIPS rules and procedures com. 1986-87, publ. subcom. for The Brief 1987, chmn. use of expert witness subcom. of com. trial practice), State Bar Ariz. (com. on rules of civil practice and procedure), Maricopa County Bar Assn. (bd. dirs. 1983—, chmn. med./legal liaison com., 1987), Maricopa County Bar Found. (trustee 1984—, sec. 1986—), Nucleus (chmn. membership com. 1984-85, chmn. 1986-87), AAUW (parliamentarian, bd. dirs. Ariz. State div. 1980-82), Ariz. State U. Alumni Assn. (bd. dirs. 1980-83), Kappa Delta Pi, Assn. Trial Lawyers Am., Phoenix Assn. Def. Counsel, Ariz. Women Lawyers Assn., Def. Research Inst. (practice and procedure com.). Democrat. Episcopalian. Office: O'Connor Cavanagh et al 1 E Camelback Rd Phoenix AZ 85012

CAMPBELL, CAROLINE KRAUSE, drug company executive; b. Praha, Tex., May 5, 1926; d. Charles Joseph and Mary Victoria (Havrde) Krause; student, U. N.Mex., 1958-63; diploma Alexander Hamilton Inst., 1966-69; m. Richard E. Campbell, Dec. 30, 1946; children—Richard E., Don Michael, Scott Gary, Jonathan Miles, Candace Kay. Survey researcher Winona Research Co., Mpls., 1953-54; merchandiser, buyer Campbell Drug Inc., Albuquerque, 1961-77, gen. mgr., 1978—, pres., 1978—, dir., 1978—. Mem. Nat. Assn. Corp. Dirs., Assn. Commerce and Industry of N.Mex., C. of C. Albuquerque (bd. dirs.), Small Business Roundtable, Nat. Assn. Retail Druggists (impaired pharmacist com.), Medicine/Bus. Coalition, N.Mex. Pharm. Assn., Internat. Platform Assn., Albuquerque Symphony Women's Assn. Republican. Clubs: Albuquerque Rose Soc., Italian Cultural. Lodge: Elks. Office: Campbell Drug Inc 8252 Menaul Blvd NE Albuquerque NM 87110

CAMPBELL, CLAIRE PATRICIA, nurse, educator; b. Jan. 10, 1933; d. Hugh Paul and Clara Louise (Bell) Campbell. Student So. Meth. U., 1956-57; BS in Nursing, U. Tex. Sch. Nursing-Galveston, 1959, Family Nurse Practitioner, 1979, cert., 1984; MS in Nursing, Tex. Woman's U. Sch. Nursing, 1971. Staff nurse parkland Meml. Hosp., Dallas County Hosp. Dist., 1955-70, head nurse gen. surgery, chest surgery, neurosurgery, orthopedics, and internal medicine, until 1970; instr. nursing Tex. Woman's U. Sch. Nursing, Dallas, 1971-72; researcher nursing diagnosis, Dallas, 1972-77; family nurse practitioner pain mgmt. program Otis Engring. Health Service, Dallas, 1979-86, Dallas Rehab. Inst., 1986—; adj. asst. prof. U. Tex. Sch. Nursing, Arlington, 1976—; cons. nursing diagnosis. Author: Nursing Diagnosis and Intervention in Nursing Practice, 1st edit., 1978, 2d edit., 1984. Mem. Am. Nurses Assn., Tex. Nurses Assn. - Dist. 4, North Am. Nursing Diagnosis Assn., Sigma Theta Tau. Roman Catholic.

CAMPBELL, DEBBIE LEE MCGEE, sales representative; b. New Castle, Pa., May 16, 1954; d. Norman Rigotti and Barbara Jayne (White) Hassel; m. James Clarence Campbell. BA, U. West Fla., 1976, MA, 1980. Cert. tchr., Fla. Spl. edn. tchr. Okaloosa County Sch. Bd., Ft. Walton Beach, Fla., 1976-82; cons. D.C. Health and Co., Atlanta, 1982-84, regional reading coordinator, 1984-85, regional curriculum coordinator, fgn. language editorial adv. com. rep., regional sales rep., 1986—. Fgn. lang. editorial adv. com. rep. D.C. Heath and Co., Lexington, Mass., 1986-87. Mem. Jr. Service League, Ft. Walton Beach, Fla., 1981. Named Tchr. Yr. Okaloosa County Sch. Bd., 1979. Mem. Internat. Reading Assn., Phi Delta Kappa. Democrat. Methodist. Home: 504 Van Buren St Fort Walton Beach FL 32548 Office: DC Heath and Co 5925 Peachtree Industrial Blvd Atlanta GA 30341

CAMPBELL, DEBORAH BOSWORTH, corporate executive; b. Thierville, France; came to U.S., 1957; d. Alvin Leonard and Joyce Marlene (Craver) Bosworth; m. Grover Richard Campbell; children: Jessie, Dustin. BBA, Tex. Tech U.; MBA, Highlands U., 1978. Mgmt. intern ERDA, Albuquerque, 1977; contract specialist Dept. Energy, Albuquerque, 1977-80; sr. strategy analyst Phillips Petroleum Co., Bartlesville, Okla., 1980-82; mgr. bus. planning Telex Computer Products, Tulsa, 1983, mgr. product planning, 1983-85, mgr. corp. planning, 1985—; active Corps of Execs. SCORE, Albuquerque and Bartlesville, 1979-82. Voter registrar Tex., N.Mex., Okla., 1975—; del. conv. Rep. Party Okla., Tex., 1976, 84; Rep. Platform Com. Okla., 1984, 87. Named The N.Mex. Young Career Woman, 1978. Mem. Planning Exec. Inst. (treas., nat. del. 1984-86), Nat. Contract Mgmt. Assn. (cert. assoc. contracts mgr., treas. 1979-80), Data Processing Mgmt. Assn., N.Mex. Fedn. Bus. and Profl. Women's Clubs (state com. chmn. 1979-80), Planning Forum (speaker com. 1985-87). Republican. Roman Catholic. Club: Downtown (Albuquerque) (pres. 1978-81). Lodge: Civitan. Home: 9602 N 111 E Ave Owasso OK 74055 Office: Memorex Telex NV 6422 E 41 St Tulsa OK 74135-6192

CAMPBELL, FRANCES HARVELL, member congressional staff; b. Goldston, N.C.; d. George Henry and Evelyn (Meggs) Harvell; m. John T. Campbell, Jr., Apr. 27, 1968 (div. Aug. 1973). BS magna cum laude, U. Md., 1982. Asst. to Congressman Claude Pepper, U.S. Ho. of Reps., 1968-80, staff dir., 1980—; exec. dir., curator Mildred and Claude Pepper Library;

1st v.p. Pepper Found. Author: Young America Speaks, 1957. V.p. Dem. Women of Capitol Hill, 1982-83. Mem. Nat. Assn. Female Execs., Women in Govt. Relations, Adminstrv. Assts. Assn. Capitol Hill, Nat. Dem. Club, Internat. Platform Assn., Fla. State Soc. (bd. dirs. 1982—), Phi Kappa Phi, Alpha Sigma Lambda. Avocations: orchid culture, gourmet food preparation, gardening. Home: 6222 Hardy Dr McLean VA 22101 Office: 2239 Rayburn House Office Bldg Washington DC 20515

CAMPBELL, FRANCES MARGARET, educator; b. Chester, Eng., Dec. 23, 1945; came to U.S., 1946; d. Jack B. Campbell and Edna (Waldash) Granas. BA, U. So. Colo., Pueblo, 1972; MRE, Seattle U., 1976; PhD, Grad. Theol. Union, Berkeley, Calif., 1986. Dir. edn. Pueblo Cath. Diocese, 1969-75, Diocesan dir. edn., parish pastor, 1975-78; Diocesan dir edn. Denver Cath. Dioces, Longmont, Colo., 1978-79; assoc. faculty mem. Franciscan Sch. Theology, Berkeley, 1981-84; vis. prof. Grad. Theol. Union, Berkeley, 1985—; prof. history Allan Hancock Coll., Santa Maria, Calif., 1986—; aux. chaplain NATO Forces U.S. and West Europe, 1983—; vis. prof. Old Mission Theology Inst., Santa Barbara, 1986—; mem. inservice faculty Los Angeles Cath. Schs., 1985—; cons. Los Angeles Cath. Archdiocese, 1984—, adult edn. Denver Cath. Archdiocese, 1978-79. Author: Sacrament Theology and Instruction, 1975-78; editor Glasgow House Journal of Bioethics, 1984—; contbr. book revs. Dir., trainer, organizer Foster Parent's Assn., 1986-88, mem. bd. advisors Cath. Social Services, Lompoc, Calif., 1985-88. Moore-Maritain Soc. Hist. Research fellow, 1984. Mem. Am. Hist. Assn., Am. Cath. Hist. Assn., Hist. Soc. N.Mex., Nat. Assn. Female Execs., Internat. Assn. Women Ministers, Alpha Omicron Pi (Lamda Beta chpt.). Democrat. Home: 1063 E Balboa Dr Santa Maria CA 93454

CAMPBELL, GERALDINE CATHERINE, real estate appraiser; b. Mineola, N.Y., Sept. 12, 1942; d. Lawrence Albert and Olga Elgina (Nelson) Feron; m. Martin T. Azzara, Oct. 26, 1960 (div. June 1972); children: Todd Lawrence, Kim Katherine. BBA cum laude, U. Albuquerque, 1979. Real estate assoc. assorted, Long Island, N.Y. and Albuquerque, 1961-77; agt. IRS, Dallas, 1979-81; owner Los Lunas (N.Mex.) Bus. and Tax, 1981-84; real estate appraiser Roos Appraisal Service, Rio Rancho, N.Mex., 1985-87; pres. The Campbell Co., Rio Rancho, 1987—; estimator Sea Gull Fence Co., Medford, N.Y., 1969-74, Cardinal Fence Co., Albuquerque, 1975-76, Valley Fence Co., Albuquerque, 1976-77. Mem. Soc. of Real Estate Appraisers, Am. Soc. Appraisers, League of Women Voters (sec. 1985-86). Republican. Office: The Campbell Co PO Box 27800 Suite 116 Albuquerque NM 87125

CAMPBELL, GLENDA SUE, physical education educator; b. McAdenville, N.C., Nov. 5, 1939; d. Glenn Wilson and Juanita Virginia (Waters) C. BS, Mars Hill (N.C.) Coll., 1964; MA, Western Carolina U., 1985, cert. in adminstrn., 1988. Cert. tchr., N.C. Tchr. Buncombe County Bd. Edn., Asheville, N.C., 1964—, coach, 1964-84. Community rep. N.C. Soc. for Autistic Adults and Children , Raleigh, 1986—. Mem. NEA, N.C. Assn. Educators, Classroom Tchrs. Assn., N.C. Assn. of Health, Phys. Edn., Recreation and Dance, Assn. Suprs. Curriculum Devel., Kappa Delta Pi. Republican. Baptist. Club: Lioness. Home: 9 Toxaway St Asheville NC 28806

CAMPBELL, HEIDI LARSEN, insurance consultant; b. Milw., Feb. 11, 1962; d. Stuart Earl and Bonny Lee (Sommer) Larsen; m. D. Michael Campbell, Aug. 23, 1986. BA, U. Miami, Coral Gables, Fla., 1984, MBA, 1985. Mgr. Sara Sharpe Catering, Coral Gables, 1984-85; mktg. specialist VA, Miami, Fla., 1986; mktg. rep. Personnel One, Miami, 1986-87; brokerage cons. Provident LIfe & Accident, Coral Gables, 1987—; instr. seminars Provident Life and Accidents, Coral Gables, 1987—. Vol. leader Meth. Youth Group, Hollywood, Fla., 1984. Cert. for excellence and design Printing Industry of Am., 1985. Mem. Nat. Assn. of Life Underwriters Miami Assn. of Life Underwriters, Women's Assn. of Life Underwriters, Young Alumni Assn., N. Miami C. of C., Kappa Kappa Gamma (treas. 1985-86). Republican. Home: 5941 SW 84 St South Miami FL 33134 Office: Provident Life & Accident 2655 LeJeune Rd PH-1 Coral Gables FL 33134

CAMPBELL, HELEN LOUISE, state agency official; b. Austin, Tex., Aug. 26, 1939; d. Herbert Louis and Hattie Louise (Schwartfeger) Benner; m. R.M. Johnson, Sept. 22, 1956 (dec. June 1963); children: Ronald M., Rhonda Louise; m. Lonnie Campbell (div. 1983). Student in mgmt., Austin Community Coll., 1981-84; student, Nat. Fire Acad., Emmitsburg, Md., 1983-87, St. Edwards U., 1987—. Office mgr. E&W Inc., Austin, 1970-71; adminstrv. asst. Austin Fire Dept., 1971-87; firemen's pension commr. State of Tex., 1987—; commr. Fire Protection Personnel Standard and Edn. State of Tex., 1985. Del. State of Tex. Dem. Conv., 1982, 84; mem. adv. bd. dirs. Austin Community Coll., 1983—; pres. bd. dirs. United Action for the Elderly Inc., Austin, 1985-86; bd. dirs. Austin Groups for Elderly, 1987; chmn. State of Tex. Higher Edn. Commn. Fire Service, 1985-87; life mem. Tex. PTA. Recipient Award for Excellence United Action for Elderly, 1986, Achievement award U. Tex. YWCA, 1986. Mem. Tex. Firemen's and Fire Marshals' Assn. Baptist. Home: 2562 Stoutwood Circle Austin TX 78745 Office: Firemen's Pension Commr 3910 S 1-35 Suite 235 Austin TX 78704

CAMPBELL, JANIE LEE, patient services executive, researcher, abstractor; b. Levelland, Tex.; d. Carl Eugene and Willie Elliott (Wood) Young; m. Parshall Campbell; children: Parshalla Kay, Curtis Dale, David Lee. AA valedictorian, Phoenix Coll., 1963; BS in Nursing, Ariz. State U., 1972, MS in Nursing, 1973; PhD in Nursing, U. Ill., Chgo., 1984. RN, Ariz., Ill. Staff nurse, asst. supr. Maricopa County Gen. Hosp., Phoenix, 1963-65; asst. dir. nursing St. Luke's Hosp., Phoenix, 1965-70; asst. adminstr. nursing Maryvale Samaritan Hosp., Phoenix, 1973-74; assoc. adminstr. nursing Good Samaritan Med. Ctr., Phoenix, 1974-82; v.p. patient services St. Mary of Nazareth Hosp. Ctr., Chgo., 1984—; cons. Bertrand Goldberg Assn., Chgo., 1982—; mem. nursing research adv. bd. U. Chgo., 1985—; mem. adv. bd. Coll. Nursing St. Xavier Coll., Chgo., 1986—; adj. asst. prof. U. Ill., Chgo., 1985—. Mem. Am. Orgn. Nurse Execs., Midwest Nursing Research Soc., Environ. Design Research Assn., Nat./Ill. League for Nursing, Am. Inst. Architects (health facilities com.). Office: St Mary Nazareth Hosp Ctr 2233 W Division St Chicago IL 60622

CAMPBELL, JEAN, retired, human organization administrator; b. Fairhaven, Mass., Mar. 4, 1925; d. Elwyn Gilbert and Marion Hicks (Dexter) C. AA, Lasell Jr. Coll., Auburndale, Mass., 1944; BA, Brown U., 1946; MEd, U. Hartford, 1963. Field dir. Waterbury Area Council Girl Scouts, Inc., Waterbury, Conn., 1946-52; exec. dir. Manchester (Conn.) Girl Scouts, Inc., 1952-60; dist. dir. Conn. Valley Girl Scout Council, Inc., Hartford, 1961-63; dir. field services Plymouth Bay Girl Scout Council, Taunton, Mass., 1963-64, exec. dir., 1964-68; exec. dir. New Bedford (Mass.) YWCA, 1968-87; mem. adv. bd. Bay State Ctrs. for Displaced Homemakers, Southeastern Mass., 1982-87, Southeastern Mass. U. Women's Studies, North Dartmouth, Mass., 1987. Trustee Millicent Library, Fairhaven, 1970—; corporator New Bedford 5 Cents Savs. Bank, 1976—; bd. dirs. Greater New Bedford Concert Series, 1978—; hon. trustee St. Luke's Hosp. of New Bedford, 1986—; mem. adv. bd. Bierstadt Art Soc., New Bedford, 1987—; com. mem., past pres. Interchurch Council of Greater New Bedford, 1976—. Recipient Sidney Adams Community Service award Interchurch Council of Greater New Bedford, 1984, AAUW Achievement award, 1987; named Woman of Yr., Internat. Women's Day Com., 1987. Mem. Delta Kappa Gamma Soc. (pres. Eta chpt. 1986—). Clubs: YWCA Investment (advisor 1976—), Moneta Assocs. Investment (New Bedford) (pres. 1982-84, 86-88).

CAMPBELL, JEANNE MARIE, government relations-public affairs company executive; b. Chgo., d. John and Wilhelmina Evelyn (Powers) Kruzic; widowed; children—Keith Maclean, Scott McElroy. B.A., B.S., No. Ill. U., 1966; M.S. in Edn., 1971; M.A., Loyola U., Chgo., 1975; postgrad. Am. U., Washington. Mem. faculty Am. U., Washington, Loyola U., Chgo., 1973-77, George Washington U.; speechwriter Congressman Dan Rostenkowski, 1977-79; press sec. Congresswoman Margaret Heckler, 1979-80; v.p. New Eng. Council, Inc., Washington, 1981-85; sr. assoc. Martin Haley Cos., 1981-85; pres. Campbell-Raupe, Inc., Washington, 1985—. Vol. tutor Laubach Lit. Assn., Ill. and Washington, 1965—. Mem. Tax Coalition, Am. League Lobbyists (sec. 1983), Women in Govt. Relations. Avocation: writing. Home: 3806 N Richmond St Arlington VA 22207 Office: Campbell Raupe Inc 1010 Pennsylvania Ave SE Washington DC 20003

CAMPBELL, JILL FROST, director academic research program; b. Buffalo, July 29, 1948; d. Jack and Elaine Mary (Hamilton) Frost; m. Gregory H. Campbell, May 31, 1969; children: Geoffrey, Kimberly, Kristina. BS, SUNY, Brockport, 1970, MS in Edn., 1981. Acct. clk. bursar's office SUNY, Brockport, 1974-75, sr. acct. clk., 1975-78; instl. research asst. Instl. Research Office, Brockport, N.Y., 1978-82, asst. dir., 1982-86; personnel assoc. Personnel Office, Brockport, 1986-87; dir. contract and grant adminstrn., sponsored research dept. Brockport, 1987—. Active exec. com. Nativity Home Sch. Assn., Nativity Blessed Virgin Mary Sch., Brockport, 1985-87, sch. bd. pub. relations and mktg. com., 1985—, Friends of Brockport Athletics, 1985—; coach Brockport Youth Soccer, 1988. Grantee United Univ. Professions, 1985. Mem. Nat. Assn. Instl. Research (exec. com., co-originator and discussion leader books and current issues, 1985-87, co-author profl. file, presenter panels 1979-87), North East Assn. for Instl. Research (exec. com., sec. 1985-87, presenter panels 1978-87), SUNY Assn. for Instl. Research and Planning Officers (exec. com., presenter panels 1984-87), Nat. Council Univ. research Adminstrs., SUNY Brockport Alumni Assn., Brockport Profl. Women's Group. Home: 5129 Redman Rd Brockport NY 14420 Office: SUNY Research Found 521 Allen Adminstrn Bldg Brockport NY 14420

CAMPBELL, JUDITH LOWE, child psychiatrist; b. Indpls., Jan. 21, 1946; d. Albert St. Clair and Adele V. (Lobraico) Lowe; B.S. in Zoology, Butler U., 1967; M.D., Ind. U., 1971; m. Robert Frank Campbell, Nov. 30, 1968; children—Christiaan Robert, Kevin Lowe, Geoffrey Ford. Resident in psychiatry Ind. U. Sch. Medicine, 1971-73, fellow in child psychiatry 1973-75; asst. dir. Riley Child Guidance Clinic, Indpls., 1975-79, dir. child psychiatry consultation, liaison service to pediatrics, 1975-79; dir. child psychiatry services Riley Hosp. for Children, 1979-85; pvt. practice child psychiatry, Indpls., 1985—; child psychiatry cons. Center for Mental Health of Madison County (Ind.), Anderson, 1975-77, Lutheran Child Welfare Assn., Indpls., 1974—, Lutherwood Children's Home, Indpls., 1974—, Jewish Family and Children's Services, 1983-84, child and adolescent div. Midtown Community Mental Health Center, 1983-85; instr. Ind. U. Sch. Medicine, Indpls., 1974-75, asst. prof. dept psychiatry, 1975—. Vol., Ind. State chpt. Cystic Fibrosis Found., 1977. Recipient Physician's Recognition award in Continuing Edn. AMA, 1974, 77; Helen McQuiston award in sci., 1967. Fellow Am. Psychiat. Assn., Ind. Psychiat. Soc. (councilor 1978-80, sec. 1981-83, editor newsletter 1981-83, chmn. com. women 1983-87), Am. Burn Assn., Am. Acad. Pediatrics (Ind. br.), Am. Med. Women's Assn., Am. Acad. Child Psychiatry, Am. Assn. Psychiat. Services for Children, Smithsonian Assocs., Field Mus. Natural History, Indpls. Mus. Art, Indpls. Zool. Soc., U. Psychiat. Assocs., Pi Beta Phi, Beta Sigma Phi. Clubs: Carmel Racquet, Eastern Star, Woodland Country. Contbr. articles on child psychiatry to profl. jours. Research on emotional aspects of burns in children, craniofacial anomalies in children, also sex differences in child and adolescent population groups. Office: 7250 Clearvista Dr Suite 345 Indianapolis IN 46256

CAMPBELL, KARLYN KOHRS, speech and drama educator; b. Blomkest, Minn., Apr. 16, 1937; d. Meinhard and Dorothy (Siegers) Kohrs; m. Paul Newell Campbell, Sept. 16, 1967. B.A. (Tozer scholar), Macalester Coll., 1958; M.A. (Tozer fellow), U. Minn., 1959, Ph.D., 1968. Asst. prof. SUNY, Brockport, 1959-63, Calif. State U., Los Angeles, 1966-71; asso. prof. SUNY, Binghamton, 1971-72, City U. N.Y., 1973-74; prof. speech and drama U. Kans., Lawrence, 1974-86, chmn. women's studies, 1983-86; prof. speech-communication U. Minn., Mpls., 1986—; Gladys Borchers lectr. U. Wis., Madison 1974. Author: Critiques of Contemporary Rhetoric, 1972, Form and Genre, 1978, The Rhetorical Act, 1982, The Interplay of Influence, ed., 1987; mem. editorial bd. Communication Monographs, 1977-80, Quar. Jour. Speech, 1981-86, Philosophy and Rhetoric, 1988—; contbr. articles to profl. jours. Mem. Speech Communication Assn., Central States Speech Communication Assn., Ctr. Study of the Presidency, Phi Beta Kappa, Pi Phi Epsilon. Office: U Minn Dept Speech-Communication Minneapolis MN 55455

CAMPBELL, LOIS FOSTER, home economics educator; b. Montague County, Tex., Nov. 27, 1933; d. Lawrence C. and Seba (Slaughter) Foster; m. M.E. Campbell, Aug. 6, 1955; children: Seba Carole, Carma Annelle, Mark Eugene, Mike Edward. BS, Tex. Tech U., 1955; postgrad., Tex. Woman's U., 1985—. Cert. home economist, Tex. Educator home econs. Henrietta (Tex.) Ind. Sch. Dist., 1955-57, Burkburnett (Tex.) Ind. Sch. Dist., 1958-59; educator City View Ind. Sch. Dist., Wichita Falls, Tex., 1961-62, Wichita Falls Ind. Sch. Dist., 1966-70, Hurst Euless Bedford (Tex.) Ind. Sch. Dist., 1970—; advisor Future Homemakers Am., Euless, Tex., 1970—; with customer relations Sears Roebuck Co., Hurst, Tex., 1979—. Mem. NEA, Tex. State Tchrs. Assn., Am. Home Econs. Assn., Delta Kappa Gamma (treas. Eta Epsilon chpt. 1975-79). Democrat. Baptist.

CAMPBELL, MARGARET DILLING, elementary educator; b. Williamsburg, Pa., Dec. 20, 1941; d. Howard Dean and Sara Mildred (Baker) Dilling; m. Gerald Robert Campbell, June 15, 1963; children: Penny Lou, Timothy Robert. BE, Shippensburg State Coll., 1962; postgrad., U. Pitts.-Johnstown (Pa.), 1986-87. Cert. tchr., Pa. 5th grade tchr. Derry Twp. Schs., Hershey, Pa., 1962-63, Logan Area Schs., Altoona, Pa., 1963-64; 6th grade tchr. Williamsburg Community Schs., 1964-69, intermediate grades language arts tchr., 1981—; substitute tchr., Williamsburg, 1969-81. Active Womens' Civic Club Williamsburg, past pres.; recording sec., mem. Williamsburg PTA, 1981—. Mem. NEA, Pa. State Edn. Assn., Williamsburg Edn. Assn., Blair County Reading Assn., Internat. Reading Assn. Republican. Methodist. Home: RD 2 Box 238-A Williamsburg PA 16693 Office: Williamsburg Community Schs Sage Hill Dr Williamsburg PA 16693

CAMPBELL, MARGARET M., academic dean; b. New Orleans, Dec. 1, 1928; d. Walter and Caroline Louise (Seither) C. BA, St. Mary's Dominican Coll., 1950; MSW, Boston Coll., 1952; 3d yr. cert. clin. practice, N.Y. Sch. Social Work, 1959; DSW, Columbia U., 1970. Caseworker Charity Hosp., New Orleans, 1951-53, Cath. Social Services, San Francisco, 1953-55; supr. Spl. Service Club sect. U.S. Army Europe, 1956-58; caseworker Children's Bur., New Orleans, 1959-60, Associated Cath. Charities, New Orleans, 1960-63; lectr. Dominican Coll., New Orleans, 1961-66; spl. projects worker Associated Cath. Charities, New Orleans, 1964-65; dir. Fla. Family Ctr., New Orleans, 1965-67; asst. prof. Tulane U. Sch. Social Work, New Orleans, 1968, assoc. prof., 1971; dir. continuing edn. programs Tulane U., New Orleans, 1976-80; dir. Child Welfare Services Tng. Ctr. Region IV, New Orleans, 1979-82; dean Tulane U. Sch. Social Work, New Orleans, 1982—, prof., 1986—; chmn. various coms. sch. social work including Advanced Programs Admissions, Continuing Edn., Family and Children Task Report, Library, Ednl. Policy, Direct Services to Individuals Sequence, NASW Student Liaison, Priorities Com. Author numerous publications and articles in profl. jours. in field. Recipient Alumnae award Dominican Coll., 1970, Dominican Coll. Torchbearer award, 1985. Mem. Nat. Assn. Social Workers (chpt. pres. 1973-75, bd. dirs., treas., program dir., membership com., 1955-85; social worker of yr. Southeastern La. chpt. 1976; La. chpt. award 1978), Acad. Cert. Social Workers, Internat. Conf. on Social Welfare, New Orleans Children's Council, Child Welfare Info. Exchange Panel for La., Task Force on Adolescent Treatment Ctr., New Orleans Collaborative Tng. Program, Child Welfare League (chmn. southeastern conf. 1980-83), Council on Social Work Edn. (steering com. 1980-81, coordinator 1985), La. State Med. Soc. (geriatrics subcom. 1985-86), Nat. Council on Aging, Gerontological Soc. Am. (conf. com. 1985), Southern Gerontology Soc., Adult Protection Services Network. Office: Tulane U Sch of Social Work New Orleans LA 70118

CAMPBELL, MARIA BOUCHELLE, banker, lawyer; b. Mullins, S.C., Jan. 23, 1944; d. Colin Reid and Margaret Minor (Perry) C. Student, Agnes Scott Coll., 1961-63; A.B., U. Ga., 1965, J.D., 1967. Bar: Ga. 1967, Fla. 1968, Ala. 1969. Practiced in Birmingham, Ala., 1968—; law clk. U.S. Circuit Ct. Appeals, Miami, Fla., 1967-68; assoc. Cabaniss, Johnston and Gardner, 1968-73; sec., counsel Ala. Bancorp., Birmingham, 1973-79; sr. v.p., sec., gen. counsel AmSouth Bancorp., 1979-84, exec. v.p., gen. counsel, 1984—; exec. v.p., gen. counsel AmSouth Bank, 1984—; lectr. continuing legal edn. programs; cons. to charitable orgns. Exec. editor Ga. Law Rev, 1966-67. Bd. dirs. St. Anne's Home, Birmingham, 1969-74, chancellor, 1969-74, 80, dirs. Children's Aid Soc., Birmingham, 1970—, 1st v.p., 1988—, bd. dirs. Positive Maturity, 1976-78, Mental Health Assn., 1978-81, YWCA, 1979-80, NCCJ, 1985—, Operation New Birmingham, 1985-87, personnel com., 1987—; bd. dirs. Soc. for the Fine Arts U. Ala., 1986—; commr. Housing Authority, Birmingham Dist., 1980-85, Birmingham Partnership, 1985-86, Leadership Birmingham, 1986—; mem. pres. adv. council Birmingham So. Coll, 1988—; trustee Ala. Diocese Episcopal Ch., 1971-72, 74-75, mem. canonical revision com., 1973-75, liturg. commn., 1976-78, treas., chmn. dept. fin., 1979-83, mem. council, 1983-87, chancellor, 1987—, cons. on stewardship edn., 1981—, dep. to gen. conv., 1985, 88. Mem. Am. Corp. Counsel Assn. (bd. dirs. Ala. 1984—), State Bar Ga., Fla. Bar, Am., Ala., Birmingham bar assns., Assn. Bank Holding Cos. (chmn. lawyers com. 1986-87). Club: Mountain Brook, Downtown. Lodge: Kiwanis. Home: 141 Camellia Circle Birmingham AL 35213 Office: AmSouth Bank PO Box 11007 Birmingham AL 35288

CAMPBELL, MARTHA JEAN (JEAN F.), public relations consultant; b. Indpls., Oct. 13, 1926; d. Matthew Stanley and Rachel Nell (Campbell) Farson; m. Donald Guy Campbell, Oct. 15, 1949; children: Scott Guy, Jennifer Lee. BA, Butler U., 1962. Dir. media relations St. Joseph Med. Ctr., Phoenix, 1970-72; feature writer N.Am. Newspaper Alliance, N.Y.C., 1972-74; communications specialist Samaritan Health Service, Phoenix, 1974-77; sr. v.p. Ralph Jackson Assocs., Los Angeles, 1979-82; prin. Jean Campbell Pub. Relations, Phoenix, 1977-79, Los Angeles, 1982-87, 1988—; press sec., cons. senator Barry Goldwater, Phoenix, 1968, mayor John Driggs, Phoenix. 1969; media cons. Scottsdale (Ariz.) Pub. Schs., 1969-70, Ariz. Commn. Arts/Humanities, Phoenix, 1971-74. Recipient 1st Pl. "Lulu" award Los Angeles Advt. Women, 1978. Mem. Pub. Relations Soc. Am. (Los Angeles newsletter editor 1980, reception chmn. 1985), Publicity Club Los Angeles, LWV (dir. publs. Ind. chpt. 1960, founder, pres. Brownsburg, Ind. chpt. 1959). Republican. Presbyterian. Home and Office: 4426 E Vermont Ave N Phoenix AZ 85018

CAMPBELL, MARY KATHRYN, chemistry educator; b. Phila., Jan. 20, 1939; d. Henry Charles and Mary Kathryn (Horan) C. A.B. in Chemistry, Rosemont Coll., 1960; Ph.D., Ind. U., 1965. Instr. Johns Hopkins U., 1965-68; asst. prof. chemistry Mt. Holyoke Coll., South Hadley, Mass., 1968-74; assoc. prof. Mt. Holyoke Coll., 1974-81, prof., 1981—; vis. scholar U. Paris VIII, 1974-75, U. Paris VII, 1977-79; vis. prof. U. Ariz., 1981-82; mem. panel on grad. fellowships NSF, 1980-81. Contbr. articles to profl. jours. Fellow Woodrow Wilson Found., 1960, NSF, 1960-64, NIH, 1964-65; grantee in field. Mem. Am. Chem. Soc., AAAS, AAUP, AAUW, Sigma Xi. Office: Mount Holyoke Coll Carr Lab Dept Chemistry South Hadley MA 01075

CAMPBELL, NANCY EDINGER, nuclear engineer; b. Washington, May 9, 1957; d. Ralph Joseph and Eleanor (Brabble) Edinger; m. Larry Alan Campbell, Feb. 25, 1984. BS in Nuclear Engring. with honors, Ga. Inst. of Tech., 1978; MBA, U. Pitts., 1985. Nuclear safety engr. Westinghouse Nuclear Tech. Div., Monroeville, Pa., 1978-81; nuclear fuel proposal engr. Westinghouse Nuclear Fuel Div., Monroeville, 1981-86; nuclear fuel project engr. Westinghouse Comml. Nuclear Fuel Div., Monroeville, 1986—; chmn. hospitality, rep. nuclear fuel site div. Westinghouse Women's Career Devel. Com., Pitts., 1985-87. Speaker career day Murrysville (Pa.) Woman's Club, 1979; speaker Westinghouse engring. expo Gateway High Sch., Monroeville, 1981; assoc. advisor Westinghouse Explorer Post 258, Monroeville, 1980-81; vol. Monroeville Mall Energy Week Fair, 1981; vol. Westinghouse Nuclear Fuel Div. Open House, Monroeville, 1981. Mem. Am. Nuclear Soc., Soc. of Women Engrs., Phi Kappa Phi, Tau Beta Pi, Phi Eta Sigma. Republican. Episcopalian. Office: Westinghouse Electric Corp Nuclear Fuel Bus Unit PO Box 3912 Pittsburgh PA 15230

CAMPBELL, PATRICIA ANNE, handicrafts company executive; b. Pitts., Dec. 30; d. John A. and M. Lucille (Park) Campbell; B.S., Duquesne U., 1968; M.Ed., U. Pitts., 1969, Ph.D., 1974. Tchr., Avonworth Schs., 1968, Beaver County Community Coll., 1969, Northgate Schs., Pitts., 1974-75; mgmt. trainee Pitts. Nat. Bank, 1974-75; pres. Patpourri Enterprises, Sewickley, Pa., 1975—. Keiki concert chmn. Honolulu Symphony, 1978-80; mem. bd. Women's Symphony Assn., Honolulu, 1978-80; bd. dirs. women's guild Pitts. Ballet Theater, 1981-84. Recipient U. Pitts. Student Research award, 1974. Mem. Doctoral Assn. U. Pitts., AAUW, Pi Lambda Theta. Republican. Club: Pitts. Athletic Assn. Author: Prosocial Television Programming for Children: Expressions of Anger By Children During the Cognitive Revolution Period of development, 1974. Home: 216 Pine Rd Sewickley PA 15143

CAMPBELL, PATRICIA F., marketing professional; b. Neptune, N.J., June 17, 1955; d. John Robert and Florence T. (Connors) Sagurton; m. Joseph A. Campbell, Spet. 7, 1986. BS in Chemistry, Montclair State Coll., 1977; MS in Indsl. Pharmacy, St. John's U., 1980; MS In Bus., Columbia U., 1985. Research chemist Am. Cyanamid Co., Clifton, N.J., 1977-79, research and devel. leader, 1979-81, reseach and devel. sect. mgr., 1981-84; product devel. mgr. Wayne, N.J., 1984-86, mktg. mgr., 1986— Home: 18 Heritage Ct Morris Plains NJ 07950

CAMPBELL, ROSE JOHNSON, educator; b. Miami, Fla., Oct. 8, 1945; d. Kirk Johnson Sr.; m. Norman Newkirk, May 22, 1963 (div. Apr. 1980); 1 child, Shelly Von; m. Wilbert R. Campbell, Jan. 19, 1986. BA, Fla. A&M U., 1968; MA, William Paterson Coll., 1980. Cert. elem. tchr., N.J. Project tchr. Newark Bd. Edn., 1971-80, reading lab instr., 1980-84, coordinator, 1984—. Bd. dirs. Day Nurseries Inc., Montclair, N.J., 1983—, Montclair YWCA, 1986-87. Mem. Internat. Reading Assn., Nat. Assn. Negro Bus. and Profl. Women's Clubs Inc. (1st v.p. 1985-87, pres. N.J. unit 1988), Fla. A&M U. Alumni Assn. Democrat. Episcopalian. Home: 6 Pierson Pl Montclair NJ 07042

CAMPBELL, SALLY SIMMONS, magazine editor; b. Clearwater, Fla., Oct. 3, 1938; d. Stephen Emery and Clara Marie (Rugheimer) Simmons; m. Bruce Michael Campbell, Apr. 18, 1964; children—Stephen, Jamie. BA, Duke U., 1960. Editor Houghton Mifflin Co., Boston, 1960-65; freelance writer, Wilton, Conn., 1978-83; editor Advisory Enterprises, Armonk, N.Y., 1983-85, Gralla Publs., N.Y.C., 1985-87, Accessories mag., Norwalk, Conn., 1987 —. Contbr. articles to various publs. Recipient First Place award, Reader's Digest, 1979; Hon. mention Writing competition Writer's Digest Mag., 1983. Mem. Women in Communications (v.p. 1983-84; newsletter editor 1982-83, job bank chair 1984-85), Phi Beta Kappa.

CAMPBELL, SHERRY DAWN, small business owner; b. Longview, Tex., Dec. 10, 1951; d. Donald Woods and Wanda Allene (Russell) Braley; m. James Brian Campbell, Dec. 31, 1985. Grad. high sch., Oklahoma City. Paste up artist Evans Furniture Co., Oklahoma City, 1972-79, photo set designer, 1975-77; paste up and overlay artist Evans Furniture, Oklahoma City, 1981-85; TV set designer Adco Advtg. Co., Oklahoma City, 1976-79, exec. electronic media, 1976-79, TV and radio copywriter, 1976-79, producer and director, 1976-79; owner Tile Designs, Oklahoma City, 1979-85; prin. Campbell Bros., Oklahoma City, 1984—, Victorian Lady Stained Glass Co., Oklahoma City, 1987—. Episcopalian. Home: 94 W Shore Dr Lake Hiwassee OK 73007 Office: Campbell Bros Rt 1 Lake Hiwassee OK 73007

CAMPBELL, SUSAN LEE, accountant; b. Danville, Va., Aug. 15, 1956; d. Edward Ross and Mildred (Finny) Burnette; m. James Franklin Campbell, Sept. 8, 1979. BS in Acctg., Va. Poly. Inst., 1978. CPA, Cert. Internal Auditor. Staff acct. Peat Marwick, Roanoke, Va., 1978-79; staff auditor City of Roanoke, 1979-81; EOP auditor Atlantic Mut. Ins. Co., Roanoke, 1981-83, audit supr., 1983-84, audit mgr., 1984-85, gen. auditor, 1985-87, v.p., auditor, 1987—. Mem. Inst. Internal Auditors (pres. S.W. Va. chpt. 1982-83, bd. dirs. 1983-85, vol faculty 1980-82), Va. Soc. CPA's, Am. Inst. CPA's, Am. Mgmt. Assn. Republican. Methodist. Club: Piedmont Ski. Office: Atlantic Mut Ins Co PO Box 4657 Roanoke VA 24015-0657

CAMPBELL, SUSAN PANNILL, banker; b. Richmond, Va., May 28, 1947; d. Raymond Brodie and Lucie Courtice (McDonald) C. A.B., Coll. William and Mary, 1969; M.Ed., U. Va., 1970, postgrad., 1974-75; postgrad. Summer Inst. of Coll. Admissions, Harvard U., 1972. Counselor, instr. Thomas Nelson Community Coll., Hampton, Va., 1970-71; asst. dean admissions U. Va., Charlottesville, 1971-78; banking officer, asst. v.p., mgr. Tex. Commerce Bank, Houston, 1978-82; asst. v.p. First City Nat. Bank, Houston, 1982-85, v.p., 1985—. Loaned exec. United Way, Houston, 1978; v.p. EnCorps, div. Houston Symphony League, 1981-82, pres., 1982-83, bd. dirs., 1983-85; bd. dirs. Houston Symphony League, 1982-83; bd. advisors Houston Symphony Soc., 1982-87. Honor award scholar Mary Baldwin Coll., Staunton, Va., 1965-66. Mem. Nat. Assn. Bank Women, Am. Symphony Orch. League (vol. council), Coll. William and Mary Alumni Assn., Kappa Alpha Theta. Democrat. Presbyterian. Office: First City Nat Bank Houston PO Box 2557 Houston TX 77252

CAMPBELL, SUZANN KAY, physical therapy educator; b. New London, Wis., Apr. 19, 1943; d. Martin J. and Virginia May (Schoenrock) Reetz; m. Richard T. Campbell, Feb. 6, 1965; children: Dianne Elizabeth, Deborah Carol. BS in Phys. Therapy, U. Wis., 1965, MS, 1968, PhD in Neurophysiology, 1973. Lic. phys. therapist; cert. neurodevelopmental therapist; cert. Brazelton instr. Staff therapist Central Wis. Colony, Madison, 1965-68; inst. U. Wis.-Madison, 1968-70; asst. prof. phys. therapy U. N.C., Chapel Hill, 1972-77, assoc. prof., 1977-84, prof., 1984-87; prof. phys. therapy and community health scis. U. Ill., Chgo., 1987— , Charles E. Culpeper fellow in med. scis., 1985-87. Editor: Pediatric Neurologic Physical Therapy, 1984; editor Phys. and Occupational Therapy in Pediatrics jour., 1979—; mem. editorial adv. bd. Churchill Livingstone Pubs., N.Y.C., 1983—; contbr. articles to profl. jours. Mem. Am. Phys. Therapy Assn. (adv. council on phys. therapy edn. 1983-86, research fellow 1980, Golden Pen 1978, research award pediatrics sect. 1984, Worthingham fellow 1987, Disting. Educator award edn. sect., 1988), Wis. Phys. Therapy Assn. (pres. 1971-72), N.C. Phys. Therapy Assn. (treas. 1984-85). Democrat.

CAMPBELL, VERONICA MARIE, auditor, govt. ofcl.; b. Phila., Aug. 30, 1952; d. Charles F. and Virginia M. (Hibbits) C.; B.A., Barat Coll., Lake Forest, Ill., 1973. With Office Insp. Gen., Dept. Agr., 1973-82, auditor-in-charge fgn. ops. staff, Washington, 1979-82; supervisory auditor Office of Insp. Gen., U.S. Dept. Interior, 1982-84; asst. dir. Washington audit office Office Insp. Gen., Dept. Labor, 1984-85, supervisory auditor nat. office, 1985-87, regional Insp. Gen. N.Y. audit office Insp. Gen. Dept. Labor, 1987—. Mem. Assn. Govt. Accts., Delta Epsilon Sigma, Kappa Gamma Pi. Roman Catholic. Office: 201 Varick St Room 871 New York NY 10014

CAMPBELL, VIRGINIA JONES, accountant; b. Topeka, Oct. 12, 1943; d. Arnold R. and Ruth D. (Cress) Jones; m. William Finley Campbell, Nov. 6, 1969; children: Sean Findlay, Colin Jason, Caitlin Paige. BSBA, U. Tenn., Knoxville, 1965. CPA, Tenn. Supr. Peat, Marwick, Mitchell and Co., Memphis, 1965-71; asst. bursar U. Va., Charlottesville, 1971-73; acct. Mann & Co., Stamford, Conn., 1980-82; controller Stamford Computer Group, 1982-83; dir. fin. Vista Ventures (The Vista Group), New Canaan, Conn., 1983—. Mem. Am. Inst. CPA's.

CAMPEL, CHRISTINE RUCH, chemical company executive; b. Yonkers, N.Y., Dec. 14, 1947; d. Emil Jr. and Edythe Evelyn (Powers) Ruch; m. Gary Philip Campel, July 23, 1943 (div. Oct. 1982). BS in internat. bus., U. Bridgeport, Conn., 1987. Sales rep. Stauffer Chem. Co., Westport, Conn., 1976-79, sr. sales rep. Latin Am., 1979-82, mgr. product sales, 1982-84; regional sales mgr. chem. products group Chesebrough-Pond's, Inc., Westport, 1984-88; export mgr.Latin Am. Borg-Warner Chems., Parkersburg, W.Va., 1988—. sec., bd. dirs. Sun Rise Hill Condominiums, Norwalk, Conn., 1979-81; sec. West End Action, Bridgeport, 1985; sponsor mayor's re-election campaign, Bridgeport, 1985-86. Mem. Nat. Com. on Internat. Trade (participant Trade Reform Bill com. 1986—), Ad Hoc Coalition Against Pre-Inspection Agys., Venezuelan Inter-Am. C. of C. . Lutheran. Home: 930 Juliana St Parkersburg WV 26101

CAMP-LEIKEN, NANCY, public relations executive; b. Honolulu, Sept. 14, 1948; d. Joseph Martin and Elizabeth Hyers (Reitz) Camp. BFA, Ill. Wesleyan U., Bloomington, 1971; MS in Info. Scis., Ill. State U., Normal, 1974. Mem. faculty Ill. Wesleyan U., 1971-72; cons. social rehab. Schultz & Assocs., Bloomington, Ill., 1972-74; mem. faculty Ill. State U., 1974-76; communications specialist Mennonite Health Care Assn., Bloomington, 1976-79; dir. pub. relations Ill. Agrl. Assn., Bloomington, 1979-85; founder, prin. McCullough Pub. Relations, 1985—. Author: Farm in the School, 1981; author, producer (video documentary) Dancing with Nature, 1987; contbr. articles, photog. studies to profl. publs. Chmn. pub. relations McLean County United Way, 1981, McLean County residential crusade Am. Cancer Soc., 1981-82; mem. adv. bd. Bro-Menn Health Care, Inc., 1987—. Recipient Pub. Relations Soc. Am. Silver Anvil award, 1986. Mem. McLean County Dance Assn. (co-founder 1976, bd. dirs. 1976-80), Agrl. Relations Council Am., Public Relations Soc. Am. (accredited mem.), Nat. Assn. Female Execs. Home: Route 2 Box 71 Eureka IL 61530

CAMPO, SANDRA LUCY, university official; b. Detroit, Mar. 16, 1938; d. Norman Haire and Mary Catherine (McCorry) Sarvis; m. Alfredo Campo, Sept. 20, 1958; children—Kevin Frederick, Keith Charles. Ph.B., U. Detroit, 1962; M.Ed., Wayne State U., 1969. Tchr., Royal Oak (Mich.) Sch. System, 1960-63, Toms River (N.J.) Sch. System, 1976-79; gen. office supr. LUTC, Washington, 1979-81, exec. asst. to v.p., 1981; mgr. Ethics Resource Ctr., Washington, 1981-82; mgmt. trainee Southland, Alexandria, Va., 1982; adminstrv. asst. to dean Med. Sch., Georgetown U., 1982—; ednl. rep. NEA, Royal Oak, 1962. Sec., Welcome Wagon, Toms River, 1976; co-chmn. meeting Toms River Hawks Internat. Soc., 1978; trustee bd. Graeser Acres Plat III, St. Louis, 1973-75; founder Graeser Acres Self-Help Com., St. Louis, 1974; parish adv. bd. St. Mary's Catholic Ch., Alexandria, 1985-88. Mem. AAUW (v.p. 1976-77, focus rep. 1982), Georgetown U. Women's Assn. (rec. sec. 1985-86, activities chmn. 1985—, pres. 1986—). Republican. Club: Fort Belvoir (Va.). Home: 3410 Ramsgate Terr Alexandria VA 22309

CAMRON, ROXANNE, editor; b. Los Angeles; d. Irving John and Roslyn (Weinberger) Spiro; m. Robert Camron, Sept. 28, 1969; children: Ashley Jennifer, Erin Jessica. B.A. in Journalism, U. So. Calif., 1967. West Coast fashion and beauty editor, Teen mag., Los Angeles, 1969-70; sr. editor Teen mag., 1972-73, editor, 1973—; pub. relations rep. Max Factor Co., 1970; asst. to creative dir. Polly Bergen Co., 1970-71; lectr. teen groups; freelance writer. Active Homeowners Assn. Mem. Women in Communications., Am. Soc. Exec. Women. Address: 8831 Sunset Blvd Los Angeles CA 90069

CANADA, REBECCA SHELTON, controller; b. Kansas City, Mo., June 12, 1948; d. Dean Joseph and Martha Jane (Wheeler) Shelton; m. Brian Joseph Benson, June 7, 1968 (div. Dec. 1985); 1 child, Eleanor Blair Benson; m. James Reed Canada Jr., Oct. 11, 1986; stepchildren: Elizabeth Lynn, Eric Reed. BS in Acctg. and Econs., U. N.C., Greensboro, 1973. CPA, N.C. Sr. audit A.M. Pullen & Co. (name now McGladrey, Hendrickson & Pullen), Greensboro, 1975-79; asst. controller Westminster Co., Greensboro, 1979-85; asst. v.p., controller ea. region Westminster Co., Jacksonville, N.C., 1985—. Campaign treas. David Hoch for Dist. Ct. Judge, Greensboro, 1976; treas., bd. dirs. Greensboro YWCA, 1980-82, Women's Profl. Forum, Greensboro, 1983-84, Greensboro Unitarian Ch., 1984-85. Mem. Am. Inst. CPA's, Nat. Assn. Accts., Piedmont Chpt. CPA's. Democrat. Office: Westminster Co 308 Western Blvd Jacksonville NC 28540

CANAVAN, ELLEN MCGEE, state legislator; b. San Antonio, Dec. 26, 1941; d. Edward Francis and Eleanor Mary (Mullen) McGee; B.A., Regis Coll., 1963; M.Ed., Boston Coll., 1975, C.A.E.S., 1978; M.P.A., Harvard U., 1985; m. M. Christopher Canavan, Jr., Apr. 18, 1965; children—Elizabeth Ann, Michael Edward. Personnel asst. Avco-Everett Research Lab., Everett, Mass., 1963-65; dir. rehab. Mass. Rehab. Commn., Chestnut Hill, 1977-78; dir. community edn. Norfolk Mental Health Assn., Norwood, Mass., 1978-80; mem. Mass. Ho. of Reps., 1980—, mem. coms. on banking, human services, elderly affairs. Mem. Gov.'s Spl. Commn. on Mental Health Facilities, Gov.'s Spl. Commn. on Violence Against Children, Spl. Commn. on Alcohol and Drug. Edn.; bd. dirs. YMCA; adv. bd. Glover Meml. Hosp., Mount Pleasant Hosp.; mem. Town Meeting, 1976—, chmn. spl. com. on mental health, 1976-77; mem. Needham (Mass.) Planning Bd., 1975-80. Mem. Nat. Fedn. Republican Women, Today's Women, Mass. Caucus Women Legislators, Mass. Legislators Assn., Boston Women, Nat. Conf. State Legislatures, Council State Govts., Women's Network (chmn.). Roman Catholic. Club: Brae Burn Country. Office: Room 22 State House Boston MA 02133

CANE, MARILYN BLUMBERG, lawyer, educator; b. Rockville Center, N.Y., Feb. 26, 1949; d. Howard Godfrey and Lily Ruth (Goldberg) B.; m. Edward Michael Cane, Dec. 24, 1970; children—Daniel Eric, Jonathan Marc Howard. B.A. magna cum laude, Cornell U., 1971; J.D. cum laude, Boston Coll., 1974. Bar: N.Y. 1975, U.S. Dist. Ct. (so. dist.) N.Y. 1975, U.S. Ct. Appeals (2d cir.) 1976, Conn. 1977, Fla. 1981. With Reavis & McGrath, N.Y.C., 1974-76, Badger, Fisher & Assocs., Greenwich, Conn., 1977-80; counsel Corp Components. div. Gen. Electric Co., Fairfield, Conn., 1980-81; with Gunster, Yoakley & Assocs., Palm Beach, Fla., 1981-83; asst. prof. law Nova U., Fort Lauderdale, Fla., 1983-85, assoc. prof. law, 1985-88, prof. law, 1988—. Contbr. articles to profl. jours. Dir. Jewish Community Day Sch. Palm Beach County, West Palm Beach, Fla., 1983—; mem. adv. com. Conn. Banking Commn., Hartford, 1979-81; trustee Temple Beth Torah, Wellington, Fla., 1985-87. Woodrow Wilson fellow designate, 1971. Mem. ABA, Fla. Bar Assn., Order of Coif. Home: 530 S Lakeside Dr Lake Worth FL 33460 Office: Nova Univ Law Ctr 3100 SW 9th Ave Fort Lauderdale FL 33315

CANEVA-BIGGANE, TERRI DENISE, sales manager; b. Brush, Colo., Apr. 17, 1955; d. Eugene Lee and Bonnie Jean (Scott) Caneva; m. Dennis James Biggane, Sept. 27, 1986. BA in Speech Communications, U. Denver, 1976, MA in Organizational Communications, 1978. Sales rep. Sandoz, Inc., East Hanover, N.J., 1979-80; sales trainer Sandoz, Inc., Colorado Springs, Colo.; regional sales mgr. Critikon, Inc. div. Johnson & Johnson, Tampa, Fla., 1980-83; product specialist Critikon, Inc. div. Johnson & Johnson, San Francisco; sales mgr. Howmedica div. Pfizer, Rutherford, N.J., 1983-84; with Hosp. Sattelite Network, 1984-88; regional sales mgr. Los Angeles, 1984-87; product specialist Boston; area mgr. Denver; mgr. Diatek, Inc., San Diego, 1988—. Mem. Nat. Orgn. Female Execs. Democrat. Methodist. Home: 6503 N Military Trail Suite 2304 Boca Raton FL 33496

CANFIELD, DEBRA BETH MCKAY, information systems manager; b. Phila., Mar. 22, 1955; d. Stanley A. and Ruth Lillian (Clemenson) McKay; m. Christopher Dwight Canfield, Aug. 20, 1977. BS, Houghton Coll., 1976; MS, Syracuse U., 1977. Cert. internal auditor, systems profl. Instr. bus. adminstrn. Houghton (N.Y.) Coll., 1978-79; lectr. Coll. William and Mary, Williamsburg, Va., 1980; internal auditor Colonial Williamsburg (Va.) Found., 1980-81, fin. analyst, 1981-82; systems analyst Dairylea Coop., Inc., Syracuse, N.Y., 1983, mgr. mgmt. info. systems, 1984—. Internal auditor Oswego (N.Y.) Alliance Ch., 1985-86, treas., 1987—. Mem. Am. Acctg. Assn., Inst. Internal Auditors, Beta Gamma Sigma, Beta Alpha Psi. Mem. Christian and Missionary Alliance. Home: Rural Rt 2 Box 182 Fulton NY 13069 Office: Dairylea Coop Inc 831 James St Syracuse NY 13203

CANFIELD, LYNDA RAE, writer; b. Elmira, N.Y., June 15, 1947; d. Raymond Frank and Doris Rae (Kilbourne) C.; m. William U. Hensel, IV, Sept. 10, 1967 (div. Oct. 1975); children—Jason William, Aaron David. B.A., Albany State U., 1969; M.S., Pa. State U., 1972. Cert. psychologist, Wis. Psychologist, Madison Pub. Schs., 1972-77; realtor Lyons Romo Inc., Tucson, 1978-83; writer Bus. Publs., Tucson, 1983—. Contbr. articles on tourism, sci., bus. to mags. Pres. bd. Avra Water Coop., Avra Valley, Tucson, 1982—; pres. Picture Rocks Fire Aux., 1978-80. Recipient Merit award Met. Tucson C. of C. Rodeo Com., 1985. Mem. Internat. Platform Assn. Democrat. Roman Catholic. Avocations: softball; banjo. Home: 9800 W Rudasill Rd Tucson AZ 85743

CANGUREL, SUSAN STONE, personnel executive; b. Madison, Wis., Sept. 11, 1946; d. John Mather and Lois Marie (Wiessinger) Murray; m. Melih Cangurel; children—Lora Rae, Julie Lynn. Student U. Wis., 1964-66, U. Wis., Milw., 1976-78, U. Tex., El Paso, 1981-84. Adminstrv. asst. Madison C. of C., 1967-72; mgr. processing dept. Kensington Mortgage & Fin. Corp., Milw., 1972-73, gen. mgr. adminstrn., 1973-75, asst. v.p., 1975-76, v.p., 1976-79; asst. v.p., internal auditor Mortgage Investment Co., El Paso, 1979-81, v.p. loan adminstrn., 1981-85; mgr. personnel services Summa Corp., Las Vegas, 1985—. Mem. Am. Soc. Personnel Adminstrs. Nat. Assn. Female Execs., Inst. Internal Auditors, Am. Mgmt. Assn. Author poems and short stories. Home: 2329 Mohigan Way Las Vegas NV 89109

CANN, NANCY TIMANUS, retail yacht sales executive; b. Balt.; d. E. Frank Timanus and Ruth G. (Herman) Schell; m. Jerrold R. Cann, Mar. 25, 1967; 1 child, Justin Ronald. Student, Balt. Bus. Coll., 1967. Pres. Crusader Yacht Sales, Inc., Annapolis, Md., 1982—. Mem. Yacht Architects and Brokers Assn. (mem. membership com. 1987-88), Bayfarers (chmn. 1987-88, bd. dirs. 1988—). Home and Office: 922 Klakring Rd Annapolis MD 21403

CANN, SHARON LEE, health science librarian; b. Ft. Riley, Kans., Aug. 14, 1935; d. Roman S. and Cora Elon (George) Foote; m. Donald Clair Cann, May 16, 1964. Student Sophia U., Tokyo, 1955-57; B.A., Sacramento State U., 1959; M.S.L.S., Atlanta U., 1977. Cert. health scis. librarian. Recreation worker ARC, Korea, Morocco, France, 1960-64; shelflister Library Congress Washington, 1967-69; tchr. Lang. Ctr., Taipei, Taiwan, 1971-73; library tech. asst. Emory U., Atlanta, 1974-76; health sci. librarian Northside Hosp., Atlanta, 1977-85; library cons., 1985-86; librarian area health edn. ctr., learning resource ctr. Morehouse Sch. Medicine, 1985-86; edn. librarian Ga. State U., 1986—. Editor Update, publ. Ga. Health Scis. Library Assn., 1981; contbr. articles to publs. Chmn. Calif. Christian Youth in Govt Seminar, 1958. Named Alumni Top Twenty, Sacramento State U., 1959. Mem. ALA, Med. Library Assn., Spl. Library Assn. (dir. South Atlantic chpt. 1985-87), Ga. Library Assn. (spl. library div. chmn. 1983-85), Ga. Health Scis. Library Assn. (chmn. 1981-82), Atlanta Health Sci. Library (chmn. 1979), Am. Numis. Assn., Am. Overseas Assn. Club: Toastmasters (Atlanta) sec.-treas. 1983-84). Home: 5520 Morning Creek Circle College Park GA 30349

CANNAVINO, DIANE MARIE, human resources director; b. Pitts., Mar. 8, 1951; d. James Anthony and Gloria Marie (Lamb) Diamond. BS in Phys. Edn., Health and Recreation, Slippery Rock (Pa.) State Coll., 1973; MBA, Pepperdine U., 1987. Mgr. employment U. Pitts. Med. Ctr., 1974-79; employment and tng. specialist Master Builders div. Martin Marietta Corp., Cleve., 1979-81; mgr. employee relations Leaseway Trans. Corp., Cleve., 1981-83, regional mgr. human resources, 1983-87; group dir. human resources and productivity Leaseway Trans. Corp., Secaucus, N.J., 1987—. Mem. Mchts. and Mfrs. Assn., Am. Soc. Personnel Adminstrs. Democrat. Roman Catholic. Home: 109 E Shearwater Ct Suite 4B Jersey City NJ 07305 Office: Leaseway Trans Corp 400 Plaza Dr Secaucus NJ 07096

CANNON, MARJORIE, newspaper advertisement manager; b. Ada, Okla., Oct. 13, 1925; d. Luther erastus and Bonnie Lee (Wood) Lewis; m. Laurence Eugene Cannon, Sept. 4, 1949; children: Deborah Ann, Patrick Owen. Grad. high sch., Haileyville, Okla. With McAlester (Okla.) News Capital Newspaper, 1944-51; classified mgr. The Norman (Okla.) Transcript Newspaper, 1965—. Campaign worker Dem. state rep. campaign, 1979,83. Mem. Norman Hi-Noon (v.p. 1973-74, Woman of Yr. 1983). Episcopalian. Office: The Norman Transcript 215 East Comanche Norman OK 73069

CANNON, MARY ELLEN, finance company executive, controller; b. Washington, Oct. 16, 1956; d. Leslie Junior and Joanne (Tana) Kinney; m. Mark Whitten Cannon, May 22, 1976; children: Erik R., Scott C., Kevin M. BS in Acctg., U. Md., 1977. CPA, Md. Bookkeeper Olson Research Assocs. Inc., Greenbelt, Md., 1977-78, acct., 1978-80, controller, 1980-85, v.p., controller, 1985—; sec., treas., bd. dirs. Edgewater Corp., Greenbelt, 1979—; bd. dirs. Chillum Sheet Metal, Inc., Bladensburg, Md. Mem. Am. Inst. CPA's, Md. Assn. CPA's. Roman Catholic. Office: Olson Research Assocs Inc 6305 Ivy Ln Greenbelt MD 20770

CANNON, NANCY GLADSTEIN, lawyer, insurance agent; b. San Francisco, Dec. 1, 1941; d. Richard and Caroline (Decker) Gladstein; m. Robert L. Cannon, Dec. 21, 1971 (May 1979). BA, San Francisco State U., 1964; JD, U. West Los Angeles, 1980. Tchr. San Bruno (Calif.) Park Schs., 1964-69; tchr. Inglewood (Calif.) Unified Schs., 1969-75, pres., 1973-75; exec. dir. Henrico Edn. Assn., Richmond, Va., 1975-76; assoc. Bernard Lehrer Assocs., Beverly Hills, Calif., 1980-81; agt. Blue Cross So. Calif., Woodland Hills, 1981-84, State Farm Ins. Co., Pacific Palisades, 1984—; owner Cannon Ins. Agy., Pacific Palisades, 1984—. Del. Dem. Nat. Convention, Chgo., 1968; mem. bd. govs. Pacific Palisades Civic League, 1987—. Mem. Pacific Palisades C. of C., Santa Monica C. of C., Women's Internat. Network. Republican. Lodge: Soroptomists. Office: Cannon Ins Agy 1027 Swarthmore Pacific Palisades CA 90272

CANNON, PATRICIA A., social worker; b. N.Y.C., Jan. 12, 1940; d. Donald F. and Dorothy (Donovan) C. B.A., Marywood Coll., 1961; M.S.W., Fordham U., 1963. Social worker Cardinal McClockey Home, White Plains, N.Y., 1963-66, Bridgeport Bd. Edn. (Conn.), 1966-68, Cath. Charities, Bridgeport, 1968-72, Hall Neighborhood House, 1972-76; asst. dir. social work Bridgeport Hosp. (Conn.), 1976—. Fellow Orthopsychiat. Assn.; mem. Nat. Assn. Social Workers (diplomate). Democrat. Roman Catholic. Home: 242 Sunwood Dr Huntington CT 06484 Office: Bridgeport Hosp 267 Grant St Bridgeport CT 06610

CANNONE, ROSALIE A(NTOINETTE), lawyer; b. Elizabeth, N.J., June 28, 1943; d. Nicola and Anna (LaMonica) C. B.A., Rutgers U., 1965; J.D., Seton Hall U., 1977. Bar: N.J. 1977, U.S. Dist. Ct. N.J. 1977, U.S. Supreme Ct. 1983. Employment interviewer N.J. State Dept. Labor and Industry, Elizabeth, 1965-66; tchr., supr., reading specialist Elizabeth Sch. Dist., 1966-77; atty. Office Gen. Counsel, Prentice-Hall, Inc., Englewood Cliffs, N.J., 1977-81; asst. gen. counsel Alfa-Laval, Inc., Ft. Lee, N.J., 1981-87; sec. bd. dirs. Imo, Inc., Ft. Lee, 1984-85, Stal Refrigeration, Ben Saleem, Pa., 1982-83; sec. bd. dirs. Celleco, Inc., Atlanta, 1982-87; asst. sec. Alfa-Laval, Inc., Ft. Lee and subs., 1981-87; with Pirelli Cable Corp., Union, N.J., 1987—. Mem. ABA, N.J. Bar Assn., Union County Bar Assn., Am. Arbitration Assn. (arbitrator). Office: Pirelli Cable Corp 800 Rahway Ave Union NJ 07083

CANNON-SMITH, LUCINDA KAY, home health care administrator, nurse; b. Washington, Ind., July 2, 1956; d. Joseph Walter and Jacqueline June (Stotts) C.; married (div. 1986); m. Scott Alan Smith, May 8, 1987. BS in Health Occupations Edn., U. So. Ind., 1985. Staff nurse ICU Deaconess Hosp., Evansville, Ind., 1981-82; health-nutrition coordinator Head Start Program, Evansville, 1982-83; clin. research assoc. Bristol-Meyers Co., Inc., Evansville, 1983-85; adminstr., dir. Partners Home Health, Inc., Evansville, 1985-87; dir. registry services Vis. Nurse Services, Inc., Atlanta, 1987—; dir. cardiac rehab. YMCA, Evansville, 1981-84; cons. in field. Recipient Clin. and Ednl. Achievement award Zion United Ch. of Christ, 1980. Mem. Nat. Assn. of Female Execs., U. So. Ind. Varsity Club, Deaconess Sch. of Nursing Alumni Assn. Home: 5035 Carole Pl Stone Mountain GA 30087 Office: Vis Nurse Services Inc 3080 McCall Dr Atlanta GA 30340

CANTARUTTI, TRACEY LERCH, management consultant, marketing specialist; b. Rock Island, Ill., Apr. 4, 1955; d. Donald Roy and Dorothy Jean (Myers) Lerch; m. Robert Cantarutti, May 21, 1983; children: Michael, Angela. BA in Spanish, U. Ill., Urbana, 1977; cert., Alliance Francaise, Paris, 1979; M in Internat. Mgmt., Am. Grad. Sch. of Internat. Mgmt., 1980. Asst. to cultural attache Inst. of North Am. Studies, Barcelona, Spain, 1978-79; grad. asst. Am. Grad. Sch. of Internat. Mgmt., Glendale, Ariz., 1980; mktg. analyst Motorola, Inc., Schaumburg, Ill., 1981-82, mktg. planner, 1982-84, sr. product planner, 1984-86; sr. cons. Chgo. Cons. Group, Arthur Young, 1986-87, mgr., 1987—. Vol. Septemberfest Com. March of Dimes, Schaumburg, 1984-86; vol. village election support Schaumburg United Party, 1987. Recipient Amalio Suarez fellowship Am. Grad. Sch. of Internat. Mgmt., 1980, Celia Howard scholarship Ill. Fedn. Bus. and Profl. Women, 1980. Mem. Woodfield Bus. and Profl. Women's Club (treas. 1987—), Am. Mktg. Assn., Nat. Assn. Female Execs. Office: Arthur Young 1 IBM Plaza Chicago IL 60611

CANTER, MARY EVELYN, utilities executive; b. St. Louis; d. Leland and Eva (Olle) Nichols; m. Robert G. Canter (div. 1986); children: Randall, Sandra K. Canter Worthington. Grad. high sch., Riverview, Mo. Various clerical positions St. Louis, 1956-62; office supr., sec. Pub. Water Supply Dist. #1 of Jefferson County, Arnold, Mo., 1967-77, office mgr., 1977—. Mem. Am. Water Works Assn. (banquet coordinator, 1981—, chair pub. relations 1986-87), Jefferson County Mgrs. Assn. (sec. 1977-86), Mo. Rural Water Assn., Mo. Water and Sewerage Conf., Arnold C. of C. Office: Pub Water Supply Dist #1 Jefferson County PO Box 277 Arnold MO 63010

CANTER, MATHILDA BUSHEL, psychologist; b. N.Y.C., June 8, 1924; d. Harry and Bertha (Lewin) Bushel; m. Aaron H. Canter, July 2, 1944; children: Rachelle Joan, Steven Barry. BA, Bkln. Coll., 1943; MA, Ariz. State U., 1961, PhD, 1965. Cert. psychologist, Ariz. Intern VA Hosp., Phoenix, 1965-66; pvt. practice clin. psychology Phoenix, 1966—; psychol. cons. Maricopa County Juvenile Ct., Phoenix, 1966-71, Florence Crittenton Services Ariz., Phoenix, 1970-86, Jewish Family Children's Service, 1985-86. Fellow Am. Psychol. Assn. (Disting. Psychologist award div. psychotherapy 1987, div. ind. practice); mem. Am. Assn. State Psychology Bds. (Roger C. Smith award 1986), Ariz. Psychol. Assn. (treas. 1977-78), Ariz. Acad. Club: Charter 100. Home: 4035 E McDonald Dr Phoenix AZ 85018 Office: The Drs Canter PC 3900 E Camelback Suite 111 S Phoenix AZ 85018

CANTLIFFE, JERI MILLER, art educator, artist; b. Alliance, N.C., Nov. 25, 1927; d. Rufus Faye Miller and Viola Elizabeth (Ireland) Miller Smith; m. Lawrence R. Cantliffe Jr., Sept.1, 1949; children: Eileen M., David L., Geri Lyn, Lisa Ann, Jonathan M. BA, Meredith Coll., 1949; M in Art Teaching, Wesleyan U., 1967; student, Paier Sch. Art, New Haven, 1974-76. Designer Stephenson Appliance Co., Raleigh, N.C., 1949-50; lab. asst. N.C. State Coll., Raleigh, 1950, Hoffman-LaRoche Pharms., Clifton, N.J., 1951-52; art tchr. Horace Wilcox Tech. Sch., Meriden, Conn., 1962-66; work shop tchr. Park & Recreation Dept., Haddam, Conn., Wallingford, Conn., 1970-84, YWCA, Meriden, 1970-85, Middletown (Conn.) Art Guild, 1970-84, Community Art Ctr., Kensington, Conn., 1977-79; free lance artist specializing in home portraits, 1980—. One woman shows include Cen. Bank, Meriden, 1977, 79, 82, Meriden Pub. Library, 1981,84 (commd. artist, Women of Yr. in Arts award 1979), Cheshire (Conn.) Pub. Library, 1982, Phoenix Mut. Life Ins. Co., Hartford, Conn., 1982, N. Haven (Conn.) Pub. Library, 1983, 86, Greene Art Gallery, Guilford, Conn., 1984, Meredith Coll., Raleigh, 1984, Lord Proprietor's Inn, Edenton, N.C.; juried mem. shows include Salamagundi, N.Y.C., New Haven Paint & Clay, Friends of New Britain (Conn.) Mus., Meriden Arts & Crafts (Frederick Flatow award 1979, Butler Paint award 1980, Alan Reid Meml. prize watercolor 1986), Middletown (Conn.) Art Guild (1st prize watercolor 1977, 78), Brush & Palette, New Haven, Milford (Conn.) Fine Arts, Mt. Carmel Art Assn., Hamden, Conn., Wis. Watercolor Show, Glastonbury (Conn.) Art Guild, The New Group, New Haven, Conn. Classic Arts, Conn. Acad. Fine Arts, Am. Penwomen, Faifield, Conn.; invitational shows include Art-on-the Mountain, Wilmington, Vt., Wesleyan Showcase, Middletown Showcase (Most Popular award 1979), AAUW Art Show, Soundview Ann. Art Show; illustrator Meriden Calendar, Meriden City Hall Christmas card. Co-chmn. Commn. on Arts, Meriden, 1975-76. Recipient Redstone Mfg. award "Mum" Art Festival, Bristol, Conn., 1978, Best in Show award Middletown Ann. Winter Show, 1978, Judges Tri-color award Community Art League, Kensington, 1978, Most Popular Vote award Middletown Showcase, 1979, Rick Ciburi 1st prize award Cheshire Art League, 1981, Best in Show (watercolor) Bridgeport Art League, 1982; named Woman of Yr. in Arts Meriden Girls Club, 1982, Meriden-Record Jour., 1981, Meriden YWCA, 1983, Meredith Coll., 1984. Mem. AAUW, (past Meriden br. art chmn., State Art Chmn., program and gallery benefit chair Rotary Exchange program 1955-87), Salmagundi, Am. Pen Women (pres. Fairfield County br.), New Haven Paint & Clay Soc., Conn. River Valley Embroiderers Guild. Congregationalist. Lodge: Rotary.

CANTOR, ANNA RAE (ANNE R. CANTOR), artist, art educator; b. West New York, N.J., Dec. 9, 1914; d. Jacob Morris and Pauline (Horowitz) C. Student Art Students League, N.Y.C.; B.A., Hunter Coll., 1937; M.F.A., Rutgers U., 1966. Cert. tchr. N.J. Art tchr. Long Branch Bd. Edn., N.J., 1948-75. One woman shows include Little Gallery, New Brunswick, N.J., 1966, 79, The Garrett, Red Bank, N.J., 1972, Caldwell (N.J.) Coll., 1979, NOHO Gallery, N.Y.C., 1987; exhibited in group shows at Guild Creative Arts, Shrewsbury, N.J., Nat. Gallery, N.Y.C., Lever House, N.Y.C., Summit (N.J.) Art Ctr. (now N.J. Ctr. for Visual Arts), Hunterdon Art Ctr., Clinton, N.J., Montclair (N.J.) State Coll., Silvermine Guild Artists, New Canaan, Conn., Montclair (N.J.) Art Mus., Morris Mus. Arts and Scis., Morristown, N.J., Monmouth Mus., Lincroft, N.J., New Jersey State Mus., Trenton;

represented in permanent collections Rutgers U., Douglass Coll., Hunterdon Art Ctr., N.J. State Mus., Monmouth Coll., Pfizer Corp., J&J Distbg. Corp., Jane Voorhees Zimmerli Art Mus. of Rutgers U. Mem. Bradley Beach Bd. Edn., N.J., 1981—. Recipient purchase prize Hunterdon Art Ctr. 12th Nat. print exhbn., 1968, N.J. State Mus., 1971, Monmouth Coll. 1973 Arts Festival. Mem. Nat. Assn. Women Artists (graphics award 1969, 74), Printmaking Council N.J.

CANTOR, ELEANOR WESCHLER, medical association executive; b. N.Y.C., Dec. 30, 1913; d. Samuel Peter and Anna (Rauchwerger) W.; m. Alfred Joseph Cantor, June 9, 1938; children—Pamela Corliss, Alfred Jay. B.A., Hunter Coll., N.Y.C., 1938. Producer radio quiz show CBS, N.Y.C., 1936-41; exec. officer Internat. Acad. Proctology, N.Y.C., 1948—, Internat. Bd. Proctology, 1950—; co-founder Acad. Psychosomatic Medicine, 1954.

CANTOR, MURIEL G., sociologist, educator; b. Mpls., Mar. 2, 1923; d. Leo and Bess Goldsman; m. Joel M. Cantor, Aug. 6, 1944; children: Murray Robert, Jane Cantor Shefler, James Leo. B.A., UCLA, 1964, M.A., 1966, Ph.D., 1969. Lectr. dept. econs. and sociology Immaculate Heart Coll., Los Angeles, 1966-68; faculty Am. U., Washington, 1968—; instr. Am. U., 1968-69, asst. prof. sociology, 1969-72, assoc. prof., 1972-76, dept. chmn., 1973-75, 77-79, prof., 1976—; vis. prof. communication studies UCLA, 1982; cons. agencies including NIMH; cons. Corp. for Public Broadcasting, 1974-75, 80-81. Author: The Hollywood TV Producer: His Work and His Audience, 1971, 2d edit. with new intro., 1987, Prime Time Television: Content and Control, 1980, (with Phyllis L. Stewart) Varieties of Work Experience, 1974, (with Phyllis L. Stewart) Varieties of Work, 1982, (with Suzanne Pingree) The Soap Opera, 1983 (with Sandra Ball-Rokeach) Media, Audiences, and Social Structure (Premio Diego Fabbri award 1988), 1986; editor Nat. SWS newsletter, 1977-78. Bd. dirs. Population Inst., 1978-80; trustee WETA, 1972-76. NIMH grantee, 1979-81. Mem. Am. Sociol. Assn., D.C. Sociol. Soc. (pres. 1977-78, Stewart A. RIce Merit award 1987), Sociologists for Women in Society, Eastern Sociol. Soc. (exec. council 1981-84). Home: 8408 Whitman Dr Bethesda MD 20817 Office: Am U Dept Sociology Washington DC 20016

CANTOR, PAMELA CORLISS, psychologist; b. N.Y.C., Apr. 23, 1944; d. Alfred Joseph and Eleanor (Weschler) C.; m. Howard Feldman, Sept. 11, 1969; children: Lauren Jaye, Jeffrey Lee. BS cum laude, Syracuse U., 1965; postgrad. in medicine, Johns Hopkins U., 1969-70; MA, Columbia U., 1967, PhD, 1972; postgrad., Harvard U.-Children's Hosp. Med. Ctr., 1973-74. Instr. Radcliffe Inst., Harvard U., 1977-78; assoc. prof. psychology Boston U., 1970-80; pvt. practice clin. psychology, Chestnut Hill, Mass., 1980—; faculty Med. Sch., Harvard U.; lectr. in field, also TV and radio appearances. Author: Understanding A Child's World- Reading in Infancy through Adolescence, 1977; cons. editor: Suicide and Life-Threatening Behavior; columnist: For Parents Only; contbr. chpts. to handbooks and numerous articles to profl. jours. Apptd. mem. Mass. Gov.'s Office for Children Statewide Adv. Bd., 1980—; adv. bd. Samaritans of Boston; pres. Nat. Com. Youth Suicide Prevention; mem. HHS Presdl. Task Force on Youth Suicide. Mem. Am. Psychol. Assn., Am. Assn. Suicidology (pres. 1985-86), Am. Orthopsychiat. Assn., Mass. Psychol. Assn., Am. Assn. Suicidology (bd. dirs.). Home: 65 Essex Rd Chestnut Hill MA 02167

CANTRELL, ANDREA, library administrator; b. Springfield, Mo., Jan. 1, 1948; d. A.J. Cantrell and Wilma (Snowden) Cave; m. James D. Hawkins, June 22, 1968 (div. 1977); m. Robert L. Clark, Jr., May 23, 1981 (div. 1985). B.A., Am. U., 1970; M.L.S., U. Md., College Park, 1971. Young adult services librarian Thomas Jefferson Regional Library, Jefferson City, Mo., 1971-72; reference librarian Springfield-Greene County Library (Mo.), 1972-74; coordinator Library resources Mo. State Library, Jefferson City, 1974-78; chief cons. service Wash. State Library, Olympia, 1978-79; dir. Joplin Pub. Library (Mo.), 1979-81; dir. library resources div. Okla. Hist. Soc., Oklahoma City, 1981-85; spl. collections librarian U. Ark., Fayetteville, 1985—. Contbr. articles to profl. jours. Mem. ALA (chmn. staff devel. com. 1977-78; genealogy com. 1983-85), Ark. Library Assn. (chmn. Coll. and Univ. div. 1986-87), Assn. Specialized and Coop. Library Agys. (chmn. 1978-79), Mo. State Library Assn. (mem. various coms.), Zeta Tau Alpha. Lodge: Soroptimist Internat. Office: Spl Collections Dept U Ark Libraries Fayetteville AR 72701

CANTRELL, COLEEN SHARON, nursing administrator; b. Williamsport, Pa., Feb. 8, 1952; d. William Francis and Natalie Elizabeth (Musser) Caldwell; 1 child; Christopher William Cantrell. BS in Nursing, Indiana U. of Pa., 1974. Commd. 1st lt. U.S. Army Nurse Corps, 1974, advanced through grades to capt., 1980; orthopedic staff nurse U.S. Army Nurse Corps, Fort Polk, La., Seoul, Korea, 1974-77, head nurse urology, Fort Bragg, N.C., 1977-78, evening, night supr., 1978-79, infection control nurse, 1979-80; head nurse urology St. John's Regional Med. Ctr., Joplin, Mo., 1981-84, staff nurse, 1980-81, dir. med. nursing service, 1984—. Asst. leader Explorer Scouts MoKan council Boy Scouts Am., 1984-85, 87-88. Serves as maj. USAR. Recipient U.S.A. Commendation award, 1977, 80, cert. of award St. John's Regional Med. Ctr., 1983. Mem. Am. Nurses Assn., Mo. Assn. Nursing Service Adminstrs., Mo. Nurses Assn. (bd. dirs. local dist. 1985-87, treas. 5th dist. 1988—), Oncology Nursing Soc., Res. Officer Assn. Lutheran. Avocations: playing piano, camping, reading. Office: St Johns Regional Med Ctr 2727 McClelland Blvd Joplin MO 64804

CANTRELL, LAVONNE OPAL (LEE), water treatment company executive; b. Pontiac, Mich., Dec. 27, 1935; d. Archiebald Hugh and Pearl Marie (Heath) Warden; m. Willis Walter Cantrell, Sept. 11, 1979. AA in Aerospace Tech. with honors, Glendale (Calif.) Community Coll., 1975. Lic. comml. pilot, FAA. Telegrapher Western Union Telegraph Co., Pontiac and Rochester, Mich., 1955-57; surgery aide Dr.'s Hosp., Cleve., 1958-60; dep. sheriff Los Angeles County Sheriff's Dept., 1967-71; aircraft mechanic Airresearch Aviation Co., Los Angeles, 1978-79; owner Hill Country Services, Kendalia, Tex., 1982—; pres. L&W Water Systems, Inc., Kendalia, 1985—. Res. dep. sheriff Kendall County Sheriff's Dept., Boerne, Tex., 1981—. Served with USN, 1960-67. Mem. Water Quality Assn., Am. Water Works Assn., Ninety Nines, Wirly Girls, Am. Legion (adjudant 1983-86, comdr. 1986-87), Alpha Gamma Sigma. Republican. Mormon. Home: PO Box 302 Kendalia TX 78027 Office: L&W Water Systems Inc 106 Fawn Circle Kendalia TX 78027

CANTWELL, ALICE CATHERINE, industry lobbyist; b. Bar Harbor, Maine, Mar. 30, 1927; d. John Francis and Bridget Mary (Finnegan) C. BA, Russell Sage Coll., 1972. Stenographer, office asst. Pub. Health Nursing Assn., Bar Harbor, 1945-46; stenographer for advt. news Cities Service Oil Co., N.Y.C., 1946-47; legal sec. Law Office Ralph C. Masterman and chmn. State of Maine Rep. party, Bar Harbor, 1947-51; sec. purchasing then sec. plant ops. Allegheny Ludlum Steel Corp., Watervliet, N.Y., 1952-61; from sec. to mgr. NE regional govtl. relations Ford Motor Co., Albany, N.Y., 1961—; mem. steering com. Associated Industries of Mass., Boston, 1985—; mem. various coms. Bus. Council of State of N.Y., Albany, 1981—. Mem. AAUW. Clubs: City of Albany, Ladies of Charity, University. Lodge: Soroptomists. Office: Ford Motor Co 111 Washington Ave Suite 206 Albany NY 12210

CANTY, MARY LOUISE, publishing company executive; b. Somerville, Mass., Mar. 14, 1934; d. Cornelius Francis and Mary Ann (McCarthy) C.; With New Eng. Telephone Co., Boston, 1951-62; office mgr., purchasing agt. Cambridge Plating Co. (Mass.), 1962-65; with Shelby Pub. Corp., Boston, Mass., 1965-87 ; cons. Boston, 1987—. John Liner Letter . Roman Catholic. Club: Irish Am. Office: 210 Lincoln St Boston MA 02111

CAPEHART, LYNNE CAROL, lawyer, educator; b. Ann Arbor, Mich., Dec. 3, 1941; d. Richard Gildart and Frances Miriam (Holmes) Fowler; m. Barney Lee Capehart, Sept. 2, 1961; children: Thomas David, Jeffrey Donald, Cynthia Diane. BS in Math., U. Okla., 1962; JD, U. Fla., 1977. Bar: Fla., 1977. Computer analyst Air Force Cambridge Research Lab., Bedford, Mass., 1963-64; research assoc. U. Fla., Gainesville, 1978-81, instr. Law Sch., 1981-82, asst. dir. legal writing, 1982—; pro bono atty. Sierra Club, Gainesville, 1978—. Author: (with B.L. Capehart and J.F. Alexander) Florida's Electric Future, 1982; contbr. articles to profl. publs. Mem. governing bd. St. John's River Water Mgmt. Dist., Palatka, Fla., 1979-87, sec., 1981-87; chair Oklawaha Basin Bd., 1985-87; mem. Orange County (Fla.) Planning and Zoning Bd., 1972; mem. bd. suprs. Alachua County Soil and Water Conservation Dist., Gainesville, 1979-80; mem. Gainesville Energy Conservation Adv. Commn., 1978-81, chair, 1980-81. Mem. ABA, Fla. Bar, Sierra Club (pro bono atty. Gainesville chpt. 1978—, v.p. 1979-81, medal 1982), Phi Beta Kappa. Democrat.

CAPELL, CYDNEY LYNN, editor; b. Jacksonville, Fla., Dec. 20, 1956; d. Ernest Clary and Alice Rae (McGinnis) Capell; m. Garrick Philip Martin, July 16, 1983 (div. Jan. 1988). B.A., Furman U., 1977. Mktg. rep. E.C. Capell & Assocs., Greenville, S.C., 1977-80; sales rep. Prentice-Hall Publs., Cin., 1980-81; sales, mktg. rep. Benjamin/Cummings, Houston, 1981-83; sales rep. McGraw-Hill Book Co., Houston, 1983-85, engring. editor, N.Y.C., 1985-87; acctg. and infosystems editor Bus. Pubs., Inc., Plano, Tex., 1988—; editor lit. mag. Talon, 1972; news editor Paladin newspaper, 1977. Named Rookie of Yr., McGraw-Hill Book Co., 1985. Mem. Women in Pub., Women in Communications, NOW, Nat. Assn. Female Execs., Mensa. Republican. Avocations: tennis, ballet.

CAPERTON, DEE KESSEL, state legislator; b. Ripley, W.Va.; d. Oliver D. and Catherine (Hartman) Kessel; m. William Gaston Caperton III, Dec. 4, 1965; children: William Gaston IV, John Ambler. BA in Lit. and Polit. Sci., W.Va. U., 1964, MA in Guidance Counseling, 1979; postgrad., Marshall U., 1978; PhD in Counseling, U. Pitts., 1983. Interior decorator Stone & Thomas, Charleston, 1974-76; founder, prin. Caperton Devel. (interior decorating firm), Charleston, 1976-79; intern individual and group counseling Charleston Job Corps, 1978-79; intern group therapy, behavior med. unit Charleston Area Med. Ctr., 1979; psychology intern, researcher Charleston Area Med. Ctr. and W.Va. U, 1983; mem. W. Va. Ho. of Delegates, 1986-88; aide Hon. Ken. Hechler, Congressman, 1960. Founder kindergartens under Fed. Community Action Program Charleston and Emmons, W.Va., 1965, 66; charter mem., bd. officer Vandalia Housing Ctr., 1968-73; founder, pres. Charleston Children's Theatre, 1977-79; bd. dirs. Charleston Domestic Violence Ctr.; mem. adv. com. Women's Health Ctr., Charleston, 1979; mem. adv. council Charleston Job Corps; del. White House Conf. on Children and Youth, 1960; bd. visitors Coll. Creative Arts W.Va. U.; mem. W.Va. Coll. Grad. Studies Found. Mem. Am. Psychology Assn., W.Va. Psychology Assn. Office: PO Box 708 Charleston WV 25323-0708

CAPKO, JUDY, management and marketing consultant; b. Ravenna, Ohio, May 17, 1942; d. Charles Vernon and Mildred Kathryn (Cady) Bentz; m. C. Joseph Capko, Sept. 15, 1962; children: Joseph, Christopher, Cheryl. Student, Moorpark (Calif.) Coll., 1976-79. Mgr. bus. Arthritis Ctr. of the Oaks, Thousand Oaks, Calif., 1975-79; owner, cons. Profl. Mgmt. Concepts, Newbury Park, Calif., 1979—; lectr. U. So. Calif., Los Angeles, 1985, UCLA, 1986. Mem. PTA Manzanita Sch., Newbury Park, 1978-84, Sequoia Intermediate Sch., Newbury Park, 1984-86; mem. bd. rev. Boy Scouts Am., Newbury Park, 1985; bd. dirs. Friends Ventura County Pub. Relations Commn. on Women, 1984-85. Mem. Nat. Assn. Exec. Women. Republican. Roman Catholic. Lodge: Soroptomist (pres. 1984-85). Office: 3525 Old Conejo Rd Suite 119 Newbury Park CA 91320

CAPLE, LYNDA JUNE, real estate executive; b. Kingston, N.Y., June 23, 1939; d. Lewis Harry and Madeline Lois (Schoonmaker) Marz; m. Anthony Grimaldi, 1958 (div. 1974); children: Anthony Jr., Karin Eller; m. Stanley Caple, Oct. 21, 1975. BS, Rochester Inst. Tech., 1963, Barry U., Miami, Fla., 1983. Pres. Grimaldi Real Estate, Kingston, N.Y., 1963-73; dir. sales The Kenilworth, Bal Harbour, Fla., 1974-75; pres. AMC Real Estate, Boca Raton, Fla., 1975-76; mgr. dept. real estate appraisal Am. Savs. & Loan Assn., Delray Beach, Fla., 1976-83; asst. v.p. Am. Realty Cons., Hollywood, Fla., 1984-85; mktg. mgr. So. Fla. div. Pulte Home Corp., Ft. Lauderdale, 1986-87; pres. Questmark Realty Ltd. subs. Questmark Cos., West Palm Beach, Fla., 1987—; cons. various corps., banks and lending institutions, trusts, ins. cos., govtl. agencies, real estate investors and developers, 1975-87. Mem. Boca Raton Bd. Realtors, Ulster County Bd. Realtors (sec. 1970-72, Soc. Real Estate Appraisers (assoc.), Fla. Home Builders Assn. Club: Wiltwyck Country (Kingston).

CAPLIK, KAREN MARIE, insurance underwriter; b. New Britain, Conn., Jan. 25, 1954; d. Edward and Veronica (Gorski) Bogden; m. James F. Caplik, June 14, 1986. BS in Mktg., U. Conn., 1976; MBA, U. Hartford, 1983. Supr. office ops. Allstate Ins. Co., Farmington, Conn., 1976-77, automation trainer, 1977-78, adjuster casualty claims, 1978-79; mktg. rep. The Hartford Ins. Group, East Hartford, Conn., 1979-83; cons. product devel. Reinsurance div. The Hartford Ins. Group, Hartford, Conn., 1983-86; sr. treaty underwriter Hartford Re Mgmt., Hartford, 1986—. Mem. Conn. Ins. Mktg. Assn. (treas. 1981-82, sec. 1982-83, v.p. 1983-84, 84-85, pres. 1985-86). Office: Hartford Re Mgmt Co Hartford Plaza Hartford CT 06115

CAPLIN, JO ANN, communications company executive; b. Indpls.; d. Irvin and Mildred Shirley (Brodsky) C. B.A., U. Mich.; M.A., Yale U., NYU. TV producer ABC News, N.Y.C., 1972-79, CBS News, N.Y.C. and Washington, 1979-85; pres. Caplin Communications, Inc., N.Y.C., 1986—; instr. New Sch. for Social Research, N.Y.C., 1980-81. Producer numerous TV shows, including: (documentary) Incest: The Best Kept Secret, 1979 (Emmy award 1980); (series) 30 Minutes, 1978-82 (Emmy award 1982), 20/20, CBS Mag., HBO Consumer Reports Spl. Bd. dirs. Nat. Found. for Advancement in the Arts, 1985—. Mem. Nat. Acad. TV Arts and Scis., Nat. Assn. Female Execs.

CAPLOW, HARRIET MCNEAL, art history educator; b. Highland Park, Ill., July 26, 1928; d. Morley Daniel and Julia (Allison) McNeal; m. Theodore Caplow (div. 1964); children: James McNeal, Julie Hughes, Firenze Caplow. MA, Columbia U., 1966, PhD, 1970. Asst. prof. art history Ind. State U., Terre Haute, 1967-72, assoc. prof., 1972-78, prof., 1978—. Author: Michelozzo, 1977; contbr. articles to profl. jours. Bd. dirs. Debs Found., Terre Haute, 1974—, Vigo Preservation Alliance, Terre Haute, 1980—, Council on Domestic Abuse, Terre Haute, 1985—. Ind. State U. research grantee, 1976, 86. Mem. Coll. Art Assn., Hist. Landmark Found. Home: 825 S 7th St Terre Haute IN 47807 Office: Ind State U Dept Art Terre Haute IN 47809

CAPO, HELENA FRANCES, comedienne; b. N.Y.C., July 29, 1959; d. Frank Remo Capo and Rose Nellie (Aguilar) Richards; m. William Patterson, Oct. 18, 1986. BA, Queens Coll., 1981. Engr., disc jockey Sta WQMC-AM, N.Y.C., 1980; writer Sta. WBLS-FM, N.Y.C., 1984-86; assoc. editor Laugh Factory Mag., Los Angeles, 1985—; pres. Precision Production Inc., N.Y.C., 1985—; producer N.Y.C. 1st Official Comedy Day, 1984; tchr. Learning Annex, N.Y.C., 1984; creator Availiabilities Hotline, N.Y.C., 1985. Author: Training Your Pet Flea, 1984, Dogslapping, 1987; video tape Microwave Sex, 1988; record album Rappin' Mae, 1985. Named Worlds Fastest Talker Guinness Book World Records, N.Y.C. and London, 1989. Roman Catholic. Office: Precision Productions Inc 85-20 167th St Jamaica NY 11432

CAPODILUPO, ELIZABETH JEANNE HATTON, public relations executive; b. McRae, Ga., May 3, 1940; d. Lewis Irby and Essee Elizabeth (Parker) Hatton; grad. Dale Carnegie Inst., 1976; m. Raphael S. Capodilupo, Jan. 21, 1967. Sec., A.R. Clark Acct., Fernandina Beach, Fla., 1958-59; receptionist, girl Friday, Channel 13, Sta. WNDT-TV, N.Y.C., 1960-62, Coy Hunt and Co., N.Y.C., 1962-69; clk. Woodlawn Cemetery, Bronx, N.Y., 1969-71, historian, community affairs coordinator, 1971—, editor Woodlawn Cemetery News newsletter, 1979—, asst. to pres., 1984, also dir. pub. relations; grad. asst. Dale Carnegie Inst., 1977-78. Chairwoman Ann. Adm. Farragut Honor Ceremony, Bronx, 1976—; chairperson Toys for Needy Children, 1983-88; bd. dirs. Bronx Mus. Arts, v.p., 1983-84; pres. Bronx Council Arts, 1987-88; mem. adv bd Salvation Army, 1985, Bronx Arts Ensemble, 1985; bd. mgrs. Bronx YMCA, 1985; bd. dirs. Bronx Urban League, 1985; bd. dirs. Bronx Council on the Arts, 1985, pres. 1987-88. Recipient awards, including award citation VFW, 1976, Voice of Democracy Program judge's citation, 1980, Disting. Community Service award N.Y.C. Council; named Woman of Yr., YMCA, Bronx, 1986, Woman of Yr., Network Orgn. of Bronx Women, 1986; cert. appreciation Dale Carnegie Inst., 1977; Outstanding Citizenship award Bronx N.E. Kiwanis Club, 1981; Service to Youth award YMCA of Bronx, 1983; recipient proclamation City Council of N.Y.; Outstanding Cemeterian award Am. Cemetery Assn., 1987-88; Citation of Merit Bronx Borough Pres.'s Office, 1988; Spl. Hons. for Outstanding Vol. Work Ladies Aux. Our Lady of Mercy Med. Ctr.; named Hon. Grand Marshall Bronx Columbus Day Parade, 1987-88. Mem. Bronx County Hist. Soc., Network Orgn. Bronx Women, Women in Communication, Bronx C. of C. (sec. 1988). Methodist. Clubs: Bronx YMCA (life mem.), N.Y. Press, Italian Big Sisters, Women's City, Order Eastern Star. Researcher Woodlawn Cemetery's Hall of Fame. Office: Woodlawn Cemetery PO Box 75 Bronx NY 10470

CAPOLUNGO, BARBARA ANN, customs officer; b. Mpls., Jan. 27, 1933; d. George Charles and Signa Amanda (Sherve) Larsen; children: Ronald G. Burghall, Brandt E. Burghall, Dirk F. Burghall. BA magna cum laude, U. Calif., San Diego, 1973; MSW, U. Calif., Berkeley, 1977. Social worker Ct. Dependency div. Dept. Pub. Social Services, Riverside, Calif., 1978; community devel. intern City of Oakland (Calif.), 1976-77, planning cons., 1977, mgmt. and budget analyst, 1977-78; inspection and control officer U.S. Customs Service, San Ysidro, Calif., 1978-80, San Francisco, 1980—. Bd. dirs. San Diego Interfaith Housing Found., 1979-80; mem. allocation com. panel United Way of San Diego County, 1978-80; mem. exec. com. Alameda County Supr., Oakland, 1977-78; legis. com. Alameda County chpt. Nat. Assn. Social Workers, 1977-78. Fellow U. B.C., Vancouver, Can., 1975; Adminstrn. on Aging grantee U. Calif. Berkeley, 1975; Outstanding Service award Oakland Econ. Devel. Council, 1970. Mem. Federally Employed Women, Nat. Assn. Social Workers. Democrat. Mem. United Ch. of Christ. Home: 4 Admiral Dr Apt 233 Emeryville CA 94608 Office: US Customs Service San Francisco Dist 555 Battery St San Francisco CA 94104

CAPONE, ANNETTE, editor. BA, Pa. State U., 1966. Articles editor Seventeen mag., 1971-76; assoc. articles editor Ladies' Home Jour., 1979-81; assoc. editor Mademoiselle, 1981-83; editor-in-chief Redbook mag., 1983—. Mem. Women in Communications. Office: Redbook Magazine 224 W 57th St New York NY 10019

CAPONE, MARGARET LYNCH, civic worker, parliamentarian; b. Wilkinsburg, Pa., May 21, 1907; d. John Edward and Anna Freda (Dunstrup) Lynch; m. Carmen R. Capone, July 21, 1936 (dec. May 1983); children—David Michael, Mary Ann Capone Sperling, Donald William. Student U. Pitts., 1925-33, 1949-53, Carnegie Inst. Tech., 1955-56. Parliamentarian Pa. Nurses Assn., 1960-68, Allegheny County Law Wives, Pa., 1975—; treas. Allegheny County LWV, 1965-69, v.p., 1969-73, pres., 1973-79, parliamentarian, 1979—, historian, 1980; parliamentarian St. Lucy Guild to Blind, Pitts., Allegheny County Lawyers Aux., Diocese Council Cath. Women, Marian Manor Guild; cons. parliamentarian. Author: So You've Joined A Club, 1954; Parliamentary Pointers, 1972. Editor Clea News, 1954-72. Named Woman of Yr., Clea News, 1973; Personality of Yr., Pitts. chpt. K.C., 1979. Mem. Nat. Assn. Parliamentarians (profl. registered parliamentarian, local pres. 1959-61, state pres. 1963-64, nat. v.p. 1977-79), Am. Inst. Parliamentarians (cert. profl. parliamentarian), Duquesne U. Women's Guild. Republican. Roman Catholic. Lodges: K.C. Women's Guild, Toastmistresses (pres. local club 1950-51, nat. bd. dirs. 1953-63, nat. sec. 1954-56, nat. v.p. 1956-57, editor Toastmistress Mag. 1958-62). Home: 6625 Woodwell St Pittsburgh PA 15217

CAPOZZI, CAROLYN ANN, computer systems director; b. Jamestown, N.Y., Apr. 6, 1947; d. Elmer Herbert and Goldie (Tomaswick) Davis; m. William Joseph Capozzi, Oct. 30, 1970; children: James, William. AAS, Jamestown Community Coll., 1967; BA, SUNY, Albany, 1969. Statistician N.Y. State Higher Edn. Services Corp., Albany, 1964-74, sr. research analyst, 1974-77, data processing project assoc., 1977-82, supr. data processing, 1982-84, dir. systems devel., 1984—. Mem. Assn. Systems Mgmt., Data Processing Mgmt. Assn. Roman Catholic. Office: NY State Higher Edn Services Corp 99 Washington Ave Albany NY 12055

CAPPELLO, EVE, development consultant; b. Sydney, Australia, Dec. 4, 1922; d. Nem and Ethel Shapira; came to U.S., 1940, naturalized, 1944; A.A., Santa Monica City Coll., 1972; B.A., Calif. State U.-Dominguez Hills, 1974; M.A., Pacific Western U., 1977, Ph.D., 1978; children—Frances Soskins, Alan Kazdin. Singer, pianist, Los Angeles, 1958-78; pvt. practice profl. and personal devel., corp. and employee tng., Los Angeles, 1976—; instr. Calif. State U. Extension, Dominguez Hills, 1977-86; Mt. St. Mary's Coll., U. of Judaism, U. So. Calif., Loyola Marymount U., 1986—; founder, dir. A-C-T Inst.; invited lectr. World Congress Behavior Therapy, Israel, U. Melbourne, Australia. Mem. Calif. State U.-Dominguez Hills Alumni Assn., Women's Internat. Network (founder, 1st pres.), Inc., Assn. Advancement Behavior Therapy, Assn. Behavioral Analysis, Alpha Gamma. Author: Let's Get Growing, 1979; The Professional Touch, 1983; Dr. Eve's Garden, 1984; Act, Don't React, 1985; The Game of the Name, 1985; newspaper columnist, 1976-79; contbr. articles to profl. jours. Home: 10600 Eastborne Ave #16 Los Angeles CA 90024 Office: PO Box 25544 Los Angeles CA 90025

CAPSALIS, BARBARA DAMON, banker; b. Washington, Apr. 22, 1943; d. Wallace Carver and Gertrude Marie (Larson) Damon; m. John N. Capsalis, Aug. 7, 1965. B.S. cum laude in Math, Ohio U. Dep. commr. N.Y.C. Dept. Gen. Services; div. exec. fin. services div. Chem. Banking Corp., N.Y.C. Recipient Catalyst Women of Yr. award, Woman of Achievement award YWCA. Office: Chem Bank 277 Park Ave 4th Floor New York NY 10172

CAPUTO, ANNE SPENCER, information science educator; b. Eugene, Oreg., Jan. 14, 1947; d. Richard J. and Adelaide Bernice (Marsh) Spencer; m. Richard Philip Caputo, July 15, 1977; 1 child, Christopher Spencer Caputo. B.A. in History, Lewis and Clark Coll., Portland, Oreg., 1969; M.A., U. Oreg., 1971; M.A.L.S., San Jose State U., 1976. Librarian San Jose State U., Calif., 1972-76; online instr. DIALOG Info. Services, Palo Alto, Calif., 1976-77, chief info. scientist, Washington, 1977-85, mgr. classroom instrn. program, 1986—; asst. prof. info. sci. Catholic U. Am., Washington, 1978—; online cons. Nat. Com. Library-Info. Sci., Washington, 1980-82; bd. dirs. ASK!, Washington, 1981—. Author: Brief Guide to DIALOG Searching, 1979. Contbr. articles to profl. jours. Named Info. Sci. Tchr. of Yr., Catholic U. Am., 1983. Mem. Am. Soc. for Info. Sci. (officer, chair Potomac Valley chpt. 1985-86), ALA, Spl. Library Assn., D.C. Library Assn., Am. Assn. Sch. Librarians. Republican. Episcopalian. Avocation: photographing architectural details on National Trust buildings. Home: 5314 26th Rd N Arlington VA 22207 Office: DIALOG Info Services 1901 N Moore St Suite 809 Arlington VA 22209

CAPWELL, BOBBI LOU STORSETH, educator; b. Amarillo, Tex., Oct. 19, 1956; d. S.L. and Marjorie Lou (McPhillips) Storseth; m. Thomas Wayne Capwell, July 24, 1981; 1 child, Jamie Nicole. AS, Amarillo Coll., 1977; BS, Tex. Women's U., 1979. Cert. tchr. Tex. Tchr. Perryton (Tex.) Ind. Sch. Dist., 1979-84, Pampa (Tex.) Ind. Sch. Dist., 1984-85, St. Vincent de Paul Cath. Sch., Pampa, 1985-87, Hereford (Tex.) Ind. Sch. Dist., 1987—. Author, illustrator: Alphabeasts, 1985. Mem. Woodrow Wilson PTA, 1984-85. Mem. Tex. State Tchr. Assn., Tex. Cath. Educators Assn., Bus. Profl. Women (sec. Perryton chpt. 1979-81), Beta Sigma Phi (treas. 1986-87). Republican. Baptist. Home: 111 Star Hereford TX 79045 Office: St Vincent de Paul Cath Sch 2300 N Hobart Pampa TX 79065

CARAM, DOROTHY FARRINGTON, educational consultant; b. McAllen, Tex., Jan. 14, 1933; d. Curtis Leon and Elena (Santander) Farrington; m. Pedro C. Caram, June 7, 1958; children—Pedro M., Juan D., Hector L., Jose M. B.A., Rice U., 1955, M.A., 1974; Ed.D., U. Houston, 1982; postgrad. U. Madrid, 1957. Tchr., Houston Ind. Sch. Dist., 1955-56, 1956-60, St. Mark's Episcopal Sch., Houston, 1964-65; substitute tchr. St. Vincent De Paul Cath. Sch., Houston, 1965-68; mgr. med. office, Houston, 1983; dir. Fed. Home Loan Bank, Little Rock, 1976-82; pres. Inst. Hispanic Culture, Houston, 1983, chmn. bd., 1987, Houston Ednl. Excellence Program, 1980; mem. task force Tex. Edn. Agy., 1981—; mem. adv. council Nat. Inst. Neurol. and Communicative Disorders and Health, 1972-76. Mem. council Miller Theater, Houston, 1976—; bd. dirs Houston Pops, 1983—; mem. Task Force Quality Integrated Edn., Houston, 1972; bd. dirs. Houston Lighthouse of Blind, 1982, United Way Tex. Gulf Coast; mem. Civil Commn. Houston, 1983—. Mem. Houston Area Tchrs. Fgn. Lang., MLA, Southwestern Social Sci. Orgn., Southwestern Council Latin Am. Studies. Roman Catholic. Club: Cedars (pres. 1978) (Houston) Home: 3106 Aberdeen Way Houston TX 77025

CARAPELLOTTI, SANNA LENE PETRELLA, health science association administrator; b. Steubenville, Ohio, Aug. 20, 1954; d. Patrick Joseph and Santa Jane (Scaffidi) Petrella; m. Paul Patrick Carapellotti, Dec. 20, 1986, 1 child, Anna. BA in Psychology, Coll. Steubenville, 1976; MS in Sch. Psychology, Duquesne U., Pitts., 1980; cert., Inst. Children's Literature, Redding, Conn., 1986. Counselor Ceta Youth Programs, Steubenville, 1977-80; child devel. specialist Community Mental Health Services, St. Clairsville, Ohio, 1980-82; psychologist Peace River Ctr. for Personal Devel., Lakeland, Fla., 1982-84; supr. parenting services Peale River Ctr. for Personal Devel., Lakeland, Fla., 1984-86; co-owner Your Time, Lakeland, 1984-86; v.p. Am. Inst. Health and Nutrition, Lakeland, 1986—; model All-Star Prodns., 1987—; cons. Child Advocacy Network Organized for Protection, Information and EducationServices' Project Lakeland, 1986—, Big Bros./Big Sisters, Lakeland, 1986; mem. state adv. bd. Cyesis Alternative Edn. Program, Lakeland, 1983, East Coast Migrant Headstart Assn., Haines City, Fla., 1986. Co-author: Journey for Health, 1986. Vol., group leader Alternatives for Living in Violent Environments, Steubenville, 1978-79. Mem. Nat. Assn. Exec. Women (chairperson edn. com. Lakeland chpt. 1986-87), Am. Bus. Women's Assn. (chairperson edn. com.), Polk County Mental Health Assn. Democrat. Roman Catholic. Office: Am Inst Health and Nutrition Lakeland FL 33802

CARBERRY, DEIRDRE, ballerina; b. Manhasset, N.Y., Nov. 7, 1965; d. Larry Paul and Marilyn (Monsour) C. Student pub. schs., Fla., pvt. schs., Fla. and N.Y.C. Corps Am. Ballet Theatre, N.Y.C., 1980-83, soloist, 1983—. Youngest person to join Am. Ballet Theatre to dance solo and prin. roles, prin. artist, U.S., Europe, Mid-East, S.Am., Cen. Am., 1979—. Dance ptnrs. have included Mikhail Baryshnikov, Fernando Bujones, Patrick Bissell, Kevin McKenzie; created lead female role in world premier The Little Ballet (choreographed for her and Mikhail Baryshnikov by Twyla Tharp, 1983). Videotapes include: Tharp by Baryshnikov, ABT at the Met, ABT in San Francisco, Sleeping Beauty, Baryshnikov Dances Balanchine, all televised on PBS. Toured U.S. with Baryshnikov and Co., 1984, 85, 87. Recipient Silver medal 1st U.S. Internat. Ballet Competition, Jackson, Miss., 1979; Harkness House scholar, 1978-79, N.Y. State Dance Summer program scholar, 1979, Sch. Am. Ballet scholar, 1979-80. Office: Am Ballet Theater 890 Broadway New York NY 10003

CARBINE, SHARON, lawyer, coporation executive; b. Bryn Mawr, Pa., Feb. 14, 1950; d. Thomas Joseph and Mary Teresa (Loftus) Carbine. B.A., Temple U., 1972, J.D., 1974, LL.M. in Taxation, 1977. Bar: Pa. 1974, Tex. 1981; C.P.A., Tex., Pa. Atty., Altemose Cos., Center Square, Pa., 1973-75; law clk. presiding justice Ct. Common Pleas, Phila., summer, 1975; tax atty. Provident Mut. Life Ins. Co., Phila., 1975-77, Emhart Corp., Farmington, Conn., 1977-78; tax sr. Peat Marwick Mitchell & Co., Phila., 1978-79; legal counsel to gov.'s chief energy advisor Tex. Energy and Natural Resources Adv. Council, Austin, 1979-80; tax atty. Sun Co., Inc., Dallas, 1980-82; sole practice, Haverford, Pa., 1983-84; tax atty. Ebasco Services Inc., N.Y.C., 1983-84; sole practice law, King of Prussia, Pa., 1985-88; asst. treas., mgr. corp. taxation PQ Corp., Valley Forge, Pa., 1988—; dir. Quaker City Japanning and Enameling Co., Inc., Phila., Vol., Republican Party, 1964—; mem. Jaycees, Phila., 1978-79, Austin, Tex., 1979-80; bd. dirs. Republican Women of the Main Line, Bryn Mawr, Pa., 1983. Mem. Pa. Bar Assn., Montgomery Bar Assn., Delaware County Bar Assn., Phila. Bar Assn., Delaware County Atty.-C.P.A. Forum, Brehon Law Soc. Roman Catholic. Lodge: Rotary (King of Prussia). Home: 110 Linwood Ave Ardmore PA 19003 Office: Valley Forge Exec Mall PO Box 840 Valley Forge PA 19482-0840

CARBONE, KERRY LYNN, data processing executive; b. Brighton, Mass., Sept. 28, 1956; d. Thomas Paul and Elizabeth Ann (O'Neill) Kendrick; m. Anthony Paul Carbone, Oct. 10, 1981. AA, Lasell Jr. Coll., 1976. Asst. nurse Quincy (Mass.) Oral Surgery, 1972, Dolman-Delagado System of Patterning, Westwood, Mass., 1973; asst. tchr. Downey Elem. Sch., Islington, Mass., 1974; mgr. Robin Hood's Barn Inc., Westwood, 1976-80; asst. mgr. Johnny Appleseeds Inc., Westwood, 1980-84; exec. sec. Kessler Installation, Dedham, Mass., 1985; exec. sec., computer programmer, office mgr. H&H Assocs. Inc., Norwood, Mass., 1985—. Roman Catholic.

CARD, CARI (PATRICIA), food product executive; b. Hollywood, Calif., Feb. 25, 1941; d. James Donald and Dorothy (Davies) North; m. Ben. F. Card, Aug. 25, 1962 (div. 1984); children: Ben F. Jr., Carol. BA, Calif. State U., Fullerton, 1971, postgrad., 1976. Cert. secondary tchr., Calif. Tchr., dept. chmn. Bell Jr. High Sch., Garden Grove, Calif., 1972-76; sales women Nolan Real Estate, Laguna Beach, Calif., 1977-78; chmn. gift shop South Coast Med. Ctr., 1985-86; pres., owner Bogart's Yogart, Laguna Hills, Calif., 1987—; lectr. in field. Contbr. articles to profl. jours. Mem. Orange County Art Edn. Assn. (bd. mem. 1976-77), Laguna Hills C. of C. Republican. Presbyterian. Club: Ebell (bd. dirs. 1986-87). Home: 25562 Rue Terr Laguna Niguel CA 92677 Office: Bogart's Yogart 23537 Moulton Pkwy Laguna Hills CA 92653

CARDAMONE, MARGARET MARY, lawyer; b. Norristown, Pa., Apr. 15, 1949; d. Joseph J. and Camelia (Sirianni) C. B.A., U. Steubenville, 1971; J.D., U. Notre Dame, 1974. Bar: Pa. 1974. Law clk. to judge Ct. Common Pleas, Montgomery County, Norristown, 1974-75; asst. dist. atty. Berks County, Reading, Pa., 1976-77; staff atty. Criminal Procedural Rules Com., Phila., 1978-79; asst. regional counsel EPA, Phila., 1979—. Bd. dirs. Whitpain Hills Homeowners Assn., Center Square, Pa., 1982—. Mem. ABA, Montgomery County Bar Assn., Delta Zeta. Republican. Roman Catholic. Clubs: Wissahickon Skating, Notre Dame (Phila.). Home: 1750 Skippack Pike Townhouse 1313 Center Square PA 19422 Office: EPA 841 Chestnut Bldg Philadelphia PA 19107

CARDIN, SHOSHANA SHOUBIN, non-profit organization administrator, consultant; b. Tel Aviv, Oct. 10, 1926; came to U.S., 1927; d. Sraiah and Chana (Barbalot) Shoubin; m. Jerome Stanley Cardin, August 17, 1948; children: Steven Harris, Irene Marcia, Nina Beth, Sanford Ronald. Student, Johns Hopkins U., 1942-45; BA, UCLA, 1946; MA, Antioch U., 1979; LHD (hon.), Western Md. Coll., 1985. Tchr. elem. schs. Balt., 1946-50; pres. Fedn. of Jewish Women's Org., Md., 1965-67; sec. Voluntary ActionCtr. Cen. Md., 1973-75; pres. women's div. Assn. Jewish Charities and Welfare Fund, Balt., 1975-77, Council of Jewish Fedns., N.Y.C., 1984-87; gov. Jewish Agy. for Israel., 1985—; dir. Calvert Telecommunications Corp., 1976-81. Co-Editor: Leadership Logic, 1974, Volunteerism: Moving into the 1980's, 1979, Stategies for Success-Surviving the New Federalism, 1982; contbr. editor, author of numerous pubs. Bd. dirs. Am. Jewish Joint Distbn. Com., United Israel Appeal, United Way Cen. Md., 1983-85, Health Welfare Council Cen. Md., 1980-85, Jewish Community Ctr. Balt., 1970-76, Balt. County Gen. Hosp. Aux., 1972-74, Park Sch. Parent's Assn., 1966-71, Md. Assn. Mental Health, 1965-66, March of Dimes Balt. Chpt., 1966-68, Levindale Ladies Aux., 1961-65, Chizuk Amuno Sch. Bd., 1963-65; Balt. Jewish Council, 1963-70, 1980-82 (sec. 1967-70) ; pres. Chizuk Amuno PTA, 1964-65, Jewish Community Ctr. Assocs. 1969-71 (exec. com. 1969—); chmn. Md. State Employment and Trng. Council, 1979-83, Md. Vol.Network, 1980-82, Md. Comm. Women, 1974-79 (commr. 1968-79); vice chmn. Gov.'s Vol. Council, Maryland Women's Conf., 1977; trustee United Jewish Appeal, Nat. Retinitis Pigmentosa Found., Loyola-Notre Dame Library, 1980-84, Balt. Hebrew Coll., 1979-82, Antioch U., 1977-78, Nat. Assn. Comms. for Women, Edn. and Research Fund, 1976-77; sec. Voluntary Action Ctr. Cen. Md., 1973-76 (exec. com. 1971-76); commr. Md. Comm. Human Relations, 1979-82; coordinator Women's Fair Balt., 1975; co-founder Women Together, 1973 (exec. com. 1973-76); co-chmn. Md. Interfaith Conf. Peace, 1966; del. Md. Constln. Conv., 1967; mem. Md. Jr. League (hon. life). Recipient Louise Waterman Wise award Am. Jewish Congress, 1970, Citizen Civics Affairs award B'nai B'rith, 1968, Jimmie Swartz medallion, 1983, Governor's Citation State of Md., 1982, Cert. of Merit U.S. Congress, 1979, Cert. of Distinguished Citizenship State of Md., 1969; named Outstanding Citizen of Md. Jewish War Vets., 1978, Woman of Yr. B'nai B'rith Women Md., 1967, one of Women of Dinstinction Fashion Group Balt. Inc., 1975, Honored and Outstanding Citizen City of Balt., 1969; inductee Md. Jewish Hall of Fame Jewish Hist. Soc. Md., 1979; Organizational and Community Devel. Fellow Johns Hopkins, 1976-77. Mem. Associated Jewish Charities and Welfare Fund (pres. women's div. 1975-77, bd. dirs. 1963-85, Elkan Myers award 1977), Am. Jewish Com. (Hilda K. Blaustein award 1978), Am. Assn. Univ. Women (Named Outstanding Woman 1975), Md. Assn. Parliamentarians (bd. dirs. 1976-77), Nat. Council Jewish Women (bd. dirs. 1963-65, 1968-72, 1973-74, Hannah G. Solomon award, 1975), Assn. Voluntary Action Scholars. Democrat. Lodge: Order Eastern Star (worthy matron). Office: Council Jewish Fedns 730 Broadway New York NY 10003

CARDINAL, SHIRLEY MAE, educator; b. Morann, Pa., May 6, 1944; d. Thomas Joseph and Mary Louise (Nemish) Giza; m. Charles Edward Cardinal, June 11, 1966; children: Julie Ann, Karen Lee. BS, Lock Haven U., 1966; MEd, Pa. State U., 1970. Tchr. Bald Eagle Nittany, Mill Hall, Pa., 1966-68; tchr., supr. Pa. State U., University Park, 1968-76; tchr., chairperson State Coll. (Pa.) Area Schs., 1968-76; primetime educator Oreg.-Davis Corp., Hamlet, Ind., 1984—; instr., cons. Dept. of Edn., Indpls., 1979—, cons. energy edn., 1980-85, educator linker, 1981—, rep. prime time, 1987—; instr. Ancilla Coll., Donaldson, Ind., 1976—. Author: Energy Activities with Learning Skills, 1980. Chmn. publicity Rep. Party, Plymouth, Ind., 1983—. Recipient Mankind and Edn. award U.S. Jaycees and Ind. Jaycees, 1981. Mem. Ind. State Tchr. Assn., Marshall County Reading Assn., Pi Lamba Theta, Sigma Kappa, Tri Kappa. Republican. Roman Catholic. Club: Pa. State U. Home: 10101 Turf Ct Plymouth IN 46563

CARDINALE, KATHLEEN CARMEL, medical center administrator; b. Donegal, Ireland, July 13, 1933; came to U.S., 1958, naturalized, 1966; d. Denis and Mary (Cannon) O'Boyle; m. Anthony Cardinale, Aug. 28, 1965. RN, Walton Hosp., Liverpool, Eng., 1955; BA, Jersey City State Coll., 1971, MA, 1973. Staff nurse, acting-in-charge Manhattan Gen. Hosp., N.Y.C., 1958-59; charge nurse, acting-in-charge, Met. Hosp., N.Y.C., 1959-60; charge nurse, relief supr. Manhattan Gen. Hosp., N.Y.C., 1960-64, asst. dir. nursing, 1964-68, staffing coordinator, 1968-70; acting assoc. dir. nursing Bernstein Inst., N.Y.C., 1970; clin. supr., clin. specialist Beth Israel Med. Ctr., N.Y.C., 1971-73; asst. dir. nursing Cabrini Med. Ctr., N.Y.C., 1974-77, assoc. dir. nursing, 1977-78, v.p. nursing services, 1978—. Mem. Am. Nurses Assn., Greater N.Y. Hosp. Assn. (mem. mental hygene com.), Am. Hosp. Assn., Am. Orgn. Nurse Execs. Home: 545 E 14th St New York NY 10009 Office: 227 E 19th St New York NY 10003

CARDINALE, MARIAN FRANCES, medical technologist; b. Independence, La., June 21, 1933; d. Isadore Thomas and Rosalie Marretta Cardinale; B.S. in Zoology and Chemistry with honors, Southeastern La. U., 1955; M.B.A., U. New Orleans, 1977. Staff technologist Charity Hosp., New Orleans, 1955-56, chemistry supr., 1956-62; chemistry supr. Mercy Hosp., New Orleans, 1962-68; chief med. technologist Pendleton Meml. Meth. Hosp., New Orleans, 1968-81, lab. mgr., 1981-84, dir. lab., 1984-85, v.p. clin. services, 1985—. Trustee Blood Ctr. for S.E. La., 1986—. Mem. Am. Soc. Med. Tech. (bd. dirs. 1980-83, 85-86, pres. 1984-85), La. (pres. 1969-70), New Orleans socs. med. tech., Sierra Club. Democrat. Roman Catholic. Home: 2704 Whitney Pl #723 Metairie LA 70002 Office: Pendleton Meml Meth Hosp 5620 Read Blvd New Orleans LA 70127

CARDMAN, CECILIA, artist; b. Soveria Mannelli, Italy; d. Samuel and Maria (Mendicino) Cardman. B.F.A., U. Colo., 1934, B.A., 1934; student Instituto dei Belli Arte, Naples, Italy, 1921-23, Denver Art Mus., 1930-31, studied with Leon Kroll, Nat. Acad., 1945-46, others. Head dept. painting Mesa Coll., Grand Junction, Colo., 1930-40; one-man shows: Naples, Italy, Grist Mill Gallery, Chester, Vt., Bergdorf-Goodman, 1978, Jarvis Gallery, Sandwich, Mass., 1975, Elliott Mus., Stuart, Fla., Grand Junction, Colo., 1981; group shows include: Nat. Arts Club, 1975-76, Nat. Acad., 1945, Knickerbocker Artists, 1979, Nelson Gallery, 1937-38, Denver Art Mus., 1924-25, Nat. League Am. Pen Women, 1979, Grand Central Art Gallery, 1977, Am. Artist Profl. League, 1979-80; one-woman show Elliott Mus., Stuart, Fla., 1988. Recipient numerous awards. Mem. Jackson Heights Art Club (1st prize 1982, 2d prize 1983), Pen & Brush (dir. admissions, Emily Nichols Hatch award 1982, 1st prize 1983, pres. 1987-88), Coll. Women's Club, Salmagundi Club (Lay Jury prize 1979), Nat. League Am. Pen Women (dir.; 1st br. v.p.), Sumi-e Soc. (prize 1982, recipient soc. award 1987), Ky. Watercolor Soc., Artist Fellowship, Inc., Knickerbocker Artists, Catherine Lorillard Wolfe Art Club (pres., dir., Best in Show award 1980, named Woman of the Year 1987), Am. Artists Profl. League (nat. dir.), Allied Artists Am. (dir. publicity, bd. dirs. 1983-86), Nat. Cowboy Hall of Fame, Western Heritage Ctr. Roman Catholic. Home: 34-06 81st St Penthouse Jackson Heights NY 11372

CARDONE, BONNIE JEAN, magazine editor; b. Chgo., Feb. 21, 1942; d. Frederick Paul and Beverly Jean (Johnson) Rittschof; m. David Frederick Cardone, June 9, 1963 (div. 1978); children—Pamela Susan, Michael David. B.A., Mich. State U., 1963. Editorial asst. Mich. State Dental Assn. Jour., Lansing, 1963-64; asst. editor Nursing Home Adminstr., Chgo., 1964-65; asst. editor Skin Diver Mag., Los Angeles, 1976-77, sr. editor, 1977-81, exec. editor, photographer, 1981—. Mem. Am. Soc. Mag. Photographers, Soc. Profl. Journalists. Clubs: Santa Monica Blue Fins (treas. 1975-76, pres. 1977-78, sec. 1985-86, v.p. 1987-88), Calif. Wreck Divers. Office: Skin Diver Mag 8490 Sunset Blvd Los Angeles CA 90060

CARDOZA, ALFREIDA FARIA, real estate assessor, appraisor; b. Boston, Mar. 30, 1938; d. Alfred Gomes and Emmagean (Christmas) Balla; m. Raymond David Cardoza. Student real estate law, U. Mass., 1964, 75-77. Accredited assessor, Mass. Real estate broker Ray-Al Real Estate, East Wareham, Mass., 1964—; bookkeeper, cashier Angelo's Supermarkets, Inc., East Wareham, 1967-68; supr. Plymouth County U.S. Fed. Census, New Bedford, Mass., 1969-70; title examiner Plymouth County Registry of Deeds, Plymouth, Mass., 1973-74; assessor Town of Wareham, Mass., 1975-78; dep. assessor Town of Duxbury, Mass., 1978—. Mem. Mass. Assn. Assessing Officers (instr. 1977—, sec. edn. com. 1978-84, vice chmn. 1980, Spl. Service award 1981), Northeast Regional Assn. Assessors (sec. 1984—, conf. dir. 1987), Internat. Assn. Assessing Officers (rep. Mass. 1979-82), Plymouth County Assn. Assessors (pres. 1981-82). Democrat. Roman Catholic. Home: 36 Main Ave PO Box 156 East Wareham MA 02538 Office: Bd Assessors Town Hall 878 Tremont St Duxbury MA 02332

CARDOZA, ANNE DE SOLA, illustrator, screenwriter, artist, animator; b. N.Y.C., Nov. 18, 1941; d. Sara Nunez de Sola and Michael Cardoza. B.S. in Creative Writing, English, NYU, 1964; M.A. in Creative Writing, English, San Diego State U., 1979; diploma Hollywood Scriptwriting Inst., 1984; diploma Alexandra Inst. Painting, San Diego, 1988. Author of 33 books including In The Chips: 101 Ways to Make Money with your Personal Computer, 1985, High Paying Jobs in Six Months or Less, 1984, Understanding Robotics, 1985, Careers in Robotics, 1985, Careers in Aerospace, 1985, (novels) Psyche Squad; co-author: Winning Tactics for Women Over 40, 1988; author 17 screen plays; contbr. articles to various publs., film scripts, 2 novelettes and collections of short stories. Office: PO Box 4333 San Diego CA 92104

CARDOZO, ARLENE ROSSEN, author; b. Mpls., Jan. 12, 1938; d. Ralph and Beatrice (Cohen) Rossen; m. Richard Nunez Cardozo, June 29, 1959; children—Miriam, Rachel, Rebecca. B.A., U. Minn., 1958, M.A., 1982, postgrad., 1982—. Founder, dir. Writers Unlimited, Mpls., 1972-76, Woman at Home Workshops, Mpls., 1976-81; lectr. U. Minn. Summer Arts Study Center, 1982—; artist-in-residence Split Rock Arts Ctr., Duluth, Minn., 1985; cons. to woman at home, 1976—, manuscript and pub. industry. Author: The Liberated Cookbook, 1972, Woman at Home, 1976, Jewish Family Celebrations, 1982, Sequencing, 1986; contbr. essays, articles, reviews to Chgo. Sun Times, Mpls. Star/Tribune, Cleve. Plain Dealer, Newsday; L.J. Journalism Quar.; guest lectr. Harvard-Radcliffe U., 1982; others; guest appearances Today Show, Phil Donahue Show, Dr. Ruth Show, radio and TV, U.S. and Can. Founder, Harvard Neighbors, Cambridge, 1963-64; vol. Mpls. pub. schs., 1972—. Mem. Authors Guild, Authors League Am., Nat. Book Critics Circle (charter), Minn. Press Club, Hadassah (life). Jewish. Home: 1955 East River Rd Minneapolis MN 55114

CARDUCCI, DIANE, hospital administrator; b. S.I., N.Y., Dec. 16; d. Geremia and Amelia (Mariano) C. A.A., S.I. Community Coll., 1967; B.S., Richmond Coll., 1970, M.S., 1972; postgrad. St. John's U., 1979-82. Tchr., librarian Our Lady of Mt. Carmel, S.I., 1967-72, St. Paul, S.I., 1972-81; tchr., prin. religious edn. Immaculate Conception, S.I., 1981-82; health care program planner Sea View Hosp. and Home, S.I., 1982-84, asst. dir. hosp., 1984-85, assoc. dir. hosp., 1986—. Editor Am. Com. on Italian Migration, 1983—; active Staten Island Health System Agy., Coll. Staten Island Alumni Assn., . Chmn. bd. dirs. March of Dimes, S.I., 1985-86; bd. dirs. S.I. Hosp., 1985—, Staten Island Ctr. Ind. Living, 1986—; treas. N.Y.C. Community Bd. 1, S.I., 1975-80; sec. Northfield Local Devel. Corp., S.I., 1979-83, sec., 1982. Richmond County Bus. and Profl. Women scholar, 1982. Mem. Health Systems Agy., Am. Pub. Health Assn., N.Y. State Planning Assn., Am. Mgmt. Assn., Gateway Bus. and Profl. Women, Coll. of S.I. Alumni Assn. (Hall of Fame, Outstanding Service Alumni 1984, Outstanding Italian Woman 1985). Roman Catholic. Lodge: Lioness. Home: 4176 Richmond Ave Staten Island NY 10312

CARDWELL, SUE POOLE, reclamation services company executive; b. Clearfield, Pa., Oct. 31, 1952; d. Robert Thomas Poole and Mary B. (Edwards) (stepmother) and Patricia Alice (Coleman) (stepmother) P.; m. Charles Howard Cardwell, Nov. 24, 1979; children—Jonathon Aaron, Jacqueline Leigh. Clk.-typist Ky. Dept. Mines and Minerals, 1974; sr. reclamation insp. div. reclamation Ky. Dept. Natural Resources, Madisonville, 1974-77; pres. Reclamation Services Unltd., Inc., Madisonville, 1977—; chmn. West Ky. adv. group Office Surface Mining, Dept. Interior, 1979—; adv. bd. U. Ky. Symposium on Surface Mining Reclamation and Hydrology, also mem. exec. adv. com.; mem. Ky. Adv. Com. on Strip Mine Regulation, 1979—; mem. exec. bd. Ky. Task Force on Exploited and Missing Children; bd. dirs., sec. Ky. Alliance for Missing and Exploited Children; mem. Rep. Senatorial Inner Circle, 1984—. Served with WAC, 1972-73. Named hon. Ky. col.; named to W.Va. Ship of State. Mem. West Ky. Coal Operators Assn. (dir.), West Ky. Assn. Gen. Contractors, Hazardous Materials Control Research Inst., Mining and Reclamation Council Am. (chmn. reclamation subcom.), Profl. Reclamation Assn. Am. (bd. dirs., charter), World Safety Assn., W.Va. Surface Mine Assn., Nat. Reclamation Assn. West Ky., West Ky. Constrn. Assn. of Associated Gen. Contractors, West Ky. Sonstrn. Assn. (bd, dirs.); contbg. editor Ky. Coal Jour. Office: 12 Hartland Ave Madisonville KY 42431

CAREY, CARLA JOANNE, savings and loan association executive; b. Watertown, S.D., Sept. 27, 1945; d. Wayne Beaudette and Grace Norma (Lowry) Clausen; m. David Dale Weaver Feb. 12, 1965 (div. Nov. 1975); children: Michael Dale, Charles Edmund, Victoria Joyce; m. Shelby Gene Carey, Nov. 17, 1975; 1 child, Michael Alan. Student, Wenatchee Valley Coll., 1963-64, Am. Inst. Banking, 1975-76, Inst. Fin. Edn., 1980-86. Paying, receiving teller Seattle First Nat. Bank, Wenatchee, Wash., 1965-67, Security Bank Wash., Wenatchee, 1975-78; head teller Community Savings & Loan, Wenatchee, 1979-80; savings/retirement account counselor Capital Savings & Loan, Wenatchee, 1980-81; savings officer, asst. v.p. Ea. Wash. Savings & Loan, East Wenatchee, 1982-85, v.p. personnel and adminstrn., 1985-88; sec., fair mgr. Chelen County Fair, Cashmere, Wash., 1988—. Pres. Children's Orthopedic Guild, 1972-75; mem. citizen's adv. council-Eastmont Sch. Dist., 1985; chmn., bd. trustees Apple blossom Festival, 1987—; mem. citizen's adv. com. City of East Wenatchee, 1987. Mem. Nat. Assn. Bank Women (award & scholarship chmn. 1984-85, v.p. 1985-86, pres. 1986—), East Wenatchee Dist. C. of C. (exec. dir. 1986—), Am. Soc. Personnel Adminstrn., Am. Mgmt. Assn., Nat. Assn. Female Execs., Women's Bowling Assn. (pres. bd. dirs. 1975-80). Republican. Lutheran. Office: Chelen County Fair Westcott Dr Cashmere WA 98815

CAREY, CATHERINE ELLEN, small business owner; b. Burlington, Mass., May 18, 1941; d. Clarence William and Mary Aglae (Dube) Ingalls; m. Edward Francis Carey, Sr., Oct. 7, 1973; 1 child, Edward F., Jr. Student, Northeastern U., 1970-73, Essex Agricultures Tech., Rowley, Mass., 1977-78, Whittier Regular Vocat. Sch., Merrimac, Mass., 1980, Custom Decorating Inst., Santa Ana, Calif., 1980-84. Asst. bookkeeper High Carbon & Wire Corp., Millbury, Mass., 1965-68; pub. relations New Eng. Newspaper Supply Co., Millbury, 1968-69; tech. aide Mitre Corp., Bedford, Mass., 1969-74; tailor, restorer of heirloom gowns Rowley, Mass., 1979—. Contbg. editor New England Bride Mag., 1984—. Mem. Nat. Assn. Female Execs., Nat. Trust, Wenham Hist.Assn. and Mus., Inc., Rowley C. of C. (bd. dirs., sec. 1983—). Roman Catholic. Home and Office: Rowley MA 01969

CAREY, ERNESTINE GILBRETH (MRS. CHARLES E. CAREY), author, lecturer; b. N.Y.C., Apr. 5, 1908; d. Frank Bunker and Lillian (Moller) Gilbreth; m. Charles Everett Carey, Sept. 13, 1930; children: Lillian Carey Clark), Charles Everett. B.A., Smith Coll., 1929. Buyer R. H. Macy & Co., N.Y.C., 1930-44, James McCreery, N.Y.C., 1947-49; lectr., book reviews, syndicated newspaper articles, 1951. Co-recipient (with Frank B. Gilbreth, Jr.) (Prix Scarron French Internat. humor award for Cheaper by the Dozen 1951), (with Lillian Moller Gilbreth) (McElligott medallion Assn. Marquette U. Women 1966); Author: Jumping Jupiter, 1952, Rings Around Us, 1956, Giddy Moment, 1958, (with Frank B. Gilbreth, Jr.) Cheaper by the Dozen, 1949, Belles on Their Toes, 1951; also mag. articles and book revs. Bd. dirs. Right to Read, Inc., 1968—, co-chmn., 1967; lay adv. com. Manhasset (N.Y.) Bd. Edn.; trustee Manhasset Pub. Library, 1953-59, v.p., 1956-59; trustee Smith Coll., 1967-72. Montgomery award Friends of Phoenix Public Library, 1981. Mem. Authors Guild Am. (life mem., mem. guild council 1955-60), P.E.N. Republican. Conglist. Clubs: North Shore, Smith College (L.I.) (asst. chmn. scholarship com. 1950-59); Smith Coll. (N.Y.); Smith College Phoenix (Phoenix) (vice chmn. scholarship com. 1967), 7 College Conf. Council (Phoenix). Home: 6148 E Lincoln Dr Paradise Valley AZ 85253

CAREY, GERTRUDE MARIE, librarian, handwriting analyst, educator; b. Lowell, Mass., Aug. 5, 1946; d. Elliot James and Gertrude (Gendreau) C. BA in History, U. Lowell, 1968, EdM, 1973; MS in Library Sci., La. State U., 1969; MBA, N.H. Coll., 1983. Cert. librarian, document examiner, graphoanalyst. Librarian Town of Tewksbury, Mass., 1970-78; ptnr., pres. JTC Cons., Acton, Mass., 1979—; instr. U. Lowell, 1978, 79, 84; prof. N.H. Tech. Coll., Manchester, 1985—. Contbr. articles to newspapers, profl. jours. Mem. World Assn. Document Examiners, Internat. Graphoanalysis Soc., Mass. Chpt. of Internat. Graphoanalysis Soc. (pres. 1977-78), Evidence Photographers Internat. Council, Cath. Alumni Club (pres. Boston chpt. 1980-82, Nashua, N.H. chpt. 1977-78, CACer of yr. award 1981). Home: 194 Nesmith St Lowell MA 01852 Office: JTC Cons PO Box 743 Acton MA

CAREY, JANE QUELLMALZ, printing company executive; b. Albany, N.Y., May 6, 1952; d. Henry and Marion Agar (Lynch) 1979. Student, Stephen's Coll., 1969-70; cert., Katherine Gibbs Sch., Boston, 1971. Sec. to headmaster St. Agnes Sch., Albany, 1971-72; exec. sec. Dwight Bldg. Co., Hamden, Conn., 1972-73; v.p. Q Corp., U.S. Agt. for WHO Publs., Albany, 1973-77, pres., 1978—, 1986—. Bd. dirs. Next Step, Inc., Albany, 1976-79, Mohawk Hudson Humane Soc., Menands, N.Y., 1988—. Mem. Printing Industries East/Cen. N.Y. (bd. dirs. 1985—), Am. Assn. World Health (bd. dirs. 1977-78), Alumnae Assn. Doane Stuart Sch. (bd. dirs. 1988). Episcopalian. Clubs: Traffic (N.Y.C.), Hudson River (Albany). Home: 12 Strathomre Dr Loudenveill NY 12221 Office: Boyd Printing Co Inc 49 Sheridan Ave Albany NY 12210

CAREY, JEAN MARIE, management consulting executive; b. Charleston, W.Va., June 2, 1943; d. Edward H. and Marian (Lendved) Lebeis; m. Robert W. Carey, Nov. 1971; 1 child, Megan Rose. BA, Pa. State U., 1965. Programmer Pa. Mutual Life Ins., Phila., 1967-68; sr. analyst/programmer U. Pa., Phila., 1969-72; sr. systems analyst Acme Markets, Phila., 1972-74; programming mgr. Bryn Mawr Coll., Pa., 1976-77; project adminstr. Smith Kline Beckman, Phila., 1977-83; project mgmt. cons. Arco Chem. Co., Phila., 1983-88; chief exec. officer Carey Project Orgn., Ardmore, Pa., 1988—; chmn. Systems Methodology Users Mid-Atlantic, 1984-86, PMI Systems Tech. Papers, 1983; co-dir. Cobol project, U. Pa., Phila., 1969-72; lectr. in field. Contbr. articles to profl. jours. Bd. dirs. Scan/Child Abuse Treatment Ctr., Phila., 1983—, Danceteller/Dance Theater, Phila., 1985—, Family and Community Service of Delaware County, 1987—. Recipient Excel award, Arco, 1986. Mem. Project Mgmt. Inst. Soc. of Friends. Home and Office: Carey Project Orgn 663 Cricket Ave Ardmore PA 19003

CAREY, JEANNE GRACE, computer consulting firm executive; b. N.Y.C., Apr. 19, 1957; d. Richard John and Ruth (Brown) C. Student, SUNY, Oswego, 1980. Sales rep. Computerland of Ithaca, N.Y., 1981-83; store mgr. CompuShop, San Jose, Calif., 1983-85; account rep. Computerland of San Francisco, 1985-86, CPT Corp., San Francisco, 1986-87; owner, computer cons. The Computer Link, San Francisco, 1987—, Optimum Computing, Inc., San Francisco, 1987—. Mem. Summit Workshops Inc.

CAREY, KATHRYN ANN, corporate philanthropy, advertising and public relations executive, editor, consultant; b. Los Angeles, Oct. 18, 1949; d. Frank Randall and Evelyn Mae (Walmsley) C.; m. Richard Kenneth Sundt, Dec. 28, 1980. BA in Am. Studies with honors, Calif. State U.-Los Angeles, 1971. Tutor Calif. Dept. Vocat. Rehab., Los Angeles, 1970; teaching asst. U. So. Calif., 1974-75, UCLA, 1974-75; claims adjuster Auto Club So. Calif., San Gabriel, 1971-73; corp. pub. relations cons. Carnation Co., Los Angeles, 1973-78; cons., adminstr. Carnation Community Service Award Program, 1973-78; pub. relations cons. Vivitar Corp.; sr. advt. asst. Am. Honda Motor Co., Gardena, Calif., 1978-84; exec. dir. Am. Honda Found., 1984—; mgr. Honda Dealer Advt. Assns.; cons. advt., pub. relations, promotions. Editor: Vivitar Voice, Santa Monica, Calif., 1978, Honda Views, 1978-84, Found. Focus, 1984 ; asst. editor Frickies Research Digest; contbg. editor Newsbriefs, Am. Honda Motor Co., Inc. employees mag.; Calif. Life Scholarship Found. scholar, 1967. Mem. Advt. Club Los Angeles, Pub. Relations Soc. Am., So. Calif. Assn. Philanthropy, Council Founds. of Washington, Airline Owners and Pilots Assn., Am. Quarter Horse Assn., Los Angeles Soc. for Prevention Cruelty to Animals, Greenpeace, German Shepherd Dog Club Am., Ocicats Internat., Am. Humane Assn., Elsa Wild Animal Appeal. Democrat. Methodist. Office: PO Box 2205 Torrance CA 90509-2205

CAREY, MARCIA J., medical transcription service executive; b. Willmar, Minn., Feb. 13, 1941; d. Franklin N. and Thelma L (Portinga) Fanberg; m. Donald L. Carey, June 23, 1962 (div. May 1976); children: Michelle C., Matthew S. Student, Trinity Coll., 1959-61, Calif. State U., Chico., 1961-62. Cert. med. transcriptionist; accredited record technician. Med. transcriptionist Hillcrest Hosp., Petaluma, Calif., 1972-73; med. care evaluation coordinator Santa Teresa Community Hosp., San Jose, Calif., 1973-79; med. transcriptionist San Jose, 1979-84; dir. pub. relations Dictation West, South San Francisco, Calif., 1984-85, dir. ops., 1985-87; pres. United Transcription Services, San Jose, 1987—. Mem. Am. Assn. Med. Transcription, (treas. 1981, v.p. 1982, bd. dirs. 1979-82, pres. South Bay chpt. 1979-81, 85-86), Am. Med. Record Assn. Home: 6283 Channel Dr San Jose CA 95123 Office: United Transcription Services 5899 Santa Teresa Blvd San Jose CA 95123

CAREY, MARGARET THERESA LOGAN, newspaper education consultant; b. Phila., May 8, 1931; d. Michael Francis and Margaret Mary (Meehan) Logan; m. William Emmett Carey, June 21, 1952; children: William Edward, Michael Patrick, Peggy Ann. AA, Bucks County Community Coll., 1968; student, Temple U., 1968-69; BS, U. Bridgeport, 1971; MEd in Reading, U. N.C., 1973. Reading resource tchr. Wake County Sch. Dist., Raleigh, N.C., 1971-76; newspaper in edn. cons. The News & Observer, Raleigh, 1976-77; ednl. cons. U.S. News and World Report, Washington, 1977-78; newspaper in edn. cons. N.Y. Times, N.Y.C., 1978, Times Newspaper, Trenton-Princeton, N.J., 1979—; cons. N.J. Dept. Edn., Trenton, 1978-79. Editor, founder (children's page) Funtimes, 1981—, (supplement) Create-An-Ad, 1984—. State rep. for N.J. Am. Newspaper Pubs. Assn. Found., Reston, Va., 1983—; dir. Reading Is Fundamental, Washington, 1984—. Mem. Internat. Reading Assn. (literacy 1986), N.J. Reading Assn. (award 1986), Tri-County Reading Assn. (award 1984), N.J. Assn. for Lifelong Learning, Mercer County Assn. for Lifelong Learning, N.J. Press Assn. (chmn. newspaper in edn. com. 1983—), Greater Trenton Literacy Coalition (chairperson). Roman Catholic. Clubs: Princeton Ski, Princeton Racquet. Office: Times Newspaper 500 Perry St Box 847 Trenton NJ 08605

CAREY, MARY VIRGINIA, writer; b. New Brighton, Cheshire, Eng., May 19, 1925; d. John Cornelius and Mary Alice (Hughes) Carey; B.S., Coll. of Mt. St. Vincent, 1946. Editorial asso. Coronet Mag., N.Y.C., 1948-55; asst. editor publs. Walt Disney Productions, Burbank, Calif., 1955-69; author: Mystery of the Flaming Footprints, 1971; Mystery of the Singing Serpent, 1972; Mystery of Monster Mountain, 1973; Secret of the Haunted Mirror, 1974; Mystery of the Invisible Dog, 1975; Mystery of Death Trap Mine, 1976; Mystery of the Magic Circle, 1978; Mystery of the Sinister Scarecrow, 1979; Mystery of the Scar-Faced Beggar, 1981; Mystery of the Blazing Cliffs, 1981; Love is Forever, 1975; Step-by-Step Candlemaking, 1972; Step-by-Step Winemaking, 1973; The Owl Who Loved Sunshine, 1977; Mystery of the Wandering Caveman, 1982; Mystery of the Missing Mermaid, 1983; Mystery of the Trail of Terror, 1984; The Gremlins Storybook, 1984; Mystery of the Creep-Show Crooks, 1985; A Place for Allie, 1985, The Case of the Savage Statue, 1987, The Mystery of the Cranky Collector, 1987; editor: Grandmothers are Very Special People, 1977; author: (with George Sherman) A Compendium of Bunk, 1976. Mem. Author's Guild, Soc. Children's Book Writers, PEN. Roman Catholic. Address: 3748 Birch St Ventura CA 93003

CAREY, NANCY BUNTING, telecommunications executive, lawyer; b. Salisbury, Md., Apr. 18, 1949; d. Asher Burton and Pauline (Bunting) C. AB, Mt. Holyoke Coll., 1971; JD, Temple U., 1974. Bar: Md., 1974, Pa., 1974, D.C., 1975. Intern U.S. Rep. Donald Riegle, Washington, 1969; law clk. Cathel and Ewell, Ocean City, Md., 1972, 73; atty. Broadcast Bur. Renewal Br. FCC, Washington, 1974-75, atty. office of Gen. Counsel, Legal Research and Treaties, 1975-77, legal asst. to Commr. Abbott Washburn, 1977-82; dir. Fed. and Regulatory Liaison MCI, Washington, 1982-85; v.p. human resources United Telephone System, Inc., Overland Park, Kans., 1985-87; v.p. intrastate revenues United Telecommunications, Inc., Overland Park, 1987; v.p. mktg. U.S. Sprint, Kansas City, 1987—; bd. dirs. United Telephone System, Inc., Overland Park, United Telephone NW, Hood River, Oreg., United Telephone Midwest Group, Kansas City, United Telephone Ind., Inc., Warsaw, United Telespectrum, Kansas City, United Telephone Systems, Inc., Overland Park. Bd. dirs. WGR Leader Found., Washington; mem. Bus. Ptnrs., Inc., Washington. Mem. ABA, D.C. Bar Assn., Women in Govt. Relations (dir. Leader found. 1985-87), Nat. Women's Coalition, Personnel Mgmt. Assn., Nat. Assn. Female Execs. Republican. Methodist. Office: US Sprint 8140 Ward Pkwy Kansas City KS 64114

CAREY, SARAH COLLINS, lawyer; b. N.Y.C., Aug. 12, 1938; d. Jerome Joseph and Susan (Atlee) Collins; m. James J. Carey, Aug. 28, 1962 (div. 1977); 1 child, Sasha; m. 2d John D. Reilly, Jan. 27, 1979; children—Sarah, Katherine. B.A., Radcliffe Coll., 1960; LL.B., Georgetown U., 1965. Bar: D.C. 1966, U.S. Supreme Ct. 1977. Soviet specialist USIA/U.S. Dept. State, 1961-65; asso. Arnold & Porter, Washington, 1965-68; asst. dir. Lawyers Com. for Civil Rights, Washington, 1968-73; ptnr. Adams Duque & Hazeltine and predecessor cos., Washington, 1973-87, Heron, Burchette, Ruckert & Rothwell, Washington, 1987—; cons. Ford Found., 1975-83, Carnegie Corp., 1984-88. Contbr. articles to profl. jours. Bd. dirs. New Transcentury Found., Washington, 1982—, Overseas Edn. Fund., 1982—, Inst. for Soviet-Am. Relations, 1983—, Carribean Cen. Am. Action, 1987—, Georgetown U. Sch. Law Inst. for Pub. Representation, 1971-85, Am. Arbitration Assn., 1975-82, Vis. Nurses Assn., 1976-81. Mem. ABA (internat. law com.), D.C. Bar Assn. (sect. internat. law), Womens Bar Assn., Washington Internat. Trade Assn., others. Democrat. Office: Heron Burchette Ruckert & Rothwell 1025 Thomas Jefferson St NW #700 Washington DC 20007

CAREY, WENDY LOUISE, environmental scientist, consultant; b. Balt., Sept. 28, 1954; d. Mervyn Lee and Louise (Otto) C.; m. Anthony P. Pratt, Oct. 21, 1978; children: Jamie Carey, Elizabeth Bradfield, Bo Griffith. BS in Geology magna cum laude, St. Lawrence U., 1976; MS in Marine Studies, U. Del., 1979. Marine cons. Coll. Marine Studies U. Del., Lewes, 1979-81; environ. cons. Coastal & Estuarine Research, Inc., Lewes, 1981—. Co-Editor: Geology of Delaware, 1977, Beach Process in Delaware, 1985; contbr. articles to profl. jours. Industry Ptnrs. scholar U. Del., 1977-79. Mem. Nat. Assn. Environ. Profls., Soc. Wetland Scientists, Del. Acad. Scis., Atlantic Estuarine Research Soc., Phi Beta Kappa. Office: Coastal & Estuarine Research Inc Marine Studies Complex Lewes DE 19958

CARGIN, CONNIE LOESCH, nursing home administrator; b. Jefferson City, Mo., Nov. 1, 1955; d. Norman Richard and Donnabell Roseanne (Fischer) Loesch; m. Thomas Clad Cargin, Sept. 13, 1980. BBA, Cen. Mo. State U., 1976; MBA, U. Mo., Kansas City, 1987. CPA, Mo.; licensed nursing home adminstr. Semi-sr. auditor Mo. State Auditor's Office, Jefferson City, 1976-79; sr. auditor Baird, Kurtz & Dobson, Kansas City, 1979-82; adminstr., chief fin. officer Kingswood Manor, Kansas City, 1982—. Mem. Statue of Liberty-Ellis Island Found., N.Y.C., 1983-87. Mem. Am. Inst. CPA's, Am. Bus. Women's Assn. (pres., v.p., treas. 1980-87), Mo. Soc. CPA's, Kansas City C. of C. (mem. bus. edn. com., v.p. mem. com.), Alpha Omicron Pi (mem. alumni chpt. corp. bd.). Club: Overland Park Athletic. Office: Kingswood Manor 10000 Wornall Rd Kansas City MO 64114

CARIC, HELEN LORA, health science specialist; b. Skopje, Macedonia, Yugoslavia, Jan. 1, 1939; d. Miladin and Hedy (Hem) Milicevic; m. Ernst Anzbock, Dec. 14, 1959 (div. 1971); children: Harald, Evelyn; m. Ranko Caric, Nov. 3, 1973 (div. 1981); 1 child, Peter. gen. agt. Intern Cons. Exchange, San Diego, Calif., 1986; minister Universal Ctr. New Age Consciousness, Inc., Monroe, N.Y., 1985—. Mem. Am. Massage Therapy Assn., Alliance of Massage Therapists, Inc., Universal Spiritualist Assn., N.Y. State Soc. Med. Massage Therapists, Orange County C. of C., Ea. Orange County C. of C. Home: Linden Motel Linden Ct Greenwood Lake NY 10925 Office: Universal Ctr New Age Consciousness Inc 101 Stage Rd Monroe NY 10950

CARLEN, SISTER CLAUDIA, librarian; b. Detroit, July 24, 1906; d. Albert B. and Theresa Mary (Ternes) C. AB in Library Sci., U. Mich., 1928, MA in Library Sci., 1938; LHD (hon.), Marygrove Coll., 1981, Loyola U., Chgo., 1983; LittD (hon.), Cath. U. of Am., 1983. Asst. librarian St. Mary Acad., Monroe, Mich., 1928-29; asst. librarian Marygrove Coll., Detroit, 1929-44; librarian Marygrove Coll., 1944-69, library cons., 1970-71; on leave as index editor New Cath. Ency., 1963-67, Cath. Theol. Ency., 1968-70; library cons. Rome, 1971-72; library cons. St. John's Provincial Sem., Plymouth, Mich., 1972-80, librarian emeritus, 1980-82, scholar-in-residence, 1982-85, archivist, 1985—; supr. orgn. and servicing Community Center Libraries staffed by vols.; bd. dirs. Corpus Instrumentorum, Inc., v.p., 1969-70; mem. instructional materials com. Mich. Curriculum Study; cons. McGraw Hill Ency. World Biography, 1968-72, World Book Ency., 1969-70. Author: Guide to Encyclicals of the Roman Pontiffs, 1939, Guide to the Documents of Pius XII, 1951, Dictionary of Papal Pronouncements, 1958; editor: Papal Encyclicals, 1740-1981, 1981; Editor: column At Your Service, Cath. Library World, 1950-52, Reference Book Rev. Sect, 1952-64, 66-72, Books for the Home column; monthly news release, Nat. Cath. Rural Life Conf., 1952-61; adv. bd.: The Pope Speaks, 1953—, Pierian Press; contbr.: Catholic Bookman's Guide, 1961, Dictionary Western Chs, 1969, Ency. Dictionary of Religion, 1979, Translatio Studii, 1973. Trustee Marygrove Coll., Detroit, 1976-79, vice chmn. bd., 1977-79. Recipient Disting. Alumna award U. Mich. Sch. Library Sci., 1974. Mem. ALA (council 1958-61, 68-71), Cath. Library Assn. (chmn. com. membership 1946-49, chmn. Mich. unit 1952-54, chmn. coll. and univ. sect. 1954-56, chmn. publs. com. 1961-62, pres. 1965-67), Bibliog. Soc. Am., Nat. Fedn. Cath. Coll. Students (moderator nat. lit. commn.), Spl. Libraries Assn., Mich. Library Assn. (chmn. coll. sect. 1956-57, chmn. recruiting com. 1959-60), Soc. Am. Archivists, Am. Friends of Vatican Library (v.p.), Phi Beta Kappa, Phi Kappa Phi, Beta Phi Mu. Home: 610 W Elm Ave Monroe MI 48161 Office: 2305 Sandalwood Circle #101C Ann Arbor MI 48105

CARLETON, JOYCE CECILIA, corporate executive; b. Boston, May 6, 1943; d. Peter John and Cecilia (DeMello) Muslawski; m. Gary Ralph Carleton, June 5, 1970. Grad. High Sch., Winslow, Maine. File clk. Keyes Fibre Co., Waterville, Maine, 1961-62, payroll clk., 1961-62, accounts receivable bookkeeper, 1962-64, head cashier, 1964-70; bookkeeper Southeastern Electronics, Ft. Lauderdale, 1970-71; bookkeeper Ike's Carter Pools, Ft. Lauderdale, 1971-75, treas., controller, 1975—. Republican. Roman Catholic. Home: 326 Sunshine Dr Coconut Creek FL 33066

CARLETON, MARY RUTH, television news anchor, broadcasting educator; b. Sacramento, Feb. 2, 1948; d. Warren Alfred and Mary Gertrude (Clark) Case. B.A. in Polit. Sci., U. Calif.-Berkeley, 1970, M.J., 1974. Television news anchorwoman, reporter Sta. KXAS-TV, Ft. Worth, 1974-78, Sta. KING-TV, Seattle, 1978-80; TV news anchorwoman Sta. KOCO-TV, Oklahoma City, 1980-84; news anchor, reporter Sta. KTTV-TV, Los Angeles, 1984-87; news anchor KLAS-TV, Las Vegas, 1987—; broadcast instr. U. Okla., 1981-82, Okla. Christian Coll., 1981-83. Trustee World Neighbors, 1983—; bd. dirs. Meadows Aux., 1982—, The Forum, 1982-86. Named Communicator of Yr., Okla. Wildlife Fedn., 1983; Women in Communication Byliner, 1984; recipient Broadcasting award UPI, 1981, Emmy award, Los Angeles, 1987; named Okla. Woman in News, Hospitality Club, 1981. Mem. Women in Communications (Clarion award 1981). Democrat. Episcopalian. Office: KLAS-TV 3228 Channel 8 Dr Las Vegas NV 89109

CARLIN, LEE JACOBS, stock broker; b. Denver, Oct. 23, 1943; d. John H. and Betty Lee (Lyons) Jacobs; m. Palmer W. Carlin; children: Bridget, Tanya. BA, Cornell U., 1965; PhD, John Hopkins U., 1971; cert., Coll. Fin. Planning, Denver. Pres. Carlin Textiles, Boulder, Colo., 1972-80; stock broker Boettchel & Co., Boulder, 1980-87; branch office mgr., v.p. Piper, Jaffray & Hopwood Inc., Boulder, 1988—. Contbr. articles to profl. jours. Mem. Internat. Assn. Fin. Planners, C. of C., Boulder. Home: 2209 4th St Boulder CO 80302

CARLING, LAURIE JEANNE, sales executive; b. Moberly, Mo., Nov. 14, 1960; d. Jacques Cameron and Marye Lou (Dickey) Meyers; m. Lee R. Carling, Nov. 22, 1978 (div. Jan. 1984). Student, Wichita State U., 1978-83, Lansing Community Coll., 1984-85. Adminstr. Home Owners Warranty, Wichita, Kans., 1978-82; staff asst. Wichita Builders Assn., 1978-83; sec. Great Plains Industries, Wichita, 1983-84; account mgr. Allied Office Interiors, Lansing, Mich., 1984—. Editor Builder's Digest, 1978-82, Great Plains Ventures News., 1982. Driver Meals on Wheels, Wichita, 1976; active Big Bros./Big Sisters, Wichita, 1980. Mem. Nat. Assn. Female Execs., Literacy Vols. Am. Republican. Roman Catholic. Home: 900 Long Blvd #403 Lansing MI 48911 Office: Allied Office Interiors 1048 Pierpont Suite 10 Lansing MI 48911

CARLISLE, LILIAN MATAROSE BAKER (MRS. E. GRAFTON CARLISLE, JR.), author, lecturer; b. Meridian, Miss., Jan. 1, 1912; d. Joseph and Lilian (Flournoy) Baker; student Dickinson Coll., 1929-30, Pierce Coll. Bus. Adminstrn., 1930-31; B.A., U. Vt., 1981, M.A., 1986; m. E. Grafton Carlisle, Jr., Jan. 9, 1933; children: Diana, Penelope. Legal sec. A. W. Sanson, Phila., 1931-35; adminstrv. sec. RAF Ferry Command, Montreal, Que., Can., 1942; exec. staff mem. in charge collections, research Shelburne (Vt.) Mus., 1951-61; exec. sec. Burlington Area Community Health Study, 1963, coordinator, 1964; asst. coordinator Vt. Mental Retardation Planning Project, 1965; project dir. 4-county Champlain Valley Medicare Alert, 1966; dir. public relations Champlain Valley Agrl. Fair, 1968-77; lectr. U. Vt. Elder Hostel program, 1976-77, mem. faculty Vacation Coll., 1980-83. Pres., Burlington Community Council for Social Welfare, 59-61, 71-73; chmn. bd. Interfaith Sr. Citizens, 1977-79; justice of peace, 1979-81; pres. Chittenden County Extension Adv. Com., 1977-78; lay mem. Gov.'s Conf. on Problems of Aging for White House Conf., 1960; chmn. publs. com. Vt. Bicentennial Commn., 1974-77; mem. Gov.'s Commn. on Mobile Homes, 1973-79; mem. Vt. Ho. of Reps., 1968-70. Recipient Community Council Disting. Citizen award, 1978. Mem. Vt. (trustee, chmn. mus. com. 1967), N.Y. (faculty seminar) Chittenden (pres. 1969-72, editor Heritage Series of 10 books about Chittenden County towns 1972-76) hist. socs., Vt. Old Cemetery Assn., Vt. Folklore Soc., League Vt. Writers (dir. 1962; v.p., pres. 1967-69). Am. Pen Women (pres. Green Mountain br. 1980-82), Order Women Legislators (pres. Vt. br. 1972-74), Chi Omega. Conglist. Club: Zonta (pres. 1964-65). Co-author: The Story of the Shelburne Museum, 1955; Profile of the Community, 1964; Environmental and Personal Health of the Community, 1964; Vermont Clock and Watchmakers, Silversmiths and Jewelers, 1970; also numerous catalogs on collections at Shelburne Mus.; editorial cons. Burlington Social Survey, 1967; contbr. articles to profl. jours. Home: 117 Lakeview Terr Burlington VT 05401

CARLISLE, MARGO DUER BLACK, federal agency administrator; b. Providence; d. Thomas F. Jr. and Margaret MacCormick Black; m. Miles Carlisle; children: Mary, Tristram Coffin. BA, Manhattanville Coll. Legis. asst. Senator James A. McClure, Washington, 1973; staff mem. budget commn. task force U.S. Senate, Washington, 1974-75, exec. dir. steering com., 1975-80; staff dir. Senate Rep. Conf., Washington, 1981-85; exec. dir. Council for Nat. Policy, Washington, 1985-86; Asst. Sec. Defense, legis. affairs Dept. of Defense, Washington, 1986—; staff dir. nat. security and fgn. policy subcoms. for Rep. platform, 1984, Washington. Author articles on govt. policy; adv. bd. Nat. Security Record, 1987—. Trustee Phila. Soc., Washington, 1987—. Roman Catholic. Club: Nantucket (Mass.) Yacht. Home: 3221 Garfield St Washington DC 20008 Office: Dept of Defense Legis Affairs The Pentagon Washington DC 20310

CARLISLE, VERVENE (VEE), banker; b. Salt Lake City, Apr. 23; d. Garnett W. and Lulu (Erickson) C. Grad. Granite High Sch., Salt Lake City. With Fgn. Service, U.S. State Dept., Manila, Rome and Bermuda; with Tracy-Collins Bank & Trust, Salt Lake City, 1970—, v.p., 1978—; mem. Utah Ho. of Reps., 1971-72, 75-76, 77-78; mem. Gov.'s Adv. Council on Consumer Credit, 1980; mem. UN Bd., 1981. Mem. community adv. bd. Sch. Social Work U. Utah; mem. adv. com., adv. bd. Jr. League; vice chmn. Salt Lake County Democratic Party, 1970-75; commr. Gov.'s Commn. on Status of Women; bd. dirs. Contemporary Arts Group; mem. Group Relations Ongoing Workshops. Recipient Disting. Woman award Womens Conf. Womens Resource Ctr. U. Utah, 1975; named Woman of Achievement Utah Fedn. Bus. and Profl. Womens Clubs, 1978-79; recipient Spl. award Utah Heritage Found., 1979; Susa Young Gates award Utah Womens Polit. Caucus, 1983, Women Helping Women award Soroptimists of Salt Lake City, Utah's Most Admired Woman award Women's Info. Network, 1984, Ordinary People's award, 1984. Mem. Utah Heritage Found., Utah State Hist. Soc. (hon.), Salt Lake Bus. and Profl. Womens Club, LWV, Salt Lake C. of C. (past chmn. Women in Bus. com.). Clubs: U. Utah Town and Gown; Salt Lake Exchange, Salt Lake City Bus. and Profl. Women's. Home: 777 East S Temple 7C Salt Lake City UT 84102 Office: Tracy-Collins Bank and Trust 107 S Main St Salt Lake City UT 84111

CARLOUGH, LINDA SUSAN, small business owner; b. Suffern, N.Y., Mar. 8, 1956; d. Edith (Burnham) Carlough. Grad., Katharine Gibbs Sch., 1976; BS in Bus., Boston U., 1987. Adminstrv. asst. Commonwealth Inst. Medicine, Boston, 1976-77, Boston U., 1977-83, Hotel Intercontinental, Boston, 1983-84; asst. to pres. Infocom, Inc., Cambridge, Mass., 1984-86; pres., owner, operator Lincar, Inc., Cambridge, 1986—. Trustee Arborway Gardens, Jamaica Plains, Mass., 1982—. Recipient disting. alumnae award Katharine Gibbs Sch., Boston, 1986. Mem. Mass. Retailers Assn., New Eng. Convenience Store Assn. Presbyterian. Office: Lincar Inc 215 First St Cambridge MA 02142

CARLSEN, DEBORAH EILEEN BETTRAY, data base administrator; b. Chgo., Nov. 6, 1956; d. Theodore Walter and Patricia Ann (Knorr) Bettray; divorced; 1 child, Alana Lee. B.S. in Mgmt., Ill. Inst. Tech., 1978. CPA, Mich., Calif. Jr. systems analyst Milw. R.R., Chgo., 1978-79; programmer/analyst St. Paul Fed., Chgo., 1979-80; data base adminstr. Schwinn Bicycle, Chgo., 1980—. Mem. Nat. Assn. Female Execs., Assn. Systems Mgmt., Chgo. Area Software A.G. User's Group (co-chairperson Chgo. area). Roman Catholic. Office: Schwinn Bicycle Co 217 N Jefferson Chicago IL 60606

CARLSEN, JANET HAWS, insurance company owner, mayor; b. Bellingham, Calif., June 16, 1927; d. Lyle F. and Mary Elizabeth (Preble) Haws; m. Kenneth M. Carlsen, July 26, 1952; children: Stephanie L. Bagnani, Scott Lyle, Sean Preble, Stacy K., Spencer J. Cert., Armstrong Bus. Sch., 1945; student, Golden Gate Coll., 1945-46. Office mgr. Cornwall Warehouse Co., Salt Lake City, 1950-55, Hansen's Ins., Newman, Calif., 1969-77; owner Carlsen Ins., Gustine, Calif., 1978—. Mem. city council City of Newman, 1980-82, mayor, 1982—; bd. dirs. ARC, Stanislaus, Calif., 1982—; vice chair Dem. Cen. Com., Calif., 1983—. Morman. Club: Booster (Newman). Lodge: Soroptimist Internat. Home: 1215 Amy Dr Newman CA 95360 Office: City of Newman 1200 O Sts Newman CA 95360

CARLSEN, JUNE MARIE, banker; b. Milton, Mass., Oct. 5, 1959. Fgn. corr. First Nat. Bank of Boston, 1980-82, fgn. exchange investigator, 1982-84, sr. fgn. exchange investigator, 1984-85, mgmt. trainee, 1985-86, fgn. exchange ops. officer, 1986-88, mgr. fgn. exchange investigations and control, 1988—. Mem. Boston Bankers Assn., Nat. Assn. Female Execs. Congregationalist. Lodge: Order Eastern Star. Office: First Nat Bank of Boston 100 Federal St Boston MA 02105

CARLSEN, LAURIE BETH, trade association manager; b. Milton, Mass., Feb. 10, 1961; d. Mervin L. and Marion A. Carlsen. BS, U. R.I., 1982. Sec. Fidelity Investments, Boston, 1982-83, regional office adminstr., 1983-85, nat. conf. coordinator, 1985-87, mgr. trade shows and confs., 1987—. Mem. Internat. Exhibitors Assn., Meeting Planners Internat. Office: Fidelity Investments 82 Devonshire St Boston MA 02109

CARLSON, CHARLOTTE BOOTH, technical illustrator; b. Brigham City, Utah, July 1, 1920; d. Robert Edwin and Mary Alice (Carhartt) B.; m. Gerald Luther Carlson, Nov. 11, 1943 (div. June 1969); children: Joel Koch, Elaine Marie Seldner, Kris Donald. Student, Omaha U., 1937-39; cert. in Engring., Nebr. State U., 1941; student, Fine Arts Ctr., Colorado Springs, 1941-42. Background painter, title bd. operator Alexander Film Co., Colorado Springs, 1943-44; draftsman Bell Telephone Co., N.Y.C., 1944-47; founder Carlson Graphic Services, Princeton, N.J. Contbr. poetry to local newspapers. Mem. Soc. Friends. Lodge: Order of Eastern Star (organist 1984-86, line officer 1986—). Home: 5F Holly House Princeton NJ 08540

CARLSON, DALE BICK, author; b. N.Y.C., May 24, 1935; d. Edgar M. and Estelle (Cohen) Bick; B.A., Wellesley Coll., 1957; children—Daniel Carlson, Hannah Carlson. Author children's books, adult books 1961—, including: Perkins the Brain, 1964; The House of Perkins, 1965; Miss Maloo, 1966; The Brainstormers; 1966; Frankenstein, 1968; Counting is Easy, 1969; Your Country, 1969; Arithmetic 1, 2, 3, 1969; The Electronic Teabowl, 1969; Warlord of the Genji, 1970; The Beggar King of China, 1971; The Mountain of Truth (Spring Festival Honor book, named Am. Library Assn. Notable Book), 1972; Good Morning Danny, 1972; Good Morning, Hannah, 1972; The Human Apes, 1973 (named Am. Library Assn. Notable Book); Girls Are Equal Too, 1973 (named Am. Library Assn. Notable Book); Baby Needs Shoes, 1974; Triple Boy, 1976; Where's Your Head?, 1977; The Plant People, 1977; The Wild Heart, 1977; The Shining Pool, 1979; Lovingsex for Both Sexes, 1979; Boys Have Feelings Too, 1980; Call Me Amanda, 1981; Manners that Matter, 1982; The Frog People, 1982; Charlie the Hero, 1983; 1984-85: The Jenny Dean Science Fiction Mysteries, The Mystery of the Shining Children; The Mystery of the Hidden Trap; The Secret of the Third Eye; The James Budd Mysteries; The Mystery of Galaxy Games; The Mystery of Operation Brain, 1984-85, Mystery's Husbands, 1988; others. Vice pres. Parents League of N.Y., editor-in-chief Parents League Bull., 1967-72. Mem. Authors League Am., Authors Guild, Nature Connection. Address: 307 Neck Rd Madison CT 06443

CARLSON, DELORES LEE, computer consultant; b. Kansas City, Kans., Sept. 3, 1944; d. Raymond William and Muriel Juanita (Loveall) C. Grad. in Bus. Adminstrn. and Data Processing, Avila Coll., 1977. Br. head USMC Cen. Design and Programming Activity, Kansas City, Mo., 1973-86; regional mgr. Planning Analysis Corp., Overland Park, Kans., 1986—. Served with USAF, 1964-66. Mem. Assn. for Systems Mgmt., Kansas City Quality Assurance Assn., Nat. Assn. Female Execs., Am. Bus. Women's Assn. Office: Planning Analysis Corp 8400 W 110th St Suite 200 Overland Park KS 66210

CARLSON, DORIS STEWART, entrepreneur; b. Moorcroft, Wyo., Jan. 3, 1930; d. Frank Royal and Della Maud (Torbert) Stewart; m. Roy W. Carlson, Sept. 10, 1949 (dec. 1974); children: Ronald Roy, Michael Alan, Nikki Carlson Niemen, Christine Carlson Brannan. Student, Sheridan Coll., 1968-69. Owner, operator Stewart #5 Ranch, Sheridan, Wyo., 1974—, Carlson's Unltd. Clothing & Sporting Goods Store, Gillette, Wyo., 1975-85, D. Stewart Subdiv., Moorcroft, 1979—. Sec.-treas. Community Theatre, Gillette, 1974. Recipient Congl. award Wyo. State Art Conv., Laramie, 1973. Mem. Am. Quarter Horse Assn. (participation in races and shows), Wyo. Artist Assn., Wyo. Racing Assn., Wyo. Writers Assn., Sheridan C. of C., Beta Sigma Phi. Republican. Home and Office: Box 639 Moorcroft WY 82721

CARLSON, HELEN LOUISE, educator; b. Duluth, Minn., Oct. 20, 1940; d. Erling Emil and Ethel Florence (Lindberg) Nelson; BS summa cum laude, U. Minn., Duluth, 1961, MA, 1975; PhD, U. Minn., Mpls., 1981; m. Gordon Jerome Carlson, Aug. 4, 1961; children: David J., Amy L., John D. Elem. tchr., pub. schs., Brockton, Mass., St. Paul and La Mesa, Calif., 1961-66;

tchr. early child care provider, 1970-75; research asst. U. Minn., Duluth, 1975-77, instr., 1977-81, asst. prof. profl. edn., 1981—, head dept. child and family devel., 1984—, assoc. prof. child and family devel., 1986—; cons. St. Mary's Child Care Center, 1981-82, Midwest Regional Trainer Communication Model, 1982; bd. dirs. Duluth Early Childhood Consortium, 1981-82; mem. adv. bd. Duluth Community Schs. Parent and Family Life Programs, 1980-82, U. Minn. at Duluth Child Care Center, 1980-82; mem. edn. adv. bd. Duluth Head Start, 1979-80; adv. bd. Dean's Grant, U.S. Office Edn., Nat. Council Social Studies, Early Childhood, State history curriculum devel. project. Ednl. Devel. Program grantee, 1981-82, 82-87, 85-87, U. Minn. grantee, 1986-87; grantee Northwest Area Found.lic. tchr., Minn. Instr. designer, interactive videodisc for edn. core curriculum, 1985—. Mem. Nat. Assn. Edn. Young Children, Nat. Council Social Studies (nat. research bd.), Phi Delta Kappa (research grantee 1978; treas. chpt. 1978-81, v.p. chpt. 1981-82), Alpha Delta Kappa. Contbr. articles to profl. jours. Research, presentation, articles in alt. service delivery models for learning disabled children; social interactions of infants and toddlers and their parents, 1982, and others. Home: 4918 Jean Duluth Rd Duluth MN 55803 Office: U Minn 140 Montague Hall Duluth MN 55812

CARLSON, JANE ELLEN, advertising executive; b. Washington, Jan. 25, 1949; d. Charles Gerald and Jane Elizabeth (McCarty) C.; m. Robert Goldstein, July 23, 1977 (div. 1985); m. Paul W. Schooley Jr., Oct. 1987. BA in Polit. Sci., U. Miss., 1971. Mgr. tng. Am. Express Co., Memphis, 1972-74, N.Y.C., 1974-76; dir. mktg. Transworld Airlines, Inc., N.Y.C., 1976-86; mgmt. supr. Wells, Rich, Greene, Inc., N.Y.C., 1986-88, sr. v.p., 1988—; travel cons. Durant, Inc., N.Y.C., 1986. Democrat. Presbyterian. Home: 21 Maple Tree Ave Stamford CT 06906 Office: Wells Rich Greene Inc 9 W 57th St New York NY 10019

CARLSON, JANET LYNN, chemistry educator; b. Mpls., Aug. 31, 1952; d. Donald S. and Katheryn F. (Kubo) Maeda; m. James G. Carlson, June 26, 1976. BA, Hamline U., 1974; PhD, Stanford U., 1978. Asst. prof. Macalester Coll., St. Paul, 1978-87, assoc. prof., 1987—. Contbr. articles to profl. jours. Office: Macalester Coll 1600 Grand Ave Saint Paul MN 55105

CARLSON, JEANNIE ANN, writer; b. Bklyn., Jan. 13, 1955; d. Lloyd Arthur and Ruth Frances (Riley) C.; 1 child, Carl Philip; m. H. Daniel Hopkins, Dec. 16, 1987. B.A., Randolph-Macon Woman's Coll., 1977. Mktg./editing rep. Harris Pub., White Plains, N.Y., 1982; adminstrv. asst. Ray Fried Assocs., Inc., Eastchester, N.Y., 1980-84; proofreader Nat. Pennysaver, Elmsford, N.Y., 1983-84; feature writer Asbury News, Crestwood, N.Y., 1983-84; chief writer Profl. Resume and Writing Service, St. Petersburg, Fla., 1984-87; exec. writer, pres. Viking Communications, Inc., 1987—; feature writer Ashbury News, Crestwood, N.Y., 1983-84; editorial asst. Children's Rights Am., Largo, Fla., 1984; pub. relations coordinator The Renaissance Cultural Ctr., Clearwater, Fla., 1985; affiliate writer City News Service; com. mem. work area on communications Pasadena Community Ch., St. Petersburg, Fla., 1986-88. Recipient Golden Poet award World of Poetry, 1985, 88, Silver Poet award, 1986, Recognition award Nat. Soc. Poets, 1979, poetry awards Internat. Publs., 1976-77, Achievement Certs. Profl. Resume and Writing Service, 1985, 86, 87, 5 World of Poetry awards of merit, 1983 (2), 85, 87, 88. Mem. City News Service (affiliate writer), Nat. Assn. Female Execs. Methodist. Avocations: theatre, culinary arts. Office: Viking Communications Inc 300 31st St North Suite 214 Saint Petersburg FL 33713

CARLSON, JODI WRIGGLESWORTH, recreation department superintendent; b. Anchorage, Mar. 2, 1950; d. Frank L. and Geri L. (Woodford) Wrigglesworth; m. Rodney Reed Carlson, Apr. 5, 1980; children: Whitney Reed, Taylor Blake. BS, U. No. Colo., 1972, MA, 1980. Cert. leisure profl.; cert. instr. Jazzercise, Inc. Dir. recreation Town of Hudson, Wis., 1972-73; adminstrv. asst. Golfam. Corp., Lafayette, Calif., 1973; leader dept. recreation City of Longmont, Colo., 1973-74, supr. recreation, 1974-76, supt. recreation, 1976—. Mem. Nat. Recreation and Parks Assn. (profl.), Colo. Parks and Recreation Assn. (recreation sect. chair 1975-76, treas. 1977-78, mem.-at-large 1985-86, chair ann. conf. 1986, Pres.'s award 1977, Outstanding Young Profl. 1978, Danford scholar 1978). Office: Longmont Recreation Dept 700 Longs Peak Ave Longmont CO 80501

CARLSON, JONE ELEANORE, editor, publisher; b. Chgo., Aug. 7, 1939; d. John Edwin Carlson and Irene Dorothy (Novak) Carlson Brown; m. William H. Besosa, Aug. 10, 1958 (div.); m. Emile F. Mouhot, Nov. 28, 1965 (dec. Dec. 1965); m. Conrad Arthur Lippmann, May 26, 1969 (dec. 1972); children: Anne Victoria Cremeans, Maria Besosa, Daniel Nater, Gregory-John Lippmann. Student, Barry U., 1959; BBA, Alexander Hamilton Inst., 1962; AA in Criminal Justice, Broward Community Coll., 1977. Interior designer J.E. Carlson & Assocs., N.Y., Ariz., Calif., Colo., Nev. and Fla., 1962-75; pres. J.E. Carlson & Assocs., Ft. Lauderdale, Fla., 1973—; v.p. Le Anne Cosmetics, Los Angeles, 1968-73; chief administrator law enforcement testing ctr. Broward County, Ft. Lauderdale, 1974-77; gen. mgr. Canam Assocs., Hollywood, Fla., 1984-86; editor-in-chief People Searching News, Ft. Lauderdale, 1986—. Mem. Ft. Lauderdale Coll. com., 1970; coordinator Law Enforcement Cadet Corps., Ft. Lauderdale Boy Scouts Am., 1974-77; bd. rep. Nova U. Law Sch., Ft. Lauderdale, 1976; warrant officer Navy League Cadet Corps, Ft. Lauderdale, 1984-85. Recipient Outstanding Civic Contbn. award City of Ft. Lauderdale, 1963, Outstanding Leadership award Boy Scouts Am., 1976, Outstanding Contbn. award Broward County Chiefs of Police Assn., 1976; named one of Women Right Now, Glamour Mag., 1987. Mem. Am. Adoption Congress, N.Y. Parents Against Drugs, Criminal Justice Educators Assn., Adopting Legislation for Adoption Rights Movement (sec. 1987). Democrat. Roman Catholic. Office: JE Carlson & Assocs PO Box 22611 Fort Lauderdale FL 33335-2611

CARLSON, JUDITH ELIZABETH, nurse; b. Penn Yan, N.Y., Aug. 26, 1946; d. Frank and Carmaletta (Wyman) Van De Mortel; R.N., Highland Hosp. Sch. Nursing, 1967; m. Dennis R. Carlson, June 3, 1967 (div.); children—Hope Stephanie, Christiaan Dennis. Staff nurse surg. unit Oceanside (Calif.) Community Hosp., 1967; staff nurse med. unit E.J. Noble Hosp., Canton, N.Y., 1968; staff nurse emergency room Corning (N.Y.) Community Hosp., 1968-70, New Hanover Meml. Hosp., Wilmington, N.C., 1972-75; staff nurse coronary care unit Duke U. Med. Center, Durham, N.C., 1975, head nurse urology clinic, supr. catheter audit team, 1976-83, head nurse dept. community and family medicine, 1983—; mem. faculty Travenol Labs., Inc., Deerfield, Ill., 1981. Author: Treating Infection, 1984. Co-leader, leader Girl Scouts, 1975-78, profl. com. Triangle chpt. Am. Cancer Soc., 1987-88. Mem. Am. Urology Allied Assn. Democrat. Methodist. Club: Duke Faculty (sec. bd. dirs. 1982-84). Home: 5604 Genesee Dr Durham NC 27712 Office: Duke U Med Ctr Box 3886 Durham NC 27710

CARLSON, LINDA BLEW, communication training executive; b. Perryton, Tex., Feb. 27, 1945; d. Doyle Debs and Nona Agnes (Gay) Thompson; m. Gary D. Blew, June 28, 1972 (div. Nov. 1983); m. Thomas Stanford Carlson, Dec. 10, 1983; children by previous marriage: Sonya Michelle, Sara Danielle. BA, U. Utah, 1972. Exec. v.p. Effective Learning Systems, Salt Lake City, 1975-78; exec. coordinator Constnl. Law Assn., Salt Lake City, 1978-80; dir. Camelot Internat. Trading Assn., Salt Lake City, 1979-80; exec. trustee Brentwood Mgmt., Salt Lake City, 1980-81; dir. Effectiveness Tng. Cons., Charleston, W.Va., 1981-83; founder, pres., chmn. bd. Focus I., Inc., Dallas, 1984—; founder, exec. v.p. Psy-Kinetics, Dallas, 1984—, creative dir., 1985—. Author: Splotches; co-author: How to Stop Talking to Brick Walls, 1986. Teaching fellow U. Utah, 1973. Office: Focus I Inc PO Box 1914 Denton TX 76202

CARLSON, LORAINE BELLE, writer; b. Los Angeles, May 6, 1923; d. Leon Cumings and Belle (Fowles) Fleener; m. Cecil C. Spencer, June 1946 (div. 1951); m. Neil W. Carlson, Dec. 1958. BA, U. Redlands, 1944; postgrad., U. So. Calif., 1950-53. Writer sci. and tech. material Hughes Aircraft Co., Culver City, Calif., 1953-58, 64-66, head publ. group, 1956-58; writer sci. and tech. material TRW-Space Tech. Labs., Manhattan Beach, Calif., 1966-68; free-lance writer 1968—. Author: Mexico: An Extraordinary Guide, 1971, The Traveleer Guide to Mexico City, 1978, The Traveleer Guide to Yucatan and Guatemala, 1980, The Traveleer Guide to Yucatan, 1982. Home: 2021 W Homer St Chicago IL 60647

CARLSON, MARY SUSAN, lawyer; b. Lincoln, Nebr., Nov. 2, 1949; d. Arnold Emil and Mary (Lloyd) C.; m. Gerald Phillip Greiman, May 2, 1982; children: David Carlson, Nora Carlson. AA, Cottey Coll., 1970; BFA in Edn., U. Nebr., 1972; postgrad., Notre Dame Law Sch., Tokyo, 1974; JD, U. Nebr., 1976. Bar: Nebr. 1977, D.C. 1979, U.S. Supreme Ct. 1986, Mo., 1988. Staff law clk. to presiding justice U.S. Ct. Appeals (8th cir.), St. Louis, 1976-78; assoc. Kilcullen, Smith & Heenan, Washington, 1978-79; trial atty. Guam land claims litigation U.S. Dept. Justice, Agana, 1981; trial atty. civil div. U.S. Dept. Justice, Washington, 1980-86; vis. asst. prof. law Washington U., St. Louis, 1987—. Mem. ABA, Mo. Bar Assn., D.C. Bar Assn, NOW, Nat. Abortion Rights Action League. Office: Washington U Sch Law One Brookings Dr Box 1120 Saint Louis MO 63130

CARLSON, NANCY LEE, English language educator; b. Spokane, Wash., June 1, 1950; d. Alfred William and Geneva May (Conniff) C. BS, Wash. State U., 1973; MEd, curriculum specialist, Ea. Wash. U., 1987. Tchr. Stevenson-Carson Sch. Dist., Wash., 1973-74, Spokane Sch. Dist., 1974—. Bd. dirs. Spokane Civic Theater, 1986—, Spokane Human Services Adv. Bd., 1986—; treas. Inland Empire for Africa, Spokane, 1985-86; vice chmn. ea. Wash. phone bank for Sen. Dan Evans, Spokane, 1984. Mem. NEA, Nat. Council Tchrs. English, Wash. Council Tchrs. English, Assn. for Supervision and Curriculum Devel., Am. Mgmt. Assn., Wash. State U. Alumni Assn. (area rep. 1987—). Republican. Presbyterian. Office: Sch Dist #81 Rogers High Sch E 1622 Wellesley Spokane WA 99207

CARLSON, PATRICIA WARREN, superintendent of schools; b. Milford, Del., Feb. 26, 1947; d. Albert Downes and Elva Frances (Grogan) W.; m. Gary W. Carlson, Aug. 8 (div.); m. Michael Robert Ciccarelli, Dec. 8, 1984; 1 child, Eric. BA in English, Hood Coll., 1969; MEd, Bridgewater (Mass.) State Coll., 1978, C.A.G.S. Adminstrn. Lead., 1986; postgrad., U. Mass., 1986—. Home: 14 Thoreau Circle Beverly MA 01915 Office: North Shore Regional Vocat Tech High Sch 20 Balch St Beverly MA 01915

CARLSON, RIA MARIE, public relations executive, writer; b. Los Angeles, Apr. 8, 1961; d. Erick Gustaf and Roberta Rae (Bandelin) C.; m. James Bradley Gerdts, May 19, 1985. BA cum laude, U. So. Calif., 1983. Assoc. producer NBC, Burbank, Calif., 1982-85; account exec. Kerr & Assocs. Pub. Relations, Huntington Beach, Calif., 1985-86; pub. relations mgr. Orange County Performing Arts Ctr., Costa Mesa, Calif., 1986-88; dir. pub. relations and mktg. Bowers Mus., Santa Ana, Calif., 1988—; free lance writer, 1985—. Scriptwriter award ceremony Latin Bus. Assn., 1985; author, editor newsletter Am. Sch. Food Service Assn. Bus. Report, 1985-86; assoc. editor Revue mag., 1987; contbr. articles to publs; cast mem. Disneyland, Anaheim, Calif. Prodn. asst. Profiles in Pride, Black History Month, Burbank, 1985. Named one of Outstanding Young Women in Am., 1985. Mem. AAUW (dir. pub. relations, br. officer), Women in Communications, Nat. Assn. Female Execs., Am. Film Inst., U. So. Calif. Alumni Assn., Blackstonians Pre-Law Hon. Soc. (life), Calif. Scholarship Fedn. (sealbearer, life). Republican. Roman Catholic. Avocations: writing short stories, reading, skiing, softball, travel. Office: Bowers Museum 2002 N Main St Santa Ana CA 92706

CARLSON, ROBERTA ELAINE, banker; b. Hartford, Conn., July 31, 1960; d. Carl Richard and Helen Louise (Zaltkauskus) C. Grad. high sch., Hartford. Teller Soc. for Savs. Bank, West Hartford, Conn., 1978-79, sr. teller, 1979-81, sr. teller, then supr., 1981-85; sr. service banker Newington, Conn., 1985-87; br. mgr. Wethersfield, Conn., 1987-88; customer service mgr. BayBank, Simsbury, Conn., 1988—. Mem. Lithuanian Am. Choral Soc., 1975-78, U. Hartford Civic Chorus and Orch., West Hartford, 1982-83. Mem. Am. Inst. Banking. Republican. Roman Catholic. Office: BayBank 744 Hopmeadow St Simsbury CT 06070

CARLSON, WILDA MAY, real estate sales agent; b. Rome, N.Y., Dec. 10, 1920; d. Percy Lloyd and Pearl Jessie (Huey) Bucklin; R.N., Buffalo Deaconess Hosp. Sch. Nursing, 1942; Public Health Nurse, SUNY, Buffalo, 1961; m. LeRoy E. Carlson, June 14, 1947; children—Nancy Carlson Stone, Carol Carlson Yannie. Admissions, supr. nurse W.C.A. Hosp., Jamestown, N.Y., 1942-45; indsl. nurse Proto Tool Co., Jamestown, 1963-65, 70-72, Marlin Rockwell div. TRW Corp., Falconer, N.Y., 1969-70; real estates saleswoman, 1973-74, 77—; dir. Fenton Park Nursing Home, 1965-67; nurse Chautauqua County Resource Center, Jamestown, 1981-82. Pres., Kiantone Mothers Club, Stillwater Ch.; Republican com. woman Kiantone Twp., 1950. Jamestown Vis. Nurse Assn. grantee, 1960-61. Mem. Chautauqua County Grad. Nurses Assn. Club: Women's Bus. and Profl. (Marvin) House. Home: 512 Barr St Jamestown NY 14701

CARLTON, CLAUDIA DOWDY, library automation consultant; b. Richmond, Va., May 20, 1955; d. Carroll Burns and Caroline Byerly (Putney) Dowdy; m. Marvin McCray Spencer, May 17, 1973 (div. June 1980); m. James John Carlton, June 28, 1983; children: Justin Stafford, Amy Shay. BS in Art Edn. and Library Sci., Longwood Coll., 1976. Librarian Cumberland County (Va.) Schs., 1976-79, Goochland County (Va.) Schs., 1979-80; media specialist Seminole County Schs., Sanford, Fla., 1980-81; software cons. Follett Library Book Co., Crystal Lake, Ill., 1981-83; pvt. practive library automation cons. Fla., 1983—. Leader Girl Scouts U.S.A., Cumberland, Va., 1976-77; coordinator Boy Scouts Am., 1977-79; pres. Cumberland County PTA, 1977-78; mem. pub. relations com. Cumberland Vol. Rescue Squad, 1979-80. Mem. NEA, Va. Edn. Assn., Ga. Library/Media Dirs., Fla. Assn. Instrnl. Materials. Home and Office: PO Box 426 Howey-in-the-Hills FL 32737

CARMAN, LAURALEE, computer company executive, consultant; b. Phoenix, May 28, 1964; d. John W. Peters and Janet May (Muder) Hiscoe; m. Brian S. Carman, July 23, 1983. Student, Portland (Oreg.) Community Coll., 1980-82. Asst. project mgr. No. Telecom, Santa Maria, Calif., 1981-82; customer service Savenet, Portland, 1982-84; acct. exec. Finzer Bus., Portland, 1984-86; western sales mgr. Abaton Tech., San Francisco, 1986-87; prin. DTP Cons., San Francisco, 1986-87; western sales mgr. DEST Corp., San Francisco, 1987—. Mem. Nat. Assn. Female Execs. Home: 239 LaPera Circle Danville CA 94526 Office: Dest Corp 1201 Cadillac Ct Milpitas CA 95035

CARMICHAEL, CHARLOTTE MARIE BREEDEN, telecommunications executive; b. Warrenton, Va., Mar. 24, 1945; d. Albert Aldine and Winnie (Hensley) Breeden; m. Michael William Carmichael, Feb. 6, 1965; children: Kathy Lynn, Bryan William. BS with High Honors, Va. Commonwealth U., 1967; postgrad., U. Va., 1971-72. Owner Intercontinental Telecommunications, Inc., Houston, 1983—, Honolulu, 1987—; owner Carmichael Communications Cons., Inc., Houston, 1982—, ITI of Utah, Salt Lake City, 1985—. Mem. Nat. Assn. for Female Execs., Am. Soc. of Profl. and Exec. Women. Republican. Mormon. Office: ITI 4900 Woodway Suite 950 Houston TX 77056

CARMICHAEL, DEBORAH MURRAY, agricultural engineer; b. Raleigh, N.C., June 13, 1956; d. Hubert Leon and Julia Nell (Guy) Murray; m. Carson Carmichael III, May 19, 1984. BSAE, N.C. State U., 1979. Registered profl. engr., N.C. Engr. Aeroglide Corp., Cary, N.C., 1980-83, design engr., 1983-84, project engr., 1984—. Mem. Am. Soc. Agrl. Engrs. Democrat. Baptist. Home: 3018 Churchill Rd Raleigh NC 27607 Office: Aeroglide Corp 965 E Chatham St Cary NC 27511

CARNAHAN, FRANCES MORRIS, magazine editor; b. Evergreen, Ala., Oct. 28, 1937; d. Houston DeLeon and Rene Vester (Bass) Morris; m. Peter Malott Carnahan, Feb. 13, 1960; children—Brian Morris, Edmund Malott. Student, U. Ala., 1956-58. With Mobile Press-Register, 1956-58, H.L. Green Co., N.Y.C., 1958-60, J.H. Lewis Advt. Agy., Mobile, 1960-61; with Early Am. Life mag., Hist. Times, Inc., Harrisburg, Pa., 1972—; editor Early Am. Life, 1975—. Costume designer, Harrisburg Community Theatre, 1961-71, Gov. Pa. Sch., 1976-77; Author articles. Mem. Am. Soc. Mag. Editors. Home: 1524 Greening Ln Harrisburg PA 17110 Office: Early American Life Box 8200 2245 Kohn Rd Harrisburg PA 17105

CARNES, JAN JAY, secondary educator; b. Cambridge, Ohio, May 19, 1956; d. Harold Clark and June Elaine (Thomas) Armstrong; m. Richard Kim Carnes, Dec. 9, 1955; 1 child, Benjamin Clark. AA, Muskingum Tech. Sch., 1976; BS, Ohio State U., 1979. Bus. tchr. Gahanna (Ohio)-Jefferson Pub. Sch., 1980-88. Republican. Mem. Christian Ch. Home: 425 S Spring Rd Westerville OH 43081

CARNES, LORRAINE, engineer, manufacturing company executive; b. Flint, Mich., Nov. 13, 1950; d. Lawrence and Johnnie Mae (Walls) Metcalfe; widowed; children—William Craig II. B.S., Cen. Mich. U., 1985. Sec. S.O.D.A.T., Flint, 1974-75; mortgage rep. Gen. Mortgage Co., Flint, 1974-75; labor relations staff BOC Metal Fab., Grand Blanc, Mich., 1983-84, supr. of hourly prodn., 1976-84, departmental planner, 1985—, quality of work life coordinator, 1983-86; sr. engr. indsl. engring. dept. 1986—. Mem. Ind. Bus. Girls Assn., Big Sisters Assn., Am. Mgmt. Assn., Nat. Assn. for Female Execs. Democrat. Roman Catholic. Clubs: Flint Golferetts (sec. 1984—). Avocations: golf, modeling, bartending, reading, sewing. Home: 1514 Wabash Ave Flint MI 48505 Office: Cadillac Car Div 10800 S Saginaw St Grand Blanc MI 48439

CARNESOLTAS, ANA-MARIA, lawyer; b. Havana, Cuba, Feb. 9, 1948; came to U.S., 1962; d. Manuel Ramon and Zenaida de las Mercedes (Enriquez) Carnesoltas. B.A., U. Calif.-Santa Barbara, 1970; J.D., Loyola Law Sch., Los Angeles, 1978. Bar: Calif. 1978, Fla. 1979. Dep probation officer Probation Dept., Santa Barbara, Calif., 1970-73; personnel analyst Dept. Personnel, Los Angeles, 1973-77; dep. dist. atty. Dist. Atty.'s Office, Los Angeles, 1978-80; asst. U.S. atty. U.S. Atty.'s Office, Miami, Fla., 1980-82; pvt. practice law, Miami, 1982-83; asst. city atty. City Atty.'s Office, Miami, 1983-85; pvt. practice, Coral Gables, Fla., 1985—; lectr. YMCA, Miami, 1983—; adj. prof. Fla. Internat. U.; hearing officer Dade County Pub. Schs., Miami, 1985—. Bd. dirs. Am. Heart Assn., Miami, 1983-86, YWCA, 1987—, Alzheimer's Disease and Related Disorders Assn., 1987. Named Disting. Advocate, Loyola Law Sch., 1978. Mem. Calif. Probation Parole and Corrections Assn. (v.p. 1972-73), Cuban Am. Attys. Council (sec. 1979-80), Cuban Am. Bar Assn. (dir. 1983, 88, sec. 1984), Dade County Bar Assn., ABA, Fla. Assn. Women Lawyers, Assn. Trial Lawyers Am., Fed. Bar Assn. Democrat. Roman Catholic. Club: Latin Bus. and Profl. Women's (pres. 1984-85), Cuban Women's. Office: City Attys Office 169 E Flagler St Suite 1101 Miami FL 33131

CARNEVALE, FRANCA NELKEN, trade co. exec.; b. Rome, Feb. 10, 1937; came to U.S., 1968, naturalized, 1977; d. Leone Boris and Annita (Budin) Nelken; D. Pharm. cum laude, Rome U., 1959; m. Dario Carnevale, Feb. 28, 1959; children—Daniela, Flavia, Fulvia, Dario. Pharmacology tchr. Rome U., 1952-62; researcher on drugs, Suez Hosp., Egypt, 1963, Beirut (Lebanon) Italian Hosp., 1964-65; researcher children's allergies Bucharest Children's Hosp., 1966; internat. coordinator European lit. and publs. Pharmacology Inst. of Rome, Des Plaines, Ill., 1970; internat. coordinator S.Am. lit. and publs. Pharmacology Inst. of Bogota (Colombia), Miami, Fla., 1972; exec. v.p. Dafra Internat., Inc., Miami, 1978—; tchr., cons.; dir. Mem. Pharmacist Assn. Rome. Roman Catholic. Clubs: Ionosphere, B.A. Exec., Sons of Italy.

CARNEVALE, SALLY LONDON, textile sales and marketing executive; b. Newark, Mar. 17, 1954; d. Allen Jay and Elaine (Rose) London; m. Louis Michael Carnevale, May 25, 1980. B.S. in Textiles and Chemistry, U. Del., 1976; M.B.A., U. Wis., 1978. Consultant/auditor, Business Advisory Center, Wausau, Wis., 1977-78 Market planner Celanese Corp., Charlotte, N.C., 1978-80, market research analyst, Celanese Fibers operations, N.Y.C., 1980-82, planning coordinator, 1982-83, fiber sales and home furnishings merchandising rep., 1983-84; product mgr. home furnishings Collins & Aikman Corp., N.Y.C., 1984-85, nat. sales mgr. home furnishings, 1985-87, dir. sales, 1987—. Mem. Big Bro./Big Sister Program, Newark, Del., 1973-76, program coordinator, Madison, Wis., 1976-78; vol. tutor Dept. Social Services, various locations, 1975-80; Com. mem., life mem. Hadassah, Teaneck, N.J., 1981-84. Mem. Am. Mktg. Assn., Am. Field Service Mu Kappa Tau. Home: 253 E Palisade Ave Englewood NJ 07631 Office: Collins & Aikman Corp 210 Madison Ave New York NY 10016

CARNEY, CLAIRE T(HERESE), real estate executive; b. New Bedford, Mass., June 18, 1922; d. Philippe and Rose Anna (Belhumeur) Galipeau; m. Hugh J. Carney, Feb. 19, 1944 (dec. May 1962); children: Patrick, Doreen, Mark, Hugh Jay. BA, Southeastern Mass. U., 1973. Dep. collector IRS, New Bedford, 1945-47; cost acct. Morse Twist Drill and Machine Co., New Bedford, 1961-68; treas. Claremont Mgmt., New Bedford, 1968—, Claremont Devel. Assocs., Boston, 1968—, Claremont Corp., New Bedford and Boston, 1968—. Chair Town of Dartmouth Hist. Commn., 1979-88; trustee Old Dartmouth Hist. Soc., 1981—, New Bedford Whaling Mus., 1986—; trustee, vice-chmn., treas. Southeastern Mass. U., Dartmouth, 1981—; mem. adv. bd. New Bedford Symphony Orch., 1985-88, Mass. Soc. for Prevention of Cruelty to Children, 1987-88; advisor Bierstadt Art Soc., 1986-87. Named 1st Woman of Yr., YWCA Tribute, 1984. Mem. Cath. Womens Club, Southeastern Mass. Alumni Assn. (ex-officio 1979-88, service award 1982). Home: 966 Tucker Rd Dartmouth MA 02747 Office: Claremont Regency 800 Pleasant St Boston MA 02110

CARNEY, DAWN MARIE, psychologist, therapist; b. Vancouver, B.C., May 10, 1962; d. Leonard Robin and Carol Irene (Reed) C. Student, So. Meth. U., 1984. Biofeedback therapist Med. Clinic, Dallas, 1984—. Crisis counselor Suicide & Crisis Ctr., Dallas, 1985—. Mem. Biofeedback Soc. Am. (cert.), Delta Gamma. Republican. Episcopalian. Club: Canadian. Home: 4425 Travis #114 Dallas TX 75205

CARNEY, KAY, actress, director, educator; b. Rice Lake, Wis., Aug. 2, 1933; d. Rexford Hugh and Margot Caroline (Haanstad) C.; B.S., U. Wis., 1955; M.A., Mt. Holyoke Coll., 1958; postgrad. Centre du Théâtre National, 1970, Columbia U. and Case-Western Res. U., 1957-63; Creative Arts fellow U. Colo., 1963. Actress performing in London, Paris, Istanbul, Ankara, Tel Aviv and Nicosia, 1970-72, performing in Off Off-Broadway! An Anthology with Kay Carney, N.Y.C., Chgo., San Francisco, Vancouver, Balt., Phila., Boston and various U.S. colls., 1973—, The Mothers by Maria Irene Fornes, Ubu Repetory Theatre, N.Y.C., 1987; performed Tonques, 1985, Camptown Ladies, 1986, Age of Enlightenment, 1986, Vacancy, 1987; dir.: Mourning Pictures, Broadway and Lenox Arts Center, 1974, A Pretty Passion, Interart Theatre, N.Y.C., 1982, Quilt Pieces, Theatre of Open Eye, N.Y.C., 1983, Superwoman Bites the Dust, Playwright's Platform, Boston, 1984, The Mothers, Ubu Repetory Theatre, Airport, Theater at St. Peter's, 1988, A Good Time, Playwright's Horizons, N.Y.C., 1988, numerous others; tchr. acting, directing and psychophys. work Hunter Coll., Henry St. Playhouse, SUNY, Purchase, U. Calif.-Santa Cruz, 1977-80; assoc. prof. dept. theatre Smith Coll., Northampton, Mass., 1980-82, Bklyn. Coll., 1983-87; tchr. Ensemble Studio Theatre Inst., 1987; condr. workshops for profls. in U.S. and abroad; organizer, trainer La Mama theatre groups, Paris and Tel Aviv; bd. dirs. Bear Rep. Theatre, 1977-79; performed with Open Theater, 1965-67; seminarian with Jerzy Grotowski, 1970. Moratorium organizer, performer Angry Artists Against the War, 1966-70; mem. Performing Artists for Nuclear Disarmament, 1981—, St. Clements Arts in Religious Action Com., 1972-75; organizer Bay Area Women in Theatre Orgn., 1978-80. Kosciuszko Found. grantee, 1979; SUNY Research Found. grantee, 1976. Mem. Soc. Stage Dirs. and Choreographers, Actors Equity, AFTRA, East Central Theatre Conf., Women and Theatre Program, Assn. for Theatre in Higher Edn. (presenter nat. convs.), League Profl. Theatre Women/N.Y. Democrat. Episcopalian. Contbr. articles to profl. jours.

CARNEY, PATRICIA, Canadian legislator, president treasury board; b. Shanghai, China, May 26, 1935; d. John James and Dora (Sanders) C.; two children. B.A. in Econs. and Polit. Sci., U. B.C., Can., 1960, M.A. in Comml. and Regional Planning, 1977. Econ. journalist various publs. 1955-70; owner, cons. Gemini North Ltd., Vancouver, B.C., Can., 1970-80, Yellowknife, N.W.T., Can., 1971, Alta., Can., 1971; mem. Can. Ho. of Commons, Ottawa, Ont., 1980—, minister of state, 1981, minister fin., 1983, minister energy, mines and resources, 1984-86, minister for internat. trade, 1986-88, pres. Treas. Bd., 1988—; mem. planning and priorities com.; mem. fgn. def. cabinet com. Recipient Can. Women's Press award, 1968, 3 MacMillan Bloedel Ltd. awards. Mem. Assn. Profl. Economists B.C., Can. Inst. Planners. Office: House of Commons, Parliament Bldgs, Ottawa, ON Canada K1A 0A6

CARNEY, PHILLITA TOYIA, marketing communications management company executive; b. Chgo., Apr. 18, 1952; d. Phillip Leon Carney and Margaret Clarice (Ewing) Brown. Student, U. Utah, 1971-74; BS in Bus., Westminster Coll., 1976. Corp. tng. dir. U&I Sugar Corp., Salt Lake City, also Moses Lake, Wash., 1976-77; program coordinator Div. on Aging, Seattle, 1977-78; bus. devel. officer Del Green Assoc., Foster City, Calif., 1978-79; regional v.p. Equitec Fin. Group, San Francisco, Irvine and Oakland, Calif., 1979-84, United Resources, Oakland, San Francisco, Nev., 1984-86; owner, mgr. Carney & Assocs., Oakland, 1986; regional v.p. Eastcoast Ops. Benefits Communications Corp. div. Great West Life Assurance Co., Washington, 1986-87; nat. dir. enrollment services, nat. plan adminstr. U.S. Conf. Mayors Fringe Benefits Program, MCW Internat., Ltd., 1988—; dir. Total One, San Francisco; corp. cons., advisor Am. Intermediation Services, San Francisco, 1986; nat. dir. communications and enrollment services for U.S. Conf. Mayor's flexible benefits plan MCW Internat., Ltd., 1988—; cons. Washington Literacy Council; sr. bus. cons., ptnr. Performance Strategies Inc., San Diego, 1986. Moderator, creator pub. affairs radio program, 1975-76 (Best Pub. Affairs Program award Nat. Pub. Radio 1976). Del. White House Conf. on Small Bus., Washington, 1986; mem., lobbyist Concerned Women for Am., 1987. Recipient award Am. Legion, 1970, DAR, 1970. Fellow Am. Biog. Inst. Research Assn. (assoc., nat. advisor); mem. Internat. Assn. Fin. Planning, Women Entrepreneurs, Internat. Biog. Ctr., Bus. and Profl. Women, Sales Mktg. Exec. Assn., Zonta Internat. (pres. 1985—). Avocations: jogging, swimming, reading, writing. Home: 1200 N Nash St Apt #1155 Arlington VA 22209

CARNEY, SUSAN MARGARET, marketing professional; b. Detroit, Apr. 14, 1960; d. Patrick Grover and Margaret Mary (Flynn) C. BA in History, U. Mich., Dearborn, 1986. Paralegal Bodman, Longley & Dahling, Detroit, 1982-85; pub. relations coordinator Am. Motors Gen. div. LTV Aerospace and Def. Co., Livonia, Mich., 1985, pub. relations rep., 1986; pub. relations and advt. rep. Am. Motors Gen. div. LTV Missiles and Electronics Group, South Bend, Ind., 1986—. Mem. Assn. U.S. Army. Roman Catholic. Office: LTV Missiles & Electronics Group Am Motors Gen Div 701 W Chippewa South Bend IN 46614

CARNIE, MARY CATHERINE, television station executive; b. Clayton, Ala., Oct. 25, 1938; d. Ories Kendall and Harriet Catherine (Scheffer) White; m. Gary Miles Carnie, Dec. 22, 1958 (div. May 1969); 1 child, Kendall Joanne. Cert. in Acting, Pasadena Playhouse Coll. Theatre Arts, 1959. Profl. actress Turn of the Century Cabaret Theatre, El Paso, Tex., 1962-73; co-author stage play A Story Of Tender Love, Or Mass Entanglement In The Tender Trap, 1964; continuity asst. KROD-TV, El Paso, 1968-69; drama critic El Paso Jour., 1977-78; continuity dir. KDBC-TV, El Paso, 1969—; continuity/promotion mgr. KDBC-TV, El Paso, 1982—; tchr.'s aide El Paso Pub. Schs., 1967; researcher Biog. Dictionary, Notable Women in Am. Theatre, 1982; scriptwriter Your Chamber and You, 1981, Your Zoo Needs You, 1973. Contbr. articles to profl. jours. Mem. task force Cultural Planning Project, El Paso, 1985; dir. edn. El Paso Zool. Soc. Bd., 1974; bd. dirs. Delta Day Care Ctr., 1973-78; mem. scholarship com., vocat. placement adv. com. El Paso/Ysleta Ind. Sch. Dist., 1979—; ruling elder Presbyn. Ch., 1971-77. Flat Rock Playhouse scholar, 1960. Mem. Actor's Fund Am. (life), Broadcasting Promotion and Mktg. Execs., Tex. Press Women (recording sec. 1983-85), Nat. Fedn. Press Women. Club: United Presbyn. Women. Avocations: reading; traveling. Home: 315 S Ascarate St El El Paso TX 79905 Office: KDBC-TV 2201 Wyoming El Paso TX 79903

CARON, BLANCHE ALICE, real estate executive; b. Lowell, Mass.; d. Wilmer A. and Alice Lena (CingMars) Paquette; m. Gerard Caron, Feb. 6, 1959 (div.); children: Catherine Benedetto, Linda Tompkins, David, Rodney. Clk. Macartney's, Lawrence, 1956-57; with prodn. dept. Western Electric, North Andover, Mass., 1957-82; sales assoc. Blinn Realty, Inc., Derry, N.H., 1978-84, v.p., 1984—; dir. relocation Blinn Realty Inc. Gallery Homes, Derry. Mem. Nat. Assn. of Realtors, Salem Area Bd. of Realtors (chmn. hospitality com. 1987—, chmn. Am. home week com. 1987—, mem. pub. seminars, mem. safety thru songs 1987—, dir.), N.H. Assn. Realtors (chmn. community service). Roman Catholic. Office: Blinn Realty Inc Gallery of Homes 1 N Main St Derry NH 03038

CARON, VIVIENNE MARIE, educator, nun; b. Chathan, Ont., Can., Jan. 13, 1928; d. Adelard Joseph and Anne Rovina (Gamble) C. B. of Sacred Music, Pius X Sch. of Liturgical Music, Manhattanville Coll., 1967; B.A., U. Windsor, 1969. Joined Ursuline Sisters, Roman Catholic Ch., 1947. Tchr. Ont. Sch. Systems, 1951-63; dir. sisters formation Ursuline Sisters, Chatham, Ont., 1963-67, choir dir. Ursuline Sisters and Students, 1963-72; religious superior Ursuline Sisters, Toronto, Ont., 1973-78, Tecumseh, Ont., 1979-81; adminstr., religious superior Ursuline Sisters, Brescia Coll., London, Ont., 1981-85; tchr. French and world religions Brennan High Sch., Windsor, Ont., 1985—. Producer, dir. record Praise God, 1964. Chmn. religious assts. Young Christian Students, London diocese, 1960-66; mem. liturgical music commn., London, 1960-68.

CARON-PARKER, LAURA MARIE, occupational therapist; b. Seattle, July 27, 1959; d. Carles William and Gwendolyn Mary (Carlson) C. BA in Occupational Therapy, Coll. St. Catherine, St. Paul, 1981. Registered occupational therapist. Mem. occupational therapy staff Meml. Med. Ctr., Long Beach, Calif., 1982; occupational therapist Marina Profl. Services, Long Beach, 1982-84; mem. occupational therapy staff Meml. Health Techs., Long Beach, 1983-84, coordinator stroke rehab. team, 1983-84; dir. occupational therapy Intermountain Health Care Rehab. Services, Orange, Calif., 1984-87, regional coordinator Los Angeles area, 1987-88; regional coordinator Los Angeles area Intermountain Health Care Therapy Mgmt., Orange, 1988—; cons. Am. Heart Assn., Los Angeles, 1986—; founder, coordinator Gerontic Network, Los Angeles, 1987—; co-founder, coordinator P.D.R. Walkers, Los Angeles, 1987—; recruiter Coll. St. Catherine, Newport Beach, Calif., 1983—; occupational therapist Marinal Profl. Services, 1982-84. Mem. Am. Occupational Therapy Assn., Occupational Therapy Assn. Calif. (pub. relations liaison 1986-87, key person to legislature 1987— SELAC chpt., govt. affairs subcom. 1988—), Los Angeles Occupational Therapy Dirs. Forum, World Fedn. Occupational Therapy, Am. Soc. on Aging, Nat. Citizen's Coalition for Nursing Home Reform, Inst. for Profl. Health Service Adminstrs. (charter mem.). Home: 2021 Ocean Ave #225 Santa Monica CA 90405 Office: IHC Therapy Mgmt 1915 W Orangewood Ave Suite 212 Orange CA 92668

CAROPRESO, SANDRA ANN, small business owner, art appraiser; b. Pittsfield, Mass., Jan. 25, 1943; d. Harry and Angeline Thersa (Sarocco) MacDonald; m. Louis Edward Caropreso, May 30, 1961; 1 child, Anthony Louis. Cataloger Berkshire County Hist. Soc., Pittsfield, Mass., 1968-70; owner, appraiser Caropreso Gallery, Lee, Mass. Mem. Berkshire County Antique Dealers (bd. dirs. 1967-85, 80-86), Lee C. of C. (bd. dirs. 1981-84). Republican. Roman Catholic. Home and Office: Capreso Gallery 134 High St Lee MA 01238

CAROSCIO, GIOVINA THERESA, social services administrator; b. Elmira, N.Y., Mar. 30, 1951; d. william Joseph and Edith T. (Manocchio) C. AA, Corning (N.Y.) Community Coll., 1971; BS, Cornell U., 1973. Vol. VISTA, Jonesboro, Ark., 1973-74; outreach worker Econ. Opportunity Program, Elmira, 1974-75; supr. Tri-County Action Council, Inc., Painted Post, N.Y., 1975, exec. dir., 1975-79; co-dir. Office of Human Devel., Elmira, 1979-82; exec. dir. Finger Lakes Office of Social Ministry, Geneva, N.Y., 1982—; mem. adv. council N.Y. Dept. Labor, Albany, 1986—; bd. dirs McAuley Inst., Washington, Rural Opportunities, Inc., Rochester, N.Y. Office: Finger Lakes Social Ministry 110 Exchange St Geneva NY 14456

CAROSELLI, MARLENE, education consultant; b. Balt., June 18, 1943; d. Patrick Renato and Elvira Josephine (Ciaccia) C. BA, SUNY, Albany, 1965; MS, SUNY, Brockport, 1974; EdD, U. Rochester, 1980. Cert. ednl. adminstr./tchr. Tchr. Rochester (N.Y.) City Sch. Dist., 1968-80; property mgr. Trizec Properties, Los Angeles, 1981-84; instr. UCLA Extension Program, Nat. U., 1984—; dir. Ctr. for Profl. Devel., 1984—; cons. Lockheed, U.S. Dept. Def., Northrop Corp., Garrett AiResearch, Rockwell, Hughes Aircraft, U.S. Office of Personnel Mgmt., TRW Corp., Magnavox Corp., U.S. Dept. Interior, 1984—; cons. English adv. bd. Sci. Research Assocs. edn. subs. IBM, 1976; speaker in field. Author: The Language of Leadership; contbr. articles to profl. English and edn. jours. Named English Tchr. of Yr. N.Y. State English Council, 1975. Mem. Mensa. Office: 10305 Summertime Ln Culver City CA 90230

CAROUSSO, DOROTHEE HUGHES, author, lecturer, genealogist; b. Winthrop, Mass., Oct. 4, 1909; d. Patrick Lawrence and Luella (Nowell) Hughes; student pub. schs., St. Agnes Acad., College Point, N.Y., Kurt's Bus. Sch., Los Angeles; L.H.D. (hon.), Combs Coll., 1968; m. Georges Carousso, Dec. 31, 1930; 1 dau., Dorothee Nowell (Mrs. George Neil McKinnon). Author: (fiction) Open Then the Door, 1942; Sports Afield, 1960; (TV plays) Climax, Studio One; also fiction, verse in Collier's, Household, All-Story, Gothic Stories, mags., Woman's Home Companion, Canadian Home Jour.; geneal. works have appeared in Geneal. Mag. N.J., Pa. Geneal. Mag., Nat. Geneal. Soc. Quar., Md. and Del. Genealogist, N.Y. Gen. and Biog. Record, New Eng. Hist. and Geneal. Register; book critic Bklyn. Eagle. Fellow Geneal. Soc. Pa. (hon. v.p.); mem. Hist. Soc. Pa., Nat. Geneal. Soc., Nat. Soc. Colonial Dames Am., D.A.R., Desc. Colonial Clergy, Colonial Daus. 17th Century, Bucks County Writers Guild, New Eng. Historic Geneal. Soc., N.Y. Geneal. and Biog. Soc., Suffolk County Hist. Soc., Smithtown Hist. Soc., Daus. Utah Pioneers, Pa. Soc. New Eng. Women, Library Co. Phila. Address: 64 Cygnet Dr Smithtown NY 11787

CAROZZOLO, SHIRLEY JEAN, clergywoman; b. Buffalo, Nov. 21, 1935; d. Albert A. and Jean Louise (Hanna) La Chiusa; m. Vito A. Carozzolo, Sept. 17, 1966; children—Michael John Kurban, David Charles Kurban. Various secretarial positions, 1953-55, 68-74; office mgr. Haney Erection Services Inc., Tonawanda, N.Y., 1975-76, corp. sec., 1976-84, EEO officer, 1980-84; ordained minister of gospel Full Gospel Assemblies Internat.; corp. sec.-treas. New Covenant Evang. Ministries Inc., 1984-87; fin. adminstr. World Outreach Conf., 1985; treas. New Covenant Tabernacle, 1985—. Mem. Niagara Frontier Subcontractors Assn. (membership chmn. 1978), Leadership Council Western N.Y., Prison Fellowship local Council of Western N.Y., Am. Mgmt. Assn., Am. Soc. Profl. and Exec. Women, Christian Ministries Mgmt. Assn. (1st v.p. 1985-87), Nat. Assn. Ch. Bus. Adminstrs., Christian Found. for the Performing Arts (treas. 1986-87). Republican. Club: Zonta (1st v.p. 1979-81, pres. 1981-82). Home: 426 Ashford Ave Tonawanda NY 14150 Office: 1 World Ministries Ctr Buffalo NY 14223

CARPENTER, ANGIE MARY, small business owner, editor; b. Bay Shore, N.Y., Sept. 30, 1943; d. Joseph and Ida (Gullo) Linarello; m. Joe David Carpenter, Apr. 13, 1964; children: Richard, Robert. Student, Nassau Community Coll., 1962-63. Office mgr., graphic designer, typographer Merrick (N.Y.) Typographers and Maverick Pubs., 1966-76; founder, v.p. AC Typesetters and Printing, Inc., West Islip, N.Y., 1976—. Editor, pub., co-founder West Islip Record, 1986—; columnist The Graphic, The Beacon, 1985-87. Chmn. publicity com., trustee Babylon/West Islip Windmill Com., Inc., Babylon, N.Y., 1986—, ASK US, 1987—; trustee West Islip After-Sch.-Care program, 1987—; vice chmn. West Islip Youth Enrichment Services, 1986-87; mem. govt. action council L.I. Assn., 1987; mem. recycling panel Town of Islip, 1987; chairperson TOI Blue Ribbon Com. on Recycling, 1987-88. Mem. West Islip C. of C. (v.p., mchts. dir. 1982-84, pres. 1985, 86, 87, 88). Republican. Roman Catholic. Office: AC Typesetters & Printing Inc 620 Union Blvd West Islip NY 11795

CARPENTER, BEVERLEY DERDEN, clothing industry executive; b. San Antonio, Mar. 19, 1940; d. Max Albert and Nan Hearne (Beverley) Derden; m. Clinton Courtney Carpenter, May 1, 1965 (div. 1977); children: Peter Brenton, James Bradley. BA, Mich. State U., 1961. Bilingual tchr. Harlingen (Tex.) Ind. Sch. Dist., Harlingen, Tex., 1867-71; owner/operator Flower Village, Rio Hondo, Tex., 1971-77; office mgr. Levi Strauss & Co., Harlingen, 1978-80; adminstrv. mgr. Levi Strauss & Co., San Antonio, 1980—; bd. dirs. Bexar County Opportunities Industrialization Ctr. Indsl. Council, San Antonio, 1985—. Advisor Community Involvement Team Levi Strauss & Co., 1978-80, Rio Grande Valley Meth. Youth Council, Weslaco, Tex., 1964-65; task force chmn. Gov.'s Com. on Phys. Handicaps, Harlingen, 1966-67; pres. Rio Grande State Hosp. Vol. Services, Harlingen, 1965, 67; bd. dirs. Am. Cancer Soc., Harlingen, 1965-68. Republican. Methodist. Lodge: Altrusa (San Antonio). Office: Levi Strauss & Co 5827 Hwy 90 West San Antonio TX 78227

CARPENTER, CAROL SETTLE, banker; b. Schenectady, Oct. 22, 1953; d. Carl Oscar and Ursula Elsen (McEldowney) Settle; m. R. Jay Carpenter, May 4, 1985. BBA, Rochester Inst. Tech., 1975. Mgmt. trainee Lincoln First Bank, Rochester, N.Y., 1976-77; investment sec. Blyth Eastman Dillon, Scottsdale, Ariz., 1977-79; stockbroker E.F. Hutton, Scottsdale, 1979; stockbroker Rauscher Pierce Refsnes, Scottsdale, 1979-81; exec. v.p. RL Kotrozo Inc., Scottsdale, Ariz., 1981-85; asst. v.p. United Bank Ariz., Phoenix, 1985—. Staff vol. Crisis Nursery, Phoenix, 1987. Mem. Nat. Assn. Female Execs., Phi Gamma Nu. Republican. Presbyterian. Clubs: Plaza (Phoenix) (promotion chmn. 1986—, membership devel. 1988—), Phoenix Country. Avocations: composing music, golf. Home: 374 E Verde Ln Phoenix AZ 85012 Office: United Bank 3300 N Central Ave Phoenix AZ 85012

CARPENTER, CHRISTY, public relations executive; b. Washington, Dec. 15, 1949; d. Leslie Elisha and Liz (Sutherland) C. BA, Brown U., Providence, 1972; JD, Am. U., Washington, 1975. Law clk. to presiding justice U.S. Supreme Ct., Washington, 1976-77; spl. asst. to asst. sec. of commerce, U.S. Dept. Commerce, Washington, 1977-79; dir. market devel. Warner Amex Cable Communications, N.Y.C., 1979-84; mgr. market devel. Trintex Corp., White Plains, N.Y., 1984-86; dir. internat. devel. Telaction Corp., N.Y.C., 1986-87; v.p. Hill & Knowlton, N.Y.C., 1987—. Apptd. bd. dirs. Women's Action Alliance, N.Y.C., 1988—; del. Albert Gore Presdl. Campaign, N.Y.C., 1988; fundraiser U.S. Senatorial Candidates, N.Y.C., 1984-88. Democrat. Home: 50 Central Park W New York NY 10023 Office: Hill & Knowlton 420 Lexington Ave New York NY 10017

CARPENTER, CYNTHIA LOUISE, aerospace engineer; b. Quantico, Va., Sept. 15, 1962; d. Thomas Michael and Kathleen Louise (LaRoche) C. BS, Tex. A&M U., 1984; MSE, U. Ala., Huntsville, 1987. Indsl. engr. City Arlington, Tex., 1983; aerospace engr. NASA, Marshall Space Flight Ctr., Huntsville, 1984—. Contbr. articles to profl. jours. Troop leader north Ala. council Girl Scouts U.S., Huntsville, 1987. Mem. Huntsville Assn. Tech. Soc. (bd. dirs. 1987), Nat. Space Club, Am. Inst. Aero. and Astronautics (young mem. dir. 1987). Office: NASA/ Marshall Space Flight Ctr MAil Stop KA81 Marshall Space Flight Ctr AL 35812

CARPENTER, DEBRA ANN, insurance executive; b. Detroit, Oct. 1, 1951; d. William Richard and Valeria Pauline (Stankiewicz) Sitek; m. Wayne Forrest Carpenter, Nov. 24, 1978; 1 child, Travis Wayne. BA, U. Mich., 1973. CLU; chartered fin. cons. Med. asst. Alan B. Cohen MD, Warren, Mich., 1973-74; office mgr. Baer Enterprises, Southfield, Mich., 1974-75; asst. br. mgr. Provident Life, Southfield, 1975—. Mem. Greater Detroit Assn. Life Underwriters (past pres. 1984-85), Internat. Assn. Fin. Planners (bd. dirs. 1987—). Roman Catholic. Home: 663 S Spinningwhell Bloomfield Hills MI 48013 Office: Provident Life & Accident 26261 Evergreen #170 Southfield MI 48076

CARPENTER, DENESE MARELLÉ, counselor, educator; b. Memphis, Sept. 1, 1955; d. Robert L. and Opal L. (Taylor) C. BS, Tenn. State U., 1978, MS in Psychology, 1982. Nursing technician Bapt. Hosp., Nashville, 1979-81; asst. resident hall dir. Tenn. State U., Nashville, 1982-84; counselor, coordinator, lectr. Fisk U., Nashville, 1984-86, counselor, 1986-87, dormitory dir., 1988—. Vol. tchr. State Jr. Coll., 1988. Delta Sigma Theta.

CARPENTER, DOROTHY FULTON, state legislator; b. Ismay, Mont., Mar. 13, 1933; d. Daniel A. and Mary Ann (George) Fulton; B.A., Grinnell Coll., 1955; m. Thomas W. Carpenter, June 12, 1955; children—Mary Ione, James Thomas. Tchr. elem. schs., Houston, and Iowa City, 1955-58; mem. Iowa Ho. Reps., 1980—, asst. minority floor leader, 1982—. Pres. Planned Parenthood of Iowa, 1970; bd. dirs. Planned Parenthood Fedn. Am., 1977-80; fin. chmn. Episcopal Diocese of Iowa, 1979-80. Recipient Grinnell Coll. Alumni award, 1980. Mem. NOW, Common Cause. Republican.

CARPENTER, ELIZABETH SUTHERLAND, journalist, author, equal rights leader; b. Salado, Tex., Sept. 1, 1920; d. Thomas Shelton and Mary Elizabeth (Robertson) Sutherl; m. Leslie Carpenter, June 17, 1944; children: Scott Sutherland, Christy. B.J., U. Tex., 1942; hon. doctorate, Mt. Vernon Coll. Reporter, UP, Phila., 1944-45; propr. with husband of news bur. representing nat. newspapers Washington, 1945-61; exec. asst. to Vice Pres. Lyndon B. Johnson, 1961-63; pres. sec., staff dir. to Mrs. Johnson, 1963-69; v.p. Hill & Knowlton, Inc., Washington, 1972-76; cons. LBJ Library, Austin, Tex.; asst. sec. Dept. Edn., 1980-81; co-chmn. ERAmerica, 1976-81. Author: Ruffles and Flourishes, 1970, Getting Better All The Time, 1987. Recipient Woman of Year award in field of politics and pub. affairs Ladies Home Jour., 1977. Named to Tex. Women's Hall of Fame, 1985. Mem. Nat. Women's Polit. Caucus (founding mem., nat. policy council 1971—), Women's Nat. Press (pres. 1954-55), Alpha Phi, Theta Sigma Phi (Nat. Headliners award 1962). Clubs: Press (Washington); Headliners (Headliner award), Univ. (Austin). Home and Office: 116 Skyline Dr Austin TX 78746

CARPENTER, JANETH TURNER, systems engineer; b. Barry County, Mo., Dec. 1, 1928; d. Otto Wilson and Adah Gladys (Jaques) Turner; m. Paul Bruce Carpenter, June 12, 1954; 1 child, Jana. AB, U. Mo., 1950, MEd, 1952; PhD, Fla. State U., 1959. Counselor U. Mo., Columbia, 1952-54; clin. psychologist Cen. State Hosp., Indpls., 1954-55; research psychologist VA, Biloxi, Miss., 1959-60; human factors scientist Ramo-Wooldridge, Canoga Park, Calif., 1960-62, Systems Devel. Corp., Santa Monica, Calif., 1962; systems engr. Hughes Aircraft Co., Fullerton, Calif., 1962-76; campaign mgr. Carpenter Campaign Com., Cypress, Calif., 1976-84; sr. systems engr. Hughes Aircraft Co., Fullerton, 1984-87, mgr. tech. staff, 1987—. Patentee in field, 1962. Mem. Am. Psychol. Assn., Phi Beta Kappa, Psi Chi, Sigma Xi. Democrat. Office: Hughes Aircraft Co MS 606/K221 PO Box 3310 Fullerton CA 92634

CARPENTER, KAREN HANSEN, banker, small business owner; b. Melrose, Mass., Feb. 18, 1943; d. Oscar Martin and Winifred (Walker) Hansen; m. G. John Carpenter, Oct. 27, 1966; children: Katherine Alice, Julia Helen. BA in Latin, Wellesley Coll., 1965; MA in Human Behavior, U.S. Internat. U., 1973. Classics tchr. San Diego State Bishop's Sch., 1965-68; cons. Pub., Exec. Search, Los Angeles, 1968-71; dir. devel. U. Calif., Irvine, 1971-73, Concord (Mass.) Acad., 1973-75; exec. dir. Human Services Corp., Lowell, Mass., 1975-80; cons. Comfed Savs. Bank, Lowell, 1981-82, v.p., 1982-85, sr. v.p., 1985—; pres., chief exec. officer, dir., trust officer Bay Bank, Merrimack Valley, Mass., 1988—. Bd. dirs. YWCA, Girls Club, Boys Club, Lowell, 1975-81, Lowell Devel.-Fin. Corp., 1975—, Unitas Hispanic Advocacy, Lowell, 1978—, T.E. Parker Found., Boston, 1981—, Merrimack Repertory Theatre, Lowell, 1982—. Exec. mem. Am. Mktg. Assn. Episcopalian. Home: 249 Haggett's Pond Rd Andover MA 01810 Office: Comfed Savs Bank 45 Central St Lowell MA 01852

CARPENTER, KATHLEEN ANNE, personnel specialist; b. Easton, Pa., Nov. 15, 1942; d. Roland Reeves and Felicia Catherine (Keyser) Prime; divorced; 1 child, Catherine Anne. Student, East Stroudsburg State Tchrs. Coll., 1960-63; AA, Thomas Edison U., 1986. Tchr. Easton Area Sch. dist., 1965; tchr.'s asst. Phila. Sch. Dist., 1966; clk. distbn. U.S. Postal Service, Phila., 1966-70; counselor EEO, investigator Belmawr, N.J., 1973-74; mgr. women's program ea. region Phila., 1974-79; officer security force U.S. Postal Inspection Service, Phila., 1970-72, supr. security force, 1972-73; officer dept. EEO Phila. Naval Shipyard, Dept. Navy, 1979—; instr., cons., lectr. EEO program, Phila. area, 1982—. Recipient Legion of Honor award Chapel of Four Chaplains, 1982, leadership award YWCA, 1983. Mem. Fed. Exec. Bd. EEO Officers Council (chairperson 1983-85), Fed. Mgrs. Assn., Phila. Area Navy EEO Officer Council (chairperson 1983-85). Lutheran. Home: 1638 Red Oak Rd Williamstown NJ 08094 Office: Phila Naval Shipyard Philadelphia PA 19112

CARPENTER, LINDA TART, public relations executive, academic program director; b. Panama City, Fla., Aug. 4, 1943; d. John P. Tart and Inda (King) Inskeep; m. William G. Carpenter, 1967 (div. 1971); 1 child, Adam Jason Gore; m. Peter Charles Schreyer, Oct. 19, 1985. BA in English, Fla. State U., 1965. Journalist Orlando (Fla.) Sentinel, 1972-76; freelance writer Orlando, 1976-78; publs. editor Orlando Regional Med. Ctr., 1978-82; dir. pub. info. Fla. Solar Energy Ctr., Cape Canaveral, 1982-84; dir. pub. relations and mktg. West Orange Meml. Hosp., Winter Garden, Fla., 1984-87; dir. pub. relations Sch. Continuing Edn. Rollins Coll., Winter Park, Fla., 1987—; faculty Crealde Sch. Art, Winter Park, 1985—. Mem. Fla. Pub. Relations Assn. (cert.), Internat. Assn. Bus. Communicators (pres. 1983-84), Am. Soc. Hosp. Mktg. and Pub. Relations.

CARPENTER, MARION PHYLLIS, government official; b. Seattle, Feb. 17, 1931; d. Kenneth Alden and Lora Catherine (Scott) Sprague; student U. Oreg., 1948-49; children—Linda Marie Hepler, Kenneth Frederick, Nancy Lynn. Receptionist, med. clk. Adult and Family Services, State of Oreg., McMinnville, 1964-68, assistance worker, 1968-73, supr., 1973-77, br. mgr., Florence, Oreg., 1977-86, Roseburg Adult and Family Services, 1986—. Mem. Florence Activity Center Bd., 1977-78; mem. McMinnville Planning Commn., 1975-77; asso. mother adviser Knowles Rainbow Girls, 1971-77; mem. Lane County Council Govt. Rural Transp. Com., 1981-84; mem. nat. adv. bd. Umpqua Community Action, 1988—, UCAN Clint Council, 1988—, also confidence clinic bd. 1988— strategic planning com. United Way, 1988—; vice chmn. Florence Area Coordinating Council, 1982-85, chmn., 1985-86; chmn. Florence Community Concert Assn., 1984-86; agy. bd. West Lane Hosp.'s Home Health, 1983-86, chmn., 1983-86. Mem. Oreg. Mgmt. Assn., Nat. Assn. Female Execs., Am. Mgmt. Assn., Oreg. Gerontol. Assn., Oreg. Assn. Retarded Citizens, Am. Assn. Retired Persons. Republican. Presbyterian. Clubs: Soroptimists, Jr. Matrons, Eastern Star, Daus. of Nile. Home: PO Box 1489 Roseburg OR 97470 Office: PO Box 70 Roseburg OR 97470

CARPENTER, NANCY CAROL, travel agency executive; b. Huntington, W.Va., Mar. 31, 1956; d. Leonard Cecil and Mary (Scott) Rice; m. Lonnie Theron Carpenter, May 30, 1975; 1 child, Krystal Rae. Student, Marshall U., 1975. Travel counselor Huntington (W.Va.) Auto Club, 1976-85; ticket agt. Huntington Auto Club Worldwide Travel, 1985-86; mgr. br. office Huntington Auto Club Worldwide Travel, Ceredo, W.Va., 1986—. Mem. Am. Automotive Assn. (cert. domestic travel counselor). Republican. Methodist. Lodge: Jobs Daughters (hon. queen 1974). Office: AAA World Wide Travel US Rt 60 and 2d St W Ceredo WV 25530

CARPENTER, PHYLLIS MARIE ROSENAU, physician; b. Hastings, Nebr., Aug. 2, 1926; d. Alvin Benjamin and Sophia Helen (Schmidt) Rosenau; B.S., Hastings Coll., 1948; M.D., U. Nebr., 1951; cert. Gestalt Inst. Cleve., 1970; m. Charles Robert Carpenter, Mar. 24, 1956 (dec. Mar. 1972); children—Charles Robert, Carole Rose, Lucinda Joy. Intern, St. Luke's Hosp., Chgo., 1951-52; resident in pediatrics Children's Meml. Hosp., Chgo., 1952-54; asst. med. dir., also clin. supr. EEG lab., Mcpl. Contagious Disease Hosp., Chgo., 1955-60; tchr. parenting; staff Well Baby Clinics, Infant Welfare, 1960-70; pvt. practice specializing in Gestalt therapy, preventive medicine and biofeedback, Chgo. and Clarendon Hills, Ill., 1970—; mem. staff Grant Hosp., Chgo.; lectr., workshops on stress mgmt. and biofeedback; founding fellow, mem. faculty Gestalt Inst. Chgo., 1970—, faculty chmn., 1981-83; mem. faculty Coll. DuPage, 1975-79, 83—, No. Ill. U., 1979-80, George Williams Coll., Chgo., 1979-85 ; therapist Martha Washington Alcoholic Rehab. Clinic, Chgo., 1969-75; mem. Wholistic Health Ctr. Hinsdale, 1986—. Mem. Am. Assn. Biofeedback Clinicians (cert. clinician), Am. Med. Writers Assn., Nat. Writers Club. Author articles in field. Contbg. editor Current Health mag., 1981-85 . Home: 35 Norfolk St Clarendon Hills IL 60514 Office: 35 Norfolk St Clarendon Hills IL 60514 Office: 826 W Armitage Ave Chicago IL 60614

CARPENTER, ROCHELLE (SHELLEY) KRISTINE, personnel director; b. Chgo., Sept. 9, 1951; d. George Eugene and Shirley Frances (Hammerle) Stevenson; m. Daniel Britton Carpenter, Mar. 22, 1980; 1 child, Charles Britton. BS in Organizational Behavior, U. San Francisco, 1987, postgrad., 1988—. Mgr. personnel ICL Scientific, Fountain Valley, Calif., 1978, Ortho Diagnostic Systems div. Johnson & Johnson, Irvine, Calif., 1978-82; dir. personnel A-Company, Inc. subs. Johnson & Johnson, San Diego, 1982—. Mem. adv. com. Johnson & Johnson Employee's Good Govt. Fund, 1981—, state relations subcom., 1986—. Mem. Am. Soc. Personnel Adminstrs., Am. Soc. Tng. and Devel., Am. Mgmt. Assn., Am Compensation Assn. Office: Johnson & Johnson A-Co Inc 11436 Sorrento Valley Rd San Diego CA 92121

CARPENTER, SANDRA ELAINE, educator; b. Birmingham, Ala., Jan. 26, 1950; d. Burl and Sammie J. (Mooneyham) Vines; m. William Brewer Carpenter, Aug. 28, 1971; 1 child, Daniel Burl. BA, U. Montevallo, Ala., 1972, MEd. Tchr. Montevallo Mid. Sch., 1972, Thompson Mid. Sch., Alabaster, Ala., 1972—. Sunday sch. tchr. Pelham United Meth. Ch., 1986—, mem. Council on Ministries, 1986—, dir. vacation bible sch., 1986—. Mem. NEA, Ala. Edn. Assn. (del. 1984-87), Shelby County Edn. Assn. (sec. 1984-85, bd. dirs. 1986—), Alpha Delta Kappa, Beta Lambda. Home: 1525 Sandpebble St Alabaster AL 35007

CARPENTER, SHERRY LEE, purchasing executive; b. Kansas City, Mo., Mar. 11, 1947; d. Wilbur L and Barbara J. (Casey) Scott; m. Loyce Heitman, June 1966 (div. 1970); m. David L Carpenter, Aug. 24, 1971. BSBA, Rockhurst Coll., 1977, MBA, 1985. Project acct. Huxtable-Hammond Co., Inc., Kansas City, Kans., 1975-78; auditor of accounts Kansas City (Mo.) So. Ry., 1978-81, dir. purchasing, 1981—. Alumni bd. Rockhurst Coll., Kansas City, Mo., 1986—; mem. The Cen. Exchange, Kansas City. Mem. Nat. Assn. of Purchasing Mgrs. (sec.-treas. Rail Industry Group 1986—, 2d vice chair 1988—), Railway Tie Assn., Am. Wood Preserver's Assn., Am. Council R.R. Women. Home: 7732 Haskins Lenexa KS 66216 Office: Kansas City So Railway 114 W 11th St Kansas City MO 64105-1804

CARPENTER, SUSAN KAREN, lawyer; b. New Orleans, May 6, 1951; d. Donald Jack and Elise Ann (Diehl) C. B.A. magna cum laude with honors in English, Smith Coll., 1973; J.D., Ind. U., 1976. Bar: Ind. 1976. Dep. pub. defender of Ind. State of Ind., Indpls., 1976-81, pub. defender of Ind., 1981—; chief pub. defender Wayne County, Richmond, Ind., 1981; bd. dirs. Ind. Pub. Defender Council, Indpls., 1981—, Ind. Lawyer's Commn., Indpls., 1984—; trustee Ind. Criminal Justice Inst., Indpls., 1983—. Mem. Criminal Code Study Commn., Indpls., 1981—, Supreme Ct. Records Mgmt. Com., Indpls., 1983—. Mem. Ind. State Bar Assn. (criminal justice sect.), Nat. Legal Aid and Defender Assn. (mem. Amicus com. 1984—), Nat. Assn. Defense Lawyers, Phi Beta Kappa. Office: Office of State Pub Defender 309 W Washington St Suite 501 Indianapolis IN 46204

CARPENTER-MASON, BEVERLY NADINE, executive health care quality assurance nurse; b. Pitts., May 23, 1933; d. Frank Carpenter and Thelma Deresa (Williams) Smith; m. Sherman Robert Robinson Jr., Dec. 26, 1953 (div. Jan. 1959); 1 child, Keith Michael; m. David Solomon Mason Jr., Sept. 10, 1960; 1 child, Tamara Nadina. RN. BS, St. Joseph's Coll., North Windham, Maine, 1979; MS, So. Ill. U., 1981. Staff nurse med. surgery, ob-gyn neontology and pediatrics, Pa., N.Y., Wyo., Colo. and Washington, 1954-68; mgr. clinician dermatol. services Malcolm Grow Med. Ctr., Camp Spring, Md., 1968-71; pediatric nurse practitioner Dept. Human Resources, Washington, 1971-73; asst. dir. nursing Glenn Dale Hosp., Md., 1973-81; nursing coordinator medicaid div. Forest Haven Hosp., Laurel, Md., 1981-83, spl. asst. to supr. for med. services, 1983-84; spl. asst. to supt. for quality assurance Burr. Habilitation Services, Laurel, 1984—; asst. treas. ABQAURP, Inc., Sarasota, Fla., 1988—, also bd. dirs.; cons. and lectr. in field. Contbr. articles to profl. jours. Mem., star donor ARC Blood Drive, Washington, Md., 1975—; chair nominations com. Prince Georges Nat. Council Negro Women, Md., 1984-85. Recipient awards Dept. Air Force and D.C. Govt., 1966—, Della Robbia Gold medallion Am. Acad. Pediatrics, 1972, John P. Lamb Jr. Meml. Lectureship award East Tenn. State U., Johnson City, 1988. Mem. Am. Assn. Mental Retardation (conf. lectr. 1988), Am. Coll. Utilization Rev. Physicians, Am. Bd. Quality Assurance and Utilization Rev. (mem. jour. editorial bd. 1985—, chmn. publs. com. 1987—), Assn. Retarded Citizens, Nat. Assn. Female Execs., Ladies of Distinction, Inc. (1st v.p. 1986—), Chi Eta Phi. Democrat. Baptist. Avocations: studying languages, travel, reading, writing, collecting antiques. Home: 11109 Winsford Ave Upper Marlboro MD 20772 Office: Bur Habilitation Services 3360 Center Ave Laurel MD 20707

CARPER, FREDA SMITH, bank marketing director; b. Roanoke, Va., Aug. 19, 1953; d. Samuel E. and R. Violet (Wilson) Smith; m. Charles R. Carper, June 18, 1978. AAS in Mgmt., U. Ky., Prestonburg, 1980. Sales dir. Ramada Inn, Roanoke, 1975-76; account exec. mgr. Am. Hotel Mgmt., Raleigh, N.C., 1976-78; asst. v.p., mktg. dir. Pikeville (Ky.) Nat. Bank, 1980-83; v.p. mktg. dir. 1st Fed. Roanoke (name changed to CorEast Savs. Bank), 1983—. Recipient Addy award Charleston/Huntington Ad Club, W.Va., 1982, 83. Mem. Sales Mktg. Execs. (pres. 1986-87), Sales Mktg. Execs. Internat. (regional bd. dirs. 1986-87), Advt. Fedn. Roanoke (treas. 1986-87, v.p. 1987-88, Addy award 1984), Fin. Instn. Mktg. Assn. Democrat. Baptist. Office: CorEast Savs Bank 36 W Church Ave Roanoke VA 24011

CARPER, GERTRUDE ESTHER, artist, marina owner; b. Jamestown, N.Y., Apr. 13, 1921; d. Zenas Mills and Virgie (Lytton) Hanks; m. J. Dennis Carper, Apr. 5, 1942; children—David Hanks, John Michael Dennis (dec. 1982). Student violinist Nat. Acad. Mus., 1931-41; diploma fine arts Md. Inst. Art, 1950; voice student Frazier Gange, Peabody Inst. Music, 1952-55. Interior decorator O'Neill's (Importers), Balt., 1942-44; auditor Citizens Nat. Bank, Covington, Va., 1945-46; owner, developer Essex Yacht Harbor Marina, Balt., 1955—; St. Michael's Sanctuary, wildlife preserve, Balt., 1965—; jewelry designer, 1987—. Portrait artist, 1947—; exhibited one-woman shows Ferdinand Roten Gallery, Balt., 1963, Highfield Salon, Balt., 1967, Le Salon des Nations a Paris, 1985, Ducks and Geese of North Am., 1986; exhibited group shows Md. Inst. Alumni Show, 1964, Essex Library, 1981, others. Author: Expressions for Children, 1985. Contbr. articles and poetry to ch. publs. and newspapers. Vol. tchr. of retarded persons, 1963—; leader Women's Circle at local Presbyterian chs., 1952—. Mem. Md. Inst. Art Alumni Assn. (life). Avocations: raising orchids, making tiny books, reading, poetry writing. Office: Essex Yacht Harbour Marina 500 Sandalwood Rd Baltimore MD 21221-5830

CARPER, GLENDA JOY, restaurant executive; b. San Angelo, Tex., July 21, 1939; d. Sam Bruce and Lethia (McGilvray) Lambert; B.A., West Tex. State U., 1971; m. Donald Clayton Carper, July 29, 1956; children—LaDon, Kelli Lin. Billing clk. Gen. Telephone Co., San Angelo, 1957-59; bookkeeper Margarets, Lubbock, Tex., 1959-62; sec., treas. Bearings and Materials Handling Co., Inc., Amarillo, Tex., 1968—, Bamco of Amarillo, Bamco of Dumas, Bamco of Hereford; regional mgr. Kaman Bearing and Supply, 1985-87; owner Doodle's Hamburger Stores, Inc., Amarillo, 1987—; pres. Amarillo Credit Women Internat., 1980-81, dir., also mem. pres.'s task force com.; dir. Cert. Collectors, Inc. Second v.p. Lone Star Regional Council, 1981-82, pres. Region II 1983-84, 3d v.p. 1984-85. Named Credit Woman of Yr., State of Tex., 1985. Mem. Credit Women Internat. (v.p. 1980-81, treas. 1979-80, 2d v.p. Lone Star chpt. 1985-86, 1st v.p. 1986-87, pres. Dist. 8 1987—), Credit Mgmt. Assn. Tex. (bd. dirs.), Retail Merchants Assn. Tex. (bd. dirs.), Amarillo Credit Mgmt. (bd. dirs.). Republican. Presbyterian. Home: 3908 Eaton Dr Amarillo TX 79109 Office: Doodle's Inc 3701-B Olsen Ave Amarillo TX 79109

CARPIEN, JANNET SIEGLE, corporate executive, financial planner; b. Reading, Pa., Jan. 24, 1943; d. Robert Eugene and Helen (Jablonski) Siegle; m. Alan Hugh Carpien, Oct. 4, 1969; children: Juliette M., Seth M. BS, Kutztown (Pa.) State U., 1964; postgrad., George Washington U., U. Madrid, San Diego State U. Tchr. Spanish and phys. edn. Holy Name High Sch., Rading, Pa., 1964-65; tchr. English, reading and speech Western High Sch., Washington, 1966-68; tchr. English Meml. Jr. High Sch., San Diego, 1968-70, Ballou High Sch., Washington, 1971-72; account exec. Johnston, Lemon & Co., Inc., Washington, 1976-84; corp. v.p., fin. planner Smith Barney Harris Upham & Co., 1984—; mem. adj. faculty Coll. Fin. Planning George Washington U., Denver, 1983—. Contbr. articles to profl. jours. Chmn. com. on seminar Womens Nat. Bank Adv. Bd., Washington, 1979-80, 81-84; mem. bus. com. D.C. Commn. for Women, Washington, 1982—; 1st v.p. bd. dirs. Florence Crittenton of Greater Washington, 1987. Recipient Profl. Service award Washington Pub. Accts., 1979, Pres.'s Club Profl. Achievement award Johnston, Lemon & Co. Inc., 1983. Mem. Internat. Assn. Fin. Planning (sec. 1980-81, exec. v.p. 1985-86, pres. 1986-87, Ea. regional bd. dirs. 1986—, chmn. 1988—, bd. dirs. 1987—), Stockbrokers Soc., Bond Club of Washington, Nat. Assn. Securities Dealers (broker). Democrat. Jewish. Office: Smith Barney Harris Upham & Co 1919 Pennsylvania Ave #610 Washington DC 20006

CARR, BARBARA J., hospital administrator; b. Miami, Fla., Oct. 16, 1950; d. Charles Ray and Evelena (Gordon) C.; 1 child, Charles Richard Seifert. Student, Miami Dade Jr. Coll., 1968-74, U. Miami, 1972-74, Nova U., 1982-83. Asst. dir. heart sta. Jackson Meml. Med. Ctr., Miami, 1972-76; mktg. dir. Cardio Services Union Carbide, Miami, 1976-80; adminstrv. dir. vascular services Miami Vascular Inst. Bapt. Hosp. of Miami, 1981—. Mem. Am. Heart Assn., Am. Coll. Cardiovascular Adminstrs., Am. Acad. Med. Adminstrs., Nat. Alliance Cardiovascular Techs. (v.p. 1987, state pres. 1987-88), Nat. Soc. Cardiovascular Techs. (nat. pres. 1976-78, chmn.), Am. Coll. Cardiovascular Adminstrs.

CARR, BESSIE, retired educator; b. Nathalie, Va., Oct. 10, 1920; d. Henry C. and Sirlena (Ewell) C. BS, Elizabeth City Coll., N.C., 1942; MA, Columbia U. Tchrs. Coll., 1948, PhD, 1950, EdD, 1952. Cert. adminstr., supr., tchr. Prin. pub. sch., Halifax, Va., 1942-47, Nathalie-Halifax County, Va., 1947-51; prof. edn. So. U., Baton Rouge, 1952-53; supr. schs. Lackland Schs., Cin., 1953-54; prof. edn. Wilberforce U., Ohio, 1954-55; tchr. Leland Sch., Pittsfield, Mass., 1956-60; chair math. dept., tchr. Lakeland Mid. Sch., N.Y., 1961-83. Founder, organizer, sponsor 1st Math Bowl and Math Forum in area, 1970-76; founder Dr. Bessie Carr award Halifax County Sr. High Sch., 1962. Mem. AAUW (auditor 1970-85), Delta Kappa Gamma (auditor internat. 1970-76), Assn. Suprs. of Math. (chair coordinating council 1976-80), Ret. Tchrs. Assn., Black Women Bus. and Profl. Assn. (charter mem. Senegal, Africa chpt.). Democrat. Avocations: travel, photography, souvenirs.

CARR, JACQUELYN B., psychologist, educator; b. Oakland, Calif., Feb. 22, 1923; d. Frank G. and Betty (Kreiss) Corker; children: Terry, John, Richard, Linda, Michael, David. BA, U. Calif., Berkeley, 1958; MA, Stanford U., 1961; PhD, U. So. Calif., 1973. Lic. psychologist, Calif; lic. secondary tchr., Calif. Tchr. Hillsdale High Sch., San Mateo, Calif., 1958-69, Foothill Coll., Los Altos Hills, Calif., 1969—; cons. Silicon Valley Companies, U.S. Air Force, Interpersonal Support Network, Santa Clara County Child Abuse Council, San Mateo County Suicide Prevention Inc.,Parental Stress Hotline, Hotel/Motel Owners Assn.; co-dir. Individual Study Ctr.; supr. Tchr. Edn.; adminstr. Peer Counseling Ctr.; led numerous workshops and confs. in field. Author: Learning is Living, 1970, Equal Partners: The Art of Creative Marriage, 1986, The Crisis in Intimacy, 1988; Communicating and Relating, 1984, Communicating with Myself: A Journal, 1984; contbr. articles to profl. jours. Mem. Mensa. Club: Commonwealth. Home: 440 Davis Ct #1502 San Francisco CA 94111 Office: Foothill College 12345 El Monte Los Altos Hills CA 94022

CARR, JUDITH ANN SAUNDERS, social worker; b. Charleston, W.Va., Apr. 26, 1942; d. James Allen and Grace Ann (Revels) Saunders; B.S. in Social Work, Eastern Mich. U., 1975, M.Guidance and Counseling, 1979; M.S.W., U. Mich., 1977, cert. specialist in gerontology, 1979; children—Marcia Arlene, Martin Anthony. With Ann Arbor (Mich.) Community Center, Inc., 1966—, dir. sr. citizens program, 1977—; field instr. U. Mich.; dir. Washtenaw County Area Agy. on Aging. Mem. Nat. Assn. Social Workers, Huron Valley Assn. Social Workers, Nat. Council on Aging. Home: 2918 Verle Ave Ann Arbor MI 48104 Office: 625 N Main St Ann Arbor MI 48104

CARR, MARY JO, lawyer, judge; b. Newton, Mass., Sept. 26, 1950; d. Howell Coleman and Anne (Kerr) C.; m. William J. Larson, Nov. 14, 1981. BA, Swarthmore Coll., 1972; JD, Rutgers U., 1978. Bar: Pa. 1978, U.S. Dist. Ct. (ea. dist.) Pa. 1978, N.J. 1979, U.S. Dist. Ct. (so. dist.) N.J. 1979, R.I. 1981, U.S. Dist. Ct. (so. dist.) R.I. 1984. Sole practice Phila., 1978-81, Warwick, R.I., 1981-83; probate judge City of Newport, R.I., 1983-87, city solicitor, 1986-87; with Sheffield & Harvey, Newport, 1988—; incorporator Bank of Newport, 1986—; pres. bd. dirs. Island Moving Co., Newport, 1986—. Bd. dirs. Sail Newport, 1988—. Home: 25 Cranston Ave Newport RI 02840 Office: Sheffield & Harvey Box 339 47 Long Wharf Mall Newport RI 02840

CARR, PATRICIA WARREN, adult education educator; b. Mobile, Ala., Mar. 24, 1947; d. Bedford Forrest and Mary Catherine (Warren) Slaughter; m. John Lyle Carr, Sept. 26, 1970; children: Caroline Elise, Joshua Bedford. BS in Edn., Auburn U., 1968, MEd, 1971. Tchr. DeKalb County Schs., Atlanta, 1969-70; counselor Dept. Defense Schs., Okinawa, Japan, 1972-75; tchr. Jefferson County Schs., Jefferson, Ga., 1975-76; counselor Clarke County Schs., Athens, Ga., 1976-78; tchr. Fairfax County Schs., Adult and Community Edn., Fairfax, Va., 1980—; coordinator Enrichment for Srs. Program Fairfax Area Agy. on Aging and Adult and Community Edn., 1985—; cons. State Va. Dept. Edn., 1984—, Va. Assn. Adult and Community Edn., 1987, Commn. on Adult Basic Edn., 1988; instr. George Mason U., Fairfax, 1985. Tchr. Met. Meml. United Meth. Ch., Washington, 1981—; co-leader Mclean, Va. troop Girl Scouts U.S., 1985—. Mem. Am. Assn. Adult and Community Edn., Smithsonian Nat. Assocs, Fairfax County Assn. Vol. Adminstrs. Methodist. Office: Fairfax County Adult and Community Edn 7510 Lisle Ave Falls Church VA 22043

CARR, PHYLLIS M., mortgage company executive, real estate broker; b. Bklyn., Aug. 23, 1943; d. Max and Anne (Epstein) Edelstein; divorced; 1 child, Melanie Jan; m. Stuart Burton Carr, Apr. 17, 1977. Lic. real estate broker, N.Y.; lic. mortgage broker, N.Y. Real estate agt. Heino Real Estate Inc., Bklyn., 1981-85; real estate broker Coldwell Banker/Neuhaus Realty, S.I., N.Y., 1985-87; pres. Carr Investors Planning, Ltd., S.I., 1986—; real estate broker Village Sq. Realty, S.I., 1987—. Mem. S.I. C. of C., S.I. Bd. Realtors, N.Y. State Bd. Realtors. Democrat. Jewish. Home and Office: 88 Mulberry Circle New York NY 10314

CARR, RUTH ANNE, lawyer; b. Athens, Ga., July 22, 1947; d. James Fletcher and Bennie Lou (Blakely) C.; 1 child, Lisa Raye Rissmiller. A.B., U. Ga., 1966; J.D., Woodrow Wilson Coll., 1978; LLM, 1987. Bar: Ga. 1978. Sole practice, Atlanta, 1978-80; gen. mgr. Am. Seal and Stamp Co., Atlanta, 1980-81; sole practice, Atlanta, 1981-82; atty. State of Ga., Atlanta, 1982-86, adminstrv. law judge; legal services officer Ga. Div. Mental Health/Mental Retardation, 1986—; legal services officer, dir. forensic services Ga. Div. Mental Health, Mental Retardation and Substance Abuse, 1987—; vis. tchr. Woodrow Wilson Coll., Atlanta, 1982; guest speaker DeKalb High Schs., Decatur, Ga., 1984. Bd. dirs. Terraces Condominium Assn., Atlanta, 1984. Mem. ABA, State Bar Ga., Ga. Trial Lawyers Assn., Atlanta Bar Assn., Nat. Assn. State Mental Health Attys. (state rep. 1987—). Home: 2527 Terrace Trail Decatur GA 30035 Office: Div Mental Health/Mental Retardation Room 306 878 Peachtree St Atlanta GA 30309

CARR, SANDRA GOTHAM, advertising and marketing executive, consultant; b. Tokyo, June 9, 1948; d. Fred Calvin and Evelyn (Dirr) Gotham; m. James P. Jenkins, June 15, 1970 (div. 1982); m. Dayton T. Carr, Dec. 27, 1986. Student Stanford-in-France, Tours, 1968-69; B.A., Stanford U., 1970, M.A., 1971. Account exec. Young & Rubicam Inc., N.Y.C., 1972-78, account supr., 1978-80; pres., Gotham Prodns., N.Y.C., 1980-82; v.p., mgmt. supr. Ogilvy & Mather, 1982-85; v.p. Steuben Glass, N.Y.C., 1985-88; cons. Congl. coms., FDA, FTC for exec. program Am. Assn. Advt. Agys., Washington, 1978-80; cons. Ctr. Arctic Studies Sorbonne, Paris, in U.S. and Can., 1980-82; seminar dir. N.Y. chpt. Women in Bus., N.Y.C., 1983-84. Writer and editor 4-part TV documentary script Invit! The Universal Cry of the Eskimo People, 1981. Writer speeches for Georgetown Ctr. Strategic and Internat. Studies, also newsletter for Am. Assn. Advt. Agys. Fund raiser Stanford U., N.Y.C., promotion coordinator of benefits and advt. Medic Alert, N.Y.C., 1983-84; mem. exec. com. Youth Counseling League, N.Y.C., 1984. Named to dean's list Stanford U., 1966-70. Mem. Writers Guild Am., Young Profls. Group of Fgn. Policy Assn. (organizing chmn. 1980-81), N.Y. Women in Communications. Club: Stanford (N.Y.C.). Home: 220 E 73d St New York NY 10021 Office: Steuben Glass Fifth Ave and 56th St New York NY 10022

CARR, SARA ANN LEACH, international business coordinator; b. Springfield, Mo., Nov. 13, 1936; d. Robert P. and Genevieve (Thompson) Leach; m. William A. Carr; children: Genevieve A. Dake, Bonnie Allane. BA in Bus. Law, Augusta (Ga.) Coll., 1954. Travel cons. Escort for Travel Co., Springfield, 1976—; owner Creative Catering & Gourmet Arts, Springfield, 1976—; food stylist J.C. Penney & Co., tchr. coll. photography, 1980—; cons. Mo. Egg Merchandising Council, Springfield, 1982—. Editor: Riggers' Bible, 1956. Active S.W. Mo. Mus. Assocs., Springfield Little Theater, Springfield Symphony Guild, Sister Cities Assn., Peace Through People. Home and Office: 638 S Fremont Springfield MO 65804

CARRAGHER, AUDREY ANN, state legislator; b. Jamaica Plain, Mass., Jan. 27, 1924; d. Daniel Joseph and Frances Louise (Wright) McLeod; R.N., Faulkner Hosp., 1945; postgrad. Northeastern U., 1968-76; B.Gen. Studies, U. N.H., 1978, postgrad., 1979; m. John C. Carragher, Nov. 11, 1947; children—John C., Janice, Daniel, Lawrence. Library trustee, mem. Bicentennial Commn., 1974; mem. New Eng. Bd. Library Trustees, 1975; chmn. Chelmsford Hist. Commn., 1975; mem. Growth Policy Commn., 1976; student rep. Lifelong Learning Council U. N.H., 1977; planner Nashua (N.H.) Human Services Council, 1978; mem. county Adv. Council on Aging, 1979; mem. N.H. Ho. of Reps., 1980-86; candidate N.H. State Senate, 1986—, mem. exec. dept. com., adminstrn. com., 1980-84, constl. revision com., 1980-82, subcom. chmn. for state reapportionment and for children and youth legislation, vice chmn. state instns. com., 1982-84, mem. joint com. on exec. reorgn., mem. policy com., Rep. floor leader, vice chairperson Health and human servs. com., 1984-86, mem. state/fed. relations com., 1984-86, vice chairperson joint com. on adm. sessions, 1985, elected del. N.H. Constitutional Conv., 1984-94; mem. health and human resources com. Nat. Conf. State Legislatures, 1984-86. Pres., Chelmsford Friends of Library, 1973, Rep. Women's Club of Nashua, 1980-82; bd. dirs. N.H. Sch. Vols., 1980-85; mem. State Conf. on Aging-Social Services, 1981; pres. N.H. Fedn. Rep. Women, 1986—; mem. Nat. Fedn. Rep. Women (nominating com. 1987), Nashua Fedn. Rep. Women; pres., founder Nashua Friends of Library, 1982-83; mem. planning bd. City of Nashua, 1984—, mem. long range master plan com. 1984-94; active ARC Blood Bank, 1970-82. Served with Cadet Nurses Corps, 1945. Mem. Nat. Order Women Legislators, N.H. Order Women Legislators, Vis. Nurse Assn. (exec. bd. 1987). Roman Catholic. Clubs: Vesper Country, Women's Guild of Parish. Office: Legislative Office Bldg Concord NH 03301

CARRAGHER, TRACEY ANN, insurance company executive; b. Quantico, Va., July 29, 1955; d. Frank and Eunice (Burns) C.; m. Richard Bradway Hall, Apr. 30, 1982; 1 child, Shawn Michael Carragher Hall. BA, Cen. Conn. U., 1977. Sr. underwriter Aetna Casualty & Security, N.Y.C., 1977-78, Gen. Reins. Corp., Greenwich, Conn., 1978-79; research cons. McKinsey & Co., Greenwich, 1979; asst. v.p., sr. cons. Alexander & Alexander, Greenwich, 1980-82; v.p., nat. sales dir. Anistics Inc., Greenwich, 1982-84; v.p. Alexander & Alexander, Greenwich, 1984-86, sr. v.p., 1986—; commr. New Eng. Bd. Higher Edn., Boston, 1986—. Contbr. articles to profl. jours. Campaign dir. dist. 6 Rep. Nat. Com., 1979-80; policy dir. Rep. Town Com., Woodbury, Conn., 1980-84. Mem. Ins. Women Conn., Exec. Women N.Y., Mariners Club. Republican. Roman Catholic. Club: Long Ridge. Office: Alexander & Alexander Two Pickwick Plaza PO Box 1409 Greenwich CT 06836

CARRAWAY, BARBARA OLAH, controller; b. Norfolk, Va., Feb. 15, 1942; d. Mike and Myrtle (Cahoon) Olah; m. Kenneth L. Carraway, Aug. 26, 1967; 1 child, Morgan Paige. BSBA, Old Dominion U., 1981. CPA, Va. Office mgr. Va. Carolina Tire Co., Chesapeake, 1960-74, corp. sec., 1970-74; bookkeeper Goodman and Co., Norfolk, 1974, Value Fair, Norfolk, 1974-75; office mgr. Cen. Supplies, Chesapeake, 1975-83; acct. Tidewater Agricorp. Inc., Chesapeake, 1983-84, acctg. mgr., 1984-87, controller, 1986-87, corp. sec., 1982-87; dir. fin. City of Elizabeth City, N.C., 1987—. Mem. Am. Soc. Women Accts., Am. Inst. CPA's. Baptist.

CARRÉ, SARA MCDOWELL, information systems administrator; b. Lancaster, Pa., Apr. 29, 1950; d. Robert James and Louise (Pool) McDowell; m. Edwin V. Carré Jr., Jan. 23, 1982. BA, Temple U., 1971. Cert. tchr., Pa. Acct. U. Pa., Phila., 1979-81; asst. to the dir. Univ. Press (U. Pa.), Phila., 1981-82; analysis and rev. acct. U. Pa., Phila., 1982, supr. trust acctg., 1982-83, mgr. cen. gifts processing, 1983-84; asst. dir. info. systems Fox Chase Cancer Ctr., Phila., 1985-86, dir. adminstrv. systems, 1986-87, dir. ops. and gift planning, 1987—. Mem. Nat. Assn. Female Execs., Nat. Soc. Fund Raising Execs., Am. Mgmt. Assn. Presbyterian. Office: Fox Chase Cancer Ctr Devel Office 7701 Burholme Ave Philadelphia PA 19111

CARRICK, PATRICIA MANNIES, educator; b. Peru, Ind., July 3, 1955; d. Oscar Harvey and Rachel Jane (Enyart) Mannies; m. Floyd Gregory Carrick, Nov. 27, 1982; children: Jacqueline Michelle, Christina Renée. BS, Ball State U., 1977, MA, 1980. Tchr. coach Marion Community Schs., Ind., 1977-78; grad. asst. Ball State U., Muncie, Ind., 1978-79; tchr., coach girls' track and field North Newton Schs., Morocco, Ind., 1979-80, Vigo County Sch. Corp., Terre Haute, Ind., 1980—; asst. coach girls' track Terre Haute Track Club, 1981—. Coach girls' volleyball, Vigo County Schs. 1980-83, track & field, 1981-84. Mem. Am. Fedn. Tchrs. Republican. Methodist. Clubs: Prairieton Young Homemakers, Terre Haute Track. Avocations: running, needlecrafts, cycling, aerobics. Office: South Vigo High Sch 3737 S 7th St Terre Haute IN 47802

CARRICK, SUSAN LYNN, management consultant; b. Lynwood, Calif., Nov. 5, 1947; d. David Benjamin and Valerian Elizabeth (Pelzl) Griffith; 1 child, Byron James. BA, Ariz. State U., 1970. Tchr. Upward Bound Fedl. Project, Tempe, Ariz., 1970-71; mgr. Scarborough/ Neninger, Phoenix, 1973-75; acct. exec. UniService, Inc., Phoenix, 1974-86, exec. v.p., 1986—. Mem. Phoenix Planned Parenthood, 1985—, Ariz. Echo Program, Phoenix, 1986—. Mem. Phoenix Personnel Mgmt. Assn., Am. Soc. Personnel Assn. Democrat. Roman Catholic. Office: UniService Inc 320 E McDowell Phoenix AZ 85004

CARRINGTON, CONNIE KAY, engineering educator; b. San Antonio, Apr. 23, 1952; d. Howard and Yoshi Elizabeth (Kaneshiro) C.; m. Samuel S. Russell, Dec. 22, 1983. BA in Math., U. Rochester, 1974; MS, U. Va., 1979; PhD, Va. Poly. Inst., 1983. Programmer/analyst Pratt-Whitney Aircraft Corp., East Hartford, Conn., 1974-75; programmer/analyst U. Va. Research Labs., Charlottesville, 1975-77, research engr., 1978-79; engr. Sperry Marine Systems, Charlottesville, 1977-78; asst. prof. Gen. Motors Inst., Flint, Mich., 1984, U. S.C., Columbia, 1984—. Author papers in field. Mem. AIAA (control tech. com. 1985-87), Am. Astronautical Soc. (mng. editor Jour. Astronautical Scis. 1985—). Home: 330 Grantham Rd Irmo SC 29063 Office: Univ SC Dept Mech Engring Columbia SC 29208

CARROLL, ADORNA OCCHIALINI, real estate executive; b. New Britain, Conn., Aug. 24, 1952; d. Antonio and Mary Ida (Reney) Occhialini; m. Christoper P. Buchas, Sept. 7, 1974 (div. Nov. 1982); 1 child, Jenna Rebecca; m. John Francis Carroll, Oct. 15, 1983; children: Jordan Ashley, Sean William. BA in Philosophy, Cen. Conn. State U., 1974. Lic. real estate broker, Conn. Dir. therapeutic recreation program Ridgeview Rest Home, Cromwell, Conn., 1974, Meadows Convalescent Home, Manchester, Conn., 1975, Andrew House Health Care, New Britain, 1976; owner, mgr. Liquor Locker, Newington, Conn., 1977-87; owner, broker A.O. Carroll & Co., Newington, 1985—; ptnr. Marco Realty & Devel. Co., Newington, 1978—. Mem. Nat. Assn. Realtors, Conn. Assn. Realtors (com.), Greater New Britain Bd. Realtors (sec. 1988, chmn. polit. affairs. 1988), Nat. Package Store Assn., Conn. Package Store Assn. (legis. lobbyist 1984-88, pres. 1986-88, Disting. Service award 1985), Greater Hartford Package Store Assn. (pres. 1981-82), Newington C. of C. (bd. dirs. 1987-88, chmn. legis. 1988). Home: 22 Hickory Hill Ln Newington CT 06111 Office: 982 W Main St New Britain CT 06053

CARROLL, ANN FOLEY, retail manager; b. Fitchburg, Mass., Feb. 17, 1962; d. Bernard James and Martha Jane (Hazel) Foley; m. Charles Bernard Carroll, Oct. 5, 1986; 1 child, Shannon Foley. BA in English, U. N.H., 1985. Supr. mdse. div. Lenox, Inc., Kittery, Maine, 1985, asst. mgr., 1985-86, store mgr., 1986—. Active York Hist. Soc. Mem. Kittery Bus. Council, 1986—. Democrat. Roman Catholic. Home: 113 Cluff Crossing Rd Salem NH 03079

CARROLL, BARBARA ANNE, physician, educator; b. Beaumont, Tex., Oct. 20, 1945; d. Theron Demp and Annette Ione (Anderson) C.; m. Olaf T. von Ramm. BA, U. Tex., 1967; MD, Stanford U., 1972. Intern, Stanford Hosp., Palo Alto, Calif., 1972, resident, 1973-76; research asst. Genetics Found., U. Tex., Austin, 1963-67; teaching asst. NSF Summer Biology Workshop, Austin, 1967; clinician Planned Parenthood, Santa Clara, Calif.,

1973-76; instr. extension div. U. Calif.-Santa Cruz, 1972-76, asst. prof. radiology Stanford U. Med. Sch., Palo Alto, 1977-84, assoc. prof. radiology, 1984-85; chief diagnostic ultrasound, 1977-85; assoc. prof. radiology Duke U., Durham, N.C., 1985—; cons. Searle, Santa Clara, 1977-78, Diasonics, Inc., Santa Clara, 1979-83, NIH, 1981-84, Acuson, 1984—. Contbr. articles to various publs.; reviewer numerous med. jours., 1982—; assoc. editor Radiology journ, 1986—. Bd. dirs. Planned Parenthood Santa Clara County, 1975-76. Agnes Axtell Moule Faculty scholar, 1979-84; recipient Cancer and Med. Research Found. award, 1980. Fellow Am. Inst. Ultrasound in Medicine (bd. govs 1987—); mem. Soc. Radiologists in Ultrasound, Am. Coll. Radiology, Assn. Women Radiologists, Assn. Univ. Radiologists, Venezuelan Ultrasound Soc., N.C. Ultrasound Soc. (faculty adv. 1986—), Phi Beta Kappa. Democrat. Episcopalian. Office: Duke U Med Sch Dept Radiology Box 3808 Durham NC 27710

CARROLL, BONNIE, publisher, editor; b. Salt Lake City, Nov. 20, 1941. Grad. high sch., Ogden, Utah. Owner The Peer Group, San Francisco, 1976-78; pub., editor The Reel Directory, Cotati, Calif., 1978—. Pub., editor The Reel Thing newsletter, San Francisco, 1977-78. Mem. Assn. Visual Communicators (bd. dirs. 1987—), No. Calif. Women in Film, San Francisco Film Tape Council (exec. dir. 1979-81). Office: The Reel Directory PO Box 866 Cotati CA 94928

CARROLL, DIAHANN, actress, singer; b. N.Y.C., July 17, 1935; d. John and Mabel (Faulk) Johnson; m. Monte Kay (div.); m. Fredde Glusman (div.); m. Robert DeLean, 1975 (dec. 1977); m. Vic Damone, 1987. Student, N.Y. U. Began career as model; actress: motion pictures, including Claudine (Nominated for Acad. award as best actress by the Acad. Motion Picture Arts and Scis. 1974), Carmen Jones, Porgy and Bess, Hurry Sundown, Paris Blues, The Split; on Broadway in No Strings, House of Flowers; appeared in: play Same Time, Next Year; TV series Julia, Dynasty, 1984-87; TV movies I Know Why the Caged Bird Sings, 1979, Sister, Sister, 1982. Address: care Triad Artists 10100 Santa Monica Blvd 16th Floor Los Angeles CA 90067 *

CARROLL, DONNA, educator, reading specialist; b. Long Beach, N.Y., Nov. 4, 1943; d. A. Stephen and M. Theresa (Connolly) Von Glahn; m. James Carroll, Aug. 7, 1965 (div. 1985); children: James, Christopher. BA in Elem. Edn., Mt. St. Agnes Coll., Balt., 1965; postgrad. Alaska Methodist U., 1967; MS in Reading, Adelphi U., N.Y., 1972, postgrad., 1985; postgrad. U. Valencia, Spain, 1981, Western Ill. U., 1985, Emmanuel Coll., Boston, 1985-86; profl. diploma in ednl. adminstn. and leadership, 1987, Post U., Greenvale, N.Y. Cert. educator, adminstr. N.Y. Tchr. remedial reading Long Beach Jr. High Sch., 1965-66; tchr. English, MacArthur Elem. Sch., El Paso, Tex., 1966-67; tchr. John F. Kennedy Elem. Sch., Anchorage, 1966-67; tchr. reading and writing Island Park Pub. Schs., N.Y., 1967-85; adult edn. tchr. Oceanside Pub. Schs., N.Y., 1978-79; educator Sewanhaka High Sch. Dist., L.I., N.Y., 1985-87; adminstrv. intern Elmont Meml. High Sch., L.I., 1986-87. Mem. parent adv. com. Island Park Schs., 1977-79; coordinator March of Dimes Reading Olympics, 1980-84; sec. Barnum Island Civic Assn., 1982-84; judge N.Y. State Am. Legion Aux. Scholarship, 1984. Mem. NEA, N.Y. State Tchrs. Assn., Sewanhaka Central High Sch. Dist. Profl. Assn. Republican. Roman Catholic. Avocations: collecting antiques, Hummel figurines, Lladro figurines, collector plates.

CARROLL, JEANNE, public relations executive; b. Oak Park, Ill., May 20, 1929; d. John P. and Mary (Noonan) Carroll; B.A., U. London, 1950; M.A., Northwestern U., 1951; m. Harold M. Kass, Apr. 1966. Bus. girls editor Charm Mag., N.Y.C., 1951-53; pub. relations dir. Rosary Coll., River Forest, Ill., 1953-66; chmn. publicity Am. Cancer Soc., bd. dirs. W. and S.W. Suburban Unit, 1967—; med. adminstr., asst. to Dr. Harold Kass, Oak Park, Ill., 1969—. Pub. relations counselor in Midwest for Brown U., 1962; dir. pub. relations Mundelein Coll., 1968; producer radio show for teen-agers, Chgo., 1954; lectr. sci. devels. Bell Labs. for AT&T, 1954; participant annual Sun-Times seminars for coll. journalists MacMurray Coll., Jacksonville Ill. Chmn., March of Dimes campaign for Chgo., ednl. TV Channel 11, River Forest, 1963; trustee DePaul U., Chgo., chmn. Soc. Fellows dinner; chmn. Oak Park Hosp. Ben Din Dan, 1971-80; mem. com. library Internat. Relations, 1975-82; mem. bd. Arden Shores, sch. for boys, 1984—. Recipient Excellence award for coll. brochures Am. Coll. Pubs. Com., 1957; medal of recognition for work in pub. relations Bishop Fulton Sheen, 1960; Humanitarian award Performing Arts Ctr. and Citizens Com., Chgo., 1976; award DuSalbe Mus., 1978. Mem. Ill. Assn. Coll. Admissions Counsellors (pres.), Assn. Coll. Pub. Relations Assn., Family Service Assn. Am. (past dir.), Acad. Hosp., Pub. Relations, Ill. (pres.), Chgo. (pub. relations dir., med. soc. auxs.), Oak Park Hosp. (pres. women's aux. 1986—), West Suburban Hosp. Med. Ctr. Aux. (life). Mailing Address: 712 Courtland Circle Springdale Western Springs IL 60558 Office: 715 Lake St Oak Park IL 60301

CARROLL, KATRINA, media consultant; b. Cin., Sept. 18, 1949; d. James Robert and Vergie Ellen (Liford) C.; m. Aaron Klein, Nov. 23, 1986. BA magna cum laude, Fordham U., 1983. Lic. horseback riding instr, Mass. Naturalist Ponkapoag Outdoor Ctr., Boston, 1976-80; affiliate relations Home Box Office, N.Y.C., 1980-83; media mgr. Integrated Resources, N.Y.C., 1983-86; pres. Katrina Carroll, Inc., N.Y.C., 1986—. Co-producer: (cable pilot) Mind Mysteries, 1982, What's Up?, 1982. Mem. Nat. Coalition for Homeless, N.Y.C., 1986—. Mem. Bus. Circuit N.Y.C., Nat. Assn. Exec. Females, Nat. Geog. Soc., Sierra Club, World Future Soc. (mem. com. 1986-87), Phi Kappa Phi. Democrat. Jewish. Club: The Wine Bistro (N.Y.C.). Home and Office: 80 Park Ave Suite 11K New York NY 10016

CARROLL, KIM MARIE, nurse; b. Ottawa, Ill., Feb. 13, 1958; d. John J. and Charin E. (Reilley) Marmion; m. Thomas Christopher Carroll, Aug. 25, 1979; 1 child, Christopher John. B.S.N., U. Denver, 1983; diploma Copley Meml. Hosp. Sch. Nursing, Aurora, Ill., 1979. R.N., Ill., Colo.; critical care practitioner. Staff nurse Penrose Hosp., Colorado Springs, Colo., 1979-83, asst. head nurse cardiac floor, 1983-84; asst. dir. nurses Big Meadows Nursing Home, Savanna, Ill., 1985-86, dir. nurses, 1986—. Mem. Women in Mgmt., Nat. Assn. for Female Execs., Am. Cancer Soc. (v.p. Carroll County , Ill., 1988—, pub. edn. chmn. 1987—), Beta Sigma Phi (chpt. pres. 1988-89), Sigma Theta Tau. Roman Catholic. Avocation: skiing. Home: 1709 Michigan Ave Savanna IL 61074 Office: Big Meadows Nursing Home 1000 Longmoor Ave Savanna IL 61074

CARROLL, LOIS MAE, nurse; b. Scranton, Pa., Oct. 29, 1929; d. Robert George and Mae Fietta (Richards) Fenstermacher; R.N., L.I. Sch. Nursing, Southampton, 1951; B.S. in Nursing, U. Ala., 1976, M.A., 1978; m. Joseph C. Carroll, Jan. 13, 1950; children—Joseph, Jeffrey, Robert. Staff nurse Crestwood Hosp., Huntsville, Ala., 1966-70; supr. occupational health Dunlop Tire & Rubber Co., Huntsville, 1970-78; student health coordinator No. Va. Community Coll., Manassas, 1978—, also adj. prof., chmn. coll. health and safety com.; CPR and first aid instr. Mem. Am. Assn. Occupational Health Nurses, Am. Coll. Health Assn., Bus. and Profl. Women's Club (dist. dir. 1973), Manassas Olde Town Assn., Alpha Lambda Delta. Republican. Unitarian. Home: 9301 Grant Ave Manassas VA 22110 Office: 6901 Sudley Rd Manassas VA 22110

CARROLL, MARGARET WADE, health care public relations administrator, consultant; b. Pottsville, Pa., Sept. 1, 1936; d. Lawrence Francis and Thelma Elizabeth (McCormick) W.; m. Maurice C. Carroll, Sept. 8, 1956 (div. 1976); children: Michael, Elizabeth, Eileen, Patrick. AB in English, Coll. of St. Elizabeth, 1977. Reporter The Herald-News, Passaic, N.J., 1956-57, The Daily Record, Parsippany, N.J., 1962-82; dir. pub. relations Morristown (N.J.) Meml. Hosp., 1982—. Trustee Morris County Assn. for the Retarded, Morris Plains, N.J., 1982-83; sec. Morris County Fair Housing Council, Morristown, 1966-67, also founding mem.; adv. Explorer post, Morristown, 1984—. Recipient 1st Place award N.J. Press Assn., 1967, 2d place award N.J. Press Assn., 1978, Disting. Service to Edn. award Morris County Edn. Assn., 1973. Mem. N.J. Hosp. Pub. Relations and Mktg. Assn. Home: 14 Symor Dr Convent Station NJ 07961 Office: Morristown Meml Hosp 100 Madison Ave Morristown NJ 07960

CARROLL, MARYBETH ANN, mortgage service executive; b. Magnolia, N.J., Nov. 3, 1953; d. Donald David and Irene Gertrude (Murray) C. Diploma, Rutgers Bus. Inst., 1975. Asst. office mgr. Edmund Sci., Barrington, N.J., 1972-75; asst. adminstr. Hub Beer Distbrs., Camden, N.J., 1975-86; mortgage service rep., loan officer Travelers Mortgage Services, Mt Laurel, N.J., 1986-88, sr. loan officer, 1988—. Mem. Sales and Mktg. Council of Builders League of S. Jersey, Travelers Mortgage Services Million Dollar Club. Roamn Catholic. Home: 142 Evesham Ave Magnolia NJ 08049

CARROLL, MOLLY PATRICIA, newspaper executive; b. Decatur, Ill., Sept. 29, 1957; d. H.D. Jr. and Carolyn (Kimball) Greider. BS in Mktg., U. Ill., 1979. Trainee circulation sales mgmt. Chgo. Tribune, 1979-80; dir. planning and mktg. Herald and Review, Decatur, Ill., 1980-83, mgr. advt. zone, 1983-84; dir. newspaper sales and promotions Lee Enterprises, Davenport, Iowa, 1984-88; pub. Muscatine (Iowa) Jour. subs Lee Enterprises, 1988—. Mem. task force Roy J. Carver Charitable Trust "Excellence in Edn.," devel. com. Quad City YMCA, 1986-87; bd. dirs. Quad City Arts Council, Rock Island, Ill., 1986—, Muscatine United Way, Muscatine Devel. Corp. Mem. Internat. Newspaper Advt.-Mktg. Execs., Newspaper Advt. Coop. Network, C. of C. (exec. com. cen. bus. dist., restructuring com.). Republican. Roman Catholic. Office: Muscatine Jour 301 E 3d St Muscatine IA 52761

CARROLL, PATRICIA MARY, marketing and sales executive; b. N.Y.C., Dec. 5, 1939; d. Patrick Michael and Bridget Patricia (Ginnelly) Curran; m. Thomas Michael Carroll, Jan. 26, 1963; children: Matthew Thomas, Jeanne Anastasia. BS, Fordham U., 1961; MS, Coll. New Rochelle, 1975; postgrad., NYU, 1972, CUNY, 1983—. Cert. tchr. spl. edn. and English, N.Y. Exec. confidential sec. N.Y. Daily News, 1961-66; tchr. White Plains (N.Y.) Adult Edn. Ctr. and Westchester Devel. Ctr., 1975; asst. dir. nursing and allied health edn. March of Dimes Birth Defects Found., White Plains, 1976-84; sales/mktg. mgr. Stoffel Seals Corp., Nyack, N.Y., 1984-87; mgr. mktg. McGraw-Hill, N.Y.C. and Washington, 1988—; copy editor Pergamon Press, Elmsford, N.Y., 1979; editor texts Appleton-Century-Crofts. Assoc. editor The First Six Hours of Life series, 1978-82, Prenatal Care series, 1978-82, 1978-85, Intrapartal Care series, 1980-82, The Birth Defects Original Article Series, 3 vols., 1984; editor: Concepts of Human Development (B. Raff and C. Windwer); contbr. articles to profl. jours. and newspapers. Legis. adv. com. N.Y. State Assembly, 1980-84; mem. Mamaroneck (N.Y.) Beautification Com., 1983; nominating com. for assoc. mems. Internat. Festivals Assn., 1986-87. Coll. scholar, 1957. Mem. Women In Communications (program com. 1983-86), Women's Nat. Book Assn., AAUW. Roman Catholic. Home: 171 Maple Ave Mamaroneck NY 10543 Office: McGraw-Hill Book Co Healthcare Info Ctr 1221 Ave of Americas New York NY 10020

CARROLL, PATRICIA V., child care center owner; b. Balt., June 26, 1951; d. Nelson and Gladys (Moore) Jones; m. Raymond L. Carroll; 1 child, Marcus Andre. Child care cert., Brookhaven Coll. Acct., analyst Arco Oil & Gas Co ., Dallas, 1973-87; owner, dir. Wee Care 24 Hour Child Care and Richland Acad. Day Sch., Dallas, 1987—; cons. child care C.A.P.E. Program. Mem. Millcreek Homeowners Assn., Dallas, 1985—, Nat. Polit. Congress of Women, 1984—. Recipient Significant Achievement award, Black Women Entrepreneurs, Dallas, 1988, Profl. Adminstr. Credential, Child Care Mgmt. Services, Austin, 1988. Mem. Dallas Womens Found., Nat. Assn. Female Execs., Top Ladies of Distinction, Tex. Assn. Child Care Adminstrs., Child Care Partnership. Baptist. Lodge: Order of the Eastern Star (assoc. matron 1986-88).

CARROLL, PATRICIA WHITEHEAD, computer company executive; b. Tallahassee, Fla., Oct. 20, 1954; d. Albert and Lucinda (Brown) Whitehead; m. Napoleon A. Carroll, May 28, 1979 (div. 1985). BS cum laude in Psychology, Bethune-Cookman Coll., 1977. Records supr. State Farm Ins. Co., Winter Haven, Fla., 1977-79; ins. agt. Pat Carroll Ins. Agy., Orlando, Fla., 1979-82; dir. mktg. Systems Support Corp., Washington, 1982-85, v.p., 1985—. Recipient Youth Day Appreciation award City of Titusville, 1976, Millionaire Club award State Farm Ins. Co., 1981, Million Dollar Round Table award State Farm Ins. Co., 1979, others. Mem. Nat. Assn. Female Execs., Am. Mgmt. Assn., Delta Sigma Theta. Democrat. Avocations: reading, coin and stamp collecting, outdoor sports. Office: Systems Support Corp 1140 Connecticut Ave NW Suite 120 Washington DC 20036

CARROLL, PATSY HOUSE, nurse, consultant; b. Hope, Ark., June 15, 1940; d. William Cicero and Ida Lorine (Belk) House; m. Henry C. Carroll ; children: Steven, Mark, Patti. RN, Gilfoy Sch. Nursing, Jackson, Miss., 1961; BSN, U. Miss., Jackson, 1976; MN, U. Miss., 1979. Staff nurse Miss. Bapt. Hosp., Jackson, 1961-62; office nurse Pyle-Walden Clin., Plain, Miss., 1962; occupational health nurse Jackson Tile Mfg. Co., Flowood, Miss., 1962-64; part-time staff nurse Hinds Gen. Hosp., Jackson, 1965-66; part-time office nurse Ball-Pittman Clin. for Women, Jackson, 1974-75; instr. U. Miss., 1976-82, asst. prof. nursing, 1982-85; ptnr. Profl. Nurse Cons., Inc., Jackson, 1985—; cons. continuing edn. Miss. Nurses Assn., Jackson, 1985—. Contbr. articles to profl. jours. Com. chmn. S. Jackson Civic League, 1974-82. Mem. An. Nurses Assn. (council on continuing edn.), Miss. Nurses Assn. (continuing edn. com. chmn. 1983-85), Nurse Cons., U. Miss. Alunmi Assn., U. Miss. Guardian Soc. Baptist. Home: 4001 Venus Ave Jackson MS 39212 Office: Profl Nurse Cons Inc PO Box 16874 360 Comet Dr Suite E Jackson MS 39236

CARROLL, PAULA MARIE, security company executive; b. Fresno, Calif., July 17, 1933; d. Paul Edward Mikkelsen and Helen Marie (Anderson) Mack; m. Herman S. Carroll Jr., April 25, 1954. V.p., co-owner Cen. Valley Alarm Co., Inc., Merced, Calif., 1963—. Author: Life Wish, 1986. Mem. Hospice of Merced and Mariposa Counties, Calif., 1979; pres., founder Consumers for Med. Quality Inc., Merced, 1981; chair Ombudsman, Merced, 1982-85. Recipient Celebrating Women award Merced County, 1987, Pres.'s award Calif. Trial Lawyers Assn., 1987; named Woman Distinction Soroptimist Internat., 1986; Consumers for Med. Quality grantee Calif. Trial Lawyers Assn., 1987. Mem. Western Burglar and Fire Alarm Assn., Soc. Law and Medicine, Hastings Ctr. Inst. of Soc., Nat. Assn. Female Execs. Home: 3271 ALder Ave Merced CA 95340 Office: Cen Valley Alarm Co Inc 620 W 14th St Merced CA 95340

CARROLL, RUTH LISA, manufacturing company executive; b. N.Y.C., June 7, 1962; d. Frank Louis and Veronica Karina (Valkama) C. BA in Bus. Adminstrn., CCNY, 1984. Gen. mgr. Alnoor Comml. Services Co., N.Y.C., 1984-86; chief exec. officer Alnoor Wind Systems Inc., N.Y.C., 1986—; venture fundraiser Alnoor Comml. Services, 1984-87. Mem. Am. Wind Energy Assn., Nat. Assn. Female Execs. Office: Alnoor Wind Systems Inc 48-55 43d St Woodside NY 11377

CARR-SHEPHERD, CONSTANCE, psychotherapist; b. Abington, Pa., July 8, 1932; d. Charles Lawyer and Catherine (Lee) Rines; m. Leslie McNari Carr, Sept. 3, 1956 (div. 1968); children: Mark Carr, Gary Carr; m. David Gwynne Shepherd, July 18, 1975. BA, Hunter Coll., 1955; MA, NYU, 1969; cert. in marriage and family therapy, Blanton Peale Inst., N.Y.C., 1985. Grad. faculty Bank St. Coll. Edn., N.Y.C., 1968-71; dir. tng. Agy. for Child Devel., N.Y.C., 1971-73; exec. dir. The Tchrs., Inc., N.Y.C., 1973-78; spl. asst. mayor's office City of New York, 1978-79; dir. tng. Ednl. Planning Inst., N.Y.C., 1980-81; adj. prof. Coll. New Rochelle, N.Y., 1982—; psychotherapist Riverside Ch. Pastoral Counseling Ctr., N.Y.C., 1984—. Chmn. bd. dirs. Africa's Friends in Am., 1973; deacon 1st Presbyn. Ch., N.Y.C., 1975—. Nat. Assn. Intergroup Relations Ofcls. Eleanor Roosevelt fellow, 1965. Mem. Am. Assn. for Marriage and Family Therapy (clin.), Nat. Assn. for Female Execs. Democrat. Home: 2 Washington Square Village New York City NY 10012 Office: Riverside Ch Pastoral Counseling Ctr 490 Riverside Dr New York City NY 10027

CARSEY, MARCIA LEE PETERSON, television producer; b. South Weymouth, Mass., Nov. 21, 1944; d. John Edwin and Rebecca White (Simonds) Peterson; m. John Jay Carsey, Apr. 12, 1969; children: Rebecca Peterson, John Peterson. B.A. in English Lit., U. N.H., 1966. Exec. story editor Tomorrow Entertainment, Los Angeles, 1971-74; sr. v.p. prime time series ABC-TV, Los Angeles, 1978-81; founder Carsey Prodns., Los Angeles, 1981; co-owner Carsey-Werner Co., 1982—; co-exec. producer TV series Oh Madeline, 1983; exec. producer The Cosby Show, 1984—, A Different World, 1987—. Office: Carsey-Werner Co 4024 Radford Ave Studio City CA 91064

CARSKADDEN, SUSAN ANN, accountant; b. Kirkland, Wash., July 20, 1941; d. Richard W. and Clella (Jacklin) Graham; m. William H. Carskadden, Mar. 10, 1962 (div. Mar 1972); children: Carolyn, Heather, Jay. Student, U. Wash., 1959-60, 70-72, Boise State U., 1974-76, Whitworth Coll., 1980-82. Exec. sec. Morrison-Knudsen Co., Boise, Idaho, 1974-76; asst. to pres. Neil F. Lampson Inc., Kennewick, Wash., 1976-78; asst. to project mgr. Fischbach/Lord JV, Richland, Wash., 1978-80; asst. nuclear contracts Fischbach & Moore, Satsop, Wash., 1980-82; adminstr. nuclear contracts Ebasco Services, Seattle, 1982-85, Santa Ana, Calif., 1985-87; acct. L.K. Comstock Co., Long Beach, Calif., 1987—. Mem. Am. Arbitration Assn. (arbitrator), Long Beach Convention and Visitors Council, Inc. Club: Independent (Long Beach). Home: 1000 E Ocean Blvd Apt 6 Long Beach CA 90802

CARSON, BONNIE L(OU), chemist; b. Kansas City, Kans., Aug. 11, 1940; d. Harold Lee and Lorene Marie (Draper) Bachert; student U. Kansas City, 1958-61; B.A. in Chemistry summa cum laude, U. N.H., 1963; M.S. in Organic Chemistry, Oreg. State U., 1966; m. David M. Carson, June, 1961 (div. 1973); 1 dau., Catherine (Katie) Leslie. Grad. teaching asst. Oreg. State U., 1963-66; organic chem. lab. instr. U. Waterloo, Ont., Can., 1968-69; asst. abstractor in macromolecular chemistry Chem. Abstracts Service, Columbus, Ohio, 1969-71; freelance Russian translator, 1971-73; asst. chemist Midwest Research Inst., Kansas City, Mo., 1973-75, assoc. chemist, 1975-80, sr. chemist, 1980—. Mem. Am. Soc. Info. Scientists, Am. Chem. Soc., N.Y. Acad. Sci., Soc. Environ. Geochemistry and Health, Am. Translators Assn. (pres. Mid-Am. chpt. 1984-85), Soc. Tech. Communication. Author and Editor: (with others) Trace Metals in the Environment, 1977-81, Toxicology and Biological Monitoring of Metals in Humans, 1986; contbr. in field. Home: 5501 Holmes St Kansas City MO 64110 Office: 425 Volker Blvd Kansas City MO 64110

CARSON, DONITA FAYE, accountant; b. Tell City, Ind., Oct. 10, 1956; d. Donald Henry and Naomi Faye (Richard) Cassidy; m. David Earl Carson, Dec. 27, 1975; children: David Jason, Jamie Kristine. BS in Acctg., U. So. Ind., 1983; cert. in Real Estate, Ind. U., 1984. Realtor Hollinden Realty, Tell City, 1985-87, Key Assocs., Tell City, 1987—; acct. Consol. Refineries, Troy, Ind., 1986—; substitute tchr. Tell City Sch. Corp., 1981—; lectr. Weight Watchers Kentuckiana, Louisville, 1982-84; owner Pure Water Perry County, Tell City, 1985—. Mem. Prime Time Com., Tell City, 1984—; bd. dirs., treas. Tot-Lots Inc., Tell City, 1984-85. Mem. Nat. Assn. Female Execs., Womens Bus. Initiative, Perry County League Woman Voters, Beta Sigma Phi (Woman of Yr. 1986), Mu Gamma. Lutheran. Club: Hoosier Heights Country (Tell City) (chmn. 1985, auctioneer 1984-86). Home: Box 6 Jonick Rd Tell City IN 47586 Office: Consol Refineries Inc 8 Commerce Dr PO Box 55 Troy IN 47588

CARSON, ELIZABETH HILL, civic worker; b. Des Moines, Apr. 21, 1928; d. Lee Forrest and Marian (Robbins) Hill; m. John Congleton Carson, Feb. 14, 1954; children—Elizabeth, John, Lee Hill, David, Barbara. B.A., Vassar Coll., 1950; J.D., U. Pa., 1953. Bar: Iowa 1953, U.S. Dist. Ct. (so. dist.) Iowa 1953. Atty., trust dept. Fidelity-Phila. Trust Co., Phila., 1954-55; pres. Jr. League San Diego, 1967-68, mem., 1960—, sustaining advisor community service council, bd. dirs. 1988—; founding trustee U. Calif.-San Diego Med. Aux., 1967-70; mem. Vassar Club San Diego, 1960—, pres., 1962-64; mem. La Jolla High Sch. PTA, 1970-84, pres., 1973-75; pres. La Jolla Civic Ctr. Corp., 1977—; trustee Francis Parker Sch., 1969-84; trustee Children's Health Ctr., 1970-72, La Jolla Country Day Sch., 1982-85; bd. govs. San Diego Community Found., 1982-87, corp. sec., 1982-84 ; founding dir. LEAD San Diego, 1980-87, adv. bd., 1987—; founding dir. EXCEL, 1983—; mem. State Calif. Judicial Selection Com. for San Diego County, 1966-74; mem. Las Patronas, 1970—; mem. child guidance adv. bd. Children's Health Ctr., 1969—; mem. bd. visitors U. San Diego Law Sch., 1974—; mem. San Diego Unified Schs. Racial Integration Monitoring Task Force and Program Quality Rev. Team; mem. acad. affairs com. U. San Diego; mem. task force on discipline San Diego Unified Sch. Dist., 1980-81, mem. task force on grad. requirements, 1981-84, mem. equity placement oversight com., 1985—; bd. dirs. San Diego chpt. ARC, 1985—; tax preparer H&R Block, 1986—. Mem. ABA, Iowa Bar Assn., San Diego County Bar Assn. Republican. Clubs Vassar (past pres.), La Jolla Beach and Tennis, Wednesday. Home: 1703 Soledad Ave La Jolla CA 92037

CARSON, JULIA M., state legislator; b. Louisville, July 8, 1938; 2 children. Ed. Ind. U., 1960-62, St. Mary of the Woods, 1976-78. Mem. In. Ho. of Reps., Indpls., 1972-76; mem. Ind. Senate, 1976—. Vice pres. Greater Indpls. Prog. Com.; nat. Democratic committeewoman; trustee YMCA; bd. dirs. Pub. Service Acad. Recipient Woman of Yr. Ind. award, 1974; Outstanding Leadership award AKA; Humanitarian award Christian Theol. Sem. Mem. NAACP, Urban League, Nat. Council Negro Women. Baptist. Office: Ind Senate State Capitol Indianapolis IN 46205 also: 2530 N Park Ave Indianapolis IN 46205 *

CARSON, LILLIAN G., psychotherapist; b. N.Y.C., Mar. 22, 1933; d. Joseph and Helen E. (Tucker) Gershenson; m. Ralph Carson, July 19, 1978 (dec. June 1983), children from previous marriage—Susan Gevirtz, Steven Gevirtz, Carrie Gevirtz; m. Sam T. Hurst, Dec. 11, 1984. BA, UCLA, 1968, MSW, 1970, DSW, 1979. Lic. clin. social worker, Calif. Psychotherapist parent-infant consultation program, dept. child psychiatry Cedars Sinai Hosp., Los Angeles, 1970; dir. counseling Zahm Sch. Individual Edn., Los Angeles, 1970-72; dir. clinic Los Angeles Psychoanalytic Soc., 1972-82; pvt. practice psychotherapy, Los Angeles, 1970—; case supr. So. Calif. Counseling Ctr.; instr. Calif. State Mental Health Tng. Ctr.; exec. com. dean's council UCLA Sch. Social Welfare, field instr., 1986-87; cons. Santa Monica Child Devel. Ctrs.; mem. exec. com., sec.-treas. Psychiat. Med. Group So. Calif., 1973-74; mem. profl. bd. Los Angeles County Mental Health Assn., 1974; bd. dirs. Friends of UCLA Child Care Services, 1981, adv. council; mem. adv. council Los Angeles Child Devel. Ctr., 1981-82; staff mem. Westwood Psychiat. Hosp.; invited guest 20th birthday celebration meetings Hempstead Clinic, London, 1972, participant seminar by Anna Freud, 1978. Fellow Calif. Soc. Clin. Social Work (nominating com. 1974-77), Am. Orthopsychiat. Assn.; mem. Ctr. Improvement of Child Caring, Nat. Assn. Social Workers, Acad. Cert. Social Workers, Nat. Assn. Edn. of Young Children.

CARSON, MARGARET MARIE, gas industry executive, marketing professional; b. Windber, Pa., Dec. 30, 1944; d. Peter and Margaret (Olenik) Buben; m. Claude Carson, Dec. 30, 1967 (div. 1974); m. Brian Charles Scruby, June 6, 1975; stepchildren: Debbie, Victor, Chris, Kenneth. BA, U. Pitts., 1971; MS in Mgmt., Houston Bapt. U., 1985. Petroleum analyst Gulf Oil Co., Pitts., 1973-75, crude oil analyst, 1971-74, environ. coordinator, 1974-79, mgr. oil acquistition, Houston, 1980-84, mktg. dir., 1985; sales dir. Cabot Cons. Group, Houston, 1985-86; dir. competitor analysis, Enron Corp., Houston, 1987—; adj. prof. bus tech. Houston Community Coll., 1985—. Columnist: The Collegian, 1984-85; contbr. to Cathedral Poets, 1976. Mem. Young Reps., Houston, 1980-85; sponsor Classical Guitar Soc., Houston; bd. dirs. Indiana U., Pa., 1980-81. Mem. Internat. Energy Analysts, Gas Processors Assn. (speaker tech. session 1985-86), Nat. Assn. Female Execs. Club: Univ.

CARSON, MARY SILVANO, educator, counselor; b. Mass., Aug. 11, 1925; d. Joseph and Alice V. (Sherwood) Silvano; m. Paul E. Carson, Feb. 21, 1947 (dec.); children: Jan Ellen, Jeffrey Paul, Amy Jayne. BS, Simmons Coll., Boston, 1947; MA, U. Chgo., 1961; postgrad., Ctr. Urban Studies, 1970, U. Chgo., 1970, 72, U. Minn., 1977, DePaul U., Chgo., 1980. Cert. sch. and employment counselor, Ill. Mgr. S.W. Youth Opportunity Ctr., Dept. Labor, Chgo., 1966-67; careers' counselor Gordon Tech. High Sch., Chgo., 1971-74; dir. Career and Assessment Ctr., YMCA Community Coll., Chgo., 1974-81; project coordinator Career Ctr., Loop Coll., Chgo., 1981-82; adv. bd. City-Wide Coll. Career Ctr. Bd. dirs. Loop YWCA, Chgo. Mem. Women's Share in Pub. Service (v.p.), Am. Ednl. Research Assn., Am. Counseling and Devel. Assn., Nat. Vocat. Guidance Assn., Pi Lambda Theta (chpt. pres. 1975). Club: Bus. and Profl. Women's. Home: 1050 North Point Fontana W San Francisco CA 94109

CARSON, TERESA SUE, journalist; b. Auburn, Wash., May 18, 1953; d. David Samuel and Myra Kathryn (Garner) C. BA, Vassar Coll., 1975. Asst. buyer, mgr. Macy's, N.Y.C., 1975-77; reporter Am. Banker, N.Y.C.,

1977-84; corr. Bus. Week, Los Angeles, 1984—. Vol. Downtown Women's Ctr., Los Angeles, 1985—. Democrat. Office: Business Week 3333 Wilshire Blvd Los Angeles CA 90010

CARSON, VIRGINIA HILL, oil and gas executive; b. Los Angeles, Dec. 4, 1928; d. Percy Albert McCord and Flora May (Newkirk) Schultz; m. John Carson, Dec. 30, 1950 (dec.). BA in Internat. Relations, U. Calif., Berkeley, 1949; postgrad. Stanford U., 1948, UCLA, 1951. Gen. office worker UN, San Francisco, 1949; ind. oil and gas profl., U.S., Can., Cuba, 1953-73; supr., specialist Sun Exploration & Prodn. Co., Dallas, 1978-83, profl. analyst, 1983—. Mem. Dallas Council World Affairs, 1984, Dallas Mus. Fine Arts, 1984. Nominated to Pres.'s Council Am. Inst. Mgmt., N.Y.C., 1974. Mem. Internat. Platform Assn., Altrusa Internat. Office: Sun Exploration Prodn Co PO Box 2880 Dallas TX 75221

CARSTEN, ARLENE DESMET, financial executive; b. Paterson, N.J., Dec. 5, 1937; d. Albert F. and Ann (Greutert) Desmet; m. Alfred John Carsten, Feb. 11, 1956; children: Christopher Dale, Jonathan Glenn. Student Alfred U., 1955-56. Exec. dir. Inst. for Burn Medicine, San Diego, 1972-81, adv. bd. mem., 1981—; founding trustee, bd. dirs. Nat. Burn Fedn., 1975-83; chief fin. officer A.J. Carsten Co. Inc., San Diego, 1981—. Contbr. articles to profl. jours. Organizer, mem. numerous community groups; chmn. San Diego County Mental Health Adv. Bd., 1972-74, mem., 1971-75; chmn. community relations subcom., mem. exec. com. Emergency Med. Care Com., San Diego, Riverside and Imperial Counties, 1973-75; pub. mem. psychology exam. com. calif. State Bd. Med. Quality Assurance, 1976-80, chmn., 1977; mem. rep. to Health Services Agy. San Diego County Govt., 1980; mem. Calif. Dem. Cen. Com., 1968-74, exec. com., 1971-72, 73-74; treas. San Diego Dem. County Cen. Com., 1972-74; chmn. edn. for legislation com. women's div. So. Calif. Dem. Com., 1972; dir. Muskie for Pres. Campaign, San Diego, 1972; organizer, dir. numerous local campaigns; councilwoman City of Del Mar, Calif., 1982-86, mayor, 1985-86; bd. dirs. Gentry-Watts Planned Indsl. Devel. Assn., 1986—, pres., 1987—; commencement speaker Alfred U., 1984. Recipient Key Woman award Dem. Party, 1968, 72, 1st Ann. Community award Belles for Mental Health, Mental Health Assn. San Diego, 1974, citation Alfred U. Alumni Assn., 1979. Mem. Am. Burn Assn., Nat. Fire Protection Assn. Home: 1415 Via Alta Del Mar CA 92014 Office: 6711 Nancy Ridge Dr San Diego CA 92121

CARSTENSEN, CAROL JEAN, state agency administrator; b. Cleve., Jan. 31, 1943; d. Herman Samuel and Rose (Offner) Schneider; m. Peter C. Carstensen, July 14, 1968; children: Mary, Jean, Daniel, Steven. BA with honors, U. Wis., 1965, M in Pub. Adminstrn., 1986; M in Teaching, Yale U., 1967. Caseworker Cuyahoga County Welfare, Cleve., 1966; tchr. New Haven (Conn.) Pub. Schs., 1966-68, Washington Pub. Schs., 1968-71; instr. Madison (Wis.) Area Tech. Coll., 1974-83; policy analyst Dept. Industry Labor and Human Relations, Madison, 1986-87, Dept. Health and Social Services, Madison, 1988—. Pres. Elem. Parent Group, Madison, 1981-82, 83-84, Mid. Sch. Parent Group, 1985-87, founder; founder, steering com., Citywide Parent Group, Madison, 1984-87. Recipient Outstanding Performance award State of Wis., 1986. Mem. LWV (unit pres. Dane County 1978-80). Home: 720 Orton Ct Madison WI 53703

CARSWELL, CAROL FRANCES, finance director; b. Bklyn., Mar. 5, 1939; d. Jacob S. and Shirley (Brecher) Rubin; m. Howard L. Carswell, Oct. 8, 1972. AAS in Secretarial Skills, Bklyn. Coll., 1959, BA in Econs., 1968; MS in Edn., St. John's U., 1973; postgrad., Queens Coll., 1979-80. Asst. credit mgr., bookkeeper Arista Trading Co., N.Y.C., 1958-59; exec. sec. Lehn and Fink Products Corp., N.Y.C., 1959-61; office mgr., legal sec. Vladeck, Elias, Vladeck, and Engelhard, N.Y.C., 1961-66; tchr. City of N.Y., 1967-72, 1975-76, Farmingdale (N.Y.) High Sch., 1972-73; staff acct. Holtz, Rubenstein & Co., CPA's, Melville, N.Y., 1979-81; pvt. practice acct. Sebastian, Fla., 1982-84; fin. dir. City of Sebastian, 1984—. bd. dirs. Sebastian Area County Library, 1983-84; treas., bd. dirs. ARC, Indian River County, Fla., 1984-85. Mem. Fla. Govt. Fin. Officers Assn., Fla. Mcpl. Treas.'s Assn. (bd. dirs.). Club: Pilot of Sebastian River (area treas.). Office: City of Sebastian PO Box 780127 Sebastian FL 32978

CART, PAULINE HARMON, minister, educator; b. Jamestown, Ky., Nov. 3, 1914; d. Preston L. and Frances L. (Sullivan) Harmon; m. William C. Cart, July 3, 1936; children—Charles W., David N. BS Berea Coll., 1955; MA U. Mich.-Ann Arbor, 1957, postgrad., 1957; postgrad. Ea. Mich. U., 1957, Nanjing Coll. Traditional Medicine, 1987. Cert. Tuina instr. Mgr., owner Gen. Store, Beattyville, Ky., 1936-41; def. worker Gen. Motors, Dayton, Ohio, 1941-46; tchr. Ann Arbor Pub. Schs., 1955-83, Leads Sch., Eng., 1963-64 myomassologist Coll. Natureopathic Physicians, St. Louis, 1959-84; minister, counselor Ch. of Universology, Ann Arbor, 1972—. Contbr. poems and short stories to mags. Instr. Touch for Health Found., Pasadena, Calif., 1972—, Ir. dology, Escondido, Calif., 1972—; mem. Conservative Caucus, Washington, 1973—. Mem. NEA (del. 1959, cons. 1987—), Am. Nutrition Counselors Am., Internat. Myomathetics Fedn. (sec. edn. 1985—), Assn. Mich. Myomassologists Inc. (v.p. 1987—), Federated Organic Garden & Farming of Mich. (v.p. 1985-86), Delta Kappa Pi. Republican. Avocations: painting, quilting, crafts, writing, traveling. Home: 2564 Hawks Ave Ann Arbor MI 48108 Office: 2450 Hawks Ave Ann Arbor MI 48108

CARTAGENOVA, VERONICA ESTELA, trading company executive; b. Capital Federal, Argentina, Oct. 29, 1962; d. Hugo Alberto and Nelida Josefa (Traverso) C. Translator degree, Cardenal Ferrari, Argentina, 1983; degree in Arabic, UN, 1983—. Sec. Permanente Investment Co., Argentina, 1981-83; asst. to ambassador Bahrain Mission to UN, N.Y.C., 1983-85; asst. to dir. Am.-Arab Assn., N.Y.C., 1985-86; internat. dir. Verka Trading Co., N.Y.C., 1986—; cons. Interpress S.A., Buenos Aires, 1986—. Recipient Beethoven award Ministry of Edn., 1979. Office: Verka Trading Co PO Box 20368 New York NY 10017

CARTE, SUZANNE LEWIS, educator; b. S. Charleston, W.Va., Nov. 16, 1943; d. Carson Richard and Thelma Lee (Dew) Lewis; m. John Herman Carte, Sept. 1, 1962; children—John Kevin, Jennifer Kristin, Samuel Jefferson. B.S., W.Va. State Coll., 1973; student W.Va. Coll. Grad. Studies, 1976-86. Tchr., Kanawha County Schs., Charleston, W.Va., 1978, tchr. history, 1979-81, tchr. intensive service unit, 1981, tchr. 6th grade, 1982-86, tchr. social studies, 1986—. Mem. Christian edn. commn. 1st Presbyterian Ch., St. Albans, W.Va., 1978. Mem. Kanawha Fedn. Educators/Am. Fedn. Tchrs., AAUW, Phi Alpha Theta, Kappa Delta Pi, Alpha Delta Kappa. Democrat. Avocations: fishing; reading; traveling. Home: Rt 1 Box 762 Coal River Rd Saint Albans WV 25177 Office: Hayes Jr High Sch 830 Strawberry Rd Saint Albans WV 25177

CARTER, BERYL THOMPSON, educator, municipal agency administrator; b. Washington, Apr. 9, 1942; d. J. Conroy and Ora J. (Sizer) Thompson; m. David N. Carter, Jan. 6, 1964; children: Camille, Brian. BS, U. D.C., 1962. Secondary sch. tchr. Washington D.C. Pub. Schs., 1962-64, San Diego Calif. Sch. Dist., 1964-66; personnel analyst City of Richmond, Va., 1967-69, personnel adminstr., 1969-82, dir. personnel, 1982-87, sr. asst. to city mgr., 1987-88; dir. personnel Reynolds Community Coll., Richmond, 1988—; Mem. com. Richmond Red Cross Personnel, 1979-81, chmn. 1981-82; dir. Richmond Employee Assistance Program Consortium, 1982-87. Mem. Richmond Urban League, 1980, 82, Richmond Exchangettes, 1980-83, Rosedale (Va.) Civic Assn., 1983-87. Kappa Delta Pi scholar, 1962. Mem. NAACP, Internat. Personnel Mgmt. Assn., Va. Chpt. Internat. Personnel Mgmt. Assn., Nat. Pub. Employers Labor Relations Assn., Conf. Minority Pub. Adminstrs., Nat. Forum for Black Pub. Adminstrs., Am. Mgmt. Assn. Office: Reynolds Community Coll 1701 E Parham Rd Richmond VA 23261

CARTER, CAROLYN HOUCHIN, advertising agency executive; b. Louisville, Nov. 2, 1952; d. Paul Clayton and Georgia Houchin C.; B.S.J., Northwestern U., 1974, M.S.J., 1975. Asst. account exec. SSC&B Advt., Inc., N.Y.C., 1975-76, account exec., 1976-77; account exec. Grey Advt., Inc., N.Y.C., 1977-79, account supr., 1979-81, v.p., account supr., 1981-82, v.p., mgmt. supr., 1982-85, v.p., group mgmt. supr., 1985—; mem. Nat. Advt. Rev. Bd., 1983—. Mem. U.S. council World Communications Yr., 1983. Mem. March of Dimes Media Adv. Council, 1981-84, chmn., 1985-86. Mem. Am. Mktg. Assn., N.Y. Women in Communications (pres. 1982-83, chmn. 1985-86, chmn. 1985 Matrix awards), Advt. Women of N.Y. (bd. dirs. 1987—). Office: Grey Advt Inc 777 3rd Ave New York NY 10017

CARTER, CONNIE BERNICE, small business owner; b. Idaho Falls, Idaho, Jan. 30, 1943; d. James Lazelle Carter and Bernice (Collier) Carter Buttars; m. Welby L. Huffaker, July 4, 1961 (div. 1972); children: Kim Huffaker Walker, Rayna Huffaker Williams. Grad. high sch., Rigby, Idaho. Sales rep. Sta. KUPI, Idaho Falls, 1968-70; sales mgr. Holiday Office Products, Idaho Falls, 1972-77; cons. Snelling & Snelling, Idaho Falls, 1977-81; sales rep. Martin Stationers, Idaho Falls, 1981-84; owner, mgr., counselor Carter Personnel Agy., Idaho Falls, 1984—; cons. Ideal Hardware, Idaho Falls, 1985—, Vo-Tech, Idaho Falls, 1987—. Mem. Idaho Falls C. of C., Achievers Club. Republican. Mormon. Office: Carter Personnel Agy 482 Constitution Way Idaho Falls ID 83404

CARTER, ELEANOR ELIZABETH, corporate professional, social worker; b. Durham, N.C., July 16, 1954; d. Joseph William Jr. and Sheila Dale (Swartz) C. BS in Social Work, N.C. State U., 1977. Field worker family planning Wake County Health Dept., Raleigh, N.C., 1975-76; sales rep. Bristol-Myers Products, N.C., 1977-80; regional adminstn. asst. Bristol-Myers Products, Dallas, Tex., 1980; regional trainer Bristol-Myers Products, Washington, N.C., Va., 1980; sales adminstrn. mgr. corp. hdqrs. Bristol-Myers Products, N.Y.C., 1980-81; dist. supr. Bristol-Myers Products, Cin., 1981-82; account rep. Fuji Photo Film U.S.A., Inc., Cin., 1982-83; spl. account mgr. Fuji Photo Film U.S.A., Inc., Chgo., 1983—. Mem. Nat. Assn. Female Execs., Alpha Kappa Delta. Presbyterian. Office: Fuji Photo Film USA Inc 1000 Pratt Blvd Elk Grove IL 60007

CARTER, EVELYN STEFFIE, educator; b. Hartford, Conn., Feb. 23, 1952. AA, Northeastern Christian Jr. Coll., 1972; BA in Edn., Pa. State U., 1974. Cert. tchr., N.J. Tchr. aide Migrant Edn., South Brunswick, N.J., 1969-80; tchr. South Brunswick Bd. Edn., 1974—. Mem. Nat. Assn. Female Execs., South Brunswick Edn. Assn. (pres. 1986—), Nat. Assn. Univ. Women. Home: Wynbrook W D 15 East Windsor NJ 08520 Office: Dayton Sch Georges Rd Dayton NJ 08810

CARTER, JANE FOSTER, agriculture industry executive; b. Stockton, Calif., Jan. 14, 1927; d. Chester William and Bertha Emily Foster; m. Robert Buffington Carter, Feb. 25, 1952; children: Ann Claire Carter Palmer, Benjamin Foster. BA, Stanford U., 1948; MS, NYU, 1949. Pres. Colusa (Calif.) Properties, Inc., 1953—; owner Carter Land and Livestock, Colusa, 1965—; sec.-treas. Carter Farms, Inc., Colusa, 1975—. Author: If the Walls Could Talk, Colusa's Architectural Heritage, 1988; author and editor: Colusa County Survey and Plan for the Arts, 1981, 82, 83, Implementing the Colusa County Arts Plan, 1984, 85, 86. Mem. agrl. adv. com. Yuba Coll., Marysville, Calif., 1976—, Gov's. Commn. Agriculture, Sacramento, 1979-82; del. Rep. Nat. Conv., Kansas City, Mo., 1976, Detroit, 1980, Dallas, 1984; mem. bd. trustees Calif. Hist. Soc., San Francisco, 1979—, regional v.p. 1984—; sec. State of Calif. Reclamation Bd., 1983—. Mem. Sacramento River Water Contractors Assn. (exec. com. 1974—). Episcopalian. Club: Francisca (San Francisco). Home and Office: 909 Oak St Colusa CA 95932

CARTER, JESSIE ANITA, computer science educator; b. Ft. Worth, June 3, 1948; d. William Charlie and Ella Marion (Andrews) C. BA in Math., North Tex. State U., 1970; secondary teaching cert., Tex. Christian U., 1975, MA In Edn. Supervision, 1976. Tchr. aide in math. Ft. Worth Independent Sch. Dist., 1972-73, tchr. math., 1973-85, tchr. computer literacy in gifted and talented program, 1984—. Named Outstanding Math. Tchr. Ft. Worth Independent Sch. Dist., 1973-74, Notable Woman Tex., 1984-85, Outstanding Magnet Tchr., Morningside Middle Sch., 1986-87; Sid Richardson Found. grantee, 1985, 86, 87. Mem. NEA, Internat Council for Computers in Edn., Nat. Council Tchrs. Math., Tex. State Tchr. Assn., Tex. Council Tchrs. Math., Ft. Worth Classroom Tchrs., Ft. Worth Council Tchrs. Math., Assn. for Supervision and Curriculum Devel., Nat. Soc. Tole and Decorative Painters, Ft. Worth Tole and Decorative Painters, Nat. Assn. Female Execs., Beta Sigma Phi. Democrat. Baptist. Home: 7101 Willis Ave Fort Worth TX 76116 Office: Ft Worth Independent Sch Dist 3200 W Lancaster Fort Worth TX 76107

CARTER, JOICE ANN, nutritionist, dietitian; b. Itasca, Tex., Aug. 12, 1947; d. Thomas and Viola (Scott) Rivers; m. Travis Harris (div.); m. Stedson Carter, May 15, 1969; children: Stedson (Trey), Kerri. BS in Food and Nutirition, Tex. Christian U., 1971; MS in Food and Nutrition, Tex. Woman's U., Denton, 1979; postgrad., U. Dallas, 1980—. Asst. chief dietician Harris Hosp., Ft. Worth, 1972-75; dir. nutrition LFS Sr. Citizens Services, Ft. Worth, 1975-84; nutritionist Tex. Dept. Health, Ft. Worth, 1984—; instr. Tarrant County Jr. Coll., Ft. Worth, 1975-81, U. Tex. Health Sci. Ctr., Dallas, 1981; owner Options, Fort Worth; cons. in field. Author: (handbook) Diabetic Meal Exchanges, 1986; contbr. articles to profl. jours. Mem. Am. Dietetic Assn. (named Young Dietician of Yr. 1978), Tex. Dietetic Assn., Ft. Worth Dietetic Assn. (pres. 1975), Delta Sigma Theta. Home: 4301 Pheasant Walk Fort Worth TX 76133

CARTER, JOYCE ELAINE ARNDT, writer, editor, photographer; b. Bellevue, Ohio, Jan. 9, 1944; d. Bryce Leroy Arndt and Agnes Arline (Rudicel) Arndt Chellis; student Gonzaga U., 1962-63, Phoenix Coll., 1963-66, U. Wash., Seattle, 1966-67; m. Zane Hartson Carter, Jan. 16, 1965 (div. 1971). Editor de Paul Speaks mag., St. Vincent de Paul Parish, Phoenix, 1971-74; editor Ultreya internat. mag. Mt. Claret Cursillo Center, Phoenix, 1971-72; pub. info. photographer Phoenix Coll., 1972—; free lance writer. Mem. Nat. League Am. Pen Women, Poetry Soc. Democrat. Roman Catholic. Club: Phoenix Writers (pres. 1972-73). Contbr. poetry and fiction to nat. profl. and popular publs. Home: 1725 E Catalina Dr Phoenix AZ 85016

CARTER, JUDY ANITA, food products executive; b. Searcy, Ark., Feb. 28, 1946; d. Corris Jason and Alma Lorene (Rogers) Lynch; m. George Edward Carter, Jan. 20, 1968 (div. Sept. 1979); 1 child, Edward Wayne. BS, Ark. State U., 1967; MA in Administrv. Studies, Southeastern Okla. State U., 1984. Chemist Sterling Drugs, Monticello, Ill., 1969-70; instr. chemistry Canal Zone Coll., Panama, 1975-77; chemist, group leader A.H. Robins, Monticello, 1977-80; foreman quality control Anderson Clayton Foods, Jacksonville, Ill., 1980-81; mgr. quality control Anderson Clayton Foods, Sherman, Tex., 1981-85; supr. process Anderson Clayton Foods, Sherman, 1985-87; dir. tech. Louisville Edible Oil Products, 1987—. Mem. Am. Oil Chemists Soc., Am. Chem. Soc., Am. Soc. Quality Control, Inst. Food Technologists, Bus. and Profl. Women (1st v.p. 1985-86, Individual Devel. award 1985), Nat. Assn. Female Execs. Republican. Baptist. Home: 2600 Stover Dr New Albany IN 47150 Office: Louisville Edible Oil Products 2500 S Seventh St Rd Louisville KY 40216

CARTER, LINDA ANN, telephone company executive; b. Rome, Ga., July 9, 1943; d. George Nubert and Mary Juanita (King) Cleveland; divorced; 1 child, Pamela Ann. Student, Gadsen Bus. Coll., 1962; BA in Mgmt. Basics, Auburn U., 1978; BA in Mgmt. Devel., U. Kans., 1984. Legal sec. John Wear, atty., Ft. Payne, Ala., 1962-64; probate clk. DeKalb City Probate Judge, Ft. Payne, Ala., 1964-68; comml. supr. Peoples Telephone Co., Leesburg, Ala., 1968-74; asst. comml. supr. Telephone & Data Systems, Leesburg, 1974-82, comml. mgr., 1982-86; mgr. Peoples Telephone Co., Centre, Ala., 1986—. Pres. Centre Middle Sch. PTA, 1978; commn. chmn. Cherokee County Rural Devel., 1986-87; bd. dirs. Boy Scouts Am., 1987. Named Employee of Yr. Telephone & Data Systems, Leesburg, 1983. Mem. Centre Bus. & Profl. Women (pres. 1983-84, Woman of Yr., 1983). Democrat. Mem. Ch. of Christ. Club: Cherokee County Chamber (pres. 1987-88), Centre Civitan. Home: 1101 Northwood Dr Centre AL 35960 Office: Peoples Telephone Co PO Box 900 Centre AL 35960

CARTER, LINDA SUSAN, broadcast journalist; b. Columbus, Ohio, Nov. 18, 1950; d. Edward Herman and Jane Lewis (Joseph) C.; m. Jerome Ronald Piasecki, June 5, 1976 (div. Feb. 1983); 1 dau., Amanda. B.A., Mich. State U., 1984. News dir. WAVZ-AM, New Haven, Conn., 1977-78, WABX-FM, Detroit, 1978—; news anchor WWJ-AM, Detroit, 1978-81; talk show host WXYZ-AM, Detroit, 1981-82; press sec. Office of the Gov., Lansing, Mich., 1982-83; news anchor WWJ-AM, Detroit, 1983-85; dir. pub. affairs Sta. WDIV-TV, Detroit, 1985-86, dir. editorials, 1986—. Vestrywoman, Cathedral Ch. of St. Paul, Detroit, 1982-83; mem. Rackman Symphony Choir. Mem. AFTRA (exec. bd. mem. 1982—), Nat. Acad. TV Arts and Scis., Sigma Delta Chi, Detroit Press Club. Episcopalian. Home: 1300 E Lafayette Blvd Apt 1009 Detroit MI 48207 Office: Sta UDIV-TV 550 W Lafayette Blvd Detroit MI 48231

CARTER, LISA JOYCE, paint manufacturing company executive; b. Galveston, Tex., June 1, 1959; d. Carlton and Dorothy Lee (McPeters) Pappas Kelly; m. Michael Page Carter, Aug. 19, 1978. Student N. Tex. State U., 1977, Richland Coll., 1978, U. Ark.-Little Rock, 1980, IBM Continuing Edn., 1981-82. Mktg. asst. Membership Services, Irving, Tex., 1978, tech. support asst., 1980; programmer, analyst Mail Mktg. Services, Little Rock, 1980-82; bus. broker VR Bus. Brokers, Longview, Tex., 1982-85; mgr., treas. Creative Coatings Inc., Kilgore, Tex., 1985—, also bd. dirs. Mem. Mothers Against Drunk Drivers, Longview, Tex., 1985-86, v.p. Gregg County chpt.; sec. East Tex. Area Parkinsonism Soc., 1987—. Mem. Data Processing Mgrs. Assn. Baptist. Avocations: skiing, traveling. Home: 110 E Hawkins Pkwy Apt 1102 Longview TX 75601 Office: Creative Coatings Inc 428 N Longview St Kilgore TX 75662

CARTER, MAE RIEDY, retired college official, consultant; b. Berkeley, Calif., May 20, 1921; d. Carl Joseph and Avis Blanche (Rhodehaver) Riedy; B.S., U. Calif., Berkeley, 1943; m. Robert C. Carter, Aug. 19, 1944; children—Catherine, Christin Ann. Ednl. adv., then program specialist div. continuing edn. U. Del., Newark, 1968-78, asst. provost for women's affairs, exec. dir. commn. status women Office Women's Affairs, 1978-86; adv. bd. Rockefeller Family grant project, 1979-83. Regional v.p. Del. PTA, 1960-62; pres. Friends Newark Free Library, 1968-69; mem. fiscal planning com. Newark Spl. Sch. Dist., 1972. Recipient Outstanding Service award Women's Coordinating Council, 1977, 79; Spl. Recognition award, Nat. U. Extension Assn., 1977, award for credit programs, 1971, Creative Programming award, 1971; AAUW grantee, 1968; Fulbright grantee, 1976. Mem. AAUW (past br. pres.), Women's Equity Action League, Nat. Assn. Women Deans, Adminstrs. and Counselors, NOW, Women's Legal Def. Fund, Nat. Women's Polit. Caucus. Republican. Author: (with Geis and Butler) Seeing and Evaluating People, 1982, revised, 1986, Research on Seeing and Evaluating People; also papers, reports in field. Home: 604 Dallam Rd Newark DE 19711

CARTER, MARILYN FAYE, real estate broker; b. Pampa, Tex., May 30, 1947; d. Carl Sullivan and Robin D. (Crisp) H.; m. William H. Carter, Oct. 1, 1966 (div. Apr. 1973); 1 child, Sadie Shea. Student, So. Meth. U., U. Tex., Arlington. Lic. real estate broker, Tex. Gen. mgr. G & C Properties, Irving, Tex., 1966-70; owner Toi et Mor, Inc., Dallas, 1970-71; regional dir. I.C. Deal Cos., Dallas, 1971-72; pres. The Crow Cos., Dallas, 1972-74, Relocators, Inc., Dallas, 1974-77; pres. chief exec. officer MCI Properties, Inc., Dallas, 1977-87; chief executive officer, exec. dir. RAP Real Awareness of People, Newport Beach, Calif., 1988—. Republican. Presbyterian. Home: 900 Sea Ln 58 Corona Del Mar CA 92625 Office: RAP 177 Riverside Dr Newport Beach CA 92663

CARTER, MARTHA LOUISE, securities consultant; b. Chgo., Aug. 19, 1956; d. John Henry and Aurelia Celeste (Bernard) C. BS in Math., Purdue U., 1978, BA in French, 1978; MBA in Fin., U. Pa., 1983. Systems analyst IBM Corp., Gaithersburg, Md., 1978-81, fin. analyst, 1984-87; dir. research First Montauk Securities Corp., Gaithersburg, Md., 1987-88; capital markets specialist Fed. Home Loan Banks, Wawshington, 1988—; pvt. cons. securities, Gaithersburg, 1988—; investment analyst Am. Stock Exchange, N.Y.C., 1982; mgmt. cons. Touche Ross & Co., Chgo., 1983-84. Bd. dirs. Gaithersburg Guide Youth Services, 1985—. Mem. Assn. MBA Execs., Nat. Assn. Female Execs., Bus. and Profl. Women, NOW, Nat. Women's Polit. Caucus (chpt. legis. com. 1986), LWV, Sierra Club, Nat. Geog. Soc., Phi Beta Kappa, Pi Delta Phi, Alpha Lambda Delta. Karate gold belt, 1985. Avocations: piano, bike riding, reading. Office: Fed Home Loan Banks Office Fin Washington DC

CARTER, MARY EDDIE, government adminstrator; b. Americus, Ga., Mar. 14, 1925; d. Walker G. and Esther (Stewart) C. B.A., LaGrange Coll., 1946; M.S., U. Fla., 1949; Ph.D., U. Edinburgh, 1956. Tchr. LaGrange (Ga.) Coll., 1946-47; chemist Callaway Mills, LaGrange, 1947-48; microscopist So. Research Inst., Birmingham, Ala., 1949-51; chemist West Point Mfg. Co., Shawmut, Ala., 1951-53; research asso. FMC Corp., Am. Viscose div., Marcus Hook, Pa., 1956-71; lab chief textiles and clothing lab. U.S. Dept. Agr., Knoxville, Tenn., 1971-73; dir. So. Regional Research Ctr, 1973-80; asso. adminstr. Agrl. Research Service, Washington, 1980—. Recipient Herty medal Ga. sect. of Am. Chem. Soc., 1979, Meritorious Presdl. Rank award, 1982, 87; Named Fed. Woman of Yr. City Wide Fed. Exec. Bd., 1977. Fellow AAAS; mem. Am. Chem. Soc., Am. Assn. Textile Chemists and Colorists, Inter-Soc. Color Council, Sci. Research Soc. Am., Fiber Soc., Inst. Food Technologists, Am. Assn. Cereal Chemists. Office: US Dept Agr Agrl Research Service 14th & Independence Ave SW Washington DC 20250

CARTER, MEDORA ABBOTT, project administrator; b. Washington, July 18, 1953; d. Jackson Miles and Frances Elizabeth (Dowdle) A.; m. Donald Lynwood Carter, May 14, 1983. Student Chowan Jr. Coll., 1971-72, J. Sargeant Reynolds and Va. Commonwealth U., 1973-76; grad. with honors Am. Inst. Banking, 1981. Asst. cashier, br. mgr. Dominion Nat. Bank, Vienna, Va., 1977-82; fin. analyst MCDonnell Douglas/TYMNET, Inc., Vienna, 1984-87; project adminstr. McDonnell, 1987—. Mem. Colonial chpt. Rep. Women's Club, Alexandria, Va., 1985—; del. to county and state Rep. convs., 1988; mem. membership drive com. Fairfax County C. of C., 1981, 82; treas. Kings Park Shopping Ctr. Mcht.'s Assn., Springfield, Va., 1981; page DAR 1976 Va. State Conv., also active mem.; mem. Alexandria Assn. Recipient Outstanding Achievement award Nat. Assn. Banking Women No. Va., 1981. Episcopalian. Office: McDonnell Douglas/ TYMNET Inc 2070 Chain Bridge Rd Vienna VA 22180

CARTER, MILDRED BROWN, adminstr.; b. Leo, S.C., Feb. 22, 1927; d. Eddie Washington and Hester Lessie Lee (Poston) Brown; m. Richard Bert Carter, Sept. 6, 1952; children: Paul, Mark, Janis, David. Student Pace Seminar, 1977, Dale Carnegie, 1977, Am. Mgmt. Assn., 1977. Various secretarial positions, FBI, Washington, 1943-48, adminstrv. asst., 1948-51; adminstrv. asst., office asso. dir., 1952; with Bellevue (Wash.) Sch. Dist., 1965-75; sec., registrar Hyak Jr. High Sch., 1971-75; asst. to exec. v.p. Bonneville Internat. Corp., Salt Lake City, 1975-83, exec. asst. to pres., 1983—. Mem. PTA Bd., Yakima, Wash., 1963; treas. PTA, Bellevue, 1973. Recipient Hon. Paul Harris Fellow award Rotary Internat., 1985. Mem. Soc. Former FBI Women, Beta Sigma Phi. Mormon. Clubs: Women's Century. Lodge: Soroptimists, Rotary (Paul Harris fellow 1985). Home: 2180 Elaine Dr Bountiful UT 84010 Office: Broadcast House 5 Triad Ctr Salt Lake City UT 84180

CARTER, PATRICIA PETERS, banker; b. Chgo., Oct. 14, 1941; d. Lawrence and Kathlee R. (Lyons) P.; B.A., Marycrest Coll., Davenport, Iowa, 1963; m. James Stanley Carter, Jan. 1, 1982. With Morgan Guaranty Trust Co., N.Y.C., 1969—, mgr. N.Am. research unit, 1978-81, instl. portfolio mgr., 1981—; bd. dirs. Foster Grant Corp., Pinnacle Broadcasting, Clarke Equipment. Mem. Fin. Women's Assn., N.Y. Soc. Security Analysts.

CARTER, RHONDA JEAN, medical bill collector; b. Kansas City, Kans., May 16, 1955; d. Joseph J. and Coral Ann Schmidt; m. Charles Lee Carter, Nov. 6, 1953; children: Charles III, Ryan Joseph, Jared Donald. BS in Edn., Pacific Coast Bapt. Bible Coll., 1977. Billing clk. Raleigh Hills Hosp., Miami, Okla., 1981-83; mgr. accounts receivable Hallowell Chevrolet, Fresno, Calif., 1983-84, Am. Homecare, Fresno, 1984-85; med. collector Interim Systems Corp., Profl. Nurses Bur./Am. Homecare, Fresno, 1985—. Republican. Baptist. Office: Am Homecare 705 E Locust #105 Fresno CA 93710

CARTER, ROBERTA ECCLESTON, educator, therapist; b. Pitts.; d. Robert E. and Emily B. (Bucar) Carter; (div.); children—David Michael, Daniel Michael. Student Edinboro State U., 1962-63; B.S., California State U. of Pa., 1966; M.Ed., U. Pitts., 1969; M.A., Rosebridge Grad. Sch., Walnut Creek, Calif., 1987. Tchr., Bethel Park Sch. Dist., Pa., 1966-69; writer, media asst. Field Ednl. Pub., San Francisco, 1969-70; educator, counselor, specialist Alameda Unified Sch. Dist., Calif., 1970—; master trainer Calif. State Dept. Edn., Sacramento, 1984 ; personal growth cons., Alameda, 1983—. Author: People, Places and Products, 1970, Teaching/ Learning Units, 1969; co-author: Teacher's Manual Let's Read, 1968. Mem. AAUW, Calif. Fedn. Bus. and Profl. Women (legis. chair Alameda br. 1984-85, membership chair 1985), NEA, Calif. Edn. Assn., Alameda Edn. Assn., Charter Planetary Soc., Oakland Mus., Exploratorium, Big Bros. of East Bay, Alameda C. of C. (service award 1985). Republican. Club: Commonwealth. Avocations: aerobics, gardening, travel, tennis. Home: 1516 E Shore Dr Alameda CA 94501

CARTER, ROSALYNN SMITH, wife of former President of United States; b. Plains, Ga., Aug. 18, 1927; d. Edgar and Allie (Murray) Smith; m. James Earl Carter, Jr., July 7, 1946; children: John William, James Earl III, Donnel Jeffrey, Amy Lynn. Grad., Ga. Southwestern Coll.; DHL (hon.), Morehouse Coll., 1980; LHD (hon.), Winthrop Coll., 1984; D Pub. Service (hon.), Wesleyan Coll., 1986; LLD (hon.), U. Notre Dame, 1987. Disting. centennial lectr. Agnes Scott Coll., Decatur, Ga., 1988—; dist. centennial lectr. Agnes Scott Coll., 1988—. Author: First Lady from Plains, 1984, (with Jimmy Carter) Everything to Gain: Making the Most of the Rest of Your Life, 1987. Mem. Ga. Gov.'s Commn. to Improve Service for the Mentally and Emotionally Handicapped, 1971; hon. chmn. Ga. Spl. Olympics for Retarded Children, 1971-75, Pres.'s Commn. on Mental Health, 1977-78; hon. chmn. bd. trustees John F. Kennedy Center Performing Arts, 1977-80; bd. mem. emeritus Nat. Assn. Mental Health; bd. dirs. The Friendship Force, The Gannett Co., Crested Butte Physically Challenged Ski Program; bd. advisors Habitat for Humanity; trustee The Menninger Found.; sponsor Nat. Alliance for Research on Schizophrenia and Depression. Recipient Vol. of Yr. award Southeastern Assn. Vol. Services, 1976, Vincent DeFrancis award for Outstanding Service to Humanity, Am. Humane Assn., 1979, Vol. of Decade award Nat. Mental Health Assn., 1980, Presdl. Citation, Am. Psychol. Assn., 1982, Disting. Christian Woman's award Women's Com. of the So. Bapt. Theol. Sem., 1984, Nathan S. Kline Medal of Merit, Internat. Com. Against Mental Illness, 1984, Disting. Alumnus award. Am. Assn. State Colls. and Univs., 1987, Dorothea Dix award Mental Illness Found., 1988; hon. fellow Am. Psychiat. Assn., 1984.

CARTER, RUTH B. (MRS. JOSEPH C. CARTER), association executive; b. Charlotte, Vt.; d. Ira E. and Sadie M. (Congdon) Burroughs; Ph.B., U. Vt., 1931; m. Joseph C. Carter, June 28, 1935. Prin., Newton Acad., Shoreham, Vt., 1931-35; substitute tchr. Spaulding High Sch., Barre, Vt., also Woodbury (Vt.) High Sch., 1935-36; tchr. Craftsbury Acad., Craftsbury Common, Vt., 1936-38; sales mgr., buyer Vt. Music Co., Barre, 1939-44; statistician Syracuse U., 1944-46; instr. English, Temple U., Phila., 1946-47; records clk. sec., 1947-56; tchr. English, Central High Sch., Phila., 1957, Springfield Twp. Sr. High Sch., Montgomery County, Pa., 1964-65; exec. dir. White-Williams Found., 1966-82, trustee, 1982—; chaplain Regent's Club Phila., 1986—. Recipient Humanitarian award Chapel of Four Chaplains, 1981; city council citation City of Phila., 1982. Mem. AAUW (admissions chmn. Phila. chpt. 1959-61, sec. 1961-64, treas. 1965-67), DAR (treas., historian, com. chmn., budget dir., treas., historian, com. chmn., regent Germantown chpt., 1983-86, registrar and pub. relations official 1986—), Women for Greater Phila., New Eng. Historic Geneal. Soc., Geneal. Soc. Vt., Soc. Mayflower Descs. (bd. dirs. 1983-84, sec. 1985—). Republican. Methodist. Clubs: Temple University Faculty Wives (rec. sec. 1983-86, pres. Old York group), Temple University Women's, The English Speaking Union. Author: (with Joseph C. Carter) Anchors Aweigh Around the World with Ernest Vail Burroughs, 1960, Pilgrimage to the Lovely Lands of our Ancestors, 1984. Home: 40 W Mt Carmel Ave Glenside PA 19038

CARTER, SARALEE LESSMAN, immunologist, microbiologist; b. Chgo., Feb. 19, 1951; d. Julius A. and Ida (Oiring) Lessman; B.A., National Coll., 1971; m. John B. Carter, Oct. 7, 1979; 1 child, Robert Oiring. Supr. lab. immunology Weiss Meml. Hosp., Chgo., 1973-80; lab. immunology supr. Henrotin Hosp., Chgo., 1980-84; tech. dir. Lexington Med. Labs., West Columbia, S.C., 1984—; mem. nat. workshop faculty Am. Soc. Clin. Pathologists. Mem. Am. Soc. Clin. Pathologists (subspecialty cert. in microbiology and immunology, cert. med. technologist). Researcher Legionnaires Disease and mycoplasma pneumonia World Soc. Pathologists, Jerusalem, Israel, 1980. Contbr. articles to profl. jours. Office: 110 E Medical Ln Suite 100 Columbia SC 29169

CARTER, SONDRA LYNNE, medical care facility administrator, educator; b. Camden, N.J., Dec. 31, 1954; d. Ralph Earl and Irene Venetta (Thompson) C. BS, Rutgers U., 1976, MD, 1980. Clin. instr. dept. Ob-Gyn SUNY Downstate Med. Ctr., Bklyn., 1980-81; cons. East Harlem Council Human Services, N.Y.C., 1985-86; clin. instr. dept Ob-Gyn N.Y. Med. Coll., N.Y.C., 1986—; chmn. N.Y. Med. Care Services, N.Y.C., 1986—. Mem. Vol. Services for Children, Inc., N.Y.C., 1986—; vol. Partnership for the Homeless Inc., N.Y.C., 1986—. Fellow Am. Coll. Ob-Gyn (jr.); mem. Assn. N.Y. County Med. Soc., Susan Smith McKinney Steward Med. Soc. (parlamentarian 1987-88), Rutgers Med. Sch. Alumni Assn. Anglican. Office: NY Med Care Services 449 E 58th St New York NY 10022-2397

CARTER, SUE CLAUDELLE, chamber of commerce executive; b. Ellensburg, Wash., May 7, 1944; d. Claude H. and Elsie M. (Johnson) Norton; m. Frank A. Peter, June 14, 1969 (div. 1978); m. 2d James E. Carter, Sr., Nov. 23, 1980. A.A., Wenatchee Valley Coll., 1964. Mcpl. clk. City Kenai, Alaska, 1974-78; owner Concepts Unltd., Kenai, 1978-80; sales rep. Beluga Realty, Inc., Kenai, Alaska, 1980—; exec. dir., mgr. Greater Kenai Chamber of Commerce, Kenai, 1982—; dir., sec.-treas. Homer Electric Assn., 1980—. Sec. Pioneers Alaska, Aux. 16, Kenai, 1983; mem. CAP, Kenai, 1983—. Mem. Alaska State C. of C., Kenai Peninsula Bd. Realtors, Peninsula Council Chambers. Republican. Roman Catholic. Clubs: Twin Cities Soroptimist (charter, dir. 1981); Birch Ridge Country (Soldotna, Alaska) Lodge: Order Eastern Star. Home: 36875 Chinulna Dr Box 212 Kenai AK 99611 Office: Greater Kenai C of C Box 497 Kenai AK 99611 *

CARTER, WANDA JOY, banker; b. Roxton, Tex., Mar. 19, 1932; d. Noble H. and Gertrude (Larkin) Weaver; m. Albert M. Carter, Jr., Sept. 3, 1955; children—Rickey K., Michael A. Student Tex. Tech. Coll., 1976, 78; grad. Am. Inst. Banking, Dallas, 1976; student U. Okla., 1980. With First Nat. Bank (now Republic Bank), Garland, Tex., 1957—, v.p., 1979—, loan officer, 1980—, loan losses and bankruptcy dept., 1987—. Bd. dirs. Ptnrs. in Edn., Garland, 1986. Nat. Assn. Bank Women scholar, 1975. Mem. Am. Bus. Women Assn. (woman of yr. 1975, 86, past pres., now chmn. scholarship), Nat. Assn. Bank Women (sec. 1978-79). Republican. Baptist. Avocations: crochet; reading; needlepoint. Home: 1217 Travis St Garland TX 75040 Office: Republic Bank Garland PO Box 461228 Garland TX 75046

CARTER-BANE, SHARIE ELIZABETH, social service executive; b. Honolulu, July 18, 1958; d. Norman Lee and Betty C. (Lane) C.; m. Gregory Scott Bane, Oct. 20, 1979; children—Angel Kay, Adrienne Rae. Student Ill. State U., 1976-77, Danville Jr. Coll., 1977-78. Librarian asst. Hoopeston Jr. High Sch., Ill., 1975-76; dental asst., Hoopeston, 1977-78; reporter Danville Comml. News, Ill., 1978-79; exec. dir., infor. and referral specialist Hoopeston Multi Agy., 1979— ; Author: American Anthology of Poetry, 1987. Sec., Grant Twp. United Way, 1983-86; del. White House Conf. on Aging in Am., 1980; sec. Vermilion County Aging Adv. Com., 1985—; mem. Alzheimers Related Disorders, Kankakee chpt., 1987. Mem. Vermilion Human Coalition, Nat. Alliance Info. and Referral, Nat. Assn. Female Execs. Democrat. Avocations: poetry; cooking; music; people. Home: 817 E Honeywell Hoopeston IL 60942 Office: 210 S Market St Suite 313 Hoopeston IL 60942

CARTER-CLAYTON, CONNIE LYNN, computer science technician; b. St. Louis, July 13, 1956; d. Robert Samuel and Beverly Ruth (Prevallet) C.; m. Barry Lee Clayton, Mar. 21, 1983. BS, So. Ill. U., 1978; postgrad., Rochester (N.Y.) Inst. of Tech., 1980; cert. computer sci., Washington U., St. Louis, 1985. Cartographer, programmer Def. Mapping Agy., St. Louis, 1978-85; computer tech. specialist Systems and Applied Scis., Fairview Heights, Ill., 1986—. Mem. NOW (v.p. Alton, Ill. chpt.), Optical Soc. Am., Soc. Photographic Scientists and Engrs., Am. Assn. of Am. Women, Bus. and Profl. Women. Home: 414 Henry Alton IL 62002 Office: Systems and Applied Scis 333 Salem Pl Fairview Heights IL 62208

CARTHEL, ANNE FAWVER, teacher; b. Floydada, Tex., July 7, 1952; d. Ralph Carlton and Jonnie Louise (Ely) Fawver; m. Hulon Lon Carthel, Aug 24, 1950; children: Casey Britten, Corey Brock, Cienna Beth. Student, S. Plains Jr. Coll., 1970-71, W. Tex. State U., 1971-75; BS, Wayland Bapt. U., 1979-80; cert. tchr., Tex. Tech. U., 1986-87. Tchr. English and reading Lockney (Tex.) Jr. High Sch., 1980-81; tchr. English Floydada High Sch., 1981, 86-87; tchr. elem. phys. edn. A.B. Duncan Elem. Sch., Floydada, 1986—; Coordinator Jump Rope for Heart, Floydada, 1986-88; com. mem. Dist. Goals Com., Floydada, 1986-87, Dist. Survey Com., Floydada, 1987-88, Campus Long Range Plan Co., 1987-88. Sec. Floydada Exes Homecoming, 1984-88; neighborhood chmn., 1985-88. Mem. Assn. Tex. Profl. Educators, Tex. Assn. Health, Physical Edn., Recreation and Dance, PTA, Am. Cancer Soc., Am. Heart Assn. Floydada C. of C., Delta Psi Kappa. Primitive Baptist. Home: 901 W Mississippi Floydada TX 79235

CARTIER, CELINE PAULE, librarian, administrator; b. Lacolle, Que., Can., May 10, 1930; d. Henri Rodolphe and Irene (Boudreau) Robitaille; m. Georges Cartier, Nov. 29, 1952; children: Nathalie, Guillaume. Diplome superieur en pedagogie, U. Montreal, 1948, certificats en litterature et linguistique, 1952; diplome de bibliothecaire-documentaliste, Inst. Catholique, Paris, 1962; maî trise en adminstrn. publique, Ecole Nationale d'Adminstrn. Publique, 1976; maî trise en bibliothé conomie, U. Montreal, 1982. Dir. Bibliotheque Centrale, Commn. des ecoles catholiques, Montreal, 1964-73; dir. spl. collections U. Quebec, 1973-76, dir. sector libraries, 1976-77; chief gen. library U. Laval, Que., 1977-78; gen. dir. libraries U. Laval, 1978—. Contbr. articles to profl. jours. Mem. Corp. des Bibliothecaires Profs. de Quebec, Can. Library Assn., ALA, Fedn. Internat. des Assn. de Bibliothecaires et des Bibliotheques, Assn. pour l'avancement des Scis. et des techniques de la documentation. Office: Univ Laval, Bibliotheque Cite, Universitaire Ste Foy, Quebec, PQ Canada G1K 7P4

CARTIER, DENISE MARIE, sales manager; b. Pittsfield, Mass., May 23, 1952; d. Robert E. and Mary S. (Cahill) C. AS in Environ. Studies, Berkshire Community Coll., Pittsfield, 1973; BS in Natural Resources, U. Mass., 1975. Technician GE Plastics, Pittsfield, 1977-81, analytical chemist, 1981-82, product coordinator, 1982-83, mktg. support specialist, 1983-85, tech. sales rep., 1985-86, mgr. tech. sales, 1986—. Office: GE Plastics One Plastics Ave Pittsfield MA 01201

CARTWRIGHT, MARY LOU, laboratory scientist; b. Payette, Idaho, Apr. 5, 1923; d. Ray J. and Nellie Mae (Sherer) Decker; B.S., U. Houston, 1958; M.A., Central Mich. U., 1976; m. Chadwick Louis Cartwright, Sept. 13, 1947. Med. technologist Methodist Hosp., Houston, 1957-59, VA Hosp., Livermore, Calif., 1960-67, Kaiser Permanente Med. Center, Hayward, Calif., 1967-71, United Med. Lab., San Mateo, Calif., 1972-73; sr. med. technologist Oakland (Calif.) Hosp., 1974-86; cons. med. lab. tech. Oakland Public Schs. Chmn., Congressional Dist. 11 steering com. Common Cause, 1974-77; consumer mem. Alameda County (Calif.) Health Systems Agy., 1977-78. Served with USNR, 1945-53. Mem. Calif. Soc. Med. Tech., Calif. Assn. Med. Lab. Tech. (Technologist of Yr. award 1968, 78, Pres.'s award 1977, Service award chpt. 1978, 79), Am. Soc. Med. Tech. (by-laws chmn. 1981-83), Am. Bus. Women's Assn., Nat. Assn. Female Execs. Democrat. Home and Office: 231 Depot St #8 Grass Valley CA 95945

CARTY, MARY JACINTHA, nurse; b. West Indies, Aug. 4, 1957; came to U.S., 1972; d. Thomas and Margaret Ann (Daley) C.; 1 child, Cuprice Curty. A, Manhattan Coll., 1982; student, St. Joseph's Coll., N.Y.C., 1984-86. Staff nurse Met. Hosp., N.Y.C., 1982-84, head nurse, 1984—. Served to 2d lt. USAR, 1984—. Mem. Am. Nurses Assn., N.Y. State Nurses Assn. (nursing practice com. dist. 13), Nat. Assn. Female Execs., N.Y. Black Nurses Assn., Am. Mktg. Assn. Home: 148 W 142d St Apt. #12 New York NY 10030

CARTY, RITA MARY, educational administrator, nurse; b. Pitts., Dec. 23, 1937; d. Ignatius and Frances (Brisini) Cardillo; m. Wayne Lee Carty, Aug. 20, 1966; 1 child, Gina Marie. Diploma in Nursing, Ohio Valley Gen. Hosp., McKees Rocks, Pa., 1958; BSN, Duquesne U., 1965; MSN, Cath. U., 1966, DNSc, 1977. Sch. nurse South Fayette Twp. Sch. Dist., McDonald, Pa., 1958-60; charge nurse Ohio Valley Gen. Hosp., McKees Rocks, Pa., 1960-62, instr., 1962-65; asst. prof. Cath. U., Washington, 1966-72, lectr., 1974-77; dir. nursing div. univ. affiliated program Georgetown U., Washington, 1972-74; assoc. prof., grad. program coordinator George Mason U., Fairfax, Va., 1978-81, chmn. dept. nursing, 1981-85, dean and prof. sch. nursing, 1985—. Contbr. articles to profl. jours. Mem. Luxmanor Citizens Assn., Rockville, Md., 1985—; vol. senatorial campaign Citizens for Goldwater, Md., 1987. Recipient Bice Lectureship sch. nursing U. Va., Charlottesville, 1984, Progress of Excellence award region III Nat. U. Continuing Edn., 1985. Fellow Am. Acad. Nursing; mem. Am. Nurses Assn., Va. Soc. Profl. Nursing (bd. dirs. 1985-87), Am. Assn. Coll. Nursing (bd. dirs. 1987—), Nat. League Nursing (exec. com. 1987—), Cath. U. Nurses Alumnae (pres. 1979-81), Sigma Theta Tau (1st v.p. 1970-73). Roman Catholic. Office: George Mason Univ Sch Nursing 4400 University Dr Fairfax VA 22030

CARUS, MARIANNE, magazine editor; b. Dieringhausen, Rhineland, Germany, June 16, 1928; came to U.S., 1951; d. Gunter Wilhelm Alexander and Elisabeth (Gesell) Sondermann; m. Milton Blouke Carus, Mar. 3, 1951; children—Andre, Christine, Inga. Abitur, Gymnasium, Gummersbach, Germany; M.S., U. Freiburg, Germany; post grad., Sorbonne U., Paris, U. Chgo. Editor Open Court Pub. Co., LaSalle, Ill., 1964-73; editor-in-chief CRICKET Mag., LaSalle, 1973—; gen. mgr. CRICKET Mag., 1982—; cons. editor for textbooks Open Court Pub. Co., LaSalle, 1975—. Editor, compiler: Cricket's Choice, 1974. Pres. Ill. Valley Garden Club, LaSalle, 1960; dir. Ill. Valley Community Concert Assn., LaSalle, 1960; mem. LaSalle Women's Club, 1960—. Mem. ALA (dir. ALSC div. 1982-85), Mag. Pubs. Assn., Friends of USBBY, Soc. Children's Book Writers, Friends of the CCBC, Inc., Children's Reading Roundtable. Home: 2222 Chartres St Peru IL 61354 Office: Cricket Mag 315 5th St Peru IL 61354

CARUTHERS, BARBARA SUE APGAR, physician, educator; b. Guthrie, Okla., Oct. 4, 1943; d. Wallace Duke and Gloria Jayne (Glover) McMillin; m. Charles George Caruthers, Apr. 1, 1976; 1 child, Larisa Ann. BA in Biology, Loretto Heights Coll., 1965; MS in Anatomy, U. Mich., 1968; MD, Tex. Tech. Med. Sch., 1976. Diplomate Am. Bd. Family Practice, Am. Bd. Med. Examiners. Research asst. Parke Davis, Ann Arbor, Mich., 1965-66, Aerospace Med. Labs Wright-Patterson AFB, Ohio, 1968-70; instr. anatomy dept. Tex. Tech. U. Med. Sch., Lubbock, 1972-74, resident in family practice, 1976-79, clin. asst. prof., 1980-83; physician The Pavilion, Lubbock, 1981-83; sr. physician, dir. gynecology clinic U. Mich., 1983-87, instr. dept. family practice, 1984—, med. dir. Briarwood Health Ctr., 1986—, also mem. steering com. for ambulatory care; mem. staff Meth. Hosp., St. Mary of the Plains Hosp., U. Mich. Hosp. Mem. adv. bd. Lubbock chpt. March of Dimes, 1972-74. Recipient Upjohn Achievement award, 1976, Psychiatry Achievement award, 1976; Soroptimist Internat. grantee, 1978-79, U. Mich. Dept. Family Practice Resident Teaching award, 1985, 87, 88. Mem. Am. Acad. Family Practice, Lubbock County Med. Soc., Tex. Med. Assn., Mich. Acad. Family Practice, Alpha Omega Alpha. Democrat. Mormon. Home: 883 Scio Meadow Ann Arbor MI 48103 Office: U Mich Briarwood Health Ctr 325 Briarwood Circle Ann Arbor MI 48108

CARUZZI, DENISE BEECHAM, insurance company executive; b. Washington, Mar. 16, 1947; d. Theodore Joseph and Fay Lillian (Tabke) Caruzzi; children: John Hunter, Blakely Nichelle, Forest Scott. Student, East Tex. State U., 1965-67, Tex. Tech U., 1967-68; BS in Bus. Mgmt., Boise State U., 1975. Compensation analyst Morrison-Knudsen Co., Inc., Boise, Idaho, 1975-76, supr. internat. adminstrn., 1976-77, mgr. corp. compensation, 1977-78, dir. area office, Lisbon, Portugal, 1978-79, dir. area office, London, 1979-80, dir. internat. personnel, Boise, 1980-82; asst. dir. personnel Boise, 1982-86; pres. DBW Assocs., Moraga, Calif., 1986—, Calif. Casualty Mgmt. Co., San Mateo, Calif., 1987—. Bd. dirs. Boise YWCA, 1985-87, Community Housing Resource Bd., Boise, 1984-86, Hays Shelter Home Bd., Boise, 1984-86; pres. Hays Shelter Home Aux., Boise, 1984-87; personnel cons. Boise Sr. Ctr., 1985-86, Am. Assn. on Aging, 1987; dir. No. Calif. Human Relations Council, 1987—. Mem. Human Relations Assn. Treasure Valley (bd. dirs. 1985-86), Am. Soc. Personnel Adminstrs. Internat. (v.p. 1983-87, pres. 1987—, bd. dirs. 1982—). Office: Calif Casualty Mgmt Co 1900 Alameda de las Pulgas San Mateo CA 94403-1290

CARVAJAL, MARGI ELLEN CARTER, cosmetic company executive; b. Stephenville, Tex., Dec. 21, 1932; d. Daniel Richard and Frances (Foote) Carter; m. John Loren Carvajal Sr., Dec. 29, 1950; children: John Loren Jr., David, Jean, James Thomas, Scott. BA, U. Tex., 1952. Cons. Am. Chem. Co., Midland, Tex., 1949-51, v.p., 1959-65; cons. Mary Kay Cosmetics, Charleston, W.Va., 1972-81, dir. sales, 1982-84, sr. dir., 1984—, queen recruiting, beauty cons., 1986; make-up artist Charleston Light Opera Guild, Charleston Children's Theatre. Leader Girl Scouts U.S., Ponce, P.R., 1968, Boy Scouts Am., Charleston, 1970-78;pres. Texas City (Tex.) Jr. League, 1962, Charleston LWV, 1974, Holtz Elem. Sch. PTA, 1974, 78, John Adams Jr. High Sch. Polit. Action Com., 1982, parent adv. com. George Washington High Sch.; mem. ways and means com. Charleston Hospice. Recipient History award Midland chpt. DAR, 1949. Mem. Charleston C. of C., $400,000 Unit Club, Cadillac Club. Democrat. Presbyterian. Home and Office: 1518 Mount Vernon Rd Charleston WV 25314

CARVALHO, ANNA MARIE, human resouce specialist; b. Kearny, N.J., Apr. 9, 1955; d. Manuel and Mary Frances (Souto) C. AA in Edn., Fla. Jr. Coll., 1975; BS in Edn., Western Carolina U., 1977. Health, physical edn. instr. Duval County Pub. Sch., Jacksonville, Fla., 1977-82; pres. A.Y.S., Inc., Jacksonville, 1983-85; claims service rep. Blue Cross/Blue Shield, Jacksonville, 1985, human resource devel. specialist, 1986-87, supr. tng. and devel., 1987—; cons. Duval County Sch. System, Jacksonville, 1983-85, Blue Cross/Blue Sheild, Jacksonville, 1986; ptnr. Unlimited Performance, 1988—. County coordinator Spl. Olympics, Jacksonville, 1983-85, area dir., 1985. Mem. Am. Alliance Health and Physical Edn., Am. Soc. Tng. and Devel., Nat. Assn. Female Execs., Am. Mgmt. Assn., Kappa Delta Pi. Democrat. Roman Catholic. Office: Blue Cross/Blue Shield 532 Riverside Ave Jacksonville FL 32202

CARVER, BARBARA ANN, temporary help service executive; b. Niagara Falls, Ont., Can.; came to U.S., 1955; d. Robert Leroy Housser and Rosemary (Waloshuk) Murdoch; m. John Rudy Carver, Nov. 21, 1964; children—Kevin, Christopher. Student Tarrant County Jr. Coll., Ft. Worth, 1969-71. Nurse various hosps., Tex., 1971-79; staff supr. Norrell Service, Houston, 1979-80, office mgr., 1980-81, ter. mgr., 1981-82, mgr. major accounts, 1982-83, br. mgr., 1983-84; br. mgr. Temps & Co., 1984-88, area mgr., 1988—. Recipient Robert Gibson award Norrell Services, 1981, others; named Tex. Profit Ctr. of Yr., 1987-88. Office: Temps & Co 3707 FM 1960 W S-260 Houston TX 77068

CARVER, DOROTHY LEE ESKEW (MRS. JOHN JAMES CARVER), educator; b. Brady, Tex., July 10, 1926; d. Clyde Albert and A. Maurine (Meadows) Eskew; student So. Ore. Coll., 1942-43, Coll. Eastern Utah, 1965-67; B.A., U. Utah, 1968; M.A., Cal. State Coll. at Hayward, 1970; postgrad. Mills Coll., 1971; m. John James Carver, Feb. 26, 1944; children—John James, Sheila Carver Bentley, Chuck, David. Instr., Rutherford Bus. Coll., Dallas, 1944-45; sec. Adolph Coors Co., Golden, Colo., 1945-47; instr. English, Coll. Eastern Utah, Price, 1968-69; instr. speech Modesto (Calif.) Jr. Coll., 1970-71; instr. personal devel. men and women Heald Bus. Colls., Oakland, Calif., 1972-74, dean curricula, Walnut Creek, Calif., 1974-86; instr. Diablo Valley Coll., Pleasant Hill, Calif., 1986—; communications cons. Oakland Army Base, Crocker Bank, U.S. Steel, I. Magnin, Artec Internat. Author: Developing Listening Skills. Mem. Gov's. Conf. on Higher Edn. in Utah, 1968; mem. finance com. Coll. Eastern Utah, 1967-69; active various community drives. Judge election Republican party, 1960, 64. Bd. dirs. Opportunity Center, Symphony of the Mountain. Mem. AAUW, Bus. and Profl. Womens Club, Nat. Assn. Deans and Women Adminstrs., Delta Kappa Gamma. Episcopalian (supt. Sunday Sch. 1967-69). Clubs: Soroptimist Internat. (pres. Walnut Creek 1979-80 sec., founder region 1978-80); Order Eastern Star. Home: 20 Coronado Ct Walnut Creek CA 94596 Office: Diablo Valley Coll 2085 N Broadway Walnut Creek CA 94596

CARVER, JOAN WILLSON, publishing executive, artist; b. St. Paul; d. Stuart Van Vranken and Marie (Carlson) Willson; m. Norman F. Carver Jr., Aug. 15, 1953; children: Norman III, Cristina. BA, Smith Coll., 1950; postgrad., Yale U. Sch. Architecture, 1950-53, Kyoto U., Japan, 1953-54. Architect Larson Playter Architects, Eau Claire, Wis., 1953, John W. King Assocs. Architects, Tokyo, 1954-55; designer Norman F. Carver Jr. Architect, Kalamazoo, 1958-78; v.p., treas. Documan Press Ltd., Kalamazoo, 1979—; artist Joan Willson Carver Porcelains, Kalamazoo, 1981—; instr. ceramics Kalamazoo Arts Ctr., 1983—. Editor: World Architecture Calendars, 1982-87, various architecture books, 1982-87; exhibited in group shows at Wichita (Kans.) Art Mus., Kalamazoo Art Ctr., Battle Creek (Mich.) Art Mus., Circle Gallery, Six 17 Gallery, co-founder, editor Perspecta-Yale Architecture Jour., numerous others. Sustainer Kalamazoo Jr. League, 1971—; chmn. Kalamazoo Dental Clinic, 1972; bd. dirs. Kalamazoo Symphony Orch., 1975-78. Mem. Kalamazoo Inst. Arts (bd. dirs. 1966-73, 78-84, pres. bd. dirs. 1970-73, chmn. exhbns. 1967-73, 78-87, scholarship com. 1980—), Women's Work, Mich. Potters Assn. (Mich. Ceramics award 1987). Episcopalian. Clubs: Service of Kalamazoo (pres. 1969-70), Current Events (Kalamazoo) (pres. 1982-83, treas. 1986-87). Office: Documan Press Ltd 3201 Lorraine Ave Kalamazoo MI 49008

CARVER, JUDITH RAI, surgical supply company executive; b. Chgo., May 8, 1945; d. Raymond Edwin and Meri Frances (Petolick) Anderson; m. John H. Walters III, Sept. 9, 1967 (dec. 1971); m. Joseph Wayne Carver, May 23, 1981. Diploma in Nursing, Roseland Community Hosp., Chgo., 1966; B.S. in Health Sci., Chapman Coll., 1981. Asst. operating rm. supr. West Valley Community Hosp., Encino, Calif., 1977-79; sales rep. Xomed, Inc., Jacksonville, Fla., 1979, Chaston Inc., Dayville, Conn., 1979-80; regional sales mgr. Carapace, Inc., Tulsa, 1980-81; co-owner, sales exec. Western Surg. Specialities, Benicia, Calif., 1981—. Vol. Big Sister of Solano County, Calif., 1984; pres., bd. dirs. Big Bros.-Big Sisters of Napa and Solano Counties, 1986-88. Home: 586 Capitol Dr. Benicia CA 94510 Office: Western Surg Specialities 940 Tyler St Suite 16 Benicia CA 94510

CARVER, LORETTA MYERS, professional society administrator; b. Memphis, June 24, 1939; d. Howard Henry and Gertrude Mercedes (Hill) Myers; m. John B. Carver, Apr. 1965 (div. Nov. 1972); children: Terry N. Richardson, Angela Richardson Mason. BS in Psychology and Edn. magna cum laude, Mid. Tenn. State U., 1975, MA in Psychology, 1976. Lic. psychol. examiner, Tenn. Psychol. examiner, dir. employee assistance program consultation and edn. div. Rutherford County Guidance Ctr., Murfreesboro, Tenn., 1975-84; dir. program and mem. services Tenn. Assn. Mental Health Ctrs., Nashville, 1984—; attended seminars in field, 1968-83. Mem. rev. bd. Rutherford County Ct. Foster Care. Mem. Am. Soc. Assn. Execs., Tenn. Soc. Assn. Execs., Tenn. Psychol. Assn., Southeastern Psychol. Assn., Psi Chi, Phi Alpha Theta, Kappa Delta Phi. Lodge: Soroptimists. Office: Tenn Assn Mental Health Ctrs PO Box 22659 Nashville TN 37202

CARVER, PATRICIA HALL, college administrator; b. Atlantic City, Aug. 29, 1950; d. William Bernard Hall and Gloria Clarisa (Livingston) Graham; m. Thomas Henry Miller, Jr., Mar. 8, 1975 (div. 1985); children: Thomas H., Dion Bernard; m. Robert Bruce Carver, Mar. 31, 1985. AA in Music, Atlantic Community Coll., Mays Landing, N.J., 1970; BS in Ednl. Speech Pathology and Audiology, NYU, 1972; PhD in Ednl. Adminstrn., Yeshiva U., N.Y.C., 1974; postgrad., Rutgers U., 1987—. Cert. Pub. Mgmt., N.J. Counselor Atlantic Community Coll., 1972-73, dir. of students, 1973-78; assoc. dir. mgmt. and evaluation program Atlanta (Ga.) U., 1979-80; admissions rep. Stockton State Coll., Pomona, N.J., 1981-82, dir. admissions, 1982-88; mgr. organizational devel. programs Honeywell, Inc., Pomona, 1988—; instr. numerous workshops, N.J. and Atlanta; co-founder and prin. Profl. Skills Ctr., Atlanta, 1980-83; cons. and lectr. in field. Contbr. articles to profl. jours. Mem. Galloway Bd. Edn., 1986—, Galloway Twp. PTA. Named one of Outstanding Young Women in Am. 1980, 82, 84, 85, 87. Mem. Nat. Assn. Female Execs., Nat. Ctr. Human Potential Seminars and Services, Am. Cancer Soc., Mid. States Assn., Coll. Registrars and Officers of Admissions, N.J. Assn. Coll. Admissions Counselors. Democrat. Methodist. Lodge: Soroptimists. Home: 742 Whalers Cove Place Smithville NJ 08201

CARY, ARLENE D., hotel company sales executive; b. Chgo., Dec. 19, 1930; d. Seymour S. and Shirley L. (Land) C.; student U. Wis., 1949-52; B.A., U. Miami, 1953; m. Elliot D. Hagle, Dec. 30, 1972 (div.). Public relations account exec. Robert Howe & Co., 1953-55; sales mgr. Martin B. Iger & Co., 1955-57; sales mgr., gen. mgr. Sorrento Hotel, Miami Beach, Fla., 1957-59; gen. mgr. Mayflower Hotel, Manomet, Mass., 1959-60; various positions Aristocrat Inns of Am., 1960-72; v.p. sales, McCormick Center Hotel, Chgo., 1972—. Active Nat. Women's Polit. Caucus, Internat. Orgn. Women Execs., membership promotion chmn., 1979-80, bd. dirs., 1980-81. Recipient disting. salesman award Sales and Mktg. Execs. Internat., 1977. Mem. Profl. Conv. Mgmt. Assn., Nat. Assn. Exposition Mgrs., Hotel Sales Mgmt. Assn., Meeting Planners Internat., Am. Soc. Assn. Execs., N.Y. Soc. Assn. Execs., Chgo. Soc. Assn. Execs., Ind. Hotel Alliance (sec. 1986—). Jewish. Home: 1130 S Michigan Ave Apt 3203 Chicago IL 60605 Office: McCormick Ctr Hotel 23d and Lakeshore Dr Chicago IL 60616

CARY, LISA JEANENE, infosystems specialist; b. Shirley, Mass., Jan. 2, 1961; d. Joel B. and Patricia A. (Davis) Stewart; m. Toby Lance Cary, Apr. 26, 1986. Student, Pa. State U., 1978-82, Norwalk (Conn.) State Tech., 1984—. Draftsperson Joint Med. Products, Stamford, Conn., 1985-86, computer assisted design coordinator, 1986—. Mem. Mensa. Office: Joint Med Products Corp 860 Canal St Stamford CT 06902

CARY, MARY KATHERINE, college administrator; b. Detroit, Sept. 10, 1953; d. Bernard L. and Margaret Mary (Ryan) C. BA, Aquinas Coll., 1975; MLS, U. Mich., 1976; MA, Cen. Mich. U., 1983. Librarian Grand Valley State Coll., Allendale, Mich., 1976-77; bus. librarian Coll. St. Thomas, St. Paul, 1977-79; regional librarian Cen. Mich. U., Troy, 1979-80; librarian Nat. Bank Detroit, 1980-82, compensation analyst, 1982; bus. subject specialist U. Toledo, 1983-87, asst. dir. library, 1985-87; dir. admissions and student services Sch. Info. and Library Studies U. Mich., Ann Arbor, 1988—. Compiler book: Information for International Marketing, 1986. Allocations co-chairperson United Way Gr. Toledo, 1985-87. Mem. ALA, Acad. Library Assn. Ohio (treas. 1986-87), Assn. Coll. and Research Libraries. Home: 3167 Lakehaven Dr Ann Arbor MI 48105 Office: U Mich Sch Info and Library Studies Ann Arbor MI 48109-1346

CARY, MIMI KUO, real estate investment banker; b. Hong Kong, Dec. 15, 1947; came to U.S., 1963; d. Zing-Yang Kuo and Portia (Y.L.) Sheen; m. Anthony N. Cary, Mar. 1, 1968 (div. Jan. 1980); m. William Moffat Drake, Aug. 8, 1988. AB, Radcliffe Coll., 1970. V.p. Grubb & Ellis Co., San Francisco, 1982-85; sr. v.p. Bear Stearns & Co., San Francisco, 1985-86; pres., chief exec. officer The Amerin Group, Inc., San Francisco, 1986—. Republican. Home: 1143 The Alameda Berkeley CA 94707-2551 Office: The Amerin Group Inc 41 Sutter St Suite 1563 San Francisco CA 94104

CARY, SHARON L., controller, computer installation consultant, fruit and poultry farmer; b. San Francisco, Nov. 5, 1950. Office mgr. Shamrock Motors, Mill Valley, Calif., 1975-77; acctg. clk. Sonoma Lifestyle Furniture, Rohnert Park, Calif., 1977-80; acct. Living Earth Crafts, Santa Rosa, Calif., 1980-83; controller Santa Rosa Golf and Country Club, 1983—; prin. Summit Enterprises, Calif., 1977—; cons. in field, Santa Rosa, 1970—. Author: Smooth Transition: A Guide to Your Small Business's First Computer, 1985.

CASALE, MARIA L., foundation executive, communications consultant; b. N.Y.C., Apr. 26, 1948; d. Salvatore A. and Marie E. (Faga) Casale; m. John J. Kennedy, Sept. 18, 1976; 1 child, David Casale Kennedy. B.A., Coll. New Rochelle, 1969. Social worker Villa Loretto Sch., Peekskill, N.Y., 1970-75; editorial asst. Arno Press, N.Y.C., 1976-78; program coordinator Alicia Patterson Found., N.Y.C., 1978-82, v.p. bd. dirs., 1980-87 ; treas., bd. dirs. Alicia Patterson Found., 1988; cons. in field; cons. CB Communication, N.Y.C., 1983-87. Mem. Women in Communications. Home: 574 West End Ave New York NY 10024

CASAS, LILLIAN, medical librarian; b. Cayey, P.R., Oct. 31, 1924; d. Guillermo and Maria (Llera) C.; B.A., U. P.R., 1951, M. Health Edn., 1973; M.S. in L.S., Syracuse U., 1958; m. Guillermo Lopez, May 3, 1956. Tchr. P.R. Dept. Edn. 1950; asst. librarian U. P.R. Sch. Medicine, San Juan, 1951-57, head cataloger, 1959-60, librarian, 1961-65, dir. Med. Scis. Campus Library, 1966-79; library cons., 1979—. Mem. P.R. Library Assn. (pres. 1964), Med. Library Assn. Home: 772 Gave Urb Lourdes Trujillo Alto PR 00760

CASE, APRIL OURS, industrial relations specialist; b. East Liverpool, Ohio, June 24, 1959; d. Virgil Lewis and Delores Jean (Everett) O.; m. David Byron Case, Aug. 14, 1982. BS in Psychology, Ohio State U., 1981; MA in Indsl. Relations, U. Ill., 1982. Bus. instr. U. Ky. Community Coll., Louisville, 1983, asst. prof., 1984-86; indsl. relations specialist Gen. Electric Co., Bloomington, Ind., 1986—. Mem. mktg. com. Louisville United Way, 1986; advisor Jr. Achievement, Bloomington, 1986-87. Mem. South Cen. Ind. Personnel Assn., Am. Soc. Tng. and Devel. Republican. Methodist. Home: 2520 Round Hill Ct Bloomington IN 47401

CASE, BARBARA SHARON, librarian; b. San Pedro, Calif., Nov. 21, 1946; d. Charles C. and Stella May (Pierce) Case; m. James V. Halloran III, Sept. 7, 1974. B.A., U. Calif.-Berkeley, 1969, M.L.S., 1970; postgrad. in bus. Harvard U., 1972-73. Catalog librarian U. Calif.-Santa Barbara, 1970-71; adminstrv. asst. to univ. librarian Calif. State U.-Los Angeles, 1973-76, head cataloging sect., 1976-82, mgr. cataloging services, 1982-83, coordinator library automation planning, 1982-83, asst. univ. librarian, 1984—; chairperson Calif. State U. Systemwide Bibliographic Standards Com., Long Beach, 1979-80, Systemwide Library Automation Standards Com., 1980-81, mem. Systemwide Online Pub. Access Catalog Evaluation Com., 1981—; chairperson info. resources mgmt. steering com. Calif. State U.-Los Angeles, 1986—. Mem. ALA, Calif. Library Assn., Calif. Acad. and Research Libraries. Home: 612 S Gertruda Ave Redondo Beach CA 90277 Office: Calif State U Library 5151 State University Dr Los Angeles CA 90032

CASE, ELIZABETH, artist, writer; b. Long Beach, Calif., July 24, 1930; d. Nelson and Sarah Lee (Odend'hal) Case; children: Walter J. Zwicker Jr., Keith Allen Zwicker, Pat James Cioffi, Susan Karin Cioffi. Student, French Inst., 1946, Art Students League, 1948-49, Elmira Coll., 1949-51, Syracuse U., 1951, Chaffey Coll., Ontario, Calif., Scripps Coll., Claremont, Calif., 1954. With dept. animation Walt Disney Prodns., Burbank, Calif., 1956-58; mem. faculty Lighthouse Art and Music Camp, 1961, New Hope Art Sch., Pa., 1961; asst. mgr. promotion, copywriter Reinhold Pub. Co., N.Y.C., 1962-63; copywriter Columbia U. Press, 1963; coordinator advt. Orbit Imperial Design Corp., 1964; prin., dir. Gadfly Prodns., 1969—; mem. faculty Ft. Lee Adult Sch., 1975-82; sr. copywriter/designer spl. projects coll. textbook advt. Prentice-Hall, Inc., Englewood Cliffs, N.J., 1975-77; mem. promotion and design staff Rutherford Mus., 1979; mgr. sales promotion M. Grumbacher, Inc., 1979-82; typographer Graphic Tech. Inc., N.Y.C., 1983—. USN combat artist, 1974—; one-person shows research library exhbn. facility Walt Disney Prodns., 1957-58, Swain's Gallery, New Hope, Pa., 1963, D'Alessio Gallery, N.Y.C., 1963, Gallery 8, N.Y.C., 1969, Ft. Lee Pub. Library, 1975, Ridgefield Pub. Library, 1977, Old Bridge Pub. Library, 1978, Edgewater (N.J.) Nat. Bank, 1983, Edgewater Pub. Library, 1984, Ea. Va. Med. Ctr., Norfolk, 1984; exhibited in group shows at Friends Cen., Phila., 1960, Hist. Soc. Ann. Exhbn., Philips Mill, Pa., 1962-63, Englewood Armory Show, 1967-68, Hadassah, Paramus, N.J., 1969, Bergen Community Coll., 1970, traveling exhbn. Bicentennial Am. Freedoms, 1975-76, Submarine Exhbn., Boat Show, Bergen County Mall, 1977, So. Vt. Art Ctr., 1980, Edgewater Arts Council (1st prize), 1982, Dawning Light Artists Fall Exhibit, Queens, N.Y., 1982, Bergen County Mus., 1984-85; represented in permanent collections at Washington Navy Yard Combat Art Collection, Ch. of Christ, Jersey City, Edgewater Pub. Library; executed murals at INSCON, San Dimas, Calif., 1956, Los Angeles County Hosp., 1958, Delaware Canal, New Hope, 1959; mural design Allegheny Airlines, Lumberville, Pa., 1960; mural corner Main and 202, New Hope, 1960, Lumberville Meth. Ch., 1961, swimming pool, Jerico Valley, Pa., 1961, Orbit Imperial Design Corp., N.Y.C., 1965, Fabric Shop, Ft. Lee, 1969, 72, Ch. of Good Shepherd, 1971, Old Bridge Pub. Library, 1977, History of Women Voting (triptych) for traveling exhbn. Momentous Events in American History, Nat. Soc. Mural Painters, 1980-82, History of Typography, GTI, N.Y.C., 1985, Clayton Hall Gallery, U. Del., 1985; illustrator cover Bucks County Life, Doylestown, Pa., 1961, Vanity Fair Books, 1962, Am. Scandinavian Rev., 1962, Molecular Kinetic Theory, 1963, Theory of Lanthinides and Chemical Energy, 1963, Harle Publs., 1969-70, Programmed Algebra vols. 1 and 2, 1977, vol. 3, 1979, Use and Misuse of Statistics, 1978; What Do I Do with a Major in ... (Malnig), 2d edit., 1984. Recipient Spring Concours award Art Students League, 1949, Outstanding Achievement award Elmira Coll., 1976, Merit award Edgewater Council, 1976; subject of 35-minute films The Wrong Elf, 1978, Stroke of Color, 1984. Mem. Nat. Soc. Mural Painters (publicity chmn. 1973-75, sec. 1975, dir. pub. relations 1981-83, editor newsletter 1980-81). Home and Studio: Edgewater NJ 07020-0058

CASE, KAREN ANN, lawyer; b. Milw., Apr. 7, 1944; d. Alfred F. and Hilda M. (Tomich) Case. B.S., Marquette U., 1963, J.D. 1966; LL.M., N.Y.U., 1973. Bar: Wis. 1966, U.S. Ct. Claims, 1973, U.S. Tax Ct. 1973. Ptnr. Meldman, Case & Weine, Milw., 1973-85; ptnr. Meldman, Case & Weine div. Mulcahy & Wherry, S.C., 1985-87; lectr. U. Wis., Milw., 1974-78; guest lectr. Marquette U. Law Sch., 1975-78. Pres. council Alverno Coll., 1988—. Fellow Wis. Bar Found. (dir. 1977—, treas. 1980—); mem. Milw. Assn. Women Lawyers (bd. dirs. 1975-78, 81-82), Milw. Bar Assn. (bd. dirs. 1985-87), State Bar Wis. (bd. govs. 1981-85, 87—, dir. taxation sect. 1981-87, vice chmn. 1986-87), Am. Acad. Matrimonial Lawyers, Nat. Assn. Women Lawyers (Wis. del. 1982-83), Alverno Coll. Pres.' Council, Milw. Rose Soc. (pres. 1981, dir. 1981-83), Friends of Boerner Bat. Gardens (pres. 1984—), Clubs: Professional Dimensions (dir. 1985-87), Tempo (sec. 1984-85). Contbr. articles to legal jours. Home: 9803 W Meadow Park Dr Hales Corners WI 53130 Office: 125 S Webster Madison WI 53708

CASE, SHARON LYNNE, legal professional; b. Milw., Nov. 8, 1951; d. Samuel and Pauline Matilda (Spitzer) Bentley; m. Clyde Martin Case Jr., Dec. 7, 1975; children: Rebecca Lynne, Rachel Megan. BS in Home Econs./Interior Design, So. Ill. U., 1973; BS in Elem. Edn., Coll. Great Falls, 1985. Cert. elem. and art tchr. Exec. sec. Rugg, Knopp and Lambert, Inc., New Berlin, Wis., 1973-75; legal sec. James R. Paul, Atty. at Law, Great Falls, Mont., 1975-80, Smith, Baillie & Walsh, Great Falls, 1980-84; substitute tchr. Great Falls Sch. Dist. #1, 1985-88, Vaughn (Mont.) Sch. Dist. #74, 1986-88; sales rep. Avon Products, Great Falls, 1986—; paralegal Bottomly Law Offices, Great Falls, 1988—. Editor (newsletter) Mont. Life News, 1985-88. State chairperson Mont. Luths. for Life, Great Falls, 1982-88; mem. Great Falls Right to Life, 1984—; counselor Pregnancy Help Ctr., Great Falls, 1986-87; mem., chmn. Reflections, Lewis and Clark PTA, 1986-87; sec. Peace Luth. Women's Missionary League, Great Falls, 1987-88; mem. choir Calvary Community Ch., Great Falls. Mem. Nat. Assn. Legal Profls., Mont. Assn. Legal Profls., Great Falls Assn. Legal Profls. Republican. Club: Christian Women's (Great Falls) (asst. book chmn. 1986-88).

CASEI, NEDDA, mezzo soprano; b. Balt.; d. Howard Thomas and Lyda Marie (Graupman) Casey; m. John A. Wiles, Jr., Dec. 1971 (div. May 1979); m. Samuel Strasbourger, Dec. 25, 1983 (dec. June 1987). B in Performing Arts Adminstrn., Fordham U., 1982; studied voice with, William P. Herman, N.Y.C., Vittorio Piccinini, Milan, Italy, Loretta Corelli, N.Y.C.; also student piano, langs., ballet. tchr. master classes, lectr. universities and festivals.; judge vocal competions for Metropolitan Opera, Fulbright Scholarship competition. Operatic debut Theatre Royal de la Monnaie, Brussels, 1960; with La Scala, Milan; operatic performances at Basel (Switzerland) Stadttheater, Gran Liceo, Barcelona, Teatro Carlo Fenice, Genova, San Remo, Trieste Opera, Opera du Rhin, Strasbourg, Salzburg Festspielhaus, Teatro San Carlo, Naples, Chgo. Lyric Opera, Bogota Opera, Caracas Opera, Pitts. Opera, Vancouver Opera, Cape Town Opera, Brno Opera, Bratislava Opera, Kosice Opera, Prague Opera, Miami Opera, Houston Opera, San Diego Opera, Hartford Opera, Phila. Opera, Toledo Opera, Dayton Opera, Memphis Opera, Mobile Opera, Los Angeles Opera, Boston Opera, N.J. Opera, Taipei Opera, Met. Opera, N.Y.C., 1964—; performances in various mus. festivals, concert tours, also symphonic concerts, oratorios in Europe, South Africa, Cen. Am., S.Am., Can., U.S., Far East, Middle East and Australia; performed on radio and TV in Holland, Belgium, Leipzig, Japan, U.S., German Dem. Republic, Fed. Republic of Germany, Hong Kong, Singapore; performed at White House, Washington, 1967; made various recs. Supraphon, Everest, Nonesuch, Concert Hall, others; contbr. articles to profl. jours. Coordinator mus. events and benefits for Internat. Center for the Disabled, Morningside Home and Gerontol. Acad. Recipient New Orleans Opera award, 1959, Rockefeller Found. award, 1962, 64, Community Leaders and Noteworthy Americans, 1975-76, Woman of Achievement award, 1969, Martha Baird Rockefeller awards, 1962, 64, Outstanding Young Singers award, 1959. Mem. Actor's Equity, AFTRA, Am. Guild Mus. Artists (bd. govs., nat. pres. 1983—), AFTRA, Nat. Assn. Tchrs. Singing. Office: Am Guild Mus Artists 1727 Broadway New York NY 10019

CASEL, MARY LYNN, real estate broker; b. Carthage, N.Y., Jan. 16, 1943; d. Floyd Albert and Mary Frances (Schack) Neuroth; m. Ronald Anthony Casel, Nov. 28, 1963 (div. Nov. 1977); children—Mark, Steven, Glen. Grad. Harper Method, Rochester, N.Y., 1961. Lic. real estate broker. Owner M. L. Salon, Rochester, N.Y., 1962-72; specialty tchrs.-aide Broward County, Ft. Lauderdale, Fla., 1973-77; office mgr. Broward County Voter Registration, Margate, Fla., 1977-82; real estate salesperson Pelican Bay, Daytona Beach, Fla., 1982-84, broker, 1984-86, broker, sales mgr., 1986—. Mem. adv. bd. Democratic Club, Margate, Fla., 1977-82. Mem. Nat. Assn. Realtors, Fla. Home Builders Assn., Nat. Home Builders Assn., Daytona Beach Home Builders Assn., Daytona Beach Bd. Realtors, Ft. Lauderdale Bd. Realtors, Nat. Assn. Women in Constrn. (v.p. 1988—), Nat. Assn. Female Execs. Avocations: travel, dancing, theater, real estate investments. Democrat. Roman Catholic. Home: 825 Pelican Bay Dr Daytona Beach FL 32019 Office: 101 Seahawk Dr Daytona Beach FL 32019

CASEY, BARBARA A. PEREA, state representatvie, educator; b. Las Vegas, N.Mex., Dec. 21, 1951; d. Joe D. and Julia A. (Armijo) Perea; m. Frank J. Casey, Aug. 5, 1978. BA, N.Mex. U., 1972; MA, Highland U., Las Vegas, N.Mex., 1973. Instr. N.Mex. Highlands U., Las Vegas, 1972-74; tchr. Roswell Ind. Schs., Roswell, N.Mex., 1974—; mem. N.Mex. Ho. of Reps., 1984—; instr. N.Mex. Mil. Inst., Roswell, 1977-82, Roswell Police Acad., 1984. Mem. NEA (Adv. of of Yr.), AAUW, Am. Bus. Women's Assn., N.Mex. Endowment for Humanities. Democrat. Roman Catholic. Home: 1214 E First Roswell NM 88201

CASEY, BEVERLY ANN, postmaster; b. Decaturville, Tenn., Aug. 6, 1949; d. Willie Hugh and Lillian Blanche (Ivy) Tillman; m. John Robert Casey, Jan. 19, 1969 (div. 1982); children—John Gary, Kimberly Jean. Student Jackson State Community Coll., 1982-84. Sec. State of Tenn., Western Institute, 1969-76; post office clk. U.S. Postal Service, Western Institute, 1977-82, postmaster, 1982-84; postmaster U.S. Postal Service, Pickwick Dam, Tenn., 1984—; officer-in-charge U.S. Postal Service, Michie, Tenn., 1984. Bd. dirs. Pickwick Med. Clinic, 1986; vol. Hardeman chpt. Saint Jude, Bolivar, Tenn., 1983; town chmn. Reelfoot council Girl Scouts U.S., 1980-84, activities chmn., 1980-84, recipient Appreciation award, 1983. Named Outstanding 3d Class Postmaster 380 area U.S. Postal Service, 1984; recipient Vol. Service award Cystic Fibrosis Found., Tenn. Chpt., 1982; Vol. Appreciation Cert. Western Mental Health, 1984. Mem. Nat. Assn. Postmasters of U.S., Nat. League of Postmasters (v.p. Tenn. br. 1984-86), 380 Postmasters Assn. (pres. 1983-84), U.S. Postal Service (bd. dirs. women's adv. council 1983—). Baptist. Club: Lioness. Avocations: walking; tennis. Home: PO Box 363 Pickwick Dam TN 38365 Office: US Postal Service Pickwick Dam TN 38365

CASEY, COLLEEN SUE, lawyer; b. Bridgeport, Conn., May 24, 1956; d. William Vincent and Marie Frances (Rock) C. BA, U. Calif., 1979; JD, Golden Gate U., 1982. Bar: Calif. Law clk. Law Offices Martin A. Schainbaum, San Francisco, 1980-82; lawyer Folik, Filley and Schey, San Francisco, 1982-85; in-house counsel Schrambling and Chu, San Francisco, 1985-87; assoc. Robert C. Elkus Law Corp., San Francisco, 1987—. Editor-in-chief Barrister Mag., 1985-87. Mem. ABA (del. young lawyers div. 1986, task force tax section), Calif. St. Bar Assn. (del. 1986), Am. Judicature Soc., St. Thomas Soc. Republican. Roman Catholic. Office: Schrambling and Chu 595 Market St #2660 San Francisco CA 94105

CASEY, DEBORAH MARIE, contract administrator; b. Watertown, N.Y., Feb. 5, 1959; d. Walter Henry and Beverly Jean (Young) Cote; m. John Eugene Casey, Mar. 14, 1982 (div. May 1988). Student N. Nev. Community Coll., 1978. Office mgr. Air Service Co., Reno, Nev., 1979-81, Bridgerland Motors, Kemmerer, Wyo., 1981-82; dir. profit sharing Metalogic, Phoenix, 1982—, contract adminstr., 1982—; asst. dir. mktg. Novelogic, Phoenix, 1986, dir. mktg., 1986—. Mem. Internat. Platform Assn. Office: Metalogic 275 S Black Canyon Hwy Phoenix AZ 85009

CASEY, DENISE MAPES, foundation administrator; b. Pontiac, Mich., Nov. 5, 1955; d. Francis Jennings and Ines Evelyn (McReynolds) Mapes; m. Bradford Earl Casey, Aug. 25, 1985; 1 stepchild, Sabrina Isabelle. Cert. in interpretation for hearing impaired, Ohlone Coll., Fremont, Calif., 1984. Asst. project coordinator People First of Calif., San Jose, 1980; pre-vocat. instr. Agnews Devel. Ctr., San Jose, 1980-84; vocat. instr. Community Assn. for the Retarded Inc, Palo Alto, Calif., 1984-85, asst. dir., 1985-86, dir., 1986—; agy. rep. San Jose Spl. Olympics, 1984-85; mem. service providers adv. com. San Andreas Regional Ctr., Campbell, Calif., 1986—; mem. adult services com. San Mateo County Coordinating Council on Devel. Disabilities. Contbr. articles to profl. jours. Organizer Com. to Elect John Anderson for Pres., Fremont, 1980. Mem. Autism Soc. Am., Nat. Assn. Female Execs., Calif. Assn. for Rehabilitatory Facilities, Palo Alto C. of C. Office: Community Assn for the Retarded Inc 3864 Middlefield Rd Palo Alto CA 94306

CASEY, LINDA MARIE, oil company executive; b. Dearborn, Mich., Jan. 14, 1952; d. Michael Henry and Leocadia Marie (Harkiewicz) Nowak; m. Gerald Lee Casey, June 12, 1976; children: Megan Colleen, Meredith Anne. BS in Biology and Chemistry, Ohio Dominican Coll., 1973; postgrad., Morehead (Ky.) State U., 1978-82. Cert. product safety mgr., Ky. Coorindator product safety Ashland (Ky.) Oil, Inc., Columbus, Ohio, 1973-76, sr. product safety coordinator, 1976-77; tech. asst. to v.p. Ashland (Ky.) Oil, Inc., Ashland, 1977-81, exec. asst. to v.p., 1981-83; specialist occupational health Ashland Petroleum Co., 1983-86, mgr. product safety, 1986—. Bd. dirs. Ashland Child Devel. Ctr., 1983-85. Mem. Am. Chem. Soc., Internat. Cert. Hazard Control Mgrs. Republican. Roman Catholic.

CASEY, MADELYN BENNETT, marketing professsional; b. Marksville, La., Jan. 9, 1951; d. Benjamin Clyde and Mary Frances (Taylor) Bennett; m. Gaynor Paul George, Nov. 29, 1969 (div. 1983); children: Mary, Paul; m. Johnny Carroll Casey, Dec. 21, 1984. Student, La. State U., 1968-70, La. Coll., 1980-83, 88. Mgr., cons. H&R Block, Marksville, 1970-71; tchr. Presentation Elem. Sch., Marksville, 1971-72; mgr. Shenandoah County Club, Marksville, 1972-74; owner, operator Hair by George Salon and Boutique, Marksville, 1974-82; exec. acct. Sta. KLAX-TV, Alexandria, Va., 1982-83, La. Bus. Jour., Nachitoches, 1983-85; dir. pub. relations Rapides Regional Med. Ctr., Nachitoches, 1985-87, v.p. mktg., 1987—; cons., speaker in field. Contbr. articles to profl. jours. and TV program. Active United Way. Mem. Am. Assn. Hsop. Pub. Relations, Am. Advt. Fedn., Nat. Assn. Female Execs., Am. Hosp. Assn., Am. Mgmt. Assn., Alexandria C. of C., Cen. La. C. of C. (chmn. communication). Home: 5221 Argonne Alexandria LA 71301 Office: Rapides Regional Med Ctr 211 4th St Alexandria LA 71301

CASEY, MARGUERITE, health care executive; b. Detroit, Mar. 11, 1937; d. James Edward and Margaret McGarry C. BA, Siena Heights Coll., 1963; MA, Mundelein Coll., 1972. Elem. tchr. Dominican Sisters, Ohio, Ill, Mich. and N.Y.C., 1960-70; dir. religious edn. St. Ambrose Parish, Latham, N.Y., 1971-78; staff trainer, personnel mgr., dir. human resources, community affairs, health edn. Empire Blue Cross & Blue Shield, Albany, N.Y., 1978—. Vol. Tri-County Council of Vietnam Vets., Albany, 1986-87, Cath. Cen. High Sch., Troy, N.Y., 1986-87; bd. dirs. ARC, Albany, 1985-87, Albany Coalition for Aging Services, 1986-87. Mem. Am. Pub. Health Assn., Coalition on Critical Health Issues, N.Y. State Pub. Health Assn. (bd. dirs. 1983-87), Assn. Labor, Mgmt. Adminstrs. and Cons. on Alcoholism, Albany-Colonie C. of C. (corp. del. 1987). Office: Empire Blue Cross & Blue Shield PO Box 8650 Albany NY 12208

CASEY, MARIE ANN, public relations company executive; b. Saint Louis, Sept. 28, 1956; d. Paul Edward and Marie Carolyn (Morheuser) C.; m. Kenneth Joseph Entringer, Nov. 24, 1979. BA in Polit. Sci. and Speech Communications summa cum laude, U. Mo., St. Louis, 1978. Asst. editor St. Louis Constrn. News and Rev., 1978-79, editor, 1979-83; pres. Casey Communications, Inc., St. Louis, 1983—; mem. devel. bd. Cardinal Glennon Children's Hosp., St. Louis, 1983-85; bd. dirs. KWMU-FM, St. Louis. Campaign mgr. 13th dist. Senator Wayne Goode, St. Louis, 1984; bd. dirs. Alternatives to Living in Violent Envionrs., St. Louis, 1985-87. Recipient Flair award Advt. Fedn. St. Louis, 1984, Best of Class award Mo. Lit. Awards Competition, 1985. Mem. Internat. Assn. Bus. Communicators, St. Louis Bus. Editors, Soc. Profl. Journalists, Soc. Mktg. Profl. Services (edn. com. 1986—). Roman Catholic. Club: Not Just Another Art Directors (St. Louis).

CASEY, MARIE C. (MRS. JOHN J. CASEY), managing editor; b. New Haven, Jan. 13, 1917; d. James Edward and Mary (Lonergan) Coogan; B.A., Coll. New Rochelle, 1938; m. John J. Casey, Aug. 20, 1946; 1 dau., Eileen Mary Casey Jachym. Advt. mgr. Brock-Hall Dairy, Hamden, Conn., 1946-53; mng. editor Am. Jour. Sci., Yale U., 1962—, assoc. mng. editor Radiocarbon. Sec., Rec. for the Blind, New Haven chpt., 1962-65; editor bull. ch. Women United of Conn., 1975-82. Mem. AAUW (corr. sec. Conn. div. 1963-69, past pres. local br., chmn. fellowships and scholarships coms. local br., v.p. program New Haven br. 1984-87, former editor Conn. div. Nutmeg News), Am. Field Service (former chmn.). Roman Catholic. Home: 835 Grassy Hill Rd Orange CT 06477 Office: Yale Univ Kline Geology Lab New Haven CT 06511

CASEY, PATRICIA B., accountant; b. Trenton, N.J., Sept. 1, 1949; d. William Edward and Leona Ruth (Peters) Botwright; 1 child, Michael Patrick. BS in Bus. Administrn., U. Fla., 1976, MA in Acctg., 1981; postgrad., U. Chapel Hill, 1983-85. CPA, Fla., N.C., cert. mgmt. acct., internal auditor. Supr. accounting Mid-State Fed. Savs., Ocala, Fla., 1977-79; sr. auditor McGladrey, Hendrickson and Pullen, Gainesville, Fla., 1980-81; coordinator acctg. program Atlantic Christian Coll., Wilson, N.C., 1982-86; acct. tax Narron, Holford et al, Wilson, 1985-86; mgr. audit Lynch Howard and Walker, Raleigh, N.C., 1986—; adj. instr. U. Fla., Gainesville 1981; proctor N.C. State Bd. CPA Examiners. Mem. Fla. Inst. CPA's, Am. Inst. CPA's, N.C. Assn. CPA's (active various coms.), Inst. Mgmt. Acctg., Inst. Internal Auditors, N.C. Real Estate Commn., Natl Assn. Real Estate Lic. Law Ofcls. (bd. dirs. several coms. 1985-88). Republican. Methodist. Office: Lynch Howard and Walker PO Box 17845 3605 Glenwood Raleigh NC 27619

CASEY, PATRICIA MARIE, auditor; b. Framingham, Mass., Oct. 6, 1955; d. William Francis and Eileen Theresa (McCarthy) C. BS in Mgmt. cum laude, Northeastern U., 1978; MBA, Suffolk U., 1982. Head teller Framingham Trust Co., 1975-78; br. asst. Guaranty-First Trust Co., Waltham, Mass., 1978-79; payroll asst. Baybank Newton-Waltham Trust Co., Waltham, 1979; asst. controller The Dow Service Group, Boston, 1979-80; sr. auditor Multibank Fin. Corp., Worcester, Mass., 1980-84, audit supr., Quincy, Mass., 1984-85; mgmt. cons. PMC Cons. Services, 1985-86; dir. internal audit Brandeis U., Waltham, Mass., 1986—; adj. prof. acctg. Northeastern U., Boston, 1985—. Recipient cert. of achievement Inst. Internal Auditors, 1980-81. Mem. Nat. Assn. Female Execs., Inst. Internal Auditors, Assn. Coll. and Univ. Auditors, AAUW, Nat. Assn. Bank Women (audit chmn.), Nat. Assn. Accts. Democrat. Roman Catholic. Home: 16 Paula Rd Milford MA 01757 Office: Brandeis U Office Internal Audit 415 South St Waltham MA 02254

CASH, LINDA JANE, transportation company executive; b. Portsmouth, Ohio, Feb. 17, 1950; d. Orville and Gladys Irene (James) Fisher; m. George M. Crickard, Oct. 25, 1969 (div. 1976); 1 child, Heather Lynn. Student, Ohio State U., 1968-69, Wright State U., 1986—, Indian Valley Coll., 1974. Import specialist Rogers & Brown CHB, Charleston, S.C., 1976-77, John S. James Co. CHB, Charleston, 1977-78, Harper Robinson CHB, Charleston, 1979-81; sales coordinator Transworld Shipping CHB, Toledo, 1982; account exec. Pilot Air Freight/KMA, Romulus, Mich., 1985, McLean Trucking Co., Dayton, Ohio, 1985-86, Duff Truck Lines, Dayton, 1986, Emery Air Freight, Vandalia, Ohio, 1986, Air Express Internat., Vandalia, 1987—. Vol. YWCA,

Battered Wives Shelter, Dayton, Ohio, 1987; vol. counselor Indian Valley Spl. High Sch., Ignacio, Calif., 1974. Mem. Miami Valley Internat. Trade Assn., Nat. Assn. Female Execs., Data Processing Mgmt. Assn., Traffic Clubs Internat., Delta Nu Alpha. Republican. Clubs: Upper Valley Transp., Toledo Transp., Air Express Internat. Pres's. Office: Air Express Internat 10700 Maintenance Rd Vandalia OH 45377

CASHELL, LOIS D., federal government administrator. Dep. sec. Fed. Energy Regulatory Commn., Dept. of Energy, Washington. Office: Dept of Energy Fed Energy Regulatory Commn 825 N Capitol St NE Washington DC 20426 *

CASHMORE, PATSY JOY, editor, author, consultant, educator; b. Milw., July 20, 1943; d. Anthony J. and Eva Irene (Arseneau) Peters; m. Gary Roy Cashmore, July 5, 1963 (div. Feb. 1983); children—Jay Allen, Jeffery Scott. Student U. Ill.-Chgo., 1961-62, Inst. Broadcast Arts, Milw., 1966-67, U. Wis.-Milw., 1970, U. Wis.-Madison, 1971-76; student labor studies N.Y.C. Grad. Ctr., 1978. Copy writer H. Vincent Allen & Assocs., Chgo., 1961-63; asst. program coordinator Sta.-WRIT, Milw., 1967-69; asst. news assignment editor WITI-TV, Milw., 1969-72; pub. relations asst. Deaconess Hosp., Milw., 1972-73; asst. editor Milw. Labor Press, 1973-81, editor, 1981—; voice talent on radio and TV commls.; instr., mem. faculty adv. com. U. Wis. Extension-Sch. for Workers, Madison; panelist NEH; guest Israeli govt., 1976, Govt. W.Ger., 1980, pre-NATO talks Friedrich Ebert Found., 1981, 87, Peoples Republic of China, 1983, All Union Central Council of Trade Unions of Soviet Union, 1985; study in E. Africa, 1987. Contbr. articles to nat. publs. Chmn. communications com., treas. Milw. Council on Drug Abuse, 1981-83, bd. dirs., 1984-87; bd. dir. Milw. Council on Alcoholism, 1985-88; mem. community affairs com. United Way, 1983-86; active Variety Club, 1983-87; chmn. community adv. bd. Sta.-WVTV pub. TV, 1982-85; bd. dirs. Goals 2000 Communications Com., 1983. Mem. Internat. Labor Communications Assn. (v.p. 1985, 87, Best Signed Column award 1973, Best Feature Story award 1975, award of Merit for best use of art 1982, Best Headline award 1982, First award for gen. excellence newspaper 1982, 83, 1st award Labor History best instl. profile 1986), U.S. Treasury Dept. Liberty Bell award, 1986. Mem. Midwest Labor Press Assn. (pres.), Wis. Labor Press Assn. (treas.), Indsl. Relations Research Assn. (bd. dirs.), Milw. Jr. Acd. Club (past sec.-treas.). Nat. Assn. Female Execs., Sigma Delta Chi. Clubs: Wapatule Ski (newsletter editor 1984-85), Milw. Press, Milw. Pen and Mike (Milw.). Avocations: travel; skiing; golf; swimming. Office: Milwaukee County Labor Council 633 S Hawley Rd Milwaukee WI 53214

CASMIR, MINA G. HALLIDAY, educator, consultant; b. Hamburg, Iowa, Oct. 16, 1945; d. Ralph Hoover and Florence (Hummel) Halliday; m. Fred L. Casmir. BS, Northwest Mo. State U., 1967; MS, So. Ill. U., 1968. Cert. secondary edn. tchr. and supr. Teaching asst. So. Ill. U., Carbondale, 1967-68; tchr. Belleville (Ill.) West High Sch., 1968-73; edn. cons. Ill. State Bd. Edn., Springfield, 1973-86; pvt. practice cons. Los Angeles, 1986—; active SCA Summer Conf. on Coll. Sophomore Speaking/Listening Competencies, 1987, Springfield Area Arts Council, 1981-85; advisor Ill. Arts Council, 1981-86, Ill. High Sch. Theatre Festival, 1975-86. Author: Teaching Speech Today, 1979, The Arts: A Basic Component of General Education, 1983; (book series) Basic Oral Communication, 1981-82; contbr. articles on communication edn. to profl. jours. Mem. Speech Communication Assn., Am. Theatre Assn. (pres. Secondary Edn. div. 1985-86, bd. dirs. 1986-87), Ill. Theater Assn. (Annual Recognition award 1980), Ill. Speech and Theatre Assn. (Edith Harrod award 1979, Sanders Life award 1986), Theatre Educators of Am. (sec. 1987—), Assn. for Supervision and Curriculum, Internat. Communication Assn., Ill. Alliance for Arts Edn. (sec. 1975-86, Arts Edn. Service award 1987). Democrat. Methodist. Home and Office: 20139 Leadwell #3 Canoga Park CA 91306

CASON, JUNE MACNABB, musician, educator, arts administrator; b. Phila., June 21, 1930; d. Vernon C. and Eleanor (Scarlet) Macnabb; m. Roger Lee Cason, June 12, 1952; children: David Alan, Diane Louise, Nancy Lynn. Student, Eastman Sch. Music, Rochester, N.Y., 1948-52; grad., U. Houston, 1965-69; postgrad. in bus., U. Pa., 1984. Dir. youth chorus St. John's Episcopal Ch., Charleston, W.Va., 1956-63; soloist ch. and music groups, Charleston, 1957-63; founder, dir. music summer camp Episcopal Diocese W.Va., 1961-62; soloist Christ Ch. Cathedral, Houston, 1963-71, Gilbert and Sullivan Soc., Houston, 1970; pvt. tchr. voice, Houston, 1965-71, Wilmington, Del., 1971—; tchr. voice San Jacinto Coll., Pasadena, Tex., 1969-71; founder, gen. mgr., soloist Minikin Opera Co., Wilmington, 1972-87; mem. faculty Wilmington Music Sch., 1973-77; mem. Del. Pro Musica, Wilmington, 1973-77, chmn., 1975-77; dir. music Immanuel Episcopal Ch., Wilmington, 1973-75; instr. music Albert Einstein Acad., Wilmington, 1975-76; v.p. Resource Ctr. for Performing Arts, 1982-86; chmn. Music Consortium New Castle County, 1982-84. Contbr. articles to profl. jours. Recipient Theta Eta award U. Rochester, 1952. Mem. Nat. Assn. Tchrs. Singing, Del. Music Tchrs. Assn., Met. Opera Guild, Nat. Opera Service, Sigma Alpha Iota (Sword of Honor 1971). Republican. Home and Office: 1125 Grinnell Rd Wilmington DE 19803

CASPERSEN, BARBARA MORRIS, food company executive; b. Phila., Feb. 27, 1945; d. Samuel Wheeler and Eleanor May (Jones) Morris; B.A., Wellesley Coll., 1967, M.A., Drew U., 1983, M.P.H., 1986; m. Finn M.W. Caspersen, June 17, 1967. Treas., dir. Westby Corp., Wilmington, Del., 1971—, Westby Mgmt. Inc., Andover, N.J., 1967—, Tri-Farms, Inc., Andover, 1967—; pres., dir. Clark Hill Sugary Inc., Canaan, N.H., 1971-86. Bd. dirs. v.p. O.W. Caspersen Found., 1967—; trustee Hoosac Sch., 1968-76, Shipley Sch., 1980-84, Peck Sch., 1981—; bd. dirs. Drew U., 1984—, Groton Sch., 1984—, Gladstone Equestrian Assn.; trustee Hilltop Sch., 1974-83, pres., 1976-80, prin., 1980-81. Mem. English-Speaking Union U.S. (dir. 1972-73, dir. N.Y. chpt. 1970-75). Episcopalian. Club: Colony (N.Y.C.). Office: Westby Corp PO Box 800 Andover NJ 07821

CASSEL, CHRISTINE KAREN, physician; b. Mpls., Sept. 14, 1945; d. Charles Moore and Virginia Julia (Anderson) C.; AB U. Chgo., 1967; MD U. Mass., 1976. Intern, resident in internal medicine Children's Hosp., San Francisco, 1976-78; fellow in bioethics, Inst. Health Policy Studies, U. Calif., San Francisco, 1978-79; fellow geriatrics Portland (Oreg.) VA Hosp., 1979-81; asst. prof. medicine and public health U. Oreg. Health Scis. U., 1981-83; asst. prof. geriatrics and medicine Mt. Sinai Med. Ctr., N.Y.C., 1983-85; assoc. prof. medicine U. Chgo., 1985—. Woodrow Wilson fellow, 1967; Henry J. Kaiser Family Found. faculty scholar, 1982-85; diplomate Am. Bd. Internal Medicine. Fellow Am. Geriatrics Soc., ACP; mem. Physicians for Social Responsibility (dir. 1983—, pres. 1988—), Soc. Health and Human Values (pres. 1986). Author: Ethical Dimensions in the Health Professions, 1981; Geriatric Medicine: Principles and Practice, 1984; Nuclear Weapons and Nuclear War: A Sourcebook for Health Professionals, 1984. Office: Sect Gen Internal Medicine Box 12 U Chgo Pritzker Sch Medicine Chicago IL 60637

CASSEL, LAVETA JANE, infosystems specialist; b. Nov. 17, 1948; d. Orvin Edgar and Velva Opal (Raulston) Elkins. B in Bus. with honors, Calif. State U., Sacramento, 1969. Computer operator, programmer Pan Am. Airlines, San Francisco, 1969-70; mgr. data processing Fantasy Records/Films, Berkeley, Calif., 1970-76; programmer, analyst Levi Strauss & Co., San Francisco, 1976-80; mgr. data processing Bank of Am., San Francisco, 1980-81; programmer, analyst McKesson, San Francisco, 1981-84; mgr. management info. services, internat. support Apple Computer Co., Cupertino, Calif., 1984—; internat. assignment Levi Strauss & Co., Europe, 1976-80, Apple Computer Co., Toronto, Can., Australia and Europe, 1984-87. Recipient various tennis trophies from tournaments in Las Vegas, Monterry, Tahoe and No. Calif., 1972-80.

CASSEL, SYLVIA ANN, market research company executive; b. Potsdam, N.Y., June 28, 1938; d. Fredrick Mott and Lillian (Walker) C. BS, SUNY, Potsdam, 1960; postgrad., NYU, 1960-61; MBA, Baruch Coll., 1980. Systems engr. IBM, 1961-63; mgr. systems, programming Diners Club, 1963-64; mgr. data processing Katz Agy., 1965-69; mgr. spl. projects Arbitron, N.Y.C., 1970-72; mgr. computer client service Axiom/Simmons Market Research Bur., N.Y.C., 1972-78; sr. v.p. Mediamark Research Inc., N.Y.C., 1978—. SUNY fellow, 1960-61; Alcoa Found. scholar, 1956-60. Mem. Advt. Data Processing Assn. (pres. 1979-80), Am. Mktg. Assn., Advt. Women N.Y., Adnet. Republican. Club: Advt. of N.Y. Office: Mediamark Research Inc 341 Madison Ave New York NY 10017

CASSELL, CAROL ANNE, community educator; b. Buffalo, Apr. 25, 1936; d. A.J. and Dorothy (Diemert) Miller; m. Robert Edward Cassell, June 26, 1971; children by previous marriage—Don, Alisa, John, Michael Mendez; stepchildren—Lisa, Emily. BA, U. N.Mex., 1970, MPA, 1976, PhD with distinction, 1980. Dir. tng. J.B.A., Austin, Tex., 1976-79; dir. edn. Planned Parenthood Fedn. Am., N.Y.C., 1979-82; instr. U. N.Mex., 1974—; lectr. and cons. in field; cons. editor Jour. of Sex Edn. and Therapy, 1977—; invited scholar Soc. of Sci. Study of Sex, 1981; adv. bd. Nat. Family Life Edn. Network, 1981—; bd. dirs. Peer Project. Author: Swept Away, 1984, Straight From the Heart, 1986, More Sassy Women, 1988; co-editor: A Sourcebook on Sexuality Education, 1987; contbr. articles to textbooks and profl. jours. Mem. Albuquerque Task Force on Devel., 1985. Recipient Margaret Sanger award Inst. Family Research and Edn., 1979, Cert. of Recognition, Eta Sigma Gamma, 1982. Mem. Am. Assn. Sex Educators, Counselors and Therapists (pres. 1983-84), Writers Guild, Phi Kappa Phi. Democrat. Address: 7129 Edwina NE Albuquerque NM 87110

CASSELL, DANA KAY, communications company executive; b. Hornell, N.Y., Dec. 12, 1941; d. Robert William and Mayadell Louise (Reubens) Amacher; m. Don Cuddy, 1983; children—William, Denise, Jody, Robert. Copywriter Sta. WTOC-TV, Savannah, Ga., 1965-67; ins. agt. Liberty Nat. Life Ins. Co., Savannah, 1967-70; dist. mgr. LaSalle Extension U., Fla., 1972; mgr. Stuart Domestic Service (Fla.), 1974-75; pres. Cassell Communications Inc., Ft. Lauderdale, Fla., 1977—. Served with USAF, 1960-61. Mem. Internat. Bus. Writers, Nat. Writers Club, Fla. Freelance Writers Assn. (founder 1982, exec. dir. 1982—), Am. Soc. Journalists and Authors, The Am. Authors Guild, Nat. Assn. Female Execs., Fla. Press Women, Women in Communications, Nat. Assn. Ind. Pubs. (bd. advisors), Fla. Pubs. Group, Fla. Mag. Assn. Mensa. Republican. Club: The Book Group. Author: How to Advertise and Promote Your Retail Store, 1983; Making Money With Your Home Computer, 1984; contbr. over 1000 articles to various publs. Home: 3600 NW 34th St Lauderdale Lakes FL 33309 Office: PO Box 9844 Fort Lauderdale FL 33310

CASSELL, KAY ANN, librarian; b. Van Wert, Ohio, Sept. 24, 1941; d. Kenneth Miller and Pauline (Zimmerman) C. B.A., Carnegie-Mellon U., 1963; M.L.S., Rutgers U., 1965; M.A., Bklyn. Coll., 1969. Reference librarian Bklyn. Coll. Library, 1965-68; adult services cons. N.J. State Library, Trenton, 1968-71; library cons.-vol. Peace Corps, Rabat, Morocco, 1971-73; adult services cons. Westchester Library System, White Plains, N.Y., 1973-75; dir. Bethlehem Pub. Library, Delmar, N.Y., 1975-81, Huntington (N.Y.) Pub. Library, 1982-85; exec. dir. Coordinating Council Lit. Mags., N.Y.C., 1985-87; univ. librarian New Sch. for Social Research, 1987—; adj. faculty mem. Grad. Sch. Library Sci., SUNY, Albany, 1976-78, Palmer Sch. of Library and Info. Scis., Long Island U., 1986—; chmn. community adv. com. Capital Dist. Humanities Program, Albany, 1980-81; bd. dirs. Literacy Vols. of Suffolk, Bellport, N.Y., 1981-85. Mem. ALA (pres. reference and adult services div. 1983-84), N.Y. Library Assn. (pres. reference and adult services sect. 1975-76), Beta Phi Mu. Home: 252 E 7th St New York NY 10009 Office: Fogelman Library New Sch for Social Research 65 Fifth Ave New York NY 10003

CASSELMAN, CINDY L., lawyer; b. San Diego, Dec. 21, 1956; d. Laurence Casselman III and Nina Soudakoff; m. Alexander Gordon Shaw, Aug. 7, 1982; 1 child, Linsey. BA, Calif. State U., Northridge, 1977; JD, U. San Diego, 1980. Bar: Calif., U.S. Dist. Ct. (so. dist.) Calif. Assoc. corp. counsel The Hahn Co., San Diego, 1982-84, leasing atty., dir. leasing documentation, 1984—. Mem. Internat. Council Shopping Ctrs., Calif. Bar Assn., Pi Gamma Mu, Phi Kappa Phi. Office: The Hahn Co 4350 La Jolla Village Dr #700 San Diego CA 92122-1233

CASSIDY, HELEN ALEXANDER, lawyer; b. Celeste, Tex., Nov. 22, 1940; d. Athrell James and Vera (Sinclair) Alexander; m. Richard Swain Cassidy, Feb. 1, 1962 (div. Apr. 1979); 1 child, David Alexander. BA magna cum laude, Lamar U., 1963; postgrad., U. Houston, 1963-66, JD magna cum laude, 1975. Bar: Tex. 1975. Cons. spl. conf. U.S. Dept. State Internat. Women's Yr., Houston, 1977; sole practice Houston, 1975-79; asst. dir. staff counsel for inmates Tex. Dept. Corrections, Huntsville, Tex., 1979-81; judge EEO Commn., Houston, 1981-83; staff atty. Tex. Ct. Appeals (14th cir.), Houston, 1983-87, chief staff atty., 1987—; adj. prof. U. Houston, 1980, sch. law U. South Tex., 1988. Contbr. articles to profl. jours. Pres. Houston area NOW, 1971-73, nat. bd. dirs., 1974-75; chair Tex. area NOW edn. and legal fund; chair, co-founder Tex. Women's Polit. Caucus, 1972-73; conv. coordinator first nat. conf. Nat. Women's Polit. Caucus. Mem. State Bar Assn. Tex., Kappa Beta Pi, Alpha Delta Pi. Home: 8061 El Mundo Houston TX 77054 Office: Tex Ct Appeals 14th Cir 1307 San Jacinto Houston TX 77002

CASSIDY, JOAN KATHRYN, business writing consultant; b. Forest Hills, N.Y., Nov. 21, 1927; d. Joseph Leo and Frances Jean (Rohaly) C. BA in English Lit., Queens Coll., 1949; BA in Journalism, George Washington U., 1956; MA in Journalism, Am. U., 1961. Asst. editor Am. Home Econs. Assn., Washington, 1954-56; dir. pub. relations Page Communications Engrs., Washington, 1956-58; head policy and procedures dept. Naval Security Sta., Washington, 1959-78; pres. Joan K. Cassidy Assocs., Wheaton, Md., 1979—; instr. Grad. Sch. USDA, Washington, 1979-80; lectr. in pub. speaking and bus. writing. Contbr. articles to profl. jours. Commd. ensign USN, 1950, advanced through grades to capt. USNR, ret., 1976. Recipient Silver Tongue award for pub. speaking USN, 1970, Meritorious Service award Naval Security Group, Washington, 1978. Mem. Women Bus. Owners Montgomery County, Nat. Assn. Women Bus. Owners. Democrat.

CASSIDY, MARY FRANCES, educator; b. Anson County, N.C., May 6, 1934; d. William Bennett and Julia Grace Meachum; m. Samuel Lafayette Cassidy, June 5, 1955; children: Mary Glenda, Samuel Layfayette (dec. 1979). AA with honors, Brevard Jr. Coll., 1954; student, U. N.C., 1954-55; AB in Elem. Edn., U. S.C., 1960, MEd, 1969; cert., Winthrop Coll., 1977. Lic. pvt. pilot. Tchr. English and math. Hillcrest Sch., Sumter County, S.C., 1956; tchr. Camden Primary Sch., Kershaw County, S.C., 1960-67, Lugoff Elem. Sch., Kershaw County, 1967-71, Jr. Vocat. Sch., Kershaw County, 1971-72, Richland County, 1972-73, Camden Elem. Sch., Kershaw County, 1973-74; itinerant tchr. orthopedically handicapped Kershaw County, 1979—. Fed. grantee in spl. edn., 1965. Mem. NEA, S.C. Edn. Assn., S.C. Augmentative Communication Assn., S.C. Council for Computers in Edn., Council Exceptional Children. Republican. Baptist. Home: PO Box 2 Hwy 34 Lugoff SC 29078 Office: Clyde Walton Ednl Bldg 1301 DuBose Ct Camden SC 29020

CASSON, HARRIETT ANN, nurse; b. Washington, June 8, 1960; d. Samuel Mitchell and Gloria Swanson (Rogers) C. BS in Nursing, Am. U. RN. Staff nurse U. Pa., Phila., 1982-88, Nat. Rehab. Hosp., Washington, 1988—. Mem. Am. Rehab. Nurses Assn. Democrat. Episcopalian. Home: 5415 Connecticut Ave NW Washington DC 20015 Office: Nat Rehab Hosp 102 Irving NE Washington DC 20015

CASTANO, ELVIRA PALMERIO, art historian, gallery director; b. Cin., July 23, 1929; d. John and Josephine Castano; B.A., Emerson Coll., Boston, 1950; postgrad. (Cardinal Spellman scholar), Pius XII Inst., Florence, Italy, 1954-55; m. Carlo Palmerio (dec.), June 1, 1958; 1 dau., Marina. Curator, Castano Art Gallery, Boston, 1965-78; dir. Castano Art Gallery, Needham, Mass., 1978—; Vatican translator; interpreter Italian art, specialist in Macchiaioli art; Italian lang. translator. Mem. Dante Alighieri Soc., Boston, Boston Mus. Fine Arts, Brockton (Mass.) Art Mus. (adv. bd.), Fogg Art Mus. of Harvard U., Friends of Needham Library. Roman Catholic. Address: 245 Hunnewell St Needham MA 02194

CASTELLANO, DENISE CATHERINE, educator; b. Newark, Sept. 7, 1957; d. Rocco Carmine and Dolores Grace (Caprio) C. AA cum laude, Ocean County Coll., 1977; BA, Montclair State Coll., 1979, MA in Bus. Edu., 1983. Sec., receptionist Shore Ins. Co., Brick, N.J., 1979; substitute bus. tchr. Brick Twp. Bd. Edn., 1978-80; bus. tchr. Am. Tng. Services, Atlantic City, N.J., 1979-80, Brick Twp. High Sch., 1980—, Brick Adult Sch., 1985-86; coll. instr. Ocean County Coll., Toms River, N.J., 1987—. Mem. N.J. Bus. Edn. Assn., Am. Vocat. Edn. Assn., Nat. Bus. Edn. Assn., Phi Kappa Phi, Phi Beta Lambda, Kappa Delta Pi, Pi Omega Pi. Democrat. Home: 24-2 Fountain Dr Lakewood NJ 08701

CASTELLANOS, MARIA LUISA, architect, general contractor; b. Havana, Cuba, May 31, 1953; came to U.S., 1961; d. Armando I. and Maria Luisa (de la Torriente) C.; m. Eduardo Escobar, Feb. 1, 1985; 1 child, Edward. BS, Ga. Inst. Tech., 1974, MArch, 1976. Registered architect, Fla.; cert. gen. contractor. Archtl. designer Saez & Pacetti, Miami, Fla., 1976-77; architect Greenleaf & Telesca, Miami, 1977-78, Urban Architects, Miami, 1978-82; pvt. practice architect 1982-84; pres. Alligator Constrn. Corp., Coral Gables, Fla., 1984—, United Architects, Inc., Coral Gables, 1986—. Active Coalition of Hispanic Am. Women, 1983-86. Recipient Appreciation cert. Dade County (Fla.) Sch. Bd., 1986. Mem. Women's C. of C. So. Fla., Coral Gables C. of C. Democrat. Roman Catholic. Office: United Architects Alligator Constrn Corp 3003 Salzedo St Coral Gables FL 22134

CASTELLI, DOLORES BENNETT, restaurateur; b. Salamanca, N.Y., Oct. 17, 1932; d. John Albert and Genevieve Ellen (Schwind) Bennett; m. Joseph Castelli, June 27, 1931; children: Deborah Proctor, Lynda CAstelli, John Castelli. A of Arts/Scis. in Bus., Rochester Inst. of Tech., 1953. Asst. buyer Sibley's, Rochester, N.Y., 1951-55; prin., owner Candle House, Rochester, 1960-76; prin. Candle House, Newark, 1976—; v.p., owner Castelli's Village Inn, Newark, N.Y., 1976—. Founding bd. dirs. Wayne County Bus. Council, Lyons, N.Y., 1979—. Mem. Nat. Restaurant Assn., N.Y. State Restaurant Assn., Finger Lakes Women's Interest Network, Newark C. of C. (pres. 1986-87, editor newsletter 1983—), Roundtable for Women in Food Service, Finger Lakes Assn. (bd. dirs. 1982—). Republican. Roman Catholic. Home: PO Box 426 Newark NY 14513 Office: Castelli's Village Inn Rte 31 E Newark NY 14513

CASTELUCCI, ANGELA MARIE, computer systems analyst, systems operation manager; b. San Andres, Calif., Sept. 27, 1964; d. Tom D. and Mary E. (Murray) C. Student, Edison Coll., 1986—, U. South Fla., 1987—. Cert. legal sec. Paralegal, clk. Steve Studybaker, Atty., Ft. Myers, 1983-84; office mgr. Hampton, Paleveda, Attys., Naples, Fla., 1984-85; systems analyst, asst. in mktg. Advanced Micro Solutions, Ft. Myers, 1985-86; computer system ops. mgr. SW Title, Inc., Naples, 1985-86; sys. operation mgr. Chico's, Inc., Sanibel, Fla., 1986—; cons. Melco Leasing Co., Ft. Myers, 1986-87, Computerland, Ft. Myers, 1986-87; instr. Entre' Computer Co., Ft. Myers, 1984. Mem. Ft. Myers Civic Assn., 1984-85; mem. Cape Coral (Fla.) Civic Assn., 1984-85; mem. Nat. Dem. Assn., Ft. Myers, 1984—; mem. SBA, 1986—. Recipient scholarship Legal Secs. Assn., 1983. Mem. Am. Bus. Woman Assn., Nat. Assn. Female Execs. Clubs: PC Users, Cub. Office: Chico's Inc 11580 Marshwood Ln SW Fort Myers FL 33908

CASTERN, MAUREEN MILES, engineer; b. Detroit, Oct. 14, 1948; d. Ross E. and Geraldine M. (Kanaga) Polkinghorne; m. Louis J. Castern, April 3, 1971; children: Anne Christine, Katherine Mary. BS in Chem. Engring., Wayne State U., 1970; MS in Sanitary Engring., Va. Polytechnic Inst. and State U., 1985. Chem. engr. Chrysler Corp., Highland Park, Mich., 1971; process engr. Fiber Industries, Inc., Shelby, N.C., 1978-80; dir. Linc of Christian Ministries, Lincolnton, N.C., 1980-82; sanitary engr. Hayes, Seay, Mattern and Mattern, Roanoke, Va., 1985—. Recipient N.C. Vol. award Gov. of N.C., 1982. Mem. ASCE, Am. Water Works Assn., Water Pollution Control Fedn. (Va. pub. affairs com. 1986—), Tau Beta Pi. Unitarian Universalist. Home: 2913 Lockridge Rd SW Roanoke VA 24014 Office: Hayes Seay Mattern & Mattern 1315 Franklin Rd Roanoke VA 24034

CASTIGLIONE, CAROLINE JOY, manufacturing company executive; b. Royal Oak, Mich., June 25, 1923; d. Thomas Wallace and Muriel Joy (Paton) Marshall; m. Paul Castiglione (div. 1978); children: Sue Scott, Patricia, Robert. AA, Fullerston (Calif.) Jr. Coll., 1977; BA, St. Mary's Coll., 1981. Mgr. stock room Microwave Prodn. div. Eaton Corp., Sunnyvale, Calif., 1979, expediter parts and raw materials, 1980, buyer metals and chems., 1980—; pres. Chairback Haberdashery, also pvt. designer neckwear for women. Tchr. Head Start, Cocoa, Fla., 1969, Huntsville (Ala.) Mentally Handicapped Sch., 1968; leader Girl Scouts U.S., Anaheim, Calif., 1964-67; voter registrar Orange City, Anaheim, 1964-67. Mem. Purchasing Mgmt. Assn., Investment Recovery Assn. Office: Eaton Corp div Microwave Prodn 2007 Euclid Ave Palo Alto CA 94303

CASTILLEJOS, MARIA ESTELA, ophthalmologist; b. Mexico City, Nov. 12, 1948; d. Santiago and Alicia (Rios) C.; m. Jose G. Hernandez, Dec. 26, 1971; children: Santiago, Estella. Degree in Biochemistry magna cum laude, U. Mex., Mexico City, 1967, MD, 1973. Intern, Moncton Hosp., (N.B., Can.), 1972-73; resident Jewish Hosp. and Med. Ctr., N.Y.C., 1973-75, resident in ophthalmology, 1975-78; fellow Harvard U. Med. Sch., Boston, 1979-80; chief retina service Mexican Inst. Health, Mexico City, 1980-82; practice medicine specializing in opthalmology (retina), San Diego, 1982—. Fellow ACS. Home: 3906 Ave San Miguel Bonita CA 92002 Office: 6699 Alvarado Rd Suite 2201 San Diego CA 92120 also: 480 4th Ave #307 Chula Vista CA 92010

CASTILLO, MAGDALENA BAYANI, fertility clinic executive; b. Torrance, Calif., Aug. 5, 1962; d. Charles Tolete and Juliana (Bayani) C. BS in Biology and Psychology, U. Calif., Irvine, 1985. Lab. dir. Fertility Ctr. Calif., Santa Ana, 1982-85, asst. dir., 1985-87; dir. Fertility Ctr. Calif. II, San Diego, 1987—. Mem. U. Calif. Alumni Assn. Democrat. Roman Catholic. Office: Fertility Ctr Calif 6475 Alvarado Rd Suite 109 San Diego CA 92120

CASTILLO, MARY HELEN MÁRQUEZ, nurse; b. El Paso, May 27, 1936; d. José Anselmo and Irene María (Federico) Márquez; diploma St. Vincents Coll. Nursing, 1957; B.S.N., U. Tex., 1974, M.S.N., 1977; Ph.D., N.Mex. State U., 1983; m. William Richard Castillo, Dec. 28, 1957; children—Carole Angel, William Richard II, Cesar Orlando. Nurse, St. Vincents Hosp., Los Angeles, 1957; office nurse, staff nurse critical care, El Paso, 1958-61; nursing supr. Providence Meml. Hosp., El Paso, 1961-64, dir. edn. dept., 1964-65, dir. nursing services, 1965-76; assoc. prof. nursing U. Tex.-El Paso, 1976-88; dir. nursing adminstrn. specialty Vanderbilt U. Mrd. Ctr. Sch. of Nursing, 1988—; coordinator internat. studies; nursing services cons.; dir., officer, West Tex. Health Systems Agy., 1975-83; mem. Profl. Adv. Council Life Mgmt. Ctr. League United Latin Am. Citizens scholar, 1980; recipient Research award Tex. League for Nursing, 1988. Mem. U.S.-Mex. Border Health Assn. (sec.), Dirs. of Nursing Services in El Paso (chmn. 1975), Tex. Nurses Assn. (v.p., pres.) Council Hosp. Nursing Tex. Hosp. Assn., Am. Hosp. Assn., Am. Nurses Assn., Tri Delta, Phi Delta Kappa, Sigma Theta Tau (pres. Delta Kappa chpt. 1986-88). Democrat. Roman Catholic. Clubs: U. Tex. Womens Aux., El Paso Womens. Contbr. articles to profl. jours. Home: 910 Woodmont Blvd Apt 0-3 Nashville TN 37204 Office: U Tex Coll Nursing El Paso TX 79902

CASTILLO, PATRICIA CABALLERO, educational diagnostician, speech pathologist; b. El Paso, Tex., July 6, 1946; d. Jose Antonio Caballero and Rosaura (Ramirez) Garcia-Nuñez; m. Jose Castillo, July 27, 1964 (div. 1983); children: Joe, Paul, Teresa. BA, U. Tex., El Paso, 1980, MEd, 1984. Cert. in ednl. supervision, early childhood edn. for handicapped. Speech pathologist El Paso Indep. Sch. Dist., 1980-84; ednl. diagnostician Ysleta Indep. Sch. Dist., El Paso, 1984—; tutor, psychologist Dr. M.L. de Socarraz, El Paso, 1983-87. Mem. Assn. Retarded Citizens (bd. dirs.), Intercambios-Hispanic Profl. Women, Nat. Assn. Female Execs., Assn. Children Learning Disabilities, Tex. Ednl. Diagnosticians Assn., Alpha Chi. Democrat. Roman Catholic. Home: 332 Crane El Paso TX 79922 Office: Ysleta Indep Sch Dist 9600 Sims Dr El Paso TX 79925-7225

CASTILLO, ROSALINDA, association organizer; b. Detroit, Feb. 5, 1957; d. Richard Dean and Rosemary (Chavez) Bondie; m. Manolo Alejandro Castillo, Jan. 19, 1985; 1 child, Alejandro Manuel. BS, No. Ill. U., 1979, postgrad., 1983. Head tchr. YMCA, Chgo., 1979-81; facilitator Safer Found., Chgo., 1981-83, supr., 1984; program coordinator Latin Women in Action, Chgo., 1984-85; instr. Chgo. Urban League, 1985-86, placement specialist, 1986-87, M/WBE EEO compliance specialist, 1987-88, program coordinator, 1988—; rep. Hispanic Am. Constrn. Industry Assn., Chgo., 1988, Black Contractors United, Chgo., 1988; Hispanic relations rep. Nat. Assn. Women in Constrn., Chgo., 1988; dep. registrar Chgo. Urban League, Chgo., 1987. Auditor Leadership Council for Open Community, Chgo., 1987. Recipient Torch award No. Ill. U., 1979, Fellowship award No. Ill. U., 1983. Democrat. Roman Catholic. Office: Chgo Urban League 1346 S Michigan Ave Chicago IL 60605

CASTLE, CONNIE JO, police officer; b. Tyler, Tex., Nov. 10, 1953; d. Joe Edwin Castle and Alice Earl (McCullars) Bowins. Student, Stephen F. Austin Coll., 1974-75; A in Med. Tech., Tyler (Tex.) Jr. Coll., 1977, student, 1986-87; cert. peace officer, East Tex. Police Acad., 1984-87. Lab. technician Pathology Assocs. of Tyler, 1976-78; asst. chief technician Gilmer (Tex.) Hosp., 1978; spl. chemistry technician Pathology Assocs. of Longview, Tex., 1978-79; well site geologist Exploration Services, Inc., Midland, 1979-84; police officer City of Tyler Police Dept., 1984—. Recipient Gold Medal Tex. Police Athletic Fedn., 1986, Gold Medal Internat. Police Olympics, 1986. Mem. NOW, Am. Soc. Clin. Pathologists. Office: Tyler Police Dept 711 W Ferguson Tyler TX 75710

CASTLEBERRY, MARGARET JEAN, school counselor; b. Santa Anna, Tex., Oct. 22, 1940; d. Obrey Benton and Beatrice Christine (Buse) Smith; m. Billy James Castleberry, July 4, 1965; 1 child, Christi Carole. Student, Tarleton State Coll., 1959-61; BS, Tex. Tech U., 1963, MS, 1967, MEd, 1979. Tchr. home econs. Lamar Jr. High Sch., Snyder, Tex., 1963-65, Monterey High Sch., Lubbock, Tex., 1965-85; counselor Atkins Jr. High Sch., Lubbock, 1985—; color/image cons. Beauty for all Seasons, Lubbock, 1984—. Social chairperson 2d Baptist Ch. Mem. NEA, Tex. State Tchrs. Assn., West Tex. Assn. Guidance Counselors, Future Homemakers Am. (hon.), Nat. Assn. Female Execs., Am. Diabetes Assn. (bd. dirs.), Delta Kappa Gamma (state chmn.). Democrat. Baptist. Home: 6505 Oxford Ave Lubbock TX 79413 Office: Atkins Jr High Sch 5401 Ave U Lubbock TX 79413

CASTOR, ELIZABETH B. (BETTY), state education commissioner; b. Glassboro, N.J., May 11, 1941; d. Joseph L. and Gladys (Wright) Bowe; children—Katherine, Karen, Frank. B.A., Glassboro State Coll., 1963; M.A., U. Miami, 1968. Mem. Fla. Senate, Tallahassee, 1976-78, 82-86, pres. pro tem, 1985-86 and formerly; Fla. commr. of edn., Tallahassee, 1987—; Mem. Hillsborough County Bd. Commrs., Fla., 1972-76, chmn., 1975-76; mem. Hillsborough County Environ. Protection Commn., 1972-76, chmn., 1973-74; mem. exec. bd. Tampa Bay Regional Planning Council, 1972-76; mem. U. Fla. Ctr. for Govt. Responsibility, bd. dirs., 1977; mem. Hillsborough Hosp. and Welfare Bd., 1972-76, chmn., 1973-74; mem. council advisers U. South Fla. Recipient Good Govt. award Town 'N Country Jaycees, 1975, Outstanding Legislator of Yr. award FEA, 1977; numerous other awards from state edn. orgns. Mem. LWV, Athena Soc. Democrat. Lutheran. Office: The Capitol PL-08 Tallahassee FL 32399

CASTRO, CAROL ANNE, cosmetic company executive; b. Chgo., May 12, 1944; d. Walter Andrus and Betty Jane (Mueller) Brown; m. James Edward (div. Jan. 1970); 1 child, Susan Leigh. Cosmet makeover specialist Syd Simons, Chgo., 1964-66; nat. staff field technician Albert Culver, Chgo., 1966-68; mgr. midwest sales H.L.H. Aloe Vera Cosmetics, Chgo. and N.Y.C., 1971-72; mfr.'s rep. J. Fink and Assocs., Chgo., 1972-74; territory mgr. Max Factor, Chgo., 1975-76, Germaine Monteil, Chgo., 1976-80, Parfums Givenchy, Chgo., 1980-83, Chanel, Inc., Chgo., 1983—. Mem. Nat. Assn. Female Execs. Republican. Lutheran. Club: Brickyard Ski (Blue Island, Ill.) (founder, pres. 1981-83). Home: 9027 Somerset Ct Orland Park IL 60462 Office: Chanel Inc 9 West 57th St New York NY 10016

CASTRO, TERESA HARPER, small business owner; b. Chgo., July 18, 1956; d. Jene Paul and June Edith (Aleff) Harper; m. Oscar Armando Rodríguez (div. 1981); 1 child, Avelina; m. Jorge Castro, Jan. 9, 1988. AA in Opera, Fleming Coll., Florence, Italy, 1975; BA in Spanish and Portuguese cum laude, U. N.Mex., 1979. Adminstrv. asst. Latin Am. Inst., Albuquerque, 1981-83; law office mgr. Camacho & Hinkle, San Francisco, 1983; owner, founder, pres. Access Word Processing, San Francisco, 1983—; free-lance computer and word processing systems analyst, San Francisco and Phoenix, 1985—. State coordinator Truth Seekers in Adoption of Calif., San Francisco, 1985—; vol. notary pub. People With AIDS/ARC, 1985—, The AIDS Found./Shanti Project, San Francisco, 1986—; chairperson bilingual adv. bd. Buena Vista Sch., San Francisco, 1986; bd. dirs. Escola Nova de Samba, San Francisco, 1987; vol. working on reunification searches for adoptees and birth parents, Calif., N.Y., Latin Am. Mem. Nat. Assn. Female Execs., Nat. Notary Assn. Home and Office: 4394 17th St San Francisco CA 94114

CASWELL, PAULETTE REVA, lawyer; b. Chgo., June 8, 1951; d. Ben and Lillian (Cohen) Watstein; m. Michael Evidson, May 15, 1975 (div. Mar. 1979); 1 child, David Allan Philip; m. Charles Frank Caswell, III, Jan. 8, 1983. A.A., West Los Angeles Community Coll., 1971; B.A., Calif. State U.-Los Angeles, 1975; J.D., Whittier Coll., 1982; D.D. (hon.), St. Alban's Coll., San Francisco, 1974. Bar: Calif. 1982, U.S. Dist. Ct. (cen. dist.) Calif., 1983. Dir., Mensa of Los Angeles, 1977-83; sole practice, Los Angeles, 1982—; dir., founder Amicus, Los Angeles Area Ctr. Law and the Deaf; cons. Editor: Consumer Rights, 1982; author legal articles pamphlets, booklets. Legal adv. Ind. Living Ctrs.; adv. for deaf and visually-impaired. Mem. ABA, Los Angeles County Bar Assn., Legal Assistance Assn. Calif., State Bar Calif., Arts. Democrat. Jewish. Home: 645 N Gardner St Los Angeles CA 90036-5712

CATALFO, BETTY MARIE, health service executive, nutritionist; b. N.Y.C., Nov. 2, 1942; d. Lawrence Santo and Gemma (Patrone) Lorefice; children—Anthony, Philip, Lawrence, Donna. Grad. Newtown High Sch., Elmhurst, N.Y., 1958. Sec., clk. ABC-TV, N.Y.C., 1957-60; lectr., nutritionist Weight Watchers, Manhasset, N.Y., 1976-75; founder, pres. Every-Bodys Diet, Inc. dba Stay Slim, Bronx, N.Y., 1976—; dir. in-home program N.Y. State Dept. Health, N.Y.C., 1985—; lectr. in field. Author: 101 Stay-Slim Recipes, 1983, Get Slim and Stay Slim Diet Cook Book, rev. ed., 1987. Author, dir., producer: (video) Dancersize for Overweight, 1986; author, editor: (video) Eating Right For Life, 1985; author, producer: (video) Eating Habits, 1986—, (video) Isometric Techniques for Weight Reduction, 1986, (video) Patience Is a Virtue When Weight Loss is the Goal, 1986; producer, dir.: (video) Positive and Negative Diet Forces, 1987, (video) Hello It's Me and I'm Thin, 1987, (video) Dance Your Calories A-Weigh, 1987, (video) Positive and Negative Diet Forces, 1987. Sponsor, lectr. St. Pauls Ctr., Bklyn., 1981—, Throgs Neck Assn. Retarded Children, Bronx, 1985—; active ARC, LWV, United Way Greenwich, Council Chs. and Synagogues, Heart Assn., Meals on Wheels, Health Assn. Fairfield County. Named Woman of Yr., Bayside Womens Club, N.Y., 1983, O, PK Woman of Yr., 1986—, Woman of Yr. Richmond Boys Club, 1987, Woman of Yr. Bronx Press Club Assn., 1987; recipient Merit award for Service Catholic Archdiocese of Bklyn., 1985, Community Service award Sr. Citizens Sacred Heart League Bklyn./Queens Archdiocese. N.Y. State Nutritional Guidance for Children Nat. Assn. Scis. Mem. Nat. C. of C. for Women (Woman of Yr. 1987), Roundtable for Women in Food Service, Bus. and Profl. Women's Club, Pres. Council for Phys. Fitness, Nat. Assn. Female Execs. Democrat. Roman Catholic. Clubs: Mothers Sacred Heart Sch. (chairperson 1979-82); Democratic (campaign coordinator 1977-86). Avocations: reading; traveling; tennis; spending leisure time with my children. Home: 208-05 15th Rd Bayside NY 11360 also: 58 Riverside Ave Greenwich CT 06878

CATALLO, BERNA ROSE, manufacturing company executive; b. Fabrica, Philippine Islands, Oct. 27, 1936; came to U.S., 1955; d. Samuel William Real and Rose (Vail) Johnston; m. Charles A. Catallo, Apr. 25, 1987; children—Janice Michelle Devia, Debra Ann Glass, Catherine Marie Gaine. A.A. in Bus., San Francisco Coll. for Women, 1957; student Diablo Valley Coll., 1977. Asst. mgr. Stecher-Traung Credit Union, San Francisco, 1969-70; with gen. office Monsanto Chem. Co., Martinez, Calif., 1970-74; sr. buyer Systron Donner-Inertial div., Concord, Calif., 1974-80, safety systems div., Concord, 1981—; sales rep. Hi-Rel Components, Los Angeles, 1980-81. Mem. Nat. Assn. Female Execs., No. Calif. Area Small and Disadvantaged Bus. Council (assoc.), Fed./Industry Small Bus. Council (sec. 1984-85), Purchasing Mgmt. Assn. (metro chpt.), Industry Council for Small Bus. Devel. (treas. 1985-87). Democrat. Roman Catholic. Office: Systron Donner Safety Systems Div 935 Detroit Ave Concord CA 94518

CATCHINGS, YVONNE PARKS, artist, educator; b. Atlanta, Aug. 17; d. Andrew Walter and Hattie Marie (Brookins) Parks; A.B. in Art, Spelman Coll., 1955; M.A. in Art Edn., Columbia U., 1958; M.A. in Mus. Practice, U. Mich., 1970, Ph.D. in Edn., 1981; m. James A.A. Catchings, May 30, 1960; children—Andrea Yvonne Hunt Warner, Wanda Elaine Hunt McLean, James Albert A. Tchr. art Atlanta Bd. Edn., 1955-59; instr. in art spelman Coll., 1956-57; tchr. art Detroit Bd. Edn., 1959-75, art specialist, 1976—; lectr. Marygrove Coll., 1970-72; one-woman show: Black Artist South, Huntsville (Ala.) Mus., 1978; group shows: Forever Free: Art by African Am. Women, 1862-1980, traveling show, 1981; Fulbright-Hayes grantee for study, Zimbabwe, 1982; trustee Afro Am. Mus., 1970-72. Program chmn. Nat. Aux. to Nat. Dental Assn., 1966, chmn. art and craft, 1976; chmn. reception com. United Negro Coll. Fund, Detroit, 1980. Recipient Spirit of Detroit award Detroit Common Council, 1978, Mayor's award of Merit, City of Detroit, 1978; James D. Parks Art award Nat. Conf. Art, 1979. Mem. Nat. Art Edn. Assn., Nat. Conf. Artists, Your Heritage House Mus., Children's Mus., Mich. Art Therapist Assn., Phi Delta Kappa, Delta Sigma Theta (chmn. Founders Day 1965; nat. chmn. heritage and archives, mem. nat. exec. bd.). Clubs: The Links, The Moles, Smart Set, Carrousels. Author: You Ain't Free Yet Notes From a Black Woman, 1976; author geneal. publs. Home: 1306 Joliet Pl Detroit MI 48207

CATES, JEANETTE SUE, educational administrator; b. Denver, May 2, 1947; d. Harold Willis and Jean (White) Skeen; m. Robert Weldon Cates, Jan. 10, 1970; children: Stephanie, Jennifer, Victoria. BS, Trinity U., 1969; MEd, U. Tex., 1982, PhD, 1988. Auditor Arthur Andersen and Co., Houston, 1969-70; instr. basic skills Army Edn. Ctr., Bad Kissingen, Fed. Republic of Germany, 1971-73, Ton Du Chong, South Korea, 1973-74; instr. office tech. Cen. Tex. Coll., Killeen, 1974-76; dir. adult skills ctr. Cen. Tex. Coll., 1976-78, instr. office tech., 1978-80; curriculum writer Cen. Tex. Manpower Consortium, Killeen, 1980; acctg. instr. Austin Community Coll., Tex., 1981-84; coordinator computer based instrn. Austin Community Coll., 1983—; cons. Austin Community Coll., 1981-83; owner Balcones Bookkeeping and Tax Service, Austin, 1981-83, Instructional Computing Services, Austin, 1983-85. Contbr. articles to profl. jours. Bd. dirs. Anderson Mill Swim Team, Austin, 1984-87. Recipient Corvus Nat. award, Corvus Systems, Inc., San Jose, Calif., 1986. Mem. Assn. for Ednl. Communications (copyright com. 1986—), Tex. Assn. Ednl. Tech. (dir. 1986—), Tex. Computer Edn. Assn. (electronic editor 1985-87), Am. Ednl. Research Assn., Assn. Devel. of Computer-Based Instl. Systems, Am. Acctg. Assn., Phi Kappa Phi, Kappa Delta Pi. Republican. Club: Mensa. Lodge: P.E.O. Office: Austin Community Coll 1212 Rio Grande Austin TX 78701

CATES, REBECCA ANN, accountant; b. Mpls., Aug. 7, 1960; d. Lawrence Joseph and Beatrice Louise (Ludowese) C. BA, honors, Gonzaga U., 1982. CPA, Wash. Asst. acct. Peat, Marwick, Main & Co., Seattle, 1982-83, staff acct., 1983-84, sr. acct., 1984-85, supervising sr. acct., 1985-87, mgr., 1987—. Mem. Am. Women's Soc. CPA's, Women CPA's of Seattle, Washington Soc. CPA's, Nat. Assn. Female Execs., Women's Bus. Exchange. Roman Catholic. Office: Peat Marwick Main & Co 1301 5th Ave Suite 2600 Seattle WA 98101

CATHCART, LINDA LOUISE, art historian. BA in Fine Arts, Calif. State U., Fullerton, 1969; MA in Art History, Hunter Coll., CUNY, 1972. Curatorial asst. Whitney Mus. Am. Art, N.Y.C., 1975-79; curator Albright-Knox Art Gallery, Buffalo, 1979-87; dir. Contemporary Arts Mus., Houston. Contbr. essays to catalogues. Fulbright fellow Courtauld Art Inst., 1973-74. Mem. Am. Assn. Mus., Internat. Council Mus., Am. Assn. Mus. Dirs. Office: PO Box 980551 Houston TX 77098

CATHER, LETHA MAE, construction company executive; b. Stratford, Okla., May 2, 1941; d. Hollis Floyd and Lillie Lorene (Austin) Ford; diploma Draughons Sch. Bus., Oklahoma City, 1960; student Okla. State U., Okla. Bapt. U.; divorced. With Hartford Ins. Co., Oklahoma City, 1966-67; with Cowen Constrn., Inc., Tulsa, 1967—, head acctg., sec.-treas., dir., 1970—; sec.-treas., dir. Stevco Inc., Rock Ridge Devel. Co.; mem. adv. com. constrn. tech. dept. Tulsa Jr. Coll., 1977-81. Mem. Nat. Assn. Women in Constrn. (pres. Tulsa chpt. 1977-81, dist. dir. 1982-83). Democrat. Baptist. Office: 18 N Maybelle Ave Tulsa OK 74127

CATHEY, M. ELIZABETH, lawyer; b. Syracuse, N.Y., Dec. 19, 1946; d. Phil Franklin Blum and Helen Marie (Yarwood) Drew; children: Denise Anne Beving Harwood, Cynthia Marie Beving; m. Robert Heaton Cathey, July 1988. BA cum laude, (Nat. Merit scholar), U. No. Iowa, 1973; postgrad. Schoitz Hosp. Sch. Med. Tech., 1973-74; JD (research scholar), Washburn U., 1981. Quality supr. U.S. Gypsum Co., Ft. Dodge, Iowa, 1974-75, employment supr., 1975-77; realtor assoc. Toothaker Real Estate Co., Manhattan, Kans., 1978, Anderson Realty Agy., Manhattan, 1978-79; research asst. Washburn U. Sch. Law, Topeka, 1979-80; law clk. Kans. Corp. Commn., Topeka, 1980-81; bar: Kans. 1981, U.S. Dist. Ct. Kans. 1981; individual practice law, Manhattan, 1981-83; mgr. personnel K-State Union, Manhattan, 1981-83; atty. Myers & Pottroff, Manhattan, 1983—; mem. univ. staff devel. task force, 1981-83, mem. univ. appeal and rev. com., 1982-83. Active LWV, 1977-80; mem. adv. bd. 4-H Club, 1981-84, chmn., 1983-84; solicitor United Way, 1981, 82, bd. dirs., 1984—, v.p., 1987, pres., 1988, allocations chair, 1986, 87; solicitor Cancer Crusade, 1975. Mem. ABA (secs. on corps., bus., banking, real property, probate, trust, taxation, econs.), Kans. Bar Assn. (coms. on legal malpractice prevention, continuing legal edn., sects. on corp., bus., banking, real estate, probate, trust, tax), Riley County Bar Assn. (chmn. Law Day 1984, pres. 1987), Am. Trial Lawyers Assn., Kans. Trial Lawyers Assn., North Central Iowa Personnel Assn. (sec. 1976-77), Manhattan Personnel Assn., Bus. and Profl. Women, Washburn Women's Legal Forum (v.p. and pres. 1979-80), Manhattan C. of C. (various coms., Leadership award 1983), Manhattan Arts Council, Am. Legion Aux., Phi Delta Phi. Republican. Methodist. Club: Pilot (rec. sec. 1983-84, 2d v.p. 1984-85, 1st v.p. 1985-86, pres. 1986-87, dir. 1987-88). Home: 2030 Hillview Dr Manhattan KS 66502

CATHOU, RENATA EGONE, scientist, consultant; b. Milan, Italy, June 21, 1935; d. Egon and Stella Mary Egone; m. Pierre-Yves Cathou, June 21, 1959. BS, MIT, 1957, PhD, 1963. Postdoctoral fellow, research assoc. in chemistry MIT, Cambridge, 1962-65; research assoc. Harvard U. Med. Sch., Cambridge, 1965-69, instr., 1969-70; research assoc. Mass. Gen. Hosp., 1965-69, instr., 1969-70; asst. prof. dept. biochemistry Sch. Medicine, Tufts U., 1970-73, assoc. prof., 1973-78, prof., 1978-81; pres. Tech. Evaluations, Lexington, Mass., 1983—; sr. cons. SRC Assocs., Park Ridge, N.J., 1984—; sr. investigator Arthritis Found., 1970-75; vis. prof. dept. chemistry UCLA, 1976-77; mem. adv. panel NSF, 1974-75; mem. bd. sci. counselors Nat. Cancer Inst., 1979-83; ind. cons. and writer. Mem. editorial bd. Immunochemistry, 1972-75; contbr. chpts. to books and articles to profl. jours. Mem. council Boston Mus. Fine Arts. NIH predoctoral fellow, 1958-62; grantee Am. Heart Assn., 1969-81, USPHS, 1970-81. Fellow Am. Inst. Chemists; mem. Clin. Ligand Assay Soc. (mem. exec. bd. New Eng. chpt. 1987—), Am. Soc. Biol. Chemists, Am. Assn. Immunologists, AAAS, N.Y. Acad. Scis. Club: U.S. Power Squadron (Lexington). Office: 430 Marrett Rd Lexington MA 02173

CATLIN, GAIL ERICA, marketing consultant; b. Denver, July 28, 1953; d. Marvin Edward and May Betty (Baker) Johnson; m. Benjamin Shields Catlin IV, Dec. 22, 1973; 1 child, Benjamin Shields. Student, Beloit Coll., 1971-73, U. de Haute, Bretagne, France, 1973, Am. U., 1973; BA in Pub. Adminstrn., Midwestern U., 1975; M in Pub. Adminstrn., Golden Gate U., 1979. Exec. dir. Greater Sacramento Cancer Council, 1976-81; adminstrv. dir. Sutter Community Cancer Ctr., Sacramento, 1981-83; asst. dir. community relations Sutter Health System, Sacramento, 1983-84; sr. dir. mktg. Sutter Health Systems, Sacramento, 1986; mktg. cons. Cunningham Assocs., Sacramento, 1984-86; owner, pres. The Catlin Co., Sacramento, 1986-87; instr. Golden Gate U., Sacramento, 1986—; speaker to profl. groups, 1980—. Author several research studies, 1981-83. Appointee Sacramento County Children's Commn., 1985-87; founder, pres. Mothers at Work, Sacramento; founding bd. mem. Sacramento Children's Mus., 1985—. Recipient Gold Medal award Sacramento Ad Club, 1986, Blue Ribbon award Camp Fire, Inc., Sacramento, 1987. Mem. Am. Soc. Hosp. Mktg. and Pub. Relations, Calif. Assn. Hosps. and Health Systems (dir. pub. affairs). Congregationalist.

CATLIN, MARIAN WOOLSTON, physician; b. Seattle, Jan. 20, 1931; d. Howard Brown and Katharine Nichols (Dally) Woolston; B.A. cum laude, Vassar Coll., 1951; M.D. (Vassar fellow), Harvard U., 1955; m. Randolph Catlin, July 5, 1959; children—Laura Louise, Jennifer Woolston, Randolph III. Intern and resident pediatric medicine Children's Hosp., Boston, 1956; resident in psychiatry Mass. Mental Health Center, Boston, 1957-59, mem. staff children's unit, 1978-82; clin. fellow psychiatry Harvard U., 1957-59, Commonwealth fellow child psychiatry, 1975-78, clin. instr. psychiatry, 1975—; clin. instr. psychiatry Tufts U., 1957-59; pvt. practice child and adolescent psychiatry, Wellesley Hills, Mass., 1978—; speaker Rhodes House, Oxford (Eng.) U., 1961. Bd. dirs. preparatory div. New Eng. Conservatory Music, 1972-75, Parents and Children's Services. Mem. AMA, Mass. Med. Soc., Am. Acad. Child Psychiatry, Am. Psychiat. Assn., New Eng. Council Child Psychiatry (mem. chmn.), Mass. Psychiat. Soc. Episcopalian. Clubs: Vassar (mem. bd. 1963-75) (Boston); Board-Hills Garden (design cons. 1973-75) (Wellesley Hills, Mass.). Home: 314 North St Medfield MA 02052 Office: 316 Washington St Wellesley Hills MA 02181

CATOE, BETTE LORRINA, physician; b. Washington, Apr. 7, 1926; d. John Booker and Laura Beola (Adams) C.; B.S. cum laude, Howard U., 1948, M.D., 1951; m. Warren J. Strudwick, Sept. 17, 1949; children—Laura Christina, Warren J., William J. Intern, Freedmen's Hosp., Washington, 1951-52; pediatric resident Howard U. Freedman's Hosp., 1952-55; practice medicine specializing in pediatrics, Washington, 1956—; instr. bacteriology Howard U., 1955-57; mem. staff Providence Hosp., Cafritz Hosp., Columbia Hosp., Howard U. Hosp., Washington Hosp. Center; sch. health officer Dept. Health, Washington, 1960-64; clin. instr. Howard U., 1956—. Mem. D.C. Health Planning Adv. Council, 1967-77, chmn., 1973-77; chmn. D.C. Devel. Disabilities Adv. Council, 1970-74; mem. D.C. Mayor's Commn. on Food and Nutrition, 1971-72, Mayor's Commn. on Maternal and Child Health, 1978—; mem. D.C. Commn. Jud. Tenure and Disabilities, 1977—, chair, 1984—; bd. dirs. United Way of Nat. Capital Area, 1974-76, chmn. social planning com., 1974-75; bd. govs. St. Alban's Sch., 1978—; bd. dirs. D.C. Health and Welfare Council, 1968-73, pres., 1973-74; del. Democratic Nat. Conv., 1976; bd. dirs. Met. Washington Health and Welfare Council, 1970-72, Parent Council of Washington, 1974-75, Met. Med. Founds., Inc., Silver Spring YMCA, 1977-80. Mem. Am. Acad. Pediatrics, AMA, Nat. Med. Assn., D.C. Chirurg. Soc., D.C. Med. Soc., Am. Med. Women's Assn. (chmn. pediatric com. 1981-83), NAACP, Urban League, Am. Assn. Comprehensive Health Planners (dir. 1975-77), Women's Aux. Medico-Chirurg. Soc., Jack and Jill Am., Century Club of Nat. Assn. Negro Bus. and Profl. Women's Clubs (pres. 1985—), Alpha Kappa Alpha. Baptist. Clubs: Links, Carrousels, Women's Nat. Dem. Home: 1748 Sycamore St NW Washington DC 20012 Office: 5505 5th St Washington DC 20011 *

CATRI, DEBORAH BINGHAM, vocational educator; b. Niagara Falls, N.Y., July 17, 1953; d. Alfred Clifton and Jean Elizabeth (Garnham) Bingham; m. Jeffrey Allen Catri, Apr. 25, 1987. BS, Ohio State U., 1975; MEd, Bowling Green (Ohio) State U., 1978. Lic. vocat. instr. consumer homemaking, data processing; cert. vocat. dir. Tchr. high sch. Lakota Pub. Sch., Kansas, Ohio, 1975-79; faculty coop. extension service Coll. of Agr., Ohio State U., Sandusky, 1979-86; supr. State of Ohio Dept. Edn. div. Vocat. Edn., Columbus, 1986—. Mem. adv. bd. Women, Infants and Children, Sandusky, 19880-86; mem. Perkins Community Sch. Bd. Edn., 1979-84. Recipient Young Profl. award Coll. Home Econs. Ohio State U., 1987. Mem. Nat. Assn. Extension Home Economists, (state liaison recruitment com. 1981-82, pub. relations com. 1982-84, voting del. 1985), Ohio Coop. Extension Agts. Assn. (personnel com. 1981-83, pub. relations com. 1983-84), Erie County Profl. Home Economists (sec.-treas. 1980-81), Am. Vocat. Assn., Ohio State U. Alumni Assn., Phi Delta Kappa. Republican. Roman Catholic. Lodge: Zonta (pres. 1986). Home: 5656 Keating Dr Dublin OH 43017 Office: Ohio State Dept Edn Div Vocat and Career Edn 907 Ohio Depts Bldg 65 S Front St Columbus OH 43266-0308

CATTANEO, JACQUELYN ANNETTE KAMMERER, artist, educator; b. Gallup, N.Mex., June 1, 1944; d. Ralph John and Gladys Agnes (O'Sullivan) Kammer; m. John Leo Cattaneo, Apr. 25, 1964; children: John Auro, Paul Anthony. Student Tex. Woman's U., 1962-64. Portrait artist, tchr. Gallup, N. Mex., 1972; coordinator Works Progress Adminstrn. art project renovation McKinley County, Gallup, Octavia Fellin Performing Arts wing dedication, Gallup Pub. Library; formation com. mem. Multi-modal/Multi-Cultural Ctr. for Gallup, N.Mex.; one-woman shows: Gallup Pub. Library, 1963, 66, 77, 78, 81, 87, Gallup Lovelace Med. Clinic, Santa Fe Station Open House, 1981, Gallery 20, Farmington, N.Mex., 1985—; group shows include: Navajo Nation Library Invitational, 1978, Santa Fe Festival of the Arts Invitational, 1979, N.Mex. State Fair, 1978, 79, 80, Catharine Lorillard Wolfe, N.Y.C., 1980, 81, 84, 85, 86, 87, 88, 4th ann. exhbn. Salmagundi Club, 1984, 3d ann. Palm Beach Internat., New Orleans, 1984, Fine Arts Ctr. Taos, 1984, The Best and the Brightest O'Brien's Art Emporium, Scottsdale, Ariz., 1986, Gov.'s Gallery, N.Mex. State Capitol, Santa Fe, 1987, Pastel Soc. West Coast Ann. Exhbn. Sacramento Ctr. for Arts, Calif., 1988; represented in permanent collections: Zuni Arts and Crafts Ednl. Bldg., U. N.Mex., C.J. Wiemar Collection, McKinley Manor, Gov.'s Office, State Capitol Bldg., Santa Fe, Sunwest Bank. Fine Arts Ctr., En Taos, N.Mex. Mem. Internat. Fine Arts Guild, Am. Portrait Soc. (cert.), Pastel Soc. of W. Coast (cert.), Mus. N.Mex. Found., Mus. Women in the Arts, Fechin Inst., Artists' Co-op. (co-chair), Gallup C. of C., Gallup Area Arts and Crafts Council, Catharine Lorillard Wolfe Art Club of N.Y.C. (oil and pastel juried membership). Lodge: Soroptimists. Address: 210 E Green St Gallup NM 87301

CATTANI, MARYELLEN BILLETTE, financial services company executive, lawyer; b. Bakersfield, Calif., Dec. 1, 1943; d. Arnold Theodore and Corinne Marilyn (Kovacevich) C.; m. Bernard Joseph Mikell, Apr. 1, 1978; 1 child, Sarah Cattani Mikell. A.B., Vassar Coll., 1965; J.D., U. Calif.-Berkeley, 1968. Bar: N.Y. 1969, Calif. 1969. Assoc. Davis Polk & Wardwell, N.Y.C., 1968-69; assoc. Orrick, Herrington & Sutcliffe, San Francisco, 1970-74; ptnr. Orrick, Herrington & Sutcliffe, 1975-81; v.p., gen. counsel Transam. Corp., San Francisco, 1981-83, sr. v.p., gen. counsel, 1983—; mem. adv. com. U. San Francisco Inst. on Fin. Services, 1984-86; mem. vis. com. Golden Gate U. Sch. Law, San Francisco, 1983—; vice chairperson, bd. dirs. Transam. Found., 1987—. Contbg. author: Corporate Counselor's Desk Book, 1982, Litigation for Non-Litagator, 1987. Mem. pvt. sector task force on juvenile justice Nat. Council on Crime and Delinquency, San Francisco, 1985-87; trustee Vassar Coll., 1985—; bd. regents St. Mary's Coll. Calif., 1985—. Named Outstanding Woman, Equal Rights Advocates, 1984. Mem. ABA, State Bar Calif. (chmn. bus. law sect. 1980-81), Bar Assn. San Francisco, Calif. Women Lawyers, San Francisco C. of C. (bd. dirs. 1987—), Am. Corp. Counsel Assn. (bd. dirs. 1982-87), Women's Forum West (bd. dirs. 1984-87). Democrat. Roman Catholic. Office: Transamerica Corp 600 Montgomery St San Francisco CA 94111

CATTERTON, MARIANNE ROSE, occupational therapist; b. St. Paul, Feb. 3, 1922; d. Melvin Joseph and Katherine Marion (Bole) Maas; m. Elmer John Wood, Jan. 16, 1943 (dec.); m. Robert Lee Catterton, Nov. 20, 1951 (div. 1981); children: Jenifer Ann Dawson, Cynthia Lea Uthus. Student, Carleton Coll., 1939-41, U. Md., 1941-42; BA in English, U. Wis., 1944; MA in Counseling Psychology, Bowie State Coll., 1980; postgrad., No. Ariz. U., 1987—. Registered occupational therapist. Occupational therapist VA, N.Y.C., 1946-50, Anne Arundel County Health Dept., Annapolis, Md., 1967-78; cons. occupational therapist Fondo del Seguro del Estado, Puerto Rico, 1950-51, Kachina Point Health Ctr., Sedona, Ariz., 1986; dir. rehab. therapies Spring Grove State Hosp., Catonsville, Md., 1953-56; dir. occupational therapy Eastern Shore Hosp. Ctr., Cambridge, Md., 1979-85; regional chmn. Conf. on revising Psychiat. Occupational Therapy Edn., 1958-59; instr. report writing Anne Arundel Community Coll., Annapolis, 1974-78. Editor Am. Jour. Occupational Therapy, 1962-67. Active Md. Heart Assn., 1959-60; mem. task force on occupational therapy Md. Dept. of Health, 1971-72; chmn. Anne Arundel Gov. Com. on Employment of Handicapped, 1959-63; mem. gov.'s com. to study vocat. rehab., Md., 1960; com. mem. Annapolis Youth Ctr., 1976-78; mem. ministerial search com. Unitarian Ch. Anne Arundel County, 1962; curator Dorchester County Heritage Mus., Cambridge, 1982-83. Mem. Puerto Rico Occupational Therapy Assn. (co-founder 1950), Am. Occupational Therapy Assn. (chmn. history com. 1958-61), Md. Occupational Therapy Assn. (del. 1953-59), Dorchester County Mental Health Assn. (pres. 1981-84), Delta Delta Delta. Republican. Clubs: Severn Town (treas. 1965), International (publicity chmn. 1966) (Annapolis); Toastmasters, Newcomers (pres. 1986) (Sedona). Home: 100 Canyon Circle Dr #4 Sedona AZ 86336

CATTRELL, BETTY JANE, librarian; b. Wichita, Kans., Feb. 27, 1927; d. Vern Hamlin and Orpha Jane (Kerr) Welch; m. Melvin Lee Cattrell, June 26, 1945; children—Kary Lee, Keith Lane(dec.), Kelly Jane, Karla Joyce. Student Kans. Newman Coll. Periodical librarian Boeing Airplane Co., Wichita, Kans., 1952-60; librarian Unified Sch. Dist. #261, Haysville, Kans., 1961-77, Haysville Community Library, 1977—. Mem. Internat. Reading Assn. (pres. 1983—), ALA, Mountain Plains Library Assn., Kans. Library Assn.(library assoc.), DAR, VFW Aux., Assn. Am. Bus. Women. Democrat. Baptist. Home: 132 Wire St Haysville KS 67060 Office: Haysville Community Library 230 E Grand St Haysville KS 67060

CATZ, ROCHELLE ZUKOR, lawyer; b. Providence, Aug. 21, 1945; d. Jerold and Frances (Konisky) Zukor; m. Robert Steven Catz, Apr. 28, 1968 (div. 1979); children: Shawn David, Jason Alan; m. Loren Edward Bailey, Dec. 18, 1986. A.B., U. So. Calif., 1968; M.S. in Edn., 1969; J.D., Antioch Sch. of Law, 1979. Tchr. Los Angeles Pub. Schs., 1968, Laguna Salada Union Sch. Dist., Pacifica, Calif., 1969-71, Omaha Pub. Schs., 1971-73; indexer/abstractor Eric Clearing House on Tchr. Edn., Washington, 1975-76; atty. Fla. Rural Legal Services, Ft. Myers, Fla., 1979-83; pvt. practice law, Ft. Myers, 1983—; mem. Fla. Legal Services, Pub. Benefits Work Group, Tallahassee, Fla., 1980-83; mem. Aging Network, Ft. Myers, Fla., 1983. Sec., Jewish Fedn. of Lee County, 1984-85. Mem. Pa. Bar Assn., Am. Bar Assn., Fla. Bar, Lee County Bar Assn. (treas. 1986, sec. 1987, pres.-elect 1988), Nat. Orgn. Social Security Calimants Reps., Fla. Assn. Women Lawyers, Southwest Fla. Estate Planning Council. Democrat. Jewish. Clubs: Women's Network (Ft. Myers, Fla.). Lodge: Zonta, Order of Eastern Star. Office: 13161 McGregor Blvd Fort Myers FL 33919

CAUDILL, HELENE LITOWSKY, health care administrator; b. Houston, Nov. 3, 1960; d. David and May (Rose) Litowsky; m. Robert Middelton Caudill, Mar. 17, 1985. B in Indsl. Engring., Ga. Inst. Tech., 1982; postgrad., North Tex. State U., 1984—. Mgmt. engr. Mediflex Systems (now HBO), Houston, 1982-83; mgmt. engr., specialist info. ctr. Baylor Healthcare System, Dallas, 1983-86; dir. mgmt. services Presbyn. Hosp. Dallas, 1986—. Contbr. articles to profl. jours. Mem. Healthcare Info. and Mgmt. Systems Soc. (chairperson newsletter com. 1986—, membership chairperson, 1988—), Healthcare Fin. Mgmt. Assn., Inst. Indsl. Engrs., Soc. Women Engrs., Nat. Soc. for Exec. Females. Jewish. Office: Presbyn Hosp Dallas 8200 Walnut Hill Ln Dallas TX 75231

CAUDILL, MAUREEN, computer consultant; b. Portsmouth, Ohio, July 14, 1951; d. Elmon C. and Harriet L. (Sisler) C. BA, U. Conn., 1973; MAT, Cornell U., 1974. Customer engr. Raytheon Data Systems, Wellesley, Mass., 1975-78; mem. tech. sales support staff Hewlett-Packard Co., Wallingford, Conn., 1978-81; project programmer Gould Ocean Systems div., Cleve., 1982-83; sr. software engr. Data Systems div. Gen. Dynamics Co., San Diego, 1983-85; computer cons. Rockwell Internat., Hughes Aircraft Corp., Honeywell Corp., other corps., 1985—; founder, computer cons. Adaptics, San Diego, 1987—; organizer ann. meetings on neural networks, San Diego and Boston, 1987—. Author: Naturally Intelligent Systems, 1988; contbr. to profl. publs. Mem. IEEE, Internat. Neural Network Soc. (exec. dir. 1988—), Assn. Computing Machinery. Office: Adaptics 16776 Bernardo Center Dr Suite 110B San Diego CA 92128

CAULDER, MARY MEZZANOTTE, bank training officer; b. Phila., Dec. 28, 1953; d. Antonio Joseph and Dora (Ciccozzi) Mezzanotte; m. Bruce Edward Caulder, Oct. 29, 1983; children: Heather, Bruce Jr. BS in Labor Relations, LaSalle U., Phila., 1983. Bank clk. Phila. Nat. Bank, 1971-76, tng. specialist, 1976-85; tng. officer Main Line Fed. Savs. Bank, Villanova, Pa., 1986—; instr. Inst. Fin. Edn., Bucks County Community Coll., 1987—. Mem. Am. Soc. for Tng. and Devel., Internat. Assn. Quality Circles (treas. 1983-85), Nat. Assn. Female Execs. Office: Main Line Fed Savs Bank Rt 320 and Lancaster Ave Villanova PA 19085

CAUTHEN, DELORIS VAUGHAN, artist; b. Wilmington, N.C.; d. Robert S. and Margaret (Hurst) Vaughan; student U. S.C., 1950-52, Richland Art Sch., 1960-63, 75-76, Robert Brackman, Madison, Conn., 1976-77, Burnsville (N.C.) Painting in the Mountains Sch., 1980-86; student of Frank Allen, Rock Port, Mass., 1955; m. John Kelley Cauthen, Dec. 28, 1925 (dec. 1973); children—John Vaughan, Henry Jennings. One-woman shows of paintings and/or sculpture include: U. S.C., Florence, 1968, U. S.C., Aiken, 1970, Francis Marion Coll., Florence, 1980, S.C. Ednl. TV, Columbia, 1966, 70, Columbia (S.C.) Town Theater, 1960, Union County Library, Monroe, N.C., 1969, S.C. Fed. Savs. & Loan Assn., Columbia, 1979 Columbia Coll., 1981, Spring Mills, Ft. Mill, S.C., 1981, Columbia Coll., 1982: four 3 person shows Columbia Mus. Art (purchase award); numerous group shows including: Mint Mus. Art, Charlotte, N.C., 1962, 65, 66, Columbia Mus. Art, 1964, 70, 73, 77, Gibbs Art Gallery, Charleston, S.C., 1966, 67, 69, Telfair Acad. Art, Savannah, Ga., 1969, Beaufort (S.C.) Art Assn., 1969, S.C. State Fair, 1959 (blue ribbon), Columbia Coll.; represented in permanent collections: Mint Mus. Art, S.C. Nat. Bank, Columbia, U. S.C., Columbia, Columbia Mus. of Art, Columbia City Schs., Darlington (S.C.) City Schs., S.C. Gov.'s Mansion, Columbia, Spriggs Corp., Banker's Trust, Columbia, others. Mem. S.C. Gov.'s Council of Advs. on Consumer Credit, 1974-78. Recipient S.C. Nat. Bank award, 1969-73, award Beaufort Art Assn., also numerous show awards including Judges Choice, Tel air Acad. Art, 1969 Mem. Columbia Artists Guild (top winner, hon. and merit awards), Guild S.C. Artists, Internat. Soc. Artists, Trenholm Artist Guild, Dutch Fork Artist Guild. Methodist. Address: 2407 Wheat St Columbia SC 29205

CAUTHEN, HELEN INGRAM, administrator, educator; b. Neptune, N.J., Dec. 12, 1954; d. Ernest and Mae Helen (Monroe) C. BS, Del. State Coll., 1977. Tchr. cooperative edn. Neptune Pub. Sch. System, 1977-78; tchr. parochial Nativity Cath. Sch., Washington, 1978-79; adminstrv. asst., ann. mtg. coordinator Am. Pub. Health Assn., Washington, 1979-87; adminstr. meeting mgmt. Am. Coll. Ob-Gyn, Washington, 1987—. Mem. Nat. Assn. Female Execs., Am. Soc. for Assn. Execs., Profl. Conv. Mgmt. Assn., Meeting Planners Internat., Greater Washington Soc. of Assn. Execs., Delta Sigma Theta. Home: 7660 Stana Ct Lorton VA 22079 Office: Am Coll Ob/Gyn 409 12th St SWW Washington DC 20024

CAVAIOLI, LINDA ANN, fundraiser; b. Leominster, Mass., June 30, 1954; d. Riccardo Joseph and Louise (Bianchini) C. BA in Sociology, U. N.H., 1976; postgrad., Clark U., Worcester, Mass., 1987—. With United Way Am., Alexandria, Va., 1976-77; assoc. campaign and communications dir. United Way Palm Beach Country, West. Palm Beach, Fla., 1977-79; communications dir. United Way Cen. Mass., Worcester, Mass., 1980-81; assoc. campaign dir. United Way Cen. Mass., Worcester, 1981, campaign dir., 1982-85, v.p., 1986—; cons. in field. Solicitor Assumption Coll., Worcester, 1980—; mem. Worcester Area Women in Devel., 1982—, Worcester area Leadership Assn. 1984—, YWCA Exec. and Managerial Women's Network, 1986—. Democrat. Roman Catholic. Home: 22 Northridge St Worcester MA 01603 Office: United Way Cen Mass 484 Main St Suite 300 Worcester MA 01608

CAVALCANTE, MITZIE W., service company executive; b. Liberty Boro, Pa., Nov. 12, 1930; d. Glennward David and Margaret LaRue (Kier) Wunderley; m. Anthony Cavalcante Jr., Oct. 5, 1951; children: Debra Ann Beck, Jennifer Sue, Jeffrey Lee, Guy Anthony, Cari Jo Cavalcante. Student, Radford Coll., 1948-50, Pa. State U., 1968-78; cert. constrn. mgmt., U. Pitts., 1971, cert. med. technician, Pa.; lic. real estate agt. Lab mgr. Dr. Mayer Green, Pitts., 1952-65; sales mgr. Don Kepner Real Estate, Lititz, Pa., 1968-74; constrn. mgr. D. Hollinger Real Estate, Lititz, 1974-76; v.p. Century Log Homes, Lititz, 1976-81; personnel adminstr. Maas Brothers, Gainesville, Fla., 1982-83; mgr. tng. and devel. Associated Temporary Staffing, Jacksonville, Fla., 1984-87; br. mgr. Associated Temporary Staffing, N.Y.C., 1987—; cons., pub. speaker. Mem. N.Y. Mayor's Com. for Summer Jobs, N.Y.C., 1987; past pres. PTA, McKeesport, Pa., 1965. Mem. Assn. Devel. and Tng. (news editor local chpt.), Nat. Assn. Female Execs., Lancaster Women Realtors (past pres.), C. of C. Republican. Office: Associated Temporary Staffing 295 madison Ave 25th Floor New York NY 10017

CAVALLON, BETTY GABLER, interior designer; b. Waverly, N.Y., July 17, 1918; d. Wallace Frederick and Harriet (Heaton) Gabler; grad. Parsien Sch. Design, Detroit, 1939; m. Michel Francis Cavollon, Dec. 26, 1946 (dec. 1981); children—Claire, Carol (dec.); stepchildren—Michel, Mary; m. John W. Crist, Nov. 20, 1982. Fabric coordinator Montgomery Ward, 1940-46; interior designer Betty Cavallon Interiors Ltd., Stamford, Conn., 1946—. Mem. Am. Soc. Interior Designers (corp.). Republican. Episcopalian. Home and Office: 1369 Long Ridge Rd Stamford CT 06903

CAVANAUGH, ESTELLE DILG, adult educator, human resources development administrator; b. Tottenville, N.Y., May 12, 1923; d. Lynden Conrad and Ella Marie (Peterson) Dilg; m. Carl Edwin Klingler, Dec. 27, 1946 (div. Aug. 1957); children—Sally Ann Klingler Keele, Nancy Jean Klingler Shelley; m. Wallace J. Cavanaugh, June 1, 1985. B.S. in Bus. Adminstrn., U. So. Calif., 1968, M.B.A., 1972; Ed.D., UCLA, 1982. Cert. community coll. and adult edn. instr., Calif. Stenographer, supr. N.Y. Telephone Co., Albany, 1941-46; staff clk. Pacific Telephone, Los Angeles, 1947-51; exec. sec. TRW, Los Angeles, 1956-66, placement mgr., 1966-70, tng./orgn. devel. specialist, 1970-73; assoc. dir. dept. engr. sci. UCLA Extension, 1973-87, co-owner Crown Devel. and Mining Co., 1987—; prin., Cavanaugh Assocs., 1987—; instr. Grad. Sch. Edn., 1983. Contbr. in field. Patron Westchester YMCA, Los Angeles, 1949-75 ; mem. edn. com. Westchester Methodist Ch., Los Angeles, 1984—. Served with USNR, 1942-45. Recipient Woman of Achievement award Bus. and Profl. Women, El Segundo, Calif., 1977; Edn. Achievement award Calif. Soc. Profl. Engrs., 1983. Fellow Inst. Advancement of Engring.; mem. Am. Soc. Engring. Edn. (chmn. continuing profl. devel. div. 1984-85), ASTD, Nat. Univ. Continuing Edn. Assn., Am. Assn. Adult and Continuing Edn., Bus. and Profl. Women Club (v.p. 1981-83). Republican. Club: Academic Women's Assn. UCLA. Lodge: Foresters. Office: 8497 Carleton Way Los Angeles CA 90069

CAVANAUGH, SHIRLEY REIKO, air force officer; b. Honolulu, Nov. 11, 1943; d. Satoshi and Yukimi (Sawamoto) Kodani; 1 dau., Kimberly Mariko; m. E. William Cavanaugh Jr., Nov. 22, 1986. B.A., Wash. State U., 1965; M.A., U. No. Colo., 1977. Tchr. speech and English Mt. Tahoma High Sch., Tacoma, 1965-67; commd. 2d lt. U.S. Air Force, 1967, advanced through grades to lt. col., 1984; personnel officer Otis AFB, Falmouth, Mass., 1967-69, Hickam AFB, Honolulu, 1969-71, Udorn Royal Thai Air Base, Thailand, 1971-72; personnel officer Kelly AFB, San Antonio 1972-74, info. officer 1974-76; pub. affairs officer, briefing officer Wright-Patterson AFB, Dayton, Ohio, 1976-79; chief pub. affairs Yokota Air Base, Tokyo, 1979-82; chief internal info. and community relations div. Andrews AFB, Camp Springs, Md., 1982-86; dep. pub. affairs officer U.S. Forces Korea, Yongsan Army Garrison, Seoul, 1986—. Decorated Air Force Commendation medal with 2 oak leaf clusters, Meritorious Service medalwith 1 oak leaf cluster. Mem. AAUW (life, past program v.p., membership v.p. 1984-86), Women in Communications, Inc., Ben Franklin Club (charter pres. 1978-79), Air Force Assn. Mailing Address: HHC EAST PAO APO San Francisco CA 96204

CAVERS-HUFF, DASIEA YVONNE, philosopher; b. Cleve., Oct. 24, 1961; d. Lawrence Benjamin and Yvonne (Warner) Cavers; m. Brian Jay Huff, July 26, 1986. BA, Cleve. State U., 1984, MA, 1988; postgrad., U. Md., 1986—. Teaching asst. Cleve. State U., 1983-86; instr. Upward Bound program Case Western Res. U., Cleve., 1986; mem. faculty U. Md. Univ. Coll., Coll. Park, Md., 1987—. U. Md. graduate fellow, 1986-87; Ford Found. predoctoral fellow, 1987. Mem. Am. Philos. Assn., Minority Grad. Student Assn. (co-chmn. U. Md. 1987-88). Democrat. Home: 16105 Penn Manor Ln Bowie MD 20716 Office: Dept Philosophy U Md 1131 Skinner Bldg College Park MD 20740

CAVNAR, MARGARET MARY (PEGGY), business executive, former state legislator, nurse; b. Buffalo, July 29, 1945; d. James John and Margaret Mary Murtha Nightengale; B.S. in Nursing, D'Youville Coll., 1967; m. Samuel M. Cavnar, 1977; children—Heather Anne, Heide Lynn, Dona Cavnar Hambly, Judy Cavnar Bentrim. Utilization rev. coordinator South Nev. Meml. Hosp., Las Vegas, 1975-77; v.p. Ranvac Publs., Las Vegas, 1976—; ptnr. Cavnar & Assocs., Reseda, Calif., 1976—, C & A Mgmt., Las Vegas, 1977—; pres. PS Computer Service, Las Vegas, 1978—; bd. dirs. No. Nev. Bank. Mem. Clark County Republican Central Com., 1977—, Nev. Rep. Central Com., 1978-80; mem. Nev. Assembly, 1979-81; Rep. nominee for Nev. Senate, 1980; Rep. nominee for Congress from Nev. 1st dist., 1982, 84; bd. dirs., treas. Nev. Med. Fed. Credit Union; v.p. Community Youth Activities Found., Inc., Civic Assn. Am.; mem. utilization rev. bd. Easter Seals; trustee Nev. Sch. Arts, 1980-87; nat. adviser Project Prayer, 1978—; co-chmn. P.R.I.D.E. Com., 1983—; co-chmn. Tax Limitation Com., 1983, Personal Property Tax Elimination Com., 1979-82, Self-Help Against Food Tax Elimination Denial Com., 1980; mem. Nev. Profl. Standards Rev. Orgn., 1984; co-chmn. People Against Tax Hikes, 1983-84; bd. dirs. Nev. Eye Bank, 1988—. Mem. Nev. Order Women Legislators (charter, parliamentarian 1980—), Sigma Theta Tau. Club: Cosmopolitany Hers Info. (pres.). Office: PO Box 26073 Las Vegas NV 89126

CAWEIN, KATHRIN (MRS. SEABURY CONE MASTICK), artist; b. New London, Conn., May 9, 1895; d. Henry and Barbara (Franz) Cawein; M.A. (hon.), Oberlin Coll., 1966; D.F.A. (hon.), Pacific U., Forest Grove, Oreg.; student Art Students League; m. Seabury Cone Mastick, Apr. 3, 1964. Music roll editor, music interpreter with various musicians, 1911-32; tchr. County Center Work Shop, 1935-36; owner studio for children, 1950-55; one man shows; County Center, White Plains, N.Y., 1935, Village Art Center, N.Y.C., 1945, Town Hall, N.Y.C., 1950, 8th St. Playhouse, N.Y.C., 1953, Sarasota, Fla., 1973, U. Tampa (Fla.), 1973, Oberlin (Ohio) Coll., 1975, St. John's Ch., Pleasantville, N.Y., 1976, Berea (Ky.) Coll., 1977, Pacific U., Forest Grove, Oreg., 1979, 80, 81, 83, 85; exhibited group shows U.S., Eng., France, Italy, Ecuador, including Century of Progress, 1934, Tex. Centennial, 1937, World's Fair, 1939; represented in permanent collections at Met. Mus., Nat. Mus., Washington, Pa. State U., Tampa U., Oberlin Coll.; illuminated books St. Marks Ch., Van Nuys, Calif.; illuminated manuscripts Pacific U. Recipient Frank Talcott Non-Mem. prize Soc. Am. Etchers, 1936, prize for lithography Village Art Center, 1944, prize for etching Nat. Assn. Women Artists, 1947, prize for dry point Pleasantville Woman's Club, 1950, prize for etching, 1952, prize for dry point Westchester Fedn. Women's Clubs, 1951, others; Kathrin Cawein Gallery of Art named in her honor Pacific U., 1985. Mem. Nat. Assn. Women Artists, Art Students League (life), Chgo. Soc. Etchers, Soc. Graphic Artists. Home and Studio: 35 Mountain Rd Pleasantville NY 10570

CAWEIN, MARA JANE, computer programmer; b. Hamilton, Ohio, July 12, 1955; d. Stanley and Mildred (Jones) Tutas; m. David Arthur Cawein, July 15, 1974; children: Gregory, Kristina, April. BS, U. Cen. Ark., 1978. Computer programmer CCX Network, Inc., Conway, Ark., 1978-83, 84—; pvt. practice computer cons. Conway, 1983-84. Lay therapist Suspected Child Abuse and Neglect, Conway, 1983-85; vol. Meals on Wheeels, 1985—; adminstrv. bd. mem. First United Meth. Ch., Morrilton, Ark., 1986—, Sunday sch. tchr., 1986—, pastor parish relations com., 1987—. Club: May McClurkin Circle, Morrilton Country. Home: 304 E Drilling St Morrilton AR 72110

CAWLEY, GOLDA S., speech pathologist, educator; b. Salt Lake City, Apr. 29, 1938; d. Golden and Vera (Robinson) Stringham; m. Roy E. Cawley, July 15, 1960 (div. June 1971); children: Nena Susan, Eddie, Todd, Tina. BS, U. Utah, 1973, MS, 1974. Cert. speech pathologist. Speech pathology student adv. chmn. U. Utah, Salt Lake City, 1972-74; speech, lang. specialist Davis County Sch. Dist., Farmington, Utah, 1974—; asst. rep. Davis Edn. Assn., Farmington, 1984—; mem. State Licensure in Speech Pathology, 1984—; program facilitator Davis Schs., Farmington, 1984-85; com. mem. Utah Speech and Hearing Assn. Pub. Relations, 1986—. Author of various edn. publs. Del. Davis County Dem. Com., 1980; participant Cancer Assn. of Utah. Mem. NEA, Utah Speech and Hearing Assn., Council for Exceptional Children, Davis Edn. Assn., Utah Edn. Assn. Mormon. Clubs: Davis Park; Bountiful Springs. Home: 236 West Meadow Ln Centerville UT 84014 Office: Davis Sch Dist Farmington UT 84025

CAWOOD, ELIZABETH JEAN, public relations executive; b. Santa Maria, Calif., Jan. 6, 1947; d. John Stephen and Gertrude Margaret (Shelton) Dille; m. Neil F. Cawood, Jan. 4, 1975; 1 child, Nathan Patrick. BA, Whitworth Coll., 1964-68. Dir. pub. info. Inland Empire Goodwill, Spokane, Wash., 1967-72; adminstrv. asst. Northwest Assn. Rehab. Industries, Seattle, 1972-74; pres., counselor Cawood Communications, Eugene, Oreg., 1974—; pres. Women in Communications, Inc., 1981-83; adv. U. Oreg. Pub. Relations Student Soc. Am., 1986—; bd. dirs. Eugene/Springfield Met. Ptnrship. Editor: Dictionary of Rehabilitation Acronyms, (newsletters) INTERCOM, Family Communicator, Oreg. Focus, (dictionary) Work-Oriented Rehabilitation Dictionary and Synonyms, 1st and 2nd edits. Bd. dirs. Eugene Action Forum, 1981-86, Birth-to-Three, 1982-85, Lane County ARC, 1982-83, Lane County Unit Am. Cancer Soc., 1984-87, Eugene Opera, 1985-87, Joint Com. Econ. Diversification, 1985—, Lane County United Way, 1987—; bd. dirs. So. Willamette Pvt. Industry Council, 1985—, v.p., 1987-88, pres., 1988; chmn. Eugene Pvt. Industries Council, 1981-83, vice chmn. 1981-84, pres. 1987-88, chmn. Bus. Owner's Network, Eugene, 1980-81. Mem. LWV (bd. dirs. 1979), Pub. Relations Soc. Am. (bd. dirs. Columbia River chpt. 1987—), Nat. Rehab. Assn. (pres. 1980-81), Profl. Women's Network (bd. dir. Oreg. chpt. 1982), Eugene C. of C. (bd. dirs. 1980-87, econ. devel. chair 1982-83, ambassador com. chair 1984, bd. dirs. exec. com. 1984—, v.p. 1987), Mid-Oreg. Advt. Club (bd. dirs. 1985-87), Oreg. Sales and Mktg. Execs. (bd. dirs. 1985-87). Office: Cawood Communications 1200 High St Suite 21 Eugene CO 97401

CAWRSE, CELESTE POWLUS, valuation consultant; b. Fairborn, Ohio, Aug. 26, 1956; d. Jesse Tilden and Alleen (Gormley) Powlus; m. David Michael Cawrse, Aug. 27, 1977. BS, U. Tenn., 1979; MBA, NYU, 1986. Fin. planner Columbia U., N.Y.C., 1979-81, research asst., 1980-82; internal audit asst. Dean Witter Reynolds, N.Y.C., 1981-82; corp. tax mgr. R. H. Macy and Co., Inc., N.Y.C., 1982-86; real estate investment analyst, Guardian Life Ins. Co., N.Y.C., 1987—. Mem. NYU Bus. Forum, DAR, Riverside Symphony Guild, Internat. Council Shopping Ctrs. Republican. Methodist.

CAWS, MARY ANN, educator, critic; b. Wilmington, N.C., Sept. 10, 1933; d. Harmon Chadbourn and Margaret Devereux (Lippitt) Rorison; m. Peter Caws, June 2, 1956 (div. 1987); children: Matthew, Hilary. B.A., Bryn Mawr Coll., 1954; M.A., Yale U., 1956; Ph.D., U. Kans., 1962; D.Humane Letters, Union Coll., 1983. Asst. instr. Romance Langs. U. Kans., 1957-62, asst. editor univ. press, 1957-58, vis. asst. prof., spring 1963; lectr. Barnard Coll., 1962-63; mem. faculty Sarah Lawrence Coll., 1963-64; mem. faculty Hunter Coll., N.Y.C., 1966—, prof., 1969—; exec. officer comparative lit. program CUNY Grad. Ctr., 1977-79, exec. officer French program, 1979-86, Disting. prof. French and comparative lit., 1983—, prof. English, 1985—, Disting. prof. French, comparative lit., English, 1987—; Phi Beta Kappa vis. scholar, 1982-83; dir. NEH summer seminars for coll. tchrs., 1978, 85; co-dir. Peyre Inst. for the Humanities, 1980—. Author: Surrealism and the Literary Imagination, 1966, The Poetry of Dada and Surrealism, 1970, The Inner Theatre of Recent French Poetry, 1972, The Presence of Rene Char, 1976, Rene Char, 1977, La Main de Pierre Reverdy, 1979, The Eye in the Text, Essays on Perception, Mannerist to Modern, 1981, Andre Breton, 1982, The Metapoetics of the Passage, Architextures in Surrealism and After, 1982, Andre Breton, 1982, Yves Bonnefoy, 1984, Reading Frames in Modern Fiction, 1988, Edmond Gabès; contbr. articles to profl. jours.; editor: Dada-Surrealism, 1972, Le Siecle eclate, 1974, About French Poetry from Dada to Tel Quel, 1974, Writing in a Modern Temper, 1984, Textual Analysis, 1986; translator: Poems of Rene Char, 1976, Approximate Man and other Writings Of Tristan Tzara, 1975, Selected Poetry Prose of Stephane Mallarme, 1982, Selected Poems of St.-John Perse, 1983; co-translator: Poems of André Breton, 1984, Mad Love, 1987. Decorated officer Palmes Academiques, France; fellow Guggenheim Found., 1972-73, Nat. Endowment Humanities, 1979-80; Fulbright traveling fellow, 1972-73. Mem. MLA (exec. council 1973-77, v.p. 1982-83, pres. 1983-84), Am. Assn. Tchrs. French, Assn. for Study Dada and Surrealism (pres. 1982-86), Internat. Assn. Philosophy and Lit. (exec. bd. 1982—, chmn. 1984), Assn. Study Dada and Surrealism (pres. 1972-76), Acad. Lit. Studies (pres. 1985), Am. Comparative Lit. Assn. (exec. com. 1981—, v.p. 1986—, pres.-elect 1986). Home: 140 E 81st St New York NY 10028 Office: CUNY Grad Ctr 33 W 42d St New York NY 10036

CAZAN, SYLVIA MARIE BUDAY (MRS. MATTHEW JOHN CAZAN), realtor; b. Youngstown, Ohio, Nov. 17, 1915; d. John J. and Sylvia (Grama) Buday; student U. Bucharest, (Rumania), 1933-35. Youngstown Coll., 1936-38, Georgetown U. Inst. Langs. and Linguistics, 1950; m. Matthew John Cazan, July 14, 1935; 1 son, Matthew John G. Adminstrv. asst. statistics U.S. Dept. Def., 1941-52; spl. employee Dept. Justice, 1956-58; mgr. James L. Dixon & Co. Realtors, Falls Church, Va., 1959-70; mgr. Lewis & Silverman Inc., Chevy Chase, Md., 1970—. Mem. bd. Examiners Georgetown U., 1950. Bd. dirs. Magnolia Internat. Debutante Ball. Recipient Commendation and Meritorious award Dept. Justice, 1958. Mem. Gen. Fedn. Women's Clubs (pres. 1955-56), Interscholastic Debating Soc., Md. Bd. Realtors, Washington, No. Va. real estate bds. Mem. Rumanian Orthodox Ch. Home: 6369 Lakeview Dr Lake Barcroft Estates Falls Church VA 22041 Office: 8401 Connecticut Ave Chevy Chase MD 20015

CEARLEY, MARTHA HYDE, educator; b. Evansville, Ind., Oct. 14, 1957; d. Billy Dorris and Phyllis Ann (Whitten) Hyde; m. Steven Wayne Cearley, Aug. 15, 1981; children: Benjamin Vern, Sarah Caitlin. BA in Edn. magna cum laude, U. No. Colo., 1979. Cert. tchr., Colo. Intern Cherry Creek Sch. Dist., Aurora, Colo., 1979-80; tchr., mem. curriculum coms. Deer Trail (Colo.) Sch. Dist., 1980—; mem. in-service coordinating coms. East Cen. Bd. Coop. Ednl. Services, Bennett, Byers, Strasburg and Deer Trail, Colo., 1982, 84. Author: (children's plays) The Most Important Thing About Halloween, 1983, Tom Turkey's Thanksgiving Treat, 1986, Why We Hunt Easter Eggs, 1987; author, dir.: (sch. musical) The Rainbow People, 1984. mem. organizing com. St. Paul Presbyn. Ch., Aurora, 1984-86; active Sta. KCFR Pub. Radio, Denver, 1984-87, Denver Zoo, 1987. Mem. Colo. Council Internat. Reading Assn., Kappa Delta Pi. Home: 6024 S Perth St Aurora CO 80015

CEASE, JANE HARDY, state senator; b. Columbus, Miss., Jan. 23, 1936; m. Ron Cease, 1960; children—Allison, Abigail. B.F.A., Tulane U. State rep. Oreg. Legislature, Salem, 1979-85, state senator, 1985-89. Pres. Portland League Women Voters, 1971-73; chair Portland Area Women's Polit. Caucus, 1977-78, Met. Govts. Subcom. Local Govt. Com., Portland, 1979-83, Portland-Multnomah Commn. Aging Transp. Com., 1983-85; active Nat. Hwy. Safety Adv. Commn., 1980-83, Transp. and Communications Com. of Nat. Council State Legislatures, 1983-85, Oreg. Commn. Women, 1985—. Democrat. Clubs: Phoenix Rising, Parents United. Home: 2625 NE Hancock St Portland OR 07212 Office: State Capitol Salem OR 97310 *

CECCARELLI, AMANDA VALERIA, health care executive; b. Seminole, Okla., Nov. 25, 1932; d. James Dunn and Edna Pearl (Ball) Goodwin; m. Ugo M. Ceccarelli, July 5, 1960 (dec. 1962); children: Charles, Carl, Janice, Jay; m. Max M. Chilcott, Apr. 5, 1986. BS, U. Nev., Reno, 1975. Owner D&N Club, Sparks, Nev., 1962-73; research analyst aging services State of Nev., Carson City, 1975-76, research analyst health planning, 1976-77; exec. dir Cen. Nev. Rural Health Consortium, Hawthorne, Nev., 1977-86; pres., chief exec. officer Nev. Health Assocs., Inc., Hawthorne, 1985—, Medforce, Hawthorne, 1987—; cons. U. Nev. Reno, 1987—. Sec.-treas. Consol. Agys. Human Services, Hawthorne, 1987; chmn. State Health Coordinating Services Council, Carson City, 1985. Mem. Pvt. Industry Council (dir. 1983-87), Am. Pub. Health Assn., Nat. Rural Health Care Assn. (bd. dirs. 1978-85). Republican. Episcopal. Home: 101 K St PO Box 941 Hawthorne NV 89415 Office: Nev Health Assocs Inc PO Box 459 Hawthorne NV 89415

CECIL, CONNIE FAY, financial planning company executive; b. Covington, Ky., Nov. 20, 1959; d. Jack Dempsey and Viola Elizabeth (Morrison) C. CLU; chartered fin. cons. Exec. sec. Lang Kruke Fin. Group, Inc., Cin., 1977-79, service adminstr., 1979-84, exec. asst., 1984-86, v.p., 1986—. Mem. Nat. Assn. Female Execs. Baptist. Home: 2934 Chaise Ln Maineville OH 45039 Office: Lang Kruke Fin Group Inc 9549 Montgomery Rd Cincinnati OH 45242

CECIL, DORCAS ANN, property management executive; b. Greensboro, N.C., Mar. 31, 1945; d. George Joseph and Marianne Elizabeth (Zimmerman) Ernst; m. Richard Lee Cecil, June 8, 1968; children: Sarah, Matthew. BA, U. Ark., 1967. Cert. property mgr.; registered apartment mgr. Pres. B & C Enterprises Property Mgmt., Ltd., O'Fallon, Ill., 1977—. Bd. dirs. O'Fallon Pub. Library, 1983—, v.p., 1986-87, pres., 1987—; sec. St. Vincent de Paul Soc., 1987—. Mem. Inst. Real Estate Mgmt. (cert.) (v.p.

1987—, mem. nat. coms. Am. Resident Mgr. Services, Am. Resident Standards), Accredited Resident Mgr. Com. (sec. 1986, coordinator 1987), Nat. Apartment Assn., Ill. Apt. Assn., St. Louis Multi-Housing Council, Profl. Housing Mgmt. Assn., Community Assns. Inst., Nat. Assn. Realtors, Belleville Bd. Realtors, O'Fallon C. of C. (bd. dirs. 1987—, v.p. 1988—), So. Ill. Network of Women. Democrat. Roman Catholic. Office: B & C Enterprises One Eagle Ctr PO Box 403 O'Fallon IL 62269

CEDRONE, MARIE C., university department administrator. B in in Applied Scis., Boston U., 1979; M in Liberal Arts, Harvard U., 1983, M in Edn., 1988. Mem. div. Applied Scis. Harvard U., Cambridge, Mass., 1968-85, dept. administr. Peabody Mus., Dept. Anthropology, 1985—; mgmt., human resource cons. Network Dynamics, Inc., Cambridge, 1983-85. Mem. Am. Psychol. Assn. (assoc.), Mass. Psychol. Assn. (assoc.), Ea. Psychol. Assn., New Eng. Soc. Applied Psychologists, Mass. Bus. Educators Assn. Office: Harvard U Cambridge MA 02138

CELANDER, EVELYN F., biochemistry educator; b. Ottumwa, Iowa, Nov. 4, 1926; d. Roy B. and Ona M. (Talbott) Agee; m. David R. Celander, July 19, 1946 (dec. Jan. 1977); children: Andrew David (dec.), Daniel Walter, Jeananne Marie. BA in Journalism, Drake U., 1948; MS in Biochemistry, Coll. Osteo. Med. Surgery, Des Moines, 1967, DSc, 1978. Lab asst. Iowa State Commn. Blind, Iowa City, 1948-52; research assoc. U. Tex. Med. Br., Galveston, 1952-61; instr., asst. prof. Coll. Osteo. Med. Surgery, Des Moines, 1961-71; assoc. prof. biochemistry U. Osteo. Med. Health Sci., Des Moines, 1971—, head biochemistry dept., 1977—. Bd. dirs., music dir. Patricia Park United Brethren Ch., Des Moines, 1963—. Mem. AAUP, AAAS, Am. Fedn. Tchrs. (local pres. 1983—), N.Y. Acad. Scis., Am. Bus. Women's Assn. Democrat. Mem. United Brethren in Christ Ch. Office: U Osteo Med and Health Sci 3200 Grand Ave Des Moines IA 50312

CELENTANO, DONNA JEANNE, food service company executive; b. Norwalk, Conn., Feb. 16, 1954; d. Jack and Marion Lee (DeBartholomeo) C. Student, Norwalk Community Coll., 1972, Western Conn. State Coll., 1972-75. Bookkeeper Xerox Corp. Internat., Stamford, Conn., 1976-78; gen. sales mgr. Conn. Calculators, Darien, 1978-82; pres. Variety Co. Inc., Greenwich, Conn., 1982—. Vol. Muscular Dystrophy Assn., Norwalk and Greenwich, 1973—. Mem. Nat. Restaurant Assn., Nat. Assn. Female Execs. Republican. Roman Catholic. Home: 389 Rowayton Ave Norwalk CT 06854 Office: Variety Co Inc 19 St Rochs Ave Greenwich CT 06000

CELLA, LISA ANN, personnel consultant; b. Boston, Apr. 12, 1962; d. Alexander Joseph and Josephine (D'Angeli) C. BS cum laude, Suffolk U., 1984. Law clk. Boston Juvenile Ct., 1985; personnel cons. L & L Assocs., Boston, 1985-88, Baxter O'Brien & Assocs., Boston, 1988—; sale support asst. Am. Repretory Theatre, Cambridge, Mass., 1987—. Mem. Nat. Assn. Female Execs., Mass. Assn. Personnel Cons. Democrat. Roman Catholic. Home: 1 School St Suite 101 Arlington MA 02174

CELOTTA, BEVERLY KAY, psychologist; b. Monroe, La., June 16, 1944; d. Morton and Geraldine (Hermalin) Lauter; m. Robert James Celotta; children: Jennifer Ann, Daniel Wayne. BA in Psychology, Queens Coll., 1965; MS, Bkyln. Coll., 1967; PhD in Ednl. Psychology, U. Colo., 1971. Lic. psychologist, Md. Research asst. Inst. for Devel. Studies, NYU, 1967; sch. psychologist Bur. of Child Guidance, N.Y.C., 1967-69, Head Start Program, N.Y.C., 1968-69; sch. psychologist Montgomery County Pub. Schs., Rockville, Md., 1973-74, edni. researcher, 1976-77; sch. psychologist Fairfax (Va.) County Pub. Schs., 1975-76; asst. prof. counseling and personnel services dept. U. Md., College Park, 1977-83, asst. chair, 1982-83; pres. Celotta, Jacobs & Keys Assocs., Inc., Darnestown, Md., 1983—; lectr. psychology Montgomery Coll., Rockville, 1975-76; cons., speaker in field. Contbr. articles to profl. jours. Mem. Am. Psychol. Assn., Am. Assn. for Counseling and Devel., Assn. for Measurement and Evaluation in Counseling and Devel. (chair membership and program coms.), Am. Sch. Counselors Assn., Am. Ednl. Research Assn., Md. Assn. for Counseling and Devel. Home and Office: 13517 Haddonfield Ln Darnestown MD 20878

CENTER, INGRID GWYNNETH CATHERINE, government insurance manager; b. Farnham, Eng., Jan. 12, 1945; came to U.S., 1962; d. G.A. and V.G. (Jones) Bessette; student Carleton U., Ottawa, Ont., Can., 1960-61, U. Oslo, 1964; B.A., Cornell U., 1966, Assoc. in Risk Mgmt., 1981; m. Alfred M. Center, June 25, 1966; children—David Gordon, Jennifer Gwynneth Catherine. With Gen. Motors Corp., N.Y.C., 1967-68; faculty Meiji U., Tokyo, 1968-69, Gulf Tech. Coll., Bahrain, 1971-73; with Sony Corp. of Am., N.Y.C., 1976-78; budget analyst Barclays Bank of N.Y., N.Y.C., 1978-79, ins. analysts, 1980-82; risk mgr. City of Stamford (Conn.), 1982-84; dir. project risk mgmt. Ogden Corp., Stamford, 1985-86; asst. budget dir. County of Westchester (Conn.), 1986-87; Marguerite Bourgeois scholar, 1957-60; U. Oslo summer scholar, 1964. Mem. Bahrain Archaeol. Soc., Risk and Ins. Mgmt. Soc., Am. Mgmt. Assn., Pub. Risk and Ins. Mgmt. Assn., Kappa Kappa Gamma. Club: Awali Riding. Author: Batangas: The Holiday Province, 1975. Home: 97 Madison Ave Larchmont NY 10538

CERF, GENEVIEVE CHARBIN, electrical engineering educator, consultant, researcher; b. Norwich, Conn., Sept. 22, 1943; d. Roger Marc and Simonne (Lepoutre) Charbin; m. Christopher Bennett Cerf, July 8, 1972. BA, Conn. Coll., New London, 1972; MS, Columbia U., 1975, PhD, 1986. Instr. elec. engring. Columbia U., N.Y.C., 1978-83, asst. prof., 1986—, cons. Electrobiology Inc., Fairfield, N.J., 1978-84, Christopher Cerf Assocs., N.Y.C., 1981—. Contbr. articles to profl. jours. Mem. IEEE, Soc. Women Engrs., Phi Beta Kappa, Eta Kappa Nu (pres. student chpt. 1977-78). Democrat. Home: 123 W 74th St New York NY 10023 Office: Columbia U Dept Elec Engring 500 W 120th St New York NY 10027

CERTAINE, EVELYN REBECCA, retired social work adminstrator; b. Phila.; d. Lawrence and Sadie (Hall) Certaine; B.S. in Edn., Temple U., 1938, postgrad., 1960-63; M.S.W., U. Pa., 1965, postgrad., 1968. With Pa. Dept. Pub. Assistance, 1940—, now adminstrv. asst. Vol., Big Sisters, 1932-38, Armstrong Assn. (Urban League), 1932-36, ARC, USO, 1942-67, Hawthorne Neighborhood Council, 1960-63; fund raiser for alumni Sch. Social Work, 1968-79; now pvt. social work practioner; active YWCA, various other community groups; bd. dirs. Dowingtown (Pa.) Indsl. and Agrl. Sch., 1977. Recipient Hon. citation for vol. work Chapel Four Chaplains, 1965; also plaques, awards, certificates United Service Orgns., Red Cross, Dept. Army, Air Force. Mem. Nat. Assn. Social Workers, Nat. Acad. Certified Social Workers, Alpha Kappa Alpha (sec. 1942-43, reporter 1945-46). Republican. Episcopalian. Club: Temple U. Mid-City Alumni.

CERTO, MARY, nurse, consultant; b. Toledo, Sept. 13, 1951; d. Rocco and Betty (Wilcox) C.; m. Thomas Portz, June 1972 (div. 1977). BS in Nursing, U. Miami, Coral Gables, Fla., 1972; MS in Nursing, Barry U., 1986. RN, Fla. Staff nurse John Peter Smith Hosp., Ft. Worth, 1972-73; asst. head nurse, head nurse U. Miami-Jackson Meml. Med. Ctr., Fla., 1973-81; charge nurse, nurse cons. Miami Mental Health Ctr., 1979-81; nursing adminstr., asst. dir. nursing Lake Hosp. Palm Beach, Lake Worth, Fla., 1981-87; mgr. adolescent psychiat. services Pavilion, West Palm Beach, Fla., 1987—; speaker in field. Mem. Am. Nurses Assn., Fla. Nurses Assn., South Fla. Nursing Research Soc., Mental Health Assn. Palm Beach, Psychiatric Nursing Network Dade-Broward-Palm Beach County, Sigma Theta Tau. Clubs: Sportsman Paradise Scuba (Miami). Office: Pavilion 2201 45th St West Palm Beach FL 33407

CERVASSI, SUSAN MARIE, entrepreneur, writer; b. Milford, Mass., Aug. 20, 1954; d. Reno Joseph and Virginia Clotilda (Allegrezza) C. BA, Simmons Coll., Boston, 1976, MLS, 1977; MBA, Northeastern U., 1988; postgrad., Boston Coll., 1988—. Librarian Uxbridge (Mass.) Middle Sch., 1977-79, Milford (Mass.) High Sch., 1979-81; facility mgmt. asst. Leonard Morse Hosp., Natick, Mass., 1981-83; library and media dir. Turners Falls High Sch., Montague, Mass., 1983-85; analyst New England Energy, Westboro, Mass., 1985-86; mktg. asst. Yankee Atomic Electric, Framingham, Mass., 1986; entrepreneur, freelance writer San Diego, 1986—; editor for dentists and psychologists, Boston, 1983—. Mem. Phi Beta Kappa. Roman Catholic.

CESINGER, JOAN, author; b. Oswego, N.Y., July 2, 1936; d. Guy Wesley and Gladys Matilda (Redlinger) Wagner; m. John Robert Cesinger, July 7, 1956; children: Michael, Richard, Steven. BA in Edn., Northwestern U., 1957. Asst. editor, feature writer Frontier Enterprise, Vernon Town Crier, Mundelein News, Lake Zurich, Ill., 1966-69; editor Lamp of Learning, Lake Zurich, 1967-68; mag. columnist Allen Raymond Inc., Darien, Conn., 1972-77; treas., office mgr., editor Dynamic Resources, La Verne, Calif., 1980—. Author: (with others) Games and Activites for Early Childhood Education, 1967, If I Were . . ., 1975, Kindling Patriotism with Challenging Activties, 1976, Fostering Spelling Achievement with Challenging Games, 1980, American Government: Puzzles, Games, and Individual Activities, 1982, World Cultures: Puzzles, Games, and Individual Activities, 1985, World Geography: Puzzles, Games, and Individual Activities, 1985, World History: From the Fall of Rome to Modern Times, 1986, Let's Learn About Dinosaurs, 1987. Mem. World Future Soc., Brookfield West Garden (v.p. 1978-79), Nat. Penwomen's Assn., Kappa Kappa Gamma. Home and Office: 2159 Base Line Rd La Verne CA 91750

CHABROW, SHEILA SUE, English language educator; B.A., U. Miami (Fla.), 1961; student Harvard U., 1960-61, George Washington U., 1961-62, Va. Poly. Inst., 1972-74; M.S., Barry U., 1976. Writer, No. Va. Newspapers, Fairfax, 1969-73; dir. Olam Tikvah Sch., Fairfax, 1973-74; tchr. Palmetto Sr. High Sch., Miami, 1979-80; instr. psychology Barry U., Miami, 1980-81; instr. intensive English, U. Miami, Coral Gables, Fla., 1981—; V.p. Cutler Bay Estates, Miami, 1975-76; instr. English Fla. Internat. U., 1986—; v.p. Parent Co-Op. Preschools Internat., 1972-73; pres. No. Va. Co-Op. Schs., 1969-70. Mem. Women in Communications, AAUW (sec. Annandale, Va. 1972), Theta Sigma Phi. Home: 13351 SW 57th Ct Miami FL 33156 Office: U Miami Dept Intensive English Coral Gables FL 33146

CHABY, DIANE BLOCK, public relations agy. exec.; b. N.Y.C., Oct. 2, 1935; d. Irving and Tillie Block; B.A. in English, N.Y. U., 1956, M.A. in English, 1968; postgrad. Yeshiva U. Grad. Center, 1972-73, John Clarke Acad., London, 1973; m. June 3, 1956 (div.); 1 son, Alan Seth. Free-lance columnist Westwood (N.J.) News, 1961-63; tchr., cons., trainer N.Y.C. Bd. Edn., 1966-78; free-lance writer and publicist, 1978; publicist, media specialist Peter Rothholz Assos., N.Y.C., 1979, dir. media relations, 1979-81; account group supr. Van Vechten & Assocs., N.Y.C., 1981-82; founder pres. Chaby Communications, N.Y.C., 1982—; free-lance mag. writer, 1981—; condr. career change workshops; tchr. trainer, lab. mgmt. cons. Right To Read; mem. Right To Read Task Force; cons. ednl. systems. Mem. Women in Communications, Bus. and Profl. Women. Office: 6 Peter Cooper Rd New York NY 10010

CHADWELL, SUSIE, real estate broker; b. Jellico, Tenn., Aug. 26, 1940; d. Ross James and Irene (Jones) C.; m. Richard Rodriguez, May 30, 1957 (dec. Aug. 1965); children: Susan Denise, Richard. Student, U. Tampa, 1965-67, Midland Tech. Coll., 1972-73, Hillsborough Community Coll., 1975-78, Tampa Coll., 1982-83. Clk. Chad Supply, Tampa, 1977-78, sec., 1978-79; salesperson real estate Chadwell Homes, Seffner, Fla., 1979-82, Thonotosassa, Fla., 1984—; salesperson condominiums Eastfield Slopes, Thonotosassa, 1982-84; broker mortgage Susie Chadwell, Thonotosassa, 1985—; cons., tchr. in field. Mem. Beta Sigma Phi. Home and Office: 9540 Field View Cir Thonotosassa FL 33592

CHADWICK, GLORIA CONSTANCE, foundation administrator; b. Philadelphia, June 19, 1932; d. Norman and Laura Mary (Roveran) C. MBA, Boston U., 1956; M in Orgn. Mgmt., U. Santa Clara, 1968; postgrad., U. Vt., 1985—. Exec. dir. U.S. Ski Assn., Colorado Springs, Colo., 1961-71; v.p. ops. Big Sky of Mont., 1971-76; pres. Burke (Vt.) Mt. Recreation, Inc., 1976-83; commr. devel. State of Vt., Montpelier, 1982-85; dir. U.S. Olympic Tng. Ctrs., Marquette, Mich. and Lake Placid, N.Y., 1985—; v.p. Ladies Cross-County Commn. Internat. Ski Fedn., Berne, Switzerland. Pres. Lyndon State Coll. Found., Lyndonville, Vt., 1983-86. Recipient Pres. citation Lyndon State Coll., 1982. Mem. U.S. Ski Assn. (Blegen award 1983, Nat. Ski Hall of Fame 1986). Home and Office: 20 Lake Placid Club Dr Lake Placid NY 12946

CHAFEL, JUDITH ANN, education educator; b. Rochester, N.Y., Apr. 8, 1945; d. James Arthur and Florence Joan (Santangelo) C. AB, Vassar Coll., 1967; MSEd, Wheelock Coll, 1971; PhD, U. Ill., 1979. Cert. elem. tchr., Mass., N.J., N.Y. Tchr. Spruce St. Sch., Lakewood, N.J., 1972-74, Sodus (N.Y.) Primary Sch., 1974-76; grad. research and teaching asst. U. Ill., Urbana, 1976-79; vis. asst. prof. U. Tex., Austin, 1979-80; asst. prof. dept. curriculum and instrn. Ind. U., Bloomington, 1980-86, assoc. prof., 1986—; reviewer Hist. Publs. and Records Commn., Nat. Archives, Washington, 1979, Little, Brown and Co., Boston, 1982—. Editorial adv. bd. Early Child Development and Care, 1985—; reviewer and contbr. numerous articles to profl. jours. Proffitt Endowment grantee Ind. U., 1982, 88; Spencer Found. grantee for Young Scholars, 1985. Mem. Soc. Research in Child Devel.(reviewer conf. proposals 1986), Am. Ednl. Research Assn. (reviewer various conf. proposals 1984, 86, 87, nominations com. 1986), Nat. Assn. for Edn. Young Children (reviewer 1980—), Assn. Childhood Edn. Internat.(publ. com. 1982-84, bull. and pamphlets rev. editor jour., 1982-84, research com. 1984—).

CHAFIN, SARA SUSAN, school administrator; b. Huntington, W.Va., Mar. 24, 1952; d. William Albert and Margaret Irene (Stigall) C. BA, Coll. William and Mary, 1977. Tchr. The Woods Acad., Bethesda, Md., 1982-83; head tchr. Children's House Washington, 1983, The Vera Gander Montessori Sch., N.Y.C., 1984-85; adminstr., pres. The Manhattan Montessori Sch., 1985—; instr., speaker Internat. Montessori workshop, N.Y.C., 1986. Active N.Y.C. Friends and Advocates of Mentally Ill, 1985—, also newsletter, legis. coms. Mem. N. Am. Montessori Tchrs. Assn., Assn. Montessori Internat. (cert. adminstr.). Home: 342 W 85th St Apt 2C New York NY 10024 Office: The Manhattan Montessori Sch 308 W 46th St New York NY 10036

CHAGNON, LUCILLE TESSIER, career development and educational consultant; b. Gardner, Mass., June 1, 1936; d. Fred G. Tessier and Alfreda C. (Ross) Noel; m. Richard J. Chagnon, Sept. 16, 1978; children—Daniel, David. B.Mus., Rivier Coll., N.H., 1968; M.Ed., Boston Coll., 1972. Edn. specialist, N.H., 1960-76; internat. cons. Inst. Cultural Affairs, Chgo., 1973-79; staff tng. dir. CO-MHAR, Inc., Phila., 1979-81; pres., owner Chagnon Assocs., Collingswood, N.J., 1981—; mem. Collingswood bd. edn., 1985—; sr. project staff Right Assocs., Phila., 1982—; adj. grad. faculty dept. counseling psychology Temple U. Sch. Edn., Phila., 1985—. Author (with Richard J. Chagnon) The Best Is Yet to Be, 1985. Bd. dirs. Camden County Literacy Vols. of Am., 1987—, Handicapped Advocated for Ind. Living, 1988—. Mem. Assn. Supervision and Curriculum Devel., New Horizons for Learning, Earthstewards Network. Home and Office: 722 Linwood Ave Collingswood NJ 08108

CHAIKIN, BONNIE PATRICIA, lawyer; b. N.Y.C., Apr. 4, 1953; d. Max and Paula (Blechman) Chaikin. Student Cornell U., 1970-73; B.A., Hofstra U., 1974; J.D., St. John's U., 1977. Law intern Queens Supreme Ct., 1977; admitted to N.Y. bar, 1978, Fla. bar, 1979, U.S. Customs Ct. bar, 1979, U.S. Tax Ct. bar, 1979, U.S. Dist. Ct. bar for Eastern and So. dists. N.Y., 1979, U.S. Ct. Customs and Patent Appeals bar, 1979, U.S. Supreme Ct., 1986; lic. real estate broker. Law asst. firm Weingold & Berman, N.Y.C., 1977-78; assoc. Dollinger, Gonski and Grossman, Carle Place, N.Y., 1978-79; mng. atty. firm Marsha Edelman, N.Y.C., 1979-80; individual practice law, Oceanside, N.Y., 1980—; dep. county atty. Nassau County, 1982—, dep. bur. chief, Mcpl. Affairs, 1986—; profl. fashion model Other Dimensions, N.Y.C., 1980-82. Bd. dirs. Mem. Fla. Bar Assn., N.Y. State Bar Assn., Nassau County Bar Assn. (sec. immigration law com.), Nassau-Suffolk Womens Bar Assn., Am. Immigration Lawyers, ABA, N.Y. State Juvenile Officers Assn. Office: 1 West St Mineola NY 11572

CHAIT, SALLIE HOPE, space programs engineer; b. Bklyn., Aug. 18, 1953; d. Robert and Phyllis (Warren) C. AS, Nassau County Community Coll., Uniondale, L.I., N.Y., 1984; student, Hofstra U./Columbia U. Combined Studies Program, 1985—. Electronic technician Fairchild Camera & Instrument Co., Syosset, N.Y., 1979-80, Olympus Camera Corp., Syosset, 1980-83; materials-components engr. Frequency Electronics, Inc., Uniondale, 1983-86; mgr. reliability test engring. Circuit Tech., Inc., Farmingdale, N.Y., 1986-87; component/standards engr. Gull Airborne, Inc., Smithtown, N.Y., 1987; engr. space programs Fairchild-Weston Systems, Inc, Syosset, N.Y., 1987—; indsl. cert. Hi-Rel Labs., Monrovia, Calif., 1985. Mem. Masters Swim Team, N.Y.C., North Massapequa (N.Y.) Reps. Republican. Jewish. Office: Fairchild-Weston Systems Inc 300 Robbins Ln Syosset NY 11758

CHALBERG-PLUNKETT, SHERRI LINELL, corporation executive; b. Leavenworth, Kans., Mar. 10, 1960; d. Larry Allen and Esther Louise (Martin) C.; m. James Davidson Plunkett, Oct. 25, 1986. BSBA, William Jewell Coll., 1984; postgrad., Rockhurst Coll., 1985—. Personnel dir. Belger Cartage Service, Kansas City, Mo., 1984-86; v.p. Jim Plunkett, Inc., Kansas City, Kans., 1986—; chief exec. officer Wall Systems Corp., Kansas City, Kans., 1986—. Mem. HBA, NAWIC, ABC. Republican. Mem. Unity Ch. Home: 13141 W 84th St Lenexa KS 66215 Office: Jim Plunkett Inc 1304 Argentine Kansas City KS 66105

CHALMERS, JACQUELINE LOUISE, art gallery owner; b. Calgary, Alta., Can., Aug. 25, 1952; d. Robert John and Doreen Jeanette (Nichols) C. Student, Mont. State U., 1973-75, U. Calagry, 1976. Media coordinator Spruce Meadows Internat. Equestrian Ctr., Calgary, 1975-77; adminstr. agr. dept. Calgary Exhibition and Stampede, Calgary, 19788; asst. sales mgr. Transcon/Charcan Livestock services, Calgary, 1978-79; prodn. mgr. Simmental County, Calgary, 1979-80; asst. coordinator Stockmen's Found., Calgary, 1980-82; mktg. and public relations cons. Best Plumbing and Heating, Edmonton, Atla., 1983-84; cons. Suicide Prevention Provincial Adv. Com., Calgary, 1983-84; owner Gallery West, Calgary, 1985—. Contbr. articles to profl. jours. Home: Millarville, AB Canada T0L 1K0 Office: Gallery West, 476 10816 Macleod Terr S, Calgary, AB Canada T2J 5N8

CHALOVICH, PAMELA SUE, rehabilitation administrator; b. Gary, Ind., July 7, 1954; d. John Charles and Dolores Jean (Ozelie) C. BA, St. Mary's Coll., 1976; MA, Loyola Marmount U., 1979. Counselor Clare Found., Los Angeles, 1977; customer service rep. Transam. Title, 1977-78; vocat. rehab. counselor Occupational Support Service, Van Nuys, Calif., 1980-85; vocat. reahb. counselor, gen. ptnr. New Opportunities, Los Angeles, 1985—. Mem. Los Angeles County Art Mus. Mem. Am. Psychol. Assn., Calif. Psychol. Assn., Nat. Rehab. Assn., Nat. Assn. Rehab. Profls. in Pvt. Sector. Office: New Opportunities 12304 Santa Monica Blvd Los Angeles CA 90405

CHAMBERLAIN, CAROLE, mortgage company executive; b. San Francisco, Oct. 20, 1949; d. Edward and Leila Adele (Gregory) C.; m. Harold Wayne Fisher, Sept. 6, 1969 (div. July 1985); children: Clint William, Kelly Danielle, Kyle Wayne. Student, Prince George's Community Coll., 1975-78, Charles County Community Coll., 1978-80, 87. Realtor L.K. Farrall, Waldorf, Md., 1981-84; account exec. Bloomfield Mortgage, Suitland, Md., 1984-87, Waldorf, Md., 1987; br. mgr. Suitland, Md., 1988—. Editor: Pinefield Newsletter, 1979-84. Lutheran. Home: 1193A Annapolis Woods Rd La Plata MD 20646

CHAMBERLAIN, CHARLOTTE APPEL, corporate executive, economist; b. N.Y.C., Apr. 30, 1946; d. Henry and Marie (Lugscheider) Appel. Ph.D. in Econs., Cornell U., 1971. Prof. econs. Northeastern U., Boston, 1971-73; br. chief forecasting and modeling U.S. Dept. Transp., Cambridge, Mass., 1973-79; v.p., mgr. dept. econs. Glendale Fed. Savs. and Loan Assn. (Calif.), 1979-81; dir. Office of Policy and Econ. Research, Fed. Home Loan Bank Bd., Washington, 1981-83; sr. v.p. asset liability mgmt. Glendale Fed. Savs. (Calif.), 1983-85, exec. v.p. strategic planning and mktg., 1985—. Bd. dirs. Real Estate Ctr., U. Calif., Berkeley. Lehman fellow. Mem. Am. Econ. Assn., Nat. Assn. Bus. Economists, Western Econs. Assn., Phi Beta Kappa, Phi Kappa Phi. Editor Jour. Housing Fin. Office: 700 N Brand Blvd PO Box 1709 Glendale CA 91209

CHAMBERLAIN, JEAN NASH, civic organization administrator; b. Chgo., Oct. 14, 1934; d. William Edmund and Virginia Jean (La Fon) Nash; m. James Staffeld Chamberlain, Dec. 29, 1953; children: James W., William S., Caren T., Martha J. Student, U. S.C., 1951-53. Polit. dir. Tribune/United Cablevision, Huntington Woods, Mich., 1982; orgn. dir. polit. campaign, Oakland, Mich., 1983-84; dir. fin. Dan Murphy for Gov., Mich., 1985-86; exec. mgr. Greater Royal Oak (Mich.)/Oak Park C. of C., 1986—. Vice chair Rep. com., Oakland County, Mich., 1971-73; chair Rep. 18th congl. dist., 1973-77; del. Rep. Nat. Conv., Kansas City, Mo., 1976; bd. dirs. Oakland County Mental Health Bd., 1976—, chair 1984-86. Mem. U.S. C. of C., Mich. State C. of C. Roman Catholic. Club: Boys and Girls Royal Oak. Office: Greater Royal Oak/ Oak Park C of C 306 S Troy St Royal Oak MI 48067

CHAMBERLAIN, JILL FRANCES, computer company executive; b. Chgo., Mar. 25, 1954; d. Chester Emery and Mary Edythe (Hurd) C. B.A. in Math. with honors, Ill. State U., 1975; M.B.A., U. Chgo., 1981. Programmer, Arthur Andersen, Chgo., 1975-76; cons. Laventhol & Horwath, Chgo., 1976-77; fin. systems analyst U. Chgo. Hosp., 1978-80; v.p. CHI/COR Info. Mgmt., Inc., Chgo., 1980-87; systems designer GECC, Stamford, 1987—; cons. RMS Bus. Systems, Chgo., 1976-77. Mem. Delaware Valley Disaster Recovery Info. Exchange Group, Nat. Assn. Female Execs. Libertarian. Methodist. Avocations: reading; traveling; needlework. Office: GECC 3003 Summer St Stamford CT 06901

CHAMBERLAIN, JOYCE ANN, information systems consultant; b. Denver, Sept. 3, 1942; d. Kenneth Lee and Delores Anna (Schlic) C. BA, UCLA, 1966. Sci. programmer Marquardt Corp., Los Angeles, 1962-63; sr. research analyst UCLA, 1963-68; cons. Peat, Marwick, Mitchell, Los Angeles, 1968-70; supr. systems and programming Larwin, Los Angeles, 1970-75; mgr. systems maintenance Mission Equities Corp., Los Angeles, 1975-76; mgr. systems analysis Telecredit, Inc., Los Angeles, 1976-78; cons. Gottfried Cons. Inc., Los Angeles, 1978-79, Chamberlain and Assocs., Los Angeles and Seattle, 1979—. Mem. Assn. Systems Mgmt. (cert. sytems profl., data processing).

CHAMBERLIN, MARGARET ELIZABETH, marketing, advertising and public relations consultant; b. Denver, Oct. 3, 1952; d. Elmer John and Helen Claire (Kilday) Roth; m. Mark Hill Chamberlin, June 22, 1974. B.A. in Journalism, U. Okla., 1974; postgrad. in bus. adminstrn. Wichita State U., 1979-83. Account coordinator Advt. Concepts, Wichita, 1974-76; pub. relations dir. Wichita Symphony, 1976-77; dir. advt. Quik Print, Inc., 1977-78; account service copywriter Stephan Advt., Wichita, 1978-79; communications specialist KG and E, The Electric Co., Wichita, 1979-81; account exec. Lida Advt. Co., Wichita, 1981-84; asst. v.p., dir. mktg. Union Nat. Bank of Wichita, 1984-85; corp. pres. Chamberlin-Nicks, Inc., Wichita, 1985—. Bd. dirs. Child Care Assn. Wichita/Sedgwick County, 1984-85 , Friends of the Library, 1985; vol. ARC, 1982-85; bd. dirs. Wichita Children's Theatre, 1987—, Am. Heart Assn., 1987—. Recipient writing awards Kans. Press Women, 1978, 79, 81; Addy awards Wichita Advt. Fedn., 1980, 82, 83, 85, 86. Mem. Women in Communications (pres. Wichita chpt. 1978-79), Pub. Relations Soc. Am. (student liaison 1984-85, bd. dirs. 1985-86), Wichita Area C. of C. (founding pres. Upgowntowners Wichita), Advt. Fedn. Wichita, Leadership Am., Kappa Delta. Republican. Congregationalist. Home: 157 N Edgemoor Dr Wichita KS 67208 Office: PO Box 703 Wichita KS 67201

CHAMBERS, ANDREA THOMAS, real estate executive; b. Tuscaloosa, Ala., May 6, 1951; d. Oscar and Gladys (Thomas) Hurst; m. Aaron D. Chambers, Feb. 23, 1973 (div.). BS, Ala. State U., 1973, MS, 1975; cert., Ala. Assn. Realtors, 1986. Dir. U. Ala. Ctr. for Developmental Learning Disorders, 1972-73; social worker, counselor Lister Hill Med. Ctr., Montgomery, 1973-75; then social worker, counselor Brantwood Childrens' Home, Montgomery, 1975-78; then state dir. Nat. Ctr. Black Aged/Ala. Rural Srs. Employment Program, Montgomery, 1978-80; previously ednl. coordinator Behavior Sci. Assocs., Inc., Montgomery, Ala., 1980-82; real estate broker Buddy Bone ERA, Montgomery, 1982-83, Don Sawyer Group, Montgomery, 1983-86; now prin. Andrea T. Realty, Montgomery, 1986—; real estate instr., 1988. Active Montgomery Support Orgn., 1986—; community leader Ala. Dem. Party, Montgomery, 1975—, mem. Young Dems. Mem. Nat. Assn. Realtors, Ala. Assn. Realtors, Montgomery Bd. Realtors (Leadership in Residential Sales award 1986), Realtor Assocs., Womens' Council Realtors, Young Realtors Club, Nat. Assn. Women, Minority Bus. Assn., Nat. Alcoholics Counselors, Ala. Conf. Social Workers, Ala. State U.

Alumni Assn. Baptist. Home: 3882 Provost Ave Montgomery AL 36116 Office: Andrea T Realty 217 S Court St Suite 206 Montgomery AL 36104

CHAMBERS, BELYNDA GAIL, advertising and public relations executive; b. Columbia, S.C., Feb. 3, 1954; d. Earl Hoyle and Lenice Ruth (Keele) C.; m. James Joseph Nemeth, June 2, 1973 (div. Oct. 1981); children: Rebecca Dawn, Jessica Rhea. Student, Millsaps Coll., 1971, Memphis State U., 1972, N.C. State U., 1981, 83, Johns Hopkins U., 1988. Account asst. Griswold-Eshleman, Cleve., 1973-75, Wyse Advt., Cleve., 1975-76; office mgr. Willard-Starin, Raleigh, N.C., 1978-79, media dir., 1980-81, account supr., supr. graphics, 1982; copywriter, creative dir. A. J. Hopkins, Raleigh, 1981; advt. asst. CPT div. Black & Decker, Raleigh, 1982-83, mgr. advt. sales promotion CPT div., 1983-85; nat. mgr. advt./pub. relations U.S. Power Tools Black & Decker, Balt., 1985-88; pres. Chambers Concepts, Inc., Balt., 1988—. Editor, co-dir. TV commls., 1982, 85 (Clio awards 1982, 85). Active Nat. Abortion Rights League. Recipient Gov.'s Spl. Recognition award Gov. of N.C., 1980. Mem. Am. Mktg. Assn., Assn. Nat. Advertisers (com. mem. 1987—), Advt. Assn. Balt. (sec. N.C. group 1983). Republican. Roman Catholic. Club: Advt. of Washington.

CHAMBERS, BEVERLY ZIVITSKI, graphics company manager, tax consultant; b. Middletown, Conn., July 31, 1952; d. Paul and Anne (Kost) Zivitski. AA, Daytona Beach Community Coll., 1977, AS in Tech. Illustration, 1978; BS in Art Adminstrn., U. Tampa, 1985. Artist Eastern Graphics, Old Saybrook, Conn., 1973-74; sch. artist Inex, Daytona Beach, Fla., 1978; art dir. Daytona pub. and pvt. schs., Daytona Beach, 1979-80; artist Pearson & Clark, Lakeland, Fla., 1980-83; ops. mgr. Imperial Graphic, Largo, Fla., 1985-87, chief exec. officer, 1987—; tax preparer H & R Block, 1979-85. Recipient 1st prize Fla. Advt. Council, 1979. Mem. Suncoast Archel. Soc., Nat. Audubon Soc. Home: 1455 Corey Way S South Pasadena FL 33707 Office: Imperial Graphics 9075 B 130th Ave N Largo FL 33543

CHAMBERS, FRANCES MARIAN, federal agency administrator; b. Wichita, Kans., Aug. 25, 1954; d. Emil Lawrence and Helen Lucile (Rounsavell) Wulfmeyer. BA, Dartmouth Coll., 1975; MS, London Sch. Econs., 1976; postgrad., Alliance Francaise, Paris, 1976-77. Sr. staff aide Hon. Joe Skubitz, Washington, 1977-78; staff cons. House Fgn. Affairs Com., Washington, 1978—; staff dir. Task Force on Internat. Narcotics Control, Washington, 1983—; cons. Council on Religion and Internat. Affairs, 1983-85; ofcl. observer U.S. Del. to UN Trusteeship Council, 1979—. Mem. Bus. and Profl. Women Assn., DAR, Phi Beta Kappa. Presbyterian. Office: House Fgn Affairs Com 2170 Rayburn Hob Washington DC 20515

CHAMBERS, IMOGENE KLUTTS, school administrator; b. Paden, Okla., Aug. 6, 1928; d. Odes and Lillie (Southard) Klutts; B.A., East Central State U., 1948; M.S., Okla. State U., 1974, Ed.D., 1980; m. Richard Lee Chambers, May 27, 1949. High sch. math. tchr. Marlow (Okla.) Sch. Dist., 1948-49; with Bartlesville (Okla.) Sch. Dist., 1950—, asst. supt. bus. affairs, treas. Ind. Sch. Dist. 30, 1977-87, treas., 1985—; dir. Plaza Nat. Bank. Bd. dirs. Mutual Girls Club, 1981—. Mem. Am. Assn. Sch. Adminstrs., Okla. Assn. Sch. Bus. Ofcls., Assn. Sch. Bus. Ofcls. Internat., Assn. Sch. Bus. Ofcls. of U.S. and Can., Okla. Assn. Sch. Adminstrs., Okla. State U. Alumni Assn., Phi Delta Kappa. Democrat. Methodist. Home: 911 Greystone Place Bartlesville OK 74006 Office: Bartlesville Ind Sch Dist 301100 S Jennings St Bartlesville OK 74005

CHAMBERS, JOAN LOUISE, university library director; b. Denver, Mar. 22, 1937; d. Joseph Harvey and Clara Elizabeth (Carleton) Baker; m. Donald Ray Chambers, Aug. 17, 1958. B.A. in English Lit., U. No. Colo., Greeley, 1958; M.S. in Library Sci., U. Calif.-Berkeley, 1970; M.S. in Systems Mgmt., U. So. Calif., 1985. Librarian U. Nev., Reno, 1970-79; asst. univ. librarian U. Calif., San Diego, 1979-81; univ. librarian U. Calif., Riverside, 1981-85; dir. libraries Colo. State U., 1985—; mgmt. intern Duke U. Library, Durham, N.C., 1978-79; sr. fellow UCLA, summer 1982; cons. tng. program Assn. of Research Libraries, Washington, 1981; library cons. Calif. State U., Sacramento, 1982-83, U. Wyo. Contbr. articles to profl. jours., chpts. to books. U. Calif. instl. improvement grantee, 1980-81; State of Nev. grantee, 1976, ARL grantee, 1983-84. Mem. ALA, Assn. Coll. and Research Libraries (com. mem. and chmn.), Library Adminstrn. and Mgmt. Assn., Library Info. Tech. Assn., Colo. Library Assn., Resources and Tech. Services Assn., Reference and Adult Services Assn., Internat. Assn. Fin. Planners, United Way, Beta Phi Mu, Phi Lambda Theta, Kappa Delta Phi. Clubs: Sierra, Audubon Soc., Colo. Mountain. Home: 1309 Linden Lake Rd Fort Collins CO 80524 Office: Colo State U Libraries Fort Collins CO 80523

CHAMBERS, KAREN JEAN, manufacturing executive; b. Delta, Colo., Nov. 18, 1946; d. Adolf Edward Patterson and Juanita Ann (Pfiel) Mumford; d. Robert LeRoy Chambers, Sept. 4, 1963; children: Ricky Allen, Russell LeRoy. AA in Bus. Mgmt., LaSalle U., 1980. Various factory jobs Samsonite Corp., Denver, 1965-68, teleprocessing oper., 1968-71; dep. sheriff Adams County Sheriff's Dept., Brighton, Colo., 1971-73; analyst computer Samsonite Corp., Denver, 1974-77, analyst finished goods, 1977-79, supr. analysts, 1979-83, supr. analysts scrap depts., 1983-85, supr. inventory control, 1985—; cons. Micro Design Engring., Niwot, Colo., 1980. Mem. Boy Scouts Am., Erie, Colo., 1984-86. Mem. Nat. Assn. Female Exec. Republican. Baptist. Office: Samsonite Corp 11200 E 45th Denver CO 80239

CHAMBERS, LINDA DIANNE THOMPSON, social worker; b. Mexia, Tex., Apr. 21, 1953; d. Lee and Essie Mae (Hopes) Thompson; m. George Edward Chambers, Nov. 30, 1978; 1 child, Brandon. AS cum laude, Navarro Coll., Tex., 1974; BSW magna cum laude, Tex. Woman's U., 1976; postgrad. Cert. gerontology. Sam Houston U., 1982, U. Tex.-Arlington, 1987—. Mem. social work staff Dept. Human Resources, Ft. Worth, Tex., 1975, Children's Med. Ctr., Dallas, 1976, Mexia State Sch., Tex., 1976—. Pres., Raven Exquisites, Mexia, 1983-84, sec.-treas., 1984-85; mem. Tex. Hist. Found., Nat. Mus. Women in Arts, 1985—. Recipient numerous awards for scholarship and profl. excellence. Fellow Internat. Biog. Assn.; mem. Am. Sociol. Soc. (sec. 1975-76), Univ. Woman's Assn., Am. Childhood Edn. Internat., Nat. Assn. Social Workers, Nat. Assn. Female Execs., Am. Assn. Mental Deficiency, Nat. Assn. Future Women, Am. Soc. Profl. and Exec. Women, Nat. Assn. Negro Bus. and Profl. Women's Clubs, AAUW, Tex. Woman's U. Nat. Alumnae Assn., Mortar Bd. Honor Soc. (sec.-treas. 1975-76), Tex. Soc. Clin. Social Workers, Internat. Platform Assn., Internat. Assn. Bus. and Profl. Women, Tex. Assn. Clin. Social Workers, Nat. Mus. Women Arts, Los Amigos, Phi Theta Kappa, Alpha Kappa Delta. Club: Young Democrats. Avocations: Reading; gardening; gourmet cooking. Home: 102 Hardin Mexia TX 76667

CHAMBERS, LOIS IRENE, insurance agency executive; b. Omaha, Nov. 24, 1935; d. Edward J. and Evelyn B. (Davidson) Morrison; m. Peter A. Mscichowski, Aug. 16, 1952 (div. 1980); 1 child, Peter Edward; m. Frederick G. Chambers, Apr. 17, 1981. Clk. Gross-Wilson Ins. Agy., Portland, Oreg., 1955-57; sec., bookkeeper Reed-Paulsen Ins. Agy., Portland, 1957-58; office mgr., asst. sec., agt. Don Biggs & Assocs., Vancouver, Wash., 1958—, v.p. ops.; automation cons. Chambers & Assocs., Tualatin, Oreg., 1985—; chmn. adv. com. Clark Community Coll., Vancouver, 1979—. Mem. citizens com. task force City of Vancouver, 1976-78, mem. Block Grant rev. task force, 1978—. Mem. Ins. Women of S.W. Wash. (pres. 1978, Ins. Woman of Yr. 1979), Nat. Assn. Ins. Women, Nat. Users Agena Systems (charter; pres. 1987-88). Democrat. Roman Catholic. Lodge: Soroptimist Internat. (Vancouver) (pres. 1978-79, Soroptimist of Yr. 1979-80). Office: Don Biggs & Assocs 916 Main St PO Box 189 Vancouver WA 98666-0189

CHAMBERS, MARY PEYTON, state legislator; b. Poca, W.Va., Aug. 31, 1931; d. Henry Hanna and Hilda Claudia (Cary) Peyton; A.B., W.Va. Wesleyan Coll., 1952; M.A. in Spl. Edn., George Peabody Coll., 1955; m. Wilbert Franklin Chambers, July 6, 1957; children—Henry Peyton, James Erland, Jane Cary. Elem. tchr., W.Va. public schs., 1952-56; ednl. supr. Baird Childrens Center, Burlington, Vt., 1956-62; dir., counselor Upper Valley Adult Basic Edn., Lebanon, N.H., 1975—; mem. N.H. Ho. of Reps., 1972, dep. minority leader, 1974-84, minority leader, 1985—; chmn. Democratic Policy Com., 1975—. Office: N H State House Rm 306 Concord NH 03301

CHAMBERS-MEYERS, TRESSA, consultant, writer; b. Lyon, Miss., Apr. 26, 1942; d. James W. and Anna L. (Dorsey) Chambers; m. Joseph R. Meyers, Mar. 18, 1961 (div. Apr. 1983); children—Monica Denise Meyers, Jon Raymond Meyers. B.A., Eastern Wash. U., 1965. Cert. sch. tchr., Calif. Tchr., San Francisco Unified Schs., 1969-75; freelance writer, San Francisco, 1975-81; writer-cons., 1981-83; founder, pres. Thought Motivation Inst., San Francisco, 1983—. Author: Balanced Living Program 1986; contbg. author: The Stress Strategists, 1986. Mem. Mayor's San Francisco Host Com., 1979—; mem. host. com. 1984 Democratic Conv., 1983; mem. Dem. Women's Forum, 1978—. Mem. Bus. Execs. for Nat. Security (charter), World Affairs Council No. Calif. (membership com.), Nat. Assn. Female Execs., Nat. Speakers Assn., Internat. Platform Assn., Assn. Continuing Higher Edn. Roman Catholic. Club: Circlets (v.p. 1978-84). Office: Thought Motivation Inst 2966 Diamond St Suite 151 San Francisco CA 94131

CHAMBLEE, DIANA BARCROFT, education educator; b. Boston, June 30, 1944; d. Fredrick Fuller and Ruth (Jones) C.; m. Garry Thomas Pegram, Sept. 8, 1968 (div. Sept. 1976); m. Edward Bryson Poucher. BS in Edn., East Carolina U., 1966; cert. in exceptional child edn., U. N.C., MS, 1976. Cert. application and psychol. types tester. Tchr. pub. schs., Greenville and Chapel Hill, N.C. and Arlington, Va., 1966-72; exceptional child program coordinator Greenville Pub. Schs., 1972-73; project coordinator Lenior Community Coll., New Bern, N.C., 1973-74; tng. instr. East Carolina U., Greenville, 1974-76; instr. sch. edn. U. Ga., Athens, 1976-79, dir. health edn. Health Ctr., 1979-81; counseling evaluator SHAPE-NATO, Belgium, 1981-84; family therapist Detty Youth and Family Services, Lawton, Okla., 1984-85; sr. instr. U. Okla. Mgmt. Tng. Sch., Norman, 1985—; tchr. human ecology Cameron U., Lawton; cons. Personal Investment, Inc., Lawton, 1985—. Mem. Philharm. of Okla, Lawton, 1985-87. Mem. LWV, Nat. Assn. Female Execs. Democrat. Clubs: Ft. Sill (Okla.) Hunt and Polo, Ft. Sill Officers Wives. Office: Cameron U Lawton OK 73507

CHAMPAGNE, BETTY JUNE, computer analyst; b. Winnsboro, La., June 20, 1949; d. James Levi and June Amanda (Hawthorne) Mahoney; m. Peter Gerald Renz, Apr. 19, 1969 (div. 1977); children: Curtis Alan Renz, Randall Scot Renz; m. Michael Joseph Champagne, Feb. 9, 1979 (div. 1982). BA in Psychology, NE La. U., 1979. Sales, mktg. adminstr. Gen. Electric Info. Services Co., San Antonio, 1980-82; word processing, documentation specialist Conoco Inc., Houston, 1982-84; sr. tech. analyst software Transco Energy Co., Houston, 1984-87, documentation cons., 1986—; documentation specialist Morino Assocs., Inc., Vienna, Va., 1987—; documentation cons., Houston, 1986—. Vol. Am. Heart Assn., Houston, 1985, 87, Pvt. Sectors Initiative, Houston, 1987, March of Dimes Team Walk, Houston, 1985. Mem. Am. Soc. Indexers, Soc. Tech. Communication (judge 1985), Women in Communication, Women's Profl. Assn. Republican. Lutheran. Home: 18624 Walkers Choice #5 Gaithersburg MD 20879 Office: Morino Assocs Inc 8615 Westwood Center Dr Vienna VA 22180

CHAMPAGNE, ELAINE R., production company executive; b. Lowell, Mass., Feb. 1, 1955; d. Joseph Leo and Mabel Alice (Perigny) C.; m. Alexander Kiddie, Oct. 5, 1973 (div. Feb. 1, 1975). Grad., Alvirne High Sch., Hudson, N.H., 1973. Exec. producer Champagne Television Bingo Cable Show, Woburn, Mass., 1978-80; acct. exec. Sta. WNBP radio, Newburyport, Mass., 1980-81; assoc. producer Advantage Group, Wakefield, Mass., 1981-82; sales, mktg. mgr. Ipswich (Mass.) Cablevision, 1981-82; studio mgr. Hotshots Adv., Salem, Mass., 1982-86; ops. mgr. The Producers, Lawrence, Mass., 1986; v.p. ops. Nat. Prodns. Inc., Salem, Mass., 1986—; career cons. Manchester, Mass., 1986—. Active Boston Hunger Project, 1986—; participant Beyond War symposium, Wakefield, 1987. Mem. Am. Mgmt. Assn. (cert), Women North of Boston Network Orgn. (dir. 1986-87), Women West of Boston Network Orgn. Home: 28 Sch St Manchester MA 01944 Office: Nat Prodns Inc 27 Congress St Salem MA 01970

CHAMPAGNE, MARIAN GROSBERG, lawyer; b. Schenectady, Dec. 17, 1915; d. Joseph E. and Rae Grosberg; m. Herbert Champagne, Aug. 18, 1940 (dec. May 1966); children—Emily, Margot J. B.A., Smith Coll., 1936; LL.B., Albany Law Sch., 1955, J.D., 1968. Bar: N.Y. 1956. Practice with Herbert Champagne, 1956-66; assoc. Wood Morris Sanford & Hatt, 1966-71. Mem. Fla. Mental Health Bd., 1975-78, Sarasota Mental Health Clinic, 1980-82. Mem. AAUW. Republican. Unitarian. Club: Smith Alumnae (Sarasota). Author: The Cauliflower Heart, 1944; Quimby and Son, 1962; Facing Life Alone, 1964; also pub. under names Elsa Gottlieb, Mary Jonathan, Kay Ottick, others. Home and Office: 3276 Pinecrest St Sarasota FL 34239

CHAMPAGNE, WINONA ANN ZERINGUE, small company executive; b. New Orleans, Nov. 8, 1949; d. John Leonard and Phedelise Ann (Schexnaydre) Zeringue; m. Errol David Champagne, Aug. 24, 1968 (dec. Jan. 1982); children: Lance Edward, Rhett David, Chad Mark. Student, Nicholls State U., 1967-68, 72, U. So. Miss., 1970-72; BS, Old Dominion U., 1978; MBA, U. New Orleans, 1987. Cert. tchr. Educator Poquoson (Va.) Sch. Bd., 1978-80; gen. ptnr. Cooking Cousins, Hahnville, La., 1983—; adj. faculty Thomas Nelson Community Coll., Newport News, Va., 1978-79; grad. asst., U. New Orleans. Co-author: (book) Jambalaya, Crawfish Pie Filé Gumbo, 1984. Mem. PTA, Hahnville, 1984—, Supt.'s Parent Com., Luling, La., 1985—. Democrat. Roman Catholic. Home: 281 Oak St Hahnville LA 70057 Office: Univ New Orleans Lakefront New Orleans LA 70148

CHAMPION WOOD, BARBARA LOUISE, state legislator; b. Swampscott, Mass., Jan. 10, 1924; d. John Duncan and Eva Louise (Moore) Champion; m. Newall Arthur Wood, June 12, 1948; children: Gary Duncan, Craig Newall, Brian Scott, Dennis Michael, Joan Wood Unger. Diploma in Nursing, Mary Hitchcock Meml. Hosp. Sch. Nursing, Hanover, N.H., 1945; student, Simmons Coll., 1947-48. RN. Rep., mem. ho. edn. com. Vt. Gen. Assembly, Montpelier, 1981—, vice chmn. edn. com., 1983—; trustee Vt. State Colls., Waterbury, 1986—, Gifford Meml. Hosp., Randolph, Vt., 1986—; commr., Vt. rep. Edn. Commn. of the States, Denver, 1981-86. Sch. dir. Bethel Sch. Bd., Vt., 1963-85; mem.-at-large Vt. Sch. Bds. Assn., Montpelier, 1982-85. Served to 2d lt. U.S. Army, 1945-46. Mem. Am. Legion. Republican. Congregationalist. Clubs: Bethel Woman's (pres. 1976-78); Vt. Fedn. Women's Clubs (dist. pres. 1978-80). Home: Woodland Rd Bethel VT 05032 Office: Vt House of Reps State House Montpelier VT 05602

CHAMSON, SANDRA POTKORONY, psychologist; b. N.Y.C., Nov. 6, 1933; d. Daniel and Rose (Sukenik) Potkorony; m. Allan Chamson, Dec. 25, 1954 (div. 1978); children—Eugene, Amy. B.A. in Psychology, NYU, 1955; M.S. in Sch. Psychology, CCNY, 1957; Ph.D. in Psychology, Fla. Inst. Tech., Melbourne, 1983. Lic. psychologist, N.Y., clin. psychologist, N.Y. Psychologist, Anne Arundel County Schs., Anapolis, Md., 1957-58, Bur. Child Guidance, N.Y.C., 1960-64, Region VI Dist., Bergen County, N.J., 1965-84; sole practice, N.Y.C., 1985—; psychol. cons. Ramaz Sch., N.Y.C., 1974-81. Mem. Am. Psychol. Assn., N.Y. Acad. Sci., Am. Orthopsychiat. Assn. Address: Apt 18-D 200 W 86th St New York NY 10024

CHAN, CAROLYN HONG, association executive; b. Greenville, Miss., Aug. 9, 1936; d. Chuck Kun and Mamie Goza (Wy) Hong; m. Tony Quong Chan, Aug. 1, 1958; children—Tony Russell, Mamie Cassandra. B.S., Miss. U. Women, 1958; postgrad. U. N.Mex., 1960-62, 70. Clk. typist U. Ill.-Chgo., 1958; tchr. pub. schs., Chgo., 1958-59, Albuquerque, 1959-63, 65-66; pres. N.Mex. Optometric Assn. Aux., 1965-66, 84-85, membership chmn., 1966-67, scholarship chmn., 1967-68, state conv. chmn., pres. 1965-66; legis. chmn. Am. Optometric Assn. Aux., 1973-75, edn. research trustee, 1975-76, trustee bull. press, 1976-77, pres., 1978-79; pub. relations, bus. cons. CHC Enterprises, Albuquerque, 1983—. Mem. N.Mex. Arts and Crafts Fair Bd., 1968-69, Music Theatre Bd., 1965-70; treas. Albuquerque Chinese Sch., 1979-82; publicity dir. Music Theatre, 1965-67, mem. Bernalillo County Rep. Cen. Com., 1977-78; mem. media com. N.Mex. Health Edn. Coalition, 1974-75; chmn. Nat. Adv. Council Bilingual Edn., U.S. Dept. Edn., 1982-83, mem., 1981-84; mem. Mayor's Commn. on Adult Literacy, 1987—; asst. sec. Chinese Am. Citizens Alliance, Albuquerque Lodge, 1986-88, pres., 1988—. Mem. Santa Fe Opera Guild, Am. Optometric Assn., Optometric Editors Assn. (adv. bd. 1976-78), AAUW, Albuquerque Symphony Womens Assn., LWV, N.Mex. Edn. Assn., NEA, Nat. Assn. Bilingual Edn., N.Mex. Symphony Guild, Pi Lamdba Theta, Epsilon Sigma Alpha. Unitarian. Home: 8515 La Sala Grande NE Albuquerque NM 87111

CHAN, CLARA SUET-PHANG, physician; b. Swatow, Guandong, People's Republic of China, Sept. 23, 1949; came to U.S., 1969; d. Hon-Kwong and Suet-Hing (Wong) C. BS, Mary Manse Coll., 1972; MD, George Washington U., 1976. Diplomate Am. Bd. Internal Medicine, Am. Bd. Hematology, Am. Bd. Oncology. Intern U. Miami (Fla.) Hosp., 1976-77, med. resident, 1977-79; fellow hematology, oncology George Washington U., 1979-81; fellow oncoloy research City of Hope Med. Ctr., Duarte, Calif., 1981-83, instr. medicine, 1982-83; asst. chief hematology VA Med. Ctr., Washington, 1983—; asst. prof. medicine George Washington U., 1983-88, assoc. prof., 1988—; prin. investigator Stem Cell Lab. VA Med. Ctr., Washington, 1983—; project chmn. S.E. Cancer Study Group, Birmingham, Ala., 1982-85; mem. med. staff George Washington U., 1983—. Del. cancer update Citizen Ambassador program People to People Internat., 1986. Recipient Internat. Peace scholarship George Washington U. 1972-76; Med. Student Research grantee Pan Am. Health Orgn., 1974; Reader's Digest Internat. fellow United Christian Hosp., Hong Kong, 1976; research fellow VA Career Devel. program, Washington, 1981. Fellow ACP; mem. Am. Soc. Clin. Oncology, Am. Soc. Hematology, N.Y. Acad. Sci., William Beaumort Med. Soc. Home: 7001 Bybrook Ln Chevy Chase MD 20815 Office: VA Med Ctr Hematology Sect 50 Irving St NW Washington DC 20422

CHAN, CONNIE SING WAI, clinical psychologist, educator; b. Hong Kong, Jan. 16, 1954; came to U.S., 1955; d. John L.K. and Lorraine (Dunn) C.; children: Lee Gregory, Malia Claire. AB magna cum laude, Princeton U., 1976; MA, Boston U., 1979, PhD, 1981. Lic. psychologist, Mass. Staff psychologist Westboro (Mass.) State Hosp., 1979-80, South Cove Community Health Ctr., Boston, 1980-82; counseling psychologist U. Mass. at Boston, 1982-84, asst. prof. human services, 1984—; pvt. practice psychology Cambridge, Mass., 1981—; assoc. Psychologists in Pub. Safety, Boston, 1981—; consulting psychologist Juvenile Ct. Suffolk County, Boston, 1984—. Contbr. articles to profl. jours. Bd. dirs. Women's Resource Ctr. N.E. Med. Ctr., Boston, 1984—, Resist Found., Somerville, Mass., 1986—; mem. Human Rights Com. Solomon Carter Fuller Hosp., Boston, 1985—. Mem. Am. Psychol. Assn. (mem. exec. com. div. 44 1986—), Mass. Psychol. Assn. Office: U Mass at Boston Coll Pub and Community Service Boston MA 02125

CHAN, ELY ELIZABETH, accountant; b. Lautoka, Fiji, July 23, 1957; d. Chock Yee and Chan Yee (Lee) C. BBA in Mgmt., U. Hawaii, 1982; BS, Hawaii Pacific Coll., 1986. Bank officer Bank of New South Wales, Nadi, Fiji, 1976-77; fin. planning trainee IDS/Am. Express, Honolulu, 1983; sec., office mgr. Mah & Ihara, Honolulu, 1984-86; mgr., acct. Wing Hang Garment Factory, Honolulu, 1985-87; ptnr. Taxland Bookkeeping Inc., Honolulu, 1986—; freelance clothes designer Honolulu, 1985—; acct., auditor Mukai Fo & Co., Honolulu, 1987—; salesperson Liberty House of Hawaii, 1987—; rep. mem. Downtown Bus. Council, Honolulu, 1983-85. Interpreter sr. citizens, Chinese immigrants, Honolulu, 1978—; vol. Ohana-O-Rod-Tam Campaign, Honolulu, 1983—. Mem. Chinatown Mchts. Assn. (bd. dirs.), Honolulu Chinese Jaycee Women (Oustanding Spokette 1983, 84), United Chinese Labor (English sec. 1984-86), Rising Phoenix Jaycees, Chinese C. of C., Delta Mu Delta. Baptist. Office: Mukai Fo & Co 33 S King Suite 511 Honolulu HI 96813

CHAN, LINDA WAI SIM, financial and investment analyst; b. Hong Kong, Aug. 20, 1945; came to U.S., 1970, naturalized, 1975; d. Lam K.C. and Fung Ming (Chan) Leung; B.S.S. in Econs. cum laude (Cheung Chun Shun scholar), Chinese U. of Hong Kong (United Coll.), 1967; M.A. in Econs., U. Colo., 1971; m. Shu Mui Chan, June 22, 1971. Chief research statistician Far Eastern Econ. Rev., 1967-70; sr. acct. C.R. Cushing & Co., Inc., 1972-76, 78-79; asst. controller Soros Assos., N.Y.C., 1979-86, head acctg. and budgeting dept. Engring. Info., Inc., 1986-87; controller Lev Zetlin Assocs., Inc., 1987—; project asst. Econ. Research Center of Hong Kong, 1964-65. Bd. deacons Broadway Presbyn. Ch., 1979-80; bd. elders Queens Chinese Presbyn. Ch., 1981—. Lic. ins. examiner N.Y. Mem. Econ. Soc. Hong Kong, Nat. Assn. Female Execs., Leadership Found. Republican. Editor Seedling, 1964-65.

CHAN, MELANIE ROSE, aerospace engineer; b. Huntington, W.Va., Feb. 5, 1959; d. Narciso Carag Moreno and Wanda Jean (Wilson) C. BS in aerospace engring., W.Va. U., 1982; MS in Engring. Mgmt., Fla. Inst. Tech., 1986; MS in Aero. Sci., Embry-Riddle Aero. U., 1987. Aerospace engring. technician Dept. of the Navy, Cherry Point, N.C., 1982; aerospace engr. environ. control and life support systems NASA, Kennedy Space Ctr., Fla., 1983-84; aerospace engr. flight crew systems NASA, Kennedy Space Ctr., 1984—; biomed. lab. research subject NASA, Kennedy Space Ctr., 1983—. Contbr. article to profl. jour. Winner Ea. U.S. Classical Piano Competition, 1987. Mem. AIAA (council 1984-87, sec. 1987—, vice chmn. 1988—), Sigma Gamma Tau (nat. aerospacehon. 1980). Republican. Roman Catholic. Club: Hobie Fleet 45 (Cocoa Beach, Fla.). Home: 2982 Barkway Dr Cocoa FL 32926-4401 Office: Nat Aeronautics & Space Adminstrn John F Kennedy Space Ctr Kennedy Space Center FL 32899

CHANCY, VIVIAN ELIZABETH, state department manager; b. Boston, Mar. 28, 1925; d. Wesley and Mary Elizabeth (Wilson) Dixon; m. Francois Mondestin Chancy, Mar. 20, 1954; 1 child, Joette V. Ajene. A. in Bus. Adminstrn., U. Lowell, 1973; B.S. in Mgmt., Boston State Coll., 1977. Mgr. office Mass. Dept. Revenue, Brockton, 1983—. Treas. Ch. of All Nations, Boston, 1965-73, 78-80. Methodist. Club: Female Investment Venture (sec. 1978-82, co-chmn. 1986—), League Afro-Am. Women.

CHANDLER, ALICE, university president, educator; b. Bklyn., May 29, 1931; d. Samuel and Jenny (Meller) Kogan; m. Horace Chandler, June 10, 1954; children: Seth, Donald. A.B., Barnard Coll., 1951; M.A., Columbia U., 1953, Ph.D., 1960. Instr. Skidmore Coll., 1953-54; lectr. Barnard Coll., 1954-55, Hunter Coll., 1956-57; from instr. to prof. CCNY, 1961-76, v.p. instl. advancement, 1974-76, v.p. acad. affairs, 1974-76, provost, 1976-79, acting pres., 1979-80; pres. SUNY, New Paltz, 1980—; bd. dirs. Revson Found., 1979. Author: The Prose Spectrum: A Rhetoric and Reader, 1968, The Theme of War, 1969, A Dream of Order, 1970, The Rationale of Rhetoric, 1970, The Rationale of the Essay, 1971, From Smollett to James, 1980, Foreign Student Policy: England, France, and West Germany, 1985. Mem. N.Y. State Council on Humanities. Lizette Fisher fellow. Mem. Am. Assn. State Colls. and Univs. (chairperson), Regional Plan Assn. (bd. dirs. 1987), Lotos, Phi Beta Kappa. Office: SUNY Office of Pres New Paltz NY 12561

CHANDLER, DOROTHY BUFFUM, civic worker; b. Lafayette, Ill.; d. Charles Abel and Fern (Smith) Buffum; m. Norman Chandler, Aug. 30, 1922; children: Camilla (Mrs. F. Daniel Frost), Otis. Student, Stanford U., 1919-22; LHD (hon.), U. Calif., U. Judaism, U. Redlands, Hebrew Union Coll.; LLD (hon.), Occidental Coll., Mt. St. Mary's Coll., U. So. Calif.; DFA (hon.), U. Portland, Pepperdine Coll., Loyola Marymount U.; D of Arts (hon.), Art Inst. Los Angeles County. Hon. life chmn. Los Angeles Philharmonic Assn.; chmn. bd. govs. Performing Arts Council, Music Ctr. Los Angeles County; chmn. The Amazing Blue Ribbon of Music Ctr., Music Ctr. Found.; former regent U. Calif.; hon. life trustee Occidental Coll., Calif. Inst. Tech. Recipient Herbert Hoover medal Stanford Alumni Assn., Humanitarian award Variety Clubs Internat., 1974. Address: care Los Angeles Philharm Assn 135 N Grand AveBlvd Los Angeles CA 90012 *

CHANDLER, ELISABETH GORDON (MRS. LACI DE GERENDAY), sculptor, harpist; b. St. Louis, June 10, 1913; d. Henry Brace and Sara Ellen (Sallee) Gordon; m. Robert Kirkland Chandler, May 27, 1946 (dec.); m. Laci de Gerenday, May 12, 1979. Grad., Lenox Sch., 1931; pvt. study sculpture and harp. Mem. Mildred Dilling Harp Ensemble, 1934-45; instr. portrait sculpture Lyme Acad. Fine Arts, 1976—; dir. Abbott Coin Counter Co., Inc., 1941-55. Exhibited sculpture NAD, Nat. Sculpture Soc., Allied Artists Am., Nat. Arts Club, Pen and Brush, Lyme Art Assn., Mattatuck Mus., Catherine Lorillard Wolfe Art Club, Am. Artists Profl. League, Hudson Valley Art Assn., USIA, 1976-78, Lyme Art Ctr., 1979, retrospective exhbn. Lyme Acad. Fine Arts, 1987, Madison Gallery, 1987; represented permanent collections, Aircraft Carrier USS Forrestal, Gov. Dummer Acad., James

Forrestal Research Ctr. of Princeton U., Lenox Sch., James L. Collins Parochial Sch., Tex., Storm King Art Ctr., Columbia U., Forrestal Meml. Medal, Timoschenko Medal for Applied Mechanics, Benjamin Franklin Medal, Albert A. Michelson Medal, Jonathan Edwards Medal, Shafto Broadcasting Award Medal, Woodrow Wilson Sch. of Princeton U., Ga. Pacific Bldg., Atlanta, Messiah Coll., Grantham, Pa., Adlai E. Stevenson High Sch., Ill., Queen Anne's County, Md., Pace U., White Plains, N.Y., pvt. collections. Chmn. Associated Taxpayers Old Lyme, 1969-72; trustee The Lenox Sch., 1953-55; with mus. therapy div. Am. Theatre Wing, 1942-45. Recipient 1st prize Bklyn. War Meml. competition, 1945; 1st prize sculpture Catherine Lorillard Wolfe Art Club, 1951, 58, 63, Gold medal, 1969; Founders prize Pen & Brush, 1954, 76, 78, Gold medal, 1957, 61, 63, 69, 74, 76, Am. Heritage award, 1968, Solo Show award, 1961, 69, 75; Thomas R. Proctor prize NAD, 1956, Dessie Geer prize, 1960, 79, 85; Sculpture prize Nat. Arts Club, 1959, 60, 62, Gold medal, 1971; Gold medal Am. Artists Profl. League, 1960, 69, 73, 75, prize, 1981, Anna Hyatt Huntington prize, 1970, 76, Harriet Mayer Meml. prize, 1961; Gold medal Hudson Valley Art Assn., 1956, 69, 74, Mrs. John Newington award, 1976, 78; Lindsey Morris Meml. prize Allied Artists Am., 1973, Gold medal, 1982; sculpture prize Acad. Artists, 1974; Sydney Taylor Meml. prize Knickerbocker Artists, 1975; New Netherlands DAR Bicentennial medal, 1976; Tallix Foundry award, 1979; named Citizen of Yr., Town of Old Lyme, Conn., 1985. Fellow Nat. Sculpture Soc. (council 1976-85, John Spring Founder's award 1986), Am. Artists Profl. League, Internat. Inst. Arts and Letters; mem. Nat. Arts Club, Allied Artists Am., Pen and Brush, Catherine Lorillard Wolf Art Club, Lyme Art Assn. (pres. 1973-75), Council Am. Artists Socs. (dir. 1970-73), Am. Artists Profl. League (dir. 1970-73), NAD, Lyme Acad. Fine Arts (trustee 1976—). Home and Studio: 2 Mill Pond Ln Old Lyme CT 06371

CHANDLER, HARRIETTE L., marketing executive; b. Balt., Dec. 20, 1937; d. S. Lester and Reba K. Levy; m. Burton Chandler, July 12, 1959; children: Frank Levy, Victoria Jane, Edward Lee. BA, Wellesley Coll., 1959; MA, Clark U., 1963, PhD, 1963; MBA, Simmons Grad. Sch. Mgmt., 1983. High sch. history tchr. Worcester (Mass.) Pub. Schs., 1959-61; polit. sci. prof. Clark U., Worcester, 1973-76; prof. polit. sci. Tufts U., Medford, Mass., 1976-78; exec. dir. nat women's com. Brandeis U., Waltham, Mass., 1978-81; cons. Prime Computer, Natick, Mass., 1983-84; mgr. documentation tng. Adelie Corp., Cambridge, Mass., 1984-85, mgr. mktg. services, 1985-87, prin., 1987—. Author: U.S. Soviet Relations During World War II, 1982. Chmn. com. on shareholder responsibility Clark U., Worcester, Mass., 1982-86; chmn. bd. trustees Worcester Meml. Auditorium, 1987—, founding mem. Worcester Women's Polit. Caucus, Worcester, 1985, Worcester Com. Fgn. Relations. Mem. Am. Telemarketing Assn. (Telemarketing award 1986, 87), Am. Mgmt. Assn., Am. Mktg. Assn. Jewish. Home: 7 Brook Hill Dr Worcester MA 01609

CHANDLER, KARYLN DOROTHY, infosystems specialist; b. Pitts., Apr. 28, 1943; d. Wilbert and Theresa). (McClenny) Scott; m. James R. Chandler, Feb. 17, 1979; 1 child, Tina Marie. AS in Bus. Mgmt., Allegheny Community Coll., 1979. Name processor for city directory R.L. Polk Co., Cleve., 1966; keypunch operator Higbee Co., Cleve., 1968-69; keypunch operator Westinghouse Electric Corp., Forest Hills, Pa., 1970-76, sr. keypunch operator, 1976-80, fin. projects clk., 1980; supr. computer ops. Westinghouse Electric Corp., Pitts., 1980—. Mem. Assn. Female Execs. Office: Westinghouse Electric Corp 777 Penn Center Blvd Pittsburgh PA 15235

CHANDLER, LANA JEAN, data processing executive; b. Charleston, W.Va., Oct. 23, 1954; d. Luther Egustas and Wava Lee (Hemmings) C. Bus. diploma, Ctr. Coll., 1973. Sec. Kanawha Valley Bank N.A., Charleston, 1974-75, programmer trainee, programmer, 1975-79, documentalist, programmer, 1979-80, product support analyst, 1980-81, data processing documentalist, coordinator, 1981, programmer analyst, 1981-82, systems devel. officer, 1982-85, applications programming mgr., 1985-87, mgr. loan systems Kanawha Valley Bank N.A. (now One Valley Bank), Charleston, 1987—; Mem. task force Software Valley, Charleston, 1987—. Author: An Invitation to DOS JCL for Application Programmers, 1985, Putting Your Money to Work, 1986, (with others) The Student Loan Handbook, 1987; contbr. articles to profl. jours. Mem. communications com. Bus. Indsl. Devel. Corp., Charleston, 1987—. Recipient Found. George Washington Honor Medal award Freedoms Found., 1969, Jean Smith O'Connor Poetry award Morris Harvey Coll., 1972. Mem. W.Va. Poetry Soc. Baptist. Office: One Valley Bank NA One Valley Sq Charleston WV 25326

CHANDLER, LINDA CLINE, investment broker, financial consultant; b. Sioux Falls, S.D.; d. Lawrence Alphonse and Wilba Nell (Leatherwood) Dhaemers; m. Terence E. Chandler, Oct. 16, 1976. BS, Iowa State U., 1968, MA, 1972. Registered investment advisor. With Sutro & Co., San Jose, Calif., 1974—, assoc. v.p., 1977-78, v.p. investments, 1978—; pres., founder Chandler Roberts, Inc., Santa Clara, Calif., 1983—, Pacific Integrated Group, 1987—, pres., 1988—; sr. v.p. Morgan, Olmstead, Kennedy & Gardner, 1985—; assoc. gen. ptnr. Brichard Properties, Phoenix Portfolio; bd. advisors Rancon Securities; assoc. gen. ptnr. Rancon Pacific, 1988—; contbg. personal fin. editor Sta. KCSM-TV; fin. commentator Sta. KPEN; speaker in field. Contbr. articles to profl. jours. Bd. dirs. League of Women Friends. Named Fin. Planner of Yr., Am. Home Properties, 1981, 83, one of nations leading brokers Wall Street Transcript, 1982, Nation's Outstanding Fin. Planners, Consol. Capital, 1983, Number One Sales Performance Rancho Cons. Realty, 1983, 85, 86. Fin. Planner of Yr., Brichard & Co., 1985-86, Outstanding Broker of Yr., Brichard & Co., 1986, Fin. Planner of Yr., Rancon Fin., 1986. UN fellow. Mem. Santa Clara County Profl. Brokers Assn., Santa Clara County Profl. Young Women, Internat. Assn. Fin. Planners (keynote conf. speaker), AAUW, Phi Kappa Phi, Phi Delta Theta, Alpha Delta Pi. Methodist. Clubs: Sutro Century (pres.'s council 1978-81), Sutro Second Century, Sutro Pres. Office: 2900 Gordon Ave Suite 101 Santa Clara CA 95051

CHANDLER, M. TAMRA, electrical engineer; b. La Grande, Oreg., Oct. 4, 1963; d. Alan Dean and Martha Marie (Beasley) C. BSEE, Mont. State U., 1985. Electrical engr. Sohio Oil Co., Sohio Constrn. Co., Prudhoe Bay, Alaska, 1984; reliability engr. Boeing Comml. Airplane Co., Seattle, 1985-87, propulsion electronic engr., 1987—. instr. ARC, Kalispell and Bozeman, 1978-85; recruiter Boeing Employees Good Neighbor Fund, King County, 1986-87. Mem. IEEE, Nat. Assn. Female Execs., Order Engrs. Democrat. Home: 2815 Boylston Ave E #106 Seattle WA 98102 Office: Boeing Corp Propulsion Project PO Box 3707 MS 6L-55 Seattle WA 98124-2207

CHANDLER, MARGARET KUEFFNER, business educator; b. St. Paul, Sept. 30, 1922; d. Otto Carl and Marie (Schaedlich) Kueffner; m. Louis Chandler, Apr. 8, 1943. B.A. in Polit. Sci, U. Chgo., 1942, M.A. in Econs, 1944, Ph.D. in Sociology, 1948. Mem. faculty U. Ill. at Urbana, 1947-62, asso. prof. sociology and indsl. relations, 1954-62; asso. prof. sociology U. Ill. at Chgo., 1962-63, prof., 1963-65; prof. bus. Columbia U., 1965—, mem. pres.'s arbitration panel, 1977—; Fulbright research prof. econs. Keio U., Tokyo, Japan, 1963-64; lectr. Rutgers U., 1958, McGill U., 1963, Emory U., 1966, Columbia, 1962; Labor arbitrator nat. labor panel Am. Arbitration Assn., 1965—, mem. collective bargaining methods study group., 1964—; asso. mem. Center Advanced Study, U. Ill. Grad. Coll., 1964-65; asso. dir. Program Mng. Complex Techs., 1967—; mem. women's salary rev. bd., also affirmative action Commn. Columbia, 1976—; dir. program for Study Collective Bargaining in Higher Edn., 1975—; mem. N.Y. Gov.'s Panel for Dispute Resolution, 1977—; arbitrator, fact-finder N.J. Pub. Employment Relations Commn., 1975—; adminstrv. bd. Bur. Applied Social Research, 1975—; mem. spl. panel interest arbitrators, State of N.J., 1978—; mem. nat. adv. com. Nat. Center Study of Collective Bargaining in Higher Edn., 1978—; mem. state adv. council Inst. Mgmt. and Labor Relations, Rutgers U., 1982—; mem. Nat. Task Force on Teaching of Alt. Dispute Resolution Methods in Law and Bus. Schs., 1985—. Author: Labor Management Relations in Illini City, vols. 1 and 2, 1953, 54, Management Rights and Union Interests, 1964 (McKinsey Found. book award 1965), Managing Large Systems, 1971 (McKinsey Found. book award 1972); Editor-in-chief: Columbia Jour. World Business, 1972—; Contbr. articles, monograph to profl. lit. Postdoctoral fellow statistics Yale, 1953-54; Ford Found. faculty research fellow social sci. and bus. U. Chgo., 1960-61; Ford Found. grantee, 1967—; Fulbright prof. Central U. Planning and Statistics, Warsaw, Poland, 1974; Recipient Recognition award Ill. Nurses Assn., 1960. Fellow Am. Sociol. Assn., Soc. Applied Anthropology; mem. Am. Statis. Assn., Am. Econ. Assn., Indsl. Relations Research Assn. (editor research vol. 1960). Office: Columbia U Grad Sch Bus Uris Hall New York NY 10027

CHANDLER, PEGGY JAN, surgeon; b. Millen, Ga., Apr. 9, 1954; d. Billy Evans and Peggy Jean (Mallard) C. BS, Ga. So. Coll., 1975; MD, Med. Coll. Ga., 1979. Diplomate Am. Bd. Surgery. Intern then resident in gen. surgery Greenville (S.C.) Hosp. System, 1979-84; gen. surgeon Portsmouth (Va.) Naval Hosp., 1984-86, Pensacola (Fla.) Naval Hosp., 1986—. Served to lt. comdr. USN, 1984—. Mem. AMA, So. Med. Assn., Am. Mil. Surgeons of the U.S., ACS, Women Officers' Profl. Network. Republican. Methodist. Home: 10776 Pampas Trail Rd Pensacola FL 32506 Office: Pensacola Naval Hosp Pensacola FL 32512-5000

CHANDOR, KAREN KAYSER, marketing executive; b. Los Angeles, Feb. 13, 1950; d. Ernest and Kathleen (Adams) Kayser; B.A., Wellesley Coll., 1970; M.B.A., Babson Coll., 1974, also postgrad. Vice pres. Tech. Steel Corp., Newton, Mass., 1971-73; asst. v.p. Thorndike, Doran, Paine & Lewis, Boston, 1973-76; v.p. Colonial Mgmt. Assos., Boston, 1976-77; v.p. mktg. Gardner and Preston Moss, Inc., Boston, 1977-87, dir. Investment Mgmt. Cons. Assn., 1987—. Mem. corp. Babson Coll., 1982—; trustee, 1987—; trustee Mass. Eye and Ear Infirmary, 1985—. Cert. employee benefit specialist. Mem. Assn. Investment Mgmt. Sales Execs. (past bd. dirs., past pres.), Internat. Found. Employee Benefits. Home: 9 Village Hill Rd Dover MA 02030 Office: 1 Winthrop Sq Boston MA 02110

CHANEY, CAROLE ANN, human resource manager; b. Clarion, Pa., June 14, 1939; d. Frederick Leroy and Hazel Lucille (Hulings) McFadden; m. Gary Francis Chaney, June 1, 1968. Student, Coll. Notre Dame, Balt., 1975, Essex Community Coll., Balt., 1981-85. Registered profl. in human resources. Various postitions Grenier, Inc., Balt., 1967-78, personnel and office mgr., 1978-85, asst. v.p. personnel, 1985—. Mem. Am. Soc. Personnel Adminstrn., Am. Mgmt. Assn., Am. Soc. Tng. and Devel., Personnel Assn. Greater Balt. Office: Greiner Inc 2219 York Rd Suite 200 Timonium MD 21093-3111

CHANEY, SARAH (SAGE), interior design company owner; b. Columbia, Mo., Sept. 15, 1933; d. Perry William and Lota Graham (Kramer) Fletcher; m. Guy R. Chaney, Mar. 27, 1956; children: Margo N., Peter G. BA, U. Ariz., 1954. Cert. instr. in Ikebana. Travel cons. Trade Wind Tours of Hawaii, Honolulu, 1954-56; Ikebana instr. Yokosuka (Japan) Naval Base, 1968-70; lic. guide Guide Service of Washington, 1972-73-74-76; sales mgr. Ober-United Travel Agy., Fairfax, Va., 1974-79; tchr. No. Va. Community Coll., Fairfax, 1977-78; sales mgr., travel specialist Travel Ctr., Belleair Bluffs, Fla., 1980—; owner Sage Interiors, Largo, Fla., 1980—; cons. Mo. Transit Bus Co., Macon, 1956-66, various travel agys., 1977-78. Treas. El de Oro Homeowners Assn., Largo, Fla.; chmn. American-Japanese exchange programs, Girl Scouts Am., Yokosuka, 1969-70. Mem. Pacific Area Travel Assn., Suncoast Area Travel Assn. Republican. Protestant. Club: Yokosuka Officers Wives (pres. 1969, Japan). Office: Travel Ctr 575 Indian Rocks Rd N Ste B Belleair Bluffs FL 34640

CHANG, SHIRLEY (HSIU-CHU) LIN, librarian; b. Chia-yi, Taiwan, June 22, 1937; came to U.S., 1962, naturalized, 1977; d. Tzu-kun and Ying (Chang) Lin; m. Parris H. Chang, Aug. 3, 1963; children: Yvette Y., Elaine Y., Bohdan P. BA, Nat. Taiwan U., Taipei, 1960; postgrad. U. Wash., 1962-63, 1982—. Pa. State U., 1976-77 MLS, Columbia U., 1967. Library asst. Yale U., New Haven, 1964, Columbia U., N.Y.C., 1964-67; asst. reference librarian Pa. State U., University Park, 1971-75; cataloguer Australian Nat. U., Canberra, 1978; catalog and reference librarian Lock Haven U. Pa., 1979—, asst. prof., 1982—. Mem. ALA, Chinese-Am. Librarians Assn. (chmn. awards com. 1982-83), Asian/Pacific Am. Librarians Assn. Home: 1221 Edward St State College PA 16801 Office: Lock Haven U Pa Stevenson Library Lock Haven PA 17745

CHANG, SUN-YUNG ALICE, mathematics educator; b. Ci-an, China, Mar. 24, 1948; came to U.S., 1970; d. Fann Chang and Li-Ching Chern; m. Paul Chien-Ping Yang, Mar. 24, 1973; children: Ray Yang, Lusann Yang. B.S., Nat. Taiwan U., 1970; Ph.D., U. Calif.-Berkeley, 1974. Asst. prof. math. U. Md., College Park, 1977-79; prof. UCLA, 1981—; speaker Internat. Congress of Math., 1986. Sloan Found. fellow, 1977, 78. Mem. Am. Math. Soc. Office: UCLA Dept Math Los Angeles CA 90024

CHANG, TOHSOOK PAIK, librarian; b. Seoul, Korea, Oct. 15, 1936; came to U.S., 1962, naturalized, 1974; d. Yong H. and Seok (Lee) Paik; m. Sang Ike Chang, July 18, 1964; children—Albert, Eugene. B.A., Ewha Womans U., 1959; M.L.S. SUNY-Albany, 1963; postgrad. Wash. State U., 1964-65. Asst. librarian Boston U. Library, 1963-64; librarian, instr., Alaska Meth. U., Anchorage, 1970-71; instr. Ewha Women's U., Seoul, 1971-72; librarian, assoc. prof., U. Alaska, Anchorage, 1972—; bd. dirs. Anchorage Korean Lang. Sch. Found., 1981—; mem. Anchorage Sch. Dist. Bilingual, Bicultural Edn. Adv. Com., 1980—, chmn., 1982-83, 1986-87. Active First Korean Presbyterian Ch., Korean Community Anchorage. Internat. fellow AAUW, 1962-63. Mem. ALA, Alaska Library Assn. Home: 4112 Chess Dr Anchorage AK 99508 Office: U Alaska-Anchorage 3211 Providence Dr Anchorage AK 99508

CHANNING, STOCKARD (SUSAN STOCKARD), actress; b. N.Y.C.; m. David Debin, 1976. B.A. cum laude, Radcliffe Coll., 1965. Performed in exptl. drama with Theatre Co. of Boston, 1967; numerous stage appearances including Two Gentlemen of Verona, N.Y.C., San Francisco, Los Angeles, 1972-73, No Hard Feelings, Martin Beck Theatre, N.Y.C., 1973, Vanities, Mark Taper Forum, Los Angeles, 1976, Joe Egg, 1985, Woman in Mind, 1988; appeared in films including Comforts of Home, 1970, The Fortune, 1975, Sweet Revenge, 1975, The Big Bus, 1976, Grease, 1978, The Cheap Detective, 1978, The Fish that Saved Pittsburgh, 1979, Safari 3000, Without a Trace, 1983, Heartburn, 1986, Men's Club, 1986; TV films include The Girl Most Likely To, 1973, Lucan, 1977, Silent Victory: The Kitty O'Neil Story, 1979, Not My Kid, 1985; star of TV series The Stockard Channing Show, 1979-80. Office: Internat Creative Mgmt 8899 Beverly Blvd Los Angeles CA 90048 *

CHAO, ELAINE L., federal maritime commissioner. d. James S. C. and Ruth M. L. (Chu) C. AB, Mt. Holyoke Coll., 1975; MBA, Harvard U., 1979. Assoc. Gulf Oil Corp., Pitts., summer 1978; sr. lending officer Citicorp, NA, N.Y.C., 1979-83; fellow The White House, Washington, 1983-84; v.p. capital markets group Bankam., San Francisco, 1984-86; dep. maritime adminstr. U.S. Dept. Transp., Washington, 1986-88; commr. Fed. Maritime Commn., Washington, 1988—; leader Bklyn. Navy Yard, Harvard Adv. Group, 1982-83; adj. asst. prof. Grad. Sch. Bus. Adminstrn., St. John's U., 1984. Mem. selection com. Nat. Maritime Hall of Fame, Am. Mcht. Marine Mus. Found. Recipient Young Achiever award Nat. Council Women of U.S., Inc., 1986, Champion of Excellence award Chinese-Ams. U.S., Inc., 1986, award Fed. Asian Pacific Am. Council, 1987; Eisenhower Fellows Assn. fellow, 1984; named one of Outstanding Women of Am., 1987. Mem. Nat. Acad. Scis. (transp. research bd. NRC 1986—), Council on Fgn. Relations, Inc. (term mem. 1983-88), World Affairs Council, Women Transp. Seminar (hon.), Harvard Bus. Sch. Alumni Council (exec. com. 1987—), Harvard Alumni Assn. (bd. dirs. 1987—), Phi Tau Phi. Clubs: Harvard (N.Y.C.); Harvard Bus. Sch. (Greater N.Y.) (chmn. applicant relations com. 1981-83, sr. v.p. programs 1983, bd. dirs. Greater N.Y. chpt. 1983-86). Office: Fed Maritime Commn 1100 L St NW Washington DC 20573

CHAPELLE, SUZANNE ELLERY GREENE, history educator; b. Phila., Sept. 21, 1942; d. John Channing and Jessie Horn (Myers) Ellery; m. Michael Thomas Greene, Sept. 15, 1972 (dec. 1973); 1 child, Jennifer; m. Francis Oberlin Chapelle 2d, Apr. 14, 1984. BA, Harvard U., 1964; MA, Johns Hopkins U., 1966, PhD, 1970. Asst. prof. Fed. City Coll., Washington, 1968-69; asst. prof. Am. history Towson State U., Balt., 1969-71; assoc. prof. Am. history Morgan State U., Balt., 1971-75, prof., 1975—. Author: Books for Pleasure, 1976; Baltimore: An Illustrated History, 1980; sr. author: Maryland: A History of its People, 1986. Mem. Am. Studies Assn., Popular Culture Assn. (mem. bd. 1980-82), Orgn. Am. Historians, Md. Hist. Soc., Mid-Atlantic Popular Culture Assn. (pres. 1977-80), Ruxton-Riderwood Assn. (bd. govs.). Episcopalian. Club: The John Hopkins. Home: 6021 Lakeview Rd Baltimore MD 21210 Office: Morgan State U History Dept Baltimore MD 21239

CHAPIN, DIANA DERBY, city official; b. St. Joseph, Mich., Nov. 15, 1942; d. David Norman and Gladys Ruth (Henke) Derby; B.A. cum laude (Woodrow Wilson fellow), U. Mich., 1964; M.A., Cornell U., 1966, Ph.D. (Woodrow Wilson dissertation fellow), 1971; m. James Burke Chapin, Mar. 16, 1968; children—James Derby, David Sheffield. Asst. prof. Queens Coll., N.Y.C., 1969-74; dist. adminstr. 8th Congl. Dist., N.Y.C., 1974-76; asst. commr. N.Y.C. Dept. Parks and Recreation, 1978-81, Queens Borough commr., 1981-86 ; dep. commr. planning Dept. Parks and Recreation, N.Y.C., 1986—. Del. Democratic Nat. Conv., Miami, Fla., 1972; dist. leader 35th Assembly Dem. Dist., N.Y.C., 1972-78; mgr. various campaigns, 1977-78. Recipient ann. employee award N.Y.C. Dept. Parks and Recreation, 1982. Congregationalist. Contbr. articles to profl. publs. Home: 35-46 79th St Jackson Heights NY 11372 Office: 830 Fifth Ave New York NY 10021

CHAPIN, JULIE KURTZ, lawyer; b. Phila., Mar. 25, 1951; d. Louis Kurtz and Adele (Gersh) Greenfield; m. Thomas J. Chapin, May 18, 1986; children: Alexis Kate, Stephanie Lynn. Student Vassar Coll., 1968-69; B.A. and B.S. summa cum laude, U. Pa., 1971, J.D., 1974. Bar: Pa. 1974, U.S. Ct. Appeals (2d cir.) 1975, N.Y. 1976, U.S. Dist. Ct. (so. dist.) N.Y. 1976, U.S. Dist. Ct. (ea. dist.) N.Y. 1977, U.S. Ct. Appeals (D.C. cir.) 1978, D.C. 1978, U.S. Supreme Ct. 1979; cert. primary edn. Law clk. to Chief Justice Benjamin R. Jones, Pa. Supreme Ct., Phila., 1974-75; assoc. firm Hughes Hubbard & Reed, N.Y.C. and Washington, 1975-82; assoc. gen. counsel Celanese Corp., N.Y.C., 1982-87; unit mgr. Hoechst Celanese Corp., sec., legal advisor Celanese Corp. Polit. Action Com., 1984-87; mem. Hoechst Celanese Polit. Action Com., 1987—; mem. Am. Soc. Corp. Secs. N.Y.C., 1983-84, 87; adviser com. on bankruptcy and corp. reorgn. Assn. Bar City of N.Y., 1976-77. Mem. ABA (sect. corp., banking and bus. law), Fed. Bar Assn., Phi Beta Kappa, Pi Lambda Theta. Home: 418 Sked St Pennington NJ 08534 Office: Hoechst Celanese Corp Rt 202-206 North Somerville NJ 08876

CHAPIN, LINDA MARI, principal; b. Detroit, Apr. 15, 1949; d. Jack and Edith (Lacoff) C. BA, U. Mich., 1970, Ednl. Specialist degree, 1978; MA, Wayne State U., 1974. Cert. tchr.; cert. guidance counselor; cert. adminstr., supr., Mich., Md. Tchr., counselor Warren Woods (Mich.) Pub. Schs., 1970-79; dir. gifted and talented programs Ingham Intermediate Sch. Dist., Mason, Mich., 1979-84; prin. Frederick (Md.) County Bd. Edn., 1984-88; head Roeper Sch. for the Gifted, Bloomfield Hills, Mich., 1988—. Mem. Nat. Assn. Elem. Sch. Prins., The Assn. for the Gifted-Council for Exceptional Children (treas., cons. 1984—), Nat. Assn. Secondary Prins., The Assn. For the Gifted (treas. 1984-87), Council for Exceptional Children, Assn. for Supervision and Curriculum Devel. Democrat. Jewish.

CHAPIN, SUZANNE PHILLIPS, psychologist; b. Syracuse, N.Y., Aug. 9, 1930; d. Harold Bridge and Charlotte Virginia (Warner) Phillips; m. Richard Hilton Chapin, June 13, 1953 (div. 1964); children: Bruce Phillips Chapin, Linda Chapin Fry. BA, Syracuse U., 1952; MA, Columbia U., 1965. Statis. asst. Syracuse Bd. of Edn., 1952-53; psychol. examiner Stamford (Conn.) Pub. Schs., 1965-68, psychologist Head Start program, 1967-68; psychologist Southbury (Conn.) Tng. Sch., 1968-74, Onondaga Assn. for the Retarded, Syracuse, 1974, Harlem Valley Psychiatric Ctr., Wingdale, N.Y., 1974—; cons. Head Start, Syracuse, 1967-68. Mem. Danbury Women's Ctr., IMPACT Coalition for Community Progress, 1987—. Mem. Mental Health Council of Westchester County, 1986—. Democrat. Club: Sierra. Home: 29 Cornell Rd Danbury CT 06811 Office: Harlem Valley Psychiat Ctr Rt 22 Wingdale NY 12594

CHAPKIN, FRANCES, health service educator; b. Toronto, Ont., Can., Jan. 29, 1926; d. Hyman and Rebecca (Markowitz) Bernholtz; m. Arthur Isaac Chapkin; children: David, Ellen, Robert, Carole. BA with honors, U. Toronto, 1947; MEd in Adult Edn., Ont. Inst. for Studies in Edn./U. Toronto, 1971. Hebrew studies tchr., adminstr. Holy Blossom Temple, Toronto, 1945-75, Temple Sinai, Toronto, 1952-55; program developer, tutor Ryerson Poly. Inst., Toronto, 1973-82; project leader Govt. Ont., Toronto, 1975; mgr. vol. services West Park Hosp., Toronto, 1980—; speaker, discussion leader. Programmer, group facilitator Jewish Community Centre, Toronto, 1976-78; trustee City of North York (Ont.) Bd. Edn., 1972-82, vice chair, 1974-75. Mem. Ont. Assn. Dirs. of Health Care Services, Assn. Vol. Coordinators (vice chmn. 1985-87), Ont. Inst. for Studies in Edn. Alumni Assn. Home: 51 Ridgevale Dr, Toronto, ON Canada M6A 1K9 Office: West Park Hosp, 82 Buttonwood Ave, Toronto, ON Canada M6M 2J5

CHAPLICK, JAN MARY, hair designer, consultant; b. Bristol, Conn., Jan. 6, 1953; d. John James and Eva Marie (Michaud) C. Student, Conn. Sch. Hair Design, 1972, U. Hartford, 1980. Hair cons. Career Girl Beauty Salon, Bloomfield, Conn., 1972-77; mgr. Gt. Cuts Hair Studio, Hartford, Conn., 1977-79, Command Performance, Simsbury, Conn., 1979-82; stylist, make up artist New Designs, West Hartford, Conn., 1982-84; v.p. Mr. Nicks Family Hair Ctr., Brookfield, Conn., 1984-86; hair designer, colorist CACHEZ Hair Designs, Hartford, 1986—; hair cons. various co. Choreographer childrens plays. Mem. Drake Hill Mall Mchts. Assn. (pres. 1980-81), Nat. Assn. Female Exec. Home: 47 Robin Ct Middletown CT 06457 Office: CACHEZ Design 1 Civic Ctr Hartford CT 06103

CHAPLIN, BARBARA J., computer company owner, consultant; b. June 8, 1945; m. Thomas W. Chaplin; 2 daughters. BA in Langs., Rutgers U., 1966. Systems analyst Sperry Univac Corp., McLean, Va., 1980-83; pres. BTC Enterprises, Inc., Winchester, Va., 1983—; prin. Tara at Bootleg Hill Tree Farm, Winchester Va. Author: (books) Poems: 1970-77, 1979, Pat the Cat and Other Easy-to-Read Stories, 1980, Crawford: A Space Story, 1980, The Girl with Purple Eyes, 1981, Computers for Beginners Only, 1986, Resumes: What Employers Want to See, 1987, numerous tech. documents for computer corps., 1980-87. Mem. Winchester Bus. and Profl. Women, Washington Ind. Computer Cons. Assn., Nat. Assn. Female Execs., DAR, Winchester/Frederick County C. of C. (edn. com. 1987). Office: BTC Enterprises Inc PO Box 2142 Winchester VA 22601

CHAPLIN, LORELEI M., court administrator; b. Joliet, Ill., Oct. 9, 1954; d. Robert George and Margaret Cecilia (Keyser) Kirchner; m. Robert Thomas Chaplin, Sept. 13, 1978. BA in Sociology, Anthropology, Psychology, Western Ill. U., 1976, MS in Edn., 1985. Cert. parent and youth effectiveness tgn. instr., Ill. Ticket control supr. Western Ill. U. Union, Macomb, Ill., 1976-78; social worker II Ill. Dept. of Children and Family Services, Macomb, 1980-81; juvenile probation officer McDonough County Juvenile Ct. Services Dept., Macomb, 1978-80, dir., 1981—; adv. Adminstrv. Office of Ill. Courts, probation div., Springfield, 1987; bd. dirs. Ill. Dept. of Children and Family Services, Regional Youth Planning com., Peoria, 1984—, McDonough County Alcohol and Substance Abuse Network, Macomb, 1987, Greater Macomb Area Task Force Orgn. on Drug and Alcohol Abuse in Youth, 1984, peer facilitator com. chair, 1984-85, v.p. 1985; mem. Ill. Commn. on Children Community Based Children's Service Task Force, 1984; sec. Juvenile Justice Adv. Com., 1981-83, Interagy. Council, 1978-79, v.p. 1979-80. Chmn. com. Heritage Days Celebration, Macomb, 1986; bd. dirs., sec. Parents Anonymous of McDonough County, 1978-79, v.p. 1979-80. Mem. Am. Correctional Assn., Ill. Correctional Assn., Ill.Probation and Court Services Assn. (com. mem. 1987, sec. exec. com. 1985-86, membership chair 1982-84, standards com. 1981-82, nomination com. chair 1986-87), Nat. Council of Juvenile and Family Court Judges, Nat. Juvenile Court Services Assn. Home: 628 Memorial Dr Macomb IL 61455 Office: McDonough County Juvenile Court Services 130 1/2 S Lafayette Macomb IL 61455

CHAPLIN, WANDA LOUISE, aviation company executive; b. Plymouth, Wis., Aug. 23, 1950; d. Harry Rial and Carol Imogene (Betts) C. Student, Venezia Isola di Studi, Italy, 1969-70; BFA, Drake U., 1972; MA in Arts Adminstr., U. Wis., 1974. Researcher Mpls. Soc. of Fine Arts, 1972; cons. Exxon Corp., N.Y.C., 1974; community arts coordinator W.Va. Arts and Humanities Council, Charleston, 1975-76; sr. coordination spl. projects Phillip Morris Inc., N.Y.C., 1978-80; owner Du-Most, Des Plaines, Ill., 1980-83; pres. Chaplin Aviation Inc., Sheboygan Falls, Wis., 1983—. Trustee Sheboygan Found. U. Wis., 1985—; gov. appointee aeros. council Wis. Dept. Transp., Madison, 1986—. Mem. Wis. Aviation Trade Assn.

(pres. 1985-86), Wis. Aviation Hall of Fame, Nat. Air Transportation Assn., U. Wis. Alumni Club (sec. 1985-86). Republican. Congregationalist.

CHAPMAN, CAROLYN, music educator; b. Oak Park, Ill., Sept. 8, 1942; d. Edmund Earle Jr. amd Ella Mae (Bryant) C.; m. Gene Paul Cech, July 6, 1963 (div. 1980); children: Geoffrey Paul, Gary Peter, Nancy Carolyn; m. Melvin LeRoy Flood, Apr. 1980 (div. 1982); 1 child, Erik Louis. BS in Music Edn., U. Ill., 1964, MS in Music Edn., 1968; Cert., Point Loma Coll., 1983; JD, Western State U., 1988. Cert. tchr., Ill., Calif. Tchr. music Barrington and Addison (Ill.) Pub. Schs., 1964-67; tchr. history, music, math., English San Diego City Schs., 1971-87; law clk. U.S. Atty.'s Office, San Diego, 1986—; judicial law clk. El Cajon (Calif.) Ct.; curriculum developer moot ct. program Western State U., San Diego, 1985-86; organizer string orch. Dana Jr. High Sch., San Diego, 1972-80. Mem. law rev. staff Western State U., 1986. Foster parent; sponsor fgn. student exchange program. Mem. Calif. Tchrs. Assn., San Diego Tchrs. Assn., NEA, Am. Trial Lawyers Assn., Delta Theta Phi, Sigma Alpha Iota, Delta Delta Delta. Republican. Club: Lawyer's of San Diego. Home: 6521 Reflection Dr #110 San Diego CA 92124

CHAPMAN, ELEANOR HOWELLS, computer company executive; b. Durham, N.C., Feb. 19, 1938; d. John Lloyd and Callie Gertrude (Neighbors) Howells; student U. N.C.-Chapel Hill, 1960-61; div.; 1 child, Laura Ann. Bookkeeper, sec.-receptionist Ricca, Nelson and Gantt, C.P.A.s, Durham, N.C., 1958-60; legal sec. Haywood, Denny and Miller, Chapel Hill, 1961-62; sec. to dir. Cytology Lab. dept. pathology Duke U. Med. Center, Durham, 1962-63; sec. Noble Truck Leasing, Richmond, Va., 1963-64, Pitts. Plate Glass Co., Richmond, Va., 1964-65; sec. dept. biophysics Med. Coll. Va., Richmond, 1966-67, housestaff sec., 1967, departmental sec. dept. pathology, 1967-68; adminstrv. sec., asst. office mgr. Office of Chief Med. Examiner, State N.C., Chapel Hill, 1968-70; adminstrv. sec. dept. zoology U. N.C., Chapel Hill, 1970-73, adminstrv. asst. dept. chemistry, 1973-74; adminstrv. sec. div. neurology Duke U. Med. Center, Durham, N.C., 1974-77; acting adminstrv. asst. dept. neurology Baylor Coll. Medicine, 1977, adminstrv. asst., 1978-81, sr. adminstrv. asst., 1981-84; owner/operator ACE Computer Co., 1984—; part-time adminstrv. sec. Lipid Research Ctr., dept. medicine Baylor Coll. Medicine, 1985; corp. sec. Diagnostic Cardiology of Houston, 1986; research sec. div. immunology Howard Hughes Med. Inst., Houston, 1987—. P.A. Vol., Houston Gulf Coast chpt. Muscular Dystrophy Assn., 1978—, mem. exec. com., 1978-84; bd. dirs. Houston Area Parkinson Disease Soc., 1981-84; sec. Neurology A Study Sect., NIH, 1979-82; vol. Camp Mission Possible, 1981. Mem. Am. Bus. Women's Assn., Nat. Assn. for Female Execs., Beta Sigma Phi. Office: M929 Michael E DeBakey Research Ctr One Baylor Plaza Houston TX 77030

CHAPMAN, EUGENIA SHELDON, political worker, former state legislator; b. Fairhope, Ala., Jan. 10, 1923; d. Chauncey Bailey and Rose (Donner) Sheldon; B.Ed., Chgo. State U., 1944; m. Gerald M. Chapman, Nov. 24, 1948; children—George, John, Katherine, Andrew. Tchr. public schs., Cicero, Ill., 1944-47, Chgo., 1947-51; mem. Ill. Ho. of Reps., 1964-83, minority whip, chmn. human resources com., standing com. on appropriations. Mem. Dist. 214 Bd. Edn., Cook County, Ill.; del. Dem. Nat. Nominating Convs., 1972, 80; mem. Cook County Dem. Central Com., 1982—, Ill. Dem. Central Com., 1984—; chief div. sr. citizens' advocacy Office Ill. Atty. Gen., 1983—. Named Best Legislator Independent Voters. Ill., 1966, 68, 70, 74, 76, 78, 80, 82. Mem. LWV (pres. Arlington Heights 1957-59), Bus. and Profl. Women's Club. Democrat. Address: 16 S Princeton Ct Arlington Heights IL 60005

CHAPMAN, FRANCES ELIZABETH CLAUSEN (MRS. WILLIAM JAMES CHAPMAN), civic worker, writer; b. Atchison, Kans., Feb. 27, 1920; d. Erwin W. and Helen (Hackney) Clausen; BA Wellesley Coll., 1941; m. W. MacLean Johnson, Aug. 31, 1940 (dec. Nov. 1965); children—Stuart MacLean, Duncan Scott, Douglas Hamilton; m. 2d, William James Chapman, Dec. 5, 1970. Project dir. Women in Community Service, Inc., St. Louis, 1965-66; pres. Nursery Found., St. Louis, 1956-58, dir., 1953-59, 65-68; adv. com. Mo. State Children's Day Care, 1963—; chmn. day care com. Mo. Council Children and Youth, 1961, chmn. foster care sect., 1961-63; spl. asst. to the pres. Webster Coll., 1966-68. Author: Grandmother's House, 1987. Bd. dirs. New City Sch., 1967-69, Mid-County YMCA, 1967-70, St. Louis Conservatory and Sch. Arts, 1978—; mem. Mo. State Coordinating Bd. Higher Edn., 1982-86 ; mem. steering com. Mo. Council on Children and Youth, 1967-69; trustee Jr. Coll. Dist., St. Louis-St. Louis County, 1968-80, pres. bd. trustees, 1971-73, 76-77; trustee John Burroughs Sch., 1973-79, Wellesley Coll., 1976-82; bd. dirs. Assn. Governing Bds. Univs. and Colls., 1970-80, v.p., 1977-78, chmn. bd., 1978-79, hon. dir., 1982-85; bd. commrs. Nat. Commn. on Accrediting, 1971-72; bd. overseers Ctr. for Research on Women in Higher Edn. and Professions, Wellesley, Mass., 1977-82. Recipient Woman of Achievement award, St. Louis Globe-Democrat, 1965. Mem. Nat. Soc. Arts and Letters, Wellesley Coll. Alumnae Assn. (sec., dir. 1958-61). Club: Wellesley Coll. (pres. 1965-67). Home: 10 Overbrook Dr Saint Louis MO 63124

CHAPMAN, GEORGIANN EUGENIA, military officer, health care administrator; b. Ogdensburg, N.Y., Apr. 6, 1951; d. Felix Herschel Chapman and Lucille Eugenia (Ellison) Batt. AS, George Washington U., 1977. Enlisted USN, 1969, advanced through ranks to lt., 1981; head manpower mgmt. Naval Dental Clinic, Bethesda, Md., 1981-84; head outpatient adminstrn. San Diego Naval Hosp., 1984-85, pub. affairs officer, 1985-87; head adminstrn. Naval Sch. Health Scis., San Diego, 1987—. Mem. Nat. Assn. Female Execs., U.S. Naval Inst., Humane Soc. of U.S., Animal Protection Inst. of Am. Office: Naval Sch Health Scis Park Blvd San Diego CA 92134

CHAPMAN, HOPE HORAN, psychologist; b. Chgo., Feb. 13, 1954; d. Theodore George and Idelle (Poll) H.; B.S. (Ill. State scholar), U. Ill., Champaign-Urbana, 1976; M.A. (research and teaching asst.), No. Ill. U., 1979. Recreational therapist Evanston (Ill.) Ridgeview Shelter Care Home, summer 1976; psychologist Glenwood (Iowa) State Hosp. Sch., 1979-83, Gov. Samuel H. Shapiro Devel. Ctr., Kankakee, Ill., 1985-86. Active Omaha Symphonic Chorus, 1981-83; mem. Omaha Public Schs. Citizens Adv. Com., 1980-81; mem. edn. com. Anti-Defamation League, 1980-85, chmn. com. anti-Semitism and Jewish youth, 1981-84. Mem. Am. Psychol. Assn., Midwest Psychol. Assn., Am. Assn. on Mental Deficiency, Assn. for Mental Health Affiliation with Israel, Phi Kappa Phi, Psi Chi. Jewish. Contbr. papers to profl. confs., articles to jours. Home: 2027 Garden Terr Hoffman Estates IL 60195

CHAPMAN, LINDA SUSAN, theatre director; b. Spokane, N.Y., Nov. 17, 1950; d. Harold LeRoy and Nellye Ester (Unterseher) C.; m. Scott E. Hamilton, Sept. 15, 1978 (div. Dec. 1980). BFA, Ft. Wright Coll., 1973; student, Sonia Moore Studio, 1973-77. Adminstr. Theater for the New City, N.Y.C., 1980-83; gen. mgr. Wooster Group, N.Y.C., 1983—. Dir. (plays) O My Rosey Dreams, 1982, On That Day, 1984, Fall Reading Series, 1986, No Damn Good, 1987, Penguins, 1988, Don't Remind Me, 1988; asst. dir. Theater for the New City, St. Theatre, 1980-83; prodn. stage mgr. Richard Foreman, 1985. Tutor Ft. Wright Upward Bound, Spokane 1970-73, Literacy Vols. Am., Bklyn. 1978-79; tchr. Kiwanis Charitable Orgn., S.I., N.Y., 1977-78; organizer Artists Survival Festival, 1980; judge Jerome Fellowship, Playwrites Ctr., Mpls., 1988. Mem. Alliance Residence Theatres N.Y., Literary Mgrs. and Dramaturgs Am., Am. Dirs. Inst. Home: 113 W 15th St #4R New York City NY 10011 Office: Wooster Group Inc PO Box 654 Canal Sta New York City NY 10013

CHAPMAN, MARGARET ARMSTRONG, investor relations specialist; b. New Haven, Jan. 6, 1950; d. George Thompson and Patricia (Cadigan) Armstrong; m. Frank M. Chapman Jr., July 11, 1970. BBA in Prodn. Logistic Mgmt., U. Houston, 1979; postgrad., Houston Bapt. U., 1986—. Planner prodn. Reliability Inc., Houston, 1979-80, mgr. customer services, 1980-82, systems analyst, 1982-84, mgr. investor relations, 1984—. Block mgr. Whitmire for Mayor campaign, Houston, 1979-80. Mem. Am. Soc. Personnel Adminstrs. Office: Reliability Inc PO Box 218370 Houston TX 77218

CHAPMAN, MARGOT LYNN, small business owner; b. Chgo., Nov. 26, 1948; d. Allan and Shirley (Pomper) C. BFA, Pratt Inst., 1971. Fashion coordinator Carson Pirie Scott, Chgo., 1971-72; fashion dir. Sears Roebuck Co., Chgo., 1973-75; producer Foote, Cone & Belding, Chgo., 1975-76, owner Warm Hearts, Inc., Chgo., 1976-80, Chapman Sisters Calorie Counter, Chgo., 1978-84, Zoom Unlimited, Inc., Chgo., 1984—. Mktg. dir. Chgo. Repetory Dance Ensemble, 1986—. Home and Office: Zoom Unlimited Inc 79 E Elm St Chicago IL 60611

CHAPMAN, PAULA, crisis internvention hotline counselor; b. Huntingburg, Ind., Oct. 27, 1950; d. Wilfred Edward and Gladys Virginia (Hall) Lottes; m. Jerry Lowell Jones, Nov. 1965 (div. Oct. 1976); m. Brian Charles Chapman, Oct. 7, 1976; 1 child, Jerrina Loraine. Tech. cert. Ind. Vocat. Tech. Coll., 1973; A.A., U. Md. European Campus, 1980; B.S., St. Thomas Aquinas Coll., 1983; M.S., C.W. Post Coll., L.I. U., 1985. Enlisted U.S. Army, 1973, advanced to staff sgt.-E6, 1982; with Reading and Study Skills Ctr., U.S. Mil. Acad., West Point, N.Y., 1981-86, acting dir., 1984-86; vol. Orange County Mental Health Assn., 1986-88, dir. hotlines, 1988—. Author: Reading Comprehension, 1980, All You Ever Wanted to Know About Crisis Intervention and Working a 24-Hour Hotline, 1987; author booklet Study Skills, 1980; editor Rapid Reading, 1981, Tri-County Self-Help Clearinghouse Directory, 1988. Decorated Army Achievement medal. Mem. Non-Commd. Officers Assn. (sec. 1985-86), Am. Assn. for Counseling and Devel., Phi Kappa Phi. Club: Non-Commd. Officers (pres. 1985-86) (West Point). Avocations: raising pedigree poodles; travel; reading. Office: Mental Health Assn 223 Main St Goshen NY 10924

CHAPPELL, BARBARA KELLY, child welfare consultant; b. Columbia, S.C., Oct. 17, 1940; d. Arthur Lee and Katherine (Martin) Kelly; 1 child, Kelly Katherine. B.A. in English and Edn., U. S.C., 1962, M.S.W., 1974. Tchr. English, Dept. Edn., Honolulu, 1962-65, Alamo Heights High Sch., San Antonio, 1965-67; caseworker Dept. Social Services, Columbia, S.C., 1969-70; supr. Juvenile Placement and Aftercare, Columbia, 1970-72; child welfare cons. Edna McConnell Clark Found., N.Y.C., 1974-75; dir. Children's Foster Care Rev. Bd. System, Columbia, 1975-85; child welfare cons., 1985—; lectr. in field. Contbr. articles to profl. jours. Coordinator Child's Rights to Parents, Columbia, 1970-75. Epsicopalian. Home and office: 3215 Girardeau Ave Columbia SC 29204

CHAPPELL, CAROL CARRIER, hospital administrator; b. Oakland, Calif., Nov. 6, 1959; d. Vern Winans Carrier and Elizabeth Parmalee (Phillips) Lovtang. BBA, U. Nev., Reno, 1985. Library asst. Nat. Jud. Coll., Reno, 1984-85; asst. data processing coordinator Kaiser Permanente, South San Francisco, Calif., 1985-86, San Rafael, Calif., 1986; data processing coordinator Kaiser Permanente, Santa Rosa, Calif., 1987—. Chairperson United Way Fund Drive-Kaiser, Santa Rosa, Calif., 1987—. Mem. Nat. Assn. Female Execs., DAR, Delta Sigma Pi, Kai-Perm. Home: 2302 Sundance St Santa Rosa CA 95403 Office: Kaiser Permanente 401 Bicentennial Way Santa Rosa CA 95401

CHAPPLE, ABBY, consumer comunications consultant; b. N.Y.C., Aug. 17, 1939; d. Adolph Emil and Thelma (Pierce) Klueppelberg; m. Ross Victor Chapple (div.); m. Robert Alan Mewhinney (div.); m. Joe David Walker. BA, Am. U., 1961, postgrad., 1961-65. Reporter Washington Star, 1966-81; pres. Chapple/Mewhinney Assocs., Annapolis, Md., 1981-82; spl. asst. to chmn. Consumer Product Safety Commn., Washington, 1982-85; pres. Consumer Communications, Washington, 1985—. Recipient Media award Dallas Mkt. Ctr., 1978, Home Furnishngs Hall Fame, 1979, Am. Soc. Interior Designers, 1985, Chmn.'s award Consumer Product Safety Commn., 1984. Mem. Soc. Consumer Affairs Profls., Internat. Furnishings and Design Assn., Nat. Assn. Bus. Women, Pub. Relations Soc. Am. Republican. Jewish. Home: 1038 Timber Creek Dr Annapolis MD 21403 Office: Consumer Communications Box 4007 Annapolis MD 21403

CHAPPLE, F. COLLEEN, finance, real estate and computer service executive; b. Manhattan, Kans., Sept. 3, 1932; d. Frank Richardson and Mildred (Webster) McKee; m. Gordon R. Chapple, Feb. 19, 1954. Pres. Chapple Fin. Services Inc., Brentwood, Tenn., 1973-85, Chapple Computer, Inc., Brentwood, 1983-85, Chapple Fin. Services, Brentwood, 1985—; mgr. The Chapple Office Bldg., Brentwood, 1983—; founding mem. Brentwood Network, 1985—. Mem. charter study com. City of Brentwood, 1986. Recipient Exec. award Nat. Women Execs., Nashville, 1984. Mem. Brentwood C. of C. (bd. dirs. 1984—, sec. 1986-87). Home: 8110 Patrice Ave Brentwood TN 37027 Office: Chapple Fin Services Inc 5115 Maryland Way Suite 200 Brentwood TN 37027

CHAR, CARLENE MAE, information systems developer, publisher, editor; b. Honolulu, Oct. 21, 1954; d. Richard Y. and Betty S.M. (Fo) C. B.A. in Econs., U. Hawaii, 1977; M.A. in Bus. Adminstrn., Columbia Pacific U., 1984, Ph.D. in Journalism, 1985, B Gen. Studies in Computer Sci., Roosevelt U., 1986, cert. in mgmt. systems analysis and computer sci., 1986. Freelance writer, Honolulu, 1982—; editor Computer Book Rev., Honolulu, 1983—, Maeventec Software Review, Honolulu, 1985-87; producer, vendor Maeventec Books On-Line Database, Honolulu, 1987—; pub. Maeven Trek Travel Guides, 1988—.

CHARATAN, DEBRAH LEE, real estate broker; b. N.Y.C., Feb. 1, 1957; d. Joseph and Pauline (Margolius) C.; 1 child, Ben Charatan Berger. P-roperty mgr. Martin J. Raynes Devel. Corp., N.Y.C., 1974-79; v.p. Peter Lawrence Real Estate Co., Inc., N.Y.C., 1979-80; pres. Bach Realty, Inc., N.Y.C., 1980—; bd. dirs. First Women's Bank, Real Estate Bd. of N.Y.; speaker in field.; lectr. Queen's Coll., 1983, 84, instr., 1985, real estate coordinator, 1984—. Featured in articles appearing in Fortune, Inc., USA Today, Cosmopolitan, Forbes and other publs.; contbr. numerous articles to jours. in field. Active Mus. Modern Art; mem. real estate council Met. Mus. of N.Y.; bd. dirs. March of Dimes, N.Y., Queens Coll. Found.; bd. dirs., v.p., treas. Jewish Nat. Fund. Mem. Nat. Assn. Profl. Saleswomen, Nat. Assn. Realtors, Women in Sales, Assn. of Real Estate Women, Smithsonian Nat. Assn., Baruch Coll. Alumni Assn. Clubs: 61 East, Women's City. Office: Bach Realty Inc 18 E 48th St New York NY 10017

CHARATAN, MARION SHEILA, reporter; b. London, Apr. 2, 1953; d. Frederick Bernard Ephraim and Winifred Zelda (Harris) C. BA, Queens Coll., 1985. Copywriter Cappa Prodns., Huntington, N.Y., 1978-82; telemarketer, sales and publicity research asst. Cablevision, Woodbury, N.Y., 1985-86, 1985-86; reporter Stas. WRCN and WHRD, Riverhead, N.Y., 1986—; prodn. asst. Assn. Ind. Video/Film Artists, N.Y.C., 1986; actress Broadhollow Repertory, Farmingdale, N.Y., 1987. Jewish. Office: Stas WRCN/WRHD 72 Main St Riverhead NY 11901

CHARBONNEAU, RHONA MAE, state legislator; b. Lowell, Mass., Feb. 20, 1928; d. Daniel Francis and Harriette (LaSalle) Shay; m. Claude Maurice Charbonneau, 1950; children—Claudia Charbonneau Dodds, Rhona Charbonneau Wollenhaupt, Richard, Mark, Alida. Ed. U. Lowell. Pres. Car Develop Corp., 1977—; sec. Continental Acad. Hair Design, Inc., 1981—, also dir.; pres. Continental Crimping Inc.; mem. N.H. Ho. of Reps., 1982-84, N.H. Senate, 1984—. Mem. Hudson County Budget Com., N.H., 1983-85; trustee Hudson Library, 1984-85. Named Disting. Woman Leader, Nashua (N.H.) YWCA, 1985. Mem. Daus. Union Vets. Civil War (pres. 1949), Nat. Hairdressers and Cosmetologists Assn., N.H. Hairdressers and Cosmetologists Assn. (2d v.p. 1982-83), Hudson C. of C. (bd. dirs.). Republican. Lodge: Lionesses. Office: NH Senate State Capitol Concord NH 03301 also: 2 Old Derry Rd Hudson NH 03051

CHARBONNEAU, SHARON MAE, data processing administrator; b. Duluth, Minn., Jan. 31, 1953; d. Sing and Lillian (Raymond) Chinn; m. Gary W. Charbonneau, Aug. 12, 1975. BS magna cum laude, U. Minn., 1975; MS, Ind. U., 1979. Tchr. high sch. English and reading Onamia (Minn.) High Sch., 1975-76; departmental sec. Ind. U., Bloomington, 1976-79, asst. to dir./bus. mgr. div. prof. dev., 1979-82, bus. mgr. adminstrv. computing, 1982-85, asst. dir. for info. services, 1985—; corp. adv. bd. PC Week mag., 1985—; fin. cons. Cert. Auctioneers' Inst., Bloomington, 1979-81; lic. real estate broker, Ind., 1981-82. Mem. Bloomington Commn. on Status of Women, 1979-81. Mem. Nat. Assn. Female Execs., Data Processing Mgmt. Assn., AAUW (v.p., editor Bloomington newsletter 1980-82), Am. Soc. for Info. Sci., Sierra Club. Republican. Clubs: Indiana U. Womens' Faculty (bd. dirs. 1982-87, pres. 1985-86), Toastmasters. Home: 6783 Lampkins Ridge Rd Bloomington IN 47401 Office: Ind U Info Services 1000 E 17th St Bloomington IN 47405

CHARDIET, BERNICE KROLL, juvenile books publisher, editor, record and cassette producer; b. N.Y.C., Nov. 12, 1930; d. Saul and Florence Kroll; m. Oscar Chardiet-DeLaTorre, June 23, 1957; children—Simon, Jon Michel. B.A., Queens Coll., N.Y.C., 1950; Ed.M., Hunter Coll., N.Y.C., 1955. Cert. tchr. English, secondary schs. Scriptwriter, composer, jazz pianist, radio, TV, nightclubs 1950-55; tchr. high sch. English DeWitt Clinton High Sch., N.Y.C., 1955-59; promotion dir. Elem. Mags. Scholastic Inc., N.Y.C., 1964-67, editor See-Saw Book Club, 1967-80, v.p., editorial dir. Scholastic juvenile books, 1980-84, producer, dir. Scholastic records, 1967-84; v.p., ptnr. Parachute Press, N.Y.C., 1985—; cons. children's books various publishers. Author: Cis for Circus, 1971; Juan Bobo and the Pig, 1973; The Monkeys and the Water Monster, 1974; Rapunzel Retold, 1980; The Carrot-Top Mystery, 1984. Producer, dir: (rec.) Jack and the Beanstalk, 1983 (ALA Notable 1984). Mem. Authors Guild, ALA, ASCAP Internat., Pen Club, Overseas Press Club, Internat. Reading Assn., Soc. Children's Book Writers. Office: Parachute Press 200 Fifth Ave New York NY 10010

CHARKEY, CAROLYN LOUISE, newspaper executive; b. Cheyenne, Wyo., Nov. 23, 1939; d. John Frederick and Frances Louise (Riddell) LoSasso; m. Norman Alan Charkey, Feb. 22, 1959 (dec. Sept. 1979); children—Mark Alan, Martin Todd. Student, Colo. State U. Freelance writer, pub. relations cons., 1958—; continuity dir. Sta. KCOL, Ft. Collins, 1964-65; reading tutor Ft. Collins Pub. Schs., 1965-69; owner, mgr. Carolyn's Interiors, Ft. Collins and Cheyenne, Wyo., 1970-77; sect. editor Wyo. Eagle, Cheyenne, 1972-74; info. officer State of Wyo., Cheyenne, 1974-77; dir. pub. relations programs Coors Distbg. Co., Tustin, Calif., 1978-82; mgr. community relations The Orange County Register, Santa Ana, 1982—; pres. The Register Charities Inc., 1982—. Nat. trustee, bd. dirs. Leukemia Soc. Am. Inc.; bd. dirs. Orange County Community Relations Council, Indsl. League Orange County, Pacific Symphony, Chariot Champions; vice-chmn. bd. Master Chorale; pres. The Register Campership; mem. adv. bd. Starting Point; mem. adv. bd. StopGap. Mem. Mothers Against Drunk Driving, Orange County C. of C. (bd. dirs.), Orange County Press Club, Internat. Assn. Bus. Communicators (accredited), Pub. Relations Soc. Am. (accredited, pres. bd. Orange County chpt.), Orange County and Santa Ana YMCA (bd. dirs.), So. Calif. Assn. Philanthropies. Republican. Office: 625 N Grand Ave Santa Ana CA 92711

CHARLES, BEVERLY ROBERTS, health science facility administrator; b. Newark, Dec. 24, 1953; d. Malcolm and JoAnn S. (Edmonds) Roberts; m. Michael Felton Charles, June 12, 1977; 1 child, Alexis. BSJ, Northweste U., Evanston, Ill., 1975, MSJ, 1976; postgrad., U. So. Calif., 1981-8 Rosebridge Grad. Sch. Psychology, Walnut Creek, Calif., 1987—. Ass account exec. Young & Rubicam, N.Y.C., 1976-77; account exec. Young & Rubicam, N.Y.C. and Los Angeles, 1977-78; mktg. rep. Prudential Ins. Group, Century City, Calif., 1979-81; lectr. Bus. Sch. Calif. State U., Long Beach, 1981-82; exec. dir. Ortho-East: An Orthopaedic Med. Group, Berkeley, Calif., 1982—; pres. BR Computer Cons., Berkeley, 1984—; mem. No. Calif. Med. and Dental Aux., Oakland, Calif., 1982-86. Mem. Arch of Sapphires Vol. Guild, Berkeley, 1982—; v.p. bd. dirs. Berkeley Art Ctr. Assn., 1985-87, pres. bd. dirs., 1987—. Mem. Am. Mgmt. Assn. Episcopalian. Office: 2500 Milvia St Suite 114 Berkeley CA 94704

CHARLES, MARGOT GRATZ, nurse; b. Phila., June 23, 1938; d. Earl Jay and Margaret Greil (Gerstley) Gratz; B.S.N., Cornell U., 1961; m. David Jay Charles, Aug. 29, 1965; children—Daniel Jay, Margery Gratz. Staff nurse Hosp. U. Pa., Phila., 1961-62; head nurse cardiopulmonary renal research unit Einstein No. Div., Phila., 1962-64; instr. Hosp. Sch. Nursing Temple U., 1964-65; part time positions, 1965-72; instr. Miami Dade Community Coll., 1972-74; nurse epidemiologist Coral Reef Gen. Hosp., Miami, Fla., 1974-77; instr. Jackson Meml. Hosp. Sch. Nursing, Miami, 1977-78; nurse epidemiologist AMI Kendall Regional Med. Ctr., Miami, 1978-84. Treas., mem. Nat. Cert. Bd. Infection Control, 1985; pres. The Charles Connection Inc., . Unit leader LWV, 1971-72, tel. chmn. Dade County, 1972; active Boy Scouts, Girl Scouts. Mem. Assn. Practitioners Infection Control (chmn. ways and means Dade County 1977, dir. Dade County chpt. 1982-83), Fla. Practitioners Infection Control (treas. 1981-85, bd. dirs. 1986—), Beta Sigma Phi, Republican. Jewish. Home: 7701 Palmetto Ct Miami FL 33156

CHARLES, RENÉE MARGERY, interior designer; b. Lockport, N.Y., Mar. 25, 1952; d. Donnell Urban and Margery Waneta (Buchner) C. AAS in Interior Design summa cum laude, Fashion Inst. Tech., 1972; BA in Environ. Design and Architecture summa cum laude, SUNY, Buffalo, 1974. Jr. designer Steiglitz Assocs., Architects, Buffalo, 1972-73; graphics designer BOSTI, Buffalo, 1972-74; jr. designer Joan Hilliers and Co., Inc., Buffalo, 1973-74; intermediate designer Interdesign, Buffalo, 1974-77; prof. Coll. Interior Design U. Bridgeport, Conn., 1977-78; intermediate designer H.M. Keiser Assoc., N.Y.C., 1978-80; prin., owner Charles, N.Y.C., 1980—; sr. designer, assoc. M. Arthur Gensler and Assocs., Architects, N.Y.C., 1980-83; sr. project designer Caudill Rowlett Scott Sirrine, N.Y.C., 1983-85; asst. v.p. nat. facility E.F. Hutton and Co., Inc. (now Shearson, Lehman, Hutton), N.Y.C., 1985—. Kenan Ctr. Student fellow, 1970. Mem. AIA (steering com., interiors com.), Am. Soc. Interior Designers, Am. Women's Entrepreneurial Devel. Democrat. Lodge: Masons (Beloved Queen 1969-70).

CHARLESWORTH, ALDA HESS, insurance agency manager; b. Ilion, N.Y., May 2, 1932; d. Harold Vaughan and Dorothy Mary (Dockstader) Hess; m. Edward Clay Page, Mar. 29, 1959 (div. 1967); children—Susan Leigh Terry, Lauren LeRoy Page. Sec. Chgo. Pneumatic Tool Co., Utica, N.Y., 1949-50, Gen. Electric Co., Utica, 1950-51; gen. office worker Peninsula Motor Club, Bradenton, Fla., 1957-60; gen. office worker Auto Club Utah, Ogden, 1962-64, mgr. Auto Club Ins. Agy., Salt Lake City, 1966—. Sec./treas. local dist. Republican party, Magna, Utah, 1980; sec. Central Ch. of Nazarene, Salt Lake City, 1981-83; bd. dirs. Alpha Omega Christian Sch., Salt Lake City, 1981-83. Mem. Ins. Women Salt Lake City (pres. 1976-78, Ins. Woman of Yr. 1977, 81), Ind. Ins. Agts. (dir. 1981-83), Profl. Ins. Agts., Nat. Assn. Ins. Women (regional legis. chmn. 1976-77, Regional Legis. award 1977, regional dir. region VIII 1980-81, You Make The Difference award 1977). Office: Auto Club Ins Agy Inc 560 E 500 S Salt Lake City UT 84102

CHARLTON, BETTY JO, state legislator; b. Reno County, Kans., June 15, 1923; d. Joseph and Elma (Johnson) Canning; B.A., U. Kans., 1970, M.A., 1976; m. Robert Sansom Charlton, Feb. 24, 1946; children—John Robert, Richard Bruce. Asst. instr. U. Kans., Lawrence, 1970-73; legis. adminstrv. services employee State of Kans., Topeka, 1977-78, legis. aide gov's. office, 1979; mem. Kans. Ho. of Reps., 1980—.

CHARLTON, MARGARET ELLEN JONSSON, civic worker; b. Dallas, Aug. 7, 1938, d. John Erik and Margaret Elizabeth (Fonde) Jonsson; ed. Skidmore Coll., 1956-57, So. Methodist U., 1957-60; children: Emily, Erik. Civic worker, Dallas; dir. KRLD radio, Dallas, 1970-74; dir. 1st Nat. Bank, Dallas, 1976-85, vice-chmn. dirs. trust com.; trustee Meth. Hosps., 1972-82, mem. exec. com., 1977-82; dir., chmn. exec. com. Lamplighter Sch., 1967—; mem. vis. com. dept. psychology M.I.T.; mem. vis. com. Stanford U. Libraries, 1984—; bd. dirs. Winston Sch., 1973-85; bd. dirs., mem. exec. com. Episcopal Sch., 1976-83; bd. dirs. Callier Center Communication Disorders, 1967—, v.p., 1974—; chmn. Crystal Charity Ball; active Stanford Centennial Campaign (co-chmn. nat. major gifts com.), bd. dirs. Children's Med. Center, Hope Cottage Childrens' Bur., Baylor Dental Sch., Dallas Health and Sci. Mus., Dallas YWCA, Day Nursery Assn.; trustee Dallas Mus. Art; mem. collectors com. Nat. Gallery Art. Margaret Jonsson Charlton Hosp. of Dallas named in her honor, 1973. Mem. Internat. Council Mus. of Modern Art., Ctr. for Strategic and Internat. Studies. (nat. adv. bd.), mem. steering com. Stanford Centennial Campaign, 1986—, co-chmn. major gifts com., 1986—; pres. MJC Fund, Jonsson Found., Susan G. Komen Found, 1988— (mem. steering com.); trustee Southern Meth. U.; mem. adv. bd. Tiffany & Co., Dallas, 1987. Republican. Club: Dallas Women's, Tower, Crescent, Brook Hollow Golf, Dallas County.

CHARNIZON, MARLENE, editor, teacher; b. N.Y.C., Oct. 10, 1938; d. Aaron and Gertrude (Goldberg) Schweid; m. Jerome Nathan, June 14, 1959 (div. 1975); children: Walter Elliot, Jennifer. BA, CCNY, 1959. Prodn.

asst., assoc. editor Library Jour. Book Rev. R.R. Bowker Co., N.Y.C., 1971-83, founding exec. editor Small Press mag., 1983-86; freelance writer, editor, 1986—; instr. York Coll. Adult Learning Ctr., N.Y.C., 1987-88; story editor part 2 mags. The N.Y. Times, 1987—.

CHAROF, EILEEN JOAN, personnel services executive; b. Bronx, N.Y., July 2, 1947; d. Robert Gerard and Rosalie Fortuna (Nasta) Stickley; B.A. in Psychology, St. John's U., 1969; m. Alan I. Charof, Nov. 15, 1969. Regional adminstr. Am. Sign and Indicator Corp., N.Y.C., 1970-72; dir. adminstrn. Direct Mail Mktg. Assn., N.Y.C., 1972-74; mgr. Allied Temporary Service, N.Y.C., 1974-78; nat. ops. mgr. Temp Force, East Meadow, N.Y., 1978-80; v.p. Cyberway, N.Y.C., 1980-82; owner, pres. Astra Inc., 1983—. Mem. Nat. Assn. Temporary Services.

CHARPENTIER, GAIL WIGUTOW, special education school administrator; b. N.Y.C., Mar. 10, 1946; d. Jacob M. and Ethel (Israel) Wigutow; m. Peter Jon Charpentier; 1 child, Elisabeth Marie. BA, CUNY, 1967; MA, New Sch. Social Research, N.Y.C., 1976. Lic. social worker. Tchr. Spl. Service Pub. Sch., Bronx, N.Y., 1967-73; adminstr. Boston City Hosp., 1973-76; dir. Monson Devel. Ctr., Palmer, Mass., 1976; residential dir. Kolburne Sch., New Marlboro, Mass., 1976-79; dir. Berkshire Children's Community, Great Barrington, Mass., 1979—; researcher Nat. Opinion Research Ctr., N.Y.C. and Boston, 1973-76; trainer residential child care, Mass., 1978—; mem. human rights bd. Oakdale Found., Great Barrington, 1980—. Recipient Community Criminal Justice award Justice Resource Inst., 1984. Mem. Mass. Assn. Approved Pvt. Schs. (bd. dirs. 1982-84, ins. trustee 1983-87, Service award 1982), New Eng. Assn. for Child Care, Assn. for Mentally Deficient, Internat. Assn. for Retts Syndrome. Home: Orchard House Tyringham MA 01264 Office: Berkshire Children's Community 41 Taconic Ave Great Barrington MA 01230

CHARREN, GABRIELLE, dental technologist; b. Berlin, Germany, Nov. 15, 1937; came to U.S., 1959, naturalized, 1965; d. Hans Manfred and Margot (Kaufmann) Purucker; Masters degree cum laude in Dental Tech., Berufschule Hannover, W. Ger., 1959; postgrad., U. Madrid, 1970-71; 1 dau., Stefanie. Head ceramist Beverly Dental Ceramics, Beverly Hills, Calif., 1959-64; dept. mgr. Wolfsen Dental Lab., Los Angeles, 1964-66, Park Dental Lab., Inglewood, Calif., 1966-68; art. mgr., rep. artists J. Zuniga, Manolo, Coronado, Mallorca, Spain, 1968-70; disc jockey 3-lang. radio show, Mallorca, 1971-72; owner Oak Grove Dental Lab., Palo Alto, Calif., 1975-79; mgr. Capital City Dental Lab., Sacramento, 1980-81; owner Novadent Ceramics, Sacramento; condr. clinics in ceramic staining and anatomy. Pres., Parent Council, Keys Family Day Sch., Palo Alto, 1976-78; v.p. Parent Council Waldorf Sch., Sacramento, 1981—. Cert. dental technician, 1977. Mem. Nat. Assn. Dental Labs., Calif. Acad. for Dental Research and Edn., Calif. Dental Lab. Assts. (component pres. Sacramento 1983-84, dir.-at-large 1987—), Nat. Assn. Female Execs. Republican. Club: Arden Hills Swim and Tennis (Sacramento). Contbr. daily column Who's Who Daily Bull., English lang. newspaper, Mallorca, 1971-72; guest contbr. Spanish newspapers: Diario Mallorca, Balleares, 1971-79. Home: 921 Castec Dr Sacramento CA 95825 Office: Novadent Ceramics 577 Arden Town Ct Sacramento CA 95825

CHARREN, PEGGY, consumer activist; b. N.Y.C., Mar. 9, 1928; d. Maxwell and Ruth (Rosenthal) Walzer; m. Stanley Charren, June 17, 1951; children: Deborah, Claudia. BA, Conn. Coll., 1949; LLD (hon.), Regis Coll., 1978; DHL (hon.), Bank St. Coll. Edn., 1988, Emerson Coll., 1988, Tufts U., 1988. Founder, owner Art Prints, Inc., Providence, 1951-53, Quality Book Fairs, Newton, Mass., 1960-65; dir. Creative Arts Council, Newton, 1966-68; founder, pres. Action for Children's Television, Inc., Cambridge, Mass., 1968—; mem. Carnegie Commn. on Future of Public Broadcasting, 1977-79; mem. task panel on public attitudes and use of media for promotion of health President's Commn. on Mental Health, 1977-80; mem. Mass. Council on Arts and Humanities, 1980—; vis. lectr. edn. Harvard U., 1987; mem. adv. bd. project on TV advt. and children NSF; mem. adv. bd. project on devel. of programs for children with spl. needs Am. Inst. Research; bd. dirs. Child Devel. Consortium, Media Access Project, Kidsnet. Co-author: Changing Channels: Living Sensibly with Television, 1983, The TV-Smart Book for Kids, 1988; joint editor: Who is Talking to Our Children, 1973, Television, Children and the Constitutional Bicentennial, 1988; contbr. articles to profl. publs. Bd. dirs. Women's Campaign Fund., Young Audiences of Mass.; mem. adv. bd. Am. Repertory Theater. Recipient Disting. Public Info. Service award Am. Acad. Pediatrics, hon. award Motion Picture Assn., Disting. Service award Mass. Radio and TV Assn., 1974, hon. medal Conn. Coll., 1974, Helen Homans Gilbert award Radcliffe Coll., Govs. award New Eng. chpt. Nat. Acad. TV Arts and Scis., 1987; named Humanist of Yr. Ethical Soc. of Boston, 1988. Democrat. Office: Action for Childrens TV 20 University Rd Cambridge MA 02138

CHARTIER, JANELLEN OLSEN, airline inflight service coordinator; b. Chgo., Sept. 12, 1951; d. Roger Carl and Genevieve Ann (McCormick) Olsen; m. Lionel Pierre-Paul Chartier, Nov. 6, 1982; 1 child, Régine Anne. B.A. in French and Home Econs., U. Ill., 1973, M.A. in Teaching French, 1974; student U. Rouen (France), 1971-72. Cert. tchr., Ill. Flight attendant Delta Airlines, Atlanta, 1974—, French qualified, 1974—, Spanish qualified, 1977-82, German qualified, 1980—, in flight service coordinator, 1980—, European in flight service coordinator, 1983—; French examiner In-Flight Service, 1984—; interpreter Formax, Inc., Mokena, Ill., 1976-82. Bd. dirs. One Plus One Dance Co., Champaign, Ill., 1977-78. Mem. Alliance Maison Francaise de Chgo., Phi Delta Kappa, Alpha Lambda Delta. Roman Catholic. Home: 155 N Harbor Dr Apt 3506 Chicago IL 60601

CHARTRAND, MARGARET, public relations consultant; b. St. John, N.B., Can., Aug. 4, 1943; d. John Wesley and Mary Wilhelmina (Reid) Gillespie; m. John Gerard Chartrand, Nov. 5, 1965; children: Christopher, Dawn. BJ, Carleton U., 1966. Reporter Sudbury (Ont.) Star, Can., 1960-66; info. officer Can. Centennial Commn., Ottawa, Ont., 1966-67, U. Western Ont., London, 1967-71, Bell Can., Montreal, Que., 1971-72; info. dir. Ont. Coll. Art, Toronto, 1972-73; info. officer Ont. Provincial Govt., Toronto, 1973-75; pub. relations mgr. Metro Toronto Library Bd., 1976-87; pub. relations cons. MC Communications, Toronto, 1987—; sr. assoc. Cormana Inc., 1987—; speaker in field. Mem. ALA (chmn. pub. relations sect. 1987-88), Nat. Newspaper Awards Newsweek (chmn. 1985-87), Can. Pub. Relations Soc., Toronto Press Club (pres. 1984). Club: Royal Scottish Country Dance Soc. Home: 139 Carrington, Richmond Hill Can L4C 7Z1

CHASE, DAWN RENEE, social services administator; b. Jamestown, N.Y., Jan. 1, 1961; d. Clarence Alvora Chase Jr. and Nona Ann (Pattison) Urso. AB, Hamilton Coll., Clinton, N.Y., 1983. Asst. dir. Career Ctr., Hamilton Coll., 1983-85; program dir. YWCA, Jamestown, 1985-86; exec. dir. Amicae Inc., Fredonia, N.Y., 1986—; chair Rape Law Coalition, Jamestown, 1985-86; chair conf. com. Chautauqua County Commn. on Family Violence and Neglect, Mayville, N.Y., 1987. Chair Minority Voter Registration Project, Utica, N.Y., 1984, Women's History Week Consortium, Jamestown, 1986; mem. steering com., treas. N.Y. Coalition Against Sexual Assault, 1987. Recipient Mary Bargar prize Zonta, 1979; named Woman of Merit, Mohawk Valley Community Coll., 1985. Mem. NOW (v.p. Mohawk Valley chpt. 1984-85, Membership Drive award 1985), Nat. Orgn. Female Execs., Bus. and Profl. Women's Club. Democrat. Roman Catholic. Office: Amicae Inc PO Box 0023 Fredonia NY 14063

CHASE, DEBRA, educational institution administrator; b. Ashland, Ky., June 19, 1951. BA in Bus. Adminstrn., U. South Fla., 1980, BA in Psychology, 1981. Asst. mall mgr. De Bartolo Corp., St. Petersburg, Fla., 1977-80; paralegal Greene, Mann, Rowe, Esq., St. Petersburg, 1981-83; tchr., prin. MLA Acad., St. Petersburg, 1983-85; owner, adminstr. Acad. for the Gifted, St. Petersburg, 1985—. Mem. task force GTE Grand Prix, St. Petersburg, 1986; mem. Tiger Bay Polit. Club, St. Petersburg, 1985, Concerned Women for Am., 1985; pres. Noah's Ark, Inc. Mem. St. Petersburg C. of C., DAR, Mensa. Office: Acad for the Gifted 1225-9 Ave N Saint Petersburg FL 33705

CHASE, DORIS TOTTEN, sculptor, video artist, filmmaker; b. Seattle, 1923; d. William Phelps and Helen (Feeney) Totten; m. Elmo Chase, Oct. 20, 1943 (div. 1972); children: Gregary Totten, Randall Jarvis Totten. Student, U. Wash., 1941-43. lectr. tours for USIA in S.Am., 1975, Europe, 1978, India, 1972, Australia, 1986, Eastern Europe, 1987. Exhibited in one-woman shows Seligman Gallery, Seattle, 1959, 61, Gallery Numero, Florence, Italy, 1961, Internat. Gallery, Italy, 1962, Hall Coleman Gallery, Seattle, 1962, Formes Gallery, Tokyo, 1963, 70, Bangkok Ctr. Mus., Thailand, 1963, Bolles Gallery, San Francisco, 1964, Suffolk (N.Y.) Mus., 1965, Smolin Gallery, N.Y.C., 1965, Gallery Numero, Rome, 1962, 66, Collectors Gallery, Seattle, 1964, 66, 69, Tacoma Art Mus., 1967, Ruth White Gallery, N.Y.C., 1967, 69, 70, Fountain Gallery, Portland, Oreg., 1970, U. Wash. Henry Gallery, 1971, 77, Wadsworth Atheneum, Hartford, Conn., 1973, Hirshhorn Mus., Washington, 1974, 77, Anthology Film Archives, N.Y.C., 1975, 80, 83, Donnell Library, N.Y.C., 1976, 79, 83, Performing Arts Mus. at Lincoln Ctr., 1976, Mus. Modern Art, N.Y.C., 1978, 80, 87, High Mus., Atlanta, 1978, Herbert Johnson Mus., 1982, A.I.R. Gallery, N.Y.C., 1983-85, Art in Embassies, USIS, 1984-88; circulating exhbt., Western Mus. Assn., 1970-71; represented in permanent collections, Finch Coll. Mus., N.Y.C., Mus. Modern Art, N.Y.C., Seattle Art Mus., Ashai Shimbum, Tokyo, Georges Pompidou Ctr., Paris, Battelle Inst., Mus. Fine Arts Boston, Milw. Art Inst., Art Inst. Chgo., Mus. Fine Arts Houston, Frye Art Mus., Seattle, Nat. Collection Fine Arts, Smithsonian Inst., Washington, Wadsworth Atheneum, N.C. Mus. Art, Raleigh, Mus. Modern Art, Kobe, Japan, Pa. Acad. Art, Phila., Portland Art Mus., Vancouver (B.C.) Art Gallery, N.Y.C., Montgomery (Ala.) Mus. Fine Art, Hudson River Mus., N.Y.C., works represented in archival collections Ctr. for Film and Theatre Research, U. Wis., Madison, U. Wash., Seattle, works reproduced in various art mags. and books; executed monumental kinetic sculpture, Kerry Park, Seattle, Anderson, Ind., Expo '70, Osaka, Japan, Sculpture Park, Atlanta, Lake Park, Ind., Met. Mus. Art, N.Y.C., Montgomery Mus. Fine Arts, Seattle Ctr. Theater, multi-media sculpture for 4 ballets, Opera Assn. Seattle; included in, Sculpture in Park program N.Y.C., Playground of Tomorrow ABC-TV, Los Angeles; work in video, TV Exptl. Lab., Sta. WNET; TV prodns. Lies, 1980; Window, 1980, Doris Chase Dance Series produced at Bklyn. Coll., U. Mich., Ann Arbor, Sta. RTSI-TV, Switzerland, Sta. WCET-Cin., Sta. WGBH, Boston, Sta. WNYC, N.Y., NET, producer, Doris Chase Dance Series, 1971-81, Concept Series, 1980-84, Table for One (with Geraldine Page), 1985, (with Anne Jackson) Dear Papa, 1986, (with Luise Rainer) A Dancer, 1987, Still Frame, 1988. Recipient honors and awards at numerous festivals in U.S. and fgn. countries; grantee Nat. Endowment for Arts, Am. Film Inst., 1988, N.Y. State Council for Arts, Mich. Arts Council, Jerusalem Film Festival, 1987, Berlin Film Festival, 1985, 87, London Film Festival, 1986, Am. Film Inst. Festival Kennedy Ctr., 1987; subject of documentary Doris Chase: Portrait of the Artist (by Robin Schanzenbach), PBS, 1985. Mem. Actors Studio (writer, dirs. wing 1986). Address: care AFI-DWW PO Box 27999 2021 N Western Ave Los Angeles CA 90027

CHASE, HELEN LOUISE, banker; b. Waukegan, Ill., Sept. 29, 1943; d. David William and Ruth Virginia (Sawyer) C. BA, U. Ill., 1965. Sec., exec. sec. Foote, Cone and Belding, Chgo., 1965-66; various positions Continental Bank, Chgo., 1966-73, internat. banking officer, 1973-76, 2d v.p., 1976-77; Brazil rep. Continental Bank, Sao Paulo, 1977-80; 2d v.p., sect. head Far East group Continental Bank Internat., N.Y.C., 1980-81; 2d v.p. internat. div. Continental Bank, Chgo., 1981-83; v.p. N.Am. Union Trust Bank (now Signet Bank), Balt., 1983-84; v.p., mgr. internat. ops. Signet Bank, Balt., 1984—. Mem. Council on Internat. Banking. Clubs: Downtown Athletic, East Bank. Office: Signet Bank/Md 7 St Paul St 5th Fl Baltimore MD 21202

CHASE, JOYCE ELAINE, accountant, nurse; b. Benton Harbor, Mich., Dec. 4, 1931; d. Richard I. and Evelyn Pauline (Hahn) Winney; student Lake Mich. Coll., 1974-75, Mich. State Ins. Sch., 1974, A.A. in Nursing, Lake Mich. Coll., 1986; m. Ernest Arthur Chase, July 21, 1951; children—Ernest L., Arthur M., Robert J., William R., James R. Clk. Gillespie's Drug Store, Benton Harbor, 1945, WoolWorth's Store, Benton Harbor, 1946-47; bookkeeper Reeder's Bookkeeping Service, Benton Harbor, 1949; assembler VM Corp., Benton Harbor, 1950; telephone operator Mich. Bell Co., Benton Harbor, 1951; bookkeeper I & M Electric Co., Buchanan, Mich., 1952, Auto Specialties Co., St. Joseph, Mich., 1953; clk. Galien Drug Store, Galien, Mich., 1955; assembler Electro-Voice Corp., Buchanan, Mich., 1958-62; bookkeeper Chase Bookkeeping & Tax Service, Galien, Mich., 1963-78, sr. tax accountant, 1968—; ins. agt. Chase Ins. Service Center, Galien, Mich., 1974-85, registered nurse, Pawating Hosp., Niles, Mich., 1986—; emergency med. technician and ambulance driver Galien Vol. Ambulance Service, 1974—. Cub. Scout den mother S.W. Mich. council Cub. Scouts Am., 1963-69; mem. Galien Twp. election bd., 1971-78; mem. Galien Sch. Election Bd., 1971—; pres. Galien Athletic Boosters, 1969; mem. Galien High Sch., PTA, 1966—, adv. com., 1965-68. Mem. Nat. Soc. Pub. Accountants, Mich. Emergency Services Health Council, Am. Legion Aux. Republican. Methodist. Home: US Route 12 East Garwood Lake Galien MI 49113 Office: 112 N Main St Galien MI 49113

CHASE, JUNE STOKER, development professional; b. Joliet, Ill., Dec. 8, 1924; d. Paul Palmer and Elizabeth Catherine (Balbinot) Stoker; m. Lloyd Karl Chase, Jr., Sept. 19, 1953 (div. 1974); children: Paul Charles, Peter Randolph, Christopher Miles. BA in English, Coll. St. Francis, Joliet, 1946. Owner, mgr. advt. agy. Words & Graphics, Pacific Palisades, Calif., 1966-70; mng. editor Werner & Werner, Santa Monica, Calif., 1970-72, 1970-72; exec. dir. Arts in Action, Pacific Palisades, 1972-76; fund raising cons. Pacific Palisades, 1976-79; campaign coordinator Los Angeles United Way, 1979-83; dir. devel. Linden Ctr., Beverly Hills, Calif., 1984-85; cons. Wordsmith Group, Los Angeles, 1985, grants cons., 1987—; devel. dir. San Fernando Valley Council Girl Scouts U.S., Chatsworth, Calif., 1985-86; cons. in field; bd. dirs. various Los Angeles area community orgns. Exhibited Wall hangings and scuptures Palisades Art Ctr.; reviewer Artweek, Oakland, Calif.; contbr. articles to profl. jours. Recipient Wonders of Work award Los Angeles Unified Sch. Dist., 1980. Mem. Nat. Soc. Fund Raising Execs., Planned Giving Round Table So. Calif., AAUW, Nat. Assn. Female Execs. Democrat. Office: Growth Dimension/Wordsmith Group 1928 Walgrove Ave Los Angeles CA 90066

CHASE, LINDA ARVILLE, musician, writer; b. Cambridge, Mass., Jan. 14, 1953; d. Harold Francis and Irene Bernice (Sakowski) Chase; m. Richard Herbert Adams, July 22, 1974 (div. 1977); m. Michel Phillip Iodice, Apr. 22, 1985. Pvt. student of R. Fitzgerald, New Eng. Conservatory, 1959-68; student, Mass. Coll. Art, 1970, Lesley Coll., 1970-71; pvt. studies, Boston, 1971-78. Writer, pub., performed more than 200 songs; co-writer theme song for movie Once Bitten, 1985, 2 MTV videos, 1985; songwriter, movie Rad; in 1987, with David R. Currier signed with Jim Boyer. Office: Paws Music Inc PO Box 2771 Woburn MA 01888

CHASE, LORIENE ECK, psychologist; b. Sacramento; d. Walter and Genevieve (Bennetts) Eck; A.B., U. So. Calif., 1948, M.A., 1949, Ph.D., 1953; m. Leo Goodman-Malamuth, 1946 (div. 1951); 1 son, Leo; m. 2d, Allen Chase, Mar. 4, 1960 (div.); m. 3d, Clifton W. King, 1974. Psychologist, Spastic Children's Found., Los Angeles, 1952-55, Inst. Group Psychotherapy, Beverly Hills, Calif., 1957-59; pvt. practice, 1953—; v.p. VSP Exec. Relocation Consultants. Condr., Dr. Loriene Chase Show, ABC-TV, Hollywood, Calif. 1966—. Cons., Camarillo State Hosp.; bd. dirs., pres.'s circle U. So. Calif.; founding mem. Achievement Rewards for Coll. Scientists; bd. dirs. Chase-King Personal Devel. Center, Los Angeles; v.p. Chase-King Prodns. Inc., Los Angeles, Shell Beach, Calif.; exec. bd. Cancer Research Center, Los Angeles. Writer syndicated newspaper column Casebook of Dr. Chase. Served with Waves World War II. Recipient Woman of Year in Psychology award Am. Mothers Com. Mem. Diadames, Assn. Media Psychologists, Les Dames de Champagne, Dame de Rotisseur, Nat. Art Assn., AFTRA, Screen Actors Guild, Internat. Platform Assn. Clubs: Regency, Lakeside Country, Santa Maria Country. Author: The Human Miracle; columnist Westways mag. Address: 375 Palomar Shell Beach CA 93449

CHASE, MARY JANE, jewelry executive; b. Glouster, Ohio, July 16, 1938; d. Cecil Nelson and Juanita Marie (Anderson) McCafferty; grad. Andrews Sch., 1957; m. Robert Vincent Chase, Oct. 16, 1971; 1 child, Robert Vincent. Sec. to v.p. accessories div. TRW, Cleve., 1957-63; office mgr. Kaufman & Reynolds Constrn. Co., Sacramento, Calif., 1964-67; asst. to med. staff Roseville (Calif.) Community Hosp., 1967-69; asst. to v.p. ops. Intel Corp., Mountain View, Calif., 1969-70; exec. asst. to pres. Catamore Co., Inc., East Providence, R.I., 1971-74, dir. adminstrn., 1978-81, v.p. adminstrn., 1981-82; market dir. Johnson Matthey Jewelry Corp., East Providence, 1983-84, sr. mgr., 1984; v.p., sec. The Byfield Group, Inc., 1985-86; v.p. spl. markets Jewel Mktg. USA, Inc., Warwick, 1986—. Bd. dirs. Nat. Fedn. Rep. Women, 1978-81, mem. nominating com., 1979; alt. del. Rep. Nat. Conv., 1976, 80; bd. dirs. East Providence unit Am. Cancer Soc., 1979-81; mem. Meml. Hosp. Aux., 1978—. Episcopalian. Home: 201 Wilson Ave Rumford RI 02916

CHASE, VICTORIA BYLER, mechanical engineer; b. Dallas, Dec. 19, 1954; d. Edwin Carl Byler Sr. and Annie Orlena Hurlburt; m. Warren Chase, Apr. 9, 1988. BSME, So. Meth. U., 1979; postgrad., U. Tex., Dallas, 1986—. Registered profl. engr., Tex. Design drafter Tex. Instruments, Inc., Dallas, 1973-78, mech. design engr., 1979, lead mech. engr., 1983-85; project engr. Exxon Co., U.S.A., Houston, 1980-81; sr. project engr. Tyler, Tex., 1981-83; engring. mgr. Tng. Gallery, Inc., Dallas, 1986; lead packaging engr. Boeing Electronics, Inc., Irving, Tex., 1987-88; sr. mech. engr. Sci. Communications, Garland, Tex., 1988—. Mem. Tex. Soc. Profl. Engrs., Pi Tau Sigma. Presbyterian. Home: 2705 Chariot Ln Garland TX 75042

CHATER, SHIRLEY SEARS, university administrator; b. Shamokin, Pa., July 30, 1932; d. Raymond and Edna (Shamp) Sears; m. Norman Chater, Dec. 5, 1959; children: Cris, Geoffrey. Diploma, U. Pa., 1953, BS, 1956; MS, U. Calif.-San Francisco, 1960; PhD, U. Calif.-Berkeley, 1964. Asst. vice chancellor acad. affairs U. Calif.-San Francisco, 1974-77; prof. dept. social and behavioral scis. Sch. Nursing, 1973-86, vice chancellor acad. affairs, 1977-82; commr. Am. Council Edn., Washington, 1977-82, council assoc., 1982-84, mem. commn. on women; adminstr. Assn. Governing Bds. Univs. and Colls., Washington, 1984-86; pres. Tex. Woman's U., Denton, 1986—; mem. commn. on women, Am. Council on Edn., 1986—. Contbr. articles to profl. jours. Mem. adv. com. Robert Wood Johnson Found., Kellogg Nat. Fellows Program; assoc. trustee U. Pa.; bd. dirs. United Way, Denton. Mem. Women's Forum West, Denton C. of C. (bd. dirs.). Office: Tex Woman's U Office of Pres Denton TX 76204

CHATFIELD, CHERYL ANN, stock brokerage firm executive, writer; b. King's Park, N.Y., Jan. 24, 1946; d. William David and Mildred Ruth (King) C.; m. Gene Allen Chasser, Feb. 17, 1968 (div. 1979); m. James Bernard Arkebauer, Apr. 16, 1983 (div. 1987). BS, Cen. Conn. Coll., 1968, MS, 1972; PhD, U. Conn., 1976. Cert. gen. prin. securities. Tchr. Bristol East High Sch., Conn., 1968-77; adminstr. New Britain Schs., Conn., 1977-79; prof. Ariz. State U., Phoenix, 1979; stockbroker J. Daniel Bell, Denver, 1980-83, Hyder and Co., Denver, 1983-84; stockbroker, pres. Denari Securities, Denver, 1984—; tchr. investment seminars Front Range Community Coll., Denver, 1984-86; speaker women's groups, Denver, 1983-86. Author: Low-Priced Riches, 1985, Selling Low-Priced Riches, 1986, (newspaper columns) For Women Investors, 1982-84, Commentary, 1985-86; editor, founder (newsletter) Women in Securities . Project bus. cons. Jr. Achievement, Denver, 1986; trustee Orchestra of Santa Fe. Mem. Nat. Assn. Female Execs., Aircraft Owners and Pilots Assn., AAUW, N.Mex. Venture Capital Club (treas.), Kappa Delta Pi. Republican. Roman Catholic. Avocation: flying. Office: Denari Securities Inc 125 Lincoln Ave Suite 116 Santa Fe NM 87501

CHATFIELD-TAYLOR, ADELE, arts administrator, historic preservationist; b. Washington, Jan. 29, 1945; d. Hobart Chatfield-Taylor and Mary Owen (Lyon) C.-T.; m. John Guare, May 20, 1981. BA, Manhattanville Coll., 1966; MS in Historic Preservation, Columbia U., 1974; postgrad. (Loeb fellow), Harvard U., 1978-79. Archtl. historian Historic Am. Bldg. Survey, Washington, 1967; co-founder, dir. Urban Deadline Architects, Inc., 1968-73; landmarks preservation specialist N.Y.C. Landmarks Preservation Commn., 1973-74, asst. to chmn., 1974-79, dir. policy and programs, 1979-80; adj. prof. historic preservation program Grad. Sch. Architecture and Planning, Columbia U., 1976—; exec. dir. N.Y. Landmarks Preservation Found., 1980-84; dir. design arts program Nat. Endowment for Arts, 1984—; asst. dir. Neighborhood Conservation Conf. Nat. Endowment Arts, 1975; bd. dirs. Preservation ACTION, 1976-84, regional v.p., 1978-83, sec., 1983-84; trustee Ctr. for Bldg. Conservation, 1978-84; mem. U.S. del. to China, Women in Architecture, 1977, 80, U.S. del. to China, Historic Preservationists, 1982; mem. exec. com. U.S./Internat. Council on Monuments and Sites, 1979-84; mem. China adv. com. Nat. Endowment Arts, 1980-84, vice chmn. design arts policy panel, 1978-82; bd. dirs. Nat. Alliance of Preservation Commns., 1983-84; trustee Tiber Island History Mus., 1983—; guest lectr. Harvard U., MIT, Columbia U., NYU, U. Va. Contbr. articles to profl. jours. Mem. restoration com. South Street Seaport Mus., 1975-84; mem. Nat. Com. on U.S.-China Relations, 1982—; mem. lawn adv. bd. U. Va., 1982-86; bd. dirs. Greenwich Village Trust for Historic Preservation, 1983-84, Internat. Design Conf. Aspen, 1986—. Archtl. fellow Ednl. Facilities Lab Acad. Ednl. Devel., 1982-83; Rome prize Am. Acad. in Rome, 1983-84; fellow N.Y. Inst. Humanities, 1983—. Mem. Archtl. League, Nat. Trust Historic Preservation, Friends of Cast Iron Architecture, Preservation League N.Y. State, Met. Mus. Art, Vernacular Architecture Soc., Decorative Arts Soc., Nat. Council of Preservation Execs. Club: Pug Dog of Greater N.Y. Office: Nat Endowment for Arts Design Arts Program 1100 Pennsylvania Ave NW Washington DC 20506

CHAVARRIA, ROSEMARY ANN, training professional; b. Amityville, N.Y., Dec. 10, 1954; d. Andrew Anthony and Philomena Rose (Grandinetti) Sinagra; m. Thomas Joseph McCoy, Aug. 14, 1977 (div. 1982); child: Christopher Thomas; m. David Chavarria Jr., Sept. 22, 1985; stepchildren: Joey, Rebecca, Albert, Melanie, Sulema. BS in Edn., Hofstra U., 1977. Lic. tchr., N.Y., Tex. Recreation specialist, tchr. arts and crafts Dept. Parks and Recreation Town of Oyster Bay, Massapequa, N.Y., 1972-78; sub. tchr. Massapequa and Farmingdale (N.Y.) Sch. Dists., 1977-78; tchr. fifth grade Roman Catholic Diocese of Houston and Galveston, 1978-79; instr. high sch. equivalency Operation SER/CETA, Galveston, 1980-81, div. continuing edn. Galveston Coll., 1981-82; tchr. arts and crafts, pre-sch. Island Montessori Sch., Galveston, 1981-82; dir. pre-sch. Tex. Parks and Recreation, Texas City, 1982-84; tng. specialist div. employment and tng. Town of Oyster Bay, Massapequa, N.Y., 1984—. Artist various media. Committeewoman Nassau County Reps., North Massapequa Reps. 1985—. Mem. Nat. Assn. Female Execs., Civil Service Employees Assn., Nat. Congress of PTA, Hofstra U. Alumni Assn., Delta Chi Delta. Roman Catholic. Home: 222 N Wisconsin Ave North Massapequa NY 11758 Office: Town of Oyster Bay Div Employment and Tng 977 Hicksville Rd Massapequa NY 11758

CHAVERS, RUBY MARGARETT, retail company administrator; b. Russellville, Ala., Nov. 21, 1956; d. Charlie Houston and Pauline (Hubbard) Nelson; m. John Willie Chavers, Jr., June 6, 1981; 1 child, Shannon Helene. BS in Acctg., Ala. A&M U., 1979. Internal auditor Cargill, Inc., Mpls., 1979-81, asst. acctg. mgr., 1981-82; internal auditor Target Stores, Mpls., 1982-84, cash mgr., 1984-87; supr. accts. payable, 1987—. Mem. Twin Cities Cash Mgmt. Assn., Nat. Corp. Cash Mgmt. Assn., Inst. Internal Auditors, Nat. Assn. Black Accts., Nat. Assn. Female Execs., Delta Sigma Theta. Home: 3486 Pilgrim Ln N Plymouth MN 55441

CHAVEZ, CHRISTINA LINDA GARCIA, lawyer, state official; b. El Paso, Tex., Mar. 6, 1953; d. Raymond D. and Emma M. (Garcia) C. BA, N.Mex. State U., 1975; JD, Cath. U. Am., 1978. Bar: N.Mex. 1978, U.S. Dist. Ct. (N.Mex. dist.) 1978, U.S. Ct. Appeals (10th cir.) 1978. Equal employment opportunity specialist trainee Office Human Rights OEO, 1972-73; govt. intern equal employment div. N.Mex. State Planning Office, 1974; tutor, counselor Spl. Student Services, N.Mex. State U., 1973-75; summer intern The White House, Exec. Office of Pres., Washington, 1975, Dept. Labor, 1976; legal intern AYUDA para el Consumidor, Washington, 1977, Senator Pete Domenici, N.Mex., 1977; law clk. Dept. Labor, 1978; law clk., N.Mex. Supreme Ct., 1978-79; ptnr. Mitchell, Alley & Rubin, Santa Fe, 1979-83; supt. State N.Mex. Regulation and Licensing Dept., Santa Fe, 1983-86; sole practice, Santa Fe, 1987—. Trustee No. N.Mex. Legal Services, Santa Fe, 1980-81, St. Vincent's Hosp. Bd., Santa Fe, 1982-83, Santa Fe Group Homes, Inc., 1982-83, 85-86; mem. N.Mex. Women's Polit. Caucus, 1975—. Recipient Spl. Achievement and Merit award Dept. of Labor, 1976, Gov.'s award for Outstanding N.Mex. Women, 1986; named Woman in 80's, N.Mex. Women's Polit. Caucus, 1980, other honors. Mem. Internat. Fedn. Women Lawyers, NOW, Mexican Am. Women Nat. Assn., LWV, Women Execs. in State Govt., Bus. and Profl. Women, Santa Fe C. of C., Mex. Bar Assn. (mem. young lawyers div., women's legal rights sect.), First Judicial

Dist. Bar Assn. (pres. 1981). Democrat. Roman Catholic. Office: La Cone Bldg 236 Montezuma St Suite 3 PO Box 9270 Santa Fe NM 87504

CHAVEZ, MARIA ELSA, medical technologist; b. Woodland, Calif., Jan. 24, 1961; d. Eleuterio Bravo and Maria (Anaya) C. BS in Biology, U. LaVerne (Calif.), 1983; BS in Med. Tech., Calif. State, Los Angeles, 1986. Lic. clin. lab. technologist, Calif. Lab. asst. Roybal Health Ctr., East Los Angeles, Calif., 1984; med. technologist intern King/Drew UCLA Med. Sch., Los Angeles, 1987-88; med. technologist Martin Luther King Jr. Hosp., Los Angeles, 1987—. Mem. Calif. Assn. Med. Lab. Tech., Am. Soc. Clin. Pathologists (lic.), Agy. for Med. Lab. Personnel (cert.), Nat. Assn. Female Execs. Republican. Roman Catholic. Clubs: Las Rosas Debutante (Montebello, Calif.). Home: 746 S Hillview Ave Los Angeles CA 90022 Office: Martin Luther King Jr Hosp 12021 Wilmington Ave Los Angeles CA 90059

CHAVIS-BUTLER, GRACE LEE, educator; b. Charleston, S.C., Aug. 26, 1916; d. Thomas and Sarah (Lafayette) Chavis; m. E. Hardy Butler, June 15, 1974 (div. Feb. 1984); remarried, Sept. 17, 1985. Diploma in Teaching, Avery Normal Inst., 1938; BA, Am. U., 1954, MA, 1955; PhD, U. Beverly Hills, 1982. Educator Washington high schs., 1955-73; chmn. history dept. Western High Sch., Washington, 1971-73; substitute tchr. Oakland (Calif.) Pub. Schs., 1973-74; substitute instr. Los Angeles Community Coll. Dist., 1974-80, 82—. Author: Reflections on Africa, 1975; contbr. articles to newspapers, profl. jours. Mem. Friends of Vernon Br. Library, Los Angeles, 1978—, v.p., 1980-81; vol. asst. mgr. The Mankind Ctr., Los Angeles, 1978-79; coordinator Los Angeles-Lusaka Sister City Com., 1980. Served as sgt. WAC, 1943-46. Recipient Cert. of Merit Human Relations Commn., Los Angeles, 1982, Martin Luther King award So. Christian Leadership Conf. West, 1978, Annual Fin. Support award Am. U. John Fletcher Hurst Soc., Washington, 1981-82. Mem. AAUW (life mem., 1st v.p. Los Angeles br. 1978-80, Recognition of Service award Los Angeles chpt. 1979, Significant Contbn. to Edn. Found. award State div. 1984, pres. 1988-90), Am. Inst. Parliamentarians (adminstrv. lt. gov. region 7 1984-85, pres. El Camino Real chpt., Los Angeles, 1982-84, chmn. region ann. conf. 1985), Nat. Council of Negro Women (life, chmn. ann. festival com. 1976-77), Seeds of Sequoia (v.p. 1983—), Am. U. Alumni Assn. (Recognition award 1987). Democrat. Roman Catholic. Home: 3465 W 54 St Los Angeles CA 90043

CHAVOOSHIAN, MARGE, artist, educator; b. N.Y.C., Jan. 8, 1925; d. Harry Mesrob and Anna (Tashjian) Kurkjian; m. Barkev Budd Chavooshian, Aug. 11, 1946; children—J. Dean, Nora Ann. Student Art Students League, 1943, Reginald Marsh, N.Y.C., 1943, Mario Cooper, N.Y.C., 1977. Designer Needlework Arts Co., N.Y.C., 1943-44; illustrator John David Men's Store, N.Y.C., 1944-45; illustrator, layout artist Fawcett Publs., N.Y.C., 1945-47; designer, illustrator Pa. State U., University Park, 1947-49; art tchr. Trenton pub. schs., N.J., 1958-68, art cons. Title One Program, 1968-74; painting instr. Princeton Art Assn., N.J., 1974-77, Jewish Community Ctr., Ewing, N.J., 1974-85, Contemporary Club, Trenton, 1974-85, YMCA, YWCA, Trent Ctr., Trenton, 1974—; artist-at-large Alliance For Arts Edn., N.J., 1979-80; adj. asst. prof. art instr. Mercer County Coll., West Windsor, N.J., 1985—. One woman shows include Rider Coll., 1974, Jersey City Mus., 1980, N.J. State Mus., 1981, Trenton City Mus., 1984; exhibited in group shows at Douglas Coll., N.J., 1977, Bergen Mus., Paramus, N.J., 1980, 81, 82, Hunterdon Art Ctr., Clinton, N.J., 1982, Morris Mus., Morristown, N.J., 1984, Oakside Cultural Ctr., Bloomfield, N.J., 1985; represented in permanent collections N.J. State Mus., Jersey City Mus., Trenton City Mus., Morris Mus., Rider Coll., Art Mus. San Lazarre, Italy. Recipient numerous awards Union Coll., Mercer County Cultural and Heritage Commn., Phillips Mill, Am. Watercolor Soc.; named Woman of Month Woman's Newspaper of Princeton, 1984. N.J. State Council Arts fellow, 1979. Mem. Nat. Assn. Women Artists (two yr. nat. travel award 1985, recipient S. Winston Meml. award 1988), Am. Artists Profl. League (Am. Arts Council award 1973, Winsor Newton award 1980, others), Catherine Lorillard Wolfe Art Club (Bee Paper Co. award 1977, Anna Hyatt Huntington Bronze medal 1979), N.J. Watercolor Soc. (Newton Art Ctr. award 1972, Helen K. Bermel award 1984, Howard Savs. Bank award 1986-87), Painters and Sculptors Soc. (Medal of Honor, Digby Chandler medal, others), Garden State Watercolor Soc. (Triangle Art Ctr. award 1976, Grumbacher Silver medal 1981, Merit award 1982, Trust Co. award 1987), Midwest Watercolor Soc., Nat. Arts Club (John Elliott award 1988), Phila. Watercolor. Democrat. Mem. Apostolic Ch. Avocations: Piano; cooking; gardening. Home: 222 Morningside Dr Trenton NJ 08618

CHEATHAM, LOIS ANNE, small business owner; b. Sand Coolie, Mont., Oct. 4, 1933; d. Harl Lewis and Alice Emma (Johnson) Bruner; m. John Calvert Cheatham, Aug. 28, 1954; children: Robert Lee, Jacquelin Jean, Jace Louis. Diploma, St. Patrick's Sch. Nursing, 1954; cert., H&R Block, 1986; student, Missoula VoTech., 1985. RN, Mont. Nurse St. Patrick's Hosp., Missoula, 1954-59, 68-69, supr. nurse, 1970-73; farm owner Arlee, Mont., 1960-65; bookeeper Sch. Dist. #8, Arlee, 1966-67, Farmer's Union Oil Co., Arlee, 1966-67; farm owner, cattle buyer Arlee, 1977-81; with H&R Block, Ronan, Mont., 1982; owner H&R Block Franchise, Ronan, 1983—. Supr. Sunday sch., Arlee, Mont. Home: Box 204 Arlee MT 59821 Office: H&R Block PO Box 748 Hwy 93S Ronan MT 59864

CHEEVER, SUSAN LILEY, writer; b. N.Y.C., July 31, 1943; d. John and Mary Watson (Winternitz) C.; m. Robert Cowley, May, 1967 (div. 1975); m. Calvin Tomkins, II, Oct. 1, 1982; 1 child, Sarah Liley Cheever Tomkins. B.A., Brown U., 1965. Tchr., Colo. Rocky Mountain Sch., Colo., 1965-67, Scarborough Sch., N.Y., 1968-69; writer Westchester-Rockland Newspapers, N.Y., 1970-72; editor, writer Newsweek Mag., N.Y., 1974-78; free lance writer, N.Y., 1978—. Author: Looking for Work, 1980; A Handsome Man, 1981; The Cage, 1982; Home Before Dark, 1984, Doctors and Women, 1987. Guggenheim Found. fellow, 1984. Mem. Pen/Am. Ctr., Authors League. Democrat. Episcopalian.

CHEGER, JEAN GLIDDEN, sociology educator; b. Gladwin, Mich., Oct. 6, 1929; d. Harvey Knox and Marie (Szatkowski) Glidden; m. Michael Cheger, June 12, 1948; children: Cheryl Jeanne, Laura Cheger-Barnard, David Michael. BEd, Wayne State U., 1963, MEd, 1964, EdD, 1967. Tchr. Warren Woods (Mich.) Pub. Schs., 1963-65; prof. sociology Ky. So. Coll., Louisville, 1965-68; prof. sociology Delta Coll., Bay City, Mich., 1968-87, chair profl. devel., 1984-86. Author, editor Sex Regulation in Society, 1971, Pairing, 1973. Pres. Saginaw (Mich.) YMCA, 1980-83; organizer teleconf. Nat. Issues Forum, 1984-86. Mem. Am. Assn. Univ. Professors (pres. 1970s), Internat. Platform Assn., Mich. Sociol. Assn. (pres. 1970s), DAR (regent Saginaw 1987—), Order Crown Charlemagne, Nat. Soc. Colonial Dames XVIII Century, Daughters Founders and Patriots Am., Nat. Soc. Women Descendants, Ancient and Honorable Artillery Co., Am. Royal Descent, Phi Delta Kappa. Republican. Office: Delta Coll Univ Ctr Bay City MI 48710

CHELIUS, ANNE KIRBY, computer executive; b. N.Y.C., July 22, 1944; d. William Arthur and Agnes (Murphy) K.; m. Garrett Andrew Chelius; m. Garrett, Genevieve, Ginette, Geronimo, Geremy. BS, St. Joseph's Coll. for Women, 1965. Cert. data processor, N.Y.; cert. systems profl., N.Y. Tchr. Pub. System, N.Y.C., 1965-66, Gov. Clinton Sch., Poughkeepsie, N.Y., 1966-67, Dix Hills, N.Y., 1967-70; v.p. Software Enterprises Inc., Lloyd Harbor, N.Y., 1975—; pres. Seven C's Charter Corp., Lloyd Harbor, 1985—; charter mem. L.I. Venture Group. Mem. Data Process Mgmt. Assn. (pres., internat. dir.), L.I. Forum for Tech. (bd. advisors). Home and Office: 1 Dolphin's Rise Lloyd Harbor NY 11743

CHELL, BEVERLY C., lawyer; b. Phila., Aug. 12, 1942; d. Max M. and Cecelia (Portney) C.; m. Robert M. Chell, June 21, 1964. BA, U. Pa., 1964; JD, N.Y. Law Sch., 1967; LLM, NYU, 1973. Bar: N.Y. 1967. Assoc. Polur & Polur, N.Y.C., 1967-68, Thomas V. Kingham, Esq., N.Y.C., 1968-69; v.p., sec., asst. gen. counsel, dir. Athlone Industries, Inc., Parsippany, N.J., 1969-81; asst. v.p., asst. sec., assoc. gen. counsel Macmillan Inc., N.Y.C., 1981-85, v.p., sec., gen. counsel, 1985—. Mem. Assn. Bar City N.Y., Am. Soc. Corp. Secs. Home: 9 Marsh Rd Westport CT 06880 Office: Macmillan Inc 866 3d Ave New York NY 10022

CHELL, JACQUELINE ROSE, corporate secretary; b. Chgo., Aug. 5, 1941; d. Anthony and Mary (Monaco) Renda; m. Don L. Esbjornson, Sept. 3d 1960 (div. Mar. 1972); children: Deora, Cheryl, Donald. Student Oakton Community Coll., Des Plaines, Ill. Cert. profl. sec. Sec. law firm, Peoria, Ill., Winnetka, Ill.; sec. law dept. Sgt. Welch, Niles, Ill., sec. v.p.; sec. Acco Internat., Wheeling, Ill.; asst. sec. Acco World Corp., Northbrook, Ill., asst. corp. sec. Roman Catholic. Office: Acco World Corp 2215 Sanders Rd Northbrook IL 60065

CHELSTROM, MARILYN ANN, educational institution administrator; b. Mpls., Dec. 5; d. Arthur Rudolph and Signe (Johnson) C.; B.A., U. Minn., 1950; L.H.D., Oklahoma City U., 1981. Staff asst. Mpls. Citizens Com. Public Edn., 1950-57; coordinator, policies and procedures Lithium Corp. Am., Inc., Mpls., N.Y.C., 1957-62; exec. dir. The Robert A. Taft Inst. Govt., N.Y.C., 1962-77, exec. v.p., 1977-78, pres., 1978—. Editor: Teaching the Execitement of Politics in America, 1984. Active LWV, Mpls., 1950-60, N.Y.C., 1972—; charter mem. Citizens League Greater Mpls., 1952-60; del. White House Conf. on Edn., 1955; vice chmn. Minn. Women for Humphrey, 1954. Recipient Cert. of Recognition for Service to Mpls. Public Schs., Mpls. Citizens Com., 1957; named Town Topper, Mpls. Star, 1958. Mem. Am. Polit. Sci. Assn., Minn. Alumni Assn. (gov. N.Y. 1963—, pres. 1971-73; nat. dir. 1971-75), Lutheran (treas. councilman). Club: Minn. Alumni (Mpls.). Home: 155 E 38th St New York NY 10016 Office: The Robert A Taft Inst Govt 420 Lexington Ave New York NY 10017

CHEN, CONCORDIA CHAO, mathematician; b. Peiping, China; came to U.S., 1955, naturalized, 1969; d. Chun-fu and Kwie Hwa (Wong) Chao; B.A. in Bus. Adminstrn., Nat. Taiwan U., 1954; M.S. in Math., Marquette U., 1958; postgrad. Purdue U., 1958-60, M.I.T., 1961-62; m. Chin Chen, July 2, 1960; children—Marie Hui-mei, Albert Chao. Teaching asst. Purdue U., Lafayette, Ind., 1958-60; system analysis engr. electronic data processing div. Mpls.-Honeywell, Newton Highlands, Mass., 1960-63; mgmt. planning asst. Lederle Labs., Am. Cyanamid Co., Pearl River, N.Y., 1964, computer applications specialist, 1967, ops. analyst, 1967; staff programmer IBM, Sterling Forest, N.Y., 1968-73, adv. programmer Data Processing Mktg. Group, Poughkeepsie, 1973-80, mgr. systems programming and systems architecture, Princeton, N.J., 1980-82, sr. systems analyst, 1982-83, data processing mktg. cons., Beijing, 1983-88, Poughkeepsie, 1988—. Mem. ednl. council MIT. Mem. Am. Math. Soc., Soc. Indsl. and Applied Maths. Home: 12 Mountain Pass Rd Hopewell Junction NY 12533 Office: IBM Corp Internat Tech Support Ctr Dept H52/Bldg 930 PO Box 390 Poughkeepsie NY 12602

CHEN, DIANE TZE-SUN, physician; b. Chgo., Jan. 30, 1951; d. York Yueh and Irene Fei-Fei (Hu) C. BS in Chemistry, U. So. Calif., 1970; MD, NYU, 1974; MPH in Epidemiology, Columbia U., 1985. Internal medicine intern L.I. Jewish-Hillside Med. Ctr., New Hyde Park, N.Y., 1974-75; resident in neurology North Shore-Meml. Sloan-Kettering Cancer Ctr., N.Y.C., 1975-76; asst. dir. profl. services Hoffmann-LaRoche Inc., Nutley, N.J., 1976-83, dir. dept. med. epidemiology, 1983-85; adj. attending physician dept. neurology Meml. Sloan-Kettering Cancer Ctr., 1977-85; vice-dir. clin. research and head drug safety F. Hoffmann-La Roche & Co., Basel, Switzerland, 1985—. Mem. Am. Med. Women's Assn., Am. Acad. Neurology, Am. Pain Soc., Eastern Pain Assn., Internat. Assn. Study Pain, Sleep Research Soc. Office: 340 Kingsland St Nutley NJ 07110

CHENEY, LYNNE ANN, national cultural organization administrator, writer; b. Casper, Wyo., Aug. 14, 1941; d. Wayne and Edna (Lybyer) Vincent; m. Richard Bruce Cheney, Aug. 29, 1964; children: Elizabeth, Mary. BA, Colo. Coll., 1963; MA, U. Colo., 1964; PhD, U. Wis., 1970. Freelance writer 1970-83; lectr. George Washington U., Washington, 1972-77, U. Wyo., Casper, 1977-78; researcher, writer Md. Pub. Broadcasting, Owing Mills, 1982-83; sr. editor Washingtonian Mag., Washington, 1983-86; chmn. NEH, Washington, 1986—; commr. U.S. Constitution Bicentennial Commn., Washington, 1985—. Author: Executive Privilege, 1978, Sisters, 1981, Kings of the Hill, 1983; contbr. articles to periodicals including Smithsonian, Am. Heritage, Washingtonian mag. Republican. Methodist. Office: Nat Endowment Humanities 1100 Pennsylvania Ave NW Washington DC 20506

CHENG, ANNA, real estate investment executive; b. Taipei, Taiwan, Oct. 15, 1954; came to U.S., 1973; d. Nunsai and Aisun Cheng; m. Ralph Jeffrey Cowing, Dec. 15, 1984. B.A. in Econs., Whitman Coll., 1976; M.B.A., U. Santa Clara, 1981. Fin. analyst Frontier Mgmt. Corp., Menlo Park, Calif., 1977-79; real estate exec. The Fox Group, Foster City, Calif., 1980. Mem. Am. Mgmt. Assn., Fin. Mgmt. Assn., Am. Fin. Assn., Real Estate Securities and Syndication Inst., World Affairs Council, Center Democratic Instns., Asian Am. Theatre Co., San Francisco Mus. Modern Art, Smithsonian Instn., Signet Table, Mortar Bd. Contbr. articles to profl. publs. Office: 950 Tower Ln Foster City CA 94404

CHENG, VIRGINIA WAI, physician; b. Nanking, China, Jan. 1, 1944; d. Shu-Chuen and Min Fong (Liu) Cheng. B.A., Concordia Coll., 1965; B.S. in Medicine, U. N.D., 1967; M.D., Northwestern U., 1969. Intern Los Angeles County-U. So. Calif. Med. Center, Los Angeles, 1969-70, resident pediatrics, 1970-72, fellowship in pediatrics, adolescent medicine, 1972-73; mem. staff So. Calif. Permanente Group Medicine, Los Angeles, 1973—; assoc. prof. clin. pediatrics U. So. Calif. Med. Sch., Los Angeles, 1978-87, clin. prof. pediatrics, 1987—. Diplomate Am. Bd. Pediatrics. Fellow Am. Acad. Pediatrics; mem. Los Angeles Pediatrics Soc. Office: Kaiser West Los Angeles 6041 Cadillac Ave Los Angeles CA 90034

CHENHALLS, ANNE MARIE, nurse, educator; b. Detroit, May 26, 1929; d. Peter and Beatrice Mary (Elliston) McLeod; m. Horacio Chenhalls, 1953 (dec.); children—Mark, Anne Marie Chenhalls Delamater. Student Detroit Conservatory Music, 1946-47; B. Vocat. Edn., Calif. State U.-Los Angeles, 1967, B.S. in Nursing, 1968; M.A., Calif. State U.-Long Beach, 1985. R.N., Calif. Nurse, Grace Hosp., Detroit, 1951-52; pvt. duty nurse, Mexico City, 1953-54; nurse St. Francis Hosp., Lynwood, Calif., 1957-63; assoc. prof. nursing Compton Coll. (Calif.), 1964-72; health educator, sch. nurse Santa Ana Unified Sch. Dist. (Calif.), 1972-76, 79—; med. coordinator, internat. health cons. Agape Movement, San Bernardino, Calif., 1976-79; instr. community health, Uganda, 1982; med. evaluator Athletes in Action, 1979. Assoc. staff mem. Campus Crusade for Christ. Solo vocalist, Santa Ana, Orange, Seal Beach, Calif. U.S. govt. grantee, 1968. Mem. Calif. Sch. Nurses Assn., Nat. Educators Assn., Calif. Assn. Vocat. Educators, Internat. Platform Assn. Democrat. Home: 12092-69 Sylvan River Fountain Valley CA 92708 Office: Santa Ana Unified Sch Dist 1405 French St Santa Ana CA 92701

CHENNAULT, ANNA CHAN (MRS. CLAIRE LEE CHENNAULT), aviation executive, author, lecturer; b. Peking, China, June 23, 1925; came to U.S., 1948, naturalized, 1950; d. P.Y. and Isabel (Liao) Chan; m. Claire Lee Chennault, Dec. 21, 1947 (dec. July 1958); children: Claire Anna, Cynthia Louise. BA in Journalism, Lingnan U., Hong Kong, 1944; LittD, Chungang, Seoul, Korea, 1967; LLD (hon.), Lincoln U., 1970; HHD (hon.), Manahath Ednl. Center, 1970, St. Johns U., 1982, Am. U. of Caribbean, 1982; D Bus. Admin. (hon.), John Dewey U. Consortium, 1983. War corr. Central News Agy., 1944-48, spl. Washington corr., 1965—; with Civil Air Transp., Taipei, Taiwan, 1946-57, editor bull., 1946-57, pub. relations officer, 1947-57; chief Chinese Sect. Machine Translation Research, Georgetown U., 1958-63; broadcaster Voice of Am., 1963-66; U.S. corr. Hsin Shen Daily News, Washington, 1958—; v.p. internat. affairs Flying Tiger Line, Inc., Washington, 1968-76; pres. TAC Internat., 1976—; cons. various airlines and aerospace corps.; lectr., writer, fashion designer U.S. and Asia; bd. dirs. Sovran, D.C. Nat. Bank. Feature writer: Hsin Ming Daily News, Shanghai, 1944-49; Author: Chennault and the Flying Tigers: Way of a Fighter, 1963; best seller A Thousand Springs, 1962; Education of Anna, 1980; also numerous books in Chinese including Song of Yesterday, 1961, M.E.E, 1963, My Two Worlds, 1965, The Other Half, 1966, Letters from U.S.A, 1967, Journey Among Friends and Strangers, Chinese edit, 1978, China Times, Chinese-English Dictionaries. Mem. Pres.'s adv. com. arts John F. Kennedy Center Performing Arts, 1970—; Pres. Nixon's spl. rep. Philippine Aviation Week Celebration, 1973; mem. women's adv. com. on aviation to sec. transp.; v.p. Air and Space Bicentennial Organizing Com.; spl. asst. to chmn. Asian-Pacific council AmChams, mem. spl. com. transp. to sec. transp., 1972, chmn. com. for spl. transp. activities, 1972; mem. U.S. nat. com. for UNESCO, 1970—; mem. adv. council Am. Revolution Bicentennial Adminstrn., 1975-77, also mem. ethnic racial council; advisor Nat. League Families of Am. Prisoners and Missing in S.E. Asia; presdl. appointee Pres.'s Export Council, 1981, vice chmn., 1981-85; pres. Chinese Refugee Relief, Washington, 1962-70, Gen. Claire Chennault Found., 1960—; hon. chmn. Chinese-Am. Nat. Fedn., 1974—; committeewoman Washington Republican Party, 1960—; mem. Nat. Rep. Finance Com., 1969—; cons. heritage groups, nationalites div. Asian affairs Rep. Nat. Com., 1969—; chmn. Nat. Rep. Heritage Council, 1979, 87; bd. govs. Am. Acad. Achievement, Dallas; trustee Center Study Presidency, Library Presdl. Papers, 1970—, Helping Hand Found.; bd. visitors Civil Air Patrol; presdl. appointee Presdl. Scholars Commn., 1985—; bd. dirs. People to People Internat; founder Nat. Rep. Asian Assembly. Recipient Woman of Distinction award Tex. Tech. Coll., Lubbock, 1966; Freedom award Order Lafayette Washington, 1966; Freedom award Free-China Assn., Taipei, 1966; Golden Plate award as champion of democracy and freedom Am. Acad. Achievement, 1967; Lady of Mercy award, 1972; Republican of Yr. award D.C. Rep. Fedn., 1974; award of honor Chinese-Am. Citizens Alliance, 1972; Mother Gerard Phelan award, Marymount Coll., 1985, Ams. by Choice award, 1987, Press Woman's award Women of Achievement. Fellow Aerospace Med. Assn. (hon.); mem. Nat. Aero. Assn. (bd. dirs.), Nat. League Am. Pen Women, Writers Assn., Free China Writers Assn., 14th Air Force Assn. (chmn. awards com. 1969—), U.S. Air Force Wives Club, Flying Tiger Assn., U.S. C. of C. (dir. internat. policy com., council on trends and perspective), Am. Newspaper Women's Club Washington, Nat. Mil. Families Assn. (founder, chmn.), Theta Sigma Phi, others. Clubs: Overseas Press (N.Y.C.); Pisces, 1925 F Street, International, Capitol Hill, National Press, Aero, George Town, Army-Navy (Washington). Home: 2510 Virginia Ave NW Washington DC 20037 Office: TAC Internat 1511 K St NW Washington DC 20005

CHENOWETH, ROSE MARIE, librarian; b. Decatur, Ill., Jan. 22, 1953; d. Harold Everett and Jacqueline Marie (Rhodes) C. BS in Edn., Ill. State U., 1974; MLS, U. Ill., 1979. Librarian Mt. Zion (Ill.) Sch. System, 1974-78; adult services librarian Willard Library, Evansville, Ind., 1979-81; reference librarian River Bend Library System, Coal Valley, Ill., 1981-83; head of extension services Moline (Ill.) Pub. Library, 1983—. Sec. Citizens for Reproductive Choice, Quad Cities, Ill., La., 1982—; v.p, archivist Council on Community Services, Rock Island, 1983—; planning com. Literacy Council of Rock Island, Henry and Mercer Counties, Ill., 1984—; sec. 23d Ave Bus. Assn., Moline, 1985—. Mem. ALA, Illowa Library Assn., Ill. Library Assn. (pub. library sect., dir. at large 1982-84, chmn. awards com.), NOW (chair reproductive rights com. 1982-83)., Beta Phi Mu. Home: 830 15th St Moline IL 61265

CHER (CHERILYN SARKISIAN), singer, actress; b. El Centro, Calif., May 20, 1946; d. Gilbert and Georgia LaPiere; m. Sonny Bono, Oct. 27, 1964 (div.); 1 dau., Chastity; m. Gregg Allman, June 1975 (div.); 1 son, Elijah Blue. Student drama coach, Jeff Corey. Singer with husband as team, Sonny and Cher, 1964-74; star TV shows: Cher, 1975-76, The Sonny and Cher Show, 1976-77; concert appearances with husband, 1977, numerous recs., TV, concert and benefit appearances with Sonny Bono; TV appearances, ABC-TV, 1978, appearance with Sonny Bono in motion pictures, Good Times, 1966, Chastity, 1969; film appearances include Silkwood, 1983, Mask, 1985, The Witches of Eastwick, 1987, Suspect, 1987, Moonstruck (Golden Globe award 1988, Acad. award for best actress 1988), 1987; helped form rock band, Black Rose, 1979; recorded albums Black Rose, 1980, Cher, 1987. Office: care Bill Sammeth Orgn 9200 Sunset Blvd Los Angeles CA 90069 also: care Creative Artists Agy 1888 Century Park East Los Angeles CA 90067 *

CHERESKIN, VALERIE LEE, marketing professional; b. Chgo., Aug. 2, 1954; d. Samuel and Rosalie (Marks) C.; m. John William Hansen Jr., July 18, 1987. MusB, Eastern Ill. U., 1976. In sales Wurlitzer Piano and Organ, Westchester, Ill., 1976-77; office mgr. Carl Fischer, Inc., Chgo., 1977-78; regional tng. mgr. Motorola, Inc., Schaumburg, Ill., 1979-81, account mgr., 1981-83; sales exec. Motorola-Codex, Schaumburg, Ill., 1983-84; account exec. Computer Intelligence, La Jolla, Calif., 1984-87. Mem. Nat. Orgn. Women. Democrat. Club: San Diego (Calif.) Flute Guild. Home: 1364 Calle Christopher Encinitas CA 92024 Office: Chereskin Designs 7825 Fay Ave Suite 200 La Jolla CA 92037

CHERICHELLA, MARIA LOURDES TANGHAL, management relations specialist; b. Manila, Feb. 24, 1956; d. Augusto Villaseran and Maria Preciosa (Hernandez) Tanghal; m. Joseph Francis Cherichella, Aug. 17, 1986. BBA in Labor Mgmt. Relations, Pace U., 1984. Adminstr. asst. adminstrv. services dept. Exxon Corp., N.Y.C., 1978-80; personnel asst. Esso Mid. East div. Exxon Corp., N.Y.C., 1980-84, staffing analyst, 1984-86; client rep. Exxon Co. Internat., Florham Park, N.J., 1986-87; specialist internat. payroll Drexel Burnham Lambert, N.Y.C., 1987—. Mem. Nat. Assn. Female Execs. Home: 68 Woodward Ln Basking Ridge NJ 07920

CHERMAK, JANE FELINA, chemist; b. N.Y.C., Aug. 4, 1947; d. Austin Leonel and Irma P. (Katz) C.; m. Como Kit North, Dec. 15, 1983; children: Tyrus, Cyrus, Ky-ky. BS, L.I. U., 1970; DVM, U. Minn., 1986. Chemist N.Y.C. Dept. of Health, 1969-80, USDA, Chgo., 1980—. Mem. Am. Chem. Soc. Buddhist. Office: USDA @ (S Dearborn Chicago IL 60602

CHERNAK, CELESTE ARLETTE, utility executive; b. Redding, Calif., Apr. 19, 1947; d. Edwin Walter Squires and Rachel (Kinkead) Layton; m. Julius Jeep Chernak, Sept. 13, 1970, (div. 1980); children: Sean Matthew, Bret Allen. BA in Art, San Francisco State U., 1970; AA in Engring. Tech., Coll. Marin, 1980; MBA in Mgmt., Golden Gate U., 1988. Tchr. art San Rafael (Calif.) Recreation Dept., 1971-75; owner, photographer Julius Chernak Photography, Novato, Calif., 1970-76; draftsman Donald Foster Drafting, San Rafael, 1975-76; surveyor Parks Dept. Sate Calif., Inverness, 1976; electric draftsman Pacific Gas & Electric, San Rafael, 1976-78, electric engring. estimator, 1978-79; mktg. rep. Pacific Gas & Electric, Santa Rosa, 1980-85; valuation analyst Pacific Gas & Electric, San Francisco, 1985-86, budget analyst, 1986—. Dir. Mariner Green Townhomes Assn., treas. 1987—. Mem. AAUW, Pacific Coast Gas Assn. Democrat. Home: 114 Mariner Green Dr Corte Madera CA 94925

CHERNOFF, NANCY ROBIN, advertising company executive; b. New Haven, Oct. 9, 1953; d. Maxwell B. and Carol D. Chernoff. BA, Simmons Coll., 1975. Promotion and graphics asst. Houghton Mifflin Co., Boston, 1975-77; mktg. asst. Can. Dry Internat., N.Y.C., 1978-79, project mgr., 1979-80; asst. product mgr. Carter Products, Inc., 1980-81; product mgr. Boyle Midway, 1980-83; account exec. Darcy MacManus & Masius, 1983-85; sr. account exec. Geers Gross Advt., 1985-87; mgr. advt. accounts Fairchild Publs., 1987—. Recipient Effie award 1986. Mem. Am. Mgmt. Assn. Avocations: running, squash, photography, travel, reading. Home: 131 E 83rd St New York NY 10028

CHERNOW, ANN LEVY, artist, art educator; b. N.Y.C., Feb. 1, 1936; d. Edward P. and Mollie (Citrin) Levy; m. Philip Chenok, Aug. 11, 1957 (div. 1969); children: David Charles, Daniel Joshua; m. Burt Chernow, Dec. 11, 1970. MA, NYU, 1969. Instr. Mus. Modern Art, N.Y.C., 1966-71; assoc. prof., head Art Dept. Norwalk (Conn.) Community Coll., 1974—; guest lectr., instr. studio and art history Silvermine Sch. Arts, Silvermine Coll., 1968-80; vis. artist, lectr. Housatonic (Conn.) Community Coll., 1975-80; vis. artist CAP program Wesleyan U., 1979; coordinator Bicentennial Exhbn. Norwalk Community Coll., 1976. One-person shows include Aaron Berman Gallery, N.Y.C., 1979, Wesleyan U., Middleton, Conn., 1979, Beall/Lambremont Gallery, La., 1980, 81, Gallery Suzanne Maag, Zurich, Switzerland, 1980, Douglass Gallery, Rutgers, N.J., 1980. Foxhall Gallery, Washington, 1981, Farmington (Conn.) Valley Arts Ctr., 1982, Queens Coll., N.Y.C., 1982, Alex Rosenberg Gallery, N.Y.C., 1982, Mattatuck (Conn.) Mus., 1982, Schochet Gallery, R.I., 1983, Munson Gallery, Conn., 1984, 88, Snug Harbor Cultural Ctr., L.I., 1984, Stamford (Conn.) Mus., 1985, Conn. Fine Arts Mus., 1986, Katonah Gallery, N.Y., 1987, Fairfield U., Conn., 1988, Armstrong Gallery, N.Y.C., 1988; group shows include Alex Rosenberg Gallery, 1980, Mus. Contemporary Art, Sao Paulo, Brazil, 1980, Aldrich Mus., Ridgefield, Conn., 1981, Silvermine Guild, 1982, Print Club, Phila., 1983, Artists Choice Mus., Marisa Del Re Gallery, N.Y.C., 1983, Morris Mus. Morristown, N.J., 1984, John Slade Ely House, New Haven, 1985,

Munson Gallery, 1985, Stamford Mus., 1985-86, Katonah Gallery, 1986, Internat. Miniature Print Bienniale, New Canaan, 1987, Uptown Gallery, N.Y.C., others; pub. collections include Rose Art Mus. Brandeis U., Nat. Mus. Women in Arts, Washington, William Benton Mus. Art, Storrs, Conn., New Britain Mus. Am. Art, Conn., Neuberger Mus., Purchase, N.Y., Housatonic Mus. Art, Mattatauk Mus., Lehigh U. Art Collection, Pa., Utah Mus. Fine Arts, U. Ariz. Art Collection, Lyman Allyn Mus., Conn., Bruce Mus., Conn., Butler Inst. Am. Art, Ohio, Rutgers U., Hofstra U., others; reviewer art history and appreciation texts Prentice Hall, Harper & Row, others, 1984—; subject bibliographies, art mags., catalogs, jours. Named Conn. Woman of Decade in Arts UN Assn., 1987. Studio: 2 Gorham Ave Westport CT 06880 Office: Norwalk Community Coll 333 Wilson Ave Norwalk CT 06854

CHEROSKE, JANICE MCKEEVER, educator, realtor; b. Los Angeles, July 28, 1929; s. Louis C. and Lela E. (Lewis) Schildwachter; B.A., Occidental Coll., 1948; M.A., Calif. State U., Dominguez Hills, 1974; postgrad. U. So. Calif., 1975-76; m. Kirk LeRoy McKeever, July 2, 1948 (dec. 1977); children—Kevin Miles, Wendelyn; m. Robert Husek Cheroske, Mar. 20, 1982. Asst. prin. Wadsworth Year Round Elementary Sch., Los Angeles; adminstr. Highly Gifted Magnet Ctr., 1983-84; personnel commr. City of Huntington Beach, Calif., 1984—, local Coastal Commn., 1988— . instr. Calif. State U., Dominguez, 1980-83,Nat. U., Palm Springs, 1987—. Recipient Hon. Service award Avalon Council PTA, 1973; cert. reading specialist, Calif. Mem. Town Hall of Calif., World Affairs Council of Los Angeles, Kappa Kappa Iota. Office: Kennedy-Wilson Inc Realty 16561 Bolsa Chica Rd Huntington Beach CA 92649

CHERP, MARTHA HART, travel company executive; b. Tallahassee, Sept. 7, 1941; d. John Pafford Tomlinson; m. Guy Donald Cherp, Nov. 30, 1963; children: Amy, Macon, Ada, Guy II. BA, Peabody Coll., 1963. Tchr. Lincoln O.M. Sch., Grand Junction, Colo., 1963-67; owner Scott Anker's Jewelry, Grand Junction, Colo., 1977-80; owner, mgr. All Seasons Travel, Grand Junction, Colo., 1981—; tchr., owner, dir. All Seasons Travel Sch., Grand Junction, Colo., 1984—; v.p. Coors of Grand Junction, 1969—. Bd. dirs. Mesa Coll. Found., Grand Junction, 1972-82. Mem. Am. Soc. Travel Agts., Grand Junction C. of C. (bd. dirs. 1985—). Home: 448 Bookcliff Dr Grand Junction CO 81501 Office: All Seasons Travel 2424 Hwy 6 and 50 Mesa Mall Grand Junction CO 81505

CHERRY, GLORIA BARRY, lawyer; b. N.Y.C., May 5, 1935; d. Irving and Rita (Gold) Barry; m. Sheldon H. Cherry (div. May 1986); children: Sabrina, Dana, Pamela, Cara; m. Jules L. Lazar. AB, Barnard Coll., 1955; LLB, Columbia U., 1958. Bar: N.Y., N.J., U.S. Dist. Ct. N.J., N.Y. (so. and ea. dist.). Assoc. Barry & Katzman, N.Y.C., 1958-62, 75-78; instr. history Am. U. at Myrtle Beach AFB, S.C., 1962-64; staff atty. Prentice-Hall Pubs., Englewood Cliffs, N.J., 1964-67, Kwasha-Lipton Pubs., Englewood Cliffs, 1964-67; regional counsel OEO, N.Y.C., 1967-68; assoc. Shupack, Rosenfeld & Fishbein, N.Y.C., 1972-73; gen. counsel LWV of N.J., 1973-78; atty. Morrison & Morrison, Hackensack, N.J., 1978-86, Winne, Banta, Rizzi, Hetherington & Basralian, Hackensack, 1986—. V.p. Tenafly (N.J.) Bd. Edn., 1975-78, Tenafly Bd. Ethics, 1975-78. Office: Winne Banta Rizzi Hetherington & Basralian 25 E Salem Hackensack NJ 07602

CHERRY, MURIEL ELIZABETH, human resource specialist; b. N.Y.C., July 17, 1947; d. Edward Murell and Inez Mae (Bloomfield) Britt; m. Arnold Cherry, Apr. 27, 1965 (div. 1972); 1 child, Arnold Jr. B, CUNY, 1976. Cert. secondary educator. Exec. dir. Soul & Latin Theater, Inc., N.Y.C., 1970-72; human rights specialist N.Y.C. Commn. on Human Rights, 1976-78; asst. personnel dir. Urban Acad. for Mgmt., N.Y.C., 1978-79; specialist affirmative action N.Y. State Met. Trans. Authority, N.Y.C., 1980-81, asst. mgr. personnel, 1981-83, dir. recruitment and employee relations, 1984—; cons. Harmony, Opportunity, Mobility, Elevation and Equality, Inc., Bronx, 1980—, Harlem Communications, N.Y.C., 1986—; owner, designer The African Closet, Bklyn., 1987—. Author short story, 1979. Lectr. N.Y.C. women's prisons, 1985—. Baptist.

CHERRY, RONA BEATRICE, magazine editor, writer; b. N.Y.C., Apr. 26, 1948; d. Manuel M. and Sylvia Zelda C. B.A., Am. U., 1968; M.S., Columbia U., 1971. Reporter No. Va. Sun, Arlington, 1968; reporter Akron Beacon Jour., Ohio, 1969-70, Wall St. Jour., N.Y.C., 1971-72; assoc. editor Newsweek mag., N.Y.C., 1972-74; reporter N.Y. Times, N.Y.C., 1976-77; exec. editor Glamour mag., N.Y.C., 1977—; lectr. New Sch. Social Research, 1978; lectr. Sch. Continuing Edn., NYU, 1980, faculty Summer Pub. Inst., 1980, 83; faculty Reader's Digest writers' workshops; mem. research com. Internat. Women's Media Conf., 1986; mem. Nat. Mag. Awards screening com., 1980-82. Co-author: The World of American Business, 1977; contbg. author: Woman in the Year 2000; contbr. articles to publs. including N.Y. Times Sunday mag., Parade, Ms. mag., Christian Sci. Monitor; contbr. book revs. to Sunday N.Y. Times. Nat. communications council March of Dimes, 1981—. Recipient Media award Nat. Assn. Recycling Industries, 1973, Bus. Journalism award U. Mo., 1977, Am. Coll. Radiology, 1986, Writer's award Am. Soc. Anesthesiologists, 1983, Maggie award Planned Parenthood Fedn. Am., 1985, Media award Am. Coll. Radiology, 1986. Mem. Am. Soc. Mag. Editors, Women in Communications, Newswomen's Club N.Y. (v.p. 1985-87). Home: 140 Riverside Dr #8P New York NY 10024 Office: Glamour Mag 350 Madison Ave New York NY 10017

CHERRY, SANDRA WILSON, lawyer; b. Little Rock, Dec. 31, 1941; d. Berlin Alexander and Renna Glen (Barnes) Wilson; m. John Sandefur Cherry, Jr., Sept. 24, 1976; 1 dau., Jane Wilson. BA, U. Ark., 1962; JD, U. Ark. Sch. Law, 1975. Bar: Ark., 1975, U.S. Dist. Ct. (ea. dist.) Ark., 1979, U.S. Supreme Ct. 1979, U.S. Ct. Appeals (8th cir.) 1979. Tchr. social studies Little Rock Sch. Dist., 1966-70; chmn. social studies dept. Horace Mann Jr. High Sch., Little Rock, 1970-72; asst. U.S. atty. Dept. Justice, Little Rock, 1975-81, 83—; commr. Ark. Pub. Service Commn., Little Rock, 1981-83; adj. instr. U. Ark. at Little Rock Sch. Law, Little Rock, 1980. Contbr. case note to Ark. Law Rev., 1975. Pres. bd. dirs. Gaines House, Inc.; pres. U. Ark. at Little Rock Law Sch. Assn., 1980-81, bd. dirs., 1982. Mem. ABA, Ark. Bar Assn. (Ho. of Del. 1984-86, sec., treas. 1986—), Pulaski County Bar Assn., Ark. Women Lawyers Assn., Jr. League Little Rock (bd. dirs. 1974), Pi Beta Phi. Republican. Presbyterian. Home: 4100 S Lookout St Little Rock AR 72205 Office: US Atty's Office PO Box 1229 Little Rock AR 72203

CHERRYH, C. J., writer; b. St. Louis, Sept. 1, 1942; d. Basil L. and Lois Ruth (Van Deventer) C. B.A. in Latin, U. Okla., 1964; M.A. in Classics, Johns Hopkins U., 1965. Cert. tchr., Okla. Tchr. Oklahoma City Pub. Schs., 1965-77; lectr. in field. Author: novel Gate of Ivrel, 1976, Well of Shiuan, 1978, Brothers of Earth, 1976, Hunter of Worlds, 1976, The Faded Sun: Kutath, 1979, Sunfall, 1981, Star Crusade, 1980, Downbelow Station, 1981 (Hugo award for best novel 1982), The Pride of Chanur, 1982, Merchanter's Luck, 1982, Port Eternity, 1982, The Dreamstone, 1983, The Tree of Swords and Jewels, 1983, Cuckoo's Egg, 1985, Angel with the Sword, 1985; contbr. short stories to numerous mags. Woodrow Wilson fellow, 1965; recipient Hugo award for best short story, 1979. Mem. Sc. Fiction Writers Assn. (sec.), L-5 Soc. (bd. advisors), Phi Beta Kappa. Methodist.

CHERUNDOLO, MARY ANNE FRANCES, nurse; b. Taylor, Pa., May 24, 1944; d. Greno Paul and Nancy Madeline (Capalongo) Fumanti; m. Robert Francis Cherundolo, June 29, 1964; children—Jean Marie, Robert Francis, Joy Anne. Nursing diploma St. Joseph's Hosp., Balt., 1971. Cert. gerontol. nurse Am. Nurses Assn., 1984. Med.-surg. ICU nurse St. Joseph's Hosp., Balt., 1969-74; sch. health instr. Shrine Sacred Heart, Balt., 1972-74; supr. Anne Lynne Manor, Louisville, 1974, asst. dir. nursing, 1974-76; neighborhood dir. Cin. council Girl Scouts U.S.A., Aurora, Ind., 1976-78; office nurse V.J. Goel, Lawrenceberg, Ind., 1978; cardiac testing staff nurse J.C. Carter Co., Norwalk, Conn., 1979-80; staff nurse Courtland Gardens, Stamford, Conn., 1980, head nurse, 1981, asst. dir. nursing edn., 1981-83, dir. nursing, 1983-87; dir. nursing devel. PersonaCare, Stamford, 1987—; cons. Homestead, Stamford, 1981-83. Pres., Home Sch. Assn., Shrine Sacred Heart, Balt., 1973; chmn. com. Central Catholic Home Sch., Norwalk, 1982-83; area chmn. Heart Fund Assn., Norwalk, 1981. Mem. Infection Control Nurses Fairfield County, Conn. Orgn. Gerontol. Nurse Educators, Dirs. of Nurse's Council Conn. Health Care Assn., Conn. Assn. Healthcare Facilities (chmn. bd. dirs.). Roman Catholic. Club: West Norwalk Community Guild (chmn. 1978-81). Home: 175 1/2 W Norwalk Rd Norwalk CT 06850

CHESEN, CATHERINE SUE, investigative consumer reporting executive; b. Lancaster, Pa., Aug. 26, 1953; d. Irwin Somberg and Doris Marion (Schimmel) C.; m. Allen Mark Morris, June 18, 1972 (div. Mar. 1977). BS, U. Nebr., 1975; BA in Speech Pathology, MA, U. Kans., Kansas City, 1978. Speech pathologist Joan Davis Sch. Spl. Edn., Kansas City, Mo., 1975-78, Rainbow Mental Health Ctr., Kansas City, 1978-79, Clinicare Home Health Care, Kansas City, 1978-79; prin. Inter-Link of Am., Leawood, Kans., 1980-86; pres. Chesen Communications Ctr., Overland Park, Kans., 1986—. Mem. Am. Bus. Women's Assn., Kansas City Multi-Family Apt. Assn., NOW. Democrat. Jewish. Office: Chesen Communications Ctr Inc 9290 Bond #114 Overland Park KS 66212

CHESLER, VICTORIA AIMEE, publishing executive, writer; b. N.Y.C., July 8, 1957; d. Bertram Arthur and Naomi (Aronson) C.; m. Matthew Robert Kovner, July 24, 1983; 1 child, Melissa Mae Chesler Kovner. BA cum laude, Conn. Coll., 1979. Editorial asst. Biomedical Info. Corp., N.Y.C., 1979-80; editor Co-op West, N.Y.C., 1980-81; founder, pres. Manhattan Cooperator Pubs., Inc., N.Y.C., 1981, mng. editor Manhattan Cooperator, 1981-82, exec. editor, 1982—; exec. editor The Apt. Buyer's Guide, N.Y.C., 1985—; free-lance writer, 1980—. Contbr. articles to Harper's Bazaar, Ski Mag., SAAVY, Redbook mag. Mem. NOW, Real Estate Bd. N.Y., Nat. Assn. Female Execs. Avocations: skiing; sailing; tennis; travel; drawing. Office: Manhattan Cooperator Publs Inc 23 Leonard St 3d Floor New York NY 10013

CHESNEY, SUSAN TALMADGE, management consultant; b. N.Y.C., Aug. 12, 1943; d. Morton and Tillie (Talmadge) Chesney; m. Donald Lewis Freitas, Sept. 17, 1967 (div. May 1976); m. Robert Martin Rosenblatt, Apr. 9, 1980. AB, U. Calif., Berkeley, 1967. Placement interviewer U. Calif., Berkeley, 1972-74, program coordinator, 1974-79; personnel adminstr. Hewlett-Packard Co., Santa Rosa, Calif., 1982-84; pres. Mgmt. Resources, Santa Rosa, 1984—; cons. Kensington Electronics Group, Healdsburg, Calif., 1984-85, Behavioral Medicine Assocs., Santa Rosa, 1985-86, M.C.A.I., Santa Rosa, 1986-87, Bowdon Designs, Santa Rosa, 1987—, Bass & Ingram, Santa Rosa, 1988—. Mem. Sonoma County Arts Council, Nat. Assn. Female Execs. Avocations: Asian cooking, gardening, music.

CHESNUT, CAROL FITTING, economist; b. Pecos, Tex., June 17, 1937; d. Ralph Ulf and Carol (Lowe) Fitting; m. Dwayne A. Chesnut, Dec. 27, 1955; children: Carol Marie, Michelle, Mark Steven. BA magna cum laude, U. Colo., 1971. Research asst. U. Colo., 1972; head quality controller Mathematica, Inc., Denver, 1973-74; cons. Mincome Man., Winnipeg, Can., 1974; cons. economist Energy Cons. Assocs. Inc., Denver, 1974-79; exec. v.p. tng. ECA Intercomp, 1980-81; gen. ptnr. Chestnut Consortium, Las Vegas, 1981—; sec., bd. dirs. Critical Resources, Inc., 1981-83. Rep. Lakehurst Civic Assn., 1968; staff aide Senator Gary Hart, 1978; Dem. precinct capt., 1982—. Mem. Am. Mgmt. Assn., Soc. Petroleum Engrs., Am. Nuclear Soc., Am. Geophys. Union, Assn. Women Geoscientists (treas. Denver 1983-85), ACLU, NOW, Colo. Assn. Commerce and Industry, Phi Beta Kappa, Phi Chi Theta. Unitarian. Clubs: City (Denver), Century. Office: 3416 Biscaya Circle Las Vegas NV 89121

CHESS, SONIA MARY, English language educator; b. Ashton, Lancashire, Eng., Apr. 14, 1930; came to U.S., 1951, naturalized, 1963; d. Arthur and Sarah Ann (Hulme) Bradburn; m. Joseph Campbell Chess, Nov. 17, 1950; children: Denise Ann, Tanya Marie, Michele Elise, Luana Jo. BA in English Lit., U. Hawaii, Honolulu, 1970, MA, 1973. Instr. English U. Hawaii/Honolulu Community Coll., 1971—, chmn. English dept., 1980-84; tchr. cons. Hawaii Writing Project, Honolulu, 1983—. Regent, Sandwich Isle chpt. Daus. of Brit. Empire, Honolulu, 1978-80. Recipient Excellence in Teaching medal, U. Hawaii Bd. Regents, 1983; Dickens fellow, Nat. Endowment for Humanities, 1985, Hawaii Writing Project fellow, U. Hawaii Found., 1983. Mem. Hawaii Council Tchrs. English, Assn. Women in Jr. Colls., Humanities Assn. Republican. Episcopalian. Office: Honolulu Community Coll 874 Dillingham Blvd Honolulu HI 96734

CHESSHIR, BUENA MAY, accountant; b. South Charleston, Ohio, Apr. 7, 1928; d. Joseph Wiley and Laura Belle (Bussard) C. BS, Wittenberg U., 1964; MBA, Case Western Res. U., 1971; postgrad., Naval War Coll., 1979-80. Bookkeeper Crowell Collier Pub. Co., Springfield, Ohio, 1947-50; clk., typist Wright Patterson Air Force Base, Dayton, Ohio, 1950-51; voucher examiner Wright Patterson Air Force Base, Dayton, 1951-62; acct. Lewis Research Ctr. NASA, Cleve., 1964-65, Def. Logistics Agy., Cleve., 1965-72, Def. Fuel Supply Ctr., Alexandria, Va., 1972-73; acct. Def. Logistics Agy., Alexandria, 1973-77, acct., group leader, 1978—. Mem. Va. Fed. Bus. and Prof. Women (bd. dirs. 1980—, st. pres. 1984-85, chmn. st. found. 1985-87), Nat. Fed. Bus. and Profl. Women (bd. dirs. 1984-85), Old Dominion Bus. and Profl. Women (pres. 1977-78) (named Woman Yr. 1979), Am. Assn. U. Women, Am. Assn. Mil. Comptrollers. Republican. Presbyterian. Office: Def Logistics Agy Cameron Sta (DLA-CFF) Alexandria VA 22304

CHESTER, STEPHANIE ANN, lawyer, banker; b. Mpls., Oct. 8, 1951; d. Alden Runge and Nina Lavina (Hanson) C.; divorced. B.A. magna cum laude, Augustana Coll., 1973; J.D., U. S.D., 1977; postgrad. C.F.S.C., ABA Nat. Grad. Trust Sch., Evanston, Ill., 1984. Bar: S.D. 1977, Minn. 1979. Asst. counselor Minnehaha County Juvenile Ct. Ctr., Sioux Falls, S.D., 1972-73; child care worker Project Threshold, Sioux Falls, 1973-74; legal intern Davenport, Evans, Hurwitz & Smith, Sioux Falls, 1976; law clk. S.D. Supreme Ct., Pierre, 1977-78; originations dept. buyer Dain Bosworth, Inc., Mpls., 1978-79; v.p., trust officer 1st Bank of S.D., N.A., Sioux Falls, 1979-86; v.p., First Trust Co., Inc., St. Paul, 1986—; bd. dirs., mem. program com. Sioux Falls Estate Planning Council, 1983-85; Projects and research editor S.D. Law Rev., 1977; author law rev. comment. Mem. fund raising coms. S.D. Symphony, Sioux Falls Community Playhouse, Augustana Coll., 1982-83; mem. S.D. div. Nat. Women's Polit. Caucus; mem. events com. Augustana Coll. Fellows, Sioux Falls, 1984; bd. dirs. YWCA, Sioux Falls, 1984, Sioux Falls Arena/Coliseum, 1985; mem. Sioux Falls Jr. Service League, 1984. Augustana Coll. scholar, 1969-73; Augustana Coll. Bd. Regents scholar, 1973. Mem. S.D. Bar Assn., Minn. Bar Assn., ABA, 2d S.D. Jud. Circuit Bar Assn., Nat. Assn. Bank Women (state conv. com. 1983-85), Phi Delta Phi, Chi Epsilon. Republican. Lutheran. Clubs: Network, Portia (Sioux Falls). Office: First Trust Co Inc 180 E 5th St Saint Paul MN 55102

CHESTNUT, DONNA L. SHELNUT, photography laboratory executive; b. Birmingham, Ala., Sept. 16, 1952; d. J. O'Neal and Helen (Morrison) Shelnut; m. Hiram C. Stone, Jr., July 1972 (div. 1978); m. Peter John Chestnut, Jan. 26, 1980; children—Lisa R., Patricia L. Student Gadsden State Jr. Coll., Ala., 1971-72. Clk., dept. asst. mgr. Belk Hudson Co., Gadsden, 1970-71; bookkeeper, mgr. Waters Plumbing Co., Attalla, Ala., 1971-72; office mgr. Clean Rental Service, Gadsden, 1972-78, Photocraft Inc., Birmingham, Ala., 1978-79, Hallmark Constrn. Co., Birmingham, 1979-80; owner, sec.-treas. Chestnut Colour, Inc., Atlanta, 1980—; owner Chestnut Imaging Ctr., 1988—. Mem. Assn. Profl. Color Labs. Republican. Baptist. Avocations: reading; running; sewing. Home: 4399 S Landing Dr Marietta GA 30066 Office: Chestnut Colour Inc 1436 Chattahoochee Ave Atlanta GA 30318

CHEUNG, EVA YEE-WAH, banker; b. Hong Kong, Aug. 21, 1958; came to U.S., 1984; d. Tak-Kee and Kau-Ying (Lau) C. BA in Econs., Wilfrid Laurier U., Waterloo, Ont., 1981; B of Computer Sci, U. Windsor (Ont.), 1985. Comml. loan trainee United Orient Bank, N.Y.C., 1984-85, comml. loan mgr., 1985-86, loan ops. supr., 1986-87, credit analyst, 1987, comml. loan officer, 1987—. Mem. Ling Liang Ch. Office: United Orient Bank 10 Chatham Sq New York NY 10038

CHEVERS, MARGO, management consultant; b. Attleboro, Mass., Aug. 7, 1944; d. John Maurice and Merle Irene (Quinham) Hansel; divorced; children: Michelle Jeanne Turgeon, Timothy Worrall Waterman. Student, Nyack Coll., 1963, Dean Jr. Coll., 1981-86. Real estate broker Christian and Schromm Real Estate, Mansfield, Mass., 1978-79; dir. sales Sheraton Mansfield Inn and Conv. Ctr., Mansfield, 1980-85; dir. sales and mktg. Sheraton Milford (Mass.) Hotel, 1985-86; owner, pres. N.E. Leadership Enterprise, North Attleboro, Mass., 1986—; tchr. North East Cen. Coll., Westboro, 1987. Mem. Women's Success Network (program chmn. 1986—), Am. Soc. Tng. Devel., Nat. Assn. Female Execs. Club: Toastmasters (sgt. at arms 1987). Office: NE Leadership Enterprise 500 E Washington St North Attleboro MA 02760

CHEVERS, WILDA ANITA YARDE (MRS. KENNETH CHEVERS), educator; b. N.Y.C.,; d. Wilsey Ivan and Herbertlee (Perry) Yarde; B.A., Hunter Coll., 1947; M.S.W., Columbia, 1959; Ph.D., N.Y.U., 1981; m. Kenneth Chevers, May 14, 1950; 1 dau., Pamela Anita. Probation officer, 1947-55; supr. probation officer, 1955-65; br. chief Office Probation for Cts. N.Y.C., 1965-72, asst. dir. probation, 1972-77, dep. commr. dept. probation, 1978-86; prof. pub. adminstrn. John Jay Coll., 1986—; conf. faculty mem. Nat. Council Juvenile and Family Ct. Judges; mem. faculty N.Y.C. Tech. Coll., Nat. Coll. Juvenile Justice; mem. adv. com. Family Ct., First Dept. Sec. Susan E. Wagner Adv. Bd., 1966-70. Sec., bd. dirs. Allen Community Day Care Center, 1971-75; bd. dirs. Allen Sr. Citizens Housing, Allen Christian Sch., Queensboro Soc. for Prevention Cruelty to Children. Named to Hunter Coll. Hall of Fame, 1983. Mem. ABA (assoc. criminal justice com.), N.Y. Bar Assn. (juvenile justice com.), Nat. Council on Crime and Delinquency, Nat. Assn. Social Workers, Acad. Cert. Social Workers. Middle Atlantic States Conf. Correction, Alumni Assn. Columbia Sch. Social Work, NAACP, Am. Soc. Pub. Adminstrn. (dir.), Counseliers, Delta Sigma Theta. Club: Hansel and Gretel (pres. 1967-69) (Queens, N.Y.). Home: 105-62 132d St Richmond Hill New York NY 11419

CHEVIS, FELICIA KAY, mechanical engineer; b. Houston, Nov. 3, 1961; d. Ervin Joseph and Rosie Marie (Pharms) C. BS, Prairie View (Tex.) A&M U., 1985. Project mgr. Naval Intelligence Support Ctr., Washington, 1985—; mem. Fed. Women's program asst. EEO, jr. adv. bd. Naval Intelligence Support Ctr., Washington, 1986—, 1987. Tutor counselor Maple Springs Bapt. Ch., Capitol Heights, Md., 1986—. Mem. ASME, Soc. Women Engrs., Nat. Assn. Female Execs., Beta Kappa Chi, Pi Mu Epsilon. Home: 6200 Westchester Park Dr #1110 College Park MD 20740

CHEW, PAT KENT, lawyer; b. El Paso, Tex., Sept. 30, 1950; d. Richard Chuck Lum and Lillian Gay (Ng) C.; m. Robert E. Kelley. A.B., Stanford U., 1972; M.Ed. in Psychology, U. Tex.-Austin, 1974, J.D., 1982. Bar: Ill. 1982, Calif. 1985. Placement dir. U. Tex., Austin, 1975-80; cons. Career Assos., Austin, 1979-80; assoc. Baker & McKenzie, Chgo., 1982-84, San Francisco, 1984-85; adj. prof. corp. law Hastings Coll. Law, U. Calif., 1984-85; asst. prof. corp. and internat. trade U. Pitts. Sch. Law, 1985—. Author: MBA, 1982; contbr. articles to publs. Recipient Contemporary Author award Gale Pub., 1982. Mem. ABA (council mem. gen. practice sect. 1983—, chmn. gen. practice sect. com. 1982-84, liaison standing com. on career devel. 1984), Phi Kappa Phi, Beta Gamma Sigma. Office: U Pitts Sch Law 3900 Forbes Ave Pittsburgh PA 15260

CHEW-FREIDENBERG, DEANNA EILEEN, hospital administrator, statistical consultant; b. Oakland, Calif., June 13, 1952; d. George Jun and Ida Chew; m. David Howard Freidenberg, Apr. 30, 1978; 1 child, Aaron. AA, Chabot Jr. Coll., Hayward, Calif., 1973; BA, BS, Calif. State U., Hayward, 1976; MA, U. Calif., Berkeley, 1977, PhD, 1982. Adminstrv. intern Peralta Community Coll. Dist., Oakland, 1977-79; research asst., acting dean Sch. Edn. U. Calif., Berkeley, 1978-79, asst. adminstrv. analyst Office of Student Research, 1979-82, evaluation asst. Tchr. Corps. Program, 1980-81, statis. cons. MESA Program, 1981-82; head orthopedic research Orthopedic Dept., Children's Hosp., Seattle, 1983-86; dep. dir. Data Coordinating Ctr., VA Hosp., Seattle, 1986—; cons. in field. Contbr. articles to profl. jours. Grantee Wash. Assn. Retarded Citizens, 1984, Biomed. Research Children's Hosp., 1984, No. Life Ins. Co., 1986. Mem. Am. Ednl. Research Assn., Am. Statis. Assn. Office: Data Coordinating Ctr VA & Med Ctr Seattle WA 98108

CHI, LOTTA C. J. LI, computer science executive; b. N.Y.C., Dec. 5, 1930; d. Chen-pien and Han Chih (Tang) Li; m. Michael Chi, June 15, 1957; children: Loretta Elizabeth, Maxwell Michael. BS, Heidelberg Coll., Tiffin, Ohio, 1953; MS, Rutgers U., 1955. Virologist, NIH, 1956-63; dir. Chen-pien Li Meml., 1985—; pres. Chi Assocs., Inc., Arlington, Va., 1974—. Mem. N.Y. Acad. Scis., Am. Soc. Microbiologists, Nat. Assn. Women Bus. Owners, Am. Soc. Profl. and Exec. Women, Nat. Fedn. Bus. and Profl. Women's Club, Sigma Xi. Home: PO Box 769 Arlington VA 22216 Office: 2045 N 15th St Arlington VA 22201

CHIACU, KAREN M., marketing executive; b. Woonsocket, R.I., Oct. 23, 1954; d. Nicholas Vasil and Victoria (Babiana) C. BS cum laude, Boston Coll., 1976; MBA, Clark U., 1983. Mfg. mgmt. trainee Data Gen. Corp., Southboro, Mass., 1976-77; mfg. systems trainer Data Gen. Corp., Westboro, Mass., 1977-81; account mgr. Computer Sci. Corp., Newton, Mass., 1981-82; internat. application specialist G.E. Mims Systems, Burlington, Mass., 1982-84; mfg. cons. Creative Output, Milford, Conn., 1984-87; mktg. mgr. Cadre Techs., Providence, 1987—. Eastern Orthodox. Home: 217 Hope St #5 Bristol RI 02809

CHIAPPERINI, PATRICIA BIGNOLI, real estate appraiser, consultant; b. N.Y.C., Jan. 16, 1946; d. Gennaro and Giovanna (Resburgo) Bignoli; m. Joseph M. Chiapperini, Dec. 14, 1968. BS in Acctg. and Econs., St. John's U., 1968; postgrad., U. Ala., 1968, Rutgers U., 1980, Am. Inst. Real Estate Appraisers, 1983. Staff acct. Cleary, During & Co., N.Y.C., 1967-69; chief acct. Montgomery Bapt. Hosp. (Ala.), 1969-70; internal auditor Scottex Corp., N.Y.C., 1970-73; office mgr. Mid-Jersey Realty, East Brunswick, N.J., 1973-79; self-employed real estate appraiser, North Brunswick, N.J., 1979—; guest lect. Middlesex County Coll., 1979—; adj. prof. Jersey City State Coll. Chmn. Arts and Cultural Com., Milltown, N.J., 1979-83; active Am. Legion Aux., Milltown, 1973—. Recipient John Marshall award St. John's U., 1968. Mem. Nat. Assn. Ind. Fee Appraisers, Middlesex County Bd. Realtors, N.J. State Bd. Realtors, Cen. Jersey Ind. Fee Appraisers (treas. 1982-83, v.p. 1984), Am. Soc. Notaries, Monmouth County Bd. Realtors. Roman Catholic. Office: 735 Georges Rd North Brunswick NJ 08902

CHIAVARIO, NANCY ANNE, community relations executive; b. Centralia, Ill., Aug. 17, 1947; d. Victor Jr. and Alma Maria (Arsenault) C. Asst. mgr. rent supplement B.C. Housing Mgmt. Commn., Vancouver, 1975-81, adminstrv. asst., 1981-84, mgr. tenants and ops. service, 1985—, adminstrv. asst., 1986-87; commr., vice chmn. Vancouver Park Bd., 1986—. Chmn. B.C. Recreation and Parks Assn. Vols., 1986-88. Mem. Inst. Housing Mgmt. (cert. adminstr. 1983, cert. finance 1985), West End Commn. Ctr. Assn. (pres. 1985-86), Mt. Pleasant Commn. Ctr. Assn. (pres. 1981-83). Democrat. Home: 507-1945 Barclay St, Vancouver, BC Canada V6G 1L2 Office: Vancouver Bd Parks and Recreation, 2099 Beach Ave, Vancouver, BC Canada V6G 1Z4

CHICAGO, JUDY, artist; b. Chgo., July 20, 1939; d. Arthur M. and May (Levenson) Cohen. B.A., U. Calif. at Los Angeles, 1962, M.A., 1964. Co-founder Feminist Studio Workshop, Los Angeles, 1973, Through the Flower Corp., 1977. Author: Through the Flower: My Struggle as a Woman Artist, 1975, The Dinner Party: A Symbol of Our Heritage, 1979, Embroidering Our Heritage: The Dinner Party Needlework, 1980, The Birth Project, 1985; one-woman exhbns. include, Pasadena (Calif.) Mus. Art, 1969, Jack Glenn Gallery, Corona del Mar, Calif., 1972, JPL Fine Arts, London, 1975, Quay Ceramics, San Francisco, 1976, San Francisco Mus. Modern Art, 1979, Bklyn. Mus., 1980, Parco Galleries, Japan, 1980, Fine Arts Gallery, Irvine, Calif., 1981, Musee d'Art Contemporain, Montreal, 1982, ACA Galleries, N.Y.C., 1984, 85, 86; group exhbns. include Jewish Mus., N.Y.C., 1966, 67, Whitney Mus., 1972, Winnipeg Art Gallery, 1975. Address: PO Box 834 Benicia CA 94510

CHICOREL, MARIETTA S., publishing executive; b. Vienna, Austria; came to U.S., 1939, naturalized, 1945; B.A., Wayne State U., 1952; M.A., U. Mich., 1960. Chief editor Ulrich's Internat. Periodicals Directory, R. R. Bowker Co., N.Y.C., 1966-68; project mgr. Info. Scis., Inc., Macmillan Pub. Co., Inc., N.Y.C., 1968-69; pres. Chicorel Library Pub. Corp., N.Y.C., 1969-79; prof. library sci. Queens Coll., 1971-72; pres. Am. Library Pub. Co., Inc., N.Y.C., 1979—; exec. council Library Resources and Tech. Services. Bd.

govs. Booksellers League of N.Y., 1968-79. Mem. ALA (councilor), Am Soc. Info. Scientists. Office: American Library Pub Co Inc 275 Central Park W New York NY 10024

CHIDSEY, LINDA, hotel executive; b. Medina, Ohio, July 9, 1956; d. Lyman A. and Alice Leona (Packard) C. Student, Ohio State U., 1974, 78. With So. Host Hotels-Ramada Inn, 1979—; property controller So. Host Hotels-Ramada Inn, Reynoldsburg, Ohio, 1985; renovation controller So. Host Hotels-Quality Inn, Jacksonville, Fla., 1985-86; regional controller corp. office So. Host Hotels-Ramada Inn, Atlanta, 1986—. Mem. Kappa Delta. Republican. Mem. United Ch. of Christ. Home: 6401 Veterans Blvd Metairie LA 70003 Office: So Host Hotels 3260 Pointe Pkwy Suite 100 Norcross GA 30092

CHIERCHIA, MADELINE CARMELLA, management consulting company executive; b. Bklyn., Jan. 30, 1943; d. Lawrence Cataldo Carrozzo and Victoria Angel (Torchio) Carrozzo Petrisic; m. Jerry Chierchia, Oct. 3, 1959 (div. July 1975); children—Gertrude Chierchia Kraljic, Geraldine Rosalie Gorga. Student parochial schs. Bklyn. Personnel mgr. Argyle Personnel Agy., N.Y.C., 1976-77; clk. typist Atlantic Mut. Ins. Co., N.Y.C., 1977-78; sec. ARC, N.Y.C., 1978-82; mgr. D.F. King & Co. Inc. N.Y.C., 1982—. Mem. Proxy Div. Securities Industry Assn., Nat. Assn. Female Execs., Reorganization Securities Industry Assn., Am. Soc. for Profl. and Exec. Women. Democrat. Roman Catholic. Avocations: bowling; chess; reading; old movies. Office: DF King & Co 77 Water St New York NY 10005

CHILCUTT, RHONDA LYNN, fuel company analyst; b. Plainview, Tex., Aug. 24, 1948; d. Leonard Ray Ward and Evelyn Ann (Duree) Mersiovsky; m. Jimmy Harold Chilcutt, Apr. 11, 1965 (div. Nov. 1979); children: John Aden, Marc Allen. Cert. in petroleum land tech., Houston Community Coll., 1983. Analyst regulatory affairs natural gas and gas products dept. Conoco Inc., Houston. Mem. Natural Gas Men Assn. Houston, Phi Theta Kappa. Baptist. Club: Mercedes Benz of N. Am. Office: Conoco Inc PO Box 2197 Houston TX 77252

CHILD, JOY CHALLENDER, accountant; b. Newton, Kans., Apr. 23, 1952; d. Willard Alton and Daisy Dolores (Horton) Challender; m. William Chapin Child, June 30, 1979; children: Christopher, Carolyn. BBA summa cum laude, Wichita State U., 1978; MBA with honors, Clark U., 1984. CPA, Mass. Budget analyst JI Case, Wichita, 1978-79; bank auditor Shawmut Worcester County Bank, Worcester, Mass., 1979-82; staff acct. Marvin I. Lainer & Co., Worcester, 1982-85, assoc. mgr., 1985-86, ptnr., 1986—. V.p. Putnam Bapt. Women's Fellowship, 1987—; asst. treas. Putnam Bapt. Ch., 196—. Mem. Am. Inst. CPA's, Mass. Soc. CPA's, Am. Soc. Women Accts. (treas. 1985-86). Republican. Office: Marvin I Lainer & Co 390 Main St Worcester MA 01608

CHILD, JULIA MCWILLIAMS (MRS. PAUL CHILD), author, television personality, cooking expert; b. Pasadena, Calif., Aug. 15, 1912; d. John and Julia Carolyn (Weston) McWilliams; m. Paul Child, Sept. 1, 1945. BA, Smith Coll., 1934. With advt. dept. W.&J. Sloane, N.Y.C., 1939-40; with OSS, Washington, Ceylon, China, 1941-45. Hostess TV program The French Chef, WGBH-TV, Boston, from 1962, Julia Child & Co, 1978-79, Julia Child & More Co., 1980, Dinner at Julia's, PBS, 1983; occasional cooking segment Good Morning America, ABC-TV, 1980—; author: (with Simone Beck and Louisette Bertholle) Mastering the Art of French Cooking, 1961, The French Chef Cookbook, 1968, Mastering the Art of French Cooking, Vol. II, 1970, (with Simone Beck) From Julia Child's Kitchen, 1975, Julia Child & Company, 1978, Julia Child & More Company, 1979, Mastering the Art of French Cooking I & II, 1983; columnist McCall's mag., 1975-82, Parade mag., 1982-86. Recipient Peabody award, 1964, Emmy award, 1966, French Ordre de Merite Agricole, 1967, Ordre National de Merite, 1974. Office: Sta WGBH 125 Western Ave Boston MA 02134 also: care Knopf Inc 201 E 50th St New York NY 10022

CHILD, MARGARET SMILLIE, government official; b. Yonkers, N.Y., July 14, 1929; d. Harold Baxter and Marie (Maloney) Smillie; B.A., Mount Holyoke Coll., 1951; M.A., Cornell U., 1952; Ph.D., U. Md., 1972; m. James Robert Child, Dec. 30, 1955; children—Peter Truesdale, Elizabeth Baxter, Anne Margaret. Intelligence officer on Indonesia, CIA, Washington, 1952-61; editor, Monthly Indonesian Press Survey, Joint Publs. Research Service, Dept. Commerce, Washington, 1961-64; teaching asst. U. Md., College Park, 1964-68, instr. history, 1971-74; asst. prof. Am. U., Washington, 1973-75; asst. dir. div. research programs Nat. Endowment for the Humanities, Washington, 1974-82; asst. dir., chief research services Smithsonian Instn. Libraries, Washington, 1982—; cons. nat. paper preservation program Council on Library Resources, 1984-85. Office: Smithsonian Instn Libraries Washington DC 20560

CHILDERS, NEIDA GENEIEVE, nurse; b. Chgo., Dec. 18, 1940; d. Louis Phillip and Phyllis Grace (Tutt) Bebo; student St. Bernard Coll., 1972-73; A.S., John C. Calhoun Jr. Coll., 1975; m. Bobby Childers, Feb. 28, 1959; children—Susan Ann, Bobby Ray, Betty Lynn. With Ill. Bell Telephone, Chgo., 1956-57, Western Electric, Chgo., 1965-66; patient care asst. Huntsville (Ala.) Hosp., 1974-75; staff nurse Pineview (Ala.) Hosp., 1975-78; dir. nursing Flint Nursing Home, Flint City, Ala., 1978-80; supr. Med. Park Convalescent Center, Decatur, Ala., 1980-85; staff nurse Pkwy. Med. Ctr., Decatur, 1985-86, Falkville Nursing Home, Ala., 1986—. Mem. Am. Nurses Assn., Ala. Nurses Assn., Am. Heart Assn. Democrat. Baptist. Home: 600 Whispering Hills Circle Hartselle AL 35640 Office: 1306 14 Ave SE Decatur AL 35601

CHILDRESS, PHYLLIS ANN, construction executive; b. Fort Wayne, Ind., Feb. 28, 1937; d. Paschal J. and Pietrina M. (Ceccanese) Pallone; m. Kelly W. Childress, Aug. 24, 1973; children: Patricia, William, Jeffrey. B.S. in Commerce, Internat. Coll., 1955; postgrad. Pima Community Coll., 1978-80. Cert. constrn. mgr. Sec. to v.p. trust dept. Lincoln Nat. Bank, Ft. Wayne, Ind., 1955-57; sec. to pres. adminstrn. dept. Internat. Coll., Ft. Wayne, 1957-60; dir., sec. Lightning Homes, Inc., Homebuilders and Developers, Ft. Wayne, 1960-63; sec. to v.p., fin. dept., office mgr. fleet maintenance dept. N.Am. Van Lines, Inc., Ft. Wayne, 1963-71; asst. mktg. dir. ITT Electro-Optical Products, Ft. Wayne, 1972-76; asst. v.p. Empire West Builders, Inc., Tucson, 1977-80; staff constrn. mgmt. Akins Co., Tucson, 1981-82; constrn. mgr. Archtl. Div., City of Tucson, 1982-85; pres. Construction Techniques, Inc., Tucson, 1985—. Block grants advisor Tucson Community Devel. Commn., 1983—. Recipient Appreciation Cert. Nat. Assn. Women Constrn., 1978; named Sec. of Yr. Tawasi chpt. Nat. Secs. Assn., 1967; recipient plaque for outstanding service, 1977. Mem. Cholla Bus. and Profl. Women (past chpt. pres., Woman of Yr. 1986), Nat. Assn. Women Constrn. (past pres.). Democrat. Baptist. Contbr. articles to various publs. Home and Office: 2833 N Laurel Ave Tucson AZ 85712

CHILDS, ANNETTE GERTH, marketing executive; b. Chgo., Mar. 26, 1957; d. Donald Rogers and Beverly Jean (Hollman) Gerth; m. Robin Adair Childs, Mar. 24, 1979. AB in English, U. Calif., Davis, 1979; postgrad., Calif. State U., Fresno, 1986—. Copywriter Office Pub. Affairs U. Calif., Davis, 1978-79; sales assoc. Century 21 Tilley Realty, Ithaca, N.Y., 1980-82; tech. writer Grad. Sch. Bus. Calif. State U., Fresno, 1982-83; tech. and mktg. copywriter Sierra On-Line, Oakhurst, Calif., 1983-85; mgr. mktg. communications Sierra On-Line, Oakhurst, 1985-86, customer service mgr., 1986-87, consumer mktg. mgr., 1987-88; dir. ops. Cinemaware, Thousand Oaks, Calif., 1988; v.p. mktg. Mastertronic, Costa Mesa, Calif., 1988—; speaker spring meeting Software Pubs. Assn., Berkeley, Calif., 1987. Mem. Am. Mktg. Assn., Am. Mgmt. Assn., Nat. Assn. Female Execs. Democrat. Episcopalian. Office: Mastertronic Internat Inc 711 W 17th St #G9 Costa Mesa CA 92627

CHILDS, CATCHI, artist; b. Phila., Aug. 27, 1920; m. Mel Fowler, May 9, 1981 (dec. Sept. 1987); children: Charles E. Willis III, Diane Neuse, Heather Sargent. Pvt. studies with, Leon Kroll, Paul Wood and Hans Hoffman, N.Y.C., Angelo Savelli, Italy. Art instr. Manhasset, N.Y., 1965-67; artist in residence Friends Acad., Locust Valley, N.Y., 1984-85. Work includes illustrations for Internat. Sculpture Symposium book. Recipient Grumbacker awards Guild Hall Mus., First Prize Ligua Duncan Gallery, Riverside Mus., Internat. Platform Assn. Art Exhibit 1973, 76; recipient Grand Prix award Op. Democracy, 1974, grantee Dr. Maury Leibovitz Art awards Program, 1986. Mem. Nat. Assn. Women Artists (pres. 1981-83, Medal fo Honor 1966-73, First Prize 1973), N.Y. Soc. Women Artists (pres. 1985-87), Artists Equity of N.Y. (bd. dirs.), Audobon Artists. Home: 2 Grist Mill Lane Manhasset NY 11030

CHILDS, ERIN THERESE, psychotherapist; b. Redlands, Calif., Apr. 2, 1958; d. C. Russell and Maryann (Carpenter) C. B.A. cum laude, Loyola Marymount U., Los Angeles, 1979, M.A. magna cum laude, 1980; postgrad. Calif. Grad. Inst., 1982—. Lic. marriage, family and child therapist, Calif. Youth counselor II, Chino Youth Services (Calif.), 1979-81; counselor chem. dependency Behavioral Health Services, Gardena, Calif., 1981-83; pvt. practice psychotherapy, West Los Angeles, Calif., 1982—; psychotherapist, part-time cons. Thomas Aquinas Psychotherapy Clinic, Encino, Calif., 1982-84; clin. dir. Emergency Crisis Counseling, West Los Angeles, 1983; unit supr., dir. driving under the influence program Southbay unit. Behavioral Health Services, Gardena, Calif., 1984-86; treatment coordinator New Beginnings, Century City Hosp., Los Angeles, 1986-87, staff psychotherapist, 1987—; instr. community services Pierce Jr. Coll., Woodland Hills, Calif., 1983, Santa Monica City Coll. (Calif.), 1984, West Los Angeles Community Coll., Culver City, Calif., 1984. Mem. Calif. Womens' Commn. on Alcoholism. Mem. Calif. Assn. Marriage and Family Therapists, ACLU, Psychologists for Social Responsibility, Psi Chi, Alpha Sigma Nu. Democrat. Roman Catholic. Office: 2080 Century Park East Suite 1405 Los Angeles CA 90067

CHILDS, JULIE, lawyer; b. Atlanta, Oct. 5, 1950; d. Otis Lee Jr. and Eloise (Wilson) C. BA, U. Ga., 1971, JD magna cum laude, 1978. Bar: Ga. 1978, U.S. Dist. Ct. (no. dist.) Ga. 1978, U.S. Ct. Appeals (5th and llth cirs.) 1978. With McLain & Merritt, P.C., Atlanta, 1986—. State chmn. Ga. Jr. Leagues, 1985-86; bd. dirs. Dekalb Jr. League, Dekalb County, Ga., 1982-88, community v.p. 1986-87; treas., bd. dirs. Women's Resource Ctr., DeKalb County, Inc.; Decatur First Meth. Council on Ministries (chmn. 1988). Mem. Ga. State Bar Assn. (young lawyers sect.), Atlanta Bar Assn., Order of the Coif, De Kalb County C. of C. (adv. bd. adopt-a-sch. program 1982—), Leadership DeKalb. Democrat. Office: McLain & Merritt PC 1250 Tower Pl Atlanta GA 30026

CHILDS, MARJORIE M., lawyer; b. N.Y.C., July 13, 1918; d. Charles W. and Eva M. (Tarrant) C. Student Hunter Coll., 1942-46; BA in Econs., U. Calif., Berkeley, 1948; JD, U. San Francisco, 1956; LLD (hon.), Iowa Wesleyan Coll., 1973. Bar: Calif. 1957, U.S. Supreme Ct. 1969. With Office of Regional Counsel, U.S. Navy, Ft. Mason, Calif., 1957-60; asst. county counsel Humboldt County, Calif., 1960-62; sole practice, San Francisco, 1962-64, 79—; referee, commr. Juvenile dept. Superior Ct., San Francisco, 1964-79. Pres. Diamond Heights Community Assn., 1983-84. Recipient James A. Harlan award Iowa Wesleyan Coll., 1969. Fellow Am. Bar Found.; mem. ABA, Internat. Bar Assn., Lawyers Club San Francisco, Queen's Bench (pres. 1967), Bar Assn. San Francisco, Internat. Fedn. Women Lawyers, Nat. Assn. Women Lawyers . Democrat. Episcopalian. Club: Metropolitan (San Francisco). Contbr. articles to profl. jours. Home: 64 Turquoise Way San Francisco CA 94131 Office: 301 Junipero Serra Blvd #208 San Francisco CA 94127

CHILDS, SHIRLE MOONE, educational administrator; b. N.Y.C., Aug. 2, 1936; d. Harold McDaniel and Bessie Mary (Batts) Moone; m. William Childs, Sept. 5, 1971; children by previous marriage: Duane Kelby Milner, David Kent Milner. BS, U. Hartford, 1968, MS, 1970; PhD, U. Conn., 1978. Tchr., Hartford (Conn.) Public Schs., 1968-71, vice prin., acting prin. Mark Twain Elem. Sch., 1973-77, early childhood edn. specialist, 1978-84; adminstrv. asst. for instruction Teaneck (N.J.) Pub. Schs., 1984—; lectr., adj. prof., instr. Conn. Coll. for Women, Eastern Conn. State Coll., U. Hartford. Pres. bd. dirs. Women's League Day Care; trustee Hartford Conservatory; mem. Windsor Democratic Club. Rockefeller Found. fellow, 1977-78; Kettering Found. fellow, 1976-85. Mem. Nat. Assn. Edn. Young Children, Am. Assn. Sch. Adminstrs., Assn. Supervision and Curriculum Devel., Hartford Assn. Edn. Young Children, Conn. Assn. Suprs./Instrs. in Spl. Edn., Urban League, NAACP, Nat. Council Negro Women, Delta Sigma Theta (nat. sec. 1979-83), Phi Delta Kappa, Pi Lambda Theta. Methodist. Lodge: Order Eastern Star. Avocations: Chinese cooking, needlepoint. Home: 26 Regency Dr Windsor CT 06095 Office: 1 Merrison St Teaneck NJ 07666

CHILSON, NANCY LEE, educator; b. Harrisburg, Pa., July 29, 1944; d. William James and Virginia (Glidewell) C. BA, San Diego U., 1968; postgrad., UCLA, 1969-72, Pepperdine U., 1969-73. Cert. tchr. Calif. Tchr. Los Angeles Unified Sch. Dist., 1968—. Author: National Teachers Catalog of Creative Program Ideas, 1986. Grantee Los Angeles Ednl. Ptnrship. 1986, State of Calif. 1985, Marine Sci. Los Angeles Ptnrship. 1986. Mem. Los Angeles Community Action Network, Actors and Others Animals, Delta Kappa Gamma. Republican. Office: Taper Ave Elem Sch 1824 Taper Ave San Pedro CA 90731

CHILTON, ALICE PLEASANCE HUNTER (MRS. ST. JOHN POINDEXTER CHILTON), former state ofcl., vocat. counselor; b. Boyce, La., Apr. 16, 1911; d. Albert Eugene and Maggie (Texada) Hunter; B.A., La. Coll., 1930; M.S., La. State U., 1934, Ph.D., 1982, Guidance Counselor certificate, 1954; m. St. John Poindexter Chilton, Mar. 2, 1935. Tchr. secondary sch., Glenmora, La., 1931-35; with La. Div. Employment Security and USES, Baton Rouge, 1937-74, employment interviewer and supr., 1937-43, personnel officer, 1943-46, ops. analyst, 1946-55, supr. counseling and tech. services, 1955-74. Vice pres., dir. LaPlace Enterprises, Inc., Belle Pointe Enterprises, Inc. Mem. curriculum study com. East Baton Rouge, Parish Sch. Bd., 1968; rec. sec. Quota Internat., Baton Rouge, 1961-62, 2d v.p., 1963-64. Bd. dirs. YWCO. Recipient certificate of merit La. Acad. Sci., 1960. Mem. Internat. Assn. Personnel in Employment Security, Nat. Trust Historic Preservation, La. Geneal. and Hist. Soc. (pres. 1957), La. Landmarks Soc., Found. for Hist. La., Kent Plantation House, Inc. (sec.1979-81), Preservation Resource Ctr., La. Preservation Alliance (dir. 1984-86), Hist. Assn. of Cen. La. (bd. dirs. 1980-86), Phi Kappa Phi. Clubs: Campus La. State U. (Faculty Wives). Methodist. Address: 431 Belgard Bend Boyce LA 71409

CHILTON, JUDITH ANN, manufacturers representative; b. Columbia, Mo., Oct. 14, 1938; d. Otis Joseph and Lorraine (Mayol) Buchanan; m. Louis P. Hetlage, Sept. 8, 1973 (div. 1977); m. 2d Howard G. Chilton, Jr., Feb. 22, 1983. B.S. in Edn. and Speech Pathology, U. Mo., 1960; postgrad. Fla. Atlantic U., 1972. Speech pathologist Kern County Sch. Dist., Bakersfield, Calif., 1964-65; office adminstr., asst. Richard Karlson D.D.S., Pompano Beach, Fla., 1967-68; speech pathologist, area chairperson Broward County Sch. Dist., Ft. Lauderdale, Fla., 1968-73; Realtor, Century 21, Richardson, Tex., 1978; v.p. ops. Fain Sales Co., Dallas, 1978-84, pres., chief exec. officer, 1984—, also dir.; dir., v.p. ops. Med. Specifics, Inc., Dallas, 1983—. Active Northwood Republican Women, Dallas, 1980. Mem. Am. Speech, Lang. and Hearing Assn. (clin. cert.), Tex. Assn. Realtors. Roman Catholic. Home: 5304 Bent Tree Dr Dallas TX 75248 Office: Fain Sales Co 3306 Wiley Post Rd Suite 106 Carrollton TX 75006

CHILTON, MARY-DELL MATCHETT, chemical company executive; b. Indpls., Feb. 2, 1939; d. William Elliot and Mary Dell (Hayes) Matchett; m. William Scott Chilton, July 9, 1966; children—Andrew Scott, Mark Hayes. B.S. in Chemistry, U. Ill., 1960, Ph.D. in Chemistry, 1967; Dr. honoris causa, U. Louvain, Belgium, 1983. Research asst. prof. U. Wash., Seattle, 1972-77, research assoc. prof., 1977-79; assoc. prof. Washington U., St. Louis, 1979-83; exec. dir. agrl. biotech CIBA-Geigy Corp., Research Triangle Park, N.C., 1983—; adj. prof. genetics N.C. State U., Raleigh, 1983—; adj. prof. biology Washington U., 1983—. Mem. editorial bd. Bio/Tech., Jour. Molecular and Applied Genetics, Plant Molecular Biology; mem. editorial bd. proceedings of the Nat. Acad. of Scis.; contbr. articles to profl. jours. Recipient of Rank Prize for Nutrition, 1987. Mem Nat. Acad. Sci. Office: CIBA-Geigy Biotech Facility PO Box 12257 Research Triangle Park NC 27709

CHIN, CECILIA HUI-HSIN, art librarian; b. Tientsin, China; came to U.S., 1961; d. Yu-lin and Ti-yu (Fan) C. B.A., Nat. Taiwan U., Taipei, 1961; M.S.L.S., U. Ill., 1963. Cataloger, reference librarian Roosevelt U., Chgo., 1963; reference librarian, indexer Ryerson & Burnham Libraries, Art Inst. Chgo., 1963-70, head reference dept. indexer,, 1970-75; acting dir. libraries Art Inst. Chgo., 1976-77, assoc. librarian, head reference dept., 1975-82; chief librarian Nat. Mus. Am. Art and Nat. Portrait Gallery, Smithsonian Inst., Washington, 1982—. Compiler: The Art Institute of Chicago Index to Art Periodicals, 1975. Recipient award Nat. Portrait Gallery, Smithsonian Instn., 1984. Mem. ALA, Spl. Libraries Assn., Art Libraries Soc., Coll. Art Assn., Washington Conservation Guild. Office: Nat Mus Am Art & Nat Portrait Gallery Smithsonian Instn Washington DC 20560

CHIN, CINDY LAI, real estate accountant; b. Kowloon, Hong Kong, Dec. 2, 1957; d. Sau Kuen and Koon On C. BS in Acctg., CUNY, 1980; postgrad., Real Estate Inst., 1987—. Real estate acct. Milford Mgmt., Inc., N.Y.C., 1980-82; staff acct. Occidental Petroleum Corp., N.Y.C., 1983-85; client acct. Richard Ellis, Inc., N.Y.C., 1985—; cons. C&M Joint Venture, N.Y.C., 1985-86. Mem. China Inst., N.Y.C., 1986. Mem. Nat. Assn. Female Execs. Home: 85-06 Parsons Blvd Jamaica NY 11432 Office: Richard Ellis Inc 527 Madison Ave New York NY 10022

CHIN, JANET SAU-YING, data processing executive, consultant; b. Hong Kong, July 27, 1949; came to U.S., 1959; d. Arthur Quock-Ming and Jenny (Loo) C. BS in Math, U. Ill., Chgo., 1970; MS in Computer Sci., U. Ill., Urbana, 1972. System programmer Lawrence Livermore (Calif.) Lab., 1972-79; sect. mgr. Tymshare Inc., Cupertino, Calif., 1979-83, Fortune Systems, Redwood City, Calif., 1983-85; div. mgr. Impell Corp, Berkeley, Calif., 1985; pres. Chin Assocs., Oakland, Calif., 1985—; Vice-chmn. Am. Nat. Standards Inst. X3H3, N.Y.C., 1979-82, internat. rep. X3H3, 1982—. Author tech. papers to profl. publs. Mem. Assn. Computing Machinery, Nat. Computer Graphics Assn., World Computer Graphics Assn., Eurographics Assn., Sigma Xi.

CHIN, MATILDE VALLADOLID, controller, accountant; b. Iloilo, Philippines, Jan. 26, 1941; came to U.S., 1971, naturalized, 1982; d. Pablo Chin and Dulzura Valladolid. BS in Commerce, U. San Agustin, Iloilo, 1960; postgrad., NYU, 1972-76. Adminstrv. asst. A.B. Martinez Constrn., Manila, 1961-64; mgr. import div. Spark Radio Elec. Supply Pioneer Ceramics, Inc., Manila, 1964-67; exec. asst. Frank J. Elizalde, Manila, 1967-68; bookkeeper accounts br. Dept. Mcpl. Affairs, Toronto, Ont., Can., 1968-70; auditor Bur. Taxation, Toronto, 1970-71; various acctg. positions N.Y.C., 1971-84; controller Salpeter Paganucci Internat. Inc., N.Y.C., 1985—. Vol. pledge drive Pub. Broadcasting Service, 1985—; broadcast vol. In Touch Networks, Inc., 1988—. Mem. Nat. Assn. Female Execs. Roman Catholic. Club: Legion of Mary (sec. 1972-79). Home: 153 Freeman St Brooklyn NY 11222

CHIN, SUE S. (SUCHIN), artist, photographer, community affairs activist; b. San Francisco; d. William W. and Soo-Up (Swebe) Chin; grad. Calif. Coll. Art, Mpls. Art Inst., (scholar) Schaeffer Design Ctr.; student Yasuo Kuniyoshi, Louis Hamon, Rico LeBrun. Photojournalist, All Together Now show, 1973, East-West News, Third World Newscasting, 1975-78, KNBC Sunday Show, Los Angeles, 1975, 76, Live on 4, 1981, Bay Area Scene, 1981; graphics printer, exhbns. include Kaiser Ctr., Zellerbach Plaza, Chinese Culture Ctr. Galleries, Capricorn Asunder Art Commn. Gallery (all San Francisco), Newspace Galleries, New Coll. of Calif., Los Angeles County Mus. Art, Peace Plaza Japan Ctr., Calif. Mus. Sci. and Industry, Lucien Labaudt Gallery, Salon de Medici, Madrid, Salon Renacimento, Madrid, Sacramento State Fair, AFL-CIO Labor Studies Ctr., Washington, Asian Women Artists (1st prize for conceptual painting, 1st prize photography), 1978; represented in permanent collections Los Angeles County Fedn. Labor, Calif. Mus. Sci. and Industry, AFL-CIO Labor Studies Ctr., Australian Trades Council, Hazeland and Co., also pvt. collections. Del. nat., state convs. Nat. Women's Polit. Caucus, 1977-83, San Francisco chpt. affirmative action chairperson, 1978-82, nat. conv. del., 1978-81, Calif. del., 1976-81. Recipient Honorarium AFL-CIO Labor Studies Ctr., Washington, 1975-76; award Centro Studi Ricerche delle Nazioni, Italy, 1985; bd. advisors Psycho Neurology Found. Bicentennial award Los Angeles County Mus. Art, 1976, 77, 78. Mem. Asian Women Artists (founding v.p., award 1978-79, 1st award in photography of Orient 1978-79), Calif. Chinese Artists (sec.-treas. 1978-81), Japanese Am. Art Council (chairperson 1978-84, dir.), San Francisco Women Artists, San Francisco Graphics Guild, Pacific/Asian Women Coalition Bay Area, Chinatown Council Performing and Visual Arts. Chmn., Full Moon Products; pres., dir. Aumni Oracle Inc. Featured in Calif. Living Mag., 1981. Address: PO Box 1415 San Francisco CA 94101

CHIN-DAVIS, DONNA LEE, communications company executive; b. Oakland, Calif., Jan. 19, 1960; d. Doy and Jean Lin (Yip) Chin; m. Glenn George Davis, Aug. 1, 1982; 1 child, Gina Rose. BA in Broadcast Communication Arts, San Francisco State U. Receptionist, clk. Stas. KNBR, KYUU-FM, San Francisco, 1978-79; programming asst. Sta. KGO-TV, San Francisco, 1979-81; assoc. producer Glenn G. Davis Prodns., Los Angeles, 1981-85; exec. adminstr. Peer-So. Music, Los Angeles, 1983-85; co-owner Davis Communications, Richmond, Calif. Democrat.

CHINITZ, JODY ANNE KOLB, data processing officer; b. Bay City, Mich., July 8, 1953; d. Adam H. and Evelyn I. (Sylvester) Kolb; m. William A. Chinitz, Feb. 11, 1979. Student Saginaw Valley State Coll., 1972, Bklyn. Coll., 1973-76; B.A. in Russian Lang. and Lit. summa cum laude, CUNY., 1980. With personnel dept. N.Y. Life Ins. Co., N.Y.C., 1972-77, computer programmer, 1977-80; computer systems cons. Soroban Data Systems, Inc., N.Y.C., 1980-82; project leader Midlantic Nat. Bank, West Orange, N.J., 1982—. Home: 31 Norwood Ave Upper Montclair NJ 07043 Office: 95 Old Short Hills Rd West Orange NJ 07052

CHINN, GLORIA SHIZUKO, infosystems manager, banker, mathematics educator; b. Honolulu, Sept. 10, 1947; m. Donald Chinn, Mar. 22, 1975; children: Nathan, Brandon. B in Math. Edn. with high honors, U. Hawaii, 1969, M in Math. Edn., 1971. Cert. systems profl. Data processing profl. Bank Am., San Francisco, 1972-82; asst. v.p. data processing div. Bank Hawaii, Honolulu, 1982—; lectr. math. Kapiolani Community Coll., Honolulu, 1986—; mem. Data Processing adv. com. Mem. Assn. Systems Mgmt., Phi Kappa Phi, Alpha Lambda Delta. Democrat. Office: Bank Hawaii Dept #222 PO Box 2900 Honolulu HI 96846

CHINN, MAMIE MAY, state agency administrator; b. Oakland, Calif., Aug. 20, 1951; d. Bing T. and Georgia S. (Ong) C. BS in Bus., U. Nev., 1974. Loan processor First Fed. Savs. and Loan, Reno, 1974-75, loan processor supr., 1975-76, sr. loan counselor, 1977-78; jr. loan officer First Fed. Savs. and Loan, Carson City, Nev., 1976-77; loan officer State of Nev. Housing Div., Carson City, 1978-79, loan adminstr., 1979-83, dep. adminstr., 1983—; mem. media relations, ethics com. Dept. Commerce, Carson City, 1987—, exec. com. Housing and Devel. Fin. Mem. Nat. Assn. Female Execs. Clubs: Capitol City (Carson City) (sec. 1984—), Women's Bowling Assn. (bd. dirs. 1983-84), Nat. 600. Office: State of Nev Housing Div 1050 E William Suite 435 Carson City NV 89701

CHIPOURAS, SUSAN MASSINA, construction executive; b. Flushing, N.Y., July 25, 1956; d. Vincent M. and Henrietta C. (Reiber) Massina; m. Peter C. Chipouras, Aug. 18, 1979; children: Anessa, Alexis, Ariana. BCE, Manhattan Coll., 1978. Project mgr. HM Hughes Co., Inc., N.Y.C., 1978-82, v.p., 1982—. Sec. Com. for Protection of Old Brookville (N.Y.) Property Owners, 1986—. Mem. ASCE (assoc.), Nat. Assn. Female Execs., Women's Internat. Alliance, Internat. Assn. Women in Real Estate. Republican. Roman Catholic. Home: Meadow Ridge Ln Old Brookville NY 11545 Office: HM Hughes Co Inc 116 Cherry Valley Ave West Hempstead NY 11552

CHISHOLM, JUNE FAYE, clinical psychologist; b. N.Y.C., Apr. 29, 1949; d. Wallace P. and Luretta (Brawley) Chisholm; B.A., Syracuse U., 1971; M.S., U. Mass., Ph.D., 1978. Asst. prof. psychology Fordham U., 1978-84, Pace U., 1986—; practice clin. psychology, N.Y.C., 1980—; sr. psychologist Harlem Hosp., 1982—; cons. N.Y.C. Bd. Edn. Mem. Am. Psychol. Assn., N.Y. State Psychol. Assn., N.Y. Soc. Clin. Psychologists, Chamber Music Assos. Office: 260 W 72 St Suite 1-B New York NY 10023

CHISHOLM, MARGARET ELIZABETH, library director; b. Grey Eagle, Minn., July 25, 1921; d. Henry D. and Alice (Thomas) Bergman; children:

Nancy Diane, Janice Marie Lane. BA, U. Washington, 1957, MLS, 1958, PhD, 1966. Librarian Everett (Wash.) Community Coll., 1961-63; asst. and assoc. prof. edn. U. Oreg., Eugene, 1963-67; assoc. prof. edn. U. N.Mex., Albuquerque, 1967-69; prof., dean Coll. Library and Info. Sci. U. Md., College Park, 1969-75; v.p. univ. relations and devel. U. Washington, Seattle, 1975-81; Commr. Western Interstate Commn. Higher Edn., Colo., 1981-85. Served as civilian aide U.S. Army, 1978-87. Recipient Ruth Worden award U. Wash., Seattle, 1957, Disting. Alumni award St. Cloud (Minn.) U., 1977, Disting. Alumni award U. Wash., 1979, John Brubaker award Cath. Library Assn., 1987. Mem. Am. Library Assn. (v.p. 1986-87, pres. 1987-88), Nat. Assn. Pub. TV Stations (trustee 1975-84, 87). Home: 5892 NE Parkpoint Pl Seattle WA 98115 Office: U Washington Grad Sch Library & Info Sci 133 Suzzallo Library FM-30 Seattle WA 98195

CHITTY, (MARY) ELIZABETH NICKINSON, university administrator; b. Balt., Apr. 27, 1920; d. Edward Phillips and Em Turner (Merritt) Nickinson; m. Arthur Benjamin Chitty, June 16, 1946; children: Arthur Benjamin, John Abercrombie, Em Turner, Nathan Harsh Brown. BA cum laude, Fla. State U., 1941, MA, 1942; D in Civil Law, U. of South, 1988. Tchr. Fla. Indsl. Sch. for Girls, Ocala, 1942-43; psychometrist neuropsychiat. dept. Sch. Aviation Medicine, Pensacola (Fla.) Naval Air Sta., 1943-46; assoc. editor Sewanee (Tenn.) Alumni News, U. of South, 1946-62; bus. mnr. and mng. editor Sewanee Review, 1962-65, dir. fin. aid and career services, 1970-80, assoc. univ. historiographer, 1980—; freelance editor. Editor: (with H.A. Petry) Sewanee Centennial Alumni Directory, 1954-62; Centennial Report of the Registrar of the University of the South, 1959; (with Arthur Ben Chitty) Too Black, Too White (Ely Green), 1970; author (with Moultrie Guerry and Arthur Ben Chitty) Men Who Made Sewanee, 1981; columnist Sewanee Mountain Messenger, 1985—. Bd. dirs. Sewanee Civic Assn., 1979-80, 86-88; CONTACT-Lifeline of Coffee and Franklin Counties, 1981-84. Mem. Assn. Preservation Tenn. Antiquities (trustee 1985—), AAUW (pres. Sewanee br., 1975-77), Fla. State U. Alumni Assn. (dir. 1941—), Mortar Bd., Phi Beta Kappa, Phi Kappa Phi, Pi Alpha Theta, Kappa Delta. Democrat. Episcopalian. Club: EQB Faculty (sec. 1975-76, 81-85). Home: 100 SC Ave Sewanee TN 37375 Office: U of the South Sewanee TN 37375

CHITTY, JUDY HUMISTON, banker; b. Glendale, Calif., Sept. 30, 1951; d. Donald Squier and Allene (McCall) Humiston; m. Louis Anthony Chitty, Jan. 7, 1977; (div. Nov. 1985); children: Amber Cecile, Erin Louise. Student, U. Calif., Santa Barbara, 1969-72; BA in Psychology, U. Calif., Berkeley, 1973. Sec. Home Savs. of Am., Irwindale, Calif., 1974-75, research analyst, 1975-77, sr. research analyst, 1977-79, mktg. research mgr., 1980-83, product devel. mgr., 1983-85, product mgr., 1985-86, Silver Circle mktg. supr., 1986—; English instr. Berlitz Sch., Barcelona, Spain, 1979-80; mem. faculty U. So. Calif., 1984. Mem. PTA, Covina, Calif., 1983—; com. mem. Am. Heart Assn., Los Angeles, 1986—. State Calif. scholar, 1969-70. Mem. Am. Mktg. Assn., Fin. Instns. Mktg. Assn. Democrat. Mem. Ch. of Religious Sci. Avocations: walking, hiking, swimming, psychic phenomenon. Home: 20262-E Arrow Hwy Covina CA 91724 Office: Home Savings of Am 1001 Commerce Dr Irwindale CA 91706

CHIULLI, E. ANTOINETTE, lawyer; b. Pescara, Italy, Oct. 30, 1950; arrived in U.S., 1955; d. Nino and Maria (Mezzanotte) C.; m. Joseph P. Breig, Spet. 5, 1976; 1 child, Christopher J. BA, Marymount Coll., 1972; JD, Rutgers-Camden Sch. Law., 1976. Legal asst. Judge Manuel Greenberg, Atlantic City, N.J., 1976-77; sole practice Somerdale, N.J., 1978—; econ. analyst Nat. Econ. Research Assocs., N.Y.C., 1972-73; panelist Matrimonial Settlement Program, 1985. Cons. Alternatives for Women Now, Camden, 1978-80, Women's Counseling Ctr., 1981-83, Glassboro (N.J.) Coll. Together Program, 1979—, Jaycettes of Camden County, 1982. Mem. ABA, N.J. State Bar Assn., Tri County Women Lawyers, Camden County Bar Assn (family law com. 1978). Home: 1213 Heartwood Dr Cherry Hill NJ 08003 Office: 10 Grove St Haddonfield NJ 08033-1218

CHIZAUSKAS, CATHLEEN JO, retail company administrator; b. Little Rock, Dec. 26, 1954; d. Daniel John and Marilyn (Wolff) Quigley; m. Alan Michael Chizauskas, Nov. 11, 1978; 1 child, Marc Alan. Diploma in Mgmt., Simmons Coll., Boston, 1981. From clk. typist to direct materials buyer Gillette Safety Razor Co., Boston, 1972-79, buyer capital equipment, 1979, mgr. mro and purchasing services, 1979-85, adminstrv. asst. to v.p. mktg., 1985-87, exec. asst. to pres., 1987-88, assoc. brand mgr. shave creams, 1988—. Mem. Am. Mgmt. Assn., Purchasing Mgmt. Assn., Simmons Coll. Grad. Sch. Alumnae Assn. Roman Catholic. Home: 14 St Lawrence St Braintree MA 02184 Office: Gillette Co Blade/Razor div Gillette N Am Gilette Park Boston MA 02106

CHIZECK, SUSAN PHYLLIS, director, sociology educator; b. Pitts., Apr. 14, 1947; d. Aleck H. and Rosalyn Nessa (Wnuk) C.; m. William J. Pervin, May 22, 1981. BA in History, Douglass Coll., 1969; MA in East Asian Studies, Stanford U., 1972; MA in Sociology, Princeton (N.J.) U., 1975; PhD in Social Work, Rutgers U., 1983. Cert. social worker, Tex.; lic. profl. counselor, Tex. Editor dept. biochemistry Stanford U., 1972; research asst. Trenton Transit Project, Princeton, 1973-74; research assoc. N.J. Div. of Youth and Family Services, Trenton, 1974-76, mgmt. info. systems analyst, 1980; exec. dir. Research Program in Devel. Studies, Princeton, 1976-78; asst. dir. Earth House, East Millstone, N.J., 1979-80; dir. HR Assocs., Richardson, Tex., 1981-83, pres., 1983—; dir. internships U. Tex., Dallas, 1986—; mem. Worksite Health Com., Dallas, 1981-84. Contbr. articles to profl. jours. Vol. Dallas County Dems., 1984—. Mem. Sociol. Practice Assn., Assn. for Tng. and Devel., Nat. Assn. of Social Workers, Assn. of Neurolinguistic Programmers, Assn. for Humanistic Psychology, Tex. Clin. Sociology Assn. (bd. dirs. 1983—). Jewish. Home: 820 Scottsdale Richardson TX 75080 Office: U Tex Floyd Rd Dallas TX 75083-0688

CHODOROW, JOAN, psychoanalyst, dance therapist; b. N.Y.C., May 29, 1937; d. Eugene Aaronovitch and Lillian (Kleidman) C.; m. Louis H. Stewart, June 23, 1985; step-children: Daniel Stewart, Sarah Stewart. MA in Psychology, Dance Therapy, Goodard Coll., 1972; Diploma in Analytical Psychology, C. G. Jung Inst. Los Angeles, 1983; PhD in Psychology, Union Grad. Sch., 1988. Registered dance therapist, Calif. Founder, tchr. Community Dance Studio, Los Angeles, 1957-64; dance therapist Child Psychiat. County Hosp., Los Angeles, 1964-66, Lawrence Sch., Van Nuys, Calif., 1965-67; dance therapist, psychotherapist Psychiat. Med. Group, Santa Barbara, Calif., 1968-73; lectr. U. Calif., Santa Barbara, 1967-79, Community Coll., Santa Barbara, 1967-79; dance therapist Psychiat. Dept. Cottage Hosp., Santa Barbara, 1968-83; practicing psychotherapist Santa Barbara, 1973-83; practicing Jungian analyst Fairfax, Calif., 1983—; tchr. C.G. Jung Inst., San Francisco, 1983—; visiting faculty Insts. Los Angeles, Houston, Israel 1976—; dir., tchr. Dance Therapy, Santa Barbara 1975-83; faculty Active Imagination course Geneva 1984, Zurich 1985-86. Editor: What is Dance Therapy, Really?, 1973; contbr. articles to profl. jours. Mem. Am. Dance Therapy Assn. (pres. 1974-76, keynote speaker 1983), Internat. Assn. Analytical Psychol., Am. Psychol. Assn., Calif. Assn. Marriage and Family Therapists. Jewish.

CHOI, SUSAN ELLEN, librarian, consultant; b. Duluth, Minn.; d. Abe O. and Ellen E. (Wilippo) Martimo; children—Daniel, James, Joshua. B.A., Sacramento State Coll., 1970; M.A., San Jose State U., 1973. Library asst. San Mateo County Office Edn., Redwood City, Calif., 1970-71; supr. library services Santa Clara County Office Edn., San Jose, Calif., 1971—; cons. in field; ind. beauty cons. Mary Kay Cosmetics, 1987—; mem. Calif. State Data Acquisition Adv. Com., 1977-80; reference adv. bd. Coop. Info. Network, 1977-80; copyright info. officer Santa Clara County Office Edn., 1980—. Editor: Guide to Resources for Improving Schools, 1979. Mem. Am. Assn. Ednl. Communications and Tech., Am. Ednl. Research Assn., ALA, Am. Soc. Tng. and Devel., Calif. Media and Library Educators Assn. (pres. No. sect. 1982-83), Nat. Sch. Pub. Relations Assn., Peninsula Media Adminstrs., Santa Clara County Sch. Librarians Assn., Women Leaders in Edn. of Santa Clara County (pres. 1981-82). Democrat. Lutheran. Home: 7494 Bayliss Ct San Jose CA 95139 Office: Santa Clara County Office Edn 100 Skyport Dr San Jose CA 95115

CHONG, DOROTHY BIERMA, trading and consulting company executive; b. Detroit, Mar. 27, 1925; d. Charles Allen and Jessica (Griffiths) Bierma; student Los Angeles City Coll., 1942-43, U. Mich., 1946-47; m. Richard Seng-Hoon Chong, Jan. 9, 1980; step-children—David C.S., Stephen C.L., Daniel C.Y. Adminstrv. asst. to plant mgr. Monsanto Co., Trenton, Mich., 1952-65; adminstrv. asst. to pres. Adache Assocs., Inc., Engrs., Cleve., 1965-69; credit mgr. Hawaiian Crane & Rigging, Ltd., Honolulu, 1969-70; adminstrv. mgr. East Central region Booz, Allen & Hamilton, Inc., Cleve., 1970-73; v.p. Amer-Asia Trading Co., Inc., Orlando, Fla., 1973—; broker, co-owner Sungold Realty Internat., Inc., Orlando, 1979—, Sungold Decor, Inc.; dir. Crown Savs. Assn. Mem. Chinese-Am. Assn. Central Fla. (sec., dir. 1980-81), World Trade Council for Central Fla., Nat. Assn. Realtors, Fla. Assn. Realtors, Orlando Area Bd. Realtors. Presbyterian. Club: Citrus. Home: 9652 Woodmont Pl Windermere FL 32786 Office: Amer-Asia Trading Co Inc 7201 Lake Ellenor Dr Suite 112 Orlando FL 32809

CHONG, MARY DRUZILLEA, nurse; b. Fairview, Okla., Mar. 8, 1930; d. Charles Dewey and Viola Haddie (Ford) Crawford; A.A. (Bells scholarship), El Camino Jr. Coll., 1950; R.N., Los Angeles County Hosp. Sch. Nursing, 1953; B.S. in Nursing, Calif. State U., 1968; m. Nyuk Choy Chong, Aug. 24, 1952 (div. 1968); children—Anthony, Dorlinda. Staff nurse neurosurgery Los Angeles County Gen. Hosp., Los Angeles, 1957-58; staff nurse Harbor Gen. Hosp., Torrance, Calif., 1958-59, emergency room staff nurse, 1959-61, asst. head nurse, 1963-64, supr. neurosurgery intensive care unit, 1964-67, part-time relief nurse, 1967-69, head nurse chest medicine, 1969-72; instr. Licensed Vocat. Nursing program Los Angeles YWCA Job Corps., 1972-74; emergency room staff nurse mobile intensive care nurse Victor Valley Hosp., Victorville, Calif., 1974-79; dir. nursing San Vicente Hosp., Los Angeles, 1980-82, Upjohn Healthcare Services, Los Angeles, 1983-85; dir. home health services Bear Valley Community Hosp. Home Health Agy., Big Bear Lake, Calif., 1986-87; asst. dir. nursing Care West Palm Springs (Calif.) Nursing Ctr., 1988—. Leader, South Bay council Girl Scouts Am., 1968; tchr. YWCA Job Corps, 1972-74; dir. nursing Helen Evans Home for Developmentally Disabled Children, 1987—. Mem. AAUW, Nat. Assn. Female Execs., Calif. State U. Los Angeles Alumni Assn., Internat. Platform Assn. Home: PO Box 697 Lucerne Valley CA 92356 Office: 15125 E Gale Ave Hacienda Heights CA 91745

CHONKO, LORRAINE N., state legislator; b. Brunswick, Maine, Dec. 31, 1936; d. Philip J. and Rosalva M. (Pinnette) Lachance; m. John J. Chonko, June 5, 1957; children: Eva Marie Chonko Hart, John J. Jr., Jolene. Grad. high sch., Brunswick. Mem. Maine Ho. of Reps., mem. joint standing com. appropriation and fin. affairs. Address: New Lewiston Rd Pejepscot ME 04067

CHOOKASIAN, LILI, contralto; b. Chgo.; student Philip Manuel, Chgo., Ludwig Donath, N.Y.C., Armen Boyajian, Paterson, N.J.; m. George Gavejian; 3 children. Voice tchr. Northwestern U.; debut La Cieca (Gioconda), Met. Opera, 1962; roles major cos., Argentina, Canada, Hamburg, Germany, Turin, Italy, Mexico City, Barcelona, Spain, Balt., Chgo., Cin., Dallas, Ft. Worth, Houston, Miami, N.Y. City Opera, Met. Opera, Phila. Lyric Opera, Portland, San Francisco Opera, Washington; rec. artist Deutsche Grammophon; appearances with symphony orchs.; coach repertoire. Office: care Thea Dispeker Artists Reps 59 E 54th St New York NY 10022 *

CHOP, ROSE MARIE, nurse; b. Kans., Mar. 4, 1955; d. John and Helen Ann (Sachen) C.; B.S. Nursing, Fort Hays State U., 1978, postgrad. Kans. U. Med. Center, 1979-81; M.S. in Nursing, Wichita State U., 1983. With Providence-St. Margaret Health Center, Kansas City, Kans., 1973—, staff charge nurse pediatric, med.-surg. unit, 1981—; nursing supr. Lawrence Meml. Hosp. (Kans.), 1983—; staff faculty mem. Providence-St. Margaret's Health Center, 1980—; instr. CPR, 1981—; aerobic dance instr., 1981—. Mem. Am. Nurses Assn., Am. Heart Assn., Fort Hays State U. Alumni Assn. (life), Sigma Theta Tau. Democrat. Roman Catholic. Club: Croation Federal Union. Home: 3013 Bainbridge Circle Lawrence KS 66044 Office: Lawrence Meml Hosp 325 Maine Lawrence KS 66044

CHOPIN, SUSAN GARDINER, lawyer; b. Miami, Fla., Feb. 23, 1947; d. Maurice and Judith (Warden) Gardiner; m. L. Frank Chopin, Sept. 4, 1964; children: Philip, Alexandra, Christopher. BBA, Loyola U., New Orleans, 1966; JD cum laude, U. Miami, 1972; MLitt (Law), Oxford U., Eng., 1983. Bar: Fla. 1972, Iowa 1979. Sr. law clk. to presiding judge U.S. Dist. Ct. (so. dist.) Fla., Miami, 1972-73; ptnr. Chopin & Chopin, Miami, 1973-77; assoc. prof. Drake U. Law Sch., Des Moines, 1979-80; sole practice Palm Beach, Fla., 1981—. Mem. editorial bd. Fla. Bar Jour., 1975—; contbr. articles to profl. jours., legal revs. Trustee Preservation Found. of Palm Beach, 1986—. Mem. ABA, Fla. Bar Assn., Iowa Bar Assn., Fed. Bar Assn., Internat. Bar Assn., Fla. Assn. Women Lawyers, Soc. Wig and Robe, Phi Kappa Phi, Phi Alpha Delta. Democrat. Office: Northbridge Ctr Pavilion 515 N Flager Dr Suite 300 West Palm Beach FL 33401

CHORNEY, THERESA RAND, publishing company executive; b. Richmond, Va., Aug. 18, 1955; d. William Harry and Maria Theresa (McMahon) C. AA in Bus. Adminstrn., Concordia Coll., Bronxville, N.Y., 1975. Sec. to v.p. audio div. Philips Audio Video Systems Corp., Mahwah, N.J., 1973-74, exec. sec. to v.p. video div., 1974-76; sec. flight ops. Gannett Co. Inc., Rochester, N.Y., 1976-77, office mgr., flight ops., 1977-79, exec. sec. to chmn. and chief exec. officer, 1979-85; asst. to chmn. Gannett Co. Inc., Arlington, Va., 1985-86, exec. dir. adminstrn. services, 1986—. Author various children's poems. Mem. Nat. Assn. for Female Execs. Republican. Lutheran. Office: Gannett Co Inc 1100 Wilson Blvd Arlington VA 22209

CHOSTNER, CHRYSTAL LEA, manufacturing company professional; b. San Diego, Feb. 1, 1963; d. Gilbert E. Chostner and Sheila I. (Preston) Radley. BA, Lindenwood Coll., 1984. Estimator Teledyne Ryan Aero., San Diego, 1985—. Advisor Jr. Achievement, San Diego, 1985. Mem. Inst. Cost Analysis (dir. edn. 1987), Nat. Contract Mgmt. Assn., Nat. Mgmt. Assn. (co-chair scholarship fund 1985). Republican. Seventh-day Adventist. Office: Teledyne Ryan Aero 2701 N Harbor Dr San Diego CA 92138

CHOU, KAREN CHAI KWAN, civil engineering educator; research, consultant; b. Hong Kong, Dec. 10, 1955; came to U.S., 1970, naturalized 1976; d. Choi Hong and Chuen Mui (Wong) C. B.S. in Civil Engring., Tufts U., 1978; M.S., Northwestern U., 1980, Ph.D., 1983. Registered profl. engr., N.Y. Civil engring. technician C.E., U.S. Army Waltham, Mass., 1977-78; cons. Ill. Inst. Tech. Research Inst., Chgo., summer 1979; structural engr. Harza Engring. Co., Chgo., 1979-81; research assoc. Johns Hopkins U., Balt., 1982-83; asst. prof. Syracuse U., N.Y., 1983-87; assoc. prof. civil engring., 1987—. Contbr. articles to profl. jours. Vol. tutor Boston Tech. High Sch., 1978. Tufts U. Class of 1926 scholar, 1976-77, Tufts U. Albert Whittier scholar, 1977-78, Mass. Soc. for Univ. Edn. of Women scholar, 1977-78; AAUW fellow, 1982-83, U.S. Air Force-Universal Energy System fellow, 1985, 88; Northwestern U. grantee, 1978-79, 81-82, Johns Hopkins U. grantee, 1982-83, NSF grantee, 1984—, USAF grantee, 1986. Mem. Soc. Women Engrs., Am. Acad. Mechanics, Am. Concrete Inst., ASCE (bd. dirs. Syracuse sect. 1984—, newsletter editor 1984-85, sec. 1985-86, pres. 1987-88), Tau Beta Pi, Sigma Chi. Avocations: stamp collecting, volleyball, ping-pong. Office: Syracuse U Dept Civil Engring Syracuse NY 13244-1190

CHOU, MAXINE J., investment banker; b. Paiking, China, May 27, 1942; came to U.S., 1968; d. Tong-Hsiu and So-Lan (Chen) Shan; m. Peter L. Chou; children: James, Jerri. BS, Morningside Coll., 1970. Chief acct. Basle Securities Corp., N.Y.C., 1970-71, asst. treas., 1972-77, asst. v.p., controller, 1978-86; v.p., controller Swiss Bank Corp. Internat. Securities Inc., N.Y.C., 1986—; bd. dirs., treas., chmn. Internat. Ops. Assn. of Securities Industry Assn. Compliance Com. of Internat. Ops. Assocs. Mem. Wall St. Tax Assn. Office: Swiss Bank Corp Internat Securities Inc 1 World Trade Ctr Suite 9051 New York NY 10048

CHOUINARD, RITA BLOCK, financial executive; b. Utica, N.Y., Mar. 27, 1942; d. Robert Heine and Anne (Polivan) Block; m. Richard J. Choinard; student U. Miami, 1959-62, Syracuse U., 1962-64. V.p. corp. bonds Muller & Co., N.Y.C., 1973-81; agt. Barry J. Levien, Real Estate Broker, N.Y.C., 1975—; corp. bond, fixed income salesperson Wertheim & Co., N.Y.C., 1981-83; fixed income sales person Dillon Read & Co., N.Y.C., 1983—; pres. Ambit Corp., N.Y.C., 1983—; v.p. AML Park Ave. Corp., N.Y.C., 1986—. Home: 245 E 87 St Apt 3A New York NY 10128 Office: 535 Madison Ave New York NY 10022

CHOW, RITA KATHLEEN, government official; b. San Francisco, Aug. 19, 1926; d. Peter and May (Chan) C. B.S., Stanford U., 1950, nursing diploma, 1950; M.S., Case Western Res. U., 1955; profl. diploma in nursing edn. adminstrn, Columbia U., 1961, EdD, 1968; B of Individualized Studies, George Mason U., 1983. Asst. in teaching Stanford U., Calif., 1951-52; instr., dir. student health Fresno (Calif.) Gen. Hosp. Sch. Nursing, 1952-54; instr. Wayne State U. Coll. Nursing, Detroit, 1957-58; research assoc., project dir. cardiovascular nursing research Ohio State U., Columbus, 1965-68; commd. officer USPHS, 1968, advanced through grades to nurse dir., 1974; spl. asst. to dep. dir. Nat. Center Health Services Research, Health Services and Mental Health Adminstrn., HEW, Rockville, Md., 1969-73; dep. dir. manpower utilization br. 1970-73; dep. dir. Office Long Term Care; dep. chief nurse officer USPHS, Rockville, 1973-77; chief quality assurance br. div. long-term care Office of Standards and Certification, Health Standards and Quality Bur., Health Care Fin. Adminstrn., HHS, 1977-82; health sci. analyst Office Health Tech. Assessment Nat. Ctr. Health Services Research, OASH, HHS, 1982-83; dir. patient edn., asst. dir. nursing G.W. Long Hansen's Disease Ctr., USPHS, Carville, La., 1984—. Author: Identifying Nursing Action with the Care of Cardiovascular Patients, 1967, Cardiosurgical Nursing Care: Understandings, Concepts, and Principles for Practice, 1975; mem. editorial bd. Nursing and Health Care, 1983—; contbr. to publs. in field. Served with Nurse Corps U.S. Army, 1954-57. AAUW scholar; Nat. League Nursing fellow, 1959-61; recipient research grant Sigma Theta Tau, 1966; recipient Fed. Nursing Service award Assn. Mil. Surgeons U.S., 1969, citation for outstanding contbn. to cardiovascular nursing Am. Heart Assn., 1972, 79, Nursing Edn. Alumni Assn. award for distinguished achievement in nursing research Columbia U. Tchrs. Coll., 1973, Meritorious Service medal USPHS, 1977, Disting. Alumnus award Case Western Res. U. Sch. Nursing, 1979, Disting. Service medal USPHS, 1987, Artist of Life award Internat. Women's Writing Guild, 1987.

CHOYKE, PHYLLIS MAY FORD (MRS. ARTHUR DAVIS CHOYKE, JR.), ceiling systems company executive, editor, poet; b. Buffalo, Oct. 25, 1921; d. Thomas Cecil and Vera (Buchanan) Ford; m. Arthur Davis Choyke Jr., Aug. 18, 1945; children: Christopher Ford, Tyler Van. BS summa cum laude, Northwestern U., 1942. Reporter City News Bur., Chgo., 1942-43, Met. sect. Chgo. Tribune, 1943-44; feature writer OWI, N.Y.C., 1944-45; sec. corp. Artcrest Products Co., Inc., Chgo., 1958—, v.p., 1964—, founder, dir. Harper Sq. Press div., 1966—. Bonbright scholar, 1942. Mem. Soc. Midland Authors (bd. dirs.), Mystery Writers Am. (assoc.), Chgo. Press Vets. Assn., Hist. Alliance of Chgo. Hist. Soc., Phi Beta Kappa. Clubs: Arts (Chgo.); John Evans (Northwestern U.). Author: (under name Phyllis Ford) (with others) (poetry) Apertures to Anywhere, 1979; editor: Gallery Series One, Poets, 1967, Gallery Series Two, Poets—Poems of the Inner World, 1968, Gallery Series Three—Poets: Levitations and Observations, 1970, Gallery Series Four, Poets—I am Talking About Revolution, 1973, Gallery Series Five/Poets—To An Aging Nation (with occult overtones), 1977; (manuscripts and papers in Brown U. Library). Home: 29 E Division St Chicago IL 60610 Office: 500 W Cermak Rd Chicago IL 60616

CHOY-WELLER, CHERYL JEAN, lawyer; b. Troy, N.Y., May 19, 1956; d. George Donald and Eileen Bridget (Griffin) Choy; m. Robert Jay Weller. BA, SUNY, 1978; JD, Harvard U., 1982. Bar: Mass. U.S. Tax Ct. 1983, So. Dist. N.Y. 1987, Ea. Dist. N.Y. 1987, No. Dist. N.Y. 1987, We. Dist. N.Y. 1987, N.Y. 1986. Atty. Office of Chief Counsel to the IRS, Albany, N.Y., 1982-87; staff atty. Pub. Utility Law Project and Pub. Utility Law Project of N.Y., Inc., 1987—. Contbr. book revs. Recipient Rafuse award for excellence in social sci. SUNY, 1978. Mem. ABA, Nat. Assn. Female Execs., Phi Beta Kappa. Office: 12 Sheridan Ave Albany NY 12207

CHRAPKOWSKI, ROSEMARIE, chemical dependence and art therapist; b. Chgo., Dec. 8, 1935; d. Andrew H. and Charlotte D. (Poterackie) C. BFA, U. Chgo. and Sch. Art Inst. Chgo., 1959, postgrad., 1962-63, 78; student Inst. Psychiatry, Chgo., Inst. Psychoanalysis, Chgo., C.G. Jung Inst., Chgo.; grad. alcoholism counselor tng. program Grant Hosp., Chgo., 1981. Cert. alcoholism counselor, Ill.; cert sr. addictions counselor, Ill. Artist various studios and agys., from 1963; staff artist Soc. for Visual Edn., Chgo., 1965-66; supr. picture acquisitions Ency. Brit., Inc., Chgo., 1969-71; alcoholism counselor U. Ill. Alcohol Program, Chgo., 1978; sr. chem. dependence counselor Northwestern Meml. Hosp. Inst. Psychiatry, Chgo., 1979-86, expressive arts therapist, 1986—; pvt. practice therapy, Chgo., 1981—; therapist Assocs. in Jungian Psychology and Creative Therapies, Chgo., 1987—; cons., workshop presenter;instr., lectr. Interventions, Inc., Cen. State Inst. Addictions, 1986—. Exhibited paintings various galleries, from 1958. Mem. Nat. Assn. Alcoholism and Drug Abuse Counselors, Ill. Addictions Counselors Assn., Ill. Art Therapy Assn., Assn. Transpersonal Psychology, C.G. Jung Inst., Alumni Assn. Sch. Art Inst. Chgo. (life), Sierra Club, Lincoln Park Zool. Soc., Nat. Anti-Vivisection Soc. (life), Humane Soc. U.S., World Wildlife Fund, African Wildlife Found. Office: 6415 N Sheridan Rd #1208 Chicago IL 60626

CHRISCOE, CHRISTINE FAUST, industrial trainer; b. Atlanta, Oct. 29, 1950; d. Henry Charles and Shirley Faye (Birdwell) Faust; B.A., Spring Hill Coll., 1973; postgrad. Ga. State U., 1974—; m. Ralph D. Chriscoe, June 25, 1983. Trainer, Fed. Res. Bank, Atlanta, 1973-77; project mgr., tng. dept. Coca Cola U.S.A., Atlanta, 1977-79, sr. project mgr., 1979-81, mgr. tech. tng., 1981-84, mgr. sales, mgmt. and mktg. tng., 1984-85, mgr. bottler tng., 1984-85; mgr. human resources devel., 1986—. Mem. Internat. TV and Video Assn., Am. Soc. Tng. and Devel., Soc. Applied Learning Technologies; TAng. Dir's. Forum (bd. dirs.). Bd. trustees Ga. Shakespeare Festival, 1986—. Roman Catholic. Office: PO Drawer 1734 Atlanta GA 30301

CHRISLER, JOAN C., psychologist, educator; b. Teaneck, N.J., Jan. 1, 1953; d. Eugene Reed and Anna Mary (Whalen) C.; m. Christopher Bishop, Nov. 20, 1976. BS in Psychology, Fordham U., 1975; MA, PhD in Exptl. Psychology, Yeshiva U., 1986. Adj. instr. Mercy Coll., Dobbs Ferry, N.Y., 1979-85, Coll. of Mt. St. Vincetn, Riverdale, N.Y., 1979, Monroe Bus. Inst., Bronx, N.Y., 1980, Iona Coll., New Rochelle, N.Y., 1980, Ramapo Coll., Mahwah, N.J., 1980-84, Upsala Coll., East Orange, N.J., 1981-85, St. Thomas Acquinas Coll., Sparkill, N.Y., 1984, SUNY, Purchase, 1984-87, Coll. New Rochelle, N.Y., 1984-85, Bergen Community Coll., Paramus, N.J., 1984-85; asst. prof. Conn. Coll., New London, 1987—; asst. to dir. Internat. English Language Inst. Hunter Coll., N.Y.C., 1978-80; asst. to coordinator Media Ctr. Payne Whitney Psychiatric Clinic, N.Y.C., 1980-82; fieldwork in behavior therapy Creedmoor Psychiatric Ctr., Queens Village, N.Y., 1982; group therapist Health Improvement Systems, Cin., 1982-84. Dist. leader New Rochelle Dem. Com., N.Y., 1985-87; mem. Westchester County Dem. Com., White Plains, N.Y., 1985-87; v.p. Westchester NOW, White Plains, 1985-87; mem. exec. com. Westchester Women's Polit. Caucus, Mt. Vernon, N.Y., 1985-87. Mem. Assn. Women in Psychology (spokesperson 1985—), Am. Psychol. Assn., Soc. Mentrual Cycle Research, New Eng. Psych. Assn., New Eng. Women's Studies Assn. Home: 1006 Grassy Hill Rd Orange CT 06477 Office: Conn Coll Dept of Psychology New London CT 06320

CHRIST, KATHY S., cable company advertising executive, consultant; b. Hartford, Conn., July 6, 1951; d. Arthur H. and Elizabeth M. (McCombe) C.; m. Paul J. Arnini, Jan. 17, 1969 (div. Apr. 1970); 1 child, June Elizabeth. Diploma, U. Conn., 1972. Asst. to v.p. adminstrn. Nat. Telephone Co., Hartford, 1972-74; adminstrv. asst. Downtown Council, Hartford, 1974-76; exec. asst. to chmn. Imagnetics Internat., Unionville, Conn., 1977-78; sales mktg. mgr. Info-Dial, Bloomfield, Conn., 1979-80; mktg. dir. Southerby Prodn., Long Beach, Calif., 1982; account exec. to advt. sales mgr. King Videocable Co., Lake Elsinore, Calif., 1982—. Dir. pub. relations, com. mem. Hartford Easter Seals Rehab. Softball Marathon, 1980; coordinator Elsinore High Sch. Tiger Pause, 1985-86; bd. dirs. Substance Abuse Council, S.W. Riverside County, 1987-88. Mem. Cable Advt. Bur., Lake Elsinore Valley C. of C., Temecula Valley C. of C. Republican. Club: BPW (Lake Elsinore). Home: 15191 P Lincoln St Lake Elsinore CA 92330 Office: King Videocable Co 556 Birch St PO Box 989 Lake Elsinore CA 92330

CHRIST, LINDA RUTH, voluntary services executive; b. Buffalo, Aug. 3, 1949; d. Albert Louis and Edna Frances (O'Connor) C. A.A., SUNY-Buffalo, 1979; B.A. with high distinction, 1981. Adminstrv. coordinator SUNY-Buffalo Urban Ctr., 1967-73; office mgr. E.J. Meyer Meml. Hosp., Buffalo, 1973-77; account auditor Office Erie County Comptroller, Buffalo, 1977-78; adminstrv. asst. Erie County Med. Ctr., Buffalo, 1978-82, coordinator vol. services, 1982-84; asst. dir. ret. sr. vol. program Erie County, 1984—. Author, producer audio-visual tape: Rehab. Medicine: A Multidiscipline Approach, 1979, Erie County Med. Ctr. Presents: Skilled Nursing Facility, 1984. Mem. Buffalo Sesquicentennial Com., 1982; co-chmn. div. United Way of Buffalo and Erie County, 1981-84; mem. adv. bd. Literacy Vols. Buffalo and Erie County, 1985—. Mem. Buffalo Dental Assts. Soc. (hon.), Western N.Y. Dirs. Vol. Services, Vol. Adminstrs. of Western N.Y., Women in Communications (historian 1982-84, co-chmn. regional conf. 1983-85, dir., sec. 1984-88), Orgn. of Triangles (state officer N.Y. 1969-72). Lodge: Order of Eastern Star (worthy matron 1975, fin. com. 1983—, chmn. publicity 1983—). Office: Erie County Dept Sr Services 95 Franklin St Buffalo NY 14202

CHRISTEN, TAMARA MARIE, marketing executive; b. Toledo, Ohio, Aug. 13, 1961; d. Frederick Clarence and Marlene Phyllis (Kros) C. BS in Indsl. Engring., Purdue U., 1983; MBA, Pepperdine U., 1986. Supr. Los Angeles Olympic Organizing Com., 1984; sr. airline analyst McDonnell Douglas Corp., Long Beach, Calif., 1984—, bd. dirs. west personnel community service, 1987—. Mem. Inst. Indsl. Engrs. Office: McDonnell Douglas Corp 3855 Lakewood M/C 7-82 Long Beach CA 90846

CHRISTENSEN, CAROL ANN, municipal agency administrator; b. Wakefield, R.I., Aug. 15, 1937; d. Harry Paul Christensen and Ethel Mae (Gould) Rosenbalm. Student, U. R.I., Community Coll. R.I., U. Lowell. Sch. bus driver Narragansett (R.I.) Sch. System, 1968-75, dir. transp., 1975—; police officer Dept. Natural Resources, Providence, 1978; instr., cons. R.I. Dept. Transp., R.I. Dept. Edn., Providence, 1983—; instr. Community Coll. of R.I., Warwick, 1985—. Vol. South County Hosp. Emergency Room, Wakefield, 1970-80, South County Ambulance Corp., 1977-80, Narragansett Little League, 1977-82; dep. dir. Civil Def., Narragansett, 1975—; disaster chmn. ARC, Westerly, R.I., 1978—. Served with USAF, 1956-60. Recipient Cert. Appreciation Meeting St. Sch., East Providence, 1973, Cert. Appreciation South Kingstown Bicentennial Com., 1976, Citation Outstanding Pub. Service Def. Civil Preparedness Agy., 1980. Mem. Sch. Bus Owner's Assn., Nat. Assn. Emergency Med. Technicians (charter mem. 1979—), VFW (mem. ladies' aux. 1967—). Home: 892 Broad Rock Rd Peace Dale RI 02879 Office: Narragansett Sch System 55 Mumford Rd Narragansett RI 02882

CHRISTENSEN, CAROLE CECILE PIGLER, social work educator; b. Bklyn., Mar. 14, 1939; d. Samuel and Georgia Mae (Williams) Pigler; B.A. in Sociology, Howard U., 1960; M.S.W., U. Mich., 1963; D.Ed. in Counseling Psychology, McGill U., 1980; m. Torkild Vejby Christensen, Sept. 21, 1963; children—Karin, Michael, Lisa. Instr. social work Danish Sch. Social Work, 1964-66; mental health counselor Danish Women's League Counseling Service, Copenhagen, 1964-68; lectr. social work McGill U., 1970-80, asst. prof., 1980-85, mem. senate McGill U., 1983-86; bd. govs. McGill U., 1985-86; bd. dirs. Internat. YMCA, Montreal, Can., mem. Met. bd. dirs.; vis. colleague Sch. Social Work, U. Hawaii, 1987. Fulbright fellow, 1960-61, Can. Council fellow, 1977-80. Recipient Outstanding Doctoral Dissertation Biennial award, 1981. Mem. Am. Psychol. Assn., Canadian Assn. Social Workers, Am. Assn. Marriage and Family Therapy (clin.), Internat. Soc. for Intercultural Edn., Tng. and Research (governing council), Nat. Congress Black Women (Montreal region), Am. Assn. Sex Educators Counselors and Therapists (cert.), Afro-Asian Assn. Can. (co-founder), Phi Beta Kappa, Phi Kappa Phi. Office: McGill U Sch Social Work, 3506 University St, Montreal, PQ Canada H3A 2A7

CHRISTENSEN, PATRICIA ANNE WATKINS, lawyer; b. Corpus Christi, Tex., June 24, 1947; d. Owen Milton Jr. and Margaret (McFarland) Watkins; m. Steven Ray Christensen, May 28, 1977 (dec. 1985); children: Geoffrey Holland, Jeremy Ladd. BS, North Tex. State U., 1971; JD, U. Houston, 1977. Bar: Utah 1977, Tex. 1977, U.S. Dist. Ct. Utah 1977, U.S. Ct. Appeals (10th cir.) 1977, Utah Supreme Ct. 1977. Assoc. Berman & Giauque, Salt Lake City, 1977-80; ptnr. Kimball, Parr, Crockett & Waddoups, Salt Lake City, 1980—; adj. prof. law U. Utah Law Sch., Salt Lake City, 1979-81. Vision screener Nat. Soc. to Prevent Blindness, sec. exec. com., trustee, chair strategic planning com., 1985—; mem. exec. auction com., 1985-86, 1987-88, Rowland Hall St. Mark's Sch., room rep., 1985—, trustee, chair devel. com., 1987—; mem. United Methodist Ch. Mem. ABA (litigation section), Utah Bar Assn. (bar examiner, ethical adv. com., chair panel legal specialization com. litigation sect.), Tex. Bar Assn., Salt Lake County Bar Assn. (exec. com. 1979-87,, author, editor Utah Lawyers Practice Manual 1986), Women Lawyers of Utah (trustee, exec. com., chair spl. projects 1987—), Phi Delta Phi, Delta Gamma (treas. Salt Lake alumae chpt.), Alpha Lambda Delta. Office: Kimball Parr Crockett & Waddoups 185 S State St Suite 1300 PO Box 11019 Salt Lake City UT 84147

CHRISTENSEN, RACHEL RUDD, civil engineer; b. Cleve., July 28, 1953; d. Ralph C. and Carolyn (Clausen) Rudd; m. Eric H. Christensen, Oct. 29, 1952; children: Lincoln, Kyle. BSCE, U. Fla., Gainesville, 1978. Registered profl. engr. Fla. Engr. Sverdrup & Parcel, Gainesville, 1978-83; project mgr. Dyer, Riddle, Mills & Precourt, Orlando, Fla., 1984—; assoc. Dyer, Riddle, Mills & Precourt, Orlando, 1988—. Mem. Neighborhood Housing Services, Gainesville, (pres. of bd. dirs. 1982-83). Mem. ASCE., (chmn. legis. com. 1985-87). Mem. Soc. Friends. Club: Sweet Adelines (Orlando). Office: Dyer Riddle Mills & Precourt 1505 E Colonial DR Orlando FL 32803

CHRISTENSEN, SUSAN ANN, marketing product manager; b. Manitowoc, Wis., Mar. 27, 1951; d. Reinhold Frederick Jr. and Lynnette Lois (Abel) Detjen; m. Dennis James Christensen, Sept. 21, 1976 (div. 1984). Grad. high sch., Manitowoc, Wis. Cert. cen. service technician. Nurses aide for retarded Cen. Wis. Colony for Retarded, Madison, Wis., 1970-73; vet. asst. Dr. Eberhardt & Assocs., Token Creek, Wis., 1973-75; cen. service technician Madison Gen. Hosp., Madison, 1975-80; operating room materials mgr. U. Hosp. & Clinics, Madison, 1980-83; surg. instrments sales rep. Aesculap Instrument Corp., Wis., 1983-84; product mgr. Aesculap Instrument Corp., Burlingame, Calif., 1984—; pres. Advanced Travel Data, Fremont, Calif., 1987—; guest speaker Medline Industries, Nortbrook, Ill., 1981, Wis. Cen. Service Orgn., Madison, 1984, Napa Valley (Calif.) Cen. Service Orgn., 1986; sales trainer Aesculap Instrument Corp., Burlingame, 1984—; mfr. cons. Aesculap Werke, Tuttlingen, Fed. Republic Germany, 1984—; sales mgr. N.W. region Genesis Med. Corp., Ohio, 1988—. Contbr. articles to profl. jours. Big sister Home Juvenile Offenders, Middleton, Wis., 1976-77; counselor Suicide Hot Line & Drug Overdose, Madison, 1972-73. Recipient Highest Sales Dollar Achievement award Aesculap Instrument Corp., 1984. Mem. Nat. Assn. Female Execs., Assn. for Advancement Med. Instrumentation. Office: Advanced Travel Data PO Box 2188 Fremont CA 94536-0188

CHRISTENSEN, SUSAN MARY, nurse, military officer; b. San Francisco, Feb. 13, 1943; d. Kathryn Dorothy (Desin) Celentano; m. Earl Raymond Christensen, Oct. 16, 1976. RN, St. Luke's Hosp. Sch. Nursing, 1964; BS, Chapman Coll., 1981; cert., Air Command and Staff Coll., 1984. RN, Calif. Commd. as 1st lt. USAF, advanced through grades to lt. col., 1984; staff nurse obstetrics USAF, Loring AFB, Maine, 1970; from staff obstet. nurse to charge nurse labor/delivery unit Clark Regional Med. Ctr. USAF, Clark AFB, The Philippines, 1970-72; charge nurse, labor and delivery Med. Ctr., Travis AFB, Calif., 1972-74; flight nurse examiner 10th Aero Evac Squadron, Travis AFB, 1974-75, charge nurse, labor and delivery, 1975-77; charge nurse, labor and delivery Med. Ctr., Scott AFB, Ill., 1977-79; charge nurse, ob-gyn Med. Ctr., Scott AFB, 1979-80; asst. chief nurse USAF Hosp., Edwards AFB, Calif., 1980-82; chief nurse USAF Clinic, Spangdahlem, Federal Republic of Germany, 1982-85; assoc. chmn. dept. nursing Med. Ctr., Andrews AFB, Md., 1985-86; nurse cons. Tri-Services Med. Info. System Dept. of Defense, Bethesda, Md., 1986—; flight nurse examiner on last aeromedical evacuation flight from Saigon, Republic of Vietnam, 10th Aeromedical Evacuation Squadron, 1975, asst. chief nurse for space shuttle support during 2d and 3d missions, Edwards AFB, 1981, 82. Mem. Am. Nurses' Assn., Nurses Assn. Am. Coll. Ob-Gyn, Assn. Military Surgeons of U.S.A., Sr Women in the Air Force, Calif. Nurses' Assn. Roman Catholic.

CHRISTENSEN, THERESA ANN, marketing and sales specialist; b. Charleston, W.Va., June 14, 1949; d. Roy Clinton and Phyllis Jean (Short) Cobb; m. Gary J. Christensen, Oct. 27, 1968 (div. Nov. 1981). Sec. Amoco Chem. Co., Naperville, Ill., 1970-72, Borg-Warner Corp., Aurora, Ill., 1972-76; customer service mgr. Ga.-Pacific Corp., Oak Brook, Ill., 1976-82, sales rep., 1982-84; mktg. and sales specialist Hoechst-Celanese, Bayport, Tex., 1984-88, mktg. mgr., 1988—. Mem. Nat. Assn. Profl. Saleswomen, Nat. Assn. Female Execs., Plastic Drum Inst. (govt. relations com. 1984—), Soc. Plastics Engrs., NOW, Greenpeace, Am. Pub. Works Assn. Democrat. Home: 401 Lakeside Dr #111B Nassau Bay TX 77058 Office: Hoechst-Celanese 12212 Port Rd Pasadena TX 77507

CHRISTENSON, EVELYN CAROL, writer, lecturer; b. Muskegon, Mich., Jan. 31, 1922; d. Edward F. and Edna B. Luhman; A.A., Bethel Coll., St. Paul; student Moody Bible Inst., Chgo.; m. Harold Christenson, Feb. 14, 1942; children—Jan Christenson Johnson, Nancy Christenson Thompson, Kurt. Sec. to pres. Bethel Coll. and Sem., 1946-50; founding pres. United Prayer Ministries, St. Paul, 1973, chmn. bd., 1976—; internat. lectr. Australia, N.Z., Eng., Ireland, Scotland, Taiwan, Japan, India, Republic South Africa, Germany, Italy; mem. com., lectr. Am. Festival of Evangelism, Kansas City, Mo., 1981; co-prayer chmn., lectr. Internat. Council Bibl. Inerrancy, San Diego, Calif., 1982; consultation com. Internat. Conf. Itinerant Evangelists, Amsterdam, 1983; a sponsor Yr. of the Bible, 1983; mem. U.S. Nat. Prayer Com., 1983—; coordinator women's workshops Internat. Prayer Assembly, Seoul, Korea, 1984, World Vision Annual Internat. Day of Prayer, 1985; prayer leader trainer Billy Graham's Crusade, Washington, 1985; bd. reference Internat. Prayer Ministries, Inc., 1987; mem. com., prayer leader Pres's. Day of Prayer, Washington, 1986; writer; books include: What Happens When Women Pray (Top Ten list Christian Booksellers), 1975; Lord Change Me (Top Ten list Christian Booksellers), 1977; Gaining Through Losing (nat. devotional book of 1982 Evang. Christian Pubs. Assn.), 1980; What Happens When God Answers, 1986; reference cons. Internat. Prayer Ministries, Inc., 1987—; teaching cons. colls. Mem. Prison Fellowship Bd. (Washington); adv. bd. Concerned Women of Am., Berean League of Minn. Named Pacesetter of Yr., Bethel Coll., 1976; books rated top two by woman author Booksellers Jour., 1979; named Churchwoman of Yr., Religious Heritage of Am., 1980. Mem. Alumni Assn. Bethel Coll., Bethel Coll. Aux., Sem. Wives Assn. Bethel Sem. Home and Office: 4265 Brigadoon Dr Saint Paul MN 55126

CHRISTENSON, FABIENNE FADELEY, business executive; b. Washington, June 20, 1951; d. James McNelledge and Catherine Shirley (Sweeney) Fadeley; B.S. cum laude, U. Md., 1976; M.B.A. with honors, Boston U., 1979; m. Gordon A. Christenson, Sept. 16, 1979. With Gen. Electric Aircraft Engines, Evendale, Ohio, 1979—, contract adminstr., 1981, 83-84, foreman, 1981, prodn. control specialist, 1980-82, contract adminstr., 1985—, now negotiator for aircraft engine component purchases; pres. Mfg. Tng. Program, 1980. Home: 3465 Principio Ave Cincinnati OH 45208 Office: Gen Electric Aircraft Engines Mail Drop A-182C 1 Neumann Way Cincinnati OH 45215

CHRISTENSON, HELENE GOEHRING, retired accountant, auditor, budget analyst; b. Avon, S.D., May 24, 1912. B.S. in Bus. Adminstrn., U. Tulsa, 1957. Field auditor for various Honolulu C.P.A.s, 1958-64; adminstrv. asst. and fiduciary auditor Cooke Trust Ltd., 1965; auditor Naval Supply Ctr., 1967-69; acct., auditor Hdqrs. Fleet Marine Force, Pacific, 1969-81; budget and acctg. analyst Naval Constrn. Bns., Pearl Harbor, 1981-82, ret., 1982. Registered lobbyist for City, and County of Honolulu, Hawaii State Legislature 1981—; mem. Waikiki Neighborhood Bd., Honolulu, 1985; pres. Kalia, Inc., 1978—, Hawaii council Assns. Apt. Owners, 1985. Home: 425 Ena Rd Apt 906A Honolulu HI 96815

CHRISTIAN, BARBARA ANDREWS, internal auditor; b. Memphis, Apr. 11, 1960; d. Augustus Felton Andrews and Barbara Jean (Fritsch) Andrews McCuller. BBA, So. Meth. U., 1982. CPA, Tex. Mem. audit staff Arthur Young & Co., Dallas, 1982-84; audit sr. 1st Tenn., Memphis, 1984-85; audit sr. Holiday Corp., Memphis, 1985-87, audit supr., 1987—. Mem. Am. Inst. CPA's. Republican. Methodist. Office: Holiday Corp 3799 Lamar Ave Memphis TN 38195

CHRISTIAN, BETTY JO, lawyer; b. Temple, Tex., July 27, 1936; d. Joe and Mattie Manor (Brown) Wiest; m. Ernest S. Christian, Jr., Dec. 24, 1960. B.A. summa cum laude, U. Tex., 1957, LL.B. summa cum laude, 1960. Bar: Tex. 1961, U.S. Supreme Ct. 1964, D.C. 1980. Law clk. Supreme Ct. Tex., 1960-61; atty. ICC, 1961-68; asst. gen. counsel ICC, Washington, 1970-72; assoc. gen. counsel ICC, 1972-76, commr., 1976-79; partner firm Steptoe & Johnson, Washington, 1980—; atty. Labor Dept., Dallas, 1968-70. Mem. ABA, Fed. Bar Assn. (Younger Fed. Lawyer award 1964), Tex. Bar Assn., Am. Law Inst., Adminstrv. Conf. U.S., City Tavern Assn. Office: 1330 Connecticut Ave NW Washington DC 20036

CHRISTIAN, DOLLY LEWIS, civic affairs administrator; b. N.Y.C.; d. Daniel Webster and Adeline (Walton) Lewis. Dir. civic affairs equal employment affirmative action program Sperry & Hutchinson Co., N.Y.C., 1968-84; program mgr. affirmative action programs IBM Corp., 1984—. Chmn. bd. N.Y. Urban League, 1977-78, pres., 1978-84; panel of arbitrators Am. Arbitration Assn., N.Y.C., 1973—; adv. com. master's degree program in fund raising mgmt. New Sch. for Social Research, N.Y.C., 1978—; mem. mgmt. assistance com. Greater N.Y. Fund United Way, 1983—; treas. Assoc. Black Charities, 1982-84; bd. dirs. Coalition of 100 Black Women, 1981-87. Recipient scroll of honor Nat. Council Negro Bus. and Profl. Women's Clubs, 1975, community service award, 1974, ombudswoman award, 1975; youth salute to black corp. execs. award Nat. Youth Movement, 1975, corp. recipient Mary McLeod Bethune award Nat. Council Negro Women, 1976; spl. corp. recognition award Met. Council of Brs., NAACP, 1981; Named to Acad. of Achievers YWCA of N.Y. Mem. Council Concerned Black Execs. (vice chmn. 1970-77), NAACP, N.Y. Personnel Mgmt. Assn., Edges Group (v.p. 1981). Home: Jamaica NY 11435 Office: IBM Corp 2000 Purchase St Purchase NY 10577

CHRISTIAN, KAREN DORTHEA HANSEN, legislative liaison, real estate broker, educator; b. Berkeley, Calif., Mar. 18, 1938; d. Kirby Walter and Isabel Jordan (Smith) Hansen; m. William Shannon Christian, Oct. 23, 1961 (div. Oct. 1975); children—Sarah Ann, Janet Jordan. Student U. Geneva, 1956; B.A., U. Calif.-Berkeley, 1959, teaching cert., 1960; postgrad. San Diego State Coll., 1960-62. Lic. real estate broker, Calif.; cert. tchr., Calif. Tchr., Carden Pvt. Sch., Fresno, Calif., 1974-75; tchr. music Fresno Unified Schs., 1975-76; salesman Brinker Real Estate, Fresno, 1975-78, Adanalian & Jackson Real Estate, Fresno, 1978-79, Bob Johansen Realty, Fresno, 1979-80; real estate broker Karen H. Christian, Realtor, Fresno, 1980—; legislative analyst Fresno Bd. Realtors, 1982-85, also dir., 1981-83, 88-90. Mem. Republican Central Com., Fresno County, Calif., 1980-82; exec. dir. Taxpayers Assn. Fresno County, 1984—. Named Realtor-Assoc. of Year, 1979. Mem. Nat. Assn. Realtors, Calif. Assn. Realtors (dir. 1978-80, 82-84, dist. chmn. land use com. 1980-83), Fresno Area Mktg. Exchange (founder, sec. treas. 1978-79); U. Calif. Alumni Assn., LWV, Kappa Delta. Christian Scientist. Home and Office: 2539 W San Bruno Fresno CA 93711

CHRISTIAN, RACHEL LISA, computer specialist; b. Green Bay, Wis., Nov. 22, 1961; d. Roger W. and Carla Ann (Gruetzmacher) Steffel; m. Jeffrey M. Christian, Apr. 25, 1987; 1 child, Ashley Ann. Student, N.E. Wis. Tech. Inst., 1981—. Clk. invoicing and accounts receivable Algoma (Wis.) Hardwoods, Inc., 1979-81, programmer, 1981—, computer operator, 1981-85, analyst, 1985—. Mem. Data Processing Mgmt. Assn. (bd. dirs. Green Bay area), Data Mgmt. Group Green Bay. Home: 109 Steele St Apt 2 Algoma WI 54201 Office: Algoma Hardwoods Inc 1001 Perry St Algoma WI 54201

CHRISTIANS, JILL ARLETTE, chemical engineer; b. Alexandria, Va., Dec. 23, 1962; d. John Andrew and Beverly Browne (Pettit) C. BS magna cum laude, Brown U., 1984; postgrad., U. Conn., Storrs, 1985-87. Devel. engr. Polymer Composites Group, Rogers (Conn.) Corp., 1984—. Mem. Am. Chem. Soc., Am. Inst. Chem. Engrs., Am. Inst. Chemists (student research recognition found. award 1984), Soc. Women Engrs. (pres. coll. chpt. 1983-84), Nat. Assn. Female Execs., New Eng. Thermal Forum, Sigma Xi. Methodist. Home: 62 Stephen Hopkins Ct Providence RI 02904 Office: Rogers Corp Lurie R&D Bldg 1 Technology Dr Rogers CT 06263

CHRISTIANSEN, CLAIRE BETH, librarian; b. Omaha, Dec. 13, 1947; d. Charles Christian and Myra Lee (Hadan) C.; m. Timothy Allan Parrott, Aug. 30, 1969 (div. Apr. 1978); m. Kenneth Leon Hoover, Feb. 18, 1984. BA, U. Oreg., 1969, MLS, 1970. Cert. librarian, Washington. Subprofl. asst. Springfield (Oreg.) Pub. Library, 1970-71; reference librarian Missoula (Mont.) City-County Library, 1971-72, Springfield Pub. Library, 1972-73; materials selection coordinator Timberland Regional Library, Olympia, Wash., 1983; sr. community librarian Olympia Timberland Library, 1983—. Mem. ALA, Pub. Library Assn., Pacific Northwest Library Assn., Washington Library Assn., Altrusa, Delta Zeta (treas. 1968-69). Lutheran. Office: Olympia Timberland Library 8th & Franklin Olympia WA 98501

CHRISTIANSON, KAREN MARIA ANNA, lawyer; b. Milw., Mar. 10, 1949; d. Donald Edwin and Maria (Kotelnikova) Jones; m. Gary Michael Christianson, June 26, 1971; 1 son, Michael. B.S., U. Wis., 1970; J.D., U. Oreg., 1979. Bar: Oreg. 1979, Wis. 1983. Tchr., S. Milw. Sch. Dist., 1970-71, Corvallis, Oreg., 1971-76; dep. dist. atty. Linn County, Albany, Oreg., 1979-83; city atty. West Bend (Wis.), 1984—. sec., mcpl. atty. sect. Wis. League Municipalities. Mem. Planning Commn. Corvallis, 1980-83; active Benton County Democrats. Mem. Wis. State Bar Assn., ABA, U. Wis. Madison Alumni Club (pres. Washington County chpt.), Phi Delta Phi. Club: PACE.

CHRISTIE, CAROLE SULLIVAN, advertising executive; b. St. Louis; d. John Hinchey and Ann (Houlihan) Sullivan; m. Robert James Christie, Sept. 7, 1974; children: John O'Meara, Kira Ann. BA, Rockhurst Coll., 1973. Writer, designer Advt. Assocs., St. Louis, 1975; creative mgrs. mktg. rep. Breckenridge Hotels Corp., St. Louis, 1975-76; sr. writer D'Arcy, MacManus & Masius, St. Louis, 1976-83; v.p., creative dir. Gardner Advt., St. Louis, 1983-85; sr. v.p., creative dir. D'Arcy, Masius, Benton & Bowles, St. Louis, 1985—; tchr. Principles of Advt. class, St. Louis U., 1982; judge CLIO awards, 1984, Indpls. ADDIs, 1985. Author and numerous dir. numerous film, radio and TV advertisements. Recipient Silver award Internat. Film & TV Festival of N.Y., 1980, award of excellence, 9th dist. ADDIs, 1980, 83, CLIO cert. for creative excellence, 1981, 84, ANDY award Advt. Club of N.Y.,1982, two first place Marconi awards St. Louis Radio Assn., 1983, "honors" Emmy award Nat. Acad. Motion Picture Arts and Scis., 1983 Gold Ring award, cert. of excellence Bus./Profl. Advt. Assn., 1986; others. Mem. Advt. Fed. St. Louis, Nat. Assn. Female Execs. Home: 89 Aberdeen Clayton MO 63105 Office: D'Arcy Masius Benton & Bowles Gateway Tower 1 Memorial Dr Saint Louis MO 63102

CHRISTIE, LAURIE POTTER, state agency administrator; b. Harvard, Ill., Sept. 20, 1956; d. Donald Eugene and Margurita Marie (Ferrero) Potter; m. Scott Graham Christie, Nov. 15, 1980. B.A., Ind. U., 1978. Constituent analyst Ind. State Senate, Indpls., 1979; exec. dir. Ind. State Election Bd., Indpls., 1981—; campaign cons. Ind. Republican State Com., 1978-81, Ind. State Senate, 1979. Author: Instruction Manual for Precinct Officials, 1982. Campus coordinator Myers for Congress Com., Bloomington, Ind., 1974; field campaign mgr. Ind. Rep. State Com., Indpls., 1978; campaign adviser Ind. State Legis. Coms., Indpls., 1978; dep. campaign mgr. Bob Orr for Gov. Coms., 1980; campaign advisor O'Laughlin for Clk. of Cts., 1982. Named Hon. Sec. of State, Ind. Sec. of State, 1979, Sagamore of Wabash, Gov. of Ind., 1981. Mem. Internat. Orgn. Election Ofcls., Nat. Assn. Secs. of State. Methodist. Club: Valley Riders Saddle. Office: Ind State Election Bd 850 N Meridian St Indianapolis IN 46204

CHRISTIN, VIOLET MARGUERITE, retired banker; b. Chgo., Oct. 4, 1903; d. Charles A. and Eva M. (Bosse) Christin; student Northwestern U., 1936-37, Am. Inst. Banking, 1955-75; Ph.D., Colo. State Christian Coll. With Nat. Bank Austin, 1922-76, asst. sec., 1953-57, sec., 1957-65, sec., asst. v.p., 1965-75, also cons., sec. mktg. com., 1977-79. Mem. Am. Inst. Banking, Ill. Bankers Assn. (50 yr. club), Assn. Chgo. Bank Women, Nat. Assn. Bank Women, Ill. Group. Nat. Assn. Bank Women, Chgo. Financial Advertisers (life mem.; Eagle award 1977, dir., treas.; First Lady Life Mem. award 1981). Clubs: Executives, Advertising, Press (Chgo.). Home: 805 N Grove Ave Oak Park IL 60302

CHRISTOFORAKIS, SHARON LEE, medical services administrator; b. Brockport, N.Y., July 22, 1951; d. Sebastian David and Beverly Ann (Seifert) Sorce; m. Nicholas George Christoforakis, July 5, 1980; 1 child, Alexandra Rose. BA, SUNY, Brockport, 1973, MS, 1975. Asst. dean students SUNY, 1973-78; dir. housing Rosary Coll., River Forest, Ill., 1978-79; collector Citicorp, Inc., Chgo., 1980-81; collector med. service plan U. Ill., Chgo., 1982-84, supr., 1984-85, tng. coordinator, 1985, assoc. dir., 1985-87; account mgr. Interpretive Data Systems, Oakbrook Terrace, Ill., 1987—. Active Wheaton (Ill.) Hist. Preservation Council, St. Nicholas Theatre Workshop, Wheaton. Mem. Med. Group Mgmt. Assn., Ill. Med Group Mgmt. Assn., Acad. Practice Assembly. Home: 417 N President St Wheaton IL 60187 Office: Interpretive Data Systems 1901 S Meyers Rd Oak Brook Terrace IL 60146

CHRISTOLON, BLAIR KAY BIRKHOLZ, librarian; b. Oak Park, Ill., Oct. 1, 1947; d. William Howard and Evelyn Weinkauf (Mueller) Birkholz; BA, U. Denver, 1969; MLS, Brigham Young U., Provo, Utah, 1976; m. Warren Kenneth Christolon, Aug. 12, 1972; children: Christopher Warren, Niklas Winston. Librarian, Johns Hopkins U., USIS, Bologna, Italy, 1972-73; tchr. Denver public schs., 1969-74; asst. dir. children's services Weber County Library, Ogden, Utah, 1975-77; dir. govt. library Overseas Pvt. Investment Corp., Washington, 1978; library cons. Dept. Edn., Washington, 1979-82; admissions dir. Alpha-Bet Sch., Manassas, Va., 1981-85, pres., 1984-85; librarian Prince William Library, Manassas, Va., 1985—. Mem. parent adv. com. Va. Coop. Extension, 1981—, editor newsletter, 1981-85; cons. Parent Infant Handicapped Edn., 1979; v.p. Manassas Friends of Library, 1983-85. Recipient Outstanding Woman award U. Denver, 1969. Mem. ALA, Delta Gamma. Home: 8396 Briarmont Ln Manassas VA 22111

CHRISTOPHER, GRACE MARY, mechanical engineer; b. Los Angeles, Oct. 14, 1960; d. Victor and Mary (Kubota) Miyamoto; m. Edward Anthony Christopher, April 12, 1986. AA in Engring. with highest honors, Cerritos Community Coll., 1980, AA in Math. with highest honors, 1981; BS in Mech. Engring. magna cum laude, Calif. Polytechnic U., 1983; postgrad., U. So. Calif., Los Angeles, 1987—. Instrnl. aide Cerritos Community Coll., Norwalk, Calif., 1980; engring. aide Garrett AiResearch Mfg. Co., Torrance, Calif., 1980-81; mem. tech. staff 2 mechanical radar systems group Radar Systems Group, Hughes Aircraft Co., El Segundo, Calif., 1983—. Recipient Recognition award Soc. Women Engrs., 1982. Mem. Nat. Assn. for Female Execs., Alpha Gamma Sigma, Phi Kappa Phi, Tau Beta Pi, Pi Tau Sigma. Republican. Home: 2559 Plaza Del Amo #213 Torrance CA 90503 Office: Hughes Aircraft Co 2000 E Imperial Hwy El Segundo CA 90245

CHRISTOPHER, MAURINE BROOKS, writer, editor; b. Three Springs, Tenn.; d. John Davis and Zula (Pangle) Brooks; m. Milbourne Christopher, June 25, 1949. B.A., Tusculum Coll., 1941. Reporter, feature writer Balt. Sun, 1943-45; TV radio Editor Advt. Age, 1947-51, sr. editor, head broadcast dept., 1951-77; dep. exec. editor Advt. Age, N.Y.C., 1977-79, dep. exec. editor, Videotech columnist, 1979-84; producer-moderator Adbeat, syndicated radio show, 1970-78, roving editor, mem. editorial bd., Videotech columnist, 1984—. Author: America's Black Congressmen, 1971, Black Americans in Congress, 1976. Mem. Am. Women in Radio and TV (past pres. N.Y.C. chpt. cert. of merit), Assn. Study Afro-Am. Life and History. Home: 333 Central Park W New York NY 10025 Office: 220 E 42d St New York NY 10017

CHRISTO-SCHLAPP, JOI, sales promotion executive; b. Elmhurst, N.Y., June 21, 1959; d. James Anastas Jr. and Rosemarie Joan (Cannavina) Christo; m. Steven Thomas Schlapp, July 21, 1984. BS in Communication Arts, St. John's U., 1981. Network sales asst. Eastman Radio, Inc., N.Y.C., 1981-83; nat. sales asst. Hillier, Newmark, Wechsler & Howard, N.Y.C.,

1983-84, office mgr., 1984-86, promotion dir., 1986—. Mem. Internat. Radio and TV Soc. Home: 69-33 Caldwell Ave Maspeth NY 11378 Office: Hillier Newmark Wechsler and Howard 100 Park Ave New York NY 10017

CHRISTY, JENNIFER ANNE KESSLER, trade association executive; b. Lincoln, Neb., Mar. 5, 1951; d. Milton Eugene and Ardis June (Carman) Kessler; m. Logan Blair Christy, Aug. 12, 1972 (div. Mar. 17, 1981). BS in Edn., U. Neb., 1973; MA in History with distinction, Georgetown U., 1982. Title I remedial reading tchr. Montgomery County Schs., Shawsville, Va., 1974-76; librarian asst. Lincoln City Libraries, 1976-79; legis. asst. Nat. Beer Wholesalers' Assn., Falls Church, Va., 1981-82, mgr. membership services, 1982, dir. membership services, 1982—. Vol. Young Dems. Arlington County, Va., 1981-83, Christmas in April, Washington, 1988—. Mem. Nat. Women's Assn. of Allied Beverage Industries Inc., Metro D.C. Women's Assn Allied Beverage Industries Inc. (pres. 1985-87), Nat. Assn. Female Execs., Am. Soc. Assn. Execs. Greater Washington Soc. Assn. Execs., Nat. Trust for Hist. Preservation, NOW, Phi Alpha Theta (past pres. Beta Pi chpt.). Democrat. Roman Catholic. Office: Nat Beer Wholesalers Assn 5205 Leesburg Pike Suite 1600 Falls Church VA 22041

CHROMAN, SANDRA CHRISTINE, executive human resources and administration; b. Delano, Calif., Jan. 24, 1949; d. Christian Andrew and Myrtle Imogene (Kirkpatrick) C. BA, Calif. State U., Bakersfield, 1973; MBA, U. Denver, 1974. Employee relations analyst Shell Oil Co., Denver, 1974-76; personnel supr. Kaiser Aluminum, Spokane, Wash., 1976-78; dir. personnel American Sign and Indicator, Spokane, 1978-80, Nat. Semiconductor, Santa Clara, Calif., 1980-83; dir. human resources Eaton Semiconductor Equipment, San Jose, Calif., 1983-85; v.p. human resources and adminstrn. Icot Corp., San Jose, 1985—; adj. faculty Ea. Washington U., Pullman, 1978-80, City Coll., Spokane, 1978-80; bd. dirs. Santa Clara County Better Bus. Bur., San Jose, 1986—. Bd. dirs. Spokane Occupational Industries Council, 1978-80. Mem. Am. Soc. Personnel Adminstrn., Am. Soc. Tng. and Devel., Human Resource Forum (chmn.), N. Calif. Human Resource Council, C. of C. (San Jose high tech. com. 1985—). Republican. Home: 2481 Clear Spring Ct San Jose CA 95133 Office: Icot Corp 3801 Zanker Rd San Jose CA 95051-5143

CHRYSSICAS, VALERIE FOSTER, marketing and advertising agency executive; b. Newark, June 6, 1955; d. Robert Samuel and Adelaide J. (Nelson) Foster; m. Willie Alton Davis, III, June 14, 1974 (div. 1977); m. John Charles Chryssicas, Jr., Jan. 4, 1980; 1 child, Jason Christopher. Student Randolph-Macon Coll., 1973-75; B.A. in Spanish, Salisbury State Coll., 1977; M.S. in Sociolinguistics, Georgetown U., 1980. Account rep. List Am., Inc., Washington, 1980; account exec. Infomat, Inc., Rolling Hills Estates, Calif., 1981; pres. N.M.C., Inc., Newport Mktg., Newport Beach, Calif., 1982—. Office: NMC Inc and Newport Mktg 1400 Quail St Suite 180 Newport Beach CA 92660

CHRZAN-SEELIG, PATRICIA ANN, Corporate professional; b. Springfield, Mass., Mar. 3, 1954; d. Stanley Paul Jr. and Roberta Ann (Casey) Chrzan; m. Harold Cranmer Seeling, Nov. 5, 1977; children: H. Casey, Marguerite Andera. BS in Human Devel., U. Mass., 1974. Dir. YWCA, Infant Day Care Ctr., Springfield, Mass., 1974-75, Tri-Cities Info. and Referral, Petersburg, Va., 1975-77; policy analyst Office of the Sec. Human Resources, Richmond, Va., 1977-78; data specialist Dept. Mental Health/Retardation, Richmond, Va., 1978-79; programmer Sands Internat., Oakton, Va., 1979-80; programmer analyst Carter Hawley Hale, Richmond, Va., 1980; v.p. Preferred Custom Software, Wilsons, Va., 1980—. Co-chmn. St. Jude's Hosp. (Bikeathon), Blackstone, Va., 1987. Mem. Nat. Assn. Female Execs., Blackstone Woman's Club (v.p. 1985-86), Va., Blackstone Town, Hobby, and Garden Club (pres. 1987—). Home and Office: Rt 1 Box 26A Wilsons VA 23894

CHUBB-HALE, VIRGINIA MIGNON, teacher; b. Roanoke, Va., Nov. 3, 1942; d. Leon and Perneller (Delaney) Chubb; m. David Lee Hale; 1 child, Brian. BS, Bluefield State Coll., 1966; MEd, U. Va., 1972. Tchr. Amherst (Va.) County Sch. Bd., 1966-67; tchr. Roanoke City Schs., 1967-85, 86—, tchr. adult edn., 1971-75, tchr. gifted program, 1979; coordinator elementary social studies Roanoke City Sch. Bd., 1985-86. Author: Outstanding Blacks in Roanoke Past and Present, 1983. Mem. Roanoke Cath. Sch. Bd., 1970-74, Comm. on Christian Edn., 1979-82; chmn. Christian Edn., 1975-77; sponsor Safety Patrol, 1970-87, Y-Teens, 1979-81; pres., founder NW Investor; bd. dirs. Harrison Heritage and Cultural Ctr. Named Outstanding Woman SW Va., Times and World News, 1983. Mem. Roanoke Edn. Assn., Va. Edn. Assn. (Mary Hatwood Futrell award 1988), Nat. Edn. Assn., Va. Council for the Social Studies (Tchr. of Yr. award 1980), Roanoke Valley Hist. Soc., Am. Assn. for Univ. Women, Bluefield State Coll. Alumni Assn. (past pres.), NAACP, Cath. Hist. Soc., Delta Kappa Gamma. Home: 2721 Cove Rd NW Roanoke VA 24017

CHUHRAN, LINDA, elected administrative clerk; b. Ypsilanti, Mich., Aug. 28, 1949; m. Terry Edward Chuhran, Feb. 14, 1970; children: Scott Edward, Stacey Lynn. AAS in Cosmetology Mgmt., Schoolcraft Coll., 1980, AAS in Small Bus. Mgmt., 1983, AAS in Mktg. and Applied Mgmt., 1984, AAS in Gen. Bus., 1986, AAS in Gen. Studies, 1987; BA in Social Sci., Madonna Coll., 1988. Lic. cosmetologist, instr.; cert. model. Sr. clk. Allison div. G.M. Detroit, Redford, Mich., 1969; adminstrv. clk. Canton (Mich.) Township Hall, 1984—; freelance model, photgraphy cons. 1970—; cons. Photographer and Model Usage Services, Mich., 1976—; del. Southeastern Mich. Councils of Govt., 1984—. Author: booklets: 1986 Punch Card Voting System, 1986 Voter Info., Media Relations, 1987; creator computer program Absentee Voters, 1986. Adv. bd. Oakwood Hosp., Canton, 1984—; v. chairperson Republican Forum, Mich., 1986—; mem. Mich. Township Polit. Action Com., Lansing, 1986; advisor Gen. Motors Jr. Achievement, Detroit, 1975-76. Recipient Disting. Advisor award Jr. Achievement of Southeastern Mich., 1975. Mem. Schoolcraft Coll. Alumni Bd., Nat. Assn. Female Execs., Am. Mgmt. Assn., Internat. Records Mgmt. Council, Bus. and Profl. Women's Orgn., Nat. Hairdressers Assn. Home: 44184 Wiclif Ct Canton MI 48187 Office: Canton Twp Hall 1150 S Canton Center Rd Canton MI 48188

CHULAK-FISKE, DARLENE, social services administrator; b. Bridgeport, Conn., Sept. 1, 1955; d. Walter Robert and Sylvia Agnes (Bartomioli) Chulak; m. Allen Sumner Fiske, Apr. 25, 1981. AS in Mental Health, U. Bridgeport, 1975, MS in Psychology, 1980; BS in Psychology, So. Conn. State U., 1978. Cert. marriage and family therapist. Adminstrv. asst. Yale U., New Haven, 1975-76; counselor Daytop, Inc., Shelton, Conn., 1976-77; sr. counselor Liberation House, Stamford, Conn., 1977-80; dir. New Canaan (Conn.)/Darien Youth Service Bur., 1980-81; clin. supr., dir. New Canaan Youth Options, 1981-83; dir. Guilford (Conn.) Youth Services, 1983—; pvt. practice marriage and family therapist Milford, Conn., 1984—; lectr. and cons. in field. Mem. Am. Orthopsychiat. Assn., Am. Assn. for Marriage and Family Therapy (clin.). Office: PO Box 5117 Milford CT 06460

CHUN, LISA YEE-TAI, loan agent; b. Chicago Heights, Ill., Apr. 10, 1957; d. Arthur Yau Kong and Tillie Ann (Dea) C. Grad. high sch., Park Forest, Ill. Lic. real estate agt. Real estate agt. Nora West-Realtor, Oakland, Calif., 1979-85; loan agt. Home Savs. of Am., Mountain View, Calif., 1985—. Cofounder, former chairperson Asian Women, San Francisco, 1983-85. Mem. Palo Alto Bd. Realtors (affiliate, social com. 1987). Lodge: Soroptimists. Office: Home Savs of Am 749 El Camino Real Mountain View CA 94040

CHUN, WENDY SAU WAN, investment company executive; b. China, Oct. 17, 1951; came to U.S., 1975; d. Siu Kee and Lai Ching (Wong) C.; m. Wing Chiu Ng, Aug. 12, 1976. B.S., Hong Kong Bapt. Coll., 1973; postgrad. U. Hawaii-Manoa, 1975-77. Real estate saleswoman Tropic Shores Realty Co., Honolulu, 1977-80; pres., prin., broker Advance Realty Investment Co., Honolulu, 1980—; owner Video Fun Centre, Honolulu, 1981-83; pres, Asia-Am. Bus Cons., Inc., Canada, 1986—; co-owner, dir. H & N Tax, Honolulu, 1983—; bd. dirs. B.P.D. Internat., Ltd., Hong Kong. Mem. Nat. Assn. Realtors. Avocations: singing; dancing; swimming; dramatic performances. Home: Apt 3302 2333 Kapiolani Blvd Honolulu HI 96826

CHUPELA, DOLORES CAROLE, children's librarian; b. New Brunswick, N.J., Dec. 25, 1952; d. John Joseph and Cecilia Dolores (Pazdon) C. B.S., Douglass Coll., 1975; M.L.S., Rutgers U., 1984. Cert. tchr., N.J. Librarian, Edison Pub. Library (N.J.), 1979—. Author: Gates to Lands of Pleasure, 1986. Speaker civic orgns. Named Tercentennial Citizen-of-Week, Middlesex County, N.J., New Brunswick, 1983; recipient Presdl. sports award in figure skating, 1980. Mem. ALA and Assn. Library Service to Children, N.J. Library Assn., Rutgers Alumnae Assn. (speaker radio program), Children's Book Council. Democrat. Roman Catholic. Club: Princeton Skating. Contbg. author 1984 Summer Reading Club Manual. Home: 51 Latonia St Edison NJ 08817 Office: Edison Pub Library 340 Plainfield Ave Edison NJ 08817

CHURCH, IRENE ZABOLY, personnel services company executive; b. Cleve., Feb. 18, 1947; d. Bela Paul and Irene Elizabeth (Chandas) Zaboly; children: Irene Elizabeth, Elizabeth Anne, Lauren Alexandria Gadd, John Dale Gadd II. Student pub. schs. Personnel cons., recruiter, Cleve., 1965-70; chief exec. officer, pres. Oxford Personnel, Pepper Pike, Ohio, 1973—, Oxford Temporaries, Pepper Pike, 1979—; guest lectr. in field, 1974—; expert witness for ct. testimony, 1982—. Troop leader Lake Erie council Girl Scouts Am., 1980-81; mem. Christian action com. Federated Ch., United Ch. Christ, 1981-85, sub-com. to study violence in relation to women, 1983, creator, presenter programs How Work Affects Family Life and Re-entering the Job Market, 1981, mem. Women's Fellowship Martha-Mary Circle, 1980—, program dir., 1982-84, 87—; chpt. leader Nat. Coalition on TV Violence, 1983—. Mem. Nat. Assn. Personnel Consultants (cert., mem. ethics com. 1976-77, co-chairperson ethics com. 1977-78, mem. bus. practices and ethics com. 1980-82, mem. cert. personnel cons. soc. 1980-82, regional leader for membership 1987—), Ohio Assn. Personnel Consultants (trustee 1975-80, 85—, sec. 1976-77, 85—, chairperson bus. practices and ethics com. 1976-77, 81-82, 1st v.p., chairperson resolutions com. 1981-82, chairperson membership com. 1985—, 2d v.p. 1987—, Outstanding Service award 1987), Greater Cleve. Assn. Personnel Consultants (2d then 1st v.p., 1974-76, state trustee 1975-80, pres. 1976-77, bd. advisor 1977-78, chairperson bus. practices and ethics com. 1974-76, nominating com. ,1983, membership com. 1984-85, arbitration com., 1980, fundraising, 1980——, bd. dirs. 1980—, , trustee 1985—, program chair 1987—, Vi Pender Outstanding Service award 1977), Euclid C. of C. (small bus. com. 1981, chairperson task force com. evaluating funding in social security and vet.'s benefits 1981), Internat. Platform Assn., Am. Bus. Women's Assn., Nat. Assn. Temp. Services, Chagrin Valley C. of C. (leader Chagrin Blvd./East chpt. 1987—), Greater Cleve. Growth Assn. Council Small Enterprises. Lodge: Rotary Internat. (pres. 1987—),(Beachwood chpt). Home: 8 Ridgecrest Dr Chagrin Falls OH 44022 Office: Oxford Personnel Exec Commons 2945 Chagrin Blvd Pike OH 44122

CHURCH, JUDITH KATHERINE, interior design consultant; b. Invercargill, Southland, New Zealand, June 18, 1940; d. Murdo Alexander and Jean Isobel (Gardiner) McKenzie; m. Barry D. Rutherford, Oct. 23, 1959 (div. Apr. 1983); children: Megan Jane, Antony Alexander McKenzie; m. Charles H. Church Jr., Jan. 11, 1986. BA, U. Otago, Dunedin, New Zealand, 1962. Tchr. pre-sch. Leith Pre-Sch., Dunedin, 1964-68, Aldrich Meml. Nursery Sch., Rochester, Minn., 1968-76; corp. recruiter Christopher & Long, Kansas City, Mo., 1983-86; interior design cons. Trans Design, Lenexa, Kans., 1986—; early edn. lectr. Rochester (Minn.) Community Coll., 1973-76; docent, tour guide Nelson Gallery Art, Kansas City, Mo., 1977—. Pres. Jr. Women's Symphony Alliance, Kansas City, Mo., 1982-83; bd. dirs. Kansas City (Mo.) Philharm., 1982-83; mem. U. Mo. Women's Council, Kansas City, 1982—, treas. 1985-86; mem. Lyric Opera Guild; guide Kansas City Ballet Guild. Club: Cen. Exchange (Kansas City, Mo.). Home and Office: 8540 Westgate Lenexa KS 66215

CHURCH, KAREN KATHLEEN, pharmaceuticals executive; b. Longmont, Colo., Oct. 26, 1945; d. Maurice G. and Hariette E. (Gage) C. BS, U. Wyo., 1967. Label editor Abbott Labs., North Chicago, 1967-70, sr. regulatory mgr., 1973-80; sr. editor Astra Pharms., Worcester, Mass., 1970-73; assoc. dir. Hoffmann LaRoche Co., Nutley, N.J., 1980-88; dir. regulatory affairs Gensia Pharms., San Diego, 1988—; mem. faculty Ctr. Profl. Advancement, East Brunswick, N.J., 1987—. Author: Current Developments in Drug Regulations/Pharmacology, 1987. Pres. Waukegan (Ill.) Community Players, 1978. Mem. Am. Med. Writers Assn., Food and Drug Law Inst., Regulatory Affairs Profl. Soc., Drug Info. Assn. (sec. 1986-89). Office: Gensia Pharms 11075 Roselle St San Diego CA 92121-1207

CHURCH, MARTHA ELEANOR, college president; b. Pitts., Nov. 17, 1930; d. Walter Seward and Eleanor (Boyer) C. B.A., Wellesley Coll., 1952; M.A., U. Pitts., 1954; Ph.D., U. Chgo., 1960; D.Sc. (hon.), Lake Erie Coll., 1975; Litt.D. (hon.), Houghton Coll., 1980; L.H.D. (hon.), Queens Coll., 1981, Ursinus Coll., 1981, St. Joseph Coll., 1982, Towson State U., 1983, Dickinson Coll., 1987. Instr. geography Mt. Holyoke Coll., S. Hadley, Mass., 1953-57; lectr. geography Ind. U. Gary Center, 1958; instr., then asst. prof. geography Wellesley Coll., 1958-60, 60-65; dean coll., prof. geography Wilson Coll., 1965-71; assoc. exec. sec. Commn. Higher Edn., Middle States Assn. Coll. and Secondary Sch., 1971-75; pres. Hood Coll., Frederick, Md., 1975—; bd. dirs. Farmers and Mechanics Nat. Bank; cons. for Choice: Books for Coll. Libraries; co-chmn. nat. adv. panel Nat. Ctr. for Research to improve postsecondary teaching and learning, U. Mich., 1985—; mem. bd. vis. Def. Intelligence Coll., 1988—. Author: The Spatial Organization of Electric Power Territories in Massachusetts, 1960; Co-editor: A Basic Geographical Library: A Selected and Annotated Book List for Am. Colls, 1966; cons. editor, Change mag., 1980—. Bd. dirs. Council for Internat. Exchange of Scholars, 1979-80, Japan Internat. Christian U. Found. 1977—, Nat. Center for Higher Edn. Mgmt. Systems, 1980-83; bd. dirs. Am. Council on Edn., 1976-79, vice chmn., 1978-79, mem. nat. identification panel, 1977—; bd. advisors Fund for Improvement of Postsecondary Edn., HEW, 1976-79; mem. Sec. of Navy's Adv. Bd. on Edn. and Tng., 1976-80; chmn. Md. Panel on Civil Rights, 1981-82; trustee Bradford Coll., Mass., 1982-87, Peddie Sch., N.J., 1982—, Carnegie Found. for the Advancement of Teaching, 1986—; mem. pub. adv. com. Bus. and Profl. Women's Found., 1982—; chmn. bd. dirs. Medici Found., Princeton, N.J., 1985—; mem. Md. Humanities Council, 1985-86, Md. Jud. Disabilities Commn., 1985—; mem. Edn. Commn. States, 1981—; exec. com. Campus Compact: Project for Pub. and Community Service, 1986—; mem. bd. visitors Defense Intelligence Coll., 1988—. Recipient Christian R. and Mary F. Lindback Found.; Disting. Teaching award Wilson Coll., 1971. Mem. AAUW, Am. Assn. Advancement of Humanities (dir. 1979-81), Am. Assn. Higher Edn. (chmn. 1980-81, bd. dirs. 1979-83), Nat. Assn. Ind. Colls. and Univs. (bd. dirs. 1983-86), Md. Ind. Colls. and Univs. Assn. (pres. 1979-81), Assn. Am. Colls. (adv. com. project on status and edn. of women 1980-85), Women's Coll. Coalition (exec. com. 1976-80, 87—), Am. Conf. Acad. Deans (sec., editor 1969-71), Council Protestant Colls. and Univs. (bd. dirs. 1969-71), Soc. Coll. and Univ. Planning (editorial bd. 1979—), Inst. Ednl. Leadership (bd. dirs. 1982-87), Sigma Delta Epsilon. Home: Pres's House Hood Coll Frederick MD 21701

CHURCH, SONIA JANE SHUTTER, librarian; b. York, Pa., Dec. 15, 1940; d. Robert Benjamin and Eva Alverta (Horn) Shutter; m. Ernest Layton Church, May 20, 1966; children—Robert Bruce, Jennifer Grace. B.S. in Edn., Millersville Coll. 1962; M.L.S., U. Pitts., 1978. Playground supr. York City Sch. Dist., Pa., 1961; officer USMC, 1962-66; children's librarian Prunedale br. Monterey County Library, Calif., 1978-79; youth services coordinator Monterey County Library, 1979-83, 85-88, head librarian Prunedale br., 1983-85; children's services mgr. Ventura (Calif.) County Library, 1988—; writer Book Beat Column for Fortnighter Newspaper, Salinas 1983-85. Editor pamphlet: What Will we Do with the Baby? a collection of nursery rhymes and finger plays, 1977. Mem. Deferred Comp. Task Force, Monterey County, 1983—, Mgmt. Council, Monterey County, 1983—; chmn. adminstrv. com. Social Services Commn., 1983-85, chmn. ad hoc com., 1983—; coordinating com. Boy Scouts Am., Salinas, 1983-85; Children's Services Mgmt. Consortium, 1986—; tchr. Sun. Sch., Luth. Ch. Good Shepherd, Salinas, 1982—. Served to capt., USMC 1962-66. Sico scholar, 1958-62. Mem. ALA, Assn. Library Service to Children, Calif. Library Assn., Assn. Children's Librarians of No. Calif., Sch. and Pub. Librarians Assn. Monterey Bay Area, Assn. Childhood Edn. Internat., Storytellers Unltd., Am. Legion (comdr. 1984-85), Women's Internat. Bowling Congress, Women's Bowling Assn., U. Pitts. Alumni Assn., Millersville Tchrs. Coll. Alumni Assn., Beta Phi Mu, Beta Sigma Phi. Democrat. Lutheran. Home: PO Box 1124 Ventura CA 93002 Office: Ventura County Library 651 E Main St Ventura CA 93001

CHURCHMAN, JONNI LYNN, computer software executive; b. Akron, Ohio, July 27, 1952; d. Flavil Hall and Ruth Elizabeth (Helms) Fisher; m. James Catalona, July 8, 1972 (div. Mar. 1977); m. James Edmund Churchman, Nov. 20, 1982; 1 child, Gina Vanessa. Assoc., U. Akron, 1972. Programmer Ohio Edison, Akron, 1972-78; sr. programmer, analyst Republic 1st Bank (formerly 1st Nat. Bank Ft. Worth), 1978-79, project mgr. teleprocessing, 1979; customer support rep. UCCEL Corp. (name now Computer Assocs.), Dallas, 1979-81, leader tech. product, 1981-82, mgr., 1982-83, mgr. paperless item processing, 1983—, mgr. asset card and consumer transaction, 1986—, mgr. wire transfer, 1987, dir. banking products support, 1987-88. Mem. Women in Computing. Republican. Roman Catholic.

CHURCHVILLE, LIDA HOLLAND, librarian; b. Dallas, May 5, 1933; d. Norbert R. and Agnes J. (Buckley) Holland; m. Joseph J. Churchville, Oct. 6, 1952 (dec. 1974); children: Lisa, Zoe, Anthony (dec.), Stephen. BA in History, Russell Sage Coll., Troy, N.Y., 1965; MLS, SUNY, Albany, 1967. Librarian Office Legis. Research, N.Y. Senate, Albany, 1967-75; chief law library U.S. Army Library, Washington, 1975-78; coordinator fed. women's program Dept. Def., The Pentagon, 1976-78; chief library Nat. Archives and Records Services, 1978-81; reference and spl. project librarian Nat. Archives Library, 1981-83; spl. project librarian publs. unit Nat. Archives Trust Fund, 1983—. Mem. Women's Issues Task Force, 1981-83, Women's Nat. Dem. Club, 1981—, Eleanor Roosevelt Dem. Club, Greenbelt, Md.; mem. Paint Branch Unitarian Ch., Adelphi, Md. Recipient Outstanding Performance award The Pentagon, 1977. Mem. Am. Soc. Info. Sci., D.C. Library Assn., Law Librarians Soc. Washington, Soc. Am. Archivists, Nat. Women's Party, NOW, DC Online Users Group. Home: 19Q Ridge Rd Greenbelt MD 20770 Office: NEPP Nat Archives 8th and Pennsylvania Ave NW Washington DC 20408

CHURGIN, HARRIET VIVIAN, retail company executive; b. Bklyn., Aug. 3, 1936; d. Peter and Sheila (Perlow) Robbins; m. Perry R. Churgin; children—Eileen Egbert, Heidi, Sterling. Student pub. schs., Bklyn.; grad., N.Y. Inst. Tech., 1987. Owner Pretty Panties and Other Fine Lingerie, Brentwood, N.Y., 1981—. Leader Suffolk County Girl Scouts U.S.A., 1966-69; com. person Democratic Club, Islip, N.Y., 1984—; charter mem. Nat. Mus. for Women in Arts, Friends of Brentwood Pub. Library. Mem. Nat. Assn. Female Execs., NRA (assoc.), People for the Am. Way, Nat. Mus. Women in Arts (charter). Jewish. Avocations: walking; camping; fishing; swimming. Home: 588 Grand Blvd Brentwood NY 11717

CHUSID, JUDITH FRANCINE (MARKS), school psychologist, psychoanalyst; b. N.Y.C., Dec. 3, 1947; d. Harry and Phyllis A. Chusid; B.A., Queens Coll., 1971; M.A., NYU, 1974, Ph.D. (A.B.D.), 1981; P.D., St. John's U., 1978; grad. Manhattan Center for Psychoanalytic Studies; m. Dec. 12, 1982. Program supr. East N.Y. YM-YWHA, 1970; tchr. Lexington Sch. for Deaf, N.Y.C. Bd. Edn., 1971-76; instr. Adelphi U., Garden City, N.Y., 1976-80; pvt. practice psychoanalytic psychotherapy, Jackson Heights and N.Y.C., 1974—; founder, pres., chmn. bd. Positive Approaches to Sports Success Found., Jackson Heights, 1980-85; faculty Ctr. Modern Psychoanalytic Studies; former mem. teaching faculty, tng. analyst Rockland Inst. for Psychoanalysis and Psychotherapy, Suffern, N.Y.; mem. Joint Council for Mental Health; founder, pres. Positive Approaches to Sports and Performance Success, 1980; lectr. Found. of Thanotology, Columbia U.; condr. workshops, lectr. field sports psychology. Bd. dirs. Studio Elem. Sch. Co-founder, Actor's Voice, N.Y.C., 1982. Recipient Otto Klitgord award N.Y., 1967; cert. sch. psychologist, N.Y. State; cert. secondary tchr., physically handicapped tchr., N.Y. Mem. Am. Psychol. Assn., Nat. Accreditation Assn. Psychoanalysis (cert.), N.Y. State Assn. Sch. Psychologists. Contbr. articles to profl. jours.

CHUTE, MARCHETTE, author; b. Wayzata, Minn., Aug. 16, 1909; d. William Young and Edith Mary (Pickburn) C. A.B., U. Minn., 1930; Litt.D., Western Coll. for Women, 1952, Carleton Coll., 1957, Dickinson Coll., 1964. Author: Rhymes About Ourselves, 1932, The Search for God, 1941, Rhymes About the Country, 1941, The Innocent Wayfaring, 1943, Geoffrey Chaucer of England, 1946, Rhymes About the City, 1946, The End of the Search, 1947, Shakespeare of London, 1950, An Introduction to Shakespeare, 1951, Ben Jonson of Westminster, 1953, The Wonderful Winter, 1954, Stories from Shakespeare, 1956, Around and About, 1957, Two Gentle Men: The Lives of George Herbert and Robert Herrick, 1959, Jesus of Israel, 1961, (with Ernestine Perrie) The Worlds of Shakespeare, 1963, The First Liberty: A History of the Right to Vote in America, 1619-1850, 1969, The Green Tree of Democracy, 1971, P.E.N. American Center: A History of the First Fifty Years, 1972, Rhymes About Us, 1974. Exec. com. Nat. Book Com.; judge non-fiction Nat. Book Awards, 1952, 59. Recipient Author Meets the Critics award for best non-fiction of, 1950; Chap-Book award Poetry Soc. Am., 1954; N.Y. Shakespeare Club award, 1954; Secondary Edn. Bd. book award, 1954; Outstanding Achievement award U. Minn., 1957. Fellow Royal Soc. Arts; mem. Am. P.E.N. (pres. 1955-57), Am. Acad. Arts and Letters, Phi Beta Kappa. Home: 66 Glenbrook Rd Morris Plains NJ 07950

CHVANY, CATHERINE VAKAR, educator; b. Paris, Apr. 26, 1927; m. 1948; 3 children. B.A., Radcliffe Coll., 1963; Ph.D., Harvard U., 1970. Instr. Russian, Wellesley Coll., 1966-67; instr. MIT, 1967-70, lectr., 1970-71, asst. prof., 1971-74, assoc. prof. Russian, 1974-83, prof., 1983—; fellow Harvard Russian Research Ctr., 1979—. Lilly postdoctoral teaching award fellow MIT, 1975-76. Mem. Am. Assn. Advancement Slavic Studies, Linguistic Soc. Am., Am. Assn. Tchrs. Slavic and Eastern European Langs., Am. Council Teaching of Russian, Bulgarian Studies Assn. Author: On the Syntax of BE-Sentences in Russian, 1975. Co-editor: Slavic Transformational Syntax, 1974, Morphosyntax in Slavic, 1980, Gertruda Vakar. Stikhotvorenija, 1984; New Studies in Russian Language and Literature, 1987 Mem. editorial adv. bd. SEEJ, Folia Slavica, RLJ, Essays in Poetics. Contbr. articles to profl. jours. Address: MIT Bldg 14N Room 311 77 Massachusetts Ave Cambridge MA 02139

CHWATSKY, ANN (RITA), photographer, educator; b. Phila., Jan. 11, 1942; d. Jules and Gladys (Coleman) Schneider; m. Robert Schulz, June 23, 1961 (div. 1964); 1 child, Marc; m. Howard Franklin Chwatsky, Nov. 2, 1965; 1 child, Julie. BS in Art Edn., Hofstra U., 1965, MS, 1971; postgrad. L.I. U., 1973-74. Cert. tchr. Photography editor L.I. mag., 1976-80; instr. Internat. Ctr. Photography, N.Y.C., 1979-80, Parrish Art Mus., Southampton, N.Y., 1984—; mem. faculty L.I. U., Greenvale, N.Y., 1982—; coordinator master art workshop Southampton Coll., 1985, 86, 87, 88; photographs featured in Time, Newsweek, Newsday, Manchete, N.Y. Times, MD Medical Times, Photographers Gallery, London, 1985, Shakers, Nassau County Mus. Fine Arts, 1987, Greater Lafayette (Ind.) Mus. Art, 1988; group shows include: The Other, Houston Ctr. Photography, 1988, L.I. Fine Arts Mus., 1984, Women's Interart Ctr., N.Y.C., 1976, 80, Parrish Art Mus., Southampton, 1979, Internat. Ctr. Photography, N.Y.C., 1980, 82, Nassau County Mus. Fine Arts, 1983, Soho 20 Gallery, N.Y.C., 1984, New Orleans World's Fair, 1984; represented in permanent collections: Forbes N.Y.C. Midtown YWCA, Nassau County Mus. Fine Arts, Susan Rothenberg, others. Author: Four Seasons of Shaker LIfe, 1986. Bd. dirs. Rosa Lee Young Day Care Ctr., Rockville Centre, 1982-85. Recipient Estabrook Disting. Alumni award Hofstra U., 1984; Kodak Profl. Photographers award, 1984; Eastman Found. grantee, 1981-82; Polaroid grantee, 1980. Mem. Assn. Am. Mag. Profls., Picture Profls. Am., Profl. Women Photographers N.Y.C. Democrat. Jewish. Avocations: tennis; gardening; travel. Home: 85 Andover Rd Rockville Centre NY 11570 also: Sag Harbor NY 11000

CIANI, JUDITH ELAINE, lawyer; b. Medford, Mass., July 24, 1943; d. A. Walter and Ruth Alice (Bowman) C.; m. Marion M. Smith, Sept. 29, 1982. Grad., Thayer Acad., Braintree, Mass., 1961; MA, Mt. Holyoke Coll., 1965; JD, Boston Coll., 1970. Aide/press sec. Rep. James A. Burke, Washington, 1965-67; atty. Pillsbury, Madison & Sutro, San Francisco, 1970-78, ptnr., 1978—; del. Calif. Bar Conv., San Francisco, 1973-78, 83-85. Mem. San Francisco Police Commn., 1976-80, Juvenile Justice Task Force, San Francisco, 1981-83; bd. dirs. Bernard Osher Found., San Francisco, 1977—; pres. Common Fund for Legal Services, San Francisco, 1985—, Sinfonia San Francisco, 1985-86. Fellow Am. Bar Found.; mem. Bar Assn. San Francisco (bd. dirs., pres. Found. 1978—, bd. dirs. 1981-83, treas. 1987). Home: 628

Lake St San Francisco CA 94118 Office: Pillsbury Madison & Sutro PO Box 7880 San Francisco CA 94120

CIARAMITARO, LINDA ROSE, nurse, administrator; b. Gloucester, Mass., May 4, 1953; d. Samuel John and Sally Rose (Orlando) C. Diploma in Nursing, Sacred Heart Hosp., 1974; BS, Boston U., 1981; M in Nursing, U. Wash., 1985. Staff nurse Oschner Found. Hosp., New Orleans, 1976-77, Beth Israel Hosp., Boston, 1977-78; asst. head nurse Providence Hosp., Seattle, 1983-85; nurse coordinator Harborview Med. Ctr., Seattle, 1985—; cons. med. affairs dept. Nutrasweet Co., Deerfield, Ill., 1984—. Bd. dirs., vice-chair Cape Ann chpt. Boston Office for Children, 1979-81, chair child abuse and neglect com., 1979-81; bd. dirs. Epilepsy Assn. Western Wash., Seattle, 1986. Mem. Am. Nurses' Assn., Sigma Theta Tau. Democrat. Roman Catholic. Office: Harborview Med Ctr 325 9th Ave Seattle WA 98104

CIARDULLO, MARION DOROTHY, public relations specialist; b. Newport, R.I., Oct. 22, 1924; d. Benjamin and Fannie (Lack) Rudick; m. Michael Ciardullo, May 31, 1950; children—Robin Bruce, Frances Audrey. A.B., Hunter Coll., 1947; postgrad. Columbia U., 1950. Copywriter, gen. Asst. Vanguard Advt., N.Y.C., 1947-48; media specialist J. Walter Thompson, 1948-50; pub. relations coordinator Norden, United Technologies Corp., Norwalk, Conn., 1971-81; mgr. mktg. communications Safe Flight Instrument Corp., White Plains, N.Y., 1982-84; mgr. mktg. communications W.W. Gaertner Research, Inc., Norwalk, Conn., 1985—. Contbr. articles to profl. jours. Mem. Aviation/Space Writers Assn., Pub. Relations Soc. Am., Fairfield County Pub. Relations Soc., Internat. Assn. Bus. Communicators, Women in Communication. Democrat. Jewish. Home: 19 Dairy Farm Rd Norwalk CT 06851

CICCOTOSTO, HARRIET MONICA, social services administrator; b. Boston, July 7, 1946; d. Limmie S. and Regina Anna Serafin Kerlin; m. Donald Ciccotosto, June 18, 1966; 1 child, Robert. Student, Combs Coll. of Music, 1964-66, Burlington County Coll., 1982—. Activities asst. Masonic Home of N.J., Burlington, 1982-83; dir. activities Mt. Laurel (N.J.) Convalescent Ctr., 1983-84; dir. activities vol. services Evergreens Episc. Home, Moorestown, N.J., 1984-88; activities dir., cons. Greenbriar Nursing and Convalescent Ctr., Woodbury, N.J., 1988—; chaplin aide, vol. coordinator Meml. Hosp. of Burlington County, Mt. Holly, N.J., 1975-84. Mem. N.J. Acticivy Profls. Assn. (founding mem., chairperson membership com. 1987, cert. activity dir. 1987)Tri-County Activities Coordinators (sec. 1984-85, pres. 1985—), Nat. Assn. of Activity Profls. (state contact), N.J. Recreation and Park Assn., N.J. Assn. Dirs. of Vol. Services., Nat. Cert. Council for Activity Profls. Republican. Episcopalian. Home: Rt 3 Carranza Rd Tabernacle NJ 08088 Office: Greenbriar Nursing and Convalescent Ctr 190 N Evergreeen Ave Woodbury NJ 08096

CICERO, MARILYN BELLE, travel consultant; b. N.Y.C., July 16, 1931; d. Sam K. and Helen (Smith) Kass; m. Arthur Bennet Cicero, Jan. 27, 1952; children—Lori Cicero Boelig, Lois Cicero Woodbury. B.B.A., CCNY, 1953. Tchr. Burlington, Mass., Pub. Schs., 1965-69; mgr. Colpitts Travel Agy., Lexington, Mass., 1969-72, exec. v.p., 1972-80, pres., 1980—; pres. Colpitts Assocs., West Roxbury, Mass., 1975-78; pres. C and L Cons., Lexington, 1981—; v.p. Nova Assocs., Dallas, treas., 1985—; adv. bd. mem. Travel Edn. Ctr., Cambridge, Mass., Pan Am. World Airways, Boston; mem. Travel Agts. Adv. Bd. Active Women's Am. Ort. Lexington (founding pres., 1960-62). Mem. Inst. Cert. Travel Agts (life), Am. Soc. Travel Agts., Brit. Airways Travel Agts. (adv. bd. 1986), Soc. Travel Tourism Educators, Lexington C. of C. (dir., 1977—, fin. chmn., 1982—). Jewish. Home: 11 Cooke Rd Lexington MA 02173 Office: Colpitts Travel Ctr 1793 Massachusetts Ave Lexington MA 02173

CICERO, MARY BETH, marketing professional; b. Pitts., Nov. 17, 1953; d. Octavius Armand and Elizabeth Ann (Ertl) C. BS in Biology, Boston Coll., 1975, MBA in Mktg., 1980. Sales rep. Dermik Labs., Ft. Washington, Pa., 1976-80, tech. coordinator, 1980-81, mgr. sales adminstrn., 1981-82, mgr. mkt. plan, 1982-83; product mgr. Serono Labs., Randolph, Mass., 1983-84, group product mgr., 1984-85, dir. mkt. plan, 1985-88, exec. dir. mktg., 1988—. Mem. Nat. Head Injury Found., Braintree, Mass., 1985—. Recipient Diana award Nat. Wholesale Druggists' Assn., 1986. Mem. Pharm. Advt. Council, Health Care Women's Bus. Assn. Democrat. Roman Catholic. Office: Serono Labs 280 Pond St Randolph MA 02368

CICHON, PAMELA DION, lawyer; b. Raleigh, N.C., Jan. 12, 1956; d. Wallace Martin and Corinne (Adams) C. B.A. with honors, U. Fla.-Gainesville, 1976; J.D., Stetson U., 1979. Bar: Fla. 1980. Tchr., Boca Ciega Sr. High St., St. Petersburg, Fla., 1979-80; uranium landman Amoco Minerals Co., Denver also Chadron, Nebr., 1980-81; petroleum landman Profl. Energy, Inc., Denver, 1981-82; atty. Cen. Fla. Legal Services, Daytona Beach, 1982; assoc. law firm Bosek & Sills, Daytona Beach, Fla., 1983-84; assoc. law firm Foster, Ramos & Foster, Daytona Beach, Fla., 1984-85; asst. atty. gen. State of Fla., 1986—; bd. dirs. Cen. Fla. Legal Services Corp. Writer, editor newsletter Business Advisory Reports, 1980-81. Vol. lawyer Volusia County Vol. Lawyers Project, Daytona Beach, 1982—; clinic atty. Legal Advice Clinic, Daytona Beach, 1983-87. Mem. Fla. Assn. Women Lawyers, ABA, Fla. Bar Assn., Volusia County Bar Assn., Phi Delta Phi, Sigma Delta Tau. Office: Dept Legal Affairs 125 N Ridgewood Ave Daytona Beach FL 32014

CICHOSZ, JOAN MARY, probation officer; b. Winona, Minn., Sept. 12, 1939; d. Chester Charles and Dorothy Mary (Sikorski) C. BA, U. Minn., 1962, postgrad., 1962-63. Community corrections worker III Ramsey County Community Corrections, St. Paul, 1970—; mem. Criminal Justice and Chem. Dependency Interface, St. Paul, 1978, Re-Entry Services Adv. Bd., St. Paul, 1979-82, Criminal Justice Adv. Bd., St. Paul, 1980-82, Ramsey County Task Force on Women Offenders, St. Paul, 1982, Comparable Worth Com., St. Paul, 1985-86. Contbr. articles to profl. jours. Coach Holy Family Ch. Boys Baseball, St. Louis Park, Minn., 1962. Recipient Cert. of Honor Sta. KSTP, 1971. Mem. Am. Correctional Assn., Minn. Community Corrections Assn. (sec. 1987-88, Robert H. Robinson Service award 1986), Mensa. Roman Catholic. Office: Ramsey County Community Corrections 965 Payne Ave Saint Paul MN 55101

CIELINSKI, AUDREY ANN, communications specialist, free-lance writer, editor; b. Cleve., Sept. 10, 1957; d. Joseph and Dorothy Antoinette (Hanna) Cielinski. B.J. with high honors, U. Tex. at Austin, 1979. Reporter, writer Med. World News mag., N.Y.C., 1979, asst. copy chief, Houston, 1983-84; free-lance writer, editor, 1984—; editorial asst. Jour Health and Social Behavior, Houston, 1980-81; sec. dept. psychiatry Baylor Coll. Medicine, Houston, 1980-81; procedures analyst, tech. writer, tech. librarian Harris County Data Processing Dept., Houston, 1981-83; communications specialist III, Wang systems adminstr., Office of Planning and Research, Houston Police Dept., tchr. tech. writing class. Contbr. stories and articles to newspapers and mags. Recipient Commendation award, Chief of Police, Houston. Vol. writer, graphic designer, office religious edn. St. Ambrose Roman Cath. Ch., Houston, 1983—; vol. editor newsletters Greater Houston area Am. Cancer Soc. and VGS, Inc. Mem. Women in Communications, Women Profls. in Govt., Am. Med. Writers Assn., Soc. for Tech. Communication, Soc. Children's Book Writers (assoc.), Austin Writer's League, Sigma Delta Chi, Phi Kappa Phi, Alpha Lambda Delta. Home: 4250 W 34th St Apt 84 Houston TX 77092 Office: Houston Police Dept Office of Planning and Research 33 Artesian Houston TX 77002

CIENCIALA, ANNA MARIA, educator; b. Gdansk, Poland, Nov. 8, 1929; d. Andrew M. and Wanda M. (Waissmann) C.; came to U.S., 1965, naturalized, 1970; B.A., U. Liverpool, 1952; M.A., McGill U., 1955; Ph.D., Ind. U., 1962. Lectr. European history U. Ottawa, 1960-61, U. Toronto (Ont., Can.), 1961-65; asst. prof. history U. Kans., Lawrence, 1965-67, assoc. prof., 1967-71, prof. history and Soviet and Eastern European area studies, 1971—. Recipient prize Pilsudski Inst. Am., 1968; Ford Found. fellow, 1958-60; Can. Council grantee, 1963; Fulbright-Hays fellow, 1968-69; U. Kans. gen. research grantee, 1965-75, 80-81; Am. Council Learned Socs. grantee, 1980, 83; Irex fellow, Poland, 1979-80. Mem. AAUP, AAUW, Am. Assn. Advancement Slavic Studies, Am. Hist. Assn., Kosciuszko Found., Pilsudski Inst. Am., Polish-Am. Inst. Arts and Scis., Polish-Am. Hist. Assn., Hist. Preservation. Author: Poland and the Western Powers, 1938-39, 1968; From Versailles to Locarno, Keys to Polish Foreign Policy, 1919-25; editor: (with A. Headlam-Morley and R. Bryant) A Memoir of the Paris Peace Conference 1919, 1972; American Contributions to the Seventh International Congress of Slavists, 1973; contbr. articles to profl. jours. Home: 3045 Steven Dr Lawrence KS 66044 Office: Dept History U Kans Lawrence KS 60045

CIFELLI, BARBARA DORIS, real estate financial accountant; b. Chgo., Dec. 16, 1942; d. Thomas and E. Doris (Jones) C. BA, Mt. Holyoke Coll., 1964. Lic. real estate agt., N.J. Programmer AT&T Co., N.Y.C., 1964-66; systems analyst AT&T Co., Piscataway, N.J., 1967-73; dist. mgr. AT&T Co., Basking Ridge, N.J., 1973-87; pres. Home Equity Enterprises of Warren (N.J.), Inc., 1987—; real estate agt. Weichert Realtors, Basking, 1987—; mem. Rand Real Estate Corp. Mem. N.J. Women's Network, N.J. Bus. Owners. Republican. Roman Catholic. Home: 18 Stockade Rd Warren NJ 07060 Office: Home Equity Enterprises Warren Inc PO Box 4558 Warren NJ 07060-4558

CIFOLELLI, ALBERTA CARMELLA, artist, educator; b. Erie, Pa., Aug. 19, 1931; d. Charles and Adeline (Tonti) C.; m. Charles Perry Lamb, Jr., July 9, 1955; children—Mark Charles, John Jamison, Todd Vincent. Diploma in painting Cleve. Inst. Art, 1953; B.S. in Art Edn., Kent State U., 1955; M.A. in Communications, Fairfield U., 1975. Chmn. art Laurel Sch., Shaker Heights, Ohio, 1964-67; instr. painting and drawing Cleve. Inst. Art, 1967-70; arts adminstr. Conn. Commn. on Arts, Bridgeport, 1972-76; visual arts tchr. Interarts, Bridgeport, 1972-76; assoc. prof. art Sacred Heart U., Bridgeport, 1977—; prof. art Grad. Sch., Coll. New Rochelle, N.Y., 1985—; co-dir. 31st Art of the Northeast, Silvermine Guild Ctr. for Arts, Conn., 1982. One woman shows include Wilbur Gallery, Cleve., 1961, Intown Gallery, Cleve., 1963, Art Ctr., Erie, Pa., 1975, Silvermine Guild Ctr. for Arts, New Canaan, Conn., 1978, Noho Gallery, N.Y.C., 1982, Artist's Signature Gallery, New Haven, 1982, Kaber Gallery, N.Y.C., 1983, Captiva Gallery, Fla., 1984, Stamford Mus., Stamford, Conn., 1988, Conn. Gallery, Marlborough, 1988, Harmon-Meek Gallery, Naples, Fla., 1989; exhibited in group shows at Alice Nash Gallery, N.Y.C., Cleve. Inst. Art, 1967-69, Slater Meml. Mus., Norwich, Conn., 1977, Lyman Allyn Mus., Aldrich Mus. Contemporary Art, New London, Conn., 1983, Armstrong Gallery, N.Y.C., 1984, Aldrich Mus. Contemporary Art, Ridgefield, Conn., 1988; residency to live and work at Djerassi Found., Woodside, Calif., May-June 1986; represented in permanent collections Housatonic Mus. Art, Bridgport, Conn., Smithsonian Mus., Washington, numerous pub. and corp. collections. Co-campaign mgr., 1st selectman Democratic Orgn., Westport, Conn., 1977; mem. Westport Democrat Town Com., 1978-79. Recipient Best in Show award Ind. Artists, John Herron Art Mus., Indpls., 1959, Doris Kriendler award NAD, 1974; Conn. Commn. on Arts grantee, 1973-77. Djerassi Found. resident, Woodside, Calif., 1986. Mem. Women's Caucus for Art, Westport-Weston Arts Council (past officer).

CIHLAR, CHRISTINE CAROL, public relations executive; b. Milw., Feb. 25, 1948; d. Peter Joseph and Sylvia (Sunstrom) C.; m. Frederick L. Rippy Jr., July 25, 1981. BA, Luther Coll., 1970. Advt. mgr. Gazette Press, Glenwood Springs, Colo., 1970-71; prodn. mgr. Eitzen Typesetting, Denver, 1971-72; dir. pub. info. Luther Coll., Decorah, Iowa, 1972-78; proprietor, founder The Emporium, Decorah, 1975-77; regional sales rep. food service div. Hormel Co., Charlotte, N.C., 1978-80; dir. pub. affairs St. Mary's Coll. Md., St. Mary's City, 1980—. Editor: Luther Mag., 1972-78, Luther College, 1974-78, Coll. Chips, 1968-69; contbr. articles and essays to local publs. Pres. Four Seasons Homeowners Assn., Charlotte, 1979-80; bd. dirs. United Way of St. Mary's County Inc., Lexington Park, Md., v.p., 1984-88, pres. 1988—; bd. dirs. Hospice of St. Mary's Inc., Leonardtown, Md., 1984—; treas. Good Shepherd Luth. Ch., Charlotte, 1979-80. Mem. AAUW, Nat. Assn. Female Execs., Council for Advancement and Support of Edn. (forum for instl. advancement 1972—), Edn. Writers Assn., Am. Numismatic Assn. Democrat. Lodge: Rotary. Home: 29 White Elm Ct California MD 20619

CILWIK, CYNTHIA JEAN, dental marketing professional; b. Elizabeth, N.J., Aug. 5, 1953; d. John and Mary (Citsay) C. BS, Fairleigh Dickinson U., 1975, MBA, 1983. Dental hygienist N.J., 1973-76, Switzerland, 1976-78; sales mgr. IPCO Coop. Dental, Bloomfield, N.J., 1978-80; sales and mktg. mgr. IPCO Dental Prosthetics, White Plains, N.Y., 1980-86; mktg. mgr. Productivity Tng. Corp., San Jose, Calif., 1986-88; owner, cons. CJC Mktg. Assocs., Pleasantville, NY, 1988—; Clinician to Nat. Assn. Dental Labs., Alexandria, Va., 1985, Dental Lab. Conf., Phila., 1985, 86, Comml. Dental Lab. Conf., Toronto, Ont., Can., 1987. Editorial bd. Lab Management Today, Wilton, Conn., 1985-87; contbr. articles to profl. jours. Mem. Sales and Mktg. Execs. of Westchester (N.Y.), Nat. Assn. Dental Labs., Dental Lab. Conf. Roman Catholic. Home and Office: 2 Parkway Terr Pleasantville NY 10570

CIMOCHOWICZ, DIANE MARIE, naval petty officer; b. Jacksonville, Fla., Aug. 13, 1955; d. Richard Clarence and Edith Darlene (Johnson) C. AS in Mgmt., Hawaii Pacific Coll., 1986, BSBA, 1986, postgrad., currently. CPA, Philippines. Enlisted USN, 1974, advanced through grades to petty officer first class; ops. specialist USN, Naples, Italy, 1975-77; ops. specialist, instr. USN, Dam Neck, Va., 1977-78; resigned USN, 1978, reenlisted, 1980; photographer USN, San Diego, 1980-82, Honolulu, 1982—; owner ICON, Columbia, Md., 1978-79; owner, operator In Other Words, Honolulu, 1988—. Mem. Federally Employed Women, Fleet Res. Assn., Associated Photographers Internat., Hawaii Pacific Coll. Student Bus. Orgn., Delta Mu Delta. Democrat. Clubs: Lokahi Canoe, Koa Kai (Honolulu). Home: 3110 Woodward SW Wyoming MI 49509 Office: Fleet Intelligence Ctr Pacific Box 500 Pearl Harbor HI 96860

CIMOSZKO, BOGY BOGUSLAWA, communications executive, civil engineer; b. Wolkowysk, Poland, Apr. 28, 1956; came to U.S., 1977; d. Richard and Janina (Piotrowicz) C. BSCE, MIT, 1979; MBA, Harvard U., 1985. Project mgr. Exxon Chem. Co., N.J., 1980-83; mktg. dir. Boston Telecom Co., 1985—. Dir. Women and Leadership Forum, Harvard Bus. Sch., Boston, 1985; advisor, Women's Living Group, Cambridge, Mass., 1979—; trustee Weybridge Court Condo, Brookline, Mass., 1987; active Inst. Contemporary Art, Boston, 1987. Mem. Assn. MIT Women. Republican. Office: Boston Telecom Co One International Pl Boston MA 02110

CINCIOTTA, LINDA ANN, lawyer, administrator; b. Washington, May 18, 1943; d. Nicholas Joseph and Laverne (Oakley) C.; m. John P. Olguin, Aug. 4, 1979. B.S., Georgetown U., 1965; J.D., George Washington U., 1970. Bar: D.C. 1970. Assoc. Arent, Fox, Plotkin & Kahn, Washington, 1970-76, ptnr., 1977-83; dir. Office Atty. Personnel Mgmt., Dept. Justice, Washington, 1983—. Recipient U.S. Law Week award George Washington U. Nat. Law Ctr., 1970. Mem. Fed. Communications Bar Assn. (pres. 1980-81, ABA del. 1977-79), Fed. Bar. Assn., D.C. Bar Assn. Office: US Dept Justice Dir Office Atty Personnel Mgmt 10th & Constitution Ave NW Washington DC 20530

CINTRON, EMMA VARGAS, clinical psychologist, educational counselor; b. Yauco, P.R., Aug. 8, 1926; d. Jose Vargas Bocheciampi and Maria Teresa Rivera de Vargas; B.A. in Sociology summa cum laude, Inter Am. U., San German, P.R., 1973, M.A. in Counseling and Guidance summa cum laude, 1974; postgrad. in psychology Centro Caribeno Estudios Postgraduados; Ph.D. in Counseling Psychology, Columbia Pacific U., 1985; m. Jorge N. Cintron, Feb. 14, 1948; children: Lisi C. Vazquez, Ileana C. Vazquez. Weekly columnist newspaper El Mundo, San Juan, P.R., 1979—; advisor for dormitories Inter Am. U., San German, P.R., 1978-79, part time prof. dept. edn., 1976-77, cons. orientation center, 1974-76; bus. mgr. U. P.R. Law Rev., Rio Piedras, 1963-71. Author: Compartiendo Contigo Vivencias Humanas, 1987, (with others) Essays Educativos, 1985; contbr. articles to newspapers including El Mundo, Impacto, El Leon, Revista Superate, Puerto Rico Evangelico. Recipient award in journalism for newspaper work Puerto Rican Inst. Lit., 1984. Mem. P.R. Psychol. Assn., Nat. Hispanic Psychol. Assn. Am. Personnel and Guidance Assn., P.R. Guidance Assn., Phi Delta Kappa (editor Phi-De-Ka; Disting. Kappan of Yr. 1981). Methodist. Clubs: Lions (Domadoras; writing award 1985, Journalist of Yr. 1987, Quality of Life Award 1988), Altrusa, Grandmothers, San German. Contbr. articles to newspapers. Home and Office: Box 2547 San German PR 00753

CIOLLI, ANTOINETTE, librarian, retired educator; b. N.Y.C., Aug. 20, 1915; d. Pietro and Mary (Palumbo) C.; A.B., Bklyn. Coll., 1937, M.A., 1940; B.S. in L.S., Columbia U., 1943. Tchr. history and civics Bklyn. high schs., 1943-44; circulation librarian Bklyn. Coll. Library, 1944-46; instr. history Sch. Gen. Studies, Bklyn. Coll., 1944-50, asst. prof. library dept., 1965-73, assoc. prof., 1973-81, prof. emerita, 1981—; reference librarian Bklyn. Coll. Library, 1947-59, chief sci. librarian, 1959-70, chief spl. collections div., 1970-81, hon. archivist, 1981—. Mem. ALA, Am. Hist. Assn., Spl. Libraries Assn. (museum group chpt. sec. 1950-51, 52-54), N.Y. Library Club, Beta Phi Mu. Author: (with Alexander S. Preminger and Lillian Lester) Urban Educator: Harry D. Gideonse, Brooklyn College and the City University of New York, 1970; contbr. articles to profl. jours. Home: 1129 Bay Ridge Pkwy Brooklyn NY 11228

CIPRESSY, MARY ANNE, physical therapist; b. Albany, N.Y., Oct. 9, 1956; d. Vittorio Armondo and Rosemary (Saccone) C. AAS, Maria Coll., 1976; student, SUNY, Albany, 1976-79, ECC, 1986—. Registered physical therapist asst., Fla. Physical therapist asst. Eden Park Nursing Home, Albany, 1976-79, N.Y. State VA Home, Oxford, 1979-82, Fla. Home Health Services, Ft. Myers, Fla., 1982—. Pres. Concerned Youth for Cerebral Palsy, Albany, 1977-78. Mem. Am. Businesswomen's Assn., Nat. Assn. Female Execs. Club: Gulf Coast Investment (Ft. Myers). Home: 4541 Jersy Rd Fort Myers FL 33905

CIPRIANO, GRACE IRENE, estimator, nurse, stables owner; b. Youngstown, Ohio, May 13, 1925; d. Floyd Raymond and Ruth (Walter) Brown; student Bliss Bus. Coll., 1942-43; LL.B., LaSalle U., 1952; grad. nurse's tng. Youngstown Hosp. Assn., 1974; m. Otto Francis Wess, June 11, 1949 (dec. Mar. 1969); children—Raymond Francis, Shannon Grace Wess Morello, Colleen Melody Wess Bloomingdale, Honey Lucile Wess Biondillo, Alyson Rae Wess King, Carol Lynn Wess Sivley; m. James L. Cipriano, June 28, 1987. Nurse's aid St. Elizabeth Hosp., Youngstown, 1938-42; traffic clk. B.F. Goodrich Co., Akron, Ohio, 1942-43; rate clk., traffic dept. Gen. Fireproofing Co., Youngstown, 1947-49; pres., co-owner Jewels by Lady Grace, Detroit, 1949-63, Grayce's Treasure Chests, Youngstown, 1949-63, Grayce's Medicine Chests, Youngstown, 1949-63; indsl. and comml. bldg. estimator Ben Rudick & Son, Inc., Youngstown, 1963-71; freelance estimator, North Lima, Ohio, 1971—; newspaper columnist, various newspapers, 1963-68; nurse, 1974—; now staff nurse Drs. Hosp., Lake Worth, Fla.; owner Grace Wess Stables, Inc., Canfield, Ohio, 1949—. Democratic candidate for Mahoning County commr., 1973; bd. dirs. Missing Children Found., Tampa, Fla.; mem. legis. com. Palm Beach County, Mothers Against Drunk Driving. Served with WAVES, 1943-47. Mem. Am. Bus. Women's Assn. (pres. 1969-70, Woman of Yr. award 1970), Youngstown Bus. and Profl. Women's Club, U.S. Trotting Assn., Canfield Harness Horsemen's Assn., Ohio Harness Horsemen's Assn., Am. Legion, VFW, Def. Supply Assn., McGuffey Meml. Assn., Women in Constrn., Constrn. Specifications Inst., Internat. Platform Assn., Home and Sch. Assn., St. Charles Altar and Rosary Soc., Mahoning County Agrl. Soc., Am. German Club of Palm Beaches (Fla.), Youngstown Playhouse. Democrat. Roman Catholic. Lodges: Order Eastern Star (Grand Nurse of Fla. 1986-87), Grange. Home and Office: 1008 Penn Grove Lake Worth FL 33461

CIPULLO, LINDA LOUISE, sales executive; b. Hot Springs, Ark., Mar. 1, 1955; d. Ronald George and Jeanne Annmarie (Diebold) Komornik; m. Wayne E. Cipullo, Nov. 13, 1982. BA, Benedictine Coll., 1977. Asst. to coach Washington Diplomats Soccer Club, 1977-81; staff asst. to Dr. Henry A. Kissinger, Washington, 1981-82; exec. sec. Omni Internat. Hotels, Norfolk, Va., 1982-83; asst. to dir. mktg. San Luis on Galveston Isle Hotel, Galveston, Tex., 1983-84; exec. asst. Mitchell Energy & Devel. Corp., Houston, 1984-85; tourism sales mgr. Colorado Springs (Colo.) Conv. and Visitors Bur., 1985-86, dir. conv. sales, 1986-87; asst. to v.p. of sales The Benchmark Mgmt. Co., Jamesburg, N.J., 1987—; mem. adv. com. Colo. Tourism Bd., Denver, 1985—; mem. Conv. Liaison Com., Colorado Springs, 1985—. Recipient Travel Employee of Yr. award Colo. Tourism Bd., 1987. Mem. Am. Soc. Assn. Execs., Colo. Soc. Assn. Execs., Colorado Springs Soc. Assn. Execs., Meeting Planners Internat., Meeting Planners Assn. Colorado Springs (bd. dirs. 1986—), Rocky Mountain Meeting Planners Internat. Democrat. Roman Catholic. Office: The Benchmark Mgmt Co 7 Centre Dr Suite 6 Jamesburg NJ 08831

CIRCLE, MELANIE KATHERINE, marketing professional; b. Columbus, Ohio, July 22, 1961; d. John E. and Charlotte M. (Dymond) C. BS in Communications, Ohio U., 1983. Chpt. cons. Alpha Gamma Delta Nat. Fraternity, Indpls., 1983-84; asst. mktg. dir. devel. dept. City of Columbus, 1984-85; mktg. coordinator Vantage Cos., Columbus, 1985—; mem. working com. Cen. Ohio Mktg. Council, Columbus, 1984-85. Chair communications Devel. Com. for Greater Columbus, 1986-87. Mem. Pub. Relations Soc. Am., Worthington C. of C. (membership com.), Columbus C. of C. (econ. devel. com., fact finders chair, info. exchange com. 1986-87), Ohio U. Alumni Assn., Mortar Bd. Alumni Assn., Alpha Gamma Delta Alumni Assn. (province dir. 1987—). Mem. Le Club, Ltd. (Boca Raton, Fla.) (communications dir. 1984—). Home: 996 Chatham Ln Apt J Columbus OH 43221 Office: Vantage Cos 100 E Campus View Blvd Columbus OH 43085

CIRELLI, DOROTHY LOUISE, health science administrator, psychologist; b. Phila., Sept. 11, 1946; d. Mario Gerald and Hildegard Marie (Rossiger) C. BA, D'Youville Coll., Buffalo, 1968; MS, Va. Commonwealth U., 1975. Cert. alcoholism and drug counselor, Va. Psychology technician Phila. State Hosp., 1968-69, psychology supr., 1969-70; tchr. elem. Richmond (Va.) Pub. Schs., 1971; counselor Va. Commonwealth U., Richmond, 1973-75; substance abuse counselor Va. Dept. Human Resources, Arlington County, 1975-80; psychologist NIH, Bethesda, Md., 1980-84, asst. hosp. administr., 1984—; mem. task force Gov. of Va. State Adv. Commn., Richmond, 1972; cons., trainer Va. Dept. Human Resources, Arlington, 1970-72; exec. bd. dirs. Va. Assn. of Drug Programs, 1972-73; owner, dir. Options, Inc., Arlington, 1973-75. Contbr. articles to profl. jours. Mem. Nat. Assn. for Female Execs., Assn. of Healthcare Administrs., Nat. Women's Polit. Caucus, NOW, Amnesty Internat., Nat. Mus. for Women in the Arts. Democrat. Roman Catholic. Home: 7712 Hanover Pkwy #201 Greenbelt MD 20770

CIRKER, BLANCHE, publisher; b. N.Y.C., Oct. 3, 1918; d. Frank and Tillie (Jager) Brodsky; B.A., Hunter Coll., 1939; M.S.W., U. Pa., 1941; m. Hayward Cirker, Aug. 11, 1939; children—Steven, Victoria. Family social worker intake office Jewish Child Care Assn., 1948-50; med. social worker Joint Disease Hosp., N.Y.C., 1950; book pub., 1950—; now v.p. Dover Publs., N.Y.C. Mem. Otto Rank Assn. (dir.). Author: Monograms and Alphabetic Devices, 1970; Dictionary of American Portraits, 1967; Golden Age of Poster, 1971; Book of Kells, 1982; Art Nouveau Postcards, 1983; Masterpieces of the Belle Epoch, 1983. Home: 199 Woodside Dr Hewlett Bay Park NY 11557 Other: 31 E 2d St Mineola NY 11501 Office: Dover Publications 180 Varick St New York NY 10014

CIRLOT, KAY CHESHIRE, real estate executive; b. Opelika, Ala., July 27, 1940; d. Howard Clarence Cheshire and Ivy Cliff (Baxley) Weldon; m. R. Patrick Cobb, Feb. 2, 1960 (div. July 1972); m. Neal W. Cirlot Jr., Aug. 4, 1976 (div. Oct. 1979). BS in Secondary Edn., Auburn (Ala.) U., 1962; MA, So. Meth. U., Dallas, 1983; mgmt. cert., U. Ga., 1985; cert., Am. Sch. Real Estate, Montgomery, Ala., 1987. Child welfare worker State of Fla., Pensacola, 1963-68; customer service rep. Gulf Oil Corp., Atlanta, 1969-77; customer service mgr. Arkla Industries, Evansville, Ind., 1977-78; collection mgr. Southland Corp., Dallas, 1979-81; br. mgr. Comdata Inc., Houston, 1981-83; dir. properties Floribec, Internat., Montgomery, 1984-86; fin. analyst Grimmer Realty Co., Inc., Birmingham, Ala., 1987—; mem. Internat. Council Shopping Ctrs., Montgomery, 1984-88. Contbr. articles to Gulf Oil Newspaper. Organizer Mother's March on Birth Defects, Snellville, Ga., 1968; mem. Nat. Assn. Female Execs., 1984-86. Home: 3119 Melissa Way Birmingham AL 35243 Office: Grimmer Realty Co Inc 2000-B South Bridge Pkwy Birmingham AL 35209

CIRRITO, THERESA ANN, insurance executive; b. Massapequa, N.Y., Aug. 24, 1963; d. Vincent and Theresa (Brady) C. BA, Molloy Coll., 1985. Ins. counselor Govt. Employees Ins. Co., Woodbury, N.Y., 1981-84, sr. ins. counselor, 1984-85, supr. fire and allied lines, 1985-86; supr. sales and service Govt. Employees Ins. Co., Chevy Chase, Md., 1987, adminstr. sales and service, 1987—, mil. service supr., 1984—, security adminstr., 1986-87; ins. counselor selection system adminstr. Govt. Employees Ins. Co., Chevy

Chase, 1985—. Republican. Roman Catholic. Home: 29 Windbrooke Circle Gaithersburg MD 20879

CIRUCCI, CHRISTINA A., mechanical engineer; b. Easton, Pa., June 14, 1961; d. Anthony J. and Ann C. (Workman) C. BSME, Va. Poly. Inst., 1983; postgrad., U. Pitts., 1984-85. Cert. engr. in tng., emergency med. technician. Assoc. engr. Westinghouse-Bettis Atomic Power Lab., West Mifflin, Pa., 1983-86, engr., 1986—. Vol. Youth Guidance, Inc., Sewickley, Pa., 1986—; med. rescue team south, Pitts., Pa., 1987—. Marshall Hahn Engring. Merit scholar Va. Poly. Inst., 1979, Am. Foundrymen's Soc. Scholar, 1982; named one of Outstanding Young Women Am., 1986. Mem. ASME (literary resources chmn. Va. Tech. chpt. 1982-83), Biomed. Engring. Soc. (publicity chmn. 1981-82), Phi Eta Sigma. Republican. Home: 556-2A Chatham Park Dr Pittsburgh PA 15220 Office: Westinghouse-Bettis Atomic Power Lab PO Box 79 West Mifflin PA 15122

CIRUTI, JOAN ESTELLE, educator; b. Ponchatouia, La., Aug. 8, 1930; d. Joseph Aloysius and Olga (Jordan) C. B.A., Southeastern La. Coll., 1950; M.A., U. Okla, 1954; Ph.D., Tulane U., 1959. Instr. modern langs U. Okla., Norman, 1957-59; asst. prof. U. Okla, Norman, 1959-63; research asst. U.S. Office Edn., Washington, 1959-60; asst. prof. Spanish Mt. Holyoke Coll., South Hadley, Mass., 1963-66; assoc. prof. Mt Holyoke Coll., South Hadley, Mass., 1966-71; chmn. dept. Spanish Mt. Holyoke Coll., South Hadley, Mass., 1965-71; prof. Mt. Holyoke Coll., South Hadley, Mass, 1971-77; Helen Day Gould prof. Spanish Mt. Holyoke Coll., South Hadley, Mass., 1977—, dean studies, 1971-74, chmn. dept, Spanish and Italian, 1975-81, 85-86; cons. Ednl. Testing Service, 1968-79. Co-author: Modern Spanish, 2d edit., 1966, Continuing Spanish, 1967; contbg. editor, Handbook of Latin-American Studies, vol. 28, 1966, Handbook of Latin-American Studies vol. 30, 1968, Handbook of Latin-American Studies, vol. 32, 1970. Named Disting. Alumnus Southeastern La. Coll., 1973. Mem. Am. Council on Teaching Fgn. Langs., MLA (nomination adv. com. 1962-64, nominating com. 1979-80, acad. freedom com. 1980-83), Latin Am. Studies Assn. (mem. steering com. consortium Latin Am. studies programs 1969-72, com. on women 1973-74, nominating com. 1975), New Eng. Council Latin Am. Studies, Am. Assn. Tchrs. Spanish and Portuguese, AAUW. Home: 21 Jewett Ln South Hadley MA 01075 Office: Mt Holyoke Coll Dept Spanish & Italian South Hadley MA 01075

CISEK, CAROL MARIE, image and color consultant, writer; b. Syracuse, N.Y., Aug. 26, 1926; d. Fred Philip and Clara Elizabeth (Raupach) Kies; m. Richard M. Cisek, Sept. 15, 1956 (div. 1972); children—Michael, Melanie, Maria. B.A., Syracuse U., 1948; grad. Med. Technician, Buffalo Gen. Hosp., 1950. Cert. med. technician, Color Me Beautiful cons. Pub. relations dir. Minn. Dance Theatre, Mpls., 1968-71, Sci. Mus. Minn., St. Paul, 1975-76, Employers Overload, Mpls., 1977; ops. mgr. Gem Model and Talent Agy., Mpls., 1979-80; cons., owner Color Me Beautiful, Mpls., 1981—; dir. Wendy Ward program, Montgomery Ward Stores, 1973-75; contbr. fashion and beauty columns publs. Mpls., St. Paul. Bd. dirs. Minn. Dance Theatre, 1969-79; founder, bd. mem. Minn. Montessori Found. and Edina Montessori Sch., 1963-71; with pub. relations Democratic Farm Labor Feminist Caucus, Mpls. 1978-80. Mem. Fashion Group, Women in Communications (sec. Mpls. 1978-80), Minn. Press Club. Roman Catholic. Home and Office: Carol Cisek Color 3609 Rhode Island Ave S Minneapolis MN 55426

CISLER, THERESA ANN, osteopath; b. Tucson, Dec. 20, 1951; d. William George and Lucille (Seeber) C.; m. Dennis Keith Luttrell, May 1, 1954; 1 child, Daniel Collin. BS in Nursing, U. Ariz., 1974; DO, Kirksville Coll. Osteopathy, 1983. Operating room technician St. Joseph's Hosp., Tucson, 1973-74, operating room nurse, 1974-78, operating room inservice coordinator, 1978-79; intern Tucson Gen. Hosp., 1983-84; family practice and manipulation Assoc. Jane J. Beregi, D.O., Tucson, 1984-87; practice medicine specializing in osteo. manipulation Tucson, 1987—; active med. staff Tucson Gen. Hosp., 1984—, med. records chmn., 1985-87; part time med. staff Westcenter Drug & Rehab., Tucson, 1984—; vol. med. staff St. Elizabeth Hugary Clinic, 1984-87; mem. substance abuse com. Westcenter - Tucson Gen. Hosp., 1986—, osteo. concepts com., 1986—, osteo. manipulative cons., 1986—. Eucharistic minister St. Pius X Ch., Tucson, 1984-86, eucharistic minister coordinator, 1987—. Mem. Am. Coll. Gen. Practitioners in Osteo. Medicine and Surgery, Am. Osteo. Assn., Am. Acad. Osteopathy, Ariz. Osteo. Med. Assn. (alternate house of dels. 1985—), Pima County Me. Soc., Kirksville Coll. Osteopathy-Century Club, Am. Med. Soc. Alcoholism & Other Drug Dependencies. Roman Catholic. Office: 4002 E Grant Rd Suite D Tucson AZ 85712

CISNEROS, DIANA GLORIA, educator; b. Brownsville, Tex., Oct. 29, 1954; d. Oscar Pedro and Gloria Dora (Colunga) C. BE, Pan American U., 1978, MEd, 1982. Kindergarten tchr. Pharr (Tex.)-San Juan-Alamo Ind. Sch. Dist., 1978-84, Northside Ind. Sch. Dist., San Antonio, 1984—. Mem. Nat. Edn. Assn., Tex. State Tchrs. Assn., Kindergarten Tchrs. Tex., Assn. Childhood Edn. Internat., Internat. Reading Assn., Kappa Delta Pi, Mu Phi Epsilon, Kappa Delta. Home: 2885 Mabe # 1008 San Antonio TX 78251

CISNEROS, SHARON ARABELLA, social welfare activist; b. N.Y.C., Feb. 2, 1950; d. Louis Manuel Tavarez and Josephine (Polanco) Molloy; divorced; children: Manual Anthony, Josephine Marlene, Erica Krysta. Cert., SUNY, N.Y.C., 1971; student, East Seton Coll., 1986. Co-host TV show Menco Prodns., Danbury, Conn., 1982-83; advt. sales rep. Intercorp., Stamford, Conn., 1982-83; bilingual legal sec. Katz, Katz & Brand, N.Y.C., 1983-84; host, dir., producer Sheran Cisneros Prodns., Yonkers, N.Y., 1981—; pres. Yonkers Area Women's Network/The People's Network, Yonkers, 1985—. Author: AVVY Story of a Desperate Girl, 1981; Poems for a Lazy Evening, 1981; editor People to People Newspaper, 1986. Mem. Danbury Women's Network, Help Our People; pub. relations officer U.S. Air Force Aux., Yonkers, 1986. Mem. Nat. Assn. Female Execs. Lodge: Order of Rosicrucians.

CISNEY, MARCELLA, theater director, administrator; b. Altoona, Pa.; d. Moses J. and Anne (Epstein) Abels; m. Robert C. Schnitzer, June 7, 1953. Student Am. Acad. Dramatic Arts, Bennington Sch. Arts, Neighborhood Playhouse Dirs. Seminar, NYU Radio-TV Workshop. Featured on Broadway in Girls in Uniform, Lady Precious Stream; dir. Off-Broadway and summer theatres; exec. dir. Jacksonville Civic Theatre (Fla.), 1942-45; producer-dir. Pasadena Playhouse (Calif.), 1946-48, Laguna Playhouse (Calif.), Las Palmas Theatre, Hollywood, 1948-49; head coach Warner Bros. Studio, 1948; network dir. for CBS-TV, N.Y., 1950-54; lectr. advanced theatre direction Columbia, 1955; adminstr. Rockefeller Found. project for Hungarian refugee artists, 1956; adminstr., assoc. coordinator U.S. State Dept. Am. Performing Arts Programs, Brussels World's Fair, 1957-58; dir. N.Y.C. Opera, 1957-58; dir. all-star Skin of Our Teeth for Theatre Guild-State Dept. world tour, Latin Am. tour of Glass Menagerie, 1960-61; co-founder, artistic dir. Profl. Theatre Program, U. Mich., Ann Arbor, 1961-73; dir. premieres Child Buyer, 1963, An Evening's Frost, 1964, Wedding Band, 1965, Ivory Tower, 1966, Amazing Grace, 1967, The Castle, 1968, The Conjurer, 1969; dir. nat. tour An Evening's Frost, 1966, ACT West Coast premiere, 1968; producer Siamese Connections, 1971, Last Respects, 1972. Theater chmn. Westport-Weston Arts Council, 1980-86; mem. bd. Westport Arts Ctr., producer Works-in-Progress Series, 1980-88; arts cons. to pres. U. Bridgeport, 1974-83; moderator seminars White Barn Theatre, 1974-80; 1st v.p. Westport Arts Council, 1978-81; mem. (hon.) Nat. Theatre Conf. Recipient Bronze medal Israeli Minister of Culture; Gold medal for Brussels Fair Program, Spl. Pres.'s citation U. Mich., 1972; chosen Outstanding Conn. Woman Gov. of Conn., 1987.

CISSELL, LOIS ANNETTE, social services specialist; b. San Francisco, June 1, 1945; d. Carl Joseph and Eleanore Natalie (Karp) C. AA, San Jose (Calif.) City Coll., 1969; BS, Calif. State U., Hayward, 1972; postgrad., U. San Francisco. Camp dir. Oakland (Calif.) Parks & Recreation Dept., 1972; program dir. Camp Fire Girls San Diego, 1973-74; dir. Camp Coyote Community Vol. Services, Inc., San Jose, 1975-76; rehab. therapist Agnews Devel. Ctr., San Jose, 1976, 78-82, gov.'s vol. coordinator, 1977-78, asst. chief cen. services, 1982-85, adv. clients' rights, 1985—. Vol. Santa Clara (Calif.) Arts and Wine Festival, 1983—, Girls Scouts U.S., Santa Clara, 1985; mem. exec. steering com. 10 Yr. anniversary Mission Coll. Friends, Santa Clara, 1987—. Mem. Nat. Assn. for Female Execs. Democrat. Jewish. Club: Santa Clara Women's League (founder, 2d v.p. 1983-86). Lodge: Soroptimists (chair sunshine com. 1986-87).

CITRIN, JUDITH, healer, counselor, artist, educator; b. Chgo., May 29, 1934; d. Harvey and Estelle (Lieberman) Goldfeder, m. Jeremy Levin, 1954 (div. 1963); m. Phillip Citrin, 1968 (div. 1984); student Art Inst. Chgo., 1943, 47-48, U. Ill., 1951-53, Am. Acad. Art, 1953-54, Adler Inst., 1975, C.G. Jung 1979—, Esalen Inst., 1981; 1 son, Jeffrey Scott Levin. Asst. producer, researcher WTTW Channel 11, Chgo., 1963-68; freelance interior designer, jewelry designer, fabricator, clothing designer, 1963—; freelance painter and sculptor, 1968—; Reiki healer and transformational counselor, 1978—; group facilitator, tchr. Oasis Center, 1981—, Loyola U., 1984, 85, Fatima Ctr., Notre Dame, 1986; group facilitator Interface, Watertown, Mass., 1987—; dir. Transformational Travel, 1987—; facilitator Healing Circle; artist in residency Cultural Ministry, Marrakech, Morocco, 1979-80; dir. Clearing House; works exhibited Musee des Oudaias, Rabat, Morocco, 1980, Art Inst. Chgo., 1973, 77, 81, Nat. Mus. Am. Art of Smithsonian Instn., 1982, Nat. Acad. Design, N.Y.C., 1982, Chgo. Cultural Center, 1979, Mus. Art of U. Okla., 1978. Ill. Arts Council grantee, 1977; Royal Air Maroc funding grantee, 1980-81. Mem. Assn. Holistic Health, Arts Club Chgo., Spiritual Emergence Network , Am. Reiki Assn., Inst. Noetic Scis., Calif. Inst. Transpersonal Psychology. Contbg. writer to Under the Sign of Pisces, 1972; contbg. artist to Black Maria, 1972, Corona mag., 1986; contbg. editor The New Art Examiner, 1978. Home and Office: 423 Greenleaf Ave Wilmette IL 60091

CITRON, RITA LEIGH, government relations consultant; b. Dec. 20, 1950; m. Donald Lee Citron, June 6, 1982; children: Jeremy David, Ryan Elliot. BA in Polit. Sci., U. Toronto, 1977. Sr. cons. Henry R. Ross, Inc., Toronto, 1980-88; pres. Citron Cons., Toronto, 1988—. Co-author Can. govt. report Racial Diversity in Government Advertising and Communications, 1982. Club: Toastmasters (past pres. Broadview chpt.). Home and Office: 18 Montclair Ave, Toronto, ON Canada M4V 1W1

CITTON, CLARE, industrial engineering supervisor; b. Windsor, Ont., Canada, May 6, 1959; d. Antonio and Marina (Zanchetta) C.; m. Bradley Edward Lyons, Apr. 5, 1986. B. of Applied Sci., U. Windsor, 1982. Draftsperson Cold Fastener, Inc., Windsor, 1979; patents researcher Windsor Pub. Library, 1980; indstl. engr. General Motors Canada, Windsor, 1981; indsl. engr. Kellogg Salada Can., Inc., London, Ont., 1982-85; indstl. engr. supr. Kellogg Salada Can., Inc., London, 1985—. Reporter Brookfield Newsletter, London. Loaned rep. Kellogg's, United Way, London, 1984; speaker Open Doors (career planning for students), London, 1986—. Recipient entrance scholarship grant, 1978, Bd. Govs. Medal, 1982, honors, 1982, U. Windsor. Mem. Assn. Profl. Engrs. Ont., Can. Soc. Indsl. Engrs.(exec. mem. inst. relations 1984-85).

CITTY, BRENDA VINSON, accountant; b. Swainsboro, Ga., July 15, 1959; d. Mary Beatrice (Jones) Doss; m. Russell Lee Citty, May 7, 1983. BA in Acctg., Bus. Adminstrn., Elon Coll. (N.C.), 1981. Acct. Moses Cone Mem. Hosp., Greensboro, N.C., 1981-84, N.C. Gas Service div. Penn and So. Gas, Reidsville, N.C., 1984—. Co-chairman comml. III United Way Reidsville, 1985-86, comml. div. United Way Reidsville, 1986—. Mem. Jaycees (dir. Reidsville chpt.1986—, treas. 1987—, C. William Brownfield award 1986, 87, Howard Halberstadt Meml. Write Up award 1987). Presbyterian. Home: 833 Summit Ave Reidsville NC 27320

CIUFFA, BARBARA JOAN PAUL, lawyer; b. N.Y.C., June 5, 1939; d. Leo Robert and Agatha (Pugatch) Paul; m. Ben Richard Ciuffa, Sept. 2, 1961; children: Jodie Jill, Christopher Jared. BA, Alfred U., 1960; cert. computer programming, Mohawk Valley Tech. Inst., 1962; cert. elec. house wiring, Bd. Coop. Ednl. Services, 1971; MS in Elem. Edn., Hofstra U., 1965; JD, Syracuse U., 1982. Bar: N.Y. 1984. Physicist aide Nat. Bur. Standards, Washington, 1960-61; social worker Oneida County Welfare Dept., Utica, N.Y., 1961-63; tchr. elem. schs., adult edn., jails, N.Y., N.D., 1963-80; lectr. SUNY, Brockport, 1983-84; staff atty. Legal Aid Soc. Wayne County, Lyons, N.Y., 1985-87; sole practice law Newark, N.Y., 1984—. Author sch. adult remedial reading text, 1973. Spokesperson Support Concered Residents Against Pollution, Broome County, N.Y., 1975; Dem. candidate Broome county legislator, 1976, village justice, Newark, N.Y., 1984, town justice Arcadia, N.Y., 1985; core coordinator Newark Meml. Playground Com., 1985, 86; bd. dirs. Homer's Kids, Newark. Recipient grant N.Y. State Dept. Edn., 1977. Mem. ABA, N.Y. State Bar Assn., Wayne County Bar Assn., Bus. and Profl. Women (v.p., scholarship chmn., Woman of Yr. 1987). Home and Office: 133 Williams St Newark NY 14513

CIUFFO, CYNTHIA (CINDI) LOUISE, nurse consultant; b. Kewanee, Ill., Aug. 11, 1946; d. Spencer Eugene and Hazel Elizabeth (Glass) Parker; m. Lawrence Gaspare Ciuffo, July 25, 1970; children: Thomas Lawrence, Spencer Tracy. RN, Meth. Hosp. Sch. Nursing, Peoria, Ill., 1967. Lic. nurse, Calif., Ill. Operating room staff nurse Peoria Meth. Hosp., 1967-69; sr. staff nurse U. Calif. San Diego Hosp., 1969-72; operating room staff nurse Claremont Community Hosp., San Diego, 1972-74, Palomar Meml. Hosp., Escondido, Calif., 1974-77; operating room head nurse Pomerado Hosp., Poway, Calif., 1977-81; operating room supr. Rancho Bernardo Cataract Outpatient Ctr., San Diego, 1982-83; dir., cons. Cinlar-A.S.C. Enterprises, Poway, 1983-86; pres. sales and cons. Cinlar, Ltd., Poway, 1986—; cons., lectr. in field; conductor workshops, seminars in field; chmn. bd. The Gift Seminars, San Diego, 1986-88, Larco Distbrs., San Diego, 1985-88. Contbr. articles to profl. jours., mem. editorial bd. Perioperiative Nursing Quar., 1984-87. Vice chmn. The Hospice Found., San Diego, 1986-88. Recipient Cert. of Recognition Calif. Legis. Assembly, 1986, Joy Freeman award, 1987; named Outstanding Alumnus, Meth. Hosp. Sch. Nursing, 1987. Mem. Calif. Nurses Assn. (co-chmn. 1982-84, charter pres. region 2, 1985-86, 2d v.p. 1986-88), Assn. Operating Room Nurses (pres. 1975-76, parliamentarian 1977—), Nat. Assn. Parliamentarians (v.p. 1983-84). Republican. Methodist. Club: Le Tip Internat. Home: 15010 Pomerado Rd Poway CA 92064

CIULLA-SANZO, ROSALIE THERESA, personnel consultant; b. Bklyn., Apr. 8, 1961; d. Thomas Salvatore and Mary Amelia (Della-Peruta) C. AAS in Nursing, Coll. Mt. St. Vincent, 1981; BS in Computer Info. Systems, Dominican Coll., Blauvelt, N.Y., 1983. Cert. personnel cons. Nurses aide Upjohn Health Care Services, West Nyack, N.Y., 1981—; personnel cons. Analysts Internat. Corp., N.Y.C., 1983-85; mktg. rep. Software Internat. Assocs., N.Y.C., 1985-87; personnel cons. Ind. Cons. Services, 1987—. Vol. nurses's aide Sparkhill Sr. Citizen Ctr., N.Y., 1981—. Mem. Ind. Computing Cons. Assn., IBM User Group, Nat. Assn. Female Execs., Mensa. Roman Catholic. Home: 42B W 23d St Bayonne NJ 07002 Office: Ind Cons Service 150 Broadway Suite 700 New York NY 10038

CLACK, DOUGLAS MAE, data base company executive, consultant; b. San Antonio, July 10, 1943; d. Douglas Campbell and Ida Mae (Norwood) King; m. Charles Leonard Clack, Aug. 6, 1966 (div. 1973); 1 son, Charles Leonard, Jr. B.A., U. Tex.-San Antonio, 1977; MPIA, St. Mary's U., San Antonio, 1983. Engring. records clk. Southwestern Bell, San Antonio and Houston, 1970-72; clk., sec. Frost Bank, San Antonio, 1972-75; adminstr. San Antonio Independent Sch. Dist., 1977-84; owner, v.p. Diverse Data Systems, Inc., San Antonio, 1984-86 ; cons. various profl. and ednl. agencies, 1980—; instr. Tex. Edn. Agy., Austin, 1980—, Alamo Community Coll. Dist., 1984—; speaker various Tex. sch. dists., 1980—; bd. dirs. Volunteer Services, San Antonio State Chest Hosp.; instr. adult continuing edn. courses NE Ind. Sch. Dist. Contbr. articles to profl. jours. Sec. PTA, 1975-77, v.p., 1977-78; vol. ARC, 1978, Am. Cancer Soc., 1979; mem. adv. bd. Ella Austin Community Clinic, sec., 1981-84; vol. youth program New Mt. Pleasant Bapt. Ch.; mem. The Women's Coalition; mem. steering com. Women's Fair, 1985. Mem. Bus. and Profl. Women (corr. sec. 1983-85), LWV (local chair fin. com.), U. Tex. Alumni Assn., Am. Soc. Tng. and Devel., San Antonio Negro Bus. and Profl. Women, Greater Randolph Area C. of C., Alamo City C. of C., Bexar County Women's Ctr. Mentor's Program, Phillis Wheatley Alumni Assn. (charter mem., treas. 1984-85), Gamma Phi Lambda. Democrat. Club: Rising Star Internat. Tng. in Communications (charter mem.). Avocations: swimming; crafts; bicycling; exercising; reading; travel. Home: 12246 Brownstone St San Antonio TX 78233 Office: Diverse Data Systems Inc 1520 N Main Ave San Antonio TX 78212

CLAGETT, LESLIE PLUMMER, editor; b. Providence, Apr. 30, 1956; d. Robert Eugene and Peg (Hassett) Plummer; m. John Stephen Clagett, June 10, 1982. BA in English, Denison U., 1978. Mng. editor N.Y. Arts Jour., N.Y.C., 1978-81, Arts & Architecture, Los Angeles, 1981-85; assoc. editor architecture Home mag., Los Angeles, 1985—. Mem. Archtl. League, Nat. Trust for Hist. Preservation. Office: Home Mag 5900 Wilshire 15th floor Los Angeles CA 90036

CLAGHORN, TINA HOLGUIN, real estate executive; b. Las Cruces, N.Mex., Aug. 28, 1936; d. Cirilo Robledo adn Mary (Romo) Holguin; m. Chester Gerald Claghorn, June 2, 1956; children: Ronald, Julie, Karen, Brian, Audry, Kathy. Student, N.Mex. State U., 1958-59; BS, U. N.Mex., 1968, MS, 1972. Lic. real estate broker and salesman. Supr. Electro Mech. Labs., White Sands Missile Range, N.Mex., 1957-59; adminstrv. asst. Las Cruces (N.Mex.) High Sch., 1959-61; substitute tchr. Albuquerque Pub. Schs., 1968-69, tchr., 1968-77; adj. prof. U. Albuquerque, 1977-78; salesperson Hooten/Stahl, Albuquerque, 1978-80; owner, mgr. Claghorn Apts., Albuquerque, 1980-88; prin., v.p. The Foxwood Co., Albuquerque, 1984-86, pres., prin. owner, 1986—; salesperson Ansco Stephens Apt. Specialists, Albuquerque, 1980-82, Walter/Hinkle, Albuquerque, 1982-83; v.p., cons. Bus. Mgmt. Cons., Albuquerque, 1986—, Parkway Mktg. Co., Albuquerque, 1986—. Active Mile High Little League, Albuquerque, 1970, Altamonte Little League, Albuquerque, 1976; tchr. Annunciation Cath. Ch., Albuquerque, 1975; mem. Cath. Daus., Albuquerque, 1984-85, Mayor's City Devel. Kitchen Cabinet, Albuquerque, 1986-87. Mem. Nat. Assn. Realtors, Pi Lambda Theta, Alpha Delta Kappa(pres. 1976-78). Club: Leads. Lodge: Civitans (pres. Albuquerque chpt. 1985-86, pres. Great Southwest Civitan Dist. Found. 1987, Civitan of Yr. Albuquerque chpt. 1987). Home: 2732 Alcazar NE Albuquerque NM 87110 Office: The Foxwood Co 8529 Indian Scholl NE #D Albuquerque NM 87112

CLAGUE, ANN F., nutritionist; b. Muscatine, Iowa, May 31, 1928; d. Roscoe E. and Amanda D. (Hoffman) Eliason; (div.); children: Karen A. Claque-Kline, Brian L., Candace A. Garza, Kevin L. BS, Iowa State U., 1950; cert., Chgo. Art Inst., 1968; PhD, Donsbach U., 1979. Nutritionist free lance, 1979; computer artist Miller Meester Advt., Bloomington, 1987—. Author 3 books. Mem. Am. Inst. Med. Preventics, Colonial Chorale. Mem. United Ch. Christ. Address: 920 Feltl Ct #262 Hopkins MN 55343 Office: 2001 Killebrew Bloomington MN 55425

CLAIBORNE, LIZ (ELISABETH CLAIBORNE), fashion designer; b. Brussels, Mar. 31, 1929; came to U.S., 1934; d. Omer Villere and Louise Carol (Fenner) C.; m. Arthur Ortenberg, July 5, 1957; 1 son by previous marriage, Alexander G. Schultz. Student, Art Sch., Brussels, 1947, Academie, Nice, France, 1948. Asst. Tina Lesser, N.Y.C., 1949-50, Omar Khayam, Ben Reig, Inc., N.Y.C., 1950-52; designer Juniorite, N.Y.C., 1952-54, Dan Keller, N.Y.C., 1955-60, Youth Guild Inc., N.Y.C., 1960-76; designer, pres. Liz Claiborne Inc., N.Y.C., 1976—; chmn. Liz Claiborne Cosmetics, 1985—; guest lectr. Fashion Inst. Tech., Parsons Sch. Design; bd. dirs. Council of Am. Fashion Designers, Fire Island Lighthouse Restoration Com. Recipient Designer of Yr. award Palciode Hierro, Mexico City, 1976, Designer of Yr. award Dayton Co., Mpls., 1978, Ann. Disting. in Design award Marshall Field's 1985, One Co. Makes a Difference award Fashion Inst. Tech., 1985, award Council of Fashion Designers, 1986. Mem. Fashion Group. Roman Catholic. Office: Claiborne Inc 1441 Broadway New York NY 10018 *

CLAING, KAREN SCHAEFER, sales executive; b. Hartford, Conn., Aug. 15, 1952; d. William John and Fern Eloise (Sharrow) Schaefer; m. Richard George Claing, Mar. 18, 1972; 1 child, Caroline Marie. Student, Manchester Community Coll., 1973-75, Cen. Conn. Community Coll., 1985—. Clk. credit dept. Sears Roebuck, Manchester, Conn., 1969-71; clk. Met. Life Ins., Manchester, 1971-75, sr. sales asst., 1975-78; exec. sec. John A. Bailey Assocs., Inc., East Hartford, Conn., 1978-79, sales coordinator, 1979-82, asst. sales mgr., 1982-85, mgr. sales, 1985-88, gen mgr., 1988—. Coach Young Am. Bowling Alliance, East Hartford, 1982-85; Dem. com. mem. Stephen Penny for Mayor, Manchester, 1979-80, 84; advisor assembly #15 Rainbow for Girls Lodge, 1985-87. Mem. Women in Communications, Hartford Women's Network. Lodge: Order Eastern Star (worthy matron 1980-81). Home: 20 Joan Circle Manchester CT 06040

CLAMAR, APHRODITE J., psychologist; b. Hartford, Conn., Sept. 26, 1933; d. James John and Georgia (Panas) Clamar; B.A., CCNY, 1953; M.A., Columbia U., 1955; Ph.D., N.Y.U., 1978; m. Richard Cohen, June 24, 1973. Mgmt. cons., psychologist Milla Alihan Assos., N.Y.C., 1957-62; research psychologist coordinator Inst. Devel. Studies, N.Y. Med. Coll., N.Y.C., 1964; intern psychologist Bellevue Psychiat. Hosp., N.Y.C., 1964-66; asso. prof. Fashion Inst. Tech., N.Y.C., 1966-69; supervising psychologist Lifeline Center Child Devel., N.Y.C., 1966-67; chief psychologist Beth Israel Med. Center, I Spy Health Program, N.Y.C., 1967-70; dir. community-sch. mental health programs Soundview Community Services, Albert Einstein Coll. Medicine, Yeshiva U., N.Y.C., 1970-73; dir. treatment program court-related children, dept. child psychiatry Harlem Hosp.; mem. faculty dept. Psychiatry Columbia U. Coll. Physicians and Surgeons, N.Y.C., 1973-76; pvt. practice psychotherapy, N.Y.C., 1976—; cons. to public health and mental health agys., N.Y.C., 1976—; mem. faculty Lenox Hill Hosp. Psychoanalytic and Psychotherapy Tng. Program, 1982—. Fellow AAAS; mem. Soc. Clin. and Exptl. Hypnosis, Am. Psychol. Assn. (chairperson com. for women div. psychotherapy 1980-82), Soc. for Psychoanalytic Psychotherapy. Democrat. Greek Orthodox. Author: (with Budd Hopkins) Missing Time, 1981; contbr. articles in field to profl. jours. Home: 162 E 80th St New York NY 10021 Office: 30 E 60th St New York NY 10022

CLAMPITT, AMY KATHLEEN, writer, editor; b. New Providence, Iowa, June 15, 1920; d. Roy Justin and Lutie Pauline (Felt) C. B.A. with honors in English, Grinnell Coll., 1941, D.H.L., 1984. Sec., writer Oxford Univ. Press, N.Y.C., 1943-51; reference librarian Nat. Audubon Soc., N.Y.C., 1952-59; free-lance writer, N.Y.C., 1960-77; editor E.P. Dutton, N.Y.C., 1977-82; writer-in-residence Coll. William & Mary, Williamsburg, Va., 1984-85; vis. writer Amherst Coll., 1986-87. Author: (poetry) The Kingfisher, 1983; (poetry) What the Light Was Like, 1985, Archaic Figure, 1987. Guggenheim fellow, 1982-83; recipient Lit. award Am. Acad. Arts and Letters, 1984; fellow Acad. Am. Poets, 1984; mem. PEN, Editorial Freelancers Assn., Am. Acad. Inst. Arts and Letters. Democrat.

CLAMPITT, MARY O'BRIANT, government official; b. Connehatti, Miss., Feb. 18, 1931; d. Theron Russell and Ola Belle (Thompson) O'Briant; m. William Henry Clampitt, May 7, 1955; children: Russell, Henry, Amy, James. BS, U. Md., 1978, MA, 1982. Info. analyst FBI, Washington, 1951-56; editor Chief State Sch. Officers, NEA, Washington, 1976-77; editor, conf. mgr. Forum Officer, Nat. Acad. Sci., Washington, 1977-78; owner Clampitt Editorial Assocs., Chevy Chase, Md., 1970—; adminstrv. specialist White House Conf. on Aging, Washington, 1980-82; program analyst Office Insp. Gen., Health and Human Services, Washington, 1982-84; mgmt. analyst Food Safety Inspection Service, Washington, 1984—; mgr. Fed. women's program Food Safety Inspection Service, 1984—; bd. dirs. Am. Fed. Credit Union, 1985—. Bibliographer: History of State Departments of Education, 1978. Vol. Pres.'s Com. on Hiring Handicapped, 1985, Mothers Against Drunk Driving, 1985—; mem. bd. reps. Greentree Home for Children, 1986—; mem. steering com. Forums on Aging, 1987; mem. adv. com. Com. for Ctr. Planning, 1987—. Mem. Federally Employed Women, Interagy. Fed. Women's Program Mgrs., Internat. Platform Assn., Phi Kappa Phi. Republican. Baptist. Clubs: Woman's Action Taskforce (bd. dirs.), Bus. and Profl. Women's (Chevy Chase) (chair civic participation 1986—). Avocations: hiking, biking, cooking, writing songs. Home: 7114 Edgevale St Chevy Chase MD 20815 Office: Food Safety Inspection Service 14th and Independence Ave Washington DC 20815

CLANCE, PAULINE ROSE, psychology educator; b. Welch, W.Va., Oct. 19, 1938; d. George W. and Gladys (Riley) Rose; B.S. cum laude Lynchburg Coll., 1960; M.S., U. Ky., 1964, Ph.D., 1969; m. Lanier Clance, Dec. 14, 1959. Clin. psychologist G.B. Dinmick Child Guidance Clinic, Lexington, Ky., 1965; psychologist Univ. Hosp. Cleve., 1966-68, Brecksville VA Hosp., 1969-71; clin. psychologist Psychol. Services, Oberlin Coll., 1971-74; asst. prof. Oberlin Coll., 1971-74; prof. psychology Ga. State U., Atlanta, 1974—; pvt. practice clin. psychology, Atlanta, 1974—; cons. in field. Adv. bd.

Odyssey Family Service, 1979-83; mem. Com. on Minority and Poverty Groups, Coll. Entrance Examination Bd., 1972-75; peer reviewer grants nat. Endowment for Humanities, Washington, 1972-82; reviewer curriculum materials Appalachian Center for Ednl. Equity, U. Tenn., 1978. Oberlin Coll. leadership tng. grantee, 1973; Urban Life Center grantee, 1977; others. Mem. Southwestern Psychol. Assn. (pres. 1982-83), AAUP, Assn. Women in Psychology, Am. Psychol. Assn. Author: The Imposter Phenomenon: Overcoming the Fear that Haunts Your Success, 1985; contbr. articles to profl. jours. Office: Ga State U Dept Psychology Atlanta GA 30303

CLANCY, JEAN MARY, publishing executive; b. Bronx, N.Y., Nov. 28, 1962; d. Frank Anthony and Arlene Jean (Wineman) C. BSBA, SUNY, Oswego, 1984. Office mgr., pub. asst. Gordon Publs., Inc., Floral Park, N.Y., 1985—. Mem. Nat. Assn. Female Execs. Republican. Roman Catholic. Office: Gordon Publs Inc 22 N Tyson Ave Floral Park NY 11001

CLANCY, ROSALIND LEE, modeling school administrator; b. Trenton, N.J., Oct. 1, 1948; d. Florindo Peter and Elsa (Lanzi) Manganelli; m. Joseph Michael Clancy, Jr., Apr. 15, 1973. AA, Trenton Jr. Coll., 1969. Dir. Calif. Sch. Modeling and Charm, Trenton, N.J., 1972—; casting dir. Motion Picture Casting, N.Y.C., 1980-82, N.C. State Fair, 1986, Tony Conforti Theatrical Prodns., 1987—, Lawrence Richards Prodns., N.Y.C., 1987—; mem. Miss Am. Scholarship Pageant, 1975—; chmn. Shamrock Specialties, Lawrenceville, N.J., 1983—; owner Roz Clancy Photography; pres. Calif. Models Mgmt., Washington Crossing, N.J.; cons. Ladato Mgmt., N.Y.C., 1979—, Cinema Liberty Prodns., Princeton, N.J., 1974—; franchise holder Miss N.J. Venus U.S.A. Pageant, 1988—; designer, cons. Count Joseppe Fashions., N.Y.C.; judge Miss Am. Teenager, N.J., 1974—, Miss Teenage Am., N.J., 1975, preliminary Miss Universe, N.J., 1985; v.p., bd. dirs. Paint n Tape Industries; spl. host., emcee N.J. Fair Pagent, 1986, 87. Recipient Profl. Excellence award Fermi Fedn., 1974. Mem. Internat. Platform Assn., NDPA Assn. Republican. Lutheran. Clubs: Italian-Am. (Hamilton Twp., N.J.); Bordentown Yacht. Avocations: boating, sports. Office: Calif Sch Modeling & Charm 937 Brunswick Ave Trenton NJ 08638

CLAPPER, KATHRYN ACCOLA, real estate company official; b. Alton, Ill., July 14, 1942; d. Carl E. and Geraldine (Hendrickson) Accola; m. Larry R. Clapper, Jan. 20, 1963 (div. 1985); children: David Eric, Laura Kay. BA in Edn., Purdue U., 1964. Lic. real estate broker, Mo., Conn., Ill. Tchr. Mountain View (Calif.) Elem. Sch., 1964-66; saleswoman Carl G. Stifel Real Estate, St. Louis, 1972-75, Westledge Assocs., Simsbury, Conn., 1975-77, Ira E. Berry Real Estate, St. Louis, 1977-78, Re/Max Crossroads, Rolling Meadow, Ill., 1984-87; saleswoman Baird & Warner Real Estate, Palatine, Ill., 1979-84, real estate sales mgr., broker, sales assoc., 1987—. Mem. Nat. Assn. Real Estate Sales Execs. (charter nat. million dollar roundtable), Northwest Suburban Bd. Realtors (bd. dirs. 1984-87), Alpha Chi Omega (pres. Gamma Chi Gamma alumnae chpt. pres. 1986-88, Chgo. area chpt. 1987-88, Outstanding Alumnae award 1988). Republican. Home: 7 Atteboro on Auburn St Rolling Meadows IL 60008 Office: Baird & Warner Real Estate 295 N Northwest Hwy Palatine IL 60067

CLAREMON, GLENDA RUTH, lawyer; b. Beacon, N.Y., Aug. 13, 1951; d. Louis David and Sarah (Smith) Friedman; m. Robert Nolan Claremon, June 23, 1974; children: Michael, Scott, Rachel, Steven. Student, Stern Coll., 1969-70, Hebrew U., Jerusalem, 1970-71; AB, Douglass Coll., 1972; JD, Georgetown U., 1976. Bar: Md. 1976, D.C. 1977, Calif. 1981. Sole practice Silver Spring, Md., 1978-81, Sacramento, 1984-86; assoc. Waits, Britt & Wallace, Sacramento, 1981-84, Weintraub, Genshlea, Hardy, Erich & Brown, Sacramento, 1986-87; sole practice law Sacramento, 1987—. Pres. Shalom Sch. PTA, Sacramento, 1983-86. Mem. Calif. Bar Assn., D.C. Bar Assn. Home and Office: 4144 Crondall Dr Sacramento CA 95864

CLARK, ALICIA GARCIA, political party official; b. Vera Cruz, Mex., Jan. 13; came to U.S., 1970; d. Rafael Aully and Maria Luisa (Cobos) Garcia; m. Edward E. Clark, Oct. 20, 1970; 1 son, Edward E. M.S. in Chem. Engring., Nat. U. Mex., Mexico City, 1951. Chemist, Celanese Mexicana, Mexico City, 1951-53, lab. mgr., 1951-53, sales promotion mgr., 1958-65, sales promotion and advt. mgr., 1965-70. Nat. chmn. Libertarian Party, Houston, 1981-83; pres. San Marino (Calif.) Guild of Huntington Hosps., 1981-82, chmn. Celebrity Series, 1979—; Pres. Multiple Sclerosis Soc., San Gabriel Valley, Calif., 1977-78. Recipient award La Mujer de Hoy mag., 1969. Mem. Fashion Group (treas. 1969-70), Mex. Advt. Assn. (dir. 1969-70, award 1970). Club: San Marino Woman's (ways and means chmn. 1980, 87).

CLARK, ANJA MARIA, lawyer; b. Vienna, Austria, Mar. 31, 1942; came to U.S., 1966, naturalized, 1982; d. Joseph and Josephine (Mokesch) Rernboeck; m. Robert Eugene Smith, Jan. 26, 1969 (div.); m. Donald Otis Clark, Nov. 5, 1983. B.A. summa cum laude in Sociology, Oglethorpe U., 1974; M.A. cum laude in Sociology, Ga. State U., 1977; J.D., John Marshall Law Sch., 1977. Bar: Ga. 1978, D.C. 1984. Paralegal asst., Atlanta, 1976-78; sole practice, Atlanta, 1978-84; trial atty. oil and gas litigation Fed. Energy Regulatory Commn., Washington, 1985—. Recipient Benjamin Parker Law award Oglethorpe U., 1974, Cross of the Holy Land award Vatican, 1987. Mem. Ga. Assn. Women Lawyers (sec.-treas. 1981-83), State Bar Ga., ABA, Bus. Council Ga. (internat. subcom. 1981-83), Women's Bar Assn. D.C. (dir. career opportunities 1984-85). Republican. Roman Catholic.

CLARK, BETTY JEAN, state legislator; b. Kansas City, Kans., Apr. 18, 1920; d. Raymond Carlisle and Mary Priscilla (Hunt) Walker; student Ft. Hays State U., 1937-38, U. Utah, 1939-40, U. Pacific, 1942-45, Garrett Evangelical Sem., 1948; m. Homer Orville Clark, Sept. 3, 1950; children—Peggy, Mark, Paul. Dir. student program Wesley Found., Ames, Iowa, 1948-51; dir. Christian edn. First United Meth. Ch., Mason City, Iowa, 1963-75; mem. Iowa Gen. Assembly, Des Moines, 1977—. Mem. Republican Women's Task Force. Mem. Bus. and Profl. Women, Women's Polit. Caucus, LWV, Fedn. Republican Women, P.E.O. Methodist. Clubs: Ch. Women United, Federated Women's Club, Older Women's League, United Meth. Women. Author: (with Harriet Ann Daffron) Nearer to Thee, 1956. Office: State Capitol Des Moines IA 50319

CLARK, BEVERLY ANN, lawyer; b. Davenport, Iowa, Dec. 9, 1944; d. F. Henry and Arlene F. (Meyer) C.; m. Richard Floss; children—Amy and Barry (twins). Student, Mich. State U., 1963-65; B.A., Calif. State U.-Fullerton, 1967; M.S.W., U. Iowa, 1975, J.D., 1980. Bar: Iowa 1980. Probation officer County of San Bernardino, San Bernardino, Calif., 1968, County of Riverside, Riverside, Calif., 1968-69; social worker Skiff Hosp., Newton, Iowa, 1971-73; social worker State of Iowa, Mitchellville, 1973-74, planner, Des Moines, 1976-77, law clk., Des Moines, 1980-81; instr. Des Moines Area Community Coll., Ankeny, Iowa, 1974-75; gen. counsel Pioneer Hi-Bred Internat., Inc., Des Moines, 1981—. Editor: Proceedings: Bicentennial Symposium on New Directions in Juvenile Justice, 1975. Founder Mothers of Twins Club, Newton, Iowa, 1971; co-chmn. Juvenile Justice Symposium, Des Moines, 1974-75; mem. Juvenile Justice Com., Des Moines, 1974-75; mem. Nat. Offender Based State Corrections Info. System Com., Ia. rep., 1976-78; incorporator, dir. Iowa Dance Theatre, Des Moines, 1981; mem. Pesticide User's Adv. Com., Fort Collins, Colo., 1981—. Mem. ABA (subcom. on devel. individual rights in work place, termination-at-will subcom.), Iowa Bar Assn., Polk County Bar Assn., Polk County Women Atty.'s Assn., Am. Trial Lawyers Assn., Am. Assn. Agrl. Lawyers, Am. Corp. Counsel Assn. (litigation subcommittee). Home: Rural Rt 1 Box 80 Baxter IA 50028 Office: Pioneer Hi-Bred Internat Inc 400 Locust St 700 Capital Sq Des Moines IA 50309

CLARK, CAROL CANDA, museum curator, art historian, educator; b. N.Y.C., July 21, 1947; d. Henry G. Canda and Dolores C. Adam; m. Jon D. Clark, May 24, 1969 (div. Apr. 1983); m. Charles Parkhurst, July 1986. B.A. with distinction, U. Mich.-Ann Arbor, 1969, M.A., 1971; Ph.D., Case Western Res. U., Cleve., 1981 . Registrar, U. Mich. Mus. Art, Ann Arbor, 1971-72; instr. Tex. Christian U., Ft. Worth, 1975-77; curator Amon Carter Mus. Ft. Worth, 1977-84; exec. prendergast fellow Williams Coll., Williamstown, Mass., 1984-87, lectr. art history, 1984-87; assoc. prof. fine arts Amhurst (Mass.) Coll., 1987—; adj. prof. art history So. Methodist U., 1982-83; adj. curator of Am. Art, Clark Art Inst., Williamstown, Mass., 1984-87; mem. art adv. panel IRS, Washington, 1983—. Author: Thomas Moran's Watercolors, 1980; (catalogue) American Impressionist and Realist Paintings, 1978. Mem. art and architecture adv. panel Tex. Commn. on the Arts, 1981-83. Kress Found. fellow 1972-75, Collections Com. Berkshire Mus. Office: Amhurst Coll Fayerweather Hall Amherst MA 01002

CLARK, CAROL LOIS, state government agency administrator, consumer advocate, consultant; b. Salt Lake City, May 23, 1948; d. Norman W. and Lois Amanda (Colt) C. BA in English cum laude, U. Utah, 1970; MEd in Secondary Edn., 1972, PhD in Cultural Founds. of Edn., 1979; postgrad. Columbia U., summer 1980. Cert. profl. tchr., Utah, Mass. Tchr. Jordan Sch. dist., Sandy, Utah, 1972-78, 81-82; curriculum cons. Brigham Young U., Provo, 1978-79, cons., lectr., 1978—; program specialist Utah System Approach to Individualized Learning, Salt Lake City, 1980-81; consumer edn. specialist Utah Atty. Gen.'s Office, Salt Lake City, 1982-84; free-lance editor, curriculum developer Utah Office Edn., Salt Lake City, 1981-82; free-lance editor, cons. Dian Thomas Enterprises, Provo, 1981—; gov.'s adminstrv. asst. for edn. and communication, 1984-87; bd. dirs. Communications and Research Utah State Dept. Community and Econ. Devel., 1987—, Deseret Gymnasium, Salt Lake City, 1982—; mem. Fund for Improvement of Post-Secondary Edn., 1986—; mem. unproven med. practices com. Utah State Med. Assn., 1983-84; mem. Utah Ins. Consumer Action Com., 1983-84; mem. Utah Records Com., 1983-84; mem. Utah Gov.'s Securities Fraud Task Force, 1984; chmn. Utah Atty. Gen.'s Consumer Adv. Com., 1984; state del. U.S. Consumer Product Safety Commn., 1985-87; mem. Utah Higher Edn. Work group for Integrating Women into Work Force, 1985—; bd. dirs. Salt Lake City Sch. Vols., 1985—; state chair Initiative for Understanding, 1987—. Author: A Singular Life, 1974; How to Avoid Getting Ripped Off: Essential But Hard-to-Find Consumer Facts for Women, 1985; co-author: Principles of Learning, 1981; contbr.: Consumer's Resource Handbook, 1986; consumer columnist Deseret News, 1982-84, Standard-Examiner, 1983-84, Golden Age, 1983-84, Cache County Citizen, 1984, Park Record, 1984, Sun Advocate, 1984, Richfield Reaper, 1984, Vernal Express, 1984, Color County Spectrum, 1984, Provo Daily Herald, 1984; contbr. articles, poetry to various publs.; editor: The Relief Society Magazine: A Legacy Remembered, 1914-1970, 1982. Mem. gen. bd. Relief Soc., Ch. of Jesus Christ of Latter-day Saints, Salt Lake City, 1973-84, state del., 1986; acting chmn. Republican Party Voting Dist., Salt Lake City, 1977, dist. vice chmn., 1984; mem. Utah Women's Legis. Council, 1977-79; mem. Denver region Ford Consumer Appeals Bd., 1983-84; mem. planning com. Utah Ednl. Seminar, 1985—. Recipient Tchr. of Yr. award Utah State Hist. Soc., 1975, Ann. Achievement award for best consumer publ. Nat. Assn. Consumer Agy. Adminstrs., 1983; named Outstanding Young Woman from Utah, 1982, Young Woman of Achievement, Nat. Council Women, 1984; Ch. of Jesus Christ of Latter-day Saints Historian's Office fellow, 1976. Mem. Salt Lake C. of C. (bus. in edn. com.), Nat. Futures Assn. (edn. adv. com. 1984-86), Nat. Assn. Consumer Agy. Adminstrs. (Best Book award 1985), Profl. Rep. Women, Utah Women's Forum (founding mem.), Home Econs. Assn. (bd. dirs. 1985-86), Phi Kappa Phi, Alpha Xi Delta, Lambda Delta Sigma. Office: Utah Gov's Office 210 State Capital Bldg Salt Lake City UT 84114

CLARK, CAROLYN ARCHER, technologist, scientist; b. Leon County, Tex., Feb. 16, 1941; d. Ray Brooks and Dena Mae (Green) Archer; m. Frank Ray Clark, Nov. 20, 1960 (div. Oct. 1979); children: Frank Ray, Valerie Lynn, Bruce Layne. BA, Sam Houston State U., 1961; MS, Tex. A&M U., 1973, PhD, 1977. Supr., bookkeeper Republic Sewing Machine Distbrs., Dallas, 1961-65; door-to-door sales Avon Products, Inc. Bryan, Tex., 1965-72; lectr. Tex. A&M Univ., College Station, Tex., 1977, research assoc., 1977-79; sr. sci. Lockheed Emsco., Houston, 1979-82, prin. scientist 1983-85; aerospace technologist phys. scientist NASA Nat. Space Technology Lab., Houston and Stennis Space Ctr., Miss., 1986—; staff scientist Lockheed EMSCO, Houston, 1986—; cons. in field. Contbr. articles to profl. publs. Recipient Commendation for Outstanding Contbns. Lockheed, 1979-80, Commendation for Excellence, 1984; Cert. of Merit U.S. Dept. Agr. 1980; Grad. Research Fellow Tex. A&M, 1975-76; NSF co-grantee Tex. A&M, 1976-77. Mem. Am. Soc. Plant Taxonomists, Bot. Soc. Am., Am. Soc. Photogrammetry, Nat. Mgmt. Assn., Sigma Xi, Phi Sigma, Alpha Chi, Kappa Delta Pi. Republican. Avocations: sailing, scuba diving, tennis, piano. Office: Lockheed EMSCO 2400 NASA Rd 1 Houston TX 77058

CLARK, CHARLENE KERNE, development and promotion coordinator, educator; b. Thibodaux, La., Apr. 15, 1947; d. Francis Lloyd and Ethel (Walker) Kerne; B.A., U. Southwestern La., 1969; M.A., U. Ark., 1970; Ph.D., La. State U., 1974; m. William B. Clark, Dec. 22, 1972; children—Mary Frances Lyons, Eleanor Kerne. Instr. in English, U. N.C., Greensboro, 1975-77; instr. bus. communication N.C. A&T State U., Greensboro, 1976-77; vis. asst. prof. English, Tex. A&M U., College Station, 1977-78; energy info. specialist Center Energy and Mineral Resources, Tex. A&M U., 1978-84; devel. and promotion coordinator Sterling C. Evans Library, Tex. A&M U., 1984—. Mem. ALA, Citizens Hist. Preservation, Internat. Assn. Bus. Communicators, Phi Kappa Phi. Roman Catholic. Home: 2304 Burton Dr Bryan TX 77802 Office: Tex A&M U Sterling C Evans Library College Station TX 77843

CLARK, CONNIE M., educator; b. Pound, Va., Mar. 8, 1948; d. Leonard Milton Mullins and Mildred (Cantrell) Rose; m. Marvin William Clark, Apr. 22, 1976. BA in English, Clinch Valley Coll., 1970; BS in Psychology, Va. Poly. Inst. and State U., 1974; MA in Edn., Union Coll., 1975; postgrad. U. R.I., 1978, U. Va., 1984. Sec. State Farm Ins., Pound, 1966-67; tchr. Wise County Sch. Bd., Wise, Va., 1970—; pres. Appalachian Edn. Lab., Charleston, W.Va., 1986-87. Precinct worker Democratic Party, Big Stone Gap, 1977—; mem. Dem. state cen. com., 9th dist. com., Wise county com., 1987—; mem. rules com. Va. Dem. Conv., 1988; active PRIDE, 1988—, Friends of the Library; legis. asst. Va. Ho. Dels. 2d dist., 1988—. Mem. Nat. Council Tchrs. of English, Va. Edn. Assn. (Appreciation award 1985, chmn. polit. action com. 1985), uniserv standards commn. 1982-85), Va. Bus. and Profl. Women (vice dir. Dist. 1 1985-86), Wise County Edn. Assn. (legis. chmn. 1985-87), Bus. and Profl. Women (pres. Wise, Va. 1983-85, pres. elect 1987—, Dock Boggs com. 1986, state legis. com. 1986-87), AAUW (legis, chmn. Big Stone Gap 1985), Wise County C. of C. (edn. com. 1988—). Named One of Outstanding Young Women of Am., 1983. Baptist. Avocations: Reading; music; animals; outdoors. Home and Office: 330 Pearl St Big Stone Gap VA 24219

CLARK, DEBORAH LYNN, financial executive; b. Pitts., Apr. 2, 1951; d. Clyde Wilson and Norma June (Glass) McCance; m. C. Richard Clark, Feb. 16, 1973. Grad. Computer Systems Inst., Pitts., 1970; student Point Park Coll. Office mgr. Pressure Chem. Co., Pitts., 1973-74, Budget Rent-a-Car, Pitts., 1974-75; acct. G.M.A.C. Fin., Pitts., 1975-79; sole propr. Clark Color Photography, Pitts., 1977-79; office mgr. McKeever, Varga & Assocs., C.P.A.s, Pitts., 1979-82; asst. controller Park Way Studios Internat. Inc., McKees Rocks, Pa., 1982-85, asst. sec.-treas., 1984—; prin. Clark Fin. Services, 1985—; pres. Pegasus Computer Corp., 1986—; controller several corps. Mem. Assoc. Photographer Internat., Nat. Assn. Female Execs., Pa. Assn. Notaries. Home: 3229 Faronia St Pittsburgh PA 15204 Office: Park Way Studios Internat Inc 6 Loop St Pittsburgh PA 15215

CLARK, DENISE LYNN, laboratory executive; b. Norristown, Pa., Oct. 14, 1954; d. James Carl and Rose Ann (DiNofrio) C. BBA, Ursinus Coll., Collegeville, Pa., 1985; postgrad. St. Joe's U., Phila. Customer service supr. Upjohn Co., King of Prussia, Pa., 1976-80; mgr. credit and collection SmithKline Clin. Lab., King of Prussia, 1980-85; mgr. nat. credit and collection SmithKline Bio-Sci. Labs., King of Prussia, 1986-87; accounts receivable mgr. Internat. Clin. Lab., Nashville, 1987—. Mem. Nat. Assn. Female Execs., N.J. Assn. Credit Execs. Avocation: travel. Home: 2753 Apple Valley Ln Audubon PA 19403 Office: Internat Clin Lab 5 Park Plaza Nashville TN 37203

CLARK, DIANA WELLS, public relations executive; b. San Jose, Calif., Aug. 3, 1945; d. Richard Gerald and Elizabeth Maja (Foster) Wells; 1 child, Michelle Kennedy Eason. BA in English and Sociology, San Jose State U., 1966. Cert. secondary tchr., Calif. Communications coordinator Comprehensive Planning Orgn., San Diego, 1975-76; pub. info. coordinator Met. Transit Devel. Bd., San Diego, 1976-81; sr. acct. exec. Stoorza Co., San Diego, 1981-82; owner, pres. The Diana Clark Co., San Diego, 1982—. Trustee San Diego Repertory Theatre, 1985—; dir. San Diego and Imperial Girl Scouts of Am. Council, 1983-85. Mem. Soc. for Mktg. Profl. Services (dir. 1983—), Associated Gen. Contractors of Am., Pub. Relations Soc. of Am., Internat. Assn. Bus. Communicators (Excellence award 1983, 86, 87), Pub. Relations Club San Diego (Excellence award 1981, 85, 87). Office: The Diana Clark Co 110 W C St Suite 909 San Diego CA 92101

CLARK, ELEANOR, author; b. Los Angeles; d. Frederick Huntington and Eleanor (Phelps) C.; m. Robert Penn Warren, Dec. 7, 1952; children: Rosanna, Gabriel. B.A., Vassar Coll. Mem. Corp. of Yaddo. Author: novels The Bitter Box, 1946, Baldur's Gate, 1971, Dr. Heart, A Novella, and Other Stories, 1975, Gloria Mundi, 1979, Camping Out, 1986; for children The Song of Roland, 1960; non-fiction Rome and a Villa, 1952, expanded edit., 1975, The Oysters of Locmariaquer, 1964, Eyes, Etc., A Memoir, 1977, Tamrart-13 Days in the Sahara; translator: Dark Wedding (R. Sender 1982), 1943; contbr. stories, essays and revs. to numerous publs. Served with OSS, 1943-45. Guggenheim fellow, 1946-47, 49-50; recipient Nat. Book Award, 1965. Mem. Nat. Inst. Arts and Letters (award 1946). Address: 2495 Redding Rd Fairfield CT 06430

CLARK, ELIZABETH ANNETTE, insurance company department manager, data processor; b. Mpls., Oct. 6, 1934; d. Walter Burdette and Daveda Marguerite (Hansen) Garver; m. Forrest Halter, May 17, 1958 (div. Feb. 1973); children: Gregory, Linda Halter Balsiger; m. Leslie Matthew Clark, Sept. 28, 1976. AA, Montgomery Coll., 1954; AAS, Greenville (S.C.) Tech. Coll., 1973; B in Gen. Studies, Furman U., 1979; MBA, Clemson (S.C.) U., 1987. Programmer Liberty Life Ins. Co., Greenville, 1973-77, chief programmer analyst, 1977-79, systems mgr., 1979-84, mgr. quality improvement dept., 1984—; instr. computer programming part-time Greenville Tech. Coll., 1980-81. Sec. S.C./Piedmont chpt. Nat. Multiple Sclerosis Soc., Greenville, 1974-76; bd. dirs. Greenville Little Theatre, 1974-75; chmn. invitation com. Bicentennial Ball, Greenville, 1976. Fellow Life Mgmt. Inst.; mem. Life Office Mgmt. Assn. (rep. So. Systems Devel. Commn. 1985—, program chmn. 1987-88), Data Processing Mgmt. Assn., Quality Assurance Inst., Beta Sigma Phi (pres. Greenville chpt. 1975-76, v.p. council 1975-76, Woman of Yr. award 1976, Alpha-Omega award 1977), Mensa. Unitarian. Home: 121 Rockwood Dr Greenville SC 29605 Office: Liberty Life Ins Co PO Box 789 Greenville SC 29602

CLARK, ELOISE ELIZABETH, biologist, university official; b. Grundy, Va., Jan. 20, 1931; d. J. Francis Emmett and Ava Clayton (Harris) C. BA, Mary Washington Coll., 1951; PhD in Zoology, U. N.C., 1958; DSc, King Coll., 1976; postdoctoral research, Washington U., St. Louis, 1957-58, U. Calif. at Berkeley, 1958-59. Research asst., then instr. U. N.C., 1952-55; instr. physiology Marine Biol. Lab., Woods Hole, Mass, summers 1958-62; mem. faculty Columbia U., 1958-69, asso. prof. biol. sci., 1966-69; with NSF, Washington, 1969-83; head molecular biology NSF, 1971-73, div. dir. biol. and med. scis., 1973-75, dep. asst. dir. biol., behavioral and social scis., 1975-76, asst. dir. biol., behavioral and social scis., 1976-83; v.p. acad. affairs, prof. biol. sci. Bowling Green State U. (Ohio), 1983—. Contbr. articles to profl. jours. Mem. alumnae bd. Mary Washington Coll., U. Va., 1967-70; bd. regents Nat. Library of Medicine, 1973-83; mem. policy group competitive grants program U.S. Dept. Agr.; mem. White House interdepartmental task force on women and interagy, 1978-80, task force for conf. on families, 1980, mem. com. on health and medicine, 1976-80, vice chmn. com. on food and renewable resources, 1977-80; mem. selective excellence task force Ohio Bd. Regents, 1984-85; mem. Ohio Adv. Council Coll. Prep. Edn., 1983-84; mem. Ohio Inter-Univ. Council for Provosts, 1983—, chmn., 1984-85, nat. adv. research resources council NIH, 1987-89; mem. informal sci. edn. panel, NSF, 1986-88. Named Disting. Alumnus Mary Washington Coll., 1975; Wilson scholar, 1956; E.C. Drew scholar, 1956; USPHS postdoctoral fellow, 1957-59; recipient Disting. Service award NSF, 1978. Mem. Soc. Gen. Physiology (sec. 1965-67, council 1969-71), AAAS (council 1969-71, dir. 1978-82), Biophys. Soc. (council 1975-76), Am. Soc. Cell Biology (council 1972-75), Am. Inst. Biol. Scientists, Phi Beta Kappa (com. on qualifications 1985-91), Sigma Xi. Home: 1222 Brownwood Dr Bowling Green OH 43403 Office: Bowling Green State U McFall Ctr Bowling Green OH 43403

CLARK, ESTHER FRANCES, legal educator; b. Phila., Aug. 29, 1929; d. John and Lucy (Scapula) Giaccio; m. John H. Clark, Jr., June 12, 1954; 1 child, Jacqueline. B.A., Temple U., 1950; J.D., Rutgers U., 1955. Bar: Pa. 1956. Practiced in Chester, until 1976; prof. law Del. Law Sch., Widener U., Wilmington, 1976—. Assoc. editor: Rutgers U. Law Rev, 1954-55. Bd. dirs. Taylor Hosp., Ridley, Pa., Pa. Bar Inst., Lindsay Law Library. Fellow Am. Bar Found.; mem. ABA, Pa. Bar Assn. (ho. of dels.), Delaware County Bar Assn. (pres. 1982), Am. Trial Lawyers Assn., Delaware County Legal Assistance Assn. (dir. 1972-77, pres. bd. dirs. 1974-76). Roman Catholic. Home: 207 Knoll Rd Wallingford PA 19086 Office: PO Box 7474 Wilmington DE 19803

CLARK, FAYE LOUISE, drama and speech educator; b. La., Oct. 9, 1936; student Centenary Coll., 1954-55; B.A. with honor, U. Southwestern La., 1962; M.A., U. Ga., 1966; m. Warren James Clark, Aug. 8, 1969; children—Roy, Kay Natalie. Tchr., Nova Exptl. Schs., Fort Lauderdale, Fla., 1963-65; faculty dept. drama and speech DeKalb Community Coll., Atlanta, 1967—, chmn. dept., 1977-81. Pres. Hawthorne Sch. PTA, 1983-84. Mem. Ga. Theatre Conf. (sec. 1968-69, rep. to Southeastern Theatre Conf. 1969), Ga. Psychol. Assn., Ga. Speech Assn., Atlanta Ballet Guild, Friends of the Atlanta Opera, Southeastern Theatre Conf., Atlanta Artists Club (sec. 1981-83, dir. 1983—), Young Women of Arts, High Mus. Art, Phi Kappa Phi, Pi Kappa Delta, Sigma Delta Pi, Kappa Delta Pi, Thalian-Blackfriars. Presbyterian. Club: Lake Lanier Sailing. Home: 2521 Melinda Dr NE Atlanta GA 30345 Office: DeKalb Community Coll Humanities div North Campus Dunwoody GA 30338

CLARK, J. FAY SALMON, principal; b. Ft. Knox, Ky., Aug. 30, 1937; d. Wilmer Henry Salmon and Evelyn Howison (Mallicotte) Huber; m. James Thomas Clark III; children: Carol Howison, James Thomas IV (dec). BS, Longwood Coll., 1959; MEd, Coll. William and Mary, 1980; postdoctoral, Va. Poly. Inst. Cert. elem. tchr., Va., La. Tchr. elem. schs., Va. and La.; prin./bookkeeper Bel Manor Kindergarten and Nursery Sch., Paris; demonstration tchr. York County (Va.) Pub. Schs., master tchr., team leader, asst. prin., disseminator Title IV-C project, CenTex coordinator, TV tchr., basic skills coordinator, fgn. lang. elem. studies coordinator, elem. program specialist, acting dir. gifted/talented program; prin. Grafton Bethel Elem. Sch., York County; presenter workshops. Contbr. articles to profl. jours. Vol. ARC, pub. chmn.; active programs Providence Bapt. Ch.; mem. Cultural Arts in Edn. Com., Tidewater, Va.; bd. dirs. Peninsula Jr. Arts Series, 1985-87; pres. PTO, 1985-86. Mem. Am. Women in France (sec.), Peninsula Women's Network, York Mgmt. Assn. (pres. 1984-87), Va. Edn. Assn., Alliance for Invitational Edn., Internat. Reading Assn., Nat. Elem. Prins. Assn., Va. Assn. Curriculum Devel., Delta Kappa Gamma, Phi Delta Kappa. Democrat. Home: Locust Point Glass VA 23072 Office: Grafton Bethel Elem Sch 410 Lakeside Dr Grafton VA 23692

CLARK, J. JILL, advertising agency executive; b. Griffith, Ind., Nov. 2, 1938; d. John Edward and Millicent Camila (Morin) McClusky; m. Dale Walker Clark, Oct. 8, 1960 (div. Nov. 1963). Student, Northwestern U., Western Mich. U. Asst. buyer SMY, Chgo., 1973-75; buyer CPM, Chgo., 1975-79; media dir. Chase Ehrenberg & Rosene, Chgo., 1979-80; assoc. nat. regional buyer operation dir. Bozell, Jacobs, Kenyon & Eckhardt, Chgo., from 1980; now with Tampa, Fla., office Ellis Diaz/Bozell Jacobs Kenyon & Eckhardt. Office: Ellis Diaz/Bozell Jacobs Kenyon & Eckhardt 3030 N Rocky Point Dr W Tampa FL 33607

CLARK, JANE COLBY, English language educator; b. Smith County, Kans., July 22, 1928; d. Noel Barclay and Velma Matilda (Helfinstine) Colby; B.S., Kans. State U., 1951; postgrad. Colo. State U., 1955-56, U. Colo., summers 1957-59; m. William Kline Clark, May 27, 1951; children—Courtney, Hilary. Tchr. rural sch., Smith County, 1946-47; sec., home service worker ARC, Boulder, Colo., 1952-55; tchr. public schs., Manhattan, Kans., 1956-59; temporary instr. in English, Kans. State U., 1968-74, instr., 1974—, asst. dir. writing lab. dept. English, 1974-85, dir. writing lab., 1985—. Mem. Nat. Council Tchrs. English, Nat. Writing Ctrs. Assn. (exec. bd.), Midwest Writing Ctrs. Assn. (exec. bd.), Riley County Humane Soc., Mortar Bd. Alumnae, Phi Kappa Phi. Methodist. Contbr. book revs. to newspaper, Manhattan Mercury; editorial bd. The Writing Ctr. Jour. Home: 2105 McDowell Ave Manhattan KS 66502 Office: Kans State U 102 Denison Hall Manhattan KS 66506

CLARK, JANET EILEEN, political scientist, educator; b. Kansas City, Kans., June 5, 1940; d. Edward Francis and Mildred Lois (Mack) Morrissey; A.A., Kansas City Jr. Coll., 1960; A.B., George Washington U., Washington, 1962, M.A., 1964; Ph.D., U. Ill., 1973; m. Caleb M. Clark, Sept. 28, 1968; children—Emily Claire, Grace Ellen, Evelyn Adair. Staff, U.S. Dept. Labor, Washington, 1962-64; instr. social sci. Kansas City (Kans.) Jr. Coll., 1964-67; instr. polit. sci. Parkland Coll., 1970-71; asst. prof. govt., N.Mex. State U., Las Cruces, 1971-77, assoc. prof., 1977-80; assoc. prof. polit. sci. U. Wyo., 1981-84, prof., 1984—. Wolcott fellow, 1963-64, NDEA Title IV fellow, 1967-69. Mem. NEA (pres. chpt. 1978-79), Am. Polit. Sci. Assn., Western Polit. Sci. Assn. (exec. council 1984-87), Western Social Sci. Assn. (exec. council 1978-81, v.p. 1982, pres. 1985), Women's Caucus for Polit. Sci. (treas. 1982, pres. 1987), LWV (exec. bd. 1980-83, treas. 1986—), Women's Polit. Caucus, Beta Sigma Phi (v.p. chpt. 1978-79), Phi Beta Kappa, Chi Omega (prize 1962), Phi Kappa Phi. Democrat. Lutheran. Book rev. editor Social Sci. Jour., 1982-87. Contbr. articles to profl. jours. Home: 519 S 12th St Laramie WY 82070

CLARK, JOAN BRYSON, accountant; b. N.Y.C., Nov. 19, 1940; d. William Harold and Mary (Reilly) Ingram; m. Henry Noel Bryson, Aug. 1, 1959 (div. 1969); 1 child, Christopher Bryson; m. Michael William Clark, Mar. 5, 1971; 1 child, Lauren. B.B.A., Baruch Coll., 1969. C.P.A., N.Y. Acct. Nehring Bros., N.Y.C., 1960-69; audit mgr. Main Hurdman, C.P.A.s, N.Y.C., 1969-73, 76-82; controller Hughes Hubbard & Reed, N.Y.C., 1982—. Mem. Am. Inst. C.P.A.s, N.Y. State Soc. C.P.A.s, Am. Woman's Soc. C.P.A.s, Am. Soc. Women Accts. (pres. N.Y. chpt. 1977-78), Nat. Assn. Female Execs. Republican. Roman Catholic. Avocations: theater; opera; computers. Home: 500 Fort Washington Ave New York NY 10033 Office: Hughes Hubbard & Reed One Wall St New York NY 10005

CLARK, JOAN-BERRY, educational administrator; b. Troy, Ala., Dec. 10, 1939; d. Graph Hubbard and Juanita Elizabeth (Pinkney) Berry; B.S., Kent State U., 1963; postgrad. Boston U., 1965; M.S., SUNY, Brockport, 1978, cert. advanced study edn. adminstrn., 1979; m. James Clark; children—Joseph Sheldon, Karen Theresa. Tchr., Cleve. Public Schs., 1963-67, Newton (Mass.) Public Schs., 1967-69; tchr., Rochester (N.Y.) City Schs., 1971-78, elem. vice-prin., 1978-79, resource tchr., 1980-81, basic skills specialist, 1981-83, elem. vice prin., 1981-88; dir. N.Y. State Econ. Edn. Council, 1977-82; liaison Foster Grandparents, 1980-81, 1985-88. Active PTA, Parent Adv. Council, Urban League; Rochester Met. Sch. Youth adviser ARC. Recipient award Internat. Paper Co. Found., 1976, Wheelabrator Fryes Econ. award, 1978; Sears fellow, 1975. Mem. Internat. Reading Assn., Assn. Supervision and Curriculum Devel., Assn. Childhood Edn. Internat., N.Y. State United Tchrs. Human Relations Council LWV, Delta Sigma Theta. Baptist.

CLARK, JOYCE NAOMI JOHNSON, nurse; b. Corpus Christi, Oct. 4, 1936; d. Chester Fletcher and Ermal Olita (Bailey) Johnson; m. William Boyd Clark, Jan. 4, 1958; (div. 1967); 1 child, Sherene Joyce. Student, Corpus Christi State U., 1975-77. RN; cert. instrument flight instr. Staff nurse Van Nuys (Calif.) Community Hosp., 1963-64, U.S. Naval Hosp., Corpus Christi, 1964-68; asst. clin. coordinator surgery Meml. Med. Ctr., Corpus Christi, 1968—. Leader Paisano Council Girl Scouts U.S.A., Corpus Christi, 1968-74. Recipient Charles A. Mella award Meml. Med. Ctr., 1981, Paul E. Garber award CAP, 1986, cert. of appreciation in recognition of Support Child Guard Missing Children Edn. Program Nat. Assn. Chiefs of Police, Washington, 1987, Grover Loenig Aerospace award, 1986, Cert. of World Leadership Internat. Biographical Ctr., Cambridge, Eng., 1987. Mem. Am. Assn. Operating Room Nurses (v.p. 1969), Aircraft Owners and Pilots Assn., USAF Aux. CAP Air Search and Rescue (past comdr. 3d group, wing chief pilot, Sr. Mem. of Yr. 1985), Am. Fed. Police, Smithsonian Instn. Avocation: flying. Home: 1001 Carmel Pkwy #15 Corpus Christi TX 78411 Office: Meml Med Ctr Operating Room 4606 Hospital Blvd Corpus Christi TX 78405

CLARK, JUDI KAREN, school administrator; b. Anniston, Ala., Apr. 21, 1951; d. Cluster Thomas and Dorthy Dee (Williams) Hicks; m. Ronald Terry Clark, Apr. 22, 1972. BS in Edn., Jacksonville (Ala.) State U., 1981, MS in Adminstrn. and Supervision, 1986; postgrad., Jax St. U., currently. Cert. elem. tchr., Ala. Tchr. Trinity Christian Acad., Oxford, Ala., 1975-78, Sycamore (Ala.) Jr. High Sch., 1981-86; tchr. Talladega County (Ala.) Tng. High Sch., 1986-87, asst. prin., 1988—; instr. Every Child A Winner elem. phys. edn. program. Contbr. article to profl. jour., 1986. Active Ala. Leukemia Soc., Ala. Heart Assn. Recipient Tchr. Year award Sycamore PTA, 1983. Mem. NEA, Ala. Edn. Assn., Talladega County Edn. Assn. (faculty rep. 1983-86), Talladega County Elem. Phys. Educators (chmn. 1986-87), Am. Alliance for Health, Phys. Edn., Nat. Assn. Elem. Sch. Prin., Ala. Assn. Elem. Sch. Adminstrs., Ala. Council Sch. Adminstrn. and Supervision, Recreation and Dance, Ala. State Health, Phys. Edn., Recreation and Dance, Delta Kappa Gamma. Democrat. Baptist. Home: Rt 1 Box 20 L Lincoln AL 35096 Office: Talladega County Tng High Sch Rt 8 Box 212 Talladega AL 35096

CLARK, JUDITH REDMOND, editor, author; b. Mansfield, Ohio, Feb. 21, 1939; d. William Earl and Frances Marie (Frassrand) Redmond; m. Jack Palmer Clark, June 8, 1957; children—Robert Cornell, Julie Elizabeth, April Kelly, Stephanie Rachelle. Student U. Houston, 1964-68. Assoc. editor Universal News, Houston, 1977—; assoc. editor/writer Pipeline Digest, 1977—; freelance writer, photo journalist. Mem. Women in Communications, Inc. (pres. Houston profl. chpt. 1988—, v.p. 1985-86, treas. 1986-87, pres.-elect, 1987-88), Soc. Profl. Journalists, 1960 Photog. Soc. Home: 11842 Hickory Hill Ln Cypress TX 77429 Office: Universal News 1840 Ridgecrest Houston TX 77055

CLARK, JULIE ELIZABETH, airline pilot; b. Hayward, Calif., June 27, 1948; d. Ernest Ashcroft and Marjorie Edith (Johnson) C.; m. Richard Paul Ames, May 10, 1975 (div. 1980). AA, U. Calif., Santa Barbara, 1968. Cert. flight instr. Sweets Flying Service, 1975, airline transport pilot Nat. Jet Industries, 1977. Hostess Trans World Airlines, N.Y.C., 1968-70; sta. agt. Trans World Airlines, San Francisco, 1971; tchr. Enterprise (Ala.) Jr. High Sch., 1970; profl. water skier Marine World, Redwood City, Calif., 1972-74; flight attendant World Airways, Oakland, Calif., 1972-75; flight instr. USN, Lemoore Naval Air Sta., Calif., 1974-75; charter pilot Western Sierra Aviation, Fresno, Calif., 1975-77; airline pilot Golden West Airlines, Los Angeles, 1976-77, Hughes Airwest, Republic Airlines, NW Airlines, Mpls., 1977—; airshow pilot Am. Aerobatics, Cameron Park, Calif., 1980—. Author: Valley Flying, 1975; co-host TV spl. Sky Dancers, 1986; aircraft restorer, 1980—. Mem. Friends Cameron Park, 1986—, Victory Fund 1984 Airport. Mem. Internat. Social Affilliation Women Airline Pilots (charter), Airline Pilots Assn. (charter), Experimental Aircraft Assn., Warbirds Am. (most improved warbird award 1981, ladies' choice award 1984), 99's Inc. (S.W. chpt., nat. Woman Pilot Yr. 1980), T-34 Assn. (chmn. membership 1985—). Republican. Mem. Christian Fellowship Ch. Club: Confederate Air Force (col. Oakland). Home: 3114 Boeing Rd Cameron Park CA 95682

CLARK, KAREN HEATH, lawyer; b. Pasadena, Calif., Dec. 17, 1944; d. Wesley Pelton and Lois (Ellenberger) Heath; m. Bruce Robert Clark,Dec. 30, 1967; children: Adam Heath, Andrea Pelton. Student, Pomona Coll., Claremont, Calif., 1962-64; BA, Stanford U., 1964-66; MA in History, U. Washington, Seattle, 1968; JD, U. Mich., 1977. Bar: Calif. 1978. Instr. Henry Ford Community Coll., Dearborn, Mich., 1968-72; assoc. Gibson, Dunn & Crutcher, Newport Beach, 1977-86, ptnr., 1986—. Mem. dean's adv. council Chapman Coll., Orange, Calif., 1986-87, Dem. Found. Oragne County, 1988; bd. dirs. Planned Parenthood of Orange County, Santa Ana, Calif., 1979-82, New Directions for Women, Newport Beach, Calif., 1986-87. Mem. Orange County Bar Assn., Women in Bus. of Orange County (legal counsel). Office: Gibson Dunn & Crutcher 800 Newport Ctr Dr PO Box 2490 Suites 500 600 & 700 Newport Beach CA 92660

CLARK, KAREN L., security analyst; b. Summit, N.J., July 24, 1951; d. Arthur J. and Evelyn (Hansen) C. BA, Bucknell U., 1973; MBA, U. Penn., 1975. Econ. report analyst Irving Trust, N.Y.C., 1973-74; mgr. planning Internat. Paper, N.Y.C., 1976-87; security analyst, v.p. research Altman Brenner Wasserman, N.Y.C., 1987—. Bd. dirs. Southwestern Conn. Girl Scout Council, Wilton, 1982-85, fin. com. 1987—. Mem. Women in Mgmt. (founding mem. 1978). Home: 40 Ken Ct Stamford CT 06905

CLARK, MARY CATHERINE, software marketing executive; b. Estherville, Iowa, Feb. 14, 1948; d. Harold Vernon and Juanita Elizabeth (Underkofler) C.; m. V. Roy Cacciatore, Aug. 22, 1970; children: R. John, Matthew Clark. BA in Journalism, U. Iowa, 1969, MA in Am. Civilization, 1974. News editor Adelphi Univ., Garden City, N.Y., 1970-72, Molloy Coll., Rockville Centre, N.Y., 1972-73; freelance edit. cons. Freeport, N.Y., 1973-80; founder, mktg. writer TRAC LINE Software, Inc., Hicksville, N.Y., 1980—, corp. sec., 1980—; conf. speaker Am. Women's Econ. Devel. Council, N.Y.C., 1986. Contbr. articles to profl. jours. Publicity dir. LWV, Nassau County, N.Y., 1980-81; mgr. Arrows Hockey Assn., Freeport, 1986-87. Republican. Roman Catholic. Home: 826 S Long Beach Ave Freeport NY 11520 Office: TRAC LINE Software Inc 51 Alpha Plaza Hicksville NY 11801

CLARK, MARY HIGGINS, author, business executive; b. N.Y.C., Dec. 24, 1931; d. Luke J. and Nora C. (Durkin) Higgins; m. Warren Clark, Dec. 26, 1949 (dec. Sept. 1964); children: Marilyn, Warren, David, Carol, Patricia. BA, Fordham U., 1979; hon. doctorate, Villanova U., 1983, Rider Coll., 1986. Advt. asst. Remington Rand, 1946; stewardess Pan Am., 1949-50; radio scriptwriter, producer Robert G. Jennings, 1965-70; v.p., partner creative dir., producer radio programming Aerial Communications, N.Y.C., 1970-80; chmn. bd., creative dir. D. J. Clark Enterprises, N.Y.C., 1980—. Author: Aspire to the Heavens, A Biography of George Washington, 1969, Where Are the Children, 1976, A Stranger is Watching, 1978, The Cradle Will Fall, 1980, A Cry in the Night, 1982, Stillwatch, 1984, Weep No More, My Lady, 1987. Recipient Grand Prix de Litterature Policiere France, 1980. Mem. Mystery Writers Am. (pres., dir.), Authors League, Am. Soc. Journalists and Authors, Acad. Arts and Scis. Republican. Roman Catholic.

CLARK, MAXINE MARJORIE, real estate executive, small business owner; b. Southwest Harbor, Maine, Feb. 20, 1924; d. Leverett Sherman and Albra Marion (Staples) Stanley; m. John O. Clark Sr., May 6, 1955 (div. June 1983); children: Gary, Margery, Paul John O. Jr. Cert. real estate broker mgr., residential specialist. Owner Maxine M. Clark, Real Estate, Southwest Harbor, 1971—; owner, mgr. Island Watch Bed and Breakfast, Southwest Harbor, 1988—. Mem. warrent com. Town of Southwest Harbor, 1980-82, planning bd., 1983-84; bd. dirs. Harbor House Youth Ctr., Southwest Harbor, 1973-75. Mem. Nat. Assn. Realtors, Hancock Washington Bd. Realtors (pres. 1985), Nat. Mktg. Inst., Nat. Assn. Real Estate Appraisers (cert.). Republican. Club: Millay Study (Bass Harbor, Maine) (pres. 1954). Lodge: Order of Eastern Star (Grand Ruth). Office: Rt 102 Southwest Harbor ME 04679

CLARK, NANCY RANDALL, state legislator; b. Portland, Maine, May 6, 1938; d. Willis Shaw and Marthajane (Lund) Randall; B.S., Husson Coll., 1962; M.Ed., U. Maine, 1968. Tchr. bus. edn. Scarborough High Sch., 1962-67, Freeport High Sch. Maine, 1968—; mem. Maine Ho. of Reps., 1972-78; mem. Maine Senate, 1978—. Mem. exec. com. Muscular Dystrophy Assn. Maine; bd. dirs. Arthritis Found., Maine chpt.; trustee Husson Coll., Freeport Conservation Trust; asst. majority leader New Eng. Bd. Higher Edn. Recipient Vets. Service award Am. Legion Maine, 1978; named Outstanding Legislator, 1977, Woman of Yr., Bus. and Profl. Women's Club, 1982. Mem. NEA, Nat. Order Women Legislators, LWV, AAUW, Maine Tchrs. Assn. (pres. 1974-75), Bus. Edn. Assn. Maine, New Eng. Bus. Educators Assn., Brunswick Bus. and Profl. Women's Club, Freeport Hist. Soc. Democrat. Congregationalist. Lodge: Order Eastern Star. Office: State Senate Office State Capitol Augusta ME 04333 Other Address: Rt 2 Box 37 Freeport ME 04032 *

CLARK, PAMELA LYNN, insurance industry executive; b. Phila., Nov. 13, 1952; d. James J. Tinney and Roberta M. (Green) Tinney; m. Mark S. Clark, Jan. 9, 1951; children: Stacy, Ann. Student, Temple U., 1970-77. Sales mgr. Joseph H. Tyson & Co., Phila., 1979-82; sales rep. Gen. Electric div. Puritan, Johnston, R.I., 1982-84; corp. benefit adminstn. Sullivan, Garrity & Donnelly, Worcester, Mass., 1984-86; owner Clark Fin. Services, Athol, Mass., 1986—; sales agt. N.Y. Life, Phila., 1977, 86—; cons. in field. Pres., bd. dirs. Archway, Inc., Leicester, Mass., 1985—. Mem. Nat. Assn. Life Underwriters. Republican. Jewish. Office: Clark Fin Service 491 Main St Athol MA 01331

CLARK, PATRICIA DIANNE, small business owner; b. Boise, Idaho, Nov. 2, 1943; d. Carroll Langley Oldham and Wilette Jean (Paddock) Osborne; m. Bruce Allen Clark, Apr. 7, 1979; children: Virginia, Dianne, Jennifer, Kristian. Lic. realtor. Sec. Halley and Halley, Attorneys, Reno, 1970-73; agt. Red Carpet Realty, Reno, 1974-78; broker, agt. Itildo Realty, Minden, Nev., 1978-85; broker, owner Century 21 Clark Properties, Minden, 1985—. Mem. No. Nev. Devel. Authority, Carson-Douglas-Tahoe Bd. Realtors, Nat. Fed. Ind. Businesspeople, Douglas County C. of C., Nat. Brokers Community Congress (rep. 1985-87), Douglas County Century Club (charter pres.). Home: PO Box 1923 Minden NV 89423 Office: Century 21 Clark Properties 1644 Hwy 395 Minden NV 89423

CLARK, PAULA DAWNE, community services director; b. Montabello, Calif., Dec. 18, 1952; d. Charles Edward and Mary Josephine (Givens) C. BS in Phys. Edn., U. Montevallo, 1975. Asst. phys. dir. Shades Valley YMCA, Birmingham, Ala., 1977, aquatics dir., 1978-80, aquatics pre-sch. dir., 1981-83; asst. br. mgr. Reynolds SW YMCA, Louisville, 1983, exec. br. mgr., 1984—; child care dir., coordinator YMCA Greater Louisville, 1984—; bd. dirs. Humana Hosp-S.W. Mem. Assn. Profl. Dirs., Nat. Assn. Female Execs. Republican. Episcopalian. Home: 2609 Accasia Dr Louisville KY 40216 Office: Reynolds SW Br 2800 Fordhaven Rd Louisville KY 40214

CLARK, PEGGY, theatrical lighting designer; b. Balt., Sept. 30, 1915; d. Eliot Round and Eleanor (Linton) C.; m. Lloyd R. Kelley, Jan. 28, 1960. A.B. cum laude, Smith Coll., 1935; M.F.A., Yale U., 1938. Designer theatrical costumes 1938—; instr. lighting Lester Polakov Studio & Forum of Stage Design, Inc., 1965—; lectr. lighting design Smith Coll., 1967-69, Yale Drama Sch., 1969-70; Bd. counselors Smith Coll., 1961-69, pres. class of, 1935, 1970-75, 80-85; mem. adv. com. Internat. Theatre Inst. Designer settings and lighting Gabrielle, 1941, High Ground, 1951, Curtain Going Up, 1952, Agnes de Mille Dance Theatre, 1953-54; designer stage lighting: numerous plays, including Beggar's Holiday, 1946, Song of Norway, 1952; Peter Pan, 1954, Will Success Spoil Rock Hunter, 1955, Kiss Me Kate, 1955, No Time for Sargeants, 1956; designer decor: Stage Door Canteen; tech. dir.: Am. Theatre Wing; lighting and tech. dir.: other plays including Connecticut Yankee, 1942; Brigadoon, 1946, High Button Shoes, 1947, Along Fifth Avenue, 1948, Gentlemen Prefer Blondes, 1949, Pal Joey, 1951, Mr. Wonderful, Auntie Mame, Bells Are Ringing, 1956, N.Y.C. Center Musical Revivals, 1956-58, 63-68, Say Darling, 1957; prodns. Wonderful Town, Carousel, Susannah, at Brussels Internat. Expn., Flower Drum Song, 1958; lighting tech. supr.: Goodbye Charlie, 1959, Bye Bye Birdie, Unsinkable Molly Brown, Under the Yum Yum Tree, 1960, Show Girl, Mary Mary, 1961, Sail Away, 1961, Romulus, 1962, Girl Who Came to Supper, 1963, Around the World in 80 Days, 1963-64, Bajour, Poor Richard, 1965, The Rose Tattoo, 1966; designer lighting: Darling of the Day, 1968, South Pacific, 1968, Rosalinda, 1968, Jimmy, 1969, Last of the Red Hot Lovers, 1969, Sound of Music, 1970, How the Other Half Loves, 1971, The King and I, 1972, Bil Baird's Bandwagon, 1973, Bil Baird's Whistling Wizard and the Sultan of Tuffet, Pinochio, 1973, Jones Beach's Carousel, 1973, Alice in Wonderland, 1974, Winnie the Pooh, Davy Jones' Locker for Bil Baird Theatre, 1976, Student Prince and Merry Widow for Light Opera of Manhattan, 1976, Mlle. Modiste, Grand Duchess, Babes in Toyland, 1978. Recipient Smith medal, Disting. Alumnae award, 1977. Fellow U.S. Inst. Theatre Tech. (vice commr. engring. commn.; Heritage award 1985); mem. United Scenic Artists (rec. sec. 1942-47, trustee 1948-51, pres. 1968-69, v.p. 1974-76, pension and welfare trustee 1970-80, 84—), ANTA, Illuminating Engring. Soc., Yale Drama Alumni Assn. (Eastern v.p. 1970-77, pres. 1977-83), Woods Hole Protective Assn. (pres. 1978-81). Clubs: French Bull Dog of Am. (pres. 1972-86), Smith (Bklyn., N.Y.C. and Cape Cod); Woods Hole Yacht (sec. 1978-80, vice commodore 1980-81, commodore 1981-83). Home: 36 Cranberry St Brooklyn NY 11201 Summer Home: 23 Albatross St Woods Hole MA 02543

CLARK, PHYLLIS RHODA, financial executive; b. Montreal, Que., Can., Apr. 21, 1955; came to U.S., 1974; d. Hyman and Lily (Brustein) Borts; m. Craig N. Clark, Oct. 18, 1974; 1 child, Adam. BS, Drake U., 1978. Cost analyst Ruan Leasing Co., Des Moines, 1979, fin. analyst, 1980, sr. analyst, 1981, asst. dir. fin. analysis and planning, 1982; dir. fin. planning Heritage Communications Co., Des Moines, 1982-85, asst. treas., 1985-87, v.p. and treas., 1987—. Mem. Com. Golden Circle Devel. Corp., Des Moines, 1986—. Clubs: Consortium, Women's Breakfast. Office: Heritage Communications Inc 2195 Ingersoll Ave Des Moines IA 50312

CLARK, RITA MARIE, nurse; b. Grand Island, Neb., Dec. 27, 1934; d. James M. and Edna M. (Sorensen) Hill; m. Marlin D. Clark, 1951 (div. 1963); children—Lisa Anne Schultz, David M. Clark. B.S.N., U. Oreg., 1963; M.S. in Health Services, Columbia Pacific U., 1988. R.N., Calif., Oreg. Pub. health nurse Multnomah County Pub. Health Dept., Portland, Oreg., 1968-71; psychiat. nurse VA Hosp., Portland, Oreg., 1971-73; supr. nursing Valley Migrant Clinic, Woodburn, Oreg., 1972-74; dir. nursing Silverton Hosp., Oreg., 1974-76; cardiology nurse USPHS Hosp., San Francisco, 1976-77; supr. pub. health Berkeley Health Dept., Calif., 1977-79; supr. pub. health nursing, Santa Cruz, Calif., 1979-80; nurse USPHS-Indian Hosp., Red Lake, Minn., 1980-81; nurse U.S. Army, 1981-84; occupational health nurse, Ft. Lewis, Wash. Contbr. articles to profl. jours. Served as lt. comdr. USPHS, 1980-81; to maj. U.S. Army, 1981-84; to lt. col. USAR, 1984—; mem. Res. Decorated U.S. Army Meritorious Service medal. Army, 1984. Mem. Assn. Mil. Surgeons U.S., U.S. Res. Officers Assn. Democrat. Roman Catholic. Clubs: Officers (Fort Sam Houston, Tex.). Avocations: fishing; camping; travel. Home: 4418 Grandview Dr W Tacoma WA 98466

CLARK, SANDRA LEE, health facility administrator; b. Adrian, Mich., Dec. 17, 1949; d. Thomas W. III and Alice J. (Culver) Warren; m. Frank L. Clark, Sept. 1, 1974; children: Casey, Anna, Sarah. BA, Wayne State U., 1978. Social worker Zieger Hosp., Detroit, 1977-78; owner, adminstr. C.F.S. Internat., Benton Harbor, Mich., 1981—; co-owner, adminstr. MEC-1, Benton Harbor, 1983—; pres. Data Solutions, Benton Harbor, 1987—; v.p. Americare Med. Assn., Valparaiso, Ind., 1987—; co-owner, sec.-treas. Aurora Corp.; ptnr. Aurora Global Network. Co-author: (with others) Inspection. Fundraiser Twin Cities Symphony, St. Joseph, Mich., 1986, United Way, St. Joseph, 1986. Mem. Nat. Assn. Ambulatory Care (bd. dirs. Mich. chpt. 1985-86), Century Club Wayne State U., In Home Health Care Assn., Phi Beta Kappa. Republican. Home: 544 Onondaga Benton Harbor MI 49022 Office: Midwest Emergency Ctr MEC-1 872 E Napier Ave Benton Harbor MI 49022

CLARK, SANDRA LEE, real estate broker; b. Leavenworth, Kans., Dec. 21, 1942; d. John Kramer and Mary Ellen (Bradley) K.; m. Ronald Wayne Clark, June 29, 1968; 1 child, Julie Wynn. AA, Kansas City (Mo.) Jr. Coll., 1962; BA, U. Mo., Kansas City, 1965. With customer service Lee Way Motor, Kansas City, Mo., 1965-85; real estate assoc. Eugene D. Brown, Kansas City, 1985—; mem. com. Met. Real Estate Bd., Kansas City, 1986. Trustee North Kansas City Bd. Edn., 1983—; exec. dir. Parent Resource Info. and Edn., 1982-84; mem. juvenile service council PTA, Mo., 1982-84. Mem. Women Traffic and Transp. (sec. 1965-68), Am. Bus. Women (corr. sec. 1965-69); Women Council of Realtors (pres.-elect 1987-88). Democrat. Home: 6741 N Garfield St Kansas City MO 64118 Office: Sacngh Realtors 2601 Kendallwood Pkwy 119 NE 72nd St Kansas City MO 64118

CLARK, SANDRA MARIE, child care company coordinator; b. Hanover, Pa., Feb. 17, 1942; d. Charles Raymond Clark and Mary Josephine (Snyder) Clark Wierman. BS in Elem. Edn., Chestnut Hill Coll., 1980; MS in Child Care Adminstrn., Nova U., 1985. Cert. elem. tchr., Pa. Tchr. various elem. schs., Pa., 1962-75; asst. vocation directress Mt. St. Joseph Motherhouse, Chestnut Hill, Pa., 1975-76; tchr. St. Catharine's Sch., Spring Lake, N.J., 1976-77; asst. mgr. Jim's Truck Stop, New Oxford, Pa., 1977-81; adminstr. Little People Day Care Sch., Hanover, 1981—, sec., treas. bd. dirs., 1985-86; coordinator regional resource Magic Yrs. Child Care & Learning Ctrs., Inc., Hanover, 1987—; presenter Hanover Area Seminar for Day Care Employees, 1983-86; prin. St. Vincent de Paul Sch., Hanover, 1988—. coordinator sch. safety patrols St. Vincent's Sch., Hanover, 1969-75, vice-chmn. bd., 1982-84; multi-media instr. first aid ARC, Hanover, 1983-86, bd. dirs., 1984—; exec. sec. of bd. of dirs. ARC, Hanover, 1988—; 1st v.p. Hanover Area Council of Chs., 1988; validator accredidation program Nat. Acad. Early Childhood Programs, Washington, 1987—; bd. dirs. Life Shills Unltd. Handicapped Adults, 1988—; facilitator Harrisburg Diocesan Synod, Hanover, 1985-88, parish del., 1988. Pa. Dept. Pub. Welfare tng. grantee, 1986. Mem. Nat. Assn. for Edn. Young Children, Nat. Geog. Soc., Pa. Assn. for Child Care Agys., Capitol Area Assn. for Edn. Young Children, Nat. Assn. for Female Execs. Democrat. Roman Catholic. Club: Internat. Assn. Turtles (London). Home: 348 Barberry Dr Hanover PA 17331 Office: Little People Day Care Sch 500 Boundary Ave Hanover PA 17331

CLARK, SARA JANE, accounting company executive; b. South Bend, Ind., Aug. 28, 1948; d. Robert F. and Maxine (Walker) Bennett; m. William H. Clark, Oct. 2, 1976; 1 child, Kristen Marie. Adminstrv. asst. Doherty Zable & Co., Chgo., 1975-77; gen. ptnr. Bennett Clark Co., Valparaiso, Ind., 1977—; mem. LaSalle St. Cashiers, Chgo., 1979-85, 87-88, outing com. chmn., 1982, correspondence com. chmn., 1987-88. Mem. Am. Soc. Profl. Women, Am. Inst. Profl. Bookkeepers, Nat. Assn. Female Execs. Republican. Presbyterian. Avocations: reading, traveling, needlework.

CLARK, SHARON ANN, public relations professional; b. Toledo, Jan. 14, 1939; d. Stanley Joseph and Anna Dorothy (Zulka) Gosik; B.A., U. Miami, 1974; m. John H. Clark, Aug 23, 1961 (div. 1968); 1 child, Tania Elizabeth. Staff writer U. Miami (Fla.), 1970-79; dir. News Bur., U. Miami, 1979-82, assoc. dir. pub. affairs, 1982-83; mus. adminstr., 1983-87; coordinator community affairs, The Miami Herald newspaper, 1987—. Trustee, Dade Heritage Trust, 1979—; mem. Women's Com. of 100; bd. dirs. Tropical Council Girl Scouts U.S., 1987, Friends of Art, Lowe Art Mus. Mem. Women in Communication, Public Relations Soc. Am., Beaux Arts. Roman Catholic. Home: 4712 SW 67th Ave Miami FL 33155 Office: The Miami Herald Office Community Affairs One Herald Plaza Miami FL 33132

CLARK, SHERYL MARIE, nurse practitioner; b. Dallas, Nov. 12, 1944; d. William Stanford and Thelma Marie (Johnson) C.; B.S. in Nursing, U. Colo., 1967. Office nurse, supr. Dr. S.E. Wood, Charleston, S.C., 1970-72; staff nurse VA Hosp., Charleston, S.C., Long Beach, Calif., 1972-73; family nurse practitioner Family Health Program, Long Beach, Calif., 1973-78; research nurse practitioner U. Calif., Irvine, 1978-79; mgr. health services Martin-Marietta Aluminum Corp., Torrance, Calif., 1979-81; mgr. health services TRW, Redondo Beach, Calif., 1981—. Served with USNR, 1967-70. Mem. Calif. Nurses Assn. (past pres. Region 1, past chairperson interregional standing com. nurse practitioners), Am. Nurses Assn. (cert. family nurse practitioner), Am. Public Health Assn., Am. Assn. Occupational Health Nurses (cert. occupational health nurse), Calif. State Assn. Occupational Health Nurses (pres.), Harbor Area Assn. Occupational Health Nurses (pres.). Republican. Home: 2313 Hungtington Ln Unit B Redondo Beach CA 90278 Office: One Space Park S/1459 Redondo Beach CA 90278

CLARK, STEPHANIE LOUISE, educational administrator; b. Des Moines, Mar. 19, 1958; d. Reber Fields, Jr., and Elizabeth Louise (O'Master) C. BS, Ark. Tech. U., 1980; MA, Northwestern State U., Natchitoches, La., 1983, MEd, 1985. Cert. math. tchr., Ark., S.C. Math. tchr. Cabot Pub. Schs., Ark., 1980-81; Panhellenic adviser Northwestern State U., 1981-83, asst. to dir. student services, 1981-83; coordinator student services program Clemson U., S.C., 1983—, coordinator edn1. placement, 1983—. Named Outstanding mem. ATU Panhellenic Council, 1980. Mem. Am. Coll. Personnel Assn., Southeastern Assn. Sch., Coll. and Univ. Staffing, Am. Assn. Counseling and Devel. (grad. liaison 1982-83), Cardinal Key (life), Kappa Delta Pi (life), Phi Mu (life). Home: PO Box 597 West Union SC 29696 Office: Clemson U Office Ednl Services and Placement 418 Tillman Hall Clemson SC 29634-0713

CLARK, SUSAN (NORA GOULDING), actress; b. Sarnia, Ont., Can., Mar. 8, 1944; d. George Raymond and Eleanor Almond (McNaughton) C. Student, Toronto (Ont.) Children's Players, 1956-59; student (Acad. scholar), Royal Acad. Dramatic Art, London. partner Georgian Bay Prodns. Producer: Jimmy B. and Andre, 1979, Word of Honor, 1980, Maid in America, 1982; star Webster, ABC-TV; appeared in play Silk Stockings; mem. London Shakespeare Festival Co., mem. Brit. Repertory Co.; appeared in Brit. TV prodns.; co-star: Brit. premiere of play Poor Bitos; appeared in

Calif. TV prodns., including Heloise and Abelard, Hedda Gabler, starred in Taming of the Shrew; appeared in Sherlock Holmes,: Williamstown Theatre Festival, (taped for HBO), 1981; appeared in: Getting Out, Mark Taper Forum, Los Angeles, 1978; films include The Apple Dumpling Gang, Night Moves, The North Avenue Irregulars, Airport '75, Midnight Man, Porky's, Murder by Decree, Tell Them Willie Boy is Here, Skin Game, City on Fire, Madigan, Coogan's Bluff, Skullduggery, Promises in the Dark, Valdez is Coming, Showdown, Double Negative; appeared in segments of TV series Columbo, Marcus Welby, Barnaby Jones; appeared in Double Solitaire, Pub. Broadcasting System, Babe, MGM-CBS TV spl., 1975 (Emmy award), Amelia Earhart (Emmy nomination), The Choice. Mem. ACLU, Am. Film Inst. Office: care Georgian Bay Prodns 3815 W Olive Ave Suite 101 Burbank CA 91505

CLARK, SYLVIA DOLORES, business educator; b. N.Y.C., June 5, 1959; d. Barna and Eva Anna (Beniczky-Gabriel) Csuros; m. Allen Lewis Spiegel, Aug. 19, 1984. B.B.A., Bernard Baruch Coll., CUNY, 1979; M.B.A., NYU, 1982. Research analyst Kornhauser and Calene and predecessor firm, N.Y.C., 1979-80; project coordinator Gen. Foods, Inc., White Plains, N.Y., 1980-82; research assoc. Lord, Geller, Federico, Einstein, Inc., N.Y.C., 1982-83; instr. Coll. of S.I., CUNY, 1984—. Recipient Becker Family Fund Scholarship award, 1978, Baruch Coll. Alumni Assn. Scholarship award, 1979. Mem. Am. Mktg. Assn., Am. Statis. Assn., Beta Gamma Sigma (past mem. exec. bd.). Home: 62 Renwick Ave Staten Island NY 10301 Office: Coll Staten Island 715 Ocean Terr Staten Island NY 10301

CLARK-BROOKS, BRONNIE DENISE, auditor, consultant; b. Washington, Dec. 13, 1954; d. Nathaniel Depriest Clark and Kay Frances (Grandy) Clark Joyner; m. John Francis Brooks Jr., May 24, 1975; 1 child, Tynisha Asheba. AA, Strayer Coll., Washington, 1980, BS, 1982, postgrad. computer systems mgmt., U. Md., 1986—; With Riggs Nat. Bank, Washington, 1974-83; sr. EDP audit supr. First Am. Bank, Washington, 1983-85; systems acct. Fed. Home Loan Bank Bd./Fed. Savs. & Loan Ins. Corp./Fin. Assistance Div., Washington, 1985-86; EDP auditor Amtrak, Washington, 1986-88; EDP auditor Columbia First Fed. Savings and Loan Assn., Arlington, Va., 1988. Mem. Apple Grove PTA and Citizens Assn., Fort Washington, Md., 1983, Prince George's County Parent-Tchrs. and Student Assn. Mem. Strayer Coll. Alumni Assn., EDP Auditors Assn., Inst. Internal Auditors, Washington Assn. Urban Bankers (chairperson annual awards banquet 1987-88, treas. 1988-89). Baptist. Avocations: modeling, designing, reading, dancing. Office: Columbia First Fed Savings and Loan 1560 Wilson Blvd Arlington VA 22211

CLARK-CAMERON, BONNIE, construction executive; b. Sharon, Pa., Oct. 17, 1946; d. William George and Nellie Marie (Maloy) Bowman; m. Charles C. Clark, Oct. 22, 1965 (div. May 1982); children: Tonya, Paul, LaVonne; m. Ralph Lee Cameron, Aug. 22, 1986. Grad., Dave Buster Sch. Constrn., 1985. Cert. residential contractor. Realtor, salesman Metroplex, Inc., Gainesville, Fla., 1979-81; v.p. Kirkpatrick Builders, Gainesville, 1981-83, Countryside Homes of Gainesville, 1983-87; pres. Paramount Mktg. Assocs., Inc., Gainesville, 1987—; pres. Home Owners Warranty Corp, Gainesville, 1986-87. Chmn. Crime Trac, Gainesville, 1986, bd. dirs., 1981-87; pres. Mercer, Pa. PTA, 1976, 77; bd. dirs. Big Bros./Big Sisters, Gainesville, 1980-84. Mem. Fla. Assn. Realtors, Gainesville Home Builders Assn. (pres. elect 1987, pres. 1988, bd. dirs. 1984—, Assoc. of Yr. 1984), Gainesville Bd. Realtors (bd. dirs. 1984—, Assoc. of Yr. 1980), Gainesville C. of C. (bd. dirs. 1987), Swimming Boosters (pres. 1987). Home: 3400 NW 34th Terr Gainesville FL 32605

CLARKE, AMY POLAN, entertainment company executive; b. Bklyn., Nov. 16, 1950; d. Stanley Norton and Ella (Germain) Polan; m. Robert G. Clarke, Jr., Jan. 4, 1984; 1 child, Jordan Haley Polan-Clarke. Student Monmouth Coll., 1968-69. Sec., reservationist Thomas Cook Travel Agy., Short Hills, N.J., 1970-72; sec. Monarch Entertainment Bur., Inc., Montclair, N.J., 1970-71, adminstrv. asst., 1972-75, v.p., 1975—, exec. v.p., gen. mgr., 1975—. Democrat. Jewish. Avocations: antique furniture; home designing; tennis. Office: Monarch Entertainment Bur Inc 7 N Mountain Ave Montclair NJ 07042

CLARKE, AUGUSTA R., legal researcher; b. Chgo., Apr. 1, 1953; d. James Joseph and Augusta Genevieve (Guerino) Clarke; m. Allan Robert Stasica, Mar. 31, 1984. BA, Simmons Coll., 1975; postgrad., John Marshall Law Sch., Chgo., 1986—. Sales rep. Proctor and Gamble Distbn. Co., Dearborn, Mich., 1975-78; field rep. Southland Corp., Taylor, Mich., 1978-79; orgnl. mgr. Bruno Leon Assocs., Detroit, 1979-81; sales rep. Kraft Food Service, Glenview, Ill., 1982-84; legal researcher B. John Mix Jr., Chgo., 1984—. Mem. Ill. State Bar Assn., Student Bar Assn. (chmn. scholarship com., dir.-night student advisor). Office: B John Mix Jr 77 W Washington Suite 415 Chicago IL 60602

CLARKE, BARBARA LEE, marketing professional; b. St. Louis, Apr. 13, 1941; d. George Dorsey and Emmeline (Klumb) Allen; m. Patrick L. Story, Aug. 19, 1961 (div. Feb. 1973); children: Cara, Bonnie. BA, Calif. State U., Dominique Hills, 1974; MA in Health Services Adminstrn., Antioch U., 1982. Editor Law in a Free Soc., Los Angeles, 1971-73; ops. mgr. Nowell's Lighting, Inc., Sausalito, Calif., 1977-80; asst. program officer S.H. Cowell Found., San Francisco, 1980-81; cons. Women's Found., San Francisco, 1982-83; dir. mktg. I.P.M. Health Plan, Vallejo, Calif., 1983-85; v.p. mktg. French Health Plan, San Francisco, 1985—. Internat. pub. health vol. Ops. Crossroads Africa, Kenya, 1981; mem. career resource staff Alumnae Resources for Women, San Francisco, 1986—. Mem. Am. Mktg. Assn., Acad. Health Care Mktg., Calif. Assn. HMO's. Democrat. Home: 1105 Mission Ave San Rafael CA 94901 Office: French Health Plan 4131 Geary Blvd San Francisco CA 94118

CLARKE, CAROL ANTOINETTE, data processing executive; b. Bronx, N.Y., Nov. 19, 1954; d. Donald Dudley and Marie Brunhilde (Burrowes) C. BA, Fordham Coll., 1975. Specifications writer M/G Data Processing, Inc., N.Y.C., 1975-78, 1979-80, Research for Advt. and Mktg. Ltd., N.Y.C., 1978-79, Donovan Data Systems, N.Y.C., 1980-81; group head, v.p. Thor Data, Inc., N.Y.C., 1981-86; v.p. Viking group Market Probe Internat., N.Y.C., 1986-87; group head CRC Info. Systems, Inc., N.Y.C., 1987—. Democrat. Club: Scrabble (Bronx) (dir. 1982—, one of top 50 players in U.S. and Can.). Office: CRC Info Systems 435 Hudson ST New York NY 10014

CLARKE, CLAIRE DIGGS, academic counselor; b. Long Branch, N.J.; d. Jeremiah and LeeBertha (Smith) Diggs; m. David C. Clarke Jr.; 1 child: Caroletta. Student, Livingston Coll., 1948-51; BA, Knoxville Coll., 1955; postgrad., Columbia U., 1961-63; MA in Edn., Hofstra U., 1968; postgrad., U. N.H., Durham, New England Coll., Concord, N.H., 1981. Cert. tchr. English, physical, health edn., counselor edn. Tchr. Charles M. Hall Sch., Alcoa, Tenn., 1955-59, Gilbert Sch., Bklyn., 1959-61; caseworker Bur. Child Welfare of N.Y., 1961-63; tchr., cons. pub. sch. #192, Hollis, N.Y., 1963-69; guidance counselor Winnisquam Regional Sch. Dist., Tilton, N.H., 1969—, specialist assessment intellectual functioning, 1981—. Bd. dirs. Merrimack Valley Sch. Dist., 1983—; police commr. Boscawen Police Dept., 1980—. Mem. Edn. Volunteerism Employment Guild, N.H. Council Vocat. Tech. Edn. (sec. 1976—), Assn. Supervision Curriculum Devel. Lodge: Zonta Internat. (pres. 1979-81). Home: 437 Daniel Webster Hwy Boscawen NH 03303

CLARKE, EVELYN (SUSAN) MOESCH, banker; b. Zurich, Switzerland, Mar. 21, 1960; came to U.S., 1964; d. Ralph Herman and Susi (Schneeberger) Moesch; m. Nicholas Charles Clarke. BA in English, SUNY, Albany, 1982. Office mgr. N.Y. State Builders Assn., Albany, 1981-83; with Union Bank of Switzerland, N.Y.C., 1983—, credit analyst, 1986-87, account mgr., 1987—. Active Jr. League of Westchester-on-Hudson, 1987—; big sister Pleasantville (N.Y.) Cottage Sch., 1986—. Mem. Nat. Assn. Female Execs. Home: 94 Grand St Apt 1D Croton-on-Hudson NY 10520 Office: Union Bank of Switzerland 299 Park Ave New York NY 10171

CLARKE, GEORGINE R., museum director; b. Gallup, N.Mex., June 18, 1940; d. George Franklin and Mahala Ruth (Erickson) Rummage; m. Jack Clarke, July 10, 1965; children: Denise Laura, Paul Franklin. BS in Biology, U. N.Mex., 1961; MA in Psychology, Ohio State U., 1963. Asst. to dean women Ohio State U., Columbus, 1964-65; instr. psychology Fla. State U., Key West, 1966; young adult program dir. YWCA, Albuquerque, 1966-67; asst. dean women U. N.Mex., Albuquerque, 1967-68; tour organizer Dept. Music U. Ala., Tuscaloosa, 1975-77; dir. Kentuck Mus. and Art Ctr., Tuscaloosa, 1978—; judge various art festivals, 1980—; guest curator So. Highlands Handicraft Guild, Asheville, N.C., 1984; visual arts adv. panel mem. Ala. State Council, 1985—; program evaluator Miss. Arts Commn., Jackson, 1986. Contbg. editor: Atlanta Art Papers, 1986. Bd. dirs. Family Counseling Service, Tuscaloosa, 1985—. Recipient Gov.'s Arts award Ala. State Council on the Arts, 1984. Mem. Ala. Craft Council (pres.), Ala. Designer/Craftsmen (mem. standards com. 1983—), West Ala. C. of C. (bd. dirs. 1985—, award of honor 1984). Office: Kentuck Mus and Art Ctr PO Box 127 Northport AL 35476

CLARKE, GRETA FIELDS, dermatologist; b. Detroit; d. George William and Willa (Wright) Fields; B.S., U. Mich., 1962; M.D., Howard U., 1967; 1 child, Richard Clement Clarke. Resident in dermatology NYU, 1969-72, clin. instr., 1972-77; practice medicine specializing in dermatology, N.Y.C., 1972-77; dermatologist Arlington Med. Group, Oakland, Calif., 1977-79; practice medicine specializing in dermatology, Berkeley, Calif., 1979—. Bd. dirs. Bay Area Black United Fund. Diplomate Am. Bd. Dermatology. Mem. Nat. Med. Assn. (chmn. council on concerns of women physicians, chmn. region VI), Golden State Med. Assn., Am. Acad. Dermatology, San Francisco Dermatol. Clubs: Jack and Jill Am. (chpt. pres. 1984-85), Alameda-Contra Costa Links. Office: 2500 Milvia St Berkeley CA 94704

CLARKE, INGRID GADWAY, academic ombudsman, consultant; b. Bad Homburg, Hesse, Fed. Republic Germany, Sept. 21, 1942; came to U.S., 1964, naturalized, 1982; d. Johann Kajetan and Irmgard (Schneider) Rebholz; m. David Scott Clarke, Dec. 24, 1984. B.A. equivalent, Johann Wolfgang Goethe Universität, Frankfurt, Fed. Republic Germany, 1964; M.A., Memphis State U., 1965; postgrad. Tulane U., 1965-69; Ph.D., So. Ill. U., 1984. Instr. So. Ill. U., Carbondale, 1969-74, univ. ombudsman, 1974—, also chairperson bd. dirs. students' legal assistance program, 1980-86 . Mem. Carbondale Human Relations Com., 1974-76; chairperson Carbondale Fair Housing Bd., 1978-82. Fulbright scholar, 1964-67. Mem. Fulbright Alumni Assn., Univ. and Coll. Ombudsman Assn. (founder and first pres. 1985-86), Soc. Profls. in Dispute Resolution Delta Phi Alpha. Avocations: opera; tennis; skiing. Office: So Ill U Office Univ Ombudsman Carbondale IL 62901

CLARKE, KIT HANSEN, radiologist; b. Louisville, May 24, 1944; d. Hans Peter and Katie (Jones) Hansen; A.B., Randolph-Macon Woman's Coll., 1966; M.D., U. Louisville, 1969; m. Dr. John M. Clarke, Feb. 14, 1976; children—Brett Bonnett, Blair Hansen, Brandon Chamberlain; stepchildren—Gray Campbell, Jeffrey William John M. Intern, Louisville Gen. Hosp., 1969-70; resident in internal medicine and radiology U. Tenn., Knoxville, 1970-73; resident in radiology U.S. Fla., Tampa, 1973-74; staff radiologist, chief spl. procedures Palms of Pasadena, Lake Seminole hosps., St. Petersburg, Fla., 1974—. Active Fla. Competitive Swim Assn. of AAU. Diplomate Am. Bd. Radiology. Fellow Am. Coll. Radiology; mem. Fla. West Coast Radiology Soc., Radiol. Soc. N.Am., AMA, Fla. Med. Assn., Pinellas County Med. Soc., Fla. Radiology Soc. Episcopalian. Home: 7171 9th St S Saint Petersburg FL 33705 Office: 1609 Pasadena Ave S Saint Petersburg FL 33707

CLARKE, LYNN MARIE, English language educator; b. Burlington, Vt., Oct. 16, 1947; d. Robert Henry III and Martha Theresa (Jarolim) Gray; m. Paul Lewis Knaus, Jan. 20, 1968 (div. Feb. 1977); m. Michael David Clarke, June 28, 1980; children: Aaron Stephen, Benjamin David; stepchildren: Sandra, Michael Jr., Susan. AB, SUNY, Fredonia, 1969. Librarian's asst. Port Washington (N.Y.) Pub. Library, 1965-66; kindergarten, pre-first tchr. Lake Shore Cen. Schs., Angola, N.Y., 1969-72; tchr.'s aide, sub. teacher Chautauqua County Bds. Coop. Ednl. Services, 1977-78; tchr. English, gifted classes Dunkirk (N.Y.) Pub. Schs., 1978—. Mem. Chautauqua Community Chorus. Mem. Am. Fedn. Tchrs., N.Y. State United Tchrs., Dunkirk Tchrs. Assn., Advocacy for Gifted and Talented Edn. (AGATE), Women's Internat. Bowling Congress, Delta Kappa Gamma. Democrat. Episcopalian. Club: Columbus Aux. Home: 708 Washington Ave Dunkirk NY 14048 Office: Dunkirk Mid Sch 525 Eagle St Dunkirk NY 14048

CLARKE, MARY ELIZABETH, retired army officer; b. Rochester, N.Y., Dec. 3, 1924; d. James M. and Lillian E. (Young) Kennedy; student U. Md., 1962; D.Mil.Sci., Norwich U., Northfield, Vt., 1978. Joined U.S. Army as pvt., 1945, advanced through grades to maj. gen., 1978; exec. asst. to Chief of Plans and Policies, Office of Econ. Opportunity, 1966-67; comdr. WAC Tng. Bn., 1967-68; office dep. chief of staff for personnel, 1968-71; WAC staff adviser 6th Army, 1971-72; comdr., comdt. U.S. Women's Army Corps Center and Sch., 1972-74; chief WAC Adv. Office, U.S. Army Mil. Personnel Center, Washington, 1974-75, dir. Women's Army Corps, Washington, 1975-78; comdr. U.S. Army Mil. Police and Chem. Sch. Tng. Center, Ft. McClellan, Ala., 1978-80; dir. human resources devel. Office of Dep. Chief of Staff for Personnel, Washington, 1980-81, ret., 1981; hon. prof. mil. sci. Jacksonville (Ala.) State U. Mem. Def. Adv. Com. on Women in the Services, 1984—, vice chmn., 1986—. Decorated D.S.M.; recipient Toastmasters Internat. award, 1984. Mem. Assn. of U.S. Army, United States Automobile Assn. (bd. dirs. 1978—), WAC Assn., WAC Mus. Found., Bus. and Profl. Women's Club. Address: 80 Fairway Dr Jacksonville AL 36265

CLARKE, URANA, musician, writer, educator; b. Wickliffe-on-the-Lake, Ohio, Sept. 8, 1902; d. Graham Warren and Grace Urana (Olsaver) C.; artists and tchrs. diploma Mannes Music Sch., N.Y.C., 1925; certificate Dalcroze Sch. Music, N.Y.C., 1950; student Pembroke Coll., Brown U.; B.S., Mont. State U., 1967, M.Applied Sci., 1970. Mem. faculty Mannes Music Sch., 1922-49, Dalcroze Sch. Music, 1949-54; adv. editor in music The Book of Knowledge, 1949-65; v.p., dir. Saugatuck Circle Housing Devel.; guest lectr. Hayden Planetarium, 1945; guest lectr., bd. dirs. Roger Williams Park Planetarium, Providence; radio show New Eng. Skies, Providence, 1961-64, Skies Over the Big Sky Country, Livingston, Mont., 1964-79, Birds of the Big Sky Country, 1972-79, Great Music of Religion, 1974-79; mem. adv. com. Nat. Rivers and Harbors Congress, 1947-58; instr. continuing edn. Mont. State U. Chmn., Park County chpt. ARC, co-chmn. county blood program, first aid instr. trainer, 1941—; instr. ARC cardio-pulmonary resuscitation, 1976—; mem. Mont. Commn. Nursing and Nursing Edn., 1974-76; mem. Park County Local Govt. Study Commn., 1974-76, chmn., 1984-86; mem. Greater Yellowstone Coalition. Mem. Am. Acad. Polit. Sci., Am. Musicol. Soc., Royal Astron. Soc. Can., Inst. Nav., Maria Mitchell Soc. Nantucket, N.Am. Yacht Racing Union, AAAS, Meteoritical Soc., Internat. Soc. Mus. Research, Skyscrapers (sec.-treas. 1960-63), Am. Guild Organists, Park County Wilderness Assn. (treas.), Trout Unlimited, Nature Conservancy, Big Sky Astron. Soc. (dir. 1965—), Sierra Club, Greater Yellowstone Coalition. Lutheran. Club: Cedar Point Yacht. Author: The Heavens are Telling (astronomy), 1951; Skies Over the Big Sky Country, 1965; also astron. news-letter, View It Yourself, weekly column Big Skies; contbr. to mags. on music, nav. and astronomy. Pub. Five Chorale Preludes for Organ, 1975; also elem. two-piano pieces. Inventor, builder of Clarke Adjustable Piano Stool. Address: Log-A-Rhythm 9th St Island Livingston MT 59047

CLARKSON, CAROLE LAWRENCE, insurance company executive; b. Fredericksburg, Va., Dec. 18, 1942; d. Jerry Allen and Gladys Mae (Eubank) Lawrence; m. David Wendell Morris, Aug. 14, 1965 (div. 1977); 1 child, Peyton Lawrence; m. Lawrence Herbert Clarkson, Aug. 14, 1982. BA, Purdue U., 1965; postgrad., Ind. U., Indpls., 1970, U. Ill., 1971-73, U. Louisville Sch. of Bus., 1980-82. Pub. sch. tchr. various Ind., Okla., Ill., N.C., Italy, 1965-75; librarian documentation U. Louisville Computing Ctr., 1980-82, IBM Corp., Austin, Tex., 1983-85; ins. mgr. Ohio State Life Ins. Co., Columbus, 1985-88, Community Life Ins. Co., Columbus, 1988—; supervisory mgr. Ins. Inst. of Am., 1987—. Mem. Internat. Claims Assn. (assoc. life and health claims 1987), Nat. Assn. Female Execs., Purdue U. Alumni Assn. Home: 8348 Waco Ln Powell OH 43065

CLARKSON, ELISABETH ANN HUDNUT, civic worker; b. Youngstown, Ohio, Apr. 20, 1925; d. Herbert Beecher and Edith (Schaaf) Hudnut; A.B., Wilson Coll., 1947; M.A., State U. N.Y., 1973, also postgrad.; L.H.D. (hon.), Wilson Coll., 1985; m. William M.E. Clarkson, Sept. 23, 1950; children—Alison H., David B., Andrew E. With J.L. Hudson Co., Detroit, 1947-50; writer The Minute Parade, daily Sta. WGR, Detroit, 1948-50; trustee Wilson Coll., Chambersburg, Pa., 1970-83, chmn. bd. trustees 1979-82; bd. dirs. Buffalo Mus. Sci., 1972-87; bd. dirs., companion in charge Soc. Companion of the Holy Cross, 1986—; past chmn. jr. group Alright Knox Art Gallery; collector, curator Graphic Controls Corp. collection art, 1976-83; dir. Bischoff Clarkson Hudnut Corp., North Creek, N.Y., 1973-83; mem. Buffalo Art Commn., 1983—; mem. exec. bd. arts adv. council SUNY at Buffalo, 1985—; bd. dirs. N.Y. State Mus. Assoc., Albany. Recipient Trustee award for disting. service Wilson Coll., 1983. Episcopalian. Clubs: Garret, Buffalo Tennis and Squash. Author: You Can Always Tell a Freshman, 1949; also articles, dramatic presentations, archival materials Adirondack Mus., 1950-77. Home: 156 Bryant St Buffalo NY 14222 also: Windover North Creek NY 12853

CLARKSON, SHIRLEY ANNE, educational administrator; b. Sterling, Ill., Sept. 14, 1934; d. Charles S. and Juliet (Darland) Long; m. June 14, 1957 (div.); 1 child, James M. B.A., U. Chgo., 1957. Adminstr. com. for comparative study of new nations, U. Chgo., 1960-64; dir. info. office, S.E. Asia Regional Council, Ann Arbor, Mich., 1969-72; program officer Am. Council Edn., Washington, 1972-75; assoc. dir. Council Internat. Cooperation in Higher Edn., Washington, 1976-79; staff Commn. Internat. Relations, Nat. Acad. Scis., Washington, 1979-80; asst. dir. research and devel. U. Mich., Ann Arbor, 1980-87, spl. asst. to provost, v.p. acad. affairs, 1987-88, asst. to pres., 1988—. Bd. dirs. Ann Arbor Community Ctr., Ann Arbor Downtown Devel. Authority, 1985-87. Mem. Internat. Studies Assn., Council Advancement of Edn. Office: U Mich Fleming Adminstrn Bldg Ann Arbor MI 48109

CLARY, ROSALIE BRANDON STANTON, timber farm executive, civic worker; b. Evanston, Ill., Aug. 3, 1928; d. Frederick Charles Hite-Smith and Rose Cecile (Liebich) Stanton; B.S., Northwestern U., 1950, M.A., 1954; m. Virgil Vincent Clary, Oct. 17, 1959; children—Rosalie Marian, Frederick Stanton, Virgil Vincent, Kathleen Elizabeth. Tchr., Chgo. Public Schs., 1951-55, adjustment tchr., 1956-61; faculty Loyola U., Chgo., 1963; v.p. Stanton Enterprises, Inc., Adams County, Miss., 1971—; author Family History Record, genealogy record book, Kenilworth, Ill., 1977—; also lectr. Leader, Girl Scouts, Winnetka, Ill., 1969-71, 78-86, Cub Scouts, 1972-77; badge counselor Boy Scouts Am., 1978-87 ; election judge Republican party, 1977—. Mem. Nat. Soc. DAR (Ill. rec. sec. 1979-81, nat. vice chmn. program com. 1980-83, state vice regent 1986-88), Am. Forestry Assn., Forest Farmers Assn., North Suburban Geneal. Soc. (governing bd. 1979—), Winnetka Hist. Soc. (governing bd. 1978—), Internat. Platform Assn., Delta Gamma (mem. nat. cabinet 1985—). Roman Catholic. Home: 509 Elder Ln Winnetka IL 60093 Office: PO Box 401 Kenilworth IL 60043

CLASEN, LORIE CHRISTINE, banker; b. San Mateo, Calif., Oct. 1, 1957; d. Philip Albert and Joanne Louise (Eggert) C. AA with honors, Delta Jr. Coll., Stockton, Calif., 1977; BA in Social Scis. summa cum laude, Stanislaus State U., 1980. Mgmt. trainee Montgomery Wards, Stockton, 1975-79; bank teller to br. mgr. Gt. Am. First Savs. Bank, Sacramento, 1979-88; asst. v.p. Gt. Am. First Savs. Bank, Fresno, Calif., 1988—. Democrat. Office: Gt Am Savs Bank 7025 N Marks Ave Fresno CA 93711

CLASTER, BARBARA LEINER, psychologist; b. Cleve., Feb. 11, 1931; d. Philip A. and Della Florence (Berkowitz) Leiner; m. Jay B. Claster, Apr. 28, 1963; 1 child, Saundra Margaret. AB, Ohio U., 1953; MA, Northwestern U., 1954, PhD, 1966. Licensed psychologist, Pa., Mass. Psychologist Div. Counseling Penn. State U., University Park, 1961-64; practicing psychology Pa., 1966-68, 1975—; staff asst. to v.p. student affairs Penn. State U., University Park, 1968-71, coordinator tutoring Edn. Opportunity Program., 1971; psychotherapist, assoc. staff mem. Postgrad. Cen. Mental Health, N.Y.C., 1973—. Convenor, bd. dirs. task force Mental Health Profl. Cen. Pa. 1978-79, chmn. interdisciplinary com. 1982-84; organizer, chmn. Women's Forum State Coll. 1977-79; bd. dirs. task force Centre County Legal Services Inc. 1971-72. Fellow Postgrad. Cen. Mental Health, 1973—. Mem. AAAS, Am. Orthopsychiat. Assn., Am. Psychol. Assn., Assn. Women Sci., Feminist Therapy Inst. Inc., Mass. Psychol. Assn., N.Y. Acad. Sci., N.Y. Soc. Clin. Psychol., N.Y. St. Psychol. Assn. Democrat. Jewish. Home and Office: 1065 Park Ave New York NY 10128

CLASTER, JILL NADELL, university administrator, history educator. d. Harry K. and Edith Lillian Nadell; m. Millard L. Midonick, May 24, 1979; 1 child from previous marriage, Elizabeth Claster (dec.). B.A., NYU, 1952, M.A., 1954; Ph.D., U. Pa., 1959. Instr. history U. Pa., 1956-58; instr. ancient and medieval history U. Ky., Lexington, 1959-61; asst. prof. U. Ky., 1961-64; adj. asst. prof. classics NYU, N.Y.C., 1964-65; asst. prof. history NYU, 1965-68, assoc. prof., 1968-84, prof., 1984—, acting undergrad. chmn. history, 1972-73, dir. M.A. in liberal studies program, 1976-78; asso. dean Washington Sq. and Univ. Coll., 1978, acting dean, 1978-79, dean, 1979-86; bd. dirs. Hebrew Immigrant Aid Soc., Turtle Bay Music Sch. Author: Athenian Democracy: Triumph or Travesty, 1967, The Medieval Experience, 1982; Contbr. articles to profl. jours. Danforth grantee, 1966-68; Fulbright grantee, 1958-59. Mem. Am. Hist. Assn., Medieval Acad. Am., Archaeol. Inst. Am., Medieval Club N.Y., Women's Forum. Home: 32 Washington Sq W New York NY 10011 Office: NYU Dept History 19 University Pl New York NY 10003

CLAUS, CAROL JEAN, computer software company executive; b. Uniondale, N.Y., Dec. 17, 1959; d. Charles Joseph and Frances Meta (Fichter) C.; m. Armand Joseph Gasperetti, Jr., July 7, 1985. Student pub. schs., Uniondale. Asst. mgr. Record World, L.I., N.Y., 1977-82, mgr. Info. Builders Inc., N.Y.C., 1982—. Mem. Nat. Assn. Female Execs. Democrat. Roman Catholic.

CLAUSEL, NAN DONEY, communications executive; b. Houston, Aug. 24, 1926; d. Louden Charles and Mary Nan (Gaynor) Doney; student Mary Baldwin Coll., 1943-44, Barnard Coll., 1945-47; B.S., U. Houston, 1948; m. Calvin L. Clausel, Jr., Oct. 19, 1951 (div. 1965); children—Caroline Clausel Peter, David Louden. Public relations dir. Houston Soc. for Prevention Cruelty to Animals, 1965-66; promotion copy chief Houston Post, 1966-67; promotion copywriter St. Petersburg (Fla.) Times & Ind., 1967-69; asst. promotion mgr., promotion coordinator San Antonio Light, 1969-83, asst. dir. promotion and pub. affairs, 1983-85; owner Clausel & Co., Creative Services, San Antonio, 1985—; free-lance music reviewer, 1973-80. Active San Antonio Symphony Mastersingers, 1981—. Mem. Women in Communications, San Antonio Advt. Fedn. (dir. 1979-81), Mensa. Republican. Episcopalian. Home and Office: 272 Emporia Blvd San Antonio TX 78209

CLAUSEN, BETTY JANE HANSEN, association executive; b. Brooklyn, Wis., Oct. 25, 1925; d. Arthur John and Kathryn (Hefty) Hansen; B.A., Beloit Coll., 1947; m. Henry Albert Clausen, Jan. 31, 1948 (div. 1976); 1 son, Scott Alyn. Psychometric sec., Vocat. Counseling Bur., Rockford (Ill.) Coll., 1947-48; classified ad-taker Beloit (Wis.) Daily News, 1948-49; copy-writer WROK, Rockford, 1955-60; tchr. elementary schs., Rockford, Elmhurst, Ill., 1960-61; exec. mgr. Melrose Park (Ill.) C. of C., 1961-67; mng. dir. S.W. Sr. Center, Parma Heights, Ohio, 1967-77; exec. dir. Sr. Citizens, Inc., Hamilton, Ohio, 1977—. Founder, pres. Easter Seal Parents Group Rockford, 1957-60, project chmn. Villa Park, Ill., 1963-65; treas. Easter Seal Aux., 1965-66; treas. United Cerebral Palsy, Rockford, 1959-60, bd. dirs. Ill. Soc., 1959-60; co-chmn. 53-Minute March, Elmhurst, 1963; pres. Freeman Sch. PTA., Rockford, 1959-60; chmn. exceptional child PTA, Elmhurst, 1962-66; hon. life mem. Ill. PTA.; mem. S.W. Community Resource Council, 1968-77, Butler County Council on Aging, 1977-83; bd. dirs. Council Exceptional Children, New Neighbors League, S.W. Ceveland chpt., 1967; mem. council on aging Cin. Area Adv. Council, 1979-83. Named Citizen of Week, Elmhurst Press, 1966. Mem. Ill. C. of C., Ill. Assn. C. of C. Execs., West Suburban Council Chambers, Ohio Assn. Sr. Citizens, Delta Delta Delta. Club: Altrusa. Methodist. Home: 1224 Beissinger Rd Hamilton OH 45013 Office: 140 Ross Ave Hamilton OH 45013

CLAVREUL, GENEVIEVE MARCELLINE, management consultant; b. Paris, May 18, 1940; d. Marcel Henri and Emilie (Cauchois) Clavreul; children—Patricia, Christina, James E., Eric P. B.A. in Psychology, Columbus (Ga.) Coll., 1976, M.Ed., 1977; M.A. in Pub. Adminstrn., Calif. State U.-Bakersfield, 1979; Ph.D. in Mgmt., Beverly Hills U., 1983. Registered nurse, Ga., Calif., S.D. Head nurse Med. Ctr. Columbus (Ga.), 1974-77; asst. dir.

nursing Sioux Valley (S.D.) Hosp., 1977-78; dir. nursing San Joaquin Community Hosp., Bakersfield, 1978-79; coordinator quality assurance Cedar-Sinai Med. Ctr., Los Angeles, 1978; pres. mgmt. cons. firm Catalyst Concept Mgmt. Cons., Los Angeles, 1978—; cons., lectr. U. Calif.-Irvine, Stanford U., State N.J., Calif. State U.-Bakersfield, Phoenix U., Columbus Coll.; internat. cons. in AIDS; creator World Immunological Network, 1987, exec. dir. hosp. satellite network. Recipient award for best grad. paper So. Sociol. Assn., 1975. Mem. Hosp. Council So. Calif., Calif. Hosp. Assn., Assn. Western Hosps., Am. Soc. Healthcare Edn. Tng., Hollywood C. of C., West Hollywood C. of C. Beverly Hills C. of C. Author: Keep Those Nurses, 1982; contbr. articles to profl. jours. Home and Office: 4119 Los Feliz Blvd Suite 9 Los Angeles CA 90027

CLAWSON, BARBARA NELLE, home economics educator; b. Ackley, Iowa, Mar. 16, 1935; d. Charles and Hazel Gleda (Hosler) C. BS, Iowa State U., 1957, PhD, 1973; MS in Home Econs., U. N.C., Greensboro, 1962. Tchr. Mason City (Iowa) High Sch., 1958-60, Grimsley High Sch., Greensboro, 1961-62; asst. prof. State U. Coll., Oneota, N.Y., 1962-64; dir. Instructional Materials Ctr., Tex. Tech U., Lubbock, 1968-70; research asst. prof. U. N.C., Greensboro, 1964-68, assoc. prof. home econs., 1973-80, prof., 1980-83, prof., chair dept. home econs. edn., 1983-88; evaluation cons. State Dept. Pub. Instrn., Raleigh, N.C., 1979-81. Contbr. articles to profl. jours. Chairperson Bread for the World, Greensboro, 1984-86. Mem. Am. Home Econs. Assn. (chair internat. sect. 1983-85), Am. Vocat. Assn. (editor Jour. Vocat. Home Econs 1985—), Am. Ednl. Research Assn. Democrat. Presbyterian. Home: 3208 C Regents Park Ln Greensboro NC 27405 Office: U NC 224 Stone Greensboro NC 27412

CLAWSON, DEBRA MAUREEN, accountant; b. Tulsa, Aug. 1, 1961; d. John Dale Platzer and Maureen M. McGirl; m. James Robert Clawson, June 4, 1983. BA in Acctg., U. Minn., Duluth, 1983. Acct. March of Dimes Birth Defect Found., Louisville, 1983—. Mem. Nat. Assn. Accts. (assoc. dir. 1986-87). Club: Toastmasters (Elizabethtown, Ky.) (charter). Home: 5488 E Jamison St Fort Knox KY 40121 Office: March Dimes Birth Defects Found 4801 Sherburn Ln Louisville KY 40207

CLAWSON, ROXANN ELOISE, college administrator, computer company executive; b. Dallas, Oct. 15, 1945; d. Robert Wellington Clawson and Jeannette Irene (Rodenhauser) Clawson Clayton. BFA, Mich. State U., 1968. Library asst. Cooper Union, N.Y.C., 1970-75, asst. librarian, 1976-82, asst. to dean, 1985—; pres. Standing By Wordprocessing, N.Y.C., 1982—; v.p. Word Group, N.Y.C., 1984—; computer cons., 1986—. Mem. Nat. Assn. Female Execs., N.Y. Personal Computer Group. Democrat. Lutheran. Avocation: administration.

CLAXTON, HARRIETT MAROY JONES, educator, retired; b. Dublin, Ga., Aug. 27, 1930; d. Paul Jackson and Maroy Athalia (Chappell) Jones; m. Edward B. Claxton, Jr., May 27, 1953; children—E. B. III, Paula Jones. AA, Bethel Woman's Coll., 1949; AB magna cum laude, Mercer U., 1951; MEd, Ga. Coll., 1965. Social worker Laurens County Welfare Bd., Dublin, 1951-56; high sch. tchr., Dublin, 1961-66; instr. Middle Ga. Coll., Cochran, 1966-71, asst. prof. English, lit. and speech, 1971-85, assoc. prof. 1985-86; research tchr. Trinity Christian Sch., 1986, sr. English tchr., 1986-87; part-time tchr., Ga. Coll., 1987, Emanuel County Jr. Coll., 1988. Contbr. articles to profl. jours. and newspapers; editor Laurens County History, II, 1987. Pres. bd. Dublin Assn. Fine Arts, 1974-76, 82-84, Dublin Hist. Soc., 1976-78; mem. Laurens County Library Bd., 1960-68; chmn. Dublin Hist. Rev. Bd., 1980-85. Named Woman of Yr., St. Patrick's Festival, Dublin, 1979; recipient Outstanding Service award Cancer Soc., Dublin, 1985. Mem. DAR (regent, state, dist. and nat. awards), Sigma Mu, Alpha Delta Pi, Phi Theta Kappa, Chi Delta Phi, Delta Kappa Gamma. Democrat. Baptist. Clubs: Woman's Study (pres.), Erin Garden (pres.) (Dublin). Home: 101 Rosewood Dr Dublin GA 31021

CLAY, CAROLYNE, metallurgist; b. Chgo., Apr. 30, 1952; d. Calvin and Leanet (May) C. B.S., Rensselaer Poly. Inst., 1974; M.S., MIT, 1976, Metall. Engr., 1978. Research asst. MIT, Cambridge, 1975-77; research metallurgist Ford Motor Co. Sci. Research Lab., Dearborn, Mich., 1977-79; sr. metallurgist Kaiser Aluminum & Chem. Co.-Trentwood Works, Spokane, Wash., 1979-85; staff metallurgist Kaiser Aluminum & Chem. Co.-Trentwood Works, 1985-87, prodn. gen. foreman, 1988—; vis. com. MIT Material Sci. and Engring. Corp., 1978. Recipient Karl T. Compton award, 1977; recipient Scott MacKay award, 1974. Mem. Am. Soc. Metals, AIME, Nat. Soc. Profl. Engrs., NAACP, Sigma Xi, Delta Sigma Theta. Congregationalist. Office: Trentwood Works PO Box 15108 Spokane WA 99215

CLAYBORNE, BRENDA LANE, city agency official, fraud investigator, social worker; b. N.Y.C., Dec. 24, 1950; d. James Walter and Ruth Richetta (Wellons) Lane; divorced; children—James Byrd Clayborne, Crystal Jeaneen Betts. B.A. in Sociology, Norfolk State U., 1974; M.S.W., 1979. Asst. dir. placement service Norfolk State U., Va., 1978; social worker Norfolk Social Services, 1979-81, fraud investigator, 1981—; v.p., pub. relations coordinator Betts & Assocs., Virginia Beach, Va., 1985—; chairperson City Mgr.'s Employee Relations Com., Norfolk, 1983—. Vol. Am. Cancer Soc., Virginia Beach and Chesapeake, Va., 1982, 85, Sr. Citizen Olympics, Norfolk, 1985. Mem. Norfolk Mcpl. Employees Fed. Credit Union (bd. dirs.), Va. Council on Social Welfare (bd. dirs.), Womens Quar., Nat. Assn. for Welfare Research and Stats., United Council on Welfare Fraud, Phi Delta Kappa. Baptist. Avocations: outdoor sports, especially football; cooking; creative writing. Home: 2020-B Brookland Dr Chesapeake VA 23324 Office: City of Norfolk 220 W Brambleton Ave Norfolk VA 23510

CLAYTON, EVELYN WILLIAMS, company executive; b. Durham, N.C., Feb. 11, 1951; d. Virge and Inez Florence (Jordan) Williams; m. Archie L. Clayton, Mar. 1, 1972 (div. May 1975); 1 child, Dorel. Student Durham Tech. Inst., 1969-71, Durham Bus. Coll., 1971-72, U. N.C.-Chapel Hill, 1977-81; A.B.A., Durham Tech. Inst., 1971. Fiscal officer Durham County Health Dept. (N.C.), 1974-82; dir. fin. MedVisit Inc., Butner, N.C., 1982—; exec. dir., pres. EC & Assocs., fin. mgmt. and cons. firm, Durham, 1982—. Mem. Durham Com. on Affairs of Black People; cubmaster, Pack 442, Boy Scouts Am.; active congl. campaign Kenneth B. Spaulding, 1985. Mem. N.C. Assn. Home Care (treas. 1980-83), N.C. Public Health Assn., NAACP. Democrat. Baptist. Home: 36 Burgess Ln Durham NC 27707 Office: EC & Assocs 2514 University Dr Durham NC 27707

CLAYTON, FRANCES ANNE, computer and mathematics educators; b. Teaneck, N.J., Jan. 2, 1940; d. Leo J. and Dorothy (Buckley) Fitzpatrick; children from previous marriage: Gregory, Andrew, Robert; m. Thaddeus G. Clayton, June 8, 1979; children: Greg, Maryellen, Doug. BA, Immaculata (Pa.) Coll., 1962; MA in Edn., William Paterson Coll. of N.J., Wayne, 1987. Elem. tchr. Jefferson Sch., Bergenfield, N.J., 1962-63, Clarkstown Cen. Sch. Dist. #1, New City, N.Y., 1963-70; instr. computer curriculum devel. St. Margaret's Sch., Morristown, N.J., 1983-86; instr. computer/math. curriculum devel. Rockaway Twp. (N.J.) Schs., 1986—; computer instr. Rockaway Twp. Schs., Jersey City State Coll., 1988—; chmn. edn. dept. Morristown Woman's Club, 1984-86. Contbr. articles to profl. jours. Chmn. dept. Jr. Woman's Club of Westwood, N.J., 1968-74, v.p. 1973-74, pres. 1974-75; mem. bd. edn. St. Andrew's Parish, Westwood, 1968-72; co-chmn. Benefit Horseshow Chilton Hosp., N.J., 1975-77. Mem. Nat. Edn. Assn., N.J. Edn. Assn., Rockaway Twp. Tchrs. Assn., Internat. Council for Computers in Edn., Assn. Supervision and Curriculum Devel. Roman. Catholic. Home: 1 Bradwahl Dr Convent Station NJ 07961 Office: Stony Brook Sch Hibernia NJ 07866

CLAYTON, JOAN BENNETT, real estate executive, writer; b. Chaleroi, Pa., Oct. 27, 1931; d. Frederick Calvin and Lena Margaret (Atkins) Bennett; m. Charles Winston Clayton, June 7, 1957; children—Charles Winston III, Clay Worthington, Cole Whitney, Elizabeth Hope. B.A., Rollins Coll., 1957. Pres. J.B.C. Corp., Winter Park, Fla., 1979-83; columnist Central Fla. Sun, Maitland, Fla., 1980-81; broker, salesman Clayton's Realty, Winter Park, 1981—. Author: Peas in a Pod, 1979; Unto You, 1982. Contbr. articles to profl. jours. Pres. Orlando Day Nursery, 1968-69; mem. exec. bd. Women of Fla. Symphony Soc.; pres. Winter Park Cotillion, 1973-74; pres. Fern Creek PTA, 1970-71; mem. central Fla. bd. Fellowship Christian Athletes, 1982-85, 87, 88, head adminstrv. com., 1984-85; sustaining mem. Council of 101 Orlando Mus. Art; bd. dirs. Orlando Union Rescue Mission, 1987. Mem. Orlando Bd. Realtors, Christian Poetry Assn. Am., Fla. Freelance Writer's Assn., Phi Mu. Republican. Baptist.

CLAYTON, MARY JO, advertising consultant; b. Georgetown, Ky.; d. Jesse L. and Nettie (Lutz) C. B.A. in English And Math., Meredith Coll. Copy supr. Foote, Cone & Belding, N.Y.C., 1960-66; copy group head Grey Advt., N.Y.C., 1967-70; v.p., copy supr. Ketchum, MacLeod & Grove, Inc., N.Y.C., 1970-76; sr. v.p., creative group head Benton & Bowles, Inc., N.Y.C., 1976-83; with Wells, Rich, Greene, Inc., N.Y.C., 1983-84; free lance advt. cons. 1985—; writer TV commls. for Digital Equipment Corp., Procter & Gamble, Shiseido Cosmetics, Revlon Cosmetics, Clairol, Johnson & Johnson. Democrat. Baptist.

CLAYTON, SALLY JANE, lawyer; b. St. Louis, June 2, 1927; d. Harold Sylvester and Martha May (Sager) Pfeffer; m. Michel Ely Cressaty, Nov. 12, 1949 (div. 1956); m. Charles Frederick Clayton, May 30, 1956; children—Ann Harper, Thomas Henry. B.A., U. Ill., 1948; cert. U. Paris, 1949; J.D., St. Louis U., 1980. Bar: Ill. 1980. Receptionist, Ford Found., N.Y.C., 1953-54; asst. buyer Famous Barr Co., St. Louis, 1955-56; tchr. Sch. Dist. 9, Lebanon, Ill., 1956-77; assoc. Delmar O. Koebel, Lebanon, 1980-87; sole practice, Lebanon, 1987—. Treas., Lebanon Edn. Assn., Sch. Dist. 9, 1974-75, Lebanon Citizens Assn., 1975; Republican candidate for state's atty., St. Clair County, Ill., 1984; bd. dirs. Call for Help Found., Belleville, Ill., 1984—. Recipient Disting. Service award in govt. and politics Clair County YWCA, 1985; French Govt. scholar, 1948. Mem. ABA, Ill. Bar Assn., St. Clair County Bar Assn., Metro East Women's Bar Assn., Assn. Trial Lawyers Am., Phi Beta Kappa, Phi Kappa Phi, Alpha Lambda Delta. Presbyterian. Home: 937 Belleville St Lebanon IL 62254 Office: 939 Belleville St Lebanon IL 62254

CLAYTON, VANESSA RAYE, personnel director; b. Opelausas, La., Mar. 25, 1957; d. Albert and Gladys Joseph; m. Louis Clayton, Nov. 30, 1955. BS, Grambling U., 1980; MBA, Miami U., 1982. Personnel dir. Buffalo Savs., Houston, 1982-84, Savs. of Am., Houston, 1984; exec. personnel dir. Colonial Savs., Houston, 1984—; v.p. personnel dir. TCF Banc Savs. (merger Colonial Savs.), Houston, 1982—; bd. dirs. Security Bank, Houston, 1983—; sec. Youth Personnel U. Houston, 1985—. Author: We The Minority, 1985. V.p. Big Sister of Tex., 1982; mem. Mayor's Task Force, 1986; founder, v.p. Black Youth Today, 1987—. Mem. Women As One, Houston Personnel Assn. (v.p. 1985-86), Minority Guidance to Employment (sec. 1985—). Home: 14 Greenway Plaza 9R Houston TX 77046 Office: TCF Banc Savs 6400 Savoy Houston TX 77036

CLEAR, CAROLYN HILL, sales executive; b. Memphis, May 21, 1937; d. Owen Landale and Sylvia Mae (Walter) Hill; B.J., U. Mo., 1959; children—Stacey Alan, Sylvia Lee. Asst. to asst. advt. dir. MFA Ins. Cos., Columbia, Mo., 1958, 59-60; traffic directory, copywriter, on-air announcer Sta. WENE, Endicott, N.Y., 1960-61; weekly columnist, advt. salesman Fort Bend Mirror, Stafford, Tex., 1970-71; advt. sales rep., promotion dir., nat. accounts mgr. Suburbia, Houston, 1972-76; dir. rep., advt. sales, mgr. directory sales Southwestern Bell, Houston, 1976-80, staff mgr. directory premise tng., 1981-83, div. sales mgr. Southwestern Bell Yellow Pages Inc., St. Louis, 1984-85, dir. sales and mktg. adminstrn., 1985-86 ; dir. corp. tng. Southwestern Bell Publs., 1986-87; div. sales mgr. Southwestern Bell Yellow Pages Inc., Wichita, Kans., 1987—. Counselor, Youth Emergency Hot Line. Recipient Gold Key award Southwestern Bell, 1977. Republican. Presbyterian. Home: 2871 Tallgrass Wichita KS 67226 Office: 2044 Woodlawn Suite 200 Brittany Ctr Wichita KS 67226

CLEAR, LEE WILLIAMS, school psychologist; b. Charlotte, N.C., Mar. 30, 1956; d. John R. and Sarah (Hicks) Williams; m. William Phillip Clear, Jr., July 10, 1982; children: William Phillip III, Nicholas Andrew. BA, Winthrop Coll., 1978; MA, Mid. Tenn. State U., 1981. Sch. psychologist Jefferson County Sch. System, Danridge, Tenn., 1983-84, Knoxville (Tenn.) City Sch. System, 1984-87, Knox County Sch. System, Knoxville, 1987—. Mem. Nat. Assn. Sch. Psychologists, Tenn. Assn. Sch. Psychologists. Presbyterian. Home: 1814 Holston River Rd Knoxville TN 37914 Office: Knox County Sch System Psychol Services 101 E 5th Ave Knoxville TN 37917

CLEARY, BERYL BOARDMAN, nurse; b. Sayre, Pa., May 7, 1926; d. Erwin W. and Mildred (Haight) Boardman; m. James G. Cleary, Aug. 15, 1954; 1 child, Michael. BS in Nursing Edn., U. Pa., 1951, MEd, 1953. Staff nurse Robert Packer Hosp., Sayre, 1947-48, nursing sch. instr., 1972—; instr. U. Pa. Hosp., Phila., 1951-58; nursing sch. instr. U. Pa., Phila., 1966-72. Mem. Am. Nurses Assn., Sigma Theta Tau. Republican. Roman Catholic. Home: 391 Main St Owego NY 13827

CLEARY, BEVERLY ATLEE (MRS. CLARENCE T. CLEARY), author; b. McMinnville, Oreg.; d. Chester Lloyd and Mable (Atlee) Bunn; m. Clarence T. Cleary, Oct. 6, 1940; children—Marianne Elisabeth, Malcolm James. B.A., U. Calif., 1938; B.A. in Librarianship, U. Wash., 1939. Children's librarian Yakima, Wash., 1939-40; post librarian Regional Hosp., Oakland, Calif., 1942-45. Author: Henry Huggins, 1950, Ellen Tebbits, 1951, Henry and Beezus, 1952, Otis Spofford, 1953, Henry and Ribsy, 1954, Beezus and Ramona, 1955, Fifteen, 1956, Henry and the Paper Route, 1957, The Luckiest Girl, 1958, Jean and Johnny, (1959) Hullabaloo ABC, 1960, Emily's Runaway Imagination, 1961, Henry and the Clubhouse, 1962, Sister of the Bride, 1963, Ribsy, 1964, The Mouse and the Motorcycle, 1965, Mitch and Amy, 1967, Ramona the Pest, 1968, Runaway Ralph, 1970, Socks, 1973, Ramona the Brave, 1975, Ramona and her Father, 1977 (Honor Book for U.S., Internat. Bd. and Books for Young People), Ramona and Her Mother, 1979, Ramona Quimby, Age 8, 1981, Ralph S. Mouse, 1982, Dear Mr. Henshaw, 1983, Ramona Forever, 1984, Lucky Chuck, 1984, The Ramona Quimby Diary, 1984, Two Dog Biscuits, 1985, The Real Hole, 1985, Beezus and Ramona Diary, 1986, Janet's Thingamajigs, 1987, The Growing Up Feet, 1987, A Girl from Yamhill, 1988. Recipient Laura Ingalls Wilder award Children's Services div. ALA 1975, Newbery Honor Book award 1978, 82, Regina medal Cath. Library Assn. 1980, Am. Book award, 1981, Golden Kite award Soc. Children's Book Writers, 1983, Christopher award, 1983, 84, George C. Stone award Claremont Colls, 1983, Newbery medal, 1984, Hans Christian Andersen medal nominee, 1984, Everychild award Children's Book Council, 1985. Am. Book award, 1981, George C. Stone award Claremont Colls., 1983, Newberry Honor Books, 1977, 83. Mem. Authors Guild of Authors League Am. Address: care William Morrow 105 Madison Ave New York NY 10016

CLEARY, JEAN MARIE, accountant; b. Jersey City, Apr. 5, 1964; d. Brian Patrick and Barbara (Murray) C. BA, Rutgers U., 1986. Sec. Pelosi Med. Ctr., Bayonne, N.J., 1982—; acct. Robert Doria and Co. CPA's, Bayonne, 1986—, Donohue & Gironda, CPA's, Jersey City, 1987—; acctg. cons. Pelasi Med. Ctr., 1987—. Mem. Nat. Assn. Female Execs., Rutgers U. Alumni Assn. Roman Catholic. Home: 47 E 45 St Bayonne NJ 07002

CLEARY, MANON CATHERINE, artist, educator; b. St. Louis, Nov. 14, 1942; d. Frank and Crystal (Maret) Cleary. B.F.A., Washington U., St. Louis, 1964; M.F.A., Tyler Sch. Art, Temple U., 1968. Instr. fine arts SUNY-Oswego, 1968-70; from instr. to assoc. prof. D.C. Tchrs. Coll., Washington, 1970-78; from assoc. prof. to prof. art U. D.C., 1978-85, acting chmn. dept. art, 1985-86; one woman shows at Mus. Modern Art Gulbenkian Found., Lisbon, Portugal, 1985, Iolas/Jackson Gallery, N.Y.C., 1982, Osuna Gallery, Washington, 1974, 77, 80, 84, U. D.C., 1987, Tyler Gallery SUNY at Oswego, 1987, others; group exhibits include Twentieth Century Am. Drawings: The Figure in Context, Traveled Nat. Acad. Design, 1984-85, others. Artist-in-residence Herning Hojskole, Denmark, 1980, Ucross Found., Wyo., 1984; recipient faculty research award, U. D.C., 1983. Mem. Coll. Art Assn., NEA, Pi Beta Phi. Democrat. Presbyterian. Home: 1736 Columbia Rd NW Apt 402 Washington DC 20009 Office: U DC Art Dept 916 G St NW Washington DC 20001

CLEEK, JUDY ANN, English as a second language educator; b. Martin, Tenn., Sept. 19, 1948; d. Vernon B. and Golda B. (Sullivan) Bynum; m. William Donnell Cleek, Sept. 19, 1970; children: Laurel Leigh, Ashley Donnell. BA, Union U., 1969; BS, Memphis State U., 1972; cert. in TESOL, Georgetown U., 1983, U. Tenn., 1986. Grad. asst. English-Memphis State U., 1969-70, 71-72; tchr. Union City (Tenn.) High Sch., 1973-76; English as a second lang. educator U. Tenn., Martin, 1981—; French club dir. Union City High Sch., 1973-76, drama club dir., 1975-76; social coordinator Internat. Programs, Martin, librarian, 1985—. Contbr. articles to profl. jours. Sec. Parent-Tchr. Orgn., 1987. Recipient Outstanding Tchr. award International Programs U. Tenn., 1983. Mem. Internat. and Tenn. Tchrs. of English to Speakers of Other Langs., Delta Kappa Gamma. Baptist. Home: Rt Box 323 Dresden TN 38225 Office: U Tenn at Martin Gooch 144 Martin TN 38238

CLEEREMAN, JOAN ANN, engineer; b. Waukesha, Wis., Nov. 11, 1960; d. Maurice James and Grace Dorothy (Schimmelpenny) McCarthy; m. Kevin Christopher Cleereman, Aug. 13, 1983. B in Computer Sci., Math. with honors, U. Wis., 1983. Computer programmer Sperry Corp., St. Paul, 1984-85; computer aided design engr. Unisys Corp., St. Paul, 1985—. Mem. Nat. Assn. Female Execs. Home: 8250 Sunnyside Rd Minneapolis MN 55432

CLELAND, AUDRY JAYE, training administrator; b. Atmore, Ala., Aug. 13, 1932; d. Robert Lee and Minnie Lee (Sasser) Jaye; m. Vinson Oran Cleland, Jr., Apr. 10, 1953. A.A., Pensacola (Fla.) Jr. Coll., 1978; B.A., U. West Fla., 1981; M.S. in Pub. Adminstrn., Troy (Ala.) State U., 1983. Claims rep. Wash. State Employment Service, Colville, 1958-61; bookkeeper Jaye Trucking Co., Atmore, 1962-64; mgmt. asst. U.S. Air Force, Randolph AFB, Tex., 1964-68, Weisbaden AB, W.Ger., 1968-74; edn. technician DANTES (Def. Activity for Nontraditional Edn. Support), Pensacola, 1974-83; tng. adminstr. Navy Comptroller Standard Systems Activity, Pensacola, 1983—. Editor: Guide to External Degree Programs, 1982; Guide for Establishing and Operating an Adult Learning Center, 1983. Recipient Spl. Achievement award Def. Activity for Non-Traditional Edn. Support, 1983, hon. EEO award Naval Edn. and Tng. Program Devel. Ctr., 1981, Chief Naval Edn. and Tng., 1981. Mem. Am. Soc. Tng. and Devel. Republican. Baptist. Clubs: Spin Off Toastmistress (pres. 1979), Federally Employed Women (pres. Pensacola 1980). Lodge: Eastern Star.

CLEM, ELIZABETH ANN STUMPF, music educator; b. San Antonio, July 9, 1945; d. David Joseph and Elizabeth Burch (Wathen) Stumpf; m. D. Bruce Clem, June 17, 1972; children: Sean David, Jeremy Andrew. BA in Music Edn., St. Mary-of-the-Woods (Ind.) Coll., 1970; MEd, Drury Coll., Springfield, Mo., 1979. Elem. tchr. St. Christopher Sch., Speedway, Ind., 1970-71; elem. and jr. high sch. tchr. Indpls. Sch. System, 1971-72; elem. tchr. Augusta (Ga.) Sch. System, 1972-73, Wabash (Ind.) Sch. System, 1976-77; pvt. practice piano tchr. Wabash, Ind., 1975-77, Honolulu, 1983-86, Burke, Va., 1986—. Dist. fund raiser rep. Wabash chpt. Am. Cancer Soc., 1975; leadership coordinator Wabash council Girl Scouts Am., 1976; music coordinator Ft. Shafter Sacred Heart Chapel, Honolulu, 1985-86. Mem. Nat. Guild Piano Tchrs., No. Va. Music Tchrs. Assn., Springfield Music Club. Republican. Roman Catholic. Home and Office: 6316 Wilmington Dr Burke VA 22015

CLEMENT, BETSY KAY, computer company executive; b. Columbus, Ohio, Oct. 12, 1952; d. Harold Francis and Carley June (Davidson) Snider; m. Laurence Peter Clement, July 10, 1981. B in Music, U. Fla., 1975; M in Music, New Eng. Conservatory, 1979. Singer Musicana Enterprises, Inc., Vero Beach, Fla., 1975-77; opera singer N.Y.C., 1979-83; asst. to programming dir. Showtime/The Movie Channel, N.Y.C., 1983-84; asst. to program guide dir. United Satellite Communications, N.Y.C., 1984; founding ptnr. Mobile Word Assocs., N.Y.C., Tampa, Fla., 1985—; cons. Time, Inc., N.Y.C., CBS TV Research, N.Y.C., Cosmopolitan Personnel, N.Y.C., Computerlands of Tampa Bay, Anheuser-Busch Inc., Medicaid Div. HRS State of Fla. Developer computer tng. courses, workbooks, reference manuals, programs. Mem. Nat. Assn. Female Execs., Ind. Computer Cons. Assn., Sigma Alpha Iota, Sigma Kappa. Home: 3120 Buckview Ln Brandon FL 33511 Office: Mobile Word Assocs PO Box 1123 Brandon FL 34299-1123

CLEMENT, HOPE ELIZABETH ANNA, librarian; b. North Sydney, N.S., Can., Dec. 29, 1930; d. Harry Wells and Lana (Perkins) C. B.A., U. of King's Coll., 1951; M.A., Dalhousie U., 1953; B.L.S., U. Toronto, 1955. With Nat. Library of Can., Ottawa, Ont., 1955—; chief nat. bibliography div. Nat. Library of Can., 1966-70, asst. dir. research and planning br., 1970-73, dir. research and planning br., 1973-77, assoc. nat. librarian, 1977—. Editor: Canadiana, 1966-69. Mem. Can. Library Assn. Office: Nat Library Can, 395 Wellington St, Ottawa, ON Canada K1A 0N4

CLEMENT, JACQUELINE PARKER, school administrator; b. Feb. 28, 1931; d. Donald C. Parker and Helen (Reininger) Parker Barnes; m. M.O. Clement. B.A., Mt. Holyoke Coll., 1952; postgrad. U. Calif.-Berkeley, 1953-56; M.Ed., Am. U., 1968; Ed.D., Harvard U., 1974; hon. degree, Lesley Coll., 1978. Dir., advisor Follow through Headstart, Lebanon, N.H., 1967-71; with div. adminstrn. N.H. State Dept. of Edn., Concord, 1971; asst. supt. Supervisory Union 22, Hanover, N.H., 1973-75; asst. supt. curriculum and instrn., Brookline, Mass., 1975-78; supt. schs., Lincoln, Mass., 1978-82; head The Winchester-Thurston Sch., Pitts., 1982—. Author: (with Mark Shedd) The Costs of Educational Innovation, 1972; Sex Bias in School Leadership, 1975; contbr. articles to profl. jours. Bd. dirs. Pitts. Youth Symphony, 1984; trustee Cambridge Sch., Weston, Mass., 1980. NEH fellow Stanford U., 1976; Dept. Econs. fellow U. Calif., 1953-54. Mem. Am. Assn. Sch. Administrs., Middle States Assn. Colls. and Schs. (adv. com.), Nat. Assn. Independent schs. (edn. issues commn.), Pa. Assn. of Independent Schs. (exec. com.), Pitts. Fund for Arts Edn. (bd. dirs.), Exec. Women's Council of Greater Pitts. Inc., Am. Ednl. Research Assn., Assn. for Supervison and Curriculum Devel., Cultural Edn. Collaborative (bd. dirs.). Office: The Winchester-Thurston Sch 555 Morewood Ave Pittsburgh PA 15213

CLEMENT, JANICE FAYE, nursing administrator; b. Norfolk, Nebr., Aug. 19, 1946; d. Allen Edward and Hilda Bernice (Stange) Reeves; m. Roger Allen Clement, Oct. 6, 1968 (dec. July 1974). R.N., Meth. Sch. Nursing, Omaha, 1967; B.S. in Nursing, magna cum laude, Creighton U., 1978; M.S. in Nursing, U. Nebr., 1981. With Meth. Hosp., 1967-68, 70-83, asst. head nurse, 1974-77, staff devel. nurse, 1977-81, dir. staff adminstrv. services, 1981-83; pub. health nurse Wichita-Sedgwick County Health Dept., Wichita, Kans., 1970-72; dir. nursing Meth. Med. Ctr., St. Joseph, Mo., 1983-84, Broadlawns Med. Ctr., Des Moines, 1984—; adj. clin. faculty nursing Drake U. Nursing, Des Moines, 1986—, mem. adv. bd., 1984—, Cen. Campus Practical Nursing, 1984—; mem. adv. bd. Des Moines Area Community Coll. Dist., 1987—, Des Moines Area Community Coll. Nursing Bd., 1987—. Mem. Am. Nurses Assn., Iowa Nurses Assn., Nat. League Nursing, Iowa League Nursing (treas. 1987—), Am. Orgn. Nurse Execs., (Iowa chpt.), Central Iowa Nursing Leadership Conf. (pres. 1985—), Colloquium Nursing Leaders Central Iowa, Iowa League for Nursing (treas. 1987—), Iowa Orgn. Nurse Execs. (treas. 1987), Iowa Hosp. Assn. Council on Patient Services, 1988—, Am. Mgmt. Assn., Sigma Theta Tau. Republican. Methodist. Avocations: flying, sewing, golfing, walking, reading. Home: 764 Knolls Ct West Des Moines IA 50265 Office: Broadlawns Med Ctr 18th and Hickman Rd Des Moines IA 50314

CLEMENT, JEAN M., public relations professional; b. Great Barrington, Mass., Sept. 22, 1948; d. Francis J. and Harriet M. (Hotchkiss) Ebitz; divorced; 1 child, Derek Scott. AS in Liberal Studies, Berkshire Community Coll., 1977; BS in Mass Communication magna cum laude, Boston U., 1979; postgrad., Babson Coll., 1987—. Dir. advt. and pub. relations Berge's Realtors, Salem, N.H., 1979-80; dir. advt. and promotion Gen. Ginema Theatres, Chestnut Hill, Mass., 1980-83; specialist employee communications Computervision Corp., Bedford, Mass., 1983-84, specialist sales promotion, 1984-85; rep. pub. relations Thermo Electron Corp., Waltham, Mass., 1985-87; free-lance pub. relations and promotion Framingham, Mass., 1985—; mgr. pub./community relations Stop & Shop Supermarket Co., Boston, 1987-88; sr. pub. relations specialist Codex Corp., Canton, Mass., 1988—. Bd. dirs. Greater Boston Diabetes Soc., Brookline, Mass., 1986—. Mem. Publicity Club Boston (bd. dirs. 1983-85, chair Bell Ringer awards com. 1984, editor newsletter 1984-85, awards).

CLEMENT, KATHERYN (KITTY), adoption agency director, consultant, trainer; b. Little Rock, Ark., Jan. 6, 1924; d. Louis Wangelin and Dorothy Louise (Butler) Fuess; m. William Crutcher Clement, July 28, 1945 (div. 1979); 4 sons, William, Louis, Peter, Richard. B.A., Tex. Women's U.,

Denton, 1945; M.S.S.W., U. Tex.-Arlington, 1971. Cert. social worker, Tex. Social worker Homes of St. Mark, Houston, 1967-69, Presbyn. Children's Home, Dallas, 1969-71; cons. therapist Child Study Ctr., Ft. Worth, 1971-74; supr. Harris County Child Welfare, Houston, 1974-79; field cons. Child Welfare League, N.Y.C., 1979-80; dir. Spaulding for Children, Houston, 1980—; trainer Dept. Human Resources State of Tex., 1981—. Co-author: Reaching Out, 1980; contbr. article to conf. Recipient Outstanding Woman award YWCA, Harris County, Tex., 1979; Dept. Health & Human Services grantee, 1982. Fellow N.Am. Ctr. Adoption, Child Welfare League Am., ACLU, Unitarian Universalist Women's Orgn., Tex. Abortion Rights Action League, Harris County Women's Polit. Caucus. Democrat. Unitarian. Club: Houston City Breakfast (sec., 1983-84). Home: 3700 Wakeforest Apt 56 Houston TX 77098 Office: Spaulding for Children 4219 Richmond Houston TX 77027

CLEMENT, KATHI DEE, physician, educator; b. Malden, Mo., Aug. 16, 1951; d. John Elton and Lois Lorraine (Moore) C. BS, S.E Mo. State U., 1973; MD, U. Mo., 1979. Diplomate Am. Bd. Family Practice. Intern in family practice U. Wyo., Casper, 1979-80, resident in family practice, 1980-82, chief resident in family practice, 1981-82; practice medicine specializing in family practice Sundance, Wyo., 1982-84; asst. prof. family medicine U. Wyo./Cheyenne Family Practice Ctr., 1984-87, U. Tenn., Memphis, 1988—; mem. Bd. Pub. Health, Laramie County, Wyo., 1987—. Bd. dirs. YWCA, Cheyenne, 1985—, Casey Family Ctr., Cheyenne, 1986—, Cheyenne Health Fair, 1985. Fellow Am. Acad. Family Physicians; mem. Wyo. Med. Soc., Wyo. Acad. Family Physicians (alt. del. 1982-84, del. 1984—), Am. Med. Women's Assn., Laramiey County Med. Soc. Democrat. Methodist. Home: 563 Vinton Square Memphis TN 38104 Office: U Tenn-Memphis Healthplex 1121 Union Ave Memphis TN 38104

CLEMENT, SHIRLEY GEORGE, educational services executive; b. El Paso, Tex., Feb. 14, 1926; d. Claude Samuel and Elizabeth Estelle (Mattice) Gillett; m. Paul Vincent Clement, Mar. 23, 1946; children—Brian Frank, Robert Vincent, Carol Elizabeth, Rosemary Adele. BA in English, Tex. Western Coll., 1963; postgrad. U. Tex., El Paso, N.Mex. State U.; MEd in Reading, Sul Ross State U., 1987. Tchr. lang. arts Ysleta Ind. Schs., El Paso, 1960-62; tchr. adult edn., 1962-64, tchr. reading/lang. arts, 1964-77; owner, dir. Crestline Learning Systems, Inc., El Paso, 1980—; dir. tutorial for sports teams U. Tex., El Paso, 1984; dir. continuing edn. program El Paso Community Coll., 1985; mem. curriculum com. Ysleta Ind. Schs., El Paso, 1974; mem. Right to Read Task Force, 1975-77; mem. Bi-Centennial Steering Com., El Paso, 1975-76; lectr. on reading. Author: Beginning the Search, 1979; contbr. poems to Behold Texas, 1983. Treas. El Paso Rep. Women, 1956; facilitator Goals for El Paso, 1975; mem. hospitality com. Sun Carnival, 1974, Cotton Festival, 1975. Mem. Internat. Reading Assn. (pres. El Paso County council 1973-74), Assn. Children with Learning Disabilities (tchr. 1980), Poetry Soc. Tex. (Panhandle Penwomen's first place award 1981), El Paso C. of C., Assn. Gifted and Talented, Chi Omega Alumnae (pres. 1952-53). Mem. Unity Sch. of Christianity. Avocations: dressmaking, tailoring, needlecraft, writing, singing. Home: 825 De Leon St El Paso TX 79912 Office: Crestline Secondary Sch and Tutor House 481 N Resler St D & E El Paso TX 79912

CLEMENT, YVONNE MADELINE, librarian; b. Tacoma, Wash., June 17, 1924; d. Cecil Edward and Madeline Edith (Wink) DeGuire; m. Ralph Louis Clement, Jr., June 25, 1949 (dec. Dec. 1969); children—Lawrence E., Catherine E. Gilbert, Mary Susan Clement Zimmerman, Michele Y. Clement Cates, David L. BA Holy Names Coll., Spokane, Wash., 1946; B.A.L.S., Rosary Coll., 1947. Asst. br. librarian Tacoma Pub. Library (Wash.), 1947-49; br. asst. Salt Lake County Library, Salt Lake City, 1967-69, br. librarian, 1969-71, assoc. dir., 1971-86. Author: (with B.M. Hepworth) Utah Libraries: Heritage and Horizons, 1976. Bd. dirs. Utah council Camp Fire, Salt Lake City, 1983-84. Lodge: Zonta.

CLEMENTS, JOYE ARLINE, health care administrator; b. Boston, July 23, 1936; d. Raymond Eugene and Arline M. (Ison) Moreau; m. Richard A. Meuse, July 11, 1953 (div. 1972); children: Darlene Trombly, Thomas, Richard; m. Walter E. Clements, Aug. 15, 1975 (dec.); 1 child, Douglas. Student, No. Essex Coll., 1971-80; BS in Nursing, Northeastern U., 1980. Cert. Am. Coll. Health Care Adminstrs. Dir. nursing Winthrop House, Medford, Mass., 1980-82; exec. dir. Elder Care Services Inc., Rowley, Mass., 1982-84; pres., chief exec. officer Briarcliff Inc., Gloucester, Mass., 1984—; mem. state regulators com. Mass. Fedn. Nursing Homes, 1986—, Blueprint 2000 com. Commonwealth of Mass., 1987-88, adv. com. nursing home and rest home regulations Mass. Dept. Pub. Health, 1988. Author: (manual) Quality Assurance, 1983. Mem. Rest Home Orgn. Mass. (pres. 1987-88), Nat. Bus. and Profl. Women (chpt. v.p. f1980-81, chpt. pres. 1981-82, Woman Yr. 1984), Cloucester C. of C., Cape Ann C. of C. (steering com. bus. women 1987-88). Roman Catholic. Home: 46 Summer St Gloucester MA 01930 Office: Briarcliff Inc PO Box 1151 Gloucester MA 01930

CLEMINSHAW, HELEN K. MARIE, psychologist, educator; b. Elizabeth, N.J., May 16, 1938; d. Fred A. and Helen W. (Bittner) Kronseder; m. John G. Cleminshaw, June 24, 1960; children: John David, Suzanne Christine. BS, Rutgers U., 1960; MA, Kent (Ohio) State U., 1972, PhD, 1977. Lic. psychologist, Ohio. Sch. psychologist Maple Heights (Ohio) Schs., 1972-75; assoc. prof. psychology U. Akron, Ohio, 1976-88, prof., 1988—; psychologist Hudson (Ohio) Psychol. Assocs., 1980—; dir. Child Life Specialist Tng. Program, Akron, 1979—, Ctr. Family Studies, Akron, 1981—. Co-editor: Alcoholism: New Perspectives, 1983; contbr. articles to profl. jours. U. Akron faculty research grantee, 1978-79, 87-88, grantee NIMH, 1979-84, AAUW Ednl. Found., 1986—, Ohio Dept. Mental Health, 1987-88. Mem. Am. Psychol. Assn., Nat. Council Family Relations, Assn. for Care of Children's Health. Office: U Akron Schrank Hall S 215 Akron OH 44325

CLEMMONS, FRANCES ANNE MANSELL (MRS. SLATON CLEMMONS), insurance company official; b. Camden, Miss., Dec. 21, 1915; d. Otho Franklin and Pearl (Dunlap) Mansell; m. Rowe Sanders Crowder, Dec. 17, 1938 (div. Mar. 1954); children—Rowe Sanders, Frances Elizabeth; m. Slaton Clemmons, Nov. 21, 1965. BS Belhaven Coll., 1937, MusB, 1937. Owner, operator Crowder Art Gallery, Jackson, Miss., 1946-50; dept. mgr., buyer Valley Dry Goods Co., Vicksburg, 1954-56; with Social Security Adminstrn., 1956-84, asst. dist. mgr., Rome, Ga., 1962-84; MEDICARE hearing officer Prudential Ins. Co. Am., 1984—. Charter mem. Citizens Adv. Council on Energy, bd. dirs., 1986—; mem. Rome Little Theatre, Rome Community Concert Assn., Rome Symphony Heritage Soc., Rome Area C. of C., Floyd County Personnel Bd., Salvation Army Aux., Internat. Platform Assn. Democrat. Presbyterian. Club: Quota Internat. Inc. (pres. Rome 1974-76, dist. 8 lt. gov. 1979-80, gov. 1980-82, bd. dirs. 1984-86). Home: 412 E 3d Ave Rome GA 30161

CLENDANIEL, ANNE LUCILLE EVANS, communications consultant; b. Harrington, Del., Aug. 30, 1918; d. John Franklin and Bertha (Collison) Evans; student U. Del., 1936-37, spl. courses in writing, leadership and communications; m. Harry Edgar Clendaniel, Jr., Sept. 6, 1941 (div. 1985); children—Mary Catherine, John Evans. Exec. sec. Beacom Bus. Coll., 1939; legal sec., tax dept. duPont Co., 1939-45, Maguire, Voorhees & Wells, Orlando, Fla., 1943-45; vol., study group leader Great Books, 1945-61; legal sec. Young, Conaway, Stargatt, 1962-63; dir. communications Episcopal Diocese of Del., 1963-73; exec. dir. Del. chpt. Arthritis Found., Wilmington, 1974-84; bd. dirs. Del. Sr. Cons., 1984-86. Mem. Del. Press Women, Profl. Staff Assn. Arthritis Found. U. Del. Div. Continuing Edn. Acad. of Lifelong Learning Faculty and Council. Republican. Club: Wilmington Quota (pres. 1977-78), Contbr. poetry and verse, to newspapers, mags., anthologies, 1939-55; founder, writer Communion Diocesan paper, 1967-73; author The Arthritis Report, 1974-84; editor DSC newsletter, Tech. and Mgmt. Services newsletter

CLEVELAND, MARCIA JOAN, lawyer; b. Holyoke, Mass., May 4, 1946; d. Arthur Burdett and Alice Marion (Craven) C.; m. Daniel W. Paul; children—Ingrid Kirsten, Aaron Samuel. B.A. with honors in History, Wellesley Coll., 1968; J.D., Yale U., 1971. Staff atty. Queens Legal Service, L.I., 1971-72; coordinating atty. Commn. Action for Legal Service, N.Y.C., 1972-74; sr. staff atty. Natural Resources Def. Counsel, N.Y.C., 1974-79; bur. chief Environ. Protection Bur., N.Y. Atty. Gen.'s Office, N.Y.C., 1979-84; asst. atty. gen. Maine Atty. Gen.'s office, 1985—; adj. prof. Columbia Sch. Pub. Health, N.Y.C., 1979-80, Rutgers Law Sch., Newark, N.J., 1982-84. Mem. exec. com. Ind. Neighborhood Democrats, Bklyn., 1969-76.

CLEVELAND, PEGGY R., cytotechnologist; b. Cannelton, Ind., Dec. 9, 1929; d. "Pat" Clarence Francis and Alice Marie (Hall) Richey; cert. U. Louisville, 1956; B. Health Sci., U. Louisville, 1984; m. Peter Leslie Cleveland, Nov. 25, 1948 (dec. 1973); children—Pamela Cleveland Litch, Paula Cleveland Bertloff, Peter L. Cytotechnologist cancer survey project NIH, Louisville, 1956-59; chief cytotechnologist Parker Cytology Lab., Inc., Louisville, 1959-75; mgr. cytology dept. Am. Biomed. Corp., 1976-78, Nat. Health Labs., Inc., Louisville, 1978—; clin. instr. cytology Sch. Allied Health U. Louisville, 1980—, cytology adv. com., 1980-81, chmn., 1982, ednl. coordinator Nat. Health Labs., Inc. with cytology program U. Louisville; owner, operator Broke N. Bent Farm thoroughbred horse breeding and racing. Mem. Am. Soc. Clin. Pathologist (cert. cytotechnologist), Internat. Acad. Cytology (cert. cytotechnologist), Am. Soc. Cytology (pilot program continuing edn. certification), Horseman's Benevolent and Protective Assn. Democrat. Roman Catholic. Home: Route 1 Box 393 Lanesville IN 47136 Office: Nat Health Labs Inc Louisville KY 40202

CLEVELAND, SUSAN ELIZABETH, library administrator, researcher; b. Plainfield, N.J., Mar. 14, 1946; d. Robert Astbury and Grace Ann (Long) Williamson; m. Stuart Craig Cleveland, Aug. 21, 1971; children—Heather Elizabeth, Catherine Elisa. B.A., Douglass Coll., Rutgers U., 1968; M.L.S., Rutgers U., 1969. Acquisitions librarian Jefferson U., Phila., 1970-71; biomed. librarian VA Hosp., Hines, Ill., 1972; med. cataloger U. Ariz., Tucson, 1973-74; dir. U. Pa. Hosps. Library, Phila., 1974-87; exec. dir. C.L.U. Assocs., 1987—; cons. in field, Phila. USPHS fellow, Detroit, 1969-70; recipient Chapel of 4 Chaplains Legion of Honor. Mem. Med. Library Assn. (Phila. chpt.), Spl. Library Assn. Club: Caravan. Home: 612 N Hobart Dr Laurel Springs NJ 08021

CLEVEN, CAROL CHAPMAN, state legislator; b. Hanover, Ill., Nov. 2, 1928; d. Edward William and Vivian (Stausser) Chapman; m. Walter Arnold Cleven, children: Kern W., Jeffrey P. BS, U. Ill., 1950, postgrad. Elem. sch. tchr. Derinda Ctr, Ill., 1946-47; with research staff U. Ill., Urbana, 1950-56; exec. dir. Crittenton Hasting House, Brighton, Mass., 1975-86; mem. Ho. of Reps. of Mass. Great and Gen. Ct., Boston, 1987—, edn. com., HUD com., fed. fin. assistance com., Commn. on Indoor Air Pollution; mem. Ho. Reps. Task Force on AIDS, Mass. Caucus of Women Legislators. Chmn. Chelmsford (Mass.) Sch. Com., 1969-87, mem. elem. needs com., 1969-71, sch. bldg. com., 1971-76; mem. adv. bd. Camp Paul for Exceptional Children, 1987; past pres. Lowell (Mass.) YWCA, Lowell Coll. Club.; mem. Merrimack River Watershed Council, Mass. Coalition for Pregnant and Parenting Teens, Alliance for Young Families. Mem. Mass. Assn. Sch. Coms., Friends of the Library, Chelmsford Hist. Soc., Chelmsford LWV, Florence Crittenton League of Lowell, Phi Sigma, Sigma Delta Epsilon. Congregationalist. Home: 4 Arbutus Ave Chelmsford MA 01824 Office: State House Room 36 Boston MA 02133

CLEVENGER, PENELOPE, association executive; b. Denver, Dec. 6, 1940; d. Harold Friedland and Charlotte (Glatt) Friedland Beskin; m. Willie K. Clevenger, Oct. 15, 1961 (div.). A.A., Stephens Coll., 1960. Office mgr. Malcolm S. Gerald, Chgo., 1977-79; personnel mgr. Rolm/Midwest, Chgo., 1979-82; office adminstr. Nutech Engrs., Chgo., 1982-83; office mgr. Am. Acad. Orthopaedic Surgeons, Chgo., 1983-85; dir. adminstrn. Telecommunications Industry Assn. (formerly U.S. Telecommunications Suppliers Assn.), Chgo., 1985—. Bd. dirs. Ctr. Tng. and Rehab. of Disabled, Chgo., 1981-84; vol. Northwestern Meml. Hosp., 1985—. Mem. Am. Soc. Assn. Execs., Am. Soc. Personnel Adminstrn. Democrat. Jewish. Home: 233 E Wacker Dr Apt 3913 Chicago IL 60601 Office: Telecommunications Industry Assn 150 N Michigan Ave Suite 600 Chicago IL 60601

CLEVENGER, SANDRA KAY, educator; b. Grand Rapids, Mich., Aug. 24, 1947; d. Philip and Beverly Jane (Storz) Elve; A.A., Grand Rapids Jr. Coll., 1967; B.A., Mich. State U., 1973, M.A. in Spanish, 1974; Ph.D., NYU, 1987; children—Tracy Jo, Amy Sue; m. Charles Clevenger, May 27, 1983. Grad. asst. Mich. State U., 1973-75; instr. Calvin Coll., Grand Rapids, 1975-81, asst. prof., 1981-83, assoc. prof., 1983-88, prof., 1988—. Mem. Am. Assn. Tchrs. Spanish and Portuguese. Home: 1981 South Shore Dr Holland MI 49423 Office: Calvin Coll Spanish Dept Grand Rapids MI 49506

CLEVER, ELAINE COX, information services consultant; b. N.Y.C.; d. Russell Scarlott and Estelle Ruth (Gilliland) Cox; m. Fred E. Clever, Feb. 18, 1944; 1 child, Eric Conrad. BA, Pa. State U., 1944; MS, Drexel U., 1962; cert., IBM Systems Research Inst., 1962; postgrad., Drexel U., 1976-78. Instr. reading Avon Sch., Barrington, N.J., 1954-59; librarian Woodland Sch. Barrington, 1959-63; librarian Haddon (N.J.) High Sch., 1963-64; head circulation dept. Temple U. Library, Phila., 1964-81; curator spl. collections WPVI-TV, 1981-85, curator contemporary culture, 1985—; v.p. Berrywood Internat., Inc., 1984—, ptnr. Answers/Info. Brokers, 1982—. Bd. dirs. Temple U. Cinematheque, Phila. Office Edn. grantee, 1969-70. Mem. AAUP (membership chmn. 1979—, nat. council 1980-83, v.p. chpt.), Nat. Assn. Women Bus. Owners (editor Greater Phila. newsletter), Nat. Com. Pay Equity (collective bargaining and organizing com.), Nat. Librarians Assn. (cert. standards com.), Theta Sigma Phi, Beta Phi Mu. Mem. Society of Friends. Clubs: Peale, Engrs. (Phila.). Office: Answers/Info Brokers PO Box 2194 Haddonfield NJ 08033

CLEVER, LINDA HAWES, physician; b. Seattle; d. Nathan Harrison and Evelyn Lorraine (Johnson) Hawes; m. James Alexander Clever, Aug. 20, 1960; 1 child, Sarah Lou. A.B. with distinction, Stanford U., 1962, M.D., 1965. Diplomate Am. Bd. Internal Medicine, Am. Bd. Preventive Medicine in Occupational Medicine. Intern Stanford U. Hosp., Palo Alto, Calif., 1965-66; resident Stanford U. Hosp., 1966-67, fellow in infectious disease, 1967-68; fellow in community medicine U. Calif., San Francisco, 1968-69; resident U. Calif., 1969-70; med. dir. Sister Mary Philippa Diagnostic and Treatment Center, St. Mary's Hosp., San Francisco, 1970-77; chmn. dept. occupational health Pacific Presbyn. Med. Center, San Francisco, 1977—; clin. prof. medicine U. Calif. Med. Sch., San Francisco; NIH research fellow Stanford U. Sch. Medicine, 1967-68; mem. San Francisco Comprehensive Health Planning Council, 1971-76, dir., 1974-76; mem. Calif.-OSHA Adv. Com. on Hazard Evaluation System and Info. Service, 1979-85, Calif. Statewide Profl. Standards Rev. Council, 1977-81, San Francisco Regional Commn. on White House Fellows, 1978-81, 83-88, chmn., 1979-81. Contbr. articles to profl. jours. Trustee Stanford U., 1972-76, 81—, v.p., 1985—; trustee Marin Country Day Sch., 1978-85; bd. dirs. Sta. KQED, 1976-83, chmn., 1979-81; bd. dirs. Independent Sector, 1980-86, vice chmn., 1985-86; bd. dirs. San Francisco U. High Sch., 1983—, chmn. 1987-88. Fellow ACP (gov. No. Calif. region 1985-89, chmn.-elect bd. govs. 1988-89); mem. Inst. Medicine of Nat. Acad. Scis., Calif. Med. Assn., Calif. Acad. Medicine, Am. Public Health Assn., Am. Occupational Medicine Assn., Western Occupational Medicine Assn., Am. Acad. Occupational Medicine, Chi Omega. Club: Stanford U. Women's (San Francisco) (dir. 1971-80). Office: 2351 Clay St San Francisco CA 94115

CLEWIS, CHARLOTTE WRIGHT STAUB, educator; b. Pitts., Aug. 20, 1935; d. Schirmer Chalfant and Charlotte Wright (Rodgers) Staub; student Memphis State Coll., 1953-54, U. Wis., 1957-59; BA, Newark State Coll., 1963; MAT, Loyola Marymount U., 1974; m. John Edward Clewis, Aug. 11, 1954; 1 dau., Charlotte Wright. Asst. to dir., housemother Leota Sch. and Camp, Evansville, Wis., 1957-59; tchr. math. Rahway Jr. High Sch. (N.J.), 1963-70; tchr. math. Torrance (Calif.) Unified Sch. Dist., 1970—, coordinator math. dept., 1977—, mem. math. steering com., 1978-83, 86—, mem. proficiency exam writing com., 1977—; mem. instructional materials rev. panel State of Calif., 1986. Sec., pres. Larga Vista Property Owners Assn., 1975-84; mem. Rolling Hills Estates City Celebration Com., 1975-81; treas. adult leaders YMCA, Metuchen, N.J., 1967-69; bd. dirs. Peninsula Symphony Assn., 1978-84; commr. Rolling Hills Estates Parks and Activities, 1981—, chmn., 1985. Named Tchr. of Year, Rahway Jr. High Sch., 1966; recipient Appreciation award PTA, 1984, Hon. Service award PTA, 1986. Mem. Nat. Council Tchrs. Math., Calif. Math. Council. Club: Philipides Track (sec. 1980-82, pres. 1982-83) (Los Angeles). Avocations: marathon running, camping, reading, computers. Home: 1 Gaucho Dr Rolling Hills Estates CA 90274 Office: Calle Mayor Mid Sch 4800 Calle Mayor Torrance CA 90505

CLIFF, JANE, biologist; b. Denver, Dec. 8, 1950; d. Edward Parley and Kathryn (Mitchell) C. BA, Lawrence U., 1972; MS, U. Minn., 1976. Community edn. instr. Hennepin County Vo-Tech., Mpls., 1977-78; biol. technician Wis. Dept. Natural Resources, Baldwin, Wis., 1978, U.S. Fish & Wildlife Service, Bemidji, Minn., 1979; forestry technician U.S. Forest Service, Blackduck, Minn., 1979-82; wildlife biologist U.S. Forest Service, Cass Lake, Minn., 1982-86; dist. wildlife biologist U.S. Forest Service, Blackduck, 1986—. Contbr. articles to profl. jours. Mem. NOW, Wildlife Soc., Nat. Wildlife Fedn., Wilson Soc., Am. Ornithol. Union, Nature Conservancy, Minn. Women's Consortium. Office: US Forest Service Blackduck Ranger Sta Blackduck MN 56630

CLIFFORD, DEBBIE J., finance professional; b. Torrance, Calif., July 7, 1957; d. Chester and Ruth Opel (Bonebrake) C.; m. Roger Lee Belsher, June 20, 1987. Student, El Camino Jr. Coll., 1976-77. Payroll supr. Filtrol, Los Angeles, 1978-82; payroll adminstr. mag. book div. ARA Services, Los Angeles, 1982-85; payroll supr. Epson Am. Inc., Torrance, 1986—; adv. bd. Automatic Data Processing, Boston, 1986-87, cons. users conf., 1987. Mem. Am. Payroll. Assn. Democrat. Home: 2008 Gates Ave Redondo Beach CA 90278 Office: Epson Am Inc 23600 Telo Ave Torrance CA 90505

CLIFFORD, DONNA E., tax professional; b. Norwood, Mass., Dec. 22, 1947; d. Ward Irving and Barbara Alice (Batchelder) C. BA, U. Mass., 1970; postgrad., Northeastern U., 1974-75, Suffolk U., 1976-80. Supr. underwriting research unit Sun Life of Can., Wellesley, Mass., 1973-78; sales assoc. Century 21 Tucker REalty, Randolph, Mass., 1978-79; asst. bookkeeper Ware Radio Supply Corp., Brockton, Mass., 1979-80; bookkeeper Bradford Hotel, Boston, 1980-83; owner, mgr. Clifford Assocs., Stoughton, Mass., 1980—; Fin. cons. Ch. of the Larger Fellowship, Boston, 1984—. Treas. Lifearts, Inc., Hanover, 1986—, First Parish Universalist Ch., Stoughton, 1985—. Mem. Nat. Assn. Enrolled Agents, Mass. Soc. Enrolled Agents, Nat. Assn. Tax Practitioners, Nat. Assn. Female Execs. Democrat. Office: 55 Pearl St Stoughton MA 02072

CLIFFORD, ETH, author, editor; b. N.Y.C., Dec. 25, 1915; m. David Rosenberg, Oct. 18, 1941; 1 dau., Zipporah. Editor, David-Stewart Pub. Co., Indpls., 1961-79; cons. editor, author Unified Coll. Press, Indpls., 1974-79; lectr. on children's books. Author: (juveniles) Red is Never a Mouse, 1960; (with Willis Peterson) Wapiti, 1961; (with Raymond Carlson The Wind Has Scratchy Fingers, 1961; The Magnificant Myths of Man, 1972; The Year of the Three Legged Deer (Booklist award Friends of Am. Writers 1973), 1972; Search for the Crescent Moon, 1973; Burning Star, 1974; The Wild One, 1974; Show Me Missouri, 1975; The Curse of the Moonraker, 1977; The Rocking Chair Rebellion, 1978; Look at the Moon, Help I'm a Prisoner in the Library; The Killer Swan (Library of Congress Children's Book of Yr. 1980); The Dastardly Murder of Dirty Pete; (adult books) Go Fight City Hall (included in anthology), 1949; Uncle Julius and the Angel with Heartburn (included in anthology), 1951; contbg. editor, author spl. materials for ednl. books, encys., dictionaries, Just Tell Me When We're Dead (Sequoyah award, Honor award, W.Va.), Harvey's Horrible Sanke Disaster, 1984 (Honor award), The Remembering Box, 1985 (listed one of Most Outstanding Books of Yr.), I Never Wanted to be Famous, 1986, Harvey's Marvelous Monkey Mystery, 1987, The Man Who Sang in the Dark, 1987. Recipient Young Hoosier Book award. Mem. Authors Guild, Children's Reading Round Table, Soc. Children's Book Writers, Book Group of S. Fla. Address: care Scott Meredith Lit Agy 845 3d Ave New York NY 10022

CLIFFORD, GARRY CARROLL, publishing executive; b. Washington, May 25, 1934; d. Thomas Patrick and Agnes (McGarry) Carroll; m. George Clifford, Jr. (dec. Aug. 1985); children: George III, Thomas Carroll, Eamon M. Grad., Carleton U., Ottawa; postgrad., Marymount U., Rome. Reporter Ottawa Jour., 1956-59; press officer Kennedy Campaign, Washington, 1960; freelance writer People mag., Chevy Chase, Md., 1961-74; corr. Time, Inc., Washington, 1974-80; bur. chief People mag., Washington, 1980—. Bd. trustees Lab. Sch. Washington, 1984—. Roman Catholic. Home: 146 Grafton St Chevy Chase MD 20815 Office: People Mag 1050 Connecticut Ave NW Washington DC 20036

CLIFFORD, GERALDINE MARIE JONCICH (MRS. WILLIAM F. CLIFFORD), educator; b. San Pedro, Calif., Apr. 17, 1931; d. Marion and Geraldine (Mustacich) Joncich; m. William F. Clifford, July 12, 1969. A.B., UCLA, 1954, M.Ed., 1957; Ed.D., Columbia U., 1961. Tchr. San Lorenzo, Calif., 1954-56, Maracaibo, Venezuela, 1957-58; researcher Inst. Lang. Arts, Tchrs. Coll., Columbia, 1958-61; asst. prof. edn. U. Calif. at Berkeley, 1962-67, asso. prof., 1967-74, prof., 1974—, asso. dean, 1976-78, chmn. dept. edn., 1978-81, acting dean Sch. Edn., 1980-81, 82-83. Author: The Sane Positivist: A Biography of Edward L. Thorndike, 1968, The Shape of American Education, 1975, Ed Sch: A Brief for Professional Education, 1988. Macmillan fellow, 1958-59; Guggenheim fellow, 1965-66; Rockefeller fellow, 1977-78. Mem. History Edn. Soc., Am. Ednl. Studies Assn., Phi Beta Kappa, Pi Lambda Theta. Home: 2428 Prince St Berkeley CA 94705

CLIFT, ANNIE SUE, nursing educator; b. Newbern, Tenn., Nov. 29, 1931; d. James L. and Mollie Sue (Gelzer) C.; B.S.N., U. Tenn. Sch. Nursing, 1954; cert. Tokyo Sch. Japanese Lang., 1964; M.R.E., Southwestern Bapt. Theol. Sem., 1967; student Union U. Extension, 1955-56, Memphis State Coll., 1956; M.N. in Rehab., Emory U., 1969. Gen. duty staff nurse John Gaston Hosp., Memphis, 1954-55; staff nurse Memphis and Shelby County Public Health Dept., Memphis, 1955-56; supr., asst. dir. nurses Parkview Hosp., Dyersburg, Tenn., 1956-59, acting dir. nurses, 1958; charge nurse (part-time) Harris Hosp., Fort Worth, 1959-60, W.I. Cook Meml. Hosp. Center for Children, Fort Worth, 1960; missionary nurse, fgn. mission bd. So. Bapt. Conv., Richmond, Va., 1961-75; gen. duty nurse Japan Bapt. Hosp., Kyoto, 1964-66, ednl. dir., 1966-67; instr. (part-time) Japan Bapt. Sch. Nursing, Kyoto, 1966-67; charge nurse, in-service dir. Jibla (Yemen) Bapt. Hosp., 1969-71; clin. instr. ob-gyn. Japan Bapt. Sch. Nursing, Kyoto, 1971-72, exec. dir., 1971-72; asst. prof. nursing U. Tenn., Martin, 1973-81, assoc. prof., 1981-88, prof., 1988—. Missionary, Fujisawa (Japan) Bapt. Ch., 1962-64; youth dir. Kyohoku Bapt. Mission, Kyoto, 1964-67; ednl. dir. Kitayama Bapt. Ch., Kyoto, 1971-72; instr. English as second lang. various schs. and hosps. in Japan, 1962-66, 71-72; Children's Sunday sch. tchr. Emmaus Bapt. Ch., 1972-77; dir. Acteens Dyer Bapt. Assn., 1976-77. Mem. Am. Nurses Assn., Tenn. Nurses Assn., Assn. Rehab. Nurses, Am. Congress Rehab. Medicine. Baptist. Contbr. book revs. on rehab. and phys. medicine to profl. publs. Home: Route 2 Box 10 Newbern TN 38059 Office: U Tenn Dept Nursing Martin TN 38238

CLIFT, ULYSSINE GWENDOLYN GIBSON (MRS. JOSEPH WILLIAM CLIFT), social worker; b. Port Arthur, Tex., Aug. 12, 1937; d. Ulysses Grant and Matilda Louise (McShann) Gibson; B.A., Fisk U., 1958; M.A., U. Chgo., 1960; m. Joseph William Clift, Aug. 10, 1963; children—Kory Grant, Nathalie Louise-Gibson. Med. Social worker social service dept. U. Tex. Med. Br., Galveston, 1960-65; caseworker Family Service, Berkeley, Calif., 1965-67; dist. dir. Family and Childrens Service Assn., Dayton, Ohio, 1967-69; caseworker, field work supr. Family Service, Berkeley, Calif., 1969-72; field work supr. U. Calif., Berkeley, 1969-72; pvt. practice, 1972—Chmn. function and service com., Lincoln Center, Oakland; bd. dirs. Lincoln Child Fin. sec. No. Calif. Med., Dental and Pharm. Assn. Aux.; sec.), Sinkler-Miller Med. Assn. Aux.; vol. Samuel Merritt Hosp., Oakland, Am. Heart Assn. Lic. clin. social worker. Mem. Nat. Assn. Social Workers (diplomate), Acad. Cert. Social Workers, No. Calif. Med., Dental, Pharm. Assn. Aux. (fin. sec.), Sinkler-Miller Med. Assn. Aux. (sec.), Alameda-Contra Costa Links, Inc., Jack and Jill AM., Inc., Alpha Kappa Delta, Alpha Kappa Alpha. Home: 14030 Broadway Terr Oakland CA 94611 Office: 3300 Webster St Suite 308 Oakland CA 94609

CLIFTON, ALMA CHRISTINA (TEENA), municipal administrator, consultant; b. Indpls., Feb. 8, 1925; d. Henson Raymond and Alma Christina (Sellars) De Bruler; m. John Robertson Clifton, Nov. 3, 1945; children: John Robertson, Christina Alma. Student, UCLA, 1943, U. So. Calif., 1944, Los Angeles Harbor Coll., 1961-63. Engring. draftsman Northrop Corp., Hawthorne, Calif., 1943-47; city mgr. City Rolling Hills, Calif., 1964-82; cons. Clifton Assoc., Napa, Calif., 1984—. Councilwoman 1957-64, City

Rolling Hills Estates, mayor pro tem 1960-62, mayor 1963-64, Com. Mayors, Los Angeles, 1960-64; trustee Torrance Meml. Hosp., 1980-82. Named Woman Year Germaine Montiel, Los Angeles/N.Y.C., 1975. Mem. League Calif. Cities (exec. com. city mgrs. dept. 1975-77), Internat. City Mgmt. Assn. (range rider 1982—) disting. service award 1985, life mem. award 1982). Clubs: Los Angeles Philharmonic (Palos Verdes, Calif.), Napa Valley Quilt. Home: 21 Lemon Ct Napa Valley CA 94558 Office: Clifton Assocs 21 Lemon Ct Napa Valley CA 94558

CLIFTON, ANNE RUTENBER, psychotherapist; b. New Haven, Dec. 11, 1938; d. Ralph Dudley and Cleminette (Downing) Rutenber; B.A., Smith Coll., 1960, M.S.W., 1962; m. Roger Lambert Clifton, Sept. 9, 1961; 1 dau., Dawn Anne. Psychiat. case worker adult psychiatry unit Tufts-New Eng. Med. Center, Boston, 1962-68, supr. students, 1967-68; pvt. practice psychotherapy, Cambridge, Mass., 1966—; supr. med. students, staff social workers out-patient psychiatry Tufts New Eng. Med. Center, 1973—, also mem. exec. bd. Women's Resource Center, interim co-dir., 1986—. Lic. clin. social worker, Mass. asst. clin. prof. psychiatry Tufts U. Med. Sch., 1974—, research dept. psychiatry, 1966-68, 73, 77—. Mem. Acad. Cert. Social Workers, Nat. Assn. Social Workers, Phi Beta Kappa, Sigma Xi. Clubs: Cambridge Tennis, Mt. Auburn Tennis. Contbr. articles to profl. jours. Home: 126 Homer St Newton Center MA 02159 Office: 20 University Rd Cambridge MA 02138

CLIFTON, JUDY RAELENE, assn. adminstr.; b. Safford, Ariz., Nov. 8, 1946; d. Ralph Newton and Fayrene (Goodner) Johnson; student Biola Coll., 1964-65; BA in Christian Edn., Southwestern Coll., 1970; married. Editorial asst. Accent Publications, Denver, 1970-73; expediter Phelps Dodge Corp., Douglas, Ariz., 1974-78; exec. asst. So. Ariz. Internat. Livestock Assn., Inc., Tucson, 1978-81; supt.'s sec. Phelps Dodge Corp., 1981—; sec. exec. bd. PAC, Phelps Dodge, 1985—. Mem. adv. bd. Ariz. Lung Assn.; mem. Am. Security Council, 1979—; leader 4-H, Douglas; mem. Rep. Nat. Com., 1978—, Conservative Caucus, 1979—. Recipient Am. Legion Good Citizen award, 1964, DAR award, 1964. Mem. DAR, Nat. Assn. Evangelicals, U.S. Tennis Assn., Nat. Assn. Female Execs., Inc., So. Ariz. Internat. Livestock Assn., AAUW, Eagle Forum, Freedon Found., N.Mex. Eagle Forum, Mus. N.Mex. Found., Sigma Lambda Delta. Baptist. Clubs: Trunk & Tusk, Pima County Republican, Centre Ct., Westerners Internat., So. Ariz. Depression Glass, Tucson Tennis, Rep. Senatorial. Home: PO Box 301 Animas NM 88020

CLIFTON, PATRICIA DAVIS, educational administrator; b. Miami, Fla., Apr. 3, 1945; d. Roy Lee and Rachel Susan (Pinder) Davis; m. Ivery D. Clifton, May 28, 1967; children—Kalisa Nicole, Kelli Rochelle. B.S., Tuskegee Inst., 1967; M.Ed., U. Ill., 1975; Ed.S., U. Ga., 1979. Tchr., Petersburg Pub. Schs. (Va.), 1967-70, Prince Georges County Pub. Schs. (Md.), 1970-71, Urbana Sch. #116 (Ill.), 1972-75; dir. reading center Champaign Schs. (Ill.), 1975-76; reading supr. Clarke County Sch. (Ga.) Dist. 1976-80, coordinator elem. and middle schs., Athens, 1980-83, coordinator middle schs., 1982-87; principal Hilsman Middle Sch., Athens, 1987—. Mem. Internat. Reading Assn., Assn. Supervision and Curriculum Devel., Phi Delta Kappa, Phi Kappa Phi, Kappa Delta Pi, Delta Sigma Theta. Democrat. Methodist. Home: 305 Idylwood Dr Athens GA 30605 Office: Hilsman Mid Sch 870 Gaines School Rd Athens GA 30605

CLIFTON, SANDRA ANN DAVIS, resources manager; b. Louisville, Feb. 1, 1938; d. Hal Jr. and Annie Laura (White) Scott; married; children: Terri, Valori, David, Traci, Chris, Sherri. AA, Ventura Coll., 1981, AS, 1982; BS, U. LaVerne, 1985. Clk. typist FTC, Washington, 1955, U.S. Army Fin. Ctr., Indpls., 1956-57, Alameda (Calif.) Naval Air Sta., 1960-61, San Francisco Naval Shipyard, 1962-63; typist City of San Diego, 1964-66; cashier to office mgr. Levitz Furniture Co., Oxnard and Northridge, Calif., 1971-73; clk. typist Naval Ship Weapon Systems Engring. Sta., Pt. Hueneme, Calif., 1974-75, mgmt. asst., 1975-78; with Dept. Energy, Las Vegas, Nev., 1988—; cert. instr. Prevention of Sexual Harassment courses, Pt. Hueneme, 1981—. Mem. Blacks in Govt., Ventura County, v.p., 1985—; mem., vice-chmn., chmn. EEO com., Pt. Hueneme, 1976—; participant Savings Bond Campaign, 1977, MESA Program, 1979, Summer Work Experience Program for Students, 1982, Career Devel. Day, 1983. Named Toastmistress of the Yr., Pt. Hueneme, 1978, Woman of the Yr. Naval Ship Weapon Systems Engring. Sta., Pt. Hueneme, 1980; recipient EEO cert. of achievement, Pt. Hueneme, 1979, plaque of achievement, 1981, sustained superior performance awards Naval Ship Weapons Systems Engring. Sta., 1981, 82, Naval Constrn. Bn. Ctr., 1985, 86, letters of appreciation for Combined Fed. Campaign, Naval Ship Weapon Systems Engring. Sta. and Naval Constrn. Bn. Ctr., 1976, 77, 79, 80, 83, 84, 85, 86, Blacks in Gov. Leadership award, Ventura County chpt., 1987, Black Affairs Com. award, Naval Constrn. Bn. Ctr., 1987, Outstanding Personal EEO Contbn. award, Naval Constrn. Bn. Ctr., 1987. Mem. Am. Soc. Mil. Comptrollers, Fed. Mgrs. Assn., Nat. Assn. for Female Execs. Office: Naval Constrn Bn Ctr Supply Dept Port Hueneme CA 93043

CLINE, CAROLYN JOAN, plastic and reconstructive surgeon; b. Boston; d. Paul S. and Elizabeth (Flom) Cline. B.A., Wellesley Coll., 1962; M.A., U. Cin., 1966; Ph.D., Washington U., 1970; diploma Washington Sch. Psychiatry, 1972; M.D., U. Miami (Fla.) 1975. Research asst. Harvard Dental Sch., Boston, 1962-64; research asst. physiology Laser Lab., Children's Hosp. Research Found., Cin., 1964, psychology dept. U. Cin., 1964-65; intern in clin. psychology St. Elizabeth's Hosp., Washington, 1966-67; psychologist Alexandria (Va.) Community Mental Health Ctr., 1967-68; research fellow NIH, Washington, 1968-69; chief psychologist Kingsbury Ctr. for Children, Washington, 1969-73, sole practice clin. psychology, Washington, 1970-73; intern internal medicine U. Wis. Hosps., Ctr. for Health Sci., Madison, 1975-76; resident in surgery Stanford U. Med. Ctr., 1976-78; fellow microvascular surgery dept. surgery U. Calif.-San Francisco, 1978-79; resident in plastic surgery St. Francis Hosp., San Francisco, 1979-82; practice medicine, specializing in plastic and reconstructive surgery, San Francisco, 1982—; cons. VA Hosp. Stanford U., Palo Alto. Contbr. articles to profl. jours. Mem. Am. Bd. Plastic and Reconstructive Surgery (cert. 1986). Address: 450 Sutter St Suite 2433 San Francisco CA 94108

CLINE, GLORIA, property management executive; b. Dallas, Nov. 16, 1953; d. Gerald Joseph and Joan (Brimberry) Cline; m. Russell Lee Poynor, May 14, 1977 (div. 1987). AS, Richland Coll., 1974; BS in Mktg. and Merchandising, Baylor U., 1977. Interior decorator DuBois Furniture Co., Waco, Tex., 1977-79; asst. closer Plano (Tex.) Title Co., 1979; mgr. office Appleton Electric Co., Dallas, 1979-80; tech. asst. Electronic Data Systems, Dallas, 1980-82; mgr. office, leasing asst. Collin Creek Mall Mgmt. Co., Plano, 1982-84; pres., dir. property mgmt. Ctr. Park Devel., Dallas, 1984—. Judge, bd. dirs. Miss Plano, Little Miss beauty contests, 1986. Named Miss Plano, MIss State Fair Tex., 1972. Mem. Internat. Council Shopping Ctrs., Inst. Real Estate Mgmt., Am. Mktg. Assn. (v.p.-sec. 1975-77), Bus. Profl. Women (publicity com. 1984-86), Bldg. Owners Mgrs. Assn., Women's Div. C. of C. (social com. 1985), Delta Delta Delta (pub. relations com. 1974-77). Republican. Baptist. Home: 906D South Weatherred Richardson TX 75080

CLINE, JOYCE NAN, sporting goods company executive; b. Raymondville, Mo., Feb. 13, 1929; d. Andy P. and Hazel Irene (Deweese) Johnson; m. Donald Holt White, Feb. 15, 1948 (dec. Sept. 1966); m. 2d, Harold Lloyd Cline, May 31, 1969. Diploma Draughons Bus. Coll., 1948. Gen. office staff Rawlings Sporting Goods, Willow Springs, Mo., 1956-57, office mgr., 1957-72, asst. plant mgr., 1972-82; personnel mgr. Mo. Regional Warehouse, Mo., Tenn., N.Y. and Springfield, 1982—. Bd. dirs. Willow Springs Ambulance Bd., 1970-74. Democrat. Methodist. Club: PEO. Lodge: Order of Rainbow (worthy advisor 1941-45). Avocations: hiking; wild flower enthusiast. Home: Route 1 Box 255 Willow Springs MO 65793 Office: Rawlings Sporting Goods Co 1859 Intertech Dr Fenton MO 63026

CLINE, KIMBERLY RENE, college administrator, lawyer; b. Morganton, N.C., July 26, 1959; d. Homer Irwin and Clara Bell (Miller) C. BS, U. N.C., 1981; MBA, Hofstra U., Hempstead, N.Y., 1986, JD, 1986. Dist. mgr. CIBA Geigy Corp., Summit, N.J., 1984-88; asst. v.p. Hofstra U., 1988—. Home: PO Box 10 Valley Stream NY 11582

CLINE, LUCILLE GLASSER, management company executive; b. Boston, Nov. 23, 1927; d. Abraham Albert and Ruth (Stoleski) Glasser; m. Penneth Melvin Cline, Mar. 10, 1946 (dec. Apr. 1976); children: Steven, Joni, Hope. Student, Boston U., 1943-46. Asst. property mgr. Payne Assocs., Inc., Newton, Mass., 1976-80, property mgr., 1980-83, pres., chief exec. officer, 1983—. Mem. Temple Emanuel, Brandeis U., Beth Israel Hosp., Children's Hosp., Dana-Farber Cancer Ctr., Am. Jewish Com., Am. Jewish Cong., Am. Friends Hebrew U., Multiple Sclerosis Found., Muscular Distrophy Found. Recipient Good Works award Am. Cancer Soc., 1982, 86. Mem. Internat. Council Shopping Ctrs., Newton-Needham C. of C. Democrat. Jewish. Club: Spring Valley Country (Sharon, Mass.). Lodge: NOEML. Office: Payne Assocs Inc 51 Winchester St Newton MA 02161

CLINE, PAULINE M., educational administrator; b. Seattle, Aug. 25, 1947; d. Paul A. and Margaret V. (Reinhart) C. B.A. in Edn., Seattle U., 1969, M.Ed., 1975, Ed.D., 1983. Cert. tchr., prin., supt., Wash. Tchr., Marysville High Sch., Wash., 1969-70; tchr./adminstr. Blanchet High Sch., Seattle, 1970-78; asst. prin. Edmonds High Sch., Wash., 1978-84; prin. College Place Middle Sch., Edmonds, 1984-85, Mountlake Terrace High Sch., Wash., 1985—; cons. Mem. Mountlake Terrace Centennial Commn., 1985-87; chair Assumption Sch. Bd., Seattle, 1977. IDEA Kettering fellow, 1984, 86, 87. Mem. South Snohomish County C. of C., Nat. Assn. Secondary Sch. Prins., Assn. Wash. Sch. Prins., Edmonds Prins. Assn., Assn. Supervision and Curriculum Devel., Phi Delta Kappa. Roman Catholic. Club: Women's University (Seattle). Lodge: Rotary (charter, treas. Alderwood club). Avocations: skiing; kayaking; backpacking. Office: Mountlake Terr High Sch 21801 44th Ave W Mountlake Terrace WA 98043

CLINE, RUTH ELEANOR HARWOOD, translator; b. Middletown, Conn., Oct. 31, 1946; d. Burton Henry and Eleanor May (Cash) Harwood; A.B., Smith Coll., 1968; M.A., Rutgers U., 1969; cert. translation from French, Georgetown U., 1978; m. William R. Cline, June 10, 1967; children—Alison, Marian. Reviewer, U.S. Dept. State, Washington, 1975—. V.p. Smith Coll. Class of 1968. Mem. Am. Translators Assn. (cert. in French, Spanish and Portuguese), MLA, Internat. Arthurian Soc. Episcopalian. Translator English verse: Yvain; or the Knight with the Lion (Chretien de Troyes), 1975; Perceval; or the Story of the Grail (Chretien de Troyes), 1983. Home: 5315 Oakland Rd Chevy Chase MD 20815

CLINGERMAN, KAREN SLANIKA, financial analyst; b. Mpls., Apr. 14, 1954; d. Raymond Anthony and Mary Ann (Kornovich) Slanika; m. Thomas Burdette, May 22, 1976; children: Michael Thomas, John Anthony. AA in Bus., Kirkwood Coll., 1983; BS in Acct. magna cum laude, Mt. Mercy Coll., 1985. Cashier Bank of Nev., Las Vegas, 1975-77; loan clk. First Security Bank of Idaho, Mt. Home, 1977-80; asst. staff acct. Iowa Electric Light and Power, Cedar Rapids, 1984-85, asst. internal auditor, 1984-85; fin. analyst Rockwell Internat., Cedar Rapids, 1984-85, sr. fin. analyst, 1986—. Mem. Nat. Contract Mgmt. Assn., Am. Bus. Women's Assn, Nat. Female Execs., Internat. Women's Air and Space Mus., Phi Theta Kappa, Kappa Gamma Pi. Democrat. Roman Catholic. Home: Rt 1 Box 269C Solon IA 52333 Office: Rockwell Internat 400 Collins Rd 124-225 Cedar Rapids IA 52498

CLINKSCALES, ANNA LEE JAMES, civic leader, public relations consultant; b. Balt., Aug. 8, 1931; d. Jesse and Margaret James; children—Alfred Jr., Angela, Antonio Jose. B.A., U. Md., 1973. Pres., Am. White House, Balt.; pres., founder Abraham Lincoln Reading and Tutoring Group, Balt.; founder, dir. Community Services Info Ctr., Balt.; owner Original Design by Anna (Swedish embroidery), Balt., 1976-77. Writer pilot program Stay In Sch. (Youth Opportunity award Pres. Lyndon B. Johnson, 1967). Convenor First Job Corps for Girls, Balt. (cited by OEC for outstanding service); chmn. first coordinating council Women in Community Service; former mem. steering com. Interracial and Interreligious Council W. Balt.; former bd. dirs. Balt. chpt. NAACP, Balt. Neighborhoods Inc., Greater Balt. Com., Allendale-Lynhurst Neighborhood Assn.; pres. Md., Nat. Council Negro Women. Recipient award Nat. Council Negro Women, 1967; honored by Pres. U.S., 1972, 73. Mem. Colonial and Indian Am. Cultures Internat. (coordinator, founder, dir. 1983), Colonial and Indian Am. Crafts Internat. (coordinator, founder, dir. 1983), Cultural Relations Internat. (coordinator 1983), Hobbies and Crafts Assn. (founder, dir.). Democrat. Roman Catholic.

CLINTON, KATHERINE LOUIS, systems engineer; b. Albany, Ga., Sept. 20, 1954; d. Johnny James Sr. and Juliette (Allen) Slaton; m. Walker Arthur Clinton, June 11, 1977 (div. 1983); 1 child, Walker Andreas. AA in Mathematics, Albany Jr. Coll., 1974; BA in Mathematics, Albany State Coll., 1977; MS in Computer Sci., Fla. Inst. Tech., Melbourne, 1983. Electronics engr. NASA, Kennedy Space Ctr., Fla., 1977-83; sr. systems engineer E-Systems, Inc., Falls Church, Va., 1983—; cons. in field. Mem. dir. The Media Arts Ctr., Washington, 1986—, pub. relations dir., 1986—. Recipient Group Achievement award NASA, 1980, 83; named one of Outstanding Young Women of Am., 1984. Fellow Nat. Assn. Female Execs., Internat. TV Assn., Am. Entrepreneur Assn.; mem. Nat. Tech. Assn. (officer 1982—, chpt. pres. 1985—, nat. sec. 1987-88). Democrat. Home: 1419 Kingstream Dr Herndon VA 22070

CLIVER (KRIENKE), KENDRA-JEAN, art dealer, artist; b. Plainfield, N.J.; d. Edwin Kendall and Estelle (Blaine) C., m. Douglas Elliott Krienke, July 21, 1973. B.A., Drew U., postgrad. NAD. Freelance portrait painter, 1970-75; art restorer, 1970—; art framer, designer, 1974—; owner, mgr. Whistler Gallery, Inc., Basking Ridge, N.J., 1974—; arranger, catalogue artist exhbns.; commd. Douglas Coll., U.S. Steel Co. Recipient Purchase award Drew U., 1968. Office: PO Box 362 Basking Ridge NJ 07920

CLOAR, PATRICIA ANN SANDSTEAD, artist, illustrator; b. Harrison, Ark., Sept. 22, 1932; d. Ronald Dennis and Eva Jewell (Pumphrey) Sandstead; m. Vincent M. Harrington III, Oct. 7, 1951 (div. Jan. 1973); children: Barbara Ann, Eve Elisabeth; m. Carroll Cloar. Student, Cottey Coll., 1948-49, U. Ark., 1949-51; B in Secondary Edn., Ark. State U., 1959. Prin. Pat Cloar, Inc., Memphis, 1976—; cons. Memphis Brooks Mus. Art, 1976—, Memphis State U., 1985—, Fontaine House: curator various exhbns. Memphis Brooks Mus. ARt, 1982, 85; lectr. in field. Illustrator: The Caring Woman, 1985; one-woman shows include Oates Gallery, Memphis, 1982, McCarty Gallery, Monteagle, Tenn., 1983, Leu Gallery, Nashville, 1985, 86, Memphis Brooks Mus. Art, 1986, The Round Table, Memphis, 1986, 87, Albers Fine Art Gallery, Memphis, 1987. Recipient award Tombigbee Women Miss., 1984. Mem. ASCAP. Democrat. Presbyterian. Home and Office: 235 S Greer St Memphis TN 38111

CLOHESY, STEPHANIE J., agency administrator, consultant; b. Morgantown, W.Va., Sept. 23, 1948; d. Edward John and Josephine (Pytlak) Jagucki; m. William Warren Clohesy, June 19, 1971. BA, Loyola U., 1970. Adminstrv. dir. Ctr. for Policy Research, N.Y.C., 1972-77; exec. dir. NOW Legal Def. and Edn. Fund, N.Y.C., 1977-85; dir. Fund for the Future Fgn. Policy Assn., N.Y.C., 1985-87; program dir. Kellogg Found., 1987&; cons. Internat. Ctr. for Family Medicine, Buenos Aires, 1985—, Conciencia, Buenos Aires, 1985—, Bus. and Profl. Women, Inc., Buenos Aires, 1985—; bd .dirs. OEF Internat., Washington. Bd. dirs. Resources for Children with Spl. Needs, N.Y.C., 1980—, Ensemble Studio Theatre, N.Y.C. Nat. Leadership fellow Kellogg Found., 1983-86. Mem. Women in Devel., Spanish Inst. N.Y. Home: 230 W 107th St Apt 5C New York NY 10025 Office: Fgn Policy Assn 205 Lexington New York NY 10016

CLOPINE, MARJORIE SHOWERS, librarian; b. N.Y.C., June 25, 1914; d. Ralph Walter and Angelina (Jackson) Showers; m. John Junior Clopine, June 19, 1948 (div.); m. Frank Mason Storck, Sept. 14, 1985. B.A., Pa. State U., 1935; M.S., Drexel U., 1936; M.S., Columbia U., 1949. Gen. asst. Library, Drexel U., Phila., 1937-42; asst. librarian Gen. Chem. Div., Allied Chem. Corp., Morristown, N.J., 1943-46; bibliographer U.S. Office Tech. Services, Washington, 1946; med. librarian VA Hosp., Washington, 1946-49; asst. librarian U.S. Naval Obs., Washington, 1949-52, librarian, 1952-63; asso. librarian Bethany (W.Va.) Coll., 1967-69; asso. librarian Marine Research Lab. Fla. Dept. Natural Resources, St. Petersburg, 1971-73; cons. in astronomy Dewey Decimal Classification Editorial Office, Library of Congress, Washington, 1956. Chmn., Community Improvement program, Fla. Dist. 14, Gen. Fedn. Women's Clubs, 1980-82; library cons. Garden Center, Oglebay Park, Wheeling, W.Va., 1965-69. Alice B. Kroeger Meml. scholar, 1935-36. Mem. AAUW, Inst. Retired Execs. and Profls., Women's Resource Ctr. of Sarasota, Friends of the Arts and Scis., Internat. House, Nat. Assn. Ret. Fed. Employees, Spl. Libraries Assn., Beta Phi Mu. Clubs: Women's of Sarasota. Contbr. articles to profl. jours. Home and Office: 8400 Vamo Rd Apt 540 Sarasota FL 34231

CLOSE, ELIZABETH SCHEU, architect; b. Vienna, Austria, June 4, 1912; came to U.S., 1932, naturalized, 1938; d. Gustav and Helene (Riesz) C.; m. Winston A. Close, 1938; children—Anne Miriam (Mrs. Milton Ulmer), Roy Michel, Robert Arthur. Student, Technische Hochschule, Vienna, 1931-32; B.Arch., Mass. Inst. Tech., 1934, M.Arch., 1935. Draftsman Oscar Stonorov, Architect, Phila., 1935-36; designer Magney & Tusler, Mpls., 1936-38; partner, architect Elizabeth and Winston Close (changed to Close Assos., Inc., 1969), Mpls., 1938—; instr. Mpls. Sch. Art, 1936-37; instr. design U. Minn. Sch. Architecture, 1938-39. Prin. works include Garden City Devel, Brooklyn Center, Minn., 1957, Duff House, variety structures Met. Med. Center Complex, 1960-75, Golden Age Homes, 1960, Peavey Tech. Center, Chaska, Minn., 1970, Gray Freshwater Biol. Inst., Orono, Minn., 1974, U. Minn. Music Bldg., Mpls., 1985. Bd. dirs. Civic Orch. Mpls., 1951-68; bd. dirs. Minn. Opera Co.; past pres. New Friends Chamber Music; mem. Commn. on Minn.'s Future. Recipient Honor award Pub. Housing Adminstrn., 1964; hon. mention F.D. Roosevelt Meml. competion, 1960; named Outstanding Woman of Yr., YWCA, 1983. Fellow AIA (dir. Mpls. chpt. 1964-69, jury of Fellows 1986-87); mem. Minn. Soc. Architects (pres., Honor award 1975), Minn. Hist. Soc. (jury bldg. competition 1986). Home: 1588 Fulham St Saint Paul MN 55108 Office: Close Assocs Inc 3101 E Franklin Ave Minneapolis MN 55406

CLOSE, GLENN, actress; b. Greenwich, Conn., Mar. 19, 1947; d. William and Bettine Close; m. Cabot Wade (div.); m. James Marlas, 1984; 1 child, Annie Maude Starke. B.A., Coll. William and Mary, 1974. Joined New Phoenix Repertory Co., 1974; made Broadway debut in Love for Love, also appeared in The Rules of the Game, The Member of the Wedding, 1974-75 season; other repertory and regional theater appearances; appeared in Broadway musicals Rex, Barnum, 1980-81 (nominated Tony award); other theater roles include The Singular Life of Albert Nobbs, off-Broadway, 1982 (Obie award), Childhood, 1985, one performance oratorio Joan of Arc at the Stake, 1985; Broadway appearances in the Real Thing, 1984-85 (Tony award for best actress in drama), Benefactors, 1986; films include The World According to Garp, 1982 (nominated for an Oscar), The Big Chill, 1983 (nominated for an Oscar), The Natural, 1984 (nominated for an Oscar), The Stone Boy, 1984, Maxie, 1985, Jagged Edge, 1985, Fatal Attraction, 1987; TV films inlcude Too Far To Go, 1979, Orphan Train, 1979, Something about Amelia, 1984 (nominated for an Emmy), Stones for Ibarra, 1988, Les Liasons Dangereuses, 1988. Mem. Phi Beta Kappa. Office: care Creative Artists Agy Inc 1888 Century Park E Suite 1400 Los Angeles CA 90067

CLOSE, JOANN PATRICIA, electrical engineer; b. Washington, May 19, 1960; d. Richard Thomas and Jena Ethel (Larson) C. BSEE, MIT, 1982. Intergrated cir. designer Analog Devices Semiconductor, Wilmington, Mass., 1982—. Patentee in field. Mem. IEEE. Office: Analog Devices 804 Wodurn St Wilmington MA 01887

CLOSE, KAREN ELIZABETH, marketing company executive, educator; b. Chgo., Oct. 5, 1951; d. Gordon Ralph and Ruth (Kernwein) C. BFA cum laude, U. Ariz., 1973. Creative dir. Progressive Communications, Colorado Springs, Colo., 1976-78; art dir. PRACO Advt., Colorado Springs, 1978-80; creative dir. Erickson-Fuller Advt., Aspen, Colo., 1980-81; pres., owner Close Communications, Inc., Denver, 1982—; exec. distbr. Nuskin Internat., 1987—; instr. evenings Colo. Inst. Art, Denver, 1987—. Design corp. identity packages, 1987—. Active Big Sisters/Little Sisters, United Way, Denver, 1986; v.p. mktg. Jr. Golf Acad., Colo. 1987—. Mem. Nat. Safety Council, Denver C. of C. (spl. olympics com.), Kappa Alpha Theta (scholarship chmn.). Episcopalian. Club: Denver Athetic (medalist). Avocations: painting, playing piano and guitar, skiing, tennis. Office: Close Communications 2561 S Jersey Denver CO 80222

CLOUD, DOLORES ONA, educator; b. Ponemah, Minn., Aug. 6, 1941. Diploma in bus. tng., Haskell Inst., Lawrence, Kans., 1962; student, U. Minn., Bemidji (Minn.) State U. Tchr., coordinator ojibwe lang. pogram An. Indian S, U. Minn., 1969-74; tchr., coordinator ojibwe tchrs., tng. and linguistic workshop Bemidji State U., 1974—; cons. South St. Paul Schs., 1973-74, Interstate Research Assocs., Indian Day Care Project, Washington, 1973, Bur. Indian Affairs, 1972, Nat. Indian Edn. Assn., 1971; chmn. adv. council St. Paul Arts and Scis. Mus., 1973-74, panel speaker Nat. Indian Edn. Conf., Seattle, 1975; mem. Red Lake Edn. Task Force, tng. for Title IV staff Minn. Dept. Edn., also tng. for curriculum devel., coordinator Indian adult basic edn. program. Bd. Dirs. Ams. for Indian Opportunity, 1970-73; mem. Red Lake Band Chippewa Indians, Red Lake (Minn.) Indian Reservation; chairpersonSenate Dist. #4 Dems., Minn., 1982-83, treas. 1983, del. 1980, 82, 84, 86. Mem. Nat. Indian Edn. Assn., Am. Indian Student Assn. (pres. U. Minn. chpt., 1970-71, dir. 73-74, co-recipient FICRES Exemplory award 1988). Mailing address: 2824 Timberlane Way SW Bemidji MN 56601

CLOUDT, FLORENCE RICKER, architectural products company executive; b. Houston, July 12, 1925; d. Norman Hurd and Sallie Lee (St. Louis) Ricker; m. William Sandford Pottinger, Dec. 28, 1946 (div. Jan. 1975); children—Norman Sandford, Margaret Halliday; m. Frank Winfield Cloudt, Aug. 12, 1977 (div. May 1982). B.F.A., Tulane U., 1946. Founder, pres. Florence Pottinger Nursery Sch., Atlanta, 1955-56; tchr. Montgomery County Schs., Md., 1956-60; master tchr. The Nat. Cathedral Sch., Washington, 1960-62; founder, pres. Florence Pottinger Interiors, Atlanta, 1962-78; co-founder, v.p. Focal Point, Inc., Atlanta, 1970-78, pres., 1978—; mem. decorative arts adv. bd. Nat. Trust for Hist. Preservation, Washington, 1985-87; mem. adv. bd. family bus. forum Kennesaw Coll., 1987—. Producer pub. service TV program: Jr. League of Washington, 1957-62. Bd. dirs. Atlanta Landmarks, 1972—, Atlanta Preservation Council, 1988; sec. Roswell Hist. Soc., Ga., 1972-74; bd. advisors Atlanta Preservation Ctr., 1979, trustee, 1980—; mem. adv. bd. Family Bus. Forum, 1988. Recipient Industry Found. award Am. Soc. Interior Designers, 1982; Outstanding Service award Atlanta Preservation Soc., 1983. Mem. Women Bus. Owners. Republican. Episcopalian. Club: Women Commerce (Atlanta). Avocations: painting; writing. Office: Focal Point Inc 2005 Marietta Rd NW Atlanta GA 30318

CLOUTIER, PATRICIA AYOTTE, human resource administrator; b. Franklin, N.H., Mar. 9, 1938; d. Antonio D. Ayotte and Cecile (Bourque) Flanders; divorced; children: Michael, David, Scott, Donald. A in Court Reporting, Johnson & Wales Coll., 1975. Co-owner franchise Montgomery Ward Catalogue Store, Concord, N.H., 1968-70, Laconia, N.H., 1969-70; court reporter Jordan and Connelly, Manchester, N.H., 1975-76; co-owner Apartment House, Cape Canaveral, Fla., 1977-79; sec., med. staff coordinator Wuesthoff Meml. Hosp., Rockledge, Fla., 1978-85; human resource adminstr. Sheaffer Eaton, Pittsfield, Mass., 1986—; real estate agent Sunshine Realty, Titusville, Fla., 1980-84. Canvasser Heart Fund Dr., Concord, 1969; chair ARC, Rockledge, 1985. Mem. Nat. Assn. Female Execs., Sheaffer Eaton Mgmt. Club. Republican. Roman Catholic. Club: Hilton Hotel 9-5. Home: 247 E Harbor Rd Adams MA 01220 Office: Sheaffer Eaton 75 S Church St Pittsfield MA 01201

CLOVER, LOUISE SUZETTE, lawyer; b. Glendale, Calif., Mar. 11, 1954; d. Floyd Wesley and Sara Evelyn (Mulvehill) C. A.A., Glendale Community Coll., 1974; B.A., U. So. Calif., 1976; J.D., UCLA, 1979. Bar: Calif. 1979. Research asst. UCLA, 1978; law clk. to judges, Los Angeles, 1980-82; assoc. Adams, Duque & Hazeltine, Los Angeles, 1983-87; asst. U.S. atty. U.S. Atty.'s Office, Los Angeles, 1987—; prin. Clover Properties, Glendale, Calif., 1973—. recipient Am. Jurisprudence award Bancroft-Whitney Co., San Francisco, 1978. Mem. ABA, Los Angeles County Bar Assn. (coms.), Los Angeles Women Lawyers Assn. (bd. govs. 1981-82, appointive office 1982-83), Alpha Gamma Delta Alumnae Assn. (editor U. So. Calif. chpt. 1982-83). Democrat. Club: Altrusa. Home: 330 Lawson Pl Glendale CA 91202 Office: U S Atty's Office 312 N Spring St Los Angeles CA 90012

CLOYD, FRANCES SPEARS, real estate broker, consultant; b. Dallas, Apr. 11; d. William Thomas and Leilah (Pelt) Spears; m. Marshall Sadler Cloyd, Feb. 14, 1942; children: Marshall, Malcolm. BA, So. Methodist U., 1929, JD, 1931, LLM, 1959. Guest lectr. So. Meth. U. Law Sch., Dallas, 1960-61; assoc. Ebby Halliday Comml. Real Estate; v.p. Day Realty, Dallas, 1979-81; real estate cons. Dallas, 1981—. Bd. dirs. Dallas Grand Opera

Assn.; adv. chmn. Southwestern Hospitality Bed. Met. Opera, Mem. women's com. Dallas Theater Ctr., 1960—; mem. women's com. Dallas Civic Opera Soc., Dallas Art Mus. League, Dallas Mus. Fine Arts. Mem. ABA, Nat. Assn. Realtors, Internat. Real Estate Fedn., Nat. Arbitration Assn. (mem. panels), Tex. Bar Assn., Tex. Bd. Realtors, Dallas Bar Assn., Dallas Bd. Realtors, Daus. Republic of Tex., Pi Beta Phi. Clubs: Dallas Country, Dallas Woman's, Dallas Dinner Dance, Dallas Garden; Thalia; Carrousel; Cadence.

CLUTTER, MARY ELIZABETH, government official; b. Charleroi, Pa.; BS, Allegheny Coll., 1953, DSc, 1976; MS, U. Pitts., 1957, PhD in Botany, 1960; Research assoc. Yale U., 1961-73, lectr. biology, 1965-78, sr. research assoc., 1973-78; program dir. NSF, Washington, 1976-81, sect. head, 1981-84, div. dir., 1984-85, 87—, sr. sci. adviser, 1985-87. Mem. AAAS (bd. dirs. Washington), Am. Soc. Cell Biology, Am. Soc. Plant Physiologists, Soc. Devel. Biology, Assn. Women in Sci. Office: NSF 1800 G St NW Washington DC 20550

CLUTTER, PAULA DUZMATI, counselor; b. Bridgeport, Conn., Dec. 14, 1946; d. Paul Peter and Florence Rita (DeLeo) D.; m. George A. Clutter, Sept. 28, 1974. BA cum laude, St. Joseph Coll., 1968; MA, George Washington U., Washington, 1969; postgrad., U. Va., 1971-77. Personnel asst. U. Bridgeport (Conn.), 1968; guidance dir. Immaculata Preparatory Sch., Washington, 1969-74; employment interviewer Va. Employment Commn., Alexandria, 1975-78, employment counselor, 1978-83; job seeking skills program coordinator Va. Dept. Rehabilitative Services, Falls Church, Va., 1983—; speaker and participant at govt. social service seminars. Mem. Am. Assn. Counseling and Devel., Nat. Employment Counselors Assn. Office: Va Dept Rehabilitative Services 2831 Graham Rd Falls Church VA 22042

CLYBURN, ROSE MARY REED, marketing manager; b. New London, Conn., July 31, 1954; d. Raymond Morgan and Bernice Joan (Zaugg) Reed; B.S. in Zoology, U. R.I., 1976; M.B.A. in Fin., Northwe. U., 1984; m. Collins G. Clyburn, Aug. 14, 1982. Market research trainee PPG Industries Chems. Group, Pitts., 1976-77, field sales rep., Houston, 1977-78, sales rep. Chems. div., Chgo., 1978-80, sales devel. rep. splty. products unit, Chgo., 1980-83, market research assoc. Chems. Group, Pitts., 1983-86, product mgr. Chems. Group, 1986—. Advisor Pitts. Jr. Achievement, 1976-77. Mem. Soc. Plastic Engrs., Soc. Petroleum Engrs., Chem. Market Research Assn., Vinyl Inst. Home: 2484 Corteland Dr Pittsburgh PA 15241 Office: One PPG Pl 35W Pittsburgh PA 15272

CLYMORE, SUE ALLISON, accountant; b. Portsmouth, Va., Apr. 19, 1959; d. Robert Stetson Perry and Shirley Carole (York) Dickter; m. Ray Allen Clymore Jr., June 12, 1982. BS in Acctg., Loyola Marymount U., 1981. CPA, Calif. Sr. auditor Touche Ross and Co., Los Angeles, 1981-85; fin. rep. mgr. Thrifty Corp., Los Angeles, 1985-86; sr. fin. analyst Toyota Motor Credit Corp., Torrance, Calif., 1987-88, adminstr. systems devel., 1988—. Mem. Am. Inst. CPA's, Calif. Soc. CPA's, Nat. Assn. Female Execs., Am. Soc. Women Accts. Republican. Methodist. Office: Toyota Motor Credit Corp 1515 W 190th St Torrance CA 90509-2958

COADY, MARY MARTHA, lawyer; b. Toronto, Ont., Can., Apr. 13, 1932; d. Charles Joseph and Margaret Theresa (Dunn) C. BA (hons.), Carleton U., Ottawa, 1976; LLB, U. Ottawa, 1979. Bar: Ont. 1981. Freelance translation contractor 1974-80; researcher Kent Commn., 1980-81; sole practice Ottawa, 1981—; with vis. tchrs. service Ottawa Bd. Edn., 1975-81. Chmn. Ottawa Psychiat. Rev., 1986—. Mem. Ottawa-Carleton Med./Legal Soc., County of Carleton Law Assn., Amnesty Internat., The Thomas More Lawyer's Guild Ottawa, Royal Commonwealth Soc., Criminal Lawyers Assn., Assn. des juristes d'expression francaise de l'Ontario, Advocates Soc. Office: 200-77 Metcalfe St, Ottawa, ON Canada K1P 5L6

COAKLEY, LYNN KESTEN, publishing executive; b. N.Y.C., May 30, 1952; d. Arthur H. and Dorothy K. Kesten; m. Terrence M. Coakley; children: Lauren Kaitlyn, Shannon Clare. BA, Cornell U., 1974. Exec. dir. Am. Helicopter Soc., Washington, 1977-81; v.p. Army Aviation Publs. Inc., Westport, Conn., 1981—. Office: Army Aviation Publs Inc 49 Richmondville Ave Westport CT 06880

COAKLEY, PATRICIA DAVIS VAUGHN, educator; b. Henderson, Ky., Feb. 22, 1941; d. Ralph Harold and Burnell (Willett) Vaughn; m. Douglas Price Coakley, June 21, 1963; children: Karen Lynn, Douglas Price. B, Murray State U., 1963, M, 1964, postgrad., 1975. Cert. secondary tchr., Ky. Grad. asst. Murray State U., 1963-64; dir. recreation Ky. Dam State Park, Gilbertsville, 1962, 64; phys. edn. Hancock Place High Sch., Lemay, Mo., 1964-65; tchr. Grand Rivers (Ky.) Sch., 1965-68; tchr. remedial program Barkley Boys Camp, Gilbertsville, 1968-69; tchr. Gilbertsville Elem., 1975-79; tchr. phys. edn. Sharpe (Ky.), Calvert City (Ky.) and Gilbertsville Elem. Schs., 1979-83; tchr. gifted North Marshall Jr. High, Calvert City, 1983—; instr. Career Tng. Ctr., Calvert City, 1969-70; developer gifted and talented program Marshall County Schs., Benton, Ky., 1982-83; commr. girls Little League Softball, Calvert City, 1981; instr. inservice Marshall County Schs., Benton, 1982-86. Pres. Calvert City Swim Team, 1983-84; chmn. Epsilon Sigma Alpha Benefit Bide Ride, 1976, participant Follies Benefit, Calvert City, 1980, 81, 82; chmn. Golf Tourney for Rescue Squad, Calvert City, 1982. Mem. NEA, Marshall County Edn. Assn., Ky. Edn. Assn., Commonwealth Inst. Tchrs., Ky. Assn. for Gifted Edn., Nat. Assn. for Gifted Edn., Relief Soc. (pres. 1985-87), Kappa Delta Phi, Alpha Omicron Pi, Epsilon Sigma Alpha. Democrat. Mormon. Home: Rural Rt 3 Box 233 Calvert City KY 42029

COAN, BEVERLY HOLLOWAY, administrative title clerk; b. Franklin, Ky., Aug. 31, 1954; d. Bruce Conrad and Estelle Marie (Knight) Holloway; m. David Lee Botts (div. Mar. 1983); children: Nichole Marie, Shawn Conrad; m. William James Coan; 1 child, Brice William. Receptionist Fredericks Acctg., Hialeah, Fla., 1970-72; nurses aid Palm Springs Gen. Hosp., Hialeah, 1972-73; asst. acct. Mondex Realty, Miami, Fla., 1973-74; sec. Audrain Med. Ctr., Mexico, Mo., 1974-79; with advtg. dept. Mexico (Mo.) Ledger, 1979-81; ins. salesperson Western-Southern Life Ins. Co., Mexico, 1981-84; mgr. Wal-Mart, Titusville, Fla., 1984-87; adminstrv. title clk. Space Coast Chrysler-Plymouth-Dodge, Titusville, 1987; sec. Dr B. Kohn, Titusville, Fla., 1987—. Mem. Mid-Mo. Artists Club (pres. 1981-83). Club: Greater Fedn. Women's (Mex.). Office: Dr B Kohn 1029 Garden St Titusville FL 32796

COATES, DIANNE KAY, social worker; b. Adrian, Mich., Jan. 4, 1945; d. John Milton Yaw and Margaret Esther (Skinner) Yaw-Carpenter; widow; 1 child, Cindi Kae McCarty. Student Jackson Bus. U., Mich., 1962-63; AA with honors, Macomb Community Coll., Warren, Mich., 1977; BA with high distinction, Madonna Coll., Livonia, Mich., 1979; MSW, Wayne State U., 1982; postgrad. Internat. Grad. Sch., St. Louis, 1984. Cert. social worker, Mich. Nat. service officer Mil. Order of the Purple Heart, Detroit, 1973-80; psychology technician VA Med. Ctr., Allen Park, Mich., 1980-84; clin. cons. HOMEBASE, Detroit, 1983-85; clin. social worker Community Counseling Assocs., Adrian, Mich., 1983, Roseville, Mich., 1983-87; clin social worker, Regional Psychiat. Hosp. Ypsilant, Mich., 1987—; area rep. Edn. Found. Fgn. Study, 1987—; ind. contract therapist Renaissance West Community Mental Health Services Clinic, Detroit, 1988—; vol. HAVEN, Pontiac, Mich., 1986-87; group counselor Survivors of Homicide Detroit, 1981-82. Mem. Nat. Assn. Social Workers (diplomat), Nat. Acad. Cert. Social Workers, Mich. Mental Health Assn., Social Work Assn. Madonna Coll. (co-founder), Mich. Alcohol and Addiction Assn., Wayne State U. Alumni Assn., Vietnam Vets. Am. (hon. life assoc. mem.). Lodges: Ladies Aux. Mil. Order of Purple Heart (region 2 v.p. 1985-86), Ladies Aux. VFW, Ladies Aux., DAV. Home: 1502 Elias Westland MI 48185

COATNEY, SHARON ANN, librarian; b. Kansas City, Kans., June 12, 1946; d. William H. and Irene M. (Vallis) Smith; m. Jeffery Richard Coatney, Apr. 2, 1966; children: Mark Stephen, Rachel Ann. BS, U. Kans., 1973; MLS, Emporia State U., 1982. Tchr. lang. arts Linwood (Kans.) Jr. High, 1973-84; library media specialist Linwood Schs., 1984-87, Oak Hill Elem. Sch., Overland Park, Kans., 1987—; sec. KAW Valley Regional Inservice Council, Lawrence, 1985-86; evaluator North Cen. Assn. Evaluation team, St. Mary's, Kans., 1987. Founder Citizens for Community Schs., Marquette, Kans., 1986-87; trustee Linwood Community Library, 1980-87, treas. 1986 87. Kans. Network Bd grantee, 1986, 87. Mem. NEA, Kans. Assn. Sch. Librarians, Kans. Assn. of Edn. and Communication Techs. Republican. Baptist. Home: Box 38 Linwood KS 66052 Office: Oak Hill Elem Sch Blue Valley Dist #229 Overland Park KS 66204

COATNEY, SHERRY KAY, cartographer; b. Pinckneyville, Ill., Jan. 10, 1960; d. Willis E. and Thelma E. (Millikin) C.; m. David H. Niemi, Sept. 1, 1984. BA, U. Wis., 1982. Coordinator, estimator Rand McNally & Co., Skokie, Ill., 1982-84; cartographer The Nakata Planning Group, Colorado Springs, 1984-85, Analytical Surveys, Inc., Colorado Springs, 1985—. Mem. Am. Congress on Surveying and Mapping. Methodist. Home: 1355 Becky Dr Colorado Springs CO 80921 Office: Analytical Surveys Inc 1935 Jamboree Dr Colorado Springs CO 80920

COBB, CAROLYN ANN, communications consultant; b. St. Louis, Feb. 21, 1950; d. Vincent Atlee and Margaret Elizabeth (Ottinger) Knopp; m. Richard Joseph Cobb, Aug. 7, 1976; children: Richard Joseph, Cassandra Ann. BA, Harris Tchrs. Coll., 1973; MA, Webster Coll., 1975. Tchr. St. Louis Pub. Schs. 1973-74; programmer Gen. Am. Life, 1974-75, Mercantile Trust Co., N.A. 1975-78; programmer/analyst Mo. Pacific R.R. 1979-81; data base adminstr. staff specialist Southwestern Bell, St. Louis 1981-84; sr. cons. CAP Gemini Am., 1984-87; sr. cons. Codd & Date Cons. Group, 1987-88; pres., C2 Cons. Corp., 1988—. Editor: Fundamentals of Data Communications and Networking. Fin. chmn., mem. various coms. United Ch. of Christ, Oakville, Mo., also softball and volleyball coach, mem. choir and adult fellowship; youth group leader Grace United Ch. of Christ; adviser Drop-In Ctr.; data processing adviser Explorer Post, Boy Scouts Am. Mem. Assn. Systems Mgmt., Data Processing Mgmt. Assn., Assn. Women in Computing (charter), Heart of Am. DB2 Users Group (founder), St. Louis DB2 Users Group (participant DB2 forum Dallas), Southeastern DB2 Users Group, SYBase Users Group, St. Louis Oracle Users Group, Britton Lee Users Group, Kappa Delta Pi. Republican. Home: 6520 Galewood Ct Saint Louis MO 63129 Office: 13035 Olive St Rd Suite 119 Saint Louis MO 63141

COBB, CAROLYN JANE, service executive; b. Harrisburg, Pa., Aug. 20, 1943; d. Edward John and Doris May (Magel) Swerk; m. Don Rickey Hall, June 1, 1961 (div. Dec. 1979); m. Phil Allison Cobb, July 10, 1981; children: Jon David, Allison C. Weaver. BFA cum laude, U. Tex., 1964. Tchr. NE Ind. Sch. Dist., San Antonio, 1964-66, Austin (Tex.) Ind. Sch. Dist., 1966-68; illustrator Tex. Employment Commn., Austin, 1968-77, instructional media technician, 1977-78, staff services asst., 1978-80, mgr. design/graphics, 1980—; v.p. Cruise Line Assocs., Inc., Austin, 1985—. Works adopted by Am. Greetings card co., 1981. Mem. Nat. Assn. Cruise Only Agencies (founding), Internat. Assn. Personnel in Employment Security (State award 1974), Nat. Assn. Female Execs., So. Watercolor Soc. (award 1983), Alpha Lambda Delta. Episcopalian. Home: 2610 Chowan Way Round Rock TX 78681 Office: Cruise Line Assocs Inc 3508 Far West Blvd #110 Austin TX 78731

COBB, CHRISTINE MARIE, accountant; b. Hot Springs, Ark., Aug. 30, 1952; d. Louis Madison and Josephine Marie (Campagna) Cobb. B.S. B.A. with honors, U. Ark., 1974. C.P.A., Tex. Analyst, sr. analyst Gulf Oil, Houston, 1974-81, dir., 1981-83; owner Christine M. Cobb, C.P.A., Houston, 1983—; lectr. in field. Mem. Am. Inst. CPA's (personal fin. planning div.), Soc. of CPA Fin. Planners, Tex. Soc. CPA's (chmn. com.), Houston C. of C., Alpha Chi Omega (pres. 1973-74). Republican. Methodist. Club: Ninety-Nines. Office: 11 Greenway Plaza Suite 1420 Houston TX 77046

COBB, ELIZABETH ANN, health maintenance group administrative director; b. Birmingham, Ala., July 16, 1949; d. Jack Maurice and Evelyn (Watts) Franklin; m. Lester Cobb, Aug. 6, 1971 (div. Sept. 1976); 1 child, Jennifer Leann. B in Social Sci., Samford U., 1984; postgrad., U. Ala., 1986—. Mem. Ala. Assn. Health Maintenance Orgns. (bd. dirs. 1985—, v.p., adv. com. 1985-86), Birmingham C. of C. (health and edn. council 1985—), Nat. Assn. Female Execs., Am. Mgmt. Assn., Nat. Mgmt. Assn., Phi Kappa Phi. Mem. Unity Ch. Home: 400 St Charles St Birmingham AL 35209 Office: Health Maintenance Group 936 S 19th St Birmingham AL 35205

COBB, PATRICIA ANN, lawyer; b. Dalton, Pa., Apr. 10, 1958; d. Paul B. and Anne Marie (Dabelko) C.; m. Paul E. Granahan, Nov. 3, 1984. BA in History magna cum laude, U. Scranton, 1980; JD, Syracuse U., 1983. Bar: PA, 1983, U.S. Dist. Ct. (mid. dist.) Pa., 1983. Compliance officer, in-house counsel First Nat. Bank Carbondale, Pa., 1983—; v.p., in-house counsel First Nat. Bank Carbondale, 1987—; instr. Am. Inst. Banking, 1987. Editor law rev. Syracuse Jour. Internat. Law and Commerce, 1982-83. Vol. Everhart Mus. Scranton, Pa., 1979-80; mem. Friends of Everhart, 1981—. Mem. ABA, Pa. Bar Assn., Am. Inst. Banking. Democrat. Roman Catholic. Home: Rt 1 Dalton PA 18414 Office: First Nat Bank Carbondale 41 N Main St Carbondale PA 18407

COBB, RUTH, artist; b. Boston, Feb. 20, 1914; d. Charles Edward and Bessie (Cohen) C.; m. Lawrence Kupferman, Apr. 29, 1937; children: Nancy Rose, David. Diploma, Mass. Coll. Art, 1935. One-woman shows, Shore Gallery, Boston, 1958, 60, 63, 65, 70, DeCordova Mus., Lincoln, Mass., 1955, Art Unlimited Gallery, San Francisco, 1961, Cober Gallery, N.Y.C., 1962, 65, 67, McNay Mus., San Antonio, 1966, Phila. Art Alliance, 1962, Galerie Moos, Montreal, Que., Can., 1969, Witte Mus., San Antonio, 1967, Harold Ernst Gallery, Boston, 1974, 75, 76, Midtown Gallery, N.Y.C., 1981, 82, Foster Harmon Gallery, Sarasota, 1984, Francesca Anderson Gallery, Boston, 1984, 87; represented in permanent collections, Boston Mus. Fine Arts, Brandeis U., Butler Inst. Am. Art, Munson-Williams-Proctor Inst., Addison Gallery Am. Art, Va. Mus. Fine Arts, DeCordova Mus., Tufts U.; featured in TV program Artist At Work, 1981; work featured in Am. Artist mag., 1979. Recipient awards Pa. Acad. Fine Arts, 1967, awards Allied Artists N.Y.C., 1966. Mem. Am. Watercolor Soc. (award), New Eng. Watercolor Soc., Allied Artists Am. (award), NAD (award).

COBB, SHIRLEY ANN, public relations specialist, journalist; b. Oklahoma City, Jan. 1, 1936; d. William Ray and Irene (Fewell) Dodson; m. Roy Lampkin Cobb, Jr., June 21, 1958; children: Kendra Leigh, Cary William, Paul Alan. BA in Journalism with distinction, U. Okla., 1958, postgrad., 1972; postgrad., Jacksonville U., 1962. Info. specialist Pacific Missle Test Ctr., Pt. Mugu, Calif., 1975-76; corr. Religious News Service, N.Y.C., 1979-81; splty. editor fashion and religion Thousand Oaks (Calif.) News Chronicle, 1977-81; pub. relations cons., Camarillo, Calif., 1977—; sr. mgmt. analyst pub. info City of Thousand Oaks, 1983—. Contbr. articles to profl. jours. Trustee Ocean View Sch. Bd., 1976-79; pres. Pt. Mugu Officers' Wives Club, 1975-76; bd. dirs. Camarillo Hospice, 1983-85. Recipient Spot News award San Fernando Valley Press Club, 1979. Mem. Pub. Relations Soc. Am., Sigma Delta Chi, Phi Beta Kappa. Republican. Clubs: Las Posas Country, Town Hall of Calif. Home: 2481 Brookhill Dr Camarillo CA 93010 Office: 2150 W Hillcrest Dr Thousand Oaks CA 91360

COBB, SUE MCCOURT, lawyer, educator; b. Los Angeles, Aug. 18, 1937; d. Benjamin Arnold and Ruth (Griffin) McCourt; m. Charles E. Cobb, Jr., Feb. 28, 1959; children—Christian McCourt, Tobin Templeton. B.A., Stanford U., 1959; J.D., U. Miami, 1978. Bar: Fla. 1978, U.S. Dist. Ct. (so. dist.) Fla. 1980. Tchr., Crystal Springs Sch. for Girls, Hillsborough, Calif., 1960-68; assoc. Greenberg, Traurig, Askew, Hoffman, Lipoff, Rosen & Quentel, P.A., Miami, Fla., 1978-83, ptnr., 1983—; chmn. bd. Fed. Res. Bank Atlanta, Miami br., 1984, 86, 88. Chmn., Dade County Super Bowl Authority, 1982-87; bd. dirs. Ransom-Everglades Sch., 1976-86; Expo 500, Miami, 1982-84; dir. United Way Dade County. Mem. ABA, Fla. Bar, Dade County Bar Assn., Nat. Assn. Bond Lawyers, Republican. Clubs: Boca Raton, Ocean Reef, Grove Isle, Indian Creek. also: 3030 K St NW Washington DC 20007 Office: Greenberg Traurig et al 1221 Brickell Ave Miami FL 33131

COBB, SUSAN CLASON, communications consultant; b. Bakersfield, Calif., Sept. 6, 1953; d. Wilmer Lincoln and Mabel (Montgomery) Clason; m. John Leonard Cobb, Jan. 6, 1979; children: Trevor Clason, John Christopher. BA in Communications, Brigham Young U., 1977. Audio journalist Mut. Broadcasting Network, Washington, 1977-79; asst. dir. pub. relations Ch. Jesus Christ of Latter-day Saints, Washington, 1979-82; cons., trainer U.S. Office Personnel Mgmt., Dallas, 1982—; speaker, seminar leader Nat. Sec. Week, 1984-88. Contbr. articles to profl. jours., 1983-85. Chmn. rapid response com. s.w. region Reagan for U.S. Pres. campaign, 1984; vol. dir. pub. relations Ch. Jesus Christ Latter-day Saints, Plano, Tex., 1985-87; mem. strategic planning com. Plano Sch. System, 1987. Mem. Internat. Tng. in Communication (pres. 1985-86), Nat. Assn. for Female Execs. Republican. Mormon.

COBBS, DOROTHY LEE, association professional, educational consultant; b. Olive Branch, Ill., Dec. 6, 1946; d. Alvin and Willie Mae (Peck) James. B.A., U. Ill., 1971; M. Profl. Studies, Cornell U., 1975. Multihosp. systems specialist Am. Hosp. Assn., Chgo., 1976—; pres. Cobbs & Assocs., Chgo., 1983, Assoc. Mktg. Services, Chgo., 1982—. Author: Egyptian Diagram, 1975; co-author: Financial Growth and Diversigication of Hospitals and Multihospital Systems; newsletter editor Directory Multihosp. Systems, 1981, merit cert., 1982; contbr. articles on health care to profl. jours. Mem. Young Execs. in Politics, Chgo., 1983; mem. minority recruitment Com. Cornell U. Edmund J. James scholar, 1966. Mem. Nat. Assn. Health Services Execs., Am. Assn. Preferred Provider Orgns. (bd. dirs.), Nat. Assn. Female Execs., Internat. Platform Assn. Alpha Lambda Delta. Democrat. Club: Cornell U. (Chgo.). Home: 421 E 45th Pl Chicago IL 60653

COBEY, VIRGINIA BRANUM, interior designer, civic leader; b. Chgo.; d. Albert Marshall and Hope (Engelhard) B.; m. James Alexander Cobey, Aug. 1, 1942; children—Hope Cobey Batey, Christopher Earle, Lisa. A.A., Stephens Coll., 1939; B.F.A. in Drama, U. Iowa, 1941. Hostess, Stage Door Canteen, N.Y.C., 1942-43; mem. Am. Theatre Wing, N.Y.C., 1942-43; actress Little Theater of the Rockies, 1939-40; asst. buyer I. Magnin, Los Angeles, 1943-44; stylist Macy's, N.Y.C., 1945; owner, designer Virginia Cobey Art/Antiques, Pasadena, Calif., 1978—. Bd. dirs. Women's Council KCET-PBS, Los Angeles, 1968; v.p. Pasadena Art Alliance, 1971-73; chmn., bd. dirs. Friends of Occidental Coll., Los Angeles, 1975-76; bd. dirs. Costume Council Los Angeles County Mus. Art, 1981-82, Friends of Vielles Maisons Françaises, Los Angeles, 1986—; bd. dirs. Internat. Student Ctr., UCLA, 1985—; founder, chmn. Southwestern Affiliates Southwestern Sch. Law, 1983-85, recipient plaque, 1985. Ford Found. grantee, 1971—. Mem. Mus. Contemporary Art Los Angeles (patron), Beta Sigma Phi, Pi Beta Phi. Republican. Episcopalian. Clubs: Valley Hunt (Pasadena), Smoke Tree Ranch.

COBEY BLACK, journalist; b. Washington, June 15, 1922; d. Elwood Alexander and Margaret (Beall) Cobey; m. Edwin F. Black; children: Star, Christopher, Noel, Nicholas, Brian, Bruce. BA, Wellesley Coll., 1944; postgrad., U. Hawaii. Exec. sec. to Irene, designer Metro-Goldwyn-Mayer, 1944; actress Fed. Republic Germany, 1945-46; women's editor Washington Daily News, 1947-50; columnist Honolulu Star Bull., 1954-65, Honolulu Advertiser, 1972-84; cons. HEW, Peace Corps, 1960-61; v.p. Mandalay Imports Corp.; bd. dirs. Pacific and Asian Affairs Council, 1986—, Honolulu Com. on Fgn. Relations, 1987—. Author: Birth of A Princess, 1962, Iolani Luahine, 1986; travel editor Bangkok World, 1968-69; publicist CBS-TV series Hawaii Five-O, 1978. Mem. Hawaii State Commn. on Status of Women, 1978-86. Democrat. Episcopalian. Clubs: Nat. Press, Royal Bangkok Sports, Outrigger Canoe, Waialae Country. Office: Mandalay Halekulani Hotel 2199 Kalia Rd Honolulu HI 96815

COBURN, KATHRYN, academic administrator; b. Atlanta, Dec. 17, 1943; d. Leslie Leonce and Isabelle (McMurray) Charbonnet; m. Richard Gardner Coburn, June 26, 1975 (div. Nov. 1984); children: Colleen Marie, Rachel Mary. AB, U. S. Fla., 1970. Tchr. Hudson (Fla.) Sr. High Sch., 1969-75; adminstr. Baylor Coll. Medicine, Houston, 1975—; cons. Coburn Cons., Houston, 1986—. Vol. The Life Tng., Houston, 1983, course supr., 1985; lay minister Christ Ch. Cathedral, Houston, 1984-87; grants writer Omega House Hospice, Houston, 1986—; mem. adv. bd. The Peace Project, Houston, 1986—. Served with USAF, 1962-64. Fla. State scholar, 1967. Mem. Am. Mgmt. Assn., Am. Assn. Female Execs., Nat. Council of Univ. Research Adminstrs., Soc. Research Adminstrs. Democrat. Episcopalian. Office: Baylor Coll Medicine Ctr Biotech 4000 Research Forest Dr The Woodlands TX 77381

COBURN, MARJORIE FOSTER, psychologist, educator; b. Salt Lake City, Feb. 28, 1939; d. Harlan A. and Alma (Ballinger) Polk; m. Robert Byron Coburn, July 2, 1977; children—Robert Scott Coburn, Kelly Anne Coburn, Polly Klea Foster, Matthew Ryan Foster. B.A. in Sociology, UCLA, 1960; Montessori Internat. Diploma honor grad. Washington Montessori Inst., 1968; M.A. in Psychology, U. No. Colo., 1979; Ph.D. in Counseling Psychology, U. Denver, 1983. Licensed clin. psychologist. Probation officer Alameda County (Calif.), Oakland, 1960-62, Contra Costa County (Calif.), El Cerrito, 1966, Fairfax County (Va.), Fairfax, 1967; dir. Friendship Club, Orlando, Fla., 1963-65; tchr. Va. Montessori Sch., Fairfax, 1968-70; spl. edn. tchr. Leary Sch., Falls Church, Va., 1970-72, sch. adminstr., 1973-76; tchr. Aseltine Sch., San Diego, 1976-77, Coburn Montessori Sch., Colorado Springs, Colo., 1977-79; pvt. practice psychotherapy, Colorado Springs, 1979-82, San Diego, 1982—; cons. spl. edn., agoraphobia, women in transition. Mem. Am. Psychol. Assn., Am. Orthopsychiat. Assn., Phobia Soc., Council Exceptional Children, El Paso Psychol. Assn., Calif. Psychol. Assn., Acad. San Diego Psychologists, AAUW, NOW, Mensa. Episcopalian. Lodge: Rotary. Contbr. articles to profl. jours.; author: (with R.C. Orem) Montessori: Prescription for Children with Learning Disabilities, 1977. Office: 826 Prospect Suite 201 La Jolla CA 92037

COBURN, PEGGY ANN, municipal official; b. Dayton, Ohio, Dec. 7, 1946; d. Hager Wilford and Edna Lorraine (Williams) Stamper; m. Chester Coburn Jr. (dec.); 1 child, Cristi. Grad.high sch., Camargo, Ky., 1964. Cert. class III water distbn. system operator, Ky. Mgr. water system City of Jeffersonville, Ky., 1970—, city clk., 1970—. Contbr. columns to local newspapers, 1984—. Precinct chmn. Young Dems. of Ky., Jeffersonville, 1970-75, Jeffersonville Dems., 1978—; sec. Camargo PTO, 1978-80; mem. Wilderness Road Girl Scout Council, Camargo, 1978-83, Am. Cancer Soc., 1980—; bd. dirs. Gateway Health Assn., 1986-87, Montgomery County Sch. Heritage Commn., 1985-87; sec. Jeffersonville HomeMakers, 1986—; vol. Gateway Early Childhood Devel. Ctr.; chairperson Com. for Montgomery County Sch. Mus. Named Ky. Col., 1976. Mem. Ky. City Clks. Assn., Ky. Rural Water Assn. Home: Rt 2 Box 253 Jeffersonville KY 40337 Office: City of Jeffersonville PO Box 127 Jeffersonville KY 40337

COCANOWER, LIANA CHERYL, lawyer; b. Salt Lake City, June 19, 1953; d. Elbert Ernest and Dorothy June (Smith) Miller; m. Michael A. Thiessen, Aug., 1973 (div. 1975); m. Michael Andrew Maher, Oct. 15, 1975 (div. Feb. 1981); m. David Lehman Cocanower, Sept. 21, 1983; children—Michael Whitten, Joseph Charles, Emily Elizabeth. B.E., Western Wash. State Coll., 1973; J.D., McGeorge Sch. Law, U. Pacific, 1979; LL.M. in Taxation, NYU, 1980. Bar: Calif. 1979, Ariz. 1980. Assoc. Lewis and Roca, Phoenix, 1980-85, ptnr., 1985-87; assoc. Storey & Ross, 1987—. Served with USAF, 1975-76. Mem. ABA (tax sect., com. small bus., chmn. subcom. on publs.. real property, probate and trust div., vice chmn. com on spl. problems of bus. owners), Calif. State Bar, Ariz. State Bar (cert. tax specialist, tax sect.), Phi Delta Phi. Republican. Presbyterian. Home: 202 E McLellan Blvd Phoenix AZ 85012 Office: Storey & Ross 4742 N 24th St Ct One 4th Floor Phoenix AZ 85016

COCHRAN, ADA, data specialist, writer; b. Lost Creek, Ky., Dec. 21, 1933; d. Shade And Doshie (Combs) Fugate; m. Alan Cochran, Oct. 1, 1956; children: Debra, Evangeline, William. Student Am. U., Kent, Ill., 1957-62; AA, Community Coll. La Plata, 1972. Dental office mgr. Dr. Arthur F. Furman, Brandywine, Md., 1968-77; data mgr. FCC, Washington, 1978—. Contbr. articles to profl. jours. Mem. Bapt. Womens Group, (pres. 1964-65). Served with USA 1956-57. Mem. So. Md. Writer's Vineyard (founder, dir. 1986—), Writer's Inst., Freelance Writer's Assn. Democrat. Clubs: Toastmaster, (pres. 1986-87), Writer's, (dir. 1985—). Home: 1003 Tyler Ct Waldorf MD 20601 Office: Cochran's Corner PO Box 2036 Waldorf MD 20601

COCHRAN, CAROLYN, librarian; b. Tyler, Tex., July 13, 1934; d. Sidney Allen and Eudelle (Frazier) C.; m. Guy Milford Eley, June 1, 1963 (div.). B.A., Beaver Coll., 1956; M.A., U. Tex., 1960; M.L.S., Tex. Woman's U., 1970. Librarian, Canadian (Tex.) High Sch., 1970-71; rep. United Food Co.,

Amarillo, Tex., 1971-72; librarian Bishop Coll., Dallas, 1972-74; interviewer Tex. Employment Commn., Dallas, 1975-76; librarian St. Mary's Dominican, New Orleans, 1976-77; librarian DeVry Inst. Tech., Irving, Tex., 1978—; with Database Searching Handicapped Individuals, Irving, 1983—; vol. bibliographer Assn. Individuals with Disabilities, Dallas, 1982-85. Mem. Am. Coalition of Citizens with Disabilities, 1982—, Assn. Individuals with Disabilities, 1982-86, Vols. in Tech. Assistance, 1985—, Radio Amateur Satellite Corp., 1985-86. HEW fellow, 1967; honored Black History Collection, Dallas Morning News, Bishop Coll., Dallas, 1973. Mem. ALA, Spl. Library Assn. Club: Toastmistress (pres. 1982-83) (Irving). Reviewer Library Jour., 1974, Dallas Morning News, 1972-74, Amarillo Globe-News, 1970-71. Office: DeVry Inst Tech 4250 N Beltline Rd Irving TX 75038-4299

COCHRAN, JACQUELINE LOUISE, financial/management executive; b. Franklin, Ind., Mar. 12, 1953; d. Charles Morris and Marjorie Elizabeth (Rohrbaugh) C. BA, DePauw U., 1975; MBA, U. Chgo., 1977. Fin. analyst Pan Am World Airways, N.Y.C., 1977-79, Gen. Bus. Group W. R. Grace & Co., N.Y.C., 1979-80; sr. fin. analyst Gen. Bus. Group div. W. R. Grace & Co., N.Y.C., 1980-81, mgr. fin. analysis, 1981-82, dir. fin. planning and analysis, 1982-85; v.p. fin. Am. Breeders Service div. W. R. Grace & Co., DeForest, Wis., 1985-87, v.p. feed ops., 1987—. Recipient Women of Distinction award Madison (Wis.) YWCA, 1987; named to Acad. Women Achievers YWCA N.Y., 1984. Mem. Am. Soc. Profl. & Exec. Women, U. Chgo. Women's Bus. Group, Dane County United Way Key Club, Mortar Bd., Phi Beta Kappa, Alpha Lamba Delta, Delta Delta Delta (advisor scholarship com. Madison chpt. 1985—, treas. 1986—). Republican. Methodist. Office: Am Breeders Service 6908 River Rd DeForest WI 53532

COCHRAN, LYNNE ANN, educator, remedial specialist; b. Carroll, Iowa, Mar. 1, 1945; d. Norman North and Dorothy Mae (Dean) Hoft. B.A., Briar Cliff Coll., 1971; M.A. in Spl. Edn., Ariz. State U., 1979. Cert. elem. and spl. edn. tchr., Ariz. Tchr. St. Edward Sch., Waterloo, Iowa, 1968-70; tchr. Chino Valley Sch., Ariz., 1971-77, program developer, 1974-76; spl. edn. tchr. Tuba City Pub. Jr. High Sch., Ariz., 1978-82; spl. edn. tchr., dept. chmn. Tuba City High Sch., 1983-86, curriculum developer, 1984-85; remedial specialist Eagles' Nest Mid-Sch., 1986—; founder, pres. Unltd. Learning Enterprises, Inc., Tuba City, 1983-85. Probation aide Waterloo Juvenile Ct., 1970-71; vol. instr. Prescott Spl. Olympics 1977-78; local coordinator Tuba City Spl. Olympics, 1978-80. Mem. Council Exceptional Children, Assn. Children with Learning Disabilities, Ariz. Edn. Assn., NEA, Tuba City Unified Edn. Assn. (pres. 1985-86), Delta Kappa Gamma. Democrat. Avocations: reading; piano; camping; hiking; writing. Office: Eagles' Nest Mid-Sch PO Box 67 Tuba City AZ 86045

COCHRAN, OLIVE LEIGH MYATT, retired educational administrator; b. Monroe, La., Sept. 8, 1907; d. Webster Andrew and Martha Fidelia (Morton) Myatt; m. Raymond Nevitt Cochran, June 4, 1940 (dec. Jan. 1985); children: Kathleen, Susan (Mrs. Susan C. Mingledorff). Student, La. State Normal Coll., 1923-25; kindergarten cert., Harris Tchrs. Coll., 1926; BS cum laude, La. State U., 1942; MEd, N.E. La. U., 1962. Tchr. rural schs., Ouachita Parish, La., 1925-27, Georgia Tucker Elem. Sch., Monroe, 1927-43, 55-62; tchr., owner Cochran Nursery Sch., 1949-51; supr. elem. edn. Monroe Sch. System, 1962-67, dir. elem. curriculum, 1967-73; organizer first spl. edn. classes Monroe schs., 1964; supr. spl. edn. Monroe City schs., 1964-73; ret., 1973. Active CD. during World War II. Mem. Internat. Reading Assn. (dir. local unit 1970-73), Assn. Childhood Edn. Internat. (br. pres. 1967-71, treas. 1971-83), La. Assn. Childhood Edn. Internat., AAUW, Delta Kappa Gamma, Sigma Tau Delta. Republican. Baptist. Home: 1105 N 7th St Monroe LA 71201

COCHRAN, SANDRA LYNN, veterinarian; b. Columbus, Miss., Nov. 10, 1953; d. George Alton and Clifton Jean (Bell) C. BS in Animal Sci., Miss. State U., 1975; DVM, La. State U., 1978. Pvt. practice vet. medicine Highland Falls, N.Y., 1981-83, Victoria, Tex., 1984—; owner, mgr. Acres of Animals Boarding Kennel, Victoria, 1984—. Served to capt. U.S. Army, 1978-81. Mem. Am. Vet. Med. Assn., Am. Animal Hosp. Assn. Home and Office: Acres of Animals Boarding Kennel Box 256 Victoria TX 77901

COCHRANE, JANET TERESA, furnishings and design company executive; b. N.Y.C., Feb. 23, 1946; d. Arthur Irwin and Patricia Sonya (Green) C. BS, Mercy Coll., 1964. Ops. mgr. Edward Don & Co., Ft. Lauderdale, 1964—. Mem. Nat. Assn. Female Execs. Republican. Roman Catholic. Club: Miami Country. Office: Edward Don & Co 2200 WS45th St Fort Lauderdale FL 33312

COCHRANE, PEGGY, architect, writer; b. Alhambra, Calif., July 9, 1926; d. E. Elliott and Gladys (Moran) C.; B.A., Scripps Coll., 1945; postgrad., U. So. Calif., 1951-52, Columbia U., 1954; m. Hugh Bowman, Nov. 24, 1954 (div.). Job capt. Kahn and Jacobs, N.Y.C., 1954-55; project architect Litchfield, Whiting, Panero & Severud, Teheran, Iran, 1956; archtl. designer Daniel, Mann, Johnson and Mendenhall, Los Angeles, 1956-59; individual practice architecture, Sherman Oaks, Calif., 1966—. Recipient Architecture prize Scripps Coll., 1945. Mem. Assn. Women in Architecture (life), Union Internationale des Femmes Architects. Republican. Episcopalian. Club: Dionysians (S. Pasadena). Author (musical) Mayaland, 1979; (play) I Gave at the Office, 1980; The Witch Doctor's Manual, 1984; The Witch Doctors' Cookbook, 1984; mem. editorial bd. Los Angeles Architect, 1978—; contbr. to Contemporary Architects. Office: 14755 Ventura Blvd Suite 1-626 Sherman Oaks CA 91403

COCHRANE, RUTH KARCHER, hospital laboratory administrator; b. Phillipsburg, N.J., June 8, 1957; d. Clarence Alfred and Doris May (Riffle) Karcher; m. Kevin Joseph Cochrane, May 24, 1981. BS, Douglass Coll., 1979. Med. technologist Muhlenberg Hosp., Plainfield, N.J., 1979-83; instr. hematology Muhlenberg Hosp., Plainfield, 1983-85, lab. supr., 1985-87; supr. hematology St. Clares Riverside Hosp., Denville, N.J., 1987-88, St. Luke's Hosp., Bethlehem, Pa., 1988—. Recipient Ingrid Brekke Nelson award Muhlenberg Hosp. Sch. Med. Tech., 1979. Mem. Am. Soc. Clin. Pathologists (cert.). Presbyterian. Home: 2112 Treeline Dr Easton PA 18042 Office: Saint Luke's Hosp 801 Ostrum St Bethlehem PA 18015

COCKE, HILDA GIBSON, industrial engineer; b. Pittsylvania, Va., Apr. 16, 1931; d. Joseph Robert and Annie Doris (Gibson) Gibson; m. Frank Curtis Cocke, June 2, 1951 (div. 1980); children—Carol Anne, Frank, Jr., David. Student U. Va.-Danville, 1964-66, Danville Tech. Inst., 1966-70. Timekeeper Dan River, Inc., Danville, 1951-52, specification clk., 1952-59, office supr., 1959-73, dept. indsl. engr., 1973-80, mill mgr. indsl. engr., 1980-85, sr. indsl. engr., 1985—. Mem. Luncheon Bus. and Profl. Women's Club (pres. 1970-71; Woman of Yr. 1970), Internat. Mgmt. Club, Phi Sigma Alpha (pres. 1971-72; Woman of Yr. 1969). Club: Starwood Garden (pres. 1981-83). Avocations: arts, crafts. Home: 152 Woodberry Dr Danville VA 24540

COCKER, BARBARA JOAN, marine artist, interior designer; b. Uxbridge, Mass.; A.A., Becker Jr. Coll., 1943; student Mt. St. Mary Coll., 1944-45, Clark U., 1945, N.Y. Sch. Interior Design, 1965-67. Owner, operator Barbara J. Cocker, Interior Design, Rumson, N.J., 1966—; owner Barbara J. Cocker Paintings of the Sea Gallery, Nantucket, Mass., 1975-86; tchr. adult edn. courses in interior design, 1965-68; artist, pvt. instr. marine art; pres. Maximus Praetorius Corp., Nantucket, Mass., 1979—; one-man shows marine paintings: Little Gallery, Barbizon, N.Y., 1971, Old Mill Assn., 1971, Pacem en Terris Gallery, N.Y.C., 1972, Central Jersey Bank & Trust Co., Rumson, 1971, 72, 74, 77, 79, Little Gallery, Nantucket Art Assn., 1975, 77, 79, 81, 84, 87, Caravan House Galleries, N.Y.C., 1975, 79, Guild of Creative Art, Shrewsbury, N.J., 1976, 81, 85, 88, IBM Corp., N.J., 1977, South St. Seaport Mus., N.Y., 1977, 80, Provident Nat. Bank, Phila., 1978, Gallery 100, Princeton, 1978, Bell Telephone Research Labs., 1982, 86, AT&T, 87, Midlantic Bank, N.J., 1988, Art Alliance N.J., 1983, Gilpin House Gallery (Va.), Swain Art Gallery, N.J., 1984; group shows include: Burr Artists N.Y., Guild Creative Art N.J., Composers, Authors and Artists Am. NAD, Salmagundi Club N.Y.C., Monmouth Coll. Festival of Arts, Caravan House Galleries, Pen and Brush Club, N.Y.C., N.Y.C., Lever House Galleries, N.Y.C., Nat. Arts Club, N.Y.C., Ocean County Artists Guild, N.J. Named Woman of Yr. Zonta Internat., 1986. Mem. Catharine Lorillard Wolfe Arts Club, Am. Artists Profl. League, N.Y. Guild Creative Arts, Nantucket Art Assn., Composers, Authors and Artists Am., Allied Artists Am., Monmouth Arts Found. (N.J.), So. Vt. Artists Inc., Pen and Brush Club (N.Y.C.). Address: 3 Rumson Rd Rumson NJ 07760 Other: Paintings Of Sea Studio Old South Wharf Box 574 Nantucket MA 02554

COCKRELL, DEBRA ANN, realtor, consultant; b. Rantoul, Ill., July 13, 1950; d. Veryl Clayton and Geraldine Marie (McConnell) Hewitt; m. John C. Sherrard, June 5, 1971 (div. July 1976); m. Franklin D. Cockrell, June 6, 1981; children: Matthew Franklin, Michael Allen. AAS, Parkland Coll., Champaign, Ill., 1970. Advt. asst. Needham, Harper & Steers, Inc., Chgo., 1970-71; ins. dept. head Citizens Bldg. Assn., Urbana, Ill., 1975-77; mem. staff Joint Cruise Missiles Project, Urbana, 1978; project head Vitro Labs., Silver Spring, Md., 1978-81; sr. system analyst Advanced Tech. Co., Reston, Va., 1981-86; realtor, bookkeeper, cons. Jackson-Temple, Inc. Realtors, Vienna, Va., 1987—; owner, cons. Computer Profl. Mgmt., Inc., Vienna, 1983—; cons., bookkeeper Carol Paris Brown, Inc. Realtors, Vienna, 1986—. Co-editor: (software manual) The Property Manager, 1984. Mem. Nat. Assn. Realtors, Nat. Exec. Females, Va. Assn. Realtors. Methodist. Home: 8600 Dellway Ln Vienna VA 22180 Office: CPMI 8600 Dellway Ln Vienna VA 22180

COCKRELL, PEARL HAND, writer; b. Gadsden, Ala., Jan. 2, 1921; d. Arthur H. and May (Jones) Hand; m. Harold R. Cockrell, May 11, 1946; children—Pamela Cockrell White, Jan Cockrell Mitchell, Donis C. Schweizer. Student Massey Bus. Coll., Cleve. State Community Coll., Chattanooga State Community Coll. Author: poems Sing On, America, 1976; Of Men and Seasons, 1978. Contbr. to mags. including Sci. of Mind, Home Life, Modern Maturity, Music Ministry, Grit, Vol. Gardener, Tenn. Voices, The American, Ch. Musician, Progressive Farmer, Nat. Daffodil Jour., Missionary Messenger, Am. Camellia Jour., Poet's Monthly, Encore, Pen Woman, Old Hickory Rev., Pegasus, The Sampler, Prize poems Nat. Fedn. State Poetry Socs., Clover Collection Verses, Sandcutters, Rose Garden, Garden Prayers, Alalitcom, others. Weekly columnist So. Democrat, 1973-80. Recipient Tenn. Fedn. Garden Clubs, Inc. Poet Laureate award, 1973, 74, 75, 76, 77, Am. Legion award, 1974, Freedom Found. at Valley Forge award, 1976, 1st place poetry awards Nat. Fedn. State Poetry Socs., 1974 (2), 79, Authors and Artists Club Chattanooga, 1972, Ala. Writers Conclave Lit. Competition, 1975, 77, 78, Mid S. Poetry Festival, 1976, 77, 78 (2), 80, 81 (2), 84, Nat. Contest Ky. State Poetry Soc., 1976, Nat. Contest Utah State Poetry Soc., 1977, Deep S. Writers and Artists Assn., 1978, Dalton Creative Arts Guild, Ga., 1981, Nat. Contest Fla. State Poets Assn., 1985, 1st place prize Ann. Contest Poetry Soc. Tenn., 1986 (2), 1987 (2), numerous other awards. Mem. Nat. League Am. Pen Women (historian Chickasaw br., Tenn. State Letters awards 1975, 77, 81), Tenn. Writers Guild (past v.p.), Cleve. Creative Arts Guild (1st place awards 1973, 74 (2), 79, Catriona Dow plaque 1974). Home and Office: 916 62d St Ct W Bradenton FL 34209

COCO, SALLY HAHN, veterinarian; b. Corpus Christi, Tex., May 10, 1954; d. Roy Emmit and Mary Jo (Middleton) Hahn; m. Lambert Baldwin Coco, Jr., Dec. 18, 1977; children: Lindsay Bridges, Stephanie Hahn. Student Nicholls State U., 1971-73; D.V.M., La. State U., 1979. Lic. veterinarian, La., Tex. Veterinarian, owner Westside Vet. Clinic, De Ridder, La., 1979—; relief veterinarian, 1979-82; profl. commentator pet health series on local TV sta. Frequent guest speaker Beauregard Parish Schs.; mem. Nat. Rep. Com.; bd. dirs. Beauregard Meml. Hosp., Beauregard Community Concerns. Recipient La. State U. Sch. Vet. Medicine Alumni of Yr. award, 1986. Mem. Am. Vet. Assn. (sec. student chpt. 1977-78), AVMA, La. Vet. Med. Assn., Central La. Vet. Med. Assn., La. State U. Vet. Alumni Assn. (pres.-elect 1981-83, pres. 1983-85), Am. Assn. Women Veterinarians, Young Women's League (v.p. 1986, pres. 1987). Republican. Baptist. Home: Star Route 1 Box 34 De Ridder LA 70634 Office: Westside Vet Clinic Star Rt 1 Box 34 De Ridder LA 70634

COCRON, GLORIA JEANNE, mental health administrator; b. Phila., Apr. 26, 1943; d. Donald George and Eunice Josephine (Miller) MacLennan; m. Ronald Robert Cocron, Feb. 8, 1964 (div. Dec. 1982); children: Lisa Anne, Cheryl Ann. Student, West Chester (Pa.) U., 1962-63; AAS with honors in Human Services, Montgomery County Community Coll., Blue Bell, Pa., 1977; student, NYU, 1987—. Case mgr., residential coordinator Penn Found. for Mental Health, Inc., Sellersville, Pa., 1978-81; residential dir. Lenape Valley Found., Doylestown, Pa., 1981—. Mem. Nat. Assn. Female Execs. Presbyterian. Office: Lenape Valley Found 500 N West St Doylestown PA 18901

CODDING, PEGGY ANN, music educator, therapist; b. Denver, Mar. 11, 1953; d. James Leland Codding and Betty June (Currence) Danyew. B in Music Edn./Therapy, Phillips U., 1975; MM, Fla. State U., 1982, PhD, 1985. Registered music therapist. Lectr. music therapy U. Wis., Eau Claire, 1979-82; research assoc. ctr. music research Fla. State U., Tallahassee, 1985-86; dir. music therapy Ohio U., Athens, 1986—; cons. music therapy, Athens, 1982—. Contbr. articles to profl. jours. Active various orgns. for handicapped. Mem. Nat. Assn. Music Therapy (assembly of delegates 1982, 87), Music Educator's Nat. Conf. Office: Ohio U Sch of Music Athens OH 45701

CODDINGTON, DENISE EASTLAKE, area manager; b. Erie, Pa., Mar. 9, 1954; d. John Locke and Marion Claire (Hanhauser) Eastlake; m. Paul Frank Coddington, Aug. 13, 1983; 1 child, Melissa Ann Braun. Area supr. Spence Mgmt. Services, Warren, Ohio, 1976-82; area mgr. Pizza Hut of Am., Inc., Nashua, N.H., 1983—. Mem. Nat. Assn. Female Execs. Home: 91 Eastside Dr Concord NH 03301 Office: Pizza Hut of Am Inc 6 Coliseum Ave Nashua NH 03063

COE, BERNICE, film company executive; b. N.Y.C.; d. Joseph Emanuel and Clara Gertrude (Rosenthal) Cohn; m. Barrie Stavis, May 17, 1950; children: Alexander Mark, Jane Devon. BA, Vassar Coll.; MA, Columbia U. V.p. sales and mktg. Sterling TV, Inc., N.Y.C., 1946-61; mgr. ea. sales TV div. Walter Reade Org., N.Y.C., 1961-70; pres. Coe Film Assocs., Inc., N.Y.C., 1970—. Bd. advs. NYU Sch. Continuing Edn., 1985—. Mem. Women in Film, Women in Cable, Am. Women in Radio and TV, Nat. Council Families and TV (exec. bd.), Nat. Acad. TV Arts and Scis., Assn. Internat. Film Animation. Avocations: reading, theater, concerts, operas, sailing.

COE, DOLORES FRANCES, human resources executive; b. Ft. Dix, N.J., Aug. 7, 1953; d. William Durr Coe. A in Applied Sci., Montgomery Coll., 1982; BS, U. Md., 1985; MBA, Loyola Coll., Balt., 1987. Recruiter Marriott Health Care Service, Washington, 1975-76; tng. mgr. Marriott Food Service Mgmt., Washington, 1976-79, dir. human resources, 1979-86; dir. human resources Marriott Bus. Food Service, Washington, 1986—; bd. dirs. Marriott Employee Credit Union, Washington, 1978-83. Republican. Morman. Office: Marriott Corp 819 10 One Marriott Dr Washington DC 20058

COE, ILSE G., lawyer; b. Koenigsberg, Germany, May 28, 1911; came to U.S., 1938, naturalized, 1946. Referendar, U. Koenigsberg, 1935, JSD, 1936; LLB, Bklyn. Law Sch., 1946. Bar: N.Y. 1946. Dir. econ. research Internat. Gen. Electric Co., Berlin, 1936-38; asst. to sales promotion and advt. mgr. Ralph C. Coxhead Corp., N.Y.C., 1940-44; law clk. Mendes & Mount, N.Y.C., 1944-46; assoc. Hill, Rivkins & Middleton, N.Y.C., 1946-50, McNutt, Longcope & Proctor, N.Y.C., 1950-52, Chadbourne, Hunt, Jaeckel & Brown, N.Y.C., 1952-54; asst. v.p., asst. trust officer Schroder Trust Co. and J. Henry Schroder Banking Corp., N.Y.C., 1954-76; dir., sec., editor Fgn. Tax Law Assn., Inc., L.I., 1945-55; tchr. Drakes Bus. Sch., N.Y.C., 1946-49; lectr. on estate planning to ch., women's and bar assn. groups, 1947—; tutor literacy vols., 1977-79; lectr. wills trusts and estates and photography Pace U., St. Francis Coll. Life mem. exec. bd. Active Retirement Ctr., Pace U., v.p., 1980-81, pres., 1982-85; Rep. county com. woman, 1948-50; former deacon, now ruling elder, chmn. investment com. 1st Presbyn. Ch., Bklyn.; v.p., chair house com. Florence Ct. Corp. Coop. Recipient Human Relations award NCCJ, 1979. Mem. Bklyn. Women's Bar Assn. (past treas., sec., bd. dirs. 1960—), Protestant Lawyers Assn. of N.Y. Inc. (sec. 1960-75, 1st v.p. 1976-77, pres. 1978-88, lifetime pres. emeritus 1988—), Internat. Fedn. Women Lawyers, Bklyn. Heights Assn., Bklyn. Hist. Soc. (investment com.), N.Y. Color Slide Club (by-laws chmn. 1983—, bd. dirs. 1973-74), Bklyn. Mus., Bklyn. Botanic Garden, others. Home: 187 Hicks St Brooklyn Heights NY 11201

COE, LINDA MARLENE WOLFE, small business owner, photographer; b. Logan, Ohio, Apr. 5, 1941; d. Kenneth William and Mary Martha (Eddy) Wolfe; m. Frederic Morrow Coe, Sept. 15, 1962; children: Christopher, Jennifer, Peter, Michael. BFA, Columbus Coll. of Art and Design, 1978. Freelance photographer Columbus, 1978—; sec., receptionist Plaza Dental, Columbus, 1983; sec. Worthington (Ohio) Dental Group, 1983-85; owner Custom Corp. Gift Service, Worthington, 1985—; bd. trustees Met. Women's Ctr., Columbus, 1986—. Docent trainee Columbus Mus. Art, 1982-83; mem. Worthington Arts Council, 1982, 83, 85, 87. Mem. Nat. Assn. Profl. Saleswomen, Columbus Bus. and Profl. Women, Columbus C. of C., Worthington C. of C. (com. mem. 1985—). Republican. Roman Catholic. Home: 320 E South St Worthington OH 43085 Office: Giftshopper 5757 Olentangy Blvd Worthington OH 43085

COE, SHERRI M., accountant; b. Bronx, Feb. 10, 1953; d. Irving E. Kovalsky and Selma (Becker) Denino; m. Frank Matthew Coe, Oct. 10, 1976; children: Stacey, Matthew. BA in Acctg., Rollins Coll., 1982. Various computer positions Mercedes Benz, N.Y.C., 1975-76; acct. Taylor and Assocs., Satellite Beach, Fla., 1982—, also bd. dirs.; cons. Donna's Haircrafters, Satellite Beach, 1984—, Indialantic Studio, Fla., 1984—. Treas., class mother PTO, Satellite Beach, 1983. Democrat. Jewish. Home: 295 Wilson Ave Satellite Beach FL 32937 Office: Taylor and Assocs 1355 S Patrick Dr Satellite Beach FL 32937

COELHO, JUDITH CAROL PRICE, medical technologist; b. Shelbyville, Ill., Aug. 20, 1942; d. Maurice Ray and Naomi Aileen (Milner) Price; B.S. in Med. Tech., Millikin U., 1970; cert. in med. tech. St. Mary's Sch. Med. Tech., 1969; m. Patrick S. Coelho, Jan. 16, 1971; children—Kawiki, Uilani. Lab. technician State of Ill. Dept. Agr., div. feeds, fertilizer and standards, 1961-63; lab. asst. Shelby County Meml. Hosp., Shelbyville, Ill., 1963-67, St. Mary's Hosp., Decatur, Ill., 1967-68, staff med. technologist, 1969-70; lab. supr. Molokai (Hawaii) Gen. Hosp., 1970-81; staff technologist Blood Bank of Hawaii, Honolulu, 1981-83; lab. supr. Pawaa Med. Lab., 1985-87; supr. lab. Kahuku Hosp., 1987—; instr. in field. Mem. infection control com. Molokai Gen. Hosp., sec., 1975-81, vice chairperson, mem. safety com., 1980-81; mem. safety com. Blood Bank of Hawaii, 1982; v.p. Kaunakakai Sch. PTA, 1979, pres., 1980-81; Cub Scouts leader, 1981—; tchr. Bible Sch., 1981—, vol. tchr. asst., 1983-84; sec. Pearl Harbor Ch. of Christ, 1984-85. Mem. Am. Soc. Med. Tech., Hawaii Soc. Med. Tech. (scholarship chairperson 1977-78). Mem. Chs. of Christ. Clubs: Malia Alanon, Molokai Saddle (sec. 1981).

COFFEE, CHARLENE DAUGHERTY, accountant; b. Athens, Tenn., Feb. 3, 1943; d. Charles McGee and Alma (Millsaps) Daugherty; B.S., U. Tenn., Knoxville, 1964; m. Joe Donald Coffee, Apr. 9, 1966 (div. Mar. 1986). Buyer trainee Castner-Knott Co., Nashville, 1964-66; asst. buyer, buyer Harvey's, Nashville, 1966-67; mdse. control clk., supr. Sears Roebuck, Nashville, 1967-73, acctg. mgmt. trainee, 1973-74, mem. point of sale implementation team So. ter., 1974-77, controller acctg. and processing center, Atlanta, 1977-80, staff asst., field report consolidation, Chgo., 1980-81, staff asst. acctg. policy and procedure, 1981-83, sr. staff asst. acctg. services, 1983-86; hdqrs. dept. controller, 1986-87; mgr. support services Sears Payment Systems, Inc. Ops. Ctr., Gray, Tenn., 1987—. Vice-pres. council Ch. of the Living Christ-Lutheran, 1985-86; dist. bd. dirs. Family Care Services Met. Chgo., 1984-87. Mem. DAR (rec. sec. Sarah's Grove chpt. 1985-86), AAUW, Delta Zeta. Home: 214 E 8th Ave Johnson City TN 37601 Office: Sears Payment Systems Inc Rt 16 Grays Station Rd Gray TN 37615

COFFEE, SUE, marketing communications manager; b. Alliance, Nebr., Sept. 23, 1954; d. Bill Brown and Virginia Claire (Kennedy) C. BA in English, Doane Coll., 1976; MS in Mktg., No. Ill. U., 1979. Grad. asst. No. Ill. U., Dekalb, 1977-79; nat. programs coordinator HDR Infrastructure, Inc., Omaha, 1980-87; mgr. mktg. communications Kiewit Constrn. Group, Inc., Omaha, 1987-88; mktg. pubs. mgr. HDR Engring., Inc., Omaha, 1988—. Contbr. articles to profl. jours. Bd. dirs. Jr. League of Omaha, 1987-88, editor JLO This Month, 1987-88; bd. dirs. adv. council Adults Basic Edn., Omaha, 1985-86, United Way Vol. Bur., 1986-87 vol. & mem. Nat. Pub. Radio KIOS, Omaha. Mem. Am. Pub. Works Assn. (com. chmn., editor Nebr. News 1984—). Office: HDR Engring Inc 8404 Indian Hills Dr Omaha NE 68114

COFFEE, VIRGINIA CLAIRE, civic worker, former mayor; b. Alliance, Nebr., Dec. 8, 1920; d. James Maddigan and Adelaide Mary (Forde) Kennedy; BS, Chadron State Coll., 1942; m. Bill Brown Coffee, June 21, 1942; children—Claire, Sara, Virginia Anne, Sue. High sch. prin., Whitman, Nebr., 1942; bookkeeper Coffee & Son, Inc., Harrison, Nebr., 1965—, officer, 1967—, pres., 1987—; mayor City of Harrison, 1978-80. Leader, Girl Scouts U.S.A., 1953-63; mem. Harrison Elem. Sch. bd., 1958-64; mem. liaison com. Chadron State Coll., 1975—; pub. relations chmn. Nebr. Cowbelles, 1968; sec. NW Stock Growers, 1971-73; corp. officer Ft. Robinson Centennial, 1973—; officer Gov.'s Ft. Robinson Centennial Commn., 1973-75; hon. gov. Nebr. Centennial, 1967; chmn. Sioux County Bicentennial, 1973-77; trustee Nebr. State Hist. Soc. Found., 1975—, Village of Harrison, 1973-80; bd. dirs. Harrison Community Club, Inc., 1983-86, officer, 1984-86. Mem. Nebr. State Hist. Soc. (life, dir. 1979-85, 2d v.p. 1982-84, 1st v.p. 1984-85, com. for marker to honor Harrison centennial 1985-86), Sioux County Hist. Soc. (v.p., bd. dirs. 1987—, 83-84, past pres., Sioux county history book com. 1985-86, contbr. articles, dir., v.p. 1987), Wyo. Hist. Soc. Cardinal Key Honor Frat. Roman Catholic. Clubs: Sioux County Cowbelles, Nebr. Cowbells, Ladies Community, Harrison Community Inc. Contbr. articles to area newspapers; chmn. compilation com. book Sioux County Memoirs of Its Pioneers, 1967; coordinator Harrison sect. book Nebraska Our Towns, 1988. Address: PO Box 336 Harrison NE 69346

COFFELT, IDONNA, artist; b. Blackwell, Okla., Jan. 19, 1929; d. Wilber J. and Frances (Curfman) Groom; m. Guy D. Coffelt, June 5, 1948; children: Mark Allen, Todd David, Gregory Lee, Paul Scott. Student, U. Houston, 1967-68; BS in Elem. Edn., North Tex. State U., 1970; postgrad., East Tex. State U., 1971-72; student, Baum Sch. of Art-Barnstone Studios, Allentown, Pa., 1981-86. Cert. elem. tchr., Tex.; cert. spl. edn. tchr., Calif.; cert. art edn. tchr., Pa. Tchr. Moravian Acad., Bethlehem, Pa., 1976-81; juror Bethlehem Palate Club, 1982. One-woman exhbns. include Bethlehem Fine Arts Commn., 1986, Lehigh County Community Coll., 1985; represented in permanent collections DuPont Am. Olean; exhibited in group shows at Bethlehem Palette Club (Binney and Smith award 1986), Catherine Lorillard Wolf Club (accepted juried exhbn. 1984), Salmagundi Club, 1983, 88, Watercolor Art Soc., Houston, Hill Country Arts Found., Fine Arts Ctr. Taos (N.Mex.). Vol. tchr. Allentown (Pa.) Sch. Dist., 1975, LAISD, 1973; campaign recruiter Channel 39, 1981. Spl. edn. grantee, 1974. Mem. Lehigh (Pa.) Art Alliance (pres. 1982, bd. dirs. 1976-86), Hill Country Arts Found., Waterloo Art Soc., San Antonio Watercolor Group, Watercolor Art Soc.-Houston (accepted in juried exhbn. 1984, 85). Republican. Home and Office: Tierra Linda Ranch HCR5 Box 574-607 Kerrville TX 78028

COFFEY, BARBARA EILEEN, corporate executive; b. Bristol, Conn., Sept. 24, 1949; d. John James and Anna (Valencis) C. BS, Nova U., 1987; postgrad., Fla. Atlantic U., 1988—. Coordinator inside sales Tex. Instruments, Ft. Lauderdale, Fla., 1975-78; mem. mfg. engineering support staff Modular Computer, Ft. Lauderdale, 1978-79; product mgr. Arrow Electronics, Ft. Lauderdale, 1980-83; sr. acct. exec. Dielco Electronics, Ft. Lauderdale, 1984-86; pres. Cypress Components, Ft. Lauderdale, 1986—. Donor Broward Blood Ctr., Ft. Lauderdale. Mem. Women in Electronics (pres., founder 1984-86), Electronic Networking. Democrat. Roman Catholic. Home: 1827 Middle River Dr Fort Lauderdale FL 33305

COFFEY, BARBARA JORDAN, magazine editor, writer; Fashion editor Vogue Mag., N.Y.C., 1959-64; advt. writer Young & Rubicam, N.Y.C., 1965-67; writer Glamour Mag., N.Y.C., 1967-74, copy chief, 1974—, also mng. editor; books include: Glamour Health and Beauty Book, 1973; Glamour's Success Book, 1979; Beauty Begins at 40, 1984; How To Dress 10 Pounds Thinner, Look 10 Years Younger, 1988. Adv. bd. Women's Research and Edn. Inst., Washington. Mem. Am. Soc. Mag. Editors, Fashion Group, Women in Communication. Office: Glamour Magazine Condé Bldg 350 Madison Ave New York NY 10017

COFFEY, HELEN ELIZABETH, physicist; b. Chelsea, Mass., Nov. 17, 1944; d. Timothy Patrick and Helen Williamina (Stevens) C. BS, Merrimack Coll., 1966; MS, U. Colo., 1969. Mem. staff MIT, Cambridge, 1969-70; physicist NOAA, Boulder, 1972—, br. chief solar and high atmosphere br., 1977—; sec. Internat. Ursigrams and World Days Service, 1981—. High Altitude Obs. Astrogeophysics fellow, 1966-67. Mem. Internat. Astronom. Union (commn. X working group internat. programs), Am. Geophys. Union (treas. Front Range br. 1985-87), Am. Meteorol. Soc., Am. Astron. Soc., AAAS, Colo. Coordinating Council of Women's Orgns. (corr. sec. 1983-84), Sigma Xi (treas. Boulder chpt. 1985-86, sec. 1986-87, v.p. 1987—). Democrat. Roman Catholic. Club: Zonta of Boulder County (v.p. 1981-82, pres. 1983-84). Editor: Solar-Geophysical Data, 1977—; geomagnetic and solar data table Jour. Geophys. Research, 1981—.13 . Home: 7659 Nikau Dr Longmont CO 80501 Office: World Data Center A Solar Terrestrial Physics NOAA E/G C2 325 Broadway Boulder CO 80303

COFFEY, JANICE HELEN, dental hygienist; b. Chgo., Sept. 7, 1936; d. Frank Richard and Katherine Wilma (Natke) Lankin; m. Harold Daniel Coffey Jr., June 16, 1956; 1 child, Michael Daniel. AAS, Prairie State Coll., 1971. Registered dental hygienist. Dental asst. Dr. Jack Amran, DDS, Chgo. Heights, Ill., 1964-69; registered dental hygienist Dr. R.N. Tanis, DDS, Calumet City, Ill., 1971-72, Ludeman Devel. Ctr., Park Forest, Ill., 1972-84; owner, employment counselor, personnel placement coordinator, office mgmt. cons. JHC Assocs., Ltd., Chgo. Heights, 1984—; speaker South Suburban Dental Hygienists Soc., Chgo. Heights, 1986, publicity chmn., 1987; educator Ludeman Devel. Ctr., Park Forest, 1984—. Author: Career Directions for Dental Hygienists, 1985. Mem. Ill. Dental Hygienists Assn. (treas. 1974-76, v.p. 1976-77,pres. 1978-79), Am. Dental Hygienists Assn. (del. 1974-79), Alpha Alpha Omega.

COFFEY, JENNIFER LYNN, graphic designer; b. Hamilton, Ohio, Nov. 16, 1958; d. Willis Ralph and Angie C. BS in Design magna cum laude, U. Cin., 1982. Graphic designer The GNU Group, Houston, 1982-84; sr. designer Westinghouse Electric Corp., Pitts., 1984—. Designer local dance groups, youth symphony group, Pitts., 1986. Recipient Printing Industries award, 1985. Mem. Am. Inst. Graphic Artists, Soc. Environ. Graphic Designers, Soc. Typographic Artists. Office: Westinghouse Electric Corp 11 Stanwix St #1057 Pittsburgh PA 15222

COFFEY, KATHRYN R(OBINSON) (KAY), civic worker. m. Clarence W. Coffey; children: Clarence William, Kathryn Ann. BS in Govt., West Tex. State U., 1937. Active Lakeview Presbyn. Ch., New Orleans, 1944—, deacon, 1968-71, bd. dirs. kindergarten and nursery sch., 1965-68; mem. com. on home and family nurture Presbytery South La., 1967-69; mem. exec. com., chmn. dept. relation to pub. schs. Greater New Orleans Fedn. Chs., 1970-76; mem. Presbyn. campus life com. Presbytery New Orleans, 1978-82; mem. various coms. Orleans Parish (La.) Sch. Bd., 1953-77; active PTA, including bd. dirs. New Orleans Council, 1956-75, pres., 1965-67, v.p., chmn. legis. services and pres. Dist One La., 1967-72, mem. legis. com. Nat. Congress, 1969-72; mem. New Orleans Pub. Library Bd., 1956-62; v.p., chmn. membership com. Civic Council New Orleans, 1952-75; organizer, exec. sec. New Orleans Citizens for Support of Pub. Schs., 1968-76; bd. dirs., mem. coms. La. Assn. Mental Health, 1968-71; mem. La. Commn. Law Enforcement and Adminstrn. Criminal Justice, 1968-70; pres. La. Orgns. for State Legis., 1972-76; com. mem., bd. dirs. regional adv. group La. Regional Med. Program Inc., 1970-76; numerous activites for gifted edn. and spl. edn., including: founder, v.p., legis. chmn. Greater New Orleans Spl. Edn. PTA, 1971-77; mem. exec. com. La. Adv. Council for Learning Disabilities, 1972-76; co-chmn. Speak Out for Spl. Children, New Orleans, 1972-77; mem. Task Force for Implementation of Act 368 of 1972, La., 1972-76; spl. hearing officer Fed. Dist. Ct., New Orleans, 1973-77; chmn. La. Adv. Com. for Gifted and Talented, 1973-76; pres., organizer Assn. Gifted and Talented Students Inc., 1973-86; editor newsletter, 1973-81, contbg. editor, 1981-87; com. mem., chmn. nomination com. La. Gov.'s 4-C Policy Bd., 1974-77; project reader Office Gifted and Talented, Office Edn., 1975-76; mem. La. Coalition on Handicapped, 1975-88; mem. U. New Orleans Task Force on Gifted and Talented, 1976-82; regional rep. La. Gov.'s White House Conf. on Handicapped, 1977; bd. dirs. Nat. Assn. Gifted Children, 1977-86; mem. La. Gov.'s Adv. Com. on Edn. of Handicapped, 1978-81; mem. adv. bd. Gifted Advocacy Info. Network, 1979-83; mem. adv. bd. Inst. Gifted and Talented Edn., N.J. Dept. Edn., 1978-81; rev. editor Jour. Edn. of Gifted, Assn. for Gifted, 1980-82; vice-chmn. bd. dirs. La. Sch. for Math., Sci. and the Arts, Natchitoches, 1981-85, chmn. bd., 1985-87; mem. adv. bd. Gifted Children's Newsletter, 1981—; mem. Gov.'s Adv. Com. Ednl. Block Grants. Recipient Life Membership in La. PTA, Edward Hynes PTA, 1954; cert. of merit Mayor New Orleans, 1969; life Membership of Nat. Congress Parents and Tchrs., New Orleans Council PTA's, 1970; award for outstanding service Gov.'s Commn. on Law Enforcement and Adminstrn. Criminal Juvenile Deliquency Com., 1970; Outstanding Scouter award Greater New Orleans Fedn. Chs., 1972, Outstanding Citizen award Council Exceptional Children, 1974; award for outstanding service Dir. Office Gifted and Talented, Office Edn., 1976; award of appreciation Assn. Gifted and Talented STudents, 1980, award for outstanding service Isnt. Gifted and Talented Edn., N.J. Dept. Edn., 1980; named Hon. Senator, Lt. Gov. and Pres. of La. Senate, 1975; award for outstanding service Inst. Arts and Humanities Inc., Kansas City, Mo., 1982; Conv. Parent of Yr., Nat. Assn. Gifted Children, 1982; award for service to bd. dirs. Nat. Assn. Gifted Children, 1987; Spl. Edn. Pioneer award for outstanding contbn. to edn. for children La. Dept. Edn., 1987; Kathryn Robinson Day declared by Mayor of Natchitoches, Nov. 19, 1987; awarded "hon. student" status, 1987; awarded Nth degree award Northwestern State U. La., Natchitoches, 1987; U. New Orleans Library designated Kay Coffey Archives, 1987. Home: 59 Oceanaire Dr Rancho Palos Verdes CA 90274

COFFIE, PATRICIA ROSE, library director; b. Des Moines, Nov. 20, 1940; d. John Floyd Ballard and Nellie Gertrude (Fredregill) Spratt; m. Frazier Lee Coffie, Sept. 11, 1960 (div. June 1, 1975); children: Daniel Guy, Christopher John; m. John J. Doeppke, Nov. 17, 1984 (div. Nov. 1985). BA, Drake U., 1963; MA of Library Sci., U. Iowa, 1976. Lang. arts tchr. Des Moines Pub. Sch. System, 1963-64; adminstrv. asst. Manned Spacecraft Ctr., Houston, 1966-67; vol. librarian Friendswood (Tex.) Pub. Library, 1965-67, first paid librarian, 1965-67, trustee, 1968-69; dir. Waverly (Iowa) Pub. Library, 1976—; Mem. steering com. Iowa Gov.'s Pre-White House Conf. on Library Info. Services, Des Moines. bd. trustees Friendswood Pub. Library, 1968-69; mem. planning com. Waverly Homecoming 1986. Mem. ALA, Am. Assn. Univ. Women, Iowa Library Assn. (v.p., pres. elect 1987—), Nat. Assn. for Preservation and Perpetuation of Storytelling, Northlands Storytelling Network (bd. dirs. 1980—, pres. 1985), Waverly C. of C. (edn. com. 1978, tourism com. 1982). Home: 502 Second St SE Waverly IA 50677 Office: Waverly Pub Library 100 Second St SW Waverly IA 50677

COFFILL, MARJORIE LOUISE (MRS. WILLIAM CHARLES COFFILL), civic leader; b. Sonora, Calif., June 11, 1917; d. Eric J. and Pearl (Needham) Segerstrom; A.B. with distinction in Social Sci., Stanford U., 1938, M.A. in Edn., 1941; m. William Charles Coffill, Jan. 25, 1948; children—William James, Eric John. Asst. mgr. Sonora Abstract & Title Co. (Calif.), 1938-39; mem. dean of women's staff Stanford, 1939-41; social dir. women's campus Pomona Coll., 1941-43, instr. psychology, 1941-43; asst. to field dir. ARC, Lee Moore AFB, Calif., 1944-46; partner Riverbank Water Co., Riverbank and Hughson, Calif., 1950-68. Mem. Tuolumne County Mental Health Adv. Com., 1963-70; mem. central advisory council Supplementary Edn. Center, Stockton, Calif., 1966-70; mem. advisory com. Columbia Jr. Coll., 1972—, pres., 1980—; pres. Columbia Found., 1972-74, bd. dirs., 1974-77; mem. Tuolumne County Bicentennial Com., 1974—; active PTA, ARC. Pres., Tuolumne County Republican Women, 1952—, asso. mem. Calif. Rep. Central Com., 1950. Trustee Sonora Union High Sch., 1969-73, Salvation Army Tuolumne County, 1973—; bd. dirs. Lung Assn. Valley Lode Counties, 1974—. Recipient Pi Lambda Theta award, 1940; Outstanding Citizen award C. of C., 1974, Citizen of Yr. award, 1987. Mem. AAUW (charter mem. Tuolumne County br., pres. Sonora br. 1965-66). Episcopalian (mem. vestry 1968, 75). Home: 376 E Summit Ave Sonora CA 95370

COFFIN, SUE ANN, personnel trainer; b. San Francisco, Jan. 2, 1947; d. Fred W. and Alice Pauline (Gess) White; m. Stephen Duane Coffin, Mar. 19, 1967; children: Dana Michelle, Jennifer Lee. Student, Warner Pacific Coll., 1965-66, Portland State U., 1966-69, Oreg. State U., 1969-70; BA in Bus. Mgmt., Calif. Coast U., 1985. Asst. personnel mgr. Gen. Foods, Woodburn, Oreg., 1972-75; exec. asst. Creative Fin. Planning, Salem, Oreg., 1979-80; service rep., initial tng. instr. AT&T/PNB, Salem and Fremont, Calif., 1981-86; vocat. trainer Marion County Ednl. Service Dist., Salem, 1987—. Chmn. bd. dirs. Residential Alternative Housing for Head Injured; co-chmn. South County adv. bd. for vocat. program. Mem. Nat. Assn. Vocat. Mgrs. Spl. Needs Program, Oreg. Assn. Vocat. Mgr. Spl. Needs Program, Oreg. Transition Team for Spl. Needs, Vocat. Adv. Com. Republican. Home: 9536 Parrish Gap Rd Turner OR 97392

COFFMAN, DIANE CAROL, escrow company executive; b. Inglewood, Calif., June 3, 1953; d. O. Galen and Janet Carol (White) Coffman; children: Janene Elyse, Geraght Denton. Grad. high sch., Costa Mesa. Calif. Sec. Walker and Lee Escrow, Costa Mesa and Whittier, Calif., 1971-73; mgr., officer Transpacific Escrow, Cerritos, Calif., 1973-76; escrow officer Treeco Escrow, Costa Mesa, 1976-77; mgr., sr. officer Laguna Escrow, Laguna Beach, Calif., 1979-80; mgr., sr. officer, v.p. Hallmark Escrow, Huntington Beach, Calif., 1980; sr. officer Freelanced, Orange County, Calif., 1980-83; mgr., sr. officer Associated Escrow, Mission Viejo, Calif., 1978-79, 83-85; owner Escrow Relief Services, Mission Viejo, 1986—; instr. Coastline Community Coll., 1976-77. Mem. Orange County Escrow Assn. (active). Republican. Office: Escrow Relief Services P.O. Box 4288 Mission Viejo CA 92690

COFFMAN, EMILY JEANNE, marketing executive; b. Victoria, Tex., Nov. 5, 1953; d. Carl and Carrie W. (Brotherton) C. Cert. polit. studies Institut d'Etudes Politiques, Paris, 1974; B.A. in Polit. Sci. and French, Rice U., 1975; postgrad. U. Tex., 1975-76. Research asst. U. Tex. Ctr. Energy Studies, Austin, 1976-77; bilingual sec. Pullman Kellogg Co., Houston, 1978; adminstrv. asst. Golemon & Rolfe Assocs., Houston, 1978-80; Publs. coordinator CM, Inc., Houston, 1980-81; mktg. coordinator The Mayan Group Inc., Houston, 1981-84; mktg. coordinator Carter & Burgess, Inc., Houston, 1984-87; mktg. dir. The White Budd Van Ness Partnership, 1987-88; v.p. M.L. Payton & Assocs., Inc., 1988— . Contbr. articles to profl. publs. Mem. Women in Communications, Inc. (chpt. pres. 1984-85, regional v.p. 1986—), Nat. Assn. Female Execs., Soc. Mktg. Profl. Services., Rice Bus. and Profl. Women (1st v.p. 1987—). Methodist. Office: M L Payton & Assocs Inc 1880 S Dairy Ashford #505 Houston TX 77077

COFFMAN, ORENE BURTON, hotel executive; b. Fluvanna, Va., Mar. 13, 1938; d. John C. and Adele (Melton) Burton; m. John H. Emerson, Aug. 5, 1955 (div. 1972); 1 child, Norman Jay; m. Mack H. Coffman, Oct. 26, 1986. Degree in hotel and motel mgmt., Michigan State U., 1966-70. Cert. hotel mgr., Mich. State U., 1970. Telephone operator Colonial Williamsburg (Va.) Hotel, 1962-64; room clk. Colonial Williamsburg (Va.) Hotel, 1964-68; mgr. front office Colonial Williamsburg (Va.) Hotel, 1968-83; asst. mgr. Williamsburg Inn, 1983—; pres. Colonial Williamsburg Employees Fed. Credit Union, 1980-85. Mem. Am. Hotel Motel Assn. (nat. acctg. award 1970). Democrat. Baptist. Office: Williamsburg Inn PO Box B Williamsburg VA 23187

COFONE, FRANCES JOANN, accountant; b. Newark, Dec. 15, 1961; d. Angelo Joseph and Antonietta (Via) C. BA, Lafayette Coll., 1983. Asst. bookkeeper Del Enterprises, Livingston, N.J., 1981, inventory clk., Totowa, N.J., 1982; jr. tax acct. Prudential Ins. Co., Newark, 1983, acctg. reviewer, Roseland, N.J., 1983-84, asst. acctg. analyst, 1984-85, staff auditor, 1985-86, sr. auditor, 1986—. Coach Lafayette Coll. Equestrien Team, Easton, Pa., 1986—. Fellow Life Mgmt. Inst.; mem. Am. Inst. CPA's, N.J. Soc. CPA's, Am. Women's Soc. CPA's, Nat. Assn. Female Execs., Intercollegiate Horse Show Alumni Assn. (bd. dirs. 1985—, sec.-treas. 1984-86). Home: 5 Freeman St Roseland NJ 07068 Office: Prudential Ins Co 72 Eagle Rock Ave East Hanover NJ 07936

COGAN, KATHERINE STILES, artist, writer; b. Camden, N.J., July 29, 1942; d. George Henry and Violet (Wiley) Stiles; children—Eileen Cogan, Cathleen, Kelleen. B.A. in Art Edn., Glassboro State Coll., 1973; cert. Pa. Acad. Fine Arts, 1984; postgrad. Tyler Sch. Art, 1974-75, Phila. Coll. Art, 1973-80, Temple U., 1975-76. Cert. art tchr., N.J. Tchr. art Cherry Hill High Sch., N.J., 1973-80; freelance photographer, writer, 1973—; adj. mem. art faculty Gloucester County Community Coll., Sewell, N.J., 1976; admissions asst. Pa. Acad. Fine Arts, Phila., 1985. Contbr. article series to Pa. Acad. Alumni Newsletter, 1984—, series of articles with photography and revs. on arts Art Matters mag., 1984—. Coordinator Art In City Hall, Phila's. first mcpl. art gallery, 1986—; elected bd. mem. Pa. Acad. Fine Arts Alumni Assn., 1986-87. One-woman show Kling Gallery, 1986, 87, Muse Gallery, 1986; group shows include Pa. Acad. Fine Arts Student Ann., Phila., 1983-84, Temple U., Phila., 1984, Third St. Gallery, Phila., 1984, 1st Ann. Creative Artists Network Exhbn., Phila., 1984, Pa. Acad. Fine Arts 8th Ann. Fellowship Exhbn., Phila., 1985, Muse Gallery Anniversary Exhbn., Phila., 1985, Cheltenham 4th Ann. Juried Invitational Exhbn., Pa., 1985, Painted Bride Art Ctr., Phila, 1987; represented in permanent collections MacDonalds Corp. Hdqrs., Ill., Smith, Kline & Beckman Corp., ARA Corp.; numerous pvt. collections Phila. Cresson travel scholar Pa. Acad. Fine Arts, 1983. Mem. Pa. Acad. Fine Arts Alumni Assn. Avocations: running; tennis; swimming; dance.

COGBURN, PATRICIA ANN, banker; b. Atoka, Okla., May 5, 1947; d. Amos Jackson Daniel and Juanita (Groves) Weaver; m. Thomas Wayne Cogburn, Oct. 5, 1968 (div. 1985); 1 child, Heath Bradley. Student, Tarrant County Jr. Coll., Ft. Worth, 1979; grad., U. Wis. Sch. Banking, 1981, U. Okla. Comml. Lending Sch., 1985. Teller, proof operator Pinemont Bank, Houston, 1969; sec. 1st State Bank, Rio Vista, Tex., 1969-72; with acctg. dept. TransAm. Van Lines, Ft. Worth, 1972; v.p., cashier Benbrook State Bank, Ft. Worth, 1972-81; exec. v.p. 1st Nat. Bank of Burleson, Tex., 1981—, also bd. dirs.; rep. Am. Inst. Banking, Ft. Worth, 1974-80. Bd. dirs. Am. Heart Assn., Johnson County, Tex., 1984—, pres. 1985-86. Mem. Nat. Assn. Bank Women (sec., treas. 1978-81, scholarhip 1987). Republican. Office: First Nat Bank of Burleson PO Box 699 Burleson TX 76028

COGGESHALL, JANICE R., city mayor; b. Trenton, N.J., June 27, 1935; d. James Clendenin and Geraldine (Badenoch) Reddig; m. Richard Edwin Coggeshall, Nov. 29, 1958; children: John, Heidi, James, Joshua. BA, Wellesley Coll., 1957. Mem. council City of Galveston, Tex., 1979—, mayor, 1984—; chmn. women mayors subcom. to U.S. Conf. Mayors, 1986—. Presbyterian. Office: City of Galveston Box 779 City Hall Galveston TX 77553

COGGIN, CHARLOTTE JOAN, cardiologist, educational administrator, educator; b. Takoma Park, Md., Aug. 6, 1928; d. Charles Benjamin and Nanette (McDonald) Coggin; B.A., Columbia Union Coll., 1948; M.D., Loma Linda U., 1952, M of Pub. Health, 1987; Intern, Los Angeles County Gen. Hosp., Los Angeles, 1952-53, resident in medicine, 1953-55; fellow in cardiology Children's Hosp., Los Angeles, 1955-56, White Meml. Hosp., Los Angeles., 1955-56; research assoc. in cardiology, house physician Hammersmith Hosp., London, 1956-57; resident in pediatrics and pediatric cardiology Hosp. for Sick Children, Toronto, Ont., Can., 1965-67; cardiologist, co-dir. heart surgery team Loma Linda (Calif.) U., asst. prof. medicine , 1961-73, asso. prof., 1973—, asst. dean Sch. Medicine Internat. Programs, 1973-75, assoc. dean, 1975—, co-dir., cardiologist heart surgery team missions to Pakistan and Asia, 1963, Saigon, Vietnam, 1974, 75, to Saudi Arabia, 1976—, China, 1984, Hong Kong, 1985; mem. Pres's. Advisory Panel on Heart Disease, 1972—. Appointed to Med. Quality Rev. Com.-Dist. 12, 1976-80. Recipient award for service to people of Pakistan City of Karachi, 1963, Medallion award Evangelismos Hosp., Athens, Greece, 1967, Gold medal of health South Vietnam Ministry of Health, 1974, Charles Elliott Weinger award for excellence, 1976, Wall Street Jour. Achievement award, 1987; named Honored Alumnus Loma Linda U. Sch. Medicine, 1973, Outstanding Women in Gen. Conf. Seventh-day Adventists, 1975, Alumnus of Yr., Columbia Union Coll., 1984. Diplomate Am. Bd. Pediatrics. Mem. Am. Coll. Cardiology, AMA (physicians adv. com. 1969—) Calif. Med. Assn. (com. on med. schs., com. on member services), San Bernardino County Med. Soc. (chmn. communications com. 1975-77, mem. communications com. 1987-88, editor bull. 1975-76), Am. Heart Assn., AAUP, Med. Research Assn. Calif., Calif. Heart Assn., AAUW, Am. Acad. Pediatrics, World Affairs Council, Internat. Platform Assn., Calif. Museum Sci. and Industry MUSES (Outstanding Woman of Year in Sci. 1969), Am. Med. Women's Assn., Loma Linda Sch. Medicine Alumni Assn. (pres. 1978), Alpha Omega Alpha, Delta Omega. Author: Atrial Septal Defects, motion picture (Golden Eagle Cine award and 1st prize Venice Film Festival 1964); contbr. articles to med. jours. Democrat. Home: 11495 Benton St Loma Linda CA 92354 Office: Loma Linda U Med Ctr Loma Linda CA 92354

COGGINS, CYNTHIA ANNE, special education teacher; b. Greenville, S.C., Apr. 29, 1954; d. Harry Edwin and Hazel Leonia (Edwards) C. BA, Furman U., 1976, MA, 1980. Cert. tchr., S.C. Tchr. emotionally handicapped Athens Elem. Sch., Travelers Rest, S.C., 1976-77; tchr. emotionally handicapped Arrington Elem. Sch., Greenville, 1977-80, tchr. learning disabilities, 1980—. Mem. Greenville Civic Chorale, 1980-81; deacon First Bapt. Ch., Greenville, 1984-87; bd. dirs. North Greenville Mental Health Clinic, 1977-78. Named one of Outstanding Young Women of Am., 1983, 85, 87, Outstanding Young Woman of S.C., 1987, Arrington Elem. Tchr. Yr., 1986-87, Greenville County Tchr. Yr., Greenville Council for Exceptional Children, 1986-87. Mem. S.C. Council for Exceptional Children (S.C. Tchr. Yr. 1987, sec. 1980-82, treas. 1983-86, v.p. 1986-87, pres.-elect 1987—, pres. chpt. 877 1982-83), Delta Kappa Gamma (Alpha Eta chpt.). Home: 14 Batesview Dr Greenville SC 29607 Office: Arrington Elem Sch 921 N Franklin Rd Greenville SC 29609

COGHLAN, MARY ELLEN, commercial real estate appraiser; b. Jersey City, June 18, 1954; d. James Joseph and Mary Deloros (Rotar) C. BA, Ramap Coll., 1976. Assoc. appraiser Coghlan Appraisal Co., Ramsey, N.J., 1976-81; appraiser Mfrs. Hanover Trust, N.Y.C., 1982-83; sr. appraiser Cushman & Wakefield N.J., Lyndhurst, 1983—. Supporter Greenpeace, Washington, 1988—. Recipient N.Y. Soc. Real Estate Appraisers scholarship, 1983. Mem. Assoc. Meadowlands Bd. Realtors, Am. Soc. for Prevention of Cruelty to Animals, Titanic Hist. Soc. Roman Catholic. Home: 19 Spanktown Rd Warwick NY 10990 Office: Cushman & Wakefield NJ 1099 Wall St Lyndhurst NJ 07071

COHEN, ANNE SILBERSTEIN, psychotherapist, clinical social worker; b. Balt., Aug. 12, 1928; d. Louis M. and Marie Rita (Adlin) Silberstein; B.A., Goucher Coll., 1949; M.A., Montclair State Coll., 1974; M.S.W., Rutgers U., 1975; cert. N.J. Acad. Group Psychotherapy, 1976-78; postgrad. N.Y. Center for Psychoanalytic Tng., 1978—; cert. in psychoanalytic psychotherapy; m. Robert J. Cohen, Sept. 7, 1952; children—Laura Marjorie, Michael Louis. Social worker children's div. Dept. Public Welfare, Balt., 1950-53, Children's Protective Services, Pa. Soc. to Protect Children from Cruelty, Phila., 1953-56; mem. staff Social Work Family Life Improvement Project, Rutgers U. Grad. Sch., New Brunswick, N.J., 1964-68; social worker Catholic Family and Community Services, Paterson, N.J., 1974-75; psychotherapist, clin. social worker Essex County Guidance Center, East Orange, N.J., 1975-83; pvt. practice psychotherapy, marriage and family counseling, Livingston, N.J., 1980—. Mem. planning com. Mental Health Assn. N.J., 1980; bd. dirs. Community Psychiat. Inst. Inst., East Orange, N.J.; trustee Community Mental Health Ctr. of Oranges, Maplewood and Millburn, N.J., 1983—. Lic. marriage counselor, N.J. Fellow Am. Orthopsychiat. Assn., N.J. Soc. Clin. Social Work; mem. N.J. Acad. Group Psychotherapy, N.J. Soc. Clin. Social Work (dir., membership chairperson), Nat. Assn. Social Workers (cert., diplomate), Am. Assn. Marriage and Family Therapists, N.J. Assn. Women Therapists, N.J. Psychol. Assn., Soc. for Advancement Self-Psychology (cert.), Nat. Registry Health Care Providers, LWV, Nat. Council Jewish Women. Jewish. Office: Roosevelt Plaza 2 W Northfield Rd Suite 305 Livingston NJ 07039

COHEN, AUDREY C., college president; b. May 14; d. Abe Cohen and Esther Cohen Morgan; children—Dawn Jennifer, Winifred Alisa. B.A. magna cum laude, U. Pitts., 1953; postgrad. in polit. sci. and edn. George Washington U., 1957-58. Founder, pres. Coll. Human Services, N.Y.C., 1964—, Am. Council Human Service, 1974—; exec. dir. Women's Talent Corps., 1964-68; founder, pres. Part-Time Research Assocs., 1958-64; lectr. in field; cons. Commn. Occupational Status Women in Nat. Vocat. Guidance Assn. Contbr. articles to profl. jours. Active subcom. higher edn. N.Y.C. Partnership; chmn. Com. on Yr. 2000, N.Y. World Future Soc.; nat. adv. com. Horizons-Bicentennial Commn.; mem. planning com. Hemispheric Congress Women, Miami, Fla., 1975-76; chmn. Nat. Task Force on Women, Edn. and Work, 1975; active Manhattan Borough Pres.'s Adv. Com. on Health Careers for Disadvantaged, Pub. Edn. Assn. Project for Restructured Edn. System N.Y.C. Recipient Stanley M. Isaacs award Am. Jewish Com., 1969; George Champion award Chase Manhattan Bank, 1970; Disting. Vis. prof. award U. Mass., 1975; Ednl. Devel. Cert. of Achievement award Atlantic Richfield Co., 1979; Otty award Our Town newspaper, 1981; Mina Shaughnessy scholarship award U.S. Office Edn., 1983; Empire State award, 1984-85; Outstanding Leadership in Higher Edn. award Commn. Ind. Colls. and Univs., 1984-85. Mem. Support Services Alliance, Inc. (bd. dirs.), Fin. Women's Assn., Am. Jewish Com. (exec. com., bd. dirs.), council Higher Ednl. Instns. Clubs: Economic, Harvard, Lotos, Women's Forum. Home: 37 E 67th St New York NY 10014 Office: Coll Human Services 345 Hudson St New York NY 10014 •

COHEN, BETH FAYE, librarian; b. Providence, R.I., Mar. 3, 1961; d. Alex and Lillian Eunice (Talmanson) C. BA, SUNY, Binghamton, 1982; M in Library Sci., UCLA, 1986. Librarian Los Angeles Regional Family Planning Council, 1984—; cons. health clinics and health orgns. in area of info. mgmt. Office of Family Planning Contract Agys. in Los Angeles County, 1986—, AIDS Project of Los Angeles, 1986—. Mem. Assn. for Population/Family Planning Libraries and Info. Ctrs., Spl. Library Assn. Home: 1416 Armacost Ave #1 Los Angeles CA 90025 Office: Los Angeles Regional Family Planning Council 3600 Wilshire Blvd Suite 600 Los Angeles CA 90010

COHEN, CARLA LYNN, publisher; b. N.Y.C., Feb. 27, 1937; d. Barnet and Florence (Skolnick) Ellowis; children—Beth Diane, Jeffrey. Student Clark U., Adelphi U. Editor, Oceanside (N.Y.) Beacon, 1975-77; adminstrv. asst. pub. relations Bd. Suprs. Nassau County, 1977-78; pres. Carla Cohen Communications, Oceanside, N.Y., pres. Cotar Publs., Nassau Borders Papers, Floral Park, N.Y., 1981—; editor Voters Guide, Lawrence, N.Y., 1979-80. Grand Marshall Meml. Day parade, 1986. Recipient Patriotic Service award VFW, 1976; Outstanding Achievement award Am. Cancer Soc., 1976-77; Pub. Service award USAF, 1983; named Woman of Yr., B'nai B'rith, 1985, Sons of Italy, 1985. Mem. C. of C. (v.p. 1982—), LWV (v.p. 1979), Internat. Platform Assn. Republican. Jewish. Office: PO Box 155 Franklin Square NY 11010

COHEN, CYNTHIA FRYER, management educator; b. Atlanta, Aug. 21, 1952; d. Robert Collins Fryer III and MaryAnne (Montfort) Pait; m. Murray Elliott Cohen, Oct. 16, 1975. BBA, U. Ga., 1974, MBA, 1975; PhD, Ga. State U., 1980. Research cons. The Urban Inst., Washington, 1978; asst. prof. mgmt. U. Houston-Clear Lake, 1979-82; asst. prof. U. South Fla., Tampa, 1982-85, assoc. prof., 1985—, acting assoc. dean, dir. grad. studies, 1986—; systems engr. Electronic Data Systems, Dallas, 1975-77. Contbr. articles to profl. jours. Vol. Christmas Adopt a Family, Tampa, 1984-85, Radio Reading Service, Tampa, 1983-84. Named one of Outstanding Young Women of Am., 1980. Mem. Acad. Mgmt., Indsl. Relations Research Assn., Am. Arbitration Assn., Am. Arbitration Assn. (labor panel 1985—). Office: U South Fla Coll Bus Adminstrn Tampa FL 33620

COHEN, DENISE JODI, athletic director; b. N.Y.C., Mar. 14, 1961; d. Howard Leonard and Shirley (Alpert) C. BA, Bucknell U., 1983; MA, Adelphi U., 1987. Asst. coach basketball Molloy Coll., Rockville Centre, N.Y., 1983-84; dir. athletics Molloy Coll., Rockville Centre, 1984—; asst. mgr. tickets, media cons. U.S. Tennis Assn., N.Y.C., 1983-84, media cons., 1985—; dir. athletics Whitestone (N.Y.) Youth Ctr., 1986—; asst. to dir. ops. World Championship Tennis, 1985—, commr. Empire State Conf., 1985—; founder, organizer Molloy Coll. Women's Basketball League, 1988. Mem. Nat. Assn. Coll. Dirs. Athletics, Coll. Sports Info. Dirs. Am., Met. Colls. Athletic Dirs. Assn. (treas. 1988), Nat. Assn. Female Execs., Omicron Delta Kappa. Office: Molloy Coll 1000 Hempstead Ave Rockville Centre NY 11570

COHEN, DIANE BERKOWITZ, lawyer; b. Vineland, N.J., June 11, 1938; d. Myer and Ida Mae (Subin) Berkowitz; m. Robert H. Cohen, June 11, 1958 (div. Dec. 1980); children: Ronald Jay, Stuart Daniel, Amy Suzanne; m. Samuel Gerstein, Aug. 5, 1984. AA magna cum laude, Fairleigh Dickinson U., 1958; BA summa cum laude, Glassboro State Coll., 1976; JD, Temple U., 1979. Bar: Pa. 1979, N.J. 1980, U.S. Ct. Appeals (3d cir.) 1981. Assoc. Lewis Katz, Cherry Hill, N.J., 1979-81, Steven D. Weinstein, Cherry Hill, 1981-83; sole practice Collingswood, N.J., 1983-85; ptnr. Gerstein, Cohen & Kurtzman PA, Haddonfield, N.J., 1985—; active ethics com. N.J. Supreme Ct. Vice chmn. Allied Jewish Appeal, Cherry Hill, 1968-72; v.p. Nat. Council Jewish Women, Haddonfield, 1969-71; bd. dirs. Planned Parenthood Assn. Camden County, N.J., 1982—. Mem. ABA, N.J. Bar Assn., Camden County Bar Assn. (chmn. women lawyers com., mem. jud. appointment com.), Assn. Trial Lawyers Am. Office: Gerstein Cohen & Kurtzman PA 20 Kings Hwy W Haddonfield NJ 08033

COHEN, DONNA EDEN, lawyer; b. Harlingen, Tex., Oct. 23, 1956; d. Gerald Myer and Annette Rose (Rodman) C. Student, U. Hawaii, 1976-77; BA, U. Mass., 1978; JD, Suffolk U., 1981. Bar: Mass. 1981, U.S. Dist. Ct. Mass. 1982, U.S. Ct. Appeals (1st cir.) 1982. Assoc. Gilman, McLaughlin & Hanrahan, Boston, 1981—; of counsel Gerald M. Cohen, Andover, Mass., 1986—; counsel Commonwealth Mass. Purchasing Agt., Boston, 1982. Mem. Gov.'s Prepaid Legal Services Com., Boston, 1982—; bd. dirs. Am. Heart Assn., Needham, Mass., 1983-87. Mem. ABA, Mass. Bar Assn., Boston Bar Assn., Assn. Trial Lawyers Am. (v.p. Suffolk chpt. 1979-81), Mass. Acad. Trial Attys. (lectr. continuing legal edn. seminar 1982—). Democrat. Jewish. Office: Gilman McLaughlin & Hanrahan 470 Atlantic Ave Boston MA 02210

COHEN, ELISABETH POSNER, brokerage house executive; b. Washington, June 17, 1939; d. Stanley Irving Posner and Lillian (Kahn) Posner-Wallace; m. Robert Stuart Cohen, June 18, 1961 (div. Jan. 1986); children: Rachel C. Smith, Suzanne M. Cohen. BA, Smith Coll., 1961. Disability examiner Social Security Adminstrn., N.Y.C., 1961-62; realtor Hugh T. Peck Properties, Potomac, Md., 1973-87; account exec., stockbroker Ferris and Co., Inc., Washington, 1986—; pres. The Posner-Wallace Found., Washington, 1983—. Head alumni fund Sidwell Friends Sch., Washington, 1971-74; chpt. area F bd. dirs. Parents without Ptnrs., Washington, 1983-84; mem. Washington Hebrew Congregation. Mem. Nat. Assn. Realtors (GRI). Clubs: Smith of Washington, Amex, Economists. Home: 11213 Powderhorn Dr Potomac MD 20854 Office: Ferris and Co Inc 1720 Eye St NW Washington DC 20006

COHEN, ESTHER RHEA, business executive, civic leader; b. Chgo., Sept. 13, 1937; d. Max and Dora (Feldman) Wolf; m. Melvyn M. Kupetz, Aug. 21, 1956 (div. July 1973); children: Debra Lynn Ehr, Sandra Kupetz; m. Melvin Aaron Cohen, Oct. 23, 1973; stepchildren: Nisa Levy, Devra H., Justin D. Student, U. Colo. Pres., gen. mgr. A.K. Glass Co., Denver, 1973-79; pres., gen. mgr., also bd. dirs. ABC Glass Co., Denver, 1980—, A.K. Car Co., Denver, 1977—; sec., bd. dirs. Generic Water Co., Denver, 1981—, T.A.D. Co. Inc., Denver, 1981—. Founder, pres., bd. dirs. Golda Meir Meml. Assn., Denver, 1981—; sec., bd. dirs. Com. to Save Golda's Home, Denver, 1984—; founder, sec., bd. dirs. Safe Cars and Trucks Now Inc., Denver, 1981—; ex-officio mem. Auraria Higher Edn. Ctr. Golda Meir House Rev. Panel, Denver, 1987—. Mem. Ind. Auto Dealers Assn., Glass Dealers Assn., Women's Bus. Owners Assn. Democrat. Jewish. Lodge: B'Nai B'rith. Office: Golda Meir Meml Assn PO Box 9693 Denver CO 80209

COHEN, FRANCINE THOMAS, human resources director; b. Guildford, Surrey, Eng., June 19, 1944; d. Myrddyn and Martha Louisa (Rouse) Thomas; children: Naomi, Joshua, Natalie. BA, Douglass Coll., 1977. Project asst. Elizabeth T. Lyons & Assoc., New Brunswick, N.J., 1977-80; personnel mgr. Ctr. for Profl. Advancement, East Brunswick, N.J., 1980-83, Fisher-Stevens, Inc., Totowa, N.J., 1983-84; coordinator Middlesex County Coll., Edison, N.J., 1984-86; asst. v.p. human resources Perth Amboy (N.J.) Savs., 1986—. Bd. dirs., Women Aware-Abused Women's Shelter, Middlesex County, N.J., 1979-82, pres. 1981-82. Mem. Am. Soc. Personnel Adminstrn. (sec. 1983-84). Jewish. Home: 261 South Adelaide Ave Highland Park NJ 08904 Office: Perth Amboy Savs 210 Smith St Perth Amboy NJ 08862

COHEN, GLORIA ERNESTINE, educator; b. Bklyn., July 6, 1942; d. Victor George and Marion Theodosia (Roberts) C. B.S. in Edn., Wilberforce U., 1965; M.A. in Elem. Edn., Adelphi U., 1975; Profl. Diploma in Ednl. Adminstrn., L.I. U., 1984; M.S. in Edn., Bklyn. Coll., 1986. Tchr. Bd. Edn., Bklyn., 1965—; case worker Dept. Welfare, Bklyn., 1965—. Mem. Northwest Civic Assn., Freeport, N.Y., 1973—, Roosevelt-Freeport Civic Assn., Freeport, 1984—. Mem. NOW, Assn. for Supervision and Curriculum Devel., Nat. Alliance of Black Sch. Educators, Inc., Bklyn. Reading Council of Internat. Reading Assn., N.Y. State Reading Assn., Assn. Black Educators of N.Y., Nat. Assn. Female Execs., Inc., Zeta Phi Beta, Kappa Delta Pi. Democrat. Roman Catholic. Clubs: FSO Internat. (Jamaica, N.Y.); Freeport Indoor Tennis. Avocations: tennis; skiing; swimming. Home: 4 Sterling Pl Freeport NY 11520 Office: Bd Ed PS 149 700 Sutter Ave Brooklyn NY 11207

COHEN, HARRIET NEWMAN, lawyer; b. Providence, Dec. 8, 1932; d. Morris and Marion Newman; B.A. in Latin and Greek, Barnard Coll., 1952; M.A. in Latin and Greek (Tuition scholar), Bryn Mawr Coll., 1953; J.D. cum laude, Bklyn. Law Sch., 1974; 4 daus. Bar: N.Y. 1975, Fed. Ct. 1975, U.S. Supreme Ct. 1982. Assoc. Squadron, Gartenberg, Ellenoff & Plesent, N.Y.C., 1974-76, Phillips, Nizer, Benjamin, Krim & Ballon, N.Y.C., 1976-80, Golenbock & Barell, N.Y.C., 1980-83; ptnr. Golenbock and Barell, 1984-86, Solin & Breindel, 1986—; tchr. domestic relations law Continuing Edn. div. CUNY, 1980—, adv. bd., 1982—; lectr. Assn. Bar City N.Y., 1982, N.Y. Women's Bar Assn., 1981, 82, N.Y. State Trial Lawyers Assn., 1981, 82, ABA, 1986; apptd. to N.Y. Child Support Commn., 1984—; mem. jud. screening bd. Ct. Appeals, 1985, 86. Author: The Equitable Distribution Law in Divorce: The New York Experience. Mem. N.Y. Women's Bar Assn., (v.p. 1983-84, pres. 1985-86), Assn. Bar City N.Y., N.Y. State Bar Assn., Bklyn. Law Rev. Alumni Assn. (trustee 1981—), Women's Bar Assn. State of N.Y. (dir. 1983-86), Coalition on Women's Legs. Issues (co-chair 1986—). Office: 501 Fifth Ave 3d floor New York NY 10017

COHEN, IDA BOGIN, export-import executive; b. Bklyn.; d. Joseph and Yetta (Harris) Bogin; student St. Johns U.; B.S., N.Y.U.; m. Barnet Gaster, June 26, 1941 (div. May 1955); m. 2d, Savin Cohen, Aug. 30, 1964. Sec.-treas. J. Gerber & Co., Inc., N.Y.C., 1942-54, v.p., dir., 1954-73; pres., dir. Austracan U.S.A., Inc., N.Y.C., 1960-73; v.p. Parts Warehouse, Inc., Woodside, N.Y., 1970-72, sec.-treas., 1972-84; also engaged in pvt. investments. Contbr. articles to South African Outspan, newspapers. Home: 12 Shorewood Dr Sands Point NY 11050

COHEN, JERI FRIED, recruiting service executive; b. Passaic, N.J., July 22, 1956; d. Jules Robert and Arlyne (Levinson) Fried; m. Jeffrey Arnold Cohen, Oct. 23, 1983. BS in Econs., Rutgers U., 1978; postgrad., Fordham U., 1982-83. Registered sales asst. Merrill Lynch Pierce Fenner & Smith, Inc., N.Y.C., 1978-80; trust officer Citibank, N.Y.C., 1980-83; v.p., dir. trust and investment, executive recruiter A-L Assocs., Inc., N.Y.C., 1983—, sr. v.p.; guest lectr. Rutgers U., 1982-83; cons. in field. Mem. Nat. Assn. Female Execs., Nat. Assn. Bank Women, Am. Mgmt. Assn., Alpha Zeta.

COHEN, JOYCE E., state senator, business executive; b. McIntosh, S.D., Mar. 27, 1937; d. Joseph and Evelyn (Sampson) Petik; children: Julia Jo, Aaron J. Grad., Coll. Med. Tech., Minn., 1955; student, UCLA, Minn., 1957-78, Santa Ana Coll., Minn., 1961-62. Med. research technician dept. surgery U. Minn., 1955-58; dept. tech. U. Calif., 1958-59, dept. bacteriology, 1959-61; med. research scientist Allergan Pharms., Santa Ana, Calif., 1961-70; ptnr. Co-Fo Investments, Lake Oswego, Oreg., 1978—; mem. Oreg. Ho. of Reps., Lake Oswego, Oreg., from 1979, now Oreg. state senator, from 1979. Vice chmn. State Energy Policy Rev. Commn., 1977-78; chmn. legis. rules and ops. com. Oreg. Ho. of Reps., 1979-80, housing and urban devel. com. and judiciary subcom., chmn. senate bus., housing and fin. com., senate trade and econ. devel. com., jud., bus. housing and fin., agrl. and natural resources and rules com., ins. task force, veteran's affairs, labor, jud., enviroment and hazardous materials coms.; mem. Oreg. Criminal Justice Council; mem. Jud. Br. State Energy Policy Rev. Com., 1979; mem. Gov.'s Commn. on Child Support Enforcement, 1985. Woodrow Wilson Lecture series fellow, 1988. Mem. Assn. Family Conciliation Cts., Citizens Council of Cts., LWV, Oreg. Environ. Council, Oreg. Women's Polit. Caucus. Democrat. Office: Oregon State Senate Salem OR 97310

COHEN, JUDITH LEVITT, psychologist; b. N.Y.C., Nov. 9, 1948; d. Arthur Harris and May (Grinovsky) Levitt; m. Ira Morton Cohen, June 11, 1972; children: Melinda Brooke, Ilana Suzanne. BA in Spaish magna cum laude, Queens Coll., 1969; MA in Psychology, Ga. State U., 1975, PhD in Orgnl. Communication, 1981; postgrad., U. Pitts. Law Sch., 1987—. Instr. Spanish N.Y.C. Bd. Edn., 1969-72, Richmond County Bd. Edn., Augusta, Ga., 1972-73; pvt. practice mgmt. cons. Atlanta and Franklin, N.C., 1973—; spl. asst. to adminstr. Ga. Office of Fair Employment Practices, Atlanta, 1978; asst. prof. bus. adminstrn. Brenau Coll. Gainesville, 1982-83, vis. asst. prof. bus. and psychology depts., 1987; vis. lectr. in community dentistry Emory U., Atlanta, 1983; asst. prof. mgmt. cons. Western Carolina U., Cullowhee, N.C., 1983-84; cons. in field, 1979—. Contbr. articles to profl. jours. Mem. legisl. action com. United Way, Atlanta, 1982-83; bd. dirs. Council on Battered Women, Atlanta, 1982-83; unit v.p. Am. Cancer Soc., Macon County, N.C., 1985—. Mem. Acad. Mgmt., So. Mgmt. Assn., ABA (student div.). Jewish. Office: 6154 Steubenville Pike McKees Rocks PA 15136

COHEN, LAUREN BEVERLY, lawyer; b. Passaic, N.J., Aug. 11, 1946; d. Morris and Sharon (Slaff) C.; 1 child: Renée Michelle. BA, Rutgers U., 1969; JD, Seton Hall U., 1973. Bar: N.J. Gen counsel and sec. AGFA Gevaert Inc., Teterboro, N.J., 1977-82, Lynch Corp., Fairfield, N.J., 1982-84; assoc. counsel Michael Sternlieb Esq., Hackensack, N.J., 1984-87; assoc. counsel and asst. sec. Anchor Sav. Bank, Wayne, N.J., 1987—. Mem. N.J. Bar Assn. Bergen County Bar Assn., Women Lawyers in Bergen County, Mensa. Republican. Jewish. Office: Anchor Savs Bank 1401 Valley Rd Wayne NJ 07470

COHEN, LINDA SCHNABL, administrator; b. Phila., Sept. 19, 1952; d. Martin and Helen (Koehler) Schnabl; m. Robert J. Cohen, Aug. 14, 1982. BA, Villanova U., 1974. Mktg. asst. Internat. Mill Service, Inc., Phila., 1974-76; advance person The White House, Washington, 1976-77; dir. tng. Rep. Nat. Com., Washington, 1977-79; cons. Event Mgmt., Washington, 1979-80; dep dir. purchasing 1981 Pres. Inaugural Com., Washington, 1980-81; spl. asst. to sec. U.S. Dept. Commerce, Washington, 1981-82; spl. asst. to dir. U.S. Dept. Health and Human Services Office of Community Services, Washington, 1982-84; asst. mgr. Housing Devel. Corp., Grand Cayman, Brit. West Indies, 1984-85; v.p. Cohen Assocs., Ltd., Grand Cayman, 1986—. Mem. Miami Internat. Press Club, Nat. Assn. Female Execs. Republican. Roman Catholic. Home: PO Box 2066 George Town, Grand Cayman British West Indies Office: Cohen Assocs Ltd 250 Catalonia Ave Suite 702 Coral Gables FL 33134

COHEN, LOIS GORDON, infosystems specialist; b. Balt., Oct. 31, 1943; d. Sylvan Bernard and Miriam Marcella (Kellert) Gordon; m. Ronald Gene Cohen, Aug. 15, 1965 (div. July 1986); children: Randee Dawn, Craig Kellert. BA, George Washington U., 1965; postgrad., U. Md., 1986. Systems analyst EG&G, Rockville, Md., 1978-80; mgmt. analyst Tracor, Inc., Rockville, 1980-84; quality assurance mgr. Caci, Inc., Gaithersburg, Md., 1984-87; integrated logistic support analyst Norden Service Co., Gaithersburg, 1987—. Editor local newsletter, all tech. documentation USAF Consolidated Space Ops Ctr., Gaithersburg, 1984-87. Named Outstanding Vol. Montgomery County Pub. Schs., 1976-77. Mem. Soc. Tech. Communication, Nat. Assn. Female Execs., Soc. Logistic Engrs., Women's Am. ORT. Clubs: Regency (Norfolk, Va.) (v.p. 1965-66); 100 (Silver Spring, Md.) (sec. 1972-74). Office: Norden Service Co 200 Professional Dr Gaithersburg MD 20879

COHEN, MARY ANN, judge; b. Albuquerque, July 16, 1943; d. Gus R. and Mary Carolyn (Avriette) C. BS, UCLA, 1964; JD, U. So. Calif., 1967. Bar: Calif. 1967. Ptnr. Abbott & Cohen, P.C. and predecessors, Los Angeles, 1967-82; judge U.S. Tax Ct., Washington 1982—. Mem. ABA (sect. taxation), Legion Lex. Republican. Office: US Tax Ct 400 2nd St NW Washington DC 20217

COHEN, MAXINE SHAW, educator; b. N.Y.C., Oct. 20, 1948; d. David and Esther (Rochelman) Shaw; m. Arnold Joseph Cohen, Aug. 24, 1969; children: Jason, Rochelle. BA, U. Vt., 1970; MS in Advanced Tech., SUNY, Binghamton, 1982, postgrad., 1986—. Programmer, analyst Eastman Kodak Co., Rochester, N.Y., 1970-76; from adj. instr. to asst. prof. Broome Community Coll., Binghamton, 1978-81; programmer, analyst computer ctr. SUNY, Binghamton, 1981-82, lectr., 1982-83, instr. div. community programs, 1983-86, div. dir. computer sci., info. sci., 1985-87; systems engr. I Singer Link Corp., Binghamton, 1984. Contbr. articles to profl. jours. Legis. chair, mem. arts and edn. Homer Brink PTA, Endwell, N.Y., 1982-85; speaker West Presbyn. Ch., Binghamton, 1986. Recipient Chem. Rubber award Am. Chem. Assn., Burlington, Vt., 1966; SUNY grantee, 1985. Mem. IEEE (computer soc.), Assn. for Computing Machinery (vice chair N.Y. So. Tier chpt. 1983-84, chairperson 1984-86). Jewish. Lodge: Temple Concord Sisterhood (chairperson gift shop Binghampton chpt. 1979-80, 84-85). Home: 871 Rosewood Terr Endwell NY 13760 Office: SUNY Binghamton Vestal Pkwy Binghamton NY 13901

COHEN, MELANIE ROVNER, lawyer; b. Chgo., Aug. 9, 1944; d. Millard Jack and Sheila (Fox) Rovner; m. Arthur Wieber Cohen, Feb. 17, 1968; children—Mitchell Jay, Jennifer Sue. A.B., Brandeis U., 1965; J.D., DePaul U., 1977. Bar: Ill. 1977, U.S. Dist. Ct. (no. dist.) Ill., U.S. Ct. Appeals (7th cir.). Law clk. to justice U.S. Bankruptcy Ct., 1976-77; instr. secured and consumer transactions creditor-debtor law DePaul U., Chgo., 1980—; ptnr. Antonow & Fink, Chgo., 1977—. Mem. Supreme Ct. of Ill. Atty. Registration and Disciplinary Commn. Inquiry Bd., 1982-86, hearing bd., 1986—. Panelist, speaker. Bd. dirs., v.p. Brandeis U. Nat. Alumni Assn., 1981—; life mem. Nat. Women's Com., 1975—, pres. Chgo. Chpt., 1975-82; mem. Glencoe Caucus (Ill.), 1977-80. Mem. ABA, Ill. State Bar Assn., Chgo. Bar Assn. (chmn. bankruptcy reorganization com. 1983-85), Commenal Law League, Ill. Trial Lawyers Assn. Contbr. articles to profl. jours. Home: 167 Park Ave Glencoe IL 60022 Office: Antonow & Fink 111 E Wacker Dr Chicago IL 60601

COHEN, NANCY MAHONEY, lawyer; b. Boston, July 14, 1941; d. Gerald Murray and Margaret (Callahan) Mahoney; m. William Cohen, Aug. 8, 1976; 1 child, Margaret Emily. AB, Emmanuel Coll., 1963; JD, Stanford U., 1975. Bar: Calif. 1975. Asst. gen. counsel Bendix Forest Products Corp., San Francisco, 1976-81; assoc. Brown & Bain, Phoenix, Ariz., 1981; counsel Syntex Corp., Palo Alto, Calif., 1982-86; sr. counsel Syntex Corp., Palo Alto, 1986—; bd. dirs. Syntex Corp. Fed. Credit Union, Palo Alto. Chmn. Rental Housing Mediation Task Force, Palo Alto, 1972-74; mem. All Saints Vestry, Palo Alto, 1985-88. Mem. ABA, Calif. Bar Assn., Am. Corp. Counsel Assn. Office: Syntex Corp 3401 Hillview Ave Palo Alto CA 94304

COHEN, RACHELLE SHARON, journalist; b. Phila., Oct. 21, 1946; d. Hyman and Diane Doris (Schultz) Goldberg; m. Stanley Martin Cohen, June 22, 1968; 1 dau., Avril Heather. B.S., Temple U., Phila., 1968. Editor, Somerville Jour. (Mass.), 1968-70; reporter Lowell Sun (Mass.), 1970-72, AP, Boston, 1972-79; state house bur. chief Boston Herald Am., 1979-80, editorial page editor, 1980-82; editorial page editor Boston Herald, 1982—. Office: Boston Herald 1 Herald Sq Boston MA 02106

COHEN, RITA S., real estate broker; b. Montreal, Ont., Can., Jan. 11, 1934; came to U.S., 1959, naturalized, 1964; d. Meyer and Annie (Black) Friedman; student Sir George Williams Coll., ed. Grad. Realtors Inst.; m. Arthur Cohen, May 29, 1956; children—Mara Susan, Dana Sherril, Marcia Gayle. mgr. inst. Bluepring Realty, White Plains, N.Y., 1970-76; vice pres., relocation dir. Robert Martin's Condo Mart Inc., Hartsdale, N.Y., 76-82; pres. Rita Cohen Realty Services Ltd., White Plains, N.Y., 1982—, resale div. Condos Plus, 1983—; tchr. condo and coop. course for real estate brokers Pace U. and Westchester County Realty Bd. and White Plains Adult Edn. Mem. Nat. Assn. Realtors, Westchester County Bd. Realtors, Women's Council Realtors, Hadassah (v.p. edn. 1978). Jewish. Home: 12 Ritchey Pl White Plains NY 10605 Office: 220 Westchester Ave White Plains NY 10604 also: 325 N Highland Ave Ossining NY 10562

COHEN, ROBIN ELLEN, lawyer; b. N.Y.C., Aug. 23, 1955; d. Charles Solomon and Evelyn (Sweisky) C.; m. Peter T. Shapiro, June 23, 1985; 1 child, Laura Rachel. J.D. cum laude, NYU, 1981; B.S., SUNY-Stony Brook, 1976; postgrad. Sloan Kettering Div. Cornell Grad. Sch. Med. Scis., 1976-77. Bar: N.Y. 1982, U.S. Dist. Ct. (ea. and so. dists.) N.Y. 1983. Assoc. atty. corp. dept. Rosenman & Colin, N.Y.C., 1981-84, Kramer Levin Nessen Kamin & Frankel, N.Y.C., 1984-87; clk. to presiding justice appellate div. 2d Dept., N.Y. State Supreme Ct., 1979. Mem. N.Y. Women's Bar Assn., N.Y. State Bar Assn., Order of Coif. Democrat. Jewish. Home: 315 E 80th St New York NY 10021

COHEN-ADDAD, NICOLE ESTHER, pediatrician, neonatologist; b. Algiers, Algeria, Jan. 21, 1949; came to U.S., 1976, naturalized, 1981; d. Raoul and Alice (Aboucaya) Cohen-Addad. B.S., Lycée de Chantilly, France, 1966; prep. cert. med. studies, Paris, 1967; M.D., Univ. Med. Center, Pitié-Salpétrière, Paris, 1972. Intern, Beer-Sheva, Israel, 1973-74; resident pediatrics Wayne State U., Detroit, 1976-77, fellow in neonatology, 1978-80; teaching asst. pediatrics, resident pediatrics NYU, N.Y.C., 1977-78; instr. pediatrics Newark Beth Israel, 1981; instr. pediatrics Univ. Med. Sch. N.J., Newark, 1981-83, asst. prof. pediatrics, 1983—; dir. Fgn. Med. Grad. Workshop, Newark, 1983; faculty Fgn. Med. Grad. Workshop, Dearborn, Mich., 1983. Contbr. chpts. to books, articles to profl. jours. Active N.Y. County Democratic Com., 1983; vol. Village Vis. Neighbors, N.Y.C., 1983. Fellow Am. Acad. Pediatrics; mem. Am. Soc. Photobiology, Am. Med. Women's Assn., N.J. Med, Womens Assn. (pres.-elect.), AAUW, AAUP, Am. Coll. Nutrition. Jewish.sh. Home: 5 Charles St Apt 2F New York NY 10014 Office: U Med Sch NJ 185 S Orange Ave Newark NJ 07103-2757

COHEN-MANSFIELD, JISKA, psychologist, educator; b. Basel, Switzerland, Dec. 19, 1951. BA, Hebrew U., 1974, MA cum laude, 1976; MA in Clin. Psychology, SUNY, Stony Brook, 1978, PhD in Clin. Psychology, 1979. Computer programmer Mgmt. Automation Co., Ltd., Tel Aviv, 1971-72, Hebrew U. Computer Ctr., Jerusalem, 1972-75; tchr. Luria Elem. Sch., Jerusalem, 1974-75; asst. prof. Touro Coll., N.Y.C., 1979-80, Haifa (Israel) U., 1980-82; adj. asst. prof. St. John's U., N.Y.C., 1983; adj. assoc. prof. Long Island (N.Y.) U., 1983; dir. research inst. Hebrew Home of Greater Washington, 1984—; assoc. prof., dir. research Ctr. on Aging Georgetown U. Sch. Medicine, Washington, 1987—; adj. assoc. prof. George Washington U., 1984-87. Haifa U. grantee, 1981-82; NIMH grantee, 1985—. Mem. Gerontol. Soc. Am., Am. Psychol. Assn., Md. Gerontol. Assn., Nat. Conf. on Social Welfare, Israel Psychol. Assn. Office: Research Inst Hebrew Home 6121 Montrose Rd Rockville MD 20852

COHL, CLAUDIA HOPE, editor; b. Detroit, Nov. 23, 1939; d. Isaac and Jennie (Mellinoff) C. B.A., Wayne State U., 1961. Tchr. Detroit Bd. Edn., 1961-62; asst. then assoc. editor New Book Knowledge, Grolier Inc., N.Y.C., 1962-66; editor social studies Franklin Watts Inc., div. Grolier, N.Y.C., 1966-74; editor Tchr. Mag., Macnillan Inc., Greenwich, Conn., 1974-75; editor, dir. elem. dept. sch. div. Scholastic Inc., N.Y.C., 1975-77, editor-in-chief classroom mags., 1977-83; editor-in-chief, corp. v.p. Family and Home Office Computing mag., Scholastic Inc., N.Y.C., 1983—. Office: Family Computing 730 Broadway St New York NY 10003

COHN, ANN ROCHELLE, psychologist; b. N.Y.C., Apr. 16, 1941; d. Harry and Eleanor Rochelle; m. Ronald Ira Cohn, Dec. 20, 1970; 1 child, Henry Ian. BS, Temple U., 1962; PhD in Psychology, Ill. Inst. Tech., 1975. Editorial asst. Babcock & Wilcox, N.Y.C., 1962-64; creative dir. Comdine Corp., N.Y.C., 1964-68; v.p. Rowland Co., N.Y.C., 1968-70; intern psychology Ill. Masonic Med. Ctr., Chgo., 1974-75; psychologist Rehab. Inst. Chgo., 1975-77; pvt. practice clin. and cons. psychology Chgo., 1977—; media psychologist NBC Radio, Chgo., 1982—. Mem. Am. Psychol. Assn., AFTRA, Nat. Register Health Service Providers, Ill. Psychol. Assn. Office: 1030 N State St Chicago IL 60610

COHN, JANE SHAPIRO, public relations executive; b. N.Y.C.; d. Harry I. and Ann (Safanie) Shapiro; divorced; children: Theodore David, William Alan. BA, Brandeis U., 1956; postgrad., Coll. of New Rochelle, 1974-76. Dir. pub. relations Hudson River Mus., Yonkers, N.Y., 1976-79; account exec. Dudley-Anderson Yutzy Pub. Relations Agy., N.Y.C., 1979-81; dir. communications Haines Lundberg Waehler, N.Y.C., 1981—; cons. Inst. Contemporary Art, Phila., 1983. Mem. AIA (assoc. 1988, speaker annual conv.), Pub. Relations Soc. Am., Internat. Assn. Bus. Communicators, Art Table, Soc. for Mktg. Profl. Services (bd. dirs. N.Y. chpt. 1988—), Am. Mktg. Assn. (panelist ann. conv. 1987, moderator profl. services sect. ann. conv. 1988). Democrat. Jewish. Office: Haines Lundberg Waehler 115 5th Ave New York NY 10003

COHN, MILDRED, biochemist, educator; b. N.Y.C., July 12, 1913; d. Isidore M. and Bertha (Klein) Cohn; B.A., Hunter Coll., 1931, Sc.D. (hon.), 1984; M.A., Columbia U., 1932, Ph.D., 1938; Sc.D. (hon.), Women's Med. Coll., 1966, Radcliffe Coll., 1978, Washington U., St. Louis, 1981, Brandeis U., 1984, U. Pa., 1984, U. N.C., 1985; m. Henry Primakoff, May 31, 1938; children—Nina, Paul, Laura. Research asst. biochemistry George Washington U. Sch. Medicine, 1937-38; research assoc. Cornell U., 1938-46; research assoc. Washington U., 1946-50, 51-58, assoc. prof. biol. chemistry, 1958-60; assoc. prof. biophysics and phys. biochemistry U. Pa. Med. Sch., 1960-61, prof., 1961-78, emeritus 1982—, Benjamin Rush prof. physiol. chemistry, 1978-82; sr. mem. Inst. Cancer Research, Phila., 1982-85; Chancellor's disting. prof. biophysics U. Calif., Berkeley, spring 1981; vis. prof. biol. chemistry Johns Hopkins U. Med. Sch., 1985—; research assoc. Harvard U., 1950-51; established investigator Am. Heart Assn., 1953-59, career investigator, 1964-78. Recipient Garvan medal; Cresson medal Franklin Inst., 1976; award Internat. Assn. Women Biochemists, 1979; Nat. Medal Sci., 1982, Chandler medal Columbia U., 1986. Mem. Am. Philos. Soc., Nat. Acad. Scis., Am. Chem. Soc. (Remsen award 1988), Harvey Soc., Am. Soc. Biol. Chemists, Am. Biophys. Soc., Am. Acad. Arts and Scis., Phi Beta Kappa, Sigma Xi, Iota Sigma Pi. Editorial bd. jour. Biol. Chemistry, 1958-63, 67-72. Office: U Pa Med Sch Dept Biochemistry and Biophysics Philadelphia PA 19104-6089

COHN, VIRGINIA S., public relations executive; b. Bklyn.; d. Lewis Henry and Beatrice Rita (Grouse) Saper; m. N. Burton Tretler, Feb. 7, 1940 (div. 1961); children: Amy Tretler Lynn Silverman, Richard Sterling; m. Julian M. Cohn, July 6, 1961 (dec. 1974). Grad. Ann-Reno Inst., N.Y.C., Bklyn. Coll. With various advt. agys., Miami, Fla., 1962-68; dir. advt., pub. relations Modernage, Miami, 1968-69, Bauder Coll., Miami and Ft. Lauderdale, Fla., 1970-84; owner, mgr. Two In Prodn., Miami, 1984-86; dir. pub. info. Hartford Easter Seal Rehab. Ctr., Conn., 1986—. Contbr. articles to mags., profl. jours. Mem. Fashion Group Miami (treas. 1974-75), Internat. Soc. Interior Designers, Advt. Fedn. Greater Miami (pres. 1974-75, named Advt. Personality of Yr. 1975), Greater Hartford Advt. Club, Hartford Women's Network, Am. Acad. Advt., Women in Communications (bd. dirs. cen. Conn. chpt.). Avocation: writing.

COHOWICZ, LUCY ANN, owner home construction business; b. N.Y.C., Mar. 11, 1950; d. Albert LaGrutta and Ruth Mae (Stanke) Porcelli; m. Michael C. Cohowicz, May 10, 1986; children: Christina-Lee Queler, Adam Eliot Queler, Robert Michael. Grad. high sch., L.I., N.Y., 1979. V.p. sales div. J&L Plastics Corp., Bklyn., 1971-72; pres. Plachem Plastics Corp., College Point, N.Y., 1972-74; owner, pres. Spunky's Boutique, Inc., Floral Park, N.Y., 1974-77, Six Love, Inc., L.I., 1974-75, Lucy and Co., Inc., Floral Park, N.Y., 1975-78; owner, v.p. Coler Custom Homes, Inc., Stroudsburg, Pa., 1983—. Fundraiser Coma Recovery Assn., Floral Park, 1980. Mem. Floral Park C. of C. (pres. 1975-76), Pocono Mt. C. of C. (mem. bldg. com. 1984—), Am. Builders' Assn. (Pocono Chpt.), Wedgewood Soc. Republican. Roman Catholic. Home: 62 Penn Estates East Stroudsburg PA 18301 Office: Coler Custom Houses Inc 1013 W Main St Stroudsburg PA 18360

COIGNEY, MARTHA WADSWORTH, theatre executive; b. N.Y.C., June 21, 1933; d. Charles and Martha Clay (Hollister) Wadsworth; m. Rodolphe Lucien Coigney, Dec. 27, 1969; 3 stepchildren. BA, Vassar Coll., 1954.

Exec. sec. Actors Studio, N.Y.C., 1956-59; asst. to pres. Teleprompter Corp., N.Y.C., 1960-61; adminstrv. and prodn. asst. to theatrical producer Roger L. Stevens (Nat. Endowment for Arts), 1962-65; asst. dir. Internat. Theatre Inst. U.S., N.Y.C., 1966-69, dir., 1969—, mem. internat. body exec. com., 1971—, v.p., 1981-87, pres., 1987—. Contbr. articles to profl. publs. Mem. theatre panel N.Y. State Council of Arts, 1976-79, chmn., 1978-79; mem. internat. panel Nat. Endowment for Arts, 1979-80; bd. dirs. Theatre of Latin Am., 1973-79. Decorated officier Ordre des Arts et des Lettres (France), 1978. Mem. Nat. Theatre Conf. (pres. 1982-84), Actors Theatre St. Paul (adv. council internat. program). Club: Cosmopolitan. Home: 1200 Fifth Ave New York NY 10029 Office: Internat Theatre Inst 220 W 42nd St New York NY 10036

COIN, SHEILA REGAN, management consultant; b. Columbus, Ohio, Feb. 17, 1942; d. James Daniel and Jean (Hodgson) Cook; m. Tasso H. Coin, Sept. 17, 1967 (div.); children: Tasso, Alison Regan; m. Robert James Hall, Feb. 28, 1987. BS, U. Iowa, 1964. RN Staff nurse VA Hosp., Boston, 1964-66; field rep. ARC, Chgo., 1966-67, adminstr., 1967; asst. div. dir. Am. Hosp. Assn., sec. Am. Soc. Hosp. Dirs. Nursing, Chgo., 1967-69; owner Coin & Assocs., Chgo., 1975-77; ptnr. Coin, Newell & Assocs., Chgo., 1977—; instr. dept. continuing edn. Loyola U., Chgo., 1975-77, Rock Valley Coll. Mgmt. Inst., Rockford, Ill., 1978-80, Ill. Central Coll. Inst. Personal and Profl. Devel., Peoria, 1979—, Triton Coll. Continuing Edn., River Grove, Ill., 1983-86, No. Ill. U. Continuing Edn., DeKalb, 1983—. Vol. Art Inst., Chgo., 1968-69; mem. Chgo. Beautiful Com., 1968-73; chmn. Mayor Daley's Chgo. Beautiful Awards Project, 1972; mem. jr. bd. Girl Scouts Assn., Chgo., 1975-76; mem. jr. governing bd. Chgo. Symphony Orch., 1971—, pres., 1977-78; governing mem. Orchestral Assn., Chgo., 1977-81; bd. dirs. Mid-Am. chpt. ARC, Chgo., 1979-81, vice chmn. 1986—; bd. dirs. Chgo. dist., 1981—, chmn. fin. devel. com., 1982-85, vice chmn. dist. bd., 1986—; dir. Com. for Thalossemia Chgo. Bd., 1981-82; mem. Women's bd. Nat. Com. Prevention Child Abuse, Chgo., 1981-82; mem. State of Ill. Disabled Persons Advocacy Div. Consumers Task Force, 1988—. Mem. Am. Mgmt. Assn., Am. Soc. Tng. and Devel., Ill. Tng. and Devel. Assn. Democrat. Roman Catholic. Avocations: piano, tennis, national and international travel, spectator sports, family activities. Home: 1037 W North Shore Ave Chicago IL 60626 Office: Coin Newell & Assocs 919 N Michigan Ave Chicago IL 60611

COKER, CLAUDIA GERMAINE, savings and loan executive; b. Walnut Ridge, Ark., Jan. 6, 1953; d. Zack Tiley and Germaine Marie (Piantoni) C. BS, Ark. State U., 1975. Cashier Harps Supermarket, Walnut Ridge, 1972-73, Rorex Supermarket Hoxie, Ark., 1973-74; office mgr. Higginbotham Burial Ins., Walnut Ridge, 1975; clk. typist Crane Co., Jonesboro, Ark., 1975-76; savs. and loan examiner Fed. Home Loan Bank Bd., Little Rock, 1976-85; Savs. and loan examiner Fed. Home Loan Bank, Dallas, 1985-87; v.p., regulatory compliance officer, United Fed. Savs. and Loan, Jonesboro, Ark., 1987—. Mem. Leadership Jonesboro 1988. Recipient Civil Services Beta award Fed. Home Loan Bank Bd., 1978. Bd. dirs. United Way, Jonesboro; bd. trustees United Way Craighead County. Mem. Assn. Bus. Profl. Women (1st v.p. Downtown Jonesboro chpt. 1988-89), Fin. Mgrs. Soc., Nat. Assn. Female Execs. Baptist. Clubs: Confederate Air Force (security detachment)(Harlingen, Tex.); Razorback Wing (security detachment)(Pine Bluff, Ark.). Avocations: counted cross stitch, knitting, needlepoint, reading, collecting depression glass. Home: 2723 C Greenbriar Dr Jonesboro AR 72401 Office: United Fed Savs and Loan 515 West Washington Jonesboro AR 72401

COKER, ELIZABETH BOATWRIGHT (MRS. JAMES LIDE COKER), author; b. Darlington, S.C., Apr. 21, 1909; d. Purves Jenkins and Bessie (Heard) Boatwright; m. James Lide Coker, Sept. 27, 1930; children: Penelope, James Lide. A.B., Converse Coll., 1929; postgrad., Middlebury Coll., 1938. Asso. prof. English Appalachian State U., Boone, N.C., 1971-72. Author: Daughter of Strangers, 1950, The Day of the Peacock, 1952, India Allan, 1953, The Big Drum, 1957, La Belle, 1959, Lady Rich, 1963, The Bees, 1968, Blood Red Roses, 1977, The Grasshopper King, 1981; Contbr. mag. articles, poems. Mem. Hartsville Sch. Bd., 1939-49; sec., dir. Blowing Rock Horse Show Assn., 1943-49; dir. United Cerebral Palsy of S.C.; mem. nat. bd. Med. Coll. Pa.; trustee Converse Coll.; nat. adv. council I.S.S. Mem. Poetry Soc. Ga., AAUW, P.E.N., S.C. Poetry Soc., Authors Guild, Acad. Am. Poets, S.C. Hist. Soc., Garden Club Am., Caroliniana Soc. (exec. council 1983—). Republican. Episcopalian. Clubs: Springdale Hall (Camden, S.C.); Hound Ears (Blowing Rock, N.C.). Home: 620 W Home Ave Hartsville SC 29550

COLABELLA, BETTY MARIE, engineering company executive; b. Mt. Carmel, Pa., May 27, 1925; d. Philip Christ and Edith Lavinia Wagner; student public schs. Mount Carmel, Pa.; m. Alfred V. Colabella, Jr., Aug. 28, 1945; children—Alfred V. III, Robert Clark, Edith Ann, Scott Michael. Sec.-treas. A.V. Colabella Engrs., Bordentown, N.J., 1955—, also dir. Mem. Bordentown Bd. Edn., 1965-75, pres., 1968-69, 73-74. Mem. Profl. Engrs. Soc. Mercer County Aux. (pres.), PTA Bordentown (pres.), Republican. Home: 19 Prince St Bordentown NJ 08505 Office: 138 Farnsworth Ave Bordentown NJ 08505

COLAGUORI, JUNE CAROL, cosmetics marketing executive; b. Pitts., Oct. 17, 1955; d. Julius Ceasar and Margaret (Hauerlesko) Bilecky. Student, U. Pitts, Wheeler Bus. Sch., Pitts., Forbes Tech. Sch., Pitts. Account exec. Jhirmack, Inc., Pitts., 1980; mktg. asst. Gen. Nutrition Corp., Pitts., 1981, mgr. mktg., 1982-83, mgr. promotions, 1984, new product buyer, 1985, mgr. new bus. and new product devel., 1986; dir. mktg. Moxie Industries div. ICN Pharms. Corp., Anaheim, Calif., 1986-87; mktg. cons., Los Angeles, 1987; mgr. mktg. div. skincare, haircare and fragrance products Merle Norman Cosmetics, Los Angeles, 1988—. Mem. Nat. Assn. Female Execs., Pitts. Advt. Club, Personal Dynamics Inst. (cert.). Episcopalian. Office: 11039 Begonia Fountain Valley CA 92708 also: 9130 Bellanca Ave at Arbor Vitae Los Angeles CA 90045

COLAIANNI, BARBARA MCPHAIL, retail music executive; b. Jackson, Miss., Nov. 2, 1951; d. Arthur Peter and Betty Lee (Bane) Colaianni; m. Robert David McPhail, Dec. 1970 (div. Jan. 1973); 1 child, Melissa Gwenn. B of Music cum laude, Columbus (Ga.) Coll., 1974, MEd summa cum laude, 1981. String orchestra tchr. Muscogee County Schs., Columbus, 1974-84; salesperson Colaianni Music Co., Columbus, 1985—, v.p., 1986—. Mem. faculty Musemont Fine Arts Camp, Jekyll Island, Ga., 1974; violinist, solo violin various orchs., symphonies throughout Ga.; dir. Musicians For Hire, Columbus, 1985—; organized and conducted The Columbus Symphony Youth Orch., 1978-79. Mem. Music Educators Nat. Conf., Nat. Fedn. Music Clubs, Ga. Fedn. Music Clubs (com. chmn. 1987—), Ga. Music Tchrs. Assn., Ga. Music Educators Assn. (dist. chmn. 1981-82, adjudicator 1983—, Honor award 1983, 84), Nat. Sch. Orch. Assn., Am. String Tchrs. Assn. Club: Orpheus (pres. Columbus chpt. 1985-87). Home: 5801 Windsor Dr Columbus GA 31909 Office: Colaianni Music Co 1010 13th St Columbus GA 31901

COLAMARINO, KATRIN BELENKY, lawyer; b. N.Y.C., Apr. 29, 1951; d. Allen Abram and Selma (Burwasser) Belenky Lang; m. Leonard J. Colamarino, Mar. 20, 1982; m. Barry E. Brenner, June 1, 1974 (div. June 1979); 1 dau., Rachel Erin. B.A., Vassar Coll., 1972; J.D., U. Richmond, 1976. Bar: Ohio 1976, U.S. Ct. Apls. (Fed. cir.), 1982. Staff atty. AM Internat. Inc., Cleve., 1976-78; atty. Lipkowitz & Plaut, N.Y.C., 1980-81; atty. Docutel Olivetti Corp., Tarrytown, N.Y., 1981-84; atty. NYNEX Bus. Info. Systems, White Plains, N.Y., 1984-85; corp. counsel, sec. Logica Systems, Inc., N.Y.C., 1986—. Class agt. Fieldston Sch., N.Y.C., 1980—, exec. bd. Ethical Fieldston Alumni Assn., 1980—, v.p. 1987—; alumnae council rep. Vassar Coll., 1982-86. Mem. Assn. Bar City N.Y., Westchester Fairfield Corp. Counsel Assn. Office: Logica Data Architects Inc 666 3d Ave New York NY 10017

COLAMARINO, MARY ANN, public relations administrator; b. Rochester, N.Y., Oct. 9, 1953; d. Nicholas and Carmella (Cottone) C. Student, Monroe Community Coll., 1972-74, St. John Fisher Coll., 1977-80, Empire State Coll., 1987—. Adminstrv. asst., offset printer Girl Scouts U.S. Genesee Valley, Inc., Rochester, 1972-76; asst. publicity St. John Fisher Coll., Rochester, 1977-80, editor, writer Alumni News, 1979-80; asst. devel., coordinator pub. relations Threshold Ctr. for Alternative Youth Services, Inc., Rochester, 1981, editor, writer Heartbeat newsletter, 1986—, staff chair pub. relations/mktg. com., 1987—; cons. Matt Talbot Ministries, Rochester, 1987—. Cons. Rochester/Antiqua and Barbuda Ptnrs. of Ams., 1984-86. Roman Catholic. Home: 1011 University Ave Rochester NY 14607

COLBERT, ANNETTE DARCIA, silver company executive; b. Tulsa, Oct. 24, 1959; d. Buel and Bonnie Helen (Pickens) C.; 1 child, Siobhan Nicole. Student, Devry Inst., Dallas, 1979, Oklahoma City U., 1986. Tech. rep. Xerox Corp., Oklahoma City, 1979-80; field engr. NCR Corps., Oklahoma City, 1980; chief exec. officer Silver Merchants Ltd., Oklahoma City, 1981—. Fund raiser U.S. C. of C., Oklahoma City, 1985-86; project dir. Embassy Inc., Oklahoma City, 1986-87. Mem. Am. Mgmt. Assn., Am. Metal Assn., Gold and Silver Inst. Republican. Home: 7501 S Sherwood #2 Oklahoma City OK 73159 Office: Silver Merchants Ltd 6161 N May #25W Oklahoma City OK 73111

COLBERT, LINDA ELAINE, nurse; b. Merced, Calif., Aug. 15, 1947; d. William Ralph and Elaine R. (Murray) Phelps; B.S., Calif. State U., Fresno, 1969, M.S.N., 1984. m. Gary Colbert, Aug. 24, 1968; children—Tamara, Rebecca, Valerie. Staff nurse Valley Med. Center, Fresno, Calif., 1969-72; night supr. Coalinga (Calif.) Dist. Hosp., 1973-75, dir. nurses, 1978-83; pvt. practice as family nurse practitioner, 1984—; coordinator med. assisting and emergency med. tech. program W. Hills Coll., 1975-78. Bd. trustees Coalinga Dist. Hosp., 1975-76.

COLBURN, JANET LOUISE, data processing administrator; b. Rahway, N.J., Nov. 6, 1942; d. Cleaveland Fisher and Virginia (Seager) C.; m. Alan S. Newman, June 3, 1963 (div. Dec. 1968); children: Brian, Russell. BA in Classical Langs., Muhlenberg Coll., 1964. Mgr. data processing ops. Nat. Tool & Mfg. Co., Kenilworth, N.J., 1972-75; supr. data processing Mailing Services Inc., Hillside, N.J., 1975-79; mgr. data processing Whitestone Products, Piscataway, N.J., 1979-86, Lladró USA Inc., Carlstadt, N.J., 1986—; microcomputer cons. Ad-A-System, Garwood, N.J., 1979—, personal computer cons., Passaic, N.J., 1987—. Com. mem. N.J. chpt. Save the Children, 1984-85. Mem. NOW, Data Processing Mgmt. Assn., Am. Mgmt. Assn. Republican. Presbyterian. Office: Lladró USA Inc 303 Paterson Plank Rd Carlstadt NJ 07072

COLBURN, JULIA KATHERINE LEE, educator; b. Columbus, Ohio, Feb. 8, 1927; d. Fred Merritt and Lillian May (Getrost) Lee; m. Joseph Linn Colburn, Sept. 5, 1947; children—Joseph Linn, Jr., David Laird, Andrew Lee, Julia LeeAnne. B.S. in Edn., Ohio State U., 1948. Library asst. Columbus Pub. Library, 1945-48, Ohio State U. Library, Columbus, 1945-47; life ins. acct. Nationwide Ins., Columbus, 1949-50; substitute tchr. Columbus Pub. Schs., 1965-69, 79-81; vol. resource person Columbus Pub. Schs., 1979—. Author: Ohio Daughters of 1812, The Six Who Signed, Christmas at Valley Forge; editor, compiler (state pub.) Star and Anchor, 1983-85 (nat. first award, 1984, 85). Presiding judge Franklin County Bd. Elections, Columbus, 1959—; pres. Linden Jr. Civic Club, Columbus, 1953, Rhapsody Unit, Columbus Symphony, 1975-77, Arlington Park PTA, Columbus, 1963-64, Linden-McKinley Jr.-Sr. High PTA, Columbus, 1964-66, Northland High PTA, Columbus, 1972-73; organizing pres. Lazarus Cancer Ray, Columbus, 1953; leader Northland council Girl Scouts U.S., 1968-70; vol. Vision Ctr., Columbus, 1969-72 (Named Vol. of Yr. 1971); v.p. Linden United Meth. Women, Columbus, 1965-66, pres. 1966-68, various coms. 1963—; pres. Meth. Youth Fellowship, Columbus, 1944-45; adminstrv. bd. Linden United Meth. Ch., Columbus, 1944-45, 52—, choir soloist, mem., 1945—, Sun. sch. tchr., 1959—, spl. membership awards 1971, 77; dist. chmn. Christian Global Concerns Columbus North Dist. United Meth. Women, 1973-77. Recipient Silver Good Citizenship medal Ohio Soc. SAR, 1978, Medal of Appreciation, Benjamin Franklin chpt. SAR, 1978. Mem. Ohio Geneal. Soc. (speakers staff 1978—), First Families of Ohio, DAR (Good Citizenship cert. 1945, state rec. sec. 1983-86, state vice regent 1986—, various offices and coms. 1976—), Children of Am. Revolution (sr. pres. state 1976-78, sr. nat. rec. sec. 1982-84, various coms. 1974—; Ohio Service award, 1979, maj. benefactor 1986), U.S. Daus. of 1812 (parliamentarian, chmn. nat. membership 1985-88, state pres. 1983-85, treas. Nat. Hdqrs. Endowment Trust Fund, 1988—), Colonial Dames XVII Century (state first v.p. 1985-87), Daus. Colonial Wars (state historian 1984-86, nat. vice chmn. 1983—), Women Desc. Ancient and Honorable Arty. Co. (state rec. sec. 1983-86, state pres. 1986—), Daus. Am. Colonists (Old Trails chpt. treas. 1981-85, vice regent 1985-87, regent 1987—), New Eng. Women (pres. Columbus colony 1984-87, nat. chmn. 1987—), Colonial Daus. Seventeenth Century, Daus. Union Vets., Zeta Phi Eta. Republican. Club: Ohio Fedn. Women's (trustee, chmn. 1974-83). Lodges: Order of Eastern Star (star point 1961-62), Linden Lawanis (Kiwanis Aux. pres. 1964). Avocations: genealogy; music; writing. Home: 1887 Northcliff Dr Columbus OH 43229

COLBURN, LESLIE CARSON, small business owner; b. Princeton, N.J., Dec. 21, 1948; d. Marlin S. and Ethel (Southgate) Carson; m. Edward J. Colburn; children: Kevin, Sara. BS, Va. Commonwealth U., 1971; MBA, N.H. Coll., 1984. Supr. St. Joseph Hosp., Nashua, N.H., 1973-78; instr. U. N.H., Manchester, 1979-82; bus. mgr. Colburn Constrn., New Boston, N.H., 1976—; acct. Matthew Thornton Health Plan, Nashua, 1984-85; pres. Beautiful Skier, Inc., New Boston, 1986—. vice chair New Boston Sch. Bd., 1985—. Office: Beautiful Skier Inc 130 McCurdy Rd Box 550 New Boston NH 03070

COLBURN, NORMA ELAINE WHEELER, city official; b. St. Johnsbury, Vt., June 26, 1933; d. Clayton Wallace and Ida Minerva (Lang) Wheeler; student Burdett Coll., 1951, Rutgers U., 1968; m. James Austin Colburn, Jan. 19, 1952; children—Candice Margaret, James Austin. Registered mcpl. clk., N.J. Exec. sec. Oswald L. Sanborn C.P.A.'s, Ridgewood, N.J., 1952; exec. sec. archtl. div. Am. Brakeshoe Co., Mahwah, N.J., 1952; postal clk. U.S. P.O., Lyndon Center, Vt., 1956-60; partner Colburn's Store, Lyndon Center, Vt., 1956-60; corr., feature writer Burlington (Vt.) Free Press, 1959-60; dep. borough clk., ct. clk., Allendale, N.J., 1968-70, sec. planning bd., dep. water collector, 1969-70, borough clk., 1970—, borough adminstr., 1972—. Active Girl Scouts U.S.A., 1965-66. Recipient Time Mag. Current Events award, 1950, 51. Mem. Municipal Clks. Assn. N.J., Bergen County Municipal Clks. Assn., Internat. Inst. Municipal Clks. Mem. Order Eastern Star. Home: 310 Brookside Ave Allendale NJ 07401 Office: Office City Clk City Hall Allendale NJ 07401

COLBY, ANNE, psychologist; b. Galveston, Tex., Feb. 10, 1946; d. Malcolm Young and Emily Jane (Armacost) C.; m. William V.B. Damon; 1 dau., Caroline Colby. B.A., McGill U., 1968; Ph.D., Columbia U., 1972. Research assoc., lectr. Harvard U., Cambridge, Mass., 1972-80; dir. Henry A. Murray Research Center of Radcliffe Coll., Cambridge, 1980—; dir. research Clin. Devel. Inst. Lic. psychologist, Mass. Mem. Nat. Council for Research on Women (dir.). Author: The Measurement of Moral Judgment, 1987. Office: Radcliff Coll H A Murray Research Ctr 10 Garden St Cambridge MA 02138

COLBY, MARVELLE SEITMAN, educator, administrator; b. N.Y.C., Oct. 31, 1932; d. Charles Edward and Lily (Zimmerman) Seitman; m. Robert S. Colby, Apr. 11, 1954 (div. Apr. 1979); children: Lisa, Eric; m. Selig J. Alkon, Dec. 6, 1986; m. Selig J. Alkon, Dec. 6, 1986. BA, Hunter Coll., 1954; MA, U. N.Colo., 1973; PhD in Pub. Adminstrn., Nova U., 1977; cert., Harvard Grad. Sch. Bus., 1979. V.p. SE Region URC Mgmt. Services Corp., Washington, 1972-77; dir. devel. Hunter Coll. Woman's Ctr. Community Leadership, N.Y.C., 1977-78; dir. tng. and career devel. Girl Scouts U.S., N.Y.C., 1978-79; dir. Overseas Tour Ops. Am. Jewish Congress, N.Y.C., 1979-81; chief exec. officer Girl Scout Council Greater N.Y.C., 1981-82; adminstr., assoc. prof. bus. mgmt., chmn. bus. mgmt. and acctg. div. Marymount Manhattan Coll., N.Y.C., 1982—; adj. prof. N.Y.U., 1986—; mem. exec. com. Assn. Recreation Mgmt., N.Y.C., 1981; cons. Rockport Mgmt., Washington, 1974-78. Author: Test Your Management IQ, 1984; co-author: Lovejoy's Four Year College Guide for the Learning Disabled, 1985; contbr. articles to profl. jours. Chmn. Met. Dade County Commn. Status Women, Miami, 1975-77; chief planner Met. Dade County U.S. SBA 1st annual conf. Future Women Bus., 1977. Named to Hunter Coll. Hall of Fame, 1986. Mem. Acad. Mgmt., Hunter Coll. Alumni Assn. (bd. dirs. 1978—), Phi Delta Kappa. Republican. Jewish. Club: Lotos (mem. literary com. 1983—). Home: 242 E 72d St New York NY 10021 Office: Marymount Manhattan Coll 221 E 71st St New York City NY 10021

COLBY, MARYGRACE, athletic director; b. San Diego, Nov. 9, 1933; d. Elliott Gillette and Harriett Elizabeth (Leverich) C. BS in Edn., U. Ariz., 1955; MA in Edn., Calif. State U., Sacramento, 1964. Tchr. Madera (Calif.) High Sch., 1955-58; camp dir. Camp Fire Inc., Sacramento, 1958-60; tchr., coach El Camino High Sch., Sacramento, 1960-63; dir. women's athletics Santa Clara (Calif.) U., 1963—; mem. various coms. Santa Clara U., 1975—. Water safety instr. ARC, San Jose, Calif., 1963-86; active Santa Clara/Santa Cruz Council Camp Fire Inc., 1979—; mem. adv. com. Nat. Wheel Chair Competition, Santa Clara, 1986—. Recipient Nat. Service award ARC, 1973, Women of Achievement award San Jose Mercury News, 1974, Luther Gullick award Camp Fire Inc., 1985, John Collier award, 1986; inductee Athletic Hall of Fame Santa Clara U., 1982. Mem. Am. Assn. Health, Phys. Edn., and Recreation, Calif. Assn. Health, Phys. Edn., and Recreation, Nat. Sports Found., Nat. Assn. Female Execs., U.S. Tennis Assn., Delta Delta Delta (Stars in our Crescent award 1984). Republican. Presbyterian. Home: 118 Timber Cove Dr Campbell CA 95008 Office: Santa Clara U Santa Clara CA 95053

COLBY-HALL, ALICE MARY, Romance studies educator; b. Portland, Maine, Feb. 25, 1932; d. Frederick Eugene and Angie Fraser (Drown) C.; m. Robert A. Hall, Jr., May 8, 1976; stepchildren: Philip, Diana Hall Goodall, Carol Hall Erickson. B.A., Colby Coll., 1953; M.A., Middlebury Coll., 1954; Ph.D., Columbia U., 1962. Tchr. French, Latin Orono (Maine) High Sch., 1954-55; tchr. French Gould Acad., Bethel, Maine, 1955-57; lectr. French Columbia U., 1959-60; instr. romance lit. Cornell U., Ithaca, N.Y., 1962-63; asst. prof. Cornell U., 1963-66, assoc. prof., 1966-75, prof. romance studies, 1975—. Author: The Portrait in Twelfth Century French Literature: An Example of the Stylistic Originality of Chrétien de Troyes, 1965; mem. editorial bd.: Speculum, 1976-79, Olifant, 1974—. Fulbright grantee, 1953-54; NEH fellow, 1984-85; recipient Médaille des Amis d'Orange, 1985. Mem. Modern Lang. Assn., Medieval Acad. Am. (councillor 1983-86), Internat. Arthurian Soc., Société Rencesvals, Académie de Vaucluse, Phi Beta Kappa. Republican. Conglist. Home: 308 Cayuga Heights Rd Ithaca NY 14850 Office: Cornell U Dept Romance Studies Ithaca NY 14853

COLDIRON, KAREN SUE, banker; b. Greensburg, Ind., Mar. 16, 1940; d. Gordon Calvin and Ruth Helen (Anderson) Emly; m. James William Coldiron, Sept. 19, 1959; 1 child, Jeffrey William. Grad. Sch. of Banking, U. Wis., 1981. with Irwin Union Bank, Columbus, Ind., 1959—, v.p., 1982-88, sr. v.p., 1988—; instr. Am. Inst. Banking., Columbus, Ind., 1976-79; dir. Ind. Clearing House, Indpls., 1983—. Bd. dirs. Shelter for Victims of Domestic Violence, Columbus. Named Woman of Yr., Am. Bus. Women, 1977. Mem. Ind. Bankers Assn. (chmn. com.), Bus. and Profl. Women (state officer 1978, local pres. 1981-82), Nat. Assn. Bank Women (nat. bd. dirs., local, nat. officer 1979-86, nat. sec. 1984-85). Republican. Home: 13211 E SR 46 Columbus IN 47203 Office: Irwin Union Bank PO Box 929 500 Washington St Columbus IN 47203

COLE, ADELAIDE MEADOR, physical education educator; b. Hinton, W.Va., June 6, 1923; d. Vollmer Aden and Josephine Florence (Ratliff) Meador; m. James Lewis Cole, Nov. 29, 1964; children: John, Alexandra, Mary Adelaide, Tanya Sean. AB, Marshall Coll., 1946; MA, Duke U., 1947; EdD, Columbia U., 1950. Instr. phys. edn. Columbia U., 1950; prof. Cedarville (Ohio) Coll., 1951-52; assoc. prof. Pan Am. Coll., Edinburg, Tex., 1953-60, Calif. Western U., San Diego, 1960-61, N.Mex. Highlands U., Las Vegas, 1961-65; prof. emeritus phys. edn. Ball State U., Muncie, Ind., 1967-86, dir. grad. studies Sch. Phys. Edn., 1971-82, also adminstrv. asst. to chmn. sch., 1977-82. Recipient ARC Outstanding Service award, 1958. Mem. AAHPERD (Midwest chmn. research sect. 1981, Midwest chmn. resolutions com. 1984-86), Ind. Assn. for Health, Phys. Edn., Recreation and Dance (sec. 1981-86, Honor award 1985), LWV, DAR (regent Sarah Winston Henry chpt. 1983-85), Sigma Sigma Sigma, Phi Delta Kappa, Pi Lambda Theta. Democrat. Episcopalian. Lodges: Elks, Eagles, Rotary. Home: 968 Mary Lee Ave New Castle IN 47362

COLE, BARBARA JACOBS, dietitian; b. Fordyce, Ark., Apr. 5, 1953; d. Lenwood Sr. and Janie (Gipson) Jacobs; m. Lewis Charles Cole, Jan. 12, 1980. BS, Ouachita Bapt. U., Arkadelphia, Ark., 1975. Intern VA Hosp. and Med. Ctr., Little Rock, 1975-76; dir. dietary services Ark. Sch. for Blind, Little Rock, 1976—. Vol. Sickle-Cell Anemia Found., Little Rock, 1976—. Recipient Service award Kiwanis, 1985. Mem. Am. Dietetic Assn., Am. Sch. Food Service Assn. (regional dir. Southwest 1986—, chmn. resolutions and bylaws com. 1984-86, nominating com. 1988—, pub. communications com. 1988—), Ark. Dietetic Assn., Am. Sch. Food Service Assn. (mem. nominating com. 1988—, pub. communications com. 1988—, regional dir. SW 1986-88), Ark. Sch. Food Service Assn. (pres. elect 1982-83, pres. 1983-84, leadership 1984), Federated Women (pres. elect 1984-85, pres. 1985-86, regional dir. SW dist. 1986-88), Delta Sigma Theta. Democrat. Baptist. Lodge: Eastern Star. Home: 3 Poydras Dr Little Rock AR 72211 Office: Ark Sch for Blind 2600 W Markham Little Rock AR 72203

COLE, BETTY LOU MCDONEL SHELTON (MRS. DEWEY G. COLE JR.), judge; b. Elwood, Ind., June 5, 1926; d. Bernard Miller and Vee Marie (Robertson) McDonel; student Ind. U., 1947-50, LL.B., 1969; student Ball State U., 1964-65; m. Elbert Shelton, Dec. 13, 1944; children—Steven Elbert, Jeanette Louise; m. 2d, Dewey G. Cole, Jr., Dec. 24, 1975. Admitted to Ind. bar, 1969, Fed. Cts., 1969; practiced in Muncie, Ind., 1969—; pvt. practice Betty L. Shelton Law Office, 1970-78; sr. ptnr. firm Dunnuck, Cole, Rankin and Wyrick, Muncie, 1978-80; judge Delaware County Superior Ct., 1980—. Mem. Am., Nat. Assn. Women Judges, Ind. Bar Assn., Muncie Bar Assn., Ind. Judges Assn., Am. Trial Lawyers, Ind. U. Law Alumni Assn., Nat. Assn. Women Judges, LWV (league pres. 1963-64), Bus. and Profl. Women. Clubs: Delaware Country (Muncie), Riley-Jones. Office: Del County Courthouse 100 W Main St Muncie IN 47305

COLE, CLAUDIA ANN, educational association administrator; b. Ravenna, Ohio, Aug. 1, 1947; d. Allen P. and Pauline M. (Carpenter) Hensley; divorced. BS in Elem. Edn., Kent (Ohio) State U., 1969; MS in Ednl. Adminstrn., Akron (Ohio) U., 1975; M in Labor and Human Relations, Ohio State U., 1984. Tchr. pub. sch. Hudson, Ohio, 1969-76; cons. in instructional and profl. devel. Ohio Edn. Assn., Columbus, 1977-84, uniserv cons., negotiator, 1981-84; exec. dir. Del. State Edn. Assn., Dover, 1984-87, Ariz. Edn. Assn., Phoenix, 1987—; cons. C & D Assocs., Columbus, 1981-84; past pres. Greater Akron Edn. Assn. Pres.'s Council, 1975; bd. dirs. Horace Mann Ins. Co., Springfield, Ill. Mem. Gov.'s Task Force on Edn., Del., 1985-87; pres. Multiple Sclerosis Soc., Columbus, 1980-84; com. mem. Del. State Bd. Edn., Dover, 1985-86. Recipient Helen Wise award Del. State Edn. Assn., 1987, Order of Excellence award Del. State Bd. Edn., 1987, Merit award Del. State Supt.'s Office, 1987; honored by resolution Del. Senate and Ho. of Reps., 1987. Mem. Am. Mgmt. Assn., Am. Soc. Assoc. Execs., Bus. and Profl. Women's Assn. (bd. dirs. 1981-84). Office: Ariz Edn Assn 2102 Indian School Rd Phoenix AZ 85015

COLE, CONNIE JEAN, fiscal director; b. Monroe, Mich., July 27, 1947; d. Harry Carl Lymond and Bonnie (Smith) Koch; m. Delbert Raymond Cole, Mar. 25, 1967 (div. Sept. 1977); children: Delbert R., Jr., Jeffery Scot. Grad. high sch., Monroe, 1965. Sec. Boyles Galvanizing Co., Monroe and Louisville, 1968-73; clk. payroll Econ. Opportunity, Inc., Monroe, 1974-75; technician computer ops. Conn. Mut. Life Ins. Co., Monroe, 1975-76; mgr. personnel Monroe County Opportunity Program, 1976-78; acct., officer affirmative action Council on Chem. Abuse, Reading, Pa., 1978-79; fiscal dir. Econ. Opportunity Council of Reading and Berks County, Inc., Reading, 1979—; cons., trainer 55-Plus Club, Reading Sch. Dist., Berks County Intermediate Unit, Consumer Action, 1980—. Recipient Outstanding Staff head Start Policy Council, 1985. Mem. Parents Without Ptnrs. (v.p. Monroe chpt. 1976-78). Republican. Home: 338 Main St Bernville PA 19506 Office: Econ Opportunity Council of Reading and Berks County Inc 229 N Fourth St Reading PA 19601

COLE, DEBRA LYNNE, elementary educator; b. Houston, Sept. 14, 1955; d. John Willie Jr. and Mercer Josephine (Jenkins) C. BS cum laude, Tex. So. U., 1978, MS, 1987. Child devel. lab. student asst. W.R. Banks Child Devel. Lab., Houston, 1975-76; art instr. Bunnyland A-Cat-A-Me, Houston, 1976-

77; head tchr. and asst. to dir. Pilgrim Day Care Ctr., Houston, 1977-79; tchr., 3d grade gifted student instr. Houston Ind. Sch. Dist., Houston, 1980—; mem. Houston Area Assn. for Edn. Young Children, Houston, 1976-79, State Dept. Human Resources, Houston, 1977-79, Houston Ind. Sch. Dist., Houston, 1979-86. Vol. Carter-Mondale Presdl. Campaign, Houston, 1976, United Negro Coll. Fund Telethon, Houston, 1985; mem. PTA, Houston, 1980—, Getsename Bapt. Ch. Young Singles Com., Houston. Named one of Outstanding Young Educator Houston Ind. Sch. Dist., 1981, 84; Nat. Dean's List Ednl. Communications Inc., Northbrook, Ill., 1977-78. Mem. NEA, Houston Tchrs. Assn., Tex. State Tchrs. Assn., Tau Sigma Upsilon (treas. 1976-77, pres. 1977-78), Assn. Childhood Edn. Internat. (v.p. 1976-77, pres. 1977-78). Home: 8743 Othello St Houston TX 77029

COLE, DIANE JACKSON, textile manufacturing company executive; b. Amesbury, Mass., Sept. 14, 1952; d. Robert Keith and Lois Elizabeth (Fogg) Jackson. B.F.A. cum laude, U. N.H., 1974; student U. London, Sir John Cass Coll. Art, London, Richmond Coll., Surrey, Eng. Owner Diane Jackson Cole Handweaving, Kennebunk, Maine, 1974—; pres. Kennebunk Weavers, Inc., 1981—. Contbr. articles to profl. jours., mags. Exhbns. include: Fiber Invitational, Milw., 1977, Currier Gallery Art, N.H., 1981, League N.H. Craftsmen, 1983. Mem. Profl. Crafts Orgn. Maine (newsletter editor 1978, sec. 1979, v.p. 1980), League N.H. Craftsmen, Nat. Bath, Bed and Linen Assn. Republican. Avocations: swimming, sailing, skiing, reading. Home: 9 Grove St Kennebunk ME 04043 Office: Kennebunk Weavers Inc Box A Canal St Suncook NH 03275

COLE, ELMA PHILLIPSON (MRS. JOHN STRICKLER COLE), social welfare executive; b. Piqua, Ohio, Aug. 9, 1909; d. Brice Leroy and Mabel (Gale) Phillipson; m. John Strickler Cole, Oct. 3, 1959. AB, Berea Coll., 1930; MA, U. Chgo., 1938. Various positions in social work, 1930-42; dir. dept. social service Children's Hosp. D.C., Washington, 1942-49; cons. pub. cooperation Midcentury White House Conf. on Children and Youth, Washington, 1949-51; exec. sec. Nat. Midcentury Com. on Children and Youth, Washington, 1951-53; cons. recruitment Am. Assn. Med. Social Workers, 1953; assoc. dir. Nat. Legal Aid and Defender Assn., 1953-56; exec. sec. Marshall Field Awards, Inc., 1956-57; dir. assoc. orgns. Nat. Assembly Social Policy and Devel., 1957-73; assoc. exec. dir. Nat. Assembly Nat. Vol. Health and Social Welfare Orgns., 1974; dir. edn. parenthood project Salvation Army, 1974-76, asst. sec. dept. women's and children's social services, 1976-78, dir. research project devel. bur., 1978—, mem. Manhattan adv. bd., 1975—, sec., 1984—, mem. hist. commn., 1978—, mem. exec. com., 1988—; cons. nat. orgns. Golden Anniversary White House Conf. on Children and Youth, 1959-60; mem. adv. council pub. service Nat. Assn. Life Underwriters and Inst. Life Ins.; mem. judges com. Louis I. Dublin Pub. Service awards, 1961-74; v.p. Blue Ridge Inst. So. Community Service Execs., 1977-79, mem. exec. com., 1979-81; mem. awards jury Girls Clubs of Am., 1981—; mem. adv. bd. Nat. Family Life Edn. Network, 1982—. Mem. com. public relations and fund raising Am. Found. for Blind Commn. on Accreditation, 1964-67; mem. task force on vol. accreditation Council Nat. Orgns. for Adult Edn., 1974-78; mem. adv. bd. sexuality edn. project Ctr. for Population Options, 1977—; sec., bd. dirs. James Lenox House and James Lenox House Assn., 1985—; bd. dirs. Values and Human Sexuality Inst., 1980—. Mem. Pub. Relations Soc. Am. (cert.), Nat. Assn. Social Workers (cert.), Nat. Conf. Social Welfare (mem. pub. relations com. 1961-66, 69-82, chair adminstrn. sect. 1966-67), Jr. League Washington, Pi Gamma Mu, Phi Kappa Phi. Club: Women's of N.Y. Home: 19 Washington Sq N New York NY 10011 Office: 120 W 14th St New York NY 10011

COLE, HELEN, state senator; b. Tishomingo, Okla., July 13, 1922; m. John Cole; 2 children. Mem. Okla. Ho. of Reps., 37-39th sessions; mem. Okla. Senate, 1984—. Active Cleveland County Republican Women's Club. Mem. Yukon C. of C., Am. Legion Aux. Office: Okla Senate State Capitol Oklahoma City OK 73105 Other Address: 104 Briarwood Moore OK 73160

COLE, JANE BAGBY, librarian; b. Tulsa, May 23, 1931; d. Walter James and Mary Frances (Eakin) Bagby; m. Bruce Herman Cole, June 7, 1953; children—Rosemary Neilsen, Dorothy Domrzalski, Robert Bagby, Frances. B.A., Grinnell Coll., 1953; M.A., U. Chgo., 1977. Library asst. Elem. Dist. 101, Western Springs, Ill., 1961-71, library aide, 1973-75; librarian Elem. Dist. 102, La Grange, Ill., 1975-77, River Forest Jr. High Sch., Ill., 1977-79; audio-visual dir. Elem. Dist. 7, Phoenix, 1980-83; library dir., curator Desert Bot. Garden, Phoenix, 1983—; discussion leader Gt. Books Found., Chgo., 1965-79, Phoenix, 1981—. Editor Saguaroland Bull., 1984-86. Precinct worker senatorial campaign, Cook County, Ill., 1966-67, Maricopa County, Ariz., 1980. Mem. ALA, Spl. Libraries Assn., Ariz. Paper and Photograph Conservation Group, Council Bot. and Hort. Libraries. Office: Desert Bot Garden 1201 N Galvin Pkwy Phoenix AZ 85008

COLE, JOAN HAYS, social worker, clinical psychologist; b. Pitts., Sept. 4, 1929; d. Frank L. Wertheimer and Edith H. Einstein; BA, Western Res. U., 1951; MSSA in Social Work, Case Western Res. U., 1962; PhD, Wright Inst., 1975; m. Robert M. Wendlinger, June 1984; children: Geoffrey F. Cole, Douglas R. Cole, Peter Hays Cole. Social group worker Alta House Settlement House, Cleve., 1958-59; housing dir. Cleve. Urban League, 1961-62; dir. Citizens for Safe Housing, Cleve., 1963; housing dir. United Planning Orgn., Washington, 1963-68; asst. prof. community orgn. U. Md., Balt., 1968-72; asso. prof. Lone Mountain Coll., San Francisco, 1975-78; psychotherapist, supr., organizational cons., Berkeley, Calif., 1977—; cons. various public and vol. social welfare, health and housing agys., 1969—; mem. adj. faculty Union Grad. Sch. and Antioch West Coll., 1978-80; lectr. U. Calif. Sch. Social Welfare, Berkeley, 1980-84; mem. faculty Berkeley Psychotherapy Inst., 1981—, pres., 1983-85. NIMH grantee, 1971-72, Sr. Social Work Career Devel. grantee, 1973-75. Fellow Soc. Clin. Social Work, Am. Orthopsychiat. Assn.; mem. Nat. Assn. Social Workers, Soc. Study of Social Issues, ACLU, NOW, Acad. Cert. Social Workers, Nat. Conf. on social Welfare and Psychotherapists for Social Responsibility. Home: 1377 Campus Dr Berkeley CA 94708 Office: 1905 Berkeley Way Berkeley CA 94704

COLE, JOHNNETTA BETSCH, academic administrator; b. Jacksonville, Fla., Oct. 19, 1936; d. John Thomas and Mary Frances (Lewis) Betsch; m. Robert Eugene Cole (div. 1982); children: David, Aaron, Ethan. Student, Fisk U., 1953; BAin Anthropology, Oberlin Coll., 1957; MA in Anthropology, Northwestern U., Evanston, Ill., 1959, PhD, 1967. Instr. U. Calif., Los Angeles, 1964; dir. black studies Wash. State U., Pullman, 1969-70; prof. anthropology U. Mass., Amherst, 1970-83, assoc. prof. undergrad. edn., 1981-83; vis. prof. Hunter Coll., N.Y.C., 1983-84, dir. Inter-Am. Affairs Program, 1984-87, prof. anthropology, 1985-87; pres. Spelman Coll., Atlanta, 1987—; pres. Internat. Women's Anthropology Conf.; mem. editorial bd. The BlackScholar; bd. dirs. The Feminist Press. Author, editor: Anthropology for the Eighties, 1982, All American Women, 1986, Anthropology for the Nineties, 1988. Mem. adv. com. Liberal Edn. Fellow Am. Anthrop. Assn.; mem. Assn. Black Anthropologists. Baptist. Home: Spelman Coll Reynolds Cottage 350 Spelman Ln SW Atlanta GA 30314 Office: Spelman Coll Office of the Pres 350 Spelman Lane SW Atlanta GA 30314

COLE, KAREN LORRAINE, operating engineer; b. Norco, Calif., Apr. 12, 1954; d. William G. Willis and Lorraine Ruth (Buratti) Willis-Beisner; children: Cirdon Brion, Vanna Alia. Apprentice, Trade Tech. Coll., Los Angeles, 1980-84, Journeyman Grad., 1984. Apprentice engr. Cushman & Wakefield, Los Angeles, 1980-83, Bank of Calif., 1983-84, chief operating engr., 1984—. Active Boy Scouts Am. Mem. Nat. Assn. Female Execs., Bldg. Owners and Mgrs. Assn., Local 501 Internat. Union Operating Engrs. (Apprentice of Yr. award 1984). Avocations: design and construction of stained-glass windows, scuba diving, off-road driving. Office: Cushman & Wakefield Calif Inc 515 S Flower St Suite 2200 Los Angeles CA 90071

COLE, KATHERINE IONE, market research professional; b. Atlanta, July 30, 1949; d. Henry Grady Cole and Lois Ann (Fentress) Wilbur; m. John Edwin Sherman, May 9, 1987. BA, Columbia Coll., 1971; MBA, North Tex. State U., 1976, postgrad., 1977-79. Research asst. M/A/R/C/ Inc., Dallas, 1973-75; ind. mktg. research cons. Denton, Tex. and Fresno, Calif., 1976-81; teaching fellow North Tex. State U., Denton, 1977-79; assoc. prof. Calif. State U., Fresno, 1979-81; dir. mktg. Mammoth Pub. and Advt., Mammoth Lakes, Calif., 1982-83; pres. MarkeTec Inc., Reno, 1984—; lectr. U. Nev., Reno, 1984-86; cons. in field. Contbr. articles to profl. jours. Bd. dirs. Nev. St. Fair, 1988—; pres. Sierra Nev. council Girl Scouts U.S., Reno, 1987—, sec., 1986-87, bd. dirs. 1986. Mem. Am. Mktg. Assn. no. Nev. chpt. (v.p. membership 1987-88, v.p. administrn. 1988—), Mktg. Research Assn., Reno-Sparks C. of C., Leadership Reno Program, Delta Sigma Pi (faculty advisor 1980-81). Mem. Christian Ch. Office: MarkeTec Inc PO Box 9058 Reno NV 89507

COLE, L(ILLA) JO, technical writer; b. Beaufort, N.C., July 1, 1936; d. Carl Kenneth and Iva Ella (Harris) Wright; m. Donald Alan Cole, Jan. 2, 1981. BA in English, Greensboro Coll., 1958; MA in Journalism, Am. U., 1969. Reporter Greensboro (N.C.) Record, 1956-58; correspondent Group Hospitalization, Inc., Washington, 1958-61; editorial asst. Nat. Planning Assn., Washington, 1962-64; editor Planning Research Corp., Washington, 1964-69; dir. tech. services Computer Scis. Corp., Silver Spring, Md., 1969-81; writer Satellite Bus. Systems, McLean, Va., 1981-86, IBM Corp., Bethesda, Md., 1986—. Home: 8011 Grand Teton Dr Potomac MD 20854 Office: IBM 10401 Fernwood Rd Bethesda MD 20817

COLE, LORELEI HELENA, accountant; b. N.Y.C., Jan. 29, 1942; d. Frank John and Elise Elvira (Edenfield) Amato; children: Adrienne Lee, Kimberleigh Suzanne. BBA cum laude, U. Miami, 1972. Sr. acct. Town of Surfside, Fla., 1964-68; acct. to sr. mgr. Peat Marwick Mitchell and Co., Miami, 1968-76; sr. mgr. N.Y.C., 1976-78; ptnr. Chgo., 1978-87. Treas. Chgo. Coaltion for the Homeless, 1986-87. Mem. Am. Inst. CPA's, Fla. Inst. CPA's, Ill. Inst. CPA's, Pi Kappa Phi, Beta Gamma Sigma, Beta Alpha Psi. Clubs: The Economic, Women's Athletic (Chgo.). Home and Office: 628 W Sheridan Rd Chicago IL 60613

COLE, SALLY DIANE, corporate secretary, controller; b. Chgo., Jan. 29, 1943; d. Lowell Wade and Florence Margaret (Schnoor) Stout; m. Lawrence Cole, June 19, 1960 (div. Jan. 1973); children: Margaret, John, Teresa, James, Bobbette, Jeffrey. AA, San Jose City Coll., 1978; BS, San Jose State Coll., 1980. Sr. staff acct. Quezada, Navarro and Co., San Jose, Calif., 1980-82; acctg. mgr. Cambridge Systems Group, Santa Clara, Calif., 1982-85; controller, corp. sec. Micro-MRP, Inc., Foster City, Calif., 1985—. Pres. parent assn. Bachrodt Sch., San Jose, 1977-79; lobbyist Calif. State Senate, Sacramento, 1984-85; freespeech messenger 2 local TV stas., San Jose, 1984. Scholar Profl. Bus. Women's Assn., 1977. Mem. Nat. Assn. Female Execs., Nat. Assn. Accts., Nat. Assn. Controllers-Counsels. Democrat. Home: 5427 Colony Green Dr San Jose CA 95123 Office: Micro-MRP Inc 1065 E Hillsdale Blvd Foster City CA 94404

COLE, SHERRELL MILLER, auditor; b. Jackson, Tenn., Aug. 27, 1958; d. Raymond E. and Ellis (Cobb) Miller; m. F. Joseph Cole, June 27, 1982; 1 child, Stephen Russell. AS, Jackson State Community Coll., 1978; BS, U. Tenn., Martin, 1980. Auditor II Tenn. Dept. Revenue, Jackson, 1981-87, auditor III, 1987—. Presbyterian. Club: Woodland Hills Golf and Country (Jackson). Office: Tenn Dept Revenue 225 Madison Box 44 Jackson TN 38301

COLE, SUE KATHRYN, records manager; b. Dallas, Dec. 12, 1947; d. Harry Roosevelt and Kathryn (Conibear) Cole. BS, Tex. Tech. U., 1970. Records analyst Tenneco Inc., Houston, 1971-75; contract adminstr. Pullman-Kellogg, Houston, 1975-81; micrographics coordinator Dallas County Community Coll. Dist., 1983-84, dist. records mgr., 1984—; cons. in field, Dallas. Mem. Willow Falls Restoration Com., Dallas, 1987. Mem. Assn. Records Mgrs and Adminstrs. (chair legisl. com., bd. dirs. 1986-87), Assn. of Info. and Image Mgmt., Soc. Am. Archivists, Tex. Jr. Coll. Tchrs. Assn., Bus. Forms Mgmt. Assn., Am. Philatelic Soc. Republican. Methodist. Club: Single Adults. Office: Dallas County Community Coll Dist 4343 N Hwy 67 Mesquite TX 75150

COLE, SUSIE CLEORA, government employee relations official; b. Bloomsburg, Pa.; d. Harry E. and Chloe Ann (McKinstry) Cole; m. Richard Edward Miller, July 31, 1959 (div. Aug. 1977); 1 child, Terri Lee Miller; m. Gerald Edward Nelson, Feb. 18, 1978 (div. June 1982). Student in history No. Va. Community Coll., 1982; also govt. courses. With Dept. Navy, Washington, 1957-74, clk., technician U.S. Dept. Navy, Washington, 1957-67, Navy mil. pay regulations specialist, 1962-71; mgr. error detection and reduction for mil. pay, allowances and travel program 1967-71, fiscal acct. 1971-74, fiscal clk. Dept. State, Washington, 1975-77, sr. retirement claims examiner, 1977-83, employee relations officer, 1983—, also mgr. fed. health benefits program and mgr. fed. life ins. program, 1983—. Active Citizen's Band Radio Club, Fairfax, Va., 1974-82, Retarded Children's Ctr., Fairfax, 1981-82. Recipient various govt. awards, including Sustained Exceptional Achievement award Dept. State, 1983, 84, 85, 86, 87. Mem. Nat. Assn. Female Execs. Democrat. Avocations: reading; travel; history; music; art. Home: 4605 John Tyler Ct Apt 104 Annandale VA 22003 Office: US Dept State Bur Personnel Office Employee Relations 2201 C St NW Washington DC 20520

COLE-BALES, LISA MICHELE, sales executive; b. Kansas City, Mo., Jan. 4, 1955; d. Richard Thomas and Norma Lea (Riggs) Cole; m. Mitchell Aldon Bales, Sept. 20, 1987. BA in English Journalism, U. Mo., Kansas City, 1977. Contract specialist Midwest Research Inst., Kansas City, 1977-78; supply rep. Hotz Co., Kansas City, 1978-80; sales rep. Standard Havens, Kansas City, 1980-81; hosp. rep. Abbott Labs., Columbia, Mo., 1981-82; hosp. specialist Abbott Labs., Kansas City, 1982-85; area sales mgr. Home Med. Support Services, Inc., Kansas City, 1985—. Legis. liason Jr. Women's Symphony Alliance, Kansas City, 1985-86; arts and crafts dir. Kansas City Hist. Found. Spirit Festival, 1984-86. Mem. Nat. Assn. Profl. Saleswomen (pres. Kansas City chpt. 1984-85, chairperson corp. mem. nat. bd. 1985-86), Nat. Assn. Female Execs. Club: Cellarmasters (Kansas City). Home: 9409 Valley Garden Dr Kansas City MO 64139 Office: Home Med Support Services Inc 8428 Melrose Kansas City MO 66214

COLEHOUR, JEAN MARIE, insurance company executive; b. Mpls., May 15, 1954; d. Clement August and Mary Elizabeth (Kunst) Kreger; m. William Wardwell Colehour, Oct. 12, 1974; children: Valerie Jean, Colin William. Cert. in programming and ops., Minn. Sch. Bus., 1973; AA in Bus. Adminstrn. with honors, Miami (Fla.) Dade Community Coll., 1986; student, U. Miami, 1986—. Computer operator No. States Power Co., Mpls., 1973-74, claims examiner, 1974-76; claims examiner Employee Benefit Claims, Inc., Mpls., 1976-78, John Alden Life Ins. Co., Mpls., 1978-79; claims supr. John Alden Life Ins. Co., Miami, 1979-84, claims system analyst, 1984-85, mgmt. info. systems mgr., 1985-86, project mgr., 1986, instr. Life Office Mgmt. Assn., 1986-87; dir. ops. John Alden Risk Mgmt. Services, Miami, 1986—. Cons. Jr. Achievement of Greater Miami, 1986-87. Fellow Life Office Mgmt. Assn. Democrat. Roman Catholic. Home: 10304 Fairway Heights Blvd Miami FL 33157 Office: John Alden Risk Mgmt Services PO Box 527750 Miami FL 33152-7750

COLEMAN, AGNES ELAINE, home economist; b. Montgomery, Ala., Sept. 30, 1959; d. Jewel Bryant and Willie Agnes (Steele) C. BS, Tuskegee (Ala.) U., 1981. Cert. home economist. Asst. county agt. Ala. Cooperative Extension Service, Livingston, 1981—, 4-H agt., 1981-87. Mem. Beautification Bd., Sumter County, Ala., 1983—. Nominated one of Outstanding Young Women Am., 1986. Mem. Ala. Assn. Extension 4-H Agts., Am. Home Econs. Assn., Ala. Home Econs. Assn., Coalition 100 Black Women, Epsilon Sigma Phi, Delta Sigma Theta. Club: Crimson and Creme (Livingston). Home: PO Box 1233 Livingston AL 35470 Office: Ala Coop Extension Service 24 Washington St PO Drawer H Livingston AL 35470

COLEMAN, ANNETTE WILBOIS, biology educator; b. Des Moines, Iowa, Feb. 28, 1934; d. Fred J. and Agnes D. Wilbois; m. John R. Coleman, July 26, 1958; children—Alan, Benjamin, Suzanne. B.A., Columbia U., 1955; Ph.D., U. Ind., 1958. Postdoctoral fellow Johns Hopkins U., Balt., 1958-61; research associate U. Conn., 1961-63; research assoc. Brown U., Providence, 1964-72, asst. prof. biology research, 1972-76, asst. prof., 1976-80, assoc. prof., 1980-84, prof., 1984—, Stephen T. Olney prof. natural history, 1984—. NSF postdoctoral fellow, 1955-58, 58-60; Guggenheim fellow, 1983-84, recipient Provasoli award, 1985, Darbaker award, 1986. Fellow N.Y. Acad. Scis.; mem. Bot. Soc. Am., Soc. Protozoologists, Phcol. Soc. Am. (pres. 1981-82). Office: Brown U Bio-Med Dept Providence RI 02912

COLEMAN, BEATRICE, intimate apparel company executive; b. Jersey City, N.J., 1916. Grad. Barnard Coll., 1938. Chmn., pres., Maidenform, Inc., N.Y.C. Named to Working Woman mag. Hall of Fame, 1987. Office: Maidenform Inc 90 Park Ave New York NY 10016 *

COLEMAN, BETHANY BALDWIN, insurance executive; b. Miami, Dec. 4, 1950; d. C. Jackson and Mary Susanne (Bonner) Baldwin; m. Carl Randolph Coleman, May 27, 1983. Student U. Ala., 1969-72. Lic. property and casualty ins. agt., life ins. agt., claims adjuster, Fla. Claims adjuster Liberty Mut. Ins. Co., Miami, 1973-75, Kemper Ins. Co., Miami, 1975-76; asst. to pres. Baldwin Ins. Agy., Miami, 1976—, also bd. dirs. Trustee Expo 500: 1992 Columbus Exposition, 1982—; Miami chairperson Nat. Family Bus. Council, 1983-84, bd. dirs., 1983; mem. citizens adv. bd. Bloomingdale's So. Fla., 1984—; mem. Orange Bowl Com., Miami, 1985—; mem. new tequestians com. Hist. Mus. of So. Fla., 1985—; chairwoman dinner com. Big Brothers/Big Sisters Greater Miami, 1986-87; mem. Doctors Hosp. Found. bd., 1987—. Mem. Fla. Assn. Ind. Agts., Nat. Assn. Security Dealers, Ind. Ins. Agts. of Dade County, Greater Miami C. of C. (com. for United Way 1985), U. Ala. Alumni Assn., Phi Beta Phi. Clubs: Generation of Miami (pres. 1983-84, chmn. 1984-85), Riviera Country (Coral Gables, Fla.); Palm Bay, New World Ctr., U. Miami Hurricane (bd. dirs.), Bankers, (Miami). Home: 1532 Dorado Ave Coral Gables FL 33146 Office: Baldwin Ins Agy Inc 840 Biscayne Blvd Miami FL 33132

COLEMAN, DEBORAH ANN, computer company executive; b. Providence, Jan. 22, 1953; d. John Austin and Joan Mary Coleman. BA, Brown U., 1974; MBA, Stanford U., 1978; PhD in Engring. (hon.), Worcester (Mass.) Poly., 1987. Prodn. supr. metals and controls Tex. Instruments, Attleboro, Mass., 1974; fin. mgmt. tng. program Gen. Electric, Providence, 1974-76; gen. acctg. supr., fin. system analyst components group Hewlett-Packard, Cupertino, Calif., 1978-79, cost acctg. supr. instrument group, 1980, fin. mgr. tech. computer group, 1981; controller Macintosh project Apple Computer, Cupertino, 1981-82, div. controller Macintosh project, 1982-83, sr. fin. controller Apple 32 product group, 1983-84, ops. mgr. Macintosh div., 1984, dir. ops. Macintosh div., 1985, v.p. ops., 1986-87, chief fin. officer, v.p. fin., 1987—; dir. worldwide mfg. Apple Computer, Fremont, Calif., 1985, v.p. worldwide mfg., 1985-86; v.p. ops. Apple Computer, Fremont, 1986-87, chief fin. officer, v.p. fin., 1987—; bd. dirs. Claris Software, Mountain View, Calif. Advisor Harvard U. Bus. Sch.; bd. dirs. Resource Ctr. for Women, Palo Alto, Calif., 1986—. Mem. Stanford Inst. Mfg. and Automation (indsl. advisor 1985-87), Com. 200, APICS. Democrat. Roman Catholic. Office: Apple Computer Inc 20525 Mariana Ave Cupertino CA 95014

COLEMAN, DONNA ANN, former state legislator; b. Sao Paulo, Brazil, Mar. 11, 1949; d. John M. and Donna (Hendricks) C.; BS, U. Utah, 1974; MBA, Washington U., St. Louis, 1985; corp. sec.-treas., dir., fin. officer Engineered Fire Protection, Inc., St. Louis, 1977—, bd. dirs., trustee employee profit sharing trust. Mem. Mo. Ho. of Reps., 1981-82, 83-84; dir. speakers bur. Mo. Citizens Council, 1979-80; del. Mo. Rep. Conv., 1980, 84; mem. Mo. Rep. Platform Com., 1984; chmn. Mo. Ho. of Reps. Rep. Caucus Campaign Com., 1983-84; appointed 2 yr. term 1986-87, reappointed 3 yr. term , 1988 vice chmn. Mo. Council Women's Econ. Devel. and Tng. Mormon. Home: 2449 Baxton Way Chesterfield MO 63017

COLEMAN, JANE DWIGHT DEXTER, communications executive; b. Boston, Aug. 24, 1942; d. Franklin and Mianne (Palfrey) Dexter; m. Peter S. Coleman, Aug. 18, 1969; 1 son, Dan C. A.B., Barnard Coll., 1965; M.Phil., Ph.D., Columbia U., 1976. Adj. lectr. Hunter Coll., 1974-75; mgr. program analysis CBS Broadcast Group, 1976-77, dir. program analysis, east, 1977-80; mgr. Sta. WINS, N.Y.C., 1980-81; v.p., gen. mgr. Sta. WIND, Chgo., 1981; pres. Oberland Prodns., N.Y.C., 1982-84; assoc. dir. adminstrn. Gannett Ctr. for Media Studies, 1985—. Mem. Nat. Acad. TV Arts and Scis., Internat. Radio and TV Soc. Office: Columbia U Gannett Ctr Media Studies 2950 Broadway New York NY 10027

COLEMAN, JEAN BLACK, nurse, physician assistant; b. Sharon, Pa., Jan. 11, 1925; d. Charles B. and Sue E. (Dougherty) Black; m. Donald A. Coleman, July 3, 1946; children: Sue Ann Coleman Lynn, Donald Ashley. RN, Spencer Hosp. Sch. Nursing, Meadville, Pa., 1945; student Vanderbilt U., 1952-54. Nurse, dir. nursing Bulloch Meml. Hosp., Statesboro, Ga., 1948-51, nurse supr. surgery, 1954-67, dir. nursing, 1967-71; physicians asst., nurse anesthetist to Robert H. Swint, Statesboro, 1971—; mem. physician assts. adv. com. Bd. Med. Examiners Ga., 1987-89. Named Woman of Yr. in Med. Field, Bus. and Profl. Women, 1980. Mem. Am. Nurses Assn., Ga. Nurses Assn., Am. Acad. Physicians Assts., Ga. Assn. Physicians Assts. (bd. dirs. 1975-79, v.p. 1979-80, pres. 1980-81). Democrat. Roman Catholic.

COLEMAN, JUDITH, library director; b. Indpls., July 29, 1947; d. Jack Leroy and Mercedes Louise (Thompson) C. BA, Barnard Coll., 1969; MLS, Columbia U., 1971; MBA, Kent (Ohio) State U., 1987. Dir. Bellevue (Ohio) Pub. Library, 1975-79, Tuscarawas County Pub. Library, New Philadelphia, Ohio, 1979-85, Euclid (Ohio) Pub. Library, 1986—; mem. State Bd. Library Examiners State Library Ohio, Columbus, 1983-86; instr. Cleve. Area Met. Library System Kent State U., 1986. Mem. Pub. Library Financing and Support Com., Columbus, 1983-86, Euclid Devel. Corp., 1986—. Mem. AAUW, Am. Library Assn., Ohio Library Assn. (bd. dirs. 1981-83, v.p., pres.-elect 1988-89). Democrat. Presbyterian. Club: Women's City (Cleve.). Home: 814 E 236th St Euclid OH 44123 Office: Euclid Pub Library 621 E 222d St Euclid OH 44123

COLEMAN, KATHREN TEMPA, real estate agent; b. Denver, Feb. 13, 1910; d. Ralph and Tempa Mae (Rainwater) Eggleston; m. Clarence E. Pederson, July 17, 1941 (dec.); stepchildren: Thomas R. Pederson, Richard L. Pederson; m. Kenneth Jack Coleman Sr., May 13, 1960. Student, U. N.Mex., 1927-28, U. Tex., El Paso, 1976-77; grad., Dale Carnegie Coll., 1987. Lic. real estate agt. Real estate agt. Hovious Assocs., Inc. (now Coldwell Banker Hovious Assocs., Inc.), El Paso, 1975—. Mem. El Paso Symphony Guild, 1983-84; election inspector, El Paso, 1982. Mem. Nat. Assn. Realtors (women's council 1979, Tex. Gov. 1983), Women's Council Realtors (Tex. Dist. v.p 1984, treas. 1985, sec. tex. chpt. 1986, pres. Tex. chpt. 1988), El Paso Bd. Realtors (bd. dirs.), Tex. Assn. Realtors (bd. dirs.), Am. Inst. Parliamentariansm Grad. Realtors Inst., Leadership Tng. Inst. Presbyterian. Clubs: Trepac 99, Million Dollar Producers. Office: Coldwell Banker Hovious Assocs Inc 5801 Acacia Circle El Paso TX 79912

COLEMAN, LILLIAN SIMONS, editor, writer; b. Atlanta, Jan. 26, 1955; d. Henry Mazyck and Martha Jane (Mack) Simons; m. John Dozier Coleman III, Nov. 29, 1975; children: Keating Simons, Lillian Marshall. BA in English, Columbia (S.C.) Coll., 1977; M in Mass Communications, U. S.C., 1980. Instr. journalism U. S.C., Sumter, 1979-82; communications mgr. Assn. for Edn. in Journalism and Mass Communications, Columbia, 1982-84, asst. editor, 1984-87, editor, 1987—; freelance writer, photographer Richland Northeast newspaper, Columbia, 1978-79, Sandlapper mag., Columbia, 1980-82, Carolina Lifestyle mag., Columbia, 1983. Pres. St. Teresa's Guild-St. John's Episcopal Ch., Columbia, 1985-86; pub. relations chmn. Holiday Market, Columbia, 1987; vol. editor Adoption Agy. newsletter, Columbia, 1988. Mem. Assn. Jr. Leagues (Columbia league), Kappa Tau Alpha. Republican. Home: 629 Springlake Rd Columbia SC 29206 Office: Assn for Edn in Journalism and Mass Communications 1621 College St Columbia SC 29206

COLEMAN, MARILYN (ADAMS), poultry science consultant; b. Lancaster, S.C., Mar. 27, 1946; d. Coyte and Jill J.D. (Lyon) Adams; B.S. in Biology, U. S.C., 1968; Ph.D. in Physiology, Auburn U., 1976; postgrad. U. Va., summer, 1971, 72, Va. Poly. Inst., 1972; m. George Edward Coleman III, Jan. 27, 1968; children—Jill Ann Marie, George Edward IV. Teaching asst. U. S.C., 1967-68; research technician Va. Poly. Inst. and State U., Blacksburg, 1968, teaching asst. biology, 1970-72; tchr. biology and basketball coach Brunswick County (Va.) Pub. Schs., 1968-69; research asst. poultry sci. Auburn (Ala.) U., 1973-76; asst. prof. poultry sci. Ohio State U.,

Columbus, 1977-81, adj. asso. prof., 1982—; propr. MAC Assos., Columbus, Ohio, 1974—; cons. to poultry industry throughout U.S. and 60 fgn. countries, 1974—. Pianist, New Cut Presbyn. Ch., Lancaster, 1960-64; tchr.'s aide Mountview Baptist Ch., Upper Arlington, Ohio, 1964. Nat. winner 4-H, 1964; NSF grantee, 1967, 71-72. Named Top 10 Young Execs., Esquire Mag., 1985. Mem. Poultry Sci. Assn., Am. Physiol. Assn., World Poultry Sci. Assn., Assn. of Southeastern Biologists, Auburn U. Alumni Assn., U. S.C. Alumni Assn., Sigma Xi, Phi Sigma. Republican. Contbr. numerous articles on poultry sci. to profl. publs. Home and Office: 2532 Zollinger Rd Columbus OH 43221

COLEMAN, MARY LOUISE, medical laboratory administrator; b. Harrison, Miss., Dec. 1; d. Clyde and Mattie (Smith) Cadney; m. Clarence Ray Coleman, Feb. 12, 1972; 1 child, Shani Rashida. Student So. U., Baton Rouge, 1966-70; diploma in cytotech. Mount Sinai Hosp., Chgo., 1971. Registered Cytotechnologist. Cytotechnologist Pathology lab. Meml. Hosp., Gulfport, Miss., 1971-74, Meth. Hosp., Memphis, 1974-76, Mercy Hosp., Vicksburg, Miss., 1977-79; founder, lab. supr. So. Lab., Fayette, Miss., 1980—; asst. adminstr. Medgar Evers Home Health, Fayette, 1983-85. Trustee Copiah-Jefferson Regional Library, Fayette and Hazlehurst, 1985; campaign mgr. Sammy White for chancery clk. Jefferson County, 1983. Mem. So. Assn. Cytotechnologists, Miss. Soc. Cytopathologists, Am. Soc. Clin. Pathologists, Am. Entrepreneurs Assn., Am. Mgmt. Assn. Democrat. Roman Catholic. Avocations: tennis; dancing; traveling; sewing. Office: So Lab Inc 414 Rodney Rd Fayette MS 39069

COLEMAN, NANCY LEE, insurance company executive; b. Coleman, Tex., Jan. 17, 1943; d. Fred E. and Minnie (Craig) C.; m. Gerald W. Timmins, Jan. 18, 1964 (div. Apr. 1972); m. Jerry W. Coleman, May 19, 1973. Student, San Angelo (Tex.) Coll., 1962. Claim auditor Life Ins. of the Southwest subs. Halliburton Co., Dallas, 1964-67, supr., 1967-73, claim mgr., 1973-77, asst. v.p. claims and adminstrn., 1977-78, v.p. claims, 1978-84, group v.p. claims, 1984-87; v.p. claims Health Econs. Corp. subs. Halliburton Co., Dallas, 1987—. Mem. Life Office Mgmt. Assn., So. Claims Assn., Southwest Ins. Assn. (asst. sec. 1975-76, sec.-treas. 1977, bd. dirs. 1977-78), Internat. Claims Assn. (subchmn. edn. com., exec. com. 1980-83, registration com. 1983-85, nominating com. 1985, pub. relations com. 1986-87, group issues com. 1986-87, future directions com. 1986-87, student Life Mgmt. Inst. claims edn. program). Republican. Methodist. Office: Health Econs Corp 1300 W Mockingbird Ln Dallas TX 75247

COLEMAN, NANCY LEE, television and motion picture executive; b. La Jolla, Calif., Mar. 28, 1953; d. James Francis and Dorothy (Powell) C. Student in acting, Am. Acad. Dramatic Arts, 1969-71; student, Emerson Coll., 1971-75; BFA in Film Prodn., NYU, 1982. Dir. traffic and communication Ong. & Assocs. Inc., N.Y.C., 1977-80; freelance lighting designer, dir., theater technician, N.Y.C., 1980-83; asst. to mgr. of post prodn. Cable Health Network, N.Y.C., 1983; asst. to dir. of mktg. Columbia Pictures Internat. TV, N.Y.C., 1983-85, supr. fin. services, 1985-86, mgr. TV sales-adminstrn., 1986—; resident writer/dir. Inroads Multimedia Art Ctr., N.Y.C., 1982-83. Author, dir.: (play) Stroke of Time, 1983; dir. cabaret show Debra Moreno Show, 1982-83. Mem. Nat. Assn. Female Execs., Nat. Acad. TV Arts and Scis., Am. Film Inst. Office: Columbia Pictures Internat TV 711 Fifth Ave New York NY 10022

COLEMAN, PAMELA ABEL, educator; b. Pensacola, Fla., Sept. 23, 1953; d. Darrel W. Sr. and Helen M. (Burke) Abel; m. Timothy Stewart Coleman, Aug. 12, 1972; children: Meredyth Nicole, Margaret Kathleen. BA, U. Mo., 1975, M in Edn. Adminstrn., 1980, postgrad. Cert. elem. adminstrn. Tchr. Blue Springs (Mo.) R-IV Sch. Dist., 1975—; instr. Longview Community Coll.; overseas exchange tchr., U.K. Contbr. articles in field. Treas. Community Edn. Assn., 1976-77; active Just Say No campaign, 1987, Girl Scouts Mid-Continent Council; dir. children's ch. Aldersgate Meth. Ch., 1988, sunday sch. tchr., 1985-88; cons. Girl Scouts U.S., 1986-88, del. to bd. dirs., 1986-87, Daisy Troop Leader, 1987-88, Jr. Troop Leader, 1983-88, pub. relations person, 1987, host person Juliette Low Camp for Handicapped Girls, 1986. Recipient Edn. Citation award. Mem. Nat. Middle Sch. Assn., Mo. Middle Sch. Assn., Pi Lambda Theta, Phi Delta Kappa. Home: 4065 Camelot Lee's Summit MO 64082

COLEMAN, REBECCA LYNN, lawyer; b. Erwin, N.C., Dec. 27, 1954; d. Halford Hartwell and Rebecca Ann (Stallings) C.; m. William McIver Cameron III, Nov. 6, 1982. BS in Indsl. Relations and Polit. Sci., U. N.C., 1977; JD, Campbell U., 1980. Bar: U.S. Dist. Ct. (ea. dist.) N.C. 1980, U.S. Supreme Ct. 1983. Sole practice Richlands, N.C., 1981-83; ptnr. Cameron and Coleman, Jacksonville and Richlands, 1983—. Active Onslow County Dems., 1986—; mem. Onslow County Mus. Found. Mem. Nat. Assn. Female Execs., Fourth Jud. Dist. Bar Assn., Onslow County Bar Assn., Soroptimist of Jacksonville. Methodist. Office: Cameron and Coleman 118 Old Bridge St PO Box 1117 Jacksonville NC 28540

COLES, ANNA LOUISE BAILEY, nursing administrator, college dean; b. Kansas City, Kans., Jan. 16, 1925; d. Gordon Alonzo and Lillie Mai (Buchanan) Bailey; children—Margot, Michelle, Gina. Diploma, Freedmen's Hosp. Sch. Nursing, 1948; B.S. in Nursing, Avila Coll., Kansas City, Mo., 1958; M.S. in Nursing, Cath. U. Am., 1960, Ph.D. in Higher Edn., 1967. Instr. VA Hosp., Topeka, 1950-52; supr. VA Hosp., Kansas City, Mo., 1952-58; asst. dir. in-service edn. Freedmen's Hosp., Washington, 1960-61; adminstrv. asst. to dir. nursing Freedmen's Hosp., 1961-66, assoc. dir. nursing services, 1966-67, dir. nursing, 1967-69; dean Coll. Nursing, Howard U., Washington, 1968-86, dean emeritus, 1986—; cons. Gen. Research Support Program, NIH, 1972-76, VA health care com. NRC-Nat. Acad. Scis., 1975-76, VA Central Office continuing edn. com., 1976—; pres. Nurses Examining Bd., 1967-68; mem. Inst. Medicine, Nat. Acad. Scis., 1974—; Mem. D.C. Health Planning Adv. Com., 1968-71, Tri-State Regional Planning Com. for Nursing Edn., 1969, Health Adv. Council, Nat. Urban Coalition, 1971-73. Contbr. articles to profl. jours. Bd. dirs. Iona Whipper Home for Unwed Mothers, 1970-72; bd. dirs. Nursing Edn. Opportunities, 1970-72; trustee Community Group Health Found., 1976-77, cons., 1977—; bd. regents State Univ. System Fla., 1977; adv. bd. Am. Assn. Med. Vols., 1970-72. Recipient Sustained Superior Performance award HEW, 1962; Meritorious Public Service award Govt. of D.C., 1968; Avila Coll. medal of honor, 1969. Mem. Nat. League Nursing (dir.), Am. Nurses Assn., Freedmen's Hosp. Nursing Alumni Assn., Am. Congress Rehab. Medicine, Am. Assn. Colls. of Nursing (sec. 1975-76), Sigma Theta Tau, Alpha Kappa Alpha. Home: 6841 Garfield Dr Kansas City KS 66102 Office: Howard U Coll Nursing 2400 6th St NW Washington DC 20059

COLES, DONNA REED, mental health administrator; b. Cleve., June 19, 1951; d. Henry and Frances (Hollingshead) Reed; divorced; children: Danielle A., Michael E. BA, U. Dayton, 1979, MA, 1985. Coordinator Eastway Corp., Dayton, Ohio, 1980-84; dir. Battered Women Project, Dayton, 1984-85; project coordinator Good Samaritan Hosp., Dayton, 1985-88; organizational cons. Donna Reed Coles' Consultation Services, Dayton, 1985—; dir. growth services Eastway Corp., Dayton, 1988—; mem. adv. bd. Victims Support Resources, Dayton, 1986—. Mem. Dayton Women's Coalition, 1984-86. Named one of Outstanding Young Woman in Am., 1985. Mem. Dayton Assn. Black Psychologists (sec. 1983-86), Miami Valley Psychol. Assn. Democrat. Home: 4644 Saint John's Ave Dayton OH 45406

COLES, LORRAINE MCCLELLAN, vehicle maintenance analyst; b. Chgo., Nov. 1, 1929; d. Wiley and Cornelia (Robinson) Packnett; m. Sam Taylor, Feb. 10, 1947 (div. 1962); children: Diana, Arvetta Lorraine, Samuel Joseph, Conella Elizabeth. Student, Truman Coll., Chgo., 1980, Loop Coll., 1982-84, U. Okla. Postal Acad., Norman, 1981-83. Asst. forelady Diana Sportswear, Chgo., 1951-52; sr. balancer Spiegel's, Inc., Chgo., 1959-60; intermittent claims examiner Ill. Dept. of Labor, 1963-72; with U.S. Postal Service, Chgo., 1960—, supt. delivery and vehicle maintenance, 1986—. Mem. Scheme Rev. Com., Chgo., 1986—. Mem. Nat. Assn. Female Execs., Nat. Geographic Soc., Black Bus. and Profl. Women Assn., League Women Voters, Presbyn. Women's Assn. (sec. 1986—). Home: 233 E Wacker Dr Chicago IL 60601

COLGATE, DORIS ELEANOR, sailing school executive, retail store executive; b. Washington, May 12, 1941; d. Bernard Leonard and Frances Lillian (Goldstein) Horecker; m. Richard G. Buchanan, Sept. 6, 1959 (div. Aug. 1967); m. 2d, Stephen Colgate, Dec. 17, 1969. Student Antioch Coll., 1958-60, NYU, 1960-62. Research supr. Geyer Moyer Ballard, N.Y.C., 1962-64; adminstrv. asst. Yachting Mag., N.Y.C., 1964-68; v.p. Offshore Sailing Sch. Ltd., N.Y.C., 1968-78, pres., Ft. Myers, Fla., 1978—; chief exec. officer On and Offshore, Inc., Ft. Myers, 1984—; v.p. Offshore Travel, Inc., City Island, 1978-88. Author: The Bareboat Gourmet, 1983. Contbr. articles to profl. jours. Mem. Royal Ocean Racing Club, Am. Women's Econ. Devel. Corp. (adv. bd. 1980-86). Club: Doubles (N.Y.C.). Avocations: sailing, photography, writing, cooking. Home: 1555 San Carlos Bay Dr Sanibel FL 33957 Office: Offshore Sailing Sch Ltd Box 08130 Fort Myers FL 33908

COLGATE, KATHLEEN BISHOP, insurance company product manager; b. Louisville, Jan. 27, 1953; d. Herman Henry Jr. and Geneva (Collins) Bishop; m. Kent Richey colgate, Sept. 10, 1977; children: Khristian Wayne, Lacey Ann. BA in Edn., U. Ky., 1975. Playground supr. Metro Parks Dept., Louisville, 1976; salesperson European Health Spa, Louisville, 1976-77; program coordinator McDonald's of Louisville, 1977-78; fundraising coordinator Nat. Multiple Sclerosis, Louisville, 1978-80, field rep., 1980-81; project coordinator Capital Holding, Louisville, 1982-84, supr., 1984-86, product mgr., 1987—. 2d lt. CAP, Louisville, 1978-84; treas. Suburban Christian Ch., Louisville, 1980-81. Named Ky. Col., State of Ky., 1980. Fellow Life Office Mgmt. Assn.; mem. Am. Mktg. Assn., Nat. Assn. Female Execs., U. Ky. Marching Band Alumni, Delta Psi Kappa, Delta Zeta, Alpha Theta Alumni. Republican.

COLIN, GEORGIA TALMEY, interior designer; b. Boston; d. George Nathan and Rose (Broad) Talmey; m. Ralph Frederick Colin, June 2, 1931 (dec.); children—Ralph Frederick, Pamela Talmey Colin Harlech. Student Smith Coll., 1928, U. Genoble (France), 1927. Co-ptnr., Talmey Inc., Interior Designers, N.Y.C., 1928-54, pres., 1954—. Sec. Young Peoples Concert Com. of N.Y. Philharmonic Soc., 1940-49; mem. vis. com. Smith Coll. Mus. Art, 1951-70, chmn., 1954-57; bd. counselors Smith Coll., 1954-57. Mem. Am. Inst. Interior Designers, Decorators Club, Nat. Soc. Interior Designers, Am. Soc. Interior Designers. Home and Office: 941 Park Ave New York NY 10028

COLLADO, LISA, artist, writer; b. Washington, June 24, 1944; d. Emilio Cabriel and Janet (Gilbert) C.; m. Octavio M. Nunez, Feb. 8, 1969 (div. 1974); children: Lisa Erendira Nunez, Gabriela Esperanza Nunez, Janet Flor de Lys Nunez; m. Malcolm W. Ford III, Aug. 24, 1974 (div. 1977). BA, SUNY, 1985. Represented by St. Peters Ch., N.Y.C. Represented in permanent collections Rutgers U., Egyptian Tourist Office. Recipient Award of Merit U. Del., 1981. Mem. N.Y. Artists Equity Assn., Nat. Assn. Women Artists, Orgn. Ind. Artists. Republican. Episcopalian. Home and Office: 920 Park Ave Apt #2A New York NY 10021

COLLARINI SCHLOSSBERG, ANTOINETTE MARIE, psychologist; b. N.Y.C., Apr. 12, 1950; d. Attilio and Ann (Pecoraro) Collarini; m. Harvey Schlossberg. BA, Fordham U., 1972; MS, Hunter Coll., 1974; M in Philosophy, Columbia U., 1982, PhD, 1982. Lic. psychologist, N.Y. Research assoc. City of Yonkers, N.Y., 1972-74; research dir. City of Mt. Vernon, N.Y., 1974-76; program adminstr. Westchester County Youth Bur., White Plains, N.Y., 1976—; pvt. practice psychology Forest Hills, N.Y., 1983—; exec. dir. Westchester County Youth Bur., White Plains, N.Y., 1988—; research and orgnl. cons., Westchester County, 1976—. Educator various civic and community groups, Westchester County, 1976—; vice chair Westchester Task Force on Adolescent Depression and Suicide. NIMH trainee, 1972-74, 79-80. Mem. Am. Psychol. Assn., New York State Psychol. Assn., Am. Soc. for Pub. Adminstrn. (chpt. v.p. 1986-87, pres. 1987—), Nat. Assn. for Female Execs.

COLLART, MARIE ETHEL, association executive; b. Clarksburg, W.Va., Nov. 23, 1945; d. Richard C. and Ethel Collart; B.S., Ohio State U., 1967, M.S., 1970, Ph.D., 1979. Cert. fund-raising exec. Legis. agt., Ohio. Staff nurse Case Western Res. U. Hosp. Cleve., 1967-70; instr. Sch. Nursing Ohio State U., Columbus, 1971-72, dir. computer assisted instrn. program devel., 1972-73; dir. Ohio Thoracic Soc., 1973-81, dir. prof. edn. Ohio Lung Assn., 1973-81, pres., exec. dir. Central Ohio Lung Assn., 1981—; adj. asst. prof. Ohio State U. Allied Medicine div. Med. Coll., 1981—; mem. advanced faculty Creative Edn. Found. SUNY, Buffalo, 1975—; chmn. health medicine and safety category Columbus Internat. Film Festival, 1981—. Mem. City Upper Arlington Cultural Arts Com., 1971—; trustee Columbus Community Cable Access Bd.; judge Taft Broad-casting Jefferson Awards, 1986. Recipient Allied Health Profl. Educator award Am. Lung Assn., 1976, Chris Bronze plaque Columbus Internat. Film Festival, 1977, Hattie Lazarus award; named a Woman of Achievement YWCA, 1987. Mem. Am. Thoracic Soc., Assn. Ednl. Communication Technicians, Health Scis. Communications Assn., Nat. Soc. Fund Raising Execs., Upper Arlington C. of C., Phi Delta Kappa, Sigma Theta Tau. Republican. Club: Columbus Met. Photography: Nursing Care of Adults and Orthopedic Conditions (Leona Mourad), 1979. Home: 4063 Fairfax Dr Columbus OH 43220

COLLETT, JOAN, librarian; b. St. Louis; d. Robert and Mary (Hoolan) C.; m. John E. Dustin, Nov. 19, 1983. B.A. magna cum laude, Maryville Coll., 1947; M.A., Washington U., St. Louis, 1950; M.S. in L.S, U. Ill., Urbana, 1954. Regional cons. W.Va. Library Commn., Spencer, W.Va., 1954-56; instr. Rosary Coll., River Forest, Ill., 1956-57; head extension dept. Gary (Ind.) Public Library, 1957-64; librarian Grailville Library, 1965; regional librarian USIA, Latin Am., Africa, 1966-78; exec. dir. librarian St. Louis Public Library, 1978-86; library dir. Great Neck (N.Y.) Library, 1986-87, CUNY Grad. Ctr. Mina Rees Library, N.Y.C., 1988—. Mem. ALA (councilor 1986—). Office: CUNY Grad Ctr Mina Rees Library 33 W 42d St New York NY 10036

COLLETTE, CAROLYN PENNEY, English language educator; b. Boston, Aug. 2, 1945; d. George Kenneth and Mary (Takessian) Penney; m. David Raymond Collette, July 9, 1967; children—Matthew, Andrew. A.B., Mt. Holyoke Coll., 1967; M.A., U. Mass., 1969, Ph.D., 1971. With Mt. Holyoke Coll., South Hadley, Mass., 1970—, asst. prof., 1972-77, assoc. prof., 1977—; prof. 1986—, dir. freshman English, 1986-87. Contbr. articles to profl. jours. Woodrow Wilson fellow, 1967; NDEA fellow, 1969; NEH summer fellow, 1976. Mem. MLA, Medieval Acad. Am., William Morris Soc., Modern Humanities Research Assn., Phi Beta Kappa, Phi Kappa Phi. Episcopalian. Office: Mount Holyoke Coll Dept English South Hadley MA 01075

COLLETTE, FRANCES MADELYN, tax consultant, lawyer; b. Yonkers, N.Y., Aug. 5, 1947; d. Morris Aaron and Esther (Gang) Volbert; m. Roger Warren Collette, Dec. 25, 1971; children: Darren Roger, Bonnie Frances. B.Ed. summa cum laude, SUNY-Buffalo, 1969; J.D., cum laude, U. Miami, 1980. Bar: Fla. 1980. Employment counselor Fla. Bur. Employment Security, Miami, 1969-73; unemployment claims adjudicator Fla. Bur. Unemployment Claims, Miami, 1973-77; pres. Fla. Unemployment, tax and personnel cons. Unemployment Services Fla., Inc., Miami, 1977—. Mem. Printing Industry S. Fla., Fla. Pest Control Assn., Better Bus. Bur. S. Fla. (1st v.p. 1980-81, bd. govs., 2d vice chmn. 1981-82), Nat. Platform Soc. Jewish. Office: Unemployment Services Fla Inc 7220 SW 39th Terr Miami FL 33155

COLLETTE, RENÉE ANN, nurse; b. Ashtabula, Ohio, Mar. 18, 1951; d. Tony Goiello and Helen (Simon) C.; m. G. John Balogh, Apr. 25, 1980. BA in Sociology, Kent (Ohio) State U., 1973; BS in Nursing, U. Akron, 1986. RN, Ohio. Paraprofl. trainer Portage County Drug Edn. and Crisis Intervention Ctr., Kent, 1972-77, treas., bd. trustees; paraprofl. trainer counseling and group resources Kent State U., 1973-77; casework coordinator Residential Intervention Ctr., Akron, Ohio, 1975-76; exec. dir. Akron Rape Crisis Ctr., 1976-79; RN Cleve. Clinic Found., 1986—, Akron City Hosp., 1986—; instr. Honor and Exptl. Coll., Kent State U., 1977-78. Registrar bd. elections Summit County, Ohio, 1986; mem. Coalition Revision Nurse Practice Act., Ohio, 1986. Recipient Mary Gladwin award U. Akron, 1986. Fellow Emergency Nursing Assn., Am. Assn. Critical Care Nurses, U. Akron Collegiate Nursing Club (pres. 1985-86), Sigma Theta Tau. Democrat. Roman Catholic. Home: 5840 Woodley Ct Ashtabula OH 44004 Office: Akron City Hosp Emergency Dept 525 E Market St Akron OH 44304

COLLETTI, LORRAINE FRANCES, psychologist; b. Detroit, Oct. 4; d. George Lisecki and Irene (Rama) Rovinski; m. John B. Colletti; children: Lisa, Renee, John Chris. BA, Marygrove Coll., 1958; MA, Wayne State U., 1970, PhD, 1977. Lic. psychologist, Mich. Sch. psychologist Ferndale/Berkley (Mich.) Schs., Grosse Pointe (Mich) Schs.; asst. prof. ednl. psychology Wayne State U., Detroit; residing psychologist Kingswood Hosp., Ferndale, Mich.; pvt. practice psychology Grosse Pointe; cons. psychologist Human Synergistics, Plymouth, Mich., 1981—, dir. clin. services, 1985—, exec. v.p. clin. services programs; cons. psychologist Montgomery Clinic, Bloomfield, Mich., 1979—, Social Services Detroit. Contbr. articles to profl. jours. Founder, bd. dirs. N.E. Child Guidance Clinics, Detroit, 1975-82, sec., 1978. Grantee U.S. Govt., 1979, State of Mich., 1979. Mem. Am. Psychol. Assn., Am. Soc. for Tng. and Devel., Mich. Psychol. Assn. (treas. 1983-85), Lakeshore Psychol. Assn. (founding pres. 1978-80), Art Assn. Founders Soc., Grosse Pointe Art Assn., Jr. Womens' Symphony Assn. Republican. Roman Catholic. Club: Detroit Country. Office: Human Synergistics 39819 Plymouth Rd Plymouth MI 48170

COLLIER, ALEXIS CHRISTINA, psychology educator; b. Norton, Va., July 10, 1951; d. S. Alexander and L. Belle (Robinett) Collier; BS, Va. Poly. Inst. and State U., 1973; postgrad. Princeton U., 1973-74; PhD, U. Wash., 1976; postdoctorate studies, Wright State U., 1986-87. Teaching and research asst. Princeton U., 1973-74, U. Wash., Seattle, 1974-76; asst. prof. psychology Ohio State U., Columbus, 1976-82, assoc. prof., 1982—; vis. assoc. prof. Wright State U., Dayton, Ohio, 1986-87; cons. to profl. jours. 1976—. NIMH grantee, 1980, mem. grant rev. com., 1981-84. Mem. Am. Psychol. Assn., Eastern Psychol. Assn., Midwestern Psychol. Assn., Psychonomic Soc., Internat. Soc. Devel. Psychobiology, NOW, Colony-Mortar Board, Alpha Lambda Delta, Sigma Xi, Phi Kappa Phi, Delta Zeta. Democrat. Baptist. Club: Columbus Met. Lodge: Order Eastern Star. Contbr. articles to psychol. jours. Home: 5015 Hibbs Dr Columbus OH 43220 Office: 1885 Neil Ave Mall Columbus OH 43210

COLLIER, CHARLOTTE MAE MEIER, publishing company executive; b. Wooster, Ohio, Sept. 24, 1947; d. Ferris Thorld and Sarah Edith (Johnson) Meier; m. John Edward Collier, Dec. 27, 1971; children: Elda Mae, John Icel. Student Case Western Res. U.; 1965-67; BA, U. Mass., 1969, MA, 1971, PhD, 1978. Project mgr. Chilton Research Services, Radnor, Pa., 1980-81; research mgr. Springhouse Corp., Pa., 1981-84, dir. research, 1984—; chair research com. Assn. Bus. Pubs., N.Y.C., 1985-86; mem. Advt. Research Found., N.Y.C., 1984—. Contbr. articles and papers to profl. lit. Mem. Montgomery County Task Force on Older Adults, Pa., 1971-78, sec., 1977; cons. on aging programs Southeastern Pa. Lutheran Synod, Phila., 1980. Univ. fellow U. Mass., 1969-72; Gerontol. Soc. fellow, 1979-80. Mem. Am. Mktg. Assn., Am. Hosp. Assn., Nat. Assn. Home Care, Phi Beta Kappa. Democrat. Lutheran. Avocation: bicycling. Office: Springhouse Corp 1111 Bethlehem Pike Springhouse PA 19477

COLLIER, DIANE HOSPODKA, architect; b. Omaha, Sept. 9, 1955; d. Jerome Frank and Beverly Jean (Potach) Hospodka; m. Don Wilson Collier, June 20, 1952; children: Don Wilson Jr., Mattie Katherine. BS in Archtl. Studies, U. Nebr., 1977; MArch, U. Tex., Arlington, 1980. Registered architect, Tex. Archtl. intern Beran and Shelmire Architects, Dallas, 1979-82; tenant constrn. mgr. Prentiss Properties, Dallas, 1982—; cons. Summa Devel., Las Vegas. Mem. LL Hotchkis Pre-Sch. PTA. Mem. AIA, Tex. Inst. Architects, Dallas Inst. Architects, Dallas Women in Architecture, Comml. Real Estate Women. Office: Prentiss Properties 1717 Main Suite 5000 Dallas TX 75201

COLLIER, ELLEN CLODFELTER, foreign policy specialist; b. Lawrence, Kans., Oct. 19, 1927; d. Harve Malone and Martha June (Lambert) Clodfelter; m. Edwin Collier, May 25, 1951; children: Stephen Harve, Martha Lambert Collier Riva, Sarah Reiner Munsey, John Reiner, Catherine Fiorello. BA cum laude with high distinction, Ohio State U., 1949; MA, Am. U., 1951; grad., Nat. War Coll., 1978. Analyst U.S. fgn. policy fgn. affairs div. Congl. Research Service, Library of Congress, Washington, 1949-55, analyst U.S. fgn. policy, 1960-69, specialist, 1969—, head spl. project sect., 1972-75, head fgn. issues and nat. policy sect., 1975-76, head global issues sect., 1976-77; mem. staff subcom. on disarmament U.S. Senate Fgn. Relations Com., 1955-59. Author govt. reports; editor: Congress and Fgn. Policy, 1979-86. Mem. Internat. Studies Assn., Am. Soc. Internat. Law, Soc. Internat. Devel., Exec. Women in Govt., Phi Beta Kappa, Pi Sigma Alpha. Club: Potomac Pedalers. Office: Library Congress Congl Research Service Washington DC 20540

COLLIER, GWENDOLYN MURIEL, real estate executive; b. Jackson, Tenn., Nov. 5, 1944; d. James Alexander and Lula (Baskerville) C. AA, Florissant Valley Community Coll., St. Louis, 1982; BS, Washington U., 1987. Lic. real estate broker. Mgr. advt. St. Louis Argus Newspaper, 1975-82; radio account exec. Unity Broadcasting Co., N.Y.C., 1982-86; mgr. property Interstate Realty Mgmt. Corp., St. Louis, 1986—. Mgr. campaign, organizer 21st Ward Orgn., St. Louis, 1979-80. Mem. Nat. Assn. Female Execs., Nat. Assn. Real Estate Brokers, NAACP, Mensa. Democrat. Office: 60 N Ewing Saint Louis MO 63103

COLLIER, KATHLEEN (KATHY) ELLEN, program director, educator; b. Sioux Falls, S.D., Oct. 11, 1946; d. Norman Luglan and Irma Jean (Kosters) Halverson; m. Donald Harold Collier, June 20, 1975; children: Lee, Lana. BA, Augustana Coll., 1968; MA, U. S.D., Vermillion, 1970. Tchr. Clara City (Minn.) High Sch., 1968-69; legal sec. T.R. Johnson and Patrick Lacey, Attys., Sioux Falls, S.D., 1970-72; instr., program dir. Colo. NW Community Coll., Rangely, 1972—; sec. Rocky Mountain Archery, Rangely, 1967-69. Examiner U.S. Govt. Civil Service, Rangely, 1973-86; advisor Phi Beta Lambda, Rangely, 1974—; mem. Spl. Services Adv. Com., Rangely, 1985—; mem. Arts Council, Rangely, 1987—, mem. Historical Soc., 1987. Mem. Colo. Assn. Coll. Instructional Dirs., Assn. Curriculum Dirs., Nat. Bus. Edn. Assn., Nat. Vocat. Assn., Colo. For and About Bus. (sec. bus. and office adv. com.), Mountain Plains Bus. Edn. Assn. Democrat. Lutheran. Home: 226 Crest Rangely CO 81648

COLLIER, NORMA JEAN, public relations executive; b. Yankton, S.D.; d. Guy L. and Elizabeth J. (Donegan) Collier. Student George Washington U., Los Angeles City Coll., U. Md.-Seoul, Korea. Exec. sec. Universal Studios, Universal City, Calif., 1955-58, Leo Burnett Advt. Co., Hollywood, Calif., 1958-60; adminstrv. asst. Survey & Research Co., Seoul, 1960-63; exec. asst. John E. Horton Assocs., Washington, 1963-72; exec. asst. Doremus & Co., Washington, 1972-74; account exec. Doremus/West, Los Angeles, 1974-79, v.p., 1979-85; v.p., acting mgr. Doremus/Los Angeles Advt., 1985-87; sr. v.p., gen. mgr. Doremus/Los Angeles Advt., 1987—. Recipient Letter of Appreciation, Republic of Korea, 1963. Mem. Los Angeles Advt. Club, Women in Communications (dir. chpt.). Republican. Roman Catholic. Club: Hollywood Studio (pres. 1957-58, house council). Home: 11147 Huston St North Hollywood CA 91601 Office: Doremus/Los Angeles Advt 11755 Wilshire Blvd Los Angeles CA 90025

COLLIER-EVANS, DEMETRA FRANCES, personnel executive; b. Nashville, Dec. 18, 1937; d. Oscar Collier and Earllee Elizabeth (Williams) Collier-Sheffield; m. George Perry Evans, Dec. 21, 1966; 1 child, Richard Edward. AA in Social Sci., Solano Community Coll., Suisun City, Calif., 1974; BA in Social Sci., Chapman Coll., Orange, Calif., 1981. Cert. tchr., Calif. Specialist placement, case responsible person employment devel. dept. City of San Diego, 1975-82; vocat. tchr. San Diego Community Coll., 1982-83; specialist placement N.J. Job Service, Camden, 1984-86, mgr. job bank, 1985; specialist placement Abilities Ctr., Westville, N.J., 1987—; cons. Bumble Bee Canning Co., San Diego, 1982. Developer women's seminar Women's Opportunity Week, City of San Diego, 1982, network seminar Fed. Women's Week, City of Phila., 1986. Bd. dirs. Welfare Rights Orgn., San Diego, 1982; mem. Internat. YWCA. Served with USAF, 1956-59. Recipient Excellence cert. San Diego Employer Adv. Bd., 1981, Leadership cert. Nat. U., San Diego, 1981. Mem. Black Advs. State Service (charter, corr. sec. San Diego chpt. 1981-82), Nat. Assn. Female Execs., AAUW, NAACP (life, rec. sec. San Diego 1982), Chapman Coll. Alumni Assn., Alpha Gamma Sigma. Democrat. Avocation: calligraphy. Office: Abilities Ctr 790 N Delsea Dr Westville NJ 08093

COLLING, CATHARINE MARY, nurse, hospital administrator; b. Broomfield, Colo., Jan. 15, 1909; d. Patrick and Margaret Mary (Ryan) Kirby; m. Anthony Joseph Colling; 1 child, Mary Helen Colling Nightingale. BA, Ursuline Coll., 1934. RN, Calif. Supr. Mary's Help Hosp., 1945-50; adminstrv. indsl. nurse Standard Oil Co. of Calif., San Francisco, 1951-62; ward conservator Bank of Am. Trust Dept., 1964-67; instr. indsl. nursing Univ. San Francisco, 1954-69; adminstr. White Sands Convalescent Hosp., Pleasant Hill, Calif., 1967-70, Hillhaven Lawton Convalescent Hosp., San Francisco, 1970—. Recipient numerous nursing awards. Mem. Am. Coll. Nursing Home Adminstrs., No. Calif. Assn. Indsl. Nurses, Western Indsl. Nurses, Calif. Nurses Assn., Catholic Nurses Assn., Mary's Help Hosp. Alumni Assn., Calif. Assn. Hosp. Facilities. Republican. Roman Catholic. Office: Hillhaven Inc 1575 7th Ave San Francisco CA 94122

COLLINGWOOD, BARBARA, banker; b. Pitts., Dec. 18, 1942; d. Howard W. and Harriet M. (Weber) C. AA, Rider Coll., 1962; BA in Bus. Adminstn., Fla. Internat. U., 1983. Administv. asst. Ea. Air Lines Inc., Miami, 1967-73; administv. asst. to pres., chmn. S.E. Bank, Miami, 1974-84, asst. v.p., asst. corp. sec., 1984-87, v.p., asst. corp. sec., 1987. Dir. Miami Design Preservation League, 1987. Mem. Am. Soc. Corp. Secs. Club: City Miami. Home: 525 Coral Way Coral Gables FL 33134 Office: SE Bank 1 SE Fin Cen Miami FL 33131

COLLINS, ANN ELIZABETH AVERITT (MRS. GALEN FRANKLIN COLLINS), civic leader; b. Peru, Ind., July 28, 1934; d. Robert Chancellor and Cleo (Hite) Averitt; m. Galen Franklin Collins, Sept. 30, 1956; children: Galen Robert, Amelia Lynn, Scott Franklin, Daniel Chancellor. BA, Fla. Internat. U. Free-lance writer, 1972—. Co-editor: (soc. page) Elkhart (Ind.) Truth, 1955-56; musical compositions include Why Am I Old?, Little Boy, My Dear Son, Color, Willows, Soldier Boy, Is That Your Voice I Hear?. Mem. Elkhart Civic Theatre, 1957-60, Chenango County (N.Y.) Community Players, 1960-63; co-founder Dogwood Playhouse, Bristol, Va.-Tenn., 1964, bd. dirs., 1964-69; co-founder Collero Puppets, Bristol, 1967; coordinator, specialist sr. citizen ctr. recreation program div. parks and recreation City of Lynchburg, Va., 1983—; dir. Christian edn. United Ch. Christ, Miami, 1978-82. Home: 1431 Club Dr Lynchburg VA 24503

COLLINS, BARBARA ANN REED, reporter, editor; b. South Pittsburg, Tenn., Mar. 8, 1937; d. Jacob Harding and Estelle Leslie (Young) Burroughs; m.; children: Roberta Ann, Frank Edward. Student, Northwestern U., 1954, U. Ala., 1955-56. Freelance writer, 1964-66; bur. chief Norwich Bull. (Conn.), 1966-68; staff writer The Day, New London, Conn., 1968—; pub. relations cons. New London County Daycare, 1982-83; founder Caretaker's Support Group, Groton, Conn., 1986—. Author: A Time to Remember, 1976. Mem. Big Bros./Bis Sisters Southeastern Conn., 1985—. Recipient Herbert Bayard Swope Meml. award 3d pl., 1978; Nat. Merit award Sudden Infant Death Syndrome Found., 1970. Mem. Noank Hist. Soc. (pres. 1972-73, 79-80, past program chmn., past sec., founder), Southeastern Conn. Women's Network, Sigma Delta Chi. Independent. Methodist. Lodges: Soroptimist (bd. dirs. 1988—), Kiwanis, Emblem. Office: 47 Eugene O'Neill Dr New London CT 06320

COLLINS, BARBARA ANNE, minister, business educator; b. Dallas, May 8, 1935; d. Paul Norton and Pauline (Coats) Henderson; m. Philip Linn Collins, June 16, 1956; children: Stephen-Andrew-Paul, Jeffrey Linn, Byron Keith. BBA, So. Meth. U., 1955; BTh, Fountain Gate Bible Coll., 1980. Ordained to ministry, 1980. Legal sec. Scurry, Scurry & Pace, Dallas, 1955-56; tchr. bus. Pflugerville (Tex.) High Sch., Dallas, 1956-57; legal sec. Hutchison, Shipp & Guinn, Dallas, 1959-60; sec., bd. of elders Fountain gate Ministries, Dallas and Plano, 1976—, dir. Alms Ministry, 1980—; tchr. bible Fountain Gate Bible Coll., Dallas and Plano, 1974-86, dean of student affairs, 1983—. Del. State Rep. Conv., Dallas, 1986, numerous county and state Rep. convs. Mem. Sigma Kappa (pres. SK Corp. Bd. of Tex. 1960-63, Nat. Pledge Trainer, 1963-70). Home: 912 Tanglewood Plano TX 75075 Office: Fountain Gate Ministries 2501 Custer Rd Plano TX 75075

COLLINS, BARBARA CLARK, retail company personnel executive; b. Orange, N.J., Oct. 2, 1953; d. John Anthony and Patricia O. (Horner) Clark; m. Richard Dwight Collins, Jan. 16, 1982. B.S. in Mgmt. Sci., Rutgers U. Coll., 1984. Exec. sec. to exec. v.p. Ronson Corp., Bridgewater, N.J., 1976-79; exec. asst. to pres. Egon Zehnder Internat., N.Y.C., 1979-80; personnel mgr. Adamas Carbide Corp., Kenilworth, N.J., 1980-84; v.p. human resources Van Heusen Factory Stores div. Phillips-Van Heusen Corp., Piscataway, N.J., 1984—. Mem. Internat. Assn. Personnel Women (bd., pres. 1987—), Nat. Assn. Female Execs., N.J. Women's Network. Avocations: Horseback riding; skiing; reading; golf. Home: 33 Edgewood Terr Bridgewater NJ 08807 Office: Van Heusen Factory Stores PO Box 2206 New Brunswick NJ 08903

COLLINS, BETTYE FINE, realtor; b. Hanceville, Ala., Oct. 11, 1936; d. Joseph Lloyd and Bertha Evora (Thompson) Fine; m. Bill R. Collins, Sept. 5, 1954; children: David Brian, Kimberly Dee. Realtor assoc. Chambers Realty, Birmingham, Ala., 1977-79, Lowder Realty, Birmingham, 1979-81, Johnson, Rast & Hays, Birmingham, 1981-84; assoc. broker Re/Max Realty, Birmingham, 1984—. Mem. Birmingham City Council, 1981-87, Nat. League Cities FAIR Com., 1986-88; state del. White House Conf. on Libraries, Washington, 1980; bd. mem. Birmingham City Sch. System, 1974-81; bd. dirs. So. Mus. Flight, Birmingham, 1986-88, Community Affairs Com., Birmingham, 1987-88, Birmingham Festival of Arts Com., 1987-88, Operation New Birmingham, 1987-88. Mem. Birmingham Area Bd. Realtors Million Dollar Club (life). Republican. Baptist. Home: 504 Red Bud Dr Birmingham AL 35206 Office: Re/Max Realty East Inc 623 Red Lane Rd Birmingham AL 35215

COLLINS, CARDISS, congresswoman; b. St. Louis, Sept. 24, 1931; ed. Northwestern U.; m. George W. Collins (dec.); 1 son, Kevin. Stenographer, Ill. Dept. Labor; sec. Ill. Dept. Revenue, then accountant, revenue auditor; mem. 93d-100th Congresses from 7th Ill. Dist., 1973—, mem. Govt. Ops. com., Energy and Commerce com.; chmn. Manpower and Housing com., former majority whip-at-large; past chmn. Congressional Black Caucus; former chmn. Mems. of Congress for Peace through Law. Bd. dirs. Greater Lawndale Conservation Commn., Chgo. Mem. NAACP, Nat. Council Negro Women, Chgo. Urban League, Alpha Kappa Alpha. Baptist. Democrat. Office: US Ho Reps 2264 Rayburn Washington DC 20515 *

COLLINS, CAROL DESORMEAU, research scientist, consultant; b. Schenectady, N.Y., Dec. 9, 1854; d. Henry William and Lila Barbara (DiLorenzo) Desormeau; m. John J. Collins III, Aug. 19, 1978; children: Ashley D., Brandon D. BS, U. Vt., 1976; MS, Rensselaer Poly. Inst., 1978, PhD, 1980. Undergrad. teaching asst. U. Vt., Burlington, 1975-76; grad. teaching asst. Rensselaer Poly. Inst., Troy, 1976-77, grad. research asst., 1977-80, post doctoral assoc., 1980-81; sr. scientist Biol. Survey N.Y. State Mus., Albany, 1981—; cons. U.S. Corps Engrs., Vicksburg, Miss., 1980, Tenn. Valley Authority, Norris, 1980; invited scientist advanced research workshop NATO, Roscoe, France, 1986. Editor: Lake George Ecosystem, 3, 1983; contbr. articles to profl. jours. Bd. dirs. Lake George (N.Y.) Assn., 1981—, Lake Champlain com., 1985-87; bd. trustees Lake George Assn., Fund, 1982—. Research grantee NSF, 1985-87. Mem. Psychol. Soc. Am., Am. Soc. Limnology and Oceanography, North Am. Lakes Mgmt. Soc. Roman Catholic. Home: 29 Schuyler Hills Rd Loudonville NY 12211 Office: NY State Mus Sci Biol Survey Albany NY 12230

COLLINS, CATHERINE LOUISE, police officer; b. Logansport, Ind., Jan. 27, 1959; d. Walter Norman and Barbara Jean (Crockett) C.; 1 child, Christopher Aaron. A in Criminal Justice, Ind. U., 1980; student, Ind. Law Enforcement Acad., 1981. Police officer Logansport Police Dept., 1980—; assoc. advisor Boys Scouts Am. Law Enforcement Explorers, Logansport, 1986—. Safety counselor Boy Scouts Am., Logansport, 1980—. Named one of Outstanding Law Enforcement Officer of Yr., Breakfast and Evening Exchange Clubs, 1980. Mem. Ind. Drug Enforcement Assn. (bd. dirs. 1986—), Ind. U. Alumni Assn. (life), Bus. and Profl. Women Club (pres. 1986-87, coll. scholarship 1980, Outstanding Young Woman of Am. 1982, 86, Young Career Woman 1983), Fraternal Order of Police (sec., treas. 1986—). Republican. Methodist. Office: Logansport Police Dept 601 E Broadway Logansport IN 46947

COLLINS, CATHY DIANE, educator; b. Madison, Wis., Dec. 11, 1948; d. Charles Douglass and JoAnn Neva (Jiru) Zinke; 1 child, Michael Evan Donegan. BS in Elem. Edn., Lamar U., 1970; M in Elem. Edn., North Tex. State U., 1974; PhD in Curriculum and Instrn., U. Wis., 1976. Elem. tchr. Beaumont (Tex.) Independent Sch. Dist., 1970-71, Oklahoma City Independent Sch. Dist., 1971-72, Azle (Tex.) Independent Sch. Dist., 1972-74; research asst. U. Wis., Madison, 1974-76; asst. prof. So. Ill. U., Carbondale, 1976-77; asst. prof. edn. Tex. Christian U., Ft. Worth, 1977-81, assoc. prof., 1981—; founder Ednl. Research Dissemination Co., 1987—; cons. sch. dists., 1974—. Author: Time Management for Teachers, 1987; co-author Stanford Early Sch. Achievement Test, 1976—; contbr. numerous articles to profl. jours. Vol. Harris Hosp., Ft. Worth, 1978-79, aerobics tchr., 1986—; judge Springtown (Tex.) Women of Yr., 1985—; bd. dirs. Gateway Pvt. Sch., Ft. Worth, 1987. Named one of Outstanding Young Women Am., 1978, 81, 85, Outstanding Community Leader, 1977, 81, Disting. Tchr. 1985, Tex. Christian U. Mem. Nat. Assn. Female Execs., Nat. Reading Conf. (chairperson field council 1982—), Internat. Reading Assn. (chairperson spl. interest group 1985—), Tarrant County Mental Health Assn. (bd. dirs. 1987—). Office: Tex Christian U Sch of Edn PO Box 32925 Fort Worth TX 76129

COLLINS, DIANA JOSEPHINE, psychologist; b. Potsdam, N.Y., Apr. 27, 1944; d. Philip Joseph and Janet Dorothy (Lynke) C.; grad. with high honors, SUNY; Psy.D., Mass. Sch. Profl. Psychology, 1981. Psychologist, N.H. Hosp., Concord, 1974-79; asst. dir. forensic unit, 1979-80; founder, dir. Victim/Witness Service County of Hillsborough, Manchester, N.H., 1980-84; pvt. practice, North Chelmsford, Mass.; adj. assoc. prof. U. N.H., 1974; adj. assoc. prof. Antioch Coll. of New Eng. Mem. AAUW, N.H. Psychol. Assn., Mass. Psychol. Assn., Eastern Psychol. Assn., Internat. Assn. Psychotherapists and Counselors, Internat. Platform Assn., Am. Assn. Female Execs., Roman Catholic. Home: RFD 2 Contoocook NH 03229 Office: 85 Tyngsboro Rd Box 2036 North Chelmsford MA 01863

COLLINS, DOROTHY SMITH, librarian; b. Nacogdoches, Tex., July 25, 1934; d. A.V. and Betty (Yarborough) Smith; m. Julius A. Collins, July 14, 1957 (dec.). BA in Sociology, Prairie View (Tex.) A&M U.; MA in Elem. Edn., Tex. So. U.; MLS, U. So. Calif. Tchr. U.S. Dependant Sch., Schwabisch, Fed. Republic Germany; tchr., librarian Cleve. Pub. Schs.; tchr. Westside Elem. Sch. Dist., Lancaster, Calif.; librarian Antelope Valley/Palmdale High Sch. Dist., Lancaster; coordinator research and reference ctr. San Diego Office Edn. Chmn. edn. and speakers bur. Save Our Heritage Orgn., 1986—; pres., bd. dirs. San Diego chpt., United Scleroderma Found, 1983—; v.p. San Diego Pres. Council, 1987—; alumni Leadership Edn. Awareness Devel., 1986—. Mem. Nat. Soc. for the Study of Edn., Nat. Council of Adminstrv. Women in Edn. (co-chmn. Woman of the Yr. 1978—), Nat. Staff Devel. Council, Assn. Supr. and Curriculum Devel., Am. Library Assn. (reference and adult services div. 1984-87), Am. Ednl. Research Assn. Home: 6267 Rockhurst Dr San Diego CA 92120 Office: San Diego County Office Edn 6401 Linda Vista Rd San Diego CA 92111

COLLINS, EARLEAN, state legislator; b. Rolling Fork, Miss.; m. John Grant, July 31, 1978; 1 child, Dwarrye. BA in Sociology, U. Ill., Chgo. Owner, realtor Collins Realty & Ins., Chgo., 1969-72; social service adminstr. State of Ill., Chgo., 1972-76, elected state senator, 1977—; bd. dirs. Nat. Caucus of Black Legislators, Westside Bus. Assn. of Chgo., Nat. Conf. State Legislators. Sponsor Unwed Mothers United, Chgo., 1977—, Collins Queenettes, Chgo., 1977—, Westside Progressive Women's Orgn., Chgo., 1980—. Named Outstanding Legislator Ill. Hosp. Assn., Best Legislator Ill. Bus. and Profl. Women's Assn. and Ill. Edn. Assn. Mem. Intergovtl. Coop. Council, Operation PUSH, Ill. Job Tng. Council, NAACP, Conf. Women Legislators. Democrat. Baptist. Office: 9th Senatorial Dist 5943 W Madison Chicago IL 60644

COLLINS, EILEEN LOUISE, economist; b. Chillicothe, Ohio, Dec. 15, 1942; d. Theodore Milton and Louise Alma (Suess) C.; B.A. (regional scholar), Bryn Mawr Coll., 1964; M.A., U. Wis., Madison, 1967, Ph.D., 1975. Lectr. dept. econs. U. Waterloo (Ont., Can.), 1971-73; asst. prof. dept. econs. Barnard Coll., N.Y.C., 1975-76; asst. prof. dept. econs. Fordham U., N.Y.C., 1976-78; economist NSF, Washington, 1978-86, sr. economist, 1986—. Editor: American Jobs and the Changing Industrial Base, 1984. Author papers and reports in field. Recipient NSF Outstanding Performance award, 1979, 81, 83, 84; NIMH fellow, 1969-71; Nat. Inst. Public Affairs fellow, 1966-67. Mem. Am. Econ. Assn., AAAS, Nat. Tax Assn., Washington Philos. Soc., Washington Women Economists. Club: Nat. Economists (v.p. seminars 1986). Office: NSF 1800 G St NW Room L-611 Washington DC 20550

COLLINS, GWENDOLYN BETH, educational administrator; b. Akron, Ohio, Dec. 28, 1943; d. Emmert Samuel and Lillice Elizabeth (Matthews) Shaffer; m. Charles F. Collins, Feb. 10, 1969 (div. 1976); 1 child, Holly Marie. BA, Case Western Res. U., 1971. Social worker Ohio Div. Pub. Welfare, Akron, Cleve., 1970-72; social services dir. Smithville-Western Care Ctr., Wooster, Ohio, 1975-76, social work cons., 1976; social worker Edwin Shaw Hosp., Akron, 1976-78; clin. treatment services coordinator The Blick Clinic for Devel. Disabilities, Tallmadge, Ohio, 1978; co-adminstr. The Sun Ctr. Inc., Akron, 1979-81; exec. dir. Canton Area Regional Health Edn. Network, 1981—; project dir. Region VII Cancer Registry, 1984—; health program devel. cons., 1986—; mem. continuing med. edn. com. Aultman Hosp. Mem. adv. com. Camp Y-Noah, 1985-86. Dept. Health and Human Services Grantee, Canton, 1986—. Mem. Cancer Control Consortium of Ohio (cancer incidence mgmt. com. 1986—), Canton Women's Roundtable, Stark County Women's Network, Nat. Assn. Female Execs. Republican. Home: 126 Bennington Rd Akron OH 44313 Office: Canton Area Regional Health Edn Network 1320 Timken Mercy Dr NW Canton OH 44708

COLLINS, JILL HARRISON, finance manager, small business owner and operator; b. Boise, Idaho, Aug. 18, 1957; d. Robert Maurice Harrison and Elsie Louise (Otto) C. Student, Contra Costa Jr. Coll., 1975-77, Diablo Valley Jr. Coll., 1977-80; cert., L.B.'s Sch. Bartending, 1980. Mgr., trainer Foodmaker, Inc., Hayward, Calif., 1974-80; co-owner,operator T.J.'s Catering, Pleasant Hill, Calif., 1978-80; mgr. Am. Recreation Ctrs., Pinole, Calif., 1980-81; asst. ops. mgr. Dobb's Houses Inc., Oakland, Calif., 1982-82; fin. mgr. Richmond (Calif.) Kawasaki, 1983-85, Dexter Enterprises, San Rafael, Calif., 1985-87; owner, operator Jill Collins Ins. Agy., El Sobrante, Calif., 1984—; cons. Home Improvement Unltd., Union City, Calif., 1987—; rep. Gt. Am. Motorcycle Show, San Francisco, 1978-80; speaker Foodmaker Inc., 1983-84; creator variousTV, radio, newspaper advertisements, 1980-85. Co-designer software program Motorcycle Finance, Ins., 1984. Mem. Ams. for Legal Reform, U.S. Olympic Com., 1987—. Mem. Nat. Assn. for Female Execs., Nat. C. of C. for Women, Am. Mgmt. Assn., Women on Wheels; Modified Motorcycle Assn. (gold card, guest speaker 1984,86). Home: 1921 Elm Ave Las Vegas NV 89101

COLLINS, JOAN HENRIETTA, actress; b. London, May 3, 1933; came to U.S., 1954; d. Joseph William and Elsa (Bessant) C.; m. Ronald S. Kass, Mar., 1972 (div.); 1 child, Katie; m. Anthony Newley (div.); children: Cynara, Sacha; m. Peter Holm, 1985 (div.). Films include: I Believe in You, Girl in the Red Velvet Swing, Rally Round the Flag Boys, Island in the Sun, Seven Thieves, Road to Hong Kong, Sunburn, The Stud, Game for Vultures, The Bitch, The Big Sleep, The Good Die Young, 1954, Land of the Pharoahs, 1955, The Bravados, 1958, Esther and the King, 1960, Warning Shot, 1967, The Executioner, 1970, Tales from the Crypt, The Bawdy Adventures of Tom Jones, 1975; theater appearance in The Last of Mrs. Cheyney; TV films include: The Man Who Came to Dinner, The Moneychanger, Paper Dolls, The Wild Women of Chastity Gulch, The Cartier Affair, The Making of a Male Model, Her Life as a Man; miniseries: Sins, Monte Carlo; star TV series: Dynasty, 1981—; author: Past Imperfect (autobiography), 1978, Katy, A Fight for Life, Joan Collins Beauty Book. Recipient Emmy award, Golden Globe award.

COLLINS, JOANNE ANITA, accounting educator; b. Chgo., Aug. 2, 1946; d. Elmer and Lucille Ann (Dombrowski) C. BS in Math., Ill. Inst. Tech., 1968, MBA, 1970; PhD in Acctg., Northwestern U., 1976. CPA, Ill.; cert. mgmt. acct.; cert. cost analyst; cert. tax acct. Mem. staff EDP ops. Internat. Harvester, 1965-70; instr. Ill. Inst. Tech., Chgo., 1969-73; fin. analyst Continental Can Co., 1970-73; econ. analyst Sargent & Lundy, 1973; asst. prof. acctg. Wharton Sch., U. Pa., Phila., 1976-82; prof. acctg. Calif. State U., Los Angeles, 1982—; cons. in field. Contbr. articles to profl. jours. Recipient Alumni award Ill. Inst. Tech., 1968; Legion of Honor, Chapel of Four Chaplains, 1980. Mem. Am. Acctg. Assn., Am. Inst. CPA's, Nat. Assn. Accts. (Author of Yr. Los Angeles chpt. 1983-85), Inst. Mgmt. Acctg., Am. Women's Soc. of CPA's (charter mem. Los Angeles chpt.), Am. Soc. Women Accts., ACLU, Calif. Soc. CPA's, Mensa, Beta Alpha Psi, Phi Eta Sigma, Sigma Iota Epsilon, Beta Gamma Sigma. Democrat. Unitarian-Universalist. Home: 8328 Rush St Rosemead CA 91770 Office: Calif State U 5151 State University Dt Los Angeles CA 90032

COLLINS, KATHLEEN ANN, educator; b. Stevens Point, Wis., Oct. 14, 1932; d. Bernard Vincent and Emily Mae (Klish) Sommers; m. William Arnold Collins, Aug. 4, 1956; children: Timothy William, Lynn Mary. BS, U. Minn., Duluth, 1954. Cert. tchr., Wis., S.D. Tchr. bus. edn. Webster (Wis.) Pub. Schs., 1954-55, Jefferson (S.D.) Pub. Schs., 1955-56, Wisconsin Rapids (Wis.) Pub. Schs., 1969—; chmn. dept. bus. edn. West Jr. High Sch. and East Jr. High Sch., Wisconsin Rapids, 1969—; with vocat. edn. curriculum Wisconsin Rapids Pub. Schs., 1984—. Bd. dirs. United Way, Wisconsin Rapids, 1986—, sec., 1987. Named Wisconsin Rapids Sch. Dist. Tchr. of the Yr., 1982. Mem. AAUW, Nat. Bus. Edn. Assn., Wis. Bus. Edn. Assn., Delta Kappa Gamma (sec. 1982-85). Roman Catholic. Office: West and East Jr High Sch 311 Lincoln St Wisconsin Rapids WI 54494

COLLINS, KATHLEEN ELIZABETH, pharmaceutical company official; b. Rock Island, Ill., Jan. 14, 1951; d. A. Phillip and Henrietta (Zeis) C.; m. David Mark Hasenmiller, June 23, 1973 (div. June 1975). Fgn. student degree, U. Grenoble, 1970; student, Barat Coll., 1968-70, U. Wis., 1970-71; BA in French and English, St. Ambrose Coll., Davenport, Iowa, 1972; postgrad. secondary edn., Augustana Coll., Rock Island, 1975, U. Iowa, 1979, 84. Sales clk. Scharff's Dept. Store, Bettendorf, Iowa, 1970-72; teller Moline (Ill.) Nat. Bank, 1972-73; mgr. Music Box, Rock Island, 1973-74, Disc Records, Moline, 1974-75; with quality assurance dept. U.S. Army, Savannah, Ill., 1975-76; sales rep. Burroughs Wellcome Co., Research Triangle Park, N.C., 1976-81; vol. nutritionist Peace Corps, Niger, 1981-82; sales rep. Phil Collins Co., Rock Island, 1982-85; med. rep. Lederle Labs., Overland Park, Kans., 1985—. vol. Big Bros./Big Sisters, Moline, 1984-85, Pathway Hospice, Luth. Hosp., Moline, 1984-86, 88. Mem. Quad Cities Pharm. Assn. (treas. 1978, 86, v.p. 1979, sec. 1987, sec./treas. 1988), Jr. League Quad Cities. Roman Catholic. Clubs: Davenport, Outing (Davenport). Home: 906 Slavens Manor Bettendorf IA 52722 Office: Lederle Labs 10955 Lowell St Suite 900 Overland Park KS 66210

COLLINS, KATHLEEN MACNAUGHTON, home health care nursing executive; b. Rochester, N.Y., Nov. 15, 1954; d. Charles Malcolm and Bobbi Ann (Thompson) Macnaughton; m. Wayne Lee Collins, May 29, 1976; children: Sarah Moore, Jennifer Wells. BS in Nursing magna cum laude, Syracuse U., 1976; postgrad., Villanova U., 1987—. Staff nurse Our Lady of Lourdes Hosp., Camden, N.J., 1976-77; staff nurse, child abuse coordinator Gloucester County Vis. Nurse Assn., Woodbury, N.J., 1977-80; asst. supr. Gloucester County Vis. Nurse Assn., Woodbury, 1980-81, supr., 1985-87; staff nurse Moorestown (N.J.) Vis. Nurses, 1982-85, v.p., 1987—. Mem. N.J. State Nurses Assn., Tech. Adv. Com. of Home Health Agy Assembly of N.J., Sigma Theta Tau. Home: 3 Boothby Dr Mount Laurel NJ 08054

COLLINS, LINDA ROSS, personnel director; b. McCaysville, Ga., Dec. 12, 1951; d. Clifford H. and Ruth (King) Ross; m. Steve A. Collins, Dec. 12, 1970. Grad. high sch., Blue Ridge, Ga., 1969. From clk./typist to personnel specialist Cities Service Co., Copperhill, Tenn., 1970-84; personnel specialist Cities Service Co., Copperhill, 1979-84, supt. personnel, 1984-85, dir. personnel, 1985—; treas. C&H Marine, Inc., Morganton, Ga., 1986—. Mem. Am. Soc. Personnel Adminstrn., Nat. Assn. Female Execs. Baptist. Club: Fountains (N.Y.C.). Home: PO Box 152 Morganton GA 30560 Office: Tenn Chem Co Ocoee St Copperhill TN 37317

COLLINS, LYNN ARNETHA, engineer; b. N.Y.C., Dec. 4, 1953; d. James Edward and Elsie Elenor (Durant) Lassiter; m. Michael Anthony (div. 1987); 1 child, Latosha. AA, Queensborough Community Coll., 1974; BA, Bklyn. Coll., 1976; postgrad., N.Y. Theol. Sem., 1986—. Registered profl. engr., N.Y. Jr. programmer N.Y. State Dept. Environ. Conservation, Albany, 1976-77; programmer Wildcat Corp., N.Y.C., 1977-78; programmer, analyst No. Telecom Inc., West Palm Beach, Fla., 1978-79; sr. programmer analyst bus. dept. Dade County Sch. Bd., Miami, Fla., 1979-80; sr. computer analyst Consol. Edison, N.Y.C., 1980-83; sr. systems programmer Chem. Bank, N.Y.C., 1983-85, systems engr., 1985—, also testing services technician, 1985-87; v.p. Evang. Computers, Inc., N.Y.C., 1984—. Co-convenor Urban Seminarians Youth Ministry, N.Y.C., 1985; sec. N.Y. Theol. Sem. Student Council, N.Y.C., 1986-88, pres. 1988—; mem. People for Andrew Jenkins, Queens, N.Y., 1982—, Episc. Black Caucus, N.Y., 1987—; instr. South Hempstead Congl. Ch., 1985-87, active leadership, 1987. Recipient Recognition Leadership Service award Urban Seminarian Youth Ministry, Service and Mission award, N.Y. Theol. Sem., 1988, Cuban Ministry award, 1988. Mem. Episc. Black Caucus N.Y., Nat. Conf. for Black Seminarians. Democrat. Home: 82 W Clinton Ave Roosevelt NY 11575 Office: Chemical Bank 55 Water St New York NY 10041

COLLINS, MARCIA FREUCHTEL, materials engineer, chemist; b. Detroit, Apr. 19, 1948; d. Charles Andrew and Ethel Mary (Greig) Freuchtel. BS in Chemistry, U. Mich., 1969; MS in Material Sci. and Engring., Rutgers U., 1983. Instr. Allegheny Schs., Pa., 1970; research asst. Koppers Co., Monroeville, Pa., 1971; tech. dir. Liquid Crystal Ind., Turtle Creek, Pa., 1971-74; research scientist Alcoa Tech. Ctr., Alcoa Center, Pa., 1974-77; scientist Am. Hoechst, Somerville, N.J., 1978-83; research and devel. materials engr. Teledyne Water Pik, Ft. Collins, Colo., 1983-87, mgr. clin. research, 1987—; cons. Liquid Crystal Ind., Turtle Creek, 1972-74; mem. affiliate faculty dept. mech. engring. Colo. State U., Ft. Collins, 1984—; instr. materials engring. elem. sch. Contbr. articles to profl. jours.; patentee in field. Warden Town of Hampton, N.J., 1976; vice chmn. Homeowners Action Com., Hampton, 1976; dir. Amateur Astronomers, Clinton, N.J., 1977-78; chmn. com. creditors of Colo. Indsl. Bank, 1987. Mem. Am. Chem. Soc. (Cert Merit 1987), Soc. Plastics Engrs., Air Pollution Control Assn. (mem. com. 1984—), Nat. Assn. Environ. Professionals. Avocations: antiques, art, creative writing, show horses, photography. Office: Teledyne Water Pik 1730 E Prospect St Fort Collins CO 80524

COLLINS, MARGARET HELEN, pathologist; b. Bronx, N.Y., July 5, 1950; d. Michael Robert and Catherine (Murray) Collins. B.S. summa cum laude, Fordham U., 1972; M.D., Georgetown U., 1977. Diplomate Am. Bd. Pathology. Intern pathology Cornell U.-N.Y. Hosp., N.Y.C., 1977-78, resident in pathology, 1978-80; chief resident in pediatric pathology Columbia-Presbyn. Med. Ctr., N.Y.C., 1980-82, research resident in pediatric pathology, 1982-83, asst. prof. clin. pathology, 1983—. Contbr. research articles to med. jours. Research fellow N.Y. Lung Assn., 1983-85, Am. Lung Assn., 1985-87. Mem. AMA, Am. Med. Women's Assn., Internat. Acad. Pathology, N.Y. Acad. Scis., AAAS, Am. Thoracic Soc., Women's Med. Assn. N.Y.C., Soc. Pediatric Pathology, Phi Beta Kappa. Democrat. Roman Catholic. Office: Babies Hosp Dept Pathology Div Developmental Pathology 3959 Broadway Box 37 New York NY 10032

COLLINS, MARIANNE NELSON, psychologist; b. Batavia, N.Y., Oct. 24, 1942; d. Leonard and Violet Marie (Pedersen) Nelson; divorced; children: Cathy Lee, Robert Jeffrey. BA, La. State U., New Orleans, 1973; MA, Ohio State U., 1975, PhD, 1977; postgrad., Wright State U., 1982. Lic. psychologist, Ohio. Asst. prof. Ohio State U., Columbus, 1978-81; asst. prof. Wright State U., Dayton, Ohio, 1982-83, clin. prof., 1983—; pvt. practice psychology Columbus, 1982—; cons. to various bus., edn. and govt. orgns. Ohio State U. fellow, 1973-77. Mem. Am. Psychol. Assn., Ohio Psychol. Assn., Cen. Ohio Cons. Psychologists. Office: 2000 W Henderson Rd Suite 340 Columbus OH 43220 also: 94 N High St Suite 170 Dublin OH 43017

COLLINS, MARTHA LAYNE, former governor; b. Shelby County, Ky., Dec. 7, 1936; d. Everett Larkin and Mary Lorena (Taylor) Hall; m. Bill Collins, July 3, 1959; children: Stephen Louis, Marla Ann. Student, Lindenwood Coll.; B.S., U. Ky., 1959. Formerly tchr. Fairdale High Sch., Louisville, Seneca High Sch., Louisville, Woodford County Jr. High Sch., Versailles; former lt. gov. State of Ky., 1979-83, gov., 1983-87; exec. in residence U. Louisville Sch. of Bus., 1988—; pres. Martha Layne Collins &

Assocs., Lexington, 1988—; sec. Ky. Edn. and Humanities Cabinet; chmn. Nat. Conf. Lt. Govs., 1982-83, So. Growth Policies Bd., 1986-87, So. Regional Edn. Bd., 1985, Nat. Govs.' Task Force on Drug and Substance Abuse, 1986, So. Growth Policies Bd., 1987; bd. dirs. Eastman-Kodak Co., Inc., Rochester, N.Y., R.R. Donnelley & Sons, Chgo., Bank of Louisville. Mem. Woodford County (Ky.) Democratic Exec. Com.; mem. Dem. Nat. Com., 1972-76; chmn. Dem. Nat. Conv., San Francisco, 1984; former coordinator Women's Activities for State Dem. Hdqrs.; del. Dem. Nat. Conv., Miami, 1972, Mid-term charter Conf., Kansas City, 1974; mem. credentials com. Dem. Nat. Com. Vice Presdl. Selection Process Commn., co-chair credentials com. Dem. Nat. Conv., Atlanta, 1988; Ky. chairwoman 51.3 Com. for Carter, 1976; mem. Ky. Dem. Central Exec. Com.; sec. Ky. Dem. Party; elected clk. Ct. of Appeals, 1975; clk. Supreme Ct. Ky., 1975; past tchr. Sunday sch.; mem. Ky. Commn. on Women; exec. dir. Ky. Friendship Force; mem. Dem. Nat. Com. Policy Commn. and Fairness Commn.; hon. chmn. bd. USO of Ky. Inc.; hon. co-chmn. Parents Against Child Exploitation; mem. adv. bd. Lexington Child Abuse Council; bd. govs. Dream Factory. Mem. So. Gov.'s Assn. (chmn. 1987), Woodford County Jaycee-ettes (past pres.), U. Ky. Alumni Assn., Women's Missionary Union (past pres.), Nat. Conf. Appellate Ct. Clks., Psi Omega Dental Aux. (past pres.). Baptist. Clubs: Bus. and Profl. Women's, Order Eastern Star. Office: PO Box 11890 Lexington KY 40578-1890

COLLINS, MARVA DELOISE NETTLES, educator; b. Monroeville, Ala., Aug. 31, 1936; d. Alex L. and Bessie Maye (Knight) Nettles; m. Clarence Collins, Sept. 2, 1960; children: Patrick, Eric, Cynthia. B.A., Clark Coll., 1957; B.A. (hon.), Howard U., 1980; D.H.L. (hon.), Wilberforce U., 1980, Chgo. State U., 1981; D.Hum. (hon.), Dartmouth Coll., 1981. Founder, tchr. Westside Prep. Sch., Chgo., 1975—. Subject of numerous publs. including Marva Collins' Way, 1982; subject of feature film Welcome to Success: The Marva Collins Story, 1981. Mem. Pres.'s Commn. on White House Fellowships, from 1981. Recipient numerous awards including: Reading Found. Am. award, 1979; Sojourner Truth Nat. award, 1980; Tchr. of Yr. award Phi Delta Kappa, 1980; Am. Public Service award Am. Inst. for Public Service, 1981; Endow a Dream award, 1980; Educator of Yr. award Chgo. Urban League, 1980; Jefferson Nat. award, 1981. Mem. Alpha Kappa Alpha. Baptist. Club: Executive. Office: Westside Prep Sch 4146 Chicago Ave Chicago IL 60641 *

COLLINS, MARY, Canadian legislator; b. Vancouver, B.C., Can., Sept. 26, 1940; d. Fredrick Claude and Isabel Margaret (Copp) Wilkins; children: David, Robert, Sarah. Student, U. B.C., Queen's U., Kingston, Ont., Can. Mem. Can. Ho. of Commons, 1984—. Trustee Queen's U. Mem. Bus. and Profl. Women's Club, North Vancouver C. of C. Mem. Progressive Conservative Party. Address: 540 Besserer Ave, Ottawa, ON Canada K1N 6C7 *

COLLINS, MARY ALICE, psychiatric social worker; b. Everett, Wash., Apr. 20, 1937; d. Harry Edward and Mary (Yates) Caton; B.A. in Sociology, Seattle Pacific Coll., 1959; M.S.W., U. Mich., 1966; Ph.D., Mich. State U., 1974; m. Gerald C. Brocker, Mar. 24, 1980. Dir. teenage, adult and counseling depts. YWCA, Flint, Mich., 1959-64, 66-68; social worker Catholic Social Services, Flint, 1969-71, Ingham Med. Mental Health Center, Lansing, Mich., 1971-73; clin. social worker Genesee Psychiat. Center, Flint, 1974-82, Psychol. Evaluation and Treatment Ctr., East Lansing, Mich., 1982-84; pvt. practice, East Lansing, 1984—; instr. social work Lansing Community Coll. and Mich. State U., 1974; vis. prof. Hurley Med. Center, 1979-84; cons. Ingham County Dept. Social Services, 1971-73; instr. Mich. State U., 1987. Advisor human relations Youth League, Flint Council Chs., 1964-65; sec. Genesee County Young Democrats, 1960-61, pres. Round Lake Improvement Assn., 1984-87. Mem. Nat. Assn. Social Workers, Acad. Cert. Social Workers, Registry Clin. Social Workers, Registry Health Care Workers, Phi Kappa Phi, Alpha Kappa Sigma. Contbr. articles to profl. jours. Home: 5945 Round Lake Rd Laingsburg MI 48848 : Lansing MI 48823

COLLINS, MARY BETH, association executive; b. Detroit, Jan. 3, 1925; d. James Edward and Mildred Ina (Barding) Hughes; B.A., Manhattanville Coll. Sacred Heart, 1947; M.A., Ariz. State U., 1970; m. Taber Loree Collins, Aug. 7, 1947; children—Louise Collins Lindsay, James, Suzanne, Mary Beth Collins Brenner, Mildred Collins Hittner, Marguerite Collins Zeller, Miriam Collins Huston, Frank, Jesse, Kathleen Collins Cheo, Martha DeVault. Community services coordinator Alcohol and Drug Abuse div. Ariz. Health Dept., Phoenix, 1967-68, acting dir., 1968-70; coordinator City of Phoenix Drug Control, 1970-73; exec. dir. Drug Action Coalition, Montgomery County, Md., 1973-74; exec. dir. Community Orgn. for Drug Abuse Control, 1974-76; adminstr. Office Substance Abuse Services, Mich. Dept. Pub. Health, Lansing, 1977-78; chmn. N.Y. State Commn. Prevention and Edn. of Alcohol and Substance Abuse, Albany, 1978-79; exec. dir. Internat. Assn. Prevention Programs, 1974—. Pres. Ariz. Family, Inc., 1970-71; bd. dirs. Community Orgn. for Drug Abuse Control, 1969-73; mem. adv. bd. Good Samaritan Hosp., Mental Health Services; mem. bd. Nat. Coordinating Council on Drug Edn., 1974-76. Mem. Internat. Council on Alcoholism and Addictions, Drugs, Alcohol and Women's Health Coalition (regional chmn.), Ariz. Alumnae of Sacred Heart (founding pres. 1963-64), Pi Lambda Theta. Home: PO Box 1825 Cave Creek AZ 85331 Office: PO Box 812 Carefree AZ 85377

COLLINS, MARY ELLEN KENNEDY, librarian, educator; b. Pitts., Feb. 28, 1939; d. Joseph Michael and Stella Marie (Kane) Kennedy; m. Orpha Collins. BA, Villa Maria Coll., 1961; MLS, U. Pitts., 1970, PhD, 1980. Tchr., Pitts. Catholic Schs., 1962-65; tchr., Anne Arundel County Schs., Annapolis, 1965-67; legal sec., firm Joseph M. Kennedy, Pitts., 1967-70; cataloger Newport News (Va.) Library System, 1970-71, reference librarian Glenville (W.Va.) State Coll., 1971-80; asst. prof. library sci. Ball State U., Muncie, Ind., 1980-83; reference librarian, asst. prof. Purdue U., West Lafayette, Ind., 1983—. Contbr. articles to profl. jours. Sec. Presbyn. Ch., 1973-74, pres., 1974-76, bd. deacons, 1979-80; chmn. library com., Muncie, 1981-83; mem. belle com. W.Va. Folk Festival, 1973-80. Recipient Title III advanced study grant, 1977-78. Mem. ALA (reference books rev. com. 1979-82, profl. devel. com. 1983-87, mem. Ednl. Behavioral Scis. Sect.-Problems of Access and Control of Ednl. Materials 1984-88), Ind. Library Assn., Spl. Libraries Assn., Assn. Coll. and Research Libraries, Am. Assn. U. Profs., Assn. Ind. Media Educators, Assn. Am. Library Schs., AAUW (corr. sec. 1981-82), Delta Kappa Gamma, Sigma Sigma Sigma. Republican. Office: Purdue U HSSE Library West Lafayette IN 47907

COLLINS, MYRTIS COCHRAN, librarian; b. Langdale, Ariz., Jan. 14, 1953; d. George and Nan Cochran; m. Michael Van Collins. BA, Ala. State U., 1974; MS, Purdue U., 1975; MLS, U. Mich., 1981. Tech. asst. Purdue U., West Layfayette, Ind., 1974-80; asst. librarian Tex. A&M U., College Station, 1981-83, U. Calif., Berkeley, 1984—. Contbg. author: Afro Americana, 1984, (microfiche) Curriculum Collection Index. Mem. ALA, Calif. Assn. Reference Librarians, Nat. Assn. Female Execs., Alpha Kappa Delta. Office: Univ Calif Main Library Gen Reference Service Berkeley CA 94720

COLLINS, NANCY ALENE, retail store manager; b. Lincoln, Neb., July 14, 1956; d. Gordon Denzel and Betty Lucille (Allen) C.; m. Thomas D. Holtgrewe, Oct. 7, 1978 (div. Dec. 1984); m. James Alan Donoho, Feb. 14, 1988. Grad. high sch., Lincoln, 1974. Salesperson World Radio, Lincoln, 1974-77, Fred Wilson Jewelers, Lincoln, 1977-78; shipping and receiving supr. Seiferts, Lincoln, 1978-80; salesperson J.C. Penney Ins. Corp., Lincoln, 1980-81, Lincoln Office Equipment Co., 1981-85; dist. sales mgr. Brandeis, Omaha, 1985-86; mgr. fine jewelry dept. Apco Merchandising Corp., Lincoln, 1986-87; mgr. Wallpapers for Less, Lincoln, 1987-88; recruiter, acct. exec. Mgmt. Recruiters, Lincoln, Nebr., 1988—. Mem. Women in Sales. Republican. Home: 4511 South St #2 Lincoln NE 68506

COLLINS, NANCY WHISNANT, foundation administrator; b. Charlotte, N.C., Dec. 20, 1933; d. Ward William and Marjorie Adele (Blackburn) Whisnant; m. James Quincy Collins Jr., Apr. 25, 1959 (div. 1974); children: James Quincy III, Charles Lowell, William Robey; m. Richard F. Chapman, May 29, 1982. Student, Queens Coll., Charlotte, 1951-53; AB in Journalism, U. N.C., 1955, MS in Personnel Adminstrn., 1967; postgrad., Cornell U., 1955-56. Personnel asst. R.H. Macy & Co., Inc., N.Y.C., 1955; jr. exec. placement dir. Scofield Placement Agy., San Francisco, 1956-57; free-lance journalist, London, Paris, and Frankfort, Fed. Republic Germany, 1957-59; program dir. Girl Scouts U.S., Hampton, Va., 1959-61; dir. tour, Tokyo, Hong Kong, Singapore, 1965-66; asst. dir. Sloan Exec. Program, Stanford (Calif.) U., 1968-78; asst. dir. Hoover Instn., 1979-81; asst. to pres. Palo Alto (Calif.) Med. Found., 1981—; bd. dirs. Am. Healthway Systems. Author: Professional Women and Their Mentors, Women Leading: Making Tough Choices on the Fast Track, 1988; contbr. articles, short stories and poems to mags. and newspapers. Mem. council Trinity Epsicopal Ch., Menlo Park Calif., 1975-80; fundraiser Cornell U., N.Y.C., 1975-81; exec. council Stanford area council Boy Scouts Am., 1980-81; mem. San Mateo County Charter Rev. Com.; mem. personnel bd. City of Menlo Park, 1979—; mem. women's program bd. Coro Found.; trustee Pacific Grad. Sch. Psychology; sec.-treas. Chapman Research Fund; bd. dirs. Santa Clara County council Girl Scouts U.S. Grantee Richardson Found., 1967; Cornell U. fellow. Mem. AAUW, Am. Mgmt. Assn., Peninsula Profl. Women's Network (adv. council), Nat. Alliance Profl. and Exec. Women (speakers' bank), Catalyst, Kappa Delta. Clubs: Overseas Press, Commonwealth. Home: 1850 Oak Ave Menlo Park CA 94025 Office: Palo Alto Med Found Office of Pres 400 Channing Ave Palo Alto CA 94301

COLLINS, PEGGY ANN, medical writer; b. Denver, Dec. 5, 1948; d. Arthur Roland and Lanita Elaine (Pitts) C. Student, Rockmont Coll., 1967-69; diploma, Colo. Coll. Med. Assts., 1970; BS, Met. State Coll., 1976. Legisl. liaison Health Med. Services of Colo., Denver, 1977; assoc. dir. Aspen Health Resources, Denver, 1977, 78; state info. officer State and Fed. Assocs. Report Service, Washington, 1978-80; editorial assoc. Am. Jour. of Sports Medicine, Columbus, Ga., 1980-81; free lance writer, editor Denver, 1981—; sec. U. Colo. Health Sci. Ctr., Denver, 1986—. Contbr. articles to profl. jours.; mem. editorial bd. Jour. Operating Room Research Inst., Denver, 1983. Rep. precinct committeewoman, Denver, 1986—. Mem. Am. Med. Writers Assn. (pres. 1986-87), Council of Biology Editors. Republican. Baptist. Home: 4324 Eaton St Denver CO 80212 Office: U Colo Health Scis Ctr 4200 E 9th Ave Box B-175 Denver CO 80262

COLLINS, SARAH FRENCH, librarian; b. Greensboro, N.C., Jan. 23, 1945; d. Merton Byron and Elizabeth Louise (Hale) French; m. Glenn Patrick Collins, Aug. 10, 1968; children—Brian Patrick, Alexander Hale. BA Grinnell Coll., 1967; MS with honors, Columbia U., 1978. Reference librarian Leonia (N.J.) Pub. Library, 1978-80, asst. dir, 1980-86; dir. N.J. Hist. Soc. Library, 1986—. Mem. ALA, N.J. Library Assn., Am. Assn. for State and Local History, Mid-Atlantic Archives Conf., Preservation and Conservation Adv. Bd. to State Librarian, State Hist. Records Adv. Bd., Beta Phi Mu. Home: 109 Gordonhurst Ave Upper Montclair NJ 07043 Office: NJ Hist Soc 230 Broadway Newark NJ 07104

COLLINS, SHERRY, public affairs administrator; b. Yonkers, N.Y., July 21, 1960; d. Ernest Joseph and Mary Edith (Dannelly) B.; m. Paul Collins, June 27, 1987. BA in Journalism, Pace U., 1982; postgrad., CUNY, 1984-86; student, NYU, 1986-87. Reporter, asst. to publisher Times Pub. Co., Yonkers, 1978-79; compositor, proof reader The Herald Statesman, Yonkers, 1979-81; asst. media planner Winner Communications, N.Y.C., 1981-82; adminstrv. sec. for v.p. and account group Young and Rubicam Internat., N.Y.C., 1982; asst. to pub., reporter Fashion Calendar Internat., N.Y.C., 1982-84; asst. to publisher Western Pub., N.Y.C., 1984, asst. to editor in chief Golden Books, 1984-86; adminstrv. aide pub. affairs Columbia U., N.Y.C., 1986—; dir. pub. relations Miss America Westchester County Pageant, Scarsdale, N.Y., 1982-82. Vol. Valentine Assn. for the Handicapped, 1978-81; mem. Intergenerational Advocates for the People, Yonkers, 1972, Mayor's Youth Adv. Com., Yonkers, 1975-78, Mayor's Community Relations Com., Yonkers, 1978-81, Yonkers Hist. Soc., 1981; corp. coordinator March of Dimes, 1984-86. Mem. Exec. Female Soc., Bus. and Profl. Women's Club (scholar 1978), NOW, Sigma Delta Chi (pres. 1978-84). Democrat. Roman Catholic. Home: 141-10 82d Dr Apt 235 Briarwood NY 11435 Office: Columbia U Pub Affairs 810 Uris Hall New York NY 10027

COLLINS, SYLVA HEGHINIAN, statistician; b. Aleppo, Syria, Oct. 9, 1948; came to U.S., 1972; d. Manasé and Ovsanna (Cholakian) Heghinian; m. John Barrett Collins, June 29, 1980; children: Susan, John Jr., Michael. BS in Math., Am. U., Beirut, 1971; MA in Math., Boston U., 1973, PhD in Math., 1977; MS in Computer Sci., NYU, 1982. Research statistician Lederle Labs., Pearl River, N.Y., 1977-79; asst. dir. Ayerst Labs., N.Y.C., 1979-81, assoc. dir., 1981-84; dir. statistics, data systems Miles Pharms., West Haven, Conn., 1985—. Contbr. numerous articles to profl. jours. Mem. Am. Statis. Assn., Soc. Clin. Trials, Biometric Soc., Drug Info. Assn. Home: 5 Arrowhead Rd Westport CT 06880

COLLINS, SYLVIA DOLORES, nurse, health promotion consultant; b. Phila., Nov. 17, 1934; d. Frank Edward and Catherine Florence (Sanford) Durnell; m. David Curtiss Collins, Sept. 29, 1951; 1 child, Dawn Catherine. BS in Nursing, U. Pa., 1959; MEd, Temple U., 1973. RN, Pa. Cons. Phila. Health Plan, 1976-79; instr. In-Service Edn. Luth. Home, Phila., 1977-79; staff nurse ACT Drug Rehab., Phila., 1981-82; cons. for health promotion Phila Corp. for Aging, 1981—; vis. lectr. Community Coll., Phila., 1978-80; Gwynedd Mercy Coll., Gwynedd Valley, Pa., 1985-86, U. Pa. Nursing Grad. Students. Sec. Gratz St. Neighbors, Phila., 1984-86; mem. Phila. Council on Neighborhoods, 1985. Mem. Am. Cancer Soc. (profl. edn. com.), Pub. Edn. Comn. Arthritis Assn., Am. Public Health Assn., Phila. County Nurses Assn. (corr. sec. 1981-84), Ethnic Nurses of Color (v. chmn. 1984-86), NAACP (life), Alpha Kappa Alpha, Omega Omega, Chi Eta Phi. Democrat. Baptist. Office: Phila Corp Aging 111 N Broad St Philadelphia PA 19107

COLLINS, THERESA ANN, theater manager; b. Middlesboro, Ky., Nov. 10, 1957; d. Joseph Sherman Collins and Anna Ruth (Cosby) Spradlin. BA, U. Ky., 1978. Asst. mgr. Golden Gate Theatre, San Francisco, 1979-82; mgr. Curran Theatre, San Francisco, 1982—, Orpheum Theatre, San Francisco, 1985—. Mem. AAUW, Nat. Assn. Female Execs. Democrat. Office: Curran Theatre 445 Geary St San Francisco CA 94102

COLLINS, WINIFRED QUICK, organizational executive; b. Great Falls, Mont.; m. Howard Lyman Collins (dec.). B.S., U. So. Calif., 1935; grad. Harvard-Radcliffe Program in Bus. Adminstrn., 1938; M.A., Stanford U., 1952. Commd. ensign U.S. Navy, 1942, advanced through grades to capt. 1962; personnel dir. Midshipman's Sch., Smith Coll., 1942-43; asst. chief Naval Personnel for Women, 1957-62; ret.; nat. v.p. U.S. Navy League, 1964-70, nat. dir. and chmn. nat. awards com., 1964—; nat. dir. Ret. Officers Assn.; former cons. HEW; former trustee Helping Hand Found.; former mem. Sec. Navy's Bd. Advs. and Tng. of Naval Personnel; dir. CPC Internat., Inc., 1977-84, chmn. employee investment com., mem. audit, exec. compensation and exec. coms.; bd. dirs. Inter Sea Fast Craft Co.; trustee U.S. Naval Acad. Found., 1977—. First v.p. Republican Women of D.C. Decorated Legion of Merit, Bronze Star; recipient Navy's Disting. Civilian Pub. Service award, 1971, Disting. Service award Navy League of U.S., 1973. Club: Harvard Grad. Bus. Sch. Washington (past dir.). Home: Harbour Sq 540 N St SW Washington DC 20024

COLLINS-EILAND, KAREN WISLER, psychologist; b. Oklahoma City, Mar. 25, 1949; d. Charles C. and Frances Joan (Higgins) Wisler; B.A. with honors, Stephen F. Austin State U., Nacogdoches, Tex., 1973; M.A., Tex. Christian U., 1978, Ph.D., 1979; m. David C. Eiland. Asst. prof. Dickinson (N.D.) State Coll., 1979-80; research asst. prof. psychiatry U. Tex. Med. Br., Galveston, 1980-81, asst. prof. dept. ob-gyn and sr. asso. Office Ednl. Devel., 1981-85; asst. prof. dept. psychiatry and behavirol scis., 1986—; cons. Med. Educators and Galveston Ind. Sch. Dist., 1981—. Contbr. articles to profl. jours. Mem. Am. Psychol. Assn., Am. Ednl. Research Assn., Sigma Xi, Psi Chi, Alpha Kappa Delta, Alpha Chi, Delta Zeta. Methodist. Office: Med Br U Tex Box 62 Galveston TX 77550

COLLINS-JORDAN, JANET, psychiatric therapist; b. Buffalo, Oct. 8, 1955; d. George William and Janet (Gibbons) Collins; m. James Allen Jordan, Nov. 1, 1986. BSBA, Purdue U., 1977. Therapist Imperial Point Med. Ctr., Ft. Lauderdale, Fla., 1977-79, dir. therapy, 1979—; mental health counselor Jordan psychiatry, Ft. Lauderdale, 1983—; sr. staff editor The Daily Exponent, 1975-77; v.p. Henderson Mental Health Aux. V.p. Hospice Care of Broward, Ft. Lauderdale, 1985—, Broward County Libraries Byblos, 1987—, Ft. Lauderdale, (Fla.) Mus. of Art, Opera Guild; chair Philharmonic Soc., Ft. Lauderdale, 1986—. Named one of ten Best Dressed, Broward County, 1986. Mem. Fla. Parks and Recreation Assn. (therapeutic div.), Pi Beta Phi, Omicron Delta Kappa. Republican. Roman Catholic. Office: 2340 NE 53 St Fort Lauderdale FL 33308

COLLINSWORTH, FRANCES MARIANNE, cytotechnologist; b. Lay, Colo., July 17, 1921; d. Charles Howard and Mary Campbell (Brodie) Webb; B.S., Colo. State U., Ft. Collins, 1943; grad. Parkland Hosp. Sch. Cytotechnology, Dallas, 1969; m. J.D. Collinsworth, Aug. 4, 1945; 1 son, Ross Brian. Tchr. home econs. Sidney (Nebr.) High Sch., 1943-44; stewardness United Airlines, 1944-45; tchr. sci. Taipei Am. Assn. Sch., Tien Mou, Taiwan, 1959-61; chief cytotechnologist, sr. instr. Parkland Meml. Hosp., Dallas, 1969-70; supr. dept. cytology Damon Lab., Phoenix, 1982-84, Humana Hosp. Vol., ARC, 1959-65. Mem. Am. Soc. Cytology, Am. Soc. Clin. Pathologists, Am. Soc. Cytotechnology, Ariz. Cytology Assn., Colo. State U. Alumni Assn., Nat. Ret. Tchrs. Assn. Democrat. Episcopalian. Club: Delta Delta Delta. Home: 310 E Sharon Ave Phoenix AZ 85022 Office: 1947 E Thomas Rd Phoenix AZ 85016

COLLISON, DIANE WITTROCK, communications executive; b. Carroll, Iowa, May 11, 1939; d. Michael August and Alberta Ernestine (Marcucci) Wittrock; m. David Michael Collison, Nov. 28, 1959 (div.); children: Christopher, Lucia, Charles, Nicholas, Paul, Michael. BA, Iowa State U., 1979, postgrad., 1979-80. Communications dir. Rep. State Cen. Com., Des Moines, Iowa, 1979-80; dir. communications, media Des Moines, Iowa, 1980-82; organ. dir. Gov. Iowa campaign, Des Moines, Iowa, 1982-83; pvt. practice public speaker Iowa, Colo., 1983—; polit. cons. Rep. Party Iowa, Des Moines, Iowa, 1983-85; arts mgmt. Denver Symphony Orch., 1985-87, Boulder Philharm. Orch., Boulder, Colo., 1985-87; telecommunications specialist US West Communications, Denver, 1987—; regional coordinator, Women in Bus. Conf., Des Moines, 1984; pub. speaker Nat. Edn. Ctr, Midwest Div., Des Moines, 1983-84, Boulder (Colo.) County YWCA, 1985— Passages, Inc., Denver, 1986. Created workshop and seminar, Transitions, 1983. Pres. Am. Field Service Foreign Exchange Program, Iowa, 1977; regional rep. Ames Internat. Orch. Fest Assn., 1977-78; mem. Colo. steering com. Dole Presdl. Campaign, 1987-88; bd. dirs. Am. Lung Assn. of Iowa, 1978-79. Mem. Colo. Fedn. Arts, Nat. Assn. Female Execs., Metro Denver Arts Alliance, Soviet Sister City Project, Nat. Speakers Assn. (cert.). Roman Catholic. Home: 801 Pennsylvania Apt 207 Denver CO 80203

COLLOM, PATRICIA ANNE, hospital administrator; b. N.Y.C., June 27, 1947; d. Edward J. and Elizabeth M. (Farrell) Kiernan; m. John A. Collom; 1 child, Kriste Ashley. Student Fordham U., 1984. Departmental mgr. NYU Med. Ctr., N.Y.C., 1972-76, adminstr., 1984—; spl. asst. to v.p. N.Y.C. Health and Hosp. Corp., 1976-78; asst. to dep. dir. Bellevue Hosp., N.Y.C., 1978-80; asst. to pres. S. Masuda, Inc., N.Y.C., 1980-82; departmental mgr. Beekman Downtown Hosp., N.Y.C., 1982-84 . Mem. Nat. Assn. Female Execs., Am. Mgmt. Assn. Democrat. Roman Catholic. Avocations: painting; reading. Office: NYU Med Ctr Affiliation Office 550 1st Ave New York NY 10016

COLMAN, WENDY, occupational therapist; b. Flushing, N.Y., July 6, 1950; d. Leo M. and Ray (Fine) C. BS, Tufts U., 1972; MA, NYU, 1977, PhD, 1984. Occupational therapist Extended Family Ctr., San Francisco, 1973-74; cons. child abuse San Francisco, 1974-75; sr. occupational therapist Roosevelt Hosp., N.Y.C., 1975-77; adj. instr. occupational therapy dept. NYU, 1977-80; asst. prof. occupational therapy dept. Boston U., 1980-83; dir. grad. edn. occupational therapy, dept. assoc. prof. Temple U., Phila., 1984-87; evaluation research coordinator Nat. Inst. Adolescent Pregnancy, Phila., 1986—; cons. curriculum design Kean Coll. N.J., Union, 1985—; cons. spl. projects, vice provost for research and grad. studies Temple U., Phila., 1987—. Contbr. articles to profl. jours. Mem. Am. Occupational Therapy Assn., World Fedn. Occupational Therapy, Pa. Occupational Therapy Assn. Home and Office: 209 Royal Ave Wyncote PA 19095

COLOMB, BETH ANNE, social worker; b. Phila., Oct. 12, 1959; d. Herman Dannemann and Margaret Katherine (Gustafson) C. BS in Psychology and Sociology, Guilford Coll., Greensboro, N.C., 1981; MEd in Counseling, U. N.C., Greensboro, 1984. Cert. counselor. Social worker Youth Care, Inc., Greensboro, 1984-85, Nexus/Guilford County Mental Health Program, Greensboro, 1985—; part-time counselor, 1986—. Active Another Way, Greensboro, 1983-86. Mem. Am. Mental Health Counselors Assn., Am. Assn. Counseling and Devel., N.C. Assn. Counseling and Devel. Presbyterian. Office: Nexus 415 N Edgeworth St Greensboro NC 27401

COLOMBI, MARIA PAOLA, pediatric cardiologist; b. Milan, May 31, 1934; d. Camillo and Renata (Giussani) C. Degree in Medicine and Surgery magna cum laude, U. Milan, 1958; Postgrad. Cert. in Cardiology with grande distinction, Univ. Libre de Brussels, 1962; postgrad., U. Turin, Italy, 1963. Asst. Inst. Solvay de Physiologie de l'Univ. Libre de Brussels, 1959-63; attending staff Dept. Cardiology Hosp. St. Pierre, Brussels, 1961-62; assoc. in pediatric cardiology Deborah Heart and Lung Ctr., Brown Mills, N.J., 1974-75, attending staff, 1975-82, asst. chief, dir. clin. pediatric cardiology, 1982-85, acting chief pediatric cardiology, 1986-87, chief pediatric cardiology, 1987—; clin. asst. prof. dept. pediatrics Coll. Medicine and Dentistry of N.J., Rutgers Med. Sch. Robert Wood Johnson, 1976—; cons. dept. pediatrics Our Lady of Lourdes Hosp., Camden, N.J., 1976—, 1976—; asst. div. pediatric cardiology Cooper Med. Ctr., Camden, 1982, cons., 1983-87. Fellow Am. Acad. Pediatrics; mem. Am. Heart Assn. (sci. counsel disease in young). Office: Deborah Heart and Lung Ctr Dept Pediatric Cardiology Trenton Rd Brown Mills NJ 08015

COLÓN, DENISE CASSANDRA, telecommunications executive; b. N.Y.C., Feb. 1, 1952; d. Isaac Tillman and Julia (Simmons) Jackson; (div. 1988); children: Denise Regina, Lana Autumn. Student, Marymount Coll., N.Y., 1982. Cons. telecommunications various co., N.Y.C., 1980-82; pres., chief exec. officer Colón Tele-Consultants Inc., N.Y.C., 1982—; cons. U.S. Dept. Labor U.S., 1986-87, Permanent Mission Guinea to UN. H.E.M. Saliou Coumbassa, 1985-87. Author: Controlling Corporate Telecommunications Costs, 1985. Mem. Am. Mgmt. Assn., Soc. Telecommunications Cons., Nat. Assn. Female Execs., Double Image Theatre. Democrat. Roman Catholic. Office: Colon Tele Comm 47-28 210th St Bayside NY 11361

COLÓN, LYDIA M., banker, small business owner, financial consultant; b. Santurce, P.R., June 2, 1947; d. Angel Luis and Lydia Maria (Pagán) Colon. BA magna cum laude, Marymount Manhattan Coll., 1978. Admissions office supr. NYU, N.Y.C., 1965-70; asst. v.p. Chem. Bank, N.Y.C., 1971-85; sr. assoc. First Washington Assocs., Arlington, Va., 1985-87; owner LMC Internat., 1987—. Co-author: Innovations in Industrial Competitiveness at the State Level, 1985, Guide to State Capital Formation, 1984. Vice chmn. N.Y. State Adv. Council for Minority and Women-Owned Bus. Enterprise, 1984-87; mem. ARC Minorities Initiative Task Force, 1985-87, N.Y. Bus. Devel. Corp. Gov.'s Task Force N.Y., 1985; trustee Community Service Soc., N.Y., 1985-87; mem. Gov.'s Task Force on Work and the Family, 1988—; co-founder Nat. P.R. Women's Caucus, Inc. Recipient Woman of the 80's award U.S. Dept. of Housing & Urban Devel., 1985, Polit. Sci. Gold medal Marymount Manhattan Coll., N.Y., 1978. Mem. Nat. Assn. Bank Women, Nat. Conf. Puerto Rican Women, 100 Hispanic Women of N.Y.C.

COLONEL, SHERI LYNN, advertising agency executive; b. Bklyn., Sept. 3, 1955; d. Irwin Murray Glaser and Rosalind (Mendelson) Krasik; m. Peter T. Colonel, Sept. 20, 1981. B.A. in Psychology, SUNY-Cortland, 1977. Account exec. Ted Bates Co., N.Y.C., 1978-80; account exec. SSC&B Advt. (name now LINTAS), Inc., N.Y.C., 1980-82, v.p. account supr., 1982-83, v.p. mgmt. supr., 1984, sr. v.p. mgmt. supr., 1985—. Home: 280 Park Ave S New York NY 10010 Office: LINTAS 1 Dag Hammarskjold Plaza New York NY 10017

COLOSI, GINGER (VIRGINIA) L., banker; b. Artesia, N.Mex., Dec. 7, 1946; d. Isom Gentry Warren and Bette Virginia (Houchin) Nesbitt; m. Francis Rosario Colosi, Oct. 18, 1964; children: Michael, Robert, Elizabeth. AA in Bus. Adminstrn., Quin Sigamond Community Coll., 1981; student, Assumption Coll., Worcester, Mass. Dept. clk. Riley Stoker, Worcester, 1981-82; receptionist R.E. Jarvis Co., Southboro, Mass., 1982-83; dept. clk. Conifer Computer Service, Worcester, 1983-84; exec. sec. Guaranty

Bank and Trust, Worcester, 1984, supr., 1984-86; mgr. Bank New Eng., Worcester, 1986—. Mem. LWV, Digital Gold Key Group (pres. 1984-86), Daughters Isabella, Nat. Assn. Bank Women (printing chmn. 1987—), New Eng. Telecommunications Assn. Roman Catholic. Club: Shrewbury Women's. Home: 40 Holman St Shrewsbury MA 01545 Office: Bank New Eng 370 Main St Worcester MA 01608

COLSON, ARDANNA ORAN, entertainment company administrator; b. Beaumont, Tex., Mar. 31, 1953; d. Sippy Wallace and Mildred (Griffin) Long; 1 child, Miguel Joseph Colson Jr. Student, Marymount Palos Verdes Coll., 1970-71, Calif. State U., Long Beach, 1971, 73-75, Calif. State U., Los Angeles, 1986; BS in Bus. Adminstrn., U. Redlands, 1987. Asst. bookkeeper Valet Parking Service, Inc., Los Angeles, 1976-80; supr. bus. mgmt. Jamner, Pariser & Meschures, Los Angeles, 1980-87, Stevland Morris, Burbank, Calif., 1987—. Mem. Nat. Notary Assn., Nat. Assn. for Female Execs. Democrat. Office: Stevland Morris 4616 Magnola Blvd Burbank CA 91505

COLSON, ELIZABETH FLORENCE, anthropologist; b. Hewitt, Minn., June 15, 1917; d. Louis H. and Metta (Damon) C. BA, U. Minn., 1938, MA, 1940; MA, Radcliffe Coll., 1941, PhD, 1945; PhD (hon.), Brown U., 1978, D of Sociology, 1979; D.Sc., U. Rochester, 1985. Asst. social sci. analyst War Relocation Authority, 1942-43; research asst. Harvard, 1944-45; research officer Rhodes-Livingstone Inst., 1946-47, dir., 1948-51; sr. lectr. Manchester U., 1951-53; assoc. prof. Goucher Coll., 1954-55; research assoc., assoc. prof. African Research Program, Boston U., 1955-59, part-time, 1959-63; prof. anthropology Brandeis U., 1959-63; prof. anthropology U. Calif.-Berkeley, 1964-84, prof. emeritus, 1984-87; vis. prof. U. Zambia, 1987; Lewis Henry Morgan lectr. U. Rochester, 1973. Author: The Makah, 1953, Marriage and the Family Among The Plateau Tonga, 1958, Social Organization of the Gwembe Tonga, 1960, The Plateau Tonga, 1962, The Social Consequences of Resettlement, 1971, Tradition and Contract, 1974; jr. author Secondary Education and the Formation of an Elite, 1980, Voluntary Efforts in Decentralized Management, 1983, sr. author For Prayer and Profit, 1988; sr. editor: Seven Tribes of British Central Africa, 1951; jr. editor People in Upheaval, 1987. Fellow Ctr. Advanced Study Behavioral Scis., 1967-68, Fairchild fellow Calif. Inst. Tech., 1975-76, AAUW travelling fellow. Fellow Am. Anthrop. Assn., Brit. Assn. Social Anthropologists, Royal Anthrop. Inst. (hon.); mem. Nat. Acad. Sci., Am. Acad. Arts and Scis., Am. Assn. African Studies, Soc. Woman Geographers, Phi Beta Kappa. Office: Dept Anthropology U Calif Berkeley CA 94720

COLVIN-DONALD, JOCELYN ELAINE, military officer; b. Smyrna, Tenn., July 6, 1955; d. John Campbell and Rosa Lee (Weatherly) Colvin; m. Edward Gregory Donald, July 5, 1985; 1 child, Rashida Y. Colvin. Student, Xavier U., 1973-77; BS in Biology, Auburn U., 1979; student, Officer Tng. Sch., Lackland AFB, Tex., 1979-80; cert. in profl. mil. edn., Trans. Officer Sch., 1980, Squadron Officer Sch., 1985. Commd. 2d lt. USAF, 1980, advanced through grades to capt., 1984; chief asst. trans. div. Williams AFB, Ariz., 1980-82; duty officer Osan AFB, Korea, 1982-83; chief plans and programs br. Wurtsmith AFB, Mich., 1983-86; chief Pacific plans br. Scott AFB, Ill., 1986—. Mem. Nat. Assn. Female Execs., Nat. Def. Trans. Assn., Delta Sigma Theta. Office: HQ Mil Airlift Commd Scott AFB IL 62225

COLWELL, RITA ROSSI, reasearch scientist, microbiologist, educator; b. Beverly, Mass., Nov. 23, 1934; d. Louis and Louise (Di Palma) Rossi; m. Jack H. Colwell, May 31, 1956; children: Alison E.L., Stacie A. BS with distinction, Purdue U., 1956; PhD, U. Wash., 1961; DSc (hon.), Heriot-Watt U., Edinburgh, Scotland, 1987. Asst. research prof. U. Wash., Seattle, 1961-64; guest scientist div.applied biology NRC of Can., 1961-63; vis. asst. prof. biology Georgetown U., Washington, 1963-64, asst. prof. biology, 1964-66, assoc. prof., 1966-72; prof. microbiology U. Md., College Park, 1972—, dir. sea grant program, 1977-83, acting dir. Ctr. for Environ. and Estuarine Studies, 1980-81; v.p. acad. affairs U. Md. System, 1983-87; dir. Md. Biotech. Inst., 1987—; cons., adviser to Washington area communications media, Congressman and legislators, 1978—; external examiner various univs. abroad, 1964—; mem. coastal resources adv. com. dept. natural resources State of Md., 1979—; mem. numerical data adv. bd. NCR, 1973-76, ocean scis. bd., 1977-80; del. 20th Gen. Assembly, Internat. Union Biol. Scis., Finland, 1979; U.S. del. 16th Assembly, Internat. Council of Sci. Union, Washington, 1976; mem. Nat. Sci. Bd., 1984—. Author: (manual numerical taxonomy) Collecting the Data, 1970, (with M. Zambruski) Rodina-Methods in Aquatic Microbiology, 1972, (with L.H. Stevenson) Estuarine Microbiology Ecology, 1973, (with R.Y. Morita) Effect of the Ocean Environment on Microbial Activities, 1974, (with A. Sinsky and N. Pariser) Marine Biotechnology, 1983, Vibrios in the Environment, 1985; contbg. author: Marine and Estuarine Microbiology Laboratory Manual, 1975; mem. editorial bd.: Microbiology Ecology, 1972—, Applied and Environ. Microbiology, 1969-81, Johns Hopkins U. Oceanographic Series, 1981-83, Revue de la Found. Oceanographique Ricard, 1981—, Oil and Petromchem. Pollution, 1980—; assoc. editor: Can. Jour. Microbiology, 1972-75; editor-in-chief: Marine Tech. Soc. Jour., 1981—; contbr. numerous articles on marine microbiology and ecology to sci jours. Mem. Gov's. Sci. Adv. Council, State of Md., 1979—; bd. dirs. Upper Bay Survey Dept. Natural Resources, State of Md., 1974-75. Recipient Outstanding Woman on Campus award U. Md., 1979. Fellow AAAS, Grad. Women in Sci., Can. Coll. of Microbiologists, Am. Acad. Microbiology (mem. ad hoc com. on environ. microbiology 1978-79), Washington Acad. Scis. (bd. mgrs. 1976-79), Sigma Delta Epsilon; mem. Am. Soc. Microbiology (mem. various sci. coms. 1961—, pres. 1984-85, chmn. program com. REGEM-1 1988; Fisher award 1985), World Fedn. Culture Collections, U.S. Fedn. Culture Collections (governing bd. 1978-88), Am. Inst. Biol. Scis. (bd. govs. 1976-82), Marine Tech. Soc. (exec. council 1982-88), Am. Oceanic Soc., Classification Soc. of Eng., Soc. for Invertebrate Pathology, Am. Soc. Limnology and Oceanography, Atlantic Estuarine Research Soc., Estuarine and Brackish Water Scis. Assn., Am. Littoral Soc., Soc. for Indsl. Microbiology (bd. govs. 1976-79), Classification Research Group of Eng., Soc. for Gen. Microbiology of Eng., Phi Beta Kappa, Sigma Xi (Ann. Achievement award 1981, Research award 1984). Home: 5010 River Hill Rd Bethesda MD 20816

COLY, LISETTE, foundation executive; b. N.Y.C., Apr. 6, 1950; d. Robert Raymond and Eileen (Lyttle-Garrett) C.; 1 child, George Robert Damalas. BA cum laude, Hunter Coll., 1973. Sec. Parapsychology Found., Inc., N.Y.C., 1972-75, assoc. editor, 1975—, v.p., 1978—. Assoc. editor Parapsychology Rev. and Procs. Ann. Internat. Parapsychology Found. Confs., 1978—. Office: 1 Parapsychology Found Inc 228 E 71st St New York NY 10021

COLYER, CHARLOTTE ELIZABETH, business executive; b. St. Albans, N.Y., Jan. 9, 1943; d. Ralph H. and Charlotte E. (Farrell) C. Student, SUNY, Buffalo, 1960-63; BFA, St. Thomas Aquinas, Sparkill, N.Y., 1976. Art tchr. Archdiocese of N.Y., N.Y.C., 1972-79; customer service mgr. MWM Dexter, W. Nyack, N.Y., 1979-81; dist. sales mgr. Avon Products, Inc., Newark, 1981-83; customer service, prodn. coordinator Lorell Press, Avon, Mass., 1983-85; customer service mgr. ComWeb Graphics, Rockland, Mass., 1985-86, sales mgr., 1986—; chmn. bd. dirs. CEI Cons., Weymouth, Mass. Mem. Nat. Assn. Female Execs. (charter), Graphic Arts Sales Found. (cert.), South Shore C. of C. Club: Eagle Ridge Country. Home: 7111 Golden Eagle Ct #511 Fort Myers FL 33912 Office: Comweb Graphics PO Box 393 10 Commerce Rd Rockland MA 02370

COMAI, CHERYL ANN, environmental test company executive; b. North Adams, Mass., Dec. 5, 1949; d. Rena (Franceschetti) C. BA in Social Work, Our Lady of the Elms, 1971; MBA, U. R.I., 1983. English tchr., supr. Autonomous U. Guadalajara, Mex., 1972-74; personnel cons. Dennis & Dennis Personnel, Huntington Beach, Calif., 1975-76; mgr. Act II, Providence, 1976-79; med. office mgr. Dr. Peter Small, Charlestown, R.I., 1980-82; research assoc. John Brown/Leesona, Warwick, R.I., 1983; asst. dir. Robotics Ctr., U. R.I., Kingston, 1983-85; dir. planning Advanced Tech. Systems, East Providence, R.I., 1985-87; v.p. Sweet Micro Systems, Cranston, R.I., 1987—; cons. Small Bus. Devel. Ctr., Kingston, 1985—; co-chmn. human resources R.I. Techn. Council, Providence, 1986—. Bd. dirs. YWCA, Central Falls, R.I., 1986—. Mem. Nat. Assn. Female Execs., South County Women's Network (mem. steering com. 1984—). Home: 65 Edgewater Rd Narragansett RI 02882

COMBS, ANN RULEY, lawyer, nurse; b. Cin., Aug. 24, 1952; d. Louis Barnett and Carolyn Ann (Hayes) Ruley; m. Mark Edward Combs, June 24, 1978; children—Sarah Avery, Derek Edward. B.S. in Nursing, U. Mich., 1974; J.D., So. Meth. U., 1977. Bar: Ohio 1977; R.N., Ohio. Nurse Children's Hosp., Cin., 1977; assoc., Kohnen, Patton & Hunt, Cin., 1977-78, 1982—; sole practice, Columbus, Ohio, 1978-81; lectr. Ohio Hosp. Assn., 1982, various Cin. and Ky. hosps., 1982—, Tri State Perinatal Nurses Assn., Ohio, 1983, U. Cin. Sch. Law, 1984, Columbia Union Coll. Nursing, Palmer and Assocs., Inc., Creative Mgmt. Corp., Profl. Edn. Systems, Inc.; presenter mock depositions to area hosps., 1984—. Mem. ABA, Am. Nurse Attys. Assn., Ohio Bar Assn., Ohio Assn. Civil Trial Attys., U. Mich. Alumni Assn., Delta Theta Tau, Sigma Theta Tau, Chi Omega. Republican. Methodist. Home: 7650 Driftwind Ct Cincinnati OH 45242 Office: Kohnen Patton & Hunt 4500 Carew Tower 441 Vine St Cincinnati OH 45202

COMBS, BETTY JANE, educator; b. Nassau County, N.Y., Dec. 18, 1932; d. Raymond George and Elsie Jane Elliott; B.A., Pace U., 1972; M.A., Manhattanville Coll., 1976; M.S., Pace U., 1980; m. LeRoy Charles Combs, Mar. 22, 1952; children—Donald Charles, David Charles, James Robert, Jeffrey Raymond. Dir., Meml. Nursery Sch., White Plains, N.Y., 1959-68; substitute tchr., Westchester County, N.Y., 1968-72; dir. Lab Sch., asst. prof. early childhood edn. Pace U., Pleasantville, N.Y., 1972—. Vice pres. PTA, 1970-71; vice chmn. North Castle Republican Town Com., 1976—. Mem. Nat. Assn. Edn. Young Children, Assn. Supervision and Curriculum Devel., Nat. Assn. Early Childhood Educators, Phi Delta Kappa, Pi Lambda Theta (pres. 1985—). Methodist. Home: 23 Washington Pl North White Plains NY 10603 Office: Pace U Sch Edn Pleasantville NY 10570

COMBS, BRENDA CHRYSTEL, computer programmer; b. Fargo, N.D., Jan. 14, 1953; d. Virgil Booker T. and Eva Charles (Hooks) Combs; B.A. in Psychology, U. Redlands, 1975. Tchr., Monrovia (Calif.) High Sch., 1975-83; computer programmer So. Calif. Gas Co., Los Angeles, 1983—; minority relations rep. Calif. Tchrs. Assn., 1981-82; sch. rep. Monrovia Tchrs. Assn., 1980-81. Mem. Calif. Tchrs. Assn., Nat. Assn. Female Execs., Black Data Processing Assocs. (treas. Los Angeles chpt. 1987-88, 88-89), Pi Lambda Theta. Home: PO Box 61156 Pasadena CA 91106 Office: Box 3249 Terminal Annex Los Angeles CA 90051

COMBS, JANET LOUISE, sales and advertising company executive; b. Houston, Jan. 13, 1959; d. James Lee and Mary Lynn (Woolley) Combs. B.S. in Bus. Adminstrn., U. Ark., 1981. With Exxon Chem. Co., Houston, 1981-82; account exec. Promotional Products Co., Houston, from 1982, asst. v.p., 1982-86, v.p., 1986—. Mem. Houston Young Profl. Reps. Mem. Spring Branch Meml. C. of C., Girls' Cotillion, Mortar Bd., Blue Key, Houston C. of C., Kappa Alpha Theta (Founder's Meml. scholar 1980-81), Beta Gamma Sigma, Alpha Mu Alpha, Omicron Delta Kappa. Republican. Methodist. Home: 12611 Trail Hollow Houston TX 77024 Office: Promotional Products Co 1700 W Belt N Houston TX 77043

COMBS, JULIA CAROLYN, oboist; b. Topeka, July 11, 1950; d. Joe Denton and Fay Magel (Meshew) C.; Mus.B., Memphis State U., 1972, Mus.M., 1974; D.M.A., North Tex. State U. Sch. Music, 1985; m. William Barney Stacy, Aug. 2, 1981. Oboist, solo English horn Memphis Opera Theater, 1971-74; 2d oboist Memphis Symphony, 1972-74; solo English horn Norfolk (Va.) Symphony, 1974-75; prin. oboe Norfolk Opera, 1974-75, U.S. Army Chamber Orch., 1975-78; assoc. prof. oboe U. Wyo., Laramie, 1978—; oboist New World Wind Quintet, 1978—; oboe and oboe d'amore soloist, 1976—. Served with U.S. Army, 1975-78. U. Wyo. grantee, 1981, 84; recipient John P. Ellbogen Meritorious Classroom Teaching award U. Wyo., 1983; Beatrice Gallatin Beuf Golden Apple teaching award U. Wyo. Mem. Internat. Double Reed Soc., Nat. Assn. Coll. Wind and Percussion Instrs., Women in the Arts (founding mem.), Music Educators Nat. Conf., DAR, Puppeteers Am., Union Internat. de la Marionnette, Sigma Alpha Iota, Pi Kappa Lambda, Phi Kappa Phi, Alpha Lambda Delta. Home: 1912 Custer Laramie WY 82070 Office: PO Box 3037 Univ Sta Music Dept U Wyo Laramie WY 82070

COMBS, MARY JIM, educator; b. Carrollton, Ga., Dec. 13, 1933; d. Lewis Lee and Floy Burson Combs; B.S. in Home Econs., Ga. State Coll. for Women, 1955; M.Ed., U. Ga., 1963, Ed.S., 1967, Ed.D., 1974; m. Curtis E. Tate, Jr., Aug. 28, 1977; stepchildren—C. Emory, Milton O. Tchr., Cedartown (Ga.) High Sch., 1955-58, Carrollton (Ga.) High Sch., 1958-66; research asst. in vocat. edn. U. Ga., Athens, 1966-68, asst. prof., tchr. educator in home econs., 1968—. Mem. Ga. Assn. Future Homemakers Am. (hon.), Phoenix Soc., NEA, AAUP, Am. Home Econs. Assn., Ga. Home Econs. Assn., Am. Vocat. Assn., Ga. Vocat. Assn., Nat. Assn. Tchr. Educators for Vocat. Home Econs., Home Econs. Edn. Assn., Ga. Assn. Educators, Phi Upsilon Omicron, Phi Kappa Phi, Kappa Delta Pi, Delta Kappa Gamma. Contbr. articles to profl. publs. Home: 130 Wells Dr Athens GA 30606 Office: 624 Aderhold Hall U Ga Athens GA 30602

COMDEN, BETTY, writer, dramatist, lyricist, performer; b. Bklyn., May 3, 1919; d. Leo and Rebecca (Sadvoransky) C.; m. Steven Kyle, Jan. 4, 1942; children: Susanna, Alan. Student, Bklyn. Ethical Culture Sch., Erasmus Hall High Sch.; B.S., N.Y. U. Writer, performer nightclub act, Revuers; writer: (with Adolph Green) book and lyrics Broadway shows On the Town, 1944-45, Billion Dollar Baby, Two on the Aisle, Bells are Ringing, Fade-Out—Fade-In, Subways are for Sleeping, A Doll's Life, 1982 (Tony award); (with Adolph Green) lyrics for Hallelujah, Baby!; screenplays Auntie Mame, Good News, The Barleleys of Broadway, Singin' in the Rain, others; screenplay and lyrics for On the Town, Bells Are Ringing, Its Always Fair Weather, What a Way to Go; co-author: book for Applause, 1970; lyricist, dir.: (with Adolph Green) book for "Lorelei", 1973; book and lyrics On the 20th Century, 1978; appeared in: On the Town, 1944; performed with Adolph Green in show of their works, 1959, 77; also appeared in play Isn't it Romantic, 1983, in movie Garbo Talks, 1985, The Bandwagon. Recipient Donaldson award and Tony award for Wonderful Town, as co-lyricist best score 1983; Tony award for Hallelujah, Baby, as co-writer best score 1968; Tony award for Applause 1970; Tony award for lyrics and book On the 20th Century; Woman of Achievement award NYU Alumnae Assn. 1978; N.Y.C. Mayor's award Art and Culture 1978; named to Songwriters Hall of Fame 1980, Theatre Hall of Fame. Mem. Dramatists Guild (council, v.p. Dramatists Guild Fund). Office: care The Dramatists Guild 234 W 44th St New York NY 10036

COMEAU, JOANNE HADFIELD, bank advertising executive; b. Providence, Mar. 12, 1952; d. Howard Vincent and Dorothy Anne (Griffin) Hadfield; m. Arthur Bill Comeau, Apr. 11, 1981; 1 child, Elizabeth. BA in Speech Communication, U. R.I., 1974. Procedure writer Liberty Mut. Ins. Co., Boston, 1974-76; account exec. Creamer Inc. Advt., Providence, 1977-82; dir. mktg. Notre Dame Hosp., Central Falls, R.I., 1983; asst. v.p. mktg. Fleet Nat. Bank, Providence, 1984-87, v.p., advt. dir., 1987—. Recipient Unit of Yr. award for Pub. Info., R.I. div. Am. Cancer Soc., 1984. Mem. R.I. Ad Club. Avocations: racquetball, reading, acting/community theatre. Home: 221 Mountain Laurel Dr Cranston RI 02920 Office: Fleet National Bank 111 Westminster St Providence RI 02903

COMEAU, PEGGY, professional association executive; b. Los Angeles, May 10, 1943; d. Nicholas Thomas and Catherine Mary (Fink) Sagalewicz; m. Robert F. Comeau, Aug. 31, 1968 (div. Sept. 1985); 1 child, Michelle. BA in Econs., Santa Clara (Calif.) U., 1965; MA in Econs., Am. U., 1969. Tchr. Peace Corps, Turkey, 1965-67; econometrician J.M.T. Assocs., Philippines, 1969-70; sr. economist Ops. Research Inc., Washington, 1970-72; assoc. Messer Assocs., Washington, 1972-74; economist Dept. Labor, State of Hawaii, Honolulu, 1975-76; analyst Dept. Finance, State of Hawaii, Honolulu, 1976-81; dir. office of info. and complaints, exec. asst. to mayor City and County of Honolulu, 1981-85; exec. v.p. Hawaii Assn./Honolulu Bd. Realtors, 1985—. Co-author: Area Handbook on Turkey, 1968. Mem. Lanikai Community Assn., Kailua, Hawaii, 1975-85, Eileen Anderson Campaign Com., Honolulu, 1980, 84, Hawaii chpt. ARC, Honolulu, 1983-84; mem. bd. Girl Scout Council of the Pacific, Honolulu, 1987-88; 1st v.p. Girl Scouts U.S.A. Council of the Pacific, Honolulu, 1988—. State of Calif. scholar, 1961-65. Mem. Nat. Assn. Realtors (mem. various coms.), Orgn. Women Leaders, Honolulu C. of C. (legis. com.). Democrat. Roman Catholic. Club: Honolulu. Office: Hawaii Assn/Honolulu Bd Realtors 505 Ward Ave Honolulu HI 96814

COMELLA, PATRICIA ANN EGAN, government official, lawyer, consultant; b. N.Y.C., Jan. 26, 1941; d. John J. and Helen (Courtois) Egan; m. August John Comella, May 30, 1964; 1 son, Christopher. BA, Hofstra U., 1962, JD, Georgetown U., 1987. Mathematician, NASA Goddard Space Flight Ctr., Greenbelt, Md., 1962-75; policy analyst Office of Policy Evaluation, U.S. Nuclear Regulatory Commn., Washington, 1975-79, br. chief Office of Standards Devel., 1979-81, dep. div. dir. Office Nuclear Regulatory Research, 1981-84; sr. regulatory assurance specialist Battelle Meml. Inst., Washington, 1984-86; licensing mgr. Roy F. Weston, Inc., Washington, 1986-87; atty. Newman & Holtzinger, Washington, 1987—.

COMET-EPSTEIN, SHARON, college administrator; b. Cleve., Oct. 25, 1950; d. Sol S. and Fay (Shochet) Comet; B.S. cum laude, Ohio State U., 1972; M.S., Case Western Res. U., 1974, Ph.D., 1985; m. Robert E. Epstein, Sept. 1, 1974; children—Adam Scott, Rachel. Instr., Columbus Jr. Theatre Arts, summer 1971; instr., designer allied health scis. Ohio State U., Columbus, 1971-72; ednl. project dir. Sch. Dentistry Case Western Res. U., Cleve., 1972-76, dir. ednl. resources and public affairs, 1976-85, asst. prof., 1986—; ednl. dir. Western Res. Geriatric Ctr., 1986-87; mgmt. cons., 1982—. Contbr. articles to profl. jours; editor Focus, 1975-77, Off the Cusp, 1976-78; nat. speaker in field. Mem. Jewish Nat. Fund Young Leadership, Hadassah, Orgn. Rehab. through Tng. Recipient 40 Under Forty award Cleve. Jewish News, 1987-88, 2d place award Health Scis. Communications Assn., 1974. Mem. Women in Communications, Health Scis. Communications Assn., Profl. Ethics Dentistry Network, Am. Soc. Tng. and Devel., Am. Assn. Dental Schs. Jewish. Office: 2123 Abington Rd Cleveland OH 44106

COMFORT, JEAN FISHER, catering company executive; b. Milw., Nov. 26, 1960; d. Lewis Hamilton Fisher and Patricia Neale (Pryor) Whittaker; m. Brian David Comfort, June 6, 1981; 1 child, Chandra Marie. BS in Hotel, Restaurant and Travel, U. Mass., 1985. Kitchen asst. mgr. Hungry U Restaurant, Amherst, Mass., 1980-81; food mgr. Andy's Restaurant, Amherst, Mass., 1982-83; mental retardation technician food services Belchertown (Mass.) State Sch., 1983-85; supr. food and purchasing Sky Chefs-Airline Catering, Boston, 1985-87; food mgr. Marriott Inflite, East Boston, Mass., 1987—; researcher on employment of mentally handicapped U. Mass., Amherst, 1984-85, resulting in course, 1986. Mem. Internat. Food Service Exec. Assn., Assn. Female Execs., Nat. Inst. Food Industries (cert. in sanitation). Office: Marriott Inflite Logan Internat Airport 5 Wood Island Park East Boston MA 02128

COMFORT, PRISCILLA MARIA, personnel director; b. Ft. Dix, N.J., Feb. 20, 1947; d. Jennie Rita (Manes) McGuire; children: James, Aimee. BS, Montclair State Coll., 1969; MEd, Trenton State Coll., 1980. Cert. tchr., N.J., cert. guidance counselor, N.J., CPM-State of N.J., N.J. Secondary Guidance Cert. Tchr. Burlington (N.J.) Twp. and City Schs., 1969-72; employment service interviewer N.J. Dept. Labor and Industry, Trenton, 1972-74; prin. career devel. specialist N.J. Dept. Civil Service, Trenton, 1974-76, personnel technician, 1976-79; dir. personnel services Stockton State Coll., Pomona, N.J., 1979—. tchr. CCD Assumption Ch., Pomona, 1981-84, mem. CCD adv. bd., 1983-84; active Little League, PTO, 1977-84; personnel adv. bd. Atlantic City, 1985, Big Brothers, Big Sisters, 1988. Recipient YWCA T.W.I.N. award, 1987, Mgmt. Merit award, 1985, 86. Mem. Am. Soc. Pub. Adminstrs., Cert. Pub. mgrs. Assn. of N.J., Atlantic County Personnel Assn., N.J. Assn. of Affirmative Action in Higher Edn (panelist), N.J. Coll. and Univ. Personnel Assn. (sec., treas. 1986-87, vice chair 1987-88, chair-elect 1988—), N.J. Personnel Council, Atlantic City C. of C. (adv. bd., personnel task force, 1985). Roman Catholic. Office: Stockton State Coll Jim Leeds Rd Pomona NJ 08240

COMPISENO, DEBORAH LORAINE, marketing professional; b. St. Louis, Oct. 6, 1956; d. Francis Eugene and Catherine Marie (Stoops) Scott; m. Gregory Scott Calvert, July 9, 1977 (div. Mar. 1981); m. Nicholas Anthony Compiseno, July 31, 1981; children: Katherine Anne, Kristy Kay. Student, St. Louis U., 1973-74; cert. secretarial sci., Southeast Mo. State U., 1977; BS in Bus. Mgmt., Tarkio Coll., 1984. Asst. bus. devel. coordinator Sverdrup Corp., St. Louis, 1985-86; mktg. coordinator Geotech. Engrs., Inc., Winchester, Mass., 1986-87, Boeing Co., Lexington, Mass., 1987-88; mktg. analyst McDonnell Douglas Built Environment Technologies, St. Louis, 1988—. Cons. classroom Jr. Achievement's Project Bus. Program, Florissant, Mo., 1985; leader Girl Scouts USA, Ferguson, Mo., 1985-86, cookie chmn., 1985. Mem. Soc. for Mktg. Profl. Services (edn. com. 1987—). Roman Catholic. Home: 2020 Cordoba Dr Florissant MO 63033

COMPO, SANDRA IRENE, law librarian; b. Camden, N.J., Dec. 22, 1950; d. Peter and Vera (Bush) C. BA, Rutgers U., Camden, 1973; MLS, Drexel U., 1977. Supr. Rutgers U. Law Sch. Library, Camden, 1973-77; media specialist Camden Bd. Edn., 1977-80; law librarian Consol. Rail Corp., Phila., 1980—; corp. resources instr. Inst. for Paralegal Tng., Phila., 1987—. Contbr. chpt. (with others) to book: Occupational Hearing Loss, 1987. Mem. Greater Phila. Law Librarians Assn. (del. Camden 1987, legal research instr. 1981—). Democrat. Eastern Orthodox. Home: 504 Almonesson Ave Westville NJ 08093 Office: Consol Rail Corp Six Penn Center Suite 1138 Philadelphia PA 19103

COMPTON, ANN WOODRUFF, news correspondent; b. Chgo., Jan. 19, 1947; d. Charles Edward and Barbara (Ortlund) C.; m. William Stevenson Hughes, Nov. 25, 1978; children: William Compton, Edward Opie, Ann Woodruff, Michael Stevenson. B.A., Hollins (Va.) Coll., 1969. Reporter, anchorwoman WDBJ-TV (CBS), Roanoke, Va., 1969-70; polit. reporter, state capitol bur. chief WDBJ-TV (CBS), Richmond, Va., 1971-73; fellow Washington Journalism Center, 1970, trustee, 1978—; network radio anchorwoman ABC News, N.Y.C., 1973-74; White House corr. ABC News, Washington, 1974-79, 81-84, congl. corr., 1979-81, 84—; mem. adv. bd. Gannett Found. Ctr. for Media Studies, Columbia U., 1984—. Trustee Hollins Coll., 1987—. Named Mother of Yr., Nat. Mother's Day Com., 1987. Mem. White House Corrs. Assn. (dir. 1977-79), Radio-TV Corrs. Bd. (chmn. 1987). Office: ABC News 1717 DeSales St NW Washington DC 20036

COMPTON, JULIA PORTER, nursing home administrator; b. Nashville, Dec. 4, 1944; d. William Claude and Julia Elise (McRory) Porter; m. Charles Jonathan Couey, May 24, 1963 (div. Feb. 1973); children—Elizabeth Dawn, Margaret Ann; m. 2d, Learon Winston Compton, Jan. 27, 1975; 1 dau., Kristy Lynn. Student Huntingdon Coll., 1962-63. Lic. nursing home adminstr., Ala. Activities supr. Marengo Nursing Home, Linden, Ala., 1970-72; adminstr. Phenix City Nursing Home (Ala.), 1973-74, Parkwood Health Facility, Phenix City, 1974-84, Canterbury Health Facility, Inc., Phenix City, 1984—; cons. activities, 1973—. Mem. health com. Russell County Extension Service, Phenix City; bd. dirs. Phenix City Girls' Club, 1986—. Mem. Am. Coll. Nursing Home Adminstrs., Phenix City C. of C. Baptist. Home: 1309 Thayer Dr Phenix City AL 36867 Office: Canterbury Health Facility 1720 Knowles Rd Phenix City AL 36867

COMPTON, MARY BEATRICE BROWN (MRS. RALPH THEODORE COMPTON), public relations exec., writer; b. Washington, May 25, 1923; d. Robert James and Abia Eliza (Stone) Brown; grad. Thayer Acad., Chandler Sch., Leland Powers Sch. Radio, TV and Theatre, Boston, 1942; m. Ralph Theodore Compton, Mar. 18, 1961, step-children—Ralph Theodore, Patricia (Mrs. William R. Schnitzler). Radio program dir. Converse Co., Malden, Mass., 1942-45; head radio continuity dept. Sta. WAAB, Yankee Network, Worcester, Mass., 1945-46; asst. dir. radio Leland Powers Sch. Radio, TV and Theatre, Boston, 1946-49, dir., 1949-51; program asst. Sta. KNBH, Hollywood, Calif., 1951-52; v.p. Acorn Film Co., Boston, 1953-54; dir. women's communications, editor Program Notes, radio interviewer NAM, 1954-61. Celebrities pub. relations Nat. Citizens for Nixon, 1968, Kennedy Ctr. Pub. Info., 1985—. Mem. Soc. Old Plymouth Colony Descs., Magna Carta Dames, Smithsonian Instn. Assos., Nat. Trust for Hist. Preservation. Clubs: Congressional Country (Bethesda, Md.), Brooke Manor Country (Rockville, Md.). Home: 3428 Chiswick Ct Silver Spring MD 20906

COMPTON, SUSAN LANELL, retired librarian; b. Batesville, Ark., Aug. 20, 1917; d. Thomas Smith and Susan (Whitlow) Compton. BS in Edn., Ark. State Tchrs. Coll., 1939; BS in Library Sci., Peabody Coll. Tchrs., 1948. Asst. cataloger U. Ark. Gen. Library, Fayetteville, 1948-49; head catalog dept. Ark. Library Commn., Little Rock, 1949-77, chief cataloger, bibliographer, indexer, 1977-79; free-lance writer. Mem. Nat. League Am. Pen Women (v.p., program chmn. Ark. Pioneer br. 1972-74, pres. 1974-76), AAUW, Am. Library Assn. (life), Ark. Hist. Assn., Ark. Fedn. Women's Clubs. Author: Beauty Transient & Other Poems, 1969; Looking Forward to a New Day, 1984. Contbr. to Collier's Ency., 1970-76; editor quar. library bull. Ark. Libraries, 1949-74. Mem. ALS. Christadelphian. Home: 620 N Oak St Little Rock AR 72205

COMRAS, REMA, library director; b. N.Y.C., Oct. 26, 1936; d. Manuel and Zita (Kessel) C.; B.A., U. Fla., 1958; M.L.S., Syracuse (N.Y.) U., 1960; m. Jose Simonet, June 22, 1981. Librarian, Queensborough (N.Y.) Pub. Library, 1960-61, Spl. Services, U.S. Army, W.Ger. and France, 1962-64; asst. head librarian City of Hialeah (Fla.), 1964-73, library dir., 1973—. Mem. ALA, Fla. Pub. Library Assn., Dade County Library Assn., Beta Phi Mu. Office: Hialeah John F Kennedy Library 190 W 49th St Hialeah FL 33012

COMRIE, SANDRA MELTON, human resource executive; b. Plant City, Fla., Sept. 15, 1940; d. Finis and Estelle (Black) Melton; children: Shannon Melissa, Colleen Megan. BA, UCLA, 1962, grad. exec. program, 1984. Div. mgr. City of Los Angeles, 1973-77, asst. personnel dir., 1977-84; v.p. Transam. Life Cos., Los Angeles, 1984—; bd. dirs. Found. for Employment and Disablity, Sacramento, Calif.; mem. Asian Pacific Employment Task Force, Los Angeles, 1986—. Bd. dirs. Los Angeles Urban League, 1985—, Vols. of Am.-Los Angeles, 1985—; active United Way Downtown Bus. Consortium, Child Care Task Force, Los Angeles, 1985-86.; mem. adv. bd. Los Angeles City Child Care, 1987—. Recipient Young Woman of Achievement award Soroptimists of Los Angeles, 1979. Mem. Internat. Personnel Mgmt. Assn. (mem. assessment council, co-chair program com. for 1982 nat. conf., chair human rights com. 1983, pres. 1985), Human Resources Round Table, So. Calif. Personnel Mgmt. Assn., Personnel Testing Council, Personnel and Indsl. Relations, Inc., Los Angeles Area C. of C. (human resources com. 1986—). Democrat. Lodge: Soroptimists (pres. Los Angeles chpt. 1983-84). Office: Transam Life Cos 1150 S Olive St Los Angeles CA 90015

COMSTOCK-BUSSELL, CAROL ELLEN, small business consultant; b. Pennyan, N.Y., Apr. 13, 1954; d. Wilbur Richard and Margaret Louise (Dunning) C.; m. Robert Steven Bussell, May 23, 1987. BS, Cornell U., 1976; MS, Ithaca Coll., 1983. Cert. early childhood edn. tchr., N.Y., Ind. Mgr. capital budget Commins Engine Co., Jamestown, N.Y., 1983-85; cons. small bus. affairs Piano Technicians, Indpls., 1985—; bus. mgr. Bussell Piano Service, Indpls., 1987—; freelance artist, writer Jamestown, Indpls., 1977—; instr., lectr. Jamestown Community Coll., 1979-84., Ivy Tech. Coll., 1987—. Editor newsletter Nat. Acctg. Assn., Jamestown, Warren, N.Y., 1985; columnist local newspaper, 1979-80. Bd. dirs. YMCA, Jamestown, 1982-83. Mem. Women In Communications (bd. dirs. 1978-79). Republican. Presbyterian. Club: Doll Study (Jamestown). Home and Office: 224 West Banta Rd Indianapolis IN 46217

CONAGHAN, DOROTHY DELL, state legislator; b. Oklahoma City, Sept. 24, 1930; d. John Joseph and Wilhelmina Elizabeth (Boyer) Miller; student U. Okla., 1949-51; m. Brian Francis Conaghan, June 10, 1951 (dec. Apr. 1973); children: Joseph Lee, Charles Alan, Roger Lloyd; m. Robert K. Chiles, Aug. 15, 1986. Mem. Okla. Ho. of Reps., 1973-86, minority caucus sec., 1977-82, asst. minority leader, 1983-86. Bd. dirs. Alpha II, 1973-86, Community Liaison Council Juvenile Services, Ponca City, Okla., 1983-84, Alcohol, Drug Abuse and Community Mental Health Planning and Coordinating Bd., 1984-86, Okla. Christian Found., 1984-89; trustee Okla. chpt. Leukemia Soc. Am., 1985-87; pres. Washington Sch. PTA, Tonkawa, 1965, Okla. Christian Found., 1988; vice chmn. Kay County Republican Com., 1960-64, 6th Dist. Congl. Rep. Com., 1967; del. Rep. Nat. Conv., 1968; 3d vice moderator Christian Ch. (Disciples of Christ), 1986-88; lay mem. Okla. Health Planning Commn., 1988—. Recipient Women Helping Women award Ponca City Soroptimist Club, 1975, hon. mem., 1978. Mem. Nat. Order Women Legislators, Am. Legis. Exchange Council (state dir.), Tonkawa C. of C., Am. Legion Aux., P.E.O., Okla. Alliance for Artisans (v.p., bd. dirs.), Beta Sigma Phi (hon.). Clubs: Delphi Study, Order Eastern Star (past matron), Soroptomists Internat. of Ams. (hon.).

CONANT, DORIS KAPLAN, sculptor, civic worker, real estate developer; b. Phila., Apr. 28, 1925; d. Benjamin A. and Rae (Shander) Kaplan; B.A., U. Pa., 1945; postgrad. U. Havana, 1945, Art Inst. Chgo., 1962; m. Howard R. Conant, Dec. 14, 1947; children—Alison, Howard, Meredith Ann. One man shows Glenview Pub. Library, Northbrook Library,; exhibited in group shows Art Inst. Chgo. Sales and Rental Gallery, Design Unlimited, New Horizons in Sculpture, Old Orchard Art Fair, Lake Forest Coll. Exhbn. Sec. to consul Argentine Consulate, Phila., 1945-47; sec., dir. Interstate Steel Co., Des Plaines, Ill., 1948—; organizer proposed 1st Women's Bank Chgo.; dir. Upper Ave. Nat. Bank, Chgo., 1976-81; founder, v.p. Urban Innovations Ltd.First pres. ERA Ill.; mem. Chgo. Network.; bd. dirs. Chgo. Found. for Women, 1986—. Recipient Glenview Brotherhood award, 1965; named one of outstanding women P.U.S.H., 1975. Clubs: Carlton, East Bank. Home: 736 Greenacres Glenview IL 60025 also: 180 E Pearson St Chicago IL 60611 Office: 444 N Wells St Chicago IL 60610

CONANT, MARY PLACIDA, hospital administrator; b. Modesto, Calif., Apr. 5, 1910; d. Daniel Frederick and Magdaleine Anne (Kaal) C.; grad. St. Mary's Coll. Nursing, San Francisco, 1931; B.S., San Francisco Coll. Women, 1936. Joined Sisters of Mercy, Roman Catholic Ch., 1931; nursing supr., instr. St Mary's Coll. Nursing, San Francisco, 1936-42, dir. nursing, 1942-52, receptionist, 1982—; adminstr. Notre Dame Hosp., San Francisco, 1952, St. Joseph's Hosp., Phoenix, 1953-65, Mercy Hosp. and Med. Center, San Diego, 1965-74, exec. dir., 1974-77; adminstr. Mercy Hosp., Bakersfield, Calif., 1976-82; bd dirs. Notre Dame Hosp., San Francisco, 1952-53; pres. bd. dirs. St. Joseph's Hosp., Phoenix, 1953-65, Mercy Hosp., San Diego, 1965-77, Mercy Hosp., Bakersfield, 1976-82. Recipient Disting. Pub. Service award Maricopa County (Ariz.) Med. Soc., 1962; Disting. Leadership and Service award NCCJ, 1972; Disting. Service award Comprehensive Health Planning Assn. San Diego and Imperial County, 1976; Cert. of Recognition Calif. State Legislature, 1977; Recognition award City of San Diego, 1977; registered nurse, Calif., Ariz. Fellow Am. Coll. Hosp. Adminstrs. Home: 3250 19th Ave San Francisco CA 94132

CONANT, SHARI, insurance company executive; b. Cleve., Nov. 12, 1947; d. Rudy Lewis and Christine Barbara (Testman) Jaros; m. Donald Richard Conant, Dec. 23, 1967; children: Donald R. II, Amy Dawn. AA in Underwriting, Ins. Inst. Am., 1981; postgrad., Life Office Mgmt. Inst., 1983, Am. Coll., 1986. Cert. profl. ins. salesperson, 1981. Claims clk. CNA Ins. Co., Cleve., 1966-67; underwriter Fireman's Fund Ins. Co., Cleve., 1967-70, Beacon Mut. Ins. Co., Columbus, Ohio, 1976-79; sales mgr. Avon Co., Columbus, 1972-76; underwriter for farm owners Country Mut. Ins. Co., Bloomington, Ill., 1979, property tng. coordinator, 1979-80; coordinator agy. tng. info. Country Cos., Bloomington, 1980-81, agt. tng. specialist, 1981—. Sec., treas. McLean Soccer Referees Assn., Normal, Ill., 1984—, Cen. Ill. Soccer Ofcls. Assn., Springfield, 1988—; mem. Twin City Civic Newcomers, Normal, 1979—. Named one of Outstanding Young Woman of Am., 1983. Mem. Bloomington-Normal Ins. Assn. (sec. 1979-81, treas. 1981-84, v.p. 1984-85, pres. 1985-86, Assoc. of Yr. award 1986), Nat. Assn. Ins., Chartered Life Underwriters, Bloomington-Normal Life Underwriters, Nat. Assn. Life Underwriters, Nat. Assn. of Ins. Women. Democrat. Lutheran. Home: 1203 Valentine Dr Normal IL 61761 Office: Country Companies 1701 Towanda Ave Bloomington IL 61701

CONAWAY, JANE ELLEN, educator; b. Fostoria, Ohio, July 9, 1941; d. Robert and Virginia Conaway; B.A. in Elem. Edn., Mary Manse Coll., Toledo, 1966; M.Ed. in Elem. Edn., U. Ariz., 1969; postgrad. in reading, U. Toledo, 1975-77; postgrad. U. Wis., 1977—. Tchr. Sandusky public schs., Ohio, 1966-67, Bellevue City Schs., Ohio, 1969-70; coordinator 1st grade small group instrn. program St. Marys Grade Sch., Sandusky, 1970-71; tchr. Chpt. I remedial reading Eastwood Local schs., Pemberville, Ohio, 1971-86, also dist. dir. Right to Read program. Mem. NEA, Wis. Edn. Assn., Middleton Edn. Assn., Madison Area Reading Council, Delta Kappa Gamma. Cert. as reading specialist in diagnostic and remedial reading, Wis. Home: 6701 Woodgare Rd Middleton WI 53562 Office: Middleton Cross Plains Sch Dist Middleton WI 53562

CONAWAY, WILBERINA, government official; b. New Orleans, Jan. 20, 1956; d. Neil Jacob and Wilberina (DeSilva) C. BBA magna cum laude, Albany State Coll., 1979; degree, Am. U., 1986. Supply systems analyst Naval Research Lab., Washington, 1979-81, contract specialist, 1981-88, contracting officer, 1988—. Sunday sch. tchr., mem. gospel chorus, youth ministry, youth chorus, mass choir LeDetroit Bapt. Ch., Oxon Hill, Md., 1982—, mem. fin. com., 1985—, pres. gospel chorus, 1987—, numerous other positions; adult asst. Girl Scouts U.S.A., 1985—, numerous other positions. Recipient letter of appreciation Naval Research Lab., 1981, 83, 84, 87, 88, Nat. Alliance Bus., 1982, Allen U., 1982, cert. of appreciation LeDetroit Bapt. Ch., 1985; named Better Chance scholar Phillips Exeter Acad., 1971, McCormick scholar Albany State Coll. Found., 1979; Kellogg Found. grantee, 1979. Mem. Nat. Contract Mgmt. Assn., Nat. Assn. Female Execs., Nat. Honor Soc., Alpha Kappa Mu. Home: 1101 Kennebec St Apt 204 Oxon Hill MD 20745 Office: US Naval Research Lab 4555 Overlook Ave SW Washington DC 20375-5000

CONCEPCION, ISIS LILIBETH, anesthesiologist; b. Concepcion, Panama, July 4, 1955; came to U.S., 1956; d. Adam and Ismenia (Lezcano) Concepcion. M.D., Universidad Autonoma de Guadalajara, Mexico, 1975. Lic. physician/surgeon, N.Y., Calif., Mont. Rotating intern Regina Gen. Hosp. (Sask., Can.), 1976-77; community health physician Universidad Autonoma de Guadalajara (Mexico), 1977-78; rotating intern Moncton Hosp., New Brunswick, Can., 1978-79; resident in anesthesiology St. Vincent's Hosp., N.Y.C., 1980-82; fellow dept. anesthesiology and critical care medicine Meml. Sloan Kettering Cancer Ctr., N.Y.C., 1983-84, asst. clin. anesthesiologist, 1984—. Mem. AMA, N.Y. County Med. Soc., Am. Soc. Anesthesiologists, N.Y. State Soc. Anesthesiologists (alt. del. dist. #2 1986), Internat. Anesthesia Research Soc., Nat. Assn. Residents and Interns. Home: 240 E 79th St New York NY 10021 Office: Meml Sloan Kettering Cancer Ctr 1275 York Ave New York NY 10021

CONDIE, CAROL JOY, anthropologist, research facility administrator; b. Provo, Utah, Dec. 28, 1931; d. LeRoy and Thelma (Graff) C.; m. M. Kent Stout, June 18, 1954; children: Carla Ann, Erik Roy, Paula Jane. BA in Anthropology, U. Utah, 1953; MEd in Elem. Edn., Cornell U., 1954; PhD in Anthropology, U. N.Mex., 1973. Edn. coordinator Maxwell Mus. Anthropology, U. N.Mex., Albuquerque, 1973, interpretation dir., 1974-77; asst. prof. anthropology U. N.Mex., 1975-77; cons. Albuquerque, 1977-78; pres. Quivira Research Ctr., Albuquerque, 1978—; cons. anthropologist U.S. Congl. Office Tech. Assessment, chair Archeol. Resources Planning Adv. Com., Albuquerque, 1985-86; leader Crow Canyon Archeol. Ctr. field seminars, 1986—. Author: The Nighthawk Site (LA 5685), a Pithouse Site on Sandia Pueblo Land, Bernalillo County, New Mexico, 1982, Five Sites on the Pecos River Road, 1985; co-editor: Anthropology of the Desert West, 1985; also articles. Mem. Downtown Core Area Schs. Com., Albuquerque, 1982. Ford Found. fellow, 1953-54. Fellow Am. Anthrop. Assn., mem. Soc. Am. Anthropology (chmn. Native Am. Relations com. 1983-85), N.M. Archeol. Council (pres. 1982-83), Maxwell Mus. Assn. (bd. dirs.), Las Arañas Spinners and Weavers Guild (pres. 1972). Democrat. Home: 1809 Notre Dame NE Albuquerque NM 87106 Office: Quivira Research Ctr 3017 Commercial NE Albuquerque NM 87107

CONDIT, (ELEANOR) LOUISE, retired museum director; b. Balt., May 7, 1914; d. George Smith and Bessie Blaine (Madeira) C.; m. Frederic G. M. Lange, Sept. 19, 1946. A.B., Vassar Coll., 1935; A.M., Columbia, 1941. Carnegie grant for study edn. museums of Brit. Isles, Scandinavia, Germany, France, Netherlands, summer 1939; supr. edn. Bklyn. Children's Mus., 1935-42; supr. Jr. Mus. Met. Mus. Art, 1943-61, asst. dean charge Jr. Mus., 1961-68, asso. in charge Jr. Mus., 1968-72, mus. educator in charge Jr. Mus., 1972-80, dep. vice dir. ednl. affairs, 1974-78, dep. dir. ednl. affairs, 1978-80; active mem. U.S. Nat. Com. for Internat. Council Museums, 1972-78. Incorporator Bergen Community Mus., Hackensack, N.J. Mem. Am. Assn. Museums (council 1957-63, v.p. 1960-63), Museums Council N.Y.C. (sec.-treas. 1960-65, vice chmn. 1977-78), Archaeol. Inst. Am. (dir. N.Y. chpt. 1973-77), N.Y. Film Council, Am. Assn. Youth Museums (pres. 1972-74), Inst. Study Art in Edn. (dir. 1974-78), Phi Beta Kappa. Home: 1203 Emerson Ave Teaneck NJ 07666

CONDOS, BARBARA SEALE, real estate investment consultant, broker; b. Kenedy, Tex., Feb. 24, 1925; d. John Edgar and Bess Rochelle (Ainsworth) Seale; m. George James Condos, Dec. 24, 1955 (dec.); 1 child, James Alexander. MusB magna cum laude, Incarnate Word Coll., San Antonio, 1946. Lic. real estate broker, Tex. Ptnr., chief exec. officer Mountain Top-V.I. Devel. Properties, V.I., 1977-85; ptnr. Condos & Rhame, San Antonio, 1976—, Investment Realty Co., San Antonio, 1978—; pres. Hallmark Realty, Inc., San Antonio, 1978—. Choreographer, dancer San Antonio Youth Concerts; actress San Antonio Little Theatre-Patio-Players 1948—. Trustee San Antonio Little Theatre, 1953-76; trustee Incarnate Word Coll., 1977—, vice chair, 1980-82; mem. council McNay Mus., 1986—, chair 1987—; chair council McNay Art Inst., 1988—; bd. dirs. San Antonio Performing Arts Assn., 1978—. Mem. Internat. Real Estate Fedn., Internat. Inst. of Valuers, Real Estate Securities and Syndication Inst., Tex. Assn. Realtors, San Antonio Bd. Realtors. Club: The Argyle (San Antonio). Avocation: painting. Home: 217 Geneseo Rd San Antonio TX 78209 Office: Investment Realty Co 1635 NE Loop 410 San Antonio TX 78209

CONDRA, NORMA LEE, newspaper owner and publisher; b. Russell, Ky.; d. Pem Burton and Lottie Lee (Edleman) Kuhn; children: David, Cynthia Condra Snyder. Student U. Tenn. Pub. Country Hot Line News, Nashville, 1977-79, Wilson World, Lebanon, Tenn., 1979-80; founder, pub. Town & Country Courier, Nashville, 1981—, Hendersonville (Tenn.) Free Press, 1975—; pub. Goodlettsville Free Press, Madison Free Press, White House Free Press; bd. dirs. Dominion City Bank. Chmn. Hendersonville Arts Council, 1978-79; mem. Sumner County Literacy Bd. Mem. Nat. Fedn. Ind. Bus. (Tenn. adv. bd.), White House Conf. Small Bus. (Tenn. del.), Suburban Newspapers of Am. (bd. dirs. 1981-85), Hendersonville C. of C. (bd. dirs., pres.-elect 1982). Republican. Methodist. Club: Tenn. Women's Golf Assn. (pres. 1980-82), Hillwood Country, Bluegrass Country (Hendersonville). Home: 106 Christopher St Nashville TN 37205 Office: Hendersonville Free Press 131 Sanders Ferry Rd Hendersonville TN 37075

CONDRILL, JO ELLARESA, logistician, speaker; b. Hull, Tex., Oct. 25, 1935; d. Freddie and Ida (Donatto) Founteno; m. Edwin Leon Ellis, Jan. 9, 1955 (div. 1979); children—Michael Edwin, James Alcia, Resa Ann, Thomas Matthew; m. Donald Richard Condrill, Sept. 21, 1980 (div. 1985). BS in Bus. Adminstrn., Our Lady of the Lake U., 1982; grad. Logistics Exec. Devel. Course, Army Logistics Mgmt. Ctr., 1985; MS in Pub. Adminstrn., Cen. Mich. U., 1987. Cert. seminar coordinator. Sec. USAF, Wiesbaden, Fed. Republic Germany, 1968-73; sec. mil. tng. ctr. USAF, San Antonio, 1973-77; editorial asst. Airman Mag., San Antonio, 1978; mgmt. analyst San Antonio Air Logistics Ctr., San Antonio, 1979-82; inventory mgr. ground fuels Detachment 29, Alexandria, Va., 1982-83; logistics plans officer Mil. Dist. Washington, 1983-85, chief logistics plans ops. and mgmt., 1985-88, hdqrs. dept. of the army staff, 1988—; owner Seminars by Jo, Alexandria, Va., 1984-86; specialist logistics mgmt. Dep. Chief Staff Logistics Info. Mgmt. Div. Hdqrs. Dept. Army, 1988—; field instr. Golden State U., Los Angeles, 1985-86, field instr. Fairfax County Adult Edn., Springfield, Va., 1984; vol. aide ARC Wilford Hall Hosp., San Antonio, 1978; constn. drafter KC Women's Aux., San Antonio, 1977; den mother Boy Scouts Am., San Antonio, 1967; docent Nat. Mus. Am. History, 1988. Recipient Cert. of Achievement, Dept. Army, 1984; Best Speaker award Def. Logistics Agy. Mem. Soc. Logistics Engrs., Federally Employed Women (Pentagon I chpt. treas. 1987-88), Assn. U.S. Army, Internat. Platform Assn., Am. Soc. Pub. Adminstrn., Nat. Assn. Female Execs. Republican. Roman Catholic. Club: Toastmasters (area gov. 1984-85, div. lt.-gov. 1988—). Home: 5904 Nount Eagle Dr #317 Alexandria VA 22303

CONE, MARTHA CAROLINE, television production executive; b. Columbus, Ohio, Apr. 11, 1933; d. Francis Edward and Freda Katherine (Ehlers) Clymer; student Ohio State U., 1951-52; children—Denise Danielle Buyaky, David Douglas DeVoe. Asst. to program mgr. Sta. WLW-C-TV, Columbus, Ohio, 1952-53, Sta. WBNS-TV, Columbus, 1953-55; dir. women's programming Sta. WPTA-TV, Ft. Wayne, Ind., 1963-65; asst. to dir. press/publicity Sta. KNBC-TV, Los Angeles, 1965-69; comml. mgr. Lawrence Welk Show, Don Fedderson Prodns., Los Angeles, 1971-77; prodn. mgr.-syndication ops. West Coast, Mark Goodson Prodns., Los Angeles, 1977—. Res. police officer City of Burbank (Calif.), 1979; vol. Burbank Community Hosp.; bd. dirs. Burbank Community Healthcare Found. Republican. Club: Foothill Civitan (Burbank, Calif.). Office: Mark Goodson Prodns 6430 Sunset Blvd Los Angeles CA 90028

CONERLY, ERLENE BRINSON, chemist; b. Jackson, Miss., Nov. 16, 1938; d. Alvin Bryan and Erlene (Brinson) C. BS, Millsaps Coll., 1959; MS in Tech. Mgmt., Am. U., 1978. Chemist NIH, Bethesda, Md., 1962-78; research biologist Dynamac, Rockville, Md., 1979-80; chemist U.S. EPA, Washington, 1980—. Mem. Assn. Official Analytical Chemists. Democrat. Episcopalian. Office: US Environ Protection Agy 401 M St SW TS 769 C Washington DC 20460

CONEY, CAROLE ANNE, accountant; b. Berkeley, Calif., Aug. 11, 1944; d. Martin James and Ida Constance (Ditora) Skuce; m. David Michael, June 20, 1964 (div. 1985); children: Kristine Marie, Kenneth Michael. BS cum laude, Calif. Poly. U., 1985, postgrad., 1985—. Acct., asst. sec.-treas. Surety Ins. Co., La Habra, Calif., 1973-76; bookkeeper Homemakers Furniture, Downers Grove, Ill., 1976-79; office mgr., acct. Helen's Pl. Printing, Upland, 1979-80; bookkeeper Vanguard Cos., Upland, 1980-82; dir. acctg. Coll. Osteopathic Medicine of Pacific, Pomona, Calif., 1982—; tax cons., instr., H&R Block, Portland, Oreg., 1969-71. Pres. Brea/La Habra Newcomers, 1975; treas. Alta Loma (Calif.) Com. to Elect Robert Neufeld, 1981. Mem. Nat. Assn. Coll. and Univ. Bus. Officers, Assn. Coll. and Univ. Auditors, Nat. Assn. Female Execs., Council Fiscal Officers, Delta Mu Delta, Alpha Iota. Democrat. Roman Catholic. Lodge: Soroptimists. Home: 9521 Konocti St Cucamonga CA 91730 Office: Coll of Osteopathic Medicine of the Pacific Plaza Pomona Pomona CA 91766-1889

CONFORTI, JOANNE, advertising executive; b. N.Y.C., Apr. 17, 1944; d. Ralph and Josephine (Amico) C. Student, Bklyn. Coll., 1961-63. Trainee, Gen. Motors, N.Y.C., 1960-62, adminstrv. asst., 1962-66, personnel asst., 1966-70; staff asst. Bozell & Jacobs, Inc., N.Y.C., 1973-75, personnel and office mgr., 1975-77, personnel and office v.p., 1977-79, human resources dir., v.p., 1979-81, corp. human resources dir., sr. v.p., from 1981, now exec. v.p. corp. human resources. Mem. Advt. Women of N.Y. Home: 252 E 61st St New York NY 10021 Office: Bozell Jacobs Kenyon & Eckhardt 40 W 23d St New York NY 10010 *

CONGALTON, SUSAN TICHENOR, lawyer; b. Mt. Vernon, N.Y., July 12, 1946; d. Arthur George and M. Marjorie (McDermott) Tichenor; m. Christopher William Congalton, May 29, 1971. BA summa cum laude, Loretto Heights Coll., 1968; JD, Georgetown U., 1971. Bar: N.Y. 1972, Ill. 1986. Assoc. Reavis & McGrath, N.Y.C., 1971-78, ptnr., 1978-85; v.p., gen. counsel, sec. Carson Pirie Scott & Co., Chgo., 1985-87, sr. v.p. fin. and law, sec., 1987—. Mem. bd. of overseers IIT Chgo.-Kent Coll. of Law, 1985—; mem. bus. adv. council U. Ill. at Chgo. Bus. Sch. Mem. ABA, Am. Corp. Counsel Assn., Am. Soc. Corp. Secs. Office: Carson Pirie Scott & Co 36 S Wabash Chicago IL 60603

CONGER, MARY LANE, county official; b. Shelbyville, Tenn., July 1; d. Jacob Thomas and Grace (Howard) Lane; m. John Beall Conger, Apr. 14, 1940; children—John Beall, Jr., Malinda Conger Gibson. B.S., Middle Tenn. State U.; postgrad. U. Tenn.-Nashville, Peabody Coll., U. Tenn.-Knoxville. Classroom tchr. Bedford County Dept. Edn., Shelbyville, 1938-40; tchr. Lincoln County Dept. Edn., Fayetteville, Tenn., 1949-80, Headstart coordinator, 1965-70 (summers); commr. Lincoln County, Tenn., 1978—. Bd. dirs. Fayetteville-Lincoln County Library, 1978-86, Lincoln County Cancer Soc., 1982—; sec. Lincoln County Law Enforcement Com., 1978-82, Lincoln County Solid Waste Com., 1982-86, Lincoln County Fin. Com., 1982-86, Lincoln County Budget Com., 1986-89; active Lincoln County Democratic Women, 1950—; chmn. Lincoln County Bi-Centennial Celebration, 1976. Recipient Freedoms Found. of Valley Forge Nat. Classroom Tchr's. award, 1960. Mem. Lincoln County Ednl. Assn. (pres. 1977-78), NEA, Tenn. Retired Tchrs. Assn., Tenn. County Commrs. Assn., Lincoln County Farm Bur. (bd. dirs.), Mimosa Home Demonstration Club (v.p. 1983—), Round Dozen Lit. Club, Lincoln County Museum Assn. (bd. dirs. 1985—), Lincoln County Hist. Soc. (editor 4 editions of jour., 1983—, pres. 1984-86, v.p. 1987-88), Alpha Kappa Lit. Club (pres. 1948-50), Delta Kappa Gamma (chpt. pres. 1980-82). Methodist. Avocations: needlework; rug hooking; rug braiding; restoring family home. Home: Rt 5 Box 338 Fayetteville TN 37334 Office: Lincoln County Seat Rt 5 Box 338 Fayetteville TN 37334

CONKLIN, LYNN SUMMERS, utilities commission executive; b. Balt., Feb. 4, 1936; d. Harry Ricks and Doris Louise (Sturm) Summers; A.A., Valencia Community Coll., 1981; B. G.S., Rollins Coll., 1983; children—Vicky Lee, David Travis. Cert. systems profl., office automation profl. Office mgr. Norrell Temporary Service, Winter Park, Fla., 1976-77, clerical div. mgr., 1977-79; office systems supr. Martin Marietta Data Systems, Orlando, Fla., 1979-80, office automation system adminstr., 1980-83; sr. customer rep. integrated office applications Harris Corp., Melbourne, Fla., 1983-85, mgr. e-mail mktg. and support Martin Marietta Data Systems, Orlando, Fla., 1985-88; supt. records mgmt. Orlando Utilities Commn., 1988—. Lectr. in field. Mem. Assn. Info. Systems Profls., Gamma Phi Beta. Home: 5324 Burning Tree Dr Orlando FL 32811 Office: 500 S Orange Ave Orlando FL 32811

CONLAN, IRENE ESTELLE, health care administrator; b. Emmett, Idaho, Sept. 25, 1935; d. Carl O. Danielson and Mona A. Cardwell; m. John B. Conlan, Sept. 13, 1968; children: Christopher, Kevin. BS in Nursing, The Cath. U. Am., 1964, MS in Nursing, 1965. Dir. St. Anthony Sch. Nursing, Oklahoma City, 1965-66; mem. faculty Coll. Nursing Ariz. State U., Tempe, 1966-67, Sch. Nursing No. Ariz. U., Flagstaff, 1966; dir. nursing adminstrn. St. Luke's Hosp Med. Ctr., Phoenix, 1967-72; asst. dir. div. emergency med. services and health care facilities Ariz. State Health Dept., Phoenix, 1987—; cons. grant rev. office child and family services HHS, Washington, 1985, office adolescent pregnancy, 1986—. Author: Women We Can Do It, 1976; co-author: 1984 and Beyond, 1984. Pres. Scottsdale Rep. Women, 1978; mem. Los Rancheros Rep. Women, Scottsdale, 1986—, St. Luke's Service League, Phoenix, 1970—. Mem. Nat. Assn. Female Execs., Nat. Speakers Assn., Sigma Theta Tau. Home: 7439 E Willowrain Ct Scottsdale AZ 85253 Office: Ariz Dept Health Div Emergency Med Services and Health Care 701 E Jefferson Phoenix AZ 85034

CONLEY, LAKITA, artificial intelligence and computer specialist; b. Washington, May 21, 1955; d. John C. and Ruby M. (Holloway) C. BA in Biol. Sci., Communication, George Washington U., 1978, MS in Med. Engring., 1987. Clin., research biologist NIH, Bethesda, 1974-79; clin. biologist G.W. Med. Ctr. Transplantation Lab., Washington, 1979-84; tech. cons. Washington, 1984-86; knowledge engr. George Washington Inst. Artificial Intelligence, Washington, 1986; field knowledge engr. Teknowledge, Inc., Rockville, Md., 1986—; free-lance cons. ind. artificial intelligence firms, Washington, 1986—, Time-Life Books, N.Y.C., 1986. Speaker in field. Bd. dirs. Washington Free Clinic, 1980-82. Mem. IEEE, Computer Soc., Am. Assn. Artificial Intelligence, Soc. Human Factors, Delta Sigma Theta. Office: Teknowledge Inc 15200 Shady Grove Rd Rockville MD 22031

CONLEY, SHARON, health and safety services executive; b. Fortress Monroe, Va., July 25, 1947; d. Irving Lionel and Irma Marie (Pierce) C.; m. William Steven Vernarec, Apr. 23, 1977 (div. Apr. 1985). Student, Westminster Choir Coll., 1972-75, Middlesex County Coll., Edison, N.J., 1980-82; BSBA, Tusculum Coll., 1987. Tng. tech. Internat. Tech. Corp., Edison, 1982-83, tng. support coordinator, 1983-85, environ. tech., 1985-86; nat. tech. coordinator Internat. Tech. Corp., Knoxville, Tenn., 1986-87, tech. and adminstrv. mgr., 1987—. V.p. Young Dem. Soc., Williamsburg, 1972; mem. Bd. Registry and Election 6th Dist., Trenton, 1979. Mem. Am. Mgmt. Assn., Nat. Assn. Female Execs. Unitarian. Office: Internat Tech Corp 312 Directors Dr Knoxville TN 37923

CONLEY, SHEILAH RICHARDS, small business owner, musician; b. Chattanooga, Sept. 14, 1952; d. Floyd Henry and Minnie Jean (McCurdy) H.; m. Richard Donovan Waskom, Dec. 11, 1976 (div. May 1978); m. Robert S. Conley, Oct. 17, 1987. BS in Speech, Mid. Tenn. State U., 1976, BS in English, 1976. Asst. pub. relations dir. Mem. Hosp., Chattanooga,

1976-80; free-lance vocalist, pianist Chattanooga, Atlanta, 1976—; owner, corp. sec. Cherokee Steel Supply, Lithonia, Ga., 1986—; cons. For Children Only, Chattanooga News-Free Press, 1978. Founder, editor Mem. Hosp. Newspaper, 1977-80; contbg. writer Chattanooga News-Free Press, 1977-79; author tunes and lyrics, 1983. Treas. Young Reps., Murfresboro, Tenn., 1974; speaker Chattanooga Bus. Profl. Womens's Club, Chattanooga, 1979; recruiter, soloist Mid. Tenn. State U., 1974-76; vocalist, pianist, New Bethel Bapt. Ch., 1967-8. Recipient Govs. Talent award, Gov. Winfield Dunn, Tenn., 1975, Young Careerist award, Chattanooga Bus. Profl. Club, 1979, New Outstanding Talent of Ga., Ga. Senators, 1984; Honorable Mention, Ga. Songwriters awards, 1987. Mem. Ga. Songwriters Assn., Atlanta Regional Minority Purchasing Council. Republican. Home: 512 Rockborough Terr Stone Mountain GA 30083

CONLEY, SUSAN B., medical school faculty pediatrician; b. Coldwater, Mich., Feb. 3, 1948; d. Kenneth D. and Mary F. (Spence) C. MD, U. Mich., 1973. Instr. Washington U. Med. Sch., St. Louis, 1977-78; asst. prof. pediatrics U. Tex. Med. Sch., Houston, 1978-84, assoc. prof. pediatrics, 1984—; med. adv. bd. Nat. Kidney Found. Southeast Tex. Fellow Am. Acad. Pediatrics; mem. Am. Soc. Nephrology, Am. Soc. Pediatric Nephrology. Office: U Tex Med Sch 6431 Fannin Houston TX 77025

CONLEY, SUSAN ELIZABETH, lawyer; b. Stillwater, Minn., May 15, 1952; d. Bernard David and Florence Mita Marie (Uzpen) C.; m. Charles E. Petry, Aug. 17, 1973 (div. Feb. 1978); 1 child, Joseph Miguel. BA in French, U. Minn., 1970, JD, 1978. Staff atty. So. Minn. Regl. Legal Services, St. Paul, 1979-84; exec. dir., mng. atty. Centro Legal, Inc., St. Paul, 1984-87; asst. regional counsel dept. justice No. Region of Immigration and Naturalization Service, Twin Cities, Minn., 1987—; guest lectr. U. Minn. Law Sch., Mpls., 1986—; bd. dirs., treas. Hispanos en Minn. Mem. Nat. Tb Sclerosis Assn., Winfield, Ill., 1981—, Hispanic Health Care Coalition, St. Paul, 1984-86, Assn. Retarded Citizens, St. Paul, 1986—; bd. dirs./treas. Hispanos En Minn., St. Paul, 1983—; bd. dirs./sec. Westside Health Ctr., St. Paul, 1984-86. Mem. Am. Immigration Lawyers Assn. Minn. and Dakotas Chpt. (sec./treas. St. Paul chpt. 1986-87). Roman Catholic. Office: Immigration and Naturalization Service Bishop Henry Whipple Fed Bldg Fort Snelling Twin Cities MN 55111

CONLIN, JOANNE, writer, corporate administrator; b. Mt. Holly, N.J., July 11, 1955; d. George Albert and Margaret Laura (Rainier) Conlin; m. Dennis Charles Haller, Apr. 2, 1982 (div. Dec. 1987). Degree with honors, Blair Sch. for Journalism, 1972; AA in Journalism, Burlington County Coll., 1977; BA in Journalism/Communications, Temple U., 1981; postgrad., Monmouth Coll., 1988—. Reporter, writer Tampa (Fla.) Tribune Newspaper, 1973-74; asst. mgr. customer service govt. systems div. Western Union, 1974-80; sr. tech. writer GTE Info. Systems, 1980; from sr. tech. writer to mgr. advt. and promotion Threshold Tech. Inc., 1980-81; specialist mgmt. info. systems documentation Datamedia Corp., 1981; from writer assoc. to programs adminstr. Okidata, Mt. Laurel, N.J., 1982-87; writer phone, computer systems AT&T, Middletown, N.J., 1987—. Contbr. articles to profl. jours. Recipient award Burlington County Editors, 1977; named best printer documentation PC Mag., 1985. Mem. Nat. Soc. for Tech. Communications (sr. mem., award of excellence 1987), Project Mgmt. Inst., Nat. Assn. for Female Execs. (bd. dirs.). Episcopalian. Home: 26 Center Ave Burlington NJ 08016 Office: AT&T 200 Laurel Ave Middletown NJ 07748

CONLIN, PATRICIA PETERS, banker; b. Santa Monica, Calif., Sept. 17, 1943; d. John Dennis and Dorothy (Tydeman) Peters. A.B. magna cum laude, Cornell U., 1965; A.M. in Econs., Stanford U., 1966. With Morgan Bank, N.Y.C., 1966—, asst. treas., 1968-70, asst. v.p., 1970-73, v.p., 1973-84, sr. v.p., 1984—. Office: Morgan Guaranty Trust Co 23 Wall St New York NY 10015

CONLIN, ROXANNE BARTON, lawyer; b. Huron, S.D., June 30, 1944; d. Marion William and Alyce Muraine (Madden) Barton; m. James Clyde Conlin, Mar. 21, 1964; children: Jacalyn Rae, James Barton, Deborah Ann, Douglas Benton. B.A., Drake U., 1964, J.D., 1966, M.P.A., 1979; LL.D. (hon.), U. Dubuque, 1975. Bar: Iowa 1966. Assoc. firm Davis, Huebner, Johnson & Burt, Des Moines, 1966-67; dep. indsl. commr. State of Iowa, 1967-68, asst. atty. gen., 1969-76; U.S. atty. So. Dist. Iowa, 1977-81; assoc. firm James, Galligan & Conlin, P.C., 1983—; gen. counsel Legal Def. and Edn. Fund, NOW, 1985-86, pres., 1986—; adj. prof. law U. Iowa, 1977-79; guest lectr. numerous univs. Chmn. Iowa Women's Polit. Caucus, 1973-75, del. nat. steering com., 1973-77; cons. U.S. Commn. on Internat. Women's Year, 1976-77. Contbr. articles to profl. publs. Nat. committeewoman Iowa Young Democrats; also pres. Polk County Young Dems., 1965-66; del. Iowa Presdl. Conv., 1972; Dem. candidate for gov. of Iowa, 1982; nat. policy chmn. John Glenn for Pres. Com., 1983-84; bd. dirs. Riverhills Day Care Center, YWCA; chmn. Drake U. Law Sch. Endowment Trust, 1985-86 ; bd. counselors Drake U., 1982-86; pres. Civil Justice Found., 1986—. Recipient Iowa Civil Liberties Union award, 1974, Iowa Citizen's Action Network award, 1987, others; named to Iowa Women's Hall of Fame, 1981; scholar Readers Digest, 1963-64, Fischer Found., 1965-66. Mem. ABA, Iowa Bar Assn., ACLU, Common Cause, Assn. Trial Lawyers Iowa (bd. dirs.), Assn. Trial Lawyers Am. (chmn. consumer and victims coalition com. 1985-87, chair edn. dept. 1987-88), Women's Equity Action League, NOW (bd. dirs. 1986—, gen. counsel legal def. and edn. fund 1985-86, pres. legal def. and edn. fund 1986—), Phi Beta Kappa, Alpha Lambda Delta, Chi Omega (Social Service award). Office: 610 Equitable Bldg Des Moines IA 50309-3790

CONLON, JOYCE ISABELLE, small business owner; b. Lawrenceburg, Ind., Feb. 25, 1949; d. Theodore Lamont and Margaret Elizabeth (Lamb) Penn; m. Joseph Martin Conlon, Nov 7, 1970; children: Joy, Jason. BA, Ind. U., 1976. Sales rep. L.M. Berry and Co., Warsaw, Ind., 1978-80, supr. sales, 1980-82, mgr. sales, 1982-88; owner Ape Over You/Celebrations, Warsaw, 1988—. co-chmn. Rep. Cen. Com., Warsaw, 1983, v. precinct committeeman 1981-83, clk. election bd. 1981, 83; fund dr. person United Way L.M. Berry and Co. 1983-86. Mem. Warsaw Econ. Devel. Commn., Nat. Assn. Female Execs., Kosciusko County Nat. Assn. Female Execs. (founding mem. 1987), Am. Soc. Profl. Exec. Women, LWV, Bloomington and Warsaw, Am. Assn. U. Women. Home: 116 Tyner Warsaw IN 46580 Office: Ape Over You/Celebrations 106 E Center St Warsaw IN 46580

CONLON, KATHRYN ANN, county official; b. Mankato, Minn., July 30, 1958; d. Ralph Raymond and Joan Margaret (Meyer) Walter; m. James Alan Conlon, Oct. 1, 1977; children—Jessica Marie, Brian Michael. Student Mankato Vocat. Sch. Teller Mankato Credit Union, 1977; clk. Nicollet County Credit Bur., Minn., 1977-78; abstracter Lorna Holmquist, St. Peter, Minn., 1978-82; dep. recorder, abstracter Nicollet County, 1982-84, county recorder, abstracter, 1984—, sec. to dept. heads, 1985, chmn. dept. heads, 1986. Mem. Spina Bifida Assn. Minn., 1981—, Spina Bifida Assn. Southwest Minn., 1983—; bd. dirs. Children's Central Child Care, 1985-87. Mem. Minn. Assn. County Recorders, VFW Aux., Am. Legion Aux., St. Peter Area C. of C. Avocations: handcrafting; camping; volleyball; racquet ball. Home: Rt 3 Box 116 Saint Peter MN 56082 Office: Nicollet County Recorder PO Box 493 Saint Peter MN 56082

CONLON, VICKI LYNN, accountant; b. Clintonville, Wis., May 28, 1952; d. Victor Carl and Harriet Elizabeth (Hurley) Desens; divorced; children: Patrick J., Rebecca E., Jillian E., Jennifer L. Cert. in fin. statements, U. Wis., Oshkosh. cert. tax preparer. Tax cons. H&R Block, Pitts., Calif., 1970; owner H&R Block, Ripon, Wis., 1971-78, DD Assocs., Ripon, 1979-83; pres. Gemini II Inc., Ripon, 1984—. Mem. Nat. Assn. Female Assn., Ripon Bus. and Profl. Women's Club (pres. 1982-83), Ripon C. of C. (bd. dirs. 1974-84). Office: Gemini II Inc 107 Watson PO Box 182 Ripon WI 54971

CONN, ALICE LYNNE, fundraiser; b. Washington, Jan. 8, 1959; d. Jackie Ray and Margaret Alice (Duvall) Conn; m. Gary Gerard Myzick, Jan. 5, 1985. BS in Journalism, U. Md., 1981. Logistics coordinator Moshman & Assocs., Bethesda, Md., 1981-82; dir. devel. Epilepsy Found. Am., Landover, Md., 1982-86; coordinator spl. events Orphan Found., Washington, 1986; dir. devel. Columbia Hosp. for Women, Washington, 1987—. Named one of Outstanding Young Women Am., 1984. Mem. Nat. Assn. Female Execs., Nat. Soc. Fundraising Execs., Nat. Assn. Hosp. Devel., Bus. and Profl. Women, Delta Delta Delta. Republican. Methodist. Home: 1526 Warfield Rd Edgewater MD 21037

CONN, CATHERINE CHAMPION, real estate executive; b. Los Alamos, N. Mex., Dec. 29, 1946; d. Glenn Reeves and Theresa (Verre) Champion; m. John C. Conn, Jr., July 1, 1967; 1 child, Terri. BA, Colo. Women's Coll., 1969. Lic. real estate salesperson, 1985. Staff tchr. Grand Forks (N.D.) Schs., 1970-74; team leader Grand Forks Pub. Schs., 1974-75; sales assoc. The Vaughan Co., Albuquerque, 1985—; bd. dirs. Remington Homes, Albuquerque, 1986. Mem. Albuquerque Bd. Realtors (top 2%). Republican. Episcopalian. Home: 451 Live Oak Lane NE Albuquerque NM 87122 Office: The Vaughan Co Realtors 11501 Montgomery NE Albuquerque NM 87111

CONNAIR, NANCY J., travel administrator; b. Dayton, Sept. 28, 1936; d. Arthur Lloyd and Edith Catherine (Stomps) Ostendorf; m. Russell Lee Johnson, Oct. 12, 1957 (div. Feb. 1983); children: Russell, Jr., Laura L., Julie L., Tracey A.; m. Timothy Joseph Connair, May 11, 1984. Grad. high sch., Dayton, Ohio, 1954. Cert. travel counselor. Asst. mgr. group tours Miami Valley Automobile Club, Dayton, 1977-86; mgr. group tours Toledo Automobile Club, 1986—; speaker Dayton/Montgomery County Conv./ Visitor Bur., 1987. Vol. Franciscan Life Ctr., Toledo, 1986-87, Sta. WGTE-TV and WGTE-FM, Toledo, 1987; mem. tourism adv. council Toledo Conv./Visitor Bur., 1987. Mem. Nat. Tour Assn. (cert., membership com. 1986-87). Roman Catholic. Office: Toledo Automobile Club 2271 Ashland Ave Toledo OH 43620

CONNEIGHTON, VICKI DAVIS, management professional, bookkeeper; b. Springfield, Ohio, June 10, 1958; d. Phillip Dale and Joyce Elizabeth (Morris) Davis; m. Patrick Michael Conneighton, Aug. 16, 1980; 1 child, Ashley Elizabeth. Grad. high sch., Edgewood, Ky., 1976. Office clk. Mid-States Cinemas, Cin., 1975-77, Kelly Girl Temporary Service, Cin., 1977-78; bookkeeper, jewler J.C., Inc., Crescent Springs, Ky., 1978-82; bookkeeper Fla. Tile Ceramic Ctr., Blue Ash, Ohio, 1982-85, office mgr., bookkeeper, 1986—; controller Containerport of Cin., 1985-86. Mem. Nat. Geog. Soc., Nature Conservancy. Club: Mädel Klub (Cin.) (pres. 1983-86). Home: 212 W 68th St Cincinnati OH 45216 Office: Fla Tile Ceramic Ctr 10850 Millington Ct Cincinnati OH 45242

CONNEL, CAMILLE MARY, advertising and marketing professional; b. St. Paul, May 28, 1959; d. Allan Archibald and Geraldine Francis (Rice) C. BA in French with highest honors, Macalester Coll., 1981; cert. in Japanese, Middlebury Coll., 1986; MA in Advt., U. Minn., 1988. Tchr. ESL English Lang. Services, St. Paul, 1981-82, Mombusho, Japanese Ministry Edn., Kanagawa, 1982-84; internat. mktg. communications adminstr. 3M Co., St. Paul, 1985-87; acct. exec. Kuschner Assocs., Inc., Mpls., 1988—; mem. Women's Assn. Minn. Symphony Orch. advt. sales com. Mem. Minn. Bus. Indsl. Advt. Assn. Home: 900 Summit Apt 210 Minneapolis MN 55403

CONNELL, ELSIE MAUREEN, medical office administrator; b. Kilgore, Tex., June 4, 1933; d. A. C. and Georgia Alice (Burton) McGraw; m. Gerald Davis Connell, Jan. 24, 1983; m. Dan Phillip Broadwater, May 5, 1954 (div. May 1980); children—Jack Phillip, Charles Wayne, Shelly Dee. Nurse, Gregg Meml. Hosp., Longview, Tex., 1958-59, Laird Meml. Hosp., Kilgore, 1959-70; receptionist Internal Medicine Assocs., Longview, 1970-71, ins. coordinator, purchasing agt., 1971-72, office mgr., 1972-76, bus. mgr., 1976—. Pres., Mathers Aux. Kilgore Baseball, 1970, 72; treas. bd. dirs. Kilgore Boys Baseball, 1972. Mem. Internal Medicine Adminstrs., Am. Coll. Med. Group Mgmt. Assn., Med. Group Mgmt. Assn., Med. Adminstrs. Tex. Republican. Baptist. Home: 708 Florey St Kilgore TX 75662 Office: Internal Medicine Assocs 701 N 6th St Longview TX 75601

CONNELL, KATHLEEN SULLIVAN, state government official; b. Newport, R.I., May 24, 1937; d. Lawrence Francis and Margaret (Byrnes) Sullivan; m. Gerald Connell, June 11, 1960; children: Lawrence, Margaret, Kathleen. BS in Nursing magna cum laude, Salve Regina Coll., 1958; postgrad., Boston Coll., U. R.I., R.I. Coll. Registered nurse Newport Vis. Nurses Assn., 1958-61; health educator Newport Sch. Dept., 1970-86; sec. of state State of R.I., Providence, 1987—; pres., bd. dirs. Shake-a-Leg, Inc. Mem. Middletown Sch. Com. 1965-76, chmn. 1972-76; mem. Middletown Town Council 1977-83, vice-chmn. 1981-83; active Save the Bay, Aquidneck (R.I.) Goals Group, Aquidneck Ecology; mem. council nominating com. Newport Girl Scouts of U.S.; bd. dirs. Vis. Nurse Service of Newport County; vice-chmn. R.I. Dem. Com.; mem. Dem. Women's Caucus, Middletown Charter Rev. Commn.; mem. Dem. Nat. Com. Recipient awards R.I. Library Assn., Vol. Services for Animals, John F. Kennedy Ctr. for Performing Arts, Very Spl. Arts Assn.; named Alumnus of Yr. Salve Regina Coll., 1987. Mem. Am. Nurses Assn., R.I. State Nurses Assn., R.I. Sch. Nurses Assn., NEA, R.I. Edn. Assn., LWV, Women's Network, Vietnam Vets. of Am. (assoc.), Newport Irish Heritage Soc. (bd. dirs.), Nat. Conf. State Legislatures (com. labor and edn.), Delta Kappa Gamma. Home: 233 Tuckerman Ave Middletown RI 02840 Office: Office Sec of State 217 State House Smith St Providence RI 02903

CONNELL, LINDA MARIE, dietitian; b. Williamsport, Pa., Jan. 30, 1957; d. Gerald Thomas and Marlot Wilma (Klein) C. BS in Dietetics, U. Ariz., 1980, MS in Dietetics, 1983. Dietician Tucson Med. Ctr., 1982-83; dietician Canyon Ranch Resort, Tucson, 1983-86, dir. nutrition services, 1986—; nutrition cons., Tucson, 1982—. Author (column) Restaurant Revealing, 1986; contbr. articles to profl. jours. Mem. Am. Dietetic Assn., Nat. Council Against Health Fraud, Ctr. for Sci. in Pub. Interest, Am. Running and Fitness Assn., Sports and Cardiovascular Nutritionists. Home: 2016 E Water St Tucson AZ 85719 Office: Canyon Ranch Resort 8600 E Rockcliff Rd Tucson AZ 85715

CONNELL, MARY JANE, lawyer; b. Pontiac, Mich., Mar. 11, 1947; d. Jerry J. and Louise (Newburg) Connell. BA, U. Mich., 1969; MA, Northwestern U., 1970; JD cum laude, Fordham U., 1982. Bar: N.Y. 1983, Hawaii 1985. Tchr., South Middle Sch., Grand Rapids, Mich., 1970-72; exec. sec. Goodman Theatre, Chgo., 1972-74; legal asst., office sec. Weissberger & Harris, N.Y.C., 1974-81, Gottlieb, Schiff, Ticktin, Sternklar & Harris, N.Y.C., 1981-82; assoc. Cravath, Swaine & Moore, N.Y.C., 1982-85, Carlsmith, Wickman, Case, Mukai & Ichiki, Honolulu, 1985—. Mem. ABA, N.Y. State Bar Assn., Hawaii Bar Assn., Alpha Omicron Pi. Office: Carlsmith Wickman Case Mukai & Ichiki PO Box 656 Honolulu HI 96809

CONNELL, SHIRLEY HUDGINS, public relations director; b. Washington, Oct. 5, 1946; d. Orville Thomas and Mary (Beran) H.; m. David Day Connell, Dec. 13, 1980 (div. 1985). BA, U. R.I., 1968, MA, 1970. Clk., editor MGM Studios, Culver City, Calif., 1970-72; scriptor, talent Monarch Records, Studio City, 1972-73; communications specialist U. So. Calif., Los Angeles, 1973-81; dir. pub. relations Six Flags Movieland, Buena Park, Calif., 1981-82, Donald J. Fager & Assocs., N.Y.C., 1982—; cons. Children's TV Workshop, N.Y.C., 1978. Pres. bd. trustees Oaks at North Brunswick Condominium Assn., 1987—; founding mem. Mcpl. Services Com., North Brunswick; mgr. Animal Rescue Force, North Brunswick, 1988—; apptd. mem. environ. com. Twp. of North Brunswick. Contbr. articles to profl. jours.; contbg. editor Greater N.Y. Doctor's Shopper mag., 1987—. Mem. Nat. Assn. Female Execs., Marine Tech. Soc. (vice chmn. 1980-81). Clubs: Oceanic Soc. (bd. dirs. 1979-81), Los Angeles Press. Avocations: photography, reading, swimming, wood finishing, writing.

CONNELL, SUZANNE (SPARKS) MCLAURIN, retired librarian; b. Bennettsville, S.C., Sept. 12, 1917; d. John Bethea and Aleine (McLeod) McLaurin; A.B., Woman's Coll. of U. N.C., 1938; A.B. in L.S., U. N.C., 1940; 1 child, John Alexander (dec.). Library asst. Mt. Pleasant br. D.C. Public Library, Washington, 1940-41; post librarian Camp Sutton, N.C., 1943-44; post librarian McGuire Gen. Hosp., Richmond, Va., 1945-46, chief librarian McGuire VA Hosp., 1946-52, 59-62; chief librarian VA Hosp., Lake City, Fla., 1952-56; cataloger, chief books acquisitions, chief books circulation, asst. chief documents acquisitions Air U. Library, Maxwell AFB, Ala., 1956-59; head extension, head circulation Greensboro (N.C.) Public Library, 1962-63; reference librarian, asst. and acting base librarian Marine Corps Base, Camp Lejeune, N.C., 1963-66; part time cataloger Wilmington (N.C.) Public Library, 1967-75. Past vol., ARC, U.S. Naval Hosp., Marine Corps Base, Camp Lejeune, N.C., local hosp. and nursing home. Mem. ALA (pres. assn. hosp. and instn. libraries 1955-56), Phi Beta Kappa. Methodist. Contbr. articles to Brit. and Am. periodicals. Home: 502 Brunswick St Southport NC 28461-3706

CONNELLY, ALICE C., restaurateur; b. Chgo., Sept. 30, 1954; d. John J. and Dorothy (Day) C. BS in Chemistry, Northwestern U., Evanston, Ill., 1975. Credit mgr., gen. sec. Stouffers Hotels, Oakbrook, Ill., 1975, kitchen supr., 1975-76; restaurant supr. Mohawk Enterprises, Joliet, Ill., 1976-78; prodn. supr. Stouffers Mgmt. Foods, Evanston, Ill., 1978; account mgr. Stouffers Mgmt. Foods, Milw., 1978-82; dist. mgr. Canteen Co. div. TW Services, Chgo., 1982—. Roman Catholic. Home: 522 S Williston St Wheaton IL 60187 Office: TW Services Canteen Co Div 216 W Diversey Elmhurst IL 60126

CONNELLY, MARCIE LEMAY, executive; b. Worcester, Mass., Nov. 15, 1949; d. Norman J. and Beatrice (Lacoste) Lemay; m. David Lynn, 1987; 1 child, Brennan. BA, Anna Maria Coll., Paxton, Mass., 1971; postgrad. bus. adminstrn., Rivier Coll., Nashua, N.H., 1982-84. Adminstrv. asst. AEC Corp., Hudson, N.H., 1980-82, product mgr., 1982-84, mgr. mktg., 1984, dir. mktg., 1984-85, dir. sales West div., 1985; dir. sales and mktg. CDX Corp., Aurora, Colo., 1985-86, exec. v.p., 1986-87, pres., chief exec. officer, 1987—. Democrat. Home: 16835 E Harvard Pl Aurora CO 80013 Office: CDX Corp 10691 E Bethany Dr Suite 900 Aurora CO 80013

CONNER, JANET CHESTELYNN, financial broker; b. Albany, Ky., Nov. 24, 1953; d. Kathleen (Stearns) C. Student, Purdue U. V.p. mktg. Brandon Polo Club, Fla., 1981-82; asst. Puller Mortgage, Indpls., 1982-83; pres., owner Excalibur Fin., New Castle, Ind., 1983—. Appointed mem. Ind. Venture Capital Conf., Indpls., 1983. Named Hon. Lt. Gov., Lt. Gov. Mutz of Ind., 1983. Mem. Nat. Assn. Women Bus. Owners, Network Women in Bus., Nat. Assn. Sec. Services, Internat. Enterpreneurs Assn., Delta Sigma Pi. Republican. Methodist. Clubs: Brandon (Fla.) Polo; Ind. Sanyo Users (Indpls.) (chmn.). Avocations: polo, business, fox-hunting, computers, airplanes. Home: PO Box 48 New Castle IN 47362

CONNER, SUSAN PUNZEL, history educator; b. Madison, Wis., Sept. 29, 1947; d. Ferdinand Frederick August and Mabel Katherine (Zellhoefer) Punzel; m. Ronald Joseph Conner, June 1, 1968. B.A. in History, Armstrong State U., 1969; M.A. in History, Fla. State U., 1974, Ph.D. in History, 1977. Instr., chmn. social sci. Calvary Day Sch., Savannah, Ga., 1969-72; instr. Ga. Tech. Inst., Atlanta, 1977-78; assoc. prof. history Tift Coll., Forsyth, Ga., 1978-82, prof. history, 1982—, Fuller E. Callaway prof. history, 1985-86, Ruth Scarborough prof. hist., 1986-87; asst. prof. Cen. Mich. U., Mt. Pleasant, 1987—; chair social scis., 1978-85, chair div. arts and scis., 1985—, dir. archives, 1978-87; cons. nat. register nominations, Forsyth, 1980—. Contbr. chpt. to books, articles to profl. jours. Bd. dirs. Middle Ga. Archives, Macon, 1983-86; bd. dirs. Monroe Hist. Soc., Forsyth, 1983-85; sec.-treas. Monroe County C. of C., 1983-84, pres., 1984-85. Recipient NEH Newberry Summer Inst. award, 1978; Ga. Endowment to Humanities Semiquincentenary grantee, 1983; NEH travel grantee, 1985; Hist. Preservation Leadership award Ga. Clean Community Com., 1983. Mem. Ga. Assn. Historians (pres. elect 1987), Am. Hist. Assn. Consortium on Revolutionary Europe, Soc. French Hist. Studies, Ga. Trust Historic Preservation, AAUW (grant honoree). Methodist. Club: Forsyth Woman's (pres. 1982-84). Home: 1506 Ridge St Mount Pleasant MI 48858 Office: Cen Mich U History Dept Mount Pleasant MI 48859

CONNERLY, DIANNA JEAN, business official; b. Urbana, Ill., June 7, 1947; d. Ellsworth Wayne and Imogene (Sundermeyer) Connerly; student Ill. Comml. Coll., 1967. Bookkeeper, Jerry Earl Pontiac, 1968-72; officer mgr. Jack Nicklaus Pontiac, 1972-76; office mgr. Simon Motors Inc., Palm Springs, Calif., 1977-83; bus. mgr., 1983—. Mem. Am. Bus. Women's Assn. (pub. relations dir. Trendsetter chpt. 1983—). Office: 78611 Highway 111 LaQuinta CA 92253

CONNERY, CAROL JEAN, marketing executive; b. Amarillo, Tex., Oct. 22, 1948; d. William Wayne and Joyce Jean (Forney) Connery; A.A., Christian Coll., 1969; B.J., U. Tex., Austin, 1971. Cert. neuro-linguistic practitioner. Asst. dir. admissions Columbia (Mo.) Coll., 1971-80; exec. dir. nat. office Teenworld Scholarship Program, Overland Park, Kan., 1980-82; account exec. Mktg. Communications, Inc., Lenexa, Kans., 1983-86; account supr. Krupp/Taylor USA, Dallas, 1986—; cons. in field. Mem. Mid-Am. Soc. Assn. Execs., Columbia Coll. Alumni Assn., Direct Mktg. Assn. of Tex., Zeta Tau Alpha, Phi Theta Kappa (past nat. v.p.). Methodist. Home: 9002 Cumberland Dr Irving TX 75063 Office: Krupp/Taylor USA 545 E Carpenter Freeway Suite 1400 Irving TX 75062

CONN-LEVIN, NANCY BARBARA, health educator, writer, researcher; b. Newark, Mar. 16, 1952; d. Ralph Irving and Gertrude (Zacks) Conn; B.A., Sarah Lawrence Coll., 1974; postgrad. Princeton U., 1974-75; M.A., Goddard Coll., 1980; m. Eric M. Levin, Dec. 17, 1972; 1 dau., Amanda Conn-Levin. Cons. women's health, Manahawkin, N.J., 1976-80; cons. Ocean County Coll., CEA of Ocean County, Ocean County NOW, Women's Counseling and Community Services, Childbirth Edn. Assn. Ocean County, La Leche League of Tuckerton, 1977-80; dir. Health Info. Assocs., Inc., Plantation, Fla., 1982-85; adult educator Broward County Sch. Bd. (Fla.), 1983-85; adj. faculty Broward Community Coll., 1984-85; cons. Broward County Library; writer, researcher on health promotion, Ocean, N.J., 1986—. Mem. Nat. Women's Health Network, Am. Public Health Assn., Internat. Childbirth Edn. Assn., Am. Assn. for Counseling and Devel. Compiler women's health info. and resources; developer, producer audio tape for relaxation tng. Wellness Through Relaxation, 1985. Office: Health Info Assocs PO Box 163 Oakhurst NJ 07755

CONNOLLY, ELIZABETH ANNE, market professional; b. Hackensack, N.J., Nov. 16, 1957; d. Richard Thomas and Helen Pauline (Jurik) C. BA, William Patterson, 1979; MA, NYU, 1981, PhD, 1986. Dir. mktg. and edn. The Equitable, West Orange, N.J., 1985—. Mem. Sociologists in Bus. Home: 10 Brewster Ave Ridgefield Park NJ 07660 Office: The Equitable 155 Prospect Ave West Orange NJ 07052

CONNOLLY, MARGARET THERESA, real estate broker; b. County Monaghan, Ireland, Aug. 31, 1942; came to U.S., 1959, naturalized, 1966; d. Terrence and Elizabeth (McGivney) Clarke; m. Thady J. Connolly, Apr. 24, 1965; children—Francis J., Christine M. Grad. Diakin Sch. Real Estate, N.Y., 1976; cert. Empire Sch. Real Estate, 1983. Pres., Connolly Realty Co. doing bus. as Active Realty, Washingtonville, N.Y., 1976—. Mem. Internat. Assn. Real Estate Appraisers, Nat. Assn. Female Execs. Democrat. Roman Catholic. Avocations: painting; gardening. Home: MD 1-Rt 208 Washingtonville NY 10992 Office: Active Realty RD 2 Rt 208 Washingtonville NY 10992

CONNOLLY-O'NEILL, BARRIE JANE, interior designer; b. San Francisco, Dec. 22, 1943; d. Harry Jr. and Jane Isabelle (Barr) Wallach; m. Peter Smith O'Neill, Nov. 27, 1983. Cert. of design, N.Y. Sch. Interior Design, 1975; BAF in Environ. Design, Calif. Coll. Arts and Crafts, 1978. Profl. model Brebner Agy., San Francisco, 1963-72; TV personality KGO TV, San Francisco, 1969-72; interior designer Barrie Connolly & Assocs., Boise, Idaho, 1978—. Best Interior Design award Mktg. and Merchandising Excellence, No. Calif., 1981, 1984;, Sales and Mktg. Council, San Diego, 1985, 86; Best Residential Design award Boise Design Rev Com., 1983;, Grand award Best in Am. Living, Nat. Assn. Homebuilders, River Run, Boise, 1986. Mem. Mannequin League of Marin. Home: 2188 Bluestem Ln Boise ID 83706

CONNOR, CONSTANCE GIBSON WEHRMAN, social secretary, publisher, writer; b. Harrisburg, Pa., May 7, 1935; d. William and Lucile Elisabeth (Phillips) Gibson; m. Philip William Wehrman, Nov. 1955 (div. 1978); children: William Thomas, Holly Elizabeth, Philip Gibson; m. Robert T. Connor, Nov. 1978 (div. 1985). AA, Centenary Coll. Women, 1956; student, U. Va., Naples, Italy, 1974, U. Md., 1975, No. Va. Community Coll., 1978. Tchr. Bangkok, Thailand, Key West, Fla. and Fairfax County,

Va., 1966-70; art importer Gibson Wehrman Imports, Charleston, S.C. and Falls Church, Va., 1972-75; protocol officer Dept. of State and White House, Washington, 1981-83; owner ind. pub. co. Falls Church, 1970—; social sec. Embassy of Can., Washington, 1983—; founder, publisher Mil. Travel News, Travel News, Arlington, Va., 1970—; instr. English, 1975. Author: World Travel Guide, 1970, Join the Jet Set on Military and Retirement Pay. Wardrobe mistress Bob Hope Vietnam Christmas Show, 1967; com. mem. Reagan/Bush inauguration, 1980-81, 84-85; vol. Pres.'s Adv. Com. on Arts, John F. Kennedy Ctr. for Performing Arts, 1987; active CARE, ARC, United Service Orgns. Home: 1530 N Key Blvd Apt 230 Arlington VA 22209 Office: Embassy of Canada 1746 Massachusetts Ave NW Washington DC 20036 also: Mil Travel News Box 9 Oakton VA 22124

CONNOR, ELIZABETH NANCY, library director; b. Bay Shore, N.Y., Nov. 16, 1955; d. Arthur Richard and Beatrice Marie (Rudnic) C. BA, SUNY, Geneseo, 1977, MLS, 1978. Supr., announcer Sta. WGSU-FM, Geneseo, 1975-78; disc jockey Sta. WMJQ-FM, Rochester, N.Y., 1977-78; ednl. devel. coordinator Allegany Community Coll., Cumberland, Md., 1978-80; head evening services Welch Med. Library at Johns Hopkins U., Balt., 1980-84; med. librarian, satellite TV coordinator Greater Balt. Med. Ctr., 1984-88; clin. librarian King Faisal Specialist Hosp. and Research Centre, Riyadh, Saudi Arabia, 1988—; cons. Leland Meml. Hosp., Riverdale, Md., 1986. Book reviewer Library Jour., 1981; co-author annotated bibliography Diagnosis and Treatment of Sex Offenders, 1982. Organizer Greater Balt. Med. Ctr. Holiday Food Drive, 1986, 87. Mem. Health Sci. Communications Assn., Med. Library Assn., Md. Assn. Health Scis. Librarians. Democrat. Office: Greater Balt Med Ctr 6701 N Charles St Baltimore MD 21204

CONNOR, JO ANN, association administrator, executive; b. Pitts.; d. Charles Melvin Connor and Millicent (Jackson) Reed. BA in Music, Oakwood Coll., 1970; MusB, MA, Mich. State U., 1975, postgrad. Mgr., sec. Flint (Mich.) Br. NAACP, 1964-66; tchr. music, Beecher Schs., Flint, 1970-71; acct. U. Mich., Flint, 1971-72; personnel specialist Lansing (Mich.) Pub. Schs., 1975-76, coordinator fed. program, 1976-80; exec. dir. Ronnoc Ednl. Cons., Flint, 1980-85; pres. Ronnoc Inc., Flint, 1985—; Exec. dir. World Trade Women, Flint, 1986—, editor directory, 1986. Mem. Mayor's City-Wide Adv. Commn., Flint, 1986. Mem. Nat. Assn. Female Execs., Am. Soc. of Assn. Execs., Small Bus. Assn. of Mich. (legisl., membership coms. 1986—), Flint Women's Forum (chair internal communication 1986—), Econ. Club Detroit, Econ. Bus. Assn., Flint Area C. of C., Women Bus. Owners Council. Office: Ronnoc Inc 2712 N Saginaw St Suite 201 Flint MI 48505-4480

CONNOR, MARGO (MARGARET BIGGS), sales executive, consultant; b. Washington, June 23, 1943; d. Herbert Stetser and Margaret Johnson (Biggs) Murphy; m. James Robert Connor, July 12, 1969; 1 child, Meredith Lauren. BA in Chemistry, U. N.C., 1965. Research assoc. Harvard Med. Sch., Boston, 1965-66; assoc. scientist Polaroid Corp., Cambridge, Mass., 1966-74; pres., owner Margo Connor Interiors, Wellesley, Mass., 1972—; promotional cons. Ultima II Inc., N.Y.C., 1975-77; mktg. mgr. Ionomet Co. Inc., Brighton, Mass., 1978-79; co-mgr. documentation Computer Identics Inc., Canton, Mass., 1982-84; sr. communications specialist Prime Computer Inc., Natick, Mass., 1984-86, sales mgmt. tng. mgr., 1986—, regional ednl. cons., 1986—; bd. dirs., broker, cons. Charterhouse Devel. Corp., Wellesley, 1985—. Troop Leader Girl Scouts U.S., Wellesley, 1980—; bd. dirs. Youth Pro Musica, Natick, 1988—, John Oliver Chorale, Boston, 1988—; mem. Tanglewood Festival Chorus Boston Symphony Orch., 1972, Jr. League of Boston, 1973—. Congregationalist. Home: 12 Brook St Wellesley MA 02181 Office: Prime Computer Inc Prime Park Natick MA 01760

CONNOR, WILDA, management specialist; b. Pleasantville, N.J., Apr. 9, 1947; d. Herman Smith and Rubina (Miraglilo) Cooney; m. James J. Connor Jr., Nov. 5, 1966; 1 child, James J. III. BSBA cum laude, Glassboro (N.J.) State Coll., 1985; postgrad., Rutgers U., 1987—. Employee services coordinator Drug Outpatient Program, Collingswood, N.J., 1976-78; mgmt. specialist Camden County Ctr. Addictive Diseases, Lakeland, N.J., 1978-86; adv. mem. Camden County Ctr. Addictive Diseases, Lakeland, 1984—, Local Adv. Com. Alcoholism, Camden, 1987—. Com. fund raiser Camden County Dem. Congl. Campaign, Stratford, N.J., 1986. Mem. N.J. Assn. Alcoholism Counselors, N.J. Substance Abuse Cert. Bd. (cert. 1987 MSA), LWV (Camden County, N.J. chpt.). Roman Catholic. Home: 228 E Vasey Ave PO Box 226 Lindenwold NJ 08021 Office: Camden County div Alcoholism 2101 Ferry Ave Suite 204 Camden NJ 08104

CONNORS, DORSEY, television and radio commentator, newspaper columnist; b. Chgo.; d. William J. and Sarah (MacLean) C.; m. John E. Forbes; 1 dau., Stephanie. B.A. cum laude, U. Ill. Floor reporter WGN-TV Republican Nat. Conv., Chgo., Democratic Nat. Conv., Los Angeles, 1960. Appeared on: Personality Profiles, WGN-TV, Chgo., 1948, Dorsey Connors Show, WMAQ-TV, Chgo., 1949-58, 61-63, Armchair Travels, WMAQ-TV, 1952-55, Homeshow, NBC, 1954-57, Haute Couture Fashion Openings, NBC, Paris, France, 1954, 58, Dorsey Connors program, WGN, 1958-61, Tempo Nine, WGN-TV, 1961, Society in Chgo, WMAQ-TV, 1964; writer: column Hi! I'm Dorsey Connors, Chgo. Sun Times, 1965—; Author: Gadgets Galore, 1953, Save Time, Save Money, Save Yourself, 1972, Helpful Hints for Hurried Homemakers, 1988. Founder Ill. Epilepsy League; mem. woman's bd. Children's Home and Aid Soc., mem. women's bd. USO. Mem. AFTRA, Screen Actor's Guild, Nat. Acad. TV Arts and Scis., Soc. Midland Authors, Chgo. Hist. Soc. (guild com., costume com.), Chi Omega. Roman Catholic. Office: Chgo Sun Times 401 N Wabash Chicago IL 60611

CONNORS, ELIZABETH ANN, university administrator; b. Bristol, Pa., June 1, 1951; d. August J. and Elizabeth R. (Carrelli) Heim; m. Thomas Connors, June 2, 1973 (div. 1982); children: Christine, Thomas M. BA, Antioch U., 1987; postgrad., Phila. Coll. Textiles and Sci., 1987—. Coordinator, adminstrv. asst. dept. pharmacology The Med. Coll. Pa., Phila., 1980-82, research adminstr. dept. microbiology and immunology, 1982-87; bids, contracts adminstr. McNeil Pharm., Phila., 1987-88; methods, procedures analyst AEL Def. Corp., Lansdale, Pa., 1988—. Mem. Profl., Bus. and Single Network, Nat. Council Univ. Research Adminstrs., Hatfield (Pa.) C. of C. Democrat. Roman Catholic. Home: 602 Wendy Way Hatfield PA 19440 Office: AEL Def Corp 305 Richardson Rd Lansdale PA 19446

CONNORS, NEILA ANN, education educator; b. Lenox Dale, Mass., Apr. 2, 1953; d. George Edward and Helen Irene (Mooney) C.; m. George Carrol Sneller, Apr. 19, 1986. BS, St. Leo Coll., 1974; MS, Fla. State U., 1981, PhD, 1986. Tchr. Lacoochee (Fla.) Elem. Sch., 1975-77, Astoria Park Elem. Sch., Tallahassee, Fla., 1977-85; middle sch. cons. Fla. Dept. Edn., Tallahassee, 1980-85; asst. prof. Valdosta (Ga.) State Coll., 1985—; cons. in field, 1985—. Vol. Valdosta Jr. High Sch., 1986—. Mem. Nat. Assn. of Secondary Sch. Prins., Nat. Middle Sch. Assn. (trustee 1986—), Assn. Supervision and Curriculum Devel., Am. Assn. Sch. Adminstrs. (NCIL com. 1986—), Ga. Middle Sch. Assn. (editor newsletter, exec. sec. 1987—), Phi Kappa Phi (v.p. 1984-86), Phi Delta Kappa (steering com. 1984-86). Democrat. Roman Catholic. Lodge: Lions (sch. bd. liaison 1986—, Quest rep. 1986—). Home: 5611 Lunker Ln Tallahassee FL 32303 Office: Valdosta State Coll 100 B Edn Ctr Valdosta GA 31698

CONOLEY, JOANN SHIPMAN, educational administrator; b. Bartlesville, Okla., July 19, 1931; d. Joe and Frances Loomis (Wall) Shipman; B.S. in English and Edn., Midwestern State U., Wichita Falls, Tex., 1968, M.S. in English and Edn., 1971; postgrad. Tex. A&M U., 1978—; m. Travis A. Conoley, Oct. 29, 1976; children by previous marriage—James F. Lane, Joe Scott Lane, Kimberly Diane Lane. Tchr. 3d grade Queen of Peace Sch., Wichita Falls, 1968-69, lang. arts team leader, jr. high sch. Wichita Falls Public Schs., 1969-74; fed. programs dir., reading coordinator Rockdale (Tex.) Public Schs., 1974-78, adminstrv. asst. to supt., 1978-79, asst. supt. adminstrn. and instrn., 1979—; reading cons. ALCOA, 1977—; cons. U.S. Dept. Edn. Secondary Sch. Recognition Program, 1987. Bd. dirs. Rockdale Public Library, 1975-79, pres., 1976-77; bd. dirs. Am. Cancer Soc. Cert. elem. and high sch. tchr., reading/lang. arts coordinator, reading cons., adminstr., Tex. Mem. NEA, Tex. State Tchrs. Assn., Nat. Council Tchrs. English, Internat. Reading Assn., Assn. Compensatory Edn. Tex. (exec. bd. 1977-83), Assn. Supervision and Curriculum Devel., Alpha Chi, Delta Kappa Gamma, Kappa Delta Pi. Home: 405 Bounds St Rockdale TX 76567 Office: Box 632 Rockdale TX 76567

CONOVER, NELLIE COBURN, retail furniture company executive; b. Lebanon, Ohio, Dec. 21, 1921; d. Frank C. and Isabel (Murphy) Coburn; student public schs.; m. Lawrence E. Conover, Jan. 11, 1941; children—Lawrence R., Carol, David C., Constance, Christina. Co-founder, 1949, since exec. sec.-treas. Larry Conover Furniture & Appliance, Inc., and predecessor, Milford, Ohio, also trustee co. pension fund. Mem. Milford C. of C., Cin. Hist. Soc., Milford Hist. Soc., DAR. Democrat. Roman Catholic. Address: 438 Main St Milford OH 45150

CONRAD, LOLA IRENE, religious association administrator; b. Dayton, Ohio, May 14, 1943; d. Basil Henry and Jeanette Mae (Goins) Fourman; m. Gary F. Arnett, Feb. 17, 1962 (div. Aug. 1973); children: Rick G., Janie Lynn; m. Duane E. Conrad, June 28, 1978. Student, Sinclair Coll., 1973—. Owner Verona (Ohio) Cafe, 1970-73; adminstrn. sec. Gen. Council on Ministries United Meth. Ch., Dayton, 1973-86, dir. council ops., 1987—. Mem. Nat. Assn. Cert. Profl. Secs., Profl. Assn. United Meth. Ch. Secs., Cert. Profl. Sec. Acad. (cert.), Religious Conf. Mgmt. Assn., Nat. Assn. Female Execs. Republican. Office: United Meth Ch Gen Council on Ministries 601 W Riverview Ave Dayton OH 45406

CONRAD, SALLY, state legislator; b. Palmer, Mass., Mar. 1, 1941; m. David Conrad; 1 child. B.A., Boston U., 1963, M.Ed., Northeastern U., 1967. Mem. Vermont Senate, 1985—; mem., Champlain Valley Women's Polit. Caucus.Unitarian Universalist. Office: State Senate Office State Capitol Montpelier VT 05602 Address: 35 Wilson St Burlington VT 05401 *

CONROY, ROSE MAUREEN, firefighter; b. Nevada City, Calif., Oct. 5, 1953; d. David Kearin and Catherine Cecila (Dalton) C. BA in Phys. Edu., U. Calif. Davis, 1975. Cert. tchr., Calif. Firefighter City of Davis, 1979-85, fire capt., 1985—. Democrat. Roman Catholic. Home: PO Box 1605 Davis CA 95617

CONSIDINE, ANN-MARIE GWIAZDOWSKI, chemical consultant; b. Norwich, Conn., Feb. 7, 1962; d. Peter Paul and Helen Carol (Bujnowski) Gwiazdowski; m. Matthew Andrew Considine, Aug. 8, 1986. BA cum laude, Conn. Coll., 1984; postgrad., N.Y. Inst. Fin., 1984, U. Conn., 1986. Jr. analyst Bear, Stearns & Co., N.Y.C., 1984-85; account exec. Data Resources div. McGraw Hill, Stamford, Conn., 1985-87; cons. Data Resources div. McGraw Hill, Phila., 1987—. Mem. Nat. Assn. Bus. Economists, Conn. Coll. Alumni Assn. (interviewer 1984—). Republican. Roman Catholic. Home: 331 S 18th St Philadelphia PA 19103 Office: Data Resources div McGraw Hill 1234 Market St Philadelphia PA 19107

CONSIDINE, JILL, banker. m. Martin Rettinger; 1 child, Danielle. BS in Biology, St. John's U., 1965, LLD (hon.), 1986; postgrad. in biochemistry, Bryn Mawr Coll., 1965-67; M.S., Grad. Sch. Bus., Columbia U., 1980. V.p. Chase Manhattan Bank, N.Y.C., 1971-81, Bankers Trust, N.Y.C., 1981-83; pres., chief exec. officer The First Women's Bank, N.Y.C., 1984-85; supt. banks N.Y. State Banking Dept., N.Y.C., 1985—. Office: NY State Banking Dept 2 Rector St New York NY 10006

CONSIDINE, SUSAN MARY, manufacturing executive; b. Queens, N.Y., Jan. 21, 1958; d. Richard Thomas and Mary Michael (Zappulo) C. Diploma in Nursing, Samaritan Hosp., Troy, N.Y., 1979; BS, SUNY, Utica, 1981; postgrad., Rensselaer Poly. Inst., 1987—. RN. RN St. Elizabeth Hosp., Utica, 1980-81, Marcy Psychiat. Ctr., Utica, 1981-84; sales mgr. Lincoln Logs Ltd., Chestertown, N.Y., 1984-86, with market research dept., 1986, v.p., 1986—, also bd. dirs. Mem. Nat. Assn. Female Execs. Home: Rural Rt 1 Box 485A Chestertown NY 12817 Office: Lincoln Logs Ltd 1 Riverside Dr Chestertown NY 12817

CONSILIO, BARBARA ANN, court administrator; b. Cleve., June 22, 1938; d. Joseph B. and Anna E. (Ford) C. BS, Kent State U., 1962; MA, U. Detroit, 1973. Cert. social worker, Mich. Tchr. Chagrin Falls (Ohio) High Sch., 1962-64; probation officer Macomb County Juvenile Ct., Mt. Clemens, Mich., 1965-68, asst. casework supr., 1968-74, dir. children's services, 1974-79; mgr. foster care Oakland County Juvenile Ct., Pontiac, Mich., 1979-83; ct. adminstr. Oakland County Probate Ct., Pontiac, 1984—. Bd. dirs. Children's Charter Cts. of Mich., Lansing, 1984-87, Statewide Adv. Bd. on Sexual Abuse, Lansing, 1986—, Havenwyck Hosp., Auburn Hills, 1986—, Orchards Children's Services, Southfield, 1987, Oakland County Council of Children at Risk, Pontiac, 1987—; mem. Nat. Women's Polit. Caucus, N.Y.C. Mem. Nat. Council of Juvenile and Family Ct. Adminstrs. Group, Mich. Probate Register's Assn., Mich. Juvenile Ct. Adminstrs. Assn., Nat. Assn. Ct. Mgrs. Home: 4045 Chestnut Hill Troy MI 48098

CONSTABLE, ELINOR GREER, diplomat; b. San Diego, Feb. 8, 1934; d. Marshall Raymond and Katherine (French) Greer; m. Peter Dalton Constable, Mar. 8, 1958; children: Robert, Philip, Julia. B.A., Wellesley Coll., 1955. Mem. staff Dept. Interior, 1955-71, Dept. State, 1955-71, OEO, 1955-71; sr. assoc. Transcentury Corp., Washington, 1971-72; with Dept. State, Washington, 1973-77, dir. investment affairs, 1978-80; dep. asst. sec. Internat. Fin. and Devel., 1980-83, dep. asst. sec. for econ. and bus. affairs, 1983—; capital devel. officer US AID, Pakistan, 1977-78. Office: Am Embassy APO New York NY 09675-8900 *

CONSTANT, PATRICIA REED, lawyer; b. Chandler, Ariz., Mar. 14, 1949; d. Charles William and Patricia (Elliott) Reed; m. Anthony F. Constant, Oct. 12, 1976 (div. 1981); children—Rebecca Kay, Jennifer Leigh. B.A. summa cum laude, Tex. A&I U., 1976; J.D., U. Tex., 1979. Bar: Tex. 1979, U.S. Dist. Ct. (so. dist.) Tex. 1980, U.S. Ct. Appeals (5th cir.) 1984. Assoc. Wood & Burney, Corpus Christi, Tex., 1979-85, ptnr., 1985—. Bd. dirs. Beautify Corpus Christi Assn., 1981-85; mem. Corpus Christi Bldg. Standards Rev. Bd., 1984—. Mem. ABA, Tex. Bar Assn., Nueces County Bar Assn. (sec. 1980-81), Nueces County Young Lawyers Assn. (dir. 1982-84, pres. 1984-85). Democrat. Episcopalian. Home: 3335 San Antonio Corpus Christi TX 78411 Office: Wood & Burney One Shoreline Plaza 300 N Tower PO Box 2487 Corpus Christi TX 78403

CONSTANTINAU, WALEA LOKELANI, infosystems specialist; b. Honolulu, June 7, 1962; d. Renau Petros and Regina (Bachmann) C. BA, U. Hawaii, 1985. Journalist tech. services The Dir. Connection Co., Honolulu, 1985; ops. mgr. Digi-Tech Alarm Systems, Honolulu, 1983-86; instr. Computer Support Ctr., Internat., Honolulu, 1986; program specialist Kapiolani Community Coll., Honolulu, 1987—. Contbr. articles to profl. jours. Recipient Journalism award Am. Heart Assn., 1980. Mem. Nat. Forensic League, Nat. Thespian Soc., Women in Communication, Communication Alumni Assn.

CONSTANTINI, JOANN M., utility administrator; b. Danbury, Conn., July 30, 1948; d. William J. and Mathilda J. (Ressler) C. B.A., Coll. White Plains, N.Y., 1970; student Central Conn. State Coll., 1977-78, U. Hartford, 1985—. Cert. records mgr., 1987. Psychiat. social worker N.Y. State Dept. Mental Hygiene, Wassaic, 1970-73; with Northeast Utilities, Hartford, Conn., 1973-88, methods analyst, 1979-82, records and procedures mgmt. adminstr., 1982-88, cert. records mgr., 1987—; dir. My Sisters Place, 1984-87. Bd. dirs. Meriden YWCA, Conn., 1978-79; vol., 1984—. Mem. Assn. Record Mgmt. and Adminstrs. (sec. 1984-85, bd. dirs., 1984-86, chair industry action com. for pub. utilities, 1986—), Assn. Image and Info. Mgmt. (dir. 1984-86), Electric Council New Eng. (chair records mgmt. com. 1985-87), Coll. White Plains Alumnae Assn., Nat. Trust for Hist. Preservation, Inst. Cert. Records Mgrs. Democrat. Roman Catholic. Club: Northeast Utilities Women's Forum. (treas. 1983-85). Avocations: antiques; gardening; traveling; collecting cookbooks. Home: 13600 Portpatrick Ln Matthews NC 28105

CONSTANTINO-BANA, ROSE EVA, nursing educator, researcher; b. Labangan Zamboanga del Sur, Philippines, Dec. 25, 1940; came to U.S., 1964; naturalized, 1982; d. Norberto C. and Rosalia (Torres) Bana; m. Abraham Antonio Constantino, Jr., Dec. 13, 1964; children—Charles Edward, Kenneth Richard, Abraham Anthony, III. B.S. in Nursing, Philippine Union Coll., Manila, 1962; M.Nursing, U. Pitts., 1971, Ph.D., 1979; J.D., Duquesne U., Pitts., 1984. Lic. clin. specialist in psychiatric-mental health nursing, registered nurse. Instr. Philippine Union Co., 1963-65, Spring Grove State Hosp., Balt., 1965-67, Montefiore Sch. Nursing, Pitts., 1967-70; instr. U. Pitts., 1971-74, asst. prof., 1974-83, assoc. prof., 1983—, chmn. Senate Athletic Com., 1985-86; project dir. grant div. of nursing HHS, Washington, 1983-85; bd. dirs. Internat. Council on Women's Health Issues, 1986—. Author: (with others) Principles and Practice of Psychiatric Nursing, 1982. Contbr. chpts. to books and articles to profl. jours. Mem. Republican Presdl. Task Force, Washington, 1980, Rep. Senatorial Com., Washington, 1980. Mem. Am. Nurses Assn., Pa. Nurses Assn., Nat. League Nursing, ABA, U. Pitts. Sch. Nursing Alumni Assn., U. Duquesne Law Alumni Assn., Sigma Theta Tau, Phi Alpha Delta. Seventh-Day Adventist. Avocations: cooking, playing the piano. Home: 6 Carmel Ct Pittsburgh PA 15221 Office: U Pitts Sch Nursing 467 Victoria Bldg Pittsburgh PA 15261

CONTE, ANDREA, retail executive, health care consultant; b. Great Barrington, Mass., Feb. 13, 1941; d. Louis William and Rosalie (Salvini) C.; m. Philip Norman Bredesen, Nov. 22, 1974; 1 child, Benjamin Conte. BS in Nursing, U. Wash., 1968; MBA, Tenn. State U., 1983. RN. Nurse various hosps. and med. ctrs., Mass. and Calif., 1961-68, Vis. Nurse Service, Boston, 1968-70; clin. coordinator RMP Boston City Hosp., 1970-72; trainer computer systems Searle Medidata, Lexington, Mass., 1973-75; dir. nursing mgmt. services Hosp. Corp. Am., Nashville, 1975-78; cons. various health care cos., Nashville, 1978-81; mgr. Ernst and Whinney, Nashville, 1981-83; pres. Conte Philips, Nashville, 1983—. Bd. dirs. Family and Children Services, 1988—. Mem. Internat. Assn. Cooking Profls., Nat. Assn. Splty. Food Trade, Nashville C. of C. Republican. Roman Catholic.

CONTE, MARYANNE MICCHELLI, radio station executive; b. Newark, June 15, 1959; d. Mario R. and Lucy C. (Attanasio) Micchelli, m. Andrew Conte, June 28, 1987. B.A., Rutgers U., 1981. Sales asst. Sta.-WNBC, N.Y.C., 1981-84, account exec., 1985—; account exec. Sta.-WHN, N.Y.C., 1984-85; speaker Fairleigh Dickenson U., Teaneck, N.J., 1985-86, career seminars YWCA, N.Y.C., 1985-86. Mem. Advt. Club North Jersey, Nat. Assn. Female Execs., Internat. Radio and TV Soc., Radio Club Am., N.Y. Market Radio Broadcasters Assn., Rutgers Alumnae Assn. Roman Catholic. Club: Rutgers of N.Y. (N.Y.C.). Avocations: photography; tennis; travel; music. Home: 221 Harrison St A18 Nutley NJ 07110 Office: NBC 30 Rockefeller Plaza Room 293 New York NY 10020

CONTI, JOY FLOWERS, lawyer; b. Kane, Pa., Dec. 7, 1948; d Bernard A. Flowers and Elizabeth (Tingley) Rodgers; m. Anthony T. Conti, Jan. 16, 1971; children: Andrew, Michael, Gregory. BA, Duquesne U., 1970, JD summa cum laude, 1973. Bar: Pa. 1973, U.S. Dist. Ct. (we. dist.) Pa. 1973, U.S. Ct. Appeals (3d cir.) 1976. Law clk. Supreme Ct. Pa., Monessen, 1973-74; assoc. Kirkpatrick & Lockhart, Pitts., 1974-76, 1982-83, ptnr., 1983—; prof. law Duquesne U., Pitts., 1976-82; hearing examiner Pa. Dept. State, Bur. Profl. Occupation and Affairs, 1978-82; chairperson search com. for judge of U.S. Bankruptcy Ct., Western dist. Pa., 1987. Contbr. articles to profl. jours. Mem. hearing com. Supreme Ct. Pa., 1982—; v.p. Com. for Justice Edn., Pitts., 1983-84; mem. Leadership Pitts., 1987-88. Named One of Ten Outstanding Young Women in Am., 1981; recipient Award of Achievement, Pa. Bar Assn., 1982, 87. Mem. ABA (ho. of dels. 1980-86), Pa. Bar Assn. (ho. of dels. 1978—, corp. banking & bus. law sect. council 1983-87, chmn. commn. comml. law, chairperson civil rights and responsibilities com. 1986—), Allegheny County Bar Assn. (adminstrv. v.p. 1984-86, chairperson corp. banking and bus. law sect. 1987—, treas. 1988—). Club: Rivers (Pitts.). Democrat. Roman Catholic. Home: 106 Barnwood Ln Pittsburgh PA 15237 Office: Kirkpatrick & Lockhart 1500 Oliver Bldg Pittsburgh PA 15222

CONTI, SANDRA GREGG, insurance company executive; b. Peoria, Ill., June 4, 1957; d. Darwin Eugene and Marianne Elizabeth (Schwerer) Gregg; m. Alexander John Conti, Jan. 5, 1980. BS in Bus., Iowa State U., 1979; MBA, Ill. Benedictine Coll., Lisle, 1988. Adminstrv. asst. Scot Lad Foods, Lansing, Ill., 1980-81; compensation analyst Witt Assocs., Oak Brook, Ill., 1981-83; regional mgr., v.p. Fin. Corp. Am., Chgo., 1983-86; br. ops. mgr. Gen. Star Mgmt. Co., Chgo., 1986—. Mem. Nat. Assn. Female Execs. Republican. Roman Catholic. Office: Gen Star Mgmt 300 S Riverside Plaza Suite 2000N Chicago IL 60606

CONWAY, JILL KATHRYN KER, former college president; b. Hillston, New South Wales, Australia, Oct. 9, 1934; d. William Innis and Evelyn Mary (Adames) Ker; m. John James Conway, Dec. 22, 1962. B.A., U. Sydney, Australia, 1958; Ph.D., Harvard U., 1969; hon. degrees, St. Thomas (N.B.) U., 1974, Mt. Holyoke Coll., 1975, Amherst Coll., 1976, York U., Toronto, 1977, U. N.H., 1977, Westfield State Coll., 1979, Mt. St. Vincent U., Halifax, N.S., 1980, Wesleyan U., 1980, U. Mass., 1981, Williams Coll., 1982, Queen's U., 1983, U. Toronto, 1984, McGill U., 1984, Potsdam Coll., SUNY, 1986, Providence Coll., 1987. Lectr. history U. Toronto, Ont., Can., 1964-68, asst. prof., 1968-70, assoc. prof., 1970-75, v.p., 1973-75; pres. Smith Coll., Northampton, Mass., 1975-85, Sophia Smith prof., 1975-85; vis. scholar MIT, 1985—; bd. dirs. Merrill Lynch Co., Arthur D. Little, Inc., Colgate-Palmolive Co., Brascan, Nike, Inc., Allen Group Inc.; adv. bd. IBM Asia Pacific, 1986. Author: The Female Experience in Eighteenth and Nineteenth-Century America: A Guide to the History of American Women, 1982, Women Reformers and American Culture, 1987. Trustee Hampshire Coll., Northfield Mt. Hermon Sch.; former trustee Clarke Sch. for Deaf, Coll. Retirement Equities Fund, Acad. of Music, Northampton; bd. dirs. Ctr. Communications. Mem. Am. Hist. Assn., Can. Hist. Assn., Am. Antiquarian Soc. (pres.). Home: 125 Canton Ave Milton MA 02186 Office: MIT Program in Sci Tech & Society Cambridge MA 02139

CONWAY, KATHRYN LOUISE, university media administrator; b. Henry County, Va., Jan. 30, 1950; d. Richard Earl and Josephine Hope (Leftwich) C.; B.F.A., U. N.C., Chapel Hill, 1975, M.A. in Communications, 1985, cert. univ. mgmt. devel. program, 1981; cert. profl. mgmt. Young Execs. Inst., 1983. Advt. writer Sta. WTOB, Winston Salem, N.C., 1969; research asst. U. N.C., Chapel Hill, 1971, 73, photographer Photo Lab., 1974-75, assoc. dir. Media and Instructional Support Ctr., 1976—, dir. telecommunications devel., 1982-85, dir. Classroom Techs. Service Ctr., 1986—; chairperson bd. Sta. WXYC-FM; mem. steering com., interim bd. dirs. N.C. Public Radio Assn.; lead actress Desperadoes, Pocket Theatre, off-off-Broadway, 1978, The Fate of my Joy teleplay Sta. WUNC-TV, Chapel Hill, 1978; mem. Chapel Hill Adv. Com. on Cable TV, 1979; mem. adv. com. on planning process U N.C., Chapel Hill; lectr. in field. Mem. Am. Mgmt. Assn. (cert. Fundamentals Data Communication), Microelectronics Ctr. N.C. (curricula adv. com.), Functional Working Group in Video (N.C. Microelectronics Ctr.), Assn. Ednl. Communications and Techs., U. N.C. Mgrs. Assn. (pres. 1983-86). Democrat. Home: Route 9 Box 361 Chapel Hill NC 27514 Office: 111 Abernathy Hall Chapel Hill NC 27599

CONWAY, LEORA, trucking company executive; b. London, June 21, 1953; arrived in Can. 1962; d. Theodore David and Esther (Fein) C. BA, U. Toronto, Ont., Can., 1977. Pub. relations rep. Molson's Breweries, Toronto, Ont., Canada, 1977-80; pvt. practice design, art work Toronto, 1983; account rep. RSB Advt. & Design, Toronto, 1980; v.p. RSB Advt. & Design, 1981-82; communications coordinator CP Trucks, Willowdale, Ont., 1984-86, supr. pub. relations & advt., 1986—. Author, editor, designer, photographer, illustrator: CP Truck News, 1985—. Mem. Can. Inst. Traffic & Transp. Jewish. Clubs: Toronto & North York Hunt, Buttonville, Markham, Ont. Office: CP Trucks, 2255 Sheppard Ave E, Willowdale, ON Canada M2J4Y1

CONWAY, MARY ELIZABETH, nursing educator, university dean; b. Albany, N.Y., Nov. 4, 1923; d. Paul H. and Elizabeth J. (Miller) C. Student, Syracuse U., 1941-43; B.S. in Nursing, Columbia U., 1947; M.Nursing Adminstrn., U. Minn., 1958; Ph.D. in Sociology, Boston U., 1972. Supr. surg. services Mass. Gen. Hosp., Boston, 1953-57; asst. dir. nursing Albany (N.Y.) Med. Center, 1958-63; dir. nursing Monroe Community Hosp., Rochester, N.Y., 1963-65; cons. nurse Bur. Hosp. Nursing, N.Y. State Health Dept., Albany, 1965-68; assoc. prof. Boston U. Sch. Nursing, 1972-76; chmn. Boston U. Sch. Nursing (D.Nursing Sci. program), 1972-76; dean Sch. Nursing, U. Wis., Milw., 1976-80, Med. Coll. Ga., Augusta, 1980—; cons. Sch. Nursing, SUNY, Albany, 1975-76, Russell Sage Coll., Troy, N.Y., 1973-77; chmn. nurse adv. council to SSS, N.Y. State, 1966-68; dir. study of nursing Republic of China 1985. Editorial bd.: Jour.

Research in Nursing and Health, 1977. Mem. N.Y. Gov.'s Adv. Council on Vocat. Rehab., 1966-68; bd. dirs. Health Services Rensselaer Area, Troy, 1966-68, United Way Greater Milw. Allocations Bd., 1976-80. Recipient citation Pres. U.S., 1965-68; HEW grantee, 1979-80. Fellow Am. Acad. Nursing (pres. 1980-81); mem. Sigma Xi, Sigma Theta Tau (Mary Tolle Wright award 1985). Home: 1308 Jamaica Ct Augusta GA 30909 Office: Sch Nursing Med Coll Ga Augusta GA 30912 *

CONWAY, MAUREEN ANN, management consultant; b. Hoboken, N.J., July 25, 1945; d. Michael A. and Margaret (Spiegel) C.; B.A., William Paterson Coll., 1966; M.A., Montclair State Coll., 1971; M.B.A., Temple U., 1980. Tchr. math. high sch., Palisade Park, N.J., 1966-68; mem. tech. staff Bell Tel. Labs., Whippany, N.J., 1968-75; dir. info. systems IUIMC, Phila., 1975-83; dir. ops. CCA, Boston, 1983-88; program mgr. Apollo Computer IMC, Chelmsford, Mass., 1988— . Bd. dirs. Penns Landing Sq. Condominium, 1977-83. Mem. IEEE, Assn. Computing Machinery, Am. Mgmt. Assn., Beta Gamma Sigma. Office: CCA Four Cambridge Ctr Cambridge MA 02142

CONWAY, RITA MARIA, utilities executive; b. Santurce, P.R., Dec. 6, 1953; d. Guido and Rosella (Di Franco) Gnocchi; m. Timothy Lee Conway, May 26, 1984; 1 child, Anthony Baer. BBA, U. P.R., 1974; student, U. Rome, 1975; MS in Mgmt., Fla. Internat. U., 1978. CPA, Fla. Fin. analyst Southeast Bank, Miami, Fla., 1976, sr. acctg. analyst, 1977; sr. cons. Price Waterhouse & Co., CPA's, Miami, 1978; mgmt. analyst Fla. Power & Light Co., Miami, 1979, contracts coordinator, 1980-82, sr. contracts coordinator, 1983-84, mgr. corp. contracts, 1985—. Vol. counselor Switchboard of Miami, 1978-81; active Humane Soc. of Greater Miami, 1978—. Mem. Nat. Assn. Accts., Am. Inst. CPA's, Fla. Inst. of CPA's, Nat. Assn. Female Execs. Republican. Roman Catholic. Office: Fla Power and Light Co 9250 W Flagler St Miami FL 33174

CONWAY DE MACARIO, EVERLY, immunologist; b. Buenos Aires, Argentina, Apr. 20, 1939; came to U.S., 1974; d. Delfin E. and Maria Gloria (Benatuil) Conway; PhD in Pharmacy, Nat. U. Buenos Aires, 1960, PhD in Biochemistry, 1962; m. Alberto J. L. Macario, Mar. 16, 1963; children—Alex, Everly. Research fellow Nat. Acad. Medicine Argentina, Buenos Aires, 1962-63; head lab. oncology and immunology Argentinian Assn. against Cancer, Buenos Aires, 1966-77; chief immunology Sch. Medicine, Buenos Aires, 1967-68; research fellow dept. tumor-biology Karolinska Inst., Stockholm, 1969-71; sr. research scientist Lab. Cell Biology, NRC Italy, Rome, 1971-73; vis. scientist Internat. Agy. Research on Cancer, WHO, Lyon, France, 1973-74; vis. scientist Brown U., Providence, 1974-76; research scientist Lab. Immunology, N.Y. State Dept. Health, Albany, 1976—; prof. Sch. Pub. Health Scis., 1986—, mem. admissions com., 1986—. Recipient Prof. J. M. Mezzadra award Nat. U. Buenos Aires, 1969; Travel award to Eng., 2d Internat. Immunology Congress, 1974; Gold medal Argentinian Soc. Biochemistry, 1980; Hans Osterman Found. grantee, Sweden, 1969; Sir Samuel Scott of Yews Trust grantee, Sweden, 1970; Winifred Cullis grantee Internat. Fedn. Univ. Women, 1972; NATO research grantee, 1975, 81; Dept. Energy grantee, 1981, 84; Travel awardee to China, 1985, to Peru, 1987. Mem. Scandinavian Soc. Immunology, Italian Assn. Immunologists, French Soc. Immunology (travel award 1974), Am. Assn. Immunologists (chmn. com. on status of women 1980-86, edn. com. 1982-87, travel award to Australia 1977), Am. Soc. Microbiology. Co-editor: Monoclonal Antibodies Against Bacteria, 1985—, Microbial Gene Probes, 1988; assoc. editor profl. jour., 1986—; contbr. articles to profl. jours.; patentee microcircle system, microsample holder and carrier. Home: 18 Carriage Rd Delmar NY 12054 Office: Wadsworth Center Labs and Research Lab Immunology Empi re State Plaza Albany NY 12201

CONWELL, ESTHER MARLY, physicist; b. N.Y.C., May 23, 1922; d. Charles and Ida (Korn) C.; m. Abraham A. Rothberg, Sept. 30, 1945; 1 son, Lewis J. B.A., Bklyn. Coll., 1942; M.S., U. Rochester, N.Y., 1945; Ph.D., U. Chgo., 1948. Lectr. Bklyn. Coll., 1946-51; mem. tech. staff Bell Telephone Labs., 1951-52; physicist GTE Labs., Bayside, N.Y., 1952-61; mgr. physics dept. GTE Labs., 1961-72; vis. prof. U. Paris, 1962-63; Abby Rockefeller Mauze prof. M.I.T., 1972; prin. scientist Xerox Corp., Webster, N.Y., 1972-80; research fellow Xerox Corp., 1981—; cons., mem. adv. com. engring. NSF, 1978-81. Author: High Field Transport in Semiconductors, 1967, also research papers; mem. editorial bd. Jour. Applied Physics; Proc. of IEEE. Fellow IEEE, Am. Phys. Soc. (sec.-treas. div. condensed matter physics 1977-82); mem. Soc. Women Engrs. (Achievement award 1960), Nat. Acad. Engring. Office: 800 Phillips Rd Webster NY 14580

CONWELL, THERESA GALLO, insurance company executive; b. Utica, N.Y., Mar. 6, 1947; d. Ernest and Anna (Caiazzo) Gallo; m. Charles Ray Conwell, Aug. 19, 1978. B.S.Ed., SUNY-Potsdam, 1968; M.A.Ed., SUNY-Cortland, 1978; Cert. tchr., N.Y.; C.L.U.; chartered fin. cons., registered rep. Tchr. pub. schs., Clinton, N.Y., 1969-78, Portland, Conn., 1978-80; supr. mktg. services Phoenix Mut. Life Ins. Co., Hartford, Conn., 1980-82, assoc. mgr. agt. tng., 1982-84, mgr. agt. tng., 1984-85, dir. agt./mgmt. devel., 1985—; speaker to small bus. orgns., women's groups, N.Y., New Eng., 1986—. Mem. New Eng. Tng. Dir.'s Assn., Nat. Assn. Life Underwriters, Internat. Assn. Fin. Planners, Women's Life Underwriters Council, Nat. Assn. Female Execs., Nat. Assn. Securities Dealers (registered rep. tchr. pub. schs.), NOW. Democrat. Avocations: tennis; golf; swimming; aerobics; reading. Home: 7 Diane Dr Cromwell CT 06416 Office: Phoenix Mut Life Ins Co One American Row Hartford CT 06115

CONWELL, VIRGINIA DONLEY, librarian; b. Carlsbad, N.Mex., Jan. 3, 1921; d. William Guy and Frances Acree (Guthrie) Donley; m. Robert E.M. Conwell, Aug. 8, 1943 (dec. 1958); children—Elizabeth Conwell Shapiro, Virginia Conwell Hall. A.B., U. N.Mex., 1944; library credential U. So. Calif., 1962. Librarian, Montebello (Calif.) Unified Sch. Dist., 1962-86. Files chmn. Downey Alumnae Panhellenic, 1978—; del. Calif. Dem. Cen. Com., 1986—; mem. Women's com. for Downey Symphony. Mem. Calif. Media and Library Assn., Mortarboard, Chi Omega, Phi Alpha Theta. Democrat. Episcopalian. Clubs: Army Navy Country, Downey Alumnae Panhellenic. Address: 8132 Primrose Ln Downey CA 90240

COOK, ALICE HANSON, industrial and labor relations specialist, educator; b. Alexandria, Va., Nov. 28, 1903; d. August Theodore and Flora Alice (Kays) Hanson; 1 child, Philip J.; 1 adopted child, Thomas F. Bernstein. BA, Northwestern U., 1924; student, J.W. Goethe Universität, Fed. Republic Germany, 1929-31; LittD (hon.), William James Coll., 1982; DSc (hon.), Northwestern U., 1087. Social worker St. Louis and Indpls., 1924-25; group worker YWCA, Chgo. and Phila., 1927-29, 31-37; adult edn. tchr. Univ. Extension, Phila., 1928-48; trade union staff Congress Insl. Orgns., Phila., 1937-39; with U.S. fgn. service Austria and Fed. Republic Germany, 1947-52; prof. Cornell Univ., Ithaca, N.Y., 1952-72; freelance writer, researcher and cons. Ithaca, 1972—. Author: Union Democracy, 1964, Japanese Trade Unionism, 1966, Working Women In Japan, 1981, Comparable Worth, 1983. Mellon scholar Wellesley Coll., 1979. Mem. Indsl. Relations Research Assn., Internat. Indsl. Relations Assn., Assn. Asian Studies, AAUP, Soc. for Study of Social Problems. Club: Internat. of Japan (Tokyo). Home: 766 Elm St Ithaca NY 14850

COOK, ANN JENNALIE, English language educator; b. Wewoka, Okla., Oct. 19, 1934; d. Arthur Holly and Bertha Mabelle (Stafford) C.; children: Lee Ann Harrod, Amy Ceil Harrod; m. John Donelson Whalley, Sept. 10, 1975. B.A., U. Okla., 1956, M.A., 1959; Ph.D., Vanderbilt U., 1972. Instr. English U. Okla., 1956-57; tchr. English N.C. and Conn., 1958-61; instr. So. Conn. State Coll., 1962-64; asst. prof. U. S.C., 1972-74; adj. asst. prof. Vanderbilt U., 1977-82, assoc. prof., 1982—; exec. sec. Shakespeare Assn. Am., 1975-87; co-chair Shakespeare in Am. Theater Conf. Author: Privileged Playgoers of Shakespeare's London, 1981; asso. editor: Shakespeare Studies, 1973-80; mem. editorial bd.: Medieval and Renaissance Drama in Eng, Shakespeare Quar., Shakespeare Studies; contbr. articles to profl. publs. Trustee Folger Shakespeare Library, Shakespeare-Santa Cruz Festival, Internat. Shakespeare Assn. Recipient Letseizer award, 1956, Nat. Leadership award Delta Delta Delta, 1956; Danforth fellow, 1966-72, Folger summer fellow, 1973, Donelson fellow, 1974-75; Rockefeller Found. fellow, 1984, Guggenheim Found. fellow, 1984-85. Mem. Internat. Shakespeare Assn. (chair), Shakespeare Assn. Am., Modern Lang. Assn., AAUP, Shakespeare Inst., Soc. Values in Higher Edn., Renaissance Soc. Am., Southeastern Renaissance Soc., Phi Beta Kappa. Episcopalian. Home: 91 Valley Forge Nashville TN 37205 Office: Vanderbilt U Dept English Nashville TN 37235

COOK, APRIL BETH, retail store executive; b. Seattle, June 28, 1955; d. Donald Irvin and Sheila Beth (Buche) C.; m. Paul Victor Young, Mar. 23, 1975 (div. Aug. 1979). AA in Music Edn., Shoreline Community Coll., Seattle, 1973; cert. psychiat. nursing, Baylor U., 1974; postgrad. in theology and psychology, Concordia Coll., Milw., 1980—. With Tandy Leather Co., 1979—, store mgr., St. Petersburg, Fla., 1980-81, Tampa, Fla., 1981-83, product mgr., Ft. Worth, 1983-85, warehouse supr., 1985-86, store mgr., Spokane, Wash., 1986—, also hazardous materials specialist, 1983—; bd. dirs. N.W. Leadership Lab., 1987—, mem. exec. bd., 1988-89, corp. treas. Speaker Service-Youth Career Guidance, Tampa, 1981-83; sch. speaker Explorer Post, Longhorn council Boy Scouts Am., 1983-85. Served to pfc. U.S. Army, 1973-75. Mem. Nat. Assn. Female Execs., Christian Bus. Women's Assn. Republican. Lutheran. Avocations: leathercraft, singing, nationally rated umpire. Home: PO Box 7242 Spokane WA 99207 Office: Tandy Leather Co E 18 Indiana Ave Spokane WA 99207

COOK, BETH MARIE, software company professional; b. Electra, Tex., Jan. 4, 1933; d. Charles Bolivar Allen and Ida Marie (Nelson) Burton; m. William H. Cook, May 30, 1955 (div. Nov. 1981); children: David M., Dianne M. Gleason. Student, Rockmont Coll., 1951-54; BA, Antioch U. West, 1981. County coordinator office econ. opportunity Upper Arkansas Council, Salida, Colo., 1974-76; dir. area agy. on aging Upper Arkansas Council/Dept. Social Services div. State of Colo., 1976-80; specialist community devel. Mountain Plains Congress Sr. Orgns., Denver, 1980-82; sr. adminstrv. asst. Digital Research Inc., Monterey, Calif., 1983-85, asst. to pres., 1985-87, retail rep., 1987-88; co-owner, ptnr. Scotia Gallery, Monterey, Calif., 1983-86; chief operating officer MiniSoft, Inc., Phoenix, 1988—; hostess Sr. Sound-Off show Sta. KVRH, Salida, 1978-80; cons. Devel. Assocs. Inc., Denver, 1982. Columnist Buena Vista Alpine Gazette, 1979-80, Mountain Plains Gazette, 1981. Coordinator crisis intervention line Chaffee County Community Crisis Ctr., Salida, 1976-80; committeewoman Chaffee County Dem. Cen. Com., Salida, 1979-80; speaker, mem. program com. Colo. Gov.'s Conf. on Aging, Denver, 1980. Recipient Human Devel. Service award HHS, 1980; named Woman of Yr. Chaffee County Bus. & Profl. Women's Club, 1978. Mem. Am. Assn. Retired Persons, Colo. Gerontol. Soc., Summit Profl. Orgn. Inc., Nat. Assn. for Female Execs. Presbyterian. Office: MiniSoft Inc 2265 E Becker Ln Suite 201 Phoenix AZ 85028

COOK, BETTE WALKER PHILPOTT, real estate investment company executive; b. Loma Linda, Calif., Mar. 6, 1941; d. Reed CLemens and Dortha (Pace) Walker; m. Donlad M. Cook, Dec. 30, 1982; children: Jane, Anne, James, Daniel, Philpott. BA in Psychology, UCLA, 1964. Personnel testing specialist N.Am. Aviation, El Segundo, Calif., 1964; kindergarten tchr. Am.-Nicaraguan Sch., Managua, Nicaragua, 1975-76; real estate sales person Ackerman Real Estate Services, Washington, 1976-78; v.p. Internat. Investment Counsel, Los Angeles, 1978-83, Sundance Homes Calif., Inc., Los Angeles, 1983-85, Internat. Capital Mgmt., Beverly Hills, 1985—. Mem. AAUW, Assn. Am. Fgn. Service Women. Home: 1714 Fleur Dr San Marino CA 91108 Office: 9944 Santa Monica Blvd #250 Beverly Hills CA 90212

COOK, BLANCHE MCLANE, artist; b. Moulton, Iowa, July 1, 1901; d. Alva Randolph and Eva (Wynn) Mclane; m. Harry Christian Cook, Feb. 19, 1938 (dec. 1983); m. Rankin A. Nebinger, May 4, 1984. Honor grad., Phila. Sch. Design for Women, 1928; student, Temple U., 1929; BA, Cen. Wash. U., 1959, MA, 1965. Tchr. Phila. Sch. Design and Baldwin Sch., 1928-29; free-lance comml. artist 1928—; with irrigation dept. Yakima County Treas., Wash., 1930-34, chief dep. treas., 1934-40; pvt. instr. art 1930—; art instr. Yakima Valley Jr. Coll., 1933-48, 57-58; portrait painter, 1928—; art instr., counselor Moxee Elem. Sch., Yakima, 1959-60; art instr. Wilson Jr. High Sch., Yakima, 1961-66, chmn. art dept., 1962-66. Works exhibited at Larson Gallery, Yakima, 1954-63, Seattle Art Mus., Woessner Gallery, Studio Gallery, Palace Legion of Honor, San Francisco, Spokane (Wash.) Art Gallery, others; represented in permanent collections Seattle Art Mus., Frye Mus., Yakima Valley Coll. Home: Madison House 21500 72d Ave W Edmonds WA 98020

COOK, BLANCHE WIESEN, history educator, journalist; b. N.Y.C., Apr. 20, 1941; d. David Theodore and Sadonia (Ecker) Wiesen. B.A., Hunter Coll., 1962; M.A., Johns Hopkins U., 1964, Ph.D., 1970. Instr. Hampton Inst., Va., 1963; instr. Stern Coll. for Women, Yeshiva U., N.Y.C., 1964-67; prof. history John Jay Coll., CUNY, 1968—; producer, broadcaster program stas. WBAI and KPFK, N.Y.C. and Los Angeles, 1978—; vis. prof. UCLA, 1982-83; syndicated journalist; bd. dirs. Women's Fgn. Policy Adv. Council. Author: Crystal Eastman on Women and Revolution, 1978, Declassified Eisenhower, 1981, Biography of Eleanor Roosevelt, 1988; sr. editor: The Garland Library of War and Peace, 360 vols., 1970-80; contbr. articles to various publs. Appointed to com. on documents for fgn. relations U.S. Dept. State, 1986—. Faculty fellow CUNY, 1978-84. Mem. Orgn. Am. Historians (co-chair freedom of info. com.), Am. Hist. Assn., Coordinating Com. Women in Hist. Profession (pres. N.Y.C. chpt. 1969-71), Berkshire Women Historians, Soc. Historians Am. Fgn. Relations, Conf. on Peace Research in History (bd. dirs., v.p.), Women's Internat. League for Peace and Freedom, Pi Sigma Alpha, Phi Alpha Theta. Office: CUNY Dept History John Jay Coll 445 W 59th St New York NY 10019

COOK, CHARLOTTE DASHER, rehabilitation counselor; b. Nashville, Ga., Sept. 11, 1948; d. Johnny Vestus and Alma Lee (Griner) Dasher; m. James Mitchell Cook, Sept. 1, 1984; children: Lynne Michele, Tina Marie, Jodie Ann. AA, DeKalb Jr. Coll., 1972; BS, Ga. State U., 1974; MEd, U. Ga., 1977. Encode operator 1st Nat. Bank, Atlanta, 1966-67; stenographer II, State Dept. Edn., Atlanta, 1967-70, stenographer III, 1970-71; rehab. intern State Dept. Human Resources, Augusta, Ga., 1974-76, counselor I, Tifton, Ga., 1976-80, sr. rehab. counselor, 1980—; mem. Spl. Edn. Adv. Council, Tifton, 1976—, mem. adv. com. for Handicapped, Fitzgerald, Ga., 1979—, mem. adv. com. Vocat. Edn., Tifton, 1983—; pres.-elect Council for Exceptional Children, Tifton, 1983-84. Bd. dirs. Tift County Assn. for Retarded Citizens, 1979—; projects chmn. Tiftarea Civitan, 1981—; Sunday Sch. tchr. 1st Bapt. Ch., Tifton, 1982—; Spl. Olympics coordinator Tift County, 1982—; Recipient Service awards Tiftarea Civitan, 1982-83, Honor Key, 1983, Cert. Recognition Tifton Jr. Womens Club, 1984, Lewis Hine award Nat. Child Labor Com., 1985; named Handicapped Profl. Woman of Yr., Tifton Pilots Club, 1988. Mem. Ga. Rehab. Counseling Assn. (sec.-treas. 1983-84, pres. SW Dist. chpt. 1980-81, program chmn. 1985, pres.-elect 1988, Currie Counselor of Yr. 1982), Nat. Rehab. Assn., Am. Soc. Personnel Adminstrs. Democrat. Baptist. Home: Rt 4 Box 2390 Tifton GA 31794 Office: Div Rehab Services PO Box 1629 Room 314 Tifton GA 31793

COOK, CINDY KAYE, pharmaceutical company researcher; b. Milw., Aug. 7, 1952; d. Harold Frederick and Ruth Marion (Kassulke) Hasse; m. Thomas Judd Cook, Oct. 10, 1988. BS in Biology, U. Wis., Oshkosh, 1974, MS in Biology, 1982. Quality control chemist Seven-Up Bottling Co., Oshkosh, 1975-76; research analyst U. Wis/Fox Valley Water Quality Planning Agy., Oshkosh, 1980-81; electronic microscopy asst. U. Wis., Oshkosh, 1980-81; instr. biology and chemistry Mt. Senario Coll., Ladysmith, Wis., 1982-84, asst. prof., 1984-85; clin. trial analyst Boehringer Ingelheim Pharmaceuticals, Ridgefield, Conn., 1986-87, med. research assoc., 1987—; disting. lectr. Lake Superior Assn. Colls. and Univs., 1984-85. Mem. grants review panel Charles A. Lindbergh Fund, Summit, N.J., 1984—. Grantee Charles A. Lindberg Fund, 1983. Mem. Am. Soc. Microbiology, Am. Water Resources Assn., Wis. Assn. Ind. Colls. and Univs. (legis. liaison 1983), Sigma Xi. Office: Boehringer Ingelheim Pharmaceuticals 90 East Ridge Ridgefield CT 06877

COOK, DIANE G(REFE), management consultant; b. Ft. Bragg, N.C., Aug. 13, 1943; d. Richard William and Marjorie Louise (Sine) G.; m. Gary M. Cook, Sept. 3, 1966; children—Christian M., Lauren S. B.A., Smith Coll., 1965. Program dir. N.Y.C. Commn. to UN and Consular Corps, 1968-70; exec. dir. Internat. Visitors Info. Service, Washington, 1971-74; v.p. Nat. Council for Internat. Vistors, Washington, 1981-83, pres. 1983-84; now pres. Diane Cook Assocs., Internat. Network Assocs., Golden, Colo.; bd. dirs. Telecommunications Coop. Network, N.Y.C.; founder, officer of bd. Tulsa Council for Internat. Visitors, 1976-83; mem. exec. com. Meridian House Internat., Washington, 1983-84; nat. adv. council Experiment in Internat. Living, Brattleboro, Vt., 1979—. Author speaker in field. Pres. Assn. of Seven Colls. of Tulsa, 1978-80; chmn. Tulsa Humanities Com., 1980-82; mem. pub. sector Okla. Found. for Humanities, Oklahoma City, 1981-83; mem. Mayor's Com. on Internat. Visistors, Washington, 1972-74. Community internat. fellow USIA, 1981; recipient Commendation award, U.S. Dept. State, 1974, Mayor's award, Washington, 1974. Mem. Am. Soc. Tng. and Devel., Am. Mgmt. Assn., Denver Com. on Fgn. Relations, Inst. Internat. Edn. Republican. Club: Smith Coll. (pres. Tulsa 1977-83). Office: Diane Cook Assocs 1692 S Sand Lily Dr Golden CO 80401

COOK, DORIS MARIE, accountant, educator; b. Fayetteville, Ark., June 11, 1924; d. Ira and Mettie Jewel (Dorman) C. BS in Bus. Adminstrn., U. Ark., 1946, MS, 1949; PhD, U. Tex., 1969. CPA, Okla., Ark. Jr. acct. Haskins & Sells, Tulsa, 1946-47; instr. acctg. U. Ark., Fayetteville, 1947-52, asst. prof., 1952-62, assoc. prof., 1962-69, prof., 1969-88, univ. prof. and Nolan E. Williams lectr. in acctg., 1988—; mem. Ark. State Bd. Pub. Accountancy, 1987—. Contbr. articles to profl. jours. Mem. Ark. Bus. Assn. (editor newsletter 1982-85), Am. Acctg. Assn. (chair nat. membership 1982-83, chair Arthur Carter Scholarship com. 1984-85, chair membership Ark. chpt. 1985-87), Am. Inst. CPA's, Am. Women's Soc. CPA's, Ark. Soc. CPA's (v.p. 1975-76, pres. NW Ark. chpt. 1980-81, sec. Student Loan Found. 1981-84, treas. Student Loan Found. 1984—, chair pub. relations 1984-88), Acad. Acctg. Historians (trustee 1985-87, mem. review bd. 1984—), Ark. Fedn. Bus. and Profl. Women's Clubs (treas. 1979-80), Mortar Bd., Beta Gamma Sigma, Beta Alpha Psi (editor nat. newsletter 1973-77, nat. pres. 1977-78), Phi Gamma Nu, Alpha Lambda Delta, Delta Kappa Gamma (sec. 1976-78, pres. 1978-80), Phi Kappa Phi. Club: Fayetteville Bus. and Profl. Women's (pres. 1973-74, 75-76, Woman of Yr. 1977). Home: 1115 Leverett St Fayetteville AR 72703 Office: U Ark Dept Acctg Fayetteville AR 72701

COOK, ELIZABETH ANN, public relations executive; b. Texarkana, Ark., Oct. 9, 1943; d. Robert Monroe and Flossie Inez (Gilmore) Abston; m. Richard Keck Cook, Feb. 5, 1966; 1 child, Elizabeth Ashley. BA, U. Tex., 1965. Adminstrv. asst. Lockheed-GA. Co., Atlanta, 1966-67; asst. account exec. Harris & Weinstein Advt., Atlanta, 1967-68; asst. dir. corp. communications Kaneb Services, Inc., Houston, 1970-79; owner, pres. Cook & Assocs., Inc., Houston, 1981—; lectr. Rice U., Houston, 1985—; advisor pub. relations Houston Rockets, 1987—. Mem. campaign com. Judge Michael McSpadden, Houston, 1986; dir. pub. relations Sunshine Kids, Houston, 1987—; pub. relations affiliate George Bush Campaign, Houston; honorary bd. mem. March of Dimes, Houston, 1988. Mem. Pub. Relations Soc. Am., Press Club of Houston, Houston Fin. Council for Women. Republican. Clubs: The Houstonian, Lakeside Racquet and Athletic (Houston). Office: Cook & Assocs Inc 2732 Virginia Houston TX 77098

COOK, FRANCES D., diplomat; b. Charleston, W.Va., Sept. 7, 1945; d. Nash and Vivian Cook. B.A., Mary Washington Coll. of U. Va., 1967; M.P.A., Harvard U., 1978. Certificats d'Etudes, Université d'Aix-Marseille (France), 1966. Commd. fgn. service officer Dept. State, 1967; spl. asst. to R.S. Shriver, ambassador to France, 1968-69; mem. U.S. Del. Paris Peace Talks on Viet-Nam, 1970-71; cultural affairs officer, consul Am. Consul Gen., Sydney, Australia, 1971-73; cultural affairs officer, first sec. Am. Embassy, Dakar, Senegal, 1973-75; personnel officer for Africa USIA, Washington, 1975-77; dir. office public affairs African Bur. Dept. State, Washington, 1978-80; ambassador to Republic of Burundi, 1980-83; consul gen. Alexandria, Egypt, 1983-86; dep. asst. sec. of state Dept. State, Washington, 1986-87, dir. Office of West African Affairs, 1987—. Recipient various honor awards Dept. State. Mem. Am. Fgn. Service Assn., Council on Fgn. Relations, Washington Alumni Council Kennedy Sch. Harvard U. Club: Harvard of N.Y.C. Office: Office West African Affairs Dept State Room 4250 Washington DC 20520

COOK, JUDITH ELLEN, marketing executive; b. Raleigh, N.C., Dec. 25, 1959; d. John Oliver and Ruth Ellen (Mohr) C. BS, Am. U., 1982; MS, London Sch. Econs., 1983. Mktg. adminstr. The Washington Workshops Found., 1980-82; mgr. mktg. and promotion The Economist, N.Y.C., 1984-87; pvt. practice mktg. communications N.Y.C., 1987—; bd. dirs. The Wall Street Workshops Found., N.Y.C. Intern U.S. Rep. Ike Andrews, Washington, 1977, U.S. Senate Com. on Judiciary, Washington, 1980, Dem. Nat. Com., Washington, 1981; fundraiser Nat. Women's Polit. Caucus, Washington, 1979. Mem. Am. Friends of London Sch. Econs., Landmarks West. Jewish. Home and Office: 350 W 55th St #2M New York NY 10019

COOK, JUDITH WENDY MORLEY, manager; b. Bromley, England, Apr. 28, 1952; d. William George Brown and Sadie Lillian (Morley) Darkins; m. Rodney Dewitt Cook, June 3, 1978. Diploma, Queen Secretarial Coll., 1970-71. Personal asst. Tomatin Distillers, London, 1971-73; company sec. McTryn Ltd., London, 1973-75; travel trade counselor U.S. Embassy, London, 1975-76, adminstrv. sec., 1976-79; adminstrv. asst. Lincoln (Nebr.) Jour., 1979-80; adminstrv. mgr. Weinberg and Weinberg, Lincoln, 1980-87; dir. adminstrn. Protocad, Inc., Colorado Springs, Colo., 1987—; leader seminars, Lincoln, Lancaster County Nebr., 1983; instr. office support staff U. Nebr., Lincoln, 1985. Mem. Adminstrv. Mgmt. Soc. (3d v.p.), Networking and Edn. for Women, Twig Daniels Network (exec. com.). Republican. Episcopalian. Office: ProtoCad Inc 1050 Elkton Dr Colorado Springs CO 80907

COOK, LINDA DARLENE, nurse; b. Yokosuka, Japan, Sept. 6, 1954; came to U.S., 1955; d. Vernon Leroy and Kazue (Hashimoto) Morrison; m. Mitchell Edward Bailey, May 26, 1979 (div. Oct. 1981); m. Clyde David Cook, Aug. 10, 1983. AS, Modesto (Calif.) Community Coll., 1976; BS, Calif. State U., Sonoma, 1982; MBA, Coll. Notre Dame, Belmont, Calif., 1987. Cert. emergency nurse, Calif. Charge nurse emergency dept. Scenic Gen. Hosp., Modesto, 1976-78; staff nurse emergency dept. Kaiser Found. Hosp., San Rafael, Calif., 1978-79; office nurse mgr. Mitchell E. Bailey, MD, Healdsburg, Calif., 1979-80; staff nurse emergency dept. Santa Rosa (Calif.) Meml. Hosp., Calif., 1981-84; coordinator emergency room Pacific Med. Ctr., Seattle, 1983-84; asst. clin. nursing coordinator Stanford (Calif.) U. Hosp., 1984-85, staff nurse III, 1985-87; asst. dir. nursing Chope Community Hosp., San Mateo, Calif., 1987—; v.p. bd. dirs., phone counselor Resolve, San Rafael, 1987. Recipient Achievement award Bank of Am., 1973. Mem. Emergency Nurses Assn., Nat. Assn. for Female Execs. Democrat. Club: Stanford Macintosh Users Group. Office: Chope Community Hosp 222 W 39th Ave San Mateo CA 94403

COOK, MARSHA EICHENBERG, religious organization administrator; b. Jefferson City, Mo., Dec. 3, 1943; d. Barnett Samuel and Iona Katherine (Hudson) E.; m. Duane Wilbert Cook, Nov. 29, 1980; 1 child, Joshua Barnett. BS in Edn., U. Mo., 1965; M in Religious Edn., So. Bapt. Theol. Sem., Louisville, 1969. Tchr. speech, drama and debate, pub. high sch. Buchannan County Schs., St. Joseph, Mo., 1965-67; dir. weekday activities 4th Ave. Bapt. Ch., Louisville, 1968-69; dir. Christian Social Ministries Etowah Bapt. Assn./So. Bapt. Home Mission Bd., Gadsden, Ala., 1969-76, Wilmington (N.C.) Bapt. Assn./So. Bapt. Home Mission Bd., 1977—, Bapt. State Conv. N.C., Wilmington, 1977—; sr. adult cons. So. Baptist Sunday Sch. Bd., 1978—; adv. conversational English/literacy New Hanover and Pender Cos., N.C., 1977—, Christian life and pub. affairs New Hanover and Pender Cos., 1985—. Contbr. articles to Ch. Tng. and Recreation mags.; contbr. to several books on recreation. Chmn. adv. council Ret. Sr. Vol. program, New Hanover County, 1980—; co-chmn., then chmn. Fetal Alcohol Task Force, New Hanover County, 1985-87; chmn. Nursing Home Community Adv. Bd., New Hanover County, 1980-87; active Community Council Women's Correctional Facility, New Hanover County, 1977—, chmn., 1978-81; dir. Summer Recreation Programs for Inner City, Wilmington, 1977—; mem. adult Sunday sch. benevolence com. Wrightsboro Bapt. Ch., Wilmington, also adult Sunday sch. mission leader. Mem. So. Bapt. Social Services Assn., So. Bapt. Assn. for Ministries of Sr. Adults, Nat. Assn. Female Execs. Office: Wilmington Bapt Assn 610 S College Rd Wilmington NC 28403 Home: 2 Logan Dr Castle Hanye NE 28429

COOK, MARY JOENE, accountant; b. Marlow, Okla., Dec. 30, 1943; d. Woodrow and Joan (Jones) Lambert; m. Sidney Wayne Cook, Aug. 2, 1963; children: Shawn, Cindy, Amy. BBA in Acctg., Midwestern State U., Wichita Falls, Tex., 1979. CPA, Tex. Asst. v.p., acctg. mgr. 1st Wichita

Nat. Bank, Wichita Falls, Tex., 1979-83, sr. v.p., treas. Ind. Am. Savs. Assn., Irving, Tex., 1983-85; pres. Ind. Am. Fin. Mgmt., Irving, 1985-86; co-owner Genesis Mktg. Group, Arlington, Tex., 1986—. Tchr. Sunday sch. Grace Luth. Ch., Arlington; mem. Arlington PTA. Mem. Am. Inst. CPA's, Tex. Soc. CPA's, Alpha Chi. Republican. Lutheran. Club: Officer's Wives (Carswell AFB, Ft. Worth).

COOK, MARY LYNN B., counselor; b. Portales, N. Mex., June 3, 1934; d. C.D. and Mary Ann (Wilhite) Bostick; m. Curtis Clifton Cook; children: Glen André, Cheryl Lynn. Student, So. Meth. U. Sec. City Dallas, Alameda County, AA, various cities, 1951-58; head dept. Froug's, Tulsa, 1965-71; office asst. Tulsa Area Safety Council, 1972, dir. driver improvement, 1973-79, mgr. tng., 1979-80; pres. Okla. Tng. Systems Inst., Owasso, 1980—; lectr. on pub. safety various schs., civic orgns., industries, 1973-80; lectr. traffic safety, substance abuse, 1980—; tchr. Defensive Driving, 1973-80. Author: Driver Improvement, 1980 (ann. revisions), Substance Abuse, 1980 (ann. revisions), Feathered Companions, 1988. Lctr. defensive driving course and alcohol/drug substance abuse courses to schs., civic orgns., law enforcement agencies, private industry. Mem. Nat. Assn. Female Exec., Okla. Assn. DUI Sch. Adminstr., Cage Bird Soc. Okla., Avicultural Soc. Okla., Aeapornis and Budgerigar Soc. Office: Okla Tng Systems Inst 9999 N 112th E Ave (Rear) Owasso OK 74055

COOK, NANCY W., state legislator; b. May 11, 1936. Ed. U. Del. Mem. Del. Senate from 15th Dist.; mem. Kent County Dem. Com. Democrat. Office: PO Box 127 Kenton DE 19955 *

COOK, REBECCA JOHNSON, lawyer, educator; A.B., Columbia U., 1970; M.A., Tufts U., 1972; M.P.A., Harvard U., 1973; J.D., Georgetown U., 1982. Bar: D.C. 1982. Dir. law program Internat. Planned Parenthood Fedn., London, 1973-78, legal adviser 1982—; assoc. firm Beveridge, Fairbanks and Diamond, 1980; cons. U.S. Congress, 1978-81; mem. legal counsel office The Upjohn Co., 1981-82; asst. prof. faculty of law U. Toronto, 1987—; asst. prof. clin. pub. health Columbia U., N.Y.C., 1983-87, staff atty. devel. law and policy program Ctr. for Population and Family Health, 1983-87. adj. faculty Humphrey Inst. Pub. Affairs, U. Minn., 1985-87; dep. dir. Internat. Women's Rights Action Watch, 1986-87. Contbr. articles to profl. jours. Bd. dirs. Operation Crossroads Africa, 1972-74, Pathfinder Fund, 1978—, Assn. for Vol. Surg. Contraception, 1982-87, Internat. Projects Assistance Service, 1982—; mem. adv. com. on depo provera AID, 1978-80; adv. bd. Program for Intro. and Adaptation of Contraceptive Tech., 1982—, standing com. study of ethical aspects of human reproduction Internat. Fedn. Gynecology and Obstetrics, 1986—; U.S. del. 2d World Conf. on Nat. Parks, 1972; mem. Mass. Citizens Com. for Environ. Affairs 1972. Office: U Toronto, Faculty of Law, Toronto, ON Canada M5S 2C5

COOK, RUNETT HORTENSE, consultant, educator; b. Phila., Oct. 29, 1942; d. Henry T. and Helen L. (Herring) Cook. B.S., Cheyney Coll., 1964; M.A., Tchrs. Coll. N.Y.C., 1969; postgrad. Oxford U., 1973; Ph.D., Walden U., 1979. Social worker Women's Hosp., Phila., 1967-68; adminstr., supr. N.Y. Bd. Edn., N.Y.C., 1968—; prof. early childhood Columbia U., N.Y.C., 1972-74, CUNY, 1973-74, Coll. for Human Services, N.Y.C., 1973-74; lectr. Seton-Hall, Orange, N.J., 1971-72; founder, owner Swan, Inc., N.Y.C., 1978—. Author collection of poems Women of the 70's and 80's, 1982. Contbr. articles, paper to workshops. Founder, bd. dirs. More For Black Women, N.Y.C., 1978—. . Recipient Chapel of Four Chapels award Temple U., 1974. Mem. Doctorate Assn. N.Y., Black Women Female Network, Nat. Council Tchrs. English, Working Woman, Black Women's Polit. Orgn., Nova Polit. Orgn., Nat. Women's Polit. Caucus, Nat. Women's Health Network, Nat. Inst. Women of Color, Nat. Assn. Female Execs., Am. Women Econ. Devel. Orgn., Phi Delta Kappa, Epsilon Delta Chi. Democrat. Baptist. Clubs: Comdrs., Eagles. Lodges: Order of Eastern Star, Rose of Sharon. Home: 419 E 76th St Apt 5-A New York NY 10021

COOK, RUTH E., utilities commissioner, former state legislator; b. Berlin, Nov. 11, 1929; d. Samuel and Ilse (Meyer) Mohr; student N.Y. U.; m. John Oliver Cook, Oct. 31, 1954 (dec.); children—Roger Mohr, Judith Ellen. Exec. dir. State Council for Social Legis.; mem. N.C. Ho. of Reps., 1974-83, mem., chmn. appropriations base budget com. on human resources, vice-chmn. appropriations base budget com., vice-chmn. appropriations expansion budget com., vice-chmn. human resources com., vice-chmn. mental health com.; chmn. N.C. Housing Programs Study Commn., 1981-82; mem. Gov's Task Force on Sci. and Tech.; commr. N.C. Utilities Commn. 1983—. Bd. dirs. N.C. Housing Finance Agy., Women's Center Raleigh; chmn. N.C. Council for Hearing Impaired; exec. dir. State Council Social Legislation, 1966-74; charter mem. Raleigh Interch. Housing Corp., 1966-69. Mem N.C. Consumers Council (pres. 1977), Raleigh Wake LWV (past pres.), Women Execs. in State Govt., Women Execs. State Gov., Arts Advocates N.C. (bd. dirs.), N.C. Ctr. Pub. Policy Research (bd. dirs.). Office: NC Utilities Commn 430 N Salisbury St Raleigh NC 27602

COOKE, ANN MARIE, purchasing executive; b. Newark, Aug. 25, 1936; d. Frank Cooke and Mary Donegan. Diploma in Exec. Mgmt., Drake Coll., Newark, 1955; student, Seton Hall U., 1955-56. Purchasing agent Robert McKeown Co., Livingston, N.J., 1958-64; asst. purchasing agent Charms Co., Bloomfield, N.J., 1964, purchasing agent, 1968-73; dir. purchases Charms Co., Freehold, N.J., 1973, corp.v.p., 1977—. Eucharistic minister St. Gabriels Roman Cath. Ch., 1983—. Mem. Purchasing Mgmt. Assn. N.J. (100 Plus Club 1984), Nat. Assn. Purchasing Mgrs. (cert.). Club: Plainfield Ski (Clark, N.J.) (dir. 1970-71, 73-74). Office: Charms Co 41 Hwy 34 S Colts Neck NJ 07722

COOKE, BARBARA AYRES, association executive; b. Mpls., Dec. 4, 1936; d. Paul Revere and Mildred (Davidson) Ayres; m. Ralph F. Montgomery, Aug. 17, 1958 (div. 1969); m. James F. Cooke, May 14, 1975. B.S., Ind. U., 1959. Tchr., Indpls. Pub. Sch. System, 1959-61; found. exec. Continental Ill. Nat. Bank and Trust of Chgo., 1969-74; exec. dir. ARC, Berrien County, St. Joseph, Mich., 1975-77, Mid. Am. ARC, Chgo., 1977-87; exec. dir. Washtenaw County Am. Cancer Soc., Ann Arbor, Mich., 1988—; adj. prof. Aurora U., Ill., 1985-86. Author: Leadership Portfolio, 1977. Mem. women's bd. Muncie Symphony, Ind., 1968; pres. Women's Aux. Ball Meml. Hosp., Muncie, 1968; bd. dirs. Thresholds, Chgo., 1973, Reading Is Fundamental, Chgo., 1973. Recipient Pelican award (2), Mid. Am. ARC, 1984, 85. Mem. Nat. Assn. Female Execs. Home: 1451 Wisteria Dr Ann Arbor MI 48104 Office: Am Cancer Soc 2500 Packard Rd Ann Arbor MI 48104

COOKE, BARBARA LYNN, news production company executive; b. Mpls., May 22, 1956; d. Newell Orval and Jane Ann (Lobstein) Gaasedelen; m. Jeffrey Allen Cooke, Feb. 17, 1985. B.A., U. Minn., 1979; M.A., U. Kans., 1986. Sales acct. Modern Mdse., Mpls., 1979-83; media traffic coordinator Baxter Advt., Mpls., 1983-84; self-employed prodn. coordinator, Mpls., 1986—. Mem. Nat. Assn. Female Execs., Radio TV News Dirs. Assn., Alpha Phi. Avocation: flying; writing. Home and Office: 433 S 7th St #1927 Minneapolis MN 55415

COOKE, DOROTHY HELENA COSBY, mathematics educator, counselor; b. Gloucester, Va., Jan. 8, 1941; d. Calvert Luchal and Pagie Florene (Dedmon) Cosby; m. Nathaniel Randolph Cooke, Sept. 2, 1961; 1 child, Nathaniel Randolph, Jr. B.S. in Math. Edn., Va. Union U., 1963; M.A. in Math. Edn., Hampton Inst., Va., 1970, M.A. in Guidance and Counseling, 1976; cert. Advanced Grad. Studies in Counselor Edn., Va. Poly. Inst. and State U., Blacksburg, 1981; D. Edn. in Counselor Edn. and Student Personnel Services, 1982. Secondary math. tchr. Va. pub. schs. 1963-71; instr. math. Rappahannock Community Coll., Glenns, Va., 1971-75, asst. prof. math. and counseling 1975-77, assoc. prof. math. and counseling, dir. student spl. services, 1977-82, prof. math. and counseling, dir. student spl. services, 1982—; cons., lectr. Rappahannock Community Coll., Glenns, 1971—, dir spl. services, 1977-86, dir. student personnel services, 1986—. Past mem. adv. com. Spl. Edn. Gloucester County Pub. Sch. System, Va.; bd. dirs. Gloucester chpt. ARC; mem. NAACP, non-resident mem. Lancaster and Northumberland Counties Devel. Services (Lands, Inc.), Kilmarnock, Va., past mem. local, state and nat. PTAs; past dir. Christian Edn. Bethel Bapt. Ch., Sassafras, Va.; mem. Gloucester County Sch. Bd. Selection Commn. Recipient Grad. Asst. for Minority Virginians Va. State Council Higher Edn. Mem. Am. Assn. Counseling and Devel., Va. Assn. Ednl. Opportunity Personnel, Mid-Eastern Assn. Ednl. Opportunity Personnel, Minority Affairs Coalition Va., Va. Counselors' Assn., Va. Assn. Non-White Concerns, So. Regional Council Black Am. Affairs, Assn. Community and Jr. Colls., Eastern Regional Counselors Adv. Council, Rappahannock Community Coll. Instl. Reps., Bd. Nat. Council Black Affairs, Am. Assn. Community and Jr. Colls., Kappa Delta Pi, Delta Psi Omega. Democrat. Avocations: singing, dramatic activities. Home: Rt 6 Box 4525 Gloucester VA 23061 Office: Rappahannock Community Coll Glenns VA 23149

COOKE, NOREEN ANN, elementary educator, consultant; b. Waltham, Mass., Oct. 14, 1943; d. Warren William and Alice Noreen (Van Wart) C.; m. Dennis A. McCluggage, Dec. 19, 1970 (div. Jan. 1978). BS in Edn., Mass. State Coll., Framingham, 1965. Cert. elem. tchr., Mass., Alaska. Tchr. 3d grade Juneau (Alaska) Borough Sch. Dist., 1965-66, tchr. 1st grade, 1966-68, tchr. 2d grade, 1970-87; tchr. 1st grade Lake Washington Sch. Dist., Kirkland, Wash., 1968-70; rep. dist. Alaska State Writing Consortium, Juneau, 1986—, cons., 1987—. Author: My Juneau Adventure, 1984; editor Alaska State Writing Consortium jour. Shaping the Landscape, 1988. Mem. Dem. Nat. Com., Washington, 1984, Juneau Arts & Humanities Council, 1985—, Big Bros./Big Sisters of Juneau, Inc., 1986—. Mem. Juneau Edn. Assn. (pres. 1980-81, named tchr. of yr. 1986-87), Nat. Edn. Assn. (bd. dirs. Alaska chpt. 1981-83), Belleek Collector's Soc. Democrat. Roman Catholic. Home and Office: 9459 Berners Ave Juneau AK 99801

COOKE, PANDORA MORGAN, insurance company executive; b. Dalton, Ga., July 8, 1952; d. Edwin Marshall Morgan and Winnie Elizabeth (Harkins) Stone; m. Robert G. Cooke, Jan. 30, 1973; 1 child, Robert Gene Jr. AA in Merchandising, Massey Jr. Coll., 1972; grad., Ala. Real Estate Inst., 1975; BS, Samford U., 1986. CLU; Chartered Fin. Cons.; registered investment advisor, fin. planner. Mgr. Ups n Downs, Atlanta, 1971-73; co-owner Pandora's Sewing Box, Sylacauga, Ala., 1973-78; pres. Diversified Plans, Inc., Sylacauga, 1976—; bd. dirs. Occupational Services, Inc., Sylacauga. Mem. Soc. for CLU's, Internat. Assn. Fin. Planners, Ala. Assn. Life Underwriters (v.p. Sylacauga 1985-86), Women's Life Underwriters Confedn., Bus. and Profl. Women's Club. Democrat. Baptist. Office: Diversified Plans Inc PO Box 2130 Sylacauga AL 35150

COOKE, SARA GRAFF, marketing company executive; b. Phila., Dec. 29, 1935; d. Charles Henry and Elizabeth (Mullin) Brandt; m. Peter Fischer Cooke, June 29, 1963; children: Anna, Peter Jr., Frances Elizabeth, Sara Reynolds, Laina Koorting. AA, Bennott Coll., 1955; BE in Child Edn., Westchester State Tchrs. Coll., 1956. Asst. to tchr. 1st grade The Woodlyn Sch., 1956-58; tchr. Sara Birchor's Kindergarten, Germantown, Pa., 1958-62, Chestnut Hill (Pa.) Acad., 1962-63, Tarleton Sch., Devon, Pa., 1963-64; with F.C.I. Mkyg. Co-ordinators Inc., N.Y.C., New Canaan, Conn., 1986—. Mem. bd. auxiliary Children's Hosp. Phila., 1970-76, mem. women's bd., 1977-87; mem. commonwealth bd. Med. Coll. Pa., 1984-87. Mem. Pa. Assn. Hosp. Auxiliaries (health rep.). Republican. Presbyterian. Clubs: Acorn, Jr. League Phila., The Sustainers Jr. League Garden, Phila. Cricket. Office: 529 E Gravers Ln Philadelphia PA 19118

COOKE, VICKY B., vocational school administrator; b. Bakersville, Ohio, May 8, 1937; d. John O. and Tamara (Pauli) Braswell; m. John R. Cooke, June 16, 1965 (div. 1970). BS in Social Work, Fla. State U., 1964; MEd., Auburn U., 1973. With U.S. Civil Service, Tokyo, 1953-55; sec. U.S. Army, Ft. Rucker, Ala., 1963-67; typing instr. U.S. Army, Pirmasens, Germany, 1967-69; instr. Russian U.S. Army, Ft. Benning, Ga., 1970-78; sec. U.S. Army, Ft. Benning, 1973-74; instr. Russian Columbus (Ga.) Coll., 1985; vocat. evaluator, recruiter Columbus (Ga.) Tech. Inst., 1974—, head dept. Work Sta. Evaluation Ctr., 1975-77; owner Oasis Night Club, Wicksburg, Ala., 1963-65; faculty advisor Columbus Tech. Student Council, 1982-85. Coordinator Red Cross Blood Dr., Columbus Tech., 1980—, United Way for Columbus Tech., 1983, 84; mem. Mayor's com. for Employment of the Handicapped, Urban League Adv. Council, 1979-81. Am. Vocat. Assn., Ga. Vocat. Assn., Nat. Assn. of Vocat. Edn. Spl. Needs Personnel, Ga. Assn. of Vocat. Edn. Spl. Needs Personnel (sec. 1980-82), Muscogee Literacy Assn. (chmn. 1980-81), Urban League (chmn. edn. div. adv. com. 1979-81). Presbyterian. Clubs: Altrusa (Columbus) (v.p. 1981-82). Home: 1905 Oakland Ave Columbus GA 31903 Office: Columbus Tech Inst 928 45th St Columbus GA 31995

COOKE-GLASNER, MARY KAY, nurse; b. Wichita, Kans., June 27, 1952; d. Bernard C. and Elnora M. (Osman) Van Arsdale; m. Dennis W. Cooke, June 3, 1972 (div. 1977); m. James Charles Glasner, May 14, 1983; children: Jamie Kay, Jordan Thomas. A.A., Butler County Community Coll., Kans., 1972; B.S.N., Wichita State U., 1986, MSN Friends U., 1988. Lic. critical care nurse, emergency nurse; lic. paramedic; prehosp. trauma life support instr. coordinator. Nurse asst. Susan B. Allen Hosp., El Dorado, Kans., 1966-72; staff nurse Wesley Med. Ctr., Wichita, 1972-74, head nurse, 1974-75; charge flight nurse Life Watch/Wesley Med. Ctr., 1975-80, chief flight nurse, program dir. 1980—. Mem. Assn. Critical Care Nurses, Nat. Flight Nurses Assn. (liaison com. 1985-86). Club: Ashbeams (com. chair 1986). Office: Wesley Med Ctr 550 N Hillside Wichita KS 67214

COOK-RUSSELL, DEBORAH ANNE, manufacturing executive, personnel administrator; b. Oneida, N.Y., Apr. 7, 1956; d. Merton Edward and Anne Delores (Whipple) C.; m. John F. Russell, Aug. 20, 1987. AAS in Journalism, SUNY, Morrisville, 1976. Reporter Syracuse (N.Y.) Post Standard, 1977; clk. San Antonio Express News, 1978-79; personnel asst. USPHS Hosps., Galveston and Nassau Bay, Tex., 1979-81; personnel administr. Reef Industries Inc., Houston, 1981-84, asst. mgr. personnel, 1984-86, mgr. personnel, 1986-87, v.p. personnel, sales, 1987—, v.p., 1987—. Contbr. various articles to N.Y. newspapers. Mem. Am. Soc. Tng. and Devel. Republican. Office: Reef Industries Inc PO Box 33248 Houston TX 77233

COOL, KIM PATMORE, retail executive, needlework consultant; b. Cleve., Feb. 1, 1940; d. Herman Chester Earl and Eva (Geneau) Patmore; m. Kenneth Adams Cool Jr., Mar. 12, 1963; 1 child, Heidi Adams. BA in Econs., Sweet Briar Coll., 1962; postgrad., Case Western Reserve U., 1962-63. Test adminstr. Pradco, Cleve., 1962-63; pvt. needlework cons. Cleve., 1970-72; retail v.p., treas., custom designer And Sew On, Inc., Cleve., 1973—, exec. v.p., treas., 1982—; tchr. Wellesley Coll. Continuing Edn. Program, 1986; lectr. seminar on mktg. needlepoint for Nat. Needlework Assn.; pub. Fredericktown Rress, Md. Artist collector quality custom hand-painted canvases; co-author: How to Market Needlepoint—The Definitive Manual, 1988. Rep. committeeman Cuyahoga County, Shaker Heights, Ohio, 1964-72. Mem. Nat. Needlework Assn. (charter assoc. retail), Embroiderers Guild of Cleve. (bd. dirs. 1980-82), Am. Profl. Needlework Retailers, S.E. Yarncrafters Guild, Nat. Standards Council Am. Embroiderers, U.S. Figure Skating Assn. (nat. judge gold and senior competitions 1967—, sect. precision judge), Sweet Briar Coll. Alumnae Assn. (nat. bd. dirs. Upper Midwest region 1965-66, class sec. 1988). Republican. Baptist. Clubs: Cleve. Skating, Mayfield Country (Cleve.). Home: 14500 Washington Blvd University Heights OH 44118 Office: And Sew On Inc 2243 Warrensville Ctr University Heights OH 44118

COOLEY, HILARY ELIZABETH, business manager; b. Leesburg, Va., May 8, 1953; d. Thomas McIntyre and Helen Strong (Stringham) C. BA in Econs., U. Pitts., 1976; postgrad. in bus. adminstrn., Hood Coll., Frederick, Md., 1985—. Mgr. Montgomery Ward, Frederick, 1976-80, merchandiser, 1980-82; asst. bus. mgr. Arundel Communications, Leesburg, 1982-84; bus. mgr. Loudoun Country Day Sch., Leesburg, 1984-85, bd. trustees, 1987—; controller Foxcroft Sch., Middleburg, Va., 1985-87. Correspondent Loudoun Times Mirror, Leesburg, 1985—. Area chair Keep Loudoun Beautiful, Leesburg, 1983—; pres. Waterford (Va.) Citizen's Assn., 1985-86, Waterford Players, 1986-88; hon. bd. dirs. Waterford Found., Inc., 1980—, Loudoun Hist. Soc., Leesburg, 1987. Mem. Fin. Officers Group, Penn Hall Alumnae Assn. (pres. 1987-88), Loudoun County C. of C. Democrat. Episcopalian. Home and Office: 602 Lee Pl Frederick MD 21701

COOLEY, LEE (MORRISON), writer, choreographer; b. N.Y.C., Oct. 3, 1918; d. Henry and Ann (Rosan) Morrison; m. Donald Meyer, June 3, 1940 (div. Sept. 1948); m. Leland F. Cooley, Aug. 6, 1953 (div. June 1982). Student, N.Y. Sch. Applied Design for Women, 1937; student ballet arts, Carnegie Hall, N.Y.C., 1940-50; BA, U. Calif., Irvine, 1983. Ballet Met. Opera, N.Y.C., 1939—; tchr. ballet for srs. Oasis Sr. Ctr., Newport Beach, Calif., 1985; tchr., author, lectr. Univ. De Catholique, Angers, France, 1979; Verano Internat. Irvine Sch. Dist., 1983; Leisure World, Laguna Hills, Calif., 1984. Dancer, Actress: Films with Warner Bros., Fox, and others, 1940-43, in Broadway Musicals, 1943-50; choreographer: CBS-Perry Como Show, Mel Torme-Peggy Lee Show, Vic Damone, and others; author: The Simple Truth About Land Investment, 1965, The Retirement Trap, 1966, Land Investment U.S.A., 1973, How to Avoid the Retirement Trap, 1974, Premedicated Murder, 1975, (with Miriam Spear) Redesigning Your Life, 1987. Dir. publicity U. Calif. Irvine Friends of the Library, 1966-70; bd. dirs. Peoples Clinic, Santa Ana, Calif., 1979-87; bd. dirs. United Way, Orange County, Calif., 1984-85. Mem. Poets, Essayists, and Novelists, U. Calif. Irvine Alumni Assn. Home: 30861 Driftwood Dr South Laguna CA 92677

COOLEY, MARIE SZPIRUK, financial company executive; b. Gnezno, Poland, Dec. 20, 1935; came to U.S., 1950; d. Pavlo and Taisia (Bohdaniw) Szpiruk; m. Victor Cooley, Sept. 19, 1954; children: George, Oleg, Paul. Student, CUNY, 1955-56, Montgomery Coll., 1975, Am. U., 1975-77; BS, U. Md., 1982. Purchase clk. Am. U., Washington, 1975-77; asst. internal auditor Citizens Savs. Bank, Silver Spring, Md., 1977-83; asst. v.p., sec., treas. First Citizens Mortgage Corp., Silver Spring, 1984—; pres. Ukrainian Washington Fed. Credit Union, 1984-86, treas., 1986—. Mem. Dumka Choir, N.Y.C., 1953-55; v.p. St. Olga's Sisterhood, Washington, 1970; instr. Ukrainian Easter Eggs White House Exhibits, 1975-80. Mem. Millennium of Ukrainian Orthodoxy, Ukrainian Assn. of Washington, The Smithsonian Assn. Ukranian. Office: First Citizens Mortgage Corp 12510 Prosperity Dr Silver Spring MD 20904

COOLIDGE, MARTHA, film director; b. New Haven, Aug. 17, 1946. Dir. films:Valley Girl, 1983, The City Girl, 1983, Joy of Sex, 1984, Real Genius, 1985, Plain Clothes, 1988, documentary David: Off and On, 1972,lMore Than a School, 1973, Old Fashioned Woman, 1974, Not A Pretty Picture, 1976 (all 3 won Am. Film Festival awards); dir. TV shows Sledge Hammer pilot episode, 3 episodes The Twilight Zone. Address: care William Morris Agency 151 El Camino Beverly Hills CA 90212

COOLIDGE, MARTHA HENDERSON, environmental specialist; b. Cambridge, Mass., Jan. 26, 1925; d. Robert Graham and Lucy (Gregory) Henderson; m. Harold Jefferson Coolidge, May 26, 1972 (dec. Feb. 1985). Student, Smith Coll., 1942-43; BA, Radcliffe Coll., 1946; MA, Harvard U., 1956. Asst. sec. China Program Harvard U., Cambridge, Mass., 1948; adminstr. Fulbright Program Inst. Internat. Edn., N.Y.C., 1949-50, assoc. dir. GARIOA program, 1950-51; staff mem. Ctr. for Internat. Studies at MIT, Cambridge, 1953-54; exec. sec. The Japan Soc. of Boston, 1958-62; asst. to mng. dir., dir. film services Ednl. Devel. Inc., Watertown, Mass., 1963-65; program dir. for internat. exchanges Smithsonian Instn., Washington, 1965-66; edn. assoc. Cen. Atlantic Regional Edn. Labs., Washington, 1966-68; sr. assoc. for edn. The Conservative Found., Washington, 1968-70; ednl. assoc. Pub. Broadcasting Environ. Ctr., Washington, 1970-71; vol., bd. dirs., exec. com. Coolidge Ctr. for Environ. Leadership, Cambridge, 1983—, vice chmn., 1983-85; temp. staff Student Adaption Study MIT, 1962-63; cons. social studies curriculum project Harvard Grad. Sch. of Edn., Cambridge, 1964-65; adv. com. INFORM, N.Y.C. Author articles in field. Bd. dirs. Lincoln Filene Ctr. for Citizenship and Pub. Affairs Tufts U., Medford, Mass.; affiliate Dudley House, Harvard U.; council mem. New Eng. Aquarium, Boston. Grantee Yenching Inst., 1958; Fulbright scholar Tokyo U., 1957-58. Episcopalian. Clubs: Cosmos (Washington); Somerset, Women's Travel, Harvard Travelers'. Home: 38 Standley St Beverly MA 01915 Office: The Coolidge Ctr for Environ Leadership 1675 Massachusetts Ave Cambridge MA 02138

COOMBS, C'CEAL PHELPS (MRS. BRUCE AVERY COOMBS), air company executive, civic worker; b. nr. Portland, Oreg.; d. Perry Edwin and Flora (Gowey) Phelps; B.S., U. Idaho, 1929; student Wash. State Coll., 1941; m. Bruce Avery Coombs, Nov. 28, 1929; children—Keith Avery, Glinda C'Ceal (Mrs. Nick E. Mason). Tchr. pub schs., Idaho, 1929-30; adminstrv. asst. Coombs West-Air Co. and Coombs Flying C Ranches, Yakima, Wash., 1945—; lobbyist for civic activities Wash. Legislature, 1947—; notary pub., Wash., 1960—. Del. White House Conf. on Children and Youth, 1960, Wash. State White House Conf. on Edn., 1955; mem. Wash. Citizens Council, Nat. Council on Crime and Delinquency, 1956—; bd. dirs., mem. exec. com. Wash. State Council Crime and Delinquency, 1956—, chmn., 1970-71, recipient Spl. State award, 1972, 76; mem. Allied Sch. Council Wash. 1951-53; mem. Western regional scholarship com. Ford Found., 1955-57; chmn. regional dist. Wash. Cities Legislation, 1960; chmn. Yakima County Sch. Bd., 1957-59; mem. Yakima County Health Dept., 1959-60; city councilwoman Yakima, 1959-61, asst. mayor, 1960; mem. Wash. Library Commn., 1960, 64-68, 72—, vice chmn., 1965-70, 75-76, recipient gov's. citation, 1976; del. UNESCO Conf. on Crime and Delinquency, Kyoto, Japan, 1970, Caracus, Venezuela, 1980; del. to Internat. Library Assn., Toronto, 1968, Washington, 1975, del. to worldwide seminar, Seoul, 1976, London, Brussels, 1977; del. Internat. Fedn. Libraries, Manila, 1980; trustee Wash. 4-H Found., 1960-79, chmn., 1969—, hon. trustee, 1979—; bd. mem. Wash. State Friends of Libraries, 1976, pres., 1977; mem. bd. Yakima County Law and Justice. Recipient Outstanding Citizen award Western Correctional Assn., 1974. Mem. Am. Library Trustee Assn. (regional dir. 1962—, pres. 1967-68), C. of C., Oreg., Idaho, Elmore County, Washington County, Calif. hist. socs., Windsor (Conn.) Hist. Assn. (life), Friends of Tewkesbury Abbey Eng. (life), Daus. Am. Colonists, Founders and Patriots, New Eng. Hist. Geneal. Soc., Conn. Hist. Soc., Dorchester (Mass.) Antiquarian and Hist. Soc., Conn. Soc. Genealogists, Ft. Simcoe Restoration Soc. (life), ALA (internat. trustee citation 1966, mem. bd. 1972—, council 1967-68, 71-72), Pacific N.W. (chmn. trustee sect. 1962-63), Wash. (chmn. 1960, trustee award 1967) library assns., Nat. Soc. Crown of Charlemagne, LWV, Allied Arts Council, Broadway Theatre League, Nat., Am., aviation assns., P.E.O., Federated Women, Colonial Dames (state rec. sec., pres. local chpt.), Altrusa, Nat. Soc. Magna Charta Dames, Descs. of Conqueror and His Companions, Friends of N.Y.C. Library. Home: 11430 Mieras Rd Yakima WA 98901

COON, MARGARET ELIZABETH, horticultural educator; b. East Liverpool, Ohio, Mar. 31, 1931; d. Oscar and Margaret Dora (Kaiser) Harbaugh; m. Jack Frederick Coon, Sept. 8, 1956. Student, Pa. State U., 1949-51; BS, Ohio State U., 1953, MS, 1971. Cert. interior horticulturist and pesticide applicator. Mng. editor Am. Rose Soc., Columbus, Ohio, 1954-64; tech. asst. hort. Ohio State U., Columbus, 1965-74, coordinator home hort. ctr., 1974-76; instr. hort. Calif. Poly. Inst., Pomona, 1976-78; interior horticulturist Environ. Care, Inc., Armstrong Garden Ctrs., Santa Ana and Monrovia, Calif., 1978-83; tech. writer Ameron, Brea, Calif., 1983—; judge All-Am. Rose Selections, Columbus, 1972-76; supt./judge Youth Gardens Ohio State Fair, 1964-76; instr. UCLA, 1981—, Cuyamaca Coll., El Cajon, Calif., 1985—, Mt. San Antonio Coll., Walnut, Calif., 1987—, various other interiorscape workshops in Ariz., Calif., Oreg., Tex. Contbr. artilces to profl. jours; photographer, editor: Practical Horticulture, 1980. Mem. Sr. Citizens Housing Task Force, Upland, Calif., 1977-80; advisor North Orange Co. Reg. Occupational Program, Anaheim, Calif., 1980—; mem. Ohio State U. Traffic and Parking Commn., 1969-71. Victor H. Ries fellow, 1969-71. Mem. Am. Soc. Hort. Sci., Am. Hort. Soc. (chpt. sec. 1981-84), Garden Writers Assn. Am., Interior Plantscape div. of Am. Landscape Contractors Assn., Profl. Interior Plantscape Assn., Nat. Assn. Female Execs., Nat. Paint and Coatings Assn., High Hopes Investment Club. Democrat. Presbyterian. Home: 1384 Erin Ave Upland CA 91786 Office: Ameron Protective Coatings 201 N Berry St Brea CA 92621

COONEY, BARBARA, illustrator, author; b. Bklyn., Aug. 6, 1917; d. Russell Schenck and Mae Evelyn (Bossert) C.; m. Guy Murchie, Dec. 1942 (div. Mar. 1947); children: Gretel, Barnaby; m. Charles T. Porter, July 16, 1949; children: Charles Talbot, Phoebe. B.A., Smith Coll., 1938; student, Art Students League, 1940; PhD (hon.), Fitchburg State Coll., 1988. Author, illustrator: Miss Rumphius, 1982, The Little Juggler, 1961, Little Prayer, 1967, Christmas, 1967, Little Brother and Little Sister, 1982, Island Boy, 1988; illustrator numerous children's books. Served to 2d lt. Women's Army Corps, World War II. Recipient Caldecott medal for Chanticleer and the Fox, 1958, U. So. Miss. medal, 1975, Smith Coll. medal, 1976, Caldecott medal for Ox-Cart Man, 1980, Am. Book award, 1983.

COONEY, JANE MARGARET, trade association executive; b. Montreal, Que., Can., Mar. 18, 1943; d. Robert C. and Florence (Nugent) Hanson; m. Patrick E. Cooney, Sept. 4, 1967 (div. 1984). BA, Marianopolis Coll., Montreal, 1963; BLS, U. Toronto, 1964, MLS, 1974. Reference librarian Calgary (Can.) Pub. Library, 1964-65; circulation librarian McGill U., Montreal, 1965-66; dep. head Metro Toronto Bus. Library, 1966-69; assoc. instr. U. Toronto, 1975-79; mgr. info. ctr. Bank Commerce, Toronto, 1969-83; v.p. Bank Mktg. Assn., Chgo., 1983-86; exec. dir. Can. Library Assn., Ottawa, 1986—; mem. editorial bd. Canadian Business Index, Toronto, 1978-83. Contbr. articles to profl. jours. Adv. bd. Seneca Coll., Toronto, 1978-82; bd. dirs. Metro Chgo. council Campfire , 1983-85. Recipient Alumni Jubilee award U. Toronto, 1983. Mem. Spl. Libraries Assn. (past bd. dirs., Mem. of Yr. award 1983), Am. Soc. Assn. Execs., Inst. of Assn. Execs., Am. Library Assn. Clubs: Nat. Press, Rideau Tennis and Squash; Can. of Chgo. (bd. dirs. 1986). Office: Can Library Assn, 200 Elgin St, Ottawa, ON Canada K2P 1L5

COONEY, JOAN GANZ, broadcasting executive; b. Phoenix, Nov. 30, 1929; d. Sylvan C. and Pauline (Reardan) Ganz; m. Timothy J. Cooney, 1964 (div. 1975); m. Peter G. Peterson, 1980. BA, U. Ariz., 1951; hon. degrees, Boston Coll., 1970, Hofstra U., Oberlin Coll., Ohio Wesleyan U., 1971, Princeton U., 1973, Russell Sage Coll., 1974, U. Ariz., Harvard U., 1975, Allegheny Coll., 1976, Georgetown U., 1978, U. Notre Dame, 1982, Smith Coll., 1986, Brown U., 1987. Reporter Ariz. Republic, Phoenix, 1953-54; publicist NBC, 1954-55, U.S. Steel Hour, 1955-62; producer Channel 13/WNET; pub. affairs documentaries Channel 13/WNET, N.Y.C., 1962-67; TV cons. Carnegie Corp. N.Y., N.Y.C., 1967-68; exec. dir. Children's TV Workshop (producers Sesame Street, Electric Company, others), N.Y.C., 1968-70; pres., trustee Children's TV Workshop (producers Sesame Street, Electric Company, others), 1970—; trustee Channel 13/Ednl. Broadcasting Corp.; dir. Xerox Corp., Johnson & Johnson, Chase Manhattan Corp., Chase Manhattan Bank N.A., Met. Life Ins. Co. Mem. Pres.'s Commn. on Marijuana and Drug Abuse, 1971-73, Nat. News Council, 1973-81, Council Fgn. Relations, 1974—, Pres.'s Commn. for Agenda for 80's, 1980-81, Adv. Com. for Trade Negotiations, 1978-80; mem. Gov.'s Commn. on Internat. Yr. of the Child, 1979, Carnegie Found. Nat. Panel on High Sch., 1980-82. Recipient numerous awards for Sesame Street and other TV programs including Nat. Sch. Pub. Relations Assn. Gold Key 1971; Disting. Service medal Columbia Tchrs. Coll., 1971; Soc. Family Man award, 1971; Nat. Inst. Social Scis. Gold medal, 1971; Frederick Douglass award N.Y. Urban League, 1972; Silver Satellite award Am. Women in Radio and TV; Woman of Yr. in Edn. award Ladies Home Jour., 1975; Woman of Decade award, 1979; NEA Friends of Edn. award; Kiwanis Decency award; NAEB Disting. Service award; 5th Women's Achiever award Girl Scouts U.S.A.; Stephen S. Wise award, 1981; Harris Found. award, 1982; Ednl. Achievement award AAUW, 1984; Disting. Service to Children award Nat. Assn. Elem. Sch. Prins., 1985; DeWitt Carter Reddick award Coll. Communications, U. Tex.-Austin, 1986. Mem. NOW, Nat. Acad. TV Arts and Scis., Nat. Inst. Social Scis., Internat. Radio and TV Soc., Am. Women in Radio and TV. Office: Children's TV Workshop 1 Lincoln Plaza New York NY 10023

COONEY, KATHRYN ANNA, travel company executive; b. Boston, May 2, 1953; d. Kenneth Francis and Patricia (Sullivan) Cooney. Student, Wellesley Coll., 1971-72; BA, Harvard U., 1980. Dir. Kelly Services, Troy, Mich., 1978-81; v.p. product planning and devel. Trans National, Inc., Boston, 1981—.

COONEY, PATRICIA R., civic worker; b. Englewood, N.J.; d. Charles Aloysius and Ruth Jeannette (Foster) McEwen; m. J. Gordon Cooney, June 8, 1957; 1 child, J. Gordon, Jr. Grad. Katharine Gibbs Sch., 1948; student Fordham U., 1950-51. Blood bank chmn. Strafford Village Civic Assn., 1968-69, sec., 1970-71; vice chmn. Spl. Gifts Com. Cath. Charities Appeal of Archdiocese of Phila., 1980—, chmn. 1985; mem. Council of Mgrs. Archdiocese of Phila., 1982—, sec., exec. com., 1983—; bd. dirs. Cath. Charities of Archdiocese of Phila., 1984—, sec., exec. com., 1988—; bd. dirs. Village of Divine Providence, Phila., 1982—, sec., 1983-85; bd. dirs. St. Edmond's Home for Crippled Children, Phila., 1984—, Don Guanella Village of Archdiocese of Phila., 1984—; mem. Women's Com. Wills Eye Hosp., 1973—, mem.-at-large, 1st v.p.; mem. Women's Aux. St. Francis Country House, Darby, Pa., 1976—, treas., 1978-82; exec. com. United Way of Southeastern Pa., 1984—, sec., 1986—; bd. dirs. Chapel of Four Chaplains, 1984—. Decorated Cross Pro Ecclesia et Pontifice, 1982. Republican. Roman Catholic. Avocations: reading; tennis; sailing. Home: 320 Gatcombe Ln Bryn Mawr PA 19010

COOPER, CAROL DIANE, publishing executive; b. Williamsport, Pa., Aug. 14, 1953; d. Ray Calvin and Norma Jane (Steiger) C. BA, Colgate U., 1975; cert. in pub., Radcliffe Coll., 1975; MA, Syracuse (N.Y.) U., 1977. Editorial and promotion asst. St. Martin's Press, N.Y.C., 1977-78, sales rep., 1978-79; dir. sales Clearwater Pub. Co., Inc., N.Y.C., 1979-80, dir. mktg., 1980-81, v.p., 1981-83; exec. v.p. K.G. Saur Inc., N.Y.C., 1983-87; with Bowker Saur Div. R.R. Bowker & Co Div.Reed Pub. USA, N.Y.C., 1987—; also bd. dirs. R.R. Browher & Co Div.Reed Pub. USA, N.Y.C. Mem. Am. Library Assn. (com. microform standards research and tech. standards div. 1986). Office: KG Saur Inc 175 5th Ave New York NY 10010

COOPER, CHRISTINE ANN, insurance broker, consultant; b. Oakland, Calif., Aug. 5, 1952; d. Robert Earl and Jean Louise (Warren) C; m. Thomas E. Hawkins, July 14, 1974 (div. 1981). A.A., Diablo Valley Coll., 1972; B.A., U. Calif.-Davis, 1975. Rater, United Pacific Ins., Fresno, Calif., 1975-77; supr. Lundberg & Assoc., Fresno, 1977-81; office mgr. L.T. Petersen Ins., Fresno, 1981-83; account exec. Corroon & Black, Sacramento, 1983-85; owner, broker Christine A. Cooper Ins., Sacramento, 1985—; Editor Capitol News & Views newsletter, 1985—. Bd. dirs. Ins. Women of Sacramento, 1985—; mem. Sacramento Women's Network, 1984—. Mem. C. of C., Profl. Ins. Agts. Democrat. Episcopalian. Avocations: creative writing, piano, sewing, softball, sailing, backpacking, skiing. Home: 2800 Matheson Way Sacramento CA 95864 Office: 510 8th St Sacramento CA 95814

COOPER, CLARINDA RYNN, retail company executive; b. Bloomington, Ind., Mar. 6, 1955; d. Dale Dallas and Catherine (Starbuck) C. B.A., Ind. U., 1978. Sales rep. Sears Roebuck & Co., Bloomington, Ind., 1974-80; asst. mgr. K-Mart, Speedway, Ind., 1980-81; salesperson FAS Auto Works, Bloomington, 1982; retail mgr. Deb Shops, Inc., Bloomington, 1982-86, dist. mgr., 1986-87, retail mgr., 1987—; cons. Ind. U. Sch. Arts and Scis., Bloomington, 1985—. Mem. Nat. Assn. Female Execs., Career Track. Republican. Mem. Ch. of Christ. Avocations: music; reading; calligraphy; photography; fashion. Home: 612 W Allen St Bloomington IN 47401

COOPER, DEBORAH ROBINSON, hydraulic engineer, researcher; b. Jackson, Tenn., July 9, 1958; d. Juvernia A. and Cathon (Jones) R.; m. Walter Jerome Cooper. BS, Miss. State U., 1982. Civil engr. Waterways Expt. Sta., Vicksburg, Miss., 1982-83, hydraulic engr., 1983-85, research hydraulic engr., 1985—. Mem. Nat. Assn. Female Execs., Soc. Am. Mil. Engrs., Blacks in Govt., Am. Soc. Civil Engrs. (publicity chmn.), Chi Epsilon, Delta Sigma Theta (publicity chmn.). Democrat. Methodist. Club: WES Castle. Home: 605 Cain Ridge Rd Apt H3 Vicksburg MS 39180 Office: USAE WES 3909 Halls Ferry Rd Vicksburg MS 39180

COOPER, DEBRA LYNN, management consultant; b. Havre de Grace, Md., Aug. 23, 1957; d. Elmer Lewis and Dollye Loise (Armacost) C. BS, U. Md., 1980, MBA, 1986. Office mgr. BioClin. Systems, Inc., Columbia, Md., 1980-85; exec. asst. Maxam Techs., Inc., Landover, Md., 1985; mgmt. analyst Syscon Corp., Washington, 1985—. Mem. Md. Fedn. Bus. and Profl. Women (long range planning com. 1987), Coll. Park Bus. and Profl. Women (editor newsletter 1983-84, 2d v.p. 1984-86, pres. 1987—). Democrat. Home: 9006 Saffron Lane Silver Spring MD 20901 Office: Syscon Corp 1050 Thomas Jefferson St NW Washington DC 20007

COOPER, DIANNE LYNN, marketing executive; b. Columbus, Ohio, Aug. 9, 1950; d. Franklin Monroe and Katherine (Lochner) Frohnauer; m. Steven Lee Cooper, Sept. 24, 1974. B.S. in Mktg., Miami U., Oxford, Ohio, 1972. Project dir. Burgoyne, Inc., Cin., 1972-74; mgr. info. services Cin. C. of C., 1974-77; project dir. Burke Market Research, Cin., 1977-79; asst. mgr. research dept. Sive Assocs./Y & R, Cin., 1979-85; mgr. market research First Nat. Bank of Cin., 1985-87; dir. market research, Northwestern Meml. Hosp., Chgo., 1987—. Recipient Mktg. Research award, 1986. Mem. Am. Mktg. Assn. (pres. Cin. chpt. 1985-86), Phi Beta Kappa. Republican. Lutheran. Office: NMH 303 E Superior St Chicago IL 60611

COOPER, DOLORES A., real estate professional, consultant, small business owner; b. Phila., Feb. 12, 1935; d. Daniel Mellor and Anne (Howard) C. BSBA, Widener U., 1983. Sec., travel coordinator Westinghouse Elec. Corp., Lester, Pa., 1953-86; owner, pres. DC Relocation Assistance Co., Bookhaven, Pa., 1986—; real estate sales assoc. Coldwell Banker Real Estate. Contbr. articles to profl. jours. Mem. Nat. Assn. Female Execs., Soc. Cert. Profl. Secs., Nat. Writers Club, Del. County C. of C., Phi Kappa Phi, Alpha Sigma Lambda. Republican. Roman Catholic. Office: DC Relocation Assistance Co PO Box 937 Brookhaven PA 19015

COOPER, DONA HANKS, story analyst, consultant; b. Oklahoma City, Nov. 5, 1950; d. Charles William and Betty Hopkins (Cragen) C. B.A., Am. U., 1972; postgrad. U. Minn., 1972-73. Caseworker U.S. Senator Marlow W. Cook, Washington, 1973-74, U.S. Congressman Benjamin A. Gilman, Washington, 1974-75; artistic dir. Am. Soc. Theatre Arts, Washington, 1975-79; mng. dir. Ensemble Studio Theatre, Los Angeles, 1979-81; story analyst Metro Media, Hollywood, Calif., 1981-82, NBC, Burbank, Calif., 1982-87; dir. story dept. NBC, 1987—, HBO, Los Angeles, 1984-85; dir. Oliver Hailey's Playwrighting Group, Los Angeles, 1982-85; radio drama cons. Radio Am., Washington, 1986; cons. Edgar Scherick Assocs., Los Angeles, 1985. Author plays: The Works of Lizzie Borden, 1981, California Calico, 1982, The Lone Star State, 1983, Rules of the House, 1984, Bosom Buddies, 1986. Sponsor Christian Children's Fund, 1983—. Mem. Nat. Assn. Female Execs., Dramatist Guild (assoc.), Phi Beta Phi. Democrat. Avocations: quilting; researching women's roles in Am. history. Home: Star Rt Box 8068 Frazier Park CA 93225 Office: NBC 3000 W Alameda #C108 Burbank CA 91523

COOPER, DORIS JEAN, market research executive; b. N.Y.C., Dec. 17, 1934; d. James N. and Georgina N. (Cassidy) Breslin; student Sch. of Commerce, N.Y. U., 1953-55, Hunter Coll., 1956-57; m. S. James Cooper, June 17, 1956; 1 son, David Austin. Asst. coding supr. Crossley S-D Surveys, N.Y.C., 1955-57; asst. field supr. Trendex, Inc., N.Y.C., 1957-59; coding dir. J. Walter Thompson Co., N.Y.C., 1960-63, Audits & Surveys, N.Y.C., 1964-65; pvt. practice cons., N.Y.C., 1965-73; pres. Cooper Services, Hastings-on-Hudson, N.Y., 1973—; cons. market research prodn. problems. Mem. Am. Mktg. Assn. (N.Y. chpt.), Nat. Bus. Women Owners Assn., Am. Assn. Opinion Research (N.Y. chpt.), Hastings C. of C. Republican. Episcopalian. Office: Cooper Services 419 Warburton Ave Hastings-on-Hudson NY 10706

COOPER, IRMGARD MARIE, employment company executive; b. Tiesendorf, Fed. Republic Germany, June 29, 1946; came to U.S. 1950; d. Richard A. and Ruth (St. Ville) Carter; m. Clyde W. Cooper Sr., Sept. 5, 1974; stepchildren: April D., Clyde W. Jr. BS, DePaul U., 1968; MS, No. Ill. U., 1976, postgrad., 1980. Cert. tchr., Ill. Personnel cons. Zinzer Personnel Co., Chgo., 1968-70; bus. tchr. Providence-St. Mel High Sch., Chgo., 1968-69; bus. tchr., job coordinator Jones Met. High Sch., Chgo., 1970-83; pres. Insta-Temps Temporaries, IMC Services, Inc., Chgo., 1985—; cons. Hobbit Travel Internat., Chgo., 1983—; mentor Membership program DePaul U., Chgo., 1986—, Women Employed Career Links Program, Chgo., 1988; panelist in field. Recipient Recognition award Chgo. City-Wide Coll., 1987; named one of Chgo. Up and Coming Bus. and Profl. Women Dollars and Cents mag., 1988. Mem. DePaul Alumni Assn. (cert. appreciation 1988), Chgo. Bus. Edn. Assn. (chmn. membership 1984-86, 1st v.p. 1986-87, pres. 1987-88, Enos C. Perry Service award 1982), Nat. Bus. Edn. Assn. (chmn. hospitality com. 1982), Ill. Vocat. Edn. Assn. (life), Chgo. Exec. Network (sec.-treas. 1986—), Nat. Assn. Women Bus. Owners (mem. programs com. 1988), Ill. Assn. Black Women Bus. Owners (exec. bd. 1988). Democrat. Roman Catholic. Home: 333 E Ontario Apt 309B Chicago IL 60611 Office: IMC Services Inc 333 E Ontario Suite 307B Chicago IL 60611

COOPER, JANE TODD, poet, writer, educator; b. Bklyn., Dec. 24, 1943; d. John Curtis and Margaret E. (Johnston) C.; m. William Hudson Shoff; children: Donald Charles Taylor, Eamon Robert Taylor, Savannah Elizabeth Cooper-Ramsey. Student U. Pitts., 1965-68; BA in Lit., Duquesne U., 1965. Research asst. U. Pitts., 1966; instr. high sch., Pitts., 1967-73; ednl. dir. drug and alcohol treatment facility Pa. Dept. Corrections, Camp Hill, 1974-78; project trainer domiciliary care, dept. behavioral sci. Pa. State Coll. Medicine, Hershey, 1979-80; dir. primary health care projct Elizabethtown Hosp., Pa., 1980-81; mgr. personal care boarding home provider tng. project, dept. family and community medicine Pa. State Coll. Medicine, Hershey, 1982; cons. Pa. Dept. Aging, Pa. Dept. Pub. Welfare, Pa. Council on Arts, 1979—, others; coordinator Fellow in Arts Mgmt. Program, 1985-87; free lance writer, Harrisburg (Pa.) and Phila., 1979—; mem. steering com. Women in the Arts, Harrisburg, 1979-83; coordinator Eye Poets Reading Series, Lancaster, Pa., 1985-87, Manchester Craftsmen's Guild Reading Series, Pitts., 1988-89. Author: (poetry) Entering Pisces, 1985; editor: AR-TREACH, 1984, Home Management for Personal Care Boarding Home Providers, 1982; edit. bd. Shooting Star Rev., 1987—; poetry and prose pub. in lit. jours. and anthologies; poet, poetry adv. bd., Geraldine R. Dodge Found., Madison, N.J., 1987—; mem. poetry selection com. Gershman YM-YWHA, Phila., 1988—. Artist in residence N.J. State Arts Council, Pa. Council on the Arts, 1982—; Carroll scholar, 1964-65; Warner Lambert/Nat. Merit scholar, 1961-65. Mem. Poets and Writers, Acad. Am. Poets. Home: 339 S 4th St Philadelphia PA 19106

COOPER, JOSEPHINE SMITH, public relations executive; b. Raleigh, N.C., Aug. 2, 1945; d. Joseph W. and Marie (Peele) S.; BA in bus. and econs., Meredith Coll., Raleigh, 1967; MS in mgmt. Duke U., 1977. Program analyst Office of Air & Quality Planning and Standards EPA, Research Triangle Park, N.C., 1968-78, environ. profl. specialist Office of Research and Devel., Washington, 1978-80; mem. profl. staff majority leader Howard H. Baker, Jr., U.S. Senate Com. on Environ. and Public Works, Washington, 1980-83; asst. adminstr. for external affairs EPA, Washington, 1983-85; asst. v.p. for environ. and health program Am. Paper Inst., Washington, 1985-86; sr. v.p. for policy Synthetic Organic Chem. Mfrs. Assn., Washington, 1986-88; sr. v.p., dir. environmental policy Hill & Knowlton, Washington, 1988—; treas. RTP Fed. Credit Union, 1969-72, pres., 1975; pres. Women's Council on Energy and Environment, 1986-88, Nat. Council on Clean Indoor Air, 1988—. Congressional fellow, 1979-80. Mem. Federally Employed Women (treas., pres. 1972-77), Women in Govt. Relations. Mem. Disciples of Christ. Club: Cts. Royal Racquetball. Office: 1330 Connecticut Ave Suite 300 Washington DC 20036

COOPER, LINDA GROOMES, consumer products company executive; b. Jacksonville, Fla., June 1, 1954; d. Benjamin H. and Freddie (Lang) Groomes. BS in Math., Fla. State U., 1974; MBA in Fin., Ind. U., 1977. Staff asst. career devel. Hallmark Cards, Inc., Kansas City, Mo., 1977-78, budget analyst, 1978-80, sr. budget analyst, 1980-81, mktg. budget adminstrn. mgr., 1981-83, mgr. sales adminstrn., 1983-85, dir. minority affairs, 1985—; mem. Hallmark Polit. Action Com. Mem. exec. com. Def. Adv. Com. on Women in the Services, Washington, 1985—; bd. dirs. YMCA, Kansas City, 1987—. Named one of Outstanding Young Women in Am., 1979, Black Achiever in Bus. and Industry, So. Christian Leadership Conf., Kansas City, 1983. Mem. Black MBA Assn., Nat. Assn. Mkt. Developers (sec. 1985—, v.p. 1986—), Mo. C. of C. (Edn. Council), NAACP, Greater Kansas City Black Econ. Union (chair bd. dirs. 1988), Alpha Kappa Alpha. Democrat. Protestant. Office: Hallmark Cards Inc 2501 McGee Kansas City MO 64108

COOPER, LOUISE FRAN, psychotherapist, management consultant; b. N.Y.C., Dec. 23, 1944; d. Samuel William and Ruth May (Handelson) C.; 1 child, Daniel. BA in Psychology and Philosophy, Queens Coll., 1965; postgrad., Smith Coll., 1965-66; MSW, Hunter Coll., 1968. Cert. social worker, N.Y. Pvt. practice psychotherapist various locations, 1968-80, pvt. practice mgmt. cons., 1981—; pres. Copwood Assocs., Poughkeepsie, N.Y., 1982—; psychotherapist to numerous cos. and orgns. including MGM Studios, 1968, Tufts U., 1972, Danbury Fed. Penitentiary, 1973-74, Ulster County Soc. Guidance Counselors, 1976, N.Y.C. Bd. Edn., 1980, mem. faculty, 1964-65; mgmt. cons. to Castle Point VA Hosp., 1981, 83, IBM, 1981, 84, Dutchess County Community Coll., 1981, 83, 87, mem. faculty, 1981-84; mgmt. cons. Rotron Industries, 1983, N.Y. State Dept. Social Services, 1984, 85, 86, Nat. Bank of Highland, 1985, Ulster County Mental Health Assn., 1986, profl trainer; mgmt. cons. AT&T, 1986, 87, U.S. Mil. Acad., 1987, Gov.'s Office N.J., 1987, various others; bd. dirs. Acorn Ctr.; mem. faculty Forest Hills Adult Edn. Ctr., 1971, Bklyn. Coll., 1971, G.R.O.W., 1972, Adelphi U. Sch. Social Work, 1976, SUNY, Albany, 1976-80, Coll. New Rochelle Sch. New Resources, 1981-84, New Sch. Social Research, 1983-87; profl. trainer Dutchess County Mental Health, Pope Pious XIII, Inst. Human Devel., Dutchess County Mental Health, Community Cultural Ctr. Hopewell Junction; lectr. L.I. Consultation Ctr., SUNY, New Paltz, Consultation Ctr. for Women, Bard Coll., N.Y. Assn. Health Profls.; speaker numerous confs. and workshops in field. Author: Jour. of Alternatives in Higher Edn., 1970-73; founder, contbr. Interface. Developer, therapist village project Jewish Family Services, 1968-69; asst. dir. Colony House Head Start United Neighborhood Houses, 1969-70; supr., designer services Contact Ednl. Alliance, 1970-72; developer programs Manhattan Community Ctr., 1966-67, East Bronx Community Ctr., 1967-68; founder, therapist New Way Ctr., 1972-75. Mem. N.Y. Inst. Psychotheraoy and the Arts, N.Y. Inst. Gestalt Therapy, Mid-Hudson Humanistic Psychology Assn., Am. Soc. Tng. and Devel., Am. Women Econ. Devel. Corp., N.Y. State Soc. Clin. Social Work Psychotherapists. Democrat. Jewish.

COOPER, MARGERY WILKENS, investment company executive; b. Glen Cove, N.Y., May 14, 1947; d. Robert George and Caroline L. (Jones) Wilkens; m. Daniel S. Cooper, May 6, 1967; 1 child, Christopher S. AA, Mt. Vernon Jr. Coll., 1967; BS, Russell Sage Coll., 1976. Registered securities rep. Chief fin. officer D.S. Cooper and Co., Troy, N.Y., 1981-87. Bd. dirs. Albany Boys' Club, Albany Hist. Soc., St. Peter's Women's Assn., pres. Albany Jr. League. Republican. Episcopal.

COOPER, MARILYN MACE, finance company executive; b. Los Angeles, Aug. 9, 1950; d. William O. and Margaret E. (O'Connor) Mace; m. William E. Cooper, Apr. 18, 1970 (div. 1982); children: Bill, Ryan, Sean. BA in Math magna cum laude, Calif. State U., 1971, MA in Edn., 1975; MBA in Fin., U. So. Calif., Los Angeles, 1985. Math instr. San Gabriel (Calif.) High Sch., 1972-77; programmer, analyst So. Calif. Edison, Rosemead, 1977-80; with Security Pacific Automation Co., Los Angeles, 1980—, bank card ops. exec., 1987—. Bd. dirs. San Gabriel Sch. Dist., 1985—, bd. pres., 1987, 88. Mem. Los Angeles County Trustees Assn., Calif. Sch. Bd. Assn., Nat. Assn. Female Execs., Phi Kappa Phi. Democrat. Roman Catholic. Office: Security Pacific Automation Co 611 N Brand Blvd Glendale CA 91203

COOPER, MARY ADRIENNE, publishing executive; b. Bklyn., Jan. 27, 1927; d. James H. and Helen (Hofeditz) C. BSBA, SUNY, Albany, 1948; postgrad. in bus., NYU, 1949-50, Columbia U., 1976. With McGraw Hill, Inc., N.Y.C., 1953—, asst. v.p. corp. fin. ops., 1973-75, v.p. corp. fin. ops., 1975-76, v.p. adminstrv. services, 1976-84, v.p. fin. services, 1984-85, sr. v.p. adminstrv. services, 1985-86, sr. v.p. corp. affairs, exec. asst. to Chief Exec. Officer, chmn., 1986—. Mem. Fin. Execs. Inst. (com. on govt. liaison N.Y.C. chpt., bd. dirs. 1986—). Roman Catholic. Avocations: golf, biking, reading, travel. Office: Mc Graw-Hill Inc 1221 Ave of the Americas New York NY 10020

COOPER, MARY ANN, radio station executive; b. Albany, N.Y., Sept. 4, 1956; d. Lewis Anker and Rosalyn Joy (Weinberg) Aronowitz; m. John Ritchie Cooper, Oct. 5, 1980. BS cum laude, SUNY, Albany, 1978. Adminstrv. asst. Sta. WQBK, Albany, 1977-79, account exec., 1979-83, regional account exec., 1983-84, sales mgr., 1984-86; account exec. Sta. WGY-WGFM, Schenectady, N.Y., 1987—. Photographer major rock concerts, 1985. Chmn. Child Abuse Prevention Month of April, N.Y., 1987, Capital dist. chpt. Soaring Spirits of Am. Women in Radio and TV, treas. 1982-84, v.p., 1984-86, pres., 1986—; fundraiser Project Equinox, Albany, 1985-86. Mem. Am. Women of Radio and TV, Inc. (chair profl. devel. com. 1987—, co-chair N.E. area conf. Albany chpt. 1987), The Ad Club (treas. 1985—). Democrat. Avocations: photography, tennis, reading, nautilus. Office: Sta WGY WGFM PO Box 1410 Schenectady NY 12301

COOPER, PAMELA ELAINE, human resources administrator, psychologist; b. Bozeman, Mont., June 20, 1949; d. Clee Scott and Dorothy Jane (Gilbert) C.; m. William J. Cook, 1987. BS in Psychology, Mont. State U., 1970; MS in Psychology, Pa. State U., 1974, PhD in Psychology, 1978. Instr. U. Conn., Storrs, 1974-78, asst. prof., 1978-82; compensation adminstr. Combustion Engring., Inc., Windsor, Conn., 1982-85, mgr. compensation and orgn. planning, 1985—. Contbr. articles on psychology to profl. jours. NIMH fellow, 1982-83. Mem. Am. Assn. Personnel Adminstrn., Am. Psychol. Assn., Am. Compensation Assn., Soc. Indsl. Psychology, Hartford Mfr.'s Assn., Phi Kappa Phi, Sigma Xi, Delta Gamma. Office: Combustion Engring Inc 1000 Prospect Hill Rd Windsor CT 06095

COOPER, PATRICIA ANN, journalist, educator, researcher, consultant; b. N.Y.C., Nov. 7, 1953; d. Leslie M. and Louise E. (Macklin) C.; m. James P. Nichols, Aug. 7, 1976 (div. Feb. 1980). Student CUNY, 1972-75; BS in Journalism and Edn., L.I. U., 1977; student Tchrs. Coll. Columbia U., 1979, Bank St. Coll. Edn., 1980. Community reporter, City Scene Newspaper, N.Y.C., 1977; research/editorial asst. Dun's Rev., N.Y.C., 1977-78; tchr. West Side Montessori Sch., N.Y.C., 1978-80; reporter The Pensacola Voice, Fla., 1980-81; adminstrv. asst. Signature Clothing Corp., N.Y.C., 1981; tchr. Langston Hughes Child Devel. Ctr. (now Morningside II Headstart Ctr.), N.Y.C., 1981-82; library inf. asst. Telephone Reference unit N.Y. Pub. Library, 1982-85; freelance writer, N.Y.C., 1985—, temporary perdiem tchr. N.Y.C. Bd. Edn., 1985—; temporary adminstrv. asst. Bread for the World, N.Y.C., 1986; edn. cons. Nat. Urban League, N.Y.C., 1985-87; researcher United Negro Coll. Fund Inc., Capital Resources Devel. Program, N.Y.C., 1986—. Author, assoc. editor BlackWorks Mag., 1977. Mem. Nat. Assn. Female Execs., Found. for Christian Living, Black Film Makers Found., Nat. Com. for Citizens in Edn. Baptist. Avocations: singing; painting; writing poetry; films; reading. Home: 253 W 72d St Apt 1807 New York NY 10023

COOPER, PATRICIA ANN, historian, educator; b. Blacksburg, Va., Aug. 29, 1949; d. Byron Nelson and Elizabeth (Doyne) C. BA, Wittenberg U., 1969; MA, U. Md., 1973, PhD, 1981. Post-doctoral fellow Smithsonian Inst., Washington, 1982; historian Service Employees Internat. Union, Washington, 1983; asst. prof. of history Drexel U., Phila., 1985-88, assoc. prof., 1988—, bd. dirs. Women's Studies com., 1985—. Author: Once a Cigar Maker, 1987. Bd. dirs. U. City Arts League, Phila., 1987—. U.S. Dept. Labor grantee, 1979-80; recipient Drexel U. Research Scholar award 1987. Mem. Orgn. Am. Historians, Am. Hist. Assn., Pa. Hist. Soc., Oral History in the Mid-Atlantic Region (pres., 1983). Office: Drexel U Dept History Politics 33rd and Chestnut Sts Philadelphia PA 19104

COOPER, PATRICIA DAWKINS, association executive; b. Houston, Feb. 5, 1944; d. Austin Eli and Sarah Lorraine (Rountree) Dawkins; B.A., Columbia Coll., 1965; children from previous marriage—Catherine Sloane, Sarah Riley, Patricia Daily. Appointments sec. to Congressman Tom Gettys, Washington, 1965; tchr. Lugoff (S.C.) Elem. Sch., 1967-68, Camden (S.C.) Elem. Sch., 1969-70; ombudsman State of S.C., 1970-73; asst. dir. Carolina Cup and Colonial Cup Internat., Camden, 1973-87; adminstr. Camden Feed Co., 1973-87; office mgr. Camden Tng. Center, thoroughbreds, 1973-87; asst. sec. Mulberry Resources, Inc., 1980-82; sec.-treas. Equistar Products Co., 1980-87; mktg. dir. Holiday Inn of Lugoff-Camden, Holiday Inn of Sumter, S.C., 1987—. Bd. dirs. Kershaw County Fine Arts Center; sustaining mem. Camden Jr. Welfare League; mem. Inaugural Class, Leadership Kershaw County, 1986-87, participant Statewide Program, 1987-88; adv. com. Charleston Steeplechase; mem. Santee-Lynches Council Govts., 1987-88; bd. dirs. Kershaw County unit Am. Cancer Soc., 1980—; chmn. bd. dirs. Kershaw unit Am. Heart Assn., 1984-86 ; bd. dirs. Palmetto Balloon Classic, 1983-86; mem. Bd. Appeals, City of Camden, 1985-87; vice chmn. Kershaw County Tourism Adv. Com., 1987-88; adminstrv. bd. Lyttleton St. United Meth. Ch., Camden, 1986-88. Mem. Nat. Steeplechase and Hunt Assn., Nat. Hay Assn., Greater Kershaw County C. of C. (v.p. pub. affairs 1983-86), Thoroughbred Assn. S.C. (sec.-treas. 1986-88). Democrat. Methodist. Clubs: Camden Country, Sprindale Hall. Home: 409 Laurens Ct Camden SC 29020 Office: Holiday Inn PO Box 96 Lugoff SC 29078

COOPER, PATRICIA JACQUELINE, lawyer; b. Detroit, Feb. 6, 1958; d. Donald and Aileen Cooper. BA, Vassars Coll., 1978; JD, U. San Francisco,

Hastings, 1981. Bar: D.C. 1982. Assoc. Costello Assocs., Washington, 1981-82; atty. VA, Washington, 1982-83; sole practice Washington, 1983—; atty. Ground Floors Mgmt., Washington, 1983—. Gen. counsel Nat. Missing Child Search Soc., Inc. Mem. ABA (entertainment and sports law com.), Songwriters Assn. of Washington, Women in Music, Women's Bar Assn., Am. Women Composers (nat. bd. dirs. 1982—). Home and Office: PO Box 12011 Arlington VA 22209

COOPER, RUTH, psychologist, health facility administrator; b. Mar. 11, 1918; m. Harry Cooper, Jan. 11, 1936; children: Joyce, Mel. BA summa cum laude, Queen's Coll., 1950; MA, Columbia U., 1957, PhD, 1959. Lic. psychologist, Fla., N.Y. Psychology intern VA, N.Y.C., 1956-59; sr. psychologist City Hosp. Ctr., Elmhurst, N.Y., 1959-64; chief psychologist City Hosp. Ctr., Elmhurst, 1964-70; cons. psychologist Lee Mental Health Ctr., Ft. Myers, Fla., 1970-74; exec. dir. Lee Mental Health Ctr., Ft. Myers, 1974—; pvt. practice psychology Naples, Fla., 1964—; mem. Gov.'s Council on Drug Abuse, Gov.'s Council on Teen-Age Suicide; bd. dirs. Alzheimer's Disease and Related Disorders, AIDS Com., Fla. Council Community Mental Health Ctrs. Mem. Am. Psychol. Assn., Fla. Council Community Mental Health Ctr. (bd. dirs. 1986—), Phi Beta Kappa. Office: Lee Mental Health Ctr PO Box 06137 Fort Myers FL 33906

COOPER, RUTHIE MAE, charitable organization executive; b. Greenwood, Miss., Apr. 11, 1948; d. Olive L. and Elouise (Shields) C. BS in Edn., Ind. U., 1971; M Pub. Adminstrn., Ball State U., 1974, Ind. U., Purdue U., 1980. Coordinator manpower Office Econ. Opportunity Allen County, Ft. Wayne, Ind., 1971-72; dir. edn., youth incentives Urban League Madison County, Anderson, Ind., 1972-74; program asst. dept. human resources City of Ft. Wayne, 1974-81, assoc. planner, coordinator contract mgmt. CETA, 1974-81; mgr. office, customer service Bus. Revenue Systems Am., Ft. Wayne, 1981-82; substitute tchr. Ft. Wayne Community Schs., 1983-86; asst. dir. planning, allocation, research United Way Allen County Inc., Ft. Wayne, 1986—; sole proprietor Office Cleaning Services, Ft. Wayne, 1981-85. Sec., bookkeeper Greater Mount Eria Baptist Ch., Ft. Wayne, 1983—. Mem. Nat. Assn. Female Execs. (Ft. Wayne chpt.), Nat. Assn. Negro Bus. Profl. Women (2d v.p. 1984-85), Ind. State Minority Women's Network (parliamentarian 1986—), Ft. Wayne Minority Women's Network (pres. 1984-85, achievement award 1986).

COOPER, SUSAN CAROL, environmental, safety and health professional; b. Milw., Dec. 25, 1939; d. Carroll Arthur and Edith Estelle (Hicks) Brooks; m. William Randall Cooper, June 20, 1964; children: Darin Benbrook, Carol Kimberly, Ryan Randall. BS in Biology, U. Wis., Milw., 1962; MS in Physiology, Wash. State U., 1966; PhD in Physiology, U. Idaho, 1972. Sr. lab. technician Dept. Vet. Pathology, Wash. State U., Pullman, 1965-68; postdoctoral assoc. dept. chemistry U. Idaho, Moscow, 1972-74, vis. prof. chemistry, 1974; instr. facilitator for gifted/talented Highland Sch. Dist., Craigmont, Idaho, 1975-76; program dir. YWCA, Lewiston, Idaho, 1977-78; support asst. Exxon Nuclear Idaho Corp., Idaho Falls, 1983; engr. Exxon Nuclear Idaho Corp. and Westinghouse Idaho Nuclear Co. Inc., Idaho Falls, 1983-84; environ. engr. Westinghouse Idaho Nuclear Co. Inc., Idaho Falls, 1984-86, mgr. environ., safety and health, 1986—. Contbr. articles to profl. jours. Mem. presenting team Marriage Encounter, 1980—; preacher, lay reader, lay Eucharistic minister Episc. Ch., Idaho, 1984—; singer Idaho Falls Opera Theater, 1983-85, St. John's, Idaho Falls, 1983—, St. Mark's, Idaho Falls, 1985—; mem., historian Mayors Com. for Employment Handicapped and Older Worker, Idaho Falls, 1983-86; campaigner United Way, Idaho Falls, 1985-86, group leader, 1986-87; del. Dem. Conv., Boise, Idaho, 1976. NSF fellow, 1963, NDEA fellow, 1963-65; Nat. Assn. Geology Tchrs. scholar, 1980. Mem. Assn. Engring. Geologist, Am. Nuclear Soc. (mem. environ. affairs subcom. Idaho chpt. 1986—), Nat. Assn. Female Execs., Idaho Assn. Profl. Engrs. Club: Snow Dragon Judo (Idaho Falls). Lodge: Toastmasters (pres. local chpt.). Home: 582 Cambridge Dr Idaho Falls ID 83401 Office: Westinghouse Idaho Nuclear Co Inc Box 4000 WCB E2 MS-3412 Idaho Falls ID 83403-3412

COOPER, VICTORIA ANN, magazine editor; b. Boston, Dec. 27, 1945; d. Thaddeus Walter and Alice Isabel (Kittredge) Kowilcik; m. Kent Leland Groninger, Oct. 12, 1968 (div. Feb. 1980); children: Jennifer Louise, Heather Louise; m. David Lawrence Cooper, May 5, 1985. BA, Emmanuel Coll., 1967; student, Cornell U., 1968-69, U. Colo., 1980-82. Manuscript editor MIT, Cambridge, 1967-68; publs. editor Cornell U., Ithaca, N.Y., 1968-70; mng. editor Boulder (Colo.) Monthly, 1979; editor Sunday mag. Boulder Daily Camera, 1980-84, mem. writing staff, 1980-83; editor Empire mag. The Denver Post, 1985-86; editor Boulder County Bus. Report, 1987—; book editor Westview Press Co., Boulder, 1976-78. Office: Boulder County Bus Report 1830 N 55th St Boulder CO 80301

COOPERPERSON, ELLEN DONNA, university administrator, consultant; b. Bklyn., Mar. 28, 1946; d. Samuel and Eve (Satz) Bloom; m. Norman Cooperman, Nov. 24, 1965 (div. 1972); 1 child, Brian Cooperman. M.A. in Human Resource Devel. and Tng., Goddard grad. program Vt. Coll. at Norwich U., Montpelier, 1983. Prin. Beachbrook Sch., bklyn., 1970-72; br. mgr. Hershey Foods Corp., Farmingdale, N.Y., 1972-75; ops. mgr. Multi-Media Films, Babylon, N.Y., 1975-78; exec. dir. women's ednl. and counseling ctr. SUNY-Farmingdale, 1978—; cons. Human Resource Devel. and Tng. Ctr., Farmingdale, 1978—; mem. adj. faculty Cornell U., Farmingdale, N.Y., 1979-85; coordinator women's project C. W. Post Coll., Brentwood, N.Y., 1979-85. Producer/dir. films: Women Now, 1974; Yes Baby, She's My Sir, 1978. Del. NOW, N.Y., 1975-77, White House Commn., N.Y., 1978. Recipient Human Services award Office County Exec., Suffolk County, N.Y., 1983, proclamation Office County Exec., Nassau County, N.Y., 1984. Mem. L.I. Ctr. for Bus. and Profl. Women (bd. dirs. 1980-81), Am. Soc. Tng. and Devel., Internat. TV Assn. Office: SUNY Women's Ednl and Counseling Ctr Farmingdale NY 11735

COOPERSMITH, BONNIE SUE, psychotherapist, program coordinator; b. Bklyn., Dec. 8, 1958; d. Herbert Joel and Arlene (Rifkin) C. AAS, Farmingdale U., 1977; BA, Albany (N.Y.) State U., 1979; EdM, Springfield (Mass.) Coll., 1980, postgrad., 1981. Crisis worker Emergency Services, Springfield, Mass., 1979-83; crisis therapist Westfield (Mass.) Crisis Program, 1983, program coordinator, 1983—; crisis worker Franklin/Hampshire Community Mental Health Ctr., Northampton, Mass., 1986—. Grantee Springfield Coll., 1980. Jewish. Office: Crisis Program 55 Broad St Westfield MA 01085

COOPERSMITH, SHIRLEY ANN, insurance company executive; b. Kansas City, Mo., Feb. 4, 1944; d. Louis and Yetta (Swartz) Agronin, m. Henry Joseph Coopersmith, Sept. 3, 1970 (div. 1978); children: Marc Daniel, Stacy Janine. AAS, Kans. City Jr. Coll., 1963; student, U. Alberta, 1964. Project mgr. Optigan Inc., Compton, Calif., 1971-72; cons. Tustin, Calif., 1972-78; sr. mktg. analyst Basic Four Corp., Irvine, Calif., 1978-80; regional mgr. Data Solutions Inc., Santa Ana, Calif., 1980-82; info. resources mgr. Pacific Nat. Ins. Co., Fullerton, Calif., 1982—. Pres. Tustin Village II, 1984-85, bd. dirs. 1985-86. Mem. Data Processing Mgmt. Assn. (legis. com. 1985-86), Calif. State Homeopathic Med. Soc., Internat. Found. Homeopathy. Libertarian. Office: Pacific Nat Ins Co 15661 Redhill Ave Tustin CA 92680

COOVERT, BARBARA JUNE, book publishing executive; b. Muncie, Ind., July 10, 1934; d. John Thomas and Helen Sylvia (DeVerse) C. BA in Bus., Ball State U., 1959. Graphic artist Ball Corp., Muncie, 1953-59; gen. mgr. Sparks Printing and Mailing Co., Chgo., 1959-61; v.p., gen. mgr. Bernard Black Printers, Chgo., 1961-64; v.p. advt. Scott, Foresman & Co., Glenview, Ill., 1964—. Treas. Mary Thompson Hosp. Corp., 1982—, pres., 1987—; bd. dirs. Chgo. Health Resources, 1984—, Near West Med. Assn., 1984—. Mem. Am. Mgmt. Assn., Chgo. Direct Mktg. Assn., North Shore Profl. Women. Office: Scott Foresman and Co 1900 E Lake St Glenview IL 60025

COPE, ALICE NELSON, educator; b. Jacksonville, Fla., Apr. 25, 1941; d. Robert Clifton and Olivia (Brobston) Nelson; m. Phillip Scott Cope, June 16, 1979. BA, Jacksonville U., 1964, MA in Teaching, 1968, postgrad. in computer edn., 1987—. Cert. elem. tchr., Fla. Tchr. Clay County Schs., Orange Park, Fla., 1968—, specialist computers, 1986—; instr. computers Clay County Community Edn., Orange Park, 1984—; cons. Tchr. Edn. Ctr., Jacksonville, 1984—; curriculum devel., coordinator, instr. Clay County Summer Inst., 1984—; developer, instr. computer applications course for blind Clay County Schs., Orange Park, 1985—, developer computer curriculum, instr. Staff Devel.; computer coordinator Orange Park Elem. Sch.; adj. prof. U. North Fla., Jacksonville, 1985—, Jacksonville U., 1988. Named finalist Tchr. of Yr., Clay County, 1987, runner-up Fla. Instructional Computing Tchr. of Yr., Fla. Assn. Ednl. Data Systems, 1987, Fla. Instructional Computing Tchr. of Yr., Fla. Assn. Ednl. Data Systems and Fla. Assn. for Computers in Edn., 1988; received commendation City Council Jacksonville, 1988. Mem. NEA, Fla. Teaching Profession, Fla. Assn. Computers in Edn. (Clay County pres. 1987, Dist. pres. 1988), Clay County Edn. Assn. Democrat. Episcopalian. Home: 4600 Julington Creek Rd Jacksonville FL 32223 Office: Clay County Schs 1401 Plainfield Ave Orange Park FL 32073

COPE, DEBORAH MCMANUS, administrative secretary; b. Port Sulphur, La., Dec. 25, 1958; d. Billy Ray and Marian Trevillion (Folendore) McManus; m. Charles L. Cope Jr., Sept. 1, 1979. BS, Ga. State U., Atlanta, 1984. Sr. sec. office ednl. media Ga. State U., Atlanta, 1981-83, adminstrv. sec. office ednl. media, 1983—. Soprano Smyrna (Ga.) Community Chorus, 1978-79; mem. Fernbank Sci. Ctr., Atlanta, 1985-86, Greenpeace, Atlanta, 1987—; tutor First Bapt. Ch. Tutorial Program, Decatur, Ga., 1986, 87. Democrat. Baptist.

COPE, ESTHER SIDNEY, history educator; b. West Chester, Pa., Sept. 10, 1942; d. Robert Wellington and Jane Davis (Stanton) C. BA, Wilson Coll., 1964; MA, U. Wis.-Madison, 1965; PhD, Bryn Mawr Coll., 1969. Instr. history Ursinus Coll., Collegeville, Pa., 1968-70, asst. prof. history, 1970-75; asst. prof. history U. Nebr., Lincoln, 1975-76, assoc. prof., 1976-81, prof., 1981—, chmn. dept. history, 1982—; bd. dirs. Yale Ctr. Parliamentary History, New Haven, 1981—. Mem. Nebr. Com. for Humanities, 1987. Author: Life of a Public Man, 1981, Politics Without Parliments, 1986; Editor: Procs. of Short Parliament 1640, 1977. Fellow Royal Hist. Soc.; mem. Am. Hist. Assn., Conf. Brit. Studies (rec. sec. 1975-81), Internat. Commn. on Hist. Rep. and Parliamentary Instns., Berkshire Conf. Women Historians, Phi Beta Kappa. Mem. Soc. of Friends. Office: U Nebr Dept History Lincoln NE 68588

COPE, NANCY ELIZABETH, television news producer; b. Woodbury, N.J., Dec. 4, 1952; d. William Fox and Kathryn Florence (Pime) C. B.S., U. Tenn., 1974. News reporter, editor Houston News Service, 1975-78; news assignment editor Sta. KHOU-TV, Houston, 1978-79; news producer Sta. KTRK-TV, Houston, 1979-86, exec. producer, 1987—. Mem. Soc. Profl. Journalists, NOW, Internat. Platform Assn., Radio-TV News Dirs. Assn. Office: KTRK-TV 3310 Bissonnet St Houston TX 77005

COPELAND, CAROLYN ABIGAIL, university dean; b. White Plains, N.Y., May 5, 1931; d. Robert Erford and Mary Terwilliger; B.A. (CEW scholar), U. Mich., 1973, M.A. (Rackham Grad. Student scholar), 1979; m. William E. Copeland, Aug. 16, 1964; children—Rob Cameron, Diana Elizabeth Bosworth. With dean's office Coll. Lit., Sci. and Arts, U. Mich., Ann Arbor, 1967—, asst. dean, 1980-84, assoc. dean, 1984—. Mem. Mortar Bd., Phi Beta Kappa (v.p. Alpha chpt. 1984-86, pres. Alpha chpt. 1986-88). Author: Tankas from the Koelz Collection, 1980; Walter Norman Koelz, A Biography, in progress. Research in Buddhist art history. Home: 520 Darwin Rd Pinckney MI 48169 Office: U Mich Ann Arbor MI 48109

COPELAND, ELAINE WILSON, data processing analyst; b. Ft. Worth, Sept. 16, 1944; d. Phillip Loren and Artie Inez (Neel) Wilson; m. Robert J. Copeland, Aug. 17, 1963 (div. 1983); children: Karen Kay Prince, Donna Lynn Copeland-Nay. BS in Bus., Info. Systems, U. Colo., Denver, 1984. Sec. Hartford Life Ins. Co., Dallas, 1964-66, St. George's Episcopal Ch., Dallas, 1976-77; technician data processing Manville Corp., Denver, 1980-81, assoc. analyst, 1984-85, analyst data processing, 1985—; fin. technician 1st Interstate Bank, Denver, 1982-84. Chmn. precinct Rep. Party Tex., Dallas, 1970-76. Recipient Silver Spark award Camp Fire Girls, Denver, 1982. Mem. Soc. Info. Mgmt., Data Processing Mgmt. Assn. (v.p. publicity 1986—, asst. editor newsletter 1985-86), Jaycee-Ettes (hon. lifetime mem.), Grand Prarie (Tex.) C. of C. (Newcomer Yr. 1971). Episcopalian. Club: St. Paul's Ultreya (Lakewood, Colo.) (lay leader 1987-88). Office: Manville Corp PO Box 5108 Denver CO 80217-5108

COPELAND, KAREN LEE, television executive; b. Chgo., Jan. 14, 1946; d. Hymen and Blanche (Feder) Cohen; m. Donald Copeland, May 30, 1974 (div. 1984). Student, Drake U., 1964-66; B.F.A., Columbia Coll., Chgo., 1968. Mem. prodn. staff WLS-TV, Chgo., 1967-69, exec. producer, 1969; freelance producer, dir., Los Angeles, 1969-73, programs include: The David Frost Show, The Della Reese Show, The Bob Hope Show, Christmas Around the World, 1970-71; staff producer WMAQ-TV, NBC, Chgo., 1973-81, mgr. programming, 1981; programs include: NBC Salutes Chic Chicago, Small World; dir. programming WNBC-TV, NBC, N.Y.C., 1981—, exec. producer spls.: Ask the Governors, Atomic High School, The Foxfire Glow, Town Meetings, Blacks: Present and Accounted For, Christmas in Rockefeller Center. Recipient Emmy award as producer Ask the Governors; Chgo. Emmy award for Best Spl. Event Program, NBC Salutes Chic Chicago, Strictly Business. Mem. Directors Guild Am., Nat. Assn. TV Programming Execs., Internat. Radio and TV Soc., Nat. Acad. TV Arts and Scis. (bd. govs. N.Y. chpt.). Address: Program Dir Sta WNBC-TV 30 Rockefeller Plaza New York NY 10020

COPELAND, LULLAWEEN, small business owner; b. Wilder, Tenn., Jan. 27, 1931; d. D. Cravens Jr. and Bessie Ellen (Reneau) Cravens; m. Roscoe C. Copeland, Mar. 14, 1953.; children: David L. Dorothy Sue, Michael Stephen. Grad high sch., Livingston, Tenn. Typist Wright-Patterson AFB, Fairborn, Ohio, 1952-56; prin. Lullaween's Hairdressers, Dayton, Ohio, 1961-69; instr. cosmetology Continental Beauty Sch., Dayton, 1969-72; prin., dir. Continental Beauty Sch., Piqua, Ohio, 1972—. Contbr. articles to profl. jours. Mem. Rep. Presdl. Task Force, Washington, 1981-87. Mem. Nat. Assn. Cosmetology Arts and Scis., Nat. Assn. Cosmetology Schs. Mem. Ch. Christ. Home: 4450 Needmore Rd Dayton OH 45424

COPELAND, MARY ELLEN, nurse; b. Atlanta, Sept. 14, 1957; d. Harold William and Mary Liz (Jones) C. AA, Freed-Hardeman Coll., 1978; BS in Nursing, Harding U., 1981. RN. Staff RN St. Vincent Infirmary, Little Rock, 1982, Piedmont Hosp., Atlanta, 1982-87, Hoag Meml. Hosp., Newport Beach, Calif., 1987—; wellness coordinator Pepperdine U., Malibu, Calif., 1987—. Mem. Am. Heart Assn., Nat. Assn. Female Execs., Nat. Wellness Assn., Sigma Theta Tau. Mem. Ch. Christ. Home: 165 Silver Leaf Dr Fayetteville GA 30214

COPELAND, MAXINE, system analyst, consultant; b. Jackson, Tenn., Aug. 5, 1956; d. Emma Louise (Randolph) Copeland. BBA in Fin., U. Wis., Milw., 1979. Sr. programmer analyst So. Co. Services, Atlanta, 1980-85; software systems cons. Am. Software, Inc., Atlanta, 1985-86; systems analyst RFC Intemediaries, Inc., Atlanta, 1986—; v.p. fin. Another Wear, Atlanta, 1986-88; cons. CAP Gemini Am., Atlanta, 1988—. Mem. Black Data Processing Assocs. (treas. 1987-88). Home: 1192 Winston Dr Atlanta GA 30032

COPELAND, SHIRLEY ANN HAMANN, travel counselor; b. Cleve., Mar. 27, 1929; d. John Henry and Gertrude Augusta (Southam) Hamann; m. George Meredith Copeland, Sept. 24, 1955; children: Constance S., Carol E., Patricia Green. BA, Flora Stone Mather, Case Western Res. U., 1951. Cert. travel counselor. Account exec. Herald Advt., Cleve., 1953-58; v.p. Jensen Travel Service, Shaker Heights, Ohio, 1975-77; pres. Jensen Travel Service, Shaker Heights, 1977—; mem. travel agt. adv. bd. Pan Am. Airways, Midwest region, 1984—. Pres. Chagrin Valley Women's Republican Club, Cuyahoga County, 1964-66; chmn. Sch. Levy Com., Chagrin Falls, 1972, 73; deacon Valley Presbyterian Ch., 1985-87; capt. Chagrin Recreation Ctr. women's tennis team, 1974-76. Mem. Mortar Bd., Phi Beta Kappa. Clubs: Cleve. Yacht (Rocky River, Ohio); Chagrin Valley Athletic, Chagrin Valley Jaycee Wives (pres. 1961). Home: 368 Bentleyville Rd Chagrin Falls OH 44022 Office: Jensen Travel Service Inc 20600 Chagrin Blvd Shaker Heights OH 44122

COPENHAVER, IDA LOUISE, chemical information company executive; b. Johnson City, Tenn., Oct. 19, 1945; d. Lawrence L. and Ida L. (Wolff) C.; m. James L. Ginter. BA in Chemistry, Agnes Scott Coll., 1967; MS in Chemistry, Emory U., 1969. Asst. editor Chem. Abstracts Services, Columbus, Ohio, 1969-72, assoc. editor, 1973-76, sr. assoc. editor, 1976-78, mgr. processing coordination, 1978, mgr. product specifications and services, 1978-86, mgr. phys.-inorganic-analytical chemistry, 1986—. Com. chair, bd. dirs. Jr. League, Columbus, 1969—, CALL, Columbus, 1980-83; pres., com. chair, bd. dirs. CALLVAC Services, Columbus, 1984—; sec., bd. dirs Columbus Area Leadership Program, 1977-83; steering com. chair Skills Bank, Columbus, 1982-86; bd. dirs. Columbus Literary Council, 1987—; trustee Conostoga, Columbus Literacy Council; bd. of zoning and planning Upper Arlington, 1988—. Recipient Pres. award Jr. League Columbus, 1985, CALP Columbus Area Leadership award, 1985, Mayor's award City of Columbus, 1988; named one of 10 Outstanding Young Citizens, 1977. Mem. Am. Chem. Soc., Am. Soc. Info. Sci. Clubs: Columbus Met., YWCA. Home: 2448 Edington Rd Columbus OH 43221 Office: Chem Abstracts Service PO Box 3012 Columbus OH 43210

COPESS, JOYCE TRAVIS, association executive; b. Lamar, Colo., Jan. 29, 1947; d. Morris Eugene and Mildred Marie (Neary) T.; m. Richard Dee Copess, Sept. 19, 1970. B.A., Colo. State U., 1969; postgrad. U. No. Colo., 1970-73, Ill. State U., 1976-81. Staff asst. in mgmt. communications State Farm Ins., Bloomington, Ill., 1969-81; staff v.p. edn. and communications Inst. Real Estate Mgmt. of Nat. Assn. Realtors, Chgo., 1981—; cons., lectr. in field. Mem. Pub. Relations Soc. Am., Internat. Bus. Communications, Women in Communications. Office: Inst Real Estate Mgmt 430 N Michigan Ave Chicago IL 60611

COPLAND, ELIZABETH ANN, radiologist, nuclear medicine; b. Norman, Okla., Oct. 29, 1951; d. George Victor and Martha Rosalee (Shock) C. BS, Okla. State U., 1973; MD, U. Okla., 1977. Diplomate Am. Bd. Radiology, Am. Bd. Nuclear Medicine. Intern U. Okla. Health Scis. Ctr., Oklahoma City, 1977-78; resident in radiology Bapt. Med. Ctr., Oklahoma City, 1978-81; radiologist Okmulgee (Okla.) Meml. Hosp., 1981-83, Wichita Gen. Hosp., Wichita Falls, Tex., 1983-85; fellow in computed typography and ultrasound William Beaumont Hosp., Royal Oak, Mich., 1985-86, resident in nuclear medicine, 1986-87; dir. nuclear medicine, radiologist St. Joseph Mercy Hosp., Ann Arbor, Mich., 1987—. Mem. Soc. Nuclear Medicine, Radiol. Soc. N.Am., Am. Coll. Radiology, Am. Inst. Ultrasound in Medicine, Am. Assn. Women Radiologists. Presbyterian. Home: 5159 Christine Dr Ann Arbor MI 48103 Office: St Joseph Mercy Hosp 5301 E Huron River Dr Ann Arbor MI 48106

COPLEY, HELEN KINNEY, newspaper publisher; b. Cedar Rapids, Iowa, Nov. 28, 1922; d. Fred Everett and Margaret (Casey) Kinney; m. James S. Copley, Aug. 16, 1965 (dec.); 1 child, David Casey. Attended, Hunter Coll., N.Y.C., 1945. Assoc. The Copley Press, Inc., 1952—, chmn. exec. com., chmn. corp., dir., 1973—, chief exec. officer, sr. mgmt. bd., 1974—; chmn. bd. Copley News Service, San Diego, 1973—; chmn. editorial bd. Union-Tribune Pub. Co., 1976—; pub. The San Diego Union and The Tribune, 1973—. Chmn. bd., trustee James S. Copley Found., 1973—; mem. Friends of Internat. Center, La Jolla, La Jolla Mus. Contemporary Art, La Jolla Town Council, Inc.; life patroness Makua Aux.; life mem., San Diego Hall of Sci.; mem. San Diego Soc. Natural History Scripps Meml. Hosp. Aux., Life mem. Star of India Aux., Zool. Soc. San Diego; mem. YWCA; hon. chmn., bd. dirs. Washington Crossing Found.; trustee, mem. audit and compensation com. Howard Hughes Med. Inst. Mem. Inter Am. Press Assn., Am. Newspapers Pubs. Assn., Calif. Press Assn., Am. Soc. Newspaper Editors, Am. Press Inst., Calif. Newspaper Pubs. Assn., Greater Los Angeles, Nat., San Diego, San Francisco press clubs, Sigma Delta Chi. Republican. Roman Catholic. Clubs: Aurora (Ill.) Country; Army and Navy (D.C.); San Diego Yacht, Univ., La Jolla Beach and Tennis, La Jolla Country, Kona Kai (San Diego). Office: PO Box 1530 La Jolla CA 92038

COPLEY, SHARRON CAULK, educator; b. Columbia, Tenn., Oct. 2, 1947; d. Tom English and Beulah (Goodin) Caulk; children—Christopher, George English, Steffenee. BA George Peabody Coll. Tchrs., 1970; MS Vanderbilt U., 1980; EdS Mid. Tenn. State U., 1986. Tchr., Ft. Campbell Jr. High Sch., Ky., 1970-71, Whitthorne Jr. High Sch., Columbia, Tenn., 1977-86, Spring Hill (Tenn.) High Sch., 1986—; chmn. edn. Homecoming '86 Maury County Schs., Columbia, 1984-86. Mem. Maury County Edn. Assn. (pres. 1983-84), Tenn. Edn. Assn., NEA, AAUW (pres. Tenn. div. 1983-85), Nat. Council Tchrs. English, Phi Delta Kappa. Mem. Ch. of Christ. Home: 1090 Rolling Fields Columbia TN 38401 Office: Spring Hill High Sch School St Spring Hill TN 37174

COPLEY, SUSAN M., painter, sculptor; b. Bklyn., Mar. 31, 1939; d. George L. and Amy Rebecca (Meirowitz) Schwartz; m. Stanford S. Copley, Sept. 27, 1958; children: Jocelyn, Melissa, Jason. Student, Pratt Inst., 1956-58, Basel, Switzerland, 1958-60; BFA, SUNY, Buffalo, 1974, MFA, 1978. bd. dirs. Arts Council, Buffalo, 1987—; guest lectr. Western N.Y. Inst., June, 1987; TV interview Artscene, Buffalo, 1985. Solo exhbns. include Carriage House Gallery, Buffalo, 1978, Chautauqua (N.Y.)Inst. Am. Art, 1980, Hallwalls, Buffalo, 1982, Art Inst. Boston, 1983, Malton Gallery, Cin., 1983, Capen Gallery SUNY Buffalo, 1984, Roberson Ctr. Arts & Scis., Binghamton, N.Y., 1984, Barbara Gillman Gallery, Miami, Fla., 1986, Rubiner Gallery, West Bloomfield, Mich., 1986; group exhbns. include 44th Cooperstown (N.Y.) Nat. Exhbn., 1979, Columbia (Mo.) Coll., 1980, Albright-Knox Art Gallery Buffalo, 1980, 81, 82, 84, 85, Western N.Y. Exhbn., 1980 (3d prize), 82, 84, More-Rubin Gallery, Buffalo, 1981, Breame Gallery, Mpls., 1981, George Frederic Gallery, Rochester, N.Y., 1981, Zaner Gallery, Rochester, 1982, 3 Rivers Nat., Pitts., 1982, Burchfield Art Ctr., Buffalo, 1982, 88 (seven-artist collage), Barbara Gillman Gallery, 1983, Theodore Roosevelt Nat. Hist. Site, Buffalo, 1983, Albany Inst. History & Art, 1984, Jack Gallery, N.Y.C., 1984, Buscaglia-Castellani Art Gallery, Niagara Falls, N.Y., 1985, Rubiner Gallery, 1985, 86, Butler Inst. Am. Art, Ohio, 1987, New Visions Gallery, Ithaca, N.Y., 1988, Barbara Schuller Gallery, Buffalo, 1988, Rubiner Gallery, West Bloomfield, Mich., 1988; included in permanent collections Albright-Knox Gallery, Roberson Ctr. Arts & Scis., Buscaglia-Castellani Gallery, numerous corps., hotels, others; commns. include Empire Bank, Goldome Bank. Recipient Bronze award, 1979, Goldome Bank award, 1983 Buffalo Soc. Artists; recipient Herdman award SUNY, Buffalo Soc. Artists Exhbn., 1980. Mem. Buffalo Soc. Artists (bd. dirs. 1985-88, group exhibitor 1979, 80, 83), The Women's Group. Home: 117 Ruskin Rd Buffalo NY 14226 Studio: 296 Bryant St Buffalo NY 14222

COPP, LAUREL ARCHER, nursing educator, administrator; b. Sioux Falls, S.D., 1931; m. John Dixon Copp. BS in Nursing Edn., Dakota Wesleyan U., 1956; M.Nursing, U. Pitts., 1960, Ph.D., 1967; P.H.S.M. cert., Harvard U. Bus. Sch., 1973. Assoc. prof. nursing Pa. State U., 1966-72, acting head nursing dept., 1971-72; chief nursing research VA Central Office, Washington, 1972-75; prof., dean Sch. of Nursing U. N.C., Chapel Hill, 1975—; vis. prof. Georgetown U., Washington, 1974-75, U. Tex.-Arlington, summer 1982; lectr. in field. Editor: The Patient Experiencing Pain, 2d edit., 1981, Recent Advances in Nursing: Care of the Aging, 1981, Recent Advanced in Nursing: Perspectives in Pain, 1985; editorial bd. Nursing and Health Care; overseas adviser Jour. Advanced Nursing; editor Jour. Profl. Nursing, 1988—; contbr. articles to profl. jours., chpts. to books. Recipient commendation VA, 1975, Disting. Alumni award Dakota Wesleyan U., 1982, U. Pitts., 1982. Fellow Am. Acad. Nursing; mem. Am. Assn. Colls. Nursing, Am. Nurses Assn., Nat. League for Nursing, Va./Carolinas Doctoral Consortium, N.C. Council Baccalaureate Deans. Office: U NC Chapel Hill Sch Nursing CB# 7460 107 Carrington Hall Chapel Hill NC 27599

COPPEDGE, HELEN LUCE, retail executive; b. Macon, Ga., Aug. 7, 1947; d. George Edgar and Willouise (Butts) Luce; m. Edward Paul Coppedge (div. Mar. 1980); 1 child, George Laurence. BA, Fla. State U., 1969. With Rich's Design Studio, Atlanta, 1970-72; pres. Peachland Consortium, Inc., Ft. Valley, Ga., 1986—, Camellia & Main, Inc., 1987—; personal investor, 1972—; bd. dirs. Blue Bird Body Co., Ft. Valley, Cardinal Investment Co., Ft. Valley. Dir. South Ga. United Meth. Home Aging, 1986—, Peach County Hosp. Authority, Ft. Valley, 1986—, also dir. capital campaign com., 1985—; bd. dirs. United Meth. Gen. Bd. Global Ministries, 1984-88, Forum for Scriptural Christianity, Wilmore, Ky., 1972—. Recipient Athena award Peach County C. of C., Ft. Valley, 1986, Resolution of Commendation, Ga. Ho. of Reps., Atlanta, 1987. Methodist. Home and Office: 305 Knoxville St Fort Valley GA 31030

COPPOLECHIA, YILLION CASTRO, educational facility administrator. naturalized; AA, Miami-Dade Community Coll., 1968; BA in French and German Lang. and Lit., cum laude, U. Miami, Coral Gables, Fla., 1971, MA in French Lang. and Lit., 1973, EdD in Adminstn. Higher Edn., 1984; postgrad., Fla. Atlantic U., U. Miami, Barry U., 1976-79. Adj. instr. Wolfson Campus, Miami-Dade Community Coll., 1972-75, coordinator bilingual program, 1975-78, chmn. bilingual dept., 1978-79, founding assoc. dean Div. Bilingual Studies, now Interam. Ctr., 1979-84, acting dean adminstrn., 1984-85, dean for community and bus. relations, North Campus, 1985-86, exec. dir. Miami Book Fair Internat., Wolfson Campus, 1986—; evaluator various colls. for Higher Edn. Commn. Middle States Assn. Colls. and Schs., 1980—; testifier on bilingual edn. State of Fla. Postsecondary Edn. Planning Commn, 1984; mem. planning coms., coordinator symposium various ednl. confs.; keynote speaker seminar Hispanic Orgn. Pvt. Entrepreneurs (Project HOPE), April, 1987; participant Leadership Miami, 1986. Mem. dropout prevention adv. council, participant bus. and industry subcom. Dade County Pub. Schs., 1984-86; appointed Hialeah Community Leaders Colloquia, 1985—; vol., mem. elderly services rev. panel, United Way Dade County, 1986-87. Named one of top ten Women of Yr. for 1978 Cuban Women's Club, Inc., 1978, one of Outstanding Miami-Dade Community Coll. adminstrs. U. Tex. Austin Community Coll. Leadership Program, 1985; recipient Cert. of Honor Student Congress Miami-Dade Community Coll., 1975-76, 78-79, Civic Leadership Cert. Miami Lions Club, 1978, Cert. of Honor Women's Com. of 100, 1978, commendation awards for ednl contbns. Mayor Met. Dade County, 1977, Mayor of City of Miami, 1977, plaque for dedicated service Miami-Dade Community Coll., 1985; grantee Fund for Improvement Postsecondary Edn., 1984-85. Mem. Am. Council for the Arts, Latin Bus. and Profl. Women's Club (bd. dirs., bus. sec. 1987-88), Coalition of Hispanic Am. Women (bd. dirs., mem. various coms 1987-88, plaque award 1987), Fla. Assn. Community Colls., Nat. Council Instructional Adminstrs., Nat. Assn. Bilingual Edn., Fla. Coalition Hispanic Educators. Office: Miami-Dade Community Coll 11011 SW 104th St Miami FL 33176

COPPS, SHEILA MAUREEN, member of parliament; b. Hamilton, Ont., Can., Nov. 27, 1952; d. Victor Kennedy and Geraldine (Guthro) C.; m. Richard Dennis Marrero, July 6, 1985; 1 child, Danelle Lauran Copps Marrero. BA in French, English with hons., U. Western Ont., London, 1970-74; postgrad., Université de Rouen, France, 1972-73, McMaster U., Hamilton, 1976-77. Reporter Ottawa Citizen, 1974-76, Hamilton Spectator, 1977; asst. Liberal Leader Stuart Smith, Hamilton, 1977-81; M.L.A. Liberal Party, Toronto, 1981-84; member of parliament Liberal Party, Ottawa, 1984—. Author: Nobody's Baby, 1986. Roman Catholic. Home: 144 Sherman South, Hamilton, ON Canada L8M 2P7 Office: House of Commons, Room 440C, Ottawa, ON Canada L8M 2P7

COQUILLA, BEATRUZ HORDISTA, dermatologist, army officer; b. Angequera, Bohol, The Philippines, May 9, 1948; came to U.S., 1955; d. Agapito Morgia and Alfonsa (Hordista) C. BS, U. Santo Tomas, Manila, 1970, MD, 1974. Diplomate Am. Bd. Dermatology. Commd. maj. U.S. Army, 1979; intern Fitzsimons Army Med. Ctr., Aurora, Colo., 1979-80; gen. med. officer 125th Med. Detachment, Korea, 1980-81; gen. med. officer, phys. asst. preceptor, brigade surgeon Evans Army Hosp., Ft. Carson, Colo., 1981-82; resident in dermatology Brooke Army Med. Ctr., Ft. Sam Houston, Tex., 1982-85; chief dermatology Womack Army Community Hosp., Fayetteville, N.C., 1985-87, Gen. Leonard Wood Hosp., Ft. Leonard Wood, Mo., 1988; assigned to Acad. Health Scis. Advanced Officers Course, Ft. Sam Houston, 1987-88, U.S. Army-Baylor Health Adminstrn. Program, San Antonio, 1988—. Contbr. articles to med. jours. Fellow Am. Acad. Dermatology; mem. AMA, Assn. Mil. Dermatologists, Fayetteville Bus. and Profl. Women. Roman Catholic. Home: 8715 Carrington San Antonio TX 98239

CORAH, DEBORAH JEAN, respiratory therapist; b. Los Angeles, May 27, 1960; d. Ronald Bruce and Dorothy Jean (Meier) Dahlstrom; m. Paul Frank Corah, June 26, 1982. Student, Oreg. State U., 1978-81; Assocs. of Respiratory Therapy, Mt. Hood Community Coll., 1986. Registered Respiratory Therapist, Oreg. Respiratory therapy asst. St. Vincent Med. Ctr., Portland, Oreg., 1981-83, respiratory therapy technician, 1983-86, cert. respiratory therapy technician, 1986-88; registered respiratory therapist St. Vincent Med. Ctr., Portland, 1988—; cert. respiratory therapy technician Portland Adventist Med. Ctr., Portland, 1986-88; respiratory therapy clin. instr. Mt. Hood Community Coll., Portland, 1987—. Mem. Am. Assn. Respiratory Care, Oreg. Edn. Assn. Republican. Roman Catholic.

CORAY, STEPHANIE MARY, nurse, career development officer; b. Crosby, Eng., May 17, 1938; d. Harold Joseph and Joan Hilda (Beer) McCann; m. Stephen A. Coray, (div. 1976); 1 child, Patrick Kael. RN, Queen of Angels Sch. of Nursing, 1959; BA, Calif. State U., Northridge, 1966; MBA, Pepperdine U., 1973. RN, Calif. Nurse pvt. physician, Oxnard, Calif., 1959-63, Oxnard Elem. Sch. Dist., 1963-71; employee devel. specialist Pacific Missile Test Ctr., Point Mugu, Calif., 1973-82, head career devel. div., 1982—; gen. ptnr. Achievement Inst. for Women, Oxnard, 1976-79; exec. chair Ventura County Combined Fed. Campaign, Point Mugu, 1985-87. Named Outstanding Woman of Yr., Bus. and Profl. Womens Club, 1977; recipient Chairperson's and Leadership awards Combined Fed. Campaign, 1985, 86. Mem. Am. Soc. Tng. and Devel., Am. Mgmt. Assn., Internat. Personnel Mgmt. Assn.

CORAZZINI, TERESA ANN, business consultant; b. Scranton, Pa., Oct. 22, 1962; d. Edmund Louis and Ketherine Margaret (DeStefano) C. BS in Pub. Adminstrn., U. Scranton, 1984, postgrad., 1984—. Mgr. Sylvia's Continental Cuisine, Inc., Scranton, 1984-87; bus. cons. Small Bus. Devel. Ctr. U. Scranton (Pa.), 1988—. Mem. Nat. Assn. Female Execs., Pi Gamma Mu, Alpha Mu Gamma, Pi Sigma Alpha. Democrat. Roman Catholic. Home: 1606 Sanderson Ave Scranton PA 18509

CORBETT, BARBARA LOUISE, advertising agency executive; b. Sioux City, Iowa, May 6, 1947; d. Bayliss and Shirley Louise (Wiese) Corbett; m. Henry F. Terbrueggen, Nov. 22, 1976. B.A. in Polit. Sci., Antioch Coll., 1969. Cert. bus. communicator. Copywriter, J.L. Hudson Co., Detroit, 1969-72, Patten Co., Southfield, Mich., 1972-73; copywriter/producer Campbell Ewald, Detroit, 1973-75; free lance writer, 1975-76; pres. Corbett Advt., Inc., Rochester, Mich., 1977—; tchr. Barbizon Sch., Southfield, 1979; prof. advt. Oakland Community Coll., 1980-82; judge Detroit News Scholastic Writing Awards competition, Detroit, 1979-80, 11th ann. BPAA Pro-Comm. awards, 1985; lectr. in field. Recipient award for Ad of the Year, J.L. Hudson Co., 1971; Merit award Seklemian, 1971; Gold Award Creative Advt. Club of Detroit, 1974; others. Mem. Greater Rochester C. of C. (past dir.), Indsl. Marketers of Detroit (past pres.), Mich. Advt. Agcy. Council (past pres.), Midstates Agy. Network (past pres.), Adcraft. Republican. Unitarian. Home: 6175 Sheldon Rd Rochester Hills MI 48064 Office: Corbett Advt Inc 555 Barclay Circle Dr Suite 100 Rochester Hills MI 48063

CORBETT, RUTH ALLEEN, artist, writer; b. Northville, Mich., Jan. 24, 1912; d. Howard James and Rhoda Alice (Fuller) C.; m. Roy Brent, Feb. 23, 1958; children: Jana Loi Janczarek, Paton. Student, Cranbrook Acad., 1932, Meinzinger Found. Art Sch., 1935-36, Famous Writer's Sch., 1967-69. Illustrator Simons-Michelson Advt. Co., Detroit, 1935-37, Bass-Luckoff, Inc., Detroit, 1937-39, Detroit Times, 1939-40, Canfield Assocs., Detroit, 1947-53, Dow Chem Co., Midland, Mich., 1950-53, Creative Services, Detroit, 1953-56, Parke-Davis Pharm. Co., Detroit, 1954-56, H.J. Heinz Co., 1950, Mich. Bell Telephone Co., 1954-56, Detroit Edison Co., 1950-53, various automobile mfg. cos., 1947-53; advt. illustrator Universal Pictures Co., Universal City, Calif., 1956-74; tchr. art as pvt. tutor, also adult classes Pontiac (Mich.) High Sch., 1933-34; freelance artist and writer; exhibitor, lectr. on movie advt. art, writing books, 1979. One woman show Freeman Gallery, Montrose, Calif., 1964; group shows Art Instrn., Mpls., 1935-65; columnist, cartoonist Sun City (Calif.) Times; executed mural Pontiac C. of C., 1934; author, illustrator: Daddy Danced the Charleston, 1970, Dying for a Cigarette?, 1976 (Nonfiction Book award Nat. Writers Club 1976), Some Doctors Make Me Sick, 1980 (Book award 1980), Diary of a Hill Hugger, 1982 (Nat. Writers Club awards 1982), Some of My Best Friends Can Fly, 1983, Art as a Living, 1984, How to Be a Professional Line Artist, 1987, Film City, 1988; contbr. numerous articles on motion picture advt. to various mags. Recipient Grand prize, numerous 1st prizes Art Instrn., Mpls., 1935-64, 1st, 2d, 3d prizes San Fernando Valley Club, 1961-63, "Women Helping Women" award Soroptimusts, 1987. Mem. Soc. Illustrators, Nat. Writers Club, Sun City Creative Writer's Group, Arts and Crafts Guild, Pontiac Sketch Club (pres. 1932-33), San Fernando Valley Art Club, Canyon Lake Art Assn. (2 awards for water color). Republican. Mem. Methodist-Episcopalian Ch. Home: 25681 Sun City Blvd Sun City CA 92381

CORBIN, KAREN SUE, management consulting company executive; b. N.Y.C., Dec. 12, 1945; d. Arnold L. and Claire Cynthia (Rothenberg) C.; BS, NYU, 1967, MA, 1971. With Xerox Corp., 1973-86, mgr. office systems cons. program, Dallas, 1977-79, br. mgr., Chgo., 1979-81, mgr. dealer sales planning, Dallas, 1981-82, mgr. mktg. ops., 1982-83, nat. mgr. customer support and edn., 1983-84, nat. systems support mgr., 1985-86; pres. Advanced Resource Mgmt., Dallas, 1986—. Mem. Internat. Customer Service Assn., Am. Mgmt. Assn., Am. Soc. Tng. and Devel., Assn. Women Entrepreneurs Dallas, Phi Beta Kappa. Home and Office: 17659 Sun Meadow Dr Dallas TX 75252

CORBIN, KRESTINE MARGARET, author, fashion designer, columnist; b. Reno, Apr. 24, 1937; d. Lawrence Albert and Judie Ellen (Johnston) Dickinson; m. Lee D. Corbin, May 16, 1959 (div. 1982); children: Michelle Marie, Sheri Karin. BS, U. Calif., Davis, 1958. Asst. prof. Bauder Coll., Sacramento, 1974—; columnist Sacramento Bee, 1976-81; owner Creative Sewing Co., Sacramento, 1976—; pres., chief exec. officer Sierra Machinery Corp., Sparks, Nev., 1983—; nat. sales and promotion mgr. Westwood Retail Fabrics, N.Y.C., 1985—; bd. dirs. No. Internat. Bank, 1988—, F.S.C. Mgmt. Services Ltd., 1988—; cons. in field. Author: Suede Fabric Sewing Guide, 1973, Creative Sewing Book, 1978, (audio-visual) Fashions in the Making, 1974; producer: (nat. buyers show) Cream of the Crewn Collections, 1978—, Style is What You Make It!, 1978-83. Mem. Crocker Art Gallery Assn., 1960-78, Rep. Election Com., Sacramento, 1964, 68. Mem. Home Economists in Bus., Am. Home Econs. Assn., Internat. Fashion Group, Women's Fashion Fabrics Assn., Nat. Tool Builders Assn., Omicron Nu. Address: PO Box 435 Reno NV 89504 Office: Sierra Machinery Inc 1651 Glendale Rd Sparks NV 89431

CORBIN, RORI COOPER, therapeutic recreation specialist, educator, consultant; b. N.Y.C., July 30, 1951; d. Charles Kneeland and Rose Elizabeth (Maggio) Cooper; m. William Ogden Corbin Jr., Apr. 19, 1980; children: Drew Cooper, Laurel Foxworth. BA, SUNY, Purchase, 1973; MA, NYU, 1980. Cert. therapeutic recreation specialist. Sr. recreation therapist N.Y. State Letchworth, Thiells, 1975-86; cons. Corbin & Corbin Cons., Monroe, N.Y., 1986—; cons. behaviorist Optifast program Nyack (N.Y.) Hosp.; cons. behaviorist, researcher joint obesity study U. Pa. and Sandoz Pharms.; mem. guest faculty Keane Coll., N.J., 1981; instr., trainer N.Y. Office Mental Retardation/Developmental Disabilities, 1981-82; bd. dirs. optifast program Our Ladry of Mercy Med. Ctr., Bronx, N.Y. Writer, editor newsletter: The Fourth "r", 1983-85. NYU fellow, 1979-80; N.Y. State grantee, 1979-80. Mem. Nat. Recreation and Parks Assn., N.Y. State Recreation and Parks Soc., Nat. Assn. Female Execs., Internat. Platform Assn. Republican. Roman Catholic. Avocations: gardening, bicycling, reading, camping. Home and Office: 61 Pine Tree Rd Monroe NY 10950

CORCORAN, ANN M., radio show host; b. Honesdale, Pa., Sept. 9, 1939; d. Gladys Alene (Collins) C.; m. Stanley Mark Ericsson, May 15, 1971. Student public schs. Waymart, Pa. and N.Y. Revenue coordinator Am. Airlines, N.Y.C., 1963-67; supr. spl. sales, 1967-73, analyst budget and cost control, 1973-78; v.p. Americsson Enterprises, Hawley, Pa., Balt., 1979—; producer Balt. Women's News Mag., 1982-85, radio host, 1985—; mgmt. cons. Cellta Corp. Balt., 1984—; bd. dirs. Jencor Prodns., Baltimore, Md., 1986—. Chmn. Cable TV task force Balt. NOW, 1983—, treas., 1979-82; Md. rep. NOW, 1984-86, citywide v.p. 1986—. Md. Croquet Soc. (v.p. pub. realtions 1986—). Avocations: sailing, sewing, sketching, croquet. Office: Americsson Enterprises 116 W University Pky #110 Baltimore MD 21210

CORCORAN, KRISTINE DOROTHY, lawyer; b. Milw., Sept. 25, 1958; d. Ned W. Pack and Evelyn Dorothy Flach; m. James Webster Corcoran, May 28, 1983. B.A., Marquette U., 1979; J.D., Drake U., 1982. Bar: Iowa 1983, Nebr. 1983. Assoc., Robert E. Conley, P.C., Des Moines, Iowa, 1983, Harold J. Crawford & Assocs., Des Moines, 1983—. Mem. ABA, Nebr. Bar Assn., Iowa State Bar Assn., Polk County Bar Assn., Polk County Women's Attys., Phi Alpha Delta, Sigma Sigma Sigma, Pi Sigma Alpha, Phi Alpha Theta. Home: 536 43d St Apt 1 Des Moines IA 50312 Office: Harold J Crawford & Assocs 850 Insurance Exchange Bldg Des Moines IA 50309

CORCORAN, MARIAN, artificial intelligence researcher; b. N.Y.C., June 7, 1952; d. William Joseph and Anna Gertrude (Zurl) C. BA summa cum laude, L.I. Univ., 1974; MS in Computer Sci., Poly. U. N.Y., 1984, postgrad., 1984—. Tchr. The Strategakis Sch., Athens, Greece, 1976-79; computer researcher Cold Spring Harbor (N.Y.) Lab., 1982-84; acad. assoc. in artificial intelligence Poly. U. N.Y., Bklyn., 1986—; v.p., founder Artificial Intelligence Group at Poly., Farmingdale, N.Y., 1985—. Book reviewer Prentice-Hall, Inc., Englewood Cliffs, N.J., 1985—; contbr. articles to mags., profl. jours. Research grantee Unisys Corp., 1986, Ctr. for Advanced Tech. in Telecommunications, 1987—; named Outstanding Alumni L.I. Univ., 1983. Mem. IEEE, Am. Assn. for Artificial Intelligence, Assn. for Computing Machinery, Spc. Mgmt. Artificial Intelligence Resources and Tech. (assoc. fin. services 1987). Home: 919 Van Buren Ave Franklin Square NY 11010 Office: Polytechnic U Dept Computer Sci Rt 110 Farmingdale NY 11735

CORCORAN, MARY BARBARA, language educator; b. Pasadena, Calif., May 22, 1924; d. George Ernest Morrison and Ina Pearl (Thomas) Phippen; m. James Leonard Corcoran, Dec. 22, 1956; children: Ann Morrison, Elizabeth Phippen DedGroodt. BA, Wellesley Coll., 1946; MA, Radcliffe Coll., 1949; postgrad., U. Munich, 1949-50; PhD, Bryn Mawr Coll., 1958. Translator U.S. War Dept., Nuremberg, Fed. Republic of Germany, 1946-47; prof. German Vassar Coll., Poughkeepsie, N.Y., 1953—, 1977—; part-time instr. Wellesley (Mass.) Coll., 1947-48. Translator: The Romantic Fairy Tale, 1964. Mem. Am. Assn. Tchrs. German, AAUP, MLA. Mem. United Ch. of Christ. Home: 11 Overlook Rd Poughkeepsie NY 12603 Office: Vassar Coll German Dept Poughkeepsie NY 12601

CORCORAN, MAUREEN ELIZABETH, lawyer; b. Iowa City. B.A. cum laude, U. Iowa, 1966, M.A., 1967; J.D., Hastings Coll. of Law, 1979. Bar: Calif. 1979, U.S. Ct. Appeals (9th cir.), 1979, U.S. Dist. Ct. (no. dist.) Calif., 1979, U.S. Dist. Ct. (cen. dist.) Calif., 1979, US. Ct. Appeals (D.C. cir.) 1983. Assoc. Hassard Bonnington Rogers & Huber, San Francisco, 1979-81; spl. asst. to gen. counsel HHS, Washington, 1981-82; spl. asst. U.S. atty. U.S. Dept. Justice, Washington, 1983; gen. counsel U.S. Dept. Edn., Washington, 1984-86; of counsel Pillsbury, Madison & Sutro, San Francisco, 1987—; speaker at health law mtgs. Editorial bd.: Jour. of Compensation and Benefits; contbr. articles on health law to profl. jours. Mem. ABA (Forum on Health Law), Calif. State Bar Assn., Nat. Health Lawyers Assn., Calif. Soc. for Health Care Attys. Office: Pillsbury Madison & Sutro 225 Bush St San Francisco CA 94104

CORDEIRO, PAULINE ANN, advertising agency executive, instructor; b. Fall River, Mass., Aug. 29, 1958; d. Bruce and Florence M. (Burkhardt) C.; m. Kenneth L. Johnson, Apr. 15, 1978 (div. Jan. 1981). AA, St. Petersburg Jr. Coll., 1979; BS in Polit. Sci. and Journalism, Eckerd Coll., 1982; postgrad., Goddard U., 1982—. Prodn. coordinator Poynter Inst. Media Studies, St. Petersburg, 1980-82; camera supr. VAL-PAK Direct Mktg., St. Petersburg, 1982-85; ops. dir. Smith Cordeiro Advt., St. Petersburg, 1985—; mem. faculty Dept. Leisure Services, St. Petersburg, 1980-87; cons. Pinellas County Sch. System, St. Petersburg, 1982-84. Author: Women in Khaki, 1985; contbr. articles to profl. 1982-84. Instr. ARC, St. Petersburg, 1979—; mem. exec. bd. Pinellas County Dems., St. Petersburg, 1981—. Served with USMC, 1977-80. Mem. NOW, LWV, Women Press Assn., Women in Media. Democrat. Lutheran.

CORDELL, LADORIS HAZZARD, judge; b. Ardmore, Pa., Nov. 19, 1949; d. Lewis Randall and Clara Beatrice (Jenkins) Hazzard; divorced; children—Cheran Denise, Starr Lynn. B.A., Antioch Coll., 1971; J.D., Stanford U., 1974. Bar: Calif. 1975, U.S. Dist. Ct. (no. dist.) Calif. 1975. Sole practice, East Palo Alto, Calif., 1975-82; asst. dean Stanford Law Sch., 1978-82; judge Mcpl. Ct., Santa Clara County, San Jose, Calif., 1982—, presiding judge, 1985-86. Mem. policy bd. Ctr. for Research on Women, Stanford U., 1980-82; chairperson bd. dirs. Manhattan Playhouse, East Palo Alto, 1980, East Palo Alto Community Law Project, 1983—; bd. dirs. Nat. Conf. on Women and Law, 1980, United Way Santa Clara County, 1986—, Police Activities League, 1986—; mem. governing com. Ctr. for Jud. Edn. and Research, 1986—. Mem. Calif. Judges Assn., Calif. Assn. Black Lawyers, Calif. Women Lawyers, Nat. Assn. Women Judges, Nat. Bar Assn. Democrat. Contbr. articles to profl. jours. Office: Santa Clara County Mcpl Ct 200 W Hedding San Jose CA 95110

CORDELL, SHARON DOLORES, accountant; b. Clear Lake, S.D., Nov. 12, 1949; d. Darwin S. and Dolores M. (Hartsell) Meis; m. Leroy Robert Cordell, Oct. 7, 1967; children: Bruce, Brian, Laurie. Assoc. Bus., Internat. Correspondence Sch., Scranton, Pa., 1981. Office mgr. Tomlinson Bldg. Ctr., Watertown, S.D., 1970-77, H&R Block, Watertown, 1975-77; acct. Cooks, Inc., Watertown, 1977-78, McGladrey Hendricksen & Co., Watertown, 1978-83, Larry A. Jerde, CPA, Watertown, 1983-85; pvt. practice acctg. Watertown, 1985—. Chmn. membership com. Girl Scouts U.S., Watertown, 1981-84. Mem. Am. Inst. CPA's (S.D. rep. state legis subcom. 1986—), S.D. Soc. CPA's (C. of C. govt. affairs com., vice-chmn. legis. com., Lake Area Bus. and Profl. Women (pres. 1982-84). Democrat. Roman Catholic. Office: 806 S Maple St Watertown SD 57201

CORDER, BILLIE FARMER, clinical psychologist, artist; b. Dundee, Miss., Sept. 12, 1934; d. Lee Kennith and Jimmy Louise (Hawkins) Farmer; B.S., Memphis State U., 1957; M.A., Vanderbilt U., 1959; Ed.D., U. Ky., 1966; student Memphis Acad. Art, 1959, Sch. Design, N.C. State U., 1971-75; m. Robert Floyd Corder, July 11, 1961. Intern, U. Tenn. Sch. Medicine, Memphis, 1959; staff psychologist Eastern State Hosp., Lexington, Ky., 1960-65, Child Guidance Clinic, Lexington, 1965-67; asst. prof. psychology Inter-Am. U., P.R., 1967-68; dir. psychology adolescent day care Area Community Mental Health Center, Washington, 1968-70; dir. psychol. services Alcoholic Rehab. Center, Butner, N.C., 1970-71; co-dir. psychol. services in child psychiatry Dix Hosp., Raleigh, N.C., 1971—; mem. adv. bd. Raleigh Developmental Evaluation Clinic, 1976—; adj. faculty psychology dept. N.C. State U., Raleigh, 1975—, U. N.C. Sch. Medicine, 1975—. Mem. Wake County Youth Adv. Bd., 1979-80; mem. adv. com. Raleigh Arts Commn.; bd. dirs. Haven House for Children, Nazareth House for Children. Recipient best research award N.C. Dept. Mental Health, 1965, cert. of appreciation Washington Tchrs. Assn., 1969; numerous awards for art, including Purchase award N.C. Mus. Art, 1976, awards N.C. Watercolor Soc., 1978, 79; numerous research grants. Mem. Am. Psychol. Assn., Southeastern Psychol. Assn., N.C. Psychol. Assn., Am. Assn. Psychiat. Services for Children (program chmn. 1976-77), Raleigh Artists Guild, Raleigh Fine Arts Soc., N.C. Art Soc., Women's Equity Action League. N.C. Women's Polit. Caucus, Durham Artists Guild, N.C. Watercolor Soc. (v.p.), AAUW. Democrat. Baptist. Club: Raleigh Racquet. Contbr. articles to profl. jours.; dir. editorial bd. N.C. Jour. Mental Health, 1974—; adj. editorial rev. bd. Hosp. and Community Psychiatry, Quar. Jour. Studies on Alcohol. Office: Child Psychiatry Clinic Dix Hospital Raleigh NC 27611

CORDERO DE DE LA MADRID, PALOMA, wife of President of Mexico. m. Miguel de la Madrid Hurtado, June 27, 1959; children: Margarita, Miguel, Enrique, Federico, Gerardo. Address: Palacio Nacional, 06220 Mexico City Mexico *

CORDERY, SARA BROWN, educator; b. Chester, S.C., Feb. 4, 1920; d. William and Fannie (Halsey) Brown; m. Albert Theodore Cordery, Mar. 30, 1947. BS, S.C. State U., 1942; MA, Columbia U., 1946, EdD, 1957. Statis. analyst Quartermaster Corps, U.S. Army, Washington, 1942-45; tchr., div. chairperson, prof., registrar, dir. alumni affairs, dir. Centennial Celebration, dir. instnl. self-study, assoc. dir. instnl. devel., spl. asst. to pres. Barber-Scotia Coll., Concord, N.C., 1947-73; prof. Sch. Bus. and Mgmt., Morgan State U., Balt., assoc. dean, 1976-85, acting dean, 1980-82; cons. Walkers and Monroe, Inc. Mem. youth motivation task force Nat. Alliance of Bus.; chair nat. com. of self-devel. United Presbyn. Ch., U.S., 1979-84; pres. Balt. Presbyterial, 1985-88. Mem. Am. Bus. Communication Assn., Assn. Tchr. Educators, Assn. Supervision and Curriculum Devel., AAUP, Nat. Bus. Edn. Assn., Eastern Bus. Tchrs. Assn., Fedn. Negro Women (pres. Concord, N.C.), United Presbyn. Women, Delta Sigma Theta. Club: Sponsors (Balt.). Home: 2718 Meredith Rd White Hall MD 21161 Office: Morgan State U Cold Spring Ln and Hillen Rd Baltimore MD 21239

CORDES, LOVERNE CHRISTIAN, interior designer; b. Cleve., Feb. 13, 1927; d. Frank Andrew and Loverne Louise (Brown) Christian; m. William Peter Cordes, Nov. 14, 1959; children: Christian Peter, Carey Pomeroy. B.S., Purdue U., 1949. Owner, mgr. Loverne Christian Cordes, Chagrin Falls, Ohio, 1967—; tchr. John Carroll U., Cleve., 1976-77. Interior designer, Fred Epple Co., Cleve., 1949-67. Fellow Am. Soc. Interior Designers, AIA, Nat. Home Fashion League (past pres. Ohio chpt.), Am. Inst. Interior Designers (past pres. Ohio chpt., nat. bd. dirs. 1969-75, nat. v.p. East Central region 1972-75, nat. exec. bd. 1972-75, recipient 1st Presdl. citation 1973, 74, 75), mem. Soc. Collectors Dunham Tavern Mus. (bd. dirs. 1961-62), Dunham Dames (past pres.), Western Reserve Hist. Soc., Cleve. Mus. Art, Cleve. Garden Center, Chagrin Falls Hist. Soc., Nat. Trust for Historic Preservation, Internat. Platform Assn., Arcadian, Kappa Kappa Gamma. Republican. Congregationalist. Clubs: Chagrin Valley Country, Dogwood Garden. Address: 60 S Franklin St Chagrin Falls OH 44022

CORDINGLEY, MARY JEANETTE BOWLES (MRS. WILLIAM ANDREW CORDINGLEY), social worker, psychologist, artist; b. Des Moines, Jan. 1, 1918; d. William David and Florence (Spurrier) Bowles; student Stephens Coll., 1936; B.A., Carleton Coll., 1939; postgrad. U. Denver, 1944-45; M.A., U. Minn., 1948; grad. art student, 1963; M.A. in Psychology Pepperdine U.; m. William Andrew Cordingley, Mar. 17, 1942; children—William Andrew, Thomas Kent, Constance Louise. Co-pub. Univ. News, 1939-40; with U.S.O. Travelers Aid Service, 1942-44; mem. Jr. League, Des Moines, 1943, bd. dirs., sec. Mpls., 1951-56; clinic psychiat. social worker U. Minn. Hosp., 1947-48; social worker community service project neuropediatrics U. Minn., 1964-65; med. dir. med. sch. service Mont. Deaconess Hosp., 1970-74; instigator, pres. Original Pioneer Prints Notepaper Co.; paintings in variety of galleries and traveling shows; exhibited in numerous one man shows Chas. Russell Gallery, Mont., Student Union U. Minn., Nat. Biennial League Am. Pen Women, 1968, 70, U. Mont., 1974, Mont. Traveling Exhibit, 1966-67, Mus. of the Rockies hist. show, 1976, Bergen Art Guild, 1976-78, 87, Russell Auction, 1977; graphic artist in metal etchings, represented Des Moines Art Center, other galleries; therapist Mental Health Center, 1977-82. Organizer, Hazeltine Nat. Golf Club Womens Assn., 1962-64, I. & R. Center, 1967; pres. adv. bd. Mont. State U.; past mem. bd. dirs. United Way, Youth Guidance Home. Recipient various awards. Mem. Nat. Assn. Social Workers, State Arts Council, Acad. Certified Social Workers (art instr.). Co-author: Series on Mont. Instns. Home: 7525 Gainey Ranch Rd #133 Scottsdale AZ 85258 Also: 7525 Gainey Ranch Rd #183 Scottsdale AZ 85258

CORDOVA, KAREN SUE, fastener industry professional; b. Walsenburg, Colo., Nov. 1, 1951; d. Moses Efren and Rachel Linda (Martinez) C.; 1 child, Elizabeth Kathleen Riley. BA summa cum laude, U. Calif., Irvine, 1975, MBA, 1984. Dir. undergraduate scholarship program U. Calif., Irvine, 1975-77; salesperson Cordova Bolt, Buena Park, Calif., 1978-81; account rep. Unisys Corp., Irvine, 1984-88, Cordova Bolt, 1987—. Troop leader Girl Scouts U.S., Irvine, 1982-84; active Irvine Coordinating Com. for the Arts, 1984, Young Reps., Orange County, Calif., 1986-87. Mem. Los Angeles Fastener Assn., Assn. Computing Machinery, U. Calif. Irvine Grad. Sch. Mgmt. Alumni (bd. dirs. 1986-87), Phi Beta Kappa. Club: Contemporary (Newport Harbor Art Mus., Newport Beach, Calif.). Home: 5 Robinsong Irvine CA 92714 Office: Cordova Bolt 5601 Dolly Buena Park CA 90621

CORDOVA, LAURA ANN, property manager; b. Indpls., Sept. 5, 1959; d. Edward Samuel and Cynthia Tobin (Bash) Brantner; m. Randall Keith

Cordova, Sept. 15, 1984. BA in Edn., Ind. U., 1981. Lic. real estate agt., N.Mex. Property mgr. Barrett & Stokely, Albuquerque, 1981-84; real estate salesperson Ansco-Stephens Ltd., Albuquerque, 1984-85; property mgr. CBS Property Services Inc., Albuquerque, 1985—. Campaign asst. Albuquerque Reps., 1986. Mem. Multiple Housing Assn., Albuquerque C.of C., Downtown Jaycees (officer, fin. v.p., Jaycee of Quarter Springboard of Yr. award 1986), Ind. U. Alumni Assn., Kappa Delta. Episcopalian. Home: 10409 Manzanillo NE Albuquerque NM 87111

CORDY, GAIL ELLEN, geohydrologist; b. Sacramento, Dec. 18, 1951; d. Donald Irving and June Marie (Box) Cordy. BS in Geology, Calif. State U., Sacramento, 1975; exchange student, U. Dundee, 1974-75; MS in Geology, Ariz. State U., 1978. Registered geologist, Calif. Geologist City of Scottsdale (Ariz.), Long Range Planning, 1976-77; staff geologist Dames and Moore, Phoenix, 1977-79; engring. geologist U.S. Bur. of Reclamation, Phoenix, 1979-80, Nev. Bur. Mines and Geology, Reno, 1981-83; instr. geology Calif. State U.-Fullerton, 1983; geohydrologist Water Resources div. U.S. Geol. Survey, Salt Lake City, 1984—. Chmn. worship Cen. Christian Ch., Salt Lake City, 1985-87. Mem. Am. Water Resources Assn. (publicity com. 1987), Utah Geol. Assn. (sec. 1985-86), Nat. Water Well Assn., Royal Scottish Country Dance Soc. (tchr. 1976—). Democrat. Office: US Geol Survey Water Resources 1745 W 1700 S Salt Lake City UT 84104

CORE, MARY CAROLYN W. PARSONS, radiologic technologist; b. Valparaiso, Fla., Dec. 8, 1949; d. Levi and Mary Etta (Elliott) Willey; m. Joel Kent Core, Aug. 3, 1979; 1 child, Candace W. Parsons. Student, Peninsula Gen. Hosp. Sch. Radiologic Tech., Salisbury, Md., 1969, U. Del. Extension, 1969-73, Del. Tech. Community Coll., 1973-79, St. Joseph's Coll., 1983-86, BSBA, 1987. Technologist, Peninsula Gen. Hosp., Salisbury, 1967-72, tech. dir. edn. Sch. Radiologic Tech., 1973-75; technologist Johns Hopkins Hosp., 1972-73, Nanticoke Meml. Hosp., Seaford, Del., 1975-79; adminstrv. chief technologist, imaging depts. Shady Grove Adventist Hosp., Rockville, Md., 1979-81; dir. dept. radiol. scis. Anne Arundel Diagnostics, Inc., then chief ops. officer Anne Arundel MRI (Magnetic Resonance Imaging), Annapolis, Md., 1981—. Recipient twin awards YWCA, 1988. Mem. Cen. Md. Council Girl Scouts U.S. Mem. Md. Soc. Radiologic Technologists (pres. 1980-81, sr. bd. mem. 1982-83, various awards including 1st Pl. Essay awards 1974, 76, 84, 87), Am. Hosp. Radiology Adminstrs. (v.p. 1984-85, chmn. by-laws com. 1984-85, statis. resources com. 1985-86), Am. Mgmt. Assn., Radiology Bus. Mgrs. Assn., Nat. Assn. Female Execs., Eastern Shore Dist. Radiologic Technologists (pres. 1976-78). Republican. Methodist. Home: 1907 Harcourt Ave Crofton MD 21114 Office: Franklin and Cathedral Sts Annapolis MD 21401

CORELL, BELLE OLIVER, educator, club and civic worker, writer; b. Suffolk, Va., July 30, 1902; d. Samuel Columbus and Eureka (Ashburn) Oliver; m. James Wesley Simmons, Apr. 27, 1926 (div. Apr. 1929); children—Belle Oliver (Mrs. Wm. E. Traver II), John Oliver; m. Harold Clifford Hart, Oct. 15, 1934 (dec. July 1937); m. Archibald Gerald Corell, Nov. 2, 1974 (dec. Aug. 1980). Student Mary Washington Coll., Fredericksburg, Va., 1920-22; A.B., George Washington U., 1944. Tchr., Martha Washington Coll., Abingdon, Va., 1922-23, Harpers Ferry (W.Va.) High Sch., 1923-24, Hopewell (Va.) High Sch., 1924-26, 28-29; asst. prin., Tenacre and Wellesley, Mass., 1938-39; asst. state service officer Dept. Public Welfare, Richmond, Va., 1929-31; adminstrv. asst. Dept. Justice, Washington, 1931-33; sec. NRA, Fed. Emergency Relief Adminstrn., U.S. Govt., 1933-34; nat. def. WPB, Washington, 1940-44; exec. sec. woman's aux. Episcopal Diocese Mass., Boston, 1945-48; asso. John M. Hancock, Lehman Bros., N.Y.C., 1948-54. Pres. Boston chpt. U.D.C., 1945-47, 58-59, rec. sec. gen., 1955-57, mil. meml. awards com., 1959-62; pres., Wellesley Council Ch. Women, 1958-60; mem. bd. Northfield League, 1955-64; bd. dirs. Mass. N.E. Grenfell Assn.; sec. Belleair Beach Property Owners Assn., 1965-68; dir. Bellaire Beach Park Bd., 1978-79; dir. altar guild Calvary Episcopal Ch. Mem. DAR (regent Amos Mills chpt. Wellesley 1961-63), Mary Washington Coll. Alumnae Assn. (pres. 1941-44), AAUW, Belleair Beach Garden Club (pres. 1967-69), Federated Hills Garden Club (rec. sec. 1956, pres. 1961-62, sustaining mem.), Power Squadron of CAP. Episcopalian. Clubs: Bath (St. Petersburg Beach, Fla.); No. Lake George Yacht. Author: Footprints (history of the establishing in 1959 the United Daughters of the Confederacy award at the U.S. Air Force Acad. honoring and memorializing Lt. Gen. Claire L. Chennault for his exceptional contribution toward developing and strengthening the air power of the U.S. Awarded annually to a graduate cadet ranking in basic scis.). Address: 117 5th St Belleair Beach FL 34635

COREY, ESTHER MARIE, church administrator; b. Providence, Jan. 26, 1927; d. Anders Ludvig and Emily Lenore (Jacobsen) Schroder; m. Hugh MacLeod Corey, May 17, 1958; children: Bonnie Jeane, Barry Hugh. Student, New England Bible Coll., 1954. Licensed to ministry, Assemblies of God, 1934. Dir. Christian edn. Assemblies of God Ch., New Eng. Dist., 1954-59; co-pastor Assemblies of God Ch., Quincy, Mass., 1960-68; dir. Missionette Girls Club Assemblies of God Ch., So. New England, 1968-78, dir. women's ministries, 1978-87, dir. ministry wives, 1987—; organizer retreats, convs., seminars Assemblies of God. Office: Assemblies of God So New England Dist Hdqr Ctr PO Box 535 Sturbridge MA 01566

COREY, MARY BETH, writer, account executive; b. Worcester, Mass., Apr. 20, 1960; d. Joseph Michael and Ellen (Flatley) C. BA in English, Coll. of the Holy Cross, Worcester, Mass., 1982. Copywriter Cahners Exposition Group, div. Cahners Pub. Co., Stamford, Conn., 1982-86; editor, doublelife Doubleday & Co., Inc., N.Y.C., 1986-87; proposal writer Flack & Kurtz Consulting Engrs., N.Y.C., 1987-88; writer, account exec. The Creative Services Group, N.Y.C., 1988—. Roman Catholic. Office: 83 Riverside Dr New York NY 10024

COREY, RAYE W., financial executive; b. Moline, Ill., Mar. 9, 1941; d. Raymond W. Corey and Maye (Louise) Stablein; m. James R. Pappas, Sept. 8, 1962 (div.); children: Deborah Lynn, James R. Jr.; m. Cyril Barlow, Jan. 2, 1986; 1 child, Joanna Elizabeth. BA, Webster Coll., Webster Groves, Mo., 1961. Ins. mgr. Booz, Allen & Hamilton, Florham Park, N.J., 1975-79; pres. Corey Fin. Group, Ft. Lauderdale, Fla., 1979—, Pension & Benefit Cons., Ft. Lauderdale, 1984—; benefit mgr. Pantry Pride, Ft. Lauderdale, 1980-81; asst. v.p. Wolper Ross, Miami, Fla., 1981-82; assoc. cons. Herget & Co., Ft. Lauderdale, 1982-84; exec. v.p. Pension & Benefit Cons., Ft. Lauderdale, Fla., 1984—. Mem. Nat. Assn. Female Execs., Nat. Assn. Tax Practicioners, Network Connection, So. Fla. Employees Benefits Council, Sales and Mktg. Execs. Office: Pension & Benefit Cons 1280 S Powerline Rd Suite 5 #407 Pompano Beach FL 33069

CORKILL, DOLORES LOYD, educator; b. Roanoke, Va., Dec. 19, 1942; d. Ernest Lorenzo Loyd and Eunice (White) Wheeler; m. Bertram Eugene Corkill Jr., June 19, 1965. BS in Edn., Radford Coll., 1965; MEd in Reading, Duke U., 1978. Tchr. Roanoke County Sch. System, 1965-69, Knightstown (Ind.) Sch. System, 1969-70, Jefferson County Schs., Louisville, 1970-72, Durham (N.C.) County Schs., 1972—. Active PTA, Durham, 1965—, sec. 1983—. Mem. NEA, N.C. Assn. of Educators (bldg. rep.), Internat. Reading Assn. (treas. Durham County Council 1980—), N.C. Assn. of Gifted and Talented, , Delta Kappa Gamma, Phi Delta Kappa. Republican. Baptist. Office: Hope Valley Elem Sch 3023 University Dr Durham NC 27707

CORLETT, DONNA JEAN, education educator; b. Seattle, Sept. 28, 1934; d. J. Earl and Margaret N. (Whitehall) Broyles; divorced; 1 child, Shannon Hayes. BA, U. Idaho, 1956; MEd, U. Oreg., 1964; EdD, U. Portland, 1969. Cert. tchr., Wash. Tchr. pub. schs. Wash. and Idaho, 1955-64; instr. Portland (Oreg.) State U., 1964-66, asst. prof., 1968-74, assoc. prof., 1974—; hon. juror, bd. dirs. Nat. Forum Ednl. Adminstrn. and Supervision Jour., Baton Rouge, 1983-87. Contbr. articles to profl. jours. Chmn. bd. trustees CableCom TV, Vancouver, Wash., 1980-81. U. Portland summer research grantee, 1987, U. Portland Alumni research grantee, 1987-88. Mem. Nat. Assn. Tchr. Educators (elections and nominations com. 1986—, mem. pres.'s council 1986—), N.W. Assn. Tchr. Educators (conf. chair 1987, pres. 1987-88), AAUW (v.p.), Phi Delta Kappa (local v.p. 1981-82). Democrat. Club: Willamette Writers (Portland). Office: U Portland 5000 N Willamette Blvd Portland OR 97203

CORLEY, JEAN ARNETTE LEISTER, infosystems executive; b. Charleston, S.C., June 16, 1944; d. William Audley and Arnette (Mason) Leister; widowed; children: Arnette Elizabeth, Daniel Lee. BS, Med. Coll. Ga., 1970; MBA, M of Pub. Adminstrn., Southeastern U., 1980. Various positions health care orgns., Augusta, Ga., 1960-70; office mgr., counselor Info. Ctr. for Alcohol and Drug Abuse, Augusta, 1970-71; planner health care systems Nat. Med. Assn. Found., Washington, 1971-72; research assoc., systems analyst GEOMET, Inc., Gaithersburg, Md., 1972-74; dir. med. records Georgetown U. Hosp., Washington, 1974-80; dir. med. info. systems Lahey Clinic Med. Ctr., Burlington, Mass., 1980-84; sales mgr. Code 3 Health Info. Systems/3M, Boston, 1984—. Contbr. articles to profl. jours. Mem. adv. com. LaBoure Coll., Dorchester, Mass., 1983—, various colls., 1973-80; campaign worker Dukakis for Gov., 1982. Mem. Am. Med. Records Assn. (mem. program com. 1977-80, chmn. 1981-82, fed. health program adv. com. 1978-80, computerized health info task force, 1983-87), D.C. Med. Records Assn. (pres. 1975), New Eng. Med. Records Conf. (exec. dir. 1984—), Women in Info. Processing, LWV, Common Cause. Democrat. Presbyterian. Home: 71 Lowell St Andover MA 01810 Office: Code 3 Health Info Systems/3M 155 Fourth Ave Needham Heights MA 02194-2796

CORLEY, JOYCE, personnel executive; b. Schenectady, Jan. 10; d. J. Edmund and Jean (Hausman) C. Assoc. Sci., Harcum Jr. Coll., 1962; postgrad. Temple U. Med. asst. Bryn Mawr Med. & Diagnostic Clinic Ltd. (Pa.), 1962-66; sec. Calif. Computer Products, Bala Cynwya, Pa., 1966-70, Drexel Firestone, Phila., 1970-71; exec. sec. IU Internat., Phila., 1972-76; adminstrv. asst. Peat, Marwick Mitchell & Co., 1976-81, mgr. personnel services, 1981—. Mem. central allocations com. United Way, 1983-85, mem. sr. services rev. com., 1984-85, com. corp. edn. Am. Cancer Soc., 1988—. Mem. Nat. Assn. Female Execs., Human Resources Profl. Assn. (bd. dirs. 1985—, treas. 1986-88 v.p. adminstrv. services 1988—), Am. Soc. Personnel Adminstrs., Delaware Valley Corp. Travel Mgrs. Assn. Republican. Office: Peat Marwick Mitchell & Co 1600 Market St Philadelphia PA 19103

CORLEY, MARTY FRANCES, construction executive; b. Central City, Ky., Feb. 25, 1956; d. J.C. and Emily Frances (Geelhood) C. BS, U. Tex., 1978. Owner Fretz Tennis Ctr., Dallas, 1979-83; v.p. sales and mktg. The Corley Co., Inc., Forest, Va., 1983—. Mem. Nat. Assn. Homebuilders, Nat. Assn. Realtors, Womens Resource Ctr., Community Assns. Inst., Lynchburg C. of C. Home: 411 Lake Vista Dr Forest VA 24551 Office: The Corley Co Inc 200 Lake Vista Dr Forest VA 24551

CORLEY, MARY JUNE, art director; b. Auburn, Ala., Oct. 8, 1951; d. Tom Edward and Mary Will (Simpson) C. BFA, Auburn U., 1973. Asst. art dir. HBM Creamer, Boston, 1973-75; art dir. McDonald & Little, Atlanta, 1975-76; free-lance art dir. Atlanta, 1976-78; ptnr., co-creative dir. Corley & Day, Atlanta, 1979-82; free-lance art dir. Atlanta, 1983—. Recipient Boston Hatch award Boston Advt. Club, 1974, ANDY Award for Excellence Advt. Club N.Y., 1975, One Show Gold award Art Dirs. Club N.Y., 1975, Award for Excellence Communications Arts Annual, 1975, 84, Nat. ADDY Gold award AM. Advt. Fedn., 1984, Regional ADDY Gold award Atlanta Advt. Club, 1984, 86, Show South Gold award Art Dirs. Club Atlanta, 1985 Regional ADDY Silver award Atlanta Advt. Club, 1986. Mem. Humane Soc. U.S., Nexus Contemporary Art Ctr., Fund for Animals Silver Circle Club.

CORMAN, BONNIE, psychologist; b. Providence, Nov. 3, 1942; d. Bernard Harold and Gertrude (Weinstein) Podrat; m. Marvin L. Corman; children: John Mayer, Alexander Stern. BA, U. Penn., 1964; MA, Harvard U., 1967, Boston Coll., 1981. Lic. marriage, family, and child counselor. Bd. dirs. Laguna Blanca Sch., Santa Barbara, Calif., 1982-83, dir. guidance, 1983—; Bd. dirs. Santa Barbara Sch. and Counseling Service. Bd. dirs. Lobero Theatre, Santa Barbara, Calif., 1983-87; exec. bd. Santa Barbara Arts Council, 1985—; adv. bd. Human Relations Inst., Santa Barbara, 1987. Mem. Am. Psychol. Assn., Calif. Psychol. Assn., Nat. Assn. Coll. Admission Counselors, Calif. Assn. Marriage, Family, Child Counselors, Brown U. Alumni Assn., Harvard U. Alumni Assn., U. Penn. Alumni Assn., U. Penn. Club (chmn. 1982). Office: Laguna Blanca Sch 4125 Paloma Dr Santa Barbara CA 93110

CORMIER, ROBIN ANDREA, defense consulting company administrator; b. Alexandria, Va., Jan. 28, 1961; d. Robert Adrien and Edith Mae (McCauley) Willett; m. Robert Hanley Cormier Jr., Mar. 16, 1985. BA in English, Va. Poly. Inst. State U., 1982. Research asst. Mgmt. Cons. and Research, Falls Church, Va., 1982-83; editor Analytic Services, Inc., Arlington, Va., 1983-85, dep. publs. mgr., 1985-86, publ. mgr., 1986—. Mem. Soc. Tech. Communications, Nat. Assn. Female Execs. Home: 7917 Birchtree Ct Springfield VA 22152

CORMIER, SHARON ANN, manufacturing executive; b. Cambridge, Mass., July 2, 1951; d. Fred Albert and Helen Mary (Boosahda) Hamwey; m. Dennis Edward Cormier, May 5, 1974; 1 child, Brian Edward. BA in Math., Boston Coll., 1973. Inventory control clk. C&K Components, Inc., Newton, Mass., 1973-74, buyer, 1974-76, purchasing agt., 1976-88. Mem. Syrian Orthodox Ch. Home: 31 Shirley Rd Stoughton MA 02072 Office: C&K Components Inc 15 Riverdale Ave Newton MA 02158

CORN, LESLIE JOAN, producer, director, writer, programming executive; b. N.Y.C., Mar. 30, 1949; d. Peter and Jacqueline (DuVal) C. Student Northwestern U., 1966-68; B.A. in English, Finch Coll., 1970; M.A. in Psychology, New Sch. for Social Research, 1976. Radio interviewer Australian Broadcasting Commn., Sydney, 1970; asst. to writers Tonight Show, NBC-TV, N.Y.C., 1971, Burbank, Calif., 1971; assoc. producer Parent's Mag. Films, N.Y.C., 1972; asst. nationally syndicated show Living Easy with Dr. Joyce Brothers, N.Y.C., 1973; assoc. producer various TV commls., N.Y.C., 1974, RKO-TV documentary Inflation: A Few Answers, 1974; producer CARE's Internat. Children's Party, 1974; prodn. assoc. Money Maze, ABC-TV, N.Y.C., 1974-75; producer, dir. Miller-Brody Prodns., N.Y.C., 1975-78; dir. program and pub. services ABC Radio Network, N.Y.C., 1979-80, dir. program prodn., 1980-81; dir. programming CBS Radio Networks, 1981-83; pres., chief exec. officer Arielle Prodns. Internat., Ltd., N.Y.C., 1984—; producer, dir., writer Love Notes radio spl., 1984—; producer, dir. Erma Bombeck in Motherhood: The Second Oldest Profession radio feature series, 1984-86, Leo Buscaglia in Loving Each Other radio feature series, 1985; dir., adapter books on tape for Warner Audio Publishing, including Rebecca (du Maurier), I the Jury (Spillane), Reflex (Francis), Brain (Cook), also dir. To Your Scattered Bodies Go (Farmer), Mosby's Memoirs (Bellow); producer, dir. adapter books on tape for Bantam Audio Pub. including Changing (Liv Ullmann), Yeager: An Autobiography, Mission: Success! The Greatest Salesman in the World Part Two (Og Mandino), And So It Goes (Linda Ellerbee), Suspects, (Caunitz), (A Christmas Carol, (Sir John Cmelgua), Sun Signs, Living through Personal Crisis, Over the Edge (Kellerman), Soulmates (Stearn), Newman Communications including The New! Improved! Bob and Ray Boon (Bob Elliott and Ray Goulding), Smart Cookies Don't Crumble (Sonya Friedman), Listen for Pleasure including The Magician of Lublin (Isaac Bashevis Singer); Wiley Sound Business including Getting New Clients (Connors and Davidson), programming cons. Warner Communications, N.Y.C. and Columbus, Ohio, 1976-78; panelist Nat. Emmy awards, 1974-77, nominations panelist children's programming, 1977; vis. lectr. NYU Sr. Seminar, 1980, Spiritual Frontiers Fellowship, 1984, 85, Folio, 1987. Mem. Internat. Radio and TV Soc. (bd. govs. 1977-81), Nat. Acad. Rec. Arts and Scis., Mensa, Spiritual Frontiers Fellowship (programming com. 1984—), Delta Delta Delta. Office: Arielle Prodns Internat Ltd 265 E 66th St Suite 32-B New York NY 10021

CORN, MARILU ALDRICH, art gallery director, portrait artist; b. Phila., Feb. 28, 1931; d. Truman H. and Helen-Mar (Gloninger) Aldrich; m. Robert A. Dauber, Feb. 28, 1953 (div. 1972); children: Craig Aldrich, Mark Christopher, Jeffrey Curtis (dec.), Anita Germaine; m. Donald J. Corn, Aug. 1972 (div. 1977). Student Phila. Bus. Coll., 1952. Sales cons. Center Art Galleries, Honolulu, 1976-81; asst. mgr. Vorpol Galleries, Laguna Beach, Calif., 1983; gallery mgr. Simic Galleries, Inc., Carmel Calif., 1984-86, Gateway Galleries, LaJolla, Calif., 1986—. Vol., Humane Soc., Honolulu, 1980. Mem. Nat. Assn. Female Execs., Nat. Assn. Realtors, Hawaiian Malacol. Soc. Republican. Mem. Ch. of Religious Sci. Clubs: Kaneohe Yacht (Hawaii); Chandon (Yountville, Calif.). Avocations: shell collecting, scuba diving. Home: 3330-150 Caminito East Bluff La Jolla CA 92037 Office: Gateway Gallery 1025 Prospect St Suite 200 La Jolla CA 92037

CORN, WANDA M., fine arts educator; b. New Haven, Nov. 13, 1940; d. Keith M. and Lydia M. (Fox) Jones; m. Joseph J. Corn, July 27, 1963. B.A., NYU, 1963, M.A., 1965, Ph.D., 1974. Instr. art history Washington Sq. Coll., NYU, 1965-66; lectr. U. Calif.-Berkeley, 1970, vis. asst. prof., 1976; lectr. Mills Coll., Oakland, Calif., 1970, vis. asst. prof., 1971, asst. prof., 1972-77, assoc. prof., 1977-80; assoc. prof. Stanford U., Calif., 1980—; vis. curator Fine Arts Mus., San Francisco, 1972, 73, 76; vis. curator Mpls. Inst. Arts, 1983-84, Grant Wood travelling exhbn. to Whitney Mus. Am. Art, N.Y.C., Art Inst. Chgo., Fine Arts Mus. San Francisco. Author: The Color of Mood, American Tonalism, 1880-1910, 1972; The Art of Andrew Wyeth, 1973; Grant Wood: The Regionalist Vision, 1983. Contbr. articles to profl. jours. Commr. Nat. Mus. Am. Art, 1988—. Ford Found. fellow, 1966-70; recipient Graves award 1974-75; Smithsonian fellow, 1978-79; Woodrow Wilson fellow, 1979-80; Stanford Humanities Ctr. fellow, 1982-83, Regents fellow Smithsonian Inst., 1987; Am. Council Learned Socs. grantee, 1982, 86; research assoc. Smithsonian Instn., 1983—; Phi Beta Kappa scholar, 1984-85. Mem. Coll. Art Assn. (bd. dirs. 1970-73, 1980-84, editor Registry of Vis. Scholars and Artists, 1971-74, program chmn. ann. meeting, 1981, mem. numerous coms.), Women's Caucus for Art, Am. Studies Assn. (nat. council 1986-89), Assn. Historians of Am. Art. Office: Stanford U Dept of Art Stanford CA 94305

CORNBLEET, AILEEN GAIL HIRSCH, English language and social studies educator; b. Chgo., Nov. 8, 1946; d. Irving Carlton and Anne (Pitlov) Hirsch; m. David H. Cornbleet, Aug. 18, 1968; children: Jonathan M., Jocelyn F. BE summa cum laude, U. Wis., 1968; interpreter's degree in German/History, U. Heidelberg, Fed. Republic Germany, 1970; M in Secondary Edn. summa cum laude, Boston U., 1972. Instr. Heidelberg Am. High Sch., 1968-75, Temple Sholom, Chgo., 1976—; instr. ESL Oakton Community Coll., Skokie, Ill., 1986-87; supervising tchr. MA students Nat. Coll. Edn., 1987—. Sec. Orgn. Rehab. Tng., Lincolnwood, Ill., 1980-82; mem. Lincolnwood Sch. Bd. Dist. #74, Ill., 1982—. Recipient Master Tchr. award Bd. Jewish Edn., 1986. Fellow Ill. Assn. for Supervision and Curriculum Devel., Phi Alpha Theta, Pi Lambda Phi. Home: 6532 N Christiana Lincolnwood IL 60645

CORNELIUS, CATHERINE PETREY, college president; b. Lakeland, Fla., May 3, 1941; d. Thomas Burch and Carolyn (Petrey) C. BA, Rollins Coll., 1963, MA in Teaching, 1966; EdS, U. Fla., 1976, EdD, 1978. Cert. educator/adminstr., Fla. Tchr. Spanish, history Orange County Pub. Schs., Orlando, Fla., 1963-67; instr. fgn. lang. Seminole Community Coll., Sanford, Fla., 1967-73, dir. coop. and career edn., 1973-78; dir. arts and scis. Daytona Beach (Fla.) Community Coll., 1978-79, v.p. acad. affairs, 1979-84; pres. South Fla. Community Coll., Avon Park, 1984—. Author: (with others) Experiential Education, 1983. Bd. dirs. Highlands Art League, Sebring, Fla., 1985-87, Fla. Endowment Fund for Higher Edn., Tampa, 1985—, Walker Meml. Hosp., Avon Park, 1986—. Named Educator of Yr. Sebring C. of C., 1987; recipient disting. alumni service award, 1988, Nat. Pacesetter award Nat. Council for Community Relations, 1988. Mem. Am. Assn. Higher Edn., Am. Assn. Community/Jr. Colls., Fla. Assn. Community Colls. (pres. 1986, Service award 1986), Fla. Council Pres. (chmn. 1987-88), Highlands Council of 100 (pres. 1986-88), Phi Delta Kappa (pres. 1983-84, Service award 1984). Methodist. Lodge: Rotary (Avon Park Breakfast Club). Office: South Fla Community Coll 600 W College Dr Avon Park FL 33825

CORNELIUS, LINDA LOUISE, advertising executive; b. Buffalo, Mar. 7, 1953; d. Adam Edward, Jr. and Virginia Elizabeth (Becker) Cornelius. B.A. summa cum laude, U. Pa., 1975, M.B.A., 1979. Asst. account exec. Ogilvy & Mather Advt., N.Y.C., 1979-80, account exec., 1980-82, account supr., 1982, v.p., account supr., 1983-84, v.p., mgmt. supr., 1984-87, sr. v.p., 1987—. Mem. Phi Beta Kappa. Office: Ogilvy & Mather Advt 2 E 48th St New York NY 10017

CORNETT, LAUREEN ELIZABETH, photographer; b. San Diego, Nov. 14, 1946; d. Clarence Alex and Barbara Ann (Mesku) Lane; m. Bruce Walter Cornett, Oct. 17, 1981; children: Cherie Ann, Robert Michael, John David. Student, San Diego State U., 1964-70. Exec. sec. Boyle Engring., San Diego, 1964-69, Design Cons., San Diego, 1969-71; owner Laureen's Secretarial Service, San Diego, 1979-83; exec. sec. Covi Corp., San Diego, 1979-83; owner Word Processing Co., San Diego, 1982-84; owner, photographer Panoramix, San Diego, 1984—. Photographer for brochures, newspaper ads. Mem. Communicating Arts Group San Diego, San Diego C. of C., Better Bus. Bur. Democrat. Methodist. Office: Panoramix PO Box 15323 San Diego CA 92115

CORNING, JOY COLE, state legislator; b. Bridgewater, Iowa, Sept. 7, 1932; d. Perry Aaron and Ethel Marie (Sullivan) Cole; m. Burton Eugene Corning, June 19, 1955; children: Carol, Claudia, Ann. BA, U. No. Iowa, 1954. Cert. elem. tchr., Iowa. Tchr. elem. sch. Greenfield (Iowa) Sch. Dist., 1951-53, Waterloo (Iowa) Community Sch. Dist., 1954-55; mem. Iowa Senate, 1984—; bd. dirs. Iowa Nat. Bankshares, Midway Bank & Trust. Pres. Cedar Falls (Iowa) Sch. Bd., 1975-83, Iowa Talented and Gifted, Des Moines, 1975-77; mem. adv. bd. Waterloo Theatre, Cedar Arts Forum; bd. dirs. Iowa Housing Fin. Authority, Des Moines, 1981-84, Iowa Assn. Sch. Bds., Des Moines, 1983-84, Iowa Peace Inst., 1987—; mem. Edn. Commn. of States, 1987—. Named Citizen of Yr., Cedar Falls C. of C., 1984; recipient Alumni Achievement award U. No. Iowa, 1985. Mem. AAUW, LWV, Delta Kappa Gamma. Republican. Mem. United Ch. of Christ. Office: 1017 Oak Park Blvd Cedar Falls IA 50613

CORNIUK, JOAN E., chemical technician; b. Cleve., Nov. 25, 1956; d. Ernest Walter and Stella Mary (Miklauz) Mance; m. Scott Charles Corniuk; children: Jessica, Cameron. Student, Lakeland Community Coll., 1976-86. Inspector Gen. Electric, Cleve., 1978-80, material handler, 1980-83, frost process analyst, 1983-88, sec. motivation com., 1985-87, mem. edn. coordination com., 1986; chem. technician Hall Chem. Co., Wickliffe, Ohio, 1988—. Mem. PTA, Mentor (Ohio) Soccer Assn., 1987, St. John Vianney Parish, Mentor, 1984-87; mem. local com. Boy Scouts Am., 1987-88. Mem. Nat. Assn. for Female Execs. Republican. Roman Catholic. Home: 6517 Carter Blvd Mentor OH 44060 Office: Hall Chem Co 28960 Lakeland Blvd Wickliffe OH 44092

CORONA, DOROTHY FRANCES, nursing educator, consultant; b. Yakima, Wash., Feb. 12, 1927; d. Dietrich D. and Dorothy Radar (Ettinger) Funk; m. Benjamin Corona, Jr., Mar. 19, 1955 (div. 1957); 1 child, Lani Louise. BS, Whitworth Coll., 1948; M in Nursing, Western Reserve U., 1951; MS in Nursing, Case Western Res. U., 1964. RN, Tex. Dir. nursing Deaconess Hosp., Spokane, Wash., 1956-62; assoc. prof. nursing Ariz. State U., Tempe, 1964-72; assoc. prof. nursing U. Tex., San Antonio, 1972-77, El Paso, 1977—; vis. assoc. prof. Boston U., 1983-84. Dir. Planned Parenthood, El Paso, 1984-86. Recipient Mildred McIntyre award Am. Heart Assn., 1978. Mem. Ariz Nurses Assn. (v.p. 1970-71, Nurse of Yr. dist. 8, 1969), Tex. Nurses Assn. (pres. local dist. 1984-86). Club: Pilot (El Paso) (pres. 1981-82). Office: U Tex 1101 N Campbell St El Paso TX 79902

COROPOFF, MARY HELEN, educational specialist; b. Dover, N.H., May 20, 1925; d. Abraham Ead Dowaliby and Helen Josephine Aberizk; m. Morris Coropoff, Sept. 6, 1958. AA, Los Angeles City Coll., 1950; BA, Los Angeles State Coll., 1952, MA in Elem. Supervision, 1960; MA, Calif. Luth. Coll., 1978. Tchr. Lawndale (Calif.) City Schs., 1952-56; tchr. Los Angeles City Schs., 1956—, specialist reading, 1968-77, 84-85, resource specialist, 1985—; tchr. Los Angeles State Coll., 1961-68; tng. tchr. Los Angeles State Coll., U. So. Calif., 1961-68. Guest expert (TV show) Vision and You, 1985. Bd. dirs. Am.-Arab Anti-Discrimination Com., Los Angeles, 1986-87. Recipient hon. service award PTA, 1983. Mem. Los Angeles Reading Assn. Home and Office: 3900 Olympiad Dr Los Angeles CA 90043

CORPORON, NANCY ANN, marketing executive; b. Independence, Kans., Nov. 11, 1949; d. Lewis Leonard and Helen Maxine (Church) Corporon. B.M. in Music Performance, Oklahoma City U., 1971; M.B.A., NYU, 1985. French hornist, 1970-85; mgr. mktg. Am. Express Co., 1987—; assoc. Mgmt. Practice Cons. Ptnrs., 1985-87; cons. Urban Bus. Assistance Corp., N.Y.C., 1981-83, v.p., 1983-84; music dir. N.Y Community Marching Band, N.Y.C., 1979-81; founder, pres. Trimusicangle, Inc., N.Y.C., 1979-82. Recipient Cardinal Key, Oklahoma City U., 1971, Sword of Honor Sigma Alpha Iota, 1971. Mem. Pi Kappa Lambda. Home: 350 W 85th St Apt 57 New York NY 10024

CORREA, EILEEN ISRAEL, clinical psychologist; b. New Orleans, Sept. 26, 1950; d. Norman Charles and Jeannette (Simison) Israel; BS, U. Southwestern La., 1972; MS (USPHS grantee 1973-75), U. Ga., 1975, Ph.D., 1977; m. John Henry Correa, Jan. 28, 1978; 1 child, John Bernard. Psychologist, Biloxi (Miss.) Gulfport VA Med. Center, 1977-79; acting chief psychology service New Orleans VA Med. Ctr., 1980-81, clin. psychologist, 1979-88, dir. psychology tng. program, 1981-83; clin. psychologist Ochsner Clinic, New Orleans, 1988—. Mem. Am. Psychol. Assn., Assn. Advancement Behavior Therapy, Southeastern Psychol. Assn. Democrat. Roman Catholic. Office: Ochsner Clinic Dept Psychiatry 1514 Jefferson Hwy New Orleans LA 70121

CORREA, ELSA ISABEL, psychiatrist; b. Guayaquil, Ecuador, Jan. 8, 1941; came to U.S., 1973; d. Telmo O. and Victoria L. (Franco) Abril; B.S., San Marcos U., Lima, Peru, 1964; M.D., 1971; m. Pelayo Correa, 1962; children—Patricia, Luz, Elsa, Fernando, Christopher, Jennifer. Intern, St. Mary of Nazareth Hosp., Chgo., 1974-75; resident Spring Group Hosp., Balt., 1975-77, Johns Hopkins Hosp., Balt., 1977-79; clin. and research fellow in psychiatry Johns Hopkins U. Sch. Medicine, Balt., 1977-81, asst. prof. psychiatry, 1981—; practice medicine specializing in psychiatry, Balt., 1977—; psychiatrist, mem. staff Johns Hopkins Hosp., Balt. City Hosp., 1977—; dir. acute psychiat unit Balt. City Hosp. (now Francis Scott Key Med. Ctr.), 1982—, asst. chief psychiatry, 1981—. Diplomate Am. Bd. Psychiatry and Neurology. Mem. Am. Psychiat. Assn., Md. Psychiat. Soc. Roman Catholic. Office: Francis Scott Key Med Ctr Dept Psychiatry 4940 Eastern Ave Baltimore MD 21224

CORREA, NORMA LEE, management consultant; b. Houston, Dec. 24, 1946; d. Leslie Norman Highsmith and Pauline Amelia (Krauel) Smith; m. Carlos Lozano Correa, June 11, 1966 (div. Nov. 1983); children: Patrisha Michelle, Carlos Alessandro; m. Kenneth L. Bales, Dec. 28, 1987. Grad. high sch., Houston. Exec. sec. Pennzoil Co., Houston, 1966-70; sec. legal Edwards, Belk, Hunter, and Kerr, El Paso, Tex., 1970-72; mgr. Correa and Assocs., Houston, 1972-77; self-employed Slick Ups by Tootsie, Mex., 1977-82; coordinator order service Westech Gear Co., Houston, 1983-85; administv. asst. to v.p. J.V. Davis and Assocs., Houston, 1985-86; dir. administn. Langosta De Tallulah (La.) Inc., 1986—; corp. sec., bd. dirs. Langosta De Tallulah, Inc., 1987—. Mem. USA Asla Inc. (bd. dirs., corp. sec. 1987), Nat. Assn. Female Execs. Episcopalian. Office: Landosta De Tallulah Inc 418 Hwy 601 Tallulah LA 71282

CORREIA, MARY BETH, music educator; b. Everett, Mass., Apr. 6, 1952; d. Joseph and Mary Lorraine (Huntley) Forni; m. Stephen Arthur Correia, Apr. 18, 1976; children: Timothy John, Ryan Elizabeth. MusB magna cum laude, U. Lowell, 1974; postgrad., Fitchburg State Coll., 1987—, MFA in Edn. summ cum laude, 1988. Elem. music specialist, field base coordinator F.J. Dutile Elem Sch. Billerica (Mass.) Pub. Schs., 1974-81; music specialist Reading (Mass.) Pub. Schs., 1981-86; elem. music specialist Dutile and Hajjar Elem Schs. Billerica Pub. Schs., 1986—; soprano soloist, Stoneham, Mass., 1966—; pvt. tchr. piano, voice Piano Lab., Melrose, Mass., 1977-81; Horace Man tchr. 1986-88; asst. choral conductor Reading Symphony "Noah's Fludde", 1986; cooperating supr. student teaching practicums U. Lowell, 1974-81, 86—; adj. faculty. 1986—; dir. elem. musical theatre groups, 1974-84, 86—; initiator elem. choral exchange concert program, 1981-84. Mem. Wildwood Sch. PTO, Burlington, Mass., 1986—; coordinator-initiator Intergenerational Concerts, Billerica, 1986-88; tchr. Confraternity Christian Doctrine St. Malachy's Ch., Burlington, 1986-87, choir-soloist, 1983—. Arts Lottery grantee, 1987. Mem. Music Educators Nat. Conf., Mass. Music Educators Assn., U. Lowell Alumni Assn. (life). Roman Catholic. Office: FJ Dutile Elem Sch Treble Cove Rd Billerica MA 01862

CORRELL, HELEN BUTTS, botanist, researcher; b. Providence, R.I., Apr. 24, 1907; d. George Lyman and Albertine Louise (Christiansen) B.; m. Donovan Stewart Correll (dec. 1983); children: Louise, Stewart, Selena, Charles. AB, Brown U., 1928, AM, 1929; PhD, Duke U., 1934. Instr. Smith Coll., Northampton, Mass., 1929-31, Wellesly (Mass.) Coll., 1934-39; assoc. prof. U. Md., Towson, 1956; research assoc. Tex. Research Found., Renner, 1959-65, co-investigator aquatic plant research, 1966-71; collaborator Fairchild Tropical Garden, Miami, Fla., 1973—. Co-author: Aquatic and Wetland Plants of the Southwestern United States, 1972, 2dn. ed. 1975, Flora of the Bahama Archipelago, 1982; editor: Wrightia Botanical Jour., 1959-63; contbr. articles to profl. jours. Chmn., Library Bd., Richardson, Tex., 1965-70. Recipient disting. alumna citation Brown U., 1983, Marjory Stoneman Douglas award Fla. Native Plant Soc., 1985. Mem. adv. council, Nat. Arboretum, Washington, 1974-79; mem. The Bahama Trust, So. Appalachion Botanical Club, Soc. for Econ. Botany, Soc. Woman Geographers, Friends of Fairchild (v.p. 1986-87, pres. 1987—), Sigma Xi, Phi Beta Kappa. Methodist. Club: Altrusa (officer 1964-71). Home: 216 E Ridge Village Dr Miami FL 33157 Office: Fairchild Tropical Garden 10901 Old Cutler Rd Miami FL 33156

CORRENTI, MARY JANE, data processing executive; b. Jefferson City, Mo., Oct. 8, 1957; d. Dale Ray and Pauline (Bond) Currence; m. Thomas Michael Correnti, Mar. 6, 1982; 1 child, Brian Dale. BS in Math., S.W. Mo. State U., 1979. Drafting clk. engring. dept. Southwestern Bell Telephone, Eldon, Mo., 1978-79; asst. staff mgr. info. systems and accounts payable systems dist. Southwestern Bell Telephone, St. Louis, 1980-82, staff specialist info. systems and accounts payable systems dist., 1982-84, systems supr. info. ctr. payroll and personnel systems dist., 1985-87, supr. mktg. and directory systems, 1987—. Mem. fin. com. Concord Trinity United Meth. Ch., St. Louis, 1986-87, mem. worship com., 1987. Mem. Profl. Women Southwestern Bell Telephone (charter; mem. membership com. 1986, treas. 1987). Office: Southwestern Bell Telephone One Bell Ctr 16-T-7 Saint Louis MO 63101

CORRIGAN, CAROL A., municipal judge; b. Stockton, Calif., Aug. 16, 1948; d. Arthur Jospeph and Genevieve Catherine (Green) C. BA, Holy Names Coll., 1970; postgrad., St. Louis U., 1970-72; JD, U. Calif., San Francisco, 1975. Dep. dist. atty. Office DIst. Atty. Alemeda County, Oakland, Calif., 1975-85; asst. prof. law U. Calif. Hastings Coll. Law, San Francisco, 1981-87, U. Calif., Berkeley, 1984-87; sr. dep. dist. atty. Office Dist. Atty. Alameda County, Oakland, 1985-87; mcpl. ct. judge Oakland, Piedmont and Emeryville Jud. Dist., Oakland, 1987—; adj. prof. sociology and polit. sci. Holy Names Coll., Oakland, 1976-80; vis. prof. law U. Puget Sound Sch. Law, Tacoma, 1981; spl. cons. Pres.'s Task Force on Victims of Crime, Washington, 1982, White House Conf. on Drug Free Am., 1988; mem. Pres.'s Commn. on Organized Crime, Washington, 1983; mem. faculty, cons. Nat. Inst. Trial Advocacy, South Bend , Ind., 1982—, Alaska Dept. Law, Fairbanks, 1983, Hawaii Dist. Atty. and Pub. Def.'s Office, Honolulu, 1981-83, Nat. Coll. Dist. Attys., Houston, 1984-87; trustee Holy Names Coll., 1987—. AUthor: Report Task Force on Victims of Crime, 1982, book chpts.; contbr. articles to profl. jours.; editor Point of View, 1981-84. Bd. dirs. Goodwill Industries of East Bay, Oakland, 1984—, St. Vincent's Day Home, Oakland, 1984—; mem. adv. bd. St. Mary's Community Ctr. for Elderly, Oakland, 1985—. Mem. ABA, Calif. State Bar Assn., Alameda County Bar Assn., Asia Found. (advisor 1987), Calif. Dist. Attys. Assn. (bd. dirs.). Roman Catholic.

CORRIGAN, CATHERINE MARY, infosytems analyst; b. Bronx, N.Y., Aug. 31, 1964; d. Edward and Bridget (Collins) C. Student in Mktg. NYU. Market research analyst Am. Internat. Group, N.Y.C., 1982-86; programmer, analyst Marcus Schloss & Co., Inc., 1986—. Mem. Nat. Assn. Female Execs. Avocations: horseback riding; softball; tennis; skiing; water-skiing. Home: 20-20 29th St Astoria NY 11105 Office: Marcus Schloss & Co Inc One Whitehall St 19 Floor New York NY 10004

CORRIGAN, LYNDA DYANN, banker; b. Selmer, Tenn., Nov. 24, 1949; d. A. Sammuel and Eunice (Burks) Davis; m. Paul James Corrigan Jr., Nov. 27, 1976. BBA, Mid. Tenn. State U., 1978; MBA, U. Tenn., 1979; JD, Nashville Sch. Law, 1984. CPA, Tenn.; bar: Tenn. 1985. Sr. v.p. First Am. Corp., Nashville, 1980—; faculty Am. Inst. Banking, Nashville, 1982—; mem. Nat. Panel Consumer Arbitrators, Nashville, 1985-87. Pres. Buddies of Nashville, 1985; treas. Mid.-East Tenn. Arthritis Found., Nashville, 1982-85, Floyd Cramer Celebrity Golf Tournament, Nashville, 1981-84; bd. dirs. Nashville Br. Arthritis Found., 1980-87. Recipient Leadership award Mid.-East Tenn. Arthritis Found, 1985, Gold award Nashville Jaycees, 1981. Mem. ABA (mem. tax com. 1987—), Nashville Bar Assn. (mem. tax com. 1986—), Tennessee Taxpayers and Mfrs. Assn., (mem. tax com. 1986—), Tenn. Soc. CPA's. Home: 806 Fountainhead Ct Brentwood TN 37027

CORRIGAN, MAURA DENISE, lawyer; b. Cleve., June 14, 1948; d. Peter James and Mae Ardell (McCrone) C.; m. Joseph Dante Grano, July 11, 1976; children: Megan Elizabeth, Daniel Corrigan. BA with honors, Marygrove Coll., 1969; JD with honors, U. Detroit, 1973. Bar: Mich., 1974. Jud. clk. Mich. Ct. Appeals, Detroit, 1973-74; asst. prosecutor Wayne County, Mich., Detroit, 1974-79; asst. U.S. atty., Detroit, 1979—, chief appellate div., 1979-86; chief asst. U.S. atty., 1986—; vice chmn. Mich. Com. To Formulate Rules of Criminal Procedure, Mich. Supreme Ct., 1982—; mem. com. on standard jury instrns. State Bar Mich., 1978-82; lectr. Mich. Jud. Inst. sixth cir. Judicial Workshop, Inst. Continuing Legal Edn., ABA-Cin. Bar Litigation Sects., Dept. Justice Advocacy Inst. Contbr. chpt. to book, articles to legal rev. Vice chmn. Project Transition, Detroit, 1976—; mem. Citizens Adv. Council Lafayette Clinic, Detroit, 1979-87; bd. dirs. Detroit Wayne County Criminal Advocacy Program, 1983-86. Recipient award of merit Detroit Commn. on Human Relations, 1974, Dir.'s award Dept. Justice, 1985. Mem. ABA, Women Lawyers Assn., Mich. Bar. Detroit Bar. Home: 721 Balfour Rd Grosse Pointe Park MI 48230 Office: US Atty Ea Dist Mich 817 Federal Bldg Detroit MI 48226

CORROTHERS, HELEN GLADYS, government criminal justice official; b. Montrose, Ark., Mar. 19, 1937; d. Thomas and Christene (Farley) Curl; m. Edward Corrothers, Dec. 17, 1968 (div. Sept. 1983); 1 child, Michael Edward. AA in Liberal Arts magna cum laude, Ark. Bapt. Coll., 1955; BS in Bus. Adminstrn. Mgmt., Roosevelt U., 1965; grad. officer leadership sch. WAC Sch., 1965; grad. Inst. Criminal Justice, Exec. Ctr. Continuing Edn., U. Chgo., 1973; postgrad. Calif. Coast U., 1981—. Enlisted U.S. Army, 1956, advanced through grades to capt., 1969; chief mil. personnel Hdqrs. and Hdqrs. Co., U.S. Army, Ft. Meyer, Va., 1965-67; dir. for housing Giessen Support Ctr., Fed. Republic Germany, 1967-69; resigned, 1969; social interviewer Ark. Dept. Corrections, Grady, 1970-71, supt. women's unit, Pine Bluff, 1971-83; chief commr. U.S. Parole Commn., Burlingame, Calif., 1983-85, U.S. Sentencing Commn., Washington, 1985—; instr. corrections U.Ark.-Pine Bluff, 1976-79; mem. bd. visitation Jefferson County Juvenile Ct., Pine Bluff, 1978-81; bd. dirs. Vols. in Cts., 1979-84, Vols. Am., 1985-88; mem. Am./Can. study team, Mexican penal system Am. Correctional Assn., Islas Marias, Mex., summer 1981; mem. Ark. Commn. on Crimes and Law Enforcement, 1975-78. Mem. Ark. Commn. on Status of Women, 1976-78; bd. dirs. Com. Against Spouse Abuse, 1982-84. Recipient Ark, Woman of Achievement award Ark. Press Women's Assn., 1980, Human Relations award Ark. Edn. Assn., 1980, Outstanding Woman of Achievement award Sta.-KATV-TV, Little Rock, 1981, Correctional Service award Vols. Am., 1984, William H. Hastie award Nat. Assn. Blacks in Criminal Justice, 1986. Mem. Am. Correctional Assn. (treas. 1980-86, v.p. 1986-88), U.S. Attorney Gen.'s Correctional Policy Study Team, 1987, N.Am. Assn. Wardens and Supts., Ark. Law Enforcement Assn., Nat. Assn. Female Execs., Nat. Council on Crime and Delinquency, Am. Soc. Criminology, Ark. Sheriff's Assn. (hon.), Delta Sigma Theta (local sec. 1976-79, local parliamentarian 1983-84). Baptist. Avocations: reading, music. Office: US Sentencing Comm 1331 Pennsylvania Ave NW Washington DC 20004

CORSBERG, DOROTHY JEAN, humanities educator; b. Greeley, Colo., July 25, 1924; d. John Hermon and Inez Christine (Salberg) Corsberg; B.A., Colo. State Coll., 1946, M.A., 1952; postgrad. U. No. Colo., 60-81. Tchr., Oakesdale Consol. High Sch., Oakesdale, Wash., 1946-49; mem. faculty Northeastern Jr. Coll., Sterling, Colo., 1949-87, dean women, 1949-62, chmn. humanities div., 1962-83, instructional dir. gen. studies, 1983-87; prof. emeritus, 1987; critical reader/reviewer for ednl. materials; N.E. Colo. field cons. Colo. Humanities Program, 1982; mem. Colo. State Dept. Adv. Bd. Social Studies, 1966-68; chmn. Anna C. Petteys Scholarship Com., 1971-86; mem. rural libraries and humanities com. Colo. Planning and Resource Bd., 1982-83. Bd. dirs. Community Concert Assn., 1971-81. Named Outstanding Female Educator, U. No. Colo., 1968, Community Coll. Faculty Mem. of Yr., State Bd. Community Colls. and Occupational Edn. in Colo., 1981-82. Mem. NEA, Colo. Assn. Higher Edn. (program chmn., dir. 1965-67, NIC rep., Colo. core transfer curriculum faculty task force 1986-87), Colo. Assn. Coll. Instructional Dirs., P.E.O. Democrat. Home: 1113 Beattie Dr Sterling CO 80751

CORSI, DEBORAH ERANDA, editor; b. McKeesport, Pa., May 6, 1953; d. Adolph J. and Francesca S. (D'Arliano) C. A.A.S., No. Va. Community Coll., 1980; B.A., Marymount Coll., 1984. Sec. Northwestern Mut. Life Ins. Co., Arlington, Va., 1971-72, adminstrv. asst., 1972-79; editorial asst. Smithsonian Mag., Washington, 1979-80; editorial and promotion asst. Smithsonian Instn. Press, 1981-83, editor, 1984-85; editor Jour. Alcohol Studies, 1986-87; freelance editor, 1987—. Roman Catholic. Home: 4306 Warner Ln Chantilly VA 22021

CORT, DIANA, social worker; b. N.Y.C., Oct. 27, 1934; d. Arthur and Augusta Deutsch; B.S., N.Y.U., 1955; M.S.W., Columbia U., 1957; m. Leonard Van Arsdale, Sept. 17, 1978; children by previous marriage—Hayley, Daniel. Clinician, Payne Whitney Clinic, N.Y. Hosp., N.Y.C., 1957-59, psychiat. clinic Jewish Bd. Guardians, N.Y.C., 1959-61; founder, pres. Big Six Towers Nursery Sch., N.Y.C., 1962-67; dir. intake and social service L.I. Consultation Center, Forest Hills, N.Y., 1966-84, clin. dir., coordinator clin. services, 1984-86; supr., faculty mem. L.I. Inst. Mental Health, 1973-86; adminstr. Bleuler Psychotherapy Ctr., Forest Hills, 1986-87; cons. in social work Bergen Ctr. for Child Devel., 1981—; dir. Seniors Option Service, Allendale, N.J., 1980—. Mem. Nat. Assn. Social Workers, N.Y. Soc. Clin. Social Workers. Address: 97 17 64th Rd Forest Hills NY 11374

CORTA, NANCY RUTH, nurse; b. Gorman, Tex., Feb. 15, 1957; d. Dale Newton and Perelene Ruth (Wright) Johnson; m. Peter Joseph Corta. BSN, Tex. Woman's U., Denton, 1980. Staff nurse Baylor U. Med. Ctr., Dallas, 1980-81; charge nurse ICU/CCU DeLeon Hosp., Tex., 1981-82; staff nurse MICU/CCU VA Med. Ctr., Phoenix, 1982-83; staff nurse Harris Hosp. Meth., Ft. Worth, 1983-84, Tex. Dept. Health, Stephenville, 1984—. Mem. Tex. Women's U. Alumni Assn., Epsilon Sigma Alpha. Lodge: Order Eastern Star. Home: Rt 2 Box 192 DeLeon TX 76444 Office: Texas Dept Health PHR-5 2301 Northwest Loop Suite B Stephenville TX 76401

CORTES, GUADALUPE MALDONADO, educator; b. Laredo, Tex., Aug. 28, 1941; d. Rogelio and Ramona (Diaz) Maldonado; m. Luis Cortes, Dec. 18, 1960; children: Maria Jesus, Sara Alicia, Luis Jr. BBA, Laredo State U., 1979, BS in Secondary Edn., 1984; MPA, LaSalle U., 1988. Cert. tchr., Tex., Mich. Comptroller Tex. Migrant Council, Laredo, 1974-81; adminstr. Laredo Kidney Ctr., Laredo, 1981-82; cons. Domingo A. and Esther A. Lara M.D.'s, Laredo, 1984—; adminstrv. aide Adolfo G. Garcia M.D., Laredo, 1981—; tchr. Laredo Ind. Sch. Dist., 1982—. Pres. Laredo Kidney Found., 1981—; del. Webb County Dems., Laredo, 1982. Mem. Nat. Assn. for Female Exec., AAUW, Tex. Tchrs. Assn. (del.), Tex. Tchrs. Assn. Hispanic Caucus. Club: Mercy Reg Med. Ctr. Aux. Home: 3304 Mier Laredo TX 78043 Office: Laredo Kidney Found 1020 E Calton Rd Rear Laredo TX 78041

CORTES, NANCY, professional association executive, contract administrator; b. Bklyn., Sept. 1, 1952; 1 child, Daryl James Howard. BA, Bklyn. Coll., 1974; JD, Antioch U., 1982. Exec. dir. Sunset Bay Community Services, Inc., Bklyn., 1983-86; exec. v.p. Mount Dora (Fla.) C. of C., 1986-87; contract compliance officer Fla. Dept. Transp., DeLand, 1987—. Human relations facilitator, 72d Precinct Community Patrol Program, Bklyn., 1983-86; mem. area policy bd., N.Y.C. Community Devel. Agy., 1983-86; judicial del. Second Judicial Dist., 51st Assembly., Bklyn., 1985. Home: 2019 Adelia Blvdt Deltona FL 32725 Office: Fla Dept of Transp 719 S Woodland Blvd De Land FL 32720

CORTEZ, SANDRA RINEL, business owner; b. Tegucigalpa, Honduras, Dec. 21, 1949; came to U.S. 1965, naturalized, 1985; d. Samuel and Herminia (Ochoa) Quan; m. Emilio Cortez, Nov. 11, 1972; children: Daniel, Emilio, Claudia. Grad. Met. Bus. Coll., 1968. Exec. sec., interpreter Harza Engring. Co., Chgo., 1975-78; exec. sec. Eagle Internat. Mfg., Brownsville, Tex., 1979-80, Hunt Pan Am Aviation, Brownsville Internat. Airport, 1981-82; gen. mgr. Brownsville Communications, Tex., 1982-84; owner, gen. profl. mgr. Profl. Sectl. Services and Translation Bur., 1982—. Author: Manual for Telephone Operators, 1982—. Mem. Am. Heart Assn. (devel. chmn. Region 14), Ct. Interpreters and Translators, Nat. Assn. Female Execs., Bus. and Profl. Women. Republican. Roman Catholic. Avocations: reading, gourmet cooking, music. Home: 217 Alan-A-Dale Brownsville TX 78521 Office: Profl Secretarial Services and Translation Bur 302 Kings Hwy Suite 210 Brownsville TX 78521

CORWIN, JOYCE ELIZABETH STEDMAN, construction company executive; b. Chgo.; d. Cresswell Edward and Elizabeth Josephine (Kimbell) Stedman; student Fla. State U., U. Miami; m. William Corwin, May 1, 1965; children—Robert Edmund Newman, Jillanne Elizabeth Newman. Pres. Am. Properties, Inc., Miami, Fla., 1966-72; v.p. Stedman Constrn. Co., Miami, 1971—; owner Joy-Win Horses, Gray lady ARC, 1969-70; guidance worker Youth Hall, 1969-70; sponsor Para Med. Group of Coral Park High Sch., 1969-70. Hostess, Rep. presdl. campaign, 1968; aide Rep. Nat. Conv., 1972. Salzburg fellow, 1988. Mem. Dade County Med. Aux. (chmn. directory com. 1970), Fla. Psychiat. Soc. Aux., Vizcayans, Fla. Morgan Horse Assn., Fla. Thoroughbred Breeders Assn. Clubs: Coral Gables Junior Women's (chmn. casework com. 1959-63), Golden Hills Golf and Turf, Royal Palm Tennis, Heritage, Golden Hills Golf & Turf, Royal Dames of Ocala. Home: 5780 SW 59 Ave Miami FL 33143 Other: Windrift Farm Rt 1 Box 239 F Reddick FL 32686

CORWIN, RITA JEAN, sales executive; b. Casa Grande, Ariz., May 22, 1951; d. Howard Throop and Barbara (Catron) Christensen; m. Bruce James Corwin, Aug. 31, 1968; children: Christina, Troy. Student, U. Alaska, 1987—. Computer sales exec. Dictation Systems, Inc., Kansas City, Mo., 1975-80; mgr. sales Barrett Office Supply, Anchorage, 1980-85; sales exec. Gen. Communications, Inc., Anchorage, 1986-87; account exec. Olympic Broadcasting Sta. KGOT, Anchorage, 1987—. Counselor Youth for Christ Crisis Hotline Intervener, Anchorage, 1986-88; vol. Anchorage Olympic Organizing Com., 1987—; exec. dir. Miss SouthCen. Alaska Scholarship Pageant, Anchorage, 1987, Miss Anchorage Scholarship Pageant, 1988. Recipient Outstanding Community Service award Nat. Mother/Daughter Pageant, 1986, Outstanding Directorship award Miss Alaska/Am. Program, 1988. Mem. Am. Bus. Women's Assn. (dirs. ways and means com. 1986-87, pres. 1987-88), Nat. Exec. Women's Assn. Republican. Home: 12100 Forelands Circle Anchorage AK 99515

CORY, BEVERLY JANE WEST, computer programmer; b. Middletown, Ohio, Apr. 2, 1959; d. James Edward and Irma Louise (Bailey) W.; m. Robert Baxter Cory, June 27, 1987. Cert. computer programming, Columbus Paraprofl. Inst., 1983; BS in Natural Resources cum laude, Ohio State U., 1982. Cashier, administrv. asst. McDonald's Univ. City, Columbus, Ohio, 1982-83; instr. word processing Bliss Coll., Columbus, 1983; lead computer operator Liebert Corp., Columbus, 1983-86, computer programmer, 1986-87; computer programmer Sears Roebuck Acceptance Corp., Greenville, Del., 1987—. Mem. The Wildlife Soc., 95 Club, Alpha Lambda Delta, Phi Eta Sigma, Gamma Sigma Delta. Home: 1 Sandalwood Dr Apt 12 Newark DE 19713

CORY, PAMELA MITCHELL, marketing professional; b. Seattle, Mar. 25, 1961; d. William Frederick and Mary Ann (Henneberger) Mitchell; m. Stephen Douglas Cory, Aug. 25, 1984. BA in Journalism and Sociology, U. Wash., 1983; MBA, Gonzaga U., 1986; postgrad., Seattle U., 1986—. Pub. relations rep. Providence Med. Ctr., Seattle, 1982-84, Restaurant Assn. Wash., Seattle, 1984; mktg. communications rep. Key Tronic Corp., Spokane, Wash., 1984-86; communications specialist Intermec Corp., Lynnwood, Wash., 1986—; free-lance writer various radio and TV stas., Wash., 1980-86; mktg. cons. Greenwood & Assocs., Spokane, 1984-86. Editor hosp. newsletter, 1982-84; contbr. articles to profl. jours. Communications specialist Spokane Inland Empire Found., Spokane, 1984-86; loaned exec. United Way Spokane, 1985. Mem. Internat. Exhibitors Assn., MBA Assn., Bus. and Profl. Women's Assn., Jr. League Spokane and Seattle, Delta Gamma. Roman Catholic. Club: Toastmasters Internat. Home: 1012 NE 71st Seattle WA 98115 Office: Intermec Corp PO Box 360602 Lynnwood WA 98046

CORYEA, CHERYL JEAN, controller; b. Emmetsburg, Iowa, May 16, 1951; d. Chester Earnest and Sylvia Marie (Moore) Cornwell; m. James Armand Coryea II, Apr. 5, 1975 (div. July 1987); 1 child, James Armand III. BSBA, Morningside Coll., Sioux City, Iowa, 1973. CPA, Minn. Staff acct. Price Waterhouse & Co., Mpls., 1973-75; sr. auditor Dayton Hudson Corp., Mpls., 1975-78; fin. analyst Ellerbe, Inc., Mpls., 1978-79, acctg. mgr., 1979-84, corp. controller, 1984—. Mem. Minn. Soc. CPA's. Republican. Methodist. Office: Ellerbe Inc One Appletree Square Minneapolis MN 55420

COSMANO, RHODA, social services administrator; b. N.Y.C., July 13, 1947; d. Jac Carl and Ruth Blanche (Rosenberg) Kaufman; m. Anthony J. Cosmano, Aug. 24, 1969 (div. 1984). BA in Sociology, SUCB, Buffalo, 1969; MEd in Personnel and Counseling, SUNY, Buffalo, 1971; MSW, Ariz. State U., 1983. Counselor, youth worker Lafayette Community Ctr., Buffalo, 1967-70, social work dir., 1970-72; counselor Compass House Runaway Ctr., Buffalo, 1972-73; caseworker Dept. Econ. Security, Phoenix, 1973-76, licensing cons., 1976-85, program evaluator child protective services, 1985, mgr. residential licensing, 1985-86, supr. child protective services, 1986—; trainer Therapeutic Phys. Intervention, Phoenix, 1983—; community mediator Community Mediation Program, Phoenix, 1986—, family mediator, 1987—. Bd. dirs. Glendale (Ariz.) Community Council, 1987. Mem. Nat. Assn. Social Workers (chair community services com. 1986—, mem. steering com., state bd. 1987—), Nat. Acad. Family Mediators. Office: Dept Econ Security PO Box 6123 146C Phoenix AZ 85005

COSSIO, MARIA-JESUS, mathematics educator; b. Santander, Spain, Mar. 13, 1935; d. Rafael Garcia and Emilia Cossio. Lic. in Physics, Univ. Complutense, Madrid, 1958; MA in Math., Boston Coll., 1965; EdD, Columbia U., N.Y.C., 1977. Tchr. Pace High Sch., Opa-Locka, Fla., 1963-67; supr. math. and sci. Archdiocese of Miami (Fla.), 1967-72; adj. instr. John Jay Coll. CUNY, N.Y.C., 1973-76; bilingual adj. instr. math. Montclair (N.J.) State Coll., 1976-77, Mercy Coll., Dobb Ferry, N.Y., 1976-77; assoc. prof. math No. Va. Community Coll., Manassas, 1977-78; asst. prof. math. La Guardia Community Coll. CUNY, L.I., N.Y., 1978-85, assoc. prof., 1985—; cons. Zeus Mag., Madrid, 1987—; bd. dirs. Solidaridad Humana, Inc., N.Y. Mem. 3d World Faculty and Staff Assn. La Guardia Coll. CUNY, 1980—. Fellow Institutum Divi Thomae, Cin., 1958-60, NSF fellow, 1971; grantee CUNY, 1980. Mem. Nat. Council Tchrs. in Math., Math. Assn. Am., Nat. Assn. Devel. Edn., N.Y. Metro Assn. Devel. Edn. Democrat. Roman Catholic. Office: La Guardia Community Coll/ CUNY 31-10 Thomson Ave Long Island NY 11101

COSSITT, JENNIFER, Canadian legislator; b. Regeal, Yorkshire, Eng., June 22, 1948; d. Nathaniel Charles and Jean (Sorrell) Birchall; m. Thomas Charles Cossitt (dec.), Jan. 5, 1980. Pres. E.C. Cossitt Co. Ltd.; chmn. Thomas C. Cossitt Found.; mem. from Leeds-Grenville Can. Ho. of Commons, 1982—. Mem. Brockville Theatre Guild. Mem. Progressive Conservative Party. Anglican. Club: Brockville Golf and Country. Address: PO Box 97, Brockville, ON Canada K6T 5V7 *

COSTA, CATHERINE AURORA, state senator; b. Bklyn., Mar. 21, 1926; d. Salvatore and Matilde (Giumporcaro) Bravo; m. Joseph P. Costa, Sept. 7, 1946; children—Nicholas, Theodore, Nadine. Freeholder, Burlington County (N.J.), 1972-83; mem. N.J. Gen. Assembly, 1982-83; mem. N.J. Senate, 1984—. Founder, Willingboro Library (N.J.), 1959, trustee, 1962-66; bd. dirs., chmn. Willingboro Zoning Bd. Adjustment, 1969-73. Named N.J. Mother of Yr., 1976; Citizen of Yr., VFW, Willingboro, 1982; recipient Soil Conservation Supr. award N.J. Assn. Natural Resource Dists., 1973. Democrat. Roman Catholic. Home: 32 Twig Ln Willingboro NJ 08046 Office: Legislative Office 11 W Broad St Burlington NJ 08016 *

COSTA, H. MARIE, writer; b. Burbank, Calif., Aug. 27, 1951; d. Larry and Betty Lee (Kesling) C.; m. William Yon Regan, June 8, 1985; stepchildren: Vesla Danielle, Andria Corinne. Student, Met. State Coll., 1987—. Staff writer Denver Monthly Mag., 1980-81; dir., head writer Sound Off, Los Angeles, 1981-82; freelance writer Denver, 1982—. Author: Adult Literacy/Illiteracy in the U.S.: A Handbook for Reference and Research, 1988; co-author: A Micro Handbook for Small Libraries and Media Centers, 1983, 2d edit., 1986; contbr. articles to profl. jours. Vol. Citizens for Romer, Denver, 1986. Mem. Soc. for Children's Book Writers (bd. dirs. 1986-87, newsletter editor), No. Colo. Writers Workshop. Democrat. Home and Office: 12255 W Ohio Pl Lakewood CO 80228

COSTA, MARY, soprano; b. Knoxville, Tenn.; student Los Angeles Conservatory of Music. Film voice of Sleeping Beauty by Walt Disney; appeared TV commls., 1955-57; debut Los Angeles Opera, 1958, in La Boheme, San Francisco Opera, 1959, as Violetta in La Traviata at Met. Opera, N.Y.C., 1964; appeared Glyndebourne Opera House, Royal Opera House Covent Garden, Teatro Nacional de San Carlos, Grand Theatre de Geneve, Vancouver, Lisbon, Kiev, Leningrad, Tbilisi, Boston, Cin., Hartford, Newark, Phila., San Antonio, Seattle; toured U.S. with Bernstein's Candide; appeared English prodn. Candide; revival Bernstein's Candide at John F. Kennedy Center for Performing Arts, 1971; tour Soviet Union, 1970; Bolshoi debut in La Traviatta, 1970; starring role motion picture The Great Waltz, 1972; appeared internat. recitals, orchs.; v.p. Hawaiian Fragrances, Honolulu, 1972. Vice pres. Calif. Inst. Arts. Named Woman of yr., Los Angeles, 1959; recipient DAR Honor medal, 1974, Tenn. Hall of Fame award, 1987; Mary Costa Scholarship established at U. Tenn., 1979. Address: care Calif Artists Mgmt 1182 Market St Suite 418 San Francisco CA 94102

COSTANTINO, LORINE PROTZMAN, woodworking co. exec.; b. Chattanooga, Feb. 8, 1921; d. John Edgar and Rosa Jane (Ellis) McClelland; student U. Balt., U. Ill.; m. Conrad Protzman, 1937 (dec. 1958); children—Rosa Lorine, Charles Conrad, James Paul, Sharon Lee; m. 2d, Anthony A. Costantino, Feb. 27, 1960. With Conrad Protzman, Inc., Balt., 1954—, pres., chief exec., 1958—; developer apprenticeship programs for woodworking industry. Mem. Archtl. Woodworking Inst. (dir.), Bldg. Congress and Exchange Balt., Am. Sub-Contractors Assn., Nat. Assn. Women Bus. Owners, Iota Lambda Sigma (hon. mem. Nu chpt.). Republican. Roman Catholic. Club: Hillendale Country. Office: Conrad Protzman Inc 2325 Banger St Baltimore MD 21230

COSTELLO, DAWN ELIZABETH BARNES, nurse, municipal administrator; b. Allentown, Pa., Dec. 7, 1940; d. Earl O. and Thelma (Walp) Barnes; m. Robert G. Costello, May 12, 1962; children: Michael R., Kelly L. BS in Nursing, U. Pa., 1962, postgrad., 1987—; MEd, Temple U., 1967; EdD in Adminstrn., Lehigh U., 1973. Nurse Allentown Sch. Dists., 1963-67; dir. research and records Lehigh County Community Coll., Schnecksville, Pa., 1972-74; assoc. dir. nursing Sacred Heart Hosp., Allentown, 1974-78; assoc. dir. personal health service City of Allentown, 1979-81; dir. nursing Coaldale (Pa.) Hosp., 1981—; 1st dir. pub. health nursing Bi-City Health Bur., Allentown and Bethlehem, Pa., 1979; adv. bd. Advanced Degree program Lehigh County Community Coll., 1987—, LDN program Carbon County Vocat.-Tech. Inst., Jim Thorpe, Pa., 1981-84; cons. Northwestern Ctr., Schnecksville, 1978—. Mem. adv. bd. Am. Heart Assn. Bethlehem, 1974-78; sec., bd. dirs. Vols. in Am. Day Care, Allentown, 1972-78. Mem. Pa. Orgn. Nurse Execs. (pres. Eastern region 1988—), Lehigh Valley Assn. for Learning Disabilities (pres. 1981-83). Republican. Roman Catholic. Home: RD #1 Box 240-A Schnecksville PA 18078 Office: Coaldale Gen Hosp 7th St Coaldale PA 18218

COSTELLO, DEBBIE W., graphic designer; b. Hanover, N.H., July 18, 1953, d. Edgar F. and Virginia (Lee) C. BA, Middlebury (Vt.) Coll., 1976; postgrad., U. Calif., Berkeley, 1979-81. Ptnr., graphic designer, editor Black Oyster Press, San Francisco, 1980—; graphic designer Ligature, Inc., Chgo., 1982-83, McDougal, Littell, Evanston, Ill., 1983-85; graphic design mgr. Scott, Foresman and Co., Glenview, Ill., 1985—. Author, designer: Looking In, 1977; editor, designer: From Shadows Emerging: An Anthology of the Bay Area, 1981, From the Island, 1982. Recipient Graphic Design U.S.A. award, 1986, 87. Mem. Feminist Writer's Guild, Chgo. Book Clinic (Book Design award 1986). Home: 3654 N Bosworth Chicago IL 60613 Office: Scott Foresman and Co 1900 E Lake Ave Glenview IL 60025

COSTELLO, EILEEN MARIE, insurance company executive; b. Camden, N.J., May 3, 1949. BA, Holy Family Coll., 1971; MPA, Rutgers U., 1988. CIE, 1988, CPCU. From rate analyst trainee to ins. analyst I 1972-85, asst. chief of rating, 1985—, instr. CPCU, 1986-88; instr. CPCU N.J. Dept. Ins., 1986-87. Mem. CPCU's Soc., Cert. Pub. Mgrs. Soc., Am. Soc. for Pub. Adminstrn., Nat. Assn. Female Execs. Roman Catholic. Home: 101 Oak Pines Blvd Pemberton NJ 08068 Office: NJ Ins Dept 20 W State St CN 325 Trenton NJ 08625

COSTELLO, JOAN, psychologist; b. Lawrence, Mass., Jan. 16, 1937; d. William Agustine and Helen Mary (Dolfe) C.; B.S., Boston Coll., 1959; M.S., Ill. Inst. Tech., 1963, Ph.D., 1967; 1 dau., Cathleen. Clin. psychologist Cath. Charities Chgo., 1960-70; research scientist Ill. Inst. Juvenile Research, 1964-70; asst. prof. Yale U., 1970-77; dean, Erikson Inst., Chgo., 1977-79; assoc. prof. Sch. Social Service Adminstrn., U. Chgo., 1979-85, dir. Chapin Hall Forum, 1985—; pvt. practice clin. psychology, 1985—; cons. U.S. Dept. Health and Human Services. Mem. Am. Psychol. Assn., Soc. Research Child Devel., Am. Orthopsychiat. Assn., AAAS. Office: 1535 Lake Cook Rd Suite 305 Northbrook IL 60025

COSTELLO, LORETTA ELIZABETH, realty firm executive; b. Jamaica, N.Y., Aug. 11, 1941; d. Peter F. and Loretta E. (McDermott) C. B.A., U. Md., 1963. Saleswoman, Lanier Bus. Products Co., N.Y.C., 1979-80; sales real estate N.K. Benjamin Realty Co., Forest Hills, N.Y.C., 1980-83; owner Town House Mgmt. Co., N.Y.C., 1982—; owner, broker Castleberry Realty Co., Rego Park, N.Y., 1984—, Forest Hills, N.Y., 1986—; residential apt. mgr. Com. mem. Concerned Citizens for Better Bayside, Queensboro Hill Neighborhood Assn., Flushing. Recipient various realty awards. Mem. Nat. Assn. Female Execs., Nat. Assn. Realtors, N.Y. State Assn. Realtors, L.I. Bd. Realtors (appraisal div., mortgage/banking, profl. standards coms. 1985—, polit. action com.), Forest Hills C. of C. Office: Castleberry Realty Co 62-57 Woodhaven Blvd Rego Park NY 11374 also: 117-16 Queens Blvd Forest Hills NY 11375

COSTELLO, MARY, consulting company executive; b. Omaha, Oct. 25, 1940; d. Patrick Francis and Margaret Helen (Costello) Henry; m. Donald F. Costello, Sept. 2, 1961; children—Maureen, Rick, Dan, Peter, Tom, Ben, Meg. B.A. in Sociology, Duchesne Coll., 1964. Vice pres. Costello & Assocs., Lincoln, Nebr., 1970—; reporter, editor Sun Papers, Lincoln, 1970-80; editor Tafelspitz Mag., Vienna, Austria, 1981—. Author: The Mary Costello How to Get a Job Book, 1988; weekly column Over the Coffee Cup (1st place award Nat. Suburban Newspaper Assn., 1985, Nat. Fedn. Press Women 1975—). Bd. dirs. Cedars Found. Children's Home, Lincoln, 1984—; pres. Alzheimer's Disease and Related Disorders Assn., Lincoln, 1988—. Mem. Nebr. Press Women, Nat. Press Women. Office: Costello & Assocs 4710 S 33d St Lincoln NE 68506

COSTIGAN, MAUREEN, lawyer; b. Trenton, N.J., Nov. 7, 1956; d. Augustus John and Ellen (O'Connell) C.; m. John W. Van Schaik. B.A. magna cum laude, Cabrini Coll., 1978; J.D., Cath. U. Am., 1981; LL.M., Villanova U., 1984. Bar: D.C. 1981, N.J. 1982, U.S. Dist. Ct. N.J. 1982, U.S. Tax Ct., 1985, U.S. Dist. Ct. D.C. 1987. Law clk. Arnold D. Berkeley Esq., Washington, 1980; assoc. Gerard F. Long Esq., Bridgewater, N.J., 1982-83, Malsbury & Armenante, Allentown, N.J., 1981-86, Law Offices Robert M. Adler, Washington, 1986—. Bruckman scholar, 1977-78. Mem. ABA, N.J. Bar Assn., D.C. Bar Assn. Home: 3600 Connecticut Ave NW Apt 307 Washington DC 20008

COTE, LOUISE ROSEANN, art director, designer; b. Quincy, Mass., Sept. 16, 1959; p. John Anthony and Theresa Janet (Oriola) Burke; m. Robert Andrew Cote, Aug. 6, 1983. BA, Bridgewater (Mass.) State Coll., 1981. Forms and graphics designer Shawmut Bank of Boston, N.A., 1981-86; art dir. Allied Aftermarket div. Allied-Signal, Inc., East Providence, R.I., 1986—; freelance designer Paine Webber Properties, N.Y.C., 1986-87. Roman Catholic. Office: Allied-Signal Inc Allied Aftermarket Div 105 Pawtucket Ave East Providence RI 02906

COTÉ, NANCY MARIE, computer company executive, columnist; b. Weehawken, N.J., Jan. 9, 1954; d. Conrad Robert and Anna Betti (Habenstein) Nurge; m. William Fredrich Firla, Oct. 20, 1973 (div. May 1979); 1 child, Kirsten Michelle; m. Mark David Coté, May 22, 1982; children: Sarah Janette, Danielle Marie. Student, Cen. Conn. State U., 1972-73, 82. Underwriter Mass Mut. Life Ins. Co., Springfield, Mass., 1973-79; sr. underwriter INA/AETNA, Phila., 1979-80, Conn. Gen., Bloomfield, Conn., 1980-82; owner NCM Enterprises, Torrington, Conn., 1982-84; pres. Ind. Computer Support, Inc., Avon, Conn., 1984—. Contbr. articles to newspapers. Mem. fin. com. St. Mathew Luth. Ch., Avon, 1986—. Recipient Nothing Succeeds Like Success award Assn. of Entrepreneurial Women, 1987. Mem. Assoc. Entrepeneurial Women (bd. dirs. 1987—). Republican. Lutheran. Office: Ind Computer Support Inc 23 Barbara Rd Bristol CT 06010

COTE, SALLY SPILKER, infosystems specialist; b. Huntington, W.Va., Nov. 16, 1946; d. Norman David and Nancy Ann (Gracie) S; m. Francis (Frank) Loyal Cote, Mar. 14, 1980. BS in Math., U. Ky., 1968; MBA, U. Detroit, 1983. Systems programmer analyst, supr. Ford Motor Credit Co., Dearborn, Mich., 1968-84, systems prodn. and devel. mgr., 1984-86, systems sect. supr. fin. staff, 1986-87, systems office mgr. office gen. counsel, 1987—. Active Dearborn Hills Civic Assn., 1983—. Presbyterian. Office: Ford Motor Co Office Gen Counsel Parklane Towers West Suite 820 Dearborn MI 48126

COTE-BEAUPRE, CAMILLE YVETTE, artist, educator; b. Worcester, Mass., May 21, 1926; d. Harvey and Blanche (Trahan) Cote; B.A. cum laude, Am. Internat. Coll., 1949; cert. in fine arts, Walker Studio Group, 1952; M.S., U. Bridgeport, 1967. Dir. arts and crafts South End Community Center, Springfield, Mass., 1955-58; art tchr. YWCA, Springfield, 1958-61; dir. workshops Hall Neighborhood House, Bridgeport, Conn., 1961-64, Jewish Community Center, Bridgeport, 1964-69; tchr., chmn. art dept. Notre Dame High Sch., Fairfield, Conn., 1970—; one-woman shows: Bridgeport Cath. Center, 1978, Creative Mind Gallery, Stratford, Conn., 1978, Burroughs Library, Bridgeport, 1979, Trumbull (Conn.) Library, 1981, St. Vincent's Hosp., Bridgeport, 1981, St. Joseph Manor, Trumbull, 1981; group shows include: Stamford (Conn.) Mus., 1977, Slade Mus., Norwich, Conn., 1975, Mus. Sci. and Industry, Bridgeport, 1974, Sacred Heart U., Bridgeport, 1979, Fairfield (Conn.) U., 1979, 56th grand nat. Am. Artists Profl. League, others; represented in permanent collections: Eastern Conn. State Coll., Trumbull Library Assn., St. Vincent's Hosp., St. Joseph's Manor. Mem. Conn. Classic Artists, Diocesan Bridgeport Edn. Assn., Newtown Soc. for Creative Arts, Am. Portrait Soc., Acad. Artists Assn., Nat. Arts Club, Conn. Pastel Soc. Home: 12 Melon Patch Ln Monroe CT 06468 Office: Notre Dame High Sch 220 Jefferson St Fairfield CT 06430

COTNEY, DEBORAH HOLDER, non-profit organization executive; b. Chattanooga, July 20, 1950; d. James Elam and Virginia Nell (Henson) Holder; m. William Russell Cotney, Dec. 17, 1977; 1 child, Lauren Amanda. BA, David Lipscomb Coll., 1972; MS, U. Ala., 1976. Tchr. Jackson Co. Bd. Edn., Bridgeport, Ala., 1972-73; grad. asst. U. Ala., Tuscaloosa, 1973-74; instr. David Lipscomb Coll., Nashville, 1974-77; dir. Elmore County Head Start, Montgomery, Ala., 1978-79; dir. programs Community Day Care and Comprehensive Social Service Assn., Memphis, 1979-82; pres. Sr. Citizens Services, Inc., Memphis, 1982—. Mem., visitation leader Ch. of Christ, Covington, Tenn., 1982—; com. chmn. Jr. Auxiliary, Covington, 1985—; provider rep. Shelby County Social Services Adv. Council, Memphis, 1985—; mem. Memphis State U. Human Services Co-Op, 1986—; appointed rep. City of Memphis Human Services Adv. Council, 1987; grad. Leadership Memphis, 1987, mem. selection com., 1988; strategic planning com. United Way Greater Memphis, 1988—. Mem. United Way Execs. Assn. (sec.-treas. 1986—), Tenn. Conf. on Social Welfare, Nat. Council of Sr. Citizens, Jaycettes (v.p. 1985). Office: Sr Citizens Services Inc 203 Beale St Suite 300 Memphis TN 38103

COTTEN, CATHERYN DEON, medical center international advisor; b. Erwin, N.C., Apr. 13, 1952; d. Ben Hur and Minnie Lee (Smith) C. BS in Anthropology, Duke U., 1975. Asst. internat. advisor Med. Ctr. Duke U., Durham, N.C., 1975-76; internat. advisor Med. Ctr. Duke U., Durham, 1976—. Mem., bd. dirs., tutor Durham Literacy Council, 1985—; mem. internat. com. Durham County ARC, 1987—. Recipient cert. recognition So. Regional Council Black Am. Affairs, Atlanta, 1985. Mem. Nat. Assn .Fgn. Student Scholar Affairs (govt. regulations adv. com. 1985—). Club: Altrusa (Durham) (pres. 1987-89). Office: Med Ctr Duke U Durham NC 27710

COTTER, SHIRLEY ANN, financial planner; b. Slim River, Malaysia; came to U.S., 1974; naturalized, 1987; d. Isaac V. and Ivy (D'Cruez) Pereira; m. Gary W. Cotter, Dec. 11, 1982. RN, Queen Mary's Hosp., Sidcup, Kent, Eng., 1965; postgrad., Sussex Maternity Hosp., Brighton, Eng., 1965, Dartford Hosp., Kent, Eng., 1966, McGill U., Montreal, Que., 1974. Med. adminstr. U.S. Peace Corps., Kuala Lumpur, Malaysia, 1969-73; RN intensive care unit Meml. Med. Ctr., Corpus Christi, Tex., 1974-76, Spohn Hosp., Corpus Christi, 1976-78; registered rep. Investors Diversified Services, Inc., Mpls., 1979-83; branch mgr. WZW Fin. Services, Inc., Shawnee Mission, Kans., 1983-84; registered rep. The Planner's Securities Group, Inc., Atlanta, 1985—; v.p. Cotter & Cotter Fin. Group, Corpus Christi, 1984—, Cotter & Cotter Risk Mgmt. Corp., Corpus Christi, 1985—, Cotter & Cotter Fin. Cons., Inc., Corpus Christi, 1984—. Mem. Internat. Assn. Fin. Planning (dir. 1986—), Inst. for Cert. Fin. Planners (provisional mem. 1983-85). Office: Cotter & Cotter Fin Group 705 MBank Center North Corpus Christi TX 78471-0801

COTTER, VERONICA IRENE, hotel executive; b. Altoona, Pa., June 2, 1949; d. William John and Joan Elmyra (Pennington) C.; m. Kenneth Brown, Sept. 12, 1971 (div. Mar. 1977); 1 child, Jennifer Alena. BS, Northeastern U., Boston, 1978. With nat. group sales office The Sheraton Corp., Boston, 1978-79; with sales tng. program The Sheraton Boston, 1980; account exec. Billings (Mont.) Sheraton, 1980; corp. sales mgr., account exec. Sheraton Columbus, Ohio, 1980-82; sr. account exec. Sheraton Steamboat Springs, Colo., 1982-83; mgr. sales Sheraton Charleston, S.C., 1983-84; dir. sales Sheraton Denver Airport Hotel, 1985-86; sr. account mgr. Sheraton Grande Hotel, Los Angeles, 1986—; instr. mktg. Am. Coll. Hotel Restaurant Mgmt. Area advisor Jr. Achievement, Nashville, 1985; vol. Buddy at AIDS Project, Los Angeles. Mem. Am. Soc. Assn. Execs., Meeting Planners Internat., Hotel Sales and Mktg. Assn. (pres. 1988—), Greater Washington Soc. Assn. Execs. Democrat. Roman Catholic. Office: Sheraton Grande Hotel 333 S Figueroa St Los Angeles CA 90071

COTTONE, SUZANNE WRIGHT, plastics company owner; b. Columbus, Ohio, Dec. 5, 1946; d. Harold Edgar and Helen (Miller) W.; m. David Paul Cottone, Dec. 18, 1982. BA, U. Evansville, 1971; MBA, So. Meth. U., 1975. Communications asst. Whirlpool Corp., Evansville, Ind., 1971-73, mgr., 1975-81; gen. supr. Whirlpool Corp., Evansville, 1981-85; supr. Whirlpool Corp., Benton Harbor, Mich., 1972-74; owner Cottone Corp., Chandler, Ind., 1985—; also Evansville, Ind. Active Met. Evansville Progress Com., 1982-83; pres. Evansville Civic Theatre, 1983, chmn. adv. bd. Salvation Army, Evansville, 1987; bd. dirs. Deaconess Hosp. Found., Evansville, 1986-87. Republican. Mem. United Ch. Christ. Office: Cottone Corp 1511 N Garvin St Evansville IN 47711

COTTRELL, JANET ANN, retail executive; b. Berea, Ohio, Dec. 2, 1943; d. Carmen and Hazel (French) Volpe; m. Melvin M. Cottrell, Mar. 2, 1963; children: Lori A., Gregory C. Student, Los Angeles State Coll., 1961-63. Lic. ins. agt., Calif. Loan processing Eastern Lenders, Covina, 1962-64; asst. bookkeeper Golden Rule Discount Stores, Rosemead, Calif., 1964-66; acctg. supr. Walter Carpet Mills, Industry, Calif., 1967-69; co-owner M.C. Specialties Inc., Industry, Calif., 1969-78, Covina (Calif.) Kawasaki, 1978-84; v.p., controller M.C. Specialties Inc., Covina, 1984—; active various coms. relating to promotion, safety and advancement of the recreational vehicle and auto industry, So. Calif., 1981—. Mem. com. Miss Covina Pageant, 1986—, presdl. task force, nat., 1982—, Rep. nat. com., 1986—. Mem. Covina C. of C., Calif. Motorcycle Dealers Assn., Nat. Auto Dealers Assn., Internat. Jet Ski Boating Assn. Republican. Lodges: Rotary (top prize short story 1958), Rions. Office: MC Specialties Inc 1017 W San Bernardino Rd Covina CA 91722

COTTRELL, MARY-PATRICIA TROSS, banker; b. Seattle, Apr. 24, 1934; d. Alfred Carl and Alice-Grace (O'Neal) Tross; m. Richard Smith Cottrell, May 17, 1969. BBA, U. Wash., 1955. Systems service rep. IBM, Seattle, also Endicott, N.Y., 1955-58, customer edn. instr., Endicott, 1958-60, 62-65, edn. planning rep., San Jose, Calif. and Endicott, N.Y., 1960-62; cons. data processing, Stamford, Conn., 1965-66; asst. treas. Union Trust Co., Stamford, 1967-68, asst. v.p., 1969-76, v.p., 1976-78, v.p., head corp. services, 1978-83; v.p. corp. fin. services Citytrust, Bridgeport, Conn., 1983—. Chmn., bd. dirs. Family and Children's Aid of Greater Norwalk (Conn.), 1986-87; bd. dirs. Gaylord Hosp., 1986-87, Bridgeport Housing Services, New Eng. Network, Inc.; trustee New Money Inst., Washington. Mem. Electronic Funds Transfer Assn. (vice chmn., bd. dirs., chmn. bd. dirs. 1983-84), Fairfield County Bankers Assn. (dir., pres. 1984-85), West Norwalk Assn. (bd. dirs.). Republican. Roman Catholic. Club: Grad. Office: Citytrust 961 Main St Bridgeport CT 06601

COUCH, ALICE MAE, nursing home administrator, practical nurse; b. Genoa, Ohio, Jan. 22, 1936; d. Thomas William and Marie (Croston) Charlton; m. Earl Dean Couch, Oct. 16, 1954; children—George Gilbert, Andrew Dean, Larry William. Student W.Va. U., 1968, 70. Lic. practical nurse, W.Va.; lic. nursing home adminstr., W.Va. News reporter, Steubenville Herald, Ohio, 1953-55; clerical positions Valley Haven Rest Home, Wellsburg, W.Va., 1957-68, nurse, adminstr., 1968-72, owner, adminstr., 1972—; sec. W.Va. Health Care, Charleston, 1972-74, pres., 1974-76, 81-83, bd. dirs., 1983—; bd. dirs. New Martinsville Health Care, W.Va., 1982—, Lewis Wetzel Nursing Home, New Martinsville, 1980-83. Hon. bd. dirs. Brooke County Soc. Crippled Children and Adults, W.Va., 1984; mem. exec. com. Republican Party, Brooke County, 1979-80, adv. council Med. Fund Services W.Va. Dept. Human Services, 1975—, chairperson, 1986-87. Recipient Presdl. citation Am. Health Care Assn., 1976; Service award W.Va. Dept. Health, 1977; Better Life award W.Va. Health Care, 1977; Outstanding Service award W.Va. Health Care, 1980. Mem. W.Va. Health Systems Agy., W.Va. State Healthwide Coordinating Council, W.Va. Health Care Assn. Republican. Mem. Disciples of Christ Ch. Club: Wellsburg Jr. Woman's. Lodges: Women of Moose. Avocations: gardening; handicrafts; collecting English commemorative pieces. Home and Office: RD 2 Box 44 Wellsburg WV 26070

COUCH, CYNTHIA MARIE, social service director, consultant; b. Newark, Oct. 14, 1946; d. Leroy Rase and Elizabeth Mary (Graham) C.; children: Kevin Leroy, Keith Lawrence. BA in Pyschology, Caldwell Coll., 1977. Cons., employment specialist Urban League Hudson County, Jersey City, 1984-85; cons., community coordinator Hub Program for Women's Self-Employment, Newark, 1985-86; cons., coordinator displaced homemaker program Wise Women's Ctr., Newark, 1986-87; founder, exec. dir. Women's Employment Network N.J., Newark, 1985—; cons., community coordinator debtor's anonymous program N.Y. Women's Edn. Ctr., N.Y.C., 1985—; coordinating dir. CMC Devels., Newark, 1985—; cons. Vanguard Mothers, Newark, 1985—. Founder, pres., trustee Newark Urban Women's Ctr. Mem. Internat. Black Women Congress.

COUCHMAN, MARY CATHERINE, administrative assistant; b. Centerville, Iowa, Aug. 24, 1945; d. George Richard and Genevieve Catherine (Rash) Mincks; m. Gary Joe Couchman, Nov. 7, 1965; children: Duane Lee, Troy Dean. Student, N.E. Mo. State U., 1963-65, Indian Hills Community Coll., 1965, Parsons Coll., Mt. Pleasant, Iowa, 1971. Sec. various orgns., 1962-66, 75-77, 77-82; sch. tchr. substitute R 3, Unionville, Mo., 1974-77; adminstrv. asst. Rathbun Area Mental Ctr., Centerville, 1982—, support staff coordinator, 1983—. Mem. Community Betterment Com., Seymour, Iowa, Extension Council Wayne County, Corydon, Iowa, 1984-86; pres. United Meth. Women, Seymour, fin. chmn. United Meth. Ch., Seymour, 1985-87. Named one of Outstanding Young Women of Am., 1971. Mem. Nat. Assn. Female Execs., Beta Tau Delta. Republican. Club: Rainbow (Seymour) (worthy advisor 1962-63). Home: Rural Rt #1 Box 77 Seymour IA 52590 Office: Rathbun Area Mental Health Ctr 211 E State Centerville IA 52544

COUGHLAN, MARLEE TURNER, health resort executive, children's camp executive; b. Bronxville, N.Y., Feb. 16, 1933. B.A. in Polit. Sci., Stanford U., 1954. Elem. tchr. Palo Alto City Schs. (Calif.), 1954-56, Los Angeles City Schs., 1966-72; co-founder CKT Assocs., Topanga, Calif., 1975, ptnr., 1975-86; co-founder, pres. No. Pines Health Resort Raymond, Maine, 1979—, also dir.; v.p., co-founder Kingsley Pines Camp, Raymond, 1983—, adv. council Maine Mcpl. Assn.; mem. Town of Raymond Planning bd.; pres. LWV of Maine. Home and Office: Route 85 Box 279 Raymond ME 04071

COUGHLIN, CAROLYN MARY, vice president of operations; b. Marysville, Calif., Nov. 29, 1957; d. William Renwick and Mary Alice (Hewlett) Green. BS, U. Calif., Davis, 1979. Pvt. practice foods cons. San Francisco, 1979-83; test kitchen home economist Busse & Cummins Advt., San Francisco, 1980-82; store mgr. Mrs. Fields Cookies, Park City, Utah, 1983; multi-store mgr. Mrs. Fields Cookies, Park City, 1983-84, dist. mgr., 1984-85, v.p. operations, 1985—. Republican. Presbyterian. Office: Mrs Fields Cookies 2391 Butano Dr Sacramento CA 95825

COUGHLIN, ELIZABETH ANN, union official, consultant; b. Americus, Ga., Oct. 1, 1945; d. Sammie Raymond and Ruth Willie (Missledine) Simmons; m. Richard Paul Coughlin, Aug. 21, 1965. BA in Social Sci., St. Mary's Coll., 1978. Cert. employed assistance profl. Sr. med. abstractor Kaiser Hosp., Oakland, Calif., 1965-74; union rep. Office and Profl. Employees Union 29, Emeryville, Calif., 1974-76; cons. Nat. Council on Alcoholism, San Francisco, 1976-80, Simmons Coughlin Ltd., Oakland, 1980-88, sec.-treas., 1988—. Office and Profl. Employees Union 29, Emeryville, 1982—; mem. wage bd. State Calif. Indsl. Welfare Commn., Sacramento, 1976; co-chair Calif. Women's Commn. on Alcoholism, San Francisco, 1976-79; lectr., faculty mem. U. San Francisco, Duke U., U. Utah, Vista Coll., 1977-83; cons. State Calif., Sacramento, 1978-79. Prin. co-author: You Know You're a Peace Officer's Wife When, 1978. Editor The 29er, 1982-83. Mem. Friendship Force Internat., San Francisco, 1984—. Recipient Past Pres. award Past Pres. Com. of Peace Officers' Wives' Club Affiliated Calif., 1978, Resolution of Spl. Pub. Honor and Highest Commendation, Calif. Legislature, 1980, Disting. Service award Nat. Council on Alcoholism, San Francisco, 1981; named Unionist of Yr., Alameda County Labor Council, Oakland, Calif., 1980. Mem. Assn. Labor/Mgmt. Adminstrs. and Cons. on Alcoholism, Problems of Alcoholism in Labor and Mgmt. (bd. dirs. 1984—). Avocations: world travel; reading. Home: 6121 Buenaventura Oakland CA 94605 Office: Office and Profl Employees Union 29 1475 Powell St Emeryville CA 94608

COUGHLIN, SISTER MAGDALEN, college president; b. Wenatchee, Wash., Apr. 16, 1930; d. William Joseph and Cecilia Gertrude (Diffley) C. B.A., Coll. St. Catherine, Mpls., 1952; M.A., Mount St. Mary's Coll., Los Angeles, 1962; Ph.D., U. So. Calif., 1970; L.H.D. (hon.), Loyola Marymount U., 1983. Joined Sisters of St. Joseph, Roman Catholic Ch., 1956. Tchr. history Alemany High Sch., San Fernando, Calif., 1960-61; tchr. history St. Mary's Acad., Los Angeles, 1961-63; asst. prof. history Mount St. Mary's Coll., Los Angeles, 1963-70, dean acad. devel., 1970-74, pres., 1976—; provincial councilor Sisters of St. Joseph, Los Angeles, 1974-76; trustee Marianne Frostig Ctr., Los Angeles, 1976—, also bd. dirs.; trustee St. Catherine's Coll., Mpls., 1982—; bd. dirs., vice chmn. Calif. Council for Humanities, 1984—. Pres. Commn. on Status of Women, Los Angeles, 1984—; bd. dirs. Doheny Found., 1987—, Frostig Ctr. for Learning Disabilities. Fulbright scholar U. Nijmegen, 1952-53; Haynes dissertation fellow, 1969-70. Mem. Calif. Hist. Soc., Am. Hist. Soc., Fulbright Alumni Assn., Women in Bus., Women's Trusteeship, Assn. Ind. Calif. Colls. (bd. dirs. 1979), Ind. Colls. So. Calif. (bd. dirs. 1976), Am. Council Edn. (bd. dirs. 1986—), Phi Alpha Theta, Pi Gamma Mu, Delta Epsilon Sigma. Home and Office: Mount Saint Mary's Coll 12001 Chalon Rd Los Angeles CA 90049

COULIS, KAREN MARIE, lawyer; b. Ann Arbor, Mich., Nov. 24, 1950; d. Charlton Thomas and Betty Lorraine (Kapanka) Campbell; m. Paul Thomas Coulis, Sept. 11, 1977; children: Thomas Charlton, Stephanie Danielle. BA, U. Dayton, 1973; JD, Valparaiso U., 1976. Bar: Ind. 1976, U.S. Dist. Ct. (so. dist.) Ind. 1976, U.S. Dist. Ct. (no. dist.) Ind. 1978. Dep. prosecutor Porter County Prosecutor's Office, Valparaiso, Ind., 1976-78, Lake County Prosecuter's Office, Crown Point, Ind., 1979—; asst. bd. atty. Lake County Welfare Dept., Gary, Ind., 1978-79; liaison to Lake County Welfare Dept., Crown Point, 1979—; legis. chmn. Lake County Child Abuse Task Force, Griffith, Ind., 1981—; instr. Ind. Prosecuting Atty.'s Council, 1986; mem. Lake County Legal Issues Task Force, 1985—. Author: Tenant's Rights, 1972. 1st v.p. N.W. Ind. Symphony Women's Assn., Gary, 1981—. Recipient Brother Albert Rose award U. Dayton, 1973. Mem. ABA, Ind. Bar Assn., Phi Alpha Delta, Pi Sigma Alpha. Greek Orthodox. Home: 1330 Brookside Dr Munster IN 46321

COULSON, TRACY NOREEN, marketing director; b. Wichita, Kans., May 31, 1957; d. William Derald Tarrant and Irma Noreen (Hays) Jacoby; m. John Michael Coulson, June 30, 1984; children: Courtney Erin, Kylie Paige. BA, Wichita State U., 1979. Prodn. coordinator Stephan Advt. Agy., Wichita, 1978-81, account service, 1981-83; mktg. dir. Towne West Sq., Wichita, 1983-85, Towne East Sq., Wichita, 1985—; trainer Melvin Simon & Assocs., Wichita, 1985—. Vol. Wichita Area Girl Scout Council, 1979—; bd. dirs. Summer Jobs for Teens, Wichita, 1987. Mem. Internat. council Shopping Ctrs. (cert.) (Maxi award for advt.), Wichita Advt. Club (bd. dirs. 1983-86), Delta Delta Delta (pres. 1983-84). Home: 415 S Roosevelt Wichita KS 67218 Office: Towne East Sq 7700 E Kellogg Suite 1300 Wichita KS 67207

COULSON, ZOE ELIZABETH, food processing executive; b. Sullivan, Ind., Sept. 22, 1932; d. Marion Allan and Mary Anne (Thompson) C. B.S., Purdue U., 1954; A.M.P., Harvard Bus. Sch., 1983. asst. dir. home econs. Am. Meat Inst., Chgo., 1954-57; account exec. J. Walter Thompson Co., Chgo., 1957-60; creative consumer dir. Leo Burnett Co., Chgo., 1960-64; mag. editor-in-chief Donnelley-Dun & Bradstreet, N.Y.C., 1964-68; food editor Good Housekeeping Inst., N.Y.C., 1968-76, dir., 1976-81; v.p. Campbell Soup Co., Camden, N.J., 1981—; dir. Rubbermaid Inc. Author: Good Housekeeping Illustrated Cookbook, 1981; Good Housekeeping Cookbook, 1972. Trustee Cooper Hosp./Univ. Med. Ctr. Named Disting. Alumnae, Purdue U., 1971. Mem. Women's Econ. Bus. Alliance (bd. govs.), Kappa Alpha Theta Alumnae Assn. Republican. Presbyterian. Avocation: meso-Am. and Southwestern archaeology. Home: 220 Locust St Philadelphia PA 19106 Office: Campbell Soup Co Campbell Place Camden NJ 08103-1799

COULTON, MARTHA JEAN GLASSCOE (MRS. MARTIN J. COULTON), librarian; b. Dayton, Ohio, Dec. 11, 1927; d. Lafayette Pierre and Gertrude Blanche (Miller) Glasscoe; student Dayton Art Inst., 1946-47; m. Martin J. Coulton, Sept. 6, 1947; children—Perry Jean, Martin John. Dir., Milton (Ohio) Union Public Library, 1968—. Active, West Milton (Ohio) Cable TV Com. Named Outstanding Woman Jaycees, 1978-1979. Mem. ALA, Ohio Library Assn., Miami Valley Library Orgn. (sec. 1981, v.p. 1982, pres. 1983), Internat. Platform Assn., West Milton C. of C., DAR. Home: 1910 N Mowry Rd Pleasant Hill OH 45359 Office: 560 S Main St West Milton OH 45383

COULTRIP, CHRISTINE ANN, police officer; b. Syracuse, N.Y., Mar. 21, 1954; d. Richard William and Ann Elizabeth (Brembeck) C. B in Criminal Justice, U. Toledo, 1976, EdM, 1984. Supr. security J.C. Penney Co., Toledo, 1976-77; police officer Rossford (Ohio) Police Dept., 1977—. Mem. Rossford Police Patrolman's Assn. (sec. 1980-85, 87—). Office: Rossford Police Dept 99 Hillsdale Rossford OH 43460

COUNIHAN, DARLYN JOYCE, educator; b. Cumberland, Md., May 1, 1948; d. Joseph Paul and Clara Kathryn (Miller) C.; m. Mark W. Chambré, Jan. 20, 1979. AB, Hood Coll., 1970, MA, 1982; postgrad., U. Md., 1971-73. Tchr. math. Cabin John Jr. High Sch., Montgomery County, Md., 1970-75, coach girls volleyball team, 1975; math. resource tchr. Takoma Park (Md.) Jr. High Sch., 1975-77, Ridgeview Jr. High Sch., Gaithersburg, Md., 1977-81; math. tchr. Kennedy High Sch., Silver Spring, Md., 1982-84; magnet math. tchr. Takoma Park Intermediate Sch., 1984—, also math. team coach; mem. Area 3 adv. council Montgomery County Pub. Schs., 1972-73; coach boys basketball team Montgomery County Recreation Assn., 1971. Co-author geometry textbook. Recipient various acad., athletic awards in high sch., coll.; NSF grantee, 1971-72. Mem. Am. Fedn. Tchrs., Women in Edn., Montgomery County Math. Tchrs. Assn., Nat. Council Tchrs. Math., Phi Kappa Phi. Clubs: Capts. Cove Golf and Yacht, Lake Holiday Country. Home: 13900 Zeigler Way Silver Spring MD 20904 Office: Takoma Park Intermediate Sch 7611 Piney Branch Rd Silver Spring MD 20910

COUNSELMAN, ELEANOR FREY, psychologist, educator; b. Oakland, Calif., Jan. 6, 1946; d. Boyd Gallatin and Eleanor Marie (Horning) Frey; m. Charles Claude Counselman III, June 25, 1966; children: Catherine Marie, Charles Boyd. BA, Wellesley Coll., 1966; MEd, Boston U., 1967, EdD, 1971. Diplomate Am. Bd. Profl. Psychology; lic. psychologist, Mass. Coordinator testing Boston U. Counseling Ctr., 1970-75, coordinator tng., 1975-78; postdoctoral fellow Wellesley (Mass.) Human Relations Service, 1978-79; faculty mem., supr. Boston Inst. for Psychotherapy, 1979—, coordinator clin. consultation, 1985—; pvt. practice psychotherapy Belmont, Mass., 1979—; cons. Mass. Rehab. Commn., Boston, 1970-73, Cambridge Police Dept., 1983. Mem. Belmont Town Meeting, 1982—; trustee Belmont Day Sch., 1983—; Sunday sch. tchr. All Saint's Episcopal Ch., Belmont, 1979—. Mem. Am. Psychol. Assn., Mass. Psychol. Assn., Am. Orthopsychiat. Assn., Am. Group Psychotherapy Assn. Republican. Home and Office: 123 Radcliffe Rd Belmont MA 02178

COUNTEE, SANDRA FLOWERS, rehabilitation services administrator; b. Oklahoma City, Feb. 15, 1943; d. LeRoy and Minnie Ola Flowers; m. Harry J. McNeill. BS, Kans. U., 1965; MS, Columbia U., 1975; MPA, NYU, 1979, PhD, 1983. Cert. social worker, N.Y.; lic. occupational therapist, N.Y. Staff occupational therapist D.C. Gen. Hosp. Community Mental Health, 1965-68; supr. occupational therapy Columbia U.-Harlem Hosp. Ctr. N.Y.C., 1968-76, chief occupational therapy, 1976-78; asst. prof., dir. field work edn. Temple U., Phila., 1978-81; dist. mgr. N.Y. Commn. Blind and Visually Handicapped, N.Y. State Dept. Social Services, N.Y.C., 1981-82; dist. mgr. Office of Vocat. Rehab., N.Y. State Dept. Edn., White Plains, 1982—; clin. instr. rehab. medicine Columbia U., 1977-78; cons. Trinity Ch. and St. Margaret's House Devel., N.Y.C., 1979; adj. prof. L.I. U., 1988—. Adv. bd. Community Home Health Services of Phila., 1980-81; mem. Westchester County Pvt. Industry Council, 1983—, Westchester County Council Disabled, 1983—; mem. bd. mgrs. Nyack YMCA, 1985-87. Mem. Am. Pub. Health Assn., Am. Soc. Pub. Adminstrn., Am. Occupational Therapy Assn. Home: 107 S Highland Ave South Nyack NY 10960

COUPERWHITE, FIONA MARY, business administrator; b. Birmingham, Eng., Jan. 7, 1948; came to Can., 1980; d. Arthur Kennedy and Janet (Mackay) Hill; m. Alan Laird Couperwhite, Apr. 25, 1980. Dip. in Commerce, Heriot Watt U., Edinburgh, Scotland, 1970. Exec. sec. Ellis & Co., Glasgow, Scotland, 1970-76; mgmt. exec. Scotwork, Ltd., Glasgow, 1976-79; exec. sec. Daily Record and Sunday Mail, Glasgow, 1979-80, Can. Trust, Calgary, 1980-84; mgr. adminstrn. Ind. Petroleum Assn. of Can., Calgary, 1984-88, Can. States Energy, Calgary, 1988—. Mem. Parkinsons Soc. So. Alberta, Calgary, 1984—. Office: Can States Energy, 1220 144 4 Avenue SW, Calgary CAN T2P 3N4

COURSHON, CAROL BIEL, civic worker; b. Cleve., Sept. 5, 1923; d. Maurice and Rita (Glueck) Biel; student Wesleyan Coll., Macon, Ga., 1941-42; m. Arthur Howard Courshon, Feb. 20, 1943; children—Barbara Mills, Deanne. With Washington Savs. & Loan Assn., Miami Beach, Fla., 1979-80, chmn. adv. bd., 1979-80, dir., 1980-82. Chmn. hotel-motel div. Mothers March Dimes, 1948-53; co-chmn. bus. div. Greater Miami Heart Fund campaign, 1977-78; bd. dirs. Children's Service Bur. of Dade County, 1960-70, Family Service Assn. Am., 1977-84, United Family and Children's Service (now Family Counseling Services), Dade County, 1970—; mem. adv. com. U. Miami-Jackson Meml. Children's Hosp. Ctr., 1983—; vol. tchrs. aide handicapped Dade County (Fla.) public schs., 1956-81; del. Democratic Nat. Conv., 1968; adv. bd. Jefferson Nat. Bank, Miami Beach, 1981—. Mem. Nat. Savs. and Loan League (exec. women's group 1979-83), Nat. Council Jewish Women (v.p. Bay div. 1953-55), Hadassah. Office: 301 41st St Miami Beach FL 33140

COURT, KATHRYN DIANA, editor; b. London, Dec. 23, 1948; came to U.S., 1976; d. Ian Howard and Elizabeth Irene (Freeman) Onslow; m. David Court, Mar. 25, 1972; m. Jonathan Coleman, July 8, 1978. B.A. in English with honors, U. Leicester, 1970. Editor William Heinemann Ltd., London, 1971-76; editor Penguin Books, N.Y.C., 1977-79; editorial dir. Penguin Books, 1979-83; editor-in-chief Viking Penguin Inc., 1984-87, v.p., sr. exec. editor, 1987—. Mem. Assn. Am. Pubs. (mem. freedom to publish com.). Office: 40 W 23d St New York NY 10010

COURTIER, LOUISE BASILE, data processing executive; b. Burgettstown, Pa., Oct. 30, 1935; d. William M. and Marina (Panzica) Basile; m. Richard G. Courtier (div. 1979); children: Candace M. Quintana, Cherie L. Student, San Diego State U., 1952-54. Exec. sec. Gen. Atomic, San Diego, 1958-66; mktg. coordinator Calbiochem, San Diego, 1971-77; asst. to pres. ISSCO, San Diego, 1977-78, dir. contracts, 1978-85, v.p., 1985-87; nat. account mgr. Computer Assocs., San Diego, 1987—. Bd. dirs. Master Chorale, 1986—, Mingei Folk Art Mus., San Diego, 1985—, Serenity House, Escondido, 1968-75. Mem. Internat. Tng. in Comunication (pres. San Diego chpt. 1984), Assn. Data Processing Service Orgns., Nat. Contract Mgmt. Assn. Office: Computer Assocs Inc 10505 Sorrento Valley Rd San Diego CA 92121

COURTNER, DEBORAH JO, banker; b. Topeka, Kans., Apr. 4, 1949; d. Forest and Eva Louise (Grigsby) C.; m. Allan C. Northcutt, Nov. 1, 1975 (div. Apr. 1986). Student, Kans. State Tchrs. Coll., 1967-69; BS in Journalism, Kans. State U., 1971; student, Wichita State U., 1976-77; MBA, Columbia U., 1979. Publs. editor Kans. Power and Light Co., Topeka, 1971-73; info. asst. Southwestern Bell Telephone Co., Topeka, 1973-75; info. supr. Southwestern Bell Telephone Co., St. Louis, 1975; pub. relations cons. Northcutt Pub. Relations, Wichita, Kans., 1977; management trainee Citibank, N.Y.C., 1979-80; asst. product mgr. Citicorp Homeowners, Inc., St. Louis, 1980-81; product devel. mgr. Citicorp Person-to-Person, St. Louis, 1981-84, product tng. mgr., 1984-87, chief of staff second mortgage ops., 1987—; mktg. cons. Circle Am. Tours, St. Louis, 1987. Violinist Topeka Civic Symphony, 1971-73; mem. Jr. League, St. Louis, 1982-85. Mem. Topeka Press Women (pres. 1972-73), Women in Communications (regional conf. planning chmn. 1973). Home: 1130 Terrace Dr Saint Louis MO 63117 Office: Citicorp Person to Person 670 Mason Ridge Center Dr Saint Louis MO 63141

COURTNEY, LISA SMITH, nurse; b. Bennington, Vt., June 9, 1954; d. Calvin Coolidge and Ina Beatrice (Christina) S.; m. Michael W. Courtney, Oct. 28, 1979. A in Applied Sci., Salem Coll., 1974; BA in Health Sci. Adminstrn., St. Mary's Coll., 1983; MA in Health Sci., San Jose State U., 1986. RN. Nurse ICU Grafton (W. Va.) City Hosp., 1974-75, head nurse in labor, delivery, 1975-76; nurse emergency dept. Dr.'s Hosp. of Prince Georges County, Lanham, Md., 1976-78; nurse operating room, post-anesthesia recovery The St. Joseph Hosp., Nashua, N.H., 1978-80; nurse ICU, CCU, hemodialysis quality assurance, edn. cons. Santa Teresa Community Med. Ctr., San Jose, Calif., 1980—. Mem. adminstrv. staff Hayward Outlaws minor league profl. football team. Mem. Am. Assn. Critical Care Nurses, Nat. Assn. Female Execs. Democrat. Roman Catholic. Office: Santa Teresa Community Med Ctr 250 Hospital Pkwy San Jose CA 95119

COURTNEY, NORMA ISABELLE, systems analyst; b. New Albany, Ind., Oct. 17, 1927; d. William and Mary Isabelle (Emery) Hagmann; B.S. in Computer Sci., Wright State U., Dayton, Ohio, 1975; M.B.A., U. Dayton, 1985; m. Robert Lee Courtney, Dec. 2, 1950; children—Deborah Lynn Courtney Smyth, Ellen Ann Courtney Irvin, Jennifer Lee Courtney Lightcap, Lisa Marie Courtney Blommel. With C.E., U.S. Army, Louisville, 1945-46, Ky. Actuarial Bur., Louisville, 1947-52; with NCR Corp., Dayton, 1976-86, sr. prin. systems analyst, 1981-86, project leader, 1983-85; with Bass, Inc., Dayton, 1986—. Home: 615 Meadowview Dr Centerville OH 45459 Office: 2211 Arbor Blvd Dayton OH 45439

COURTOIS, CHRISTINE ANN, counseling psychologist; b. Providence, Aug. 29, 1949; d. Normand Albert and Dorice Irene (Dufort) Courtois; B.A. in History and Secondary Edn. (R.I. State scholar, Herbert Pell award), R.I. Coll., 1971; M.A. in Counseling (grad. asst., fellow), U. Md., 1973, Ph.D., 1979. Asst. dir. Orientation Office, U. Md., 1975-77, counseling psychology intern Counseling Ctr., 1977-78, counselor, 1978-80; with Counseling and Testing Center, Cleve. State U., 1978-80; counseling psychologist U. Md., 1980-81, GAO, Washington, 1981-82, Women's Med. Center, 1981-83; pvt. practice counseling psychology, Washington, 1981—; adj. faculty George Mason U., 1982, U. Md., 1983-84. Trustee Cleve. Rape Crisis Center, 1979-80; co-founder, dir. Univ. Women's Crisis Hotline, U. Md., 1972-76. Mem. Am. Psychol. Assn., D.C. Psychol. Assn., Am. Assn. Counseling and Devel., Am. Mental Health Counselors Assn., Md. Psychol. Assn., Nat. Orgn. Victim Assistance. Democrat. Author book; contbr. articles to profl. jours. Office: 3 Washington Circle #206 Washington DC 20037

COURTOT, MARILYN EDITH, management executive; b. Plainfield, N.J., Mar. 17, 1943; d. Anthony Roland Hopcroft and Marion Edith (Schoenly) Hopcroft Rowen; m. George C. Courtot, Aug. 20, 1966 (div. Nov. 1981). BA in English, U. Md., 1965; MLS, Cath. U. Am., 1972. Programmer Prudential Ins. Co., Newark, 1965-66, Dept. Army, Lawton, Okla., 1966-68; systems analyst IBM Corp., Gaithersburg, Md., 1968-71; sr. systems analyst Library of Congress, Washington, 1971-73; adminstrv. dir. U.S. Senate, Washington, 1973-81, asst. sec., 1981-86; dir. standards and tech. Assn. Info. and Image Mgmt., Silver Spring, Md., 1986—. Editor: Glossary of Micrographics, 1982; contbr. articles to profl. jours. Recipient cert. of appreciation Nat. Micrographics Assn., 1973-74, 77, 80, Pres.'s award Capitol chpt., 1978, award of merit Fed. Govt. Micrographics Council, 1977; named Outstanding Grad, Cath. U., Coll. Library Sci., 1987. Fellow Assn. for Info. and Image Mgmt.; mem. Continuing Library Edn. Network and Exchange, Info. Policy Discussion Group, Fed. ADP Users Group, Assn. Secs.-Gen. of Parliaments, White House Conf. on Libraries and Info. Service (adv. com. 1979), Nat. Commn. on Libraries and Info. Service (pub./pvt. sector task force 1979-81), Fed. Office Automation Conf. (adv. com. 1980-84), Beta Phi Mu. Lodge: Zonta. Office: Assn Info and Image Mgmt 1100 Wayne Ave Suite 1100 Silver Spring MD 20910

COUSINOW, JEAN ANN, home health care executive; b. Pontiac, Mich., Aug. 10, 1942; d. Edward Robert and Helen Janet (Mills) C. BA, Cen. Conn. State Univ., 1973. Supr. Salvation Army, Hartford, Conn., 1972-73; asst. coordinator Home Health Aide Service Waterbury (Conn.) Vis. Nurses Assn., 1973-77, asst. dir., 1977-79, v.p. spl. services, 1979-82; v.p. Waterbury br. Vis. Nurse and Home Care, Inc., 1983-85; v.p. growth and communication VNA Group, Inc., Plainville, Conn., 1985—; pres. VNA Health Resources, Inc., Plainville, 1985—. Mem. Conn. Assn. for Home Care (bd. dirs. 1982-84, chmn. mktg. com. 1982-84). Democrat. Office: VNA Group Inc 146 New Britain Ave Plainville CT 06062

COUTANT, PAMELA KINNEY, insurance company executive, opera singer; b. Balt., Sept. 26, 1953; d. F. Stanley and M. Eileen (Schott) Kinney; m. Paul E. Coutant, Oct. 1, 1983 (Mar. 1986). BS, Towson State U., 1976; MusM, North Tex. State U., 1980. Night mgr. Swensen's Ice Cream, Denton, Tex., 1977-78; clk. Mr. Gatti's Pizza, Denton, 1978-79, Russell's Dept. Store, Denton, 1979-80, Dillard's Dept. Store, Ft. Worth, 1980; new bus. clk. Transport Life Ins. Co., Ft. Worth, 1980-82, supr. data entry, 1982-84, mgr. data entry/control, 1984-88, supr. ops. scheduling, JCL/Setup specialist, 1988—. Artist in residence Ft. Worth Opera, 1986—; stage dir. several operas, 1977-78; mem. Dallas Opera Chorus, 1986—, Dallas Lyric Opera Co., 1988—. Vol. Van Cliburn Found.; chmn. employee campaign United Way, 1987-88. Mem. Am. Guild Mus. Artists, Mu Phi Epsilon, Sigma Delta Pi. Democrat. Presbyterian. Office: Transport Life Ins Co 714 Main St Fort Worth TX 76102

COUTANT, SHEILA COUNIHAN, marketing professional, counselor; b. Long Beach, Calif., Feb. 15, 1940; d. John Laurence and Frances Meredith (Weathersbee) Counihan; m. Edward W. Coutant (div. May 1982); children: Carol Anne, Deborah Meredith. BS, U. Conn., 1978. Owner Clothes Hut, North Stonington, Conn., 1970-73; mgr., travel agt. Stonington Travel, 1973-77; project coordinator U. Conn., Storrs, 1979-80; asst. dir. recruitment ARC Blood Services, Farmington, Conn., 1980-87; v.p. devel., communications, mktg. Easter Seals, Uncasville, Conn., 1987—; ind. coll. counselor Future Focus Assocs., Stonington, Conn., 1985—. vice chmn. Zoning Bd. Appeals, North Stonington, 1979-82, North Stonington Pub. Health, 1982-85; bd. dirs. Easter Seals, 1987—. Club: Women Sales (New Haven). Lodge: Zonta, (vice chmn. 1981-83). Home: 11 Old Colony Rd North Stonington CT 06359 Office: Easter Seal Rehab Ctr 154 Norwich-New London Turnpike Uncasville CT 06382

COUTTS-MINERS, CARLA BOND, graphic designer, marketing professional; b. Abington, Pa., June 25, 1943; d. Charles H. and Marion (Carlo) Bond; m. Charles R. Coutts, Sept. 14, 1976 (divorced); children: Sydney Anne, Charles Andrew; m. William J. Miners, Mar. 2, 1988. BFA, Moore Coll. of Art, 1964. Art dir. FineFrock, Bice & Goebel, San Francisco, 1964-66, Brit. Auto Parts, San Francisco, 1966-67; from art dir. to mng. editor to pub. Bucks County Panorama Mag., Doylestown, Pa., 1971-75; advt. dir., creative dir. Peddler's Village, Lahaska, Pa., 1975—; small bus. owner C.M. Assocs., Doylestown, 1975—. Contbr. articles to profl. jours.; artist in field; designer in field. Named Desktop Pub. of Yr., Macuser Mag., 1986. Mem. Cen. Bucks C. of C. (chmn. tourism 1978-79, pub. relations com. 1975—, Outstanding Contbns. 1982). Republican. Roman Catholic. Clubs: Windjammers Sailing (N.J.) (cruising dir. 1987). Office: CM Assocs 120 S Main Doylestown PA 18901

COUTURE-HARTMAN, T(HIRA) J(ANE), advertising executive; b. South Bend, Ind., Oct. 21, 1953; d. Harold Charles and Thora Jane (Deepe) Mays; m. Dennis A. Couture, May 20, 1972 (div. Apr. 1986); children: Ryan A., Casey A.; married Apr. 16, 1988. Grad. high sch., South Bend. Receptionist sta. WPTA-TV, Ft. Wayne, Ind., 1972-74; media mgr. Bonsib, Inc., Ft. Wayne, 1974-78; media mgr., account exec. Tri-State Advt., Warsaw, Ind., 1979—; speaker FF Club Chgo., 1985; media cons., Northern, Ind., 1980—. Mem. com. YMCA, Warsaw. Mem. Am. Bus. Women's Assn., Nat. Assn. for Female Execs. Presbyterian. Club: Volleyball (Warsaw). Office: Tri-State Advt 307 S Buffalo St Warsaw IN 46580

COVEL, BARBARA ALICE, human resources manager; b. Boston, Nov. 10, 1958; d. John Joseph and Alice Barbara (Caldwell) C. BS in Edn., Fitchburg State Coll., 1980; Cert. in Personnel, Bentley Coll., 1986. Cert. spl., elem. tchr., Mass. Tchr. resource room Ayer (Mass.) Pub. Schs., 1980; tchr. human resources Malden (Mass.) Pub. Schs., 1981; adminstrv. asst. Genetics Inst., Cambridge, 1981-83, human resources mgr., 1983-87, dir. human resources, 1987—. Chairperson human resources com. Mass. Biotech Council, Boston, 1987-88, bd. dirs., 1988—; mem. adv. bd. biomed. and lab. scis. program Boston U., 1987, 88. Mem. Am. Mgmt. Assn., Indsl. Biotech. Assn. (chairperson human resources 1988), Kappa Delta Pi (charter). Home: 355 Park Terrace Dr Stoneham MA 02180

COVER, EVA KATHERINE (NAST) TIMRUD, communications director, association executive; b. Kansas City, Mo., Apr. 7, 1946; d. Herbert Wilbur and Katherine Hall (Evans) Timrud; m. Thomas James Riley, Nov. 30, 1968 (div.); m. Jehu Fell Cover, May 23, 1982. B.J. in Advt., U. Mo., 1968. Editor, Waddell & Reed Inc., Kansas City, Mo., 1968-70; copywriter Berry World Travel, Kansas City, 1970-71, Western Auto, Kansas City, 1971-72; editor Nat. Sch. Supply and Equipment Assn., Arlington, Va., 1973-78, dir. communications, 1978-80; dir. communications Internat. Bus. Forms Industries, Inc., Arlington, 1980—. Author: The World of Business Forms, 1983; exec. editor, pub. Forms Mfg. mag., 1987—. Pub. relations dir. Univ. Theatre, U. Mo., Columbia, 1966-67. Recipient Roy A. Roberts scholarship Kansas City Star, 1964-68; Curator's scholarship U. Mo., 1964-66, honors cert., 1966. Mem. Women in Communications, Inc. (dir. Washington profl. chpt. 1983-85), Internat. Assn. Bus. Communicators, Alpha Gamma Delta (1st v.p. 1966-67), Sigma Alpha Iota. Republican. Office: Internat Bus Forms Industries Inc 2111 Wilson Blvd Suite 350 Arlington VA 22201

COVEY, NORMA SCOTT, travel service executive; b. Cambridge, Mass., Feb. 16, 1924; d. Irving Osgood and Leah (Crowell) Scott; m. Myles Edward Covey, July 8, 1950; children: Chrisann and Cynthia (twins). BE, Boston U., 1950. Tchr. East Hartford (Conn.) Schs., 1947-57; mgr., owner, pres. Myles Travel, Glastonbury, Conn., 1975—; bd. dirs. C&W Mfg., Glastonbury; computer instr. Conlin-Hallissey Travel Sch., Glastonbury, 1984-86. Columnist for 3 local newspapers. Vol. Foster Parents Plan Outreach Group, 1984—. Mem. Am. Soc. Travel Agts., Internat. Airlines Travel Agts. Assn., Cruise Lines Internat. Assn., Pacific Area Travel Assn., Bus. and Profl. Women, Nat. Assn. Female Execs. Republican. Congregationalist. Club: Boston U. Alumni. Home: 174 Carriage Dr Glastonbury CT 06033 Office: Myles Travel Agy 13 Welles St Glastonbury CT 06033

COVILLE, KATHERINE RUTH, illustrator; b. Syracuse, N.Y., Dec. 7, 1951; d. Kenneth Merrill and Jill Aileen (Sherlitz) Dietz; m. Bruce Ferrington Coville, Oct. 10, 1969; children: Orion Sean, Cara Joy, Adam Benjamin. Grad. high sch., Phoenix, N.Y. Illustrator: (children's books) The Foolish Giant, 1978, Sarah's Unicorn, 1979, The Peasant and the Fly, 1980, The Skull in the Snow, 1981, Hob Goblin and the Skeleton, 1982, The Monster's Ring, 1982, The Scary Halloween Costume Book, 1983, The Incredbile Cat Caper, 1985, Casey's Counting Party, 1985, Mostly Micheal, 1987, Short and Shivery, 1987, Read Aloud Bible Stories from the Old Testament, 1987, The Picolinis, 1988, The Pudgy I Love You Book, 1988. Democrat.

COVINGTON, ANN K., judge; b. Fairmont, W.Va., Mar. 5, 1942; d. James R. and Elizabeth Ann (Hornor) Kettering; m. James E. Waddell, Aug. 17, 1963 (div. Aug. 1976); children—Mary Elizabeth Waddell, Paul Kettering Waddell; m. Joe E. Covington, May 14, 1977. B.A., Duke U., 1963; J.D., U. Mo., 1977. Bar: Mo. 1977, U.S. Dist. Ct. (we. dist.) Mo. 1977. Asst. atty. gen. State of Mo., Jefferson City, 1977-79; ptnr. Covington & Maier, Columbia, Mo., 1979-81, Butcher, Cline, Mallory & Covington, Columbia, 1981-87; bd. dirs. Mid Mo. Legal Services Corp., Columbia, 1983-87; chmn. Juvenile Justice Adv. Bd., Columbia, 1984-87. Bd. dirs. Ellis Fischel State Cancer Hosp., Columbia, 1982-83; chmn. Columbia Indsl. Revenue Bond Authority, 1984-87; trustee United Meth. Ch., Columbia, 1983-86. Mem. Boone County Bar Assn. (sec. 1981-82), ABA (family law sect.), Mo. Bar. Home: 1109 Falcon Dr Columbia MO 65201 Office: 1300 Oak St Kansas City MO 64106

COVINGTON, EILEEN QUEEN, educator; b. Washington, May 25, 1946; d. Louis Edward and Evelyn (Travers) Q.; m. Norman Francis Covington; children—Norman, Marina, Deanna, Trena. BS, D.C. Tchrs. Coll., 1971; postgrad. George Washington U., 1978-81. Tchr., coach Evan Jr. High Sch., D.C. Pub. Schs., 1971; tchr., coach Woodrow Wilson High Sch., Washington, 1971—, chmn. phys. edn. dept., 1971-75, 1977-81, 1984-87, athletic dir., 1988—; cons. Coaches Assn., Washington, 1973-76. Named Coach of Yr., Eastern Bd. Ofcls., 1977, Nat. Coaches Assn. 2d Region, 1982, 86, Winningest Coach Washington Coaches Assn., 1982, Coach of Yr. U.S., 1986, Coach of Yr., Washington Post, 1987; recipient Billie Jean King award Women Sports and Am. Fedn. Coaches, 1980-81. Mem. D.C. Coaches Assn. (v.p. volleyball 1981-83), D.C. Assn. Health, Phys. Edn. Athletics, D.C. High Sch. Coaches Club. Home: 7601 Ingrid Pl Landover MD 20785 Office: Woodrow Wilson High Sch Nebraska and Chesapeake Sts NW Washington DC 20016

COVINGTON, JUANITA LOUISE, nurse; b. Bklyn., Sept. 28, 1949; d. John Louis and Beatrice G. (Wright) Harrison; m. Clarence Covington Jr., Aug. 20, 1966 (div. 1971); children: Christina, Sharanda. BS, CUNY, N.Y.C., 1977. RN, N.Y.C. Nurse Flower Fifth Ave. Hosp., N.Y.C., 1977; nurse Luth. Med. Ctr., Bklyn., 1977-87, asst. nursing care coordinator, 1979-87; nurse Internat. Coma Recovery Program, Bklyn., 1987—. Mem. Sigma Theta Tau (mem. com.), Theta Eta. Democrat. Methodist.

COVINGTON, LYNN HOFFMAN, government agency administrator; b. Beckley, W.Va., May 6, 1944; d. John Emerson and Mattie E. (Aaron) Hoffman; m. Brodie Charles Covington, Oct. 20, 1973; children: Chip, Cassy. BS in Bus. Adminstrn., Concord Coll., Athens, W.Va., 1966. Auditor GAO, Washington, 1966-69, Hdqrs. 8th Army, Dept. Army, Seoul, Republic of Korea, 1969-70; mgmt. analyst VA, Washington, 1970-80; dir. program evaluation services VA, 1980-86, dir. paperwork mgmt. and regulations service, 1986—; chmn. Evaluation Dirs.' Forum, Washington, 1983-86; mem. seminar on improving govt. productivity U. So. Calif., 1986—; mem. adv. bd. Info. Resources Adminstrn. Council, Washington, 1987—; speaker profl. confs. Mem. Am. Evaluation Assn., Canadian Evaluation Assn., New Eng. Orgn. Research Soc., Nat. Assn. Female Execs., So. Md. Democratic Club, Cobb Island (Md.) Citizens' Assn., Friends of Kennedy Ctr. Baptist. Home: Route 254 Cobb Island MD 20625

COVINGTON, PATRICIA ANN, educator, university administrator, director, artist; b. Mount Vernon, Ill., June 21, 1946; d. Charles J. and Lois Ellen (Combs) C.; m. Burl Vance Beene, Aug. 10, 1968 (div. 1981). BA, U. N.Mex., 1968; MS in Ed., So. Ill. U., 1974, PhD, 1981. Lab dir. Anasazi Origins Project, Albuquerque, 1969; tchr. pub. schs., Albuquerque, 1969-70; teaching asst. So. Ill. U., Carbondale, 1971-74, prof. art, 1974-88, adminstr. in admissions, 1988—; dir. Artist of the Month for U.S. rep. Paul Simon, Washington, 1974-81; vis. curator Mitchell Mus., Mount Vernon, Ill., 1977-83, judge Mitchell Mus., Dept. Conservation; panel mem. Ill. Arts Council, Chgo., 1982; faculty advisor European Bus. Seminar, London, 1983; edn. cons. Ill. Dept. Aging, Springfield, 1978-81, Apple Computer, Cupertino, Calif., 1982-83. Exhibited papercastings in nat. and internat. shows in Chgo., Fla., Calif. Tenn. N.Y. and others, 1974—; author: Diary of a Workshop, 1979, History of the School of Art at Southern Ill. Univ. at Carbondale, 1981. Bd. dirs. Humanities Council John A. Logan Coll., Carterville, Ill., 1982-88. Grantee Kresge Found., 1978, Nat. Endowment for the Arts, 1977, 81; named Outstanding Young Woman of Yr. for Ill., 1981. Fellow Ill. Ozarks Craft Guild (bd. dirs. 1976-83); mem. Ill. Higher Edn. Art Assn. (chmn. bd. dirs. 1978-88), Nat. Assn. Female Execs., NOW, Sphinx Hon., Phi Kappa Phi. Presbyterian. Home: 352 Lake Dr Rt 6 Murphysboro IL 62966 Office: So Ill U Admissions and Records Carbondale IL 62966

COWAL, VIRGINIA DOROTHY, computer programmer; b. Newmarket, Ont., Can., Jan. 11, 1960; came to U.S., 1963; d. Roy Frank and Dorothy W. (Taylor) C. AA in Bus. Data Processing, Fulton-Montgomery Community Coll. Mgr. computer ops. Vogel Van & Storage Inc., Albany, N.Y., 1984-86; computer operator Beech-Nut Nutrition Corp., Canajoharie, N.Y., 1986—. Home: 76 Grove st Amsterdam NY 12010

COWAN, AIMÉE GRACE, insurance broker; b. West Monroe, La., Oct. 9, 1939; d. Floyd Taylor Partin and Lettie Christine (Smith) Walker; m. Thomas Johnson Gilbert, Apr. 4, 1955 (div. Aug. 1961); children: Dennis, Mike, Ann, Kathy; m. Herbert Cameron Cowan Sr., Aug. 21, 1961 (div. Jan. 1970); children: Irene, Laura, Herbert Jr. Student, NE La. State U., 1960-61, U. Tex., 1971-77, S.W. Tex. State U., 1977-79. Various sales positions Westmore Cosmetics, Kraft Hosiery, Austin, Tex. area, 1968-73; with med. records dept. Tex. Dept. Mental Health Retardation, Austin, 1973-76; with clin. records dept. Austin-Travis County Mental Health, Austin, 1976-77; ins. agt. Southland Life Ins. Co., Austin, 1979-80, Protective Life Ins. Co., Austin, 1980-81; collectibles broker Keep NEAT Things Source, Austin, 1985—; ins. broker, agt. Investors' Asset Mgmt., Austin, 1987—; appraiser Writing-Relating Items to Enjoy, Austin, 1984—. Mem. Tex. Assn. Life Underwriters. Presbyterian. Home and Office: 10003 Woodland Village Dr Austin TX 78750

COWAN, RUTH, counselor; b. East Orange, N.J., Feb. 22, 1929; d. Henry Seldon and Edith Lucille (Shaw) C. BS in Edn., Trenton (N.J.) State Coll., 1951; JD, John Marshall Law Sch., 1962; MS in Edn., Chgo. State U., 1972. Tchr., counselor Chgo. Bd. Edn., 1958—. Democrat. Home: 2146 E 96th St Chicago IL 60617

COWDEN, JULIANAN, steel company executive; craftsman; b. Midland, Tex.; d. Robert Edwin and Jett (Baker) Cowden; student Hockaday Jr. Coll., 1940-41; B.A., U. Tex., 1944. Rancher, oil investments JAL Co., Alvarado, Tex., 1950—, chmn. bd., 1970—; treas. J & M Steel Co., Inc., Ft. Worth, 1971—. Instr. jewelry and silversmith Ft. Worth Art Center, 1963-66; exhibited jewelry and sculpture in one-man shows at Simpson Gallery, Amarillo, 1969, Sq. House Mus., Panhandle, 1971; exhibited in group shows at Ft. Worth Art Center, Carlin Gallery, Mus. Internat. Folk Art, Santa Fe, Wichita Falls (Tex.) Art Mus., Tex. Tech U. Mus., Lubbock, Artist's Jamboree, San Antonio. Trustee, past pres. Tex. Sch. Bd. Assn.; mem. adv. com., mem. tech. and telecommunications systems adv. com. Tex State Bd. Edn.; mem. Fed. Relations Network; pres. Alvarado Ind. Sch. Dist. Bd., 1966-86; mem. Nat. Fedn. Republican Women; sustaining mem. Rep. Party, 1979—; mem. Rep. Senatorial Inner Circle; mem. Task Force Com. on Sch./Coll. Articulation; trustee Hockaday Sch., 1971-73; bd. dirs. Christian Heritage Found.; Mem. Nat. Sch. Bd. Assn., Tex. Designer Craftsmen, U. Tex. Ex-Students Assn. (life), Tex. Artists Craftsmen Guild (pres. 1970-72), S. W. Cattleraisers Assn., Ranch Heritage Assn., West Tex. C. of C. (dir.), Zeta Tau Alpha, Phi Delta Kappa. Episcopalian. Clubs: Amarillo, Fort Worth. Home: PO Box 305-308 Alvarado TX 76009

COWEN, SONIA SUE, university administrator; b. Wichita Falls, Tex., Sept. 30, 1952; d. Jackson Thompson and Shirley Isabel (Skerritt) C.; B.A. magna cum laude, East Wash. U., 1973; M.F.A. in Creative Writing, U. Mont., 1975; postgrad. U. Utah, 1981-82, Gonzaga U., 1983—. Grants adminstr. Eastern Wash. U., Cheney, 1978-81, 82, asst. to v.p. and provost, 1982-83, acad. projects adminstr., 1983—; registered ski instr., 1985-88; dir. Moving Ahead, 1985-86; mem. adj. faculty, 1979, exec. sec. N.W. Inst. for Advanced Study, 1978-81, 82—; teaching asst. U. Mont., Missoula, 1974-75; instr., head journalism program Coll. of Siskiyous, Weed, Calif., 1975-76; spl. asst. in adminstrn. Ednl. Service Dist. 101, Spokane, Wash., 1976-78; teaching fellow U. Utah, Salt Lake City, 1981-82; freelance writer; cons. grants and contracts to hosps. and state govts. Del. to Mont. State Land Use, 1974, Bend in the River Council, 1974-75; publicity chmn. Wash. State 4th Ann. Very Spl. Arts Festival for Handicapped Children and Adults, 1978, Nat. Theatre of Deaf Spokane Tour, 1978. Recipient Gov.'s Commendation, State of Wash., 1979, also named Outstanding Woman of Yr., 1979; recipient Leadership award YWCA, 1985; named Key Person, United Way of Spokane County, 1984; scholar Bread Loaf Writers Conf., 1973. Mem. Nat. Council Univ. Research Adminstrs., Nat. Assn. Coll. and Univ. Bus. Officers, Nat. Assn. Univ. Women Deans, Adminstrs. and Counselors, Am. Assn. State Colls. and Univs., LWV, Nat. Assn. Exec. Females (network dir. 1985-86), Profl. Ski Instrs. Am. Club: Panhandle Yacht, North Star Yacht (Coeur D'Alene, Idaho). Author: (with B. Mitchell and L. Triplett) Something About China, 1971; contbr. poems to various publs. Home: PO Box 172 Cheney WA 99004 Office: Eastern Washington U Cheney WA 99004

COWLES, MILLY, educator; b. Ramer, Ala., May 29, 1932; d. Russell Fail and Sara (Mills) C. B.S., Troy State U., 1952; M.A., U. Ala., 1958, Ph.D. (grad. fellow), 1962. Tchr. pub. schs. Montgomery, Ala., 1952-59; asst., then assoc. prof. Grad. Sch. Edn. Rutgers U., 1960-66; assoc. prof. U. Ga., 1966-67; prof., dir. early childhood devel. and edn. Sch. Edn., U. S.C., Columbia, 1967-73; assoc. dean, prof. Sch. Edn., U. Ala., Birmingham, 1973-80; dean, prof. Sch. Edn., U. Ala., 1980-87, Disting. Prof. edn., 1987—; Dir. Williamsburg County Schs. Career Opportunity Program, 1970-73; cons. So. Edn. Found., Atlanta, Ga. Inst. Higher Edn. U. Ga., also numerous sch. systems throughout Northeast and South. Editor, contbg. author: Perspectives in the Education of Disadvantaged Children, 1967; co-author: Taming the Young Savage, Developmental Discipline. Bd. dirs. S.C. Assn. on Children Under Six, 1969-73. Recipient Outstanding Public Educator award Capstone Coll. Edn. Soc. U. Ala., 1977, Outstanding Alumna award Troy State U., 1984. Mem. Am. Ednl. Research Assn., Soc. for Research Child Devel., AAAS, AAUP, Nat. Council Tchrs. English, Internat. Reading Assn., Assn. for Supervision and Curriculum Devel. (mem. council on early childhood edn. 1969—, dir. 1978-82), Nat. Assn. for Edn. Young Children, Assn. for Childhood Devel. Internat., So. Assn. Children Under Six (bd. dirs. 1985-87), Ala. Assn. Young Children (pres. 1984-85), Ala. Assn. for Colls. for Tchr. Edn. (pres. 1986-88), Ala. Assn. Supervision and Curriculum Devel. (pres. 1985-86), N.Y. Acad. Scis., Kappa Delta Pi (chpt. treas. 1964-66), Kelta Kappa Gamma. Home: 4000 Rock Ridge Rd Birmingham AL 35210

COWLES, REGINA G., educator; b. Birmingham, Ala., July 1, 1956; d. Johnny F. Davis and Betty S. (Mehaffey) Bloom; m. Robert John Segovia, Aug. 17, 1979 (div. 1982); children: Robert Frank, Benjamin James, Katherine Elizabeth; m. Roger Babb, 1986. Student, Ind. U., 1976-77; BA in English, Mundelein Coll., Chgo., 1979. News writer, intern Sta. WGN, Chgo., 1978-79; newscaster, writer, producer Sta. WAAC, Terre Haute, Ind., 1979-80; coordinator women's resource ctr., editor newsletter Ind. State U., Terre Haute, 1981; gen. assignment reporter Terre Haute Star, 1981-82; reporter labor environment Port Arthur (Tex.) News, 1982-85; tchr. journalism, Nederland (Tex.) High Sch., 1987—. Recipient 3d place award Hoosier Press Assn., 1982, UPI award, 1983, AP 3d place award, 1984, Tex. Press Assn. award, 1984. Democrat.

COWLING, REBECCA ANN, biochemist; b. Kermit, Tex., Aug. 13, 1956; d. Ben Edward and Doris Patricia (Lovelace) C.; m. Bennie Lee Pressly, July 26, 1986; 1 stepchild, Jason. BA in Biochemistry, U. Tex., 1980; PhD in Biochemistry, Tex. A&M U., 1987. Research asst. Midland (Tex.) Cert. Reagent Co., 1980-81; teaching asst. Tex. A&M U., College Station, 1981-85, research asst., 1982-87, vis. lectr., 1985-87, postdoctoral research assoc., 1988—. Contbr. articles to profl. jours. Field counselor Alpha Xi Delta, Indpls., 1979-80. Dorothy M. Nichols Sci. research grantee, 1986. Mem. AAAS, Am. Chem. Soc., Am. Inst. Chemists, Phi Lambda Upsilon.

COWLISHAW, MARY LOU, state legislator; b. Rockford, Ill., Feb. 20, 1932; d. Donald George and Mildred Corinne (Hayes) Miller; m. Wayne Arnold Cowlishaw, July 24, 1954; children: Beth Cowlishaw McDaniel, John, Paula. BS in Journalism, U. Ill., 1954. Mem. editorial staff Naperville (Ill.) Sun newspaper, 1977-83; mem. Ill. Ho. of Reps., Springfield, 1983—, minority spokesman elem. and secondary edn. com., mem. joint Ho.-Senate edn. reform oversight com., 1985—. Author: This Band's Been Here Quite a Spell, 1983. Mem. Naperville Dist. 203 Bd. Edn., 1972-83, Ill. Citizens Council on Sch. Problems, Springfield, 1985—. Recipient 1st pl. award Ill. Press Assn., 1981, commendation Naperville Jaycees, 1986; named Best Legislator Ill. Citizens for Better Care, 1985, Woman of Yr. Naperville AAUW, 1987. Mem. Am. Legis. Exchange Council, Conf. Women Legislators, Nat. Fedn. Rep. Women, DAR. Methodist. Home: 924 Merrimac Circle Naperville IL 60540 Office: 41st Dist State Rep 552 S Washington St #119 Naperville IL 60540

COWPER, MARY GASKINS, retired home economist; b. New Bern, N.C., Mar. 16, 1923; d. William Ottis and Mittie Irene (Becton) Gaskins; m. George Pulaski Cowper, May 17, 1952 (dec. Aug. 1985); children: Ottis Riddick, William Neal, Edith Dell. BA in Home Econs., E. Carolina U., 1943. Cert. home economist. Cryptographic clk. U.S. Army Signal Corps, Arlington, Va., 1943-45; tchr. Craven County Schs., Brigeton, N.C., 1945-46, Dover, 1948-50; tchr. Edenton (N.C.) City Schs., 1946-47; home econs. extension agt. N.C. Agrl. Extension Service, Elizabeth City, 1950-51, Gatesville, 1951-53, 67-88, Edenton, 1965-67. Active Gates County Am. Cancer Soc., 1957—; county rep. Area Health Planning Orgn., Edenton, 1968-73; sec. Gates County Council on Status of Women, Gatesville, 1984-85; mem. Gates County Hist. Soc. Mem. Nat. Assn. Extension Home Economists (pub. affairs com. 1985-86, disting. service award 1982), N.C. Assn. Extension Home Economists (pres. NE dist. 1972, chmn. dist. com. 1974, 76-79, 83-84, Best Newsletter award 1972), N.C. Home Econs. Assn. (chmn. NE region 1980, liaison to state family life council 1983-86, chmn. state family relations com. 1983-84). Democrat. Episcopalian. Clubs: Gatesville Women's (v.p., pres. 1957-59). Home: PO Box 92 Gatesville NC 27938

COX, ANN RAESE, professional association executive; b. Charlotte, N.C., Sept. 18, 1945; d. George Phillip and Carol (Fields) Raese; m. Frank G. Lake III (div. Oct. 1972); 1 child, Frank G. IV; m. William S. Cox IV, Nov. 26, 1976. BS in Nursing, Ga. State U., Atlanta, 1974; MS in Nursing, Emory U., 1975. Staff nurse Piedmont Hosp., Atlanta, 1966-72, asst. prof. Emory U. Sch. Nursing, Atlanta, 1975-82; dir. edn. Am. Assn. Occupational Health Nurses, Atlanta, 1982-84, dir. profl. affairs, 1984-86, assoc. exec. dir., 1987—; cons. United Way Metro Atlanta, 1984—. Author: Women's Health Protocols, 1985 (Book the Yr. 1985). Mem. Am. Soc. Assn. Execs. (cert.), Ga. Soc. Assn. Execs. (bd. dirs. 1987—, leadership award 1984). Office: AAOHN 50 Lenox Pointe Atlanta GA 30325

COX, BARBARA ROOSE, public relations executive; b. Houston, Mar. 15, 1951; d. Kenneth E. and Patsy L. (Hinsley) Roose; m. John B. Goss Jr. (div. Apr. 1979); children: Benjamin Jason, Christopher John; m. James O. Cox III, Sept. 28, 1979. Student, U. Houston, 1969-75. Claims rep. State Farm Ins., Houston, 1969-73; adminstrv. asst. S.W. Bancshares Inc., Houston, 1973-77; account exec. Mel Anderson Communications, Houston, 1978-79; v.p. James Cox Inc., Houston, 1979-82, also bd. dirs.; pres. Barbara Cox Pub. Relations, Houston, 1982-83; account supr. Daniel J. Edelman Inc., Houston, 1983-85, v.p., 1985-86, sr. v.p., 1986—. Advisor to pres. Houston Jaycees, 1987; bd. dirs. First United Meth. Ch., Houston, 1985-86; chmn. pub. relations com. Houston Ballet Nutcracker Market, 1986; publicity chair Mayor's Ball/Houston Internat. Festival, 1985. Mem. Pub. Relations Soc. Am. (Silver Anvil 1985, Excalibur awards Houston chpt. 1985, 87). Clubs: Houston City, Gov.'s, Forum (Houston); Quail Valley (Missour City, Tex.). Office: Daniel J Edelman Inc One Greenway Plaza Suite 700 Houston TX 77046

COX, BRENDA GALE, statistician; b. Princeton, W.Va., May 16, 1948; d. Ernest Monroe and Mona Virginia (Dove) C. BA magna cum laude, Concord Coll., 1970; MS, Va. Polytechnic Inst. and State U., Blacksburg, 1974, PhD, 1977. Statistician Research Triangle (N.C.) Inst., 1977-81, sr. statistician, 1981-85, dept. mgr., 1985—. Author: Methodological Issues for Health Care Surveys, 1985; contbr. articles to profl. jours. Fellow NIH, 1972-74. Mem. Am. Statis. Assn. (pres. N.C. chpt. 1984-85, council rep. 1985-86, sec., treas. survey research methods sect. 1986-88, dist. 5 gov. 1986-88), Biometrics Soc. (regional adv. bd. 1986-88), Am. Assn. for Pub. Opinion Research, Pi Mu Epsilon. Democrat. Baptist. Office: Research Triangle Inst PO Box 12194 Research Triangle Park NC 27709

COX, BRENDA SUSAN, marketing manager; b. Tulsa, Sept. 18, 1952; d. Benjamin Franklin and Mildred Violet (Uran) C. BS, U. Tulsa, 1974; postgrad., Fairleigh-Dickinson U., 1980-83. Rep. profl. sales USV Labs., Tuckahoe, N.Y., 1976-79, assoc. clin. research, 1979; assoc. dir. Oxford Research Internat. Corp., Clifton, N.J., 1979-83; product mgr. Automated Microbiology Systems, Inc., San Diego, 1984-85, Creative Computer Applications, Inc., Calabasas, Calif., 1986-87; dir. sales, mktg. Westland Software House, Calabasas, Calif., 1988—; Lectr. Ctr. for Profl. Advancement, East Brunswick, N.J., 1980-83. Author: Good Clinical Practices, 1987. Lectr. Am. Heart Assn., Glen Ridge, N.J., 1982-83. Mem. Med. Mktg. Assn., Nat. Assn. for Female Execs., So. calif. Women for Understanding (writer newsletter 1987). Republican. Baptist. Club: Wilderness Women (Los Angeles).

COX, CAROL ANN, transportation executive; b. Shenandoah, Pa., Sept. 29, 1950; d. Stanley Joseph and Julia (Whitecavage) Wozniewicz; m. George Fredrick Hahn, July 5, 1969 (div. 1980); 1 child, Michelle Lynn; m. Robert Earl Cox, July 26, 1980. Diploma, TLC Travel Inst., Pennsburg, Pa., 1986. Lab. technician Philco-Ford, Inc., Spring City, Pa., 1969-71; parking enforcement officer Pottstown (Pa.) Police Dept., 1973-75; sec., billing clk. Cates Ford, Inc., Pottstown, 1975-77; corrections mail insp. Graterford (Pa.) Correctional Inst., 1977-83; decorator cons. Princess House, Inc., Reading, Pa., 1983-86; asst. mgr. Avante Apts., Gilbertsville, Pa., 1985-86; travel agt. Village Travel, Montgomeryville, Pa., 1986, Chadwick Travel Ltd., Pottstown, 1986-88; travel coordinator Hewlett-Packard Corp., Valley Forge, Pa., 1988—; cruise escort Chadwick Travel Ltd, Pottstown, 1987-88. Mem. Internat. Assn. Travel Agts. Roman Catholic. Home: 950 Jackson St Pottstown PA 19464

COX, CATHLEEN RUTH, zoologist, educator; b. Vallejo, Calif., Oct. 20, 1948; d. Charles W. and Betty A. (Born) Cox; B.A., U. Calif.-San Diego, 1970, Ph.D., Stanford U., 1976; m. William S. Bain, Dec. 14, 1985. Postdoctoral fellow Am. Mus. Natural History, N.Y.C., 1976-78; research assoc. Barnard Coll., N.Y.C., 1978-79; research zoologist UCLA, 1979-82; asst. prof. Calif. State U.-Northridge, 1980-84 ; dir. research Los Angeles Zoo, 1981—. Recipient W.C. Allee award Animal Behavior Soc., 1976; NSF research grantee, 1978. Mem. Am. Assn. Zool. Parks and Aquaria, Am. Ornithol. Union, Animal Behavior Soc., Am. Primatol. Soc. Contbr. articles to profl. jours. Office: 5333 Zoo Dr Los Angeles CA 90027

COX, ELIZABETH LARTER, state agency administrator, researcher; b. East Orange, N.J., Sept. 20, 1927; d. William H.D. and Josenia Elizabeth (Larter) C. BA, U. Vt., 1949; MA, NYU, 1952, postdoctoral, 1953; M in Library Sci., Pratt Inst., 1986. Librarian Saturday Rev. mag., N.Y.C., 1959-72; editorial project coordinator Chicorel Library Pub. Corp., N.Y.C., 1973; sales asst. Straus Communications, N.Y.C., 1974-78; editorial coordinator Vollmer Assocs., Inc., N.Y.C., 1979; dir. N.J. Research and Info. Service, Summit, 1979—; librarian Editor & Publisher mag., N.Y.C., 1981-82; program devel. specialist N.J. Dept. Community Affairs div. on Aging, Trenton, 1983—. Author: (audio-visual) Aging in New Jersey, 1986; editor directory Statewide Benefits on Aging bulletin, 1986—, other div. pubs., 1987—; compiler for handbook Women's Resource Directory, 1986. Pres. Union County Women's Polit Caucus, 1978-80; alt. del. Rep. Nat. Conv., Detroit, 1980, New Orleans, 1988; mem. choir Women's Polit. Caucus N.J., 1982-84, sec. Rep. task force Nat. Women's Polit. Caucus, 1985—; chair Union County Adv. Bd. on Status Women, Elizabeth, N.J., 1982-87; chmn. Summit Rep. City Com., 1985—. Recipient New Counties award Nat. Assn. Counties, 1979, Citation Outstanding Meritorious Service, City of Summit, 1979. Mem. Newspaper Guild (chair rep. assembly 1974-78), Spl. Libraries Assn., Am. Polit. Sci. Assn., Communication Workers Am. Episcopalian. Home: 390 Morris Ave Summit NJ 07901

COX, JOY DEAN, business executive; b. Oklahoma City, Sept. 13, 1940; d. Wordy John Neely and Ethel (Russell) Neely Biggs; m. Sidney Lee Johnson, Sept. 10, 1958 (div. 1963); m. Ronald Gene Cox, Sept. 22, 1964; children: Ronald D., Beverly Kay, Jeffrey Wilson. Student pub. schs., Oklahoma City. Long-distance operator S.W. Bell Telephone Co., Oklahoma City, 1958-59, Los Angeles, 1959-60; clk. John Pilling Shoes Oklahoma City, 1960-62; cashier Dial Fin. Co., Houston, 1966; file clk., typist N. Am. Ins. Co., Oklahoma City, 1966-67; bookkeeper, co-owner farm and ranch operation, 1969—; co-owner/operator Apco Service Sta. and Bulk Fuel Plant, Taloga, Okla., 1972-75, D&R Service & Supply Co., Panola, Okla., 1979—; co-owner Panola Store, 1980-85; dealer/co-owner Cox Chevrolet, Wilburton, Okla., 1985; Pres. Taloga Extension Homemakers, 1971-73, sec.-treas., 1973-75; entertainer Latimer County Rest Homes, Wilburton, 1978—; leader Latimer County 4-H, Wilburton, 1979—. Recipient Leadership award Latimer County 4-H, 1983. Democrat. Avocations: camping, boating, sewing, cooking, reading. Office: D&R Service and Supply PO Box 55 Panola OK 74559

COX, JOYCE PRATHER, data processing executive; b. Washington, Aug. 13, 1944; d. Wesley Bernard andLois Marie (Burroughs) Prather; m. Gordon Cox, Sept. 20 1963 (div. 1981). BA, Empire State Coll., Albany, N.Y., 1976. Mgr. data systems Dept. City Planning, N.Y.C., 1971-73; mgr. personnel adminstrn. Human Resources Adminstrn., N.Y.C., 1973-78, dir., ops., 1978-80; communications analyst 1st Atlanta Bank, 1980-84; area staff mgr. Wang Labs., Atlanta, 1984-85, br. mgr., 1985-86, data processing specialist, 1986-87; owner Prather Assocs., Inc., Atlanta, 1987—. Mem. Nat. Assn. Female Execs. (dir. Atlanta chpt. 1984—), Am. Mgmt. Assn., Atlanta C. of C. Home and Office: 2692 Stardust Trail Decatur GA 30034

COX, MARLENE MILLICAN, nurse, rehabilitation counselor; b. Hanceville, Ala., July 8; d. Marl Maston and Mattie (Freeman) Millican; m. Robert Wimberly, II, July 24, 1982; children—Marla C. Dykes, Gena C. Reid. B.S.N., Samford U., 1975; A.D. Nursing Jefferson State Jr. Coll., 1968; cert. health care adminstrn. U. Ala.-Birmingham, 1974. Claims examiner Blue Cross Blue Shield Ala., Birmingham, 1955-60; R.N., East End Meml. Hosp., Birmingham, 1968-70, Bapt. Med. Ctr., 1970-72; coordinator ICU, Cooper Green Hosp., Birmingham, 1972-75; dist. mgr. Internat. Rehab., Birmingham, 1976-82; pres. Ind. Rehab. Cons., Birmingham, 1982—. Mem. Exec. Female Assn., Assn. Rehab. Nurses, Ala. Claims Assn., Pvt. Rehab. Suppliers Ga. Home: 5543 Circlestone Ln Stone Mountain GA 30088

COX, MARY LINDA, paper distribution company executive; b. Alton, Ill., July 3, 1946; d. William M. and Helen (Winters) C. B.A., McKendree Coll., 1970; M.B.A., So. Ill. U., 1977; postgrad. date St. Louis U., 1984—. Exec. dir. Girl Scouts U.S.A., 1969-76; instr. So. Ill. U., Edwardsville, 1976-80; mgr. Smith-Scharff, St. Louis, 1980-81; account exec. AT&T, Tulsa, 1981-82; pres. Mo. Disposable Products, St. Louis, 1982—. Media specialist Tenn. Republican party, 1974; mem. fin. com. Greater St. Louis council Girl Scouts U.S.A.; mem. youth panel United Way St. Louis; mem. City of Wood River planning commn. Mem. Central Bus. Assn. (v.p. 1985), Beta Gamma Sigma (chpt. pres. 1978-79). Office: Mo Disposable Products 2649 Washington St Saint Louis MO 63103

COX, SHARON DYER, banker; b. Waxahachie, Tex., Feb. 11, 1949; d. Ray and Betty (Hart) Williams Dyer; m. Charles E. Cox, Sept. 3, 1978. B.S. in History, U. Tex.-Arlington, 1970. Dealer cashier Paine, Webber, Jackson & Curtis, Dallas, 1971-73; sec.-interviewer Tex. Am. Bank, Dallas, 1973-76, asst. personnel dir., 1976-80, v.p., personnel dir., 1980-82, sr. v.p., 1982—, Dallas region human resources coordinator, 1983. Mem. Am. Soc. Personnel Adminstrs., Dallas Personnel Assn., Nat. Assn. Bank Women. Republican. Methodist. Office: Tex Am Bank of Dallas 100 Exchange Park Dallas TX 75235

COX, THELMA BANKS, educational consultant; b. Cambridge, Md., July 21, 1928; d. Charles Monroe and Ida Mae (Slacum) Banks; BS, Morgan State U., 1948, MS, 1972; PhD, Union Grad. Sch., Cin., 1980; m. Leonard Cox, June 25, 1949. Social caseworker Phila. Dept. Public Assistance, 1949-50; sci. tchr., Annapolis, Md., 1949-50; English tchr., Balt., 1950-65, reading tchr., 1965-66, dept. head, 1966-67, coordinator community schs., 1967-68, spl. projects coordinator, 1968-72, project mgr., 1972-73, regional supt., 1973-79, asst. supt. intergovtl. relations, 1980-83; mem. Md. Council Higher Edn., 1970-76, State Bd. Higher Edn., 1976-86. Pres., Girl Scouts of Cen. Md., 1982-86; bd. dirs. Girl Scouts of U.S.A., 1985-87. Named Woman of Yr., Greyhound Bus Co., 1972. Mem. Am. Assn. Sch. Adminstrs., Nat. Assn. Black Sch. Educators, Delta Sigma Theta. Democrat. Editor: The Heritage of the Baltimore Chapter of Delta Sigma Theta, 1979. Home: 3344 Dolfield Ave Baltimore MD 21215

COX, WILMA BEATY, marketing and communications executive; b. Spokane, Wash., June 27, 1929; d. Robert Wilbur and Ruth Aseneth (Duran) Dudley; m. Robert S. Cox, Jr., Apr. 25, 1958 (div.); children: Charles Thomas, Leslee Ann Cox Stout, Robert Sayre, Nancy Elizabeth, Kristina Suzanne. BA, San Jose State U., 1972, MA, 1976. Cert. tchr., Calif. Asst. to dir. Crocker Art Gallery, Sacramento, 1973-74; dir. Pub. info. U. Calif.-Davis Sch. Medicine, 1974-76; dir. pub. affairs East Conn. State Coll., Willimantic, 1976-79; dir. pub. info. Bryn Mawr Coll., Pa., 1979-80; dir. pub. relations U. Puget Sound, Tacoma, Wash., 1980-83; dir. univ. communications Santa Clara U. (Calif.), 1983-85; dir. mktg. and communications Leisure Care, Inc., Bellevue, Wash., 1985-87, Village Concepts, Inc., Federal Way, Wash., 1987—; owner, operator Benchmark Communications,

Redmond, Wash., 1987—; cons. Hopkins Art Ctr., Dartmouth Coll., N.H., 1978; chairperson Com. on Publs. Standards, State of Conn., 1978-79. Author art catalogs. Bd. dirs. Crocker Art Gallery Assn., Sacramento, 1974-76; charter mem. communications group No. Calif. Cancer Program, Stanford, 1974-76; charter mem. bd. dirs. Sacramento Cancer Council, 1975-76; bd. dirs. San Jose State U. Art Alumni Assn., 1983-86. Recipient Best Mus. Pub. award, Western Assn. Museums, 1976; Disting. Service award La Sangre Latina, Hispanic Soc. ECSC, 1979. Mem. Council Advancement and Support of Edn. (CASE, exceptional achievement award periodicals program 1983, exceptional achievement award total publs. program 1983; chairperson publs. track 1985, Gold medal individual recruiting, Gold medal program pubs. 1985), Women in Communications (sec. Tacoma-Olympia chpt. 1980-83), Internat. Bus. Communicators, Phila. Pub. Relations Assn. (mem. peer awards com. 1980), Phi Kappa Phi. Democrat. Home: 6479 137th Av NE #358 Redmond WA 98052 Office: Village Concepts Inc 34004 16th Ave S Suite 200 Federal Way WA 98003

COX, WINONA JUNE, corporate administrator; b. Ft. Worth, Jan. 23, 1936; d. Gus Matthew and Opal Lee (Warden) Richey; m. Elmer Clinton Cox, Dec. 22, 1956; children: Gina Renae, Eric Matthew, Van Clinton, Christopher Wade, Richey Shay. BA in Sociology, North Tex. State U., 1979, BA in Psychology, 1981. Exec. sec. Pioneer Life Ins., Ft. Worth, 1956-58; mfg. supr. Tex. Instruments, Dallas, 1965-81, tng. mgr., 1983-87, div. tng. mgr., 1987—. Sec. Am. Cancer Soc., Wise County, 1966; v.p. PTA Chico (Tex.) Ind. Sch., 1965. Republican. Baptist. Home: 1505 Ave C Denton TX 76205

COX-SHOOP, SANDRA LEE, sales representative, nurse; b. Reno, Nev., Dec. 4, 1944; d. John William and Frances (Williams) Shoop; m. James Leslie Cox, Aug. 27, 1962; children: Christa Louise, Nathaniel Lewis. BS in Nursing, Covenant Coll., 1971. RN, Ala. Office nurse Huntsville (Ala.) Clinic, 1966-68; head ob-gyn nursing Woman's Hosp., Chatanooga, 1968-71; indsl. nurse Teledyne-Brown Engring., Huntsville, 1971-78; family nurse practitioner Nat. Health Service Corp., Atlanta, 1979-81; sr. sales sales rep. Wyeth-Ayerst Labs., Huntsville, 1981—. Pres. Eagle Forum, Huntsville, 1971-78; pres., founder Pregnancy Hot Line, Huntsville, 1981-84, counselor, advisor, 1984—. Mem. Am. Drug Travelers Assn., Nat. Assn. Female Execs., Madison County Pharm. Assn., Lauderdale and Colbert Pharm. Assn., Sigma Theta Tau (v.p. 1979—). Republican. Presbyterian. Home and Office: Wyeth-Ayerst Labs 1717 Club View Dr NW Huntsville AL 35816

COY, ARVEL JEAN, computer operations executive, music consultant; b. Chickasha, Okla., June 29, 1951; d. Orville Columbus and Dessie Mae (Wilson) Sutterfield; m. Richard Earl Coy, April 20, 1968; children: Karla Jeanne, Richard Earl II. AA in Music, Luther Rice Coll., 1973; BA in Music Edn., Sterling (Kans.) Coll., 1978; MA in Indsl. and Organizational Psychology, MS in Indsl. Relations, U. New Haven, 1987. Computer operator Bapt. Hosp., Oklahoma City, 1969-69; data entry operator Human Resource Research Orgn., Alexandria, Va., 1969-73; organist Groveton Bapt. Ch., Alexandria, 1971-73; data entry operator Standard Oil of Ind. (Amoco), Kansas City, Mo., 1973-75; vocal music tchr. Sterling (Kans.) Pub. Schs., 1978-79; data entry supr. data systems div. Gen. Dynamics, Groton, Conn., 1980-83; computer ops. supr. data systems div. Gen. Dynamics, Quonset Point, R.I., 1983—; vis. prof. Sterling Coll., 1978-79; cons. music So. New Eng. Bapt. Assn., Ledyard, Conn., 1979-84, Christian Bookstore of New Eng., West Warwick, R.I., 1986—, sec., treas. corp., 1986—. Musical accompanist to Brigadoon, 1969, 76; performer organ recital, 1973, vocal recital, 1978. Asst. dir. Pawtuxet Valley Community Chorus, 1988—. Recipient Sterling 100 award Sterling Coll. Alumni, 1987. Baptist. Home: 22 Riverside Ave West Warwick RI 02893 Office: Gen Dynamics Data Systems Div Quonset Point Facility North Kingstown RI 20852

COYNE, DONNA MARIE, marketing and advertising executive; b. Bklyn., Apr. 19, 1954; d. Carmelo Francis and Natalie Marie (Ryan) Failla. AS, So. Vt. Coll., 1974; BBA, U. Tex., Arlington, 1983. Purchasing specialist Am. Airlines, N.Y.C., 1977-79; purchasing agt. Am. Airlines, Dallas/Ft. Worth, 1979-80, gen. purchasing agt., 1980-81, supr. direct mail, 1981-82, specialist sales promotion, 1982-83, mgr. direct mail, 1983-84, mgr. frequent traveler promotion, 1984-86, nat. product mgr. comml. sales, 1986-88, mgr. domestic advt., 1988—. Active Jr. Achievement, Dallas, 1986—, Big Bros./Big Sisters, Dallas, 1986—, Ronald McDonald House, Dallas, 1988—, Dallas Symphony Assn., 1988—. Mem. Nat. Passenger Traffic Assn., Nat. Mus. Women in the Arts. Office: Am Airlines Dallas-Fort Worth Airport PO Box 619616 Dallas TX 75261-9616

COYNE, JOANNE DENISE, account coordinator; b. Oakland, June 13, 1958; d. Lloyd Denise and Nancy Josephine (Jacobberger) C. BA in Psychology, U. Calif., Berkeley, 1980. Personnel specialist Timesavers, San Francisco, 1980-81; traffice mgr. Ketchum Advt., San Francisco, 1981-84; account exec. Fischer Assoc. Advt. Agy., San Francisco, 1984-85; account coordinator Foote, Cone & Belding Advt. Agy., San Francisco, 1986—. Office: Foote Cone & Belding Advt Agy 1255 Battery St San Francisco CA 94111

COYNE, M. JEANNE, state supreme court justice; b. Mpls., Dec. 7, 1926; d. Vincent Mathias and Mae Lucille (Steinmetz) C. BS in Law, U. Minn., 1955, J.D., 1957. Bar: Minn. 1957, U.S. Dist. Ct. Minn. 1957, U.S. Ct. Appeals (8th cir.) 1958, U.S. Supreme Ct. 1964. Law clk. Minn. Supreme Ct., St. Paul, 1956-57; assoc. Meagher, Geer & Markham, Mpls., 1957-70, ptnr., 1970-82; assoc. justice Minn. Supreme Ct., St. Paul, 1982—; mem. Am. Arbitration Assn., 1967-82; mem. bd. conciliation Archdiocese St. Paul and Mpls., 1981-82; instr. U. Minn. Law Sch., Mpls., 1964-68; mem. Lawyers Profl. Responsibility Bd., St. Paul, 1982; chmn. com. rules of civil appellate procedure Minn. Supreme Ct., St. Paul, 1982—. Editor: Women Lawyers Jour., 1971-72. Mem. ABA, Minn. State Bar Assn., Nat. Assn. Women Lawyers, Nat. Assn. Women Judges, Minn. Women Lawyers Assn. (dir.), U. Minn. Law Alumni Assn. Office: Minn Supreme Ct 230 State Capitol Saint Paul MN 55155 *

COYTE, CAROLINE R., contracts administrator, writer; b. Panama C.Z., June 9, 1951; d. Hugh Wayne and Gloria (Scott) Randel; student Am. U., 1969-71, George Washington U., 1972-73; B.A. in Polit. Sci., U. Ariz., 1973; grad. Western State U. Coll. Law, 1984; m. Michael Alan Coyte, June 26, 1978; 1 child, Alistair Jeremy. Profl. staff/writer U.S. Senate Republican Policy Com., Washington, 1973-77; legis. asst./speechwriter U.S. Senator Cliff Hansen, Washington, 1977-78; dir. legislation Nat. Asphalt Pavement Assn., Washington, 1979-80; with Wickes Cos., San Diego, 1981-82, corp. govt. affairs analyst, 1982; with ICA Mortgage Corp., La Jolla, Calif., 1984-86; with Mgmt. Analysis Co., Del Mar, Calif., 1986—. Mem. Nat. Contracts Mgmt. Assn. Presbyterian.

COZART, ALETA DELORIS, municipal government official; b. Noblesville, Ind., Aug. 11, 1946; d. James Lee and Leta Marie Nolton; divorced; 1 child, Lance. ABA, Ind. U.-Purdue U. at Indpls., 1973; BA in Bus. Adminstrn. and Social/Behavioral Scis. with honors, U. South Fla., 1975; M in Pub. Adminstrn. with honors, Golden Gate U., 1979. Adminstrv. asst. to cen. services dir. City of Clearwater, Fla., 1976-77, asst. cen. services dir., 1977-78, acting cen. services dir., 1978, asst. to city mgr.; dep. adminstrv. officer Monterey County, Salinas, Calif., 1987—; interim dir. library City of Clearwater, 1980, pub. affairs dir., lobbyist and intergovtl. dir.; owner beauty salon, Tampa, Fla., 1985—; cons. Tampa chpt. Nat. Orgn. Indsl. Office Park Developers, 1985-86. v.p. Leadership Pinellas, Clearwater; active Vision Cable Community Access com., GTE Community Adv. Panel. Mem. Internat. City Mgrs. Assn., Fla. Women's Network, Nat. Assn. Female Execs. Club: Tiger Bay (Pinellas County, Fla.). Lodge: Soroptimists. Office: Monterey County Adminstrv Office 855 E Laurel Salinas CA 93905

COZZOLINO, DOROTHY MARIE, law librarian; b. Flushing, N.Y., Jan. 9, 1938; d. William George and Anna Amelia (Brignole) Aramini; student U. Conn., 1955-58; B.S. in Geography, Trenton State Coll., 1973; M.S., Drexel U., 1975; m. Joseph M. Cozzolino, Nov. 30, 1957; children—Suzan, Alison, Matthew. Asst. librarian U.S. Ct. Appeals 3d Circuit, Phila., 1975-79, chief librarian, 1979-88. Trustee, Morrisville (Pa.) Vis. Nurse Assn., 1972-75; fin. chairperson, treas. Morrisville Jr. Women's Club, 1970-74. Mem. Am. Assn. Law Libraries, Greater Phila. Law Library Assn. (treas. 1979-81, dir. 1978).

CRABB, BARBARA BRANDRIFF, federal judge; b. Green Bay, Wis., Mar. 17, 1939; d. Charles Edward and Mary (Forrest) Brandriff; m. Theodore E. Crabb, Jr., Aug. 29, 1959; children: Julia Forrest, Philip Elliott. A.B., U. Wis., 1960, J.D., 1962. Bar: Wis. 1963. Assoc. Roberts, Boardman, Suhr and Curry, Madison, 1968-70; research asst. Law Sch. U. Wis., 1968-70; research asst. Am. Bar Assn., Madison, 1970-71; U.S. magistrate Madison, 1971-79; U.S. dist. judge Western Dist. Wis., 1979—, chief judge, 1980—; mem. Gov. Wis. Task Force Prison Reform, 1971-73. Membership chmn., v.p. Milw. LWV, 1966-68; mem. Milw. Jr. League, 1967-68. Mem. ABA, Nat. Council Fed. Magistrates, Nat. Assn. Women Judges, State Bar Wis., Dane County Bar Assn., U. Wis. Law Alumni Assn. Home: 741 Seneca Pl Madison WI 53711 Office: US Dist Ct PO Box 591 Madison WI 53701 *

CRABTREE, CLARISSA CHRISTINE, human resources professional; b. Vienna, Austria, Oct. 8, 1948; d. Dallas Henry and Liselotte (Kabrna) C.; m. Carlos Lira Coppo, Apr. 30, 1972, (div. 1977); 1 child, Vanessa Lira. Student, Columbia U., NYU, 1966-68. Asst. dir. social activities Foreign Student Ctr. Columbia U., N.Y.C., 1969-72, student services asst., 1972-79; asst. mgr. office support services Grad. Sch. Bus. Columbia U., N.Y.C., 1979-81; employment mgr. Del Labs, Farmingdale, N.Y., 1981-85; dir. human resources Four Seasons Solar Products, Holbrook, N.Y., 1985—. Mem. Nat. Orgn. Female Exec., Am. Assn. Personnel Adminstn., L. I. Personnel Soc., Miller Place Hist. Soc. Lutheran. Office: Four Seasons Solar Prod 5005 Veterans Meml Hwy Holbrook NY 11741

CRAFT, AIMEE JO, transportation rate analyst; b. Newton, Iowa, Oct. 14, 1960; d. Ivan John Craft and Mary Kay (Stevens) Saxe. AS, Des Moines Area Community Coll., Ankeny, Iowa, 1983. Sr. programmer-analyst Ruan Transp. Corp., Des Moines, 1984-85, info. specialist, 1985-87, rate analyst, 1987-88; div. adminstrv. coordinator Ruan Transp. Corp., Dallas, 1988—. Mem. Research Inst. Am., Nat. Assn. Female Execs. Methodist. Home: 2508 Park Village Dr Apt #814 Arlington TX 76014

CRAFT, PEARL SARAH DIECK SERBUS, free-lance writer, former editor; b. Riverdale, Ill.; d. Emil Edwin and Pearl (Kaiser) Dieck; m. Gerald Serbus, Jan. 26, 1946 (dec. Aug. 1969); children—Allan Lester, Bruce Alan, Curt Lyle; m. James E. Craft, Jan. 16, 1974 (dec. June 1984). Mem. home econs. staff, writer Chgo. Herald Examiner, 1934-39; operator test kitchen Household Sci. Inst., Mdse. Mart, Chgo., 1940-45; free-lance writer grocery chains, Chgo., 1945-49; Riv.-Dolton corr. Calumet Index, Chgo., 1953-58, editorial asst., 1958-60, asst. editor, 1960-68, editor, 1968-72; with Suburban Index, Chgo., 1959-72, editor, 1960-72; mng. editor Index Publs., 1972-74; free lance writer, 1974—. Public relations vol. New Hope Sch., 1959-67; bd. dirs. United Fund of Riverdale, Roseland Mental Health Assn., Thornton chpt. Am. Field Service. Recipient Disting. Service Meml. scroll PTA, 1959, Sch. Bell award Ill. Edn. Assn., 1965, Outstanding Citizen award Chgo. South C. of C., 1972. Named Outstanding Civic Leader Am. Mem. Ill. Woman's Press Assn. (past pres. Woman of Distinction 1968, recipient 46 state awards, 3 nat. awards), Ark. Press Women, Nat. Fedn. Press Women (pres. parley past presidents 1981, dir. protocol), Riverdale (v.p. 1966-68), Chgo. South (v.p., dir.) chambers commerce. Home: 1421 N University Apt N-215 Little Rock AR 72207

CRAHAN, ELIZABETH SCHMIDT, medical association administrator; b. Cleve., Oct. 6, 1913; d. Edward and Margaret (Adams) Schmidt; student Wellesley Coll., 1931-32; B.Arch., U. So. Calif., 1937, M.L.S., 1960; m. Kenneth Acker, 1938 (div. 1968); children—Margaret Miller Johanningmeier, John Acker, Steven Acker, Charles Acker; m. 2d, Marcus E. Crahan, Dec. 16, 1968. Reference librarian Los Angeles County Med. Assn., 1960-61, head reference librarian, 1961-67, asst. librarian, 1967-78, dir. library services, 1978—. Founder, Med. Library Scholarship Found., 1967; pres. Friends of the UCLA Library, 1977-79. Mem. Spl. Libraries Assn., Med. Library Assn., Med. Library Group, So. Calif. and Ariz., Med. Mus. Assn., Am. Inst. Wine Food. Office: 634 S Westlake Ave Los Angeles CA 90057

CRAIG, BARBARA ANNE, educator, consultant; b. Arlington, Va., Sept. 25, 1949; d. Harry Edward and Ethel (Wolfe) Born; m. John Steven Craig, Oct. 23, 1971. BS in Langs., Georgetown U., 1971; MS in English, Edn., Radford U., 1976. Research asst., writer Gen. Services Adminstrn., Washington, 1971-72; instr. in English New River Community Coll., Dublin, Va., 1976-77; program asst. Montgomery County Pub. Library, Christiansburg, Va., 1976-77; instr. of English Broward County Schs., Ft. Lauderdale, Fla., 1978-79; mag. editor Fichera Publs., Margate, Fla., 1981; realtor Boone and Co., Roanoke, Va., 1983-86; cons. Resources for Profl. Effectiveness, Roanoke, 1986—. Tutor Literacy Vols. of Am. in Roanoke Valley, 1986—, newsletter editor, 1987—. Recipient Nat. Def. Fgn. Lang. scholarship Middlebury Coll., 1970. Mem. Am. Soc. Tng. and Devel., Roanoke Network for Profl. and Managerial Women. Mem. Baha'i Faith. Home: 3428 Londonderry Ct SW Roanoke VA 24018 Office: Resources for Profl Effectiveness PO Box 20808 Roanoke VA 24018

CRAIG, DOROTHY LOUISE, publisher; b. San Antonio, Tex., Jan. 28, 1921; d. Henry P. and Henrietta B. (Michon) Ehrhardt; m. Roy M. Craig, 1941 (dec. 1979); children—Celeste, Bernadette, Jennifer; m. James C. Drain, Apr. 18, 1981. Grad San Antonio Vocat., Tech. Sch., 1937. Bookkeeper, Stamford Am. newspaper (Tex.), 1950-58, acct., buyer, 1958-62, advt. acct., 1962-69; asst. to publisher, 1969-78, pub., pres., 1978—. Active Ind. Democratic party politics, 1977—. Mem. Tex. Press Assn., West Tex. Press Assn. Mem. Christian Church (Disciples of Christ). Clubs: Pierian, Tex. Fedn. Women's (pres. Mesquite dist. 1984-86). Office: Stamford Am 124 E Hamilton St Stamford TX 79552

CRAIG, GAIL HEIDBREDER, architect, educator; b. Balt., Jan. 20, 1941; d. Gerald August and Ora Henderson (Longley) Heidbreder; m. Val Dean Craig, Jan. 19, 1985; children: Laura Temple Cook, John Temple. BA, Stanford U., 1966, postgrad., 1975-78. Registered architect, Calif. With various firms 1969-85; owner Gail Craig, AIA, Porterville, Calif, 1985—; instr. Calif. Community Colls., Kern County, 1985—. Mem. AIA, Internat. Conf. Bldg. Offcls., Porterville C. of C. (bd. dirs. 1985-87), Main St. Inc. (bd. dirs. 1988—). Lodge: Zonta. Office: 639A N Main St Porterville CA 93257

CRAIG, JUDITH, clergywoman; b. Lexington, Mo., June 5, 1937; d. Raymond Luther and Edna Amelia (Forsha) C. BA, William Jewell Coll., 1959; MA in Christian Edn., Eden Theol. Sem., 1961; MDiv, Union Theol. Sem., 1968; DD, Baldwin Wallace Coll., 1981; DHL, Adrian Coll., 1985. Youth dir. Bellefontaine United Meth. Ch., St. Louis, 1959-61; intern children's work Nat. Council of Chs. of Christ, N.Y.C., 1961-62; dir. Christian edn. 1st United Meth. Ch., Stamford, Ct., 1962-66; inst. adult basic edn. N.Y.C. Schs., 1967; dir. Christian edn. Epworth Euclid United Meth. Ch., Cleve., 1969-72, assoc. pastor, 1972-76; pastor Pleasant Hills United Meth. Ch., Middleburg Heights, Ohio, 1976-80; conf. council dir. East Ohio Conf. United Meth. Ch., Canton, 1980-84; bishop United Meth. Ch., Detroit, 1984—; mem. Nat. Task Force on Itineracy, 1977-80; responder to World Council of Chs. (document on Baptism, Eucharest and Ministry 1975); gen. conf. delegate 1980, 84. Contbr. articles to ministry mags. Bd. dirs. YWCA, Middleburg Heights, 1976-80. Recipient Citation of Achievement William Jewell Coll., 1985. Mem. Internat. Women Minister's Assn. Office: United Meth Ch 155 W Congress Suite 200 Detroit MI 48226

CRAIG, KAREN LYNN, certified public accountant; b. Detroit, Mar. 17, 1959; d. John and Corinne (Legel) C.; m. Robert A. Steshetz, May 3, 1986. A. in Commerce, Henry Ford Community Coll., 1980; B.S. in Bus. and Acctg., Wayne State U., 1982. C.P.A., Mich., Calif. Cost and staff acct. Wilson Dairy Co., Detroit, 1982-83, sr. acct., 1983-84, acting controller, 1984; staff acct. Coopers & Lybrand, Detroit, 1984-85, sr. acct., 1986-87, supr. acct., Newport Beach, Calif., 1987—. Mem. Mich. Assn. CPA's, Nat. Assn. Female Execs. Avocations: music; photography; baseball. Office: Coopers & Lybrand One Newport Pl 1301 Dove St Newport Beach CA 92660

CRAIG, LEONE ERIN, government official; b. Sydney, Australia, May 10, 1945; came to U.S., 1946; d. James Robert and Iris Gralton (Adams) C. AA in Social Sci., Imperial Valley Coll., 1972. Letter carrier U.S. Postal Service, El Centro, Calif., 1966, clk., 1967-80, officer-in-charge, Winterhaven, Calif., 1978-79, Postmaster, Westmoreland, Calif., 1980-82, Calipatria, Calif., 1982-86, Imperial, Calif., 1986—; com. mem. U.S. Postal Service Women's Program, Palm Springs, Calif., 1976-81, San Bernardino, Calif., 1981—. Bd. dirs. Imperial Valley Coll. Mus. Soc., El Centro, Calif., 1983-85; guide Mich. Artrain, El Centro, 1983; mem. planning commn. City of Calipatria, 1986-88. Mem. Nat. Assn. Postmasters U.S., Nat. League Postmasters U.S., Imperial County Postmasters' Assn. (pres. 1981-82, 87—, sec./treas. 1982-87). Republican. Office: Postmaster US Postal Service 116 N Imperial Ave Imperial CA 92251-9998

CRAIG, LEXIE FERRELL, educator, career vocational and guidance counselor; b. Halls, Tenn., Dec. 12, 1921; d. Monroe Stancil and Hester May (Martin) Ferrell; m. Philip L. Craig, May 19, 1951; children: Douglas H., Laurie K., Barbara J. BS magna cum laude, George Peabody Coll., Vanderbilt U., 1944; MA with honors, Denver U., 1965; postgrad. Colo. U., 1972—, Colo. State U., 1964—, U. No. Colo., 1964—. Cert. local vocat. adminstr., vocat. guidance specialist, vocat. bus. specialist, vocat. home econs. specialist, reading specialist, nat. recreation dir. specialist. Danforth grad. fellow, counselor Mich. State U., East Lansing, 1944-46; nat. student counselor, field dir. student counseling dept. higher edn. Am. Bapt. Conv., summer service career projects dir. U.S. and Europe, 1946-51; coordinator religious and career activities counselor, Colo. U., 1951-52; tchr. home econs., phys. edn., counseling, dist. 96, Riverside, Ill., 1952-54; substitute tchr., psychometrist, reading specialist part time, Deerfield, Ill., 1956-59; substitute tchr. Littleton (Colo.) Dist. VI, 1961-63, guidance and career counselor Littleton Pub. Schs., 1963-67, 68-86, career devel. specialist, guidance counselor spl. assignments state and nat., Gov.'s Youth 2000 Task Force Com., 1985—, also mem. vocat. needs and assessment com., 1988—; dir., counselor YWCA Extension Program, Job Corps, Denver, 1967-68; tchr. adult edn. home econs. evenings, 1963-66; mem. Colo. State Career Task Force, 1973-77; vol. home econ. cons. Colo. State U extension office. Lay conf. rep. Meth. Ch. Pastor/Parish Commn.; vol. sr. citizens programs United Meth. Ch., Littleton Community Ctr.; chmn. membership com. St. Andrew United Meth. Ch., Colo. Ch. Women United; mem. Greater Denver Frienship Force; bd. dirs. Career Awareness Council Boy Scouts Am., Metro Denver; also mem. Colo. Career Awareness Council; bd. dirs. So. Suburban Recreation, Littleton Community Arts Ctr.; adv. council Powell PTO, 1981-84; adv. council SEMBCS area vocat. schs.; mem. local caucus com. Republican Party; mem. Dist. Environ. Sci. Council. Didcott scholar, 1942; mem. AVS adv. council Early Childhood Edn., Health Occupation, Restaurant Arts and Coop Career Devel., 1970—; Danforth home econs. and leadership scholar, 1943; Am. Leadership Camp Found. scholar, Shelby, Mich., 1942-45; Hildegarde Sweet Scholar, 1983; recipient Sullivan award and grant, named outstanding grad., 1944; named Littleton Mother of Year, 1977, Colo. Vocat. Counselor of Yr., 1978, Colo. Vocat. Guidance Assoc. Counselor of Yr., 1984; recipient plaque for recruiting and career guidance Navy and Air Force, 1980, Clifford G. Houston award, 1985, Outstanding award Boy Scouts of Am. Career Awareness Council, 1986, Recognition Gold Pin award United Meth. Ch. Women, 1988. Mem. NEA, AAUW, Colo. Edn. Assn., Littleton Edn. Assn., Am. Vocat. Assn., Colo. Vocat. Assn., Am. Assn. Counseling and Devel., Colo. Assn. for Counseling and Devel. (exec. bd.), Nat. Career Devel. Assn. (membership chmn.), Colo. Career Devel. Assn. (past pres., membership chmn.), Nat. Vocat. Guidance Assn. (Colo. rep.), Am. Assn. Retired Persons, Colo. Retired Sch. Employees Assn., Arapahoe County Retired Tchrs., Colo. Sch. Counselors Assn., Am. Field Service (pres. Littleton chpt.), Lit. Book Club Littleton Arts Ctr., Home Economists in Homemaking (Littleton and Bega, Australia clubs), Phi Delta Kappa, Delta Kappa Gamma Alpha Delta (chpt. pres.), Delta Pi Epsilon (past pres.), Pi Omega Pi (past pres.), Pi Gamma Mu (past pres.), Kappa Delta Pi (past pres.). Clubs: Order Eastern Star, Country Western Dance. Editor, pub. Join in a Song, 1949; editor The Church Follows Its Youth, 1950, curriculum units in consumer edn., home econs., careers, parenting classes.

CRAIG, MYRITA PARKER, communications company executive; b. Joliet, Ill., Aug. 11, 1954; d. Kenneth P. and Myrita H. (Milligan) Parker; m. Alfred B. Craig, Aug. 8, 1981. B.A., U. Iowa, 1976. Account rep. AT&T, Cin., 1978-79, staff mgr. corp. planning, Chgo., 1980, ops. mgr., 1981, nat. account exec., Cin., 1981-82, nat. account mgr., 1982-85; asst. v.p. Cin. Bell Enterprises, 1985-87, v.p., 1987—. Author: Chapter Relations Handbook, 1977; Decolores, 1982. Pub. relations dir. Big Bros./Big Sisters, Joliet, Ill., 1977-78; com. chairperson Hyde Park Community United Methodist Ch., Cin., 1981-84; bd. dirs. Camp Fire Inc., Cin., 1984. Harry S. Bunker journalism scholar U. Iowa, Iowa City, 1975. Mem. Nat. Assn. Female Execs., Women in Communication, Am. Assn. Profl. and Exec. Women, Cin. C. of C., Delta Gamma (chpt. adviser 1981-84). Home: 930 Morris St Cincinnati OH 45206 Office: Cin Bell Enterprises 201 E 4th St Cincinnati OH 45202

CRAIG, VIRGINIA SUSAN, college director; b. Fulton, Mo., Dec. 16, 1949; d. Allan Jr. and Rita Maxine (Sweet) C. BS, U. Colo., 1971, MA, 1973; MEd, Antioch U., 1976. Counselor Nat. Ctr. Child Abuse, Denver, 1972-74; exec. dir. Boulder (Colo.) Children's Ctr., 1974-79; dir. devel. Oglala Lakota Coll., Kyle, S.D., 1979-81; dir. instl. strengthening Black Hills State Coll., Spearfish, S.D., 1981—; commr.-at-large No. Cen. Assn., Chgo., 1986; cons. in field; owner Media Assocs., Spearfish, 1986. Mem. S.D. Strip Mining Awareness Coalition. Democrat. Club: Congl. Home: 130 W Dakota St Spearfish SD 57783

CRAIK, PEGGY SUE, nursing educator; b. Kansas City, Mo., Apr. 5, 1943; d. Jack L. and Bettie J. (Iba) Hayes; m. Willis R. Craik, Oct. 16, 1976; children: Jacquelyn, Raelynn, William. BSN, Ft. Hays State U., 1965; MS, Tex. Women's U., 1978. Staff, charge nurse Southwest Med. Ctr., Liberal, Kans., 1965-66; supr. Ochletree Gen. Hosp., Perryton, Tex., 1966-67; dir. nursing Sr. Village, Perryton, 1967-68; mem. faculty Northwest Tex. Hosp. Sch. Nursing, Amarillo, 1968-69; head nurse High Plains Bapt. Hosp., Amarillo, 1969-72; dir. staff devel. U. Tex. Med. Br., Galveston, 1972-75; asst. adminstr. King's Daus. Hosp., Temple, Tex., 1975-79; assoc. prof. U. Mary Hardin-Baylor, Belton, Tex., 1980—; cons. Meml. Med. Ctr. W.Mich., Ludington, St. John's Hosp., Redwing, Minn., Cen. Counties Ctr. Mental Health/ Mental Retardation, Temple; clin. preceptor Tex. Women's U., Denton; mem. adv. bd. Girling's Home Health Services, Temple. Contbr. book chpt., articles to profl. jours. Instr. CPR Am. Heart Assn., first aid ARC. AAUW scholar, 1965. Mem. Am. Nurses Assn., Tex. Nurses Assn. (v.p. dist. 7, 1981-83), Nat. Assn. Female Execs., Sigma Kappa, Nu Sigma Lambda. Republican. Presbyterian. Office: U Mary Hardin-Baylor 9th & College St Belton TX 76513

CRAIN, D'ANN DEYONG, dancer, director; b. Lawton, Okla., Feb. 4, 1956; d. Robert Leon and Juanita Frankie (Ashton) DeYong; m. Russell Dean Crain, Dec. 21, 1981. Student, Calif. Inst. Arts, 1974-75, Oklahoma City U., 1978-80. Prin. dancer Lawton (Okla.) Civic Ballet, 1968-74, Prairie Dance Theatre, Oklahoma City, 1981-85; artist-in-residence State of Okla., 1984—; inst. artist Harwelden Inst., Tulsa, 1986—; co-artistic dir. Three Dancers Plus, Colorado Springs, 1986—; co. dancer Three Dancers Plus, Colo. and Okla., 1986—; cons., master artist Project Arts in Math., Putman City Schs., Oklahoma City, 1986-88; audition panel artist State Arts Council of Okla., 1988. Choreographer: (sacred dances) For the Beauty of the Earth, 1982, Create in Me a Clean Heart, 1985, Now the Silence, 1988; (modern dance) In Our Heads, 1988. Recipient Disney artist scholarship Calif. Inst. of the Arts, Valencia, 1974. Mem. Nature Conservancy, Sierra Club, Sacred Dance Guild, Mid-Am. Dance Network, Okla. Alliance for Arts in Edn. Republican. Presbyterian. Home: 1133 NW 50th St Oklahoma City OK 73118

CRAIN, MRS. GERTRUDE RAMSEY, publishing company executive. m. G.D. Crain Jr. (dec. Dec. 15, 1973); 2 sons: Keith, Rance. Asst. treas. Crain Communications Inc., Chgo., 1941-61, sec., 1943-74, treas., 1961-74, chmn. bd., 1974—. Named to Working Woman Hall of Fame, 1987; recipient Magnificent medal Mundelein Coll., Chgo., 1988. Office: Crain Communications Inc 740 N Rush St Chicago IL 60611 *

CRAMER, ELSIE RINDT, health company director; b. Neuheuser, Fed. Republic of Germany, Dec. 19, 1940; came to U.S., 1959; d. Rudolf Rindt and Adele (Reichert) Defort; m. John William Cramer, June 26, 1959 (div. Aug. 1983); 1 child, Drew. Cert. family nurse practitioner and physician's asst., U. Calif., Davis, 1977-78; BA, Sonoma State U., 1983; M in Pub. Adminstrn., U. San Francisco, 1985. RN, Calif. Staff nurse Mad River Community Hosp., Arcata, Calif., 1974-76; asst. head nurse intensive care unit The. Gen. Hosp., Eureka, Calif., 1976-77, supr. nursing, 1977-78; asst. head nurse Marin Gen. Hosp., Greenbrae, Calif., 1978-79, supr. adminstrv. nursing, 1979—; dir. patient care services West Contra Costa Community Health Care Corp., Richmond, Calif., 1979—; coordinator PSRO, Santa Rosa, Calif., 1975-76; family nurse practitioner Arcata Open Door Clinic, 1977-78; instr. CPR Am. Heart Assn., San Rafael, Calif., 1980—; mgmt. cons. MLK Health Plan, Richmond, 1986—. Cons. health Richmond Unified Sch. Dist., 1980—, Lao Family Community Inc., Richmond, 1982—, Farmer's Market, Richmond, 1985—. Mem. Nat. Assn. Nurse Practitioners in Family Planning, Calif. Coalition Nurse Practitioners, Nat. Assn. for Female Execs., AAUW, AAL, Beta Sigma Phi (sec. 1963-65). Republican. Lutheran.

CRAMER, JUDITH ANN, court adminstrator; b. Cleve., Aug. 20, 1941; d. Charles Camden Ernst and Audrey Helen (Peck) Pelz; m. Wilbur Ray Hawkins, Feb. 15, 1965 (div. Aug. 1976), 1 child: Myrrha; m. Robert Michael Cramer, Mar. 11, 1978; children: Lisa, Cami, Cara, Robert Sean, William Robert. BS in Polit. Sci. and Langs., Wittenberg U., 1962; BS in Edn., Bowling Green State U., 1963; MS in Program in Social Work, Ohio State U., 1968; MS in Pub. Adminstrn., U. Dayton, 1980. Caseworker Welfare Dept., Columbus, 1964-65, Children's Services Bd., Dayton, 1965-67, Ohio Youth Commn., Dayton, 1967-69; juvenile probation officer Shelby County, Sidney, Ohio, 1969-70; adminstr. Montgomery County Retarded Children's Program, Dayton, 1970-71, dir. resident home for mentally retarded, 1971-72; dep. dir. ct. planner grants adminstrn. Criminal Justice Program Miami Valley Planning Commn., Dayton, 1972-78; co-founder, dir. MonDay Community Correctional Inst., Dayton, 1978-80; ct. adminstr. Montgomery (Ohio) County Ct. of Common Pleas, 1980—; faculty Nat. Jud. Coll. U. Nev., 1984—; guest faculty U. Dayton, 1984—; cons. EMT Bur. Justice Assistance, Washington, 1985—; founder, 1st bd. dirs. MonDay Correctional Instn., Dayton, 1978-80; bd. dirs. Nat. Ctr. for State Cts. Author: House Bill 1000 Community Corrections, 1979, school partnership program School Awareness Brochure, 1986; producer TV show And Justice for All, 1986. Bd. dirs. Mental Retardation, Dayton, 1976-78; chmn. Criminal Justice Policy Bd. Miami Valley Regional Planning Commn.; mem. Montgomery County Fin. Com., Dayton, 1985—, Montgomery County Records Ctr., 1984—, Stingers Soccer Club, Dayton, 1985—, Englewood Co-ed Adult Soccer (coach 1987—). Recipient Leadership Dayton award, 1978, Disting. Pub. Service award, WKEF TV, 1979, Outstanding Leadership award Corrections Club Sinclair Coll., 1979, Career Acad. award Dayton Career Acad., 1985, Leadership award Ohio Supreme Ct., 1986, Disting. Service award Nat. Ctr. State Cts., 1988. Mem. Ohio Assn. Ct. Adminstrn. (past pres. 1984), Nat. Assn. Ct. Adminstrn. (bd. dirs. 1985), Nat. Assn. Ct. Mgmt. (v.p. 1985, pres. elect 1986, pres. 1986—), ABA (assoc., com. delay reduction 1986), Delta Gamma. Republican. Methodist. Club: Gem City Sweet Adelines (Dayton). Office: Montgomery County Ct Common Pleas 41 N Perry Dayton OH 45422

CRAMER, ROXANNE HERRICK, educator; b. Albion, Mich., Apr. 24; d. Donald F. and Kathryn L. (Beery) Herrick; m. James Loveday Hofford, Jan. 29, 1955 (div.); children—William Herrick, Dana Webster, Paul Christopher; m. 2d Harold Leslie Cramer, Apr. 20, 1967. Student, U. Mich., 1952-55; B.A., U. Toledo, 1956; Ed.M., Harvard U., 1967; doctoral candidate Va. Poly. Inst. and State U., 1984—. Tchr. Wayland (Mass.) Pub. Schs., 1966-70, Fairfax County (Va.) Pub. Schs., 1970—; tchr./team leader Gifted/Talented program, 1975—; coordinating instr. Trinity Coll., Washington, 1978; nat. coordinator gifted children programs Am. Mensa, Ltd., 1981-84. Mem. Nat. Assn. Gifted Children, Am. Assn. Gifted Children, Coalition for Advancement Gifted Edn. (bd. dirs. 1982-84), World Council Gifted and Talented Children, Intertel Found., Inc. (bd. dirs., mem. Hollingworth award com. 1979—, now chmn.), Fairfax County Assn. Gifted, NEA, Va. Edn. Assn., Fairfax Edn. Assn., Mensa, Phi Delta Kappa. Club: Harvard (Washington). Contbr. articles to profl. jours. Home: 4300 Sideburn Rd Fairfax VA 22030 Office: Louise Archer Gifted Ctr 324 Nutley St NW Vienna VA 22180

CRANDALL, CONNIE ALICE, educational director; b. Salt Lake City, Oct. 3, 1949; d. James Neal and Ruth Elaine (Hultquist) Foulks; m. Jay Thomas Crandall, Aug. 17, 1977 (div. 1981). BA, Westminster Coll., 1973; MA, U. Utah, 1976. Adminstrv. asst. UBTL Inc., Salt Lake City, 1976-83, State of Utah Sci. Advisor, Salt Lake City, 1983-84, U. Utah, Salt Lake City, 1984-85; program dir. continuing edn. Rocky Mountain Ctr. for Occupational and Environ. Health, Salt Lake City, 1985—. Mem. Meeting Planners Internat., Nat. Assn. Female Execs. Democrat. Lutheran. Office: U Utah RMCOEH Bldg 512 Salt Lake City UT 84112

CRANDALL, JUDITH ANN, publishing company executive; b. Milw., Aug. 20, 1948; d. Robert Joseph and Fern Alice (Stevens) Neulreich; m. P. Henry, Apr. 3, 1969 (div. 1970); m. Jerry C. Crandall, July 4, 1976. Student, U. Ariz., 1966-68. Mgr. advt. Mattel Toys, Hawthorne, Calif., 1968-72; mgr. Peterson Galleries, Beverly Hills, Calif., 1974-76; dir. Saddlebrook Gallery, Santa Ana, Calif., 1978-82; prin. Eagle Editors, Ltd., Sedona, Ariz., 1983—; bus. mgr. Women Artists Am. West, 1982. Editor AeroBrush; writer SW Art mag., Houston, 1972-83. Home: PO Box 2606 Sedona AZ 86336 Office: Eagle Editions Ltd PO Box 1830 Sedona AZ 86336

CRANDALL, PATRICIA IRENE, lawyer; b. Rhinelander, Wis., Apr. 28, 1945; d. John Edward and Irene Selma (Koskelin) Cerney; m. Thomas Dwane Crandall, Aug. 28, 1965 (div. 1976); m. Jack Donald Brenton, Nov. 23, 1982. BS, Ind. U., 1969; MS, U. Wis., 1973; JD, Gonzaga U., 1977. Bar: Wash. 1977, U.S. Dist. Ct. (ea. dist.) Wash. 1978. Tchr. Notre Dame High Sch., Milw., 1970-71, Holy Rosary Sch., Milw., 1970-73; communications specialist Human Relations Council Greater Harrisburg, Pa., 1973-74; assoc. Shine, Rein, Stiles, Spokane, Wash., 1977-78; assoc. Lukins & Annis, P.S., Spokane, 1978-81, prin., 1981—, mem. exec. com., 1986—; bd. dirs. Wash. Soc. of Hosp. Attys.; adj. faculty Whitworth Coll., Spokane, 1986. Bd. dirs. Profl. Resource Options, Spokane, 1983—, sec. 1986-87; atty. team capt. United Way Campaign, 1984. Mem. ABA, Am. Acad. Hosp. Attys., Wash. Bar Assn. (chairperson code of profl. responsibility 1981-82, chairperson clients security funds com. 1983-85, spl. dist. counsel 1985—), Spokane County Bar Assn. (trustee 1982-84). Club: Spokane. Home: 2424 S Magnolia Spokane WA 99204 Office: Lukins & Annis PS 1600 Washington Trust Ctr Spokane WA 99204

CRANDELL, MARJORIE MALLORY, advertising executive; b. Hartford, Conn., June 3, 1957; d. Charles W. Jr. and Patricia (Higbie) C. Student, Oberlin Coll., 1975-76; BS in Communications, Boston U., 1979. Account coordinator Lynn Jeffery & Co., Boston, 1978-80; assoc. dircet mail mgr. H.E. Harris & Co., Boston, 1980-82; account supr. Kobs & Brady Advt., Inc., N.Y.C., 1982-86, Mallory Communications, N.Y.C., 1986-87; dir. direct mktg. Found. for Commemoration of U.S. Constn., N.Y.C., 1987—; dir. Underwriters, Inc., San Francisco, 1985—. Author: Waterfront Vacations, USA, 1987. Chairperson memberships Carnegie Hill Neighborhood Assn., N.Y.C., 1987—. Mem. Internat. Radio and TV Soc., Cable TV Advt. and Mktg. Assn. (award 1985), Direct Mktg. Assn. (leader award 1986). Episcopalian.

CRANE, BARBARA JOYCE, publishing company executive, author; b. Trenton, N.J., June 2, 1934; d. Herman and Elizabeth (Stein) Cohen; m. Stuart G. Crane, Aug. 27, 1956; children: Susan Jill, Patricia Lynne. BA, Vassar Coll., 1956. Tchr. Trenton Pub. Schs., 1956-58; prin. Little People's Sch., Yardley, Pa., 1964-66; reading cons. Newtown Friends Sch., Pa., 1967-68, Trenton State Coll., 1968-69; dir. Demonstration Sch., Trenton State Coll., 1969-70; pres. Crane Pub. Co., Trenton, 1968—; mem. social, polit. concerns com. Nat. Assn. Bilingual Edn., Washington, 1980. Author: (reading systems) Categorical Sound System, 1977, Crane Reading System: BASIC Program, 1977-82, Spanish Crane Reading System, 1981-87, Pacer Program; (test) Crane Oral Dominance Test, 1976; contbr. articles to various publs. Bd. dirs. Inst. New World Archaeology, Chgo., 1981—. Grantee Vassar Coll., 1967-68, Trenton State Coll., 1968-69, State N.J., 1968, N.Y. State Framework Com. for Spanish Lang. Arts. Mem. Internat. Reading Assn., Nat. Assn. Bilingual Edn. Clubs: Vassar College, Metedeconk River Yacht. Home: 1909 Yardley Rd Yardley PA 19067 Office: Crane Pub Co 1301 Hamilton Ave Trenton NJ 08629

CRANE, JANET GRAY, association executive; b. Villa Rica, Ga., Oct. 9, 1953; d. James David Sr. and Norma Ruth (Lee) Gray; m. Stephen Winston Crane, Dec. 18, 1971; 1 child, Alexander Gray. AB in Journalism, Ga. State U., 1974. Dir. publs. Ga. Sch. Bd. Assn., Atlanta, 1974-76, asst. exec. dir., 1976-80; meetings adminstr. Tech. Assn. of the Pulp and Paper Industry, Atlanta, 1980-81, membership promotional adminstr., 1981-82, mem. services mgr., 1982-84; dir. communications Tech. Assn. of the Pulp and Paper Industry, 1984—. Contbr. articles to profl. jours. Mem. Ga. Soc. Assn. Execs. (v.p. edn. 1984-85, v.p. programming 1985-86, pres. 1986-87), Am. Soc. Assn. Execs. (cert.), Council Engring. and Sci. Soc. Execs. Office: Tech Assn Pulp and Paper Industry PO Box 105113 Atlanta GA 30348

CRANE, KEENAN DURKIN, human resource consultant, therapist; b. Phila., Jan. 6, 1944. AA cum laude, Montgomery County Community Coll., 1975; BA in Psychology magna cum laude, Rosemont Coll., 1978; MS in Exptl. Psychology, Villanova U., 1980, MS in Counseling and Human Relations, 1981; PhD, Temple U., 1988. Cert. practitioner in psychodrama. Asst. psychodramatist Interim House, Mt. Airy, Pa., 1980-81, Horsham Clinic, Ambler, Pa., 1981-82; therapist Alliance for Creative Devel., Quakertown (Pa.) Hosp., and Landsdale, Pa., 1982-85; pvt. practice, individual and group therapy Villanova, Pa., 1985—; founding mem., bd. dirs., chairperson mgmt. cons. firm DHORS (Devel. of Human and Organizational Systems), Villanova; part-time prof. Temple U., Del. County Community Coll., 1984-88; adminstrv. asst. Ctr. for Intergenerational Learning, group leader Inst. on Aging, Temple U., 1988; cons. trainer group therapy, psychodrama Jefferson Med. Sch., Sacred Heart Hosp., Haverford, Pa., Del. Valley Soc. Group Psychotherapy, Drug and Rehab. Ctr., Seabrook (N.J.) House; spl. lectr. West Chester (Pa.) U., Widener U.; cons. in group dynamics Interim House. Mem. Assn. Counseling and Devel., Am. Assn. Group Psychotherapy (psychodrama and sociometry research com.), Eastern Psychol. Assn., Delta Epsilon Sigma, Kappa Delta Pi. Home and Office: DHORS 1208 Spring Mill Rd Villanova PA 19085

CRANE, LINDA RUTH, public relations director; b. Halifax, N.S., Canada, Sept. 17, 1952; d. Alfred Robert and Muriel Catherine (Scott) C. BA, York U., Downsville, Ont., 1974; BEd, U. Western Ont., London, 1976. Tchr. Toronto Bd. Edn., 1976-78; sales rep. Ma Cherie Ltd., Hamilton, Ont., 1978-79; asst. show mgr. Can. Nat. Sportsmen's Shows, Toronto, 1979-83; mgr. info. services Can. Nat. Sportsmen's Shows, 1983-84; show mgr. Toronto Internat. Boat Show, 1985-87; dir. pub. relations Can. Nat. Sportsmen's Shows, 1987—; v.p. pub. relations, cons. Mgmt. Info. Bookkeeping and Reporting Systems, Toronto. Editor newsletter VISTA, 1984-85; author articles in field. Mem. Can. Assn. Exhibition Mgrs., Can. Pub. Relations Soc. Conservative. Club: RBI Group, Toronto. Office: Can Nat Sportsmen's Shows, 595 Bay St Suite 1010, Toronto, ON Canada M5G 2C2

CRANE, LYNN CAROL, accountant; b. Chardon, Ohio, Mar. 16, 1954; d. Richard James Buchan and Esther (Hatten) Bly; m. Peter M. Crane III, Sept. 25, 1976; children: Peter M. IV, Pamela Morgan. BS, Ohio State U., 1976; MBA, Ohio U., 1979. CPA, Ohio. Phys. therapist Profl. Therapeutic Services, Inc., Dayton, Ohio, 1976-77; office mgr. 7-Up, Pepsi Bottling Co., Athens, Ohio, 1979; acctg. instr. Ohio U., Athens, 1980, 85; staff acct. Armstrong & Smith, CPA's, The Plains, Ohio, 1980-84; pvt. practice acctg. The Plains, 1984—. Service unit dir. Girl Scouts U.S., Athens, 1976—; treas. SE Ohio Victim/Witness Assistance Program, Athens, 1987—. Named Nat. Intercollegiate Women's Pistol Champion Nat. Rifle Assn., 1975. Mem. Am. Inst. CPA's, Ohio Soc. CPA's, Nat. Alliance Homebased Bus. Women (chair 1985, pres.). Republican. Roman Catholic. Home and Office: 17 Johnson Rd The Plains OH 45780

CRANE, PAULA LOUISE, management consultant; b. Akron, Ohio, Dec. 28, 1957; d. Anthony Barnum and Dolores Anne (Magusiak) C. BS in Systems Analysis, U. Miami, 1978; postgrad., 1982—. Programmer, analyst S.E. Data Processing, Miami, 1980-83; sr. fin. analyst S.E. Bank, N.A., Miami, 1983-84; sr. systems analyst Metro Dade County, Miami, 1984; owner, dir. Crane Data Systems, Inc., (formerly Sabco, Inc.), Coral Gables, Fla., 1983-87; owner, pres. Sabco of Miami, Inc., Coral Gables, 1984-87; sr. mgmt. cons. Peat, Marwick, Main & Co., Miami, 1987—. Vol. Am. Cancer Soc., Miami Grand Prix, Miami Motor Sports, Ronald McDonald House. Mem. U. Miami Alumni, Delta Delta Delta Alumni (treas. Miami 1984-86, pres. 1986—). Roman Catholic. Club: Progress. Avocations: photography, ballet, scuba diving, wine, travel. Home: 2180 Brickell Ave Apt 6 Miami FL 33129 Office: Peat Marwick Main & Co 1 Biscayne Tower 2 S Biscayne Blvd Miami FL 33131 also: Two Biscayne Blvd Miami FL 33131

CRANE, PHYLLIS, artist; b. San Diego, Apr. 14, 1903; d. William Anderson and Mabel (Ray) C.; B.S., U. So. Calif., 1935, M.A., 1945; postgrad. Noyes (N.Y.) Sch. Rhythm and Creative Arts Studios, Portland, Conn., 1955. Tchr. schs. Pasadena, Calif., 1927-56, Peekskill, N.Y., 1958-60, Brewster, N.Y., 1960-62; co-program presenter Nature Moods to numerous clubs in N.Y.C. and Westchester County, 1979-84; one-woman shows: Contemporary Artists Gallery, Kingston, Jamaica, 1971, Dawson's Grist Mill Gallery, Chester Depot, Vt., 1974, 76, Port Chester (N.Y.) Library Gallery, 1975, Wood Pavalion Gallery, White Plains, N.Y., 1978; group shows include: Nat. Arts Club, 1965-79, Hansen Galleries, 1979, Pen and Brush Galleries, 1978-82, Sotheby Parke Bernet Galleries, 1980, 81, Custom House Mus., World Trade Center, 1981, Lever House, 1980, 82, Salmagundi Club (all N.Y.C.), Burr Artists, Newhouse Galleries, Snug Harbor Cultural Ctr., S.I., N.Y., 1984, Am. Mus. Yorktown, Va., 1986; Eleanor Gay Lee's Gallery Found., N.Y.C., Pen & Brush, N.Y.C.; represented in permanent collections U.S., Europe; chmn. art shows No. Westchester, 1969-72, 77; co-chmn. art shows Hendrick Hudson Library, Montrose, N.Y., 1977; chmn. art show Lever House, N.Y.C., 1982. Bd. dirs. YWCA. Anglo-Am. Acad. hon. fellow, 1980. Mem. Pen and Brush (Emily Nichols Hatch award 1979, dir. 1980-85), Nat. League Am. Pen Women, Composers, Authors and Artists Am. (corr. sec. 1978-80), Burr Artists, Gotham Artists, DAR, Pi Beta Phi, Delta Kappa Gamma. Author: Fundamental Exercises Most Beneficial for Relaxation, 1943; contbr. articles in field to profl. jours. Home and Studio: Boscobel Point Croton-on-Hudson NY 10520

CRANE, TERESA GAYLE, real estate management company executive; b. Ft. Worth, Oct. 11, 1948; d. Arthur Joseph and Agnes Isabelle (Edwards) Faram; m. Gilbert O. Crane, June 8, 1968 (div. Jan. 1986); 1 child, Caren Jenelle. Student, Cypress (Calif.) Coll., 1967-68. Sales agt. Century 21 Loughry, Ft. Worth, 1980; mgr. property Dal Worth Mgmt. Co., Ft. Worth, 1981-83; mgr. property Nat. Real Property Services, Inc., Ft. Worth, 1983-85, gen. mgr., 1985-86, pres., 1986; v.p. Angeles Real Estate Mgmt., Ft. Worth, 1986—. Mem. Downtown Ft. Worth, Inc. mktg. com., 1987. Mem. Nat. Assn. for Female Execs., Bldg. Owners and Mgrs. Assn. (v.p. 1986, pres. 1987), S.W. Region Bldg. Owners and Mgrs. Assn. (bd. dirs. 1987). Republican. Presbyterian. Club: Headliners (Ft. Worth) (ex-officio mem. bd. dirs. 1986, 87). Home: 7701 Greengage Dr Fort Worth TX 76133 Office: Angeles Real Estate Mgmt Co 309 W 7th #815 Fort Worth TX 76102

CRANEY, MYRNA, accountant; b. Brackenridge, Pa., Feb. 24, 1936; d. Ralph I. Howells and Margaret E. (Bavetz) Mivec; m. Patrick M. Craney, June 19, 1954; children: Michael P., T. Bryan, Kathleen E. BS, U. So. Ind., 1980. CPA, Ind. Acct. Geo. S. Olive & Co., Evansville, Ind., 1976-81; accountant Harding & Shymanski, Evansville, Ind., 1981-83; ptnr. Craney & Wilson, Evansville, 1983-86, Brown, Smith & Settle, Evansville, 1986—; lectr. U. So. Ind., Evansville, 1981-84. Mem. Am. Inst. CPA's, Ind. CPA Soc., Women's Bus. Initiative. Club: Oak Meadow Country (Evansville). Office: Brown Smith & Settle 777 Oak Hill Rd Evansville IN 47711

CRANFORD, EULA FORREST, health science administrator, retired; b. Stanly County, N.C., Sept. 24, 1923; d. Claude Columbus and Gertie Ann (Chandler) Forrest; m. John Henry Cranford, July 4, 1942; children: Brenda Mae, Barbara Gail. Cert., Vocat. Rehab. Tng. Sch., Cleve., 1967, Stanly Tech. Coll., Albemarle, N.C., 1975, Human Services, Cen. Piedmont Coll., 1974. Acting dir. Stanly County Vocat. Workshop, Inc., Albemarle, 1966-67, exec. dir., 1967-85; dir. adult day program Assn. for Retarded Citizens, Inc., Albemarle, 1985-87. Pres. N.C. Shelter Workshops, Inc., 1977, treas., 1973, pres. adminstrv. practice div., 1976, sec., treas., 1974; vol. Albemarle Cancer Soc., Heart Fund, Cystic Fibrosis Soc., Spl. Olympics, Assn. for Retarded Citizens, 1988—; mem. N.C. Easter Seal Soc. (bd. dirs. 1976-77, adv. com. 1976-77, VIP award 1978, 79); pres. Albemarle United Methodist Women, 1988, dist. coordinator Christian Social Concerns, 1988—. Recipient Community Service award Stanly County C. of C. Mem. N.C. Rehab. Assn. Facility (pres. chpt. I 1977, Citation of Merit award, 1973). Democrat. United Methodist. Lodge: Civitan (Stanly Actioneers chpt. v.p. 1985-86, pres. 1986-87, Citizen of Yr. award 1970, 71). Home: 1625 W Park Ave Albemarle NC 28001 Office: Assn for Retarded Citizens Inc 730 Greenwood St PO Box 68 Albemarle NC 28002-0068

CRANK, RUTH ELIZABETH, financial planning executive, life insurance executive, manufacturing company executive, employment agency executive; b. Sidney, Ohio, Aug. 18, 1938; d. Charles Max Stephenson and Mildred Katherine (Hoover) Stephenson Foresythe; m. Robert G. Crank, Dec. 2, 1978; children—Rochelle, Roxanne, Troy, Juliana, Trent, Dominique. Dir. sch. project and ctr. U. Dayton, Father Phillip Hoelle, Ohio, 1971; field mgr. Avon Co., Cin., 1972-74; life ins. agt. N.Y. Life Ins. Co., Dayton, 1974—; pres. Crank, Crank & Assocs., Dayton, 1982—; speaker in field; cons. in field. Leader Buckeye Trails council Girl Scouts U.S. lead Drill Team, Cheerleading Camps., 1964-74; founder Woodman Play Sch.; mem. Better Bus. Bur. Named Ace of Yr., N.Y. Life, 1975, Star & Exec. council, 1974-84, Centurim, 1974-1984; mem. Women's Million Dollar Round Table; first woman ins. agt. recognized by Dayton Gen. Mgmt. and Mgrs. Life Assn. for outstanding work, 1976. Mem. Dayton C. of C. Republican. Roman Catholic. Avocations: riding scooter, small motorcycle; playing organ; camping; swimming. Home and Office: Crank & Crank 4837 Kentfield Dr Dayton OH 45426

CRANMER-BRISKEY, KAREN SUE, editor; b. St. Joseph, Mich., Sept. 11, 1948; d. Raymond J. and Eris J. (Jacobsen) Piotroski; m. Jerry Burke Cranmer, Nov. 30, 1968 (div. Mar. 1981); 1 son, Colin Sean; M. Robert Joseph Briskey; July 28, 1984. Student Purdue U., 1966-68; B.S. cum laude, U. Minn.-Duluth, 1971. Cert. elem. tchr. Elem. tchr., Duluth, 1971-72; apt. mgr. Hallmark Village Apts., Clarksville, Ind., 1972-73; substitute tchr., Duluth, 1974-75; prodn. mgr. Harcourt Brace Jovanovich, Duluth, 1975-76, prodn. supr., 1976-79; mng. editor Hearing Instruments, 1979—. Author: Annual Survey of Hearing Aid Dispensing, 1980-88. Mem. Am. Auditory Soc., Am. Med. Writers' Assn. Home: 370 Ardmore Rd Des Plaines IL 60016 Office: 131 W 1st St Duluth MN 55802

CRANSTON, MARY B., lawyer; b. Palo alto, Calif., Dec. 29, 1947; d. James Alfred and Bettye (Luhnow) Bailey; m. Harold David Cranston, Aug. 15, 1970; children: Susan Anne, John David. AB in Polit. Sci., Stanford U., 1969, JD, 1975; MA in Psychology, UCLA, 1970. Bar: Calif., 1977. Assoc. atty. Pillsbury, Madison & Sutro, San Francisco, 1975-82, ptnr., 1983—; faculty Nat. Inst. Trial Advocacy, San Francisco, 1986—, Calif. Continuing Edn. of the Bar, 1985—, The Rutter Group, 1984—. Contbr. articles to profl. jours. Mem. Calif. Com. on Women in Law, San Francisco and Los Angeles, 1985-86; bd. dirs. Legal Services for Children, San Francisco, 1983-87. Mem ABA Found. (chmn. Sherman Act com. of antitrust sect. 1986—), Calif. Bar Assn., San Francisco Bar Assn. (bd. dirs.), Stanford U. Alumni Assn. Club: Cap & Gown (Stanford) (treas. 1974-75). Office: Pillsbury Madison & Sutro 225 Bush St San Francisco CA 94104

CRASWELL, ELLEN, state senator; b. Seattle, May 25, 1932; m. Bruce A. Craswell, 1953; children—Richard Bruce, James Arthur, Patricia Louise Craswell Johnson, Jill Ellen Craswell Solano. Student U. Wash. Mem. Wash. State Senate, pres. task force to sec. edn. Am. Legis. Exchange Council; dir. Gt. N.W. Fed. Savs. and Loan. Bd. dirs. Seattle Hearing and Speech Clinic. Republican. Baptist. Club: Altrusa. Office: Office of the State Senate State Capitol Olympia WA 98504 *

CRAVENS, JOAN PEMBERTON, editor; b. Portland, May 20, 1939; d. Paul Arthur and Naomi Amelia (Henry) P.; m. Hamilton Cravens, June 17, 1961; children: Heather, Christopher. BA, U. Wash., 1961; MA, Ohio State U., 1968. Instr. English. Iowa State U., Ames, 1968-69; free-lance writer, crafts designer Ames, 1972-77; book editor crafts Meredith Corp. div. Better Homes/Gardens, Des Moines, 1977-88—; mng. editor Meredith Corp. div. Craftways Publs., Richmond, Calif., 1988—. Bd. dirs. Ames Pub. Library, 1974-80; founder, pres. The Laurel Tree Sch., Ames, 1974-76. Office: Craftways Publs 4118 Lakeside Dr Richmond CA 94806

CRAW, GLENNA YVONNE, elementary educator; b. Canton, Okla., Jan. 18, 1930; d. Lyman Glen and Iva Mae (Bair) Ziller; m. Edwin Arthur Craw, Oct. 23, 1954; children: Cynthia, Cari, Catherine, David. BA in Music Edn., Okla. Coll. Women, 1952; M in Elem. Edn., U. Ariz., 1966. Music tchr. specialist Clovis (N.Mex.) Pub. Schs., 1952-56; classroom elem. tchr. Tucson Pub. Schs., 1956-57, elem. music helping tchr., 1957-58; intermediate helping tchr. Tucson Pub. Sch., 1965-67, classroom elem. tchr., 1959-65, 67—. Co-author: Arizona for Young People, 1968. Elem. choral dir. First Meth. Ch., Tucson, 1957-59; choir dir. Hope Meth., 1969-81; player agt. Little League, Inc., Tucson, 1969-73, pres., 1973-83, softball commr., 1979-82, assoc. dist. adminstr., 1982-84. Named one of Outstanding Elem. Tchrs. Am. Tchrs. of Am., 1972. Mem. Ariz. Philatelic Rangers (dep. sheriff for outstanding service 1983), Friends of Library, Alpha Delta Kappa. Methodist. Home: 217 W Bilby Rd Tucson AZ 85706

CRAWFORD, AMANDA CLEMENTS, food products executive; b. Gastonia, N.C., June 15, 1960; d. Charles A. Jr. and Nancy (Kiser) C. BS in Biology, Belmont (N.C.) Abbey Coll., 1982. Technician microbiology Gasten Meml. Hosp., Gastonia, 1980-82; asst. lab. mgr. Dixie Yeast Corp., Gastonia, 1982-84; research chemist ICI Americas, Inc., Charlotte, N.C., 1984-85; quality assurance mfg. mgr. Frito Lay, Inc., Charlotte, 1985-87; rep. tech. sales Remel, Inc., Lenexa, Kans., 1987—. Mem. Nat. Assn. Female Execs., Beta Beta Beta. Democrat. Methodist. Home: 11118 Harrowfield Rd Pineville NC 28134

CRAWFORD, ANN MACCOLLOM, journalist; b. Sterling, Mass., Apr. 8, 1927; d. Donald Bingham and Marjorie (Stiles) MacCollom; m. H. Vance Crawford, Jan. 24, 1948; children: Joel, Peter. BA, Wellesley Coll., 1947. Corr. Sta. WAGM, Presque Isle, Maine, 1953-55; script writer Impcomation, Sterling Forest, N.Y., 1960-63; reporter Rockland Jour. News, Nyack, N.Y., 1965-67; reporter, editorial writer, columnist Bergen Record, Hackensack, N.J., 1963-65, 67-81, asst. editor, 1981—. Recipient Deadline Writing award Soc. of Silurians, N.Y.C., 1973. Mem. Beta Beta Beta. Office: Bergen Record 150 River St Hackensack NJ 07601

CRAWFORD, CAROL ANNE, marketing executive; b. San Francisco, Jan. 17, 1945; d. Kenneth H. and Marcella (Schloesser) C. B.A., San Jose State U., 1967; M.B.A. in Mktg., Golden Gate U., 1985. Food publicist J. Walter Thompson, San Francisco 1967-70; asst. mktg and sales promotion dir. Eastridge Shopping Ctr., San Jose, Calif., 1970-72; consumer info. specialist Carl Byoir & Assocs., San Francisco, 1972-78; account supr. Ketchum Pub. Relations, San Francisco, 1978-80; v.p., dir. pub. relations Grey Advt., San Francisco, 1980-82; dir. corp. communications S&O Cons., San Francisco, 1982-84; mgr. mktg. and pub. relations GTE Sprint, 1984-86; dir. pub. relations U.S. Sprint, 1986; prin. Crawford Communications, 1986—; instr. pub. relations Golden Gate U., 1987; cons., lectr. in field, 1987—. Bd. mgrs. YMCA, Embarcadero, 1980-82. Mem. Pub. Relations Soc. Am. (past chpt. pres.), Am. Women in Radio and TV (past chpt. membership chmn.), Home Economists in Bus. (past chpt. chmn., past chmn. nat. pub. relations); Commonwealth Club. Home and Office: 423 Lansdale Ave San Francisco CA 94127

CRAWFORD, CAROL TALLMAN, government executive; b. Mt. Holly, N.J., Feb. 25, 1943; m. Ronald Crawford; children: Timothy, Jeffrey, Richard. B.A., Mt. Holyoke Coll., 1965; J.D. magna cum laude, Washington Coll. Law, Am. U., 1978. Bar: Va. 1978, D.C. 1979. Legis. asst. to Senator Bob Packwood Washington, 1969-75; assoc. firm Collier, Shannon, Rill & Scott, Washington, 1979-81; exec. asst. to chmn. FTC, Washington, 1981-83, acting exec. dir., 1982, dir. bur. consumer protection, 1983-85; assoc. dir. econs. and govt. Office Mgmt. & Budget, 1985—; sr. advisor Reagan-Bush Transition Team, 1981. Trustee Barry Goldwater Chair of Am. Instns., Ariz. State U., Phoenix, 1983—. Mem. ABA, D.C. Bar Assn., Va. Bar Assn., Phi Delta Phi. Republican. Office: OMB 246 Old Exec Bldg Washington DC 20503

CRAWFORD, ELLEN SUE, federal agency administrator; b. Detroit, Aug. 11, 1946; d. Richard Mark and Norma Ellen (Wheeler) Ross; children: Barney Lee, Leilani Kim. BS in Geology, Austin Peay U., Clarksville, Tenn., 1984, AS in Mgmt., 1984; modeling cert., Barbizon Internat., Louisville, 1987. Talent agt. U.S. Army Morale Support Unit, Europe, 1974-77; owner, operator Pyramid Dance Studio, Clarksville, Tenn., 1977-82; activity chmn. Latter Day Saints, Clarksville, 1982-84; instr. U.S. Army Sch. System, Ft. Campbell, Ky., 1984-85; freelance fashion model Louisville, 1985—; terrain analyst Def. Mapping Agy., Louisville, 1985—; illustrator children's books. Mem. DAR, Internat. Tng. and Communication Assn. (voting chmn. 1986—), Clarksville C. of C., Am. Fedn. TV and Radio Artists, Screen Actors Guild (asst. editor 1987), Nat. Assn. Female Execs., Fedn. for Employed Women, Alpha Kappa Psi. Democrat. Mem. Ch. Jesus Christ of Latter Day Saints. Clubs: Clan Ross Assn., Pensacola Officers, Shadlin Kempo Assn. (instr. 1987—). Home: 3201 Leith Ave #106 Louisville KY 40218 also: 203 Kings Deer Clarksville TN 37042

CRAWFORD, GAY JOHNSTON, communications executive; b. N.Y.C., Dec. 1, 1943; d. William Dickson and Jessianna Louise (Holmes) Johnston; m. Roy Patrick Crawford, June 11, 1966; children—David William, Katharine. Student U. Salzburg (Austria), 1962; A.A. with honors, Bradford Coll., 1963; A.B. with honors, U. Calif.-Berkeley, 1965. Reporter, club and fashion editor Berkeley (Calif.) Gazette, 1965; spl. asst. editor Oakland Tribune (Calif.), 1965; editorial asst., writer San Diego mag., 1965-66; writer, pub. info. specialist U. Calif.-San Diego, La Jolla, 1966-68; free lance writer/editor, San Jose, Calif., 1968-69; community relations dir. KNTV, San Jose, 1969-85; pub. relations cons. Sta. KTEH PBS-TV, 1986; v.p. HomeSearch NuCom Communications of Calif., 1987; media cons., 1987—. Editor: Discovering Santa Clara Valley, 1973; Tailoring for Women, Step by Step, 1974. Bd. dirs., founder Hospice of the Valley, San Jose, 1979—; adv. bd. Children's Health Council, San Jose, 1982—, Coro Found., 1982—, Resource Ctr. for Women, 1984—; pres. bd. dirs. Santa Clara County unit Am. Cancer Soc., 1982-84; communications dir. United Way of Santa Clara County. Named Outstanding Woman Journalism Student, Bay Area chpt. Theta Sigma Phi, 1965, Woman of Achievement, San Jose Mercury News, 1973, recipient Vol. Recognition award Midpeninsula Girls' Club, Palo Alto, 1977. Mem. Women in Communications (Woman of Achievement Far West region 1983), Pub. Relations Roundtable, Santa Clara County Broadcasters Assn. Republican. Episcopalian. Home: 14711 Aloha Ave Saratoga CA 95070

CRAWFORD, JEAN ANDRE, counselor; b. Chgo., Apr. 12, 1941; d. William Moses and Geneva Mae (Lacy) Jones; student Shimer Coll., 1959-60; BA, Carthage Coll., 1966; MEd, Loyola U., Chgo., 1971; postgrad. Nat. Coll. Edn., Evanston, Ill., 1971-77, Northwestern U., 1976-83; m. John N. Crawford, Jr., June 28, 1969; cert. counselor Nat. Bd. Cert. Counselors, elem. edn., spl. edn. and pupil personnel services, Ill. Med. technologist, Chgo., 1960-62; primary and spl. edn. tchr. Chgo. Pub. Schs., 1966-71, counselor maladjusted children and their families, 1971-88; counselor juvenile first-offenders, 1968-88; vocat. counselor, 1988—. Vol. Sta. WTTW-TV; vol. counselor deaf children and their families; counselor post-secondary students. Mem. Ill. Assn. Counseling and Devel., Am., Ill. sch. counselors assns., Council Exceptional Children, Am. Assn. Counseling Devel., Coordinating Council Handicapped Children, Shimer Coll. Alumni Assn. (sec. 1982-84), Phi Delta Kappa. Home: 601 E 32d St Chicago IL 60616 Office: 3233 W 31st St Chicago IL 60623

CRAWFORD, LINDA SIBERY, lawyer, educator; b. Ann Arbor, Mich., Apr. 27, 1947; d. Donald Eugene and Verla Lillian (Schneck) Sibery; m. Leland Allardice Crawford, Apr. 4, 1970; children: Christina, Lillian, Leland. Student, Keele U., 1969; BA, U. Mich., 1969; postgrad., SUNY, Potsdam, 1971; JD, U. Maine, 1977. Bar: Maine 1977, U.S. Dist. Ct. Maine 1982, U.S. Ct. Appeals (1st cir.) 1983. Tchr. Pub. Sch., Tupper Lake, N.Y., 1970-71; asst. dist. atty. State of Maine, Farmington, 1977-79; asst. atty. gen. State of Maine, Augusta, Maine, 1979—; ptnr. The Forensic Cons. Group, Lexington, Mass., 1988—; legal advisor U. Maine, Farmington, 1975; legal counsel Fire Marshall's Office, Maine, 1980-83, Warden Service, Maine, 1981-83, Dept. Mental Health, 1983—; instr. trial adv. course Harvard Law Sch., Cambridge, Mass., 1987; teaching team—; instr. trial advocacy course Harvard U. Law Sch.; ptnr. The Forensic Cons. Group. Mem. Natural Resources Council, Maine, 1985—; bd. dirs. Diocesan Human Relations Council, Maine, 1977-78, Arthritis Found., Maine, 1983-88. Named one of Outstanding Young Women of Yr. Jaycees, 1981. Mem. ABA, Maine Bar Assn., Kennebec County Bar Assn., Assn. Trial Lawyers Am., Maine Trial Lawyers Assn., Nat. Health Lawyers Assn., Nat. Assn. State Mental Health Attys. (treas. 1984-86, vice chmn. 1987—), Bus. and Profl. Womens Club. Home: 25 Winthrop St Hallowell ME 04347 Office: Forensic Cons Group 17 Patriots Dr Lexington MA 02173

CRAWFORD, LYNN SIERGIEJ, banker; b. Summit, N.J., Mar. 14, 1940; d. Edward J. and Veronica C. (Birofka) Siergiej; m. Joseph M. Crawford, June 24, 1961; children: Colleen, Kevin, Jody, Terry, Kelly, Jacky. Student, U. Ariz., 1957-61; BA in Bus. Adminstrn., Rosary Coll., 1982; diploma, U. Okla., 1983, U. Colo., 1986. From trading desk clk. to v.p. retail banking, ops. and mktg. Pioneer Bank, Chgo., 1978—. Pres. Circle 31 Oak Park-River Forest (Ill.) Infant Welfare Soc., 1980; 1st v.p. Austin Bus. Council, Chgo., 1982-86. Mem. Nat. Assn. Bank Women, Assn. Chgo. Bank Women, Bank Mktg. Assn., Chgo. Fin. Advertisers, Hispanic Fedn. Ill. Cs. of C. (bd. dirs.), North-Pulaski C. of C. (pres. 1983-87). Home: 846 Monroe River Forest IL 60305 Office: Pioneer Bank 4000 W North Ave Chicago IL 60639

CRAWFORD, MARY LOUISE PERRI, naval officer; b. Grand Haven, Mich.; d. Louis and Helen Marie (Buckley) Perri; m. Keith Eugene Crawford, Feb. 23, 1974 (dec. Oct. 1986); children—Matthew Perri, Michael Kirk. A.A., Muskegon County Community Coll., 1969; B.A., U. Mich., 1971. Commd. ensign U.S. Navy, 1972, advanced through grades to comdr., 1987; pub. affairs officer Naval Air Sta., Key West, Fla., 1974-77, adminstrv., personnel officer Naval Air Res. Detachment, Patuxent River, Md., 1977-78, adminstrn. br. head Strike Aircraft Test Directorate, Naval Air Test Ctr., Patuxent River, 1978-80, ops. watch officer Command Ctr., Comdr.-in-Chief Naval Forces Europe Staff, London, 1980-84, officer-in-charge Personnel Support Activity Detachment, Patuxent River, 1984-86; engring. officer Chief Test and Evaluation Div., Strategic C3 Systems Directorate, Ctr. for Command, Control, and Communications, Def. Communications Agy., Washington, 1986—. Mem. AAUW, Women's Overseas Service League, U. Mich. Alumni Assn. Roman Catholic. Avocation: painting, ballet. Office: Def Communications Agy Ctr Command Control Communications Test & Evaluation Div Washington DC 20305-2000

CRAWFORD, MURIEL LAURA, lawyer, author, educator; b. Bend, Oreg., Oct. 10, 1931; d. Mason Leland and Pauline Marie (DesIlets) Henderson; m. Barrett Matson Crawford, May 10, 1959; children—Laura Joanne, Janet Muriel, Barbara Elizabeth. Student, U. Calif., Berkeley, 1958-60, 67-69; B.A. with honors, U. Ill., 1973; J.D. with honors, Ill. Inst. Tech./Chgo.-Kent Coll. Law, 1977. Bar: Ill. 1977; C.L.U.; Chartered Fin. Cons. Atty., Washington Nat. Ins. Co., Evanston, Ill., 1977-80, sr. atty., 1980-81, asst. counsel, 1982-83, asst. gen. counsel, 1984-87, assoc. gen. counsel, sec., 1987—. Author: (with Greider and Beadles) Law and the Life Insurance Contract, 1984, also articles. Recipient Am. Jurisprudence award Lawyer's Coop. Pub. Co., 1975; 2d prize Internat. LeTourneau Student Med.-Legal Article contest, 1976; Bar and Gavel Soc. award Ill. Inst. Tech./Chgo.-Kent Student Bar Assn., 1977. Mem. ABA, Ill. Bar Assn., Chgo. Bar Assn., Am. Corporate Counsels Assn., Ill. Inst. Tech./Chgo.-Kent Alumni Assn. (dir. 1981—) Republican. Congregationalist.

CRAWFORD, NORMA VIVIAN, nurse; b. Cleveland, Tex., Dec. 29, 1936; d. Ira Wesley and Lizzie Augusta (Godejohn) C.; m. Arthur B. Crawford, Sept. 20, 1956 (dec.); children: Pamela, Desiree. Lic. vis. nurse, Lee Jr. Coll., 1971-72; RN, Cumberland County Coll., 1977; BSN, U. Mary-Hardin Baylor, 1986. Charge nurse Patrick Henry Hosp., Newport News, Va., 1972-73; staff nurse Salem (N.J.) County Nursing Home, 1975-77, Nicholson Nursing Home, Penns Grove, N.J., 1977; nurse ICU, Metroplex Hosp., Killeen, Tex., 1977-79; dir. nurses Wind Crest Nursing Ctr., Copperas Cove, Tex., 1979-82; staff nurse supr., unit mgr. med./surg. unit, supr., home health nurse, dir. home health Metroplex Hosp., Killeen, Tex., 1979-87, dir., 1988—. Baptist. Club: Order of Eastern Star. Home: 604 Yucca Dr Copperas Cove TX 76522 Office: PO Box 10219 Killeen TX 76547-0219

CRAWFORD, PRISCILLA RUTH, social psychologist; b. Ferndale, Mich., Oct. 13, 1941; d. Ernest Henry and Ethel Ruth (Huth) Thomas; m. Thomas Earl Crawford, June 10, 1963 (div.). B.A., Butler U., 1962; postgrad. (Fulbright scholar) Goethe U., Ger., 1963; M.A. in Sociology (fellow), Ohio State U., 1965, Ph.D. (NIMH fellow), 1970. Mem. faculty sociology dept. Bklyn. Coll., 1966-67, Ind. U., Indpls., 1967-70; adj. faculty Roosevelt U., Chgo., 1974-77, Ind. U./Purdue U., Indpls., 1978—; research assoc. Gary (Ind.) Income Maintenance Expt., Ind. U. Northwest, 1970-73; cons. human resource and orgn. devel., Chgo., 1973-77; dir. human resource devel Ind. State Dept. Mental Health, Indpls., 1978-84, dir. edn. and tng., 1984-86, dir. ops. research, policy analysis, 1986—; vol. cons. numerous womens's groups, 1977—; cons. to state agys., So. Regional Edn. Bd., Nat. Orgn. Human Service Educators, NIMH, 1978—; mem. tng. adv. com. Ind. State Personnel Dept., 1983—; mem. adv. com. M.S. in Nursing degree program Ind. U. Sch. Nursing, 1982—; adv. com. Lic. Practical Nursing Initiative, 1981. Bd. dirs. Ind. Conf. Social Concerns, 1979-81; mem. Gov.'s Spl. Grant Com., Ind. Employment Tng. Council, 1981-82; mem. adv. bd. Program in Ind. Living, 1980-82; mem. adv. com. Indpls. Preschs., Inc., 1982—; mem. planning com. Ind. U. Sch. Medicine Women's Health Research Inst., 1986—; mem. planning com. Women in the Year 2000; bd. dirs. Women's Agenda for Action, 1981-83. Mem. Am. Sociol. Assn., Midwest Sociol. Soc., North Central Sociol. Assn., Am. Mgmt. Assn., Nat. Assn. State Mental Health Program Dirs. (mem. human resources com. 1986—), N.Y. Acad. Sci., Ohio Acad. Sci., Ind. Acad. Social Scis. (dir. 1978-81, 84—), Inst. Noetic Scis., AAUP, Phi Kappa Phi, Alpha Lambda Delta. Home: 1653 E Kessler Indianapolis IN 46220

CRAWFORD, SANDRA KAY, lawyer; b. Henderson, Tex., Sept 23, 1934; d. Obie Lee and Zilpha Elizabeth (Ash) Stalcup; m. William Walsh Crawford, Dec. 21, 1968; children—Bill, Jonathan, Constance, Amelia, Patrick. B.A., Wellesley Coll., 1957; LL.B., U. Tex., 1960. Bar: Tex. 1960, U.S. Supreme Ct. 1965, Colo. 1967, Ill. 1974. Asst. v.p.-legal Hamilton Mgmt. Corp., Denver, 1966-68; v.p., gen. counsel, sec. Transamerica Fund Mgmt. Corp., Los Angeles, 1968; cons. to law dept. Met. Life Ins. Co., N.Y.C., 1969-71; counsel Touche Ross & Co., Chgo., 1972-75; v.p., assoc. gen. counsel Continental Ill. Bank, Chgo., 1975-83; sr. div. counsel Motorola, Inc., Schaumburg, Ill., 1984; corp. atty. Sears Roebuck & Co., 1985—. Mem. ABA, Ill. State Bar Assn., Colo. Bar Assn., Tex. Bar Assn. Clubs: Saddle & Cycle, Carlton (Chgo.). Home: 3900 S Mission Hills Rd Northbrook IL 60062

CRAWFORD, SARAH CARTER, broadcast executive, media consultant; b. Glen Ridge, N.J., Oct. 3, 1938; d. Raymond Hitchings and Katherine Latta (Gribbel) Carter; m. Joseph Paul Crawford III, Sept. 10, 1960 (div. 1966). BA, Smith Coll., 1960. Media dir. Kampmann & Bright, Phila., 1961-64; sr. media buyer Foote, Cone & Belding, N.Y.C., 1964-69; assoc. media dir. Grey Advt., Los Angeles, 1969-75; account exec., research dir. Sta. KHJ-TV, Los Angeles, 1975-76; mgr. local sales Sta. KCOP-TV, Los Angeles, 1977-82; gen. sales mgr. Sta. KTVF-TV, Fairbanks, Ak., 1982—; bd. dirs. Vista Travel, Fairbanks; mem. adv. com. Golden Valley Electric Corp., Fairbanks, 1984-86; career cons. small bus. devel. ctr. Tanana Valley Community Coll., Fairbanks, 1986-87. Vice chmn. Fairbanks Health and Social Service Commn., 1986—; pres. Fairbanks Meml. Hosp. Aux.; bd. dirs. Fairbanks Downtown Assn. Mem. Fairbanks Womens Hockey Assn., Fairbanks Womens Softball Assn. Republican. Episcopalian. Home: 518 Juneau Fairbanks AK 99701 Office: Sta KTVF-TV Box 950 Fairbanks AK 99707

CRAWFORD, SUSAN JEAN, lawyer, federal government official; b. Pitts., Apr. 22, 1947; d. William Elmer Jr. and Joan Ruth (Bielau) C.; m. Roger W. Higgins; 1 child, Kelley S. BA, Bucknell U., 1969; JD, New Eng. Sch. Law, 1977. Bar: Md. 1977, D.C. 1980. History tchr., coach Radnor (Pa.) High Sch., 1969-74; assoc. Burnett & Eiswert, Oakland, Md., 1977-79; ptnr. Burnett, Eswert and Crawford, Oakland, 1979-81; prin. dep. gen. counsel U.S. Dept. Army, Washington, 1981-83, gen. counsel, 1983—; asst. states atty. Garrett County, Md., 1978-79; instr. Garrett County Community Coll., 1979-81. Del. Md. Forestry Adv. Commn., Garrett City, 1978-81, Md. Commn. for Women, Garrett City, 1980-83; chair Rep. State Cen. Com., Garrett City, 1978-81. Mem. ABA, Md. Bar Assn., D.C. Bar Assn., Fed. Bar Assn., Am. Arbitration Assn., Bus. & Profl. Women. Presbyterian. Office: US Dept Army Gen Counsel(SAGC) The Pentagon Washington DC 20310

CRAWFORD-JONES, CANDACE KAY, retail executive; b. Austin, Tex., Dec. 7, 1959; d. Bobby Dalton and Kathryn Sue (Mangrum) Crawford; m. Linza Joseph Jones Jr., Jan. 9, 1982 (div. Jan. 1987); 1 child, Clayton. B of Journalism, U. Tex., 1982. With reprodn. and drafting dept. Tex. State Dept. Hwys. and Pub. Transp., Odessa, Tex., 1982-84; co-owner Crawford Well Service, Inc., Kermit, Tex., 1984—, Longhorn Well Service, Inc., Kermit, 1984—, Longhorn Prodn. Co., Kermit, 1984—; owner, mgr. The Fashion Shop, Kermit, 1986—; reporter, photographer The Winkler County News, Kermit, 1985. Mem. Nat. Assn. Female Execs., Retail Mchts. Assn., Beta Sigma Phi. Republican. Lutheran. Home and Office: Box 1153 Kermit TX 79745

CRAWFORD-KUMMER, SONDRA, printing/fund-raising company executive, consultant; b. Balt., July 12, 1950; d. Donald Revere and Phyllis Edna (Finck) Crawford; m. Charles A. Kummer III, Mar. 17, 1979. Student Edinboro State U. Sec. RT&A Assocs., Balt., 1977-78; sec. Barton-Cotton, Inc., Balt., 1978-79, adminstrv. asst., 1979-81, mem. sales service staff, 1981-82, v.p. sales, 1982—, fund-raising cons., 1982—, v.p. in Balt. Mem. Nat. Assn. Female Execs., Nat. Cath. Devel. Council, Nat. Soc. Fund-Raising Execs. Republican. Presbyterian. Avocations: snow skiing, water skiing, basketball, yoga, meditation. Home: 6229 Gilston Park Rd Baltimore MD 21228 Office: Barton-Cotton Inc 1405 Parker Rd Baltimore MD 21227

CRAWLEY, JANE CAROLYN, business educator; b. Campbellsville, Ky., Nov. 17, 1950; d. J.B. and Elizabeth (Perkins) C. BS, Ea. Ky. U., 1972, MA, 1974. Bus. educator Ky. Bus. Coll., Lexington, 1972-74, LaBelle High Sch., Fla., 1974-76, Cyesis Ctr., Ft. Lauderdale, Fla., 1979, Ft. Lauderdale Coll., 1979, Fla. Coll. Bus., Pompano Beach, 1979-83, Broward County Sch. Bd., Fla., 1983-84; instr. visually handicapped Broward County Sch. Bd., 1976-78; bus. and computer educator Businessland, Ft. Lauderdale, 1984—; dir. edn. Fla. Coll., 1981-83; ednl. cons. Hammel Coll., 1983. Recipient cert. of Recognition for outstanding service aiding in finding missing children Broward County Sheriff's Dept., 1985; commd. Ky. Col., Gov. of Ky., 1988. Mem. Am. Council of Blind, Visually Handicapped Transcribers Assn. Republican. Baptist. Home: 2389 NE 30th Ct Lighthouse Point FL 33064 Office: Businessland 830 E Oakland Park Blvd Fort Lauderdale FL 33334

CRAWLEY, NANCY ANN, real estate broker; b. Pawtucket, R.I., July 18, 1946; d. Andrew Martin and Marion (Dumore) C. AS, Miriam Hosp., 1971; BA, R.I. Coll., 1976. Radiological technologist Miriam Hosp., Providence, 1969-72; collection supr. Sears Roebuck & Co., Warwick, R.I., 1975-79; new account mgr. Sears Roebuck & Co., Syracuse, N.Y., 1980-81; credit mgr. Sears Roebuck & Co., Altoona, Pa., 1981-82; collection mgr. Sears Roebuck & Co., White Plains, N.Y., 1982-86; real estate broker Albert-Better Homes & Gardens, Warwick, 1986—. Chair United Way, 1983-86; fundraiser GOP Fund Congl. VIP, Washington, 1984—. Mem. Nat. Assn. Female Execs. Roman Catholic. Home: 5300 Post Rd East Greenwich RI 02818

CRAYNE, NANCY ANN, data processing consultant; b. Toledo, Aug. 27, 1942; d. Richard Vernor and Arlene Edna (Thull) Crayne; BS, Bowling Green (Ohio) State U., 1964; MBA, Oakland U., Rochester, Mich., 1986. Analytical chemist Stauffer Chem. Co., Adrian, Mich., 1964-76; ind. computer programming cons., Westland, Mich., 1976-78; systems analyst Ford Motor Co., Dearborn, Mich., 1978-81; project mgr. Powderhorn Assocs., Hamtramck, Mich., 1981-82; computer cons. Mich. Cons. in Data Processing, Birmingham, Mich., 1982-84; computer cons. Charles Davis & Assocs., Detroit, 1984-86, Analysts Internat., Inc., 1986—. Mem. Nat. Assn. Female Execs., Mich. Profl. Women's Network (pres. 1981-82).

CREECH, CAROLE B., accountant; b. Indpls., Sept. 3, 1948; d. James M. and Charlotte Lois (Wright) Beckham; m. James L. Creech, Sept. 12, 1986. BS, Ball State U., 1970; postgrad., Purdue U., 1974-77. Staff acct. Pub. Service Co. of Ind., Plainfield, 1970-75, power analyst, 1975-80, sr. power analyst, 1980-83, supr. power office, 1983—. Bd. dirs. Midland House, Inc., Indpls., 1982—; bd. dirs. 2d Ch. of Christ Scientist, Indpls., 1976-78, reader, 1979-81. Club: Cen. Ind. Shetland Sheepdog (Indpls.). Office: Pub Service of Ind 1000 E Main St Plainfield IN 46168

CREECH, SANDRA KAY, college administrator; b. San Antonio, Tex., Mar. 23, 1947; d. Bill G. and Frieda Maurine (Sanders) C.; 1 child, Colleen Dee Havican. B.S. in Math., U. Houston, 1972; MPA in Govt. Info., Southwest Tex. State U., 1985; postgrad. Tex. A&M U. Adminstrv. asst. Dow Chem. Co., Houston, 1969-72; data processing dir. Jetero Constrn. Co., Houston, 1972-74; programmer-analyst Fannin Bank, Houston, 1974-75; sr. systems analyst Nat. Supply Co., Houston, 1975-79; dir. adminstrv. info. services Temple Jr. Coll., Tex., 1981—; cons.; presenter at profl. meetings. Mem. Edn. Planning Com., Hewitt, Tex., 1985-86. Mem. Tex. Jr. Coll. Tchrs. Assn., Assn. Studies in Higher Edn., Waco Hist. Found. Baha'i. Office: Temple Jr Coll 2600 S 1st St Temple TX 76643

CREED, BETTY DETTWILER, artist, educator; b. Cin., Apr. 15, 1935; d. Walter Percival and Betty Ethel (Calerdine) Dettwiler; m. Thomas Gary Creed, Aug. 27, 1955; children: James Thomas, Elizabeth Lynn, Richard Thomas. Student, Purdue U., 1953-55; BA, U. South Fla., 1981, MFA, 1984. Tchr. watercolors and advanced painting classes U. South Fla., Tampa, 1983-84, asst. acad. advisor Art dept., 1985, adj. lectr. Art Dept. Coll. Fine Arts, 1986, docent, edn. coordinator Art Galleries, 1984-87; tchr. workshop Gulfcoast Art Ctr., Bellair, Fla., 1987. One-woman shows include South Fla. Jr. Coll., Avon Park, 1982, Soho South Gallery, Safety Harbor, Fla., 1985, Fla. Gulf Coast Art Ctr., Bellair, 1987; exhibited in group shows at Soc. Four Arts 44th ann. exhbn., Palm Beach, Fla., 1982, Two Centers Show, St. Petersburg, Fla., 1983, Miller Pappas Gallery, Tampa, 1983, Gallery 600, Largo, Fla., 1984, Loch Haven Art Ctr. Juries Exhbn., Orlando, Fla., 1984 (Merit award), Deland (Fla.) Mus., 1984, 85, Barbara Gillman Gallery, Miami, Fla., 1984, Arrowmont Sch., Gatlinburg, Tenn., 1984, Festival of States Juried Exhbn., St. Petersburg, 1985, 87, Valencia Coll., Orlando, 1985, U. Tampa Scarfone Gallery, 1985, Las Damas Invitational Art Exhibit, Tampa, 1986, Fla. Ctr. for Contemporary Art, Tampa, 1986, Tampa Mus. West, 1986, Zaner Gallery, Rochester, N.Y., 1986, Fla. West Coast Women's Caucus Art, St. Petersburg, 1987, U. South Fla., 1987; painter for calendars and Christmas cards. Mem. art coalition com. Women's Survival Ctr., Tampa, 1982; bd. dirs. Fla. Ctr. for Contemporary Arts, Tampa, 1980-87, v.p., 1981-82, chmn. exhbn. com., 1980. Fellowships U. South Fla., 1981-82. Mem. Women's Caucus for Art (West coast chpt.), Kappa Alpha Theta. Republican. Methodist. Home: 5133 S Nichol St Tampa FL 33611 Office: care Univ S Florida Art Gallery 4202 Fowler Ave Tampa FL 33620

CREEK, ELEANOR BERRY, addictions specialist, paralegal; b. Washington, Mar. 27, 1950; d. Jessie James and Alice (Thompson) Berry; m. Rustin Knight Fielding, Sept. 20, 1981 (div. Aug. 1985). BA in Psychology, U. Md., 1984, BS in Paralegal Studies, 1986; postgrad., Bowie U., 1988—. Cert. paralegal, 1986. Clk. technician Manpower, PGC Govt., Upper Marlboro, Md., 1971-75; chief editor Human Resources PGC Govt., Upper Marlboro, 1975-77; counselor Commn. for Women PGC Govt., Upper Marlboro, 1977-81; addiction specialist Health Dept. PGC Govt., Riverdale, Md., 1981—; freelance paralegal, Md., 1986—. Notary pub. Prince George's County, Md., 1975—. Served with USAR, 1975—. Recipient Humanitarian award, USAR, 1981. Democrat. Roman Catholic. Home: 2318 W Rosecroft Village Cir Oxon Hill MD 20745

CRENSHAW, MARGARET PRICE, lawyer; b. Eugene, Oreg., Apr. 16, 1945; d. Warren Charles and Lillian Irene (Shidell) Price; B.A., Stanford U., 1967, M.A., 1968; J.D., Georgetown U., 1975; m. Albert Burford Crenshaw, Aug. 11, 1973; children—David Ollinger, Caroline Abbey. Bars: D.C. bar 1975, U.S. Ct. Appeals 1976, U.S. Ct. Claims 1976, U.S. Supreme Ct. 1983. Reporter Eugene Register-Guard, 1965, 66; press asst. Californians for Humphrey San Francisco, 1968; newswoman AP, New Haven, Conn., 1969; press asst. Rep. Jeffery Cohelan, Washington, 1969; research writer Congl. Quar., Washington, 1969-70; asst. editor Washington Post, 1970-72; law clerk firm Harrison, Lucey, Sagle & Solter, Washington, 1974-75; legis. counsel Senator Philip A. Hart, Washington, 1975-77; legis. counsel Senator Paul S. Sarbanes, Washington, 1977; asso. firm Brownstein, Zeidman & Schomer, Washington, 1977-79; counsel Senate Subcom. on Govt. Efficiency and the D.C., 1979-81, minority chief counsel, 1981-85, minority staff dir. Senate Com. on Govtl. Affairs, 1985-87; v.p. Govt. Retirement and Benefits, Inc., Alexandria, Va., 1987—; adj. prof. journalism U. Md., College Park, 1975. Trustee Capitol Hill Day Sch., Washington, 1984-87. Ford Found. fellow, 1967-68. Mem. ABA, D.C. Bar Assn., Women's Bar Assn. D.C. Democrat. Episcopalian.

CRENSHAW, MARVA LOUISE, lawyer; b. DeFuniak Springs, Fla., Sept. 21, 1951; d. Lewis and Helen (Anderson) Crenshaw; m. Norman P. Campbell, Dec. 30, 1977; children: Kalinda I., Kamaria A. BS in Polit. Sci. with honors, Tuskegee Inst., Ala., 1973; J.D., U. Fla., Gainesville, 1975. Bar: U.S. Dist. Ct. (mid. dist.) Fla., 1978, U.S. Ct. Appeals (11th cir.) 1978. Asst. state's atty. Dade County State's Atty. (Fla.), Miami, 1976-78; mng. atty. Bay Area Legal Services, Tampa, Fla., 1978-84, dep. dir., 1984—; cons. tng. adv. com. Fla. Legal Service, Tallahassee, 1982-84. Vice pres. bd. dirs. Suicide and Crises Ctr., Tampa, 1983-84, pres., 1984-85, also mem. Aux. Mem. ABA, Hillsborough County Bar Assn. (chmn. county ct. civil rules com. 1984-85, mem. mock trial com. 1987—), Fla. Bar Assn., George Edgecomb Bar Assn., Nat. Inst. Trial Advocacy, Delta Sigma Theta. Democrat. Baptist. Home: 14522 Wessex St Tampa FL 33625

CRENSHAW, MARY ELLEN, accountant; b. Fostoria, Ohio, Jan. 22, 1944; d. Ellis Duane and Grace Arlington (Ketcham) Gooch; m. James Allen Crenshaw; children: James Ellis, Jacqueline Marie. BA in French, U. Ill., 1965, MA in English, 1967; BS in Acctg., So. Ill. U., 1983. CPA, Ill. Instr. English So. Ill. U., Carbondale, 1969-70; sec. Litton Industries, Palo Alto, Calif., 1974, Boise Industries, Palo Alto, 1975; substitute tchr. Carbondale Community High Sch., 1976-80; instr. bus. communications So. Ill. U., 1984; acct. Chas. H. Petersen and Co., Mountain View, Calif., 1984-85, So. Ill. U., 1985; pvt. practice acctg. Carbondale, 1985—. Tchr. bible Jehovah's Witnesses, Carbondale, 1973-74, 75-84, 85—, Palo Alto, 1974-75, 84-85. Mem. Am. Inst. CPAs, Nat. Assn. Tax Preparers, Phi Beta Kappa, Beta Gamma Sigma.

CRENSHAW, TENA LULA, librarian; b. Coleman, Fla., Dec. 15, 1930; d. Herbert Joseph and Nellie Jackson (Wicker) Crenshaw; B.S., Fla. So. Coll., 1951; postgrad. U. Fla., 1952-55; M.L.S. (Univ. scholar), U. Okla., 1960. Tchr. pub. schs., Coleman, Fla., 1952-55, St. Petersburg, Fla., 1955-57, Houston, 1957-59; tech. librarian Army Rocket & Guided Missile Agy., Redstone Arsenal, Huntsville, Ala., 1960-61; acquisitions librarian Martin Marietta Corp., Orlando, Fla., 1961-64; reader services librarian John F. Kennedy Space Center, NASA, Fla., 1964-66; research information analyst, specialist, Lockheed Missiles and Space Co., Palo Alto, Calif., 1966-68; head services to pub. A.W. Calhoun Med. Library, Emory U., Atlanta, 1969-78; dep. dir. Louis Calder Meml. Library, U. Miami (Fla.) Sch. Medicine, 1979-80; head edn. library U. Fla., Gainesville, 1980-84; librarian Westinghouse Electric Corp., Orlando, 1984-86; chief librarian tech info. ctr. U. Cen. Fla., Orlando, 1986-87, librarian contracts and grants, 1987—; chmn. Fla. State adv. Council on Libraries. Mem. Spl. Libraries Assn. (treas. S. Atlantic chpt. 1970-72, chmn. membership com. 1973, v.p. 1973-74, pres. 1974-75, mem. resolutions com. 1975-76, nominating com. biol. scis. div. 1974-75, chmn. 1977-78), Med. Library Assn. (mem. conf. planning com. So. regional group 1973-74, membership com. 1977-79 by laws rev. com. 1979-80), Southeastern (mem. new directions com. 1972-74, chmn. spl. libraries sect. 1974), Ga. (careers in librarianship com. 1974-77), Fla. library assns., D.A.R., Alpha Delta Pi, Kappa Delta Pi. Democrat. Episcopalian. Home: Vestavia Lake Apts F 208 1100 S Delaney Ave Orlando FL 32806 Office: U Cen Fla U Libraries Orlando FL 32816-0666

CRESPIN, REGINE, soprano; b. Marseilles, France; d. Henri and Margherite (DiMeirone) C. Student, Lycée Français, Conservatoire de Paris. Appeared in: numerous operas including Lohengrin, Mulhouse, France, 1950, Paris, 1951, N.Y.C., 1964, Tosca, Il Trovatore, Otello, Die Walkuere, Oberon, Fidelio, Der Rosenkavalier, Marseilles, Le Nozze di Figaro, Paris, 1956, Dialogues of the Carmelites, 1957, Parsifal, 1958, Ballo in Maschera, 1958, Fedra, Milan, Italy, 1959, Die Walkuere, Vienna, 1959, Der

Rosenkavalier, Berlin, 1960, as the Marshallin, London, 1961, Les Troyens Paris, 1961, Penelope, Buenos Aires, 1961, Otello, Ballo in Maschera, Die Walkuere, Der Rosenkavalier, Vienna, also Rosenkavalier, N.Y.C., 1962, Flying Dutchman, N.Y.C., 1962, Ballo in Maschera, N.Y.C., 1962, La Vestale, N.Y.C., 1962, Herodiade, N.Y.C., 1963, Fidelio, Ballo in Maschera, Tannhauser, Fidelio, Chgo., 1963, Carnegie Hall, 1973, Met. Opera, 1973, Carmen, Met. Opera, 1975, Cavalleria Rusticana, San Francisco Opera, 1976, Dialogues of the Carmelites, Met. Opera, 1977, 78, soloist, N.Y. Philharmonic, 1964-65, appeared in recital, Hunter Coll., 1965. Office: Herbert H Breslin 119 W 57th St New York NY 10019

CRESS, JEAN ELIZABETH, television executive; b. Sacramento, Nov. 10, 1951; d. Earl Sylvester and Nancy Louise (Cress) Gimblin. Student, Sacramento City Coll., 1969-70, Calif. State U., Sacramento, 1974-75. Dir. pub. affairs Sta. KRTH, Los Angeles, 1978-79; promotion and advt. dir. Roaring Camp R.R., Felton, Calif., 1981; news dir. Sta. KMFO, Aptos, Calif., 1981-82, program dir., 1982-84, gen. mgr., 1984-85; sales and mktg. mgr. Group W Cable, Santa Cruz, Calif., 1985-86; promotion dir. Sta. KCBA-TV, Salinas, Calif., 1986-87; dir. mktg. Am. Cablesystems, Pomona, Calif., 1987-88; affiliate mgr. The Z Channel, Santa Monica, Calif., 1988—. TV hostess Cinema Classics, Sta. KRUZ-TV, 1985-86, Focus-35, 1986-87. Bd. dirs. Film Commn., Santa Cruz, 1985-87. Recipient Sam Seagull award Monterey Ad Club, 1985. Democrat. Episcopal. Office: Z Channel 1545 26th St Santa Monica CA 90404

CREWS, JUDITH CAROL, educator; b. Sanford, N.C., Apr. 30, 1948; d. Thomas Tengene and Pearl Irene (Douglas) Edwards; m. Richard Lee Crews, Oct. 12, 1967. AA, Long Beach Community Coll., 1973; BFA, Calif. State U., Long Beach, 1976; postgrad., U. San Francisco, 1979-80; MA in Edn., Calif. State U., Los Angeles, 1984. Cert. elem., secondary, spl. edn. tchr. Tchr. ceramics Mid-Cities Assn. for Retarded, Compton, Calif., 1976-80; art prof. Compton Coll., 1977-80; spl. edn. tchr. Hillside Ctr., Long Beach, 1980, Hillside Devel. Learning Ctr., La Canada, Calif., 1980-82, Westminster (Calif.) High Sch., 1982—; facilitator drugs Westminster High Sch., 1984—; grant writer Mid-Cities Assn. and Westminster High Sch., 1976—; coordinator spl. edn. dept. Westminster High Sch., 1985—; cons. Orange County Drug Abuse, Westminster, 1985—. Contbr. articles to profl. jours. Sec. Council for Exceptional Children, Orange County, Calif., 1986—; mem. Nat. Fedn. for Drug Free Youth, Washington, 1986—; bd. dirs. Huntington Beach Unified High Sch. Dist. Alcohol/Substance Abuse Council, Huntington Beach, Calif., 1986-87, Westminster Alcohol/Drug Abuse Council, 1984—; support mem. Westminster High Sch. Booster Club; active Hope house. Grantee U.S. Dept Rehab., Health, Edn., Welfare, 1976, 77, 78. Mem. Am. Bus. Women's Assn., NEA, Calif. Edn. Assn., Mothers Against Drunk Driving. Democrat. Baptist. Office: Westminster High Sch 14325 Goldenwest St Westminster CA 92683

CREWS, RUTHELLEN, education educator; b. McCaysville, Ga., July 3, 1927; d. Robert Harvey and Della P. (Mason) C. B.A., Maryville Coll., 1949; M.S., U. Tenn., 1959; Ed.D., Columbia U., 1966. Tchr. English and speech Cradock High Sch., Portsmouth, Va., 1949-50; elem. tchr. Rose Sch., Morristown, Tenn., 1951-54; tchr. English and speech Morristown High Sch., 1954-58; elem. sch. librarian Knox County Schs. Materials Ctr., Knoxville, Tenn., 1958-60; supr. instrn. Knox County Schs., Knoxville, 1960-65; prof. edn. U. Fla., Gainesville, 1966—; cons. curriculum devel. in pub. schs., lectr. in field. Author: (with others) The World of Language textbook series, 1970, rev. edit., 1973; (with others) Pathfinder textbook series, 1978; contbr. articles in field of edn. to profl. jours. Mem. Nat. Council Tchrs. English, Assn. for Supervision and Curriculum Devel., Internat. Reading Assn., Delta Kappa Gamma. Home: 1719-4B NW 23d Ave Gainesville FL 32605 Office: U Fla Coll of Edn Gainesville FL 32611

CRIDER, IRENE PERRITT, educator, consultant; b. Chatfield, Ark., Apr. 29, 1921; d. Dolphus France and Eula Allan (Springer) Perritt; m. Willis Jewel Crider, Aug. 3, 1945; 1 child, Larry Willis. BA, Bethel Coll., 1944; MA, Memphis State U., 1957; EdD, Fla. State U., 1977. Cert. elem., secondary tchr., administr., Tenn. Tchr. various schs., Tenn., 1941-57; dean girls Lake Worth (Fla.) Jr. High, 1957-65; dean women Lake Worth High Sch., 1965-73; gen. instructional supr. Palm Beach (Fla.) County Pub. Schs., 1973-75; asst. prin. Jupiter (Fla.) High Sch., 1975-76; supr. interns Fla. Atlantic U., Boca Raton, 1977-83, Palm Beach Atlantic Coll., West Palm Beach, Fla., 1982-84; cons. Paris, Tenn., 1984-87; instr. edn. Bethel Coll., McKenzie, Tenn., 1987, prof. MEd Grad. Program. Contbr. articles to profl. jours. Bd. dirs., founder, charter mem. Palm Beach County Kidney Assn., 1973-86; chairperson citizens action com. Fla. Ch. Women United, 1982-84. Mem. Delta Kappa Gamma (charter pres. Beta Xi-Mu 1968-70, chmn. state com., scholarship), Phi Delta Kappa. Democrat. Methodist. Lodges: Zonta (Lake Worth) (pres. 1969-70), Order Ea. Star. Home and Office: Rt #1 Box 307 Springville TN 38256

CRIGER, NANCY S., banker; b. Ypsilanti, Mich., Apr. 16, 1951; d. Douglas D. and Edith (Nicoll) Smith; m. Dane Criger, July 9, 1982; children: Amanda L. Denomme, William G. Denomme, Jr. Student, Mich. State U., 1969-71; BS in Elem. Edn., Wayne State U., 1973. Asst. v.p. Nat. Bank of Detroit, 1978-87, Comerica Bank, Detroit, 1987—. Asst. treas. Jr. League of Detroit, 1985-86, treas., 1986-87; treas. women's assn. Detroit Symphony Orch., 1987—; mem. Assistance League N.E. Guidance Ctr. Detroit Symphony League, past bd. dirs.; mem. Friends of Greenfield Village, Detroit Inst. Arts, Detroit Artist Market, Detroit Zool. Soc., Detroit Sci. Ctr., Smithsonian Instn. Archives of Am. Art. Mem. Detroit Hist. Soc., Chi Omega. Office: Comerica Bank 211 W Fort St Detroit MI 48275-1034

CRILE, SUSAN, artist; b. Cleve., Aug. 12, 1942; d. George Jr. and Jane (Halle) C.; m. Joseph S. Murphy, May 18, 1984. Student, NYU; BA, Bennington Coll., 1965. Mem. faculty Fordham U., N.Y.C., 1972-76, Princeton (N.J.) U., 1974-76, Sarah Lawrence Coll., Bronxville, N.Y., 1976-79, Sch. Visual Arts, N.Y.C., 1976-82, Barnard Coll., N.Y.C., 1983-86, Hunter Coll., N.Y.C., 1983—; travelling rep. to Hungary and Portugal with exhbn. Am. Paintings in the Eighties, Internat. Communication Agy., Washington, 1981; lectr. Nat. Gallery, Budapest, Hungary, 1979, Gulbenkian Mus., Lisbon, Portugal, 1979; bd. dirs. Yaddo Corp. One-woman shows include Kornblee Gallery, N.Y.C., 1971, 72, 73, Fischbach Gallery, N.Y.C., 1974, 75, 77, Brooke Alexander Gallery, N.Y.C., 1975, Phillips Collection, Washington, 1975, New Gallery, Cleve., 1977, Ctr. Gallery Bucknell U., Lewisburg, Pa., 1978, Droll Kolbert Gallery, N.Y.C., 1978, 80, Ivory Kimpton Gallery, San Francisco, 1981, 84, 88, Van Straten Gallery, Chgo., 1983, Lincoln Ctr. Gallery, N.Y.C., 1983, Cleve. Ctr. for Contemporary Art, 1984, Nina Freudenheim Gallery, Buffalo, N.Y., 1980, 84, 88, Graham Modern, N.Y.C., 1985, 87, Adams Middleton Gallery, Dallas, 1986, Gloria Luria, Bay Harbor Island, Fla., 1987; exhibited in group shows at Whitney Mus. Art, N.Y.C., 1972, 82, Indpls. Mus. Art, 1972, 74, Kent State U., 1972, Art Inst. Chgo., 1972, Suffolk Mus., Stony Brook, N.Y., 1972, Corcoran Gallery Art, Washington, 1973, Va. Mus. Fine Arts, 1975, Lowe Art Gallery, Syracuse, N.Y., 1977, Boston U. Art Gallery, 1978, Inst. Art and Urban Resources, 1979, U.S.I.A., 1979, Grey Art Gallery, N.Y.C., 1979, 83, Janie C. Lee Gallery, Houston, 1979, Meml. Art Gallery, U. Rochester, 1980, Bklyn. Mus., 1980, 81, 83, Carnegie Inst., Pitts., 1981, Inst. Contemporary Art, 1981, Am. Acad. Arts and Letters, 1983, Weatherspoon Gallery, Greensboro, N.C., 1984, Edith C. Blum Art Inst., Bard Coll. Ctr., Annandale-on-Hudson, N.Y., 1984, Columbus (Ga.) Mus. Arts and Sci., 1985, Wright State U. Art Galleries, Dayton, 1985, Associated Am. Artists, 1985, Robert and Jane Meyerhoff Gallery, Md. Inst. Coll. Art, Balt., 1986, Queens Mus., 1986, Portland (Maine) Mus. Art, 1986, Mus. Fine Arts, Boston, 1986, Cleve. Mus. Art, 1987, Mt. Holyoke Coll. Art Mus., South Hadley, Mass., 1987; poster commn.: Live from Lincoln Ctr., N.Y.C., 1980, Mostly Mozart, 1985; represented in permanent collections Albright-Knox Art Gallery, Buffalo, Bklyn. Mus., Mus. Art Carnegie Inst., Pitts., Hirshhorn Mus., Washington, Met. Mus. Art, N.Y.C., Phillips Collection, Washington, Cleve. Mus. Art. Trustee Bennington Coll., 1979-81; bd. dirs. Hand Hollow Found., 1983-85. Recipient resident grant Yaddo, 1970, 71, 74-75, 78, Ingram Mertill Found. grant, 1972, MacDowell Colony resident grant, 1972; NEA fellow, 1982. Home: 168 W 86th St New York NY 10024

CRIM, CHERYL LEIGH, nurse; b. Winchester, Va., Oct. 23, 1956; d. Victor L. and Mary (Martin) C. BS in Nursing, U. Va., 1979; postgrad., Shenandoah Coll. and Conservatory of Music, 1987—. RN. Cert. psychiatric and mental health nurse. Nurse Med. Coll. Va., Richmond, 1979-80, Henrico Doctor's Hosp., Richmond, 1980-81, Winchester (Va.) Med. Ctr., 1981—. Mem. Va. Soc. Profl. Nurses. Home: Rt 1 Box 147 Clearbrook VA 22624 Office: Winchester Med Ctr S Stewart St Winchester VA 22601

CRIMMINS, BRENDA SEHNERT, educational career administrator; b. Dover, N.H., May 23, 1947; d. Frank Henry and Imogene (Lewis) Sehnert; m. T. Dale Crimmins, Sept. 2, 1967; children: Melanie Dawn, Andrea Marie, Sarah Elaine. BS, So. Ill. U., 1970, MS, 1977. Tchr. St. Louis City and County Sch. Bd., 1974-76; dir. Mobile Consumer Edn. Program St. Louis Community Coll., Florissant, Mo., 1976-79; instr. Adult Re-Entry Program Eastern Ill. U., Charleston, 1980-81; ednl. coordinator Dislocated Worker Program of Lake Land Coll., Mattoon, Ill., 1982—; cons. Consumer Products Safety Commn., St. Louis, 1978-79, St. Louis Police Acad., 1979; presenter numerous workshops; ednl. cons. St. Louis area, 1974-79, East Cen. Ill. area, 1982—. Contbr. articles to profl. jours. Vol. 4-H leader Charleston Coop. Extension Service, 1980—. Mem. Am. Home Econs. Assn. (bd. dirs. 1984), Ill. Employment and Tng. Assn., Ill. Community Edn. Assn., Ill. Adult and Continuing Edn. Assn., Phi Delta Kappa, Kappa Omicron Phi, Omicron Nu. Home: 1804 Meadowlake Dr Charleston IL 61920 Office: Lake Land Coll Dislocated Worker Program 1420 Wabash Mattoon IL 61938

CRISCUOLO, WENDY LAURA, lawyer, interior design consultant; b. N.Y.C., Dec. 17, 1949; d. Joseph Andrew and Betty Jane (Jackson) C.; m. John Howard Price, Jr., Sept. 5, 1970 (div. Apr. 1981). AB with honors in Design, U. Calif., Berkeley, 1973; JD, U. San Francisco, 1982. Space planner GSA, San Francisco, 1973-79; sr. interior designer E. Lew & Assocs., San Francisco, 1979-80; design dir. Beier & Gunderson, Inc., Oakland, Calif., 1980-81; sr. interior designer Environ. Planning and Research, San Francisco, 1981-82; interior design cons., Mill Valley, 1982—; law clk. to Judge Spencer Williams, U.S. Dist. Ct., San Francisco, 1983-84; atty. Ciros Investments, Mill Valley, 1985—. Author: (with others) Guide to the Laws of Charitable Giving, 3d rev. edit., 1983; mem. U. San Francisco Law Rev., 1983. Bd. dirs., v.p. and treas. Marin Citizens for Energy Planning; bd. dirs., treas. The Wildlife Ctr. Mem. ABA, State Bar Calif., Queen's Bench (San Francisco), Calif. Women Lawyers. Republican. Episcopalian. Club: Commonwealth (San Francisco). Avocation: creative writing.

CRISMAN, PAMELA KAY, public relations official, college administrator; b. Galesburg, Ill., Aug. 26, 1952; d. Mildrehn Carl and Norma Jean (Goodrich) Black; d. Gerald R. Crisman, Apr. 9, 1977; children: Brian Matthew, Jeffrey Ray. BS in Pub. Relations, So. Ill. U., 1974; postgrad. Sangamon State U., 1980. Pub. relations asst. Hansen Photography, Decatur, Ill., 1976; sales mgr., promotion dir. G.E. Cablevision, Decatur, 1976-78; info. and plan coordinator Decatur Mental Health Ctr., 1978-83, asst. adminstr., 1983; pub. relations dir. Lake Land Coll., Mattoon, Ill., 1983—; cons. Ill. Dept. Mental Health and Devel. Disabilities-Beneficiary Awareness Project, Springfield, Ill., 1982, Decatur Mental Health Ctr., 1984; chmn. Mental Health Pub. Awareness Com., Decatur, 1978-80. Author, dir. TV pub. service announcements, 1982; co-editor (manual) Student Assistance Programs, 1986. Mem. Pub. Relations Soc. Am. (sec. cen. Ill. chpt. 1988), Ill. Coll. Relations Council (bd. dirs. 1986, treas. 1988), Ill. Council Community Coll. Adminstrs. (sec. pub. relations commn. 1986, chmn.-elect 1988), Nat. Council for Community Relations (bd. dirs. 1988). Avocations: photography, writing. Office: Lake Land Coll State Rt 45 Mattoon IL 61938

CRISMOND, LINDA FRY, county librarian; b. Burbank, Calif., Mar. 1, 1943; d. Billy Chapin and Lois (Harding) Fry; m. Donald Burleigh Crismond, 1965 (div. Sept. 1980). B.S., U. Calif.-Santa Barbara, 1964; M.L.S., U. Calif.-Berkeley, 1965. Cert. county librarian, Calif. Reference librarian, EDP coordinator San Francisco Pub. Library, 1965-72, head acquisition, 1972-74; asst. univ. librarian U. So. Calif., Los Angeles, 1974-80; chief dep. county librarian Los Angeles County Pub. Library, Los Angeles, 1980-81; county librarian Los Angeles County Pub. Library, Downey, 1981—; Western rep. quality control council Ohio Coll.l Library Ctr., Columbus, 1977-80; mem. Am. Nat. Standards Inst., N.Y.C., 1978-80; bd. councillors U. So. Calif. Sch. Library and Info. Mgmt., 1980-83; adv. bd. mem. UCLA Library Sch., 1981—; chmn. bd. dirs. Los Angeles Pub. Library Found., 1982—. Author: Directory of San Francisco Bay Area, 1968. Named Staff Mem. of Year San Francisco Pub. Library, 1968. Mem. ALA (chmn. Percy Jury 1976-78, chmn. Gale Jury 1982-84, exec. com. resources and tech. services div. resources sect. 1980-82), Calif. Library assn. (council 1980-82), Calif. County Librarians Assn. (pres. 1984). Home: 15985 Alcima Ave Pacific Palisades CA 90272 Office: Los Angeles County Pub Library 7400 E Imperial Hwy Downey CA 90241

CRISP, RUTH HINTON, confectionary brokerage company executive; b. Winchester, Va., Sept. 11, 1944; d. Edward Raymond and Hazel Valene (Pyle) Payne; divorced; children—Teresa Anne Hinton, Paul Edward Hinton. Degree in interior design Fla. Sch. Art. Office worker Sea Cold Service, Atlanta, 1967-70; salesperson J. Reid Green Assocs., Atlanta, 1970-80; salesperson Richard Born Co., Atlanta, 1980-85, owner, pres. Ruth Crisp Assocs., Inc. doing bus. as Richard Born Co., Atlanta, 1986—; mem. broker adv. bd. Fleer Corp., 1983, Republic Tobacco Co., 1985. Named to honor roll Nat. Assn. Tobacco Distbrs., 1978. Mem. Nat. Candy Wholesale Assn. (Nat. Candy Ambassador award 1985), So. Tobacco and Candy Assn., So. Salesmen Club (v.p. 1987), Atlanta Candy and Tobacco Club (pres. 1982, Presdl. plaque 1983), Nat. Confectionary Salesmen (Ambassador award 1984, bd. dirs. 1985-86), Nat. Assn. Female Execs. Republican. Avocations: reading; theater; golf; antiques. Office: Ruth Crisp Assocs Inc 4285 Memorial Dr Suite H Decatur GA 30032

CRISPIN, MILDRED SWIFT (MRS. FREDERICK EATON CRISPIN), civic worker, writer; b. Branson, Mo.; d. Albert Duane and Anna (Harlan) Swift; student Galloway Woman's Coll., 1922-24; m. Herbert William Kochs Jr., Dec. 1, 1928 (div. Mar. 1955); children—Susan Kochs Judevine (dec.), Herbert William, Judith Ann (Mrs. Nelson Shaw); m. 2d, George Walter King Snyder, Oct. 6, 1962 (dec. 1969); m. 3d, Frederick Eaton Crispin, May 20, 1972. Bd. dirs. Travelers Aid Soc., Chgo., 1936-68, nat. dir., 1948-71; bd. dirs. U.S.O., Chgo., 1944-65, nat. dir., 1951-57; bd. dirs. John Howard Assn., 1958-67, Community Fund Chgo., 1950-56, Welfare Council Met. Chgo., 1950-56; chmn. woman's div. Crusade of Mercy, Chgo., 1964. Mem. U.S. Women's Curling Assn. (co-founder 1947, pres. 1950, founder Indian Hill Women's Curling Club, Winnetka, Ill., 1945, chmn. 1945-46), DAR, Daus. Am. Colonists. Republican. Methodist. Clubs: Saddle and Cycle, Town and Country Arts (pres. 1957-58) (Chgo.); Everglades (Palm Beach, Fla.); Venice (Fla.) Yacht; Coral Ridge Yacht (Ft. Lauderdale, Fla.); Bird Key Yacht (Sarasota, Fla.). Home: Box 1098 Osprey FL 33559

CRIST, CYNTHIA LOUISE, academic administrator; b. Waukesha, Wis., Sept. 30, 1950; d. George Philip and Evelyn Pauline (Schultz) C.; m. Andy Driscoll, June 27, 1987. BS in Edn., Ill. State U., 1972, MS in Edn., 1977. Tchr. Peoria (Ill.) Pub. Schs., 1972-78; spl. edn. tchr. North St. Paul-Maplewood Pub. Schs., Minn., 1978-82; asst. dir. Govs. Office of Sci. and Tech., St. Paul, 1983-86, acting dir., 1986-87; asst. to chancellor for policy research Minn. State U. System, St. Paul, 1987—; mem. Equity and Edn. Task Force Commn. on the Econ. Status of Women, Minn., 1984, Govs. adv. com. on tech. in edn., 1985—, Govs. adv. council on tech. for people with disabilities, 1985—. Author: (directory) High Technology in Minnesota: A Directory of Programs, Policies, and Services, 1984, Disabilities and Technology: Report of the Governor's Issue Team on Technology for People with Disabilities, 1986; editor: Interdisciplinary Methods of Teaching, 1981; contbr. articles to profl. jours. Dir. 4th Congl. Dist. Dem. Farmer Labor Party, St. Paul, 1981-85; del. Minn. State Dem. Farmer Labor Cen. Com., 1983-85; chair Ramsey County Human Services Adv. Com., Minn., 1985-87. Ednl. Policy fellow Inst. for Ednl. Leadership, 1987-88. Mem. Minn. Alliance for Sci. (bd. dirs. 1986—), Minn. Acad. Sci., Minn. Orchestral Assn. (guarantor 1985—), Minn. Wellspring (edn. and tech. com. 1981-82). Office: Minn State U System 555 Park St Suite 230 Saint Paul MN 55103

CRIST, GERTRUDE H. (MRS. HOWARD G. CRIST, JR.), civic worker; b. Barnard, S.D.; d. Jacob H. and Lillian Belle (Freeman) Hartman; student S.D. State Coll., 1936-38; m. Howard Grafton Crist, Jr., Nov. 2, 1940; children—Howard Grafton III, Douglas Freeman. Owner, partner Farm and Home Service. Dir. Columbia Bank & Trust Co. Chmn., Westmoreland County chpt. ARC, 1946, sec., 1943-45, chmn. vol. spl. services, 1944-45; dist. chmn. Cancer drive Howard County; mem. Howard County Bd. Edn., 1953-70, pres., 1963-65; bd. dirs. Howard County Tb Assn.; adv. council Catonsville Community Coll.; chmn. Emergency Civil Def. Hosp. Howard County, 1961-62; sec. Community Action Council Howard County, 1965, dir., 1966; bd. dirs. Girl Scout Council Central Md., 1967-68; mem. Md. Council Higher Edn., 1968-76, State Bd. for Community Colls., 1968-77; trustee Howard Community Coll., 1966-71, v.p., 1969-70; bd. dirs. Howard County chpt. ARC, 1973—, v.p., 1976-77; mem. Md. Bd. for Higher Edn., 1977-86, Howard County Commn. on Arts, 1975-77; v.p. Farm and Home Service, Inc., 1968-78. Mem. Md. Congress Parents and Tchrs. (life), Md. Assn. Bds. Edn. (pres. 1966, 67), Nat. Sch. Bds. Assn. (dir. 1968-71), W. Friendship PTA (sec. 1949-51), League Women Voters (county sec. 1957-59, dir. 1960-62, pres. 1959), Nat. Congress Parents and Tchrs. (hon. life mem.), Delta Kappa Gamma (hon. Alpha Beta State and Lambda chpts.). Episcopalian (vestryman; chmn. parish day sch. bd. 1970-73). Club: Cattail River Garden. Home: 13905 Burnt Woods Rd Glenelg MD 21737

CRIST, JUDITH KLEIN, film, drama critic; b. N.Y.C., May 22, 1922; d. Solomon and Helen (Schoenberg) Klein; m. William B. Crist, July 3, 1947; 1 son, Steven Gordon. A.B., Hunter Coll., 1941; teaching fellow, State Coll. Wash., 1942-43; M.Sc. in Journalism, Columbia, 1945. Civilian instr. 3091st AAFBU, 1943-44; reporter N.Y. Herald Tribune, 1945-60, editor arts, 1960-63, assoc. theater critic, 1957-63, film critic, 1963-66; film, theater critic NBC-TV Today Show, 1963-73; film critic World Jour. Tribune, 1966-67; critic-at-large Ladies Home Jour., 1966-67; contbg. editor and film critic TV Guide, 1966-88; film critic N.Y. mag., 1968-75, The Washingtonian, 1970-72, Palm Springs Life, 1971-75; contbg. editor, film critic Saturday Rev., 1975-77, 80-84, N.Y. Post, 1977-78, MD/Mrs., 1977—, 50 Plus, 1978-83, L'Officiel/USA, 1979-80; arts critic Sta. WWOR-TV Channel 9 News, 1981-87; critical columnist on Coming Attractions 1985—; instr. journalism Hunter Coll., 1947, Sarah Lawrence Coll., 1958-59; assoc. journalism Columbia Grad. Sch. Journalism, 1959-62, lectr. journalism, 1962-64, adj. prof., 1964—. Author: The Private Eye, The Cowboy and the Very Naked Girl, 1968, Judith Crist's TV Guide to the Movies, 1974, Take 22: Moviemakers on Moviemaking, 1984. Contbr. articles to nat. mags. Trustee Anne O'Hare McCormick Scholarship Fund. Recipient Page One award N.Y. Newspaper Guild, 1955; George Polk award, 1961; N.Y. Newspaper Women's Club award, 1955, 59, 63, 65, 67; Edn. Writers Assn. award, 1952; Columbia Grad. Sch. Journalism Alumni award, 1961; named to 50th Anniversary Honors List, 1963; Centennial Pres.'s medal Hunter Coll., 1970; named to Hunter Alumni Hall of Fame, 1973. Mem. Columbia Journalism Alumni (pres. 1967-70), N.Y. Film Critics Circle, Nat. Soc. Film Critics., Sigma Tau Delta. Office: 180 Riverside Dr New York NY 10024

CRISTINA, DONNA MARIE, public relations, advertising executive; b. N.Y.C., June 27, 1948; d. Anthony R. and Marie (Greco) C. AS, Fashion Inst. Tech., N.Y.C., 1968; postgrad., CUNY, 1968-69. Asst. fashion coordinator Ind. Retailors Syndicate, N.Y.C., 1968-70; fashion coordinator Frederick Atkins, Inc., N.Y.C., 1970-75; assoc. fashion dir. Bergdorf Goodman, N.Y.C., 1975-79; v.p. fashion merchandising I.M. Internat., N.Y.C., 1979-81; account exec., creative dir. Jody Donohue Assocs., N.Y.C., 1981-82; v.p., ptnr. Cristina, Gottfried and Loving, Inc., N.Y.C., 1982-84; pres. Cristina & Shafer, Inc., N.Y.C., 1984-87; v.p. sales promotion, advt., visual merchandising Adrienne Vittadini Inc., N.Y.C., 1987—. Elected to Creative Achievements in Fashion Merchandising Hall of Fame Fashion Inst. Tech., N.Y.C., 1979-80. Mem. The Fashion Group (various coms.). Democrat. Roman Catholic. Office: Adrienne Vittadini Inc 575 7th Ave New York NY 10018

CRISTO, DEBORA JO, holding company executive; b. Anadarko, Okla., June 15, 1954; d. Floyd Roger and Donna Jo (Manley) Hardesty; m. Constantine Gus Cristo, May 9, 1979; children—Paul Hardesty, Roger Alexander. B.A. in Sociology, Psychology, Anthropology, U. Tulsa, 1973. Mgr. multi-family leasing Hardesty Co., Tulsa, 1969-74, partnership adminstr., 1977-79; gen. mgr. Manley Co., Tulsa, 1974-76; exec. v.p. Resource Group Industries, Tulsa, 1979-81, Atlas Tower Corp., Vinita, Okla., 1981-83, Exomesa Corp., Tulsa, 1983—; pres. Athena Devel., Tulsa, 1982—; v.p., dir. Exomesa Financial Services, Inc., Tulsa, 1983—; v.p., chief operating officer InAm. Corp., 1986—. Co-inventor Westower Technology, 1983-84; Co-designer Computerized Videotex Network System "Dax"; 1982-84. Recipient Cert. of Achievement Okla. senator, 1970; named Woman of Year, United Earth Found., 1973. Democrat. Greek Orthodox. Office: InAmerica Corp PO Box 52550 Tulsa OK 74152

CRISWELL, ELEANOR CAMP, psychologist; b. Norfolk, Va., May 12, 1938; d. Norman Harold Camp and Eleanor (Talman) David; m. Thomas L. Hanna. B.A., U. Ky., 1961, M.A., 1962; Ed.D., U. Fla., 1969. Asst. prof. edn. Calif. State Coll., Hayward, 1969; prof. psychology Calif. State U., Sonoma, 1969—; faculty adviser Humanistic Psychology Inst., San Francisco, 1970-77; biofeedback trainer Novato Inst. Somatic Research and Tng.; mng. editor Somatics jour.; cons. Venturi, Inc., Autogenic Systems, Inc.; clin. dir. Biotherapeutics, Kentfield Med. Hosp., 1985—. Founder Humanistic Psychology Inst., 1970. Co-editor: Biofeedback and Family Practice Medicine, 1983, How Yoga Works, 1987. Mem. Am. Psychol. Assn., Biofeedback Soc. Calif. (dir.), Aerospace Med. Assn., Assn. for Transpersonal Psychology. Patentee optokinetic perceptual learning device. Office: Sonoma State U Psychology Dept Rohnert Park CA 94928

CRISWELL, KIMBERLY ANN, computer company executive, dancer; b. Los Angeles, Dec. 6, 1957; d. Robert Burton and Carolyn Joyce (Semko) C. B.A. with honors, U. Calif.-Santa Cruz, 1980. Instr., English Lang. Services, Oakland, Calif., 1980-81; freelance writer Gambit mag., New Orleans, 1981; instr. Tulane U., New Orleans, 1981; instr., editor Haitian-English Lang. Program, New Orleans, 1981-82; instr. Delgado Coll., New Orleans, 1982-83; instr., program coordinator Vietnamese Youth Ctr., San Francisco, 1984; dancer Khadra Internat. Folk Ballet, San Francisco, 1984—; dir. mktg. communications Centram Systems West, Inc., Berkeley, Calif., 1984-87; communications coordinator Safeway Stores, Inc., Oakland, 1985; dir. corp. communications TOPS, div. Sun Microsystems, Inc, 1987-88; pres. Criswell Communications, 1988—. Writer speeches articles, press releases, brochures, users manuals. Vol. coordinator Friends of Haitians, 1981, editor, writer newsletter, 1981; dancer Komenka Ethnic Dance Ensemble, New Orleans, 1983; mem. Contemp. Art Ctr.'s Krewe of Clones, New Orleans, 1983, Californians for Nonsmokers Rights, Berkeley, 1985. Mem. Internat. Assn. Bus. Communicators, Nat. Assn. Female Execs., Dance Action, Bay Area Dance Coalition, Oakland Mus. Assn., Mus. Soc. Democrat. Avocations: visual arts, travel, creative writing.

CRITCHLOW, SUSAN MELISSA, public relations executive, advertising and printing consultant; b. Gainesville, Fla., Dec. 24, 1950; d. James Carlton and Mildred Estelle (Pringle) Barley; m. Warren Hartzell Critchlow, Jr., Aug. 18, 1973. BA, U. South Fla., 1972, MA in Speech Communication with honors, 1973. Asst. dir. pub. relations Goodwill Industries of N. Fla., Inc., 1973-74; dir. pub. relations St. Luke's Hosp., Jacksonville, Fla., 1974; dir. informational services Greater Orange Park Community Hosp., Orange Park, Fla., 1974-82; pres. Susan Critchlow & Assocs., SC&A Pub. Co., Inc., Orange Park, 1976—. Mem. bd. dirs. Children's Haven. Named N.E. Fla. Bus. Communicator of Month, 1975, 78. Mem. Fla. Hosp. Assn. (bd. dirs. pub. relations council 1976-78, Gold award 1975, Silver award 1976, 78), Jacksonville Hosp. Pub. Relations Council (chmn. 1975-77), Fla. Pub. Relations Assn. (Golden Image award 1975-83), Pub. Relations Soc. Am., Jacksonville Advt. Fedn. (Addy award 1982-86). Democrat. Episcopalian. Office: 1580 Wells Rd Suite 15 Orange Park FL 32073

CRITTENDEN, SOPHIE MARIE, communications manager; b. Mansfield, Ohio, Apr. 14, 1926; d. Joseph S. and Mary Ellen (Hagerman) Wojcik; m. Robert Eugene Crittenden, Aug. 24, 1946; children: Robert J., Mark A., Christopher E., Laura Ann. Student, Coll. St. Francis, 1944-45, Ohio U., 1945-46, North Cen. Tech. Coll., 1976-78. Substitute tchr. Mansfield City Schs., 1956-62; lab. technician The Ohio Brass Co., Mansfield, 1962-68, draftsman, 1968, mgr. internal publs., 1969-78, mgr. advt., 1978-83, mgr. communications, 1983-88; cons. communications Mansfield, 1988—. Creator and shower of quilts. Com. chmn. United Way Campaign, Mansfield and Richland, Ohio, 1978; pub. relations chmn. Tribute to Women and

Industry Project, Mansfield, 1986 (award 1985). Named Mrs. Mansfield Mrs. Am. Contest, 1961. Mem. Bus. and Profl. Advt. Assn., Mktg. Club of North Cen. Ohio (dir., sec. 1987—). Republican. Roman Catholic. Club: Cen. Ohio Weavers Guild (editor). Lodge: Altrusa (pres. 1976). Home: 84 Wildwood Dr Mansfield OH 44907 Office: 84 Wildwood Dr Mansfield OH 44907

CRIVELLI, GIOCONDA MARIA CATHERINE, artist, jewelry designer; b. Florence, Italy, d. Lorenzo and Catherine Anderson (Lester) R.; student Istituto Santa Reparata, Istituto della Santissima Annunziata al Poggio Imperiale Florence; m. Eric Richards Rippel, Nov. 6, 1974; 1 child, Schoenly Shearer Alexandra. Mem. pub. relations staff S. Ferragamo, Florence, 1959-63; pub. relations fashion coordinator Irene Galitzine couture, Rome, 1963-67, Titti Brugnoli, 1967-69; owner, mgr. Gioconda, N.Y.C., 1969—; editor Harpers Bazaar, Italy, 1969-71. Mem. organizing com. Scuola d'Italia, N.Y.C., 1977; one-woman shows: Aaron Faber Gallery, N.Y.C., 1978, Martha, Park Ave, N.Y.C., 1985; painting exhbn. Essex Art Gallery, 1979; collage exhbn. Rizzoli Art Gallery, N.Y.C., 1980; collage and jewelry show Gallery Il Borro, Florence, Italy, 1981; jewelry exhbn. Am. Mus. Natural History, N.Y.C., 1980, coordinator Pompeii A.D. '79 Show, 1982, Art Students League, N.Y.C.; jewelry, sculpture exhbn. Dyansen Gallery, SoHo, N.Y., 1987; coordinator, pub. relations "Italy on Stage" art festival, 1987, N.Y.; bd. dirs. Compagnia Italiana Turismo, 1987—. Mem. Pres.'s Council Vis. Nurses, N.Y.C.; mem. coms. N.Y. Infirmary-Beekman Downtown Hosp., N.Y.C.; mem. com. Internat. Inst. Rural Reconstrn., N.Y.C.; bd. control Art Students League, 1984-87. Club: Circolo Nautico E Della Vela, Porto Ercole, Italy. Office: Art Students League 215 W 57th St New York NY 10019

CROCE, ADELE ANDREA, data processing auditor; b. July 31, 1960; d. Antonio and Victoria (Pepe) C. BA in Acctg. and Info. Systems, CUNY, Flushing, 1983. Mgmt. auditor N.Y.C. Comptrollers, 1983-86; sr. EDP auditor Fin. Info. Services Agy., N.Y.C., 1986—. Vol. Mayor's Election Com., N.Y.C., 1985. Mem. Internal Auditors Assn. Office: Fin Info Services Agy 111 Eighth Ave New York NY 10011

CROCE, ARLENE LOUISE, writer; b. Providence, May 5, 1934; d. Michael Daniel and Louise Natalie (Pensa) C. Student, Women's Coll., U. N.C., 1951-53; BA, Barnard Coll., 1955. Founder, editor Ballet Rev., 1965-78; dance critic New Yorker mag., 1973—; dance panelist Nat. Endowment for Arts, 1977-80. Author: The Fred Astaire & Ginger Rogers Book, 1972, Afterimages, 1977, Going to the Dance, 1982 (AAAL award 1979, Award of Honor for arts and culture Mayor N.Y.C. 1979), Sight Lines, 1987. Recipient Janeway prize Barnard Coll., 1955; Hodder fellow Princeton U., 1971; Guggenheim fellow, 1972, 86. Office: New Yorker 25 W 43d St New York NY 10036

CROCKER, PATRICIA LYNN, public relations professional; b. Toronto, Dec. 11, 1948; d. Richard Wellington and vera (Belsey) C. BAA, Ryerson Pub. Inst., Toronto, 1976; BEd, U. Toronto, 1971. Tchr. Scarborough Bd Edn., Toronto, 1972-76; mktg. mgr. Cuisinart-Weil Co., Toronto, 1976-79; tchr. Toronto Bd. Edn., 1979-81; owner Ad Astra, Toronto, 1981-82, Crocker Internat. Co., Toronto, 1982—. Contbr. articles to profl. jours. Recipient award of Recognition Can. pub. relations jour., 1985, 2 awards of Excellence, 1986. Mem. Can. Home Econs. Assn., Toronto Home Econs. Assn. (bd. dirs. 1985—, pres. 1984-85), Toronto Culinary Guild (bd. dirs. 1986—). Office: Crocker Internat Co Inc, 49 Spadina Ave, Toronto, ON Canada M5W 2J1

CROCKETT, ADRIENNE JONES, principal; b. Hamtramck, Mich., Dec. 7, 1946; d. Sidney Minrose and Rosa Eileen (McKinney) J.; m. John William Crockett, June 27, 1981; children: April Eileen, Brandon William. BA, U. Mich., 1969, MA, 1973. Tchr. Bloomfield Hills (Mich.) Schs., 1969-77, adminstrv. intern, 1977-78, prin., 1978—. V.p. Bloomfield Hills Adminstrv. Council, 1980-81, treas., 1986-88. Organist, St. Peters African Meth. Episc. Zion Ch., 1974-79; fin. sec., treas. Brazeal Dennard Chorale, 1973—; dir. music Resurrection United Meth. Ch., 1986—, coordinator of children, 1986; U.S. adult rep. to Leeds, Eng, for Children's Internat. Summer Village, 1974. Recipient Opportunity grant U. Mich., 1965-69. Mem. Internat. Reading Assn., Nat. Assn. Elem. Sch. Prins., Mich. Elem. and Middle Sch. Prins. Assn.(rep. to Curriculum Council), U. Mich. Alumni Club, One Hundred Club U. Mich. Home: 22950 Mapleridge St Southfield MI 48075 Office: 1101 Westview St Eastover Sch Bloomfield Hills MI 48013

CROCKETT, CATHERINE GRAYSON, lawyer, mediator; b. Norfolk, Va., Aug. 6, 1949; d. Douglas Harman and Mary Catherine (Sturgis) C.; m. Lafe Elkas Solomon, Aug. 25, 1979; children: Catherine Hannah, William David. BA, Hollins Coll., 1971; MA (fellow), U. Americas-Puebla, Mex., 1973; JD, Antioch Sch. Law, 1976. Bar: D.C. 1977, Md. 1981, U.S. Dist. Ct. D.C. 1980, U.S. Ct. Claims 1983. Adv. atty. NLRB, Washington, 1976-79; trial atty. EEOC, Washington, 1979-80; trainer divorce mediators Family Mediation Assn., Bethesda, Md., 1982-84; co-founder Nat. Center Mediation Edn., 1984; sole practice family law and divorce mediation, Bethesda, 1980—; adj. faculty Cath. U. Am., Washington, 1984—; coordinator family mediation service Cir. Ct. Montgomery County, Md., 1986—; co-dir. Nat. Ctr. Mediation Edn., 1984—; sec. bd. dirs. Family Mediation Assn., 1980-84; factfinder Montgomery County Md. Personnel Grievance System, 1982—; mem. family dispute panel Am. Arbitration Assn., 1983—. Mem. ABA, Women's Bar Assn. Md., Assn. Family and Conciliation Cts., Montgomery County Md. Bar Assn. (sec. family law sect. 1981-82). Democrat. Episcopalian. Contbg. author: Divorce Mediation: A Guide for Family Therapists, 1984; co-author: Starting Your Own Mediation Practice: A Workbook, 1985. Office: 110 N Washington St Suite 207 Rockville MD 20850

CROCKETT, ETHEL STACY, librarian; b. Mt. Vernon, N.Y., Jan. 19, 1915; d. Henry Pomeroy and Marian (Putnam) Stacy; m. Clement Wirt Crockett, Aug. 17, 1936 (div. July 1969); children: Patricia Crockett Johnson, Richard; m. Jack Howard Aldridge, June 22, 1973. B.A., Vassar Coll., 1936; M.A., San Jose State Coll., 1962; postgrad., U. Calif.-Berkeley, 1964-65, San Francisco State Coll., 1966. Children's librarian Corning (N.Y.) Meml. Library, 1958; catalog librarian Sequoia Union High Sch., Redwood City, Calif., 1960-61; gen. reference librarian, instr. San Jose (Calif.) City Coll., 1962-68; dir. library services City Coll. San Francisco, 1968-72; dir. Inst. Effective Use of Paraprofls. in Libraries, summer 1971; Calif. State librarian Sacramento, 1972-80; chmn. Chief Officers of State Library Agencies, 1974-75; mem. Nat. Council on Ednl. Stats., 1975-78; mem. adv. group on the Library to Librarian of Congress, mem. adv. council Ctr. for the Book, 1980—; mem. vis. com. Stanford U. Libraries, 1975-82; mem. adv. council Stanford Library Assos., 1978—. Vice pres. Sir Francis Drake Commn., 1974-80; bd. dirs., treas. Seadrift Property Owners Assn., Stinson Beach, Calif.; bd. dirs. Strybing Arboretum Found., San Francisco; mem. edn. com. Strybing Arboretum Soc., San Francisco, 1987—; bd. dirs. Pacific Horticulture Found., spl. events chmn., 1982—; bd. dirs. San Francisco Mus. Art, Marin Income Property Owners Assn., Stinson Beach Community Ctr., West Marin Sr. Services, 1988—; mem. vis. council Living History Centre; mem. U. Calif.-Santa Cruz Arboretum Soc., 1987—. Mem. ALA, Book Club of Calif. (dir., v.p. 1983—), Calif. Library Assn., Calif. Inst. Libraries (pres. 1973—). Club: Colophon. Home: PO Box 457 Stinson Beach CA 94970

CROCKETT, PHYLLIS DARLENE, reporter; b. Chgo., July 14, 1950; d. Leo F. Crockett and Mae (Corbin) Williams; divorced; 1 child, Adina Darlene Gittens. BA, U. Ill., Chgo., 1972; MS in Journalism, Northwestern U., 1978. Free-lance reporter AP and UPI, Raleigh and Durham, N.C., 1978-80; news writer Sta. WTTG-TV, Washington, 1981-82; free-lance writer Pacific News Service, San Francisco, 1984; producer, reporter, anchorperson Sta. WSOC, Charlotte, N.C., 1978-79, Sta. WFNC/WQSM, Fayetteville, N.C., 1979-80; exec. editor Sheridan Broadcasting Network, Washington, 1980-81; reporter Nat. Pub. Radio, Washington, 1981—; panelist Am.'s Black Forum, Washington, 1980-83; commentator Black Entertainment TV, Washington, 1987, analyst, 1987—; cons. Washington Scholastic Press Assn., others, 1982—; vis. instr. Fayetteville State U., 1980, Johnson C. Smith U., Charlotte, 1979; guest lectr. Howard U., U. D.C., Fairfax (Va.) Pub. Schs., 1980—. Mem. Nat. Assn. Black Journalists (Frederick Douglass award 1984), Washington Assn. Black Journalists (v.p. 1982), Sigma Delta Chi. Baptist. Office: Nat Pub Radio 2025 M St NW Washington DC 20036

CROCKETT-GALLO, BARBARA, dancer; b. Berkeley, Calif., Sept. 19, 1920; d. Earl Warner and Elsie Bliss (Kennedy) Wood; m. Deane Crockett, Dec. 7, 1941; children—Leslie Crockett Farrow, Allyson Deane Crockett Schwennesen; m. Albert Gallo, Nov. 23, 1978. Ed. pub. schs., Fresno, Calif. Dancer, San Francisco Ballet, 1938-43; artistic dir., instr. Crockett Dance Studio, Sacramento, 1945—; founder, 1965-86, since prin. dancer, artistic dir. Sacramento Ballet; bd. dirs. Sacramento Regional Arts Council, 1974-77; mem. dance panel Calif. Arts Council, 1981, 82, 85, 86, 88. Recipient Community Service award Sacramento Regional Arts Council. Mem. Nat. Assn. Regional Ballet (pres. 1972-74, bd. dirs. 1974-87), Pacific Regional Ballet Assn. (co-founder 1966, pres. 1975, 87). Office: 4050 Manzanita Ave Carmichael CA 95608

CROFFORD, HELEN LOIS, accountant; b. Mesa, Ariz., Sept. 1, 1932; d. Elmer Earl and Lillian Irene (Williams) C.; grad. Lamson Bus. Coll., Phoenix, 1952. Acct., Bob Fisher Enterprises, Inc., Holbrook, Ariz., 1964-78; office mgr. for physician, Holbrook, 1978-79; office mgr. Trans Western Services, Inc., Holbrook, 1979; acct., Northland Pioneer Coll., Holbrook, 1980—. Squadron comdr. CAP, 1965-67, mission coordinator, 1970-79, group comdr., 1972-77, mem. regional staff, 1977-79, wing. historian, 1984—; mem. Navajo Fair Commn., 1966-75; mem. Navajo County Natural Resource Conservation Dist., 1970—, sec.-treas., 1971-81, chairperson, 1981-88; chmn. Navajo County Emergency Service Council, 1984-87; co-chmn. Navajo County Local Emergency Planning Com., 1987-88. Mem. Ariz. Assn. Conservation Dists. (exec. bd. 1977-78, sec., 1979-80, v.p. 1981-82, pres. 1983-84, past pres. 1985), Nat. Assn. Conservation Dist. Past Pres., Nat. Assn. Female Execs., D.A.R. Democrat. Home: Box 36 Woodruff AZ 85942 Office: 1200 E Hermosa Dr Holbrook AZ 86025

CROMER, DEBBIE GAIL, marketing professional; b. Kirksville, Mo., May 5, 1951; d. Wayne E. and Teresa (Miller) C. BA in Chemistry, U. No. Colo., 1975. Analytical chemist Hazen Research, Golden, Colo., 1975-77; supr. telemktg. Hach Chem. Co., Loveland, Colo., 1977-78, product mgr., 1978-80; tech. sales rep. Eastman Kodak Co., Rochester, N.Y., 1980-83, sales devel. and mktg. specialist, 1983-85, product and market dealer specialist, 1985-86, mktg. planning specialist, 1986—. Office: Eastman Kodak Co 343 State St Rochester NY 14587

CROMWELL, FLORENCE STEVENS, journal editor, therapist; b. Lewistown, Pa., May 14, 1922; d. William Andrew and Florence (Stevens) C. BS in Edn., Miami U., Oxford, Ohio, 1943; BS in Occupational Therapy, Washington U., St. Louis, 1949; MA, U. So. Calif., 1952; cert. in health facility adminstrn., UCLA, 1978. Mem. staff, then supervising therapist Los Angeles County Gen. Hosp., 1949-53; occupational therapist Goodwill Industries, Los Angeles, 1954-55; staff therapist Vis. Nurse Assn., Phila., 1955-56; research therapist United Cerebral Palsy Assn., Los Angeles, 1956-60; dir. occupational therapy Orthopaedic Hosp., Los Angeles, 1961-67; coordinator occupational therapy Research and Tng. Ctr. U. So. Calif., Los Angeles, 1967-70, assoc. prof., 1970-76, acting chmn. dept. occupational therapy, 1973-76, mem. adv. bd. project SEARCH, Sch. Medicine, 1969-72; founding editor Occupational Therapy in Health Care jour., Pasadena, Calif., 1984-88, editor emerita, 1988—; assoc. dir. Los Angeles Job Corps Ctr., 1977-78, cons. in edn. and program devel., 1976—. Author: Manual for Basic Skills Assessment, 1960; also articles. Mem. scholarship com. Los Angeles March of Dimes, 1963-70; Bd. dirs. Am. Occupational Therapy Found., 1965-69, v.p., 1966-69; bd. dirs. Nat. Health Council, 1975-78. Served to lt. (j.g.) WAVES, 1943-46. Recipient Disting. Alumni award Washington U., 1978, Disting. Lectr. Calif. Occupational Therapy Found., 1986. Fellow Am. Occupational Therapy Assn. (pres. 1967-73); mem. Inst. Medicine of Nat. Acad. Scis., So. Calif. Occupational Therapy Assn. (pres. 1950-51, 75—), Coalition Ind. Health Professions (chmn. 1973-74), Assn. Schs. Allied Health Professions (dir. 1973-74), World Fedn. Occupational Therapists, Cwen, Mortar Bd., Kappa Delta Pi, Kappa Kappa Gamma. Address: 1179 Yocum St Pasadena CA 91103

CROMWELL, MOLLY COWAN, fundraising professional, consultant; b. Peoria, Ill., Nov. 18, 1938; d. Robert Fort Cowan and Fay Kathryn (Eastman) Sexton; m. James Hamilton Cromwell Sr.; children: James Jr., Marshall, Mary Kathryn, Graham, Amanda. BS, U. Wis., 1960. Dir. pub. relations Fairfax Symphony, McLean, Va., 1974-76; dir. fundraising Sta. WNVT-TV, Falls Church, Va., 1976-78; dir. devel. Holton-Arms Sch., Bethesda, Md., 1970-82, Georgetown Prep. Sch., Rockville, Md., 1983-88; v.p. univ. relations Marymount U., Arlington, Md., 1988—. Home: 4701 Duncan Dr Annandale VA 22003 Office: Marymount Univ 2807 N Glebe Rd Arlington VA 22207

CRONAU, REBECCA LYNN, business analyst; b. Tokyo, Aug. 9, 1962; came to U.S., 1968; d. Jackie Don Baize and Hisako (Ogawa) Ishimoto; m. Stephen Leslie Cronau, Apr. 21, 1982; 1 child, Tanya Lynn. Student, U. Pitts., 1982-87, U. Tex., 1980-82. Coordinator data mgmt. and outreach, liaison to Ctr. Continuing Edn. Health Scis. U. Pitts., 1983-87; cons. TRW-Fla. Ops. Def. Systems Group, Cape Canaveral Air Force Sta., 1987, bus. analyst, 1987—. Democrat. Roman Catholic. Office: TRW Def Systems Group PO Box 903 Cape Canaveral FL 32920

CRONENBERGER, JO HELEN, clinical laboratory science educator; b. La Grange, Tex., Mar. 17, 1939; d. Lenon Paul and Gladys Frances (Legler) C. BS, U. Tex., 1962, BA, 1962; PhD, U. Houston, 1972; postdoctoral, Max-Planck Inst., Berlin, Fed. Republic of Germany, 1972-75. Cert. med. technologist. Med. technologist Meth. Hosp., Houston, 1961-64; research asst. Baylor Med. Sch., Houston, 1964-68; dir. med. tech. U. Tex. Health Sci. Ctr., San Antonio, 1975-80, U. N.C. Med. Sch., Chapel Hill, 1980—; Editor in chief Lab. Sci. Computer Line. Lan Learning Ctr. grantee Charles Culpeper Found., 1986, 88. Fellow Robert Welch Found., Deutsche Forschungs Gemeinschaft; mem. Handi-Hams, Amateur Radio Relay League, Am. Soc. Med. Technologists (computer newsletter editor 1986—), N.C. Soc. Med. Technologists (membership com. 1986—). Republican. Methodist. Lodges: Altrusa (v.p.), Eastern Star. Home: 100 Boulder Ln Chapel Hill NC 27514 Office: Univ NC Med Sch Dept Med Tech Wing H 222 M Chapel Hill NC 27514

CRONHOLM, BEBRA TIDWELL, author, advertising and public relations consultant; b. Albertville, Ala., Nov. 6, 1952; d. Ollis Cleveland and DeMile Yvonne Tidwell. B.A. in Journalism and English, U. Ala., 1974. Continuity dir. Sta. KAUM, ABC, Houston, 1976-77; copy supr. Point Communications, Houston, 1977-81, Popejoy & Fischel Advt., Dallas, 1980; account exec. Tracy-Locke/BBDO, Dallas, 1981; owner Bebra/Writer, Dallas, 1982—. Contbr. articles to jours. in field; freelance writer for mags. Recipient 1st place in Grand Prix award Houston Ad Club, 1977; hon. mention Houston Art Dirs. Club, 1978. Mem. Women in Communications, Dallas Ad League (Silver Tops award 1983, 84), Dallas County Med. Soc. Aux. Home: 9912 Silvertree Dallas TX 75243

CRONHOLM, LOIS S., biology educator; b. St. Louis, Aug. 15, 1930; d. Fred and Emma (Tobias) Kisslinger; m. James Cronholm, Sept. 15, 1965 (div. 1974); children: Judith Frances, Peter Foster; m. Stuart E. Neff, Apr. 11, 1975. BA, U. Louisville, 1962, PhD, 1966. Faculty mem. biology dept. U. Louisville, 1973-85, dean arts and scis., 1979-85; dean arts and scis. Temple U., Phila., 1985—. Contbr. articles to profl. jours. Chmn. Human Relations Commn., Louisville, 1976-79; group capt. Dems., Valley Station, Ky., 1975-78; sec. Grass Roots Dem. Club, Valley Station, 1975; chmn. Southwestern Jefferson County Econ. Devel. Com., Valley Station, 1983-84. Recipient Pre-Doctoral fellowship NIH, 1963-66, Post-Doctoral fellowship NIH, 1967-70; named Prin. Investigator Dept. Interior, 1978-79. Mem. Nat. Assn. Land Grant and Urban Univs. (com. arts and scis. 1985-88), Council Colls. Arts and Scis., Am. Assn. Colls., Am. Assn. Higher Edn. Democrat. Jewish. Office: Temple Univ Anderson Hall Berks Mall Philadelphia PA 19122

CRONIN, KATHLEEN KAY, accountant; b. Oakland, Calif., Apr. 6, 1950; d. Roger Warren and Dorothy Mary (Campbell) Kelly; m. James Ronald Cronin, Feb. 19, 1984; children: Shannon Elizabeth, Shawn Margaret. Student, U. Tex., Arlington, 1968-70. Cashier supr. Elliott's Hardware, Dallas, 1969-76; billing and payroll specialist South-East Tex-Pack, Dallas, 1976-78; mgr. acctg. and data processing McDonald's Photo Products, Dallas, 1978-81, James Hirsch Furs, Dallas, 1981-85; comptroller Loyd-Paxton, Inc., Dallas, 1985—. Mem. Nat. Assn. Female Execs., Alliance of Design Profls. Republican. Episcopalian. Office: Loyd-Paxton Inc 3636 Maple Ave Dallas TX 75219

CRONIN, KATHRYN MARY, retail executive; b. Manhattan, N.Y., June 3, 1958; d. Harold Raymond and Mary Alice (Brassington) C. BS in Mktg., Fairfield U., 1980. Dept. mgr. Abraham and Straus, White Plains, N.Y., 1980-82, Macys, New Rochelle, N.Y., 1982-83; asst. buyer Macys, N.Y.C., 1983-84; mdse. mgr. Macys, Humble, Tex., 1984-85; buyer mens accessories Macys, N.Y.C., 1985-87, buyer mens dress shirts, 1987—. Roman Catholic. Office: Macys 151 W 34th St New York NY 10001

CRONIN, MARY PATRICIA, state official; b. Malden, Mass., Aug. 11, 1949; d. John Joseph and Ellen Teresa (Crowley) C. BS, Suffolk U., 1973, M Pub. Adminstrn., 1982. Cert. tchr., Mass. Copyright editor Allyn & Bacon Pub. Co., Boston, 1973-74, prodn. editor, 1974-78; editorial prodn. mgr. CBI-Thompson Pub. Co., Boston, 1978-82; mem. spl. com. staff Mass. Legislature, Boston, 1982-84; spl. asst. Exec. Office of Econ. Affairs, Boston, 1984-85, asst. sec., 1986—; cons. Capital Services, Washington, 1984—. Bd. dirs. Margaret Fuller House, 1987. Mem. Women in Pub. (chairperson 1975-76), 9 to 5 (chairperson 1977-78), SEIU Local 925 (steward 1977), Women for Econ. Justice (sec. 1983), Employer Supported Network (steering com. 1986—). Democrat. Roman Catholic. Home: 283 Vinton St Melrose MA 02176 Office: Exec Office Econ Afairs One Ashburton Pl Room 2101 Boston MA 02176

CRONIN, PATTI ADRIENNE WRIGHT, state agency administrator; b. Chgo., May 25, 1943; d. Rodney Adrian and Dorothy Louise (Thiele) Wright; m. Kevin Brian Cronin, May 1, 1971; 1 child, Kevin. BA, Beloit (Wis.) Coll., 1965; JD, U. Wis., 1983. Vol. Peace Corps, Turkey, 1965-67; recruiter Peace Corps, Washington, 1967-68; tchr. English Kamehameha III Sch., Lahaina, Hawaii, 1968-70, Evansville (Wis.) High Sch., 1972-77; tchr. math. and history Killian Sch., Hartford, Wis., 1977-78; tchr. English Kaiser High Sch., Honolulu, 1979-80; intern Wis. Ct. Appeals, Madison, 1983; exec. dir. waste facility siting bd. State of Wis., Madison, 1983—; founder, v.p., bd. dirs. Justice Ctr. Honolulu, 1979-82; sec., treas. Cronin Constrn. Co., Inc., Madison, 1986—. Editor: Internat. Law Jour., 1982. Bd. dirs. Neighborhood Bd., Honolulu, 1979-82. Recipient Mayor's award of outstanding achievement, City of Honolulu, 1980. Mem. Soc. Profls. in Dispute Resoultion, ABA, State Bar Wis. Office: Waste Facility Siting Bd 132 E Wilson St #201 Madison WI 53702

CRONK, VIRGINIA MAE, social services administrator, educator; b. Emmetsburg, Iowa, July 8, 1942; d. George W. and Mary V. (Swartfager) Varcoe; m. Dennis G. Cronk, Feb. 3, 1963; children: Marcus W., Scott A., Brian C. BS in Community Edn., U. Wis., 1977, MS in Adminstrn., 1980, postgrad., 1982—. Exec. dir. Vol. Ctr. of Greater Milw., 1977—; adj. prof. Cardinal Stritch Coll., Milw., 1985—; pres. Agy. Execs. Group, Milw., 1984-85. Tchr. North Shore Congl. Ch., Milw., 1978—; mem. com. Am. Heart Assn. of Wis., Milw., 1980—. Mem. Nat. Conf. on Vols. (nat. chmn. 1982-83), Nat. Assn. for Vol. Adminstrs. (bd. dirs. 1983-85), League of Women Voters (pres. 1975-77), Assn. for Vol. Adminstrn. (founder local chpt. 1980), TEMPO. Office: Vol Ctr of Greater Milw 600 E Mason St Milwaukee WI 53202

CRONKY, JEANNE ANN, child care executive; b. Oakland, Calif., May 31, 1947; d. Eugene Fletcher and Frances Elaine (Storey) Newell; m. Richard John Cronky, Oct. 17, 1980; children: Lisa, Kira, Brenna. Cert. in day care, U. Minn. Owner Jeanne's Kid's Korner, Ill., Minn., 1967—; cons. in field, 1977-86. Mem. Minn. Assn. for Edn. of Young Children, Nat. Alliance Homebased Bus. Women, Greater Mpls. Day Care Assn. (trainer 1987—), Hennepin County Family Day Care Assn. (trainer 1986—, editor Bootline News 1986-87), Minn. Licensed Family Child Care Assn. Roman Catholic. Home and Office: 7421 74th Way Brooklyn Park MN 55428

CRONN, DAGMAR RAIS, atmospheric chemistry educator; b. Vicksburg, Miss., Nov. 9, 1946; d. Wesley Edward and Sarah Margaret (Courtney) Rais; m. Robert Stuart Cronn, June 22, 1968. BS, U. Wash., 1969, MS, 1972, PhD, 1975. Teaching asst. U. Wash., Seattle, 1969-71, research asst., 1971-75; asst. research chemist Wash. State U., Pullman, 1975-79, asst. prof., 1977-79, assoc. prof., 1979-86, prof. atmospheric chemistry, 1986—, asst. program dir., 1985-86, chair environ. sci. and regional planning program, 1986-88; cons. Am. Plywood Assn., Tacoma, 1977, EPA, Research Triangle Park, N.C., 1979-81, Meteorology Research Inc., Santa Rosa, Calif., 1981, Environ. Research and Tech., Inc., Westlake Village, Calif., 1981, W.K. Kellogg Found., Battle Creek, Mich., 1985, NSF, Washington, 1986. Contbr. numerous articles to profl. jours. Kellogg Found. fellow, 1981-84, Am. Council Edn. fellow, 1988—; Welsh Fund scholar, 1965-69. Air Pollution Control Assn. (chair regional meeting 1982), Soc. Women Engrs. (nat. keynote speaker 1983), Antarctican Soc. (speaker 1986), Sigma Xi. Home: Rt 3 Box 596 Pullman WA 99163 Office: Wash State U Pullman WA 99164

CRONOGUE, CHRISTINA ELIZABETH ANDREW, English language educator; b. N.Y.C., Sept. 27, 1957; d. James William and Myrtle Hastings (Aker) Andrew; m. Ronald Peter Cronogue, Dec. 30, 1982; children: Ian Andrew, Graham Robert. BA in German, U. Hawaii, 1980; MA in English and Linguistics, Iowa State U., 1985. Translator, sec. Fedn. Internationale de Natation Amateur, Des Moines, 1981-84; English proficiency evaluator Iowa State U. Grad. Coll., Ames, 1984—; instr. English Iowa State U., Ames, 1985—. Active Fund for Animals, N.Y.C., 1982—, People for the Am. Way, 1984—. Mem. Tchrs. of English to Speakers of Other Langs., Am. Assn. Vet. Medicine Aux., Phi Kappa Phi, Pi Delta Pi, Delta Phi Alpha. Democrat. Episcopalian. Home: Star Rt 263 Currituck NC 27929

CROOK, BETTY ROSS, lawyer; b. Shreveport, La., Aug. 16, 1927; d. John H. and Edna Allison (Wallette) Ross; m. Jack P.A. Crook, Sept. 25, 1966 (dec. 1976). BS, Centenary Coll., 1947; JD, Georgetown U. 1954. Bar: Tex. 1955. Claims examiner VA Regional Office, Waco, Tex., 1966-67; asst. fin. v.p. Baylor U., Waco, 1976-81, property mgmt. assoc. office bus. affairs, 1981—. Pres. Women's Guild St. Mary's Cath. Ch., Waco, 1982-84, 87-88, chmn. liturgy commn., 1979—, sec. parish bd., 1981-85, pres. parish bd., 1980-81, 87—, mem. fin. com. 1987—; mem. legis. com. Regis-St. Elizabeth's Nursing Home, Waco, 1985; bd. trustees Reicher Cath. High Sch., 1987—. Mem. Tex. Bar Assn., Waco-McLennan County Bar Assn. Avocations: reading, ch. choir singing, polit. work. Home: 1810 Lyle Ave Waco TX 76708 Office: Baylor Univ Bus Affairs Office CSB 384 Waco TX 76798

CROOK, NANCY FAYE, real estate sales executive; b. Seminole, Okla., May 12, 1938; d. Earl Sanford and Helen Lotus (Morgan) Austin; m. Gilbert Wayne Crook, Aug. 24, 1957; children: Kevin Austin, Kirsten Ann. BS, U. Redlands, 1979. Adminstrv. asst. Valley-Wide Recreation and Park Dist., Hemet, Calif., 1972-76, gen. mgr., 1976-85; investment sales rep. Gilbert W. Crook, Riverside, Calif., 1985-87; realtor Herbert Hawkins Realtors, Pasadena, Calif., 1987—; v.p. Calif. Parks and Recreation Soc., 1979, mem. legis. com., 1980-85, bd. dirs.; bd. dirs. Workmen's Compensation Joint Powers Ins. Program. Pres. Valley Resource for Retarded, San Jacinto, Calif., 1980; mem. grants com. Hemet Valley Hosp. Found., 1981; bd. dirs. Mt. San Jacinto Coll. Found., 1983—; chair publicity Assistance League of Hemacinto, Hemet, 1987. Recipient Outstanding Community Service award Calif. State Assembly, 1985. Republican. Lutheran. Club: Soboba Country (San Jacinto). Home: 277 Pleasant St Pasadena CA 91101

CROOKS, JEAN HAYES, financial marketing executive; b. Washington, July 26, 1942; d. Lewis Wendell and Elizabeth Jane (Blyth) Hayes; m. Joseph William Crooks, Sept. 11, 1965 (div. Dec. 1982); 1 child, James Lewis; m. Michael Joseph Gora, Dec. 14, 1986. BA, Mt. Holyoke Coll., 1964; MA, Johns Hopkins U., 1965. Program analyst U.S. Dept. Commerce, Washington, 1965-67; tng. officer U.S. Office Econ. Opportunity, Atlanta, 1968-70; instr. Ga. State U., Atlanta, 1970-75; dir. corp. research Payment Systems, Inc., Atlanta, 1975-81; v.p. research Synergistics Research Corp., Atlanta, 1981—. Contbr. numerous articles to profl. jours. Mem. Amnesty Internat., 1983—. Mem. Am. Mktg. Assn., Phi Beta Kappa. Democrat. Mem. United Ch. Christ. Home: 203 14th St NE Atlanta GA 30309 Office: Synergistics Research Corp 3384 Peachtree Rd NE Atlanta GA 30326

CROOKSHANKS, BETTY DORSEY, radio station executive, state legislator; b. Rainelle, W.Va., Oct. 27, 1944; d. Talmage Lee and Gilda Marie (Sovine) Dorsey; BA, W.Va. Inst. Tech., 1968; MA, W.Va. U., 1973; m. Donald Eugene Crookshanks, Sept. 1, 1972. Sec., NIH, 1965-66; tchr., coach Fayette County Bd. Edn., Meadow Bridge, W.Va., 1968-78; life underwriter Farm Family Life Ins. Co., 1979-82; tchr. Greenbrier (W.Va.) West High Sch., 1981-84; mgr. Sta. WYKM, 1984—; mem. W.Va. Ho. of Dels., 1977—, chmn. coal mine health and safety interior com., 1987—. Mem. adv. bd. W.Va. Woman's Commn., 1977—, Greenbrier Valley Domestic Violence Com.; treas. Rupert Community Library, 1977—; bd. dirs. Seneca Mental Health/Mental Retardation Council, 1978-82, treas., 1979-80, pres., 1980-82; bd. dirs. W.Va. Health Systems Agy., 1980-82; bd. dirs. W.Va. div. Am. Cancer Soc., 1981-83; pres. Greenbrier County Cancer Soc., 1981-82; treas. Big Clear Creek Baptist Ch., 1982-85. Recipient meritorious award W.Va. div. Isaac Walton League of Am., 1978; Disting. Service award W.Va. Osteo. Sch. Medicine, 1982; named Outstanding Young Woman of W.Va., 1980, Outstanding Citizen Rupert Rotary. Mem. Order of Women Legislators, Rainelle Bus. and Profl. Women's Club (treas. 1984-86, pres., chmn. dist. 2 1986—), Delta Kappa Gamma (sec. 1980-82, 1st v.p. 1982-85). Democrat. Clubs: Quota (bd. dirs. 1981-83), Rupert Woman's (pres. 1979-80, 82-83). Lodges: Order of Eastern Star, White Shrine, Rebekah. Office: Mountain State Bd Corp Rupert WV 25984

CRORY, ELIZABETH L., educational administrator; b. Gardner, Mass., Sept. 12, 1932; d. James Quaiel and Mary (Reilly) Lupien; m. Frederick E. Crory, Aug. 21, 1954; children—Thomas, David, Ellen, Ann, Edward, Stephen. A.B., U. Mass., 1954; M.A.L.S., Dartmouth Coll., 1975. Tchr., Amherst (Mass.) Schs., 1954, Lyme (N.H.) Schs., 1972-76; mem. N.H. Ho. of Reps., 1977-87, mem. commerce/consumer affairs com., 1977-87, mem. spl. com. on med. malpractice, 1984; exec. dir. Children's Ctr. of Upper Valley, 1986—; bd. incorporators Mascoma Savs. Bank. Mem. N.H. Democratic State Com., to 1984; treas. Grafton County Dem. Com., Hanover, N.H., 1980-84; chair Women's Vote '84 Task Force, Manchester, 1984; bd. overseers Mary Hitchcock Meml. Hosp. Roman Catholic. Home: 40 Rip Rd Hanover NH 03755

CROSBY, BARBARA ANN, nurse; b. S.C., May 22, 1944; d. David Perry and Bertha Lee (Worthy) Strong; m. William Franklin Crosby, June 2, 1960; 1 child, Marcella Lorraine. AA, Community Coll. of Balt., 1978, AA in Nursing, 1978; BS in Nursing, Coppin State Coll., 1985; postgrad., Bowie State Coll., 1987—. Nurse U. Md. Med. System, Balt., 1987, nurse clinician. Com. mem. Urban League of Morgan State U., Balt., 1985-86, Gov.'s Task Force on Infant Mortality, Balt., 1986—; fin. sec. Gr. Gethsemane Bapt. Ch., Balt., 1986—. Mem. Black Nurses Balt. (sec. 1985—, chmn. 1985—, Charity award 1986), Nat. Black Nurses Assn., Chi Eta Phi (nominating com. 1987—). Home: 1014 Upnor Rd Baltimore MD 21212

CROSBY, FAYE JACQUELINE, educator, author; b. Bethesda, Md., July 12, 1947; d. Robert A. and Andrée (Cohen) Newman; m. Travis Lee Crosby, Sept. 5, 1970; children: Matthew, Timothy. BA, Wheaton Coll., 1969; postgrad., London Sch. Econs., 1973-74; PhD, Boston U., 1976. Lectr. Rhode Island Coll., Providence, 1976-77; asst. prof. Yale U., New Haven, 1977-82, assoc. prof., 1982-85; prof. Smith Coll., Northampton, Mass., 1985—. Author: Relative Deprivation and Working Women, 1982; editor: Spouse, Worker, Child, 1987; contbr. articles to profl. jours. Office: Smith Coll Northampton MA 01060

CROSS, DEBORAH JOHANSEN, art director, gallery manager; b. N.Y.C., Aug. 19, 1947; d. John (Maclane) Johansen and Mary Lee (Longcope) Johansen; m. C. Fredric Hobbs, Dec. 16, 1978 (div. Dec. 1982); m. Robert Louis Cross, Mar. 30, 1986. BA, Boston U., 1969. Editorial, publishing asst. Beacon Press, Boston, 1969-73; office mgr., promotion mgr. Glide Pub. Co., San Francsco, 1973-74; publicity promotion cons. Douglas Mount & Others, San Francsco, 1974; ptnr., promotion cons. Charlsen & Johansen, San Francsco, 1974-76; pres., promotion, mktg. cons. Johansen Bookworks, San Francsco, 1976—; art. dir., mgr. Coast Galleries, Big Sur, 1983—. Co-author Untitled, 1974; contbg. author Big Sur Women, 1985; editor Overland Through Asia, 1974. Editor newsletter Big Sur Hist. Soc., 1985—, v.p., 1986; mem. Big Sur Property Owners Assn., 1986—. Democrat. Episcopalian. Home: PO Box 244 Big Sur CA 93920 Office: Coast Gallery Hwy 1 Big Sur CA 93920

CROSS, DOLORES E., university administrator, educator; b. Newark, Aug. 29, 1936; d. Charles and Ozie (Johnson) Tucker; children: Thomas E., Jane E. BS, Seton Hall U., 1963; MS, Hofstra U. 1968; PhD, U. Mich. 1971. Asst. prof. edn. Northwestern U., Evanston, Ill. 1971-74; assoc. prof. Claremont Grad. Sch., Calif., 1974-78; vice chancellor CUNY, 1978-81; prof. Brooklyn Coll., 1978—; pres. N.Y. State Higher Edn. Service Corp., Albany, 1981-88; assoc. provost, assoc. v.p. academic affairs U. Minn., Mpls., 1988—. Bd. dirs. 100 Black Women, Albany, 1983-88; bd. dirs. Nat. Council Higher Edn. Loan Program, Washington, 1982—. Editor: Teaching in a Multicultural Society, 1978. Mem. NAACP (life), Am. Edn. Research Assn., Am. Council on Edn., Women Execs. in State Govt. Avocations: running, hiking, bicycling, theater, writing. Home: 3411 Hennepin Ave S Minneapolis MN 55408

CROSS, DOROTHY ABIGAIL, librarian; b. Bangor, Mich., Sept. 9, 1924; d. John Laird and Alice Estelle (Wilcox) C.; B.A., Wayne State U., 1956; M.A. in Library Sci., U. Mich., 1957. Jr. librarian Detroit Public Library, 1957-59; adminstrv. librarian U.S. Army, Braconne, France, 1959-61, Poitiers, France, 1961-63; area library supr., 1963, asst. command librarian, Kaiserslautern, Germany, 1963-67, acquisitions librarian, Aschaffenburg, Germany, 1967, Munich, Germany, 1967-69, sr. staff library specialist, Munich, 1969-72, command librarian, Stuttgart, Germany, 1972-75, dep. staff librarian, Heidelberg, Germany, 1975-77; chief librarian 18th Airborne Corps and Ft. Bragg (N.C.), 1977-79; chief ADP sect. Pentagon Library, Washington, 1979-80, chief readers services br., 1980-83, dir., 1983—. Mem. ALA, U. Mich. Alumni assn., Delta Omicron. Methodist. Home: 6511 Delia Dr Alexandria VA 20310-6000 Office: Pentagon Library Rm 1A526 Pentagon Washington DC 06000

CROSS, JOAN ELAINE, nurse, insurance company representative; b. Cin., June 22, 1945. Diploma in Nursing, Bethesda Hosp. Sch. Nursing, Cin., 1966. Staff nurse emergency dept. Jewish Hosp., Cin., 1966-70; nurse, team leader ICU, critical care unit Bethesda Hosp., Cin., 1970-73, critical care instr., 1978-82; staff nurse ICU Christ Hosp., Cin., 1973-78; healthcare rep., risk mgmt. services St. Paul Fire and Marine Ins. Co., Cin., 1982—. Mem. ARC, Am. Soc. Healthcare Risk Mgrs., Ohio Soc. Healthcare Risk Mgrs., Nat. Assn. Female Execs. Office: St Paul Fire and Marine Ins Co 250 W Court St Cincinnati OH 45202

CROSS, JUDITH ANN, lawyer; b. Balt., Sept. 23, 1949; d. Joseph William and Ruth Marie (Pratt) Ortman; m. Kris Roger Cross, Nov. 15, 1969. A.A., Villa Julie, 1969; B.A. magna cum laude, U. Balt., 1980, J.D. magna cum laude, 1983. Bar: Md. 1983, U.S. Dist. Ct. Md. 1983, U.S. Ct. Appeals (4th cir.) 1983. Legal sec. various firms, Balt., 1970-72; pretrial release officer Dist. Ct. Md., Balt., 1972-78; fiscal officer, legal. asst. Office Atty. Gen., Balt., 1978-80; law clk. House Counsel Liberty Mut. Ins. Co., Balt., 1980-83; intern, student prosecutor State's Atty. Office, Balt., summer 1982; trial atty. Law Offices Eugene A. Edgett, Jr., Balt., 1983—. Contbr. articles to legal jours. Mem. jud. evaluation team Sheppard and Enoch Pratt Hosp., Balt., 1972-78; mem. Ednor Gardens Community Assn., 1975—. Mem. ABA, Md. Bar Assn., Balt. City Bar Assn., Women's Bar Assn. Home: 3627 Rexmere Rd Baltimore MD 21218 Office: Law Office of Eugene A Edgett Jr 250 West Pratt St Suite 900 Baltimore MD 21201

CROSS, LAURA ELIZABETH, lawyer; b. Lathrop, Mo.; d. Pross T. and Nina (Peel) C.; A.B., Lindenwood Coll., 1923; B.Litt., Columbia Sch. Journalism, 1925; J.D., George Washington U., 1939. Bibliog. research Library of Congress, Washington, 1931-42; admitted to D.C. bar, 1940; atty. Office Chief of Engrs., U.S. Army, 1942-73; practiced in Washington, 1973—. Mem. ABA, Fed., D.C. bar assns., Am. Judicature Soc., Women in Communications, Kappa Beta Pi, Theta Sigma Phi. Home and Office: 2500 Wisconsin Ave NW Washington DC 20007

CROSS, SHELLEY ANN, neurologist, neuro-ophthalmologist; b. Beacon, N.Y., Dec. 2, 1948; d. A.J. and Anna L. (Geering) C. AB, Wellesley (Mass.) Coll., 1970; MD, Med. Coll. Pa., 1975. Intern Montreal (Can.) Gen. Hosp., 1975-76; resident in medicine Royal Victoria Hosp., Montreal, Can., 1976-78; resident in neurology Mass. Gen. Hosp., Boston, 1978-81; fellow in neuro-ophthalmology Bascom Palmer Eye Inst., Miami, Fla., 1981-82; cons. in neurology Mayo Clinic, Rochester, Minn., 1982—. Contbr. articles to profl. jours. Fellow Royal Coll. Physicians, Am. Coll. Physicians, N.A.; mem. N.Am. Neuroophthalmological Soc., Am. Acad. Neurology and Psychiatry. Office: Mayo Clinic Dept Neurology Rochester MN 55905

CROSS, SUSAN LEE, consulting actuary; b. Abington, Pa., Mar. 10, 1960; d. James Robert and Mary Elizabeth (Schleiden) Garris; m. Kevin Michael Cross, July 15, 1979. BS in Math., U. Md., 1981. Actuarial asst. The Wyatt Co., Washington, 1981-83; actuarial asst. Tillinghast a Towers Perrin Co. (formerly Tillinghast), Hamilton, Bermuda, 1984-85, asst. v.p., 1985-86; cons. actuary Tillinghast a Towers Perrin Co. (formerly Tillinghast), Vienna, Va., 1987—. Fellow Casualty Actuarial Soc.; mem. Am. Acad. Actuaries, Soc. of Actuaries (assoc.). Republican. Home: 12041 Lake Newport Rd Reston VA 22070 Office: Tillinghast 8300 Boone Blvd Suite 250 Vienna VA 22180

CROSSLAND, HARRIET KENT, portrait painter; b. Cleve., Sept. 8, 1902; d. Carl and Harriet Emily (Bacon) Dueringer; pupil of Margaret McDonald Phillips; m. Paul Marion Crossland, Sept. 20, 1959. Portrait painter, 1952—; freelance editor med. papers, 1953-70; represented in permanent collection John F. Kennedy Library, Boston. Fund raiser Am. Cancer Soc.; mem. Santa Rosa Symphony League; mem. art mus. com. Luther Burbank Center for the Arts, Santa Rosa, 1982—. Recipient award of merit Am. Cancer Soc., 1979, 84. Mem. Sonoma County Med. Assn. Aux., Am. Med. Women's Assn. (friend), Am. Cancer Soc., DAR, Stanford U. Alumni Assn. Clubs: Ret. Officers Wives, Sonoma County Press, Sat. Afternoon (Santa Rosa). Editor, illustrator: X-Rays and Radium in Treatment of Diseases of the Skin, 1967; included in The Fifty American Artists by Margaret McDonald Phillips, 1969. Prin. donor Crossland Lab. for Audiovisual Learning in Dermatology, Stanford U. Sch. Medicine. Address: 2247 Sunrise Dr Santa Rosa CA 95405

CROSSLEY, KAY FRANCES, affirmative action coordinator; b. Kansas City, Kans., Sept. 10, 1946; d. John LeRoy and Frances Esther (Karriger) Bradford; m. Michael Aaron Crossley, Apr. 8, 1966; children: John Thomas, Philip Creighton. AA, Kansas City Community Coll., 1966. With Continental Elec. Co., Kansas City, Mo., 1964-66, Fairbanks-Morse Corp., Kansas City, Kans., 1966-68, Electra-Midland Corp., Kansas City, 1968-69, Gustin Bacon/St. Gobain Corp., Kansas City, 1969, Providence-St. Margaret Health Ctr., Kansas City, 1969-73, Bulk Mail Ctr. U.S. Postal Service, Kansas City, 1974-79; account rep. Main Post Office, Kansas City, 1979-85; coordinator womens' programs Mid-Am. Dist., Shawnee Mission, Kans., 1985-86; affirmative action/equal employment opportunity coordinator State of Mo., Kansas City, 1986—. Mem. Federally Employed Women, Am. Bus. Women's Assn., Nat. Assn. Female Execs., Nat. Assn. Postal Suprs., U. Kans. Alumni Assn. Mem. Christian Church. Home: 1823 N 78th Pl Kansas City KS 66112-2052

CROSSLIN, LOUISE, real estate broker; b. Sallisaw, Okla., May 29, 1927; d. Alvon A. and Maye M. (Burton) Diffee; student Oklahoma City U., 1949, 50; m. Paul L. Crosslin, July 18, 1943; children—Alvon Paul, Norman Randy. With CRE, Tahlequah, Okla., 1952—, owner, broker, 1955—; supr. Mr. Quik Stores. Mem. Rural Water Dist., Tahlequah, 1972-75. Mem. C. of C. (sec. 1952-82), Home Builders Assn., Okla. Real Estate Commn., Am. Legion Aux., VFW Aux., Beta Sigma Phi. Democrat. Baptist. Club: Sportsmen Acres Devel. Co. (pres. 1970-82). Home: PO Box 164 Tahlequah OK 74464 Office: 400 S Muskogee Tahlequah OK 74464

CROSSWELL, CAROL FAIN, real estate developer, lawyer; b. N.Y., Jan. 27, 1953; d. William Jefferson and CArol (McCormick) C. BArch with honors, Syracuse U., 1972; JD/MBA, Washington U., St. Louis, 1985; LLD, Washington U., 1988. Registered architect, N.Y.; lic. real estate broker, N.Y., Calif.; Bar: Ill. 1986, Calif. 1988. Developer Pyramid Cos., Syracuse, N.Y., 1972-75; project mgr. Turner Constrn. Co., Inc., N.Y.C, Boston, 1975-79; midwest regional mgr. J.A. Jones Constrn. Co., Charlotte, N.C., 1979-81; mgr. Urban Investment and Devel. Co., Chgo., 1981-83; v.p. devel. project mgr. Calif. Fed. Enterprises subs. Calif. Savs. & Loan, 1986-87; chief exec. officer CBC Interests, Inc., Palos Verdes, Calif., 1987—, also chmn. bd.; ptnr. C.B.C. Properties and C.B.C. Ptnrship., 1987—. Contbr. articles to profl. jours. Mem. AIA. Home and Office: CBC Interests Inc 27429 Rainbow Ridge Rd Palos Verdes CA 90274

CROTTY, MARILYN NEUBER, educator; b. Wilmington, Ohio, Jan. 24, 1936; d. Kenneth Arthur and Lavina Iola (Norvell) Neuber; m. Martin Joseph Crotty, Nov. 26, 1958 (div. 1984). BEd, U. N.Mex., 1958. Tchr. elem. music Farmingtn (N. Mex.) Pub. Schs., 1962-63; tchr. elem. Albuquerque Pub. Schs., 1963—. Author: 33 children's stories; contbr. 17 articles to mags. Mem. Soc. Children's Book Writers, Internat. Tng. Communication, Nat. League Am. Pen Women (1st prize article contest 1985), SW Writers's Workshop, Alpha Delta Kappa. Club: Toastmasters Internat. (Competent Toastmaster cert. 1987). Home: 3733 Big Bend RD NE Albuquerque NM 87111

CROUCH, HELEN OLIVE, microbiologist; b. Norwood, N.Y., Nov. 25, 1925; d. William Nelson and Ethel Grace (Austin) C. BS, U. Bridgeport, 1981, MS, 1983. Med. technologist St. Agnes Hosp., White Plains, N.Y., 1958-62, Burke Rehab. Ctr., White Plains, N.Y., 1962-66; technician dept. labs. and research County of Westchester, Valhalla, N.Y., 1966-69, sr. technician, 1969-78, microbiologist II, 1978-84, chief microbiologist, 1984-86, sr. microbiologist, 1986—. Mem. Am. Soc. Clin. Pathologists (assoc., registered med. technologist), Am. Soc. for Microbiology. Office: Westchester County Dept Labs Hammond House Rd Valhalla NY 10595

CROUCH, MADGE LOUISE, government official; b. Winston-Salem, N.C., Sept. 21, 1919; d. Amos C. and Emma Jane (Griffith) C.; m. Sam T. Gibson, Spet. 1986. Diploma Bklyn. Meth. Hosp. Sch. Nursing, 1941; BS, Columbia U., 1947; MA, George Washington U., 1961. Mem. faculty Meth. Hosp. Sch. Nursing, Bklyn., 1941-43, 47-48; asst. dir., nat. dir. nursing blood program ARC, Washington, 1948-65; br. dir. blood and blood products, dept. dir. div. biologics evaluation Bur. Biologics, FDA, Washington, 1965-82, dept. dir. Office Biologics, Center Drugs and Biologics, 1982-87; dept. dir. Office Compliance, Ctr. for Biologics Evaluation and Research, Washington, 1987—. Served with USNR, 1943-46. Recipient Commendable awards FDA, 1974, 77, Pfizer Meml. award, 1961; Legis. fellow, 1982. Mem. Internat. Soc. Blood Transfusion. Office: 8800 Rockwall Pike Bethesda MD 20892

CROUCH, ROBYN R., lawyer; b. Lousville, Aug. 28, 1959; d. Roby E. and Clara (Lilly) C. Student, U. Ky., 1977-79; BA in Biology, U. Louisville, 1982; JD, Miss. Coll., 1985. Bar: Miss. Law clk. Hon. Wm Sebastian Moore, Jackson, Miss., 1985; atty. Schwartz & Assocs., Jackson, 1985—. Mem. ABA, Miss. Bar Assn., Am. Trial Lawyers Assn., Miss. Trial Lawyers Assn., Internat. Right of Way Assn., Jackson Young Lawyers Assn., Hinds County Bar Assn. Democrat. Roman Catholic. Home: 6300 Old Canton Rd #7-208 Jackson MS 39211 Office: Schwartz & Assocs 117 W Capitol St Jackson MS 39201

CROUCH, SOFIA CASTRO, state official, consultant, researcher; b. Lingayen, Philippines, May 11, 1931; d. Ignacio Asara-Cruz and Maria Consolacion (Bravo) Castro; came to U.S., 1951; m. Harvey Jesse Crouch, Sept. 27, 1972. B.S., Ga. State Coll. for Women, 1952; M.Ed., U. Ga., 1953, D.Ed., 1965. Dean of edn. Visayan Central Coll., Iloilo City, Philippines, 1954-63; supr. Glynn County Bd. Edn., Brunswick, Ga., 1966-68, coordinator research 9th Dist. Services Ctr., Cleveland, Ga., 1968-73; researcher Atlanta Bd. Edn., 1973-75; grant project dir. Ga. Dept. Human Resources, Atlanta, 1977—. Vol. United Way, Atlanta, 1973-76, Wyche Fowler Campaign Com., Atlanta, 1974-82, Joe Frank Harris for Gov. Com., Atlanta, 1982; del. Internat. Assembly, Williamsburg, Va., 1964. Mem. Ga. Assn. Educators (pub. relations com. 1969-71), Ga. Council Adminstrs. Spl. Edn., Assn. Suprs. and Curriculum Dirs., Atlanta Bd. Realtors, Phi Kappa Phi, Kappa Delta. Democrat. Roman Catholic. Club: Homemakers (Sandy Springs, Ga.). Lodges: Rotary Internat. (scholar 1951-53), Sandy Springs Rotary (named Lady of Yr. 1981). Home: 10766 Morris Rd Alpharetta GA 30201 Office: Profl Services Ga Retardation Ctr 4770 N Peachtree Rd Atlanta GA 30330

CROUCH-RUIZ, EVELYN, nurse, educator; b. Ponce, P.R., May 18, 1945; d. Everett Irvin and Juanita Victoria (Ruiz) C.; diploma St. Luke's Epis. Sch. Nursing, 1966; BSN cum laude, Cath. U. P.R., 1972; MSN, U. Tex., Austin, 1978, PhD in Nursing, 1987; m. Julio M. Rivera, Aug. 8, 1970; children—Evelyn Aixa, Julio Irvin, Alex Raul. Staff clin. nurse St. Luke's Episcopal Hosp., Ponce, 1966-67; clin. nurse Columbia Presbyn. Med. Center, N.Y.C., 1967-69; pvt. duty nurse, Ponce, 1969-72; nursing instr. Cath. U. P.R., Ponce, 1972-80, prof. Grad. Sch. Nursing, 1983—; cons. nursing adminstrn. edn., Ponce, 1984—; clin. nurse USPHS Hosp., Houston, 1980-81; asst. instr. U. Tex., Austin, 1981-82; cons. labor and delivery Castaner (P.R.) Hosp., Damas Hosp., Ponce, 1978-80; dir. cultural and social activities Delicias, Ponce, 1980; chmn. recruitment Coll. Profl. Nurses, Ponce, 1979-80; coordinator Assoc. Degree Nursing Program, Regional Coll., Ponce, 1980. Mem. Nat. League Nursing, Assn. Nurses Grad. Sch. (research rep.), P.R. Coll. Profl. Nurses (pres. commn. on research). Democrat. Episcopalian. Home: BE-33 4th St Urb Las Delicias Ponce PR 00731 Office: Cath Univ PR Dept Nursing Ave Las Americas Ponce PR 00731

CROUSE, JANICE SHAW, university administrator; b. Milstead, Ga., June 3, 1939; d. Charles Columbus and Sarah Ruth (Baird) Shaw; m. Gilbert Lewis Crouse, Aug. 4, 1939; children: Laura Charmaine, Gilbert Lewis Jr. AB, Asbury Coll., 1961; MA, Purdue U., 1972; PhD, SUNY, Buffalo, 1979. Tchr. Lafayette High Sch., Lexington, Ky., 1961; grad. asst. SUNY, Buffalo, 1970-72, asst. prof. communications, 1970-74; hostess TV program Focus, Buffalo, 1970-73; tchr. high sch. Taipei (Taiwan) Am. Sch., 1974-76; prof. Asbury Coll., Wilmore, Ky., 1976-81, Ball State U., Muncie, Ind., 1981-84; asst. to pres. Taylor U., Upland, Ind., 1984-85, assoc. v.p., 1985—. Contbr. articles to Christian Scholars Rev., Ind. Speech Jour., Communication Edn. Rep. Mayor's task force on coliseum, Marion, Ind., 1986, Ind. Council on Humanities, Indpls., 1984-86; mem. steering com. Hoosier Celebration '88, 1987—. Mem. Nat. Assn. Female Execs., Assn. Acad. Affairs Adminstrs., Christian Ministries Mgmt. Assn., Speech Communication Assn., Ind. Assn. Women Deans and Adminstrs. (exec. com. 1986—), Career Women's Council (pres. 1986), Oriental Missionary Soc. Internat. (exec. com., trustee 1986—), Religious Speech Communications (past holder nat. offices). Republican. Methodist. Home: 802 W South St Upland IN 46989 Office: Taylor U Office Assoc VP Reade Ave Upland IN 46989

CROUSE, LINDSAY, actress; b. N.Y.C., May 12, 1948; d. Russel and Anna (Erskine) C.; m. David Mamet, Dec. 21, 1977. BA, Radcliffe Coll., 1970. Films include: Slapshot, Between-the-Lines, All the President's Men, Prince of the City, The Verdict, Daniel, Iceman, Places in the Heart (Acad. award nomination 1985), House of Games; author: (with David Mamet) The Owl, 1987. Recipient Village Voice Obie award for Acting in Reunion, 1980. Mem. Circle Repertory Co., Atlantic Theater Co. (bd. dirs. 1984—).

CROUTER, VORIS MARGARET, accountant, consultant; b. Detroit, Nov. 16, 1938; d. William Henry and Voris Marcella (Murphy) Cassel; m. Ronnie Lee Farmer, June 1, 1957 (div. 1968); 1 child, Ronald; m. Richard Van Crouter, Nov. 29, 1969. BS in Bus. Adminstrn., Calif. State U., San Bernardino, 1982. Chief bookkeeper Atlas Fed. Savs. & Loan, Pasadena, Calif., 1960-63; office mgr. J.L.L. Inc., Corona, Calif., 1967-69; staff corp. acct. Royal Inns of Am., Inc., San Diego, 1970-74; acct. Hauer Steel Co., San Bernardino, 1976-78; pres. Attg. Services, Joshua Tree, Calif., 1980—. Bd. govs., v.p. publicity chair Hi-Desert Med. Found., Joshua Tree, 1984-88; v.p. chmn. allocations Morongo Basin United Way, Joshua Tree, 1987-88. Mem. Am. Bus. Womens Assn. (v.p. nat. dist. VI 1986-87, Woman of Yr. El Cajon chpt. 1975, Woman of Yr. Apple Valley chpt. 1982, Bus. Assoc. of Yr. Apple Valley chpt. 1988), C. of C. Morongo Basin (gen. chmn. 1987), Nat. Assn. Parliamentarians, Calif. Assn. Parliamentarians. Democrat. Presbyterian. Club: Emblem (29 Palms, Calif.); Hearts of Yucca Valley.

CROVITZ, ELAINE SANDRA, clinical psychologist; b. N.Y.C., Oct. 18, 1936; d. Sydney and Jennie (Papier) Kobrin; children—Gordon, Deborah, Sara Pi. B.A., Bklyn. Coll., 1956; M.A., Duke U., 1960, Ph.D., 1964. Instr. med. psychology, staff psychologist Duke U. Med. Center, Durham, N.C., 1963-64, assoc. med. psychology, supervising psychologist, 1964-67, asst. prof. med. psychology, 1967-75, assoc. prof., 1975—; bd. dirs. Maferr Found., N.Y.C.; vis. assoc. prof. N.C. Cen. U., Durham, 1976-79. Mem. Am. Psychol. Assn., Southeastern Psychol. Assn., N.C. Psychol. Assn., Assn. for Advancement Psychology, Internat. Council Psychologists, Internat. Assn. Applied Psychology, Nat. Register Health Service Providers Psychology, AAUW. Author: (with Elizabeth Buford) Courage Knows No Sex, 1978; author research papers; contbr. articles to profl. jours. Home: 2745 Montgomery St Durham NC 27705 Office: Duke U Med Ctr PO Box 3895 Durham NC 27710

CROW, CECILE MARIE, sales executive; b. Wichita Falls, Tex., Apr. 21, 1938; d. Edward Patrick and Frances Beatrice (Bruckner) Hopkins. BS in Psychology, North Tex. U., 1971, MS in Social Sci., 1972; postgrad., Columbia U., 1980. Tchr. Eastfield Coll., Dallas, 1972-73; rep. sales Am. Can Co., Dallas, 1973-75; exec. nat. accounts Am. Can Co., Miami, 1975-77; mgr. dist. sales Am. Can Co., Boston, 1977-78; mgr. foodservice mktg. develop. Am. Can Co., Greenwich, Conn., 1978-81; dir. sales devel. James River Corp., Norwalk, Conn., 1981-87; dir. nat. accounts James River Corp., Norwalk, 1987—. Grantee North Tex. U., 1971. Mem. Internat. Foodservice Mfrs. Assn., Round Table Women Foodservice (bd. dirs. 1986-87). Club: YMCA. Office: James River Corp 800 Conn Ave PO Box 6000 River Park Norwalk CT 06856

CROW, DEBORAH A., business executive; b. Elkins, W.Va., Aug. 23, 1960; d. Edward L. and Carol J. (Stalnaker) C. BA in Music Edn. summa cum laude, Temple U., Phila., 1982. Cert. teacher, N.J. Pa. Interviewer Chilton Research Services, Radnor, Pa., 1979; research assoc. E.L. Crow Inc., Lafayette Hill, Pa., 1979-81; drill designer Father Judge High Sch., Phila., 1979-82; color guard instr. PAL Drum and Bugle Corps, Phila., 1981-82; instrumental music teacher W. Windsor Plainsboro High Sch., Princeton Junction, N.J., 1982-84; framing coordinator Prints 'n Things, Lawrenceville, N.J., 1984-85; pres. DAC-CON, Titusville, N.J., 1985—, Canal Crafts Inc., Lafayette Hill, Pa., 1986—; judge Nat. judges Assoc., N.J., 1983-85. Recipient Citation of Merit N.J. Gen. Assembly, 1984; Presser Found. scholar, Temple U. Pres.' scholar. Mem. Nat. Assoc. Female Execs., Mid Atlantic Craft and Hobby Assoc., Ginnie Thompson Guild. Republican. Methodist. Office: Canal Crafts Inc 4126 Jackson Dr Lafayette Hill PA 19444

CROW, ELIZABETH SMITH, publishing executive; b. N.Y.C., July 29, 1946; d. Harrison Venture and Marlis (deGreve) Smith; m. Charles P. Crow, Mar. 2, 1974; children: Samuel Harrison, Rachel Venture, Sarah Gibson. B.A., Mills Coll., 1968; postgrad., Brown U., 1969-70. Editorial asst. New Yorker mag., N.Y.C., 1968-69; editorial asst., exec. editor New York mag., N.Y.C., 1970-78; editor-in-chief Parents mag., N.Y.C., 1978-88; freelance book reviewer N.Y. Times Book Rev. and Washington Post Book World; pres. Gruner & Jahr USA Pub., 1988—; v.p. Editors' Organizing Com., 1982—; screener, judge Nat. Mag. Awards, 1984—. Video and software reviewer, Video Rev. mag. Mem. media adv. council March of Dimes; mem. mng. com. Alternative Def. Project; bd. advisors The Giraffe Project; trustee Mills Coll., 1986—. Mem. Am. Soc. Mag. Editors (exec. bd.). Democrat. Club: Cosmopolitan. Office: Gruner & Jahr USA Pub 685 3rd Ave New York NY 10017

CROW, LYNNE CAMPBELL SMITH, insurance company executive; b. Buffalo, Oct. 13, 1942; d. Stephen Smith and Jean Campbell (Ruggles) Hall; m. William David Crow II, Apr. 16, 1966; children: William David III, Alexander Fairbairn, Margaret Campbell. BA, Sweet Briar (Va.) Coll., 1964; student, Am. Coll., 1986. CLU; Chartered Fin. Cons. Claims rep. Liberty Mut. Ins. Co., Bklyn. and N.Y.C., 1964-66; with McGraw-Hill Corp., N.Y.C., 1966-67; claims rep. Liberty Mut. Ins. Co., East Orange, N.J., 1967-68; sales assoc. Realty World/Allsopp Realtors, Millburn, N.J., 1981-82; field rep. Guardian Life Ins. Co., Millburn, 1982—. Bd. dirs. Jr. League of the Oranges and Short Hills, Millburn, 1979-80, Millburn LWV,

1979-80; campaign chair, bus. chair, bd. dirs. United Way of Millburn/Short Hills, 1981-88. Mem. Assn. Chartered Life Underwriters and Chartered Fin. Cons., Newark Assn. Life Underwriters (bd. dirs. 1986—), Women's Life Underwriters Confedn., Jr. League The Oranges and Short Hills. Republican. Episcopalian. Club: Short Hills (N.J.) Racquets (bd. dirs. 1980-82). Home: 22 The Crescent Short Hills NJ 07078 Office: Ferrara Assocs 181 Millburn Ave Millburn NJ 07041

CROWDER, BARBARA LYNN, lawyer; b. Mattoon, Ill., Feb. 3, 1956; d. Robert Dale and Martha Elizabeth (Harrison) C.; m. Lawrence Owen Taliana, Apr. 17, 1982; children: Paul Joseph, Robert Lawrence. BA, U. Ill., 1978, JD, 1981. Bar: Ill. 1981. Assoc., Louis E. Olivero, Peru, Ill., 1981-82; asst. state's atty. Madison County, Edwardsville, Ill., 1982-84; ptnr. Robbins & Crowder, Edwardsville, 1985-87; ptnr. Robbins, Crowder & Bader, Edwardsville, 1987—. Chmn. City of Edwardsville Zoning Bd. Appeals, 1986-87; com. mem. Edwardsville Dem. Precinct 15, 1986—; mem. City of Edwardsville Planning Commn., 1985-87. Named Best Oral Advocate, Moot Ct. Bd., 1979, Outstanding Sr., Phi Alpha Delta, 1981, Young Career Woman, Dist. XIV. Ill. Bus. and Profl. Women, 1986; recipient Parliamentary Debate award U. Ill., 1978, Alice Paul award Alton-Edwardsville NOW, 1987, Jr. Service award Edwardsville Bus. and Profl. Women, 1987. Mem. ABA, Ill. Bar Assn., Assn. Trial Lawyers Am., Phi Alpha Delta, Women Lawyers Assn. Met. East (v.p. 1985, pres. 1986), LWV, Edwardsville Bus. and Profl. Women (Woman of Achievement 1985, Jr. Service award 1987). Democrat. Home: 982 Surrey Dr Edwardsville IL 62025 Office: PO Box 451 Edwardsville IL 62025

CROWDER, JEAN CHRISTOPHER, social services administrator; b. Chgo., Aug. 19, 1950; d. Alonzo James and Mary Magdalena (Shern) C.; m. Pensacola Frye Jr., July 13, 1967 (div. Apr. 1979); children: D'Arcy Christopher Frye, Eric Patrick Frye. BS, Chgo. State U., 1977; postgrad., Ill. Inst. Tech., 1987. Pricer Allied Radio, Chgo., 1967-68; typist Travelers Ins. Co., Chgo., 1968-69; corr. Ency. Brittanica, Chgo., 1969-73; clk., typist Juvenile Detention Ctr., Chgo., 1973-77, caseworker II, 1977-79, caseworker III, 1979—. Bd. dirs., election bd., personnel bd., health com. Carole Robertson Ctr. Learning, Chgo., 1976-81; active Oak Park (Ill.) Youth Township Com., 1987—. Mem. Nat. Assn. Negro Bus. and Profl. Women's Clubs, Inc. (2d v.p. 1986-88, corr. sec. 1984-86), Nat. Assn. Female Execs., League Black Women. Democrat. Baptist. Home: 935 N Humphrey Oak Park IL 60302

CROWDER, MARY ANN, nurse; b. Buckhannon, W.V., July 11, 1961; d. Robert Charles and Arlene Anita (Hinterer) Pope; m. Franklin Delano Crowder Jr., July 24, 1982; 1 child, Laura Ann. BS in Nursing, U. W.V., 1984. RN. Nurse 1984-86; asst. nurse mgr. U. W.V. Hosp., Morgantown, 1986—. Hospice vol. Morgantown, 1984—. Republican. Roman Catholic. Home: 441 Harding Ave Morgantown WV 26505 Office: U WV Hosp Sta 52 Med Ctr Dr Morgantown WV 26506

CROWE, KITTY, data processing executive; b. Erie, Pa., Mar. 15, 1948; d. Anthony Andrew and Dorothy Mae (Merschrod) Onisko; m. Martin H. Crowe, Nov. 23, 1966; children: Remlee Meredith, Amber Melody. AS in Edn., W.Va. State Coll., 1976. Instr. fgn. lang. Loop Jr. Coll., Chgo., 1970-71; with dept. credit and collections Nat. Homes Corp., Lafayette, Ind., 1972-74; agt. real estate Estill & Greenlee, Charleston, W.Va., 1975-77; dir. field sales devel. program Digital Equipment Corp., Boylston, Mass., 1977-79, specialist logistics, 1979-81; v.p. ops. Performance Inc., Stow, Mass., 1981—. Advisor: Stop the Phone Invasion publ., 1986. Mem. Boylston Hist. Soc. (coms. bicentennial events, trainer personnel).

CROWELL, CAROL ANN, editor; b. St. Petersburg, Fla., Aug. 19, 1958; d. John Richard and Dolores (Pavick) C. BA in English, Western Carolina U., 1980, MA in English, 1982. Graduate asst. Western Carolina U., Cullowhee, N.C., 1980-82; editorial asst. Creative Computing Ziff-Davis, N.Y.C., 1984-85; assoc. editor Yourdon Press, N.Y.C., 1985-86; editor production Simon and Schuster Brady Books, N.Y.C., 1986-87; managing editor Software Div. Simon and Schuster, N.Y.C., 1987—. Contbr. articles to jours. Mem. Women's Nat. Book Assn. Office: Simon and Schuster 1 Gulf and Western Plaza New York NY 10023

CROWELL, NANCY MELZER, investment banker; b. Evanston, Ill., Oct. 29, 1948; d. Clifford Nicholas and Grace (Meier) Melzer; m. George Henry Crowell III, May 6, 1972; children: George Andrew, John Alexander, Thomas Courtney. BA, Wellesley Coll., 1970; MBA, U. Calif., Berkeley, 1979. Research analyst Merrill Lynch, Toronto, Ont., Can., 1973-75; credit analyst Citibank, San Francisco, 1975-77; research analyst Rosenberg Capital Mgmt., San Francisco, 1977-78; investment banker Dean Witter Reynolds Inc., San Francisco, 1979-87, Eberstadt Fleming Pacific Inc., San Francisco, 1987—.

CROWL, MARTHA JEAN, nurse; b. Cleve., June 13, 1941; d. Thomas Laird and Bernice (Pugh) C. Diploma in Nursing, M.B. Johnson Sch. Nursing, Elyria, Ohio, 1962; postgrad., Baldwin Wallace Coll., Berea, Ohio, Cuyahoga Community Coll., Parma, Ohio. RN, Ohio, Mass., N.C. Asst. head nurse, instr. Lakewood (Ohio) Hosp., 1963-71; operating room edn. dir. Fairview Gen. Hosp., Cleve., 1971-76; operating room supr. Luth. Hosp., Cleve., 1976-80; assoc. dir. surgery services Moore Meml. Hosp., Pinehurst, N.C., 1981-83; asst. dir. nursing Community Med. Ctr., Marion, Ohio, 1983-84; adminstr. and project coordinator Dr. John Marquardt Eye Clinic, Mansfield, Ohio, 1984-85; nat. quality assurance dir. MediVision, Inc., Boston, 1985-86; nurse cons., quality assurance dir. Carolina Eye Assocs., Southern Pines, N.C., 1981-88; corp. quality risk mgr. Eye Am., N.C. and Va., 1988—; surgical asst. adv. bd. Cuyahoga Community Coll., 1967-72; dir. operating room tech. program Fairview Gen. Hosp., 1971-76; faculty mem. Ambulatory Surgical Ctr. lecture series Carolina Eye Assocs., 1983-85; chairperson Sandhills Multi-Inst. Rev. Bd.; lectr. in field. Contbr. articles to profl. jours. Mem. Cleve. Orch. Womens Com., 1976-81; 1983; exec. bd. Great Lakes Festival Women's Com., 1976-81; bd. dirs. Health Fair, Marion, 1983. Mem. Assn. Operating Room Nurses, Assn. Opthalmic RNs, Am. Assn. Allied Health Personnel in Opthalmology, We. Res. Hist. Soc., Am. Soc. Health Care Risk Mgmt., Nat. Assn. Quality Assurance Profls., Am. Soc. Risk Mgmt. Democrat. Office: Eye Am 20 Page Rd PO Box 250 Pinehurst NC 28374

CROWLEY, ELIZABETH MARLENE, management consultant; b. LeCenter, Minn., Dec. 30, 1940; d. Roman Aloysius and Elizabeth Winifred (Cummings) Malinski; m. John Patrick Crowley, Aug. 3, 1963; children: Elizabeth J., John S., Ann B. BS in English, History, Mankato State U., 1960; MS in Orgn. Devel., U. Wis., Green Bay, 1985. English instr. various schs., Minn., Calif., Wis., 1960-69; communications instr. Northeast Wis. Tech. Coll., Green Bay, 1973-74, human resources devel. cons., coordinator, 1974-83; pres. Human Resources Devel. Cons., Green Bay, 1979-83; exec. dir. Fin. Mgmt. Concepts, Green Bay, 1983-85; asst. to pres. Univ. Bank, Green Bay, 1983-85; pres. Crowley, Lautenbach & Assocs., Green Bay, 1985—. Contbr. articles to profl. jours. Dir. Brown County Hist. Soc., Green Bay, 1978-85, YMCA, Green Bay, 1978. Mem. Assn. Mgmt. Cons. (v.p. 1987—), Am. Assn. Univ. Women (v.p. 1969-83), Am. Soc. Tng. and Devel., Ind. Bus. Assn. Wis. Roman Catholic. Office: Crowley Lautenbach & Assocs PO Box 24032 Green Bay WI 54324-4032

CROWLEY, NEELY DOWALL, broadcasting executive; b. Abington, Pa., Mar. 10, 1950; d. Robertson L. and Martha (Groome) Dowall; m. Michael E. Crowley, May 10, 1975; children: Kate Elizabeth, Megan Lynn. Student, High Point Coll., 1968-71. Field rep. Zeta Tau Alpha Nat. Frat., Indpls., 1972-74; account exec. Sta. WFPG/WIIN-Radio, Atlantic City, 1974-80; pres., SMC Inc., serving as gen. mgr. Sta. WSLT/WIBG-Radio, Ocean City, N.J., 1980—; pub. The Sun Newspaper, Ocean City, 1980—. Chairperson Ocean City Tourism Devel. Commn., 1983—, Families for Freedom of Choice, Ocean City, 1986; mem. N.J. Gov.'s Mgmt. Improvement Study Program, 1984; bd. dirs. Ocean City Task Force on Child Care, 1984—; youth coach Ocean City Recreation Dept., 1985—. Recipient Cert. of Merit, 1975, Honor Ring, 1976 Zeta Tau Alpha, Media award N.J. Foster Parents Assn., 1986; named among People to Watch in '83 Atlantic City Mag., 1983. Mem. Alliance, The Women's Network (former bd. dirs. Atlantic City), Humane Soc. Ocean City (v.p., bd. dirs. 1986—), Ocean City C. of C. (v.p., bd. dirs. 1987—, named Citizen of Yr. 1988). Office: Sta WSLT/WIBG 957 Asbury Ave Ocean City NJ 08226

CROWN, NANCY ELIZABETH, retail executive; b. Bronx, Mar. 27, 1955; d. Paul and Joanne Barbara (Newman) C.; children: Rebecca, Adam. BA, Barnard Coll., 1977, MA, 1978, MEd, 1983. Cert. tchrs. Tchr. Sachem Sch. Dist., Holbrook, N.Y., 1978-82; dir. mail order dept. Haber-Klein, Inc., Hicksville, N.Y., 1984-86, exec. v.p., corp. sec., 1984—. Mem. Nat. Assn. Female Execs., L.I. Direct Mktg. Assn., Women's Direct Response Group. Democrat. Jewish. Club: Barnard of L.I. Office: Haber-Klein Inc 376 Old Country Rd Hicksville NY 11801

CROWN, ROBERTA, artist, educator; b. N.Y.C., Sept. 9, 1946; d. Louis and Sophia (Siegal) C. B.A., Queens Coll., M.A., 1970. Art tchr. N.Y. Bd. Edn., N.Y.C., 1969—. Group shows include: Air Naval Res. Show (1st prize oils, 3d prize watercolors), 1969, East Meadow Outdoor Show, N.Y.C., 1970, Aorta, East Hampton, N.Y., 1971, United Art Group, N.Y.C., 1976, WIA Gallery, N.Y.C., 1978, 79, 80, Bklyn. Coll. (2d prize oils), 1978, One Hundred Artists Show, N.Y.C., 1979, Picture Show Gallery, N.Y.C., 1979, Contemporary Arts Ctr., 1980, Fed. S.I. Artists, Lever House, N.Y.C., 1980, Fine Arts Gallery Ocean County Coll., 1980, Panassus Gallery, Woodstock, N.Y., 1980, Gallery 14, Copenhagen, 1980, Newhouse Gallery, 1981, Queens Mus., 1981, 84, Off the Wall Show, 1982, Cork Gallery, 1983, 84, 86, 87, Nugent Gallery, Marymount Manhattan Coll., 1983, 84, Garcia Gallery, Bronx, N.Y., 1983, City Gallery, N.Y.C., 1984, Franklin Furnace, N.Y.C., 1984, Lehigh U., Bethlehem, Pa., 1984, Chgo. Gallery, U. Ill., 1984, Tokyo Met. Mus., 1984, Arsenal Gallery, 1984, 86, Art and Design High Sch., N.Y.C., 1985, Janco-Dada Mus., Ein-Hod, Israel, 1985, Passaic Community Coll., Patterson, N.J., 1986, Todd Capp Gallery, N.Y.C., 1986, Castillo Gallery, N.Y.C., 1987, WRIC Ctr., 1987, Appalachian State U., Boone, N.C., 1988, Transco Energy Gallery, Houston, 1988; one-woman shows include: Harbor Sq., Washington, 1970, Andalusia Arts, Inc. Gallery, N.Y.C., 1974, Women's Sudio Workshop Gallery, Rosendale, N.Y., 1988, others. Mem. Women in the Arts Found., Inc. (exec. coordinator 1980—), Women Caucus in Art, N.Y. State Assn. Tchrs. Art.

CROWNINGSHIELD, SHARON KAY, savings and loan executive; b. Cedar Rapids, Iowa, Dec. 1, 1948; d. Marvin John Henry and Maxine Harriet (Barlow) Rathje; student in acctg. Mesa Jr. Coll., 1974-75; m. Gary Crowningshield, Sept. 9, 1967; children—Scott, Vicki. With Home Fed. Savs. & Loan Assn., San Diego, 1968—, mgr., 1974—, v.p., 1980—, asst. controller, 1980 83, mem. polit. action coms. for fed. and state, 1980—. Mem. Fin. Mgrs. Soc. for Savs. and Loan Assn. (chpt. pres. 1985-86). Office: 5565 Morehouse Dr San Diego CA 92121

CROWTHER, JEAN DECKER, publishing executive, designer; b. Mesa, Ariz., Jan. 10, 1937; d. J. Smith and Helen (Ellsworth) Decker; m. Duane Swofford Crowther, Mar. 21, 1958; children: Don, Scott, Laura, Lisa, David, William, Sharon, Bethany. BS, Brigham Young U., 1959. Clerk Milano Music Store, Mesa, 1952-57; reserve librarian and clerk Brigham Young U. Library, Provo, Utah, 1956-60; co-owner and clerk Logan (Utah) Music and Book Co., 1961-66; mgr. shipping dept. Horizon Publishers, Bountiful, Utah, 1971-74; mgr. accounts receivable Horizon Publishers, Bountiful, 1971-76, mem. editorial bd., 1978—, div. mgr. specialty div., 1976-84; corp. v.p., bd. dirs., sec. Horizon Publishers & Distributors, Bountiful, 1981—, creative designer, 1984—. Author: Growing Up in the Church, The Joy of Being a Woman, Book of Mormon Puzzles and Pictures, A Mother's Prayer, What Do I Do Now, Mom?, Pedigree Patterns, Jesus and the Children, A Savior is Born, Prayer, Jesus of Nazareth, The Last Supper, 1987, Murphy Strikes Again, 1987. Holder various offices Hannah Holbrook Elem. Sch. PTA, Bountiful, 1967-85; vice chair Bountiful-Bethlehem Sister City Com., 1986—. Mem. Hobby Industries Am., The Nat. Needlework Assn., Christian Booksellers Assn., Latter-day Saint Booksellers Assn. Republican. Office: Horizon Pubs & Distbrs 50 S 500 W Bountiful UT 84010

CROXFORD, LYNNE LOUISE, social services adminstr.; b. Schenectady, N.Y., Nov. 9, 1947; d. Frederick William and Elizabeth Elger (Irish) C.; B.A., Kalamazoo Coll., 1969; M.P.A., Wayne State U., 1975; m. Daniel Roderick Talhelm; 2 children, Alan Frederick, Thomas Arthur. Caseworker dept. social service County of Calhoun, Battle Creek, Mich., 1969-70; caseworker, supr. County of Oakland, Pontiac, Mich., 1970-76; program specialist Mich. Dept. Social Services, Lansing, 1976-78; exec. coordinator for programming Mich. State Planning Council for Devel. Disabilities, 1978-79; staff coordinator Gov. Com. on Unification of Public Mental Health System, Lansing, 1979-80; dir. dept. social service County of Ingham, Lansing, 1980—; adv. Mich. Assn. Non-Profit Residential Facilities, 1976-78. Trustee, Unitarian Universalist Ch. of Greater Lansing, 1979-82, v.p., 1980-82; bd. dirs. Council for Prevention Child Abuse and Neglect, 1980-83; mem. Lansing Tri-County Pvt. Industry Council, 1980—. Mem. Am. Soc. Public Adminstrn. (nat. council 1986—), Am. Pub. Welfare Assn., Michigan County Social Services Assn. Club: Zonta (charter Mich. Capitol area). Contbr. in field. Home: 531 Gainsborough Dr East Lansing MI 48823 Office: 5303 S Cedar St Lansing MI 48910

CROYLE, BARBARA ANN, management consultant; b. Knoxville, Tenn., Oct. 22, 1949; d. Charles Evans and Myrtle Elizabeth (Kellam) C. BA cum laude in Sociology, Coll. William and Mary, 1971; cert. corp. tax and securities law Inst. Paralegal Tng., 1971; JD, U. Colo., 1975; cert. program mgmt. devel. Colo. Women's Coll., 1980; MBA, U. Denver, 1983. Bar: Colo. 1976. Paralegal firm Holland & Hart, Denver, 1972-73; law clk. Colo. Ct. Appeals, Denver, summer 1976; assoc. firm Shaw Spangler & Roth, Denver, 1976-77; mgr. acquisitions/lands Petro-Lewis Corp., Denver, 1977-85; mgr. strategic planning Westinghouse, Transp. Div., 1985-87; sr. mgmt. cons. Benefit Resource Mgmt. Co. (subs. Blue Cross We. Pa.), 1987—; tchr. oil and gas law Colo. Paralegal Inst., 1978, 79; arbitrator Am. Arbitration Assn.; vol. arbitrator Better Bus. Bur. Bd. dirs., vol. mediator Denver Center Dispute Resolution; bd. dirs. Women and Bus. Enterprises, Inc.; vol. Legal Info. Center, YWCA-Colo. Women's Bar. Mem. ABA, Pa. Bar Assn., Nat. Assn. Female Execs, Am. Mgmt. Assn., Soc. Profls. in Dispute Resolution. Home: 5611 Howe St Pittsburgh PA 15232 Office: Foster Plaza Bldg 8 Pittsburgh PA 15220

CROZIER, PRUDENCE SLITOR, economist; b. Boston, Oct. 27, 1940; d. Richard Eaton and Louise (Bean) S.; m. William Marshall Crozier, Jr., June 20, 1964; children—Matthew Eaton, Abigail Parsons, Patience Wells. B.A. with honors, Wellesley Coll., 1962; M.A. in Econs., Yale U., 1963; Ph.D. in Econs., Harvard U., 1971. Research asst. Fed. Reserve Bank, Boston, 1963-64; teaching fellow-tutor Harvard U., Cambridge, Mass., 1966-69; instr. Wellesley Coll., Mass., 1969-70; sr. economist Data Resources Inc., Lexington, Mass., 1973-74; bd. dirs. Mass. Health and Ednl. Facilities Authority, 1985—, Omega Fund, 1984-87. Contbr. article to profl. jour. Trustee Newton Wellesley Hosp., Mass., 1978—; overseer Center Research on Women, Wellesley, 1982-83; trustee Wellesley Coll., 1980—. Mem. Am. Econ. Assn., Boston Econ. Club, Phi Beta Kappa. Home: 41 Ridge Hill Farm Rd Wellesley MA 02181

CRUICKSHANK, SHEILA ETHEL, farmer; b. Ilford, Essex, Eng., June 26, 1937; came to U.S., 1956; d. Lesley Edward Richard and Ethel Maud (Davage) Bradley; m. Alfred William Cruickshank, May 26, 1956 (dec. 1984); children: Carol Ann Cruickshank Hoffman, William Alfred. Student, St. Mary's Convent, South Woodford, Essex. Bookkeeper Swiss Travel Service, London, 1954-56; co-owner Al Cruickshank Farming, Woodland, Calif., 1964-84; owner Cruickshank Farms, Woodland, 1984—. Coordinator, tchr. religious edn. St. Paul's Parish, Knights Landing, Calif., 1985—, pres. Altar Soc., 1986—. Democrat. Roman Catholic. Clubs: Priscilla (pres. 1978-79), Yolo Thursday (pres. 1978-79).

CRUM, KATHERINE BISHOP, art gallery director; b. Palo Alto, Calif., Dec. 10, 1941; d. Frank Crowell Bishop and Jane Verne (Greenwood) Gunn; m. David Morris Crum, May 3, 1969. BA in English, Stanford U., 1962, MA in Hispanic, American Studies, 1964; MA in Art History, CUNY, 1972; PhD in Art History, Columbia U., 1984. Owner, art dealer Nicholas Wilder Gallery, Los Angeles, 1964-69; dir. Glassboro (N.J.) State Coll. Gallery, 1972-73; dep. dir., curator of exhibitions Inst. for Research in History, N.Y.C., 1980-83; dir. Baruch Coll. Gallery CUNY, 1983—; bd. dirs. Inst. Research History, 1985—. Author: Figural Art of the New York School (catalogue); editor: World View of Art History. Vestry mem. Grace Ch., N.Y.C., 1977-83. Fellow Inst. Research History. Democrat. Episcopalian. Office: Baruch Coll Gallery 135 E 22d St New York NY 10010

CRUMB, JEANMARIE LARSON, educational administrator; b. Fairbanks, Alaska, June 21, 1945; d. Albert Elmer and Alice Elizabeth (Gurtler) Larson; m. Lewis F. Crumb, Jan. 21, 1978 (div. May 1986). BA, U. Alaska, 1968; EdM, Harvard U., 1975. cert. secondary educator, superintendant, Alaska. Statewide coordinator edn. program Alaska Fedn. Natives, Anchorage, 1971-72; project asst. Alaska State Operated Schs., Anchorage, 1972-74; pres., exec. dir. Cook Inlet Native Assn., Anchorage, 1975-77; field services coordinator Alaska Native Found., Anchorage, 1978; curriculum devel. specialist Anchorage Sch. Dist., 1975, dir. community relations, 1979-85, spl. asst. to supt. for community relations, 1985—; instr. U. Alaska, Anchorage, 1975; cons. Larson & March Cons. Assocs., Anchorage, 1980-82, Crumb/Sappier Cons., Anchorage, 1987; bd. dirs. Alaska Children's Services, Anchorage, 1986—; chmn. Native Adv. Com. 1973-74. Editor Anchorage Sch. Dist. Parent Handbook, 1982. Pres. Alaska State Council for Career and Vocat. Edn., Juneau, 1982-83. Mem. Alaska Native Edn. Assn. (pres. 1985-87, treas. 1987-88), Nat. Sch. Pub. relations Assn. (hon. mention 1982). Office: Anchorage Sch Dist 4600 Debarr Ave Anchorage AK 99504

CRUMBO, MINISA, artist; b. Tulsa, Sept. 2, 1942; d. Woodrow and Lillian (Hogue) C.; student Tex. Western U., El Paso, 1961-62, U. Colo., Boulder, 1970-71, Taos (N.Mex.) Acad. Fine Arts, 1972-74, Sch. Visual Arts, N.Y.C., 1974-75, Wasatch (Utah) Acad.; children—Woody Carter, Cris Carter. One-woman shows: Gilcrease Inst. Am. History and Art, Tulsa, 1976, Tulsey Town Gallery, Tulsa, 1975, USSR, 1978-79, Roy Clark Ranch Party-TV Spl., 1976, Pottawatomie Agrl. and Cultural Center, Shawnee, Okla., 1977, Okla. Gov.'s Spl. Showing, 1976, Adobe Gallery, Las Vegas, 1977; traveling exhbn. Indian Art Show, U. Oreg., 1977; other exhbns.; Pushkin Mus., Moscow, Montreux (Switzerland) Jazz Festival, 1979, Harwelden, Tulsa, 1979, Oklahoma City U., 1981, Independence (Kans.) Community Coll., 1981, Native Am. Women in Art, Kans. Mus. History, 1984, Native Am. Women Show, Indian Ter. Gallery, Sapulpa, Okla., 1985, Exhbn. Mus. Ethnography, Budapest, Hungary, 1988; represented in permanent collections at Heard Mus., Phoenix, Gilcrease Inst. Am. History and Art, Philbrook Art Center, Tulsa, U. Tulsa Art Center, Pushkin Mus., Moscow, Wasatch Acad., Oklahoma City U., Baker U., Baldwin, Kans., Independence (Kans.) Community Coll., also pvt. collections in U.S. and Europe; guest artist instr. Taos Pueblo Day Sch. Center; designer, instr. Native Am. Studies program Wasatch Acad., Utah. Recipient Graphics award for pencil drawing Creek Woman, 29th Am. Indian Exhbn. at Philbrook Art Center; Disting. Alumni award Wasatch Acad., 1980; Disting. Service award Baker U., 1982. Home: 17351 Sunset Blvd #403 Pacific Palisades CA 90272-4198 Office: PO Box 4003 Beverly Hills CA 90213

CRUME, NANCY ANN, account supervisor; b. Dallas, July 1, 1960; d. Albert Theodore and Shirley (Cleveland) Nemecek; m. Carter Lynn Crume, Sept. 21, 1985. BA cum laude, U. North Tex., 1982. Account coordinator Moeller/Baker Co., Dallas, 1981-82; account exec. Rosenberg & Co. Advt., Dallas, 1982-84; account supr. Crume/Coker Advt., Dallas, 1984-88. Vol. youth counselor, parent/adolescent mediator Urban Services Casa De Los Amigos, Dallas, 1984—; chair Lakewood/Hollywood Heights Neighborhood Dist., Dallas, 1987—; vol. tchr., adminstrv. bd. Highland Park United Meth. Ch., Dallas, 1985—; speaker devel. exchange Nat. Pub. Radio, Dallas, 1987. Mem. Bus. Profl. Advt. Assn., Alpha Delta Pi. Methodist. Office: McCann-Ericksont 10860 N Central Expressway Dallas TX 75231

CRUMP, JANICE ELLIOTT, librarian; b. Albert, Okla., May 25, 1932; d. Jewel Homer and Goldie Mae (Hamilton) Elliott; m. Kenneth E. Crump Sr., Nov. 26, 1952; children: Kenneth E. Jr., Kathy Lynn. BA, U. Okla., 1953; student, Okla. U., Norman, 1969-70; MEd, SW Okla. State U., 1973. Cert. secondary tchr., library sci. Minister's sec. First Presbyn. Ch., Chickasha, Okla., 1953-55; clk. typist U.S. Army, Ft. Sill, Okla., 1956-58; social worker Dept. of Human Services, Chickasha, 1963-67; tchr. Apache (Okla.) Pub. Schs., 1968-70, sch. librarian, 1970-80; tchr. Chickasha Jr. High Sch., 1980-84; librarian Chickasha Mid. Sch., 1984—. Mem. First Presbyn. Ch. choir, Chickasha, 1963-67, 80—; mem. Jr. Social Workers, Chickasha, 1965-67; mem. Long Range Sch. Improvement Task Force, Chickasha, 1984-85. Mem. NEA, Okla. Edn. Assn., Apache Edn. Assn. (sec. 1970-72), Chickasha United Tchrs. Assn. (bldg. rep. 1982-84), ALA, Okla. Library Assn. Democrat. Home: 23 Dusky Valley Ln Chickasha OK 73018 Office: Chickasha Mid Sch 1000 S 9th Chickasha OK 73018

CRUMP, JOCELYN VENECIA, air force officer; b. Montgomery, Ala., Aug. 16, 1962; d. James Cecil Jr. and Thelma Venecia (Pickett) C. BA, Howard U., 1984. Cert. Laubach tutor for illiterate adults. Commd. 1st lt. USAF, 1984; dep. dir. pub. affairs 314th tactical airlift wing USAF, Jacksonville, Ark., 1984—. Mem. Air Force Assn., Nat. Assn. Female Execs., Pub. Relations Soc. Am., Airstreamers Internat. Tng. in Communication Assn. (2d v.p., 1986-87, pres. 1987-88), Delta Sigma Theta (Outstanding Young Woman award 1988). Democrat. Home: 1900 Oakwood Dr Apt 160 Jacksonville AR 72076 Office: USAF Pub Affairs Div 314th Tactical Wing Little Rock AFB AR 72099-3602

CRUMPTON, SANDRA ANN, financial services company executive; b. Greenville, S.C., Oct. 12, 1945; d. James Albert and Elizabeth Mae (Surett) C. BA, Mich. State U., 1968; postgrad. U. Calif.-Berkeley, 1976-77, Am. U., 1972-74. Cert. tchr., Mich., Calif.; cert. adminstr., Calif. Tchr., Okemos (Mich.) Pub. Schs., 1968-70, Crete (Ill.) Pub. Schs., 1970-72; master tchr. Am. Community Sch., Athens, Greece, 1972-74; bus. dir. Crested Butte, Colo., 1974-76; mktg. rep. data processing div. IBM, San Francisco, 1977-80; dir. customer support Walker Interactive Products, San Francisco, 1980-85; v.p. prodn. ops. SEI Corp., Chgo., 1985—; Mem. Am. Mgmt. Assn., Nat. Assn. Female Execs., Women in Bus., AAUW, Women's Exec. Network, Chgo. Council on Fgn. Relations, Alliance Française. Republican. Clubs: Corp. Connections Exec., Execs. of Chgo. Office: 2 N Riverside Plaza Suite 500 Chicago IL 60606

CRUTCHER, DIANE MARIE, social services organization executive; b. Canton, Ill., Aug. 28, 1948; m. C. William Crutcher, Aug. 31, 1968; children: Amie Carol, Mindie Lea. BS in Psychology, Ill. State U., 1985, postgrad., 1986—. Co-founder Cen. Ill. Down Syndrome Orgn., Normal, 1973—; exec. dir. Nat. Down Syndrome Congress, Park Ridge, Ill.; Coordinator Nat. Down Syndrome Congress Convs., 1977—; co-chair First Internat. Down Syndrome Conv., 1980-81, Second Internat. Down Syndrome Conv., 1982-83; prin. investigator Down Syndrome State-of-the-Art Conf., 1985; mem. Infant Doe Com., 1982—; mem. nat. adv. com. Am. Acad. Pediatrics, 1984—; mem. pres.'s com. on handicapped Sub. on Employment of Mentally Retarded, 1985—, Gov.'s Council Rehab. Services, 1987—; numerous other coms. on down syndrome and child mental behavior; lectr. in field; speaker numerous confs. Co-editor New Perspectives on Down Syndrome, 1986; contbr. articles to profl. jours. Mem. Parent/Prefl. Liaison Com., Unit 5 Sch. Dist., Normal, 1986—; mem. Least Restrictive Environ. Task Force, 1986; mem. Regulations Task Force, 1986. Named Career Woman of Yr., Bloomington-Normal, Ill., 1983. Mem. Am. Assn. Mental Deficiency (chair steering com. 1981-83), Ill. Alliance Exceptional Children, Cen. Ill. Down Syndrome Orgn., Down Syndrome Spl. Interest Group (chair steering com.), Nat. Down Syndrome Congress. Home: 1310 Heritage Rd E Normal IL 61761 Office: Nat Down Syndrome Congress 1800 Dempster St Park Ridge IL 60068-1146

CRUZ, KATHLEEN COYLE, rehabilitation administrator, consultant; b. Bklyn., Nov. 12, 1944; d. Owen Thomas and Helen (Stotz) Coyle; m. Manolo S. Cruz, Mar. 12, 1972; 1 child, James M. A in Advt., Bklyn. Coll., 1963, BA in Sociology, 1967; MEd in Rehab. Counseling, NYU, 1969; diploma, N.Y. Inst. Photography, 1980. Cert. master therapeutic recreation specialist. Dir. recreation Shore View Nursing Home, Bklyn., 1970-73, Waring Nursing Home, Bronx, 1973-75; cons. 13 hosps. N.Y.C., 1975-78; dir. leisure services Valley Psychiat. Hosp., Chattanooga, Tenn., 1978-84; dir. adult program Signal Ctr., 1984—; cons. A&D programs Suma Corp., Hixson, Tenn., 1987—; pres., founder Nursing Home Recreation Assn. Bklyn., 1972. Author: Wellness. Sec., Tenn. Govs. Com. on Employment of Handicapped, 1987-88; mem. Venture Task Force on Disabled, 1987—.

Recipient 2d Place Photography award N.Y. Inst., 1960. Mem. Nat. Therapeutic Recreation Soc., Am. Soc. Trainers and Developers, Nat. Assn. Female Execs. Home: 6265 Fairview Rd Hixson TN 37343

CSERNOVICZ, BARBARA ANN, personnel administrator; b. Chgo., Mar. 8, 1933; d. Clarence and Elsa (Jamison) Gump; m. Lajos Csernovicz, 1964 (div. 1981); children: Lynda, Michael. BA, MacMurray Coll., 1954; MSIR, Loyola U., 1983. Office mgr. Am. Arbitration Assn., Chgo., 1978-81; with personnel dept. City Colls., Chgo., 1981-82; with retirement office Loyola U., Chgo., 1982-83; personnel asst. David Berg, Chgo., 1983-84; asst. personnel mgr. Guernsey Dell Co., Chgo., 1984-85; personnel mgr. Service Plastics, Elk Grove Village, Ill., 1986—. Mem. Friends of Lincoln Park, Chgo., 1986—; bd. dirs. Francis W. Parker Sch. Alumni, 1979—. Mem. Indsl. Relations Assn. (treas. 1986-87). Club: Taurino de Chgo. (newsletter editor 1984—).

CUADRA, DOROTHY ELIZABETH, lawyer; b. Washington County, Kans., Dec. 5, 1932; d. Gilbert H. and Nan Ellen (Smith) Stanbrough; m. Emilio L. Cuadra, 1957 (div. Mar. 1965); 1 child, Dione Catherine. BS in Engring., UCLA, 1959, MS in Engring., 1965; JD, U. Va., 1977. Bar: Alaska, Va., D.C. Research engr. The Marquardt Corp., Van Nuys, Calif., 1959-63, The Boeing Co., Seattle, 1965-66; sr. research engr., cons. Wyle Labs., El Segundo, Calif., 1966-71; dep. program devel. office of noise control U.S. EPA, Washington, 1971-74; assoc. Robertson, Monagle & Eastaugh P.C., Juneau, Alaska, 1977—, also bd. dirs., mgmt. com. Author numerous poems; contbr. articles on noise control to profl. jours. Mem. assembly science and tech. adv. council Calif. Legislature, 1970, science adv. com. Alaska Eskimo Whaling Commn., 1980-82; pres. League Women Voters Juneau, 1981-82; bd. dirs. League Women Voters Alaska, 1984. Amelia Earhart Graduate fellow Zonta Internat., 1963-64, 75-76; recipient pub. service commendations Los Angeles City Council, 1971, Calif. Legislature, 1970-71. Mem. ABA (law student div., Silver Key award com. environ. law 1977), Alaska Bar Assn., Acoustical Soc. Am. (Alaska region coordinator 1977—). Democrat. Jewish. Home: 9151 Skywood Ln Juneau AK 99801 Office: Robertson Monagle & Eastaugh PC PO Box 1211 Juneau AK 99802

CUBALCHINI, LINDA SHARON, engineer; b. Chgo., Dec. 4, 1956; d. Richard and Virginia Catherine (Rigoni) C. BS in Zoology, Western Ill. U., 1978. Cert. quality engr., Ill.; cert. reliability engr., Ill. Lab. analyst quality control dept. J. L. Prescott Co., South Holland, Ill., 1979-81; packaging technician quality control dept. Econs. Lab., Joliet, Ill., 1981-84; quality engr. corp. quality assurance dept. Viskase Corp., Chgo., 1984—, reliability engr. Mem. Am. Mgmt. Assn., Am. Soc. for Quality Control (publicity chmn. host com. 38th ann. congress 1984, newsletter editor Chgo. sect. 1984—, instr. Ednl. Inst. 1986—, sr. 1987), Nat. Found. for Advancement Women in Careers (west suburban chpt.), Young Irish Fellowship, Joint Civic Com. of Italian-Ams. (young adult div.). Roman Catholic. Office: Viskase Corp 6855 W 65th St Chicago IL 60638

CUDA, LYNNE ROSE, data processing executive; b. Chicago Heights, Ill., June 4, 1951; d. Paul Pasquale and Frances Elverina (Gabriel) DeProsperis; m. James Paul Cuda, Aug. 4, 1973; 1 child, Carla Marie. BS in Advt., U. Ill., 1973; M in Computing Sci., Tex. A&M U., 1978. Programmer, analyst Agy. Records Control, Inc., College Station, Tex., 1978-82; asst. research sci. Tex. Transp. Inst., College Station, 1982-85; programming mgr. Hillcrest Bapt. Med. Ctr., Waco, Tex., 1985-88; systems anayst State of Mont., 1988—; systems analysis cons. Tex. Aeros. Commn., Austin, 1984-85. Mem. Delta Delta Delta. Roman Catholic. Home: 4 Gardner Park Dr Bozeman MT 59715 Office: State Personnel Div Helena MT 59620

CUDLIPP, ALICE VERNER, health care executive; b. Richmond, Va., Nov. 1, 1941; d. Joseph Henry and Mary Irene (Mills) C. BA, Bridgewater (Va.) Coll., 1962; MA, U. Richmond, 1968. Tchr., dept. head Chesterfield (Va.) County Pub. Schs., 1967-71, Nansemond County Pub. Schs., Va., 1962-66; v.p. Smithdeal-Massey Coll., Richmond, 1974-78; instr. J. Sargeant Reynolds Coll., Richmond, 1982-84; asst. to v.p. patient services Columbia Hosp., Milw., 1982-84; pres., chief exec. officer Med. Placement Services Inc., Milw., 1984—; pres. Cons. Resources, Inc., Richmond, 1974-81; gen. ptnr. Courtland Ltd., Richmond, 1981—; pres. chief exec. officer Shafer Rand Assocs., Inc., Glendale, Wis., 1987—; cdir. David A. Linney, Inc., Milwaukee, 1987—; cons. and lectr. in field. Mem. Clovernook Homeowners Assn.; ruling elder North Shore Presbyn. Ch., Shorewood, Wis., 1988—. Named one of Outstanding Young Women of Am., U.S. Jaycees, 1974; DuPont fellow U. Va., 1972. Mem. Columbia Coll. Nursing Alumni Assn. (chmn. 1984-85), Nat. League Nursing, Southeastern Wis. Home Health Assn., Am. Mgmt. Assn., Nat. Assn. for Home Care, Wis. Home Care Orgn., Nat. Assn. Female Execs., Am. Pub. Health Assn., Phi Delta Epsilon, Alpha Psi Omega, Delta Kappa Gamma. Club: YMCA (Brown Deer, Wis.). Office: Med Placement Services Inc 710 N Plankinton Ave Milwaukee WI 53203

CULBERTSON, EVE HOWARD, office epuipment executive; b. Slaton, Tex., Mar. 10, 1940; d. Wallace Master and Catherine Mozell (Fulbright) Howard; m. Dan Ray Culbertson, Feb. 16, 1980. BS, Tex. Tech U., 1962. Sec. Ling and Co., Dallas, 1965-73; underwriter personal lines Royal Ins. Co., Dallas, 1973-83; pres. AMES, Shreveport, La., 1984—. Mem. Assn. Ind. Mailing Equipment Dealers, Shreveport C. of C. Republican. Baptist. Office: AMES 2545 Midway Shreveport LA 71108

CULBERTSON, FRANCES MITCHELL, psychology educator; b. Boston, Jan. 31, 1921; d. David and Goldie (Fishman) Mitchell; m. John Mathew Culbertson, Aug. 27, 1947; children: John David, Joanne, Lyndall, Amy. BS, U. Mich., 1947, MS, 1949, PhD, 1955. Lic. clin. psychologist, Wis. Clin. child psychologist Wis. Diagnostic Ctr., Madison, 1961-65; chief clin. psychologist dept. child psychiatry U. Wis., Madison, 1965-66; resident psychologist NIMH, Berkeley, Calif., 1966-67; psychologist Madison Pub. Schs., 1967-68; prof. psychology U. Wis., Whitewater, 1968—; clin. psychologist Mental Health Assocs., Madison, 1987—; clin. psychologist Counseling and Psychotherapy Assn., Madison, 1982—; clin. hypnotherapy cons. Family Achievement Ctr., Oconomowoc, Wis., 1984—. Author: Voices in International School Psychology, 1985. Mem. Dane County Mental Health Bd., Madison, 1980-82. Fellow Am. Psychol. Assn.; mem. Madison Hypnotherapy Soc. (pres. 1986—), Internat. Council Psychologists (pres. 1979), Nat. Assn. Sch. Psychologists, Sigma Xi, Pi Lambda Theta. Home: 5305 Burnett Dr Madison WI 53705 Office: U Wis Dept Psychology N Prairie Whitewater WI 53190

CULBERTSON, KATHERYN CAMPBELL, lawyer; b. Tom's Creek, Va., Aug. 14, 1920; d. Robert Fugate and Mary Campbell (Leonard) C. B.S., East Tenn. State U. (1940); B.S. in L.S, George Peabody Library Sch., 1942; J.D., YMCA Night Law Sch., Nashville, 1968. Bar: Tenn. 1969. Librarian Bur. Ships Tech. Library, U.S. Navy Dept., Washington, 1945-49, 51-53; librarian Lincoln Elementary Sch., Kingsport, Tenn., 1949-50, 51, Regional Library, Tenn. State Library and Archives, Johnson City, 1953-61; dir. extension services library Met. Govt. Nashville and Davidson County, Tenn, 1961-71; state librarian and archivist State of Tenn., Nashville, 1972-82; practice of law Nashville; mem. library com. Pres.'s Com. on Employment of Handicapped, 1966-86; Nat. Bus. and Profl. Women's Found., 1968-70; pres. Tenn. Fedn. Bus. and Profl. Women's Clubs, 1974-75. Contbg. author: Encyclopedia of Education, 1966; Editor: YMCA Alumni Assn. Bull, 1970-71. Named One of Five Women of Yr. Nashville Banner-Davidson County Bus. and Profl. Women's Club, 1979. Mem. Tenn. Bar Assn., Nashville Bar Assn., ALA, Southeastern Library Assn., Tenn. Library Assn., D.A.R. Republican. Club: Nashville Bus. and Profl. Women's (past pres.). Home: 800 Glen Leven Dr Nashville TN 37204 Office: 1506 Church St Suite 4 Nashville TN 37203

CULBRETH, JUDITH ELIZABETH, digital systems engineer; b. Greenville, S.C., Apr. 28, 1943; d. Judson Grady and Doris (Hamilton) C.; m. Elliott Shugar, Apr. 23, 1988 ; 1 child, Martin. BS, Furman U., 1965; PhD, U. Md., 1972. Assoc. dir. Diagnostic Labs., Charlotte, N.C., 1972-80; engr. Gen. Electric, Wilmington, N.C., 1980—. Contbr. articles to profl. chemistry jours. Mem. Am. Chem. Soc., Am. Assn. Clin. Chemistry, Sigma Xi, Mensa. Democrat. Home: 121 Watauga Rd Wilmington NC 28403 Office: Gen Electric M/CK54 PO Box 780 Wilmington NC 28402

CULBRETH, LUANN JANINE, radiologic technologist, educational consultant; b. Chattanooga, Sept. 26, 1961; d. Richard M. and Dorothy I. (Jones) Carter; m. Stephen A. Culbreth, Mar. 20, 1982. AS, Chattanooga State Coll., 1981; B Med. Sci., Emory U., 1984; MEd, Ga. State U., 1986. Cert. radiologic technologist. Staff radiol. technologist Emory U. Hosp., Atlanta, 1981-84; instr. Sch. Radiology Grady Meml. Hosp., Atlanta, 1984-87; instr. Magnetic Resonance Imaging Emory U., 1987—; adj. faculty Chattanooga State Coll., 1988—. Judge Ga. Occupational Award of Leadership, Atlanta, 1985-86. Mem. Am. Soc. Radiologic Technologists, Ga. Soc. Radiologic Technologists (faculty speaker Student and Grad. Technologists' Seminar 1988), Atlanta Soc. Radiologic Technologists, Assn. Educators in Radiol. Scis., Nat. Assn. Female Execs. Republican. Baptist. Home: 1376 Oakengate Dr Stone Mountain GA 30083 Office: Magnetic Resonance Edn Ctr Emory U PO Box 23853 Atlanta GA 30322

CULHANE, GAYLE PATRICIA, educator; b. Utica, N.Y., Apr. 16, 1941; d. Gerald Henry and Gladys Marjorie (Cooley) Nelbach; m. J. Michael Van Strander (div.); children: Kitren Van Strander, Adrianne Van Strander, Karla Van Strander; m. R. Brendan Culhane; 1 child, Brendan Gale. BA in Math, Coll. of St. Rose, 1963; postgrad., SUNY, Cortland, 1969-71. Tchr. math 7th and 8th grade Hazard St. Sch., Solvay, N.Y., 1963-64; tchr. math 7th through 9th grade East Syracuse (N.Y.) High Sch., 1964-65; tchr. math 9th grade Jamesville-DeWitt (N.Y.) High Sch., 1967-68; tchr. math 7th grade Jamesville-DeWitt Mid. Sch., 1968-71; computer coordinator Holy Cross Sch., Rochester, N.Y., 1983-86; computer coordinator, tchr. St. Theodore Sch., Rochester, 1984—, Holy Ghost Sch., Rochester, 1986—; computer coordinator St. Cecilia Sch., Rochester, 1984-85; computer cons. Guardian Angel Sch., Rochester, 1987. Mem. edn. com. Holy Cross Parish, Rochester, 1982-84, sec. council, 1986-87, v.p. council, 1987—; sec. Parish Pastoral Council, 1986-87, v.p. 1987-88, pres. 1988—. Mem. Assn. Math. Tchrs. N.Y. State. Roman Catholic. Office: St Theodore Sch 170 Spencerport Rd Rochester NY 14606

CULLEN, JONNA LYNNE, public/government relations executive; b. Memphis, Oct. 10, 1941; d. John Nolan Cullen Jr. and Louise (Bunnell) Shipp. Student, U. Miss., 1959-61. Asst. minority counsel U.S. Ho. of Reps. Com. on Rules, Washington, 1967-81; dir. legis. affairs Office Mgmt. and Budget, Washington, 1981-83, U.S. Pres.'s Commn. on Cen. Am., Washington, 1983; pres. J. L. Assocs., Alexandria, Va., 1983—. Dir. congl. relations Rep. Conv., Rep. Nat. Com., 1987—; donor mem. Nat. Women's Mus., Washington, 1987. Mem. The Charter 100 (founder mem. Washington Metro chpt., pres. 1984), Pres.'s Commn. on Sr. Exec. Service Compensation, 1987-88. Baptist. Club: Capitol Hill. Home and Office: 217 N Pitt St Alexandria VA 22314

CULLEN, KARON NUNNALLY, public relations executive; b. Richmond, Va., Jan. 27, 1947; d. Moses Washington and Alice Maude (Emory) Nunnally; B.A., Mary Baldwin Coll., 1968; postgrad Radcliffe Coll. Pub. Sch., 1968. Dir. publicity Americana Hotels, Inc., N.Y.C., 1970-71; dir. public relations Princess Hotels Internat., N.Y.C., 1971-74; chmn. Cullen and Taylor, Ltd., N.Y.C., 1974-82; pres. Cullen and Casey, Ltd., N.Y.C., 1982-85; exec. v.p. Good Relations, Inc., N.Y.C., 1985-86. Bd. dirs. Irvington House for Med. Research, N.Y.C.; bd. dirs. Manhattan Theatre Club, N.Y.C. Mem. Public Relations Soc. Am., Soc. Am. Travel Writers (sec. N.Y.C. chpt.), Pride and Alarm (public relations corp. leaders N.Y.C.). Club: Doubles (N.Y.C.).

CULLEN, LYNN, reporter; b. Green Bay, Wis., Jan. 18, 1948; d. Norman and Shirlyn (Ross) Miller; m. William Lee Cullen, June 4, 1972 (div. 1980). Student, Northwestern U., 1966-69, Neighborhood Playhouse Sch. Theatre, N.Y.C., 1969-71; BA, U. Wis., 1975. Corr. state govt. Sta. WLUK-TV, Green Bay, 1974-75; anchor, host talk show Sta. WISC-TV, Madison, Wis., 1975-81; feature reporter Sta. WTAE-TV, Pitts., 1981-87; host The Lynn Cullen Show, Pitts., 1987—; feature reporter Pitts. Steelers, 1985—. Bd. dirs. Bread and Roses mag., Madison, 1979, Ctr. for Victims of Violent Crime, Allegheny County, Pa., 1987; vol. TV outreach Vol. Action Ctr., Pitts, 1982-85; host telethon United Cerebral Palsy, s.w. Pa., 1984—; mem. Anti-Defamation League Media Com., Pitts., 1984—. Recipient Clarion award Women in Communications, 1982, Golden Quill award Pitts. Press Club, 1982, 83, 86, 1st place award Pa. AP Broadcasters Assn., 1983, 85, Printer's Devil award Women in Communications, 1984. Office: Sta WTAE-TV 400 Ardmore Blvd Pittsburgh PA 15221

CULLER, KRISTINE KRINER, communications personnel executive; b. Chambersburg, Pa., Sept. 21, 1957; d. Paul Kinter and Geraldine Foltz (Carr) Kriner; m. Randy Brian Culler, Aug. 18, 1979. BA in Psychology, Indiana U. of Pa., 1979; MBA, Shippensburg (Pa.) U., 1987. Service rep. ea. group United Telephone System, Chambersburg, 1979-83; mgmt. trainee ea. group United Telephone System, Carlisle, Pa., 1983-84, human resources planning adminstr. ea. group, 1984—; sec. bd. dirs. United Telephone Employees Fed. Credit Union, Carlisle, 1985-87. Youth counselor First United Meth. Ch., Chambersburg, 1979—, Sunday sch. tchr., 1983-87. Republican. Home: 3507 Eagle Dr Chambersburg PA 17201

CULLIMORE, JACQUELINE (ANGELA), insurance company administrator; b. Jacksonville, Fla., Jan. 12, 1946; d. James David and Jacqueline Joyce (Peters) Koon; m. Daniel Micheal Cullimore, Oct. 5, 1963 (div. June 1967); children: Charles Martin, Kelly Rae Cullimore Howard. Grad. high sch., Jacksonville, 1982. Sect. dir. profl. services Scottie Pharmacy, Jacksonville, 1968-75; with Blue Cross Blue Shield Fla., Jacksonville, 1975—, sr. analyst, 1983-87, mgr. Durable Med. Equipment, 1987—. Democrat. Office: Blue Cross Blue Shield Fla Inc 532 Riverside Ave Jacksonville FL 32202

CULLINGFORD, HATICE S., chemical engineer; b. Konya, Turkey, June 10, 1945; came to U.S., 1966; d. Ahmet and Emine (Kadayifcioglu) Harmanci. Student, Mid. East Tech. U., 1962-66; BS in Engring. with high honors, N.C. State U., 1969, PhD, 1974. Registered profl. engr., Tex.; cert. mgr. Statis. clk. Research Triangle Park Inst., 1966; reactor engr. AEC, Washington, 1973-75; spl. asst. ERDA, Washington, 1975; mech. engr. Dept. Energy, Washington, 1975-78; staff mem. Los Alamos Nat. Lab., 1978-82; sci. cons., Houston, 1982-84; ECLSS test bed mgr. Johnson Space Ctr., NASA, Houston, 1984-85, sr. project engr. advanced tech. dept., 1985-86, sr. staff engr. div. solar system exploration, 1986-88, asst. div. advanced devel., 1988—; mem. internal adv. com. Ctr. for Nonlinear Studies Los Alamos Nat. Lab., 1981; organizer tech. workshops, sessions at soc. meetings; lectr. in field. Editor, author tech. reports; contbr. articles to profl. jours.; patentee in field. Mem. curriculum rev. com. U. N.Mex., Los Alamos, 1980. Recipient Woman's badge Tau Beta Pi, 1968, ERDA Spl. Achievement award, 1976, Inventor award Los Alamos Nat. Lab., 1982; Cities Service fellow, 1969-72. Mem. Am. Nuclear Soc. (sec.-treas. fusion energy div. 1982-84, vice chmn. South Tex. sect. 1984-86, mem. local sects. com. 1986—), Am. Inst. Chem. Engrs. (organizer, 1st chmn. No. N.Mex. club 1980-81, chmn. low-pressure processes and tech. 1981—), Am. Chem. Soc., Fusion Power Assocs., Internat. Assn. Hydrogen Energy, AIAA, NSPE, Soc. for Risk Analysis (organizer, sec. Lone Star chpt. 1986—), No. N.Mex. Chem. Engrs. Club, Engrs. Council Houston (councilor, sec. energy com.), Sierra Club, Phi Kappa Phi, Pi Mu Epsilon. Club: Houston Orienteering.

CULP, BONNIE E., manufacturing company executive; b. Phila., Feb. 21, 1957; d. George and Elizabeth (Reeb) Raslovick; m. Lamont Raymond Culp, May 9, 1981; 1 child, Allan Michael. Student, Temple U., 1983—. With Honeywell, Inc., Ft. Washington, Pa., 1976—; customer service adminstr. Honeywell, Inc., 1981-84, contracts adminstr., 1984-85, field ops. adminstr., 1985—; computer cons. Honeywell, 1983—. Participant Spl. Olympics, Ambler, Pa., 1985, 86, 87, 88. Mem. Am. Bus. Women's Assn. (pres. 1984-85, Woman of Yr. 1986), Nat. Assn. Female Execs. Republican. Office: Honeywell Inc 1100 Virginia Dr Fort Washington PA 19034

CULP, MILDRED L., corporate executive, syndicated columnist, broadcaster; b. Ft. Monroe, Va., Jan. 13, 1949; d. William W. and Winifred (Stilwell) C. BA in English, Knox Coll., 1971; AM Div., U. Chgo., 1974, PhD in History of Culture, 1976. Coll. faculty, adminstr. 1976-81; dir. Exec. Résumés, Seattle, 1981—; pres. Exec. Directions Internat., Inc., Seattle, 1985—. Columnist Seattle Daily Jour. Commerce, syndicated, 1981—, Singer Media Corp., 1987; radio commentator, Seattle, featured on TV; contbr. articles and book revs. to profl. jours. Admissions advisor U. Chgo., 1981—; adv. bd. Nat. Alliance Mentally Ill, 1987. Mem. U. Chgo. Seattle Alumni Club (bd. dirs., 1982-86), Network Exec. Women (bd. dirs 1981-82), SOS/CAMI. Home and Office: Exec Directions Internat Inc 3313 39th Ave W Seattle WA 98199

CULVERHOUSE, RENEE DANIEL, management educator; b. Tuskegee, Ala., Nov. 10, 1950; d. Gerald Lee and Janelle (Dyson) Daniel; m. Charles E. Culverhouse III, May 27, 1978; 1 child, Danielle Renee. BA in Fgn. Langs., Auburn U., 1972, postgrad., 1972-73; JD, Cumberland Sch. Law, 1978. Bar: Ala., 1979. Assoc. Dinsmore, Waites & Stovall, Birmingham, Ala., 1978-81; asst. prof. Auburn U., Montgomery, Ala., 1981-86; undergrad. coordinator Auburn U., Montgomery, 1985—, assoc. prof., 1986—; cons. EEOC. Montgomery, 1983-84. Contbr. articles to profl. jours; abstract editor Jour. of Direct Mktg. Bd. dirs. Acad. and Athletic Excellance, Montgomery, 1985—, David Gries Meml. Found., Montgomery, 1986—; adv. bd. Montgomery AIDS Outreach. Mem. Atlantic Mktg. Assn., Am. Bus. Law Assn., Ala. Acad. Scis., So. Bus. Law Assn., Southeastern Bus. Law Assn., Southwestern Social Scis. Assn., Pi Sigma Epsilon. Home: 651 Carol Villa Dr Montgomery AL 36109 Office: Auburn U at Montgomery Sch Business Montgomery AL 36193

CUMMINGS, CONSTANCE, actress; b. Seattle; d. Dallas Vernon and Kate Logan (Cummings) Halverstadt; m. Benn Wolfe Levy, 1933; children: Jonathan, Jemina. Chmn. Young People's Theatre Panel; mem. Arts Council, 1963-69. Broadway debut Treasure Girl, 1928; London debut Sour Grapes, Repertory Players, 1934; film debut Movie Crazy, 1932; appeared on radio, TV, films, theatre; joined Nat. Theatre Co., 1971; appeared in London stage prodns.: Madame Bovary, 1937; Romeo and Juliet, 1939, Saint Joan, 1939, The Petrified Forest, 1942, Return to Tyass, 1950, Lysistrata, 1957, The Rape of the Belt, 1957, Who's Afraid of Virginia Woolf?, 1964, Justice is a Woman, 1966, Fallen Angel, 1967, Nat. Theatre Co., A Long Day's Journey Into Night, 1972, The Cherry Orchard, 1973, The Circle, 1975, Mrs. Warren's Profession, Vienna, 1976, Wings, U.S., 1978, London, 1979 (Tony award 1979), Hay Fever, 1980, The Golden Age, 1981, The Chalk Garden, N.Y.C., 1982, The Glass Menagerie, N.Y.C., London, 1984, The Glass Menagerie, 1985, (one woman show) Fanny Kemble, 1986, Crown Matrimonial, 1987, others; performed in Claudel-Honnegar oratorio St. Joan at the Stake, Albert Hall, London, 1949, Peter and the Wolf, Albert Hall, 1955, Wings on Am. pub. TV; dir. Royal Ct. Theatre. Recipient Obie award, 1979, Drama Desk award, 1979; decorated Comdr. Brit. Empire. Mem. Brit. Actors Equity (mem. council), Royal Soc. for Encouragement of Arts and Commerce. Mem. Labour Party. Club: Chelsea Arts.

CUMMINGS, CONSTANCE PENNY, public relations executive; b. Morristown, N.J., Feb. 12, 1948; d. Renwick Speer and Juliana Diane (Novotny) C.; B.A., U. Md., 1970. With Kaiser Aluminum, Washington, 1970-71, Manning, Selvage & Lee, pub. relations, Washington, 1971-77; dir. pub. relations Sheraton Washington Hotel, 1977-82, area dir. pub. relations Sheraton Corp., Washington, 1982-84, dir. pub. relations N.Am., 1984-87, Sheraton Corp. Hotels, Md., Va., Washington, 1987—. Recipient Sheraton Corp. Pres. award, 1978, Pub. Relations award, 1981, 82, 87. Bd. dirs. Big Sisters of Met. Washington, 1984. Mem. Am. News Women's Club (pres. 1982-83), Am. Women in Radio and TV (pres. chpt. 1976), Pub. Relations Soc. Am. (dir. 1977). Contbr. articles in field. Office: Sheraton Corp 2660 Woodley Rd NW Washington DC 20008

CUMMINGS, ERIKA HELGA, management consultant; b. Offenbach, Federal Republic of Germany; came to U.S., 1978; d. Erwin and Edith (Trunski) Maier; m. Robert H. Cummings, Dec. 1970; 1 child, Marisa Anne. BS in Bus. Adminstrn., Calif. State U., Bakersfield, 1982; M in Internat. Mgmt., Am. Grad. Sch. Internat. Mgmt., Glendale, Ariz., 1983. Inflight supr. Trans World Airlines, Paris; internat. ops. mgr. Cooper LaserSonics, Santa Clara, Calif., 1984-85; sales mgr., club mgr. Oaks Club, Osprey, Fla., 1985-86; bus. cons. Suncoast Bus. Investments, Sarasota, Fla., 1986—. Mem. Nat. Assn. Female Execs., Beta Gamma Sigma.

CUMMINGS, JEANETTE GLENN, gerontologist, social worker, nursing home administrator; b. Cyrene, Ga., Aug. 11, 1949; d. Asbery and Euzera (Humphrey) Glenn; BS, Tuskegee Inst., 1972; MSW. (Univ. fellow), Atlanta U., 1973; gerontology leadership cert. Ga. State U., 1983; m. Jesse Cummings, Dec. 30, 1978. Dir. resident services Wesley Homes Inc., Atlanta, 1973-78; sr. citizen planner/coordinator Cen. Savannah River Area Planning Commn., Augusta, Ga., 1979, dir. Area Agy. on Aging, 1979—; cons. on group work with elderly, organizing social service programs. Mem. Mental Health/Mental Retardation Assn., Augusta; mem. exec. bd. Leadership Augusta; participant Leadership Ga., trustee; mem. Sr. Enrichment Assn., Augusta, Ga. Council on Aging. Elected Employee of Yr., Cen. Savannal River Area Planning Commn., 1980; named Social Worker of Yr. Augusta unit Nat. Assn. Social Workers, 1982; Citizen of Yr. Sr. Enrichment Assn., 1982; Disting. Alumni award Ga. State U. Gerontology Ctr., 1986, Gateopeners award Augusta Black History Assn., 1986. Mem. Nat. Assn. Social Workers, Acad. Cert. Social Workers, Ga. Gerontology Soc. (pres., Louis Nemark award 1986), Southeastern Assn. Area Agy. on Aging, Nat. Assn. Found. Execs., Delta Sigma Theta. Democrat. Mem. Unity Ch. Club: Tuskegee Alumni. Home: 2715 Vernon Dr W Augusta GA 30906 Office: 2123 Wrightsboro Rd Augusta GA 30904

CUMMINGS, KATHLEEN, medical systems administrator; b. Oak Park, Ill., July 16, 1947; d. Mark Joseph and Margaret (Lamping) C.; m. Thomas James Knight, Jr., May 2, 1970 (div. Jan. 1982); children—Brandy Lynn, Thomas James III; m. Alvin L. Jones, Nov. 23, 1983. B.F.A., Quincy Coll., 1969. Service rep. Ill. Bell Telephone Co., Chgo., 1970-73; collection mgr. Gen. Telephone Answering Service, Chgo., 1973-75; sr. collector Children's Meml. Hosp., Chgo., 1975-80; bus. officer mgr. Seton Med. Ctr., St. Joseph's Hosp., Chgo., 1981-83; sr. legal investigator Hayt, Hayt, & Landau, Evanston, Ill., 1983-84; office mgr. Shared Med. System, Oak Park, Ill., 1985—. Campaign vol. Democratic Party, Chgo., 1982. Roman Catholic. Avocations: jogging; photography. Home: 7928 S Brandon Chicago IL 60617

CUMMINGS, MARY MARIAM EISELE, clinical psychologist; b. Chgo., Oct. 3, 1939; d. Charles Wesley and Blanche Mae (Kennell) Eisele; 1 child, John Miller Adam. BA, Radcliffe Coll., 1962; MA, U. Ariz., 1970, PhD in Psychology, 1973. Cert. psychologist, Ariz. Tchr. high sch. Valley Sch. Girls, Tucson, 1963-66; clin. psychologist student counseling service U. Ariz., 1972-76, asst. dir., 1976-85, assoc. dir., 1985-86, acting dir., 1980, dir. univ.-wide honors program, 1980-85, lectr. psychology, 1974-76; program coordinator Adult Edn. Ctr., U. N.Mex., Los Alamos, 1987—. Co-founder Tucson Gilbert and Sullivan Theatre, 1966, bd. dirs., 1966-71; alumni interviewer Harvard-Radcliffe Admissions Office, 1976—; adminstrv. bd. St. Francis in the Foothills Meth. Ch., 1978-81; mem. Ariz. Opera Co.; v.p. Los Alamos Guild of the Santa Fe Opera. Recipient Faculty Achievement award U. Ariz. Alumni Assn., 1983; NIMH fellow U. Ariz. Mem. Am. Psychol. Assn., Ariz. Psychol. Assn., N.Mex. Psychol. Assn., Internat. Transactional Analysis Assn., Nat. Collegiate Honors Council, Catalyst Network Nat. Women's Info. Democrat. Episcopalian. Office: U N Mex Los Alamos br Los Alamos NM 87544

CUMMINS, KATHRYN LEWIS, museum director; b. Chgo., Oct. 14, 1908; d. Floyd Watson and Ina Catherine (Steckert) Lewis; m. Glen James Cummins (dec.); 1 child, David Lewis. BS, Cen. Mich. U., 1950; postgrad., U. Mich., 1952. Tchr. Pub. Schs., Midland, Mich., 1928-32, 42-52; social worker Midland County Red Cross, 1936-39; chem. analyst Dow Chem. Co., Midland, 1939-42; exec. sec. Midland County Hist. Mus., 1952-70, dir., 1970-86. Editor, contbr. Midland Log mag., 1921-70. Tchr. 1st Bapt. Ch., Midland. Named Citizen of Yr. Civitan Club, 1976; honoree Mich. State Hist. Soc., 1974, Mich. State Sen., 1976. Mem. Am. Assn. Mus., Am. Assn. State and Local History, AAUW (honors with named gift 1987), Mich. Mus. Assn., Mich. Edn. Assn., Mich. Cen. U. Alumnus, Am. Bus. Women (past pres., Woman of Yr. 1981).

CUMMINS, PATRICIA ANN, real estate specialist, educator; b. Portland, Maine, Sept. 29, 1945; d. Arther M. and Eunice G. (Swan) Peterson Griggs; m. Gerald D. Cummins, July 4, 1964 (div. 1971); children: Mark David, Christine Diane, Scott David. AA, San Diego City, 1967; BA, Nat. U., 1977, MBA, 1977; D in Bus. Adminstn., U.S. Internat. U., 1980. Real estate broker Carlton Oaks Realty and Investment, Santee, Calif., 1967-86, Century 21 Dahl-Lollis, Santee, Calif., 1987; tax acct. Larson CPA, San Diego, 1966-86, asset mgr. Mesa Mortgage, San Diego, 1970-80; bus. prof. U.S. Internat. U., San Diego, 1980-82; instr. Grossmont Coll., El Cajon, Calif., 1982. Author: (with others) Inside Secrets IRS, 1981, Tax Dictionary, 1981; producer broadway mus., San Diego, 1980. Active Boy Scouts Am., Pop Warner youth softball league, Santee, 1972-80; dir. Calif. Performing Arts, San Diego, 1980—; reader 1st Ch. Christ Scientist, Lakeside, Calif. Mem. Nat. Assn. Realtors, Calif. Assn. Realtors, Nat. Rifle Assn., Planned Parenthood, Santee C. of C., Calif. Performing Arts (dir. 1980—). Republican. Clubs: Flying, Los Ancianos. Home: PO Box 187 Santee CA 92071

CUMMINS, SUSAN AMY, financial analyst; b. Norfolk, Va., July 22, 1957; d. Harold and Virginia (Nelson) C. BBA in Polit. Sci. with honors, Memphis State U., 1979; MBA, Vanderbilt U., 1985. Analyst office mgmt., br. mgr. fin. Burroughs Corp., Nashville and Atlanta, 1979-81; mgr. cost acctg. Procter & Gamble Co., Memphis, 1981-82; mgr. fin. planning and analysis No. Telecom Co., Dallas and Raleigh, N.C., 1985—. Owen Merit scholar Vanderbilt U., Nashville, 1985. Mem. AAUW, Am. Assn. MBA Execs., Phi Kappa Phi. Mem. Ch. of Christ. Office: No Telecom Co Bell No Research div 35 Davis Dr Research Triangle Park NC 27709

CUNDY, CHRISTINE KAY, program administrator; b. Fond du Lac, Wis., Apr. 25, 1960; d. Calvin Lewis and Gertrude Rose (Wenger) C.; 1 child, Ashley Rose Houston. A in Acctg., Moraine Park Tech. Inst., 1980; BBA summa cum laude, Lakeland Coll., 1982. Mktg. research coordinator Med. Engrng. Corp., Racine, Wis., 1983-84, media coordinator, 1984-85; media coordinator Nationwide Advt. Service, Phoenix, 1985; purchasing and prodn. coordinator CPA Services, Inc., Brookfield, Wis., 1986—, office mgr., 1987; program adminstr. Info. Mktg. div. Frank Mayer and Assocs., Grafton, Wis., 1987—. Home: N5265 County Rd P Rubicon WI 53078 Office: Info Mktg 1975 Wisconsin Ave Grafton WI 53024

CUNNANE, PATRICIA S., medical facility administrator; b. Clinton, Iowa, Sept. 7, 1946; d. Cyril J. and Corinne Spain; m. Edward J. Cunnane, June 19, 1971. AA, Mt. St. Clare Coll., Clinton, Iowa, 1966. Mgr. Eye Med. Clinic of Santa Clara Valley, San Jose, Calif. Mem. Med. Adminstrs. Calif. Polit. Action Com., San Francisco, 1987. Mem. Med. Group Mgmt. Assn., Am. Assn. Med. Assts., Nat. Notary Assn., Resource Ctr. for Women, Nat. Assn. Female Execs., Exec. Women Internat. (v.p. 1986-87, pres. 1987—), Profl. Secs. Internat. (sec. 1979-80), Am. Soc. Ophthalmic Adminstrs., Am. Health Care Execs. Roman Catholic. Home: 232 Tolin Ct San Jose CA 95139 Office: Eye Med Clinic of Santa Clara Valley 220 Meridian Ave San Jose CA 95126

CUNNIFF, MARY TERESA, business executive; b. Boston, Nov. 16, 1950; d. John Patrick and Marie-Theresa (Riccelli) Rose; m. James Walter Cunniff, Nov. 21, 1971; children: Ann-Marie, Teresa Jean, Sean James. Treas., J.W. Cunniff Co., 1971-81; pres., treas. Berniff Industries, Inc., Stoughton, Mass., 1983—, chmn. bd., 1983—, also dir. Dir. vols.; pres., owner J.M.C. Enterprises, Inc., 1988—. Goddard Hosp., Stoughton, 1969-71. Mem. C. of C. (bd. dirs., pres.). Democrat. Roman Catholic. Address: 309 Morton St Stoughton MA 02072 also: JMC Enterprises Inc 25 Brock St Stoughton MA 02072

CUNNINGHAM, ANDREA LEE, public relations executive; b. Oak Park, Ill., Dec. 15, 1956; d. Ralph Edward and Barbara Ann C.; m. Rand Wyatt Siegfried, Sept. 24, 1983. BA, Northwestern U., 1979. Feature writer Irving-Cloud Pub. Co., Lincolnwood, Ill., 1979-81; account exec. Burson-Marsteller Inc., Chgo., 1981-83; group account mgr. Regis McKenna Inc., Palo Alto, Calif., 1983-85; founder, owner, pres. Cunningham Communication Inc., Santa Clara, Calif., 1985—. Mem. Am. Electronics Assn., U.S. C. of C. Republican. Office: Cunningham Communication Inc 2350 Mission Coll Blvd Suite 900 Santa Clara CA 94022

CUNNINGHAM, ANNA VERNICE, social worker, social services administrator; b. Buena Vista, Miss., Jan. 1, 1923; d. Bud and Mary Cunningham. Cert., Okolona (Miss.) Jr. Coll., 1944; AB, Tougaloo (Miss.) Coll., 1946; postgrad. in social work, St. Louis U., 1950; MSW, Washington U., St. Louis, 1955. Social worker St. Louis Welfare Dept., 1950-54, Inst. for Juvenile Research, East St. Louis, Ill., 1954-55; psychotherapist Columbus (Ohio) State Hosp., 1955-57; case worker Family and Children's Services of St. Louis, 1957-62; instr. field work Sch. of Social Services St. Louis U., 1962-63; case worker Jewish Family and Community Services, Chgo., 1963-74; dir. day care ctr. Martin Luther King/ Afro Family Services, Chgo., 1974-75; service dir. United Charities of Chgo., 1975-81; dir. profl. services Family and Children's Service, Pitts., 1982—; cons. head start program Ebony Mgmt., Inc., Chgo., 1981-82; team leader and peer reviewer Council on Accreditation, N.Y.C., 1983—; rev. of proposals Adam Hall Rev. Com., Rockville, Md., 1987. Charter mem. Nat. Mus. of Women in the Arts; mem. Mayor's Commn. on Families, Pitts., 1987. Mem. Nat. Assn. Social Workers (del. 1980-81), Internat. Council on Social Welfare, Internat. Fedn. of Social Workers, Am. Orthopsychiat. Assn. Home: 320 Fort Duquesne Blvd #5-J Pittsburgh PA 15222 Office: Family and Children Services 921 Penn Ave Pittsburgh PA 15222

CUNNINGHAM, BRIDGET EUGENIA, medical records administrator; b. Detroit, June 28, 1952; d. Eugene B. and Consuella V. (McSmith) C. AS, East Los Angeles Coll., 1979; student, UCLA, 1980, 86, Coll. St. Scholastica, 1987—. Med. records coder Los Angeles County.-U. So. Calif. Med. Ctr., 1979-81; cancer case abstractor Los Angeles Coll.-U. So. Calif. Med. Ctr., 1981-84, tumor registry supr., 1984-86; dir. med. records Alhambra Hosp., Rosemead, Calif., 1986—. Vol. worker health fair Am. Cancer Soc., Pasadena, 1984-86. Mem. Nat. Assn. Female Execs., Am. Med. Records Assn., Nat. Assn. Med. Staff Services, So. Calif. Med. Library Assn., Patient Care Assessment Council, So. Calif. Tumor Registry Assn. (treas. 1986). Democrat. Roman Catholic. Club: Sierra (Los Angeles). Home: 5107 N Rosemead #19 San Gabriel CA 91776

CUNNINGHAM, CAROLYN KATHRON, equal employment opportunity manager; b. Waukegan, Ill., Dec. 25, 1952; d. Lawrence and Thelma Louise (Vernon) C.; children: Melinda Katrice, Stephanie Rae. BS, U. Ill., 1975. Community service coordinator Lake County Urban League, Waukegan, 1976-77, dir. econ. devel. and employment, 1977-79; equal employment opportunity specialist Office for Civil Rights HHS, Chgo., 1979-85; equal employment opportunity mgr. N.E. Region Naval Med. Command, Great Lakes, Ill., 1985—; Mem. equal employment opportunity com. Fed. Exec. Bd., Chgo., 1985—. Bd. dirs. Lake County Urban League, Waukegan, 1986—. Mem. Nat. Assn. Female Execs. Office: Naval Med Command NE Region Bldg 384 Great Lakes IL 60088-0052

CUNNINGHAM, DEBRA JO, marketing executive; b. Parkersburg, W.Va., Mar. 12, 1957; d. Darrel Vincent and Dora Marie (Collins) C. AAS, Parkersburg Community Coll., 1977. Nursing sec. Camden-Clark Hosp., Parkersburg, 1977-81, mktg. sec., 1981-83, community relations coordinator, 1983-85, mktg. asst. dir., 1985—. Mem. Am. Mktg. Assn., Profl. Women's Assn. (bd. dirs. 1983), Parkersburg C. of C. (acting pub. relations chmn. 1985). Office: Camden Clark Hosp 800 Garfield Ave Parkersburg WV 26101

CUNNINGHAM, DOROTHY RUTH, savings and loan executive; b. Ashland, Ky., Nov. 23, 1951; d. Clayton Allen and Jamie Sue (Rogers) Cunningham; m. Coy Edward Simmons Jr., Aug. 2, 1986. B.S. in Acctg. magna cum laude, U. Balt., 1981, postgrad., 1985—. C.P.A., Md. Word processing supr. R.M. Towill Corp., Honolulu, 1971-73; real estate reviewer Prudential Ins. Co., Balt., 1973-78; real estate investment analyst Equitable Life Assurance Soc. U.S., Balt., Washington, 1978-83; v.p. Chevy Chase Savs. Bank, Md., 1983—; instr. Am. Inst. Banking, 1988—. Vol. Nat. Aquarium in Balt., 1982-85. Mem. Comml. Real Estate Women (pres. and founder Balt. chpt. 1985-86, nat. steering com. 1986-87, nat. bd. dirs. 1987—), Mortgage Bankers Assn. Wash. and Md., Nat. Assn. Indsl. and Office Parks, Urban Land Inst., Am. Inst. Real Estate Appraisers. Avocations: home renovation; racquetball; reading; computers. Home: 21 Donzi Ct Severna Park MD 21146 Office: Chevy Chase Savs Bank 2360 W Joppa Rd Suite 205 Chevy Chase MD 21093

CUNNINGHAM, KARIN OLSEN, editor; b. Dallas, Oct. 15, 1959; d. Kenneth Bruce and Marilyn (Jennings) O. Grad., Okla. State U., 1981. Editor, sales rep. Country Club Publs., Oklahoma City, 1981. Contbr. articles to profl. jours. Big Sister, Big Bros.-Big Sisters, Oklahoma City, 1984-85; mem. Citizens Adv. Council, Am. Inst. Cancer Research, Washington, 1984; communications dir. United Way of Cen. Okla., Oklahoma City, 1988. Mem. Women in Communications (pres. 1980-81), Sigma Delta Chi, Pi Beta Phi. Republican. Mem. Dutch Reform Ch. Home: 11550 N May Apt 107 Oklahoma City OK 73120 Office: Country Club Publs 6531 Classen Blvd Oklahoma City OK 73116

CUNNINGHAM, MARIE-CLAIRE, real estate executive; b. Washington, June 25, 1963; d. William J. and Patricia A. (Sloan) C. BS, NYU, 1985. Asst. Wertheim and Co., N.Y.C., 1981-82; asst. Citibank N.A., N.Y.C., 1982-83, asst. to ret. pres., 1983-84; analyst real estate Corp. Property Investors, N.Y.C., 1984—. Conttbr. articles to profl. jours. Mem. NOW, Nat. Assn. Female Execs., Nat. Assn. Young Profl. Women (dir. 1985). Democrat. Roman Catholic. Home: 230 W 79th St #124 New York NY 10024 Office: Corp Property Investors 305 E 47th St New York NY 10017

CUNNINGHAM, MARY C., respiratory therapy educator; b. Lansing, Mich., May 30; d. Phillip Karl and Elisabeth (Ivanick) Alber; m. Robert E. Cunningham, Feb. 6, 1965; children: Kristin, Erika. Cert. as registered respiratory therapist, Lansing Community Coll.; BBA, Northwood Inst. Registered respiratory therapist. Adminstrv. asst. McKendry Realty, Lansing, 1973-76; asst. dir. food and beverage Long's Conv. Ctr., Lansing, 1976-78; acct. cons. Mktg. Resource Group, Lansing, 1978-80; respiratory therapist Ingham Med. Ctr., Lansing, 1980-84; admissions counselor Johnson and Wales Coll., Lansing, 1985-86; instr. respiratory therapy Lansing Community Coll., 1986—; pres. Tetragon, Lansing, 1985—; chief operating exec. Tetragon, Lansing, 1985—. Author: The Found Lunch, 1987, Rejection, Rebuild, and False Praise and Other Upbeat Topics, 1984. Mem. Mich. Soc. for Respiratory Care, Am. Assn. for Respiratory Care, Nat. Assn. Female Execs., Am. Bus. Womens' Assn., Phi Theta Kappa. Republican. Roman Catholic.

CUNNINGHAM, MARY ELIZABETH, venture capital company executive; b. Portland, Maine, Sept. 1, 1951; d. Shirley (Sears) C.; m. William Joseph Agee, June 5, 1982; children: Mary Alana, William Nolan. BA, Wellesley Coll., 1973; MBA, Harvard U., 1979; postgrad. Trinity Coll., Dublin, 1972; DHL (hon.), Franklin Pierce Coll., 1983. Asst. treas. Chase Manhattan Bank, N.Y.C., 1974-77; corp. v.p. strategic planning Bendix Corp., Southfield, Mich., 1979-80; exec. v.p. planning, corp. v.p. strategic planning Joseph Seagram & Sons, N.Y.C., 1981-84; pres., chief operating officer Semper Enterprises, Inc., Osterville, Mass., 1982—; exec. dir. The Nurturing Network, Inc.; v.p. Lojack Corp. Author: Powerplay, 1984; contbr. articles to profl. jours. Bd. dirs. Franklin Pierce Coll., Rindge, N.H., 1983—, Marymount Manhattan Coll., N.Y.C., 1983-88, Alternatives to Abortion Internat., Aguinas House, YMCA of Cape Cod; bd. advisors council Collegiate Research Services, Inc., Jour. Bus. Strategy; mem. strategic planning com. The Conf. Bd.; mem. United Negro Coll. Fund, Women's Equity Action League; mem. women's forum, nat. corp. adv. bd. NOW Legal Def. and Edn. Fund; mem. adv. com. Com. for Nat. Security; chmn.'s advisor U.S. Congl. Adv. Bd. Recipient Econ. Equity award Women's Equity Action League, N.Y.C., 1982; named to YWCA's Acad. Women Achievers, 1980. Mem. Am. Mgmt. Assn., Phi Beta Kappa. Roman Catholic. Clubs: Commonwealth of Calif. (San Francisco); Economic (N.Y.C.); Women's Economic (Detroit). Home: Oyster Harbors Osterville MA 02655 Office: Semper Enterprises Inc PO Box 2001 Oyster Harbors Osterville MA 02655

CUNNINGHAM, RHONDA CECIL, psychologist, testing center administrator; b. Jackson, Miss., Dec. 23, 1952; d. Fred Douglas and Margie Bernice (Fairley) C. BA, Dillard U., 1974; MA, U. Houston, 1978, PhD, 1980. Lic. psychologist, Tenn. Asst. prof. clin. psychology Meharry Med. Coll., Nashville, 1980-86; dir. counseling and testing ctr. Fisk Univ., Nashville, 1986—; cons. Dept. Psychiatry Meharry Med. Coll., 1980, Care Unit, Comp. Care Inc., Newport Beach, Calif., 1985-86, Children, Youth, and Family Services Meharry Community Mental Health Ctr., Nashville, 1986—, Rehab Care Meharry-Hubbard Hosp., 1987—. Editor: Harmony newsletter, 1987. Grantee U.S. Children Bur., 1984, 85, 86. Mem. NAACP, Americans for Substance Abuse Prevention, Am. Psychol. Assn., Am. Assn. for Counseling and Devel., Tenn. Psychol. Assn., Nashville Psychol. Inst., Delta Sigma Theta. Democrat. Roman Catholic. Home: 2826 Lake Forest Dr Nashville TN 37217

CUNNINGHAM, VICKI FRANCES, publishing executive; b. Houma, La., Aug. 27, 1963; d. Charles and Joyce Rita (Guidry) C. Student, Nicholls State U., 1981-86, Spring Hill Coll., 1983. Pub. Gulf Oil Field Service Co., Inc., Houma, 1978-87, sec., treas., 1987—; real estate assoc. Century 21, Houma, 1982; instr. Nicholls State u., Thibodaux, La., 1984; pvt. practice law clk., abstractor, La., 1984-86; pub., pres. Faces South Pubs., Inc., Kenner, La., 1986—; cons. small pubs., New Orleans, 1987—. Contbr. articles to profl. jours. Active dept. econ. devel. U. New Orleans, 1988—, small bus. devel. ctr., 1988—. Mem. Nat. Assn. Female Execs., Venture Capital Club New Orleans (assoc.). Roman Catholic. Home: 310 Estate Dr Houma LA 70364

CUPP, ANETA JOAN, educator; b. Bonham, Tex., Dec. 30, 1940; d. Emmett Morgan and Hattie Fay (Taylor) Northcutt; m. Charles Daniel Cupp, Mar. 8, 1980; 1 son, Daniel Emmett, B.Mus., North Tex. State U., 1963; M.Ed., U. Houston, 1983. Sec. health workshop North Tex. State U., Denton summer 1963; recreation music dir. Parks and Recreation Dept. Houston, summers 1964, 65, 66, 68; tchr. elem. itinerant music Houston Ind. Sch. Dist., 1963-80; elem. music tchr. Luther Burbank Elem. Magnet Sch., Houston, 1980—. Program dir. PTA, 1963-80, program cons., 1980-84. Jim Collins scholar Corsicana Sr. High Sch., 1959. Named Tchr. of Year, Houston Ind. Sch. Dist., 1976, named to Hall of Honor, 1984. Mem. Houston Music Educators, Houston Tchrs. Assn., Congress Houston Tchrs., Tex. State Tchrs. Assn. Mem. Ch. Jesus Christ of Latter-day Saints. Home: 1237 Althea Houston TX 77018 Office: Burbank Elem Sch 216 Tidwell Houston TX 77022

CUPPLES, JANET CUMMINGS, business executive; b. Burnsville, Miss., Dec. 22, 1942; d. James E. and Juanita (Hale) Cummings; m. David C. Linton, May 21, 1961 (div. 1984); 1 child, Jeffory Mark; m. Thomas Gilbert Cupples, Mar. 5, 1984. Student, NE Miss. Jr. Coll., 1960-61, Memphis State U., 1975-76, Sheffield Tech. Ctr., Memphis, 1984-85. Property owner, Burnsville, 1974—; mem. bus. adv. com. Sheffield Tech. Ctr., 1987. Coeditor Internat. Heritage Bull./Newsletter. Vol. Memphis Brooks Mus. Art, 1980—; mem. exec. com., pub. info. officer Bldg. Bridges for A Better Memphis, 1985—; pres. Eagle Watch Assn.; founder Janet C. Cupples Citizenship awards, Memphis City Inter-City Sch., Student Leadership award, Memphis City Schs.; founder, chair women's com. on crime, City of Memphis, 1985—, chair Heritage-City of Memphis, chair internat. heritage program, 1987, 88—, Ethnic Outreach Neighborfest, 1988; hon. mem. city council, 1987; donor, exec. com. Women of Achievement, Inc., Memphis, 1986; mem. speakers bur. United Way of Greater Memphis, Friends of Shelby County Library, 1986—, YWCA; chair ethnic outreach com. Neighborfest, Memphis, 1987, chairperson exec. com. 1988; ambassador Memphis Internat. Heritage Commn., 1988; youth mentor Memphis Youth Leadership Devel. Inst.; internat. coordinator Neighborfest '88; chairperson Internat. Heritage City of Memphis, 1987, Ethnic Outreach Neighborfest, 1988. Contbr. articles to newspapers. Recipient 4 certs. of recognition Memphis City Council, 1986-88, Outstanding Service to Pub. Edn. award, 1986, merit award City of Memphis, 1987; named Outstanding Female Participant, Neighborhood, Inc., 1987; named Woman of Achievement 1988 Bd. Mem. Nat. Assn. Female Execs., NOW (2d v.p. Memphis chpt. 1987, del. nat. conf. 1987, 2d v.p.), Network Profl. Women's Orgn., NCCJ, Rep. Career Women, Memphis Peace and Justice Ctr., Women's Polit. Caucus Tenn. Methodist. Avocations: community service, writing, teaching. Office: 3021 Eagle Dr Memphis TN 38115

CURCURUTO-ROSE, FELICIA ELVIRA, consultant; b. N.Y.C., Dec. 12, 1951; d. Philip and Jane Amy (Monroe) Curcuruto; m. Kari Olavi Nieminen, July 27, 1974 (div. Oct. 1981); m. Michael Dale Rose, Jan. 10, 1982; 1 child, Breana Munro. Student Pierce Jr. Coll., 1972; BA in Drama, U. So. Calif., 1975. Bookkeeper, sec. Philip Curcuruto Chiropractic Corp., Van Nuys, Calif., 1972-77; freelance performer, Hollywood, Calif., 1968-77; assoc. producer Headshop, Kaiser Broadcasting, Hollywood, 1970-72; pub. relations, producer, writer Saquirius Prodns., Century City, Calif., 1977-80; freelance pub. relations, Los Angeles, 1981; property mgr. Middlegate Corp., San Francisco, 1982; cons. Dalicia Enterprises, Inc., Los Angeles, 1983—; propr. Firewind, Healdsburg, Calif., 1986—; lectr. metaphysical and health confs., 1987. Producer, actress: Viva! Felicia!, 1969. Author: I'll Be Missing You, 1984, Daughter of a God, 1986; Tools for the Healing Arts, 1987. Mem. Nat. Assn. Female Execs., Am. Fedn. TV and Radio Artists, Am. Film Inst., Ind. Feature Project, DAR (past regent), U. So. Calif. Alumni Assn. Republican. Unitarian. Club: Clan Munro Assn. Avocations: hiking, dancing, needlepoint, latchhooking, tapestries, crocheting, knitting, reading.

CURIE, EVE, author, lecturer; b. Paris, Dec. 6, 1904; d. Pierre (Nobel prize winner for work in radium 1903) and Marie (Skiodowska) (Nobel prize winner in radio-active substances, 1903, in chemistry 1911) Curie; B.S., Ph.B., Sevigne Coll.; D.H.L. (hon.), Mills Coll., 1939, Russell Sage Coll., 1941; Litt.D. (hon.), U. Rochester, 1941; Hartwick Coll., 1983; m. Henry Richardson Labouisse, Nov. 19, 1954. Took up study of music and gave first concert as pianist, Paris, 1925; later concerts in France and Belgium; mus. critic for Candide (weekly jour.) for several years; also wrote articles on motion pictures and the theater; made first visit to U.S. with mother, 1921; on 2d visit lectured in 10 U.S. cities (speaks English, French and Polish), 1939; witnessed fall of France, 1940, went to London to work for cause of Free France; came to U.S., 1941, lectured on war in France and Eng.; because of pro-ally activities deprived of French citizenship by Vichy Govt., 1941. Served in Europe with Fighting French as officer in Women's div. of army; one of pubs. Paris Presse (daily), resigned to return to ind. writing, 1949. Spl. adviser Sec. Gen., NATO, 1952-54. Decorated Chevalier Legion of Honor (France), 1939; Polonia Restituta (Poland), 1939; Croix de Guerre (France), 1944. Author: Madame Curie (selection of Lit. Guild, Jr. Guild, Book-of-the-Month Club, Scientific Book of the month; Nat. book award for non-fiction), 1937; Journey Among Warriors (Lit. Guild Selection), 1943. Home: 1 Sutton Pl S New York NY 10022

CURLE, ROBIN LEA, computer software industry executive; b. Denver, Feb. 23, 1950; d. Fred Warren and Claudia Jean (Hardina) C.; m. Lucien Ray Reed, Feb. 23, 1981 (div. Oct. 1984). BS, U. Ky., 1972. Systems analyst 1st Nat. BAnk, Lexington, Ky., 1972-73, SW BancShares, Houston, 1973-77; sales rep. Software Internat., Houston, 1977-80; dist. mgr. Uccell, Dallas, 1980-82; v.p. Info. Sci., Atlanta, 1982-83; v.p. sales TesserAct, San Francisco, 1983-85, Foothill Research, San Francisco, 1986-87; v.p. sales and field ops. Natural Language, Inc., Berkeley, Calif., 1987-88; pres., founder Curle Cons. Group, Berkeley, 1988—. Mem. U. Ky. Alumni Assn., Delta Gamma (pres. 1969). Republican. Presbyterian. Home and Office: 140 Arguello Blvd San Francisco CA 94118

CURLER, (MARY) BERNICE (MRS. ALBERT ELMER CURLER), writer; b. Los Angeles, Dec. 4, 1915; d. Charles Ether and Josephine Babetta (Meier) Davis; student Woodbury Coll., 1934-35; m. Albert Elmer Curler, Apr. 10, 1938; children—Daniel Jay, Dawna Dee. Freelance writer of short stories and articles for various nat. mags. including McCalls, Parents Mag., Modern Maturity, Success Unlimited, Progressive Women, Christian Sci. Moniter, Small World, Ladys Circle, Chevron USA, Writer's Digest, National Enquirer, 1957—; author: (play) Mazle's Red Garter, 1962; Story of a Medal, 1976; contbg. author: Creative Congregations, 1972. Instr. article writing Cosumnes River Evening Coll., Sacramento, 1971-82; asst. dir. Sierra Writing Camp; condr. writing seminars. Recipient Achievement award Sacramento Regional Arts Council. Mem. Calif. Writers Club (pres. 1960-61, dir. 1960—, Jack London award 1981), Am. Soc. Journalists and Authors. Home and Office: 8156 Waikiki Dr Fair Oaks CA 95628

CURLEY, KATHLEEN FOLEY, management educator; b. Boston, Dec. 1, 1950; d. John Joseph and Mary Anna (Flavin) Foley; m. Robert A. Curley Jr., June 10, 1972; children: Christine Foley, Elizabeth Foley, Margaret Foley. AB in Econs. cum laude, Smith Coll., 1972; MBA, Harvard U., 1976, D in Bus. Adminstrn., 1981. Research asst. case writer Harvard Grad. Sch. Bus. Admnstrn., Cambridge, Mass., 1977-80, sr. research assoc. U.S. forest service project, 1981-82; instr. computer resource exec. edn. program Harvard Grad. Sch. Bus. Admnstrn., Cambridge, 1982; instr. prodn. and ops. mgmt. Harvard Grad. Sch. Bus. Admnstrn., Boston, 1980; asst. prof. mgmt. info. Northeastern U., Boston, 1982-86, assoc. prof. mgmt. info. systems, 1986—; lectr. in field; cons. Xerox Corp. 1982, Polaroid, 1982-83, IBM Corp., 1983, Nolan, Norton & Co., 1981—, Lotus Devel. Corp., 1987—, Dove Assocs., 1985, Massport, Honeywell Corp, 1983-84. Author: Word Processing: First Step to the Office of the Future?, 1983; contbr. articles to profl. jours. Research grantee Coll. Bus. Adminstrn., 1983, Provost's Fund, Nolan Norton & Co., 1984-85, Ballinger Press, 1985. Mem. Assn. for Computing Machinery, Am. Decision Scis. Inst., Soc. for Info. Mgmt. Home: 29 Pioneer Rd Hingham MA 02043 Office: Northeastern U Coll Bus Adminstrn 214 Hayden Hall 360 Huntington Ave Boston MA 02115

CURPHY-BURMONT, RHONDA JUNE, management consultant; b. Omaha, Nebr., Aug. 10, 1946; d. Bill and M. Nadine (Calton) Curphy; m. Walter Martin Shetskie, Oct. 5, 1974 (div. June 1983); 1 child, Christopher Ashley; m. Frederick Julius Burmont, May 25, 1986. Student, Tex. Tech U., 1965, Tex. Tech U., 1967, U. Okla., 1966. Dental asst. Donald L. Baker, D.D.S., Denver, 1970-71; ins. adminstr. and sec. Village Inn Corp. Hdqrs., Denver, 1971-73; ins. broker and sec. Gaspar-Jones Ins. Agy., Denver, 1973-75; adminstrv. asst. Management, Inc., Denver, 1975-81, Blue River Valley Corp., Denver, 1981-84; contract adminstr. Chaparral Industries, Inc., Denver, 1984-85; v.p. and cons. Burmont & Assocs. Internat., La Jolla, Calif., 1985—. Active Mile High United Way, Denver, 1983; Am. Def. Preparedness Assn., Washington, 1983-85. Mem. Greater San Diego C. of C., San Diego Venture Capital Group. Republican. Office: Burmont & Assocs Internat 7825 Fay Ave Suite 200 La Jolla CA 92037

CURRAN, CAROL ANNE, commercial real estate company official; b. San Francisco, Nov. 2, 1943; d. Andrew Joseph and Verna Maude (Woodman) Geiser; A.A. in Bus., City Coll. San Francisco; A.A. in Bus. Adminstrn., Foothill Coll.; B.S. in Bus. Adminstrn., San Jose State U., M.B.A., 1978; teaching credential Calif. Community Coll. System, 1980. Employee recruiter, employment rep., asst. mgr. Pacific Telephone Co., San Francisco, 1962-65; with Stanford U., 1965-68; with mktg. dept. Varian Assocs., Palo Alto, Calif., 1968-71; with Michael C. Fields, Menlo Park, Calif., 1971-72; adminstrv. asst. engrng. div., editor co. newsletter Time/Data Corp., Palo Alto, Calif., 1972-74; ind. cons. Olson Labs., Anaheim, Calif., 1977-78; office bldg. specialist, sr. sales cons. Coldwell Banker Comml. Real Estate Services, San Jose, Calif., 1978—. Trustee Music and Arts Found. Santa Clara County 1984-85; mem. City of San Jose Mayor's Econ. Devel./Image Bd., 1986. Named Office Bldg. Broker of Yr., San Jose C. of C., 1982; named to Comml. Real Estate Hall of Fame, City of San Jose, 1986. Mem. Assn. South Bay Brokers (dir. 1981). Office: Coldwell Banker Comml Real Estate 226 Airport Pkwy Suite 150 San Jose CA 95110

CURRAN, HILDA PATRICIA, social worker; b. Patterson, N.J., Jan. 15, 1938; d. James Patrick and Hilda Lucille (Walsh) C.; m. Robert S. Kennon, Nov. 1980. AB, Hiram Coll., 1959; MSW, Ohio State U., 1963. Tchr. Cin. Bd. Edn., 1960; caseworker Franklin County Welfare Dept., Columbus, Ohio, 1960-61; mem. relocation staff Springfield (Mass.) Redevel. Authority, 1963-64; neighborhood organizer Community Council Greater Springfield, 1964-65; mem. program devel. staff United Community Ctrs., Bklyn., 1965-67; facilities devel. specialist in vocat. rehab. Mich. Dept. Edn., Lansing, 1967-70; program devel. specialist Bur. Community Services, Mich. Dept. Labor, Lansing, 1970-78, dir. Office Women and Work, 1978—. Mem. Ingham County Housing Commn., 1977-79, Ingham County Social Services Bd., 1979-82; bd. dirs., officer Big Bros.-Big Sisters Greater Lansing, 1968-82; charter mem. bd., officer Big Bros.-Big Sisters Am., 1977—, Big Sisters Internat., 1973-77, pres. 1976-77; trustee Hiram Coll., 1985—; mem. adv. bd. Salvation Army, 1986—; mem. zoning bd. appeals City of Lansing, 1986—. Recipient Diana award in govt. YWCA, 1977, ann. award for outstanding achievement Hiram Coll., 1980. Mem. Nat. Assn. Social Workers (mem. del.

assembly 1977, 81, 84, 87, fin. com. 1983—, pres. Lansing-Jackson chpt. 1978-80, Lansing-Jackson Social Worker of Yr. 1977), Acad. Cert. Social Workers, AAUW (Women as Agt. of Change award 1981), Phi Kappa Phi (life). Club: Torch (pres. 1979-80) (Lansing). Lodge: Zonta. Home: 415 McPherson Lansing MI 48915 Office: 309 N Washington St Lansing MI 48909

CURRAN, KRISTINE CHARNOWSKI, marketing executive; b. Winona, Minn., Dec. 10, 1954; d. H.J. and Louise (Golt) C.; m. Mark A. Curran, June 1, 1985. BA in Sociology, Loyola U., Chgo., 1977; MA in Sociology, U. Chgo., 1979, PhD in Sociology, 1982. Research analyst U. Chgo., 1977-81; cons. demographics City Bond Cons., Oakland, Calif., 1981-82; sr. research analyst Allstate Ins. Co., Menlo Park, Calif., 1982-84; cons. mktg. Bank Am., San Francisco, 1984-86; mgr. mktg. Pacific Bell Corp., San Francisco, 1986—. Coordinator Ogle County McGovern for Pres., Rochelle, Ill., 1972; bd. dirs. East Bay chpt. Big Bros./Big Sisters, 1988—. Mem. Am. Mktg. Assn., Am. Population Assn., Am. Sociol. Assn., U. Chgo. Alumni Assn. (bd. dirs. No. Calif. chpt. 1986—), Alpha Sigma Nu. Democrat. Roman Catholic. Club: Oakland Athletic. Home: 4507 Montgromery St Oakland CA 94611 Office: Pacific Bell Corp 2600 Camino Ramon Room 45800 San Ramon CA 94583

CURRID, CHERYL CLARKE, infosystems specialist; b. Newark, July 21, 1950; d. Charles McAleer and Evelyn (Agusta) Clarke; m. Raymond E. Currid Jr., Nov. 17, 1979; children: Raymond E. III, Justin Clarke. BA in Psychology, George Mason U., 1972, postgrad. in systems, 1976-77. Sales rep. R.J. Reynolds Co., Annandale, Va., 1975-78; sales mgr. M&M Mars Co., Annandale, 1978-82; systems mgr. Coca-Cola Foods, Houston, 1983—; bd. dirs. Connectivity Solutions 88 Personal Computer expo, Englewood Cliffs, N.J., 1987—. Mem. Software Assocs. Group (pres. 1979-82), Capital Personal Computer Users Group, Houston Area League of Personal Computer Users, Netware In Common. Republican. Home: 13731 Queensbury Houston TX 77079 Office: Coca-Cola Foods 2000 St James Pl Houston TX 77056

CURRIE, BARBARA FLYNN, state legislator; b. LaCrosse, Wis., May 3, 1940; d. Frank T. and Elsie R. (Gobel) Flynn; A.B. cum laude, U. Chgo., 1968, A.M., 1973; m. David P. Currie, Dec. 29, 1959; children—Stephen Francis, Margaret Rose. Asst. study dir. Nat. Opinion Research Center, Chgo., 1973-77; part time instr. polit. sci. DePaul U., Chgo., 1973-74; mem. Ill. Ho. of Reps., 1979—, chmn. House Democratic Study Group, 1981-83, House Com. on State Govt. Adminstrn.; co-chair Ill. Citizens Assembly, Ill. Council on Women; mem. House Energy, Environment and Natural Resources Com. Mem. adv. bd. Harriet Harris YWCA; v.p. Chgo. LWV, 1965-69; mem. ACLU, Hyde Park-Kenwood Community Conf., South Shore Commn., South Shore Hist. Soc., Ind. Voters of Ill.-Ind. Precinct Orgn., Hyde Park Coop. Soc., Ams. for Dem. Action. Named best legislator Ind. Voters of Ill., 1980, 82, 84, 86, Ethel Parker award, 1982, 86, best legislator Ill. Credit Union League; recipient Ill. Environ. Council award, Ill. Community Action Agys. award, Ill. Women's Polit. Caucus Lottie Holman O'Neill award; Outstanding Legislator Ill. Hosp. Assn., 1987; Susan B. Anthony award, honor award Nat. Trust Historic Preservation; awards Welfare Rights Coalition of Orgns., Ill. Pub. Action Council, Chgo. Heart Assn., ACLU, DAV, Delta Kappa Gamma; named Legislator of Yr., Ill. Nurses Assn., 1984, Nat. Assn. Social Workers, 1984, Ill. Women's Substance Abuse Coalition, 1984. Mem. Ill. Conf. Women Legislators, Nat. Order Women Legislators. Contbr. article to publ. Office: 2107 Stratton Office Bldg Springfield IL 62706

CURRIE, SISTER EILEEN, college president. BA in Psychology, Cabrini Coll., 1966; MA in Religious Edn., LaSalle Coll., 1976; postgrad. Bryn Mawr Coll./HERS Summer Inst., 1982, Inst. for Ednl. Mgmt./Harvard U., 1983. Tchr. religion/English, coordinator Confraternity Christian Doctrine programs, mem. vicariate religious edn. bd. Sacred Hearts of Jesus and Mary Sch., Bklyn., 1970-73, mem. parish council, 1971-77, prin., 1973-77, chairperson area cluster schs. for consol., 1975-77; tchr. Mother Cabrini High Sch., N.Y.C., 1977-81, acting prin., 1978-79, coll. advisor, 1979-80, moderator student body assn., 1979-81; dean student affairs Cabrini Coll., Radnor, Pa., 1981-82, pres., 1982—, past trustee; chairperson Apostolic Evaluation Team U.S. Provinces, Missionary Sisters of Sacred Heart, 1975-76, mem. provincial council ea. province, 1978-81; trustee St. Clare's Health Ctr., N.Y., 1981-82; mem. bd. adminstrn. Santa Cabrini Hosp., Montreal, Can., 1983—. Office: Cabrini Coll Eagle and King of Prussia Rds Radnor PA 19087

CURRIE, JULIANA WADDELL, resume service executive; b. Anniston, Ala., Jan. 12, 1953; d. William Xerxes and Minnie Lou (Mahaffey) Waddell; m. Phillip Dale Currie, May 21, 1977; children: Phillip Zachary, Liana Oakley. Student music, Jacksonville (Ala.) State U., 1985—. New accounts cons. United Bank Tulsa, 1980-81; office mgr. John Wylie Assocs., Tulsa, 1981-82; owner, operator J. Currie Assocs., Jacksonville, Ala., 1983—; lectr. tech. writing Jacksonville State U., 1984-86. Author non-fiction journalism; composer songs. Co-minister of music Christian Ctr., Anniston, 1982—. Named one of Outstanding Young Women if Am., 1985, 86. Republican. Club: Anniston (Ala.) Christian Womens' (exec. bd. 1984—). Office: J Currie Assocs PO Box 965 Jacksonville AL 36265

CURRIE, MADELINE ASHBURN, business administration educator; b. Rankin, Tex., Sept. 28; d. Herman and Ivan G. Vinson; BS, Tex. Woman's U., 1962; MA, Calif. State U., 1967; EdD, UCLA, 1974; m. Gail G. Currie; children: Robb Ashburn, Mark Ashburn, Michael Ashburn. Tchr., Edgewood High Sch., West Covina, Calif., 1962-69 ; instr. Rio Hondo Coll., Whittier, Calif., 1968-69, prof., grad. dir. Coll. Bus. Adminstrn., Calif. State Poly. U., Pomona, 1969—. Recipient award Alpha Lambda Delta; Exceptional Merit award, Meritorious Service awards Calif. State Poly. U., 1984. Mem. Grad. Sch. Edn., UCLA. Mem. Calif. Bus. Edn. Assn. (Recognition award), Tex. Woman's U. Alumnae Assn., Delta Pi Epsilon, Pi Lambda Theta, Delta Kappa Gamma (chpt. pres.), Delta Mu Delta. Office: Calif State Poly U Coll Bus Adminstrn Pomona CA 91768

CURRIER, SUSAN ANNE, computer software company executive; b. Melbourne, Victoria, Australia, Nov. 20, 1949; d. David Eric and Irene Hazel (Baker) Bruce-Smith; m. Kenneth Palmer Currier, Feb. 16, 1974. Student, Melbourne U., 1967-70. Fashion model Eileen Ford Model Agy., N.Y.C., 1971-74, Wilhelmina Models, N.Y.C., 1974-82; owner Softsync Inc., N.Y.C., 1981—. Home: 330 E 33rd St #1L New York NY 10016 Office: Softsync Inc 162 Madison Ave New York NY 10016

CURRY, KAREN ANN, dietetic technician; b. N.Y.C., June 28, 1955; d. William and Veronica (Boylan) Galante; m. Brian Micheal Curry, May 7, 1977; children—Rachel Marie, Amanda Lynn. A.A.S., Suffolk County Community Coll. Eastern Campus, 1981. Diet clk. Brookhaven Meml. Hosp., East Patchogue, N.Y., 1972-80, supr., 1980-81; supr. United Presbyterian Residence, Woodbury, N.Y., 1981-82; tech. asst. Suffolk Community Coll., Riverhead, N.Y., 1984—, also mem. adv. com. for dietetic technicians, 1985—; dietetic technician Intake, 1985—. North Shore asst. campaign mgr. Democratic campaign to re-elect John Randolph, N.Y., 1977. Mem. Am. Dietetic Assn., L.I. Dietetic Assn. Office: Suffolk County Community Coll Ea Campus Speonk-Riverhead Rd Riverhead NY 11901

CURRY, NANCY ELLEN, education educator; b. Brockway, Pa., Jan. 26, 1931; d. George R. and Mary F. (Covert) C. B.A., Grove City Coll., 1952; M.Ed., U. Pitts., 1956, Ph.D., 1972. Lic. psychologist, Pa. Tchr. public schs. East Brady and Oakmont, Pa., 1952-55; presch. demonstration tchr. Arsenal Family and Children's Center, U. Pitts., 1955-79, asso. dir., 1971-79; instr. Sch. of Health Related Professions, U. Pitts., 1956-61, asst. prof., 1961-72, assoc. prof., 1972-75, prof., 1975—, acting chmn. dept. child devel./child care, 1972-73, chmn. dept., 1973-86, program dir., prof. social work, 1986—; also mem. faculty U. Pitts Sch. Medicine and Sch. Edn.; assoc. Pitts. Psychoanalytic Inst., 1974—; Fulbright exchange tchr. North Oxford Nursery Sch., Oxford, Eng., 1957-58; asso. dir. early childhood project Edn. Professions Devel. Act, U.S. Office of Edn., 1970-74; cons. in field. Coproducer 12 films on children's play; author numerous articles on child devel. Mem. AAUP, Assn. for Care of Children in Hosps., Nat. Assn. for Edn. of Young Children, Am. Psychol. Assn., Am. Psychoanalytic Assn. Office: U Pitts 1717 CL Pittsburgh PA 15260

CURRY, TONI GRIFFIN, counseling center executive administrator, consultant; b. Langdale, Ala., June 23, 1938; d. Robert Alton and Elsie (Dodson) Griffin; m. Ronald William Curry, June 13, 1959 (div. 1972); children—Christopher, Catherine, Angela. B.A., Ga. State U., 1962; M.S.W., U. Ga., 1981. Cert. addictions counselor. Tchr. DeKalb County Bd. Edn., Atlanta, 1962-63; counselor Peachford Hosp., Charter Med. Corp., Atlanta, 1974-79; dir. aftercare, 1976-79; dir. aftercare and occupational services Ridgeview Inst., Atlanta, 1979-82; owner, dir., adminstr., counselor Toni Curry and Assocs., Inc., Atlanta, 1982—; founder, bd. dirs. Anchor Hosp., 1985—; cons., lectr. to numerous cos. and orgns.; mem. adv. bd. Peachford Hosp., Atlanta, 1982-87, Rockdale House, Conyers, Ga., 1981—, Outpatient Addictions Clinics Am., 1983-85; bd. dirs. Employee Assistance Programs Inst., 1981—; pres., mem. exec. bd. Ga. Employee Assistance Programs Forum, Atlanta, 1981-86; appointed to Gov.'s Advisory Council on Mental Health, Mental Retardation and Substance Abuse, 1987, Commn. on Drug Awareness and Prevention, 1987; chairperson Driving under Influence of Alcohol Assessment Task Force. Mem. Nat. Assn. Social Workers, Ga. Addiction Counselors Assn. (dir. 1982-86), Ga. Citizens Council Alcoholism, Assn. Labor-Mgmt. Cons. and Adminstrs. on Alcoholism (ALMACA), Nat. Assn. Alcoholisms and Drug Abuse Counselors, Mems. Guild of High Mus. Art, Kappa Alpha Theta. Home: 2112 Bucktrout Pl Atlanta GA 30338 Office: 5454 Yorktowne Dr Atlanta GA 30349 also: 5675 Peachtree-Dunwoody Rd NE Atlanta GA 30342

CURT, JEANNE DONOGHUE, modeling company executive; b. Stamford, Conn., May 9, 1941; d. George Edward and Irene Rene (Albert) Donoghue; student Marymount Jr. Coll., 1959, U. Conn., 1972; children: George Gregory, Timothy Joseph. With Conn. Modeling Agy., Stamford, 1960-65; partner Charming Way Boutique, Stamford, 1965-68; tchr. YWCA, Stamford, 1965-73; regional mgr. Community Ambassador, Ridgefield, Conn., 1973-74; instr., dir. admissions Barbizon Schs., Stamford, 1973-75, pres., 1975—, also pres. Barbizon Sch. of Westchester, White Plains, N.Y. Mem. citizens cons. com. J.M. Wright Tech. Sch., Stamford, 1978-81; dir. Barbizon Sch. and Agy., Hamilton, Bermuda, 1985—; cons. modeling schs. and agys., 1985—. Mem. Better Bus. Bur. (dir. 1979-80). Republican. Roman Catholic. Club: Landmark. Home: 316 Talmadge Hill Rd New Canaan CT 06840 Office: 26 6th St Stamford CT 06905

CURTIN, CATHERINE MARIE, foreign trade consultant, product market research and analysis consultant; b. Portland, Oreg., July 3, 1951; d. Edmond and Olive Joan (Schrantz) C. BA, U. Portland, 1973; BA, Univ. Coll., Cork, Ireland, 1976, MA, 1976. Historian Archdiocese of Portland, 1976-78; market research devel. Property Mgmt. Services Inc., Vancouver, Wash., 1978-80; adj. instr. history U. Portland, 1981—; dir. contbns. Nike, Inc., Beaverton, Oreg., 1981-84, research asst. to chmn., 1984-87; pres. CMC Research Internat., 1987—. Contbr. articles to hist. and profl. jours. Vol., Oreg. Hist. Soc., 1980, Spl. Olympics, Portland, 1981—; pres. bd. dirs. Oreg. Spl. Olympics. Mem. Am. Com. on Irish Studies, All Ireland Cultural Soc., U.S.-China Peoples Friendship Assn., N.W. China Council, Soc. Competitor Intelligence Profls. Democrat. Club: Oreg. Road Runners (Portland). Avocations: early 20th century Chinese history, Chinese lang./writing, running. Office: PO Box 10932 Portland OR 97210-0932

CURTIN, DOREEN ANN, pharmaceutical company executive; b. Belleville, N.J., July 18, 1959; d. Michael Joseph and Josephine (Coppola) Ventola; m. John Edward Curtin, Sept. 4, 1982. BA, Rutgers U., Newark, 1981, MS, 1982. Specialist clin. immunology Sandoz Pharms., East Hanover, N.J., 1983-84, adminstr. clin. relations, 1984-85, assoc. mgr. strategic bus., 1985-86, mgr. strategic bus., 1987—; mem. AGA/Industry Council, Chgo., 1985—. Mem. Nat. Assn. for Female Execs. Home: 561 Audrey Rd Landing NJ 07850 Office: Sandoz Pharms 59 Rt 10 East Hanover NJ 07936

CURTIN, JANE THERESE, actress, writer; b. Cambridge, Mass., Sept. 6, 1947; d. John Joseph and Mary Constance (Farrell) C.; m. Patrick F. Lynch, Apr. 31, 1975. A.A., Elizabeth Seton Jr. Coll., 1967; student, Northeastern U., 1967-68. Appeared in plays The Proposition, Cambridge and N.Y.C., 1968-72, Last of the Red Hot Lovers touring co., 1973; Broadway debut in Candida, 1981; author, actress Off-Broadway mus. rev. Pretzels, 1974-75; star TV series NBC Saturday Night Live, 1975-79, Kate & Allie, 1984—; appeared in films including Mr. Mike's Mondo Video, 1979, How to Beat the High Cost of Living, 1980; TV films include Divorce Wars-A Love Story, 1982, Suspicion, 1988. Recipient Emmy nomination, 1977; Emmy awards for outstanding actress in comedy series, 1984, 85. Mem. Screen Actors Guild, Actors Equity, AFTRA. Office: care Creative Artists Agy 1888 Century Park E Suite 1400 Los Angeles CA 90067 •

CURTIN, SUSAN MARIE CONNAUGHTON, writer; b. Teaneck, N.J., Aug. 5, 1943; d. Francis Joseph and Corinne (Hanley) Connaughton; children: Timothy, Molly. Student, Hunter Coll., 1963-64, Harvard U., 1968-79, Simmons Coll., 1979-81, Yeats Internat., Sligo, Ireland, 1981, U. Coll. Dublin, Ireland, 1982. Flight attendant Ea. Airlines, N.Y.C., 1964-69; photographic model and actress Maggie Inc., Boston, 1969—; v.p. F. Foster Photography, Boston, 1979-81; mgr. Phil Porcella Photography, Boston, 1975-76; ind. photo stylist Boston, 1981—. Author: Real Women Send Flowers, 1983; writer (TV show) Kate & Allie, "Dearly Beloved", 1986, The Horns, The Rage, 1988. Mem. Screen Actors Guild, Am. Fedn. Radio and TV Actors, Writers Guild Am. Democrat. Roman Catholic. Home: 350 N St #603 Boston MA 02113 Mailing: PO box 81039 Wellesley Hills MA 02181-0001

CURTIS, ALVA MARSH, artist; b. N.Y.C., June 15, 1911; d. Charles Johan and Elizabeth (Hagstrom) Berg; student Art Students League, N.Y.C., 1928-29, Grand Central Art Sch., 1934-36, N.Y. Sch. Fine Arts, 1930-31, Nat. Acad., N.Y.C., 1934-35, Columbia U., 1943-44, Yale U., 1969-70; m. Terrill Belknap Marsh, Nov. 3, 1932; children—Owen Thayer, Charles Ames, Ronald Belknap; m. Russell G. Curtis, Aug. 11, 1979; children—Russell G. Jr., William E. One woman shows: Scranton Meml. Library, Madison, Conn., 1969, Phippsburg (Maine) Library, 1964, Town and County Club, Hartford, Conn., 1976, Conn. Bank & Trust Co., Madison, 1977, 1st Fed. Savs. & Loan, Madison, 1977; group shows include: The Mariner's Mus., Newport News, Va., Va. Salmagundi Club, N.Y.C., Smithsonian Inst., Washington, 1964, 66, Internat. Maritime Art Award Show (Sculpture award), 1981, Nat. League Am. Penwomen Art Show (Sculpture award), Atlanta, 1982, Arnold Gallery, Newport, R.I., 1984, Copley Gallery, Boston, 1986, Candlewood Gallery (Sculpture award 1986), New Milford, Conn., 1986; represented in permanent collections: Swedish Club, Chgo., Conn. Bank & Trust Co., Windsor, Phippsburg Library, also pvt. collections; partner, art dir. Terrill Belknap Marsh, Assos., N.Y.C., 1934-69; lectr. in field. Vice chmn. Madison Inland Wetlands Agy., 1974-84. Mem. Am. Soc. Marine Artists, New Eng. Sculpture Assn., Nat. Arts Club, Nat. League Am. Penwomen (pres. 1978—, Greenwich br. 1958). Republican. Episcopalian. Clubs: Lyme Art Assn., Madison Winter, Garden Madison. Home: 12 Dogwood Ln Madison CT 06443

CURTIS, JEAN TRAWICK, library director; b. Washington; d. Ivory Wilson and Dannie May Trawick; divorced; children: Karen Elizabeth Phoenix, Jeffrey Lynn Phoenix. BA in Library Scis., Howard U., 1958; MLS, U. Md., 1971. Children's librarian D.C. Pub. Library, Washington, 1958-69, reader's adviser, 1965-69; field worker young adults Enoch Pratt Free Library, Balt., 1971-75, regional librarian, 1975-78, chief of extension, 1978-85; deputy dir. Detroit Pub. Library, 1986-87, dir., 1987—; Dir. New Detroit, Inc., 1987—; adv. bd. library services and constrn. act Library of Mich., 1987; bd. dirs.Southeastern Mich. League of Libraries. Mem. Am. Library Assn., Mich. Library Assn., U. Ctr. Cultural Assn. (dir. 1987—). Office: Detroit Public Library 5201 Woodward Ave Detroit MI 48202

CURTIS, JESSICA, nurse, administrator; b. Birmingham, Ala., Apr. 21, 1945; d. Clinton Curtis and Mary Anna (Barker) Winkler; m. Richard Michael Sand (div.); children: Peter Erik, Anna Armida Curtis. BA in Sociology, NYU, 1967; BS in Nursing, SUNY, Bklyn., 1975. Staff nurse Mayo Clinic-Meth. Hosp., Rochester, Minn., 1975-76, Vis. Nurses Assn. Bklyn., 1976-80; supervisory nurse Family Home Care of Bklyn. and Queens, Bklyn., 1980-84, asst. dir. for field service, 1984-85; mgr. patient services Vis. Nurses Soc. Home Care, Queens, 1985-87; supr. St. Mary's Home Care, Bklyn., 1987—. Author: Single Mother by Choice, 1987.

CURTIS, LOIS DARLENE, restaurant owner; b. San Diego, Mar. 3, 1956; d. William Ananias and Leona Pearl (Beitler) Goughnour; m. Albert Edward Curtis, July 2, 1983. BBA, Redlands U., 1987. Program asst. Riverside (Calif.) YWCA, 1974-76; biochem. lab. tech. Hancock Labs., Anaheim, Calif., 1976-81; now owner Ragamuffin's Restaurant, San Clemente, Calif. Mem. San Clemente C. of C. (visitor and conv. com.). Republican. Methodist. Home: 9462 Nautilus Dr Huntington Beach CA 92646 Office: Ragamuffin's 1527 N El Camino Real San Clemente CA 92672

CURTIS, MARIANNE LOUISE, fundraising development consultant; b. Lafayette, Ind., Aug. 9, 1952; d. Samuel Churchill and Shirley (Burns) C.; m. Larry L. Rose. BS, William Woods Coll., Fulton, Mo., 1974; MS in Pub. Recreation, Ind. U., 1976. Adminstrv. aid Lake County Parks and Recreation Dept., Crown Point, Ind., 1977-78, with pub. info., 1978-80, dir. leisure services, 1980-81; asst. exec. dir. YWCA, Lafayette, 1981-82; exec. dir. YWCA, Hanover, Pa., 1982-86; ptnr. Curtis, Coe & Co., Balt., 1986-87; fundraising dir. C.H. Bentz Assocs., Westfield, N.J., 1987—. Bd. dirs. Am. Cancer Soc., Lake County, Ind., 1979-81, Southlake (Ind.) YMCA, 1980-81. Mem. Nat. Soc. Fundraising Execs., Cen. Pa. Chpt. Fundraising Execs. Home: 46 Mulard Ct Severna Park MD 21146

CURTIS, MARY PACIFICO, advertising agency executive; b. Chgo., Feb. 22, 1953; d. Louis Enrico Pacifico and Margaret (Geneva) Peterson; m. Douglas Reid Curtis, Jan. 2, 1982. B.S., Northwestern U., 1973. Assoc. producer Panorama Prodns., Santa Clara, Calif., 1975-76; copy chief Moorhead Mktg., San Francisco, 1976-77; pres. Pacifico & Assocs. Inc., San Jose, Calif., 1977—; founder Silicon Valley Bank, San Jose, 1984—. Bd. dirs. Childrens Counseling Ctr., Santa Clara, 1980—, pres.; bd. dirs. San Jose Symphony Assn., 1984-85. Recipient San Francisco Cable Car award San Francisco Ad Club, 1978; Best in the West awards of merit, 1979, 80; Maggie award, 1980; Addy award, 1984; Joey award, 1984; Murphy award, 1984, 85, 86. Mem. San Jose Ad Club, Peninsula Women in Advt., San Jose Women in Advt., Western States Ad Agys. Assn., Am. Mktg. Assn. Roman Catholic. Avocations: photography; tennis; skiing. Office: Pacifico & Assocs Inc 2145 The Alameda Suite 101 San Jose CA 95126

CURTIS, PATRICIA ELLEN, consultant, educator; b. Buffalo, Nov. 14, 1930; d. Alfred John and Irene (Doll) C. BA in Music, Rosary Hill Coll., Amherst, N.Y., 1952; BS in Piano Performance, Julliard Sch. Music, 1955; MA in Musicology, Columbia U., 1957. V.p., sec. Economy Reduction Corp., Buffalo, 1957-67; prof. and chmn. dept. music Daemen Coll., Amherst, N.Y., 1958-75; v.p. acad. affairs, dean Daemen Coll., 1975-84; sr. assoc. McManis Assocs., Inc., Washington, 1984—; pres. Curtis Cons. Assocs., Inc., Buffalo, 1987—; trustee, treas. Community Music Sch., Buffalo, 1984-88, pres., 1988—; cons. ORS Arts Found., Buffalo Zoo, numerous other orgns., 1984—; lectr. arts to civic, profl. and ednl. orgns. Author program notes Buffalo Philharm. Orch., 1958-65. Mem. Amherst Community Edn. Adv. Council, 1985—; div. chmn. United Way, Buffalo, 1986-87. Mem. Am. Assn. Higher Edn., Am. Council on Edn., Buffalo C. of C. Office: Curtis Cons Assocs Inc Olympic Towers 300 Pearl St Buffalo NY 14202

CURZON, LISA MAE, medical association administrator; b. Edinburgh, Scotland, Nov. 29, 1947; came to Can., 1952; d. James and Ann (Shaw) Hope; m. William Nisbet (div. 1978); children: William, Angela, Blair; m. Anthony Paul Curzon; 1 child, Matthew. Sales cons. Pioneer Pools, Toronto, 1972-78; mgr. homemaking/outreach Can. Red Cross Soc., Scarborough, Ont., 1978—. Mem. George Brown Coll. Adv. Bd., Toronto, 1980—. Recipient Communication Excellence award United Way Am., 1986, Cert. of Achievement in Coop. Edn. Toronto Bd. Edn., 1987. Home: 11140 Sheppard Ave E, Scarborough, ON Canada M1B 1G2 Office: Scarborough Red Cross, 1095 Bellamy Rd N, Scarborough, ON Canada M1H 3B8

CURZON, SUSAN CAROL, library administrator; b. Poole, Eng., Dec. 11, 1947; came to U.S., 1952; d. Kenneth Nigel and Terry Marguerite (Morris) C. AB, U. Calif., Riverside, 1970; MLS, U. Wash., 1972; PhD, U. So. Calif., 1983. Spl. librarian Kennecott Exploration, San Diego, 1972-73; various positions Los Angeles County Pub. Library, Los Angeles, 1973-83, regional adminstr., 1983—; cons. Grantsmanship Ctr., Los Angeles, 1981-83; vis. lectr. Grad. Sch. Library and Info Sci. UCLA, 1986—. Columnist The Union Jack newspaper, 1985—. Mem. ALA, Calif. Library Assn. Democrat. Office: Los Angeles County Pub Library 23710 W Magic Mountain Pkwy Valencia CA 91355

CUSACK, BRENDA KELLAM, small business owner; b. Trenton, N.J., July 20, 1949; d. Brent and Ethel (McGee) Kellam; m. George W. Cusack, May 4, 1968; children: Gregory, Pamela. AS, Mercer Community Coll., 1976; BS, Trenton State Coll., 1981, postgrad., 1982—. Fin. officer State of N.J., Trenton, 1967-76; v.p., mktg. dir., co-founder G.B.G. Contstrn. Inc., Trenton, 1976—; co-founder Exec. Plus, Trenton, 1984—. Pub. relations dir. Community Edn. Adv. Council, Trenton, 1983. Recipient Cert. Appreciation, Gov. N.J., 1984. Mem. Nat. Assn. Female Execs. (network dir. 1983—), Internat. Tng. in Communications. Home and Office: PO Box 4022 Trenton NJ 08610

CUSACK, MARY JOSEPHINE, lawyer; b. Canton, Ohio, Mar. 3, 1935; d. Edward Thomas and Mary (O'Meara) Cusack; A.B, Marquette U., 1957; J.D., Ohio State U., 1959. Admitted to Ohio bar, 1959, U.S. Supreme Ct. bar, 1962. Atty. Indsl. Commn. Ohio, Columbus, 1960-61, Ohio Dept. Taxation, Columbus, 1961-65; adj. prof. family and probate law Capital U., Columbus, 1971-82; spl. counsel to Ohio Atty. Gen., 1971-82; ptnr. Cotruvo & Cusack, Columbus, 1961-79; sole practice Columbus, 1979—. Mem. Ohio Commn. on Status of Women. Fellow Ohio State Bar Found., Columbus Bar Found. (charter), Am. Bar Assn., Ohio Bar Assn. (past chmn. workmen's compensation com., mem. council dels.), Columbus Bar Assn. (profl. ethics com., adv. com. fees, workmen's compensation; mem. Women Lawyers Club Columbus (past pres.), Ohio Acad. Trial Lawyers (workmen's compensation com.), Franklin County Trial Lawyers (sec., past pres.), Nat. Assn. Women Lawyers (rec. sec., past pres.), Ohio Assn. Attys. Gen. (past pres.), Nat. Bd. trial Advocacy, Am. Arbitration Assn. (nat. panel arbitrators), Thomas More Soc., Kappa Beta Pi (past internat. pres., del. Profl. Frat. Assn.), Theta Phi Alpha. Clubs: Columbus Toastmistress (past pres.), Columbus Met., Pilot of Columbus, Inc., Press of Ohio. Home: 229 W Southington Ave Worthington OH 43085 Office: 50 W Broad St Columbus OH 43215

CUSHING, KAY SMITH, public relations executive; b. Pitts., Feb. 21, 1944; d. George Byron and Margaret Elizabeth (Smith) C.; m. Kenneth Neuhausen, May 16, 1981. BA, Lindenwood Coll., 1965. Gen. mgr. Pitts. Ballet Theatre, 1975-78; account supr. Ketchum Pub. Relations, Pitts., 1978-79, v.p., 1979-82, group mgr., 1982—, sr. v.p., 1984—. Mem. strategic planning com. United Way of Allegheny County; trustee Am. Fed. Aging Research; mem. gov.'s bd. Arthritis Found. Western Pa.; bd. dirs. Gateway to Music, Pitts. Pub. Theater. Recipient Matrix award Women in Communications, Pitts., 1983-84. Mem. Pub. Relations Soc. Am. (pres. Pitts. chpt. 1986-87; Vic Barkman award 1984), Fedn. Girls Sch. Socs. Republican. Roman Catholic. Clubs: Carnegie 100, Concordia (Pitts.). Office: Ketchum Pub Relations 6 PPG Pl Pittsburgh PA 15222

CUSHING, MARY ANN, banker; b. Bemidji, Minn., Mar. 22, 1951; d. Delmar Lee and Rosemary V. (Karels) Shull; m. Philip Lee Fisk, July 26, 1969 (div. 1977); children: Neil Lincoln, Angela Ruth; m. Roderick C. Cushing, Dec. 29, 1984. Student, Anchorage Community Coll., 1981-85, Alaska Pacific U., 1982. Sec. Nat. Bank Alaska, Ketchikan, 1976-78; loan officer Nat. Bank Alaska, Anchorage, 1981-85; loan processor Puget Sound Mut. Savs. Bank, Seattle, 1978-80; office mgr., treas. Shull Constrn., Inc., Ketchikan, 1980-81; quality control sr. analyst City Fed. Mortgage Corp., Somerset, N.J., 1985-86; regional underwriting mgr. City Fed. Mortgage Corp., Somerset, 1986-87; asst. v.p., quality control mgr. Carteret Mortgage Co., Cedar Knolls, N.J., 1987-88; asst. v.p., mgr. mortgage loan dept. First Bank, Ketchikan, 1988—; adj. lectr. Anchorage Community Coll., 1984; instr. Anchorage chpt. Am. Inst. Banking, 1985. Active Madison (N.J.) High Sch. Parent Student Tchr. Orgn., Tory J. Sabitini Sch. Parent Student Tchr. Orgn., 1985—. Mem. Nat. Assn. Female Execs. Democrat. Roman Catholic. Home: Rt 1 Box 804 Ketchikan AK 99901 Office: First Bank 331 Dock St Ketchikan AK 99901

CUSHING, PAMELA HIGLEY, municipal development executive; b. Elgin, Ill., Dec. 16, 1943; d. Philip Isidro and Helen Leonore (Bettis) Higley; m. Victor Merchant Cushing, July 8, 1967 (div. 1981); 1 child, Jason Philip. BS in Retailing, Mich. State U., 1966. Supr. Bridgeport (Conn.) Hosp., 1969-71; owner, mgr. Cushing Dressage Ctr., Neenah, Wis., 1983-85; exec. dir. Future Neenah Devel. Corp., 1985-87, Downtown Neenah Action Com., Inc., 1986-87, City Ctr. Devel. Authority, Bellingham, Wash., 1987—; cons. Internat. Downtown Assn., Washington, 1986—, Internat. Council Shopping Ctrs., 1987—, Urban Land Inst., 1987—. Contbr. articles to profl. jours. Mem. Horizon's PTA, Appleton, Wis., 1986-87, Happy Valley PTA, Bellingham, 1987-88. Home: 102 N Commercial Bellingham WA 98225 Office: City Ctr Devel Authority PO Box 5785 Bellingham WA 98227

CUSHMAN, HELEN BAKER, consultant, historian; b. Perth Amboy, N.J.; d. Ivan Franklin and Lucile (Atkinson) Baker; B.A., Barnard Coll.; postgrad. N.Y. U.; m. Robert Arnold Cushman, June 2, 1945; children—Lucinda, Robert. Route analyst Air Transport Command, Washington, 1942-44; personnel asst. Gen. Cable Corp., N.Y.C., 1944-45; sr. staff asst. to chmn. Trans World Airline, Inc., N.Y.C., 1946-50; mng. assoc. H. M. Baker Assocs., Westfield, N.J., 1958—; cons. to various corps., 1958—. Author, pub. various bus. history publications. Pres. Barnard Coll. Club North Central, N.J., 1962-64; pres. PTA, 1964-65. Recipient Literary award Am. Records Mgmt. Assn. 1972. Mem. N.J. Hist. Soc., Soc. Am. Archivists. Club: PEO. Office: Box 363 Westfield NJ 07090

CUSHMAN, ORIS MILDRED, retired nurse, hospital education administrator; b. Springfield, Mass., Nov. 22, 1931; d. Wesley Austin and Alice Mildred (Vaile) Stockwell; m. Laurence Arnold Cushman, Apr. 16, 1955; children: Lynn Ann Cushman Crandall, Laurence Arnold III. Diploma in nursing Hartford Hosp. Sch. Nursing (Conn.), 1953; BS, Western Mich. U., 1978, MA, 1980. Staff nurse Wesson Maternal Hosp., Springfield, 1953-54, acting supr., 1954-55; staff nurse Hartford Hosp., 1955-56, head nurse, 1956, staff nurse, 1957-59; staff nurse, charge nurse Reed City Hosp. (Mich.), 1961-67; supr. Meml. Hosp., St. Joseph, Mich., 1967-75, clin. supr. maternal/child health, 1975-77, dir. maternal/child health 1977-80; dir. edn. Pawating Hosp., Niles, Mich., 1980-87; ret., 1987. Sec. Women's aux. Reed City Hosp., 1964-65, v.p., 1965-66, pres., 1966-67; mem. adv. bd. on family life edn. St. Joseph Sch. Bd. (Mich.), 1979-80, Krasl Art Ctr., St. Joseph, 1987—. Mem. Nurses Assn. Am. Coll. Obstetricians and Gynecologists, Perinatal Assn. Mich., S.W. Mich. Perinatal Assn. (founding; v.p. 1979-80, pres. 1980), S.W. Mich. Healthcare Edn. Council (sec. 1983-85), Tri-County Continuing Edn. Council Southwestern Mich. (founding, chairperson 1983-84), Mich. Soc. Healthcare Edn. and Tng. (sec. 1985-86), Am. Soc. Healthcare Edn. and Tng., Mich. Health Council. Republican. Office: Pawating Hosp 31 N St Joseph Ave Niles MI 49120

CUSHMAN, SHERRY A., sales representative; b. Cuba City, Wis., June 19, 1962; d. Floyd Ernest and Constance Ann (Clemens) C. BS/BA in Agribus., U. Wis., 1984. Office asst. U. Wis., Platteville, 1980-84; record keeper pvt. farmer, Platteville, 1982-84; intern loan officer Prodn. Credit Assn., Juneau, Wis., 1983; sales rep. Ciba-Geigy Chem. Corp., Eau Claire, Wis., 1984—; sales trainer Ciba-Geigy Chem. Corp., Eau Claire, 1986—. Mem. Pres.'s Club, Phi Kappa Phi, Alpha Zeta. Home and Office: 311 River St Black River Falls WI 54615

CUSICK, MARGARET MARY, graphic designer; b. New Brunswick, N.J., June 13, 1959; d. James Joseph Jr. and Delores Jean (Whatmore) C. BA, Antioch U. West, San Francisco, 1984. Adminstrv. asst. Great Falls Devel. Corp., Paterson, N.J., 1978-80; program coordinator Greater Paterson Arts Council, 1980-81; ceramicist Cosanti (Ariz.) Origionals, 1981-82; book designer Sybex, Berkeley, Calif., 1982-83; graphic artist Wyckoff (N.J.) News, 1983-84; pres., owner Enterprise Graphic Arts, Ft. Lee, N.J., 1984-86, Cusick Design Studio, Hackensack, N.J., 1987—. Designer (book) Visicalc For Science and Engineering, 1981. Vol. Ringwood (N.J.) Manor Assn. of Arts, 1984—; mem., vol. Architects, Designers and Planners for Social Responibility. Recipient plaque Pastel Soc. Am., Ringwood Manor Assn. of Arts, 1986, Spl. award for Achievement, Dale Carnegie Found., Hackensack, 1987. Mem. Am. Inst. Graphic Arts, Self-Employed Writers and Artists Network. Libertarian. Hindu. Office: Cusick Design Studio 426 Hudson St Hackensack NJ 07601

CUSICK, PATRICIA DAULTON, insurance company executive; b. N.Y.C., Aug. 21, 1938; d. Marion Daulton and Francine (Hermansen) Martin; m. Kenneth S. Evans, June 8, 1955 (dec. 1979); 1 son, Randall Lee; m. 2d, Thomas Patrick Cusick, May 9, 1980. Personnel asst. European Exchange Service, Fontainebleau, France, 1961-64, City Water Bd., San Antonio, 1964-69; interviewer United Services Automobile Assn., San Antonio, 1969-75, EEO coordinator, 1975-83, dir. employee asst. and counseling, 1983—. Mem. Am. Soc. Personnel Adminstrs., San Antonio Personnel and Mgmt. Assn. (v.p. adminstrn. 1983, pres. 1985.) Republican. Office: United Services Automobile Assn USAA Bldg San Antonio TX 78288

CUSTER, MARY JO, university official; b. Cortland, N.Y., Aug. 1, 1955; d. Edward Daniel and Nancy Janet (Burdick) Dwyer; m. James Robert Custer, Aug. 1, 1980; 1 child, Jessica Lynn. Student, Nazareth Coll., Rochester, N.Y., 1973-75; BS in Nursing, Syracuse U., 1978, BS in Psychology, 1978. Cert. in sanitation and tng. Nat. Inst. Foodservice Industry. Service supr. dining services Syracuse U. (N.Y.), 1978-79, asst. mgr. dining services, 1979-81, dir. sanitation and tng. dining services, 1981-82, asst. to v.p. instnl. services, 1983-85, asst. to sr v.p. for student services, 1985—; lectr. in field. Contbr. articles to profl. jours. Mem. United Methodist Women's Aux., 1980—, Firemen's Aux., Cuyler, N.Y., 1980—, pres., 1987—; sec. Tioughnioga Lake Assn., 1972-80. Recipient award for disting. service Nat. Inst. Foodservice Industry, 1983. Mem. Nat. Assn. Coll. and Univ. Food Services (pubs. officer, Meritorious Service award 1983), Nat. Restaurant Assn., Am. Mgmt. Assn., Internat. Assn. Milk, Food and Environ. Sanitarians, Assn. Coll. and Univ. Housing Officers-Internat. Republican. Roman Catholic. Home: 4539 Route 13 Truxton NY 13158 Office: 606 University Ave Syracuse NY 13210

CUSTINI, JOSEPHINE, chief internal auditor; b. N.Y.C., Feb. 13, 1933; d. Louis Michael and Florence (Esposito) Festa; m. Fred Custini, Mar. 7, 1953; children: Louis, Judith. Student, Adelphi U., 1983. Chief internal auditor Maspeth (N.Y.) Fed. Savs., 1972—. Mem. L.I. Group Internal Auditors (sec. 1979-80, treas. 1981, v.p. 1982, pres. 1983), Nat. Fin. Mgrs. Assn. (bd. dirs. internal auditors div. 1982, liaison 1984-85), United Soc. Accts. and Tax Practioners of N.Y., Profl. Businesswoman Orgn., Fin. Planners Soc. (cert.). Office: Maspeth Fed Savs & Loan Bank 56-18 69th St Maspeth NY 11378

CUTHBERTSON, IDA DIENER, government agency official; b. Cleve.; d. Gottlieb John and Tess Diener. BA, Ohio State U., MA, Va. Poly. Inst. and State U. Community planner, pub. participation coordinator Soil Conservation Service, Washington; statistician Ohio Dept. Health, Columbus; research asst. Research Analysis Co., McLean, Va.; grad. research asst. Va. Poly. Inst. and State U., Reston; U.S. Congl. fellow, Washington, 1984. Recipient Superior Performance award Soil Conservation Service, Washington, 1978; Commendation award Office Mgmt. and Budget, 1979; Cert. of Achievement, Pres. of U.S., 1980; Spl. Act award Sec. Agr., 1983. Mem. Orgn. Profl. Employment of USDA (exec. v.p. 1982-85), Am. Inst. Cert. Planners (charter mem.), Soil Conservation Soc. Am. (chpt. sec. 1977), World Future Soc. Office: Soil Conservation Service USDA 14 & Independence Ave SW Washington DC 20250

CUTLER, BEVERLY WINSLOW, judge; b. Washington, Sept. 10, 1949; d. Lloyd Norton and Louise Winslow (Howe) Cutler; m. Mark Andrew Weaver, Sept. 22, 1977; children: Lucia Mary, Andrew Thaddeus, Rebecca Howe. BA, Stanford U., 1971; J.D., Yale U., 1974. Bar: Alaska 1975. Research atty. Alaska Jud. Council, Anchorage, 1974-75; atty. Alaska Pub. Defender Agy., Anchorage, 1975-77; judge Alaska Dist. Ct., Anchorage, 1977-82, Alaska Superior Ct., Palmer, 1982—. Mem. ABA, Alaska Bar Assn., Anchorage Assn. Women Lawyers, Nat. Assn. Women Judges, Nat. Assn. Women in Criminal Justice. Home: Edgerton Park Rd Palmer AK 99645 Office: Alaska Ct System 268 E Firewood Ln Palmer AK 99645

CUTLER, LAUREL, advertising agency executive; b. N.Y.C., Dec. 8, 1926; d. A. Smith and Dorothy (Glaser) C.; m. Stanley Bernstein, July 3, 1952 (div. 1983); children—Jon Cutler, Amy Sarah, Seth Perry. B.A., Wellesley Coll., 1946. Reporter Washington Post, 1946-48; copywriter J. Walter Thompson, N.Y.C., 1947-50; copy chief Wesley Assocs., 1950-56; v.p. Fletcher, Richard, Calkins & Holden, N.Y.C., 1956-63; sr. v.p., creative dir. McCann Erickson, N.Y.C., 1963-72; sr. v.p. Leber Katz Ptnrs., N.Y.C., 1972-80, exec. v.p., dir. mktg. planning, 1980-84, vice chmn., 1984-86; vice chmn. FCB/Leber Katz Ptnrs., N.Y.C., 1986—; speaker to orgns. including Assn. Nat. Advertisers, Am. Mktg. Assn., Produce Mktg. Assn., Grocery Mfrs. Am., Conf. Bd. Recipient Matrix award Women in Communications, 1985. Mem. Fashion Group. Home: 15 W 53d St New York NY 10028 Home: 145 Catalpa Rd Wilton CT 06897 Office: FCB/Leber Katz Ptnrs 767 Fifth Ave New York NY 10153

CUTLER, LAUREN ELIZABETH SAVAGE, sales executive; b. Syracuse, N.Y., July 10, 1961; d. William Edward and Patricia Noreen (Anable) Savage; m. Robert Lee Cutler, Aug. 30, 1986. BS, Clarkson U., 1983. Sales rep. Tab Products of Cen. N.Y., Cazenovia, 1983-84, Satellite Bus. Systems (div. IBM), Mpls., 1984-85; market researcher Tompkins Bros. Co., Inc., Syracuse, 1985-86; territory mgr. Monarch Marking div. Pitney-Bowes Corp., Fairfield, N.J., 1986—; corp. sec. Curran Indsl. Sales, Bayshore, N.Y., 1986—. Mem. Am. Prodn. and Inventory Control Soc. (speaker), Nat. Assn. Female Execs. Republican. Roman Catholic. Home: 105 Country Village Ln East Islip NY 11730

CUTLER, MORENE PARTEN, civic worker; b. Waxahachie, Tex., July 27, 1911; d. Bedford Taylor and Lofie Mae (Stockton) Parten; m. Robert Ward Cutler, Apr. 27, 1954. Student, Trinity U., 1929, U. Okla., 1931, U. Tex., 1933. Asst. to dir. N.Y. Sch. for Interior Decoration, N.Y.C., 1938; chief cons. Hilton Hotels Corp., Chgo., 1946-58; free-lance interior designer 1948-54. Author: Stagecoach Inn--Iron Skillet and Velvet Potholder, 1981. 1st pres., chmn. bd. dirs. Salado (Tex.) Bicentennial Commn., 1974—; bd. dirs. Cen. Tex. Bicentennial Com., 1974—; vice-chmn. Internat. Debutante Ball, N.Y.C., 1975-78; mem. Beautify Tex. Council, 1976—; chmn. Beautify Salado Com., 1979-80; founder Tex. Blubonnet Com., 1961. Recipient Tex. Good Will awards 1960—; named hon. Ellis County Hist. Mus. and Art Gallery, Waxahachie, 1967; Cen. Tex. Area Mus. trustee, Salado, 1968-75. Mem. AIA (founder N.Y. aux. chpt. 1958, citation 1966), Chautauqua Preservation Soc. (bd. dirs. Waxahachie chpt. 1975), Preservation Soc. Newport County, Salado C. of C. (bd. dirs. aux. chpt. 1974-75), Tex. Soc. Washington. Episcopalian. Club: Met. (N.Y.C.). Home: PO Box 26 Salado TX 76571

CUTLER, RUTH ELLEN LEMON, publisher; b. York, Nebr., Feb. 26, 1928; d. Harry Oliver and Ruby Elizabeth (Hartgrave) Lemon; m. Harold Max Cutler, Nov. 17, 1944 (div. 1971); children—Sheryl, Harold Max, Pamela. Student Latter-day Saints Bus. Coll., 1946. Sec., photostat operator IRS, Salt Lake City, 1951-54; sec. Purdue U. Sch. Civil Engring., West Lafayette, Ind. and engring. firms, 1954-60; exec. sec. Rico Argentine Mining Co., Salt Lake City and Rico, Colo., 1960-63; exec., legal sec. Manpower, Inc., Salt Lake City, 1959-71; owner, operator Mountain View Motel and Country Club Motel, Salt Lake City, 1963-64; exec. sec., adminstrv. asst. to clin. psychologist in pvt. practice, Salt Lake City, 1964-70; legal sec., head office staff Watkins & Faber, attys., Salt Lake City, 1971-73; adminstrv. sec. F-15 Radar div. Hughes Aircraft Co., El Segundo, Calif., 1973—; dir., v.p., sec. Cutler Enterprises, Inc., Salt Lake City, 1963-71; founder, pres., pub., dir. Gallant House Inc., Heber City, Utah, 1983—. Utah Rep. del., 1967-69; active various community drives. Mem. League Utah Writers. Home: 8628 S 300 E Sandy UT 84070

CUTLER, SEENA NORMA, psychiatric social worker; b. N.Y.C., Apr. 18, 1928; d. Nat and Rose S. Schwartz; BA, N.Y. U., Washington Sq. Coll., 1951; MSW, Columbia U., 1955; m. B. Robert Cutler, Nov. 24, 1954; children: Andrew Neale, Matthew Steven. Diplomate Clin. Social Work. Social worker Bklyn. VA Hosp., 1955-59, Roosevelt Hosp., N.Y.C., 1974-77; sr. social worker, supr. Community Health Program, Queens-Nassau, Inc., New Hyde Park, N.Y., 1977—; pvt. practice therapist; cons. VA Div. of Handicapped, Kansas City, Kans., 1976; guest lectr. Nassau County Dept. Sr. Citizens Affairs, 1980-81, Am. Cancer Soc., 1981, Am. Coll. Obstetrics and Gynecology; group therapist, various groups, 1979-81, 83-84; oncology therapist, cons., 1985-86, supr., lectr. 1981-88. Bd. dirs. and com. mem. Temple Emanuel of Gt. Neck, N.Y., 1965-86, v.p. Sisterhood, 1969-71; com. mem. Gt. Neck Public Schs., 1964-79. Recipient award, Bklyn. VA Hosp., 1959. Mem. Nat. Assn. Social Workers. Democrat. Home: 48 Berkshire Rd Great Neck NY 11023 Office: 410 Lakeville Rd New Hyde Park NY 11042

CUTSINGER, MARVA DEAN, automobile executive; b. Evansville, Ind., Aug. 10, 1932; d. Marvin Wesley and Christine (Haney) Martin; m. Larry Earl Cutsinger, Aug. 1, 1949; children: Cinda, Larry III, Candace, David, Charles. Cert. real estate agt. Advt. sec. Cutsinger Dodge, Chrysler, Plymouth, Sullivan, Ind., 1973-76; v.p. Workingman's Finance Co., Indpls., 1978—; corp. sec. Cutsinger Buick, Oldsmobile, Pontiac GMC, New Castle, Ind., 1986—; advt. cons. Fin. Co., Indpls., 1978—. Zone leader Women's Dem. Orgn., Evansville, 1960, Mother's March of Dimes, Carmel, Ind., 1985, Mental Health Assn., New Castle, 1987. Democrat. Club: Westwood Country, Country Club Indpls. Home: 3620 Rolling Springs Dr Carmel IN 46032 Office: Cutsinger Buick Olds Pontiac GMC 4701 S Memorial Dr New Castle IN 47362

CUTTER, ELIZABETH PARSONS, psychologist; b. Jefferson, N.Y., Jan. 9, 1932; d. John Raymond and Edith Louise (Hobert) Champlin; m. Edward Thomas Parsons, Dec. 22, 1951 (dec. Oct. 1972); children: Claudia Louise McClure; Catherine Eve Skogman; m. Robert Earl Cutter, June 29, 1974. BS, Wilkes Coll., 1953; MS, Pa. State U., 1959. Lic. psychologist, Wis. Psychologist Indiana (Pa.) County Guidance Ctr., 1960-62; psychologist, adminstr. Family Counseling Ctr., Kenosha, Wis., 1962-76; pres. Psychol. Assn. of Kenosha, 1976-83; supervising diagnostician Tex. Dept. Corrections, Huntsville, Tex., 1983—; cons. psychologist Taylor Children's Home, Racine, Wis., 1964-68, Racine Mental Health Clinic, Racine, 1971-72; personnel cons. Johnson's Wax Co., Racine, 1970-71. Mem. adv. com. on spl. edn., Kenosha, 1970-72; mem. steering com. Kenosha Youth Service Bd., 1973-77; bd. dirs. Outpost Youth Counselor Program, Kenosha, 1972-78. Mem. Am. Psychol. Assn. (assoc.), Nat. Bd. Profl. Counselors, Bus. and Profl. Women (pres. 1979-83). Republican. Methodist. Home: PO Box 720 Point Blank TX 77364 Office: Tex Dept of Corrections Box 83 Huntsville TX 77340

CUTTER, PORTIA LYNETTE, mathematics educator; b. N.Y.C., Dec. 28, 1938; d. JeRoyd Wiley and Portia Mae (Russell) Greene; m. James Allen Cutter Sr., Mar. 3, 1962; 1 child, James Allen. Student, Long Beach State Coll., 1962-63, Morgan State Coll., 1955-57; BA, CUNY, 1961; MS in Teaching, Memphis State U., 1972, postgrad., 1980-83. cert. math. educator, Tenn. Tchr. 7th grade Del Norte Elem. Sch., West Covina, Calif., 1961-62; tchr. algebra Vanguard Jr. High Sch., Compton, Calif., 1963-64; tchr. 7th grade math Klondike Elem. Sch., Memphis, 1965; tchr. 7th grade sci. Humboldt (Tenn.) Jr. High Sch., 1966-68; tchr. 7th and 8th grade math Georgian Hills Jr. High Sch., Memphis, 1968-71; tchr. algebra Kingsbury Jr. High Sch., Memphis, 1971—, chair math dept., 1982—. Fin. sec. Greater Faith Baptist Ch., 1975—. Office: Kingsbury Jr High Sch 1276 N Graham Memphis TN 38122

CVETKOV, ADRIANA, advertising executive; b. Sofia, Bulgaria, Dec. 9, 1950; came to U.S., 1974; d. George and Maria (Paneva) Ignatov; m. Eugene Cvetkov, Oct. 31, 1971; 1 child, Juliet. BS, U. Sofia, Bulgaria, 1973. Field research asst. Crop Protection Inst., Sofia, 1972-73; market analyst Stauffer Chem. Co., Westport, Conn., 1976-84, mgr. product, 1984-86; supr. accounts Della Femina, Travisano & Ptnrs., N.Y.C., 1986-87, Warwick Advt., N.Y.C., 1987—. Mem. ARC, Stanford, Conn., 1980. Mem. Bus. and Profl. Advt. Assn. Eastern Orthodox. Home: 27 Hartford Ave Stamford CT 06907 Office: Warwick Advt 875 3d Ave New York NY 10022

CWIRKO, TRACEY ALICE, restaurant owner; b. Englewood, N.J., Aug. 18, 1963; d. Roy Arnold Jr. and Joyce Alice (Wolff) Askling; m. Arnold Anthony Cwirko, Oct. 25, 1986; 1 child, Anthony Edwin. Assocs. in Liberal Arts, Fairleigh Dickinson U., 1985. Owner Zacchino Inc., Milton, N.J., 1985—. Mem. Omicron Nu Epsilon (sec. 1982-83, v.p. 1983-84, 84-85). Republican. Home: 51 Liberty Ln Franklin NJ 07416 Office: Zacchino Inc 5531 Berkshire Valley Rd Milton NJ 07438

CYN, T.G., writer; b. Hollywood, Calif., Feb. 29, 1948; d. Edwin Whitfield and Virginia Lou (Newcomb) McKinley; m. Gerald J. Harvey, June 26, 1970 (div. 1976); m. Stanley John Maleski Jr., Oct. 21, 1979 (div. 1984); m. Bruce B. McCulloch, Sept. 13, 1986. Student, Riverside City Coll., 1965-67, Orange Coast Coll., 1967-68. Editor Al buraag mag., 1979; freelance writer, editor Profl. Horseman, Equine Practitioner, Small Animal Practitioner, The Cons., Arabian Horse Mktg. and Bus. Rev., Washington, 1980-82; dir. publs. Am. Horse Council, Washington, 1982-84; cons. Haifa Arabians, Diamond Bar, Calif., 1983-86, Khemosabi Syndicate, Diamond Bar, 1983—; pres. T.G. Cyn & Co. Author: Tangled Mane, 1983, Gardner Bloodstock Consultant, 1980, Resilient Heart, 1985, Cowards, 1985, Tangled Mane, Vol. II, 1986, The Lonesome Pony, 1986, A New Wrinkle, 1988. Mem. Women in Communications, Internat. Arabian Horse Assn., Arabian Horse Registry Am., Am. Horse Shows Assn.

CYPESS, SANDRA MESSINGER, educator; b. N.Y.C., Jan. 5, 1943; m. Raymond Cypess, Aug. 16, 1964; children: Aaron Martin, Joshua Neil. BA, Bklyn Coll., 1963; MA, Cornell U., 1965; PhD, U. Ill., 1968. Teaching fellow U. Ill., Urbana, 1966; instr. Duke U., Durham, N.C., 1967-68; vis. asst. prof. Duke U., Durham, 1968-70; asst. prof. Point Park Coll., Pitts., 1970-74; vis. asst. prof. Carnegie-Mellon U., Pitts., 1975-76; asst. prof. SUNY, Binghamton, 1976-80, assoc. prof., dir. Latin Am. studies, 1980—; vis. prof. U. Ky., Lexington, 1973; mem. editorial bd. Latin Am. Theatre Rev., 1978—, Biligual Rev., 1985—; cons. Nat. Endowment for Humanities. Editor: Studies in Roman Languages and Literature, 1979; contbr. articles to profl. jours. Mem. MLA, Am. Assn. Tchrs. of Spanish and Portuguese, Latin Am. Studies Assn., N.E. Modern Lang. Assn. (bd. dirs. 1976-78). Office: SUNY at Binghamton Binghamton NY 13901

CYR, ELLIE R., geologist, educator; b. Cambridge, Mass., Jan. 21, 1942; d. Philip and Pauline (Nemser) Raab; m. Guy A. Cyr, Sept. 1, 1968 (div. June 1980); children: Barry, Gary. BA in Philosophy cum laude, Clark U., 1963; postgrad., U. Mass., 1965; MS in Geology, Lehigh U., 1967. Cert. geolog. scientist, sewage enforcement officer; reg. profl. geologist, S.C. City geologist Dept. Pub. Works, Bethlehem, Pa., 1966-68; geologist Rosdor Constrn., Ardsley, N.Y., 1968-69; tchr. Jewish Day Sch., Allentown, Pa., 1970-74; owner, v.p. M&E Sewerage Specialists, Inc., Nazareth, Pa., 1974-78; geologist R&G Engring. Co., Inc., Bethlehem, Pa., 1977-78; cons. geologist Macungie Pa. and Durham N.C., 1979—. Zoning officer Bushkill Township, Nazareth, 1974-76; planner Bushkill Planning Commn., 1975-78; vol. firefighter Macungie Fire Dept., 1980-86. Recipient Cert. of Merit, Nat. Assn. Home Builders, 1982; Chester Kingsley fellow, 1965. Mem. Geol. Soc. Am., Am. Inst. Profl. Geologists, Phi Beta Kappa, Sigma Gamma Epsilon, Fireman's Relief Assn. (treas. 1981-85), Carolina Geologic Soc. Democrat. Jewish. Home and Office: 529 Woodwinds Dr Durham NC 27713

CYR, LORNA JANE, marketing executive; b. N. Tonawanda, N.Y., Jan. 28, 1957; d. Lawrence Esdras and Irene Nancy (Sachuk) C. AS in Bus. Methods, SUNY, Buffalo, 1983, BS in Bus. Adminstrn., 1987. Credit clk. Nat. Assn. Credit Mgmt., Buffalo, 1975-77; sec. to v.p. The Sample, Inc., Buffalo, 1977-78; credit rep. Liberty Nat. Bank and Trust, Buffalo, 1978-79, Spencer Kellogg Div. Textron, Buffalo, 1979-82; sr. customer service rep. Spencer Kellogg/NL Chems., Buffalo, 1982-86; account exec. WYRK-FM, Buffalo, 1986, Genigraphics Corp., Phila., 1986—. Roman Catholic. Home: 9071 Mill Creek Rd Apt 2420 Levittown PA 19054 Office: Genigraphics Corp 3 Ben Franklin Pkwy Philadelphia PA 19102

CYR, SUSAN CAROL, small business owner; b. Misawa, Japan, Dec. 26, 1954; d. Thomas Roger and Priscilla Marie (Deschaine) C. Diploma, Conn. Inst. Hair Design, Hartford, 1974. Tchr. Wilford Acad., Hartford, 1975-76; stylist Headquarters Ltd., Hartford, 1974-77; owner Headquarters of Essex, Conn., 1977—; mem. Pure Logic Hair Cutting Team, 1975-77. Chair entertainment com. Flood Fair, 1984; mem. com. St. Citizen's Council, Essex; vol. Child and Family Assn., Middlesex County, 1983-87, Steamboat Dock Found., Essex, 1983-87; organizer Am. Cancer Soc. Benefit, Essex, 1987. Mem. Essex Bd. Trade, U.S. C. of C., Nat. Women's Soc., Conn. Rivery Valley Women's Network. Office: Headquarters of Essex Rt 153 Olivers Corner Essex CT 06426

CYRUS, TERIECE DYER, educational adminstrator; b. West Monroe, La., Feb. 17, 1912; d. Virge Lee and Nora (Green) Ivey; m. Isaac S. Dyer, Oct. 7, 1930; (dec.); children: Virgie Lee, Gwendolyn Marie, Nora Jean; m. Wiliam Cyrus, Dec. 29, 1960. BS, Grambling State U., 1951. Tchr. Quachita Parish Sch. Bd., Monroe, La., 1930-32, 61-71, Webster Parish Sch. Bd., Minden, La., 1940-60; dir. Westside Devel. Ctr., West Monroe, 1973—; summer dir. Headstart Program, Monroe, 1962-74. Bd. dirs. Girl Scouts U.S., Quchita Parish, 1966-73, Sr. Citizen's Ctr., West Monroe, 1979-83; v.p. Mayor's Commn. on Needs of Women, Monroe, 1986—. Recipient Merit Service award Christian Meth. Ch., 1980. Mem. NEA, LWV (pres. 1980-82), Delta Sigma Theta (treas. 1978-80). Democrat. Office: Westside Devel Ctr 1000 N Sixth St West Monroe LA 71291

CZAYA, MARY THERESA, educational administrator; b. Carteret, N.J., June 2, 1917; d. Francis and Theresa (Mezglewski) Dylag; B.S., N.J. State Tchrs. Coll., 1947; M.Ed., Rutgers U., 1957; postgrad. U. Mexico, 1958; m. Francis Czaya, June 22, 1946; 1 son, Paul. Tchr., Nathan Hale Sch., Carteret, N.J., 1940-46, Columbus Sch., Carteret, 1946-61, prin., 1961-70; prin. Washington & Cleveland Schs., Carteret, 1970-79, Minue Sch., Carteret, 1979-83. Trustee Carteret Public Library, 1972-78; mem. Middlesex County Mental Health Bd., 1961-66, Carteret Juvenile Delinquency Bd., 1974-75; trustee Middlesex County Coll., 1972-86, bd. sec., 1978-81, bd. v.p., 1981-86. Recipient cert. of merit VFW Aux., 1978. Mem. N.J. Congress Parents and Tchrs. (life), Nat. Elem. Prins. Assn., N.J. Elem. Prins. Assn., Kappa Delta Phi. Home: 75 Edgar St Carteret NJ 07008

CZEKALSKI, LONI RAVEN, air transportation systems executive; b. Atlantic City, Aug. 24, 1948; d. Zigman Stanley Czekalski and Eleanor Frieda (Schnegelberger) Raven. BA in Math., Glassboro State Coll., 1970; M in Aviation Mgmt., Embry Riddle U., 1984. Mathematician data processing div. Cen. Programming Br. Utility and Support Programming Sect., Atlantic City, 1970-71; mathematician enroute systems div. Devel. Programming Br. Engring. Programming Sect., Atlantic City, 1971-74; mathematician terminal sect. Air Traffic Control Systems div. Devel. Programming Br., Atlantic City, 1974-76, mathematician systems sect., 1976-78; computer specialist Simulation and Analysis div. Systems Integration Br., Atlantic City, 1978-81; supr. mathematician, tech. program mgr. Airborne Separation Assurance program Systems Test and Evaluation div., Atlantic City, 1981-83, Aircraft Icing program Flight Safety Research Br., Aircraft and Airport Systems Tech. div., Atlantic City, 1983-84; spl. asst. for programs Office of Dir. FAA, Atlantic City, 1984-85, operations research analyst Office Sci. and Advanced Tech., 1985—. Contbr. articles to profl. jours. Jehovah's Witness. Office: FAA Atlantic City NJ 08405

CZNARTY, DONNA MAE, educator; b. Bridgeport, Conn., Aug. 17, 1950; d. Richard W. and Dorothy Mae (Kosturko (Oefinger); m. Wiliam C. Cole, Jr., July 11, 1970; 1 child, Michael William Cole; m. Thomas Robert Cznarty, Apr. 29, 1983. BS in Edn., So. Conn. State U., 1973, MS in Edn., 1977. Lang. arts tchr. Shelton Bd. Edn., Conn., 1973-82; English tchr. Millbrook Bd. Edn., N.Y., 1985-86; mem. sales staff Hopewell Precision, Inc., Hopewell Junction, N.Y., 1986—. Mem. Internat. Platform Assn., Nat. Assn. Female Execs. Republican. Roman Catholic. Avocations: interior design, fashion, traveling, doll collecting. Home: 71 Hibernia Heights Dr Salt Point NY 12578 Office: Hopewell Precision Inc Ryan Dr Hopewell Junction NY 12533

DABNEY, ANITA ELIZABETH, real estate specialist; b. Belleville, Ill., July 27, 1951; d. Oliver Junious and Lois (Blayton) D. BS cum laude, Spelman Coll., 1973; MS, Cornell U., 1976. Mgr. neighborhood revitalization City of Buffalo Dept. Community Devel., 1978-79; community devel. rep. N.Y. Div. Housing and Community Renewal, Buffalo, 1979-81; with real estate investment dept. The Travelers Ins. Co., Houston, 1981-87, investment supr. real estate investment dept. so. regional office, 1987—. Author: Urban Homesteading in Four Cities: Potential for Urban Neighborhood Revitalization, 1976. Bd. mem., chmn. fin. com. YMCA Erie County, Buffalo, 1977-80; bd. mem., mem. housing com. Buffalo Urban League, 1979-81; mem. adv. com. Houston Met. Ministries, 1986-87; mem., coordinator polit. forums Nat. Coalition 100 Black Women, Houston, 1985-87; mem. fin. com. new sanctuary devel. Windsor Village Meth. Ch., Houston, 1986-87; founding mem. Christia Adiar Soc. Polit. Action com., 1987—. Recipient Felicitations award City of Buffalo Common Council, 1981. Mem. Houston Urban Bankers Assn. Democrat. Methodist. Club: Girl Friends, Inc. (Houston) (rec. sec. 1984-86). Office: The Travelers Ins Co Real Estate Investments 2250 Lakeside Dr Suite 500 Richardson TX 75281

DABNEY, COLETTE ELLEN, state government employee; b. Richmond, Va., Jan. 11, 1958; d. Jacob Alfred and Phyllis Lee (Godette) D. Student, Del. State Coll., 1976-77; BS, Howard U., 1980; diploma, Surety Real Estate, Richmond, 1986. Pub. relations asst. Office of Mayor, Washington, 1979; interior designer Savoir Faire Interior Design, Rockville, Md., 1979-80; asst. mgr. Design Store of Georgetown, Washington, 1981-82; mgr. Once in a Lifetime Gallery, Washington, 1982; assoc. purchasing agent Hecht Co., Washington, 1982-84; pub. relations asst. Sta. KYW, Phila., 1985; high sch. sci. tchr. King and Queen County Pub. Schs., Va., 1986; advt. statis. clk. Miller and Rhoads, Richmond, 1986-87; acctg. asst. Dept. Social Services, Richmond, 1987—; participant various seminars, Richmond, 1987; pub. relations asst. Sta. KYW, Phila., 1988. Vol. Richmond Arts Council, 1987, Childrens Hosp., Richmond, 1987; mem. Valentine Mus., Richmond, 1987. Mem. Nat. Assn. Female Execs., Am. Bus. Womens Assn., AAUW, nat. Assn. 9 to 5 Working Women (com. chair), Nat. Council Negro Women, Alpha KAppa Alpha. Baptist. Home: 7619 Wistar Village Dr Apt C Richmond VA 23228 Office: Dept Social Services 8000 Discovery Dr Richmond VA 23288

DABOLL, EVELYN LOUISE KENYON, tax and financial consultant; b. Old Mystic, Conn., Feb. 22, 1927; d. Anson Surber and L. Maude (Tinker) Kenyon; student Jackson (Miss.) Sch. Law, 1954; m. H. Merle Witt, Oct. 29, 1945 (div. Apr. 1956); m. 2d, Frederick A. Daboll, Feb. 9, 1962. Instr. traffic dept. So. New Eng. Telephone Co., New Britain, Conn. and Mystic, Conn., 1943-45; residential designer Frank Kincannon, AIA, Tupelo, Miss., 1949-51; chief dep. Chancery clk. Chancery Clk's Office, Tupelo, 1951-54; jr. partner Sadler Oil Co., Jackson, Miss., 1954-61; owner, operator Witt Enterprises, bookkeeping and secretarial services, 1961-62; adminstr. asst. Copp, Brenneman & Tighe, attys., New London, Conn., 1961-62; owner, operator Daboll Enterprises, Noank, Conn., 1963—. bd. dirs. Hobo Line Inc. Moderator, Town of Groton Rep. Town Meeting, 1969-70, rep., 1968-70; mem. Bd. Selectmen Groton, 1980-81. Mem. Nat. Assn. Tax Preparers, VFW Aux. Democrat. Baptist. Lodge: Kiwanis. Address: 206 Seneca Dr Noank CT 06340

DACE, TISH, educator; b. Washington, Sept. 13, 1941; d. Edward Durnford and Claude Marshall (Russell) Skinner; children: Hal, Ted. AB, Sweet Briar (Va.) Coll., 1963; MA, Kans. State U., 1967, PhD, 1971. Instr. Kans. State U., Manhattan, 1967-71; asst. prof. John Jay Co. CUNY, 1971-74, dep. chmn. speech and theatre, 1974-79, assoc. prof., 1975-80, chmn. speech and theatre, 1979-80; dean Coll. Arts & Scis. Southeastern Mass. U., North Dartmouth, 1980-86, prof. English, 1986—; chmn. Am. Theartre Wing Design Awards, N.Y., 1986—; mem. adv. bd. Contemporary Dramatists, London, 1986—. Author: LeRoi Jones (Imamu Amiri Baraka: A Checklist of Works by and about Him, 1971; author: (with others) Modern Theater and Drama, 1973, Black American Writers, 1978; New Eng. editor Stages, 1986—; assoc. editor Shakespearean Research & Opportunities, 1971-75; theatre critic over 400 play reviews; contbr. 90 articles to newspapers, mags. profl. jours. Recipient research stipend, NEH cand., 1987. Mem. Outer Critics Circle (exec. com. 1980-83), Am. Theatre Critics Assn., Drama Desk, Am. Soc. Theatre Research, Phi Beta Kappa (pres. Kans. chpt. 1969-70). Democrat. Office: Southeastern Mass U English Dept North Dartmouth MA 02747

DACEY, EILEEN M., lawyer; b. N.Y.C., Dec. 15, 1948; d. Gabriel A. and Mary (Breen) D.; m. Kinchen C. Bizzell, Jan. 1, 1984 B.A. in Sociology, SUNY-Stony Brook, 1970; J.D., St. John's U., 1975. Assoc. Mendes & Mount, N.Y.C., 1976-80, jr. ptnr., 1980-88; ptnr. Adams, Duque & Hazeltine, N.Y.C., 1988—. Mem. Vol. Lawyers for the Arts. Mem. ABA, Assn. Bar City N.Y. Republican. Home: 208 E 35th St New York NY 10016 Office: Adams Duque & Hazeltine 551 Madison Ave New York NY 10022

DACEY, KATHLEEN RYAN, judge; b. Boston; m. William A. Dacey (dec. Aug. 1986); 1 child, Mary Dacey White. A.B. with honors, Emmanuel Coll., 1941; M.S. in L.S., Simmons Coll., 1942; J.D., Northeastern U., 1945; postgrad., Boston U. Law Sch., 1945-46. Bar: Mass. 1945, U.S. Supreme Ct. 1957. Practiced in Boston, 1947-75; asst. atty. gen., chief civil bur. Mass. Dept. Atty. Gen., Boston, 1975-77; law clk. to justices Mass. Supreme Jud. Ct., 1945-47; U.S. adminstrv. law judge Boston, 1977—; auditor, master Commonwealth of Mass., 1972-75, Suffolk and Norfolk Counties, Mass., 1972-75; asst. dist. atty. Suffolk County, Mass., 1971-72; mem. panel def. counsel for indigent persons U.S. Dist. Ct. Dist. Mass.; lectr., speaker in field. Contbr. articles to profl. jours. Bd. dirs. Mission United Neighborhood Improvement Team, Boston; mem. Boston Sch. Com., 1945-46, chmn., 1946-47. Recipient Silver Shingle award Boston U. Sch. Law, 1980; named Alumnae Woman of Yr., Northeastern U. Law Sch. Assn., 1976. Mem. ABA (ho. of dels. 1982—, exec. com. conf. of adminstrv. law judges jud. adminstrn. div. 1987—), Internat. Bar Assn., Mass. Bar Assn., Boston Bar Assn., Norfolk Bar Lawyers Assn., Nat. Assn. Women Lawyers (pres.), Mass. Assn. Women Lawyers, Internat. Fedn. Women Lawyers, Boston U. Law Sch. Alumni Assn. (corr. sec. 1974-76), Boston U. Nat. Alumni Council. Office: SSA-OHA 10 Causeway St Room 417 Boston MA 02221-0091

DACHS, ANNE ARNOLD, health services administrator; b. San Francisco, Jan. 20, 1939; d. Leon Weaver and Irene Mae (Strutt) Arnold; m. Louis Leon Dachs, June 12, 1971. BS, U. Calif., Berkeley, 1961; MPH, UCLA, 1971. Pub. health microbiologist Dept. Pub. Health State of Calif., Berkeley, 1962-65, 67-70; vol. Peace Corps, Sandakan Sabah, Malaysia, 1965-67; assoc. dir. San Fernando Valley Health Consortium, Los Angeles, 1971-74; asst. dir., academic adminstr. UCLA, 1974-77; cons. Am. Med. Internat., Beverly Hills, Calif., 1978, v.p. profl. devel., 1979—. Contbr. articles to profl. jours. Mem. Calif. Commn. on Indsl. Innovation, Sacrament, 1982; bd. dirs. Los Angeles Bus. Labor Council, 1983-85, Friends of Observatory, Los Angeles, 1987-88; vol. exec. Los Angeles Olympic Organizing Com., Los Angeles, 1984. Recipient cert. of Achievement Los Angeles YWCA, 1985, 87. Mem. Am. Mgmt. Assn., Am. Pub. Health Assn., Am. Soc. Tng. and Devel. Democrat. Home: 5782 Calpine Malibu CA 90265

DACOSTA, JACQUELINE, advertising company executive; b. N.Y.C., Jan. 21, 1927; d. Joachim and Tirsa (Olmeda) DaC. BA in Bus. Adminstrn., Hunter Coll., 1952. Asst. exporter mgr. Morse Internat., N.Y.C., 1946-52; supr. media research Biow, Beirn, Toigo, Inc., N.Y.C., 1952-55; media research analyst Ted Bates & Co., N.Y.C., 1955-63, asst. v.p. media research, 1963-65, coordinator internat. media, 1965—, v.p., dir. media info. and analysis, 1965-78, sr. v.p., 1977-86, media dir., 1978-86, ret., 1986; pres. JDC Communications Marketing Cons., N.Y.C., 1986—; exec. v.p. AC&R-Rossi Hispanic div. Ted Bates Worldwide, 1984-85; cons. media, research, mktg., govt. and pvt. orgns.; internat. lectr. Contbr. articles to trade jours. Mem. adv. bd. Nat. Urban Coalition; bd. govs. Nat. Conf. P.R. Women, 1975-77; active P.R. Family Inst., 1977-87, 88, Hamilton Madison Settlement House, 1977—, pres., 1981, 87; bd. dirs. Bus. Council for UN Decade for Women, pres., 1979; bd. dirs. Broadcast Pioneers Found. Mem. Am. Advt. Fedn. (dir., named Advt. Woman of Yr. 1974), Advt. Research Found. (bd. dirs.), Advt. Women N.Y. (pres. 1973-74), Internat. Radio TV Soc., Internat. Radio TV Found., Hispanics in Communications (founder, pres. 1980-81). Home: 6403 Greenvale Ln Houston TX 77066 Office: JDC Communications Marketing Consultants 340 E 64th St New York NY 10021

DAEBRITZ, CHERYL ANN, bank trainer; b. Elkhorn, Wis., Oct. 15, 1949; d. George Herbert and Lorraine Hulda (Frodl) Nelson; m. Harold Robert Daebritz, Feb. 17, 1978. BS, Loyola U., 1972; PhD, Kent State U., 1975. Lectr. U. Md., Heidelberg, Fed. Rep. W. Germany, 1975-79, U. Lowell (Mass.), 1980-83; service rep. Neworld Bank, Boston, 1984-85, trainer, 1985—. Contbr. articles to profl. jours. Mem. Am. Psychol. Assn., Soc. Advancement Soc. Psychology, Am. Soc. for Tng. and Devel. Home: 75 Cedar St Malden MA 02148 Office: Neworld Bank 55 Summer St Boston MA 02110

DAEHLER-DANZIGER, KRISTA KAREN, consultant; b. Logan, Utah, Sept. 26, 1957; d. Ralph Edwin and Pat (Bigelow) Daehler; m. Gregory L. Hasler, Nov. 20, 1976 (div. 1982); m. Sanford E. Danziger, May 1, 1988. Grad. in graphic arts, Al Collins Design Sch., 1980. Cert. graphic designer, counselor, Hawaii, 1986. Tng. asst. Allison Arabians, Scottsdale, Ariz., 1976-77; tng. dir. mgr. Lake Side Farms, Rockwood, Mich., 1977-79; sales assoc. The Broadway, Phoenix, Ariz., 1979-80; art dir. The Larson Agy., Honolulu, 1980-81; pub. Common Ground Networking News, Honolulu, 1981-82; art, creative dir. Relationship Tng. Ctr. Internat., Honolulu, 1982-86; owner, dir. Design by Krista, Honolulu, 1982-87; instr. Al Collins Graphic Design Sch., Temple, Ariz., 1987-88; exec. dir. Ptnrs. in Performance, Scottsdale, Ariz., 1987—; counselor Omesa Directory, Phoenix, 1987-88. Illustrator numerous books including Past Lifes: A Key to Your Present Relationships, 1984, The Monthly Energies, 1985. Vol. Horsemanship for the Handicapped, Honolulu, 1981-82, Ch. of Universal Religions, Honolulu, 1982-86, Winners Circle Breakfast Club, Honolulu, 1982-86. Recipient Outstanding Artwork award and Outstanding Artist award, Al Collins Graphic Design Sch., 1987. Clubs: Comancheros (Kauai, Hawaii), Toastmasters (Honolulu). Office: Pntrs in Performance 3370 N Hayden Rd Suite 313 Scottsdale AZ 85251

DAFFERN, SHARI LYNN, auditor; b. Victoria, Tex., May 27, 1949; d. Arthur Edward and Dorothy Aline (Pels) Walkowiak; m. Eddie Earl Daffern, May 30, 1970. BBA, Texas Tech U, 1971. Acct., office mgr. Western Assocs., Inc., Lubbock, Tex., 1971-73; acct. Rodman Oil Co., Odessa, Tex., 1973-74; acct. Tex. Tech U., Lubbock, 1974-78, internal auditor, 1980-88; acct. Mason, Nickels & Warner, CPA's, Lubbock, 1978-79; acct., bus. mgr. La Fonda del Sol, Lubbock, 1979-80; dir. internal audit West Tex. State U., Canyon, 1988—. Mem. Tex. Assn. Coll. and Univ. Auditors, Inst. Internal Auditors (cert.). Roman Catholic. Lodge: Daus. of Nile (local v.p. 1987, pres. 1988). Home: 1028 Cimarron Canyon TX 79015

DAGG, DIANE MARIE, information processing specialist; b. Wichita, Kans., May 1, 1953; d. Ronald Martin and Bonnie Mae (Lyons) Gray; Student Kans. Wesleyan U., 1971-74; BBA in Econs., Washburn U., 1977. Adminstrv. asst. The Villages, Inc., Topeka, 1975-81; office support mgr. Office Automation Systems of Topeka, Inc., Topeka, 1981—. Actress Topeka Civic Theatre, 1975—; dancer Topeka Ballet Co., 1978; bd. dirs. Dance Arts Topeka, 1979-81, v.p.-membership, 1980-81. Named Best Actress, Alpha Psi Omega, Kans. Wesleyan U., 1972, 75; recipient 3 Renna Hunter awards Topeka Civic Theatre, 1984-85, 85-86. Democrat. Presbyterian. Office: Office Automation Systems Topeka Inc 3124 SW 29th St Ste 1 Topeka KS 66614

DAGGETT, ANDREA STUHLMAN, human resources specialist; b. Darby, Pa., Nov. 21, 1952; d. William Christopher and Ann (McFadden) Stuhlman; m. John Stephen Daggett, July 26, 1980; children: Ryan, Christopher. BS, St. Joseph's U., Phila., 1974; MEd, Boston Coll., 1977; PhD, U. Ariz., 1983. Retail mgr. Ups N Downs, Springfield, Pa., 1974-75; counselor Natick (Mass.) High Sch., 1976-78; personnel asst. U. Ariz., Tucson, 1980-81; analyst Pima County Govt. Office, Tucson, 1981-83, employment mgr., 1983, sr. analyst, 1984-85; personnel mgr. Ariz. State Sch. for Deaf and Blind, Tucson, 1985—; cons. Tohono O'Odham Nation, Sells, Ariz., 1985—, St. Luke's Home for Women, Tucson, 1986-87, Palo Verde Hosp., 1987; mem. indsl. adv. bd. Ctr. for Employment Tng., 1983-85. Mem. Am. Soc. Tng. and Devel., Am. Soc. Personnel Adminstrn., Internat. Personnel Mgmt. Assn. (publs. adv. bd.), So. Ariz. Affirmative Action Assn., Tucson Personnel Assn. Home: 3827 Lizard Rock Pl Tucson AZ 85718 Office: Ariz State Sch Deaf and Blind PO Box 5545 Tucson AZ 85703-0545

D'AGNESE, HELEN JEAN (MRS. JOHN J. D'AGNESE), artist; b. N.Y.C.; d. Leonardo and Rose (Redavid) De Santis; m. John J. D'Agnese, Oct. 29, 1942; children—John, Linda, Diane, Michele, Helen, Gina, Paul. Student CUNY, 1940-42; student Atlanta Coll. Art, 1972-76. One-man shows: Maude Sullivan Gallery, El Paso, 1964, John Wanamaker Gallery, Phila., 1966, U. N.Mex., 1967, Karo Manducci Gallery, San Francisco, 1968, Tuskegee Inst. Carver Mus., 1968, Lord & Taylor Gallery, N.Y.C., 1969, Harmon Gallery, Naples, Fla., 1970, Fountainbleau, Miami, 1970, Reflections Gallery, Atlanta, 1972, Williams Gallery, Atlanta, 1973, Atlanta Coll. of Art, 1976-80, Americana Gallery, Mineola, Tex., 1977, E. M. Howard Gallery, Amelia Island, Fla., 1978, Haitian Primitives Gallery, 1981, Highland Gallery, Atlanta, 1987, others; group shows: Musseo des Artes, Juárez, México, 1968, Benedictine Art Show, N.Y.C., 1967, Southeast Contemporary Art Show, Atlanta, 1968, Atlanta U., 1969, Red Piano Gallery, Hilton Head, S.C., Terrace Gallery, Atlanta, Ann. Bible Heritage Art Exhibit, Marietta, Ga., 1976, Nat. Judaic Theme Exhbn., Atlanta, 1976, Crystal Britton Gallery, Atlanta; represented in permanent collections: Pres. Jimmy Carter, Juarez (Mexico) Art Mus., Vatican Mus., Rome, Nassau (Fla.) County Pub. Library. Judge art show Mt. Loretto Acad., El Paso, 1967; commd. sculptor of Bob Marley in Limestone, 1985; art demonstration and lectr. Margaret Harris Sch., Atlanta, 1970; artist-in-residence Montessori Sch., Atlanta, 1978-79. Recipient Gold medal Accademia Italia delle Arti, Italy, 1979, Calvatone, 1982, Golden Flame award, 1986; 1st place sculpture award Tybee Island Art Festival, 1982, Golden Flame award Parliamento U.S.A., 1987, Golden Palette award Academia Europea, 1986, 87, Gold medal Internat. Parliament for the Arts, 1982. Mem. Nat. Mus. of Women in the Arts (chartered), Arts Alliance Amelia Island, Nat. Mus. Women in Arts (chartered). Address: 3240 S Fletcher Ave Fernandina Beach FL 32034 Studio: 14 1/2 N 4th St Fernandina Beach FL 32043

D'AGNOLO, GEORGIANNA LOLA, training executive; b. Peoria, Ill., Oct. 11, 1958; d. George Richard Lewis and Virginia Maxine (Bolding) Anderson; m. Otto (Rusty) Keith D'Agnolo, June 2, 1984. Grad. high sch., Peoria. Supply technician 182 TASGp, Peoria, 1976-79, with allowance and authorization dept., 1979-81, tng. technician, 1981-83; supply stock control 160 RMS Rickenbacker, Columbus, Ohio, 1983-85, tng. technician 160 CAM, 1986—; co-owner D.D. Discs, Columbus, 1984—; aerobic instr. YMCA, Circleville, 1986—; fitness choreographer, Circleville, 1986—. Participant various fund raising runs, 1983—. Mem. Nat. Assn. Female Execs. Home: 360 Meadow Dr Circleville OH 43113 Office: Rickenbacker ANG Base 160 CAM/MAT Columbus OH 43217

DAGUANO, KAREN MARTHA, educational administrator, consultant; b. Jersey City, Mar. 15, 1950; d. Albert and Helen Therese (Zelenty) Daguano. B.A., Jersey City State Coll., 1972; M.Ed., U. Va., 1973, Ed.D., 1981. Tchr. spl. edn. Virginia Beach City Schs. (Va.), 1973-77; asst. dir. instnl. research SUNY-New Paltz, 1981-83, dir. instnl. research, 1983-85; dir. instnl. research and planning Glassboro State Coll., N.J., 1985-87; asst. v.p. acad. affairs William Paterson Coll., Wayne, N.J., 1987—. Mem. Am. Ednl. Research Assn., Assn. Instnl. Research, Soc. Coll. and Univ. Planners, Advancement Women in Higher Edn. Adminstrn, Phi Delta Kappa. Democrat. Roman Catholic. Office: William Paterson Coll Acad Affairs Morrison Hall Wayne NJ 07470

DAHBANY, AVIVAH, psychologist; b. Bklyn., Jan. 3, 1951; d. Hyman and Esther (Levy) D.; BA, CCNY, 1974, MS, 1978. Fellow in Clin. Psychology Albert Einstein Coll. Medicine, 1976-77; psychologist Adams Sch., N.Y.C., 1977-78; dir. spl. edn., psychologist Dov Revel Yeshiva, Forest Hills, N.Y., 1978-79; psychologist Franklin Twp. Public Schs., Somerset, N.J., 1979—; adj. lectr. CCNY, 1977-78; adj. instr. Monmouth Coll., 1981, 88, Raritan Valley Community Coll., 1987—; psychol. cons. Robert Wood Johnson Meml. Hosp., Laurie Devel. Inst., Child Evaluation Ctr., 1985—. Mem. N.Y. Assn. Sch. Psychologists (chairperson student certification task force 1977-78), Am. Psychol. Assn., Nat. Assn. Sch. Psychologists, NEA. Office: Pupil Personnel Services 1755 Amwell Rd Somerset NJ 08873

DAHER, TERESA ANN, personnel director; b. Los Angeles, Sept. 12, 1952; d. Clyde Frank and Mary Virginia (Mancino) Flynn; m. John C. Nisbet, Aug., 1976 (div.); m. Donald A. Daher, July 8, 1983. Investigator Shaw Investigations, Long Beach, Calif., 1975-76; jailer, desk officer City of Inglewood, Calif., 1976-78; dep. sheriff trainer Los Angeles County, 1978; personnel dir. Latchford Glass Co., Los Angeles, 1978—. Res. police officer City of Inglewood, 1975-78; organizer, participant Adopt-a-Sch., Los Angeles, 1984—. Mem. Personnel and Indsl. Relations Assn., Am. Payroll Assn., Nat. Notary Assn., Nat. Assn. Female Execs. Roman Catholic. Office: Latchford Glass Co PO Box 01707 Los Angeles CA 90001

DAHL, ARLENE, actress, cosmetic executive, author; b. Mpls., Aug. 11, 1928; d. Rudolph and Idelle (Swan) D.; m. Marc A. Rosen; children: Lorenzo Lamas, Carole Christine Holmes, Rounsevelle Andreas Schaum. Student, U. Minn., Mpls. Inst. Art, Minn. Coll. Music, Minn. Bus. Coll. Pres. Arlene Dahl Enterprises, 1952-77; v.p. Kenyon & Eckhart, 1967-72, pres. Woman's World div., 1967-72; internat. dir. Sales and Mktg. Execs. Internat., 1972-75; fashion dir. O.M.A., 1975-78; pres. Dahlia Parfums, Inc., 1975-85, Dahlia Productions, Inc., 1978-81, Dahlmark Prodns., 1981—, Lasting Beauty Ltd., 1986—; nat. beauty advisor Sears Roebuck Co., 1970-75. Author: Always Ask a Man, 1965, 12 Beautyscope books, 1968, rev. edit., 1978, Arlene Dahl's Secrets of Hair Care, 1970, Arlene Dahl's Secrets of Skin Care, 1972, Beyond Beauty, 1980, Arlene Dahl's Lovescopes, 1983; actress: (Broadway plays) including Mr. Strauss Goes to Boston, Questionable Ladies, Cyrano de Bergerac, The Camel Bell, Blithe Spirit, Life With Father, (Broadway musical) Applause (Tony award), (films) including (debut) My Wild Irish Rose, The Bride Goes Wild, Reign of Terror, A Southern Yankee, Ambush, The Outriders, Three Little Words, Watch the Birdie, Scene of the Crime, Inside Straight, No Questions Asked, Desert Legion, Slightly Scarlet, Sangaree, Caribbean Gold, Jamaica Run, Diamond Queen, Here Come the Girls, Bengal Brigade, Kisses for My President, Woman's World, Journey to the Center of the Earth, Wicked as They Come, She Played with Fire, Les Poneyettes, Du Blé Enliases, The Land Raiders, The Way to Kathmandu, Fortune is a Woman, The Big Bank Role, Who Killed Maxwell Thorn?, (TV show) Lux Video Theatre, 1952-53; guest starring appearances on The Love Boat, Fantasy Island, Love American Style, One Life to Live, 1981-84, Night of 100 Stars, 1983, Happy Birthday Hollywood, 1987; hostess (TV series): Pepsi-Cola Theatre, 1954, Opening Night, 1958, Arlene Dahl's Beauty Spot, 1966, Arlene Dahl's Starscope, 1966, Arlene Dahl's Lovescope, 1980-82; played throughout U.S. in One Touch of Venus, The Camel Bell, Blithe Spirit, Liliom, The King and I, Roman Candle, I Married an Angel, Bell, Book and Candle, Applause, Marriage Go Round, Pal Joey, A Little Night Music, Forty Carats, Life With Father, Murder Among Friends, Night; nightclub act Flamingo Hotel, Las Vegas, Latin Quarter, N.Y.C.; internat. syndicated beauty columnist, Chgo. Tribune/ N.Y. News Syndication, 1950-70; designer sleepwear for A.N. Saab & Co., 1952-57, In Vogue with Arlene Dahl (Patterns), 1980-85. Hon. life mem. Father Flannagan's Boys Town; internat. chair Pearl Buck Found.; bd. dirs. Hollywood Mus. Recipient 8 Laurel awards Box Office Mag., Hollywood Walk of Fame star, Coup de Chapeau Deauville Film Festival award, 1982; named Best-Coiffed, 3 times, Woman of Yr., Advt. Club of N.Y.C., 1969, Mother of Yr., 1979. Mem. Author's Guild, Acad. Motion Picture Arts and Scis., Commanderie des Bontemps de Medoc, Nat. Acad. TV Arts and Scis., Internat. Platform Assn., Sierra Club, Nat. Trust Hist. Preservation, The Film Soc., Smithsonian Inst. Office: Dahlmark Prodns PO Box 116 Sparkill NY 10976

DAHL, SONDRA CHRISTINE, aerospace executive; b. Salt Lake City, Jan. 15, 1946; d. Bert Olaus and Rubye (Anderson) D. BS, U. Alaska, Anchorage, 1972. Dir. Mutual Acceptance Corp., Tacoma, Wash., 1969-74; sec. The Boeing Co., Seattle, 1974-75, computing analyst, 1975-82, aerospace exec., 1982—; pres. Excaliber Ednl. Services, Seattle, 1983—, Cameo Leasing, Inc., Seattle, 1982—; dir. First Fidelity Fin., Seattle, Advanced Prodns., Inc., Seattle. Minister Esoterian Soc., Seattle, 1985—. Mem. Nat. Assn. Female Execs. Republican.

DAHLBERG, DONNA D., auditor; b. New Haven, Oct. 14, 1959; d. Donald Kenneth and Emily Frances (Allen) D.; m. Glenn Fiorentino, Aug. 15, 1958. AS in Acctg., Quinnipiac Coll., 1986, BS in Gen. Bus., 1988. Head teller Fidelity Fed. Savs./Loan Assn., New Haven, 1978-79; service rep. Blue Cross/Blue Shield, North Haven, Conn., 1979-83, staff acct., 1983-84, internal auditor, 1984-86, EDP auditor, 1986—. Mem. Nat. Mgmt. Assn., Inst. Internal Auditors, Nat. Assn. Female Execs., Venetian Gardens Condo Assn. (pres.).

DAHLBERG, JOYCE KAREN, communications company executive; b. Mpls., Sept. 30, 1943; d. Elon Clinton and Adelynne Elizabeth (Mitchell) Tuttle; m. Curtis Leroy Dahlberg, Dec. 23, 1967; children: Eric Curtis, Curtis Elon. BA cum laude, Hamline U., 1965; postgrad. U. Minn., community colls., 1965—. Tchr. English, Ind. Sch. Dist. 281, Robbinsdale, Minn., 1965-68; patient fin. rep. Univ. Hosps., U. Minn., Mpls., 1968-70; space analyst health scis. U. Minn., Mpls., 1970-71; freelance photographer, writer, editor for bus. communications, mags., newspapers, Mpls., 1975—; freelance franchise communications cons.; speaker various confs. and meetings; instr. continuing edn., 1988—. Editor: (newsletters) Friday Council for High Potential Children, 1981— (sec. 1981-82, pres. 1985-88), Minn. Park Suprs. Assn., 1980-86; writer ednl. videotapes Osseo TV/Media Prodns., 1978-81 (Upper Miss. Ednl. Videotape Competition award 1979), also pub. relations materials, software and tech. manuals, poetry, children's stories. Active numerous coms. United Methodist Ch., Fridley, Minn., 1978—, coordinator Year of Child, 1979; active YWCA Program Council, 1975-78, No. Suburban YWCA, Mpls.; vol. tchr. OMNIBUS, Fridley Schs., 1982, mem. community edn. tchr., 1985-86, mem. parent adv. com., 1985-87, others; citizen ambassador People to People Internat. to Republic of China, 1988. Mem. Women Entrepreneur Network, Women in Communications (continuing edn. com., 1984-86), Minn. Council on Gifted and Talented (pres. Fridley chpt. 1985-88, newsletter edit. 1981—, sch. rep. 1982-84, advocate with State Ho. Reps. 1985-86), Fridley Council for High Potential Children, Freelance Communicators Network (charter, publicist), Am. Soc. Profl. and Exec. Women. Methodist. Address: 205 Rice Creek Blvd NE Minneapolis MN 55432

DAHLBERG, SOPHIA FLORANCE, insurance agent, writer; b. Tulsa, Sept. 4, 1928; d. Hayes Louis Little Bear and Lorraine Mary Ivers; student Okla. Coll. Liberal Arts, 1973; m. W. N. Overton, Dec. 30, 1944; children—Mickie Chouteau, Hayes Neil, Roger Dean, Michael Anthony, Nakomis Ann; m. 2d, Gilbert Harry Dahlberg, Oct. 29, 1960. With Smoot-Holman, Inglewood, Calif., 1950-51, N.Am. Aviation, Compton, Calif., 1959-60; restaurant mgr. Catalina Island, Calif., 1964-66; mgr. Authentic Am. Indian Singers and Dancers, 1961-64; dancer, 1944-81; bail bondsman Stuyvesant Ins., Davenport, Iowa, 1977-80; life ins. agt., Duncan, Okla., 1984—; lectr. in field. Mem. Stephens County Hist. Soc., Duncan, Okla., 1972-82. Mem. Am. Legion Aux., Okla. Hist. Soc. Democrat. Roman Catholic. Clubs: Klash-Kah-she Indian Woman's, Cher-O-Kan Gateway Soc., others. Author: The Adventures of Nakomis, 1964; Osage Indian Neosho Agency in Kansas, 1983; The Enumeration of the Osage Tribe of Indians in Oklahoma, 1983; Those Illustrious Frenchmen, 1985, Osage Indians 1878-79, 1986; A Personal Experience, 1984; author children's stories. Contbr. biographies to hist. soc. publs., articles to profl. jours. Home: Box 422 Duncan OK 73534

DAHLE, KAREN, actress, announcer; b. Paterson, N.J., Oct. 24, 1945; d. Walter R. and Marjorie L. (van Rossum) Rosendale. B.A., SUNY-Oswego, 1967; postgrad. Utica Coll. Syracuse U., 1968; cert. The Neighborhood Playhouse Sch. of Theatre, 1969-71. Tchr. English, theater and speech New Hartford Central Sch., N.Y., 1967-69; actress, announcer, N.Y.C., 1969-82; staff announcer NBC, N.Y.C., 1982—. Actress various TV series and spls.; narrator, commentator, announcer various documentary and indsl. films, radio, TV commls.; actress off Broadway, regional and stock theatres. Mem. Actors Equity Assn., AFTRA, Screen Actors Guild (nat. bd. dirs. 1978-84, exec. com. 1980-84, various coms.), Alpha Psi Omega, Alpha Delta Eta. Democrat. Unitarian. Avocations: bicycling; crafts; cooking; backgammon.

Home: 330 E 80th St New York NY 10021 Office: NBC 30 Rockefeller Plaza New York NY 10020

DAHLGREN, MARSIEA WARREN, city official; b. Long Beach, Calif., Sept. 14, 1947; d. J. Claude and Ethelyne (Yarbrough) Warren; m. Tom Boyd Yates, Dec. 11, 1971 (div. Jan. 1984); stepchildren—Karen, Steven, Kristine, Hope Melanie; m. Eric Dahlgren, May 3, 1986. B.A. U. Ala.-Birmingham, 1974, M.A., 1977, postgrad., Nova U., 1987—; Records clk. Orange County Sheriff's Dept., Santa Ana, Calif., 1968-71; adminstrv. officer, police officer U. Ala. Police Dept., Birmingham, 1971-74; adminstrv. coordinator faculty devel. Project on Teaching and Learning in Univ. Coll., U. Ala., Birmingham, 1974-76; asst. dir. aux. service U. Ala., Birmingham, 1976-78; info. mgr. Fort Collins Police Dept., Colo., 1979-82; mgr. integrated network services City of Ft. Collins, 1982-86, dir. info. and communications systems, 1986—; cons. office automation, telecommunications; instr. Colo. State U., 1982—, U. No. Colo., 1982—; cons. human aspects of tech. Author: Criminal Record Security for Colorado Criminal Justice Agencies, 1981, rev. edit., 1983. Contbr. articles to profl. jours. Mem. bus. and industry team United Way Campaign, Ft. Collins, 1984; creator Reader's Theatre, Ft. Collins Nursing Homes, 1985—. Mem. Assn. Info. Mgrs., Office Automation Soc. Internat., Urban and Regional Info. Systems Assn., Interex. Republican. Episcopalian. Avocations: stained glass design and art, scuba diving, travel, new age metaphysics. Home: 1318 Tuckaway Ct Fort Collins CO 80525 Office: City of Fort Collins 300 La Porte Ave Fort Collins CO 80521

DAHLIN, ELIZABETH CARLSON, university administrator; b. Worcester, Mass., July 26, 1931; d. Alden Gustaf and Elizabeth Christine (Peterson) Carlson; m. Douglas Gordon Dahlin, June 27, 1953; children: Christine Elizabeth, Cynthia Jean, Constance May. BA, Wellesley Coll., 1953; postgrad. Harvard U., 1953, 64; MA, George Washington U., 1971. Substitute tchr. Fairfax County, Va., 1958-77; asst. folklife specialist, concessions mgr. Smithsonian Instn., Washington, 1976-77; asst. to exec. dir. Nat. Sch. Vol. Program, Alexandria, Va., 1978-80; asst. to v.p. devel. George Mason U., Fairfax, Va., 1980-83, dir. devel., 1983-87; exec. dir. George Mason U. Found., 1983—; v.p. for univ. devel., 1987—; bd. dirs. George Mason Bank Shares, Inc.; George Mason Bank. Treas., bd. dirs. Nation's Capital Council Girl Scouts U.S., 1972-78, award, 1978; chief election judge Fairfax County Electoral Bd., 1967-75; chmn. Belle Haven precinct Mount Vernon dist. Fairfax County Democratic Com.; bd. dirs. Alexandria Symphony, 1983-88; deacon United Ch. of Christ; mem. alumni council Wellesley Coll., 1970, 81. Brown U. grad. fellow, 1953. Mem. Va. Women's Polit. Caucus, Council Advancement and Support Edn., Profl. Women's Network, Textile Mus., Smithsonian Assocs., Nat. Aviation Club, AAUW, George Washington U. Alumni Council (edn. council), Arlington C. of C. (bd. dirs. 1984—), Phi Delta Kappa. Clubs: Wellesley (bd. dirs. 1969—, treas. 1978-80, pres. 1980-82), Harvard (Washington); Fort Myer Officer's. Home: 6041 Edgewood Terr Alexandria VA 22307 Office: George Mason U Devel House 4400 University Dr Fairfax VA 22030

DAHN, VICKY LYNN, educator; b. Salt Lake City, Mar. 11, 1950; d. Frank Paul and Norma Marie (Parkin) D. BS, U. Utah, 1972, MEd, 1976. Cert. secondary tchr., Utah. Tchr. Salt Lake City Schs., 1972-78, 80-84, 86—, dist. computer coordinator, 1984-86; rep. tech. study group Nat. Supts. Network, Washington, 1983-84, computer sci. adv. com. Utah State Office Edn.; cons. Wasatch Edn. Systems, Salt Lake City, 1985-86. Mem. NEA, Nat. Council Tchrs. Math., Internat. Council for Computers in Edn., Assn. for Supervision and Curriculum Devel., Utah Council for Computers in Edn. (pres. 1987), Phi Beta Kappa, Phi Delta Kappa, Phi Kappa Phi. Mormon. Home: 1773 E Sego Lily Dr Sandy UT 84092 Office: Salt Lake City Schs 440 E 1st South Salt Lake City UT 84111

DAI, JING LING, medical writer, researcher, consultant; b. Tacoma; d. Yunan and Yet Sze Ling; m. Shenyu Dai (div.); children—Alexander M., Benjamin M. Student Temple U., 1960-63; BA in Journalism, Calif. State U., Long Beach, 1968; MPH, UCLA, 1977; CME, U. So. Calif., 1984. Exec. editor Bearing & Transmission Specialist, 1971-72; dir. publs. City of Hope Nat. Med. Ctr., Duarte, Calif., 1972-74; sr. proposal engr., writer, subcontractor for aerospace cos., 1965-66, 79-82, 86—; med. affairs research cons., Gravity Guidance, Inc., Pasadena, Calif., 1982-84; freelance writer, cons.; research cons. Musculo-Skeletal Clinic, Pasadena, 1982-84. Condr. study on premarital rubella antibody tests, 1977; contbr. articles to profl. jours. Bd. dirs., v.p. Bouggless-White Scholarship Found., Long Beach, 1967-71; publicity adviser Am. Cancer Soc., Los Angeles, 1975; adv. Metric Cert. Specialist Bd., U.S. Metric Assn., 1981—. USPHS grantee, UCLA, 1975-77. Mem. Women in Communications (chmn. careers conf., Los Angeles, 1975, award 1975), Am. Med. Writers Assn., Am. Pub. Health Assn., Nat. Assn. Female Execs., Assn. Health Services Research, Soc. Tech. Communication (chmn. ways/means, internat. tech. com. conf. 1978), Council Biology Editors, U.S. Metric Assn. (planning com. ann. conf. 1987). Home: 320 S Gramercy Place Los Angeles CA 90020

DAICHENDT, LINDA JOYCE, human resource consultant; b. Youngstown, Ohio, May 4, 1961; d. Albert Richard and Martha Jane (Hughes) D. Student, Youngstown State U., North Harris Coll. Mktg. dir. Eastwood Mall Cafaro Co., Niles, Ohio; placement dir. ATES Tech. Inst., Niles; service rep. Manpower, Inc., Youngstown; employment cons. Access Enterprises, Vienna, Va., 1988—; cons. Kent State U., Warren, Ohio. Author: Job Search Guide, 1986. Adv. bd. VA job service, 1988—. Mem. Exec. Link (founder, v.p., 1986—), Job Search Employers Com. (bd. dirs. 1986—), Healthwise Planning Com. (chair 1987), Trumbull Personnel Assn., Pub. Relations Resource Group, Niles C. of C. (cons.). Office: Access Enterprises 8605 Westwood Ctr Dr #301 Vienna VA 22180

DAILEY, COLEEN HALL, lawyer; b. East Liverpool, Ohio, Aug. 10, 1955; d. David Lawrence and Deloris Mae (Rosensteel) Hall; m. Donald W. Dailey Jr., Aug. 16, 1980; 1 child, Erin Elizabeth. Student, Wittenberg U., 1973-75; BA, Youngstown State U., 1977; JD, U. Cin., 1980. Bar: Ohio 1981, U.S. Dist. Ct. (no. dist.) Ohio 1981. Sr. library assoc. Marx Law Library, Cin., 1979-80; law clk. Kapp Law Office, East Liverpool, 1979, 1980-81, assoc., 1981-85; sole practice East Liverpool, 1985—; spl. counsel Atty. Gen. Ohio, 1985—. Pres. Columbiana County (Ohio) Young Dems., 1985-87; bd. dirs. Big Bros. Big Sisters Columbiana County, Inc., Lisbon, Ohio, 1984-86. Mem. ABA, Ohio Bar Assn., Columbiana County Bar Assn., Assn. Trial Lawyers Am., Ohio Trial Lawyers Assn., St. Clair Bus. and Profl. Women Assn. (pres. 1985-87). Democrat. Lutheran. Office: 16687 St Clair Ave PO Box 2519 East Liverpool OH 43920

DAILEY, JANET, romance novelist; b. Storm Lake, Iowa, May 21, 1944; m. William Dailey; 2 stepchildren. Student pub. schs., Independence, Iowa. Sec. Omaha, 1963-74. Author: No Quarter Asked, 1974, After the Storm, 1975, Sweet Promise, 1976, The Widow and the Wastrel, 1977, Giant of Medabi, 1978, The Bride of the Delta Queen, 1979, Lord of the High Lonesome, 1980, Night Way, 1981, This Calder Sky, 1981, This Calder Range, 1982, Stands a Calder Man, 1982, Lancaster Men, 1981, Terms of Surrender, 1982, With a Little Luck, 1982, Wildcatter's Women, 1982, Silver Wings, Santiago Blue, 1984, The Pride of Hannah Wade, 1985, The Glory Game, 1985, The Great Alone, 1986, Calder Born, Calder Bred, 1987, numerous other novels. Recipient Golden Heart award Romance Writers Am., 1981, Romantic Times Contemporary award, 1983.

DAILEY, SHARON ANN, veterinarian, nurse; b. Buffalo, Dec. 18, 1943; d. Russel P. and Gertrude A. (Hyland) D. RN, Queens (N.Y.) Hosp. Ctr. Sch. Nursing, 1966; BS cum laude, Trinity Coll. Vt., 1975; DVM, U. Pa., 1979. Head nurse ICU Abraham Jacobi Hosp., Bronx, N.Y., 1966-69; nurse clin. research UCLA Harbor Gen. Hosp., Torrance, Calif., 1969-71; nurse ICU Med. Ctr. Vt., Burlington, 1972-74; staff veterinarian Marlton (N.J.) Animal Hosp., 1979-83; staff nurse Cooper Shock/Trauma Ctr., Camden, N.J., 1983-84; owner, veterinarian Mobile Vet. Clinic, Voorhees, N.J., 1984—; mem. adv. bd. Camden County Animal Shelter, 1987—. Vol. Ambulance Squad, Voorhees, 1984-85, Town Watch, Voorhees, 1985—; mem. nat. governing bd. Trinity Coll., Burlington, 1985—. Mem. AVMA, So. N.J. Vet. Med. Assn., Soc. Aquatic Vet. Medicine.

DAILY, ELLEN WILMOTH MATTHEWS, technical writer, training analyst; b. Marfa, Tex., Aug. 13, 1949; d. Lynn Henry Sr. and Wilmoth Hamilton (Cox) Matthews; m. John Scott Daily Sr., Mar. 21, 1970; children: John Scott Jr., Kristen Michelle. BS in Physics, U. Tex., El Paso, 1971; postgrad., George Mason U., Fairfax, Va., 1980. House dir., activity counselor Southwestern Children's Home, El Paso, Tex., 1965-68; analyst Schellenger Research Found. Labs, El Paso, 1968-70; computer operator, supr. keypunch El Paso Nat. Bank, 1970-73; supr., progam analyst El Paso Sand Products, 1973-74; tech. rep. Xerox Corp., Jackson, Miss., 1975-77; product tech. specialist Xerox Corp., Jackson, 1977-79; tech. trainer Xerox Corp., Leesburg, Va., 1979-82; sr. tech. writer, tng. analyst Xerox Corp., Lewisville, Tex., 1982—; group rep. Xerox Corp., various cities, 1975—; owner Daily Delight Cattery, Chantilly, Va. and Carrollton, Tex., 1979—; co-owner J & M Answering Service, Dallas, 1983-84. Co-author: (electronic Bible verse) Verse of the Day, 1987—. Team and div. mgr. Chantilly Youth Assn., 1980-82; bd. dirs., swim team dir. Brookfield Swim Club, Chantilly, 1980-82; vol. Metrocrest Service Ctr., Carrollton, 1986—. Mem. Sigma Pi Sigma, Kappa Delta (social service dir. 1969-70). Presbyterian. Club: U. Tex. El Paso Cannoneers (sec.-treas. 1967-71); Xerox Bowling League (Lewisville, Tex.). Home: 3701 Grasmere Carrollton TX 75007 Office: Xerox Corp 1301 Ridgeview Dr MS181 Lewisville TX 75067

DAILY, FAY KENOYER, botany educator; b. Indpls., Feb. 17, 1911; d. Fredrick and Camellia Thea (Neal) Kenoyer; A.B., Butler U., 1935, M.S., 1952; m. William Allen Daily, June 24, 1937. Lab. technician Eli Lilly & Co., Indpls., 1935-37, Abbott Labs., North Chicago, Ill., 1939, William S. Merrell & Co., Ohio, 1940-41; lubrication chemist Indpls. Propellor div. Curtiss-Wright Corp., 1945; lectr. botany Butler U., Indpls., 1947-49, instr. immunology and microbiology, 1957-58, lectr. microbiology, 1962-63, mem. herbarium staff, 1949-87, curator cryptogamic herbarium, 1987—. Grantee Ind. Acad. Sci., 1961-62. Mem. Am. Inst. Biol. Sci., Bot. Soc. Am., Phycol. Soc. Am., Internat. Phycol. Soc., Ind. Acad. Sci., Torrey Bot. Club, Sigma Xi, Phi Kappa Phi, Sigma Delta Epsilon. Republican. Methodist. Co-author book on sci. history. Contbr. articles on fossil and extant charophytes (algae) to profl. jours. Home: 5884 Compton St Indianapolis IN 46220

DAIN, SANDIA ELIZABETH, interior designer; b. Syracuse, N.Y., May 3, 1955; d. Thomas Avery and Berneice (Powers) D.; m. Adrian Lambert Jr., Oct. 1, 1983. AS, Bennett Coll., Millbrook, N.Y., 1975. Interior designer Scandinavian Design, Burlington, Mass., 1975-77; design coordinator and sales mgr. Allied Store, Boston, 1977-79; interior designer Village Decorator, Sudbury, Mass., 1979-80; v.p., sr. designer Maxim's Interiors, Inc., West Newton, Mass., 1980 82; interior designer Campbell-Moreau Assocs., Inc., Boston, 1982-83; v.p., sr. designer Renovated Interiors, Inc. doing bus. as Campbell-Moreau Interiors, Boston, 1983—; instr. Bennett Coll., 1974-75, Mt. Ida Jr. Coll., Newton, Mass., 1980-82, Newton Dept. Continuing Ed., 1981-83; cons. Weather Energy Systems, Falmouth, Mass., 1979. Contbr. articles on design to Better Homes and Gardens and Money Mag., 1980-82. Vol. designer March of Dimes, Boston, 1982-83. Recipient Appreciation award Mass. March of Dimes, 1983. Mem. Am. Soc. Interior Designers (allied), Nat. Mus. Women in the Arts. Republican. Office: Renovated Interiors Inc PO Box 1187 Boston MA 02117

DAINS, JILL ALYCE, educator, freelance writer; b. Jersey City, Mar. 8, 1950; d. Joseph Keeler and Mildred Ida (Weiss) D. BS in Edn., Ball State U., 1972, MA in English and Linguistics, 1980. Bibliographer searcher Ball State U. Library, Muncie, Ind., 1972-74; tchr. English Culver (Ind.) Community Schs., 1974—. Bd. dirs. Marshall County Humane Soc., Plymouth, Ind., 1985; first violin in Fort Wayne (Ind.) Symphony Orch., 1970-75. Mem. NOW. Liberal. Home: 432 Liberty St Culver IN 46511 Office: Culver Community Schs School St Culver IN 46511

DAITCH, JACQUELINE SHIRLEY, marketing professional; b. Boston, Dec. 29, 1935; d. Harry V. and Eve (Finkelstein) Cohen; m. Burton Daitch; children: Bryan S., Barry K., Jennifer S. Tech. sales Millipore Corp., Bedford, Mass., 1974-76, tech. service adminstr., 1976-79, product specialist, 1979-81, adminstr. govt. contracts, 1981-82, nat. account mgr., 1983-84, application specialist, 1984-85, sr. application specialist, 1985-86, mgr. mktg., 1986—; bd. dirs. Ace Muffler Clinic Inc., Lowell, Mass. Mem. Nat. Assn. for Female Execs., Nat. Asbestos Council, Am. Standards Testing Materials, Mass. Environ. Health Assn., Internat. Food Tech., Nat. Soft Drink Assn. Jewish. Home: 100 Indian Ridge Rd Sudbury MA 01776 Office: Millipore Corp Ashby Rd Bedford MA 01730

DALBERG, BARBARA M., small business owner, consultant; b. Denver, Aug. 5, 1936; d. Walter B. and V. Marie (Chumley) M.; m. LeRoy E. Dalberg, July 18, 1954 (div. 1984); children: Stephen, Jeanine, Gerald. BS, U. Colo., 1956-75, MA, 1983. Registered soc. worker. Counselor Colo. Christian Services, Englewood, 1963-72, dir., 1972-74; counselor, trainer Luth. Social Service, Denver, 1974-79; area mgr. Nutri-system Weight Loss Ctrs., Denver, 1982-83; prin. Dalberg & Assoc., Denver, 1980-87; cons., trainer Dept. Interior, Denver, 1982-87; educator, trainer U. Colo., Denver, Red Rock Community Coll., Denver, Amax, Denver, 1982-87. Mem. Nat. Speakers Assn., Nat. Assn. Social Workers.

DALCH, SUZANNE MONTI, public affairs specialist; b. Alexandria, Va., July 22, 1953; d. Vincent James and Ruth Suzanne (Merson) M.; m. Walter Edward Dalch III, Oct. 17, 1987. BA, George Mason U., 1976. Supr. writer, editor U.S. Dept. State, Washington, 1977-85; pub. affairs specialist U.S. Arms Control and Disarmament Agy., Washington, 1985—. Methodist. Office: US Arms Control and Disarmament Agy 320 21st St NW Washington DC 20451

DALE, ESTHER ELLEN, insurance company executive; b. Hanover, N.H., Oct. 2, 1956; d. John Franklin and Jean Esther (Kendall) D. BA, Ft. Hays State U., 1977; MS, U. Nebr., Omaha, 1979. Time mgmt. analyst Mut. of Omaha, 1980-82, sr. time mgmt. analyst, 1982-84, tng. cons., 1984-86, specialist employee benefits, 1986—. Mem. AAUW (bd. dirs. 1987—), Personnel Assn. of Midlands (program com. 1986—). Democrat. Lutheran. Club: Symphony Usher (Omaha). Home: 4359 S 42d St Omaha NE 68107 Office: Mut of Omaha Mut of Omaha Plaza Omaha NE 68175

DALE, SHERRY LYNN, accountant; b. Spruce Pine, N.C., Dec. 8, 1960; d. John M. and Bette J. (Greene) D. BA, Hendrix Coll., 1982. CPA, Okla., Ark. Staff acct. Coopers and Lybrand, Oklahoma City, 1982; CPA Gray, Northcutt and Olson, Oklahoma City, 1982-84, Young, Jones and Battles, Oklahoma City, 1985-87; ptnr. Jones and Dale P.C., Oklahoma City, 1985—. Mem. Nat. Assn. Female Execs., Okla. Soc. CPA's, Nat. Assn. Women Bus. Owners. Republican. Club: Toastmasters (sgt.-at-arms 1986-87, treas. 1987-88). Office: Jones and Dale PC 5400 NW Grand Suite 365 Oklahoma City OK 73112

D'ALENE, ALIXANDRIA FRANCES, management consultant; b. Buffalo, Oct. 21, 1951; d. Fern (Hill) D'A.; B.A., Canisius Coll., Buffalo, 1973, M.S., 1975, M.B.A., 1980. Tchr., Buffalo public schs., 1973-76; personnel cons. Sanford Rose Assos., Williamsville, N.Y., 1976-78; mgr. benefits adminstrn. Service Systems Corp., Clarence, N.Y., 1978-80; mgr. employee relations Del Monte Corp., Walnut Creek, Calif., 1980-82; human resource mgmt. cons. H.R.S., Inc., Winston-Salem, N.C., 1982-87; corp. personnel specialist Advance Stores Co., Inc., Roanoke, Va., 1987-88; personnel dir. Alfred (N.Y.) U., 1988—. Mem. Assn. Personnel Adminstrs., Indsl. Personnel Soc., Coll. and U. Personnel Assn., Phi Alpha Theta. Episcopalian.

D'ALESSANDRO, LILLIAN JOANNE, employment services administrator; b. Rochester, N.Y., Jan. 19, 1939; d. Paul Michael and Bridget (Ronzo) Petrilli; m. Donald Anthony D'Alessandro; children: Paul, Sandra. A in Applied Sci., Rochester Inst. Tech., 1959; postgrad., Nazareth Coll., 1961-62. Buyer, mgr. Sportown, Inc., Rochester, 1959-61; tchr. Diocese of Rochester, 1961-64; supr. payroll Manpower Temp. Services, Rochester, 1979-80, supr. acctg., 1981-82, mgr. ind. services, 1982-85, dir. sales and mktg., 1985—; br. mgr. Olsten Services, Rochester, 1986—. Vol. Am. Cancer Soc., Muscular Dystrophy Assn., United Cerebral Palsy Assn. Mem. Am. Mgmt. Assn., Rochester Profl. Sales and Mktg. Assn., Rochester Sales and Mktg. Execs., Nat. Assn. for Female Execs., Rochester C. of C. Republican. Roman Catholic. Office: Olsten Services 625 Panorama Valley Office Park 14 Franklin St Rochester NY 14604

D'ALESSIO, KITTY, cosmetic and clothing co. exec.; b. Sea Girt, N.J., 1929; B.A., Upsala Coll., 1948; Formerly with B. Altman and Co., N.Y.C.; fashion cons. NBC/TV, N.Y.C.; sr. v.p., dir. Norman, Craig, and Kummel, until 1979; pres. Chanel, Inc., N.Y.C., 1979-88, vice chmn. new ventures and spl. projects, 1988—. Office: Chanel Inc 9 W 57th St New York NY 10019

DALLAIRE, MARIAN EVANS, academic administrator; b. East Providence, R.I., Jan. 13, 1959; d. Wayne Trevor and Elizabeth Angela (Spadea) Evans; m. James Brian Dallaire, Sept. 5, 1982; 1 child, Aline Elizabeth. BS in Community Devel., Springfield Coll., 1980; MS in Mgmt., Lesley Coll., 1985. Childcare worker Old Colony YMCA, Brockton, Mass., 1979-80; residence dir. Community Support Program, Holyoke, Mass., 1980-81; program dir. SE Human Resource Assn., Brockton, 1981-85, Mass. Dept. Mental Health, Brockton, 1984-85; dir. devel. Massasoit Community Coll., Brockton, 1985—; bd. dirs. Whitman (Mass.) Counseling Ctr., 1986—; mem. Old Colony YMCA, Brockton, 1966—, centennial com. 1986-87, Service to Youth award 1978. Mem. Old Colony YMCA, Brockton, 1966— (centennial com. 1986-87, Service to Youth award 1978). Mem. Community Services Gr. Brockton, Nat. Assn. Female Execs., Mass. Tchrs. Assn., Nat. and State Council for Resource Devel. Democrat. Roman Catholic. Home: 48 Thurber Ave Brockton MA 02401 Office: Massasoit Community Coll One Massasoit Blvd Brockton MA 02402

DALLE, PATRICIA ANNE-MARIE, utilities executive; b. Rochester, N.Y., Nov. 29, 1952; d. Louis Alphonse and Jean Elizabeth (Mayer) D.; m. Gary Richard Voleshen, July 30, 1988. AAS in Mktg., Monroe Community Coll., 1979; BS in Bus. Mgmt., Empire State Coll., 1983. Invoice clk. Rochester Gas and Electric Co., 1975-77, sec. to purchase agt., 1977-81, fuels coordinator, 1981—. Treas. Rochester Gas and Electric Chorus, 1980-81. Mem. Purchasing Mgrs. Assn. Rochester, Women in Energy, Akita Club Buffalo. Roman Catholic. Office: Rochester Gas and Electric 89 East Ave Rochester NY 14649

DALLMANN-SCHAPER, MARY LOUISE, technical contingency planner; b. Duluth, Minn., July 4, 1951; d. Norbert Henry and Lahja Mildred (Mykra) D. BA in Bus. Adminstrn., U. Minn., 1974; M in Mgmt. Adminstrn., Met. State U., 1987. With Norwest Info. Services, Inc., 1971-85; tech. contingency planner First Bank Corp., St. Paul, 1985-87, tech. support supr., 1987—. Mem. Data Processing Mgmt. Assn., Nat. Assn. Female Execs., Minn. Women's Network. Home: 1500 76th Ct Brooklyn Park MN 55444 Office: FBS Info Services Corp PO 64603 Saint Paul MN 55164

DALLY, BEVERLY JEAN, legal assistant; b. Akron, Ohio, Nov. 2, 1935; d. George Tilman and Julia Mae (McClure) Willoughby; m. Don I. Dally, July 10, 1955 (div. 1981); children—Bruce, Alan, Jack. Student, Hilbert Coll., Hamburg, N.Y., 1975-76, SUNY-Buffalo, 1972-75. Legal asst. Cowen & Swados, Buffalo, 1977-78, Eikenburg & Stiles, Houston, 1978-79, Foreman & Dyess, Houston, 1979-84, Michael G. Page, Atty.-at-Law, The Woodlands, Tex., 1984-85, Fulbright & Jaworski, Houston, 1985-86, Granada Corp., Houston, 1986-87, Ensource, Inc., Houston, 1988—. Contbr. article to legal publ. Mem. Houston Legal Assts. Assn. (chmn. com. 1980), Nat. Assn. Female Execs. (Houston). Republican. Methodist. Office: Ensource Inc 1001 Fannin Suite 1900 Houston TX 77002

DALLY, REBECCA POLSTON, lawyer; b. Columbus, Ga., Dec. 4, 1955; d. James Olon and Lottie Myrl (Woodham) Polston; m. Hal W. Dally, June 28, 1980; children—Patrick William, Melissa Leigh. Student Mercer U., 1973-75; B.A. cum laude, Ga. State U., 1976; J.D., U. Ga., 1979. Bar: Ga. 1979. Asst. loan coordinator Transam. Real Estate Tax Service, Atlanta, 1975-77; sole practice law, Social Circle, Ga., 1981—; spl. asst. dist. atty. Alcovy Jud. Circuit, Monroe and Covington, Ga., 1982-84; spl. asst. atty. gen., 1984—. Bd. dirs. Social Circle Hist. Preservation Soc., 1982—, The Alcove, 1986—; trustee Walton County Arts Council, 1983—, Hist. Soc. Walton County, 1984—; mem. fin. com. Social Circle Pub. Library; vol. ARC, Social Circle Nursing Home, 1980-81. Mem. ABA, Ga. Trial Lawyers Assn., Alcovy Jud. Circuit Bar Assn. (v.p. 1983-84, pres. 1984-85), Walton County Bar Assn. (v.p. 1982-83, pres. 1983-84), State Bar Ga., Social Circle Mcht. and Trade Assn., Walton County C. of C. (bd. dirs. 1988—), Phi Alpha Delta. Baptist. Home: PO Box 745 Social Circle GA 30279 Office: 137 E Hightower Trail PO Box 745 Social Circle GA 30279

DALPES, LINDA FRANCES, management firm executive; b. New Orleans, Jan. 3, 1938; d. Walter James and Frances Katherine (Jordan) Fountain. AA, Stephens Coll., 1957; BA, U. Hawaii, 1959. Cert. dental asst. Sr. claims analyst Am. Gen. Life Inc. Co., Houston, 1960-64; mgr. claims Southwest region Calif. Western States Life Ins. Co., Houston, 1964-68; mgmt. cons. Met. Agy., Houston, 1968-70; clinic adminstr. Harris & Adams, Inc., Houston, 1970-75; founder, pres. Team Coordinators, Houston, 1975—; clinician major dental meetings; internat. lectr., cons. south, southwest univs.; exec. sec. Tex. Dental Hygienists Assn., 1972-75. Mem. LWV, Am. Mgmt. Assn., AAUW, Nat. Assn. Women Bus. Owners, Nat. Assn. Female Execs. Republican. Episcopalian. Home: 120 E Fork Rd Cleveland TX 77327 Office: PO Box 1181 Cleveland TX 77327

DALRYMPLE, JEAN, theatrical producer, publicist; b. Morristown, N.J., Sept. 2, 1910; d. George Hull and Elizabeth Van Kirk (Collins) D.; m. Ward Morehouse, Mar. 31, 1932 (div. 1937); m. Philip De Witt Ginder, Nov. 1, 1951. Ed. pvt. tutors; DFA (hon.), Wheaton Coll., 1959. Bd. dirs. N.Y.C. Ctr. Music and Drama, Soldiers, Sailors and Airmen's Club, N.Y.C., Friends of the Theatre and Music Collection of Mus. City N.Y., Profl. Children's Sch., N.Y.C., N.Y. World's Fair, 1964-65, cons. Performing Arts Program, N.Y. World's Fair; dir. U.S. Performing Arts Program, Fed. Pavilion, N.Y. World's Fair; mem. adv. bd. N.C. Sch. Arts; co-moderator Working in the Theatre seminar Am. Theatre Wing, 1981—; currently pres. Light Opera of Manhattan. Actress, writer, 1926-29; publicist for John Golden, 1929-33, publicist, mgr. for artists including Jose Iturbi, Grace Moore, Lily Pons, Bidu Sayoa, Glinka Milanov, Nathan Milstein, Leopold Stokowski, 1933-44, permanent dir., N.Y. City Ctr. Theatre Co., theatre publicist Tallulah Bankhead, Mary Martin, Margaret Sullavan; Broadway plays, Ballet Russe de Monte Carlo, N.Y. City Ctr.; publicist Lewisohn Stadium concerts; prod.: Hope For The Best, 1944, Brighten the Corner, 1945, Burlesque, 1946-48, Red Gloves, 1948-49; prod., dir.: (summer cir.) The Second Man, Harvey, Voice of the Turtle, Petrified Forest, 1950-53; permanent dir. Drama Co. N.Y. City Center; prod. 4 plays starring Jose Ferrer, 1953-54, Winter Play Festival of 1954-55, What Every Woman Knows (starring Helen Hayes), The Fourposter (Hume Cronin and Jessica Tandy), Time of Your Life (Franchot Tone), Wisteria Trees (Helen Hayes), 1955, King Lear (Orson Welles), Marcel Marceau, Streetcar Named Desire, 1957 (Tallulah Bankhead); dir., Light Opera Co. N.Y. City Ctr.; producer: Carousel (spl. Christmas show); dir., producer numerous others; producer numerous TV programs and films; assoc. producer film Children of Theatre Street, 1976; producer La Casa de Te de la Luna de Agosta, U.S. Dept. State, Mexico and S.Am., 1956-57, Variations on the Same Theme (Ionesco), Guggenheim Mus., N.Y.C., 1980; coordinator U.S. Performing Arts Program, Brussels World's Fair, 1958; producer Agnes de Mille Heritage Dance Theatre; coordinator Internat. Festival Entertainment; author: September Child, 1963, Careers and Opportunities in the Theatre, 1969, Jean Dalrymple's Pinafore Farm Cookbook, 1971, The Folklore and Facts of Natural Nutrition, 1973, From the Last Row, 1975, The Complete Handbook for Community Theatre, 1977; author sketches, plays; contbr. articles to mags. and newspapers. Bd. dirs. Am. Theatre Wing, 1940—. Decorated Knight Order Crown for Brussels World's Fair work, Belgium; recipient 4 citations for City Center work from mayors of N.Y.C. Mem. Nat. Council on Arts, ANTA (bd. dirs., treas.), Friends of the Am. Theatre Wing (vice chmn.), New Dramatists. Home: 150 W 55th St New York NY 10019

DAL SANTO, DIANE, judge; b. East Chicago, Ind., Sept. 20, 1949; d. John Quentin Dal Santo and Helen (Koval) D.; m. Fred O'Cheskey, June 29, 1985. B.A., U. N. Mex., 1971; cert. Inst. Internat. and Comparative Law, Guadalajara, Mex., 1978; J.D., U. San Diego, 1980. Bar: N.Mex. 1980, U.S. Dist. Ct. N.Mex. 1980. Ct. planner Met. Criminal Justice Coordinating Council, Albuquerque, 1973-75; planning coordinator Dist. Atty.'s Office, Albuquerque, 1975-76, exec. asst. to dist. atty., 1976-77, asst. dist. atty. for violent crimes, 1980-82; chief dep. city atty. City of Albuquerque, 1983; assoc. firm T.B. Keleher & Assocs., 1983-84; judge Met. Ct., 1985-88, presiding judge Met. Ct., 1988—. Bd. dirs. Nat. Council Alcoholism, 1984,

S.W. Ballet Co., Albuquerque, 1982-83; mem. Mayor's Task Force on Alcoholism and Crime. Recipient Woman of Yr. award Duke City Bus. and Profl. Women, 1985; U. San Diego scholar, 1978-79. Mem. ABA, N.Mex. Bar Assn., Albuquerque Bar Assn., Nat. Assn. Women Judges, LWV, N.Mex. Council on Crime and Delinquency, N.Mex. Magistrate Judges Assn. (v.p.). Democrat. Home: 4139 Coe Dr NE Albuquerque NM 87110 Office: Met Ct 401 Roma NW Albuquerque NM 87103

DALTON, BARBARA ANN, nursing supervisor; b. Balt., Jan. 7, 1947; d. Harold Clifton and Doris Loretta (Reed) D. BS in Nursing, Johns Hopkins U., 1976. Staff nurse Md. Gen. Hosp., Balt., 1967-71, South Balt. Gen. Hosp., 1971-72; team leader St. Agnes Hosp., Balt., 1972-73; head nurse Good Samaritan Hosp., Balt., 1973-77, primary nurse, 1978-81; instr. Union Meml. Hosp. Sch. Nursing, Balt., 1977-78; research study coordinator Johns Hopkins Hosp. and U., Balt., 1981-82; nursing supr. C&P Telephone Co. of Md., Balt., 1982—. Mem. Am. Nurses' Assn. (cert. community health nurse), Md. Area Occupational Health Nurses Assn. (ednl. com. 1985—, bd. dirs. 1986—). Office: C&P Telephone Co of Md One E Pratt St Baltimore MD 21202

DALTON, JENNIFER FAYE, accountant; b. Maryville, Tenn., May 1, 1959; d. James Theodore Teffeteller and Melody (Potts) Allison; m. Robert Byron Dalton, Dec. 15, 1979. Student, U. Tenn., 1977-79, Coastal Carolina Community Coll., 1980-81, 84-86; BS in Mgmt., Golden Gate U., Camp Lejeune, N.C., 1982. Bookkeeper, with accounts payable dept. McMar Too, Inc., Jacksonville, N.C., 1980-83; acctg. clk. City of Jacksonville, 1983—. Alcoa Found. scholar, 1977. Mem. Gamma Beta Phi. Republican. Mem. Ch. of Christ. Club: Leatherneck Rifle and Pistol (Camp Lejeune) (sec.-treas. 1983—). Home: 1932 Greenstone Ct Midway Park NC 28544-1628

DALTON, M. THERESE, federal government administrator; b. Atlanta, Sept. 15, 1945; d. Donald F. and Anna R. (McGraw) Backe; m. Bruce R. Siecker, June 19, 1965 (div. Oct. 1980); children: David Scott, Diane Lynn; m. David L. Dalton, Sept. 10, 1983. AAS with distinction, Purdue U., 1972; BS in Nursing magna cum laude, NE La. U., 1978; MPA, George Mason U., 1981. RN, 1972. Staff and charge nurse cardiac care unit Ohio State U. Hosp., Columbus, 1972-74; vol. Am. Heart Assn., Columbus, 1975-76; research analyst Quachita Health Unit, Monroe, La., 1977-78; personnel mgmt. specialist Def. Logistics Agy., Alexandria, Va., 1979; mgmt. analyst U.S. GAO, Washington, 1980, analyst, auditor gen. govt. div., 1981-83, sr. info. systems mgmt. evaluator, info. mgmt. and tech. div., 1983-88; div. chief med. computer systems plans and evaluations VA, Washington, 1988—. Vol. budget analyst Fedn. Citizens Assns., Fairfax County, Va., 1983. Named one of Outstanding Young Women of Am., 1979. Fellow Am. Soc. Pub. Adminstrn. (GAO liaison 1982-83); mem. AAUW, Healthcare Info. and Mgmt. Systems Soc., Electronic Data Processing Auditors Assn., Nat. Assn. Female Execs., Toastmasters Internat., Smithsonian Instn. (resident assoc.), Phi Kappa Phi. Club: Toastmasters. Office: VA 004M 810 Vermont Ave NW Washington DC 20420

DALTON, PHYLLIS IRENE, library consultant; b. Marietta, Kans., Sept. 25, 1909; d. Benjamin Reuben and Pearl (Travelute) Bull; m. Jack Mason Dalton, Feb. 13, 1950. B.S., U. Nebr., 1931, M.A., 1941; M.A., U. Denver, 1942. Tchr. city schs., Marysville, Kans., 1931-40; reference librarian Lincoln Pub. Library, Nebr.; librarian U. Nebr., Lincoln, 1941-48; librarian Calif. State Library, Sacramento, 1948-57, asst. state librarian, 1957-72; pvt. library cons., Las Vegas, 1972—. Author: Library Service to the Deaf and Hearing Impaired, 1985 (Pres's Com. Employment of Handicapped award 1985). Contbr. chpt., articles, reports to books and publs. in field. Mem. exec. bd. So. Nev. Hist. Soc., Las Vegas, 1983-84; mem. So. Nev. Com. on Employment of Handicapped, 1980—; mem. adv. com. Nat. Orgn. on Disability, 1982—; bd. dirs. Friends of So. Nev. Libraries; trustee Univ. Library Soc., U. Nev.-Las Vegas. Mem. Allied Arts Council. Recipient Library Sodalitas, U. So. Calif., 1972, Alumni Achievement award U. Denver, 1977, Alumni Achievement award U. Nebr., Lincoln, 1983. Mem. ALA (councilor 1963-64, exceptional service award 1981), Assn. State Libraries (pres. 1964-65), Calif. Library Assn. (pres. 1969), Nev. Library Assn. (hon.), Internat. Fedn. Library Assns. and Instns. (chair working group on library service to prisons, mem. standing com. Sect. Libraries Serving Disadvantaged Persons 1987—), LWV, AAUW. Republican. Presbyterian. Club: Pilot (parliamentarian). Home: 205 E Harmon Ave Apt 801 Las Vegas NV 89109

DALY, FREDERICA, psychologist, educator; b. Washington, Feb. 14, 1925; d. Samuel and Geneva (Sharper) Young; m. Paul V. Martineau (dec. 1969); m. Michael E. Daly, Mar. 15, 1972. BS, Howard U., 1947, MS, 1948; PhD, Cornell U., 1956. Lic. psychologist, N.Y. Clerk War Manpower Commn., Washington, 1942-46; clin. intern Middle Valley State Hosp., Middletown, Conn., 1943-49; instr. psychology Howard U., Washington, 1950-53, research asst. Cornell U., Ithaca, N.Y., 1953-55; psychologist George Jr. Republic, Freeville, N.Y., 1955-72; assoc. prof. SUNY, Empire State Coll., N.Y.C., 1972-80; coordinator U. N. Mex. Forensic Unit, Albuquerque, 1980-81, VA Med. Ctr. Alcohol Unit, Albuquerque, 1981—. Bd dirs. Child and Family Services, Ithaca, NY, 1956-59; bd. dirs. YMCA Albuquerque, 1979-80; bd. dirs. Street Ministry, Albuquerque, 1980-81. Fellow Am. Orthopschiat.; mem. Am. Psychol. Assn., N.Y. State Psychol. Assn. Democrat. Unitarian. Home: 526 Hermosa NE Albuquerque NM 87108 Office: VA Med Ctr 2100 Ridgecrest SE Albuquerque NM 87108

DALY, JUDITH MARIE, retail executive; b. Cedar Rapids, Iowa, Dec. 2, 1950; d. Elmer Frederick and Lucille Magdalen (Bousek) Vorhies; m. James Francis Daly, Sept. 3, 1970 (div. 1979); children: Jonathan W., Jaime B. Student, U. No. Iowa, 1970, Ind. U. N.W., 1988—. Head cashier Home Hardware Co., St. Charles, Ill., 1972-73, dept. mgr., 1973-74, buyer, merchandiser, 1974-79; head buyer Home Hardware Co., West Chicago, Ill., 1979-81, v.p. purchasing, 1982-86; sr. v.p. Home Hardware Co., Portage, Ind., 1987—; also bd. dirs. Home Hardware Co., Marengo, Ill.; pres. Nationwide Wholesale Supply, Portage, Ind., 1984—. Mem. Nat. Assn. Female Execs. Avocation: golf. Home: 156 Southport Dr Valparaiso IN 46383 Office: Nationwide Wholesale Supply 6044 Central Ave Portage IN 46368

DALY, M. VIRGINIA, marketing firm executive; b. Washington, Sept. 10, 1945; d. John Jay and Mary Louise (Tinley) Daly; m. Garrett Sanderson, Nov. 1, 1982. BA Coll. Saint Elizabeth, 1967. Copywriter, Doubleday Advt., N.Y.C., 1968-74; sr. writer Bur. Nat. Affairs, Inc., Washington, 1975-76; pres. Daly Direct Mktg., Washington, 1976—. Creator nat. industrywide slogan, 1970. Vol., House of Ruth, D.C., 1978-85, Sloan Kettering Meml. Hosp., N.Y.C., 1968-70. Mem. Direct Mktg. Assn. Washington (pres. 1982-83, Profl. of Year award 1985-86), Am. News Womens Club (pres. 1986-88), Creative Guild, Womens Direct Response Group, Am. Women in radio and Television Soc. Avocations: crafts; reading; biking. Office: Daly Direct Mktg 918 16th St NW Washington DC 20006

DALY, MARY F., feminist philosopher; A.B., Coll. of St. Rose, Albany, N.Y.; A.M., Cath. U.; S.T.L., S.T.D., Ph.D., U. Fribourg; Ph.D. in Religion, U. Notre Dame. Assoc. prof. dept. theology Boston Coll. Author: The Church and the Second Sex, 1968, 3d rev. ed., 1985; Beyond God the Father, 1973, 2nd edit. rev. 1985; Gyn/Ecology, 1979, Pure Lust, 1984. Address: Boston College Dept Theology Chestnut Hill MA 02167

DALY, TYNE, actress; b. N.Y.C., 1947; d. James Daly and Hope Newell; m. Georg Stanford Brown; children—Alisabeth, Kathryne, Alexandra. Student, Brandeis U., Am. Music and Dramatic Acad. Performed at Am. Shakespeare Festival, Stratford, Conn.; films include The Enforcer, 1976, Telefon, 1977, Zoot Suite, 1982, The Aviator, 1985, Movers and Shakers, 1985; made TV debut in series The Virginian; guest appearances in various TV series, starring role in Cagney and Lacey, 1982—(Emmy awards 1983, 84); TV films include In Search of America, 1971, A Howling in the Woods, 1971, Heat of Anger, 1972, The Man Who Could Talk to Kids, 1973, The Entertainer, 1976, Intimate Strangers, 1977, Better Late Than Never, 1979, The Women's Room, 1980, A Matter of Life and Death, 1981, Your Place or Mine, 1983, Kids Like These, 1987. Office: care Camden Artists Ltd 2121 Ave of the Stars Suite 410 Los Angeles CA 90067 *

D'AMATO, JANET POTTER, artist, writer; b. Rochester, N.Y., June 5, 1925; d. Earle H. and Florence (Cowles) Potter; m. Alex D'Amato; children: Sandra D'Amato Tompkins, Donna Lee. Cert., Pratt Inst., 1946. Artist filmstrips Zaffo Studio, N.Y.C., 1946-47; display artist Regency Inc., Rochester, 1947-48; freelance artist, writer N.Y.C., 1952—. Author, illustrator 12 books; illustrator 40 books for various publishers; illustrator for various cos., including Singer Co., Pepsico, Bioessence, Radiant, Eureka Co., CBS, Lillian Vernon, McGraw-Hill Inc., Grosset & Dunlap, Inc., Prentice-Hall, Inc., Doubleday & Co., Inc., Messner, Hawthorne, Caedemon.

DAMEROW, MAE WRIGHT, retail executive; b. Northampton, Mass., Nov. 14, 1956; d. Lawrence Sheperd and Caroline Mary (La Rose) Wright; m. Robert Frederick Haley, June 10, 1978 (div. 1980); m. Frederick Wright Damerow, Aug. 7, 1981. BS in Mech. Engring., Worcester (Mass.) Poly., 1980. Assoc. engr. nuclear safety Westinghouse Electric Corp., Monroeville, Pa., 1978-80, engr. nuclear safety, 1980, shift tech. advisor Salem nuclear plant, 1980-81, engr. info. program, 1981-84, sr. engr. info. program, 1984, mgr. info. program, 1984-86, mgr. bus. relations, 1987—; speaker Campus Am., nationwide, 1979-81; bd. dirs. Energy Source Edn. Council, Washington, 1987 (bd. pres. 1988—); mem. mgmt. com. Electric Info. Council, N.D., 1987—; mem. program com. U.S. Com. for Energy Awareness, Washington, 1987—, publications subcommittee U.S. Council for Energy Awareness, 1988—. Mem. Nat. Assn. of Female Execs. Office: Westinghouse Electric Corp Energy Ctr E 511B Haymaker and Northern Pike Monroeville PA 15146

D'AMICO, ANN, urban planner, developer; b. Ottawa, Ill., Apr. 15, 1943; d. Andrew F. and Harriet Theresa (Hoffman) Loeb; m. Dennis Chesterson D'Amico, June 27, 1964; children: Brad Christopher, Rob Michael. Degree in Advt., U. Mo., Columbia, 1964. Lic. real estate broker, Tex. Dir. continuity Sta. WCVS Radio, Springfield, Ill., 1964-66; staff asst. Bond for Gov. Campaign, St. Louis, 1972; adminstrv. asst., copywriter George Johnson Advt., St. Louis, 1972-74; sales asst. KATZ, Dallas, 1974-75; account service coordinator The Bloom Agy., 1975-77; copywriter D'Amico & Assocs., 1977; media research asst. TM Communications, 1977-78; copywriter, prodn. mgr. Womack, Claypoole, Griffin Advt., 1978-79; dir. mktg. NorthPark Ctr., 1980-82; asst. gen. mgr. Valley View Ctr., 1982-85; dir. leasing, devel. Roblee Co., 1985-86; sales assoc. The Monitor Group, Dallas, 1986-87; exec. dir. The West End Assn., Dallas, 1987—. Mem. Internat. Council Shopping Ctrs., Comml. Real Estate Women, Mktg. Communications Execs. Internat., Dallas Mus. Art, U. Mo. Alumni Assn., Child Care Ptnrship. (bd. dirs.), Retail Mktg. Profls. (bd. dirs.), Hoop-D-Do (bd. dirs.), Our Friends Place, Delta Gamma. Republican. Roman Catholic. Office: The West End Assn 1801 N Lamar Suite 105 Dallas TX 75202

DAMICO, DEBRA LYNN, French and English language educator, student counselor; b. Passaic, N.J., Apr. 15, 1956; d. Nicholas Biagio and Eleanore Lorraine (Hugle) D. BA, Montclair State Coll., 1978, MA, 198*. Cert. tchr., N.J. Tchr. St. Francis Sch., Hackensack, N.J., 1978-79, Saddle Brook (N.J.) High Sch., 1979-80, St. Dominic Acad., Jersey City, 1980-84; adult basic edn./gen. edn devel. and ESL instr. Adult Learning Ctr. Montclair (N.J.) State Coll., 1974—; internat. student advisor Manhattan Coll., Bronx, N.Y., 1984—, ESL instr., 1986—; instr. Writing Inst. Adult Edn. Resource Ctr. Jersey City State Coll., 1987—. Mem. Dist. Wide Curriculum Council, Lodi, N.J., 1977-78; ch. cantor and musician. Nat. Assn. for Foreign Student Affairs grantee, 1985-86; named Outstanding Young Woman Am., 1986. Mem. N.Y. Tchrs. of ESL, Nat. Assn. Foreign Student Affairs, Metro-Internat., Am. Assn. Tchrs. French, YMCA Internat. Student Service, Kappa Delta Pi, Pi Delta Phi. Democrat. Roman Catholic. Office: Manhattan Coll 4513 Manhattan Coll Pkwy Bronx NY 10471

DAMMANN, APRIL ANSON, screenwriter; b. Los Angeles, Sept. 30, 1946; d. William Paul and Geraldine C. (Manus) Anson; m. Ronald William Dammann, Aug. 16, 1969; children: Sarah Madeleine, Joseph William. BA, UCLA, 1968; MA, U. Rochester, 1969; la licence es lettres, U. Paris, 1969. Coordinator student relations UCLA, 1969-72; staff writer Heartbeat Theatre, Los Angeles, 1978-85; exec. producer, screenwriter Am. Film Inst., Los Angeles, 1985-86; freelance writer Los Angeles, 1986—; active Creative Access program Columbia Pictures, Burbank, Calif., 1984—. Exec. producer, co-writer: (film) Rose & Katz, 1986 (Nat. Acad. TV Arts and Scis. award 1987); author various screenplays. Bd. dirs., newsletter editor Ethnic Arts Council of Los Angeles, 1972-76; bd. dirs. Art Mus. Council, Los Angeles, 1974-78, 84-86; acting dist. chairperson UCLA Scholarship Com., 1987; active Nat. Charity League, 1987. Named one of Outstanding Young Women of Am., 1970; UCLA Regents scholar, 1966. Mem. Writers Guild Am., Women in Film, Phi Beta Kappa. Republican. Presbyterian. Home and Office: 7065 Hillside Ave Los Angeles CA 90068

DAMON, CLAUDIA CORDS, lawyer; b. Heidelberg, Fed. Republic Germany, Aug. 11, 1946; came to U.S., 1952, naturalized, 1957; d. Helmuth and Jutta (Sorge) Cords; married; children: Caroline, Samuel. BA, Wellesley Coll., 1967; MA, Boston U., 1968, JD, 1974. Bar: N.H. 1974, U.S. Dist. Ct. N.H. 1974, U.S. Tax Ct. 1976. Tchr. history MacDuffie Sch. for Girls, Springfield, Mass., 1968-69; research asst. Princeton (N.J.) U., 1969-71; assoc. Sheehan, Phinney, Bass & Green P.A., Manchester, N.H., 1974-78, mem., 1979—; mem. N.H. Bd. Bar Examiners, Concord, 1980—. Chmn. Boscawen (N.H.) Zoning Bd. Adjustment, 1976—; bd. dirs. Manchester Girls Club, 1975-80, Merrimack Valley Day Care Services, Concord, 1983—, pres., 1987—, Manchester YMCA, 1986—. Mem. ABA, N.H. Bar Assn., Assn. Trial Lawyers Am., N.H. Trial Lawyers Assn., N.H. chpt. Lawyers Alliance for Nuclear Arms Control (exec. bd. mem. 1985—). Democrat. Office: Sheehan Phinney Bass & Green PA PO Box 3701 Manchester NH 03105-3701

DAMON, SARA ELLEN, chemical company executive; b. Rapid City, S.D., Sept. 22, 1926; d. Samuel and Sara Anna (Johnston) Crabb; m. Jack Almon Damon, Feb. 2, 1952; children: Alan Jay, Janice Ann, Kenneth Lew, Keith Jeffrey. BA in Journalism and Spanish, Cornell Coll., Mt. Vernon, Iowa, 1948. Teen-age program dir. YWCA, Alliance, Ohio, 1950-52; sec., treas. Damon Chem. Co., Alliance, Ohio, 1953—. Contbr. poems and articles to Sharing Mag., 1980—. Mem. Ch. Women United, chmn. com. 1982-83; council rep. Alliance of Chs., 1980—; mem. region IV council Order of St. Luke the Physician, 1982—, convenor, 1982, Alliance chpt., sec., 1983—, workshop leader, 1984—, counselor Inner Healing and Healing of Memories, 1980—, dir. ann. local healing conf., 1982—; deaconess First Bapt. Ch., 1985—, spiritual healing minister, 1982—. Republican. Club: Am. Univ. Women (charter mem., first v.p.). Home: 1100 Fernwood Blvd Alliance OH 44601 Office: Damon Chem Co Inc 12435 Rockhill NE Alliance OH 44601

DAMPIER, FRANCES MAY, educator; b. Winona, Miss., Oct. 22, 1947; d. James Sidney Purnell and Hazel (Hobbs) Walker; m. Charles Wayne Dampier, Oct. 3, 1948; children Charles Wayne Jr., Trevis, Desmond. BS in Speech Edn., Jackson State U., 1970; M in Sch. Mgmt., U. Laverne, 1985. Tchr. Sunnyvale (Calif.) Sch. Dist., 1970-85, San Jose (Calif.) Eastside Sch. Dist., 1986-87; dir. WASC accrediation com. Sunnyvale (Calif.) Sch. Dist. 1984-85, activities dir., 1983-85, multicultural dir., 1975-85. Outreach leader, group leader, sec., Emmanuel Bapt. Ch., San Jose, Calif., 1983-87; advisor Black Student Union, San Jose, 1986-87; rep. Desegregation com., San Jose, 1986-87. Named tchr. of the year Sunnyvale Sch. Dist., 1985. Mem. NAACP, Nat. Coalition Negro Women, Calif. Teachers Assn. (liason 1975-76), Black Educators of Eastside Sch Dist., Delta Sigma Theta. Democrat. Home: 2873 Westberry Dr San Jose CA 95132 Office: Piedmont Hills High Sch 1377 Piedmont Rd San Jose CA 95132

DAMSBO, ANN MARIE, psychologist; b. Cortland, N.Y., July 7, 1931; d. Jorgen Einer and Agatha Irene (Schenck) D. B.S., San Diego State Coll., 1952; M.A., U.S. Internat. U., 1974, Ph.D., 1975. Commd. 2d lt. U.S. Army, 1952, advanced through grades to capt., 1957; staff therapist Letterman Army Hosp., San Francisco, 1953-54, 56-58, 61-62, Ft. Devers, Mass., 1955-56, Walter Reed Army Hosp., Washington, 1958-59, Tripler Army Hosp., Hawaii, 1959-61, Ft. Benning, Ga., 1962-64; chief therapist U.S. Army Hosp., Ft. McPherson, Ga., 1964-67; ret. U.S. Army, 1967; med. missionary So. Presbyterian Ch., Taiwan, 1968-70; psychology intern Naval Regional Med. Ctr., San Diego, 1975, pre-doctoral intern, 1975-76, postdoctoral intern, 1975-76, chief, founder pain clinic, 1977-86; adj. tchr. U. Calif. Med. Sch., San Diego; lectr., U.S., Can., Eng., France, Australia, cons. forensic hypnosis to law enforcement agys. Contbr. articles to profl. publs., chpt. to book. Tchr. Sunday sch. Methodist Ch., 1945—. Fellow Am. Soc. Clin. Hypnosis; mem. San Diego Soc. Clin. Hypnosis (pres. 1980), Am. Phys. Therapy Assn., Calif. Soc. Clin. and Hypnosis (bd. govs.), Internat. Soc. Clin. and Exptl. Hypnosis, Am. Assn. Univ. Women, Internat. Platform Assn., AAUW, Ret. Officers Am. Republican. Club: Toastmasters (local pres.). Lodges: Job's Daus., Zonta. Home and Office: 1062 W 5th Ave Escondido CA 92025

DAMSKER, BECA, microbiologist; b. Jassy, Romania, Jan. 15, 1923; came to U.S., 1969, naturalized, 1974; d. Jacques and Rose Grünspan; M.D., Bucharest U., 1950; M.Sc., U. Montreal (Que., Can.), 1969; m. Mircea Damsker, May 11, 1944. Intern, resident and fellow, Bucharest, 1950-59; specialist physician, clin. lab. Hosp. Extrapulmonary Tb, Bucharest, 1959-63; research physician Hadassah Hebrew U., 1964-66; dir. clin. lab., Jerusalem, 1966-67; clin. lab. supr., asst. dir. Mt. Sinai Hosp., N.Y.C., 1969-80, assoc. dir. microbiology, 1980—; instr., then asst. prof. Mt. Sinai Med. Sch., 1970—. Recipient Physicians Recognition award AMA, 1971, 81, 84. Mem. Am. Soc. Microbiology, AMA, N.Y. Film Soc., Met. Mus. Contbr. articles on mycobacteriology to profl. jours. Office: 1 Gustave Levy Pl New York NY 10029

DANA, BARBARA, marketing professional; b. Washington, Aug. 22, 1943; d. Vernon Paul and Fay Kathleen (Beall) Hance; m. Frank S. Dana, Dec. 1962 (div. 1972); 1 child, Frank David; m. Charles Joseph Infosino, Apr. 2, 1976. Student, Strayer Bus. Coll., 1961-62, U. Md., 1970-72. Asst. lobbyist Miller Assocs. Inc., Washington, 1962-67; account exec. Creative Mailing Cons. Am., Capital Heights, Md., 1967-75, EU Services Inc., Rockville, Md., 1975-77; pres. Barbara Dana Assoc., Washington, 1977-83; v.p. mktg., sales Precision Web Press Corp., Upper Marlboro, Md., 1983-85; dir. corp. devel., community affairs Hosp. Sick Children, Washington, 1985-87; exec. dir., chief exec. officer Kids Inc., Arlington, Va., 1987—. V.p. Infants Acquired Immune Deficiency Disease Internat. Washington, 1987—; mem. Vol. Clearing DC, steering com. 1978—. Mem. Am. Newswomens Club, Direct Mktg. Assn. Washington, Nat. Assn. Female Exec., Arts Club Washington, Beethoven Soc. Home: 2757 Unicorn Ln NW Washington DC 20015 Office: KIDS Inc Crystal Gateway N 1111 Jefferson Davis Hwy #508 Crystal City VA 22202

DANBURG, DEBRA, state legislator; b. Houston, Sept. 25, 1951; d. Stanley and Barbara Jean (Hamilton) D.; B.A., U. Houston, 1974, J.D., 1979. Asst. dir., lobbyist Texans for ERA, 1974-75; atty. pvt. practice, Houston, 1979—; mem. Tex. Ho. of Reps., 1981—; del. Democratic Nat. Convention, 1984; co-chmn. Gary Hart for Pres. campaign, 1984; Tex. rep. Am. Council of Young Polit. Leaders, 1982. Mem. Harris County Democratic Exec. Com., 1976-80, bilateral adv. com. Cultural Exchange The Netherlands-USA, 1986. Named Outstanding feminist NOW, 1975, best legistlator Houston mag., 1981, vol. of yr. KS/AIDS Found., 1984; recipient spl. presdl. award Houston Apt. Assn., 1985. Mem. Tex. Bar Assn., Gulf Coast Conservation Assn., Ducks Unlimited Inc., Houston Bar Assn. Office: Tex Ho Reps State Capitol PO Box 2910 Austin TX 78769-2910 also: Legis Dist Office PO Box 66602 Houston TX 77266

DANCA-EASTWOOD, CHARLENE MARIE, pharmaceutical company executive; b. Chgo., Dec. 3, 1950; d. Charles Anthony and Irene Ann (Corso) D.; m. Garry Gene Eastwood, July 16, 1988. BS in Edn., No. Ill. U., 1972. Tchr. jr. high sch. Willow Springs, Ill., 1973-79; pharm. sales rep. Hoecht-Roussel Co., Chgo., 1979-81; hosp. specialist Hoechst-Roussel Co., Los Angeles, 1981-86; product mgr. Hoechst-Roussel Co., Somerville, N.J., 1986-88; sci. symposia mgr. Hoechst-Roussel Co., 1988—. Bd. dirs. Am. Diabetes Assn., Bridgewater, N.J., 1987—. Mem. Pharm. Advt. Council. Roman Catholic. Home: 5 Cambridge Rd Bedminster NJ 07921 Office: Hoescht-Roussel Pharms Rt 202 - 206 North Somerville NJ 08876

DANCE, GLORIA FENDERSON, dance studio executive, ballet administrator; b. Portsmouth, Va., Mar. 10, 1932; d. Charles Bourrell and Ottillia Lavinia (Korn) Fenderson; m. Walter Forrest Dance III, June 4, 1951; children—Walter Forrest IV, Jon Marlon, Gloria Cherie. Student pub. schs., Petersburg. Cert. promotional dir., modeling/finishing and charm sch., cosmotologist. Assoc. tchr. Boyer/Traylor Dance Acad., Richmond, Va., 1952-60; founder, owner, dir. Gloria F. Dance Sch. Dancing, Petersburg, 1960—; artistic dir. Petersburg Ballet, Inc., 1984—. Block leader Ind. Voters, Walnut Hill, 1955—; chairwoman Jr. Woman's Club, Petersburg; Va. chairwoman Petersburg Dance Festival, White House Performance, Aug. 1984; chairwoman 1985 July 4 Festival, Petersburg. Recipient hon. award Optimist Club, Colonial Heights, Va., 1950-63, Va. Hon. award Va. Nat. Dance Week, 1984, Petersburg Pub. Service award Alumni Gloria F. Dance Sch., 1980, award Best Actress-Actress/Dancer, Liot, South Pacific, Mosque, Richmond, 1950; named Miss Virginia in Miss Am. Pageant, Atlantic City, Sept. 1950; prin. judge Miss America Preliminaries, Va., Md., N.C., Tenn., 1950's-80's; Dance Library Dedication (Gloria F. Dance Collection), Petersburg Pub. Library. Mem. Dance Educators of Am., Profl. Dance Tchrs., Miss America Sorority (life). Presbyterian. Clubs: Petersburg Country; Ft. Lee Country (Va.); Battlefield Park and Racquet. Avocations: boating; swimming; snow skiing; dancing. Home: 1806 Brandon Ave Petersburg VA 23805 Office: Petersburg Ballet Inc 44 Goodwich Ave Petersburg VA 23805

DANCER-VANDECOEVERING, DANA JO, sales representative; b. Hillsboro, Oreg., Mar. 18, 1961; d. Roy Evans Dancer and Betty Jane Maxwell; m. Joseph Anthony Vandecoevering, Sept. 30, 1964. Student in modeling, John Roberts Powers Finishing Sch., 1978; BA in Communications, Linfield Coll., McMinnville. Oreg., 1983. Chpt. cons. Phi Sigma Sigma, Miami, Fla., 1983-85; sales rep. L.G. Balfour Co., Attleboro, Mass., 1985—, mem. mktg. council, 1987—. Named one of Outstanding Young Women Am., 1979, 83. Mem. Nat. Assn. Female Execs., Portland Advt. Fedn. (AD-2 Club), Portland Advt. Mus., Phi Sigma Sigma (div. pres. 1984-88, regional dir. 1988—). Home and Office: 5341 NE Farmcrest St Hillsboro OR 97124

DANCO, KATHARINE LECK, educator; b. Wilton, Conn., June 11, 1929; d. Walter Charles and Katharine (Elmendorf) Leck; m. Leon A. Danco, Aug. 25, 1951; children—Suzanne, Walter. R.N., Roosevelt Hosp. Sch. Nursing, 1950, R.N., N.Y., Ohio. Vice pres., treas. Univ. Services Inst., Cleve., 1968—, v.p., treas. Center for Family Bus., Cleve., 1973—, faculty, 1970—, seminar dir., 1971—; also dir. syndicated columnist numerous trade mags., 1978—, The Family in Bus., Cleve., 1978—. Author: From the Other Side of the Bed, 1980; contbr. articles to profl. jours. Bd. dirs. Julie Billiart Sch., Cleve., 1976—. Episcopalian. Home: 28230 Cedar Rd Pepper Pike OH 44122 Office: PO Box 24268 Center for Family Bus Cleveland OH 44124

DANCY, BONITA JOYCE, lawyer; b. Balt., Jan. 21, 1946; d. Homer Benson and Joyce (Harper) D.; m. Theron Napoleon Whitaker, July 10, 1982. BA, Morgan U., 1967; MSW, U. Md., 1971, JD, 1981; Cert. in Group Therapy, U. Chgo., 1972. Bar: Md. 1981; lic. social worker, Md. Supr. family service Md. Dept. Social Services, Balt., 1967-72; adminstr. Northwest Youth Services, Balt., 1972-81; atty. adivsor, gen. counsel HHS, Balt., 1981-82; master in chancery Balt. City Cir. Ct., 1982—; assoc. prof. sociology Coppin State Coll., Balt., 1973-75; adj. prof. Morgan State Coll., Balt., 1975-81; commr. Gov.'s Landlord Tenant Law Commn., Md., 1975—; training cons. U. Md. Sch. Social Work, Balt., 1974-75. Past pres., mem. Balt. Urban League Leaguettes, 1968—; bd. dirs. Mental Health Assn. Balt., 1983, Balt. Urban League, 1981-82, v.p. Named Vol. of Yr. Balt. Urban League, 1983. Mem. ABA, Md. Bar Assn. (v.p. pre trial diversion program 1974-80), Balt. City Bar Assn. (chair continuing legal edn. com. 1986-87, mem. exec. com. 1987—), Md. Inst. Continuing Profl. Edn. Lawyers Inc. (bd. dirs.), Nat. Bar Assn., Monumental City Bar Assn., Phi Alpha Theta, Alpha Kappa Alpha.

DANDOY, SUZANNE EGGLESTON, physician, educator; b. Los Angeles, Jan. 2, 1935; d. Leonard Lester and Catherine (Wheelwright) Eggleston; m. Jeremiah Richard Dandoy, June 14, 1958; children: Kevin, Bret, Jolyn. BA, U. Calif., Los Angeles, 1956; MD, UCLA, 1960, MPH, 1963. Diplomate: Am. Bd. Preventive Medicine. Intern, Los Angeles Harbor Gen. Hosp., Torrance, Calif., 1960-61; resident Los Angeles Health Dept., 1961-62, 63-64; epidemiologist San Diego Dept. Pub. Health, 1967-68; bur. chief Ariz. Dept. Health Service, Phoenix, 1970-73; asst. commr. Ariz. Dept. Health Service, 1973-74, asst. dir., 1974-75, dir., 1975-80; prof. health adminstrn. Ariz. State U., Tempe, 1981-85; exec. dir. Utah Dept. Health, Salt Lake City, 1985—; adj. assoc. prof. U. Utah; bd. dirs. Pub. Health Found. Editorial bd. Am. Jour. Pub. Health; contbr. articles to profl. jours. Bd. dirs. Child

Crisis Ctr., Tempe St. Lukes Hosp.; chair Nat. Vaccine Adv. Com. Dept. Health and Human Services; adv. com. on immunization practices HEW; pres. Utah Women's Forum. Recipient award Ariz. Dietetic Assn., 1976; award Maricopa County Med. Soc., 1980. Fellow Am. Pub. Health Assn., Am. Coll. Preventive Medicine; mem. AMA, Utah Med. Assn., Utah Pub. Health Assn., Phi Beta Kappa, Delta Omega. Democrat. Mormon. Home: 990 S Oak Hills Way Salt Lake City UT 84108 Office: Utah Dept Health PO Box 16700 Salt Lake City UT 84116-0700

DANFORD, ARDATH ANNE, retired librarian; b. Lima, Ohio, Feb. 11, 1930; d. Howard Gorby and Grace Rose (Klug) D. B.A., Fla. State U., 1951, M.A., 1952. Head tech. services Lima Pub. Library, 1956-60; librarian Way Pub. Library, Perrysburg, Ohio, 1960-70; asst. dir. Toledo-Lucas County Pub. Library, 1971-77, ret., 1985, dir., 1977-85; mem. adv. bd. mid-Am. Nat. Banks. Author: The Perrysburg Story, 1966. Bd. dirs. Toledo-Lucas County Council Human Services, Housing Directions of Greater Toledo, Hist. Perrysburg Inc.; mem. adv. bd. St. Charles Hosp.; mem. animal research com. Med. Coll. Ohio. Recipient Toledo Headliner award Women in Communication, 1978, Boss of Yr. award PerRoMa chpt. Am. Bus. Women's Assn., 1978. Mem. ALA, Ohio Library Assn. (Librarian of Yr. 1985). Methodist. Clubs: Toledo; Perrysburg Garden. Lodge: Zonta (Toledo) (pres. club 1975-76). Home: 1075 Cherry St Perrysburg OH 43551

D'ANGELO, RITA YVONNE, psychologist, educator; b. N.Y.C., Apr. 21, 1928; d. J. Anthony and Alice (Mignona) D'A. BA, Hunter Coll., N.Y.C., 1948; MA, Fordham U., N.Y.C., 1950, PhD, 1961. Lic. psychologist, N.Y. Clin. psychologist Cath. Charities Psychology Clinic, N.Y.C., 1950—; asst. prof. psychology Marymount Coll., Tarrytown, N.Y., 1953-57; supr. clin. psychology St. Germaines Residential Treatment Ctr., Peekskill, N.Y., 1957-62; asst. prof. L.I. U., N.Y.C., 1962-64, Hunter Coll., 1964-68; asst. assoc. full prof. CUNY, N.Y.C., 1968—; acting dir. Italian-Am. Studies CUNY, 1975-80; psychology dept. chairperson CUNY, N.Y.C., 1976-88; acting dean Coll. Social Scis. CUNY, 1976-80; mental health cons. HEW, NIMH, 1973-77. Recipient Disting. Tchrs. award CUNY, 1973. Mem. Am. Psychol. Assn., Eastern Psychol. Assn., N.Y. Soc. for Clin. Psychologists, N.Y. Acad. Scis. Office: CUNY Bronx NY 10468

DANGLADE, RUTH ELLEN, special education administrator; b. Marion, Ind., Jan. 27, 1940; d. Harold Davis and Elizabeth (Lake) Neel; m. James K. Danglade, Sept. 2, 1961 (div. Nov. 1979); children: Annette, John. BS, Ball State U., 1961, MA, 1964. Cert. elem., secondary bus., spl. edn. and speech pathology tchr., Ind. Tchr. orthopedically handicapped Muncie (Ind.) Community Schs., 1961-67, tchr. of multiply handicapped, 1969-74, tchr. learning disabled, 1976-79; spl. edn. instr. Ball State U., Muncie, 1974-79; asst. dir. spl. edn. Delaware County Spl. Edn. Coop., Muncie, 1979—; sci. curriculum cons. NSF, Muncie, 1976-78; learning disabilities cons. Ball State U., 1974-80. Bd. dirs. Delaware County Easter Seal Soc., 1967—; adv. council Ball State U. Coll. Bus., 1985—; adminstrv. bd. High Street United Meth. Ch., Muncie, 1984—, youth coordinator, 1985—. Mem. Assn. for Children with Learning Disabilities, Ind. Council Adminstrs. in Spl. Edn., Council for Exceptional Children (pres. Delaware County chpt. 1977-78), Phi Delta Kappa, Pi Beta Phi. Methodist. Office: Delaware County Spl Edn Coop 2000 S Franklin Ave Muncie IN 47304

DANGOT-SIMPKIN, GILDA ROSE, training executive, management consultant; b. N.Y.C., Aug. 18, 1952; d. Alter and Paula (Mentlik) Dangot; m. Bernard E. Simpkin, Sept. 7, 1986. BA, CCNY, 1973; cert. in tng. and devel., NYU, 1973; postgrad. Syracuse Coll. Law, 1973-74, CUNY. Cert. tchr. N.Y. Mgmt. intern Dept. Consumer Affairs, N.Y.C., 1973; tchr. N.Y.C. Bd. Edn., 1974-75; community cons. N.Y.C. Human Rights Commn., 1975-78, spl. projects cons., 1978-79, dir. info. and resource devel., 1979-80, dir. tng., 1980—; mgmt. cons. Dynamic Devel., N.Y.C., 1980—, Am. Airlines, N.Y.C., 1984—, Kings Auto, N.Y.C., 1982-83, El Al Airlines, 1984—, Sheraton Corp., 1984, Bank Hapoalim, 1985—, World Trade Inst., 1984-86, Am. cyanamid, 1986—; lectr. N.Y. Network for Learning, 1980-82, Westwinds Learning Ctr., N.Y.C., 1982—; adj. instr. Queens Coll., N.Y.C., 1984, Marymount Coll., 1985. Author: ABCs of Getting Help, 1976; So Your Organization Needs Money, 1978; How to Negotiate Anything, 1983. Founder Little Red Sch. House Community and Cultural Ctr., Inc., N.Y.C., 1978; pres. B'Nai Hashoah: Children of Holocaust Survivors, N.Y.C., 1979; founder, bd. dirs. internat. Network of Children of Survivors, N.Y.C., 1981. Recipient Gov.'s cert. for excellence in govt., 1969, Mayor's Scholarship, N.Y.C., 1983. Mem. Am. Soc. Tng. and Devel. (chmn.), Ind. Cons. Spl. Interest Group (chmn. program com.), Inter-Govt. Tng. Council, Nat. Soc. Fund-Raising Execs. (cert. of recognition 1982), The Bus. Initiatives, Orgn. Devel. Network, Phi Beta Kappa, Pi Sigma Alpha, Kappa Delta Pi.

DANIEL, BRENDA JEAN, social services administrator; b. Tunica, Miss., July 4, 1957; d. Charles Willie Lawson and Mattie Lee (Greene) Keys; m. James Daniel Jr., June 1, 1975; 1 child, Kimberly Shellette. BS in Recreation and Occupational Therapy with high honors, Memphis State U., 1978; BS in Nursing, U. Tenn., 1983; postgrade. Memphis State U., 1987—. Nurse Elvis Presley Trauma Ctr., Memphis, 1977-86, recreational and occupational therapist VA Hosp., Memphis, 1978-80; tchr., dir. Teen Parent Rehab. Program, Tunica, 1986-88; asst. adminstr. Tunica County Hosp., 1988—; tchr. spl. students City of Memphis, 1977-79; supr. Tunica Home Health Service, 1986—; pres. Nursing Unit, Clarksdale, Miss., 1987—; mem. com. on corr. youth activity City of Tunica; nurse advisor Home Health, Tunica; cons. in field. Sunday sch. tchr., bd. dirs. N.W. Ch. of God in Christ, Tunica, pres., 1987—; leader No. Miss. Dist. Fight Against Teen Pregnancy, 1986; created the first Teen Parent Program, No. Miss., 1986. Nat. Recreation scholar, 1977, Nat. Black Student Assn. scholar, 1978. Mem. Am. Vocat. Assn., Tenn. Nursing Assn., Miss. Nursing Assn., Nat. Employment Tng. Assn. Club: Exec. Women (Phila.). Lodge: Order of Eastern Star. Home: Rt 2 Box 55B Tunica MS 38676

DANIEL, CECILE MARGARET, township official; b. New Bedford, Mass., Mar. 28, 1956; d. Romeo Alfred and Leona Blanch (Lemiuex) D.; m. George Walter Waterman III, Aug. 4, 1984; 1 child, Nathan Daniel. B.A. in Polit. Sci., U. Mass., 1978; M.A. in Pub. Adminstrn., Pa. State U., 1981. Mgr. Towamencin Twp., Pa., 1981-87, Perkiomen Twp., Pa., 1987. Chairperson Task Force on Ednl. Curriculum Mgr./Council; appropriations com. United Way, 1984-86; mem. North Penn Solid Waste Commn. Mem. Pa. Assn. Mcpl. Mgrs., Southeast Pa. Mgrs. Assn., Montgomery Assn. Twp. Ofcls. (sec. 1983-85, program chair 1986), Pa. Mgr's. Ednl. Com. (chairperson 1985-86), Pa. Mcpl. Mgrs. Inst. Republican. Roman Catholic. Avocations: reading, running, tennis. Home: 1133 Black Rock Rd RD #1 Phoenixville PA 19460 Office: Perkiomen Twp 467 Gravel Park Collegeville PA 19426

DANIEL, EVELYN HOPE, university dean; b. Whitefield, Maine, Nov. 23, 1933; d. George Snowdeal and Evelyn Lura (Cole) Cunningham; m. Alfred Eugene Foulkes, Mar. 30, 1951 (div. 1956); children: Nancy Karen, George Warren; m. Harold Clifford Daniel, Jan. 1, 1957 (div. 1974); children: Jeffrey Martin, Dawn Hope. AB magna cum laude, U. N.C., Wilmington, 1968; MLS, U. Md., 1969, Ph.D., 1974. Asst. prof. Coll. Library Sci. U. Ky., 1972-74; asst. prof. Grad. Sch. Library U. R.I., 1974-76; assoc. prof., asst. dean Sch. Info. Studies Syracuse (N.Y.) U., 1976-81, dean and prof., 1981-85; dean, prof. U. N.C., Chapel Hill, 1985—; cons. ednl. radio and TV, Tehran, Iran, 1976-77, Millersville State Coll., Pa., 1983, Fgn. Service Inst., U.S. Dept. State, Washington, 1983-85, Rutgers U., 1985, Case Western Res. U., Cleve., 1985, U. So. Fla., 1986, McGill U., 1986, U. Ky., 1986, U. Iowa, 1987, Nat. Library Medicine, 1987, Emporia (Kans.) U., 1987, Ohio State U., 1988. Co-author: Reader in Library and Information Sciences, 1974, Media and Microcomputers in the Library, 1983; mem. editorial bd.: Library and Info. Sci. Research jour., 1979—; contbr. articles to profl. jours. NDEA fellow, 1968-69; recipient Sch. Library Media award, 1984—. Mem. ALA (chmn. standing com. on edn. 1980-83, coordinator Library Edn. Assembly 1980-83), N.Y. Statewide Continuing Library Edn. Adv. Com. (vice chmn. 1982-84), Assn. for Library and Edn. Sci. Educators (chmn. 1983-84). Office: U NC Sch Info and Library Sci 100 Manning Hall CB# 3360 Chapel Hill NC 27599-3360

DANIEL, GRISELDA, university administrator; b. Battle Creek, Mich., Feb. 7, 1938; d. Edward and Teritha (Faulce) Daniel; married; children—Cornell A., Gary L., Cheri A., Patrick H. B.S. magna cum laude, Western Mich. U., 1973, M.S. Adminstrn. in Higher Edn., 1980. Surg. nurse Borgess Hosp., Kalamazoo, 1958-66; attendent nurse Kalamazoo State Hosp., 1966-70; counselor trainer Coll. Gen. Studies, Western Mich. U., Kalamazoo, 1970-73, dir. Martin Luther King Jr. program, 1975-80, asst. to v.p. acad. affairs/dir. spl. programs, 1980—; supr. packaging dept. Peter Echrich & Co., Kalamazoo, 1974-75; lectr. in field. Mem. NAACP, AA Univ. Adminstrs., Nat. Assn. Female Execs., Nat. Consortium Black Profl. Devel. Home: 42818 N 30th St PawPaw MI 49079 Office: Western Mich U 2312 Adminstrn Bldg Kalamazoo MI 49008

DANIEL, LYNN MARIE (LINDA), microbiologist; b. Abilene, Tex., Aug. 19, 1944; d. James Marcus and Mary Marie (Hill) Daniel; B.S., U. Tex., 1969. Microbiologist, instr., Good Samaritan Hosp., Phoenix, 1967-70; supr., ednl. coordinator Desert Samaritan Hosp., Mesa, Ariz., 1970-73; surveyor/cons. Ariz. Dept. Health, Phoenix, 1973-76; owner, cons. Lab. Cons., Ltd., Tempe, Ariz., 1976-77; owner, pres., supr. Mobile Microbiology Services, Inc., Tempe, 1977-85; owner Microlab Spltys., 1983-85; dir. infectious disease dept. Nat. Health Labs., Phoenix, 1985-87, San Diego, 1988—; tchr. Maricopa County Jr. Colls., 1972-73; cons. in field; lectr. in field. Mem. Nat. Registry of Microbiologists, Am. Soc. Microbiology, Am. Soc. Med. Technologists. Home: 4061 Honeycutt St San Diego CA 92109 Office: 1225 S 23d St Phoenix AZ 85034

DANIEL, MARGARET MARY, municipal court administrator; b. Pittsfield, Mass., Jan. 28, 1950; d. Carmen and Mary Rose (Marra) Russo; m. Thomas J. McCarthy, June 24, 1972 (div.); children: Michael Patrick, Christopher Thomas; m. Joe Richard Daniel, Mar. 11, 1982. Student, San Jose (Calif.) State U., 1967-69, Summit Orgn., 1986—, Sierra Coll., 1987—. Dep. clk. Santa Clara Mcpl. Ct., San Jose, 1973-79; clk. courtroom Los Gatos, Calif., 1979-86; chief dep. Placer County Mcpl. Ct., Auburn, Calif., 1986—. Mem. Mcpl. Ct. Clk.'s Assn. (ct. dir. 1986—). Democrat. Office: Placer County Mcpl Ct 11544 B Ave Auburn CA 95603

DANIEL, MARVA JEANE, principal, home relations consultant; b. Buffalo, Oct. 8, 1943; d. Edmund and Beatrice Lessie (Jones) Howell; m. Marvin Lawrence Daniel, Dec. 23, 1976; children: Marcia Marie, Marion Darcel. BS, SUNY, Buffalo, 1968, MS, 1970. Cert. elem. tchr., N.Y. Instr. elem. Buffalo Bd. Edn., 1968-73, home sch. coordinator, 1973-76, human relations specialist, 1976-83, asst. prin., 1984-85, prin., 1985—; adminstrv. asst. Buffalo Sch. of Performing Arts, 1983-84; lectr. SUNY Coop. Coll. Ctr., Buffalo, 1970-73; desegregation cons. U.S. Dept. Justice Community Relations, Cherry Hill, N.J., 1977; cons. youth conf. Community Action Orgn. of Erie County, Buffalo, 1984, 85; test cons. Ednl. Testing Service, Princeton, N.J., 1985, 86, 87; facilitator trainer Effective Parenting Info. for Children, Buffalo, 1982—. Author: U.S. proposal on literacy, Linking with Literacy, 1986; co-author: U.S. Justice Dept.'s Conf. Jour., 1977. V.p. B.U.I.L.D. Orgn., Buffalo, 1975; facilitator vol. Western N.Y. Assn. for Learning Disabled, Buffalo, 1983, Parent Anonymous, Buffalo, 1985; tutor vol. Literacy Vols. of Am., Buffalo, 1986-87. Mem. Black Educator Assn., N.Y. State Fedn. of Sch. Adminstrs., Buffalo Suprs. and Cen. Office Adminstrs., Assn. for Supervision and Curriculum Devel., Smithsonian Inst., Afro-Am. Hist. Assn. Democrat. Club: Links (Erie County). Office: Buffalo Sch #77 370 Normal Ave Buffalo NY 14213

DANIEL, REBECCA SUSAN, engineer, military officer; b. South Charleston, W.Va., Sept. 17, 1959; d. Charles David and Juliet Sue (Summers) D.; m. Joey Lee McCoy, July 10, 1978 (div. June 1983); m. Gregory Scott Williams, Jan. 2, 1987. BS in Electrical and Electronic Engring., Calif. State U., Sacramento, 1985; postgrad., Embry-Riddle Aero. U., 1986—. Radio systems technician USAF, George AFB, Calif., 1978-80; radio systems instr. USAF, Keeler AFB, Miss., 1980-82; commd. 2d lt. USAF, 1985; program mgr. USAF, McClellan AFB, Calif., 1985-86, project engr., 1986—; report survey officer Sacramento Air Logistics Ctr., 1985-87. Math. and English tutor Dyer-Kelly Elem. Sch., Sacramento, 1985—. Mem. Co. Grade Officers' Council (Officer Quarter 1987), Air Force Assn., Nat. Assn. Female Execs.; Armed Forces Communications-Electronics Assn. Democrat. Home: 1371 Old West Dr Sacramento CA 95834-1412

DANIEL, YVETTE FELICE, municipal official; b. Hammond, Ind., Nov. 18, 1959; d. Donald Fredrick and Dorothy Daniel. BA, U. Denver, 1983. Asst. supr. Goodwill Rehab., Denver, 1980-82; lab. aide Kaiser Permanente, Denver, 1983; rep. mktg. Nat. Home Health Care, Houston, 1983-84, also bd. dirs.; environ. technician City of Houston, 1984-87; architect, engr. rep. Am. Standard, Inc., HOuston, 1987—. Officer Dorothy Smith Ednl. Found., Houston, 1979—; alumni admissions counselor U. Denver Alumni Assn., 1984—. Recipient Gov. Vol. award State of Tex., 1978; Katrina McCormick Barnes scholar U. Denver, 1978; named one of Outstanding Young Women of Am., 1987. Mem. Nat. Assn. Female Execs. Club: Links (Houston). Home: 9450 Woodfair 2008 Houston TX 77036

DANIEL-DREYFUS, SUSAN B. RUSSE, civic worker; b. St. Louis, May 30, 1940; d. Frederick William and Suzanne (Mackay) Russe; m. Don B. Faerber, Nov. 27, 1962 (div. Nov. 1968); 1 child, Suzanne Mackay; m. Marc Andre Daniel-Dreyfus, Aug. 9, 1969; 1 child, Cable Dunster. Student, Smith Coll., 1958-60, Corcoran Sch. Fine Arts, 1960-61, Washington U., St. Louis, 1961-62. Mng. ptnr. Communications, Inc., 1980-82; asst. dir. Harvard Bus. Sch. Fund, Cambridge, 1982-86; pres. SCR Assocs. Corp., Cambridge, 1986—; mem. bd. advisors Odysseum, Inc.; bd. dirs. Future Mgmt. Systems. Mem. St. Louis-St. Louis County White House Conf. on Edn., 1966-68; mem. Mo. 1st Gov.'s Conf. on Edn., 1966, 2d Conf., 1968; bd. dirs. Tunbridge Sch., 1973-78, St. Louis Smith Coll.; hon. bd. dirs. New Music Circle; mem. woman's bd. dirs. Washington U., New Music Circle, 1963-67; mem. woman's bd. Mo. Hist. Soc.; bd. dirs. Non-Partisan Ct. Plan for Mo., Young Audiences Inc., 1967-69; bd. dirs. Childrens Art Bazaar, 1968-70; founder St. Louis Opera Theater; chmn. Art. Mus. Bond Issue election St. Louis, 1966; jr. bd. dirs. St. Louis Symphony, 1966-68, Opportunities Indsl. Center, Boston; legis. chmn. bd. dirs. Boston LWV, 1969-72; mem. council, bd. dirs. Jr. League Boston, 1970-72, 74-76, v.p. Bd. of Family Counseling Services-Region West, Boston, 1979—; pres. Family Counseling Bd., Brookline, Mass.; bd. govs. Tunbridge Sch.; trustee Chestnut Hill Sch., Boston, Brookline Friendly Soc.; mem. steering com. ann. fund Boston Children's Hosp. Med. Center, 1980-84; v.p. Nat. Friends Bd., Joslin Diabetes Found., 1980-83; mem. corp. bd. Joslin Diabetes Ctr.; v.p. bd. dirs. Boston Ctr. Internat. Visitors, 1979-82; Boston bd. dirs. Mass. Soc. Prevention of Cruelty to Children, 1980-84; exec. v.p. Ctr. for Middle East Bus., 1978-82; pres. bd. Brookline Community Fund, 1984—; overseer Old Sturbridge Village, 1987—. Mem. Colonial Dames, Soc. Art Historians. Clubs: Women's City (dir.) (Boston); Vincent (dir.). Home: 120 Middlesex Rd Chestnut Hill MA 02167

DANIELEY, MARCIA ANN, insurance professional; b. Bonne Terre, Mo., Nov. 11, 1959; d. Donald Philip and Maxine Elizabeth (Andriano) D.; m. James Philip Pease, Apr. 30, 1988. Student, Murray (Ky.) State U., 1978-80. Rep. customer service Am. Family Ins. Agy., Farmington, Mo., 1977-80, agt., broker, 1985—; solicitor, rep. customer service Western Ins. Services, Inc., Houston, 1980-83; broker, rep. customer service Bowersox Ins. Agy., Co., St. Louis, 1983-85. Mem. art com. Literary Gourmet, 1987. Mem. Federated Women's Club Am. Home: 403 N Carleton #11 Farmington MO 63640 Office: Don Danieley Ins Agy 313 Saint Genevieve Ave Farmington MO 63640

DANIELL, ELLEN, personnel director; b. New Haven, Conn., July 14, 1947; d. Martin Haynes and Winifred (Marvin) D.; m. David H. Gelfand, Dec. 29, 1980. BA in Chemistry, Swarthmore Coll., 1969; PhD in Chemistry, U. Calif., San Diego, 1973. Postdoctoral fellow Cold Spring Harbor (N.Y.) Labs., 1974-76; asst. prof. molecular biology U. Calif., Berkeley, 1976-84; sr. sci. recruiter Cetus Corp., Emeryville, Calif., 1984-85, personnel dir., 1985—; mem. sci. adv. bd. Mills Coll., Oakland, Calif, 1985—. Contbr. articles to profl. jours. NIH, NSF, Am. Cancer Soc. grantee, 1976-84. Mem. Am. Soc. of Personnel Adminstrs., Am. Soc. Micorbiology, Am. Soc. Cell Biology, Phi Beta Kappa, Sigma Xi. Democrat.

DANIELS, ADRIENNE HELEN, computer company administrator; b. Troy, N.Y., May 7, 1942; d. Felix Frank and Vergin (Hrachian) Novak; m. Harold Irving Daniels, July 18, 1964 (div. Feb. 1981); children: Tamara Lynn, Patricia Ann. AS in Bus. Adminstrn., Schenectady County Community Coll., 1985. Mktg. sec. Albany (N.Y.) sales div. Prime Computer, 1978-79, dist. adminstr. Albany and N.Y.C., 1979-82; regional customer service adminstr. Prime Computer, Parsippany, N.Y., 1982-85, N.Y.C., 1985—. Mem. Nat. Assn. Female Execs., Naval Res. Enlisted Assn. (v.p. Albany chpt. 1986-87). Club: O.C. Ski. Home: 11 Cornell Ave Albany NY 12203

DANIELS, ARLENE KAPLAN, sociology educator; b. N.Y.C., Dec. 10, 1930; d. Jacob and Elizabeth (Rathstein) Kaplan; m. Richard Rene Daniels, June 9, 1956. B.A. with honors in English, U. Calif., Berkeley, 1952; M.A. in Sociology, 1954, Ph.D. in Sociology, 1960. Instr. dept. speech U. Calif., Berkeley, 1959-61; research assoc. Mental Research Inst., Palo Alto, Calif., 1961-66; assoc. prof. sociology San Francisco State Coll., 1966-70; chief Center for Study Women in Soc., Inst. Sci. Analysis, San Francisco, 1970-80; mem. faculty Northwestern U., Evanston, Ill., 1975—; prof. dept. sociology Northwestern U., 1975—; cons. NIMH, 1971-73, Nat. Endowment for Humanities, 1975-80, Nat. Inst. Edn., 1978-82. Editor: (with Rachel Kahn-Hut) Academics on the Line, 1970; co-editor: (with Gaye Tuchman and James Benét Hearth and Home: Images of Women in the Mass Media, 1978, (with James Benét) Education: Straightjacket or Opportunity?, 1979, (with Rachel Kahn-Hut and Richard Colvard) Women and Work, 1982, (with Alice Cook and Val Lorwin) Women and Trade Unions in Eleven Industrialized Countries, (with Teresa Odendahl and Elizabeth Boris) Working in Foundations, 1985, Invisible Careers, 1988; editor: Jour. Social Problems, 1974-78; assoc. editor: Contemporary Sociology, 1980-82, Symbolic Interaction, 1979—. Trustee Bus. and Profl. Women's Research Found. Bd., 1980-85, Women's Equity Action League Legal and Ednl. Def. Fund, 1979-81; mem. Chgo. Research Assos. Bd., 1981—. Recipient Social Sci. Research Council Faculty Research award, 1970-71; Ford Found. Faculty fellow, 1975-76; grantee Nat. Inst. Edn., 1978-79, 1979-80, NSF, 1974-75, NIMH, 1973-74. Mem. Sociologists Women in Soc. (pres. 1975-76), Am. Sociology Assn. (council 1979-81, chmn. occupations and orgns., 1987, chmn. pubs. com. 1985-87), Soc. Study Social Problems (v.p. 1981-82, pres. 1987), Soc. Study Symbolic Inter-Action. Office: Northwestern Univ Dept of Sociology 1810 Chicago Ave Evanston IL 60201

DANIELS, BEVERLY JONES, equal employment opportunity program manager; b. Memphis, May 16, 1956; d. Thomas William and Lucy Mae (Jackson) Jones; m. Carlton Timothy Daniels, Aug. 11, 1984. BBA, Memphis State U., 1979. Sr. sec. Schering-Plough Consumer Ops., Memphis, 1979-80, adminstrv. sec., 1980-82, assoc. mgr. EEO, 1982-84, mgr. EEO programs, 1984—. Mem. Memphis City Beautiful Commn., 1985-87. Mem. EEO Council Greater Memphis and Shelby City, Memphis Vol. Placement Programs (coordinator 1983—), Interpreting Services for Deaf (sec. 1983-84), Memphis Personnel Assn., Delta Sigma Theta. Office: Schering-Plough Consumer Ops 3030 Jackson Ave Memphis TN 38151

DANIELS, DORIA LYNN, manufacturing executive; b. Kent, Ohio, Apr. 22, 1951; d. Eli and Henrietta (Johnson) D. BBA, Kent State U., 1973; postgrad., Old Dominion U., 1975-76, Akron U., 1984-86. Mgmt. trainee Cardinal Fed. Savs., Cleve., 1973-74; acctg. mgr. People Savs. and Loan, Hampton, Va., 1974-77; ins. agt. John Hancock Mut. Life Ins., Hampton, 1977-79; prodn. planner Little Tikes Mfg., Hudson, Ohio, 1979—; pres., co-founder Thomas Anderson Devel. Corp., 1986. Mem. Kent (Ohio) Bd. Edn., 1987, Shade Tree Commn. Kent City Council, 1987; candidate ward 3 council seat Rep. Party, Kent, 1969, co-founder and chmn. Thomas-Anderson Devel. Corp. Kent, 1986—; mem. bd. advisors Portage County Human Services Dept., 1988. City of Kent scholar, 1969; recipient Gov.'s Recognition award Gov. of Ohio, 1986, commendation from Ohio Ho. of Reps., 1987, Ohio House of Reps. State Commendation for record service to the Kent community, 1987, Kent Edn. Assn. awards, 1988. Mem. NAACP (life, polit. advisor), Am. Prodn. Inventory Control Soc., Nat. Assn. Female Execs., Nat. Council Negro Women. Baptist. Home: 234 Dodge St Kent OH 44240 Office: Little Tikes Mfg 2180 Barlow Rd Hudson OH 44236

DANIELS, DOROTHY, writer; b. Waterbury, Conn., July 1, 1915; d. Judson Richard and Mary (Guilfoile) Smith; student Central Conn. State Coll., 1932-36; m., Oct. 7, 1937. Tng. tchr., New Britain, Conn., 1937-39; actress, 1939-40. Author 132 books under name Dorothy Daniels, 1962—, most recent including: House of Silence, 1980, Nicola, 1980, Monte Carlo, 1981, Sisters of Valcour, 1981, For Love and Valcour, 1983; seven books under name Suzanne Somers, 1961-73, including: The Caduceus Tree, 1961, Image of Truth, 1963, Romany Curse, 1971, House on Thunder Hill, 1973, Crisis at Valcour, 1985; other books under names Cynthia Cavanaugh, Angela Gray, Daniella Dorsett. Active Citizens Adv. Com. Ventura Sch., Calif. Youth Authority, Republican Women's Club. Mem. Nat. League Am. Pen Women (nat. hon.), Authors Guild, Ventura County Writers' Club.

DANIELS, FAY DOLORES, civic leader; b. Detroit, Oct. 27, 1941; d. David William and Ann Elizabeth (McMillian) Sebastian; m. Martin J. Smith, 1960; children: Cindy, Jerry, David; m. Doanld Benjamin, July 26, 1975 (div. 1978); m. Jerold Jay Daniels, Apr. 16, 1983. Student, Internat. Correspondence Sch., 1966-67, NW Coll. Bus., 1968-69, Tacoma Community Coll., 1979-81, Seattle U., 1978, U. Idaho, 1982. State coordinator Parents Anonymous, Tacoma, 1980—; dir. Crossroads Motivational Services, Sacramento. Vol. Rockefeller for Pres. Campaign, State of Oreg., 1964-74; vol. coordinator Parents Anonymous Portland, 1974-76; vol. crisis hotline, counselor Women's Emergency House Vancouver, Wash., 1976-78; planner numerous confs. on child abuse and neglect, Wash., 1978-79; trainer, cons. child abuse, spousal abuse and self-abuse Parents Anonymous, State of Wash., 1980—; vol. hotline, counselor Pierce County, Wash., 1980—; mem. Wash. State Coalition for Prevention Child Abuse/Neglect; mem. citizen's rev. bd. sexual exploitation of women and children; v.p. Wash. State Foster Care Assn. Named Woman of Yr., Tacoma Social Services, 1981. Mem. Exec. Women, Parents Support Program Calif. Roman Catholic. Home and Office: 293 Fairgrounds Dr Sacramento CA 95817

DANIELS, JANICE CISSNA, communications executive; b. Portland, Oreg., June 28, 1947; d. Wayne Robert Cissna and Gwendolyn Darlene (Rothchild) Shearer; m. Ralph Franklin Daniels, June 22, 1977; children: Colleen, Kathleen, Charles, Ralph Jr. BS in Elem. Edn., Portland State U., 1970; MBA in Gen. Mgmt., St. Edwards U., 1980. Tchr. Westside Union Sch. Dist., Lancaster, Calif., 1970-71; munitions officer USAF, Ariz. and Thailand, 1971-76; munitions inspector USAF, Bergstrom AFB, Tex., 1976-78; mgmt. analyst Houston Instrument div. Bausch and Lomb, Austin, Tex., 1980-84; data resources supr. Houston Instrument div. B&L, Ametek, Austin, Tex., 1984-87; gen. mgr. Bus. Resources, Panama City, Fla., 1987—; adv. office edn. Austin Ind. Sch. Dist., 1983-85; dir. youth edn. Holy Cross Luth. Ch., Austin, 1978-82. Contbr. articles to profl. jours. Served to capt. USAF, 1971-77; munitions staff officer USAFR, Bergstrom AFB, 1978—; maintenance staff officer USAFR, Warner Robins AFB, Ga., 1987—. Mem. Soc. for Tech. Communication, Internat. Tng. in Communication (1st v.p. 1984, 85, pres. 1986, 87, level I accreditation 1984, level II accreditation 1987), Cen. Tex. PC Users Group, Reserve Officers Assn., Alpha Omicron Pi (pledged pres. 1965, 66). Republican. Lutheran. Office: Bus Resources PO Box 15906 Panama City FL 32406

DANIELS, LAURIE JEAN, data processing executive; b. Oak Park, Ill., Mar. 19, 1954; d. William Joseph and Carol Awrey (McDonald) Moore; m. Mark Robert Daniels, Aug. 5, 1978. BA, U. Notre Dame, 1976; MPA, U. Denver, 1977. Asst. dir. personnel and budget Arapahoe County, Littleton, Colo., 1977-80; cons. Deloite Haskins & Sells, Denver, 1980-82; mgr. info. services Coseka Resources Ltd., Denver, 1982-85; dir. U.S. Info. Services Bramalea Ltd., Denver, 1985—. Democrat. Roman Catholic. Clubs: Denver Athletic (chmn. wellness com. 1986-87, mem. athletic com. 1987—). Office: Bramalea Ltd 3773 Cherry Creek N Dr #700 Denver CO 80209

DANIELS, LESLIE BETH, city ofcl.; b. Kansas City, Mo., July 14, 1951; d. Charles Lee and Helen Atanasoff D.; B.A., U. Ariz., 1972; M.A., U. Phoenix, 1981; postgrad. U. Okla. Econ. Devel. Inst., 1983. Copywriter public relations, Tucson, 1972-74, graphic artist/electronic typesetter, 1974-75, polit. campaign mgr., 1976-77; adminstrv. asst. City Mgrs. Office, City of Tucson, 1978-85; transit coordinator City of Tucson Transp. Dept., 1985—; bd. dirs. Tucson Clean and Beautiful Com. Editor, State Republican Com. newspaper, 1975-76; chmn. Pima County Young Rep. League, 1973-74; dist. 9 chmn. Pima County Rep. Central Com., 1974. Mem. Kappa Tau Alpha,

Delta Sigma Pi. Republican. Methodist. Club: Pima County Trunk 'n Tusk (publicity chmn. 1974-77). Home: 7369 E 20th St Tucson AZ 85710 Office: PO Box 27210 Tucson AZ 85726

DANIELS, MADELINE MARIE, psychotherapist, author; b. Newark, Oct. 14, 1948; d. William and Dorothy Barlow; BA cum laude, CCNY, 1971; PhD, Union Grad. Sch., Yellow Springs, Ohio, 1975; m. Peter W. Daniels, Oct. 18, 1976; children—Jonathan, Jedediah, Jeremiah. Lectr., Westchester Community Coll., also Bronx Community Coll., 1973-74; mem. adj. faculty SUNY, Purchase, 1974-76; data processing coordinator GTE Internat., 1976-78; lectr. div. continuing edn. U. N.H., 1979-87; exec. dir. Crossroads Center Human Integration, East Kingston, N.H., 1979-88; administrator Spectrum Cross-Cultural Inst. Youth Inc., East Kingston, 1988—; psychotherapist, lectr., cons. in field. Cert. ind. biofeedback practitioner. Mem. Internat. council Psychologists (area chair 1988), Am. Psychol. Assn., Biofeedback Soc. Am., Soc. Psychol. Athropology, N.H. Psychol. Orgn., Phi Beta Kappa. Author: Realistic Leadership, 1983; Living Your Religion in the Real World, 1985. Office: Crossroads Center East Kingston NH 03827

DANIELS, MILLIE (ANN), cost accounting supervisor; b. Cobleskill, N.Y., Oct. 6, 1941; d. Franklin Martin and Cornelia Ellen Holmes; m. John Carlile Daniels, Feb. 22, 1967 (div. Feb. 1976); children: Laurel Althea, Jacques Christopher. BA, St. Lawrence U., 1963; postgrad., U. Pa., 1963-64, Ga. State U., 1980-83. Tchr. Audubon (N.J.) Sch. System, 1964-67, Unionville (Pa.)-Chadds Ford Sch. System, 1967-68; clk., typist Atomic Personnel Inc., Phila., 1968-69, Hancock Paper Co., Phila., 1970-72; mgr. Ken Crest House, Phila., 1972-75; acct. Group Land Inc., Atlanta, 1975-76; office mgr. ATCO Mfg. Co., Marietta, Ga., 1976-80; gen. acctg. supr. Kraft Inc., Atlanta, 1980-86, cost acctg. supr., 1986—; recorder affirmative action task force Kraft Inc., 1985-86, mem., 1987—; mgr. Paideia Pl. Thrift Shop, Atlanta, 1984-86. Mem. Paideia Sch. Scholarship Com., Atlanta, 1984-86; leader Project Bus., 1986-87. Democrat. Office: Kraft Inc 501 Dekalb Indus Way Decatur GA 30031

DANIELS, PEARL GRAY, business educator; b. Montgomery, Ala., Sept. 10, 1926; d. Abraham Harrison and Nancy (Jones) Gray; m. Simon Duval Daniels, Oct. 20, 1974; children—Valerie G. Wheeler, Nathan G. Wheeler. A.A., Stillman Coll., 1947; B.S., Ala. State U., 1952; Ed.M., Tuskegee U., 1958. Tchr. bus. Dallas County Bd. Edn., Selma, Ala., 1951-52; sec. Tuskegee U., Ala., 1955-56, 1957-58; tchr. bus. Macon County Tng. Sch., Roba, Ala., 1955-56; sec. Howard U., Washington, 1960, U. D.C., Washington, 1961; bus. tchr. D.C. Bd. Edn., Washington, 1962-72; asst. prin. Cardozo Adult Evening Sch., Washington, 1972-73; asst. prof. Ala. State U., Montgomery, 1974—. Author: Portrait of Fred D. Gray, 1975; Freshman Orientation Study Guide Manual, 1976; Test Taking: Techniques and Practices, 2d edit., 1988. Recipient Cert. Merit Ala. Dem. Conf. 1983, Disting. Educator and Alumni award Stillman Coll. Alumni Assn., 1985; named Outstanding Woman of Yr. 1984. Fellow Inst. Devel. Ednl. Activities, 1973—, NDEA 1965. Mem. NAACP, Nat. Bus. Edn. Assn., Ala. Assn. Tchr. Educators, Kappa Delta Pi, Iota Phi Lambda, Sigma Gamma Rho. Democrat. Clubs: Montgomery City Fedn. Women's and Youth (corr. sec. 1983-85, 2d v.p. 1985—), Nancy J. Gray Federated (pres. 1980—) (Montgomery). Home: 2585 Westwood Dr Montgomery AL 36108 Office: Ala State U 915 S Jackson St Montgomery AL 36195

DANIELS, SHARON JEAN, foundation administrator; b. Ransom, Ks., Jan. 3, 1944; d. Maurice Buchanon and Mary Eliza (Buell) D.; m. Gary Michael Mulloy, July 22, 1967 (div. June 1976); m. Danny James Cassidy, June 25, 1977. Student, Mt. St. Scholastica Coll., 1962-63; BA, Ft. Hays (Kans.) State U., 1967; JD, U. Okla., 1976. Customer service rep. Mobil Oil Corp., Kansas City, Mo., 1968-73; sole practice law Oklahoma City, 1977-81; ptnr. Dennis, Daniels & Cryer, Oklahoma City, 1981-84; assoc. Rose, Schmidt, Dixon & Hasley, Pittsburgh, 1984; exec. dir. Ea. Mineral Law Found., Morgantown, W.Va., 1985—; Mem. adv. bd. nat. coal issue W.Va. Law Rev. Contbg. author: Children and the Law, 1975. Chair County Presdl. Campaign, Norman, Okla., 1968. Mem. Pa. Bar. Assn., Assn. Continuing Legal Edn. Admstrs., Alleghany County Bar, Okla. Bar Assn. (mineral law sect.), Am. Soc. Assn. Execs. (legal sect.), Assn. Continuing Legal Edn. Adminstrs., Pitts. Coalbed Methane Forum (steering com.), DAR. Democrat. Office: Ea Mineral Law Found WVa Univ Law Ctr PO Box 6130 Morgantown WV 26506-6130

DANIELS, SUZANNE MADELEINE, medical technologist; b. Worcester, Mass., July 23, 1941; d. George Edward and Ruth Bernadette (St. Martin) Brodeur; student Central New Eng. Coll. Tech., 1959-62; M.T., Worcester City Hosp. Sch. Med. Tech., 1962; m. Charles Daniels; children—Edward, Jennifer. Flight exam technician Pratt & Whitney, E. Hartford, Conn., 1962-63; sect. head chemistry/radioisotopes Mt. Sinai Hosp., Hartford, Conn., 1963-65; gen. technician Meml. Hosp., Worcester, 1965-69; blood bank supr. Milford-Whitinsville Regional Hosp., Milford, Mass., 1969-70; asst. clin. supr., sect. head chemistry Worcester Hahnemann Hosp., 1970-75; lab. supr. Weeks Meml. Hosp., Lancaster, N.H., 1975-87; clin. teaching staff Vt. Coll. Sch. Med. Lab. Technicians, 1975-87; office supr. Gulf Coast Pathology and Med. Lab. Services, Inc., Bradenton, Fla., 1987—. Mem. Am. Soc. Clin. Pathologists, Clin. Lab. Mgmt. Assn. Roman Catholic. Clubs: Twin Mt. Snowmobile, Bethlehem Country. Home: 2220 Holyoke Ave Bradenton FL 34207

DANIELSON, ELIZABETH KAY, psychology educator; b. Van Nuys, Calif., Oct. 5, 1949; d. Joe Henry and Margaret Louise (Owens) Bull; m. Scott G. Danielson, Dec. 27, 1984. BA, Baylor U., 1970; MA, U. Colo., 1977, PhD, 1982. Lic. cons. psychologist, Minn., psychologist, N.D., sch. psychologist, Minn., La. VISTA vol. Sp. Peaks Mental Health Ctr., Peublo, Colo., 1971-72; vol. Peace Corps, Khemisset, Morocco, 1974-75; sch. psychologist Northeast Colo. BOCES, Haxtun, Colo., 1978-80, Boulder (Colo.) Valley Schs., 1980-82; asst. prof. Moorhead (Minn.) State U., 1982-88, assoc. prof., 1988—; cons. Rape/Abuse Crisis Ctr., Fargo, N.D., 1986—. Mem. Nat. Assn. Sch. Psychologists (mem. exec. bd. 1986—), Am. Psychol. Assn., Am. Ednl. Research Assn., North Cen. Assn. Sch. Psychologists (pres. 1985), Colo. Soc. Sch. Psychologists (sec. 1981), Minn. Sch. Psychologists Assn. (treas. 1988—). Democrat. Episcopalian. Home: 915 2d Ave S #5 Fargo ND 58103 Office: Moorhead State U Dept Psychology Moorhead MN 56560

DANIELSON, PATRICIA ROCHELLE FRANK, urban planner; b. Manhattan, N.Y., Dec. 22, 1941; d. Maxwell and Theresa (Kleckner) Frank; m. Michael Nils Danielson, Sept. 8, 1979; m. Seymour B. Fingerhood, Sept. 15, 1963 (div. Dec. 1978); children—Karl John, Louisa Laura. A.A., Thomas Edison State Coll., 1973; M.U.P., Princeton U., 1976. policy planner Gov's Office, Trenton, 1978-80; program devel. specialist N.J. Dept. Community Affairs, Trenton, 1980-82; sr. planner Eggers Group, N.Y.C., 1982-85; pvt. research cons., Princeton, N.J., 1985-87; dir. mktg. and membership services N.J. Retail Mcht.'s Assn., 1987—. Mem. bd. trustees Thomas A. Edison State Coll., Trenton, 1978—, chmn., 1984-87. Mem. Princeton Research Forum, N.J. State Coll. Gov. Bd. Assn., Am. Soc. Public Adminstrs. Avocations: creative writing; folk music.

DANIELSON, PHYLLIS I., art school administrator, tapestry artist; b. Marion, Ind. B.A. in Art, Ball State U., 1953; MA, Mich. State U., 1960, EdS, 1966; EdD, Ind. U., 1968. One-person shows Jewish Community Ctr., Indpls., 1972, Eye-Opener Gallery, Cin., 1972, Mint Mus. Art, 1974, Herron Art Gallery, Indpls., 1974, Sloane O'Stickey Gallery, Cleve., 1974, Women in Art, West Bend, Wis., 1976; group exhbns. include Weatherspoon Gallery, Greensboro, N.C., 1969, 70, Stichery, Pa., 1971, Iowa, 1975; Matrix Gallery, Bloomington, Ind., 1972; pres. Kendall Coll. Art and Design, Grand Rapids, Mich., 1976—; asst. prof. art Ball State U., Muncie, Ind., 1966-67; asst. prof. art edn. U. N.C., Greensboro, 1968-70; assoc. prof. edn. and art Herron Sch. Art, Indpls., 1970-76. Contbr. articles to profl. jours. Mem. Nat. Art Edn. Assn., Nat. Council Art Adminstrs., Nat. Assn. Schs. Art and Design, Coll. Art Assn. Office: Kendall Coll Art and Design 111 Division Ave NE Grand Rapids MI 49503

DANKNER, LAURA ANNE, music librarian; b. Bklyn., Oct. 20, 1945; d. Alvin and Rose (Smith) Rosenthal; m. Stephen Dankner, June 3, 1973. B in Music, Ithaca Coll., 1967; M in Music, Bklyn. Coll., 1971; MLS, SUNY, Albany, 1976. Lectr. Bklyn. Coll., 1970-73; with Holliston Jr. Coll., Lenox, Mass., 1967-79, librarian, 1976-78; assoc. prof. Loyola U., New Orleans, 1979—. Author contemporary music scores revs. Mem. Music Library Assn. (edn. personnel coms. 1983—, placement officer 1986-88, bd. dirs. 1988—), Am. Library Assn., SE Music Library Assn., Assn. Coll. and Research Libraries, Mu Phi Epsilon. Office: Loyola U Music Library 6363 St Charles Ave PO Box 8 New Orleans LA 70118

DANKO, PATRICIA ST. JOHN, visual artist, writer; b. Orange, Tex., Aug. 7, 1944; d. George Milton and Rebecca Alice (McCoppin) Solomon; m. Jim Danko, Aug. 19, 1973 (dec. 1983). BA, Dominican Coll., Houston, 1965; BFA, U. Houston, 1979; postgrad. Mus. Fine Arts Sch., Houston, U. Ibero-Americana, Mexico, Mich. State U. Teaching asst. Mich. State U., East Lansing, 1966; vol. Peace Corps, Chile, 1965-68; silkscreen apprentice, printer Atelier Zárate, Buenos Aires, 1969; tchr. high sch. Orange Ind. Sch. Dist. (Tex.), 1971, Houston Ind. Sch. Dist., 1973; instr. English, English Lang. Services, Houston, 1973-75; instr. English, Spanish, Inlingua Lang. Schs., 1976; instr. Art League Houston, 1978-81; performance art writer Houston Art Scene, 1979-84, editor, 1981-84, mng. editor, 1982-83, exec. editor, 1983-84; acting Tex. editor New Art Examiner, 1985-86; contbg. editor Tex. New Art Examiner, 1986-88; ind. art hist. researcher, writer; freelance writer; visual artist, pub. collections: N.Y. Feminist Art Inst., Equinox Theatre, Houston, Chomo Uri Collective, U. Mass., Memphis-Brooks Mus. Art, Several Dancers Core Sch., Atlanta, McGlothlin Ins. Agy., Houston, Cameron Petroleum Co., Houston, Emdyne, Inc. Designer numerous artistic performances; exhbns. of artistic work to numerous museums and cultural instns. throughout U.S. Jesse H. Jones Found. scholar, 1961-65. Recipient Presdl. Commendation by Pres. Johnson for Service to U.S. and Chile, 1968; named Outstanding Young Woman of Am., OYWA Press, Chgo., 1970; Sum Arts grantee for sculpture The Matriarch as Phoenix, 1981; Shell Found. grantee for performance of Thanatopsis, 1983; grantee Ruth Chevon Found., Inc., 1987, Change, Inc., N.Y.C., 1987, Adolph and Esther Gottlieb Found. Mem. Artists Equity Assn., Contemporary Arts Mus. (Houston). Roman Catholic. Address: 2112 Dunlavy Houston TX 77006

DANN, EMILY, chemical company executive; b. Albany, Ga., July 26, 1932; d. Jesse Lyman and Evelyn (Calhoun) Dann; m. Christian A. Hansen, June 7, 1977; children: Leslie Montgomery Eagan, Ann Montgomery. BA, Huntingdon Coll., 1954; MS in Math., U. Houston, 1964; EdD, Rutgers U., 1976. Instr., Lee Coll., Baytown, Tex., 1965-67; prof. Middlesex County Coll., Edison, N.J., 1967-81; dir. human resources LCP Chem. & Plastics Co., Edison, 1981-84, systems analyst, 1986—; vis. assoc. prof. Drew U., 1984-86; cons. Title I math. program Bedminster (N.J.) Pub. Sch., 1976-77; mem. co-adj. faculty Grad. Sch. Edn., Rutgers U., 1976-81, Kean Coll., 1980-81. Contbr. articles to profl. jours. Mem. Acad. Mgmt., Orgn. Devel. Network, Am. Soc. Tng. and Devel., Am. Math. Assn., Jean Piaget Soc. Home: 1 Scenic Dr Highlands NJ 07732 Office: LCP Chem & Plastics Co Raritan Plaza II Edison NJ 08837

DANN, RONNIE, demographic survey statistician, consultant; b. Chgo., Nov. 16, 1936; d. Peter and Rose (Cummuta) Indurante; m. John Charles Dankowski, Apr. 8, 1956 (div. Aug. 1986); children: Greg Dann, Karen Perri, Sharon Worsham, Diane Savoy, Mary Dann, Rosanne Dann. AA in Behavioral Sci, Citrus Coll., Azusa, Calif., 1984; AS in Business, Citrus Coll., 1985; BA in psychology Gerontology, Calif. State U., Fullerton, 1987. Cert. tchr. Los Angeles Catholic Archdiocese. With U.S. Bur. Census, Los Angeles, 1970—, special survey technician, 1986-87, field mgr., 1988—; commr. human resources City of El Monte, Calif., 1970-71; chmn. Nativity Ch., El Monte, 1073-76; research field coordinator U. Mich., Ann Arbor 1977-79; lectr. Pitzer Coll., Claremont, Calif., 1977; psych-social technician Beverly Enterprises Hosp., Arcadia, Calif., 1987—. Precint cpt., El Monte, 1962-69; vol. Red Cross, Cancer Soc., El Monte, 1962-75; chmn. numerous ogrns. including Girl Scouts, Boy Scouts, PTA, El Monte, 1962-75; campaign chmn. Non Partisan City Election, El Monte, 1974. Named Outstanding Vol. Convalescent Hosp., Arcadia, 1986. Mem. Am. Bus. Women's Assn., Am. Pub. Health Assn., Am. Soc. on Aging, Am. Assn. Entrepreneurs, Am. Assn. Retired Persons, Am. Demographic Soc., Screen Actors Guild. Home: 727 Jenifer Glendora CA 91740 Office: US Bur Census 16300 Roscoe Blvd Van Nuys CA 91406

DANNA, JO J., publisher, author; b. N.Y.C., Apr. 4, 1925; d. Lucy (Macalusd) D.; m. David Pender (div. 1961). BA, Hunter Coll., 1948; MA, Columbia U., 1964, PhD, 1974. Elem. sch. tchr. N.Y.C. Bd. Edn., 1956-65; asst. dir., cons. Villaggio Del Superdotato, Sicily, Italy, 1967-70; asst. prof. edn. Baldwin Wallace Coll., Berea, Ohio, 1971-73; dir., writer ethnic studies curriculum edn. dept. SUNY, Albany, 1975-76; asst. prof. La Trobe U., Melbourne, Australia, 1976-79; freelance writer 1982—; pub. Palomino Press, N.Y.C., 1983—; founder Network Ind. Pubs. Greater N.Y. Contbr. articles to profl. jours. Mem. Pubs. Mktg. Assn., Com. Small Mag. Editors and Pubs. Home and Office: 86-07 144th St Briarwood NY 11435

DANNEMILLER, KATHLEEN DOUGLAS, management consulting executive; b. Detroit, Apr. 27, 1929; d. Benjamin and Kathleen (Cosgrove) Douglas; m. William F. Dannemiller, Mar. 11, 1949 (div. Dec. 1982); children: William B., David S., Robert A., Kathleen C. BA, U. Mich., 1950, MA, 1974. Cons. Trenkle Assocs., Southfield, Mich., 1969-72; asst. to v.p. for student services U. Mich., Ann Arbor, 1972-83; ptnr. Dannemiller Tyson, Inc., Ann Arbor, 1983-86; owner Dannemiller Tyson Assocs., Inc., Ann Arbor, 1986—; cons. in field. Author: MBO in Higher Education, 1975; contbr. articles to profl. jours. Founder Ark Coffeehouse, Ann Arbor, 1963—; pres., bd. edn. Ann Arbor Pub. Schs.1973-79. Mem. Nat. Tng. Labs. (profl.), Nat. Orgn. Devel. Network. Democrat. Presbyterian. Home: 3671 Eli Ann Arbor MI 48104 Office: Dannemiller Tyson Assocs 201 E Catherine Ann Arbor MI 48104

DANNER, PATSY ANN (MRS. C. M. MEYER), businesswoman, state legislator; b. Louisville, Jan. 13, 1934; d. Henry J. and Catherine M. (Shaheen) Berrer; m. Lavon Danner, Feb. 12, 1951 (div.); children: Stephen, Stephanie, Shane, Shavonne.; m. C.M. Meyer, Dec. 30, 1982. Student, Hannibal-LaGrange Coll., 1952; B.A. in Polit. Sci. cum laude, N.E. Mo. State U., 1972. Dist. asst. to Congressman Jerry Litton, Kansas City, Mo., 1973-76; fed. co-chmn. Ozarks Regional Commn., Washington, 1977-81; owner, prin. Danner & Assocs., 1981—; mem. Mo. State Senate, 1983—. Mem. Bus. and Profl. Women, AAUW, Beta Sigma Phi. Roman Catholic. Home: 6 Nantucket Court Smithville MO 64089

DANOFF-KRAUS, PAMELA SUE, shopping center development executive; b. Gallup, N.Mex., Aug. 29, 1946; d. Isadore Harry and Armida Catherine (Ceccardi) Danoff; m. Milo Joseph Warner III, Dec. 28, 1968 (div. 1974); m. Robert Warren Kraus, Nov. 30, 1985; 1 child, Jillian Amaris. BA, U. N.Mex., 1968. Lic. in real estate, Calif. Real estate rep. Kaiser Aetna, Newport Beach, Calif., 1975-76; leasing agt. Alexander Haagen Co., Roling Hills, Calif., 1976-77; dir. leasing Warren Kellogg & Assocs., Newport Beach, 1977-81, Center Devel. Co., Newport Beach, 1981-86; ptnr. Marketplace Properties, Tustin, Calif., 1986—; lectr. in field; panelist various convs., univs.; conductor seminars in field. Contbr. articles to profl. jours. Sponsor Californians Working Together to End Hunger and Homelessness, Los Angeles, 1988; mem. Orange County Performing Arts Ctr., 1983-85. Mem. Internat. Council Shopping Ctrs. (program chmn. 1987—, mem. small ctr. devel. com.), Calif. Bus. Properties Assn., Women in Retail Real Estate, Calif. Redevel. Assn., Chi Omega. Republican. Roman Catholic. Home: 9 Aspen Tree Ln Irvine CA 92715 Office: Marketplace Properties 210 W Main St #206 Tustin CA 92680

DANSER, MARY HELEN, pharmacist; b. Dawson Springs, Ky., Mar. 8, 1940; d. Maurice and Emma Louise (Thorn) Lisanby; m. Richard Allen Danser, June 8, 1963 (dec. Apr. 1976); 1 child, Richard Allen Jr. AA, Lindsey Wilson Jr. Coll., 1961; BS in Pharmacy, U. Ky., 1965. Intern U. Ky. Med. Ctr., 1965; intern, pharmacist Hubbard & Curry Druggists, Lexington, Ky., 1965-66; chief pharmacist Ky. Dept. Mental Health, Frankfort, 1966-73, Ky. Bur. Health Services, 1973-84; pharmacy services program mgr. Ky. Dept. Mental Health Cabinet for Human Resources, Frankfort, 1984—; cons. in field; instr. Coll. Law Enforcement Dept. Traffic Safety, Eastern Ky. U., 1968-84, vis. lectr.; instr. Jefferson County Police Dept., Louisville, Ky., 1985—. Mem. pastor/parish com. 1st Meth. Ch., Lexington, 1971-77, adminstrv. bd., 1972-74; chmn. com. Troop 276, Boy Scouts Am., Lexington, 1984—; youth counselor Antioch Christian Ch., 1981-86. Recipient Scouters Tng. award Boy Scouts Am., 1988; named to Hon. Order Ky. Cols., 1988. Mem. Bluegrass Pharm. Assn. (chair peer review com. 1986-87), Ky. Soc. Hosp. Pharmacists (sec. 1970), Am. Soc. Hosp. Pharmacists (panelist 1975-77). Democrat. Mem. Christian Ch. (Disciples of Christ). Methodist. Avocations: gardening, sewing. Home: 3175 Paris Pike Lexington KY 40511 Office: Dept Mental Health 275 E Main St Frankfort KY 40621

DANYLCHUK, KAREN ELIZABETH, collegiate athletic coordinator; b. Sarnia, Ont., Canada, Apr. 14, 1957; d. William and Helen E. (Hummel) D. BPE, McMaster U., 1979; MA, U. Western Ont., 1981. Lectr McMaster U., Hamilton, Ont., 1980-81; aquatics dir., phys. edn. tchr., coach Hong Kong Internat. Sch., 1982-86; coordinator women's intercollegiate athletics U. Western Ont., London, 1986—. Contbr. articles to Can. Jour. Applied Sport Sci., 1984, research quart. Exercise and Sport, 1984. Mem. N. Am. Soc. Sport Mgmt., Can. Assn. Health, Phys. Edn., Recreation, Can. Assn. Sport Scis. Office: U Western Ont, Intercollegiate Athletics, London, ON Canada N6A 3K7

DANZ, TERESA KAY, sales executive; b. Rockville Centre, N.Y., July 23, 1958; d. William and Winifred (Martin) D. AAS, Nassau Community Coll., 1978; BBA, Adelphi U., 1981. Sales rep. Durkee Food Service, San Francisco, 1981-85; dist. sales mgr. Golden Gate Food Mktg., San Leandro, Calif., 1985-88; dir. mktg. for Northern Calif. Genet-Western Brokerage Co., San Rafael, Calif., 1988—. Mem. Nat. Assn. Exec. Women, Phi Theta Kappa, Delta Mu Delta. Democrat. Roman Catholic. Home: 50 Crestline Dr #8 San Francisco CA 94131 Office: Genet-Western Brokerage Co 19 Kinross San Rafael CA 94901

DANZIG, JOAN, newspaper editor; b. Elmira, N.Y., Mar. 3, 1929; d. George Hamilton and Estelle (Saqui) Danzig; m. Joseph Krasner; children—Susan, Karin. B.A., Empire State Coll., 1975; student Elmira Coll., 1946-47; B.A., Empire State Coll., 1975. Asst. feature editor Buffalo News, 1952-60; reporter, society editor Evening Times, Sayre, Pa., 1948-51; editor Lifestyles Sect., fashion editor Buffalo News, 1960—. Recipient Page One award Buffalo Newspaper Guild, 1957, 64, Pa. Women's Press Assn., 1949, Outstanding Woman award Community Adv. Council, SUNY-Buffalo. Mem. Am. Newspaper Guild, Bus. and Profl. Women (charter pres. 1948-50), AAUW, Sigma Delta Chi. Address: The Buffalo News 1 News Plaza Buffalo NY 14240

DANZIGER, JOAN, sculptor; b. N.Y.C., June 17, 1934; d. Emanuel and Martha (Kaplan) Schwartz; m. Martin Danziger, June 17, 1958. B.F.A., Cornell U., 1954; B.F.A. (hon.), Acad. Fine Art, Rome, 1958. One woman exhbns. include: Corcoran Gallery, Washington, 1975, Calif. Mus. Sci. and Industry, Los Angeles, 1977, Muckenthal Cultural Ctr., Los Angeles, 1977, SUNY-Albany, 1978, Jacksonville Mus. Art and Sci. (Fla.), 1979, Fendrick Gallery, Washington, 1979, Terry Dintenfass Gallery, N.Y.C., 1980, Joy Horwich Gallery, Chgo., N.J. State Mus., Trenton, 1982, Benjamin Mangel Gallery, Phila., Louisiana World Expn., New Orleans, 1984, Textile Mus., Washington, 1985, Nat. Mus. Women in Arts, 1987. vis. artist, lectr. Smithsonian Instn., 1980-82; artist-in-residence AFL-CIO Labor Studies Ctr., 1975; visual arts panelist D.C. Commn. Arts and Humanities, 1974-79, 84-85; sculpture panelist N.J. State Council Arts, 1982. Commd. by Nat. Mus. Am. Art, Jacksonville Mus. Arts and Scis., Columbia Hosp., Washington, Frostburg State Coll. (Md.), George Meany Labor Studies Ctr., New Orleans Mus. Art, D.C. Conv. Ctr., Nat. Mus. Women in Arts, N.J. State Mus., Nat. Endowment Arts grantee, 1975, grantee Internat. des Arts, Paris, 1986. Mem. Artists Equity, Washington Sculptors Group (bd. dirs.). Home: 2909 Brandywine St NW Washington DC 20008

DARDEN, MARY DUNLAP, management consultant; b. Richmond, Va., Aug. 10, 1952; d. Oscar Bruton and Ann Wingfield (Johnson) D.; BS in Math. and Edn., Va. Poly. Inst. and State U., 1974; MBA, U. Richmond, 1984. Mktg. rep. IBM, Richmond, 1974-78; territorial saleswoman Swan, Inc., Richmond, 1978, dir. ops., 1978-83; pres. Cygnet, Inc., mgmt. cons., 1980-83; v.p. Lee-Darden Assocs. inc., Richmond, 1983—. Bd. dirs., sec.-treas. Va. Small Bus. Financing Authority, 1984-86; Va. del. White House Conf. on Small Bus., 1986. Named to 100 Percent Club, IBM, 1976, 77. Mem. St. Mary's Hosp. Aux., Richmond Assn. Women Bus. Owners (sec. 1983-84, pres. 1984-85). Presbyterian. Home: 4104 Park Ave Richmond VA 23221 Office: Lee-Darden Assocs Inc Santa Rosa Rd Suite 240 Richmond VA 23229

DARDEN, SUE EAGLES, librarian; b. Miami, Fla., Aug. 13, 1943; d. Archie Yelverton and Bobbie (Jones) Eagles; m. Paul Fisher Darden, Aug. 24, 1969 (dec. June 1978). B.A., Atlantic Christian Coll., Wilson, N.C., 1965; M.L.S., U. Tex., Austin, 1970. Cert. librarian, N.C., Va. Instr. Chowan Coll., Murfreesboro, N.C., 1966-68; librarian's asst. Albemarle Regional Library, Winston, N.C., 1968-69; br. librarian Multnomah County Pub. Library, Portland, Oreg., 1971-72; asst. dir. Stanly County Pub. Library, Albemarle, N.C., 1973-76; dir. Stanly County Pub. Library, 1976-80; asst. dir. Norfolk Pub. Library, Va, 1980-83; dir. Norfolk Pub. Library, 1983—. Mem. ALA (councilor Va. chpt. 1987—), Library Adminstv. and Mgmt. Assn. (pub. relations, friends, vols. and advocates com. 1985-87), Pub. Library Assn. (dir.-at-large met. library sect. 1986-87, conf. exhibits subcom. 1986-88), Southeastern Library Assn. (satff devel. com. 1986-88, Rothrock award com., 1986, sec. pub. library sect. 1982-84), Va. Library Assn. (council 1984, 87—, chmn. ad hoc conf. guidelines com. 1985-86, awards and recognition com. 1983, conf. program com. 1982). Home: 3534 Brest Ave Norfolk VA 23509 Office: Norfolk Pub Library 301 E City Hall Ave Norfolk VA 23510

DARITY, EVANGELINE ROYALL, educator, dean; b. Wilson, N.C., June 16, 1927; B.Sc. in Religious Edn., Barber-Scotia Coll., Concord, N.C., 1949; M.Ed., Smith Coll., 1969; Ed.D., U. Mass., Amherst, 1978; m. William A. Darity; children—William, Janki Evangelia. Various YWCA positions 1949-53; tchr., Egypt, N.C. and Mass., 1953-67; asst. to class deans Smith Coll., Northampton, Mass., 1968-75; v.p. student affairs Barber-Scotia Coll., 1978-79; exec. dir. YWCA, Holyoke, Mass., 1979-81; assoc. dean studies, assoc. dean 3d world affairs Mt. Holyoke Coll., South Hadley, Mass., 1981—; corp. mem. Community Savs. Bank, Holyoke. Mem. Amherst Town Meeting, 1971-80; mem. adv. bd. Community Adolescent Resource and Edn. Ctr.; trustee Barber-Scotia Coll., Concord, N.C. Mem. AAUW (br. pres. 1971-74, 86-88), Am. Assn. Counseling and Devel., Nat. Assn. Women Deans, Counselors and Adminstrs., LWV, Alpha Kappa Alpha, Phi Delta Kappa. Home: 105 Heatherstone Rd Amherst MA 01002 Office: Mount Holyoke College South Hadley MA 01075

DARKIS, MILDRED LEE MORRIS (MRS. FREDERICK RANDOLPH DARKIS), civic worker; b. nr. Salisbury, Md.; d. Elisha Purnell and Martha Florence (Bailey) Morris; A.B., U. Md., 1924; m. Frederick Randolph Darkis, Oct. 6, 1928; children—Frederick Randolph, Thomas Morris, Barbara Lee (Mrs. James Frederick Blake). Tchr. English and Am. history high sch., Pittsville, Md., 1924-25, Salisbury, 1925-28. Pres. Durram Parent-Tchr. Council, 1945-47, Hope Valley Garden Club, 1962-64; bd. dirs. Durham YWCA, 1946-48, v.p., 1948; bd. dirs. Durham Child Guidance Clinic, 1945-47, Girl Scout Council, 1944-48; chmn. woman's div. Community Chest, Durham, 1946-47. Mem. D.A.R. (N.C. chmn. nat. honor roll 1961-64, chpt. regent 1968-70), Phi Kappa Phi, Alpha Omicron Pi. Republican. Methodist (tchr. adult Bible class, v.p. Durham dist. Woman's Div. Christian Service 1957-59, steward 1960, bd. stewards 1972—). Club: Hope Valley Country. Address: 3010 Surrey Rd Durham NC 27707

DARKOVICH, SHARON MARIE, nurse; b. Ft. Wayne, Ind., Dec. 10, 1949; d. Gerald Antone LaCanne and Ida Eileen (Bowman) LaCanne Cutler; m. Robert Eliot Ness, July 17, 1971 (dec. Aug. 1976); m. Paul Darkovich, Jan. 23, 1981; 1 child, Amy Elizabeth. B.S. in Nursing, Case Western Res. U., 1973, B.A. in Psychology, 1978. R.N., Ohio. Staff nurse Univ. Hosps., Cleve., 1973, asst. head nurse, 1973-76; quality assurance coordinator St. Luke's Hosp., Cleve., 1976-83, 84—, dir. nursing, 1983-84. cons. to long-term care facilities, 1986—. Mem. Am. Nurses Assn., Greater Cleve. Nurses Assn. (mem. dist. council on practice, 1982-84), Sigma Theta Tau. Avocations: reading; needlework; sewing; camping.

DARLAND, CARMEN KIRKPATRICK, banker; b. Des Moines, June 24, 1952; d. Keith L. and Arbie (Monk) Kirkpatrick; m. Jack D. Darland, Apr. 28, 1984; 1 chld, Emily S. BA, U. Iowa, 1974, MBA, 1981. Mgmt. trainee J.C. Penney Co., Des Moines, 1974-75; personnel mgr. J.S. Brandeis & Sons, Omaha, 1975-76, corp. tng. dir., 1976-78; mktg. officer 1st Nat. Bank, Ft. Dodge, Iowa, 1978-79; mktg. officer Davenport (Iowa) Bank and Trust, 1979-83, bus. devel. officer, 1984—. Pres. Davenport Conv. and Visitors Bur., 1987, Downtown Davenport Assn., 1985-86; treas. Festival of Trees bd.; chmn. Leadership Task Force Visions for the Quad Cities Future; mem. Davenport Sesquecentennial Com., Sales Tax Referendum Com., 1985; bd. dirs. Eldridge Planning & Zoning Commn.; bd. mgrs. Community Health Ctr., Davenport, 1984-85. Recipient Mover & Shaker award Quad-City Times, Davenport, 1985. Mem. Nat. Assn. Bank Women (bd. mgrs. 1979—), Nat. Assn. Female Execs., Am. Inst. Banking, Davenport C. of C. (bd. mgrs. 1984, 87), Chi Omega. Republican. Methodist. Club: Davenport. Lodge: Rotary. Home: 711 W Spring Eldridge IA 52748 Office: Davenport Bank and Trust Co 203 W 3d Ave Davenport IA 52801

DARLING, ALBERTA STATKUS, art museum executive, marketing professional; b. Hammond, Ind., Apr. 28, 1944; d. Albert William and Helen Anne (Vaicunas) Statkus; m. William Anthony Darling, Aug. 12, 1967; children—Elizabeth Suzanne, William Anthony. B.S., U. Wis., 1967. English tchr. Nathan Hale High Sch., West Allis, Wis., 1967-69, Castle Rock High Sch., Colo., 1969-71; community vol. work, Milw., 1971—; cons. orgn. devel., Milw., 1982—; dir. mktg. and communications Milw. Art Mus., 1983—. A founder Goals for Greater Milw. 2000, 1980-84; co-chair Action 2000, 1984-86; bd. dirs., exec. com. United Way, Milw., 1982—, chair project 1985, 1984-85; founder Today's Girls/Tomorrow's Women, Milw., 1982—; pres. Jr. League Milw., 1980-82, Planned Parenthood Milw., 1982-84, Future Milw., 1983-85; vice chmn. State of Wis. Strategic Planning Council, 1988—; mem. Greater Milw. Com.'s Mktg. Task Force, 1987-88; chmn. United Way Policy Com., 1987-88; participant Bus. Ptnrs. White House Conf., 1987. Recipient Vol. Action award Milw. Civic Alliance, 1984, Community Service award United Way, 1984, Leader of Future award Milw. Mag., 1985, Nat. Assn. Community Leadership Orgn. award, 1986, Today's Girls/Tomorrow's Women Leadership award, 1987. Mem. Greater Milw. Com., TEMPO Profl. Women, Am. Mktg. Assn. (Marketer of Yr. 1984), Pub. Relations Soc. Am., Internat. Assn. Bus. Communicators. Republican. Avocations: travel, art history, contemporary Am. lit., golf, tennis. Home: 1325 W Dean Rd Milwaukee WI 53217 Office: Beckley/Myers/Flad Inc 825 N Jefferson Milwaukee WI 53202

DARLING, SHARON SANDLING, museum director; b. Mitchell, S.D., Feb. 28, 1943; d. Joseph Davis and Barbara M. (Fixmer) Sandling; m. Mikell C. Darling, Apr. 15, 1972. BA, N.C. State U., 1965; MAT, Duke U., 1967. Curator Chgo. Hist. Soc., 1972-86; dir. Motorola Mus., Motorola, Inc., Schaumburg, Ill., 1986—. Author: Chicago Metalsmiths, 1977, Chicago Ceramics and Glass, 1981, Chicago Furniture, 1984 (C.F. Montgomery award 1985). Mem. Am. Soc. Interior Designers, Am. Ceramics Art Soc., Decorative Arts Soc. Home: 225 1/2 Greenwood St Evanston IL 60201 Office: Motorola Inc 1303 E Algonquin Rd Schaumburg IL 60614

DARLINGER, COPPER, protective services official; b. Denver, Jan. 20, 1954; d. Richard Eugene and Mary Louise (VanLaningham) Kroeckel; m. James Russell, July 20, 1980. Student in criminal justice, Northwestern U., 1984—. Cert. communications specialist. Head clk. Household Fin. Corp., Denver, 1969-72, 75-76; exec. sec. Intergroup, Golden, Colo., 1972-73; adminstrv. asst. Colo. Humane Soc., Henderson, 1973-75; head trainer Wheat Ridge (Colo.) Police Dept., 1976-87, cons., 1986—; communications specialist Broomfield (Colo.) Police Dept., 1984—; co-dir. Animal Welfare Assn. Inc., Wheat Ridge, 1975-78; mem. Wheat Ridge Police Aux., 1978-80; trainer, instr. City of Wheat Ridge, 1979—. Asst. dir. Colo. Humane Soc. Women's Adv. Aux., 1973-74. Mem. Assn. Pub. Safety Communications Officers. Republican. Presbyterian. Office: Broomfield Police Dept #6 Garden Ctr Broomfield CO 80020

DARLOW, JULIA DONOVAN, lawyer; b. Detroit, Sept. 18, 1941; d. Frank William Donovan and Helen Adele Turner; m. George Anthony Gratton Darlow (div.); 1 child, Gillian; m. John Corbett O'Meara. A.B., Vassar Coll., 1963; postgrad., Columbia U. Law Sch., 1964-65; J.D. cum laude, Wayne State U., 1971. Bar: Mich. 1971, U.S. Dist. Ct. (ea. dist.) Mich. 1971. Assoc. Dickinson, Wright, McKean, Cudlip and Moon, Detroit, 1971-78; ptnr. Dickinson, Wright, Moon, Van Dusen & Freeman, Detroit, 1978—; adj. prof. Wayne State U. Law Sch., 1974-75; commr. State Bar Mich., 1977-87, mem. exec. com., 1979-83, 84-87, sec. 1980-81, v.p. 1984-85, pres.-elect 1985-86, pres. 1986-87, council corp. fin. and bus. law sect. 1980-86, council computer law sect. 1985—. Reporter: Mich. Nonprofit Corp. Act, 1977-82. Bd. dirs. Detroit Grand Opera Assn., 1978—, Hutzel Hosp., 1984—, Mich. Opera Theater, 1985—, Mich. Women's Found., 1987—; trustee Internat. Inst. Met. Detroit, 1986—; mem. Blue Cross-Blue Shield Prospective Reimbursement Com., Detroit, 1979-81; mem. allocation and rev. com. United Found., 1982-88, cen. allocation com., 1984-88, adv. bd., 1987—, priorities com., 1987—, mem. adv. bd. 1987. Fellow Am. Bar Found.; mem. Detroit Bar Assn. Found. (treas. 1984-85, trustee 1982-85), Mich. Bar Found. (trustee 1987—), Am. Judicature Soc. (bd. dirs. 1985—), Women Lawyers Assn. (pres. 1977-78), Mich. Women's Campaign Fund (charter). Democrat. Club: Renaissance (Detroit). Office: Dickinson Wright Moon et al 800 First Nat Bldg Detroit MI 48226

DARMON, VERONICA LAURIE, catering executive; b. Rabat, Morroco, Feb. 3, 1961; d. William and Camille (Benovdlz) D. BA, Brooks U., 1981. Service rep. Northwestern Nat. Life, San Francisco, 1981-82; sr. account exec. United of Omaha, San Francisco, 1982—; pres. Chez Véronique, San Francisco, 1983—; French tutor, San Francisco, 1985—. Counselor Rape Crisis of No. Calif., Walnut Creek, Calif., 1983—, group facilitator, 1984—, v.p. bd. dirs., 1984-86; counselor Planned Parenthood, Concord, Calif., 1983—, Children's Hosp., Oakland, Calif., 1985—. Vol. of the Yr. Rape Crisis of No. Calif., 1984. Mem. Nat. Assn. for Female Execs., No. Calif. Employee Benefits Council, Women's Culinary Assn. Libertarian. Jewish. Home: 2430 Hearst AveCircle Oakland CA 94602 Office: United of Omaha 2430 Hearst Ave Oakland CA 94602

DARNELL, BETTY JEAN (B.J.), small animal consultant, association executive; b. Augusta, Ga., Sept. 6, 1942; d. Rufus Eugene Randall and Martha Lee (Payne) Darnell-Bush. AS in Vet Medicine. Technician emergency room Lee County Hosp., Sanford, N.C., 1965-67; supr. vet. technicians Durham (N.C.) Animal Hosp., 1967-68; vet. technician Vine Vet. Hosp., Chapel Hill, N.C., 1968; supr. vet. technicians Rossville Vet Clinic, Chattanooga, 1968-71; owner Profl. Kennels, Ft. Oglethorpe, Ga., 1971—; stockholder Our Gang, Inc., Chattanooga, 1972-75; co-owner Us Girls, Inc., Chattanooga, 1972-74; cons. Groom & Bd. mag., Chgo., 1984-87; pub. speaker Pet Industry, 1981—. Author: mag. Jour. AVMA, 1971; author, editor: mag. Chattanoogan, 1974-76; editor mag. Clipperblade, 1979-80. Mem. Am. Boarding Kennels (regional dir. 1984-87, v.p. 1986-87, pres. elect 1987—, pres. 1987-89, Service award 1981, 82, 83), Ga. Profl. Dog Groomers (pres. 1982-83) Am. Inst. Parliamentarians. Democrat. Club: Battlefield Pilot, Civitan. Lodge: Ladies Oriental Shrine of N.Am. (High Priestess 1987-88, Bhakti Ct. #25 Atlanta, Grand Page 1988, Hon. Grand Page 1988—). Home: 1811 Old Lafayette Rd Fort Oglethorpe GA 30742 Office: Profl Grooming & Boarding Kennels 1813 Old Lafayette Rd Fort Oglethorpe GA 30742

DARNOV, SHARON ELAINE, management consultant; b. Los Angeles, July 12, 1953; d. Morris H. and Natalie R. (Rose) D.; m. Omar Maden, Aug. 26, 1983; 1 child, Remmie Maden. BA in Spanish, U. Calif., Berkeley, 1975; MA, Am. Grad. Sch. Internat. Bus., 1977. Lending officer Bank of Am., Los Angeles, 1978-79; mgr. cons. dept. Peat Marwick, Los Angeles and Washington, 1979-83; v.p. Kaplan Smith & Assocs., Washington, 1983-86; prin. Maden Tech. Cons. Inc., Falls Church, Va., 1986—. Mem. Fairfax County C. of C., Planning Forum, Fin. Mgrs. Soc. Democrat. Jewish. Office: Maden Tech Cons Inc 5203 Leesburg Pike Suite 610 Falls Church VA 22041

DARO, KAREN SUZANNE, advertising executive; b. Detroit, Apr. 2, 1954; d. Edward Richard and Theresa J. (Lewandoski) D.; m. Thomas Stedman DeMott, Nov. 30, 1974 (div. 1987); children: Matthew Thomas, Laura Theresa. Student, Schoolcraft Coll., 1972-73, Siena Heights Coll., 1973-74, Ea. Mich. U., 1974-76. Dir. recreation, education All Indian Pueblos, Pojoaque, N.Mex., 1976-77; owner, operator Casa de Colores, Santa Fe, 1977-79; project coordinator Leach Research, Inc., Santa Fe, 1979-81, mgr. ops., 1981-82, dir. consumer research, 1982-83; dir. market research Hayduk-King Advt., Santa Fe, 1983-87, sec., treas., 1984—, v.p., 1987—. Vol. Our House Crisis Ctr., Plymouth, Mich., 1971-76, adminstr., 1973-76; trainer Meth. Youth Program, Plymouth, 1975. Mem. Am. Mktg. Assn., N.Mex. Advt. Fedn., No. N.Mex. Advt. Fedn. (cons. awards 1986). Republican. Unitarian. Office: Hayduk-King Advt Inc 1219 Luisa Suite 3 Santa Fe NM 87501

DARPHIN, SARAH WINIFRED, flight attendant; b. Jennings, La., Aug. 24, 1949; d. Robert Douglas and Sarah Winifred (Gulley) D. BA, NW State U. of La., 1971. Sec. First Nat. Bank, Dallas, 1971-72, Sun Oil Co., Dallas, 1972-73; flight attendant Am. Airlines, N.Y.C., 1973-76, flight service supr., 1976-82, flight attendant, 1982—; com. chairperson quality of work life Am. Airlines, N.Y.C., 1984-86; developed and coordinated SabreComputer Tng., 1985, and Life Enhancement Sems., 1986. Creator, fundraiser, co-chairperson World Hunger Yr., Harvest for Hunger Benefit, N.Y.C., 1985, Save the Children, Am. Harvest Benefit, N.Y.C., 1986-87—, Am. Airlines Flight Attendants and Friends for Hands Across Am., N.Y.C., 1986—. Recipient Profl. Flight Attendant award Am. Airlines, 1976, 83, 85, Vol. award Starlight Found., 1987. Mem. Nat. Assn. Female Execs. Democrat. Presbyterian. Home: 408 E 65th St #4E New York NY 10021 Office: Am Airlines Internat Flight Service John F Kennedy Airport Jamaica NY 11431

DART, CAROL ANNE, consulting company executive, lobbyist; b. Bloomfield, Mo., July 21, 1950; d. Frank M. and Rita (Decelis) Hodge; B.A., Sangamon State U., 1982; m. William Edward Dart, June 28, 1974. Asst. to program dir. WICS-TV, NBC, Springfield, Ill., 1973-75; adminstrv. asst. Air Time, Inc., Chgo., 1975-76; v.p. Dart & Assocs., Springfield, 1976-78; pres. C. Dart, Cons., 1979—; cons. Hill and Knowlton Inc, R.L. Polk and Co., Ill, Polygraph Soc.; govt. affairs cons./lobbyist Juvenile Diabetes Found. 1980-81. Mem. Ill. Diabetes Adv. Council; chair 20th Congressional Dist.; active Chgo. Area Pub. Affairs Group. Mem. Am. Soc. Assn. Execs., Chgo. Soc. Assn. Execs., Women in Mgmt., Inc. (Capital City area chpt. founder 1982, nat. pres. 1984-86, dir.), Women in Government Relations, Citizens for Am., Springfield C. of C. (govt. action com.). Roman Catholic. Club: Executives (Chgo.). Office: PO Box 1964 Springfield IL 62705

DARTING, EDITH ANNE, pharmaceutical company supervisor; b. Hillsboro, Kans., Jan. 1, 1945; d. Sammuel E. and Carrie (Swehla) Jewett; m. John Ronald Darting, Aug. 8, 1979; children—Theresa Michelle, Lloyd L. Grad., Emporia State Tchrs. Coll., 1963-65. Materials insp. Sterling Drug Inc., McPherson, Kans., 1977-78, auditor, 1978-82, coordinator, 1982—. Mem. Nat. Assn. Female Execs., Am. Soc. Quality Control. Republican. Methodist. Home: 320 N Birch St Hillsboro KS 67063 Office: Sterling Drug Inc Box 1048 McPherson KS 67460

DARTY, KAY WILSON, banker; b. Grand Rapids, Mich., Aug. 25, 1942; d. James W. and Margaret (Lawrence) Wilson; m. Odis Kenneth Darty, May 29, 1960; 1 child, Mark Anthony. Grad. Am. Banking Assn. courses, U. Okla., 1984-85; grad., Memphis State U., 1985, Mid South Sch. Banking, 1985, Am. Inst. Banking, 1986. Corr. bank clk. 1st Nat. Bank, Memphis, 1960-64; asst. mgr. 1st Fed. Savs. & Loan, Ripley and Halls, Tenn., 1970-78; mgr. savs. dept. Bank of Halls, 1978-81; compliance officer 1st Citizens Nat. Bank, Dyersburg, Tenn., 1981—; instr., chmn. banking adv. com. Dyersburg State Community Coll., 1986—. Mem. Crockett County Hist. Soc., Alamo, Tenn., 1979—; sr. state organizing sec. Children of Am. Revolution, Nashville, 1982-84. Recipient Outstanding Coll. Service award, Outstanding Coll. Adv. Com. Chmn. award Dyersburg State Community Coll., 1988. Mem. DAR (vice regent Ft. Prudhomme chpt. 1986—), Am. Bus. Women's Assn., Nat. Assn. Bank Women, Nat. Assn. for Female Execs., West Tenn. Compliance Network, Am. Hist. Soc. Democrat. Office: 1st Citizens Nat Bank Mills and Court Sts Dyersburg TN 38024

DARWIN, REBECCA, magazine publishing executive; b. Chattanooga, July 5, 1953; d. Dr. William Hinton and Louise Christine (Yeattes) Wesson; m. Cress Darwin, May 24, 1980. BA, U. N.C., 1975; AS, Tobe-Coburn Sch. for Fashion Careers, 1977. Various sales and promotion positions to mktg. dir. GQ Mag., N.Y.C., 1977-85; corp. mktg. dir. The New Yorker Mag., N.Y.C., 1985-86, v.p., assoc. publisher, 1986-87, v.p., pub., 1988—. Mem. Advt. Women of N.Y., The Fashion Group. Presbyterian. Home: 110 W 86th St #10E New York NY 10024 Office: The New Yorker 25 W 43d St New York NY 10036

DASTE, KATHRYN LOUISE, management consultant; b. Los Angeles, Sept. 28, 1951; d. Richard Leonard Kater and June (Yale) Hooten; m. John Cary Daste, July 24, 1973 (div. Apr. 1978). Student music, Calif. State U., Northridge, 1969-72; BA in Mgmt., U. Redlands, 1985. Lic. minister Universal Ch. of the Master, 1979; cert. in human resources. Asst. buyer Bullock's Wilshire, Los Angeles, 1973-76; corp. mgr. recruiting and tng. Robinson's Dept. Store, Los Angeles, 1976-80; regional mgr. personnel Gen. Nutrition Ctrs., Los Angeles, 1980-82; mgr. personnel Carnation Co., Los Angeles, 1982-84; cons. bus. and mgmt., Los Angeles, 1983-85; founder, cons. Profitivity, 1985—; lectr. in field. Author: The Profitivity Process, Are You Hiring the Smile?, 1984. Practitioner Encino (Calif.) Community Ch., 1978. Mem. Am. Soc. for Tng. and Devel., Western Coll. Placement Assn. Democrat. Address: 2032 Barry Ave #D Los Angeles CA 90025

DATA, JOANN LUCILLE, pharmaceutical company executive, physician; b. N.Y.C., Apr. 20, 1944; d. John Batiste and Grace Emma (Karr) D.; m. Herman Aquilla Cantrell, Nov. 13, 1976. BS with highest honors, Purdue U., 1966; MD, Washington U., 1970; PhD, Vanderbilt U., 1977. Intern SUNY, Buffalo, 1970-71, resident, 1971-73; fellow div. Clin. Pharmacology Vanderbilt U., Nashville, 1973-75, instr. medicine/pharmacology, 1975-76; clin. research physician Bronson Clin. Investigational Unit Upjohn Co., Kalamazoo, 1976-80; med./teaching staff Southwestern Mich. Area Health Edn. Ctr., Bronson Meth. Hosp., Kalamazoo, 1976-80; asst. clin. prof. Dept. Medicine Mich. State U., East Lansing, 1978-80; sr. clin. research scientist I Burroughs Wellcome Co., Research Triangle Park, N.C., 1980-82; adj. asst. prof. pharmacology Duke U. Med. Ctr., Durham, N.C., 1982—; dir. Dept. Clin. Pharmacology Hoffmann-LaRoche, Nutley, N.J., 1982-85, v.p., dir. clin. research and devel., 1985—; adj. asst. prof. pharmacology, medicine Cornell U., N.Y.C., 1987—; lectr. in field; conductor seminars in field. Contbr. articles to profl. jours. Trustee N.J. Organ and Tissue Sharing Network Inc., 1987—. Mortar Bd. scholar, 1966. Mem. AMA, Am. Soc. Pharmacology and Exptl. Therapeutics, Am. Fedn. Clin. Resarch, Am. Med. Women's Assn., Am. Soc. Clin. Pharmacology and Therapeutics. Republican. Office: Hoffmann-LaRoche Inc 340 Kingsland St Nutley NJ 07110

DATTA, LOIS-ELLIN, government administrator; b. Paterson, N.J., June 12, 1932; d. Gerald Gershon and Martha Rose (Cohen) G.; m. Padma Rag Datta, Dec. 20, 1953; children—Tane Mohan, Eric Raman. B.A., W.Va. U., 1952, M.A., 1956; M.A., Bryn Mawr Coll., 1957, Ph.D., 1961. Researcher Gen. Electric Co., Valley Forge, Pa., 1961-63; research fellow NIH, Bethesda, Md., 1963-68; chief early childhood research U.S. Dept. HEW, Washington, 1968-72; assoc. dir. Nat. Inst. Edn., Washington, 1972-82, U.S. GAO, Washington, 1982—. Recipient Myrdal award Evaluation Research Soc. Office: GAO Room 5741 441 G St NW Washington DC 20548

DATZ, RUTH ELIZABETH, educator, musician; b. Greensburg, Pa., June 10, 1936; d. Robert Albert and Ruth Elizabeth (Bates) Datz; B.A., Indiana (Pa.) U., 1958; M.A., NYU, 1961; postgrad Pa. State U., 1962-63, U. Colo., 1971, SUNY-Potsdam, 1978. Tchr. music pub. schs., Middletown Twp., N.J., 1958-61, Tyrone, Pa., 1961-65, Ann Arbor, Mich., 1965—; counselor, recreation dir., dir. jr. girls div. Interlochen (Mich.) Nat. Music Camp, 1956-69; head womens counselor New Eng. Music Camp, Maine, 1970, 72; flutist, pit orchestras, N.Y.C., 1959-61; conductor spl. chorus, Ann Arbor Youth Chorale. Mem. Republican. Com., Tyrone, 1962-65. Mem. Music Educators Nat. Conf., Mich. Music Educators Assn., Mich. Sch. Vocal Assn., Am. Choral Dirs. Assn., Nat. Assn. Humanities Edn., NEA, Mich. Edn. Assn., Delta Omicron, Delta Zeta. Mem. United Ch. of Christ. Clubs: Ann Arbor Dog Tng., Eastern Star, Job's Daughters. Home: 1564 Barrington Pl Ann Arbor MI 48103 Office: 2727 Fuller Rd Ann Arbor MI 48105

DAUBENAS, JEAN DOROTHY TENBRINCK, librarian; b. N.Y.C., Apr. 4; d. Eduard J.A. and Margaret Dorothy (Schaffner) Tenbrinck; m. Joseph Anthony Daubenas, May 29, 1965. AB, Barnard Coll., 1962; grad. Am. Acad. Dramatic Arts, 1963; MA, N.Y. U., 1965; MLS, U. Ariz., 1972; PhD, U. Utah, 1986. Tchr., Beth Jacob Tchrs. Sem. Am., Bronx, 1965-66; caseworker, Dept. Social Services, N.Y.C., 1966-67; actress Boothbay (Maine) Playhouse, others, 1967-70; reference librarian Ariz. State U., Tempe, 1972-75; asst. librarian, asst. prof. library sci. Avila Coll., Kansas City, Mo., 1979-83; assoc. prof./librarian St. John's U., Jamaica, N.Y., 1983—. N.Y. State Regents scholar, 1958-62, U. Ariz. scholar, 1971-72. Mem. ALA, Actors Equity Assn., AAUP, Beta Phi Mu, Phi Kappa Phi. Roman Catholic. Home: 110-21 73d Rd Apt 3-G Forest Hills NY 11375 Office: Library St Johns U Grand Central and Utopia Pkwys Jamaica NY 11439

DAUGHERTY, ANN ISABEL, stockbroker; b. Lansing, Mich., May 9, 1958; d. Burton Perry and Daugherty and Jane Blanchard (Kerr) Daugherty Bremer. Student, Calvin Coll., 1976-78; BS, Mich. State U., 1980; postgrad., James Madison Coll., U. Detroit, 1982. Dir. coll. recruiting Best Inc., Southfield, Mich., 1980-81; asst. to structure settlement specialist Kidder Peabody Ltd., Detroit, 1981-82; mgmt. trainee Comerica Bank, Detroit, 1982-83; registered rep. First Investors Corp., Southfield, 1983-86; mktg. specialist Anthony Brown Devel. Co., Birmingham, Mich., 1986-87; stockbroker Smith Barney, Harris Upham and Co., Newport Beach, Calif., 1987—; Mem. Jr. League of Detroit, 1986-87, of Orange County, Newport Harbor, Calif., 1987-88. Mem. Women's Sailing Assn. Santa Monica Bay. Republican. Office: Smith Barney Harris Upham 5000 Birch St Suite 7000 Newport Beach CA 92660

D'AULNIS DE BOUROUILL, MONIQUE CHANTAL, publisher, translator, writer; b. Jakarta, Java, Indonesia, Aug. 8, 1952; came to U.S., 1979; d. Pierre Louis and Blanche (Noyon) d'A. Grad. in pub. and bookselling, Dutch Book Trade Assn., Amsterdam, The Netherlands, 1974. Editor Ploegsma, Amsterdam, 1972-78; asst. editor Gallimard, Paris, 1978; mgr. contract sales Collins, Glasgow, Eng., 1979; mgr. subs. rights Holt, Rinehart & Winston, N.Y.C., 1979-83; dir. bus. affairs and internat. rights DC Comics, Inc., N.Y.C., 1983—. Translator children's books De Kroondieven, 1975; editor, creator nat. children's book week (book award) Het Verdwenen Plakboek, 1976. Martinus Nijhoff internat. scholar Dutch Book Trade Assn., 1978. Mem. Nat. Assn. Female Execs. Club: Woman Pays (N.Y.). Office: DC Comics Inc 666 5th Ave New York NY 10103

DAUN, MARY AGNES, information systems specialist; b. Jersey City, Oct. 9, 1945; d. John Patrick and Juliana Elizabeth (Schaefer) Larney; m. James Archie Curtiss, Oct. 22, 1966 (div. 1976); m. Dennis Emil Daun, Nov. 17, 1979; 1 adopted child, Timothy Curtiss; legal guardian of Jeffrey Anderson; stepchildren: Timothy, Brian, Andrew. BS, East Stroudsburg (Pa.) State Coll., 1966; MS, Cardinal Stritch Coll., 1984. Programmer analyst Am. Motors Corp., Kenosha, Wis., 1966-69, freelance contract programmer, 1969-76, sr. analyst, 1976-77, supr. mgmt. info. systems, 1977-80; mgr. ops. Am. Motors Corp., Milw., 1980-81, mgr. systems programming, 1981-84, mgr. info. systems, 1984-87; dir. corp. info. services Am. Motors Corp., Detroit, 1987; mgr. application systems, automotive sales and parts systems Chrysler Motors Corp., Centerline, Mich., 1987—; instr. math Gateway Tech. Inst., Kenosha, 1975-76. Office: Chrysler Motors Corp 25999 Lawrence Ave Centerline MI 48015

DAUSER, KIMBERLY ANN, physician assistant; b. Detroit, Nov. 20, 1947; d. George Leonard and Jeanne (Austin) Wilke; m. Steven Kent Dauser, Nov. 10, 1983; 1 child, Aaron Thomas. AA, Pensacola Jr. Coll., 1971; BS in Medicine, physician's asst. cert. in medicine, U. Ala., Birmingham, 1976. Cert. physician's asst. Asst. mgr. Christo's, Gulf Breeze, Fla., 1966-67; teller, bookkeeper loan dept. Bank Gulf Breeze, 1967-72; med. tech. aide USN Hosp., Pensacola, 1972, physician's asst., 1972-73; physician's asst. John Kingsley, MD, Pensacola, 1976, Mountain Ctr. Health Corp., Whitesburg, Ky., 1976-78; physician's asst. N.W. Fla. Nephrology, Pensacola, 1978—, med. mgr., 1984—; physician's asst. N.W. Fla. Artificial Kidney Ctr., Pensacola, 1980-87. Fellow Am. Acad. Physician's Assts. (del. nat. meeting 1979), Nat. Commn. on Cert. Physician's Assts., Fla. Acad. Physician's Assts. (mem. jud. com. 1979-80). Democrat. Roman Catholic. Office: NW Florida Nephrology 1717 North E St Suite 501 Pensacola FL 32501

DAVENPORT, DIANNE WHITLEY, organization development consultant; b. Americus, Ga., May 29, 1949; d. Billy Allen and Annie Ruth (Daniel) Whitley; m. Thomas Francis Delaney (div. Mar. 1974); m. Daniel Garwin Davenport, Feb. 14, 1975; 1 child, Whitley Price. AB, U. Ga., 1971; MEd, Boston U., 1972; PhD, Ga. State U., 1985. Counselor, instr. behavioral sci. Reinhardt Coll., Waleska, Ga., 1974-77; dir. student devel. Reinhardt Coll., Waleska, 1978-81; grad. teaching asst. Ga. State U., Atlanta, 1982-83; mgmt., career devel. cons. Bernard Haldane Assocs., Atlanta, 1984; cons. orgn. devel. Ga. Power Co., Atlanta, 1985—. Contbr. articles to profl. jours. Mem. community adv. com. Ga. State U., Atlanta, 1987. Mem. Am. Mgmt. Assn., Am. Soc. for Tng. and Devel., Am. Assn. Counseling and Devel., Atlanta Soc. Applied Psychology, Phi Beta Kappa, Phi Kappa Phi. Democrat. Methodist.

DAVENPORT, GAIL PIERNAS, marketing administrator; b. Chgo., Dec. 6, 1951; d. Leo Frederick and Mary (Kelly) Piernas; m. Montell A. Davenport, July 14, 1979; 1 child, Adam. B in Urban Planning with hon., U. Ill., 1973. Dir. community relations Sch. Dist. 151, South Holland, Ill., 1975-81; profl. asst. for communications Am. Assn. Sch. Librarians div. ALA, Chgo., 1983-84; owner Walking and Talking Prodns., Park Forest, Ill., 1982—; mktg. coordinator Suburban Fed. Savs., Harvey, Ill., 1987—. Mem. Harvey Econ. Devel. Com., 1982-83, Harvey Bicentennial Commn., 1975-77, S. Suburban YWCA, Olympia Fields, Ill.; pres., commr. Harvey Park Dist., 1975-77; bd. dirs. S. Suburban Housing Ctr., Homewood, Ill, 1981-83. Mem. Nat. Assn. Female Execs. Methodist. Home: 415 Indiana St Park Forest IL 60466

DAVENPORT, JACQUELINE, manufacturing company executive; b. N.Y.C., Feb. 7, 1944; d. John Joralemon Davenport and Fanny Wilhemina (Barberis) Allison. Student, SUNY, 1987—. Pres., owner Transp. Ctr., Inc., Long Island City, N.Y., 1962-74; owner Commerce Realty of Houston, 1974-86; contract adminstr. Hercules, Inc., McGregor, Tex., 1986—.

DAVENPORT, PATRICIA JENNINGS, financial executive; b. Richmond, Va., Nov. 29, 1959; d. Alvin Pritchett and JoAllen (Baptist) Jennings; m. Raymond William Davenport, Oct. 5, 1985. BS, James Madison U., 1982; MBA, Marymount U., 1986. System analyst Computing Analysis Corp., Arlington, Va., 1983-84, Am. Mgmt. Systems, Arlington, 1984-86; tech. contract mgr. Logicon, Inc., Arlington, 1986-88; fin. systems analyst MCI Telecommunications, Arlington, 1988—. Mem. Nat. Assn. Female Execs., Arlington Jaycees, Info. Systems Security Assn. Office: MCI Telecommunications Corp 701 S 12th St Arlington VA 22202

DAVID, GABRIELLE, editor; b. Great Falls, Mont., May 10, 1947; d. Richard Fredrick and Ann (Hollister) D.; m. Gerald Paul Krenbiel Jr., Sept. 11, 1966 (div. June 1970); children: Paula, Gerald Paul III; m. John Gaylon Barton, Dec. 28, 1980 (div. Dec. 1986). AA, Mesa Community Coll., 1976. Bookkeeper Diamonds Gen. Office, Tempe, Ariz., 1976-77, Agro Land and Cattle, Tucson, 1977-80; editor, corp. officer David Publs. Inc., Ajo, Ariz., 1980—. Sec. Ajo Clinic Aux., 1987; bd. dirs. Ajo-Lukeville Health Service Dist., 1987-88. Mem. Ariz. Press Club, Nat. Assn. Female Execs., Ajo Dist. C. of C. (pres. 1985-86, treas. 1987-88), Jobs Tng. Ptnrship. Act Pvt. Industry Council, Desert Music Club, Ajo Roping Club, Beta Sigma Phi. Democrat. Lodge: Women of the Moose. Home: PO Box 482 Ajo AZ 85321 Office: David Pubs Inc PO B 39 Ajo AZ 85321

DAVID, JUDY BREINER, advertising and promotion consultant, writer, producer; b. Milw., May 26, 1938; d. James Mirko and Fannie (Apple) Breiner; divorced; children—Rod Alan, Donna Lyn. Student Washington U., St. Louis, 1956-58. Dir./producer amateur theatricals Empire Producing Co., Kansas City, Mo., 1959; supr. pub. relations, tours, producer and host interview show Sta. KETC-TV, St. Louis, 1959-60; freelance pub. relations writer, St. Louis, 1966-69; copywriter George Johnson Advt., Inc., St. Louis, 1968, Ridgeway Advt., St. Louis, 1969; copywriter, producer Gardner/Wells, Rich, Greene, Inc., St. Louis, 1970-74; sr. writer, producer McCann-Erickson, Inc., Atlanta, 1974-77; freelance writer, producer, promotions, cons., doing bus. as A Functional Literate, Atlanta, 1977—; judge CLIO Awards, 1982, 84, 86, 87, ADDY Awards, 1980, 81, 83, 84, 86, Hollywood Radio and TV Internat. Broadcast awards, 1984; panelist, lectr. Ga. State U., DeKalb Coll., Portfolio Ctr., various seminars and workshops; amateur performer, cartoonist, comedy writer, product designer. Author: Moonlighter's Guide to Success, 1978. Vol., Atlanta Soc. for Blind, 1975, 76, 77, Ga. Press Assn. Gridiron, 1978, 79, 80, 81, Jewish Vocat. Services, 1982, others; bd. dirs. Camp Fire Boys and Girls, Inc., 1987; mem. communications adv. bd. Atlanta Jewish Fedn., 1985, 86, 87, Interfaith Shelters for Homeless, 1984, 85, 86, 87. Named Top Writer, Atlanta Bus. Chronical Profl. Poll, 1986, hon. mention, 1987, ADWEEK All Am. Creative Team, 1982; recipient Addy awards, 1974, 75, 77, 80-85, Phoenix award, 1974, 75, 76, 78, 81, 82, Andy awards, 1976, 78, 80-83, CLIO, 1975, 81, 85, Maxi award, 1982, 83, Cable Mktg. award, 1983, Telly award, 1985, Hollywood Radio & TV Internat. Broadcast award, 1983, Internat. Radio Festival of N.Y. award, 1985, Silver Microphone awards, 1984, 86, Silver award Health Services Mktg., 1987. Mem. Atlanta Soc. Communication Artists (dir. 1974-75), Art Dirs. Club (bd. dirs. Atlanta chpt. 1986, 87, 88), Portfolio Ctr. (bd. advs. 1986, 87), Women Bus. Owners, High Mus. Soc., Greenpeace, Zool. Soc., Bot. Soc. Address: 1073 Lanier Blvd Atlanta GA 30306

DAVID, KATHERINE MAUTHE, home economist; b. New Orleans, June 28, 1955; d. Henry Frank and Earline Loretta (Landreaux) Mauthe; m. Joseph Bernie David, July 14, 1981. BS, Southeastern La. U., 1977; M in Extension Edn., La. State U., 1982. Home economist La. State U. Coop. Extension Service, St. Helena Parish, 1977-80, Lafayette Parish, 1980-82, Washington Parish, 1983—; consumer advisor McDonald Sales and Cuisinart, Lafayette, La., 1980-83. Mem. La. Assn. Extension 4-H Agents (Outstanding Young 4-H Agent award 1981, reporter 1980-81, v.p. 1981-82), Washington Parish Fair Assn. (chmn. youth bldg. 1983-87), La. Assn. Extension Home Economists. Republican. Roman Catholic. Office: La Coop Extension Service 1104 B Bene St Franklinton LA 70438

DAVID, KATHLEEN CATTRALL, training and project administrator; b. Niagara Falls, N.Y., Oct. 28, 1955; d. Charles Ronald and Janis Elizabeth (Wadsworth) Cattrall; divorced; 1 child, Christopher Leigh. BA, SUNY, Geneseo, 1977. Instr. SUNY, Brockport, 1979-81, dir. non-credit programs, 1981-85; v.p. accounts devel. Interact Assocs., Rochester, N.Y., 1985-87; tng., project mgr. Learning Internat. (Times Mirror Co.), Stamford, Conn., 1987—; chmn. Owens-Ill. Resource and Placement Ctr., various locations, 1984-85; keynote speaker Am. video and film producers, Rochester, 1987. Recipient Congl. Cert. of Honor, USA Congress, 1985. Mem. Am. Mgmt. Assn., Am. Soc. Tng. and Devel., Genesee Region Assn. Adult and Continuing Edn. (pres. 1984), Rochester Sales and Mktg. Execs., Rochester Area C. of C. Democrat. Home: PO Box 722 New Milford CT 06776 Office: Learning Internat 200 First Stamford Pl Stamford CT 06904

DAVIDOFF, DENISE TAFT, advertising executive; b. N.Y.C., Mar. 11, 1932; d. Allen Robert and Bunnee Lola (Zuckerman) Taft; m. Jerry Davidoff, Oct. 2, 1955; children—Douglass Taft, John Oliver Albert. A.B., Vassar Coll., 1953. Exec. v.p. C.A. Smith & Co., Westport, Conn., 1961-67; pres. Davidoff & Ptnrs Inc., Fairfield, Conn., 1967—; dir. Automatix, Inc., Billerica, Mass.; mem. Govs. council Am. Assn. Advt. Agys., N.Y.C., 1986. Trustee, pres. Westport Library Assn., 1973-83, Unitarian Universalist Women's Fedn., Boston, 1973-85, Unitarian Universalist Peace Network (steering com. 1984—) Phila., 1984; trustee Conn. Pub. TV, Hartford, 1975—.Democrat. Home: 109 Harvest Commons Westport CT 06880 Office: Davidoff & Ptnrs Inc Heritage Sq Fairfield CT 06430

DAVIDSON, ANNE STOWELL, lawyer; b. Rye, N.Y., Feb. 24, 1949; d. Robert Harold and Anne (Breeding) Davidson. B.A. magna cum laude, Smith Coll., 1971; J.D. cum laude, George Washington U., 1974. Bar: D.C. 1975, U.S. Supreme Ct. 1980. Asst. gen. counsel FDA, Rockville, Md., 1974-78; counsel Abbott Labs., North Chicago, Ill., 1978-79; counsel U.S. Pharm. Ops. Schering-Plough Corp., Kenilworth, N.J., 1979-83; sr. counsel Sandoz Pharms. Corp., Inc., East Hanover, N.J., 1983-86, v.p., assoc. gen. counsel, 1987—. Trustee, N.J. Pops Orch. Recipient Dawes Prize Smith Coll., 1971. Mem. ABA, Pharm. Mfrs. Assn., Food and Drug Law Inst., Proprietary Assn. (govt. affairs com.). Republican. Presbyterian. Club: Smith Coll. (pres. 1981-82). Contbr. articles to profl. jours. Office: Sandoz Pharms Corp 59 Rt 10 East Hanover NJ 07936

DAVIDSON, BARBARA TAYLOR, real estate sales agent; b. Ames, Iowa, Jan. 30, 1920; d. Harvey Nelson and Ruby (Britten) Taylor; m. Donald Thomas Davidson Sr., May 22, 1942 (dec. Oct. 1962); children: Donald Thomas Jr., John Taylor, Ann Elizabeth Davidson Costanzo. BS in Home Econs. Sci., Iowa State U., 1943. Assoc. tchr. Ames (Iowa) Pub. Schs., 1970-73; retail mgr. Gen. Nutrition Ctr., Ames, 1974-77; sales assoc. Century 21 Real Estate, Ames, 1978-82, Friedrich Realty, Ames, 1982—; cons. Delta Zeta Corp.; chmn. adv. bd. Delta Zeta Corp., Ames, 1956-62. Pres. Ames City PTA Council, 1950; leader, advisor Boy Scouts Am., Ames, 1952-58; chmn. Campfire Leaders' Assn., Ames, 1959-61; sec. bd. dirs. Campfire Girls, Ames, 1964-66; property com. United Meth. Ch., Ames, 1964-67; mem. Octagon for the Arts, Brunier Gallery, Med. Ctr. Auxiliary. Mem. Nat. Assn. Realtors, Iowa Assn. Realtors, Ames Multiple Listing Service, Nat. Home Econs. in Homemaking (chmn. fgn. student relations com.), Internat. Orch. Assn., Iowa State U. Meml. Union (life), Iowa State U. Alumni Assn. (life). Republican. Home: 1416 Harding Ave Ames IA 50010 Office: Friedrich Realty Sixth at Duff Ave Ames IA 50010

DAVIDSON, DEBORAH, utilities company executive, electrical engineer; b. Nashville, Mar. 23, 1951; d. Tuyl Kenneth and Therese (Hanley) Davidson; m. Gerald Michael Ground, July 14, 1969 (div. 1976); m. Bobby Glenn Pate, Aug. 7, 1978 (div. 1986); foster children: Lorie Ellen Lewis, Randy James Lewis. B.S. in Engring., U. Tenn., 1981. Registered profl. engr., Tenn. Audit cler, Tenn. Dept. Rev., Nashville, 1974-75; account clk. Blair, Follen, Allen, & Walker, Nashville, 1975-76; freelance wallpaper hanger, decorator, Nashville, 1976-81; materials engr. Nashville Electric Service, 1982-87, asst. mgr. purchasing, stores, 1987—. Recipient Andrew Holt scholarship U. Tenn. Alumnae, 1976-81. Mem. Internat. Assn. Quality Circle, (leader), Mensa. Republican. Roman Catholic. Club: Toastmasters Internat. Avocations: horticulture; needlework; bluegrass music. Home: 106 Jackstaff Dr Hendersonville TN 37075 Office: Nashville Electric Service 1214 Church St Nashville TN 37203

DAVIDSON, GRACE EVELYN, nursing administrator and educator; b. Wabash, Ind., Aug. 2, 1920; d. William Alexander and Jennie Lavinia (Baker) Davidson. Diploma, Columbia Presbyn. Sch. Nursing, 1942; BS, U. Minn., 1948; MA in Teaching, Columbia U., 1954, postgrad. 1963-64. Instr. Sch. Nursing, Columbia U., N.Y.C., 1948-51; assoc. prof. Skidmore Coll., Saratoga Springs, N.Y., 1954-66; asst. adminstr., dir. nursing Univ. Hosp., NYU Med. Ctr., 1966-79, assoc. prof. part-time, 1977-79, prof. 1979—; cons. nursing service adminstrn., N.Y.C., 1980—. Contbr. articles to profl. jours. Served to maj. Army Nurse Corps, 1943-46, World War II, 51-53, Korea, Res., 53-60, Ret. Recipient Alumni Fedn. medal Columbia U., 1981, Plaque for leadership in nursing NYU Med. Ctr., 1983. Mem. Nursing Edn. Alumnae Assn. Tchrs. Coll. Columbia U. (achievement award 1977), Am. Nurses Assn., Nat. League Nursing, Soc. Nursing History Council, Columbia U.-Presbyn. Hosp. Sch. Nursing Alumnae Assn. (pres. 1970-76, Disting. Alumnae award 1981), Fedn. Alumni Assn. Columbia U., Ret. Officers Assn., LWV. Republican. Presbyterian. Home: 67 Chestnut St Dumont NJ 07628

DAVIDSON, JESSICA URSULA, music educator; b. Rome, N.Y., Jan. 10, 1914; d. Jay Sidney and Lucy Adelaide (Clarke) Brown; grad. Potsdam State Coll., 1934; B.Mus. in Music Edn., U. Del., 1972, M.Ed. in Music Edn., West Chester U., 1973; Ph.D. in Secondary Edn.-Music Edn., U. Md., 1978; m. Alexander Clyde Davidson, June 8, 1936; children—Shirley Anne, Nancy Jeannette. Tchr. music Adams Center High Sch., 1934-36, 42-43; dir. music Ave. Methodist Ch., Del. 1946-75; dir. Student Nurses Choir, Del., 1965-75; tchr. piano, organ Kimball Music Co., 1967-69; tchr. music Milford Spl. Dist., Del., 1969-70; tchr. music New Castle County (Del.) Sch. Dist., 1970-77, 78-79; tchr. music edn. U. Md., 1977-78; dir. music edn. and area music program for Council on Aging, Sanders Brown Ctr. on Aging, U. Ky., 1979—. Composer: Christmas Cantata: The Birth of Christ According to Saint Luke, 1970, The Night the Christ Chil;d Came to Earth, 1965, The Greatest of These is Love, 1973, Mothers of the World, 1965, Christmas in Kentucky, 1980. Class rep. U. Del., 1977—. Mem. Music Educators Nat. Conf., Ky. State Music Edn. Assn., Nat. Ret. Tchrs. Assn., Am. Assn. Ret. Persons, Delta Kappa Gamma (chmn. music com. Newcastle, Del 1975-77, mem. program com. Lexington 1980). Republican. Methodist. Clubs: Order Eastern Star (matron 1942). Home: 339 Eagle Creek Dr Lexington KY 40502 Office: U Ky Ligon House Lexington KY 40506

DAVIDSON, JOAN KLINGEBIEL, human resources executive; b. Peoria, Ill., May 12, 1939; d. Roy William and Mildred (Stephens) Klingebiel; m. James T. Davidson, Dec. 28, 1956 (div. Sept. 1977); children: Anne Davidson McDonnell, Robert James. AA in English, Brookdale Community Coll., 1976; BA in English, Monmouth Coll., West Long Branch, N.J., 1981; MS in Indsl. Relations and Human Resources, Rutgers U., 1987. Personnel rep., exec. sec. Reynolds Metals Co., Massena, N.Y., 1961-66; asst. to v.p., treas. Brookdale Community Coll., Lincroft, N.J., 1972-76, asst. dir. personnel, 1976-80, dir. personnel, 1981-84; v.p. human resources Metaplex Mgmt. Services, Inc., Red Bank, N.J., 1984—; cons. St. Mary's Hosp., Lewiston, Maine, Vis. Nurse Assn., Middlesex County North Brunswick, N.J. Bd. dirs. Red Bank YMCA, 1983—. Mem. N.J. Coll. and Univ. Personnel Assn. (pres. 1983), N.J. Assn. Health Care Human Resources Adminstrs., N.J. Chpt. Am. Soc. Personnel Adminstrs. Republican. Presbyterian. Office: Metaplex Mgmt Services 151 Bodman Pl Red Bank NJ 07701

DAVIDSON, M. BERNICE, secretarial service executive; b. Pickering, Ontario, Canada, July 7, 1935; d. George Franklin and Annie Muriel (Dunn) Duncan; m. Frederick William DeCaire, May 23, 1953 (div. 1982); children: Lance, Rhonda, Dale, Annette. Grad. high sch., Pickering, Ont., Canada. Personnel asst. McCulloch of Canada Ltd., Toronto, Ont., 1965-70; personnel supr. Zellers Inc., Sarnia, Ont., 1970-74; adminstrv. asst. Des Parker Town Planner, Prince George, B.C., Canada, 1974-75; v.p. Beneath the Sea, Revelstoke, B.C., 1975-80; v.p. Tri-C Secretarial Services Inc., Vancouver, B.C., 1980-84, pres., 1984-87. Gov. YMCA, Vancouver, B.C., 1986—. Mem. Sales and Mktg. Execs., (exec. dir. 1984—), Western Bus. Women's Assoc., Nat. Assoc Secretarial Services, Canadian Office Services Assoc. United Church. Club: Canadian (Vancouver) (sec. 1982-87). Office: Tri-C Secretarial Services, 1250 Homer St, Vancouver, BC Canada V6B2Y5

DAVIDSON, MARCELLA SCHOOLS, food products executive; b. St. Petersburg, Fla., Mar. 27, 1952; d. James Askew and Elizabeth Marie (Preston) Schools; divorced; children: James Matthew, Ashley Elizabeth. BS, Va. Poly. Inst., 1974. Dir. compliance and quality Eberwine Bros., Inc., Suffolk, Va., 1974-76; supr. quality control Planters Nuts, Suffolk, 1976-78, mgr. packaging specifications div., 1978-79, mgr. audits div., 1979-81, mgr. material evaluation div., 1981; mgr. quality assurance and environ. affairs Hershey Chocolate Co., Stuarts Draft, Va., 1981-87; asst. to v.p. mfg. Luden's div. Hershey (Pa.) Chocolate Co., 1987—. Bd. dirs., 2d v.p. Jr. Achievement Waynesboro (Va.)/Augusta County, 1982-87; mem. Shenandoah River Basin Com., 1985-87, Future Agr. Study, Va., 1986-87. Recipient Disting. Service award of Merit Gamma Sigma Delta, 1985. Mem. Inst. Food Technologists, Va. Food Processors Assn. (bd. dirs., pres. 1980-81), Am. Soc. Quality Control, Cen. Atlantic States Assn. Food and Drug Officials (assoc. membership chmn.), Va. Mfg. Assn. (environ. affairs com. 1983-87), Va. Poly. Inst. Agr. Alumni Orgn. (bd. dirs. 1980-87), Nat. Agr. Alumni and Devel. Assn. (bd. dirs. 1985—). Office: Hershey Chocolate Co Luden's div Box 15087 Reading PA 19612

DAVIDSON, MARIE DIANE, publisher; b. Los Angeles, Mar. 6, 1924; d. Charles Casper and Stella Ruth (Bateman) Winnia; divorced, 1953; children: David William, Ronald Mark. AB, U. Calif., Berkeley, 1943; MA, Calif. State U., Sacramento, 1959. cert. secondary tchr., 1944. Tchr. Campbell (Calif.) High Sch., 1944-45; actress Pasadena (Calif.) Playhouse, 1945, U.S.O. Camp Shows, N.Y.C., 1946-47, El Camino High Sch., Sacramento, 1954-85; publisher, editor Swan Books, Fair Oaks, Calif., 1979—; actress, cons. Valley Inst. TV Assn, Sacramento, 1971; writer Crown Pubs., N.Y.C., 1969. Author: Feversham, 1969; illustrator, editor (book series) Shakespeare on Stage, 1979, Shakespeare for Young People, 1986. Mem. Author's Guild, Calif. Writer's Club, NEA, Calif. Tchrs. Assn., Pi Lambda Theta, Phi Beta Kappa. Democrat. Episcopalian. Office: Swan Books PO Box 2498 Fair Oaks CA 95628

DAVIDSON, MARY FRANCES LOGUE, protective services official; b. Balt., Aug. 26, 1958; d. Thomas Hemler and Ruth Marie (Zulauf) Logue; m. James D. Davidson, Oct.7, 1984; (step-children) Heather, Dax. BA, U. Md., 1980; cert. European Criminal Justice, U. Copenhagen, 1979. Special agt. U.S. Secret Service, 1980—; instr. USSS-MCI Computer System, U.S. Secret Service, Los Angeles, 1984-86. Leader Girl Scouts Am., Hacienda Heights, Calif., 1986-87; foster mother Chino Hills, Calif., 1986-87. Mem. Nat. Assn Female Execs. Republican. Office: US Secret Service US Courthouse Room 7100 101 W Lombard St Baltimore MD 21201

DAVIDSON, YVETTE MAIRE, accountant; b. Akron, Ohio, Dec. 14, 1941; d. Yvon and Sophia (Kozopas) Fleury; married Dec. 6, 1960; divorced 1966; 1 child, Laurele. Student, Akron U., Kent State U. Payroll clk., cashier W.T. Grant Co., Akron, Ohio, 1956-59; legal sec. Summit County Prosecuter, Akron, 1959-61, Summit County Legal Aid Soc., Akron, 1961-62; acct. Ekus Textial and Waste Co., Akron, 1962-65; cost acct. Alside's Home Div, Northfield, Ohio, 1965-66; acct. City of Akron, 1966—; agent Merkle & Kalstron Real Estate, Akron, 1961—; v.p., chmn. bd. dirs. City of Akron Credit Union, 1980—; cons. on grant mgmt., travel. Active local March of Dimes. Mem. Cleve. Metro Ski Council (trip chairperson 1980—), Bitoa Ski Club (trip chairperson, v.p. 1970-86), U.S. Recreational Skiing Assn. (voting del. 1970—), U.S. Ski Assn. (voting del. 1984—). Home: 127 Mission Dr Akron OH 44301

DAVIES, JANE B. (MRS. LYN DAVIES), architectural historian; b. Amboy, Ill., Sept. 9, 1913; d. Henry Harold and Clara May (Heermans) Badger; B.A., Wellesley Coll., 1935; M.A., Columbia U., 1942, B.S. in L.S. with high honors, 1944; postgrad. U. Mich., summer 1936, U. Wis., summers 1937, 38; m. Lyn Davies, July 18, 1942. Tchr. Monticello Prep. Sch., Godfrey, Ill., 1935-37, Kent Sch. Girls, Denver, 1937-41, Halsted Sch., Yonkers, N.Y., 1942-43; reference librarian Columbia Univ. Libraries, 1944-50, rare book cataloger, 1951-77; cons. Nat. Trust for Hist. Preservation, 1965, 87-88, Smithsonian Inst., 1967, Greensboro (N.C.) Preservation Soc., 1967-70, Historic Green Springs, 1970-73, 82, Llewellyn Park Hist. Dist., 1982-84, Hist. Hudson Valley, 1986-88; lectr. on Am. archtl. history. Am. Council Learned Socs. grantee, 1970, Am. Philos. Soc. grantee, 1970-71; NEH fellow, 1978. Mem. Soc. Archtl. Historians (sec.-treas. N.Y. chpt. 1959-67), Victorian Soc. Am. (adv. com. 1966-76), Nat. Trust Historic Preservation, Friends of Lyndhurst, N.Y. Hist. Soc., Archtl. League N.Y., Preservation League N.Y. State, Greensboro Preservation Soc. (hon.), Phi Beta Kappa, Beta Phi Mu. Presbyn. Author intro. Houston Mus. Fine Arts: The Gothic Revival Style in America, 1830-1870, 1976; Alexander Jackson Davis: Rural Residences (1837), 1980. Editorial asst. Jour. Soc. Archtl. Historians, 1964-65. Contbr. articles on Am. archtl. history to mags., jours. and Macmillan Ency. of Architects. Home: 549 W 123d St New York NY 10027

DAVIES, LOIS SHILLING, civic worker, writer; b. Troy, Ohio, June 5, 1909; d. Harry Ernest and Clara (Prugh) Shilling; m. Alfred W. Davies, June 14, 1932 (dec.); children—A. Robert, Thomas J., Matthew H. B.A., Ohio Wesleyan U., 1932. Y-Teen dir. YWCA, Piqua, Ohio, 1951-54; tchr. Miami County Schs., Ohio, 1949, 61; dir. Miami County Children's Services, 1965; exec. dir. Am. Heart Assn. Miami County, 1966-75; founder, leader, bd. dirs. Troy council Girl Scouts U.S., 1930-48; tchr. water safety ARC, 1930-48; mem. Miami County Central Democratic Com., 1970-80; bd. dirs. United Fund, Troy, 1977-81; chmn. Bd. Archtl. Rev., Troy, 1984-85. Author, interviewer oral history: Troy 1913 Flood, 1976; co-author: Some Self-Evident Truths, 1980; local history columnist Troy Daily News, 1983—. Recipient Woman of Yr. award Troy Bus. and Profl. Women's Club, 1980; Charles A. Glatt award Ohio Edn. Assn., 1982-83, Jaycee Community Service award, 1985, Troy C. of C. (instr. Leadership Troy 1984-85, Outstanding contbns. award 1900). Mem. AAUW (bd. positions 1965-80), Troy Hist. Soc. (pres. 1977-79). Methodist. Avocations: researching and documenting local history; Ohio Senior Olympics; Volksmarch. Home and Office: 113 N Market St Troy OH 45373

DAVIES, MARILYN ANNE, health science facility administrator, nurse; b. Pitts., Aug. 19, 1949; d. Harry Aloysius and Florence Catherine (Carver) Brickner; m. William Richard Charles Davies; children: William Charles, Ashley Catherine. BS in Nursing, U. Pitts., 1970, M of Nursing, 1977, PhD, 1985. RN, Pa. Staff nurse Magee-Womens Hosp., Pitts., 1970-71; clin. instr. St. Francis Gen. Hosp., Pitts., 1971-73; asst. coordinator Altoona (Pa.) Hosp. Community Mental Health Ctr., 1973-74; head nurse VA Hosp. Highland Dr., Pitts., 1974-76; sr. adminstrv. specialist Western Psychiat. Inst. and Clinic, Pitts., 1978—; cons., Pitts., 1974-87; prin. research investigator U. Pitts., 1985-87, faculty resource, student adviser 1986-87; instr. psychiatry Dept. Medicine U. Pitts., 1987. Author: (with others) Rape: Nursing Care of Victims, 1982; contbr. articles to profl. jours. Vol. Pitts. Action Against Rape, 1978-82; vice chairperson bd. trustees Dixmont State Hosp., Sewickley, Pa., 1980-83. Mem. Pa. Nurses Assn. (legis. com. 1979-82), Sigma Theta Tau (chmn. by-laws 1978). Republican. Roman Catholic. Office: Western Psychiat Inst and Clinic 3811 OHara E 504 ERC Pittsburgh PA 15213

DAVIES, OLGA G., insurance executive; b. Ukraine, Dec. 26, 1927; came to U.S., 19; d. Michael and Mary (Lohinska) Gabrysz; m. William David Davies, Nov. 12, 1950 (dec.); children—Nancy, Barbara, William. Student Rutgers U., 1975; cert. Stockton State Coll., 1976; cert. of ins. Ins. Inst. Am., 1977. Ins. underwriter Tifft, Laver & Co., Atlantic City, 1948-51; office mgr., corp. sec., ins. agt. C.J. Adams Co., Ins. Inc., Atlantic City, 1952—. Mem. Nat. Assn. Ins. Women, Ins. Women Atlantic County (pres. 1977-79). Republican. Presbyterian. Home: 112 Pennsylvania Ave Absecon NJ 08201 Office: CJ Adams Co Ins Inc 20 S Tennessee Ave PO Box 1047 Atlantic City NJ 08404

DAVILA-JOHNSTON, RUTH MARIE, computer programmer and analyst; b. Honolulu, Oct. 11, 1960; d. Daniel and Sally (Yunson) Davila; m. Johnnie Dean Johnston, Sept. 15, 1984; children: Jacob Harrison, Travis Daniel. BS, Southwest Mo. State U., Springfield, 1982. Computer programmer/analyst Marine Corps Fin. Ctr., Kansas City, Mo., 1983—. Mem. Nat. Assn. Female Execs., Southwest Mo. State U. Alumni Assn., Delta Sigma Pi. Roman Catholic. Avocations: shopping craft shows, swimming, dancing, reading. Home: 7 Belmo St Belton MO 64012 Office: Marine Corps Fin Ctr 1500 E 95th St Kansas City MO 64197

DAVION, ETHEL JOHNSON, language arts specialist; b. Raleigh, N.C., July 21, 1948; d. John Arthur and Ethel Mae (Morgan) Johnson; m. Joel Davion, Aug. 6, 1988. BA, Livingstone Coll., 1971; MA, Glassboro (N.J.) State U., 1983. Cert. tchr. English, supr. and principal. Sr. English tchr. Camden (N.J.) Bd. Edn., 1977-81; tchr. of English Westfield (N.J.) Bd. Edn., 1982-85, Union County Regional Dist. 1, Berkeley Heights, N.J., 1981-82, Hillside (N.J.) Bd. Edn., 1985-87; supr. language arts Invington Bd. Edn., N.J., 1987—; writer, researcher Collegiate Research Systems, Camden, 1976-77. Contbr. articles to jours. Bd. dirs, sec. Emmanuel Tabernacle, Linden, N.J., 1986—. Fellow N.J. Edn. Assn., Hillside Edn. Assn., Nat. Tchrs. English; mem. Linden Scholarship Guild (sec. 1985—). Democrat. Pentecostal. Clubs: Good Samaritans (Linden); Obsidian Civic (Westfield) (historian 1985—). Home: 610 E Blancke St Linden NJ 07036

DAVIS, ALICE J., municipal employee; b. Galveston, Tex., Aug. 4, 1929; d. Joseph Edward Reagan and Gertrude Bertha Reagan Zeller; m. Bob J. Davis, Oct. 22, 1948; 1 child, Paula Lynn Davis Baughman. A.A., San Jacinto Coll., 1966; B.S., Western Ill. U., 1976. With office staff various automobile dealerships, Houston, 1951-68, Yeast Printing Co., Macomb, Ill., 1974-77; clk. Office of City Clk., City of Macomb, 1977-86. Youth program leader 1st Meth. Ch., Pasadena, Tex., 1960-63; mem. choir Wesley United Meth. Ch., Macomb, 1968—, worship com., 1987-88, chmn. Alter Guild, 1987-88; area chmn. Macomb United Way, 1970-71, program chmn., 1984-85. Mem. Univ. Faculty Women, Macomb Home Econs. Assn. (pres. 1981-82, treas. 1987-88), Kappa Omicron Phi, Phi Kappa Phi, Beta Sigma Phi (treas. 1987-88), Xi Epsilon Rho (pres. 1981-82, 86-87). Lodges: Eastern Star, White Shrine, Deer. Office: Office of City Clerk City of Macomb Macomb IL 61455

DAVIS, ANGELA CECILIA, nurse; b. Arouca, Trinidad and Tobago, July 6, 1944; d. Joseph Davis and Emelda Cecilia (Jakie) Yearwood. BS in Nursing, Hunter Coll., 1982; MA, NYU, 1988. Staff nurse Mt. Sinai Hosp., N.Y.C., 1971-72, 75—, head nurse, 1972-75; educator childbirth Council Childbirth Edn. Specialists Inc., N.Y.C., 1979-83. Telephone counselor Community Sex Info., N.Y.C., 1984—; vol. advocate Rape Crisis Intervention Program Mt. Sinai Hosp., N.Y.C., 1984-86. Fellow Am. Nurses Assn., N.Y. State Nurses Assn., Sex Info. and Edn. Council U.S., Soc. for Sci. Study Sex. Democrat. Roman Catholic. Home: 1245 Park Ave #142 New York NY 10128 Office: Mt Sinai Med Ctr 1 Gustave Levy Pl New York NY 10029

DAVIS, AUDREY BLYMAN, medical sciences curator, author; b. Hicksville, N.Y., Nov. 9, 1934; d. George William Blyman and Helen Rosalie Usewack; m. Miles Davis, Aug. 6, 1960; children—Laura Helen, Allan Watson. B.S., Adelphi U., 1956; Ph.D., John Hopkins U., 1969. Sci. tchr. Sewanhaka High Sch., Floral Park, N.Y., 1956-58, Saugus (Mass.) High Sch., 1959-60; cons. Sci. Service, Washington, 1966-70; curator med. scis. Smithsonian Instn., Washington, 1967—; mus. cons. U.S. Armed Forces Inst. Pathology, Washington, 1983-84; Muetter Mus., Phila., 1979-80, Med. Mus. Indpls., 1986; cons. N.J. Med. Sch., New Brunswick, 1982; Kate Hurd Mead lectr., 1985; keynote speaker Vis. Nursing Assns., Buffalo, 1985, Omaha, 1986, Richmond, Va., 1986, Arlington, 1987; tour leader Smithsonian Assocs. trips to USSR, 1985, 86, People's Rep. China, 1984, 86. Author: Medicine and Its Technology (Choice award for outstanding acad. book 1983), 1981; Bloodletting Instruments in the NMAH, 1979; The Circulation of the Blood and Medical Chemistry in England, 1650-1680, 1974; The American Dentist: A Sociological History, 1988; contbr. articles, monographs in field to publs. Recipient Excellence Award as chairperson, editor newsletter Smithsonian Instn. Women's Council, 1982. Mem. Hist. Sci. Soc. (sec. 1982-85, council 1975-78), Am. Assn. Hist. Medicine (council 1976-79), Am. Hist. Assn., Am. Council Learned Socs, Conf. Secs. Democrat. Roman Catholic (chair fin. com. Corpus Christi Parish 1987—). Club: Bolton Swim, Tennis (Balt.) (former tennis chmn.) Office: Smithsonian Instn NMAH 5000 Washington DC 20560

DAVIS, BARBARA AVENT, government official; b. Durham, N.C., Sept. 22, 1935; d. Dallas Gaston and Elsie Amelia (Baugh) Avent; B.S. magna cum laude in Bus. Adminstrn., U. Tenn., Chattanooga, 1979, M.B.A., 1981; m. Jack Davis, May 30, 1953; 1 son, David Jack. Sec. various firms, 1953-65; with TVA, Chattanooga, 1973—, mgmt. asst., 1979-82, supr. records sales and adminstrn., 1982-85, land mgmt. specialist, 1985-86; tech. evaluator nuclear tng., 1986—. Pres. Brainerd United Methodist Women, Chattanooga, 1972-74, trustee ch., 1980-83. Mem. Nat. Mgmt. Assn., Chattanooga Symphony Guild, U. Tenn. Chattanooga Alumni Council (treas.), Alpha Soc. Home: 4604 Rocky River Rd Chattanooga TN 37416 Office: TVA Power Ops Tng Ctr PO Box 2000 Soddy-Daisy TN 37379

DAVIS, BARBARA JEAN SIEMENS, service company executive; b. Louisville, Nov. 12, 1931; d. Gustav Adolph Siemens and Alberta Jeanette (McAdams) Simon; m. Donald Elmore Davis, Aug. 4, 1950; children—Dale Montgomery, Gale Sue Davis Beaty. Mktg. and personnel mgr. Kelly Services, Louisville, 1962-65; tchr. asst. TV English, Jefferson County Schs., Louisville, 1960-70; wedding and floral designer Wedding Ring, Louisville, 1971-73; owner, designer Nook Flowers and Gifts, Memphis, 1973-75; cons. pub. relations Dixie Rents, Memphis, 1975-79; div. mgr. pres. Party Concepts, Inc., Memphis, 1980—. Author: Wedding Workshop Brides Work Book, 1984. Mem. Sales and Mktg. Execs., Am. Rental Assn. (mem. party council 1985—), Nat. Assn. Wedding Cons. (pres. 1983—); Nat. Assn. Female Execs. (dir. Memphis Network, mem. Internat. Platform Assn.). Republican. Presbyterian. Home: 2200 Admington Pl Cordova TN 38018

DAVIS, BARBARA M(AE), librarian; b. Cranston, R.I., Dec. 23, 1926; d. Harrie S. and Marguerite M. (Cameron) D.; SB in Chemistry, Brown U., 1948; MS in Library Sci., Simmons Coll., 1956. Asst. research librarian research and devel. dept. Cabot Corp., Cambridge, Mass., 1948-57, research librarian, 1957-61, research librarian Billerica (Mass.) Research Center, 1961-68, head tech. info. services, 1968-81, mgr. tech. info. center, 1981-87 . Dir. Cabot Boston Credit Union, 1956-59, 61-64, 72-78, clk., 1961-64, 72-77, v.p., 1977-78; chmn. research com. Greater Boston Young Republican Club, 1959-61. Mem. Am. Chem. Soc. (sec. div. chem. lit. 1961-65), Spl. Libraries Assn. (chmn. Boston chpt. 1965-66, chmn. chemistry div. 1971-72), Simmons Coll. Library Sch. Alumni (v.p. 1965-66). Home: 37 Drummer Boy Way Lexington MA 02173

DAVIS, BEATRICE ANNA KIMSEY, educator, civic worker; b. Oklahoma City, June 23, 1917; d. Carl Cleveland and Beatrice Mary (Rudersdorf) Kimsey; grad. Ward-Belmont Coll., 1938; m. Bruce A. Davis, Jan. 22, 1942; children: Belinda Anne Davis Pillow, Beatrice Annette Davis Orynawka, Beverly Anne Davis Steckler. BA, Vanderbilt U., 1940; MEd, Lamar U., 1973. Personnel interviewer Ft. Sam Houston, San Antonio, 1942-43; advisor Jr. Achievement, 1974-80; asst. instr. drama Watkins Night Sch., Nashville, 1939-40; substitute tchr. Port Arthur (Tex.) Ind. Sch. Dist., 1950-64; high sch. English tchr. South Park Ind. Sch. Dist., 1964—, head English dept., 1982-85; tchr. Nederland (Tex.) Ind. Sch. Dist., 1948-50. Co-author: Curriculum Guides for Reading, 1973, 81, Curriculum Guides for English, 1980; contbr. articles to mags. Pres. Port Arthur Family Services Am., 1979-81, Women's Orgn. Presbyn. Ch. of Covenant, 1988—; v.p. Jefferson High Sch. PTA; bd. dirs. Hughen Sch. for Crippled Children, Gates Meml. Library, PTA of Tyrell Elem. Sch., Port Arthur, Parliamentarians of Port Arthur, Story League of Port Arthur, Jefferson County Hist. Commn.; mem., docent SE Tex. Mus. Art, Beaumont, 1987-88; mem. Community Concert Assn. Port Arthur; 2d v.p. Vol. Adv. Bd., docent McFaddin-Ward Home, Beaumont, 1987-88, Art Mus. S.E. Tex., 1987—; mem. Women's Commn. S.E. Tex., 1985-86; bd. dirs. SE Tex. Hist. Commn. 1986—, Tyrell Library Hist. Preservation, 1988—; sec. Chpt. CP of P.E.O. Sisterhood, Port Arthur, 1987—, mem. Beaumont Opera Buffs; trustee, membership com., tchr. Presbyn. Ch. of Covenant; bd. dirs. Tyrell Restoration Geneal. Soc., Beaumont, 1987—. Served as ensign USNR, 1942-43, lt. comdr. Res. Recipient numerous awards for outstanding civic service, various ednl. stipends and grants; named Tchr. of Yr. for South Park High Sch., Tex. Agrl. and Mech. U., 1981-82. Mem. NEA, All Tchrs. Assn. Beaumont, Nat. Council Reading Tchrs., S.E. Tex. Council Reading Tchrs., Tex. Assn. for Specialists in Group Work, Sabine-Neches Personnel and Guidance Assn., AAUW (past pres. Port Arthur chpt.), Federated Women's Club (past pres. bd. Port Arthur chpt.), Rosehill Bd. (past pres.), Panhellenic Assn. (past pres. Port Arthur chpt.), Women's Orgn. Symphony Club (pres pres.). Choral Club (past pres.), Thalian Drama Group (past v.p.), Heritage Soc., Hist. Soc., Knights of Neches Aux., DAR, United Daus. Confederacy, English-Speaking Union U.S., Key Club, Sigma Kappa Alumni, Phi Lambda Phi, Phi Delta Kappa. Republican. Clubs: Reading, Port Arthur Country Club Women's Aux. (pres.). Home: 2816 35th St Port Arthur TX 77640

DAVIS, BEATRICE LYNN, management consultant; b. Berkeley, Calif., Dec. 28, 1950; d. H. Virgil and Margie (Snowden) D. BBA, U. Denver, 1973, MBA, 1974. Asst. adminstr. Davis Nursing Home, Inc., Denver, 1972-76; prof. Universidad De Santo Tomas, Bogota, Colombia, 1977-78; writer, translater Sintesis Economica, Bogota, 1978-79; prof. Universidad Los Andes, Bogota, 1979-80; mgr. Serviminas Ltd., Medellin and Bogota, 1978-81; prof. Eafit U., Medellin, 1982-84; pres. Performance Plus, Sacramento, 1986—; trainer Colo. State Dept. Health, Denver, 1975; pres. Negodiagnosticos Ltd., Medellin, 1981-85. Adv. Colo. State Legisl. Register Health/Planning Bd., Denver, 1974-75; alt. del. Denver County Rep. Convention, 1971; del. Leadership Denver, 1975. Mem. Nat. Speakers Assn. (sec. 1986—), Sacramento Women's Network (chair com. 1986—), Delta Sigma Pi (pres. 1975). Office: Performance Plus 5524 Assembly Ct Sacramento CA 95823

DAVIS, BERTHA GERMIZE, artist; b. Vilno, Lithuania; came to U.S., 1940, naturalized, 1941; d. Abraham and Dvora Germaize; student Stewart Van Orden, Pan Am. Coll., 1960-61, Fred Samualson and James Pinco, Art Inst. of San Migual Allende, Mex., 1965, Harold Phenix, 1972-73, Ed Whitney, 1973-74, Bud Shackelford, 1976, Zoltan Szabo, 1977, Morris Shubin, 1977; children—Sylvia Caplan Rawley, Doryn Davis Chervin. Owner, operator art gallery, Houston, 1969-72; asst. mgr. Art Internat., Houston, 1972-75; asst. mgr. Kirt Niven Gallery, Dallas, 1977-78; one woman shows: Pan Am. Coll., 1960, Jewish Community Center, Houston, McAllen State Bank, 1974, La Ciuldadela, Monterey, Mex., Houston Public Library, U. Tex. Health Sci. Center, Dallas, 1979, Gallery of Discovery, Dallas, 1981, Channel 13 TV Gallery, Dallas, 1981, Sol Del Rio Gallery, San Antonio, 1982, Wichita Falls, Tex., 1985, Jewish Community Ctr., 1986, Barens, Blackman, Houston, 1988, O'Kane Gallery, U. Houston, 1988, Artcetera Showing, 1988, First City Bank, Houston, 1988, also others; group shows include: Watercolor Soc. Houston, S.W. Watercolor Soc., Am. Painters in Paris, Cooperstown Art Exhibit, Issac Delgado Mus. Art, New Orleans, Corpus Christi Art Found., Salmagundi Club Art Show, N.Y.C., 1979, Dallas, Laguna Gloria Mus., Austin, Tex., 1979, 84, Catharine Lorillard Wolfe Art Club, N.Y.C., 1980, Houshangs Gallery, Dallas, 1980, Nimbus Gallery, Dallas; showings in Marsha London Gallery, N.Y.C., Nat. Design Center, N.Y.C., Fonteinbleau Gallery of N.Y., Deportive Israelita de México, Paige Gallery, 1984, Dallas S.L. Gallery, 1984; represented in permanent collection: Shell Oil Co., Houston, Transco Tower, Arthur Anderson Acctg. Co. Mem. Tex. Fine Art Assn., S.W. Watercolor Assn., Richardson Civic Art Assn., Artist Sculptors Contemporary Assn., Art League Houston, Houston Art Assn., Watercolor Art Soc. Houston, La Revue Moderne De Paris, Repetorium Artis Monte Carlo. Prin. illustrator: Open Dallas, 1976; works reproduced in various publs. Home: 8803 Jackwood St Houston TX 77036

DAVIS, BETTE RUTH ELIZABETH, actress; b. Lowell, Mass., Apr. 5, 1908; d. Harlow Morrell and Ruth (Favor) D.; m. Harmon Oscar Nelson, Jr., Aug. 18, 1932 (div.); m. Arthur Farnsworth, Dec. 1940 (dec. Aug. 25, 1943); m. William Grant Sherry, Nov. 30, 1945; 1 child, Barbara Davis; m. Gary Merrill, Aug. 1950 (div.); adopted children: Margot, Michael. Ed., Cushing Acad., Ashburnham, Mass. Began as motion picture actress, 1931; pictures include Dangerous (Acad. award Best Actress 1935), The Petrified Forest, Jezebel (Acad. award Best Actress 1938), Dark Victory, Juarez, The Old Maid, The Private Lives of Elizabeth and Essex, The Great Lie, The Bride Came C.O.D, All About Eve, 1950, Payment on Demand, 1951, Phone Call from a Stranger, 1952, The Star, 1953, The Virgin Queen, 1955, Storm Center, The Catered Affair, 1956, John Paul Jones, 1959, The Scapegoat, 1959, What Ever Happened to Baby Jane, Dead Ringer, Painted Canvas, 1963, Where Love Has Gone, Hush, Hush, Sweet Charlotte, 1964, The Nanny, The Anniversary, 1967, Connecting Rooms, 1969, Bunny O'Hare, 1970, Madam Sin, 1971, The Game, 1972, Burnt Offerings, 1977, Death on the Nile, 1979, Watcher in the Woods, 1979, The Whales of August, 1987; TV movies Sister Aimee, 1977, The Dark Secret of Harvest Home, 1978, Strangers (Emmy award 1979), White Momma, 1980, Skyward, 1980, Family Reunion, 1981, A Piano for Mrs. Cimino, 1982, Little Gloria-Happy at Last, 1982, Right of Way, 1983 (pilot) Hotel, 1983, Murder with Mirrors, 1984, As Summers Die, 1985; appeared in play The Night of the Iguana. Author: The Lonely Life, 1962; (with Michael Herskowitz) This 'N That, 1987; co-author: Mother Goddam, 1974. Recipient Am. Film Inst. Life Achievement award, Rudolph Valentino Life Achievement award, 1982, Am. Acad. Arts award, 1983, Disting. Pub. Service medal Dept. Def., 1983, Crystal award Women in Films, 1983, Cesar award French Film Inst., 1986, Order Arts et Belles Lettres, French Ministry Culture, 1986, Legion of Honor French Ministry Culture, 1987, Kennedy Ctr. Honors medallion, 1987. Office: care Gottlieb Schiff 555 Fifth Ave New York NY 10017 *

DAVIS, BETTY JEAN BOURBONIA, real estate investment executive; b. Ft. Bayard, N.Mex., Mar. 12, 1931; d. John Alexander and Ora M. (Caudill) Bourbonia; BS in Elem. Edn., U. N.Mex., 1954; children: Janice Ann Cox Plagge, Elizabeth Ora Cox. Gen. partner BJD Realty Co., Albuquerque, 1977—. Bd. dirs. Albuquerque Opera Guild, 1977-79, 81-83, 85-86, 86-87, membership co-chmn., 1977-79; mem. Friends of Art, 1978-85, Friends of Little Theatre, 1973-85, Mus. N.Mex. Found. Recipient Matrix award for journalism Jr. League. Mem. Albuquerque Mus. Assn., N.M. Hist. Soc., N.Mex. Symphony Guild, Jr. League Albuquerque, Alumni Assn. U. N.Mex. (dir. 1973-76), Mus. N.Mex. Found., Alpha Chi Omega (Beta Gamma Beta chpt., adv., bldg. corp. 1962-77). Republican. Methodist. Clubs: Tanoan Country. Lodges: Order Eastern Star, Order Rainbow for Girls (past grand worthy adv. N.Mex., past mother adv. Friendship Assembly 50). Home: 9505 Augusta NE Albuquerque NM 87111

DAVIS, BETTYE JEAN, academic administrator; b. Homer, La., May 17, 1938; d. Dan and Rosylind (Daniel) Ivory; m. Troy J. Davis, Jan. 21, 1959; children: Anthony B., Sonja D. Cert. nursing, St. Anthony's, 1961; BSW, Grambling State U., 1971. Asst. dir. San Bernardino (Calif.) YWCA, 1971-72; mental health worker Alaska Mental Hosp., Anchorage, 1972-75, child care specialist div. Social Service, 1975-80, foster care coordinator, 1980-86; bd. dirs. Anchorage Sch. Dist., 1982—. Bd. dirs. Alaska Black Caucus, Anchorage, 1980— (Polit. Awareness award 1984, Outstanding Woman in Edn. 1986), Office Pub. Advisors, 1986—, Nat. Black Caucus Black Sch. Bd. Mems., Washington, 1985—. Named Social Worker of Yr. Foster Parent Assn., 1980, Woman of Yr. Nat. Assn. Colored Women, 1981, Outstanding Woman in Edn. Zeta Phi Beta, 1985. Mem. Alaska Women Lobby (treas.), Delta Sigma Theta (Alaska chpt. pres. 1978-80). Democrat. Baptist. Club: North to Future Bus. and Profl. Women (past pres.). Home: 2240 Foxhall Dr Anchorage AK 99504

DAVIS, BILLIE JOHNSTON, school counselor; b. Charleston, W.Va., Sept. 24, 1933; d. William Andrew, Jr. and Garnet Macil (Johnston) D.; B.S., Morris Harvey Coll., Charleston, W.Va., 1954; M.A., W.Va. U., 1959. Tchr. math. Kanawha County schs., Charleston, 1954-59, counselor, 1959—; mem. public edn. study commn. W.Va. Legislature, 1980; mem. W.Va. Commn. on Juvenile Law, 1982—; bd. dirs. W.Va. Com. for Prevention Child Abuse, W.Va. Sch. Health Adv. Com. Recipient Anne Maynard award W.Va. Sch. Counselor Assn., 1986; named Am. mid./jr. high Sch. Counselor of Yr., 1987, Citizen of the Yr., Dunbar Lions Club. Mem. Am. Assn. Counseling and Devel., W.Va. Assn. Counseling and Devel. (pres. 1964-66, legis. chmn., 1974—; spl. award legis. services 1981), W.Va. Edn. Assn. (past legis. chmn.), Kanawha County Sch. Counselors Assn. (pres., legis. chmn. 1974—), Alpha Delta Kappa (past chpt. pres.), Phi Delta Kappa. Democrat. Baptist. Home: 12 Warren Pl Charleston WV 25302 Office: Dunbar Jr High Sch 1300 Myers Ave Dunbar WV 25064

DAVIS, CAROL LYN, research consultant; b. West Palm Beach, Fla., Oct. 22, 1953; d. Robert Lee and Barbara Jean (Collett) D. B.F.A., Tex. Christian U., Ft. Worth, 1975, M.A. in Am. Studies, 1977. Research and devel. product line designer Am. Handicrafts/Merribee Needlearts, Ft. Worth, 1977-81; ceramics/china sales cons. Dillard's, Ft. Worth, 1981-82, dept. mgr., 1981; dept. mgr. Stripling-Cox, Ft. Worth, 1982-83; freelance ceramic and string art designer, 1982-83; with phase III IV, V historic sites inventory of Tarrant County for Historic Preservation Council for Tarrant County (Tex.) and Page, Anderson & Turnbull, Inc., San Francisco, 1983-86; Tarrant County rep. Greater Ft. Worth Housing Starts, Texas Update, Inc., 1987—; mem. mgmt. adv. panel Chem. Week, 1981. Mem. Nat. Trust Historic Preservation, Ft. Worth Opera Assn., Royal Oak Found. Democrat. Episcopalian. Author pamphlets in field. Home: 7800 Garza Ave Fort Worth TX 76116 Office: Tex Update Inc 1221 W Campbell Rd Suite 291 Richardson TX 75080

DAVIS, CAROL LYNN, accountant; b. Orange, Calif., Mar. 8, 1963; d. Robert Stanley Davis and Patricia (Geiger) Griffo. BA, Calif. State U., Fullerton, 1988. Computer operator Graybar Electric, Los Angeles, 1981-82; clk. Tam's Stationers, Inc., Whitier, Calif., 1982-84; asst. dir. of tng. Tam's Books, Inc., Paramount, Calif., 1985, with promotions/advt., 1985-86; accounts receivable analyst McDonnell Douglas Fin. Corp., Long Beach, Calif., 1987-88; acct. Lance, Soll & Lunghard, Whittier, 1988—. Co-author: Tam's Beginning Employee's Training Manual, 1985. Mem. Nat. Assn. Accts., Alpha Delta Pi. Republican. Presbyterian. Lodge: Job's Daus. (pres. 1978-79, honored queen). Home: 10006 Melgar Dr Whittier CA 90603

DAVIS, CAROL MARIE PATTERSON, educator; b. Alexandria, La., Dec. 26, 1949; d. George Nelson and Marie (Travis) Patterson; m. Michael Lynwood Davis, Jan 15, 1972; 1 child, Bennett Lynwood. BS in Elem. Edn., La. State U., 1971; postgrad., U. North Fla. Elem. tchr. Caddo Parish Sch. Bd., Shreveport, La., 1971-72, Clay County Sch. Bd., Orange Park, Fla., 1972-79; asst. prin. Clay County Sch. Bd., Doctors Inlet, Fla., 1979-85; elem. tchr. Clay County Sch. Bd., Middleburg, Fla., 1985—. Sec. adv. com. Fleming Island Bd. County Commrs., Green Cove Springs, Fla., 1984—; mem. Jacksonville Panhellenic Soc., 1972—, United Meth. Women and Alter Guild, Orange Park, 1973—. Named one of Outstanding Tchrs. Am., 1975. Mem. NEA, Fla. Edn. Assn., Clay County Edn. Assn., Assn. Supervision and Curriculum Devel., Fla. Reading Assn., La. State U. Alumni Assn., Suzuki Music Assn. Am., Alpha Delta Kappa, Delta Gamma Alumni Assn. (pres. Jacksonville chpt. 1974-77). Republican. Methodist. Home: 345 W Shores Rd Orange Park FL 32073 Office: Clay County Sch Bd Gratio Pl Green Cove Springs FL 32043

DAVIS, CAROLYN LEIGH, psychotherapist; b. Houston, Mar. 18, 1936; d. William Harvey Speight and Veral Audra (Nunn) Speight Poole; m. John C. Rogers, June 22, 1957 (div. Nov. 1970); children: Elizabeth Leigh Porterfield, Rena Kathleen, John; m. L.B. Davis Sept. 14, 1972. Diploma in nursing, U. Houston, 1956; MSW, U. Denver, 1981; postgrad., Iliff Sch. Theology, 1987—. RN, Tex., Colo.; lic. social worker II, Colo.; cert. alcohol, drug counselor, Colo. Therapist Bethesda Mental Health Ctr., Denver, 1972-73; supr. emergency alcoholism services Denver Gen. Hosp., 1973-74; dir. alcoholism services Jefferson County Health Dept., Lakewood, Colo., 1974-78; pvt. practice psychotherapy Lakewood and Littleton, Colo., 1981—; adj. prof. Grad. Sch. Social Work, U. Denver, 1982—; cons. employee assistance program FAA, Longmont, Colo., 1984—; mem. adv. bd. Nurses of Colo., Denver, 1984—. Author: The Most Important Months of Your Child's Life: Fetal Alcohol Syndrome, 1976. Mem. Nat. Assn. Social Workers, Assn. Labor and Mgmt. Adminstrs. and Cons. on Alcoholism. Republican. Episcopalian. Office: 6909 S Holly Circle Suite 260 Englewood CO 80112 also: 720 Kipling Lakewood CO 80215

DAVIS, CHERYL MARIE, computer company executive; b. Winona, Minn., Dec. 30, 1945; d. George W. and Beverly F. (Cieminski) Wos; A.B. in English with honors in humanities, Stanford U., 1968; postgrad. Ga. State U., 1974-75, U. Tex., Austin, 1975-81; m. John Nicholas Davis, Aug. 24, 1985; child, Patrick Robert Davis; children by previous marriage—David Austin Russell, Timothy Francis George Russell, Cristi Lynn Traver, Pamela Cindy Traver. Programmer Fairchild Semiconductor, Mountain View, Calif., 1966-67; programming mgr. adminstrn. computing Stanford (Calif.) U., 1969-74; mgmt. info. systems dir. Ga. State U., Atlanta, 1974-75; software engring. mgr. INTEL, Austin, Tex., 1976-81, product mktg. mgr., 1982-84; dir. Wollongong Group, Palo Alto, Calif., 1985—; bd. dirs. Coll. and Univ. Systems Exchange, 1974-76, Info. Success Systems, 1972. Tchr. religious edn. St. Theresa Sch., 1976-78, St. Thomas More Sch., 1978-79, mem. fin. com. St. Thomas More, 1978-79. Recipient Bausch & Lomb award, 1964, Nat. Sci. Fair award, 1964. Mem. Phi Kappa Phi. Republican. Roman Catholic. Club: Stanford Alumni. Contbr. papers to profl. publs. and confs. Home: 1417 Fallen Leaf Ln Los Altos CA 94022 Office: Wollongong Group 1129 San Antonio Rd Palo Alto CA 94303

DAVIS, CHRISTINE SALKIN, market research executive; b. Los Angeles, Dec. 3, 1957; d. Arthur J. and Margaret (Moore) Salkin; m. Jerry Paul Davis, Feb. 14, 1987. BA in Communications, Va. Polytech. Inst., 1979; MBA, U. N.C., Greensboro, 1986—. Research asst. Horace Kelly & Assocs., Winston-Salem, N.C., 1980-81, project dir., 1981-82, research analyst, 1982, sr. analyst, 1982-83, v.p., 1983-87, exec. v.p., gen. mgr., 1987—; judge Nat. Agri-Mktg. Assn. awards, 1988. Vol. Samaritan Soup Kitchen, Winston-Salem, 1981-86; mem. young adult task force Moravian Ch., Winston-Salem, 1983-86. Mem. Am. Mktg. Assn. (Winston-Salem chpt. membership subcom.), Am. Mgmt. Assn. Office: Horace Kelly & Assocs 503 High St Winston-Salem NC 27101

DAVIS, COLEEN COCKERILL, educator; b. Pampa, Tex., Sept. 20, 1930; d. Charles Clifford and Myrtle Edith (Harris) Cockerill; m. Richard Harding Davis, June 22, 1952 (div. Dec. 1984); children: David Christopher, Denis Benjamin (dec. 1979). B.S., U. Okla., 1951; M.S., UCLA, 1952; postgrad. U. So. Calif., Whittier Coll., UCLA. Cert. tchr., Calif. Chmn, dept. home econs., tchr. Whittier Union High Sch. Dist., Calif., 1952-85; substitute tchr., 1985—; home tchr., 1985—, cons. 1986—; coHost America's Bed & Breakfast, Whittier, 1983—, also founder, pres., exec. dir. Contbr. articles to newspapers. Founder Children of Murdered Parents, Whittier, 1984, Coalition of Orgns. and People, Whittier, 1984, Whistle, Ltd., Whittier, 1984; chpt. leader Parents of Murdered Children, Whittier; mem. citizens' adv. bd. Fred C. Nelles Sch. Mem. Calif. Tchrs. Assn., NEA, Internat. Tour Mgmt. Inst., Whittier C. of C. (ambassador). Republican. Episcopalian. Avocation: volunteer worker. Office: CoHost America's Bed and Breakfast PO Box 9302 Whittier CA 90608

DAVIS, CYNTHIA GAIL, physician, naval officer; b. Cleve., Jan. 13, 1956; d. Donald B. and Joyce (Walters) Robertson; m. Martin Alex Davis, Apr. 10, 1980. B.A., UCLA, 1978; M.D., Uniformed Services U., 1982. Commd. ensign U.S. Navy, 1978, advanced through grades to lt. comdr., 1986; staff physician Br. Hosp., U.S. Marine Corps, Twenty Nine Palms, Calif., 1983-84; med./surg. intern U.S. Naval Hosp., San Diego, 1982-83, postdoctoral tng. in head and neck surgery, 1984—; med. officer Clinic/Hdqrs. Bn., U.S. Marine Corps Air Ground Combat Ctr., 1983-84; organizer, com. mem. biology of cancer program UCLA, 1978; vol. Cystic Fibrosis Clinic, UCLA, 1977-78. Latter Day Saints Hosp. research fellow, 1977. Mem. AMA, Assn. Mil. Surgeons U.S., Am. Acad. Otolaryngology, Am. Acad. Facial Plastic and Reconstructive Surgery, Alpha Phi. Democrat. Presbyterian. Home: 2377 Ron Way San Diego CA 92123 Office: US Naval Hosp Dept Otolaryngology San Diego CA 92134

DAVIS, DAISY SIDNEY, educator; b. Bay City, Tex., Nov. 7, 1944; d. Alex. C. and Alice M. (Edison) Sidney; m. John Dee Davis, Apr. 17, 1968; children—Anaca Michelle, Lowell Kent. BS, Bishop Coll., 1966; MS, East Tex. State U., 1971; MEd, Prairie View A&M and Mech., 1980. Cert. lifetime elem. tchr., Tex.; mid-mgmt. administrator. Tchr., Dallas pub. schs., 1966—. Coordinator, Get Out the Vote campaign, Dallas, 1972, 80, 84, 88. Recipient Outstanding Tchr. award Dallas pub. schs., 1980, Jack Lowe award for ednl. excellence, 1982; Free Enterprise scholar So. Meth. U., 1987; Constitutionalism fellow U. Dallas, 1988; named to Hall of Fame, Holmes Acad., 1979. Mem. NEA, Tex. State Tchrs. Assn., Classroom Tchrs. Dallas (faculty rep. 1971-77), Dallas County History Tchrs., Afro-Am. Daus. Republic of Tex. (founder), Zeta Phi Beta. Democrat. Baptist. Club: Jack & Jill, (Dallas) (rec. sec., v.p.). Home: 1302 Mill Stream Dr Dallas TX 75232 Office: 9339 S Polk St Dallas TX 75232

DAVIS, DENISE, controller; b. Phila., Oct. 18, 1954; d. Irvin and Frances Louise (Outlaw) Jackson. B in Acctg., Rutgers U., 1986. Rater personal lines CIGNA Corp., Phila., 1972-75; asst. to underwriters Rollins Burdick Hunter of Pa., Phila., 1976-78, acct. clk., 1978-80, sec. to treas., 1980-81, asst. to treas., 1981-82, controller, 1981—. Office: Rollins Burdick Hunter of Pa 756 Public Ledger Bldg Philadelphia PA 19106

DAVIS, DIANA GAIL, real estate executive; b. Buffalo, Sept. 9, 1943; d. William Leonard and Rosalie (Kilgore) Levay; m. John Keith Davis; children: Mark, Nicole, Robin. BS in English, U. Buffalo, 1964. Property mgr. The Sales Corp., Buffalo, 1970-78, Oxford Devel. Co., Pitts., 1978-85, Gold & Co., Inc., Pitts., 1985-87; dir. property mgmt. and leasing Wilkensburg Real Estate and Ins. Agy., Pitts., 1988—. Editor Pioneer Community Newspaper, Columbus, Ohio, 1969. Vol. Spl. Olympics, Pitts., 1978—; speaker, fund raiser Make A Wish Found. Western Pa.; mem. adv. bd. human needs and resources Municipality of Monroeville, Pa., 1988-91. Mem. Nat. Assn. Female Execs., Nat. Writers Club. Republican. Home: 1304 Woodland Dr Monroeville PA 15146 Office: Wilkensburg Real Estate and Ins Agy 1001 Wood St Pittsburgh PA 15221

DAVIS, (ALICE) DIANE WILCOX, retail executive, designer, consultant; b. Chgo., Jan. 10, 1937; d. Charles Albert and Alice-Diane (Kjellander) Wilcox; m. James Barnhart Lohr, Sept. 1, 1956 (div. 1971); m. Jean-Pierre Alexandre Radley, Aug. 30, 1973 (div. 1981); m. Richard Manchester Davis, Nov. 24, 1982; children—Alice-Diane Wilcox Lohr, Valerie Barnhart Lohr. Student Brown U., 1954-56. Asst. buyer couture, Gidding-Jenny Stores, Cin., 1968-69, buyer, 1969-71; buyer couture, Neiman-Marcus Stores, Dallas, 1971-73, Saks Fifth Ave., N.Y.C., 1973-78; v.p. wholesale-retail and pub. relations, Julio, Inc., N.Y.C., 1978-79; mgmt. cons., San Miguel De Allende, Mexico, 1979—; ptnr., designer (couture clothing) Per las de San Miguel, San Miguel de Allende, 1977—. Bd. dirs., chmn. endowment fund Centro De Crecimiento, San Miguel de Allende, 1984-85; pres. bd. dirs. La Fiesta Internacional de San Miguel Allende; chmn. La Fiesta 86, La Fiesta 87, San Miguel Ednl. Found.; bd. dirs., chmn. fundraising com. Soc. Protectora de Animales, 1987, 88, Mexican Red Cross, 1988, Patronata Pro Nino's. 1988-89. Mem. Brown U. Alumni Assn. (v.p. Cin. chpt. 1968-71). Recipient Gracias award, 1987. Avocations: bridge, skiing, Mah Jongg, breeding kitas. Address: APDO 418, San Miguel de Allende, Guanajuato Mexico 37700

DAVIS, DIXIE JO RETHERFORD, foundation administrator; b. Russiaville, Ind., Nov. 23, 1943; d. John Morris and Julia Iva (Hickman) Retherford; m. Kenneth L. Davis, Aug. 30, 1963 (div. 1983). BA, U. Colo., Boulder, 1965; MA, U. No. Colo., 1975, EdD, 1982. Probation officer Denver Juvenile Ct., 1965-67, Wyandotte County Juvenile Ct., Kansas City, Kans., 1967-70; social worker Luth. Social Services, Milw., 1970-73; rehab. counselor Services for the Blind, Denver, 1973-76; coordinator Luth. Social Services, Denver, 1976-79; dir. Adoption Resource Ctr., Denver, 1979-81; founder, exec. dir. Rocky Mountain Adoption Exchange, Denver, 1983—, also bd. dirs.; instr. Community Coll. Aurora, Colo., 1982—; pub. speaker, cons., psychotherapist, trainer Profl. Psychol. Assocs., Denver, 1982—; cons. Wyo. Childrens Soc., Cheyenne, 1985-86; trainer Adrienne Hynes Assn., Denver, 1985—; mem. adv. bd. Nat. Resource Ctr. for Adoption. Contr. articles to profl. jours. Bd. dirs. Adult Blind Home, Denver. Mem. AAUW, Adoption Exchange Assn. (pres.). Democrat. Mem. Soc. Friends. Club: Quota. Office: Rocky Mountain Adoption Exchange 5350 Leetsdale Dr Suite 10 Denver CO 80222

DAVIS, DORINNE SUE TAYLOR LOVAS, audiologist; b. East Orange, N.J., Mar. 29, 1949; d. William Henry and Evelyn Doris (Thorp) Taylor; BA, Montclair State Coll., 1971, MA, 1973; m. Warren B. Davis, Jr., Aug. 10, 1985; children—Larissa Louise, Peter Alexander. Ednl. audiologist Morris County Coll., Dover, N.J., 1974-75, Kinnelon (N.J.) Bd. Edn., 1972—, Inst. for Career Advancement, Inc., 1980-82, Dover Gen. Hosp., 1984—; pres. Hear You Are. Cert. tchr. of hearing impaired, speech correctionist, tchr. speech and drama N.J. Dept. Edn.; nursery sch. endorsement. Mem. NEA, Internat. Orgn. Educators Hearing Impaired, Am. Speech and Hearing Assn. (cert. of clin. competence in audiology), Alexander Graham Bell Assn. (pres.), N.J. Speech and Hearing Assn., Morris County Speech and Hearing Assn., N.J. Edn. Assn., Morris County Edn. Assn., Kinnelon Edn. Assn., Self Help for the Hard of Hearing, Ednl. Audiology Assn. (pres. elect). Methodist. Home: 4 Musconetcong Ave Stanhope NJ 07874 Office: Kinnelon Bd Edn Spl Services Kiel Ave Kinnelon NJ 07405

DAVIS, DOROTHY SALISBURY, author; b. Chgo., Apr. 26, 1916; d. Alfred Joseph and Margaret Jane (Greer) Salisbury; m. Harry Davis, Apr. 25, 1946. A.B., Barat Coll., Lake Forest, Ill., 1938. Mystery and hist. novelist, short story writer. Author: A Gentle Murderer, 1951, A Town of Masks, 1952, Men of No Property, 1956, Death of an Old Sinner, 1957, A Gentleman Called, 1958, The Evening of the Good Samaritan, 1961, Black Sheep, White Lamb, 1963, The Pale Betrayer, 1965, Enemy and Brother, 1967, God Speed The Night, 1968, Where the Dark Streets Go, 1969, Shock Wave, 1972, The Little Brothers, 1973, A Death in the Life, 1976, Scarlet Night, 1980, A Lullaby of Murder, 1984, Tales for a Stormy Night, 1985, The Habit of Fear, 1987. Mem. Authors Guild, Mystery Writers of Am. (former pres., recipient Grand Master award 1985). Home: Palisades NY 10964

DAVIS, ELISE MILLER (MRS. LEO M. DAVIS), author; b. Corsicana, Tex., Oct. 12, 1915; d. Moses Myre and Rachelle (Daniels) Miller; student U. Tex., 1930-31; m. Jay Albert Davis, June 27, 1937 (dec. June 1973); 1 dau., Rayna Miller (Mrs. Michael Edwin Loeb); m. 2d, Leo M. Davis, Aug. 23, 1974. Freelance writer, 1945—; merchandiser and dir. Jay Davis, Inc., Amarillo, Tex., 1956-73; instr. mag. writing U. Tex., Dallas, 1978; lectr. creative writing Baylor U., Waco, Tex., 1980, 81, 83. Mem. Am. Soc.

Journalists and Authors (bd. dirs. 1985). Author: The Answer Is God, 1955; articles to periodicals including Reader's Digest, Woman's Day, Nation's Business, others. Home: 3906 Old Mill Rd Waco TX 76710

DAVIS, ELIZABETH ANN, city official; b. Kansas City, Mo., Jan. 16, 1941; d. Samuel Wyatt Jr. and Maurita Bell (Irick) Driggers; m. Roy Edward Davis Jr., July 1, 1957; children: Scott Edward, Catherine Elizabeth, Christopher Kelly, Sean Wyatt. Student polit. sci., U. Tex., Arlington. Cert. mcpl. clk., Tex. Sec. First Nat. Bank, Ft. Worth, 1966-69; office mgr. City of Luling, Tex., 1972-73; adminstrv. sec. State of Tex., Austin, 1973-74; office coordinator City of Arlington, Tex., 1974-77; city sec. City of Granbury, Tex., 1977-83, City of Bedford, Tex., 1983—; adv. mem. mcpl. records project Tex. State Library, Austin, 1984—. V.p. Greater Green Valley Home Owners Assn., 1987—. Mem. Tex. Assn. of Elections Adminstrs., Assn. City Clks. and Secs. of Tex. (chair resolutions com. 1984, mem. retirement com. 1985, mem. legis. com. 1987), Internat. Inst. Mcpl. Clks. (cert. Advanced Acad., state mem. chmn. 1986—, conf. com. 1987, profl. status com., 1984—, fed. legis. com., 1985—, chair membership com. 1987—), North Tex. City Secs. Assn. (sec.-treas. 1985, v.p. 1986, pres. 1987), Nat. Assn. for Court Mgmt., Tex. Assn. for Ct. Adminstrn., Bedford C. of C. (crime prevention com. 1987—). Methodist. Avocations: music, gardening, reading, tennis, cooking. Home: 7720 Aubrey Ln North Richland Hills TX 76180 Office: City of Bedford PO Box 157 Bedford TX 76021

DAVIS, ELIZABETH ANN, telephone company maintenance administrator; b. Kansas City, Mo., June 5, 1950; d. Wayne Ruppert Jr. and Norine (French) Perkins; m. Frederick David Adamson, Jan. 1, 1970 (div. Feb. 1973); children: Shane Frederick, Shawnda Elizabeth. Constrn. supr. Southwestern Bell, Kansas City, Kans., 1976-77; mgmt. ctr. supr. Southwestern Bell, Kansas City, 1976-77, staff mgr. constrn. quality, 1977-79, mgr. placing, outside plant constrn., 1979-80, mgr. of splicing outside plant constrn., 1980-82; mgr. of placing, splicing outside plant constrn. Southwestern Bell, Topeka, 1982-85, mgr. outside plant maintenance, 1985-87, area mgr. installation and repair div. staff, 1987—. Mem. Am. Bus. Women's Assn., Nat. Assn. Female Execs. Office: Southwestern Bell 220 E 6th Suite 200B Topeka KS 66602

DAVIS, ELIZABETH EMILY LOUISE THORPE, visual psychophysicist, computer scientist; b. Grosse Pointe Farms, Mich., Aug. 11, 1948; d. Jack and Mary Alvina (McCarron) Thorpe; student U. Calif.-Irvine, 1966-69; B.S., U. Ala., 1972; M.A., Columbia U., 1975, M.Phil., 1976, Ph.D., 1979, M.S. in Computer Sci., 1987; m. Ronald Wilson Davis, May 16, 1969. Lectr. Am. Lit. and English composition Nei Ming Inst., Lamtin, Hong Kong, 1969-71; research fellow Columbia U., 1973-77; postdoctoral fellow N.Y.U., 1979-81, adj. asst. prof., 1981; asst. prof. exptl. psychology Oberlin (Ohio) Coll., 1981-82; research asst. prof., mem. grad. faculty Inst. for Vision Research, SUNY Coll. Optometry, 1983-87; assoc. prof. dept. visual scis., 1987—. Recipient Nat. Research Services award; fellow Hertz Found., 1983; NIH grantee, 1979-81, 84—; grantee Sigma Xi, 1979, Oberlin Coll., 1981. Mem. AAAS, Am. Psychol. Assn., Assn. Research Vision and Ophthalmology, Soc. Neurosci., Optical Soc. Am. (co-feature editor jour. 1987), N.Y. Acad. Scis., Psychonomic Soc., Sigma Xi, Pi Mu Epsilon. Author papers in field. Office: SUNY Coll Optometry 100 E 24th St New York NY 10010

DAVIS, EMMA-JO LEVEY, government executive; b. Greensboro, N.C., June 5, 1932; d. Harry Nelson and Alma (Snellen) Levey; m. Andrew Jackson Davis Jr., July 3, 1957 (div. July 1977); children: Anne Stone, Kelsie Lee. Student, Mary Washington Coll., 1949-51; AB, U. N.C., 1953; MEd, Coll. William and Mary, 1969. Tchr. local pub. schs., Gloucester, Va., 1959-61; editor U.S. Army, Ft. Eustis, Va., 1961-63, historian, 1963-67, curator Transp. Mus., 1967-80; chief curator U.S. Army, Washington, 1980—. Author: History of the U.S. Army Transportation Corps, 1967, History of the U.S. Army Transportation School, 1967. Mem. Am. Assn. Mus., Am. Assn. State and Local History, Nat. Geneal. Soc., Mensa, Council on Mil. Mus. Am. (vice chmn. 1983—). Episcopalian. Home: 309 Yoakum Pkwy #1415 Alexandria VA 22304 Office: US Army Ctr Mil History 20 Massachusetts Ave NW Washington DC 20314

DAVIS, EUNICE BEATRICE, health services administrator; b. Murphy, N.C., Feb. 11, 1936; d. William Albert Edna Mae (Martin) Hedden; m. Wallace Blackwell Davis, Aug. 26, 1960; children: Sandy, Richard, James. Student, Tri County Community Coll., 1983. With Bershire Knitting Mills, Andrew, N.C., 1959-64, Magnavox (now Baker Furniture), Andrew, 1964-67; co-adminstr. Carolina Rest Homes, Andrew, 1973—; adminstr. Davis Family Care Home, Andrew, 1986—; activity coordinator Carolina Rest Homes, Andrews, N.C., 1973—. Mem. N.C. Assn. Long Term Care Facilities (cert.), Nat. Assn. Residential Care Facilities. Republican. Baptist. Home: PO Box 671 Andrews NC 28901 Office: Carolina Rest Homes PO Box AN Andrews NC 28901

DAVIS, EVA THOMAS, civic worker; b. Ash Grove, Mo., Sept. 20, 1905; d. Charles and Ida Mae (Moser) Thomas; m. Paul D. Davis, Dec. 9, 1944. BS, Southwestern Mo. State, 1925; M, Northwestern U., 1939. Tchr., prin. Mo. Pub. Schs., 1925-40; various positions, personnel mgmt. specialist Dept. Health, Edn. and Welfare, Washington, 1940-69. Mem. Pres.' Com. on Employment of Handicapped, Washington, 1958-61, appointed White House Conf. on Aging, Washington, 1981; apptd. Long-Term Care Ombudsman Council, Tampa, Fla., chmn. council, 1986—; co-founder, bd. dirs, advocacy coordinator Alzheimers Disease Inc. of Manatee/Sarasota, Fla., 1982—; bd. dirs. West Cen. Fla. Area Agy. on Aging, Tampa, 1983—, H.O.P.E. of Manatee Inc., Bradenton, Fla., 1982-88; charter mem. Total Care Am., Inc.; apptd. supt. schs. Manatee County Affirmative Action, 1986; vol. elderly services, 1978-84. Named Outstanding Sr. Vol. of Yr. Manatee County, 1986, Citizen of Day Sta. WQSA Radio; recipient Good Neighbor award Nat. Conf. Christians and Jews. Mem. Fla. Silver-Haired Legis. (elected 1981—, speaker of house 1984-85, chmn. bd. dirs.), Internat. Fedn. on Aging, Nat. Council on Aging, Am. Soc. on Aging, So. Gerontological Assn., Fla. Council on Aging, AAUW (pres. 1977-79, Outstanding award), Am. Assn. Retired Persons, Nat. Assn. Retired Fed. Ees, People's Med. Soc., Common Cause, LWV, Library Found. Democrat. Episcopalian. Clubs: Bradenton Country (pres. women's golf 1980-82), Plaza. Home: 6303 Sun Eagle Ln Bradenton FL 34210

DAVIS, EVELYN CADENHEAD, human resource executive; b. Commerce, Tex., July 29, 1948; d. Orville Lavern and Mary Kathryn (Rogers) C.; m. John Maynard Davis, Feb. 9, 1973; children: Lauren Mary, Megan Elizabeth. BA, Mary Hardin-Baylor U., 1969; MA, North Tex. State U., 1972; MBA, U. Dallas, 1983. From flight attendant to mgr. centralized tng. Am. Airlines, Dallas, N.Y.C. and Chgo., 1972-80; co-owner Patt Walker Assoc., Dallas, 1980-81; mgr. mgmt. tng. Surgikos, Arlington, Tex., 1981-82; in-flight dir. Continental Airlines, Houston, 1982-83; dir. compensation and benefits Sky Chefs, Inc., Arlington, 1983-87; dir. corp. human resources Volume Shoe Corp., Topeka, 1987—; benefits cons. Child Care Dallas, 1987. Mem. Am. Soc. Personnel Assocs., Am. Compensation Assn. Office: Volume Shoe Corp 3231 E 6th St Topeka KS 66601

DAVIS, EVELYN CLEVELAND, academic administrator; b. Seneca, S.C., Aug. 12, 1934; d. James Benjamin and Evelyn Rebecca (Reaves) Cleveland; m. Richard L. Davis, Aug. 19, 1958 (div. 1970); children: Mark, Stuart, Carolyn. BA, Furman U., 1956; MA in Teaching, Converse Coll., 1969; EdD, Auburn U., 1975. Tchr. high sch. Ky., N.C., Tex. and S.C., 1956-65; reading specialist Denver Pub. Schs., 1966-67; chmn. dept. reading Fulmer Jr. High Sch., West Columbia, S.C., 1967-70; head dept. adult edn., instl. services Midlands TEC, Columbia, S.C., 1970-73; dir. master's program in adult edn. Memphis State U., 1975-77; dir. master's program in adult edn., learning assistance service U. N.C. Charlotte, 1977—; cons. adult edn., Charlotte, 1977—. Editor jour. Living for Learning Modules, 1977; contbr. articles to profl. jours., 1975-86. Auburn U. fellow. Mem. AAUP, Acad. Excellence Leadership Forum, Assn. Tchr. Educators, Adult Edn. Assn., Council Women Edn. Adminstrn. Republican. Lutheran. Office: U NC Charlotte Atkins 32 UNCC Sta Charlotte NC 28223

DAVIS, FLOREA JEAN, social worker; b. Crossett, Ark., Jan. 10, 1953; d. Richard Davis and Geneva (Bedford) Williams. BA in Psychology and Social Work cum laude, Park Coll., Parksville, Mo., 1975; MSW, Kans. U., 1982. Cert. tchr. social studies secondary level, lic. social worker, Kans. Asst dir. Northeast Counseling and Devel. Ctr., Kansas City, Kans., 1973, asst. dir., clin. supr. DRAG Alcohol Ctr., Kansas City, 1975-83; substance abuse counselor Johnson County Substance Abuse Ctr., Shawnee, Kans., 1983-85; clin. social worker Family & Children Services, Inc., Kansas City, 1975-88; area mgr. Agy. Heart of Am. Family Services, Kansas City, 1988—; agy.'s field practicum instr. U. Kans., Lawrence, 1976; substance abuse specialist, cons., Kansas City area, 1985—; part time instr. Avila Coll., Kansas City, Mo., 1987—. Vol. United Way Speakers Bur., 1986—. Mem. Acad. Cert. Social Workers, Nat. Assn. Female Execs., Nat. Assn. Social Workers (clin. diplomat). Home: 1529 N 29th St Apt 10 Kansas City KS 66102 Office: Heart of Am Family Services 5424 State Ave Kansas City KS 66102

DAVIS, FRANCES KAY, lawyer; b. Phila., Apr. 1, 1952; d. Francis Kaye and Ida May (Lamplugh) D. B.A., Mount Holyoke Coll., 1974; MA, Duke U., 1976; JD, Villanova U., 1983-86. Legal asst. Cozen, Begier & O'Connor, Phila., 1982-83; summer assoc. Montgomery, McCracken, Walker & Roads, Phila., 1985, assoc., 1986—. Served to capt. USAF, 1977-82. Recipient Welsh Soc. of Phila. scholar, 1984-85. Mem. ABA, Pa. Bar Assn., N.J. Bar Assn., Phila. Bar Assn.,Trial Lawyers Assn. (Trial Advocacy award, Phila. chpt., 1986).

DAVIS, FRANCES M., lawyer, corporate executive; b. 1925. Grad., UCLA, 1946; JD, U. Calif., Berkeley, 1953. Bar: Calif. 1954. Ptnr. LeProhn & LeProhn, 1960-67; asst. dean Earl Warren Legal Ctr. Calif. Coll. Trial Judges, 1968-72; assoc. Pillsbury, Madison & Sutro, 1972-75; v.p., gen. counsel Potlach Corp., San Francisco, 1975—; mem. Pvt. Industry Council of San Francisco. Bd. overseers U. Calif., San Francisco; mem. adv. bd. Sta. KOIT, San Francisco. Office: Potlatch Corp 1 Maritime Plaza PO Box 3591 San Francisco CA 94111

DAVIS, GWENDOLYN PICKLESIMER (GWEN), foundation administrator; b. Brevard, N.C., June 27, 1940; d. Louis Emory and Linda (Edney) Picklesimer; m. Charles Alfred Davis, June 9, 1962. Student, Mars Hill Coll., 1958-60; BA, Meredith Coll., 1962. Acctg. clk. N.C. State Hwy. Commn., Raleigh, 1962-63; bookkeeper Meredith Coll., Raleigh, 1963-65, chief acct., 1965-71; loan officer Coll. Found. Inc., Raleigh, 1971-73, dir. loan adminstrn., 1973-75, program adminstr., 1975-80, dir. program, 1980-82, dir. resource mgmt., 1982-83, adminstrv. dir., 1983-85, sr. v.p., 1985—. Mem. N.C. Hist. Preservation Found., Raleigh. Mem. Nat. Council of Higher Edn. Loan Programs (sec. 1973-75, program ops. com. 1978—), N.C. Assn. Student Fin. Aid Adminstrs., Meredith Coll. Alumnae Assn., Mars Hill Coll. Alumni Assn. Democrat. Presbyterian. Home: 1422 Ridge Rd Raleigh NC 27607 Office: Coll Found Inc 2100 Yonkers Rd Raleigh NC 27604

DAVIS, HELEN ANN PATRICIA, physician, ophthalmologist; b. Detroit, May 14, 1953; d. Garbe and Ethel (Jones) D.; m. William McKinley Parham III, Nov. 29, 1986. BS, U. Mich., 1974; MD, Tufts U., 1978. Diplomate Am. Bd. Ophthalmology. Intern Faulkner Hosp., Boston, 1980-81; ophthalmologist Internat. Med. Ctr., Miami Beach, Fla., 1982-83; resident Bascom Palmer Eye Inst. at U. Miami (Fla.) Med. Ctr., 1981-82; fellow Katzen Eye Group, Balt., 1983-84; assoc. chief ophthalmology Wyman Park Health Systems, Balt., 1985—. Fellow Internat. Coll. Surgeons, Am. Coll. Surgeons, Am. Acad. Ophthalmology; mem. AMA, Soc. Geriatric Ophthalmologists, Pitts. Ophthal Soc., Md. Soc. Eye Physicians and Surgeons, Balt. City Med. Soc. Roman Catholic. Office: Davis Eye Group 508 S Church St Mount Pleasant PA 15666

DAVIS, HELEN GORDON, state legislator; b. N.Y.C., Dec. 25; d. Harry Gordon and Doree Gordon; B.A., Bklyn. Coll.; postgrad. U. South Fla., 1967-70; m. Gene Davis; children—Stephanie, Karen, Gordon. Tchr., High Sch. Commerce, N.Y.C., Hillsborough High Sch., Tampa, Fla.; grad. asst. U. South Fla., 1968; mem. Fla. Ho. of Reps., 1974—, vice chmn. appropriations com., chmn. state employee pay and benefits com. Jud. chmn. Local Govt. Study Commn. Hillsborough County (Fla.), 1964; mem. Tampa Commn. on Juvenile Delinquency, 1966-69, Mayor's Citizens Adv. Com., 1966-69, Quality Edn. Commn., 1966-68, Gov.'s Citizen Com. for Ct. Reform, 1972, Hillsborough County Planning Commn., 1973-74; mem. Gov.'s Commn. on Jud. Reform, 1976; mem. employment com. Commn. Community Relations, 1966-69; by-laws chmn. Arts Council Tampa, 1971-74; 1st v.p. Tampa Symphony Guild, 1974; bd. dirs. U. South Fla. Found., 1968-74, Stop Rape, 1973-74; founder Ctr. for Women, Tampa, 1978. Recipient U. South Fla. Young Democrats Humanitarian award, 1974; Diana award NOW, 1975, Woman of Achievement in Arts award Tampa, 1975; Tampa Human Relations award, 1976, Hannah G. Solomon Citizen of Yr. award, 1980, St. Petersburg Times/Fla. Civil Liberties award, 1980, Friend of Edn. award, 1981, Fla. Network of Runaway Youth award, 1985, Ctr. for Women Leader-advocate Friend award, 1985, Nat. Assn. Juvenile Ct. Judges Appreciation award 1986, Martin Luther King award City of Tampa, 1988. Mem. LWV (pres. Hillsborough County 1966-69, lobbyist, Fla. adminstrn. of justice chmn. 1969-74), PTA (past pres.), Temple Guild Sisterhood (past pres.), Am. Arbitration Assn. Home: 45 Adalia Ave Tampa FL 33606 Office: 178 E Davis Blvd Tampa FL 33602

DAVIS, HELEN NANCY MATSON (MRS. CHAUNCEY D. DAVIS), real estate broker, civic worker; b. Zanesville, Ohio, Nov. 18, 1905; d. Austin F. and Georgianna (Hale) Matson; grad. high sch.; m. Chauncey D. Davis, May 1, 1924; children—James Harvey, Robert Lee. Real estate broker, South Bend, Wash., 1964—. Chmn. Park Bd., South Bend, 1955—; ofcl. Pacific County Bicentennial Pageant, Dedication Ft. Columbia, 1959; trustee Pacific County Hist. Soc. Named Woman of Yr. Pacific County C. of C., 1949, 61. Mem. Nat. League Am. Pen Women, Dramatists Guild Inc., Propaelaeum Study Club, Chinook Indian Tribe (hon.), The Dramatist Guild N.Y., Nat. League Am. Pen Women, Delta Kappa Gamma (hon.). Republican. Methodist. Rebekah. Club: Garden (South Bend). Composer: Washington, My Home (ofcl. state song Wash.), 1959; Eliza and the Lumberjack (mus. play) (ofcl. territorial centennial play Wash.), 1954. Home: 606 W 2d St South Bend WA 98586 Office: 705 Robert Bush Dr South Bend WA 98586

DAVIS, INGER PEDERSEN, social work educator; b. Holstebro, Denmark, Oct. 16, 1927; came to U.S., 1961; naturalized, 1970; d. Niels Aage and Ansine Wilhelmine (Larsen) Pedersen; m. Kenneth Culp Davis, 1962. BS, Statens Kursus, Copenhagen, 1948; MSW, Copenhagen Sch. Social Work, 1952; MA (U.N. fellow), U. Chgo., 1962, PhD, 1972. Dir. reference library dept. Social Affairs, Copenhagen, 1954-59; lectr. Copenhagen Sch. Social Work, 1959-61, research asst., textbook writer, 1962-64; parent counselor, caseworker Chgo. Child Care Soc., 1965-67; lectr. then asst. prof. sch. social service adminstrn. U. Chgo., 1971-76; mem. faculty sch. social work San Diego State U., 1977—, prof. social work, 1981—, also bd. dirs. found.; mem. regional steering com. Child Welfare Tng. Ctr., UCLA, 1979-82; bd. dirs. San Diego County Commn. Children and Youth. Author Adolescents Theoretical and Helping Perspectives; contbr. articles to profl. jours. Fulbright fellow, 1956, 61-62; Fed. Child Welfare Teaching grantee, 1977-82. Mem. Internat. Assn. Schs. Social Work, Council Social Work Edn., Nat. Assn. Social Workers. Office: San Diego State U San Diego CA 92182

DAVIS, JACQUELINE MARIE VINCENT (MRS. LOUIS REID DAVIS), child development educator, academic administrator; b. Birmingham, Ala.; d. Jud Fred and Marie (Yates) Vincent; m. Louis Reid Davis, July 17, 1943. A.B. cum laude, Birmingham So. Coll., 1943; M.A., Columbia, U., 1950; M.S., U. Ala., 1958, Ed.D., 1961; postgrad., U. Va., George Washington U. Tchr. Fork Union (Va.) Mil. Acad., 1943-46; tchr. Fork Union (Va.) Mil. Acad., Ft. Belvoir, Va., 1946-48; tchr., adminstrv. asst., supr. Quantica (Va.) Post schs., 1950-52; instr., prof. dept. child devel. and family life U. Ala. Sch. Home Econs., 1952-57, assoc. prof., 1957-67; prof. child devel., dir. U. Ala. Sch. Home Econs. (Child Devel. Ctr.), 1967—, mem. grad. council, adminstr. head start tng. program, dir. U. Ala. Sch. Home Econs. (Ala. Presch. Inst.), 1964—; mem. NASA scholarship selection bd. U. Ala., 1966; mem. Gov.'s Advisory Com. on Day Care, 1963-66, State Adv. Com. on Children and Youth, 1960—; coordinator Head Start supplementary tng. programs State of Ala. Contbr. articles to profl. jours. Adviser, mem. selection com. Tombigbee council Girl Scouts U.S.A., 1961-66; cons. Tuscaloosa Community Action Program, 1965-66; chmn. Ala. Advisory Com. Children and Youth 1978—. Mem. Nat. Assn. for Edn. of Young Children (mem. planning bd. 1963-64), U.S. Nat. Com. for Early Childhood Edn., World Orgn. for Early Childhood Edn., Southeastern Council Family Relations, So. Assn. Children Under Six (pres. 1961, mem. exec. bd. 1961—, chmn. 19th ann. conf.), Ala. Assn. Children Under Six (pres. 1963-64), Ala. Home Econs. Assn. (chmn. profl. sect. family life and child devel. 1963—, v.p. mem. governing bd. 1969-70), Comparative Edn. Soc., NEA, Am. Home Econs. Assn., Phi Beta Kappa, Kappa Delta Pi, Kappa Delta Epsilon. Methodist. Home: 47 Guilds Wood Tuscaloosa AL 35401 Office: PO Box 1211 University AL 35486

DAVIS, JENNIFER LOUISE BERG, university admissions counselor; b. Buffalo, May 19, 1955; d. Roger Martin and JoAnne (Bennett) Berg. BS in Gen. Family Resources, W.Va. U., 1976. Exec. trainee, staff asst. Bloomingdale's Dept. Store, Bethesda, Md., 1977-81, dept. mgr., 1981-84, employment mgr., 1984-85; admissions counselor Pa. State U., Mont Alto, 1985—, residence hall coordinator, 1985-86. Mem. Nat. Assn. for Female Execs., Pa. Coll. Personnel Assn., Pa. Assn. of Coll. Admission Counselors. Office: Pa State U Mont Alto PA 17237

DAVIS, JO ANN MARIE, educator; b. Pueblo, Colo., Sept. 24, 1956; d. Elias J. and Yolanda J. (Portlock) Umali; m. James K. Davis, July 29, 1984. AA, Columbia Union Coll., Takoma Park, Md., 1978, BS, 1978. Cert. elem. tchr., Ill., Md., Va. Tchr. Ill. Conf. Sch. Dist., Brookfield, 1978-87, Springfield (Va.) Acad., 1987, Fairfax County Pub. Schs., 1987—. Also: Lynbrook Elem Sch 5801 Backlick Rd Springfield VA 22151

DAVIS, JOANNE HERRING, foreign service officer, consultant; b. San Antonio; d. W. Dunlap and Maelan McGill (Johnson); m. Robert R. Herring (dec.); children—Beau S. King, Robin D. King, Ed., U. Tex. TV talk show hostess, editor Sta. KHOU TV, Houston, 1963-72, Sta. KPRC-TV, Houston, 1973-75; hon. consul gen. Pakistan and Morocco, Houston, 1973—; cons. LTV, WEDTECH, CONTRAVES; bd. dirs. First Bank Houston, Coronado Oil Co., Kittinger Furniture, Internat. Films Prodns. Inc.; hostess numerous fgn. ministers, princes, ambassadors including Kings of Sweden, Jordan, Morocco, Pres. of Egypt, Pres. of Pakistan, Shah of Iran, Prime Minister of Belgium, Houston. Knighted, King of Belgium; Decorated, Pres. Pakistan. Bd. dirs. Lindbergh Fund, Moroccan Am. Found., Houston Ballet, Houston Youth Symphony. Republican. Presbyterian. Clubs: Lyford Cay; Met. (N.Y.C.); Rivers Oaks Country, Ramada, Houston.

DAVIS, JOYCE NADEAN, librarian; b. Marshall, Mo., Oct. 10, 1941; d. Irvine Woodrow and Nona Myrom (Bell) D.; m. Bayard Preston Herndon, Aug. 25, 1967 (div. Nov. 1977). BA, William Jewell Coll., 1963; postgrad., Southeastern Bapt. Theol. Sem., 1963-65; MLS, U. N.C., 1967; M Div., Duke U., 1970. Subject cataloger Duke U., Durham, N.C., 1967-70; head cataloging Conn. State Library, Hartford, 1970-72; asst. head cataloging services U. Notre Dame, Ind., 1973-74; assoc. head tech. services Ferguson Library, Stamford, Conn., 1974-77; mgr. library systems support services Cin. Electronics, 1977-81; asst. dir. Bridgeport (Conn.) Pub. Library, 1981-83; asst. dir. for automated systems and tech. services Okla. State U. Library, Stillwater, 1984—; cons., Dublin, Ohio, 1982, Okla. State Dept. Vocat.-Tech. Edn., Stillwater, 1985-87; guest lectr. Simmons Coll., Boston, 1983, U. Okla., Norman, 1984. Contbr. articles to profl. jours. Mem. ALA (various coms. and assns.), Am. Soc. for Info. Sci. (chmn. Okla. chpt. 1985-86). Clubs: North Cen. Sq. Dance Dist. (singles coordinator 1987-88), Stillwater Wagon Wheels. Office: Okla State Univ Library Stillwater OK 74078-0375

DAVIS, JUDI RATLIFF, dietitian; b. San Antonio, Nov. 5, 1944; d. Wortham Wayne and Margaret (Bales) Ratliff; m. Frank Eugene Davis, Feb. 11, 1967; children: Darrell Wayne, Douglas Alexander, Deborah Michelle. BS, U. Tex., 1966; MS, Tex. Women's U., 1978. Clin. dietitian Rex Hosp., Raleigh, N.C., 1967-69; nutrition cons. nursing homes S.W. Va., 1969-70; clin. dietitian Bapt. Meml. Hosp., San Antonio, 1970-71, Park North Gen. Hosp., San Antonio, 1972-73; food and nutrition cons. The Sugar Assn., Washington, 1975-78; instr. Tarrant County Jr. Coll., Ft. Worth, 1976-78; dietitian Greenhouse Health Spa, Arlington, Tex., 1979-81; pvt. practice cons. dietitian Arlington, 1981-87; chief dietitian Fort Worth State Sch., 1987—. Author: Diabetic Meal Plan Handbook, 1987, (with others) Applied Nutrition and Diet Therapy, 1988; created several slide presentations, 1978-79. Dir. Nutrition Task Force Am. Heart Assn. Tarrant County, 1978-80. Mem. Am. Dietetic Assn., Tex. Dietetic Assn., Ft. Worth Dietetic Assn. Home: 3103 Westador Dr Arlington TX 76015 Office: Ft Worth State Sch 5000 Campus Dr Fort Worth TX 76119

DAVIS, JUDITH ANNE, accountant; b. Louisa, Va., June 3, 1963; d. John Preston and Evelyn (Bagby) D. BS, U. Richmond, 1985. CPA, Va. Sales rep. Avon Products, Richmond, Va., 1983-86; accounts receivable clk. Haywood-Clarke Buick, Richmond, 1984; jr. auditor Auditor of Pub. Accounts, Richmond, 1985-86, staff auditor, 1986-87; internal auditor County of Henrico, Richmond, 1987—. Mem. Am. Inst. CPA's, Inst. Internal Auditors. Baptist.

DAVIS, JUDITH ANNE, health care educator; b. Henderson, N.C., May 25, 1947; d. Herbert A. and Estelle (Hamlett) D. BS, High Point Coll., 1969; cert. med. technology, Bowman-Gray Sch. Medicine, Winston-Salem, N.C., 1971; PhD, U. Fla., 1980. Med. technologist Morehead Meml. Hosp., Eden, N.C., 1971-73; instr. Sandhills Community Coll., Pinehurst, N.C., 1973-76, chair Allied Health dept., 1978-80, chair Div. Health Scis., 1980-82; asst. prof., chair Health Occupations Edn. N.C. State U., Raleigh, 1982—; v.p. Nat. Cert. Agy. for Med. Lab. Personnel, Washington, 1984-85; cons. N.C. Dept. Community Colls., Raleigh, 1982—; chair Wake County Health Occupations Adv. Bd., Raleigh, 1985; mem. N.C. Health Occupations Edn. Adv. Bd., 1985—; presenter workshops. Reviewer Jour. Med. Technology, 1986-87; contbr. articles to profl. jours. Treas. Moore County Choral Soc., Southern Pines, N.C., 1980. Named Disting. Professor Sandhills Community Coll., 1981; recipient W.K. Kellogg Outstanding Young Leader in Allied Health award, 1984. Mem. Am. Soc. Allied Health Profls., Am. Soc. for Med. Technology (state pres. 1984-85, editor newsletter Filter Paper 1980-82), Assn. Clin. Pastoral Edn., Assn. for Psychol. Type, Order of St. Luke The Physician, Phi Delta Kappa, Phi Kappa Phi. Democrat. Episcopalian. Office: NC State U Dept Health Edn Campus Box 7801 Raleigh NC 27695-7801

DAVIS, JUDY ELLEN, controller; b. N.Y.C., Feb. 2, 1946; d. Irving and Miriam (Epstein) Lieberman; Richard Davis, July 29, 1969 (div. May 1978); children: Elisabeth, David; m. A.S. Rosenthal, June 12, 1988. BS, SUNY, Stoney Brook, 1967; MBA, Western Mich. U., 1978. Bank examiner N.Y. State, N.Y.C., 1967-69; fin. analyst NBC, N.Y.C., 1969-71, Studebaker-Worthington, N.Y.C., 1971-72, Columbia House, CBS, N.Y.C., 1973-74; fin. mgr. Mich. Area X Profl. Standards Rev. Orgn., Kalamazoo, 1978-83; controller Douglass Community Assn., Kalamazoo, 1983—. V.p. Hadassah, Kalamazoo, 1981-82; bd. dirs. Congl. Moses, Kalamazoo, 1983-86, Family Health Ctr., 1978-81; pres. Women's League for Conservative Judaism, Kalamazoo, 1986-88. Jewish. Office: Douglass Community Assn 1000 W Paterson Kalamazoo MI 49007

DAVIS, JUNE FIKSDAL, medical facility administrator, designer; b. Alexandria, Minn., June 18, 1944; d. Mads and Gladys Lillian Katherine (Engstrom) Fiksdal; m. Merrill Nathaniel Davis III, June 20, 1971; adopted children—Kim Geoffrey, Marc Lee. Cert. with highest honors, Am. Sch. Floral Arts, Chgo., 1965. Floral designer Fiksdal Flowers, Rochester, Minn., 1960-70; prin. floral designer, nat. design tchr. Retail Florists, Kansas City, Mo., also Houston, 1970-81; pres. owner, founder The Gables Found., Inc., Rochester, 1982—; floral designer, 1981—. Author: Floral Design (Am. Inst. Floral Design award 1974), 1973. Cellist Rochester Symphony Orch., 1960-69; bd. dirs., fin. planner United Way, 1974; real estate placement Riverplace Devel., 1980; bd. dirs. Rochester Ballet, 1975; mem. Rochester PTA; chair Symphony Ball, Rochester Symphony, 1975; coordinator music program, new pipe organ, harpsichord Unitarian Ch., 1975-81 (Outstanding Service award 1977), project pres. Walden Hill Bach Soc., 1975-82. Mem. Am. Inst. Floral Design, Bus. and Profl. Women, P.E.O. Avocations: gourmet cooking, water sports, winter sports, skiing, European travel, camping, music. Office: Gables Found Inc 300 3d Ave SE Rochester MN 55904

DAVIS, JUNE HODGE, educator; b. Phila., Jan. 25, 1955; d. Richard John and Angela Theresa (Majewsky) Hodge; m. Elbert Colville Davis, May 29, 1982; 1 child, Taryn Jane. BA, BS, U. Pa., 1976, MS, 1977, postgrad., 1977—. Cert. reading supr., Pa. Reading specialist West Deptford (N.J.) Twp. Schs., 1977-78, Samuel K. Faust Sch., Bensalem, Pa., 1978—; coordinator Reading is Fundamental project, Bensalem, 1979-86; guest lectr. U. Pa., Phila., 1980—; owner Brown Bear Co., Bensalem, 1981-85; reading and computer supr. Bucks County (Pa.) Community Coll., summers 1983—; monitor chpt. I program Pa. Dept. Edn., 1985-87; computer trainer Project Quest Bucks County Intermediate Unit, 1985-86; teaching asst. Grad. Sch. Edn. U. Pa., 1988. Contbr. articles to profl. jours. Adele C. Hickman scholar, West Chester, Pa., 1972-76. Mem. Internat. Reading Assn., Assn. for Supervision and Curriculum Devel., AAUW, Phi Beta Kappa, Pi Lambda Theta, Phi Delta Kappa. Democrat.

DAVIS, KAREN PADGETT, economist, educator; b. Blackwell, Okla., Nov. 14, 1942; d. Walter Dwight and Thelma Louise (Kohler) Padgett; 1 child, Kelly Denise. BA, Rice U., 1965, PhD, 1969. Asst. prof. econs. Rice U., 1969-70; econ. policy fellow Social Security Adminstrn., Brookings Instn., Washington, 1970-71, research assoc., 1971-74, sr. fellow, 1974-77; dep. asst. sec. for planning and evaluation/health HEW, Washington, 1977-80; adminstr. health resources adminstrn. USPHS, 1980-81; prof. Johns Hopkins U., 1981—, chmn. dept. health policy and mgmt., 1983—; vis. lectr. Harvard U., 1974-75. Author: National Health Insurance: Benefits, Costs and Consequences, 1975, Health and the War on Poverty, 1978, Medicare Policy: New Directions for Health and Long-Tern Care, 1986; assoc. editor Milbank Meml. Fund Quar., Health and Soc., 1972-77; regional editor: Health Policy, 1985—. Bd. dirs. Commonwealth Fund Commn. on Elderely People Living Alone, 1985—. Recipient John W. Gardner dissertation award Rice U., 1969. Mem. Inst. Medicine, Am. Econs. Assn., Phi Beta Kappa. Home: 414 New Jersey Ave SE Washington DC 20003 Office: Johns Hopkins U Sch Hygiene Dept Health Policy and Mgmt 624 N Broadway Baltimore MD 21205

DAVIS, KATHLEEN VIRGINIA VIRGILIO, college administrator; b. Camden, N.J., Mar. 3, 1950; d. Nicholas James Virgilio and Concetta Virginia (Startare) Virgilio Biebel; m. James Gordon Davis, Aug. 13, 1977. BS, St. Francis Coll., 1972; MA, Glassboro State Coll., 1981. Tchr., Camden City pub. schs., 1972-81; asst. dean continuing edn. Orangeburg Calhoun Tech. Coll., S.C., 1981-84; job. tng. div. coordinator Orangeburg Calhoun Tech. Coll., 1984—; edn. chmn. United Way. Mem. Orangeburg C. of C. (edn. chmn.), Am. Assn. Women in Community and Jr. Colls., S.C. Tech. Edn. Assn., S.C. Network Women in Higher Edn. Adminstrn. Republican. Roman Catholic. Home: 3129 Landing Way Orangeburg SC 29115 Office: Orangeburg Calhoun Tech Coll 3250 St Matthews Rd NE Orangeburg SC 29115

DAVIS, KATHRYN ANN, management consultant; b. Avon, Ill., Oct. 23, 1952; d. Royce Miller and Martha Jane (Welsh) D. BS in Gen. Engring., U. Ill., Urbana-Champaign, 1974, MSCE, 1975; MBA, Harvard Bus. Sch., 1986. Registered profl. engr., Wash. Project mgr. CH2M Hill, Inc., Seattle, 1977-83; mgr. tech. services ASCE, N.Y.C., 1983-84; bus. mgr. Beals and Thomas, Inc., Westborough, Mass., 1985; sr. v.p. Fogel and Assocs., Inc., N.Y.C., 1986-87; pres. Engring. Mgmt. Cons., N.Y.C., 1987-88; v.p. mktg. and planning Merritt & Harris Inc., N.Y.C., 1988—. Mem. ASCE (bd. dirs. Seattle chpt. 1981-83), Soc. Mktg. Profl. Services, Tau Beta Pi (dist. dir. 1981-83, Disting. Service award 1983). Clubs: Harvard, Harvard Bus. Sch. (N.Y.). Office: Merritt & Harris Inc 110 E 42d St 12th Floor New York NY 10017

DAVIS, KATHRYN LEOLA, labor union administrator; b. Muskogee, Okla., Apr. 23, 1954; d. Hershall Alvin and Jwell Juanita (Hale) Brown; m. Larry Dewayne Workman, Aug. 7, 1970 (div. Oct. 1978); 1 child, Tracy L. AS in Quality Control Tech., Tulsa Jr. Coll.; BS in Indsl. Technology, Northeastern State U., 1985, M in Indsl. Technology, 1987; postgrad., Tulsa U., 1988—. Cert. union counselor United Way Labor Community Services, 1979; lic. in airframe and powerplant, FAA. Machine operator Swan Hose Co., Stillwater, Okla., 1972-73; quality control inspector Dorsett Electronics/Labarge, Inc., Tulsa, Okla., 1973-74; mechanic Cessna Aircraft Co., Wichita, Kans., 1974-75; quality control lab. technician Red Devil, Pryor, Okla., 1975; mechanic McDonnell Douglas Corp., Tulsa, 1975-78, inspector, 1978-80, quality control analyst, 1980-86, structures and installations planner, 1986—; Mem. exec. bd., recording sec. UAW Local 1093, Tulsa, 1978-84, chair women's com., 1978-86, voting del. polit. action com., 1978—, voting del. community action com., 1978—, fin. sec., 1986—. Mem. community service com. Camp Fire Girls, Tulsa, 1978—, Claremore, Okla., 1980-82, Claremore Christian Fellowship Ch. Mem. Am. Soc. for Quality Control, Coalition of Labor Union Women (del. convention 1982-86), Local Union Press Assn., Epsilon Pi Tau. Democrat. Lodge: Eastern Star. Home: 201 W 20th St Owasso OK 74055 Office: UAW Local 1093 1414 N Memorial Tulsa OK 74112

DAVIS, KIMBERLY VANCE, environmental planner; b. Midland, Tex., Sept. 13, 1956; d. Claude William Floyd and Mary Frances (Ball) Beverley; m. William Clark Davis, July 28, 1984. BA, Trinity U., 1978; postgrad., NYU, 1985—. Coordinator NEH, San Antonio, 1978; supr. Acad. Press Harcourt Brace Javonovich, N.Y.C., 1978-80; internat. project coordinator CARE Internat., N.Y.C., 1980-86; environ. planner Tim Miller Assocs., N.Y.C., 1987-88; sr. project mgr. environ. assessment N.Y.C. Dept. City Planning, 1988—. Tutor Literacy Vols. Am., N.Y.C., 1984-86; chmn. Windsor Terrace Coop. Assn., Bklyn., 1985-87. Recipient Frances Sidwell award AAUW, 1974; named one of Outstanding Young Women of Am. Gen. Fed. Women's Clubs, 1987. Mem. Am. Planning Assn. (conf. asst. 1984-87), NYU Urban Planning Students' Assn. (pres.). Democrat. Presbyterian. Home: 10 Prospect Park SW Brooklyn NY 11215 Office: NYC Dept City Planning 22 Reade St New York NY 10007

DAVIS, LAURA ARLENE, foundation administrator; b. Battle Creek, Mich., Apr. 14, 1935; d. Paul Bennett and Daisy E. (Coston) Borgard; m. John R. Davis, Aug. 7, 1955; children—Scott Judson, Cynthia Ann Davis Welker. B.S., Central Mich. U., 1986. Sec., Mich. Loan Co., Battle Creek, 1952-56; legal sec. Ryan, Sullivan & Hamilton, Battle Creek, 1957-64; exec. sec. W.K. Kellogg Found., Battle Creek, 1965-76, adminstrn./program asst., 1976, fellowship dir., 1977, asst. v.p. adminstrn., asst. corp. sec., 1978-84; v.p. adminstrn., corp. sec., 1984—. Mem. word processing adv. com. Kellogg Community Coll., Battle Creek, 1982—; v.p. bd. dirs. State Tech. Inst. and Rehab. Ctr., Delton, Mich., 1983-84; pres. bd. dirs. Charitable Union, Battle Creek, 1983-85; mem. allocations panel United Way of Battle Creek, 1983; trustee Binder Park 200. Mem. Adminstrv. Mgmt. Soc. (pres. chpt. 1982-83), Soc. Office Automation Profls., Am. Mgmt. Assn. Home: 131 Hanson Dr Battle Creek MI 49017 Office: WK Kellogg Found 400 North Ave Battle Creek MI 49016

DAVIS, LAURIE ANN, advertising executive; b. Hudson, N.Y., June 22, 1953; d. Thomas Marshall and Joan (Lackman) D. BS in Mktg., U. Md., 1975. Media buyer Earle, Palmer and Brown, Washington, 1977-78; media buyer, planner Weitzman, Dym & Assocs., Washington, 1978-80; dir. advt. Subaru Atlantic Co., Columbia, Md., 1980-81; supr. planning W.B. Doner, Balt., 1981-85; v.p., media dir. Smith, Burke & Azzam, Balt., 1985-88; pres. Davis Media Group, Balt., 1988—; judge internat. broadcast awards, 1987. Winner Perfect Print Plan Contest, 1987. Mem. Advt. Assn. Balt. Democrat. Roman Catholic.

DAVIS, LILA R., public health officer; b. Balt., June 16, 1941; d. Robert P. and Lila (Norfleet) D. BA in Psychology, Mary Washington Coll., 1963; cert. in med. record adminstrn., USPHS Sch. for Med. Record Adminstrs., 1964. Chief med. record dept. DePaul Hosp., Norfolk, Va., 1964-66, Kings Daughters Children's Hosp., Norfolk, 1966-69; research analyst Norfolk Gen. Hosp., 1969-73; commd. officer USPHS, 1973, advanced through grades to capt., 1983; dep. chief med. record dept. USPHS Hosp., Norfolk, 1973-74; chief USPHS Hosp., 1974-79; chief med. record dept. USPHS Hosp., San Francisco, 1979-81; dep. dir. USPHS Health Data Ctr., Lanham, Md., 1981-83, dir., 1983-86; dir. USPHS Health Data Ctr., GWL Hansen's Disease Ctr., Carville, La., 1986—; cons. Fed. Bur. Prisons, Springfield, Mo., 1982; participant, cons. disaster med. assistance program Bur. Health Care and Delivery, Rockville, Md., 1983-86. Mem. Am. Med. Record Assn., La. Med. Record Assn., Commd. Officer Assn. USPHS, Assn. Mil. Surgeons U.S. Presbyterian. Lodge: Zonta. Office: GWL Hansens Disease Ctr Carville LA 70721

DAVIS, LORRAINE JENSEN, magazine editor; b. Omaha, Apr. 2, 1924; d. Theron R. and L. Mildred (Henkel) Jensen; m. Richard Morris Davis, Apr. 4, 1959 (dec.); 1 child, Laura Jensen. B.A., U. Denver, 1946. Copywriter Glamour mag., N.Y.C., 1946-54; prodn. editor Glamour mag., 1954-61, Vogue Children mag., N.Y.C., 1963-66. Writer, assoc. features editor, Vogue mag., N.Y.C., 1966-77; mng. editor, writer women's news column, 1977—; editor: Vogue Living and Food Guide, 1975; editorial cons.: Vogue Beauty and Health Guide, 1979-82; editor: Cooking with Colette (by Colette Rossant), 1975, Fairchild Dictionary of Fashion (by Charlotte Calasibetta), 1975, English translation Paul Bocuse's French Cooking, 1977. Recipient Disting. Citizen award Alpha Gamma Delta, 1981. Mem. NOW, Am. Soc. Mag. Editors. Democrat. Episcopalian. Club: Cosmopolitan. Home: 425 E 63d St #93 New York NY 10021 Office: Vogue Condé Nast Bldg 350 Madison Ave New York NY 10017

DAVIS, LOUISE SPIERS, educator; b. Malden, Mass., Jan. 11, 1911; d. Thomas H. and Elizabeth (Sullivan) Spiers; m. Frank L. Davis, June 24, 1939 (dec. Oct. 1952); children—Elizabeth Davis Littleton, Jane F. Davis-Gavin. A.B., Boston U., 1932, M.A., 1965; Ed.M., Tufts U., 1962; student U. London, 1966, Goldsmith Coll. London, 1966. Cert. secondary tchr., Mass. Tchr., Malden Pub. Schs., Mass., 1932-39; with Bedford Pub. Schs., 1953-73, program adminstr. social studies, 1960-73, tchr. emeritus, cons., 1973—; tchr. adult edn. program Hanscom AFB, Bedford, Mass., 1973-84; critic tchr. B.U. Tufts U., U. Mass., Boston Coll., Suffolk U.; lectr., cons. in field; mem. Mass. Dept. Edn. Nat. Council Social Studies, 1960-73; Mass. rep. Nat. Educators Conf. on Fgn. Policy, Dept. of State, Washington, 1967; Author pamplet; contbr. articles to profl. jours. Editor: Mass. Industry, 1966-67. Demonstration tchr., lectr. Newsweek Mag., 1970-73. Co-chmn. Bedford Dem. Town Com., 1976-78, coordinator, 1972-84, assoc. mem., 1984.; elected to Barnstable Dem. Town Com., 1986—; advisor Human Relations Council, 1962-63; del. Dem. State Conv., Springfield, Mass., 1982; class agt. ann. fund raising Boston U., Tufts U. Recipient Disting. Service Tchrs. medal Freedoms Found., 1970; State Citation, Dept. Edn., 1962, 63, 64, State Citation in field of human relations, Mass., 1962, 63; Coe fellow; Louise S. Davis Ann. Citizenship scholar. Mem. Mem. NEA, Mass. Tchrs. Assn., Nat. Council Social Studies, New Eng. History Tchrs. Assn., AAUW (pres. Housatonic Br. 1947-49), Tufts Alumni Assn., Boston U. Alumni Assn. Roman Catholic. Clubs: Hyannisport Yacht, Hyannis Yacht (assoc.); Boston U. of Cape Cod, Tufts U. of Cape Cod; Bedfords Woman's Community (com. chmn. 1965-70), Bedford Hist. Assn., Theta Phi Alpha, Delta Sigma Rho. Home: 36 Craigville Beach Rd PO Box 171 Hyannis Port MA 02647 Also: 1302 Piaya Azul III, Luquillo Puerto Rico oo673

DAVIS, LOURIE IRENE BELL, computer systems specialist; b. Las Vegas, N.Mex., Apr. 8, 1930; d. Currie Oscar and Minnie I. (Rodgers) Bell; m. Robert Eugene Davis, Aug. 21, 1950; children—Judith Anne, Robert Patrick. B.S., West Tex. U., 1959; student Eastern N.Mex. U., 1947-49. Cert. systems profl.; cert. data processing profl. Programmer/analyst Blue Cross/Blue Shield Okla., Tulsa, 1972-75, mgr. systems, 1977-81, dir. info. systems, 1981-82, mgr. project control, 1982-83, mgr. info. ctr., 1984-85, mgr. profl. cons. and tng., 1985-87; independent profl. cons., Tulsa, 1987; faculty devel. coordinator CAID Okla. State U., Okmulgee, 1987—; systems curriculum coordinator Tulsa Jr. Coll., 1975-76, mem. computer sci. adv. bd., 1976-83; mem. steering com. U.S. Senate Bus. Adv. Bd., 1981. Mem. budget panel United Way Tulsa, 1981-87; mem. U.S. Presidential Task Force, 1982—. Recipient Allocations Exec. Com. award, 1987. Mem. Assn. Systems Mgmt. (regional dir. 1985-86, chpt. membership chair 1982-84; internat. awards 1980, 84), Nat. Assn. Female Execs., AAUW, Tulsa Area Systems Edn. Assn. (recorder 1980-81), Alpha Chi, Mensa, Intertel (nat. acceptance com. chair 1978, dir. region VIII 1987—). Republican. Mem. Unity Ch. of Christianity, Home: 2403 W Oklahoma Tulsa OK 74127 Office: OSUTBO 444 S Mission Okmalger OK 74447

DAVIS, LUCY TOLBERT, psychologist, educator; b. Greenville, S.C.; d. Joseph Augustus and Margaret (Shirley) Tolbert; m. Ron Willson Davis, Aug. 28, 1948; children: Ronald Redd, Margaret Willson, Elisabeth Southard. BA, Erskine Coll, 1946; MA, Columbia U., 1948, EdD, 1955. Lic. psychologist, N.C. Guidance testing New Trier High Sch., Winnetka, Ill., 1948-50; exec. dir. Student Life Office Columbia U., N.Y.C., 1950-54; dir. counseling services Centennial Schs., Southampton, Pa., 1954-57; dir. pupil services Bucks County Schs., Doylestown, Pa., 1957-64; research assoc. Greater Cleve. Research Council, 1964-67; edn. dir. therapeutics Edn. Program Duke Med. Ctr., Durham, N.C., 1967-70; prof. dept. edn. Duke U., Durham, 1970—; cons. Pa. and N.C. Sch. Systems and State Depts., research assoc. Gov.'s and State's Commns., N.C. Author, editor four books; contbr. articles to profl. jours. Div. head Am. Heart Assoc. and Cancer Drives. Fellow N.C. Psychol. Assn. (program chmn. 1978); mem. N.C. Sch. Psychologist Assn.(Most Outstanding Woman 1985), Am. Psychol. Assn., Nat. council Health Care Providers. Episcopalian. Home: 705 Gimghaul Rd Chapel Hill NC 27514 Office: Duke U West Duke Bldg Durham NC 27708

DAVIS, LYDIA JOANNA, publishing executive; b. Kokomo, Ind., May 4, 1958; d. Henderson Sheridan and Ruth Vinita (Patterson) D. BA magna cum laude, Howard U., 1980. Reporter trainee Sta. WRTV-TV, Indpls., 1980-81; writer, researcher Johnson Pub. Co., Chgo., 1981-82, asst. dir. pub. relations, 1983, assoc. producer Ebony/Jet Celebrity Showcase, 1983, dir. promotion, 1983-85, v.p. promotion, 1985—. Recipient cert. Merit Circulation Direct Mail awards, 1984, Communications Excellence to Black Audiences, 1986. Mem. League Black Women, Cosmopolitan C. of C., Women's Advt. Club (Chgo.), Exec. Club (Chgo.). Mem. African Methodist Episcopal Ch. Club: Execs. of Chgo. Office: Johnson Pub Co 820 S Michigan Ave Chicago IL 60605

DAVIS, MAMIE LEE, auditor; b. Shellman, Ga., Aug. 29, 1954; d. R.L. and Lorene (Pittman) D. BS in Acctg., Fla. State U., 1977; MBA, Stetson U., 1981. CPA, Ga. Contract price analyst NASA, Kennedy Space Ctr., Fla., 1976-80; auditor U.S. Treasury Dept Bur. Alcohol, Tobacco and Firearms, Atlanta, 1980-87; auditor-in-charge U.S. Vets. Adminstrn., Office of Inspector Gen., Atlanta, 1987—. Trustee, choir mem. Ebenezer Bapt. Ch., Atlanta, 1982—. Mem. Assn. Govt. Accts. (dir. 1985—), Nat. Black MBA Assn., Am. Inst. CPA's, Ga. Soc. CPA's, Fla. State U. Alumni Assn., Fla. State U. Black Alumni Assn. (v.p. 1984—), Alpha Kappa Alpha. Democrat. Home: 1927 Young Rd Lithonia GA 30058 Office: 730 Peachtree St NE Atlanta GA 30365

DAVIS, MARCIA WELCH, interior designer; b. Atlanta, Sept. 29, 1949; d. Edward Douglas and Annie Laurie (Smith) Welch; m. James J. Davis, Oct. 23, 1971 (div. Sept. 1982). B in Visual Arts, Ga. State U., 1971. With sales, unit control depts. J.P. Allen, Atlanta, 1968-71; draftsman U.S. Exchange System, Frankfurt, Fed. Republic Germany, 1972-74; leasing mgr. Post Properties, Atlanta, 1975; interior designer Alan L. Ferry Designers, Atlanta, 1976-81; pres. Davis-Kloss Interior Design and Space Planning, Atlanta, 1981-88, Marcia Davis & Assocs., Atlanta, 1988—. Contbr. articles to profl. jours. Trustee High Mus. Decorative Art, 1986-87. Mem. Am. Soc. of Interior Designers (bd. dirs. 1986—, v.p., 1982, chair coms. 1979-83), Women C. of C. (chmn. com. 1981, 87, bd. dirs. 1982-84, Named Outstanding Chmn. 1981), Atlanta C. of C., Midtown Bus. Assn. Republican. Episcopalian. Home: 1421 Peachtree St #212 Atlanta GA 30309 Office: Marcia Davis & Assocs One Piedmont Ctr 3565 Piedmont Rd Suite 200 Atlanta GA 30305

DAVIS, MARGARET ALEXANDRA, real estate broker; b. Havana, Cuba, July 17, 1952; came to U.S., 1961.; 1 child, Seth Jon. Student, U. South Fla., 1972. Lic. real estate broker, Fla. Salesperson Lobel's Child Ctr., 1967-68; banker First Fed. Savs. & Loan, Miami, Fla., 1976-78; owner Margaret's Flea Collectibles, Charleston, S.C., 1979-81; pub. relations agent Linch Pub. Co., 1984; broker Unique Homes & Invest, Inc., Orlando, Fla., 1984—. Author, editor: It's Easy to Avoid Probate, 1984; contbr. editorials to newspapers and newsletters; lectr. to profl. orgns. Bd. dirs. Health Food Corp., Orlando, 1982-84, Human Rights Orgn.; active NOW, Womens' Network, Freedom of Choice, Orlando, 1982—; moderator Winter Park (Fla.) Roundtable, 1983—. Recipient numerous ribbons for cooking and needlework Homestead and CharlestonFairs, Merit award Orlando Drug Rehab. Counseling. Mem. Fla. Real Estate Commn., Nat. Assn. Female Execs., Latin-Am. C. of C., Notary of Am. (exec. dept.). Democrat.

DAVIS, MARGARET AMES, graphics designer; b. Derby, Conn., Apr. 7, 1957; d. Samuel Ames and Katherine Phyllis (Giovannucci) D. BA, Bard Coll., 1979; cert. in illustration, graphic design and typography, Mass. Coll. Art, Boston, 1986. Typesetter My Girl Kellie, Braintree, Mass., 1979; exec. asst. NAD Electronics, Lincoln, Mass., 1980-82; graphics mgr. NAD Electronics, Norwood, Mass., 1982—. Democrat. Roman Catholic. Home: 18 Walnut Ct Arlington MA 02174 Office: NAD Electronics 575 University Ave Norwood MA 02062

DAVIS, MARGARET BRYAN, paleoecology researcher, educator; b. Boston, Oct. 23, 1931. AB, Radcliffe Coll., 1953; PhD in Biology, Harvard U., 1957. NSF fellow dept. biology Harvard U., Cambridge, Mass., 1957-58, dept. geosci. Calif. Inst. Tech., Pasadena, 1959-60; research fellow dept. zoology Yale U., New Haven, 1960-61, prof. biology, 1973-76; research assoc. dept. botany U. Mich., Ann Arbor, 1961-64, assoc. research biologist Great Lakes Research div., 1964-70, research biologist, assoc. prof. dept. zoology, 1966-70, research biologist, prof. zoology, 1970-73; head dept. ecology and behavioral biology U. Minn., Mpls., 1976-81, prof. ecology, 1976-82, Regents prof., 1982—; vis. prof. Quaternary Research Ctr., U. Wash., 1973; vis. investigator environ. studies program U. Calif., Santa Barbara, 1981-82; mem. adv. panel for ecology, NSF, 1976-79; mem. planetary biology com. NRC, 1981-82, mem. global change com., 1987—. Mem. editorial bd. Quaternary Research, 1969-82, Trends in Ecology and Evolution, 1986—. Fellow AAAS, Geol. Soc. Am.; mem. Ecol. Soc. Am. (pres. 1987-88), Am. Quaternary Assn. (councillor 1969-70, 72-76, pres. 1978-80), Am. Soc. Limnology and Oceanography, Internat. Assn. for Great Lakes Research (bd. dirs. 1970-73), Nat. Acad. Scis. (plantary biology, global change com.), Phi Beta Kappa, Sigma Xi. Office: U Minn 107 Zool Bldg 318 Church St Minneapolis MN 55455

DAVIS, MARIAN BELLE, former museum curator, educator; b. St. Louis County, Mo., Sept. 24, 1911; d. John William and Frances Edith (Walters) D.; A.B., Washington U., St. Louis, 1932, M.A., 1935, postgrad., 1935-36; M.A., Radcliffe Coll., 1939, Ph.D., 1948. Mus. instr. Worcester (Mass.) Art Mus., 1941-44; instr. U. Tex., Austin, 1944-45, asst. prof. art, 1946-50, asso. prof., 1950-60, prof., 1960-78, prof. emeritus, 1978—, chief curator Univ. Art. Mus., 1963-78. Alice Longfellow fellow, 1940-41; U. Tex. at Austin grantee, 1951. Mem. Renaissance Soc., Coll. Art Assn. (editorial advisory bd. Coll. Art Jour., 1953-60, dir., 1951-55), Soc. Archtl. Historians, Archeol. Inst. Am., Nat. Trust, Phi Beta Kappa. Unitarian. Contbr. numerous articles, book and exhbn. revs. to art and hist. jours., to catalogues. Home: 2701 Wooldridge Dr Austin TX 78703

DAVIS, MARILYN K, management information systems director, nurse; b. Brocket, N.D., Jan. 20, 1943; d. Ivan O. and Lempi E. (Honkola) Wick; m. George W. Davis Jr., Sept. 20, 1969; 1 child, George W. IV. Diploma, St. Luke's Sch. Nursing, Fargo, S.D., 1963. Staff nurse St. Luke's Hosp., Fargo, 1964-65; staff nurse El Camino Hosp., Mt. View, Calif., 1964-65, asst. head nurse med. unit, 1965-67, head nurse med. unit, 1967-74, med. info. systems asst., 1973-74, head nurse urology unit, 1974-80, head nurse dialysis unit, 1980-82; med. info. systems dir. El Camino, Mt. View, Calif., 1983—.

DAVIS, MARINA WINN SMITH, marketing professional; b. Laredo, Tex., Aug. 30, 1945; d. Seaborn LaFayette and Lucy Curtis (Winn) Faulk; 1 child from previous marriage, Susan Ellene Smith; m. Early Clifford Davis Jr., Jan. 23, 1988. BS, U. Montevallo, 1970; postgrad., U. New Orleans, 1970-75. Supr. tng. D.H. Holmes, Co., Ltd., New Orleans, 1967-72; interior designer Stone Lumber's Kitchen and Bath, New Orleans, 1972-73, Kirschman's Interstate West, New Orleans, 1973-76; tech. editor Bell Aerospace Textron, New Orleans, 1976-77; elec. draftsman Geosource, Inc., Corpus Christi, Tex., 1979-80; owner Marina Smith Designs, Corpus Christi, 1980-85, Brighter Image Advt., Corpus Christi, 1985—; exec. v.p., dir. Hayes Research Corp., Corpus Christi, 1986—; mktg. cons. Corpus Christi, 1987—; distbr. Panel Internat., Inc., 1988—. Editor (newsletter) Holmes Store News, 1970. Advisor Jr. Achievement Co., New Orleans, 1969-70; mem. adv. bd. New Orleans East Family YMCA, 1977-78; mem. steering com. Family Outreach, Inc., Corpus Christi, 1981-83, mem. mng. bd. 1983-84. Mem. Corpus Christi C. of C., Corpus Christi Geol. Soc., Corpus Christi Pub. Relations Soc. Methodist. Office: Brighter Image Advt 320 Bayview Fed Bldg Corpus Christi TX 78474

DAVIS, MARION PEASE (MRS. PAUL DAVIS), social work administrator; b. Derby, Conn., Oct. 9, 1918; d. John Wood and Myrtle Stowe (Humphrey) Pease; m. Paul Davis, Oct. 15, 1938; children: Linda Davis Payne, Robert, Richard. BA in Psychology, U. Bridgeport, 1964; MSW, U. Conn., 1969. Cert. ind. social worker, Conn. Caseworker dept. welfare State of Conn., Bridgeport, 1964-65, social worker dept. protective services, 1965-67, supr. protective services unit, 1969-73, sr. psychiat. social worker, 1973-75, supervisory psychiat. social worker, 1975-78; dir. psychiat. social workers Greater Bridgeport Community Mental Health Ctr., 1973-82, chmn. housing com., 1974-78, mem. accreditation com., 1974-78, chmn., 1978-81, chief psychiat. social work, 1978-82; pvt. practice psychiatry, 1982—; owner Winning Combinations, 1983-86; mem. profl. adv. com. VNA, 1987—; mem. Sr. Citizens Needs Assessment Com., 1987—; sec., co-chair by-laws com. Sr. Citizens Ctr. Council, 1987—. Co-editor: Washington Sr. Ctr. News, 1987—. Mem. Nat. Assn. Social Workers (diplomate, registered clin. social worker; mem. exec. com. 1974-75, editorial com. 1975-77), Am. Assn. Marriage Family Counsellors (assoc.), Logos World Univ. Bd. (chair curriculum com. 1986-88), Huxley Inst. Biosocial Research (v.p., bd. dirs. 1978-81), Conn. Assn. Human Services, Mental Health Services Coordinating Com. (rec. sec., exec. com. 1975-82, corr. sec. 1978-82), Assn. for Research and Enlightenment (rep. study group 1963-79, 84—), Conn. Assn. Research and Enlightenment (sec. 1986-88, v.p. 1987—), Sr. Citizen's Orgn. (sec. 1987—, co-chair bylaws com. 1987), Assn. for Past Life Research and Therapy, Soc. for Clin. and Exptl. Hypnosis, Internat. Soc. Hypnosis, Nat. Guild Hypnotists, Assn. for Study Dreams, LWV (bd. dirs. 1985—, pres. 1986-88, chair agrl. study com. 1986-88 Home: Sunset Ln Washington CT 06794

DAVIS, MARJORIE ALICE, city official; b. Newton, Mass., July 1, 1917; d. Herbert Francis and Harriet Cole (Dodge) Parmenter; A.B., Wellesley Coll., 1939; spl. grad. student Radcliffe Coll., 1941; cert. Harvard U., 1940; spl. courses in social work Boston U., 1961-62; m. Charles William Davis, Aug. 31, 1940 (dec.); children—Harriet Parmenter, Charles Edwin II. Exec. dir. Mid-Essex Area council Girl Scouts U.S.A., South Hamilton, Mass., 1952-59, Greater Lynn council, 1959-63, Merrimack River council, Andover, Mass., 1963-80; mem. Wenham Bd. Selectmen, 1972—, chmn., 1977-87. Mem. Met. Area Planning Council, 1975—, sec., 1984—, mem. Mass. Com. Criminal Justice, 1974; exec. dir. Essex County Greenbelt Assn., 1980; mem. Lynn (Mass.) Area Pvt. Industry Council, 1982—, bd. dirs. Healthquarters, 1981, treas., 1982-83; v.p., 1983—, pres., 1986—; mem. ct./Community Relations Com. for Essex County, 1975; pres. Hamilton-Wenham Community Service, 1970-80, bd. dirs., 1983—; sec. United Fund of Central North Shore (v.p. United Way of Mass, 1982-88) 1969-84; mem. exec. com. Essex County Adv. Bd., 1983—, sec., 1984—; pres. Bay Area Vis. Nurses Assn., 1963-73, Bay area dir., 1983—; v.p. Mass. chpt. Children Am. Revolution, 1944; mem. Republican Town Com. Mem. Mass. Selectmen's Assn., Essex County Selectmen's Assn. (pres. 1984-85, bd. dirs.), Women Elected Mcpl. Ofcls., Mass. Mcpl. Assn. (bd. dirs.), Christ Ch. Women (pres. 1987—). Episcopalian. Clubs: Harvard (Boston); Singing Beach (Manchester, Mass.). Home: 143 Grapevine Rd Wenham MA 01984

DAVIS, MARLEEN KAY, architect, educator; b. Pitts., Apr. 24, 1952; d. Edward William and Mary Margaret (Dixon) Kay; m. Thomas Kirby Davis, Apr. 8, 1978; children: Stephen Mabon, Robert Jackson. BArch, Cornell U., 1976; MArch with honors, Harvard U., 1979. Lic. architect, N.Y., Mass. Designer Henry Schadler & Assocs., West Hartford, Conn., 1977-78, Sert Jackson & Assocs., Cambridge, Mass., 1979-80; architect Skidmore, Owings & Merrill, Boston, 1980-81; assoc. prof. architecture Syracuse (N.Y.) U., 1981—. Exhibitor recent faculty competitions, Syracuse U., 1983, 85, 86, portfolios in architecture, N.Y.C., 1983. Recipient Grand Prize award U. Miami Campus Masterplan Design Competition, 1986, Third Prize award Ft.

Lauderdale (Fla.) Riverfront Plaza Design Competition, 1982. Office: Syracuse U Sch Architecture Syracuse NY 13210

DAVIS, MARVA ALEXIS KENON, lawyer; b. Quincy, Fla., May 26, 1952; d. Harold Kenon and Thelma L. Robinson; m. Calvin C. Davis, Sept. 2, 1973. B.A. in Polit. Sci., Lincoln U., Pa., 1974; J.D., Fla. State U., 1977. Bar: Fla. 1977. Sole practice, Quincy, 1981-82, 86—; ptnr. Travis & Davis, P.A., Quincy, 1982-86; asst. gen. counsel Fla. Commn. Human Relations, Tallahassee, 1979-81; asst. pub. defender Office Pub. Defender, Tallahassee, 1977-79, 81-85; gen. counsel Community Econ. Devel. Orgn., 1982—, Midway Community Council, 1978-86; dir. Legal Services North Fla., 1981-86; city attorney, City of Midway, Fla., 1986-87. Mem. Barristers Assn. (pres. 1982-84), Fla. Bar Assn., ABA, Assn. Trial Lawyers Am., Acad. Fla. Trial Lawyers, Nat. Bar Assn. Democrat. Mem. Worldwide Ch. of God. Home: Route 1 Box 3045 Havana FL 32333 Office: 379 E Jefferson SE PO Drawer 551 Quincy FL 32351-0551

DAVIS, MARY EUGENIE, video production company executive; b. Washington, Mar. 20, 1957; d. Mitchel James and Mary (Pachuta) Burns; m. Donald C. Davis, Dec. 31, 1982. BS, Boston U., 1978; postgrad., UCLA, 1980. Audiovisual producer Bostonia Films, Boston, 1978-80, Filmline, Inc., Los Angeles, 1980; writer, audiovisual producer Trainex, Inc., Garden Grove, Calif., 1981-82; mgr. audiovisual communications Carl Larcher Enterprises, Anaheim, Calif., 1982-84; owner, producer AV Designs, Hermosa Beach, Calif., 1984—. Vol. Mus. Contemporary Art, Los Angeles, 1986-87. Recipient Nona Kirby award New Eng. Broadcasters' Assn., 1978. Mem. Am. Soc. Tng. and Devel. (High Achiever award 1984). Democrat. Roman Catholic. Office: AV Designs 1233 Hermosa Ave Hermosa Beach CA 90254

DAVIS, MARY HELEN, psychiatrist, educator; b. Kingsville, Tex., Dec. 2, 1949; d. Garnett Stant and Emogene (Campbell) D. BA, U. Tex., 1970; MD, U. Tex., Galveston, 1975. Cert. Nat. Bd. Med. Examiners, Am. Bd. Psychiatry and Neurology, Child and Adolescent Psychiatry. Intern, then resident in psychiatry SUNY, Buffalo, 1975-78; asst. prof. Med. Coll. Wis., Milw., 1980—; cons. Milw. Mental Health Cons., 1980—, Children's Service Soc., Milw., 1982—; med. dir. adolescent treatment unit Milw. Pscyhiat. Hosp., 1981-86; med. dir. Schroeder Child Ctr., 1986—. Bd. dirs. Next Generation Theater, Milw., 1988—. Fellow in Child Psychiatry U. Cin., 1975-78; named one of Outstanding Young Women of Am., 1985. Mem. Am. Psychiat. Assn., Am. Soc. Adolescent Psychiatry, Am. Acad. Child and Adolescent Psychiatry, Am. Med. Women's Assn. Baptist. Club: Univ. (Milw.). Office: Milw Psychiat Hosp 1220 Dewey Ave Wauwatosa WI 53213

DAVIS, MARY VIRGINIA, tax service specialist; b. Phila., Feb. 5, 1927; d. John Richard and Lucinda Tyson (Brown) Garmela; m. Ralph E. Davis, Nov. 1, 1958 (dec. Nov. 1975); 1 child, Ann Elizabeth Davis Kagarise. Student, Temple U., 1956-58. Sec., supr. Naval Air Material Ctr., Phila., 1944-55; adminstrv. asst. Jerrold Electronics Corp., Phila., 1955-58; sec. Pacific Vegetable Oil Corp., Vernon, Calif., 1958-60; exec. sec. Walter Motor Truck Co., Voorheesville, N.Y., 1960-61; claims clk. Social Security Adminstrn., Buffalo, 1961-63; exec. sec. Chesapeake and Ohio R.R., Cleve., 1963-65; tax preparer H&R Block, Akron, Ohio, 1974-78; tax preparer Hammer Tax Service, Akron, Ohio, 1978-80, co-owner, enrolled agt., 1980—. Treas. Franklin (Ohio) Park Civic Ctr., Franklin Twp., 1985-87. Served with USMR, 1957-58. Mem. Nat. Assn. Enrolled Agts., Ohio Soc. Enrolled Agts., Bus. and Profl. Womens Assn. Office: Hammer Tax Service 958A W Nimisila Rd Akron OH 44319

DAVIS, MAVIS CATHERINE, transportation executive; b. Newton, Ala., May 2, 1946; d. Edgar A. Turner and Dora B. (Monk) Fontenot; m. Germain Davis, Dec. 31, 1962 (div. Feb. 1975); children: Donna Jo, Dionne Rachel. Grad. high sch., Cortland, Ohio. Bookkeeper Duncan Furniture Store, Hendersonville, Tenn., 1974-75; asst. term mgr. Herbert MAterials, Nashville, 1975-78; sales rep. Dean Truck Lines, Inc., Nashville, 1978-79, Atlanta Motor Lines, Nashville, 1979-84, Burlington No. Air Freight, Nashville, 1984-85, Service Transport, Inc., Nashville, 1986; pres. M.C.D Transp. Inc., Smyrna, Tenn., 1986—. Author various poems; designer greeting cards; contbr. articles to company newsletter. Bd. dirs. Nashville Golf Classic, 1978—, Sam's Kids, Inc., Nashville, 1987; active vol. Tenn. Spl. Olympics, Nashville, 1980—, Bullshooter's Golf Tournament, Nashville, 1981-83. Mem. Nat. Assn. Female Execs., Nashville Traffic Transp. Club, Delta Nu Alpha. Baptist. Office: MCD Transp Inc PO Box 100008 Nashville TN 37210

DAVIS, MONIQUE (DEON), state legislator; b. Chgo., Aug. 19, 1936; d. James and Constance (Dutton) McKay; divorced; children: Robert Jr., Monique C. Conway. BS in Edn., Chgo. State U., 1967, MS in Guidance and Counseling, 1976. Tchr. Chgo. Bd. Edn., 1967-86, coordinator, 1986—; rep. 36th dist. Ill. Ho. of Reps., 1987—. Mem. legis. com. Chgo. Area Alliance Black Sch. Edn., 1982-84, Independent Voters of Ill.-Independent Precinct Orgns., Chgo., 1982-83; coordinator 21st ward, Citizens for Mayor Washington, 1985, 87. Recipient GRIT award Roseland Womens Orgn., 1987; named a Tchr. Who Makes a Difference PTA, 1978, 85. Mem. Chgo. Area Tchrs. Alliance (chmn.), Christian Bd. Edn. (bd. dirs. 1978-82), Phi Delta Kappa. Mem. United Ch. of Christ. Office: 9449 S Ashland Chicago IL 60820

DAVIS, NANCY ANN, city clerk; b. Indianola, Iowa, Sept. 10, 1933; d. Ralph Orlando Cline and Irene Harriett (Summy) Horridge; m. Lewis Lee Davis II, Dec. 27, 1958; children: Douglas Wilson, Paula Lee. BA, U. So. Calif., 1957. Newspaper reporter Post-Advocate, Alhambra, Calif., 1952-56; assoc. women's editor News-Press, Glendale, Calif., 1957-60; reporter, family editor Times-Press-Recorder, Arroyo Grande, Calif., part-time 1962-80; with pub. relations staff Rose Victorian Inn, Arroyo Grande, 1981-85; city clk. City of Arroyo Grande, 1984—. Mem. Criminal Justice Planning Bd., Tri-County Region, 1973-77; chairperson Human Relations Commn., South San Luis Obispo County, 1976-77, Juvenile Justice/Delinquency Prevention Commn., San Luis Obispo County, 1986-87. Mem. Internat. City Clks. Assn., Calif. City Clks. Assn., LWV. Democrat. Methodist. Home: 1431 Newport Ave Arroyo Grande CA 93420 Office: City Hall 214 E Branch St Arroyo Grande CA 93420

DAVIS, NATALIE ZEMON, history educator; b. Detroit, Nov. 8, 1928; d. Julian Leon and Helen (Lamport) Zemon; m. H. Chandler Davis, Aug. 16, 1948; children: Aaron Bancroft, Hannah Penrose, Simone Weil. BA, Smith Coll., 1949, DHL (hon.), 1977; MA, Radcliffe Coll., 1950; PhD, U. Mich., 1959; D hon., Universite Lyon II (France), 1983; DHL (hon.), Northwestern U., 1983, U. Rochester, 1986, Lawrence U., 1984, George Washington U., 1987; LLD (hon.), Tufts U., 1987, Williams Coll., 1987. Lectr. to asst. prof. Brown U., 1959-63; asst. prof. to assoc. prof. U. Toronto, 1963-71; prof. history U. Calif.-Berkeley, 1971-77; Henry Charles Lea prof. history Princeton U., 1978—. Author: Society and Culture in Early Modern France, 1975 (Berkshire Conf. spl. award 1976), The Return of Martin Guerre, 1983, Fiction in the Archives: Pardon Tales and Their Tellers in Sixteenth-Century France, 1987. Recipient teaching citation U. Calif.-Berkeley, 1974, Outstanding Achievement award U. Mich., 1975, New Eng. Hist. Assn. Media award, 1985; decorated Chevalier Ordre des Palmes Academiques France, 1976. Fellow Am. Acad. Arts and Scis.; mem. Renaissance Soc. Am., Soc. French Hist. Studies (pres. 1976-77), Am. Hist. Assn. (council 1972-75, pres. modern history sect. 1980, pres. 1987), Soc. Reformation Research, Am. Antiquarian Soc. (selected mem. 1987). Democrat. Jewish. Home: 78 Alexander St Princeton NJ 08540 Office: Dept History Princeton U Princeton NJ 08544

DAVIS, OLIVE MCFATE, trade show executive; b. Oakland, Calif., Nov. 16, 1922; d. Thomas Albert and Leana Jewel (Combs) McFate; m. Warren L. Davis, Jan. 18, 1942 (dec. 1976); children: Jean, Patricia, Larry, Allan, Bonnie. Student, Inst. Orgnl. Mgmt., 1980-82, 84-86. Ptnr. with husband in farm, Calif., 1943-69; newspaper corr. Stockton (Calif.) Record, 1968-73; urban 4-H coordinator, San Joaquin County, Stockton, 1973; writer-researcher Slow Tired & Easy R.R., Stockton, 1974-76; coordinator Cen. Valley Agrl. Expo, Stockton, 1976-77; trade show exec. Stockton C. of C., 1976—. Author: Slow Tired & Easy Railroad, 1976, Stockton Sunrise Port on the San Joaquin, 1984. Mem. Citizen Ambassador Program to China, 1987; chmn. Stockton Cultural Heritage Bd., 1981-82; regional dir. Am. Field Services, 1970-73; pres. 4-H Leaders Council, 1956; bd. dirs. Linden Devel. Commn., 1973, Linden Peters C. of C., 1974-77. Named Citizen of Yr., Linden Lions, 1973. Mem. Nat. League Am. Pen Women, Nat. Assn. Agrl. Mktg., San Joaquin County Hist. Soc. (pres. 1981-82, trustee 1987), Calif. Hist. Soc. Club: Linden Garden. Office: 445 W Weber Ave Suite 220 Stockton CA 95203

DAVIS, OLIVIA ANNE CARR (MRS. TOM LUCIAN DAVIS), author; b. Leeds, Eng., Dec. 4, 1922; d. Henry Marvell and Olive Frances Kate (Rumble) Carr; student pvt. sch., pvt. tutors; m. Tom Lucian Davis, Oct. 13, 1943; children—Sebastian, Miranda, Penelope. Came to U.S., 1951, naturalized, 1956. Sec., Mil. Intelligence, War Office, London and Oxford, Eng., 1941-44. Recipient Emily Clark Balch award Va. Quar. Rev., 1969. Mem. Authors Guild, Smithsonian Resident Assos., Nat. Trust Historic Preservation, Audubon Soc. Author: The Last of the Greeks, 1968; The Steps of the Sun, 1972; The Scent of Apples, 1973; contbr. short stories to lit. quars. and anthologies in U.S. and abroad. Home: 6828 Floyd Ave Springfield VA 22150 Office: care Curtis Brown Ltd 575 Madison Ave New York NY 10022

DAVIS, PAMELA EILEEN, banker; b. Johnstown, Pa., Feb. 29, 1956; d. William Ashley and Dorothy Eileen D. BA in Econs. cum laude, Dickinson Coll., 1978; postgrad., Bucknell U., 1981-82. Officer loan dept. Am. Bank, 1980-82, asst. v.p. SBA loan dept., 1982-83; v.p., mgr. small bus. loan dept. Meridian Bank, Reading, Pa., 1984—. Mem. Kutztown U. MBA adv. com.; treas. Berks Women's Council; bd. dirs. Berks County YWCA, chmn. long range planning com., 1986-88; chmn. City of Reading Enterprize Zone loan com. Recipient Berks County YWCA Trendsetter Yr. award, 1986. Mem. Nat. Assn Accts. (pres. Reading chpt. 1984-85, rep. Mid-Atlantic Council 1986-89), SBA (chmn. Region III Phila. Adv. Council 1988-89, Adv. of Yr. award 1986), Robert Morris Assocs., Berks Women's Network (1st v.p. and chmn. membership com. 1987-88), Berks County C. of C. (chmn. Program for Women com.). Republican. Presbyterian. Office: Meridian Bank PO Box 1102 Reading PA 19603

DAVIS, PEGGY COOPER, law educator; b. Hamilton, Ohio, Feb. 19, 1943; d. George Clinton and Margaret (Gillespie) Cooper; m. Gordon Jamison Davis, Aug. 24, 1968; 1 child, Elizabeth Cooper. BA, Western Coll. for Women, 1963; student, Barnard Coll., 1963-64; JD, Harvard U., 1968; student, N.Y. Soc. for Freudian Psychologists, 1972-73. Bar: N.Y., 1969, U.S. Supreme Ct., 1976. Law clk. to judge U.S. Dist. Ct., N.Y.C., 1972-73; asst. counsel capital punishment project NAACP Legal Def., N.Y.C., 1973-77; assoc. prof. law Rutgers U., N.J., 1977-78; assoc. prof., NYU, 1983-86, prof. 1987—; dep. criminal justice coordinator City of N.Y., 1979-80; judge Family Ct. State of N.Y., 1980-83. Contbr. articles to profl. jours. Bd. dirs. Vera Inst., N.Y.C., Com. for Modern Cts., Fund for City of N.Y. Fellow N.Y. Inst. for Humanities. Office: NYU Sch Law 40 Washington Sq New York NY 10012

DAVIS, PENELOPE ANN, lawyer; b. Kennedy, Ala., Feb. 14, 1952; d. John William and Mary Evelyn (Keenum) D.; m. Eugene B. Williams, May 10, 1984; 1 child, Lance Christopher. BS, U. Ala., 1973, MA, 1974, JD, 1978. Bar: Ala. 1978, U.S. Ct. Appeals (5th cir.) 1979, U.S. Ct. Appeals (11th cir.) 1981. Law clk. to sr. justice U.S. Ct. Appeals (5th cir.), Tuscaloosa, Ala., 1978-79; assoc. dir. Ala. Law Inst., University, 1979—; instr. Shelton State Coll., Tuscaloosa, 1982-84; adj. faculty law U. Ala., 1984—. Mem. citizen adv. com. State Jail Standard, 1981, Ala. Victim/Witness Resource Task Force, 1981-82, Ala. Domestic Violence Commn., 1981-82. Named one of Outstanding Young Women of Am., 1984. Mem. ABA, Ala. Bar Assn. Baptist. Home: 21 Englewood Dr Tuscaloosa AL 35405 Office: Ala Law Inst PO Box 1425 University AL 35486

DAVIS, PHYLLIS ALTHEA, communications supervisor; b. Carriacou, Grenada, West Indies, Oct. 29, 1937; d. Joseph Vivien Paul and Ada Rebirtha McKenzie; m. Leonard O. Davis (div. 1976); children: Trudi Karen (dec.), Darryl Arthur. Corp. sec. Mountain States Telephone and Telegraph, Denver, 1975-79, exec. sec., 1979-80; personnel supr. Bell System Ctr. for Tech. Edn., Denver, 1980-82; asst. mgr. methods, procedures Bell System Ctr. for Tech. Edn., Lisle, Ill., 1982-84; communications mgr. Hickory Ridge Conf. Ctr., Lisle, 1984-85, mktg. cons., 1985-87; supr. AT&T, Morristown, N.J., 1987—. Editor: American Poetry Athology, 3 vols., 1988; producer (videotape): Meetings & Seminars, 1986, Getting Down to Bus. 1986. Family services coordinator Mil. Dependent Families, Aviano AFB, Italy, 1964. Recipient 1st Time Exhibitor award Tng. Mag., 1986. Mem. Awareness Task Force, Meeting Planners, Inc., Am. Mgmt. Assn., Nat. Assn. Female Execs. Home: 21 Pleasant Rd Highbridge NJ 08829

DAVIS, PRISCILLA LOUISE, small business director; b. Grinnell, Iowa, Sept. 10, 1952; d. Mac Eugene and Verle G. (Schwartz) P.; divorced; children: Robert S., Christopher Paul. Grad. high sch., Phoenix. With Robert Wold Communications, Los Angeles, 1980-81; ops. coordinator Netcom Enterprises, Burbank, Calif., 1981, ops. supr., 1981-82, ops. mgr., 1982-83, asst. dir., 1983-84, dir., 1984-86; v.p. Sales Mktg. Services Optimum, Burbank, 1986-87, exec. v.p., ptnr. B&P Spacesconnection Inc., Burbank, 1987—. Mem. Soc. Satellite Profls.

DAVIS, REBECCA ANN HENRY, public adminstration executive; b. Ruston, La., Sept. 11, 1948; d. George Wayne and Vina (Greer) Henry; m. Michael P. Brown, Nov. 29, 1968 (div. June 1974); children—Christopher Douglas; m. James Harry Davis, May 12, 1976 (div. Dec. 1985). B.A., La. Tech. U., 1969; M.A., U. Okla., 1976. Regional alcoholism and drug abuse coordinator Nortex Regional Planning Commn., Wichita Falls, Tex., 1975-79; adminstrv. asst. to exec. dir. Tex. Commn. on Alcoholism (now Tex. Commn. Alcohol and Drug Abuse), Austin, 1979-81, dep. dir., 1982—. Mem. Wichita Mental Health Assn., Wichita Falls, Tex., 1976-79; coordinator Silent Friends Benefit Com., Wichita Falls, 1976-79; chair, vice-chair Citizens Traffic Safety Council, Wichita Falls, 1976-79; mem. Austin Council on Fgn. Affairs, 1984-88. Mem. Human Relations Assn., Women in Tex. Govt., Alliance Francaise, Beta Sigma Phi. Democrat. Baptist. Office: Tex Commn on Alcohol and Drug Abuse 1705 Guadalupe Austin TX 78701

DAVIS, REBECCA WING, accountant; b. Provo, Utah, Apr. 23, 1953; d. Sherman William and Martha Elayne (Hinckley) W.; m. Michael Whitaker Davis, Aug. 11, 1983; children: Margaret Jeanne, Joseph Michael, Jessica Ann. Student Brigham Young U., 1971-72; B.S., U. Utah, 1976, M.B.A., 1982. Typist, pool supr. Haskins & Sells, Salt Lake City, 1977-78; real estate salesperson Ken Mayne Inc., Salt Lake City, 1978-79; exec. sec. Eimco PMD, Salt Lake City, 1979-80; legal sec. Richard G. Cook, P.C., Salt Lake City, 1980; fin. analyst E-Systems, Inc., Salt Lake City, 1982-83; acct. U. Utah, Salt Lake City, 1983—. Campaign worker Frances Farley for Congress, Salt Lake City, 1982. Mem. Women in Communications. Democrat.

DAVIS, ROBIN SOLTIS, science editor; b. Waterbury, Conn., Jan. 13, 1959; d. Jonas Francis and Nancy Lynn (Schaal) Soltis; m. Atwood Franklin Davis IV, Mar. 28, 1987. BA, Swarthmore Coll., 1981. Research asst. Acad. Nat. Scis., Phila., 1981-83, asst. editor, 1984-86, dir. editorial services, 1986—. Mem. Nat. Assn. Female Execs. Office: Acad Natural Scis Phila 19th and the Pkwy Philadelphia PA 19103

DAVIS, RUTH MARGARET (MRS. BENJAMIN FRANKLIN LOHR), former government official, business executive; b. Sharpsville, Pa., Oct. 19, 1928; d. W. George and Mary Anna (Ackermann) D.; m. Benjamin F. Lohr, Apr. 29, 1961. B.A., Am. U., 1950; M.A., U. Md., 1952, Ph.D., 1955. Statistician FAO, UN, Washington, 1946-49; mathematician Nat. Bur. Standards, 1950-51; head operations research div. David Taylor Model Basin, 1955-61; staff asst. Office Dir. Def. Research and Engring., Dept. Def., 1961-67; asso. dir. research and devel. Nat. Library Medicine, 1967-68; dir. Lister Hill Nat. Center for Biomed. Communications, 1968-70; dir. Inst. for Computer Scis. and Tech., Nat. Bur. Standards, 1970-77; dep. undersec. def. for research and engring. 1977-79; asst. sec. resource applications U.S. Dept. Energy, 1979-81; pres. Pymatuning Group Inc., 1981—; bd. dirs. Control Data Corp., United Telecommunications Inc., Air Products and Chems., Varian Assocs., BTG, Inc., Premark Internat., Inc., Prin. Fin. Group, Ins.; trustee Consol. Edison Co. of N.Y., Aerospace Corp.; lectr. U. Md., 1955-57, Am. U., 1957-58; vis. prof. computer sci. U. Pa., 1969-72; adj. prof. U. Pitts.; cons. Office Naval Research, Washington, 1957-58; mem. Md. Gov.'s Sci. Adv. Council, 1971-77; chmn. nat. adv. council Electric Power Research Inst., 1975-76. Contbr. articles to profl. jours. Trustee Inst. Def. Analysis, bd. visitors Cath. U. Am.; adv. bd. U. Calif.-Berkeley Sch. Engring. Recipient Rockefeller Tech. Mgmt. award, 1973; Fed. Woman of Yr. award, 1973; Systems Profl. of Yr. award, 1973; Computer Sci. Man of Yr. award, 1979; Disting. Service medal Dept. Def., 1979; Disting. Service medal Dept. Energy, 1981; gold medal Dept. Energy, 1981; Ada A. Lovelace award, 1984. Fellow AIAA, Soc. for Info. Display; mem. AAAS, Am. Math Soc., Math Assn. Am., Nat. Acad. Engring., Nat. Acad. Pub. Adminstrn., Washington Philos. Soc., Phi Kappa Phi, Sigma Pi Sigma. Office: Pymatuning Group Inc 2000 N 15th St Suite 707 Arlington VA 22201

DAVIS, SANDRA IRENE, municipal service educator; b. Aurora, Ill., Jan. 29, 1949; d. Edgar Colin and Charlotte Irene (Larson) Gabel; m. James Edward Davis, Nov. 27, 1971; children: Charlyn, Gabrielle. BS in Edn., No. Ill. U., 1971, MS in Clothing and Textiles, 1974. Asst. home econs. extension advisor Lasalle County Coop. Extension Service-U. Ill., Ottawa, 1971-75, assoc. home econs. extension advisor, 1975-83, extension advisor, 1983-86, sr. advisor, 1986—. State bd. dirs. Family Community Leadership, 1987; bd. dirs. Newark Sch. Dist. 66, 1987. Mem. Nat. Assn. Extension Home Economists (disting. service award 1983, pub. affairs edn. award 1983), Ill. Assn. Extension Home Economists (peer award 1978, 82), Am. Home Econs. Assn., Ill. Home Econs. Assn. (group award 1975), Epsilon Sigma Phi, AAUW. Lutheran. Club: Newark (Ill.) Community (v.p. 1986-87). Office: La Salle County Coop Extension 125 Swanson St Ottawa IL 61350

DAVIS, SANDRA KAYE, accountant; b. Borger, Tex., Nov. 20, 1952; d. Montie Joe and Gracie (Keeton) Boyett; m. John Karl Davis, Aug. 27, 1972; 1 child, Stephen Kyle. BA in Acctg., Okla. Bapt. U., 1975. CPA, Tex. Jr. acct. Am. Fidelity Assurance Co., Oklahoma City, 1975-77; bookkeeper Child Study Ctr., Ft. Worth, 1977-78, comptroller, 1978-81, 83—; acct. Donald R. Shaw CPA, Victoria, Tex., 1981-82; comptroller Easter Seal Soc., Ft. Worth, 1982-84; fin. cons. Women's Haven Ft. Worth, 1979, Assn. Retarded Citizens, Ft. Worth, 1978; instr. bookkeeping seminars United Way Tarrant County, 1979-80. Sunday sch. tchr., Ft. Worth. Mem. Tex. Soc. CPA's, Ft. Worth Chpt. CPA's, Alpha Lambda Delta. Republican. Baptist. Home: 6904 Ritter Ln Fort Worth TX 76137 Office: Child Study Ctr 1300 W Lancaster Fort Worth TX 76102

DAVIS, SARA JANE, utility company official; b. Jackson, Mich., Feb. 24, 1948; d. Leonard William and Margery Barbara (Smith) Lashley. AA in Bus. Mgmt. and Data Processing, Lansing Community Coll., 1978; BA, Spring Arbor Coll., 1984. Computer programmer Consumers Power Co., Jackson, 1968-79, computer analyst, 1979-82, supr. software services, 1982-83, supr. energy supply systems support, 1984-85, project mgr. customer info., 1986-87, client services account mgr., 1988—. Mem. mktg. com. United Way; mem. exec. com. Employees for Better Govt. PAC; bd. dirs. Jackson Community Leadership Acad. Mem. Assn. for Systems Mgmt. (chpt. sec.), Nat. Fedn. Bus. and Profl. Women (chpt. pres.). Office: Consumers Power Co 1945 Parnall Rd Jackson MI 49201

DAVIS, SARA LEA, pharmacist; b. Knoxville, Tenn., Aug. 1, 1951; d. Horace William and Margaret Jewel (Hill) D. BS in Liberal Arts, U. Tenn., 1973; BS in Pharmacy, U. Tenn., Memphis, 1976, PharmD, 1977. Asst. mgr. Pharmaco Nuclear, Inc., Chgo., 1977-79; nuclear pharmacist Kansas City, Mo., 1979, Bapt. Meml. Hosp., Memphis, 1979-83; asst. mgr. Syncor, Inc., Washington, 1983-84; staff pharmacist Rite Aid Corp., Knoxville, 1984-87, pharmacist-in-charge, 1987—; rep. 3d High Country Nuclear Medicine Conf., Vail, Colo., 1983; mem. adv. bd. V.I.P. Home Nursing & Rehab., Knoxville, 1985-86. Mem. Am. Pharm. Assn., Acad. Pharm. Sci. (sect. nuclear pharmacy), Soc. Nuclear Pharmacy, Memphis Bus. and Profl. Women's Assn. (bd. dirs. 1982-83), Mortar Bd., Phi Beta Kappa, Phi Kappa Phi, Rho Chi, Alpha Lambda Delta. Baptist. Club: Club Leconte. Office: Rite Aid Pharmacy 1637 Downtown West Blvd Knoxville TN 37919

DAVIS, SARAH JANE, health care professional; b. Cheyenne, Wyo., Feb. 8, 1949; d. Frederick Eugene and Bernice (Deaver) Fowler; m. David Allen Davis, Dec. 21, 1968 (div. 1973); 1 child, Jacoby. Lic. realtor, Tex. Key punch operator San Antonio Coll., 1967-70; with personnel dept. Bapt. Meml. Hosp., San Antonio, 1970-71; key punch operator Frost Bank, San Antonio, 1971-72; mgr. Stop and Go, Inc., San Antonio, 1971-72; coordinator S.W. Tex. Meth. Hosp., San Antonio, 1973—; Owner Mexican Curio and Gift Shop, San Antonio, 1986—. Mem. Nat. Assn. Female Execs. Home: 1955 Larkspur #1412 San Antonio TX 78213 Office: SW Tex Meth Hosp 7700 Floyd Curl Dr San Antonio TX 78229

DAVIS, SHARRON KAY, credit reporting company executive; b. Lubbock, Tex., Mar. 27, 1953; d. Cleon Elmer and Wilma (Dawson) D.; m. (div. Sept. 1977). Diploma in fashion merchandising and bus. Bauder Fashion Coll., Arlington, Tex., 1972. Dist. sec. Gen. Electric Credit Corp., Lubbock, 1973-77; asst. to mgr. Equico Lessors, Lubbock, 1977-78; loan processor Nat. Mortgage Co., San Antonio, 1978-79; gen. mgr. Chilton Credit Reporting, Lubbock, 1979—. Local vol. worker Am. Cancer Soc., 1982—, March of Dimes, 1985. Named Mgr. of Yr., Chilton Credit Reporting, 1983. Mem. Credit Women Internat. (Boss of Yr. award 1985). Republican. Home: 4609 62d St Lubbock TX 79414 Office: Chilton Credit Reporting 6502 Slide Rd Suite 203 Lubbock TX 79416

DAVIS, STACY ADDINGTON, financial analyst; b. Texarkana, Tex., Dec. 12, 1959; d. Doyle Raymond Addington and Emma Ruth (Corbell) Eggenburger; m. George William Davis III, Aug. 30, 1986. BBA, Baylor U., 1982; MBA, Vanderbilt U., 1984. Staff cons. Mgmt. Info. Consulting div. Arthur Andersen & Co., Nashville, 1984-85; staff auditor No. Telecom, Inc., Nashville, 1985-86, fin. analyst, 1986-87, sr. fin. analyst, 1987—. Vol. Terry Holcombe Congl. campaign, Nashville, 1987. Mem. Chi Omega Alumni Assn. Republican. Presbyterian. Office: No Telecom Inc 200 Athens Way Nashville TN 37228-1803

DAVIS, SUSAN FRANCES, international real estate broker; b. Chgo., Mar. 5, 1939; d. John S. Wysocke and Patricia (Dyess) Roberts; m. George Davis, Jan. 27, 1973; 1 child, Lisa. A. BS, So. Ill. U., 1962; postgrad., San Diego State Grad. Sch., 1963-64. Elem. sch. tchr. Elk Grove Sch. Dist., Arlington Heights, Ill., 1968-74; realtor Livable Forest, Kingwoodq, Tex., 1977-82; v.p. Corp. Investment Bus. Brokers, Houston, 1985-86; owner, broker Investments Internat., Kingwood, 1983—; pres., owner Reunions with Class, Kingwood, 1987—. Mem. AAUW, Internat. Real Estate Fedn., Internat. Realtors Assn. Roman Catholic. Club: Republican Woman's (Kingwood). Home: 1726 Chestnut-Ridge Kingwood TX 77339

DAVIS, SUZANNE GOULD, small business owner; b. N.Y.C., Apr. 22, 1947; d. Lawrence Robert and Diana (Klotz) Gould; 2 children. Diploma in French Civilization Studies with honors, Sorbonne U., Paris, 1967; BA in French magna cum laude, Tufts U., 1968; MA in Teacher English Speaker Other Lang., Columbia U., 1975, MLS, 1984. Prodn. asst. James Garrett and Ptnrs., N.Y.C., 1969-70; adminstrv. asst. Alvin Toffler, N.Y.C., 1970-71; dir. mktg. Econ. Models Ltd., London, 1971; mgr. John Player Info. Bur., London, 1972-73; mgr. mktg. Berkey Film Processing, N.Y.C., 1974-75; freelance editor, translator N.Y.C., 1975-82; gen. mgr. Rosemary Scott Temps. Inc., N.Y.C., 1983-86; pres. Suzanne Davis Temps. Inc., N.Y.C., 1986—. Editor-translator: La Méthode Orange: Teacher's Manual, 1977. Mem. Arts and Bus. Council, N.Y.C., 1984—. Mem. Nat. Assn. Female Execs., Nat. Assn. Women Bus. Owners, Spl. Libraries Assn., N.Y. Assn. Temp. Services (bd. dirs. 1986-87, co-chair program com.), Murray Hill Bus. and Profl. Women's Orgn. (bd. dirs., chair scholarship com. 1985, chair young careerist award 1986-88), Beta Phi Mu. Office: Suzanne Davis Temps Inc 20 E 46th St Suite 302 New York NY 10017

DAVIS, TERRI M., communications executive; b. Binghampton, N.Y., Dec. 2, 1947; d. Michael Sr. and Patricia Ann (Bentz) Maslak; m. Thomas Leon Davis, Dec. 20, 1969; children: Eric, Annette. BS in Dietetics, Okla. State U., 1970; postgrad., Phillips U., 1978-82, 88, Coll. for Fin. Planning, 1984—. Pub. relations cons. TMD Enterprises, Tulsa, 1984-85, proprietor, cons., 1985-86; systems analyst Arrow Specialty Co. div. Masco Co., Tulsa, 1986; dir. communication services Arrow Specialty Co. div. Masco Industries, Tulsa, 1986-87, inventory control mgr., 1987—; cons. computer systems

Resonance for Women, Tulsa, 1983-86, Cascia Hall Prep Sch., Tulsa, 1986-87. Editor (newsletters) Arrow Update, Arrow News. Dir. edn. programs Kirk of the Hills Ch., Tulsa, 1976-78; cabinet advisor Camp Fire, Tulsa, 1986-87, advisor, 1984—, discovery treas., 1987—; active Mothers Against Drunk Driving. Elks Found. scholar, Endicott, 1965. Mem. Nat. Assn. Female Execs., Nat. Math Scholarship Assn., Holland Hall Parents Assn. (treas. 1982-83). Republican. Episcopalian. Lodge: Rotary. Home: 1810 E 43d St Tulsa OK 74105 Office: Arrow Specialty Co 2301 E Independence Tulsa OK 74110

DAVIS, TERRY SERFASS, psychologist; b. Los Angeles, Nov. 6, 1942; d. George Donald and Miriam Allen (Baisden) Serfass; m. Bernard Morgan; children: Sheryl Ann Barak, Janet Lee Barak. BA with distinction, U. Redlands, 1966; PhD in Clin. Psychology, U. So. Calif., 1973. Supr. field placement psychology dept. UCLA, 1973-76, dir. family rehab. coordinator project extension dept., 1976-81; out-patient counselor alcoholism, recovery service San Pedro (Calif.) Peninsula Hosp., 1979-80; lectr. health and safety Calif. State U., Los Angeles, 1975-78; pvt. practice psychology, Torrance, Calif., 1978—; dir clin. services addictive disease unit Charter Pacific Hosp., Torrance, 1981-83; coordinator alcohol/drug tng. programs extension dept. UCLA, 1978-87; ptnr., A Healing Partnership, 1987—faculty Antioch U.-West, 1981-82, instr. grad. program, 1985; clin. supr. South Bay Human Services, Torrance, 1985-86; cons. in field. Bd. dirs. CLARE Found., 1977-80, pres., 1979-80; bd. dirs. Felicity House, 1974-80, pres., 1977-78, 79-80; bd. dirs. Valley Women's Ctr., 1978-79. Mem. Calif. Assn. Alcoholic Recovery Homes (pres. Los Angeles chpt. 1979-80), Am. Psychol. Assn., Western Psychol. Assn., Calif. Psychol. Assn., Assn. Women in Psychology, Sierra Club. Office: 3246 N Sepulveda Blvd Suite 204 Torrance CA 90505

DAVIS, THELMA LORRAINE FAULKNER, retired educator, political worker; b. Columbus, Ga., June 20, 1906; d. John Asa and Amanda Louise (Hill) Faulkner; m. Lewis Herschel Davis, Mar. 21, 1926 (dec. 1970); 1 child, Lisa Erline. AB, Mercer U., 1953, MEd, 1959. Cert. elem. tchr., Ga., supervising student tchrs., Ga., reading specialist, Ga. Tchr., Ga. Pub. Schs., until 1982; reading specialist, Griffin-Spalding County, Ga., 1966-73; conv. del. World Confederation of Orgns. of Teaching Profession, various locations internationally, 6 yrs., 1963-76. Contbr. articles to profl. jours. Life mem. Ga. Congress of Parents and Tchrs., 1950-74; mem. Educators for Johnson and Humphrey, 1964-65; alt. to Democratic Nat. Conv., 1964; speaker on edn. Okla. Senate and Ho. of Reps., 1964; speaker on compulsary edn. law, tchrs.' salaries Senate and Ho. of Reps., 49 states; speaker Gov.'s Conf. on Edn., 1965; pres. LWV, Griffin, 1980-81; Griffen rep. for bd. dirs. Council on Aging of McIntosh Trail, past chmn., now sec.; vol. tchr. Griffen-Spaulding Adult Edn. Ctr., 1986—; state-at-large del. NEA Conv., Mpls., 1981. Recipient Outstanding Service award Va., 1972, La., 1974, S.C., 1976, Gov. of Ga. Vol. award, 1982. Mem. Griffin-Spalding Assn. Educators (pres. 1956-58, award for 35 yrs. of appreciated services, 1974), Ga. Assn. Educators (pres. dept. classroom tchrs. 1960-62, ann. service award 1954, award for strengthening human relationships 1982), NEA (life mem., pres. dept. classroom tchrs. 1964-65, disting. service award 1966-71, Trentholm award for human relations 1970, M.Communications for advancement of Edn. in Am. 1971), Am. Assn. Sch. Adminstrs. (hon., life), AAUW (community leadership award 1982, pres. Griffin chpt. 1982-84, sec. 1984—, Griffin rep. to Council on Aging Ret. Tchrs. Assn., Delta Kappa Gamma. Baptist. Avocations: tutoring, visiting nursing homes. Home: 19 Terracedale Ct Griffin GA 30223

DAVIS, VIKKI ANN, janitorial supply company executive; b. Troy, N.C., Apr. 17, 1952; d. Melwood L. and Ann (Norris) Davis; 1 child, William Corwin McKinney II. BS in Sociology, Edgecliff Coll., Cin., 1974; MBA, Xavier U., Cin., 1985. Sales mgr. Ross Labs., Cin., 1975-80, Johnson & Johnson, Cin., 1980-83, Ayerst Labs., Cin., 1983-85; pres. Multi-Devel. Janitorial Supply Co., Cin., 1985—. Mem. Legal Def. and Edn. Fund, Am. Mgmt. Assn., Nat. Assn. Female Execs., Nat. Assn. Minority Contractors. Republican. Presbyterian. Office: Multi-Devel Janitorial Supply 956 Wareham Dr Cincinnati OH 45202

DAVIS, WANDA ROSE, lawyer; b. Lampasas, Tex., Oct. 4, 1937; d. Ellis DeWitt and Julia Doris (Rose) Cockrell; m. Richard Andrew Fulcher, May 9, 1959 (div. 1969); 1 child, Greg Ellis; m. Edwin Leon Davis, Jan. 14, 1973 (div. 1985). BBA, U. Tex., 1959, JD, 1971. Bar: Tex. 1971, Colo. 1981, U.S. Dist. Ct. (no. dist.) Tex. 1972, U.S. Dist. Ct. Colo. 1981, U.S. Ct. Appeals (10th cir. 1981, U.S. Supreme Ct. 1976. Atty. Atlantic Richfield Co., Dallas, 1971; assoc. firm Crocker & Murphy, Dallas, 1971-72; prin. Wanda Davis, Atty. at Law, Dallas, 1972-73; ptnr. firm Davis & Davis Inc., Dallas, 1973-75; atty. adviser HUD, Dallas, 1974-75, Air Force Acctg. and Fin. Ctr., Denver, 1976—; co-chmn. regional Profl. Devel. Inst., Am. Soc. Mil. Comptrollers, Colorado Springs, Colo., 1982; chmn. Lowry AFB Noontime Edn. Program, Exercise Program, Denver, 1977-83; mem. speakers bur. Colo. Women's Bar, 1982-83, Lowry AFB, 1981-83; mem. fed. ct. liaison com. U.S. Dist. Ct. Colo., 1983; mem. Leaders of the Fed. Bar Assn. People to People Del. to China, USSR and Finland, 1986. Contbr. numerous articles to profl. jours. Bd. dirs. Pres.'s Council Met. Denver, 1981-83; mem. Lowry AFB Alcohol Abuse Exec. Com., 1981-84. Recipient Spl. Achievement award USAF, 1978; Upward Mobility award Fed. Profl. and Adminstrv. Women, Denver, 1979. Mem. Fed. Bar Assn. (pres. Colo. 1982-83, mem. nat. council 1984—, Earl W. Kintner Disting. Service award 1983, 1st v.p. 10th cir. 1986—), Colo. Trial Lawyers Assn., Bus. and Profl. Women's Club (dist. IV East dir. 1983-84, Colo. pres. 1988—), Am. Soc. Mil. Comptrollers (pres. 1984-85), Denver South Met. Bus. and Profl. Women's Club (pres. 1982-83), Denver Silver Spruce Am. Bus. Women's Assn. (pres. 1981-82; Woman of Yr. award 1982), Colo. Jud. Inst., Colo. Concerned Lawyers, Profl. Mgrs. Assn., Fed. Women's Program (v.p. Denver 1980), Dallas Bar Assn., Tex. Bar Assn., Denver Bar Assn., Altrusa, Zonta. Denver Nancy Langhorn Federally Employed Women. (pres. 1979-80). Christian. Office: Air Force Acctg and Fin Ctr AFAFC/JAL Denver CO 80279

DAVIS-BECKETT, LUANN RUTH, satellite coordinator, television producer; b. Gassville, Ark., Nov. 18, 1951; d. Harold Fenton and Ruth Leona (Harpe) Davis; m. David C. Beckett, Oct. 5, 1986. BS in Elect. Communications, Southwest Mo. State U., 1978. News anchor Sta. KMTC-TV, Springfield, Mo., 1975-76; sales mgr., reporter, announcer Sta. KICK-AM/KTTS-FM radio, Springfield, 1976-78; publ. and cultural affairs dir. Sta. KOZK-TV, Springfield, 1976-79; assignment editor Sta. KMGH-TV, Denver, Colo., 1979-81; account exec. Hill & Knowlton Pub. Relations, Denver, 1981-83; ptnr. Cordy-Davis Media/Speaker Tng., Denver, N.Y.C., 1983—; pres., bd. chmn. Video Info., Inc., Denver, 1983-86; owner, cons. L.R. Davis & Assocs., N.Y.C., 1983—; satellite coordinator CBS News, N.Y.C., 1987—; prodn. coordinator Internews Inc./P3TV, N.Y.C., 1986-87; cons. in field. TV tng. grantee Corp. Pub. Broadcasting, 1978. Mem. Nat. Assn. Bus. and Profl. Women (Colo. state pub. realtions chair1985-86), Colo. Career Devel. Ctr. (exec. bd. 1986), Internat. Assn. Broadcast Monitors, Colo. Women's Hall of Fame (founder, bd. dirs.). Home: 780 Riverside Dr Apt 10-D New York NY 10032 Office: CBS News 15 N Ferris St Irvington NY 10533

DAVIS-GROSSMAN, CAROL GAIL, organization executive; b. Newark, Jan. 8, 1952; d. Franklin Fredrick and Helen (Kabacoff) Davis; m. Stephen Fred Grossman, Oct. 5, 1980; 1 child, Genna. B.A. with honors, U. Md., 1974; M.S., Hunter Coll., 1975. Spl. investigator Prince George's County Office of Landlord-Tenant Affairs, Upper Marlboro, Md., 1974; contract adminstr. Com. of Interns and Residents, N.Y.C., 1975-82; NE regional organizer Physicians Nat. Housestaff Assn., Washington, 1977-79; exec. dir. Am. Med. Women's Assn., N.Y.C., 1982—. Mem. Am. Pub. Health Assn., Pub. Health Assn. N.Y.C., Am. Soc. Assn. Execs., N.Y. Soc. Assn. Execs., Am. Assn. Med. Soc. Execs. Office: Am Med Women's Assn 465 Grand St New York NY 10002

DAVISON, BARBARA, small business owner; b. Palmerton, Pa., Jan. 3, 1936; d. David and Lillian (Roth) Seiden; m. Maxwell E. Davison, Aug. 25, 1957; children: Mark, Andrew, Douglas. Student, Simmons Coll., 1953-55, MBA, 1984; student, Cedar Crest Coll., 1973. Travel cons. Group Travel Assocs., Allentown, Pa., 1974-80; campaign dir. State of Pa., 1980-81; stockbroker Warren York and Co., Inc., Allentown, 1981-83; v.p. ops. GTA Travel, Allentown, 1984-86; owner Resumes, etc., Allentown, 1986—; lectr. Lehigh County Community Coll., Allentown, 1987—. Mem. Nat. Assn. Profl. Saleswomen, Womens Health Ctr., Exec. Womens Council, Allentown C. of C. Home: Box 195A Rd #2 Emmaus PA 18049

DAVISON, BETSY JANE, training consultant; b. Cleve., Dec. 22, 1921; d. Alexander Stuart and Helen Eva (Chapman) D.; student Albion (Mich.) Coll., 1941-43; B.A., U. Chgo., 1943; M.A., Tchrs. Coll., Columbia U., 1952. Civilian recreation dir. U.S. Army and Air Force Overseas, 1945-55; command recreation dir. Hdqrs. U.S. Air Forces in Europe, Ger., 1956-58; coordinator student activities Kean (N.J.) Coll., 1959-66; cons. edn. and tng. Assn. Jr. Leagues, N.Y.C., 1966-70; dir. tng. Mental Health Materials Center, N.Y.C., 1971-76; tng. cons. APC Skills Co., N.Y.C., 1977-78; dir. tng. and confs. Child Welfare League Am., N.Y.C., 1979-83; tng. cons., 1983—. Mem. Am. Soc. Tng. and Devel., Am. Adult Edn. Assn., Kappa Delta Pi, Pi Lambda Theta, Delta Sigma Rho, Alpha Lambda Delta. Author tng. manuals. Home and Office: 333 E 43d St New York NY 10017

DAVISON, DOROTHY, retired urban planner; b. Boston, June 22, 1925; d. Israel and Tillie (Bloom) Goldstein; m. Sol Davison, Feb. 3, 1945; children: Scott J., Mark G. Student, Chaffey Coll., 1947, Ind. U., 1948-50, Harvard U., 1952-55, Contra Costa Coll., 1956-59, U. Calif., Berkeley, 1960; BA in Urban Studies and Community Devel., San Francisco State U., 1968; postgrad. in basic indsl. devel., Tex. Agrl. and Mech. U., 1982; postgrad. in econ., U. Okla., 1982-84. Cert. housing mgr.; lic. real estate broker, Tex. With CSC, Mass., Calif., Tex. and Fla., 1942-46; apptd. to Mayor's Citizen Adv. Com., Richmond Urban Renewal Agy., Assn. Bay Area Govts. and Richmond (Calif.) Model Cities, 1956-72; chief planner Harris County Community Devel. Agy., Houston, 1975-82, asst. dir., 1982-84, dir. research and devel., 1984-85; exec. dir. Harris County Housing Authority and Harris County Community Devel. Agy., 1985-86; cons. Tex. Agrl. and Mech. U. Agrl. Extension Resource Council, Gulf Coast regional econ. devel. com. Houston/Galveston Area Council. Nat. del. White House Conf. on Aging, 1981; Tex. del. Gov.'s Conf. Aging, 1981; chmn. housing for elderly Houston/Harris County Area Agy. Aging, 1981. Recipient cert. of merit City of Richmond, 1969, Women in Govt. cert. U. Houston, 1978, resolution and cert. of merit Harris County Commrs., 1981, 86, Profl. Community Leadership of Yr. award Harris County Extension Service, Tex. Agrl. and Mech. U., 1985. Mem. Am. Planning Assn., Nat. Assn. Housing and Redevel. Ofcls. (internat. com., Spl. Achievement award 1984), Tex. Indsl. Devel. Council, Nat. Assn. Home Builders (srs. housing com. 1984—), Nat. Inst. Sr. Housing (del. council 1985—). Address: PO Box 820609 Houston TX 77282

DAVISON, M(ARY) JO, environmental research laboratory executive, educator, writer; b. Middletown, Ohio, Nov. 8, 1935; d. Harry Edmund and Marie Angeline (Caswell) D. BS, Miami U., Oxford, Ohio, 1957; MA in Sci. Edn., Environ. Studies, Counseling & Guidance, W.Va. U., 1974. Cert. high sch. sci. tchr., W.Va., Ohio. Sci. tchr. Los Angeles Schs., 1958-61; with sales, advt. and pub. relations staff Bell and Gen. Telephone, Columbus, Ohio and Long Beach, Calif., 1962-69; sci. tchr. Summers County (W.Va.) Schs., 1970-76; sci. and environ. edn. specialist Fayette County (W.Va.) Schs., 1976-84; pres., research dir. Lambda Group, Inc., Columbus, Ohio, 1984—, Lambda of Am., Inc., Columbus, 1984—; pres., owner Lambda Environ. Tech., Morgantown, W.Va., 1987—; pres. Lambda Prodn. Corp., Dayton, Columbus, Ohio, 1987—; environ. edn. cons. Columbus City Schs., 1984—; mem. Acid Rain Adv. Com.—U.S. and Can.; exec. council mem. Tech. Alliance Cen. Ohio. Author: The Colony Trilogy, 1974, Against The Odds, 1978; contbr. articles to sci. jours.; inventor coal and water cleaning processes, microbial delivery system, process for bioremediation of acid mine water and reversal of acid rain damaged aquatic ecosystems. Advisor Women's Outreach, Columbus, 1983—; adv. com. W.Va. Dems. in State Sen. and Ho.of Reps., Oak Hill and Charleston, 1979-84; dist. rep. W.Va. Conservation Edn. Council, Oakhill, 1979-84. Recipient several Sci. and Environ. Educator of Yr. awards, 1973-84; Dept. of Energy grantee, 1985-86. Mme. Nat. Assn. Biologist, Am. Assn. Scientists, Ohio Acad. Sci. (sci. fair judge, 1983—), W.Va. Acad. Sci., Sierra Club, Nature Conservancy, NOW, Nat. Orgn. Female Execs. Home: 1709 Hickory Creek Ln Columbus OH 43229 Office: Lambda Group Inc 1445 Summit St Columbus OH 43201

DAWES, JANICE LYNN, retail executive; b. Decatur, Ill., Mar. 21, 1950; d. Alvie L. and Pearlie M. (Shephard) Paine; m. David W. Peters, June 6, 1968 (div. Oct. 1982); children: Matthew W., Antony E., Ginger A.; m. Ronald L. Dawes, Dec. 3, 1983. Student, Richland Coll., 1980-81. Owner, mgr. Dairy Queen, Salem and Watseka, Ill. and Las Vegas, Nev., 1972-77; adminstrv. asst. Mary Moppets of Las Vegas, 1977-78; asst. to v.p., dir. advt. Bachrachs Menswear Inc., Decatur, 1981-83; registered rep., agt. various ins. firms, Ill., 1983—; pres. Janice Lynn's Inc., Charleston, Ill., 1986—. Historian Charleston ARea ARts Council, 1985. Democrat. Club: Ea. Ill. U. Panther.

DAWKINS, JACQUELINN HAWKINS, infosystems specialist; b. Sacramento, Sept. 10, 1938; d. Jack Alfred Hawkins and Gladys Lynn (Shipp) Schmeckenbecher; m. Michael Stuart Dawkins, Apr. 12, 1970; children from previous marriage: Cheryl Lynn Myers (dec.), Tamara Annette Myers. BA in Pub. Adminstrn. summa cum laude, Upper Iowa U., 1982. Computer operator 437th hdqrs. squadron USAF, Charleston AFB, S.C., 1967-71; computer operator Keesler (AFB) Tech. Tng. Ctr. USAF, Miss., 1971; computer aid base suppley computer facility USAF, Keesler AFB, Miss., 1971-75, computer specialist, 1975-78, supply mgmt. analyst, 1978-79, cost and mgmt. program analyst, 1979-83, program analyst, 1983—. Vol. income tax asistance program, Keesler AFB, 1982-88. Mem. Am. Soc. Mil. Comptrollers, Inst. Cost Analysis (cert.). Republican. Home: 6349 Chaucer Dr Ocean Springs MS 39564

DAWKINS, LISA FRETER, communications specialist; b. Washington, Aug. 25, 1951; d. Theodore Henry and Elizabeth Crawford (Stout) Freter; m. David O'Shea Dawkins, Dec. 20, 1975; 1 child, Meghan Elizabeth. Student, Towson State Coll., 1969-70, Inst. Allende, San Miguel de Allende, Guanajuato, Mex., 1970-72, U. de las Americas, Cholula, Puebla, Mex., 1972-73, U. Phoenix, Denver, 1988. Asst. mgr. Henri Baby, Washington, 1969-70; salesperson Brooks Fashions, Bloomington, Ind., 1972-73; mgr. Top Hat Tuxedo Rental, Bloomington, 1973-74, La Bonita Supper Club, Denver, 1974-75; adminstrv. asst. Magic Pan Inc., Denver, 1975-79; owner B&B Liquors, Denver, 1979-81; adminstrv. asst. Gt. Amusement Emporium, Englewood, Colo., 1981-83; sec. corp. Ponderosa Homes Colo. Inc., Englewood, 1983-85; dir. pubs. Gt. Western Assn. Mgmt., Denver, 1985-88; dir. publicity and pubs. Freedom's Found. Valley Forge, Denver, 1988; adminstrv. asst. Arapahoe County Div. Employment and Tng., Englewood, Colo., 1988—. Author: (poems) The San Miguel Writer, 1970, Xalli, 1971; exec. producer Law Enforcement Torch Run for Spl. Olympics Video, 1986, script author video Torch Run for Spl. Olympics, 1987, videotaped pub. service announcements. Exec. dir. Colleagues Police for Edn., Support, Denver, 1983—; liaison Colo. Assn. Chiefs Police and Colo. Spl. Olympics, 1986-88. Mem. Nat. Assn. Female Execs., Freedoms Found. (v.p. pub. relations Valley Forgechpt.). Baptist. Home: 8163 E Phillips Circle Englewood CO 80112-3254

DAWKINS, MARVA PHYLLIS, psychologist; b. Jacksonville, Fla., Apr. 12, 1948; d. Ralph and Altamese (Padgett) D.; student U. Freiburg (W.Ger.), 1969-70; B.S., Stetson U., 1971; M.S., Fla. State U., 1972, Ph.D., 1975. Research asst. Fla. State U., Tallahassee, 1970-72; clin. intern, psychology dept. Presbyn.-St. Luke's Med. Ctr. and mental health dept. Mile Square Health Ctr., Chgo., 1973-74; staff psychologist, dir. aftercare treatment program, mental health dept. Mile Square Health Ctr., Chgo., 1974-75, staff psychologist, coordinator devel. disabilities program, 1976-79; asst. prof. psychology U. North Fla., Jacksonville, 1975-76, Rush U.-Presbyn. St. Luke's Med. Ctr., Chgo., 1976—; pvt. practice clin. psychology, 1977—; exec. dir. Inst. for Community Mental Health, 1979—. Registered psychologist, Ill. Mem. Am. Psychol. Assn., Assn. Black Psychologists. Office: PO Box 49474 Chicago IL 60649

DAWLEY, REBECCA JOAN, computer programmer; b. Eveleth, Minn., Mar. 26, 1955; d. Lloyd Ray and Betty Shirley (Larson) D. AA, Rainy River Community Coll., 1975; BS in Math., Bemidji State U., 1977. Assoc. programmer Federated Mutual Ins., Owatonna, Minn., 1977-79, programmer, 1979-81; sr. programmer Federated Mut. Ins., Owatonna, Minn., 1981-83, lead programmer, 1983-85, computer programming supr., 1985—. Mem. So. Minn. Data Processing Assn. (bd. dirs. 1983-85), Owatonna Ins. Women, Nat. Assn. for Female Execs., Bus. and Profl. Women (treas. 1987—). Club: Toastmasters. Home: 1425 Havana Rd Owatonna MN 55060 Office: Federated Mut Ins 121 E Park Square Owatonna MN 55060

DAWSON, CAROL GENE, federal official; b. Indpls., Sept. 8, 1937; d. Ernest Eugene (dec.) and Hilda Lou (Carroll) D.; m. Robert Edmund Bauman, Nov. 19, 1960 (div. 1982); children: Edward Carroll, Eugenie Marie, Victoria Anne, James Shields; m. Franklin Dean Smith, Aug. 2, 1986. BA, Dunbarton Coll., Washington, 1959, Cath. U., Washington, 1961. Staff asst. Senator Kenneth B. Keating, Washington, 1959; exec. asst. Americans for Constl. Action, Washington, 1959; exec. sec. Youth for Nixon Lodge, Washington, 1959-60; legis. asst. Rep. Donald C. Bruce, Washington, 1961-63; dep. dir., pub. info. Goldwater for Pres. Campaign and Rep. Nat. Com., Washington, 1963-64; editor, assoc. editor The New Guard Mag., Washington, 1965-66; dir. info. Am. Conservative Union, Washington, 1966-67; publs. and news analyst White House, Washington, 1969—; staff reporter Easton (Md.) Star-Democrat, 1971-72; freelance writer Easton, 1972-77; real estate salesperson Latham Realtors, Easton, 1977-80; sr. staff asst. presdl. transition U.S. Office of Personnel Mgmt., Washington, 1980-81; dep. press sec. U.S. Dept. Energy, Washington, 1981-82, dep. spl. asst. to sec., 1982-84; commr. U.S. Consumer Product Safety Commn., Washington, 1984—; editor Cath. Currents newsletter, Washington, 1969-70. Co-chmn. Nat. Coll. Young Reps., Washington, 1959-61; bd. dirs. Young Americans for Freedom, 1960-64; vice chmn. Talbot County Rep. State Cen. Com., Md., 1970-74; del. 1st Dist. Md. Rep. Nat. Conv., 1980; mem. bd. visitors Inst. Polit. Journalism Georgetown U., 1985—. Recipient Award of Merit Young Americans for Freedom, 1970. Mem. Presdl. Appointees Orgn. (exec. level IV 1984—). Roman Catholic. Clubs: Capitol Hill; The Fairfax Hunt (Great Falls, Va.). Home: 320 Canterwood Ln Great Falls VA 22066 Office: Consumer Product Safety Commn Suite 500 5401 Westbard Ave Bethesda MD 20207

DAWSON, DONNA RAE, manufacturing company executive; b. Painesville, Ohio, Jan. 25, 1952; d. Bonny Weaver and Mayme Beatrice (Davis) Simmons; m. Robert James Dawson, Aug. 23, 1969 (div. Mar. 20, 1986); children: Rodney James, Denise Rachelle. A in Applied Bus. cum laude, Lakeland Community Coll., 1982. Various positions Fasson div. Avery Internat., Painesville, 1974-78, customer service specialist, 1978 79, sales adminstrn. coordinator, 1979-81; mktg. specialist Mentor, Ohio, 1981-82; market mgr. 1983; product mgr. Painesville, 1983; bus. mgr. 1984-86, venture devel. mgr., 1987; dir. strategic planning Matrix Essentials, Solon, Ohio, 1988—; cons. Fasson Profl. Women's Network, Painesville, 1987, Northeastern Ohio Exec. Women's Network, 1987. Founding mother Sexual Assault Ctr. Lake County, Painesville, 1976, trustee, 1976-87, v.p., fund raising chmn., 1986-87; organist, choir dir. Perry (Ohio) Christian Ch., 1975—. Recipient Account Exec. of Yr. award Lake County United Way, 1987. Mem. Nat. Assn. Female Execs., Am. Soc. Profl. and Exec. Women, Women's City Club (chmn. exec. women's network 1987—). Republican. Mem. Disciples of Christ. Home: 10306 Mayfield Rd Chesterland OH 44026-2732 Office: Matrix Essentials 30601 Carter St Solon OH 44139

DAWSON, MIMI WEYFORTH (MIMI DAWSON), government official; b. St. Louis, Aug. 31, 1944; d. Francis Griffin and Jeanne (Gething) Weyforth; m. Rhett Brewer Dawson, Jan. 15, 1976; 2 children: Elizabeth Stuart, Andrew Brewer. AB, Washington U., St. Louis, 1966. Legis. asst. Rep. Richard Ichord, Mo. Dist., 1969-72, 73; press sec., legis. asst. to Rep. James Symington, Mo. Dist., 1973; press. sec. Sen. Bob Packwood, Oreg., 1973; adminstrv. asst., chief staff, legis. dir. Sen. Bob Packwood, 1975-81; commr. FCC, Washington, 1981-87; dep. Sec. U.S. Dept. of Transportation, Washington, DC, 1987—; Trustee Am. Council Young Polit. Leaders. Republican. Roman Catholic. Office: Dept of Trans Office of the Dep Sec 400 7th St SW Washington DC 20590

DAWSON, ROSE DOROTHY, educator; b. Waukesha, Wis., Feb. 16, 1931; d. Frank Peter and Rose M. (Cisler) Zaic; m. Keith W. Dawson, June 13, 1953 (dec. May 1987); children: Kenneth, Richard, Michael, Gail, Allen. BS, U. Wis., Whitewater, 1971; postgrad., U. Wis. Parkside, Kenosha. Cert. elem. tchr., Wis. Tchr. Magee Sch., Genesee Depot, Wis., 1951-53, Union Grove (Wis.) Grade Sch., 1953-54, 65—, Union Grove Middle Sch., 1965—. Mem. NEA, Wis. Edn. Assn., Union Grove Area Edn. Assn., Am. Rose Soc. Lutheran. Home: 18906 58th Rd Union Grove WI 53182

DAWSON, SUE ELLEN, publishing executive; b. Jefferson City, Mo., Dec. 19, 1955; d. Dale William and Margaret Mary (Nuernberger) Warren; m. Monty Paul Meyer (div. Sept. 1978); m. Joseph Charles Dawson Jr., Apr. 15, 1983 (div. Aug. 1988); 1 child, Meghan Lee. Grad. high sch., Bloomington, Ill. Sec. A&P Transp., Louisville, 1977-78; graphic art dir. Copy Boy Printing Co., Louisville, 1978-86; v.p. On-Line Copy & Pub. Services, Louisville, 1986—. Recipient Pub. Speaking award Dale Carnegie, 1986, Human Relations award, 1987. Mem. Entrepreneur Soc. Republican. Home: 4116 Wheeler Ave Louisville KY 40215

DAY, BEVERLY JEAN, state insurance examiner; b. Tacoma, Wash., July 29, 1942; d. Therial Etheon and Georgia Ykema (Fisher) Wright; AA, Riverside City Coll., 1962; BA, U. Md., 1969; MBA, U. Utah, 1975; m. Dallas Glenn Day, June 13, 1964; 1 child, Linda Gayle. Cert. fin. examiner and accredited record technician. Acct., Toledo Scale Corp., Riverside, Calif., 1962-64, Dikeou Bros., Denver, 1964-65, Redlands (Calif.) Community Hosp., 1965-66, Titan Constrn. Co., Denver, 1969-72; med. record technician U.S. Air Force Hosp., RAF Lakenheath, England, 1973-76; insurance examiner State of Colo. Ins. Div., Denver, 1977—, sr. ins. examiner. Recipient scholarship Am. Soc. Women Accountants, 1961. Mem. Soc. Fin. Examiners (state chmn., mem. ins. examination rev. com., bd. govs.), Am. Mgmt. Assn., Assn. M.B.A. Execs., Nat. Assn. Female Execs., Inc., Am. Med. Record Assn., AAUW. Republican. Methodist. Home: 10330 W Burgundy Ave Littleton CO 80127 Office: Div Ins State of Colo First Western Plaza Bldg 303 W Colfax Ave Suite 500 Denver CO 80204

DAY, BRIGITTE KAPITAEN, financial services company executive, trainer; b. Bad Ischl, Austria, May 8, 1951; Came to U.S., 1951; d. Joseph and Rose (Steigerwald) Kapitaen. BA, West Chester U., 1973; MBA in Fin., Drexel U., 1988. Cert. elem. edn., Pa. Program coordinator MOT Community Action Ctr., Middletown, Del., 1974; engrng. asst. Burroughs Corp., Downingtown, Pa., 1975-76; with Oxford (Pa.) Intermediate Sch., 1977-78; caseworker Kelsch Assocs., Lionville, Pa., 1977-78; mgr. tng. SEI Corp., Wayne, Pa., 1978—. Vol. patient rep. Brandywine Hosp., Coatesville, Pa., 1987, counselor Open Door, West Chester, Pa., 1972-73, archeology Valley Forge Nat. Park, 1987. Recipient Charles S. Swope award First Nat. Bank of West Chester, 1970. Mem. Am. Soc. Tng. and Devel. Roman Catholic. Clubs: Congrega (Coatesville); Women's (Brandywine) (pres.). Home: Rd 2 Box 374D Coatesville PA 19320 Office: SEI Corp 680 E Swedesford Rd Wayne PA 19087

DAY, CONNIE JO, moving company executive, consultant; b. Norfolk, Nebr., Mar. 10, 1949; d. Wayne Leonard and Marilou (Ferry) Walters; m. John Henry Day, Sept. 28, 1971; children: Nanette Marie, Brandon Wayne. Student, Nebr. Wesleyan U., 1968-69. Clk. Delcher Moving and Storage, Jacksonville, Fla., 1970-74; asst. mgr. Jaxpak, Inc., Jacksonville, 1974-78; co-owner John Day & Assocs., Norfolk, 1978—, 2001 Computer Store, Norfolk, 1981-83, OPT for the Future, Norfolk, 1986-87; advisor Bus. and Edn. Task Force on Econ. Devel., Norfolk, 1986-87; advisor entrepreneurial studies N.E. Community Coll., Norfolk, 1987—. Contbr. articles to profl. jours. Pres. Greater Nebr. Muscular Dystrophy Assn., 1984-85, Creative and Talented Children Support Group, Norfolk, 1984-85, Combined Health Agy. Dr., Norfolk, 1987—. Mem. Nat. Assn. of Female Execs., Household Good Forwarders Assn., Am. Movers Conf., Norfolk C. of C. (treas. 1985-87, v.p. 1987-88, chmn. elect 1988—), Am. Bus. Women's Assn. Democrat. Lodge: Toastmistress (v.p. Alexandria, Va. chpt. 1978-79). Home: 609 E Maple Norfolk NE 68701 Office: John Day & Assocs 1118 Riverside Blvd Norfolk NE 68701

DAY, GRACE ANNE, violinist; b. Tondo, Belgian Congo, Jan. 4, 1933, (parents Am. citizens); d. George Wesley and Ellen Irene (Peckham) Westcott; B.M., Eastman Sch. Music, 1957; m. Bernard Hoffer, June 1957; children—Kara Hoffer Day, Gilbert Hoffer; m. 2d, Robert Day, Feb. 8, 1972; adopted children—Ronald Day, Robin Day. Violinist, Rochester (N.Y.) Philharmo. Orch., 1953-58, orch. Radio City Music Hall, N.Y.C., 1964-65, N.J. Symphony, Newark, 1965-66, Toledo Symphony, 1966-67, Indpls. Symphony Orch., 1967—, Suzuki and Friends Chamber Orch., Indpls., 1980-87, Indpls. Symphony Spotlight Concerts, 1987—; mem. faculty Am. U., 1961; pvt. tchr. violin. Mem. Matinee Musical. Home: 903 W 54th St Indianapolis IN 46208

DAY, JANET LOUISE, social services administrator; b. Milw., Jan. 31, 1955; d. John Adolph and Thomasina (Rae) D. BSW, U. Wis., Whitewater, 1976; MSW, Washington U., St. Louis, 1978. Clin. med. social worker St. Joseph's Hosp., Marshfield, Wis., 1978-80, Good Samaritian Med. Ctr., Milw., 1980-83; dir. patient and family service St. Mary's Med. Ctr., Racine, Wis., 1983—; bd. dirs. Anorexia and Bulimia Support Group Bd., Racine, Mental Health of Racine, Inc.; , Daily Nursing Service Adv. Bd., Racine, Racine County Council for Children Illness/Disabilities. Mem. Nat. Assn. Social Workers, Am. Hosp. Assn. of Hosp. Social Work, Nat. Assn. Female Execs., Wis. Nat. Kidney Found., Wis. Hosp. Assn. of Hosp. Social Work, Wis. Assn. Hosp. Social Workers, Sierra Club. Office: St Mary's Med Ctr 3801 Spring St Racine WI 53405

DAY, JENNIE D., state legislator; b. Madera, Pa., Dec. 13, 1921; m. Marvin Day. Ed. Temple U. City councilwoman, Coventry, R.I., 1978-84; realtor; mem. R.I. Senate, 1985—. Democrat. Office: RI Senate State Capitol Providence RI 02903 Address: 19 Beachwood St Coventry RI 02816 *

DAY, JULIA FLAGLER, lawyer; b. Atlanta, Feb. 23, 1947; d. Thomas Thorne and Julia (Gemes) Flagler; m. Stephen Joseph Day, May 1, 1970; 1 child, Ashley Elizabeth. AB, U. Ga., 1968; JD, Lincoln U., 1979. Bar: Calif. 1979. Paralegal Ericksen, Arbuthnot, McCarthy, Kearny & Walsh, San Francisco, 1978-79, assoc., 1979-83, ptnr., mgr. office, San Jose, Calif., 1983—. Mem. ABA, Calif. Bar Assn., Santa Clara Bar Assn., No. Calif. Def. Counsel, Calif. Trial Lawyers Assn., San Jose C. of C., U. Ga. Alumni Assn. Republican. Episcopalian. Club: Commerce (San Francisco). Home: 35 Elston Ct San Carlos CA 94070 Office: Ericksen Arbuthnot McCarthy Kearny & Walsh 351 Miller St San Jose CA 95110

DAY, LINDA CHRISTINE, food products executive; b. Pasadena, Calif., Apr. 9, 1953; d. Dean Kenneth Day and Nancy Jean (Hall) Collins. BS, Calif. Poly. U., 1976, MBA, 1980; postgrad., Claremont Grad. Sch., 1982. Mgr. auditory, prodn. processing and inventory control Dunbar, Inc., City of Industry, Calif., 1972-76; home economist Hunt-Wesson Foods, Fullerton, Calif., 1977-78; sales rep. Appetizers And, Inc., So. Calif., 1979; product mgr. Knudsen Corp., Los Angeles, 1979-81; mgr. strategic planning analysis Ameron Co., Monterey Park, Calif., 1982; asst. dir. mktg. Beatrice Cos., Chgo., 1983-84; bus. unit mgr. Ocean Spray Cranberries, Inc., Plymouth, Mass., 1985; pres. JNANA Corp., San Dimas, Calif., 1986—; adj. lectr. bus. Calif. Poly. U., 1987—. Recipient Desi Advt. award Graphics Design: U.S.A., 1982. Mem. Am. Mktg. Assn., Nat. Assn. Female Execs., Phi Kappa Phi. Home: 3237 Rancho La Carlota Covina CA 91724 Office: JNANA Corp 558 Derby Rd Suite 55 San Dimas CA 91773

DAY, M. JOANNA, controller; b. Cleve., Sept. 8, 1936; d. Joseph Charles and Margaret (Peters) Tyler; m. Milton Clifford (div.); m. Allan William Day, Nov. 4, 1960; children: Gregory, Lisa Adrienne. Student, Earlham Coll., Richmond, Ind., 1954-55; BSBA in Acctg., Garfield Sr. Coll., Painesville, Ohio, 1979. CPA. Acct. Babcock & Wilcox Ind. Systems, Mentor, Ohio, 1970-75; controller Micromenex, Willoughby, Ohio, 1975-80, LCNE, Perry, Ohio, 1980-83, Mid-Con Corp., Valley View, Ohio, 1983-85, Truckpro, Valley View, 1985—; bd. dirs. Western Reserve Services, Inc., Chardon, Ohio; cons. in field. Mem. Am. Field Service, Nat. Assn. Accts. (dir. of communications 1985-87, editor newsletter), Nat. Assn Female Execs. Republican. Baptist. Home: 10210 Thwing Rd Chardon OH 44024 Office: Truckpro 5725 Canal Rd Valley View OH 44125

DAY, MARY JANE THOMAS, cartographer; b. Connors, New Brunswick, Can., Oct. 12, 1927; d. Angus (dec.) and Delina (dec.) (Michaud) Thomas; m. Howard M. Day, Jan. 17, 1923; children: Laurie Anne Day Greene, Angus Howard. BS in Geography, U. Md., 1974, BS in Bus. & Mgmt., 1977. Meteorol. aide Hangar 8 Eastern Airlines, N.Y.C., 1946-47, U.S. Weather Bur., Washington, 1948-50; cartographic aide U.S. Navy Hydrographic Office, Suitland, Md., 1950-57, cartographer, 1957-62; cartographer U.S. Navy Oceanographic Office, Suitland, 1962-72, Def. Mapping Agy., Suitland, 1972—; cartographer USNS Harkness, 1978, Indonesian Naval Personnel, Jakarta, Indonesia, 1981-82. Mem. Nat. Aeronautic Assn., Am. Soc. Photogrammetry & Remote Sensing. Club: Andrews Officers (Md.). Home: 3532 28th Pkwy Temple Hills MD 20748

DAY, MARYLOUISE MULDOON (MRS. RICHARD DAYTON DAY), appraiser; b. St. Louis; d. Joseph A. and Dorothy (Lang) Muldoon; A.B., Washington U., St. Louis, 1940; postgrad. Air U., 1958, George Washington U., 1963-64; grad. Real Estate Inst. Md., 1972; m. Richard Dayton Day, Aug. 15, 1959. Intelligence specialist U.S. Air Force, Washington, 1947-60; program officer, spl. asst. to dir. project devel. VISTA, OEO, 1965-67; v.p. Culpeper Corp., Wilmington, Del., 1955-65; with Joint Intelligence Bur., London, Eng., 1953; appraiser, cons. on antiques, fine arts, 1969—; pres. Agts. For Sales Ltd., 1974—, Marylouise M. Day, Inc., 1978—. Recipient citation U.S. Air Force, 1960. Fellow Inc. Soc. Valuers and Auctioneers (London), Am. Soc. Appraisers (chpt. 1st v.p. 1977-78, pres. 1978-79, chmn. fine arts forum 1976-78, gov. Region 3 1980-82, internat. sec. 1982-84, treas. ednl. found. 1986—); mem. Appraisers Assn. Am., Irish Georgian Soc., Winterthur Guild, Assn. Former Intelligence Officers, Delta Gamma. Club: Kenwood Golf and Country (Washington). Home: 4928 Sentinel Dr Bethesda MD 20816

DAY, NANCY JEANETTE, food products executive; b. Battle Creek, Mich., Feb. 19, 1940; d. James Theodore Ure and Evelyn Viola (MacDonald) Griffin; m. Jerry Lee Wolfersberger, June 14, 1958 (div. Apr. 1975); children: Lynda Kaye, James Bryan, Mary Anne, Scott Alan; m. Richard Keith Day, Oct. 6, 1979. Student, Kellogg Community Coll., Battle Creek, 1979—. Long distance operator Mich. Bell Telephone, Battle Creek, 1957-58; office clk. Gen. Fin., Battle Creek, 1958-59; receptionist, copywriter Sta. WBCK-FM, Battle Creek, 1959-60; sec., bookkeeper Battle Creek Country Club, 1960-62; sec. Marlo Constrn., Battle Creek, 1961-62, Miller Davis Constrn., Kalamazoo, Mich., 1962-63; with sales dept. Handleman Co., Lansing, Mich., 1963-64; continuity dir. Sta. WCEN-FM, Mt. Pleasant, 1968; supr. employee info. system Kellogg Co., Battle Creek, 1969-84, supr. employee relations systems, 1984—. Mem. Battle Creek Community Chorus, 1969—, Mich. Arthritis Found., 1987; bd. dirs. Marshall (Mich.) Civic Players, treas., 1982-83; stage mgr. Kellogg United Way Campaign, Battle Creek, 1983; co-chair Calhoun County Easter Seals, Battle Creek, 1984. Mem. Am. Bus. Women's Assn. (pres. Mitten chpt. 1973-74, pres. Creekview chpt. 1978-79, pres. Unity chpt. 1982-83, originator Calhoun area council, chair 1982, mem. nominating com. 1986, Creekview chpt.'s Woman of Yr 1979, Unity chpt.'s Woman of Yr. 1984), Nat. Mgmt. Assn. (treas. 1985-87, exec. v.p. 1987—), Beta Sigma Phi. Lodges: Elks, Ladies of Moose. Office: Kellogg Co 1 Kellogg Square PO Box 3599 Battle Creek MI 49016-3599

DAY, PEGGY JEAN, education professional; b. Nixon, Tex., July 3, 1946; d. Eugene Estle and S. Mildred (Wishert) D.; divorced; children: Jason Edmonson, Courtney Edmonson. BS, Tex. A&I U., 1968; MEd, U. Houston, 1982. Migrant ednl. liaison Edinburg (Tex.) Independent Sch. Dist., 1974-78; ednl. cons. Tex. Rehab., Gonzales, 1978, Devereaux Found., Victoria, Tex., 1983; ednl. diagnostician Harlandale Independent Sch. Dist., San Antonio, Tex., 1985—; cons. in field, 1982—. Contbr. articles on emotional disturbances and learning disabilities to profl. jours. Leader Girl Scouts Am., Victoria, 1983; chairperson Dem. Party, Victoria, 1985; activist, spokesperson Human Soc.-Man and Beast Assn., San Antonio, 1986—. Recipient Vol. award Gov. of Tex., 1983, 84. Mem. NEA, Tex. State Tchrs. Assn., Tex. Ednl. Diagnostician Assn., Tex. Suprs. Assn., Council Exceptional Assn. Mem. Unity Ch. Office: Harlandale Ind Sch Dist 902 March Ave San Antonio TX 78214

DAY, SHARON HOELSCHER, home economics educator, adult community education administrator; b. Lima, Ohio, Apr. 7, 1932; d. Oscar William and Ruby Henrietta (Feil) Hoelscher; m. Daniel L. Day, June 27, 1981. BS, Ohio State U., 1973; MA, Mich. State U., 1977; postgrad., U. Ariz., 1975, 80, Bowling Green (Ohio) State U., 1982. Cert. secondary edn. tchr., home economist. Extension home economist Ohio State U.-Coop. Extension Service, Celina, 1973-76, 78-80, U. Ariz.-Coop. Extension Service, Phoenix, 1983—; instr. Bowling Green State U., 1980-83. Community rep. Maricopa County Headstart Policy Bd., Phoenix, 1984-86, nutrition evaluator, 1984-85; mem. planning com. Ariz. Hunger Conf., Phoenix, 1986; mem. choir United Meth. Ch., 1978-87. Mem. Am. Home Econs. Assn. (New Achiever of 1987), Ariz. Home Econs. Assn. (pres.-elect 1987—, bd. dirs. 1983-87), Am. Assn. Housing Educators, Nat. Assn. Extension Home Economists (Gen. Foods media grant 1987), Ariz. Assn. Extension Home Economists (pres. 1986), Ariz. Nutrition Council, Am. Youth Hostels Orgn. Democrat. Office: U Ariz Coop Extension Service 4341 E Broadway Phoenix AZ 85040

DAY, SHERRY EADS, corporate professional; b. Houston; d. York Parrish Pope and Erlene (Whitehead) Smith; m. Donald J. Day; children: Dana, Judi Lynn, Craig, Dawn, Lisa. Student, San Antonio Coll., 1963-64, Tex. A&M U., 1964-67. Adminstr. Nurnberg Jugend Pflieger Kinder Programme, Fed. Rep. Germany, 1974-77; sr. v.p. Med. Mgmt. Assn., Temple, Tex., 1980-83; mgr. adminstn., bus. Hassmann Enterprises, Temple, Tex., 1977-83; pres., chief exec. officer Calif. Pharm. Group Inc., Med. Pharm. Inc., DP Mgmt. Inc., Dallas, 1983—. Mem. Nat. Assn. Realtors, Dallas Mus. Art, Dallas Symphony Orchestra Assn., Tex. Assn. Realtors, Am. Mgmt. Assn., Nat. Assn. Female Exec., Vail Assocs., Vail Arts Council.

DAY, TERESA, systems analyst; b. Richmond, Va., Jan. 26, 1954; d. Robert Lee and Joyce (Bryan) Warren; m. Richard W. Day, Feb. 27, 1982; 1 child, Nathan. BS in Math. and Computer Sci., Coll. of William and Mary, 1975. Programmer, analyst Hosp. Data Ctr. of Va., Norfolk, 1976-78; computer specialist NIH, Bethesda, Md., 1978-80; sr. programmer, analyst Med. Coll. of Va. Hosps., Richmond, 1980-81, mgr. patient care systems, 1981-86, systems analyst, 1986—. Office: Med Coll of Va Hosps PO Box 483 MCV Sta Richmond VA 23298-0001

DAY, TERRY LEE, real estate development executive; b. Dania, Fla., Dec. 16, 1955; d. Robert S. and Rachel I. (Dykes) D.; m. Mark G. Minnick, Sept. 14, 1974 (div. June 1976). Student, Valencia Community Coll., 1976, 79, 81. Lic. real estate broker, Fla.; lic. mortgage broker, Fla. Credit specialist Credithrift of Am., Inc., Orlando, Fla., 1976-77; loan officer Nationwide Acceptance, Orlando, 1977-79; asst. dist. credit mgr. Gen. Tire and Rubber Co., Orlando, 1979-80; leasing assoc. J.S. Karlton Mgmt., Inc., Wilmington, Del., 1980-82; v.p. fin. Complete Interiors, Inc., Altamonte Springs, Fla., 1982-87; pres. T.L. Day Properties, Orlando, Fla., 1987—. Editor UHURU mag., 1972. Active fund raising Am. Heart Assn., Orlando, 1986; mem. water quality adv. bd. City of Altamonte Springs, Fla. Mem. Nat. Assn. Female Execs., Internat. Tng. and Communications Assn. Republican. Office: 1337 W Colonial Dr Orlando FL 32804

DAYANI, ELIZABETH LOUISE CROW, nurse, educator; b. Birmingham, Ala., Apr. 28, 1950; d. Jon Killough and Flora Louise (Worthington) Crow; m. John H. Dayani, June 13, 1970; 1 son, John H. BS in Nursing, Vanderbilt U., 1971, MS in Nursing cum laude, 1972. Instr., Vanderbilt U. Sch. Nursing, Nashville, 1972-74; dir., practitioner Moore County Primary Care Center, Lynchburg, Tenn., 1974-75; family nurse practitioner Metro Health Dept., Nashville, 1975-76; asst. prof. Wayne State U. Sch. Nursing, Detroit, 1976-77; asst. prof. U. Kans. Sch. Nursing, Kansas City, 1977-81, assoc. prof., 1981-82; co-owner, exec. dir. Am. Nursing Resources, Overland Park, Kans., 1982—. Bd. dirs. Midwest Bioethics Ctr., Kans. Nurses Found.; mem. adv. bd. Cradles and Crayon; mem. Home Care Profl./Tech. Adv. Com. Joint Commn. on Accreditation of Healthcare, 1988—. Recipient Service award Moore County Health Council, 1975, Exceptional Performance award Am. Nursing Resources, 1986; named one of Outstanding Young Women Am. Good Housekeeping mag., 1985. Mem. Am. Nurses Assn., Am. Pub. Health Assn., Nat. Assn. Home Care, Nat. League Nursing, Nat. Assn. Women Bus. Owners, JCAHO (mem. home care adv. com., 1985-87), Sigma Theta Tau (Leadership award 1986). Republican. Presbyterian. Clubs: Central Exchange. Author: (with Betty R. Riccardi) The Nurse Entrepreneur, 1982; contbg. editor: The Nurse Practitioner, 1979-83, mem. editorial bd., 1983—; mem. editorial bd. Nursing Economics, 1983, assoc. editor, 1985—; mem. editorial bd. The Kansas Nurse, 1983—.

DAYER, CYNTHIA LOUISE, engineering company executive; b. Buffalo, Feb. 15, 1962; d. Roger Samuel and Roberta Anne (Allbert) D. BA, U. Mich., 1984; student, Imperial Coll. Sci. and Tech., London, 1982-83. Mgr. CK Inc., N.Y.C., 1984-85; v.p. Avcon Design Group, Inc., N.Y.C., 1985—. Mem. Nat. Assn. Female Execs., U. Mich. Alumni Assn. Democrat. Methodist. Office: Avcon Design Group Inc 139 E 33d St New York NY 10016

DAYHOFF, NANCY ELAINE, nursing educator; b. Gas City, Ind., Feb. 11, 1937; d. Frederick William and Florence Ann (Butcher) Hengstler; m. Donald Gene Dayhoff; children: Douglas, David. BSN, Indiana U., Indpls., 1958; MS in Nursing Edn., Indiana U., Bloomington, 1960, EdD, 1987. Staff nurse Parkview Hosp., Ft. Wayne, Ind., 1958-59; chief nurse Ind. Regional Med. Stroke Program, Indpls., 1968-72; instr. Indiana U., Indpls., 1960-66, asst. prof., 1966-69, assoc. prof., 1969—; pvt. practice nursing Office for Nursing Practice, Indpls., 1985—; owner Resources for Nursing, Shelbyville, Ind., 1984—. Contbr. articles to profl. jours. Mem. Health Facilities Council, Indpls., 1975-82; officer and bd. mem. Major Hosp., Shelbyville, 1976—, v.p., bd. dirs., 1986—. Miller's Merry Manor research grantee, 1986. Mem. Am. Nurses Assn., Am. Congress of Rehab., Assn. of Rehab. Nurses, Midwest Nursing Research Soc., Kappa Delta Pi, Sigma Theta Tau. Home: Rural Rt 5 Box 511 Shelbyville IN 46176 Office: Ind U Sch Nursing 610 Barnhill Dr Indianapolis IN 46223

DAYTON, REGINA LAUDI, educator; b. Cleve., Apr. 27, 1952; d. Peter Rocco and Gretchen Margaret (Schoen) Laudi; m. Timothy John Dayton, July 28, 1978. BA in Am. Studies and Social Studies in Edn., Heidelberg Coll., 1974; MA in Am. Studies, Bowling Green State U., 1975. Cert. tchr., Ohio. Tchr. social studies Nordonia City Schs., Northfield, Ohio, 1975-77, Strongsville (Ohio) City Schs., 1977—; coll. recruiter Heidelberg Coll., Tiffin, Ohio, 1974—. Dem. ward chairperson Dem., Medina, Ohio, 1980-84; lay minister Saint Francis Xavier Cath. Ch., Medina, 1980-84; pres. Huntington Colony Homeowners, Strongsville, 1985—; info. rep. U.S. Mcht. Marine Acad., Kings Point, N.Y., 1986—. Served to lt. USNR, 1980—. Mem. NEA, OEA, AAUW, LWV, Naval Res. Assn., U.S. Naval Inst. Democrat. Roman Catholic. Club: Heidelberg Coll. Women's Cleve. Home: PO Box 360742 Strongsville OH 44136-0742 Office: Strongsville City Schs 13200 Pearl Rd Strongsville OH 44136

DEA, MARGARET MARY, wholesale school supplies company executive; b. St. Albans, Vt., Feb. 8, 1946; s. Ralph Homer and Irene Mae (Trombly) Wilson; m. Eugene Michael Dea, Aug. 26, 1967; children—Francesca Meredith, Vanessa Laurel. B.A., U. Vt., 1967; student Art Students League, 1972-77, Sch. Visual Arts, 1975-77. Tchr. French, Hun Sch., Princeton, N.J., 1968-70; tchr. French, Spanish, Newark Acad., Short Hills, N.J., 1970-71; dir. reading, research and edn. Park Sch., Indpls., summers, 1968-71; exec. tng. personnel Bloomingdale's, N.Y.C., 1972-74; commn. portrait artist, Englewood, N.J., Lake Forest, Ill., 1974-79; pres. Service Plus, Inc., Fort Myers, Fla., 1979—, United So., Inc., 1983—; art designer E.M. Dea & Assocs., Inc., Fort Myers, 1984—; pres. Margaret Dea Graphics Studio, Fort Myers, 1986—. Editor, author Bloomingdale's employee mag. Faces, 1972-74. Mem. Portrait Soc. Am., Nat. Assn. Female Execs., Portrait Inst., Womens Network, Lee County Alliance Arts, Mensa (chpt. South by Southwest). Republican. Roman Catholic. Club: Jr. League Bergen County. Avocations: piano; needlework; drawing; photography. Office: Service Plus Inc 30 Mildred Dr Fort Myers FL 33901

DEA, MOON SUEY, telecommunications professional; b. Hong Kong, June 21, 1950; came to U.S., 1954; d. William and Jean Dea. BA summa cum laude, U. So. Calif., 1972, MLS, 1973; MBA, UCLA, 1982. Cert. tchr., Calif. Sr. librarian Los Angeles Pub. Library, 1977-80; tech. cons. AT&T Info. Systems, Los Angeles, 1983-85; product specialist Lexar div. United Tech. Communications Co., Westlake Village, Calif., 1985-86; product mgr. Security Pacific Network Services Co., Los Angeles, 1986-87; dir. planning analysis, Jan.-June, 1987; project mgr Security Pacific Automation Co., Los Angeles, July-Nov., 1987; adv. systems engr. IBM, Los Angeles, 1987—. Mem. adv. bd. Friends of Chinatown Library, Los Angeles, 1986—, bd. dirs. 1984-85, pres., 1983-84. Calif. State scholar, 1968-72; Calif. PTA LIbrary scholar, 1972; fellow Gen. Telephone and Electronics, 1981. Mem. Asian Bus. League, Chinese Hist. Soc., Phi Beta Kappa. Home: 1409 Sycamore Ave Glendale CA 91201 Office: IBM 355 S Grand Ave Los Angeles CA 90060

DEAL, JOANNE BAKER, free-lance writer, publicity consultant; b. Long Beach, Calif., July 17, 1955; d. Richard Gene and Grace Lorraine (Thomas) Baker; m. Thomas Everett Deal, Aug. 18, 1979; children: Sarah Joy, Hannah Melody. AA, Long Beach City Coll., 1975; BA Speech Communication and Pub. Relations, U. So. Calif., 1977; postgrad. Calif. State U.-Fullerton, 1978-79. Office mgr., research asst. U. So. Calif., Los Angeles, 1975-77; layout typist, copy editor McDonnell Douglas Corp., Long Beach, Calif., 1977-78; creative asst. K. Esterly & Assocs., La Habra, Calif., 1978, grad. asst. Calif. State U., Fullerton, 1978-79; asst. editor, publicity asst. Globe Pequot Press, Chester, Conn., 1980-82; free lance writer, Ivoryton, Conn., 1982—; multimedia cons./asst. Twentyone-hundred Prodns., Madison, Wis., 1977, Karl Karcher Entr., Anaheim, Calif., 1978; research cons., asst. Orange County chpt. Pub. Relations Soc. Am., 1978. Contbr. articles to various publs.; editor: Great New England Churches, 1982; Factory Store Guide to All New England, 1981; The Bluefish Cookbook, 1981. Advisor publicity/fundraising Refugee Resettlement Projects, Interfaith Council Old Saybrook, 1980, Lower Valley chpt. Pro-Life Council Conn., 1980-84; newsletter editor Clinton Bapt. Ch., Conn., 1983—; free lance editor Word of Life Clubs, Schroon Lake, N.Y., 1985. Mem. Women in Communications, Phi Beta Kappa, Phi Kappa Phi. Republican. Baptist. Address: 68 Mares Hill Rd Ivoryton CT 06442

DEAL, PATRICIA LOU EISENBISE, educational administrator; b. Reading, Pa., Mar. 25, 1932; d. Jasper Paul and Mae (Rozycki) Eisenbise; B.S., Albright Coll., 1954; M.A., Pacific Lutheran U., 1978; m. Robert Lee Deal, May 31, 1955; children—Robert Lee Jr., David Alan, James Edward. Tchr. aide instr.-coordinator Clover Park Vocat.-Tech. Inst., Tacoma, Wash., 1970-78, asst. to program supr. of secondary vocat. edn., 1979, career edn. asst., fed. and spl. projects asst., 1979-81, asst. dir. Elective High Sch., 1981-82, dir., 1982-84, 85, dir. Elective High Sch. and Adult Edn., 1985-87; dir. Singletree Estates, Yelm, Wash., 1981-84, 85; trustee Lakes Dist. Library, 1986-87. Recipient Community Service award United Way, 1980; honoree Clover Park Found., 1984, 85, 86. Mem. Wash. Vocat. Assn. (pres. Clover Park local unit 1981-82, legis. chmn. 1980-81, exec. bd. local chpt. 1985-86), Wash. Assn. Career Edn. (mem. exec. bd. 1980-81), Am. Vocat. Assn., C. of C., Pierce County Adminstrv. Women in Edn., South Sound Women's Network, Nat. Council Local Adminstrs., Wash. Assn. Vocat. Admnistrs. (bd. dirs. 1986-88), Internat. Platform Assn. Home: 8401 Woodlawn Ave SW Tacoma WA 98499 Office: 4500 Steilacoom Blvd SW Tacoma WA 98499

DEALMEIDA, MARCELLA J., banker; d. Floyd Francis and Ruth Elma (Cox) Craig; grad. Sch. Consumer Banking, U. Va., 1973; children—Steven Craig and Victor James (twins). Fashion model, 1941-42; tchr. of voice, piano and organ, 1943-53; with First Nat. Bank & Trust Co., Joplin, Mo., 1953-81, v.p., 1976-81; sr. v.p. Centerre Bank of Springfield (Mo.), 1981—; condr. TV program on banking and fin., 1974-75, workshops for Am. Bankers Assn., 1974-75; speaker in field. Bd. dirs. S.W. Mo. Health Systems Agy., 1975-79; mem. Gov. Mo. Adv. Council, 1971-74; exec. com. Jasper County Devel. Assn., 1969-72; vice chmn. Mo. Health Planning Council, 1976; mem. adv. council U. Mo. Health Services Research Center, U. Mo. Spl. Emphasis Health Care Tech. Center. Named to Hall of Honor, Joplin Ann. Celebration Commn., 1973. Mem. Nat. Assn. Bank Women (past chmn. Ozark group), Mo. (past chmn., dir. women's div.), Am. (adv. bd. installment loan div. 1973-79) bankers assns., Am. Inst. Banking (dir. div., bd. govs.), Joplin C. of C. (chmn. red carpet com. 1970-79). Baptist. Clubs: Briarbrook Golf and Country, Mid-Am. Press (dir. 1975—). Home: Route 2 Fair Grove MO 65648 Office: 300 S Jefferson St PO Box 1745SSS Springfield MO 65806

DEAM-DAVES, BARBARA JOAN, psychotherapist; b. Ft. Wayne, Ind., Apr. 15, 1940; d. Herman F. and Olga M. (Kasper) Wachholz; m. Richard E. Deam, Aug. 24, 1957 (div. Aug. 1977); children: Renée Elizabeth, Michele Suzanne; m. Benson Daves, June 29, 1981. BA in Psychology with highest honors, Rutgers U., 1980; MS in Social Work, Columbia U., 1981. Psychotherapist Pride of Judea, Douglaston, N.Y., 1980-84; pvt. practice psychotherapist Bayside (N.Y.) and N.Y.C., 1984—. Home: 400 E 57th St New York NY 10022 Office: 23-50 Waters Edge Dr Bayside NY 11360

DEAN, ANNA ROSE, hospital administrator; b. Boston, Mar. 22, 1940; d. Thomas and Anna Rose (Mulcahy) Donnelly; m. David Doonan, Sept. 21, 1958 (div. June 1968); children: Kathleen, Dennis, Christopher. AS, Cape Cod Community Coll., 1982, BS, Lesley Coll., 1986; MS, Lesley Coll. Grad. Sch. Mgmt., 1988. Computer programmer United Concrete Pipe Corp., Baldwin Park, Calif., 1968-71; data processing operator FMC Corp., Pomona, Calif., 1971-75; with admissions dept. Falmouth (Mass.) Hosp., 1975-79, personnel asst., 1979-81, dir. personnel, 1981-87, dir. human resources, 1987; outreach adminstr. grad. outreach div. Lesley Coll., Cambridge, Mass., 1987—; bd. trustees Rita Kendall Day Care Ctr., Falmouth, Mass., 1987—. Mem. personnel bd. Town of Falmouth, 1987; vol. Am. Cancer Soc., Hyannis, Mass., 1986, United Way Hyannis, 1987. Mem. Vis. Nurses Assn. (chair personnel com. Falmouth 1985—, trustee), Am. Soc. Hosp. Human Resources, Mass. Soc. Hosp. Human Resources, Am. Soc. Personnel, Cape Cod Personnel Assn., Southeastern Hosp. Personnel Dirs. Assn. Republican. Roman Catholic. Home: 176 Palmer Ave Apt #2 Falmouth MA 02540 Office: Falmouth Hosp Ter Heun Dr Falmouth MA 02540

DEAN, CAROL CARLSON, accountant, educator; b. Ft. Worth, Aug. 1, 1944; d. Virgil Harry and Katherine Augusta (Staring) Carlson; m. William Franklin Dean, June 17, 1966; children: William Carlson, Kelly Meredith Carlson. BBA in Acctg., Midwestern State U., Wichita Falls, Tex., 1966, MBA, 1987. Acct. Parkland Meml. Hosp., Dallas, 1966-67; mortgage intern, acct. Fed. Nat. Mortgage Assn., Dallas, 1967-69; acct., bus. mgr. Wichita Falls Cardiovascular Assocs., 1984-87; instr. Midwestern State U., Wichita Falls, 1987—. Mem. adv. bd., TEXPAC rep. Wichita County Med. Soc. Aux., 1979-80, pres., 1983-84; bd. dirs. YMCA, Wichita Falls, 1980-87, chmn. ann. membership and sustaining fund drive, 1988; chmn. Archer County Reps., Tex., 1984-87; apptd. to Com. for Health Care Reimbursement Alternatives for Tex., Mil. Acad. Appointment Com., Congl. Dist. 13, Tex. Republican. Roman Catholic. Office: Midwestern State U Div Bus Adminstrn 3400 Taft Blvd Wichita Falls TX 76308

DEAN, DEAREST (LORENE GLOSUP), songwriter; b. Volin, S.D., Oct. 4, 1911; d. John Henry and Bessie Marie Donnelly Peterson; m. Eddie Dean, Sept. 11, 1931; children: Donna Lee Knorr, Edgar Glosup II. Grad. high sch., Yankton, S.D. Bd. dirs. Acad. Country Music, Hollywood, 1960-62. Composer songs including: One Has My Name, 1948, The Lonely Hours, 1970, 1501 Miles of Heaven, 1970, Walk Beside Me, 1980. Sec. ARC, Burbank, Calif., 1943. Mem. ASCAP. Republican. Roman Catholic. Avocation: golf.

DEAN, DEBORAH GORE, federal government public relations executive; b. N.Y.C., Nov. 30, 1954; d. Gordon Evans and Mary (Gore) D. B.S., Georgetown U., 1980. Mng. editor Encore Mag., Washington, 1978-79; pub. City Life Mag., Washington, 1979-81; dir. pub. relations Global Research Internat., Washington, 1981; spl. asst. to asst. sec. Congl. Intergovtl. and Pub. Affairs, Washington, 1981-82; spl. asst. to sec. U.S. Dept. Housing and Urban Devel., Washington, 1982-84; exec. asst. to sec. HUD, 1984-87, asst. sec. for community planning and devel., 1987-88; owner Dean & Assocs. Cons., Washington, 1988—; rep. to Nat. Bldg. Mus. Bd. Trustees; bd. dirs. Neighborhood Reinvestment Corp. , Nat. Urban Coalition; mem. working group on family and working group on privitization White Ho. Domestic Policy Council; mem. Pres.' Com. on Employmentof Handicapped; adv. bd.

child abuse and neglect Dept. Health and Human Services; mem. Adult Literacy Initiative com. Dept. Edn. Editor mag. The Georgetowner, 1978, mng. editor Encore Mag., 1979; pub. City Life Mag., 1980. Speechwriter Leadership Found., Washington, 1972, 73, Gore for Gov. Campaigns, Rockville, Md., 1974, 78; vol. Reagan-Bush, Rockville, 1979-80; fundraiser The Textile Mus., Washington DC, 1984; mem. Fund Am.'s Future, Rep. Women's Fed. Forum; mem. Women's Com. for Nat. Mus. of Women in Arts. Recipient W. "Bill" Calloway Pub. Service award, Nat. Assn. Real Estate Brokers, 1986, Key to City, Providence, 1984, Key to City, Rockford, Ill., 1986, Key to City, Manchester, N.H., 1986, Key to City, Greenville, S.C., 1986, Key to City, Cleve., 1986. Mem. Nat. Press Club, Nat. Strategy Info. Ctr., Rep. Women Captiol Hill, Rep. Women of Capitol Hill, Nat. Assn. Female Execs. Roman Catholic. Home: 4201 Cathedral Ave NW Washington DC 20016 Office: Dean & Assocs 2300 M St Suite 800 Washington DC 20037

DEAN, ELIZABETH M., rehabilitation medicine educator, physical therapist; b. Birmingham, Eng., Dec. 2, 1948; came to Can., 1965; d. Cyril Lemuel and Marian Emma (Rogers) Isitt; m. Daniel Perlman, Aug. 22, 1975. BA, U. Manitoba, 1972, Diploma in phys. therapy, 1975; MS, U. So. Calif., 1978; PhD, U. Manitoba, 1987. Research asst. Can. Agr., Winnipeg, Man., Can., 1966-71; phys. therapist St. Boniface Gen. Hosp., Winnipeg, 1975-78, research assoc., 1978-79; part-time tchr. U. Man., Winnipeg, 1978-81; instr. U. of B.C., Vancouver, 1983-87, research fellow, 1985-87, phys. therapist, dir. Ergometric Performance Lab., Sch. Rehab. Med., 1985—, asst. prof. Sch. Rehab. Med., 1987—. Contbr. articles to profl. jours. and chapts. to books on phys. therapy. Post doctoral fellow, U. of B.C., 1985-87. Mem. Can. Phys. Therapy Assn., Am. Phys. Therapy Assn. Home: 3493 W 23d Ave, Vancouver, BC Canada V6S 1K2 Office: U of BC Sch Rehab Med, 2211 Westbrook Mall, Vancouver, BC Canada V6T 1W5

DEAN, ELIZABETH NATIONS, bank executive, lawyer; b. Orange, Tex., Aug. 25, 1951; d. Charles Wayne and Frances (Forsythe) D.; children: Sterling Pierce Jeffries, Travis Clark Jeffries. BA in Fine Arts, U. N.Mex., 1975, JD, 1978; grad. N.Mex. Sch. Banking, 1988. Bar: N.Mex. 1978; cert. corp. trust specialist. Trust officer, corp. trust mgr. Sunwest Bank Albuquerque, 1979—. Mem. N.Mex. Bar Assn. Office: Sunwest Bank Albuquerque PO Box 26900 Albuquerque NM 87125

DEAN, FRANCES CHILDERS, librarian; b. Parker County, Tex., Apr. 20, 1930; d. John and Audrey (Ribble) Childers; divorced; 1 dau., Deborah Jane. B.S., Tex. Woman's U., Denton, 1959, M.L.S., 1962; postgrad., U. Md. Sch. librarian pub. schs. Dallas and Fairfax, Va., 1959-63; sch. librarian, then coordinator evaluation and selection Montgomery County (Md.) pub. schs., 1963-76, dir. div. instructional materials, 1976-80, dir. dept. instructional resources, 1980—. Mem. Am. Assn. Sch. Librarians (pres. 1977-78 Intellectual Freedom award), ALA (trustee Freedom to Read Found. 1974-76), Ednl. Film Library Assn. (dir. 1980—), Children's Book Guild Washington, Assn. Supervision and Curriculum, Soc. for Sch. Librarians Internat., Beta Phi Mu. Democrat. Home: 528 Meadow Hall Rockville MD 20851 Office: Montgomery County Pub Schs 850 Hungerford Dr Rockville MD 20850

DEAN, HELEN BARBARA, sales executive; b. Roanoke, Va., Apr. 10, 1945; d. George William and Hestenia B. (Motley) Ferguson; m. Robert L. Dean, June 1972. BS, Knoxville Coll., 1967. Tchr. Hart Jr. High Sch., Washington, 1967-69; system analyst IBM, Indpls., 1969-72; adminstv. aide Ind. U., Bloomington, 1972-74; with sales mktg. dept. Redactron, Indpls., 1974-75; trainer Xerox, Chgo., 1975-77; mgr. branch support Xerox, $, 1977-79; mgr. nat. support Xerox, Dallas, 1979-82; mgr. regional sales Xerox, Chgo., 1982-85; v.p. sales service Autex Systems Inc., Wellsley, Mass., 1985—. Democrat. Presbyterian. Home: 236 Congress St Milford MA 01757 Office: Autex Systems Inc 85 Wells Ave Newton MA 02159

DEAN, JACQUELYN MARIE, federal agency administrator; b. Jersey City, Feb. 26, 1954; d. Justin Caswell Dean and Hazel Virginia (Jimerson) Dean-John. BA in English, SUNY, Fredonia, 1976; MEd, Harvard U., 1978, cert. of advanced study in human devel., 1981. Adminstrv. asst., bookkeeper Seneca Nation of Indians, Salamanca, N.Y., 1976-77, head start tchr., adminstr., 1979; head tchr. Boston Indian Council, Jamaica Plain, Mass., 1980, coordinator Wabanaki Curriculum Project, 1981-83, dir. edn. dept., 1983-84; dir. pub. info. Presdl. Commn. on Indian Reservation Econs., Washington, 1984; tng. specialist Native Am. Cons., Inc., Washington, 1984-85, tech. specialist, 1985-86; spl. asst. to Dep. to Asst. Sec. on Indian Affairs, Office of Trust and Econ. Devel. of Bur. of Indian Affairs, Washington, 1987-88; program analyst, Office of Sec. Office of Contrn. Mgmt., Washington, 1988; cons. ORBIS, Washington, 1981—, Indian edn. Boston schs., 1980-84; speaker curriculum devel. State of Maine Dept. Indian Edn., Augusta, 1987. Book reviewer Interracial Books for Children, 1986. Mem. community adv. bd. Sta. WGBH-TV, Boston, 1983-85. Recipient spl. achievement award U.S. Dept. Interior, 1985. Mem. Nat. Assn. Female Execs., Nat. Indian Council on Aging, Native Am. Pub. Broadcasting Consortium, Am. Indian Sci. and Engring. Soc. Mem. Ch. Longhouse Traditional Senecas. Home: 5543 Columbia Pike #309 Arlington VA 22204

DEAN, LOUISE DANFORTH, educator; b. St. Louis, May 1, 1933; d. Carlton Miles and Christine Alice (Danforth) D.; BA, Calif. State U., Northridge, 1971, MA with honors, 1974; EdD, Nova U., 1980; children: Deborah Louise, Lee E., Linda Gail, Laura Dean. Dir., Congl. Presch., Chatsworth, Calif., 1971-74, dir. campus child devel. ctr. Los Angeles Valley Coll., Moorpark, Calif., 1974-75, instr. child devel., 1975—; prof. Los Angeles Valley Coll., chmn. dept. family and cons. studies, 1979-86; assoc. prof. Calif. State U., Northridge, 1977; pres., past public policy chair Valley chpt. So. Calif. Edn. Young Children; bd. dirs. Child Care Consortium of San Fernando Valley, 1975-84; mem. accreditation com. Western Assn. Schs. and Colls., 1986; presenter Nat. Adv. Council on Women Hearings, 1979. Named Outstanding Calif. Home Econs. Prof. of Yr., 1984. Mem. Assn. Supervision and Curriculum Devel., Nat. Assn. Edn. of Young Children (nat. presenter 1977), Calif. Assn. Edn. Young Children (bd. dirs. 1982—, chair fin. planning com.), So. Calif. Assn. Edn. of Young Children (pres. 1985-87, chair ethics com. 1987—, editor newsletter, pres. 1984), Child Care Consortium San Fernando Valley, Consortium Internat. Edn. Travel Student Groups, 1980, World Orgn. Early Childhood Educators, NOW, Phi Kappa Phi, Kappa Kappa Gamma. Presbyterian. Home: 17808 Lemarsh St Northridge CA 91325 Office: 5800 Fulton Ave Van Nuys CA 91401

DEAN, LYDIA MARGARET CARTER (MRS. HALSEY ALBERT DEAN), author, food and nutrition consultant; b. Bedford, Va., July 11, 1919; d. Christopher C. and Hettie (Gross) Carter; m. Halsey Albert Dean, Dec. 24, 1941; children: Halsey Albert Jr., John Carter, Lydia Margarae. Grad., Averett Coll.; B.S., Madison Coll., 1941; M.S., Va. Poly. Inst. and State U., 1951; postgrad., U. Va., Mich. State U.; D.Sc., Ph.D., UCLA Med. Sch., 1985. Dietetic intern, therapeutic dietitian St. Vincent de Paul Hosp., Norfolk, Va., 1942; physicist U.S. Naval Operating Base, Norfolk, 1943-45; clin. dietitian Roanoke Meml. Hosps., 1946-51; asso. prof. Va. Poly. Inst. and State U., 1946-53; community nutritionist Roanoke, Va., 1953-60; dir. dept. nutritions and dietetics Southwestern Va. Med. Center, Roanoke, 1960-67; food and nutrition cons. Nat. Hdqrs. A.R.C., Washington, 1967—; staff and vol. Nat. Hdqrs. A.R.C., 1973—; nutrition scientist, cons. Dept. Army, Washington, 1973—, Dept. Agr., 1973—; pres. Dean Assoc.; cons., assoc. dir. Am. Dietetic Assn., 1975—; coordinator new degree program U. Hawaii, 1974-75; dir., nutrition coordinator programs HHS, Washington, 1975—; mem. task force White House Conf. Food and Nutrition, 1969—; chmn. fed. com. Interagy. Com. on Nutrition Edn., 1970-71; tech. rep. to AID and State Dept.; chmn. Crusade for Nutrition Edn., Washington, 1970—; participant, cons. Nat. Nutrition Policy Conf., 1974. Author: (with Virginia McMasters) Community Emergency Feeding, 1972, Help My Child How To Eat Right, 1973, rev., 1978, The Complete Gourmet Nutrition Cookbook: The Joy of Eating Well and Right, 1978, The Stress Foodbook, 1980, rev. edit., 1982; contbr. articles to profl. jours. Trustee World U. Fellow Am. Pub. Health Assn., Internat. Inst. Community Service; mem. Am. Dietetic Assn., Bus. and Profl. Women's Clubs (cons. 1970—, pres. 1981-82), Am. Home Econs. Assn. (rep. and treas. joint congl. com.), AAUW, Inst. Food Technologists. Home: 7816 Birnam Wood Dr McLean VA 22101

DEAN, MARGARET GENEVIEVE, lawyer; b. Bklyn., Dec. 30, 1943; d. Richard Gerard and Pearl Dorothy (Olson) D.; B.A., Hunter Coll., 1967; J.D., U. Conn., 1980; m. Norman Dean, Apr. 3, 1966; children—Peter, Richard, Dean. Bar: Conn. 1980. Research asst. dept. pediatric psychiatry Bklyn. Jewish Med. Center, 1965-66; research asst. dept. internal medicine Yale U. Med. Sch., 1974; assoc. Hartford, Conn., 1978-81; pvt. practice employment rights and labor law, New Haven, 1982—; op-editorial column writer New Haven Register; mem. women's adv. panel Sta.-WTNH-TV, New Haven, 1975-78; commentator Sta. WELI, 1976—. Mem. employment task force NOW, Tucson, 1970-71, founder New Haven chpt., 1973, cons. coordinator employment task force, 1973-77, mem. nat. ins. task force, 1976-77; co-founder Ariz. Women's Polit. Caucus, 1972; mem. public edn. com. Conn. div. Am. Cancer Soc., 1973-74; mem. citizens' adv. bd. Conn. State Police and Sex Crimes Adv. Bd., 1974-75; mem. Orange (Conn.) Democratic Town Com.; bd. dirs., chmn. legis. and by-laws com. Griffin Hosp. Aux., Derby, Conn.; mem. exec. bd. Am. Lung Assn. of Conn.; Mem. New Haven Bar Assn., Conn. Bar Assn., Roman Catholic. Home: 888 Indian Hill Rd Orange CT 06477 Office: 29 Whitney Ave New Haven CT 06510

DEAN, MARGO, artistic director; b. Ft. Worth, Dec. 9, 1930; d. Arthur Augustus and Margaret (Holliday) Webster; m. Beale Dean, Sept. 3, 1948; children: Webster Beale, Giselle Liseanne. BFA, Ward-Belmont Coll., 1947; postgrad., Tex. Christian U., 1948. Ballet appearances, Louisville, 1948, Dallas, 1947; prin. dancer, choreographer Ft. Worth Opera Ballet, 1955-60; dir. Ft. Worth Ballet Assn., 1961; artistic dir. Ballet Concerto, Ft. Worth, 1969—. Bd. dirs. Ft. Worth Symphony Orch. Mem. Southwestern Regional Ballet Assn. (pres. 1985-86, bd. dirs. 1985—), Nat. Assn. Regional Ballet. Republican. Presbyterian. Clubs: Ft. Worth, Ft. Worth Boat, Ridglea Country. Office: Ballet Concerto 3803 Camp Bowie Blvd Fort Worth TX 76107

DEAN, MARY ELISABETH, psychotherapist, engineering and chemical company executive; b. Englewood, N.J., July 21, 1933; d. Jesse Parke and Marguerite A. (Jossier) D.; m. Earle W. Orr Jr., April 23, 1957 (div. Sept. 1966); children: Mary Julitta, Gregory Dean; m. Hamed A. El-Maksoud, Nov. 17, 1985. AB, Coll. of St. Elizabeth, 1955; MS, Purdue U., 1957; PhD, NYU, 1985. Instr. Grad. Sch. Edn. Seton Hall U., West Orange, N.J., 1968-70; dir., career devel. and sch. counselor Matawan (N.J.)-Aberdeen Regional Schs., 1968-80; pvt. practice psychol. counselor Middletown, N.J., 1968-84; v.p. H and M Engring. and Chems., Cairo, Egypt, 1984—; psychotherapist Community Services Assn., Cairo, 1986—; psychol. counselor Am. Univ., Cairo, 1986—; bd. dirs. Children's Internat. Summer Villages, Egypt. Editor: Meliorism I, Meliorism II, 1981-82. Bd. dirs. Community YMCA, Red Bank, N.J., 1984. Named Univ. fellow Purdue U., 1956. Mem. Internat. Psychol. Assn., Phi Delta Kappa, Kappa Delta Pi. Republican. Home: 25 Meadow Ave Unit #66 Monmouth Beach NJ 07750

DEAN, MARY ELIZABETH, law educator; b. Washington, Jan. 8, 1947. BA, U. Mass., 1970; JD, Suffolk U., 1978; M Law in Taxation, Georgetown U., 1983. Bar: Mass. 1979, D.C. 1985, U.S. Tax Ct. 1980, U.S. Ct. Claims 1979, U.S. Supreme Ct. 1983. Atty.-adv. honors program, chief counsel's office IRS, Washington, 1978-85; assoc. Rogers & Wells, Washington, 1985-87; prof. William Mitchell Coll. Law, St. Paul, 1987—. Vol. Women's Legal Defense Fund, Washington, 1985—. Recipient Class Leader scholarship Suffolk U. Law Sch., 1977. Mem. ABA, Mass. Bar Assn., Dist. Columbia Bar Assn. Democrat. Unitarian. Home: 767 Goodrich Ave Saint Paul MN 55105 Office: William Mitchell Law Sch 875 Summit Ave Saint Paul MN 55105

DEAN, MARY T., realty company officer; b. Washington, Oct. 28, 1942; d. John Joseph and Lillian Joyce (Phillips) Dean. Student, U. Md., 1970's, Montgomery Coll., 1981-82, Am. U., Washington, D.C., 1983. Sec., U.S. Treasury Dept., 1960-67; adminstrv. asst. Arthur Andersen & Co., Washington, 1967-69, Leisure Time Industries, Inc., Washington, 1969-70, Ringling Bros. Circus, Washington, 1970-77; asst. sec. Washington REIT, Bethesda, Md., 1977-87, asst. corp. sec., 1988—; dir., sec. Boardwalk One Owners Assn., Ocean City, Md., 1982—. Mem. Nat. Assn. Secs., Nat. Assn. Female Execs., Notary Assn. Democrat. Roman Catholic. Home: 19028 Quail Valley Blvd Gaithersburg MD 20879 Office: Washington Real Estate Investment Trust 4936 Fairmont Ave Bethesda MD 20814

DEAN, SHARON LOU, information manager; b. Ithaca, N.Y., Nov. 4, 1943; d. Kermit Lewis and Lila Lee (Moravia) D.; m. Richard Stephen Chrappa. B.A., Keuka Coll., 1964; M.A., Syracuse U., 1965; M.L.S., U. Wash., 1978, cert. in bus. adminstrn., Wash. 1981. Cert. profl. librarian, Wash.; cert. secondary tchr., Wash., N.Y., Ariz. Supr. learning resource ctr. Mercer Island Sr. High Sch., Wash., 1975-77; head librarian John F. Kennedy High Sch., Seattle, 1977-81; sr. info. analyst Cigna Corp., Phila., 1982-83, mktg. cons., 1983-84, systems mgr., 1984-86, bus. cons., 1986—; pres. bus. research consulting group D&D Assocs. Contbr. articles to profl. and bus.jours. Bd. dirs. Ardmore Civic Assn., Pa., 1984-85. Recipient State of Wash. Commendation award Gov., Sec. of State, 1976. Mem. Associated Info. Mgrs., ALA (com. mem. 1978-80), SLA, Keuka Coll. Alumni Club (chmn. Phila.), Network Women Phila. Avocations: sewing; photography; reading; needlework. Office: Cigna Corp 1600 Arch St Philadelphia PA 19103

DEAN, VALLIE B., educator; b. Enterprise, Ala., Mar. 5, 1944; d. Willie K. Bechem; m. Richard D. Dean, Sr., Dec. 29, 1964; children: Richard D. II, Clifton, Mensah. Student, Southwestern Christian Coll., 1963, Hardin-Simmons U., 1965-66; BS, U. D.C., 1972, postgrad., 1975. Cert. tchr., D.C. Tchr. D.C. Pub. Sch. System, Washington, 1971-80, 87—; cons. edn. Office Employability Devel., Govt. of D.C., Washington, 1980-81; computer operator AT&T Communications, Washington, 1981-84, Bell Atlantic Corp., Washington, 1984-86; corp. officer Bechem-Deuw Mgmt., Inc., Pitts., 1986-87; tchr. math. W. Bruce Evans Jr. High Sch., Washington, 1987—; cons. edn. LABCO, Washington, 1980-86. Mem. Kettering Civic Fedn., Upper Marlboro, Mo., 1975—. Recipient Nat. Hall of Fame Pub. Service award Govt. of D.C., 1979. Mem. Homewood-Brushton C. of C., Delta Pi Epsilon (plaque 1977). Democrat. Mem. Ch. of Christ. Club: Women at Work (Fairfax, Va.). Home: 12113 Hunterton St Upper Marlboro MD 20772 Office: W Bruce Evans Jr High Sch 5600 E Capitol St NE Washington DC 20019

DE ANDA, SOCORRO, educational business manager; b. Presidio, Tex., June 18, 1945; d. Lazaro H. and Maria (Hernandez) Brito; m. Ismail de Anda Jr., Nov. 26, 1967; children: Ismael III, Marco, Dorinda. BBA, U. Tex., El Paso, 1966. Auditor Hotel Paso Del Norte, El Paso, 1966-67; sr. acct. Braddock Dunn & McDonald, El Paso, 1968-71; controller, v.p. Reinharts Furniture Inc., El Paso, 1977-84; bus. mgr. Lydia Patterson Inst., El Paso, 1984—; fundraiser, promoter Lydia Patterson Inst., 1985—; notary pub. State of Tex., El Paso, 1979—. Campaign promoter dist. atty. candidate, El Paso, 1978; mem. PTA, El Paso, 1987. Statutory scholar State of Tex., 1966; recipient Rocognition award El Paso Office of Devel., 1981. Mem. Nat. Assn. Female Execs., Nat. Assn. Profl. Mgrs., Nat. Notary Assn., El Paso C. of C., Pan Am. Golf Assn. Women. Democrat. Roman Catholic. Home: 6404 Pino Real Dr El Paso TX 79912 Office: Lydia Patterson Inst 517 S Florence El Paso TX 79901

DEANE, MARJORIE SCHLESINGER, fashion merchandising executive; b. N.Y.C., Apr. 18, 1923; d. Walter C.B. and Marjorie (Walsh) Schlesinger; m. Disque D. Deane, May 20, 1952; children: Marjorie Gregg Swain, Kathryn Morgan, Disque D. Jr., Walter L. Student, Finch Coll., 1941, Tobe Coburn, 1942. With Franklin Simon, N.Y.C., 1943-45; jr. editor Tobe Fashion Report, N.Y.C., 1945-47; accessories stylist Tobe Assocs., N.Y.C., 1956-62, chair, publisher, 1963—, owner, publisher, 1983—; bd. dirs. ednl. found. Fashion Inst. of Technology, N.Y.C.; mem. fashion com. Smithsonian Inst., Washington, 1973—. Mem. adv. council Tobe-Coburn Sch., N.Y.C., 1971—; v.p. bd. trustees Kips Bay Boy's Club, N.Y.C., 1971—; chair women's com., 1984-86; bd. dirs. Girl Scout Council of Greater N.Y., N.Y.C., 1982—, chair corp. dinner, 1983—. Recipient 1st Place Fashion Video Trends Video. Mem. The Fashion Group (head various coms., pres. 1970-71), The Com. of 200.

DEANE, SALLY JAN, public health administrator, consultant; b. Downey, Calif., Sept. 24, 1948; d. Virgil Eldred and Pearl Jan (Kettell) D. BA, Whittier Coll., 1970; MEd, Boston U., 1971, MPH, 1988. Mgr. community health Peter Bent Brigham Hosp., Boston, 1974-76; coordinator WIC program Martha Eliot Health Ctr., 1976-78; dir. S.W. Boston WIC program Shattock Hosp. Corp., 1978-80; exec. dir. Fenway Community Health Ctr., 1980-84; exec. asst. commr. Boston Dept. Health & Hosps., 1984-86; assoc. dir. spl. projects Health Policy Inst. Boston U., 1986-87; dir. ambulatory reimbursement Mass. Medicaid, 1987—; cons. Mass. Dept. Pub. Health, Boston, 1978-80, Citicorp Corp. Hdqrs., N.Y.C., 1986, Jane C. Edmonds & Assocs., Boston, 1986-87, Digital Equipment Corp., Maynard, Mass., 1987. Mem. Mayor's Task Force on AIDS, Boston, 1983-86; v.p. Trustees Charitable Donations, Boston, 1984-86; bd. dris. Bay Windows Community Newspaper, Boston, 1984-88; candidate Brookline (Mass.) Town Meeting Precinct 10, 1986. Mem. Mass. Pub. Health Assn., Am. Pub. Health Assn., Women in Health Care Mgmt. Democrat. Presbyterian. Home: 115 University Rd Brookline MA 02146-4532 Office: Commonwealth Mass Dept Pub Welfare Medicaid 600 Washington St Boston MA 02111

DE ANGELIS, DEBORAH ANN AYARS, university athletics official; b. San Diego, July 2, 1948; d. Charles Orvil and Janet Isabel (Glithero) Ayars; m. David C. De Angelis, Sept. 29, 1984. B.A., U. Calif.-Santa Barbara, 1970, Certificate in Social Services, 1972; M.S., U. Mass., 1979. Eligibility worker County Welfare Dept., Santa Barbara, Calif., 1970-73; women's crew coach Northeastern U., Boston, 1979-83, bus. mgr. women's athletics, 1983-87, asst. dir. bus., 1987—; com. mem. Women's Olympic Rowing Com., 1976-84; life trustee Nat. Rowing Found., 1984; life mem. selection com. Rowing Found. Hall of Fame, 1984—; rowing mgr. Women's Olympic Team, 1976, 80; head mgr. U.S. Olympic Festival, Syracuse, N.Y., 1981, coach, Indpls., 1982, Colorado Springs, Colo., 1983; mem. alcohol and drug awareness com. Northeastern U. Mem. Nat. Women's Rowing Assn. (Woman of Yr. award 1983), Nat. Assn. Amateur Oarsmen, Fedn. Sociétés d'Aviron (women's commn. 1978—, U.S. del. to ann. congress 1978, 80-87), U.S. Rowing Assn. (del. 1988, bd. dirs. 1985—, co-chmn. internat. div., co-chmn. events div. 1985-86, chmn. internat. div. 1986-88, women's v.p. 1985-88, mem. exec. com. 1985—, exec. v.p. 1988—). Club: ZLAC Rowing. Home: 143 Pemberton St Cambridge MA 02140 Office: Northeastern U Women's Athletics 360 Huntington Ave Boston MA 02115

DEANGELIS, LORRAINE THERESA, investment company executive; b. Bklyn., Oct. 15, 1960; d. Carl and Flora (Terranova) DeA.; m. Vincent A. Reitano, May 26, 1984. BA in Polit. Sci., Bklyn. Coll., 1982, postgrad., 1982-84; postgrad., NYU, 1985. Adminstr. labor Am. Arbitration Assn., N.Y.C., 1983-84; project coordinator Coopers & Lybrand, N.Y.C., 1984, tax asst., 1984-86; officer comml. loans The Money Store Investment Corp., Union, N.J., 1986—. Mem. Midnet. Roman Catholic.

DEANGELIS, MARGARET SCALZA, publishing executive; b. Jersey City, May 27, 1936; d. Louis Patrick and Josephine M. (Cleary) Scalza; m. David Jenkins, Sept. 30, 1951 (div. 1962); children: Alison Brittain, Cynthia Higgins, Ann; m. Henry DeAngelis, Aug. 28, 1977; children: Valerie, Brenda Falato, Louise Brine, Henry Jr. Owner Towne House Restaurant, Hackettstown, N.J., 1963-65; pres. Kinsley Assocs., Inc., Florham Park, N.J., 1966—, Kinsley Publs., Inc., Florham Park, 1972—. Mem. Nat. Assn. Sch. Bus. Ofcls., U.S. Postal Customer Council (co-chmn. 1978), Morris County Bd. Realtors, Nat. Assn. Female Execs., Hackettstown Trade Assn. (sec.-treas. 1963). Republican. Roman Catholic. Home and Office: 20 E Madison Ave Florham Park NJ 07932

DEANGELIS, SUSAN PENNY, jewelry manufacturing corporate officer; b. N.Y.C., Nov. 20, 1950; s. Milton Abraham and Anne Pearl (Fleischer) Zwilling; m. Ivo DeAngelis, July 25, 1971 (div. Feb. 1982); m. Benjamin H. Pfeffer, May 17, 1985. BA cum laude, Bklyn. Coll., 1971. Spl. projects coordinator, customer service rep. N.Y. Property Ins. Underwriting Assocs., N.Y.C., 1971-72; office mgr. Pyramid Personnel Agy., N.Y.C., 1972-73; asst. v.p. human resources Feature Enterprises Inc., N.Y.C., 1973—; cons. JWJ Enterprises, Inc., N.Y.C., 1984-85. N.Y. State Bd. Regents scholar, 1967. Mem. Nat. Assn. Female Execs., N.Y. Assn. New Ams. (pvt. sector adv. com. 1985-88). Jewish. Avocations: photography, calligraphy, painting. Home: 2258 E 27th St Brooklyn NY 11229 Office: Feature Enterprises Inc 130 W 46th St New York NY 10036

DEANGELO, MARLENE ANN, social services administrator; b. Orland, Calif., Aug. 14, 1937; d. Elmar Laurence and Gloria Arnel (Warren) Zimmerman; m. Ernest Lewis DeAngelo; children: Kippi Lynn, Scott. AA, Sierra Coll., 1973; BA, Calif. State U., Sacramento, 1979, MA, 1980. Tchr. Roseville (Calif.) Adult Ctr., 1978-81; counselor supr. Aquarian Effort Inc., Sacramento, 1981-85; program dir. Assn. Retarded Ctr. Placer County Auburn (Calif.) Activity Ctr., 1985-87; asst. dir. Aquarian Effort Inc., Sacramento, 1988—. Mem. AAUW, Sacramento C. of C., Assn. Retarded Ctr. Democrat. Club: Toastmasters (officer). Home: 5000 9th Ave Sacramento CA 95820 Office: The Aquarian Effort Inc 2015 J St #32 Sacramento CA 95814

DEARMAN, MALEAH ANNETTE, accountant; b. Anniston, Ala., Apr. 13, 1957; d. Joe Wheeler and Virginia (Morris) D.; m. Arthur Gerald Coley Jr., Sept. 7, 1980; 1 child, Graham Coley. BS in Acctg., Jacksonville (Ala.) State U., 1978. CPA, Ala. Sr. staff auditor Ernst & Whinney, Birmingham, Ala., 1978-82; sr. fin. analyst Blue Cross and Blue Shield of Ala., Birmingham, 1982-85, mgr. gen. acctg. dept., 1985—; adj. prof. Samford U., Birmingham, 1982-83. Vol. Cystic Fibrosis, Birmingham, 1982—. Mem. Am. Inst. CPA's, Am. Soc. CPA's, Nat. Assn. Accts. (treas. South Birmingham chpt. 1983-87), Nat. Mgmt. Assn. (treas. Blue Cross/Blue Shield Ala. chpt. 1985-86, bd. dirs. 1987—), Inst. Mgmt. Accts., Roebuck-Center Point Jaycettes (v.p. 1982-83, pres. 1983-84), Ala. Jaycettes (treas. 1984-85).

DEASY, THERESA, law firm financial executive; b. N.Y.C., May 19, 1958; d. Thomas Edward Deasy and Dorothy Beatrice (Federico) Deasy Cox; m. Dennis James Stanton, May 29, 1983. BS in Commerce, DePaul U., 1981; postgrad. Keller Grad. Sch. Bus. Acctg. clk. Kirkland & Ellis, Chgo., 1977-80; fin. div. clk. Talman Home Fed. Savs. & Loan, Chgo., 1980-81; staff acctg. Sachnoff Weaver & Rubenstien, Chgo., 1981-83, asst. controller, 1984-86, controller, 1987—. Vol. dir., treas. The Commons of Evanston, 1985-87; leader Ravenswood Hosp. Mental Health Ctr., Chgo., 1984 . Mem. Assn. Legal Adminstrs., Am. Soc. Women Accts., Digital Equipment Computer Users Soc., Nat. Assn. Female Execs., Chgo. Council Fgn. Relations, Ill. Notaries Assn., Assn. Legal Adminstrn., Law Office Mgrs. Assn. Avocations: travel, photography, skiing, racquetball. Home: 1408 W Norwood Chicago IL 60660 Office: Sachnoff Weaver & Rubenstein Ltd 30 S Wacker Dr 29th Floor Chicago IL 60606

DEATON, KAY DAWN, nurse, educator; b. Whitefish, Mont., Aug. 3, 1942; d. Otto Carl and Augusta (Blumentritt) Kriegel; children: Dee Ann, Cindy Denise. BSN, Tex. Christian U., 1966; MS, Loma Linda U., 1975; MA, Claremont (Calif.) U., 1982, PhD, 1983. RN. Office nurse Angelo Clinic, San Angelo, Tex., 1963-65; instr. Tex. Christian U., Ft. Worth, 1966-71; instr. Cypress (Calif.) Coll., 1975-70, telecommunications cordinator, 1979-82, assoc. dean instructional devel., 1982-86, dean instrn., 1987—, chmn. campus computer services, 1984—; bus. relations coordinator, advisor on cable TV Cypress City Council, 1981-86; chmn. ednl. cable com. Garden Grove (Calif.) City Council, 1986. Editor Highlights newsletter, 1984; producer: (film) The Baby Bath, 1968. Mem. Nat. Council Staff Program and Orgn. Devel. (regional cluster leader 1985-86, nat. mktg. com. 1986—), Assn. Calif. Community Coll. Adminstrs. Presbyterian. Home: 10561 LaDona Dr Garden Grove CA 92640 Office: Cypress Coll 9200 Valley View Cypress CA 90630

DE BELON, BARBARA JANE HUFFMAN, corporate course developer; b. Patuxent River, Md., June 16, 1949; d. Donald Smith and Harriet Priscilla (Miller) Huffman; m. Aug. 22, 1970 (div. 1981); children Brian Thomas Dunlap, Michael Ryan Dunlap; m. Edwin Belon, June 16, 1984. BS, Slippery Rock State Coll., 1971; MA, Columbia U., 1981, EdM, 1982, EdD, 1985. Curriculum devel., instr. The Day Sch., N.Y.C., 1980-83; research adminstr. Mt. Sinai Sch. of Medicine, N.Y.C., 1983-85; info mgmt, asst. staff mgr. NYNEX Bus. Info Systems Co., White Plains, NY, 1985-87, corp. adminstr., staff dir. tng., 1987; product mgr., course devel. MUST Software Internat., Norwalk, Conn., 1987—; cons., Mt. Sinai Sch. of Medicine, 1983. Mem. Westchester Choral Soc., White Plains, 1986-87. Recipient academic scholarship Columbia U., 1981-83. Mem. Nat. Assn. Female Execs., Mu Kappa Gamma, Kappa Delta Pi. Republican. Lutheran. Office: MUST Software Internat 101 Merritt 7 Norwalk CT 06856

DE BERGE, CASSANDRA STILES, banker; b. West Palm Beach, Fla., Nov. 1, 1953; d. Philip Henry and Cassandra (Quickel) Stiles; m. Robert Clanton De Berge, Nov. 19, 1977. BS in Econs., Rollins Coll., 1975; M in Internat. Mgmt., Thunderbird, Glendale, Ariz., 1976. Fin. analyst Fgn. Credit Ins. Assn., N.Y., 1976; credit analyst The Ariz. Bank, Phoenix, 1976-78, with internat. div., 1978-84; v.p. trade fin. First Interstate Bank, Ltd., San Diego, 1984—; tchr. Grossmont Coll., 1987; bd. dirs. Calif. Export Fin. Office. Mem. San Diego Dist. Export Council, 1987—. Mem. Nat. Assn. Bank Women (bd. dirs. 1986-87), World Trade Assn. of San Diego (corp. sponsor, treas. 1985-86, sec. 1987, bd. dirs. 1984—, 1st v.p. 1988), San Diego C. of C. (internat. adv. council 1984—). Office: First Interstate Bank Ltd 401 B St Suite 303 San Diego CA 92101

DEBLASIO, CAROL JOAN, petroleum engineer; b. Natrona Heights, Pa., Oct. 22, 1959; d. Louis Joseph and Margaret Katherine (Buhl) DeB. BS in Petroleum and Natural Gas Engring., Pa. State U., 1981. Field engr. Halliburton Services, Evanston, Wyo., 1981-82, Brighton, Colo., 1982-84; sales engr. Halliburton Services, Denver, 1984-85; reservoir engr. So. Calif. Gas Co., Los Angeles, 1985-86, drilling engr., 1986-87, environ. engr., 1987—. Mem. Soc. Petroleum Engrs., USCG Aux. Avocations: sailing, antiques, biking, beaching.

DEBOSKEY, DANA STEPHENS, psychologist, consultant; b. N.Y.C., Sept. 12, 1946; d. Valdane and Winifred Margaret (Rundlett) Stephens; m. William DeBoskey, Mar. 25, 1972; children: Kristina, Stephen, Christopher, Kari. BA, U. South Fla., 1968, EdM, 1970, MA, 1973; PhD, U. Tenn., 1982. Lic. psychologist, cert. sch. psychologist. Psychol., ednl. examiner Team Evaluation Ctr., Chattanooga, 1973-74, dir. psychol. services, 1974-75; psychol. examiner Drs. Bacon, Miller & Assocs., Knoxville, Tenn., 1975-79; sch. psychologist Hillsborough County Schs., Tampa, Fla., 1980-83; clin. coordinator U. South Fla. Ctr. for Children, Tampa, 1983-84; chief of neuropsychology Tampa Gen. Hosp., 1984-87; dir. neuropsychology Dana S. DeBoskey & Assocs., 1987—; cons. psychology Douglas Cherokee Headstart, Alcoa, Tenn., 1976-78, infant psychology Appalachian Regional Child Devel. Ctr., Knoxville, 1975-79, neuropsychology Fla. Diagnostic and Resource Ctr., St. Petersburg, 1984—, head injury program New Medico Rehab. Ctr., Tampa, 1987—, pain mgmt. Touchstone Phys. Restoration Ctr., Tampa, 1987—. Author: Manual for Management of Head Injury, 1985, Manual for Employers of Head Injured, 1986, Manual for Teachers of Head Injured, 1986, Manual for Homebased Cognitive Rehabilitation, 1986, Manual for Families of Pain Patients, 1986, Manual for CVA Families, 1987, Life After Head Injury: Who Am I?, 1987, Strategies for Living with Pain, 1987; also articles, assessment tools in field. Mem. Temple Terrace Ladies Aux., 1985. U. South Fla. fellow, 1968-70; recipient Creative Scholar award, 1970. Mem. Am. Psychol. Assn., Internat. Neuropsychology Soc., Nat. Assn. Sch. Psychologists, Suncoast Assn. Sch. Psychologists (sec. 1983-84), Acad. of Neuropsychology, Fla. Psychol. Assn., Nat. Registrar of Health Providers in Psychology. Democrat. Avocations: jogging, reading, youth sports. Home: 105 N Burlingame Ave Tampa FL 33617 Office: Dana S DeBoskey PhD & Assocs Tampa FL 33618

DE BRUN, SHAUNA DOYLE, investment banker; b. Boston, June 3, 1956; d. John Justin and Marie Therese (Carey) Doyle; m. Seamus Christopher de Brun, July 24, 1982; 1 child, Brendan Joseph. Student U. Salzburg, 1974-75; BA, Mt. Holyoke Coll., 1978; postgrad. Harvard U., 1981-82; M in Internat. Affairs Columbia U., 1984. Cert. fin. analyst. Assoc., Salomon Brothers, N.Y.C., 1978; research assoc. Kennedy Sch. Govt., Cambridge, Mass., 1979-80; faculty assoc. Harvard Bus. Sch., 1980-81; fgn. expert Beijing Normal U., Peoples Republic China, 1981-82; assoc. dir. N.Y. Capital Resources, N.Y.C., 1984-85; ptnr. Eppler & Co., Denver, 1985-87, pres., Teaneck, N.J., 1987—. Contract cons. Booz, Allen & Hamilton, N.Y.C., 1981-82. Columbia U. Internat. fellow, 1982; Sarah Williston scholar Mt. Holyoke Coll., 1975. Mem. N.Y. Sos. Security Analysts, AAAS, Soc. Internat. Devel., Phi Beta Kappa. Club: Harvard. Avocations: piano; horseback riding. Office: Eppler & Co Inc Glenpointe Centre W Teaneck NJ 07666

DEBUS, ELEANOR VIOLA, business management company executive; b. Buffalo, May 19, 1920; d. Arthur Adam and Viola Charlotte (Pohl) D.; student Chown Bus. Sch., 1939. Sec., Buffalo Wire Works, 1939-45; home talent producer Empire Producing Co., Kansas City, Mo., sec. Owens Corning Fiberglass, Buffalo; public relations and publicity Niagara Falls Theatre, Ont., Can.; pub. relations dir. Woman's Internat. Bowling Congress, Columbus, Ohio, 1957-59; publicist, sec. Ice Capades, Hollywood, Calif., 1961-63; sec. to controller Rexall Drug Co., Los Angeles, 1963-67; bus. mgmt. acct. Samuel Berke & Co., Beverly Hills, Calif., 1967-75; Gadbois Mgmt. Co., Beverly Hills, 1975-76; sec., treas. Sasha Corp., Los Angeles, 1976—; bus. mgr. Dean Martin, Shirley MacLaine, Debbie Reynolds; pres. Tempo Co., Los Angeles, 1976—. Mem. Nat. Assn. Female Execs., Nat. Notary Assn., Nat. Film Soc., Am. Film Inst. Republican. Lodge: Order Eastern Star. Contbr. articles to various mags. Office: Tempo Co 1900 Ave of Stars #1230 Los Angeles CA 90067

DEBUSSEY, JODY BROWN, facilities management executive; b. Balt., Mar. 9, 1958; d. Stanley Louis and Edith (Brill) Brown; m. Fred Woods Debussey, Apr. 19, 1986. BS in Environtl. Design, U. Vt., 1980; postgrad., The Pratt Inst., 1981; MS in Facilities Mgmt. and Planning, Cornell U., 1983. Facilities planner analyst Dept. Housing and Community Devel., Balt., 1982; facilities planner Towson (Md.) State U., 1983; facilities mgr. Merrill Lynch & Co., N.Y.C., 1983-85; dir. client services Monitor Facilities Mgmt. Co., Inc., N.Y.C., 1985—; cons. and lectr. in field, Burlington, Vt., 1981. Contbr. articles to profl. jours. Vol. Happy Hills Children's Hosp., Balt., 1975, Balt. Convention and Civic Ctr., Balt., 1980-87. Mem. Internat. Facilities Mgmt. Assn., Nat. Assn. Female Execs., Assn. of Women in Real Estate, N.Y. Jr. League, Alpha Zeta. Democrat. Jewish. Office: Monitor Facilities Mgmt Co 400 Park Ave New York NY 10022

DECARLO, ANGELA ROCCO, writer, journalist; b. Chgo., Sept. 11, 1947; d. Peter J. And Della (Serritella) Rocco; m. Daniel G. DeCarlo; children: Mark, Michael, Daniel. BA in Communications and Edn., Ill. Benedictine Coll., 1976. Cert. K-12 tchr., Ill. With Chgo. Tribune; journalist, cons. various publs., 1975—; columnist The Bus. Rev. Traveler Las Vegas (Nev.) Rev. Jour., 1985; dir. pub. relations, communications Ill. Coll. Optometry, Chgo., 1986; cons. Hinsdale (Ill.) chpt. Lyric Opera, 1986. Mem. Ind. Writers Chgo. Home and Office: 2718 N Vista Knoll Rd Orange CA 92667

DE CARVALHO, LINDA LEE, sales professional; b. Long Beach, Calif., Dec. 11, 1953; d. John August and Mary Amelia (Lourenco) Nunes; divorced; children: Vanessa Marie, John Daniel. Student, Cerritos Jr. Coll., 1971-74. Ops. mgr. Ecco's Pizza Inc., Long Beach, 1974-82; dir. group sales and mktg. Golf N' Stuff Devel. Corp., Norwalk, Calif., 1982—. Mem. planning com. Anything Goes A Thon, Pasadena, Calif., 1984-85; chairperson publicity St. Pancratius Parish Festival, Lakewood, Calif., 1985, 86, 87. Mem. Calif. Sch. Employees Assn., Norwalk C. of C. (treas. 1986-87, pres. 1987—). Republican. Roman Catholic. Office: GNS Devel Corp 10555 E Firestone Blvd Norwalk CA 90650

DECESARE, EILEEN GODOY, nurse executive, consultant; b. Manila, Dec. 29, 1941; came to U.S., 1964; d. Luis Solitario and Francisca (Zaide) Godoy; m. Ronald DeCesare Sr.; children: Kent, Ronald Jr., Anthony. Diploma in Nursing, St. Luke's Hosp., Quezon City, The Philipines, 1963; BSN, U. Ill., Chgo., 1976; MS, DePaul U., 1978. RN, cert. nurse adminstr. Asst. dir. nursing Howard U. Hosp., Washington, 1978-81; dep. dir. nursing D.C. Gen Hosp., 1981-84, cons. nurse, 1984-85, assoc. dir. for nursing, 1985-87, dir. nursing systems, 1987—. Contbr. papers, presentations in field. Chairperson Dean Mary Kelly Mullane Symposium U. Ill., 1978. Recipient Commendation Leadership in the Quality Assurance Program Cook County Hosp. Dept. Nursing, 1978. Mem. Philippines Nurse Assn., Am. Nurses Assn. (cert. 1984), U. Ill. Alumni Assn., Assn. Filipino Am. Nurses (bd. dirs.), Assn. Profl. and Exec. Women, DePaul U. Alumni Assn., Am. Orgn. Nurse Execs. (treas. Nat. Capitol Area chpt., Nominee Level award 1986), Am. Hosp. Assn., Council Operating Room Dirs. Met. Washington Area, Sigma Theta Tau. Roman Catholic. Home: 10300 Hunt Country Ln Vienna VA 22180 Office: DC Gen Hosp 19th and Mass Ave SE Washington DC 20003

DECESARE, PAULA DOREEN, small business owner; b. Berlin, N.H., June 29, 1936; d. William Briry and Mildred Victoria (Sloan) Raymond; m. William Joseph DeCesare, Feb. 16, 1957; children: Jay Raymond, Mark William, Brett Patrick. Student, Jackson Coll., 1954; AA in Communication, Leland Powers Sch. Broadcasting and Speech, 1955-57. Copy writer, salesperson Sta. WHVW Radio, Hyde Park, N.Y., 1963-67; mgr. real estate Mobile Home Park, Hudson, N.Y., 1967—; pres., sole incorporator Alice in Videoland Ltd., Kingston, N.Y., 1983—; mgr. real estate numerous comml. holdings, 1967—; sales agt. Equitable Life Assurance, N.Y.C., 1975-77; account exec. sales Sta. WKIP Radio, Poughkeepsie, N.Y., 1977-83. Episcopalian. Home: 36 Roosevelt Rd Hyde Park NY 12538

DE CHAMPLAIN, VERA CHOPAK, artist, painter; b. Kulmbach, Germany, Jan. 26, 1928; Am. citizen; d. Nathaniel and Selma (Stiefel) Florsheim; m. Albert Chopak de Champlain, 1948. Student, Art Students League, N.Y.C., 1950-60; spl. studies with Edwin Dickinson, 1962-64. Art dir., tchr. Emanuel Ctr., N.Y.C., 1967—. One person show Consulate Fed. Republic of Germany, N.Y.C., 1986, Fusco Gallery, N.Y.C., 1969-70, B. Altman Gallery, N.Y.C., 1982; exhibited group shows including Munich, W. Ger., 1966, Rudolph Gallery, Woodstock, N.Y., 1967, Artists Equity Gallery, N.Y.C., 1970-77, Lever House, N.Y.C., 1974, 80, 85; Avery Fisher Hall-Cork Gallery, N.Y.C., 1970, 82, 83, 84, 87, Fontainebleau Gallery, N.Y.C., 1972, 73, 74, NYU, 1978, Met. Mus., 1979, Muriel Karasik Gallery, Westhampton Beach, N.Y., 1980; represented in permanent collections Butler Inst. Am. Art, Youngstown, Ohio, Ga. Mus. Art, Athens, Slater Mus., Norwich, Conn., Webster Coll., St. Louis, Evansville Mus. Arts and Sci. (Ind.), Smithsonian Instn., Archives Am. Art, Washington; traveling exhibition in U.S, 1988—. Recipient award in portrait painting, Hainesfalls, N.Y., 1965, First Prize-World award, Acad. Italia, Parma, 1985, 87; subject of TV interview, 1984. Fellow Royal Soc. Arts (London); mem. Artists Equity Assn. N.Y., Arts Students League (life), Nat. Soc. Arts and Letters (art chmn. 1969—), Kappa Pi (life). Clubs: Woman Pays, Liederkranz City of N.Y. (trustee 1979—). Home: 230 Riverside Dr New York NY 10025

DECHELLIS, DEBORAH SUSAN, officer, assistant treasurer, bank operations manager; b. Plainfield, N.J., Jan. 16, 1960; d. Anthony and Joan Dora (Brown) DeC. BS in Elem. Spl. Edn., U. Hartford, 1982. Spl. edn. tchr. Hartford (Conn.) Pub. Schs., 1982-83, East Hartford (Conn.) Pub. Schs., 1983-84; individual retirement account ops. supr. Conn. Nat. Bank, Hartford, 1984-87; individual retirement account adminstr. Glastonburg (Conn.) Bank & Trust, 1987, mgr. fin. mgmt. service ops., 1987—; ind. edn. cons. Democrat. Methodist. Office: Glastonbury Bank & Trust Co 2461 Main St Glastonbury CT 06033

DECKER, DEBRA ELNORA, librarian; b. Williamsport, Pa., Oct. 25, 1946; d. Herman Thomas and Harriett Lucina (Mullen) Palmer; B.S., Lock Haven State Coll., 1968; M.Ed., West Chester State Coll., 1971; M.S. in Library Sci., Clarion State Coll., 1981; m. Sept. 7, 1969; 1 dau., Moana Kai. Tchr., Owen J. Roberts Sch. Dist., Pottstown, Pa., 1968-73; instr., Becker Research Learning Center, Clarion (Pa.) State Coll., 1976-80, librarian instr., Instructional Materials Center, 1980-84, serials coordinator Carlson Library, 1984—. Neighborhood chmn. Brookville Council Girls Scouts U.S., 1976-82; bd. dirs. Brookville Area United Fund, 1980-83; officer Zion United Methodist Ch., 1977—. Mem. NEA, ALA, Pa. Library Assn., Pa. Edn. Assn., Assn. Pa. State Coll. and Univ. Faculties, Phi Delta Kappa. Democrat. Home: RD 4 Box 250 Brookville PA 15825 Office: Carlson Library Clarion State Coll Clarion PA 16214

DECKER, JEAN CAMPBELL, retired financial executive; b. Chgo., Mar. 10, 1915; d. Dm and Bertha (Campbell) Decker; B.A. in Bus. Adminstrn., U. Chgo., 1937. Notary pub., Ill. With Calco Mfg. Co., Addison, Ill., 1950-85, treas., 1969-81, plan adminstr., dir. pension plan, 1976-82, cons., 1981—; treas. Gustafson Enterprises, Inc., Addison, Ill., 1971-85, dir., 1971-78, 82-85; treas. Environ, Inc., Haines City, Fla., 1971-72. Mem. U. Chgo. Alumni Assn., Phi Delta Upsilon. Republican. Home: 885 Smith St Glen Ellyn IL 60137

DECKER, JOSEPHINE I., clinic administrator; b. Barling, Ark., May 24, 1933; d. Ralph and Ada A. (Claborn) Snider; student public schs., Muldrow, Okla.; m. William Arlen Decker, Feb. 4, 1952; 1 son, Peter A. With Southwestern Bell Telephone Co., Ft. Smith, Ark., 1951-52; with Holt Krock Clinic, Ft. Smith, 1952—, bus. adminstr., 1970—. Bd. dirs. Sparks Credit Union, Adv. Council Northside and Southside high schs., Ft. Smith, Ft. Smith Girls Shelter, Ft. Smith Credit Bur. Mem. Credit Women Internat., Soc. Cert. Consumer Credit Execs. Office: Holt Krock Clinic 1500 Dodson Ave Fort Smith AR 72901

DECKER, JUDITH ELAINE, land development company executive; b. Derry, N.H., Nov. 2, 1940; d. Clayton Kent and Ariel Almina (Palmer) Gillis; m. Marshall Norman Decker, Nov. 2, 1965; children: Timothy, Jennifer, James, Wesley. Diploma, McIntosh Bus. Sch., 1958-59; BS magna cum laude, Franklin Pierce Coll., 1986. Treas. N.H. Electric, Inc., Salem, 1974-77; treas. J.E.D. Assocs., Inc., Danville, N.H., 1978-86, pres., chief exec. officer, 1986—; bd. dirs. J.E.D. Assocs., Inc., Danville, MarDec, Inc., Salem, Shalles Corp., Salem. Chmn. Thompson for Gov., Salem, 1970, Heart Fund, Salem, 1969, 70, 71; troop leader Girl Scouts of Am., Salem, 1969-72. Mem. Nat. Assn. Female Execs., Greater Haverhill C. of C., Nat. Assn. Self Employed. Republican. Home: Wesley St Danville NH 03819 Office: MarDec Inc 53 Stiles Rd Suite 105 Salem NH 03079

DECKER, VICKI LYNN, educational placement director; b. Decorah, Iowa, Sept. 13, 1951; d. Edward Clark and Fern Emma (Drager) Simpson; m. Dennis Richard Decker, ;Apr. 19, 1974; children: Sasha Simpson, Danielle Simpson. Diploma in secretarial sci., Winona Area Tech. Sch., 1971; AA, Winona (Minn.) State U., 1987; diploma in bank mktg., Bank Mktg. Assn., Boulder, Colo., 1982. Mktg. officer Norwest Bank, Winona, 1978-82, credit officer, 1982-83, officer real estate loan dept., 1983-84; dir. devel. Watkins Meth. Home Found., Winona, 1985-88; asst. dir. career planning and placement Winona State U., 1988—. Bd. dirs. Winona Area United Way, 1986—, v.p., 1987-88, pres. 1988—; trustee Winona Alliance for Youth, 1986—; commr. Winon Charter Commn., 1987—, treas. 1988—. ; mem. Archtl. Review Bd., 1988—. Named Sec. of Yr., Profl. Secs. Assn. Internat., 1977; named one of Outstanding Young Women Am., 1981. Mem. Nat. Soc. Fund Raising Execs. (bd. dirs. Upper Miss. Valley chpt. 1986—, sec. 1987—), Nat. Soc. Women in C. of C.'s (sec., bd. dirs. 1985—, charter mem. 1985, 2d v.p. 1988—), Winona Area C. of C. (bd. dirs. 1987—, v.p. 1988—). Clubs: Hiawatha Valley Corvette (bd. dirs. 1978-81, pres. 1980), YeGgadds Investment (pres. 1986). Home: 1620 Edgewood Rd Winona MN 55987 Office: Winona State U 110 Gildenmeister Winona MN 55987

DECKER SLANEY, MARY TERESA, athlete; b. Bunnvale, N.J., Aug. 4, 1958; d. John and Jacqueline Decker; m. Ron Tabb (div. 1983); m. Richard Slaney, June 1, 1985; 1 child, Ashley Lynn. Student U. Colo., 1977-78. Amateur runner, 1969—; holder several world track and field records, 1980—; winner 2 gold medals at 1500 and 3000 meter World Track and Field Championship, Helsinki, Finland, 1983; mem. U.S. Olympic teams, 1980, 84; cons. to CBS Records, Timex, Eastman Kodak. Recipient Jesse Owens Internat. Amateur Athlete award, 1982, AAU Sullivan award, 1982; named Amateur Sportswoman of the Year, Women's Sports Found, 1982, 83; Top Sportswoman A.P. Europe, 1985. Address: 2923 Flintlock St Eugene OR 97401-4660 *

DECKERT, MYRNA JEAN, social service executive; b. McPherson, Kans., Nov. 4, 1936; d. Francis J. and Grace (Killion) George; m. Ray A. Deckert, Sept. 29, 1957; children: Rachelle, Kimberly, Charles, Michael. AA, Coll. of Sequoilas, 1956; BBA, U. Beverly Hills, 1983, MBA, 1984. Youth dir. Asbury Meth. Ch., El Paso, Tex., 1960-63; teen program dir. YWCA of El Paso, 1963-69, assoc. exec. dir., 1969-70, exec. dir., 1970—; mem. Constn. com., trainer YWCA of the U.S.A., N.Y.C., 1983-86, cons. 1987; bd. dirs. InterFirst Bank-Chelmont, El Paso; bd. dirs., vice chmn. El Paso Commn. for Women, 1985-86. Mem. state dept. Human Resources D.C. Task Force, Austin, Tex., 1986, Exec. Forum Bd. Recipient Hannah Soloman Community Service award Nat. Council Jewish Women, Sertoma Club award Service to Mankind, 1974, award of Merit Adalante Mujer, 1986, Social Services award KVIA/Sunturians, 1986. Mem. Council of Agy. Execs., Exec. Forum, UTEP Profl. Network (steering com. 1983—). Methodist. Home: 4276 Canterbury Dr El Paso TX 79902

DECOTIS, DEBORAH ANNE, investment banker; b. Salem, Mass., Nov. 13, 1952; d. John and Marie (Mahoney) DeC. B.A., Smith Coll., 1974; M.B.A. (Miller scholar), Stanford U., 1978. Analyst, Morgan Stanley & Co., Inc., N.Y.C., 1974-76, assoc., 1978-81, v.p., London, 1982-84, prin., N.Y.C., 1985—. Home: 211 Central Park W New York NY 10024 Office: Morgan Stanley & Co Inc 1251 Avenue of the Americas New York NY 10020

DECOURSEY, EILEEN MARIE, industrial manufacturing company executive; b. East Orange, N.J., Sept. 20, 1932; d. Andrew A. and Mildred H. (Shields) DeC.; m. Sidney Jack McDuff, Aug. 21, 1976. BS in Edn. and Speech, Kean Coll., 1954; postgrad., NYU, 1960-61. Personnel asst. Warner-Lambert Co., Morris Plains, N.J., 1956-59; research assoc. Handy Assoc., N.Y.C., 1959-60; jr. account exec. Johnson and Higgins, N.Y.C., 1960-64; personnel supr. Time Inc., N.Y.C., 1964-66; mgr. employee benefits Bristol-Myers Co., N.Y.C., 1966-71; v.p., exec. asst. to chmn. Squibb Corp., N.Y.C., 1971-75; v.p. employee relations Manville Corp., Denver, 1975-85; pres. Exec. Research Assocs., 1985—; mem. Mgmt. and Personnel Research Council of Conf. Bd., 1978-82; bd. dirs. First Colo. Bank and Trust Co., Denver. Bd. dirs. Mile High United Way, Denver, 1976-78, Craig Hosp., Denver, 1986-87; trustee Loretto Heights Coll., Denver, 1977-85. Mem. Am. Soc. Personnel Adminstrs. (bd. dirs. 1972-78), Am. Mgmt. Assn. (human resources council 1972-78), Personnel Round Table (chair program com. 1983-84), Human Resources Round Table Group (founder, chair 1980-86), Women's Forum Colo. (bd. dirs. 1987—). Republican. Clubs: Denver Country; Garden of Gods (Colorado Springs).

DE COUX, JANET, sculptor; b. Niles, Mich., Oct. 5, 1904; d. John Charles and Bertha (Wright) de C. Former student, Carnegie Inst. Tech., N.Y. Sch. Design, R.I. Sch. Design, Chgo. Art Inst. Apprentice C.P. Jennewein, N.Y.C., 1927-29, James Earl Fraser, Westport, Conn., 1932-35; apprentice to other; resident instr. Cranbrook Acad. Art, Birmingham, Mich., 1942-45; self-employed sculptor Gibsonia, Pa., 1945—. Sculptures include Deborah Song, 1942 (Widener medal 1942), Heroic Portrait William Penn, State Capitol Pa., Harrisburgh, 1967. Fellow Tiffany Found., 1927; fellow Guggenheim Found., 1939-42; grantee Am. Acad.-Nat. Inst. Art and Letters, 1945. Fellow Nat. Sculpture Soc. (Lindsay Meml. prize 1940); academician mem. Nat. Acad. Design. Democrat. Episcopalian. Home: 3930 Dickey Rd Gibsonia PA 15044

DE CROW, KAREN, lawyer, author, lecturer; b. Chgo., Dec. 18, 1937; d. Samuel Meyer and Juliette (Abt) Lipschultz; m. Alexander Allen Kolben, 1960 (div. 1965); m. Roger Edward DeCrow, 1965 (div. 1972). B.S., Northwestern U., 1959; J.D., Syracuse U., 1972. Bar: N.Y., U.S. Dist. Ct. (no. dist.) N.Y. Resorts editor Golf Digest mag., Evanston, Ill., 1959-60; editor Am. Soc. Planning Ofcls., Chgo., 1960-61; writer Center for Study Liberal Edn. for Adults, Chgo., 1961-64; editor Holt, Rinehart, Winston, Inc., N.Y.C., 1965, L.W. Singer, Syracuse, N.Y., 1965-66; writer Eastern Regional Inst. for Edn., Syracuse, 1967-69, Pub. Broadcasting System, 1977; tchr. women and law 1972-74; nat. bd. mem. NOW, 1968-77, nat. pres., 1974-77, also nat. politics task force chmn.; cons. affirmative actio; lectr. corps., polit. groups, colls. and univs. U.S., Canada, Finland, Peoples Republic of China, Greece, USSR; nat. coordinator Women's Strike for Equality, 1970; N.Y. State del. Internat. Women's Year, 1977; candidate for mayor, Syracuse, 1969; originated Schs. for Candidates; bd. advisors Working Women's Inst.; participant DeCrow-Schlafly ERA Debates, from 1975; co-founder World Woman Watch, 1988. Author: (with Roger DeCrow) University Adult Education: A Selected Bibliography, 1967, The Young Woman's Guide to Liberation, 1971, Sexist Justice, 1974, First Women's State of the Union Message, 1977; (with Robert Seidenberg) Women Who Marry Houses: Panic and Protest in Agoraphobia, 1983; editor: The Pregnant Teenager (Howard Osofsky), 1968, Corporate Wives, Corporate Casualties (Robert Seidenberg), 1973; contbr.: articles to USA Today, N.Y. Times, Los Angeles Times, Boston Globe, Vogue, Mademoiselle, Newsday, Penthouse, Washington Post, Los Angelex Times Mag., Policy Review, Miami Herald, Internat. Herald Tribune, Social Problems; other newspapers, mags.; columnist: Syracuse New Times; recording: Opening Up Marriage, 1980. Hon. trustee Elizabeth Cady Stanton Found. Mem. Am. Arbitration Assn., Dist. Attys. Adv. Council, ACLU (Kharas award N.Y. chpt.), N.Y. State Women's Bar Assn. (chpt. dir., task force on gender bias), N.Y. State, Onondaga County bar assns., Yale Polit. Union (hon. life). Address: 7 Fir Tree Ln Jamesville NY 13078

DE CUEVAS, ELIZABETH, sculptor; b. St. Germain en Laye, France, Jan. 22, 1929 (Am. citizen); d. George and Margaret (Strong) de C.; 1 child, Deborah Carmichael. Student, Vassar Coll., 1946-48; AB, Sarah Lawrence Coll., 1952; student, Art Students League, N.Y.C., 1963-68. One-woman shows include Lee Ault Gallery, N.Y.C., 1977-78, Tower Gallery, Southampton, N.Y., 1980, Iolas-Jackson Gallery, N.Y.C., 1983-85, Guild Hall Mus., East Hampton, N.Y., 1985, Kerr Gallery, N.Y.C., 1988—; exhibited in group shows at Guild Hall, East Hampton, 1980, Art Students League of N.Y., 1982, Bruce Mus., Greenwich, Conn., 1984, 85, Tower Gallery, N.Y.C., 1984, Andre Zarre Gallery, N.Y.C., 1985, Kouros Gallery, N.Y.C. and Ridgefield, Conn., 1985, Susan Blanchard Gallery, N.Y.C., 1985-86, Ruth Vered Gallery, East Hampton, 1986-87, Benton Gallery, Southampton, 1987—, Kerr Gallery, 1988—; represented in pvt. collections. Club: Vassar of N.Y.

DECYK, ROXANNE JEAN, manufacturing company executive lawyer; b. Chgo., Nov. 5, 1952; d. Walter and Tillie (Kuzma) D.; m. John F. Chlewbowski, June 27, 1987. AB, U. Ill., 1973; JD, Marquette U., 1977. Bar: Wis. 1977, Ill. 1981. Pres. Penta Advt., Champaign, Ill., 1972-73; staff journalist Coll. Medicine U. Ill., 1973-74; assoc. Foley & Lardner, Milw., 1977-79; pres. Corp. Legal Communications, Milw., 1980-81; v.p., sec., asst. to chmn. Internat. Harvester Co., Chgo., 1981-83, v.p. adminstrn., sec., 1983-84, sr. v.p. corp. relations, 1984-86, sr. v.p. adminstrn., 1986—; dir. Lincoln Nat. Pension, Ft. Wayne, Ind. Mem. Leadership Greater Chgo., Voices for Ill. Children, The Chgo. Network United Way. Recipient Nat. Merit Scholar award Outboard Marine Corp., 1970. Mem. Econ. Club Chgo., ABA, State Bar Wis., Ill. State Bar Assn., Chgo. Network, Phi Beta Kappa. Home: 55 W Goethe #1254 Chicago IL 60610 Office: Navistar Internat Transp Corp 401 N Michigan Ave Chicago IL 60611

DEDIOS, BELINDA, financial analyst; b. San Jose, Calif., Nov. 26, 1958; d. Antonio and Eunice (Carranza) DeD. BA in Psychology, Ariz. State U., 1981; M, Am. Grad. Sch. Internat. Mgmt., 1983. Teller First Interstate Bank of Ariz., Tempe, 1980-82; fin. analyst Sperry Corp., McLean, Va., 1984-86, U.S. Sprint, Reston, Va., 1986—. Democrat.

DEEBLE, SONDRA LEE, human resource professional; b. Kingston, Pa., Mar. 7, 1942; d. George Oliver and Helen Thickla (Stanton) D.; m. Robert John Golomb, July 8, 1961; 1 child, Pamela Anne. BS in Mgmt. magna cum laude, Rider Coll., 1976; MEd in Bus. summa cum laude, Temple U., 1978; student, Columbia U., 1980-81. Asst. prof. Burlington County Coll., Pemberton, N.J., 1976-81; asst. mgr. employment and staffing Bell Atlantic Corp., Princeton, N.J., 1985—. Program chmn. Jr. League Cen. Delaware Valley, Trenton, N.J., 1986-87; vol. Princeton Med. Ctr., 1982-85. Mem. Am. Soc. Tng. Devel., Princeton Personnel Assn. Republican. Roman Catholic. Club: Hopewell Valley Golf (mwm. tennis com. 1985-86).

DEEGAN, PATRICIA RUBY, optician; b. Deshler, Nebr., May 17, 1955; d. James Nelton and Lorraine Cecile (Larmand) Fobair; m. Thomas Michael Deegan, Dec. 11, 1981; children: Sara Jeanne, Renee Alarie. Cert. optometric tech., Itasca Community Coll., 1974. Optometric technician Drs. Truax and Simpson, Albert Lea, Minn., 1974-76; optician trainee Walman Optical Co., Mpls., 1976-77; optician Dayton Hudson, Burnsville, Minn., 1977-78; div. mgr. Share Health Plan, Bloomington, Minn., 1978—. Recipient Cert. of Achievement Optifair, 1983, 84. Mem. Am. Bd. Opticianry (cert.), Nat. Acad. Opticianry, Minn. Opticians Soc. Democrat. Roman Catholic. Home: 530 Montrose Lane Saint Paul MN 55116 Office: Eyewear by Share 7920 Cedar Ave S Bloomington MN 55425

DEEL, FRANCES QUINN, librarian; b. Pottsville, Pa., Mar. 9, 1939; d. Charles Joseph and Carrie Miriam (Ketner) Q.; m. Ronald Eugene Deel, Feb. 5, 1983. B.S., Millersville State Coll., 1960; M.L.S., Rutgers U., 1964; M.P.A., U. West Fla., 1981. Post librarian U.S. Army Armor (Desert Tng. Ctr.), Ft. Irwin, Calif., 1964-66; staff librarian Mil. Dist. of Washington, 1966-67; supervisory librarian 1st Logistical Command, APO San Francisco, 1967-68; tech. process specialist Naval Edn. and Tng. Supervisory Command, Washington, 1968-77, Pensacola, Fla., 1968-77; chief tech. library USAF Armament Lab., Eglin AFB, Fla., 1977-81; dir. command libraries Air Force Systems Command (Andrews AFB), Washington, 1981—; mem. exec. adv. council Fed. Library and Info. Network, Washington, 1983-86. Mem. ALA (dir.-at-large armed forces libraries sect. Chgo. 1983-86), Spl. Libraries Assn., D.C. Library Assn. Roman Catholic. Home: 9225 Forest Haven Dr Alexandria VA 22309 Office: Air Force Systems Command/ MPSL Andrews AFB Washington DC 20334

DEEM, JANE ANN, graphic artist; b. Dayton, Ohio, Aug. 25, 1954; d. Francis Elbert and Mary Jane (Melling) D. BFA, Ohio U., 1976. Substitute art tchr. Kettering Sch. Dist., Ohio, 1976-77; prodn. supr. Subia, Inc., Hawthorne, Calif., 1977-80; prodn. mgr. Lienett Co., Inc., Los Alamitos, Calif., 1980-81; v.p., ptnr. Comml. Graffix, Los Angeles, 1981—. Democrat. Mem. Christian Ch. Avocations: music, decorating/home improvement, computers, pets, photography. Office: Commercial Graffix 5777 W Century Blvd Suite 800 Los Angeles CA 90045-5631

DEEM, NANCY LOUISE, stock brocker; b. Martins Ferry, Ohio, July 15, 1938; d. Lee and Gladys Caroline (Dienstill) Rushforth; m. Delbert William Deem; 1 child, Robert Lee. Student, Northwestern U., 1971. Sec. Thomas & Hill, Inc., Charleston, W.Va., 1967-73; loan counselor Decatur Fed. Savs. and Loan, Dalton, Ga., 1979-81; registered rep. INVEST/Decatur Fed. Savs. and Loan, Dalton, 1981—. Mem. Internat. Assn. Fin. Planning, Nat. Assn. Accts. (sec. 1984-85, v.p. communications 1986-87), Bus. and Profl. Women (treas. 1985-87, pres. 1987—), Dalton LWV (chmn. membership com. 1985-86, pres. elect 1986-87). Republican. Club: Pilot Internat. (Dalton). Home: 423 Crawford Terr Tunnel Hill GA 30755 Office: INVEST/Decatur Fed Savs Loan Box 2207 Dalton GA 30722-2207

DEEN, LESLIE, controller; b. Bradenton, Fla., Mar. 8, 1958; d. H. Broughton and Shirley Deen (Williams) Smith. Student, Harper Coll., 1983-86, Oakton Coll., 1986—. With sales dept. Bob Horsley's, Wheaton, Ill., 1975-77; controller Lake Ctr. Mgmt., Mt. Prospect, Ill., 1977—. Mem. Nat. Assn. Female Execs. Republican. Baptist. Home: 1705 Forest Cove Dr #302 Mount Prospect IL 60056 Office: Lake Ctr Mgmt 1699 Wall St Suite 114 Mount Prospect IL 60056

DEES, SANDRA KAY MARTIN, psychologist; b. Omaha, Apr. 18, 1944; d. Leslie B. and Ruth Lillian (May) Martin; m. Doyce B. Dees; B.A. magna cum laude, Tex. Christian U., 1965, M.A., 1972; postgrad. Washington U., St. Louis; postgrad., Tex. Christian U., 1987—. Adminstrv. asst./research coordinator Hosp. Improvement Project, Wichita Falls (Tex.) State Hosp., 1968-69; caseworker adoptions Edna Gladney Home, Ft. Worth, Tex., 1970-71; psychologist Mexia (Tex.) State Sch., 1971-72; sch. psychologist Ft. Worth Ind. Sch. Dist., 1971-78, program evaluator, 1978-86; pvt. counselor, 1986—; project mgr. Growth Center Project, 1975-77. Founder Alateen Group, Wichita Falls, 1969; mem. Ft. Worth Adolescent Pregnancy Bd. Dallas Tex. Christian U. Women's Club creative writing scholar, 1962-64, Virginia Alpha scholar, 1963; NASA research asst., 1965-67; USPHS trainee, 1967-68; cert. Am. Montessori Soc., 1977. Mem. Am. Ednl. Research Assn., Mental Health Assn., Mortar Bd., Mensa, Alpha Chi, Phi Alpha Theta, Psi Chi, Phi Delta Kappa. Contbr. articles to profl. publs. Home: 29 Bounty Rd W Fort Worth TX 76132 Office: 3210 W Lancaster St Ft Worth TX 76107

DEFABRITIS, ELIZABETH REEVES, architect; b. Newton, N.J., Mar. 21, 1956; d. Herbert West Reeves and Elizabeth Jane (Hubbard) Van Syckle; m. Richard Anthony DeFabritis, Oct. 1, 1983; 1 child, Marie Elizabeth. BArch, Cornell U., 1979. Registered architect, N.J. Architect Houghton Quarty Warr Architects, Newton, 1979-87; freelance, architect, hist. cons. Andover, N.J., 1987—. Mem. steering com. Kuser Mansion Inc., Sussex, N.J., 1980-81; vice chair hist. dist. adv. commn. Town of Newton, 1988. Mem. Nat. Trust for Hist. Preservation (assoc.), Delta Delta Delta. Methodist. Home and Office: 213 Main St PO Box 408 Andover NJ 07821

DEFAZIO, LYNETTE STEVENS, dancer, choreographer, educator, chiropractor; b. Berkeley, Calif., Sept. 29; d. Honore and Mabel J. (Estavan) Stevens; student U. Calif., Berkeley, 1950-55, San Francisco State Coll., 1950-51; D. Chiropractic, Life-West Chiropractic Coll., San Lorenzo, Calif., 1983, BA in Humanities, New Coll. Calif., 1986; children—Joey H. Panganiban, Joanna Pang. Diplomate Nat. Sci. Bd.; eminence in dance edn., Calif. Community Colls. dance specialist, standard services, childrens ctrs. credentials Calif. Dept. Edn. Contract child dancer Monogram Movie Studio, Hollywood, Calif., 1938-40; dance instr. San Francisco Ballet, 1953-64; performer San Francisco Opera Ring, 1960-67; performer, choreographer Oakland (Calif.) Civic Light Opera, 1963-70; fgn. exchange dance dir. Academie de Danses-Salle Pleyel, Paris, France, 1966; dir. Ballet Arts Studio, Oakland, 1960—; teaching specialist Oakland Unified Sch. Dist.-Childrens Ctrs., 1968-80; instr. Peralta Community Coll. Dist., Oakland, 1971—, chmn. dance dept., 1985—; cons., instr. extension courses UCLA, Dirs. and Suprs. Assn., Pittsburg Unified Sch. Dist., Tulare (Calif.) Sch. Dist., 1971-73; researcher Ednl. Testing Services, HEW, Berkeley, 1974; resident choreographer San Francisco Childrens Opera, 1970—, Oakland Civic Theater; ballet mistress Dimensions Dance Theater, Oakland, 1977-80; cons. Gianchetta Sch. Dance, San Francisco, Robicheau Boston Ballet, TV series Patchwork Family, CBS, N.Y.C.; choreographer Ravel's Valses Nobles et Sentimentales, 1976. Author: The Opera Ballets; A Choreographic Manual, Vols. I-V, 1986. Recipient Foremost Women of 20th Century, 1985, Merit award San Francisco Children's Opera, 1985. Mem. Profl. Dance Tchrs. Assn. Am. Author: Basic Music Outlines for Dance Classes, 1960, rev., 1968; Teaching Techniques and Choreography for Advanced Dancers, 1965; Basic Music Outlines for Dance Classes, 1965; Goals and Objectives in Improving Physical Capabilities, 1970; A Teacher's Guide for Ballet Techniques, 1970; Principle Procedures in Basic Curriculum, 1974; Objectives and Standards of Performance for Physical Development, 1975. Asso. music arranger Le Ballet du Cirque, 1964; Techniques of a Ballet School, 1970, rev., 1974; asso. composer, lyricist The Ballet of Mother Goose, 1968; choreographer: Walses Nobles Et Sentimentales (Ravel); Cannon in D for Strings and Continuo (Pachelbel), 1979. Home and Office: 4923 Harbord Dr Oakland CA 94618

DEFELICE, LOIS ANNE, religious education administrator; b. Chgo., Oct. 28, 1950; d. Nicholas J. and Grace D. (Normoyle) Weiler; m. Wayne Alan DeFelice Sr., Aug. 3, 1973; children: Wayne Alan II, Dustin, Nicholas, Elizabeth, Sean. BA, Northeastern Ill. U., 1971. Tchr. music Palatine (Ill.) Sch. Dist., 1972-74; dir. religious edn. St. William Sch., Chgo., 1976-85, St. Priscilla Sch., Chgo., 1985—. Mem. Chgo. Area Religious Edn., Nat. Cath. Educators. Home: 2228 N Nagle Chicago IL 60635

DE FILIPPO, RITA MARCELLA, budget analyst; b. N.Y.C.; d. Sal and Margaret (Jaeger) DeF. Student, Los Angeles City Coll., 1957, City Coll. San Francisco, 1975, U. San Francisco, 1976; cert. in acctg., LaSalle U., 1968. Asst. dir. advt. Gump's, Inc., San Francisco, 1959; research statistician Honig-Cooper & Harrington, San Francisco, 1960-61; salesperson Landau Realty, San Francisco, 1962-63; mgmt. analyst Oakland (Calif.) Army Base, 1978-80; budget analyst Dept. Army, San Francisco, 1980—. Recipient Outstanding Performance award Fed. Govt., 1979. Mem. Am. Bus. Women's Assn. (treas. 1978-79), Am. Soc. Mil. Comptrollers, Assn. Women in Sci., Assn. U.S. Army, Nat. Fedn. Fed. Employees (trustee 1972), World Affairs Council, Sierra Club. Home: 1348 C Scott St San Francisco CA 94115 Office: Dept of Army Presidio San Francisco San Francisco CA 94129

DEFOREST, JUNE, violinist; b. Pitts., June 30, 1939; d. William Edward and Isabel (Nameth) DeF.; m. Daniel R. Morganstern, June 19, 1966. Student Carnegie-Mellon U., 1957-60; B.Mus., Manhattan Sch. Music, N.Y.C., 1963, M.Mus., 1974. Violinist, concertmaster Joffrey Ballet, N.Y.C., Can. Opera Co. Toronto, Ont., 1968; asst. concertmaster Am. Ballet Theater, N.Y.C., 1967-70, violinist, 1971—; violinist Chgo. Lyric Opera, 1969—; violinist Am. Chamber Trio, 1975—. Mem. Internat. Congress of Symphony and Opera Musicians (del. 1983, 84, 85), Coll. Music Soc., Chamber Music Am., Am. Chamber Concerts. Address: 890 West End Ave New York NY 10025

DEFOREST, MYRA LOUISE, laboratory consultant; b. Wyatt, Mo., Oct. 1, 1955; d. Thomas Eugene and Bonnie Cleo (Tyner) Jackson; m. Byron Neely DeForest Jr., Mar. 19, 1977; children: Shawna Louise, Shannon Neely. BS in Biology, Lindenwood Coll., St. Charles, Mo., 1978. Cert. med. tech. Med. tech. ARC, St. Louis, 1978-81; blood bank supr. DePaul Hosp., St. Louis, 1981-84; clin. lab. cons. Daughters of Charity Nat. Purchasing Services, St. Louis, 1984—. Mem. Coll. Am. Pathologists, Clin. Lab. Mgmt. Assn. Baptist. Office: Daughters of Charity Nat Purchasing Services 11775 Borman Dr Saint Louis MO 63146-6902

DEFORREST, KATHRYN ANN, baking company executive; b. Port Huron, Mich., June 16, 1950; d. Calvin Arthur Mausolf and Janet Ann (Lillis) Goodrich; m. John C. Russell, Aug. 8, 1970 (div. Feb. 1982); m. Thomas N. DeForrest, Aug. 1, 1987. Student No. Ill. U., 1968-70, Elmhurst Coll., 1982—. Receptionist/switchboard operator Keebler Co., Elmhurst, Ill., 1971-74, purchasing analyst, asst. to v.p. purchasing, 1974-77, purchasing agt., 1977—. Roman Catholic. Office: Keebler Co 1 Hollow Tree Ln Elmhurst IL 60126

DEGAND, LYNNE MARIE, manufacturing company administrator; b. Evanston, Ill., Nov. 1, 1955; d. Maurice Henry and Elnora Grace (Graves-Lavis) Hofmeister; m. Arturo F. Moreschi, Sept. 15, 1979 (div. 1982); m. Richard Degand Jr., Nov. 25, 1983. Student, Knox Coll., 1972-75, Mundelein Coll., 1978; BBA, Upper Iowa U., 1985. With acctg. staff Nat. Can Corp., Chgo., 1975-87; mgr. cost acctg. Am. Nat. Can Corp., Chgo., 1987-88, ITT Bell and Gossett, Morton Grove, Ill., 1988—; cons. Chgo. Enterprise Ctr., 1987-88. Cons. Chgo. Enterprise Ctr., 1987, 88, youth motivation program Chgo. Assn. Commerce and Industry, 1980; solicitor United Way-Crusade of Mercy, 1980, 84, United Blood Services, Chgo., 1980-87, Chgo. Jr. Achievement, 1981; lobbyist Planned Parenthood Assn. Chgo., 1984; rep. Women's Career Conv., Chgo., 1980, 81. Republican. Lutheran. Home: 6B Dundee Quarter Apt 102 Palatine IL 60074 Office: ITT Bell and Gossett 8200 N Austin Ave Morton Grove IL 60053

DEGASTER, BARBARA JENNIFER, investment advisor; b. N.Y.C., Jan. 25, 1957; d. Zachary and Elizabeth (Philips) deG. BBA, U. Mass., 1979. Asst. v.p. retail sales Prescott Ball & Turben, N.Y.C., 1980-83; instl. sales Laidlaw Adams & Peck, N.Y.C., 1983-84; v.p. N.C.A. Asset Mgmt. Corp., N.Y.C., 1984-86; exec. v.p. Universal Asset Mgmt. Corp., N.Y.C., 1986—. Mem. Nat. Assn. Female Execs.

DEGENHART, PEARL C., artist, educator; b. Phillipsburg, Mont., Feb. 25; d. L.C. and Ellen (O'Neill) Degenhart; A.B., U. Mont., 1923; A.M., Columbia, 1928. Instr. art Arcata (Calif.) Union High Sch., 1928—, chmn. art dept., 1930-65; one-man shows Stafford Inn, Scotia, Calif., 1954, Humboldt State Coll., 1951; exhibited group shows San Francisco Art Assn., 1932, 37, 40; Contemporary Arts Gallery, N.Y.C., 1939; Denver, 1938; Humboldt State Coll., 1935, 45, 54; Spokane Wash., 1948; Oakland Art Gallery, 1948; Humboldt Fed. Gallery, 1966; Eureka Courthouse, 1968, Redwood Art Assn., Eureka, 1976-80, Old Town Art Guild, Eureka, 1977, San Rafael, Calif., 1978-79. Mem. Nat. League Am. Pen Women, Alpha Xi Delta, Delta Phi Delta. Contbr. to art, juvenile mags.; author children's story book. Address: Box 142 Trinidad CA 95570

DEGNAN, JANE HEALY, university administrator; b. Albany, N.Y.; d. John Francis and Ruth Elizabeth (Hughes) Healy; m. Michael J. Degnan; children—Diana, Laura, Deborah. B.A. in English, Coll. St. Elizabeth, Madison, N.J., 1962; M.A. in English, Montclair State Coll., 1973. Tchr. English, Lincoln Jr. High Sch., West Orange, N.J., 1976-81; dir., program developer Westfall Film Prodns., Madison, N.J., 1981-83; coordinator pub. relations Seton Hall U., South Orange, N.J., 1983—; pres., cons. Connor Martin Agy., West Orange, 1981—; host radio talk show Viewpoint, 1985—. Author film scripts, articles, children's stories. Democrat. Roman Catholic.

DE GÓNGORA, ADA ELENA, counseling administrator, psychologist, educator; b. Holquin, Oriente, Cuba, Dec. 6, 1940; came to U.S., 1967; d. Luis Guillermo and Ada (Artigas) De Góngora; m. Jesus Del Corro, Oct. 16, 1965 (div. 1973). D in Law, U. Havana, Cuba, 1963, PhD, 1964; EdB, U. Miami, Fla., 1973; MS, St. Thomas U. (formerly Biscayne Coll.), Miami, 1976; PhD, Columbia Pacific U., 1988. Tchr. various schs. Cuba, 1958-65; tchr. pub. schs. Miami, 1970—; adj. prof. psychology St. Thomas U., Miami, 1976-82; prof. psycohology, dept. chmn. bilingual campuses Fla. Meml. Coll., Miami, 1978—; instr. sch. ctr. for spl. instrn. Shenandoah Jr. High Sch., Miami, 1986-87, sponsor Youth Crime Watch program, 1986-87; tchr. North Shore and Ashley Manor Nursing Homes, Miami, 1984—; counselor Nicky Cruz Outreach Program, Miami, 1976-78; staff mem. Human Relations Tng. Lab., N.Y.C., 1979-80; pres. Adegon Investment Co., Miami, 1987. Contbr. numerous articles to Abdala mag.; writer poetry. Helper Melrose Community Action Assn., Miami, 1979. Recipient Trahajadores de la Patria award YMCA, 1972, Diploma Merito Docente Colegio de Pedagogos Cubanos, 1977, award Pan Am. Inst. for the Arts, 1981, Crime Watch plaque Hall fo Fame, 1988; cert. appreciation Miami Lions Club, 1981. Mem. United Tchrs. of Dade, Circulade de Cultura Hispanoamericano. Republican. Roman Catholic. Home: 17021 North Bay Rd #620 North Miami Beach FL 33161

DE GRAFFENRIED, VELDA MAE CAMP (MRS. THOMAS P. DEGRAFFENRIED), clinical laboratory executive; b. Kirwin, Kans.; d. George Robert and Laura (Woodward) Camp; student No. Ill. U., 1959-60; m. Thomas P. deGraffenried, May 23, 1942; children—Donna Rae McCaffrey, Albert Lawrence II, Nicholas Thomas. Office mgr. deGraffenried & Fisher Clin. Labs., DeKalb, Ill., 1957-64, exec. sec., 1964—, dir. pub. affairs until 1985; dir. public affairs deGraffenried Med. Cons. Service, Inc. Vice pres. Haish Sch. PTA, DeKalb, 1958-59; den mother cub scouts Chief Shabbona council Boy Scouts Am., 1957-60; supr. Teen Age Club, Louisville, 1949-50; county crusade chmn. Am. Cancer Soc. (recipient commendation, 1987), 1965, mem. exec. bd. DeKalb County, 1964—, dir. public affairs, 1970—, chmn. bd., 1978-80, chmn. Radiothon, 1972-82, 83-87, sec. DeKalb County Soc., 1969—, mem. state bd. Ill. div., 1985—. Recipient commendations Am. Cancer Soc., 1965, 74, Boy Scouts Am., 1955. Mem. DeKalb County Med. Soc. Aux. (sec. 1959-60, 76—, pres. 1973-74), DeKalb Hosp. Aux. Methodist. Home: 1208 Sunnymeade Trail DeKalb IL 60115

DEGRAFT-JOHNSON, ALTHIA FAIN, educational administrator; b. MOrristown, Tenn., July 2, 1950; d. Robert Harris and Irene (Clark) Fain; m. Alphonso Canty, May 28, 1970 (div. Dec. 1985); 1 child, Irena Catrice; m. Kwamena Gyakye deGraft-Johnson, Dec. 14, 1985. AA, Morristown Coll., 1970; BA, Carson-Newman Coll., 1974; MS, U. Tenn., 1976, EdD, 1982. Instr. English Morristown Coll., 1976-77; dir. personnel and research Motlow State Community Coll., Tullahoma, Tenn., 1977-79; asst. personnel mgr. Levi Strauss & Co., Knoxville, Tenn., 1979; asst. prof. English Knoxville Coll., 1980-81; asst. prof. English Walters State Community Coll., Morristown, 1982-84, asst. dir. Greeneville Ctr., 1982-84; assoc. prof. English Ga. Mil. Coll., Augusta, 1984-86; reading specialist SUNY, Oswego, 1986; dir. Geneva Extension Ctr. Community Coll. of the Finger Lakes, Canandaigua, N.Y., 1986-88; exec. asst. to pres. SUNY Health Sci. Ctr., Syracuse, 1988—; cons. Indsl. and Bus. Inst., Tullahoma, 1977-79, social servces dept. Morristown Housing Authority, 1977-83; cons. in field. Contbr. articles to profl. jours. Nat. Inst. of Edn. fellow, 1980-81; named one of Outstanding Young Women in Am., 1974. Mem. Nat. Assn. Female Execs., Rochester Area Colls. Continuing Edn. Com., Continuing Edn. Assn. N.Y., Delta Sigma Theta. Office: SUNY Health Sci Ctr Office of Pres 750 East Adams St Syracuse NY 13210

DE GRANDPRE, JEAN LOUIS, physicist; b. Montreal, Que., Can., May 25, 1929; arrived in U.S., 1960; d. Joseph Oscar and Orthelea (Robillard) De G. BA, U. Montreal, 1948, BSc in Physics, 1952, MSc in Physics, 1954. Engr. Canadair Ltd., Montreal, 1954-60; simulator team leader Sperry Gyroscope of Can. Ltd., Montreal, 1960-61; mgr. Douglas Aircraft Co., Santa Monica, Calif., 1961-65; mem. tech. staff Gen. Research Corp., Santa Barbara, Calif., 1965-71, Saigon, Vietnam, 1968, Bangkok, 1968-69, Denville, N.J., 1971-74; mem. tech. staff Gen. Research Corp., Huntsville, Ala., 1975—, sr. scientist, 1988—; pres. adv. com. A&M U. Sch. Tech., Huntsville, 1982-83. Contbr. over 100 tech. reports. Mem. N.W. Huntsville Civic Assn., 1985—. Societe St. Jean Baptiste grantee, 1952-54, Que. ProvincialGovt., 1950-54. Mem. IEEE, AIAA, Assn. for Computing Machinery, Can. Assn. Physicists, Operation Research Soc. of Am. (assoc.). Office: Gen Research Corp 635 Discovery Dr Huntsville AL 35806

DEGRAW, FRANCES LEE DISHMAN, lawyer, banker; b. Newport News, Va., Oct. 26, 1936; d. Robert Ernest and Charlotte Elizabeth (Bishop) Dishman; m. Edward Carleton Hurman, June 19, 1955 (div. 1965) children—Bobbi C. Kesnig, Bonni G. Sandt, Johanna L. Hurman; m. 2d Donald Xavier DeGraw, Apr. 4, 1965. B.S. B.A. with honors, Christopher Newport Coll., 1974; J.D., Marshall Wythe Law Sch., Williamsburg, Va., 1976. Bar: Va. 1977, Fla. 1977, U.S. Tax Ct. 1977, U.S. Dist. Ct. (so. dist.) Fla. 1977. Tax specialist Coopers & Lybrand, Miami, Fla., 1977-78; assoc. Bruce Scheiner P.A., Ft. Myers, Fla., 1978-79; trust officer, v.p. Flagship Bank of Tampa, Punta Gorda, Fla., 1979-83; v.p. Fla. Nat. Bank, Punta Gorda, 1984-85, Orlando, 1985—; dir. Solar Pool Heaters, Inc., 1983-84; dir. fin., instr. Fla. Inst. for Legal Assts., 1986—. Columnist Estate Advisor weekly newspaper, 1983-85; announcer daily radio program on estate advice, 1980-81. Trustee St. Joseph Hosp., Port Charlotte, Fla., 1981-85, treas., 1983-85; bd. dirs. Wesleyan Coll.-SW Fla., Port Charlotte, 1983-85, Am. Cancer Soc., Charlotte County, Fla., 1980. Mem. ABA, Va. Bar Assn., Fla. Bar Assn., Orange County Bar Assn., Charlotte County Bar Assn., Central Fla. Assn. Women Lawyers, Central Fla. Estate Planning Council. Democrat. Episcopalian. Home: 329 Gilbert Rd Orlando FL 32792 Office: Fla Nat Bank 801 N Orange Ave Orlando FL 23593

DE GRAZIA, LORETTA THERESA, oil company executive; b. Boston, May 17, 1955; d. Gaetano T.P. and Nancy R. (Serino) De G. A in Mgmt./ Mktg. magna cum laude, Newbury Coll., 1986. V.p. mktg. and sales Grimes Oil Co., Boston, 1977-85; pres. East Coast Petroleum, Boston, 1985—. Fellow New Eng. Women Bus. Owners, Nat. Assn. Women in Constrn., Greater Boston Women's Network, Nat. Assn. Female Execs. Office: East Coast Petroleum Corp 645 Morrissey Blvd Boston MA 02122-3538

DEGUIRE, KATHRYN SILBER, psychologist; b. Mankato, Minn., Nov. 16, 1932; d. Ernest Albert and Anna (John) Silber; Mus.B., Eastman Sch. Music U. Rochester, 1954; postgrad. Akademie fur Musik ünd Darstellende Kunst, Vienna, 1954-55, Upsala Coll., 1966-69; M.A., Fordham U., 1971, Ph.D., 1974; m. John Diaz, Aug. 22, 1981; 1 dau., Lise Kathryn. Pianist, organist, instr. piano, 1955-66; clin. asst. psychologist Meml. Sloan Kettering Cancer Center, N.Y.C., 1974-83; pvt. practice, N.Y.C., 1976-88, Fairfield, N.J., 1976—; lectr. Upsala Coll., East Orange, N.J., 1971-72, 78-81. Fulbright scholar, Vienna, 1954-55; USPHS grantee, 1969-71. Mem. Am. Psychol. Assn., N.J. Psychol. Assn., Soc. Psychologists in Pvt. Practice (pres. 1986). Rec. artist: Orion. Home and Office: 26 Sand Rd Fairfield NJ 07006

DE HAAN-PULS, JOYCE ELAINE, sales representative; b. Grand Rapids, Mich., Dec. 22, 1941; d. Harry Herman and Dorothy Elaine (Kikstra) DeHaan; student Calvin Coll., 1960-61; B.S. with honors, Grand Valley State Colls., 1978; postgrad. U. Sarajevo, Yugoslavia, 1978, Grad. Inst., Siedman Grad. Coll., 1979—; M in Speech Communications Wayne State U., 1986 ; children—Bruce Todd, Daniel Lane, Cristy-Ann Sara Elizabeth Puls. Owner, operator Joyce Elaine's Beauty Parlor, Grandville, Mich., 1960-64; asst. assessor City of Hudsonville, Mich., 1978; dir. displaced homemaker program Women's Resource Center, Grand Rapids, 1979-81; visual products rep. 3M Corp., Grand Rapids, 1982-85, sr. account rep., Detroit, 1985—; mem. Ottawa County (Mich.) CETA Adv. Bd. Bd. dirs. Downtown Day Care Center, Grand Rapids, 1972. Recipient cert. of appreciation Bishop of Saigon, Vietnam, 1969; Top Sales rep. 3M/US, 1983, VIP, 1983, 84, 85; Phillip Morris scholar, 1975. Mem. Internat. Visitors Council, Nat. Assn. Fgn. Students, Nat. Assn. for Female Execs., Grand Rapids Council on World Affairs, Am. Soc. Public Adminstrn. Republican. Home: 2141 Seminole Detroit MI 48214 Office: 2225 Oak Industrial Dr Grand Rapids MI 49505

DEIBLER, BARBARA ELLEN, librarian; b. Pottsville, Pa., Aug. 11, 1943; d. Samuel Elwood and Miriam Elizabeth (Houser) D. BA, Pa. State U., 1965, MS, Drexel U., 1966. Cataloger State Library Pa., Harrisburg, 1966-82, head cataloger, 1972-82, rare book librarian, 1980—, asst. coordinator collection mgmt., 1982—. Librarian Hist. Soc. Schuylkill County, 1971-77. Mem. Am. Acad. Polit. and Social Scis., Acad. Polit. Sci., Soc. Polit. Enquiries (sec. 1987—), Schuylkill County Allied Artists (dir. 1976-77), Pa. Library Assn., Hist. Soc. Pa. Baptist. Clubs: Pilot of Pottsville (rec. sec. 1974-75, dir. 1975-77), Pilot of Harrisburg (pres. 1979-81, 87-88, treas. 1978-79, dir. 1981-83, 88—, sec. 1983-85, v.p. 1985-87). Author: Pennsylvania German Barn Signs: For Protection or Just for Nice, 1978, Simplified Cataloging for Libraries, 1978, The State Library of Pennsylvania: The Philadelphia Years, 1982, Books of State: A Peripatetic Collection, 1983, A Treasure Trove of Books, 1986, How Libraries Stack Up With Authors, 1987, Anne Royall's Visit to Carlisle in 1828, 1987. Home: 2285 W Norwegian St Pottsville PA 17901 Office: State Library Pa Box 1601 Harrisburg PA 17105

DEIBLER, MARIE PHILLIPS, university media relations specialist, political activist; b. Gary, W. Va., May 20; d. George Monroe and Lura (Watson) Phillips; m. William Dan Deibler, Apr. 10, 1944 (dec.); 1 dau., Deborah Deibler Steele. AB Marshall U., 1943; postgrad. George Washington U., U. South Fla. Writer Washington Post, Washington, 1940-41, 43-44; staff writer/reporter A.P., Jacksonville, Fla., 1944-47; editor Que Pasa in Puerto Rico, San Juan, 1951-54; asst. editor U.S. Lady mag., Washington, 1961-65; editor U. Tampa mag. (Fla.), 1966-71; writer/media specialist U. South Fla., Tampa, 1972—. Author: What Every Military Kid Should Know, 1969; contbr. articles to mags. and newspapers. Bd. dirs. Hillsborough Polit. Caucus, Tampa, 1983—; bd. dirs., v.p. Friends of Temple Terrace Library (Fla.), 1978-85; mem. citizens adv. com. Met. Planning, Orgn., Tampa, 1986—; mem. USF Lecture Series com.; bd. dirs. Fla. Suncoast Writers Conf. Recipient Best Mag. in Category award Fla. Mag. Assn., 1968. Mem. Am. News Womens Club, Women in Communications. Democrat. Episcopalian. Club: Tiger Bay (Tampa). Office: U South Fla Office Pub Affairs Tampa FL 33620

DEICH, ALICE EMERSON, personnel administrator; b. Indpls., Feb. 12, 1954; d. Robert Wesley and Shirley Ann (Brodfuehrer) Emerson; m. James Dale Deich, May 25, 1973. BA in Psychology, U. Iowa, 1977; cert. in personnel mgmt., NYU, 1986. Audio-visual equipment coordinator U. Iowa, Iowa City, 1977-78, dental clinic coordinator, 1978-80; office mgr. Noble Fulfillment Corp., N.Y.C., 1980-81; personnel asst. Columbia U., N.Y.C., 1981-85, acting personnel adminstr., 1985-86; personnel adminstr. NYU libraries, N.Y.C., 1986—. Mem. Nat. Assn. Female Execs., Coll. and Univ. Personnel Assn., Am. Mgmt. Assn. Office: NYU Libraries 70 Washington Sq S New York NY 10012

DEISTER, CHRISTINE ROSEMARY, airline executive; b. Lowestoft, Eng., Apr. 16, 1949; came to U.S., 1973; d. Douglas Stephen and Vera (Mears) Smith; m. Terrence Leonard Deister, Aug. 28, 1976; 1 dau., Nicole Stephanie. Student Felixstowe High Sch., Eng.; gen. cert. edn. U. London; cert. pianoforte Royal Schs. Music. Supr. revenue acctg. Trans World Airlines, London, 1967-73, supr. air freight systems and acctg., Kansas City, Mo., 1973-79, mgr. credit ops., Kansas City, 1979-81, mgr. disbursements, Kansas City, 1981-85, dir. cash ops., 1985—; treas., corp. officer Duncourt & Assocs., Kansas City, Mo. Bus. coordinator Heart of Am. United Way, 1981. Recipient Charles C. Tillinghast award; named Employee of Yr., Controller's Dept. TWA, 1978. Mem. Internat. Concerns Com. for Children. Home: RR 27 Box 277D Parkville MO 64152 Office: TWA 11500 NW Ambassador Dr Kansas City MO 64153

DEITSCH, MARIAN MIMI, writer, editor; b. Scranton, Pa., Apr. 9, 1933; d. David T. and Florence V. (Chait) Rubin; m. Thomas A. Deitsch, Oct. 16, 1955 (dec. Nov. 1983); children—Lisa Ellen, Thomas Alan. A.B., Barnard Coll., 1954; postgrad. NYU, 1956-57, William Paterson Coll., Wayne, N.J., 1982-83. Writer, Scranton Times, 1954; asst. economist Fed. Res. Bank N.Y., N.Y.C., 1955-60; mktg. rep. Welcome Wagon Internat., Memphis, 1974-79; writer Jewish News, East Orange, N.J., 1979; editor C.H. Kline & Co., Inc., Fairfield, N.J., 1979-84, sr. cons., 1984-88 ; pub. relations mgr. Fin. Execs.

Inst., Morristown, N.J., 1988—. Author: (with others) Guide to Energy, 1981; editor: Guide to Plastics Industry, 1982; Guide to Packaging Industry, 1980; Entering Livingston, 1963; contbr. articles to profl. jours. Bd. dirs. Hemlock Farms Community Assn., Lords Valley, Pa., 1977-78, 83-85; mem. various coms., 1977-86; pres. Livingston (N.J.) LWV, 1969-71; chmn. Livingston Ednl. Liaison Com., 1968-69. Mem. Women in Communications, Chem. Mktg. and Econs. Group N.Y. of Am. Chem. Soc. (bd. dirs. 1986—). Home: 21 Coddington Terr Livingston NJ 07039 Office: Fin Execs Inst 10 Madison Ave Morristown NJ 07960

DE IULIO-CASDIA, LORI ANNE, electronics company executive; b. Dix Hills, N.Y., Feb. 20, 1961; d. Edward S. and Jeannette Anita (Boretti) De Iulio; m. Peter Casdia. Student, Oswego U., 1979-81, Hofstra U., 1981-82. Mktg. interne WYSR/Roberts Advt. Agy., Syracuse, N.Y., 1980-81; computer operator Beck/Arnley, Melville, N.Y., 1982; adminstrv. asst. Minuteman Press/Speaking of Soaps, Farmingdale, N.Y., 1982; sales exec. Glass Oven Bakery (div. of MMP), Farmingdale, 1982-83; sales exec. Arrow Electronics Inc., Hauppage, N.Y., 1983-84, product mgr., 1983-84; corp. contracts adminstr. Arrow Electronics Inc., Melville, N.Y., 1985-87; supr. corp. contracts Arrow Electronics Inc., Melville, 1987—. Vol. Jack Kemp for Pres., N.Y.C., 1987-88. Recipient Pacesetter award Arrow Electronics Inc., 1984; named Employee of the Month, Arrow Electronics Inc, Dec. 1986. Mem. Nat. Assn. Female Execs. Republican. Roman Catholic. Home: 68 Kendrick Ln Dix Hills NY 11746 Office: 25 Hub Dr Mellville NY 11747

DEJESSE, JACQUELINE RITA, optometrist; b. Darby, Pa., Feb. 8, 1954; d. Joseph Carmen and Antoinette (Marella) DeJ.; m. John W. Fisher, June 24, 1978. BS in Biology, Widener Coll., Chester, Pa., 1975; BS in Physiol. Optics, OD, Pa. Coll. Optometry, 1979. Gen. practice optometry Hunting Park Med. Ctr., Phila., 1979—; mem. staff Crozier Chester (Pa.) Hosp.; prin. Brookhaven (Pa.) Family Eye Care Ctr., 1987—. Active Cousteau Soc., 1980—, Planetary Soc., 1982—; mem. health adv. com. Rainbow Head Start Program, Phila., 1987—; mem. subcom. on med. assistance as optometric rep. from Pa., Harrisburg, 1987—. Mem. Am. Optometric Assn., Pa. Optometric Assn., Chester-Delaware County Optometric Soc. (treas. 1985-86, sec. 1987, v.p. 1988), Better Vision Inst. Democrat. Roman Catholic. Office: Hunting Park Med Office 4000 N 9th St Philadelphia PA 19140

DEJESUS-BURGOS, SYLVIA TERESA, information systems specialist; b. Rio Piedras, Puerto Rico, Jan. 13, 1941; came to U.S., 1961; d. Luis deJesus Correa and Maria Teresa (Burgos) deJesus. BA, Cen. U., Madrid, 1961. Sr. systems analyst H.D. Hudson Mfg. Co., Chgo., 1974-76; mgr. software engring. Morton Thiokol, Chgo., 1976-87; sr. mgr. systems devel. Kraft, Inc., Glenview, Ill., 1987—. Editor U. Minn. Mgmt. Info. Systems Jour., 1984—. Pres. Chgo. chpt. Nat. Conf. Puerto Rican Women, 1980-83, nat. v.p. 1981-82; bd. dirs. Midwest Women's Ctr., 1980-82, YWCA, Chgo., 1982-84, Gateway Found. Substance Abuse Prevention and Rehab., 1986-87; v.p. communications Hispanic Alliance for Career Enhancements, 1986-87, bd. dirs. 1982-84; 1st v.p. Campfire Met. Chgo., 1982, bd. dirs. 1980-82; appointed to Selective Service Bd. by Ill. Gov. James Thompson, 1982; alt. del. Dem. Nat. Conv., N.Y.C., 1980. Served with USN, 1961-64. Recipient Youth Motivation award Chgo. Assn. Commerce and Industry, 1978-82, 86, YWCA Leadership award 1980, 84. Mem. Women in Computing, Info. Systems Planners Assn., Navy League, Am. Legion. Republican. Roman Catholic. Home: 35 Wildwood Dr S Prospect Heights IL 60070 Office: Kraft Inc Kraft Ct Glenview IL 60025

DE JESUS-MCCARTHY, FE TERESA, physician; b. Samar, Philippines, Dec. 31, 1942; came to U.S., naturalized, 1978; d. Felicisimo V. and Baslia E. de J.; M.D., U. Philippines, 1966; m. Thomas J. McCarthy, Mar. 3, 1973; children—Amour Fe, Vida Linda. Practice medicine specializing in ob-gyn, Schenectady; mem. staff Bellevue Maternity Hosp. Mem. AMA, Am. Med. Women's Assn., Am. Fertility Soc., Am. Coll. Ob-Gyn, Am. Assn. Gynecol. Laparoscopists, N.Y. State Med. Soc., Med. Soc. of Schenectady County. Home: 1261 Hempstead Rd Schenectady NY 12309 Office: PO Box 1030 2210 Troy Rd Schenectady NY 12301

DEJMEK, LINDA MARIE, optometrist; b. Memphis, June 2, 1953. BS in Optometry, Ind. U., 1975, OD, 1977. Owner, operator Appleton (Wis.) Eye Clinic, 1977—. Med. illustrator System for Ophthalmic Dispensing, 1979; illustrator Diver Mag., 1985, Skin Diver mag., 1985; exhibited in group shows at Appleton Gallery Arts, 1979—. Recipient Harold Bailey Award Am. Optometric Found., 1977; named Hon. Citizen, City of Clarksville, Tenn., 1976. Mem. Am. Optometric Assn., Wis. Optometric Assn. (bd. dirs. 1988—), Fox Cities Optometric Soc. (pres. 1984-86), Wis. Fedn. Bus. Profl. Women (chmn. state membership com. 1985-86, state 1st v.p. 1986-87, pres. elect 1987—), Wis. Optometric Assn. (bd. dirs. 1987-88), State of Wis. Optometry Examining Bd., 1988—, Mid-Day Bus. and Profl. Women (treas. 1980-81, found. chmn. 1981-84, pres. 1984-86), Fox Cities C. of C. (mem. govtl. relations com. 1986-87), Appleton Jr. Women's Club (illustrator 1981-82). Office: Appleton Eye Clinic 509 Chain Dr Appleton WI 54915

DEJMEK, LUDMILA MARIE, architect; b. Prague, Czechoslovakia, Jan. 19, 1941; d. Sava and Edita (Sedlackova) Sedlacek; children: Mark, Andrea. Grad., Czech Tech. U., 1962; postgrad., U. Charles IV, Prague, 1963; grad. Acad. of Fine Arts, 1967; postgrad., L'Universite de Paris, La Sorbonne, L'Institute d'Urbanisme, 1964, L'Institute Catholique a Paris, 1967-68; MArch, Nova Scotia Tech. Coll., 1971. Constrn. supr. Steel Corp. of Kladno, Czechoslovakia, 1962-63; designer Krushen & Dailey, Waterloo, Ont., also Donald Skinner, Architect, 1967-72; architect Cen. Mortgage & Housing Corp., Hamilton, Ont., 1972-74, program mgr., 1974-76; prin., architect, engr. Dejmek Assoc., Cambridge, Ont., Can., 1976—. NRC Can. grantee, 1970-71; recipient 2000 Kcs award, City Hall, Czechoslovakia, 1967, 3000 Kcs award CSSR Embassy, New Delhi, India, 1966. Mem. Ont. Assn. Architects, Profl. Engrs. Ont., Canadian Fedn. Univ. Women. Club: Chicopee Ski. Address: 207 Main St, Cambridge, ON Canada N1S 2S6

DEJOIE, CAROLYN BARNES MILANES, educator; b. New Orleans, Apr. 17; d. Edward Franklin and Alice Philomene (Milanes) Barnes; children: Deirdre, Prudhomme III, Duan. MA, Universidad Nacional de Mexico, Mexico City, 1962; MSW, U. Wis., 1970; PhD, Union U., Cin., 1976. Cert. psychotherapist, Wis. Instr. So. U., Baton Rouge, 1962-63; asst. prof. Va. State Coll., Norfolk, 1963-66; asst. to pres. U. Wis. System, Madison, 1970-73, prof. adult edn. U. Wis., Madison, 1973—; fgn. lang cons., Mexico City, 1960-62; pvt. practice psychotherapy, 1980—; dir. Human Relations Counseling Service, 1980—; owner Sun and Shadows Pub. Co., 1987; exec. dir. Organizacion Hispana Americana, 1974-75; spl. con. on crime prevention, Nassau, Bahamas, 1985. Mem. adv. editorial bd. Jour. of Negro Edn., 1985—, Negro Ednl. Rev., 1988; editor: Readings from a Black Perspective, 1984, Racism-Sexism: The Interlock of Racist and Sexist Problems, 1986; author book of poetry: Just Me, 1980; producer, hostess TV show Innervisions Sta. WYOU, Madison, 1987, 88; contbr. articles to scholarly jours. Mem. adv. bd. Madison Met. Schs. Human Relations Council, 1975-85; mem. exec. bd. Madison chpt. ACLU, 1978-80, Council Minority Pub. Adminstrs., Madison, 1980-82; bd. dirs. Dane County Mental Health (Wis.), 1980-82. Recipient Recognition award Va. State Coll., 1962, Outstanding Woman award Zeta Phi Beta, 1975, Black Women: Achievements Against the Odds award Wis. Humanities Com., 1983, Gov.'s Spl award State of Wis., 1984, Appreciation award Madison Met. Sch. Dist., 1984, Outstanding Contbn. to Soc. award Alpha Kappa Alpha, 1984, Recognition of Service award Nat. Assn. Negro Bus. and Profl. Women, 1986, laudatory resoultion Bd. Commrs. Genessee County, Mich., 1986; Fulbright scholar, 1966-67. Mem. AAUP, AAUW, Nat. Assn. Media Women (Woman of Yr. 1985, Golden Egg Appreciation award 1987), Nat. Assn. Social Workers, NAACP (mem. exec. bd.), Nat. Congress Black Faculty, Links, Inc. Home: 5322 Fairway Dr Madison WI 53711 Office: 610 Langdon St Madison WI 53706

DEKEN, JEAN MARIE, librarian, archivist; b. St. Louis, Apr. 5, 1953; d. Cornelius John and Loretta Frances (McGuire) D.; m. James Roger Reed, Jan. 2, 1981. BA in English summa cum laude, Washington U., 1974, MA in English, 1976. Archivist Mo. Botanical Garden, St. Louis, 1975-78; mgmt. analyst Nat. Archives and Records Service, St. Louis, 1978-81, supervisory archives specialist, 1981-82; instr. of English St. Louis Community Coll., St. Louis, 1982-83; curator John W. Baringer III collections St. Louis Merc. Library, 1983-85, librarian Ralston Purina, St. Louis, 1985-86; mgr. library services Maritz, Inc., St. Louis, 1986-87; supervisory archivist Nat. Archives and Records Adminstrn., St. Louis, 1987—. Author: Henry Shaw: His Life and Legacy, 1977; contbr. articles to profl. jours. Mem. Spl. Libraries Assn., Midwest Archives Conf., Soc. Am. Archivists, St. Louis Online Users Group, St. Louis Regional Library Network. Office: Nat Archives and Records Adminstrn NPRC-CPR 11 Winnebago St Saint Louis MO 63118

DE KOONING, ELAINE, artist; b. N.Y.C., Mar. 12, 1920; d. Charles Frank and Mary Ellen (O'Brien) Fried; m. Willem de Kooning, Dec. 9, 1943. Hon. degree, Western Coll. Women, Oxford, Ohio, 1964; DFA (hon.), Moore Coll. Art, Maryland Inst.; DHL, Adelphi U. Mellon chair Carnegie Mellon U., 1969-70, Cooper Union, N.Y.C., 1976; Lamar Dodd chair U. Ga., Athens, 1976-78; Milton and Sally Avery chair Bard Coll., 1982. One-woman shows include Stable Gallery, N.Y.C., 1954, 56, Tibor de Nagy Gallery, N.Y.C., 1957, Graham Gallery, N.Y.C., 1960, 61, 63, 65, 75, U. N.Mex., 1957, Mus. N.Mex., Santa Fe, 1959, Gump's, San Francisco, 1959, Washington Gallery Modern Art, presdl. portraits, 1964, Lyman Allen Mus., New London, Conn., retrospective, 1959, Montclair (N.J.) Art Mus., 1973, Benson Gallery, Bridgehampton, N.Y., 1973, Ill. Wesleyan U., Bloomington, 1975, Coll. St. Catherine, St. Paul, 1975, Tampa Bay Arts Ctr., 1975, Grimaldis Gallery, Balt., 1980, 84, 85, Gruenebaum Gallery, N.Y.C., 1982, 86, Adelphi U., N.Y., 1984, Vered Gallery, N.Y., 1984, Gallery Silvia Menzel, Berlin, 1986, Guggenheim Gallery, Miami, Fla., 1986, Wenger Gallery, Los Angeles, 1987, others; represented in permanent collections Mus. Modern Art Loeb Ctr., N.Y.C., Kennedy Library, Cambridge, Mass., Truman Library, Independence, Mo., Elmira (N.Y.) Coll., Ark. Arts Ctr., Little Rock, Jewish Community Ctr., Bayonne, N.J., Montclair (N.J.) Art Mus., Ciba-Geigy Corp., Ardsley, N.Y., Neuberger Mus., Purchase, N.Y., Albright-Knox Gallery, Buffalo, Corcoran Gallery of Art, Washington, Hirshorn Mus. Art, Washington, Washington Gallery of Modern Art, also pvt. collections; instr., U. N.Mex., 1959, Pa. State U., 1960, Contemporary Art Assn., Houston, 1952, U. Calif. at Davis, 1963-64, Yale, 1967, Mellon chair Carnegie-Mellon U., 1969-70, U. Pa., 1970-72, Wagner Coll., 1970, U. Pa., 1971—, N.Y. Studio Sch., Paris, France, 1974—, Parsons Sch. Fine Art, 1974-76, Lamar Dodd chair U. Ga., Athens, 1976—, Mellon chair Cooper Union, 1976, Milton and Sally Avery chair Bard Coll., 1982. Office: PO Box 1437 East Hampton NY 11937

DELABARRE, PAMELA DUNN, automotive company professional; b. Florence, S.C., May 13, 1957; d. Charles Loney and Joanne (Comer) Dunn; m. Charles Mehrer DeLaBarre, Nov. 24, 1984. AA, U. S.C., 1979, BA in Interdisciplinary Studies, 1981. Auto supply mgr. S.C. Dept. Edn., Columbia, 1977-84; expeditor Gen. Motors Co., Ft. Wayne, Ind., 1986—. Mem. Nat. Assn. Female Execs., S.C. State Employees Assn. (bd. dirs. 1983). Democrat. Methodist. Office: Gen Motors Corp 12200 Lafayette Ctr Roanoke IN 46783

DE LA FRANIER, CAROL, metallurgical engineer; b. London, Ont., Can., Apr. 24, 1960; d. Paul Edward and Rita (Hamelin) D. Student, John Abbott Coll., Montreal, Que., Can., 1977-79; BS in Metall. Engring., U. Toronto, 1982. Metall. engr. Dofasco, Hamilton, Ont., 1982; sr. metall. engr. Ballard Research, Inc., Vancouver, B.C., 1983—. Contbr. articles to profl. jours. Mem. Am. Soc. for Metals. Home: 4030 Lynn Valley Rd, North Vancouver, BC Canada V7K 2T2

DE LAGUNA, FREDERICA, anthropology educator emeritus, consultant; b. Ann Arbor, Mich., Oct. 3, 1906; d. Theodore and Grace Mead (Andrus) de L. A.B., Bryn Mawr Coll., 1927; Ph.D., Columbia U., 1933; L.H.D., U. Alaska, 1981. Asst., field dir. U. Pa. Mus., Phila., 1931-35; lectr. anthropology Bryn Mawr Coll., Pa., 1938-41, asst. prof., 1941-42, 46-49, assoc. prof., 1949-55, prof. anthropology, 1955-75, prof. emeritus, 1975—; vis. lectr. or vis. prof. U. Pa., U. Calif.-Berkeley, Bryn Mawr Coll. Author: The Thousand March: Adventures of an American Boy with Garibaldi, 1930, The Archaeology of Cook Inlet, Alaska, 1934, reprinted, 1975, The Arrow Points to Murder, 1937, Fog on the Mountain, 1938, (with Kaj Birket-Smith) The Eyak Indians of the Copper River Delta, Alaska, 1938, Prehistory of Northern America as Seen from the Yukon, 1947, Chugach Prehistory: The Archaeology of Prince William Sound, 1956, 67, The Story of a Tlingit Community, 1960, The Archeology of the Yakutat Bay Area, Alaska, 1964, (with others) Under Mount Saint Elias, 3 vols., 1972, Voyage to Greenland: A Personal Initiation into Anthropology, 1977; editor: Selected Papers from the American Anthropologist, 1888-1920, 1960, 76. Recipient Lindback award for Disting. Teaching, Bryn Mawr Coll., 1975, Rochester Mus. award and fellowship, 1941, numerous fellowships including: Columbia U., 1930-31, NRC, 1936-37, Rockefeller Found., 1945-46, Wenner-Gren Found., 1949-50, Social Sci. Research Council, 1962-63; grantee Am. Philos. Soc., Arctic Inst. of N.Am., Bryn Mawr Coll., NEH, NSF, Social Sci. Research Council, U. Pa. Mus., Wenner-Gren Found. for Anthrop. Research. Fellow AAAS, Am. Anthrop. Assn. (pres.-elect, pres. 1965-67, Disting. Service award 1986), Arctic Inst. of N.Am. (hon. life); mem. Nat. Acad. Scis., Soc. for Am. Archaeology (1st v.p. 1949-50, 50th Ann. award 1986), Phila. Anthropology Soc. (pres. 1939-40), Alaska Anthrop. Assn. (hon. life), Homer Natural History Soc. (hon. life; Alaska). Democrat. Home: 830 Montgomery Ave Apt 510 Bryn Mawr PA 19010 Office: Bryn Mawr Coll Dept Anthropology Bryn Mawr PA 19010

DELAHANTY, LINDA MICHELE, dietitian; b. Boston, Feb. 8, 1957; d. John Joseph and Helen Mary (Salami) D.; m. Paul Joseph Gorski, June 14, 1987. BS summa cum laude, U. Mass., 1978; MS summa cum laude, Boston U., 1980. Adminstrv. dietitian Joslin Diabetic Camp, Charlton, Mass., 1978; nutritional research asst. Lemuel Shattuck Hosp., Jamaica Plain, Mass., 1979; nutrition educator Home Med. Service Univ. Hosps., Boston, 1980, Boston City Hosp., 1980-81; clin. dietitian Mass. Gen. Hosp., Boston, 1981—; researcher Diabetes Ctr. Mass. Gen. Hosp., Boston, 1983—; nutrition coordinator Diabetes Control and Complications Trial, N.H., 1987—; cons. New Eng. Diabetes and Endocrinology Ctr., Brookline, Mass., 1985-86; panelist NIH Consensus Devel. Conf., Bethesda, Md., 1986; assoc., lectr. Harvard U. Geriatric Edn. Ctr., 1984—. Contbr. articles to profl. jours. Named Young Dietitian of Yr. Am. Dietetic Assn., 1984. Mem. Mass. Area Rehab. Dietitians (co-chair 1983-84), Diabetes Care and Edn. Practice Group (sec. 1985-87), Mass. Geront. Nutrition Practice Group (chair 1984-85), Mass. Dietetic Assn. (chair community dietetics div. 1983-84, council on practices). Roman Catholic. Home: 18 Saybrook Rd Framingham MA 01701 Office: Mass Gen Hosp Dept Dietetics Fruit St Boston MA 02114

DELAMAR, GLORIA, author, writer; married; 5 children. BS in Early Childhood Edn., U. Pitts., 1951, postgrad., 1952. Tchr. kindergarten Pitts. Pub. Schs., 1951-55; substitute tchr. kindergarten, pub. schs., Richmond, Va., 1967-70; freelance market research supr. and interviewer, Richmond, 1970-76; free-lance pub. relations writer, 1976—; tchr. Abington Twp. Adult Edn., 1984—, Bucks County Community Coll., 1988—; tchr. writing Nat. League Am. Pen Women, Richmon, 1975, 76, Gloria Dei Creative Arts Ctr., Phila., 1977—, Unitarian Soc. Germantown's Community Enrichment Classes, Phila., 1977-81; lectr. in field to adults, children. Author: Play Aesop, 1971, Children's Counting-Out Rhymes, Fingerplays, Jump-Rope and Bounce-Ball Chants and Other Rhythms: A Comprehensive English Language Reference, 1983, Rounds Re-Sounding - Circular Music for Voices and Instruments: An Eight Century Reference, 1987, Mother Goose: From Nursery to Literature, 1987, Rounds for Voices and Simple Instruments: A Comprehensive English Language Reference; co-editor, contbg. author: Voices; contbr. articles, fillers, verses to various mags., newspapers, 1968—. Bd. dirs. Better Films and TV Council Pitts., 1963-67, Richmond Pub. Forum, Inc., 1968-76. Mem. Nat. League Am. Pen Women (pres. Richmond br. 1974-76, pres. Phila. br. 1978-80, pres. Pa. 1978-80, 80-82), Soc. Children's Books Writers, Phila. Children's Reading Round Table, Phila. Writers' Conf. (pres. 1981-82), Pi Lambda Theta.

DELAMATTER, DONNA ANNE, computer company executive; b. Lakewood, Ohio, Apr. 12, 1942; d. W. Richard and Martha Caroline (Jahnke) Hoecker; m. Thomas C. DeLamatter, Dec. 12, 1976. Cert. bus., Baldwin Wallace Coll., 1965. Exec. sec. World Pub. Co., Cleve., 1965-67, Mayor of Lakewood, 1968-72; adminstrv. asst. Saul N. Davidson & Assocs., Denver, 1973-76; adminstrv. asst. Telxon Corp., Akron, Ohio, 1977-79, asst. to v.p. sales, 1979-80, asst. sec., 1979-83, dir. personnel and adminstrn., 1980-83, v.p., 1983—, sec., 1983-84. Named one of Greater Cleve.'s Enterprising Women, 1986. Mem. Sales and Mktg. Execs. Akron. Republican. Club: Catawba Island (Port Clinton, Ohio). Home: 273 Treetop Spur Akron OH 44321 Office: Telxon Corp 3330 W Market St Akron OH 44313

DELAMIELLEURE, DEBORAH ANN, nurse; b. Detroit, Feb. 16, 1953; d. Gerald Charles and Ann (Gera) Selke; m. Gary Stanley Delamielleure, Nov. 23, 1973; children: Robin Lynn, Megan Marie. Diploma in nursing, Providence Hosp. Sch. Nursing, 1973. Staff nurse Flint Osteo. Hosp. (Mich.), 1973, Bi-County Community Hosp., Warren, Mich., 1974-75; charge nurse Bay Osteo. Hosp., Bay City, Mich., 1977-78; office nurse J.C. Gromada DO, Bay City, 1981-85; head nurse Larry J. Ross, Jr., M.D., Peoria, Ill., 1985-88; office mgr. Pediatric Assocs., Peoria, 1988—; vol. Shriners Mich. Mini-Clinic, 1981-84. Roman Catholic. Home: 1200 S Lafayette Bartonville IL 61607

DELAND, DIANE O. AMMONS, business executive; b. Redding, Calif., Jan. 3, 1940; d. Mark T. and Lucille I. (Wissert) Ammons; m. Maurice Graham DeLand, Feb. 19, 1966 (div. 1974); 1 child, Charles Maurice De Land. B.A., U. Calif.-Berkeley, 1961; Cert., Goethe Inst., Berlin, 1961; postgrad. Am. U., 1969-71. Economist, AID, U.S. Dept. State, Washington, 1962-70; sr. economist U.S. EPA, Washington, 1970-73, PBGC, Washington, 1974-76; rep. U.S. Govt. Inter-Agy. Task Force, Washington, 1978; dir. tech. programs Pension Benefit Guaranty, Washington, 1976-79; pres. Pension Corp., Los Angeles, 1979—; cons. and lectr. in field. Co-author: (tech. booklet) Guidelines on Plan Termination, 1977; Syllabus on Pension Plans, 1981. Headmaster council Indian Mountain Sch., Conn., 1984—. Named Life mem. Calif. Scholastic Soc., 1957, U.S. Pres.'s Govt. exchange scholar, 1978-79. Mem. Women in Bus., Nat. Assn. Female Execs., Am. Soc. Pension Actuaries (assoc.), Jr. League. Avocations: Painting; reading; skiing; tennis; travel. Office: Pension Corp 429 Santa Monica Blvd Suite 320 Santa Monica CA 90401

DELANEY, CATHY EILEEN, state ofcl.; b. Binghamton, N.Y., Apr. 5, 1947; d. Martin Frank and Beverly Carolyn (Hamlin) Piza; B.A., Harpur Coll., Binghamton, 1968; M.S.W., Syracuse (N.Y.) U., 1976; m. Frank L. Delaney, June 28, 1969 (div.). Public assistance caseworker Seneca County Dept. Social Services, Seneca Falls, N.Y., 1968; psychiat. social worker Willard (N.Y.) Psychiat. Center, 1968-73, Broome Devel. Center, Binghamton, 1973-74, 76; congl. legis. aide, 1975; asst. dir. bur. program and fiscal audits N.Y. State Office Mental Retardation and Devel. Disabilities, Albany, 1976-80, asst. dir. bur. program and fiscal audits, 1976-80, statewide coordinator intermediate care facilities for developmentally disabled, 1980, cert. coordinator Western County service group, 1980-83, Upstate unit dir. Bur. Cert. Control, 1983-85; dir. ICF/DD Survey and Review, 1985—; adj. instr. SUNY Sch. Social Welfare, Albany, 1982-83. Grantee HEW, 1975-76. Mem. Upstate Assn. Psychiat. Social Workers in State Schs. and Hosps. (sec. 1970), Am. Mgmt. Assn. Office: 44 Holland Ave Albany NY 12229

DELANEY, ELEANOR CECILIA COUGHLIN, educator; b. Elizabeth, N.J.; d. John C. and Eleanor C. (Fadde) Coughlin; B.S., Sch. Edn. Rutgers U., 1930, M.A., 1939; Ph.D., Columbia U., 1954; 1 son, John. Tchr. public schs., Elizabeth, N.J., 1927; prin. Woodrow Wilson Sch., Elizabeth, 1941-55; prof. Grad. Sch. Edn., Rutgers U., New Brunswick, N.J., 1955-87, prof. emeritus, 1987—, chmn. dept. ednl. adminstrn. and supervision, 1974—; vis. prof. William and Mary Coll., U. Mex., Columbia U.; ednl. cons. sch. systems, N.J., N.Y., Va., 1950—; con. U.S. Dept. State, Health and Edn., coordinator Intern-Am. Affairs. Mem. Elizabeth Charter Commn., 1960-61; chmn. Mayor's Adv. Commn. on Urban Devel., 1962-64, Elizabeth Human Relations Commn., 1968-75; mem. Elizabeth Bd. Edn., 1972-79, pres., 1973-76; mem. exec. bd. Union County chpt. ARC; mem. exec. bd. Vis. Nurse and Health Assn., 1977—; pres., 1981-85. Mem. AAUW, Nat., N.J. edn. assns., Dept. Elem. Sch. Prins., AAUP, AAAS, Am. Ednl. Research Assn., Kappa Delta Pi (counelor 1970-87, Nat. Honor Key), Pi Lambda Theta, Phi Delta Kappa. Author: Spanish Gold, Lands of Middle America, Our Friends in South America, Science-Life Series, Book 4; Persistent Problems in Education. Contbr. articles to profl. mags. Home: 220 W Jersey St Elizabeth NJ 07202

DELANEY, MARION PATRICIA, advertising agency executive; b. Hartford, Conn., May 20, 1952; d. William Pride Delaney and Marian Patricia (Utley) Murphy. BA, Union Coll., Schenectady, N.Y., 1973. Adminstrv. asst. N.Y. State Assembly, Albany, 1973-74; account exec. Foote, Cone & Belding, N.Y.C., 1974-78; sr. account exec. Dailey & Assocs., Los Angeles, 1978-81; pub. relations cons. NOW, Washington, 1981-83; account supr. BBDO/West, Los Angeles, 1983-85; v.p. Grey Advt., Los Angeles, 1985-87, San Francisco, 1987—. Del. Dem. Nat. Conv., San Francisco, 1984; v.p. NOW, Los Angeles, 1980-83, pres. 1984, advisor 1985—. Mem. Bus. and Profl. Women Assn., Los Angeles Advt. Club. Congregationalist. Home: 3682 Fillmore St San Francisco CA 94123 Office: Grey Advt 2 Embarcadero Ctr San Francisco CA 94111

DELANEY, PATRICIA JOANNE, human resources company executive; b. Hutchinson, Kans., Aug. 24, 1934; d. Ralph Raymond and Hazel Yufalla (Holland) Wright; children: Debra Jean, Daniel Norman, Denise Rene, Douglas Raymond; m. Donald Keith Delaney, May 5, 1973. Student, Am. River Coll., 1970. Fin. couselor Credit Counselors, Sacramento, 1962-70; owner, pres. Delaney & Assocs., Las Vegas (Nev.) and Reno, 1974—. Bd. dirs. PTA, Sacramento, 1963-70, Boys & Girls Clubs Am., Las Vegas, 1976—, Girl Scouts U.S., 1985-87; speaker, presenter workshops local schs., Las Vegas, 1980—, St. Readiness Prison Program, Indian Springs, Nev., 1980—; state chmn. orgns. Gov.'s Conf. for Women, Las Vegas, 1987—. Recipient Continuing Service award Sacramento PTA, 1968, hon. life membership Sacramento PTA, appreciation award Alpha Kappa Psi, 1985, numerous others. Mem. Nat. Assn. Personnel Cons. (state rep. 1986), Employment Assn. State Nev. (state chmn. 1987), So. Nev. Personnel Assn. (pres. 1986, appreciation award 1987), So. Nev. Exec. Council, Nat. Assn. Female Execs., Las Vegas C. of C. (com. 1986—). Republican. Lutheran. Club: Renaissance Women (Las Vegas) (pres. 1981). Office: 2225 Renaissance Dr Suite A Las Vegas NV 89119 Office: 1135 Terminal Way #103 Reno NV 89502

DELANO, LINDA CHRISTINE, physical education educator, coach; b. Chgo., June 6, 1953; d. William Stevens and Louise Catherine (Uccello) D. B.S.E., No. Ill. U., 1975, M.S.E., 1980. Tchr. phys. edn. Libertyville (Ill.) High Sch., 1975-87, head volleyball coach, head softball coach, 1975-87; asst. prof. phys edn., women's athletic dir., head volleyball coach Hamline U., St. Paul, 1987—; basketball assignment chmn. North Suburban Conf., Lake County, Ill., 1983-84. Contbr. articles to profl. jours. Named Athlete of Yr., Ind. Register, Vernon Hills, Ill., 1982; sec.-treas. sr. girls league No. Ill. Sr. and Jr. Fast Pitch Softball Leagues, 1981, 82, 83. Mem. U.S. Field Hockey Assn. (chmn. north central sect. 1980-82, 83-85, chmn. membership com. 1982-83), Ill. Assn. Health, Phys. Edn. and Recreation (Lake County rep. 1976-81, award 1982), AAHPERD (life), Ill. Coaches Assn. for Girls' and Women's Sports (pres. softball coaches assn. 1980-81). Home: 1266 Hubbard Ave Saint Paul MN 55104 Office: Hamline U Saint Paul MN 55704

DE LARROCHA, ALICIA, concert pianist; b. Barcelona, Spain, May 23, 1923; d. Eduardo and Teresa (De La Calle) de L.; m. Juan Torra, June 21, 1950; children: Juan, Alicia. Grad. (prize extraordinary, Gold medal), Acad. Marshall, Barcelona. Debut, Barcelona, 1929, solo recitalist, concert pianist maj. orchs. in, Europe, U.S., Can., Central and S. Am., S. Africa, N.Z., Australia, Japan; dir. Acad. Marshall, 1959—; rec. artist: Hispavox, CBS, Decca-London; records.; (Grammy award 1974, 75, 1st Gold medal Merito a la Vocacion 1972). Recipient Harriet Cohen Internat. Music award, 1968; Paderewski Meml. medal, 1961; Grand prix du Disque Acad. Charles Cros, 1960, 74; Edison award, 1968; decorated Order Civil Merit Order Isabel la Catolica, Spain). Mem. Musica en Compostela (dir.), Hispanic Soc. Am. (corr.), Internat. Piano Archives (hon. pres.). Address: care Columbia Artists Mgmt 165 W 57th St New York NY 10019

DELARYE-GOLD, ANN ELIZABETH, corporate conference executive; b. Chgo., Apr. 11, 1955; d. William Lloyd and Marjorie Mae (Davis) DeLarye; m. Michael Aleck Gold, Aug. 7, 1977. Student, Northwestern U., 1973-76, New Sch. for Social Research, 1976-78. Free-lance writer Chgo., 1982-84; dir. communications Cen. Ednl. Network, Chgo., 1984-86; v.p. Inst. for

Internat. Research, N.Y.C., 1986—; planner confs. Mike Gold Media Services, Chgo., 1976-86, field producer, 1982-84, vocal trainer, 1985-86. Contbr. articles to Chgo. Tribune, 1982-84. Chmn. tech. and tng. com., commr. Evanston (Ill.) Cable TV Regulatory Com., 1982-86. Mem. Nat. Assn. for Female Execs. Home: 2 Naples Ave East Norwalk CT 06855 Office: Inst for Internat Research 331 Madison Ave 6th Floor New York NY 10017

DE LAURENTIS, MARY ROSE, construction executive, small business owner; b. Scarsdale, N.Y., Mar. 11, 1938; d. Lawrence Leonard and Rose Ida (Calandro) Labriola; m. R. Edmond De Laurentis; children: Joseph, Edmond, Lawrence, Eleana, René Anna, Aliza. Student, Mercy Coll., White Plains, N.Y. Administrator De Laurentis Constrn. Co. Inc., Mamaroneck, N.Y., 1963—; owner Glenville Florist and Gift, Greenwich, Conn., 1984—. Mem. Nat. Assn. Female Execs., Nat. Notary Assn. (cert. notary pub., N.Y.), Profl. Women in Constrn., Women Bus. Owners Westchester, C. of C. Club: Tamarack Golf (Greenwich). Home: 26 Day Rd Armonk NY 10504 Office: De Laurentis Constrn Co Inc 335 Center Ave Mamaroneck NY 10543

DE LA VEGA, DIANNE WINIFRED DEMARINIS (MRS. JORGE DE LA VEGA), government official; b. Cleve.; d. Gerald M. and Dorothy (Philp) DeMarinis; student Case Western Res. U., 1948-50, MA, 1969; BA, U. Am., 1952; PhD in Psychology, Internat. Coll., Los Angeles, 1977; MA, Goddard Coll., 1978; m. Jorge Alejandro de la Vega, July 19, 1952; children: Constance, Francisco Javier, Alexandra. Faculty, Western Res. U., Cleve., 1961-62; instr. Instituto Mexicano-Norteamericano de Relaciones Culturales, Mexico, 1967; supr. fgn. press Mexican Olympic Organizing Com., Mexico, 1968; asst. to producer Producciones Ojo, Canal 8 TV, Mexico, 1969; exec. asst. Internat. Exec. Service Corps, Mexico City, 1969-70; asst. to dir. U.S. Internat. U. Mexico, Mexico City, 1970-75; family planning evaluator for Latin Am., AID, 1976; with dept. spl. edn. region IX Nat. Ctr. on Child Abuse and Neglect, Children's Bur., Office Child Devel., HEW, Calif. State U., 1977—. Chmn. Puppet's Jr. League, Mexico City, 1967, chmn. ways and means, 1968; sec. Tlaxcala-Okla. Partner's of Alliance for Progress, 1967—; pres. acculturating hispanic refugee children Los Angeles Unified Sch. Dist.; bd. dirs. Hot Line of Mexico City; mem. Los Angeles adv. com. 1984 Olympics. Lic. marriage and family counselor. Mem. Los Angeles chpt. Calif. Marriage and Family Therapists Assn., Flying Samaritans, Pro Salud Maternal, Transactional Analysis Assn. Club: Jr. League (Los Angeles). Home: 130 Alta Ave D Santa Monica CA 90402

DE LAY, DOROTHY (MRS. EDWARD NEWHOUSE), violinist, educator; b. Medicine Lodge, Kans., Mar. 31, 1917; d. Glenn Adney and Cecile (Osborn) DeLay; m. Edward Newhouse, Mar. 5, 1941; children: Jeffrey H., Alison Dinsmore. Student, Oberlin Coll., 1933-34, MusD (hon.), 1981; BA, Mich. State U., 1937; Artists diploma, Juilliard Grad. Sch. Music, 1941. Prof. violin The Juilliard Sch., N.Y.C., 1947—; mem. faculty Sarah Lawrence Coll., 1948-87, Meadowmount Summer Sch. Music, Westport, N.Y., 1948-70, Aspen Summer Music Sch., 1971—; Starling prof. violin U. Cin., 1974—; vis. prof. violin Phila. Coll. Performing Arts, 1977-83, New Eng. Conservatory, 1978-87; Starling prof. violin The Juilliard Sch., N.Y.C., 1988—; vis. prof. violin Royal Coll. Music, Eng., 1987—; condr. Master classes univs. and conservatories in U.S., Europe, Asia, Africa, Near East. Solo, chamber music performances in, U.S., Can., S.Am., 1937—, violinist, founder, Stuyvesant Trio, 1940-42; Contbr. articles on violins, violinists to various encys. Recipient Outstanding Artist-Tchr. award Am. String Tchrs. Assn., 1975, Highest honor citation Fedn. of Music Clubs, 1983, Gov.'s award State of Kans., 1982, Alumni Accomplishment award Mich. State U., 1984, King Solomon award America-Israel Cultural Found., 1985. Fellow Royal Coll. Music, Gt. Brit.; mem. Mu Phi Epsilon. Home: 349 N Broadway Upper Nyack NY 10960 Office: Juilliard Sch Lincoln Ctr Plaza New York NY 10023

DELCAMBRE, LOIS MARIE LUNDBERG, computer science educator; b. Mpls., July 25, 1950; d. Neil Vernon and Joyce May (Olsen) Lundberg; m. Charles R. Delcambre, Feb. 17, 1979; 1 child, Andrew Charles. BS in Math., U. Southwestern La., 1972, PhD in Computer Sci., 1982; MS in Math. Sci., Clemson U., 1974. Mgr. system design and software devel. Clemson (S.C.) U. Div. Infosystems Devel., 1974-79; asst. prof. Center for Advanced Computer Studies-U. Southwestern La., Lafayette, 1983-87, assoc. prof., 1987—. Contbr. papers to computer confs. Mem. IEEE (software mag. referee), IEEE Computer Soc., Assn. for Computing Machinery (referee database systems). Office: U Southwestern La Ctr Advanced Computer Studies PO Box 44330 Lafayette LA 70504

DEL CASTILLO, JEANNE LOUISE TAILLAC, oil industry executive; b. New Orleans, May 15, 1933; d. Roland Jean and Louise (Schwall) Taillac; m. Roberto Eduardo del Castillo (div.); children: Esther, Jeanne, Roberto, Eduardo, Tammy. Nursing student, Charity Hosp., New Orleans, 1951-52; student, various bus. mgmt. courses, 1952-86. Asst. office mgr. Ray Merc. Co., New Orleans, 1958-64; consul, maritime comml. officer Consulate Gen. Panama, New Orleans, 1964-72; mgr. McDermott Internat., Inc., New Orleans, 1972—; pres., owner Kiddie Kare Train'n Sta.; cons. Consulates of Panama, Houston, New Orleans, 1972—; coordinator Panama Maritime Licensing, 1985—. Co-chmn. Jerry Lewis Telethon, New Orleans, 1977; fundraising co-chair Annual Hanicapped Children's Easter Parade, bd. dirs. La. Sch. for Deaf, Baton Rouge, 1985—, Sta. WNNR-Radio, 1972-74, New Orleans Soccer Assn., 1969-73; pres. Costa Rica Soccer Assn., 1969-72; fundraiser Bayside Vol. Fire Dept., Bay St. Louis, Miss., 1986—; co-chmn. State Sex Edn. Handicapped Children Comn., Baton Rouge, 1986—; chmn. Handicapped Children Christmas Program. Recipient merit award Bayside Fire Dept., Bay St. Louis, 1987, New Orleans Soccer Leagues merit award, 1971. Mem. Panama Maritime Adv. Com., Panama C. of C. and Industry, U.S. C. of C. in Panama, Miss. C. of C. Republican. Roman Catholic. Home: 4413 Senac Dr Metairie LA 70003

DE LEON, LIDIA MARIA, magazine editor; b. Havana, Cuba, Sept. 10, 1957; d. Leon J. and Lydia (Diaz Cruz) de L. B.A. in Communications cum laude, U. Miami, Coral Gables, Fla., 1979. Staff writer Miami Herald, Fla., 1978-79; editorial asst. Halsey Pub. Co., Miami, 1980-81, assoc. editor, 1981, editor, 1981—, editor Delta Sky mag., 1983—. Mem. Fla. Mag. Assn., Am. Soc. Mag. Editors, Golden Key Nat. Honor Soc., Am. Assn. Travel Editors. Democrat. Catholic. Clubs: Jockey, Cricket (Miami). Office: Delta Sky 12955 Biscayne Blvd North Miami FL 33181

DELEONE, VICKY (ANNE), software technical specialist; b. Springfield, Pa., May 27, 1957; d. James Joseph and Ann Marie (Cifone) Cattafesta; m. James Francis DeLeone, Aug. 11, 1979 (div. 1982). B in Bus. Adminstrn., Temple U., 1979. Quality assurance Burroughs Corp., Downingtown, Pa., 1977, software QA, 1978, program systems analyst, 1979-81; program analyst Crocker Internal Systems, San Jose, Calif., 1981-83; systems analyst Avantek, Inc., Santa Clara, Calif., 1983-84; tech. support speclist Micro Focus, Palo Alto, Calif., 1984—; programmer cons. Fin. Group, Palo Alto, 1985-86. Active Sierra Club. Democrat. Roman Catholic. Office: Micro Focus 2465 E Bayshore Rd Palo Alto CA 94303

DELGADO, ADELA MAY, personnel resources executive; b. Akron, Ohio, Apr. 7, 1939; d. Armanté Raphael and Antonia Maria (Griego) Garduno; m. Adolfo Delgado, Aug. 23, 1963 (div. July 1971). Grad. in bus. adminstrn., Akron U., 1974. V.p., counselor Ja-Her, Inc., Canton, Ohio, 1971-82; pres. Delgado and Assocs., Inc., Canton, 1982—. Mem. Ohio Assn. Personnel Cons. (bd. dirs. 1982—, v.p. Akron chpt. 1979-82), Am. Bus. Women (chairperson membership com. 1979-87), Canton C. of C. (numerous coms.). Democrat. Roman Catholic. Home: 2632 Beverly NE Canton OH 44714

DELGADO, MADALENE LYDIA, service executive; b. Salt Lake City, Oct. 5, 1960; d. Antonio and Maria Isabel (Velasquez) D. Cert., Utah Tech. Coll., 1980, student, 1987—. Adminstrv. sec. Intermountain Health Care, Inc., Salt Lake City, 1982, exec. sec., 1982-85, asst. mgr., instr. IBM S/38 text mgmt., 1985-86, mgr., 1986-87; mktg. and sales support rep. Intermountain Health Care, Inc., Wellesley, Mass., 1987—. Mem. Nat. Assn. Female Execs. Democrat. Roman Catholic. Home: 1610 Worcester Rd 333A Framingham MA 01701 Office: Intermountain Health Care Inc 70 Walnut St Wellesley MA 02181

DELGADO, PAULETTE MARIE, construction company executive; b. Loma Linda, Calif., July 12, 1954; d. Paul O. and Marie (Olivas) D.; divorced; children: Paul, Loretta, Melinda, Andrea; remarried: Stephen A. Matich, Sept. 5, 1987. Cert. CPR. Dept. mgr. T.G.Y., Yucaipa, Calif., 1973-74; cashier, asst. mgr. Burger King, Calif., 1977-78; mgr. restaurant Delgado's, Yucaipa, 1979-80; laborer Delgado & Sons, Inc., Yucaipa, 1980-81, office mgr., 1981-83, corp. sec., 1983-86, v.p., 1986—. Mem. ASTM, Nat. Assn. Women in Constrn. (bd. dirs. 1985-87, attending chmn. 1985-86, publication chmn. 1986-87), Nat. Assn. Female Execs., Calif. State Sheriff Assn. (charter assoc.). Republican. Roman Catholic. Home: 12624 17th St Yucaipa CA 92399 Office: Delgado and Sons Inc 12600 17th St Yucaipa CA 92399

DELGADO, SANDRA GAYLE, infosystems specialist; b. Bakersfield, Calif., May 18, 1952; d. Walter Douglas Vogel and Bobbe Rhea (Davenport) Haggard; m. Stephen Charles Delgado, May 19, 1973; children: Melanie Renée, Stephen Charles II. AA, Coll. of the Sequoias, 1972. Ops. mgr. Santa Clarita Nat. Bank, Los Angeles, 1974-80; EDP mgr. Sequoia Community Bank, Sanger, Calif., 1980-87; mgr. membership processing Ednl. Employees Credit Union, Fresno, Calif., 1987—. Active Sanger Perseptive Orn. Women. Mem. Bus. and Profl. Women., Exec. Female, Calif. Credit Union League. Republican. Club: Womens Trade (Fresno). Home: 2111 Vine Sanger CA 93657 Office: Am Embassy Madrid-DEA APO New York NY 09285

DELIBES, CLAUDE BLANCHE, communications company executive; b. Paris, Sept. 20, 1932; d. Andre Jean and Simone (Barou) Seligmann; came to U.S., 1940; naturalized, 1954; B.A., Sorbonne U., Paris, 1953; m. Maurice Delibes, Dec. 31, 1961; 1 son by previous marriage, Roger Schwartz; 1 dau., Jacqueline Delibes. Editor Fairchild Publications, N.Y.C., 1961-65; pub. relations dir. West Point Pepperell Corp., N.Y.C., 1968-72; sr. account supr. The Siesel Co., N.Y.C., 1972-75; pres. Delibes Communications, Ltd., N.Y.C., 1975—. Mem. Women Execs. in Pub. Relations, Fashion Group, Advt. Women of N.Y., Nat. Home Fashions League, French-Am. C. of C. Home: 1601 3d Ave New York NY 10028 Office: 200 W 57th St New York NY 10019

DE LISI, JOANNE, communication executive, educator; b. Bklyn., June 23, 1951; d. Louis Anthony and Maria Anna (Ferrantelli) De L. BA, Hunter Coll., 1972, MA, 1977; postgrad., N.Y.U. Cert. tchr., N.Y. Asst. instr. Hunter Coll., N.Y.C., 1974-75; instr. N.Y.U., 1974-78; instr. Bklyn. Coll., 1978-82, dir. forensics, 1981-82, asst. dir. acad. prep. program, 1980-82; adjunct lctr. City U. System, N.Y.C., 1983—; cons. communication N.Y.C., 1976—; Faculty advisor Alpha Tau Omega, Blkyn. Coll., 1980-82. Contbr. artices to profl. jours. Forensics judge Am. Legion Forensics Tournament, Queens 1979; media cons. Ramsay Clark Senatorial Campaign, N.Y.C. 1974. Mem. Speech Communication Assn. (conf. chair info. com. 1980), Internat. Soc. Gen. Semantics, N.Y. Acad. Scis., N.Y. St. Speech Assn., Nat. Assn. Female Execs., Kappa Delta Pi, Phi Delta Kappa, Phi Beta Honor Soc. (publicity coordinator 1978—). Roman Catholic. Clubs: Hunter Alumni Orgn., Fencers Am. Office: PO Box 370029 Wyckoff Heights Sta Brooklyn NY 11237

DELLA-GIUSTINA, MARSHA ANN, television news producer, educator; b. Springfield, Mass., Jan. 27, 1947; d. Joseph Augustus and Jennie Delores (Subotin) Della-G.; B.A. in English, Russell Sage Coll., Troy, N.Y., 1968; M.S. in Broadcast Journalism, Boston U., 1974, Ed.D. in Media and Tech., 1985; m. John R. Wetmiller, Aug. 26, 1972. Jr. high sch. tchr., Agawam and Westfield, Mass., 1968-72; radio public affairs host-producer sta. WBZ-FM, Boston, 1973-74; TV news producer-writer sta. WCVB-TV, Boston, 1976-85; journalism program dir., asst. prof. broadcast journalism Emerson Coll., Boston, 1976—; TV news assoc. producer, writer sta. WLVI-TV, Boston, 1986—; owner, producer Giustina Prodns., Arlington, Mass., 1979—; co-chmn. Freedom of Info. Act Symposium, 1982; TV news Cons., Harvard U. News Office, Cambridge, Mass., 1986—; cons. in field. Commr., Agawam Youth Commn., 1970-72; mem. Agawam Town Meeting, 1970-72; co-chmn. reunion com. Russell Sage Coll. Alumni Class 1968, 1978-83; mem. media com. Mass. ERA Referendum Com., 1974-76; lobbyist NOW, 1973-76. Recipient Emmy award, 1977, 81, award for disting. achievement in broadcast journalism edn., 1983. Mem. Italian-Americans in Commr, Radio-TV News Dirs. Assn. Am. Women Radio and TV, Nat. Acad. TV Arts and Scis., Boston Women's Media Network, Assn. Edn. in Journalism, Internat. Radio and TV Soc., Russell Sage Coll. Alumni Assn., Soc. Profl. Journalist Sigma Delta Chi. Democrat. Home: 113 Gray St Arlington MA 02174 Office: Emerson Coll 100 Beacon St Boston MA 02116

DELLAGNENA, GAIL LYNN, computer specialist; b. Akron, Ohio, Oct. 19, 1956; d. George McInnes and Iva Gena (Ridgeway) Massie. BA in Polit. Sci., Kent (Ohio) State U., 1977. Programmer Soc. Nat. Bank, Cleve., 1982-84; programmer, analyst Ohio Savs. and Loan, Cleve., 1984-86, Coulter Electronics Inc., Hialeah, Fla., 1986—. Served with U.S. Army, 1978-82. Mem. NOW, Am. Mgmt. Assn. Democrat. Presbyterian. Home: 8520 SW 133 Ave Rd #206 Kendall FL 33183 Office: Coulter Electronics Inc 600 W 20 St Hialeah FL 33010

DELLA ROSA, SUSANN GUGLIELMO, state agency administrator; b. Providence, Sept. 6, 1950; d. Salvatore James and Rose Marie (Penacho) Guglielmo; m. Ralph T. Della Rosa, Sept. 1, 1979; children: Jason, Amy, Jocelyn. BA in Polit. Sci., Merrimack Coll., 1972. Personnel asst. R.I. Outlet Co., Providence, 1972-74; asst. exec. dir. R.I. Dem. State Com., Providence, 1983-86; sr. adminstrv. aide to atty. gen. Office Atty. Gen. R.I. State Dept., Providence, 1975-78, adminstrv. officer fiscal dept., 1979-83, asst. to atty. gen. adminstrn., 1987—. Named Providence YWCA Woman of Yr., 1987. Democrat. Roman Catholic. Lodge: Order Sons of Italy (pres. East Providence chpt. 1977-81, state fin. sec. 1981-85, state recording sec. 1985—, nat. del. 1987). Home: 60 Don Ave Rumford RI 02916 Office: RI State Dept Office Atty Gen 72 Pine St Providence RI 02903

DELLINGER, ANN COLVARD, marketing professional, editor, writer; b. Gastonia, N.C., Feb. 11, 1948; d. Eulas Phillip and Pansy Patrick (Moten) Colvard; m. C. Frank Dellinger, July 29, 1966; children: Candace, Phillip, Patti. Cert. in Communications Mgmt., Belmont Abbey Coll., 1986. Mgr. food services Belmont Abbey Coll., Belmont, N.C., 1979-80, asst. dir. food services, 1980-81; adminstrv. asst. Good Will (Pubs.) Inc., Gastonia, N.C., 1981-83, asst. editor, 1982—, mgr. incentive program, 1983-84, sales promotion mgr., 1984-86; dir. sales and mktg. wholesale div. Good Will (Pubs.) Inc., Charlotte, N.C., 1986—. Author: (with others) The Way to Go, 1985, Be the Best You Can Be, 1985. Chair ways and means com. Parkland Elem. Sch., Rochester, N.Y., 1976-77; co-pres. Sacred Heart Home Sch. Assn., Belmont, 1983-85; dir. Belmont Abbey Coll. Cheerleaders, 1981-85; bd. dirs. Belmont Abbey Coll. Athletic Found., 1981-87, v.p. bd. dirs. 1982-87. Served with CAP, 1961-65. Recipient Pacemaker of the Piedmont award The Gastonia Gazette, 1984. Mem. Charlotte Soc. Communicating Arts, Nat. Assn. Female Execs., Smithsonian Assocs., Am. Mgmt. Assn., Am. Mktg. Assn., Am. Soc. Profl. and Exec. Women, Internat. Platform Assn. Roman Catholic. Club: Newcomers (soc. dir. 1980-81). Home: 305 Amity Circle Belmont NC 28012 Office: Good Will Publishers Inc 229 N Church St Suite 400 Charlotte NC 28202

DELL'ORCO, MARILYN ROSE, educator; b. St. Louis, Aug. 6, 1939; d. Casper A. and Anne R. (Catanzaro) Montileone; m. Louis A. Dell'Orco Jr., Nov. 23, 1961; children: Louis, Michael, Philip. BA, Fontbonne Coll., 1961; MA, Maryville Coll., 1987. Educator, various levels pub. schs., Mo., 1961—, prin., 1981-82. Author: Reflections on Writing, 1981; author, editor: Understanding Grammar and Growing the Paragraph, 1986. Mem. Nat. Council Tchrs. English, Internat. Reading Assn., Mo. State High Sch. Ofcls., Greater St. Louis Tchrs. English, Phi Delta Kappa. Republican. Roman Catholic. Home: 12543 Shepherd Dr Florissant MO 63033

DELMERICO, FRANCES EUGENIA, piano educator, retired music educator; b. Battle Creek, Mich., Feb. 17, 1918; d. Frank and Laura Theodosia (Adams) Minges; m. George Gregory Delmerico, June 16, 1946 (dec. 1958); children—Daniel Adams, Bruce Eugene deMedici. B.Music in Music Edn., Mich. State Coll., 1939; postgrad. Mich. State U., Western Mich. U. Cert. tchr., Mich. Music tchr. Quincy Pub. Schs., Mich., 1939-40, Fraser Pub. Schs., Mich., 1940-42, Lakeview Consol. Schs., Battle Creek, 1942-44, Harper Creek Community Sch., Battle Creek, 1964-73, Battle Creek Pub. Sch., 1973-80; piano tchr., Battle Creek, Mich., 1980—; writer program notes Battle Creek Symphony Orchestra, 1980-85. Active Lakeview Sch. Dist. Citizens' Com., Battle Creek, 1980-81, Battle Creek Hist. Soc.; bd. dirs. Battle Creek Area United Arts Council, 1980-83, Battle Creek Community Concert Assn., 1979-83; pres. ch. council First Congregational Ch., 1983-85, pres. women's fellowship, 1986-87, pres. SW dist. Mich. chpt., 1987—; sr. adv. council to the div. bd. Leila Hosp. and Health Ctr. 1987—; Battle Creek Town Hall bd., 1985—; charter mem. Battle Creek Community Chorus, mem. ch. choir, 1940—; mem. Cereal City Bellringers. Mem. Mich. Fedn. Music Clubs (v.p. SW dist. 1987—), Battle Creek Area Music Tchrs. Assn. (v.p. 1981-83, pres. 1983-85), Mich. Music Tchrs. Assn., Music Tchrs. Nat. Assn., Area and State Ret. Sch. Personnel Assn., Battle Creek Morning Musical Club (2d v.p. 1982-83, sec. 1983-85), Battle Creek Woman's Club (v.p. 1984-85, pres. 1985-87), Delta Kappa Gamma (mem. state music com. 1976-78, co-chair 87—, Chpt. Outstanding Service cert. 1983, 2d v.p. 1984-86, pres. 1986-88, Woman of Distinction, 1987), Alpha Xi Delta, Sigma Alpha Iota. Avocations: bridge, golf, assisting with music related student activities, restoring antique furniture. Home: 160 S Minges Rd Battle Creek MI 49017

DELOFFI, AUDREY YOUNG, social worker, mental health facility administrator; b. Portland, Maine, Apr. 9, 1947; d. William G. and Elcye M. (Ross) Y.; m. Thomas v. DeLoffi, Jr., June 4, 1983. BA cum laude, U. N.H., Durham, 1969; MSW, Boston Coll., Chestnut Hill, 1974. Social worker Children's Protective Services, Worcester, Mass., 1969-73; social work intern McLean Hosp., Belmont, Mass., 1973-74; prin. clin. social worker Danvers State Hosp., Hathorne, Mass., 1977-78, clin. social work supr., 1978-79; crisis team worker Project RAP, Beverly, Mass., 1977-81; vis. lectr. Salem State Coll., Beverly, Mass., 1976—; mental health coordinator Dept. Mental Health, Lynn, Mass., 1979-81; assoc. area dir. Dept. Mental Health, Lynn, Mass., 1981-83, area dir., 1983-85; chief operating officer Met. State Hosp., Waltham Dept. Mental Health, Mass., 1985—; mem. Greater Lynn Sr. Services Adv. Bd., 1982-85; cons. Cath. Family Services, Lynn, 1981—. Mem. alumni bd. dirs. Boston Coll. Sch. Social Work, 1976-78, 80-82; bd. dirs. Social Advocates for Youth, 1975-79, pres. 1977-79; bd. dirs. Melrose Hickory Hawks Ski Club, 1976-78, sec., 1977-78; bd. dirs. Project Rap, Beverly, 1983-86; clk. Tabernacle Ch., Salem, Mass., 1985-87. Recipient Outstanding Service award Social Advocates for Youth, 1979, Outstanding Service to the Spl. Needs Citizens award Town of Greater Lynn Sr. Services, 1984. Mem. Nat. Assn. Social Workers (dir. N.E. region steering com. 1977-81, vice chmn. 1978-80), Acad. Cert. Social Workers (lic. ind. clin. social worker). Home: 7 Laurent Rd Salem MA 01970 Office: 475 Trapelo Rd Waltham MA 02254

DELONG, DEBORAH, lawyer; b. Louisville, Sept. 5, 1950; d. Henry F. and Lois Jean (Stepp) D.; m. Michael A. Marrero, Jan. 12, 1981; children—Amelie DeLong, Samuel Prentice. B.A., Vanderbilt U., 1972; J.D., U. Cin., 1975. Bar: Ohio 1975, U.S. Dist. Ct. (so dist.) Ohio 1975, U.S. Ct. Appeals (6th cir.) 1975, U.S. Supreme Ct. 1982. Assoc. Paxton & Seasongood, Cin., 1975-82, ptnr., 1982—. Contbr. articles to profl. jours. Fund raiser Jr. League Cin., Ohio, 1979-84; bd. dirs. Childrens Psychiatric Ctr., Cin., 1980-84. Mem. ABA, Ohio State Bar Assn., Cin. Bar Assn., Arbitration Tribunal U.S. Dist. Ct., Ohio, 1984. Republican. Episcopalian. Office: Paxton & Seasongood 1700 Central Trust Tower 1 W 4th St Cincinnati OH 45202

DELONG, MARILYN FISHER, real estate executive; b. Boston, Feb. 28, 1942; d. John Brookins and Frances (Wilder) Fisher; m. James B. Boynton Jr., Aug. 3, 1963 (div. Sept. 1974); children: James B. III, Jennifer Craig. BA, Rollins Coll., Winter Park, Fla., 1963. Lic. realtor, Fla. Coordinator, editor Rollins Coll. Alumni Assn., Winter Park, 1972-76; realtor Park Place Assocs., Winter Park, 1978-80, The Stephens Co., Ltd., Winter Park, 1980-82; adminstrv. sec. CNL Investment Co., Orlando, Fla., 1982-83, property mgr., 1983-87, v.p. for franchise relations, 1987—. Mem. Jr. League Orlando, 1973—, Fla. House Council, Orlando, 1979; pres. Orlando Mus. Guild, 1972-73; chmn. Rollins Coll. Ann. Fund., Winter Park, 1985. Mem. Nat. Assn. Realtors, Fla. Assn. Realtors, Orlando Bd. Realtors, Nat. Assn. Securities Dealers (registered rep.), Real Estate Securities and Syndication Inst., Rollins Alumni Assn. (bd. dirs. 1982-85, v.p. 1985), Kappa Kappa Gamma. Republican. Episcopalian. Club: The Citrus (Orlando). Home: 700 Melrose A-24 Winter Park FL 32789 Office: CNL Investment Co 400 E South St Orlando FL 32801

DELONG, MARSHA JANE, insurance company executive; b. Reading, Pa., Aug. 23, 1952; d. William Marsh and Jane Eaches DeLong. B.A., Duke U., 1974; C.P.C.U., Ins. Inst. Am., 1980. Coach swimming and diving Kutztown (Pa.) Swim Assn., summers 1968, 69; mem. pub. relations staff Kutztown Folk Festival, summers, 1970-74; mktg. rep. Aetna Life & Casualty, Reading, 1974-77, personal lines account exec., 1977-83; personal lines underwriting mgmt. CNA Ins., Reading, Pa., 1983-86, projects coordinator, 1986—; nat. exam. grader Ins. Inst. Am., 1981—. Vol. instr. Easter Seal Soc., Reading, 1976-81, coordinator pledge ctr., 1979; co. chmn. United Way of Berks County, 1981-82; bd. dirs. Flint Hill Water Co., Bowers, Pa., 1974—; vol. speaker Center City Devel. Corp., Reading, 1980—; bd. dirs. Leadership Berks, 1986—, sec., 1988, graduation coordinator, 1988. Recipient Brace for an Ace award Easter Seal Soc., 1978; named Ins. Woman of Yr., 1980. Mem. Ins. Women of Reading (past pres.), Nat. Assn. Ins. Women (regional legis. chmn. 1981), Nat. Soc. CPCU's (bd. dirs. 1986—, chpt. pres. 1984-85), Junior League of Reading, Delta Delta Delta. Republican. Mem. United Ch. of Christ. Office: CNA Ins 401 Penn St Reading PA 19601

DELONG, NANCY GLYN, journalist, public relations and communications consultant; b. Columbus, Ohio, Oct. 2, 1946; d. Glen A. and Reba Z. (Pope) DeL.; B.A. in Journalism and English, Ohio State U., 1969. Exec. dir. Tri-County Dental Health Council, Detroit, 1971-76, reporter The Detroit News, 1970-71, The Columbus (Ohio) Dispatch, 1965-68; editorial photographer, contbg. editor Amusement Bus., 1968-73; producer The Oz of Prevention, Detroit, 1971-74; partner Real to Reel 1973-77; pres. project promotion Glyn Prodn. Ltd., 1977-79; pres. N. Glynn & Assocs., Inc., Southfield, Mich., 1979-82; bus. cons., 1976—; interior designer, 1976—; assoc. Walt Peabody Advt. Service Inc., Ft. Lauderdale, Fla.; beauty cons. Mary Kay Cosmetics, Inc., Dallas, 1982-85; dir. employee assistance programs and pub. relations Shepherd Hill, Newark, Ohio, 1985-86; dir. communication, liaison CompCare Corp., Irvine, Calif. and Columbus, Ohio, 1987—. Profl. boxing judge, State of Mich. Contbr. articles to various mags.; contbg. editor Downbeat, 1966-68, Billboard, 1968-73; producer ednl. films on health and rehab.; producer, dir. Super Party '82. Address: 1990 Aberdeen Dr Columbus OH 43220

DELONG, NORMA NEILL, civic association executive; b. Gulfport, Miss., June 25, 1934; d. Joe Horace and Gertrude Olivia (Holley) Neill; children: Fred Cole III, Holley Neill. BA, Millsaps Coll., 1955; MEd, U. Miss., 1958. Cert. secondary tchr., Miss. Tchr. Laurel (Miss.) City Schs., 1955-56, South Panola County Schs., Batesville, Miss., 1956-59, Greenville (Miss.) High Sch., 1959-62; tchr., organizer Washington Sch., Greenville, 1970-76; exec. dir. Nat. Assn. Jr. Auxiliaries, Inc., Greenville, 1984—. pres. Greenville Jr. Auxiliary, 1968-69; bd. dirs. Greenville Council on Aging, 1981—, William Alexander Percy Library, Greenville, 1981—; vol. activist for Miss., 1974. Mem. Greenville C. of C. (bd. dirs.), Am. Assn. Soc. Execs., Delta Kappa Gamma. Methodist. Club: Greenville Garden (pres. 1979-81).

DELOUGHERY, GRACE LEONA, nursing educator; b. Allison, Iowa, Jan. 17, 1933; d. Ed F. and Alma K. (Kampman) Meinen; B.S., U. Minn., 1955, M.P.H., 1960; Ph.D., Claremont Grad. Sch., 1966; m. Henry O. Deloughery, Nov. 30, 1962; children—Paul Edward, Michael, Kathleen. Staff nurse Mpls. Dept. Pub. Health, 1955-59; research fellow U. Minn. Sch. Pub. Health, 1960-63; sch. nurse Val Verde Sch. Dist., Perris, Calif., part-time 1963-66; community coordinator, nurse in Title I pilot project in San Jacinto, Riverside (Calif.) County Schs., 1966, cons. Title I, 1966-67; assoc. prof. U. N.C. Coll. Nursing, 1967-68; asst. prof. U. Calif. Sch. Nursing, Los Angeles, 1968-72; dean Center Nursing Edn., Spokane, 1972-74; prof., head dept. nursing Winona (Minn.) State U., 1975-77; adminstr. Deloughery Home Sr. Adults, 1977-84; assoc. prof. Ind. U., New Albany, 1984—, Bellarmine Coll., Louisville, Ky., 1987—; participant seminars, condr. workshops, cons. in field. Recipient award for research Calif. Edn. Research and Guidance Assn., 1967. Fellow Am. Pub. Health Assn., Am. Assn. Social Psychiatry (treas. 1974-78); mem. Am. Nurses Assn., Nat. League Nursing, Am. Sch. Health Assn., Internat. Mental Health Fedn., Wash. Pub. Health Assn., Acad. Polit. and Social Sci., Acad. Polit. Sci., Pi Lambda Theta, Sigma Theta Tau. Lutheran. Club: Winona Country. Contbr. to profl. jours. Home: Route 2 Circle Dr Georgetown IN 47122

DEL PAPA, FRANKIE SUE, state official; b. 1949. BA, U. Nev.; JD, George Washington U. Bar: Nev. 1974. Sec. of state Nev., 1987—. Democrat. Office: Office Sec State Capitol Complex Carson City NV 89710 •

DEL PESCO, SUSAN MARIE CARR, judge; b. Long Beach, Calif., May 20, 1946; d. Clarence Monroe and Leona (Goings) Carr; m. Thomas W. Del Pesco, Aug. 28, 1965; children: Joseph Thomas, Nicholas Paul. Student, UCLA, 1963-65; BA, U. Calif., Santa Barbara, 1967; JD, Widener U., 1975. Bar: Del. 1975, U.S. Dist. Ct. Del. 1975, U.S. Ct. Appeals (3d cir.) 1982. Assoc. Schnee & Castle, Wilmington, Del., 1976-81; ptnr. Prickett, Jones, Elliott, Kristol & Schnee, Wilmington, 1981-88, also bd. dirs.; assoc. judge Superior Ct. Del., Wilmington, 1988—; mem. Del. Supreme Ct. Bd. on Profl. Responsibility, 1979-86, Permanent Lawyers Adv. Com. for U.S. Dist. Ct. Del., 1985—. Recipient Outstanding Alumnae award Del. Law Sch., 1987. Mem. Del. State Bar Assn. (treas. 1978-79, v.p. New Castle 1984-85, v.p. at large 1985-86, pres.-elect 1986-87, pres. 1987-88). Republican. Office: Superior Ct Del Pub Bldg 11th & King Sts Wilmington DE 19801 Office: Superior Ct Pub Bldg 11th & King Sts Wilmington DE 19801

DELPRINCE, RENEÉ ANN, service executive; b. Ashtabula, Ohio, Nov. 26, 1955; d. Albert Jr. and Marie Josephine (Sespico) DelP. BA, Point Park Coll., 1978. Security cons. Barton Protective Services, Atlanta, 1982-83; sales mgr. Continental Security Services, Atlanta, 1983-85, br. mgr., 1985-87, v.p., 1987—; v.p., co-owner Atlanta Royal Cabbies Co., Atlanta, 1984—; cons. in field, 1983—. Mem. Am. Soc. for Indsl. Security, Ga. Assn. Security Profls., Atlanta C. of C. (team player 1987). Democrat. Roman Catholic. Office: Continental Security Service 3475 Lenox Rd NE Atlanta GA 30274

DEL PRINCIPE, DONNA GRACE, lawyer; b. Chgo., Aug. 3, 1947; d. Matthew John and Grace (Stompanato) Del P.; m. Rocco M. Labellarte, Feb. 14, 1981. BA, U. Ill., 1969; JD, John Marshall U., 1980. Bar: Ill., 1980. Substitute tchr. Chgo. Bd. Edn., 1969-70; social worker Traemour Sheltered Care Home, Chgo., 1971-72; tchr. St. Mary Ctr. for Learning, Chgo., 1971-72, registrar, 1974-76; assoc. Law Offices Mark Bigelow, Chgo., 1980-81, Brodie & Reynolds, Chgo., 1981-83, Kane, Obbish & Propes, Chgo., 1986—. Mem. Chgo. Bar Assn., Women's Bar Assn. Ill., Lawyers for Alternative Work Schedules (founding dir. 1985—), Part-time Lawyers Network (founder). Office: Kane Obbish & Propes 100 W Monroe St Chicago IL 60657

DEL RIO DIAZ, ESTYNE, psychologist; b. Chgo., July 30, 1945; d. Sal Ernest and Evelyn Sandea (Del Rio) Bernhardt; m. Raul Diaz, Nov. 21, 1987. PhD, Jackson State U., 1974; postgrad., U. Pa., 1975, Robbins Research Inst., 1985. Pres. Psychelogistics Inc., N.Y.C., 1960-80; TV talk show personality various shows, N.Y.S., 1971; practicing psychologist N.Y.S., 1974—; psychologist Ghana, Africa, 1975; v.p. Jo-Del Consol. Ltd., 1976; columnist Health and Diet Times, N.Y.C., 1980; exec. producer, host Encounters, N.Y.C., 1986—. Mem. Assn. Nat. Christian Counselors, Am. Bd. Christian Psychology, Assn. Humanistic Psychology. Democrat. Club: N.Y. Health and Raquet, Century 21. Office: 30 East End Ave Apt 6B New York NY 10028

DEL SARDO, HELEN ANN, financial company representative; b. Boston, Jan. 5, 1954; d. Nick James and Mary Florence (Marino) Falce; m. Anthony Robert Del Sardo, June 25, 1982. BA in Polit. Sci., Duquesne U., 1976. Lic. securities dealer, ins. salesperson, Pa. Sr. budget analyst Allegheny County Controller's Office, Pitts., 1979-84; rep. Equitable Life Assurance Soc., Pitts., 1985-86; registered rep. Lincoln Investment Planning, Inc., Pitts., 1986-87; registered rep., assoc. Renaissance Fin. Group, Pitts., 1987—. Vol. Frank J. Lucchino for State Auditor Gen., Pitts., 1984; mem. YWCA Greater Pitts. Mem. Nat. Assn. Life Underwriters, Nat. Assn. Female Execs., Duquesne U. Alumni Assn. Democrat. Roman Catholic. Home: 2723 Brownsville Rd Apt 3 Pittsburgh PA 15227 Office: Renaissance Fin Group Foster Plaza Bldg 10 680 Andersen Dr Pittsburgh PA 15220

DE LUCCIA, EILEEN DOROTHY, day care center director, consultant; b. Paterson, N.J., Oct. 26, 1943; d. John Arthur and Dorothy Julia (Muzio) Van Vliet; m. Nicholas Sabatino De Luccia, May 19, 1974. B.A., William Paterson Coll., 1966. Certified tchr. Tchr. fifth grade North Haledon Bd. Edn., N.J., 1966-69, Wayne Bd. Edn., N.J., 1969-73; spl. edn. tchr. Oakland Bd. Edn., N.J., 1973-75; dir. Gingerbread Castle Day Sch., Oakland, 1977—; cons., Oakland, 1983—. Bd. dirs. Ramapo Bergen Animal Rescue, Inc., Oakland, 1981-82, Pet Pride, Inc., 1970—. Mem. Assn. for Childhood Edn. Internat., Oakland C. of C., Nat. Assn. Female Execs., Assn. of Early Childhood, People for Ethical Treatment of Animals, Internat. Fund for Animal Welfare, Defenders of Wildlife, Animal Protection Inst. Avocations: animal rescues; behaviorism; shelter work; tutoring; gardening. Home: 40 Venna Ave North Haledon NJ 07508 Office: Gingerbread Castle Day Sch Ramapo Valley Rd Oakland NJ 07436

DE LUCE, VIRGINIA, entertainer; b. San Francisco, Mar. 25, 1921. Student, Bishop-Lee Sch. of Theatre, Beacon Hill, Mass. Model John Roberts Powers, Harry Conover; dir. New Wrinkle Theatre; actress 20th Century Fox Film Corp., Columbia Pictures, Paramount Pictures, also commercials; pres. Soc. Prodns., Cosmic Sci. Inst., Earth Jazz, Texloid Products. Actress: (musicals and plays) including Kiss Me Kate, Brigadoon, Can Can, Pal Joey, Will Success Spoil Rock Hunter, Twelfth Night, Emperor Jones, Pygmalion and Galatea, White Iris, Leave It To Psmith, The Sacrifice, Bonanza, The Beggars' Opera, (Broadway play) Who Was That Lady, (musical revues) Vaudeville at Palace Theatre, New Faces at Royale Theatre, Chic at Orpheum Theatre, Billy Barnes' Rev. at Carnegie Hall, Have A Heart at Madison Sq. Garden; producer: (concert) Blue Dove's Many Feathers; appeared in hotel shows and cabarets including Ritz Carlton Hotel, Montreal, Can., Le Cabaret, Toronto, Can., Copacobana Palace, Rio De Janeiro, Comedy Club, N.Y.C., Twelfth Night Club, N.Y.C., Waldorf Astoria, N.Y.C., Biltmore Bowl, Los Angeles, Golden Horseshoe, Disneyland, Calif., Hotel Roosevelt, New Orleans, Scotch and Sirloin, Los Angeles, #1 Fifth Avenue, N.Y.C., Di Maggio's Yacht Club, San Francisco, Leon & Eddie's, N.Y.C., The Ballroom, N.Y.C., Mayfair, Boston, Pirates' Den, Hollywood, Calif., Trocadero, Hollywood, House of Vienna, N.Y.C., Blue Angel, N.Y.C.; appearances in TV shows including Play of the Week (NTA), Repetoire Workshop, Tonight Show, Sgt. Bilko series, others, also radio shows, local and network telethons; appeared in rodeos Leo Carillo, Roy Rogers Rodeos, Coliseum, Los Angeles; author, composer: The Boston Nod, (scripts, songs and poetry) Dallas Sal, Spider, Give All His Love to Her, Great Sun, Victory, Making Up-Silent Song, Pow Wow Smile, Saga of Jini, When Love is Near, The Thorns of Summer; author: Your Own Voice, My Learning Path, Crystal Gazing Lessons, Your Heart's Desire, Lucky Break; creator astrological paintings, datascope, delineations, Dog-O-Scope, Cat-O-Scope; also painter, fashion designer and songwriter. Mem. Rep. Town Com., Weston, Mass.; alt. Senator Silver Haired Legis., Mass.; asst. to mgr. Eisenhower-Nixon Bandwagon Hdqtrs., N.Y.C.; creator theme, chmn. entertainment Inaugural Ball Pres. Nixon; asst. coordinator, dir. pub. relations Mass. Satellite Inaugural Ball for Pres. Reagan, 1980; precinct dir. Re-elect Pres. Reagan, 1984; coordinator Dr. Richard A. Jones for Senator campaign, Weston; speaker, writer LWV Candidate Night; apptd. election officer Town of Weston, also apptd. fence viewer; author Mass. Legis. House bills; bd. dirs. Arts and Crafts Assn.; mem. Environment Task Force, Mass.; past mem. numerous other civic orgns., bds.; vol. worker, performer for charities. Named to Times Square Hall of Fame; recipient Theatre World award, Yale U. Drama Salute. Mem. Am. Guild Variety Artists, Screen Actors' Guild, Actor's Equity Assn., Am. Fedn. TV and Radio Artists, Franklin County C. of C., Am. Legion, Mass. Fedn. Rep. Women (bd. dirs.), Nat. Rifle Assn., Gun Owners' League, AIM, Am. Fedn. Astrologers.

DELUNA, DIANE GONCALVES, electrical engineer; b. Elizabeth, N.J., July 20, 1954; d. Nelson and Maria (Costa) Goncalves; m. Tommy Raymond DeLuna, Aug. 24, 1975. BSEE, Fla. Inst. Tech., 1976, MBA, 1985; MSEE, U. Calif., Irvine, 1980. Digital design engr. Rockwell Internat. Autonetics, Anaheim, Calif., 1976-80, GE Corp., Daytona Beach, Fla., 1980-83; digital designer, group leader, systems engr. govt. info. systems div. Harris Corp., Melbourne, Fla., 1983-87, program mgr. govt. aerospace systems div., 1987—; adj. faculty mem. Sch. Mgmt. Fla. Inst. Tech. Mem. Assn. Old Crows (treas. Spacecoast chpt. 1987—), Fla. Inst. Tech. Alumni Assn. (treas. 1987—), Eta Kappa Nu. Home: 4905 Fauna Dr Melbourne FL 32935 Office: Govt Aerospace Systems Div Harris Corp PO Box 94000 MS 102-4562 Melbourne FL 32902

DEL VALLE, HELEN CYNTHIA, artist; b. Chgo., Sept. 22, 1933; d. Andrew Jack and Mary Texanna (Cohen) DelValle; student Pa. Acad. Fine Arts, 1952; B.J., Northwestern U., 1960. Tchr. art, math., history, Fla., 1952-54; artist, designer, Chgo., 1954-59; free-lance artist, 1959—; group exhbns. include: Mcpl. Art League of Chgo., U. State Mus., Mid Am. Art Assn., Am. Soc. of Artists, Northshore Art Guild; one woman shows include: Balzekas Mus., Chgo., 1973, Chgo. Public Library, 1972, 73, 75, Combined Ins. Co. Am., Chgo., 1970, 71, 72, 74, 75, Am. Soc. Artists, Chgo., 1971, 1977, also others. Recipient Portraiture award, 1961, 68; internat. award for landscape painting, Switzerland, 1975; 38 merits of honor from U.S. and Europe; award Hollywood Music Co., 1984; Idaho award oriental gardening watercolor, 1984, oustanding award on water color, 1987. Mem. Am. Soc. Artists (membership chmn. 1970—, also dir., v.p.), Nat. League Am. Pen Women (Dingle award Chgo. chpt. 1971, traditional in oil award 1971, landscape in watercolor award 1973, 1st award in painting 1979, 3d place award Chgo. br. 1980, 81, award for watercolor state art show), Mcpl. Art League Chgo. (hon. mention 1973), Nat. Soc. Artists, Internat. Poetry Soc., Ill. Poetry Soc., Poets and Patrons. Author published poem Happiness, 1986, and others; poems pub. in 14 edits. New Voices in Am. Poetry. Address: PO Box 958 Chicago IL 60690

DELVENTHAL, PRISCILLA JANE, histologist; b. Chgo., July 29, 1938; d. Ralph Daniel and Geneva Mae (Walden) Esterly; student No. Ill. U., So. Ill. U.; diploma histology, St. Anthony's Hosp., Rockford, Ill., 1961; m. LeRoy Earl Delventhal, Sept. 3, 1966; children—Kathryn Lee, Lane Aaron, Daniel Albert. Tchr., Rockford, Ill., 1960-61; asst. supr. surg. pathology-histology lab. U. Colo. Med. Sch., Denver, 1961-64; head histology Lutheran Hosp., Wheatridge, Colo., 1964-65; asst. head histology Colo. State U., Ft. Collins, 1966-68; head histology lab. Pathology Lab. Assocs., Lander, Wyo., 1977-84; supr. histologist portamedic services Hooper Homes, 1978—; supr. histology and cytology labs. Lander Valley Regional Med. Ctr., 1984—. Active local Boy Scout Am.; dir. jr. choir Trinity Luth. Ch., Riverton, Wy. 1978-81, St. Johns Luth. Ch., Ft. Collins, Colo. 1967-67. Mem. Am. Soc. Clin. Pathologists (assoc.), Colo. Soc. Histotech. (charter), Nat. Soc. Histotechnology. Home: 829 Cheryl Sue Dr Riverton WY 82501 Office: 1320 Bishop Randall Dr Lander WY 82520

D'EMANUELE, MAY ANN, consulting company executive; b. Lawrence, Mass., June 21, 1934; d. Michael and Ann (Catanese) D'E. BA, Merrimack Coll., 1956. Chief ops. Alexander Proudfoot Co., Chgo., 1972-82; account exec. Inst. Mgmt. Resources, Westlake Village, Calif., 1982-85; v.p. ops. The Princeton (N.J.) Group, 1985—. Mem. Nat. Assn. Female Execs. Office: 214 Carnegie Center Princeton NJ 08540

DE MAR, LEODA MILLER, fabric and wallcovering designer, advertising design and layout artist; b. N.Y.C., May 26, 1929; d. Benjamin and Malvina (Altman) Miller; m. Robert Mathis de Mar, Dec. 30, 1955 (div. Jan. 1985); children: Victoria, Miller Mathis, Charles David. Diploma, Parson's Sch. of Design, N.Y.C., 1946-49; postgrad., Parson's Sch. of Design, Eng., France, Italy, 1949, NYU, 1950-53. Designer Joseph B. Platt, Indsl. Design, N.Y.C., 1950-53; instr. textiles Parson's Sch. Design, N.Y.C., 1953-55; freelance designer various companies, N.Y.C., 1956-62; designer Leoda de Mar, Inc., N.Y.C., 1962-74; designer, advt. cons. Woodson Wallpapers, N.Y.C., 1975-85, Richard E. Thibaut, Inc., Irvington, N.J., 1985—. Designer 1st wallpaper collection Pippin Papers, N.Y.C., 1954, 1st wallpaper collection Woodson Wallpapers, 1955, own collections Richard E. Thibaut, Inc., 1985—, fabric and wallcovering designs featured in various popular mags.; contbr. articles to mags. Recipient Creativity award Art Direction mag., 1981. Home and Office: 350 Riversville Rd Greenwich CT 06831

DE MARCO, DANA, real estate executive; b. New Brunswick, N.J., Dec. 12, 1955; d. Arthur and Rae (Yaw) De M. Grad. real estate sch., Profl. Sch. Bus., Union, N.J., 1986. Cert. real estate agt. Clk. typist County Food Stamps N.J. Welfare Dept., New Brunswick, 1974-75; sec. County Prosecuter's Office, New Brunswick, 1975-76; claims examiner Blue Cross/Blue Shield N.J., Princeton, 1976-81; exec. sec., adminstrv. asst. Action Temps, Inc., New Brunswick, 1981-82; NE/SE regional sales asst. Osborne Computer Corp., Monmouth Junction, N.J., 1982-84; north/cen. regional sales asst. Fujitsu Microsystems Am., Iselin, N.J., 1984-86; real estate agt. Sun Realty, Inc., Woodbridge, N.J., 1986-88; adminstr. office Rothe-Johnson Assocs., Edison, N.J., 1986—; real estate agt. Century 21-Golden Post Realty, Stirling, N.J., 1988—. Mem. Ambassadors for Friendship. Matawan, N.J., 1974. Mem. Nat. Assn. Female Execs., Middlesex, Hunterdon, Morris, and Somerset County Bds. Realtors, N.J. Soc. Archtl. Adminstrs., Nat. Soc. Archtl. Adminstrs. Home: 260 Grant Ave Piscataway NJ 08854 Office: Rothe Johnson Assocs 2025 Lincoln Hwy Edison NJ 08817

DEMARCO, DIANE LYNN, contractor; b. Fort Worth, June 4, 1958; d. Ronald Charles and Rita Bernice (Davis) DeMarco. BS, U. Fla., 1981. Cert. gen. contractor, Fla. Vice pres. DeMarco Homes, Boca Raton, Fla., 1981-86, pres., 1986—. Project coordiantor Boca Raton Hist. Soc., 1983-85; cons. historic Palm Beach County Preservation bd., 1984-85; pres. DeMarco Constrn., Inc., Boca Raton, 1986—; bd. dirs. St. Joan of Arc Catholic Ch. Constrn. Bd., Boca Raton, 1985; restorationist Old Town Hall, 1983-85, Raulerson House, 1986; bd. dirs. City Boca Raton Preservation Bd., 1984—, Boca Raton Bd. Realtors, 1987—. Chmn. preservation Delray Beach Hist. Soc., 1988—. Recipient Spl. Achievement award Fa. Trust for Historic Preservation, 1985, Fed. Restoration grant Fla. Dept. Stte, 1984, Leadership 84 award Boca Raton C. of C., 1984. Mem. Boca Raton C. of C. (com. chmn. 1985), Boca Raton Hist. Soc., Nat. Assn. Home Builders, Fla. Atlantic Builders Assn., Nat. Asn. Women in Constrn., Nat. Bldg. Mus., Fellowship Single Profls. (pres. 1984-85), Nat. Assn. Miniature Enthusiasts, Fla. Atlantic Builders Assn. (mem. remodeler's council 1985-87), Boca Rotan Bd. Realtors, Nat. Assn. Homebuilders, Jr. League, Sigma Lambda Chi. Republican. Avocations: doll and miniature collecting, camping, quilting. Office: DeMarco Homes Inc 290 SW 2d Ave Boca Raton FL 33432

DE MARCO, NATALIE ANNE, corporate executive; b. Easton, Pa., Feb. 2, 1961; d. Lawrence Adriano and Donna Louise (Gordon) De M. Student, Indiana U. Pa., 1979-81, Northhampton Community Coll., 1982, Broward Community Coll., 1986. Mgr. Louise's Contourella, Easton, 1982-83; reservationist Wainwright's Travel, Bethlehem, Pa., 1983-84; receptionist Finley, Kumble, Wagner et al, Miami, 1984; staff, tour dir. Royal Carribean Cruise Lines, Miami, 1986; sec. USA Express Inc., Miami, 1986, Hasting's and Hasting's, Miami, 1984-86; sec. Benthor-Sanijura Inc., North Miami Beach, Fla., 1985, pres., treas., corp. officer, 1985—. Roman Catholic.

DEMARCO, RITA LOUISE, market research administrator, consultant; b. Cleve., Oct. 26, 1949; d. Anthony Joseph and Lillian Mary (Koeth) D. B.S. in Edn., Baldwin-Wallace Coll., 1970, M.B.A., 1977. Tchr. Highland Local Schs., Cleve., 1972-77, mng. editor-Am. machinist tng. programs Beckwith & Assocs. subs. McGraw Hill, Cleve., 1977-79; mgr. ind. research and devel. and bus. devel. Gould Inc., Rolling Meadows, Ill., 1979-82; mgr. market research and planning Master Builders div. Sandoz, Cleve., 1982—; prof. William Rainey Harper Coll., Chgo., 1980-81; pres., cons. Profl. Individualized Tng. Systems, Cleve., 1982—; cons. Strategic Innovations, Cleve., 1987—. Author/editor: Upper Engine Rebuild, 1978. Contbr. articles to Bridge Repair Markets, 1983. Baldwin Wallace Coll. scholar, 1967-70. Mem. Am. Mktg. Assn. (newsletter chmn. 1980-81, 86-87), Planning Execs. Inst., Am. Soc. for Tng. and Devel., Kappa Delta Pi. Democrat. Roman Catholic. Club: Masque and Staff (Chgo.). Office: Master Builders Div Sandoz 23700 Chagrin Blvd Beachwood OH 44122

DEMARCO-KEATING, MARY LOUISE, education administrator, writer; b. Bklyn., Mar. 1, 1951; d. Vincent Edward and Bridget (Cornacchio) DeMarco; m. Robert G.M. Keating, May 19, 1984. BA, Cen. Conn. State U., 1973; MS, SUNY, Stony Brook, 1978; postgrad., CCNY, 1981-83. Elem. sch. tchr. St. Martin of Tours, Bethpage, N.Y., 1974-77; jr. high sci. tchr. N.Y.C. Bd. Edn., 1977-82; sci. coordinator N.Y.C. Bd. Edn., Bklyn., 1982-85, edn. adminstr., 1985—; writer N & N Pub. Co., Middleton, N.Y., 1987—. Sec. Beverly Square West Block Assn., Bklyn., 1984—; vol. Prospect Park Environ. Ctr., Bklyn., 1984—, Bklyn. Botanical Garden, 1986; liaison Bklyn. Community Council, 1987—. Mem. Elem. Sch. Sci. Assn. (workshop leader 1985—), Sci. Tchrs. Assn. N.Y. (workshop leader 1985—). Democrat. Roman Catholic.

DEMAREE, BETTY, artist, educator; b. Denver, Oct. 19, 1918; d. Nathaniel and Margaret Elizabeth (Sanderson) Wolfson; m. Dean Clay DeMaree, Jan. 15, 1962; 1 stepchild. Student Cooper Union Sch. Art, 1938-41. Textile designer Am. Textile Co., N.Y.C., 1940-43; self-employed greeting card designer, Los Angeles, 1945-48; self-employed designer, Bolivia, 1948-53; self-employed custom ceramics designer, Denver, 1954-65; self-employed painter, tchr., Denver, 1967—; condr. numerous workshops; judge various art shows; bd. dirs. Rocky Mountain Nat. Watermedia Soc. ann. exhbn. Exhibited in group shows at Southwestern Watercolor Soc., Dallas, 1968-84, Am. Watercolor Soc., N.Y.C., 1976-80, San Diego Watercolor Soc. and Traveling Show, 1983, Ky. Watercolor Soc., 1984-87, Allied Artists Am., N.Y.C., 1977-87; Rocky Mountain Nat. Watermedia Exhbn., 1975-85, Gallery A, Taos, N.Mex., Cason Gallery, Helena, Mont., La Porta Gallery, Englewood, Colo., Art of Denver Gallery, Paint Horse Gallery, Breckinridge, Colo., Parker-Blake Galleries, Amparo Galleries, Denver, Scotsdale, Ariz.; represented in permanent collections Los Alamos Nat. Lab., United Bank of Denver, Mason, Reuler and Peake, Denver, Central Bank and Trust, Denver, Colo. State U., Fort Collins, Rocky Mountain Energy Corp., Broomfield, Colo., Dwight Energy Data, Natkin & Co., Englewood, Denver, James Ins. Co., Denver, Sheraton Hotel, Ft. Lauderdale, Fla., Combs-Gates Airport, Denver, Harris Bank and Trust, Scottsdale, Utah State U., Logan, Glendale (Colo.), Jefferson County Bank, Lakewood, Colo., Dental Groupothers. Mem. Southwestern Watercolor Soc. (named Best of Show 1969, selected for travelling show 1969), Am. Watercolor Soc. (Emily Lowe Meml. award 1976), Allied Artists Am. (John Young-Hunter award 1977, Winsor Newton award for watercolor 1978), Audubon Artists Am., Rocky Mountain Nat. Watermedia Soc., Colo. Watercolor Soc. Denver Artists Guild, Colo. Artist Assn. (award 1981, Best of Show award 1986), San Diego Watercolor Soc. Republican. Christian Scientist. Home and Office: Betty DeMaree Studio 4725 W Quincy Ave Denver CO 80236

DE MARNEFFE, BARBARA ROWE, small business owner; b. Boston, June 2, 1929; d. H.S. Payson and Florence Van Arnhem (Cassard) Rowe; m. James Hopkins, Oct. 9, 1954 (div. 1969); m. Francis de Marneffe; stepchildren: Peter, Daphne, Colette. BA, Vassar Coll., 1952; postgrad., Boston U., 1959. Tchr. Chapin Sch., N.Y.C., 1952-54; adminstrv. asst. to dean Sch. of Indsl. Mgmt. MIT, Cambridge, Mass., 1959-60; asst. pub. relations dir. Peter Bent Brigham Hosp., Boston, 1960-61, pub. relations dir., 1961-63; pub. relations cons. Diabetes Found. and Joslin Clinic, Boston, 1963-64; pub. relations dir. McLean Hosp., Belmont, Mass., 1964-68; pres. de Marneffe Selections, Cambridge, 1978—. Contbr. articles to profl. jours. Trustee, v.p. Archives of Am. Art of the Smithsonian Inst., Washington, , chmn. New Eng. com., 1982-88, chmn. Ellis Meml. Settlement House Antiques Show Radio and TV publicity, 1985-86; v.p., bd. dirs. McLean Hosp. Aux., Belmont, Mass.; bd. dirs. officer Family Counseling Service of Cambridge; Mass. Rep. State Committeewoman; exec. sec. Cambridge Rep. City Committee, 1956-57; pub. relations dir. Peabody for Congress Campaign, Newton, Mass., 1968; bd. dirs. Nat. Com. on the Treatment of Intractable Pain, Washington D.C., Friends of McLean Hosp., Belmont, Peterborough Players, Peterborough, N.H. Mem. Jewelers of Am., Inc., Cambridge C. of C. (pub. affairs mgr. 1975-78). Club: Vassar (v.p. Boston chpt.). Home and Office: 126 Coolidge Hill Cambridge MA 02138

DE MARR, MARY JEAN, English language educator; b. Champaign, Ill., Sept. 20, 1932; d. William Fleming and Laura Alice (Shauman) Bailey. B.A., Lawrence Coll., 1954; M.A., U. Ill., 1957, Ph.D., 1963; postgrad., Universitaet Tuebingen, 1954-55, Moscow State U., 1961-62. Asst. prof. English Willamette U., 1964-65; asst. prof. English Ind. State U., 1965-70, asso. prof., 1970-75, prof., 1975—. Co-author: Adolescent Female Portraits in the American Novel, 1961-81: An Annotated Bibliography, 1983, The Adolescent in The American Novel Since 1960, 1986; Am. editor: Annual Bibliography of English Language and Literature, 1979—. Recipient Fulbright assistantship, 1954-55. Mem. MLA, Modern Humanities Research Assn., AAUP, Nat. Council Tchrs. English, ACLU, Phi Beta Kappa, Phi Kappa Phi. Home: 594 Woodbine Dr Terre Haute IN 47803 Office: Dept English Ind State U Terre Haute IN 47809

DEMARS, CARON EMERSON, insurance specialist; b. Rock Springs, Wyo., Oct. 18, 1955; d. Eugene Reynders and Mildred Evelyn (Bohmont) E.; m. Bruce David DeMars, Aug. 11, 1984. BS, U. Wyo., 1978. Claims adjuster Crawford and Co. Ins. Adjusters, Great Falls, Mont., 1978-79; adjuster-in-charge Rawlins, Wyo., 1979-80; field claim rep. State Farm Ins., Sheridan, Wyo., 1980, sr. field claim rep., 1981-82; specialist arson State Farm Ins., Casper, Wyo., 1982-85; reinsp., trainer State Farm Ins., Colorado Springs, Colo., 1985—. Bd. dirs. Wyo. Girl Scout Council, Green River, 1974, Crimestoppers Cen. Wyo., Casper, 1982-85; chair publicity Sheridan County Reps., 1980-82, Jr. League El Paso County, 1988—. Mem. Western Ins. Info. Service (Wyo. coordinator level III 1987), Bus. and Profl. Women (chair young careerist com. 1985, state Outstanding Young Career Woman 1984), Nat. Assn. for Female Execs., VFW (aux.), Kappa Delta Alumnae Assn. (editor 1988-89). Republican. Mem. Unity Ch. Club: Toastmasters (pers. Casper chpt. 1984-85, ednl. v.p. Colorado Springs chpt. 1987, Competent Toastmaster 1983, pres. Colo. Springs chpt. 1988-89). Home: 5025 Whip Trail Colorado Springs CO 80917 Office: United Services Automobile Assn 1485 Kelley Johnson Blvd Colorado Springs CO 80918

DE MASSA, JESSIE G., media specialist. BJ, Temple U.; MLS, San Jose State U., 1967; postgrad., U. Okla., U. So. Calif. Tchr. Palo Alto (Calif.) Unified Sch. Dist., 1966; librarian Antelope Valley Joint Union High Sch. Dist., Lancaster, Calif., 1966-68, ABC Unified Sch. Dist., Artesia, Calif., 1968-72; dist. librarian Tehachapi (Calif.) Unified Sch. Dist., 1972-81; also media specialist, free lance writer, 1981—. Contbr. articles to profl. jours. Mem. Statue of Liberty Ellis Island Found., Inc. Fellow Internat. Biog. Assn.; mem. Calif. Media and Library Educators Assn., Calif. Assn. Sch. Librarians (exec. council), AAUW (bull. editor, assoc. editor state bull., chmn. publicity 1955-68), Nat. Mus. Women in Arts (charter), Hon. Fellows John F. Kennedy Library (founding mem.). Home: 9951 Garrett Circle Huntington Beach CA 92646

DEMATTEO, GLORIA JEAN, insurance saleswoman; b. Perth Amboy, N.J., May 23, 1943; d. John J. and Helena (Elias) Kancz; m. Ronald D. DeMatteo, Feb. 20, 1965 (div. Nov. 1987); children: Douglas J., Keith G. Student, Berkeley Sch., 1961. Exec. sec. Rhodia Inc., New Brunswick, N.J., 1961-65; real estate saleswomen Mid-Jersey Realty, East Brunswick, N.J., 1974-79; pntr. Realty World Garden of Homes, East Brunswick, 1979-81; spl. agt. Prudential Ins. Co., Woodbridge, N.J., 1981—. V.p. Belcourt Condo Assn., North Brunswick, N.J., 1987-88. Mem. Nat. Assn. Life Underwriters (Nat. Sales Achievement award 1988, Nat. Quality award 1987). Home: 1144 Schmidt Ln North Brunswick NJ 08902 Office: Prudential Ins Co 1 Woodridge Ctr Woodbridge NJ 07095

DEMBECK, MARY GRACE, artist, writer; b. N.Y.C., Oct. 29, 1931; d. August and Lucia Louisa (De Sanctis) Menghini; m. John Francis Dembeck, June 14, 1958; children: Christine Elizabeth, John Francis Jr. Student, St. John's U., N.Y.C., 1950-51, Fordham U., 1951-52, Fairfield U., 1982-83; studies with, Charles Reid, Daniel Green, John Mc Clelland, Leonard Everett Fisher, John C. Pellew and Mary Ann Hoberman, Conn., N.Y., 1974-82. Artist, pres. Pinafore, Ltd., Westport, Conn., 1987—. works exhibited at Eagle Tower Gallery, Stamford, Conn., 1979, 80, Nat. Acad. Design, N.Y.C., 1981, Westport Nature Ctr., Westport Ctr. Arts, 1983-85, Rowayton (Conn.) Arts Ctr., 1983-87 (acrylic award 1983), Trumbull (Conn.) Library, 1985-87, Gallery Four, Norwalk, Conn. 1986, Norfield Art Show, Weston, Conn., 1987, Fairfield (Conn.) U., 1987; contbr. light verse, humor and poetry to mags., newspapers including Nat. Wildlife Fedn's. Ranger Rick Mag., Westport News, 1979-83, Banker's Newsletter, 1985, Wall Street Jour., 1985—; creator cartoon character "Harriet", illustrator Carousel mag.; panelist local radio, cable TV arts/humor discussions. Designer Mass book cover St. Patrick's Cathedral, N.Y.C., 1977—; judge children's poetry and short story Trumbull Arts Festival, 1986—; mem. Westport Hist. Soc., Westport Women's Club (awards for acrylics 1985, 86, 87); artist mem. Italian Apostolate Archdiocese N.Y.C. Recipient Nat. Pub. Radio award, 1987. Mem. Rowayton Arts Ctr., Westport Ctr. for the Arts, Nat. League of Pen Women (poetry award 1983, best humorous poem 1984) Nat. Soc. Painters in Acrylic & Casein (assoc.), Westport Hist. Soc., Brontë Soc. (life). Roman Catholic.

DEMBER, JEAN WILKINS, civic worker, civil rights advocate; b. Bklyn., Jan. 29, 1930; d. William H. and Marie (Benson) Wilkins; m. Clarence R. Dember, Apr. 15, 1950; children: Clarence, Judith, Regina, Lila, Theresa, Zelie. M of Human Service, Lincoln U., Pa., 1988. Curator Dember-Webb African Am. Heritage Workshop, Copiague, N.Y., 1970—; advocate, chair L.I. Day Care Services Inc., 1985-87; advocate of the poor, 1970—. Author: Sex Isn't Strawberry Jam, 1975, Black Lines in Poetry, 1973, Growing Pains, 1978. Nat. del. Black Polit. Assembly, Gary, Ind., 1972-82, Rainbow Coalition, Washington, 1984-86, Coalition Against Genocide, Chgo., 1978; advocate Suffolk County (N.Y.) Econ. Opportunity Council, 1968-85; candidate Suffolk County Legis., 1975-77; mem. Nat. Black Lay Cath. Caucus, Suffolk County del., 1970—, sec.-treas., 1978-79, Evangelist award, 1982; Black Congl. Caucus oganizer nat. hearings on police brutality; lobbyist Ciminal Justice Braintrust; bd. dirs. Cath. Interracial Council, 1984—; minority adv. com. N.Y. State Office of Mental Health. Recipient awards Service to Christ's Mission St. Martin of Tours, L.I., 1969, Meritorious Service Am. Legion, 1968, Outstanding Service Greenhaven Preson NAACP, 1974, 78, Outstanding Contribution S.C. Human Rights Commn., 1975-80, Community Service Nassau County Black History, 1977, Polit. Leadership Gordon Heights Cultural Assn., 1981, Kuumba Creativity Our Lady Charity Ch., 1975, Civic Activities Cen. L.I. NAACP, 1978, Outstanding Service Union Black Collegians, 1981, Poetess, Pub. Servant, Humanitarian Chi Rho chpt. Omega Psi Phi, 1982, Martin Luther King Lifers' Com. Auburn Prison, 1982, Jupiter Hammond, L.I. Black History Month, 1985, Dedicated Service Nat. Office Black Caths., 1982. Mem. N.Y. State Assn. Human Services. Democrat. Home and Office: 5 Jefferson St Copiague NY 11726

DEMBIAK, DOROTHY ANN, recreational association executive, financial executive; b. Passaic, N.J., Oct. 17, 1946; d. Stanley Dembiak and Florence Czaikoski. Grad. The Kimberley Sch., Montclair, N.J.; B.S., Fairleigh Dickinson U., 1968, B.A. in Edn., 1974. Tchr. cert. N.J. Tchr. reading and math., jr. high sch., 1976-78; staff acct. Melnor Industries, Moonachie, N.J., 1968-75; acctg. rep., office mgr. Sedata Systems, Ft. Lauderdale, Fla., 1979-81; controller Capital America, Ft. Lauderdale, 1981-83; controller Nat. Golf Found., North Palm Beach, Fla., 1983-85; controller, asst. sec. of bd. govs. Evergreen Golf Country Club, 1985—. Mem. Nat. Assn. Accts. Office: Evergreen Country Club 4225 SW Bimini Circle Palm City FL 34990

DEMELLO, BARBARA ALICE, educator; b. Summit, N.J., June 16, 1947; d. Gerald Allen and Elizabeth Alice (Kelly) Larson; m. Richard Joseph DeMello, Sept. 2, 1972. BS, SUNY, Geneseo, 1969; Assoc. in Computer Sci., Newbury Jr. Coll., 1980. Cert. tchr., Mass., N.Y. Elem. tchr. Corfu, N.Y., 1969-71; spl. needs tchr. New Bedford, Mass., 1975—; computer dir. for students and adults at elem. level New Bedford Sch. Dept., 1984—. Dir. sports YWCA, New Bedford, 1978; leader Girl Scouts Am., Dartmouth, Mass., 1983. Mem. NEA, Mass. Tchrs. Assn., New Bedford Educators Assn., South Bedford County Women's Bowling Assn. (bd. dirs. 1980—, sec. 1987—). Roman Catholic. Office: New Bedford Sch Dept County St New Bedford MA 02740

DE MERE-DWYER, LEONA, medical artist; b. Memphis, May 1, 1928; d. Clifton and Leona (McCarthy) De Mere; BA, Rhodes Coll., Memphis, 1949; M.Sc., Memphis State U., 1984; m. John Thomas Dwyer, May 10, 1952; children—John, DeMere, Patrice, Brian, Anne-Clifton DeMere Dwyer, McCarthy-DeMere Dwyer. Med. artist for McCarthy DeMere, Memphis, 1950-80; pres. Aesthetic Med. & Forensic Art, 1984—; speech therapist, Memphis, 1950-82; lic. embalmer, funeral dir., 1981; lectr. on med. art univs., conf., assns.; cons. in prostheses Vocat. Rehab. Services; bereavement counselor. Organizer Ladies of St. Jude, Memphis, 1960; active Brooks Art Gallery League of Memphis; leader Confraternity of Christian Doctrine, St. Louis Cath. Ch., 1966-67; vice dir. Tellico Hist. Found., 1980-80; mem. exec. bd. Chickasaw council Boy Scouts Am.; active Republican campaign coms. Lic. Fedn. Internationale de'Automobile, (internat. car racing), 1972; recipient Disting. Service award Gupton-Jones Coll. Mortuary Sci., 1981; Silver Sons of the Am. Revolution medal, 1985. Mem. Assn. Med. Illustrators, Am. Assn. Med. Assts., Emergency Dept. Nurses Assn., Am. Physicians Nurses Assn., Am. Soc. Plastic and Reconstructive Surgeons Found. (guest mem., cons.), Women in Law (chmn. assos.), FORUM, Nat. Death Edn. Soc., Exec. Women Am., Brandeis U. Women, DAR (1st v.p. regent 1980), UDC (pres. Nathan Bedford Forrest chpt.), Cotton Carnival Assn. (chairperson children's ct. 1968-70), Pi Sigma Eta, Kappa Delta (adv.), Kappa Delta Pi. Clubs: Tennessee, Royal Matron Amaranth (Faith Ct.), Sertoma (1st female mem. Memphis, 1st female life mem. Sertoma Internat.) (Memphis). Contbr. articles to profl. jours. Home: 660 W Suggs Dr Memphis TN 38119

DEMERS, JUDY LEE, university dean, state legislator; b. Grand Forks, N.D., June 27, 1944; d. Robert L. and V. Margaret (Harming) Prosser; m. Donald E. DeMers, Oct. 3, 1964 (div. Oct. 1971); 1 child, Robert M.; m. Joseph M. Murphy, Mar. 5, 1977 (div. Oct. 1983). BS in Nursing, U. N.D., 1966; MEd, U. Wash., 1973, postgrad., 1973-75. Pub. health nurse Govt. D.C., 1966-68, Combined Nursing Service, Mpls., 1968-69; instr. pub. health nursing U. N.D., Grand Forks, 1969-71, assoc. dir. Medex program, 1970-72, dir., family nurse practitioner program, 1977-82, assoc. dir. rural health, 1982-85, dir. undergrad. med. edn., 1982-83, assoc. dean, 1983—; research assoc. U. Wash., Seattle, 1973-76; cons. Health Manpower Devel. Staff, Honolulu, 1975-81, Assn. Physician Asst. Programs, Washington, 1979-82; site visitor, cons. AMA-Com. Allied Health Edn. Accreditation, Chgo., 1979-81. Author: Educating New Health Practitioners, 1976; mem. editorial bd.: P.A. Jour., 1976-78; contbr. articles to profl. jours. Sec., bd. dirs. Valley Family Planning and Edn. Ctr., Grand Forks, N.D., 1982—; exec. com., bd. dirs. Agassiz Health Systems Agy., Grand Forks, 1982-86; mem. N.D. Ho. of Reps., 1982—, N.D. State Daycare Adv. Com., 1983—, Mayor's Adv. Com. on Police Policy, Grand Forks, 1983-85, N.D. State Foster Care Adv. Com., 1985—, N.D. State Hypertension Adv. Com., 1983-85, Gov.'s Com. on DUI and Traffic Safety, 1985—, Statewide Adv. Com. on AIDS, 1985—. Recipient award Alpha Lambda Delta, 1963, Pub. Citizen of Yr. award N.D. chpt. Nat. Assn. Social Workers, 1986; U. Wash. regional med. program service fellow, 1972-73; U. Wash. Kellogg Allied health fellow, 1972. Mem. Am. Nurses Assn., N.D. Nurses Assn. (mem. cabinet on edn. and practice 1982-86, Nurse of Yr. 1983), Am. Pub. Health Assn., Am. Ednl. Research Assn., N.D. Pub. Health Assn., N.D. Mental Health Assn., Assn. for Retarded Citizens, NOW, ACLU, LWV, Pi Lambda Theta, Sigma Theta Tau. Democrat. Home: 1826 Lewis Blvd Grand Forks ND 58201 Office: U ND Sch Medicine 501 Columbia Rd Grand Forks ND 58201

DEMERY, HAZEL GURLEY, nurse; b. Lexington, Tenn., Sept. 20, 1922; d. Marshall Tilliman and Effie (Beecham) Gurley; m. James B. Demery, July 18, 1942 (div. 1973); 1 child, Martha Ann. Student pub. schs., Blytheville, Ark. Head nurse Robinson Clinic, Manila, Ark., 1941-42, Congers Clinic, Lexington, 1942-43, Dickerson Clinic, Hartford, Ky., 1949-50; supt. nurses Blytheville Hosp., 1943-45, chief surg. nurse, 1945-46; office nurse M.H. Moseley, Eddyville, Ky., 1953-59, W.H. England, Grand Rivers, Ky., 1967—; indsl. nurse Reed Crushed Stone, Co., Inc., Grand Rivers, 1972—. Mem. bd. Community Mental Health, Mayfield, Ky., 1975-76, Livington County Hosp., Salem, Ky., 1975-76, Nashville Regional Red Cross Blood Program, 1976-79. Pres. Grand Rivers PTA, 1967-68; chmn. Livingston County Blood Program, 1961—; hon. clk. Ct. of Appeals, 1975; country chmn. Democratic party. Mem. Ch. of Christ. Club: Lake City Homemakers (pres. 1960-61) (Grand Rivers). Lodge: Eastern Star (worthy matron 1958-59). Home: Lake City Grand Rivers KY 42045 Office: Dr WH Englands Clinic Main St Box 158 Grand Rivers KY 42045

DEMETRIADES, DESPINA GUS, real estate executive, writer; b. Gastonia, N.C.; d. Gus George and Athena (Leventis) D.; B.A. in Psychology, Columbia U., 1966; M.A. in Counselor Edn., Appalachian State U., Boone, N.C., 1967. Instr., Lynchburg (Va.) Coll., 1967-69; dir. inservice edn. Gastonia Meml. Hosp., 1970-77; edn. coordinator Catawba/Wateree Health Edn. Consortium, Lancaster, S.C., 1977-78; pres., devel. analyst Profl. Devel. Systems, Gastonia, 1978-82; edn. dir. Wesley Long Community Hosp., Greensboro, N.C., 1982-84; sales/tech. freelance writer, Greensboro, 1984—; real estate appraiser. Mem. Women's Forum of N.C., LWV. Greek Orthodox. Home: 4314 Big Tree Way Greensboro NC 27409 Office: PO Box 18311 Greensboro NC 27419

DEMEZA, KIMBERLY FOX, marketing, public relations executive; b. Miami, Fla., Aug. 15, 1958; d. Elliot Zolman and Janet Elizabeth (Lewis) Fox; M. Mark Kim DeMeza, May 22, 1982. BS in journalism, U. Fla., 1980. Asst. to pub. relations rep. University Computing Co., Dallas, 1980-81; dir. pub. relations March of Dimes, Dallas, 1981-82, James Archer Smith Hosp., Homestead, Fla., 1982-86; dir. mktg. Saint Francis Hosp., Miami Beach, Fla., 1986—. Bd. dirs. S. Dade County unit Am. Cancer Soc., 1985-88; vol. Dade County Assn. for Retarded Citizens, 1982-85; mem. Homestead Civitan Internat., 1983-86; grad. Leadership Miami, 1987. Named Rookie of the Year Am. Cancer Soc., S. Dade County unit, 1986. Bd. dirs. Pub. Relations Soc. Am.; mem. Am. Soc. Hosp. Mktg. and Pub. Relations (cert. mem.), S. Fla. Hosp. Pub. Relations and Mktg. Assn. (pres.), Am. Mktg. Assn., Fla. Hosp. Assn. Pub. Relations and Mktg. Council (bd. dirs.). Democrat. Home: 14231 SW 155 St Miami FL 33177 Office: 250 W 63d St Miami Beach FL 35141

DEMIK, ANITA LORRAINE, executive secretary; b. Aurora, Ill., Oct. 11, 1945; d. Thorsten Oscar and Emily Kristine (Sorensen) Ostergren; m. Robert A. DeMik, Sept. 11, 1965; children—Thor Arnold, Michael James, Todd Arthur. Cert. profl. sec. Legal sec. McDermott, Will & Emery, Chgo., 1977-81; adminstrv. asst. Sch. Social Service, U. Chgo., 1981-82; legal sec., dept. coordinator Kirkland & Ellis, Chgo., 1982-84; legal sec., legal asst. Bell, Boyd & Lloyd, Chgo., 1984—; v.p., sec. Atina, Inc., Park Forest, Ill., 1984-86; exec. sec. Morgan Stanley & Co., Chgo., 1986—. Author papers on secretarial professionalism and ethics. Guest speaker EPA, Chgo., 1984-85; guest instr. Catherine Bus. Coll., Chgo., 1985; speaker Archdiocese Carousel of Learning, Chgo., 1985. Mem. Profl. Secs. Internat. (sec. 1982-83, v.p. 1983-84, pres. 1984-85, membership chmn. 1985-86, Chgo. chpt.; chmn. retirement ctrs. trust ctr., Ill. div., 1986—; del. internat. conv. Toronto 1964, alt. internat. conv. Louisville 1965), Nat. Assn. for Exec. Women. Democrat. Lutheran. Club: Will County Extension (pres. 1972-73) (Beecher, Ill.). Avocations: computers; writing. Home: 439 Homan Ave Park Forest IL 60466 Office: Morgan Stanley & Co Inc 440 S La Salle Chicago IL 60605

DE MILLE, AGNES, choreographer. d. William Churchill and Anna (George) de M.; m. Walter F. Prude, June 14, 1943; 1 son, Jonathan. A.B. cum laude, U. Calif.; Litt.D. (hon.), Mills Coll., 1952, Russell Sage Coll., 1953, Smith Coll., 1954, Western Coll., 1955, Hood Coll., 1957, Northwestern U., 1960, Goucher Coll., 1961, Clark U., 1962, UCLA, 1964, Franklin and Marshall, 1965, Western Mich. U., 1967, Nasson Coll., 1971; L.H.D., Dartmouth Coll., 1974, Duke U., 1975, U. N.C., 1980, NYU, 1981. Dance recitalist U.S., Eng., France, Denmark, 1928-42; choreographer and dancer The Black Crook, 1929; choreographer (film) Romeo and Juliet, 1936; (musicals) Nymph Errant, 1933, Hooray for What, 1937, Oklahoma, 1943, One Touch of Venus, 1943, Bloomer Girl, 1944, Carousel, 1945, Brigadoon, 1947, Gentlemen Prefer Blondes, 1949, Paint Your Wagon, 1951, The Girl in Pink Tights, 1954, Goldilocks, 1958, Juno, 1959, Kwamina, 1961; (ballets) OBeah Black Ritual, 1940, Three Virgins and a Devil, 1942, Drums Sound in Hackensack, 1941, Rodeo, 1942, Tally-Ho, 1944, Fall River Legend, 1948, The Harvest According, 1952, Oklahoma (film), 1955, The Wind in the Mountains, 1965, The Four Mary's, 1965; choreographer, dir. Allegro, 1947; dir. Rape of Lucrecia, 1949, Out of this World, 1950, Come Summer, 1969; choreographer (musical) 110 In the Shade, 1963; head Agnes de Mille Dance Theatre, presented by S. Hurok, 6 mos. tour, 126 cities, 1953-54, Agnes de Mille Heritage Dance Theater, 1973, 74, Conversations About the Dance, 1974, 75, Omnibus lectrs. and ballets, 1956-57; choreographer for Ballet Russe de Monte Carlo, 1942, Royal Winnipeg Ballet, 1972; author: Dance to the Piper, 1952, And Promenade Home, 1958, To A Young Dancer, 1962, The Book of the Dance, 1963, Lizzie Borden Dance of Death, 1968, Dance in America, 1970, Russian Journals, 1970, Speak to Me, Dance with Me, 1974, Where the Wings Grow, 1978, America Dances, 1980, Reprieve, 1981. Contbr. to McCalls, Atlantic Monthly, N.Y. Times mag., Vogue, Good Housekeeping, Esquire, Horizon mags. Recipient N.Y. Critics prize, 1942-46, Donaldson award, 1943-47, Madamoiselle merit award, 1944, Antoinette Perry award, 1947, 62, Lord and Taylor award, 1947, Dancing Masters award of merit, 1950, Dance Mag. award, 1957, Capezio award, 1966, Handel award Mayor N.Y.C., 1976, Kennedy award Pres. U.S., 1980, Commonwealth award in dramatic arts, 1980, Nat. Medal of Arts, 1988; named Woman of Yr. by Am. Newspaper Woman's Guild, 1946, named to Theatre Hall of Fame, 1973; Agnes de Mille Theatre, N.C. Sch. Arts, Winston-Salem named in her honor 1975. Mem. Soc. Stage Dirs. and Choreographers (pres. 1965-66). Office: Harold Ober Assocs 40 E 49th St New York NY 10017 *

DEMILLION, JULIANNE, health fitness trainer, rehabilitation consultant; b. Monessen, Pa., Dec. 20, 1955; d. William Vincent and Enise Mary (Tocci) DeM. B.A., B.S., U. Pitts., 1977; cert. massage therapist Phoenix Therapeutic Massage Coll., 1985. Mgr. program devel. Exclusively Women Spas, Scottsdale, 1977-81; self-employed exercise therapist, Scottsdale, 1981-83, self-employed personal trainer, Scottsdale, 1983—; cons. in field, City of Phoenix, 1981—. Mem. Scottsdale Ctr. for the Arts Assn., 1984. Mem. Am. Massage Therapy Assn., Ariz. Massage Therapy Assn. (sec.-treas. 1986—), Internat. Dance and Exercise Assn., Nat. Assn. Female Execs., Circulo-Systems Ltd., Am. Coll. Sports Medicine.

DEMILT, CELESTE LAUREL WOSCHKE, telecommunications marketing executive; b. Washington, Oct. 3, 1959; d. Ernest Fredrick and Eleonore Laurel (Ulrich) W.; m. Robert Franklin DeMilt Sr., Sept. 17, 1983 (div. 1988); 1 stepchild, Robert Franklin III. BS in Mktg., U. Md., 1981. Fin. planner Suburban Planning Corp Finl., Rockville, Md., 1981; account exec. Chesapeake & Potomoc Telephone Co., Washington, 1981, AT&T Communications, Washington, 1983, Chesapeake & Potomac/Bell Atlantic, Washington, 1985-87; sr. mktg. rep., east coast rep. Am. Telecorp., Inc., Vienna, Va., 1987—. Mem. Am. Mktg. Assn., Nat. Assn. Female Execs., Women in Sales, Women's Sports Fund. Office: Am Telecorp 8300 Boone Blvd 5th Fl Vienna VA 22180

DEMIZIO, JOANNE LENA, health physicist; b. Ft. Bragg, N.C., Oct. 25, 1956; d. Francis B. Greenwald and Lena (Mosca) Beauchamp; m. Steven John DeMizio, May 14, 1983; 1 child, Steven Daniel. BS in Radiol. Physics and Health Sci., Manhattan Coll., 1978; postgrad., N.J. Inst. Tech., 1980, Rutgers U., 1982-83. Assoc. engr. Am. Electric Power, N.Y.C., 1978-83; nuclear analyst Consol. Edison Co., N.Y.C., 1983-87; staff hazardous materials analyst N.Y.C. Dept. Environ. Protection, 1987—. Mem. Am. Nuclear Soc., Nat. Assn. for Female Execs. Republican. Roman Catholic.

DEMLER, LINDA KASS, corporate manager; b. Pocatello, Idaho, Feb. 17, 1954; d. Theodore Edwin and Pauline Therese (Gaudreau) Kass; m. Frederick Russel Demler, Aug. 26, 1976; 1 child, Todd Frederick. B.S. cum laude in Psychology, Pa. State U., 1976. Dining mgr. Holiday Inn, State College, Pa., 1976-77; restaurant mgr. Corner Room, State College, 1977-78; acctg. mgr. Heim, Heckendorn & Bruce, State College, 1978-80; div. mgr. N.Y. Life Ins. Co., N.Y.C., 1980—. Active Republican Nat. Com., Washington, 1985—. Mem. Nat. Assn. Female Execs., Am. Mgmt. Assn., Chi Omega, Psi Chi, Alpha Lambda Delta. Home: 4 Effingham Rd Yardley PA 19067

DEMMING, SHEREE ROOKE, human resources administrator; b. Glens Falls, N.Y., Apr. 29, 1956; d. George and Betty (Phillips) Rooke; m. Bruce M. Demming, May 20, 1978; children: Kristin, Lauren. BA, Purdue U., 1978, MS in Indsl. Relations, 1979. Personnel intern Ross Gear div. TRW, Lafayette, Ind., 1979; personnel intern Indsl. and Energy sector TRW, Cleve., 1980, mgr. human relations Replacement Parts and Internat. Trade div., 1980-83; mgr. human relations Oilwell Cable div. TRW, Lawrence, Kans., 1983—; leader seminars, Kans., 1980—. Contbr. articles to profl. jours. Home: Rt 2 Box 125 Lawrence KS 66046 Office: TRW Oilwell Cable Div PO Box 945 2400 Packer Rd Lawrence KS 66044

DEMONG, PHYLLIS, painter, writer, illustrator; b. Washington, Mar. 3, 1920; d. Frank Elliott and Minne Belle (White) Hickman; m. Francis L. Demong, Mar. 24, 1941; children—Peter, Geoffrey, Thomas, Sarah. B.F.A., Syracuse U., 1940. One woman shows: Wood Mus., Montpelier, Vt., The Munson Gallery, New Haven, Conn., The Peel Gallery, Danby, Vt., Middlebury Coll., Gallery Two, Woodstock, Vt., Munson Gallery, Chatham, Mass., St. Pauls Cathedral, Burlington, Vt.; group shows include: Everson Mus., Syracuse, N.Y., Meml. Gallery, Rochester, N.Y., Roberson Mus. Biennial, Binghamton, N.Y., Stratton (Vt.) Arts Festivals; represented in permanent collections: Munson Williams Proctor Inst., Utica, N.Y., Everson Mus., Marine Midland Trust Co., Syracuse, Cooperstown Art Assn. (N.Y.), Central Presbyn. Ch., Rochester, N.Y., Vt. Fed. Savs., Burlington, Vt. Author, illustrator: Celebearties & Other Bears, 1979; It's A Pig World Out There, 1980; Rare & Undone Saints, 1981; designer: Bakery Lane Soup Bowl, 1978. Recipient Artist of N.Y. Purchase award Munson Williams Proctor Inst., 1966; Purchase award Marine Midland Everson Mus., 1967; George Arents medal Syracuse U., 1974; Vt. Artists 1st prize Norwich U., 1978. Mem. So. Vt. Artists, No. Vt. Artists, Cooperstown N.Y. Art Assn., Associated Artists of Syracuse (Gordon Steele Meml. medal), Provincetown Art Assn. Democrat. Episcopalian. Home: PO Box 70 Middlebury VT 05753

DEMONTIER, PAULETTE LAPOINTE, chemist; b. Milw., Jan. 12, 1948; d. Paul Wilfred and Gladys Marie (Graf) LaPointe; m. Roger Heber DeMontier, June 9, 1969 (dec. June 1986). BS, U. Miami, Coral Gables, Fla., 1970; MS, U. Miami, 1972, PhD, 1985; postgrad., Kennedy-Western U., 1986-87. Lic. clin. chemist, Fla. Lab. asst. TLC Corp. subs. Eastman Kodak, Miami, Fla., 1969-71; lab. supr. Tocci Labs., Inc., Miami, 1971-72; asst. organic chemist Coulter Electronics, Hialeah, Fla., 1972-75; analytical chemist Coulter Diagnostics, Hialeah, 1976-80; research scientist Dade Baxter Travenol, Miami, 1981-86, staff analytical chemist, 1986—; pres., chief chemist, cons. Indsl. Assocs., Miami, 1980—. Patentee chems.; contbr. articles to sci. jours. Task force mem. NOW, Miami, 1986. Recipient Dade Sci. Contbn. Citation Am. Dade County, 1985. Mem. Am. Chem. Soc. (mem. analytical div. 1974—, women chemists com. 1985—), Am. Assn. for Clin. Chemistry (chmn. Fla. sect. 1985-86, membership chmn. 1987), S. Fla. Chromatography Discussion Group. Office: Dade Baxter Travenol PO Box 520672 Miami FL 33152

DEMPSEY, BARBARA JEAN, broadcast producer, consultant; b. Winchester, Mass., June 10, 1953; d. John Thomas and Irene (Geremonte) D. BA cum laude, Adelphi U., 1975. Lic. radiotelephone operator. Producer, host talk show Sta. WVBF-WKOX FM-AM, Boston, 1979-81; news anchor, reporter Sta. WGGB-TV, Springfield, Mass., 1979-80; pub. info. officer Essex County Dist. Atty's Office, Salem, Mass., 1979-80; media coordinator Coalition for Auto Ins. Reform, Boston, 1980-83; producer, news reporter Sta. WTAG-Radio, Worcester, Mass., 1983-84; press sec. Michael Connolly for U.S. Senate, Boston, 1984; mgr., media relations Arnold Pub. Relations, Boston, 1986-87; media, pub. relations cons. Marblehead, Mass., 1985-87; news anchor, reporter Sta. WXLO-FM, Worcester, 1988—; talk show host Sta. WBSM-Radio, New Bedford, 1981-82; regional stringer UPI, Worcester and Boston, 1983-84; instr. seminars in field; free lance writer. Producer: The Collins Report Sta. CATV, Arlington, Mass., 1985-86; host, writer, producer: Cancer Today Sta. CATV, Winchester, 1986. Bd. dirs. Quanapowitt Players, Reading, Mass., 1978-81; press sec. Evelyn Murphy for Lt. Gov. Com., Boston, 1986; press liaison Mass. State Dem. Convention, Springfield, 1986; reporter town election coverage Sta. CATV, Winchester, 1987; active Women's Polit. Caucus, 1987, Marblehead Little Theatre. Mem. The Women's Network, Iota Beta Sigma. Home and Office: PO Box 310 Manchester NH 03102

DEMUTH, NINA LEWIS, chemical air sterilization company executive; b. Benton, Ill., July 14, 1921; d. William Henry and Agnes Clara (Landreth) Lewis; m. Herbert Willard Demuth, Feb. 16, 1947; 1 child, Nina Dale (dec.). Student Nassau Coll., 1976—. With Barbour Co., Inc., St. Louis, 1939-47, v.p., 1943-47; pres. Demuth Co., Garden City, N.Y., 1948—, Demuth Service Corp., Garden City, 1955—, Demuth Devel. Corp., Garden City, 1958. Contbr. articles to profl. publs. Mem. Parenteral Drug Assn. (bd. dirs. 1977-79), Parenteral Drug Assn. Found. for Pharm. Scis. (incorporator 1979, pres. 1979-83, bd. dirs. 1979—, treas. 1984—), Huguenot Soc. Methodist. Office: PO Box 242 Garden City NY 11530

DEMYAN, JEANNE RAUCH, veterinarian; b. Columbia, S.C., Nov. 1, 1951; d. Jacob Elton and Edna Mae (Long) Rauch; divorced. BS with honors, Clemson U., 1972; DVM, U. Ga., 1976. Assoc. veterinarian Johnson McKee Animal Hosp., Salisbury, Md., 1976; zoo veterinarian Riverbanks Zoo, Columbia, S.C., 1976; research assoc. Squibb Inst. Med. Research, New Brunswick, N.J., 1976-78, dir. lab. animal medicine, Princeton, N.J., 1978; owner Travelers Rest (S.C.) Animal Hosp., 1979—; mem. adv. council North Greenville Hosp., Travelers Rest, 1981-83; dancer Greenville Concert Ballet, 1983-84. Mem. AVMA, Greenville Vet. Med. Assn., Am. Holistic Veterinary Med. Assn., Internat. Veterinary Acupuncture Soc., NOW (convenor 1st S.C. chpt. 1971, pres. 1972). Episcopalian. Club: Target Investment (pres. Greenville chpt.). Office: Travelers Rest Animal Hosp 409 Old Buncombe Rd Travelers Rest SC 29690

DENATALE, CAROLE EGAN, lawyer; b. Buffalo, Dec. 10, 1954; d. John Lloyd and Dorothy (Nigro) Egan; m. Richard Grimes DeNatale, Aug. 18, 1979. B.A. magna cum laude, Mt. Holyoke Coll., 1976, J.D., SUNY-Buffalo, 1979. Bar: N.Y. 1980, Ariz. 1980, U.S. Dist. Ct. (so. and ea. dists.) N.Y. 1985. Law clk. Diebold & Millonzi, Buffalo, 1978-79; assoc. John Lloyd Egan, Buffalo, 1979-80, Cates & Roediger, Phoenix, 1980-81, Kuhn, Muller & Bazerman, N.Y.C., 1982-84, Kane, Dalsimer, Kane, Sullivan & Kurucz, Levy, Eisele & Richard, N.Y.C., 1984—. Sarah Williston scholar, Mt. Holyoke Coll., 1973; Mary Lyon Scholar, 1976. Recipient Jessie Goodwin Spaulding Prize, Mt. Holyoke Coll., 1974, Cornelia Catlin Coulter Prize, 1975, Jean Renneisen Toub Prize, 1976. Mem. ABA, N.Y. State Bar Assn., State Bar Ariz., N.Y. Patent, Trademark and Copyright Law Assn., Jr. League, Phi Beta Kappa. Office: Kane Dalsimer Sullivan et al 711 3d Ave 20th Floor New York NY 10017

DENBOW, JOANN ANITA, computer science administrator; b. San Francisco, June 11, 1960; d. Richard Eugene and Tomiko (Kawamoto) D.; m. Dante Osvaldo Servin, June 18, 1978 (div. Dec. 1980); 1 child, Dante II. AS, San Diego City Coll., 1985. Legal dept. analyst Imperial Savs. Assn., San Diego, 1985-86; project control coordinator ICA Service Corp., San Diego, 1986—. Mem. San Diego Legal Sec. Assn., Nat. Assn. Female Execs. Republican. Baptist. Office: ICA Service Corp 8807 Complex Dr San Diego CA 92123

DEN BRABER, JOYCE ELAINE, controller, accountant; b. LaPorte, Ind., July 21, 1947; d. Hyle K. and Virginia M. (Sharp) Claflin; m. John C. Den Braber, Jan. 6, 1968; 1 child, Todd J. BS in Acctg., Mich. State U., 1975; ABA, Stonier Grad. Sch. of Banking, U. Del., 1986. CPA, Ind., Mich. Sr. acct. Bristol Leisenring and Co., Coldwater, Mich., 1975-79; acct., audit mgr. Guy Wiley Jr. and Co., Bloomington, Ind., 1979-82; v.p., controller Monroe County Bank, Bloomington, 1982—, dir., 1983—; sec., treas. Monroe Bancorp, Bloomington, 1984—, also bd. dirs. Author: Bus. and Tax Planning Quar., 1987. Active Bloomington Progress Council, 1984—; mem. fin. com. Bloomington Hosp., 1985—, adv. council, 1985—; mem. fin. com. First United Meth. Ch., 1985—; sec., treas. Bloomington Downtown Parking Devel. Corp., 1985. Mem. Nat. Assn. Accts. (mem. of yr. 1982, 84), Am. Inst. CPA's, Mich. Assn. CPA's, Ind. Assn. CPA's. Office: Monroe County Bank 210 E Kirkwood Ave Bloomington IN 47401

DENCH-CALLOWAY, GWENDOLYN ETHEL, financial director; b. Phila., June 30, 1940; d. Richard and Mary Frances (Jackson) Smith; m. Eustice V. Dench, Mar 4, 1970 (div. Sept. 1975); 1 child, Richard J.; m. James M. Calloway, Nov. 16, 1981. B in Acctg., Howard U., 1961. Fin. cons. Govt. Virgin Islands, St. Thomas, 1969-76, Office Criminal Justice, Washington, 1976-78; fin. officer Inner Voices, Washington, 1978-83; sr. cons. Arawalk Cons., Arlington, Va., 1982-83, sr. analyst, 1983-84; asst. dir. fin. Community Coll. Balt., 1983-84, asst. dir. financing, 1984-85; self employed fin. cons. Silver Springs, Md., 1985-86, fin. dir. DC Housing Fin. Agy., Washington, 1986—. Mem. Nat. Hook Up of Black Women, NAACP. Lodge: Lions (dir. Ebony Fashion Show, 1973-76, Citizens award 1976). Home: 809 Caddington Ave Silver Spring MD 20901 Office: 1401 New York Ave NW Washington DC 20005

DENDA, AKEMI, marketing executive; b. Niigata, Japan, Feb. 20, 1959; came to U.S., 1977; d. Hiroshi and Eiko (Maeda) Denda; m. Thomas George Wetherington, Aug. 9, 1986. AA, Bee County Coll., 1979; BA, George Washington U., 1981, MBA, 1984. Congl. intern Congressman Henry B. Gonzalez, Washington, 1980, Senator Edward Kennedy, Washington, 1981; adminstrv. asst. IBM, Fujisawa, Japan, 1981, lab. asst., 1982; congl. fellow Senator Frank Murkowski, Washington, 1983; research assoc. Tech. Analysis Group, Washington, 1983-84; asst. to v.p. Motorola Inc., Washington, 1984-85, analyst internat. trade, 1985-87; planner internat. markets AT&T, Basking Ridge, N.J., 1987—; prof. bus. George Mason U., Fairfax, Va., 1987. Active tele-campaign Reagan for Pres. of U.S., Washington, 1984; bd. dirs. George Washington U. Sch. Bus., Washington, 1985. Recipient award Tex. Phi Theta Kappa. Mem. George Washington U. Alumni Assn. (com. chmn. 1986). Episcopalian. Office: AT&T PO Box 7000 Basking Ridge NJ 07920

DENEAULT, MAUREEN ISDEPSKI, art educator, puppeteer; b. Acushnet, Mass., Mar. 4, 1942; d. Frank James and Mary Elizabeth (Soltys) Isdepski; m. Louis A.L. Deneault, June 13, 1970; children: Ethan Albert Nathan, Sarah Elaine Alexandra. B.F.A., Southeastern Mass. U., 1969, M.F.A., 1971; M.Ed., Bridgewater State Coll., 1972, postgrad., 1982—. Cert. spl. subject tchr. (art), librarian. Library aide, Southeastern Mass. U., North Dartmouth, 1968-69, teaching asst. graphic arts, 1969-71; tech. illustrator Raytheon, Inc., Newport, R.I., 1969; graphic designer MI Studio Graphics, New Bedford, Mass., 1969—; sch. librarian Joseph H. Martin Sch., Taunton Pub. Schs., East Taunton, Mass., 1973-81, set designer music dept., 1975-81, elem. art tchr. Taunton Pub. Schs., Taunton, Mass., 1983—; dir., puppeteer, puppet designer, instr. Puppetree Playhouse, New Bedford, 1981—; teaching asst. library sci. Bridgewater State Coll. (Mass.), 1982-83; instr. art edn. Southeastern Mass. U., 1986; set designer Taunton Children's Theatre, 1979; instr. puppetry, Southeastern Mass. U., 1982. Author/illustrator: Regenesis: 1971, Wandering..., 1969, Lowicz-Style Wedding Design, 1973 (spl. award), Nicolas Copernicus, 1973 (hon. mention); instructional manuals: Puppetry Titles: The Basic Mouth Puppet, The Basic Hand Puppet, 1981, The Priest's Vestments, 1983, The Bishop's Vestments, 1984, The Deacon's Vestments, 1984. Advt. designer. co-chmn. Internat. Fair segment of Whaling City Festival, New Bedford, 1973. City of New Bedford scholar, 1965-69. Mem. ALA, Puppeteers Am., New Eng. Ednl. Media Assn., EEA, Mass. Tchrs. Assn., Taunton Educators Assn., Nat. Art Edn. Assn. Episcopalian. Club: Polish Women's Bus. and Profl. rec. sec. New Bedford 1972-73). Home and Office: 87 Harvard St New Bedford MA 02746

DENES, MAGDA, psychologist. came to U.S., 1950; d. Gyula and Margaret (Indig) D.; m. Michel Radomisli, May 1963 (div. Jan. 1975); children: Gregory John, Timothy Evan. BA, CCNY, 1956; MA, Boston U., 1958; PhD, Yeshiva U., 1961; cert. psychoanalysis, psychotherapy, NYU, 1964. Lic. psychologist, N.Y. Pvt. practice psychoanalysis, psychotherapy N.Y.C., 1961—; clin. prof. supr. tng. analyst Inst. Psychol. Studies Adelphi U., Garden City, 1969—, Inst. Advanced Psychol. Studies, 1970—; sr. cons. VA, N.Y.C., 1971-73; assoc. clin. prof. supr. and tng. analyst NYU, N.Y.C., 1972—; cons. ABC-TV FYI Pub. Service program, 1980-84; mem. faculty, supr. dept. psychiatry Mt. Sinai Sch. Medicine, N.Y.C., 1981—. Author: In Necessity and Sorrow: Life and Death in an Abortion Hospital, 1976; contbr. articles to profl. jours., newspapers and mags. Fellow Am. Psychol. Assn. (various coms.); mem. N.Y. Soc. Clin. Psychologists (pres. 1978-79), N.Y. State Psychol. Assn. (pres. 1986-87). Club: Williams Coll. Home: 40 E 84th St New York NY 10028 Office: 125 E 87th St New York NY 10128

DENHARTIGH, CARLA RUTH, accountant; b. Wauwautosa, Wis., June 17, 1952; d. Henry Paul and Marjorie Ruth (Eye) D. Student, U. Wis.-Parkside, Kenosha, 1970-72; BBA, U. Wis., Whitewater, 1974. CPA, Wis. Staff acct. Hammill & Co., Racine, Wis., 1974-84; audit mgr. Clifton, Gunderson & Co., Racine, 1984—; bd. dirs. Career Industries Inc., Racine. Trustee Atonement Luth. Ch., Racine, 1980-84; tchr. Gateway Tech. Inst., Kenosha, 1978. Mem. Am. Inst. CPA's, Wis. Inst. CPA's (health and social services com. 1987—, various coms. 1979-86), AAUW, Racine Bus. and Profl. Women (2d v.p.). Office: Clifton Gunderson & Co 222 Main St Suite 200 Racine WI 53403

DENINNIS, MICHELE, automobile company specialist; b. Rochester, N.Y., Apr. 15, 1962; d. Antonio and Mary (Amato) DeN. A in Secretarial Studies, Bryant & Stratton Bus. Inst., 1982. Personnel specialist in employee devel. and tng. Rochester (N.Y.) Products div. Gen. Motors Corp., 1981—. Democrat. Roman Catholic. Home: 9 Wyndover Rd Rochester NY 14616

DENIO, LENA SUE, medical administrator; b. Martins Ferry, Ohio, June 7, 1955; d. William Harold and Geraldine E. (Long) Carpenter; children: Matthew, Benjamin, Andrew. BS in Allied Health Professions, Ohio State U., 1977. Med. technologist clin. labs. Ohio State U., Columbus, 1976-80, research assoc. neurology dept., 1986-87, program mgr. neurology dept., 1987—; med. technologist Internal Medicine Assn., San Diego, 1980-81, Sacred Heart Gen. Hosp., Chester, Pa., 1981-82; supr. lab. Wannamaker & Pritchard, Charleston, S.C., 1983-86. Contbr. articles to profl. jours., 1985—. Mem. Am. Soc. Clin. Pathologists (cert.), Am. Acad. Neurology, Am. Epilepsy Soc., Assocs. Clin. Pharmacology (publs. com. 1986—), Nat. Assn. Female Execs., Nat. Orgn. Mothers of Twins, (grants com. 1987), Charleston Mothers of Twins (pres. 1986-87). Republican. Methodist. Home: 1590 Northam Rd Columbus OH 43221

DENISON, KATIE CLARY, nurse, consultant; b. Helena, Ark., June 25, 1948; d. Joseph William Denison and Martha (Williams) Ragsdale. BS in Nursing, U. Tenn., Memphis, 1971; MBA, U. Denver, 1984. RN. RN City of Memphis Hosp., 1971-76; cardiovascular nurse Surg. Group for Thoracic and Cardiovascular Diseases, Memphis, 1976-80, Drs. Elliott & Halseth, P.C., Denver, 1980-82; mktg. dir., grad. bus. programs U. Denver Sch. Bus. and Pub. Mgmt., 1984-86; pvt. practice cons. Denver, 1984—; rep. Grad. Mgmt. Admissions Council. Mem. Am. Assn. Critical Care Nurses.

DENKER, BERYL SYLVESTER, controller; b. Boston, Aug. 2, 1938; d. Arthur F. and Catherine B. (MacMillan) Sylvester; m. James M. Denker, Sept. 6, 1958; children: Karen, Jeffrey. BS in Humanities and Math., MIT, 1960; postgrad. in Acctg. and Fin., Northeastern U., Boston, 1978-83. Project engr. D.S. Kennedy Co., Cohasset, Mass., 1958-60, Antenna Systems, Inc., Hingham, Mass., 1960-63; asst. treas. Nutron Corp., Hingham, 1968-83; controller, treas. Blake Films, Inc., Boston, 1983—. Ednl. counselor MIT Alumni Council, Cambridge, Mass., 1982—. Office: Blake Films Inc 160 Southampton St Rear Boston MA 02118

DENMEAD, DORIS LOUISE, medical facility administrator; b. N.Y.C., Feb. 17, 1933; d. Robert William and Florence Mary (Hunt) Tobin; m. James Gordon, Oct. 19, 1958; 1 child, Linda Mary. BBA, St. John's U., N.Y.C., 1954; MBA, Columbia U., 1975. Sr. pub. acct. Harris, Kerr, Foster and Co., N.Y.C., 1959-63; asst. controller John Hay Whitney, N.Y.C., 1963-71; instr. acctg. Drake Coll., Plainfield, N.J., 1971-75; fin. analyst Gen. Learning Corp., Morristown, N.J., 1975-76; internal fiscal auditor Seton Hall U., South Orange, N.J., 1976-77; controller Am. Cancer Soc., Union, N.J., 1978-80, Bonnie Brae Sch. for Spl. Boys, Millington, N.J., 1980-82; fiscal coordinator U. Medicine and Dentistry of N.J., Piscataway, N.J., 1982—. Nat. Assn. Female Execs., Accts. for Pub. Interest, Soc. Bus. and Profl. Women (pres. Somerset N.J. chpt. 1974-75, 77-78) Am. Legion Aux (v.p. Warren, N.J. club 1986-87). Democrat. Roman Catholic. Home: 33 Mountain Ave Warren NJ 07060 Office: U Medicine and Dentistry Robert Wood Johnson Med Sch 675 Hoes Ln Piscataway NJ 08854

DENMON, MELANIE PATRICIA, insurance executive; b. Springhill, La., Jan. 22, 1954; d. Thomas Winton and Marjorie Loyce (Crisp) D. BA in Speech Pathology and Audiology, U. Southwestern La., 1976. Mgr. ins. brokerage, cons., agy. supr. Charles D. Bernard Agy., Ltd./Transamerica Life Ins. Services, Lafayette, La., 1979—. Col. Staff of Gov. David C. Treen, Baton Rouge, 1980; mem. Acadiana Arts Council, Lafayette Ballet Co. Mem. Nat. Assn. Female Exec., Nat. Assn. Life Underwriters (mem. women life underwriters conf.), Acadiana Assn. Life Underwriters of Nat. Assn. Life Underwriters, Lafayette Fine Arts Assn.,. Republican. Methodist. Home: 200 Lodge Dr Unit #110 Lafayette LA 70506 Office: Charles D Bernard Agy Ltd 102 Jomela Dr Lafayette LA 70503

DENNEE, JEAN MARGARET, educator; b. Stratford, Wis., Aug. 27, 1946; d. Myron J. and Eleanore B. (Strigel) D. BS, U. Wis., Whitewater, 1968, MS in Teaching, 1974; EdD, Utah State U., Logan, 1981. Bus. instr. Milw. Pub. Schs., 1968-84; asst. prof. Western Carolina U., Cullowhee, N.C., 1984-87, Eastern Ill. U., Charleston, 1987—; bus. instr. Milw. Area Tech. Coll., 1977-78. Contbr. articles to profl. jours. Mem. Nat. Bus. Edn. Assn., N.C. Bus. Edn. Assn. (audit com. 1987), Milw. Tchrs. Edn. Assn. (speaker 1981), Office Tech. Mgmt. Assn. (speaker Milw. area 1981, bd. dirs. 1984), Assn. Info. Systems Profls., Assn. Suprs. and Curriculum Devel., Assn. Ednl. Communications Devel. (instrnl. com. 1987). Republican. Roman Catholic. Office: Eastern Ill U Coll Edn Charleston IL 61920

DENNER, VALERIE LOUISE DAINO, nurse; b. N.Y.C., July 21, 1952; d. Albert and Violet Louise (Acanfora) Daino; m. Alan Matthew Denner, May 29, 1976; children: Tami Danielle, Robert Albert. Diploma in nursing YWCA/Bklyn.-Cumberland Med. Ctr., 1972; AS, Genesee Community Coll., 1975; BA, SUNY-Albany, 1980. Staff nurse Albany Med. Ctr., N.Y., 1972-73, Hosp. of St. Raphael, New Haven, 1976-77; nursing instr. Quinnipeac Coll., Hamden, Conn., 1977-79; nurse Med-Staff, Boston, 1979-81; br. adminstr. Nurse World, Inc./Home Care Am. div. of Cosmopolitan Care Corp. Amex, Orlando, 1981-88, corp. v.p., 1985-86; pres., founder Sun Shine Temporaries, 1988—; mgmt. cons. Cosmopolitan Care Corp./Norell Health Care, 1988—; mem. med. adv. bd. Hospice of Cen. Fla., Orlando, 1984-85, Kimberly Clark Corp., Balt., 1986—; lectr. LPN Assn. of Orlando, 1986; founder, ltd. ptnr. Home Med. Services, 1984; founder, v.p. B. Daino Constrn., 1983, Investiclaim, Inc., 1986; founder, pres. Respiratory Therapy Inc., 1985; cons. Orlando Physicians Network Inc., 1987-88. Asst. producer CBS 60 Minutes program, Sharon, Mass., 1980-81; author: How to Choose Home Health Care Services, 1986. Founder Hosp. of St. Raphael Physician Spouse Assn., 1976-79; pres., founder Citizens Action Group for Protection of Buyers of Newly Constructed Homes, 1979-81. Mem. Orlando C. of C., Am. Nurses Assn., Fla. Nurses Assn. (del. 1983), Nat. Assn. Female Execs., Nat. Assn. for Notary Pubs., Orange County Med. Aux. Republican. Avocations: designing and building houses; numismatics; skiing; swimming. Home: 9162 Kilgore Rd Orlando FL 32819 Office: Sun Shine Temporaries LC 7380 Sand Lake Rd Suite 541 Orlando FL 32819

DENNICK, ROBIN LEE, producer; b. Greensburg, Pa., May 12, 1955; d. Clinton William and Olga Evelyn (Backstrom) D. BA in Theater and Film, Pa. State U., 1976. Dir. WKEF-TV, Dayton, Ohio, 1980-84; producer, dir. Greater Dayton Pub. TV, Inc., 1984—. Mem. Five Oaks Neighborhood Improvement Assn., 1984—; staff mem. Re-elect Mayor Paul Leonard Com., Dayton, 1985. Mem. Women in Communications Inc., Columbus, Dayton, Cin. Chpt. Nat. Acad. TV Arts and Scis. (bd. govs.). Democratic. Methodist. Home: 123 Rockwood Ave Dayton OH 45405 Office: WPTD-TV 2563 S Gettsburg Ave Dayton OH 45418

DENNING, SUSAN KAY, social services administrator; b. Rapid City, S.D., May 26, 1952; d. Glenn Jordan and Margaret Jean (Gehres) D. BA, Kent State U., 1979. Cert. peace officer instr., Ohio. Correctional counselor Portage County Juvenile Group Home Court, Ravenna, Ohio, 1979, program coordinator, 1979-80, grantwriter, interim dir., 1980; emergency services coordinator Drug Edn. and Crisis Intervention Ctr., Kent, Ohio, 1980-86; exec. dir. Cleve. Rape Crisis Ctr., 1986—, also bd. dirs.; bd. dirs. Ohio Council Info. and Referral Providers, Columbus, Ohio, 1983-84, West Side Women's Ctr., Cleve., 1986—; mem. exec. com. Council Health and Social Agencies, Portage County, 1983-85. Co-author: self-evaluation instrument for crisis intervention ctrs. and info. and referral agencies, 1986. Recipient Ohio Drug Studies Inst. scholarship Drug Edn. and Crisis Intervention Ctr., Kent, 1978, Hall of Fame award Drug Edn. and Crisis Intervention Ctr., 1980. MEM. NOW, Nat. Abortion Rights Action League, Ohio Abortion Rights Action League, Cleve. Abortion Rights Action League, Ohio Coalition Against Sexual Assault, Ohio Citizens Council, Ohio Council Fund Raising Execs., Nat. Coalition Against Sexual Assault. Democrat. Unitarian. Office: Cleve Rape Crisis Ctr 3101 Euclid Ave Suite 711 Cleveland OH 44115

DENNIS, BARBARA WALDRON, psychiatric social worker, educator; b. Bklyn., Nov. 9, 1945; d. Joseph Grove and Ruth Delilah (Sanford) Waldron; 1 child, Justin Grove. BA in Psychology, U. S.C., 1968, MSW, 1972. Social worker Assoc. Social Agys., Columbia, S.C., 1969-70, Family Service Assn., Columbia, 1972-74; clin. social worker William S. Hall Psychiatric Inst., Columbia, 1974-77; clin. social worker, supr. S.C. State Hosp., Columbia, 1977-81, dir. social work admission unit, 1981-85; dir. social work, activity therapies and edn. Charter Pines Hosp., Charlotte, N.C., 1985-87, dir. partial hospitalization and counseling ctrs., 1987—. Mem. dist. steering com. South Piedmont, 1987—. Mem. Nat. Assn. Social Workers (bd. dirs. 1977-79, 1987—), Acad. Cert. Social Workers (mem. exec. com.), Epsilon Sigma Alpha (pres. alpha alpha chpt. 1980). Democrat. Club: Altrusa (Charlotte). Home: 6928 Old Post Rd Charlotte NC 28212 Office: Charter Pines Hosp 3621 Randolph Rd Charlotte NC 28211

DENNIS, DONNA, sculptor; b. Springfield, Ohio, 1942. One-person exhbns. include: Hotels, West Broadway Gallery, N.Y.C., 1973, Donna Dennis, Wilcox Gallery, Swarthmore Coll., Pa., 1974, Subway Stations and Tourist Cabins, Holly Solomon Gallery, N.Y.C., 1976, City Station and Country Stops, JFK Ctr. Performing Arts, Washington, 1977, Maquettes and Drawings, Adler Gallery, Los Angeles, 1978, Donna Dennis, Holly Solomon Gallery, N.Y.C., 1978, Three Sculptures by Donna Dennis, Contemporary Arts Ctr., Cin., 1979, Donna Dennis, Sullivant Gallery, Ohio State U., Columbus, 1980, Drawings and Maquettes, Holly Solomon Gallery, N.Y.C., 1980, N.Y. and N.J., Holly Solomon Gallery, 1980, Maquettes and Drawings, Locus Solus Gallery, Genoa, Italy, 1981, Mad River Tunnel, Entrance and Exit, Dayton, 1981, Holly Solomon Gallery, N.Y.C., 1983, Abe Adler Gallery, Los Angeles, 1983, Moccasin Creek Cabins, Outdoor Installation, Moccasin Creek, Aberdeen, S.D., 1983, Night Stops, Neuberger Mus. SUNY-Purchase, 1985, Deep Stas., U. Mass.-Amherst, 1985, Deep Sta., Bklyn. Mus., 1987, 26 Bars, Richard Green Gallery, N.Y.C., 1987; group exhbns. include: numerous galleries, N.Y.C., 1972-75, most recent: Venice Bienale, Italy, 1984, numerous others; set designer: Midsummer's Night Dream, 1973; TV Interviews: Gulliver's Travels series, 1979, CBS Cable Network, 1981, Manhattan Cable TV, 1986. Pub. service grantee N.Y. State Creative Artists, 1975, 81, Am. Acad. and Inst. Arts and Letters grantee, 1984; N.Y. Found. Arts, 1985; fellow NEA, 1977, 80, Guggenheim Found., 1979. Address: 131 Duane St New York NY 10013

DENNIS, HELEN MARION, gerontologist, educator; b. Lansdale, Pa., Aug. 27, 1940; d. Eric and Hedy (Gruenberg) Gutman; m. Lloyd B. Dennis, Dec. 1, 1963; children: Lauren, Susan. BA, Pa. State U., 1962; Ma, Calif. State U., Long Beach, 1976. Asst. coordinator data analysis George Washington U., Washington, 1965-69; dir. project, research assoc., lctr. Andrus Gerontology Ctr. U. So. Calif., Los Angeles, 1976—. Editor: Retirement Preparation, 1984, Fourteen Steps in Managing an Aging Work Force, 1988; contbg. author books on aging; mem. editorial bd. Retirement Planning Jour., 1984—. Mem. exec. bd., trustee Temple Menorah, Redondo Beach, Calif., 1981-85; mem. exec. bd. Los Angeles Council Careers Older Americans, 1985—; mem. adv. bd. Project Reinvest, Coro Found., Los Angeles, 1985. Mem. Internat. Soc. Pre-Retirement Planners (nat. pres. 1986-87, pres. So. Calif. chpt. 1983-85), Am. Soc. Aging, Gerontol. Soc. Am. Home: 347 Via el Chico Redondo Beach CA 90277 Office: U So Calif Andrus Gerontology Ctr Los Angeles CA 90089

DENNIS, JUANITA, microbiologist; b. New Orleans, June 2, 1929; d. Lawrence Alphonse and Brunetta (Williams) Dennis; B.A., Dillard U., 1951; Cert. in Med. Tech., U. Calif., San Francisco, 1954; Med. technologist Kaiser Found. Hosp., Oakland, Calif., 1954-55; microbiologist virology Viral and Rickettsial Diseases Lab., State Dept. Health Services, Berkeley, Calif., 1955—, supr., 1981—. Mem. Am. Soc. Microbiology, No. Calif. Assn. Am. Soc. Microbiologists, No. Calif. Assn. Public Health Microbiologists, Profl. Photographers of Am., Inventors of Calif. Contbr. articles to profl. jours. Patentee in field. Home: 1225 Derby St Berkeley CA 94702 Office: 2151 Berkeley Way Berkeley CA 94704

DENNIS, LYNETTE COLLEEN, contract administrator; b. Des Moines, Aug. 27, 1946; d. Benjamin W. and Vernette L. (Ronnenberg) D.; children: Eric Marshall, Jason Robert; m. Barry C. Myers, Oct. 17, 1986. B.S., N.W. Mo. State U., 1968; M.A., Antioch Sch. Law, Washington, 1985. Notary public. Ct. services Fairfax County sheriff, Va., 1978-80; adminstrv. mgr. Tech. Applications, Falls Church, Va., 1980-81; contract adminstr. Advanced Tech., Reston, Va., 1981-83; sr. contract analyst Maxfield Assocs. Ltd., Arlington, Va., 1983-85; sr. contract planner Wheeler Industries, Arlington, 1985-86; program mgr., Integrated Systems Analysts, 1986—. Adminstr., Glenside Counseling Ctr., Glendale Heights, Ill., 1976-77; proprietress Red Bank Farm, Charlottesville, Va. Mem. Profl. Women's Network, AAUW. Avocations: furniture and house restoration (owner, restorer Red Bank Farm, Fork Union, Va.), investments. Home: Rt 1 Box 48A Fork Union VA 23055

DENNIS, ROBBIE SMAGULA, sales promotion and advertising manager; b. Dover, Del., Oct. 15, 1957; d. Thomas David and Billie Jo (Talkington) Smagula; m. Mark Steven Dennis, May 26, 1979 (div. May 1982); 1 child, Gregory Steven. BS in Marine Biology, Tex. A&M U., 1978. Tech. writer Tex. Trans. Inst., College Station, Tex., 1978-80; documentation coordinator Genentech, Inc., South San Francisco, Calif., 1980-82; sr. tech. writer Cen. & South West Services, Inc., Dallas, 1982-88; sales promotion mgr. Computer Assocs. (formerly UCCEL Corp.), Dallas, 1988; with corp. communications J. Driscoll & Assocs., Dallas, 1988—; tech. cons., editor Tex. Trans. Inst. TOTSEA Jour., 1979-80. Mem. Soc. Tech. Communication (Best of Show and Excellence Achievement award 1985, 86), Internat. Assn. Bus. Communicators, Nat. Assn. Female Execs. Home: 9941 Miller Rd #1060 Dallas TX 75238 Office: J Driscoll & Assocs 15851 Dallas Pkwy Dallas TX 75248

DENNIS, SHARON J., social service administrator; b. York, Pa., Apr. 22, 1948; d. Paul F. and Florence A. (Macheski) Woolridge; m. Richard A. Dennis Jr., June 19, 1969; children: Jessica Rae, Brooke Alexis. BA in Theatre and Speech Edn., Coll. Artesia, 1970; MA in Counseling, Ball State U., Muncie, Ind., 1980. Service rep. Mountain States Telephone, Albuquerque, 1970-72; field registrar U. Md. European Div., Landstuhl, Fed. Republic Germany, 1978-79; asst. field dir. ARC, Landstuhl, 1979-80; asst. dir. family service ARC, Washington, 1981-84; asst. sta. mgr. ARC, Alameda Naval Air Sta., 1985-86; dir. emergency services ARC, El Paso, Tex., 1986—. Loaned exec. United Way, Washington, 1983-84, El Paso, 1986-87, 87-88, active loaned exec. alumni assn., El Paso, 1986—; chairperson adv. bd. Montgomery County Mental Health Assn., Olney, Md., 1983-84; scholarship chairperson Bus. and Profl. Women's Club, Olney, 1983-84; active health service auxiliary William Beaumont Hosp. Mem. Am. Bus. Women's Assn. (v.p.), Nat. Assn. Female Execs. Democrat. Home: 11268 Signal Ridge El Paso TX 79936 Office: ARC 9211 Montana El Paso TX 79925

DENNISTON, MARJORIE MCGEORGE, educator; b. Coraopolis, Pa., Mar. 21, 1913; d. Chauncey Kirk and Elsie (George) McGeorge; m. Delbert Dicks Denniston, Dec. 25, 1942 (dec. 1973); 1 child, Robert Bruce. Student Ohio U., 1931-33; B.A., Westminster Coll., 1936; postgrad. U. Kans., 1959, Western Ill. U., 1962, 64. Elem. tchr. county schs., West Pittsburg, Pa., 1936-42, New Castle Sch. System, Pa., 1942, 51-78; vol. aid Pa. Assn. Retarded Children, Jameson Hosp., Law County Home, 1983—. Mem. AAUW, LWV (bd. dirs. New Castle 1986—), Delta Kappa Gamma. Republican. Presbyterian (trustee ch., New Castle, 1986—). Clubs: College (pres. 1987—), Woman's (parliamentarian Lawrence County fedn. 1984—, sec. 1986—). Avocations: photography, coin and rock collecting, volunteering, book reviewing, travel. Home: 331 Laurel Blvd New Castle PA 16101

DENNISTON, PAMELA BOGGS, organizational development consultant; b. San Diego, Feb. 15, 1948; d. Warren Leo and Edna Mae (Hippensteel) Boggs; m. John Henry Cynkar, July 26, 1969 (div. 1973); m. Warren Kent Denniston Jr., Mar. 20, 1980; step children—Julie, Warren, Edward, Scott. AA, Coll. DuPage, 1984; BA in Applied Behavioral Sci., Nat. Coll. Edn., 1985; MA, Loyola U., 1987. Sales cons. ARA Services, Des Plaines, Ill., 1977-78; regional sales mgr. Canteen Corp., Chgo., 1978-79; nat. mktg. mgr. Borg-Warner Leasing, Schaumburg, Ill., 1979-81; owner, cons. Adv. Mgmt. Systems, Downers Grove, Ill., 1981-86; ptnr. Eating Disorders Treatment Ctr., 1986-87; pres. Aretê Inc., 1987—; owner, mgr. Boggs Homemade Ice Cream Shoppe, Downers Grove, 1980-86; pres. Aretê, Inc., Naperville, Ill., 1987—; cons. Downers Grove C. of C., 1981-87; mem. planning Commn. Village of Downers Grove, 1984-86; vol. Indian Boundary YMCA, Downers Grove. Mem. Naperville C. of C. Club: Soroptomist. Avocations: travel; sailing; camping; hiking. Home: 805 Biltmore Naperville IL 60540 Office: Aretê 1 Naperville Plaza Naperville IL 60540

DENNO, ZETTA LEE, social services administrator; b. Pueblo, Colo., Apr. 22, 1943; d. Clarence Loyd P. and Myrtle Louise (McFerren) Bewley; m. Robert E. Everhart, Feb. 13, 1965 (div. 1975); children—Tod Alan, Shelly Anne, Karen Marie; m. Roy Joseph Denno, Aug. 12, 1977; stepchildren—Roy Scott, Randy Michael. Student Columbia Pacific U. Youth dir. Rochester YWCA, N.Y., 1972-81; pres. Parents Without Ptnrs., chpt., 1975-76; program coordinator Regional Parents Without Ptnrs., 1976-77; youth employment specialist Genesee Settlement House, Rochester, 1981-82, family services coordinator, 1982—. Bd. dirs. Twelve Corners Day Care Ctr., Rochester, 1978—, Parents Anonymous of Rochester, 1978-86; co-chmn. adv. com. Monroe County Blue Cross, 1986-87, vol. counselor Health Assn., 1987—. Mem. Nat. Assn. Female Execs., Nat. Assn. Edn. Young Children, Internat. Platform Assn. Methodist. Club: Altrusa. Home: 930 Garden Ln Webster NY 14580 Office: Genesee Settlement House Inc 10 Dake St Rochester NY 14605

DENNY, BONNIE ELIZABETH, banker; b. Shelby County, Ind., May 16, 1935; d. James Albert and Valeria Ethel (Gregory) Kelley; student public schs.; m. Billy Denny, Sept. 25, 1953. With State Bank of Waldron (Ind.), 1953-85, asst. cashier, 1974-78, asst. v.p., 1978-85; asst. v.p. Central Ind. Bank N.A., 1985-87. Democrat. Baptist. Home: Box 92 Waldron IN 46182 Office: Box 7 Waldron IN 46182

DENNY, JUDITH ANN, lawyer; b. Lamar, Mo., Sept. 18, 1946; d. Lee Livingston and Genevieve Adelpha (Falke) D.; BA, La. Tech. U., 1968; JD, George Washington U., 1972; m. Thomas M. Lenard, May 29, 1976; children: Julia Lee, Michael William. Bar: D.C. 1973. Asst. spl. prosecutor Watergate Spl. Prosecution Office, Washington, 1973-75; pros. atty. U.S. Dept. Justice, 1975-78; dir. div. compliance U.S. Office Edn., HEW, 1978-80; acting asst. insp. gen. for investigations U.S. Dept. Edn., 1980; dep. dir. policy and compliance, office of revenue sharing U.S. Dept. Treasury, Washington, 1980-83, counselor to gen. counsel, 1983—. Mem. D.C. Bar Assn. Home: 3214 Porter St NW Washington DC 20008 Office: 15th & Pennsylvania Ave NW Washington DC 20220

DENNY, JULIE, marketing executive; b. N.Y.C., Apr. 19, 1940; d. Thomas Gwinn and Mayme Lillian (Tatum) D.; m. Harold Frank Clark, July 7, 1962; children: Tobin Denny, Gregor Tatum. BA, Mt. Holyoke Coll., 1962. Mktg. mgr. Dow Jones Info. Services, Princeton, N.J., 1982-86; mgr. mktg. sales McGraw-Hill Info. Network, N.Y.C., 1986—; founding bd. dirs. The Audiotex Group, 1986—. Contbr. articles to profl. jours. Mem. Rent Control Commn., Princeton, 1979; trustee Trinity Counseling Service, Princeton, 1984—; chair Youth Commn., Princeton, 1985—. Mem. Info. Industry Assn. (mktg. cons. 1983—), Women in Communications. Democrat. Episcopalian. Home: 130 Mercer St Princeton NJ 08540 Office: McGraw-Hill 1221 Ave of the Americas New York NY 10020

DENNY, SUANNE EMILY, medical technologist; b. Rochester, N.Y., Feb. 27, 1947; d. Crawford Alfred and Doris Catherine (Coventry) D.; A.A.S., Rochester Int. Tech., 1967, B.S., 1969; cert. med. tech. St. Mary's Sch. Med. Tech., 1969; postgrad. U. Rochester Med. Sch., 1972, 74, 76, 80. Staff technologist St. Mary's Hosp., Rochester, 1969-70; technologist Soldiers and Sailors Meml. Hosp., Penn Yan, N.Y., 1970-78, sr. technologist, 1978-80, supr. hematology and blood bank dept., asst. lab. supr., 1980-84; technologist, sr. hematologist Animal Reference Labs., Houston, 1984-86 ; hematology supr. Kelsey-Seybold, Houston, 1987-88, Brown & Assocs. clin. labs, 1988—; instr. Finger Lakes Shared Edn. and Tng. Program; cons. technologist Rushville Community Clinic; instr. Keuka Coll. Active Career Day programs Penn Yan Acad., 1976-80; mem. youth com. Penn Yan Area Council of Chs., 1974; deacon 1st Presbyn. Ch., Penn Yan, 1977-80, ruling elder, 1983-84. Mem. Am. Soc. Med. Tech., Tex. State Soc. Med. Tech., Am. Soc. Clin. Pathologists (registered med. technologist, specialist in hematology, clin. lab. scientist), Nat. Assn. Female Execs., Am. Soc. Prevention Cruelty to Animals, Intern Wildlife Coalition, World Wildlife Fund (charter mem.), Animal Protection Inst. Am., Defenders of Wildlife, Greenpeace, Seal and Whale Rescue Funds, Nat. Humane Edn. Soc., Internat. Fund Animal Welfare, African Wildlife Leadership Fund, Center for Environ. Edn., Alpha Sigma Alpha. Democrat. Home: 1011 S Kansas La Porte TX 77571 Office: 1213 Hermann Dr Houston Tx 77030

DENOYER, LINDA KAY, astrophysicist, educator; b. Hollywood, Calif.; d. Donald Benjamin and Wanda Bonita (Sinsell) DeN.; m. Peter J. Davies, Aug. 5, 1976; children: Kenneth, Caryn. BA, U. Wis., 1963; PhD, Cornell U., 1972. Lectr. Cornell U., Ithaca, N.Y., 1978-79, sr. research assoc., 1980-81, vis. fellow, 1984—; instr. Ithaca Coll., 1981; adj. prof. Colgate U., Hamilton, N.Y., 1982-83; asst. prof. U. Minn., Mpls., 1984; cons. sci. software Spectrum Assocs., Ithaca, 1985-86. Contbr. articles to astrophys. and astron. jours. Marie Curie fellow AAUW, Cavendish Lab., Cambridge, Eng., 1976-77; NSF vis. prof. Colgate U., Hamilton, N.Y., 1982-83. Mem. Am. Astron. Soc. Home: 755 Snyder Hill Ithaca NY 14850 Office: Cornell U 522 Space Scis Bldg Ithaca NY 14853

DENSLOW, DEBORAH PIERSON, educator; b. Phila., May 2, 1947; d. Merrill Tracy Jr. and Margaret (Aiman) D.; m. James Tracy Grey III, Nov. 24, 1972 (div. Dec. 1980); 1 child, Sarah Elizabeth. BS, Gwynedd Mercy Coll., 1971. Tchr. Willingboro (N.J.) Bd. Edn., 1971—; union rep. Burlington County Edn. Assn., Willingboro, 1981-82, Willingboro Edn. Assn., 1981-82. Rep. committeewoman 1st ward, Morrisville, Pa., 1985—; Rep. candidate for borough council, Morrisville, 1985; borough chmn. Am. Cancer Soc., Morrisville, 1986—. Mem. NEA, Parents Without Ptnrs. (bd. dirs. Mercer County, N.J. chpt. 1981-82, sec. 1982-84). Presbyterian. Home: 1206 Ohio Ave Morrisville PA 19067

DENSLOW, SUZETTE POUPORE, municipal government official, educator; b. Richmond, Va., Sept. 24, 1956; d. Ray A.H. and Suzanne (Bergot) P.; m. Theodore North Denslow, III, Aug. 9, 1980 (div. Nov. 1985). Student, U. Va., 1974-76, MPA, 1981; BS in Urban Studies, Va. Commonwealth U., 1979. Systems and budget analyst City of Charlottesville, Va., 1980-82; sr. legis. analyst Joint Legis. Audit and Rev. Commn., Richmond, 1982-84, City of Richmond, 1984-86; research dir. Va. Mcpl. League, Richmond, 1986—; mem. adj. faculty urban studies and planning dept. Va. Commonwealth U., 1985—, mem. adj. faculty pub. adminstrn., 1987—. Vol. tutor Literacy Forum, Richmond, 1986; vol. reader Va. Voice Radio, Richmond, 1986. Mem. Pub. Fin. Pubs., Inc. (bd. dirs. 1986—), Am. Soc. Pub. Adminstrs. (budgeting and fin. mgmt. com. 1982-87, Va. chpt. council), Va. Analysts Network. Roman Catholic. Home: 715 W 33d St Richmond VA 23225 Office: Va Mcpl League 13 E Franklin St PO Box 12203 Richmond VA 23241

DENSMORE, ANN, writer, speech pathologist/audiologist, marketing executive; b. Los Angeles, Nov. 24, 1941; d. Ray B. and Margaret M. (Walsh) D.; B.S. cum laude, UCLA, 1963; M.A. in Communicative Disorders, Calif. State U., 1975; student Cape Cod Conservatory of Arts, 1977-79, Harvard U. graphics-architecture program, 1980—; children—Kristin Ann, Jennifer Ann. Tchr., Santa Monica (Calif.) Unified Sch. Dist., 1973-74; speech pathologist Kennedy Child Study Center, 1975-76; audiologist VA Hosp. Sepulveda, Calif., 1976-77, New Eng. Rehab. Hosp., Woburn, Mass., 1978; audiology cons. Wellesley (Mass.) Public Schs., 1979; speech pathologist Framingham (Mass.) Public Schs., 1979; speech pathologist and audiologist The Learning Center for Deaf Children, Framingham, 1978-80; dir. ann. fund Babson Coll., 1981-83; asst. dir. devel. Lakey Clinic Med. Ctr., 1984-86; assoc. dir. corp. relations Harvard Med. Sch., 1986—; speech counselor corp. execs. Malkenna/Jandl Assoc., Inc., 1983—; free-lance photographer, 1979—; v.p. U.S. sales Boston Corp.; exhibited photographs Copley Soc. of Boston, 1979-80. Contbr. articles to Boston Globe, 1986—. Lic. speech pathologist and audiologist Calif. Mem. Am. Speech and Hearing Assn. (cert. clin. competence, speech pathologist-audiologist), Artists Assn. of Nantucket, Nat. Assn. Security Dealers. Copley Soc. of Boston. Episcopalian. Home: 9 Roanoke Wellesley MA 02181

DENSON, JOAN LEWIS, psychotherapist; b. Chicago, Nov. 2, 1937; d. Bernard Richard and Reva (Smith) Lewis; m. Michael M. Denson, Jan. 2, 1963 (div. Feb. 1973); 1 child, David. J. BA in History, Roosevelt U., 1960; MA in Edn., Calif. State U., 1971; MA in Psychology, Antioch U., 1981; PhD in Clin. Psychology, Internat. Coll., 1983. Lic. marriage and family counselor, calif. Elem. edn. tchr. Chgo. Bd. Edn., 1961-67; secondary edn. tchr. Los Angeles Bd. Edn., 1972-78, tchr. ESL, 1978-80; psychotherapist, clin. dir. Joan Denson, PhD & Assocs., Los Angeles, 1981—; supr. Maple Counseling Ctr., Beverly Hills, 1985-87. Mem. Soc. Clin. Research (v.p. 1983-85, Service award 1985), Calif. Assn. of Marriage & Family Therapists, Nat. Assn. for Counseling and Devel., Am. Women in Psychology, ACLU, NOW. Office: 1355 Westwood Blvd #214 West Los Angeles CA 90024

DENTON, EMMA MANEY, landscape design appraiser; b. Hiawassee, Ga., Nov. 25, 1905; d. Milton M. and Missouri (Eller) Maney; student pvt. schs., Hiawassee; m. James Young Denton, May 20, 1920 (dec. Jan. 1982); children—J.C., Evelyn Isabel Denton Groves, Ruth Elois Denton Anderson, J. William, Emma Jean Denton Anderson. Assoc. cashier Bank of Hiawassee, 1936-70, cashier, 1970—, dir., 1950—. Chmn. county drive Am. Cancer Soc., 1944-60; adult Sunday sch. tchr. various locations, 1934—; flower show judge. Recipient Service award Am. Cancer Soc., 1977; Emma Denton Day, Bank of Hiawassee, 1979; nat. awards flower shows. Mem. DAR, Friendship Community Club, Hiawassee Garden Club (charter mem., pres. 1960—), State Garden Club Ga. (hon. life), Nat. Council Garden Clubs (life). Baptist. Address: Bank of Hiawassee Main St Hiawassee GA 30546

DENTON, GISELE ANN, advertising executive; b. Italy, Oct. 21, 1937; d. Erasmus R. and Amelia Claire (Finamore) P.; m. L. Karl Denton, Aug. 26, 1961; children: Lewis K. II, Lance Kip. BSBA in Stats., U. Denver, 1961. Media liaison Saturday Evening Post mag., div. Curtis Pub. Co., Phila., 1955-58; mgr. merchandising Valspar Corp., Denver, 1961-66; v.p., media dir. Henderson, Bucknum, Denver, 1967-72, Barickman Advt., Denver, 1972-80, Doyle Dane Bernbach Advt., Denver, 1980-86, DDB Needham Worldwide, Denver, 1986—. Del. Arapahoe County Reps., Aurora, Colo., 1976-86, Douglas County Reps., Castle Rock, Colo., 1984-88; vol. Colo. Heart Assn., Colfax Project, Excelsior House, Denver, 1970-87; chmn. publicity com. Mother Cabrini Shrine, Golden, 1986-87. Mem. Nat. Acad. TV Arts and Scis. (treas. 1986-88), Denver Advt. Fedn. (sec. centennial com. 1988), Colo. Broadcasters Assn. (assoc.), AAUW (treas. local chpt. 1978-80), Il Circolo Italiano (v.p. 1980-87). Republican. Roman Catholic. Home: 4910 Hwy 67 Sedalia CO 80135 Office: DDB Needham Worldwide Denver 4582 S Ulster St #1101 Denver CO 80237

DENTON, TERESA LEAH, health care executive; b. Point Pleasant, N.J., Sept. 4, 1957; d. Raymond George and Susan Beatrice (Johnson) Schroeder; m. Shawn W. W. Denton, Mar. 5, 1980; children: Melissa, Jeff, Jennifer, Joey. Student, Monmouth Coll., Haheman Coll.; BS in Nursing, Mich. State U.; postgrad., Broward Community Coll. With Claremont Care Ctr., Point Pleasant, 1975-76; owner Life Care Nursing, Inc., Pembroke Pines, Fla., 1982—, Lifecare Med. Co., Pembroke Pines, Fla.; cons. in field; pvt. practice underwater photography. Mem. Rep. Nat. Com., Washington, 1986, Mchts. Crime Watch, Pembroke Pines, 1986. Mem. Nat. Assn. Female Execs., Bus. Against Drugs, Police Benevolent Assn., Greenpeace, Smithsonian Soc., Couteau Soc. Roman Catholic. Club: Emerald Hills Country, Turnberry Country (North Miami, Fla.).

DENVER, EILEEN ANN, editor; b. N.Y.C., Nov. 16, 1942; d. Daniel Joseph and Katherine Agnes (Boland) D. B.A., Coll. New Rochelle, 1964; certificate, Radcliffe Sch. Pub., 1964; M.A., Ind. U., 1967. Editorial asst. Mass. Inst. Tech. Tech. Review, Boston, 1965-66; instr. English St. Peter's Coll., Jersey City, 1967-70; assoc. editor, writer Am. Home mag., N.Y.C., 1971-75; asst. editor Consumer Reports, Mt. Vernon, N.Y., 1975-77; asst. mng. editor Consumer Reports, 1977-79, mng. editor, 1979—. Home: 345 W 21st St New York NY 10011 Office: Consumer Reports 256 Washington St Mount Vernon NY 10553

DEO, ROSALIE ANN (LEA), personnel trainer, educator; b. Creston, Iowa, Sept. 2, 1949; d. Ernest Johnson and Jean Ruth (Lisk) McCaslen; m. Duane Allyn Deo, June 28, 1968; children: Christopher, Ryan. BS, NW Mo. State U., 1973, MBA, 1974. Instr. NW Mo. State U., Maryville, 1974-75; mgmt. trainer St. Luke's Hosp., Kansas City, Mo., 1975-78; supr. personnel adminstrn. St. Luke's Hosp., Kansas City, 1979-84, spl. projects mgr., 1984-86, edn., tng., and devel. instr., 1986—; owner, pres. Med. Mgmt. Resources Inc., Shawkee, Kans., 1987—; cons. various small bus., Kansas City; adj. assoc. prof. Webster U., Kansas City, 1975—. Orgn. cons. The Lighthouse, Kansas City, 1985; mem. Citizens for Excellence in Edn., Shawnee, 1986; cons. Something Beautiful TV show, 1986. Mem. Am. Soc. Tng. and Devel., Nat. Assn. Female Execs. Republican. Baptist.

DE OLARTE, GLORIA ACOSTA, plastic surgeon; b. Cali, Colombia, July 28, 1948 (came to U.S., 1973); d. Marco T. and Blanca (Perez) Acosta; m. Felipe Olarte, May 26, 1973; 1 dau., Natalia. M.D., U. Antioquia, 1971. Diplomate: Am. Bd. Plastic Surgeons, 1980. Intern Bapt. Meml. Hosp., Houston, 1973-74; resident gen. surgery, Albany (N.Y.) Med. Ctr., 1974-77, plastic surgery, 1977-79; staff microsurgery Ralph Davis Med. Ctr., San Francisco, 1979, craniofacial Hosp. Enfants Malades, Paris, 1979-80; pvt. practice plastic surgery, Pasadena, Calif., 1981—. Mem. Am. Med. Women's Assn., Am. Soc. Plastic and Reconstructive Surgery, AMA, Calif. Med. Assn. Contbr. article to profl. jours. Office: 65 N Madison Ave Suite 606 Pasadena CA 91101 also: 11411 Brookshire Ave Downey CA 90241

D'EOR-HYNES, DANIELLE DEBORAH, employment agency executive, day care firm executive; b. Watertown, N.Y., Aug. 10, 1953; d. Miles Delosse Wright and Marie Anne Jeanette Aubin; m. Keith Crayton, Aug. 10, 1976 (div. Oct. 1980); m. Mark Francis Hynes, Jan. 3, 1981; children: Nicole Marie, Greta Colette. Student Monroe Community Coll., 1977-78, Canisius Coll., 1979-80, U. Md. Lic. day care dir., Maine. Sales and repair mgr. Auto City of Buffalo, 1979-80; adminstrv. asst. Nissho-Iwai Am. Corp., N.Y.C., 1980-81, House of Three Real Estate Devel., Portsmouth, N.H., 1984-85; owner, operator FreeLance Temps-Network, Cape Neddick, Maine, 1983-87, Nippersinker Licensed Day Care, Neddick, 1985-87; media advt. account exec., Seacoast Life Mag., Hampton, N.J., 1987—; exec. asst. to sr. v.p. mktg., sales and consumer affairs, Nat. Sea Products, Inc., Portsmouth, 1986—; adminstrv. asst. to pres. Bank N.H., Portsmouth, 1987—; active mem. Maine Food Program, Augusta, 1985—. Author picture book: Mommy Works, Daddy Works, 1985; editor, mixer cassette/picture book: The Story of Whistles, 1986. Leader Rochester council Girl Scouts U.S., 1979; bd. for fund raising Seacoast United Way Found.; bd. dirs. Ballet New Eng., Portsmouth. Mem. Nat. Assn. Female Execs., Portsmouth C. of C. Lutheran. Avocations: reading, writing, aerobics, skiing. Home: c/o M/Sgt Mark F Hynes, USAF Band Glen Miller Hall, Einesiedlerhoff Federal Republic of Germany Office: Seacoast Life Mag Chases Pond Rd Cape Neddick ME 03902

DEPALMA, KIMBERLY ANNE, financial executive; b. Louisville, Nov. 26, 1955; d. James Wayne and Betty Jane (Felts) Roney; m. Richard Joseph DePalma, June 17, 1978; children: Maria, Richard. AS in Nursing, U. Louisville, 1977; BS in Nursing, SUNY, Albany, 1982; cert. in fin. planning, Coll. for Fin. Planning, 1984. Cert. fin. planner, Pa., Ohio, N.J.; RN, Pa. Ohio, N.J. Nurse ICU St. Luke's Hosp., Cleve., 1977-79; indsl. nurse Gulf Oil Corp., Phila., 1980; nurse emergency room Jersey Shore Med. Ctr., Neptune, N.J., 1981; nurse Richard DePalma D.P.M., Brick, N.J., 1982—; fin. planner Fin. Alternatives, Lanoka Harbor, N.J., 1986—. Tchr. Epiphany Cath. Ch., Brick, 1987—. Republican. Home: 484 K Herbert Ln Brick NJ 08724

DE PAUW, LINDA GRANT, history educator; b. N.Y.C., Jan. 19, 1940; d. Phillip and Ruth (Marks) Grant. B.A., Swarthmore Coll., 1961; Ph.D., Johns Hopkins U., 1964. Asst. prof. history George Mason Coll.-U. Va., Fairfax, 1964-65; spl. asst. to archivist U.S. Nat. Archives, Washington, 1965-66; asst. prof. history George Washington U., Washington, 1966-69, assoc. prof., 1969-75, prof. Am. history, 1975—. Editor-in-chief, project dir. Documentary History of the First Fed. Congress, 1966-84; author: The Eleventh Pillar: New York State and the Federal Constitution, 1966, Founding Mothers: Women of America in the Revolutionary Era, 1975, Remember the Ladies, 1976, Seafaring Women, 1982; editor, pub. Minerva: Quar. Report on Women and the Mil., 1983—, writer/producer "Minerva on the Air" (armed forces radio), 1987—. Founder, coordinator The Minerva Ctr., 1986—. Woodrow Wilson fellow, 1961. Mem. Am. Hist. Assn. (Beveridge award 1964), Am. Mil. Inst., Authors Guild, Coordinating Com. on Women in Hist. Profession, Inter-Univ. Seminar on Armed Forces and Soc., Women in Internat. Security, Orgn. Am. Historians, So. Hist. Assn., U.S. Naval Inst. Home: 1101 S Arlington Ridge Rd Arlington VA 22202 Office: George Washington U Dept History Washington DC 20052

DEPAUW, MARY ELIZABETH, psychologist; b. Chgo., Dec. 2, 1948; d. Charles Anton and Beata Marie (Gough) Janovsky; B.S., Loyola U., Chgo., 1970; M.Ed., U. Mo.-Columbia, 1977, Ph.D., 1980; m. A. Philip DePauw, III, Sept. 6, 1969; children—A. Philip, Elizabeth B. Fin. aid asst. U. Chgo. Grad. Sch. Bus., 1972-75; student personnel intern Center for Student Life, U. Mo., Columbia, 1977-78, counselor intern Counseling Services, 1978-80; dir. counseling and career devel. St. Mary's Coll., Notre Dame, Ind., 1980—, adj. asst. prof. psychology, 1981—. Mem. Women's Assn. of S. Bend (Ind.) Symphony, 1981-86; mem. aux. St. Joseph County Med. Soc., 1980—; bd. dirs. St. Joseph County Mental Health Assn., 1982-86, v.p. adminstrn., 1984-86, mem. bd. edn. St. Joseph High Sch., 1985-88, v.p., 1986-88; dir. tng. Abuse Assault and Rape Crisis Center, Columbia, 1978-79. Mem. Am. Psychol. Assn., Ind. Psychol. Assn., Am. Assn. Counseling and Devel., Am. Coll. Personnel Assn., AAUW, Phi Delta Kappa, Phi Mu, U. Mo. Alumni Assn. Roman Catholic. Author: (with Robert Callis, Sharon K. Pope) Ethical Standards Casebook, 3rd edit., 1982. Contbr. articles to profl. jours. Home: 15099 Hunting Ridge Trail Grancer IN 46530 Office: 165 LeMans Hall Saint Marys Coll Notre Dame IN 46556

DE PONTE, VELMA ALANA, health care executive; b. Los Angeles, Jan. 13, 1949; d. Clell Millard and Virginia Yvonne (Roberts) Thomas; 1 child, Deris Jermaine Flenoil (dec.). BA magna cum laude, U. So. Calif., 1969; MA in Pub. Adminstrn. with honors, Calif. State U., Long Beach, 1978. Social worker Los Angeles County Dept. Pub. Social Services, 1969-71, eligibility worker, 1971-74, supr. eligibility worker, 1974-76, children's treatment cons., 1976-79; personnel analyst Los Angeles County Dept. Personnel, 1979-81; adminstrv. analyst Los Angeles County Chief Adminstrv. Office, 1981-83; exec. asst. to exec. dir. Los Angeles County Human Relations Commn., 1983-87; spl. asst. to dep. dir. Los Angeles County Health Services Adminstrn., 1987—. Mem. Am. Massage Therapy Assn., Am. Soc. Pub. Adminstrn., Calif. Women in Govt., Assn. Black Women Mgrs., Nat. Assn. Female Execs. Seventh Day Adventist.

DERBY, ANNE RAFTERMAN, biomedical engineer; b. N.Y.C., Feb. 1, 1949; d. Nathan Joseph and Phyllis Fannie (Kerner) Rafterman; A.B., Barnard Coll., 1969; M.S., Columbia U. Sch. Engring. and Applied Scis., 1971; m. Jeffrey Haskell Derby, Sept. 13, 1970; children—Nina Rafterman, Suzanne Rafterman. Clin. engr. dept. surgery Bronx (N.Y.) VA Hosp., 1971-75; chief bio-med. engring. Bronx VA Med. Center, 1975-81; dep. dir. facilities engring. service Nat. Insts. Environ. Health Scis., NIH, Research Triangle Park, N.C., 1981-84; dir. hosp. computer info. services Rex Hosp., Raleigh, N.C., 1984-85; product mgr. Atwork Corp., Chapel Hill, N.C., 1986—; asst. in surgery Mt. Sinai Sch. Medicine, CUNY, 1973-82; cons. hosp. planning, biomed. engring. Adv. council Girl Scouts U.S.A. NSF fellow, 1964-65; VA research fellow, 1973-76. Mem. N.Y. Acad. Scis., IEEE, Assn. Advancement Med. Instrumentation. Democrat. Jewish. Contbr. articles to profl. jours., 1972—. Office: Atwork Corp 700 Eastowne Dr Chapel Hill NC 27514

DERBY, CHERYL ANN, insurance company writer; b. Paterson, N.J., Jan. 19, 1946; d. Elles Mayo and Sarah Emma (Steele) D. BA, Elmira Coll., 1967; MBA, NYU, 1982. Tchr. Ramsey (N.J.) High Sch., 1967-70; contbns. analyst Met. Life Ins. Co., N.Y.C., 1970-83, fin. writer investments dept., 1983—; editor MetLife Investments mag., 1983—. Fellow Life Mgmt. Inst. (bd. dirs. Greater N.Y. chpt. 1984—, pres. 1986, nat. adminstrv. com., mktg. subcom. 1985-88); mem. Elmira Coll. Alumni Club of N.J. (exec. bd. 1982-87). Methodist. Office: Met Life 1 Madison Ave New York NY 10010

DEREBERY, VIRGINIA JANE, occupational medicine physician; b. San Angelo, Tex., Jan. 9, 1953; d. Jean Carlat and Jacqueline (Nodler) D.; m. William Hershey Tullis, Feb. 28, 1982; children: Brandt, Gabriel. Student U. Okla., 1974, M.D., 1978. Diplomate Nat. Bd. Med. Examiners. Intern, Mercy Med. Ctr., Denver; resident in occupational medicine U. Cin. Sch. Medicine; dir. Holly Health Services, Denver, 1979-82; dir. occupational medicine dept. Merced County Med. Ctr., Calif., 1982-86 ; sole practice, Austin, Tex. ; med. dir. Phoenix Alcohol Treatment Unit, Merced, 1983—; council mem. Commn. Pub. Health, Denver Med. Soc., 1981-82; bd. dirs. St. Joseph Hosp. Occupational Med. Council, 1981-82. Contbr. articles to profl. jours. Mem. Am. Occupational Medicine Assn., Western Occupational Med. Assn. (del. 1983), Travis County Med. Soc. Republican. Home: 3906 Glengarry Austin TX 78731 Office: 1600 W 38th Suite 132 Austin TX 78731

DERESHIWSKY, MARY IRENE, statistician; b. New Haven, May 27, 1952; d. Adam and Filomena (Zarowska) D. BS in Edn. Math., So. Conn. State U., 1974; MS in Acctg., U. New Haven, 1977; PhD in Bus. Adminstrn., U. Mass., 1985. Asst. prof. acctg. U. New Haven, 1975-78; research assoc. U. Mass., Amherst, 1977-85; computer cons. No. Ariz. U., Flagstaff, 1985—, statis. research specialist Inst. Human Devel., chief statistician research project Ctr. for Excellence in Edn., 1987—. Contbr. articles to profl. jours. Resource coordinator, lectr. Am. Diabetes Assn., Flagstaff, 1986—. Mem. Am. Acctg. Assn. (delegate 1983), Am. Statis. Assn., Caucus Women in Stats., Nat. Assn. Accts. Home: 1200 S Riordan Ranch Rd Apt 13 Flagstaff AZ 86001

DE RIEMER, CYNTHIA DIANN, college administrator; b. San Antonio, Aug. 3, 1950; d. Thomas Joseph and Josephine (Lempa) Krzywonski; m. Daniel Louis De Riemer, Dec. 28, 1971. BA in English, St. Mary's U., 1971; MEd, U. Tenn., Chattanooga, 1978; PhD, U. Tenn., 1986. Tchr. St. James (Mo.) Jr. High Sch., 1971-72; registrar, tchr. Giessen (Fed. Republic of Germany) Am. Sch., 1973-76, with pub. relations dept. U. Tenn., Chattanooga, 1976-78, trainee adminstrn., 1978-79, asst. dir., faculty instl. research dept., 1979-81, asst. prof. communication, 1981-86; head div. State Tech. Inst., Memphis, 1986, dept. chmn. mid-mgmt. tech., 1987—. Contbr. articles to Essence, other profl. jours. and newspapers. Mem. Internat. Assn. Bus. Communicators (v.p. Chattanooga chpt. 1982-86), Assn. for Edn. in Journalism & Mass Communication, World Affairs Council, Council for Internat. Visitors, LWV (pres. Chattanooga chpt. 1985-86), Chattanooga C. of C. (chair spl. events com. Cen. City Council 1980-82, bd. dirs. 1981), Kappa Tau Alpha. Roman Catholic. Office: State Tech Inst Memphis 5983 Macon Cove Memphis TN 38134

DE RIEMER, JANE THOMPSON, market research company owner, consultant; b. York, Pa., Apr. 27, 1919; d. Theodore Gregg and Gladys Ruth (Dickey) Thompson; m. James Dorman Carty, Sept. 30, 1944 (dec. Oct. 1945); m. 2d, William Breckinridge DeRiemer, May 26, 1956; children—Lysbet True, Jan Gregg, Peter Breckinridge. B.S., Drexel U., 1941. Owner, analyst J. DeRiemer Assocs., Inc., Wilmington, Del., 1969—. Bd. dirs., chmn. pub. relations Mental Health Assocs., Wilmington; bd. dirs., cofounder, state coordinator Reach to Recovery, Am. Cancer Soc. Del., recipient Terese Lasser award, 1982. Mem. Am. Mktg. Assn., Mktg. Research Assn., Wilmington Women in Bus. (chmn. 1983—). Republican. Episcopalian. Clubs: Country of Wilmington, Rodney Square (Wilmington). Home: Box 187 RD 3 Hockessin DE 19707 Office: Jane DeRiemer Assocs Inc 107 Stratton Dr Hockessin DE 19707

DER MANUELIAN, LUCY, Armenian art and architecture educator; b. Arlington, Mass. A.B. in English lit., Radcliffe Coll.; M.A. in Art History, Boston U., 1975, Ph.D. in Art History, 1980. Head teaching fellow Boston U., 1975-76; vist. lectr. Framingham State Coll., 1979-80; archivist, Armenian Archtl. Archives Project, 1979-84; lectr. Armenian art and architecture Tufts U., Medford, Mass., 1984—, McGill U., Montreal, Can., 1987—, Harvard U., 1989; mus. cons. Dartmouth Coll., 1979; acad. lectr. univs. and colls. including Poly. Inst., U. Erevan, USSR, U. Aarhus, Denmark, Courtauld Inst., Eng., McGill U., U. Mich., U. Pa., Harvard U., Brown U., Chgo. U., Columbia U., Northeastern U., UCLA, Dartmouth Coll., Wellesley Coll., Mt. Holyoke Coll., Queens Coll.; lectr. mus., cultural and community orgns. U.S. and abroad; author/narrator 3 TV documentaries on Armenian art. Author: Armenian Architecture, 4 vols., 1981-88; Dictionary of the Middle Ages, 1982—, The Gregorian Collection-Armenian Rugs, 1983, Weavers, Merchants and Kings: The Inscribed Rugs of Armenia, 1984, contbr. to publs. in field including: Dictionary of the Middle Ages, Classical Armenian Culture, 1982, Medieval Armenian Culture, 1984, others. Exchange fellow to USSR, 1977-78; fellow Bunting Inst., Radcliffe Coll., 1971-73; Samuel H. Kress grantee, Boston U., 1975, 78; research grantee Nat. Assn. for Armenian Studies and Research to USSR, 1972, 78; sr. scholar grantee Am. Council Learned Socs./Soviet Acad. Scis., 1983; recipient Jack H. Kolligian award Nat. Assn. Armenian Studies and Research, 1981, Boyan award Armenian Students Assn.; named to Boston U. Acad. Disting. Alumni, 1986; Accademia Tiberina of Rome, 1987.

DEROSA, MARY CATHERINE, obstetrician-gynecologist, educator; b. Utica, N.Y., Dec. 13, 1952; d. Humbert Francis and Anne Theresa (Cavallo) DeRosa. B.A. summa cum laude, Western Md. Coll., 1974; M.D., SUNY-Syracuse, 1978. Resident U. Rochester (N.Y.), 1978-82. Attending physician ob-gyn Genesee Hosp., Rochester, 1982—; clin. instr. ob-gyn. Strong Meml. Hosp., U. Rochester, 1982—; cons., mem. Therapeutic Alternatives Social Abuse, Rochester, 1983; lectr. Jewish Family Services, Rochester, 1982-83. Mem. Med. Soc. State N.Y., Monroe County Med. Soc., Beta Beta Beta, Alpha Omega Alpha. Roman Catholic. Office: 220 Alexander St Rochester NY 14607

DEROSA, ROSE MARIE, chef; b. N.Y.C., Feb. 7, 1929; d. Paul Joseph and Caroline (Tiziano) DeR.; children: Dianne, Carolyn. BA, Pace Coll., 1950; MA, NYU, 1961. Cert. tchr., N.J. Office: 112 La Roche Ave Harrington Park NJ 07640

DERRICK-WHITE, ELIZABETH, marketing consultant; b. Atlanta, Dec. 11, 1940; d. Andrew O. and J. Elizabeth (Rawlins) Derrick; m. Oct. 1958 (dec.); 1 child, Deborah Helene. LLB, U. New South Wales, Australia, 1974. Pres. Edmund Strange Assocs. Ltd., Atlanta, 1958-62; gen. mgr. Associated Brokerage Corp., Atlanta, 1962-66; trust officer Stewart Title Co. Ga., Atlanta, 1964-66; mgr. advt. Barkers Inc., N.Y.C., 1967-68; pres. White, Hufham and Young Ltd., Atlanta, 1978-82; creative dir. Effective Letters Party Ltd., Johannesburg, Rep. South Africa, 1982-83; mktg./creative dir. J. Walter Thompson, Lintas, Ogilvey & Mather Direct, Johannesburg, 1983-84; dir. Vineyard Christian Ctr. for Psychologically Stressed, Johannesburg, 1984-85; dir. mktg. Design Co., Atlanta, 1985-86; counselor Genesis Christian Ctr., Johannesburg, 1983-84; mktg. dir. Response Products, Atlanta, 1988, D & G Research and Mktg., 1988. Author: Home Care for the Long Term Patient, 1979. Founding mem. Individual Rights Party, Australia, 1978; mem. nat. congl. Rep. com., 1980; mem. Am. Security Council, 1979-86, Caritas Ministry Team, Johannesburg, 1984-88, Team Ministeries, St. Pat's Episcopal Ch., Atlanta, 1988, Women's Caucus, Emory U., 1988; assoc. sister Order of St. Benedict Ch. Eng. Mem. Direct Mktg. Assn. Australia (dir. mktg. group 1974-76), Cons. Assn. (founder, pres.), Direct Mktg. Assn. S.E. (organizer), Commonwealth Journalists Assn. African Desk (pres., ops. officer bridge to S.A. 1983-85), Orgn. Counter-Terrorism Specialist. Home: 1785 N Decatur Rd Atlanta GA 30307 Office: 1785 N Decatur Rd #5 Marietta GA 30307

DERRY, PATRICIA MARIE, corporate communications specialist; b. N.Y.C., Nov. 5, 1952; d. Walter Francis and Marie Patricia (Ryan) D. BA with honors, Mich. State U., 1974; postgrad., U. Mich., 1976-84. Tchr. Wyandotte (Mich.) Jr. High Sch., 1974-75, Romulus (Mich.) High Sch., 1975-76; tchr. St. Mary of Redford, Detroit, 1976-79, chmn. English dept.,

1978-79; chmn. English dept. Royal Oak (Mich.) Shrine, 1979-80, audit personnel Peat, Marwick, Main & Co., Detroit, 1980-84, communications dir., 1984-86; communications dir. Peat, Marwick, Main & Co., Montvale, N.J., 1986—; mktg. cons. Tax Info. Mgmt. & Edn. Soc., Park Ridge, N.J., 1987—. Mem. Am. Mgmt. Assn., Women in Communications, Western Metro Detroit Mich. State U. Alumni (bd. dirs. 1984-86, pres. 1986). Roman Catholic. Home: 11-21 Oxford Dr Valley Cottage NY 10989 Office: Peat Marwick Main & Co Three Chestnut Ridge Rd Montvale NJ 07645

DERSH, RHODA E., management consultant, business executive; b. Phila., Sept. 10, 1934; d. Maurice S. and Kay (Wiener) Eisman; m. Jerome Dersh, Dec. 23, 1956; children: Debra Lori, Jeffrey Jonathan. BA, U. Pa., 1955; MA, Tufts U., 1956; MBA, Manhattan Coll. Sch. Bus., 1980. Interpreter, Consul of Chile, 1954-57; various teaching and staff positions Albright Coll., Mt. Holyoke Coll., Amherst Coll., Marple Newtown Sch., 1957-64; systems designer Systems Inc., Reading, Pa., 1964-67; pres., chief exec. officer Profl. Practice Mgmt. Assocs., Reading, 1976—; pres., chief exec. officer Pace Inst.; chief exec. officer Pace Inst., Reading, 1981—; pres., chief exec. officer Pace Mgmt., Inc., 1983—; pres. Wordserv, 1984—, State Bd. Pvt. Lic. Schs., 1987—; cons. dir. pub. sch. budget study project City of Reading, 1967-78, chmn. comprehensive community plan task force, 1973-75, chmn. pub. service cons. project, 1980—; panel chmn. budget allocations United Way, 1974-76; del. White House Conf. on Children Youth, 1970; co-founder World Affairs Council, Reading and Berks County, 1963-65; chmn. Berks County Com. for Children Youth, 1968-72; commr. Trial Ct. Nominating Commn. of Berks County (Pa.), 1982-84; bd. dirs. United Way of Berks County, 1984-87; chmn. programs Leadership Berks; mem. Bd. of Pvt. Lic. Schs., Pa., 1987—. Recipient grant AAUW Ednl. Found.; Outstanding Womens award Jr. League Reading; Trendsetter award YWCA, 1985; accredited ind. cons. Mem. Inst. Community Affairs (exec. com. 1975-79), Pa. Assn. Pvt. Sch. Bus. Adminstrs. (bd. dirs. 1985—), LWV, Berks County C. of C. (bd. dirs. 1983-86, chmn. edn. com. 1983-85), AAUW, Am. Mgmt. Assn., Am. Acad. Ind. Cons. (pres. 1978-80), Nat. Com. Citizens in Edn., Am. Acad. Polit. Social Sci., Nat. Assn. Female Execs., Reading and Berks C. of C (bd. dirs., chmn. edn. com., Entrepreneur of Yr. 1985). Lodge: Rotary. Author: The School Budget is Your Business, 1976, Business Management for Professional Offices, 1977, The School Budget: It's Your Money, It's Your Business, 1979, Improving Public School Management Practices, 1979, Part-Time Professional and Managerial Personnel: The Employers View, 1979; contbr. articles to profl. jours. Office: 606 Court St Reading PA 19601

DERUBERTIS, PATRICIA SANDRA, software company executive; b. Bayonne, N.J., July 10, 1950; d. George Joseph and Veronica (Lukaszewich) Uhl; m. Michael DeRubertis, 1986. BS, U. Md., 1972. Account rep. Gen. Electric Co., San Francisco, 1975-77; tech. rep. Computer Scis. Corp., San Francisco, 1977-78; cons., pres. Uhl Assocs., Tiburon, Calif., 1978-81; cons. mgr. Ross Systems, Palo Alto, Calif., 1981-83; v.p. Distributed Planning Systems, Calabasas, Calif., 1983—. Troop leader San Francisco council Girl Scouts U.S., 1974; participant Women On Water, Marina Del Rey, Calif., 1983. Mem. Nat. Assn. Female Execs., Delta Delta Delta. Democrat. Club: San Fernando Valley Yacht (Marina Del Rey, Calif.). Office: Distributed Planning Systems 23632 Calabasas Rd Suite 107 Calabasas CA 91302

DERUYTER, AVIS JEAN, cultural organization administrator; b. Morris, Minn., June 10, 1943; d. John and Freda Louise (Erdman) Van Otterloo; m. Willard R. DeRuyter, July 23, 1966 (div. Mar. 1986). BA, U. Minn., Morris, 1965; postgrad., Adelphi U., 1968-69. Adminstrv. asst. U. Utah, Coll. of Medicine, Salt Lake City, 1971-76, Exec. Devel. Ctr., Wellesley, Mass., 1976-77; asst. dir. Harvard Sch. Pub. Health, Boston, 1977-79; exec. asst. Am. Nurses' Assn., Kansas City, Mo., 1980-81; co-owner, v.p. Tri-City Airways, Inc., Pasco, Wash., 1981-83; exec. dir. Mid-Columbia Girl Scout Council, Richland, Wash., 1983—; mem. spl. com. on membership strategies Girl Scouts U.S.A., N.Y.C., 1985-86. Mem. Columbia Chorale, Richland, 1984—. Mem. Richland C. of C., Soroptimist Internat. (pres. Pasco-Kennewick 1983-84). Republican. Presbyterian. Home: 1966 Mahan Ave Richland WA 99352-2121 Office: Mid-Columbia Girl Scout Council 710A George Washington Way Richland WA 99352-4211

DESA-MATOS, MARTA TERESA, bilingual elementary educator; b. Mayagûez, P.R., Sept. 23, 1950; d. Benjamin and Eugenia (Negrón) Desa; m. Reinaldo Matos-Molero, Nov. 8, 1980; children: Mónica, Javier. BA in Social Sci., U. P.R., Mayagûez, 1972; MA in Edn., U. Hartford, Bloomfield, Conn., 1973; 6th yr. diploma, Cent. Conn. State U., 1984; postgrad., U. Conn., Storrs, 1986—. Cert. elem., reading cons.; cert. in suprvision, adminstrn. Bilingual tchr. Hartford (Conn.) Bd. Edn., 1972—, tchr. kindergarten, 1974-75, tchr. elem. sch., 1975-87, chmn. sch. inservice com., 1986-87; mem. Conn. Dept. Edn. Social Studies Com., Content Validation Com., 1986—. Election moderator-interpreter City Hartford, 1985; active Fred D. Wish Sch. PTO, 1985—. Tchr. Corps. fellow, 1972-74. Mem. Am. Fedn. Tchrs. (union rep. Hartford chpt. 1985—, cert. achievement 1987), Conn. Orgn. Profl. Devel., Internat. Reading Assn. (Greater Hartford Area Council). Roman Catholic.

DESANTIS, JANET MARIE, marketing professional; b. Syracuse, N.Y., Sept. 25, 1961; d. Frank John and Rosemary (Simonetta) DeS. BA magna cum laude, Wellesley Coll., 1983; postgrad., U. Rochester, 1988—. Intern treasurer's dept. Eastman Kodak Co., Rochester, N.Y., 1981; intern customer equipment services Eastman Kodak Co., Rochester, 1982, planner sensitized good production, 1983-85, analyst mkt. intelligence, 1985-86, analyst bus. research/stategic planning, 1986—. Mem. Am. Production and Inventory Control Soc., Rochester Wellesley (undergrad. chmn. 1983-87), Phi Beta Kappa. Office: Eastman Kodak Co 343 State St Rochester NY 14650

DESANTIS, JUDITH MARIAN, army officer; b. Hoboken, N.J., June 14, 1956; d. Irmo Mario and Julia Marie (Gialanella) DeS.; m. Kenneth John Hlavac, Sept. 5, 1976 (div. Feb. 1985). Student Canisius Coll., Buffalo, 1974-76; B.S., Columbus Coll., Ga., 1979; M.B.A., Fla. Inst. Tech., 1986. Commd. 2d lt. U.S. Army, 1979; advanced through grades to capt., 1983; adjutant 3d Infantry div. Arty., Kitzingen, Ger., 1980-82; adjutant U.S.A. Trasana, White Sands Missile Range, N.Mex., 1982-84, co. comdr., White Sands Missile Range, 1984-85, adjutant logistics officer Recruiting Bn., Ft. Monmouth, N.J., 1985-86, dep. affairs officer, Ft. Drum, N.Y., 1987—. Decorated Commendation medal, Achievement medal, Parachute Wings. Mem. Assn. U.S. Army, Nat. Assn. Female execs. Democrat. Roman Catholic. Avocations: needlepoint; reading; tennis; basketball; softball. Home: PO Box 137 Fort Drum NY 13602 Office: US Army Pub Affairs Office Ft Drum New York NY 13602

DESANTIS, LYDIA ANN, nursing educator, anthropologist; b. Monongahela, Pa., Nov. 30, 1939; d. Frank and Albertina (Ferrari) DeS. R.N., Allegheny Gen. Hosp., 1960; B.S. in Nursing, U. Pitts., 1963, M. Nursing Edn., 1967; M.A., U. Wash., 1976, Ph.D., 1979. Staff nurse Allegheny Gen. Hosp., Pitts., 1960-61, instr., 1963-66; instr. U. Pitts., 1967-68, Duke U., Durham, N.C., 1968-69; asst. chief nurse edn. Project Hope, Jamaica, 1969-71; research assoc. U. Wash., Seattle, 1972-76; project coordinator Fred Hutchinson Cancer Research Ctr., Seattle, 1976-78; dir., dean Frontier Sch. Midwifery and Family Nursing, Hyden, Ky., 1979-81; assoc. prof. nursing U. Miami, Fla., 1982—. HEW grantee, 1974-75. Mem. Am. Anthropol. Assn., Am. Nurses Assn., Am. Pub. Health Assn., Nat. Council for Internat. Health, So. Anthropol. Assn., Am. Assn. for World Health, Council on Nursing and Anthropology, Transcultural Nursing Soc., Sigma Theta Tau. Office: U Miami Sch Nursing Royce Bldg D2-5 1755 NW 17th Ave Miami FL 33136

DESCHAINE, BARBARA RALPH, real estate broker; b. Syracuse, N.Y., Feb. 16, 1930; d. George John and Dora Belle (Manchester) Ralph; children by previous marriage: Olav Bernt Kollevoll, Kristan George Kollevoll, Eric John Kollevoll; m. Bernard Richard Deschaine, May 23, 1981. BA, St. Lawrence U., 1952; postgrad. Pa. State U., 1969-72; grad. Pa. Realtors Inst., 1973; student Realtors Nat. Mktg. Inst., 1974-75. Salesman Brose Realty, Easton, Pa., 1967-72, assoc. broker/mgr., 1973, broker, owner, 1974-85; broker, mgr. John W. Monaghan Corp. Realtors, 1985—; mem. Pa. Real Estate Polit. Edn. Com. Bd. dirs. Easton Area C. of C., 1973-79, v.p. organizational improvement, 1975-76, v.p. econ. devel., 1976-77, pres., 1977-79; mem. Greater Easton Corp. Strategy Group, 1977-78; mem. Northampton County Revenue Appeals Bd., 1984—; trustee Easton area YMCA, 1984—. Mem. Nat. Assn. Realtors, Pa. Assn. Realtors, Bethlehem Bd. Realtors, Eastern Northampton County Bd. Realtors (bd. dirs. 1973—, sec. 1977, v.p. 1980-81; Realtor of Yr. 1978), Realtors Nat. Mktg. Inst., Homes for Living Network (state chmn. 1980), Nat. Assn. Female Execs., Sales and Mktg. Execs. (bd. dirs. Easton area chpt. 1976—; Disting. Sales award 1982), Phi Beta Kappa. Republican. Presbyterian. Home: 330 Paxinosa Rd W Easton PA 18042 Office: 131-133 N 4th St Easton PA 18042

DESCOTEAUX, CAROL J., academic administrator; b. Nashua, N.H., Apr. 5, 1948; d. Henry Louis and Therese (Arel) D. BA, Notre Dame Coll., 1970; MEd, Boston Coll., 1975; MA, U. Notre Dame, 1984, PhD, 1985. Jr. high sch. instr., dir. religious studies St. Joseph's Sch., North Grosvenordale, Conn., 1970-73; jr. high sch. tchr., dir. religious edn. Notre Dame Sch., North Adams, Mass., 1973-77; jr. high sch. instr. Sacred Heart Sch., Groton, Conn., 1977-78; chairperson religious studies discipline U. Notre Dame, Grad. Theol. Union, Notre Dame, Ind., 1982-83, 84-85; pres. Notre Dame Coll., Manchester, N.H., 1985—; trustee King's Coll., Wilkes-Barre, Pa., 1987—; pres. Fedn. of Holy Cross Colls., 1985—; mem. adv. bd. Manchester Christian Life Ctr., 1978-80; treas. N.H. Coll. and Univ. Council, Manchester, 1985—; trustee N.H. Higher Edn. Assistance Found., 1986—. Mem. Manchester United Way campaign, 1985—; bd. incorporators, mem. ethics com., instl. research com. Cath. Med. Ctr., Manchester, 1986—. Named Disting. Woman Leader of Yr., So. N.H. region YWCA, 1985. Mem. Am. Acad. Religion, Coll. Theology Soc. Am., N.H. Women's Forum, Soc. Christian Ethics, AAUW, N.H. Women in Higher Edn. Democrat. Roman Catholic. Office: Notre Dame Coll Office of the Pres 2321 Elm St Manchester NH 03104

DE SERBINE BAHRAWY, LISA, German language educator, nurse; b. Hannover, Fed. Republic Germany, Mar. 6, 1929; arrived in U.S., 1963; d. Wilhem Georg de Serbine and Luise Anna Sophie (Tott) Lindemann; m. Ibrahim Bahrawy, May 2, 1953; children: Ramsey Ali, Jens Adly, Dina Birgitta. RN, London, 1953; BA summa cum laude, Tufts U., 1978, MA, 1979; PhD in German, Harvard U., 1987. RN Mass., N.H.; cert. educator Mass., N.H. Nurse King Edward Meml. Hosp., London, 1953-54; health and sci. instr. The Brit. Sch., Port Said, Egypt, 1954-56; nurse Taunton (Mass.) State Hosp., 1963-64, Boston State Hosp., 1964-66, VA Hosp., Bedford, Mass., 1966-67, Danvers (Mass.) State Hosp., 1970-72; lectr. German Tufts U., Medford, Mass., 1978—; free-lance translator. Active PTA, Bedford, 1967-73, Georgetown, Mass., 1973-77, LWV, Bedford, 1967-73. Mem. MLA, AAUP, Am. Assn. Tchrs. German, Women in German, Am. Council on Teaching Fgn. Langs., Goethe Soc., Austro-Am. Soc., Bon Secours and Lawrence Gen. Hosps Aux.; founding mem. Am. Psychiat. Assn., Bd. Mental Health. Lutheran. Club: Tufts (Boston). Home: 281 Main St North Andover MA 01845 Office: Tufts U Medford MA 02155

DESFOSSES, HELEN ROBERTA, political scientist, university official; b. Dover, N.H., Apr. 24, 1945; d. Robert Louis and Agnes Mary (Mater) D.; 1 child, Adam Robsohn Cohn. BA, Mt. Holyoke Coll., 1965; MA, Harvard U., 1967; PhD, Boston U., 1971. Chmn. Soviet and East European Studies, Boston U., 1970-72; chmn. dept. govt. Emmanuel Coll., Boston, 1972-74; research fellow Harvard U. Russian Research Ctr., 1974-76; assoc. dean Coll. Arts, Scis. and Letters, U. Mich., Dearborn, 1976-78; dean undergrad. studies and asst. v.p. acad. affairs SUNY, Albany, 1978-82, assoc. v.p. research and ednl. devel., 1982-83, dir. pub. policy program, 1983-84, chmn. dept. pub. affairs and policy, 1984—; cons. Internat. Communications Agy., Fgn. Service Inst., Refugee Policy Group, Roosevelt Ctr. for Policy Studies, Forum Inst., Voice of Am., Def. Intelligence Coll., Bus. Execs. for Nat. Security (exec. com., bd. dirs.); Ctr. for Women in Govt., 1979-83. Author: Soviet Policy Toward Black Africa, 1972, Socialism in the Third World, 1975, Soviet Population Policy, 1981. Bd. dirs. Detroit Urban League, 1977-78, Washington Park Theatre Co., 1984-88, Project Equinox, 1986—; chmn. Commn. on Peace and Justice, Diocese of Albany, 1981-85; active Albany YWCA, 1985-88; bd. dirs. Mercy House, 1985—, pres., 1987—; sec. bd. trustees Albany Pub. Library, 1986—. Fellow NDEA, 1967-70, AAUW Coretta Scott King, 1969-70, Population Council, 1974-75, Ford Found., 1975-76, Andrew W. Mellon Found., 1980; Nat. Acad. Scis. exchange scholar, 1975. Mem. Am. Polit. Sci. Assn., African Studies Assn., Am. Assn. Advancement Slavic Studies, ACLU (state bd. Mich. chpt. 1977-78), NAACP (legal redress com. Albany 1979-85), Albany Colonie Regional C. of C., AAUW. Democrat. Roman Catholic. Office: SUNY Milne 107 135 Western Ave Albany NY 12222

DESHOTELS, ANNETTE CAMILLE, television studio technician; b. Mamou, La., May 22, 1959; d. Wilfred Joseph and Leonie Theresa (Fontenot) D.; m. Reginald Charles Mitchell, Nov. 9, 1984. Lic. 1st class, Fed. Communications Commn. Studio technician Sta. KLFX-TV, Lafayette, La., 1978-79; technician, supr. Sta. KMEX-TV, Los Angeles, 1979-82; tech. dir. Sta. KCBS-TV, Los Angeles, 1982-87, Sta. CBS-TV, Los Angeles, 1987—. Mem. Internat. Brotherhood Elec. Workers. Democrat. Office: CBS 7800 Beverly Blvd Los Angeles CA 90036

DE SILVA, HOMITA, manufacturing company executive; b. Colombo, Sri-Lanka, May 29, 1952; Came to Can., 1981; d. Harry and Elsie (Kularatne) Wijesekera; m. Tissa DeSilva, July 6, 1978. Gen. Cert., Musaeus Coll., Colombo, 1970. Cert. in Accountancy. Contract accountant Johnson Control Systems, London, 1976-79; fin. acct. Tefal (UK) Ltd., London, 1979-80; product acct. Carnation Foods Ltd., London, 1980-81; controller Millard Lister Sales, Scarborough, Ont., Can., 1983; corp. acct. Eaton Bay Fin. Services, Toronto, 1984-85; asst. controller Bay Mills Homeshield Div., Brampton, Ont., 1985—. Mem. Inst. Cost Mgmt. Accts. (assoc.), Inst. Adminstrv. Accts. Office: Bay Mills Homeshield Div, 75 Bramalea Rd, Brampton, ON Canada L6T 2X1

DESIMONE, RORY JEAN, small business owner; b. N.Y.C., Mar. 25, 1941; d. Joseph and Lee (Giardelli) DeS.; m. William Andrew D. Hammer Jr., Dec. 16, 1972; children: Craig Simon, Alexander Joseph. BA, Marymount Coll., 1962; postgrad., NYU, 1965-72. V.p. MacKay-Shields Fin. Corp., N.Y.C., 1962-80, cons., 1980-81; v.p. Medico Corp., Gainesville, Fla., 1981-82; pres., owner Children's Computer Co. Div. Compu-TOTS, Gainesville, 1983—; ptnr., owner Dynamic Didactic Developware, Gainesville, 1985—; cons. computer various cos. Author software packages. Mem. adv. bd. Fla. Instructional Computing Conf.; bd. dirs. Children's Resource Ctr.; Coach Youth Soccer. Mem. So. Assn. Children Under Six, Assn. Ednl. Data Systems, Am. Ednl. Research Assn., Nat. Acad. Early Childhood Programs, Pilot Internat. (co-chair projects 1984-85, chair safety 1985—, Regional Safety award 1984-85, Nat. Grant Safety 1984-85, 85-86), Math. Assn. Am., Internat. Assn. Computing Edn., Nat. Council Tchrs. Math., Fla. Assn. Computing Edn., Fla. Pub. Interest Research Group, Apple Programmer's and Developer's Assn. Republican. Roman Catholic. Clubs: APPLE Co-op (Wash.); Internat. Apple User Group (Mass.). Home: 1016 NW 112th Terr Gainesville FL 32606 Office: Dynamic Didactic Developware 4300 NW 23 Ave Suite 216 Gainesville FL 32606

DESISTI, JOAN KAY, nurse, educator; b. Harrison County, Ind., Sept. 10, 1941; d. Anderson Dewey and Florence Marie (Haas) Williar; m. Michael Joseph DeSisti, Nov. 21, 1964 (dec. May 1985); children: Ann Marie, Michael Joseph. Cert. in rehab. nursing. Staff nurse St. Mary's Hosp., Evansville, Ind., 1964-65; office nurse Drs. Austin and Coleman, Evansville, 1965-66; sch. nurse/aid Sch. Dist. #47, Crystal Lake, Ill., 1980-81, learning disabilities tchr., aid, 1981-82; utilization rev. nurse Good Shepherd Hosp., Barrington, Ill., 1982-83; instr. McHenry County Coll., Crystal Lake, 1984—, nurse coordinator, 1986—; area coordinator Coll. of St. Francis, Joliet, 1981-82. Contbr. poetry to mags. Vol. Sr. Citizens Council, Crystal Lake, 1966-79, Crystal Lake sch. dist., 1977-78; tchr. St. Theresa Confraternity of Christian Doctrine, Billerica, Mass., 1975-76. Mem. McHenry County Nurses Assn. (pres. 1986-87, bd. dirs. 1984—). Republican. Roman Catholic. Office: McHenry County Coll Rt 14 and Lucas Rd Crystal Lake IL 60012

DESJARLAIS, ERIKA ELSE, management analyst; b. Hamburg, Federal Republic Germany, Oct. 28, 1934; came to U.S.; d. Friedrich Heinrich Paul Franz and Else Anna (Klussman) Fehrke; m. Leo Raymond Desjarlais, 1956 (dec. 1956); 1 child, Raymond Marcel; m. Richard Alexis Poirier, 1959 (div. 1985); 1 child, Denise Simone. AA, Monterey Peninsula Coll., 1975; BA, Antioch U., 1980; postgrad., Donsbach U., 1982. Office asst. A. Rienaecker, Goslar, Fed. Republic Germany, 1952-53, J. Wenig, Oker, Fed. Republic Germany, 1953; clk. Konsumgenossenschaft "Nordhanz", Goslar, 1953-55; clk. typist 2d Can. Inf. Brigade, Soest, Fed. Republic Germany, 1956; purchasing clk. U.S. Army Quartermaster Market Ctr., Frankfurt, Fed. Republic Germany, 1957-58; sec./translator V Corps Hdqrs., Frankfurt, 1958-59; accounts maintenance clk. USAF So. Command, Panama Canal Zone, 1968-69; sec. U.S. Army Combat Devels. Experimentation Ctr., Ft. Ord, Calif., 1970-83, mgmt. analyst, 1983—; correctional officer Sheriff's Office, Salinas, Calif., 1974-75. Mem. Fed. Women's Program Adv. Com., Ft. Ord, Calif., 1975-88; mem. Advocate Governing Bd., Rape Crisis Ctr., Monterey, 1980-82; commr. Commn. on Status of Women, Monterey County, 1986-88, Affirmative Action Commn., 1986-88; advocate Women Against Domestic Violence, 1980-81, Monterey Rape Crisis Ctr., 1980-82; active YWCA. Mem. nat. Assn. Female Execs., Am. Soc. Mil. Comptrollers, Internat. Tng. in Communication Inst., Am. Nutrition Cons. Assn. Libertarian. Evangelical-Lutheran. Club: Monterey Bay Hot Jazz Soc. (publicity chmn. 1978, corres. sec. 1977). Home: 335 Parson Circle Marina CA 93933 Office: USA TEXCOM Expirimentation Ctr Attn: ATEC-RF Fort Ord CA 93941-7000

DESKIN, FREDA DIANE, education educator; b. Pasadena, Calif., June 7, 1948; d. R.B. and Bessie Maxine (Raines) Jones; m. Bobby Ray Deskin, June 17, 1966; 1 child, Samuel Hardin. BS in Edn., Cen. State U., Edmond, Okla., 1970; MEd, U. Okla., 1986, postgrad., 1987—. Cert. elem., secondary tchr., Okla. Tchr. Okla. City Pub. Schs., 1970-71, Lexington (Okla.) Pub. Schs., 1972-75; tchr., gymnastics coach Whitebead Schs., Pauls Valley, Okla., 1975-82; coordinator gifted edn. Pauls Valley Mid. Schs., 1982-85; coordinator spl. projects Dept. Edn. State of Okla., Oklahoma City, 1985-87; adj. prof. U. Okla., Norman, 1986—; cons. Edn. Tng. Cons., Norman, 1987—, Wright Group, San Diego, 1987—; dir.,creator Space Acad. Am., Oklahoma City, 1986—; speaker Aerospace Found. Okla., 1986—; mem. speakers bur. Challenger Ctr., Washington, 1986—; advisor newsletter Countdown, 1987—; instr. Garvin County Community Edn., 1979-85. Regional editor nat. jour. Educators, Today, Touching Tomorrow, 1986—. Pres. Aerospace Found. Okla., 1986—; dir. jr. high Sunday sch. 1st Bapt. Ch., 1982-85; sec. Garvin County chpt. Okla. Edn. Polit. Action, 1979-81; co-founder Okla. Olympics Mind, bd. dirs., 1978-84; bd. dirs. Youth-Adult Theatre, Pauls Valley, 1981-85. Leadership Enrichment Program scholar, 1987; named Okla. Tchr. in Space NASA, 1985, Space Ambassador NASA, 1985, Whitebead-Pauls Valley Tchr. Yr., 1977, 84, Educator Yr., 1976; recipient Nat. Scholastic All-Am. award, 1988. Mem. Assn. Supervision Curriculum Devel., Okla. Edn. Assn. (v.p. 1979-81, pres., sec. Garvin County chpt. 1979-81), Whitebead Edn. Assn. (pres. 1981, founder), Delta Kappa Gamma. Republican. Lodge: Order Eastern Star. Home: 3208 Dove Crossing Dr Norman OK 73072 Office: U Okla 820 Van Fleet Oval Norman OK 73019

DESKIN, RENEE JEAN, mechanical engineer; b. Peoria, Ill., Dec. 27, 1958; d. Frank Hoke and Martha Ella (Kirby) Riddle; m. Gregory Lee Deskin, June 30, 1960. BSME, Purdue U., 1982. Student engr. Hughes Aircraft, El Segundo, Calif., 1978-82; engr. Ford Aerospace, Newport Beach, Calif., 1982-83, database adminstr., 1983-86, research engr., 1986—. Mem. ASME. Republican. Office: Ford Aerospace Ford Rd M/S 6/J200 Newport Beach CA 92658

DESOMOGYI, AILEEN ADA, retired librarian; b. London, Nov. 26, 1911; d. Harry Alfred and Ada Amelia (Ponten) Taylor; immigrated to Can., 1966; B.A., Royal Holloway Coll., U. London, 1936, M.A., 1939; M.L.S., U. Western Ont., 1971; m. Leslie Kuti, Nov. 22, 1958; m. 2d, Joseph DeSomogyi, July 8, 1966. Librarian in spl. and public libraries, Eng., 1943-66; sr. instr. Nat. Coal Bd., 1957; charge regional collection S.W. Ont., Lawson Library, U. Western Ont., 1967-71; cataloger Coop. Book Centre Can., 1971; mem. staff E. York (Ont.) Public Library, 1971-74; librarian Ont. Ministry Govt. Services Mgmt. and Info. Services Library, 1975-78, Sperry-Univac Computer Systems, Toronto (Ont.) Central Library, 1980-81. Fellow Internat. Biographical Assn.; Mem. Internat. Platform Assn., English Speaking Union, Can. Orgn. for Devel. Through Edn., Royal Can. Geog. Soc., Consumers Assn. Can., Can. Wildlife Fedn., Ont. Humane Soc., Internat. Fund Animal Welfare, Endangered Animal Sanctuary, U. Western Ont. Alumni Assn., Royal Holloway and Bedford New Coll. Assn., Am. Biog. Inst. Research Assn. (dep. gov., nat. bd. advisors), Can. Mental Health Assn., John Howard Soc., Met. Toronto Zool. Soc., Toronto Humane Soc. Roman Catholic. Contbr. articles to profl. jours. Home: 9 Bonnie Brae Blvd, Toronto, ON Canada M4J 4N3

DESPAIN, SARA ELLEN, product designer; b. Lexington, Ky., Sept. 3, 1949; d. Clell Ford and Rebecca (Perry) DeS. BA, U. Ky., 1971; cert. in diamond grading, Gemological Inst. Am., 1988. Owner, mgr. Sara DeSpain Designer/Goldsmith, Nags Head, N.C., 1974—. Mem. Soc. N.Am. Goldsmiths, Am. Crafts Council, Outer Banks C. of C. Republican. Home and Office: PO Box 986 Nags Head NC 27959

DESPALATOVIC, ELINOR MURRAY, history educator; b. Cleve., Aug. 10, 1933; d. Clyde Eugene and Janet Hamilton (Page) Murray; m. Marijan Despalatovic, Aug. 18, 1962; children: Pavica Catherine, Mirna Susan. BA, Barnard Coll., 1955, MA, Columbia U., 1959, PhD, 1969. Lectr. in history U. Mich., Ann Arbor, 1962-63; researcher Yale U., New Haven, 1963-65; instr. Conn. Coll., New London, 1965-86, asst. prof., 1968-74, assoc. prof., 1974-79, prof., 1979—, chmn. dept. history, 1980-84, Bridida Ardenghi Pacchiani prof., 1986; mem. E. European Selection com. IREX, N.Y.C., 1973-76, 87—. Author: Ljudevit Gaj and the Illyrian Movement, 1975; editor: How the People Live, 1981; contbr. articles to profl. jours. Mem. Conn. Humanities Council, Middletown, Conn., 1980-86. Fulbright Hays fellow, 1955-56, 72, 78-79, 85-86; Ford Found. fellow, 1957-61; IREX fellow, 1972, 78-79, 85-86. Mem. Am. Hist. Assn., Am. Assn. for Advancement of Slavic Studies, Am. Assn. for Croatian Studies (v.p. 1980-86), AAUP, Am. Soc. for SE European Studies, Phi Beta Kappa. Home: 111 Nameaug Ave New London CT 06320 Office: Conn Coll Dept History New London CT 06320

DESPRES, GINA HELEN, lawyer; b. Sydney, Australia, Sept. 28, 1941; came to U.S., 1964, naturalized, 1972; d. George Alfred and Winifred Florence (Bush) Eviston; B.A. with honors (Commonwealth scholar 1960-64), U. Sydney, 1964; postgrad. (NDEA fellow 1966-68), U. Calif., Berkeley, 1965-70; J.D., UCLA, 1974; m. John Despres, Sept. 23, 1964; children—Sarah, Naomi. Bar: Calif. 1974, D.C. 1976. Atty. firm Irell & Manella, Los Angeles, 1974-75; mem. firm Caplin & Drysdale, Washington, 1976-77; with Dept. Energy, 1977-79, dir. internat. energy and energy security policy, 1978-79; counsel, tax and internat. affairs U.S. Senator Bradley of N.J., 1979—. Bd. editors UCLA Law Rev. 1973-74. Mem. D.C. Bar Assn. Author articles in field. Office: 731 Hart Senate Office Bldg Washington DC 20515

DESROCHES, DIANE BLANCHE, English language educator; b. Webster, Mass., Nov. 17, 1947; d. Victor Joseph and Rose Blanche Blouin; m. Roger John DesRoches, Aug. 27, 1966 (div. Apr. 16, 1974); 1 child, Bill. AA, Mesa Coll., 1976; BA in English magna cum laude, San Diego State U., 1979, MA, 1981. Cert. lang. arts, lit. and basic English edn. instr., Calif. community colls. Instr. ESL, substitute Am. Lang. Inst., ESL Inst., San Diego, Calif., 1982, San Diego Community Coll., 1982—; instr. ELS Inst. Coll. English Lang., San Diego, 1982—. Author: (short story) Something Special, 1979, Cinderella of the 80's; (software) Basic MAP Reading Skills, 1981, (reading comprehensive series) Comprehension Plus, 1982, (student assessment system) CASAS, 1982, (puzzles) The Seven Warning Signs of Cancer, 1981, Poisons Around the Home, 1980, Some Poisonous Plants, 1980, numerous other Dell Word Search Puzzlesand Recipes, 1980—; contbr. articles to mags.; translator: ABC of Ecology, 1982. Recipient Gregg award Gregg Inst., 1965; fellow State of Calif., 1979, DB Williams San Diego State U., 1979. Mem. Phi Kappa Phi, Psi Chi, Pi Delta Phi. Democrat. Roman Catholic. Home and Office: 2029-F Cerrissa Ct San Diego CA 92154

DES ROSIERS, KATHLEEN ANN, public relations executive; b. Oakland, Calif., Aug. 19, 1945; d. George Albert and Katherine Jane (Dragich) D.; m. Allan David Katz, Apr. 12, 1969 (div. 1974). BA, Viterbo Coll., 1967. Appointments sec. to Mayor Office of Mayor, Los Angeles, 1973-82; acct. supr. Fleishman-Hillard, Inc., Los Angeles, 1982-85, v.p., 1985—. Recipient

Prisms Merit award Los Angeles chpt. Pub. Relations Soc. of Am., 1986. Mem. Women in Pub. Affairs (chair 1986), Los Angeles Pub. Affairs Officers Assn., Los Angeles Area C. of C. (govt. affairs 1982—). Club: Los Angeles Athletic. Office: Fleishman Hillard Inc 444 S Flower St Los Angeles CA 90071

DESSASO, DEBORAH ANN, association legislative specialist, freelance writer; b. Washington, Feb. 6, 1952; d. Coleman and Virginia Beatrice (Taylor) D.; student public schs., Washington; AS in Bus. Adminstrn., Southeastern U., 1986. Clk.-stenographer FTC, Washington, 1969-70; sec. NEA, Washington, 1970-72; sec. Nat. Ret. Tchrs. Assn./Am. Assn. Ret. Persons, Washington, 1972-79, assoc. adminstrv. specialist, 1979-80, adminstrv. specialist, 1980—; founding mem., sec. Andrus Fed. Credit Union, 1980. Mem. Nat. Assn. Female Execs. Mem. Worldwide Ch. of God. Home: 3052 Stanton Rd SE Washington DC 20020 Office: 1909 K St NW Washington DC 20049

D'ESTE, MARY ERNESTINE, health administration executive; b. Chgo., Apr. 1, 1941; d. Ernest Gregory and Mary (Turcich) D'E. Student, Mundelein Coll., 1958-61. Sec. MMM, Bedford Park, Ill., 1961-69, Michael Reese Med. Ctr., Chgo., 1969-73; adminstrv. asst. Thomas Jefferson U., Phila., 1973-85, divisional adminstr., 1985-86; adminstr. dept. cardiothoracic surgery Hahnemann U., Phila., 1986—; v.p. Cardiac and Thoracic Surgeons, PC, Phila., 1986—. V.p. archtl. review com. Homeowners Assn., Marlton, N.J., 1979-85. Mem. Med. Group Mgmt. Assn., Am. Assn. Notaries, Nat. Assn. Female Execs. Roman Catholic. Office: Hahnemann U Hosp Broad and Vine MS 111 Philadelphia PA 19102-1192

DE SZALAY, HELGA KERSTEN, medical technologist; b. Stolp, Germany, Oct. 9, 1936; came to U.S., 1961; d. Gottfried A. and Erna A. (Renius) K.; m. Csaba J. de Szalay, July 1, 1962; children: Péter J., Ferenc A., Krisztina K. Cert. med. technologist, U. Frankfurt/Main, Fed. Republic Germany, 1957; BS in Biology, SUNY, Saratoga Springs, 1982; MS in Immunology, L.I. U., 1988. Cert. lab technician, N.Y.; cert. technologist in chemistry; clin. lab. scientist/chemistry. Research technician NYU Med. Ctr., N.Y.C., 1961-63; technician North Shore Univ. Hosp., Manhasset, N.Y., 1971-75; sr. technician North Shore Univ. Hosp., Manhasset, 1975-78, technologist, 1978-86, sr. technologist, 1986—; tchr. of med. technology North Shore Univ. Hosp., Manhasset, 1982-86. Contbr. articles to profl. jours. Mem. N.Y. Acad. Scis., Am. Soc. Clin. Pathologists, Am. Soc. for Med. Tech., Internat. Assn. Med. Lab. Techonologists. Lutheran.

DETERMAN, SHERI MAE, marketing manager; b. Dallas, June 13, 1954; d. Bruce Herbert and Norma Mae (Schumer) Verran; m. Ronald Howard Determan, Sept. 29, 1979. BS in Bus. Adminstrn., Calif. State U., Northridge, 1979; MS in Bus. Adminstrn. and Mktg., 1982. Advt. coordinator Action Industries, Los Angeles, 1978-79; account mgr. NCR Corp., Los Angeles, 1979-82; mktg. mgr. M/D Systems, Inc., Encino, Calif., 1982-88; product mgr. Interactive Systems Corp., Santa Monica, Calif., 1988—; profl. ice skater Ice Follies, toured U.S., Can., 1972-74. Recipient Wall St. Jour. award, 1979, Arco Acad. Excellence award, 1981. Mem. Beta Gamma Sigma.

DETERT-MORIARTY, JUDITH ANNE, civic worker, graphic artist; b. Portage, Wis., July 10, 1952; d. Duane Harlan and Ann Jane (Devine) Detert; m. Patrick Edward Moriarty, July 22, 1978; children—Colin Edward, Eleanor Grace. Student U. Wis.-Madison, 1970-73, U. Wis.-Green Bay, 1984-88. Cert. in no-fault grievance mediation, Minn. Legis. sec., messenger State of Wis. Assembly, Madison, 1972, 74-76; casualty-property div. clk. Capitol Indemnity Corp., Madison, 1976-77; sec./credit clk. comml. credit div. Affiliated Bank of Madison, 1977-78; word processor consumer protection div. Wis. Dept. Agr., Madison, 1978; graphics arts composing specialist Moraine Park Tech. Inst., Fond du Lac, Wis., 1978-79; prodn. asst. West Bend News, 1980-83; free-lance artist Picas, Pictures and Promotion (formerly Detert Graphics), 1978-88; art and promotional publs. dir. Michael G. & Co., Albert Lea, Minn., 1988—; community services instr. Austin (Minn.) Community Coll., 1988—; devel. assoc. Riveredge Nature Ctr., Inc., Newburg, Wis., 1983-84; dir. fund-raising and program devel., Voluntary Action Ctr. of Washington County, West Bend, 1984-86; devel. cons. West Bend Hospice Program, 1985. Vol. activities include: Austin Pub. Schs. Omnibus Program polit. cartooning instr. Dane County vol. Udall for Pres., 1976; Washington County campaign coordinator Nat. Unity Campaign for John Anderson for Pres., 1980; Washington County ward coordinator Earl for Gov., 1982; Washington County campaign chmn. Peg Lautenschlager for Wis. state senate, Washington County ward coordinator Mondale/Ferraro, 1984; sec., newsletter editor Dem. Party of Manitowoc County, Wis., 1986; publicity coordinator Wis. Intellectual Freedom. Coalition, 1981; founding exec. bd. mem., newsletter editor Moral Alternatives, Catholics for a Free Choice Wis. community contact; bd. dirs., v.p. Wis. Pro-Choice Conf., 1981-82; pres., founder People of Washington County United for Choice, 1981-83; bd. pres. Planned Parenthood of Washington County, 1984-85, newsletter editor, mem. coms., 1980-85; bd. mem. Montessori Children's House, West Bend, 1983-85, newsletter editor, com. chmn.; artist LWV Washington County, 1984-86; newsletter artist, artist Friends of Battered Women, West Bend, 1983-86; appointed to Austin Human Rights Commn, 1987-88; fundraiser Victims Crisis Ctr., 1987. Mem. Nat. Assn. Female Execs., Women in Communications, Dem. Party Minn. (Mower County precinct chmn., affirmative action officer, 1988—), Minn. Womens Polit. Caucus, Population Inst., NOW (newsletter editor Dane County 1977-78, coordinator Wis. state reproductive rights task force 1982-84, coordinator reproductive rights task force North Suburban Chpt., 1981-84, Minn. pub. relations coordinator, 1987—). Avocations: Reading; hand spinning and knitting; world wide correspondence; antiques. Home: 1810 2d St NE Austin MN 55912

DETMAR, GINA LOUISE, school system administrator; b. S.I., N.Y., May 3, 1949; d. Joseph and Grace Vivian (Brown) Sargente. BS in Edn., Wagner Coll., 1971, MS in Edn., 1972; MA in Urban Affairs and Policy Analysis, The New Sch. for Social Research, 1987; post grad. studies in Bus. Adminstrn., Baruch Coll. City U., 1987—. Tchr. pub. schs. N.Y.C., 1971-82; coordinator spl. projects, pub. affairs N.Y.C. Bd. Edn., 1982, spl. asst. to exec. dir. pupil services, 1983, asst. to the chancellor, 1983-84; dir. Tchr. Summer Bus. Industry Program, Bklyn., 1984—; liaison for the Tchr. Industry Program, N.Y.C. Ptnrship., 1985—. Mem. Com. to re-elect Borough pres. Lamberti, S.I., 1985. Recipient Mayor's scholarship City of N.Y., 1984—. Mem. Fgn. Lang. Instrs. Assn., U.S. Seaplane Pilot's Assn., Internat. Orgn. for Licensed Women Pilots, Chinese-Am. Soc., Am. Mgmt. Assn. Democrat. Episcopalian. Club: Cambridge Flying Group. Office: NYC Bd Edn 65 Court St Brooklyn NY 11201

DE TORNYAY, RHEBA, nurse, university dean emeritus, educator; b. Petaluma, Calif., Apr. 17, 1926; d. Bernard and Ella Fradkin; m. Rudy de Tornyay, June 4, 1954. Student U. Calif., Berkeley, 1944-46; diploma, Mt. Zion Hosp. Sch. Nursing, 1949; A.B., San Francisco State U., 1951, M.A., 1954; Ed.D., Stanford U., 1967; Sc.D. (hon.), Ill. Wesleyan U., 1974; L.H.D. (hon.), U. Portland, 1974. Faculty San Francisco State U., 1957-67, prof. nursing, 1966-67, chmn. dept., 1959-67; asso. prof. U. Calif. Sch. Nursing, San Francisco, 1968-71; prof. U. Calif. Sch. Nursing, 1971; dean, prof. Sch. Nursing, UCLA, 1971-75; dean emeritus, prof. U. Wash., Seattle, 1975—; dir. Clin. Nurse Scholars Program, Robert Wood Johnson Found. Author: Strategies for Teaching Nursing, 1971, 3rd edit., 1987, Japanese transl., 1974, Spanish edit., 1986. Mem. Am. Nurses Assn., Am. Acad. Nursing (charter fellow, pres. 1973-75), Inst. Medicine (governing council 1979-81), Soc. Health and Human Values, Nat. League for Nursing (dir. 1976-79). Office: Sch Nursing SM-24 U Wash Seattle WA 98195

DETRE, KATHERINE MARIA, physician; b. Budapest, Hungary, Apr. 28, 1926; came to Can., 1949; d. Ignac and Irene (Lefkovits) Drechsler; m. Thomas P. Detre, Sept. 16, 1956; children: John, Anthony. Student, U. Med. Sch., Budapest, 1945-49; BA, Queens U., Kingston, Ont., Can., 1950, MD, 1952; MPH, Yale U., 1964, PhD, 1967. Rotating intern Kingston Gen. Hosp., Queens Kingston, Ont., Can., 1952-53; resident in internal medicine Queen Mary Vets. Hosp. McGill, Montreal, 1953-56; research assoc. hematology Yale U., New Haven, 1956-60, lectr. in biometry, 1968-74; biostatistician VA Cooperative Studies Program, West Haven, Ct., 1967—; assoc. prof. U. Pitts., 1974-79, prof. epidemiology, 1979—; clin. adv. bd. NIH, Bethesda, Md., 1977-78, epidemiology and disease control com. 1983—; research com. B Nat. Heart, Lung and Blood Inst., Bethesda, 1978-82. Contbr. 132 articles to profl. jours. Named Woman in Sci. Chatham Coll., 1987; internat. student scholar Queens U., 1949-52. Fellow Council on Epidemiology (chmn. 1981-83), Am. Coll. Epidemiology; mem. Am. Statis. Assn., Biometric Soc. (regional adv. bd. 1978-81), Soc. Clin. Trials (bd. dirs. 1981-85), Am. Epidemiology Soc. Office: U Pitts 130 DeSoto St A531 Pittsburgh PA 15261

DETTERMAN, DEBORAH ALLYNN, accountant; b. Bklyn., Oct. 3, 1951; d. Herbert Allen and Mary Eleanor (Van Ness) Wortmann; m. Paul Eric Detterman, Oct. 26, 1985. B.S., Fairleigh Dickinson U., 1984. Actuarial supr. Bankers Nat. Life Ins. Co., Parsippany, N.J., 1969-76; staff acct. Bobst Champlain, Inc., Roseland, N.J., 1976-82; staff acct., controller Blonder-Tongue Labs., Inc., Old Bridge, N.J., 1982-86 ; asst. corp. controllerSteinway Musical Properties, Inc., Newton, Mass, 1986— . Treas., North Jersey Walk for Mankind, West Caldwell, N.J., 1980-81. Dir. youth choir Presbyn. Ch. West Caldwell, 1980-82. N.J. Soc. C.P.A.s scholar, 1982. Mem. Delta Mu Delta, Phi Omega Epsilon. Presbyterian. Office: Steinway Mus Properties Inc 120 Wells Ave Newton MA 02159

DE TUEDE, CATHERINE, executive recruitment consultant; b. Brookline, Mass., Feb. 15, 1951; d. James Kerr and Villa (Hodgkins) Tweedie; m. Alexander Drummond Close, Mar. 21, 1969 (div. Apr. 1978). BA in Am. Studies, Manhattanville Coll., 1977; MLS, Columbia U., 1981. Asst. librarian Greenwich (Conn.) Library, 1978-81; reference librarian Perrott Library, Greenwich, 1981-82; research assoc. Halbrecht Assocs., Stamford, Conn., 1982-83, dir. research, 1983-85; cons. Haskell & Stern Assocs., Inc., N.Y.C., 1985—; cons. Bush-Holley House Greenwich Hist. Soc., 1979-80. Vol. Arts Council, Greenwich, 1980-81. Mem. Am. Shakespeare Theatre (chmn. benefit com. 1975-76), Nat. Audubon Soc. (vol. 1974), Columbia U. Alumni Club. Republican. Episcopalian. Home: 4 Lafayette Ct 4A Greenwich CT 06830 Office: Haskell & Stern Assocs Inc 529 5th Ave New York NY 10017

DETURK, PAMELA ELIZABETH, educator, consultant; b. Phila., Aug. 26, 1946; d. Clarence Newton and Myrtle (Stauffer) Herb; m. Jay Ralph DeTurk, June 8, 1968; children: Nathan Jacob, Benjamin Levi. AS, Harcum Jr. Coll.; BS in Elem. Edn., St. Joseph U.; MEd, U. Colo. Tchr. Bryn Mawr (Pa.) Pre-Sch., 1966-68, Boyertown (Pa.) Area Sch. Dist., 1968-70; tchr. trainable mentally retarded Mahoning County Sch. for Retarded, Youngstown, Ohio, 1970-76, El Paso Sch. Dist. #11, Colorado Springs, Colo., 1976—; cons., tutor PHD Learning Systems, Inc., Colorado Springs, 1982—; v.p. JMJ Imports, Inc., Colorado Springs, 1985—; ptnr. Rampart Kennels, Colorado Springs, 1981—. Mem. Airedale Terrier Club of Am. (mem. nominating com. 1976—), Colorado Springs Kennel Club (corresponding sec. 1978-80). Lutheran. Home: 5977 Templeton Gap Rd Colorado Springs CO 80918 Office: Bristol Elem Sch 890 N Walnut St Colorado Springs CO 80905

DEUBERRY, LAURA ANNE, college administrator; b. St. Paul, Aug. 23, 1948; d. William N. and Neenann A. (Burns) D. Student, St. Mary's Coll., Mpls.; AA, Metro State Coll. Materiel mgr. Divine Redeemer Hosp., South St. Paul, Minn., 1972-76; buyer The Webb Co., St. Paul, 1976-83; dir. purchasing accounts payable, receiving and stores Coll. of St. Thomas, St. Paul, 1983—. Singer St. Paul Opera Workshop, 1974-75, Coppertones, Mpls., 1979-82; advisor St. Paul Jr. Achievement, 1977-82; vol. Little Bros. of the Poor, Mpls., 1985; mem. St. Paul Jr. League, 1986—. Recipient Community Leader award St. Paul YWCA, 1983. Mem. Nat. Assn. Purchasing Mgmt., Nat. Assn. Ednl. Buyers (regional pres. 1986, editorial bd. 1986—, Leader award 1986), Twin City Purchasing Mgmt. Assn. (seminar chairperson 1984-86, chair bus. edn. found. com. 1987, Recognition award 1986), Associated Colls. of Twin Cities (chairperson joint purchasing com. 1986). Office: Coll of St Thomas 2115 Summit Ave Box 5045 Saint Paul MN 55105

DEUMAN, LEANNE BARNES, lawyer; b. Sault Ste. Marie, Mich., Oct. 7, 1951; d. Wayne Gordon and Anne (Welsh) Barnes; m. Gary Wayne Deuman, Apr. 25, 1981. B.A. cum laude in English Lang. and Lit., Lake Superior State Coll., 1975; J.D. cum laude, Thomas M. Cooley Law Sch., 1982. Bar: Mich. 1982. Bus. mgr. E.U.P. Mental Health Bd., Sault Ste. Marie, Mich., 1976-79; assoc. Thomas J. Veum, P.C., Sault Ste. Marie, 1982—. Trustee, First United Presbyn. Ch., 1984—; bd. dirs. Salvation Army; of counsel Sault Symphony Assn. Recipient Disting. Student Alumni award T.M. Cooley Law Sch., 1982; Ga. Emery Scholar, Mich. Fedn. Bus. and Profl. Women's Club, 1979-82. Mem. Mich. Bar Assn., Mich. Trial Lawyers Assn., Women Lawyers Assn. Mich., 50th Jud. Dist. Bar Assn. (pres. 1985-86), NOW, Chippewa Baroque Soc., Bus. and Profl. Women's Club. Presbyterian. Lodge: Rotary. Office: Thomas J Veum PC 216 Ashman St Sault Sainte Marie MI 49783

DEUSS, JEAN, librarian; b. Chgo.; d. Edward Louis and Harriet (Goodwin) D. B.A., U. Wis., 1944; M.S., Sch. Library Service, Columbia U., 1959. Cataloger library N.Y.C. Council Fgn. Relations, 1959-61; head cataloger research library Fed. Res. Bank N.Y., N.Y.C., 1961-68; asst. chief librarian Fed. Bank N.Y., N.Y.C., 1969-70, chief librarian, 1970-85. Editor Banking and Fin. Collections, Spl. Collections, vol. 2, No. 3, 1983. Mem. U. Wis. Found., 1977—, bd. dirs., 1983—. Mem. Spl. Libraries Assn. (assoc. treas. 1967-70, pres. N.Y. chpt. 1971-72, bd. dirs. 1972-76). Episcopalian. Home: 260 W 12 St New York NY 10014

DEUTSCH, FLORENCE ELAYNE GOODILL, nursing and health care consultant; b. San Diego, Aug. 1, 1923; d. George Ehrlich and Beatrice Marie (Urick) Goodill; m. Edward Thomas Deutsch, June 27, 1953 (dec.); 1 son, George Edward. Student, San Diego State Coll., 1942-43; B.S.N., Villa Maria Coll., 1948; diploma in nursing Evanston Hosp., Northwestern U., 1947; M.Ed., Edinboro U., 1961. Staff nurse St. Vincent Hosp., Erie, Pa., 1947; clin. instr.-supr. Hamot Med. Ctr., Erie, 1948-58, dir. edn., 1958-62, dir. Sch. Nursing, 1962-66, asst. adminstr., dir. Sch. Nursing, 1969-73; exec. dir. Florence Crittenton Home, Erie, 1966-69; asst. adminstr., dir. nursing Capitol Hill Hosp., Washington, 1974-79; assoc. adminstr. profl. services Millcreek Community Hosp., 1980-82; v.p. nursing East Liverpool City Hosp. (Ohio), 1982-87; lectr., cons. on nursing and nursing law. Past bd. dirs. Columbiana County Cancer Soc. Served with USNR, 1948-53. Named Most Outstanding Nurse Erie County, 1969. Mem. Nat. League Nursing, Am. Orgn. Nurse Execs., Am. Soc. Law and Medicine, Sigma Theta Tau, Delta Kappa Gamma. Republican. Presbyterian. Editor: Penn League News, 1968-70; contbr. articles to profl. jours. Address: 3207 Georgian Ct Erie PA 16506

DEUTSCH, NINA, concert pianist, actress; b. San Antonio, Mar. 15; d. Irvin and Freda Deutsch; B.S., Juilliard Sch. Music; M.M.A., Yale U., 1973. Concert pianist, 1958—; recording artist Vox Prodns.; only woman to record complete solo piano music of Charles Ives, 1976; recs. include: piano arrangement of Variations on Am. (Ives); freelance writer on music for N.Y. Times, UPI and mags., 1974—; music cons. Joe Franklin Show, WOR-TV, 1975—; entertainer Home Lines Cruises, N.Y.C., 1987—; exec. v.p. Internat. Symphony. Author: (play) Portrait of Clara Wieck Schumann. Bd. dirs. Metzner Found. for Overseas Relief; Ft. Lee coordinator Channel 13, 1974. Grantee Nat. Endowment for Arts, 1975, Phillips Petroleum Found., 1982; Tanglewood fellow, 1966; recipient award for Am. music Nat. Fedn. Music Clubs, 1975; Oberlin Coll. scholar. Mem. Music Critics Assn., Publicity Club N.Y., Dramatist Guild, Music Critics Assn. Avocations: swimming, baking. Home: 410 Hazlitt Ave Leonia NJ 07605

DEUTSCH, SYLVIA, municipal official; b. Bklyn., July 9, 1924; d. Nathan and Dora (Siegel) Schatz; m. Leon Deutsch, Dec. 21, 1946; children: Jack, Nathaniel Mark, Jeremy Joseph. AB cum laude, Bklyn. Coll., 1947. Exec. dir. Proportional Representation Ednl. Project, 1969-70; dir. N.Y. Met. Council, Am. Jewish Congress, 1972-78; edn. cons. ,1972-78, nat. dir. field ops. and membership, 1978-81; mem. N.Y.C. Planning Commn., 1972-81, chair, 1987—; chair N.Y.C. Bd. Standards and Appeals, 1981-87; dir. N.Y.C. Dept. City Planning, 1987—. Mem. Mayor's Commn. Taxi Regulatory Issues, 1981-82; v.p., chmn. legis. com. United Parents Assns., 1967-72, chmn. orgn. dept. and high schs., 1962-67; mem. Citizens Commn. City U., 1969-71; co-founder, exec. v.p. Com. for Pub. Higher Edn., 1966-74; mem. Mayor's Commn. Status of Women, 1976-79. Named Alumna of Yr., Bklyn. Coll., 1974; recipient Community Service award NCCJ, 1976, Nat. award Girls' Clubs of Am., 1988. Jewish. Office: NYC Planning Commn 22 Reade St New York NY 10007

DEUTZ, NATALIE RUBINSTEIN, consultant; b. Plymouth, Mass., Sept. 26; d. Louis and Lillian Rubinstein; student Simmons Coll., 1937, Modern Sch. Applied Art, 1938-40; m. Nov. 29, 1947 (dec.). Fashion buyer Wm. Filene's Sons Co., Boston, 1940-47; asst. to corp. pres. Columbia Textiles, Inc., N.Y.C., 1956-68; dir. John Robert Powers Sch., N.Y.C., 1968-72; v.p., nat. dir. fashion merchandising, dir. advt. workshop Barbizon Internat., Inc., N.Y.C., 1972-83; cons., 1983—. Mem. Nat. Acad. TV Arts and Scis., Screen Actors Guild, AFTRA.

DEVANEY, CYNTHIA ANN, real estate broker, elementary school teacher; b. Gary, Ind., Feb. 6, 1947; d. Charles Barnard and Irene Mae (Nelson) Burner; m. Harold Verne DeVaney, Nov. 23, 1974 (dec. 1981). BS, Ball State U., 1970, MS, 1972; postgrad., Ind. U., Gary, 1974-76. Cert. real estate broker, Ind. Real estate broker Century 21 McColly Realtors, Merrillville, Ind., 1979-86, Better Homes and Gardens McColly Realtors, Merrillville, 1986—; tchr. Merkley Elem. Sch., Highland, Ind., 1969—. Leader Project Charlie Drug Program, Highland, 1987—; active Schubert Theater Guild, Chgo. Mem. Calumet Bd. Realtors (bd. dirs.), Nat. Bd. Realtors. Democrat. Methodist. Clubs: Million Dollar, Innsbrook Country, Match Point Tennis. Home: 607 E 78th Pl Merrillville IN 46410 Office: McColly Better Homes & Gardens 9143 Indianapolis Blvd Highland IN 46322

DEVAUGHN, DONNA MICHELLE, insurance company executive; b. Houston, Sept. 20, 1954; d. Canary and Louise (Robinson) DeV. BBA, So. Meth. U., 1977. Assoc. mgr. acctg. and payroll Prudential Ins. Co., Inc., Houston, 1980-83; adminstrv. mgr. claims and billing Prudential Health Care Plan, Inc. subs. Prudential Ins. Co., Inc., Memphis, 1983-84, dir. adminstrn. Prucare of Memphis div., 1984-86; dir. health care mgmt. Prudential Health Care Systems, Inc. subs. Prudential Ins. Co., Inc., Memphis, 1987—; preceptor for health adminstrn. grad. internship program Memphis State U., 1985-86. Vol. Big Bros./Big Sisters United Way Agy., Houston and Memphis. Mem. Nat. Assn. Female Execs., Delta Sigma Theta. Democrat. Methodist. Lodge: Heralds of Jericho. Office: Prudential Ins Co Inc 845 Crossover Ln Suite 220 Memphis TN 38117

DEVILLE, VICKI LYNNE, commercial real estate broker; b. Portland, Oreg., Sept. 5, 1950; d. Byron Paul and Alice Gertrude (Ely) Brocksen; m. Gary Raymond McGrew, Sept. 11, 1971 (div. 1978); children: Jason Alan, Justin Scott; m. Paul Irving deVille, July 13, 1985; stepchildren: Tricia, Melany, Landon. BS, Portland State U., 1973. Lic. elem. tchr., Oreg. Elem. sch. tchr. Portland Pub. Schs., 1973-75; mortgage loan processor Equitable Savs. and Loan, Portland, 1876-77; adminstrv. asst. The Robert Randall Co., Portland, 1976-79; comml. mktg. mgr. Chgo. Title Ins., Portland, 1979-83; comml. real estate broker Norris, Beggs & Simpson, Portland, 1983-84, Monroe & Friedlander, Honolulu, 1984-87; owner Vicki deVille Hidden Treasures Shopping Excursion, Honolulu, 1987—. Recipient Project award Monroe & Friedlander, Inc., 1985. Mem. Nat. Asssn. Realtors, Honolulu Bd. Realtors, Profl. Women's Network. Republican. Clubs: Pilot, Ladies Who Invest and Perhaps Speculate (Honolulu). Home and Office: 201 Poipu Dr Honolulu HI 96825 other: Monroe & Friedlander 220 S King St #1800 Honolulu HI 96813

DEVINE, DORIS MARION, nurse; b. Guelph, Ont., Can., Aug. 7, 1946; d. Malcolm Angus and Wilma Irene (Watson) Moffat; m. William James Devine, Oct. 19, 1974; 1 child, Luanne Marie. Diploma in Nursing, Guelph Gen. Hosp., 1968; student, Conestoga Coll., 1978-81, U. Waterloo, 1984-86. RN, Can. Nurse Edmonton (Alta.), Milton (Ont.), Guelph (Ont.), Can., 1968-72; head nurse Guelph Gen. Hosp., Can., 1972-78; supr. nurses Gen. Hosp., Guelph, Ont., Can., 1978-87, employee health nurse, 1982-87, asst. staff edn., 1986087; nurse Wellington Indust. Med. Services, Guelph, Ont., Can., 1987—; tchr. Candy Stripers, Gen. Hosp., Guelph 1982-86. Canvasser Ont. Heart Found., Guelph 1987. Mem. Coll. Nurses Ont., RN Assn. Ont., occupational Nurses Assn. Ont., Nurse's Alumni Assn. (pres. 1986-88). Liberal. Mem. United Ch. Home: 16 Penni Pl, Guelph CAN N1H 7L2

DE VINE-KIRK, VALARIA ANN, entrepreneur; b. Chgo., June 14, 1951; children: Stacy, Stephen, Scott. Student, So. Ill. U., 1969, Lewis U., 1976-77. Asst. gen. mgr. Hilton-Stauffers, Chgo., 1970-73; v.p. Universal Temperature Control, Glendale Heights, Ill., 1974-77; sales rep. Matthew-Bender & Co., N.Y.C., 1977-79, D & S Pubs., Clearwater, Fla., 1979-80; assoc. pub., bus. mgr., pub. cons. Rep-Insider mag., Ft. Lauderdale, Fla., 1980-81; pres. Galaxy Distbg., Inc., Charlotte, N.C., 1982-87, Trailers by Squires, Inc., Matthews, N.C., 1988—; lectr., cons. small bus. Mem. Nat. Assn. Female Execs. Home: 3031 Shallowood Ln Mathews NC 28105 Office: Trailers by Squire Inc 3709 Gribble Rd Matthews NC 28105

DEVINEY, ELIZABETH CATHERINE, psychotherapist; b. New Brunswick, N.J., Apr. 16, 1943; d. Elton Taylor and Frances Kathleen DeV. BS, Trenton State Coll., Ewing, 1964; MA, Jersey City State U., 1971; MSW, Rutgers U., 1972; postgrad., Fielding Inst. Cert. tchr. handicapped; lic. marriage consellor. Tchr. East Brunswick (N.Y.) Pub. Schs., 1965-66; founder, dir. Rutkowski Sch. Emotionally Disturbed Children, New Brunswick, N.J., 1967-76, adminstr. Morristown (N.J.) Mem. Hosp., 1976-86, dir. child & adolescent services, 1976-86; pvt. practice psychotherapist Bernardsville, N.Y., 1982—; sheep breeder Clover Hill Farm, Flemington, N.Y., 1976—; cons. N.J. Assn. Brain Injured Children, 1974-78, Dept. Youth & Family Services, Somerset and Hunterdon counties, 1982—. Contbr. articles to profl. jours. Mem. Nat. Assn. Soc. Workers, (cert.), N.J. Battered Women's Assn. (pres. 1978-80). Office: Flemington Ctr Psychotherapy Clover Hill Farm Flemington NJ 08822

DEVIVO, ANGE, small business owner; b. Bay Shore, N.Y., Oct. 20, 1925; d. Romeo Zanetti and Karolina (Hodapp) King; m. John Michael DeVivo, Dec. 30, 1950; 1 child, Michael. Student, Washington Sch. for Secs., N.Y.C., 1945-46. Sec. Am. Airlines, N.Y.C., 1946-51; exec. sec. W.C. Holzhauer, N.Y.C., 1951-52; dist. sales mgr. Emmons Jewelers, Inc., Bound Brook, N.J., 1952-53; adminstrv. sec. Mercy Hosp., Charlotte, N.C., 1973-81; pres. Secs., Plus, Convs., Plus, Charlotte, 1983—; com. chair Bus. Opportunity Network, Charlotte, 1987. Active Human Services Council, Charlotte, 1984-88, Emergency Med. Services Adv. Council, Charlotte, 1981—, Charlotte Women's Polit. Caucus, 1972—, Mecklenburg Evening Rep. Women's Club, Charlotte, 1970—, citizen's adv. com. Conv. and Vis. Bur., Charlotte, 1986—; mem. chamber com. Small Bus. Council, 1983-86, 88. Recipient Order Long Leaf Pine award Gov. of N.C., 1974. Mem. Women Bus. Owners, Meeting Planners Internat., Meeting Cons. Network, Greater Charlotte C. of C. (minority/women bus. entrepreneurs 1988). Roman Catholic. Office: Secs Plus/Conventions Plus 2 Fairview Plaza Suite 620 5980 Fairview Rd Charlotte NC 28210

DEVLIN, DIANE MARIE, nurse; b. Bucks County, Pa., Dec. 17, 1957; d. Elmer and Josephine (Mazeika) Glaum; m. James V. Devlin; 1 child, Monica. BSN, Trenton (N.J.) State Coll., 1982; diploma, Abington Sch. Nursing, 1978. Cert. childbirth tchr. Staff nurse Abington (Pa.) Meml. Hosp., 1978-82; dir. nursing services Home Cross, Phila., 1982-83; pub. health nurse Bucks County Dept. Health, Bristol, Pa., 1983-85; pvt. practice nursing, cons. Levittown, Pa., 1985—. Mem. AAUW (bd. dirs. Bucks County 1984), Am. Nurses Assn., Am. Soc. Psychoprophylaxis, Pa. Nurses Assn., Lower Bucks C. of C., Sigma Theta Tau. Republican. Roman Catholic. Home and Office: 55 Idlewild Rd Levittown PA 19057

DEVLIN, LAURA MARIE, lawyer; b. Chgo., Mar. 30, 1959; d. Thomas H. and Geraldine M. Devlin; m. Justin D. Smock, Feb. 14, 1987. BA, U. Ill., Champaign, 1980; JD, Ind. U., 1983. Bar: Ill. 1983. Atty. Hyatt Legal Services, Matteson, Ill., 1984; ptnr. Devlin & Smock, South Holland, Ill., 1984—; speaker South Holland Pub. Library, Calumet City (Ill.) Pub. Library, Ill., Evergreen Park (Ill.) Pub. Library. Mem. ABA, Ill. Bar Assn., Chgo. Bar Assn., South Suburban Bar Assn. Office: Devlin & Smock 837 E 162d South Holland IL 60473 Other: Devlin & Smock 7725 W 159th St Tinley Park IL 60477

DEVLIN, MARY KATHLEEN, information management consultant; b. Portland, Oreg., Aug. 17, 1946; d. Donald Eugene and Laura W. Devlin. BS, Lewis and Clark Coll., 1968, MAT, 1971; MLS, U. Oreg., 1976. Service rep. Pacific N.W. Bell Co., Portland, 1969-70; approval program mgr. Richard Abel and Co., Ltd., London, 1971-75; trade mgr. Gerald Duckworth & Co., Ltd., London, 1975; spl. services librarian U. Portland, Oreg., 1977-78, tech. services librarian, 1978-80; tech. librarian Portland Gen. Electric, 1980-82, mgr. library services, 1982-84, mgr. Info. Ctr., 1984-88, info. mgmt. cons., 1988—; instr. library automation Maryhurst Coll., Oreg., 1981, instr. mgmt. info. systems, 1988; del. Oreg. Gov.'s Conf. on Libraries and Info. Sci., 1978. Author: (pamphlet) At the Crossroads, 1984; editor Directory of Spl. Libraries in Oreg. and S.W. Wash., 1978. Mem. Commn. on Futures Research, Salem, 1987; chairperson fire bur. adv. com. City of Portland, 1988—; bd. dirs. Columbia-Willamette Futures Forum, Portland, 1984-85; mem. adv. bd. Econ. Info. Network, Salem, Oreg., 1986—; pres. bd. dirs. Oreg. Library PAC, 1986-87; active Communications Era Task Force, Action Linkage, Conf. of Corridors. Mem. Oreg. Library Assn. (pres. 1984-85), Pacific N.W. Library Assn. (bd. dirs. 1980-82, Oreg. rep. 1980-82), Spl. Libraries Assn. (bd. dirs. Oreg. chpt. 1977-78), Soc. for Info. Mgmt., OCLC Peer Council, Stumptown Cloggers. Democrat. Avocations: reading, film theater, skiing. Office: 921 SW Morrison Suite 531 Portland OR 97205

DEVNEY, JAYN ANNE, mental health facility administrator; b. Dover, Ohio, Apr. 10, 1955; d. Donald Leroy and Dorothy Mae (Purkey) Fisher; m. Gregory Allen Devney. BA in Sociology, Kent State U., 1977; MBA, Ashland Coll., 1984. Intake worker dept. human services Tuscarawas County, New Philadephia, Ohio, 1975-77; dir. alcohol program dept. health Tuscarawas County, Dover, Ohio, 1979-81; mental health intake worker Community Profl. Services, Dover, Ohio, 1977-79; assoc. dir. Tuscarawas-Carroll Mental Health Bd., New Philadelphia, 1981-85, exec. dir., 1985—. Bd. dirs. Personal Family Counseling, 1979-81, Eastern Ohio Regional Alcoholism Council, 1984—, United Day Care, New Philadelphia, 1985—, Sagamore Hills (Ohio) Children's Pschiat. Hosp., 1987-1990. Mem. Ohio Assn. Community Mental Health Bds. (exec. com. 1987-88), Mental Health Adminstrs. Republican. Home: 423 W 7th St Dover OH 44622 Office: Tuscarawas-Carroll Community Mental Health Bd County Rd 21 S PO Box 522 New Philadelphia OH 44663

DE VORE, DENISE ELLEN, marine biologist, researcher; b. N.Y.C., May 2, 1955; d. Bert and Laura Esther (Borrego) De V. B.S. in Biology and French, Coll. Mt. St. Vincent, 1977; M.S. in Biology, Adelphi U., 1979; postgrad. in Marine Scis., U. P.R., 1980—. Teaching asst. dept. biology Adelphi U., 1977-79; research assoc. U. Md., 1979; research asst. Ctr. Energy and Environ. Research Dept. Marine Scis. U. P.R., Mayaguez, 1980-81, 83-86 ; profl. chem. cons. Mayaguez Water Treatment, 1980, 81. Contbr. articles to profl. jours. Vol. tutor for high sch. students in Sci. Fair 1981-84. Vol. judge for regional and state high sch. sci. fairs, 1985, 86. Grantee Sigma Xi., 1984, 86; named Outstanding Young Women of Am., 1980. NSF trainee, 1981-83; Slocum-Lunz Found. grantee, 1983. Mem. AAAS, Internat. Soc. Toxinology, Internat. Soc. Chem. Ecology, Sigma Xi, Alpha Mu Gamma, Beta Beta Beta. Editor departmental newspaper, 1984-85. Home: 326 Tejas St San Gerardo Rio Piedras PR 00926 Office: U PR Dept Marine Scis PO Box 5000 Mayaguez PR 00708

DEVOSS, VICKI RAE, educator; b. Red Oak, Iowa, Oct. 19, 1946; d. George Watson and Hillis Lorene (Peterman) DeV. BBA in Math. and English, Moorhead (Minn.) State U., 1969; MA in Math. Edn., Stanford U., 1977; cert. in spl. edn. learning disabilities, Mankato (Minn.) State U., 1978. Tchr. Jurupa Unified Sch. Dist., Riverside, Calif., 1969-70; tchr. vocat. high sch. Mpls., 1970-75; tchr. Work Opportunity Ctr., Mpls., 1975—, chair dept., 1975-85; active West Area Achievement Project Mpls. Pub. Schs., 1980, mem. citywide testing com., 1985-87. Author (coursebook) Mathematics Used in Occupations; (with others) math. coursework, tests. Vol. Save the Children Craft Shop, Mpls., 1986-87. NSF scholar, 1972-74. Mem. Nat. Council Tchrs. of Math., Minn. Council Tchrs. Math., Mpls. Math Club, Urban Math. Collaborative. Office: Work Opportunity Ctr 2908 Colfax S Minneapolis MN 55408

DE VRIES, BARBARA KAY, systems manager, consultant; b. Angleton, Tex., June 2, 1957; d. Glenn Lester and Esther Annie (Reavis) DeV.; m. Keith T. Dean, Aug. 16, 1975. BA in Physics, Tex. A&M U., 1977, BA in Chemistry, 1977; BS in Math., Tex. A & M U., 1978; MA in Math., U. Calif., Berkeley, 1979. Instr. math Tex. A & M U., College Station, 1977-78; instr. math, physics U. Calif., Berkeley, 1978-79; programmers, system analyst TRW, Inc., Redondo Beach, Calif., 1979-81; system analyst, cons. TMI, Inc., Dallas, 1981-82; mgr. project SEI Corp., Dallas, 1983; sr. system analyst Shared Fin. Systems, Dallas, 1983-84; mgr. Shope Assocs., Inc., Dallas, 1984—. Com. mem. Farmers Branch (Tex.) Task Force, 1983-84. Recipient scholarship United Daughters of the Confederacy, 1974, Houston A & M Mothers, 1977-78, grant Welch Found., 1976-77. Mem. Mensa, Pi Mu Epsilon. Republican. Methodist. Home: 14353 Tanglewood Dr Farmers Branch TX 75234 Office: Shope Assocs Inc 8204 Elmbrook Dr Suite 217 Dallas TX 75247

DE VRIES, MARGARET GARRITSEN, economist; b. Detroit, Feb. 11, 1922; d. John Edward and Margaret Florence (Ruggles) Garritsen; m. Barend A. de Vries, Apr. 5, 1952; children: Christine, Barton. B.A. in Econs. with honors, U. Mich., 1943; Ph.D. in Econs., MIT, 1946. With IMF, Washington, 1946-87, sr. economist, 1949-52, asst. chief multiple currency pratices div., 1953-57, chief Far Eastern Div., 1957-59, econ. cons., 1963-73, historian, 1973-87; professorial lectr. econs. George Washington U., 1946-49, 58-63. Author: (with Irving S. Friedman) Foreign Economic Policy of the United States in the Postwar, 1947, (with J. Keith Horsefield and others) The International Monetary Fund, 1945-1965, Twenty Years of International Monetary Cooperation, 3 vols., 1969, The International Monetary Fund, 1966-71, The System Under Stress, 2 vols., 1977, The International Monetary Fund, 1972-78, Cooperation on Trial, 3 vols., 1985, The IMF in a Changing World, 1945-85, 1986, Balance of Payments Adjustment, 1945-86: The IMF Experience, 1987; contbr. articles to profl. jours. Recipient Disting. Alumni award U. Mich., 1980, Cert. of Appreciation George Washington U., 1987, Outstanding Washington Woman Economist award, 1987; AAUW scholar, 1939-42; U. Mich. Univ. scholar, 1942; MIT fellow, 1943-46; Ford Found. grantee, 1959-62. Mem. Am. Econ. Assn., Washington Women Economists Assn., U. Mich. Alumni Assn., MIT Alumnae Assn., Phi Beta Kappa, Phi Kappa Phi. Mem. United Church of Christ. Home: 10018 Woodhill Rd Bethesda MD 20817 Office: IMF 700 19th St NW Washington DC 20431

DEW, JOAN KING, author; b. Columbus, Ga., June 24, 1932; d. Henry Grady and Vivian Pauline (Cook) King; m. Clifford Dew (div.); children—Clifford L., Jr., Michael David; m. 2d. Albert Schmitt (div.); children—Christopher, Thomas. Student, Fla. State U., 1949-51; reporter, feature writer Ft. Lauderdale (Fla.) Daily News, 1950-56; editor Nassau (Bahamas) Guardian, 1956-58; stringer UPI, Bahamas, 1956-58; copy chief Art and Publicity, Ltd., Kingston, Jamaica, 1958-60; feature writer, author column Male Call, Valley Times Today, North Hollywood, Calif., 1960-66; freelance writer, Hollywood, Calif., 1966-77, Nashville, 1977—. Author: Singers and Sweethearts: The Women in Country Music, 1977; Stand By Your Man: The Autobiography of Tammy Wynette, 1978; Minnie Pearl, The Autobiography of Minnie Pearl, 1980; 3 books on wine and food, 1984-88, Christmas 1987, 1987, Follow Your Heart (with David Fox) 1988; columnist Nashville Tennessean, 1988; contbr. numerous articles to nat. mags. Office: PO Box 150904 Nashville TN 37215

DEW, LINDA SUE, health science facility administrator; b. Bastrop, La., Aug. 21, 1956; d. Jewel Clinton and Christien Cora (Hughes) D. Student, La. Tech. U., 1974-75; AAS, Tidewater Coll., 1977. With counter sales Taylor Rentals, Portsmouth, Va., 1977-80, party cons., 1978-80; asst. mgr. Patient Aids & Party Rentals, Norfolk, Va., 1980-81; gen. mgr. Aids for Health Care, Norfolk, 1983-87; div. mgr. Medequip Ctr. Inc., Norfolk, 1987; pres., owner Rehab Health Care, Norfolk, 1987—; cons. Hosp. Corp. Am., Nashville, 1987—; v.p. Home Care Systems Inc., Portsmouth, 1988—; bd. dirs. Albemarle Home Care Systems., Elizabeth City, N.C. Mem. Health Industry Digest Assn. Democrat. Mem. Ch. of Christ. Home: 2920 Seashore Point Virginia Beach VA 23454 Office: Rehab Health Care 5873 Poplar Hall Dr Norfolk VA 23502

DEWALD, GRETTA MOLL, county official; b. Kutztown, Pa., Oct. 26, 1929; d. Lloyd A. and Olga (Wuchter) M.; m. Charles Frederick DeWald, Dec. 20, 1951; children—Michael S., Jonathon G., Henry L., Janie P., Joseph C. BA, Agnes Scott Coll., 1950. Tchr. secondary schs. Eastman City Schs., Ga., 1950-51, Bass High Sch., Atlanta, 1951-52; project exec. sec. Appalachian project Day Care and Child Devel. Council Am., Atlanta, 1971-73; researcher Ga. Senate, Atlanta, 1973-74; community relations officer Met. Atlanta Rapid Transit Authority, 1976-77, bd. dirs., 1977; dir. women's div. Democratic Nat. Com., Washington, 1977-80; exec. asst. to chief exec. officer and bd. commrs. DeKalb County, Decatur, Ga., 1981—. Aide to commr. DeKalb Bd. Commrs., 1974-77. Mem. Ga. Commn. on Volunteerism, 1970-74, Ga. Women's Adv. Com., 1972-74, Nat. Adv. Com. of Women, 1977-80. Chmn., DeKalb County Dem. Com., 1972-74, 4th Congl. Dist. Ga. Com., 1974-76; campaigner, Peanut Brigade, N.H., Vt., Md., Ohio, Wi., Fla., Pa., 1976; del. Dem. Nat. Conv., 1972, 74, 76, 80; mem. adv. bd. Ga. Women's Polit. Caucus, 1983—; So. regional coordinator Dem. Task Force, Nat. Women's Polit. Caucus, 1983-85; organizer, mem. adv. bd. DeKalb Women's Network, 1983—; bd. dirs. DeKalb Library System, 1981—; bd. dirs. DeKalb Humane Soc., 1985-88; bd. dirs. Our House, Inc., 1987-88; mem. Women's Resource Ctr. DeKalb. Mem. Nat. Assn. County Adminstrs., Ga. Council County Adminstrs. and Mgrs. (v.p. 1986—), Nat. Assn. Counties (steering com. intergovtl. relations 1981—, mem. women ofcls. chpt.), Women's Council Nat. Assn. Counties, Assn. County Commrs. Ga. (bd. dirs. 1986-88), County Adminstrs. Ga. (pres. council 1986-88), City-County Mgrs. Assn. Ga., Abigails (organizer). Presbyterian. Home: 1096 DeLeon Ct Clarkston GA 30021 Office: New Court House 9th Floor Commn Office 456 N McDonough St Decatur GA 30030

DEWBERRY, BETTY BAUMAN, law librarian; b. Dallas, Jan. 18, 1930; d. William Allen Bauman and Julia Ella (Owen) Hurt; m. James A. Dewberry Jr., Mar. 22, 1952 (div. Apr. 1976); children: Mary Julienne, Jennifer Camille, Robert Bruce. BA, U. Tex., 1951; MLS, Tex. Women's U., 1982. Asst. librarian Johnson & Swanson, Dallas, 1979-85, dir. libraries, 1985—. Mem. Am. Assn. Law Libraries, Southwestern Assn. of Law Librarians, Dallas Assn. Law Librarians, Spl. Libraries Assn. Democrat. Presbyterian. Club: Lakeside Browning.

DEWBERRY, CLAIRE DEARMENT, engineering librarian; b. Youngstown, Ohio, Oct. 12, 1937; d. Eugene Howard and Ruth (Bright) DeA.; m. Carl R. Meinstereifel, 1956 (div. 1964); children—Paul, Dawn; m. Olin Jerry Dewberry, Jr., 1974 (div. 1979). B.S., Clarion State U., 1967; M.L.S., Ga. State U., 1977. Cert. library media specialist, Ga. Librarian Henry County, Stockbridge, Ga., 1967-69; head librarian Russell High Sch., East Point, Ga., 1969-84; engrig. librarian Rockwell Internat., Duluth, Ga., 1984—; rep. GIDEP, Corona, Calif., 1984—. Author newsletter: Blueline. Mem. Spl. Libraries Assn., Mensa, AIAA. Democrat. Avocations: computers; flea market selling; writing. Home: 5623 Cobb Meadow Norcross GA 30093 Office: Rockwell Internat Corp 1800 Satellite Blvd Duluth GA 30136

DEWEERD, ANNETTE MAE, nursing director; b. Holland, Mich., Mar. 13, 1933; d. Raymond and Elizabeth (Dreyer) DeW. BS in Nursing, U. Mich., 1959, M of Guidance and Counseling, 1972. RN. Psychiatric attendant nurse Pine Rest Christian Hosp., Grand Rapids, Mich., 1951-55, nursing supr., pediatric clin. instr., 1959-61, dir. clin. support services, 1961—, mem. sr. mgmt. team, 1983; past nurse cons. North Shore Community Mental Health Ctr., Muskegon, Mich.; cons. Project Rehab., Grand Rapids, 1980. Mem. Am. Orgn. Nursing Execs. Mem. Sunshine Christian Reformed Ch. Home: 6181 Kran Ave SE Grand Rapids MI 49508 Office: Pine Rest Christian Hosp 300 68th St Grand Rapids MI 49508-6999

DEWEESE, ANITA FAYE, corporate executive, controller; b. Mansfield, Ohio, Oct. 22, 1936; d. S. Edward and Margeret R. (McFadden) Sites; m. Robert P. Hoeffler, Aug. 14, 1954 (div. Oct. 1969); m. J. George DeWeese, Apr. 4, 1972; children: Steven, Debra, Jane. Grad. high sch., Upper Arlington, Ohio, 1954. Sec. Westinghouse Elect. Corp., Mansfield, 1954-58; bookeeper Bob Hoeffler Tile Co., Mansfield, 1958-68, Kleshinski & Reister, CPA's, Mansfield, 1968-69; accounts payable clerk Servisteel Corp., Mansfield, 1969-71; credit mgr. accounts payable Sanchez Enterprises, Inc., Mansfield, 1971-74; controller, corp. treas. Weiss Industries (formerly Mansfield Tool & Die Co.), 1974—. Named Tribute to Women and Industry honoree YWCA, 1987. Mem. Nat. Assn. Accts. Home: Rt 1 Ross Rd PO Box 452 Bellville OH 44813 Office: Weiss Industries 2480 N Main St PO Box 157 Mansfield OH 44903

DEWEY, ANNE ELIZABETH MARIE, lawyer; b. Balt., Mar. 16, 1951; d. George Daniel and Elizabeth Patricia (Mohan) D.; m. Peter Michael Barnett, Aug. 27, 1977; children: Brendan M., Andrew P. BA, Mich. State U., 1972; JD, U. Chgo., 1975; grad., Stonier Grad. Sch. Banking, East Brunswick, N.J., 1983. Bar: D.C. 1976. Atty. FTC, Washington, 1975-78; atty. enforcement div. Comptroller of Currency, Washington, 1978-81, sr. atty. office legis. counsel, 1981-83; sr. atty. dist. office Comptroller of Currency, Dallas, 1983-86; sr. atty. legal adv. services div. Comptroller of Currency, Washington, 1986; assoc. gen. counsel corp. and adminstrv. law Farm Credit Adminstrn., McLean, Va., 1986-87, gen. counsel, 1987—. Tchr. St. Rita's Ch., Dallas, 1984-85. Mem. ABA, D.C. Bar Assn., Women in Housing and Fin. (bd. dirs. 1982-83). Roman Catholic. Home: 833 Fontaine St Alexandria VA 22302 Office: Farm Credit Adminstrn Office Gen Counsel 1501 Farm Credit Dr McLean VA 22102-5090

DEWEY, PAT PARKER, radio station executive, composer; b. Berkeley, Calif., Jan. 27, 1923; d. George and Mildred (Johnston) Parker; student Sullins Jr. Coll., 1940-41; Mus.B., U. Miss., 1943; m. Grayson Headley, Dec. 30, 1946 (dec. 1961); m. 2d, M. Lee Williams, Dec. 18, 1964 (div.); 1 son, Philip Lee Williams; m. Ralph B. Dewey, Dec. 26, 1976. Woman's dir. radio sta. WNNT, Warsaw, Va., commentator daily women's program, Chat with Pat, 1952-60, now owner, pres. radio station WNNT AM-FM; partner WKWI-FM, Kilmarnock, Va.; asst. soc. editor Jackson Daily News, 1943-44. Composer: concerto for piano and orch., Rhapsody of Youth, performed by Nat. Air Force Symphony, Washington, Lisner Auditorium, 1947, guest pianist with Nat. Air Force Symphony, 1964, 75; (song) Cotton Picking Blues, featured in several musicals in Miss., Washington; (song) Maid of Cotton, used as theme song Nat. Cotton Council, 1945-51; (song) Lucky X, ofcl. song Chi Omega. Chmn., Red Cross water safety program, Lancaster County, Va., 1950-56; mem. exec. com. Jr. Assembly, Washington; jr. chmn. Home Hospitality Com., Washington, 1943-46; jr. chmn. UN Club activities, Washington, 1943-48. Mem. Am. Women in Radio and Television (dir. Va. 1962-65), Nat. Soc. Arts and Letters (music chmn. Washington chpt. 1964-65), Va. Assn. Broadcasters, Internat. Platform Assn., Nat. Assn. Am. Composers and Conductors, Women's Com. for Nat. Symphony Orch., Chi Omega, Delta Beta Sigma, Sigma Alpha Iota, Alpha Psi Omega. Episcopalian. Clubs: Friday Morning Music; Debutante of Miss., Women's (chmn. music div. Lancaster County, Va. 1956-60); Washington; Kenwood Golf and Country; Kenwood Garden; Tides Inn Chesapeake; Congl. Golf; Indian Creek Yacht and Country. Home: 6211 Garnett Dr Chevy Chase MD 20815 Home: Steamboat Landing Irvington VA 22480 Office: Radio Sta WNNT Warsaw VA 22572

DEWINE, SUE, communication educator; b. Xenia, Ohio, June 27, 1944; d. Gilbert and Eva (Kepley) Ogilvie; m. Mike DeWine, Aug. 20, 1966; children: Leigh Anne, James Gilbert. BA, Miami U., Oxford, Ohio, 1966, MA, 1967; PhD, Ind. U., 1975. Teaching asst. Miami U., 1966-67; instr. Miami U., Middletown, Ohio, 1967-72, sr. instr., 1972-75; teaching assoc. Ind. U., Bloomington, 1975-77; asst. prof. communications Ohio U., Athens, 1977-80, assoc. prof., 1980-85, prof., 1985-88, dir. Sch. Interpersonal Communication, 1988—; pres. Communications Cons., Athens, 1972—; mem. and office holder numerous coms. with Ohio U.; cons. to industry, govt.; speaker commencement Ohio U., 1987. Author: (with Jackie Rumbly) Ten Designs for Integration in Experience Based Learning Environments, 1976, (with Lynn Phelps) Interpersonal Communication Journal, 1976, (with Tom Tortoriollo and Steve Blatt) Communication in the Organization: An Applied Approach, 1978, (with others) Women in Organizations, 1983; editor Ohio Speech Jour., 1980-82; contbr. numerous articles to profl. jours. Cochmn. Athens Taxpayers for a Service Orientated Budget; mem. exec. bd. PTO; asst. leader Girl Scouts U.S., Athens; mem. Civitan. Named Outstanding Tchr., Ind. U., 1977, Outstanding Grad. Faculty Mem., 1986; Ohio U. grantee, 1984. Mem. Internat. Communication Assn. (exec. bd. 1980-84, chmn. orgnl. communication div. 1984—), Speech Communication Assn. (exec. bd. 1980-84), Am. Soc. Tng. and Devel. (chpt. advisor), Cen. States Speech Assn., Ohio Speech Communication Assn., Am. Psychology Assn., Acad. Mgmt., LWV. Home: 8 York Dr Athens OH 45701 Office: Ohio U Sch Interpersonal Communication Kantner Hall Athens OH 45701

DEWITT, BECKY JANE, computer systems analyst; b. Corona, Calif., Nov. 3, 1954; d. Cletus James and Daphne Adele DeWitt. BA in Comparative Lit., San Diego State U., 1976; BS in Computer Sci., Coleman Coll., 1982. Dir. mktg. Sand Mfg., San Diego, 1978-81; computer programmer Manor Enterprises, Vista, Calif., 1981-82; systems analyst Electronic Data Systems Inc., San Diego, 1982-84; systems analyst cons. Lemon Grove, Calif., 1984—. Mem. Nat. Assn. Female Execs. Democrat. Home and Office: 8365 Broadway #25 Lemon Grove CA 92045

DEWITT, EVELYN YVONNE, school district accountant; b. Denver, Oct. 11, 1946; d. Arby Lahoma and Audra Delores (Mann) Litton; m. John Phillip DeWitt, Dec. 7, 1968 (div. Feb. 1985); children: Richard Dean, Heather Dawn. BS, Phillips U., 1964; postgrad., Western State Coll. of Colo., 1979, U. Colo., 1981, Regis Coll., 1985-87. Bookkeeper Mullins Neon Sign Co., Denver, 1968; accounts payable bookkeeper Dave Cook's Sporting Goods Co., Denver, 1969; bookkeeper Monarch Leasing Service Co., Denver, 1970-71; asst. treas. Fountain Valley Sch., Colorado Springs, Colo., 1971-76; head bookkeeper Widefield Sch. Dist. #3, Colorado Springs, 1976-81, supr. of bookkeeping, 1981-86, dist. acct., 1986—; supervisory com. mem. Dist. #3 Fed. Credit Union, Colorado Springs, 1985—; pres. Widefield Adminstr.'s Constituency, 1983-85, sec., treas. 1985—. Deaconess First Christian Ch., Colorado Springs, 1985, deacon 1986-87. Mem. Assn. of Sch. Bus. Ofcls. (sch. fin. research com. 1983—), Rocky Mountain Assn. of Sch. Bus. Ofcls., Colo. Assn. of Sch. Execs., Am. Edn. Fin. Assn. Democrat. Club: Rawhide (treas. 1987). Lodge: Eagles (pres. 1975-77). Home: 126 Bradley St Colorado Springs CO 80911 Office: Widefield Sch Dist #3 1820 Main St Colorado Springs CO 80911

DEWITT, MARY SCHILLER, marketing consultant; b. Chgo., Aug. 25, 1948; d. Robert Baldwin and Helen (Rossman) DeW. AA, Coll. of DuPage, 1968; BA in Edn., U. Wis., Whitewater, 1969. With customer relations dept. John M. Smyth Furniture, Oak Brook, Ill., 1968-71, Wiggs Furniture, Bloomfield Hills, Mich., 1971; dir. pub. relations Hotel de las Hadas, Manzanillo, Mex., 1972; dir. promotion Ramco-Gershenson, Southfield, Mich., 1973-75; dir. mktg. Homart Devel. Co., Florence, Ky., 1975-76, Melvin Simon & Assocs., Inc., Hurst, Tex., 1976-79; pres. Mary DeWitt Co., Ft. Worth, 1979-85; v.p. mktg. Southmark Comml. Mgmt., Dallas, 1986-87; prin. DeWitt Group, Dallas and Ft. Worth, 1988—. Participant Foster Parents Plan, Inc., Warwick, R.I., 1986—; mem. publicity com. Friends of Euless (Tex.) Library, 1987—. Recipient award of excellence Jones Report, 1978. Mem. Internat. Council Shopping Ctrs., Pub. Relations Soc. Am., Tarrant County Mktg. Profls., Advt. Club Ft. Worth, Tulsa Advt. Fedn. Democrat. Episcopalian. Home: 1905 Cripple Creek Dr Euless TX 76039

DEXTER, DALLAS-LEE, insurance executive, consultant; b. Rockville Center, N.Y., Nov. 30, 1950; d. David D. and Jane (Nesbitt) D.; m. Leonard Eugene Carter, Nov. 6, 1975 (div. 1982). Student numerous dance courses; B.S., Mills Coll., 1972; M.A., Tchrs. Coll. Columbia U., 1974; postgrad. Nat. U. Mex., 1974, Lesley Coll., 1974, Fgn. Service Inst., 1977, Johns Hopkins Sch. Advanced Internat. Studies, 1982, Middle East Inst., 1982-83, U. N.C., 1982-86. Cert. ins., securities, teaching. Tchr. Am. Sch., Hawalli, Kuwait, 1975-76, Copenhagen Internat. Sch., 1977-79, Rygaards Internat. Sch., Hellerup, Denmark, 1980-81; mktg. contractor Nat. Right to Work Com., 1986—, 21st Century Telemedial Mktg. Services, Inc., 1986, sales mgr. Best Programs, Inc., Arlington, Va., 1987—; cons. Mark V Assocs., Inc., N.Y.C., 1982-86, Success, Inc., Palm Beach, Fla., 1985-86, Resources Planning Systems, 1983-86, Mgmt. Engring. Affiliates, Calabasa, Calif., 1984, Aerojet Gen., Washington, 1983; ednl. cons. Mayors Program on Summer Youth Employment, Washington, 1986, Islamic Saudi Acad. of Kingdom of Saudi Arabia, Dunn Loring, Va., 1986-87; mktg. cons. Nat. Right to Work Com., Springfield, Va., 1986—; cons., adminstr. Kingdom Of Saudi Arabia: Islamic Saudi Acad., 1986-87; sales rep. First Investors Corp., Arlington, Va., 1985-86; assoc. Potomac Ins. and Fin. Planning Group, Rockville, Md., 1985—; mgr. telesales div. Best Programs, Inc., Arlington, Va., 1987—; dancer Twyla Tharp Dance Co., 1969-70, James Cunningham Co., 1970, others; . Campaign worker Reagan-Bush, Washington, 1983-84; active Rock Creek Women's Republican Club, Chevy Chase Women's Rep. Club, Montgomery County Rep. Club, Nat. Fedn. Rep. Women; mem. women's com. Nat. Symphony Orch.; charter mem., sponsor Assn. of Friends of Mus. Modern Art of Latin Am. Mem. Nat. Assn. Life Underwriters, U.S. C. of C., D.C. Life Underwriters Assn., Nat. Assn. Female Execs. (network dir. 1985—), Internat. Educators Inst., World Affairs Council, Soc. for Internat. Devel., Middle East Inst., Middle East Studies Assn., Nat. Acad. TV Arts and Scis., Am. Def. Preparedness Assn., Air Force Assn., AAUW, Phi Delta Kappa. Unitarian. Clubs: Renaissance Women, Columbia Univ., University. Avocations: Travel; theatre; music; dance; painting. Home: 1280 21st St NW Washington DC 20036 Office: Best Programs Inc 2700 S Quincy St Suite 200 Arlington VA 22206

DEXTER, HELEN LOUISE, dermatologist, consultant; b. Cin., July 28, 1908; d. William Jordan and Katherine (Weston) Taylor; A.B., Bryn Mawr Coll., 1930; M.D., Columbia U., 1937; postgrad. U. Cin. Coll. Medicine, 1948-50; m. Morrie W. Dexter, Jan. 27, 1937; children—Katharine, Helen Dexter Dalzell, Elizabeth Taylor Dexter Potsubay, William Taylor. Intern, Jersey City Med. Center, 1938-39; internist Cin. Babies Milk Fund, Maternal Health Clinic, 1938-45; clinician U. Cin. Med. Sch., 1938-48, lectr. dept. dermatology, 1948-53; practice medicine specializing in dermatology, Clearwater, Fla., 1954—; dermatology cons. VA, 1955—; investigation of carcinogenic effects of shale oil U.S. Bur. Mines, Rifle, Colo., 1950. Mem. Clearwater Power Squadron Aux.; bd. dirs. Girls Clubs Pinellas County; commr. Town of Belleair, 1980. Recipient Ina Clay trophy Intercollegiate Ski Champion, 1928-30. Mem. AMA, Soc. Investigation Dermatology, Am. Acad. Dermatology, S.E. Dermatol. Assn. (v.p. 1963-64), Fla. Dermatol. Soc. (pres. 1959), Fla. Soc. Dermatology (pres.), Noah Worcester Dermatol. Soc., Am. Archaeol. Soc., Pan-Am. Dermatol. Soc., Soc. Tropical Dermatology. Presbyterian. Club: Clearwater Yacht Carlovel Yacht. Contbr. articles to profl. jours. Address: 409 Bayview Dr Belleair FL 34616

DEXTER, VIVIAN ANN, electronic manufacturing company executive; b. Rochester, N.Y., Feb. 19, 1942; d. Holmer Alvin and Tina Laura (Monroe) Fry; m. William Deville Dexter, May 25, 1962 (div. June 1975); 1 child, Vivian Ann II. BA, Elmira Coll., 1978; MA, N.C. State U., 1983. Engaged in staff mgmt. Corning Glass Works (N.Y.), 1960-77; mfg. mgmt. Corning Glass Works (N.Y.), Raleigh, N.C., 1977-80; instr. V.I. Coll., St. Thomas, N.C., 1980-81; sr. foreman AVX Corp., Myrtle Beach, S.C., 1981-82, employment mgr., 1982-83, quality circle facilitator, 1983—. Mem. Leadership Grand Strand III, Myrtle Beach, 1983, United Way Horry County, Myrtle Beach, 1983—; bd. dirs. Citizens Against Spouse Abuse, Myrtle Beach, 1982—. Recipient 1st place award Indsl. Safety Commn., Raleigh, 1979. Mem. Internat. Assn. Quality Circles (cert.), Am. Bus. Women's Assn., Organizational Dynamics Making Things Better (cert.), Am. Personnel Assn., Word Processing Assn. Democrat. Club: Toastmasters. Home: PO Box 1942 Myrtle Beach SC 29578 Office: AVX Corp PO Box 867 Myrtle Beach SC 29578

DEYOUNG, KAREN JEAN, journalist; b. Chgo., Jan. 4, 1949; d. Edward Leonard and Jeanette K. (Clausen) DeY.; B.S. cum laude in Journalism and Communication, U. Fla., 1971. Features writer St. Petersburg (Fla.) Times, 1972-74; freelance reporter, Western Africa, 1974-75; Latin Am. corr. Washington Post, 1977-80, dep. fgn. editor, 1980-81, fgn. editor, 1981-85, London Bur. chief, 1985—. Recipient Disting. Service award fgn. reporting Sigma Delta Chi, 1979, Fgn. Corr. award Inter-Am. Press Assn., 1979; Maria Moors Cabot award Columbia U., 1981. Address: 1150 15th St NW Washington DC 20071

DEYOUNG, LILLIAN JEANETTE, nurse, educational administrator; b. Ogden, Utah, July 26, 1926; d. Peter and Gertrude (Dallinga) DeY. R.N.,

Dee Meml. Sch. Nursing, Utah, 1947; B.S. in Nursing Edn., U. Utah, 1950, M.S. in Ednl. Adminstrn., 1955, Ph.D. in Ednl. Adminstrn, 1975. Asso. dir. nursing edn. Latter Day Saints Hosp., Salt Lake City, 1954-55; dir. Sch. of Nursing, instr. St. Luke's Hosp. Sch. of Nursing, Denver, 1955-72; asso. prof., curriculum coordinator Intercollegiate Center for Nursing Edn., Spokane, Wash., 1972-73; asst. dir. nursing service U. Utah Med. Center, Salt Lake City, 1973-75; prof., dean Coll. of Nursing, U. Akron, Ohio, 1975-88; cons. Duquesne U. Sch. Nursing, 1980, Youngstown State U. Dept. of Nursing, 1979; mem. State of Ohio Bd. of Nursing Edn. and Nurse Registration, 1979-83, v.p., 1980-82, pres., 1982-83. Author: Dynamics of Nursing, 4th edit., 1981, 5th edit., 1985. Active ARC; mem. exec. com. bd. trustee Akron Gen. Med. Ctr., exec. bd. Huntington Nat. Bd., 1986. Isobel Robb scholar, 1974-75; recipient pearl pin Am. Nurses Assn., 1972; named Colo. Nurse of Yr., 1965. Mem. Ohio League for Nursing, Ohio Nurses Assn. (dir. 1977-81), Am. Assn. Collegiate Nursing (by—laws com. 1980—). Mormon. Office: College of Nursing Univ Akron Akron OH 44325

D'HARNONCOURT, ANNE, museum director. m. Joseph J. Rishel, June 19, 1971. B.A., Radcliffe Coll., 1965; M.A. with distinction, Courtauld Inst. Art, U. London, 1967. Curatorial asst. Phila. Mus. Art, 1967-69; asst. curator 20th Century art Art Inst. Chgo., 1969-71; curator 20th Century art Phila. Mus. Art, 1971-82, the George D. Widener dir., 1982—. Organizer: (with McShine) exhbn. Marcel Duchamp, 1973-74, (with others) Philadelphia: Three Centuries of American Art, 1976, Eight Artists, 1978, (with Percy) Violet Oakley, 1979, Futurism and the International Avant-Garde, 1980, (with Sims) John Cage: Scores and Prints, 1982; author: (with Walter Hopps) Etant Donnes. . .Reflections on a New Work by Marcel Duchamp, 1969, The Cubist Cockatoo: Preliminary Exploration of Joseph Cornell's Hommages to Juan Gris, 1978. Office: Phila Mus Art 26th St and Benjamin Franklin Pkwy PO Box 7646 Philadelphia PA 19101

DHOLAKIA, RUBY ROY, management educator; b. Calcutta, India, Feb. 16, 1948; came to U.S. 1963; d. Somendra Nath and Saila Rani Roy; BS in Bus. Adminstrn., U. Calif., Berkeley, 1967, MBA, 1969; PhD, Northwestern U., 1976; m. Nikhilesh Dholakia, Aug. 30, 1974; children: Ritik, Nishita. Mktg. analyst Wells Fargo Bank, San Francisco 1969; asst. prof. Indian Inst. Mgmt., Calcutta 1970-73, 76-78; vis. faculty Indian Inst. Mgmt., Ahmedabad, 1977-79; assoc. prof. Kans. State U., 1979-81; assoc. prof. U. R.I., 1981-84, prof., 1984—; cons. in field of consumer research and telecommunications marketing. Am. Mgmt. Assn. fellow, 1975; AAAA fellow 1982. Mem. Am. Mktg. Assn., Assn. Consumer Research. Contbr. articles in field to profl. jours. Office: U RI Ballentine Hall Kingston RI 02881

DHONDT, LINDA JEAN, pension consultant; b. Lyons, N.Y., Aug. 6, 1946; d. Maurice B. and Madeline (Pierson) D. Student, Adrian Coll., 1964-66; BS in Math., SUNY, Oswego, 1968; postgrad., SUNY, Brockport, 1970-71. Clerical underwriter Aetna Life & Casualty, Rochester, N.Y., 1968-69; tchr. Lackawanna (N.Y.) High Sch., 1971-72; clk. Houston 1st Savs., 1972-74; clk. Allied Bank Tex., Houston, 1974-77, adminstr. asst., 1977-79; analyst Custom Benefit Services, Houston, 1979-81; pension cons. Moreland, Black & Assocs., Houston, 1981—. Mem. Am. Soc. Pension Actuaries. Methodist. Office: Moreland Black & Assocs 13201 Northwest Freeway Suite 504 Houston TX 77040

DHONDY, SUSAN SCHEREZADE, marketing manager, dietitian; b. Bombay, Nov. 7, 1958; d. Sarosh Savak and Rita Ann (Shaw) D. AA, Tallahassee (Fla.) Community Coll., 1982; BS, Fla. State U., 1984. Dietetic aide Westminster Oaks, Tallahassee, 1983-85; dietetic intern VA Med. Ctr., San Francisco, 1985; catering coordinator Park Plaza Hotel, Oakland, Calif., 1985-86; sales mgr. Holiday Inn, San Francisco, 1986—. Asst. Sr. Citizen Meal Program, Tallahassee, 1984; helper Meals on Wheels, Tallahassee, 1984; mem. Oakland Airport Ctr., Inc., 1985—; Oakland Convention and Visitors Bur., 1985—. Mem. Am. Dietetic Assn. (cert.), Hotel Sales and Mktg. Assn., Oakland C. of C., San Leandro C. of C., Golden Key Nat. Hon. Soc. Democrat. Office: Holiday Inn - Fin Dist 750 Kearny St San Francisco CA 94108

DIAMANTOPOULOS, WINONA JEANNE, financial company executive; b. Lincoln, Neb., Mar. 21, 1943; d. Harold Winfred Spink and Pauline (Heckman) Camp; m. Ronald Dean Jones, Feb. 7, 1965 (div. May 1978); children: Carrie Waldron, Christopher Pace; m. David Arthur Diamantopoulos, Apr. 6, 1980. BA, U. Nebr., 1965. Market research Kearfott Systems, Wayne, N.J., 1965-66; reporter Matzner Pubs., Wayne, N.J., 1966-67, Ridgewood (N.J.) News, 1967-68; editor Trends Newspapers, Riverdale, N.J., 1968-71; ops. mgr. JBS Assocs., Ringwood, N.J., 1978-85; ops. dir. Credit Services of Am., Wayne, 1985—. Bd. dirs. Ringwood Bd. Edn., Ringwood, N.J., 1984-87; mem. Lakeland Juvenile Conf., Passaic County, N.J., 1982-85, com. mem. Ringwood Dem. Club, 1984—. Recipient 1st place award women's editor N.J. Press Assn., 1969, reporting, 1970; named to Com. of 400 N.J. Sch. Bd. Assn., 1986. Democratic. Presbyterian. Club: Cupsaw Beach (Ringwood) (pres. 1982-83). Home: 91 Cedar Rd Ringwood NJ 07456

DIAMOND, ADELINA, writer; b. Chgo., Oct. 9, 1927; d. Herbert C. and Jennie (Friedman) Lust; A.B., U. Chgo., 1947; M.P.A., N.Y. U., 1972, postgrad., 1981; m. Edwin Diamond, Dec. 5, 1948; children—Ellen, Franna, Louise. Sportswear buyer Mandel Bros., Chgo., 1947-49, advt. copywriter, 1949-50; fashion reporter Womens Wear Daily, Chgo., 1950-52; editor Hyde Park Herald, Chgo., 1953-56; assoc. Center for Housing Partnerships, N.Y.C., 1970-72; Eastern public affairs rep. U. Chgo., 1972-78; dir. public relations Carnegie Council on Children, 1978-81; cons. Children's Def. Fund, 1978-81; founding mem. Women U.S.A., Friends of NOW, N.Y.C.; founder, chairperson Friends of ERA. Home: 20 Waterside Plaza New York NY 10010

DIAMOND, DOROTHY BLUM, author, editor; b. N.Y.C., Sept. 7, 1919; d. Asher and Lily (Williams) Blum; m. Walter H. Diamond, June 15, 1947. B.A. with highest honors, Wellesley Coll., 1940; M.S., Columbia U., 1941. Reporter, Newark Star-Ledger, 1941; assoc. editor Young Am. mag., N.Y.C., 1941-42; sr. editor, columnist Tide mag., N.Y.C., 1942-47, 55-59; columnist Printers Ink, N.Y.C., 1959-61, Modern Floor Coverings, N.Y.C., 1958-63; author: Tax Havens of the World, 1974; Tax-Free Trade Zones of the World, 1976; International Tax Treaties of All Nations, 1976; Capital Formation and Investment Incentives Around the World, 1983, also supplements; contbr. articles to mags. and newspapers. Mem. Merchandising Execs. Club (award 1958), World Trade Writers Assn., Phi Beta Kappa. Club: Wellesley-in-Westchester (past bd. dirs.), Columbia U. Alumni (Westchester County). Home: 9 Old Farm Ln Hartsdale NY 10530 Office: Overseas Press & Cons 9 Old Farm Lane Hartsdale NY 10530

DIAMOND, ELAYNE FERN, interior designer, small business owner; b. Newark, July 1, 1945; d. Charles Ronald and Louise Pearl (Fern) Newman; m. Stanley Diamond, Nov. 20, 1965; children: Garrett L., Robin Fern. Student, N.Y. Sch. Interior Design, 1963-67. Pres. Elayne Diamond Interiors, Union, N.J., 1964—; owner, pres. Novelty Express, Union, Springfield, Totowa, N.J., 1975-80, Personalitees, Beach Haven, N.J., 1978-84, Put Togethers, Surf City, N.J., 1979-81, Designer's View Inc., Greenbrook, N.J., 1988—; cons. in field; designer, owner Yellow Brick Rd., Inc., Springfield, Beach Haven, 1975-79; cons. to constrn. cos., window mfgs., N.J., 1969—; distbr. Energy Controls, Springfield, 1985-86. Contbr. designs to trade and comml. mags., various home tours, newspaper articles, 1964—. Fund raiser Ctr. Sch. for the Learning Disabled, N.J., Am. Cancer Soc., others. Mem. Allied Bd. Trade.

DIAMOND, JOAN, principal; b. Los Angeles, July 19, 1942; d. David Martin and Juliet (Feldman) Diamond; m. Stuart Frank Greenfeld, July 21, 1963 (div. 1977); 1 child, Andrea Hana. BA, U. Calif., Berkeley, 1964, cert. in teaching, 1965, MA, 1970, cert. standard teaching, 1976, cert. standard adminstrn., 1978. Tchr. Los Angeles Unified Sch. Dist., 1965-68, Piedmont (Calif.) Sch. dist., 1971-72; dir. Options for Women, Oakland, Calif., 1972-73; tchr. in charge Title IVC Fed. Project: Pre-Sch., Richmond, Calif., 1973-76; program specialist Contra Costa County, Concord, Calif., 1983-84; resource, reading specialist San Ramon Valley (Calif.) Unified Sch. Dist., 1976-81, adminstrv. asst., 1981-83, principal, 1984—. Contbr. articles to profl. jours. Mem. Assn. Calif. Sch. Adminstrs., Learning Alternatives Resource Networks, (bd. dirs. 1986—), Nat. Council of Adminstrv. Women in Edn., Calif. Soc. Edn. Program Auditors and Evaluators, Bus. Edn. Roundtable (chair adopt-a-sch. com. 1985—). Democrat. Jewish. Lodge: Soroptimists (Woman of Distinction award 1987). Home: 139 Wilding Lane Oakland CA 94618 Office: Bollinger Canyon Sch 2300 Talavera Dr San Ramon CA 94583

DIAMOND, JONI LYNN, psychotherapist; b. Cin., Apr. 1, 1956; d. Sidney David and Elaine Shirley (Gindy) D. BSW, Ohio State U., 1977; MSW, Atlanta U., 1980. Lic. clin. social worker, Calif.; diplomate in clin. social work. Evaluation cons., trainer S.E. Regional Support Ctr. A.L. Nellum and Assocs., Atlanta, 1979-80; social worker Coosa Valley (Ga.) Community Mental Health Ctr., Cartersville, 1980-81; program dir. Vols. of Am., Los Angeles, 1981-83, Gateways Hosp. and Mental Health Ctr., Los Angeles, 1983-86; psychotherapist Balog Med. Group, Pasadena, Calif., 1984-87; program mgr. Drug/Alcohol Recovery Team, Pasadena, 1986-87; psychotherapist Balog Inst. Assocs., Glendale, Calif., 1987—; pvt. practice psychotherapy North Hollywood, Calif., 1987—; mem. adv. bd. Nursing Services Internat., Beverly Hills, Calif., 1986-87; cons. in field. Mem. Women's Referral Service, Calif. Attys. for Criminal Justice. Mem. Nat. Assn. Social Workers (cert., bd. dirs. 1987—), Bus. and Profl. Women (exec. bd. dirs., 1st v.p. 1986-87, pres. 1987—), So. Calif. Jewish Communal Workers, Jewish Prisoners (mem. adv. bd.), Escalon Group (hon., bd. dirs. 1981—, program chmn. 1984-85). Home: 12352-2 Runnymede St North Hollywood CA 91605 Office: 12501 Chandler Blvd Suite 202 North Hollywood CA 91607

DIAMOND, KIMBERLEY SUE, securities investment executive; b. Houston, Oct. 4, 1955; d. Louis Elliott II D. and Tommy Sue Smith. Student, U. Tex., 1975; BA magna cum laude, San Francisco State U., 1979. Lic. securities registered rep. Stockbroker Dean Witter Reynolds, Inc., Los Angeles, 1979-80, Smith Barney, Harris Upham and Co., Inc., Newport Beach, Calif., 1980-81; mktg. dir. Wall St. Cons. Group, Inc., Newport Beach, Calif., 1981-82; fin. counselor CIGNA Fin. Services Co., Newport Beach, Calif., 1982-83; account exec. E.F. Hutton and Co., Inc., Long Beach, Calif., 1983-84; investment exec. Bank America Capital Markets Group, Los Angeles, Calif., 1984—. Mem. Nat. Assn. Female Execs., Women of Wall St. (v.p. 1983-84), Delta Gamma. Home: PO Box 3249 Long Beach CA 90803

DIAMOND, SUSAN Z., management consultant; b. Okla., Aug. 20, 1949; d. Louis Edward and Henrietta (Wood) D.; AB (Nat. Merit scholar, GRTS scholar), U. Chgo., 1970; MBA, DePaul U., 1979; m. Allan T. Devitt, July 27, 1974. Dir. study guide prodn. Am. Sch. Co., Chgo., 1972-75; publs. supr. Allied Van Lines, Broadview, Ill., 1975-78, sr. account services rep., 1978-79; pres. Diamond Assocs. Ltd., Melrose Park, Ill., 1978—; condr. seminars Am. Mgmt. Assn. Mem. Nat. Assn. Accts., Adminstrv. Mgmt. Soc., Assn. Records Mgrs. and Adminstrs., Internat. Records Mgmt. Council, Records Mgmt. Soc. Gt. Britain, Bus. Forms Mgmt. Assn., Nuclear Info. and Records Mgmt. Assn., Nat. Fire Protection Assn., Assn. Info. and Image Mgmt., Delta Mu Delta. Author: How to Talk More Effectively, 1972; Preparing Administrative Manuals, 1981; How to Manage Administrative Operations, 1981; How to be an Effective Secretary in the Modern Office, 1982; Records Management: A Practical Guide, 1983; co-author: Finance Without Fear, 1983; editor Mobility Trends, 1975-78; contbr. numerous articles to profl. jours. Office: 2851 N Pearl Ave Melrose Park IL 60160

DIAZ, ANTOINETTE, investment broker; b. Los Angeles, July 16, 1943; d. Tony and Candelaria (Baca) D. Student, East Los Angeles Coll., 1962; degree, N.Y. Inst. Fin., 1970. Broker asst. Rutner Jackson & Gray, Los Angeles, 1969-70; exec. asst. Jefferies & Co, Los Angeles, 1970-72; acct. exec. Rosenthal & Co., Beverly Hills, Calif., 1976, Econ. Systems, Century City, Calif., 1976-77, Shearson Am. Express, Sherman Oaks, Calif., 1978-79, Clayton Brokerage, Westwood, Calif., 1979-80; sr. acct. rep. Monex Internat., Newport Beach, Calif., 1980—; mem. Commodity Futures Trading Commn., 1976. Contbr. articles to profl. jours. Mem. Nat. Futures Assn., N.Y. Futures Exchange, Chgo. Bd. Trade, Nat. Assn. Securities Dealers, Pres.'s Council of Newport Beach. Roman Catholic. Office: Monex Internat 4910 Birch St Newport Beach CA 92660

DIAZ, MAGNA M., librarian, educator; b. N.Y.C., Mar. 20, 1951; d. Jose Enrique Rodriguez and Juanita (Diaz) Rodriguez Garcia; m. Ramon A. Diaz, Jr., May 1, 1976. 1 dau., Joana Marie. B.A., U. P.R., 1972; postgrad. Community Coll. Phila., 1978, Temple U., summer 1979, 80; M.L.S., Rutgers U., 1980. Tchr. English Pub. Sch. Bd., P.R., 1972-76; bilingual cataloger Temple U., Merit Ctr., Phila., 1980; bilingual librarian Camden Free Pub. Library (N.J.), 1980-81; children's librarian Free Library Phila., 1981-82, bilingual librarian, 1983—, tchr. library sci. Sch. Dist. Phila. Vare Middle Sch.; sch. librarian Phila. Vare Mid. Sch. Pub. Sch. System; reference librarian Community Coll. Phila., 1982; chairperson Spanish com. Free Library Phila., treas. Coordinating Council Human Services, 1986-88, AMR (Hispanic Adv. Com. 1986-88), coordinator Nat. Assn. to Promote Library Services to the Spanish Speaking, Recipient HEW scholarship, 1980. Mem. ALA (assoc.). Democrat. Lutheran. Home: 5243 Horrocks St Philadelphia PA 19124 Office: Sch Dist Phila Vare Mid Sch 24th and Snyder Philadelphia PA 19145

DIAZ, SALLY ANN, town clerk, treasurer; b. Evansville, Ind., Aug. 9, 1935; d. Raymond John and Dorothy Jeanette (Peck) Kincaid; m. Luis S. Diaz, Nov. 24, 1956; children: David Ray, Kathryn Ann. Reporter The Evansville Press, 1953-59, bur. chief, 1959-75. Clk.-treas. Town of Newburgh, Ind., 1976—; pres. PTA, 1975-76, com. chmn., sec. v.p. for fund raising, 1972-75; trustee Newburgh United Meth. Ch., 1972-74, adminstrv. bd., originator and columnist ch. newsletter, ch. historian, 1985—. Recipient Appreciation award Town of Newburgh, 1982, William C. Griffin Meml. award, Boonville (Ind.) Jaycees, 1984; named to Council of Sagamores of the Wabash Gov. of Ind., 1988. Mem. Ind. League Mcpl. Clks. and Clk.-Treas., Warrick County Fraternal Order of Police, Hist. Newburgh, Inc., VFW Aux. Home: PO Box 446 Newburgh IN 47629 Office: Town of Newburgh Town Hall PO Box 6 Newburgh IN 47630

DIBARTOLOMEO, DIANE LYNN, communications executive; b. Chgo., Feb. 21, 1956; d. Rebell Clarence and Lucille (Calonico) DiB. AA, William Rainey Harper Community Coll., Palatine, Ill., 1975; grad., Sch. Mortgage Banking, Washington, 1981; B of Communications, DePaul U., Chgo., 1986—. Reporter Chgo. Tribune, 1974-76; br. collection mgr. Fleet Mortgage (formerly Mortgage Assocs.), Milw., 1977-79; br. collection mgr. Sears Mortgage Corp., Lincolnshire, Ill., 1979, foreclosure supr., 1979-81, cashiering mgr., 1982-84, tng. mgr., 1985-86, corp. communications mgr., 1986—. Mem. Internat. Assn. Bus. Communicators, Nat. Assn. Realtors, Mortgage Bankers Assn. Office: Sears Mortgage Corp 300 Knightsbridge Pkwy Lincolnshire IL 60069

DIBBLE, ELIZABETH JEANE, lawyer, educator; b. Hammond, Ind., May 26, 1958; d. Harold Richard and Janet Deliah (Lane) Elsey; m. John Taylor Dibble, June 7, 1980; children: James Taylor, Katherine Elizabeth. BS in Learning Disabilities magna cum laude, MacMurray Coll., Jacksonville, Ill., 1979; JD, So. Ill. U., 1983. Bar: Ill. 1983. Tchr. learning disabilities Sedgwick (Kans.) Sch. System, 1979-80; atty. Powless & Brocking, Marion, Ill., 1984-85, Randy Patchett & Assoc., Marion, 1985-86; sole practice Marion, 1987—; part-time lectr. So. Ill. U., Carbondale, 1985—. Fundraiser Rep. Party, Williamson County, Ill, 1986; bd. dirs. So. Ill. Epilepsy Found., Mt. Vernon, 1984-86; mem. Episcopal Ch. Women; religious edn. dir. St. James Episcopal Ch., Marion, 1983-86. Cartwright scholar for women MacMurray Coll., 1976-79. Mem. Williamson County Bar Assn., Ill. State Bar Assn., Nat. Assn. Female Execs. Republican. Home: 1513 N State St Marion IL 62959 Office: 208 N Market St PO Box 394 Marion IL 62959

DIBELLA, LUCY LEOLA, police investigator; b. Nashville, Tenn., Jan. 19, 1951; d. Morris Thomas and Joyce (Eaton) Brandon. Grad. high sch., Nashville. Began as computer programmer Nat. Life and Accident Co., Nashville; police officer Nashville Met. Police, 1978-82, police officer/investigator, 1982—. Mem. Tenn. Assn. Women Police (v.p. 1984-87), Internat. Assn. Women Police, Internat. Assn. Identification. Office: Nashville Met Police Dept 200 James Robertson Pkwy Nashville TN 37201

DIBENEDETTO, LYNNE PAGE, communications company executive; b. Durham, N.C., Oct. 10, 1956; d. Millard Wilson Page and Carol Ann (Lynn) Van Hise; m. Mark DiBenedetto, Oct. 2, 1982. BS in Home Econs., U. N.C., Greensboro, 1977. Comml. loan asst. First Union Nat. Bank, Durham, 1978; office mgr. Daly, Joyce & Borsari Law Firm, Washington, 1979-82; asst. recruitment coordinator Gardere & Wynne Law Firm, Dallas, 1983-86; office mgr. Gray and Co. Pub. Communications, Dallas, 1986-87; v.p. Cozart Communications (pub. relations and pub. affairs cons.), Dallas, 1987—. asst. dir. I Have A Dream Found.-Dallas, 1987; active Dallas Symphony Orchestra Innovators, 1985-87; mem. Tex. Women's Alliance, 1986—. Mem. Craft Guild, Omicron Nu. Republican. Home: 3128 Oliver St Dallas TX 75205 Office: Cozart Communications 2 Turtle Creek Village Suite 900 Dallas TX 75219

DIBONA, KATHLEEN DRABIK, school board administrator; b. Buffalo, May 2, 1947; d. Joseph and Alice (Gorski) Drabik; m. Dennis David DiBona, Apr. 20, 1985. BS, SUNY, Buffalo, 1969; MS, Nova U., 1979, EdS, 1985. Cert. tchr., adminstrn & supervision. Tchr. Erie County Sch. Bd., Buffalo, 1968-74; recreation supr. Ft. Lauderdale (Fla.) Recreation Dept., 1974-75; dir. YMCA, Coral Springs, Fla., 1975-76; prin. Pottery Workshop, Wilton Manors, Fla., 1977-79; tchr. Sch. Bd. of Broward, Ft. Lauderdale, 1979-84, tchr., exceptional student, 1984-85, edn. program specialist, 1985-86, staff devel. adminstr., cons., 1986—. Author: (book, project) Strategies for the Socially Maladjusted Student, 1985, (Exemplary Distinction), 1985. Vol. Assist the Elderly, Inc., Pembroke Pines, Fla. Recipient Master Tchr. award State of Fla., 1985-86. Mem. Nat. Staff Devel. Council, Fla. Assn. Staff Devel., Broward County Tchr. Edn. Council, Nat. Council of States for Inservice Edn., Phi Delta Kappa. Democrat. Roman Catholic. Office: Sch Bd Broward County 1005 E Broward Blvd Fort Lauderdale FL 33301

DICAPUA, RAE M., assistant postmaster; b. Bklyn., Feb. 22, 1948; d. Edmund B. and Constance J. (Longo) DiC. BBA, SUNY, Farmingdale, 1967; cert. in travel agt. studies, Poh Inst., Queens, N.Y., 1973; student, CUNY, 1976; cert. in tng. and devel., U.S. Postal Service Mgmt. Acad., Bethesda, Md., 1982. Acctt. supr. Singer Corp., Syosset, N.Y., 1970-72; med. receptionist Dr. E.B. DiCapua, Massapequa, N.Y., 1972-74; accounts receivable clk. Mitsubishi Internat., N.Y.C., 1974-75; accounts payable specialist U.S. Postal Service, N.Y.C., 1975-76; distbn. clk. U.S. Postal Service, Port Richey, Fla., 1977-79, window clk. instr., 1979-80, supr. mails and delivery, 1980-84, supt. postal ops., 1984—; Mem. Nat. Women's Conf. U.S. Postal Service, Orlando, Fla., 1980-81. Mem. North Shore Animal League, N.Y.C., 1981-85, Jasmine Lakes Civic Assn., Port Richey, 1984-86; advisor Greater N.Y. Women's Sports Assn.; capt. Leukemia Soc. for West Pasco County, Port Richey, 1983; founder, pres. Nat. Orgn. for Women Pasco County chpt., 1985-86. Mem. Nat. Assn. Postal Suprs., Nat. Assn. Female Execs. Democrat. Roman Catholic. Home: 9502 Blackwood Dr New Port Richey FL 34654-1905 Office: US Postal Service 8101 Washington St Port Richey FL 34668-1905

DICARLO, SUSANNE HELEN, financial analyst; b. Greensburg, Pa., Nov. 24, 1956; d. Wayne Larry and Clara Emogene (Weaver) Gower; m. John Joseph DiCarlo, June 21, 1980; children: Sarah Rose, Kristen Marie. BS in Acctg., Va. Inst. Tech., 1978. Auditor U.S. Army Audit Agy., Ft. Monroe, Va., 1978-79; acct. technician Fleet Combat Tng. Ctr., Virginia Beach, Va., 1980-82, supervisory auditor, 1982-83; fin. analyst Comml. Activity Mgmt. Team, Norfolk, Va., 1983—; fed. women's program mgr. Fleet Combat Tng. Ctr., 1980-83. Creator newsletter Fed. Women's Program Manager, 1980-83. Club: Seaside Mountaineers (Va. Beach) (treas. 1986—). Home: 4013 Dillaway Ct Virginia Beach VA 23456

DICCIANI, NANCE KATHERINE, chemical engineer; b. Phila., Oct. 18, 1947; d. Augustine Joseph and Josephine Cecila (Maggiano) D.; m. Joseph William Kunz, Oct. 31, 1970 (div. 1984). B in Chem. Engring., Villanova U., 1969; MS in Chem. Engring., U. Va., 1970; PhD in Chem. Engring., U. Pa., 1977, MBA, 1986. Registered profl. engr., Pa. Engr. Phila. Water Dept., 1971-72, supt., 1972-74; with Air Products and Chems., Inc., Allentown, Pa., 1977—, dir. research and devel., 1984-86, gen. mgr., 1986—; mem. adv. com. U. Va., Charlottesville, 1987—. Contbr. articles to tech. publs.; patentee in field. Mem. Allentown Com. on Sci. Edn., 1984-85, adv. com. Allentown Women's Health Ctr., 1987. Mem. Am. Inst. Chem. Engrs., Soc. Women Engrs. (nat. adviser 1984-86, Achievement award 1987). Home: 2862 Rolling Green Pl Macungie PA 18062 Office: Air Products and Chems Box 538 Allentown PA 18105

DICK, CHARLOTTE A., academic administrator; b. Ft. Worth, Jan. 31, 1944. BS in Sociology, Tex. Woman's U.; postgrad. in Edn., Tex. A&M U.; cert., Research Inst. of Am. Tchr. Killeen (Tex.) Ind. Sch. Dist., 1968-70; sec. Dept. Agrl. Econs. Tex. A&M U., 1970-72, sr. sec. to dept. head, 1972-74; exec. sec. to dept. head Office of Continuing Edn. and Tex. Engring. Extension Service Tex. A&M U. System, 1974-78, asst. to dir., 1979—; cons. office mgmt., 1980—. Sec. First Meth. Ch., Killeen, 1968-70; chmn., mem. exec. bd. Vocat. Office Edn. Adv. Com., Coll. Station Ind. Sch. Dist., 1985, Tex. A&M U. Communications Com., Computer Users Group, 1986; mem. adminstrv. applications group Tex. A&M U.; mem. Gov.'s Citizen Assistance Office Tex. Engring. Extension Service Rep.; coordinator United Way activities Tex. Engring. Extension Service; chmn., mem. vocational edn. adv. bd. Coll. Sta. Ind. Sch. Dist., 1988; pres. Tex. A&M U. Computer Users Group, 1988. Recipient Plaque of Appreciation Coll. Sta. Ind. Sch. Dist. Mem. Am. Bus. Women's Assn., Nat. Assn. Females Execs., Brazos Valley Personnel Assn., Phi Chi Theta, Alpha Kappa Delta. Office: The Tex A&M Univ System Tex Engring Extension Service College Station TX 77843-8000

DICK, NANCY E., former lieutenant governor; b. Detroit, July 22, 1930; m. Stephen Barnett; children: Margot, Timber, Justin. B.A. in Resort Mgmt., Mich. State U. Worked in resort mgmt., conv. dir., interior design, bookkeeping; mem. Colo. Gen. Assembly, 1974-79, vice chmn. transp. and energy com.; lt. gov. State of Colo., 1979-86; fin. chmn. Fedn. Rocky Mountain States; mem. adv. panel U.S. Oil Shale Environ. Com., 1974-78; del. Nat. Democratic Party Convention, 1980; mem. Fordham Planning Commn., U.S. Health Care Cost Containment, 1981; Rocky Mt. bd. dirs. Inst. Internat. Edn., 1980-87; exec. bd. Gov.'s Interstate Indian Council, 1981-83; chmn. regional selection White House Fellows, 1981, panelist, 1979-80; chmn. Colorado-Human Indsl. Conf. Planning Com.; del. Women's Leadership Conf. on Nat. Security. Trustee Denver Symphony Assn.; hon. chmn. Friends of the Urban League; mem. rural health com. Colo. Med. Soc., 1975-76; exec. bd. U.S. Army War Coll., 1981. Recipient Disting. Alumni award Mich. State U., 1980; recipient Florence Sabin award Colo. Pub. Health Care Assn., 1980, Outstanding Alumnus award Coll. Bus., Mich. State U., 1981, Outstanding Citizen Nat. Rural Primary Care Assn., 1981, Found. scholarship Nat. Ctr. Creative Leadership, 1981. Democrat. *

DICKENS, DEBORAH SEABRON, federal agency program administrator; b. Mpls.; d. William Manson and Nevada (Thornton) Seabron; m. Nathaniel Augustus Dickens, Jr., Nov. 2, 1983. BA, Howard U., 1970. Urban intern HUD, Washington, 1973-75; consumer advisor Pres.'s Rent Adv. Bd., Washington, 1975-77; fair housing specialist Community Housing Resource Bd. program, Washington, 1978-80, nat. coordinator, 1980-86, affirmative mktg. team leader, 1986—. Author: (booklet) A Tenants Guide to Federal Rent Controls, 1975; contbr. articles to profl. jours. Recipient Cert. Spl. Achievement HUD, 1978, 80; Cert. Outstanding Performance HUD 1984, 85. Mem. HUD Women's Caucus, Am. Bus. Women's Assn., Nat. Assn. Female Execs., Zeta Phi Beta. Home: 1703 Taylor St NW Washington DC 20011 Office: US Dept HUD 451 7th St SW Room 5244 Washington DC 20011

DICKENS, DORIS LEE, psychiatrist; b. Roxboro, N.C., Oct. 12; d. Lee Edward and Delma Ernestine (Hester) D.; B.S. magna cum laude, Va. Union U., 1960; M.D., Howard U., 1966; m. Austin L. Fickling. Intern, St. Elizabeth's Hosp., Washington, 1966-67, resident, 1967-70; staff psychiatrist, dir. Mental Health Program for Deaf, St. Elizabeth's Hosp., Washington, after 1970-87; psychiatrist, med. officer Community Mental Health Ctr., D.C. Commn. on Mental Health, 1987—; mem. faculty Howard U. Coll. Medicine, Washington, 1982—. Bd. dirs. Nat. Health Care Found. for Deaf. Diplomate Nat. Bd. Med. Examiners. Mem. Am. Psychiat. Assn., Washington Psychiat. Soc., Alpha Kappa Mu, Beta Kappa Chi. Author: How and When Psychiatry Can Help You, 1972; You and Your Doctor; contbg.

author: Hearing and Hearing Impairment, Counseling Deaf People: Research and Practice. Home: 12308 Surrey Circle Dr Tantallon MD 20022 Office: 2700 Martin L King Ave Washington DC 20032

DICKENS, DORIS LEE (MRS. AUSTIN LECOUNT FICKLING), psychiatrist; b. Roxboro, N.C., Oct. 12; d. Lee Edward and Delma Ernestine (Hester) Dickens; B.S. magna cum laude, Va. Union U., 1960; M.D., Howard U., 1966; m. Austin LeCount Fickling, Oct. 15, 1975. Intern, St. Elizabeth's Hosp., Washington, 1966-67, resident, 1967-70; staff psychiatrist, dir. Mental Health Program for Deaf, St. Elizabeth's Hosp., Washington, 1970-87. Bd. dirs. Nat. Health Care Found. for Deaf; med. officer Region 4 Community Mental Health Ctr., Washington, Commn. on Mental Health, 1987—. Recipient Dorothea Lynde Dix award, 1980; diplomate Nat. Bd. Med. Examiners. Mem. Am. Psychiat. Assn. (achievement awards bd. 1988—), Washington Psychiat. Soc., Alpha Kappa Mu, Beta Kappa Chi. Author: How and When Psychiatry Can Help You, 1972; You and Your Doctor; contbg. author: Hearing and Hearing Impairment, 1979; contbg. author Counseling Deaf People, Research and Practice. Home: 12308 Surrey Circle Tantallon MD 20022 Office: 833 Moraga Dr Los Angeles CA 90049

DICKENS, VERA JOSIE, beauty supply company executive; b. Dixon, Mo., Nov. 27, 1933; d. Thomas Leddel and Lydia Louise (Tackett) Bacon; m. Harold Freddie Dickens, June 4, 1949; children—Harold Joseph, William Lee. Br. mgr. Midwest Beauty Supply, Jonesboro, Ark., 1964-76; mgr. Cache Beauty Supply, Jonesboro, 1976-83, corp. pres., 1983—. Mem. Beauty and Barber Supply Inst. Mem. Christian Ch. Lodge: Eastern Star. Office: Cache Beauty Supply Inc 2826 E Highland Dr Jonesboro AR 72401

DICKERSON, BETTY JEAN, nurse; b. Cotton Plant, Ark., Dec. 16, 1936; d. Laurence Von and LaVerne Roddy; A.A. in Nursing, Ind. U., 1971; B.S. Nursing, Purdue U., 1976; M.S. in Restorative Nursing Govs. State U., 1980; m. Robert E. Dickerson, Jan. 8, 1954; children—Carolyn, Edward, Monteena. Staff nurse Our Lady of Mercy Hosp., Dyer, Ind., 1971; staff nurse pediatrics St. Mary Med. Center, Gary, Ind., 1971-75, asst. dir. nursing service, 1975-83, asst. adminstr. nursing services, 1983-86, instr. heart-lung assessment, 1977-79; instr. med. secs. Marion Bus. Coll., 1973-74; clin. nurse instr. Ind. U. N.W., 1980-81. Bd. dirs. Ind. U. N.W., 1981—, v.p., 1985-86, pres., 1986-87; bd. dirs. Hospice N.W. Ind., 1981—, 3d v.p., 1985-86, 86-87, 2d v.p., 1987—, The Ambassadors. Recipient Outstanding Nurse of Yr. award Ind. U., 1971, Very Spl. Person award Ind. U. N.W. Sch. Nursing, 1984. Mem. Ind. State, Am. nurses assns., Nat. League Nursing, Ind. U., Purdue U., Govs. State U. alumni assns., Ind. U. Nurses Soc. (alumni), Young Women's Christian Council. Author hosp. pediatrics teaching manual, 1974.

DICKERSON, BEVERLY CAROL, computer sales representative; b. Monroe, N.C., Mar. 26, 1944; d. Andrew Jackson and Margaret Gwendolyn (McCorkle) D.; m. Thomas Denny O'Neal, Aug. 26, 1966 (div. May 1982); 1 child: Lauren Kinney; m. Ronald Segal, Mar. 30, 1985. AB, Wellesley Coll., 1965; MA in Teaching, Duke U., 1966; MBA, NYU, 1981. Programmer, analyst U. Ky., Lexington, 1968-69; systems programmer Keydata Inc., Watertown, Mass., 1969-71; cons. SDI Ltd., Ottawa, Ont., Can., 1971-73, Albany, N.Y., 1973-74; project mgr. Albany Med. Coll., 1974-75; cons. Princeton, N.J., 1975-76; project mgr. EDUCOM, Princeton, N.J., 1976-79; communications rep. AT&T Co., Parsippany and Somerset, N.J., 1979-82; with sales AT&T Co., Washington, 1982-88. Contbr. articles to profl. jours. NSF scholar 1966. Mem. Assn. Computing Machinery, Sierra Club. Home: 11003 Oakton Woods Way Oakton VA 22124 Office: AT&T 1825 I St NW Suite 800 Washington DC 20006

DICKERSON, EVELYN PITMAN, controller; b. Spruce Pine, N.C., Sept. 13, 1949; d. Lee Jim and Helen Louise (Autry) Pitman; m. James D. Riggan Sr., Mar. 7, 1969 (div. 1976); 1 child, James; m. George Norman Dickerson, Sept. 22, 1979. Student, Vance-Granville Community Coll., 1981, Internat. Corr. Sch./Ctr. for Degree Studies, 1981-83. Office mgr., acctg. clk. La.-Pacific Corp., Henderson, N.C., 1981-84; controller Perry Builders Inc., Henderson, 1984—, corp. sec., 1981—, also bd. dirs. V.p. Vance County Am. Cancer Soc., Henderson, 1972; pres. Womens Missionary Union-Tungsten, Henderson, 1984-86, Tungsten Bapt. Ch., Henderson, 1985—. Mem. Nat. Assn. for Female Execs. Republican. Home: Rt 4 Box 186EE Henderson NC 27536 Office: Perry Builders Inc Raleigh Rd PO Box 589 Henderson NC 27536

DICKERSON, JULIE BRADSHAW, temporary personnel company executive; b. Atlanta, June 25, 1957; d. Richard Boyd and Mary Ann (Bagwell) Bradshaw; m. William Edward Dickerson; children: Corey Alan, Landon Bradshaw. Cert. emergency med. technician. Group examiner Provident Gen. LGH, Atlanta, 1976-78; group claims mgr. Gulf Group Services, Atlanta, 1978-81; group claims examiner Fireman's Fund, Atlanta, 1981-82; pres., owner Temp. Ins. Personnel, Atlanta, 1982-86; pres. Atlanta Ins. Profls., 1986—, Internat. Ins. Personnel, Atlanta, 1987—. Mem. Nat. Ins. Women's Assn., So. Loss Assn., Atlanta Claims Assn., Atlanta Ins. Agts., Atlanta C. of C. Democrat. Baptist. Office: Internat Ins Personnel Inc 880 Johnson Ferry Rd NE Suite 565 Atlanta GA 30342

DICKERSON, NANCY HANSCHMAN, television producer, news correspondent; b. Milw.; d. Frederick R. and Florence (Conners) Hanschman; m. Claude Wyatt Dickerson, Feb. 24, 1962 (div. 1983); children: Elizabeth, Ann, Jane, Michael, John. Student, Clarke Coll., Dubuque, Iowa; grad., U. Wis., 1948; postgrad., Harvard U.; HHD, Am. Internat. Coll., Springfield, Mass.; ArtsD, Pine Manor Coll., 1988. Sch. tchr. Milw.; staff asst. Senate Fgn. Relations Com., Washington; producer CBS News, 1956-60, 1st woman news corr., 1960-63; news corr. NBC, 1963-70; news analyst Inside Washington (syndicated nationally for TV stas.), 1971—; producer spl. syndicated TV programs, pres. Dickerson Co., 1971—; polit. commentator Newsweek Broadcasting Service; founder, exec. producer Television Corp. Am., 1980—; reporter Pres. Kennedy's funeral, Republican and Democratic convs., Civil Rights March on Washington, Kennedy, Johnson and Nixon inaugurations; represented Pub. Broadcasting Corp. (on all-network Conversation with Pres. Nixon), 1970; lectr; commentator Fox TV News, 1986—. Author: Among Those Present, 1976. Trustee Am. U. Recipient Collegian award LaSalle Coll., Phila; Spirit of Achievement award Albert Einstein Coll., Yeshiva U.; Sigma Delta Chi award Boston U.; Pioneer award New Eng. Women's Press Assn.; Assoc. fellow Pierson Coll., Yale, 1972—; Peabody award for 1982 TV program on Watergate; Silver Gavel award for 1982 TV program on Watergate ABA. Mem. Radio-Television News Analysts. Club: Washington Press (past v.p.).

DICKERSON, PAMELA MAY, writer; b. Orange, Calif., June 6, 1961; d. Joseph Beattie, III and Norma May (Miller) D. BBA, BA in English summa cum laude, Chapman Coll., 1980. Free-lance writer, editor, Garden Grove, Calif., 1980-84; documentation mgr. Am. Data Industries, Irvine, Calif., 1984—. Contbr. articles to progl. jours. Mem.Laguna Moulton Playhouse, Laguna Art Mus., Dollar Dames Investment Group, Nat. Assn. for Female Execs., Soc. for Tech. Communication, Islamic Computer Soc., Orange County Islamic Soc. (mem. publs. com. 1982—), Smithsonian Assocs. Democrat. Muslim. Avocations: reading, theater.

DICKERSON, PAMELA SUE, health care executive; b. Coshocton, Ohio, June 8, 1948; d. Ned Martin and Mary Lou (Henderson) Patterson; m. Timothy Owen Dickerson, June 28, 1969; children: Annette Marie, Marcus Glenn. BSN, Old Dominion U., 1974; MS, Ohio State U., 1978; graduate, Westerville Area Leadership Program, 1986. RN, Ohio. Staff, charge nurse Coshocton County Hosp., 1969; instr. Norfolk (Va.) Gen. Hosp., 1974-76, Columbus (Ohio) Tech. Inst., 1978-82; chief exec. officer Life Wise, Westerville, Ohio, 1982—; cons. U.S. Army Hosp., Bremerhaven, Fed. Republic Germany, 1970-72; instr., specialist ARC, various locations, 1970-82; founder, past bd. dirs. Chem. People, Gahanna, Ohio. Contbr. articles to profl. jours. Trustee Community Improvement Corp., Gahanna, 1983-87; active Westerville (Ohio) South Music Boosters, 1985—; bd. dirs. Community Counseling Ctr., Gahanna, 1983-86. Mem. Am. Nurses Assn., Nat. League for Nursing, Ohio Nurses Assn., Nurse Entrepreneur Assembly, C. of C., Sigma Theta Tau. Avocations: walking, reading, crafts. Home: 412 Cherrington Rd Westerville OH 43081 Office: Life Wise 647C Park Meadow Rd Westerville OH 43081

DICKEY, CATHY SUE, school administrator; b. Cleve., Feb. 2, 1948; d. George Nickolas and Ruth (Delau) Basen; m. Richard Carver (div. Dec. 1981); children: Jessica, Melissa Joines; m. Benjamin Shepard Dickey, Jr., June 19, 1982; stepchildren: Benjamin III, Elizabeth. AB, Ohio U., 1969; MS in Sch. Adminstrn., Calif. State U., Hayward, 1986. Cert. tchr. social studies; cert. sch. adminstrv. service, Calif. Tchr. social studies Parma (Ohio) City Schs., 1969-75; educator jail Contra Costa County Schs., Pleasant Hill, Calif., 1979-84; coordinator jail edn. Contra Costa County Sheriff's Office, Martinez, Calif., 1982-83; cons. edn. San Quentin State Prison, 1983-84; tchr. history, English Liberty Union High Sch., Brentwood, Calif., 1984-85, vice prin., 1985—; cons. Sch./Law Enforcement Ptnrship Cadre, Sacramento, 1986—. Author: Educational Quality Circles, 1985. Chairperson, facilitator East Contra Costa County Juvenile Justice Com., 1986—. Mem. Assn. for Supervision and Curriculum Devel., Assn. Calif. Sch. Adminstrs. Club: Commonwealth (San Francisco). Lodge: Soroptimists. (bd. dirs. 1987—). Office: Liberty Union High Sch Dist 850 Second St Brentwood CA 94513

DICKEY, DIANE COLERIDGE, marketing professional; b. DuBois, Pa., Mar. 26, 1945; d. Raymond Roosevelt and Hilda (Finch) D. AB, Bucknell U., 1966; MFA, Cath. U., Washington, 1969. Pub. relations rep. W. Colston Leigh, Inc., N.Y.C. and Beverly Hills, Calif., 1973-79, DCD & Assocs., North Hollywood, Calif., 1980-82; account exec. Fin. Mgmt. Cons., Inc., Sherman Oaks, Calif., 1983—; Producer Actors Alley Theater, Sherman Oaks, 1976-77, R-Kane Prodns., Los Angeles, 1978. Writer The Making of Star Trek documentary, 1978. Office: Fin Mgmt Cons Inc 15233 Ventura #611 Sherman Oaks CA 91403

DICKEY, JULIA EDWARDS, management and promotional consultant; b. Sioux Falls, S.D., Mar. 6, 1940; d. John Keith and Henrietta Barbara (Zerell) Edwards; student DePauw U., 1958-59; A.B., Ind. U., 1962, M.L.S., 1967, postgrad., 1967—; m. Joseph E. Dickey, June 18, 1959; children—Joseph E., John Edwards. Asst. acquisitions librarian Ind. U. Regional Campus Libraries, 1965-67; head tech. services Bartholomew County Library, Columbus, Ind., 1967-74; dir. reference services Southeastern Ind. Area Library Service Authority, Columbus, 1974-78, exec. dir., 1978-80; pres. Jedco Enterprises, 1981—; legis. strategy chmn. Ind. Library Coop. Devel., 1975; dir. Ind. Library Trustees Assn. Governance Project, 1982. Mem. Columbus exec. bd. Mayor's Task Force on Status of Women, 1973—; del. Ind. Sch. Nominating Assembly, 1973-75, 75-77; sec. bd. dirs. Human Services Inc. (Bartholomew, Brown and Jackson Counties community action program), 1975, pres., 1976, 77, 78; mem. adv. council Ind./Nat. Network Study, 1977-78; bd. dirs. Columbus Women's Center; precinct coordinator Vols. For Bayh, 1974; sheriff Columbus 1st precinct, 1975, clk., 1976-77, insp., 1978, judge, 1980-83; treas. Hayes for State Rep. Com., 1978, 82, 84, 86. Named Outstanding Young Woman Am., 1973. Mem. ALA, Ind. Library Assn. (dist. chmn. 1972-73, chmn. library edn. div. 1980-81, ad hoc com. on legis. effectiveness, 1982, various coms.), Library Assts. and Technicians Round Table (chmn. 1968-69), Tech. Services Round Table (chmn. 1971-72, sec. library planning com. 1969-72), AAUW (pres. 1973-75), Bartholomew County Library Staff Assn. (pres. 1975-76), Exptl. Aircraft Assn. (charter pres. chpt. 729 1981, pres. Ind. council 1982—, major achievement award Oshkosh), 1983), Ind. EAA Council (pres. 1982—), Antique Airplane Assn., First Tuesday, Psi Iota Xi. Club: Zonta. Home and Office: 511 Terrace Lake Rd Columbus IN 47201

DICKINSON, CATHERINE SCHATZ, microbiologist; b. Cin., Jan. 6, 1927; d. Ralph Marvin and Mabel (Dare) Schatz; student U. Cin., 1944-46, postgrad. 1952; A.B., Miami U., Oxford, Ohio, 1948; m. Willard C. Dickinson, Jr., June 23, 1956; children—Kellie Dare, Bradley Clark. Supr., Bacteriology Lab., Children's Hosp., Cin., 1948-53; supr., sect. head Microbiology Lab., Ochsner Found. Hosp., New Orleans, 1953—; lectr. in field. Mem. New Orleans Area Soc. for Microbiology (pres. 1979), Am. Soc. Microbiology, Am. Soc. Clin. Pathologists (specialist in microbiology), New Orleans Soc. Microbiology, Nat. Registry for Microbiologists, Delta Zeta. Episcopalian. Club: Order Eastern Star. Home: 10001 Hyde Pl River Ridge LA 70123 Office: 1516 Jefferson Hwy New Orleans LA 70121

DICKINSON, JANE W. (MRS. E.F. SHERWOOD DICKINSON), club woman; b. Kalamazoo, Sept. 27, 1919; d. Charles Herman and Rachel (Whaler) Wagner; student Hollins Coll., 1938-39; B.A., Duke U., 1941; M.Ed., Goucher Coll., 1965; m. E.F. Sherwood Dickinson, Oct. 23, 1943; children—Diane Jane Gray Clem, Carolyn Dickinson Vane. Exec. sec. Petroleum Industry Com., Balt., 1941-43; exec. sec. Sherwood Feed Mills Inc., Balt., 1943-79. Mem. exec. com. Children's Aid Md., 1960-61; mem. bd. women's aux. Balt. Symphony Orch., 1958-60; dist. chmn. Balt. Cancer Drive, 1958; dist. chmn. Balt. Mental Health Drive, 1957; co-chmn. Balt. United Appeal, 1968; bd. mgrs. Pickersgill Retirement Home. Mem. Alpha Delta Pi. Republican. Episcopalian. Clubs: Three Arts (sec. 1958-60, bd. govs. 1960-64, 67—, pres. 1970-72) (Balt.); Women's (bd. govs. 1960-64, 86-88) (Roland Park); Cliff Dwellers Garden. Home: 1708 Killington Rd Baltimore MD 21204

DICKINSON, JOANNE WALTON, lawyer, writer; b. Windsor, N.C., Nov. 17, 1936; d. John Odell and Lois (King) Walton; m. Charles Cameron Dickinson III; children: Richard E.P. Eaton, John W.T. Eaton, Edward V.H. Eaton. Student Wake Forest Coll., 1961-62; BA, W.Va., U., 1975, JD, 1978. Bar: W. Va. 1978. Actress, W.Va., 1968-78; contbg. editor Victorian Poetry W.Va. U., Morgantown, 1970-75; assoc. Love, Wise, Robinson & Woodroe, Charleston, W.Va., 1978-82; adj. prof. U. Charleston, 1982—; prof. Hebei Tchrs. U., Shijiazhuang, Hebei Province, People's Republic China, 1983-84; lectr. Erikson Ctr./Harvard Med. Sch., 1985—; lead articles editor W.Va. Law Rev., Morgantown, 1977-78; asst. editor Mountain State Press, Charleston, 1980-83. Bd. dirs. Women's Health Ctr., Charleston, 1980-81; bd. dirs. Legal Aid Soc., Charleston, 1980-81. Winner 1st prize Nathan Burke Competition ASCAP, W.Va., 1977; nominee for Best Supporting Actress W.Va. U., Morgantown, 1974. Fellow Royal Soc. Arts; mem. W.Va. State Bar Assn., ABA, Phi Beta Kappa. Clubs: University (Wichita Falls, Tex.); Harvard (Boston), Athenaeum (Boston). Contbr. articles to profl. jours. Home: 2100 Santa Fe #903 Wichita Falls TX 76309 Mailing Address: 1111 City National Bldg Wichita Falls TX 76301-3309

DICKMAN, VIRGINIA MYERS (MRS. RONALD), legal secretary; b. Tampa, Fla., Oct. 1, 1940; d. Thomas B. and Virginia Kathryn (Robinson) Kirby; student public schs. Sec. to Walter Burnside, Jr., Tampa, 1958-61; sec. Hughes Aircraft Co., Newport News, Va., 1961-62; sec. Lifsey & Johnston, Attys., Tampa, 1962-66, Shackleford, Farrior, Stallings & Evans, Tampa, 1966—. Named Legal Sec. of Yr. Tampa Legal Secs. Assn., 1977-78, 87-88. Mem. Nat. Assn. Legal Secs., Fla. Assn. Legal Secs. (del. state conv. 1979-81, 84, ways and means chmn. 1980-81, corr. sec. 1981-82), Tampa Legal Secs. Assn. (pres. 1978-79, gov. 1979-81, legal edn. co-chmn. 1980-81, historian 1982, 85, public relations chmn., parliamentarian 1981-88, fundraiser chmn. 1982-88), Presbyterian. Home: 2917 Harborview Ave Tampa FL 33611 Office: Shackleford Farrior Stallings & Evans PO Box 3324 Tampa FL 33601

DICKOVER, JOY JUNE, small business owner; b. White Plains, N.Y., Aug. 17, 1950; d. Alan Frederick and June (Crolly) D. AS, Garland Coll., 1970; BA, Boston U., 1972; postgrad., Notre Dame Coll., 1987. Asst. dir. occupational therapy Health Care Manor, Dover, N.H., 1972-73; head tchr. Greater Manchester (N.H.) Child Care Assn., 1973-74; day care dir. Community Action Program, Concord, N.H., 1974-76; supr. office child support enforcement State of N.H., Hillsboro County, 1977-84; mktg. counselor Pleasantview Retirement Community, Concord, 1985-86; owner Superior Word Processing Services, Concord, 1985—; owner, cons. A Touch of Color, Concord, 1987—; exec. v.p. N.H. Bus. Jour., Concord, 1987—. Mem. Bus. and Profl. Women Concord (chmn. pub. relation 1986—, Woman Achievement 1986), Am. Mgmt. Assn., Am. Pub. Welfare Assn., Am. Assn. Counseling & Devel., Am. Assn. Art Therapists, New Eng. Assn. Art Therapists, N.H. Day Care Dirs. Assn., N.H. Assn. Counseling Devel., Concord C. of C. Presbyterian. Office: A Touch of Color PO Box 458 Concord NH 03301

DICKSON, CAROL WARD, training and development administrator; b. Radford, Va., Dec. 27, 1951; d. George truman and Margaret Ann (Hall) Ward; m. Brian Douglas Dickson, Apr. 28, 1984; 1 child, Christopher Ward Dickson. BA in English, Wake Forest U., 1972; MS in Mgmt., Frostburg State Coll., 1985. Rep. customer service Tektronix, Inc., Blue Bell, Pa., 1973-74, supr. support services, 1974-79; staff asst. to regional mgr. Gaithersburg, Md., 1979-80, specialist mgmt. devel. tng., 1980-84; tng. adminstr. Fairchild Space Co., Germantown, Md., 1984, supr. mgmt. devel. and tng., 1984-88, mgr. tng. and devel., 1988—. Mem. Am. Soc. Tng. and Devel. Republican. Baptist. Club: Toastmasters (pres., sec.-treas. NUS chpt., founder Fairchild chpt. 1986, pres. 1986—; Competent Toastmaster award 1986, named Area Pres. of Yr. 1986-87). Home: 301 W College Terr Frederick MD 21701 Office: Fairchild Space Co 20301 Century Blvd Germantown MD 20874

DICKSON, EVA MAE, credit bureau executive; b. Clarion, Iowa, Jan. 16, 1922; d. James and Ivah Blanche (Breckenridge) D. Grad. Interstate Bus. Coll., Klamath Falls, Oreg., 1943. Reporter, Mchts. Credit Service, Klamath Falls, 1941, mgr., 1973—; credit dept. Montgomery Ward, Klamath Falls, 1941-42; bookkeeper Heilbronner Fuel Co., Klamath Falls, 1942; stenographer City of Klamath Falls, 1943, bookkeeper, office mgr., 1943-52; owner, operator All Star Bus. Service, Klamath Falls, 1953-58, Ace Mimeo Service, Klamath Falls, 1958-73; mgr. Mchts. Credit Service, 1973-87; customer service rep. CBI/Credit N.W., 1987—. Bd. dirs. United Way, Klamath Falls, 1980—; sec. Klamath Community Concert Assn., 1956—; treas., mems. chmn. Klamath County chpt. Am. Cancer Soc.; bd. dirs., treas. Hope in Crisis; mem. Klamath County Centennial Com., 1982, Unification for Progress Joint Planning Com., 1985; mem. nursing adv. com. Oreg. Inst. Tech., 1982—; mem. Klamath Employment Tng. Adv. Com., 1983-86; bd. dirs., sec., treas. Klamath Consumer Council; sec. Unified City for Progress Task Force, 1983-84, Snowflake Winter Festival, 1984—. Recipient Bronze Leadership award Assoc. Credit Burs., Inc., 1976. Mem. Consumer Credit Assn. Oreg. (pres. 1984-85), Credit Women Internat. (treas. dist. 10 1984-85, 2d v.p. dist. 10 1987-88), Assoc. Credit Bur. Pacific N.W. (pres. 1981-82), Assoc. Credit Bur. Oreg. (pres. 1978-80), Klamath Basin Credit Women-Internat. (pres. 1976-78), Soc. Cert. Consumer Credit Exec., Internat. Consumer Credit Assn., Klamath County C. of C. (pres. 1979, ambassadors com. 1980—0, Nat. Fedn. Bus. and Profl. Women's Club (chmn. nat. fin. com. 1983-84, nat. fin. com. 1982-83), Oreg. Fedn. Bus. and Profl. Women's Club (state pres. 1971-72), Klamath Falls Bus. and Profl. Women's Club (pres. 1966-67, 76-77), DAR (past regent local chpt.). Republican. Presbyterian. Club: Quota (pres. 1958-59, dist. gov. 1969-70). Avocations: painting, traveling.

DICKSON, FLORA SPECTOR, government official; b. Buenos Aires; came to U.S., 1950, naturalized, 1960; d. Goodman Max and Rose C. (Herzlich) Spector; children: Glenn, Errol, Robert. Student, Columbia U., 1950; AA, Miami Dade Community Coll., 1963; BA, U. Miami, 1965, MA, 1968, postgrad., 1968-69; M of Pub. Adminstrn., Fla. Internat. U., 1986. Teaching fellow U. Miami, 1967-68; instr. Spanish Miami Dade Community Coll., 1968-69; social worker, pub. assistance eligibility specialist Fla. Dept. Health and Rehab. Services, Coral Gables, 1969-80, dist. XI staff adv. council rep., 1977-78, sec., 1979, adminstrv. asst. client relations office, 1980-82, residential placement coordinator for dist. program Office Devel. Services, Miami, 1982-84, human services program analyst Adult Congregate Living Facilities, 1984-85. Sec. Temple Zamora, Coral Gables, Fla., 1974; pres. Friends Unltd., Temple Beth Am. South Miami, Fla., 1975; facilitator Solo Ctr. Dade County Mental Health Assn., 1977—; vol. Cedars of Lebanon Health Care Ctr.; active various community drives. NDEA/HEW fellow, U. Miami, 1965. Mem. Friends Hispanic Am. Lit., AAUW, Sigma Delta Pi, Iota Tau Alpha. Democrat. Jewish. Office: Office Licensure and Cert Dept Human Resource Services 5190 NW 167th St Miami FL 33014

DICKSON-PORTER, CLAUDIA BLAIR, librarian; b. Memphis, Oct. 22, 1925; d. Walton Avery and Annie Laurie (Tate) Tucker; B.S., U. Nebr., Omaha, 1964; M.L.S., N. Tex. State U., Denton, 1971, Ph.D., 1979; m. Benjamin A. Dickson, June 5, 1945 (div.); children—Susan Dickson Morrison, Andrea Dickson Darby, Donna Dickson Stephens, Reid W., Bryan A.; m. 2d, William G. Porter, Feb. 8, 1978. Tchrs. schs. in Nebr. and Hawaii, 1964-71; librarian Nat. Assn. Retarded Citizens, Arlington, Tex., from 1971; dir. Regional Office TAS VI, Research and Tng Center in Mental Retardation Tex. Tech. U.; dir. planning Tex. Planning Council for Devel. Disabilities, Tex. Dept. Mental Health/Mental Retardation, 1979-80; program specialist Office of Devel. Disabilities, Office of Human Devel., Fed. Region VI, Dallas, 1980-82, grants mgmt. specialist Office of Fiscal Ops., 1982-83; Head Start Community rep. Adminstrn. for Children, Youth and Families, 1983-84; program specialist So. Region Adminstrn. on Developmental Disabilities, Fed. Region VI, 1984—; tchr. community services courses El Centro Jr. Coll., Dallas Recipient Disting. Alumnus award North Tex. State U., 1984. Mem. Spl. Libraries Assn., Southwestern, Tex. library assns., Am. Assn. Mental Deficiency, Council Exceptional Children, Soc. S.W. Archivists, Local History Soc., Phi Delta Kappa. Author, compiler in field. Home: 2413 Lakeside Dr Arlington TX 76013 Office: 1200 Main Tower Dallas TX 75202

DIDION, JOAN, author; b. Sacramento, Calif., Dec. 4, 1934; d. Frank Reese and Eduene (Jerrett) D.; m. John Gregory Dunne, Jan. 30, 1964; 1 child, Quintana Roo. B.A.,, U. Calif.,, Berkeley,, 1956. Assoc. feature editor Vogue mag.,, 1956-63; former columnist Saturday Evening Post; former contbg. editor National Review; now freelance writer. Novels in clude: Run River, 1963, Play It As It Lays, 1971, A Book of Common Prayer, 1977, The White Album, 1979, Democracy, 1984; book of essays Slouching Towards Bethlehem, 1969; non-fiction Salvador, 1983, Miami, 1987; co-author: screenplays for films The Panic in Needle Park, 1971, A Star Is Born, 1976. Recipient 1st prize Vogue's Prix de Paris, 1956, Morton Dauwen Zabel prize AAAL, 1978; Breadloaf Writers Conf. fellow, 1963. •

DIDOMENICO-MASSEI, DOROTHY ANN, cytotechnologist; b. Blossburg, Pa., Aug. 19, 1941; d. George Houk Gurnsey and Ann (Mahosky) Verdolini; m. Leo J. Massei; children—Monica Angela Cole, Damien Anthony. Cert., Sch. Cytotech., Thomas Jefferson Med. Coll., 1960; student Va. Commonwealth U., evenings 1972-84. Cytotechnologist, Thomas Jefferson Med. Coll., Phila., 1960-61, 66-68; chief cytotechnologist Mercy Cath. Med. Ctr., Darby, Pa., 1968-70, St. Luke's Hosp., Richmond, Va., 1970-73; supr. cytology dept. Physician's Pathology Lab., Richmond, 1971-76, Retreat Hosp., Richmond, 1973-85; owner, mgr. DiDomenico Cytological Service, Inc., Richmond, 1976-85; sect. chief, cytology dept. Henrico Doctors Hosp., Richmond, 1985—; mem. profl. edn. com. Va. div. Am. Cancer Soc., 1976-78. Contbr. articles to mags. Am. Cancer Soc. scholar, 1959. Mem. Va. Soc. Cytology (mem. founding com., exec. com., 1st pres. 1976-77, chmn. bd. dirs. 1976-78, pres. 1987—, chmn. nominations com. 1987, pres. 1987-88), Internat. Acad. Cytology, Am. Soc. Clin. Pathologists, Am. Soc. Cytology, Am. Soc. for Cytotech. (regional dir. 1986-87, chmn. membership com. 1987), So. Assn. Cytotechnologists. Avocations: reading, swimming, cross stitch. Office: 2211 E Parnam Rd Richmond VA 23228

DIDRICKSON, LOLETA ANDERSON, state legislator; b. Chgo., May 22, 1941; d. J. Henning and Ruth (Anderson) Anderson; m. Charles E. Didrickson, June 17, 1961; children: Abby, Charles E. Jr., John. Student U. Ill., 1958-61; BA, Governors State U., 1974. Legis. aide state senator 1979-82; gen. mgr. Titan Jack Mfg., Chicago Heights, 1981-82; mem. Ill. Ho. of Reps., 1982—; minority spokesperson labor and commerce com.; mem. appropriations I, elem. and secondary edn., registration and regulation coms.; appointee Legis. Research Unit. Mem. Jr. League Am.; pres. Homewood-Flossmoor (Ill.) High Sch. Parents Bd., 1981; v.p., bd. dirs. Prairie State Coll. Found., Chicago Heights, 1982-83; mem. Ill. Dangerous Drugs Adv. Council, Chgo., 1985—; bd. dirs. Y-Me Breast Cancer Orgn., Homewood, Ill., 1984—, Ingall's Meml. Hosp., South Suburban Focus Council, Operation Snowball Region II, Cook County Bd. Nat. Rep. Women; alt. del.-at-large Rep. nat. conv., 1984; chairperson Ill. Elected Officials for Reagan-Bush, 1984; pres. Rich Twp. Rep. Women's Club . Recipient Friend of Edn. award Ill. State Bd. Edn., 1985, Treasure award South Suburban Focus Council, 1986, Outstanding Citizen awrd South Suburban Assn. Commerce and Industry, 1987, Legislator of Yr., Ill. Nurses Assn., 1987, Women of Achievement award, Women in Mgmt., 1987. Mem. Taylor Inst., South Suburban Assn. Commerce, LWV. Home: 1111 Brassie Ave Flossmoor IL 60422 Office: 2023 Ridge Rd Homewood IL 60430

DIE, ANN MARIE HAYES, psychologist, educator; b. Baytown, Tex., Aug. 15, 1944; d. Robert L. and Dorothy Ann (Cooke) Hayes; m. Jerome Glynn Die, June 5, 1971; 1 child, Meredith Anne. BS with highest honors,

Lamar U., 1966; MEd, U. Houston, 1969; PhD, Tex. A&M U., 1977. Cert. tchr., psychologist. Tchr. Deer Park, Tex., 1966-71, team leader, 1969-71; tchr. Lexington, Ky., 1971-73; asst. prof. dept. psychology Lamar U., Beaumont, Tex., 1977-82, assoc. prof., dir. Psychol. Clinic, 1982-86, dir. grad. programs in psychology, 1981-86, Regents prof. Psychology, 1986, pres. Faculty Senate, 1985-86; pvt. practice clin. psychology Beaumont, 1979-87; adminstr. adolescent residential unit Mental Health/Mental Retardation of S.E. Tex., 1979-80; cons. in field; coordinating bd. Tex. Coll. and Univ. System Internship, 1986. Contbr. articles to profl. jours. Active community adv. com. Beaumont State Ctr. Human Devel., 1981-88, Mental Health/Mental Retardation S.E. Tex., 1981-87; participant Nat. Identification Program for Women, Am. Council on Edn., 1985; bd. dirs. Beaumont Civic Opera, Lamar U. Meth. Student Ctr. Fellow Coll. William and Mary, 1986-87; recipient Regents Merit award, 1979, Coll. Health and Behavioral Sci. Merit award, 1982. Fellow Am. Council on Edn.; mem. Am. Psychol. Assn., Southwestern Psychol. Assn., Family Services Assn. (bd. dirs. 1988—), Tex. Psychol. Assn. (dir. div. of psychologists 1986), SE Tex. Psychol. Assn. (treas. 1978-79, 79-80, pres. 1983), Tex. Council Family Relations, Nat. Council Family Relations, Mental Health Assn. Jefferson County, Nat. Register Health Service Providers in Psychology, Beaumont Art Mus. Methodist. Home: 855 Belvedere Dr Beaumont TX 77706 Office: Lamar U PO Box 10036 Beaumont TX 77710

DIEDERICH, SISTER ANNE MARIE, college president. BA in English, Ursuline Coll. for Women, 1966; MA in Edn., John Carroll U., 1975; PhD, Ohio State U., 1988. Joined Order St. Ursula, Roman Cath. Ch. Tchr. Villa Angela Acad., Cleve., 1966-70, asst. prin., 1971-76, prin., 1976-82; tchr. Beaumont Sch. for Girls, 1982-84; pres. Ursuline Coll., Pepper Pike, Ohio, 1986—. Dan H. Eikenberry scholar Ohio State U., 1985; William R. and Marie A. Flesher fellow Ohio State U., 1986. Mem. Ohio Tchr. Edn. and Adv. Commn., Phi Kappa Phi. Office: Ursuline Coll Office of the Pres 2550 Lander Rd Cleveland OH 44124

DIEDERICHS, JANET WOOD, public relations executive; b. Libertyville, Ill.; d. J. Howard and Ruth (Hendrickson) Wood; B.A., Wellesley Coll., 1950; m. John Kuensting Diederichs, 1953. Sales agt. Pan Am. Airways, Chgo., 1951-52; regional mgr. pub. relations Braniff Internat., Chgo., 1953-69; pres. Janet Diederichs & Assocs., Inc., pub. relations cons., Chgo., 1970—; advisor Apparel Industry Bd, Inc.; lectr. Harvard U.; mem. exec. com. World Trade Conf., 1983, 84. Com. mem. Nat. Trust for Historic Preservation, 1975-79, Marshall Scholars (Brit. Govt.), 1975-79; trustee Northwestern Meml. Hosp., 1985—; bd. dirs., mem. exec. com. Chgo. Conv. and Visitors Bur. 1978-87; bd. dirs. Internat. House, U. Chgo., 1978-84, Com. of 200, 1982-84, Latino Inst., 1986—, Chgo. Network, 1987—; com. mem. Art Inst. Chgo., 1980-83; mem. exec. com. Vatican Art Council Chgo., 1981-83; pres. Jr. League Chgo., 1968-69. Mem. Nat. Acad. TV Arts and Scis., Soc. Am. Travel Writers, Chgo. Assn. Commerce and Industry (bd. dirs. 1982—, exec. com. 1985—), Pub. Relations Soc. Am., Pub. Relations Exchange, Publicity Club Chgo., Chgo. Network. Clubs: Economic, Mid-Am. (dir. 1977-79), Woman's Athletic (Chgo.). Office: Janet Diederichs & Assocs 333 N Michigan Ave Chicago IL 60601

DIEDRICK, KAREN ALEICIA, construction executive; b. Kingston, Jamaica, Jan. 28, 1961; d. Keith Aloysius and Marjorie (Ergas) Thompson; m. Peter Vernon Diedrick, Feb. 14, 1981; children: Raina, Roxanne, Danielle. A, Alpha Comml. Coll., 1978; AA, Palm Beach Jr. Coll., 1986. Sec. to pres. Wallachs of Fla., Miami, 1979-80; sec. to chief exec. officer Grand Bahama Hotel, Riviera Beach, Fla., 1981; exec. sec. Post, Buckley, Schub & Jernigan, West Palm Beach, 1981-82; office mgr. Craven Thompson & Assocs., West Palm Beach, 1982-83; sec., treas. K&P Distbg., Inc., West Palm Beach, 1983—; pres. Permits Plus, West Palm Beach, 1987. Mem. NRA. Republican. Roman Catholic. Clubs: Everglades Pistol and Rifle. Home: 14369 Paddock Dr West Palm Beach FL 33411 Office: Fountains of Palm Beach 6674 Fountains Circle Lake Worth FL 33467

DIEHL, CAROL LOU, library director; b. Milw., Aug. 10, 1929; d. Gilbert Fred and Erna Lou (Braeger) Doepke; m. Russell Phillip Diehl, Aug. 8, 1953; children: Holly Lou Diehl Nelson, Jeffrey Phillip. BS, U. Wis., Madison, 1951; MA, U. Wis., Oshkosh, 1971. Tchr. English, library Port Washington (Wis.) High Sch., 1951-54, Minoqua (Wis.) High Sch., 1954-55; librarian Ozaukee High Sch., Fredonia, Wis., 1964-65, Vernon County Tchrs. Coll., Viroqua, Wis., 1965-67; library media coordinator Manawa (Wis.) Sch. Dist., 1973-77; dir. library media services Sch. Dist. of New London, Wis., 1977—; v.p. Council on Library and Network Devel., Madison, 1979—; pres. Lake Forest Bd. Dirs., Eagle River, Wis., 1987—. Author: (with others) School Library Media Annual, 1985-87; news corr. Appleton (Wis.) Post Crescent, 1971—; contbr. articles to profl. jours. Mem. Fox Valley Symphony League; mem. exec. com. Waupaca County Grand Ole Party. Fellow Internat. Downtown Execs. Assn.; mem. Am. Library Assn. (legis. com. 1986—), Am. Assn. of Sch. Libraries (legis. chmn. 1987—), Wis. Sch. Library Assn., Wis. Library Media Assn. (pres. 1980, fedl. coordinator 1987—), Assn. of Wis. Sch. Adminstrs. (edn. services commn. 1986—), Wis. Edl. Media Assn. (leg. com. 1986—), Phi Delta Kappa. Republican. Lutheran. Club: Futurae (Manawa, Wis.). Office: Sch Dist of New London 901 W Washington St New London WI 54961

DIELEONORA, MARY BETH, sales executive; b. Hazeltown, Pa., Feb. 13, 1947; d. John M. and Janette L. (Baskin) Potcner; m. Louis A. DiEleonora, Apr. 22, 1978. BA, Wesley Coll., Dover, Del., 1966. Personnel asst. Turbo Machine Co., Lansdale, Pa., 1966-73; pub. relations asst. I-T-E Imperial Corp., Spring House, Pa., 1973-76; sales promotion mgr. Gould Inc., Spring House, 1976-84, AMP, Valley Forge, Pa., 1984—. Contbr. articles to profl. jours. Mem. Internat. Exhibitors Assn. Republican. Office: AMP 440 Swedesford Rd Valley Forge PA 19399

DIENER, BETTY JANE, university administrator; b. Washington, Sept. 15, 1940; d. Edward George and Minnie (Feild) D. AB, Wellesley Coll., 1962; MBA, Harvard U., 1964, DBA, 1974. Account exec. Young & Rubicam, Inc., N.Y.C., 1964-70; product mgr. Am. Cyanamid Co., Wayne, N.J., 1970-72; asst. dean, Sch. Bus. Case Western Res. U., Cleve., 1974-79; dean Sch. Bus. Adminstrn., Old Dominion U., Norfolk, Va., 1979-82; sec. commerce and resources Commonwealth of Va., Richmond, 1982-86; prof. mktg. Old Dominion U., Norfolk, Va., 1986-87; provost, vice chancellor acad. affairs U. Mass., Boston, 1987—. Contbr. articles to profl. publs. Commr. Norfolk Indsl. Devel. Authority, 1979-82; mem. Citizens Council for Chesapeake Bay, 1986-87; bd. dirs. Norfolk Conv. and Visitors Bur., 1979-82, Norfolk C. of C., 1979-82, Greater Norfolk Corp., 1986-87, Va. Orch. Group, 1982-87, Va. Stage Co., 1986-87, Karamu House, 1975-79, Womenspace, 1975-79, Rapid Recovery, 1975-79, Woodruff Hosp., 1975-79; adviser Jr. Achievement, 1963-64, Plans for Progress, 1968-70, Leadership Met. Richmond, 1980-82; adv. com. on state and local govt. programs John F. Kennedy Sch. Govt., Harvard U. Named Outstanding Working Woman, Glamour Mag., 1979, one of 10 Outstanding Career Women of Decade, Glamour Mag., 1984; recipient Honor award Soil Conservation Soc., 1984. Democrat. Clubs: Women's City of Cleve. (bd. dirs. 1976-79); Harbor, Town Point (Norfolk); Ocean Reef (Key Largo, Fla.). Office: U Mass at Boston Harbor Campus Boston MA 02125

DIENER, JENNIFER FLINTON, health care services executive; b. Medford, Mass., Nov. 19, 1945; d. Edgar William and Doris (Holt) F.; m. Roger Diener, Nov. 29, 1985. B.A., Radcliffe Coll., 1967; M.B.A., Harvard U., 1972. Editorial asst. Addison-Wesley, Reading, Mass., 1967-69; asst. fund dir. Radcliffe Coll., Cambridge, Mass., 1969-70; with Am. Med. Internat., Beverly Hills, Calif., 1972—; sr. v.p. Am. Med.l Internat., Beverly Hills, Calif., 1983—. Bd. dirs. Santa Monica Arts Found., Los Angeles Chamber Orch. Mem. Orgn. Women Execs. Club: Regency. Office: 414 N Camden Dr Beverly Hills CA 90210

DIERAUF, LESLIE ANN, veterinarian, consultant; b. Boston, Feb. 7, 1948; d. Curtis John and Adeline M. (Kirk) D. BS in Microbiology, English cum laude, U. Mass., 1970; DVM, U. Pa., 1974; postdoctoral, U. Calif., Davis, 1974-77. Lic. vet. Calif., Nev., N.Y., Vt.; cert. community coll. tchr., Calif. Instr. physiology U. Calif., Davis, 1976-77; staff vet. Elk Grove (Calif.) Vet. Clinic, 1977, Midtown Animal Hosp., Sacramento, 1978-79, Marin County Vet. Emergency Clinic, San Rafael, Calif., 1979-87; independent cons. 1988—; staff vet. Calif. Marine Mammal Ctr., Ft. Cronkhite, 1979-82, dir. vet. services, 1982-84, bd. sci. advisors, 1984—; instr. animal health tech. Western Sch. Allied Health Professions, Sacramento, 1977-79; cons. Marine Mammal Cons. Services, Novato, Calif., 1985—; cons. Naval Ocean Systems Ctr., 1984—, Calif. Marine Mammal Ctr., 1984—, Pribilof Island Fur Seal Program, 1981-84, San Francisco Zoo, 1979-84, Calif. State U., Hayward, 1979-84, ; bd. sci. advisors West Quoddy Marine Research Sta., Lubec, Maine, 1979—; bd. examiners Calif. Dept. Consumer Affairs, 1978-85. Mem. editorial bd. Diseases of Aquatic Organisms, 1985—; contbr. articles to profl. jours. Mem. com. to Save Squaw Valley Meadow; dir. Calif. Marine Mammal Ctr. Run for Seals; mem. Wildlife Care Assn., Sacramento, Sacramento Jr. Sci. Mus., Sacramento Community Orch., Sacramento Intramural Softball and Volleyball; vol. Belchertown State Hosp., Vet. Assistance, Nicaragua, 1988. Recipient Erickson Ednl. Found. award 1982-83; Thouron scholar U. Pa., 1974, U. Pa. scholar 1970-73; U. Calif., Davis grantee 1974-76; U. Calif. fellow, 1974-75, Teaching fellow U. Calif., 1975-77. Mem. AVMA (editorial asst. 1986), Calif. Vet. Med. Assn. (editorial asst. 1988—), Internat. Assn. Aquatic Animal Medicine (pres. 1986-87), Soc. Marine Mammalogy, Am. Assn. Wildlife Vets., Am. Animal Hosp. Assn., Am. Assn. Avian Vets., Women's Vet. Med. Assn., Marin County Vet. Med. Assn., Wildlife Disease Assn., Calif. Vet. Med. Assn., Am. Assn. Vet. Immunology, Calif. Acad. Scis., Calif. Marine Mammal Ctr., Friends of Sea Otter. Democrat. Episcopalian. Home and Office: PO Box 2925 Olympic Valley CA 95730

DIERDORF, LEISA MARIE, investments administrator; b. Weirton, W.Va., Sept. 3, 1960; d. Russell Wayne and Margaret Verna (Hall) Johnson; m. Ronald Gene Dierdorf Jr., Dec. 24, 1978; children: Rhonda Jean, Krystal Marie. BBA, Ottawa U., 1987. Mgr. Bisanti Bldg. Services, Akron, Ohio, 1980-83; owner D & M Bldg. Services, Canton, Ohio, 1982-84; mgr. Village Green Assocs., Bowling Green, Ohio, 1983—; agt. DiSalle Real Estate Co., Bowling Green, Ohio, 1984—. Author poetry (Silver Poet award 1986). Active Wood County Humane Soc., Bowling Green, 1983—, Gold Club Animal League, North Shore, Calif., 1985—; vol. Toledo Zoo. Mem. Nat. Assn. Realtors, Am. Entrepreneurs Assn., Wood County Bd. Realtors, Bowling Green C. of C., Nat. Assn. Real Estate Owners Inc.

DIERINGER, CINDY SUE, physician; b. Canton, Ohio, Mar. 2, 1949; d. Frank Melvin and Mary Ruth (Van Orman) D. BS in Chemistry, Grove City Coll., 1971; MS in Pharmacology, W.Va. U., 1973, PhD in Pharmacology, 1976; MD, U. N.C., 1982. NIH predoctoral fellow W.Va. U. Dept. Pharmacology, Morgantown, 1972-76; staff fellow, research scientist Nat. Inst. Environ. Health Scis., Research Triangle Park, N.C., 1976-78; internal medicine resident Richland Meml. Hosp., Columbia, S.C., 1982-85; physician, chief emergency dept. Providence Hosp., Columbia, 1985—. Contbr. articles to profl. jours. Mem. Eastminster Presbyn. Ch. Choir, Columbia, 1983—, Ch. Handbell Choir, 1986—. Mem. AMA, Am. Med. Women's Assn., Am. Coll. Physicians, S.C. Med. Assn., Columbia Med. Soc., N.Y. Acad. Scis., So. Med. Assn., Sigma Xi. Republican. Office: Providence Hosp 2435 Forest Dr Columbia SC 29204

DIERS, CYNTHIA DELL, health service human resources operations director; b. Houston, Nov. 9, 1952; d. Loy Dell and JoRita (Mitchell) Kaltwasser; m. Kenneth W. Diers, Mar. 11, 1972. BS in Bus. Services Tech., U. Houston, 1983. Supr. human resources info. services Pennzoil Co., Houston, 1972-84; dir. human resource ops. M. D. Anderson Cancer Ctr. U. Tex., Houston, 1985—. Mem. Assn. Human Resource Systems Profls. (founding, pres. Houston chpt. 1983-84, v.p. Walnut Nat. Creek chpt. 1986—, Mem. of Yr. 1984), Personnel Adminstrs. of Tex. Sr. Colls. and Univs. Lutheran. Office: MD Anderson Cancer Ctr 1515 Hocombe Houston TX 77030

DIESTELKAMP, DAWN LEA, laboratory data processing specialist; b. Fresno, Calif., Apr. 23, 1954; d. Don and Joy LaVaughn (Davis) Diestelkamp. B.S. in Microbiology, Calif. State U.-Fresno, 1976, M.S. in Pub. Adminstrn., 1983. Lic. clin. lab. technologist, Calif.; cert. clin. lab. dir. Clin. lab. technologist Valley Med. Ctr., Fresno, Calif., 1977-82, quality control coordinator, 1983-84; cons., instr. in field. Mem. Nat. Assn. Female Execs. Democrat. Office: 445 S Cedar Ave Fresno CA 93702

DIETEL, JODY LYNNE, personnel consultant; b. Mpls., Dec. 10, 1957; d. Lenn Edward and Elsa Ruth (Grunke) D.; m. Stephen J. Bovy, Aug. 9, 1980 (div. 1982). BA in Psychology, Bethel Coll., 1979. Asst. accts. cons. Prudential Ins. Co., Mpls., 1979-84; cons. The Wyatt Co., Mpls., 1984-87, Treacy and Rhodes Cons., Solana Beach, Calif., 1987—. Mem. Minn. Chem. Dependency Assn., Nat. Assn. Female Execs. Baptist. Office: Treacy and Rhodes Cons 462 Stevens Ave Suite 308 Solana Beach CA 92075

DIETEMANN, DORIS E., health science association executive; b. Bridgeport, Conn., Feb. 24; d. Norman Ellsworth and Bertha (Bruce) Little; m. Aloys A. Dietemann, May 22, 1964. ThD, Bernadean Coll., 1973; M, Emerson Coll., Can., 1980. Diplomate Am. Bd. Naturopathic Medicine. With Savs. and Comml. Banking, New Haven, Conn., 1949-53; rep. Phoenix Mutual Life, Hartford, Conn., 1953-60; coordinator Religious Research Found., Los Angeles, 1960-63; v.p., researcher Dietemann Research Found., 1968-86; owner, pres. Acad. Health Scis., Los Angeles, 1975—; mgmt. cons. Valentine G. Birds, MD Inc., 1986—. Coordinator, Travel/Ednl. Program for Edn. Abroad, 1987—. Mem. Western Mining Council (v.p. Los Angeles chpt. 1979—), Internat. Naturopathic Assn. (pres., exec. dir.), Internat. Myomassethics Fedn. (pres., bd. mem. 1971—), Calif. Fedn. Massage (pres., exec. dir. 1971—). Republican. Episcopalian.

DIETRICH, MARTHA JANE (SHULTZ), genealogist; b. Brazil, Ind., Aug. 19, 1916; d. Charles Russell and Florence Delilah (McIntire) Shultz; grad. Ind. State U.; m. E(arl) Donald Dietrich, June 17, 1939; children—Florence Ann Dietrich Harris, Jean Carol Dietrich Litterst, Charles Donald. Clk., CSC, Washington, 1937-43; personnel officer Armed Forces Med. Library, Washington, 1948-54; personnel staffing specialist Navy Dept., Washington, 1954-70, ret., 1970; profl. free lance genealogist, College Park, Md., 1970—. Cert. Am. lineage specialist; authorized Bd. Cert. of Genealogists, Washington. Mem. Ky. Hist. Soc. (life), Ind. Hist. Soc., Clay County (Ind.) Geneal. Soc., Somerset County (Pa.) Geneal. Soc., Geneal. Soc. Pa., DAR, Nat. Officers Club (bd. dirs. Eastern region 1988—), DAR, (state registrar 1973-76, state vice regent 1976-79), Md. DAR (state regent 1979-82, hon. state regent 1982—), Md. State DAR Officers Club, Colonial Dames XVII Century Nat. Officers Club (registrar gen. 1974-79), Daus. Am. Colonists (state chmn. 1977-79), Daus. Colonial Wars, UDC, Daus. of 1812, Sons and Daus. of Pilgrims, Magna Charta Dames, Order Crown of Charlemagne (registrar gen. 1982—, hon. registrar gen. life 1986), Soc. Ind. Pioneers (life), Order Ky. Cols., Clan MacIntyre Assn. (genealogist 1978-84), Daus. Barons of Runnymede, Colonial Dames XVII Century (state pres. D.C. state soc. 1975-77, acting registrar gen. 1974-75, registrar gen. 1975-79, service awards 1977, 78), Soc. Ky. Pioneers, Colonial Daus. Seventeenth Century, Flagon and Trencher (life), Kappa Kappa, Kappa Kappa Kappa (Ind.). Episcopalian. Home and Office: 4616 Guilford Rd College Park MD 20740

DIETRICH, SUZANNE CLAIRE, instructional designer; b. Granite City, Ill., Apr. 9, 1937; d. Charles Daniel and Evelyn Blanche (Waters) D.; B.S. in Speech, Northwestern U., 1958; M.S. in Pub. Communication, Boston U., 1967; postgrad. So. Ill. U., 1973—. Intern, prodn. staff Sta. WGBH-TV, Boston, 1958-59, asst. dir., 1962-64, asst. dir. program Invitation to Art, 1958; cons. producer dir. dept. instructional TV radio Ill. Office Supt. Pub. Instruction, Springfield, 1969-70; dir. program prodn. and distbn., 1970-72; instr. faculty call staff, speech dept. Sch. Fine Arts So. Ill. U., Edwardsville, 1972—, grad. asst. for doctoral program office of dean Sch. Edn., 1975-78; research asst. Ill. public telecommunications study for Ill. Public Broadcasting Council, 1979-80; cons. and research in communications, 1980—; exec. producer, dir. TV programs Con-Con Countdown, 1970, The Flag Speaks, 1971. Roman Catholic. Home: 1011 Minnesota Ave Edwardsville IL 62025

DIETZ, JANIS CAMILLE, manufacturing company executive; b. Washington, May 26, 1950; d. Albert and Joan Mildred (MacMullen) Weinstein; m. John William Dietz, Apr. 10, 1981. BA, U. R.I., 1971; MBA, Calif. Poly. U., Pomona, 1984. Customer service trainer People's Bank, Providence, 1974-76; salesman, food broker Bradshaw Co., Los Angeles, 1976-78; salesman Johnson & Johnson, Los Angeles, 1978-79, Gen. Electric Co., Los Angeles, 1979-82; regional sales mgr. Leviton Co., Los Angeles, 1982-85; nat. sales mgr. Jensen Gen. div. Nortek Co., Los Angeles, 1985-86; retail sales mgr. Norris div. Masco, Los Angeles, 1986-88; nat. sales mgr. Thermador Waste King div. Masco, Los Angeles, 1988—; sales trainer, Upland, Calif., 1985—; instr. Calif. Poly. U., 1988—. Dir. pub. relations Jr. Achievement, Providence, 1975-76. Recipient Sector Service award Gen. Electric Co., Fairfield, Conn., 1980, Outstanding Achievement award, 1988. Mem. Nat. Assn. Female Execs., Sales Profls. Los Angeles (v.p. 1984-86). Unitarian. Club: Toastmasters (adminstrv. v.p. 1985). Avocations: sewing, running. Office: Thermador Waste King 5116 District Blvd Los Angeles CA 90040

DIFATE, HELEN KESSLER, architect; b. Mt. Vernon, N.Y., Jan. 23, 1942; d. Lawrence Victor and Helen de Forestal (McKernan) Kessler; m. Victor George DiFate, Jr., June 5, 1966; children—Eric Victor, Kristen Helen. BA, Coll. New Rochelle, 1963; BArch, Cooper Union, 1968. Designer, Bro. Cajetan J.B. Baumann O.F.M. Architect, FAIA, N.Y.C., 1962-70; project dir. Philip J. Wilker Architect & Assocs., Bronxville, N.Y., 1970-71; designer Robert A. Green & Philip G. McIntosh AIA, Architects, N. Tarrytown, N.Y., 1971-72; architect Fleagle and Kaeyer, Architects, Yonkers, N.Y., 1972-74, Anselevicius/Rupe/Assocs., St. Louis, 1974-75; architect Helen Kessler DiFate AIA Architect, St. Louis, 1971—; part time faculty engr. div., archtl. option, St. Louis Community Coll. Meramec, 1975-76, also mem. drafting and design tech. adv. com.; mem. Women's Assn. of St. Louis Symphony Soc., Friends of St. Louis Art Mus., Friends of St. Louis Sci. Mus. Registered architect, N.Y., Mo., Ill.; cert. Nat. Council Archtl. Registration Bds. Mem. AIA (corp. mem.; dir. Westchester, N.Y. chpts., 1974, officer St. Louis chpt. 1984, 85), Mo. Council Architects (bd. dirs.), Mo. Bd. for Architects, Profl. Engrs. and Land Surveyors, Alliance of Women in Architecture, Clayton (Mo.) C. of C. Roman Catholic. Archtl. project published in books: Buildings Reborn: New Uses, Old Places (Barbaralee Diamonstein), 1978, The Building Art in St. Louis: Two Centuries (George McCue), 1981.

DIGGS, CAROL BETH, marketing executive; b. Lubbock, Tex., Feb. 26, 1949; d. Billy Horace Diggs and Adele Frieda (Krueger) Weinberger; m. Aloy Louis Ruland Jr., Oct. 10, 1981. B.A. with honors, Okla. U., 1970; M.A., George Washington U., 1974; postgrad. Johns Hopkins U., 1974-76. Tchr. Norman (Okla.) Pub. Schs., 1970-71; promotion asst. Johns Hopkins U. Press, Balt., 1976-77, tng. asst. 1st Nat. Bank Md., Balt., 1977-78, mktg. coordinator, 1978-79, br. adminstrn. officer, exec., 1979-83, product mgmt. exec., 1983-85, sr. product mgmt. exec., 1985-87; asst. v.p. Signet Bank Md., Balt., 1987—. Contbr. poetry Anthology of Modern Poets, 1969. Mem. Balt. Symphony Chorus, 1976-83, bd. dirs., 1979-81; ch. promotion coordinator Md. Bicentenniel Fund, Balt., 1983; editor The Tower, Ch. of the Messiah, Balt., 1982-84; mem. adv. bd. Md. Ch. News, Bishop Claggett Ctr. Eastern Star scholar, Okla. U., 1967, E.K. Gaylord scholar, 1967, 69; fellow George Washington U., 1972-74, Johns Hopkins U., 1974-76. Mem. MLA, Nat. Assn. Bank Women, Alpha Lambda Delta, Sigma Delta Pi (treas. 1973-74). Republican. Home: 2118 Oak Lodge Rd Baltimore MD 21228 Office: Signet Bank Md 7 Saint Paul St Baltimore MD 21203

DIGIAMARINO, MARIAN ELEANOR, zoning and code specialist; b. Camden, N.J., July 23, 1947; d. James and Concetta (Biancosino) DiG. BS in Mgmt., Rutgers U., 1978. Clk. and stenographer transp. div. Dept. of Navy, Phila., 1965-70, sec., 1970-73, realty asst. Profl. Devel. Ctr.. program, 1973-75, realty specialist, 1975-81, supervisory realty specialist, head acquisition and ingrant sect., 1981-85, supervisory realty specialist, mgr. ops. br., 1985—; instr. USNR, Phila., 1983. Contbr. articles to profl. jours. Mem. AAUW, Soc. Am. Mil. Engrs., Nat. Assn. Female Execs., Phi Chi Theta (pres. Del. Valley chpt. 1984-86, nat. councillor 1984, nat. fundraising com., pres. and corr. sec. (Alpha Omega chpt. 1976-78). Office: Dept of Navy Northern div Naval Facilities Engring Command Real Estate div U S Naval Base Philadelphia PA 19112

DIGIOVANNI, ELEANOR ELMA, scaffold installation company executive; b. Long Island City, N.Y., May 14, 1944; d. Charles and Josephine (Laureni) DiG. Student Queensboro Coll. Collector Atlas/Re/Sun Ins. Co., N.Y.C., 1965-69; instr. Oak Manor Equitation, Weyers Cave, Va., 1970-76; dispatcher, salesperson Safway Steel Products, Long Island City, N.Y., 1977-83; ops. mgr. York Scaffold, Long Island City, 1983—. Mem. Mus. Natural History, Nat. Assn. Female Execs., Women in Constrn., Internat. Platform Assn. Democrat. Roman Catholic. Avocations: reading, horseback riding, needlepoint. Home: 14-34 30th Rd Astoria NY 11102 Office: York Scaffold Equipment Corp 37-20 12th St Long Island NY 11101

DIGIULIO, JOAN MARIE, psychotherapist, educator; b. Joliet, Ill., Oct. 6, 1937; d. John Ferry and Mary Kolman; m. Robert A. DiGiulio, June 9, 1962 (dec. May 1984); 1 child, Katrina. BA, Coll. St. Francis, Joliet, 1959; MA, U. Chgo., 1962; PhD, Case Western Res. U., 1986. Cert. social worker. Marriage and family therapist Family Counseling Service, Aurora, Ill., 1963-67; field instr. U. Pitts., 1970-72; psychiat. social worker Tipp. County Mental Health Ctr., West Lafayette, Ind., 1967-69; clin. supr. Family Service Agy., Youngstown, Ohio, 1969-72, cons., 1973—; pvt. practice marriage and family therapy Youngstown, 1974—; assoc. prof. Social Work Youngstown State U., 1976—. Contbr. articles in social casework and child welfare to profl. jours. Mem. Nat. Assn. Social Work, Am. Assn. for Marriage and Family Therapy (clin.). Office: Youngstown State U Wick Ave Youngstown OH 44512

DI GREGORIO, DEBRA GWEN, communications company executive, editor, writer; b. Louisville, Ky.; d. Francois and Dorli Maltilde (Hoenigsburg) Di G. Cert., U. Nice, France, 1975; BA in Contemporary Arts, Ramapo Coll. N.J., Mahwah, 1978. Pub. relations dir. Bergen Community Mus., Paramus, N.J., 1980-81; writer The Record, Hackensack, N.J., 1981-82; asst. editor Am. Health Mag., N.Y.C., 1982-83; freelance writer, editor, Ridgewood, N.J., 1983-85; pres., owner Camarés Communications, Inc., Ridgewood, 1985—. Author cover stories Family Computing Mag., 1984, 85. Independent Democrat. Avocations: cross country skiing, kite flying, writing, acting. Home: 136 Union St Ridgewood NJ 07450 Office: Camares Communications 4 Franklin Ave Ridgewood NJ 07450

DIGUISEPPE, DOROTHY ROSE, organization development specialist; b. Pottstown, Pa., Nov. 25, 1958; d. Sabatino Joseph and Gertrude (Jablonski) DiG. BA magna cum laude, Kutztown U., 1980; MA, W. Chester U., 1982. Project cons. Green-Herman Assocs., Washington, 1983; mgmt. cons. Alexander Proudfoot Co., West Palm Beach, Fla., 1983-84; employee devel. specialist Carpenter Technol. Corp., Reading, Pa., 1985-86, org. devel. specialist, 1986—; mgmt. asst. Gagliardi Bros. Inc., West Chester. 1982. Exec. adv. Jr. Achievement, Reading, 1987—. Named Outstanding Young Woman Am., 1985-86. Mem. Am. Soc. for Tng. and Devel., Am. Soc. for Performance Improvement, Nat. Assn. for Female Execs. Republican. Home: Valley View Apts. Amhurst #9 Pottstown PA 19464 Office: Carpenter Technol Corp PO Box 14662 Reading PA 19612-4662

DIIANNI, DONNA ANNETTE BRYANT, textile executive; b. Walhalla, S.C., Nov. 18, 1960; d. James Coy and Mary Evelyn (Alexander) Bryant; m. William Joseph DiIanni, Aug. 9, 1986. BS in Textile Chemistry, Clemson U., 1983; MS in Textile Tech., Inst. Textile Tech., Charlottesville, Va., 1987. Mgmt. assoc. Milliken & Co., Pendleton, S.C., 1983-85, Dye Lab. div. Burlington Industries, Altavista, Va., 1987—. Contbr. articles to profl. jours. Mem. YMCA, Altavista, Va., 1987—. Recipient Merit award S.C. Textile Mfrs. Assn., 1983. Mem. Am. Assn. Textile Chemists and Colorists, Phi Psi (v.p. 1986-87). Club: Altavista Country. Office: Burlington Industries Klopman Fabrics Div Altavista VA 24517

DILAPO, JANE THOMPSON, retail market owner; b. Buffalo, Dec. 3, 1945; d. C. Robert and Ruth Naomi (Rogers) Thompson; m. John H. McKeever, June 23, 1962 (div. Jan. 1982); 1 child, Kathlene Jane Feltz; m. Jonathan K. Dilapo, May 29, 1982. Student, Erie Community Coll., 1966. Lab. technician Buffalo Clin. Lab., 1967-70, Our Lady of Victory Hosp., Buffalo, 1971-73, Springville (N.Y.) Med. Group, 1973-76; owner Wholesale, Retail Tool Co., Buffalo, 1977-81; co-owner Remodeling/Woodworking Co., Buffalo, 1981-83, Produce Market, Deerfield Beach, Fla., 1983—. Mem. Deerfield (Fla.) C. of C. Republican.

DILEONARDI, JOAN WALL, social services administrator, researcher; b. Chgo., Oct. 20, 1935; d. Patrick Joseph Wall and Nora (Campbell) Jacoby; m. Robert J. DiLeonardi, June 14, 1958 (div. Feb. 1976); children: Robert, Mary (dec.), Jean. BA, De Paul U., 1956; PhD, U. Ill., 1982. Research dir. Omni Youth Services, Wheeling, Ill., 1975-76; research dir. Children's Home and Aid Soc., Chgo., 1979-82, v.p., 1982—; instr. Inst. for Clin. Social Work, Chgo., 1983—, U. Chgo., 1986-87; part-time tchr. various univs., Chgo. area, 1975—; local advisor Info. Tech. Resources, Chgo., 1983-87; peer reviewer Administrn. for Children, Youth and Families, HHS, Washington, 1982-87; cons. in field. Author: Evaluating Child Abuse Prevention Programs, 1982, What to do When the Numbers Are In, 1987; contbr. articles to profl. jours.; presenter in field. Pres. NW Suburban Day Care Ctr., Des Plaines, Ill., 1968-77; vol. Earthwatch; trustee Mensa Edn. and Research Fedn., Phila., 1984-87; bd. dirs. Rainbow Hospice, Des Plaines, 1986—, The Harbor, Des Plaines, 1987—. NIMH fellow, 1978-80. Mem. Nat. Assn. Social Workers (bd. dirs. 1981-83, del. 1982-83, instr. 1979—), Child Welfare League.

DILIBERTO, TENA JO, accountant, consultant; b. Birmingham, Ala., Dec. 17, 1958; d. Joseph Anthony and Josephine Catherine (Toro) D. BBA, Samford U., 1981. Cashier, clk. Birmingham Apothecary, 1973-76; cashier, reservationist Brookwood Med. Ctr., Birmingham, 1976-81; staff acct. Borland, Benefield, Crawford, Webster and Jeffares, CPA, PC, Birmingham, 1980-85; corp. acct. Health Ventures, Inc., Birmingham, 1985—. Mem. Am Soc. Women Accts. (bd. dirs. 1986-87). Republican. Roman Catholic.

DILKS, ELIZABETH THOMAS S., poet, clubwoman; b. North Merion, Bryn Mawr, Pa., July 21, 1917; d. Benjamin and Elizabeth Jones (Thomas) Shank; m. John Henry Dilks, June 17, 1945; student Louis Shenk Voice Studios, Phila., 1939-42, Pison Acad. of Appreciation of Arts, Phila., 1941-43, Taylor Coll., Phila., 1943-45. Author, illustrator poetry: His and Hers, 1976, A Drop in the Bucket; contbr. poetry to mags. and various anthologies in American Poetry, Contemporary Poets of America. Recipient Soc. Disting. Am. award, 1976; poem hung at Christian C. Sanderson Mus. Fellow Internat. Acad. Poets, The World Literary Acad. Eng. (hon.); mem. Acad. Am. Poets and Writers, Pa. Acad. Fine Arts, Poets and Writers N.Y., Nat. League Am. Pen Women (Phila. chpt.), Internat. Platform Assn., Acad. Am. Poets, Christian C. Sanderson Mus. (life), DAR (Downtown chpt.), Chester County Library, G. Wilson Peale House, Phila. Clubs: Whitford Country (Exton, Pa.), Mercedes-Benz of Am. Home: 394 Carlton Pl Exton PA 19341

DILL, ANNE HOLDEN, educator; b. Poplarville, Miss., Mar. 7, 1920; d. James Houston and Florence Elizabeth (Henley) Holden; B.S., U. Ala., 1954, M.A., 1955, Ed.S., 1970; m. Elmer Dill, Jan. 25, 1941; children—Winston Elmer, Jane Anne, Caroll Elizabeth Dill Norman. High sch. tchr. in Ga., 1958-65; instr. Western world lit. U. Ga. Center, Dublin, 1965-66; instr. English, Gadsden (Ala.) Jr. Coll., 1966-83. Mem. Nat. Council Tchrs. English, NEA, AAUW, S.Central MLA, Southeastern Conf. English in Two-Year Colls., Conf. Coll. Composition and Communication, Ala. Coll. English Tchrs. Assn., Ala. Council Tchrs. English, Ala. Jr. Coll. Assn., Ala. Edn. Assn., DAR (regent James Gadsden chpt. 1983—), Children of Am. Revolution, Princess Noccalula Soc. (sr. organizing pres.), Ala. Hist. Soc., Etowah Hist. Soc. Democrat. Baptist. Clubs: Gadsden Woman's, Gadsden Music. Home: 850 Walnut St Gadsden AL 35901

DILL, MARY ALYSON, information analyst; b. Aug. 30, 1951; d. William A. and Marjorie Croft D. BLS, Edinboro (Pa.) State U., 1973; MS in Instl. Communications, Shippensburg (Pa.) State U., 1979; MLS, Case Western Res U., 1982. Librarian elem. schs. Bd. Cooperative Ednl. Services, Stamford, N.Y., 1973-76; librarian West Point Elem. Sch. U.S. Mil Acad., N.Y.C., 1976-81; info. specialist, records analyst Sohio Info. Ctr., Cleve., 1981-83; info. analyst Standard Oil Corp. (formerly Sohio Info. Ctr.), Cleve., 1983—. Mem. ALA, Library Adminstrn. Mgmt. Assn., Library Info. Tech. Assn. Home: 2156 Evans Court Apt 202 Falls Church VA 22043

DILLARD, ANNIE, author; b. Pitts., Apr. 30, 1945; d. Frank and Pam (Lambert) Doak; m. Gary Clevidence, 1980; 1 child, Cody Rose; stepchildren: Carin, Shelly. B.A., Hollins Coll., 1967, M.A., 1968. Columnist The Living Wilderness, Wilderness Soc., 1973-75; contbg. editor Harper's mag., N.Y.C., 1973-85; scholar-in-residence Western Wash. U., Bellingham, 1975-78; disting. vis. prof. Wesleyan U., 1979-83, adj. prof., 1983—, writer in residence, 1987—; Phi Beta Kappa orator Harvard/Radcliffe, 1983; mem. U.S. Writers' del. UCLA U.S.-Chinese Writers' Conf., 1982; mem. U.S. Cultural Del. to China, 1982. Author: (poems) Tickets For A Prayer Wheel, 1974; (novels) Pilgrim at Tinker Creek, 1974 (Pulitzer prize for gen. nonfiction 1975), Holy the Firm, 1978, Living by Fiction, 1982, Teaching a Stone to Talk, 1982, Encounters with Chinese Writers, 1984, An American Childhood, 1987. Mem. Nat. Com. on U.S.-China Relations, 1982—. Recipient N.Y. Presswomen's award for excellence, 1975, Wash. Gov.'s award for contbn. to lit., 1978; grantee Nat. Endowment for Arts, 1980-81, Guggenheim Found., 1985-86. Mem. Poetry Soc. Am., Authors Guild, Nat. Citizens for Public Libraries, Phi Beta Kappa. Address: care Blanche Gregory 2 Tudor City Pl New York NY 10017

DILLARD, JOAN HELEN, financial executive; b. Balt., June 12, 1951; d. Anthony Joseph and Frances Helen (Waclawski) Bartynski; m. Gordon Earl Dillard, Apr. 21, 1984; 1 child, Valerie Kay. A.A., Anne Arundel Community Coll., Md., 1973; B.A., U. Md., 1977; M.B.A., U. Balt., 1984. Instr. music Acad. Music, Glen Burnie, Md., 1972-77; cash mgr. Johns Hopkins Hosp., Balt., 1979-83, Md. Casualty Co., Balt., 1983-85; 2d v.p., asst. treas. Am. Gen. Corp., Houston, 1985—. Mem. Nat. Corp. Cash Mgmt. Assn., Houston Cash Mgmt. Assn. (v.p. 1986, pres. 1987), Nat. Assn. Corp. Treas. Office: Am Gen Corp 2929 Allen Pkwy Houston TX 77019

DILLARD-MCGEOCH, M. ANNE, marketing professional; b. Montgomery, Ala., Mar. 20, 1950; d. William Barney and Martha Robert (Pugh) Dillard; m. Richard Arthur McGeoch, Sept. 7, 1985. BA, Agnes Scott Coll., 1972. Actress, model, tchr. Alliance Children's Theater, Atlanta, 1971-76; mgr. mktg. Nat. Linen Service, Atlanta, 1977-79; divisional healthcare specialist Nat. Healthcare Linen Service, Atlanta, 1979-83, dir. mktg. and sales, 1983—. Bd. dirs. Collier Condominium Assn., Atlanta, 1983, 87, pres., 1984-86. Mem. Am. Mktg. Assn. (exec. council 1986—), Am. Fedn. Health Services, Am. Hosp. Assn., Nat. Assn. Female Execs. Methodist. Home: 264 Batre Ln Mobile AL 36608 Office: Nat Healthcare Linen Service 1180 Peachtree St NE Atlanta GA 30309

DILLEHAY, PAMELA ANN, marketing communications professional; b. Berkeley, Calif., Feb. 2, 1957; s. Ronald Clifford and Valerie Ruth (Sherborne) D. B.A., U. Calif.-Santa Cruz, 1980. Translator/writer/counselor Choice Med. Clinic, Santa Cruz, Calif., 1980-82; writer KSCO Radio, Santa Cruz, 1982; mktg. programs analyst Cygnet Tech., Inc., Sunnyvale, Calif., 1983-86; public relations specialist Borland Internat., Scotts Valley, Calif., 1986-88; copy editor Technix Mag., 1988—. Counselor Planned Parenthood, Santa Cruz, 1977-80; peer advisor U. Calif.-Santa Cruz, 1980. Undergrad. research grantee U. Calif.-Santa Cruz, 1979. Avocations: scuba diving; stained glass; volleyball. Office: Borland Internat 4585 Scotts Valley Dr Scotts Valley CA 95066

DILLEMUTH, DOROTHY KATHERINE, academic administrator; b. Buffalo, Apr. 10, 1927; d. Harry C. and Ivy Dorothy (Mashford) Waltman; m. Irwin C. Dillemuth (div. Nov. 1978); children: Charles, Ivy Dillemuth Perrault, Michael C. BS in Edn., SUNY, Buffalo, 1949, M in Edn., 1964. Tchr. Maryvale Sch. Dist., Cheektowaga, N.Y., 1949-52; from tchr. to supr. testing and guidance Grand Island (N.Y.) Sch. Dist., 1953-78, acting supt. schs., 1978-79; supt. schs. Greene (N.Y.) Cen. Sch. Dist., 1980-82, Conneaut Sch. Dist., Linesville, Pa., 1982-85, Chartiers-Houston (Pa.) Sch. Dist., 1985—. Office: Chartiers-Houston Sch Dist 2080 W Pike St Houston PA 15342

DILLINGHAM, MARJORIE CARTER, foreign language educator; b. Bicknell, Ind., Aug. 20, 1915; m. William Pyrle Dillingham, (dec. 1981); children: William Pyrle (dec.), Robert Carter, Sharon Dillingham Martin. PhD in Spanish (Delta Kappa Gamma scholar and fellow), Fla. State U., 1970. High sch. tchr., Fla.; former instr. St. George's Sch., Havana; former mem. faculty Panama Canal Zone Coll., Fla. State U., U. Ga., Duke U.; dir. traveling Spanish conversation classes abroad. U.S. rep. (with husband) Hemispheric Conf. on Taxation, Rosario, Argentina. Named to Putnam County Hall of Fame, 1986. Mem. Am. Assn. Tchrs. Spanish and Portuguese (past pres. Fla. chpt.), Fla. Edn. Assn. (past pres. fgn. lang. div.), La Sociedad Honoraria Hispanica (past nat. pres.), Fgn. Lang. Tchrs. Leon County, Fla. (pres.), Delta Kappa Gamma (pres.), Phi Kappa Phi, Sigma Delta Pi, Beta Pi Theta, Kappa Delta Pi, Alpha Omicron Pi, Delta Kappa Gamma. Home: 2109 Trescott Dr Tallahassee FL 32312

DILLMAN, LINDA WILSON, marketing executive; b. Boston, Aug. 3, 1940; d. Francis Stone and Edith (Tuttle) Wilson; m. David McKnight Dillman, Feb. 8, 1964 (div. 1982); children—Jennifer Cox Dillman, Edith Stone Dillman. B.S., Northwestern U., 1963. Writer, Sta. WGN Radio & TV, Chgo., 1963-65; press info. dir. Sta. WBBM Radio, Chgo., 1965-67; devel. officer Spertus Coll. Judaica, Chgo., 1975-76; dir. pub. relations North Suburban Blood Ctr., Glenview, Ill., 1976-81, North Suburban Health Resources, Glenview, 1976-78; dir. mktg. Blood Ctr. No. Ill., Glenview, 1981-87; dir. mktg. Life Source, Glenview, 1987—; cons. and lectr. in field. Contbr. articles to profl. jours. Bd. dirs. First Congregational Ch., Wilmette, Ill., 1980—; mem. community adv. com. Northwestern Program on Women, Evanston, Ill., 1982—. Mem. Women in Communications (pres.-elect 1981-82, pres. 1982-83, del., mem. coms.), Assn. Blood Donor Recruiters, Northwest Press Club (pres. 1980-82), Am. Mktg. Assn., Avocations: writing; photography; figure skating; travel. Office: Life Source 1255 N Milwaukee Ave Glenview IL 60025

DILLON, MOLLY, banker; b. Utica, N.Y., Feb. 13, 1949; d. Dennis T. Dillon and Mildred Marion Foley; m. Thomas P. Menson; 1 child, John Kelly Bartholomew. AB, Cornell U., 1970. Mgr. Union Dime Savs. Bank, N.Y.C., 1970-73, asst. sec., 1973-75, br. mgr., asst. v.p., 1975-76; v.p. Middlebury br. Bank of Vt., 1977-81; v.p. pvt. banking Bank Vt., Burlington, 1981-83, v.p. mktg., 1983-85, sr. v.p., 1985—; pres. Bank of Vt. Trust and Investment Group, 1988. Bd. dirs. Burlington YMCA, 1985—; treas. Addison County United Way, Middlebury, 1979-81, bd. dirs., 1979-81. Mem. Internat. Assn. Fin. Planners, Nat. Orgn. Bank Women (pub. affairs chmn. 1986—), Vt. Bankers Assn. (exec. com. 1987-90). Home: Box 361 Rd 2 Hinesburg VT 05461 Office: Bank Vt 148 College St Burlington VT 05401

DILLON, SANDRA LYNN, dietitian, educator; b. Birmingham, Ala., Aug. 8, 1943; d. Harvey Drennen Rollings and Pauline (Harville) Dowling; m. Roy L. Dillon, Aug. 29, 1964 (div. Apr. 1985); children: Michael Wess, John Rollings, Jennifer Lynn. BS in Foods and Nutrition, Auburn (Ala.) U., 1965; MA in Allied Health Edn., U. Ala., Birmingham, 1986. Psychiat. dietitian U. Ala. Hosp., Birmingham, 1966-68, clin. research dietitian, 1974-75, asst. dir., 1975-80, assoc. dir., 1980—, asst. prof. nutrition scis., 1985—; clin. dietitian St. Vincent's Hosp., Birmingham, 1969-70; dir. dietetics Horizon Med. Facilities, Birmingham, 1970-74; adv. com. Cooking Light, So. Living, Birmingham, 1986—. Editor: Cookbook for Diabetics and Their Families, 1984; contbr. articles to profl. jours. Mem. Am. Dietetic Assn., Ala. Dietetic Assn. (bd. dirs. 1980—, award 1987), Ala. Food Service Expn. (bd. dirs. 1984—). Episcopalian. Home: 3401 Talheim Circle Birmingham AL 35216 Office: U Ala Hosp 619 19th St S Birmingham AL 35233

DILLON, VALERIE GERARD, anesthesiologist; b. Albuquerque, Feb. 14, 1953; d. George and Rhianwen (Roberts) Gerard; m. Stephen Darrell Dillon, Aug. 7, 1976; 1 child, Cariad Susan. BS, U. N.Mex., 1975, MD, 1980. Resident U. N.Mex. Hosps., Albuquerque, 1980-81; resident in anesthesiology U. Tex. Southwestern Parkland Hosp., Dallas, 1981-83; staff mem. Presbyn. Hosp., Albuquerque, 1983—. Mem. Am. Soc. Anesthesiologists, N.Mex. Soc. Anesthesiologists, Greater Albuquerque Med. Soc., Phi Beta Kappa. Democrat. Office: Presbyn Hosp 500 N Oak NE Suite 106 Albuquerque NM 87106

DILWORTH, BRENDA LEE, social services administrator; b. Brampton, Ont., Can., July 18, 1958; d. Lorne Maxwell and Anne Dale (Fendley) Widdess. BA in Social Scis. and Psychology, U. Guelph, Ont., 1981. Residential counsellor Met. Toronto Assn. for the Mentally Retarded, Ont., 1981-82; residential counsellor Brampton/Caledon Assn. for the Mentally Retarded, 1982-84, residential mgr., 1984—. Office: Brampton/Caledon Assn for the Mentally Retarded, 29 Haggart Ave S, Brampton, ON Canada L6Y 2C2

DILWORTH, LINDA GAIL, systems administrator, consultant; b. Ocala, Fla., June 2, 1954; d. Lawrence E. and Pauline (Nelson) Parkey; m. Jerome G. Dilworth, Aug. 16, 1975; 1 child, J. Glendon II. B.S., Fla. A&M U., 1975; M.P.A., Fla. State U., 1978, postgrad., 1981—. Fiscal asst. State of Fla., Tallahassee, 1979-80, mgmt. analyst, 1980-82, mgmt. analyst supr., 1982-84, systems project coordinator, 1984-85, systems project adminstr., 1985—; office systems cons., 1982—. Chmn. bd. Bond Community Ventures, 1983; sec. Nat. Council Negro Women, 1985. Recipient Woman of Yr. award Am. Bus. Women's Assn., 1985. Mem. Am. Soc. Pub. Adminstrn. Democrat. Baptist. Clubs: Am. Bus. Women's Assn. (pres. 1984-85), Delta Sigma Theta (treas. 1985-87, pres. 1987—). Avocations: sewing; reading; chess. Office: The Capitol Office State Comptroller Div Info Systems Tallahassee FL 32301

DIMAGGIO, PATRICIA EICHLER, media manager; b. Rochester, Pa., Feb. 28, 1952; d. Harry S. Eichler and Grace Louise (Jones) Kay; m. Robert Michael, Dec. 7, 1970 (div. Nov. 1980). Student, Duquesne U., 1965-68, Clarion U., 1970-71, Bluefield State U., 1984. Comml. teller 1st Nat. Bank Bluefield, W.Va., 1973-75; talk show host Sta. WHIS-TV, Bluefield, 1975-77; account mgr. Sta. WHIS-AM-FM, Bluefield, 1977-80; sales mgr. Sta. WHIS, Bluefield, 1980-83; nat. sales mgr. Adventure Communications, Inc., Bluefield, 1983-85; station mgr. Adventure Communications, Inc. Sta. WHIS/WHAJ, Bluefield, 1985—; asst. instr. Dale Carnegie Courses, Bluefield, 1985-87; Nat. Telethon Host March of Dimes Found., Charleston, 1985-86. Mem. budget rev. bd. Greater Bluefield United Way, 1986-88; lay minister Luth. Mountain Ministries, Wytheville, Va., 1987—; mem. reading com., actress Summit Theatre, 1974—; vol. advisor W.Va. March of Dimes, Charleston, 1982-85. Mem. Communicators Roundtable of the Virginias (bd. dirs. 1986—), Bluefield Sales Execs. Club (bd. dirs. 1986-87, v.p. 1987-88, pres. 1988—), W. Va. Broadcaster's Assn. (bd. dirs. 1987—), Greater Bluefield C. of C. Club: Quota (bd. dirs. 1984-86). Home: 2625 Grandview Ave Bluefield WV 24701

DIMAIO, VICTORIA LEE, art gallery director; b. Newport Beach, Calif., Oct. 21, 1955; d. James Vincent and Virginia Sue (Chambers) DiM. Student, Occidental Coll., 1974; AA, San Diego Coll. Bus., 1977. Stenographer Harrell Brunson Cert. Shorthand Reporters, San Diego, 1978-81, Hutchins Ct. Reporters, Santa Ana, Calif., 1981; dir. art gallery, editor newsletter Galeria Capistrano, San Juan Capistrano, Calif., 1981—; cons. TV series The Human Journey, Costa Mesa, Calif., 1986—. Contbr. articles to arts jours., 1983-85. Patron S.W. Mus., 1987. Recipient Acheivement in Lit. award Bank of Am., San Diego, 1973. Mem. Nat. Mus. Women in Arts, Mus. Contemporary Art, Mothers Against Drunk Driving, Occidental Coll. Bus. Assocs. Club: Charter 100 (La Jolla, Calif.). Office: Galeria Capistrano 31681 Camino Capistrano San Juan Capistrano CA 92675

DIMAIO, VIRGINIA SUE, gallery owner; b. Houston, July 6, 1921; d. Jesse Lee and Gabriella Sue (Norris) Chambers; AB, U. Redlands, 1943; student U. So. Calif., 1943-45, Scripps Coll., 1943, Pomona Coll., 1945; m. James V. DiMaio, 1955 (div. 1968); children: Victoria, James V. Owner, dir. Galeria Capistrano, San Juan Capistrano and Santa Fe, N.Mex., 1979—; founder Mus. Women in Arts, Washington; cons., appraiser Southwestern and Am. Indian Handcrafts; lectr. Calif. State U., Long Beach; established ann. Helen Hardin Meml. scholarship for woman artist grad. Inst. Am. Indian Art, Santa Fe, also ann. Helen Hardin award for outstanding woman artist at Indian Market, S.W. Assn. on Indian Affairs, Santa Fe. Recipient Bronze Plaque Recognition award Navajo Tribal Mus., 1977. Mem. Indian Arts and Crafts Assn., S.W. Assn. Indian Affairs, Heard Mus., San Juan Capistrano C. of C. Republican. Roman Catholic. Office: 31681 Camino Capistrano San Juan Capistrano CA 92675 also: 409 Canyon Rd Santa Fe NM 87501

DIMASO, ANGELA ANN, real estate developer; b. Chgo., Feb. 18, 1939; d. Philip and Louise Ann (Defalco) D.; m. Gerald J. Dimaso (div. 1975); children: Philip Gerald, Lou Ann Geralyn, Michele Marie. BA, DePaul U., 1960, MA, 1962, PhD, 1965; postgrad., Triton Coll., 1968, 71. Psychologist, dir. Internat. Guild Hypnotist, Chgo., 1961-71; mgr. sales Homestead Realty, Oak Park, Ill., 1971—; condo developer Homestead Realty, Oak Park, 1976—, dir. devel., 1978—; cons. Dimaso Enterprises, Chgo., 1984—; dir. Shanti Internat., Chgo. Co-author: Childbirth with Hypnosis, 1960. Co-founder of Horizon Orgn. Developmentally Disabled Children; active in equal fights issues and aid to needy, Operation Breadbasket; precinct capt. Nat. Democratic Orgn., Elmwood Park, Ill., Oak Park, 1988—. Recipient Pres. award Ill. Assn. Realtors, 1982. Mem. NOW, Women Real Estate, Oak Park Bd. Realtors, N.W. Bd. Realtors, Italian-Am. Nat. Orgn. Roman Catholic. Home: 138 S Clinton St Oak Park IL 60302 Office: Homestead Realty 6968 W North Ave Chicago IL 60635

DIMICK, NINA GRACE, software company executive, educator; b. Richmond, Vt., Sept. 3, 1949; d. Howard Alboro and Marion Kate (Dike) D.; m. Earle William Hill, Jan. 17, 1972 (div. Apr. 1976); children—Janet Lea, Stephen Howard, B.A., Johnson State Coll., 1983; M.Acctg. Info. Systems, U. West Fla., 1984. Computer lab. mgr. Johnson State Coll., Vt., 1982-83; tchr. Coastal Tng. Inst., Pensacola, Fla., 1983-84, Community Coll. Vt., Barre, 1984—; mgr. quality control Datamann, Inc., Wilder, Vt., 1984—, dept. jr. vp., 1987—. Author: How to Choose a Computer for Small Business, 1984. Editor: Guide to JSC Computer Room, 1983. Named Pres. of Yr., Vt. VFW Aux., 1980, 81, 86; recipient Second Highest Chmn. award Nat. VFW Aux., 1981, 86. Mem. Nat. Assn. Female Execs., Assn. Masters Bus. Arts, Data Processing Mgmt. Assn. (pres. 1981-83); Golden Past Pin 1983). Republican. Mennonite. Avocations: painting with watercolors; horseback riding. Home: HCR 35 Box 146 Woodstock VT 05091 Office: Datamann Inc Wilder VT 05088

DIMINO, SYLVIA THERESA, educator, educational administrator; b. N.Y.C., June 6, 1955; d. John Anthony and Elena (Berardeca) D. BA, St. John's U., 1977; M in Pub. Adminstrn., NYU, 1980, MA in Elem. and Secondary Edn., 1982, cert. advance studies in ednl. adminstrn., 1986. Cert. elem. and secondary tchr., sch. administrator N.Y. Traffic coordinator Creamer Inc., N.Y.C., 1977-79; tchr. St. Patrick's Sch., N.Y.C., 1979-82; tchr. IS 131, Manhattan, N.Y.C., 1984—, adminstr., coordinator, 1985—. Mem. Nat. Orgn. Female Execs., Nat. Orgn. Women in Adminstrn., Bus. Cir. N.Y., Nat. Council Administrv. Women Edn.. Roman Catholic. Office: IS 131 Manhattan 100 Hester St New York NY 10002

DIMMICK, CAROLYN REABER, federal judge; b. Seattle, Oct. 24, 1929; d. Maurice C. and Margaret T. (Taylor) Reaber; m. Cyrus Allen Dimmick, Sept. 10, 1955; children: Taylor, Dana. BA, U. Wash., 1951, JD, 1963; LLD, Gonzaga U., 1982, CUNY, 1987. Bar: Wash. Asst. atty. gen. City of Seattle, 1953-55; pros. atty. Kings County, Wash., 1955-59, 60-62; sole practice Seattle, 1959-60, 62-65; judge U.S. Dist. Ct. Wash., 1965-75, U.S. Superior Ct., 1976-80; justice Wash. Supreme Ct., 1981-85; judge U.S. Dist. Ct. (we. dist.) Wash., Seattle, 1985—. Recipient Matrix Table award, 1981, World Plan Execs. Council award, 1981, others. Mem. Am. Judges Assn. (gov.), Nat. Assn. Women Judges, World Assn. Judges, ABA, Wash. Bar Assn., Am. Judicature Soc. Clubs: Wash. Athletic, Wingpoint Golf and Country, Harbor. Office: US Dist Ct 911 US Courthouse 1010 5th Ave Seattle WA 98104

DIMOND, KENDRA LYNN, lawyer; b. Harrisburg, Pa., Oct. 12, 1947; d. Albert Kenneth and Spacha (Zaikoff) Dimond; m. Frederick Samuel Faber, June 21, 1969 (div. 1976); 1 child, Elena Marie. BA, Gettysburg Coll., 1969; MA, Pa. State U., 1973; JD, Dickinson Law Sch., 1979. Bar: Pa. 1979. Tchr. French West Shore Sch. Dist., Lemoyne, Pa., 1969-73; asst. prof. Charleston (S.C.) Coll., 1974-75; law clk. Commonwealth Ct., Harrisburg, 1979-80; dep. dist. atty. Dauphin County, Harrisburg, 1980-82; dep. atty. gen. Office of Atty. Gen., Harrisburg, 1982—, regional dir. Medicaid fraud control, 1985-88; assoc. Duane Morris and Heckscher, Harrisburg, 1988—. Mem. ABA, Pa. Bar Assn. (v.p., sec. criminal law sect.), Dauphin County Women Lawyers. Eastern Orthodox. Home: 5202 Royal Dr Mechanicsburg PA 17055 Office: Duane Morris and Heckscher The Payne Shoemaker Bldg 240 N Third St 10th Floor Harrisburg PA 17108-1003

DINEEN, DIANE M., library administrator. BA, U. Guelph, 1969; M in Lib. Sci., U. Western Ont., London, 1971; MBA, York U., Toronto, 1986. Librarian Windsor (Ont.) Pub. Lib., 1972-74; chief librarian Newcastle Pub. Lib., Bowmanville, Ont., 1975-79; head cen. lib. Mississauga (Ont.) Pub. Lib., 1980—. Mem. Am. Lib. Assn., Can. Lib. Assn., Ont. Lib. Assn. Lodge: Zonta. Office: Mississauga Pub Lib, 110 Dundas St W, Mississauga CAN L5B1H3

DINEHART, JUDITH ANN, psychiatric hospital administrator, social work consultant; b. Gloversville, N.Y., Dec. 14, 1947; d. Clinton George and Helen Elizabeth (Weaver) D. BA, SUNY, New Paltz, 1969; MSW, Fla. State U., 1972. Tchr. Lexington Tng. Ctr., Johnstown, N.Y., 1969-70; psychiat. social worker Ga. Regional Hosp., Savannah, 1972-79, unit dir., 1979-83, dir. adult mental health, 1983—; social work cons. Effingham County Hosp., Springfield, Ga., 1973—; Glenvue Nursing Home, Glennville, Ga., 1975-80. Organizer, leader 1st parent edn. group in Ga. for parents of mentally retarded children attending tng. ctr., 1972; mem. Community Task force to Locate Housing for Mentally Ill, Savannah, 1982. Mem. Nat. Assn. Social Workers, Ga. Assn. Hosp. Social Workers, Acad. Cert. Social Workers, Nat. Humane Soc., Audubon Soc. Democrat. Unitarian. Home: 5010 Spartan Dr Savannah GA 31404 Office: Ga Regional Hosp PO Box 13607 Savannah GA 31416

DINELL, NINA ALIX, treasurer; b. Rinteln, Federal Republic of Germany, Mar. 21, 1949; d. Ike and Eugenie (Gutsche) Dinell. BA in Pub. and Internat. Affairs, George Washington U., 1970; cert. in Program for Mgmt. Devel., Harvard U., 1978; MBA, Fordham U., 1982. Treas.'s asst. GAF Corp., N.Y.C., 1972-74; asst. v.p. Bank of Calif., San Francisco, 1974-76; asst. treas. Supermarkets Gen. Corp., Woodbridge, N.J., 1976-82; treas. M&M/Mars, Hackettstown, N.J., 1982-87, The Great Atlantic and Pacific Tea Co., Inc., Montvale, N.J., 1987—; alumni advisor Fordham U. Grad. Sch. Bus., 1982—, Harvard U. Grad. Sch. Bus., 1982—; faculty mem. Cash Mgmt. Inst., 1983—. Cons. editor: Jour. Cash Mgmt., 1982—. Mem. Nat. Assn. Corp. Treas. (bd. dirs.), N.Y. Treas.'s Group (treas. 1986-88, pres. 1988—), Women's Econ. Roundtable (mem. program com. 1987-88). Club: Harvard Bus. Sch. of N.Y. (mem. vol. cons. group 1986—). Home: 7 E 86th St New York NY 10028 Office: The Great A&P Tea Co Inc 2 Paragon Dr Montvale NJ 07645

DINETTA, DIANNE CONNELL, financial consultant; b. Wilmington, Del., Sept. 23, 1951; d. Clinton Robert and Kathleen Elizabeth (Kelly) Connell; m. Joseph Michael DiNetta, Sept. 23, 1978; 1 child, Edward. BA, Douglass Coll., 1984; MBA, Rutgers U., 1985. With human resources Warner Cosmetics, Somerset, N.J., 1981-82; corp. planning analyst Merck & Co., Inc., Rahway, N.J., 1984-86; fin. cons. Arthur D. Little Valuation, Edison, N.J., 1986—. Mem. Opera Guild at Florham, Madison, N.J., 1986-88; bd. dirs. Watchung Arts Council, 1984, 85-86. Mem. The Planning Forum, Rutgers U. Women in Bus. Republican. Home: 380 Johnston Dr Watchung NJ 07060

DINEZZA, JANICE HELEN, advertising executive; b. Buffalo, Mar. 21, 1953; d. Gregory Joseph and Helen Genevieve (Hermon) DiNezza. Student Erie Community Coll., 1971-72; B.A., Southwestern U., Tucson, 1983. Office mgr. R. H. Stark Co., Buffalo, 1974-76; media dept. mgr. Healy Schutte & Comstock, Ltd., Buffalo, 1976-80; v.p., dir. media Tavco Mktg. and Media, Buffalo, 1980; media research dir. Cable Time Network, Inc., Buffalo, 1980-82; pres. DiNezza Media Services, Buffalo, 1982-83; group media supr. Healy-Schutte & Comstock Advt., Ltd., Buffalo, 1983-86; advt. supr. McDonald Corp., Detroit, 1986—. Pub. service advt. coordinator Erie County Citizens Com. Sexual Assault, 1979-86; writer, producer, numerous TV comms. and radio announcements on program services and needs of Vol. Supportive Advocate Program, 1979-86; mem. Committees' Speakers Bur., 1980-86; solicitor trainer, retail div. United Way Campaign Buffalo and Erie County, 1981-82. Named top 100 Young Women in Nation Good Housekeeping Mag. Mem. Women in Communications (pres. 1981-84, nat. dir., v.p. region 1984-86, nat. v.p., fin., 1986—), Nat. Acad. of TV Arts & Sci., Nat. Orgn. Italian Am. Women, C. of C. (vice chmn. com.), Women in

Cable. Republican. Roman Catholic. Home: 23434 Park Pl Southfield MI 48034

DINGLE, SUSAN, library educator; b. Kankakee, Ill., Aug. 31, 1950; d. Harold Eugene and Julia Martha (Condon) Dingle; m. Gerald Howard Cliff, June 30, 1975 (div. Feb. 1984). AB, U. Ill., 1972, MS, 1975, postgrad., 1981—. Sessional reference librarian U. ALberta, Edmonton, Can., 1975-76; pub. services librarian Grant MacEwan Community Coll., Edmonton, 1976-77; librarian Alberta Alcoholism & Drug Abuse Commn., Edmonton, 1977-81; assoc. editor Grad. Sch. Library and Info Sci. U. Ill., Urbana, 1981-86; fellow Grad. Sch. Library and Info Scis. U. Ill., Urbana, 1986-87; asst. prof. Coll. Library Sci. Clarion U., Pa., 1987—. contbr. articles to profl. jours. Mem. ALA, LWV, Am. Soc. for Info Sci. (chair local arrangements 1979), Spl. Libraries Assn., U. Ill. Alumni Assn. (life), Beta Phi Mu. Democrat. Mem. Soc. of Friends. Office: Clarion U of Pa Coll Library Sci Clarion PA 16214

DINGUS, ANITA CRAVEN, manufacturing executive; b. Houston, Tex., Sept. 24, 1956; d. Albert Lee and Peggy Anita (McCombs) C.; m. Harold Phillip Dingus, Mar. 10, 1979; 1 child, Edythe Elizabeth. BA in French magna cum laude, Emory and Henry Coll., 1978; BBA, MS in Acctg., Appalachian State U., 1980. CPA, Va. Sr. acct. Peat, Marwick, Mitchell & Co., Roanoke, Va., 1980-83; exec. v.p., gen. mgr. Salem (Va.) Vent Internat., Inc., 1983-87, mng. dir. mfg. and adminstrv. functions, 1987—; cons. Blue Ridge Pkwy. Assn. C. of C., Roanoke, 1983. Mem. Am. Women's Soc. CPA's Southwest Va. (v.p. 1985-86), Am. Inst. CPA's, N.C. Assn. CPA's, Roanoke Valley C. of C. Affiliates, Beta Alpha Psi, Beta Gamma Sigma. Methodist. Home: Rt 1 Box 107 Troutville VA 24175 Office: Salem Vent Internat Inc PO Box 885 Salem VA 24153

DINKINS, CAROL EGGERT, lawyer; b. Corpus Christi, Tex., Nov. 9, 1945; d. Edgar H., Jr. and Evelyn S. (Scheel) Eggert; m. O. Theodore Dinkins, Jr., July 2, 1966; children: Anne, Amy. B.S., U. Tex., 1968; J.D., U. Houston, 1971. Bar: Tex. 1971. Adj. asst. prof. law U. Houston Coll. Law, also prin. asso. Tex. Law Inst. Coastal and Marine Resources, U. Houston, 1971-73; assoc., then partner firm Vinson & Elkins, Houston, 1973-81, 83-84, 85—; asst. atty. gen. land and natural resources Dept. Justice, 1981-83, dep. atty. gen., 1984-85; chmn. Pres.'s Task Force on Legal Equity for Women, 1981-83; mem. Hawaiian Native Study Commn., 1981-83; dir. Nat. Consumer Coop. Banks Bd., 1981, ELI; bd. dirs., chmn. govt. and pub. affairs com. Nat. Ocean Industries Assn. Author articles in field. Chmn. Tex. Gov.'s Task Force Coast Mgmt., 1979, Tex. Gov.'s Flood Control Action Group, 1980-81; bd. dirs. U. Houston Law Ctr. Found., 1985—, Energy and Environ. Study Inst., Houston Mus. of Natural Sci., Tex. Nature Conservancy. Mem. ABA, State Bar Tex., Houston Bar Assn., Tex. Water Conservation Assn., Houston Law Rev. Assn. (dir. 1978—), Fed. Bar Assn. (bd. dirs. Houston chpt. 1986—). Republican. Lutheran. Office: Vinson & Elkins 3300 First City Tower 1001 Fannin Houston TX 77002

DINKINS, JANE POLING, management consultant, EDP specialist; b. Van Wert, Ohio, Oct. 11, 1928; d. Doyt Carl and Kathryn (Sawyer) Poling; BBA, So. Meth. U., 1974. Stewardess, instr. stewardesses, chief stewardess Am. Airlines, 1946-50; exec. sec., adminstrv. asst. Southland Royalty Co., Ft. Worth, 1956-63; exec. sec. Charles E. Seay, Inc. and C.W. Goyer, Jr., Dallas, 1963-68; systems analyst, programmer Southland Life Ins. Co., Dallas, 1968-69, 1st. Nat. Bank, Dallas, 1969-72, Occidental Life Ins. Co., Los Angeles, 1972-73; systems analyst, programmer Pacific Mut. Life Ins. Co., Newport Beach, Calif., 1973-74, mgr. mut. fund subs., 1975; systems analyst, programmer Info. Services Div. TRW, Orange, Calif., 1975-79; EDP auditor Union Bank, Los Angeles, 1979; sr. EDP auditor Security Pacific Nat. Bank, Glendale, Calif., 1979-80, asst. v.p., Los Angeles, 1981; mgmt. cons. Automation Program Office, Fed. Res. Bank, Dallas, 1982-85; pres. Poling & Assocs., Inc., 1985—. Mem. Am. Mgmt. Assn., EDP Auditors Assn., Quality Assurance Inst. (cert. quality analyst), Data Processing Mgmt. Assn., Sigma Kappa. Republican. Methodist. Club: University (Dallas). Home and Office: 5990 Arapaho Rd Apt 3D Dallas TX 75248-3712

DINNERSTEIN, MYRA, university official; b. Phila., Apr. 19, 1934; d. Ben and Kathryn (Sharp) Rosenberg; m. Leonard Dinnerstein, Aug. 20, 1961; children—Andrew, Julie. A.B., U. Pa., 1956; M.A., Columbia U., 1963, Ph.D., 1971. Assoc. editor Ency. Yearbook, Grolier Pub. Co., N.Y.C., 1960-63; dir. women's studies U. Ariz., Tucson, 1975—, dir. S.W. Inst. for Research on Women, 1979—; mem. Ariz. Council on Humanities, Phoenix, 1975-80, 83—; Ariz. state coordinator Am. Council on Edn., Washington, 1978-80; dir. Nat. Council for Research on Women, N.Y.C., 1982—. Editor: Changing Perspectives on Menopause, 1982; contbr. articles to profl. jours. Pres. nat. adv. bd. New Directions for Young Women, Tucson, 1981. Recipient Faculty Achievement award U. Ariz. Alumni Assn., 1980; citation award Mortar Bd. U. Ariz., 1981; Faculty Recognition award Tucson Trade Bur., 1982; named to Mortar Bd. Hall of Fame, U. Ariz., 1985. Mem. Nat. Women's Studies Assn., Am. Hist. Assn., Phi Beta Kappa. Democrat. Jewish. Office: U Ariz 102 Douglass Bldg Tucson AZ 85721

DINSMORE, ROBERTA JOAN, library director; b. Phila., Sept. 30, 1934; d. Bert Faust and Emma Baker (Keen) Maier; m. Ray W. Dinsmore Sr., Oct. 20, 1956; children: Ray Wilson Jr., Jeffrey Maier, Debra Joan, Matthew Bert. BA, Pa. State U., 1956. Proofreader Aluminum Co. Am., Pitts., 1957-60; office mgr. Dinsmore, Lithographer, Punxsutawney, Pa., 1969—; dir. Punxsutawney Meml. Library, 1978—; free-lance writer Greenburg (Pa.) Tribure Rev., 1980-81; adult edn. tchr. Jeff Tech., Reynoldsville, Pa., 1981-82. Head hostess Welcome Wagon Internat., Memphis, 1976-80; ch. librarian Punxsutawney Presbyn. Ch., 1985—, mem. Jefferson County Constitution Com.; tchr. adult discussion class; chairperson numerous orgns. Mem. ALA, Pa. Library Assn., Pa. Citizens for Better Libraries, Clarion Dist. Library Assn. (pres. 1984-86), AAUW (Woman of Yr. 1987), Punxsutawney Area Hist. and Geneol. Soc., Inc. (sec. bd. dirs., charter mem.), Bus. and Profl. Women, Friends of Library, Punxsutawney Area Hosp. Auxiliary, Goschenhoppen Historians. Republican. Presbyterian. Club: Garden (past pres. Punxsutawney chpt.), Irving (past pres.). Lodge: P.E.O. Home: 808 E Mahoning St Punxsutawney PA 15767 Office: Punxsutawney Meml Library 301 E Mahoning St Punxsutawney PA 15767

DINTELMAN, SHARON FAYE, school system administrator; b. Dewitt, Ark., Feb. 28, 1949; d. James Lloyd and Bernice Maxine (Parker) Clemons; m. George Edward Dintelman, (div. Mar. 1984); children: Amy Lynn, Russell Barrett. BEd, U. Ark, Monticello, 1969; MEd, U. Ark, 1982; postgrad., U. Cen. Ark. Cert. elem. tchr., Ark, elem. prin., curriculum specialist. Tchr. elem. Dollarway Sch. Dist., Pine Bluff, Ark., 1970-73; tchr. elem. Stuttgart (Ark) Pub. Schs., 1976-81, prin., 1981-86; dir. curriculum Searcy (Ark) Pub. Schs., 1986—; cons. in field; mem. audio-visual selection com. Ark. Dept. Edn., Little Rock, 1985, elem. council mem., 1986—; dir. fed. programs Searcy Pub. Sch. Mem. Community Orgn. for Drug Edn., Stuttgart, 1980-86, Ark. Advocates for Children and Families, Little Rock, 1980—; chairperson Ark. County Child Abuse Task Force, Stuttgart, 1984-86. Mem. Nat. Assn. for Supervision and Curriculum Devel., Ark. Assn. for Supervision and Curriculum Devel., Nat. Staff Devel. Council, Ark. Staff Devel. Council, Nat. Assn. Female Execs., Nat. Assn. Fed. Program Adminstrs., Ark. Assn. Fed. Program Adminstrs., DAR, Phi Delta Kappa, Alpha Chi. Methodist. Home: 200 Western Hills Dr Searcy AR 72143 Office: Searcy Pub Schs 801 N Elm Searcy AR 72143

DINUNZIO, BEVERLY ANN, reading educator; b. Sharon, Pa., May 3, 1934; d. John and Josephine (LaRussa) Marmo; m. Nicholas J. DiNunzio, July 28, 1956; children: Anamarie DiNunzio Rayburn, Patricia Ann, John Mark. BFA, Ohio U., 1952-56; postgrad., Pa. State U., New Kennsington, 1958-59, U. Pitts., 1959-61. Cert. reading tchr., Pa. Grade level chairperson Highlands Sch. Dist., Natrona Heights, Pa., 1965—, reading chairperson, 1968—; Bd. dirs. Tarentum (Pa.) Motor Sales, Inc., West-Mar Land Co., Inc., Tarentum. Mem. Allegheny Valley Hosp. Aux., Natrona Heights, 1961-70, Natrona Heights Rep. Women; sec. Women's Civic Club of Allegheny Valley, 1962-66, 68-70. Mem. Nat. Automotive Dealers Assn., Pitts. Auto Dealers Assn., NEA, Pa. State Edn. Assn. (del. 1968-74), Highlands Edn. Assn. (rep. 1962-68, sec. 1968-74), Zeta Tau Alpha Alumni. Republican. Roman Catholic. Home: 1204 Calisle St Natrona Heights PA 15065

DION, NANCY LOGAN, health care administrator, management consultant; b. Bayonne, N.J., July 15, 1941; d. Walter Parker and Ethel B. (Kreiss) Logan; 1 son, Kenneth W. Diploma in nursing Bayonne Hosp., 1961; B.S., Fla. Internat. U., 1974, M.S. in Mgmt., 1976; postgrad. in bus. adminstrn. Nova U., 1980. Indsl. nurse AT&T, N.Y.C., 1966; pvt. duty nurse, Miami, Fla., 1967-69; dir. nursing Long Term Care Facility, Miami, 1969-72; nursing supr. Jackson Meml. Hosp., Miami, 1972-75, asst. adminstr., 1975-79; patient services dir. South Fla. State Hosp., Hollywood, 1979-85, adminstr., 1985—; adj. prof. Fla. Internat. U., Miami, 1979-81, Nova U., Ft. Lauderdale, Fla., 1980-82; mgmt. cons. U. Miami Hosp., 1979—; textbook resource cons.. Mem. Acad. Mgmt., Nat. Assn. Quality Assurance Profls., Fla. Assn. Quality Assurance Profls. (v.p. 1985-88), Dade County Assn. Quality Assurance Profls. (v.p. 1983-84, pres. 1984-86), Am. Coll. Hosp. Adminstrs., Am. Coll. Health Care Execs. Roman Catholic. Home: 11401 NE 8th Ave Miami FL 33161

DIOSEGY, ARLENE JAYNE, lawyer, consultant; b. Pitts., Sept. 13, 1949; d. William Cornelius and Rosemarie Arlene (Voivoda) D.; m. Charles Richard Mansfield, Apr. 11, 1981; 1 child, Corey Redling. BA, Allegheny Coll., 1971; JD, Temple U., 1974. Bar: Pa. 1974, U.S. Dist. Ct. (mid. dist.) Pa. 1974, U.S. Supreme Ct. 1980, Colo. 1981, U.S. Dist. Ct. (ea. dist.) Colo. 1981, N.C. 1987, U.S. Cir. Ct. (4th Cir.) 1987. Assoc. Smith & Roberts, Harrisburg, Pa., 1974-75; asst. atty. gen. Pa. Dept. of Edn., Harrisburg, 1975-77; chief counsel Gov.'s Council on Drug and Alcohol Abuse, Harrisburg, 1977-80; acting dir. legal affairs and risk mgmt. U. Colo. Health Scis. Ctr., Denver, 1980-81; asst. univ. counsel Duke U. Med. Ctr., Durham, N.C., 1981-85, adj. asst. prof. grad. dept. health adminstrn., 1983-87; v.p. legal services Coastal Group Inc., Durham, 1985-87; assoc. Faison and Brown, Fletcher and Brough, Durham, 1987—; cons. Colo. Dept. Health, Denver, 1980-81. Bd. dirs. YWCA, Durham, 1984-87; mem. fin. com. Epworth Ch., Durham, 1984-87. Mem. Am. Acad. Hosp. Attys., Am. Coll. Legal Medicine (assoc.-in-law), Nat. Health Lawyers Assn., ABA, N.C. Bar Assn. (sec. health law program com. 1983-84, vice chmn. 1984-85, chmn. 1985-86, 86-87, mental health law com.), Durham Bar Assn., N.C. Soc. Health Care Attys. (legis. com. 1983, program chmn. 1983, bd. dirs. 1985). Republican. Methodist. Office: Faison and Brown Fletcher and Brough PO Box 2800 Durham NC 27705

DI OTTAVIO, ROSE SCHOLASTICA, acquisition consultant; b. West Chester, Pa., July 11, 1950; d. Carlo Arthur and Lena Rose (Mammarella) Di O. BS, U. Pitts., 1971, MS, 1972. Research asst. Regional Comprehensive Health Planning Council, Inc., Phila., 1973-75, planning assoc., 1975-77; sr. planning assoc. Health Systems Agy. S.E. Pa., Inc., Phila., 1977, dep. dir., 1977-81; cons. Plante & Moran, Southfield, Mich., 1981-83; v.p. devel. Horsham Psychiat. Group, Ambler, Pa., 1983-84; exec. v.p., dir. Capital Home Care Group, North Wales, Pa., 1984-86; regulatory cons. Albert Einstein Med. Ctr., Phila., 1984-86; acquisition cons. Venture Investment Profls., 1986—; founder, pres. Health Ventures Ltd., 1986—; bd. dirs. Fox Ridge Manor, 1988. Chairwoman Met. Home Health Services, Inc., Horsham, Pa., 1985-86. Senatorial scholar, 1969-71. Mem. U. Pitts. Alumni Assn., Assn. Research and Enlightenment, Amnesty Internat., Nat. Assn. Female Execs., Found. Health Care Mgmt., Am. Soc. Profl. and Exec. Women, Career Guild. Office: Health Ventures Ltd 9 E Moreland Ave Philadelphia PA 19118

DIOUM, THERESE ELAINE, human resources executive; b. Indpls., Aug. 19, 1945; d. Bernard and Elaine (Glenn) Wisdom; m. Mamadou Dioum, Jan. 15, 1970 (div. 1979); 1 child, Djenaba. Student, Marian Coll., 1963-64. Regional personnel officer West Africa region Citibank, Abidjan, Ivory Coast, 1977-83; corp. personnel mgr. Amfac, Inc., San Francisco, 1984—. Mem. Am. Soc. Personnel Adminstrs., Northern Calif. Human Resources Council, Bay Area Network Profls.

DIPASQUALE, EDA SUSAN, marketing executive; b. Pitts., Feb. 19, 1960; d. Henry John and Rita Ann (Hohman) DiP. BS cum laude, W.Va., 1982. Personnel coordinator Schneider, Inc., Pitts., 1982-83; account mgr. NCR Corp., New Brunswick, N.J., 1983-85; assoc. dir. mktg. Carnegie Ctr. Assn., Princeton, N.J., 1985-87; v.p. Strategis Asset Valuation & Mgmt., Plymouth Meeting, Pa., 1987—. Prin. oboist Rutgers Community, Westminster Orch., 1985-88. Recipient Cert. of Appreciation Am. Heart Assn., 1985, Greater Princeton Jaycees, 1986, 87, 88, Cert. of Merit March of Dimes, 1986. Mem. Nat. Hist. Preservation Assn., W.Va. U. Alumnae, Nat. Assn. Corp., Real Estate Execs., Princeton Area C. of C., Lower Bucks County C. of C., Nat. Assn. Female Execs. Republican. Roman Catholic. Home: 13-5 Bennett Pl Holland PA 18966

DIPPO, CATHRYN SUZETTE, mathematical statistician, researcher; b. Palmyra, N.Y., Aug. 1, 1947; d. Gordon Jack and Alice Louise (Clarke) D. BS, George Washington U., 1969, PhD, 1981; MS, U. Mich., 1970. Math. statistician Bur. of Census, Washington, 1970-75; sr. math. statistician Bur. of Labor Stats., Washington, 1975—. Mem. Am. Statis. Assn., Washington Statis. Soc., Internat. Assn. of Survey Statisticians, Mid-Atlantic Germanic Soc., Nat. Genealogy Soc. Office: Bur of Labor Stats 441 G St NW Room 2126-GAO Bldg Washington DC 20212

DIRK, LISA, executive assistant; b. Washington, Oct. 5, 1956; d. Robert Anthony and Elsi Mae (Updyke) Brenkworth; m. Douglas Michael Dirk, June 12, 1976; children: Robert Anthony, Adam Michael. BA in Criminal Justice, Moorhead State U., 1981; postgrad. N.D. State U., 1981. Sec. Harmon Glass Co., Fargo, N.D., 1976-78, N.D. State U., Fargo, 1978-81; owner Handloader Heaven, Fargo, 1981-83; exec. asst. Fargo Glass & Paint Co., 1983—. Mem. Nat. Assn. Women in Constrn., Nat. Assn. Female Execs. Methodist. Avocations: reading, needlepoint.

DIRKS, VICKIE ELLEN, accountant, consultant; b. Mpls., Jan. 21, 1953; d. Robert Waldo and Georgina Mae (Olson) D. BS in Engring. Sci., U. Minn., 1975, BS in Electronic Sci., 1978. CPA, Minn. Internal auditor Bemis Co. Inc., Mpls., 1978-79, cost acct., acctg. supr., 1979-80, staff acct. to controller, 1980-81; fin. mgr. commodities div. Harvest States Co., St. Paul, 1981-83; sr. acct. DataMyte Inc., Minnetonka, Onn., 1983-84; supr. acctg., mgr. credit DataMyte Inc., Minnetonka, 1984-85, mgr. fin./MIS and credit, 1985—. Cons. Spl. Olympics College Heights, Mpls., 1985-86; chmn. campaign com. Zaccardi for Office, College Heights, 1987. Mem. Am. Inst. CPA's, Am. Soc. CPA's, Nat. Assn. Accts., Nat. Assn. Credit Mgrs., Twin Cities PC Users Club, Am Legion Aux. (charter), VFW (charter), AWSCPA (chmn. pub. relations com. Mpls. chpt. 1986-87). Office: DataMyte Inc 14960 Industrial Rd Minnetonka MN 55345

DISALVO, JO-ANN M., automotive company executive; b. Bronx, N.Y., Oct. 20, 1953; d. Joseph and Rachel DiS.; m. Richard B. Houghton, Nov. 9, 1979 (div.). Automobile sales rep., fin. mgr. Chisulli Orgn., N.J., 1978-81; corp. fin. and aftersell dir., cons., recruitor and mem. motors mgmt. support staff Sansone Dealer Group, Neptune, N.J., 1981—. Home: 1 Scenic Dr Suite 702 Highlands NJ 07732 Office: Sansone Dealer Group Motors Mgmt 3301 Rt 66 Neptune NJ 07753

DI SANTO, GRACE JOHANNE DEMARCO, poet; b. Derby, Conn., July 12, 1924; d. Richard and Fannie De Marco; m. Frank Michael Di Santo, Aug. 30, 1946; children: Frank Richard, Bernadette Mary, Roxanne Judith. Student in journalism, NYU, 1941-43; AB in English, Belmont Abbey Coll., 1974. Newswriter Australian Assn. Press, N.Y.C., 1942-43; staff reporter Ansonia Sentinel, Derby, 1943-45; feature writer, drama critic Bridgeport Herald, New Haven, 1945-46; editor monthly bull. Pa. State Coll. Optometry, Phila., 1947-48; free-lance writer, 1949-54; founder, pres. bd. dirs. Investors Ltd., Morganton, N.C., 1966-67; freelance writer. Author: (poetry) The Eye is Single, Portrait of the Poet as Teacher: James Dickey; contbr. The Dream Book: An Anthology of Writings by Italian-American Women. Pres., Burke County chpt. N.C. Symphony Soc., 1968-70; mem. exec. bd. Community Concerts Assn., 1962-71; trustee N.C. Symphony Soc., 1965-68, 69-70, North State Acad., Hickory, N.C., 1974—; bd. advisors Belmont Abbey Coll., 1986—. Recipient Oscar Arnold Young Meml. award, 1982. Republican. Roman Catholic. Clubs: Grandfather Golf and Country (Linville, N.C.); Mimosa Hills Golf. Address: 218 Riverside Dr Morganton NC 28655 Other: Grandfather Golf And Country Club Linville NC 28646

DISCHBEIN, DONNA ELAINE, small business owner; b. New Bedford, Mass., Dec. 30, 1945; d. Owen Joseph and Veronica (Baldwin) Dowd; m. Thomas E. Cranmer, Mar. 1, 1968 (div. Feb. 1981); 1 child, Brenda; m. David F. Dischbein, Oct. 16, 1982; children: Michael, Jefferey, Seth. AA, Fullerton (Calif.) Coll., 1966; BA, So. Utah State Coll., 1982. Tchr. Archdiocese of Los Angeles, 1966-78; technician U.S. Postal Service, Long Beach, Calif., 1974-76; tchr. Sevier County Pub. Schs., Richfield, Utah, 1981-82; prin. AA Row Wrecking and Salvage, Cedar City, Utah, 1982—; mgr. Los Angeles We. Union, 1969-74. Pres. Alter Soc. Christ the King Ch., Cedar City, 1986. Mem. Internat. Reading Assn., Assn. Recycling and Dismantling, Beta Sigma Phi (sec. 1983, pres. 1985). Republican. Roman Catholic. Lodge: Ladies of Elks (local pres. 1985, 88). Home: 3690 Cottonwood Dr Cedar City UT 84720 Office: AA Row Wrecking & Salvage 2481 N 580 W Cedar City UT 84720

DISENHAUS, HELEN ELIZABETH, lawyer; b. Washington, Nov. 2, 1948; d. Nathan and Henrietta (Weiss) Disenhaus; m. Brian Girard Driscoll, Sept. 11, 1977; children—Daniel Benjamin, David Michael. A.B., Mt. Holyoke Coll., 1970; M.A.T., Wesleyan U., Conn., 1972; J.D., Yale U., 1977. Bar: D.C. 1977. Tchr. English, Glastonbury (Conn.) High Sch., 1971-74; atty. law firm Dow, Lohnes & Albertson, Washington, 1977-87; of counsel Swidler & Berlin, 1987—; pres. D.C. chpt. Am. Women in Radio and TV, 1982-83, bd. dirs., 1983-84, nat. v.p. govt. industry affairs, 1984-86, sec.-treas., 1986—; mem. exec. com. Yale Law Sch., 1983-84. Sarah Williston scholar, 1968. Mem. D.C. Bar Assn., Women's Bar Assn. D.C., Fed. Communications Bar Assn., ABA, Yale Law Sch. Assn. D.C. (pres. 1982-83), Phi Beta Kappa. Jewish. Club: Yale (N.Y.), Mt. Holyoke Club (Washington). Office: Swidler & Berlin Chartered 3000 K St, NW Suite 300 Washington DC 20007

DISHAROON, BARBARA SCHAEFFER, college administrator; b. Balt., Dec. 1, 1946; d. Richard Carl and Clara (Valianti) Schaeffer; m. Donald Douglas Disharoon, Jan. 4, 1969; children: Eric Douglas, Grant Douglas. BS in Early CHildhood Edn., Towson (Md.) State U., 1978; MEd, Western Md. Coll., 1984. cert. tchr., Md. Tchr. Christian Pre-Sch. Program, Westminster, Md., 1976-78, William Winchester Elem. Sch., Westminster, 1979-82; supr. student tchrs., adj. instr. Western Md. Coll., Westminster, 1983—, asst. registrar, 1985-86, registrar, 1987—. Reader adv. panel Arithmetic Tchr. Mag., 1984-85; contbr. articles to ednl. jours. dir. publicity September Song, Westminster, 1979-85; bd. dirs. Carroll County Assn. for Retarded Citizens, Westminster, 1984-86. Mem. AAUW, Am. Assn. Coll. Registrars and Admissions Officers, Middle States Assn. Coll. Registrars and Admissions Officers, Kappa Delta Pi, Phi Delta Kappa. Democrat. Roman Catholic. Office: Western Md Coll Elderdice Hall Westminster MD 21157

DISHMAN, MELANIE GAY, copywriter, freelance writer; b. Phoenix, Oct. 9, 1956; d. George Austin and Joanne (Gay) D. Student, Tex. Christian U., 1974-75; BS in Speech, Lamar U., 1988. Supr. front desk Hyatt Regency Hotel, Dallas, 1979-81; mgr. catering Grand Hotel, Houston, 1981-83; adminstrv. v.p. mktg. Hotel Mgmt. Inc., Houston, 1983-85; owner, mgr. Kitchenworks Catering, Houston, 1985-86; copywriter Ann Lee & Assocs., Beaumont, Tex., 1986—. Contbr. articles to mags. Sec., bd. dirs. Tex. Energy Mus., Beaumont, 1987—; mem. Jr. League Beaumont. Mem. Profl. Communication Assn., Art Mus. S.E. Tex. Presbyterian. Home: 280 Summerwood Beaumont TX 77706 Office: Ann Lee & Assocs 6th and North Sts Beaumont TX 77704

DISHMAN, PATRICIA LOUISE, public relations executive; b. Ft. Worth, Oct. 20, 1939; d. Hubert Clinton and Cora Ophelia (Wood) D. B.S., Hardin Simmons U., 1962; M.A., U. Okla., 1969. Asst. editor So. Bapt. Radio-TV Commn., Ft. Worth, 1962-63; adult program and pub. relations dir. Midland YMCA, Midland, 1964-68; dir. pub. relations and devel. Midland Meml. Hosp., 1969-81; editor, pub. Petro plex Focus Mag., Midland, 1983-85; owner, mgr. Write Communications, Midland, 1981-86, dir. pub. relations St. Joseph's Hosp. and Health Ctr., Paris, Tex., 1986—. adv. bd. Paris (Tex.) Salvation Army. Author: Ten Who Overcame, 1966; contbr. articles to profl. jours. Mem. Indian Arts and Crafts Assn., Paris C. of C., Projecto Huasteco Sonrisa Alegre Internat., Tex. Hosp. Soc. Pub. Relations/Mktg.; Am. Hosp. Soc. Pub. Relations/Mktg., Cath. Hosp. Assn. Republican. Baptist. Avocations: photography; camping.

DISIMILE, MARY ANNE, telecommunications administrator; b. Rockville Center, N.Y., Aug. 3, 1948; d. Peter John and Regina (Shade) Combatti; m. Robert John Disimile, Aug. 3, 1969 (div. 1987); 1 child, Christopher Michael. Degree in Liberal Arts, Suffolk Community Coll., 1980. Rep. N.Y. Telephone Co., N.J. Bell, N.Y.C., 1966-71, 80-82; regional sales mgr. IBC/MegaRing, Hauppauge, N.Y., 1984-87; mktg. mgr. OST, Bohemia, N.Y., 1987—. mem. Women in Telecommunications Assn. Home: 16 Woodleigh Ct Holbrook NY 11788 Office: OST Sycamore Plaza Bohemia NY 11716

DI STEFANO, ANNA MARIA, educator; b. Lawrence, Mass., July 29, 1947; d. Charles C. and Carmela Rose (Coppa) Di S. AB, Trinity Coll., Washington, 1969; MEd, Boston U., 1972, EdD, 1977. Employee relations specialist Dept. Navy, Washington, 1970-71; counselor, social studies tchr. Brookline (Mass.) Pub. Schs., 1974-78; asst. prof. Washington U., St. Louis, 1978-83; program dir. The Fielding Inst., Santa Barbara, Calif., 1983—; adminstrv. dir. Project Turnabout, Charlestown, Mass., 1971-73; pvt. practice mediation, Santa Barbara, 1985—. Contbr. 10 articles to profl. jours. Mem. Women's Community Bldg., Santa Bararba, 1983—; bd. dirs. New City Sch., St. Louis, 1979-83, Peace Resource Ctr., Santa Barbara, 1986—. Named one of Outstanding Young Women Am., 1982; Am. Council on Edn. fellow, 1987—. Mem. Am. Psychol. Assn., OD Network, Nat. Assn. for Women Deans, Adminstrs. and Counselors, Nat. Women's Studies Assn., Assn. for Women in Psychology. Democrat. Unitarian-Universalist.

DITHRIDGE, BETTY, civic worker; b. Los Angeles, Sept. 11, 1920; d. Thomas Edward and Louise (Miles) Mitchell; m. Andrew Morrison Dithridge, May 11, 1940; 1 child, Andrew Morrison Jr. Student, UCLA, 1937-39. Boy scout and cub scout leader Los Angeles Orphan's Home Soc., 1952-69, sec. extension com., 1959-61, chmn., 1966-68; vol. worker USO; mem. Los Angeles Jr. Philharmonic Com., 1949—; active Symphonies for Youth Concerts, 1958-59; founder, chmn. San Marino Protection Com., 1971-72; sec. Los Angeles County Grand Jury, 1974-75; bd. dirs. Pasadena chpt. ARC, 1961-62, Vol. Service Bur. Pasadena; bd. dirs., treas. Wilshire Community Police Council, 1979-81; mem. citizens adv. com. Los Angeles Olympics Organizing Com., 1982-84; dir. Capistrano Bay Community Services Dist., 1987—. Recipient awards for work with local youth groups. Mem. Wilshire C. of C. (chmn. women's bur. 1957-59), Los Angeles C. of C. Assocs. Los Angeles City Coll., Orange County Marine Inst., Friends of Huntington Library, D.A.R., Friends of San Juan Capistrano Library, San Juan Capistrano Hist. Soc., Los Angeles Grand Jurors Assn., Alpha Phi, Sigma Alpha Iota. Home: 35411 Beach Rd Capistrano Beach CA 92624

DITTRICH, JACLYN ROBERTA, accountant; b. Denver, May 15, 1953; d. Dan Eugene and Janette Roberta (Wirth) Jones; m. Robert George Dittrich, Nov. 24, 1979; children: Jordan Robert, Kyle Eugene. BA, Ft. Lewis Coll., 1975. Jr. acct. Robert McKenna CPA, Durango, Colo., 1975-76; staff acct. Louis L. Fox & Co. CPAs, Denver, 1976-77; acct. Doran Peck CPA, Denver, 1977-79; pvt. practice acct. Denver, 1980—. Mem. Am. Inst. CPA's, Colo. Inst. CPA's. Republican. Home and Office: 11524 Steele St Thornton CO 80233

DITUCCI, DIANNA LYNN, advertising executive; b. Dallas, Mar. 11, 1964; d. John M. and Mary Ellen (Monfredo) DiT.;. BA in Advt., Mktg. and Spanish, Stephen F. Austin State U., 1985. Advt. asst. Kerri Tate Advt., Nacogdoches, Tex., 1984-85; pub. relations asst. United Way, Nacogdoches, 1985; account coordinator Thompson Recruitment Advt., Dallas, 1985; account exec. J. Walter Thompson, Dallas, 1986-88, Stern/Monroe Advt, Dallas, 1988—. Mem. Ad-2 Dallas. Republican. Home: 4300 Rosemeade #1917 Dallas TX 75252

DITZION, GRACE, artist, playwright, songwriter; b. Montreal, Que., Can.; B.A., Hunter Coll.; M.A., NYU; children—Lynn Shaw, Bruce. Tchr.,

N.Y.C. Bd. Edn., 1937-74; exhibited in one woman shows at Mus. of the Air (Cable TV), 1977, Nat. Arts Club, 1977, Westchester Community Coll., 1977, Salmagundi Club (award for sculpture), 1977, 1st Fed. Savs. Bank, 1979; group shows include Nat. Acad., Allied Artists of Am., Springfield Mus., Ponce Mus., P.R., Pittsfield Mus., Hudson Valley Art Assn., Chung-Cheng Cultural Center, St. John's U., Lincoln Center Cork Gallery, others; represented in permanent collections at Milford (Conn.) Fine Arts Council, Auburn (N.Y.) Community Coll., City U. Grad. Center, U. Hawaii; mem. awards jury Washington Sq. Outdoor Art Exhibit, 1977-79, NCCJ, 1977; vice-chmn. awards jury Salmagundi Art Club, 1978, 79, 80; cons. Womanart Gallery, 1976-78; TV appearances The Price Is Right, Mid-day Live Show, Richard Roffman Focus Show, 1977, 78. Recipient numerous art awards including 1st prizes, Gold medal, Purchase prize, Award of Excellence, Council Am. Artists Socs. award, Award of Merit. Mem. Am. Artists Profl. League, Artists Fellowship, Inc., Am. Portrait Soc., Nat. Arts Club, Internat. Beaux Arts Club of Performing Arts, Internat. Soc. Artists, Women's Press Club of N.Y.C. Important works include portrait of author on dust jacket of book, Club, 1974; (plays) A Moment of Truth, The Decision, A Dream Within a Dream, Sliding on a Rainbow, No Escape. Home and Studio: 3635 Johnson Ave New York NY 10463

DIX, LINDA SKIDMORE, science and engineering program administrator, editor, consultant; b. Salisbury, Md., July 15, 1948; d. David Donaldson Skidmore Sr. and Mabel Frances Matthews Shockley; m. Charles Raymond Dix, Sep. 13, 1969; 1 child, Lara. BA, Loyola Coll., Balt., 1972; MEd, Salisbury (Md.) State Coll., 1982. Advanced profl. Md. State Dept. Edn. Tchr. secondary schs. Balt., 1972-73; tchr. James M. Bennett Sr. High Sch., Salisbury, 1973-77, coordinator English dept., 1978-81; adminstrv. asst. Commn. Human Resources Nat. Research Council, Washington, 1981-82; adminstrv. assoc. Office Sci. Engring. Personnel Nat. Research Council, Washington, 1982-84, adminstrv. officer, 1984-87, program officer, 1987—; instr. English Salisbury State Coll., 1979; cons. leadership trng. program for women Md. State Tchrs. Assn., Balt., 1978-81, Anne Arundel County Pub. Schs., Annapolis, Md., 1982—. Editor: Women: Their Underrepresentation and Career Differentials in Science and Engineering, 1987, Minorities: Their Underrepresentation and Career Differentials in Science and Engineering, 1987; contbr. articles to profl. jours. Active Chesapeake Bay Found.; Sunday school tchr.; original appointee Wicomico County Commn. Women, 1977-81; Severna Park (Md.) United Methodist Ch. 1985—. Recipient cert. of Appreciation Wicomico County Bd. Edn., 1980; named Outstanding Young Woman Wicomico County Jaycees, 1977. Mem. Am. Ednl. Research Assn. (spl. interest group on women and edn.), Nat. Coalition for Women and Girls in Edn., Am. Women in Sci., Am. Legion Aux., Nat. Trust Hist. Preservation, Am. Assn. Univ. Women, Nat. Mus. Women Arts (charter), NEA, Md. State Tchrs. Assn. (chair women's caucus 1977-78, human rights com. 1979-81, meritorious service, 1978, 80), Wicomico County Edn. Assn. (pres. 1979-81), Amnesty Internat. Democrat. Club: Arundel Plaza (Severna Park). Home: 64 Arundel Beach Rd Severna Park MD 21146 Office: Nat Research Council Office Sci & Engring Personnel 2101 Constitution Ave NW Washington DC 20418

DIXON, ALEXANDREENA DELAIDA, correctional services administrator; b. Bronx, N.Y., Aug. 16, 1945; d. Samuel R. Dorsett and Janet Frances (Mardell) Fritz, stepdaughter Urias McKinley Fritz; children: Delaina A., Deshala T. BA in Sociology, Upsala Coll., 1967; MA in Urban Studies, Occidental Coll., 1974; MPA, John Jay Coll. Criminal Justice, 1984. Probation officer N.Y.C. Office of Probation, 1967-72; parole officer N.Y. State Div. of Parole, N.Y.C., 1972-73; equal employment specialist N.Y. State Dept. Correctional Services, Albany, 1974-75, dir. inmate grievances, 1975-79; assoc. dir. standards Am. Correctional Assn., College Park, Md., 1979-81; dir. standards review N.Y.C. Dept. Correction, 1981-82, dir. classification, 1982-85; dir. Parole Transition Project Return Found., N.Y.C., 1985-86; coordinator family services Bedford Hills (N.Y.) Correctional Facility, 1986-88; asst. dep. supt. Sin Sing Correctional Facility, Ossining, N.Y., 1988—; cons. Ramapo Counseling Ctr., Spring Valley, N.Y., 1986—; adj. prof. Ramapo Coll., Mahwah, N.J., 1987. V.p. Black Polit. Caucus of Rockland, Spring Valley, N.Y., 1982—; mem. adv. bd. Town Parks and Recreation, Suffern, N.Y., 1983—; mem. Community Services Bd., Pomona, N.Y., 1983—; leader Rockland County Dist. 11, N.Y.C., 1986—; sec. Suffern Democratic Party, 1986—. Fellow Nat. Urban Fellow, Inc.; mem. Am. Correctional Assn., Am. Soc. Pub. Adminstrs., Conf. of Minority Pub. Adminstrs. (local chpt. pres. 1975-76), Alpha Kappa Alpha. Methodist. Home: 76 Ramapo Ave Suffern NY 10901

DIXON, CAROLE, merchandise mart director; b. Gainsville, Tex., Mar. 21, 1943; d. George C. and Ann C. (Wistrand) Dixon; ed. Keuka Coll., Penn Yan, N.Y., N.Y. U. Real Estate Inst.; children—Kristin, Shaun. Real estate sales No. Westchester Land Co., Pound Ridge, N.Y., 1970-76; exec. dir. N.Y. Mdse. Mart, N.Y.C., 1979—; dir. N.Y. Tabletop Assn. Bd. dirs. 23d St. Assn. Mem. Nat. Home Fashions League, World Assn. Mart Mgrs. Contbr. articles to profl. jours. Home: 25 W 81st St New York NY 10024 Office: NY Mdse Mart Office of Exec Dir 41 Madison Ave New York NY 10010

DIXON, DEBORAH DARLENE, marketing executive; b. Barnwell, S.C., Oct. 6, 1964; d. Wendell Irvin and Karen Darlene (Spitzer) D. Student, Columbia Coll., 1982-83, 84-85, U.S.C., 1985-86. Fashion advisor, buyer Ormond Stores, Inc., Columbia, S.C., 1983-84; resale sec. Internat. Soc. of Cert. Electronics Technicians, Ft. Worth, Tex., 1984; customer service rep. Tex. Electric Service Co., Ft. Worth, 1984-85; dir. telemarketing Am. Computer Profls., Columbia, S.C., 1985, asst. to v.p. sales, mktg. coordinator, 1985—; telemktg. cons. E.I. de Nemours-DuPont, Charlotte, N.C., 1987—, Tele-techniques for Profit Workshop, Atlanta, 1987, Advanced DOS & dBASE III with Entrè. Hostess Rep. Presdl. Banquet, Columbia, 1984; vol. Soc. for Prevention of Cruelty to Animals, Columbia, 1986; asst. youth dir. Jackson Creek Bapt. Ch. Mem. Nat. Assn. Female Execs., Am. Mgmt. Assn., Starduster Little Sister Orgn., Kappa Sigma. Republican. Baptist. Lodge: Lions (queen 1982-83). Home: 1825 St Julian Pl Apt 16E Columbia SC 29204 Office: Am Computer Profls 1777 St Julian Pl Columbia SC 29204

DIXON, DOROTHY BEATRICE, school administrator; b. Albert Lea, Minn., June 1, 1921; d. Peter Bernard and Elsie Leonora (Sybilrud) Hoidale; m. James George Dixon, Jr., Aug. 14, 1941; children: Richard, Paula, Paul, James III, Peter, Deborah. Student, Biola Coll., Los Angeles, 1941-43. Dir. Grace Brethren Christian Schs., Temple Hills, Md., 1965—; dir. Grace Brethren Christian Schs., Clinton and Calvert, Md., 1986—, also cons., 1987—. Author: (bible studies series) Pleasing Him, 1951, His Own, 1961, Hidden Beauty, 1973, How Mature?, 1987. Republican. Office: Grace Brethren Christian Sch 6501 Surratts Rd Clinton MD 20735

DIXON, MARY ELLEN, personnel consultant; b. Olney, Ill., Nov. 8, 1940; d. Charles D. and Harriet (Dotson) Combs; m. Larry L. O'Dell, July 1, 1958 (div. 1968); children: Debra, Gary; m. William J. Dixon, May 1, 1976. AS in Bus., Olney Cen. Coll., 1940; BS, Ea. Ill. U., 1971; MS in Indsl. Relations, Loyola U., Chgo., 1985; cert. in data processing, Harper Coll., 1983. Personnel adminstr. Booz, Allen & Hamilton, Chgo., 1974-77; personnel mgr. ITW, Chgo., 1977-80, Sara Lee, Chgo., 1980-83; dir. personnel TSR, Inc., Lake Geneva, Wis., 1983-85; cons. William M. Mercer-Meidinger Hansen Inc., Chgo., 1985—. Mem. Am. Soc. Personnel Adminstrn., Am. Compensation Assn., Assn. Human Resource Systems Profls. Republican. Home: 3908 W Lakeshore Dr Wonder Lake IL 60097 Office: Mercer-Meidinger Hansen 222 S Riverside Plaza Chicago IL 60606

DIXON, ORA WRIGHT, research microbiologist; b. Monroe, La., July 27, 1950; d. Henry Hudson and Legertha Marie (Thompson) Wright; m. Clark Andrew Dixon Jr., June 4, 1977; children: Michael Sean, Rachel Annette, Clark Andrew III. BS, So. U., La., 1972. Instr., counselor Ala. Luth. Acad. & Coll., Selma, 1973; biol. technician Ea. Fish Disease Lab., Kearneysville, W.Va., 1973-77; research microbiologist Nat. Fisheries Ctr., Kearneysville, 1977—. Contbr. articles to profl. jours. Asst. organizer N.Am. Found. Marcel Marceau France, 1982; scouting coordinator Shenandoah council Boy Scouts Am., 1984-88; troop leader Shawnee Council Girl Scouts U.S., 1986-88; active W. Va. U. Extension Service 4-H Com. Recipient Spl. Achievement award U.S. Fish and Wildlife, 1981, plaques Boys and Girls Scouts, 1984-88. Mem. Am. Fisheries Soc. (Potomac chpt.), Federally Employed Womens Assn. (pres. Shenandoah Valley chpt. 1984-85), Nat. Assn. Femal Execs. (network dir. 1985-86), Toastmasters Internat. (historian 1987), NAACP, Bus. and Profl. Women Assn. Democrat. United Methodist. Club: Loyal Ladies. Office: Nat Fisheries Ctr Leetown Box 700 Kearneysville WV 25430

DIXON, RITA HURT, educational administrator; b. Harlan, Ky., Mar. 21, 1938. B.A., Georgetown Coll., 1960; M.Ed., Xavier U., 1967; postgrad. Va. Poly. Inst. and State U., Radford U., James Madison U. Tchr. French, Oakwood High Sch., Dayton, Ohio, 1960-61, Worthington High Sch., Ohio, 1961; mem. personnel staff Kimberly Clark Corp., West Carrollton, Ohio, 1962-64; French and English tchr. West Carrollton High Sch., 1964-67, counselor, 1967-69; coordinator counseling and testing New River Community Coll., Dublin, Va., 1975-83, dir. student devel., 1983—; presenter workshops, seminars in field; rep. for New River Community Coll. to Nat. Identification Program in Higher Edn.; chmn. bd. dirs. Community Coll. Ministries, 1985—. Mem. Va. Personnel and Guidance Assn., New River Personnel and Guidance Assn. (pres. 1980), Va. Counselors Assn. (dir. grant project), Am. Personnel and Guidance Assn., New River Community Coll. Women's Orgn. (pres. 1979-80), Wytheville Community Coll. Faculty Wives (pres. 1979-80), Nat. Assn. Female Execs., Phi Delta Kappa. Home: 880 Mountain View Dr Wytheville VA 24382

DIXON, SHERRIE ROSEN, banker; b. N.Y.C., Oct. 14, 1955; d. Irving and Gertrude (Chernick) Rosen; m. James T. Dixon, June 26, 1976; 1 child, Alexandra J. BS, Northwestern U., Evanston, Ill., 1972-76; JD, Loyola U., Chgo., 1979. Bar: Ill. 1979. Asst. tax counsel No. Trust, Chgo., 1979-80; asst. trust officer Chemical Bank, N.Y.C., 1981-83, trust officer, 1984-87, sr. trust officer, 1987—. Mem. planned giving com. Arthritis Found., Hudson Valley chpt. Mem. Westchester County Bar Assn., Westchester Estate Planning Council, Jr. League of Westchester on the Sound, Larchmont LWV (fin. dir.). Jewish. Home: 96 N Chatsworth Ave Larchmont NY 10538 Office: Chemical Bank Trust Dept 30 Rockefeller Plaza New York NY 10112

DIXON, SHIRLEY JUANITA, restaurant owner; b. Canton, N.C., June 29, 1935; d. Willard Luther and Bessie Eugenia (Scroggs) Clark; m. Clinton Matthew Dixon, Jan. 3, 1953; children: Elizabeth Swanger, Hugh Monroe III, Cynthia Owen, Sharon Fouts. BS, Wayne State U., 1956; postgrad. Mary Baldwin Coll., 1958, U. N.C., 1977. Acct., Standard Oil Co., Detroit, 1955-57; asst. dining room mgr. Statler Hilton, Detroit, 1958-60; bookkeeper Osborne Lumber Co., Canton, N.C., 1960-61; bus. owner, pres. Dixon's Restaurant, Canton, 1961—; judge N.C. Assn. Distributive Edn. Assn., state and dist., 1982—; owner Halbert's Family Heritage Ctr., Canton. V.p. Haywood County Assn. Retarded Citizens Bd., 1985—; bd. commrs. Haywood Vocationals Opportunities, 1985—; dist. dir. 11th Congl. Dist. Democratic Women, 1982—; state Teen-Dem. advisor State Dem. party, 1985—; del. 1988 Dem. Nat. Conv., Atlanta; alderwoman Town of Canton, N.C.; vice-chair Gov.'s Adv. Council on Aging, State N.C., 1982—; 1st v.p. crime prevention Community Watch Bd., State N.C., 1985, 86; mem. Criminal Justice Bd., N.C. Assembly on Women and the Economy; chair. Western N.C. Epilipsey Assn., Haywood County N.C. Mus. Historu, 1987—; co-chair Haywood County Commn. on the Bi-Centennial of Constn., 1987—; bd. dirs. Canton Recreation Dept., Western N.C. Alzheimers and Related Disorders Assn., 1987—, N.C. Conf. for Social Services, 1987—. Recipient Outstanding Service award Crime Prevention from Gov., 1982, Gov.'s Spl. Vol. award, 1983, Outstanding Service award N.C. Community Watch Assn., 1984, Community Service award to Handicapped, 1983-84, Outstanding Service award ARC, 1988; named Employer of Yr. for Hiring Handicapped N.C. Assn. for Retarded Citizens, 1985. Mem. NOW, Women's Polit. Caucus, Nat. Assn. Female Execs., Internat. Platform Assn., Women's Forum N.C., Canton Bus. and Profl. Women's Club (pres. 1974-79; Woman of Yr. 1984). Democrat. Episcopalian. Club: Altrusa. Avocation: softball club. Home: 104 Skyland Terrace Canton NC 28716 Office: Dixon's Restaurant 30 N Main St Canton NC 28716

DIXON MORLOCK, NANCY LORETTA, medical consultant; b. Hagerstown, Md., Nov. 10, 1948; d. James Elmer and Eva Mildred (Cooney) Gaver; m. Wayne W. Dixon, July 12, 1969 (div. 1986); m. James Howard Morlock, May 29, 1987. BS, Mount Saint Mary's, Emittsburg, Md., 1982; MA, Hood Coll., 1985; diploma in Nursing, Sinai Hosp., Balt. RN, lic. real estate agt., Md. Tech. legal cons. Annapolis, Md., 1987—; med. cons. Balt., 1988—; cons. Forensic Techs. Internat., 1988—, various law firms; adminstrv. med. legal trial asst. Marvin Ellin, Esq., 1984-88. Author newspaper series Am. Heart Assn. risk factors, lectr., 1982. Mem. Washington County Heart Assn. (bd. dirs. 1980-85, chmn. Nursing Edn. com. 1978-83). Democrat. Lutheran. Home and Office: 1110 Old County Rd Severna Park MD 21146

DLOUHY, ANNETTE STEPHANIE, advertising and public relations executive, consultant; b. Cleve., Apr. 19, 1952; d. Ruth Stephanie (Dlouhy) V. AA, Dyke Coll., 1974, BS in Mktg., 1988. Sec. Dyke Coll., Cleve., 1972-74; exec. sec. Bearings Inc., Cleve., 1974-80, adminstrv. asst., 1980-82, advt. mgr., 1982-85, mgr. advt. and pub. relations, 1985, dir. advt. and pub. relations, 1985-87; prin. Designs by Dlouhy, Independence, Ohio and Naples, Fla., 1987—. Mem. adv. bd. Make-a-Wish Found. of N.E. Ohio, Cleve., 1986; mem. Dirs. Circle, Cleve. Mus. of Art; lector/eucharistic minister St. Paul's Shrine, Cleve., 1983—; leadership devel. program Fed. Cath. Community Services, 1986, trustee; trustee Cath. Charities Corp., 1988—. Named one of Outstanding Young Women in Am, 1986. Mem. Exec. Women Internat., Bus. Profl. Advertisers Assn., Citizen's League. Roman Catholic. Club: Cleve. City, Press of Cleve. also: 1826 Kings Lake Blvd Suite 103 Naples FL 33962

DMYTRYSHAK, CAROLE ANN, banker; b. Altoona, Pa., Mar. 16, 1942; d. Michael and Dorothy Bernice (Garman) D.; B.S. in Math., Drexel U., Phila., 1965; M.S. in Computer Sci., Pratt Inst., 1972. With Bankers Trust Co., N.Y.C., 1967-85, sr. v.p., head div. br. banking, European Am. Bank, Uniondale, N.Y. 1985—; cons. in field. Mem. Bank Mktg. Assn., N.Y. Map Soc., NOW. Home: 118 E 19th St New York NY 10003 Office: European Am Bank EAB Plaza Uniondale NY 11555

DOAK, JANICE ASKEW, banker; b. Houston, Jan. 18, 1925; d. Andrew Miller and Cleo Elizabeth Askew; B.B.A., U. Tex., Austin, 1944; m. Ira Kennedy Doak, Dec. 9, 1944; children—Barbara Sue, Carolyn M. With Bank of Houston, 1949—, cashier, 1960-62, v.p., cashier, 1962-74, v.p., 1974-86, sr. v.p., 1986—. Vol. worker St. Luke's Episcopal Hosp., 1973—; docent Harris County Heritage Soc. Mem. Nat. Assn. Bank Women, Am. Inst. Banking (past dir. Houston chpt.), Credit Women Internat. (pres. Lone Star council 1986), Credit Reps. Assn. Greater Houston Banks (bd. dirs.), Houston Credit Women (pres. 1977-78, 84-85), Am. Bus. Women's Assn. (pres. Houston charter chpt. 1980-81), Fedn. Houston Profl. Women (v.p. 1982-83, honoree) Alpha Chi Omega. Episcopalian. Clubs: Altrusa (pres. 1967-68) (Houston), Order Eastern Star (worthy matron). Office: Bank of Houston 5115 Main St Houston TX 77002

DOBBINS, BETSY JANE, communications center director; b. Hopkinsville, Ky., Nov. 24, 1950; d. Russell Burke and Earlene (Robertson) King; m. Lawrence Randolph Dobbins, Aug. 17, 1979 (div. Nov. 1985); children: Tina Michele, Kathy Marie, Randi Renee, Amanda Beth. Student, Austin Peau State U.; A in Applied Sci. in Bus. Mgmt., Hopkinsville Community Coll., 1988. Trainee radio dispatcher Hopkinsville/Christian County Communication Ctr., 1976, class B radio dispatcher, 1976-77, class A dispatcher, 1977-80, lt. tng. officer, dispatcher, 1980-83, capt., dispatcher, 1983-85, asst. dir., 1985—; dir. tng. Pub. Safety Tng. Ctr. (dir. Hopkinsville/Christian County Communication Ctr.), 1983-85. Instr. Commn. on Fire Protection, 1983—, CPR ARC, Christian County, Ky., 1985—. Mem. Associated Pub. Safety Communication Officers (v.p. 1983, pres. Ky. chpt. 1984, pres. 1985). Democrat. Baptist. Lodge: Fraternal Order Police (trustee 1978). Office: Hopkinsville Christian County Communications Ctr 116-A W 1st St Hopkinsville KY 42240

DOBBS, LINDA LEE, state agency administrator; b. San Francisco, Oct. 7, 1948. BA in Sociology, Calif. State U., Los Angeles, 1973; MSEd, U. So. Calif., 1980. Cert. community coll. student personnel worker, instr. psychology, counselor, basic pupil personnel services, Calif. Cons. affirmative action Los Angeles Community Coll. Dist., 1979; fin. aid analyst Occidental Coll., Los Angeles, 1979; officer employment devel. State of Calif., El Monte, 1970-80; employment program counselor, San Fernando, 1980—; chairperson No. Valley Occupational Ctr., 1983—; mem. career adv. com. Los Angeles Mission Coll., 1983—; speaker, lectr. in field. Vol. Found. for the Jr. Blind, Los Angeles, 1978, Ctr. for Study of Drug Abuse, Tarzana Psychiat. Hosp., 1979; counselor Immaculate Conception Home for Girls, Los Angeles, 1972, McKinley Jr. High Sch., Pasadena, Calif., 1973; apptd. mem. Calif. Sate Spl. Projects Team, Valencia, Calif., 1985. Recipient appreciation award Los Angeles Unified Sch. Dist., 1982. Mem. Calif. State Employees Assn., Internat. Assn. Personnel in Employment Security (sec. Los Campadres chpt. 1984-85), LWV, U. So. Calif. Alumni Assn. Avocation: collecting international embassy posters. Office: 1520 San Fernando Rd San Fernando CA 91340

DOBELIS, INGE NACHMAN, editor; b. Würzburg, Germany, Nov. 16, 1933; came to U.S., 1938, naturalized, 1951; d. Rudolf Hugo and Resi (Hamburger) Nachman; B.A. in English, U. Ga., 1956; m. Miervaldis C. Dobelis, May 4, 1969; 1 son, Arthur N. Editorial positions Buttenheim Publs. and Crowell-Collier, 1956-64; copy editor Gen. Book div. Readers Digest, N.Y.C., 1965-72, asso. editor, 1973-79, sr. editor, 1979-85, sr. staff editor, 1985—. Exec. bd., officer Murray Hill Democratic Club, 1968-74; exec. bd. Community Bd. No. 6, N.Y.C., 1973-78, sec., 1976, chmn. health and hosps. com., 1974-78; trustee, officer Brotherhood Synagogue, 1983—; mem. N.Y. Dem. County Com., 1967-74. Mem. Phi Beta Kappa. Assoc. editor: Reader's Digest Family Encyclopedia of American History, 1975; Reader's Digest Family Health Guide and Medical Encyclopedia, 1976; Reader's Digest Illustrated Guide to Gardening, 1978; editor: Readers Digest Family Legal Guide, 1981; Quick and Thrifty Cooking, 1984; Magic and Medicine of Plants, 1986; Great Recipes for Good Health, 1988. Club: Nat. Arts (N.Y.C.). Home: 201 E 17th St New York NY 10003 Office: 750 3d Ave New York NY 10016

DOBERVICH, BETTY ANN, transportation executive; b. St. Cloud, Minn., Sept. 12, 1944; d. Robert Eugene and Lila Luvern (Leifson) Rasmusson; m. Richard A. Walvatne, June 14, 1964 (div. Aug. 1979); children: Randal A. Walvatne, Robb R. Walvatne; m. Paul David Dobervich, Apr. 24, 1982; 1 child, Matthew Eli. Student, Fergus Falls (Minn.) Jr. Coll., 1962-63. Sec. Arneson and Co., Fargo, N.D., 1963-65; loan auditor, advisor student loans Moorhead (Minn.) State Bank, 1972-76; exec. sec. Steiger Tractor, Inc., Fargo, 1976-82; tchr. piano Fargo, 1982-86; owner Select Services, Fargo, 1985-86; account exec. MidAm. Long Distance Co., Fargo, 1986-87; mktg. rep., exec. dir. sales and mktg. execs. Lewis Truck Lines Inc., Fargo, 1987—; lectr. in field. Active Concerned Parents for Edn., Fargo, 1984; bd. dirs. Am. Cancer Soc., Fargo, 1985; mem. Congressman Dorgan Com., Fargo, 1987, also cons. on welfare law status. Mem. Fargo C. of C. Democrat. Lutheran. Home: 1705 42d St SW Fargo ND 58103 Office: Lewis Truck Lines Inc 4001 12th Ave N Fargo ND 58102

DOBLE, DEBRA KAREN, accountant; b. Hollywood, Calif., July 24, 1958; d. Clifford Carl and Ann Louise (Greatbanks) Wallgren; m. Michael Lloyd Doble, Sept. 14, 1980. BS in Bus. Adminstrn. and Info. Systems with honors, Calif. State U., Hayward, 1981. CPA. Bookkeeper United Grocers, Ltd., Oakland, Calif., 1978-80, Lee Devel. Co., Inc., San Pablo, Calif., 1980-82; sr. acct. Sallmann, Jones & Wright, Pleasanton, Calif., 1982-87; pvt. practice acctg. Pinole, Calif., 1987—. Mem. Nat. Assn. Accts. (pres. 1988—, v.p. 1985-88, treas. 1984-85, manuscripts dir. 1983-84, Dist. Service award 1987, named Most Valuable Mem. 1984, 85), Calif. State Soc. CPA's (MAS com. 1985—), Am. Inst. CPA's. Republican. Baptist.

DOBLER, NORMA (MRS. CLIFFORD DOBLER), state legislator, civic worker; b. Haines, Oreg., May 2, 1917; d. Lester and Bessie (Bircket) Woodhouse; student U. Cin., 1935-37; B.S. in Bus., U. Idaho, 1939; m. Clifford Dobler, June 14, 1941; children—Sharon Louise Dobler Vega, Carol Marie Dobler Harris, Terry Lee. Sec. to registrar U. Idaho, 1939-41; sec. to judge, Caldwell, Idaho, 1945; sec. Am. Express Co., Seattle, 1943; lab. technician U. Idaho Coll. Forestry, Moscow, 1963-69; mem. Idaho Ho. of Reps., 1973-77, Idaho Senate, 1977-87 ; mem. health and human services com. Nat. Conf. State Legislators; mem. Idaho Bd. Tax Appeals, 1987—; mem. Idaho Job Tng. Coordinating Council; mem. Idaho Developmental Disabilities Adv. Council, 1977-81; chairperson Gov.'s Task Force Independence, alternative nursing homes; mem. Commn. on Nursing and Nursing Edn.; mem. State Edn. Equity Com., 1986—, State Adv. Council on Aging, 1986—. Mem. LWV, 1951—, bd. dirs. Moscow, 1953-68, pres. Idaho, 1968-71; county adv. bd. trustee Moscow Sch. Dist., 1963-69, vice chmn., 1966-69; bd. dirs. Idaho Sch. Trustees Assn., 1969; leader 4-H Club, 1951-64; pres. Moscow PTA, 1958-59, life mem. Recipient Service award Idaho Home Economists, 1979; Conservation Legislator of Yr. award Idaho Wildlife Fedn., 1984; named Citizen of Yr. Nat. Assn. Social Workers, Idaho chpt., 1980; Outstanding Alumna award dept. home econs. U. Idaho, 1984; Conservation Legislator of Yr. award Idaho Wildlife Fedn., 1984. Mem. AAUW (hon.), Delta Kappa Gamma (hon.). Methodist (pres. Woman's Soc. Christian Service 1972, supt. ch. sch. 1953-65, mem. ofcl. bd. 1953-67, 72). Home: 1401 Alpowa St Moscow ID 83843

DOBRIANSKY, PAULA JON, government official; b. Alexandria, Va., Sept. 14, 1955; d. Lev Eugene and Julia Kusy D. BS summa cum laude, Sch. Fgn. Service, Georgetown U., 1977; MA, Harvard U., 1980, postgrad., 1980—. Adminstrv. aide Dept. Army, Washington, 1973-76; staff asst. Am. embassy, Rome, 1976; research asst. joint econ. com. U.S. Congress, Washington, 1977-78; NATO analyst Bur. Intelligence and Research, Dept. State, Washington, 1979; staff mem. NSC, White House, Washington, 1980-83, dep. dir. European and Soviet affairs, 1983-84, dir. European and Soviet affairs, 1984-87; dep. asst. sec. of state for Human Rights and Humanitarian Affairs, 1987—; assoc. Ctr. for Internat. Affairs, Harvard U., Cambridge, Mass. Fulbright-Hays scholar, 1978; Rotary Found. fellow, 1979; Ford Found. fellow, 1980. Mem. Internat. Inst. Strategic Studies, Am. Polit. Sci. Assn., Council on Fgn. Relations, Phi Beta Kappa, Phi Alpha Theta, Pi Sigma Alpha. Club: Harvard (bd. dirs. 1982-85) (Washington). Office: Dept of State Human Rights & Humanitarian Affairs 2201 C St NW Washington DC 20520

DOBRONSKI, AGNES MARIE, state legislator; b. Detroit, Apr. 21, 1925; d. Clarence Robert and Agnes Frieda (Franz) Dobronski; m. James Z. Cichocki, June 27, 1987; stepchildren: Thomas, Jerry. BS, Detroit Coll. Bus., 1970; MA, Eastern Mich. U., 1975. Bus. mgr. Dearborn (Mich.) Pub. Schs., 1943-80; exec. dir. Retirement Coordinating Council, Lansing, Mich., 1980-85; mem. Mich. Ho. of Reps., 1987—. Trustee Dearborn Bd. Edn., Henry Ford Community Coll., 1980-86. Recipient Disting. Alumna award Detroit Coll. Bus., 1974, Disting. Citizen award Henry Ford Community Coll., 1987; named Sch. Adminstr. of Yr. Dearborn PTA Council, 1978. Democrat. Lutheran. Home: PO Box 1948 Dearborn MI 48121 Office: House of Reps State Capitol Lansing MI 48909-7514

DOCKRY, BERNADETTE THERESE, personnel manager; b. Flemington, N.J., Mar. 4, 1959; d. Joseph Michael and Margaret Madeleine (McAndrew) D. BA, Marymount Coll., Tarrytown, N.Y., 1982. Personnel asst. Sheraton Ctr. Hotel, N.Y.C., 1982-83, personnel adminstr., 1983-85; asst. dir. personnel N.Y. Penta Hotel, N.Y.C., 1985-87; coordinator personnel Young Adult Inst., N.Y.C., 1987—. Sr. vol. Covenant House Under 21, N.Y.C., 1984—. Mem. Nat. Assn. Female Execs. Democrat. Roman Catholic. Home: PO Box 296 Milford NJ 08848 Office: Young Adult Inst 460 W 34th St New York NY 10001

DOCKRY, NANCY K., producer; b. Niagara Falls, N.Y., Mar. 24; d. Walter Edward Cazen and Adolpha (Jacek) Dezik; m. John Dockry, Aug. 19, 1961 (div. Aug. 1968). BS, Syracuse U., 1958; PhD, Columbia U., 1961. Freelance writer 1956-60; with corp. tng. program ABC, 1960-62; with Dancer, Fitzgerald and Sample, 1962-70; v.p. advt. Am. Home Products, 1970-75; office sr. agt. William Morris Agy., N.Y.C., 1975-76; office sr. agt., v.p. William Morris Agy., Los Angeles, 1975-78; sr. v.p. Nephi Prodns., 1978-79; v.p. TV MCA-Universal, 1979-80; v.p. Time-Life TV Inc., 1980-81; v.p. TV Columbia Pictures Inc., 1981-82; sr. v.p. Jay Bernstein Prodns., 1983-85; ind. producer Dockry Prodns., 1985—; bd. dirs. Entertainment Industries Council, Los Angeles and Washington; cons. Tree Music Pub., Nashville, 1980—. Producer Maneaters, Cheapshow, The Plant Family, Gauguin, Masada, Galactica, Minnesota Strip, Nobody's Perfect, Semi-Tough, The Bunker, The Wall, Mom the Wolfman and Me, Dial M for

Murder, Baker's Dozen, Night Heat, The Blue and the Gray, Shadow Riders, Be-At-Rice, Ripley's Believe It or Not, Money on the Side, Ain't Misbehavin', Malibu, Mickey Spillane's Mike Hammer, Susan Hayward, Suddenly A Stranger, Two By Two, Houston Knights, Johnny Aladdin, The Great Diamond Robbery, Clash of Eagles, The America's Cup, Last Cheaters, Stiff, Harry, Stranger Dangers. Panel mem. Pres. Commn. on Whitehouse Fellows, Los Angeles, N.Y.C., Washington. Mem. TV Acad., Motion Picture Acad. Republican. Office: Sotela Pictures 9000 Sunset Blvd Los Angeles CA 90069

DOCTEUR, BEVERLY MARIA, controller; b. Niagara Falls, N.Y., July 10, 1946; d. Idio Peter and Rosina Maria (Tolarico) Grazzini; m. Gerald John Docteur, Jan. 17, 1970; children: Kelli Ann, Rose Marie. BS summa cum laude, SUNY, Plattsburgh, 1979. Asst. mgr. Marine Midland Bank, N.A., Albany, N.Y., 1967-81; instr. Albany Bus. Coll., 1980-83, Clinton Community Coll., Plattsburgh, 1979; corp. controller Regal Art Press of Troy (N.Y.) Inc., 1983—. Mem. Friends of Lindenwald, Kinderhook, N.Y., 1983—; asst. coach Bethlehem Soccer Club, Delmar, N.Y., 1986—. Mem. Printing Industry of Am., Albany, 1983—. Home: 10 Venture Terr Glenmont NY 12077 Office: Regal Art Press of Troy Inc Industrial Park Rd Troy NY 12180

DODD, DARLENE MAE, nurse, air force officer; b. Dowagiac, Mich., Oct. 11, 1935; d. Charles B. and Lila H. Dodd; diploma in nursing Borgess Hosp. Sch. Nursing, Kalamazoo, 1957; grad. U.S. Air Force Flight Nurse Course, 1959, U.S. Air Force Squadron Officers Sch., 1963, Air Command and Staff Coll., 1973; BS in Psychology and Gen. Studies, So. Oreg. State Coll., 1987, postgrad., 1987; Commd. 2d lt. U.S. Air Force, 1959, advanced through grades to lt. col., 1975; staff nurse, Randolph AFB, Tex., 1959-60, Ladd AFB, Alaska, 1960-62, Selfridge AFB, Mich., 1962-63; Cam Rahn Bay Air Base, Vietnam, 1966-67, Seymour Johnson AFB, N.C., 1967-69, Air Force Acad., 1971-72; flight nurse 22d Aeromed. Evacuation, Tex., 1963-66; chief nurse Danang AFB, Vietnam, 1967; flight nurse Yokotu AFB, Japan, 1969-71; clin. coordinator ob/gyn and flight nurse, Elmendorf AFB, Alaska, 1973-76; clin. nurse coordinator obstetrics-gynecology and pediatric services USAF Med. Center, Keesler AFB, Miss., 1976-79, ret., 1979. Decorated Bronze Star, Meritorious Service medal, Air Force Commendation medal (3). Mem. So. Oreg. Hist. Soc., DAV, Ret. Officers Assn., Vietnam Vets. Am., VFW, Uniformed Services Disabled Retirees, Psy Chi, Phi Kappa Phi. Clubs: Psychology, Women of Moose. Home: 712 W 1st St Phoenix OR 97535

DODD, DEBORAH JANE, military contracting officer; b. Longmont, Colo., Oct. 11, 1947; d. John Jerome and Margaret Cora (Slee) D. BA, U. Colo., 1969; cert. teaching, Keane Coll., 1971; MS, San Jose State U., 1975. Vista vol. Palatka, Fla., 1969-70; tchr. N.J. Urban Edn. Corp., Newark, 1971-72, English Conversation Circle, Tokyo, Japan, 1972-73; camp dir. Baker Beach Golden Gate Nat. Recreation Area, San Francisco, 1975; recreation therapist Casa Grande (Ariz.) Rehab. Ctr., 1975-76; office mgr., counselor Tucson Rape Crisis Ctr., 1976-78; customs inspector U.S. Customs Service, Nogales, Ariz., 1978-81; elem. edn. tchr. Salome Show-Low Schs., Ariz., 1981-82; contract negotiator and contracting officer USAF, McClellan AFB, Calif., 1982—; gen. ptnr. Wymer and Assocs., Citrus Heights, Calif., 1986—. Mem. Calif. Native Plant Soc., Sacramento Minerology Soc., Fossils for Fun, Phi Beta Kappa. Democrat. Home: 8100 oak Ave Citrus Heights CA 95610

DODDS, CHRISTINE CHAMBERS, travel executive; b. Champaign, Ill., May 11, 1962; d. Donald Chambers Dodds and Martha (Sanford) Munitz. BS in Bus. Mgmt., San Diego State U., 1984. Asst. restaurant mgr. Hyatt Regency, Long Beach, Calif., 1984; adminstrv. asst. Catering and Transp., Newport Beach, Calif., 1984-85; group mgr. Conlin-Dodds Group Tours, Winston-Salem, N.C., 1985—. Sec. N.C. Sch. Arts Assocs. Bd., Winston-Salem, 1986—, captain annual fund drive, 1987; mem. Endow-A-Seat Bd. Stevens Ctr., Winston-Salem, 1987. Mem. Nat. Assn. Female Execs., San Diego State U. Bus. Alumni Assn., San Diego State U. Alumni Assn., Southeastern Contemporary Art Assn., Piedmont Craftsmen Inc. Democrat. Presbyterian. Home: 1409 Pilot View Dr #1 Winston-Salem NC 27101

DODDS, CLAUDETTE LA VONN, broadcast consultant; b. Lenapah, Okla., Sept. 2, 1947; d. Willie Lee and Dora (Harrell) Davis; m. Donald Howard Dodds, Jan. 14, 1965 (div. June 1982); children: Clarence Adam, Donyielle Alana, Erin Michelle. AAS with honors, Kennedy-King Coll., 1984. Newscaster, newswriter Sta. WKKC-FM, Chgo., 1983-84, news dir., 1984-85, program and music dir., 1985, sta. mgr., 1985-87; research asst. Vernon Jarrett Chgo. Sun Times, 1988—; mem. adv. com. Coll. Broadcasting, 1985-87; cons. Chicago Nite Life, 1985-87, Hayes & Co., 1986—, Morning Show/Danny Jack Sta. KWEZ, Monroe, La., 1986—, Sta. WKKC-FM, Future Records, 1988—; music researcher Let's Dance, Chgo., 1986—. Producer (TV spl.) Messiah, 1985; producer, writer (radio and TV spls.) Dr. Martin Luther King, 1985-86; producer, hostess (radio spls.) Englewood Parade, 1986, Bud Billiken Parade, 1986; mag. music reporter, 1987—. Mem. Dem. Student Task Force, Chgo., 1984, Student Disciplinary Bd. Chgo., 1986—; coordinator Concerned Students for Broadcasting Equipment, 1984. Mem. Ill. Broadcasters Assn., Broadcasters Edn. Assn., Communications Arts Guild (corr. sec. 1982-83), Phi Theta Kappa. Clubs: WKKC Social (Chgo.) (treas., founder 1983-84), Broadcasting (Chgo.) (staff adv. 1985-86). Lodges:Order of Eastern Star, Heroines of Jericho. Home and Office: 305 W 69th St Chicago IL 60621

DODDS, SUZAN LEE, electronics corporation executive; b. Frankin, Pa., Dec. 22, 1956; d. Wayne Edward and Catherine Virginia (Jawdy) D. BSin Computer Sci. and Biology, U. Pitts., 1978. Computer programmer On-Line Systems, Inc., Pitts., 1978-79; mgr. East End Food Cooperative, Pitts., 1979-81; computer programmer Prose Computer Services, Pitts., 1981-83, Allegheny Computer Services, Pitts., 1983-84; pres. Alliance Systems, Inc., Pitts., 1984 . Democrat. Office: Alliance Systems Inc 1016 N Canal St Pittsburgh PA 15215

DODERER, MINNETTE FRERICHS, state legislator; b. Holland, Iowa, May 16, 1923; d. John A. and Sophie S. Frerichs; B.A., U. Iowa, 1948; m. Fred H. Doderer, Aug. 5, 1944; children—Dennis, Kay Lynn. Mem. Iowa Ho. of Reps. 1964-69, 80—, minority whip, 1967-68, chairperson ways and means com., 1983—; mem. Iowa Senate, 1969-79, pres. pro tem, 1975-76; vis. prof. Stephens Coll., Iowa State Coll. (both 1979); vice-chairwoman Iowa Interstate Cooperation Commn., 1965-66; Vice-chairwoman Democratic Party Johnson County, 1957-60; mem. Dem. Nat. Com., 1968-70, Dem. Nat. Policy Council Elected Ofcls., 1973-76; chairwoman Iowa del. Internat. Women's Del. Bd. fellows Iowa Sch. Religion. Recipient Disting. Service award Iowa Edn. Assn., 1969; mem. Iowa Women's Hall of Fame, 1978. Mem. LWV, Delta Kappa Gamma (hon.). Democrat. Methodist.

DODGE, MADELINE RUTH WHEELAN, learning center administrator; b. Pueblo, Colo., July 24, 1929; d. Theodore Charles and Ruth Madeline (Caulfield) Wheelan; m. James E. Dodge, Feb. 21, 1952; children—Arlene, Kathleen, James, Jr., Thomas. Student Wash. State U., 1947-49; B.A., U. Wash., 1970. Asst. tchr. U. Wash., Seattle, 1965-67, head tchr., 1967-70, supr., 1970-71, dir., 1971-76, cons., 1979-80; instr. North Seattle Community Coll., 1978; dir., owner Christopher Robin Learning Ctr., 1976—; cons. Model Cities Seattle U., 1971-75, various colls., univs., head start programs. Contbr. articles to profl. jours. Vol. Juvenile Ct., King County Guardian Ad Litem Program, 1978—. Office: Christopher Robin Learning Ctr 7016 35th NE Seattle WA 98115

DODGE, MARGARETHA GERBERT, construction company executive; b. Mannheim, Baden, Germany, Nov. 17, 1929; came to U.S., 1954; d. Gotthold Nikolaus and Helene (Gebhardt) Gerbert; m. Arthur Byorn Dodge Jr., Dec. 18, 1953; children: Arthur Byron III, Andrew Nikolaus. Degree in Performing Arts, Hochschule Music, Heidelberg, Fed. Republic Germany, 1951; degree in Music History, U. Heidelberg, 1953. Opera singer Staats Theater, Detmold, Fed. Republic Germany, 1951-52; mgr. U.S. Hdqrs. Clubs and Messes, Heidelberg, 1952-54; pres., owner Gerbert Ltd., Lancaster, Pa., 1976—; pres. ABD Partners; v.p. Dodge Cork Co., Lancaster, 1981—. Pres. St. Joseph Hosp. Aux.; bd. dirs. Vol. Info. and Referral Service, Jr. League, Lancaster. Mem. Constrn. and Specifiers Inst., Cork Inst. Am. Republican. Roman Catholic. Office: Gerbert Ltd PO Box 4944 651 High St Lancaster PA 17604

DODSON, SIDNEY LEE, crafts company executive; b. Richmond, Va., July 17, 1953; d. Beverly Barham and Martha Annette (Warriner) D. Student, Greensboro Coll., 1971-73; BS in Art Edn., East Carolina U., 1975, M of Art Edn., 1978. Instr. art Southampton Acad., Courtland, Va., 1975-76, Lewis Chapel Jr. High Sch., Fayetteville, N.C., 1977-79; v.p. Old Buttermould Pattern Products, Inc., Franklin, Va., 1979-83, pres., 1983—. Mem. Nat. Assn. Female Execs., Museum Store Assn., Am. Crafts Council, Earthwatch. Republican. Baptist. Home and Office: Old Buttermould Pattern Products 722 Clay St PO Box 551 Franklin VA 23851

DOEZEMA, MARIANNE, art historian; b. Grand Rapids, Mich., Sept. 8, 1950; d. Charles William and Geraldine Frances (Slopsema) D.; m. Michael Andrew Marlais, Dec. 29, 1977. B.A., Mich. State U., 1973; M.A., U. Mich., 1975, postgrad. Boston U. Instr. dept. art history and edn. Cleve. Mus. Art, 1976-79, asst. curator, 1980-81; curator of edn. Ga. Mus. Art, Athens, 1981-83, assoc. dir., 1983-85. Author: American Realism and the Industrial Age, 1980. Contbr. articles to profl. jours. Presdl. U. Grad. fellow Boston U., 1985-86; Luce Found., 1987—. Mem. Coll. Art Assn. Am. Office: Ga Mus Art U Ga Jackson St Athens GA 30602

DOHERTY, ANNA MARIE, magazine editor; b. Baldwin, N.Y., Oct. 28, 1929; d. Dennis James and Helen Elizabeth (Koch) Doherty; A.A., Immaculata Coll., 1949; cert. Traphagen Sch. Interior Design, 1950. Asso. food editor This Week mag., N.Y.C., 1952-66, N.Y. Herald Tribune, 1952-66; acting food editor N.Y. World Jour. Tribune, 1966-67; food editor, columnist Suffolk Sun, L.I., N.Y., 1967-69; with Family Circle mag., N.Y.C., 1970—, sr. editor, dir. editorial services, 1971-79, women's service editor, 1979—, editor Cashing In consumer column, 1980-87, Mary Ellen Tips column, 1979-88, Quick Fix column, 1988—; editor, writer Quick Sew column, 1988—; food industry cons., 1965—; free lance food writer, 1966—. Fellow N.Y.C. Ballet; mem. Internat. Fund for Monuments (Venice Com.), Met. Mus. Art, Nat. Trust for Hist. Preservation, Am. Mus. Natural History, Met. Opera Guild, Smithsonian Instn. Club: Newswomen's (dir. N.Y.C. 1970-72). Editor, author: Family Circle's 429 Great Gifts To Make, 1977. Contbr. articles to profl. jours. Home: 154 E 61st St New York NY 10021 Address: 4080 Peconic Bay Blvd Laurel NY 11948 Office: 110 Fifth New York NY 10011

DOHERTY, SISTER BARBARA, academic administrator; b. Chgo., Dec. 2, 1931; d. Martin James and Margaret Eleanor (Noe) D. Student, Rosary Coll., 1949-51; BA in Latin, English and History, St. Mary-of-the-Woods Coll., 1953; MA in Theology, St. Mary's Coll., 1963; PhD in Theology, Fordham U., 1979. Tchr. Jr. and Sr. High Schs., Ind. and Ill., 1953-63; asst. prof. religion St. Mary-of-the-Woods Coll., Ind., 1963-67, 71-75, pres., 1983—; provincial supr. Chgo. Province of Sisters of Providence, 1975-83; summer faculty NCAIS-KCRCHE, Delhi, India, 1970. Author: I Am What I Am, 1981, Make Yourself an Ark, 1984; editor: Providence: God's Face Towards the World, 1985; contbr. articles to New Cath. Encyclop. Vol. XVII, 1982. Pres. Leadership Terre Haute, Ind., 1985-86; bd. regents Ind. Acad., 1987—; bd. dirs. 8th Day Cen. for Justice, Chgo., 1978-83. Arthur J. Schmidt Found. grantee, 1967-71. Mem. Women's Coll. Coalition (nat. bd. dirs. 1984—), Assoc. Colls. Ind., Ind. Colls. and Univs. of Ind., Assn. Am. Colls., Leadership Conf. of Women Religious of USA (program chairperson nat. assembly 1982-83). Democrat. Roman Catholic. Home and Office: St Mary-of-the-Woods Coll Office of the President Saint Mary-of-the-Woods IN 47876

DOHERTY, EILEEN PATRICIA, university administrator, educator; b. Astoria, N.Y., Aug. 21, 1952; d. Joseph John and Joan Ellen (Conway) D.; m. Robert A. Ungar, June 11, 1988. B.A., St. John's U., 1974, M.B.A., 1978, postgrad. Sch. of Law, 1986—; M.A., Columbia U., 1976, Ed.M., 1985. Asst. to dean admissions St. John's U., Jamaica, N.Y., 1974-75, asst. to dir. instnl. research, 1975-76, asst. dean Evening & Weekend Coll., 1976-80, asst. dean Coll. Bus. Adminstrn., 1980-81, assoc. dean St. Vincent's Coll., dir. Evening and Weekend sessions, 1981—, adj. prof. econs., 1978—. Assoc. editor: The Forum, 1987—. Hosp. vol. ARC, N.Y.C., 1967; rep. of city comptroller Steinway Bus. Improvement Dist., Astoria, N.Y., 1982—; mem. Queens Community Planning Bd., 1980-83. Mem. ABA (law student div. rep.), N.Y. State Bar Assn., Queens County Bar Assn., N.Y. Area Pub. Affairs Profls., Am. Assn. Higher Edn., Am. Econ. Assn., Am. Mktg. Assn., Am. Fin. Assn., Am. Soc. for Tng. and Devel., Phi Delta Kappa, Psi Chi, Kappa Delta Pi, Phi Delta Phi, Pres. Soc. Alumni Assn. (rec. sec. 1983—). Roman Catholic. Home: 150-16 17th Ave Whitestone NY 11357 Office: St Johns U 113 Bent Hall Jamaica NY 11439

DOHERTY, ELIZABETH C., hospital administrator, educator; b. Pitts.; d. Roger Joseph and Frances Mary (Callaghan) Doherty Smith. BS, Seton Hill Coll., Greensburg, Pa., 1965; MEd, Duquesne U., 1972; PhD, U. Pitts., 1976. Registered Dietitian , 1967. Nursing instr. Montefiore Hosp., Pitts., 1969-72; dir. dietetic edn. Alleghany County Community Coll., Pitts., 1972-78; dir. grad. edn. Sharecorp, Pitts., 1978-82; pres. Personal Devel. Assn., Pitts., 1977-86; acct. mgr. med. div. Mgmt. Recruiters, Pitts., 1985-86; quality assurance dir. Equitable Group and Health Ins., Pitts., 1986; quality assurance coordinator Eye and Ear Hosp., Pitts., 1987—, Falk Clinic U. Pitts., 1987—; instr. and cons. in field; adj. prof. masters health adminstrn., Coll. St. Francis, Pitts. Author: (audio cassette) Your Quality Assurance Program Can Be Statistically Significant, 1980; Contbr. articles to profl. jours. Arbitrator Better Bus. Bur., Pitts., 1985—. Recipient Edn. award Internat. Food Research Services Ctr., 1972, Notable Americans award Am. Biog. Inst., 1976, 77, numerous govt. grants for ednl. devel. Fellow Am. Biog. Inst.; mem. Nat. Assn. Quality Assurance Profls., Nat. Assn. Female Execs., Pitts. Conn. (exec. dir. 1985-87), Conn. Profl. Quality Assurance Soc. Roman Catholic. Home: 605 Shady Ave Pittsburgh PA 15206 Office: Eye and Ear Hosp 230 Lothrop St Pittsburgh PA 15213

DOHERTY, EVELYN MARIE, data processing consultant; b. Phila., Sept. 26, 1941; d. James Robert and Virginia (Checkley) D. Diploma, RCA Tech. Inst., Cherry Hill, N.J., 1968. Freelance data processing programmer N.J., 1968-81, data processing cons. ednl., banking, transp., mfg., medical, pub., food wholesaling and brokerage community, 1981—. Contbr. articles in field. Chairwoman Collingswood (N.J.) Dems.. founder Babe Didikson Collingswood Softball Team for Women. Mem. Data Processing Mgmt. Assn. (chairperson, mem. ednl. com., bd. dirs. N.J. chpt., 1980—). Roman Catholic. Office: PO Box 3780 Cherry Hill NJ 08003

DOHERTY, JOSEPHINE VARLEY, computer company executive; b. N.Y.C., Mar. 1, 1940; d. Michael and Elizabeth (O'Donnell) Varley; B.A. (N.Y. State Regents scholar 1958-62), Marymount Manhattan Coll., 1962; M.A., St. John's U., 1970; m. William G. Doherty, Aug. 15, 1970; children—Katherine Varley, Andrew Attwood. English tchr. St. Catherine Acad., Bronx, 1962-67; English dept. adminstr. Christ the King High Sch., boys' div., Queens, N.Y., 1967-72; KEN-MAC div. mgr. Aspen Systems Corp., N.Y.C., 1977-80; dir. procedures and tng. Am. Legal Systems, N.Y.C., 1980-82, mgr. computerized projects, 1982, regional mgr., 1982-85, corp. services mgr., 1985-86; dist. adminstrv. mgr. Burn's Internat. Security, 1987—. Lic. English tchr., N.Y. Mem. Nat. Assn. Female Execs, Am. Mgmt. Assn. Office: 97-45 Queens Blvd Suite 1008 Forest Hills NY 11374

DOHERTY, KAREN ANN, corporate executive; b. Elizabeth, N.J., July 6, 1952; d. Eugene Nason Godfrey and Helen L. (Andersen) D.; m. Jonathan Kent Tillinghast, June 17, 1972 (div. Oct. 1978). Account exec. The John O'Donnell Co., N.Y., 1979-80; conservation rep. Sierra Club, N.Y., 1980-81; asst. dir. membership Am. Mgmt. Assn., N.Y., 1981—. Mem. Am. Soc. Profl. and Exec. Women, Women's Econ. Roundtable, Trinity Coll. Alumnae Assn. (bd. dirs. N.Y. chpt. 1981-83), Sierra Club (exec. com. N.Y.C. group 1979-82). Democrat. Roman Catholic. Home: 375 Riverside Dr #11AA New York NY 10025 Office: Am Mgmt Assn 135 W 50th St New York NY 10020

DOHERTY, MARY CUSHING, lawyer; b. Evanston, Ill., Apr. 22, 1953; d. F. John and Margaret Louise (Wolf) Cushing; m. James Francis Doherty, Aug. 20, 1977; children—John Francis, Margaret Rose. B.A., U. Del., 1975; J.D., Villanova U., 1978. Bar: Pa. 1978, N.J., 1978, U.S. Dist. Ct. (ea. dist.) Pa. 1978, U.S. Dist. Ct. N.J. 1978. Assoc. Abrahams and Loewenstein, Phila., 1979-87, ptnr. 1987—; also lectr., course planner Pa. Bar Inst., Pa. Bar Assn., others. Contbr. articles to Pa. Law Jour., 1981. Mem. staff Pre-Cana Counselling, Roman Cath. Chs., 1981—; counselor UNITE of Jeanes Hosp., Phila., 1984, bd. dirs., 1985-86, v.p., 1986-87, chair bd. dirs., 1987—. Minerva Schultz Found. grantee, 1978. Fellow Am. Acad. Matrimonial Lawyers; mem. Phila. Bar Assn. (chmn. family law sect. 1985, del. bd. govs. 1986), ABA, N.J. Bar Assn., Hidden Meadow Community Assn., Bus. Women's Network. Roman Catholic. Office: Abrahams & Loewenstein One Montgomery Plaza Suite 700 Norristown PA 19401

DOHERTY, MICHEL GEORGE, alcohol and drug treatment facility administrator; b. Erie, Pa., Dec. 7, 1930; d. David Lloyd and Marie (Morris) George; m. William K. Rodstein, June 10, 1952 (dec. Apr. 1969); children: William Michael, Michael William; m. Edward L. Doherty, Aug. 14, 1982; m. Edward L. Doherty. M in Human Service Adminstrn., Lincoln U., Oxford, Pa., 1981. Cert. addiction profl., Pa., Fla. Addiction counselor Livingren Found., Eldington, Pa., 1974-75; clin. dir. Vitae House Inc., Glenmoore, Pa., 1975-80; clin. dir., dir. spl. programs, projects coordinator med. students Temple U. Horsham Hosp., Ambler, Pa., 1980-83; exec. dir., chief exec. officer Roxbury, Shippensburg, Pa., 1983-84; dir. substance abuse div. First Hosp. Corp., Norfolk, Va., 1982; exec. dir., chief exec. officer The Cloisters at Pine Island, Pineland, Fla., 1984—; mem. Nat. Credentialing Commn. of Alcohol Counselors, Washington, 1978-84; co-chairperson Nat. Women's Support Network, Washington, 1982-83. Contbr. articles to newspaper and mags. Bd. dirs. alcohol/drug abuse task force Springfield (Pa.) High Sch., 1983. Recipient Outstanding Accomplishment in Field award N.Am. Women's Commn. on Alcohol/Drug Abuse, 1979. Mem. Nat. Assn. Drug/Alcohol Counselors (v.p. 1978), Pa. Addiction Counselors Assn. (pres. 1978-79, Outstanding Contbn. award 1979), Assn. Labor Mgmt. & Adminstrn. Del. Valley (v.p. 1981-83), LWV, Bus. and Profl. Women. Republican. Unitarian. Home: 5341 SW 11th Ave Cape Coral FL 33914 Office: The Cloisters at Pine Island Waterfront Dr Box 1616 Pineland FL 33945-1616

DOHERTY, ROSALIE MICHELLE, marketing executive; b. Phila., Sept. 1, 1961; d. John Joseph and Mary Patricia (Bonner) D. BS in Mktg. and Fin., La Salle Coll., 1983. Mktg. rep. Phila. Fed. Credit Union, 1983-86, mgr. mktg., 1986—. Mem. Chestnut Street Assn., Phila. , 1987. Mem. Phila. Chpt. Credit Unions (youth ambassador 1985-86, sec. bd. dirs. 1987—), Pa. Credit Union League (youth ambassador 1986-87, Full Family Mktg. award, Credit Union Publs. award 1987), Fin. Mktg. Assn. Credit Union Execs. Democrat. Roman Catholic. Home: 728 E Ontario St Philadelphia PA 19134 Office: Phila Fed Credit Union 1206 Chestnut St Philadelphia PA 19107

DOI, MARY ELLEN, research chemist, laboratory administrator; b. Memphis, Mo., Jan. 15, 1933; d. Earl Edward and Beulah Mae (Leach) Tucker; m. Minoru Doi, June 16, 1962; 1 child, Paul Edward. BS, Northeast Mo. State U., 1953. Cert. med. technologist, 1957. Tchr. chemisty, biology Princeton (Mo.) High Sch., 1953-54; tchr. sci. Evans Jr. High Sch., Ottumwa, Iowa, 1954-56; lab. technician Shelby County Hosp., Shelbyville, Ill., 1957-58; med. chemist Barnes Hosp., St. Louis, 1958-60; research chemist Monsanto Chem. Co., St. Louis, 1960-63; chief chemist, dir. lab. E.S. Erwin and Assocs., Tolleson, Ariz., 1963—. Active Rep. campaign, 1976. Mem. Am. Chem. Soc., Assn. Official Analytical Chemists, Ariz. Assn. Cert. Labs. Republican. Methodist. Club: Bus. and Profl. Women (Maryvale, Glendale, Ariz.) (past sec.-treas., v.p., pres., Woman of Yr. 1974, 79). Home: 5963 W Hazelwood Phoenix AZ 85033 Office: Nutrition-Lab Services PO Box 237 Tolleson AZ 85353

DOKA, JANET ANN, health project director; b. Passaic, N.J., June 28, 1952; d. Joseph William and Gladys Teresa (Agner) D. BA, Fairleigh Dickinson U., 1974. Tng. seminars and pub. relations adminstr. Am. Soc. TV Cameramen, Sparkill, N.Y., 1974-77; free-lance health reporter, producer United Artists Columbia Cable TV Co., Oakland, N.J., 1977; med. mktg. communications coordinator Clark-O'Neill, Inc., Fairview, N.J., 1977-80; mktg. mgr. Med. Econs. Co., Oradell, N.J., 1981-82; project dir. Planned Parenthood of Bergen County, Hackensack, N.J., 1982—; cons. mktg. and patient edn. Bklyn. Lung Ctr., 1987—. Mem. Nat. Assn. Female Execs., Am. Soc. Assn. Execs. Democrat. Roman Catholic. Home: 23 Miller St Saddle Brook NJ 07663

DOKUPIL, INEZ LOTT, real estate and investments executive; b. New Orleans, Dec. 14, 1937; d. H. Alvin and Edna M. (Joiner) Lott; m. Harold T. Dokupil, Oct. 15, 1960; children: Elizabeth, Michael. BS, Baylor U., 1958. Lab. asst. Tex. Children's Hosp., Houston, 1956; sec. H.A. Lott, Inc., Houston, 1957, Am. Nat. Bank, Houston; researcher Tenneco, Houston, 1959-63; ptnr. Lott Properties, Houston, 1979—. Research grantee Johns Hopkins U., 1958. Republican. Mem. Ch. of God. Home: 11911 Doncaster Houston TX 77024

DOLAN, MARYANNE MCLORN, writer, educator, lecturer; b. N.Y.C., July 14, 1924; d. Frederick Joseph and Kathryn Cecilia (Carroll) McLorn; m. John Francis Dolan, Oct. 6, 1951; children—John Carroll, James Francis McLorn, William Brennan. B.A., San Francisco State U., 1978, M.A., 1981. Tchr. classes and seminars in antiques and collectibles U. Calif.-Berkeley, U. Calif.-Davis, U. Calif.-Santa Cruz, Coll. of Marin, Kentfield, Calif., Mills Coll., Oakland, Calif., St. Mary's Coll., Moraga, Calif., 1969—; tchr. writing Dolan Sch., 1978 ; owner antique shop, Benicia, Calif., 1970—. Author: Vintage Clothing, 1880-1960, 1983; Collecting Rhinestone Jewelry, 1984; weekly columnist The Collector, 1979—; contbr. articles to profl. jours. Mem. AAUW, Internat. Soc. Appraisers, Calif. Writers Club, Internat. Platform Assn. Republican. Roman Catholic. Home: 138 Belle Ave Pleasant Hill CA 94523 Office: 191 West J St Benicia CA 94510

DOLAN-GREENE, COLLEEN, academic affairs and personnel administrator; b. Omaha, Jan. 20, 1948; d. James Ralph and Mary Irene (Dunn) Dolan; m. Walter Raleigh Greene III, Apr. 10, 1976; 1 child, Nicholas James, 1 stepchild, Walter Raleigh IV. BA, Mt. St. Scholastica Coll., 1970; MA, U. Tex., Austin, 1973; IEM, Harvard U., 1986. Labor relations mgr. Oakland U., Rochester, Mich., 1973-76; dir. personnel U. Detroit, 1976-80; asst. personnel dir. Employment and Human Resource Devel., Ann Arbor, Mich., 1980-83; asst. dir. personnel U. Mich., Ann Arbor, 1983-87, personnel adminstr., 1980-87, asst. v.p. acad. affairs, 1987—; personnel adminstr. U. Mich., Ann Arbor, 1980-87. Author: (book chpt.) Handbook of Faculty Bargaining, 1977, Coping With Faculty Reductions, 1981. Mem. allocation com. Washtenaw United Way, Ann Arbor, 1983-86; bd. dirs. Huron Valley Girl Scout Council, Ypsilanti, Mich., 1982—, pres., 1985-88; mem. personnel's com. First Unitarian-Universalist Ch., Detroit, 1984-85. Fellow L.B. Johnson Sch. Pub. Affairs, 1971-73; recipient Pres.'s Mgmt. award Huron Valley Girl Scout Council, 1985. Mem. Am. Soc. for Personnel Adminstrn. (v.p., bd. dirs. region 10 1984-86, v.p., bd. dirs. Area III 1987), Detroit Personnel Mgmt. Assn. (pres. 1984-86), Acad. for Academic Personnel Adminstrs. (pres. 1975-76), Coll. and Univ. Personnel Adminstrs. (collective bargaining council 1976-80), Indsl. Relations Research Assn., Nat. Assn. Women's Deans. Democrat. Home: 2295 W Boston Blvd Detroit MI 48206 Office: U Mich 4048 Fleming Adminstrn Bldg Ann Arbor MI 48109-1340

DOLE, ELIZABETH HANFORD, Republican campaigner, former secretary of transportation; b. Salisbury, N.C., July 29, 1936; d. John Van and Mary Ella (Cathey) Hanford; m. Robert Joseph Dole (U.S. Senator from Kans.), Dec. 6, 1975. B.A. with honors in Polit. Sci., Duke, 1958; postgrad., Oxford (Eng.) U., summer 1959; M.A. in Edn., Harvard U., 1960, J.D., 1965. Bar: D.C. 1966. Staff asst. to asst. sec. for edn. HEW, Washington, 1966-67; practiced law Washington, 1967-68; assoc. dir. legis. affairs, then exec. dir. Pres.'s Com. for Consumer Interests, Washington, 1968-71; dep. dir. Office Consumer Affairs, The White House, Washington, 1971-73; commr. FTC, Washington, 1973-79; chmn. Voters for Reagan-Bush, 1980; dir. Human Services Group, Office of Exec. Br. Mgmt., Office of Pres.-Elect, 1980; asst. to Pres. for pub. liaison 1981-83; sec. U.S. Dept. Transp., 1983-87; with Robert Dole for Presdl. Campaign, 1987-88; mem. nominating com. Am. Stock Exchange, 1972. Bd. overseers Comprehensive Career Ctr. Duke U., 1983—; mem. bd. visitors Duke U. Sch. Bus., 1988—; hon. chmn. bd. overseers Duke U. Comprehensive Cancer Ctr., 1988—; mem. vis. com. John

F. Kennedy Sch. Govt. Harvard U., 1988—. Recipient Arthur S. Flemming award U.S. Govt., 1972, Humanitarian award Nat. Commn. Against Drunk Driving, 1988, Disting. Alumni award Duke U., 1988; named one of Am.'s 200 Young Leaders, Time mag., 1974, one of World's 10 Most Admired Women, Gallup Poll, 1988. Mem. Delta Delta Delta, Phi Beta Kappa, Pi Lambda Theta, Pi Sigma Alpha. Office: Dept of Transp Office of Sec 400 7th St SW Washington DC 20590

DOLE, GRACE FULLER, librarian, artist; b. Cambridge, Mass., Sept. 20; d. John Soper and Margaret Fernald Dole; m. Paul E. Kohler, Jan. 22, 1944; (div. May 1946); 1 dau., Margaret K. Nicholson. B.A., Bryn Mawr Coll., 1944; M.L.S., Columbia U., 1954. Library cert., N.Y. Tchr. French, librarian Low-Heywood Sch., Stamford, Conn., 1948-50; sch. librarian Greenwich Library (Conn.), 1950-53; librarian reference dept. N.Y. Pub. Library, N.Y.C., 1954-56; asst. librarian, then librarian Benton & Bowles, Inc., N.Y.C., 1956-62; reference librarian Ferguson Library, Stamford, 1962-64; librarian U. Conn. Library, Stamford, 1964-75, library specialist, 1975—; mem. Library Adminstrs. group Fairfield County (Conn.), 1974-75; exhibited Chinese brushwork in various shows. Mem. Assn. Coll. and Research Libraries, ALA, Spl. Libraries Assn. (treas. Hudson Valley chpt. 1984-86), English Speaking Union, Pen and Brush, Fairfield County Panhellenic Alumnae Assn. (treas. 1987-88). Clubs: Catharine Loriallard Wolfe Art (bd. dirs. 1975-78), Margret Fernald Dole Contemporary Art (pres. 1975—); Nat. Arts, Pen and Brush (N.Y.C.); Indian Harbor Yacht (Greenwich). Home: 503 W Lyon Farm Dr Greenwich CT 06830 Office: U Conn Scofieldtown Rd Stamford CT 06903

DOLIN, LONNY H., lawyer; b. Youngstown, Ohio, Jan. 24, 1954; d. Lawrence Joseph and Sonya (Sacks) Heselov ; m. Raphael Dolin, June 19, 1976; children: Nathaniel, Brooke. AB, Georgetown U., 1976; JD, Cath. U., 1979. Bar: Vt. 1980, N.Y. State Bar 1984, U.S. Dist. Ct. (we. dist.) N.Y. 1984. Assoc. Downs, Rachlin & Martin, Burlington, Vt., 1979-81; sole practice Burlington, 1981-84; assoc. Harris, Beach, Wilcox, Rubin & Levey, Rochester, N.Y., 1984—; of counsel to U.S. Congressman Fred J. Eckert, N.Y., 1985—; bd. dirs. Monroe County Legal Services Corp. Mem. Pittsford Town and County Com., N.Y., 1983—, Town of Pittsford Bd. of Zoning Appeals, N.Y., 1984—; chmn. Monroe County Comparable Worth Task Force, Rochester, 1985—, Fred J. Eckert Women's Adv. Council, Rochester, 1985—; del. The Jud. Dist. N.Y., Rochester, 1985; bd. dirs. Nat. Council Jewish Women. Recipient Corpus Juris Secundum award West Pub. co., 1979. Mem. ABA, Vt. Bar Assn., N.Y. Bar Assn., Monroe County Bar Assn., Greater Rochester Women's Bar Assn. (treas. 1986), Assn. Trial Lawyers Am., N.Y. State Trial Lawyers Assn. Republican. Home: 22 Fletcher Rd Pittsford NY 14534 Office: Harris Beach et al 130 E Main St Rochester NY 14604

DOLINICH, CHRISTINE, artist; b. Elizabeth, N.J., Feb. 24, 1950; d. Anton J. and Irene Marie (Kutay) D. Student, Oxford U., England, 1970-71; BA in Studio Art, Rutgers U., 1973; postgrad., Westminster Choir Coll., 1984, 86. Dir. Union County Conservatory, Rahway, N.J., 1987, Linden (N.J.) Art and Music Studio, 1983-87; critiquer Union County Teen Arts Festival Union Coll., Cranford, N.J., 1986, 87. Exhibited in group shows at Los Angeles Women's Ctr., Houston U., Utah U., 1977, Newark Mus., 1982, City Without Walls Gallery, Newark, 1982, 83, 84, 85, 86, Morris Mus., Morristown, N.J., 1987; one-woman shows include Caldwell (N.J.) Coll., 1976, 82, Middlesex Coll. Art Gallery, Edison, N.J., 1985, Douglass Coll. Women Artists Series, 1986-87, Rutgers U., New Brunswick, N.J., 1987; artists books Rutgers U., U. of Delaware, Newark Library, New Brunswick, 1982-83. Fellow N.J. State Council on the Arts, 1984-85; recipient First prize Art with Mus. Subjects Cover Contest. Mem. AAUW (radio host Sta. WFMU Women in Music and Art Series 1984-85, lectr., slide and tape presentation Women in Art and Music 1985), Women's Caucus for Art, Music Tchr. Nat. Assn. (1st prize Am. Music Tchr. 1981, 83) , Piano Tchrs. Soc. Am. Home: 322 Mitchell Ave Linden NJ 07036 Studio: 45 E Milton Ave Rahway NJ 07065

DOLLAR, SANDRA MARIE, marketing and communication executive; b. Phila., Feb. 10, 1949; d. Francis William and Marion Beatrice (Gross) D.; B.A., Bryn Mawr Coll., 1971. Asst. to advt. mgr. Theodore Presser Co., Bryn Mawr, Pa., 1971-72; freelance writer, 1972-73; editor, publicity coordinator AMP Spl. Industries, Valley Forge, Pa., 1973-75; public info. coordinator Peirce Jr. Coll., Phila., 1975-76; Vistas editor Roswell (N.Mex.) Daily Record, 1977-78; publs. coordinator Penn Mut. Life Ins. Co., Phila., 1979-80; mgr. editorial services CIGNA Corp., Phila., 1980-84; dir. mktg. and communication Huggins Fin. Services, Inc., Phila., 1984-87; pres. Sandra Dollar & Assocs., Inc., 1987—. Mem. pub. relations com., co. communications subcom. United Way S.E. Pa., 1983. Recipient Mary Swindler award, Mary Windsor award Bryn Mawr Coll., 1969, Media award N.Mex. div. Am. Cancer Soc., 1977, Guy Rader award N.Mex. Med. Soc., 1977, Communicators award United Way Am. and SE Pa., 1980, 81, 82, Bell Ringer award Bus./Profl. Advt. Assn., 1981, Neographics Gold award, 1986, Bryn Mawr Coll. alumnae regional scholar, 1967-71; Pa. State scholar, 1967-70. Mem. Internat. Assn. Bus. Communicators (program chmn. 1982-84), Mktg. Communication Execs./Phila., Phila. Ctr. City Proprietors. Office: 6 Maple Terr Cherry Hill NJ 08002

DOLMAN, HARRIETT GAILYN, rehabilitation services administrator; b. Montgomery, Ala., Nov. 11, 1949; d. James Benjamin Sr. and Clee Bennie (Robinson) D. BS in Sociology, Tuskegee Inst., 1972; MS in Occupational Therapy, Columbia U., 1982. Caseworker Rockland Psychiat. Ctr., Orangeburg, N.Y., 1973-74, tchr., 1974-77, rehab. worker, 1977-81, occupational therapist, 1982—, sr. occupational therapist, 1982-84, program coordinator, 1984-86; dir. occupational therapy Middletown (N.Y.) Psychiat. Ctr., 1986—; adj. faculty Orange County Community Coll., Middletown, 1983-87, Dominican Coll., Blauvelt, N.Y., 1987; advisor Occupational Therapy Program Dominican Coll., Blauvelt, 1984-87. Mem. Am. Occupational Therapy Assn., N.Y. State Occupational Therapy Assn. (v.p. Hudson Taconic dist. 1987-88), Nat. Black Occupational Therapy Caucus, Nat. Assn. Female Execs., Assn. Occupational Therapy Adminstrs. Democrat. Methodist. Office: Middletown Psychiat Ctr 141 Monhagen Ave Middletown NY 10940

DOLOREY, SISTER MARY, nun, college administrator. BS in Biology, Coll. Misericordia, Dallas, Pa.; MA in Ednl. Adminstrn., Fairfield U.; postgrad., Syracuse U. Prin. Our Lady of Pilar High Sch., Rio Piedras, P.R.; registrar Alvernia Coll., Reading, Pa., 1978-79, pres., 1982—. Office: Alvernia Coll Office of the Pres Reading PA 19607

DOLPHIN, BETH JAN, computer company executive; b. N.Y.C., July 29, 1958; d. Arnold Lazarus and Renee (Eichenbaum) Kantor; m. Richard David Mann, Nov. 16, 1980 (div. Feb. 1983); m. M. Craig Dolphin, July 20, 1986. Student, Sullivan City Community Coll., Loch Sheldrake, N.Y., 1976-77, Columbia U., 1978-79. Coop. advt. coordinator Lady Manhattan, N.Y.C., 1983-84; tech. support specialist Mgmt. Systems, Inc., Glenbrook, Conn., 1984-85; office systems rep. Harris/Lanier, Tarrytown, N.Y., 1985-86; pres., owner, cons. The PC Learning Curve, Inc., Larchmont, N.Y., 1986—; cons., lectr. New Rochelle (N.Y.) Pub. Library. Vol. Lenox Hill Hosp., N.Y.C. Mem. Nat. Assn. Female Execs. Republican. Jewish. Home: 120 Pelham Rd New Rochelle NY 10805 Office: The PC Learning Curve Inc PO Box 1045 Larchmont NY 10538

DOLSON, MARY JO DE PAUL, tax administrator; b. Youngstown, Ohio, Mar. 5, 1958; d. Phillip Arthur and Anna Joyce (Barrett) DePaul; m. Timothy Joseph Dolson, Nov. 29, 1986. BSBA in Acctg., Youngstown State U., 1981. State tax auditor Ohio Dept. Taxation, Cleve., 1981-84; tax analyst Coopers and Lybrand, Cleve., 1984-85; state and local income tax manager Am. Greetings Corp., Cleve., 1985—. Mem. Nat. Assn. Accts., Cleve. Tax Club, Cleve. Jaycees.

DOLSON, VIVIAN ANTOINETTE, sales executive; b. Chgo., July 17, 1925; d. Werner Henry and Lillian Rose (Ghilardi) Steger; student DePaul U., 1943-46; m. Sept. 10, 1948 (div.); children—Bill, David. Asst. registrar DePaul U., 1952-55, exec. sec., 1955-58; asst. personnel dir. Stat. Tabulating Co., Chgo., 1958-61; owner, operator Dolson Market Research, Chgo., 1961-75; dist. sales mgr. for Ill. and Wis., Borroughs/Lear Siegler Co., Chgo., 1975-78, asst. nat. sales mgr., Kalamazoo, 1978-81; nat. sales mgr. Marvel Metal Products, Chgo., 1981-84, pres. Dolson Associates, Inc., Honolulu, 1984—; career cons. Triton Jr. Coll. Mem. Am. Market Research Assn., Nat. Office Products Assn. Am. Mgmt. Assn., Mfr. Assocs. Nat. Assn. Club: Soroptomists Internat. Home and Office: Dolson Assocs 3138 Waialae Ave Apt 218 Honolulu HI 96816

DOMAN, JANET JOY, association executive; b. Phila., Dec. 16, 1948; d. Glenn J. and Hazel Katie (Massingham) D. Student, U. Hull, England, 1969-70; BA, U. Pa., 1971. Cert. tchr. Clinician Inst. Achievement Human Potential, Phila., 1971-74; dir. English Early Devel. Assn., Tokyo, 1974-75; dir. Evan Thomas Inst. Early Devel., Phila., 1975-77, Inst. Achievement of Intellectual Excellence, 1977-80; vice dir. Inst. Achievement Human Potential, 1980-82, dir., 1982—; internat. lectr. treatment of brain injured children and superiority. Chair Child Brain Devel., United Steelworkers Am., 1987. Recipient Gold medal Centro de Reabilitacion Nosa Senhora da Gloria, Rio de Janeiro, 1974, Brit. Star Brit. Inst. Achievement Human Potential, 1976, Sakura Korosho medal Japanese Inst. Achievement Human Potential, 1977, statuette with pedestal Internat. Forum Human Potential, 1980. Office: 8801 Stenton Ave Philadelphia PA 19118

DOMASH, DIANNE JOY, psychologist, nutritional consultant; b. N.Y.C., July 30, 1959; d. Norman and Zelda (Senft) D. B.S., C.W. Post Coll., 1979, profl. diploma, 1986; M.S., Hofstra U., 1980; Ph.D., U.S. Internat. U., San Diego, 1983. Lic. psychologist; cert. nutritional cons.; cert. paramedic; registered hypnotherapist. Psychologist, U.S. Internat. U., 1980-82, San Diego City Schs., 1981-83, Sachem Cen. Sch. Dist., Holbrook, N.Y., 1984—; exec. dir. LIFE, Gt. Neck, N.Y., 1984—, assoc. program dir. Stresscare Systems, NLYLCL, 1988—. Firefighter, paramedic Port Washington Fire Dept., N.Y., 1985—; exec. dir. Nutrition For You Inc., N.Y.C., 1988; cons. nutrition, fitness and stress mgmt.; instr. CPR Gt. Neck United Community Fund, other seminars; guest speaker, radio and TV programs; trainer, instr. Stresscare, Great Neck, N.Y.: pres. Nutrition for You, Great Neck; vol. North Shore Univ. Hosp., Manhasset, N.Y.; instr. CPR ARC; spl. task force on adolescent suicide; pres. Successful Living Strategies, Gt. Neck, editor newsletter SLS Newsbrief, Nutrition for You. Mem. Am. Psychol. Assn., N.Y. State Psychol. Assn., Suffolk County Psychol. Assn., Am. Assn. Sex Educators, Counselors, and Therapists, AADE, AACD, IPA, Nassau County Psychol. Assn. (mem. exec. bd. 1984-85), Fire Fighters Benevolent Assn., Nat. Rifle Assn., Am. Ednl. Research Assn., Am. Assn. Sex Educators and Therapists, Am. Counseling and Guidance Assn., Internat. Cops for Christ, Phi Delta Kappa. Avocation: photography. Home: PO Box 4289 Great Neck NY 11027

DOMBRO, MARCIA WINTERS, nurse, educational administrator; b. Clinton, Minn., Dec. 14, 1940; d. Benton Jay and Thelma Elizabeth (Roth) Winters; BSN, U. Wash., 1963; MS in Adult Edn., Fla. Internat. U., 1976, postgrad. 1985—; m. Roy S. Dombro, Sept. 10, 1967; children: Rayna Lisette, Meryl Elana. Public health nurse Seattle-King County Health Dept., 1964-66, N.Y.C. Dept. Health Bur. Nursing, 1966-67; head nurse home care unit Bellevue Hosp., N.Y.C., 1967-68; asst. clin. instr. in obstetrics City Hosp. at Elmhurst, N.Y.C., 1968; clin. instr. obstetrics Miami-Dade Community Coll., 1973-74; instr. U. Miami Sch. Nursing, 1976-80; dir. dept. nursing edn. Baptist Hosp. Miami (Fla.), 1980—; adj. faculty U. Miami Sch. Nursing, 1984—; tchr. sex edn. for schs., civic groups, parent edn. groups. Active ERA, NOW, Miami. Mem. Nurses Assn.-Am. Coll. Ob-Gyn. (sec.-treas. Dade County 1985—), Am. Nurses' Assn., Nat. League for Nursing, Am. Soc. Psychoprophylaxis in Obstetrics (cert. childbirth instr. 1970, coordinator South Fla. 1976-81), Am. Soc. Health Edn. and Tng. Jewish. Author: Post Partum for the Childbirth Educator-A Programmed Text, 1976; contb. articles to profl. jours.; co-producer audiovisual kit: Born Sexy, 1976; computer program on teenage pregnancy, 1986. Home: 9841 SW 123d St Miami FL 33176 Office: 8900 N Kendall Dr Miami FL 33176

DOMBROWSKI, ANNE WESSELING, microbiologist, researcher; b. Cin., Jan. 26, 1948; d. Robert John and Margaret Mary (Bell) Wesseling; m. Allan Wayne Dombrowski, Apr. 17, 1982; children: Amy, Alicia. BA summa cum laude, Xavier U., 1970; MS, U. Cin., 1972, PhD, 1974. Fellow Scripps Clinic & Research Found., La Jolla, Calif., 1974-76; sr. research microbiologist Merck & Co., Inc., Rahway, N.J., 1976-87, research fellow, 1987—. Contbt. articles to profl. jours. Mem. Soc. Indsl. Microbiology (sec. 1982-85), Am. Soc. Microbiology, Am. Assn. Advancement Sci., Soc. Gen. Microbiology.

DOMEISEN, MICHELLE ANNE KEANE, investment, real estate executive; b. Pitts., Sept. 10, 1955; d. John Edgar and Janet Marie (Mackall) K.; B.A. in Urban Affairs, U. Pitts., 1977, M.B.A., 1982. TV account exec. Sta. KDKA-TV2, Pitts., 1977-84; brokerage rep. Oliver Realty, 1984—. Bd. dirs. Western Pa. chpt. Nat. Hemophilia Found.; mem. assocs. council U. Pitts. Grad. Sch. Bus. Anna R.D. Gillespie scholar, 1976-77; Pa. Senatorial scholar, 1976-77. Mem. Greater Pitts. Bd. Realtors, Omicron Delta Kappa, Chi Omega, Rho Lambda. Home: 416 Virginia Ave Pittsburgh PA 15215 Office: 2800 Two Oliver Plaza Pittsburgh PA 15222

DOMEK, CASSANDRA JANE, management consultant; b. Thief River Falls, Minn., Dec. 1, 1948; d. Donald Vincent and Jonella Jean (Larson) D. BA in Social Work, Moorhead State U., 1970. Investigator Minn. Human Rights Dept., St. Paul, 1971-75, conciliator, supr., 1976-77; EEOC/affirmative action dir. First Bank System, Mpls., 1975-76; asst. mgr. affirmative action, mgr. corp. employment Gen. Mills., Inc., Mpls., 1977-81; v.p. employee relations Wallpaper To Go (subsidiary. Gen. Mills, Inc.), Hayward, Calif.; pvt. practice mgmt. cons. San Francisco, 1981—. Vol. San Francisco Symphony, 1987—; mem. No. Calif. Human Resources Council, 1981—. Mem. San Francisco C. of C.

DOMINA, JUDY MAE, retail executive; b. Broken Bow, Nebr., May 30, 1951; d. Harley Richard and Ollie Rosetta (Nielsen) Hanson; m. David A. Domina, June 5, 1970; children: Thurston Alan, Salesia. BS in Edn., U. Nebr., 1972. Tchr. Dist. 39, Ashton, Nebr., 1970-72, Lincoln (Nebr.) Pub. Schs., 1972-73, Hickman Hills (Mo.) Pub. Schs., 1973-74, Norfolk (Nebr.) Pub. Schs., 1974-75; dir. Big Bros./Big Sisters Inc., Norfolk, 1975-76; owner Flowers on the Mall, Norfolk, 1977—; mgr. office Domina Law Firm, Norfolk, 1982-85; owner Little Professor Book Ctr., Norfolk, 1986—; speaker, cons. OPT for the Future, Norfolk, 1986—. Mgr. Nixon for Mayor Campaign, Norfolk, 1982, Domina for Gov., Norfolk, 1986—; vice chmn. Madison County Dems., Norfolk, 1987; bd. dirs. Norfolk Library Bd. Mem. Sunset Plaza Merchant's Assn. (bd. dirs., v.p. 1978-82,), Nat. Assn. Female Execs., Norfolk C. of C. Lutheran. Home: 110 S 12th Norfolk NE 68701 Office: Edgar Dell & Co Inc Sunset Plaza Norfolk NE 68701

DOMINGUEZ, VIRGINIA ROSA, anthropologist; b. Havana, Cuba, Jan. 5, 1952; d. Jorge Jose and Lilia Rosa (de la Carrera) Dominguez. BA, Yale U., 1973, MPhil., 1975, PhD, 1979. Jr. fellow Harvard U. Soc. of Fellows, Cambridge, Mass., 1976-79; asst. prof. dept. anthropology Duke U., Durham, N.C., 1979-87, dir. undergrad. studies anthropology dept., 1983-84, 87—, assoc. prof., 1987—; cons. The Ford Found., N.Y.C., 1976-80, The Kettering Found., Dayton, 1977-78; vis. prof. sociology and anthropology Hebrew U., Jerusalem, 1984-85; lectr. in field. Author: From Neighbor to Stranger: The Dilemma of Caribbean Peoples in the U.S., 1975, White By Definition: Social Classification in Creole Louisiana, 1986; co-author: The Caribbean and Its Implications for the U.S., 1981; contbr. articles to profl. jours. Expert witness various subcoms. U.S. Congress, 1978-80; tutor Durham Literacy Council, 1987—. Fellow The Mellon Found., 1981-82; grantee Social Sci. Research Council, 1981-82; recipient Fulbright award, 1984-85. Mem. Inst. Cuban Studies (bd. dirs.), Am. Anthrop. Assn., Soc. for Cultural Anthropology, Israel Anthrop. Assn., Am. Ethnol. Soc., Latin Am. Studies Assn. (program com. 1980-82), AAUW (guest panelist 1986-88), Phi Beta Kappa. Democrat. Club: Elihu (New Haven). Office: Duke U Dept Anthropology Durham NC 27706

DOMINIAK, GERALDINE FLORENCE, accountant; b. Detroit, Sept. 28, 1934; d. Benjamin Vincent and Geraldine Esther (Davey) D. BS, U. Detroit, 1954, MBA, 1956; PhD, Mich. State U., 1966. CPA, Mich. Audit supr. Coopers & Lybrand, 1958-63; asst. prof. U. Detroit, 1965-68; assoc. prof. Mich. State U., 1968-69; prof. acctg. Tex. Christian U., Ft. Worth, 1969—, chmn. dept. acctg., 1974-83; Arthur Young prof. acctg. Fla. A&M U., 1977. Author: (with J. Edwards and T. Hedges) Interim Financial Reporting, 1972, (with J. Louderback) Managerial Accounting, 1975, Managerial Accounting, 3d edit., 1978, Managerial Accounting, 5th edit., 1988. Ford Found. fellow, 1964-65. Mem. Am. Inst. C.P.A.s, Am. Acctg. Assn., Assn. Govt. Accts., Nat. Assn. Accts., Am. Woman's Soc. C.P.A.'s, Tex. Soc. C.P.A.'s, AAUP, ACLU, Beta Alpha Psi, Beta Gamma Sigma. Roman Catholic. Home: 4401 Cardiff St Fort Worth TX 76133 Office: Tex Christian U Sch Bus Fort Worth TX 76129

DOMINICK, ANN RUBIN, financial analyst; b. New Orleans, Jan. 8, 1958; d. Harold and Nathalee (Bluhm) Rubin; m. Patrick Lawler Dominick, June 7, 1987. BA, Smith Coll., 1980; MBA, Vanderbilt U., 1982. CPA, La. Acct. Price Waterhouse, New Orleans, 1982-84; fin. analyst Mid. South Services, New Orleans, 1984-85, Freeport-McMoran, New Orleans, 1985-86; sr. financial analyst Lightnet, Washington, 1987—. Named one of Outstanding Young Women Am., 1985. Mem. Am. Inst. CPA's, Va. Soc. CPA's, Women in Telecommunications. Democrat. Jewish. Office: Lightnet 600 E Jefferson St Rockville MD 20852

DOMINIQUE, LISE MARIE, broadcasting executive, radio personality; b. Lake Forest, Ill., Mar. 5, 1956; d. Nazaire Louis and Eleanor (Steffin) D. B.S. in Radio and TV, U. Ill., 1978. Sales rep. Staffbuilders, San Jose, Calif., 1979-80; account exec. Marquez-Ramirez Advt., San Jose, 1980; morning disc jockey Sta.-KRVE, Los Gatos, Calif., 1981-83; evening air personality Sta.-KHTT, San Jose, 1983-85, news dir., 1983-85, news dir. Stas.-KSJO/KHTT, 1984-85; weekend morning air personality Sta. KEEN-AM, San Jose, 1985; relief news asst. Sta. KSAN-FM, Oakland, Calif., 1985; relief weather person Sta. KICU-TV, San Jose, 1985; traffic reporter for KCBS-San Francisco Traffic Central, Hayward, Calif., 1985-86; news dir., traffic reporter Sta. KEZR-FM, San Jose, 1986—; weekend news anchor Sta. KGO-AM, San Francisco, 1987. Mem. Radio-TV New Dirs. Assn. Home: 1279 Curtiss Ave San Jose CA 95125

DOMM, ALICE, lawyer; b. Phila., May 22, 1954; d. William Donald and Alice Frances (Day) D.; m. RIchard Coles Grubb, Sept. 26, 1987. B.A., Gettysburg Coll. (Pa.), 1976; J.D., Rutgers U., 1981. Bar: N.J. 1981, Pa. 1981. Atty., juvenile sect. chief Office of the Pub. Defender, New Brunswick, N.J., 1982—; assoc. prof. Glassboro Coll. (N.J.), 1980-81. Bd. dirs. Police Athletic League, New Brunswick, 1982-85; mem. Middlesex County Youth Services Commn., New Brunswick; mem. Gov.'s Council on Child Abuse and Neglect, Middlesex County, Gov.'s com. childrens Services Planning Juvenile Justice Subcom.; mem. Middlesex County Commn. Child Abuse and Missing Children, Criminal Justice Planning Com. Middlesex County. Mem. ABA, N.J. Bar Assn. (trustee, chairperson young lawyers com.), Middlesex County Bar Assn., Middlesex County Women's Bar Assn. (steering com., treas., gov.'s com. on Children Services Planning), Assn. Criminal Def. Lawyers N.J. Office: Office of the Public Defender 172 New St New Brunswick NJ 08903

DOMMEL, DARLENE HURST, writer; b. Charles City, Iowa, July 11, 1940; d. Roy and Elsie (Hopkes) Hurst; B.S. with high distinction, U. Minn., 1963, M.S., 1965, grad. exec. program Grad. Sch. Bus. Administrn., 1972; postgrad. So. Meth. U., 1976-77; m. James H. Dommel, Oct. 15, 1961; children—Diann, Christine, David. Pub. health nurse Combined Nursing Service, Mpls., 1963-64; contbr. articles on pottery to various collectors and antiques mags., 1967—; organizer, exhibitor of art pottery display touring fin. instns. in upper midwest, 1976—; lectr. and cons. health care, antiques, journalism; health care specialist Health Services Research Center, St. Louis Park Med. Center, 1978-79; instr. Augsburg Coll., 1979-81. Mem. Minn. Adv. Task Force on Epilepsy, 1981-83, State Council for Handicapped, 1982-84, Dept. Pub. Welfare Adv. Council on Mental Retardation and Phys. Disabilities, 1982-84; mem. profl. adv. com. Epilepsy Found. Minn., 1984—. Mem. Mpls. Inst. Arts. USPHS trainee, 1964-65; Sigma Theta Tau scholar, 1962-63; Martha Ripley scholar, 1961-62: U. Minn. Sch. Nursing Found. scholar, 1962. Mem. AAUW, U. Minn. Alumni Assn., Nat. Writers Club, Nat. League for Nursing (regional assembly constituent leagues for nursing. exec. com. 1985-87), Minn. League for Nursing (pres. 1983-85). Gethsemane Luth. Ch. Women, Am. Art Pottery Collectors Assn., Sigma Theta Tau, Delta Delta Delta. Lutheran. Home: 510 Westwood Dr N Golden Valley MN 55422

DONAGHY, DEBRA ANN, controller; b. Pasco, Wash., Feb. 9, 1957; d. Martha S. (Mantel) Rice; m. Michael James Donaghy, July 12, 1986. AA, Columbia Basin Coll., 1977; BA, Whitworth Coll., 1979; MS in Taxation, Gonzaga U., 1987. CPA. Staff acct. Christie, Lyle and Co., Spokane, Wash., 1978-81, Aspaas, Simmons and Lochmiller, Spokane, 1981-83; corp. controller Jones Wholesale Florist, Spokane, 1983-88; fin. acct. Ernest and Julio Gallo Winery, Modesto, Calif., 1988—. Mem. Am. Soc. Women Accts. (nat. sec. 1987—, pres. 1984-85), Am. Inst. CPA's, Wash. Soc. CPA's. Republican. Presbyterian. Lodge: Order of Eastern Star. Office: E & J Gallo Winery PO Box 1130 Modesto CA 95353

DONAGHY, MELANIE SUSAN, sales director; b. London, Mar. 26, 1960; came to U.S., 1981; Diplome A'Honneur Comite Interprofessionnell Des Vins De Bourgogne. Statistician Bank of Eng., London, 1976-78; with internat. loan adminstrn. 1st Nat. Bank Boston, London, 1978-80; supr. internat. loans Tex. Commerce Bancshares, London, 1980-81; cons. wine Martin Weiner Selections, Los Angeles, 1982-84; dir. nat. sales Marine Trading Cons., San Francisco, 1984-87, pres., 1987—. Mem. Soc. Wine Educators. Home: 99 Brodea San Rafael CA 94501

DONAHUE, LAURA KENT, state senator; b. Quincy, Ill., Apr. 22, 1949; d. Laurence S. and Mary Lou (McFarland) Kent; m. Michael A. Donahue, July 16, 1983. B.S., Stephens Coll., 1971. Mem. Ill. State Senate, Quincy, 1981—. Mem. Lincoln Club of Adams County, Ill. Fedn. Republican Women. Mem. P.E.O. Lodge: Altrusa. Office: 400 Maine St Quincy IL 62301 *

DONAHUE, LINDA WHEELER, academic administrator; b. Derby, Conn., Nov. 21, 1941; d. Wilson Chatfield and Beatrice (Smith) Wheeler; m. Raymond Maurice Farrell, July 17, 1965 (div. 1977); 1 child, Sarah Elizabeth; m. James John Donahue Jr., Dec. 30, 1977; 1 child, James John III. BS, Nasson Coll., 1963; MS, U. Bridgeport, 1967. Assoc. prof. Mattatuck Community Coll., Waterbury, Conn., 1976-80; prof. English and humanities Mattatuck Community Coll., Waterbury, 1980-84, dir. acad. div. arts and humanities, 1984—. Contbr. articles to profl. jours. Mem. Roosevelt Warm Springs (Ga.) Found., 1960—, Gazette Internat. Polio Newworking Inst., St. Louis, 1975—, Polio Survivors Found., Downey, Calif., 1977—, Conn. Coalition Citizens with Disabilities. Mem. Conn. Heads of English Depts., Nat. Council Tchrs. English, Nat. Assn. Female Execs., Assn. Exec. Educators, AAUW, Congress Conn. Community Colls. (pres. 1985—), Phi Theta Kappa. Congregationalist. Home: 294 Jeremy Swamp Rd Southbury CT 06488 Office: Mattatuck Community Coll Div Arts and Humanites 750 Chase Pkwy Waterbury CT 06708

DONAHUE, SUZANNE MARY, writer, film producer; b. N.Y.C., June 1, 1956; d. John Francis and Fumiko (Tanioka) D. AB in Psychology, U. So. Calif., 1977, MFA in Cinema Prodn., 1980, PhD in Communication, Cinema, 1984. Producer Learning Corp. Am., N.Y.C., 1981-82; with Columbia Pictures, Burbank, Calif., 1985; writer Univ. Microfilms Internat. Research Press, Ann Arbor, Mich., 1986; screenwriter Los Angeles, 1986—. Author: American Film Distribution: The Changing Marketplace, 1986.

DONALD, AIDA DIPACE, publishing executive; b. Bklyn., Apr. 19, 1930; d. Victor E. and Bessie (Catania) DiPace; m. David Herbert Donald; 1 child, Bruce Randall. AB cum laude, Barnard Coll., 1952; MA, Columbia U., 1953; PhD, U. Rochester, 1961. Instr. history dept. Columbia U., N.Y.C., 1955-56; editor Mass. Hist. Soc., Boston, 1960-64, Johns Hopkins U. Press, Balt., 1972-73; social scis. editor Harvard U. Press, Cambridge, Mass., 1973-79, exec. editor, 1979—. Editor: John F. Kennedy and the New Frontier, 1966, (with David Herbert Donald) Charles Frances Adams Diary, 2 vols., 1965. Mem. various coms. NEH. Columbia U. Dibblee fellow, 1952-53, U. Rochester fellow, 1953-55, 56-57, Oxford U. Fulbright fellow, 1959-60. Fellow AAUW; mem. Am. Hist. Assn., Orgn. Am. Historians, Polit. Sci. Assn. Am. Office: Harvard Univ Press 79 Garden St Cambridge MA 02138

DONALD, CLARA PHILLIPS, educator; b. Nashville; d. Ezra and Lucy (King) Phillips; m. Grady H. Donald, June 21, 1953; children—Grady H., Jr., Michael T., Angelyn Yvonne. B.S., Tenn. State U., 1956; M.A., Columbia U., 1974. Missionary advisor, tchr. religion, Jamaica, 1954; tchr., Holloway High Sch., Murfreesboro, Tenn.; 1954-55; tchr. Nashville Pub. Sch., 1959-66; tchr. Pub. Sch. Dist. 8, Bronx, N.Y., 1966—; exptl. tchr. Peabody Coll.; Head Start dir. summer programs, Bronx, 1966, 67; head tchr. Pre-Sch. program Pub. Sch. 140, Bronx, 1969-71; Chmn. Consumer Affairs Com., Bronx Planning Bd. 4, 1978; pres. missionary soc. mem. Deaconess bd. Greater Victory Bapt. Ch. Mem. United Fedn. Tchrs. (chmn. sch. chpt.), Baptist Ministers Wives Assn., Nat. Edn. Assn., Alpha Kappa Alpha. Avocations: Bible study; reading; traveling.

DONALD, DONNA KAY, home economist; b. Keokuk, Iowa, June 24, 1952; d. Leonard Seyb and Rosemary Blanche (Barr) Mohr; m. David Eudean Donald, Jan. 27, 1979; stepchildren: Michele, Tina, Angela. Student, Columbia (Mo.) Coll., 1970-71; BS, U. Mo., 1974; MA, Drake U., 1985. Home economist Iowa State U. Extension Service, Wayne and Appanoose Counties, 1974—; dir. county extension Iowa State U. Extension Service, Corydon, 1987—. Editor: The Reporter, 1986-88. Lay leader United Meth. Ch., Promise City, Iowa, 1982-84, chair pastor parish relations com., Seymour, Iowa, 1986-88. Mem. Am. Home Econs. Assn. (cert.), Iowa State U. Extension Assn. (pres. home econs. sect. 1982, Achievement award 1977), Nat. Assn. Extension Home Economists (editor, nat. bd. dirs. 1986-88, Achievement Communications awards 1975—). Republican. Club: P.E.O. (Seymour). Home: Rt 1 Promise City IA 52583

DONALDSON, DARCY MILLER, publishing executive; b. Glen Ridge, N.J., June 17, 1953; d. Paul Richardson and Susan (Alling) Miller; m. James R. Donaldson III, Feb. 6, 1988. Co-founder, assoc. pub. Mus. Mag., N.Y.C., 1979-83; pub. Crop Protection Chemicals Reference, N.Y.C., 1983-85; assoc. pub. Chief Exec. mag., N.Y.C., 1986-87, pub., 1987—. Mem. ASCAP, Advt. Women of N.Y. Democrat. Episcopalian. Office: Chief Exec Mag 205 Lexington Ave New York NY 10016

DONALDSON, E. LISBETH, education specialist, research associate; b. Nordegg, Alta., Can., Oct. 29, 1940; d. W. Wallace Donaldson and Gladys Irene (Metheral) Wilson; m. Allan Pyesmany, Aug. 19, 1960 (div.). Diploma in Physiotherapy, U. Alta., 1960; BA in History with honors, U. B.C., Vancouver, 1971; MA in Communications, Simon Fraser U., 1979; post-grad., U. Toronto, 1987—. Physiotherapist various locations in Can. and Los Angeles, 1960-77; sales, pub. relations rep. Douglas-McIntyre Pub. Co., Vancouver, 1977-79; instr. English Douglas Coll., New Westminster, Coquitlam and Maple Ridge, B.C., 1981-86; research fellow York U., Toronto, 1987—; research asst. Ont. Inst. Studies Edn., Toronto, 1987—; instr. Can. Studies King Edward Campus Vancouver Community Coll., 1980-84, communications B.C. Inst. Tech., Burnaby, 1980; curriculum devel., tchr. Work-And-Learn program Surrey (B.C.) Sch. Bd., 1982-84; coordinator Youth Tng. Option program Langley (B.C.) Sch. Dist. 35, 1985-86; coordinator Vol. Tng. Services for Expo '86, Vancouver, 1986; cons. Kanawa (Ont.) Internat. Mus., 1983-87. Author short stories, telescripts; playwright Ian and Irving, 1980; contbr. articles to mags. and newspapers. Skills mktg. trainer Fitness-Amateur Sport Can.; coordinator Cross-Can. Water Relay. Mem. Can. Assn. for Studies in Ednl. Adminstrn., Can. Recreational Canoeing Assn. (pres.). Club: Voice of Women. Home: 344 Cranbrooke Ave, Toronto, ON Canada M5M 1N3

DONALDSON, LORAINE, economics educator; b. Clearwater, Fla.; d. Lonnie Milton and Lois Lorene (Young) D. BSBA, U. Fla., 1960, MA, 1961; D in Bus. Adminstrn., Ind. U., 1965. Asst. prof. Ga. State U., Atlanta, 1964-66, assoc. prof., 1966-70, prof. econs., 1970—; cons. econs., 1964—. Author: Development Planning Ireland, 1966, Economic Development, 1984; contbr. numerous articles to profl. jours. Vol. Scottish Rite Hosp., Atlanta, 1983—, Sheperd Spinal Ctr., Atlanta, 1983—; mem. Pine Hills Civic Assn., Atlanta, 1972—. Mem. Am. Econ. Assn., Soc. Internat. Devel., Am. Assn. U. Profs. Democrat. Office: Ga State U Univ Pl Atlanta GA 30303

DONALDSON, MARCELINE MALICA, consulting company executive; b. New Orleans, Oct. 25, 1937; d. Maurice and Doris Gaynelle (Taylor) D.; grad. N.Y.C.; grad. Program for Mgmt. Devel., Harvard, m. Robert A. Bennett; children—Elise Karen Leon, Malica Aronowitz, Michelle, Jacqueline Aronowitz. Owner, Ma-Li-Kai, Inc., Mpls., 1965-69; stock broker Dain, Kalman & Quail, Inc., Mpls., 1969-71; sales and mktg. with Pillsbury Co., Mpls., 1972-73; owner, pres. Donaldson & Assocs., Inc., Wayzata, Minn., 1973-77; sales/mktg. IBM, after 1977; pres. cons. firm. Precinct chmn. Republican Party, 1974-79; mem. nat. fund raising com. Black Women's Community Devel. Found.; nat. bd. NOW, 1973-75; fund raiser legal def. fund NAACP. Mem. Acad. Mgmt., Needlework Guild Minn., Cin. Art Mus., Harvard Bus. Sch. Club Cin. (v.p.). Republican. Episcopalian. Home: 49 Hawthorne St Cambridge MA 02138

DONALDSON, MARY MURDOCK, business analyst, marketing professional; b. Bronxville, N.Y., Apr. 12, 1958; d. William George and Josephine (Murdock) D. BSCE, Bucknell U., 1980. With Burns and Roe, Oradell, N.J., 1980—, civil and mech. engr., 1980-84, strategic planner, bus. analyst, 1984-87, market planner, 1985-87; dir. corp. planning and devel. Vicon Recovery Systems, Butler, N.J., 1987—. Mem. Exploring Exec. Com., Bergen County, N.J., 1984—; v.p. Pond Ridge Condominium Assn., Park Ridge, N.J., 1985—. Recipient Tribute to Women and Industry award, 1986. Mem. Internat. Soc. for Planning and Strategic Mgmt., NSPE, TWIN Mgmt. Forum. Office: Vicon Recovery Systems 10 Park Place Butler NJ 07405

DONATH, THERESE (PHYLLIS THERESE FREEMAN), artist, writer; b. Hammond, Ind., Dec. 14, 1928; d. Arthur Max and Lillian Louise (Donath) Helfer; children from previous marriage: Mark, Alex, Kim; m. Jefferson Richardson Scoville, 1986; step-children: Suzanne, Michelle, Thomas; student Monticello Coll., 1946-47; B.F.A., St. Joseph's Coll., 1975; additional study Oxbow Summer Sch. Painting, Immaculate Heart Coll., Hollywood, Calif., Penland, N.C., Haystack, Maine.Interviewer, producer Viewpoint, Sta. WLNR-FM, Lansing, Ill., 1963-64; reporter, columnist N.W. Ind. Sentinel, 1965; freelance writer Monterey Peninsula Herald, 1981-85; contbg. author Monterey Life mag. 1981-84; asst. dir. Michael Karolyi Meml. Found., Vence, France, 1979; one-woman shows include: Ill. Inst. Tech., Chgo., 1971; group shows include: Palos Verdes (Calif.) Mus., 1974, Los Angeles Inst. Contemporary Art, 1978, Mus. Contemporary Art, Chgo., 1975, Calif. State U., Fullerton, 1973, No. Ill. U., DeKalb, 1971, Bellevue (Wash.) Mus. Art, 1986-87; represented in permanent collections including Kennedy Gallery, N.Y.C., also pvt. collections; creative cons. Aslan Tours and Travel, 1983-85; instr., lectr. Penland, N.C., 1970, Haystack Mountain Sch., Deer Isle, Maine, 1974, Sheffield Poly., Eng., 1978. Bd. dirs., sec. Mental Health Soc. Greater Chgo., 1963-64; exec. dir. Lansing (Ill.) Mental Health Soc., 1963-64. Recipient awards No. Ind. Art Mus., 1966, 70, 71, 73; grantee Ragdale Found., Lake Forest, Ill., 1982. Represented in The Mirror Book, 1978; author: Before I Die; contbr. articles to profl. jours., newspapers; illustrator: Run Computer Run, 1983. Office: Mixed Media Rt 3 Box 74 Vashon Island WA 98070

DONATINI, LYNN MARIE, marketing professional; b. Canton, Ohio, Aug. 26, 1955; d. Dino and Pauline Jane (Capuano) D. BS, Bowling Green (Ohio) State U., 1981; MS in Journalism, Ohio U., 1982. Purchasing agt. Consumer Pub. Co., Inc., Canton, 1973-76; sales rep. Copeco, Inc., Canton, 1976-77; copywriter Consumer Direct, Inc., Canton, 1982-84, comml. producer, 1984—, mktg. v.p., 1987—. Mem. Direct Mail Mktg. Assn. (ECHO award 1985), Electronic Mktg. and Media Assn. Democrat. Pentacostal. Office: Consumer Direct Inc 1375 Raff Rd SW Canton OH 44750

DONATO, LORETTA ANN, advertising executive; b. Scotch Plains, N.J., Aug. 7, 1947; d. Albert Samuel and Frances Janet (Dello-Russo) D.; m. Stewart W. Lunn, Jan. 24, 1987. BA, Marquette U., 1969. Dir. continuity Sta. WPAT, Patterson, N.J., 1969-72; asst. dir. legal clearance Grey Advt., Inc., N.Y.C., 1972-80, dir. legal clearance, 1980-82, v.p., 1982—. Vol., Am. Mus. Natural History, N.Y.C., 1982—, N.Y. Philharm. Orch., 1984—, boarder baby program St. Luke's-Roosevelt Hosp., 1987—; mem. ad hoc com. Marquette U., 1986—. Office: Grey Advt Inc 777 3d Ave New York NY 10017

DONEGAN, JANE BAUER, history educator, author; b. Bklyn., Sept. 24, 1933; d. Henry William and Mary E. (Barlow) Bauer; m. Denis I. Donegan, Jan. 16, 1956 (div.); children—Stuart Barlow, Jennifer Barlow; m. Robert A. Huff, Mar. 6, 1981. B.A., Syracuse U., 1954, M.A., 1959, Ph.D., 1972. Grad. asst. Syracuse U., Maxwell Sch., 1955; tchr., chair Fabius (N.Y.) Central Sch., 1955-59, 60-62; tchr. Deposit (N.Y.) Central Sch., 1959-60; prof. history, coordinator women's studies Onondaga Community Coll., Syracuse, N.Y., 1962—; reviewer NEH pub. programs, Washington, 1979-82; panelist NEH Edn. Programs, Washington, 1980, NEH Profl. Nominating, Washington, 1980; mem. SUNY Commn. on Hon. Degrees, Albany, 1983-86. Author: Women and Men Midwives, 1978; Hydropathic Highway to Happiness, 1986. Contbr. articles to profl. jours. NEH research fellow, Washington, 1980-81; NEH grantee, Washington, summer 1977; faculty research fellow SUNY Research Found., Albany, 1978; recipient trustees' recognition award Onondaga Community Coll., 1980; named Unsung Heroine of 1986 NOW Cen. N.Y. Mem. Orgn. Am. Historians, Am. Assn. for History of Medicine, Soc. for Social History of Medicine, Am. Hist. Soc., Upstate N.Y. Women's History Conf. Office: Onondaga Community Coll Dept Social Scis Syracuse NY 13215

DONELSON, ANGIE FIELDS CANTRELL MERRITT, real estate executive; b. Hermitage, Tenn., Dec. 2, 1914; d. Dempsey Weaver and Nora (Johnson) Cantrell; student public and pvt. schs., Hermitage, Nashville; m. Gilbert Stroud Merritt, Dec. 15, 1934 (dec.); 1 son, Gilbert Stroud; m. 2d, John Donelson, Jr., VII, Apr. 23, 1966 (dec.); step-children—John, Agnes Donelson Williams (dec.), William Stockley. Pres., So. Woodenware Co., Nashville, 1955-61, So. Properties, Co., Inc., Hermitage, 1961—. Chmn. comml. flower exhibits Tenn. State Fair, 1951; committeewoman and v.p. Davidson County Agrl. Soil and Conservation Community Com., 1959-60; bd. mem. Nashville Symphony Assn., 1961-64, regional council mem., 1977-79; chmn. bd. Nashville Presbyn. Neighborhood Settlement House; founding bd. mem. Davidson County Cancer Soc.; bd. mem. Nashville Vis. Nurse Service; dist. chmn., speakers bur. Am. Red Cross. Proclaimed First Lady Donelson-Hermitage Community, 1986. Mem. Vanderbilt U. Aid, Peabody Coll. Aid, Tenn. Hist. Soc., Descs. of Ft. Nashboro Pioneers (bd. dirs. 1984-87), English Speaking Union. Presbyterian. Clubs: Ladies Hermitage Assn. (dir. 1949—), DAR, (chpt. regent 1941), Lebanon Rd. Garden Club (pres. 1947), Horticulture Soc. Davidson County (v.p. 1949). Clubs: Ravenwood Country, Centennial, Belle Meade. Contbr. to books and mags. on history of Tenn. Home: Stone Hall Stones River Rd Hermitage TN 37076 Office: Lebanon Rd Hermitage TN 37076

DONHAM, CINDY LOU, marketing and sales professional; b. Cape Girardeau, Mo., Feb. 19, 1957; d. William Lewis and Arbutus (Wright) D. BS in Bus., Miami U., Oxford, Ohio, 1979. Sr. acctg. clk. Standard Brands, Inc., San Francisco, 1978-79; fin. planner Pacific Mut. Life Ins. Co., San Francisco, 1980-81; mgr. Bank One of Milford, Ohio, 1981-84, Fifth Third Bank, Cin., 1984-86; mgr. mktg. CBS Personnel, Cin., 1986—. Clermont County liaison coordinator Cin. Regatta, 1986; chairperson publicity com. March of Dimes Northeast area Jail n'Bail, Cin., 1987. Mem. Nat. Assn. Female Execs., Greater Cin. C. of C. (Cin. inst. small enterprise program com. 1982-84), Clermont County C. of C. (transp. com. 1984-86). Home: 8439 Island Pines Pl Maineville OH 45039

DONISON, DEBORAH ROSE, psychologist; b. Windsor, Ontario, Can., Nov. 19, 1954; d. Peter Anthony and Theresa Beatrice (Barsona) D. BA, U. Windsor, 1976; MA summa cum laude, Ea. Ill. U., 1978; PhD summa cum laude, U. Detroit, 1984. Masters level psychologist community mental health services St. Mary's Gen. Hosp., Timmins, Ont., 1979-81; intern dept. child psychiatry Mt. Carmel Mercy Hosp., Detroit, 1982-83; intern dept. child psychology Henry Ford Hosp., Detroit, 1983-85, staff clin. psychologist, 1985—, clin. supr., 1986—. Mem. Am. Psychol. Assn., Mich. Psychol. Assn., Mich. Soc. for Psychoanalytic Psychology. Roman Catholic. Home: 18091 Muirland Detroit MI 48221

DONISTHORPE, CHRISTINE ANN, state senator; b. Christina, Mont., May 31, 1932; d. Lambert A. and Ludmilla (Hruska) Benes; m. Oscar Lloyd Donisthorpe, 1951; children—Paul, Karen, Bruce, Brian. Student U. Mont., 1951-53, San Juan Coll., N.Mex. Real Estate Sch., 1958-70. Pres. Bd. of Edn., Bloomfield, N.Mex., 1975-81; mem. N.Mex. State Senate, 1979—, mem. edn. com., 1979, fin. com., 1980, edn. study com., 1981; mem. Bd. Realtors San Juan County, 1978-81. Adv. bd. Salvation Army, 1970-75; active C. of C. Recipient U.S. Soil and Water Conservation award, 1967; Hon. State Future Farmers Adv. award, 1975. Mem. N.Mex. Hay Growers Assn. Republican. Methodist. Address: PO Box 746 Bloomfield NM 87413 *

DONLEY, BARBARA ELLEN, nurse anesthetist; b. Burlington, Wis., Sept. 1, 1932; d. Arthur W. and Lillian C. (Luhn) Juranek; R.N., St. Francis Sch. Nursing, 1953; cert. registered nurse anesthetist St. Francis Sch. Anesthesia, 1954; B.A., Redlands U., 1976; M.Sci. Health Care Mgmt., Calif. State U., Los Angeles, 1980; m. Clifford A. Donley, June 15, 1963; children—Timothy A., Jennifer A. Staff nurse anesthetist Misericordia Hosp., Milw., 1954-62, Kaiser Permanente, Los Angeles, 1962-65, Bellflower, Calif., 1965-70, chief nurse anesthetist, 1970-80, dept. adminstr., 1980-88, reitred; clin. supr., didactic lectr. Kaiser Permanente Sch. Anesthesia, 1972-75; instr. CPR, 1975-77. Tchr. religious edn. jr. high level St. Cyprian Catholic Ch., Long Beach, Calif., 1977-84. Mem. Am. Assn. Nurse Anesthetists, Calif. Assn. Nurse Anesthetists, Greater Los Angeles Heart Assn. Republican. Roman Catholic.

DONLEY, BETTIE LOUX, editor, writer; b. Drexel Hill, Pa., Nov. 5, 1931; d. Frank Turner and Elizabeth Ida (Kauffman) Loux; B.S., Pa. State U., 1953. Prodn. coordinator, editorial research Nat. Geog. Soc., Washington, 1959-69; editor World Traveler mag., dir. publs. Alexander Graham Bell Assn. for Deaf, Washington, 1969-76; free-lance book editor/writer, 1976-87; mng. editor The Magnificent Foragers, A Zoo for All Seasons (Smithsonian Books), Aural Habilitation, Mainstreaming (A. G. Bell), Fundamentals of Aquatic Toxicology, Health Care for Women Internat., Particulate Sci. and Tech., 1983-84; editor Cheshire Homes News, 1985-87; dir. publs. Gerontol. Soc. Am., Washington, 1987—; contbr. Nat. Geog. children's atlases. Mem. forum White House Conf. Children, 1970. Recipient award for picture story Ednl. Press Assn. Am., 1970, award for layout, 1971, award for one-theme issue, 1973, Eleanor Fishburn award for outstanding contbn. to internat. understanding among readers, 1971. Mem. Women in Communications, Ednl. Press Assn. Am., Council Biology Editors, Washington Book Pubs., Washington Ind. Writers, Smithsonian Assos., Alpha Gamma Delta. Democrat. Episcopalian. Editor Grace Ch. Messenger, 1971—. Home: 1217 Woodside Pkwy Silver Spring MD 20910

DONNALLY, PATRICIA BRODERICK, fashion editor; b. Cheverly, Md., Mar. 11, 1955; d. James Duane and Olga Frances (Duenas) Broderick; m. Robert Andrew Donnally, Dec. 30, 1977. B.S., U. Md., 1977. Fashion editor The Washington Times (D.C.), 1983-85, The San Francisco Chronicle, 1985—. Recipient Atrium award, 1984, 87, Lulu award, 1985, 87. Mem. San Francisco Fashion Group, Inc. Avocation: travel. Home: 1 Lansdale San Francisco CA 94127-1608 Office: The San Francisco Chronicle 901 Mission St San Francisco CA 94103

DONNELLY, BARBARA SCHETTLER, medical technologist; b. Sweetwater, Tenn., Dec. 2, 1933; d. Clarence G. and Irene Elizabeth (Brown) Schettler; A.A., Tenn. Wesleyan Coll., 1952; B.S., U. Tenn., 1954; cert. med. tech., Erlanger Hosp. Sch. Med. Tech., 1954; postgrad. So. Meth. U., 1980-81; children—Linda Ann, Richard Michael. Med. technologist Erlanger Hosp., Chattanooga, 1953-57, St. Luke's Episcopal Hosp., Tex. Med. Center, Houston, 1957-58, 1962; engrng. research and devel. SCI Systems Inc., Huntsville, Ala., 1974-76; cons. hematology systems Abbott Labs., Dallas, 1976-77, hematology specialist, Dallas, Irving, Tex., 1977-81, tech. specialist microbiology systems, Irving, 1981-83, coordinator tech. service clin. chemistry systems, 1983-84, coordinator customer tng. clin. chemistry systems, 1984-87, supr. clin. chemistry tech. services, 1987-88, clin. chemistry customer support ctr., 1988—. Mem. Am. Soc. Clin. Pathologists (cert. med. technologist), Am. Soc. Microbiology, Nat. Assn. Female Execs., U. Tenn. Alumni Assn., Chi Omega. Contbr. articles on cytology to profl. jours. Republican. Methodist. Home: 204 Greenbriar Ln Bedford TX 76021 Office: 1921 Hurd St Irving TX 75061

DONNELLY, MARY ELIZABETH, mining company executive; b. Jersey City, July 15, 1951; d. John William and Rita Constance (Dillon) Sweeney; m. Raymond O'Brien II, Dec. 23, 1974 (div. Mar. 1981); children: Raymond III, Andrew Dillon; m. James Dennis Donnelly, May 21, 1983; children: Shannon Elizabeth, Allison James. BA, Trinity Coll., 1973. Leg. asst. Gulf Oil Co., Washington, 1973-74; staff asst. Office Chief Justice U.S. Supreme Ct., Washington, 1974-75; asst. dir., asst. editor Supreme Ct. Historical Soc., Washington, 1975-79; asst. to v.p. nat. affairs Anheuser Busch Co., Washington, 1979-81; analyst leg. Newmont Mining Corp., Washington, 1981-84, asst. dir. gov. relations, 1984-86, dir. gov. relations, 1987—; bd. trustee scholarship Trinity Coll., Washington 1969-73. Chmn. Internat. Eye Found. Annual Eye Ball, Washington 1987. Mem. Women Mining (v.p. 1987—), Women Gov. Relations (bd. dirs., sec. 1984-86), Women Energy and Environ. Club: Columbia Country. Home: 11012 Waycroft Way North Bethesda MD 20852 Office: Newmont Mining Corp 1233 20th St NW Washington DC 20036

DONNELLY, ROSE ANN, educator; b. Bklyn., Feb. 21, 1925; d. James John and Madeline Lillian (La Tuga) Garone; m. Albert Joseph Donnelly, July 16, 1955. B.A., Barnard Coll., 1948; M.A., Columbia U., 1949, Ed.D., 1957. Tchr., Bklyn. Public Schs., 1950-56, tchr. in charge, 1956-57, asst. prin., 1958-67, prin., 1967-85, exec. dir. funded and spl. programs, 1985—. Served with WAC, 1945-46. Mem. Assn. Supervision and Curriculum Devel., Edn. Assn. of N.Y.C. Educators, Nat. Council Adminstrv. Women in Edn., Council Suprs. and Adminstrs. (dist. 21 treas.), N.Y.C. Assn. Supervision and Curriculum Devel., Bklyn. Reading Council, Internat. Reading Council, Assn. Compensatory Educators. Club: Barnard Coll. (L.I.). Contbr. articles to profl. jours. Home: 149 Beach 141 St Belle Harbor NY 11694 Office: 345 Van Sicklen St Brooklyn NY 11223

DONNER, ALICE WILKINSON, social worker; b. Phila., July 5, 1922; d. William MacIlhenny and Mary (Yost) Wilkinson; B.S. in Edn., U. Pa., 1944; M.A., Villanova (Pa.) U., 1975; M.S.W., Temple U., Phila., 1977; m. William T. Donner, Apr. 12, 1946; children—William W., Marda Elisa, Mary Alice, Margot Ramona. Diplomate Clin.Social Work. Elementary sch. tchr., 1944-50; renal social worker Abington (Pa.) Meml. Hosp., 1977—. Bd. dirs. Jenkintown Day Nursery, 1966-75, treas., 1969-71, v.p., 1972-74; bd. dirs. Montgomery County Homemaker Home Health Aide, 1965-74, v.p., 1970-72. Mem. Nat. Assn. Social Workers, Acad. Cert. Social Workers, Council Nephrology Social Workers. Home: 314 Wellington Terr Jenkintown PA 19046 Office: Abington Meml Hosp Abington PA 19001

DONNER, JUDITH FRIZZELL, editor, writer, marketing professional; b. Anaheim, Calif., Oct. 22, 1958; d. Norman Richard and Thelma Virginia (Josephson) Frizzell; m. Phillip Louis Donner, Aug. 12, 1984. Grad. high sch., 1976. Editor, mktg. dir. Arnett Press, Anaheim, 1986—. Mem. Nat. League of Am. Pen Women. Democrat. Office: Arnett Press PO Box 4179 Anaheim CA 92803

DONOGHUE, ELIZABETH MARION MACMAHON (MRS. FLORENCE JOSEPH DONOGHUE), emerita museum curator; b. Castleisland, Kerry, Ireland, Nov. 9, 1896 (parents Am. citizens); d. James and Johanna Mary (Brosnan) MacMahon; B.A., Calvin Coolidge Coll., 1955, M.A., 1956; m. Florence Joseph Donoghue, Apr. 17, 1963 (dec. July 1970). Acct., Boston Wool Trade, 1914-33; tchr. Everett (Mass.) High Sch., 1934-63; trustee Wenham (Mass.) Hist. Assn. and Mus., Inc., 1956—, curator dolls, 1960-82. Driver, Red Cross Motor Corps, Boston, 1939-41, Civilian Def. Motor Corps, Everett, 1941-43. Mem. Antique Toy Collectors Am., Doll Club Gt. Britain, Doll Collectors Am., Emerald Isle, L.I., Ginny doll clubs, League Cath. Women, Mus. Fine Arts Boston, Nat. Ret. Tchrs. Assn., United Fedn. Doll Clubs, Am. Irish Hist. Soc. (life), Christ Child Soc. (life), Soc. Preservation N.E. Antiquities (life), Yesteryears Doll Mus. (life), Eire Soc. Boston (life, editor Bull. 1954-64), Worcester Art Mus., Boston U. Alumni Assn. Contbr. articles to profl. jours. Home: 86 Bradford St Everett MA 02149

DONOGHUE, MILDRED RANSDORF, educator; b. Cleve.; d. James and Caroline (Sychra) Ransdorf; m. Charles K. Donoghue (dec. 1982); children: Kathleen, James. Ed.D., UCLA, 1962; J.D., Western State U., 1979. Asst. prof. edn. Calif. State U.-Fullerton, 1962-66, assoc. prof., 1966-71, prof., 1971—. Author: Foreign Languages and the Schools, 1967, Foreign Languages and the Elementary School Child, 1968, The Child and the English Language Arts, 1971, 75, 79, 85; co-author: Second Languages in Primary Education, 1979; Contbr. articles to profl. jours., Ency. of Edn. Mem. Nat. Council Tchrs. English, Am. Dialect Soc., Am. Ednl. Research Assn., AAUP, Nat. Soc. for Study of Edn., Am. Assn. Tchrs. Spanish and Portuguese, Internat. Reading Assn., Nat. Assn. Edn. Young Children, Orange County Med. Assn. Women's Aux., Authors Guild, Phi Beta Kappa, Phi Kappa Phi, Pi Lambda Theta. Office: Calif State U Dept Elem Edn Fullerton CA 92634

DONOHO, BETTY SUE, electric company executive; b. Hendersonville, N.C., Oct. 12, 1935; d. Daniel Wade and Leila (Allison) Brittain; m. Tom J. Donoho, Apr. 6, 1959; children: Daniel, Susan E. Student, U. N.C., 1965-86. V.p., dir. fin. dept. Asheville Electric Co. Inc., N.C., 1962—; owner, mgr. Warehouse Beauty Ctr., Asheville, 1981—. Chmn. pub. relations com. A.C. Reynolds Mid. Sch., Asheville, PTA, 1978, pres., 1979, sec. adv. bd., 1980-81; active Jerry Silverman Scholarship Com., 1986-87. Mem. Nat. Assn. Female Execs., Sub-Contractors Am. Democrat. Baptist. Home: 124 Gashes Creek Rd Asheville NC 28805 Office: Asheville Electric Co Inc 950 Fairview Rd Asheville NC 28813

DONOHUE, EDITH M., continuing education coordinator, consultant; b. Balt., Nov. 10, 1938; d. Edward Anthony and Beatrice (Jones) McParland; m. Salvatore R. Donohue, Aug. 23, 1960; children: Kathleen, Deborah. BA, Coll. Notre Dame, Balt., 1960; MS, Johns Hopkins U., 1981, CASE, 1985. Dir. pub. relations Coll. Notre Dame, Balt., 1970-71, asst. dir. continuing edn., 1978-81, dir. continuing edn., 1981-86; coordinator program bus. and industry Catonsville Community Coll., Baltimore County, Md., 1986-88; mgr. tng. and devel. Sheppard Pratt Hosp., Balt., 1988—. Co-editor, contbg. author career devel. workshop manual, 1985. Pres. Cathedral Sch. Parents Assn., 1972-74; asst. treas., treas. Md. Gen. Hosp. Aux., 1975-78; dir. Homeland Assn., 1978-81; regional rep., leader Girl Scouts Cen. Md., 1975-76; dir. sect. Exec. Women's Network, Balt., 1983-85; adv. bd. Mayor's Com. on Aging, 1981-86; dir. Md. Assn. Higher Edn., 1985—. Recipient Mayor's Citation, City of Balt. Council, 1985. Mem. Am. Assn. Tng. and Devel (bd. dirs.), Am. Assn. Counseling and Devel., AAUW (dir., v.p. 1980-83), Chi Sigma Iota, Phi Delta Kappa. Democrat. Roman Catholic. Lodge: Order Sons of Italy in Am. Avocations: tennis, theatre, aerobics, handcrafts, symphony, opera. Home: 5420 Springlake Way Baltimore MD 21212 Office: Sheppard Pratt Hosp 6501 N Charles St Baltimore MD 21285

DONOHUE, HELEN SHAY, speech pathologist, audiologist; b. Ansonia, Conn., Jan. 26; d. Thomas Francis and Margaret (Buckley) Shay; B.S., So. Conn. State Coll., 1948; M.A., Columbia U., 1958; profl. diploma U. Bridgeport, 1961; m. Thomas C. Donahue, Dec. 7, 1943 (dec. Oct. 1984). Speech and hearing therapist New Haven Public Schs., 1958-68; pvt. practice speech pathology, audiology, Hamden, Conn. and Boca Raton, Fla., 1969—; cons. in field. Bd. dirs. Riviera Civic Assn., 1975. Mem. Am. Speech and Hearing Assn. (cert. clin. competence), AAAS, AAUW, Pi Lambda Theta. Home: 1414 Whitney Ave D 1 Hamden CT 06517

DONOVAN, CAROL ANN, state agency administrator; b. Tampa, Fla., Feb. 19, 1947; d. Leonard Augusta and Jane Ruth (Lyman) Swinney; m. Ralph H. Donovan Jr., Feb. 6, 1981 (div.). BA, U. South Fla., 1971. Tchr. Pinellas County Sch. Bd., St. Petersburg, Fla., 1971-73; bookkeeper N.Am. Ins. Agy., St. Petersburg, 1974-75; pub. assistance eligibility specialist Dept. Health and Rehab. Services, State of Fla., St. Petersburg, 1975-82, supr., 1982-83, state program supr., 1983—; tax cons. H&R Block, St. Petersburg, 1974-76, 81-83. Mem. Rep. Exec. Com., St. Petersburg, 1973-79. Mem. Nat. Welfare Fraud Assn., Am. Pub. Welfare Assn., United Council Welfare Fraud, Nat. Assn. Female Execs. Episcopalian. Home: Rt 2 Box 383A

Tallahassee FL 32301 Office: State of Fla Dept Health and Rehab Services 1317 Winewood Blvd Tallahassee FL 32301

DONOVAN, DEBORAH CAROLYN, chemical company executive; b. Binghamton, N.Y., Jan. 10, 1951; d. Robert Frances and M. Carolyn (Hamilton) D.; 1 child, Rachael Donovan Wander. BA, SUNY, Buffalo; M of Pub. Adminstrn. in Fin. Mgmt., Temple U., 1975; JD, U. Del., 1978. Bar: Del., Tenn. Ct. rep. Phila. Ct. Common Pleas, 1972-74; asst. supt. Newark (Del.) Sch. Dist., 1974; dist. rep. Congressman Pierre S. du Pont, Washington, 1974-77; spl. asst. to Del. Gov. du Pont Dover, 1977; exec. dir. Ingergovtl. Task Force, Wilmington, Del., 1977-79; dep. atty. gen. Office Atty. Gen., Wilmington, 1979; atty., area mgr., dir. state govt. affairs The Du Pont Co., Wilmington and Nashville, 1979—; instr. U. Del., Newark, 1979-80; sec.-treas. Fla. Chem. Industry Council, Tallahassee, Tenn. Bus. Roundtable, Nashville; adj. prof. Massey Graduate Sch. Bus. Bd. dirs. Tenn. Assn. Planned Parenthood, Nashville Planned Parenthood; sec. bd. dirs. YMCA of Del., 1979-83. Mem. Tenn. Bar Assn., Nashville Bar Assn., Tenn. chpt. Am. Corp. Counsel Assn., Del. Bar Assn., Del. Assn. Pub. Adminstrn. (pres. 1979-80). Unitarian-Universalist. Home: 3733 Estes Rd Nashville TN 37215 Office: The Du Pont Co 501 Union Bldg Suite 401 Nashville TN 37219

DONOVAN, DONNA MARIE, marketing and advertising professional; b. Phila., Oct. 6, 1945; d. Donald Sager and Rita Eleanor (Campbell) D.; m. Garner L. Lewis II, Aug. 19, 1967 (div. 1971); 1 child, Maura Lynn; m. Kenneth R. Thornley, Oct. 26, 1984. BA in Bus. Adminstrn., Dunbarton Coll., 1967; postgrad., Western New Eng. Coll., 1967. Communications specialist Gerber Sci. Instrument Co., South Windsor, Conn., 1972-74; pub. info. officer Commn. on Status of Women, Hartford, Conn., 1974; mgr. communications TMI Systems Corp., Cambridge, Mass., 1974-76; mgr. bus. devel. Arrowstreet, Inc., Cambridge, 1976-77; dir. sales promotions Black & Webster, Inc., Waltham, Mass., 1977-79; dir. mktg. communicatins Tool div. Litton Industries, New Britain, Conn., 1979-80; account exec. The Graphic Ctr., Bloomfield, Conn., 1980-81; sr. copywriter Adams, Rickard and Mason Advt., Glastonbury, Conn., 1981-82; pres. Really Good Copy Co., West Hartford, Conn., 1982—. Copywriter, creative dir. numerous ads, brochures, radio spots, others. Justice of the Peace, Windsor, Conn., 1972-74; chairperson Town Day Celebration Weekend, Arlington, Mass., 1978; vol. writer Oak Hill Sch. for Blind, Hartford, 1986-87. Mem. Bus. and Profl. Advt. Assn. (v.p., bd. dirs. 1986), Women in Communication. Clubs: Conn. Art Dir.'s (v.p., bd. dirs. 1982-87), Hartford Advt., Fairfield County Ad. Home and Office: Really Good Copy Co 76 Whiting Ln West Hartford CT 06119

DONOVAN, GERTRUDE ANN, obstetrician-gynecologist; b. St. John's, Nfld., Canada, Mar. 6, 1953; d. Gerald Justin and Mary Martha (Roche) Donovan; Joseph Gordon Coyle, July 6, 1984. BMSc, Meml. U. Nfld., St. John's, 1975, MD, 1977. Intern, then resident in ob-gyn McMaster U., Hamilton, Ont., Canada, 1977-82; locum tenens in ob-gyn United Arab Emirates and Ontario, Canada, 1982-83; cons. ob-gyn King Faisal Hosp., Khamis Mushayt and Riyadh, Saudi Arabia, 1983-84; cons. ob-gyn Hahira, Ga., 1985-86, Northborough, Mass., 1986—. Fellow Royal Coll. Surgeons. Office: 112 Main St Northborough MA 01532

DONOVAN, LOWAVA DENISE, data processing director; b. Galesburg, Ill., Mar. 27, 1958; d. Richard Eugene and Lowava Jeanine (Squire) Corbin; m. James Dean Rutledge, June 17, 1977 (div. May 1981); 1 child, Tiffany Michelle; m. Neal Edwin Donovan, July 9, 1983. Computer operator cert., Carl Sandburg Coll., 1977, student, 1976-86; student, IBM Edn., Chgo., 1979-87. Keypunch operator Fin. Industry Systems, Galesburg, Ill., 1977-79; computer operator Solution Assocs., Peoria, Ill., 1979-80; programmer, data processing mgr. May Co., Galesburg, 1980-81; programmer Kirkendall Gen. Offices, Galesburg, 1981-82; programmer, data processing mgr. Munson Transp., Monmouth, Ill., 1982-85, programmer/analyst, dir. data processing, 1985-87, dir. mgmt. info. systems, 1987—; bd. dirs. Windwood Water Systems, Galesburg. Bd. dirs. Windwood Water Systems, Galesburg, 1986-87. Mem. Nat. Assn. Female Execs. Baptist. Office: Munson Transp PO Box 428 Monmouth IL 61462-0428

DONOVAN, MARGARET, student services administrator; b. Yankton, S.D., Jan. 1, 1950; d. Robert Bauerle and Norma Louise (Miller) D. BA in Psychology, Loretto Heights Coll., Denver, 1973; MS in Counseling and Personnel, Drake U., 1986. Cert. substance abuse counselor II, Iowa. Service worker II div. youth services State of Colo., Denver; probation officer Woodbury County Juvenile Ct., Sioux City, Iowa; mental health, substance abuse advocate Woodbury County Ct., Sioux City; dir. chem. dependency treatment ctr. Winnebago Indian Reservation; residential dir. Intersect. United Advanced Planning Ctr., Des Moines; now pvt. practice Des Moines. Mem. edn. com. Interfaith Resources, Sioux City, 1982-83. Mem. Nat. Rehab. Counseling Assn., Nat. Rehab. Assn., Iowa Mental Health Assn., Substance Abuse Assn. of Iowa, Nat. Assn. Student Personnel Adminstrs., Nat. Assn. Alcoholism and Drug Abuse Counselors, Women's Cultural Collective. Home and Office: PO Box 12076 Des Moines IA 50321

DONOVAN, MARIE PHILLIPS, television executive; b. Detroit; m. Tom Donovan; children: Kathleen Marie, Kevin Thomas. Student, Wayne U. Profl. actress Actors Equity Assn., N.Y.C., AFTRA, N.Y.C.; bus. mgr. Dirs. Service Inc., N.Y.C., exec. v.p., treas. Mem. Nat. Assn. Female Execs. Clubs: Cavendish, Am. Contract Bridge League (life master).

DONOVAN, MARTHA JANE, educator, consultant; b. Boston, May 23, 1946; d. Daniel Michael and Martha Alice (Webber) Sullivan; m. James Bernard Donovan Jr., June 29, 1969; children: Matthew, Jason, Daniel. BS in Edn., Boston U., 1968. Cert. tchr., Mass. Tchr. and coach Franklin (Mass.) Pub. Schs., 1968-74; tchr. and soccer coach Norfolk (Mass.) Pub. Schs., 1974-75; health edn. cons. Norwood Hosp. Comprehensive Alcoholism Program-Southwood Community Hosp., Norfolk, Mass., 1986—; research asst. Consortium for Primary Prevention fo Substance Abuse, Norfolk, 1986—; cons. Am. Cancer Soc. Pub. Edn. Com. Norwood Hosp.; asst. coordinator Consortium for the Primary Prevention of Substance Abuse Southwood Hosp., Norfolk, 1986—. Pres. PTA, Norfolk, 1982-84; chmn. Drug Alcohol Awareness Com., Norfolk, 1983-85; active Norfold Sch. Com., 1984—, sec. 1984-86, King Philip Regional Sch. Com., Wrentham, Mass., 1987—; coach youth soccer league, 1979—; den leader Cub Scouts of Am., Norfolk. Recipient Namesake of Spirit award Franklin High Sch., 1974-77. Mem. Mass. Assn. Sch. Coms. Republican. Episcopalian. Home: 144 Boardman St Norfolk MA 02056 Office: Consortium of Southwood Hosp 111 Dedham St Norfolk MA 02056

DOODY, BARBARA PETTETT, computer specialist; b. Cin., Sept. 18, 1938; d. Philip Wayne and Virginia Bird (Handley) P.; student Sinclair Coll., Tulane U.; 1 son, Daniel Frederick Reasor, Jr. Owner, mgr. Honeysuckle Pet Shop, Tipp City, Ohio, 1970-76; office mgr. Doody & Doody, C.P.A.s, New Orleans, 1976-77, computer ops. mgr., 1979—; office mgr. San Diego Yacht Club, 1977-79. Mem. DAR, UDC, Jamestown Soc., Magna Charta, So. Dames, Colonial Dames of 17th Century, Nat. Soc. Daughters of 1812. Republican. Lutheran. Home: 16 Cypress Covington LA 70433 Office: 1160 Commerce Bldg New Orleans LA 70112

DOOLEY, ANN ELIZABETH, magazine and newspaper editor; b. Mpls., Feb. 19, 1952; d. Merlyn James and Susan Marie (Hinze) Dooley; m. John M. Dodge, May 8, 1983. BA in Journalism, U. Wis., 1974. Free-lance journalist 1974-75; photo editor C.W. Communications, Newton, Mass., 1975-77, writer, photographer, 1977-79; editor Computerworld O A, Framingham, Mass., 1979-83; editorial dir. Computerworld Focus, Framingham, 1983—; speaker, chmn. mem. editorial adv. bd. various computer confs. Mem. Pub. Relations Soc. Am., Women in Communications (sec. 1982-84). Office: Computerworld Focus 375 Cochituate Rd Framingham MA 01701

DOOLEY, JO ANN CATHERINE, publishing company executive; b. Cin., Nov. 24, 1930; d. Joseph Frank and Margaret Mary (Flynn) Dooley; ed. U. Cin., 1966. Clk., Castellini Co., Cin., 1949-52; IBM operator Kroger Co., Cin., 1952; asst. acct. Gardner Publs., Inc., Cin., 1953-67, treas., sec., 1967—, dir., 1983—, v.p. fin., 1986—, also trustee employees profit sharing trust, trustee retirement trust. Mem. Am. Soc. Women Accts. (govt. mgr. Woman CPA 1979-81, nat. pres. 1982-83, treas. 1984—, trustee Ednl. Found., achievement award), Cin. Women's Forum, Nat. Assn. Female Execs. Roman Catholic. Office: 6600 Clough Pike Cincinnati OH 45244

DOOLEY, MARY AGNES, college president; b. Sommerville, Mass., Mar. 5, 1923; d. Richard and Mary A. (O'Neill) D.; B.A., Elms Coll., 1944; M.A., Assumption Coll., 1960, L.H.D. (hon.), 1982; Doctorat d'Université, U. Paris, 1968; LL.D. (hon.) Am. Internat. Coll., 1981; D.Ministry, St. Louis U. Aquinas Inst., 1983; Litt.D. (hon.), Fitchburg State Coll., 1985. Joined Congregation of the Sisters of St. Joseph, 1944; tchr. St. Joseph's High Sch., North Adams, Mass., 1946-65; chmn. lang. dept. Elms Coll., Chicopee, Mass., 1968-70, pres., 1979—; pres. Leadership Conf. Women Religious U.S., Washington, 1978-79; pres. Congregation Sisters of St. Joseph, Springfield, Mass., 1971-79; corporator Community Savs. Bank, Holyoke, Mass., trustee, 1984-87. Recipient Disting. Alumna award Elms Coll., 1979, Human Relations award NCCJ, 1988; decorated chevalier dans l'Ordre des Palmes Academiques (France), 1981; named Woman of Yr., Chicopee Bus. and Profl. Women's Club, Woman of Yr. Greater Springfield C. of C., 1987. Mem. Assn. Cath. Colls. and Univs. (dir. 1980-85), Leadership Conf. Women Religious, Delta Epsilon Sigma. Roman Catholic. Contbr. articles in field to profl. jours.

DOOLITTLE, DIANE LEWIS, electronic engineer; b. Meriden, Conn., May 13, 1959; d. William Blair and Mary Alice (Cowing) D. BS in Math., Monmouth Coll., 1982; BS in Electronic Engring., 1987; postgrad. in elec. engring., Fairleigh Dickinson U., 1988—. Prodn. control analyst Wheelock Signals, Inc., Long Branch, N.J., 1982-83; quality control mgr. Molecu Wire Corp., Farmingdale, N.J., 1983-84; communications-system engr. Semcor, Inc., Farmingdale, 1984-87; systems analyst Teledyne Brown Engring., Tinton Falls, N.J., 1987—. Mem. IEEE, Army Aviation Assn. Am.

DOOLITTLE, EVELYN HARRISON, controller; b. Bryn Mawr, Pa., Nov. 14, 1957; d. Robert Drew and Evelyn (Berkley) Harrison; m. Thomas Butler Doolittle III, Sept. 6, 1980. BA in Am. Studies, Speech Communication, U. Va., 1980; MBA in Mktg., Ga. State U., 1986. Legis. aide State Rep. Dorothy Felton, Atlanta, 1980-81; from sales mgr. to controller Rich's Dept. Store, Atlanta, 1981-88, control and ops. mgr., 1988—. Mem. Am. Mktg. Assn. (asst. v.p. career devel. group Atlanta chpt.), Colonial Dames, Delta Gamma. Republican. Club: Atlanta Tennis Assn. Home: 24 Dunwoody Springs Dr Atlanta GA 30328 Office: Rich's Dept Store 1300 Cumberland Mall Atlanta GA 30339

DOOLITTLE, SHEILA ROSE, investment executive; b. Detroit, Aug. 31, 1956; d. Leonard George and Rosemary (Macaulay) Rose; m. Douglas Burklin Doolittle, May 28, 1988. BA in Mgmt. and Bus. with deptl. honors, Barat Coll., 1980. Registered commodity broker. Asst. to pres. Goldsholl Assocs., Northfield, Ill., 1980-81; mgr. Miller-Jesser Inc., Chgo., 1981-83; ptnr. Hugo Securities, N.Y.C., 1983-85; portfolio mgr. Gofen an Glossber Inc., Chgo., 1985—; mem. Chgo. Merc. Exchange, 1983-85. Fundraiser Lawrence Hall Sch. for Boys, Chgo., 1980—; mem. Sheffield Neighborhood Assn. Mem. Nat. Futures Assn., Chgo. Bot. Gardens, Chgo. Art Inst. Home: 1035 W Webster Ave Chicago IL 60614

DOORY, ANN MARIE, lawyer, legislator; b. Yonkers, N.Y., Aug. 19, 1954; d. Gerard R. and Patricia M. Lowe; m. Robert Leonard Doory Jr., Sept. 29, 1979; children: Brian Robert, Elizabeth Lowe. BA in Polit. Sci., Towson State U., 1976; JD, U. Balt., 1979. Bar: Md. Counsel to majority leader Md. State Senate, 1981; vol., arbitrator Better Bus. Bur., 1984-86; chm. bd. York Woodbourne Action Area and York Rd. Planning Com. Md. Ho. of Dels., 1982—, zoning chairperson Homeland Assn., 1984-86, v.p. Homeland Assn., 1987—. Mem. Dem. State Cen. Com. 43d Legis. Dist., Baltimore City, 1982—, 3d Dist. Citizens for Good Govt., Baltimore City, issues and legis. com., Mayors Drug Abuse Adv. Council, Baltimore City, 1983-86. Mem. Women's Bar Assn., Md. Bar Assn. Democrat. Roman Catholic. Home: 112 Taplow Rd Baltimore MD 21212 Office: Ho of Dels 321 Lowe House Office Bldg Annapolis MD 21401

DOPP, ALICE FLORENCE, librarian; b. Detroit, Oct. 28, 1931; d. Kenneth Wilton and Florence Caroline (Gabriel) Marsh; m. James Wellington Dopp, Jr., Aug. 1, 1969; m. Harold Lewis Allen, Aug. 1, 1953 (div. July 1960); 1 child, Laurie Jeanne. B.A., Wayne State U., 1965; M.L.S., U. Mich., 1967. Reference librarian Detroit Pub. Library, 1967-69; cataloger San Luis Obispo (Calif.) City Library, 1970-73; head tech. services San Luis Obispo City/County Library, 1973-78; head tech. services Las Vegas-Clark County Library Dist., 1981—; cons. San Luis Obispo Friends of Library, 1975-78; organizer, cons. Second Edit. Book Store, Las Vegas, 1982-83. Art tchr. local 500, United Auto Workers, Detroit, 1964; bd. mem. Detroit Pub. Library Staff Credit Union, Detroit, 1968; chmn. Internat. Inst. Supper Club, Detroit, 1967. Mem. ALA, Mich. Library Assn., Calif. Library Assn., Nev. Library Assn. (chmn. S.O.U.P. 1983-84), Black Gold Tech. Services Com. (chmn. 1977-78), AAUW. Democrat. Lutheran. Club: Silver Queens Investment (acctg. ptnr. 1981-83) (Las Vegas). Office: Las Vegas-Clark County Library Dist 1401 E Flamingo Rd Las Vegas NV 89119

DORA, JOAN TERESA, municipal clerk; b. Jersey City, Jan. 7, 1935; d. Samuel Francis and Helen Elizabeth (Curry) Kaminsky; m. Ewald Dora, Feb. 6, 1960; children—Deborah Ann, Walter John. Student County Coll. Morris-Randolph, N.J., 1970-73, Rutgers U., 1978—. Cert. mcpl. clk., N.J. Bookkeeper, office mgr. Lake Hopatcong Water Corp., High Ridge Water Co./High Ridge Sewer Co., N.J., 1970-77; acct. Lieberman & Co., Newton, N.J., 1977-78; mcpl. clk. Borough of Hopatcong, N.J., 1978—. Trustee, corp. sec. U.S. Land & Utilities, N.Y.C., 1973-77; chairperson Hopatcong Woman's Club Community Improvement Program, 1982—, Hopatcong Constnl. Bicentennial Com., 1987—. Recipient Merit award Rotary Club, 1982, Citizenship award, Rotary Club, 1985. Mem. Hopatcong C. of C. (pres. 1982-84), N.J. Fedn. Bus. and Profl. Women (asst. treas. 1982-83), Sussex County Mcpl. Clks. Assn. (pres. 1981-82), Mcpl. Clks. Assn., Internat. Inst. Mcpl. Clks., Hopatcong Econ. Devel. Commn. Clubs: Hopatcong Women's, N.W. Morris Bus. and Profl. Women's (pres. 1982-83), Deborah Hosp. Found. (1st v.p. 1982-83). Avocations: walking; golf. Home: PO Box 112 Hopatcong NJ 07843 Office: Borough Hopatcong Mcpl Bldg River Styx Rd Hopatcong NJ 07843

DORAN, DORIS JEANNE, librarian; b. Chambersburg, Pa., July 19, 1932; d. John Franklin and Kathleen Elmira (Cooke) Fraker; m. Francis Joseph Doran, Feb. 5, 1955; children: Brenda Lou, Polly Ann. B.S., Wilson Coll., 1954; MLS, U. Md., 1970, postgrad., 1976-77. Asst. buyer Joseph Horne Co., Pitts., 1955-56; dir. research library Sears Roebuck & Co., Chgo., 1956-58; project officer contracts John I. Thompson Co., Washington, 1967-69, staff asst. to v.p. info. sci. div., 1969-70; program officer grants div. Nat. Library of Medicine, Bethesda, Md., 1970-79, program analyst Office of Dir., 1980-82; project dir. Nat. Med. Audiovisual Center, 1979; asst. for network devel. VA, Washington, 1982-84; co-owner, treas., gen. mgr. Gilran Lighting Products, Springfield, Va., 1969-87; project mgr. Preservation Microfilm Project, REMAC Info. Corp., 1987-88, Nat. Library Medicine; acquisitions specialist Nat. Tech. Info. Service, 1988—. Mem. Am. Library Assn., Med. Library Assn., Nat. Assn. Female Execs. Home: 4816 Cloister Dr Bethesda MD 20852 Office: 7518H Fullerton Rd Springfield VA 22153

DORAN, JUDITH ANN, military professional; b. Chgo., June 18, 1953; d. Walter Stanley and Katherine Veronica (Butler) Grabowski; m. Patrick George Doran, May 6, 1978; children: Diane Michelle, Padraic Scott. BA, Chapman Coll., 1984. Enlisted USAF, 1972; advanced through grades to master sgt. 1984; vet. specialist USAF Clinic, McChord AFB, Wash., 1972-75; vet. technician USAF Hosp., Fairchild AFB, Wash., 1975-79; instr. Noncommd. Officer Ctr., Elmendorf AFB, Ala., 1979-83; instr. Leadership and Mgmt. Devel. Ctr., Maxwell AFB, Ala., 1983-84, dir. noncommd. officer prep. course instr. course, 1984-85, chief noncommd. officer prof. milit. edn. research, 1985-86; deputy dir. Family Support Ctr., Elmendorf AFB, 1986—. Recipient Outstanding Achievement award Profl. Mil. Edn., 1984. Mem. Air Force Sgts. Assn., Non-commd. Officers Assn. Republican. Roman Catholic. Office: Family Support Ctr 21 CSG FS Elmendorf AFB AL 99506

DORAN, KAREN CATO, lawyer, clinical social worker; b. Tucson, May 26, 1952; d. Benjamin Ralph and Wilma Lucille (Roberts) Cato; m. James Peter Doran, Dec. 29, 1975; children: Paul Tyler, Timothy James, Elizabeth Lee. BA, Duke U., 1974; MSW, Boston Coll., 1976; JD, U. Va., 1983. Bar: Va. 1983. Clin. social worker Denver State Sch., Taunton, Mass., 1976-77; asst. dir. Danville-Pittsylvania Mental Health Ctr., Danville, Va., 1977-79, clin. dir., 1979-80; instr. Averett Coll., Danville, 1979; assoc. Christian, Barton, Epps, Brent & Chappell, Richmond, Va., 1983-84; sole practice law, Richmond, 1984—; examiner Va. Licensing Bd., Richmond, 1980-82. Columnist Danville register, 1979-80. V.p. Va. Law Women, Charlottesville, 1980-83. Recipient NIMH award Boston Coll., 1975-76; Outstanding Young Women Am. award Jaycees, 1979; Dillard fellow U. Va., 1981-83. Mem. Nat. Assn. Social Workers, Acad. Cert. Social Workers, Va. State Bar Assn., Va. Bar Assn., ABA, Richmond Bar Assn., Duke U. Alumni, Delta Delta Delta. Home: 524 Williamsdale Dr Richmond VA 23235

DORAY, ANDREA WESLEY, marketing consultant, agency owner, writer; b. Monte Vista, Colo., Oct. 4, 1956; d. Dant Bell and Rosemary Ann (Kassap) D.; m. Paul Dean Doray, Nov. 25, 1978. BA, U. No. Colo., 1977. Cert. post secondary tchr. Asst. advt. mgr. San Luis Valley Publ. Co., Monte Vista, 1977-78; mktg. dir. Stuart Scott & Assocs. (formerly Philip Winn & Assocs.), Colorado Springs, 1978-80; sr. v.p. Heisley Design and Advt., Colorado Springs, 1980-85; pres., creative dir. Doray Doray, Monument, Colo., 1985—; account services dir. Praco Ltd., Advt., Colorado Springs, 1987-88; owner, ptnr. Davis, Doray, McGuill Advt., Colorado Springs, 1988—; pt. time instr. Pikes Peak Community Coll., Colorado Springs, 1983-86;project bus. cons. Jr. Achievement, Colorado Springs, 1985-86; mem. mktg. adv. council Pikes Peak Community Coll., Colorado Springs, 1985—; spkr. Colorado Springs C. of C. Small Bus. Council, 1985, Pikes Peak Advt. Fedn., Colorado Springs, 1986—; guest lectr. Colo. Mountain Coll., 1982-84, U. So. Colo., 1983, Pikes Peak Community Coll, 1983—. Author: The Other Fish, 1976, Oil Painting Lessons, 1986, Coming to Terms, 1986, Roger Douglas, 1987; contbg. editor Colorado Springs Bus. Mag., 1984-86; creative writer World Cycling Fedn. Championships, Colorado Springs, 1986. Mem. mktg. adv. council Pikes Peak Community Coll., Colorado Springs, 1985-88; chmn. Colorado Springs Local Advt. Review Program, 1985; chmn., advt. pub. relations task force exec. com. U.S. Olympic Hall of Fame, 1986; mem. State Legis. Alert and Action Coalition, 1985-87; spkr. Nat. Council for Community Relations, Orlando, Fla., 1988. Named one of Colorado Springs Leading Women, Colorado Springs Gazette Telegraph, 1984, Outstanding Young Woman of Yr., State of Colo., 1986, Outstanding Young Alumna, U. No. Colo., 1987. Mem. Pikes Peak Advt. Fedn. (pres. 1984-86, Advt. Person of Yr. award), Am. Advt. Fedn. (chmn. dist. 12 legis. com. 1985—, pub. relations com. 1986, Silver medal award 1986), Colorado Springs C. of C. (advt. roundtable). Office: Davis Doray McGuill PO Box 1228 Monument CO 80132-1228

DORE, BONNY ELLEN, film and television production company executive; b. Cleve., Aug. 16, 1947; d. Reber Hutson and Ellen Elizabeth (McNamara) Barnes; m. James Llewellyn Metz, Feb. 20, 1977 (div. Aug. 1986); m. Sanford Astor, May 22, 1987. BA, U. Mich., 1969, MA, 1975. Cert. tchr., Mich. Dir., tchr. Plymouth (Mich.) Community Schs., 1969-72; gen. mgr. Sta. WSDP-FM, Plymouth, 1970-72; prodn. supr. pub. TV N.Y. State Dept. Edn., 1972-74; producer TV series Hot Fudge Sta. WXYZ-TV, Detroit, 1974-75; mgr. children's programs ABC TV Network, Los Angeles, 1975, dir. children's programs, 1975-76, dir. prime time variety programs, 1976-77; dir. devel. Hanna-Barbera, Los Angeles, 1977; v.p. devel. and prodn. Krofft Entertainment, Los Angeles, 1977-81, Centerpoint Prodn., Los Angeles, 1981-82; pres., owner in assn. with Orion TV The Greif-Dore Co., Los Angeles, 1983-87, Bonny Dore Prodns. Inc., Los Angeles, 1988—. Producer (TV series) The Krofft Superstar Hour, 1978 (2 Emmy awards 1979), (mini-series) Sins, 1986, (comedy series CBS) First Impressions, 1987-88, (mini-series HBO) Sister Ruth, 1988, numerous others; exec. producer (mini-series) Sister Ruth, 1988-89). Named Outstanding Young Tchr. of Yr., Cen. States Speech Assn., 1973; Cert. of Appreciation, Gov. of Mich., 1985, City of Beverly Hills, Calif., 1985. Mem. Women in Film (v.p. 1978-81, pres. 1980-81), Women in Film Found. (trustee 1981—), Acad. TV Arts and Scis., Beverly Hills C. of C. (cons. 1985), Exec. Roundtable Los Angeles (trustee 1987—). Home: 15150 Dickens Condo 307 Sherman Oaks CA 91403 Office: Orion TV Studios 1888 Century Park E 6th Floor Los Angeles CA 90067

DORF, ANITA KAY, health facility administrator; b. Hollywood, Calif., June 17, 1945; d. Ralph Ormand and Romeyn Virginia Elizabeth (Holm) Dove; m. David Julius Dorf, June 23, 1967; children: Tanya Leanne, Mindy Nicole. BA, Bethany Coll., Lindsborg, Kans., 1967; MS, Kans. State U., 1976, PhD, 1985. Tchr. English, speech, drama Bonner Springs (Kans.) High Sch., 1967-68; instr. ABE/GED U.S.D. 305, Salina, Kans., 1973-78; dir. edn. St. John's Hosp., Salina, 1975-82, Asbury Hosp., Salina, 1980-82; cons. mgmt. devel. Wesley Med. Ctr., Wichita, 1982-84, mgr. manpower productivity, 1984-87, dir. edn., 1987—; speaker in field 1976-87. Editor: Education Coordinator's Man., 1976. Mem. adv. com. Salina Area Vocat.-Tech. Sch., 1981-82, community edn. com. YWCA, Salina, 1980-81, steering com. Project Growing in Families Together, Wichita, 1986—, Wichita Plan for Ednl. Excellence Task Force, 1985-86. Mem. Kans. Assn. Hosp. Edn. Coordinator (pres. 1981-82, bd. dirs. 1976-84, 86—), Am. Assn. Adult and Continuing Edn., Am. Soc. Tng. and Devel., Am. Soc. Healthcare Edn. and Tng., Kans. Forum Women Healthcare Execs. (founder, bd. dirs.), LWV, Delta Kappa Gamma, Beta Rho. Republican. Lutheran. Office: Wesley Med Ctr 550 N Hillside Wichita KS 67214

DORFMAN, KAREN K., corporate consultant, lecturer; b. Indpls., Mar. 3, 1950; d. John and Margie King; B.A., U. Tex., 1972; M.A., Ind. U., 1976. Sales rep. John H. Harland Co., 1979—; guest lectr. Ind. U.-Purdue U., 1977—. Mem. various clubs. Home: 5678 N Meridian Indianapolis IN 46208

DORFMAN, LISA ANN, nutritionist, consultant, educator; b. New Hyde Park, N.Y., Feb. 5, 1961; d. Walter and Melanie (Safane) Shapiro; m. Robert Alan Dorfman, May 1, 1982; 1 child, Rebecca Elizabeth. BS in Dietetics and Nutrition, Fla. Internat. U., 1983, MS in Dietetics and Nutrition, 1984. Registered dietitian, Fla. Cons. Nutrition Assocs. of Am., Inc., Miami, Fla., 1983—, pres., 1983—, also bd. dirs.; nutritionist Doral Saturnia Internat. Spa Resort, Miami, 1987—; pres. Food Fitness Internat., Inc., 1987—; counselor, educator Anorexia and Bulimia Resource Ctr., Coconut Grove, Fla., 1983-87, Humana Hosp. Biscayne, North Miami Beach, Fla., 1984-86; clin. nutritionist Canteen Corps. of S. Fla. State Hosp., Hollywood, 1985-86; pub. health nutritionist U. Miami-Jackson Meml. Hosp., 1984-85; instr. Miami Dade Community Coll., 1986—; counselor, cons. Piedmont Airlines, Miami, 1986—; counselor, instr. Inst. of Eating Behaviors, Miami, 1986—. Author: The Tropical Diet, 1986; (curriculum guide) Close to You-Anorexia Nervosa and Bulimia, 1987; co-producer, co-host TV series Dr. Green's Kitchen, 1986-87; co-host, co-producer Food Fitness, Sellkirk Communications, Inc., Hot Talk, Sta. WHQT, Miami. Mem. Am. Dietetic Assn., Fla. Dietetic Assn., Miami Dietetic Assn., Soc. Nutrition Edn., South Fla. Cardiovascular and Sports Nutritionists (sec. 1985—), Am. Anorexia/Bulimia Assn. of Fla. (founder local chpt., pres., bd. dirs. 1984—), Am. Heart Assn. (com. mem. 1984-88); pub. relations chair, cons. Nutritionists Practice Group, 1988-89. Jewish. Home: 151 Crandon Blvd #334 Key Biscayne FL 33149 Office: Nutrition Assocs of Am Inc 5975 Sunset Dr Suite 601 Miami FL 33143

DORFMONT, LINDA BERNICE, industrial engineer, consultant; b. Los Angeles, Feb. 9, 1947; d. Elmer and Bernice Alberta (Bechestobill) D. BA, Calif. State U., Long Beach, 1968; MBA, U. So. Calif., 1975. Cert. mfg. engr. With Hughes Aircraft Co., Los Angeles, 1969—; prin. Linda Dorfmont E.A., Lawndale, Calif., 1983—; cons. Calif. State U., Fullerton and Northridge, 1984—. Contbr. articles to profl. jours. Mem. Inst. Indsl. Engrs. (sr., v.p. 1977-78, pres. 1979-80, chmn. annual conf. 1985, bd. dirs.), Calif. Soc. Enrolled Agts. (bd. dirs.), Productivity Ctr. S.W. (bd. dirs. 1977-83). Libertarian. Byzantine Catholic. Club: Toastmasters. Home: 11638 Truro Hawthorne CA 90250 Office: Hughes Aircraft Co PO Box 92426 R1O/10066 Los Angeles CA 90009

DORIAN, JOANNE, advertising executive; b. N.Y.C., Feb. 28, 1955; d. John Mesrobian and Margaret (Melkonian) D. BA, Queens Coll., 1977; MA, Adelphi U., 1979. Substitute tchr. N.Y.C. Bd. Edn., 1977-79; sec.

Cahners Pub. Co., N.Y.C., 1979-80, info. card sales mgr., 1980-81, sales mgr., 1981—. Mem. Nat. Assn. Female Execs., Am. Students Assn. Republican. Am. Apostolic. Office: Cahners Pub Co 249 W 17th St New York NY 10011

DORIAN, NANCY CURRIER, educator; b. New Brunswick, N.J., 1936; d. Donald Clayton and Edith (McEwen) D. B.A. summa cum laude, Conn. Coll. for Women, 1958; postgrad., Yale U., 1959-60; M.A., U. Mich., 1961, Ph.D. (Rackham fellow), 1965. Lectr. Bryn Mawr Coll., Pa., 1965-66, asst. prof. linguistics in German and anthropology, 1966-72, assoc. prof., 1972-78, prof., 1978—, William R. Kenan Jr. prof., 1980-85; vis. lectr. U. Pa., 1966, 70, U. Kiel, 1967-68. Author: East Sutherland Gaelic, 1978, Language Death, 1981, Tyranny of Tide, 1985; asst. editor Internat. Jour. of the Sociology of Language; assoc. editor Language; contbr. articles to profl. jours. Fulbright scolar, W. Ger., 1958-59; NSF grantee, 1978-79. Mem. Linguistic Soc. Am., Internat. Linguistic Assn., Eastern States Celtic Assn. Democrat. Unitarian. Office: Bryn Mawr Coll Dept German Bryn Mawr PA 19010

DORIS, DERA CHARLENE, coroner; b. Opp, Ala., Dec. 25, 1944. AA in Psychology, U. Alaska, 1980. Sec. City of Crestview, Fla., 1964-74; med. sec. Bayberry Hosp., Hampton, Va., 1972-74; probate sec. Alaska Ct. System, Anchorage, 1974-83, dep. coroner, 1981-83, coroner, 1983—. Mem. Internat. Assn. Coroners and Med. Examiners. Republican. Club: Eagle River Running. Home: 19411 Eagle River Rd Eagle River AK 99577 Office: Alaska Ct System 941 W Fourth Ave Anchorage AK 99501

DORKO, WENDY LYNN, automobile dealership executive; b. Sarnia, Ont., Can., Feb. 10, 1959; came to U.S., 1973; d. Zoltan Joseph and Beverly Charlotte (Lyons) D. BA in Psychology, U. Akron, 1981. Adminstrv. asst. Polysar Rubber Services, Akron, Ohio, 1981-84; bartender, mgr. Ryan's Park Place, Honolulu, 1985-86; research asst. Naval Ocean Systems Ctr. div. SEACO, Inc., Kailua, Hawaii, 1986-88, bioscientist, 1986-88; dir. customer relations Tony Honda Pearlridge, Aiea, Hawaii, 1988—; asst. test dir. U.S. Navy, Key West, Fla., summer 1987, San Diego, 1987-88. Recipient Outstanding Performance award Naval Ocean Systems Ctr., 1987. Home: 322 Aoloa St PH05 Kailua HI 96734 Office: Tony Honda Pearlridge 98-051 Kamehameha Hwy Aiea HI 96701

DORLAND, BYRL BROWN, civic worker; b. Greenwich, Utah, Apr. 25, 1915; d. David Alma and Ethel Myrle (Peterson) Brown; teaching cert. Brigham Young U., 1937; B.S., Utah State Coll., Logan, 1940; grad. John Robert Powers Sch. Profl. Women, N.Y.C., 1980; m. Jack Albert Dorland, June 11, 1944; children—Lynn Elise Dorland Trost, Lee Allison. Sch. tchr., Utah, 1937-39, 40-42; restored Washington Irving's graveplot in Sleepy Hollow Cemetery, North Tarrytown, N.Y. (named Nat. Hist. Landmark 1972); nat. dir. Washington Irving Graveplot Restoration Program, 1968—, designer landmark plaque for grave; mem. Nat. Council State Garden Clubs, 1959—; pres. Potpourri Garden Club, Westchester, N.Y., 1966—; nat. chmn. for graveplot programs Washington Irving Bicentennial, 1983-84; dir. Dorland Family Graveyard Restoration, N.J. Hist. Landmark, 1983—. Recipient May Duff Walters trophy Nat. Council State Garden Clubs, 1974; nat. trophy Nat. Historic Landmark Com., 1974; citation Keep Am. Beautiful, 1974. Mem. Nat. Trust for Historic Preservation (Pres.'s award 1977), Nat. Historic Soc. Am., Gen. Soc. Mayflower Desc., Internat. Washington Irving Soc. (founder, pres. 1981—), Nat. Assn. for Gravestone Studies (hon.), Herb Soc. Am., DAR. Home and Office: 10 Castle Heights Ave Tarrytown NY 10591

DORMAN, HATTIE LAWRENCE, management consultant, former government agency official; b. Cleve., July 22, 1932; d. J. Lyman and Claire A. (Lenoir) Lawrence; m. James L. Dorman, May 16, 1959; children—Lydia, Lynda, James Lawrence. Student Fenn Coll. (Cleve. State U.), part time 1950-58, D.C. Tchrs. Coll., 1960-64, Dept. Agr. Grad. Sch., 1968-69; BA, Howard U., 1987. Clk., tax specialist, mgmt. analyst, supr., staff advisor IRS, Washington, 1954-79; spl. asst. to dep. asst. sec. adminstrn. Dept. Treasury, Washington, 1978-79; dep. dir. Interagency Com. on Women's Bus. Enterprise, SBA; Task Force on EEO, Dept. Treasury 1978-79; mem. Pres.'s Task Force on Women Bus. Owners, from 1979, now ret.; trainer and speaker in field. Sec. Linton Hall Guild, 1978-80; chmn. trainer, cons., leader Girl Scout Service Unit, 1971-80; ofcl. observer Nat. Women's Conf., Houston, 1977; bd. dirs. YWCA, 1957-62; mem. planning com. Black Women's Summit, 1981; mem. Vestry Register, St. Paul's Episcopal Ch., 1981—. Recipient spl. achievement award Commr. IRS, 1978, thanks badge Girl Scout Nation's Capital, 1977, recognition cert. for work in Christian edn. St. Paul's Episcopal Ch., 1976, Mary McLeod Bethune Centennial award Nat. Council Negro Women, 1975, other awards and certs. of appreciation. Mem. Am. Soc. Public Adminstrs., Federally Employed Women, Alumni Fed. Exec. Inst. Club: Delta Sigma Theta. Journalist Neighbor's Inc., 1969-71.

DORMAN, LYNDA BROWNELL, retail store manager; b. Monterey, Calif., July 20, 1944; d. Harold Cox and Loris Irene (Miller) Brownell; m. Richard Morris Dorman (div.); children: Kelley Ann, Brent William. Student, Fla. So. Coll., Lakeland. Model Rheinauers, Ocala, Fla., 1976-82, cons., fashion coordinator, 1976-87, mgr., fashion dir., 1985—; fashion coordinator Maas Bros., Ocala, 1982-85; #*#*#*. Editor Fashion Editor mag., 1978. Mem. Children's Service League, Ocala, 1969-87. Mem. Fashion Group, DAR. Republican. Methodist. Office: Rheinauers 2005 E Silver Springs Blvd Ocala FL 32671

DORN, JENNIFER LYNN, political campaign professional; b. Grand Island, Nebr., Dec. 7, 1950; d. Harold Clarence and Ethel Agnes D.; m. David James Oldfield (div. Oct. 1980). B.A., Oreg. State U., 1973; M.P.A., U. Conn., 1977. Account exec. J.R. Tendler Assoc., Woodbridge, Conn., 1974-75; legis. asst. Senator M. Hatfield, Washington, 1977-81; com. staff Senate Appropriations, Washington, 1981-83; spl. asst. Sec. Elizabeth Dole, Washington, 1983-84; dir. Comml. Space Transp., Washington, 1984-85; assoc. dep. sec. U.S. Dept. Transp., Washington, 1985-87; dir. Office of Elizabeth Dole Dole for President Campaign, Washington, 1987. Bd. dirs. Washington Women's Network, 1982-85. Mem. Nat. Space Club (bd. dirs. 1985—), Oreg. Women's Forum. Republican. Lutheran. Home: 2248 Washington Ave #103 Silver Spring MD 20910

DORN, WANDA FAYE, talent agent; b. Little Rock, May 23, 1945; d. Jesse Dorn and Daisy Mae (Washington) Dorn-Jones; m. Donald Hayman, Nov. 22, 1966 (div. June 1986); 1 child, Deon Horace. Grad., Crest Modeling Sch., Chgo., Patricia Vance Sch. Modeling, Chgo., 1966; AA, Chgo. Coll. Commerce, 1970; grad. tchr. tng. program, John Robert Powers Modeling Agy., Chgo., 1979. Lic. fashion cons., retailer, modeling sch. adminstr. and instr. Sec. numerous banks and ins. cos., Chgo., 1963-66; ct. reporter Superior Cts., San Jose, Oakland, Calif., 1973-83; instr. Marnee Jones Modeling Sch., San Jose, Calif., 1980; freelance writer San Jose-Peninsula Metro, 1982-86; fashion writer San Francisco Sun Reporter, 1982-86; owner, founder A'Dorn Studios, San Jose, Los Angeles, 1979—; lectr., instr. modeling and personal improvement; coordinator fashion prodns.; founder Black Model of Yr. Pageant, 1982; producer, host weekly talk show Society Pages, 1986—. Author: Your Most Important Accessory - Your Appearance, 1984. Recipient Outstanding Community Service award Human Relations Com. of Santa Clara, 1986, Community Service award San Jose C. of C.; appointed to Fine Arts Commn., Mayor and City Council of San Jose, 1986—. Mem. Calif. Ct. Reporter's Assn., NOW, NAACP, Nat. Council Negro Women, Inc. (past v.p., chmn. fundraising com., chmn. bylaws com., chmn. internat. com.), South Bay Black Women's Network (past pres., chmn. hotline com., chmn. structure com., founding mem.), Black Concerns Assn. (past v.p., chmn. new faces program), Black Media Coalition, Black Filmmakers Hall of Fame. Office: A'Dorn Studios 1901 Avenue of the Stars Suite 1774 Century City CA 90067 also: PO Box 21668 San Jose CA 95151

DORNBUSH, VICKY JEAN, medical billing systems executive; b. Willowick, Ohio, Aug. 12, 1951; d. Charles W. and Josephine H. (Palumbo) Rader; m. Eric D. Erickson, Oct. 22, 1972 (div. June 1974); m. Thomas Dornbush, Dec. 29, 1979 (div. 1987); 1 child, Dana. Student, Kent State U., 1969-72, San Jose State U., 1982-84. Accounts receivable clk. MV Nursery, Richmond, Calif., 1975-76; accounts receivable and computer supr. Ga. Pacific, Richmond, 1976-78; acct. Ga. Pacific, Tracy, Calif., 1978-79, Crown-Zellerbach, Anaheim, Calif., 1979-80; acct. Interstate Pharmacy Corp., San Jose, Calif., 1981-83, controller, 1983-85; gen. ptnr. Med. Billing Systems, San Jose, 1984—; seminar trainer Systems Plus, Mountain View, Calif., 1987—. Mem. San Jose Civic Light Opera, 1987—, San Jose Repertory Co., 1986—. Mem. Women in Bus. Republican. Methodist. Office: Med Billing Systems 255 W Julian St #403 San Jose CA 95110

DORNER, VIRGINIA MARY, travel agency executive; b. Milw., Mar. 18, 1939; d. John Henry and Ruth Hope (Nowatney) Wynhoff; m. John Robert Dorner, Apr. 30, 1960 (div.); children: Michael John, Denise Marie, Scott Patrick. Student, U. Wis., Madison, 1957-59, Milw. Inst. Tech., 1961, Jefferson Community Coll., Watertown, N.Y., 1973-76; entrepreneurial program diploma, U. Tex., San Antonio; grad., SABRE computer key coordinator program. Chmn. N.Y. Bd. Assessment Rev., Watertown, N.Y., 1976-79; travel cons. Gelco Travel Services, San Antonio, 1982-84, mgr., 1984-85; real estate agt. Rosow & Kline, San Antonio, 1980; pres. Travel Focus, Inc., San Antonio, 1985—. Chmn. Good Neighbor Program, San Antonio; bd. dirs., pres. PTA; sec. Mt. Laurel Service and Tax Study Com.; mem. Total Living Complex; mem. State Legis. Task Force., U. Tex. San Antonio Entrepreneurial Leadership Program, 1987-88. Mem. Bus. Roundtable, North San Antonio C. of C. (mem. sports com., mem. Diplomats, mem. urban affairs com., tourism com.), Greater San Antonio C. of C. (tax equity com.), San Antonio Leads Exchange (pres.), Bons Vivant. Republican. Clubs: Los Amigos, World Affairs Council (San Antonio). Home: 3422 Wellsprings Dr San Antonio TX 78230 Office: Travel Focus Inc 613 NW Loop 410 Suite 350 San Antonio TX 78216

DORNER-ANDELORA, SHARON A. HADDON, educator; b. Morristown, N.J., Nov. 3, 1943; d. William P. and Eleanor (Dygert) Haddon; BA in Bus. Edn., Montclair State Coll., 1965, MA in Bus. Edn., 1970, MA in Guidance and Counseling, 1978; EdD in Vocat.-Tech. Edn., Adminstrn. and Supervision, Rutgers U., 1982; m. Robert Andelora, Feb. 17, 1985: children—Wendy, Meridith. Tchr., Morris Knolls High Sch., 1965-70; tchr. Katherine Gibbs Sec. Sch., Montclair, N.J., 1973-74; tchr. Leonia (N.J.) High Sch., 1974-75; tchr. bus. Woodcliff Sch., Woodcliff Lake, N.J., 1976—, adminstrv. intern to supt., 1980—; tchr. adult sch. Sussex Vocat. Sch., County Coll. Morris, Randolph, N.J. Judge, Election Bd., Montclair, 1972-82. Mem. Assn. Supervision and Curriculum Devel., Am. Vocat. Assn., Am. Vocat. Research Assn., N.J. Vocat. Assn., NEA, N.J. Edn. Assn., Bergen County Edn. Assn., Woodcliff Lake Edn. Assn. (sec. 1976-84), N.J. Bus. Edn. Assn., Nat. Bus. Edn. Assn., Eastern Bus. Tchrs. Assn., Consumers League (dir. 1979—), N.J. Coll. Ednl. Leaders (v.p. 1985—, treas. 1983-84, Northeastern regional rep. 1982-83), Northeast Coalition Ednl. Leaders, Delta Pi Epsilon (pres. Beta Phi chpt. 1979-80, v.p. 1978-79, sec. 1976-78, newsletter editor 1974-76, nat. com. 1980-84, nat. council rep. 1981—, chmn. nat. com. 1982-84, nat. historian 1987—), Sigma Kappa (nat. alumnae province officer 1977-81, nat. alumnae dist. dir. 1981—), Phi Delta Kappa (pres. 1980-82 treas. 1975-79, 82-84, council del. 1977-80, 84-86, research rep. 1986—), Omicron Tau Theta (pres. Delta chpt. 1987-88, v.p. 1986-87, nat. parliamentarian 1986-88). Lodges: Daus. of Nile, N.J. Eastern Star. Mem. adv. bd. Today's Sec., 1981-82. Home: 28 College Ave Upper Montclair NJ 07043 Office: 134 Woodcliff Ave Woodcliff Lake NJ 07675

DORO, MARION ELIZABETH, political scientist, educator; b. Miami, Fla., Oct. 9, 1928; d. George and Alma (Carram) D. B.A., Fla. State U., 1951, M.A., 1952; Ph.D. (Bennett fellow), U. Pa., 1959. Instr. polit. sci. Wheaton Coll., Norton, Mass., 1958-60; Ford Found. Area Studies fellow U. London, Kenya, Africa, 1960-62; asst. prof. Conn. Coll., New London, 1962-65; assoc. prof. Conn. Coll., 1965-70, prof., 1970—, Lucy Marsh Haskell prof. govt., 1983—, dir. grad. studies, 1975-79, chmn. dept. govt., 1981-84, 87—. Editor: (with N. Stultz) Governing in Black Africa, 1970, 2d edit., 1986, Africa Contemporary Record; mem. editorial bd.: African Studies Rev.; contbr. articles and book revs. to profl. jours. Fulbright fellow Makerere U., Kampala, Uganda, 1963-64; sr. research fellow Radcliffe Inst., Cambridge, Mass., 1968-69; vis. research fellow, Am. Philos. Soc. grantee East Africa Inst. Social Sci. Research, 1971-72; AAUW Am. fellow, sr. assoc. St. Anthony's Coll., Oxford U., 1977-78; vis. faculty fellow Yale U., 1984-85. Mem. Am. Polit. Sci. Assn. (publ. com. 1987—), N.Eng. Polit. Sci. Assn. (chmn. status women com. 1972-75, exec. council 1973-75), Northeast Polit. Sci. Assn. (exec. council 1974-76, 82-84), African Studies Assn. (dir. program nat. meetings 1976), AAUP, AAUW, Soc. Fellows Radcliffe Inst. (exec. council 1979-84), Phi Beta Kappa, Phi Kappa Phi, Pi Sigma Alpha. Office: Conn Coll PO Box 1457 New London CT 06320

DORR, LORNA BITGOOD, librarian; b. New London, Conn., May 2, 1941; d. Royal Earl and Frances Allen (Minson) Bitgood; m. Darwin Dorr, Apr. 25, 1964 (div. Mar. 1984); children: Benjamin Paul, Christopher Joseph. BA, Alfred U., 1963; postgrad. U. Coll., Washington U., St. Louis, 1973-74, Mars Hill Coll., 1980-82; MLS, U. S.C., 1985. Elem. music tchr., Newburgh (N.Y.) Public Schs., 1963-65; library asst. R. M. Strozier Library, Fla. State U., 1965-67, acting head circulation div., 1968-69; book orderer dept. ind. study U. Minn., 1967-68; swimming instr. Asheville (N.C.) YWCA, 1978; circulation supr. Meml. Library, Mars Hill Coll., 1979-82; chief reference asst. Ramsey Library U. N.C., Asheville, 1982-85; reference librarian Western Carolina U., 1986—. Mem. Brevard (N.C.) Chamber Orch., 1979-84; mem. Asheville Symphony, 1981-83; former mem. bd. dirs., com. chmn. Community Center for Arts, Asheville. Mem. ALA, N.C. Library Assn., Western N.C. Library Assn., Beta Phi Mu. Episcopalian. Home: PO Box 2403 Cullowhee NC 28723

DORSCH, ROBERTA FUNK, association executive; b. Balt., July 9, 1943; d. Edward Joseph and Roberta E. (Harris) Funk; m. Dennis Edward Dorsch, Apr. 26, 1969; 1 child, Brenda Jean. Student U. Md., 1961-63; cert. Johns Hopkins Hosp., 1967. Staff cytotechnologist Johns Hopkins Hosp., Balt., 1962-69, Meml. Hosp. Easton, Md., 1969-71; sr. cytotechnologist Johns Hopkins Hosp., 1971-75, VA Hosp., Balt., 1975-78, Sacred Heart Hosp., Cumberland, Md., 1978-80; field dir. Shawnee Girl Scout Council, Martinsburg, W.Va., 1981—; tchr. swimming Cash Valley Sch., La Vale, Md., 1980—; tchr. water ballet Cumberland Dept. Parks and Recreation, 1980-82, Frostburg Dept. Recreation, 1983-86. Contbr. articles to profl. jours. Bd. dirs. Allegany County unit Am. Cancer Soc., 1979-81, 82—, mem. pub. edn. com. Md. div., 1984—; exec. com. PTA, Cash Valley Elem. Sch., 1980-82; mem. rev. bd. selections com. Allegany/Garrett County Foster Care, 1986—; mem. state adv. com. Office of Children and Youth, 1987—; active youth activities Ellerslie United Meth. Ch., 1979—; mem. Allegany County Children's Council, 1984—, pres., 1985-86; active Allegany County Chem. People, 1983-85, Md. Alcohol Drug Resource Team of Allegany County, 1985—. Mem. Am. Soc. Cytology, Md. Assn. Cytotechnologists (pres. 1974-76), Am. Soc. Clin. Pathologists, Am. Soc. Cytotechnologists. Clubs: Frostburg Badminton (v.p. 1981-82). Republican. Roman Catholic. Address: PO Box 358 Ellerslie MD 21529

DORSETT, CORA MATHENY, librarian; b. Camden, Ark., July 15, 1921; d. Walter Stanton and Cora (Smith) Matheny; B.S. in Edn. summa cum laude, Centenary Coll. La., 1963; M.S. in L.S. (Grad. fellow), U. Miss., 1965, Ph.D., 1972; postgrad. U. Okla., 1973. Tchr. pub. schs., Shreveport, La., 1963-64; dir. Pine Bluff and Jefferson County Pub. Library, Pine Bluff, Ark., 1965-86. Librarian Emerita, cons., 1987—; bd. dirs. Pine Bluff Community Art Center, 1966-67; mem. steering com. Pine Bluff-Jefferson County Am. Revolution Bicentennial Celebration, 1975-76. Recipient Social Sci. award Chi Omega, 1963. Mem. Am., Ark., Southeastern library assns., Jefferson County Hist. Assn., Kappa Delta Pi, Phi Delta Kappa, Alpha Chi. Episcopalian. Home: 1305 W 35th Ave Pine Bluff AR 71603

DORSETT, PATRICIA JEAN, educator, consultant; b. New Castle, Ind., May 26, 1935; d. George Meredith and Margaret (Bryan) Poole; m. Carroll Edwin Cleek, Jan. 8, 1954 (div. 1976); children: Cynthia Anne Cleek, Patricia Jill Cleek, Deborah Susan Cleek, David Carroll Cleek; m. John Ford Dorsett, Feb. 11, 1978. BS in Edn. cum laude, Ga. State U., 1982, MS in English Edn., 1986. Cert. tchr., Ga. Pres. Direct Systems Corp., Orchard Park, N.Y., 1969-72; coordinator reservations and travel Ciba-Geigy Corp., Greensboro, N.C., 1975-78; pvt. practice travel cons. Conyers, Ga., 1979-81; cons. property mgmt. and bus. P&J Assocs., Conyers, 1980—; tchr. language arts Cousins Mid. Sch., Covington, Ga., 1983—; sec.-treas. P&J Assocs., 1979—. Editor: (newsletter) St. Mark's Caller, 1964-69, The Voter, 1982-87, Direct Systems Corp. Mail Order Catalog, 1969-72. Pres. Coop. Nursery Sch., Orchard Park, 1961-62; leader 4-H Club, Orchard Park, 1964-74; active Rockdale (Ga.) Arts Alliance. Mem. LWV (first pres. Rockdale County chpt. 1982-83, fin. chair 1984-85, sec. 1986-87, adminstrv. v.p. 1987—, Outstanding Service award 1986, chair natural resources 1987—, bd. dirs. 1987—), Ga. Assn. Educators, Ga. Internat. Reading Assn., Ga. Council Tchrs. of English, Nat. Fedn. Womens Clubs (chair scholarship fund 1974-75), Village Writers Group, Phi Alpha Theta. Episcopalian. Home: 1460B Pine Log Rd Conyers GA 30207 Office: P&J Assocs 954 S Main St Conyers GA 30207

DORSEY, RHODA MARY, college president; b. Boston, Sept. 9, 1927; d. Thomas Francis and Hedwig (Hoge) D. BA magna cum laude, Smith Coll., 1949, LLD, 1979; BA, Cambridge (Eng.) U., 1951, MA, 1954; PhD, U. Minn., 1956; LLD (hon.), Nazareth Coll. Rochester, 1970; DHL (hon.), Mount St. Mary's Coll., 1976, Mount Vernon Coll., 1979, Coll. St. Catherine, 1983, Johns Hopkins U., 1986, Towson State U., 1987. Mem. faculty Goucher Coll., Towson, Md., 1954—; prof. history Goucher Coll., 1965-68, dean, v.p., 1968-73, acting pres., 1973-74, pres., 1974—; lectr. history Loyola Coll., Balt., 1958-62, Johns Hopkins, 1960-61; dir. U.S. Fidelity & Guaranty Co., Balt., Chesapeake & Potomac Tel. Co. Md., Noxell Corp., First Nat. Bank Md. Bd. dirs. Am. Friends of Cambridge U., 1978—; mem. Md.-D.C. Com. on Selection Rhodes Scholars; bd. dirs. Gen. German Aged Peoples Home, Balt., 1984—. Recipient Outstanding Woman Mgr. of 1984 U. Balt. Women's Program in Mgmt. and WMAR-TV, Outstanding Achievement award U. Minn. Alumni Assn., 1984; Andrew White medal Loyola Coll., 1985; named in survey of peers as one of 100 Most Effective Coll. and Univ. Pres. in U.S., Chronicle of Higher Edn., 1986. Mem. Md. Ind. Coll. and Univ. Assn. (chmn. bd.). Clubs: Smith, Hamilton St. (Balt.); Cosmopolitan (N.Y.C.). Home: Goucher Coll President's House Towson MD 21204

DORTCH, SUSAN MADELINE, educator; b. Phila., Nov. 5, 1951; d. Ulester L. Mahoney and Flora (Blair) Simmons; m. Eulas C. Dortch, Feb. 10, 1983; children: Candace Alexis, Brandon Edward, Bryan Vincent. BS in Edn. and Infancy, Temple U., 1976; postgrad., U. Md., 1988—. Tchr. nursey Phila. Bd. of Edn., 1976-83, tchr. kindergarten, 1983-85; tchr. kindergarten Prince Georges County (Md.) Bd. of Edn., 1986, tchr. 2d grade, 1986—; union rep. Phila. Tchr. Union, 1981-82. Active local PTA, 1986—; mem. Phila. Zool. Soc., 1983—. Mem. Prince Georges County Edn. Assn.

DORWARD, JUDITH A., food company executive; b. Hazleton, Pa., Apr. 16, 1941; d. Eugene Joseph and Dorothy Cecelia (Shields) McNertney; m. Douglas Dean Owens, Apr. 15, 1961 (div. 1968); children: Kevin Patrick, Kelly Shawn; m. Clifford Dorward, July 4, 1969 (div. 1974). AA, Lehigh County Community Coll., 1979; BA, Muhlenburg Coll., 1984; grad. in statis. process control, Process Mgmt. Inst., Inc., Mpls., 1986. Customer service clk. Pa. Power & Light Co., Allentown, 1959-61; mgr. Merle Norman Cosmetic Studios, Allentown and Bethlehem, Pa., 1968-70; adminstrv. clk. Pillsbury Co., East Greenville, Pa., 1970-85, mgr. ops. prodn., 1985-87, mgr. distbn. and prodn. control, 1987—. Former voting machine operator Lehigh County, Slatington, Pa.; held various offices Gen. Fedn. of Women's Clubs. Mem. Phi Beta Kappa. Democrat. Roman Catholic. Home: 1249 Knossos Dr Apt 5 Whitehall PA 18052 Office: Pillsbury Co Pillsbury Rd East Greenville PA 18041

DORWART, MARY L., lawyer; b. Sidney, Nebr., July 10, 1948; d. Clinton Bonaventure and Lucille Marguerite (Keller) D.; 1 child, Lisa. JD, Creighton U., 1971. Bar: Nebr. 1972, Minn., 1982. Lawyer Fed. Land Bank Omaha, 1972-76; office counsel Chgo. Title Ins. Co., Omaha, 1976-80, Kansas City, Mo., 1980-81, Bloomington, Minn., 1981—. Mem. Nebr. State Bar Assn., Minn. State Bar Assn. Office: Chgo Title Ins Co 8000 Town Line Ave Bloomington MN 55438

DOSEN, SUSAN GAIL, speech and language coordinator; b. Duluth, Minn., July 4, 1951; d. Oliver Gust and Dorothy (Kampa) Mackley; m. James Anthony Dosen, June 23, 1972; children: Jessica Ann, Anthony Oliver. BS, U. Minn., 1973, MA, 1975. Cert. speech & lang. pathologist, early childhood spl. edn. tchr., spl. edn. supr. Spl. needs cons. Project Head Start, Va., Minn., 1974-75; speech, lang. clinician Mid-Range Spl. Edn. Coop., Chisholm, Minn., 1975-78, coordinator, 1978—. Mem. AAUW (pres.), Minn. Speech/Hearing Assn. (policy council 1984-86), Am. Speech, Lang. and Hearing Assn., Early Childhood div. of Council for Exceptional Children, Minn. Adminstrs. for Spl. Edn. Lodge: Elks (bd. dirs. 1980-83). Home: 506 Highland Dr Hibbing MN 55746

DOSPIL-JULIAN, MARGARET LOUISE, management consultant; b. Chgo., Oct. 14, 1958; d. Felix Charles Jr. and Astrid Margarethe (Keipper) Dospil; m. Scott Charles Julian, Sept. 8, 1984. BSCE, Bradley U., 1980; MS in Indsl. Engring., Northwestern U., 1985. Design engr. Universal Oil Products, Des Plaines, Ill., 1980-83; mgmt. cons. Touche Ross & Inc., Chgo., 1984—; cons. on ch. renovation. Dancer, singer USO, 1980-82. Named Miss Heart of Ill., Miss Ill./Miss Am. contest, 1980, recipient Spl. Judge's award, 1980. Mem. Nat. Assn. for Female Execs., Northwestern U. Tech. Alumni Assn. Roman Catholic. Home: 7355 N Winchester Chicago IL 60626

DOSS, DONNA SUE, software engineer; b. Dearborn, Mich., June 18, 1961; d. Norman Eugene and Carolyn Ann (Weber) Caldwell; m. Robert James Doss, May 22, 1982. BS, Eastern Mich. U., 1984. Computer programmer Morgan Electric, Inc., Southfield, Mich., 1984-85; software engr. Automated Systems div. Volvo N.Am. Corp., Sterling Heights, Mich., 1985—. Mem. Nat. Assn. Female Execs., Inc., Golden Key, Phi Kappa Phi. Presbyterian. Avocations: tennis, reading, collecting Depression Era glassware. Home: 7962 Harding St Taylor MI 48180 Office: Volvo NAm Corp 7000 Nineteen Mile Rd Sterling Heights MI 48078

DOSS, ERICE ELAINE, psychologist, educator, consultant; b. Nashville, July 29, 1952; d. Woodrow Wilson Doss and Birdie Mae (Northington) D. BS, Tenn. State U., 1973; MS, U. Tenn., 1975; EdD, Vanderbilt U., 1985; spl. study Ga. Inst. Tech., 1986-87. Team coordinator Tenn. Dept. Mental Health Retardation, Arlington, 1975-77; outreach social worker, Nashville, 1977-78, adminstrv. rev. officer, 1978-80, program specialist, 1980-84; counseling intern Ga. State U., Atlanta, 1984-85; counseling psychologist Ga. Inst. Tech., Atlanta, 1985—; spl. study Ga. Inst. Tech., 1986-87; adj. assoc. prof. Atlanta U., 1982—; . cons. Industry Edn. Connection, 1987—, Personal Resource Design, Inc., Atlanta, 1985-86; writer Nat. Baptist Pub. Bd., Nashville, 1982-83, 85—. T.B. Boyd fellow Nat. Bapt. Pub. Bd., 1983; named one of Outstanding Young Women in Am., 1985; recipient Most Outstanding Faculty of Yr. award Ga. Inst. Tech, 1987. Mem. Am. Assn. Counseling Devel., Assn. Mental Health Counselors, Atlanta Mental Health Assn. Assn. Non-White Concerns, Assn. Black Psychologists, Southeastern Psychol. Assn., Assn. Social and Behavioral Scientists, Kappa Kappa Gamma (scholar), Alpha Kappa Alpha. Avocations: reading, writing, singing, sports, pub. speaking. Mailing Address: 5761 Wells Circle Stone Mountain GA 30088 Office: Ga Inst Tech Dir Student Affairs Atlanta GA 30332

DOSS, JUDITH HARRIS, country club executive; b. Memphis, Dec. 7, 1934; d. Wiley Chasteen and Irene Randle (Hodges) Harris; student Memphis State U., 1952-53, seminars U. Tenn., Nashville, 1971-76, Tenn. State U., 1978-81, Vanderbilt U., 1982, Gourmet's Oxford (Eng.) Center for Mgmt. Studies, 1982, Lo Scaldavivande Cooking Sch., Rome, 1983; m. Leslie Doss, Jr., 1953 (div. 1973); children—Leslie Walter III, Randle Elizabeth. Sec., receptionist James W. Stewart, investor, Dixie Oil Co., 1971-75; food service dir. The Webb Sch., Bell Buckle, Tenn., 1976-83; mgr. Plantation Country Club, Pharr, Tex., 1983-87; gen. mgr. Graymere Country Club, Columbia, Tenn., 1987—; mem. 3d Nat. Conf. Nutrition, 1980, Nat. Food Policy Conf., Washington, 1982. Pres. Hillwood Presbyn. Ch. Women, Nashville, 1968-70; mem. Nashville Symphony Guild. Mem. Colonial Dames Am. (chpt. dir. 1981-83), Ladies Hermitage Assn. (life), Cheekwood Fine Arts Center, Assn. Tenn. Antiquities, Nat. Assn. Female Execs., Club Mgrs. Assn. Am. Internat. Wine Soc., Pharr C. of C., Tex. Restaurant Assn., Orgn. Women Execs. (v.p. 1986-87), DAR, Alpha Gamma Delta. Clubs: Shelbyville Women's, Zonta (chpt. bd. dirs. 1986-87). Contbr. to The Webb Cookbook, 1977, 79. Home: 2013 Union Dr Columbia TN 38401 Office: Graymere Club Country Club Ln Columbia TN 38401

DOTY, DELLA CORRINE, financial consultant; b. Marshalltown, Iowa, Apr. 12, 1945; d. Edwin Francis and Della Edna (Keller) Mack; B.S.B.A. in Acctg., Drake U., 1967; m. Philip Edward Doty, Dec. 23, 1967; children—Sarah Corrine, Anne Elizabeth. Audit staff Alexander Grant & Co., C.P.A.s, Denver, 1967-71; controller Valley View Hosp. and Med. Center, Denver, 1971-75; rate rev. specialist Colo. Hosp. Assn., Denver, 1975-79; pvt. fin. cons., Littleton, Colo., 1979—; lectr. in field. Dir., asst. treas. YWCA of Metro Denver, 1972-74; bd. dirs. Colo. Heart Assn., 1974-82; chmn., bd. dirs. Families First, Inc., 1988—; mem. Jr. League of Denver, 1979—, v.p. mktg., 1985-86; sec. Littleton Pub. Schs. Bldg. Authority, 1983-86; active various charitable orgns.; v.p. fin. and housing Alpha Phi Internat., 1974-78, trustee, 1980-86; dir., treas. Alpha Phi Found., 1978-86. Recipient Founders Merit award Healthcare Fin. Mgmt. Assn., 1976, 83, Outstanding Vol. award Jr. League of Denver, 1984; C.P.A., Colo. Mem. Am. Inst. C.P.A.s, Colo. Soc. C.P.A.s, Hosp. Fin. Mgmt. Assn., Alpha Phi (Ursa Major award 1980). Republican. Baptist. Contbr. articles to profl. jours. Address: 5981 S Coventry Ln W Littleton CO 80123

DOUBLEDEE, SARA LYNN, nurse, educator; b. Laural, Miss., Mar. 28, 1946; d. James Raymond and Sarah Frances (Ruffin) D. ADAS, Kellogg Community Coll., 1967; BS in Nursing, No. Mich. U., 1972, MA, 1974; MS in Nursing, Wayne State U., 1977; PhD, Mich. State U., 1986. RN, Mich. Staff nurse Community Hosp., Battle Creek, Mich., 1967-68; staff nurse, head nurse Hutzel Hosp., Detroit, 1968-71; staff nurse Health Ctr. No. Mich. U., Marquette, 1971, asst. prof. nursing, coordinator continuing edn. dept. nursing, 1972-88, prof. nursing, coordinator continuing edn. for nurses, 1988—; dir. grad. programs nursing, No. Mich. U., Marquette, 1988—. Bd. dirs. Lake Superior Hospice Assn., Marquette, 1985—. Mem. Mich. Nurses Assn. (chairperson 1986-88), Marquette Alger Dist. Nurses Assn. (chairperson 1975-77, Nurse of Yr. 1980), Am. Legion Aux., Phi Kappa Phi, Sigma Theta Tau. Presbyterian. Office: No Mich U Dept Nursing Marquette MI 49855

DOUGAN, DIANA LADY, federal agency executive; b. Dayton, Ohio, Jan. 13, 1943; d. Harold Wendell and Elaine (Staggers) Lady; m. J. Lynn Dougan, Nov. 30, 1968; children: Gavin Marriott, Elena Lady. BA in Indsl. Psychology and English, U. Md., 1964; postgrad., U. Utah, 1969-70; grad. advanced mgmt. program, Harvard U., 1979. Asst. chief clk. Md. State Legis., Annapolis, 1965, 66; free lance mktg. pub. relations cons. N.Y.C., Washington, 1965-66; mktg., promotions dir. Time Inc., N.Y.C., 1966-68; ptnr. Dougan and Assoc., Salt Lake City, 1970-81; dir. Corp. for Pub. Broadcasting, Washington, 1976-83; coordinator, dir. for internat. communications and info. policy Dept. State, Washington, 1983—; nat. adv. bd. Ctr. for Study of Presidency, 1987—; chmn. numerous U.S. dels. on telecommunications and info. policy. Exec. producer pub. affairs TV series Way of Art, 1970-72, Pub. Broadcasting System TV and Nat. Pub. Radio program The MX Debate, 1981 (Peabody award 1981); producer Pub. Broadcasting System TV spl. The Nutcracker, 1975, 76, 77. Bd. dirs. U.S. Film and Video, 1978-82; mem. nat. adv. bd. Ballet West, 1987—; mem. gubernatorial commn. on exec. reorgn. Utah, 1980-83; mem. Utah Telecommunications Task Force, 1978. Recipient Md. Disting. Citizen award Gov. Md., 1965; named Hon. Citizen of Korea, 1965, Utah Woman of Yr. AAUW, 1978, Outstanding Woman in Communications, Women in Communications, 1980. Republican. Office: Dept of State Internat Communication & Info 2201 C St NW Washington DC 20520

DOUGHER, CATHERINE ANNIE, retail store executive; b. Scranton, Pa., Feb. 6, 1947; d. William Gary and Veronica (Duffy) Gray; m. James Michael Dougher, Nov. 27, 1969; children: William, Veronica, Timothy, Andrea, Amanda. Student, Lackawanna Jr. Coll., 1978-80. Asst. bookkeeper Kingswood Restaurant and Gourmet Family Restaurant, Chinchilla, Pa., 1977-80; payroll clk. Jacobson Hat Co., Inc., Scranton, Pa., 1980-84; bookkeeper James Dougher Plumbing & Heating, Scranton, 1984-87; owner, mgr. Renaissance Woman, Scranton, 1987—. Mem. Scranton C. of C., Am. Bus. Women's Assn. Democrat. Roman Catholic. Home: 714 Prescott Ave Scranton PA 18510 Office: Renaissance Woman 1403 Mulberry St Scranton PA 18510

DOUGHERTY, BARBARA CAROLYNE, utility company insurance administrator; b. Elizabeth, N.J., May 9, 1937; d. Alexander Joseph and Marie Louise (Buchwald) D.; m. Peter R. Madorma (div. July 1958); children: Keith R., Kim L. Madorma DiPaolo; children from previous marriage: Kelli A. Gencsy, Kevin A. Gencsy. Model Barbizon Agy., N.Y.C., 1954-58; sec. Hartig Extruders, Mountainside, N.J., 1958-61, Albert, Frank, Gunther Law Advt., N.Y.C., 1961-65; legal sec. Rinaldo and Rinaldo, Elizabeth, N.J., 1965-77, office mgr., 1973-77; legal asst. Elizabethtown Gas Co., Elizabeth, 1977-87, ins. adminstr., 1987—. Bd. dirs. Rahway (N.J.) Day Care Ctr., 1984—, sec., 1986-87, v.p., 1987—; mem. exec. com. Rahway YMCA, 1985—, sec. bd. dirs, 1985—. Mem. Union County Legal Secs., C. of C. Roman Catholic. Home: 6 Tisbury Ct Scotch Plains NJ 07076 Office: Elizabethtown Gas Co 1 Elizabethtown Plaza Elizabeth NJ 07207

DOUGHERTY, BONNIE JOAN, property management company executive; b. Newark, Dec. 20, 1950; d. William Martin and Alice Ella (Campbell) D. BA in Psychology, Monmouth Coll., 1971. Lic. real estate broker, Colo., N.Mex.; lic. real estate salesman, Ariz. Asst. mgr. Viewmont Village Apts., Scranton, Pa., 1972-74; resident mgr. Levering & Reid, Houston, 1976-78; v.p. Allen Assocs., Denver, 1978-83; v.p. adminstrn. Arthur Assocs., Albuquerque, 1983; regional property mgr. Empire West Cos., Tucson, 1984; mgr. Tucson br. Evans Withycombe, Tucson, 1985—; instr. Nat. Apt. Assn., Denver, 1981-83, El Paso, Tex., 1984. Pres., Pier Point Homeowners Assn., Aurora, Colo., 1982. Mem. Nat. Assn. Female Execs., Ariz. Multi Housing Assn., Nat. Apt. Assn., Inst. Real Estate Mgmt. (cert. property mgr. 1983). Lodge: Eastern Star. Avocations: swimming, collecting Southwest Indian Art. Office: Evans Withycombe 1600 N Kolb #220 Tucson AZ 85715

DOUGHERTY, JUNE EILEEN, librarian; b. Union City, N.J., Mar. 27, 1929; d. Robert John and Jane Veronica (Smith) Beyrer; B.A. in Edn., Peterson State Coll., 1967; postgrad. Rutgers U. Sch. Library Sci., 1959-69; m. Donald E. Dougherty, Dec. 2, 1946; 1 son, Glen Allan. With A. B. Dumont, Paterson, N.J., 1950-54; sch. librarian St. Paul's Elementary Sch., Prospect Park, N.J., 1957—; dir. North Haledon (N.J.) Free Pub. Library, 1957—; sec.-treas. Dougherty & Dougherty, Inc., North Haledon, 1968—. Den mother Boy Scouts Am., 1954-57; mem. Gov. N.J.'s Tercentenary Com., 1962-64. Mem. Am., N.J., N. Haledon library assns., Cath. Library Assn., N.J. Libraries Roundtable, Bergen-Passaic Library Club, Friends N. Haledon Library. Roman Catholic. Club: St. Paul's Social. Home: 155 Westervelt Ave North Haledon NJ 07508 Office: 129 Overlook Ave North Haledon NJ 07508

DOUGHERTY, MOLLY IRELAND, organization executive; b. Austin, Tex., Oct. 3, 1949; d. John Chrysostom and Mary Ireland (Graves) D. Student Stanford U., 1968-71, Grad. Theol. Union, Berkeley, 1976; B.A., Antioch U. W., 1979. Tchr., fundraiser Oakland Community Sch., Calif., 1973-77; assoc. producer, asst. editor film Nicaragua: These Same Hands, Palo Alto, Calif., 1980; free lance journalist, translator, Nicaragua, 1981; ednl. programs dir. Found. for Open Co., Berkeley, 1982-83; assoc. producer, film: Short Circuit: Inside the Death Squads; exec. dir. Vecinos, A Tex. Inter-Am. Initiative, Austin, Tex., 1984—. Bd. dirs. Nat. Immigration Refugee and Citizenship Forum, Washington, 1985-88. Home: 1100 Claire Ave Austin TX 78703 Office: Vecinos A Tex Inter-Am Initiative PO Box 4562 Austin TX 78765

DOUGHERTY, SHYRL LYNNETTE, food service director; b. Santa Ana, Calif., Dec. 20, 1944; d. Virgil Roy and Ruth Evelyne (Critzer) Winn; m. Robert Segraves Dougherty; 1 child, Rochelle Louise. AA, Santa Ana Jr. Coll., 1964; BA, Calif. State U., Long Beach, 1966, MA, 1967. Registered dietitian, Calif. Intern in dietetics St. Mary's/Mayo Clinic, Rochester, Minn., 1968; supervisory dietitian Food Mgmt. Systems Co., Los Angeles, 1968-69; dietitian Healthcare Nat. Dietary Systems, Inc., Los Angeles, 1969-76; dir. food services Montebello (Calif.) Unified Sch. Dist., 1976—. Pub., editor health care manuals. Recipient Ozzie award, 1987. Mem. Am. Dietetic Assn., Calif. Sch. Food Service Assn. (sec. 1983-85, pres.-elect 1987—), So. Calif. Sch. Food Service Assn. (sec. 1981-82, pres. 1982-83). Office: Montebello Unified Sch Dist 123 S Montebello Blvd Montebello CA 90640

DOUGHERTY, URSEL THIELBEULE, communications, marketing executive; b. Rotenburg, W. Ger., July 30, 1942; naturalized U.S. citizen, 1965; d. Hugo and Margarete (Marquardt) Thielbeule; B.A. summa cum laude in Polit. Sci., Cleve. State U., 1971; M.A. in Polit. Sci., U. Wis., 1972; M.B.A. in Fin., Case Western Res., 1982; m. Erich A. Eichhorn, Jan. 3, 1979. Journalist maj. daily, women's mag., Germany, 1962-66; assoc. editor Farm Chems., 1967; publs. mgr. Trabon Systems, 1967-68; research analyst Legis. Council, State of Wis., 1972; pub. relations adminstr. to mgr. pub. info. Eaton Corp., Cleve., 1972-84; dir. pub. affairs Freightliner/Mercedes-Benz Truck Co., Washington, 1984-87, v.p. Chmn.'s Office, 1987—; cons. small bus. Trustee, Lake Erie council Girl Scouts U.S.A., 1975-82, Sr. Citizen Resources, 1978-81; ambassador Jr. Achievement, 1979; steering com. YWCA Career Women of Achievement, 1981; adv. bd. Women's Career Networking, 1980-84; trustee, chmn. fin. com. Young Audience Greater Cleve., 1982-84. Mem. Women in Communications, Sales and Mktg. Execs. Cleve., Public Relations Soc. Am., Detroit Press Club, Cleve. Inst. Art, Am. Exec. Women, Pub. Affairs Council. Home: 1510 Crest Rd Cleveland Heights OH 44121 Office: Freightliner Corp Chairman's Office Washington DC 20090

DOUGLAS, CYNTHIA LYNN, pathologist; b. Appleton, Wis., Oct. 7, 1952; d. Richard Richard and Shirley Ann (Cole) Douglas. BA summa cum laude, Cen. Wash. State U., Ellensburg, 1975; MD, U. Wash., 1978. Resident U. Wash. Med. Ctr., Seattle, 1979-82; co-dir. lab. Twin Cities Community Hosp., Templeton, Calif., 1983-85, dir., 1985—; locum tenens coroner Chelan County Coroner office, Wenatchee, Wash., 1982-83; locum tenens lab. dir. N.W. Med. Lab., Seattle, 1982-83; labs. insp. Coll. Am. Pathologists, 1982; lectr. U. Wash., high schs. and community groups; investigator causes of post-operative granulomas, 1979, transcutaneous oxygen monitoring in high risk pregnancies, 1981. Contbr. articles to profl. jours., short stories to mags. Recipient Physician Recognition award AMA, 1984—, 4th Place Afgan Crochet award SLO County Fair, 1986. Fellow Coll. Am. Pathologists, Am. Soc. Clin. Pathologists; mem. Calif. Med. Assn., Hypnosis Soc. (Cen. Coast chpt.), San Luis Obispo County Med. Soc., San Luis Obispo Pathology Soc. (pres. 1985-88), Women's Med. Soc. (utilization rev. chmn. 1985, tissue and transfusion 1983—, infection control com. 1984—, chmn. 1988), Paso Robles C. of C., Cousteau Soc., Greenpeace. Avocations: piano, knitting and crocheting, softball. Home: 932 Walnut Dr Paso Robles CA 93446 Office: Twin Cities Community Hosp-Lab 1100 Las Tablas Rd Templeton CA 93465

DOUGLAS, ELIZABETH G., real estate broker; b. Wilmington, N.C., Aug. 2, 1920; d. Eugene Earl and Margaret G. (Johnson) Graham; m. Charles Gwynne Douglas Jr., Apr. 15, 1915; children: Charles G. III, Margaret Douglas Frank, Eugenia D. O'Brien. BA magna cum laude, Beaver Coll., 1940. Cert. sec. tchr., Pa. Head English dept. Hopkinton (N.H.) High Sch., 1966-72; pres., owner Decoy House Real Estate, Hopkinton, 1972—. Contbr. articles to profl. jours. Pres. Concord (N.H.) Bd. of Realtors, 1984, chmn. gov. affairs com. 1985-87; dir. Tri-State Grad. Realtors Inst., Concord, 1978-83. Named Realtor of Yr., Concord Bd. Realtors, 1985. Mem. N.H. State Assn. Realtors (mem. com. 1986-87), New England Cert. Residential Brokers (ambassador 1986-87), Women's Council of Realtors (pres. N.H. chpt. 1985, state gov. 1986, v.p. Concord chpt. 1987, Woman of Yr. 1987). Republican. Episcopalian. Club: Hopkinton Woman's (1st v.p., membership chmn.), RTB Investment (Concord) (pres. 1985-87). Home: Gould Hill Rd Hopkinton NH 03229 Office: Decoy House Realtors Fountain Square Hopkinton NH 03229

DOUGLAS, MARION JOAN, labor negotiator; b. Jersey City, May 29, 1940; d. Walter Stanley and Sophie Frances (Zysk) Binaski; children: Jane Dee, Alex Jay. BA, Mich. State U., 1962; MSW, Sacramento State Coll., 1971; MPA, Calif. State U.-Sacramento, 1981. Owner, mgr. Linkletter-Totten Dance Studios, Sacramento, 1962-68, Young World of Discovery, Sacramento, 1965-68; welfare worker Sacramento County, 1964-67, welfare supr., 1968-72, child welfare supr., 1972-75, sr. personnel analyst, 1976-78, personnel program mgr., 1978-81, labor relations rep., 1981—; cons. State Dept. Health, Sacramento, 1975-76; cons. in field. Author/editor: (newsletter) Thursday's Child, 1972-74. Presiding officer Community Resource Orgn., Fair Oaks, Calif., 1970-72; exec. bd. Foster Parent's Assn., Sacramento, 1972-75; organizer Foster Care Sch. Dist. liaison programs, 1973-75; active Am. Lung Assn., 1983-87; rep. Calif. Welfare Dirs. Assn., 1975-76; county staff advisor Joint Powers Authority, Sacramento, 1978-81; mem. Mgmt. Devel. Com., Sacramento, 1979-80; vol., auctioneer KVIE Pub. TV, Sacramento, 1970-84, 88—; adv. bd. Job and Info. Resource Ctr., 1976-77; spl. adv. task force coordinator Sacramento Employment and Tng. Adv. Council, 1980-81; vol. leader Am. Lung Assn., Sacramento, 1983-86 Calif. Dept. Social Welfare ednl. stipend, 1967-68, County of Sacramento ednl. stipend, 1969-70. Recipient Achievement award Nat. Assn. Counties, 1981. Mem. Mgmt. Women's Forum, Indsl. Relations Assn. No. Calif., Indsl. Relations Research Assn., Nat. Assn. Female Execs., Mensa. Republican. Avocations: real estate, nutrition. Home: 7812 Palmyra Dr Fair Oaks CA 95628 Office: County of Sacramento Dept Personnel Mgmt 700 H St Sacramento CA 95814

DOUGLAS, MICHELLE, medical records administrator; b. Gary, Ind., Mar. 26, 1961; d. William James and Dorothy Mae (Adkisson) D. BS, Indiana U., Indpls., 1985. Dir. med. records Cermak Health Services, Chgo., 1985-86; mgr. med. records Cook County Hosp., Chgo., 1986; dir. med. records and utilization rev. dept. Mary Thompson Hosp., Chgo., 1986-87, dir. utilization rev., 1987-88; dir. med. records Chgo. Osteo. Hosp., 1988—. Recipient Gertrude Gunn award Fore Found., Indpls., 1985, Cheer Quild award Univ. Hosps., Indpls., 1985. Mem. AMA, Ind. Med. Record Assn., Ill. Med. Record Assn., Chgo. Vicinity Med. Record Assn., Alpha Kappa Alpha. Democrat. Baptist. Home: 532 Ralston St Gary IN 46906 Office: Chgo Osteo Hosp 5200 S Ellis Chicago IL 60615

DOUGLAS, SUSAN, data processing specialist, consultant; b. Chgo., Oct. 29, 1946; d. Lawrence and Phoebe Fern (Sibbald) D.; m. John D. Hauenstein, Dec. 21, 1972 (div. June 1975). BA, U. Iowa, 1972; postgrad., U. Wis., Whitewater, 1985. Project coordinator Westinghouse Learning Corp., Iowa City, Iowa, 1967-75; echocardiology technician Chgo. Osteo. Hosp., 1975-78; systems programer, analyst Household Fin. Corp., Prospect Heights, Ill., 1978-81; applications analyst Burdick Corp., Milton, Wis., 1981-84; cons. Edgerton, Wis., 1984—. Mem. Data Processing Mgmt. Assn., System 38 User's Group. Episcopalian. Home and Office: 8203 Hwy 184 Edgerton WI 53534

DOUGLASS, ENID HART, educational director; b. Los Angeles, Oct. 23, 1926; d. Frank Roland and Enid Yandell (Lewis) Hart; m. Malcolm P. Douglass, Aug. 28, 1948; children: Malcolm Paul Jr., John Aubrey, Susan Enid. BA, Pomona Coll., 1948; MA, Claremont (Calif.) Grad. Sch., 1959. Research asst. World Book Ency., Palo Alto, Calif., 1953-54; exec. sec., asst. dir. oral history program Claremont Grad. Sch., 1963-71, dir. oral history program, 1971—, history lectr., 1977—; mem. Calif. Heritage Preservation Commn., 1977-85, chmn. 1983-85. Contbr. articles to hist. jours. Mayor pro tem City of Claremont, 1980-82, Mayor, 1982-86; mem. planning and research adv. council State of Calif., mem. city council, Claremont, 1978-86; founder Claremont Heritage, Inc., 1977-80, bd. dirs., 1986—. Mem. Oral History Assn. (pres. 1979-80), Southwest Oral History Assn. (founding steering com. 1981, J.V. Mink award 1984), Nat. Council Pub. History, LWV (bd. dirs. 1957-59). Democrat. Home: 1195 Berkeley Ave Claremont CA 91711 Office: Claremont Grad Sch Oral History Program 900 N College Ave Claremont CA 91711

DOUGLASS, RAMONA ELIZABETH, medical sales professional; b. N.Y.C., Aug. 15, 1949; d. Howard William and Lena Verona (Belle) D. Student, Colo. Sch. Mines, 1966-68; BS in Physical Sci., Colo. State U., 1970. Adminstrv. asst. S.E. Queens Community Corp., Queens, N.Y., 1970-71; research editor Encyclopedia Britannica, Chgo., 1971-73; sales rep. Scott Foresman Co., Glenview, Ill., 1973-75, Am. Sci. Products, McGaw Park, Ill., 1975-78; mgr. New Eng. territory Hollister, Inc., Libertyville, Ill., 1978-81; mgr. midwest region Precision Dynamics Corp., San Fernando, Calif., 1981—; ptnr. Douglass/Sherod-Winter Assocs., Chgo., 1986-88. Contbr. poetry) Great Am. Poetry Anthology, 1987. Founding mem. The Nat. Alliance Against Racist & Polit. Repression, Chgo., 1972; bd. dirs., chair publicity The Biracial Family Network, Chgo., 1987—. Mem. Nat. Assn. Female Execs., Nat. Network Women Sales. Democrat. Home: 3952 N Southport Box 178 Chicago IL 60613 Office: Precision Dynamics Corp 13880 Del Sur San Fernando CA 91340-3490

DOUMAS, GENA KATHLEEN, controller; b. Winston-Salem, N.C., Nov. 27, 1963; d. Nick Harold and Susan Ellen (Ledwith) D. BS in Bus. Computers, Davidson County Community Coll., 1984. Computer programmer Precision Part Systems, Inc., Winston-Salem, 1984-85, controller, 1986—; computer oerator Stroh Container, 1985-86; ptnr., office mgr. Artisan Prodns. Ltd., Winston-Salem, 1986—. Republican. Greek Orthodox. Home: 3155 Stratford Rd Winston-Salem NC 27103 Office: Precision Part Systems Inc 3401 Indian Ave Winston-Salem NC 27105

DOURAS, CAROLE LYNN, personnel director; b. El Paso, Tex., Dec. 4, 1944; d. William O. Jr. and Martha L. (Hutchinson) Johnson; m. James H. Douras, June 6, 1965 (div. Feb. 1978); children: Jenny Rebecca, Alison Lynn. BS, Wayne State U., 1966, MBA, 1985. Tchr. Detroit Bd. Edn., 1966-67; corp. tng. exec. J.L. Hudson Co., Detroit, 1967-68; exec. sec. Detroit Police Officer's Assn., 1976-77; personnel asst. Mich. HMO, Detroit, 1977-79; personnel dir. John V. Carr and Son, Inc., Detroit, 1979—. Mem. personnel com. Camp Fire Detroit Area Council. Mem. Internat. Assn. Personnel Women (Det. chpt. treas. 1984-85, pres. 1986-87), Detroit Grand Prix Assn., Riverfront West Bus. Dist. Assn. (sec. 1985-86, pres. 1988). Office: John V Carr & Son Inc 1600 W Lafayette Detroit MI 48216

DOUTHIT, AUDREY HOLZER, social worker; b. Cin., May 2, 1925; d. William Frederick and Emma Elizabeth Holzer; B.A., U. Cin., 1946; M.A., U. Chgo., 1948; m. Harold Henry Douthit, July 17, 1948; 1 dau., Susan Emily Douthit Hollinberger. Social worker Presbyn. Hosp., Chgo., 1948-50; dir. social service dept. Drake Meml. Hosp., Cin., 1952-56; intake supr. Marion County Assn. Retarded Citizens, Indpls., 1966-78; dir. admissions New Hope Found. of Ind., Indpls., 1978-85; grad. student supr. Ind. U. Pres., So. Club of Indpls., 1976; mem. North Group Indpls. Symphony, Indpls. Mus. of Art. Mem. Nat. Assn. Social Workers, Acad. Cert. Social Workers (diplomate), Kappa Alpha Theta. Republican. Presbyterian. Home: 8120 N Brent Ave Indianapolis IN 42640

DOUTHITT, SHIRLEY ANN, insurance agent; b. Mexia, Tex., Feb. 21, 1947; d. Othello Young and Hazel Lorene (Corley) Thompson; m. A. Dwane Douthitt, Nov. 24, 1966; 1 child, Steven Dwane. Student, Leonard's Tng Sch., Houston, 1979; student Tex. local recording agts. licensing course, Austin, Tex., 1980; student farmers ins. group tng. program, Austin, 1980; student life underwriters trng course, Tyler, Tex., 1987. Lic. ins. agt. Sec. Lindsey & Newsom Ins. Adjusters, Palestine, Tex., 1965-73, J. Herrington Ins. Agy., Palestine, 1973-76, Ramsey Ins. Agy., Palestine, 1976-79; agt. Farmers Ins. Group, Palestine, 1979—. Recipient Bus. Woman of Yr. Palestine Profl. Bus. Women, 1983. Mem. Nat. Assn. Female Execs. Office: Shirley Douthitt Ins Agy 3507 W Oak PO Box 7000 Palestine TX 75802

DOUVILLE, JUDITH ANN, information scientist, chemist; b. N.Y.C., Nov. 3, 1937; d. Frank Peter and Helene Elizabeth (Wagner) Piliero; m. Phillip Raoul Douville, Jan. 31, 1959; children: Christina E. Douville Shaw, Suzanne T., Gabrielle M. AAS, Concordia Jr. Coll., Bronxville, N.Y., 1957; BA, U. Conn., 1959, MS, 1965; MLS, U. R.I., 1971. Instr. chemistry Annhurst Coll., Woodstock, Conn., 1965-66, Ea. Conn. State U., Willimantic, Conn., 1967-70; instr. chemistry Cen. Conn. State U., New Britain, 1966-67, serials librarian, 1970-72; mng. editor Info. Sci. Abstracts, New Haven, 1972-75; circulation mgr. Info. Sci. Abstracts, Albany, N.Y., 1978-81; info. scientist Metals Info. Ctr. Olin Corp., Albany, 1975-78; tech. librarian TRC Environ Cons. Inc., East Hartford, Conn., 1978-86; pres., owner NdS Info. Cons., Middletown, Conn., 1980—; abstractor Chem. Abstracts Service, Columbus, Ohio, 1961-78; adj. prof. U. R.I., Kingston, 1980-81; mem. faculty Sch. Library Sci., SUNY-Albany, 1984; sci. cons. Books for Coll. Libraries, 1986—. Compiler book Guidelines and Suggested Title List for Undergraduate Chemistry Libraries, 1982; editor HazChem Alert jour., 1986—; contbr. articles to profl. jours. Mem. Am. Chem. Soc., Spl. Libraries Assn., AAAS, Am. Soc. Indexers (newsletter editor 1985-87, Air Pollution Control Soc., Sigma Xi. Home: 23 Virginia Dr Middletown CT 06457 Office: NdS Info Cons 23 Virginia Dr Middletown CT 06457

DOVE, PATRICIA HOLLY, business/marketing consultant, housekeeping company executive, realtor; b. Mineola, N.Y., Dec. 27, 1949; d. Ronald Garrett and Ruth (Clarke) D.; stepdau. E. Lois Dove; student Forbes Trail Tech. Inst., 1967; B.S. in Chemistry cum laude, City U. N.Y., 1974; M.B.A., Babson Coll., 1981; m. George M. Patton, Feb. 7, 1970 (div. 1979). Lic. real estate salesperson, Calif. Research chemist, product mgr. Collaborative Research, Inc., Waltham, Mass., 1974-78; asst. to dir. corp. devel. Thiokol Corp., Newtown, Pa., 1979; asst. to comptroller Vac Hyd Processing Co., Woburn, Mass., 1979; nat. accounts sales rep. Millipore Corp., Bedford, Mass., 1980-81; sales and mktg. cons., Acton, Mass., 1981, Piedmont Calif., 1982-83; life ins. rep., service mgr. COPA/ITT Life Ins. Co., San Mateo, Calif., 1983; mktg. mgr. Strata GM Corp., Santa Clara, Calif., 1983-84; owner P.H. Dove Enterprises, Santa Clara, 1984—; realtor Los Altos (Calif.) Bd. Realtors, 1987— . Mem. Bus. and Profl. Women Boston (Nike award 1980), Am. Soc. Profl. and Exec. Women, Nat. Assn. Female Execs., AAUW. Address: 1809 Joan Way Apt 10 Santa Clara CA 95050

DOVE, RITA FRANCES, English language educator, writer; b. Akron, Ohio, Aug. 28, 1952; d. Ray A. and Elvira E. (Hord) D.; m. Fred Viebahn, Mar. 23, 1979; 1 child, Aviva Chantal Tamu Dove-Viebahn. BA summa cum laude, Miami U., Oxford, Ohio, 1973; postgrad., Universität Tübingen, Fed. Republic of Germany, 1974-75; MFA, U. Iowa, 1977; LLD (hon.), Miami U., Oxford, Ohio, 1988. Asst. prof. English Ariz. State U., Tempe, 1981-84, assoc. prof., 1984-87, prof., 1987—; writer-in-residence Tuskegee (Ala.) Inst., 1982; lit. panelist Nat. Endowment for Arts, Washington, 1984-86, chair poetry grants panel, 1985. Author: (poetry) The Yellow House on the Corner, 1980, Museum, 1983, Thomas and Beulah, 1986 (Pulitzer prize 1987); (short stories) Fifth Sunday, 1985 (Callaloo award 1986); mem. editorial bd. Nat. Forum, 1984—; assoc. editor Callaloo, 1986—; adv. and contbg. editor Gettysburg Rev., 1987—, TriQuarterly, 1988—. Commr. The Schomburg Ctr. Research in Black Culture, N.Y. Pub. Library, 1987—. Presdl. scholar, 1970; Fulbright/Hays fellow, 1974-75; research fellow U. Iowa, 1975, teaching/writing fellow U. Iowa, 1976-77; grantee Nat. Endowment for Arts, 1978; Guggenheim Found. fellow, 1983, Mellon fellow, 1988—; recipient Lavan Younger Poet award Acad. Am. Poets, 1986; Gen. Electric Found. award, 1987. Mem. PEN, Poetry Soc. Am., Associated Writing Programs (bd. dirs. 1985-88, pres. 1986-87), Phi Beta Kappa, Phi Kappa Phi. Office: Ariz State Univ Dept of English Tempe AZ 85287

DOVEL, MICHELLE, engineer; b. Annapolis, Md., Feb. 24, 1962; d. William Lawrence and Jean Ann (Hughes) D. BS in Computer Engring., Tulane U., 1984; postgrad., Fla. Inst. Technology, 1987—. Customer service Software Solutions, Metairie and Baton Rouge, La., 1984-85; test equipment engr. Martin Marietta, Orlando, Fla., 1985—. Mem. Assn. Female Execs., T.U. Engrs. Home: 4723 White Willow Ln Orlando FL 32808 Office: Martin Marietta Aerospace Sand Lake Rd Orlando FL 32855

DOVRING, KARIN ELSA INGEBORG, author, playwright; b. Stenstorp, Sweden, Dec. 5, 1919; came to U.S., 1953, naturalized, 1968; grad. Coll. Commerce, Gothenburg, Sweden, 1936; M.A., Lund (Sweden) U., 1943, Ph.D., 1951; Phil. Licentiate, Gothenburg U., 1947; m. Folke Dovring, May 30, 1943. Journalist several Swedish daily newspapers and weekly mags., 1940-60; tchr. Swedish colls.; research assoc. of Harold Lasswell Yale U., New Haven, 1953-78; fgn. corr. Swedish newspapers, Italy, Switzerland, France and Germany, 1956-60; vis. prof. Internat. U., Rome, 1958-60, Gottingen (W.Ger.) U., 1962; lectr. numerous univs. including Yale U., U. Wis., McGill U., U. Iowa; research assoc. U. Ill., Urbana, 1968-69; free-lance writer, journalist, 1960—; radio and TV interviews; books include Songs of Zion, 1951, Land Reform as a Propaganda Theme, 3d edit. 1965, Road of Propaganda, 1959, Optional Society, 1972; Frontiers of Communication, 1975, (short stories) No Parking This Side of Heaven, 1982; Harold D. Lasswell: His Communication with a Future, 1987; Forked Tongue? Body-Snatched English in Political Communications, 1988, contbr. numerous articles to mags.; writer Ill. Alliance to Prevent Nuclear War, radio theater. Recipient Swedish Nat. award for short stories Bonniers Pub. House Stockholm, 1951; lit. awards Internat. Acad. Leonardo da Vinci, Rome, 1982-83. Mem. NOW, Société Jean Jacques Rousseau (hon. life), Inst. Freedom of Press (life asso.). Democrat. Address: 613 W Vermont Ave Urbana IL 61801

DOW, JEAN LOUISE, school system business manager; b. Mattoon, Ill., Dec. 20, 1955; d. Paul Leroy and Maria (Brandlhofer) Smith; m. Chris Alan Pfeiffer, June 1, 1974 (div. Nov. 1979); 1 child, Lisa Marie; m. Bradley Ray Elder, Sept. 4, 1982 (div. Mar. 1985); m. John W. Dow, Aug. 1, 1986. B.S. in Bus., Eastern Ill. U., 1977, M.B.A., 1980. Office mgr. ED Buxton & Assocs., Charleston, Ill., 1974-77; personnel mgr. Unibuilt Structures, Charleston, 1977-80; bus. mgr. Eastern Ill Area Spl. Edn., Mattoon, 1980—. Ill. Assn. Sch. Bus. Ofcls. (scholarship 1984, com. mem. 1984—), Assn. Sch. Bus. Ofcls., Ill. Adminstrs. Spl. Edn. Republican, Kappa Delta Pi. Baptist. Avocations: sewing; jogging; swimming; racquetball; tennis.

DOW, LESLIE WRIGHT, communications company executive, writer, photographer; b. N.Y.C., Apr. 28, 1938; d. Charles Leslie Kerr and Margaret Scott (MacArthur) Wright; m. William Arthur Dow, Aug. 8, 1987; 1 child, John M. Haywood Jr. AA, Colby-Sawyer Coll., 1957; cert., Katharine Gibbs Sch., 1958. Prodn. asst. Time, Inc., N.Y.C., 1958-60; exec. asst. Jefferson-Standard Broadcasting Co., Charlotte, N.C., 1960-68, G.B. Wilkins Inc., Charlotte, 1981-83; pres., pub. relations cons. Wright Communications, Inc., Charlotte, 1983—. Contbr. photography to mags. and profl. jours.; contbr. articles to mags. Bd. dirs. Charlotte Symphony Women's Assn., 1964-71, Charlotte Symphony Orch., 1965—; mem. Aux. of the Mint Mus., Charlotte, 1965—. Mem. Am. Soc. Interior Designers (pub. relations dir. Charlotte 1984—), Nat. Assn. Female Execs., Am. Bus. Women's Assn., Am. Soc. Mag. Photographers, Profl. Photographers of N.C. Republican. Episcopalian. Home and Office: 3721 Pelham Ln Charlotte NC 28211

DOW, LOIS WEYMAN, physician; b. Cin., Mar. 11, 1942; d. Albert Dames and Elsie Marion (Krug) Weyman; m. Alan Wayne Dow, July 23, 1966 (div. Aug. 1979); children: Elizabeth Suzanne, Alan Wayne. BA summa cum laude, Cornell U., 1964; MD cum laude, Harvard U., 1968. Diplomate Am. Bd. Internal Medicine, Am. Bd. Hematology, Am. Bd. Med. Oncology. Intern Bronx Mcpl. Hosp. Ctr., N.Y.C., 1968-69; resident in internal medicine Presbyn. Hosp., N.Y.C., 1969-70; instr., research assoc. U. Tenn., Memphis, 1972-73, asst. prof., 1973-74; research assoc. in hematology and oncology St. Jude Children's Research Hosp., Memphis, 1974-77, asst. mem., 1977-80, assoc. mem., 1980-88; assoc. prof. pediatrics U. Tenn., Memphis, 1983—; mem. staff St. Jude Children's Research Hosp., Bapt. Mem. Hosp., 1972-88, Wilmington Med. Ctr., 1988—; cons. Nat. Cancer Inst. Contbr. articles to profl. jours. Fellow ACP, Am. Soc. Clin. Oncology; mem. Am. Fedn. Clin. Research, Am. Soc. Hematology, Am. Assn. for Cancer Research, Internat. Soc. Exptl. Hematology. Clubs: Harvard Radcliffe (Memphis), Club of Mid-South. Office: Delaware Clin and Lab Physician Suite 129 Med Arts Pavilion 4745 Stanton-Ogletown Rd Newark DE 19713

DOW, MARY ALEXIS, financial executive; b. South Amboy, N.J., Feb. 19, 1949; d. Alexander and Elizabeth Anne (Reilly) Pawlowski; m. Russell Alfred Dow, June 19, 1971. B.S. with honors, U. R.I., 1971. C.P.A., Oreg. Staff acct. Deloitte, Haskins & Sells, Boston, 1971-74; sr. acct. Price Waterhouse, Portland, Oreg., 1974-77, mgr., 1977-81, sr. mgr., 1981-84; chief fin. officer Copeland Lumber Yards Inc., Portland, 1984-86; ind. cons. in field, 1986—. Mem. council and fin. com. Oreg. Mus. Sci. and Industry; bd. dirs., exec. com. chair budget com. Oreg. Trails chpt. ARC; mem. budget rev. com. Multnomah County. Mem. Am. Inst. CPAs, Oreg. Soc. CPAs, Fin. Execs. Inst. Roman Catholic. Clubs: City (bd. govs.), University (Portland), Multnomah Athletic. Contbr. articles to profl. publs.

DOWBEN, CARLA LURIE, lawyer, educator; b. Chgo., Jan. 22, 1932; d. Harold H. and Gertrude (Geitner) Lurie; m. Robert Dowben, June 20, 1950; children: Peter Arnold, Jonathan Stuart, Susan Laurie. AB, U. Chgo., 1950; JD, Temple U., 1955; cert., Brandeis U., 1968. Bar: Ill. 1957, Mass. 1963, Tex. 1974, U.S. Supreme Ct., 1974. Assoc. Conrad and Verges, Chgo., 1957-62; exec. officer MIT, Cambridge, Mass., 1963-64; legal planner, Mass. Health Planning Project, Boston, 1964-69; assoc. prof. Life Scis. Inst., Brown U., Providence, 1970-72; asst. prof. health law U. Tex. Health Sci. Ctr., Dallas, 1973-78, assoc. prof., 1978—; ptnr. Brice and Mankoff, Dallas; cons. to bd. dirs. Mental Health Assn., 1958-86, Ft. Worth Assn. Retarded Citizens, 1980—, Advocacy, Inc., 1981-85. Contbr. articles to profl. jours.; active in drafting health and mental health legis., agy. regulations in several states and locat govts. Mem. ABA, Tex. Bar Assn., Dallas Bar Assn., Nat. Health Lawyers Assn., Hastings Inst. Ethics, Tex. Family Planning Assn. Quaker. Home: 7150 Eudora Dr Dallas TX 75230 Office: Brice and Mankoff 300 Crescent Ct Dallas TX 75201-1841

DOWDNEY, DONNA LEE, communications executive, educator; b. Chgo., Apr. 13, 1943; d. Donald Scott and Clarice Dolores (Pineau) Smyth; m. William Clayton Dowdney Jr., Aug. 19, 1967; children: Deborah Lee, David Scott. BA, Wheaton Coll., 1965; MA in Teaching, Ind. U., 1968; PhD, Columbia Pacific U., 1984. Cert. tchr. Tchr. Columbus (Ind.) Sr. High Sch., 1966-68, Ohlone Coll., Fremont, Calif., 1968-69; instr. various adult schs. and colls., Calif., 1969—; pres. Writing Enterprises Internat., Palo Alto, Calif., 1978—, Nautical Enterprise Internat., Palo Alto, 1987—; seminar presentor various orgns. Co-author: How to Write and Publish Articles in Nursing, 1986 (award); contbr. articles to profl. jours. Mem. Am. Med. Writers (speaker), Soc. Tech. Communication (speaker), Am. Bus. Communication Assn. (speaker), Calif. Writer's Club (Writer of Month 1985), Royal Overseas League, Royal Oak Found., No. Calif. Marine Assn., Calif. Yacht Brokers Assn. Club: Coyote Point Yacht. Home and Office: 1150 Newell Rd Palo Alto CA 94303-2997

DOWDY, HELEN MARIE, educational administrator; b. Macon, Ga., Mar. 10, 1930; d. Manly Calvin and Eriel Marie (Merriman) Britt; m. Lemuel Stroud Dowdy, Sept. 5, 1953; children—Lemuel David, Donald Manly. A.A., Mars Hill Coll., 1950. Cert., N.C. Pub. Mgr. Program. Sec. First Citizens Bank, Raleigh, N.C., 1950-53, N.C. State U., Raleigh, 1953-55; adminstrv. asst. N.C. Dept. Curriculum Study, Raleigh, 1959-63; adminstrv. asst. N.C. Dept. Community Colls., Raleigh, 1963-77, spl. asst. to pres., 1977—; cons. N.C. Employees Tng. Ctr., Raleigh, 1974-76; mem. adv. com. N.C. Employee Suggestion System, 1978—. Vice pres. Cary Jr. Woman's Club (N.C.), 1964. Mem. N.C. Assn. Ednl. Office Personnel (pres. dist. 10, 1977-78, scholarship fund named in her honor 1979), Am. Bus. Womens Assn. (chmn. edn. com. Cary chpt. 1979-80), Women in Mgmt. Democrat. Lutheran. Lodge: Soroptomists. Office: NC Dept Community Colls 200 W Jones St Raleigh NC 27603

DOWLEN, BETTY GREEN, director senior citizen center; b. Sheboygan, Wis., Oct. 26, 1929; d. William and Elsie (Hazen) Green; m. Robert Poppe, Jan. 10, 1951 (dec.); m. John Roe Dowlen, Nov. 20, 1956. Grad. high sch., Sheboygan. Med. historian Sheboygan Clinic, 1948-55; dir. Cathrine Edmondson Sr. Citizen Ctr., Clarksville, Tenn., 1975—. Vol. various community orgns., Clarksville, 1957-77. Democrat. Methodist. Home: Rt 2 Box 114 Clarksville TN 37093 Office: Cathrine Edmondson Sr Citizen Ctr 343 Pageant Clarksville TN 37040

DOWLING, DOROTHY RITA, communications company executive; b. Bklyn. Oct. 4, 1944; d. Leonard Thomas and Dorothy Mary (Steer) D.; m. James Thomas O'Neill, June 14, 1980. B.A., Montclair State Coll., 1966; postgrad. AT&T exec. M.S. program, Pace U., 1978-80. Researcher Ogilvy & Mather, N.Y.C., 1967-69; dir. research Einstein Assocs., N.Y.C., 1969-73; bus. analyst Xerox Corp., Rochester, N.Y., 1973-75; with mktg. dept. AT&T, Basking Ridge, N.J., 1975-84; dir. advt. and promotions NYNEX Corp., White Plains, N.Y., 1984-88, dir. product planning, 1988—. Home: 308 Glenbrook Rd Stamford CT 06906 Office: NYNEX Corp 1113 Westchester Ave White Plains NY 10604

DOWLING, JACQUES MACCUISTON, sculptor, painter, writer; b. Texarkana, Tex., Oct. 19, 1906; d. Charles Edward and Viola John (Estes) MacCuiston; Tchrs. Certificate, Coll. Marshall, 1923; studied art Loyola U., Frolich's Sch. Fine Art, Los Angeles, NAD, Art Students League, N.Y.C.; Ph.D., Colo. State Christian Coll. One woman shows include Fedn. Dallas Artists, 1950, 52, Rush Gallery, 1958, Sartor's Gallery, 1958, Sheraton-Dallas Hotel, 1960, Dallas Meml. Auditorium, 1960; exhibited in group shows at Dallas Mus. Fine Arts, Mus. of N.Mex., Fedn. Dallas Artists, Sartor's Galleries, Ney Art Mus., Oak Cliff Soc. of Fine Arts, Sartor's Gallery, Shuttles Gallery, Sheraton-Park Internat. Platform Assn., 1966-68, Phillips Mills Art Assn., 1967-74, Yardley Ann. Exhbn., 1968-73, Tinicum Art Festival, 1968, Woodmere Art Gallery (life mem.), 1972-74, others; selected sculpture 1st S.W. ann. show Mus. N.Mex., 1958; represented in permanent collections several corps., many pvt. homes. Recipient 1st Sculpture Fedn. Dallas Artists, 1950-54, pinned (all awards jewels), 1961; Recipient Sweepstakes award SW Ann. Art Show, 1953, Hon. Cert. award Dallas Fed. Bus. Assn., 1964; two 1st awards N.J. Fedn. Womens Clubs, 1972, two 1st award, 1974, 1st and 2d award 1975, Gold medal Accademia Italia, 1979, Golden Centaur award Accademia Italia, 1982, Gold medal Internat. Parliament (U.S.A.) of Safety and Peace, 1983, Centro Studi e Ricerche delle Nazioni, Parma, Italy, 1986, statue of victory, 1983; Oscar d' Italia, Accademia Italia, 1985; named Cavalier of Arts, Accademia Bedriacense, 1985, many others, including 3 awards for journalism, 1962-63; 2 Golden Flame awards World Parliament (U.S.A.), 1986. Fellow Internat. Inst. Arts and Letters (life); mem. Cousteau Soc. (founding), U.S. Chess Fedn., Am. Contract Bridge League, Internat. Acad. Lit., Arts and Sci. (hon. life mem., Tommaso Campanello with gold medal award 1972), C. of C. South Hunterdon (charter). Republican. Episcopalian. Mem. Order Eastern Star (past grand officer; past matron). Address: 2005 Halmrock Pl Sun City Center FL 33570

DOWLING, JEANNINE MARIE, manufacturing company executive; b. N.Y.C., Nov. 19, 1952; d. William Donald and Jeanne Dolores (Millet) Dowling; student Mich. State U., 1970-71, Harpur Coll., 1971-72; B.A., cum laude, SUNY, 1974; m. Michael E. Twomey, Sept. 20, 1980; 2 children. Dir. pub. info. N.Y. State Div. Human Rights, N.Y.C., 1975-78; mgr. pub. affairs programs Philip Morris, Inc., N.Y.C., 1978—. Dep. press sec. N.Y. State Carter Presdl. Campaign, 1974-75; mem. N.Y.C. Commn. on Status of Women, 1979—. Recipient Industry award Nat. Conf. Puerto Rican Women, 1981. Mem. Women in Communications (chmn. Matrix com. 1983), Public Relations Soc. Am., Women in Govt. Relations, N.Y. Public Affairs Profls., Nat. Women's Polit. Caucus, Lifelong Learning Council, Women's Econ. Round Table, Internat. Assn. Bus. Communicators, Women's Equity Action League. Office: Philip Morris 120 Park Ave New York NY 10017

DOWLING, MARY ANN, banker; b. N.Y.C., May 23, 1947; d. Christopher Patrick and Mary (Wilson) D.; 1 child, Danielle Marie. BA in Math., Herbert H. Lehman Coll., 1969; MBA in Fin., Pace U., 1978. With St. Vincent's Hosp., N.Y.C., 1970-72; asst. sec. corp. div. European Am. Bank and Trust Co., N.Y.C., 1972-78, asst. treas. Dutch sect., 1978-79; asst. v.p. N.Y. corp. sect. Bank of Am., N.Y.C., 1979-81, v.p. fin. markets cons. and tng., 1981-83, v.p., mgr. fgn. exchange cons. and sr. fgn. exchange advisor, 1983-84, v.p., mgr. treasury systems support, 1984-87, v.p., dir. tng. for global trading, 1987—. Mem. Nat. Assn. Female Execs., NOW, Career Links. Democrat. Roman Catholic.

DOWLING, NADINE VALERY, college administrator, educator; b. Weymouth, Mass., Feb. 14, 1947; d. Clayton Ellsworth and Alise (Rostan) D. BS with high honors, Northeastern U., 1978, MBA, 1983, postgrad., 1986—; postgrad., Harvard U., 1986. Asst. dir. personnel Northeastern U., Boston, 1972-84, mem. faculty coll. bus., 1980—; exec. dir. human resources/affirmative action Emerson Coll., Boston, 1984—; cons. Whale Communications, N.Y.C., 1978-80, Images, Hull, Mass., 1982—. Founder New Eng. Retirement Planners Council, 1974; chmn. employment com. Gov.'s Adv. Council for Affirmative Action, Boston, 1986—; mem. personnel bd. Town of Hull. Mem. Personnel Mgrs. Council (dir. pub. relations 1985-86, personnel bd. Town of Hull 1988), Internat. Assn. Personnel Women (editor newsletter 1982-83, pub. relations com. 1983-84), Nat. Assn. Female Execs. (dir. network 1985-86), Am. Soc. Personnel Adminstrs., Mass. Assn. Affirmative Actions Profls., Coll. and Univ. Personnel Assn. (dir. pub. relations 1984), Small Coll. Personnel Mgr.'s Assn. (founder), Fringe Benefits Adminstrs.' Council (founder), Greater Boston C. of C. (speaker Bus. Expo 1985). Democrat. Methodist. Home: 24 Halvorsen Ave Hull MA 02045 Office: Emerson Coll 100 Beacon St Boston MA 02115

DOWLING, ROSEMARIE, human resources executive; b. N.Y.C., Nov. 1, 1934; d. Patrick Bradley and Bridget (Duggan) McGowan; children: Michael Thomas, Kathleen Mary, Margaret Ann, Thomas Vincent, Barbara Ellen, Anne Elizabeth. AA, Queensborough Community Coll., Queens, N.Y., 1973; student, Queens Coll. Supr. William Esty Co., Inc., N.Y.C., 1954-55; clk. U.S. Postal Service, Far Rockaway, N.Y., 1968-80, foreman mails, supr. sta. ops., women's program coordinator L.I. dist., 1978-82; profl. spec. trainee NE region U.S. Postal Service, N.Y.C., 1982-83; dir. mgmt. sectional ctr. U.S. Postal Service, Hicksville, N.Y., 1983-86, field div. dir. human resources, 1986—. Mem. Golden Key Assn., Mensa (pres., v.p., sec. Greater N.Y. club 1979-87). Democrat. Roman Catholic.

DOWNEY, D'ANN BARBARA, contract administrator, business consultant; b. Medford, Oreg., Feb. 16, 1940; d. Myron Marcus and Marianna (Koepsell) D. BA in Econs., Calif. State U., Hayward, 1979; postgrad., UCLA, 1980-81, Golden Gate U., 1986—. Proposal analyst Stanford (Calif.) U., 1969-73, asst. research adminstr., 1973-75, contracts officer, 1975-80; sr. contracts adminstr. Jet Propulsion Lab., Pasadena, Calif., 1980-81; sr. subcontract buyer GTE-Govt. Systems Corp., Mountain View, Calif., 1981-85, procurement specialist, 1985—; cons. NCI, Bethesda, Md., 1973-79. Mem. Nat. Contract Mgmt. Assn., Soc. Research Adminstrs. Republican. Mormon.

DOWNEY, DEBORAH ANN, systems specialist; b. Xenia, Ohio, July 22, 1958, d. Nathan Vernon and Patricia Jaunita (Ward) D. Assoc. in Applied Sci., Sinclair Community Coll., 1981, student, 1986—. Jr. programmer, project mgr. Cole-Layer-Trumble Co., Dayton, Ohio, 1981-82; sr. programmer, analyst, project leader Systems Architects Inc., Dayton, 1982-84, Systems and Applied Sci. Corp., Dayton, 1984; systems programmer, analyst Fairborn, 1987—; analyst Unisys, Dayton, 1984-87; cons. computer software M&S Garage/Body Shop, Beavercreek, Ohio, 1986-87. Mem. Nat. Assn. for Female Execs., Am. Motorcyclist Assn., Sinclair Community Coll. Alumni Assn., Cherokee Nation Okla., Cherokee Nat. Hist. Soc. Democrat. Mem. United Ch. of Christ.

DOWNEY, LISA JANIS, data processing manager; b. Toppenish, Wash., Oct. 23, 1957; d. William W. and Juliana (Putney) Smith; m. Kevin W. Downey, Aug. 8, 1981; 1 child, Shawn C. Sec., legal aide King County Pros. Atty.'s Office, Seattle, 1977-79; graphics artist Boeing Co., Seattle, 1979-80; computer tech. aide, programmer Boeing Co., Tukwila, Wash., 1980-85; resource mgr. ESCA Corp., Bellevue, Wash., 1985-86, product support mgr., 1986—. Office: ESCA Corp 13208 Northup Way Bellevue WA 98005-2091

DOWNHAM, TAMARA SUE, real estate executive; b. Lafayette, Ind., Sept. 22, 1962; d. Robert Henry and Sally (Ingleman) D.; stepfather: William E. Miller. BA, Wheaton (Ill.) Coll., 1984. Exec. v.p. corp. accounts Spencer Realty Co., N.Y.C., 1984—; singer, actress N.Y. area, 1986—. Mem. Nat. Assn. Female Execs. Methodist. Office: Spencer Realty 274 Madison Ave New York NY 10016

DOWNING, CHRISTINE ROSENBLATT, theology educator; b. Leipzig, Germany, Mar. 21, 1931; came to U.S., 1935; d. Edgar Fritz and Herta (Fischer) Rosenblatt; m. George Downing, June 9, 1951, (div. Jan. 1978); children: Peter, Eric, Scott, Christopher, Sandra; m. River Malcolm, Sept. 2, 1984. BA, Swarthmore Coll., 1948; PhD, Drew U., 1966; MA, U.S. Internat. U., 1982. From instr. to assoc. prof. religion and psychology Rutgers U., New Brunswick, N.J., 1963-75; prof., chmn. dept. religious studies San Diego State U., 1974—; mem. core faculty Calif. Sch. Profl. Psychology, Pomona, 1974—. Author: The Goddess, 1981, Journey Through Menopause, 1987, Psyche's Sisters, 1988; co-author: Face to Face to Face, 1975; contbr. articles to profl. jours. Fellow NEH, 1982-83. Fellow Soc. Values in Higher Edn. (bd. dirs. 1966-81); mem. AAUP, Am. Acad. Religion (pres. 1973-74). Office: San Diego State U Dept Religious Studies San Diego CA 92182

DOWNING, DOROTHY JEAN, nurse practitioner; b. Omaha, June 9, 1928; d. Alvin Carl and Bessie Pearl (Williams) Wegeman; m. Jerome Grant Downing, Sept. 22, 1950; children: Jerome Grant II, Judith L. Jeanine A. BS in Nursing magna cum laude, Metro. State Coll., Denver, 1977; adult nurse practitioner degree, U. Colo., Denver, 1977. RN, Colo. Surgical nurse St. Anthony Hosp., Denver, 1950-51, Children's Hosp., Denver, 1951-52; supr. Hermitage Nursing Ctr., Alexandria, Va., 1963-64; staff nurse Vis. Nurse Service, Fairfax, Va., 1964-66; sch. nurse Denver Pub. Schs., 1968-69; dir. Casa Del Nursing Ctr., Lakewood, Colo., 1969-74; staff adult nurse practitioner Geriatric Med. Mgmt. Clinic, Denver, 1976-78, Metro. State Coll. Student Health Clinic, Denver, 1978-84; nursing cons., educator 1984—; asst. prof. nursing Denver U., 1982-84; lectr., cons. Met. State Coll., 1987; cons. Colorado Coll., Colorado Springs, 1984-85; presenter stress mgmt. sems. Contbr. articles to profl. mags. Mem. bd. of diaconate Ch. in the Wildwood, Green Mountain Falls, Colo. Club: Officer's Wives (Colorado Springs Air Force Acad.). Home and Office: PO Box 5252 Woodland Park CO 80866

DOWNING, LINDA L(OU), radio sales executive; b. Smith Center, Kans., Dec. 2, 1954; d. Forrest Jack Bock and Laneta Fern (Gilbert) Bock Karsting; m. Richard Lynn Johnson, Aug. 5, 1973 (div. July 1980); 1 child, Cody Ryan; m. Michael J. Downing, July 10, 1987; stepchildren: Alussa, Courtney. Degree in fashion merchandising Patricia Stevens Sch., Wichita, Kans., 1973. Asst. mgr. J. M. McDonald Co., Concordia, Kans. and Holdredge, Nebr., 1979-81; store mgr. Salking & Linoff Inc., Concordia and Sioux City, Iowa, 1982-83; account exec. Sentry Sta. KSEZ, Sioux City, 1983-84; sales mgr. Sta. KGLI, Cardinal Communications, Sioux City, 1984-85, gen. sales mgr. Stas. KGLI/KWSL, 1985-88; gen. mgr. KKRC/KKFN Radio Stas.-Vaughn Broadcasting, Sioux Falls, S.D., 1988—. Mem. Ad Club Sioux City, Nat. Assn. Female Execs. Home: 3728 Jones Sioux City IA 51104 Office: KKRC/KKFN 1704 S Cleveland Sioux Falls SD 57103

DOWNING, LYNDA, mortgage company executive; b. Hollywood, Calif., Jan. 10, 1949; d. Joseph Richard and Patricia Anita (Olson) Angelotti; m. John Jeffrey Downing, July 19, 1969; children: Joseph Scott, Kimberly Lynn, Lisa Michelle. AA, Moorpark Coll., 1967; cert. paralegal, Calif. Coll. Paralegal Studies, 1972; cert., Calif. Sch. Mortgage and Banking, 1979. Pvt. practice litigation paralegal Encino, Calif., 1975-79; asst. br. mgr. Transamerica Mortgage, San Diego, 1980-84; br. mgr., asst. v.p. Investors First Mortgage, San Diego, 1984-87; br. mgr. Coldwell Banker Mortgage, Encinitas, Calif., 1987—. Mem. Mortgage Bankers Assn., Assn. Profl. Mortgage Women, Nat. Assn. Female Execs. Democrat. Home: 2616 Sunset Hills Escondido CA 92025 Office: Coldwell Banker Mortgage 191 N El Camino Real Encinitas CA 92024

DOWNING, MARGARET MARY, newspaper editor; b. Altoona, Pa., June 3, 1952; d. Irvine William and Iva Ann (Regan) D. B.A. magna cum laude, Tex. Christian U., 1974. Reporting intern Corpus Christi Caller Times, summer 1973; reporter, bur. chief Beaumont Enterprise & Jour. (Tex.), 1974-76, Dallas Times Herald, 1976-80; reporter, asst. city editor, asst. bus. editor Houston Post, 1980—. Mem. Press Club of Houston (pres. 1984, bd. dirs. 1982-85), Greater Houston Hunter-Jumper Assn., Sigma Delta Chi. Episcopalian. Home: 6216 Community Dr Houston TX 77005 Office: Houston Post 4747 SW Freeway Houston TX 77001

DOWNS, BRANDI ELIZABETH, artist; b. McComb, Miss., Aug. 11, 1932; d. Jack Denson and Martha Ethel (Bornman) Hammack; B.F.A., Miss. State Coll. Women, 1955; m. William K. Douglas, Dec. 23, 1956 (div. Mar. 1986); children—Martha Anne, William K. Jr., Christine Rachel. Artist, WLBT-TV, Jackson, Miss., 1955, Gorden Marks Advt., Jackson, 1955-57, Dallas Times Herald, 1957-58, Whaley Studio, Dallas, 1958; art dir. Jiffy Printing, Dallas, 1958-59; tchr. art Dallas Public Schs., 1959-62; one-man shows Municipal Art Gallery, Jackson, 1955, French Quarter Gallery, New Orleans, 1967—71, Sheraton Gallery, San Juan, P.R., 1968, La Concia Gallery, San Juan, 1972, Our Lady of Holy Cross, 1971, San Geronimo Gallery, San Juan, 1973, French Quarter Design, New Orleans, 1974-75, Symmetry Gallery, New Orleans, 1976-77; exhibited in group shows Norfolk (Va.) Mus., 1953, Nat. Kappa Pi Exhbn., 1954. Recipient 1st prize Colonial Dames Art award, Columbus Miss., 1954; 1st prize Allison Wells, 1955; silver medal Tommaso Campanella Soc., Rome, 1970, Gold medal, 1972. Mem. Am. Artist Profl. League, Soc. N.Am. Artists, Jackson Sq. Lic. Artists. Home: 828 Orleans St New Orleans LA 70116 Office: 1136 Bourbon St New Orleans LA 70116

DOWNS, KATHLEEN ANNE, hospital department director; b. Toledo, Sept. 20, 1951; d. Keith Landis and Cecelia Josephine (Wood) Babcock; m. Michael Brian Thomas, July 17, 1971 (dec. Oct. 1973); m. David Michael Downs, Aug. 8, 1981. Student, San Diego Mesa Coll., 1968-70, Union for Experimenting Colls. and Univs., 1988—. Cert. med. staff coordinator. Sec. Travelodge Internat., Inc., El Cajon, Calif., 1970-73; intermediate stenographer City of El Cajon, 1973-77; adminstrv. asst. MacLellan & Assocs., El Cajon, 1977-78; sr. sec. WESTEC Services, Inc., San Diego, 1978; adminstrv. sec. El Cajon Valley Hosp., 1978-80; asst. med. staff Grossmont Dist. Hosp., La Mesa, Calif., 1980-83, coordinator med. staff, 1983-87, dir. med. staff services, 1987—; tchr. The Vogel Inst., San Diego, 1986. Mem. Nat. Assn. Med. Staff Services, Calif. Assn Med. Staff Services (pres. San Diego chpt. 1986-87, treas. San Diego chpt. 1984-86), Nat. Assn. for Female Execs. Office: Grossmont Dist Hosp PO Box 158 La Mesa CA 92044

DOWNS, LINN HEDWIG, computer company executive; b. Binghamton, N.Y., June 16, 1954; d. Charles William and Nancy Linn (Nellis) Downs; m. Donald Yukio Endo, Aug. 24, 1985. B.A., Pa. State U., 1976, MS, Nazareth Coll., 1980, postgrad. SUNY, Brockport, 1978-80. Cert. tchr., N.Y. Spanish tchr. Methacton Sch. Dist., Fairview Village, Pa., 1976-77; tchr. Ibero-Am. Action League, Rochester, N.Y., 1977-78; computer assisted translator Xerox Corp., 1978-82; research and devel. mgr. computer aided translation Cyaliphase Corp., Vienna, Va., 1982; computer aided translation sales mgr. Stenograph Corp., Skokie, Ill., 1982-83; mgr. computer aided translation Burroughs Corp., Detroit, 1983-85; v.p. Te Corp., Campton, N.H., 1985—; adv. bd. Wayne State U., 1984—. Contbr. articles to profl. jours. Mem. Am. Translators Assn. (panelist Washington 1982, chmn. machine translation subcom. 1984-86), Soc. Tech. Communication, Translators and Interpretors Edn. Soc. (panelist BYU 1983), Translators Guild, Assn. Computational Linguists, Inst. Linguists, N.Y. State Permanente. Home: 48 Treeline Thornton NH 03223 Office: Te Corp PO Box 140 Campton NH 03223

DOWNS, NANCY ELIZABETH, social worker; b. Marcus Hook, Pa., July 17, 1937; d. James Leon and Beatrice Ada (Roberts) D. BA in Sociology, Wheaton (Ill.) Coll., 1959; MSW, U. Pa., 1962. Social worker child care service County of Delaware, Media, Pa., 1959-65; dist. supr. family and community service County of Delaware, Media, 1969-81; social worker outpatient clinic Haverford (Pa.) State Hosp., 1966-68; pvt. practice social work Media, 1974-76; social worker United Cerebral Palsy Delaware County, Swarthmore, Pa., 1982—; chmn. staff personnel com. and grad. student supr. Family and Community Service Delaware County, 1974-75. Recorded album as mem. religious singing group Jes' Friends. Youth leader, tchr., music dir. Marcus Hook Baptist Ch., Linwood, Pa., 1959-65; restorer 1860 French Victorian house, Media and throughout Delaware County, Pa., 1975-83; vol. in teaching and music Crum Lynne (Pa.) Bapt. Ch., Elwyn Inst., Media, 1965-74. Mem. Nat. Assn. Social Workers (chmn. recruitment com. Brandywine Valley chpt. 1964), Acad. Cert. Social Workers, Nat. Assn. Social Workers Register Clin. Social Workers, Nat. Assn. Female Execs. Office: United Cerebral Palsy Delaware County 401 Rutgers Ave Swarthmore PA 19081

DOYLE, BARBARA ANN, engineer, consultant; b. Boston, Feb. 19, 1948. BA, U. Mass., 1977; MEd, Lesley Coll., 1979. Educator Lynnfield (Mass.) Schs., 1979-80; data processing supr. G.T.E. Sylvania, Westboro, Mass., 1980-83; sr. cons. Booz-Allen & Hamilton, Bedford, Mass., 1983-86; engr. Gen. Electric, Burlington, Mass., 1986—. Mem. gov.'s task force Com. on Edn., Boston, 1985-86; mem. Hugh O'Brien Youth Leadership, Boston, 1984-87. Mem. Nat. Assn. Female Execs., Armed Forces Communications and Elecronics Assn. Office: Gen Electric Rt 62 Burlington MA 01803

DOYLE, BEVERLY ANN, special education educator, psychologist; b. Hamburg, Iowa, Nov. 1, 1945; d. Robert Avery and Eunice Rose (Barsch) Scrimsher; m. Wayne Ralph Oppenheim, Mar. 7, 1960. BS, Iowa State U., 1967; MS, U. Nebr., Omaha, 1971; PhD, U. Nebr., 1977. Cert. sch. psychologist; cert. mental retardation tchr., Nebr. Tchr. Omaha Womens Job Corp., 1967, 69; dept. supr. Glenwood (Iowa) State Hosp., 1969-71; specialist learning disabilities Meyer Childrens Rehab. Inst., Omaha, 1971-77; asst. and assoc. prof. Creighton U., Omaha, 1977—; ednl. therapist Omaha Psychiat. Assn., 1985—. Contbr. articles to profl. jours. Mem. human rights rev. com. Boys Town Inst., Omaha, 1986—. Grantee Creighton U., 1979, 82, Am. Assn. Colls. for Tchr. Edn., 1984; U. Nebr.-Omaha fellow, 1971. Mem. Council for Exceptional Children, Consortium for Spl. Edn., Nebr. Assn. for Children with Learning Disabilities, Orton Soc. (pres. 1987—). Home: 5203 Izard St Omaha NE 68132 Office: Creighton U 2500 California St Omaha NE 68178

DOYLE, CONSTANCE TALCOTT JOHNSTON, physician; b. Mansfield, Ohio, July 8, 1945; d. Frederick Lyman IV and Nancy Jean Bushnell (Johnston) Talcott; m. Alan Jerome Demsky, June 13, 1976; children—Ian Frederick Demsky, Zachary Adam Demsky. B.S., Ohio U., 1967; M.D., Ohio State U., 1971. Diplomate Am. Bd. Emergency Medicine. Intern, Riverside Hosp., Columbus, Ohio, 1971-72; resident in internal medicine Hurley Hosp. and U. Mich., Flint, 1972-74, emergency physician Oakwood Hosp., Dearborn, Mich., 1974-76, Jackson County (Mich.) Emergency Services, 1975—; survival flight physician U. Mich. helicopter rescue service, 1983—; disaster cons., co-chmn. emergency med. services disaster com. Region II EMS, 1978-79; course dir. advanced cardiac life support and chmn. advanced life support com. W.A. Foote Meml. Hosp., Jackson, 1979—, others; clin. instr. emergency services, dept. surgery U. Mich., 1981—; instr. Jackson County Emergency Med. Technician refresher courses, Jackson Community Coll. Bd. dirs. Jackson County Heart Assn., 1979-83. Fellow Am. Coll. Emergency Physicians (Mich. disaster com., dir. Mich. 1979—, chmn. Mich. disaster com. 1979-85, mem. nat. disaster med. services com. 1983-85, chmn., 1987-88; cons. disaster mgmt. course Fed. Emergency Mgmt. Agy., 1982—, treas. 1984-85, emergency med. services com. 1985, pres. 1986-87, councillor 1986—); mem. ACP, Am. Med. Women's Assn., Mich. Assn. Emergency Med. Technicians (bd. dirs. 1979-80), Mich., Jackson County med. socs., Sierra Club. Jewish. Contbg. author: Clinical Approach to Poisoning and Toxicology, 1983; contbr. articles to profl. publs. Home: 1665 Lansdowne Rd Ann Arbor MI 48105 Office: WA Foote Hospital East Emergency Dept Jackson MI 49201

DOYLE, DOROTHY ANGELA, consulting firm executive, writer; b. Orange, N.J., Aug. 22, 1935; d. Michael Edward and Angelina (Battista) Palmieri; m. William J. Doyle, Oct. 3, 1953; children—Lisa, Jeffrey. A.A., Broward Community Coll., Davie, Fla., 1971; B.A. in English, Fla. Atlantic U., 1974. Substitute tchr. Broward County Schs., Ft. Lauderdale, Fla., 1974-75; freelance writer, Miramar, Fla., 1977—; owner, mgr. Dorothy Doyle, Pembroke Pines, Fla., 1982; v.p. communications Mfrs. Support Services Corp., Atlanta, 1983—. Contbr. articles to mags. Organizer, communications coordinator Alzheimer's and Related Disorders Assn., Ft. Lauderdale, 1980, now mem. Ga. chpt.; troop organizer Girl Scouts U.S.A., Broward County, 1969. Mem. Women in Communications, Assn. Women Entrpreneurs, Phi Theta Kappa. Republican. Roman Catholic. Clubs: Toastmasters (Hollywood, Fla.) (ednl. v.p. 1978). Office: Mfrs Support Services Corp 600 Houze Way Suite 2D Roswell GA 30076

DOYLE, ELIZABETH ARLINE, marketing executive, nurse; b. Bronx, Nov. 29, 1950; d. Joseph Edward and Angelina (Rullo) McL.; m. Jim Doyle; 1 child, Christopher. BS in Nursing, Hunter Coll., 1972. Registered profl. nurse, N.Y. Staff nurse ICU and coronary care unit Peninsula Hosp. Ctr., Edgemere, N.Y., 1971-72; charge nurse ICU Peninsula Hosp. Ctr., Edgemere, 1972-74; program instr. enterostomal therapy edn. Roswell Park Meml. Inst., Buffalo, 1974-78; nurse, enterostomal therapist, assoc. nursing care coordinator Westchester County Med. Ctr., Valhalla, N.Y., 1978-80; sales rep. Convatec, A Squibb Co., Princeton, N.J., 1980-82, product mgr., 1982-86, sr. product mgr., 1986-88, dir. market planning, 1988—. Mem. Internat. Assn. Enterostomal Therapists, Nurse Cons. Assn., Inc. Republican. Roman Catholic. Office: Convatec A Squibb Co CN 5254 Princeton NJ 08543-5254

DOYLE, IRENE ELIZABETH, electronic sales executive, nurse; b. West Point, Iowa, Oct. 5, 1920; d. Joseph Deidrich and Mary Adelaide (Groene) Schulte; m. William Joseph Doyle, Feb. 3, 1956. R.N., Mercy Hosp., 1941. Courier nurse Santa Fe R.R., Chgo., 1947-50; indsl. nurse Montgomery Ward, Chgo., 1950-54; rep. Hornblower & Weeks, Chgo., 1954-56; v.p. William J. Doyle Co., Chgo., 1956-80, Ormond Beach, Fla., 1980—. Served with M.C., U.S. Army, 1942-46. Mem. Electronic Reps. Assn. Republican. Roman Catholic. Club: Oceanside Country (Ormond Beach).

DOYLE, JAYNE ANNE, small business owner; b. Biddleford, Maine, Nov. 9, 1958; d. Donald Charles and Constance Frances (Robinton); m. Donald Scott Krimpler, June 13, 1987. Student, No. Essex Community Coll., 1980-81. Mgr. traffic Sta. WHAV-FM, Haverhill, Mass., 1980-81; dir. media Cooper/GK Advt., Exeter, N.H., 1981-83; account exec. Eagle Advt., Manchester, N.H., 1983-85; dir. mktg. Nat. Video, Manchester, 1985-86; owner, chief operating officer White Star Advt., Manchester, 1986—. Author/dir. radio commercial for Sanders Lobster Co., 1982 (1st place Graniteer advt. award); dir./producer music jingle for Ctr. of N.H./Holiday Inn, 1984 (1st place Graniteer advt. award). Vol. Easter Seals/Goodwill, Manchester 1984-87; corp organizer Easter Seals Telethon, Manchester, 1986; fundraiser Cancer Soc., Manchester, 1984, Big Bros./Big Sisters, Nashua, N.H. 1985, Manchester, N.H., 1987. Recipient certs. of appreciation N.H. Coll., 1987, 88. Mem. Nashua C. of C., Manchester C. of C., Nat. Assn. Female Execs., N.H. Ad Club, Vintage Triumph Register (zone rep. 1982-84). Republican. Roman Catholic. Club: Amherst Country (asst. mgr. 1985). Home: 66 Moody St Manchester NH 03103 Office: White Star Advt 103 Bay St Manchester NH 03104

DOYLE, JUDITH E., editor; b. St. Louis, Feb. 1, 1949; d. Edward I. and Cornelia Ester (Taylor) Davidson; m. Patrick J. Doyle, Jan. 13, 1973 (div. Mar. 1987); children: Kathleen Taylor, Joshua Edward, Megan Davidson. BJ, U. Mo., 1971. Reporter Palm Beach Times, West Palm Beach, Fla., 1972-73; tchr. Palm Beach Prepratory Sch., North Palm Beach, Fla., 1973; reporter Orlando (Fla.) Sentinel Star, 1973-80; editor ECI/The Capitol Group, Tallahassee, 1986-88; reporter Capitol Bur. Tallahassee Democrat, 1988—. Bd. dirs. PTA Kate Sullivan Elem. Sch., Tallahassee, 1985—, Planned Parenthood of Tallahassee, 1985—. Democrat. Jewish. Home: 2783 Armistead Rd Tallahassee FL 32312 Office: Tallahassee Democrat 277 N Magnolia Dr Tallahassee FL 32301

DOYLE, JUDITH STOVALL, real estate executive; b. Dothan, Ala., Apr. 19, 1940; d. E.H. and Justine (Knowles) Stovall; m. John P. Doyle Jr., Aug. 22, 1964; children: John Patrick III, Michael D., Julie A. BS, Miss. State Coll. for Women, 1961. Tchr. math., jr. high sch., Gulfport, Miss., 1961-62; asst. dir. dept. pub. relations SUNY-Buffalo, 1962-64; tchr. math., jr. high schs., Alexandria, Va., 1964-65, Auburn, N.Y., 1970-71; realtor, assoc. Mosher Real Estate, Auburn, 1972-80; owner, mgr. real estate property, Auburn, 1977—. Active, past pres. Mercy Aux., Auburn; chairperson Owasco Bd. Assessment Rev., N.Y., 1976—; mem. Sacred Heart Parish Council, Auburn, 1985—; bd. dirs. Unity House, Auburn, 1985-87. Democrat. Roman Catholic. Lodge: Ancient Order Hibernians (charter mem. Ladies Aux. 2).

DOYLE, JUDITH WARNER, marriage and family therapist, corporate executive, consultant; b. Los Angeles, Aug. 18, 1943; d. Raymond Ross Manley and Sarah Virginia (Pletcher) Manley Flint; 1 child, Brennan Corey. B.A., Calif. State U.-Long Beach, 1975, M.S., 1977. Counselor Calif. State U., Long Beach, 1976-78; case mgmt. supr. Bridge/Boys Club, Wilmington, Calif., 1978-80, ElMonte Sr. Citizens Ctr., Calif., 1979-81; dir. counseling services Gay/Lesbian Community Service Ctr., Orange County, Calif., 1985-88 ; owner, therapist Judith Doyle MFCC, Long Beach, 1978—; cons. Aids Response Program, Garden Grove, Calif., 1985-88 ; med. adv. bd. Aids Service Found., Costa Mesa, Calif., 1985-88 ; exec. dir. One in Long Beach Inc., 1988—;Golden mem. Long Beach Lambda Democratic Club, 1980—; chmn. So. Calif. Women for Understanding, Los Angeles, 1981-85; pres., bd. dirs. Long Beach Lesbian and Gay Pride Inc., 1983—; apptd. mem. Calif. State Commn. Econ. Devel. Task Force, 1984-85. Recipient Woman of Yr. award Lambda Democratic Club, 1981, Christopher Street W., 1986; Spl. Person award Press/Telegram, 1985; Myra Riddell Service award So. Calif. Women for Understanding. Mem. Calif. Assn. Marriage and Family Therapists (bd. dirs. 1981-85, pres. 1985-86, named Disting. Clin. Mem. 1988), Nat. Assn. Female Execs., ACLU, Greenpeace, People for the Am. Way, Nat. Mus. Women in the Arts (charter), Mus. Contemporary Art (charter), Calypso Soc. Avocations: dancing; theatre; volleyball; softball. Office: 4041 E 4th St Long Beach CA 90814

DOYLE, SISTER MARY ANNE, religious organization administrator; b. Boston, Mar. 17, 1943; d. Walter Andrew and Loretta Mary (Burgoyne) D. AB in Math. cum laude, Regis Coll., 1967; MS in Nuclear Physics, Ohio State U., 1973, PhD in Nuclear Physics, 1976. joined Sisters of the Congregation of St. Joseph. Lectr., asst. prof. physics Regis Coll., Weston, Mass., 1975-82, dir. research ctr., 1978-80, research physicist, prin. investigator Research Ctr., 1982-85; asst. prof. Wellesley (Mass.) Coll., 1980-81; adminstrv. resident Carney Hosp., Boston, 1985-86; assoc. dir. Office of Synod Archdiocese Boston, 1986—; vis. scientist accelerator lab. U. Lowell, Mass., 1977-78; facilitator, cons. congregations of religious women, 1979—. Contbr. articles to profl. jours. Mem. Am. Geophys. Union, Am. Phys. Soc., Stoneham Citizens for Peace. Roman Catholic.

DOYLE, MICHELLE LEAH, sales executive; b. San Bernadino, Calif., Oct. 19, 1949; d. James Earl and Dorothy (Holt) Sturtevant. BS in Communications, U. Calif., Santa Barbara, 1973; MS in Psychology, Calif. State U., Hayward, 1975; PhD in Psychology, U. So. Calif., 1981; MBA, Northeastern U., 1987; postgrad., Harvard U. Asst. dir. pub. relations Alta Bates Hosp., Berkeley, Calif., 1971-73; psychologist Contra Costa County, Concord, Calif., 1973-75; prof. Psychology Coll. of Alameda (Calif.), 1975-78, Boston Coll., 1978-80; psychologist Childrens Hosp., Boston, 1978-80; psychologist pvt. practice Marblehead, Mass., 1980-83; founder, chief exec. officer, pres. Interface, Inc. (now subs. of Avatar Tech.), Marblehead, 1983—; founder, chief exec. officer Matrix Communications (now subs. of Avatar Tech.), Marblehead, 1984—; dir. sales, officer Avatar Tech., Hopkinton, Mass., 1986—. Author: (book) Nice, 1975. Psychologist Friends For All Children, Vietnam, 1975, Orphan Airlift, San Francisco, 1975. Mem. AMA, Phi Beta Kappa. Republican. Lutheran. Club: Colonial Fitness Ctr. Home: 57 Pleasant St Marblehead MA 01945 Office: Avatar Tech Inc 99 South St Hopkinton MA 01748

DOYLE, PATRICIA A., advertising agency executive; b. Rockville Centre, N.Y., Sept. 16, 1953; d. Thomas Edward and Anita (Maurer) D. BA in Sociology, St. Mary's Coll., 1975; MA in Sociology, Ind. U., 1977. V.p. dir. ops. Sturm Research Inc., N.Y.C., 1977-81; research supr. Ogilvy & Mather Inc., N.Y.C., 1981-83, v.p., assoc. research dir., 1983-85, sr. v.p., planning and research dir., 1985—; mem. N.Y. operating bd. Ogilvy & Mather Inc., 1986—. Mem. Am. Mktg. Assn. (chair judging 1987), Ind. U. Alumni, St. Mary's Alumni. Roman Catholic. Office: Ogilvy & Mather Advt Inc 2 E 48th St New York NY 10017

DOYLE, SHEILA WITMER, optometrist; b. Ridley Park, Pa., Oct. 14, 1948; d. Clement J. and Madeleine (Groff) McGovern. BS in Human Ecology and Biology summa cum laude, U. Md., 1970; OD, Pa. Coll. of Optometry, 1978. Designer Bulder-Whaley Assocs., Chevy Chase, Md., 1970-74; optometrist Stamford, Conn., 1978-84, Norwalk, Conn., 1984—. Mem. Am. Optometric Soc., Conn. Optometric Soc., Nat. Homeopathic Soc., Beta Sigma Kappa. Home: 8 Fort Point St #2 Norwalk CT 06855 Office: 350 Connecticut Ave Norwalk CT 06854

DOYLE, SHEILAH ANNE, nurse, counselor; b. Toronto, Ont., Can., Sept. 5, 1952; came to the U.S. 1956; d. Benard and Gladys (DeVeau) McGillivary; m. William J. Doyle Jr., April 15, 1972; children: Kelly, Kevin, Kristin. Student, Thornton Community Coll., 1981, Gov.'s State U., Ill. Lic. practical nurse; cert. pharmacoligist. Legal sec. Michael & Richard Daley Law Office, Chgo., 1971-73; sec. Eriksen & Olson Architects, Palos Heights, Ill., 1973-74; nurse Oak Forest (Ill.) Hosp., 1981-82; nurse, oncology Ingalis Hosp., Harvey, Ill., 1982-87; nurse, counselor Interventions/Crossroads, Oak Lawn, Ill., 1987—, Careunit of DuPage, Downers Grove, Ill., 1988; Counselor Ill. Substance Abuse; sec. preschool, 1979. Tchr. Catholic catechism, 1972; worker state rep. Terry Steczo, Ill., 1974, Sen. Philip Rock, Ill.; facilitator Aunt Martha's Youth Service Ctr., Park Forest, Ill., 1985; bd. dirs. Homeowners Assn. Palos Park, Ill., 1987. Democrat. Roman Catholic. Home: 12857 S Mill Rd Palos Park IL 60464 Office: CareUnit of DuPage 21 W 251 64th St Downers Grove IL 60517

DOYLE, SUE ELLEN, state association executive; b. Wichita, Kans., May 19, 1949; d. William Thomas and Helen Francis (Rose) James; children: Brandee Michelle, Amber Lea. BA, Coll. Emporia, 1971. Dir. continuity Great Empire Broadcasting, Wichita, 1980-84; dir. pub. affairs Kans. Credit Union League and Affiliates, Wichita, 1984-85, asst. v.p., 1986-87, v.p., 1987—. Mng. editor Directions, 1984—, Focus, 1984—; (newsleter) From The Capital, 1987—. Foster parent Kans. State Assn. Foster Parents, Wichita, 1985—; ct.-apptd. spl. adv., Wichita, 1986—. Mem. Assn. Credit Union League Execs., Kans. Soc. Assn. Execs. Republican. Baptist. Office: Kans Credit Union League and Affiliates 8410 W Kellogg Wichita KS 67209

DOYLE, THERESA LIPARI, real estate executive, public relations specialist; b. Long Beach, Calif., Aug. 27, 1957; d. Joseph and Joyce Lorraine (Wagle) Lipari; m. Timothy Xavier Doyle, June 26, 1982. BA, Calif. State U., Fullerton, 1980. Fundraising asst. Am. Heart Assn., Santa Ana, Calif., 1980; account exec. Kerr & Assocs. Pub. Relations, Huntington Beach, Calif., 1980-83; dir. mktg. Covington Homes, Fullerton, Calif., 1983-86; dir. sales and mktg., Covington Homes, Orange County, Calif., 1986, v.p. sales and mktg., 1986—; pub. relations cons. Am. Heart Assn., 1980-84, Family Crisis Ctr., Orange County, 1980-83. Recipient Outstanding Pub. Relations award Publicity Club Los Angeles, 1980, 3 Mem. Inst. Residential Mktg. awards Nat. Assn. Home Builders, 1986. Mem. Women in Communications, Inc. (Outstanding Mag. Article award 1980, Outstanding Pub. Relations award 1980), Bldg. Industry Assn. (dir. sales and mktg. 1984-86, 5 Major Achievment in Merchandising Excellence awards, 1984-85), Nat. Assn. Female Execs., Southern Calif. Women in Advertising, Calif. State U., Fullerton Alumni Assn. Republican. Roman Catholic. Office: Covington Homes 1748 W Katella Ave Suite 103 Orange CA 92667

DOYLE, VERLA DOHERTY (MRS. JACOBS H. DOYLE), club woman; b. Franklin, Pa., Aug. 12, 1912; d. Wilbur Felix and Walza (Magee) Doherty; A.B., St. Francis Xavier Coll. Women, 1936; m. Jacobs H. Doyle, Nov. 10, 1951. Case worker Pa. Dept. Pub. Assistance, Franklin, 1937-41; with USO, Nat. Catholic Community Service, 1941-47, successively asst. club dir., club dir., rep. Tenn. maneuvers, 1943-44, traveling dir. S.E. region U.S., 1944-46; exec. sec. Cath. Youth Orgn., Nashville, 1949-51; bd. dirs. Nashville Diocesan Council Cath. Women, 1951—, sec., 1955-57, pres., 1959-61; nat. youth chmn. Nat. Council Cath. Women, 1958-62; del. Pres.'s White House Conf. Children and Youth, Washington, 1960; bd. dirs. Cath. Youth Orgn., Nashville, 1951-55, Nat. Multiple Sclerosis Soc., Nashville chpt., 1963-64. Alternate del. Democratic Conv. from Tenn., 1952, 56. Mem. Cath. Daus. Am., Cheekwood Cultural Center, St. Xavier Coll. Alumnae, Tenn., Nashville bar auxs. Clubs: Richland Country, Newman (dir. 1963-64), Colonna (treas. 1956, pres. 1958-60) (Nashville). Address: 6117 Robin Hill Rd Nashville TN 37205

DOYLE-BRENNAN, ADRIENNE PAULA, marketing executive; b. Dublin, Ireland, June 26, 1957; came to U.S., 1961; d. Christopher James and Pauline Rita (Ryan) Doyle; m. Henry George Brennan, June 13, 1987. BA in Social Ecology, U. Calif., Irvine, 1980; MA in Counseling Psychology, Chapman Coll., Orange, Calif., 1984. Cert. tchr., Calif. Asst. therapist Care Unit Hosp., Orange, 1980-81; police officer Los Angeles Police Dept., 1981-86; with mktg. personnel dept. Pola Prodns., Irvine, Calif., 1985; pres. The Profl. Image, Inc., Newport Beach, Calif., 1985—; cons. Am. Acad. Cosmetic Surgery, Pacific Palisades, Calif., 1986—. Active Big Sis. of Los Angeles, 1985—; Assn. Treatment Services Ctr., Costa Mesa, Calif., 1987—. Republican. Roman Catholic. Home: 1137 Granville Dr Newport Beach CA 92660 Office: The Professional Image Inc 359 San Miguel Dr #303 Newport Beach CA 92660

DRADDY, ELIZABETH, lawyer; b. N.Y.C., Aug. 13, 1957; d. Joseph and Patricia (Shea) D. AB, Mt. Holyoke Coll., 1979; postgrad., London Sch. Econs., 1979-80; JD, Fordham U., 1984. Bar: N.Y. 1985, U.S. Dist. Ct. (so. and ea. dists.) N.Y. 1985. Legis. analyst office of budget Mayor's Office, N.Y.C., 1981—; assoc. Cusack & Stiles, N.Y.C., 1984-87; asst. gen. counsel Phoenix House, N.Y.C., 1987—. Mem. ABA, County Lawyers Assn., N.Y. State Bar Assn. Home: 209 W 13th St New York NY 10011 Office: Phoenix House 164 w 74th St New York NY 10023

DRAGE, STARLA RAE, fashion designer; b. Santaquin, Utah, Oct. 1, 1932; d. Andrew William and Vera Mae (Chatwin) Larsen; m. James Don Drage, Feb. 3, 1951; children: William Joe, Julia Ann, Callene, Darrell Edward. Seamstress Jolene Co., Provo, Utah, 1959, fore-lady, 1960-61; designer, pattern grader Little Gems, Provo, 1961-63; pattern grader Jolene Co., 1963-82, purchasing and prodn. coordinator, 1978-83, designer 1st patterns, 1984—. Mem. Nat. Assn. Female Execs. Office: Jolene Co 1050 W 350 S Provo UT 84601

DRAGOUN, MARY MARGARET, corporate planning professional; b. Omaha, Dec. 6, 1944; d. Stephen Henry and Marjorie Lois (Gerlach) D. BS, St. Norbert Coll., 1967; MA, Fairfield U., 1980. Registered med. technologist. Staff med. technologist Emory U. Hosp., Atlanta, 1968; vol. med. technologist Peace Corps, Brazil, 1968-73; lab. educator Project Hope, Brazil, 1974-75; staff med. technologist St. Vincent's Hosp., Bridgeport, Conn., 1976-81; asst. dir. planning/evaluation Save The Children Fedn., Westport, Conn., 1981-83; analyst strategic planning, mgr. corp. planning Am. Fed. Bank, Greenville, S.C., 1984—; trainer health edn. Peace Corps, Frogmore, S.C. Mem. Planning Forum, Nat. Assn. for Female Execs., Alpha Delta Theta (founding pres. DePere chpt. 1965-66). Office: Am Fed Bank PO Box 1268 Greenville SC 29602

DRAKE, BARBARA LEIGH, banker; b. Richmond, Va., Mar. 14, 1950; d. Wilbert Smith and Dorothy Bell (Hollins) Priddy; m. James Ronald Kennedy, June 28, 1969 (div. 1973); m. Charles Brittain Drake III, Dec. 14, 1977; children: Jennifer Ann, Carolann Brittain. BA in Mgmt., Bus. Adminstrn., La. State U., 1982. Sec. 1st and Merchants Bank, Richmond, 1970-71, personnel officer, 1974-83; sec. VEPCO, Norfolk, Va., 1971-73, Norfolk A/C Corp., 1973-74; v.p. Sovran Fin. Corp. (merger 1st and Merchants Bank and Va. Nat. Bank), Norfolk, 1984—. Coordinator vols. March Dimes TeamWalk, 1987, 88; fund raiser Eastern VA Med. Coll., 1985; vol. United Way Campaign, 1975-83, Norfolk. Mem. Nat. Assn. Banking, Am. Soc. Personnel Adminstrn. (chmn. accreditation 1987), Am. Inst. Banking (pres. 1981-82, past v.p., sec.), Tidewater Personnel Assn. (pres. 1985-87, chmn. regional conf. 1983, superior merit award 1987). Republican. Methodist. Office: Sovran Bank NA 2 Commercial Pl Norfolk VA 23510

DRAKE, CHARLENE, city comptroller; b. Chgo., Aug. 8, 1952; d. Charles LeRoy and Catherine (Watson) D. BS, No. Ill. U., 1974. Exec. sec. Village of Robbins, Ill., 1974-77, asst. treas., 1978-81; jr. acct. Wilson & Gills, CPA, Chgo., 1977-78; adminstrv. asst. Modern Health and Rapid Therapy, Inc., Markham, Ill., 1981-83; comptroller City of Harvey, Ill., 1983—. Mem. Pride of Robbins Temple, 1978—; bd. dirs. Robbins Community Ctr., treas., 1975-81; bd. dirs. Robbins Pub. Library Dist., 1976-80, United Way of Robbins, 1980—; charter mem. Community Woman Interested in Drug Edn.-W.I.D.E., 1987—. Named one of Outstanding Young Women Am., 1981. Mem. Ill. Mcpl. Treasurers Assn. (bd. dirs. 1986-88), Mcpl. Tresurers Assn. of U.S. and Can., No. Ill. U. Black Alumni Assn. (treas. 1984-88), Robbins Alumni Assn. (pres. 1987-88, numerous other offices 1980—, Service award 1981-82), Nat. Assn. for Female Execs., Zeta Phi Beta, Zeta Tau Zeta (numerous regional and state offices 1972—, numerous awards 1981, 86, Zeta of Yr. 1987). Democrat. Baptist. Home: 332 E 147th Pl Harvey IL 60426 Office: City of Harvey 15320 Broadway Harvey IL 60426

DRAKE, LENORE MAE, grant administrator; b. Orland, Calif.; m. John E. Drake. BS in Social Sci., So. Oreg. Coll., 1968; MS in Psychology, N.Mex. Highlands U., 1969; postgrad., Ariz. State U., 1974, 77-78, Am. U., Cairo, 1975. Staff psychologist Cumberland County Guidance Ctr., Millville, N.J., 1969-71, Yuma (Ariz.) Guidance Clinic, 1971-73; govt. relations specialist Middle East Systems and Devel., Inc., Cairo, 1974-76; dir. Profl. Rehab. Mgmt., Phoenix, 1977-80; program mgr. Rehab. Services Adminstrn., Yuma, 1980-86; dir. Ariz. Supported Employment Project, Rehab. Services Adminstrn., Phoenix, 1986—; mem. com. Ariz. State Dept. Edn. Project, Phoenix, 1986—. Chair subcom. Phoenix Mayor's Com. Employment of Handicapped, 1981-82. Home: 69 W Willetta Phoenix AZ 85003

DRAKE, LYNN ANNETTE, physician; b. Albuquerque, Aug. 4, 1945; d. Olen Lester and Lucille Susan (Henry) Drake; BA, Adams State Coll., 1966, MA, 1967; MD, U. Tenn., 1971. Instr. math. Adams State Coll., Alamosa, Colo., 1966-67; intern City of Memphis Hosp., 1971-72, resident in dermatology, 1972-75, chief resident, 1974-75; mem. faculty dept. medicine, div. dermatology U. Tenn. Center Health Scis., also Med. Practice Group, Inc.; asst. prof. dermatology Emory U., Atlanta; chief dermatology VA Med. Center, Atlanta; dir. devel., policy and planning Mass. Gen. Hosp.; with dept. dermatology Harvard Med. Sch.; chmn. chemosurgery task group VA; instr. advanced cardiac life support Am. Heart Assn.; mem. emergency room com. St. Joseph Hosp. Vol., Am. Cancer Soc., 1973-75; dir. policy and planning dept. dermatology and Wellman Labs Photomedicine Harvard, Mass. Gen. Hosp., Boston, 1988—. Diplomate Am. Bd. Dermatology (chmn. com. health care quality assurance 1984—). Robert Wood Johnson Health Policy fellow, 1986-87. Fellow Am. Acad. Dermatology (bd. dirs. 1987—); mem. Soc. for Investigative Dermatology, Am. Acad. Dermatology (com. on health planning), Women's Med. Assn., ACP, Ga. Dermatology Soc., Atlanta Dermatology Soc. (program chmn.), Am. Assn. Med. Colls., Council Acad. Scis., Women's Dermatology Soc. (housestaff liaison com., nominating com., pres. 1984-86). Dermatology Found. Home: One Longfellow Pl #2418 Boston MA 02114

DRAKE, MIRIAM ANNA, librarian, educator; b. Boston, Dec. 20, 1936; d. Max Frederick and Beatrice Celia (Mitnick) Engleman; m. John Warren Drake, Dec. 19, 1960 (div. Dec. 1985); 1 child, Robert Warren. BS, Simmons Coll., Boston, 1958, MLS, 1971; postgrad., Harvard U., 1959-60. Assoc. United Research, Cambridge, Mass., 1958-61; with mktg. services Kenyon & Eckhardt, Boston, 1963-65; cons. Boston, 1965-72; head research unit libraries Purdue U., West Lafayette, Ind., 1972-76, asst. dir. libraries, prof. library sci., 1976-84; dir. libraries, prof. Ga. Inst. Tech., Atlanta, 1984—. Author: User Fees: A Practicle Perspective, 1981; mem. editorial bd. Coll. and Research Libraries Jour., 1985—, Libraries and Microcomputers Jour., 1983—; contbr. chpts. to books, articles to profl. jours. Recipient Alumni Achievement award Simmons Coll., 1985. Mem. ALA (councilor at large 1985—), Am. Mgmt. Assn., Am. Soc. Info. Sci., Spl. Libraries Assn. (H.W. Wilson award 1983). Office: Ga Inst Tech Library Atlanta GA 30332

DRAKE, SUSAN FREIMER, telecommunications consultant; b. Bklyn., May 23, 1946; d. Leo and Beatrice (Samuels) Freimer; m. Stanley Rosenzweig, July 16, 1967 (div. Oct. 1981); m. Richard P. Drake, Nov. 15, 1981. BA, Bklyn. Coll.-CUNY, 1967. Communications cons. N.Y. Telephone, N.Y.C., 1970-75; communications analyst Nat. Telephone Planning Corp., Yonkers, N.Y., 1975-78; sr. cons. Peat, Marwick Mitchell & Co., N.Y.C., 1978-79; dir. Los Angeles ops. Contel Info. Systems, Great Neck, N.Y., 1979-82; owner, mgr. Suritel Assocs., Los Angeles, 1982—. Contbr. articles to profl. jours. Bd. dirs., residential chmn. Am. Cancer Soc., Yonkers, 1977-78. Mem. Internat. Orgn. Women in Telecommunications, Valley Interchange of Entrepreneurial Women (founding dir., pres. 1982-86), Nat. Assn. Female Execs. Avocations: skiing, sailing. Home: 17246 Braxton St Granada Hills CA 91344

DRASKOVICH, ZLATANA JENNIE, educator; b. Bklyn., Dec. 20, 1948; d. Roy L. and Nancy Corinne (Thompson) Brundidge. BS, Purdue U., Hammond, Ind., 1969, MS in Edn., 1978; MA in German, Purdue U., Lafayette, Ind., 1971. Cert. tchr. German and math. grades 7-12, Ind. Shop math. educator Hammond Vocat.-Tech. High Sch., 1971-78; math. educator Hammond High Sch., 1978-86, Morton Sr. High Sch., Hammond, 1986—. Creator Miniature Egyptian Music Salon, 1984. Judge Sci. Fair Purdue U. Calumet, Hammond, 1970—; sponsor German Club Hammond Vocat.-Tech.

High Sch., 1971-78, Calculator Tournament Ind. U., Gary, 1975—; class sponsor Hammond Pub. Schs., 1972-86; dir. Math Calculator Olympiad, Hammond, 1987—. Recipient 10 Years Sci. Fair Judge award Purdue U. Calumet, 1979. Mem. Nat. Council Tchrs. Math., Gary Area Council Tchrs. Math., AAUW (chairperson judges Calumet chpt. 1975—, treas. 1974-76), Am. West Indian Assn., Inc., Purdue Alumni Assn. (life). Serbian Orthodox. Home: 3736 Johnson St Gary IN 46408 Office: Morton Sr High Sch 6915 Grand Ave Hammond IN 46323

DRAUDEN, GAIL, psychologist; b. Joliet, Ill., Jan. 13, 1948; d. Floyd and Marian (Krieger) D. BA, U. Iowa, 1968; PhD, U. Minn., 1980. Psychologist test validation ctr. State of Minn., St. Paul, 1973-76; sr. researcher employee relations Honeywell Corp., Mpls., 1979-82; prin. cons. Gail Drauden & Assocs., Mpls., 1983—. Mem. Am. Psychol. Assn., Soc. Indsl. Orgnl. Psychologists. Office: PO Box 8128 Minneapolis MN 55408

DRAZIN, LISA, real estate investment banker, financial consultant; b. Washington, Nov. 26, 1953; d. Sidney and Bernice Ann (Jeweler) D. A.B. with honors, Wellesley Coll., 1976; M.B.A., George Washington U., 1980. Chartered Financial Analyst. Securities analyst Geico, Inc., Chevy Chase, Md., 1982; mng. prin. Jefferson Securities Ltd., Bethesda, Md., 1983; chmn., chief exec. officer Drazin & Co., Inc., Bethesda, 1985—, Drazin Properties, Inc., Bethesda, 1985—, Drazin Securities, Inc., Bethesda, 1985—; affiliate Montgomery County Bd. Realtors; bd. dirs. Fed. Home Loan Bank. Founder, Ivy Connection, Washington, 1982. Mem. Nat. Trust for Historic Preservation. Fellow Fin. Analysts Fedn.; mem. Nat. Assn. Securities Dealers (exec. rep.), Nat. Assn. Realtors, Comml. Investment Real Estate Council, Realtors Nat. Mktg. Inst., Wash. Soc. Investment Analysts, Inc., Beta Gamma Sigma. Club: Wellesley (interns coordinator, recent grads. rep. 1981-84) (Washington). Office: Drazin & Co Inc 6403 Kirby Rd Bethesda MD 20817

DREBLOW, DARLENE DEMARIE, psychology educator; b. N.Y.C., Oct. 24, 1952; d. Joseph and Elizabeth (Cardella) DeMarie; m. Lewis Maxwell Dreblow; 1 child, Charles Joseph Dreblow. BA cum laude, Marietta (Ohio) Coll., 1974; MEd, Ohio U., 1978; MS, U. Fla., 1985. Tchr. 1st grade Caldwell (Ohio) Exempted Village Schs., 1974-77, tchr. learning disabilities, 1978-80; tchr. 2d grade Marietta City Schs., 1980-82; asst. prof. of psychology Muskingum Coll., New Concord, Ohio, 1987—. Mem Women's Resource Ctr., Betsy Mills Club, Marietta, 1979-82, v.p. 1981-82. Mem. Internat. Reading Assn., Am. Psychol. Assn. (assoc.), Southeastern Psychol. Assn., Soc. Research Child Devel., Muskingum Area Joint Chpt. Council Exceptional Children (pres. 1979-80), Phi Kappa Phi. Office: Muskingum Coll Dept Psychology New Concord OH 43762-1199

DREISKE, JANE DIANE, hotel entrepreneur; b. Antigo, Wis., Sept. 2, 1942; d. William Daniel and Freida Violet (Helmig) Wendt; children: Daniel Raymond, Joseph Robert. Cert. of Completion, Humbolt Inst., Mpls., 1961. Teletypist Pan Am Airways, San Francisco, 1961-63; exec. sec. Dee Tozar Advt., Redwood City, Calif., 1963-64; claims adjuster Glen Slaughter & Assocs., Oakland, Calif., 1964-65; office mgr. Dr. Liechti, MD, Rheem, Calif., 1965-67; owner, operator Imperial "400" Hotel, El Cajon, Calif., 1967-68, El Rancho Motor Hotel, Torrance, Calif., 1969-71; exec. sec. Toyota Motor Distbr., Torrance, 1969-71, Motorola, Denver, 1971; owner, operator Chalet Lodge Motor Hotel, Tarzana, Calif., 1971-75, Casa Blanca Motor Hotel, Palm Springs, Calif., 1975-76, Best Western Date Tree, Indio, Calif., 1976—, Travelodge Motor Hotel, Rancho Bernardo, Calif., 1977-79; owner operator Travel lodge Motor Hotel, Palm Springs, 1978-82; owner, operator Lotus Inn & Casino, Las Vegas, 1982-84, Western Host Motor Hotel, Palm Springs, 1983—, Desert Inst. of Travel, Palm Desert, Calif., 1985—, Desert Travel, Palm Desert, 1986—. Chmn. Indio's Second Ann. Hot-Air Baloon Festival, 1984-85; co-chmn. Desert Bicycle Classic 1st and 2d, 1985-86. Mem. Best Western Internat. (gov. 1980—), C. of C. (dir./sec. 1983-86). Club: Palm Desert Women's. Home: 73-860 Grapevine St Palm Desert CA 92260 Office: Best Western Date Tree Motor Hotel 81-909 Indio Blvd Indio CA 92201

DRENNAN, DONNA JANE, lawyer; b. Champaign, Ill., Mar. 4, 1944; d. Walter E. and Marcella (Cavanaugh) Judson; children: Judson W., James B. BA, Ind. U., 1965, JD, 1969; LLM, Georgetown U., 1975. Bar: Ind. 1969, D.C. 1971, U.S. Supreme Ct. 1973. Asst. to gen. counsel Fed. Power Commn., Washington, 1972-73; gen. counsel for policy Fed. Property Council, Washington, 1973-74; spl. asst. Fed. Power Commn., Washington, 1974-76; atty. FERC, Washington, 1976-79; ptnr. McDermott, Will & Emery, Washington, 1979-82, Pillsbury, Madison & Sutro, Washington, 1982-88, Wunder & Diefenderfer, Washington, 1988—. Mem. FERC Transition Team, Pres. Elect Reagan, Wsahington, 1980-81, Presidential Pvt. Sector Task Force, Washington, 1982. Mem. ABA (chmn. adminstrv. law sect., natural resources law and pub. utility law sects.), Fed. Energy Bar Assn. (exec. council 1981-84). Club: Georgetown (Washington). Home: 5801 Hillburne Way Chevy Chase MD 20815 Office: Wunder & Diefenderfer 1615 L St NW Suite 650 Washington DC 20036

DRENNAN, JILL CHRISTINE, aerospace company engineer; b. Cheyenne, Wyo., Feb. 21, 1960; d. Alan Edward and Nancy Jane (Bond) Fuller; m. Russell Dwain Drennan, May 23, 1981. BS in Tech., U. Houston, 1982. Electronic tech. Litton Resources Systems, Houston, 1980-82; engr. Ford Aerospace and Communications, Houston, 1982-84, research and devel. engr., 1984—. Lutheran. Club: Sabishii Hoshi Akita of Tex. (Houston) (treas. 1987—); Levis and Lace Sq. Dance (sec. 1987-88). Office: Ford Aerospace and Communications 1322 Space Park Dr CC5 Houston TX 77058

DRESCHER, JOAN E., author, illustrator; b. N.Y.C., Mar. 6, 1939; d. Joseph Manley and Elizabeth (Straub) McIntosh; m. Kenneth W. Drescher, June 11, 1960; children—Lisa, Kimberly, Kenneth. Student, Rochester Inst. Tech., 1958-59, Parsons Sch. Design, 1960-63, Art Students League, 1964. Tchr. writing Cambridge Ctr. for Adult Edn. (Mass.), Cambridge Art Assn., 1973-78, Mass. Coll. Art, Boston, 1975-76, Art Inst. Boston, 1977-79, Lesley Coll., Cambridge, 1979-81; artist-in-residence Hingham Pub. Schs., 1984, Kingston and Milton pub. schs., 1982-83, China Trade Mus., Milton, Mass., 1983; lectr. in field. Author, illustrator: Max and Rufus, 1982; I'm in Charge, 1981; The Marvelous Mess, 1980; Your Family, My Family, 1980; Tell Me Grandma/Tell Me Grandpa, 1979; What Are Daisies for, 1975; My Mother's Getting Married, 1985; Your Doctor, My Doctor, 1985; illustrator: Horrible Hannah, 1980; Follow that Ghost, 1979; Bubbles and Soap Films, 1979; The Other Place, 1978; Nonna, 1975, others; murals executed Parents and Childrens Services, Boston, 1982, The Children's Hosp., 1988, St. Anne's Hosp., Fall River, Mass., Meml.-Sloan Kettering Hosp., N.Y.C., 1986-87. Recipient Illustration award N.Y. Acad. Sci., 1980; Social Studies award, 1980. Mem. Soc. Illustrators, Soc. Childrens' Book Writers, Authors Guild. Address: 23 Cedar St Hingham MA 02043

DRESCHER, JUDITH ALTMAN, library director; b. Greensburg, Pa., July 6, 1946; d. Joseph Grier and Sarah Margaret (Hewitt) Altman; m. Robert A. Drescher, Aug. 10, 1968 (div. 1980); m. David G. Lindstrom, Jan. 10, 1981. AB, Grove City Coll., 1968; MLS, U. Pitts., 1971. Tchr. Hempfield Sch. Dist., Greensburg, 1968-71; children's librarian Cin. Pub. Library, 1971-72, br. mgr., 1972-74; dir. Rolling Meadows (Ill.) Pub. Library, 1974-79, Champaign (Ill.) Pub. Library, 1979-85, Memphis/Shelby County Pub. Library and Info. Ctr., 1985—; cons. HBW Assocs., Dallas, 1986—. Mem. Rhodes Coll. Commn. on 21st Century, Memphis, 1986—, 100 for the Arts, Memphis, 1986—, Leadership Memphis, 1987—; bd. dirs. Literacy Council Memphis, 1986—. Recipient Govt. Leader award U. Ill. YWCA, 1981. Mem. ALA (chair intellectual freedom com. 1986-87), Tenn. Library Assn., Memphis Library Council, Beta Phi Mu. Democrat. Mem. United Ch. of Christ. Lodge: Rotary. Home: 1505 Vance Memphis TN 38104 Office: Memphis Shelby County Pub Library & Info Ctr 1850 Peabody Ave Memphis TN 38104

DRESKIN, JEANET STECKLER, painter, medical artist, educator; b. New Orleans, Sept. 29, 1921; d. William Steckler and Beate Bertha (Burgas) Steckler Gureasko; m. E. Arthur Dreskin, May 9, 1943; children—Richard Burgas, Stephen Charles, Jeanet Dreskin Haig, Rena Dreskin Schoenberg. B.F.A., Newcomb Coll., 1942; grad. cert. in med. art Johns Hopkins U., 1943; M.F.A., Clemson U., 1973; student Art Students League, N.Y.C., Art Inst. Chgo., 1946, Balt. Mus. Fine Art, 1943, Staff artist Am. Mus. Natural History, N.Y.C., 1943-45, U. Chgo. Med. Sch., 1945-50; mem. faculty Mus. Sch. Art, Greenville, S.C., 1950-52, 62—, dir., 1968-75; adj. prof. art U. S.C. at Mus. Sch. Art, 1973—; mem. faculty Govs. Sch. for Arts, Greenville, 1980—; condr. workshops, lectr. in art edn., 1970-88; mem. arts adv. bd. S.C. State Mus., Columbia, 1984-89; workshop leader art dept. U. Ga., 1985; rep. by Fay Gold, Atlanta, Hampton III, Taylors, S.C., also by Etchings Internat., N.Y.C., Art South Gallery, Washington. Group shows Butler Inst. Am. Art, Youngstown, Ohio, 1974, 83, Chataugua Exhbn. Am. Art, N.Y., 1970, Nat. Mus. Illustrators, N.Y.C., 1986; represented in permanent collections Nat. Mus. Am. Art, Washington, S.C. State Art Collection, Columbia, Ga. Mus. Art, Greenville County Mus. Art, Guild Hall Mus., East Hampton, N.Y., Gibbes Art Gallery, Charleston, S.C., Columbia Mus. Art, Tex. Fine Art Assn., Sunrise Valley Mus., Charleston, W.Va., Beaufort Mus., S.C., Kate Shipworth Mus. at U. Miss., McDonald Corp. Coll., Chgo., N.C. Nat. Bank Coll., Asheville (N.C.) Mus. Art; exhibited at Butler Inst. Am. Art, 1974, 83, Nat. Mus. of Ill., N.Y.C., 1986, Nat. Print and Drawing, Clemson U., 1987; Contbr. med. drawings to various publs. Mem. community Found. Greenville, 1968-84, chmn. projects com., 1968-76; historian Rose Ball, Greenville, 1972-89; bd. dirs. Charity Ball, 1971-89. Recipient Kaplan award Nat. Assn. Painters in Casein, 1969, 71; Keenen award Am. Contemporary Exhbn., Palm Beach, Fla., 1970. Mem. Guild S.C. Artists (invitational exhibit, 1988, pres. 1970-71, bd. dirs. 1981-86, numerous awards 1965, 67, 68, 71, 73, 84), S.C. Watercolor Soc. (pres. 1983-84, bd. dirs. 1985—), So. Watercolor (So. Watercolor-Mabry award 1981, numerous other awards), So. Graphics Council (invitational exhibits 1975-77, v.p. 81-83, treas. 1988—), Nat. Assn. Women Artists (S.C. membership chmn. 1970—), Nat. Assn. Med. Illustrators, Am. Contemporary Artist, Greenville Artists Guild (pres. 1956-58, 63, bd. dirs. 1954-83). Avocation: sailing. Home: 60 Lake Forest Dr Greenville SC 29609 Office: Mus Sch Art 420 College St Greenville SC 29601

DRESSELHAUS, MILDRED SPIEWAK, engineering educator; b. Bklyn., Nov. 11, 1930; d. Meyer and Ethel (Teichteil) Spiewak; m. Gene F. Dresselhaus, May 25, 1958; children: Marianne, Carl Eric, Paul David, Eliot Michael. A.B., Hunter Coll., 1951, D.Sc. (hon.), 1982; Fulbright fellow, Cambridge (Eng.) U., 1951-52; A.M., Radcliffe Coll., 1953; Ph.D. in Physics, U. Chgo., 1958; D.Engring. (hon.), Worcester Poly. Inst., 1976; D.Sc. (hon.), Smith Coll., 1980, N.J. Inst. Tech., 1984; Doctorat Honoris Causa, U. Catholique de Louvain, 1988. NSF postdoctoral fellow Cornell U., 1958-60; mem. staff Lincoln Lab., MIT, 1960-67, prof. elec. engring., 1968—, asso. dept. head elec. engring., 1972-74, prof. physics, 1983—; Abby Rockefeller Mauzé vis. prof. MIT, 1967-68, Abby Rockefeller Mauzé prof., 1973-85, Inst. prof., 1985—, dir. Ctr. for Materials Sci. and Engring., 1977-83; vis. prof. dept. physics U. Campinas (Brazil), summer 1971, Technion, Israel Inst. Tech., Haifa, Israel, summer 1972, Nihon and Aoyama Gakuin Univs., Tokyo, summer 1973, IVIC, Caracas, Venezuela, summer 1977; lectr. Am. Carbon Soc., 1982; chmn. steering com. of evaluation panels Nat. Bur. Standards, 1978-83; mem. Energy Research Adv. Bd., 1984—; bd. dirs. The Alliance Fund, Rogers Corp., Quantum Chem. Corp. Contbr. articles to profl. jours. Bd. govs. Argonne Nat. Lab.; mem. governing bd. NRC, 1984-87. Named to Hunter Coll. Hall of Fame, 1972; recipient Alumnae medal Radcliffe Coll., 1973, Killian Faculty Achievement award, 1986-87. Fellow Am. Phys. Soc. (pres. 1984), Am. Acad. Arts and Scis., IEEE, AAAS (bd. dirs. 1985—); mem. Nat. Acad. Engring. (council 1981-87), Soc. Women Engrs. (Achievement award 1977), Nat. Acad. Scis. (council 1987—, chmn. engring. sect. 1987—); corr. mem. Brazilian Acad. Sci. Home: 147 Jason St Arlington MA 02174 Office: Mass Inst Tech Cambridge MA 02139

DRESSER, ROBERTA LEAZENBY, microbiologist; b. Fayette, Mo., Sept. 30, 1940; d. James Daniel and Mary Ann (Bates) Leazenby; B.A., U. Mo., 1961, B.Med.Sci., 1963, M.S. in Med. Microbiology, 1968; m. Steven T. Dresser, Dec. 17, 1959 (dec. Aug. 1973); children—Sara, Steven M., Todd, Thomas; m. 2d, Louis A. Kaufman, Dec. 30, 1977. Various clin. lab. positions with U.S. Army, USPHS and VA hosps., 1963-74; commnd. officer USPHS, 1974—; microbiologist div. in vitro diagnostic device standards Bur. Med. Devices, FDA, 1974-80, supervisory program analyst Office Asso. Dir. Standards, 1980-82, spl. asst. for regulatory analysis, 1982-83, analyst, div. planning and evaluation Ctr. for Devices and Radiol. Health, 1983-87; spl. asst. for internat. affairs, exec. sec. Internat. Conf. Med. Device Regulatory Authorities, Ctr. for Devices and Radiol. Health, 1987—. Mem. vestry All Saints Episcopal Ch., San Francisco, 1973-74. Mem. Internat. Soc. for Tech. Assessment in Health Care, Am. Soc. Microbiology, Am. Soc. Clin. Pathologists, Federally Employed Women, Commd. Officers Assn., Nat. Assn. Female Execs., Children Am. Revolution (officer 1980—). Democrat. Home: 2128 Edgewater Pkwy Silver Spring MD 20903 Office: 5600 Fishers Ln Rockville MD 20857

DREW, BETTY BERG, parliamentarian, civic worker; b. Green Bay, Wis., May 27, 1929; d. Walter Richard and Viola Marion (Holz) Berg; m. Dale Robert Drew, June 3, 1950; children—Laura Jane, John Robert, Thomas Richard, James Berg. Diploma in Nursing, Wesley Meml. Hosp. Sch. Nursing, 1950. Registered profl. parliamentarian, Mich. Judge for high sch. parliamentary competitions, local, state and nat. levels, Mich., 1978—; organizer coalition of State Organ Donor Agencies, Ann Arbor, Mich., 1982-88; lectr. for parliamentary unit Oakland-Birmingham, Mich., 1983—. Officer PTO, Bloomfield Hills, Mich., 1970, 77; mem. Bloomfield Republican Women's Club. Mem. AMA Aux. (speaker of house 1984-86), Mich. State Assn. Parliamentarians (officer 1983—), Nat. Assn. Parliamentarians, Mich. State Med. Soc. Aux. (pres. 1983-84), Women's Nat. Farm and Garden Assn. (Vernor br. pres. 1977-78), P.E.O. (pres. chpt. 1985-87). Republican. Congregationalist. Avocations: Golf; knitting; sewing; bridge; piano. Home: 4454 Barchester Dr Bloomfield Hills MI 48013

DREW, CHARLOTTE EMAGENE, educator, accountant; b. Beckley, W.Va., June 16, 1935; d. Charley D. and Hazel Virginia (Wyrick) Hodges; m. Marlee Drew (div. 1975); children: Reginald, Victor, Sue Ellen, Shoska. BS, U. Cen. Fla., 1975; cert. in vocat. office edn., State of Fla., 1975. Tchr. South Seminole Mid. Sch., Casselberry, Fla., 1977, 79—; pvt. practice acctg. Maitland, Fla., 1983—; instr. acctg., fed. tax Orlando (Fla.) Coll. Mem. NEA, Seminole Ednl. Assn., Fla. Vocat. Assn., Phi Beta Lambda. Democrat. Home: 833 Leopard Trail Winter Springs FL 32708

DREW, ELIZABETH, journalist, television commentator; b. Cin., Nov. 16, 1935; d. William J. and Estelle (Jacobs) Brenner; m. J. Patterson Drew, Apr. 11, 1964 (dec. 1970); m. David Webster, Sept. 26, 1981. B.A., Wellesley Coll., 1957; L.H.D., Hood Coll., 1976, Yale U., 1976, Trinity Coll., 1978, Reed Coll., 1979, Williams Coll., 1981; LL.D., Georgetown U., 1981. Writer editor Congl. Quar., 1959-64; free lance writer 1964-67; Washington editor Atlantic Monthly, 1967-73; host TV interview program Thirty Minutes With, 1971-73; commentator Agronsky & Co., Post-Newsweek TV and radio stas. (named changed to Inside Washington, 1988), 1973—; corr. New Yorker Mag., Washington, 1973—. Author: Washington Journal, 1975; American Journal, 1977; Senator, 1979; Portrait of An Election, 1981; Politics and Money, 1983; Campaign Journal, 1985; contbg. author various mags. and jours. Recipient award for excellence Soc. Mag. Writers, 1971, Wellesley Alumnae Achievement award, 1973, DuPont award, 1973, Mo. medal, 1979, Sidney Hillman award, 1983, Ambassador of Honor award Books Across the Sea, 1984, Literary Lion award N.Y. Pub. Library, 1985, Edward Weintal prize, 1988. Home: 3112 Woodley Rd Washington DC 20008 Office: 1717 Massachusetts Ave NW Room LL220 Washington DC 20036

DREW, KATHERINE FISCHER, history educator; b. Houston, Sept. 24, 1923; d. Herbert Herman and Martha (Holloway) Fischer; m. Ronald Farinton Drew, July 27, 1951. B.A., Rice Inst., 1944, M.A., 1945; Ph.D., Cornell U., 1950. Instr. history Rice U., 1946-48; asst. history Cornell U., 1948-50; mem. faculty Rice U., 1950—, prof. history, 1964—, Harris Masterson, Jr. prof. history, 1983-85, Lynette S. Autrey prof. history, 1985—, chmn. dept. history, 1970-80; editor Rice U. (Rice U. Studies), 1967-81, acting dean humanities and social scis., 1973. Author: The Burgundian Code, 1949, Studies in Lombard Institutions, 1956, The Lombard Laws, 1973; Editor: Perspectives in Medieval History, 1963, The Barbarian Invasions, 1970; also articles.; bd. editors: Am. Hist. Rev., 1982-85; Contbr.: Life and Thought in The Middle Ages, 1967. Guggenheim fellow, 1959; Fulbright scholar, 1965; NEH Sr. fellow, 1974-75. Fellow Mediaeval Acad. Am. (mem. council 1974-77, 2d v.p. to pres. 1985-87, del. to Am. Council Learned Socs. 1977-81); mem. Am. Hist. Assn. (council 1983-86), Am. Soc. Legal History, So. Hist. Assn. (vice chair, chair European sect. 1986-88), Phi Beta Kappa. Home: 509 Buckingham Houston TX 77024

DREW, NADINE WRIGHT, college official; b. Timmonsville, S.C., Sept. 11, 1954; d. Norman P. and Maxine (Wilson) Wright; m. Antonius M.A. Drew, Nov. 24, 1979; children—Andre Marcus, LaKesha Alaina, Lenneice Antonia, Marla Aurellia. B.S. in Bus. Adminstrn., Barry U., 1976, B.S. in Mktg./Mgmt., 1976. Legis. asst. to Senator Bob Graham, Miami, Fla., 1976-78; adminstrv. asst. Hunt/Meyer Community Relations, Miami, 1978-80; dir. pub. affairs and publs. Fla. Meml. Coll., Miami, 1980—; pub. relations dir. Nat. Speakers Bur., 1984—. Mem. Internat. Bus. Assn. Communicators, Women in Communications, The Edn. Network, Pub. Relations Soc. Am., Nat. Assn. Univ. Women. Democrat. Mem. Ch. of God. Home: 552 NW 45th St Miami FL 33127 Office: Fla Meml Coll 15800 NW 42nd Ave Miami FL 33054

DREW, SHIRLEY DELORES, insurance company executive; b. Mobile, Ala., Mar. 13, 1932; d. Charles Edward and Gertrude Elizabeth (Hansen) Coleman; m. Lewis Gordon Drew, Aug. 28, 1959 (div. 1977); chilren: Curtis Wayne, Timothy Gordon. Student, Huffsteler Bus. Coll., 1949-50. With Am. Family Life Assurance Co., Mobile, 1970—, dist. mgr., 1981-85, sales assoc., 1985—. treas. Mobile chpt. Altrusa Internat., 1983; charter mem. Rep. Task Force, Washington, 1986, Statue of Liberty-Ellis Island Com., 1986. Mem. Nat. Assn. Life Underwriters, Nat. Assn. Female Execs., Am. Bus. Women's Assn. (pres. 1985-86, named Woman of Yr. 1985-86), Exec. Women's Froum. Baptist. Home: 4154 Stanford Rd Mobile AL 36618 Office: Am Family Life Assurance Co 750 Downtower Blvd Mobile AL 36609

DREYER, LYNN MARIE, social service executive; b. Mpls., May 3, 1958; d. Earl E. and Marlene (Olson) D.; m. Bryan E. Bruchhof, June 18m 1983. A in Mus., BA in Psychology and Social Work cum laude, Concordia Coll., 1980; postgrad., Moorhead State U. Dir. victum assistance program Blue Earth County Human Services, Mankato, Minn., 1980-84; exec. dir. Rape and Abuse Crisis Ctr., Fargo, N.D., 1984-88; mgr. human resources Great Plains Software, Fargo, N.D., 58107; instr. emergency leadership program Moorhead (Minn) State U., 1986—. Mem. N.D. Coalition Sexual Assault Services (pres. 1987—), Inter Agy. Execs. Non Profit Orgns. (pres.), Minn. Coalition Sexual Assault Services (sec. 1983-84), Fargo-Moorhead Personnel Assn. (v.p.), Bus. and Profl. Women, Am. Soc. for Personnel Adminstrn., Female Execs. Assn., Nat. Coalition Battered Women's Services, Fargo C. of C., Nat. Orgn. for Women. Democrat. Lutheran. Lodge: Zonta. Office: Great Plains Software Fargo ND 58107

DREYER, SUSAN MARIE, educator, food service executive; b. Palatine, Ill., May 13, 1959; d. Franklin Delano and Barbara Ann (Schrank) D.; 1 child, Andrew Franklin. Cert. restaurant mgmt., Harper Coll., Palatine, 1982; cert. banking, fin. and credit, Harper Coll., 1986. Mgr. Denny's Restaurant, Schaumburg, Ill., 1983; & Denny's Restaurant, Hanover Park, Ill., 1983-84, Hoffman Estates, Ill., 1984—; instr. Triton Coll., River Grove, Ill., 1986—. Author: (poems) Good-Bye to Seniors, 1977, Natural Highs, 1977. Mem. Nat. Honor Soc., Spanish Honor Soc., Rolling Meadows C. of C. (vendor 1980-81), Phi Theta Kappa. Republican. Roman Catholic. Home: 420 W Palatine Rd #3 Palatine IL 60067 Office: Denny's Restaurant 1175 N Roselle Rd Hoffman Estates IL 60195

DREYFUSS, NANCY MATIS, speech pathologist; b. Chgo., Sept. 20, 1954; d. Jacob David and Rosalie Bette (Metzger) Matis; m. David Michael Dreyfuss, June 7, 1988. B.A., Columbia U., 1976; M.S., Tchrs. Coll., Columbia U., 1978. Staff speech pathologist diagnosis, program planning, treatment of multiply handicapped pre-sch.-age children St. Agnes Hosp., White Plains, N.Y., 1978-82; sr. speech pathologist infant/toddler devel. program North Shore Univ. Hosp., Westbury, N.Y., 1982—; pvt. practice speech therapy, 1983—. Chmn. Young Adults Forum, Congregation Rodeph Sholom, 1983—. Mem. N.Y. Speech and Hearing Assn., Am. Speech and Hearing Assn. (cert. clin. competence), N.Y.C. Speech/Lang./Hearing Assn. Home: 25 Central Park W New York NY 10023 Office: North Shore Univ Hosp Dryden St Westbury NY

DRIESSEN, KAREN RAE, librarian; b. Missoula, Mont., Jan. 24, 1941; d. George Alexander Chestnutt and Helen Marie (Oertel) Gross; m. Jon J. Driessen, Aug. 20, 1961; children: Renée, Eric. BA, U. Mont., 1965; MLS, U. Denver, 1967. Cert. librarian, Colo., Mont. Dir. library processing Adams County Sch. Dist. #50, Westminster, Colo., 1967-69; dir. library purchasing and processing Missoula County High Sch. Dist., Mont., 1969-70; media cataloger instructional materials service U. Mont., Missoula, 1973-74, lectr., media cataloger sch. of edn., 1974-76, media librarian, asst. prof. instructional materials service, 1976-81, media librarian/assoc. prof. instructional materials service, 1981—; faculty sch. of edn. U. Mont., Missoula, 1985-86, audio visual com., chmn. producer contact project, 1985-87; chmn. producer/library relations subcom., 1988—; Mont. rep. Western Library Network Bibliographic Standards Com., Olympia, Washington, 1981-84; cons. audio visual cataloging Mont. U. System, various campuses, 1982—. Contbr. articles to profl. jours. Vol. Am. Heart Assn., Am. Cancer Soc., March of Dimes, Missoula, 1969—. Grantee Mont. State Library, 1986, U.S. Dept. Edn., 1985-86. Mem. Am. Library Assn. (audio visual com., producer, project chmn. 1985-87), Assn. Coll. and Research (librarian 1987) Assn., Mont. Library Assn. (corr. sec. 1984-85, conf. co-chmn. 1981), ACRL (vice chmn., chair elect Mont. chpt. 1987), Online Audiovisual Catalogers (cataloging policy com. 1988—). Home: 2301 Cloverdale Dr Missoula MT 59803 Office: U Mont Instructional Materials Service Missoula MT 59812

DRIGGINS, CLAUDIA JEAN, organization executive; b. Atlantic City, Aug. 19, 1950; d. Alvin Jackson and Emily Elizabeth (Hamilton) D. BA, Bradley U., 1972. Field exec. Kickapoo Council Girl Scouts U.S., Peoria, Ill., 1972-76; program and pub. relations dir. Irish Hills Council Girl Scouts U.S., Jackson, Mich., 1976, exec. dir., 1976-79; exec. dir. Badger Council Girl Scouts U.S., Beloit, Wis., 1979-84, Great River Council Girl Scouts U.S., Cin., 1984—. 2d v.p. LWV, Beloit Wis., 1981-83, pres. 1983-84; community vol. YWCA, Beloit, 1983; mem. Altrusa Club, Cin. and Beloit, bd. dirs. 1983-84; bd. dirs. Cin. United Way, 1987-88; mem. bd. edn. Met. C.M.E. Ch., Cin., 1986—; mem. Leadership Cin., Class XI, 1987-88; div. leader Cin. United Way. Named Vol. of the Month, Beloit Daily News, 1984. Mem. Assn. Girl Scout Exec. Staff (sect. IV program chmn. 1978-81, nat. nominating com. 1981-84), Council of Agy. Execs. (program chmn. Cin. chpt. 1985, 2d v.p. 1986, 1st v.p. 1987), LWV. Club: Womens City (Cin.). Home: 3236 Ashwood Dr Cincinnati OH 45213 Office: Gt Rivers Girl Scout Council Inc 4930 Cornell Rd Cincinnati OH 45242

DRIGGS, MARGARET (MRS. HOWARD R. DRIGGS), educator; b. Kansas City, Kans., June 30, 1909; d. William Foster and Lillian Edith (Landers) Brazier; m. J.W. Quarrier, Nov. 26, 1933 (div. July 1945); children: John Chilton, Philip Harrington, Camille Elizabeth; m. Howard R. Driggs, Sept. 26, 1933 (dec.). AB, U. Kans., 1930; postgrad. Hofstra Coll., 1960, Grad. Sch. Library Sci., Pratt Inst., 1964-65. Contbr. Kansas City Star and Johnson County (Kans.) Herald, 1930-33; editor Am. Trails Series, filmstrips; nat. dir. pub. relations Am. Pioneer Trails Assn., 1948; chmn. pub. relations NYU Faculty Women's Club, 1950-54; nat. 1st v.p. Assn. Parents and Friends Kings Point, 1957-58; mem. Nat. Council Coll. Publs. Advisers, 1958; staff adviser Nexus (yearbook), Hofstra Coll., 1961; mem. faculty Westover Sch., Middlebury, Conn., 1964-65; dir. devel. pub. relations, asst. to dean Cathedral Sch. of St. Mary, Garden City, N.Y., 1965, also yearbook adviser; chmn. guides N.J. Gov.'s Mansion, 1975-82; chmn. docents N.J. Hist. Soc., 1982-86; curator Driggs Collection of Americana. Mem. women's council Hofstra Coll., 1959-60; mem. U.S. Com. for UN Children's Fund, 1957; mem. Friends of Princeton Univ. Library, 1975; mem. Princeton Med. Ctr.Aux.; chair civilian hostesses 15th Ann. U.S. Army Mus. Conf., Princeton, 1986. Recipient Disting. Service citation Am. Pioneer Trails Assn., 1943, medals Am. Yearbook, Columbia Scholastic Press Assn., 1970, pin for vol. work in Princeton, 1976, French-Am. Alliance medal, cert. and hist. house tile award N.J. Hist. Soc., 1984; Margaret Brazier Driggs Collection of Americana established at U. Kans., 1953, at Hofstra Coll., 1961. Mem. ALA, Internat. Platform Assn., Assn. Coll. and Research Libraries, Princeton Hist. Soc., Nat. Trust Hist. Preservation, Smithsonian Assocs., Women's Bd. of N.J. Hist. Soc., Met. Mus. Art, Women's Coll. Club

Princeton, Amiga of Orgn. of Am. States, Pi Delta Epsilon (grand councilman 1960-61). Clubs: NYU; Faculty (hon. life), Present Day (Princeton), Gold Medal (pin and citation for achievement 1930-1980, Kans.). Editor: New Light on Old Glory, 1950, Pitch Pine Tales, 1951, Nick Wilson, 1951, George, The Handcart Boy, 1952, The Old West Speaks, 1956, When Grandfather Was a Boy and Western Cowkid, 1957 (all by Howard R. Driggs); contbg. editor Nat. Assn. Ind. Schs. Archives, Harvard, 1965; editor and photographer Vive Rochambeau, Vive Washington. Home: 135 Princeton Arms S Cranbury NJ 08512

DRILL, BARBARA ANN, music educator; b. Duncan, Okla., Nov. 11, 1933; d. John Knox and Lula Ann (Hatley) Bowling; m. Lewis Stewart Drill, June 12, 1971; children by previous marriage—Daniel Knox Kiniry, John Michael Kiniry. B.Mus., So. Meth. U., 1955. Tchr. music Dallas Ind. Schs., 1955-58, 67-70; pvt. tchr. piano and organ, Dallas, 1955—; organist Casa View Christian Ch., Dallas, 1978—; accompanist Dallas Girls Chorus, 1982—; tchr. music Hockaday Sch., Dallas, 1983—; dir. children's choir Cara View Christian Ch., 1982—; accompanist various festivals, recitals, 1955—; organist/accompanist Tex. Ch. Choir Chorale European Tour, 1985. Recipient Recognition for outstanding contbn. to program for talented and gifted, Dallas Ind. Sch., 1977. Mem. Dallas Music Tchrs. Assn., Tex. Music Tchrs. Assn., Music Tchrs. Nat. Assn., Choristers Guild, Assn. Disciple Musicians, Tex. Music Educators Assn., Am. Guild Organists, Gamma Phi Beta. Republican. Home: 8635 Hackney Ln Dallas TX 75238 Office: Hockaday Preparatory Sch 11600 Welch Rd Dallas TX 75229

DRINNON, DORIS JEAN, dietary professional; b. Gray, Ky., Apr. 29, 1930; d. Jack S. and Margaret (Sevier) Grace; m. Ralph E. Drinnon; children: Cheryl Butler, Jackie Leah Wert, Robert Garfield II. Student, Lincoln Meml. U., 1946-47, Lake Sumpter Jr. Coll., 1965-66; cert., U. Fla., 1985-86. Tchr. Bell County Sch. Bd., Pineville, Ky., 1947-48, Wise (Va.) County Sch. Bd., 1952-54; dietician Norton (Va.) Gen. Hosp., 1959-61; with sales Walling's Ladies Wear, Leesburg, Fla., 1962-68; educator nutrition U. Ga. Extension, Cordele, Ga., 1976-82; supr. dietary Cordele Royal Care Health Ctr., 1984-87. Writer Cordele Dispatch, 1988; feature writer (weekly column by-line) Meanderings; author poetry. Chmn. Am. Cancer Soc., Cordele, project dir. Shrine Hosp. Atlanta, St. Jude's Childrens Hosp. Bike-A-Thon, Cordele; bd. dirs. Cordele Hotel/Motel Tax Adv. Com.; pres. Harris Star Class 1st United Meth. Ch. Mem. Internat. Platform Assn., Nat. Mus. Women in Arts, Nat. Trust for Hist. Preservation, Dietary Mgrs. Assn. (cert.), Writer's Guild. Democrat. Methodist. Club: Pilot Internat. (chmn. projects com., v.p., pres.-elect 1976—). Lodge: Order Eastern Star (matron local chpt. 1959-60). Home and Office: 902 17th Ave Cordele GA 31015

DRISCOLL, ANITA MARIE, banker; b. Chgo., Aug. 22, 1953; d. Clement Joseph and Maria T. (Matilla) D.; m. George M. Feiger; children: Lola E. Feiger, Natasha I. Feiger. BA in Econs. magna cum laude, Am. U., 1975; MBA, Stanford U., 1979. Staff economist Congl. Budget Office, Washington, 1975-77; cons. to Wharton product group Wharton Econ. Forecasting Assn., Boeing Computer Services, Washington and McLean, Va., 1977; v.p. corp. fin. First Boston Corp., N.Y.C., 1979-83; v.p. mortgage fin. First Boston Corp., San Francisco, 1983-85; sr. v.p., chief fin. officer Fed. Home Loan Bank of San Francisco, 1986—. Mem. adv. bd. Low Income Housing Fund, San Francisco, 1986—. Kurth Found. fellow, 1971, Robert Thorson Meml. fellow, 1978. Club: Metropolitan (San Francisco). Office: Fed Home Loan Bank of San Francisco 600 California St San Francisco CA 94108

DRISCOLL, SISTER BRIGID, college president; b. N.Y.C.; d. Daniel Driscoll and Delia Duffy. B in Math., Edn., Marymount Manhattan Coll., 1954; M in Math., Cath. U., 1957; PhD in Math., CUNY, 1967; EdD (hon.), Siena Coll. Joined Religious of Sacred Heart of Mary, Roman Cath. Ch., 1954. Prof. math., assoc. acad. dean, dir. continuing edn. Marymount Coll., Tarrytown, N.Y., founder Weekend Coll., 1975, pres., 1979—; mem. Commr. of Edn.'s Adv. Council on Post-Secondary Edn. in N.Y. State; trustee Commn. on Ind. Colls. and Univs. Bd. dirs. Girl Scouts U.S., Phelps Meml. Hosp. Ctr., North Tarrytown, N.Y., Axe-Houghton Funds, bd. dirs. Westchester/Putnam chpt. United Way, mem. nat. vol. involvement com. 2d Century Initiative; mem. Statue of Liberty/Ellis Island Commn.; trustee Marymount Sch., N.Y.C. Named Woman of Yr. Sleepy Hollow C. of C., 1982; honored for disting. service Westchester (N.Y.) chpt. NCCJ; NASA fellow, 1967. Mem. Assn. Cath. Colls. and Univs. (bd. dirs., chairwoman Neylan Commn.), Commn. on Ind. Colls. and Univs. (trustee). Office: Marymount Coll Office of the Pres Tarrytown NY 10591-3796

DRISCOLL, CONSTANCE FITZGERALD, educator, author; b. Lawrence, Mass., Mar. 29, 1926; d. John James and Mary Anne (Leecock) Fitzgerald; A.B., Radcliffe Coll., 1946; postgrad. Harvard U., U. Hartford (Conn.), U. Bridgeport (Conn.), Worcester (Mass.) State Coll.; m. Francis George Driscoll, Aug. 21, 1948; children—Frances Mary, Martha Anne, Sara Helene, Maribeth Lee. Secondary sch. tchr., North Andover, Mass., 1946 48; book reviewer N.Y.C. and Boston pubs., 1955-64; asst. conf. edn. dir. U. Hartford, 1964-68; lectr. Pace U., N.Y.C., 1973-74; edn. commentary Radio WVOX, New Rochelle, N.Y., 1974-75; asst. ednl. adv. Nat. Girl Scouts, 1972-74; pres., owner, dir. Open Corridor Schs. Cons., Inc., Bronxville, N.Y., 1972—, pres., dir. Open Corridor Schs., Inc., Oxford, Mass., 1984—; creator in-service edn. programs pub. schs., Norwalk, Conn., 1983—; assoc. Worcester State Coll. (Mass.) 1984—, Fitchburg State Coll., 1986-87; cons. in-service tchr. edn. programs, Norwalk, Yonkers, N.Y., 1987—; tutor, cons. Wincester County sch. dist., 1989—. Author curriculum materials. Recipient Educator award Nat. Council ARC, Washington, 1985, Edn. award Nipmuc Am. Indian Council, Webster, Mass, 1985. Home: 338 Main St Oxford MA 01540 Office: Box 564 Oxford MA 01540

DRISCOLL, GENEVIEVE (JEANNE) BOSSON, mgmt. and orgn. devel. cons.; b. Pitts., Mar. 26, 1937; d. George August and Emma Haling Bleichner; B.S. cum laude, Fla. State U., 1959; postgrad. program for specialists in orgn. devel. Nat. Tng. Labs., 1970. m. John Edwin Bosson, June 17, 1959; 1 son, Matthew Edwin; m. 2d Frederick Driscoll, Oct. 7, 1972; stepchildren—Jennifer Locke, Cynthia Hall, Molly Davis, Julie Ann. Planning asst. Center for Planning and Innovation, Dept. Edn. State of N.Y., 1967-71, planning cons. So. Tier Regional Office for Ednl. Planning, Elmira, N.Y., 1971-72; tng. dir. Neusteters, Inc., Denver, 1973-74; orgn. devel. specialist CONNECT, Inc., N.Y.C., 1975-77; cons. Robert H. Schaffer & Assos., Stamford, Conn., 1977-80; partner Driscoll Cons. Group, Williamstown, Mass., 1980—; sales tng. mgr. Sheaffer Eaton, Pittsfield, Mass., 1983, mgr. human resources and orgn. devel., 1983—; cons. in field. Office: 24 Lee Terr Williamstown MA 01267

DRISCOLL, JEANNE BAKER, business manager; b. Pipestone, Minn.; d. John B. and Marie Helena (Kallemeyn) B.; m. John Paul Driscoll, Mar. 20, 1971; children: Emily Vida-Marie, Gillian Paula-Jean. BA, U. Minn., 1969; MEd, Pa. State U., 1973, PhD, 1978; bus. cert., U. Pa., 1980. Cert. counselor, career counselor. Admissions counselor U. Minn., Morris, 1969-71; career counselor Pa. State U., State Coll., 1971-75, counselor of edn. faculty, 1975-78; dir. placement and transfer Quinsigamond Community Coll., Worcester, Mass., 1979-80; dir. grad. programs Fitchburg (Mass.) State Coll., 1981-82, dir. career services, 1982-87; v.p. for adminstrn. Babcock Galleries, N.Y.C., 1987—; adj. grad. faculty Fitchburg State Coll., 1978-87. Author: Optimizing Women's Leadership Skills, 1974; contbr. articles to profl. jours. Pres. Mental Health Assn., Fitchburg, 1983; review bd. mem. United Way, Fitchburg, 1984-85; v.p. First Parish Ch., Fitchburg, 1985-86. Mem. Am. Assn. for Counseling and Devel. (career info. service reviewer 1983—), Nat. Career Devel. Assn. (del. 1976, 77), New Eng. Assn. for Sch., Coll., and Univ. staffing (treas. 1985—), Mass. Pub. Coll. Career Planning and Placement Assn. (pres. 1985-86), Ea. Coll. Personnel Officers (presenter 1986). Office: Babcock Gallery 140 E 83d St New York NY 10028

DRISCOLL, JEANNE MARIE, restaurant owner; b. Huntington, N.Y., June 10, 1956; d. Donald John and Doris Margaret (Welch) D. BA, Boston Coll., 1978. Asst. dept. mgr., dept. mgr. gourmet foods Bloomingdale's Dept. Store, N.Y.C., 1978-82, restaurant mgr., 1982, buyer, fresh foods, Michel Guérard, 1982-84; nat. sales mgr. Gourmet Resources Internat. Inc., N.Y.C., 1984; dir. mktg. Piret's specialty restaurants VICORP, San Diego, 1985-87; prin. J.M. Driscoll Corp., San Diego, Calif., 1987—. Recipient Award of Excellence Wine Spectator, Calif., 1986. Mem. Am. Mktg. Assn., Am. Inst. Wine and Food. Office: Piret's Mission Hills 902 W Washington St San Diego CA 92103

DRISCOLL, JEANNE WATSON, nurse; b. Bronx, N.Y., Aug. 23, 1949; d. Robert Ernest and Lorraine Jane (Rittereiser) Watson; m. David John Driscoll, Aug. 18, 1973; children: Lorraine, Kathleen. BS in Nursing, U. Del., 1971; MS, Boston Coll., 1975. Staff nurse New Eng. Deaconess Hosp., Boston, 1971-73; instr. Faulkner Hosp., Jamaica Plain, Mass., 1973-74, 77-78, Salem (Mass.) State Coll., 1976-77, Northeastern U., Boston State Coll., 1979-81; pvt. practice psychotherapy Boston, 1979-81; clin. nurse specialist Brigham and Women's Hosp., 1981—; childbirth educator Boston Hosp. for Women, 1979-81; founder Lactation Assocs., Weston, Mass., 1981—; pres. Lifecycle Prodns., Inc., Newton Mass., 1985—. Author: Breastfeeding Your Premature Baby, 1986. Troop leader Girl Scouts U.S.A., Boston, 1985—. Mem. Am. Nurses Assn. (cert.), Mass. Nurses Assn. (clin. practice award 1983), Nurses Assn. Am. Coll. Ob-Gyn., Nat. Assn. Female Execs., Sigma Theta Tau. Roman Catholic. Office: Brigham and Women's Hosp 75 Francis St Boston MA 02115

DRISCOLL, JOSEPHINE MARGARET, state official; b. East Helena, Mont., July 7, 1923; d. George and Josephine (Masonovich) Nick; m. William J. Driscoll, Sept. 6, 1953 (div. 1967); children—Sara Kathleen, Maureen Elaine. With Fireman's Fund Group, Helena, Mont., 1940-53, Wolfstone & Co., Seattle, 1953-57, 59-62; supr. rates and forms Mont. Ins. Dept., Helena, 1966-74, asst. chief dep., 1974-77, chief dep. ins. commr., 1977-81; asst. commr. State Oreg. Dept. Commerce, Salem, 1981, ins. commr., 1981-87; v.p. regulatory affairs, Standard Ins. Co., 1987—. Named Woman of Yr., Ins. Women's Assn., Helena, Mont., 1978. Mem. Am. Bus. Women's Assn. (pres. chpt.; Woman of Yr. 1980), Nat. Assn. Ins. Commrs. (pres. 1986). Republican. Serbian Orthodox. Office: Standard Ins Co Standard Plaza Portland OR 97204

DRISCOLL, SHIRLEY GRIFFITH, pathologist, educator; b. Pittston, Pa., Feb. 8, 1923; d. William Edmund and Margaret Helen (Underwood) Griffith; m. John J. Driscoll, Sept. 18, 1948. A.B., U. Pa., 1945, M.D., 1949. Intern Mt. Auburn Hosp., Cambridge; resident Children's Hosp., Phila., Phila. Gen. Hosp., Peter Bent Brigham Hosp., Boston Lying-in Hosp., Free Hosp. for Women, Brookline, Mass.; pathologist Boston Lying-in Hosp., 1948-65; pathologist Boston Hosp. for Women, 1965-78, pathologist in chief, 1978-81; dir. women's and perinatal div. of pathology Brigham & Women Hosp. Harvard Med. Sch.; instr. pathology Harvard U., 1958-75, prof., 1975—. Author: (with Benirschke) Pathology of the Human Placenta, 1967. Mem. AAAS, Teratology Soc., New Eng. Pediatric Pathology Group, Soc. Pediatric Pathology, Obstet. Soc. Boston, Mass. Med. Soc., New Eng. Soc. Pathology, Mass. Soc. Pathology, Internat. Soc. Gynecol. Pathology, Am. Soc. Clin. Pathologists. Office: 75 Francis St Boston MA 02115

DRIVER, PAMELA JEAN, management consultant, motivational speaker and trainer; b. Louisville, June 30, 1957; d. Stanley L. and Dorothy (Meador) K.; m. Jesse E. Driver, June 18, 1976; children—Clifford Dewayne, Jennifer Michele. B.S., U. Tenn., 1978, M.S., 1982. Dietary supr. Fort Sanders Presbyn. Hosp., Knoxville, Tenn., 1977-78; nutrition edn. project dir. Loudon County Schs., Loudon, Tenn., 1980-82, foodservice supr., 1980-83; pres., owner Driver & Assocs., Philadelphia, Tenn., 1982—; seminar, tng. presenter; trainer thousands of bank employees, 1986, other groups; editor, pub. foodservice newsletter. Chmn. March of Dimes, Heart Fund drives. Recipient 4-H Leader award Loudon County 4-H, 1981, 82, 83; Tenn. Nutrition edn. grantee, 1980-82. Mem. Nat. Restaurant Assn., Soc. Nutrition Edn. (membership coordinator Tenn. 1980-83), Am. Home Econs. Assn. (area pres. Tenn. conv. com.), Tenn. Sch. Food Service Assn. (resolutions chmn. conv. com. 1982-83), Am. Sch. Food Service Assn., Tenn. Home Econs. Assn. (conv. com.), Am. Mgmt. Assn., Tenn. Bankers Assn. (assoc.), Omicron Nu. Baptist. Home: Route 1 Philadelphia TN 37846 Office: Driver and Assocs PO Box 139 Philadelphia TN 37846

DRIVER-NEFF, BEVERLY GENE, electrical engineer; b. Clinton, La., June 28, 1960; d. Eddie C. and Ruth E. (Catherine) Driver; m. William Leon Neff, Jr., Aug. 30, 1986. BSEE, So. U., 1984. Registered engr., La. Indsl. engr. Gulf States Utilities, St. Francisville, La., 1984-85, engr. quality assurance, 1985-86, electrical engr., 1987—; cons. computer Constrn. Systems Assn., St. Francisville, La., 1986-87. Mem. Polit. Action Com., Baton Rouge, 1984—. Mem. IEEE. Democrat. Baptist. Club: Community (sec. 1980-81). Home: 11232 Neff Ln Zachary LA 70791

DROEGE, MARIE THERESE, hospital administrator; b. Washington, Mo., July 17, 1961; d. Firmin Francis D. BS in Biology, Chemistry, Quincy Coll., 1983; MHA, U. Mo., 1985. Adminstrv. fellow Mercy Hosp., Urbana, Ill., 1985-86, acting v.p. patient care services, 1986; ops. specialist Healthcor, Urbana, 1986-87; chief exec. officer Cen. Community Hosp., Clifton, Ill., 1987—. Mem. Health Care Fin. Mgmt. Assn., Am. Hosp. Assn., Mgmt. Systems Soc., Women's Bus. Council Urbana, Nat. Assn. Female Execs., Urbana C. of C. Roman Catholic. Office: Healthcor 175 S Wall St Kankakee IL 61821

DRONGOSKI, CYNTHIA, pharmacist, researcher; b. Passaic, N.J., Dec. 29, 1957; d. Frank and Gloria A. (Ortolan) D. BS in Pharmacy, Rutgers U., 1981. Registered pharmacist, N.J. Staff pharmacist Plaza Drug Mart, Lincoln Park, N.J., 1981-85; staff pharmacist Bloomingdale (N.J.) Pharmacy, 1981-86, mgr., pharmacist, 1985-86; clin. research asst. Ortho Pharm. Corp., Raritan, N.J., 1986-87, clin. research assoc., 1987—. Mem. Am. Pharm. Assn., N.J. Pharm. Assn., Passaic County Pharm. Assn., Drug Info. Assn., Rho Chi. Roman Catholic. Home: 23 Hamilton Ave Wayne NJ 07470 Office: Ortho Pharm Corp Rt 202 S PO Box 300 Raritan NJ 08869-0602

DROPKIN, SHEILA LEE, public relations executive; b. Bklyn., Jan. 27, 1934; d. Harry and Gussie (Luftschein) Engelman; m. Arthur Dropkin, May 27, 1956; children: Adam Stuart, Gayle Ellen. BA in Journalism, N.Y.U., 1954. Exec. asst. student mktg. orgn., N.Y.C., 1954-60; feature writer Surburban Newspaper Chain, Montreal, 1972-77; dir. Can. Soc. for the Weizmann Inst. of Sci., Vancouver, B.C., 1977-79; dir. nat. pub. relations Can. Shaare Zedek Hosp. Found., Toronto, 1980-87, nat. execs. dir., 1988—; cons. pub. relations Can. Hadassah-Wizo, Toronto, 1985—; feature writer Can. Jewish News, Toronto, 1979—; columnist Surburban Newspaper Chain, Montreal, 1977-82. Mem. Toronto Assn. Profls. in Jewish Communal Service (pres.), Alpha Tau Omega.

DROZDA, HELEN DOROTHY, psychiatric social worker; b. Omaha, Mar. 21, 1924; d. Joseph J. and Mary E. (Sabatka) D.;. BS, U. Nebr., 1955; MS, So. Ill. U., 1965; postgrad., Tex. Tech U., 1969, Midwestern U., 1968-69; PhD, Colo. State Christian Coll., 1973. Diplomate Clin. Social Workers; cert. social worker, advanced clin. practitioner, Tex., rehab. counselor. Supervising group counselor San Diego Probation Dept., 1956-57; health edn. dir. YWCA, Omaha, 1954-56; Y-teen dir. YWCA, Alton, Bloomington and Peoria, Ill., 1958-62; guidance dir. Acad. of Our Lady, Peoria, 1962-64, St. Teresa Acad., East St. Louis, Ill., 1964-67, Knox County Pub. Schs., Benjamin, Tex., 1967-69, Wilbarger County Pub. Schs., Vernon, Tex., 1969-70; exec. dir. Burk Guidance and Counseling Services, Burkburnett, Tex., 1970-86; social service supr. Western unit Wichita Falls State Hosp., Burkburnett, Tex., 1970-86. Named Social Worker of Yr., 1984. Mem. Am. Legion, Air Force Assn., Am. Guidance and Personnel Assn., Nat. Assn. Social Workers (past chmn. Red River unit, diplomate), Midwest Soc. Individual Psychology, Tex. Pub. Employees Assn., Tex. Social Psychotherapy Assn., Acad. Certified Social Workers, Nat. Rifle Assn., Am. Assn. Ret. Persons. Home: 820 Sheppard Rd Burkburnett TX 76354 Office: Burk Guidance and Counseling Burkburnett TX 76354

DROZDA, KIMBERLY KAY, public relations executive; b. Bainbridge, Md., Apr. 26, 1956; d. Janet G. (Vernon) Hepner; m. Richard Allen Drozda, May 19, 1977; 1 child, Scott R. BA, Am. Inst. Banking, Chgo., 1980; postgrad, LaRoche Coll., Pitts., 1982-83; postgrad., Fairfield (Conn.) U., 1984-85. Owner, operator The Best Cellar Shoppe, Dover, Ohio, 1977-81; actress N.Y., Calif., 1972—; cons. pub. relations, advt. various corps., Conn., N.Y., N.J., Calif., 1984—; pres., chief exec. officer Silverscreen Prodns., Mansfield, Ohio, 1985—; cons., dir. Madison Comprehensive High Sch., Mansfield, Ohio, 1987-88; cons. Advt. Area Media, Los Angeles, 1985-88; dir. Software Interface Internat., Independence, Ohio, 1988—. Author: (news digest Class In Style, 1988, Receptionist/Secretary's Handbook, 1988; (newsletter) Computing of Public and Private Security, 1988. Chairperson Mansfield Symphony, 1986-87; buyer, trustee Mansfield Art Ctr., 1986-87; com. chair person Downtown Mchts. Assn., Dover, 1978-83, Downtown Growth Assn., 1978-83. Mem. Screen Talent Ltd. (Extrodinary Workmanship award 1987), Nat. Orgn. Women, Profl. Bus. women Assn. (com. chmn. 1978-81). Methodist. Mktg. (Columbus, Ohio) (pres. 1987-88), Advt. Unltd. (St. Louis) (chairperson 1988-89). Office: Silverscreen Prodns PO Box 3515 Mansfield OH 44907

DRUCKER, MINDY M., editor, writer; b. Newark, Apr. 25, 1957; d. Burton and Shirley D. BA, U. Rutgers, 1979; diploma, NYU, 1983. Assoc. editor Time Capsule, Inc., N.Y.C., 1979-80; proofreader, editor Grolier Inc./The Scarecrow Press, Metuchen, N.J., 1980-83; copy editor spl. publs. House Beautiful mag., N.Y.C., 1983-86; mng. editor Hotel and Resort Industry mag., N.Y.C., 1986-87; copy editor Colonial Homes mag., N.Y.C., 1987—. Contbr. articles to various mags. Mem. Nat. Assn. Female Execs. Office: Colonial Homes Mag 1790 Broadway New York NY 10019

DRUM, JOAN MARIE MCFARLAND, federal agency administrator; b. Waseca, Minn., Mar. 31, 1932; d. Leo Joseph and Bergetthe (Anderson) McFarland; m. William Merritt Drum, June 13, 1954; children: Melissa, Eric. BA in Journalism, U. Minn., 1962; MEd, Coll. William and Mary, 1975, postgrad., 1984-85. Govt. official fgn. claims br. Social Security Adminstrn., Balt., 1962-64; freelance writer Polyndrum Publs., Newport News, Va., 1967-73; tchr. Newport News (Va.) Pub. Schs., 1975-79; writer, cons. Drum Enterprises, Williamsburg, Va., 1980-82; developer, trainer communicative skills U.S. Army Transp. Sch., Ft. Eustis, Va., 1982-86; govt. ofcl. test assistance div. U.S. Army Tng. Ctr., Ft. Eustis, 1986—; adj. faculty English dept. St. Leo Area Coll., Ft. Eustis, 1975-78; del. Communicative Skills Conf., Ft. Leavenworth, Kans., 1983; lectr. in field. Author: Ghosts of Fort Monroe, 1972, Travel for Children in Tidewater, 1974; editor: army newsletter for families, 1968-73, Social Services Resource Reference, 1970; contbr. articles to profl. jours. Chmn. Girl Scouts U.S., Tokyo, 1964-66, Army Community Service, Ft. Monroe, Va., 1967-68; chmn. publicity Hist. Home Tours, Ft. Monroe, 1971-73. Recipient numerous civic awards including North Shore Community Service award, Hialeah, Hawaii, 1966, Home Bur. Service award, 1975, Service award Girl Scouts U.S., Tokyo, 1965. Mem. Nat. Assn. Govt. Communicators, Tidewater Writers' Assn., Kappa Delta Pi. Home: 9 Bray Wood Williamsburg VA 23185 Office: US Army Tng Ctr Test Assistance Div Individual Tng Evaluation Directorate Fort Eustis VA 23604

DRUMHELLER, LINDA BETH, publishing company professional; b. Pitts., Apr. 25, 1947; d. Alfred Carroll and Alice Beth (Swift) Kraft; m. Russell L. Drumheller, July 26, 1969; children: Shelly Kim, Jeffrey Lee. Student, Dickinson Coll., 1965-66; BA in English, Pa. State U., 1969. Analyst actuarial/benefits Towers, Perrin, Forster & Crosby, Phila., 1969-76; mgr. benefit statement services Comshare, Inc., Phila., 1976-78; assoc., group mng. editor loose leaf references services Datapro Research Corp. subs. McGraw-Hill, Inc., Delran, N.J., 1978-84, dir. new product devel., 1984-87, dir. vendor database products, 1987—. Bd. dirs. Burlington County Council, Girl Scouts U.S., Westhampton Twp., N.J., 1974—. Mem. Info. Industry Assn. Home: 270 Black Baron Dr Delran NJ 08075 Office: Datapro Research Corp 1805 Underwood Blvd Delran NJ 08075

DRUMMER, DOROTHY JEAN, executive search consultant, lawyer; b. Racine, Wis., Apr. 13, 1949; d. Paul Allan and Ruth Ellen (Fanning) D.; m. W. Merriman Morton, Dec. 26, 1982; children: Michelle Morton, Brad Morton and Ben Morton. AB, Smith Coll., 1970; JD, Rutgers U., 1975. Bar: N.Y. 1976, Tex. 1986. V.p., counsel to the chmn. Am. Stock Exchange, N.Y.C., 1976-82; v.p. Am. Bus. Conf., Washington, 1980-85, exec. v.p., 1985-87, cons., 1987—; dir. Spencer Stuart, Houston, 1987—. Exec. dir. Pres.' Task Force on Pvt. Sector Initiatives, Washington, 1981-82. Mem. Houston Bar Assn., Exec. Forum (pres. 1985-86). Office: Spencer Stuart 1111Bagby St Suite 1616 Houston TX 77002

DRUMMOND, CONSTANCE ANNE, government lawyer; b. Toledo, Jan. 11, 1949; d. Charles William and Bernice Louise (Brauneck) Gaiser; children: Melissa Anne, Daniel Charles. BS, Bowling Green State U., 1972; JD, U. Louisville, 1978, LLM, 1988. Bar: Ky. 1979. Commd. capt. U.S. Army, 1980; tchr. Jefferson Ctr. for Handicapped, Toledo, 1972, Toledo Bd. Edn., 1972-76; acting v.p. Fort Knox (Ky.) Nat. Bank, 1976; legal clk. Skeeters & Bennett, Radcliff, Ky., 1976-78; sec. Stites, McElwain & Fowler, Louisville, 1979; corp. sec., advisor CoaLiquid, Inc., Louisville, 1979-80; faculty Elizabethtown (Ky.) Community /coll., 1979; mil. atty. U.S. Army, Ft. Monmouth, N.J., Republic of Panama, Honduras, 1980—, Office the Staff Judge Advocate, West Point, N.Y., 1984-87. Sun. sch. tchr. various chs., 1972-84; group leader Ft. Monmouth, N.J. 4-H Club, 1981-83. Mem. Ky. Bar Assn., Pi Omega Pi. Republican. Lutheran. Club: Eastern Star (Waterville, Ohio). Office: Chief Mil Justice Office of the Staff Judge Advocate Fort Dix NJ 08640

DRUMMOND, DOROTHY WEITZ, geography educator, writer; b. San Diego, Dec. 19, 1928; d. Frederick William and Dora (Weidenhofer) Weitz; m. Robert R. Drummond (dec. 1982); children: Kathleen, Gael, Martha. BA, Valparaiso (Ind.) U., 1949; MA, Northwestern U., 1951. Research and editorial asst. Am. Geog. Soc., N.Y.C., 1951-53; freelance writer Terre Haute, 1953—; adj. instr. geography St. Mary of the Woods Coll., Terre Haute, 1968—; adv. McGraw-Hill Text-Film div., N.Y.C., 1960-73, Agy. Instructional Tech., Bloomington, Ind., 1985—; tour leader to Republic of China, 1986—. Author: The World Today: Its Patterns and Cultures, 3d edit. 1971, People on Earth, 3d edit. 1987; creator World Patterns overhead projector transparencies, Our World Yesterday and Today. Past pres. Swope Mus. Alliance, Terre Haute; bd. dirs. Mental Health Assn., YWCA, Council on Domestic Abuse, Terre Haute. Named Fulbright scholar, Burma, 1957. Mem. Nat. Council for Geog. Edn. (bd. dirs. 1983-86, v.p., pres.-elect), Ind. Council Social Studies (bd. dirs.), Geography Educators' Network in Ind. (bd. dirs.), Assn. Am. Geographers. Home and Office: Rt 15 Box 497 West Terre Haute IN 47885

DRUMMOND, GILLIAN M., home furnishings company executive; b. Haywardsheath, Eng., Apr. 3, 1943; came to U.S., 1951; d. Bernard Gilbert and Margaret (Soot Hutcheson) D. Cert. N.Y. Sch. Interior Design, 1965; student U. Geneva, 1961-62. Asst. designer B. Altman & Co., N.Y.C., 1966-68; interior designer Tate & Hall, N.Y.C., 1968-72; Practice interior design, N.Y.C., 1972-75; mgr. customer relations Marcel Dekker Inc., N.Y.C., 1975-78; exec. dir. S.M. Hexter, N.Y.C., 1978-80; exec. dir. East Coast Winfield Design Assocs., N.Y.C., 1980-82; home furnishings cons., N.Y.C., 1982-85; pres. Gillian Drummond Inc., Wilmington N.C., 1985—. Conservative candidate N.Y. Congress, 1974; bd. dirs. Arts Council Lower Cape Fear; program chmn. St. Thomas Celebration of Arts. Mem. Decorative Fabrics Assn. (membership chmn. 1982-84), Nat. Home Fashions League, Decorative Arts Assn., Nat. Assn. Female Execs., Nat. Trust Historic Preservation, Historic Wilmington Found. Republican. Address: 115 Nun St Wilmington NC 28401 Office: 127 N Front St Wilmington NC 28401

DRUMMOND, PAULA GRIER, lawyer; b. Fort Lauderdale, Fla., Dec. 8, 1950; d. John Perkins and Jeanne (Bottomley) Grier; m. Michael A. Fruchey, Aug. 30, 1968 (div. Oct. 1972); 1 child, Cecily N.; m. Richard Wayne Drummond, June 17, 1978; 1 child, John Edward. A.A. with honors, Brevard Community Coll., 1973; B.A. summa cum laude, U. Central Fla., 1975; J.D., Fla. State U., 1978. Bar: Fla. 1978, U.S. Dist. Ct. (no. dist.) Fla. 1978, U.S. Cir. Ct. of Appeals (11th cir.) 1982, U.S. Supreme Ct. 1984. Law clk. U.S. Magistrate, No. Dist. Fla., Pensacola, 1978-80; asst. county atty. Escambia County, Fla., Pensacola, 1980-82, county atty., 1982-83; sole practice, Pensacola, 1983—. Bd. dirs. YWCA, Pensacola, 1985; active Leadership Pensacola Class of 1987; bd. dirs. Cath. Soc. Services, 1987—. Mem. ABA, Fla. Bar Assn. (exec. council local govt. law sect. 1982-83), Escambia-Santa Rosa Bar Assn. (exec. com. 1984-85, chmn. bar found. com. 1984-85), Pensacola Network Exec. Women (v.p. 1985-86, pres. 1988), Northwest Fla. Assn. Women Lawyers (pres. 1988), Leadership Pensacola Class of 1987 (curriculum com. 1987-88). Clubs: Panhandle Tiger Bay, Gulf Coast Econs. Office: 15 W La Rua St Pensacola FL 32501

DRURY, DORIS MARIE, economics educator, consultant, researcher; b. Louisville, Nov. 18, 1926; d. Coleman F. and Ursula P. (Darst) D. B.S., U. Louisville, 1955, M.B.A., 1957; M.A., Ind. U., Bloomington, 1962, Ph.D., 1964; postgrad., U. Denver Coll. Law, 1973-74. Asst. prof. econs. U. Wyo., Laramie, 1962-63; assoc. prof. La. State U., 1963-65; prof. econs. U. Denver, 1965—, chmn. div. research, 1968-71, chmn. econs., 1972-79; dir. Fed. Res. Bank, Kansas City, 1980-84, chmn. bd., 1985, chmn. audit, 1980-83; dir., chmn. audit com. Pub. Service Co., Denver, 1979—; dir., founder Women's Bank, Denver, 1977-78; dir. Colo. Nat. Bankshares, Equitable of Iowa; pres., chmn. Ctr. for Bus. and Econ. Forecasting, Denver. Author: Accidents in Coal Producing Countries, 1964, Phase II Economic Controls, 1972, Key Public Economic Issues, 1971, Construction Industry in Colorado, 1969. Mem. Gov.'s Blue Ribbon Panel on Econ. Planning, Colo., 1979-81; bd. dirs. YWCA, Denver, 1979-81. Recipient Disting. Teaching Specialist Commendation, U. Denver, 1973; Resources of the Future, Inc. fellow, 1961-62. Mem. Nat. Assn. Bus. Economists, Am. Econ. Assn., Denver C. of C. Home: 10879 E Powers Dr Englewood CO 80111 Office: U Denver CBA 2020 S Race St Denver CO 80210

DRURY, REGINA ROSE, hospital executive; b. Warsaw, Ind., Sept. 18, 1951; d. John Estel and Rosamond Elaine (Dahm) Funk; m. Gary Lynn Drury, May 1, 1976 (div. July 1986); children: Jason Eric, Julie Ann. BS in Nursing, Ind. U., Indpls., 1974; postgrad., Coll. St. Francis, Joliet, Ill. RN Ind., Tex. Emergency staff nurse U.S.A.A. Ins. Co., San Antonio, 1978-79; realtor Century 21, San Antonio, 1979-80; head nurse emergency room Michiana Community Hosp., South Bend, Ind., 1981-84; from treas. to chief exec. officer Am. Eagle Gen. Contractors, Mishawaka, Ind., 1984-85; v.p. Holy Cross Parkview Hosp., Plymouth, Ind., 1985—; instr., cons. Inner Dimensions, South Bend, 1985—. Chairperson health profl. adv. com., exec. com. No. Ind. March Dimes. Served to maj. Nursing Corps., U.S. Army, 1974-77. Mem. Am. Coll. Health Care Execs. (affiliate), Am. Orgn. Nurse Execs, Res. Officers Assn., Nat. Assn. for Female Execs., Am. Legion, Ind. Hosp. Assn. Midwestern Council Nurse Execs., Ind. Org. Nurse Execs., Nat. Assn. Female Execs.Sigma Pi Alpha. Republican. Roman Catholic. Office: Holy Cross Parkview Hosp 1915 Lake Ave PO Box 670 Plymouth IN 46563

DRYDEN, JUDY CANADAY, government official; b. Elkhart, Kans., Dec. 14, 1930; d. Lieu Pierce and Eva Maudie (Caler) Canaday; m. Donald W. Dryden, May 6, 1949 (dec.); children—Donald Wayne, Mary Anne, John Robert. Student, Iola Jr. Coll., Kans., 1947-49, Northwestern State U., Natchitoches, La., 1974. Clk.-typist spl. services U.S. Army, Ft. Polk, La., 1962-66, mil. personnel clk. testing, 1966-67, computer operator, data processing, 1967-70, computer systems analyst Mgmt. Info. Systems Office, Ft. Polk, La., 1970-74, computer specialist, Ft. Dix, N.J., 1974-76, computer specialist Hdqrs. Tng. and Doctrine Command, Info. Mgmt. Div., Ft. Monroe, Va., 1976-82, chief customer services br., Data Processing Field Office, 1982, chief customer support div., 1982-83, chief office automation and mgmt. br., 1983-85, chief accountability, acquisition and contracting, 1985-87, chief logistics support br. DOIM, 1988—. Mem. fin. com. Phoebus Bapt. Ch., Hampton, Va., 1982-85, 88, chmn., 1983, ch. clk., 1983-88. Recipient Sustained Superior Performance award Dept. of Army, 1979, Outstanding Performance award 1981. Mem. Nat. Assn. Female Execs., Assn. U.S. Army, Smithsonian Assocs., Internat. Platform Assn., Nat. Trust for Hist. Preservation. Democrat. Baptist. Home: 9 Pavilion Pl Hampton VA 23664 Office: Data Processing Field Office Bldg 117 Fort Monroe VA 23651

DRYDEN, MARY ELIZABETH, legal librarian, writer, actress; b. Chgo., Oct. 18, 1949; d. James Heard and Hazel Anne (Potts) Rule; m. Ian Dryden, Nov. 22, 1975. Student, U. London, 1969, Bath U., 1970; B.A., Scripps Coll., 1971; postgrad. U. Edinburgh, 1971-74. Head librarian Hahn, Cazier & Leff, San Diego, 1980, Fredman, Silverberg & Lewis, San Diego, 1980-83, Riordan & McKinzie, Los Angeles, 1983—; freelance photog. model, 1973—. Theatrical appearances include Antony and Cleopatra, McOwen Theatre, London, 1984, Table Manners, Los Angeles, 1985, Harliquinade, Los Angeles, 1985, Julius Caesar, Los Angeles, 1986, Witness for the Prosecution, Los Angeles, 1987, Come and Go, Los Angeles, 1988; book critic Los Angeles Times; contbr. articles to newspapers. Mem. So. Calif. Soc. Law Librarians, Am. Film Inst., Theatre Palisades, Mensa, Phi Beta Kappa. Avocations: photography, wine, architecture, fine art, languages. Office: Riordan & McKinzie 29th Floor 300 S Grand Ave Los Angeles CA 90071

DRYER, DOROTHEA MERRILL (MRS. EDWIN JASON DRYER), lawyer; b. Salt Lake City; d. George Edmund and Lillian (Chapman) Merrill; A.B., Stanford, 1936; LL.B., Yale, 1940; m. Edwin Jason Dryer, Feb. 28, 1942; children—Diana Claire Dryer Wright, Faith Ellen. Admitted to Utah bar, 1941, U.S. Supreme Ct. bar, U.S. Ct. Mil. Appeals; clk. to Chief Justice Wolfe, Utah Supreme Ct., 1941; atty. Bur. Immigration, Dept. Justice, Washington, 1941-42; practiced in Salt Lake City, 1943-47, Washington, 1948—; dep. county atty., Salt Lake City, 1947-48. Fellow Am. Assn. Criminology; mem. Am., Fed., Utah bar assns., Nat. Assn. Women Lawyers, Am. Judicature Soc., Nat. Assn. for Gifted Children, Assn. for Gifted, Oral History Assn., Kappa Kappa Gamma. Unitarian. Clubs: Jr. League Washington; Potomac Bus. and Profl. Women's; Nat. Lawyers. Home: 5126 Palisade Ln NW Washington DC 20016 Office: Farm Running Brook Farm Rt 1 Bentonville VA 22610

DRYFOOS, NANCY, sculptor; b. New Rochelle, N.Y., Mar. 28; d. Richman and Edith (Harris) Proskauer; m. Donald Dryfoos. Cert. Sarah Lawrence Coll., 1939; postgrad. Columbia U. Extension Sch., 1945-46. One-person shows include: Contemporary Arts Gallery, N.Y.C., 1952, Silvermine Guild Gallery, 1954, Wellons Gallery, 1956, Bodley Gallery, 1958, Collectors Gallery, 1960, Dime Savs. Bank, Bklyn., 1969, Lincoln Savs. Bank, N.Y.C., 1975-76, Donnell Library, N.Y.C., 1987 (pen and pen and brush show winner 1988); group shows include: Pa. Acad. Fine Arts, 1947, Syracuse Mus., 1948, Bklyn. Mus., 1952, Corcoran Gallery, 1954, Nat. Acad. Fine Arts, N.Y.C., 1952-76, Lincoln Savs. Bank, 1987, Donnell Library Ctr., 1987, others; V.p. Fine Arts Fedn. of N.Y. Contbr. articles to profl. publs. Fellow Nat. Sculpture Soc. (recording sec. 1973, bd. dirs. 1988—); mem. Allied Artists America (Medal of Honor 1978), Audubon Artists (exhbn. dir. 1983-84, asst. treas. 1987-88, prize), Am. Soc. Contemporary Artists (dir., exhbn. dir., prize), Contemporary Artists Guild (dir.), N.Y. Soc. Women Artists (dir.), Fine Arts Fedn. N.Y. (v.p.), Pen and Brush Club, Nat. Trust for Hist. Preservation, Network Visual Arts Ctr. (dir.), Brandeis Creative Arts Commn. (dir.), Artists Equity Assn. (bd. dirs. 1978-80). Avocations: printmaking, enameling. Home: 45 E 89th St New York NY 10128

DRYNAN, MARGARET ISOBEL, music teacher, retired consultant; b. Toronto, Ont., Can., Dec. 10, 1915; d. William James and Ellen (Rowney) Brown; Mus.B., U. Toronto, 1943; m. George Drynan, July 3, 1940; children—Judith, John, James. Mem. nat. exec. bd. Royal Can. Coll. after 1951, nat. 1st v.p., 1980-82, nat. pres., 1982-84; charter mem., pres. Oshawa Council for the Arts, Ont., Can., 1972-74; bd. dirs. Canterbury Singers, Oshawa, 1952-69; music supr., cons. Durham Bd. Edn., 1960-81; bd. dirs. Oshawa Symphony, 1960-80, 1st v.p., 1984-86, pres., 1986—, percussionist. Recipient award Royal Conservatory Toronto, 1975, other awards. Hon. fellow Royal Can. Coll. Organists; mem. Fedn. Women Tchrs., Can. Fedn. Adjudicators, Registered Music Tchrs. (past pres.). Anglican. Clubs: Univ. Women's (past pres.); Helicanian of Toronto. Compositions include: Songs for Judith, Why do the bells?, Including Me, Missa Brevis in F, The Fate of Gilbert Gim, The Canada Goose (operetta), British Columbia, Rainy Day Song, Superjogger, Roller-skating, November, To Mary and Joseph, Prelude and Fugue in C minor for organ. Home: 589 Pinewood St, Oshawa, ON Canada L1G 2S2

DUARTE-MARSHALL, PATRICIA, real estate and insurance broker; b. Truro, Mass., Feb. 23, 1938; d. Antone Jr. and Marjorie (Beckley) Duarte. Grad. high sch., Provincetown, Mass. Lic. ins. and real estate broker; constrn. supt. Sec. various ins. agys., Amherst, Mass., 1957-60; ins. and real estate agt. Duarte Ins. & Real Estate, Truro, 1966-78, owner, prin. agt., 1966-78; ins. risk mgr. J.L. Marshall & Sons, Inc., Pawtucket, R.I., 1979—; owner, mgr. Patricia-Duarte-Marshall Real Estate, Rockport, Maine, 1979—; restorer antique homes New Eng., Mass., 1979—. Mem., sec. Truro Planning Bd., 1965-72, chmn., 1974-78; mem. exec. com. Cape Cod Planning and Econ. Devel. Com., 1971-76; mem. re-elect Brawn for Senate Com., Camden, Maine, 1988; bd. dirs., chmn. Cape Cod chpt. Am. Heart Assn., 1963-70. Mem. Penobscot Bay Bd. Realtors, Profl. Ins. Agts. New Eng. (bd. dirs. 1974-76). Republican. Roman Catholic. Club: Internat. Women's (Camden). Home and Office: 46 Pascal Ave Rockport ME 04856 also: Skyline Dr Saint Thomas VT 00801

DUBACH-SILVIUS, DOROTHY JEAN, psychotherapist; b. Detroit; d. Merrill King and Beaulah Elizabeth (Lang) Dubach; m. David Roland Wyborny, Oct. 14, 1950 (div. 1980); children: David Grant, Lynn Alison, Scott Christopher; James Edwin Silvius, July 14, 1984. BJ, U. Mo., 1950; MSW, U. Louisville, 1979. Diplomate clin. social work. Writer, clk. Sta. WDAF Radio Sta., Kansas CIty, 1950; advt., copywriter The Fair Store, Chgo., 1950-52, Sears Roebuck & Co., Chgo., 1952-53; freelance copywriter Memphis, 1955-59, Chgo., 1960-66; advt. mgr. Connoiseur Studios, Louisville, 1967-76; therapist East Cen. Kans. Mental Health Ctr., Emporia, 1980-82; psychotherapy Chandler (Ariz.) Counseling Ctr., 1982—. Contbr. articles to profl. jours. Mem. adv. bd/ ARC. Chandler, Ariz., 1987—; bd. dirs. Chandler Golden Age Ctr., 1984-85, Chandler Area United Way, Chandler Area Council. Mem. Am. Assn. Marriage and Family Therapists (clin. 1983), Internat. Assn. for Study of Pain, Nat. Assn. Social Workers (cert. 1982, diplomate 1987), Phoenix Soc. for Clin. Hypnosis, Duplicate Bridge Assn., Delta Gamma. Office: Chandler Counseling Ctr 485 S Dobson Suite 208 Chandler AZ 85224

DUBAY, GWEN ANN, sales and marketing professional; b. Lewiston, Maine, Mar. 25, 1951; d. Ronald N. and Alice M. (Fellows) Johnson; widowed Feb. 1985; children: Ty Brandon, Tara Lee. BA in Sociology, U. Maine, Orono, 1972. Social worker State of Maine, Bangor, 1972; office mgr. S.C. Clayton Co., Marlboro, Mass., 1972-74; sec., treas. Dubay Sales & Mktg., Zionsville, Ind., 1983-85, pres., 1985—; sales adminstr. Woods Wire Products, Inc., Carmel, Ind., 1985—; vis. artist intern Ind. Arts Commn., Indpls., 1983-84. treas. PTO, Zionsville, 1982-83; vol. tchr. for gifted Eagle Elem. Sch., Zionsville, 1983-85. Republican. Methodist. Home: 200 Governors Ln Zionsville IN 46077 Office: Woods Wire Products Inc 510 Third Ave SW Carmel IN 46032

DUBÉ-KASTNER, CHERYL ANN, insurance analyst; b. Bklyn., Aug. 22, 1963; d. Arthur and Marion (Thomas) Dubé; m. George Anthony Kastner, June 28, 1986. AAS in Computer Applications, NYU, 1988. Asst. mgr. Fayva Shoes subs. Moorse Shoe Corp., Ridgewood, N.Y., 1981-82; sec. M. Castellvi Inc., N.Y.C., 1982-83; reinsurance technician Sentry Reinsurance, N.Y.C., 1983; info. specialist Kidder, Peabody & Co., N.Y.C., 1983-85; syndicate acct. Drexel Burnham Lambert, N.Y.C., 1985-86; sr. analyst Cameron & Colby Co., Inc., N.Y.C., 1986—. Asst. editor: (mag.) Hocus Pocus, 1980. Mem. Nat. Assn. Female Execs. Republican. Office: Cameron & Colby Co Inc 7 World Trade Ctr New York NY 10048

DUBIN, ELLEN ZAWEL, corporate communications executive; b. N.Y.C., Oct. 20, 1938; d. Joseph and Leona (Snitkoff) Richman; B.A., City U. N.Y., 1970; postgrad. Yeshiva U., 1972, A. K. Rice Inst. Group Dynamics, 1974; children : Alyssa Zawel, Leigh Zawel, Reva Zawel, Joshua Zawel. Community advocate, 1961-73; consumer ombudsperson Washington supermarket div. Greenbelt Consumer Services, Silver Spring, Md., 1974-76; founding pres. Nat. Consumers Congress, Washington, 1973-76; pres. Zawel Assos., Inc., Harrington Park, N.J., 1976-78; v.p. external affairs The Stop and Shop Cos., Inc., Boston, 1978-83; pres. E.Z. Dubin Assocs., Sharon, Mass., 1983-87; dir. corp. communications Polymer Tech. Co., 1987—; bd. dirs. Nat. Consumer Resource Center, 1976-80. Bd. dirs. Mass. Assn. Mental Health. Mem. Food Mktg. Inst., Public Relations Soc. Am., Am. Nat. Metric Council, Soc. Consumer Affairs Profls., Pi Sigma Alpha.

DUBIN, KAREN HARRIS SULLIVAN, retail chain executive; b. St. Louis, Dec. 12, 1954; d. William Clinton and Elsie (Jackson) Harris; B.F.A., S.W. Mo. State U., 1976; m. Michael Dubin, Jan. 23, 1988; 1 child, Lauren Marie Sullivan. Dept. mgr. Famous-Barr, St. Louis, 1976-77, dept. mgr. budget store, 1977, asst. buyer designer sportswear and accessories, 1977-78, dept. mgr. designer sportswear, dresses, furs, coats, FB Ltd., Frontenac, Mo., 1978-79, dept. mgr., 1979-80, sr. asst. buyer, 1980-81; dist. mgr. Libson's, Inc., St. Louis, 1981, dir. store supervision, 1981-82, asso. gen. mdse. mgr., 1982, gen. mdse. mgr., 1982-83; dist. mgr. J. Riggins Corp., 1983; buyer, mdse. mgr. Strawberry Fields div. S. Mizrahi Sons, 1983—. Mem. Alpha Delta Pi. Roman Catholic. Office: 9753 Preston Trail W Ponte Vedra Beach FL 32082

DUBLIN, ELVIE WILSON, clinical psychologist; b. Athens, Greece, May 18, 1937; d. Anthony I. and Rosa (Protecdicos) Nicolopoulos; m. John Wilson, Oct. 29, 1958 (div. 1967); children: David, Toni; m. James Dublin, Dec. 21, 1973 (div. 1978). BA, Ind. U., 1966, PhD, 1972. Cons. Hospitality House Nursing Home, Bedford, Ind., 1972-73; psychotherapist Choice, Inc., 1973-79, sec.-treas., 1973-79; pres. Studentworld, Inc., 1978-81; pvt. practice psychology, Bloomington, Ind., 1979—; Arabian horse breeder, founder, owner Tall Oaks Arabians, 1980—; bd. dirs. Midwestern Psychotherapy Inst., 1977. Trainee NSF, 1965-67, USPHS, 1967-70. Mem. Am. Psychol. Assn., Ind. Psychol. Assn., Assn. Advancement Psychology, Internat. Arabian Horse Assn., Arabian Horse Registry of Am. (assoc.), Phi Beta Kappa. Clubs: Arabian Jockey, Ind. Arabian Horse (chair racing com. 1986—). Home: 9401 E St Rd 46 Bloomington IN 47401 Office: 4151 E 3d St Bloomington IN 47401

DUBOE, EILEEN, real estate executive; b. Chgo., Dec. 27, 1936; d. William Abel and Bess (Katz) Romanek; m. Burton Vern DuBoe, June 23, 1957; children: Robert Neil, Wendy Lynn. BA with honors, Northwestern U., 1957. Traffic mgr. Henry I. Christal Co., Chgo., 1957-62; ptnr. DuBoe Devel. Co., Skokie, Ill., 1974—. PTA del. Dist. 63 Sch. Bd., Des Plaines, Ill., 1969-73; mem. Morton Grove Beautification Com., 1970-72. Jewish. Club: Little City (treas. 1966-70). Office: DuBoe Devel Co 5301 W Dempster Skokie IL 60077

DUBOIS, DELORES MAE, librarian; b. Winnebago County, Wis., Aug. 24, 1934; d. Carlton John and Mary Josephine (Nehring) Hoffmann; m. Wilbur F. DuBois, Jan. 12, 1961. BA, Carroll Coll., 1957; MLS, U. Washington, Seattle, 1970. Tchr. Horicon (Wis.) Sch. Dist., 1957-59, Adak (Alaska) Naval Air Station, 1959-60, Seattle Sch. Dist., 1960-61, Highline Sch. Dist., Washington, 1961-62; reference librarian King County Library System, Federal Way, Washington, 1970-75, head librarian, 1975—. Named Citizen of Month Federal Way C. of C., 1976. Mem. ALA, Wash. Library Assn. Republican. Lodge: Soroptimist (sec. 1986—). Home: 10011 Occidental Ave S Seattle WA 98168 Office: Fed Way Library 848 S 320th Federal Way WA 98003

DUBREUIL, DANA ROSENTHAL, banker; b. Ottawa, Ont., Can., July 6, 1945; d. Robert Workman and Shirley Natalie (Snaith) Rosenthal; m. Jean-Pierre Dubreuil. BA with honors, Bishop's U., Lennoxville, Que., 1967; cert. fin. counselor, Northwestern U., 1982; postgrad., Harvard U., 1984. Registered rep. Nat. Assn. Securities Dealers. Trust officer First Nat. Bank of Boston, 1975-76, sr. trust officer, 1976-82, v.p., then sr. mgr., 1982—; guest lectr. Radcliffe Coll., Cambridge, Mass., 1980—. Bd. advisors div. pub. charities Office Atty. Gen. Commonwealth of Mass., Boston, 1980-84; dir., chmn. devel. com. Sch. Vols. for Boston, 1985—; bd. advisors Sta. WBZ-TV Fund for Arts, Boston, 1982-84; reviewer United Way of Massachusetts Bay, Boston, 1981—; advisor Oxfam Am., Boston, 1984-85. Recipient citations Boy Scouts of Am., 1980, United Way of Mass., 1986. Mem. Harvard Bus. Sch. Assn. (pres. Class of '84 program for mgmt. devel. 1986—), Assn. Grantmakers of Mass. (bd. dirs. 1976-84). Home: 153 W Newton St Boston MA 02118

DUBROW, JOYCE CAROL, report processor, purchasing consultant; b. Detroit, Oct. 27, 1928; d. Harvey and Ruth (Levien) Melvin; m. Samuel Rupert Kramer, July 12, 1951 (div. 1957); children—Roberta Anne, Jeffrey Mark; m. Leonard Dubrow, Jan. 20, 1959 (div.); 1 son, John Steven. Student UCLA, 1948. Self-employed mcht., Kramer's of Honolulu, 1951-57; bookkeeper J. A. Cappuccilli, Syracuse, N.Y., 1960-66, G. H. Miner Co., Syracuse, 1967-70; tax processor, purchasing agt. Ernst & Whinney, Syracuse, 1970—; self-employed builder J. C. & Assocs., Syracuse, 1983—; cons. internat. duty drawback D&D Assocs., Syracuse and Boston, 1981; actress film South Pacific, 1957. Aide to disabled Home Aides Central N.Y., Inc., Syracuse, 1974—; campaign mgr. Town Dewitt Bd. Nominee, Syracuse, 1980-81. Served as hon. capt. to maj. ROTC, 1943-44. Democrat. Jewish.

DUBUC, MARY ELLEN, educator; b. N.Y.C. July 20, 1950; d. Patrick Joseph and Catherine (McKenna) Reynolds; BA cum laude (scholar), Marymount Manhattan Coll., 1972; MA, Columbia U., 1973; cert. advanced grad. studies R.I. Coll., 1985; m. Leo Dennis Dubuc Jr., Sept. 9, 1978; children: Brian Robert, Kimberly Ann. Spl. edn. tchr. Cardinal Cushing Sch., Hanover, Mass., 1973-76, Ferncliff Manor Sch., Yonkers, N.Y., 1976-77; program coordinator Bronx Devel. Services, 1977-78; dir. edn. R.I. Assn. Retarded, Woonsocket, 1978-84, spl. edn. cons., 1984—. Fed. trainee, 1971, 72. Mem. N.Smithfield PTA, 1986—. Mem. Assn. Severely Handicapped, R.I. Assn. Retarded Citizens, Nat. Assn. Female Execs., R.I. Assn. Adult and Continuing Edn. (v.p. pub. relations 1986-89), Alpha Chi. Democrat. Roman Catholic. Office: No RI Chpt RIARC Inc 80 Fabien St Woonsocket RI 02895

DUCKETT, BARBARA RUTH, hospital administrator; b. Fall River, Mass., Feb. 13, 1945; d. John Gallagher and Doris Selina (Chapman) D.; m. James Joseph Matthews, Nov. 12, 1966 (div. June 1977); m. John David McPeake, Oct. 7, 1985. Diploma in nursing, Children's Hosp. Sch. Nursing, Boston, 1966; BA with honors, U. Fla., 1975; MS, Antioch New Eng. Grad. Sch., 1984. RN. Staff nurse, head nurse supr. Boston Children's Hosp., 1966-71; staff nurse Boulder (Colo.) Meml. Hosp., 1971-72; pediatric nurse clinician Shands Med. Ctr. U. Fla., Gainesville, 1972-75, grad. teaching asst., 1975-76; dir. nursing Beech Hill Hosp., Dublin, N.H., 1978-87; v.p. clin. services Beech Hill Hosp., Dublin, 1986-88, exec. v.p., 1988—; adj. faculty Keene (N.H.) State Coll., 1985—; surveyor Commn. on Accreditation of Rehab. Facilities, Tucson, 1986—. Chairperson planning council Monadnock United Way, Keene, 1985—, bd. dirs., 1986—. Mem. Am. Orgn. Nurse Execs., Am. Nurses Assn., Am. Coll. Addiction Treatment Adminstrs., N.H. Nurse's Assn. (commn. on nursing practice 1987—), Phi Beta Kappa. Democrat. Home: Upper Jaffrey Rd Dublin NH 03444 Office: Beech Hill Hosp New Harrisville Rd Dublin NH 03444

DUCKOR, ANITA SPERRY, manager economic development; b. Pine City, Minn., Dec. 3, 1945; d. Thomas E. and Marjory Cowling (Stuck) Sperry; m. Michael John Duckor, Oct. 11, 1963 (div. Oct. 1980); 1 son, Brent Michael; m. Richard R. Pollick, Sept. 11, 1982. B.S. in Bus. with highest honors and distinction (Outstanding Grad. award), San Diego State U., 1979. Residential mktg. coordinator San Diego Gas & Electric Co., 1979-80, comml./indsl. mktg. coordinator, 1981-82; conservation planning analyst/project leader No. States Power Co., Mpls., 1982-83; mgr. energy services NORENCO Corp., Mpls., 1983-86, dir. energy services, 1986-87, v.p. energy services, 1987, mgr. Econ. Devel. No. States Power Co., 1987—, also bd. dirs. Mem. Nat. Assn. Energy Services Cos. (bd. dirs. 1983-87 , v.p. 1985-86, pres. 1986-87), Am. Mgmt. Assn., Am. Mktg. Assn., Minn. Indsl. Devel. Assn., Minn. High Tech. Council, Minn. Women's Network (bd. dirs. 1985-87, exec. mem.), NOW, Phi Kappa Phi, Beta Gamma Sigma, Sigma Iota Epsilon. Office: No State Power Co 414 Nicollet Mall Minneapolis MN 55401

DUCKWORTH, CAROL KAY, university administrator, consultant; b. Wichita, Kans., Apr. 21, 1941; d. Elmer Floyd and Cynthia Ruth (Dodson) D. BA, Okla. Baptist U., 1965; MSE, Ark. State U., 1975; postgrad., U. Ark. Cert. secondary adminstr., counselor, vocat. prof., human relations trainer/coordinator. Tchr. bus. Midway High Sch., Denton, Kans., 1965-69; tchr., counselor, dir. cooperative edn. Green Forest (Ark.) High Sch., 1969-72; prof. bus. adminstrn., computer sci. Weatherford (Tex.) Coll., 1972-75; dir. cooperative edn. North Ark. Community Coll., Harrison, Ark., 1975-80; prof. computer sci. bus. adminstrn. North Ark. Community Coll., Harrison, 1976-87; asst. registrar Kans. State U., Manhattan, Kans., 1980-84; counselor Rogers (Ark.) High Sch., 1984-87; registrar U. Ozarks, Clarksville, Ark., 1987—; cons. grant reader U.S. Office Edn., Washington, 1980-83, cons. grant writer numerous nationwide univs., 1976—. Author: Individualized Instruction in the Business Education Classroom, Computerized Instruction in Advanced Development. Named Outstanding Bus. Student Okla. Bapt. U., 1965. Mem. Am. Assn. Bus. Women (pres. 1979, 86-87), Phi Delta Kappa (pres. 1980-81 v.p. 1986), Phi Beta Kappa (v.p. 1975). Republican. Baptist. Lodge: Order of Eastern Star (conductress 1987—). Home: 350 North Giles PO Box 434 Gentry AR 72734

DUCKWORTH, KIM PELTO, marketing executive; b. Fresno, Calif., Dec. 15, 1956; d. William Armos and Marjorie Mae (Haninger) Pelto; m. David Paul Duckworth, Aug. 16, 1986. BA in Communications, Stanford U., 1978. Asst. dir. membership club Westin Internat. Hotel, San Francisco, 1978; mktg. trainee IBM, Palo Alto, Calif., 1978-79, mktg. rep., 1979-82; account mktg. rep. IBM, San Francisco, 1982-83; adv. staff IBM, White Plains, N.Y., 1983-85; mgr. mktg. IBM, Sunnyvale, Calif. 1985—. Active Young Reps. Los Gatos; precinct leader United Way, Palo Alto, 1985, vol. canvasser White Plains, 1984; vol. Am. Heart Assn., March of Dimes, Los Gatos, Calif., 1988—. Mem. Stanford Alumni Assn., Female Exec. Assn. Republican. Episcopalian. Clubs: Stanford (Los Gatos), Los Gatos Athletic. Office: IBM 455 W Maude Ave Sunnyvale CA 94086

DUCO, JOSEPHINE DIANE, title insurance company financial executive; b. Detroit, Apr. 28, 1947; d. Henry Leopold and Antoinette (Bono) D. B.A. in Sociology, U. Mich., 1969; M.B.A. with distinction in Acctg., L.I. U., 1981. Head teller Am. Savs. Bank, N.Y.C., 1975-77, customer service rep., 1977-78, acct., 1978-79; staff acct. Radio City Music Hall, N.Y.C., 1980; chief acct. N.E. region Am. Title Ins. Co., N.Y.C., 1980-81, asst. regional controller, 1981-83, regional controller, 1983—, v.p., 1984—, asst. sec., 1986—. Mem. Nat. Assn. Accts. (mem. of yr. 1986-87), Nat. Assn. Female Execs., AAUW, LWV. Office: Am Title Ins Co 675 3d Ave New York NY 10017

DUCOTE, MARJORIE ELLEN, chemist, researcher; b. Chattanooga, Oct. 28, 1938; d. David S. and Beatrice Allene (Harrell) Tate; m. Calvin L. Cucksee, Jan. 1, 1962 (div.); 1 child, Brian E.; m. Jere D. Ducote Sr. (dec. March 1986); children: Melissa L., Jesse H. AB, U. Chattanooga, 1959; student, U. Tenn., 1959-60, Southeastern Inst. Tech., 1984-86. Research and devl. chemist Eastman Chem. Products, Kingsport, Tenn., 1960-62; chemist Newport News (Va.) SS&DD Co., 1962-64; research chemist U.S. Army MICOM, Huntsville, Ala., 1964—; facilitator CPO-EEO Program, Ala.; investigator U.S. Army Grievance Investigation, Ala. Instr. karate YMCA, 1978-80, instr. self def. U. Ala., Huntsville, 1979. Recipient Mary Jane Hearn award Toastmistress, 1984, two U.S. Army MICOM Sci. and Engring. awards, 1979, 84. Mem. Federally Employed Women (pres. 1986-87), Am. Def. Preparedness Assn., VFW,Am. Legion Aux. Club: Toastmistress (pres. 1984). Lodge: Elks. Home: 2037 Bankhead Pkwy Huntsville AL 35801 Office: US Army MICOM AMSMI-RD-PR-T Gladstone Arsenal AL 35898-5249

DUCY, PATRICIA CORNELIA, financial executive; b. Bklyn., July 17, 1945; d. Clement Ambrose and Ellen Catherine (O'Brien) D. Student, Ottumwa Heights Jr. Coll., 1963-64, George Washington U., 1967-69, No. Va. Community Coll., 1980-83, USDA Grad. Sch., Washington, 1983-84. Mgr. staffing audit dept. Arthur Andersen & Co., Washington, 1973-75; comptroller The Co. Inkwell, Arlington, Va., 1976-78; registrar Antioch Sch. Law, Washington, 1978-79; dir. fin. and adminstrn. SRA Corp., Arlington, Va., 1979-81; mem. staff com. govt.-univ. relations Nat. Acad. Scis., Washington, 1981-83; dir. fin. and adminstrn. Advanced Systems Devel. Inc., Arlington, Va., 1983—; cons. in field. Vol. J.F. Kennedy Campaign, Bethesda, Md., 1960, Georgetown U. Hosp., Washington, 1960-63; sec. D.C. chpt. Am. Jr. Red Cross, 1962; prodn. coordinator Am. Light Opera Co., Washington, 1964-67; del. Citizen Ambassador Program to China, 1988. Recipient 500-hour award Georgetown U. Hosp., 1961. Mem. Am. Mgmt. Assn., Nat. Bus. and Profl. Women's Orgn., Am. Soc. Personnel Adminstrs., Nat. Assn. Female Execs., Nat. Orgn. Victim Assistance, Ams. for Legal Reform. Democrat. Roman Catholic. Office: Advanced Systems Devel Inc 1701 N Fort Myer Dr Suite 1101 Arlington VA 22209

DUDA, CATHY, automotive company executive; b. Oshawa, Can., Dec. 10, 1959; d. Paul and Anna D. B in Indsl. Adminstrn., Gen. Motors Inst., Flint, Mich., 1983; MBA, U. Windsor, Ont., 1984. Paint forward planning com. Gen. Motors of Can., Oshawa, 1984-85, prodn. paint supr., 1985-86, gen. supr. quality, 1986-87, area mgr. trim and hardware, 1987—; co-op.

student recruiter Gen. Motors of Can., 1983, new employee interviewer, 1984-86, affirmative action rep., United Auto Worker's local com., 1985-86. Treas. Jr. Achievement, Oshawa, 1982, advisor, 1981. Mem. Mgmt. Honor Soc. (v.p. 1983). Home: 504 Stewart St, Whitby CAN LIN3V4 Office: Gen Motors of Can, 215 William St E, Oshawa CAN LIG IK7

DUDEK, NANCY KAY, lawyer, real estate consultant; b. Los Angeles, Oct. 5, 1955; d. Joseph and Amy Kay (Kay) D. JD, U. West Los Angeles, 1982. Bar: Calif. 1982. Escrow officer Escrow Systems, Inc., Los Angeles, 1973-82; sole practice Los Angeles, 1982-84; counsel Eiger Group, Beverly Hills, Calif., 1984-86; lawyer, cons. real estate Burlington Properties, Inc., Los Angeles, 1986—; bd. dirs. Moskowitz Fin. Services, Los Angeles; pres., bd. dirs. Burlington Properties Inc., Los Angeles, 1986—. Poet various publs., 1970-75. Docent S.W. Mus. Mem. ABA (real property sect., bus. law sect., taxation sect.), MENSA.

DUDICS, SUSAN ELAINE, interior designer; b. Perth Amboy, N.J., Oct. 22, 1950; d. Theodore W. and Joyce M. (Ryals) D. BS in Sociology, W.Va. U., 1972; postgrad. Rutgers U., 1975-78, U. Calif., Irvine, 1979-81, Can. Coll., 1981—. Programmer Prudential Life, Newark, 1972-73; sr. systems analyst Johnson & Johnson, New Brunswick, N.J., 1973-78, Sperry Univac, Irvine, Calif., 1978-80; sr. systems analyst, project leader Robert A. McNeil, San Mateo, Calif., 1981-83; design dir. TransDesigns, Woodstock, Ga., 1982—. Contbr. articles to profl. jours. High sch. mentor Directions, San Francisco, 1985-86. Mem. Women Entreprenuers (membership com., treas. 1983-88), Cen. N.J. Alumni Assn. (assoc. sec., founder, pres.), Delta Gamma. Recipient awards TransDesigns, Woodstock, Ga., 1984, 85, 86, 87. Avocations: skiing, sewing, scuba diving, ballet, hand crafts. Office: Celestial Designs/TransDesigns 19 Molimo Dr San Francisco CA 94127

DUDINSKY, VIRGINIA KAY, newspaper editor; b. Warren, Ohio, Nov. 3, 1949; d. Calvin Coolidge and Doris Marie (Owen) Patchin; children—Thomas Allen, Stephanie Lynn. Student Kent State U., 1976-77; Cosmotologist, Isabelle Sch. Beauty, 1969. Office mgr. sales White Real Estate, Munson, Ohio, 1977-78; editor's asst. The Valley News, Orwell, Ohio, 1979-81, editor, 1981—; real estate assoc. Steve J. Jozsa Realty, Orwell, 1979—; news editor The Gazette, Jefferson, Ohio, 1986—; editor The Gazette and Sentinel, 1987—. Mem. Ohio Newspaper Assn. Democrat. Roman Catholic. Home: 13 Chaffee Dr Orwell OH 44076 Office: The Gazette 46 W Jefferson St Jefferson OH 44047

DUDLEY, ELIZABETH HYMER, security manager; b. Hibbing, Minn., Mar. 12, 1937; d. Howard Golden and Esther Juliette (Wanner) Hymer; m. Richard Walter Dudley, 1962. BA Brown U., 1959; postgrad. U. Calif., Berkeley. With AT&T Bell Labs., Murray Hill, N.J., 1959—, systems programmer, personnel info., 1965-67, systems analyst, personnel info., 1967-71, sr. systems analyst, mgmt. info. and adminstrv. systems, 1971-77, applications systems coordinator mgmt. info. and adminstrv. systems, 1977-78, group supr. affirmative action compliance and reports, 1978-81, group supr. service ops. system support group, 1982-84, mgr. security, 1984-85, mgr. govt. security, 1986—. Mem. Nat. Security Indsl. Assn., Women's Rights Assn. (treas. 1977, v.p. 1978), Am. Soc. Indsl. Security, Nat. Classification Mgmt. Soc., Brown Network. Club: Pembroke Coll. of N.J. (publicity chmn. 1965-69, v.p. 1969-70). Office: AT&T Bell Labs Whippany Rd Whippany NJ 07981

DUDLEY, EVELYN KAY, state legislator; b. Brazil, Ind., June 23, 1935; d. Alvin Ross and Daisy (Snell) Mercer; m. Thomas F. Dudley; children: Stephen Webb, Andria Pasch Whaley, Brittanie Kay Harner. Grad., Indpls. Meth. Hosp. Sch. Nursing. Mem. Okla. State Senate, 1987—. Past pres. Prairie Queen PTA, Oklahoma County Dental Aux. Address: 6501 S Barnes Oklahoma City OK 73159 *

DUDLEY, MARY CATHERINE, advertising executive; b. Wausau, Wis., Jan. 27, 1953; d. Richard David and Eileen (Deneen) Dudley; B.A., Tex. Christian U., 1975; m. William David Stotesbery, June 21, 1975. Reporter, Austin (Tex.) Am.-Statesman, 1975-78; polit. columnist Tex. Woman Mag., Austin, 1978-80; media cons., mktg. mgr. Austin Conv. Bur., Austin C. of C., 1980-82; sr. promotion specialist Bausch & Lomb, Austin, 1982-84, mktg. promotion mgr. Houston Instrument div., 1984-86; v.p. Fellers and Gaddis, Austin, 1986—; cons. in field. Bd. dirs. Center for Battered Women, Austin, 1981-83; vol. coordinator Austin Symphony Sq., 1980-81, mem., 1980—; mem. Austin Commn. on Status of Women, 1978-79. Recipient Med. Reporting award Tex. Med. Assn., 1977. Mem. Women in Communications (chpt. bd. dirs. 1979-80), Tex. Soc. Assn. Execs., Austin Sister City Assn. Roman Catholic. Office: Tellers and Gaddis 2211 South IH35 Austin TX 78753

DUDLEY, SHERRY ATHLENE, personnel director; b. Los Angeles, Mar. 11, 1939; d. Sammy Mahan and Elma Lois (Sutton) Becker; m. Charles T. Dudley, Nov. 4, 1961; children: Kathleen Ann Thompson, Michael Charles. Asst. v.p. Century Bank, Phoenix, 1976-81, v.p. br. adminstrn., 1981-84, v.p. dir. personnel, 1984—. Vol. docent Heritage Sq. Guide, Phoenix, 1985—; active Tempe (Ariz.) Sister Cities. Mem. Ariz. Bankers Assn. (personnel com. 1984—), Phoenix Personnel Mgmt. Assn., Am. Soc. Personnel Administrs., Western Pension Conf. Presbyterian. Home: 434 E Carter Dr Tempe AZ 85282 Office: Century Bank 3225 N Central Ave Phoenix AZ 85012

DUER, ELLEN ANN DAGON (MRS. T. MARSHALL DUER, JR.), physician; b. Balt., Feb. 3, 1936; d. Emmett Paul and Annie (Sollers) Dagon; A.B., George Washington U., 1959; M.D., U. Md., 1964; postgrad. Johns Hopkins U., 1965-68; m. Lyle Jordan Millan IV, Dec. 21, 1963; children—Lyle Jordan V, Elizabeth Lyle, Ann Sheridan Worthington.; m. T. Marshall Duer, Jr., Aug. 23, 1985. Intern, Union Meml. Hosp., Balt., 1964-65; resident anesthesiology Johns Hopkins Hosp., Balt., 1965-68, fellow in surgery, 1965-68; practice medicine specializing in anesthesiology, Balt., 1968—; attending staff Union Meml. Hosp., Church Home and Hosp., Franklin Sq. Hosp., Children's Hosp., James Lawrence Kernan Hosp., Balt., 1982—; co-chief anesthesiology James Kernan Hosp., 1983—, med. dir. outpatient surgery dept., 1987—; faculty Church Home and Hosp., Balt., 1969—, affiliate cons. emergency room, 1969—, mem. med. audit and utilizations com., 1970-72, mem. emergency and ambulatory care com., 1973-74, chief emergency dept., 1973-74; cons. anesthesiologist Md. State Penitentiary, 1971; fellow in critical care medicine Md. Inst. Emergency Medicine, 1975-76; mem. infection control com. U. Md. Hosp., 1975—; instr. anesthesiology U. Md. Sch. Medicine, 1975—; staff anesthesiologist Mercy Hosp., 1978—, audit com., 1979-80, 82; med. dir. outpatient surgery Kernan Hosp., 1987—. Mem. AMA, Am. Coll. Emergency Physicians, Met. Emergency Dept. Heads, Am., Md. socs. anaesthesiologists, Balt. City Med. and Chiurgical Soc., Internat. Congress Anaesthesiologists, Internat. Anaesthesia Research Soc., Am., Md. horse shows assns. Clubs: L'Hirondelle; Annapolis Yacht; Chesapeake Bay Yacht Racing Assn. Episcopalian. Address: 1011 Wagner Rd Ruxton MD 21204

DUERR, DIANNE MARIE, physical education educator, professional sports medicine consultant; b. Buffalo, July 14, 1945; d. Robert John and Aileen Louise (Scherer) D. BS in health and phys. edn., SUNY, Brockport, 1967; cert., SUNY, Oswego, 1982; postgrad., Canisius Coll., 1970-71. Cert. tchr., N.Y. Tchr. North Syracuse (N.Y.) Sch. Dist., 1967—; cons. sport med. Dept. Orthopedic Surgery SUNY Health Sci. Ctr., Syracuse, 1982—; coordinator Scholastic Sports Injury Reporting System project, SUNY, 1985—; creator sports medicine and human performance ctr., SUNY, 1988. Author: SSIRS Pilot Study Report, 1987, SSIRS Fall Study Report, 1988; creator SUNY Sports Med. Human Human Performance Ctr., 1988, Scholastic Sports Injury Reporting System, 1985. Co-chmn. Sports Medicine USA, Amateur Athletic Union, Nat. Jr. Olympic Games, Syracuse, 1987, vol. Sports Medicine Empire State Games, Syracuse, 1987, active Girl Scouts U.S.; YMCA. Mem. Am. Coll. Sports Medicine, AAHPERSD, Am. Fedn. Tchrs., N.Y. United Tchrs., North Syracuse Tchrs. Assn. Home: 4825 Norstar Blvd Apt 124 Liverpool NY 13088 Office: SUNY Dept Orthopedic Surgery 550 Harrison Ctr Syracuse NY 13202

DUERR-LEVINE, DIANE, marketing executive; b. Tulsa, Mar. 8, 1938; d. Arthur and Reta (Reeves) Duerr; B.A. in Math., U. Mich., 1960; M.B.A., Columbia U., 1962; m. Matthew A. Levine, June 9, 1963; children: Arielle, Sarsh. Systems engr. Xerox Corp., N.Y.C., 1963-64; products mgr. Lever Bros. Corp., N.Y.C., 1964-68; sr. br. mgr. Am. Home Products Corp., N.Y.C., 1968-71; account supr. Honig-Cooper Herrington (now Foote Cone/ Honig), San Francisco, 1971-72; v.p. advt. and sales promotion Continental Airlines, Los Angeles, 1973-76; dir. mktg. and communications San Francisco Bay Area Transit Dist., 1976-78; pres., founder Inst. Health Mgmt., San Francisco, 1978-85; prof. San Francisco State U., 1982-85. Bd. dirs. Greybridge, Palo Alto, Calif., Pacific Select Corp., San Francisco; chmn. membership com. Bus. Adv. Bd., San Francisco State U., chmn. membership com.; cons. Solar Energy Research Inst., No. Calif. Coalition for ERA. Mem. Columbia U. Grad. Sch. Bus. Alumni Assn., Kappa Kappa Gamma, Beta Gamma Sigma. Recipient numerous mktg. and advt. awards. Democrat. Mem. Soc. of Friends. Author: Executive Edge, 1981; Vital Living after Fifty, 1982.

DUFF, RUTH ELEANOR, retired educator; b. Alexander County, Ill., Dec. 19, 1934; d. Richard Ernest and Ruth Ethel (Dickerson) D.; B.S. in Edn., S.E. Mo. State Coll., 1961; M.S. in Edn., So. Ill. U., 1968, Ph.D. (Coll. Edn. dissertation fellow 1972), 1973. Primary and elem. sch. tchr., Ill., 1954-65; dir. demonstration presch. program Alexander County Sch. Dist. I, 1965-68; instr., Head Start regional tng. officer So. Ill. U., 1968-70, instr., dir. Head Start supplementary tng., 1970-72; asso. prof. early childhood edn. U. S.C., Columbia, 1973-74, coordinator early childhood edn., 1974-79, asst. dean acad. affairs, 1979-80, asst. dean students and programs Coll. Edn., 1980-82, asst. dean tchr. edn., 1982-83, assoc. dean, 1983-86, prof., 1981-82; sec. Midlands Human Resources Devel. Commn., 1980-86; mem. Gov. S.C. Interagy. Coordinating Council Early Childhood Devel. and Edn., 1980-86, Gov. S.C. Adv. Com. Early Childhood Devel. and Edn., 1980-86. Fellow, tchr. tng. for disadvantaged, summer 1970. Mem. Assn. Childhood Edn. Internat., U.S. Nat. Com. Early Childhood Edn., Organization Mondiale pour l'Education Prescolaire, Nat. Assn. Edn. Young Children, So. Assn. Children Under Six, S.C. Assn. Children Under Six, Soc. Research Child Devel., Phi Delta Kappa. Co-author: The Parent-Teacher Bond: Relating, Responding, Rewarding, 1978; Early Childhood Education, 1980; others. Contbr. articles to profl. jours., chpts. to books. Home: 2612 Monroe St Columbia SC 29205 Office: USC Coll Edn Columbia SC 29208

DUFF, SUSAN ELAINE, programmer analyst; b. Mobile, Ala., Feb. 8, 1963; d. Brian Eugene and Mary John (Varner) D. BS in Computer Sci., U. South Ala., 1984, MBA, 1988. Programmer analyst Internat. Paper Co., Mobile, 1984—; cons. Jr. Achievement, Mobile, 1986-87. Active United Way, Mobile, 1984-85; asst. advisor computer sci. post Explorers, Mobile, 1984; tchr. Sunday Sch., Cottage Hill Bapt. Ch., Mobile, 1985-86. Home: 6075-6 Grelot Rd Mobile AL 36609 Office: Internat Paper Co PO Box 160707 Mobile AL 36616

DUFFEE, BEVERLY ANN, educator; b. Sharon, Pa., Apr. 18, 1946; d. Kenneth Ira and Edith Belle (Farringer) Duffee; B.A., Roberts Wesleyan Coll., 1968; M.A., Calif. State U., 1973. Personnel adminstr./programmer Newport Electronics, Santa Ana, Calif., 1973-77; personnel counselor Dennis & Dennis Personnel Services, Santa Ana, 1978; sales sec. Gould Inc., Auto. Battery Div., Irvine, Calif., 1979-81; chmn. dept. English, tchr. music, art, drama Leffingwell Christian Jr./Sr. High Sch., Norwalk, Calif., 1981—; instr. English, Biola U., La Mirada, Calif., 1984-85. Mem. World Gospel Mission, Alpha Kappa Sigma. Republican. Methodist. Home: 8811 Park St Space 98 Bellflower CA 90706 Office: 11032 Leffingwell Rd Norwalk CA 90650

DUFFIE, ESSIE COLEMAN, fisheries biologist; b. Tallahassee, May 26, 1951; d. Palmore and Ida Bell Coleman; m. Howard Duffie, Sept. 23, 1983; 1 child, Tanisha T. Coleman. BS, Fla. A&M U., 1974; postgrad., U. Miami, 1975-76. Biol. technician NOAA Nat. Marine Fisheries Service, Miami (Fla.) Lab., 1974-77, fisheries biologist, 1978—, mgr. EEO Black program, 1979—. Pres. Fed. Exec. Bd. Black Council, Miami, 1980-81; mem. Nat. Black Child Devel. Inst. Mem. NAACP, Am. Inst. Fishery Research Biologists (assoc.), Nat. Assn. Female Execs., Family Christian Assn. Am. (bd. dirs. 1980—, chairperson program com. 1987—), Blacks in Govt. (pres. 1981-82), Am. Fedn. Govt. Employees. Democrat. Baptist. Club: Y's Women (Miami) (pres. 1984-85). Home: 1481-102 NE 150th St Miami FL 33161 Office: NOAA Nat Marine Fisheries Service 75 Virginia Beach Dr Miami FL 33149

DUFFY, BARBARA ANNE, non-profit corporation executive; b. Providence, May 14, 1958; d. Thomas Joseph and Barbara Anne (Molloy) D. BA, U. R.I., 1980; MEd, R.I. Coll., 1982. Cert. tchr., kindergarten - 6th grades. Intern Tchr. Corps, Pawtucket, R.I., 1980-82; job specialist Jobs Bay State Graduates, Boston, 1982-84; employee resource advisor Mass. Youth Teen Unemployment Reduction Network, Brockton, 1984-85; pres. Universal Leasing, Pawtucket, 1985—; exec. dir. Mass. Youth Teen Unemployment Reduction Network (My Turn, Inc.), Brockton, Mass., 1985—. Mem. Brockton Sch. Dept., 1986. Mem. Metro South C. of C., (personnel council 1986), Kappa Delta Pi. Democrat. Roman Catholic. Home: 82 Hamlet St Pawtucket RI 02861 Office: Mass Youth Teen Unemployed Red Network Inc 43 Crescent St Brockton MA 02401

DUFFY, BRENDA FREEBURG, business researcher; b. Jamestown, N.Y., May 10, 1949; d. Milton Walter and Elsie June (Howell) F.; m. Richard Allen Duffy, Nov. 27, 1971; children: Jennifer, Matthew. BA, SUNY, 1971. Research assst. Machinery and Allied Products Inst., Washington, 1972—. Sec. Nat. Neurofibromatosis Found. (Met. Washington chpt.), 1984—, fed. liaison bd. dirs., 1987—; leader Girl Scout troop, Alexandria, Va., 1984—. Mem. Spl. Libraries Assn. Roman Catholic. Home: 7110 Vantage Dr Alexandria VA 22306 Office: Machinery & Allied Products Inst 1200 18th St NW Washington DC 20036

DUFFY, ESTHER RODGERS (MRS. ROGER FRANCIS DUFFY), librarian; b. Pitts., Aug. 14, 1911; d. Arthur Gregory and Charlotte Catherine (Nagle) Rodgers; B. Music and B.S. in Music Edn., Seton Hill Coll., 1932; postgrad. U. Pitts., 1933, Carnegie Inst., 1935, Simmons Coll., 1941-42; m. Roger Francis Duffy, Nov. 14, 1945; children—Katherine, Mary Anne, Roger. Instr. music coll. Misericordia, Dallas, Pa., 1932-37; music librarian Cornell U., Ithaca, N.Y., 1937-41; asst. music librarian Columbia U., N.Y.C., 1942-43; research librarian OSS, State Dept., 1943-44, Balkans outpost rep. Office War Info., 1944-46, Balkans regional rep. USIS, 1946; asst. to pres. Juilliard Sch. Music, N.Y.C., 1947-49; asst. to mng. dir. U.S. Internat. Book Assn., N.Y.C., 1945-47; librarian fine arts Greenwich (Conn.) Library, 1961-81. Mem. adv. com. Greenwich Sr. Center. Mem. Greenwich Arts Council, AAUW, Kappa Gamma Pi. Home: 2 Peters Rd Riverside CT 06878

DUFFY, EVELYN GROENKE, clinical nurse specialist, consultant; b. London, Mar. 30, 1953; came to U.S., 1953; d. John Herman and Marcella Irene (Engelman) Groenke; m. Mark Elton Duffy, Aug. 7, 1976; 1 child, Patrick Sean. B.S., Baylor U., 1975; M.S., U. Wis.-Madison, 1981. R.N., Ohio, Wis., Tex.; cert. geriatric nurse practitioner. Staff nurse Ohio State U. Hosp., Columbus, 1975-76; team leader Vis. Nurse Service, Madison, Wis., 1976-79; nurse practitioner William S. Middleton Meml. VA Hosp., Madison, 1981-84; clin. nurse specialist VA Med. Ctr., Cleve., 1985—; clin. preceptor U. Wis.-Madison, 1981-84. Bd. dirs. Calvary Luth. Chapel, Madison, 1977-78, sec. Calvary Luth. Women, 1980-81. Recipient Performance award VA, 1982. HEW traineeship, 1979-81. Mem. Am. Nurses Assn., Gerontol. Soc. Am., Madison Dist. Nurses Assn. (chmn. pub. relations com., 1983-84), Wis. Nurses Assn. (bd. dirs. nurse practitioner council 1981-83), Vis. Nurse Service Staff Assn. (sec. 1978-79). Sigma Theta Tau. Avocations: stained glass; running; sailing; cross country skiing; gourmet cooking.

DUFRESNE, JERILYN CLARE, social services executive; b. Quincy, Ill., Aug. 2, 1947; d. Edward Arthur and Elaine Catherine (Kuhlman) Bozarth; m. Phillip Burns, Sept. 2, 1967 (div. Mar. 1978); m. John R. Dufresne, Aug. 23, 1980 (div. June 1983); children: Robert, Jill. Student, Quincy Coll., 1965-67; BS summa cum laude, Troy State U., 1979; M of Social Work, Washington U., St. Louis, 1984. Rehab. counselor Goodwill Industries of Chattahoochie Valley, Inc., Columbus, Ga., 1977-79; caseworker Chaddock, Quincy, Ill., 1979-81; team coordinator Chaddock, Quincy, 1981-82, asst. to v.p., 1982-83, dir. tng., 1984-85, unit dir., 1986-86, dir. research program devel., 1986—. Co-chair Pax Christi, Quincy, 1986—; mem. Diocesan Justice and Peace Commn., Springfield, Ill., 1985—, Govt. Affairs Commn. Child Care Assn., Springfield, 1987; chmn. Social Action Commn., Quincy, 1987—; pres. St. Francis Parish Council, Quincy, 1988—. Mem. Acad. of Cert. Social Workers, Nat. Assn. of Social Workers, Child Care Assn. of Ill., Ill. Council on Tng. (treas. 1986—). Democrat. Roman Catholic. Home: 709 Oakland Ave Quincy IL 62301 Office: Chaddock 205 S 24th St Quincy IL 62301

DUFRESNE, MAUREEN MCLAUGHLIN, corporate supervisor; b. Johnstown, Pa., May 20, 1957; d. Donald Francis and Marie Adeline (Potter) McLaughlin; m. Joseph Stevens Dufresne, Apr. 23, 1983. BS in Mgmt., St. Francis Coll., Loretto, Pa., 1979. Adminstrv. paralegal sec. CIA, McClean, Va., 1980-83; security adminstr. Ge. Electric Corp., King of Prussia, Pa., 1983-84; security edn. specialist Ge. Electric Corp., King of Prussia, 1984-85, mgr. security awareness, 1986-87; supr. security and adminstrv. support Ge. Electric Corp., Reston, Va., 1987—. Mem. The Exec. Female, Phi Beta Kappa. Republican. Roman Catholic. Home: 801 Suffield Dr Gaithersburg MD 20878 Office: Gen Electric 1840 Michael Faraday Dr Reston VA 22090

DUGAN, AMY KELCHNER, government press secretary; b. Harrisburg, Pa., Dec. 13, 1957; d. Rodney Clair and Joan Elaine (Laubach) Kelchner; m. J. Scott Dugan. BA in Communications, Mansfield State Coll., 1979. Writer gov.'s commn. on Three Mile Island Commonwealth of Pa., Harrisburg, 1979-80, info. specialist dept. environ. resources, 1980-81, spl. project coordinator dept. environ. resources, 1981-82, mktg. specialist Pa. Hist. and Mus. Commn., 1982-84; dep. press sec. dept. corrections Commonwealth of Pa., Camp Hill, 1984-87; press sec. Pa. Ins. Dept., Harrisburg, 1987—; cons. speaker's tng. AT&T, Harrisburg, 1984-86. Dept. coordinator State Employees United Way Campaign, Harrisburg, 1985-86. Mem. Nat. Assn. Female Execs., Mansfield U. Alumni Assn. (trustee, bd. dirs., 1981-87, sec.-treas. Harrisburg chpt., 1983—), Delta Zeta (pres. 1983-85, v.p. 1981-85, editor 1985-87). Methodist. Office: Pa Ins Dept 1326 Strawberry Sq Harrisburg PA 17120

DUGAN, KIMIKO HATTA (MRS. WAYNE ALEXANDER DUGAN), anatomist, educator; b. Kyoto City, Japan, Oct. 21, 1924; came to U.S., 1948, naturalized, 1956; d. Shinzo and Sano (Hatta) Hatta; student U. Md., 1957-58; B.A., Okla. Coll. Women, 1961; M.S., U. Okla., 1965, Ph.D., 1970; m. Wayne Alexander Dugan, Aug. 18, 1947 (dec. Aug. 1971). Grad. fellow dept. anatomy Sch. Medicine, U. Okla., Oklahoma City, 1964-69, instr. dept. anat. sci. Coll. Medicine, 1969-71, asst. prof., 1971-78, asso. prof., 1978—. Recipient Undergrad. Chemistry Achievement award Okla. Coll. Women, 1960; elected to U. Sci. and Arts Okla. (formerly Okla. Coll. Women) Alumni Hall of Fame, 1977. Mem. Am. Assn. Anatomists, AAAS, AAUW, Okla. Acad. Sci., Am. Chem. Soc., Am. Soc. Zoologists, Electron Microscopy Soc. Am., N.Y. Acad. Sci., Internat. Soc. Developmental Comparatvie Immunology, Sigma Xi. Episcopalian. Home: 1139 NW 63d St Oklahoma City OK 73116 Office: U Okla Health Scis Ctr Coll Medicine Dept Anat Scis PO Box 26901 Oklahoma City OK 73190

DUGGAN, CAROL COOK, researcher; b. Conway, S.C., May 25, 1946; d. Pierce Embree and Lillian Watkins (Eller) Cook; m. Kevin Duggan, Dec. 29, 1973. B.A., Columbia Coll., 1968; M.S., U. Ky., 1970. Reference asst. Richland County Pub. Library, Columbia, S.C., 1968-69, asst. to dir., 1970, chief adult services, 1971-82; dir. Maris Research, Columbia, 1982—; lectr. mem. Friends of Richland County Pub. Library, 1977—, Greater Columbia (S.C.) Literacy Council, 1973—; parish relations com. Washington St. United Meth. Ch., Columbia, 1986—. Recipient Sternheimer award, 1968. Mem. ALA (councilor 1980-82, chmn. state membership com. 1979-83), S.C. Library Assn. (sec. 1976, exec. bd. 1976, 78-82), S.C. Pub. Library Assn. (pres. 1980-81), Beta Phi Mu. Methodist (exec. bd. United Methodist Women 1983—, worship com. 1985-86, mem. history and archives com. 1988—). Club: PEO (pres. 1983-85 , chmn. amendments and recommendations com. 1983-85, historian 1986-87, treas. State conv., 1987-88), Columbia Coll. Afternoon of S.C. Home: 2101 Woodmere Dr Columbia SC 29204

DUGGAN, CATHERINE MARIE, investment services executive; b. St. Louis, June 15, 1949; d. William Joseph and Fern Beatrice (Dodson) D.; 1 child, Christina Jennifer. Lic. real estate assoc., Calif.; registered mortgage underwriter. Salesperson, Schauer Realty, Los Angeles, 1975-76; sales mgr. Property Store, Los Angeles, 1976-77; cons. Expert Realtor, Los Angeles, 1977-79; ptnr. Duggan, Ruggieri & Co., Los Angeles, 1979-82; v.p. Am Cal Co., Los Angeles, 1982—. Mem. Apt. Owners Assn., Nat. Assn. Female Execs., Calif. Mortgage Bankers Assn., Young Mortgage Bankers, Nat. Assn. Rev. Appraisers and Mortgage Underwriters. Roman Catholic. Avocation: Tang Soo Do karate. Office: Am Cal Co 4730 Woodman St Suite 220 Sherman Oaks CA 91423

DUGGINS, MARIAN BARBER, nurse administrator; b. Eden, N.C., Jan. 13, 1925; d. Odell Hillard and Autney (Hughes) Barber; m. William Paul Duggins, June 24, 1949; children: Eva Ruth Haywood, William Odell. Student, Bob Jones U., 1942-43; RN, N.C. Bapt. Hosp., 1946; cert. in pub. health, U. N.C., 1947. Staff nurse Forsyth County Health Dept., Winston-Salem, N.C., 1947-51, nurse adminstr., 1957-59; clinic coordinator Forsyth County Mental Health Dept., Winston-Salem, 1959-74; treatment coordinator Mandala Psychiat. Hosp., Winston-Salem, 1974-78; nurse supr. New Hanover County Health Dept., Wilmington, N.C., 1978-80; nurse adminstr. New Hanover County Health Dept., Wilmington, 1980—; cons. Forsyth County Half-Way House, Winston-Salem, 1960-74, Goodwill Industries, Winston-Salem, 1961-74. Co-author Nurses Teach Mothers, 1949. Pres. Prince Ibraham PTA, Winston-Salem, 1962, Mineral Springs PTA, 1968; chair Operation Santa Claus, John U. Hosp., Butner, N.C., 1965; mem. awards selection com. YWCA, Wilmington, 1986. Recipient Margaret B. Dolan award N.C. Pub. Health Nurse, 1986. Mem. N.C. Pub. Health Assn. (Service award 1984, Outstanding Career Achievement award 1986, program chair ea. dist. 1984-85, program chair maternal child health sect. 1986-87), Forsyth County Mental Health Assn. (chair 1965-66). Republican. Baptist. Home: 3851 Malvern Rd Wilmington NC 28403 Office: New Hanover County Health Dept 2029 S 17th St Wilmington NC 28401

DUGICK, ANGELA EVA MARIE, real estate finance executive; b. Luneburg, W. Ger., Aug. 9, 1949; d. Erwin Richard and Maria Aloysia (Fucik) Kruse; came to U.S., 1953, naturalized, 1960; student Case Western Res. U., 1967-70; B.A. in Econs., U. Alaska, 1977; m. Joseph Dugick, July 11, 1970; 1 child, J. Paul. Econs. researcher Cook Inlet Region, Inc., an Alaska native corp., Anchorage, 1976, mgr. research and analysis, 1976-79, spl. projects coordinator, 1979-81; devel. mgr. Quadrant Devel. Co., Anchorage, 1981-84; v.p. income property Alaska Mut. Bank, 1984-86; asst. v.p. income property Banner Banc, Dallas, 1986-87; asst. v.p. real estate fin. Southmark Corp., Dallas, 1987—. Bd. dirs. Overall Econ. Devel. Commn., Mat-Su Borough, 1977-80; chmn. zoning subcom. Anchorage Land Use Task Force; mem. Anchorage Econ. Devel. Commn., 1985-86. Mem. Nat. Assn. Bus. Economists, Anchorage Bd. Realtors (bd. dirs. 1983-85), Alaska Mortgage Bankers Assn., Dallas Mortgage Bankers Assn. Republican. Roman Catholic. Home: 2305 Covington Lane Plano TX 75023 Office: Southmark Corp 1601 LBJ Freeway Suite 720 Dallas TX 75234

DUHME, CAROL MCCARTHY, civic worker; b. St. Louis, Apr. 13, 1917; d. Eugene Ross and Louise (Roblee) McCarthy; A.B., Vassar Coll., 1939; m. Sheldon Ware, June 12, 1941 (dec. 1944); 1 son, David; m. 2d, H. Richard Duhme, Jr., Apr. 9, 1947; children—Benton (dec.), Ann, Warren. Tchr. elem. sch., 1939-41, 42-44; moderator St. Louis Assn. Congregational Chs., 1952; dir. Christian edn. First Congregational Ch., St. Louis, 1987—, trustee, 1964-66, mem. ch. council, 1974-75, 88—, bd. deaconesses, 1978-81, bd. deacons, 1982-85, chmn. bd. Christian Edn., 1988—; former bd. dirs. Community Music Schs., St. Louis, Community Sch., Ch. Women United, John Burroughs Sch., St. Louis Bicentennial Women's Com., St. Louis Jr. League; pres. St. Louis Vassar Club; pres. bd. dirs. YWCA, St. Louis, 1973-76; bd. dirs. North Side Team Ministry, 1968-84, Chautauqua (N.Y.) Instn., 1971-79, mem. adv. council to bd., 1987—; Mo. Bapt. Hosp., 1973—; exec. com. bd. dirs. Eden Theol. Sem., 1981—, presdl. search com. 1986—; sec. bd. dirs. UN Assn., St. Louis, 1976-84; pres. bd. dirs. Family and Children's Service Greater St. Louis, 1977-79; mem. chancellor's long-range planning com. Washington U., 1980-81, mem. Nat. Council, Sch. Social Work, 1987—;

chmn. Benton Roblee Duhme Scholarship Fund; pres., trustee Joseph H. and Florence A. Roblee Found., St. Louis, pres. 1984—; chmn. Chautaugua Bell Tower Scholarship Fund. Mem. corp. assembly Blue Cross Hosp. Service of Mo., 1978-86. Recipient Mary Alice Messerley award for volunteerism Health and Welfare Council St. Louis, 1971; Vol. of Yr. award, YWCA, 1976; Woman of Achievement award St. Louis Globe Democrat, 1980. Home: 8 Edgewood Rd Saint Louis MO 63124

DUKAKIS, KATHARINE (KITTY), wife of governor of Massachusetts, civic worker. d. Harry Ellis Dickson; m. John Chaffetz (div.); 1 child, John; m. Michael Dukakis, 1963; children: Andrea, Kara. Former modern dance tchr., TV reporte; dir. Pub. Space Ptnrships. Project Harvard U., Cambridge, Mass. Former mem. U.S. Commn. on the Holocaust; former chmn. Mass. Gov.'s Adv. Com. on Homeless. Democrat. Jewish. *

DUKAKIS, OLYMPIA, actress; b. Lowell, Mass., June 20, 1931; d. Constantine S. and Alexandra (Christos) D.; m. Louis Zorich; children: Christina, Peter, Stefan. Grad. in phys. therapy, Boston U. Co-founder, artistic dir. The Whole Theatre Co., Upper Montclair, N.J., 1970—. Appeared in plays La Ronde, Buzzards Bay Summer Theatre, 1957, The Breaking Wall, The Trojan Women, The Cherry Orchard, N.Y. Shakespeare Festival, Peer Gynt, The Marriage of Bette and Boo, others; Broadway plays include The Aspern Papers, Social Security, The Night of the Iguana; films include The Idolmaker, King of America, Moonstruck, 1987 (Acad. award Best Supporting Actress, 1988). Del. Dem. Nat. Convention, 1988. Recipient 2 Obie awards, Los Angeles Film Critics award, 1988. Mem. Screen Actors Guild, Am. Fedn. TV and Radio Artists. Address: care The Whole Theatre Co 544 Bloomfield Ave Upper Montclair NJ 07042 *

DUKE, CAROL MICHIELS, real estate broker; b. Alexandria, La., Sept. 2, 1944; d. Leo A., Sr. and Elva L. (Wilson) Michiels; m. M. Carey Duke, Jr., Apr. 23, 1971; 1 child, Perrianne. Student in personnel mgmt. Nichols State U., 1974-77; grad. Dale Carnegie Inst., Realtors Inst. Lic. real estate broker, Tex.; lic. notary pub., Tex.; cert. residential broker. Officer mgr. Bayou Constrn. Co., Houma, La., 1974-76; realtor, mgr. Glynn & Assoc. Realtors, Houma, La., 1976-79; owner, broker Century 21 Real Estate One, Houma, 1979-81; v.p., mgmt. cons. Century 21 of Tex. and La., Houston, 1981-82; v.p., gen. mgr. Doyle Stuckey Realtors, Houston, 1982-83; broker/mgr. Gary Greene Realtors, Better Homes & Gardens, Houston, 1983-85, Better Homes and Gardens Real Estate Service, Des Moines, 1985— ; com. mem. Farm and Land Inst., Austin, 1972—; seminar condr.; chmn. conv. booth Realtors Nat. Home Builders, Houston, 1983. Editor Training and Policy Manual, 1982. Local chmn. Easter Seal Soc., Houma, 1979. Recipient Top Listing award, numerous Top Quarterly awards La. Dist. of Century 21, 1980, Yearly Top Goal award, Yearly Bottom Line award, Top Prodn. award, numerous Top Quarterly awards, Better Homes & Gardens, Houston, 1983, 84. Mem. Houston Bd. Realtors (edn. com. 1984-85), Tex. Assn. Realtors (realtor/builder, sec. 1983—), Nat. Assn. Realtors, Realtors Nat. Mktg. Inst., West Houston C. of C., Jaycee Jaynes (state bd. dirs. 1976-77, sec. 1977-78). Democrat. Roman Catholic. Home and Office: 13807 Aspen Hollow Houston TX 77082

DUKE, CLAIRE DIANE, civic leader, real estate broker; b. Barre, Vt., Sept. 22, 1935; d. Alexander Marcel and Margaret Lucien (Leclerc) Laferriere; m. David Carroll Duke, July 26, 1958; children: Douglas, Brian, Gary, Ellen, Kenneth, Susan. Grad. high sch., Barre. Lic. realtor. Pres. Berg, Carmolli and Kent Real Estate, Barre, 1981—; trustee Cen. Vt. Service Properties Inc., Montpelier 1985—. Pres. Barre Town Sch. Assn. 1971; campaign mgr. Ledbetter U.S. Senate 1980; pres. Vt. Fedn. Rep. Women 1976-80; dir. Nat. Fedn. Rep. Women, Washington 1976-80; mem. Gov. Commn. Status Women, Montpelier, Vt. 1976-80; exec. dir. Vt. Rep. Party, 1978-79. Mem. Cen. Vt. C. of C., Cen. Vt. Bd. Realtors, Vt. Assn. Realtors, Nat. Assn. Realtors. Roman Catholic. Lodge: Rotary. Office: Berg Carmolli and Kent Real Estate Corp 83 N Main St PO Box 628 Barre VT 05641

DUKE, ELLEN KAY, computer marketing executive, community activist; b. Indpls., June 7, 1952; d. Richard Thomas and Ruby Mae (Wright) D. Student Chapman Coll., Orange, Calif., 1972; B.S. in Pub. Affairs, Ind. U.-Bloomington, 1975; postgrad. Portland State U., 1980-81. Cert. Dale Carnegie Pub. Speaking Instr., 1987—; News reporter, Salem Statesman, Corvallis, Oreg., 1976-78; com. adminstr. Oreg. State Legislature, Salem, 1979-80; pub. involvement coordinator Met. Regional Service Dist., Portland, 1981-82; account mgr. Thunder & Visions, Portland, 1982-83; project asst. Amdahl Corp., Sunnyvale, Calif., 1983-84; spl. project coordinator Computerland Corp., Hayward, Calif., 1984—; producer, lead facilitator Sage, Inc., Walnut Creek, Calif., 1982—. Co-author: (ednl. film) Communication Skills, 1975. Chairperson Corvallis Budget Commn., Oreg., 1978; commr. Hayward Library, Calif., 1985—, Alameda County Consumer Affairs, Oakland, 1985; rep. Nat. Democratic Conv., N.Y.C., 1982. Named Able Toastmaster Toastmasters Internat., 1981. Mem. Nat. Assn. Female Execs., Am. Mktg. Assn. Club: Sierra, (San Francisco). Office: Computerland 2901 Peralta Oaks Ct Oakland CA 94605

DUKE, JUDITH SILVERMAN, author; b. Portchester, N.Y., Mar. 27, 1934; d. Herbert Francis and Fannye (Cohen) Silverman; m. Alan Duke, Mar. 2, 1968; 1 child, Sharon. BA, Cornell U., 1955; postgrad. in bus. adminstrn., NYU. Research asst. Boni Watkins, Jason & Co., N.Y.C., 1955; statistician Nat. Footwear Mfrs. Assn., Washington, 1956-59; head research dept. Lefcourt Realty Corp., N.Y.C., 1959-60; asst. to dir. market research Life mag., 1960-70; abstracter-indexer Morningside Assos., Pleasantville, N.Y., 1973-75; free-lance writer, 1976—. Author: The Children's Literature Market, 1977 1982, 1977, The Religious Communications Market, 1978-1983, 1978, Children's Books and Magazines, 1979, The Business Information Markets, 1979-1984, 1979, The Technical, Scientific and Medical Publishing Market, 1981-86, 1981, The Technical Scientific and Medical Publishing Market, 1985, Religious Publishing and Communications, 1981; mng. editor: U.S. Book Publishing Yearbook and Directory, 1981-82, 1982; editor: The Knowledge Industry 200, 1983; asst. editor Advanced Tech. Libraries, DataBase Alert, 1983-85; assoc. editor Data Base Alert, 1985—, Advanced Technology Libraries, 1985—. Address: 6 Carriage Hill Millwood NY 10546

DUKE, PATTY (ANNA MARIE DUKE), actress; b. N.Y.C., Dec. 14, 1946; d. John P. and Frances (McMahon) Duke; m. John Astin, 1973 (div. 1985); m. Michael Pierce, March 15, 1986. Grad., Quintano's School for Young Profls. Pres. Screen Actors Guild, 1985—, lecturer Am. Film Inst., 1988. TV appearances include Armstrong Circle Theatre, 1955, The Prince and the Pauper, 1957, Wuthering Heights, 1958, U.S. Steel Hour, Meet Me in St. Louis, 1959, Swiss Family Robinson, 1958, The Power and the Glory, 1961, (series) Patty Duke Show, 1964-66, Before and After, 1979, Women in White, The Baby Sitter, The Women's Room, All's Fair, 1981-82, Something So Right, Best Kept Secrets, September Gun, (series) It Takes Two, 1983, (TV film) A Time to Triumph, George Washington: The Forging of a Nation, 1984, Fight for Life, numerous others; theatrical appearances include The Miracle Worker, 1959-61, Isle of Children, 1962; motion picture appearances in The Miracle Worker, 1962 (Acad. award as best supporting actress 1963), Valley of the Dolls, 1967, Me, Natalie, 1969 (Golden Globe award as best actress 1970), My Sweet Charlie, 1970, Captains and the Kings, 1976, The Miracle Worker, 1979; co-author Surviving Sexual Assault, 1983, Call Me Anna, 1987. Nat. corp. council Muscular Dystrophy Assns. Am. Recipient Emmy Awards, 1964, 69, 76, 79. Mem. AFTRA. Office: care The Agy 10351 Santa Monica Blvd Suite 211 Los Angeles CA 90025 *

DUKE, VERONICA MURRAY, social worker; b. Cape May, N.J., Sept. 28, 1931; d. Thomas Patrick and Cora Beatrice (Davies) Murray; student U. Tampa, 1949-51; B.S., U. Fla., 1953; M.S.W., U. Mo., 1959; m. Alvah G. Heideman, Jr., 1955 (div. 1976); children—Alvah G. III, Sara Elizabeth; m. 2d, George Duke, Jr., 1979. Caseworker, Hillsborough County, Tampa, Fla., 1954-56; caseworker State of Mo., Fulton, 1956-59; chief social worker Mo. State Sch., 1959-60; psychiat. social worker State of Alaska, Anchorage, 1970-72; chief social worker Alaska Psychiat. Inst., U. Alaska, Anchorage, 197287; pvt. cons., Anchorage, 1987—; field instr. U. Wash.-Yeshiva U. Republican Committeewoman, Columbia, Mo., 1969; pres. Camp Fire Girls Council, 1969-70. Served as ensign USNR, 1953-54: Korea. Diplomate Nat. Assn. Social Workers; mem. Soc. Dirs. Hosp. Social Work, Acad. Cert. Social Workers, U.S. Ski Assn., Mo. Alumni Assn., Clin. Social Work Registry, Circle of Friends, U. Pacific. Republican. Episcopalian. Clubs: Soroptimists, Women's of Am. Home: 1710 Eastridge Dr Anchorage AK 99501 Office: 2900 Providence Rd Anchorage AK 99508

DUKERT, BETTY COLE, television producer; b. Muskogee, Okla., May 9, 1927; d. Irvan Dill and Ione (Bowman) Cole; m. Joseph M. Dukert, May 19, 1968. Student, Lindenwood Coll., St. Charles, Mo., 1945-46, Drury Coll., Springfield, Mo., 1946-47; B.J., U. Mo., 1949. With Sta. KICK, Springfield, Mo., 1949-50; adminstrv. asst. Juvenile Office, Green County, Mo., 1950-52; with Sta. WRC-TV-NBC, Washington, 1952-56; assoc. producer Meet the Press, NBC, Washington, 1956-75; producer Meet the Press, NBC, 1975—; mem. Robert F. Kennedy Journalism Awards Com., 1978-82. Trustee Drury Coll., Springfield, Mo., 1984—. Recipient Disting. Alumna award Drury Coll., 1975; Disting. Alumni award U. Mo., 1978; Ted Yates award Washington chpt. Nat. Acad. TV Arts and Scis., 1979; Pub. Relations award for pub. service Am. Legion Nat. Comdrs., 1981. Mem. Am. Women in Radio and TV, Am. News Women's Club, Radio/TV Corrs. Assn., Women's Forum Washington, Soc. Profl. Journalists (dir. 1983-84), Silver Circle Broadcasting, Nat. Acad. TV Arts and Scis. Club: Nat. Press. Office: NBC News 4001 Nebraska Ave NW Washington DC 20016

DUKES, JOAN, state legislator; b. Tacoma, Wash.. Mem. Oreg. State Senate. Democrat. Address: Rt 2 Box 503 Astoria OR 97103 *

DUKES, REBECCA WEATHERS (BECKY), musician, singer, songwriter; b. Durham, N.C., Nov. 21, 1934; d. Elmer Dewey Weathers and Martha Rebecca (Kimbrough) Weathers-Hall; m. Charles Aubrey Dukes Jr., Dec. 20, 1955; children: Aurelia Ann, Charles Weathers, David Lloyd. BA, Duke U., 1956. Lic. elem. sch. tchr. Tchr. Durham City Schs., 1956-57; sec. USMC, Arlington, Va., 1957-58; tchr. Arlington County Schs., 1958-59; office mgr. Dukes and Kooken, Landover, Md., 1976; musical performer Washington and various locations, Va., Md., 1982—. Vocal student Todd Duncan; pianist, vocalist Back Alley Restaurant Lounge, 1982;orginal program, A Life Cycle in Song, presented throughout mid-Atlantic states and Washington; full operatic solo recital, 1983; featured performer benefit for Nat. Symphony Orch.; frequent performer pvt. functions, athletic, civic, religious and cultural events including appearances at Capitol Ctr., Cole Field House, George Washington U., Smith Ctr.; operatic solo concert with pianist Glenn Sales, 1985; benefit appearance U. Md. Concert Series, 1986, 87; holds copyrights for over 70 original songs including Between the Lovin' and the Leavin', Covers of My Mind, Gentle Thoughts (lead song Nat. Capitol Area Composers Series), Headin' Home Again, I Would Like to Be Reborn, Miss You, Tears, You Played a Part in My Life; author: (poems) Pottery. Pres. Nat. Capitol Law League, Washington, 1976-77; pres. women's group, deacon Riverdale Presby. Ch., Hyattsville, Md., 1968-70; chmn. event honoring wives of Supreme Ct. justices, 1981; mem. women's com. Nat. Symphony, 1980—. Recipient Friend of Yr. award Md. Summer Inst. for Creative & Performing Arts U. Md., 1986; named hon. trustee Prince George's (Md.) Arts Council, 1984—. Mem. Songwriter's Assn. Washington, William Preston Few Assn. of Duke U. Republican. Clubs: Founders of Duke U.; Pres.' of U. Md.; Univ. (Balt.). Home and Office: 7111 Pony Trail Hyattsville MD 20782

DULA, MARTHA ALYCE, health care administrator; b. Spartanburg, S.C., Sept. 25, 1945; d. A. Cecil and Alice (Roberts) D. BA, U. N.C., Asheville, 1966; MA, U. N.C., Chapel Hill, 1967. Instr. SUNY, Oneonta, 1968-70; research asst. Harvard Bus. Sch., Cambridge, Mass., 1970-73; cons. Cambridge Research Inst., Inc., 1973-77; exec. dir. Met. Boston Hosp. Council, 1977-84; prin. Brewster/Lowe Group, Inc., Boston, 1984-86; v.p. planning and mktg. Horizon Health System, Inc., Bethlehem, Pa., 1986—. Mem. Am. Mktg. Assn., Am. Soc. Health Care Planning and Mktg., Am. Acad. Health Care Mktg., Internat. Health Econ. and Mgmt. Assn. Home: 1426 Moravia St Bethlehem PA 18015 Office: Horizon Health System Inc 60 W Broad St Bethlehem PA 18018

DULANY, ELIZABETH GJELSNESS, university press administrator; b. Charleston, S.C., Mar. 11, 1931; d. Rudolph Hjalmar and Ruth Elizabeth (Weaver) Gjelsness; m. Donelson Edwin Dulany, Mar. 19, 1955; 1 son, Christopher Daniel. B.A., Bryn Mawr Coll., 1952. Proofreader, editor Books in Print, R.R. Bowker Co., N.Y.C., summers 1948-51, mng. editor, summer 1952; med. sec., editor dept. pediatrics U. Mich. Hosp., Ann Arbor, 1953-54; editorial asst. E.P. Dutton & Co., N.Y.C., 1954-55; editorial asst. U. Ill. Press, Champaign, 1956-59, asst. to editor, 1959-60, asst. editor, 1960-67, asso. editor, 1967-72, mng. editor, 1972—, asst. dir., 1983—. Democrat. Episcopalian. Home: 73 Greencroft Champaign IL 61821 Office: U Ill Press 54 E Gregory St Champaign IL 61820

DULA-WILSON, CAROLYN, service company executive; b. Lenoir, N.C., Mar. 24, 1956; d. Charles Barber and Gertrude (Felder) Dula; m. Darryel Ray Wilson, June 29, 1984. B.S., N.C. A&T State U., 1978. Customer service rep. So. Bell, Greensboro, N.C., 1978-79; restaurant mgr., Atlanta and Decatur, Ga., 1979-84; auto leasing agt., Atlanta, 1984—. Sec. Know-Your-Neighbor Club, Atlanta, 1982. Recipient T. Austin Finch scholarship Thomasville Industries, N.C., 1974. Mem. Intown Bus. Assocs., Nat. Assn. Female Execs.

DULLIEN, STARLEY BEATRIX, wholesale tour operator; b. Wiesbaden, Hessen, W. Ger., July 26, 1951; d. Milan Nicholas and Martha Henriette (Zwinkau) Drakulich; m. Thomas Klaus-Dieter Dullien, Jan. 2, 1975; 1 son, Daniel Claudio Didier. BA, U. Utah, 1974; Teaching Cert. in Multilingual/Multicultural Edn., U. Utah, 1976. Conf. dir. Nat. Network for Bilingual Edn., Salt Lake City, 1976-77; assoc. tchr. U. Utah, Salt Lake City, 1974-79; transfer agt. Western Capital and Securities, Salt Lake City, 1979-82; promotion dir. Saltair Resort, Salt Lake City, 1982-83; sec., treas. Starbar, Inc., Salt Lake City, 1982-83; pres. Stardust, Inc., Salt Lake City, 1983-84; gen. mgr. E.T. World Travel, Inc., Salt Lake City, 1984-87; pres. Voyagers, Salt Lake City, 1988—; dir. Les Chic Orgn., Salt Lake City, 1977-79, Jazzin' Dance Co., Salt Lake City, 1982-83; title VII curriculum coordinator Nat. Network for Bilingual Bicultural Edn., Salt Lake City, 1976. Performance grantee Utah Arts Council, 1982. Mem. Phoenix Conv. Bur., Salt Lake Conv. Bur., Nat. Tour Assn., Foremost West. Democrat. Office: 936 S 200 W Salt Lake City UT 84101

DUMAS, RHETAUGH ETHELDRA GRAVES, nursing school dean; b. Natchez, Miss., Nov. 26, 1928; d. Rhetaugh Graves and Josephine (Clemmons) Graves Bell; m. A.W. Dumas, Jr., Dec. 25, 1950; 1 child, Adrienne. BS in Nursing, Dillard U., 1951; MS in Psychiat. Nursing, Yale U., 1961; PhD in Social Psychology, Union Grad. Sch. 1, Union for Experimenting Colls. and Univs., Cinn., 1975; also various other courses; D.Public Service (hon.), Simmons Coll., 1976, U. Cin., 1981. Instr. Dillard U., 1957-59, 61; research asst., instr. Sch. Nursing Yale U., 1962-65, from asst. prof. nursing to assoc. prof., 1965-72, chmn. dept. psychiat. nursing, 1972; dir. nursing Conn. Mental Health Ctr., Yale-New Haven Med. Ctr., 1966-72; chief psychiat. nursing edn. br. Div. Manpower and Tng. Programs, NIMH, Rockville, Md., 1972-76; dep. dir. Div. Manpower and Tng. Programs NIMH, 1976-79, dep. dir., 1979-81; dean U. Mich. Sch. Nursing, 1981—; dir. Group Relations Confs. in Tavistock Model; cons., speaker, panelist in field; fellow Helen Hadley Hall, Yale U., 1972, Branford Coll., 1972; dir. Community Health Care Ctr. Plan, New Haven, 1969-72; mem. U.S. Assessment Team, cons. to Fed. Ministry Health, Nigeria, 1982; mem. adv. com. Health Policy Agenda for the Am. People, AMA, 1983—; cons. NIH Task Force on Nursing Research, 1984; mem. Nat. Commn. on Unemployment and Mental Health, Nat. Mental Health Assn., 1984-85; mem. com. to plan maj. study of nat. long-term care policy Inst. Medicine, 1985; mem. adv. com. to dir. NIH, 1986-87. Author profl. monographs; contbr. articles to profl. publs.; mem. editorial bd. Community Mental Health Rev., 1977-79, Jour. Personality and Social Systems, 1978-81, Advances in Psychiat. Mental Health Nursing, 1981. Bd. dirs. Afro Am. Center, Yale U., 1968-72; mem. New Haven Bd. Edn., 1968-71, New Haven City Demonstrations Agy., 1968-70, Human Relations Council New Haven, 1961-63. Named Disting. Alumna Dillard U., 1966; recipient various awards, including cert. Honor NAACP, 1970, Disting. Alumnae award Yale U. Sch. Nursing, 1976, award for outstanding achievement and service in field mental health D.C. chpt. Assn. Black Psychologists, 1980. Fellow A.K. Rice Inst., Am. Coll. Mental Health Adminstrs. (founding), Am. Acad. Nursing (charter, pres. 1987—); mem. Am. Nurses Assn., Nat. Black Nurses Assn., Am. Public Health Assn., Inst. Medicine of Nat. Acad. Scis., Urban League, Nat. Acad. of Scis. Inst. of Med., NAACP, Sigma Theta Tau, Delta Sigma Theta. Office: U Mich Sch Nursing Ann Arbor MI 48109

DUMAS, SANDRA LEE, personnel executive, personnel consultant; b. Malone, N.Y., Mar. 27, 1957; d. Leonard James and Myrtle Lucille (Beverlin) Dumas. A.S., NYU-Canton, 1976; student Tunxis Community Coll., 1977-79. Receptionist N.W. Enterprises, Malone, 1972; receptionist, sec. Wasley Products, Inc., Plainville, Conn., 1973, time study estimator, 1974-76; prodn. control clk., 1976-77, personnel asst., 1977-79, asst. personnel mgr., 1979-82, personnel mgr., 1982—; cons. Wasley Lighting, Essex, Conn., 1982—, Precision Molding, New Britain, Conn., 1985—. Bd. dirs. United Way of Plainville, 1985-88, campaign chairperson, 1987—; bd. dirs. Wheeler Clinic, Inc., Plainville, 1984—; trustee UAW Local 376 Union Welfare Fund, Hartford, Conn., 1984-88; crisis intervention counselor Help Line, Plainville, 1983-84; rape crisis counselor YWCA, New Britain, Conn., 1984-85; Strike Back Against Crime rep. Strike Back, New Haven, 1984—; cons. Jr. Achievement Project Bus., Plainville, 1986; advisor Coop. Work Experience, Bristol Eastern High Sch., 1982-85. Recipient Outstanding Young Woman award Jaycee Women, Bristol, Conn., 1984, Conn. Outstanding Young Citizens award WFSB Channel 3, Conn. Jaycees, 1985, Proclamation, Mayor City of Bristol, 1985. Mem. Nat. Assn. Female Execs., Am. Soc. Personnel Adminstrn., Internat. Found. Employee Benefit Plans, Nat. Safety Council, Mfrs. Hartford County, Conn. Bus. and Industry Assn. Democrat. Roman Catholic. Club: Jr Women's (co-chmn. health and safety 1977-78) (Bristol). Avocations: bowling; swimming. Office: Wasley Products Inc Plainville Indsl Park Plainville CT 06062

DUNAVAN, ILENA ABRAMS LENI, travel firm operations manager; b. Bklyn., May 13, 1938; d. Sidney Charles and Lilian Lucille (Lustgarten) Abrams; m. Lawrence A. Dunavan, Dec. 16, 1974. BA, U. Fla., 1960. Classroom tchr. various schs., U.S. and abroad, 1960-67; hosp. field dir. ARC, Washington, 1967-76; travel cons. Montgomery Village Travel, Gaithersburg, Md., 1983-84, Gelco Travel Services, Rockville, Md., 1984-85; mgr. Montgomery Travel Ctr., Gaithersburg, 1985-86; ops. mgr. Travelogue, Inc., Washington, 1986—. Mem. adv. council Kaiser-Permanente Med. Ctr., Gaithersburg, 1982-85; leader Jr. Girl Scouts USA, Gaithersburg, 1982-83. Named one of Outstanding Young Women Am., 1973. Mem. Inst. Cert. Travel Agts., Pacific Area Travel Assn., Upper Montgomery C. of C. Democrat. Jewish. Office: Travelogue Inc 1111 19th St NW Suite 206 Washington DC 20036

DUNAWAY, FAYE, actress; b. Bascom, Fla., Jan. 14, 1941; d. John and Grace D.; m. Peter Wolf, Aug. 7, 1974; m. Terrence O'Neill; 1 son. Student, U. Fla., Boston U. An original mem. Lincoln Center Repertory Co.; appeared off-Broadway in Hogan's Goat; played Bonnie in motion picture Bonnie and Clyde, 1967; appeared in motion pictures: Hurry Sundown, 1967, The Happening, 1967, The Thomas Crown Affair, 1968, A Place For Lovers, 1969, Little Big Man, 1970, Doc, 1971, The Getaway, 1972, Oklahoma Crude, 1973, The Three Musketeers, 1973, Chinatown, 1974, Three Days of the Condor, 1975, Network, 1976 (Academy award for best actress), The Voyage of the Damned, 1976, The Towering Inferno, 1976, The Eyes of Laura Mars, 1978, The Champ, 1979, The First Deadly Sin, 1980, Mommie Dearest, 1981, The Wicked Lady, 1982, Supergirl, 1984, Barfly, 1987, others; TV movies include: After the Fall, 1974, The Disappearance of Aimee, 1976, Evita Peron, 1981, Ellis Island, 1986, 13 at Dinner, 1985, Beverly Hills Madame, 1986; appeared in play The Curse of an Aching Heart, 1982. Recipient Most Promising Newcomer Award Brit. Film Acad., 1968. *

DUNAWAY, FRANCES LOUISE, public aid casework supervisor; b. Chgo., June 11, 1933; d. Sam and Gladys Emma (Hornbeak) D.; m. Allen Adams, May 12, 1951 (div. Oct. 1964); children: Karen, Jerome, Bernard, Kenneth, Adams; m. Edwin Hoskins, Feb. 1, 1969 (dec. Jan. 1978). Student, DePaul U., 1950-51, Crane Coll., 1965. Supr. pub. aid casework State of Ill. Foster parent Chgo. Youth Ctr., 1978; pres., organizer Springfield Block Club, 1971; pres. Our Lady of Sorrows Cath. Council 1985-87, treas. 1987—. Office: State of Ill Dept Pub Aid 4105 W Chicago Ave Chicago IL 60651

DUNBAR, CHERYL DOSS, nurse; b. Birmingham, Ala., July 1, 1953; d. Daniel Edward and Mable Lee (Bennett) Doss; m. Jerome Lee Dunbar, Sept. 4, 1976 (div. May 1986); 1 child, Aprille. Student, Old Dominion U., 1971-74; BS, U. Ala., 1976. Staff nurse Washington Hosp. Ctr., 1976-77; staff nurse Sentara Norfolk (Va.) Gen. Hosp., 1977-79, clin. coordinator, 1979-86; adminstrv. asst. head nurse Norfolk (Va.) Gen. Hosp., 1986—; preceptor Norfolk State U., 1986—, Old Dominion U., Norfolk, 1986-87. Mem. Va. Perinatal Assn., Nat. Perinatal Assn., Nurse Assn. Ob-Gyn., Clin. Coordinator Com. (pres. 1984-85), Delta Sigma Theta (Dem. campaign promotion 1974). Baptist. Home: 844 Main Creek Rd Chesapeake VA 23320

DUNBAR, ISOBEL MOIRA, former environmental scientist; b. Edinburgh, Scotland, Feb. 3, 1918; d. William and Elizabeth Mary (Robertson) D. B.A., Oxford U., 1939, M.A., 1948. With div. earth sci. Can. Def. Research Bd., Ottawa, Ont., 1947-78, dir., 1975-77, sr. scientist, 1977-78; mem. Can. Environ. Adv. Council, 1972-78. Contbr. articles to profl. jours. Recipient Centennial award Can. Meteorol. Service, 1971; Massey medal Royal Can. Geog. Soc., 1972; Decorated Order of Can., 1976. Fellow Royal Soc. Can., Arctic Inst. N. Am. (gov. 1966-69), Royal Can. Geog. Soc. (dir. 1974-84); mem. Internat. Glaciological Soc. Home: Rural Rt 1, Dunrobin, ON Canada K0A 1T0

DUNBAR-WEBB, EVELYN LOUISE, computer systems business owner, consultant; b. New Haven, Apr. 6, 1954; d. Marshall Nelson and Evelyn Louise (Clinton) D.; m. John Henry Webb, Aug. 9, 1986; children: Jennifer Ann, Heather Merri. Student, U. New Haven, 1972, Monegan Community Coll., Norwich, Conn., 1983-84, Conn. Coll., New London, 1984—. Travel cons. Tours, Inc., Cheshire, Conn., 1972-73; credit collector W.T. Grant Co., Wrightstown, N.J., 1973-74; data entry clk. Thomas G. Faria Corp., Uncasville, Conn., 1982-83; sec., office mgr. adminstrv. partial hospitalization program Lawrence & Meml. Hosps., New London, Conn., 1983-84; sec., office mgr. planning dept. Lawrence & Meml. Hosps., New London, 1984-85; computer systems' cons. Gremlin Systems, Old Lyme, Conn., 1985—; seminar cons. Conn. Small Bus. Devel. Ctr., New London and Groton, 1987—. Designer software Rental Realty Management, Accounting Systems Management, 1986; mem. Conn. River Valley Women's Network. State of Conn. scholar, 1972; Conn. Coll. scholar, 1984, 86-87. Mem. Nat. Assn. Female Execs., NOW, Am. Assn. Entrepreneurial Women, Conn. River Valley Women's Network, Old Saybrook C. of C. Episcopalian. Club: Fitness Unltd. Health. Home and Office: 126 Boston Post Rd Old Lyme CT 06371

DUNCAN, ANN HUBERTY, university administrator; b. Sacramento, Sept. 21, 1933; d. Martin R. and Gertrude (Turner) Huberty; m. John B. Duncan, June 30, 1957 (div. July 1971); children—Robert Martin, Kenneth Ross. BA, U. Calif.-Berkeley, 1956; MA, Calif. State U.-Hayward, 1977; EdD, Pepperdine U., 1988. Cert. tchr. Personnel dir. Calif. Sch. Employees Assn., 1974-75; assoc. personnel analyst City of Oakland, Calif., 1975-76; dir. employer-employee relations City of Livermore, Calif., 1976-80; pres. mgmt. cons. firm Duncan & Assocs., Los Angeles and Castro Valley, Calif., 1980-88; asst. dir. Ctr. Ednl. Leadership, Pepperdine U., Los Angeles, 1984-85; prof. Grad. Sch. Pub. Adminstrn., J.F.K., Orinda, Calif., 1979-83; lectr. career devel. San Jose State U., 1974-84, Santa Monica City Coll., 1986—; trustee Calif. Community Colls., 1982-84. Chmn. Robert Cummings Student Loan Fund, 1970; mem. Hayward Zoning Commn., 1970-71; trustee Chabot Coll., Hayward, 1971-84, emeritus, 1984, pres. bd., 1975, 79; factfinder Pleasanton (Calif.) Sch. Dist., 1975. Recipient Pub. Service award Alameda County Sch. Bd. Assn., 1975, 79; fellow Pepperdine U., Kappa Kappa Gamma). Mem. Calif. Elected Women's Assn. for Ednl. Research (charter, state bd. dirs.), U.S.-China Peoples Friendship Assn., LWV (chpt. pres. 1968-70), Internat. Personnel Mgmt. Assn. (ethics com.), No. Calif. Personnel and Employee Relations Assn. (pres. 1979-80), Calif. Community Colls. Trustees Assn. (bd. dirs. 1982-84), Am. Assn. Community and Jr. Colls. (speaker), Kappa Kappa Kappa. Avocations: travel, reading, museums. Home and Office: 1250 Monaco Pacific Palisades CA 90272

DUNCAN, CAROL ALEXANDER, entrepreneur; b. Dallas, Oct. 1, 1939; d. John Roland and Ruth (Brown) Alexander; divorced; 1 child, Robert

Kevin Duncan. Student, North Tex. State U., 1957; So. Meth. U., 1958. Cert. vocat. evaluation specialist. Pres. Natwel Supply Corp., San Antonio, 1977-79, CD Enterprises, Dallas, 1977—, Carol Duncan Enterprises Inc., Dallas, 1978—, the Relocation Group Inc., Dallas, 1982—; bd. dirs. Carol Duncan Enterprises Inc., the Relocation Group Inc. City officer Urban Rehab. Standards Bd., 1986—; bd. dirs. Turtle Creek Manor Inc., 1986—, Dallas Women's Found., 1987—, Dallas Council Alcoholism and Drug Abuse, 1986-88. Mem. Nat. Assn. Women Bus. Owners, Am. Soc. Personnel Adminstrn., Tex. Women's Alliance, Dallas C. of C., Small Bus. Adminstrn. (dist. advocate 1983), Exec. Women Dallas (bd. dirs. 1985—), Leadership Dallas. Republican. Club: Park City (Dallas). Office: Carol Duncan Enterprises 12900 Preston Rd Suite 500 Dallas TX 75230

DUNCAN, DVENNA AVONNE, educator; b. Astoria, Oreg., Mar. 28, 1943; d. James Thomas and Grace Isobel (Leathers) D. BS, U. Oreg., 1966, MS, 1972; PhD, U. Wash., 1976. Tchr. spl. edn. Santa Barbara (Calif.) Schs., 1966-74; asst. prof. U. Pitts., 1976-81; assoc. prof. U. Vt., Burlington, 1981-83, U. Portland, Oreg., 1983—. Editor The Communicator newsletter, 1986—; contbr. articles to profl. jours. Mem. Am. Assn. Colls. Tchr. Edn. (adv. com.), Council for Exceptional Children (chmn. tchr. edn. div. 1986—), TEO (assoc. chairperson small coll. div.), Zeta Tau Alpha. Home: 2408 NE Tillamook Portland OR 97212 Office: U Portland 5000 N Willamette Portland OR 97203

DUNCAN, ELIZABETH CHARLOTTE, family counselor, educational therapist, educator, psychologist; b. Los Angeles, Mar. 10, 1919; d. Frederick John de St. Vrain and Nellie Mae (Goucher) Schwankovsky; m. William McConnell Duncan, Oct. 12, 1941 (div. 1949); 1 child, Susan Elizabeth Duncan Sturges. BA, Calif. U.-Long Beach, 1953; MA, UCLA, 1962; PhD, Internat. Coll., 1984. Dir. gifted program Palos Verdes Sch. Dist., Calif., 1958-64; TV tchr., participant ednl. films Los Angeles County, 1961-64; dir. U. So. Calif. Presch., Los Angeles, 1965-69; pvt. practice family counselor, Malibu and Ventura, Calif., 1979—; resident psychologist for film series Something Personal, 1987—; mem. Research Inst. of Scripps Clinic, La Jolla, Calif.; charter mem. Inst. Behav. Med., Santa Barbara, Calif.; TV performer: (documentary) The Other Side, 1985. Author: TV mini-series Persephone's Child, 1988. Active Chryalis Ctr., Los Angeles, 1984-86, Ventura County Mental Health Adv. Bd., Calif., 1985-86, United Way, Los Angeles, 1985-86. Recipient Emmy award for best documentary Am. TV Arts and Scis., 1976, Child Advocate of Yr. Calif. Mental Health Adv. Bd., 1987. Mem. Transpersonal Psychol. Assn., Am. Counseling and Devel. Assn., Calif. State Orgn. Gifted Edn. (sec. 1962-64). Democrat. Avocations: swimming; plays; concerts; boating; political issues, especially women and child abuse. Office: 260 Maple Ct Suite 129 Ventura CA 93003

DUNCAN, EVE CRITTENDEN, quality assurance educator; b. N.Y.C., Aug. 2, 1940; d. Harold Westle and Marie Rose (Reda) Crittenden; children: Carlton W. Cole, Julia M. AAS, Corning Community Coll., 1962. Research asst. Vanderbilt U., Nashville, 1962-80; biotech. research Corning (N.Y.) Glass Works, 1981-86, instr. quality inst., 1986—. Contbr. articles to profl. jours. Mem. CAC Nashville Bd. of Edn., 1977-80; dir. Near Westside Neighborhood, Inc., Elmira, N.Y., 1981—; leader Brownie Troop #715, Elmira, 1986—. Recipient Ten Yr. Service award Girl Scouts of Am., 1986, Citizen Recognition award NWNA, 1981, 82, 83, 84, 85, 86, 87. Mem. Assurance Soc. Quality Control, Am. Chem. Soc., Tissue Culture Soc., Beta Sigma Phi (pres. 1970, 77). Office: Corning Glass Works MP 51 02 Corning NY 14831

DUNCAN, FRANCES MURPHY, educator; b. Utica, N.Y., June 23, 1920; d. Edward Simon and Elizabeth Myers (Stack) Murphy; B.A., Barnard Coll., Columbia U., 1942; M.Ed., Auburn U., 1963, Ed.D., 1969; m. Lee C. Duncan, June 23, 1947 (div. June 1969); children—Lee C., Edward M., Paul H., Elizabeth B., Nancy R., Richard L. Head sci. dept. Arnold Jr. High Sch., Columbus, Ga., 1960-63; tchr. physiology, Spanish, Jordan High Sch., Columbus, 1963-64; tchr. spl. edn. mentally retarded Muscogee County Sch. System, Columbus, 1964-65; instr. spl. edn. Auburn (Ala.) U., 1966-69; asso. dir. Douglas Sch. for Learning Disabilities, Columbus, 1969-70; prof. edn. and spl. edn. Columbus Coll., 1970-85; ret., 1985; dir. Columbus Specialized Presch.; lectr. Troy State U., Phenix City, Ala. Past sec. exec. bd. Muscular Dystrophy Assn., 1968-70; 73-74; mem. Gov.'s Commn. on Disabled Georgians; past trustee Listening Eyes Sch. for Deaf; mem. adv. bd. Columbus Health Dept. Tng. Centers; chmn. Consumer Adv. Bd. Vocat. Rehab., Mayor's Com. on Handicapped; mem. team for evaluation and placement of exceptional children Columbus Public Schs. Fellow Am. Assn. Mental Deficiency; mem. AAUP, AAUW (pres. 1973-75, div. rec. sec. 1975—), Council Exceptional Children (legis. chmn. 1973-74), Kappa Delta Pi, Psi Chi, Phi Delta Kappa. Roman Catholic. Home: 1811 Alta Vista Dr Columbus GA 31907

DUNCAN, JANET NESTER, hospital financial adminstrator; b. Va., May 17, 1932; d. Conrad Shurl Sr. and Cloria Oleita (Turman) Nester; m. Lonnie Duncan Jr., Mar. 8, 1952; children: Kathy Lynn Duncan Smith, Richard Keith. BS, Radford U., 1986. Sec. Dalton and Poff Law Firm, Radford, Va., 1949; gen. office clk. J. Freezer & Co., Radford, 1950-51; bookkeeper Radford Community Hosp., 1951-52, adminstrv. asst., payroll coordinator, 1959-64, office mgr., 1964-79, dir. fin. counseling and collections, 1979—. Mem. Healthcare Fin. Mgmt. Assn. (cert.). Republican. Mem. Ch. of Christ. Office: Radford Community Hosp Inc 8th and Randolph Sts Radford VA 24143 Home: 1311 Madison St Radford VA 24141

DUNCAN, LINDA LEE, government personnel administrator; b. Balt., Dec. 31, 1949; d. Ervin Ryland and Betty Marie (Jones) Taylor, Jr.; m. Ray D. Charron, Oct., 1975 (div. 1979); 1 child, Jennifer Lorraine Watkins; m. Edgar D. Duncan, May 25, 1985. BA in Human Resources, St. Leo Coll., 1983. Civilian personnel officer Dobbins AFB, Marietta, Ga., 1978-80, chief labor and employee relations, EEO, and tng., 1980-82, personnel officer, 1982—, chief labor and employee relations, 1982-83, 86, employee relations specialist, 1983-85; instr. Gunter Air Force Sch., Montgomery, Ala., 1985-86. Sec., Northeast Cobb Jaycee Women, Marietta, 1984, external dir., 1985, sec., 1986; pres. Cobb Christmas, Inc. Marietta, 1985. Recipient numerous awards U.S. Air Force, 1982—. Mem. Nat. Assn. Female Execs., Federally Employed Women. Home: 2713 Macby Ave Marietta GA 30066 Office: 94 CSG/DPC Dobbins AFB GA 30069-5000

DUNCAN, MARGARET DUNSMORE (MRS. WILLIAM FOWLER DUNCAN), civic worker; b. Summit, N.J., Sept. 9, 1920; d. James and Margaret (Montgomery) Dunsmore; student Fresno State Coll., 1941; m. William Fowler Duncan, June 17, 1940; children—William Fowler, Laird Douglas, Fraser Scott. Gray lady A.R.C., Oahu, Hawaii, from 1959, chmn. vols. Langley AFB; active Heart Fund and Neuromuscular Disease drives; mem. Los Ninos Guild, Childrens Hosp. Orange County; vol. San Clemente Gen. Hosp. (Calif.); program chmn. United Presbyn. Women. Mem. Fairfax Hosp. Aux., Clans of Scotland, U.S.A., Scribe, Internat. Platform Assn., Order of Diana, League Women Voters, Beta Sigma Phi (past chpt. pres.). Republican. Presbyterian. (chmn. missionary edn. women's assn., mariner, fellowship chmn. 1973, 74, ordained deacon 1974). Clubs: Ikebana, Air Force Officers Wives (Washington); Neighborhood Garden; Wheeler AFB Officers Woman's (1st v.p. 1960) (Oahu, Hawaii); Langley Officers Wives, Langley Yacht, Langley Golf; San Clemente Garden, San Clemente Women's; Am. Wives, Am. Officers' Wives, NATO Wives. Home: 6652 17th Ave Court W Bradenton FL 33529-4631

DUNCAN, MARIA LAVONNE, communication company administrator; b. Lincoln, Nebr., Sept. 10, 1954; d. Donald Lee and Ramona Lavonne (Goebel) Dowding; m. Gerald Ray Bolin, Aug. 12, 1975 (div. Jan. 1982); 1 child, Jennifer LaVonne; Albert Chistopher Duncan, June 2, 1984; 1 child, Bryan Chistopher. BA in Psychology, U. Okla., 1976; A in Physics, Math., Rose State Coll., 1979; MBA, Oklahoma City U., 1983. Dist. mgr. Info. Specialists, Oklahoma City, 1976-77; with AT&T, Oklahoma City, 1977—, process coordinator, 1981-83, supr. equipment, 1983-87, supr. purchasing, 1987—; assoc. Abide, Oklahoma City, 1984-86; advisor Duncan Enterprises Ltd. Ptnr., Oklahoma City, 1985—. Mem. St. Eugene Ch., Oklahoma City, 1987—. Mem. Nat. Assn. Realtors (assoc.), Women Execs. Cen. Okla. (treas. 1986—), PTA. Republican. Roman Catholic. Club: Weokie (Oklahoma City) (1st v.p. 1982-83). Home: PO Box 1245 Bethany OK 73008 Office: AT&T Dept 1529 7725 W Reno Oklahoma City OK 73125

DUNCAN, PATTI LOU, lawyer; b. Altus, Okla., July 22, 1955; d. Robert Allen and Erma Lou (Parks) Duncan; m. Richard A. Capshaw, July 3, 1981; children: Christopher Sean, Courtney Anne. B.S. in Econs., U. Okla., 1976, J.D. with honors, 1980. Bar: Tex. 1980. Assoc. Johnson & Swanson, Dallas, 1980—. Contbr. articles to profl. jours. Arthur E. Lippold Scholar, 1977; Brown Oil and Gas award, U. Okla., 1980. Mem. Tex. Bar Assn., Order of Coif. Democrat.

DUNCAN, VIRGINIA BAUER, power corporation executive, television producer and director; b. Lansing, Mich., June 9, 1929; d. Theodore Irving and Maurine Virginia (Foote) Bauer; B.A., U. Mich., 1951; m. Bruce G. Duncan, Oct. 27, 1956; children—John C., Michael G., Timothy B. Producer, dir. KQED-TV, San Francisco, 1960-75; pres. Candide Prodns., Inc., San Francisco, 1966—; corp. exec. Bechtel Power Corp.; dir. Corp. for Public Broadcasting, Washington, 1975-79, First Interstate Bank of Calif., 1979—. Bd. dirs. Town Sch. for Boys, San Francisco, 1966-70; pres., Parents Assn. Marin Parents Assn. Marin County Day Sch., Corte Madera, Calif., 1971-72, mem. public media panel Nat. Endowment for Arts, Washington, 1973-79; chmn. bd. dirs. Yosemite Inst., 1974-84; trustee Katharine Branson/Mt. Tamalpais High Sch., Ross, Calif., 1975-82; assoc. council Mills Coll., Oakland, Calif., 1975—; mem. Carnegie Commn. on Future of Public Broadcasting, 1977-79; mem. Council for Arts, M.I.T., 1977-80; bd. dirs. James Irvine Found., 1979—. Recipient Edward W McQuade award for disting. programming in field of social justice, 1964; NET award for excellence for individual contbn. to outstanding television programming, 1966; Readers Digest Found. award, 1969; CINE Golden Eagle award, 1970; Emmy award Nat. Acad., TV Arts and Scis., 1971. Office: Box 18222 San Francisco CA 94118

DUNCAN, VIRGINIA IRWIN, lawyer; b. Parker Dam, Calif., May 7, 1949; d. George Gothic and Virginia E. (Dick) Irwin; m. Richard Vaughn Duncan, Jan. 25, 1971; 1 dau., Jessica Von. B.S. in Spl. Edn., No. Ariz. U., 1972, B.S. in Elem. Edn., 1972, M.A. in Spl. Edn., 1978; J.D., U. Ariz., 1983. Cert. tchr. elem. edn., spl. edn., learning disabled, gifted, mentally retarded, blind, Ariz.; bar: Ariz. 1983. Dir., instr. spl. edn. program Beaver Creek Sch. Dist., Rimrock, Ariz., 1975-78; instr. Yavapai Community Coll., Verde Campus, Ariz., 1977-78; tchr. Verde Valley Sch., Sedona, Ariz., 1978, Beaver Creek Sch., Rimrock, 1972-79; assoc. Joyce & Frankel, P.A., Sedona, 1983-88, Joyce, Levin & Duncan, 1988—; bd. dirs. Verde Valley Guidance Clinic. Recipient Am. Jurisprudence award Lawyers Coop. Pub. Co. and Bancroft-Whitney Co., 1982, Samuel M. Fegtly award U. Ariz., 1982; Am. Field Service fgn. exchange student, 1966. Mem. ABA, Ariz. Bar Assn., Phi Kappa Phi, Phi Delta Phi. Democrat. Home: PO Box 3275 Sedona AZ 86340 Office: Joyce Levin & Duncan PO Box 3984 Sedona AZ 86340

DUNCAN-TREVIRANUS, ANN, counselor, consultant, minister; b. Phila., June 27, 1935; d. William Howard and Mildredgrace (DeFerbrache) Duncan; m. William Anthony Crimmins, Aug. 21, 1954 (div.); children—Catherine, Tom, John, Hugh, Paul, Eve; m. 2d, Hamish Henry Alexander Stewart Treviranus, Dec. 26, 1983. A.D., U. Maine, 1980; ecumenical minister studies, 1983. Registered nurse, Maine, Va. Pres., filmmaker Noumena, Inc., N.Y.C., Europe, USSR 1971-73; staff nurse Eastern Maine Med. Ctr., Bangor, Maine, 1979-80; family counselor, pvt. practice hypnotherapist, Camden, Maine, 1980-82; staff nurse mental health unit Loudoun Meml. Hosp. Leesburg, Va., 1985-88; with Holistic Health/USA-Asia-Europe for Maine Holistic Health Network, Portland, 1982-83; counselor, cons. Vortex, Inc., Washington, 1982—; founder-dir. Internat. Inst. Transpersonal Diplomacy, 1985—; dir. Rev. Elizabeth Ann Bogert Meml. Fund for Study and Practice Christian Mysticism, Phila., 1983—; dir. U.S. Assocs. for Cultural Triangle of Sri Lanka, Washington, 1983-84. Originator, nat. bd. dirs. Camden/Nuwara Eliya Sister Cities Project, 1982—; mem. Crime Watch, Camden, 1982-83; spl. cons. U.S. Ambassador to Sri Lanka, Colombo, 1982-83; mem. Maine State Soc., Washington, 1982-86. Mem. Am. Holistic Nurse's Assn. (charter), Internat. Transpersonal Assn., Assn. Transpersonal Psychology, Acad. Religion and Psychical Research, Assn. Humanistic Psychology, Maine State Nurses Assn., Am. Nurses Assn., Va. State Nurses Assn.

DUNEIER, DEBRA HOPE, gemologist; b. N.Y.C., Aug. 30, 1954; d. Jacob and Anita Arkow; student Queens Coll., 1976; grad. Gemological Inst. Am., 1980; m. Dana Brad Duneier, Sept. 2, 1971; children—Jamie Troy, Danielle Taylor. With Clyde Duneier Inc., N.Y.C., 1975—, v.p. loose stone div., 1980—; lectr., seminar leader in field. Mem. Am. Gem Soc., Women's Jewelry Assn., Assn. Women Gemologists, Am. Gem Trade Assn. Retail Jewelers Am., Trends Orgn., Am. Biog. Inst. Research (bd. advisors nat. div. 1986—). Address: 1212 Ave Americas New York NY 10036

DUNHAM, ANEVA JO, educator; b. Portsmouth, Va., Mar. 20, 1938; d. Joseph William and Rachel Lorraine (Kight) D.; B.S. in Edn. cum laude, S.E. Mo. State Coll., 1960; M.Ed. in Elem. Edn., St. Louis U., 1972; M.A. in Mgmt., Webster U., 1983. Tchr., Ritenour Consol. Sch. Dist., St. Louis, 1960—; Tri-Hi-Y coordinator YMCA, Overland, Mo., 1963-68; mem. nominating com. Ednl. Employees Credit Union, 1976-77, bldg. rep., 1975—. Bd. dirs. The Connection, 1986—. Coro Found. Women in Leadership tng. award, 1984. Mem. NEA (2nd v.p. 1986—, Women's Polit. Caucus. Kappa Delta Pi, Phi Alpha Theta. Democrat. Presbyterian. Home: 16 Coach Ct Saint Peters MO 63376 Office: 4301 Edmundson Rd Saint Louis MO 63134

DUNHAM, MARTHA JUNE, roofing company executive, consultant; b. Newark, Ohio, May 31, 1954; d. Harold Justus and Elinor Rose (Eschman) D.; 1 child, Anastasia Jean Dunham Parker. Grad. high sch., Granville, Ohio. Social service worker various sites, Oakland, Calif., 1972-79; service and project mgr. Fidelity Roof Co., Oakland, 1979-85; pres., founder Tech. Roof Services, Pleasant Hill, Calif., 1985-88; estimator Enterprise Roofing Services Inc., Concord, Calif., 1988—; cons. Longs Drug Stores of Calif., 1985-88, USN, 1986-88, U.S. Postal Service, 1986-88; pres. adv. bd. Oakland Feminist Women's Health Ctrs., Calif., 1986-87; active Tech. Roofing Services USSSA Softball Team League, 1987—. Recipient Valuable Service award Oakland Feminist Women's Health Ctr., 1982, Outstanding Apprentice award Bay Area Counties Roofing Apprenticeship Tng. Program, 1982, Valuable Service award Advs. for Women, 1985. Mem. Nat. Assn. Gen. Contractors, Tradeswomen Inc., Bldg. Industry Assn., Nat. Roofing Contractors Assn., Roofers Waterproofers and Allied Workers Local Union. Democrat. Club: Big C Athletic. Office: Enterprise Roofing Service Inc 2400 Bates Ave Concord CA 94320

DUNHAM, RUBY LUELLA, financial analyst; b. Kansas City, Mo., Aug. 25, 1937; d. Walter Killian Pflaum and Hazel Mae (Stookey) Ferguson; m. Orrin Loraine Dunham, Apr. 17, 1954 (div. 1976); children: Bertie Phay Loraine, David Eugene, Kevin Scott. BS in Elem. Edn., Mo. Western State Coll., 1974. Cert. elem. tchr., Mo. Mgr. office Glad Rents Inc., Gladstone, Mo., 1974-75; credit analyst E.F. Selby Co., North Kansas City, 1975-78; mgr. credit Cook Paint-Varnish Co., North Kansas City, 1978-81; dist. mgr. credit Lee Apparel Co., Shawnee Mission, Kansas, 1981-86; asst. mgr. credit Denrich Leasing Corp. formerly Westinghouse Credit Corp., Kansas City, Mo., 1986—; cons. Splty. Item Distbrs., North Kansas City, 1981-86, executor-owner, 1965-70. Leader study Christian Women's Fellowship, 1979-74; v.p. East Platte Sch. PTA, sec. 1969; leader 4-H Club, Kansas City, 1972-74, silver service award, 1974. Office: Denrich Leasing Corp 8330 Ward Pkwy Kansas City MO 64141

DUNHAM, SARA LYNNE, dental hygienist; b. Milw., June 4, 1948; d. Roy Henry and Helen Marie (Wagner) Dunham. Student E. Tenn. State U., 1967, U. Tenn.-Memphis, 1970; BS in Dental Hygiene U. Tenn., 1984. Lic. dental hygienist, Ga., N.C. Pvt. practice dental hygiene, Atlanta, 1970-83; pres. Am. Dental Hygienists Assn. Found., Chgo., 1983-84, chmn. bd., 1983-84; nat. dir. practice resources Dental One, Atlanta, 1984-87; interior designer Panache Interior Design, Atlanta, 1988—. Contbr. articles to profl. jours. Mem. Atlanta High Mus. Art, Atlanta Children's Guild. Named Outstanding Young Women of Am., 1982. Mem. Ga. Dental Hygienists Assn. (pres. 1973-74), Atlanta Dental Hygienists Assn. (pres. 1972-74), Am. Dental Hygienists Assn. (trustee 1977-80, 2d v.p. 1980-81, 1st v.p. 1981-82, pres.-elect 1982-83, pres. 1983-84, vice chmn. polit. action com. 1979-80), Nat. Assn. Female Execs., Sigma Phi Alpha. Republican. Methodist Office: Am Dental Hygienists Assn 444 N Michigan Ave Suite 3400 Chicago IL 60611

DUNIO, DONNA KAY, religious organization director, municipal official; b. Alexandria, La., Oct. 31, 1946; d. Robert Lowell and Cumie Violet (Wolfe) Demaree; m. Philip Michael Dunio, Feb. 5, 1966; children: Paul Brian, Cumie Carol. Student, U. Scranton, Pa., 1982—. Dist. mgr. Wm. Taylor, Inc. subs. Elaine Powers Corp., Scranton, Wilkes-Barre, Pa., 1972-74; exec. asst. Moses Taylor Hosp., Scranton, 1974-76; med. asst. Thomas H. Armstrong, M.D., Carlisle, Pa., 1976-78; mem. mgmt. team Spa Health and Fitness Ctrs., Exton, Pa., 1978-81; community liaison, dir. Allied Services, Scranton, 1982-84; exec. dir. United Chs. NE Pa., Scranton, 1984-87; exec. asst. mayor City of Scranton, Pa., 1987—; mem. church and Society com. Wyoming Conf. United Meth. Ch. Bd. dirs. Urban Ministries/St. Anthony's Shelter, Ne Pa. Goodwill Industries, SHINE, Interfaith Found., Womens's Employment Program, Moscow United Meth. Ch., local UN Assn., Scranton Interfaith Friends; mem. local PTA, ; mem. Steamtwon Bd., Downtown Scranton Bus. Assn., Deutsch Bd., Mayor's 504 Task Force, Lackawanna Arts Council, Scranton Library Bd., Leadership Lackawanna. Named NE Woman of Week The Scranton Times, 1985; recipient Women's Recognition award Scranton YWCA, 1986. Mem. Scranton C. of C. (visitors and conv. bur.), Council on Ministries, Tri-County Migrant Assn., Deutsch Inst. Sabbath, Loaned Exec. Alumni Assn., Alpha Sigma Lambda (pres.), Alpha Upsilon (Nat. Honor Soc. scholar 1987-88), Delta Tau Kappa. Republican. Home: RD 2 104 Hollow Dr Moscow PA 18444 Office: City Hall Scranton PA 18503

DUNKEL, FLORENCE VACCARELLO, entomologist; b. Kenosha, Wis., Oct. 10, 1942; d. Vincent James and Mildred (Behr-Naegeli) Vaccarello; m. Thomas Beatty Dunkel, Dec. 27, 1964 (div. 1982); children: Anne-Marie C., Alexander J., Marylynn S.; m. Robert Eller Diggs, June 20, 1987. Student, Lawrence U., 1960-62; BS in Zoology, U. Wis., 1964, MS in Zoology, 1966, PhD in Entomology, 1969; grad. studies, U. Minn., 1973-75. Research fellow dept. entomology U. Minn., St. Paul, 1975-84; team leader USDA Office Internat. Cooperation, People's Republic China, 1982; project dir. internat Agril. programs U. Minn., 1983-87; pres., cons. Internat. Postharvest Systems, Inc., Minnetonka, Minn., 1985—. Vis. Scholar Nat. Acad. Scis. Zhongshan U., 1981; recipient numerous grants for research 1977—. Mem. AAAS, Entomol. Soc. Am. (reviewing editor), Am. Soc. Mammalogists, Am. Assn. Cereal Chemists, Sigma Xi, Gamma Sigma Delta. Club: PEO Sisterhood. Home: 12016 Douglynn Dr Minnetonka MN 55343 Office: U Minn Underground Space Ctr Civil and Mineral Engring Minneapolis MN 55455

DUNKER, LAVONNE BERNIECE, technician nurse; b. Albert Lea, Minn., Apr. 16, 1931; d. Herman Albert and Stella Elizabeth (Larson) Luthe; m. Lowell Herman Dunker, June 21, 1949 (div. 1975); children—Katherine Boylan, Krystal Frink Steven, Julie Wilson. BS in Community Service, Bemidji State U., 1975. Program clk. ASCS, Wadena, Minn., 1965-67; bookkeeper Verndale (Minn.) Bank, 1966-69; sch. health technician Wadena Pub. Schs., 1970-78; house dir. Kappa Kappa Gamma, U. Minn., Mpls., 1978-87; nurse St. Williams Nursing Home, Parkers Prairie, Minn., 1987—; technician Phys. Measurements, Inc., Mpls., 1983-86; camp nurse Herzl Camp, Webster, Wis., summers 1984, 85, 86. Mem. Human Services Task Force, Mpls., 1980-81; govt. agy. monitor United Way Mpls., 1979-81; organizer, project leader 4-H, Wadena, 1960-76; sponsor, chaperone Alateen Teen Ctr., 1970-75. Lutheran. Republican. Home: 218 E Main St Eagle Bend MN 56446 Office: St William's Nursing Home Parkers Prairie MN 56361

DUNLAP, ELLEN S., museum and library administrator; b. Nashville, Oct. 12, 1951; d. Arthur Wallace and Elizabeth (Majors) Smith; m. Arthur H. Dunlap, Jr., Dec. 27, 1972 (dec. 1977); m. Frank Armstrong, May 11, 1979; 1 child, Libbie Sarah. B.A., U. Tex., Austin, 1972, M.L.S., 1974. Research assoc. Humanities Research Ctr. U. Tex., Austin, 1973-76, research librarian, 1976-83; exec. dir. Rosenbach Mus. and Library, Phila., 1983—; dir. Conservation Ctr. for Art and Hist. Artifacts, Phila., 1985—, Greater Phila. Cultural Alliance, 1985—; mem. exec. com. Phila. Area Consortium Spl. Collections Libraries, 1985—. Mem. ALA. Clubs: Grolier (N.Y.C.); Philobiblon (Phila.). Home: 13 Dickens Ln Mount Laurel NJ 08054 Office: Rosenbach Mus and Library 2010 Delancey Pl Philadelphia PA 19103-6584

DUNLAP, MELODY DAWN, publishing company executive; b. Watseka, Ill., June 13, 1959; d. Glendon Jack and Nilo Jo (Bright) Moore; m. Ronald Eugene Dunlap, Aug. 13, 1977 (div. Aug. 1980). AA, Kankakee (Ill.) Community Coll., 1978; BA, U. Tampa, Fla., 1982. Auditor Hillsbrough County Sch. Bd., Tampa, 1983; asst. ops. dir. Houston Gamblers Football Team, 1983-84; acct. Colo. Nat. Bank, Denver, 1984-85; adminstr. Syntrex, Inc., Los Angeles, 1986-86; bus. mgr. Jacksonville (Fla.) Bus. Jour., 1986—, also sec.-treas. bd. dirs. Tchr., interviewer Learn to Read Program, Jacksonville, 1986-87, big sister Big Bros. and Big Sisters, Jacksonville, 1987. Mem. Nat. Assn. Women Execs. Democrat. Lodge: Civitan. Office: Jacksonville Bus Jour 1851 Executive Ctr Dr #227 Jacksonville FL 32207

DUNLAP, SUSAN, social agency administrator; b. Washington, Jan. 1, 1953; d. Richard Morrison and Edith Jane (Boone) D. BA, Wheaton Coll., 1975; cert., Devel. Tng. Inst., 1985. Exec. dir. The Centre Inc., Chgo., 1976-81; asst. dir. Midwest Women's Ctr., Chgo., 1982-86, exec. dir., 1986—; Bd. dirs. Community Workshop on Economic Devel., 1986; adv. bd. dirs. Women's Bus. Devel. Ctr., 1986. Mayoral appointee Chgo. Pvt. Industry Council, Chgo., 1986, Mayor's Commn. on Women's Affairs, Chgo., 1987. Mem. Women in Charge (bd. dirs. 1986), Henry Horner Homes Mothers Guild (hon. 1985), Logan Square Neighborhood Assn. Democrat. Office: Midwest Women's Ctr 53 W Jackson Blvd Suite 1015 Chicago IL 60604

DUNLAVEY, MARY ANN, police captain; b. Keokuk, Iowa, Mar. 14, 1929; d. Ralph Anthony and Ruth Irene (Cramer) Wilkens; m. Richard Emile Dunlavey, Aug. 12, 1948; children—Michael R., Mark A., Cheryl A., James P. A.A. in Adminstrn. Criminal Justice, Ill. Central Coll., 1971; B.S. in Adminstrn. of Criminal Justice, Bradley U., 1973, M.A. in Counseling, 1975; M.A. in Adminstrn. of Criminal Justice, Sangamon State U., 1978; Cert. Delinquency Control Inst. U. So. Calif., 1980; cert. Bus. Mgmt., Bradley U., 1979; cert. Sr. Mgmt. Inst. for Police, 1986. Police officer Peoria Police Dept., Ill., 1964-69, police sgt., 1969-77, police lt., 1977-82, police capt., 1982—. Contbr. articles to profl. jours. Mem. Internat. Police Mgmt. Assn. (bd. dirs., founding mem.), Peoria Police Benevolent and Protective Assn. (local and state). Avocations: aerobics, gardening, crafts, biking, fishing. Home: 4904 Lionel Ct Mapleton IL 61547 Office: Peoria Police Dept 542 S W Adams St Peoria IL 61602

DUNMEYER, SARAH LOUISE FISHER, health care consultant; b. Ft. Wayne, Ind., Apr. 13, 1935; d. Frederick Law and Jeanette Blose (Stults) Fisher; m. Herbert W. Dunmeyer, Sept. 9, 1967; children: Jodi, Lisa. BS, U. Mich., 1957; MS, Temple U., 1966; EdD, U. San Francisco, 1983. Lic. Clin. Lab. Technologist, Calif. Instr. med. tech. U. Vt., Burlington, 1966-67; instr. med. tech. Northeastern U., Boston, 1967-68, instr. lab. asst. program, 1968-70; educator, coordinator sch. med. tech. Children's Hosp., San Francisco, 1970-73; dir. continuing edn. program Pacific Presbyn. Med. Ctr., San Francisco, 1974-82; project mgr., cons. Peabody Mktg. Decisions, San Francisco, 1983-87; sr. research assoc. Inst. for Health and Aging, U. Calif., San Francisco, 1986—; external cons. Health Care Consulting Services, San Francisco, 1987—; seminar presenter Am. Assn. Blood Banks, San Francisco, 1976, Am. Soc. Clin. Pathologists, Miami Beach, Fla., 1977, Ann. Meeting of Am. Soc. Med. Technology, Atlanta, 1977; site surveyor Nat. Accrediting Agy. for Clin. Lab. Scis., Chgo., 1974-80. Contbr. articles to profl. jours. Vol. French-Am. Internat. Sch., San Francisco. Mem. Women Health Care Execs. of Northern Calif., Am. Soc. on Aging, Am. Pub. Health Assn., Health Care Forum, San Francisco Med. Tech. Soc. Club: U. Mich. Alumni (San Francisco).

DUNN, ANNE ROBERTS, optical engineer; b. Champaign, Ill., Nov. 23, 1940; d. Howard Creighton and Elizabeth (Clifford) Roberts; m. Karl Lindemann Dunn, June 24, 1967. BS, Beloit Coll., 1962; MS, Rensselaer Poly. Inst., 1965, PhD, 1969. Research physicist Teledyne Brown Engring., Huntsville, Ala., 1969-76; engr. McDonnell Douglas Astronautics Co., Huntsville, 1976-78; sr. optical engr. Nichols Research Corp., Huntsville, 1978—. Contbr. articles on solar physics and military infrared data analysis to profl. jours. Mem. Am. Astronomical Soc., AAAS. Home: 1044 Joe Quick Rd Hazel Green AL 35750

DUNN, CAROLYN ANN, business services company owner; b. Baton Rouge, Apr. 23, 1950; d. Vincent and Flora (Jones) D. BS, Southern U., 1972; MBA, Rutgers U., 1975. Fin. analyst Rutgers Investment Co., Newark, 1975-77; asst. product mgr. Standard Brands Inc., N.Y.C., 1977-80; mgr. product Welch Foods Inc., Westfield, N.Y., 1981-83, Esselte Pendaflex Inc., Garden City, N.Y., 1983-84; pres., owner Copy-Type Services, Kew Gardens, N.Y., 1984—; cons. DUN-WA Assocs., Kew Gardens. 1984—. Vol. UNICEF, N.Y.C. 1986. Mem. Nat. Assn. Female Execs., Nat. Black MBA Assn. (named outstanding entrepreneur 1987, v.p. N.Y. chpt. 1988). Democrat. Baptist. Home: 123-60 83rd Ave Apt 7S Kew Gardens NY 11415

DUNN, DAPHNE VERONICA, nurse; b. Montego Bay, Jamaica, Oct. 2, 1933; d. John Wong and Ethlyn Louise Haldane; m. Raymond Rudolph Dunn, May 16; children: Tanya, Brian. Degree in nursing, U. W.I., Jamaica, 1956, degree in nursing adminstrn., 1977. Staff nurse U. Coll. Hosp., Kingston, Jamaica, 1956-57, 60-62; sister U. Coll. Hosp., Kingston, 1962-70, supr., 1970-83; pvt. duty nurse St. Joseph's Hosp., Kingston, 1958-60; lic. practical nurse St. Vincent's Nursing Home, Montclair, N.J., 1985-86, charge nurse, 1986—. Mem. Jamaica Operating Theatre Nurse League (life, founder, pres. 1975-77), Nurses Assn. of Jamaica (v.p. 1981-83). Roman Catholic. Home: 155-30 SW 109 Terr Miami FL 33196

DUNN, DARLENE SHEREE, nurse; b. Chgo., Aug. 23, 1956; d. Bruce Wallace and Alma Eileen (Sheridan) D.; m. Eric Dale Bergsten, Nov. 22, 1980 (div. 1986); m. Timothy Darrell Green, Sept. 10, 1988. AS, Ill. Central Coll., 1977; BS, Bradley U., 1980; MS, Coll. St. Francis, 1986. RN. Critical care nurse Meth. Med. Ctr., Peoria, Ill., 1980; employee health dir. Carle Clinic Assn., Urbana, Ill., 1981, cardiac rehab. mgr., 1982—, cons., lectr., 1982—; clin. instr. exercise physiology U. Ill., Urbana, 1984—. Contbr. articles to profl. jours.; presenter TV documentary on fitness. Mem. Am. Coll. Hosp. Adminstrs., Am. Heart Assn., Nat. Assn. Female Execs., Cen. Ill. Soc. Health Edn. and Tng., AAUW, Sigma Theta Tau, Sigma Zeta, Phi Theta Kappa. Republican. Home: 311 Royal Ct Champaign IL 61821 Office: Carle Clin Assn 602 W University Ave Urbana IL 61801

DUNN, ELIZABETH FREDERICKA, marketing executive; b. Balt., Sept. 15, 1945; d. Frederick Thomas and Elizabeth Daisy (Taylor) D. BS, Pa. State U., 1969; MS, Bucknell U., 1970; PhD, Temple U., 1977; postdoctoral, U. Pa., 1981. Sr. market analyst Colonial Penn group, Phila., 1977-79; market planner Phila. Health Plan, 1979-81; cons. Towers, Perrin, Forster and Crosby, Phila., 1982-85; corp. v.p. mktg. and planning West Jersey Health System, Camden, N.J., 1985—; cons. in field. Editorial bd. Guest Relation in Practice, Phila., 1985—. Founding dir. Pa. Women's Campaign Fund, Harrisburg, 1981, Women's Bail Fun, Phila., 1985; bd. dirs. Phila. YWCA, 1983-85. Recipient Jasper award, 1986. Mem. Am. Mktg. Assn. Office: West Jersey Health System Mt Ephraim Ave Camden NJ 08104

DUNN, IMA CHARLENE (DEBBIE), special education educator; b. Pueblo, Colo., Jan. 29, 1941; d. William Arthur and Fern Evelyn (Traylor) Gant. AA, U. So. Colo., 1960; BA in Elem. Edn., U. No. Colo., 1962; postgrad., U. N.M.; MA in Spl. Edn., Cen. State U., 1966; EdD in Spl. Edn., U. No. Colo., 1973; postgrad., Western State Coll., 1975, Ft. Hays State U., 1981. Tchr. Albuquerque Pub. Schs., 1962-65; instr. U. So. Colo., Pueblo, 1966-68; specialist in field experiences U. No. Colo., 1971-73; secondary reading coordinator Pueblo Sch. Dist. #70, 1968-71, coordinator of secondary edn., 1973-74, dir. spl. services, 1974—; lectr., instr. Okla. Council for Exceptional Children, 1966, Colo. Reading Assn. Conv., 1967, U. No. Colo., 1972, Adams State Coll., Alamosa, Colo., 1973; cons. South Cen. Bd. Cooperative Services, 1974-75, Giles Inservice Tng. Model, 1974-75, Right-to-Read, Colo., 1974, Giles Edn. Cen., 1977. Contbr. articles to profl. jours. Mem. NEA, AAUW, Cen. State Univ. Alumni, Assn. Sch. Curriculum Devel. (Pueblo chpt. sec., treas. 1974-75), Colo. Assn. Sch. Execs., Council for Exceptional Children (Pueblo chpt. pres. 1975-76), Council for Adminstrs. Spl. Edn., Am. Assn. Sch. Adminstrs., Internat. Platform Assn., Kappa Delta Pi, Phi Delta Kappa, Pi Lambda Theta. Republican. Methodist. Lodge: Easter Star (grand rep. 1984-87). Home: 229 W Orman Pueblo CO 81004-1837 Office: Pueblo Sch Dist #70 24951 E Hwy 50 Pueblo CO 81006

DUNN, JESSIE JOYCE, psychotherapist, consultant; b. Pineville, Mo., July 16, 1930; d. Silas and Lucretia (Packwood) Clark; m. Robert E. Dunn, Dec. 13, 1958 (div. 1970); 1 child, Jonathan. BA in Soc. and Justice magna cum laude, U. Wash., 1974, MSW, 1977. Counselor Salvation Army, Seattle, 1977-78; therapist Divorce Lifeline, Seattle, 1977-84; pvt. practice specializing in psychotherapy Seattle, 1980—; practicum instr. U. Wash. Sch. Social Work, 1980-81. Screen clients Mcpl. Probations and Parole, Seattle, 1974; bd. dirs. Seattle Counseling, 1973-74, v.p.; coordinator of adult single programs Univ. Unitarian Ch., Seattle, 1979-83. Mem. Nat. Assn. Social Workers, Phi Beta Kappa. Democrat.

DUNN, JOAN ELIZABETH, retail company executive; b. N.Y.C., May 27, 1947; d. Alfonso Granada and Charlotte Fitzsimmons Cunningham. BBA, Thomas Edison U., 1980. Ind. cons. in computers Washington, 1977-80; v.p. sales Ross Systems, N.Y.C., 1980-83; ind. cons. in computers N.Y.C., 1983-85; owner Nature's Touch, Bethany Beach and Lewes, Del., 1985—; bd. dirs. Del. Nat. Bank, Ocean View. Fashion writer Beachcomber mag. of Del. Mem. C. of C. (bd. dirs. 1987, 88). Home and Office: PO Box 80 Bethany Beach DE 19930

DUNN, JOANNA SOUTH, business executive; b. Roanoke, Va., June 8, 1954; d. Charles Edward and Joyce (Karlet) D. Student, Va. Commonwealth U., 1973-76; BA in History, Rutgers U., 1978; JD, Temple U., 1981. Bar: Pa. 1981, N.J. 1982. Asst. city solicitor City of Phila., 1981-84; assoc. Kraft & Hughes, Newark, 1984-85; of counsel ORFA Corp. of Am., Cherry Hill, N.J., 1985-86, v.p. project devel., 1986-87, sr. v.p. project devel., 1987—. Presbyterian. Office: ORFA Corp of Am 51 Haddonfield Rd Suite 325 Cherry Hill NJ 08002

DUNN, JOHANNA ALEXANDRA READ, investment banker, venture capitalist; b. N.Y.C., Mar. 7, 1946. B.A. summa cum laude, Barnard Coll., 1965; M.A. cum laude, Columbia U., 1967, Ph.D. magna cum laude, 1970; postgrad. The Sorbonne, U. Paris, 1969-70. With McKinsey & Co., Inc., N.Y.C., 1967; mng. editor European Bus., Paris, 1969-70; co-founder, chief bus. editor Tempo Economico, Lisbon, Portugal, 1970-74; chief fin. writer for Expresso Lisbon, 1970-74; fgn. correspondent Manchester Guardian, Portugal, 1973-74; communications cons. Citicorp, 1975-76, Norton Simon Inc., 1975-76, Council of Americas, 1975-76; communications specialist N.Y. Stock Exchange, Inc., 1976-78; exec. asst. to office of chmn. N.Y. Stock Exchange, 1978-79, asst. v.p. corp. planning, 1979-80; v.p. mktg. planning and support N.Y. Futures Exchange, 1980-81; asst. v.p. market ops. N.Y. Stock Exchange, 1981-83, asst. v.p. mktg. group, 1984-85; asst. v.p. communications dept., 1985-87; pres., chief exec. officer Stephen R. Petschek Investment Bankers, Greenwich, Ct., 1988—; cons. State Edn. Dept., State U. N.Y., 1975-81. Mem. Pres.'s Council Marymount Manhattan Coll., 1981—; mem. Cardinal's Com. of Laity for the 1980's, Archdiocese of N.Y. Woodrow Wilson vis. fellow, 1979-81; bd. dirs. Spl. Citizens Unltd. Inc., 1980—. Mem. Fin. Women's Assn., Investment Assn. N.Y., Bond Club, Wall St. Planning Group (v.p.), Phi Beta Kappa. Democrat. Presbyterian. Author: Counterpoint: A Book of Modern Poetry, Depois de 25 de Abril, Photo Exposé of 1974 Portugese Revolution; contbg. author Business: Its Nature and Environment; contbr. numerous poems to lit. publs. Avocations: hunting, horseback riding, photography, swimming, music. Home: 750 Park Ave New York NY 10021 Office: Stephen R Petschek Investment Bankers 34 Simmons Ln Greenwich CT 06830

DUNN, JOSEPHANA LEIGH, civic leader; b. Houston, Feb. 5, 1940; d. Joseph Franklin and Lonnie Marie (Rice) Burdett; m. Kenneth Michael Dunn, Feb. 27, 1960 (dec. Oct. 1982); children: Kendall Leigh, Kenneth Michael II. Student, Tex. Christian U., 1957-58, U. Houston, 1958-59. Lic. real estate salesman, Tex. Bd. dirs. Cullen Bank, Sugar Land, Tex. Pres. Ft. Bend County Am. Cancer Soc., Sugar Land, Tex., 1980-81, bd. dirs., 1980—, publicity chmn., 1981-82, chmn. ann. Fund Raiser, 1980; edn. chmn. Galveston County Jr. League, 1973-74, publicity chmn., 1976-77, Holiday Ball decorating chmn. 1970, 74, bd. dirs., 1974-75; silent auction chmn. Texans' War on Drugs Gala, Sugar Land, 1984; co-chmn. Mazda Hall of Fame Golf Tournament, 1985, 86. Mem. Fort Bend County Panhellenic Assn. (pres. 1985-86), Zeta Tau Alpha. Republican. Methodist. Club: Sugar Creek Country.

DUNN, LORETTA LYNN, lawyer; b. Owensboro, Ky, Dec. 3, 1955; d. John Edwin and Arnetta Mae (Trunnell) D.; m. Herbert S. Lunenfeld, Oct. 18, 1985; 1 child, Jack W. BA, U. Ky., 1976, JD, 1979; LLM, Georgetown U., 1983. Bar: Ky. 1979, D.C. 1984. Staff atty. U.S. Senate Com. Commerce, Sci. and Transp., Washington, 1979-86, minority counsel, 1982-86, sr. trade counsel, 1987—. named Order of Coif. Mem. D.C. Bar Assn., Ky. Bar Assn., Washington Internat. Trade Assn., Women Internat. Trade, Phi Beta Kappa. Office: Senate Commerce Com SH-428 Washington DC 20510

DUNN, MARGARET MARY COYNE, journalist; b. Pittsfield, Mass., Sept. 9, 1909; d. Robert Joseph and Margaret Jane (O'Neill) Coyne; student Berkshire Bus. Coll., Pittsfield, Mass., 1928-29; m. John Raymond Dunn, May 29, 1933 (dec.); children—Joyce Dunn Higgins, John Raymond, Joel. Freelance contbr. articles to numerous newspapers, including Boston Post, Boston Globe, The Pilot, Beverly Times, Providence Jour., The Tablet, Montreal Herald and Weekly Star, 1937—, to mags. including Better Homes and Garden, Yankee, Conn. Circle, Modern Baby, Family Digest, others; lectr. in field. Mem. Nat. League Am. Pen Women (pres. Boston br. 1968-70, 74-76, rec. sec. 1970-72, membership chmn. 1972-74, nat. charter chmn. 1974-76, mature women's scholarship com. 1978—, Mass. State pres. 1978-80, nat. auditor 1978-80, nat. roster chmn. 1978-80, nat. orgn. and bylaws chmn. 1982-84, nat. bylaws chmn., 1986-88; co-editor Fifty Year history Boston br., contbg. editor Pen Woman mag., assoc. editor 1980—, pres. Conn. valley br. 1987—, nat. bylaws chmn. 1986-88), Boston Authors Club (rec. sec. 1973, 1st v.p. 1980-82, pres. 1982-86, treas. 1986—), Dickens Fellowship (council mem. 1972—), treas. 1977—), Boston Browning Soc. Club: Women's City (heritage com.). Author: (with Barbara B. Reese) Capture of the Johnson Family (hist. pageant for Charlestown, N.H.), 1954; editor Between Branches, 1974-80. Home: 19 Pilgrim Rd Wellesley MA 02181

DUNN, MARILYN CLAIRE, insurance brokerage firm executive; b. Teaneck, N.J., May 9, 1953; d. Bernard Joseph and Claire Margaret (Langenstein) Dunn. A. in Applied Sci., Bergen Community Coll., 1972. Exec. sec. Fer. Schmetz Needle Corp., Leonia, N.J., 1972-75, Walter Dental Supply, South Hackensack, N.J., 1975-78, Heyward-Robinson Co., N.Y.C., 1978-79, Jones Lang Wootton, N.Y.C., 1979-81; personnel adminstr. Gen. Mills Toy Group, N.Y.C., 1981-85; personnel mgr. Corroon & Black Corp., N.Y.C., 1986—. Mem. parish council St. John's Roman Catholic Ch., Leonia, 1973. Mem. Nat. Assn. for Female Execs. Leonia Bowling League (sec. 1978). Home: 266 Broad Ave Apt E 1 Leonia NJ 07605 Office: Corroon & Black Corp Wall Street Plaza New York NY 10005

DUNN, MARY CATHERINE, research director; b. Norfolk, Va., Oct. 2, 1949; d. Douglas Donald Jr. and Nira Lee (Lenhart) D. Student, Mary Washington Coll., 1967-69; BA in Polit. Sci., Old Dominion U., 1971; MA, Coll. William and Mary, 1979, postgrad., 1987—. Info. planner Southeastern Va. Planning Dist. Commn., Norfolk, 1974-84; asst. v.p., dir. research Goodman Segar Hogan, Inc., Norfolk, 1984—. Chmn. Holly Homes Tour, Norfolk, 1985-86, Night on the Town, Norfolk, 1986; bd. dirs. Young Audiences Va., Norfolk, 1986. Mem. The Women's Forum (sec. 1984-86). Episcopalian. Club: Horizons Circle (sec. 1984-85). Home: 338 W Freemason St Norfolk VA 23510 Office: Goodman Segar Hogan Inc 900 World Trade Ctr Norfolk VA 23510

DUNN, MARY MAPLES, college president; b. Sturgeon Bay, Wis., Apr. 6, 1931; d. Frederic Arthur and Eva (Moore) Maples; m. Richard S. Dunn, Sept. 3, 1960; children—Rebecca Cofrin, Cecilia Elizabeth. B.A., Coll. William and Mary, Williamsburg, Va., 1954; M.A., Bryn Mawr Coll., 1956, Ph.D., 1959; L.L.D. (hon.), Marietta Coll., 1987, Amherst Coll., 1987. Faculty Bryn Mawr Coll., 1958-85, prof. history, 1974-85; acting dean Bryn Mawr Coll. (Undergrad. Coll.), 1978-79, dean, 1980-85; pres. Smith Coll., 1985—. Author: William Penn: Politics and Conscience, 1967; editor: Political Essay on the Kingdom of New Spain (Alexander von Humboldt), 1972, (with Richard S. Dunn) Papers of William Penn, vols. I-IV, 1979-87. Trustee The Clarke Sch. for the Deaf, 1985, Acad. Mus., 1985, Hist. Deerfield, Inc., 1986—, Bingham Fund for Teaching Excellence at Transylvania U., 1987—; dir. Bank of New England West, 1986. Recipient Lindbeck Found. award distinguished teaching, 1969; Fellow Inst. Advanced Study Princeton U., 1974. Mem. Berkshire Conf. Women Historians (pres. 1973-75), Coordinating Com. Women Hist. Profession (pres. 1975-77), Am. Hist. Assn., Inst. Early Am. History and Culture (chmn. adv. council 1977-80), Phi Beta Kappa. Office: Smith Coll Office of the Pres Northampton MA 01063

DUNN, PATRICIA ANN, academic coordinator, educator; b. Englewood, N.J., Mar. 17, 1942; d. Thomas Joseph and Rosanna Valerie (Cummings) D.; m. James Edward Egan, 1963 (div. 1974); 1 child, Deirdre Tracy. BA in English Edn., William Paterson Coll., 1963, MA in Communication Arts, 1974; postgrad., Montclair (N.J.) State Coll., 1988—. Cert. tchr., N.J., N.Y. Tchr. English Ind. Sch. Dist. 218, Brooklyn, 1965-66, tcher., English, humanities, 1966-67, co-chmn. dept. humanities, 1967-68; tcher. English and humanities Midland Park (N.J.) Schs., 1969—, staff devel. coordinator, 1986—; coordinator bus. workshops Women in Bus., 1983, Stress, 1983. Editor N.M. Staff Devel. Newsletter, 1988. Co-founder, coordinator Ministry for separated and divorced Caths., Montclair, 1983-86. Fellow NEA, Nat. Staff Devel. Council, N.J. Edn. Assn., Bergen County Edn. Assn. , Midland Park Edn. Assn. (rep. council). Democrat. Roman Catholic. Club: Garden State Ski (Maywood, N.J.). Office: Midland Park High Sch 250 Prospect St Midland Park NJ 07432

DUNN, PATRICIA ELLEN, marketing and sales executive; b. Norwalk, Conn., Mar. 3, 1958; d. M. Joseph and Catherine (Clayton) D. BA in Govt., Wheaton Coll., 1980. New bus. underwriter MONY, N.Y. C., 1980-81, pension termination specialist, 1981-82, pension service rep., 1982-83; northeastern account exec. CNA, N.Y. C., 1983-84; cons. Johnson & Higgins, N.Y. C., 1984-86, mktg. cons., 1986; dir. mktg. and sales/cons. The Wyatt Co., N.Y.C., Stamford, Conn., Upper Montclair, N.J., 1986—. Mem. Women in Employee Benefits. Club: Wheaton (N.Y.C.). Home: 539 E 81st St Apt 2G New York NY 10028 Office: The Wyatt Co 99 Park Ave New York NY 10016

DUNN, SANDRA PUNCSAK, transportation executive; b. Melbourne, May 28, 1946; d. Frank and Thelma May (Maher) Puncsak; (div. 1978); m. Roger G. Dunn, Feb. 24, 1983. BA in Environ. Design, U. Calif., 1968; MA in Spl. Edn., San Francisco St. U., 1970; MA in Counseling and Guidance, Lewis and Clark Coll., 1974; certificate, Brookings Inst., 1983; postgrad., Columbia U. Dir. project Community Experiences for Career Edn., Tigard, Oreg., 1973-78; dir. dep. ctr. Portland (Oreg.) Job Corps Ctr., 1978; mgr. mktg. edn. div. Ea. and Western regions Singer Co., Washington, 1978-81; mgr. corp. pub. affairs Kaiser Aluminum and Chemical Corp., Oakland, Calif., 1981-84; dir. exec. edn. Pacific Telesis Group, San Francisco, 1984-85; asst. exec. dir. consumer affairs, acting dep. exec. dir. Dallas Area Rapid Transit, 1985-88; assoc. v.p., dir. univ. relations So. Meth. U., Dallas, 1988—. Past pres. Calif. St. Council Vocat. Edn.; past chmn. Gov.'s Task Force on Youth Employment; mem. Leadership Tex., 1987; trustee Tex. council Girl Scouts U.S.; bd. dirs. Dallas chpt. Am. Diabetes Assn., USA Film Festival, Dallas. Recipient Twin award Nat. YWCA, 1983, Presdl. White House award, 1984, Matrix award; named Rising Star, Dallas-Ft. Worth Home and Garden Mag., 1987. Mem. Tex. Pub. Relations Assn. (Best Texan award 1985-86), Tex. Women's Alliance, Exec. Women Dallas. Home: 3628 Binkley Ave Dallas TX 75205

DUNN, SUSAN, singer; b. Malvern, Ark., July 23, 1954. BA, Hendrix Coll., 1976; MM, Ind. U., 1980. Profl. debut in Aida with Peoria (Ill.) Opera Co., 1982; La Scala, Milan, debut in Aida, 1986; Carnegie Hall debut in Die Walkure concert performance; other significant appearances include Requiem (Verdi), N.Y. Choral Soc., 1983, La Forza del Destina (Verdi), Lyric Opera, Chgo., 1988, Un Ballo in Maschera (Verdi), Vienna State Opera, 1988, Il Trovatore, Washington Opera, San Diego Opera; also performances with leading symphony orchs.; recordings of Mass in C (Beethoven), Gurrelieder (Schoenberg), Wagner and Verdi Arias. Recipient Met. Opera Nat. Council award, 1981; winner Phila. Opera Co./Pavarotti Internat. Vocal Competition, 1981, WGN-Ill. Opera Competition, 1983; G.B. Dealey first prize Dallas Morning News-Dallas Opera, 1983; Richard Tucker award, 1983. Mem. Mu Phi Epsilon. Office: care Herbert H Breslin Inc 119 W 57th St New York NY 10019

DUNN, VIRGINIA ROSE (GINGER), securities brokerage executive; b. Gardner, Mass., June 30, 1940; d. Henry Roger and Vivian June (Rouleau) Denis; m. James Edward Dunn, Sept. 19, 1959 (div. Aug. 1984); children: Debra Lynn, James Edward Jr., Jennifer Gaye, Clayton Scott. Grad. high sch., Alexandria, Va. Sec. CIA, Langley, Va., 1958-62; exec. asst. LogEtronics, Inc., Springfield, Va., 1964-69; office mgr. Witherspoon & Lane, Arlington, Va., 1969-77; gen. mgr. Wagonwerks, College Park, Md., 1978-79; sec. Internat. Money Mgmt., Greenbelt, Md., 1979-84, office mgr., 1984-85, v.p. ops., 1985-86, exec. v.p., 1986—, also bd. dirs.; bd. dirs. Internat. Money Mgmt. Corp., Greenbelt, Summit Capital Group, Inc. Mem. Am. Mgmt. Assn., Internat. Assn. Fin. Planners, Nat. Assn. Female Execs. Republican. Office: Internat Money Mgmt 6301 Ivy Ln #514 Greenbelt MD 20770

DUNNAVAN, CAROL CHAMBLIN, educator; b. Maysville, Ky, Feb. 5, 1954; d. Kenneth Harold and Anna Elizabeth (King) Chamblin; m. Jay Calvin Dunnavan, July 7, 1979; 1 child, Elizabeth Ann. Student Cin. Bible Coll., 1972-74; B.A., Morehead State U., 1976, M.A., 1980, Rank I in Edn., 1985. Cert. elem. tchr., Ky. Tour guide Washington Hist. Soc., Ky., 1972-75; tchr. Washington Elem. Sch., Maysville, 1976-78, Mason County Elem. Sch., Maysville, 1978-80; tchr. Straub Elem. Sch., Maysville, 1980—; supervising tchr. for student tchr. tng. Morehead State U., 1980, 83-84, 86, 88; tchr. in film Emergency Preparedness, Ky. Dept. Edn., 1983; activities demonstrator on Edn. Notebook, TV Program, 1985. Active Germantown Christian Ch., Ky., 1975—, Maysville-Mason County PTA., 1976—; camp counselor Northward Christian Assembly, Falmouth, Ky., 1973. Named Outstanding Elem. Tchr. at Morehead State U. Sci. Fair, 1981, 84. Mem. Commonwealth Inst. for Tchrs. (distinguished mem.), NEA, Eastern Ky. Edn. Assn., Mason County Edn. Assn., AAUW, Kappa Delta Pi. Democrat. Club: Mason County Homemakers. Avocations: Interior decorating; floral arranging; needlework; reading. Home: Route 3 Box 610-A Maysville KY 41056 Office: Straub Elem Sch 387 Chenault Dr Maysville KY 41056

DUNN-CAVELLIER, BRIDGET THERESE, insurance executive; b. Highland Park, Mich., Aug. 2, 1963; d. John Joseph and Barbara Ann (Asbury) D.; married, Oct. 1987. Grad. high sch., Troy, Mich. Cert. ins. agt. Receptionist Amerisk Corp., Troy, 1981-83, mgr. life and health ins., 1983-86, salesperson, 1985—; pres. Amerisk Fin. Services Corp., Troy, 1987—. Mem. Nat. Assn. Female Execs., Oakland County C. of C. Republican. Roman Catholic. Office: Amerisk Fin Services Corp 1191 W Long Lake Rd Troy MI 48098

DUNNING, KAREN ELLEN, electronics manufacturing company executive; b. Danville, Ill., Mar. 16, 1956; d. Thomas Wesley and Sarah Anne (Lewis) D. B.B.A. in Fin., Fla. Atlantic U., 1979, M.B.A., 1981. Researcher, Fla. Atlantic U., Boca Raton, Fla., 1979-81, cons., research assoc., 1981-85; research analyst asst. IBM, Boca Raton, 1985-86, Motorola, Inc., 19—; free-lance computer programmer and cons., Boca Raton, Fla., 1983—; adj. instr. fin. Fla. Atlantic U. Mem. Beta Gamma Sigma, Phi Kappa Phi. Republican. Avocations: golf; tennis; woodworking; mechanic; running. Home: 8176 A Thames Blvd Boca Raton FL 33433 Office: 8000 W Sunrise Blvd Fort Lauderdale FL 33322

DUNPHY, MAUREEN ANN, educator; b. Springfield, Mass., Feb. 25, 1949; d. Donald J. and Mary C. (Tabb) Milbier; m. Terrence Michael Dunphy, June 30, 1979. BSE, Westfield State Coll., 1971, MEd, 1975, Cert. Advanced Grad. Study, 1988. Tchr. Thornton Burgess Intermediate Sch., Hampden, Mass., 1971-75; reading specialist, dept. head W. Springfield (Mass.) Jr. High Sch., 1975—. Mem. Long Range Bldg. Needs Com., Westfield, 1986-87. Mem. Pioneer Valley Reading Council (pres. 1977-79), Mass. Reading Assn. (dir. 1977-81), W. Springfield Edn. Assn. (negotiations sec.), Mass. Tchrs. Assn., Hampden Co. Tchrs. Assn. Home: 282 Steiger Dr Westfield MA 01085

DUNWIDDIE, CHARLOTTE, sculptor; b. Strasbourg, France, June 19, 1907. Student, Acad. Fine Arts, Berlin, Mariano Benlliure, Madrid, Alberto Lagos, Buenos Aires, Argentina. Nat. Academician. Editorial bd.: Nat. Sculpture Rev; One-woman shows, Kennedy Galleries, N.Y.C., Salon de Bellas Artes, Buenos Aires, Nat. Horse Show, Madison Sq. Garden, N.Y.C., Aqueduct Racetrack, N.Y.C.; Pimlico Racetrack, Balt., Nat. Arts Club, N.Y.C., group shows include, NAD, N.Y.C., Nat. Sculpture Soc. N.Y.C., Allied Artists Am., N.Y.C., Am. Artists Profl. League, N.Y.C., Hudson Valley Art Assn., Pen and Brush, N.Y.C.; represented in permanent collections including, Mus. Brookgreen Gardens, Myrtle Beach, S.C., Marine Corps Mus., Washington, Mus. Am. Art, New Britain, Conn., O'Bannon Hall, USMC, Quantico, Va., Sem. of Redemptorist Fathers, Suffield, Conn., Ch. of Good Shepherd, Lima, Peru, Nuncio Palace, Lima, also pvt. collections. (Recipient numerous awards including 15 gold medals.). Fellow Allied Artists, Nat. Sculpture Soc. (pres. 1982—), Royal Soc. Arts (London); mem. Am. Artists Profl. League, Pen and Brush (pres. 1964-68). Club: Cosmopolitan.

DUPEY, MICHELE MARY, free-lance copywriter; b. Bronx, N.Y., Feb. 26, 1953; d. William B. and Sandra Nancy (Raia) D.; m. Daniel Michael Gieser, July 14, 1980. BA, Montclair State Coll., 1975; postgrad. NYU, 1981. Product analyst Internat. Playtex, Paramus, N.J., 1975-79; child care counsellor Bergen Residential Ctr., Rockleigh, N.J., 1979-80; asst. to editor Standard & Poor's Corp., N.Y.C., 1981-84; sec. DDB Needham Worldwide Inc. Advt. (formerly Doyle Dane Bernbach Advt. Co.) N.Y.C., 1985-87; freelance copywriter, Jersey City, 1987—. Contbr. articles to profl. publs. Mem. NOW (pres. local chpt. 1982-83, 84-86. chmn. fin. com. N.J. orgn. 1984-85, chmn. fund raising com. 1984-85, mem. N.J. state bd. 1982-86), Women's Direct Response Group (writer newsletter), N.Y. Open Ctr. (ad writer catalog promotion). Democrat. Roman Catholic. Home and Office: 217 7th St Jersey City NJ 07302

DUPLESSIS, SUZANNE, Canadian legislator; b. Chicoutimi, Que., Can., June 30, 1940; d. Jean-Julien and Pearl (Tremblay) Fortin; m. Maurice Duplessis, Dec. 26, 1959; children: Jean-Maurice, Claude. BA, Laval U. Alderman Ste.-Foy, Que., 1981-84; mem. Can. Ho. of Commons, 1984—; v.p. Can. sect. Interparliamentary Union. Bd. dirs. Que. Opera Found. Mem. Ste.-Foy C. of C., Que. Provincial Assn. for Progressive Conservative Party (1st v.p. 1979—). Roman Catholic. Club: Richelieu. Address: 1070 Long Sault, Sainte-Foy, PQ Canada G1W 3Z9 *

DUPONT, FRANCES MARGUERITE, plant physiologist; b. Duluth, Minn., May 23, 1944; d. John Francis and Florence Marguerite (Anderson) Milne; m. Gene F. DuPont, July 15, 1969 (div. Dec. 1980). BA, U. Calif., Berkeley, 1965; MA, UCLA, 1971; PhD, U. Calif., Riverside, 1979. Cert. high sch. tchr. Tchr. Peace Corps, Gulu, Uganda, 1965-68, Homer High Sch., Alaska, 1971-72; lab. technician med. genetics Harbor Gen. Hosp., Torrance, Calif., 1973-74; research asst. U. Calif., Riverside, 1975-79; research assoc. Cornell U., Ithaca, N.Y., 1979-81, ARCO Plant Cell Research Inst., Dublin, Calif., 1981-83; plant physiologist USDA, Albany, Calif., 1983—. Mem. edit. bd. Journal Plant Physiology; contbr. articles to profl. jours. USDA grantee, 1986-88; U.S.-Israel Bilateral Agr. Research and Devel. Fund grantee, 1987-89. Mem. AAAS, Am. Soc. Plant Physiologists. Office: USDA Agrl Research Service Western Regional Research Ctr 800 Buchanan St Albany CA 94710

DUPONT, MILLICENT KATHRYN (KAY), speaker; b. Cedartown, Ga., June 14, 1950; d. Hamilton B. and Kathryn (Millican) duP.; m. Jeffrey E. Disend, Mar. 26, 1983. BA, Samford U., 1978. Office mgr. Robert B. Staats, Atty., Panama City, Fla., 1970-73; exec. legal sec. Hare, Wynn, Newell, Newton, Birmingham, 1973-76; legal asst. Berkowitz, Lefkovitz, Patrick, Birmingham, 1976-79; v.p., owner duPont and Disend Inc., Atlanta, 1980—; sec. adv. bd. Auburn (Ala.) U., 1984—, Kennesaw Coll., Atlanta, 1983—. Author Illusions and Dreams, 1976, Don't Let Your Participles Dangle in Public!, 1983; contbr. articles to profl. jours. Chair pub. relations Am. Cancer Soc., Marietta, Ga., 1984-85; vol. trainer United Way, Atlanta,

1986; del. Rep. Convention, Atlanta, 1987, 88. Mem. Internat. Platform Assn., Nat. Speakers Assn., Ga. Speakers Assn. (v.p. 1983-84), Nat. Assn. for Female Execs. Club: Toastmasters. Office: duPont and Disend 2137 Mt Vernon Rd Atlanta GA 30338

DUPPSTADT, JOHNNA LYNN GALLETT, accountant, consultant; b. Dumas, Tex., May 11, 1952; B.S., No. Ariz. U., 1975. Accounting technician Dept. of the Army, Yuma, Ariz., 1978-82, operating acct., 1982-84, cost acct., 1984-85, supervisory operating acct., 1985-87, supr. cost acct., 1987—. Mem. Am. Bus. Women's Assn. (v.p. 1986—), Fed. Women's Program (asst. mgr. 1985-86), Am. Soc. Mil. Comptrollers (treas. 1984-85) Assn., U.S. Army, Nat. Assn. Female Execs. Democrat. Methodist. Avocations: gourmet cooking, collecting books. Home: PO Box 902 Yuma AZ 85364

DUPRE, CONSTANCE LOUISE, lawyer; b. N.Y.C., July 23, 1933; d. John David and Mary Edith (Pfautz) Pierson; m. Louis Dupre, Dec. 18, 1965 (div. Dec. 1974); 1 son, Christian. B.A., Dunbarton Coll., 1953; M.A., Georgetown U., 1960, J.D., 1966. Bar: D.C. 1967, U.S. Supreme Ct, 1979. Law clk. U.S. Ct. Appeals, D.C. cir., Washington, 1966-67; br. chief OEO, Washington, 1967-73; supervisory atty. EEOC, Washington, 1973-75, assoc. gen. counsel, 1975-82, legal counsel, 1982-85, program dir. region I, 1985-87; clk. of ct., D.C. cir. U.S. Ct. Appeals, Washington, 1988—. Editor, Georgetown Law Jour., 1965-66. Mem. Women's Bar Assn., Sr. Execs. Assn., D.C. Bar Assn. Democrat. Roman Catholic. Avocations: reading, hiking, needlework, hospice vol. Office: US Courthouse John Marshall Pl Washington DC 20001

DUPRE, JUDITH ANN NEIL, real estate agent, interior decorator; b. Houma, La., May 7, 1945; d. Herbert Joseph and Doris Mae (LeFouef) Neil; m. Michael Anthony Dupre, Jan. 7, 1962 (div. Aug. 1987); children: Arienne Danielle, Travis Lance. BA in Psychology, Southeast Okla. State U., 1982. Fin. mgr., supr. Gen. Fin. Loan Co., La., Colo., 1960-69; exec. sec. Progressive Bank & Trust Co., Houma, La., 1973-74; health coordinator Spring Cypress Cultural & Recreation Ctr., 1974-75; bus. mgr., buyer June Morris Boutique, Ardmore, Okla., 1978-79; actress, model David Payne Agy., Dallas, 1985—; real estate agt. Vonnie Cobb Inc. Realtors, Sugar Land, Tex., 1986—; nat. mktg. asst. North American Mortgage Co. (subs. MONY Mut. N.Y.), Houston, 1987-88. Mem. Strake Jesuit-Mothers' Club, Houston, 1985-87, St. Agnes Acad. Women's Club, Houston, 1985-87, Ft. Bend Republican Women, Sugar Land, 1985-86; chmn. Texans War on Drugs, Sugar Land, 1985-86; bd. dirs. MUD (Dist. 6), Sugar Land, 1986—, provider representative SANUS Tex. Health Plan. Mem. Cath. Daus. of the Americas, Nat. Assn. Realtors, Tex. Assn. Realtors, Assn. Profl. Mortgage Women, Alpha Chi. Roman Catholic. Clubs: Sweetwater Ladies Golf Assn., Sweetwater Country (Sugar Land). Avocations: tennis, golf, fishing, boating, dancing. Address: 4747 Nasa Rd #1 #304 Seabrook TX 77586

DUPREE, TERESA HURST, accountant, health facility administrator; b. Savannah, Ga., Feb. 29, 1952; d. Donald Bruce Hurst and R. Lea (Dilbeck) Helms; m. Marvin Vernon DuPree, Feb. 27, 1982; 1 child, Jameson Parker. BBA, U. Ga., 1974. CPA, Ga., Fla. Staff auditor Hurst, Hurst, Higginson & Shipes, CPA's, Waycross, Ga., 1974; staff acct. Richard Aboud, CPA, Jacksonville, Fla., 1975-76; acct. Gaston Photo Finishers, Waycross, 1976-77; asst. controller Beaches Hosp., Jacksonville Beach, Fla., 1977-82, fin. dir., 1982-83; hosp. chief fin. officer Hosp. Corp. Am., Jacksonville Beach, 1983—. Sec. Beaches Area Found. for the Advancement of Healthcare, Jacksonville Beach, 1979-85. Recipient Todays Woman award Village Gazette, Jacksonville, 1986. Mem. Am. Inst. CPA's, Fla. Inst. CPA's, Healthcare Fin. Mgmt. Assn. (v.p. north region 1984-86, bd. dirs. 1986-87). Club: First Coast Civitan (Jacksonville Beach) (charter). Home: 4022 Duval Dr Jacksonville Beach FL 32250 Office: Beaches Hosp 1430 16th Ave S Jacksonville Beach FL 32250

DUPREY, JANET MARIE, county official; b. Plattsburgh, N.Y., Nov. 27, 1945; d. Peter Joseph and Edna Mae Lacy; student Empire State Coll., 1979—; m. Elmer C. Duprey, Sept. 9, 1967; children—John, Michelle. Exec. sec. Eastman Kodak Co., Rochester, N.Y., 1965-66; legal sec. John L. Bell, Plattsburgh, 1966-68; legis. asst. to Sen. Ronald B. Stafford, Plattsburgh, 1968-70; co-owner Rustic Restaurant, Peru, 1967-85; mem. Clinton County Legislature, 1976-86, chmn., 1981-82; treas. Clinton County, 1986—; mem. Champlain Valley Physicians Hosp. Med. Ctr. Corp. Mem. N.Y. State Dept. Social Services Statewide Adv. Council, 1979-81; Clinton County Social Services Adv. Council, 1976-86, Office Aging Adv. Council, Child Abuse Task Force. Mem. adv. bd. Clinton County Div. for Youth; bd. dirs. Hospice Care Services, Council Community Services, Clinton County ARC; mem. SUNY-Plattsburgh Coll. Found. Mem. LWV, SUNY Plattsburgh Coll. Found., Clinton Community Coll. Found., N.Y. State Treas. Assn., Clinton County Hotel, Restaurant and Liquor Dealers Assn. (past pres.), Champlain Valley Bus. and Profl. Women's Club (Woman of Yr. award 1985), Delta Kappa Gamma (hon.). Republican. Roman Catholic. Club: Plattsburgh AFB Officers (hon.). Home: Telegraph St Peru NY 12972 Office: 137 Margaret St Plattsburgh NY 12901

DUPUIS, BONNIE JEANNE, mortgage banker; b. Oceanside, Calif., Mar. 7, 1949; d. Lawrence Joseph and Dorothy Jeanne (Foye-Rost) D.; m. William James Dynes III, Apr. 13, 1968 (div. 1977); children: William James Dynes IV, Ryan Christopher Dynes. Grad. high sch., Vista, Calif. Loan processor Bankers Mortgage Co. (now Transam.), Walnut Creek, Calif., 1969-70; office mgr., sr. loan processor Guild Mortgage Co., Oakland, Calif., 1970-72; loan processor Pacific Mortgage and Loan Co., Oceanside, 1977; br.and office mgr. Keystone Fin., Inc., Vista, Calif., 1977-78; office mgr. Approved Mortgage Corp., La Mesa, Calif., 1978-79, Sunset Mortgage Corp., Vista, 1979-80, Mission Bay Mortgage Co., Escondido, Calif., 1979-80; Office mgr. Internat. Mortgage Corp., Carlsbad, Calif., 1980-81; office and br. mgr. Allstate Enterprises Mortgage Corp., Carlsbad, 1981-82; office mgr. Meritor Mortgage Corp. W. (formerly PSFS Mortgage Corp. W.), San Diego, 1982-85, United Western Funding, Inc., San Diego, 1985, 1st Calif. Funding, Inc., Escondido, 1986; v.p. underwriting, processing, closing Ocean Pacific Fin., Escondido, 1985-88; part-owner Network Mortgage, San Marcos, 1988—; owner B.J. Dupuis Underwriting Services, Vista, 1988—. Democrat. Lutheran. Office: Network Mortgage 334 Via Vera Cruz Suite 252 San Marcos CA 92069

DUPUIS, SHARON BULLOCK, lawyer; b. Lincoln, Nebr., May 3, 1944; d. Richard Brooks, and Betty June (Martin) Bullock; m. Daniel G. DuPuis. A.A., Riverside City Coll., 1968; B.S.L., Citrus Belt Law Sch., 1976, J.D., 1978. Bar: Calif. 1978, U.S. Dist. Ct. (cen. dist.) Calif. Customer service rep. Alumax, Riverside and Joliet, Ill., 1968-70; ptnr. DuPuis & DuPuis, Fontana, Calif., 1979-85; sole practice, Fontana, 1985—. Bd. dirs. Fontana Service Ctr. ARC. Mem. Attys. for Criminal Justice Los Angeles, Attys. for Animal Rights, Inland Counties Women at Law (v.p., pres. 1987—), Valley Trial Lawyers Assn. (pres.), ABA, Calif. State Bar, San Bernardino County Bar Assn., Trial Lawyers Am., DAR, San Bernardino County Employee's Retirement Assn. (bd. dirs.), Sigma Iota Delta. Democrat. Clubs: Fontana Bus. and Profl. Women's (Woman of Achievement 1982, v.p. 1985-86, pres. 1986), Zonta. Lodge: Rotary. Office: DuPuis Law Offices 8414 Sierra Ave Fontana CA 92335

DUQUENOY, LINDA IRENE, health services administrator; b. Providence, R.I., Jan. 2, 1960; d. Dennis Matthew and Irene May (MacIsaac) Lynch; m. Gordon Charles Duquenoy, July 25, 1981; children: Katlyn Ann, Jonathan Dallas. BS in Health Services Adminstrn., Providence Coll., 1982. Exec. intern Office of the Gov. of R.I., Providence, 1980-82; adminstrv. asst. Pawtucket (R.I.) Heart Health Program, 1982-84; tng. specialist R.I. Div. of Substance Abuse, Cranston, 1984—; mem. Gov.'s Refugee Task Force, Gov.'s AIDS Adv. Com. Campaign worker Dennis M. Lynch for Mayor, Pawtucket, 1972-81; campaign vol. J. Joseph Garrahy for Gov., R.I., 1978-84; campaign worker, cons. William T. Lynch for Councilman, Pawtucket, 1986; active Gov.'s Prevention Edn. and Tng. Commn., R.I., 1984—. Mem. R.I. Joint Edn. Com. (sec., 1985—, chair 1986—), R.I. Trainers Council, R.I. Drug Cert. Bd., R.I. Chem. Dependency Profl. Cert. Bd. Democrat. Roman Catholic. Office: RI Div of Substance Abuse Substance Abuse Adminstrn Bldg Cranston RI 02920

DURALL, MARTHA LOUISE, personnel executive; b. Fairmont, W. Va., Dec. 10, 1950; d. Charles Oliver and Dorothy (Morris) McIntire; m. James Raymond DuRall, Dec. 29, 1970; 1 child, Christine Elizabeth. A.G.S., Ind. U.-Purdue U.-Indpls., 1985. Sec., Flint Osteo. Hosp., Mich., 1968-69; office mgr. pvt. physician, Mt. Morris, Mich., 1969-74; personnel sec. Westview Hosp., Indpls., 1974-76; employment coordinator Westview Hosp., Indpls., 1976-81, dir. personnel services, 1981—. Chmn. volunteer devel. com. Indpls. YWCA, 1983-88, pres. bd., 1984-85, nat. conv. del., 1985, bd. dirs., 1983-87, bd. dirs. Marion County Farm Bur. Credit Union, Indpls., 1976-78, Pvt. Industry Council, 1985-88, Pro-Health, 1985-86; vice chmn. fund drive Indpls. Mus. Art, 1983. Mem. Am. Soc. Hosp. Personnel Adminstrn., Am. Soc. Personnel Adminstrn. (dir.-at-large Ind. State Council 1987-89), Indpls. Soc. Hosp. Personnel Adminstrn., Ind. Soc. Personnel Adminstrs., Am. Osteo. Assn. (nat. del. aux.), Ind. Aux. Osteo. Physicians and Surgeons (state sec. 1982-83, v.p. 1983-84).

DURAND, CATHERINE LOUISE, probation and parole supervisor; b. Flint, Mich., May 21, 1948; d. Gerald Frederick and Joyce Leone (Sewell) D. BA in Theology, St. Louis U., 1971, MA in Bibl. Lang. and Lit., 1974. Campus minister St. Louis U., 1972-74, Marygrove Coll., Detroit, 1974; probation, parole officer Mo. Probation and Parole, St. Louis, 1975-77, asst. supr., 1977-79, dist. supr., 1979-82, sr. dist. supr., 1982—; mem. adv. bd. Higher Edn. Council on Ednl. Opportunity Ctrs., St. Louis, 1978—, Human Services Dept. St. Louis Community Coll. At Florissant, Mo., 1983—. Sister Servants of the Immaculate Heart of Mary, Monroe, Mich., 1966-74. Recipient Outstanding Service award Gov. of Mo., 1976. Mem. Am. Correctional Assn., Mo. Correctional Assn., Nat. Assn. Female Execs., Nat. Wellness Inst. Roman Catholic. Club: St. Charles Health and Racquetball. Home: 8 Hickory Hill Dr O'Fallon MO 63366 Office: Mo Probation and Parole 9165 W Florissant Ferguson MO 63136

DURAND, JO-ANN CAROL, accountant; b. Toronto, Ont., Can., Aug. 4, 1957; d. Carl Alexander and Dorothy A. (Shane) Freitag; m. Dale Thomas Durand, Nov. 21, 1981. B Commerce, Queen's U., 1979. Chartered acct., 1981. Audit controller Thorne Ernst and Whinney, Toronto, 1979-83; treasury mgr. Thomas J. Lipton, Inc., Toronto, 1983-87; corp. controller Warner-Lambert Can., Inc., Toronto, 1987—. Mem. Inst. Chartered Accts. Ont. Club: Boulevard. Home: 1847 Briarcrook Crescent, Mississauga, ON Canada L4X 1X3 Office: Warner-Lambert Can Inc, 2200 Eglinton Ave E, Scarborough, ON Canada M1L 2N3

DURANTE, ANGELA, university official, writer, editor; b. Hackensack, N.J., Nov. 20, 1949; d. Louis Anthony and Adeline (Puntolillo) D. B.A. in Comml. Art, Jersey City State Coll., 1972; M.A. Communications, Fordham U., 1979. Tchr. scholastic journalism, art dir. student publs. Paterson Diocesan Regional High Sch. System, 1972-74, 76-79; reporter, editor, designer Key to the News, paper, Kansas City, 1974-75; intern, researcher Sta. WCBS-TV, N.Y.C., 1978; corr. The Record, Hackensack, 1978-79; mgr. univ. relations Fairleigh Dickinson U., Rutherford, N.J., 1979-82; dir. news services U. Mo.-Columbia 1982-85; dir. pub. relations Fordham U., N.Y.C., 1985—; bd. judges Quill and Scroll Soc., U. Iowa, Iowa City; bd. advisors Sta. KBIA-FM, Columbia, 1983-85. Fellow Dow Jones Newspaper Fund; mem. Soc. Profl. Journalists (v.p. mid-Mo. chpt. 1977-78), Council for Advancement and Support. Edn. (scholar 1982, exceptional achievement in editorial content award dist. VI 1983, Nat. Silver medal 1985, 88), Pub. Relations Soc. Am., Women in Communications. Democrat.

DURAN-TROISE, GRACIELA, biomedical consultant, cancer research scientist; b. Buenos Aires, Argentina, Sept. 14, 1943; d. Eduardo and Melida Ethel (Troise) Duran; M.S., U. Buenos Aires, 1969, Ph.D., 1973; m. Ernest A. Montemayor, May 24, 1974 (div. 1987); 1 son, Diego. Fellow U. Buenos Aires, Argentina, 1969-70, Argentinian League for Fight Against Cancer, Buenos Aires, 1970-71; WHO fellow Curie Found. and Gustave Roussy Inst., Paris, France, 1971-73; postdoctoral fellow Nat. Cancer Inst., NIH, Bethesda, Md., 1973-76, vis. asso., 1976-78; sr. research scientist Meloy Labs., Rockville, Md., 1979-80; dir. DTM Cons., Bethesda, Md., 1981—. Bd. dirs. Hispanic Orgn. Profls. and Execs., 1981—; mem. Argentine Woman's Commn. Charity, 1978—. Mem. Am. Soc. Microbiology, AAUW, Tissue Culture Assn., AAAS, Assn. Women in Sci., Argentine Genetic Soc., Am. Transalators Assn., N.Y. Acad. Scis., San Martin Soc. Washington. Contbr. numerous articles to various publs. Home: 8610 Woodbrook Lane Chevy Chase MD 20815

DURGIN, DIANE, lawyer; b. Albany, N.Y., May 17, 1946; d. Leslie P. and Shirley A. (Albright) D. BA, Wellesley Coll., 1970; JD magna cum laude, Boston Coll., 1974. Assoc. Shearman & Sterling, N.Y.C., 1974-83; corp. sec. Ga.-Pacific Corp., Atlanta, 1983—, v.p. law, 1986—. Bd. dirs., mem. exec. and nominating coms. Alliance Theatre/Atlanta Childrens Theatre, 1985—; bd. dirs. Metro Atlanta Ch. of Red Cross, 1988—; bd. sponsors Georgian Chamber Players, Inc., 1986—. Mem. ABA, N.Y. State Bar Assn., Securities Law Com., Order of Coif. Clubs: Broad St. (N.Y.C.); Ga. Exec. Women's Network (Atlanta). Office: Georgia-Pacific Corp 133 Peachtree St NE Atlanta GA 30303

DURHAM, BARBARA, state justice; b. 1942. BSBA, Georgetown U.; JD, Stanford U. Bar: Wash. 1968. Former judge Wash. Superior Ct., King County; then judge Wash. Ct. Appeals; assoc. justice Wash. Supreme Ct., 1985—. Office: Wash Supreme Ct Temple of Justice Olympia WA 98504

DURHAM, CHRISTINE MEADERS, state justice; b. Los Angeles, Aug. 3, 1945; d. William Anderson and Louise (Christensen) Meaders; m. George Homer Durham II, Dec. 29, 1966; children: Jennifer, Meghan, Troy, Melinda, Isaac. A.B., Wellesley Coll., 1967; J.D., Duke U., 1971. Bar: N.C. 1971, Utah 1974. Sole practice law Durham, N.C., 1971-73; instr. legal medicine Duke U., Durham, 1971-73; adj. prof. law Brigham Young U., Provo, Utah, 1973-78; ptnr. Johnson, Durham & Moxley, Salt Lake City, 1974-78; judge Utah Dist. Ct., 1978-82; justice Utah Sup. Ct., 1982—; faculty Nat. Jud. coll., Reno, 1983. Fellow Am. Bar Found.; mem. ABA (edn. com. appellate judges' conf.), Nat. Assn. Women Judges (pres. 1986—), ABA, Utah Bar Assn., Am. Law Inst., Am. Judicature Soc. (bd. dirs.). Mormon. Home: 1702 Yale Ave Salt Lake City UT 84108 Office: Utah Supreme Ct 332 State Capitol Salt Lake City UT 84114

DURHAM, INEZ M., retired parish official; b. Woodville, Miss., May 30, 1909; d. John Riley and Nancy Virginia (Hastings) McCearley; m. Louis Stanley Durham, Aug. 14, 1929 (dec. Feb. 1943); children—Louis Stanley, John Weldon; m. Frank A. Bailey, Feb. 5, 1977. Student pub. schs., Fayette, Miss. Clk. of ct. East Feliciana Parish, La., 1943-80, ret., 1980. Named Woman of Yr., Krewe of Adonis, New Orleans, 1962. Mem. La. Clks. of Ct. Assn. (past mem. bd. dirs.), Hist. Soc. East Feliciana Parish (charter), Jackson Assembly, East Feliciana Pilgrimage and Garden Club, Am. Legion Aux. Democrat. Methodist. Lodge: Order Ea. Star. Home: PO Box 903 Clinton LA 70722

DURHAM, LINDA THEUNE, writer; b. Ft. Leavenworth, Kan., Nov. 11, 1951; d. Stanley William and Carol Ann (Feld) Theune; student U. Ga., 1969-70; B.A., West Ga. Coll., 1973; m. Michael Bryan Durham, Aug. 4, 1973. Sec. The Coca-Cola Co., Atlanta, 1973-75, research asst., 1975-76, research specialist, 1976-77, supr. editorial services, 1977-79, editor internal. publs., 1979-81, mgr. consumer info. center, 1981-83, mng. editor fin. communications, 1983-85, free lance writer, 1985—. Mem. Assn. to Revive Grant Park, 1980—. Nat. Merit scholar, 1969-73. Mem. Internat. Assn. Bus. Communicators. Roman Catholic. Home: 366 Oakland Ave Atlanta GA 30312 Office: 366 Oakland Ave Atlanta GA 30312

DURHAM, PEGGY J., free-lance journalist; b. Boise City, Okla., Aug. 19, 1941; d. John M. and Mildred C. (Phillips) D.; 1 dau., Erin Christine Phillips Durham. B.A. in Journalism, U. Okla., 1963. Dir. public info. U. Tulsa, 1967-70; mgr. communications Honeywell Info. Systems, Oklahoma City, 1970-75; dir. public info. Okla. Bar Assn., Oklahoma City, 1975-77; chmn. bd., partner Metro Media Ltd. Advt. Agy., Oklahoma City, 1977-78; pres. The Word Place Advt. Agy., Oklahoma City, 1978-82; pres. Okla. Feminist Enterprises, Inc., Oklahoma City, 1977-80; freelance journalist. Bd. dirs. PASEO Drug Counseling Center, Oklahoma City, 1970-73; bd. dirs., co-founder Okla. Women's Center, 1973-74; mem. ERA coalition NOW, 1973-73. Named one of Okla.'s 10 movers and shakers in women's movement Okla. Monthly Mag., 1976. Mem. Internat. Assn. Bus. Communicators, Oklahoma City Press Club, ACLU, Okla. Press Assn. Democrat. Editor Okla. Halfway House newsletter Alternatives, 1973; founder, editor Sister Advocate newspaper, Okla.'s only feminist newspaper, 1975-80; co-pub. Red Dirt Women's Press, 1987—. Home and Office: 829 NW 140th St Edmond OK 73013

DURHAM, PHYLLIS DIXON, accountant, management consultant; b. Asheboro, N.C., Jan. 9, 1950; d. Arnold Philmore Dixon and Ronnie LaRue (Greene) Bowers; divorced 1985; children: Dale, Melinda. Student, Belk Tng. Ctr., Charlotte, 1972-73, Asheboro Coll., 1981-82; AAS in Acctg., Randolph Tech. Coll., 1987, AAS in Bus. Adminstrn., 1987. Acctg. supr. First So. Savs. and Loan, Asheboro, 1982-83; sec., tres., office mgr. Profl. Ins. Services, Inc., Asheboro, 1984-87; acct., office mgr. Stewart's Sporting Goods Co., Asheboro, 1987—; pvt. practice acctg., cons. Asheboro, 1985—; cons. Profl. Ins. Services, 1984—, Telephone Answering Service, Asheboro, 1984—. Recipient Cet. of Appreciation Asheboro City Sch., 1978. Mem. Am. Soc. of Notaries, N.C. Soc. Accts., Randolph Assn. Ins. Women. Home: 111 Sterling St Asheboro NC 27203 Office: Stewart's Sporting Goods 135 Sunset Ave Asheboro NC 27203

DURHAM JONES, BONNIE DEE ROETMAN, lawyer; b. Ansted, W.Va., Oct. 5, 1935; d. Edward Terrink and Fern Catherine (McCleary) Roetman; m. Edward Allen Durham, Oct. 1, 1960 (div. 1976); 1 child, Mark Allen; m. Roger Rittenhouse Jones, Dec. 19, 1981. BS, U. Nebr., 1972; JD, Creighton U., 1976. Bar: U.S. Supreme Ct. 1983, U.S. Dist. Ct. (Nebr.) 1972, U.S. Dist. Ct. (N.C.) 1983. Asst. city prosecutor legal dept., prosecution div. City of Omaha, 1977-82; v.p., legal counsel Piedmont Record Classics, Winston-Salem, N.C., 1983—; sole practice, Winston-Salem, 1983-84; assoc. Womble Carlyle Sandridge & Rice, 1984-87; corp. counsel, U.H. Internat., Phoenix, 1987-88, legal counsel Phoenix Record Classics, 1988—; research cons. Nat. Coll. State Judiciary, Reno, 1970-71, Met. Criminal Justice Commn., Omaha, 1971-73. Author: Court Systems Analysis 4th Judicial District Court System, 1972. Pres. Nebr. PTA, Omaha, 1969; chmn. library and reading services Nat. Congress Parents and Tchrs. State Nebr., Omaha City Council, 1972; chmn. legis. com. sch. unit Nat. Congress Parents and Tchrs. 1972, pres. 1972-73; bd. dirs. Halfway House Stop-Over Homes, Inc., 1972; cons. com. mem. Omaha Pub. Schs. Self-Study and Eval., 1972-73. Recipient Service award Nat. Cystic Fibrosis Research Found., Nebr. chpt., 1963. Mem. ABA, Am. Trial Lawyers Assn., N.C. Acad. Trial Lawyers, N.C. Women Attys. Assn. Nebr. State Bar Assn., N.C. State Bar Assn., Forsyth County Bar Assn, Forsyth County Women Attys. Assn., Forsyth County Def. Attys. Assn. (v.p.), Nebr. Personnel and Guidance Assn., AAUW, Alpha Phi Sigma. Lutheran. Home: 5122 E Shea Blvd Scotsdale AZ 85254 Office: Phoenix Record Classics 12629 W Tatum Blvd Suite 612 Phoenix AZ 85032

DURHAM-MCLOUD, DIANNA, state agency director; b. Memphis, Sept. 30, 1947; d. Horace Cary and Charlotte Virginia (Cain) Goode; m. William Dawson McLoud, Jr., Aug. 26, 1978; 1 child, William Dawson McLoud III. BA in Pub. Adminstr., Purdue U., 1969; MPA, Ind. U., 1974. Community service rep. AT&T, Indpls., 1969-71; asst. dir. Urban League NW Ind., Gary, 1972-76; mgmt. asst. specialist Nat. Urban League, Chgo., 1976-79, regional coordinator, 1979-82, asst. dir., 1982-84; dep. dir. Ill. Dept. Employment Security, Chgo., 1984—. composer inspirational songs. V.p. Hull House Assn., 1982-85, also bd. dirs.; bd. dirs. Women Employed Network, 1986—, Network Black Women, 1984—; vice-chairperson Midwest Minority Womens Caucus, 1979—; co-chair UNCF Telethon, 1986; trustee, Bible instr. Ch. Christ. Recipient Outstanding Citizen award Ill. Dept. Human Rights, 1983, Disting. Service award, U.S. Dept. Labor, 1984; named one of Outstanding Young Women, 1981, Woman of the Yr. Ind. Assn. Social Service Agys., 1978. Mem. NAACP, Internat. Assn. Personnel Employment Security, Nat. Urban Affairs Council (chair telethon 1986), Delta Sigma Theta. Home: 908 Dempster St Evanston IL 60202

DURISHIN-WILLIAMS, MIKKI TERRY, small business owner, marketing professional, consultant; b. Bronx, N.Y., July 4, 1943; d. Louis Schwartzbaum and Bette (Rubinstein) Rawson. m. Gabriel Michael Durishin, June 25, 1966 (dec. Feb. 1973); 1 child, Jason Todd; m. Anthony John Williams, June 4, 1977. BS in Phys. Edn., Ithaca Coll., 1965; MBA in Hotel Mgmt., U. New Haven, 1987. Instr. various high schs., N.Y., Conn., 1965-70; choreographer, performer various theaters, univs., N.Y., Conn., 1970-76; owner gourmet catering service The Happy Cooker, N.Y., Conn., 1973-79; owner A Dance Class, Westport, Conn., 1976-87, The Body Firm, Fairfield, Conn., 1980-87, Kisses Boutique, Westport, 1982-84; founder The Mikki Williams Dancers, Westport, 1977-87; dir. dance div. Univ. Bridgeport (Conn.), 1977-78; seminar speaker, cons. Mikki Williams Unltd., 1984—; program mktg. mgr. Conn. Pub. Broadcasting System; state rep. Internat. Dance Exercise Assn., Conn., 1985—; adv. bd. mem. Reebok, New Eng., 1986—. Artistic dir. Young Americans Dance Fest. (first place award, 1987). Governing bd. Levitt Pavilion Performing Arts, Westport, 1978—; ; mistress of ceremonies Leukemia Soc., March of Dimes, Westport, Stamford, 1980—; chmn. Town of Westport 150th Birthday Celebration, 1985. Recipient Am. Regional Cuisine award Culinary Inst. Am., Hyde Park, N.Y., 1986, Showmanship, Originality award Young Ams. Invitational, Las Vegas, 1987, Presidential Sports award, 1987; named Outstanding Conn. Women Decade United Nations, 1987; Eli Whitney Entrepreneurial award, 1987. Mem. Am. Soc. Assn. Execs. (convention mgmt. 1987), Nat. Assn. Female Execs., Nat. Speaker's Assn., Am. Coll. Sports Medicine, Entrepreneural Women's Network (pres. 1987—), Am. Woman's Econ. Devel. Corp., Westport C. of C., SACIA. Democrat. Jewish. Home and Office: 40 Hermit Ln Westport CT 06880

DURKIN, DOROTHY ANGELA, university administrator; b. Glen Cove, N.Y., June 23, 1945; d. Frank Vincent and Rose Marie Durkin; ; 1 child, David Francis. BA, SUNY, Stony Brook, 1968; MA, NYU, Stony Brook, 1974. Adminstrv. asst. SUNY, Stony Brook, 1965-67; prodn. editor Holt, Rhinehart & Winston, Inc., Stony Brook, 1967-69; editor Hill & Wang Pub., Inc., N.Y.C., 1969-70; asst. dir. pub. info. NYU Sch. Continuing Edn., N.Y.C., 1970-72, asst. dean pub. affairs and student services, 1972—; cons. N.Y.C. Center for Lifelong Learning, 1974. Recipient Andy Advt. award of merit, 1972; Direct Mktg. Leadership award, 1977, 87; Nat. Univ. Continuing Edn. Assn. awards, 1978, 81-87; merit award Art Dirs. Club, 1980; Merit award Soc. of Illustrators, 1980. Mem. Am. Coll. Pub. Relations Assn. (nat. award 1973), Council for Advancement and Support of Edn. (award 1981, 82, 83, 84, 86, 87, 88, Admissions Mktg. Report awards 1986, 87, John Caples award for mixed-media consumer advtg. category, 1987 , Gold Medal TV Merit award Newspaper), Women in Communications (job chmn.), N.Y. Radio Broadcasters Assn. (Big Apple award 1985), Nat. Univ. Continuing Edn. Assn. (chmn. info. services div. 1980-81, mktg. task force 1986—), Pub. Relations Soc., Am. Demographics, Direct Mktg. Assn. (speaker, cons. coll. bd., Echo Leadership award 1987), Council for Advancement and Support of Edn. (silver medal, bronze medal 1988), Pub. Relations Soc., Am. Demographics, SUNY Alumni Assn. Office: NYU Sch Continuing Edn 126 Shimkin Hall New York NY 10003

DURKIN, ELIZABETH ANN, business executive; b. Sacramento, Dec. 11, 1959; d. Richard Joseph and Agatha M. (Palmer) D. BA, St. Anselm Coll., 1981; MA in Adminstrn., Framingham (Mass.) State Coll., 1984. Computer input operator Am. Biosci. Labs., Waltham, Mass., 1981-84; supr. accounts receivable Clin. Data, Inc., Boston, 1984-85; bus. mgr. The Family Ctr., Inc., Somerville, Mass., 1985—. Chairperson com. St. Barbara's Fall Festival, Woburn, Mass., 1986, 87. Mem. Nat. Assn. Female Execs., Am. Soc. Profl. and Exec. Women. Democrat. Roman Catholic. Club: St. Barbara's Womens (Woburn) (sec. 1985-87). Office: The Family Ctr Inc 385 Highland Ave Somerville MA 02144

DURR, JANIS JOY, home entertainment corporation executive; b. Ann Arbor, Mich., Mar. 3, 1947; d. Elwood Harry and Genevieve Joy (Southworth) Ball; m. Richard Theodore Durr, Sept. 8, 1973 (div. Aug. 1980). BA in Psychology, Monmouth Coll., 1969. Computer saleswoman LAG Drug Co., Chgo., 1976-77; regional mgr. Sales Maids of Am., Westport, Conn., 1977-78; sales rep. MST, Inc., Skokie, Ill., 1979, Northrop Data Systems Corp., Rosemont, Ill., 1979-80; video specialist MCA, Inc., Rosemont, 1980-81, regional video dir.,1981-87, dir. nat. video accounts,

MCA, Inc., Universal City, Calif., 1987—. Mellinger Found. fellow, 1966-69. Mem. NOW, Am. Film Inst., Mus. Sci. and Industry. Presbyterian. Office: MCA Inc 70 Universal City Plaza Universal City CA 91608

DURSO, EMILY FRANCES, marketing executive; b. Washington, Aug. 28, 1950; d. Thomas Anthony and Frances (Davern) D. BA in History, Georgetown U., 1973. Owner, operator Francis Scott Key Book Shop, Washington, 1973-78; spl. asst. to pub. parking adminstr. D.C. Dept. Transp. 1978-79; legis. aide to mem. D.C. City Council, 1979-80; asst. dir. D.C. Office of Bus. and Econ. Devel., 1980-83, dir. promotions, 1983-84; spl. asst. to dep. mayor for econ. devel., Washington, 1984-85; mktg. mgr. Techworld, Washington, 1985-87, v.p. mktg., 1987; bd. dirs. Fed. City Nat. Bank, 1988—; mem. exec. bd. Washington Conv. and Visitors Assn., 1982-87; bd. dirs. Internat. Visitors's Info. Service, Washington, 1983—, Mayor's Design Commn. Mem. Ward Two Dems., Washington, 1984. Bd. dirs. Washington Urban League; trustee Meridian House; mem. Design Adv. Steering Com., Washington. Home: 2153 California St NW #102 Washington DC 20008 Office: Techworld 901 8th St NW Washington DC 20001

DURST, BARBARA, non-profit association executive; b. N.Y.C., Jan. 9, 1943; d. Marc and Beatrice (Grossfeld) Durst. BA in Polit. Sci., Hunter Coll., 1964; postgrad. in pub. adminstrn., NYU. Tchr. English N.Y.C. Bd. Edn., 1964-66; specialist community relations Urban Renewal Agy., Tarrytown, N.Y., 1966-67; urban planner Hudson River Valley Community Tarrytown, 1967-69; urban renewal rep. N.Y. Div. Housing, N.Y.C., 1970; project dir. N.Y.C. Housing Preservation and Devel., 1970-79; exec. dir. NHS of Ft. Worth, Tex., 1979—. Bd. dirs. Dan Danciger Jewish Community Ctr., 1981-87, Hist. Preservation Ctr. Tarrant County, Hebrew Day Sch., Ft. Worth, 1985—, Southside Preservation League, 1986—; council mem. Englewood Community Ctr.; chair Neighborhood Adv. Council, 1985-86. Recipient Cert. of Recognition for service to Poly. Neighborhood Adv. Council, City of Ft. Worth, 1986, Senate Proclamation of Appreciation service to community; named Hon. Tex. Citizen, 1986. Fellow Nat. Trust for Hist. Preservation. Democrat. Avocations: reading, travel, needlework. Office: Neighborhood Housing Services of Ft Worth 3301 E Rosedale Fort Worth TX 76112

DUSSEAULT, MARY LOUISE, paralegal; b. Framingham, Mass., June 14, 1953; d. Frederick Joseph and Mary Louise (Claffey) D. AA, Quinsigamond Community Coll., Worcester, Mass., 1975; BS in Bus. Mgmt., U. Lowell, 1985. Sec. with Dept. of Defense, Bedford, Mass., 1975-78, acctg. technician, 1978-82; office adminstr. Zilog, Inc. (affiliate of Exxon, Inc.), Burlington, Mass., 1982-86; paralegal Marshall & Snyder, Attys At Law, Burlington, 1987—. Music minister Ch. of St. Theresa, N. Reading, Mass., 1985—. Mem. Alpha Nu Omega. Republican. Roman Catholic. Office: Marshall & Snyder Attys At Law 10 Mall Rd Suite 150 Burlington MA 01803-4199

DUTCHER, BARBARA ANN, linen services executive; b. Moose Lake, Minn., July 2, 1955; d. Vernon Ernest and Helen Elizabeth (Viita) Beck; m. Dean Mark Dutcher, June 28, 1980 (div. May 1984). AA, St. Mary's Jr. Coll., Mpls., 1975; BA in Applied Sci., U. Minn., 1980. Instr. McDonell Ctr., Mpls., 1975-78, Portland Resident, Mpls., 1978-80; supr. dir. Community Hosp. Linen Services, Mpls., 1980—; project engr. Foussard Mgmt. Services, St. Paul, 1983-86. Mem. Assn. Operating Room Nurses, Nat. Assn. Instl. Laundry Mgrs. Democrat. Lutheran. Home: 3621 Newton Ave N Minneapolis MN 55412 Office: Community Linen Services 201 Royalston Ave Minneapolis MN 55405

DUTCHER, LISA DELAYNE, construction executive; b. Grand Rapids, Mich., Apr. 7, 1956; d. Bruce Irwin and Patricia Louise (Campbell) Dutcher. Student Grand Valley State U., 1975-76, Mich. State U., 1976-77, Davenport Coll., 1977, Internat. Acad. Merchandising and Design, 1978, Rock Valley Coll., 1979, 84. Draftsman, surveyor Heritage Engring., Rockford, Ill., 1979; engr. technician II City Belvidere (Ill.), 1979-81; adminstrv. asst. City of Rockford, 1981-82, ops. analyst, 1982-86; constrn. project controller WW Facilities Group, Grand Rapids, Mich., 1987—. Rep. City of Rockford Emergency Services, 1981-86; group leader quality circle Rockford (Ill.) Pub. Works, 1983-86; mem. Rockford Interactions Teams, Rockford, 1983-86. Mem. Nat. Assn. Female Execs., Nat. Assn. Women in Constrn., Am. Bus. Women Assn. Congregationalist. Home: 51 Johns Woods Dr Rockford IL 61103 Office: WW Facilities Group 5555 Glenwood Hills Pkwy Grand Rapids MI 49508

DUTCHER THORNTON, ALICE MARILYN, musician, educator; b. Grand Rapids, Mich., Aug. 11, 1934; d. Minor David and Mary Jeanette (Croninger) Dutcher; m. William James Thornton, Mar. 3, 1984. AA, Pine Manor Jr. Coll., 1954; MusB in Voice, U. Mich., 1956, MusM in Voice, 1958; postgrad., New Eng. Conservatory, 1960-62, Goethe Inst., Blaubeuren, Fed. Republic of Germany, 1966. Instr. voice, music lit. Kans. State Coll., Pittsburg, 1959-60; chair dept. voice Pine Manor Jr. Coll., Wellesley, Mass., 1960-63; instr. voice Detroit Inst. Musical Art, 1964-66; soloist various Chs., N.Y.C., 1967-68, 69-72; mezzo soprano Nat. Artist Co., Seattle Opera, 1968-69; mgr. Wolf Trap Farm Park Co., Vienna, Va., 1972; asst. prof. voice Grand Valley State Colls., Allendale, Mich., 1972-74, Chgo. Musical Coll., Roosevelt U., 1974-84; owner pvt. studio San Antonio, 1984-86; instr. voice San Antonio Coll., 1986—; clinician Alexander technique U. Okla., Norman, 1986, Sch. Music, Okla. State U., Stillwater, 1987, Sch. Music, Sam Houston State U., Huntsville, Tex., 1987, Sch. Ch. Music, Southwestern Bapt. U., Ft. Worth, 1987, 1987, others; adjudicator Young Tex. Music Award, Conroe, 1987. Winner Am. opera auditions debut Milan teatro nuovo, 1966; debut Cin. Zoo Opera; recitals, opera and concert appearances, Can., Europe. Fundraiser San Antonio chpt. Am. Cancer Soc., 1986-87. Mem. Soc. Tchrs. Alexander Technique, N.Am. Soc. Tchrs. Alexander Technique, Nat. Assn. Tchrs. Singing (bd. dirs. Chgo. chpt. 1980-83, tchr., nat. conv. Chgo. 1986, soloist 1987), Nat. Soc. Arts and Letters (tchr.). Episcopalian. Club: Tuesday Musical (San Antonio). Home: 347 Sharon Dr San Antonio TX 78216 Office: San Antonio Coll San Antonio TX 78284

DUTIKOW, IRENE VLADIMIROVNA, librarian; b. Tallinn, Estonia, USSR, Nov. 7, 1938; came to U.S., 1951; d. Vladimir A. and Ludmilla P. (Minjaev) Vekshin; m. Wsewolod M. Dutikow, July 26, 1959; children: Ekateriana, Larissa. BA, Hunter Coll., 1970; MLS, NYU, 1975, MA, 1980. Cert. librarian, N.Y. Tech. asst. N.Y.C. Pub. Library, 1970-78, librarian, 1978-80; reference librarian, head librarian Radio Free Europe-Radio Liberty, Inc., N.Y.C., 1980—. Author: K.I. Chukovsky, 1975, 2d edit., 1979; contbr. to profl. publs.; compiler scrapbooks on Greek and Brit. royal families. Mem. ALA, Am. Assn. Advancement of Slavic Studies, Spl. Library Assn., Congress Russian Ams. (pres. Flushing chpt. 1978—), Slavic Heritage Council Am. (bd. dirs. 1979-85). Republican. Russian Orthodox. Home: 43-38 Colden St Flushing NY 11355 Office: Radio Free Europe Radio Liberty Inc 1775 Broadway New York NY 10019

DUTIL, LISE LETENDRE, construction company executive, real estate officer; b. Drummondville, Que., Apr. 13, 1947; came to U.S., 1968, naturalized, 1977; d. Roland and Rose Alma (Morin) Letendre; m. Aime Dutil, Sep. 4, 1971; children: Erica, Genevieve. BBA summa cum laude, Western New England Coll., 1986. Treas. A. Dutil, Inc., Hampden, Mass., 1974—; mgr. Dutil Real Estate Rental, Hampden, 1985—. Mem. Home Builders Assn., Rental Assn. Greater Springfield (Mass.). Club: Springfield Ski (Blandford, Mass.). Homeand Office: A Dutil Inc 44 Forest Hills Rd Hampden MA 01036

DUTKA, MINDY, sales executive; b. Yonkers, N.Y., Sept. 14, 1959; d. Robert Milton and Cynthia (Rose) D.; m. Joel A. Sweetbaum, July 8, 1984. BA in Communications, Ariz. State U., 1981. Account rep. Reuben H. Donnelley, N.Y.C., 1982-83; advanced systems specialist Pitney Bowes, N.Y.C., 1983-85; account exec. Harrison Conf. Ctr., Tarrytown, N.Y., 1985-86; dir. sales Chase Manhattan Bank, N.Y.C., 1987—. Mem. Meeting Planners Internat. Jewish. Office: Chase Devel Ctr 33 Maiden Ln New York NY 10038

DUTTON, LOIS ANN, consulting firm executive; b. Pensacola, Fla., Mar. 9, 1939; d. Cecil Ivor and Juanita (Locklear) D. B.S. in Nursing, U. N.C., 1965; M.P.H., 1966; Ph.D., U. Ala., 1984. R.N., Fla., Ala. Program dir. Alcoholism Services, Winter Haven, Fla., 1973-77; exec. dir. Tri-County Alcoholism Services, Inc., Winter Haven, 1975-80; asst. prof. U. Ala.-Birmingham, 1980-85; cons. Comprehensive Care Corp., Irvine, Calif., 1985-86; pres. Dutton Assocs., Inc, Tampa, Fla., 1985—; cons. Fla. Adv. Bd. for Profl. Alcoholism Edn. and Tng., Tallahassee, 1978-80; chairperson community health council U. Ala.-Birmingham, 1981-83. Mem. adv. task force Gov.'s Task Force for Devel. Alcoholism Program Standards, Tallahassee, 1977-80; adv. counsel Spouse Abuse Program, Lakeland, Fla., 1979-80; mem. edn. com. Am. Cancer Soc., Birmingham, 1981-85; instructional specialist ARC, Birmingham, 1984—; active Track Club, Tampa. Recipient Outstanding Faculty award U. Ala.-Birmingham sr. nursing students, 1983. Mem. Am. Nurses Assn., Am. Pub. Health Assn., Fla. Nurses Assn., Nat. Assn. Female Execs., Sigma Theta Tau, Kappa Delta Pi. Republican. Roman Catholic. Avocations: running; painting; guitar.

DUTTON, PAULINE MAE, fine arts librarian; b. Detroit, July 15; d. Thoralf Andreas and Esther Ruth (Clyde) Tandberg; B.A. in Art, Calif. State U., Fullerton, 1967; M.S. in Library Sci., U. So. Calif., 1971; m. Richard Hawkins Dutton, June 21, 1969. Elem. tchr., Anaheim, Calif., 1967-68, Corona, Calif., 1968-69; fine arts librarian Pasadena (Calif.) Public Library, 1971-80; art cons., researcher, 1981—. Mem. Pasadena Librarians Assn. (sec. 1978, treas. 1979-80), Calif. Library Assn., Calif. Soc. Librarians, Art Librarians N.Am., Nat. Assn. Female Execs., Am. Film Inst., Am. Entrepreneurs Assn., Gilbert and Sullivan Soc., Alpha Sigma Phi. Club: Toastmistress (local pres. 1974).

DUTTON, TAMARA LEA, bookstore manager; b. Colby, Kans., Oct. 4, 1948; d. Marshall W. and Ethelyn (Dimmitt) D.; m. Timothy A. Miller, Aug. 13, 1982; childre: Jesse, Abraham. AB, U. Kans., 1970. Mgr. Law Sch. Book Exchange, Lawrence, Kans., 1978—. Treas. Oread Neighborhood Assn., Lawrence, 1980-81; coordinator local polit. campaigns, Lawrence, 1979-83. Democrat. Home: 620 Indiana Lawrence KS 66044 Office: Law Sch Book Exchange 103A Green Hall Lawrence KS 66045

DUTZ, ELFRIEDE IRMA, pathologist; b. Vienna, Austria, June 23, 1926; came to U.S., 1974; d. Leopold and Valerie Kohout; m. Werner F. Dutz, Sept. 1956; children: Peter, Michael. MD, U. Vienna, 1952. Diplomate Am. Bd. Med. Microbiology. Intern Misericordia Hosp., Edmonton, Alta., Can., 1955-56; resident Nassau County Gen. Hosp., Hempstead, N.Y., 1956-58; from asst. to assoc. prof. Pahlavi U., Shiraz, Iran, 1960-68; prof. clin. pathology Med. Coll. Va., Richmond, 1974—; cons. Aramco, Dharan, Saudi Arabia, 1973-74. Author more than 70 articles and book chpts. Fellow Am. Soc. Clin. Pathologists, Am. Soc. Trop. Medicine, Am. Acad. Microbiology, Am. Bd. Pathology (specialist med. microbiology 1985); mem. Coll. Pathologists. Home: 4306 Oxford Circle W Richmond VA 23221 Office: McGuire Va Med Ctr 1201 Broad Rock Rd Richmond VA 23240

DUVA, DONNA MARIE, financial executive; b. Paterson, N.J., June 28, 1956; d. Alfred Dominick and Frances P. (D'Andrea) D. AAS, Bergen Community Coll., 1976; BBA in Acctg., Ramapo Coll., 1985. Bookkeeper Passaic County Treas. Office, Paterson, 1973-77; acctg. tutor Bergen Community Coll., Paramus, N.J., 1974-76; full charge bookkeeper Weisz Supermarket, Inc., Clifton, N.J., 1977-79; acct. Beecham, Inc., Clifton, 1980-85; chief fin. officer, controller Al Duva Enterprises, Inc., Paterson, 1976—; chief fin. officer, acctg. mgr. Power Battery Corp., Paterson, 1986—; Author newspaper editorials Paterson Evening News, 1976. Mem. N.J. Soc. Notary Pubs., Ramapo Coll. Alumni Assn., Bergen Community Coll. Alumni Assn., Nat. Assn. Female Execs. Democrat. Roman Catholic. Home: 205 Vernon Ave Paterson NJ 07503 Office: Power Battery Co Inc 543-53 E 42d St Paterson NJ 07513

DUVAL, BETTY ANN, financial publishing and news service executive; b. Springfield, Mo., May 13, 1921; d. William and Marie T. (Townsend) D. B.A. in Psychology, DePauw U., 1943. Mgr. tng. RCA, Camden, N.J., 1943-57; dir. personnel planning and devel., also other personnel positions Gen. Foods Co., White Plains, N.Y., 1957-80; v.p. staff devel. Dow Jones & Co. Inc., N.Y.C., 1980-86, sr. v.p., 1986—. Mem. greater consistory Ref. Ch., Bronxville, N.Y., 1973—. Club: Siwanoy Country (Bronxville, N.Y.).

DUVAL, CYNTHIA, museum curator; b. Port Talbot, South Wales, Oct. 6, 1932; came to U.S., 1972; d. Joseph and Esther (Goldberg) Armstrong; m. Marcel Duval, Aug. 26, 1973; 1 son, Jonathan Armstrong. Intermediate degree, Chelsea Sch. Art, London, 1953. Antiques buyer Harrod's, London, 1972-73; gen. appraiser Sotheby's, N.Y., 1973-77; lectr. Ringling Sch. Art, Sarasota, Fla., 1977-79; adminstr. Ringling program Tampa Ringling Mus. Art, Sarasota, 1979-80, sr. curator decorative arts, 1980—; advisor State Div. of Culture, 1985—; grants panelist for visual arts, Fla., 1985—; liaison to Gov.'s Mansion, Tallahassee. Author: History of Lighting and Lamps, 1972; Toys of Long Ago, 1972; The Life of a Gentleman, 1972; Love and Marriage, 1972. Author: (catalog) 500 Years of the Decorative Arts, 1984; Medieval and Renaissance Armor, 1984. Recipient Designers Image award Am. Assn. Interior Designers, 1983. Mem. Hist. House Assn., The Decorative Arts Trust, Appraisers Assn. Am. (fine and decorative arts appraiser 1977—), Am. Assn. Mus., Internat. Assn. Mus. (mem. internat. exhibitions exchange com.). Avocation: study of social history. Office: Ringling Mus Art 5401 Bayshore Rd Sarasota FL 33580

DUVAL, MARJORIE ANN, archivist; b. Leominster, Mass., Aug. 31, 1922; d. Daniel Joseph and Margaret Loretta (Desmond) D. Diploma in teaching, New Eng. Conservatory Music, 1943, MusB, 1945; MS, Simmons Coll., 1962; cert., Am. U., 1973. Tchr. music Jeanne d'Arc Acad., Milton, Mass., 1946-51; supr. recreation U.S. Civil Service, various locations, U.S., Far East, Europe, 1951-61; head librarian U. Maine, Portland, 1962-72, assoc. prof.library sci., 1967-76, archivist, 1972—; adj. prof. U. R.I., Kingston, 1978; reviewer grant proposals NEH, Nat. Hist. Publs. and Records Commn. Mem. Soc. Am. Archivists, New Eng. Archivists (pres. 1978-79), New Eng. Library Assn. (sec. coll. library sect. 1970-71), Maine Library Assn. (sec. 1971-74). Club: Altrusa (pres. Portland chpt. 1965—). Home: 32 Wildwood Blvd Cumberland Foreside ME 04110 Office: U So Maine 96 Falmouth St Portland ME 04103

DUVALL, PATRICIA ARLENE, educator; b. Pitts., June 27, 1950; d. William Richard and Willene Alberta (Goode) Addison; 1 child, Tiyonda Aikee. B.A. in Math., Carnegie-Mellon U., 1972; M.Ed., U. Pitts., 1981. Long distance telephone operator AT&T, Pitts., summers 1968-71; switchboard operator Union Nat. Bank, Pitts., summers 1972; math tchr. Allegheny Intermediate Unit, Pitts., summers, 1978-79; math skills program Chatham Coll., Pitts., 1983—; tchr. math Pitts. Bd. Pub. Edn., 1972—; math instr. Kids and Teens coll. program Community Coll. Allegheny County, summer 1986, 87; tennis coach Allegheny High Sch., Pitts., 1979-81. Mem. U.S. Tennis Assn., Nat. Assn. Female Execs., Am. Alliance for Health, Phys. Edn., Recreation and Dance. Jehovah's Witness. Avocations: stamp collecting, tennis, reading, collecting comic books, home computers.

DUVALL, SHELLEY, actress; b. Houston, 1949; d. Robert and Bobby Duvall. Actress: (films) (debut) Brewster McCloud, 1970, McCabe and Mrs. Miller, 1971, Thieves Like Us, 1974, Nashville, 1975, Buffalo Bill and the Indians, 1976, Three Women, 1977 (Cannes Film Festival Best Actress award), Annie Hall, 1977, Popeye, 1979, The Shining, 1980, Time Bandits, 1981, Roxanne, 1987, (TV movies) Bernice Bobs Her Hair, 1977, Lily, 1986, (TV episode) Twilight Zone, 1986; exec. producer: (Showtime pay TV series) Faerie Tale Theatre, 1983— (Peabody award), Shelley Duvall's Tall Tales and Legends, 1985—. Office: William Morris Agy 151 El Camino Beverly Hills CA 90069 *

DUVER-MICLOT, STEPHANIE ANNE, personnel company executive; b. Des Moines, Dec. 18, 1956; d. William Carl and Catherine Anne (Rodine) Duver; m. Jonathan Miclot; children: Carl, Susanne, Eric. BA in Journalism, Iowa State U., 1978; BA in Communications, U. West. Fla., 1982; MBA in Mktg., Nat. U., 1985; student in children's lit., Mary Wash. Coll., 1979. Tech. asst. writer The Bankers Life, Des Moines, 1978; staff editor The Havelock (N.C.) Progress Newspaper, 1980-81; staff writer, assoc. editor The Tides and Times Newspaper, Laguna Beach, Calif., 1981-84; asst. advt. coordinator Toshiba Am., Inc., Irvine, Calif., 1981-86; dir. public relations, sales & mktg. Personnel Pool of San Joaquin Valley, Inc., Fresno, Calif., 1986—; mktg. coordinator The Fresno (Calif.) Bee, 1987—; instr. Nat. Coll., Fresno, 1987—; cons. Words, Unltd., Fresno, 1987—. Mem. Nat. Assn. Female Execs., AAUW, Bus. and Profl. Women's Network.

DWINELL, ANN JONES, special education educator; b. Lowell, Mass., Oct. 28, 1934; d. George Hubert and Bridget (O'Neill) Jones; m. Roland A. Dwinell, Dec. 23, 1956; children: Theresa, Joseph, Richard, John. BA, Framingham State Coll., 1972; MEd, Lesley Coll., 1974; postgrad., Boston Coll., 1978—. Cert. Eng. tchr., moderate spl. needs instr., Mass. Spl. edn. tchr. Marlborough (Mass.) Pub. Sch., 1972-78; core chairperson Malden (Mass.) Pub. Schs., 1978-80, spl. edn. specialist, 1980—. Mem. Holliston (Mass.) Dem. Town Com., 1980—. Mem. NEA, Mass. Tchrs. Assn. (rep. 1983-85, liaison 1987—), Phi Delta Kappa. Roman Catholic.

DWORSKY, CLARA WEINER, merchandise brokerage executive, lawyer; b. N.Y.C., Apr. 28, 1918; d. Charles and Rebecca (Becker) Weiner; m. Bernard Ezra Dworsky, Jan. 2, 1944; 1 dau., Barbara G. Goodman. B.S., St. John's U., N.Y.C., 1937, LL.B., 1939, J.D., 1968. Bar: N.Y. 1939, U.S. Dist. Ct. (ea. dist.) N.Y. 1942. Law clk. Milton Ehreneich, N.Y.C., 1938-39; sole practice, N.Y.C., 1939-51; assoc. Bessie Farberman, N.Y.C., 1942; clk., sec. U.S. Armed Forces, Camp Carson, Colo., Camp Claiborne, La., 1944-45; abstractor, dir. Realty Title, Rockville, Md., 1954-55; v.p. Kelley & Dworsky Inc., Houston, 1960—; appeals agt. Gasoline Rationing Apls. Bd., N.Y.C., 1942; dir. Southlan Sales Assocs., Houston. Vol., ARC, N.Y.C.; vice chmn. War Bond pledge drive, Bklyn.; vol. Houston Legal Found., 1972-73; pres. Women's Aux. Washington Hebrew Acad., 1958-60, v.p. bd. trustees, 1959-60; co-founder, v.p. S. Tex. Hebrew Acad. (now Hebrew Acad.), Houston, 1970-75, hon. pres. women's div., 1973. Recipient Certificate award Treas. of U.S., 1943; Commendation Office of Chief Magistrate of City N.Y., 1948; Pietas medal St. Johns U., 1985. Mem. ABA (chmn. social security and fed. disability com. sr. lawyers div.), N.Y. State Bar Assn., Nat. Assn. Women Lawyers (chmn. organizer Juvenile Delinquency Clinic N.Y. 1948-51), St. Johns U. Alumni Assn. (coordinator Houston chpt. 1983-86, pres. 1986). Jewish. Clubs: Delphians Past Pres.'s, Amit Women. Lodges: B'nai B'rith Women, Hadassah. Home: 9726 Cliffwood Dr Houston TX 77096

DWYER, CARRIE ELIZABETH, securities exchange executive; b. San Mateo, Calif., Dec. 19, 1950; d. Robert Harold and Alice Marian (Daley) D.; m. Richard M. Konecky, Feb. 12, 1977; 1 child, Rachel Anne. BA, U. Santa Clara, 1973, JD, 1976. With Am. Stock Exchange, N.Y.C., 1977—, staff atty., 1977-79, legal exec. asst., 1979-80, exec. asst. to pres., 1980-85, assoc. gen. counsel, v.p., 1985-86, gen. counsel, sr. v.p., 1986—. Mem. ABA, Assn. of Bar of City of N.Y., N.Y. State Bar Assn., Investment Assn. Office: Am Stock Exchange Inc 86 Trinity Place New York NY 10006

DWYER, DORIOT ANTHONY, flutist; d. William C. and Edith (Maurer) Anthony; B.Music, Eastman Sch. Music, 1943; hon. degrees Harvard U., 1982, Simmons Coll., 1982; 1 child, Arienne. Second flutist Nat. Symphony, Washington, 1943, Los Angeles Philharm., 1945-52; 1st flutist Boston Symphony Orch., 1952—; flutist numerous chamber groups including: Boston Symphony Chamber Players, Doriot Anthony Dwyer and Friends; appeared at numerous music festivals including: Carmel Bach Festival, Berkshire Festival at Tanglewood, Rocky Mountain Music Festival; former mem. faculty Pomona Coll., New Eng. Conservatory Music; vis. prof. U. Calif. Davis, 1987; soloist, lectr. Summer Arts Festival, Calif. Poly. State U., St. Luis Obispo, 1986, Calif. State U. Fullerton Riverside, 1987, Dominguiz Hills, 1987; adj. prof. flute Boston U.; mem. faculty Berkshire Music Festival. Recipient Sanford fellowship Yale U., 1972. Mem. Nat. Council of Women, Audubon Soc. Home: 3 Cleveland Rd Brookline MA 02146 Office: care Boston Symphony Symphony Hall Boston MA 02115

DWYER, ETHEL THERESA, psychologist; b. Manchester, N.H., July 30, 1931; d. Joseph George and Florence Theresa (Kittredge) Thibodeau; Mus.B., Boston U., 1953, Ed.M., 1962, cert. advanced grad. study, 1965, Ed.D., 1968; m. John Philip Dwyer, June 22, 1957. Tchr., Miss Jacques Pvt. Sch., Manchester, 1953-54; asst. dir. Girls Club, Manchester, 1954-57; tchr. Manchester Public Schs., 1957-65; instr. edn. Boston U. Sch. Edn., 1965-66; asst. prof. psychology New Eng. Coll., Henniker, N.H., 1965-67; assoc. prof. Mt. St. Mary Coll., Hooksett, N.H., 1968-70; staff psychologist N.H. Hosp., Concord, 1968-71; ind. practice child psychology, 1970—; mem. N.H. Bd. Examiners Psychologists, 1976-77, chmn., 1977-79, investigator, 1984; mem. peer rev. com. APA/CHAMPUS, 1977-78; profl. adv. bd. N. River Sch., 1978-80, chmn., 1977; mem. teen age pregnancy/mother adv. bd. Vis. Nurse Assn. Manchester, 1978—; research asst. Boston U. Center Exceptional Children, 1962-63; curriculum cons. Concord Public Schs., 1967-68; psychologist, cons. Easter Seal Rehab. Center, 1971-72. Instr. water safety and first aid ARC; active YWCA. Diplomate sch. psychology Am. Bd. Profl. Psychology; cert. psychologist, N.H.; lic. psychologist, Mass.; listed Nat. Register Health Service Providers in Psychology. Mem. Am. Psychol. Assn., NEA (state rep. elem. educators 1965-70), Am. Ednl. Research Assn., Music Educators Nat. Conf., Eastern Psychol. Assn., New Eng. Psychol. Assn., Mass. Psychol. Assn., N.H. Dental Assn. Women's Aux., Hillsboro County Kennel Club (dir. 1980), Mu Phi Epsilon, Pi Lamda Theta. Republican. Roman Catholic. Home: 2071 N River Rd Manchester NH 03104 Office: 1480 Elm St Manchester NH 03101

DWYER, MARIE RITA ROZELLE (MRS. JOHN D. DWYER), educator; b. N.Y.C., Sept. 4, 1915; d. Charles W. and Agnes (Coyle) Rozelle; student L'Assomption, Paris, 1932-33; B.A., Notre Dame Coll., 1936; M.A., Fordham U., 1938, also postgrad; postgrad. St. Louis U.; student Sorbonne, Paris, summers 1933-37, 52; m. John D. Dwyer, Sept. 8, 1942; children—John Duncan, Joseph Charles, James Gerard, Jerome Valentine. Tchr. French, Sch. of Edn., Fordham U., N.Y.C., 1938-42, Notre Dame Coll., N.Y.C., 1939-40, Coll. of St. Rose, Albany, N.Y., 1949-53, Washington U., St. Louis, 1959-60; faculty French dept. Webster Coll., 1966-74; dir. community services Internat. Students Program, St. Louis U., 1974-83, with internat. programs, 1984—; mem. faculty Meramec Community Coll., St. Louis, 1968-70. Active community fund drives, including Greater St. Louis Fund for Arts and Edn.; bd. dirs. St. Louis Christmas Carols Assn., 1962-64, Parish Council, 1966-67; adult adviser cultural program for young adults Archdiocesan Council Cath. Youth, 1961-67; mem. Archdiocesan Council Laity Charities; chmn. internat. friendship program Archdiocesan Council of Laity of St. Louis, 1984. Mem. Am. Assn. Tchrs. French (pres. St. Louis chpt. 1955-56), Mo. Acad. Sci. (life mem., editorial staff transactions 1969-72, chmn. linguistics sect. 1970-76, past mem. exec. bd.), Alliance Française (past sec. St. Louis), Société Française (past sec.), KC Aux. (past pres.), AAAS (rep. Mo. Acad. Sci. at conv. in Mexico City 1973), Notre Dame Coll. Alumnae Assn. (past pres.), Internat. Fedn. Cath. Alumnae (past pres. Albany), Jesuit Mothers Guild (pres. 1963-65), Cath. Women's League (pres. 1964-66), Archdiocesan Council Cath. Women (mem. coms. family life teen-age code, corr. sec. 1963-64, pres. 1964-66 South Central dist., adv. council 1968—), Nat. French Honor Soc., AAUP, MLA, Mo. MLA (pres. 1961-63), Central States Conf. on Teaching Fgn. Langs., Société International de la Linguistique, Linguistic Soc. Am., Fgn. Lang. Assn. Mo. (v.p. 1973, sec. 4-Coll. Consortium (Webster, Fontbonne, Maryville and Lindenwood) 1972-73), Centro Studie Scambi Internazionali (mem. internat. com.), Smithsonian Instn. Nat. Assos., Internat. Platform Assn., Pi Delta Phi, Alpha Sigma Nu. Club: St. Louis University Faculty Women's (pres. 1956-58, dir. 1959—, v.p. 1983-84). Extensive travel for ednl. and linguistic research. Home: 526 Oakwood Ave Webster Groves MO 63119 Office: St Louis U Internat Programs 221 N Grand Blvd Room 234 Saint Louis MO 63103

DYBDAHL, JILL YVETTE, computer systems consultant; b. Freeport, Ill., Sept. 8, 1960; d. Dale Donald and Dorothy Clara (Bower) Brinker; m. Paul Clayton Dybdahl, Dec. 2, 1983; 1 child, Anna Nicole. BS in Math., U. Wis., 1983. Programmer Farm Plan Corp., Madison, Wis., 1983-85; computer cons. Computer Assistance by Dybdahl, Mt. Horeb, Wis., 1985—. Mem. YMCA, Madison. Mem. Nat. Assn. Female Execs. Republican. Evang. Lutheran. Home and Office: Computer Assistance by Dybdahl 106 S 5th St Mount Horeb WI 53572

DYCHTWALD, MADDY KENT, multimedia producer; b. Newark, Feb. 13, 1952; s. Stanley and Sally Susan (Gordet) Kent; m. Kenneth Mark Dychtwald, Nov. 24, 1983. Student in media communications, U. Wis.-Madison, 1968-70; B.A., NYU, 1974. Actress, N.Y.C. and Los Angeles, 1974-83; dir. spl. projects Dychtwald & Assocs., Emeryville, Calif., 1983-86; v.p., dir. communications Age Wave, Inc., Emeryville, 1986, v.p. communications, 1987—. Designer, producer slide shows, videos, mktg. and communication materials; author, editor: Third Age America: The Shape of Things to Come, 1988. Mem. Screen Actor's Guild, Am. Fedn. TV and Radio Actors, Am. Film Inst., Internat. Assn. Bus. Communicators (Award of Merit for logo design), Nat. Assn. Female Execs. Office: Age Wave Inc 1900 Powell St #700 Emeryville CA 94608

DYCKOFF, HEIDI MAE, accountant; b. N.Y.C., Sept. 2, 1961; d. Bernard and Beatrice D. Student, SUNY, Stony Brook, 1977-78, L.I. U., 1978-79, Kingsborough Coll., 1981. Asst. bookkeeper H&R Block, Bklyn., 1978-79, tax preparer, 1979-84, fgn. state tax preparer, dist. mgr., 1984-85; owner, acct. It's a Cinch, Ellenville, N.Y., 1985—. Author tax column, 1986-87. Mem. Nat. Assn. Female Execs., Nat. Assn. Tax Profls., Profl. Ins. Agts., E.R. Morrow Alumni Assn. (pres. 1977—). Democrat. Jewish. Office: It's a Cinch 1 Terrace Hill Ellenville NY 12428

DYER, ARLENE THELMA, retail company owner; b. Chgo., Oct. 23, 1942; d. Samuel Leo Sr. and Thelma Arlene (Israel) Lewis; m. Don Engle Dyer, July 3, 1965 (div. 1970); 1 child, Artel Terren. Cert. in mgmt. effectiveness, U. So. Calif., 1987. Community resource rep. Calif. State Employment Devel. Dept., Los Angeles, 1975-76, spl. projects rep., 1976; employment services rep. Culver City, Calif., 1977; contract writer Los Angeles, 1976-80, employment program rep., 1980—; pres. Yabba and Co., Los Angeles, 1981-83; pres., designer, cons. Spiritual Ties Custom Neckwear, Los Angeles, 1985—; pres. Dyer Custom Shirts, Blouses and Suits, Beverly Hills, Calif., 1988—; founder self-evaluation seminar. Exhibited in fashion shows, Calif., 1984—. Vol. Big Sister Gwen Bolden Found., Los Angeles, 1986; mem. Operation PUSH, Chgo., 1983; program chair Black Advs. in State Service, 1987—; leader Girl Scouts U.S., Los Angeles, 1982; Los Angeles Urban League. Mem. Nat. Alliance Homebased Businesswomen (v.p., program chair 1987), Nat. Assn. Female Execs., Calif. State Employees Assn., U. So. Calif. Alumni Assn., Los Angeles Urban League, Black Women's Forum, NAACP (Beverly Hills-Hollywood chpt.). Democrat. Club: 92d St Block. Office: Custom Shirts Blouses & Ties 8530 Wilshire Blvd Suite 404 Beverly Hills CA 90211

DYER, CAROL DICICCO, sales executive; b. Framingham, Mass., Oct. 22, 1945; d. Frank Arthur and A. Janat (Murphy) DiCicco; m. Francis Harvey Dyer, May 4, 1968. BA in Sociology, U. Mass., 1967. Child welfare caseworker Conn. State Welfare Dept., Torrington, 1967-68; retail salesperson The Bon, Seattle, 1968-69; various positions Pacific N.W. Bell, Seattle, 1969-83; staff mgr. AT&T Communications, Basking Ridge, N.J., 1983-85; v.p. sales Cybernetics Systems Internat., Coral Gables, Fla., 1985-88; dir. software products Telecom Techs., Pomona, Calif., 1988—. Loaned exec. vol. United Way, Seattle, 1976-77. Mem. Nat. Assn. for Female Execs. Club: Wash. Athletic (Seattle). Home: 2333 Brickell Ave Unit 1015 Miami FL 33129 Office: Telecom Techs 761 Corporate Ctr Dr Pomona CA 91768

DYER, DORIS ANNE, nurse; b. Washington, Jan. 14, 1944; d. William Edward and Helen Gertrude (Smith) Swain; R.N., Sibley Nursing Sch., Washington, 1964; B.S., Am. U., 1966, M.Ed., 1969; m. Robert Francis Dyer, Jr., June 27, 1970; children—Robert Francis, William Edward, Anne-Marie Helen Sallie, Scott Robertson McGavin. Mem. staff emergency medicine dept. George Washington U. Hosp., 1960-69, emergency specialist protective services clinic, 1967-70, adminstr. asst. to dir. clinic, 1970-78; nurse cons., 1987—. Trinity Coll. scholar, 1960; Lucy Webb Hayes scholar, 1964; recipient Martha Washington award Md. Soc. SAR, 1977; Community Leaders award, 1979; Washington medal, 1984, Disting. Women of Washington award 1987; decorated comdr. Order of St. Lazarus, 1984; created dame Order of Sovereign Mil. Order, 1980. Mem. Am., D.C. nurses assns., Am. Acad. Ambulatory Nursing Adminstrs., Washington Med.-Surg. Soc. Aux. (pres.), Am. U. Grads. Assn., DAR, Washington Assembly. Clubs: Washington, Annapolis Yacht, Kenwood Golf and Country. Author: Say Ah, 1971; also articles. Address: 5608 Albia Rd Bethesda MD 20816

DYER, GERALDINE (GERI) ANN, artist; b. Bklyn., Nov. 4, 1921; d. Edward and Chattie (Holmes) Bingham; m. Ralph Dyer, Oct. 1956. Student N.Y. Phoenix Sch. Design, N.Y.C., 1946-48, Bklyn. Mus. Art Sch., 1959; pvt. studies in voice with Julia Gille, 1947. Commd. U.S. Army, 1941, retired USCG, 1979. Exhibited in one-woman shows Henry Hicks Gallery, N.Y.C., 1978-79, 81, Womanart Gallery, N.Y.C., 1980, Keane Mason Gallery, N.Y.C., 1981, Esta Robinson Gallery, N.Y.C., 1983, Bklyn. Heights Br. Library, Bklyn., 1986; exhibited at numerous group shows; represented in permanent collection Samuel Schulman Inst., Bklyn. Mem. Womeninterart Ctr., Drawing Ctr., Nat. Assn. Female Execs., also galleries, mus. Club: Officers (N.Y.C.). Avocation: writing poetry.

DYER, ROSEMARY MARGARET, physicist; b. N.Y.C., May 16, 1932; d. Edward Enoch and Margaret Mary (O'Brien) Griffith; m. Glenn Lionel Dyer, Feb. 11, 1967; 1 child, Richard. B.S. in Physics Fordham U., 1954; M.S. in Meteorology, NYU, 1962; M.S. in Engring. Mgmt., Western New Eng. Coll., 1980. Sci. advisor RCA, N.Y.C., 1960-65; research assoc. McGill U., Montreal, 1965-67; atmospheric physicist U.S. Air Force, Bedford, Mass., 1967—. Contbg. editor AI Applications in Resource Management; contbr. articles to profl. jours. V.p. Nat. Fedn. Fed. Employees Local1384, 1983—. Recipient Patricia Glass award, U.S. Air Force, 1973, various tech. achievement awards, 1973, 76, 80, 82. Fellow Royal Meteorol. Soc.; mem. Am. Assn. for Artifical Intelligence, Am. Physical Soc., Am. Meteorol. Soc., Nat. Fedn. Fed. Employees (v.p. local 1384 1984-88, Sigma Xi. Avocations: travel, puzzle compiler, historical reenactments. Home: 4 Fox Run Rd Bedford MA 01730

DYER, SIMONE, real estate professional; b. Morristown, N.J., May 25, 1940; d. Edgar Wilson and Simone Marie (Vermeillet) Baxter; m. Robert Russell Dyer, Jan. 1, 1982 (div. July 1986); children: Randall Scott, Shawn Michael, Christian Daniel Schmidt. Student, So. Ill. U., 1958-59. Lic. real estate agt., Calif. Owner Offspring, Ltd., San Clemente, Calif., 1968-69; rep. cable TV Times-Mirror Inc., San Clemente, Calif., 1969-70; pub.'s rep. Multi-Lines, N.Y.C., 1970-73; mgr. hardcover books Kroch's & Brentano's Inc., Costa Mesa, Calif., 1973-74; with Dennis & Dennis Personnel, Irvine, Calif., 1974-76; rep. wine sales MLF, Carson, Calif., 1976-79; owner, editor Acton (Calif.) News, 1980-82; with gen. real estate dept. Ferne Realty, Acton, 1981-84; real estate sales mgr. West Venture Devel. Corp., Van Nuys, Calif., 1984-87; dir. sales Domus Corp., Palmdale, Calif., 1987—. Mem. Sales and Mktg. Council. Republican. Roman Catholic. Club: Lions (officer Acton chpt. 1986—). Home: 2565 Bottle Tree Dr Palmdale CA 93550 Office: Domus Corp 38338 30th St E Palmdale CA 93550

DYKE, NANCY BEARG, U.S. government official; b. Mpls., Feb. 11, 1947; d. Richard W. and Hildegarde V. Bearg; B.A., Williamette U. 1969, M.P.A. Harvard U. 1978; m. Charles W. Dyke, June 22, 1980; 2 daus. With U.S. Dept. State, 1969; with NSC, 1969-70; mem. profl. staff com. on armed services U.S. Senate, 1970-75; analyst Congressional Budget Office, 1975-77; dir. policy analysis for N. East, Africa and South Asia, U.S. Dept. Def., 1978-79; dep. asst. sec. of air force 1980; asst. to v.p. for nat. security affairs The White House, Washington, 1981-82; mem. Army Sci. Bd. Recipient Sec. Def. Meritorious Civilian Service medal 1979, Air Force Exceptional Civilian Service award 1980. Contbr. in field. Home: Office of Comdg Gen US Army Japan/IX Corps San Francisco CA 96343

DYKEMAN, WILMA, author, educator; b. Asheville, N.C., May 20, 1920; d. Willard J. and Bonnie (Cole) Dykeman; B.S. in Speech, Northwestern U., 1940; Litt.D., Maryville Coll., 1974; L.H.D., Tenn. Wesleyan Coll., 1978; m. James R. Stokely Jr., Oct. 12, 1940; children—Dykeman Cole, James R. III. Lectr. English dept. U. Tenn., Knoxville, 1975—, adj. prof., 1985—; columnist Knoxville News-Sentinel, 1962—; historian State of Tenn., 1980—; author 14 books including: The French Broad: A Rivers of America Volume, 1955, The Tall Woman, 1962, Seeds of Southern Change, 1962, The Far Family, 1966, Return the Innocent Earth, 1973, others; co-author: Neither Black Nor White, 1957; Tennessee: A Bicentennial History, 1976; Explorations, a collection of essays, 1984; contbr. articles to nat. mags. Ency. Brit.; nat. lectr. in field; dir. Merchants & Planters Bank. Trustee Berea Coll., 1971—, Phelps Stokes Fund, 1981—, U. N.C.-Asheville, 1985—. Guggenheim fellow, 1956-57, NEH fellow, 1976-77; recipient Hillman award, 1957; N.C. Gold medal for Contbn. to Am. letters, 1985. Mem. PEN, Authors Guild, So. Hist. Assn., Phi Beta Kappa, Sigma Delta Chi. Home: 405 Clifton Heights Newport TN 37821

DYKES, VIRGINIA CHANDLER, occupational therapist; b. Evanston, Ill., Jan. 10, 1930; d. Daniel Guy and Helen (Schneider) Goodman; children: Ron Lee, Chuck Lee. B.A. in Art and Psychology, So. Methodist U., 1951; postgrad. in occupational therapy Tex. Women's U., 1953; cert. ins. rehab. specialist; cert. in work adjustment and vocat. evaluation. Occupational therapist Beverly Hills Sanitarium, Dallas, 1953-55; dir. occupational and recreational therapy Baylor U. Med. Center, Dallas, 1956-60, 68—, Fla. Sanitarium and Hosp., Orlando, 1962-65; staff therapist Parkland Meml. Hosp., Dallas, 1965-68; cons. Arthritis Found., 1974—. Mem. coordinating bd. allied health adv. com. Tex. Coll. and Univ. System, 1980—; bd. dirs. Tex. Arthritis Found., chmn. patient services com., 1985—; bd. sponsors Kimball Art Mus. Named Tex. Occupational Therapist of Yr., 1985. Mem. Am. Occupational Therapy Assn. (del. Fla. 1964, Tex. 1980-88), World Fedn. Occupational Therapists (participant 8th Internat. Congress, Hamburg, Germany, 1982, del. to 10th European Congress on Rheumatology, Moscow 1983), Chi Omega. Club: Boomerang (dir. 1971—). Author: (manual) Lightcast II Splints, 1976; Adult Visual Perceptual Evaluation, 1981; contbr. articles to profl. jours. Home: 3203 Alderson Dallas TX 75214 Office: Baylor U Med Ctr 3500 Gaston Ave Dallas TX 75246

DYKSTRA-ALLISON, JANE LEA, marketing company executive, consultant; b. Oskaloosa, Iowa, July 17, 1953; d. Melvin Eldred and Lucille (Maughan) Dykstra. BS, Northeast Mo. State U., 1974; cert. in fin. planning, Coll. Fin. Planning, Denver, 1976. Regional sales mgr. Gt. Western Fin. Co., Newport Beach, Calif., 1974-78; br. mgr. Equitec Fin. Group, Newport Beach, 1978-81; sales rep. Security First Group, Century City, Calif., 1981-83; br. mgr. Bretcourt Fin. Inc., Santa Ana, Calif., 1983-84; ins. sales specialist J&H/KVI, Des Moines, 1984-87; sales cons. KBIZ-KTWA, Ottumwa, Iowa, 1987; mktg. dir. London Choate Ins. Services, Tustin, Calif., 1988—. Mem. Internat. Assn. Fin. Planning (sec. Des Moines chpt. 1986-87), Nat. Assn. Female Execs, Nat. Assn. Security Dealers, Alpha Sigma Alpha. Democrat. Roman Catholic. Home: 17266 Nisson #C Tustin CA 92680 Office: London Choate Ins 14081 Yorba St Suite 111 Tustin CA 92680

DYM, FRAN G., public relations consultant; b. N.Y.C.; d. Aaron and Goldie (Lustig) D.; m. Henry V. Goldstein, Feb. 13, 1958 (div. Dec. 1972); children—Janet, Jonathan. B.A., Hunter Coll., 1976; postgrad. NYU, 1976-78. Vice-pres. Kalmus Corp., N.Y.C., 1965-77, Keller Haver Advt., N.Y.C., 1978-79; sr. v.p. Daniel S. Roher, Inc., N.Y.C., 1979-83; pres. Dym/SR&A, Inc., N.Y.C., 1983—; cons. KLH R&D Corp., Canoga Park, Calif., 1979-82, Bang & Olufsen of Am., Mount Prospect, Ill., 1980—, dbx, Inc., Newton, Mass., 1979—, Studer Revox of Am., Inc., Nashville, 1982—, Sparkomatic Corp., Milford, Pa., 1983-88, Inter-Link Technology, Ltd., London, 1984—, Altec Lansing Consumer Products, Milford, 1986—, Finial Tech., Sunnyvale, Calif., 1986—, Lexicon Inc., Waltham, Mass., 1984-86, Audio Dynamics Corp., San Bruno, Calif., 1988—. Contbr. articles to profl. jours. Mem. Nat. Assn. Female Execs., Audio Engring. Soc., Internat. Motor Press Assn., Am. Women's Econ. Devel. Corp. Office: Dym/SR&A Inc 355 Lexington Ave New York NY 10017

DYMOND, MARY STOIK, risk manager; b. Clinton, Iowa, Oct. 31, 1952; d. Lloyd P. and Mary (Johnson) Stoik; m. Steven H. Dymond. B.A., U. S.D., Vermillion, 1975. Paralegal firm Ross Hardies, Chgo., 1975-77, firm Calkins & Kramer, Denver, 1977-79, firm Holland and Hart, Denver, 1979-81; corp. affairs adminstr., risk mgr. asst. sec. Axem Resources, Denver, 1981-87 ; asst. sec. Laser Oil Co., Axroyalty Inc.; corp. sec. Axem Found., 1981-87; risk mgr. Apache Corp., Denver, 1987—. Active Denver Sym. Orch., 1982-85, choreographer for local dance co., 1982-85. Mem. Risk Ins. Mgrs. Soc., Delta Phi Alpha, Phi Alpha Theta, Pi Beta Phi (v.p., 1974-75). Home: 1616 S Grant St Denver CO 80210 Office: Apache Corp One United Bank Bldg Denver CO 80237

DZIEDZIC, INGEBORG SVETLANA, ophthalmologist; b. Zagreb, Yugoslavia, June 6, 1952; came to U.S., 1970; d. Svetozar and Ivanka (Uhrl) Vlascic; m. John David Dzledzic, Feb. 9, 1974; children—John Jr., Stephan, Michael. Student Atlantic Coll. (Gt. Britain), 1968-70; B.S., Fordham U., 1974; M.D., Albert Einstein Sch. Medicine, Yeshiva U., 1979. Intern pediatrics Med. Coll. Pa., Phila., 1979-80; resident in ophthalmology Montefiore Hosp., N.Y.C., 1980-83; practice medicine specializing in ophthalmology, Yorktown Heights, N.Y., 1983-84, Pleasantville, N.Y., 1984—. Mem. Am. Acad. Ophthamology, Phi Beta Kappa. Roman Catholic. Office: 320 Manville Rd Pleasantville NY 10570

DZIEKAN, RENEE ANN, health services administrator; b. Milw., Oct. 6, 1955; d. Clifford Michael and Dolores Lenora (Gerard) D. BS in Nursing, U. Wis., Milw., 1978; postgrad., Cardinal Stritch Coll., 1986—. RN, Wis. Staff nurse St. Francis Hosp., Milw., 1978-79; occupational relief nurse Rexnord-Nordberg, Milw., 1978-84; staff nurse, head nurse Caterpillar Tractor, Milw., 1979-82; neonatal intensive care unit, staff, charge nurse Milw. County Med. Complex, 1982-84; relief nurse U.S. Dept. Fed. Employee Occupational Health, Milw., 1983-84; head nurse, supr. Northwestern Mut. Life Ins., Milw., 1984—; med. adv. com., corp. mem. Milw. Wellness Council, 1986—. Instr. first-aid ARC. Mem. Southeastern Wis. Assn. Occupational Health Nurses (Creative Contbns. to Practice of Nursing award 1987), Am. Assn. of Occupational Health Nurses, The Wis. Assn. on Alcohol and Drug Abuse, Nat. Assn. Female Execs. Office: Northwestern Mut Life 720 E Wisconsin Milwaukee WI 53202

EADIE, GRACE RAMSEY, corporate professional; b. Charleston, S.C., July 9, 1941; d. Jake Bailey and Dorothy Mae (Haney) Ramsey; m. Sidney Allen Eadie, July 12, 1969; children: Earle Cleveland, James Marc. A in Bus., Trident Tech. Coll., 1977; student, Nat. Coll. Edn., 1987—. Sec. Pepsi Cola Bottling Co., Charleston, S.C., 1968-69, Cath. Social Services, Panama City, Fla., 1978-79; auditor technician Gayfer's, Panama City, 1980-82; staff sec. Def. Mapping Agy., Washington, 1983-84; configuration mgmt. specialist Contel Govt. Systems div., Fairfax, Va., 1984-87; configuration mgmt. supr. Govt. Info. Systems div. PRC, McLean, Va., 1987-88; configuration mgmt. specialist Fed. and Electronic Systems Div. Gen. Electric, Reston, Va., 1988—. Vol. Panama City chpt. ARC, 1980-83. Mem. Am. Soc. Profl. and Exec. Women, Nat. Assn. Female Execs. Republican. Lutheran. Home: 10323 Yellow Pine Dr Vienna VA 22180 Office: Gen Electric 1840 Michael Fieraday Reston VA 20090

EADS, M. ADELA, state legislator; b. Brooklyn, N.Y., Mar. 2, 1920. Ed. Sweet Briar Coll. Mem. Conn. Ho. of Reps., from 1976; now mem. Conn. Senate. Republican. Mem. Conn. Bd. Edn., 1972-76. Office: Conn Senate State Capitol Hartford CT 06106 Home: R 1 Box 395 Kent CT 06757 *

EAGAN, MARIE T. (RIA), chiropractor; b. Rockville Ctr., N.Y., June 17, 1952; d. John F. and Mary (Ebner) E. BA, Goddard Coll., 1975; D in Chiropractic Medicine, N.Y. Chiropractic Coll., 1983. Pvt. practice chiropractic medicine N.Y.C., 1983—; Bd. dirs. Chalice Found., Los Angeles, 1986. Fellow N.Y. Chiropractic Assn., Am. Chiropractic Assn. Democrat. Office: 231 W 21st St #B New York NY 10011

EARGLE, JUDITH HUBBARD, mathematical statistician; b. Washington, May 11, 1944; d. John Stanley and Hazel Louise (Coore) Hubbard; m. Linwood Overton Eargle, Sept. 6, 1969 (dec. Apr. 1980). BS, N.C. State U., 1966, MS, 1980. Actuarial analyst Life of Va., Richmond, 1967-70; programmer Va. Electric and Power, Richmond, 1970; project leader Carolina Power and Light, Raleigh, N.C., 1971-79; project mgr. Fed. Home Loan Mortgage Corp., Washington, 1979-80; sr. analyst Gen. Research Corp., McLean, Va., 1980-81; fin. planning supr. Potomac Electric and Power, Washington, 1981-82; research asst. George Washington U., Washington, 1982-83; economist Small Bus Adminstrn., Washington, 1983-85, E.H. Pechan Assocs., Inc., Springfield, Va., 1985-87; math. statistician Census Bur., Suitland, Md., 1987—. Mem. Nat. Assn. Bus. Economists, Am. Soc. Personnel Adminstrs., Trout Unltd. Republican. Lutheran. Home: PO Box 488 Churchton MD 20733 Office: Census Bur Population Div Washington DC 20233

EARHART, EILEEN MAGIE, educator; b. Hamilton, Ohio, Oct. 21, 1928; d. Andrew J. and Martha (Waldorf) Magie; m. Paul G. Earhart; children: Anthony G., Bruce P., Daniel T. B.S., Miami U., Oxford, Ohio, 1950; M.A. in Adminstrn. and Ednl. Services, Mich. State U., 1962, Ph.D. in Edn., 1969; H.H.D. (hon.), Miami U., Oxford, Ohio, 1980. Tchr. home econs. W. Alexandria (Ohio) Schs., 1950-51; elementary tchr. Waterford Twp. Schs., Pontiac, Mich., 1958-65; reading specialist Waterford Twp. Schs., 1965-67; prof., chmn. family and child ecology dept. Mich. State U., East Lansing, 1968-84; prof., head dept. home and family life Fla. State U., Tallahassee, 1984—. Author: Attention and Classification Training Curriculum; co-editor spl. issue of Family Relations, 1984; contbr. chpts. to profl. jours., books. Mem. adv. bd. Lansing Com. on Children's TV; bd. dirs. Women's Resource Center, Grand Rapids, Mich. Mem. Soc. Research in Child Devel., Nat. Council on Family Relations (pres. Assn. of Councils 1987-88), Fla. Council on Family Relations (pres. elect 1985-86, pres. 1986-87), AAUW, Nat. Assn. Edn. Young Children, Assn. Childhood Edn. Internat., Am. Home Econs. Assn. (named an AHEA Leader at 75th Anniversary of assn. 1984), Internat. Fedn. of Home Economics, Mich. Home Econs. Assn. (pres. 1980-82), Fla. Home Econs. Assn. (scholarship chair 1986-88) Internat. Fedn. Home Econs., Ednl. Research Assn., Internat. Reading Assn., Phi Kappa Phi (pres.-elect 1987-88), Omicron Nu, Delta Kappa Gamma. Home: 4009 Brandon Hill Dr Tallahassee FL 32308 Office: Fla State U 213 Sandels Bldg Tallahassee FL 32306

EARLE, SYLVIA ALICE, biologist, oceanographer; b. Gibbstown, N.J., Aug. 30, 1935; d. Lewis Reade and Alice Freas (Richie) E. B.S., Fla. State U., 1955; M.A., Duke U., 1956, Ph.D., 1966. Resident dir. Cape Haze Marine Lab., Sarasota, Fla., 1966-67; research scholar Radcliffe Inst., 1967-69; research fellow Farlow Herbarium, Harvard U., 1967-75, researcher, 1975—; research assoc. in botany Natural History Mus. Los Angeles County, 1970-75; research biologist, curator Calif. Acad. Scis., San Francisco, 1976—; research assoc. U. Calif.-Berkeley, 1969-75; founder, v.p., sec.-treas., bd. dirs. Deep Ocean Tech., Inc., Oakland, Calif.; founder, v.p., sec.-treas. Deep Ocean Engring., Oakland, 1981-88, chief exec. officer, 1988—, also bd. dirs. Author: Exploring the Deep Frontier, 1980. Editor: Scientific Results of the Tektite II Project, 1972-75. Contbr. 60 articles to profl. jours. Trustee World Wildlife Fund U.S., 1976-82, council mem., 1984—; trustee World Wildlife Fund Internat., 1979-81, council mem., 1981—; trustee Charles A. Lindbergh Fund., Ocean Trust Found.; council mem. Internat. Union Conservation Nature, 1979-81; corp. mem. Woods Hole Oceanographic Inst.; mem. Nat. Adv. Com. Oceans and Atmosphere, 1980-84. Recipient Conservation Service award U.S. Dept. Interior, 1970, Boston Sea Rovers award, 1972, 79, Nogi award Underwater Soc. Am., 1976, Conservation service award Calif. Acad. Sci., 1979, Lowell Thomas award Explorer's Club, 1980, Order of Golden Ark Prince Netherlands, 1980; named Woman of Yr. Los Angeles Times, 1970, Scientist of Yr., Calif. Mus. Sci. and Industry, 1981. Fellow AAAS, Marine Tech. Soc., Calif. Acad. Scis., Explorers Club, Calif. Acad. Sci.; mem. Internat. Phycological Soc. (sec. 1974-80), Phycological Soc. Am., Am. Soc. Ichthyologists and Herpetologists, Am. Inst. Biol. Scis., Brit. Phycological Soc., Ecol. Soc. Am., Internat. Soc. Plant Taxonomists. Club: Explorers (fellow). Home: 12812 Skyline Blvd Oakland CA 94619 Office: Calif Acad Scis Golden Gate Park San Francisco CA 94118

EARLY-ODOM, ETHEL, personnel director; b. Waco, Tex., June 28, 1935; d. Leonard Franklin and Minnie Elizabeth (Cox) Pate; m. Robert Lynn Early, May 1, 1958 (div. 1971); 1 child, Ricky Lynn; m. Daniel Leon Odom, Oct. 12, 1985. Cert., Hankimer/Baylor U., 1981, Am. Mgmt. Assn., 1978, 83, Dale Carnegie Inst., Dallas, 1983, 84. Mgrs. asst. Tandy Leather Co., Waco, 1956-59; collection teller Citizen Nat. Bank, Waco, 1959-62; personnel asst. Gulf State Paper Corp., Waco, 1968-74; personnel adminstr. Chaparral Steel Co., Midlothian, Tex., 1975—; ind. personnel cons., 1988—; bd. dirs. TXI Employees Credit Union, Arlington, Tex., 1976-80. Mem. Ellis County Personnel Assn. (1st v.p. 1986-87, pres. 1988—), Midlothian C. of C. Republican. Baptist. Office: Chaparral Steel Co 300 Ward Rd Midlothian TX 76065

EARNHEARDT, RUSSELLYN ANNE, nursing administrator, marketing consultant; b. Detroit, May 29, 1946; d. Walter Joseph and Virginia Ruth (Vertuno) Kawecki; m. Thomas Richard Stackpoole, Sept. 15, 1948 (div. 1980); 1 child, Jeffrey Michael. Diploma in nursing, Grace Hosp. Sch. Nursing, 1967; BS in Nursing, Wayne State U., 1984; MS in Adminstrn., Cen. Mich. U., 1987. Staff nurse emergency room Grace Hosp., Detoit, 1967-70; staff nurse ICU-CCU Mt. Clemens (Mich.) Gen. Hosp., 1970-74, staff nurse hemodialysis, 1974-76, head nurse hemodialysis, 1976-78, dir. nursing quality assurance, 1978—. Mem. Mich. Nurses Assn., Nat. Assn. Quality Assurance Profls., Sigma Theta Tau. Home: 37639 Charter Oaks Mount Clemens MI 48043 Office: Mt Clemens Gen Hosp 1000 Harrington Mount Clemens MI 48043

EARNSHAW, JOAN SALISBURY, government revenue agent; b. Billings, Mont., Jan. 16, 1943; d. Donovan Dee and Florence (Chandler) Salisbury; m. Joseph B. Earnshaw, Mar. 27, 1965; children: Deborah, Mary. Student Mont. State U., 1960-61, Brigham Young U., 1961-62, Ariz. State Coll. (now No. Ariz. U.), spring 1963, spring 1964, U. Calif.-Berkeley, 1971—; BS in Bus. Adminstrn., Thomas Edison State Coll., 1986. Acctg. clk. Nat. Park Service, Yellowstone Nat. Park, 1960-67; clk. IRS, Phoenix, 1974-75, tax auditor, Phoenix, 1975-78; tax auditor, Farmington, N. Mex., 1978-84, revenue agt., 1984—, also site dir. Vol. Income Tax Assistance, Phoenix, 1977, Vol. Income Tax Assistance instr., Farmington, 1979—; various TV and radio appearances for IRS, 1979—; mem. speakers panel San Juan Coll., Farmington, 1980—, mem. adv. bd. dept. acctg., 1984—, instr., 1987—. Leader, fundraiser Campfire, Fontana, Calif., then Phoenix, 1971-78; fundraiser for schs., ch., 1973—; mem. Community Action Council, Phoenix, 1975-78; coordinator religious edn. Holy Trinity Parish, Flora Vista, N.Mex., 1985—. Recipient Wakan award Camp Fire, 1977, Performance award IRS, 1981, Spl. Act award IRS, 1982. Mem. Sodality of Our Lady Club. Democrat. Roman Catholic. Avocations: building underground home; herb gardening; sewing; historical research. Office: IRS 3539 E 30th Farmington NM 87401

EARP, BRENDA CAROL, medical technologist; b. Lafe, Ark., Aug. 25, 1946; d. A.G. Harrison and Clarice Beatrice (Harris) Earp; A.S., Mott Community Coll., 1966; A.B., U. Mich., 1969; cert. Hurley Med. Center Sch. Med. Technology, 1970. Lab. asst. Dr. F.W. Baske, Flint, Mich., 1966-68; substitute tchr. Flint Community Schs., 1969; med. technologist microchemistry lab. Hurley Med. Center, Flint, 1970—; lectr. in field. Vol. ARC. Named Hurley Med. Center Employee of Month, 1976, of Yr., 1977; Brenda Earp Day proclaimed by mayor of Flint, 1977. Mem. U. Mich. Alumni Assn., Hurley Med. Center Med. Technologist Orgn., Am. Soc. Clin. Pathologists. Democrat. Baptist. Contbr. articles to profl. jours. Home: 652 Vermilya Ave Flint MI 48507 Office: 1 Hurley Plaza Flint MI 48502

EARP, R(OBERTA) DIANE, foundation administrator; b. Petersburg, Va., Mar. 14, 1958; d. Robert Donald and Verenia Avalee (Bryant) E. BS in Med. Tech., Western Carolina U., 1980; cert. in specialist in blood banking, Duke U., 1983. Med. technician intern VA Med. Ctr., Asheville, N.C., 1979-80; staff immunohematologist Med. Ctr. Duke U., Durham, N.C., 1980-82; asst. dir. tech. services ARC, Columbia, S.C., 1983, dir. tech. services, 1983-87; regulatory compliance assoc. med. ops. ARC, Washington, 1987—; part-time faculty mem. Midlands Tech. Coll., Columbia, 1983-87. Mem. Am. Assn. Blood Banks, N.C. Blood Bankers Assn., Palmetto Blood Bankers Assn., (chair planning com. 1984, bd. dirs. 1984-85, chair membership com. 1986, sec. 1986-87), Internat. Soc. Blood Transfusions, Am. Soc. Clin. Pathologists. Methodist. Home: 2104 Randolph Rd Apt. 206 Silver Spring MD 20902 Office: ARC Nat Headqrs 1730 E Street NW Washington DC 20006

EASBEY, MARION MORIARTY, writer, retired telephone company official; b. New Bedford, Mass., Apr. 8, 1930; d. Walter Vincent and Marion Elizabeth (Rigby) Moriarty; B.S., U. R.I., 1947-51; student Bell System Center for Tech. Edn., 1973-86. Service rep. N.E. Telephone & Northwestern Bell, Providence and St. Paul, 1952-58; office supr. Northwestern Bell, St. Paul, 1958-63, engring. staff asst., 1963-64; engring. technician, asso. engr. and engr. Northwestern Bell, St. Paul and N.E. Telephone, Providence, 1967-79, project mgr. N.E. Telephone, Framingham, Mass., 1979-86; engr. chief clk. Northwestern Bell, 1964-67. Practical politics instr. St. Paul C. of C., 1970; Lake Elmo Precinct chmn. and county conv. del., 1973; bd. dirs., co-chmn. privacy com. ACLU. Recipient cert. of Accomplishment, CAP, 1968, cert. of Merit, 1968. Mem. Common Cause (state network chmn. 1976-79), Assn. Mgmt. Women, Nat. Assn. Female Execs., Am. Mgmt. Assn., AAUW, ACLU, NOW. Democrat Unitarian. Club: Appalachian Mountain. Home: 212 Sandy Ln Apt 201-B Warwick RI 02889

EASLEY, JACQUELINE RUTH, personnel executive; b. Ames, Iowa, Oct. 21, 1957; d. Eddie V. and Ruth (Burton) E.; m. Odell G. McGhee II. BA, Carleton Coll., 1980. Personnel adminstrn. Am. Republic Ins. Co., Des Moines, 1980-83, asst. v.p., 1093—. bd. dirs. Day Care, Inc., Des Moines, 1983—, Willkie House, Inc., Des Moines, 1983—, United Way of Cen. Iowa, Des Moines, 1984—; pres. YWCA of Greater Des Moines, 1987. Mem. Adminstrv. Mgmr. Soc., Alpha Kappa Alpha. Home: 1332 Creston Ave Des Moines IA 50315 Office: Am Republic Ins Co 6th and Keo Way Des Moines IA 50334

EASLEY, VICTORIA LYNN, news writer, columnist; b. Kewanee, Ill., Sept. 19, 1950; d. Marcia B. (Easley) Fuller; raised by grandparents John and Elaine (Sayles) E.; 1 child, Heather Elaine. Student, Kendall Coll., 1968-70, No. Ill. U., DeKalb, 1971-73; AAin Broadcast Journalism, Los Angeles Valley Coll., 1984. Promotions The Jockey Club, Los Angeles, 1982-86; pub. relations and promotions G.S.B. Fashion Designs, Los Angeles, 1982-84; columnist The Salem Reporter, Los Angeles, 1984—; corp. intern Sta. KHJ, RKO, Los Angeles, 1984; news intern Sta. KNX, Los Angeles, 1985-86; desk and prodn. asst. Sta. KFWB, Los Angeles, 1986-87, news writer, 1987—, on-air reporter, 1987—; editor Mendes Cons. Service, Los Angeles, 1986—; Vol. news writer, reporter Sta. KPFK, Los Angeles, 1987—. Contbr. articles to profl. jours., mags. Mem. Black Journalists So. Calif., Women in Radio, TV and Film, Am. Fedn. TV and Radio Artists, Wilshire Bus. and Profl. Women, Tau Alpha Epsilon. Democrat. Baptist. Home: 7540 Satsuma Ave Sun Valley CA 91352 Office: Sta KFWB 6230 Yucca St Los Angeles CA 90028

EASTER, ANITA BATCHELOR, manufacturing company executive; b. Greenville, S.C., July 22, 1944; d. Paul Raymond and Evelyn Lurlene (Massingill) Batchelor; m. Curtis Harold Easter Jr., Aug. 8, 1964; children: Shawn Curtis, Gina Anita. Diploma in Nursing, N.C. Bapt. Hosp., 1965; BS in Nursing magna cum laude, U. S.C., 1978. Staff nurse Meml. Hosp., Danville, Va., 1965-68, St. Joseph's Hosp., Asheville, N.C., 1969; nursing quality assurance coordinator Kershaw County Meml. Hosp., Camden, S.C., 1981-83; sales exec. Al Walker & Assocs., Inc., Columbia, S.C., 1984-87; bd. dirs. St. Andrews Area Council Greater Columbia C. of C., 1987—; corp. dir. Anchor Continental Inc., Columbia. V.p. membership Richlands Northeast High Sch., Columbia, 1986-87; site coordinator Columbia Bicentennial Commn., 1986; del. to Wellness Council of S.C. Midlands; mem. First 70 Task Force, Bapt. Med. Ctr., Columbia, 1986; social ministry com. Good Shepherd Luth. Ch., Columbia, 1985—. Mem. Sales and Mktg. Execs. (Disting. Sales award Columbia chpt. 1984, 86), Millwood Embroiderers Guild, Sigma Theta Tau. Lutheran. Club: Columbia Tip. Home: 3605 Greenleaf Rd Columbia SC 29206 Office: Anchor Continental Inc PO Drawer G 2000 S Beltline Blvd Columbia SC 29205

EASTERBROOK, HELEN LOUISE, bank officer; b. Cowles, Nebr., Feb. 2, 1917; d. Jesse M. and Lora Belle (Holland) Marsh; A.B., Hastings (Nebr.) Coll., 1938; M.S. in Edn., Kearney (Nebr.) State Coll., 1961; m. Carl W. Easterbrook, May 25, 1940; 1 dau., Leslie Eileen Easterbrook Holchak. Tchr. English, Nebr. high schs., 1939-58, Lab. Sch., U. No. Colo., Greeley, 1963-65; instr. English, Kearney State Coll., 1960-72; trust adminstrn. officer Platte Valley State Bank & Trust Co., Kearney, 1973-83. Mem. Nat. Assn. Bank Women (pres. Central Nebr. Group 1980-81), Am. Inst. Banking. Presbyterian. Home: 3117 10th Ave Kearney NE 68847

EASTHAM, CAROLE ANN, marketing professional; b. Jackson Heights, N.Y., Mar. 27, 1950; d. Charles Robert and Anna Marie (Jason) Rae; m. James N. Eastham Jr., June 24, 1972 (div. Feb. 1985); children: James N. III, Bradley; m. W. Todd Shera, Apr. 23, 1988. BA in Sociology, St. Bonaventure U., 1972. Activities dir. Cattaraugus County Nursing Home, Olean, N.Y., 1972-74, Old Court Nursing Ctr., Randallston, Md., 1978-82; account mgr. Nat. Film and Video, Sykesville, Md., 1983; activities dir., social service designee Breightonwood Nursing Home, Catonsville, Md., 1983-84; divisional sales mgr. M.S. Video Distbrs., Balt., 1984-87; account exec. The Dub Centre, Owings Mills, Md., 1987; dir. mktg. and pub. relations Dawson Electronics Mktg., Sykesville, 1987-88; owner C. Moore Video, Balt., 1988—. Author: Reality Orientation, 1980, Remotivation Therapy, 1984; producer video film: Activities and the Aged, 1987. Mem. Nat. Assn. for Women Execs., Video Software Dealers Assn., Am. Assn. of Polit. Cons. Democrat. Roman Catholic. Home: 3736 Springdell Ave Randallstwon MD 21133 Office: C Moore Video 7208 Windsor Mill Rd Baltimore MD 21207

EASTMAN, CAROLYN ANN, microbiology company executive; b. Potsdam, N.Y., Sept. 8, 1946; d. Frank Orvis and Irene (Rheaume) Eastman. BS in Biology, Nazareth Coll., 1968; AAS in Photography, Rochester Inst. Tech., 1976. Technician U. Rochester, N.Y., 1968-69; chemist Castle/Sybron, Rochester, 1969-79; owner, v.p. Sterilization Tech. Svcs., Rush, N.Y., 1979—; owner Fairfield Cosmetics, Rush, 1986—; ptnr. EFC Properties, 1983—. Contbr. articles to profl. jours.; patentee in field. Recipient 1st and 3d places Arts for Greater Rochester, 1977. Mem. NOW, Assn. for Advancement of Med. Instrumentation, Nat. Assn. Female Execs., Amnesty Internat., Sierra Club. Democrat. Roman Catholic. Club: Huggers Ski, Henrietta Art. Home: 6 Genesee St Scottsville NY 14546 Office: Sterilization Tech Services 7500 W Henrietta Rd Rush NY 14543

EASTMAN, LINDA SUZANNE, consulting organization executive, corporate image consultant; b. Evanston, Ill., Sept. 21, 1946; d. Robert William and Ardath Louis (Stoddard) Ellis; m. Albert Henry Eastman, Nov. 20, 1971; 1 dau., Suzanne Elisabeth. Student No. Ill. U., 1965-66, U. Louisville, 1986—. Model, Jack Winter, Chgo., 1969-71, Saks Fifth Avenue, N.Y.C., 1969; stewardess Am. Airlines, Chgo. and N.Y.C., 1969-71; owner, operator Louisville Model Agy., 1973—; pres. The Profl. Woman Network, Prospect, Ky., 1981—; corp. image cons. Author: The Professional Woman; The Teen Image Guide, 1984. Mem. Nat. Assn. Female Execs., Am. Soc. Tng. and Devel., Am. Assn. Women Bus. Owners. Republican. Episcopalian. Club: Louisville Tennis. Lodge: Zonta. Avocations: tennis, water skiing. Home: 14107 Harbour Pl Prospect KY 40059 Office: The Profl Woman Network PO Box 333 Prospect KY 40059

EASTMAN, LOUELLA JANE, telecommunications company executive; b. Sudbury, Can., Dec. 29, 1955; d. Hilliard William Henry and Elizabeth Helen Nora (Breen) Lachance; m. Douglas Kendall Eastman, June 10, 1978. B in Commerce, Queen's U., Kingston, Ontario, 1978; MBA, McMaster U., Hamilton, Ontario, 1982. Inventory control, prodn. mgr. Internat. Harvester Corp., Hamilton, 1978-81; mgr. human resource Steetley Industries, Ltd., Hamilton, 1981-83; mgr. employee relations Ontario and Western provinces No. Telecom Can. Ltd., Toronto, 1983—. Mem. food drive orgn., Toronto, 1987—. Mem. Personnel Assn. of Ontario (bd. dirs. 1986—). Office: No Telecom Can, 2920 Matheson Blvd E, Mississauga, ON Canada L4W 4M7

EASTON, JOAN MARIE, educator; b. Bklyn., May 4, 1935; d. John and Honor Angela (Sheehan) Wardenier; m. Edward R. Easton, Dec. 23, 1970; 1 child, Sean. BA, Hunter Coll., 1954, MA, 1957; postgrad. doctoral studies, NYU, 1968-74. Instr. Pace U., N.Y.C., 1963-70, asst. prof., 1970-76; spl. lectr. Univ. Coll., Cork City, Ireland, 1980-82; adj. asst. prof. Coll. Santa Fe, 1982-85, adj. assoc. prof., 1985-86, asst. dir. Sch. of Open Studies, 1984-86; assoc. prof., faculty advisor Capital U., Columbus, Ohio, 1986—; founder, headmistress The Little Sch., Schull, Ireland, 1975-82; cons. in field. vol. counselor Stop Child Abuse Now, Santa Fe, 1982-83; exec. dir. Santa Fe Girls Club, 1983-84. Recipient citation City of Santa Fe, 1983. Mem. Nat. Women's Studies Assn., Nat. Council of Tchrs. of English, Am. Assn. for Adult and Continuing Edn., AAUW, Bus. and Profl. Women (2d v.p. 1986-87). Roman Catholic. Office: Capital U Adult Degree Program Columbus OH 43209

EASTON, LORETTA J., real estate executive; b. Chgo., Aug. 30, 1959; d. Jerry W. Sandoval and Patricia A. (Martinez) Martin; m. Roger J. Easton, May 25, 1985. AS in Bus. Communications, Elgin Bus. Coll., 1979; BA in Mgmt., Ga. State U., 1985. Office mgr. Richard Heiman Advt., Atlanta, 1979-85; v.p. Roberts Properties, Inc., Atlanta, 1985—. Mem. Atlanta C. of C., Humane Soc. Republican. Presbyterian. Office: Roberts Properties Inc. 1000 Abernathy Rd Suite 1115 Atlanta GA 30328

EASTON-KIRKMAN, JANET RENE, marketing professional; b. Normandy, Mo., Mar. 23, 1960; d. John Wesley and Lois Eleanor (Gortner) E.; m. Roger Dale Kirkman, May 17, 1986. BA, U. N.C., 1979; BA in Industl. Mgmt., Mech. Engring., Purdue U., 1983; MBA, Ariz. State U., 1987. Engr. McDonnell Douglas Aricraft Co., St. Louis, 1980-81; rep.account AT&T Tech., Phoenix, 1983-85; rep. mktg. O'Neil Assocs., Tempe, Ariz., 1986; grad. asst. Ariz. State U., Tempe, 1986-87; product mgr. customer service Hewlett Packard, Mountain View, Calif., 1987-88; product mgr. LAN Products, Roseville, CA, 95678. Tchr. Mt. View Presbytarian Ch., Scottsdale, Ariz. 1987. Mem. Am. Mktg. Assn., Nat. Assn. Female Exec., Soc. Women Engrs. (pres. 1982-83, treas. 1981-82), Purdue Alumni Assn., Beta Gamma Sigma. Home: 2300 Quail Ridge W Ln #131 Roseville CA 95678 Office: 8000 Foothills Blvd Roseville CA 95678

EATON, CARLOTTA BROWNING, computer programmer, administrator; b. Radford, Va., Aug. 7, 1957; d. Connie Ray and Nina Alice (Hollandsworth) Browning; m. John Steven Eaton, June 2, 1979; 1 child, Cassandra Lovelyn. BS in Math. and Stats., Radford U., 1979; MS in Stats., Va. Tech. U., 1980; postgrad., U. N.C., 1984-86. Assoc. programmer IBM-CPD, Research Triangle Park, N.C., 1981-82; sr. assoc. engr., scientist IBM-CPD, Research Triangle Park, 1982-86, staff product planner, 1986—. Mem. Nat. Assn. Female Execs. Home: 9704 Kingsford Dr Raleigh NC 27606 Office: IBM-T57-671-1BA 11000 Regency Pkwy Cary NC 27511

EATON, EDNA DOROTHY, home health care administrator; b. Van Meter, Iowa, Mar. 21, 1938; d. Walter Clifford and Rosemarie Rose (Lienemann); m. Edward Eugene Eaton, July 1, 1962; children: David Clifford, Thomas Eugene. BS in Nursing, RN, U. Iowa, 1961. Staff nurse Shenandoah Hosp., Iowa, 1961-62, 63-65, Hamburg Community Hosp., Iowa, 1965-73; surg. supr. Grape Community Hosp., Hamburg, 1973-79, dir. nursing, 1979-87 ; health care administr. S.W. Iowa Home Health Services, Sidney, Iowa, 1987—. Bd. govs. Iowa Bd. Nursing, 1984—. Named Booster of Yr., Booster Club Sidney, 1985. Republican. Lutheran. Home: Box 429 Sidney IA 51652 Office: SW Iowa Home Health Services Box 357 Sidney IA 51652

EATON, LYNDA LOU, aircraft manufacturing company executive; b. Nevada, Mo., Aug. 31, 1946; d. Ira and Anna Mae (Welch) E.; B.S. in Chemistry, Central Mo. State U., Warrensburg, 1967; M.B.A., Pepperdine U., 1981; m. John C. Carlisle, Dec. 1980. Blood bank supr. St. Luke's Hosp., Kansas City, Mo., 1968-71; acting blood bank supr. Hoag Meml. Hosp., Newport Beach, Calif., 1971-72; blood bank supr. City of Hope Nat. Med. Center, Duarte, Calif., 1975-77; mgr. Immuno-Science, Inc., Los Angeles, 1977-82; materials mgr. Ortho Diagnostic Systems, Inc., Irvine, Calif., 1982-85; br. mgr. Douglas Aircraft Co., Long Beach, Calif., 1985—. Mem. Am. Soc. Clin. Pathology (med. technologist, specialist in blood banking), Am. Assn. Blood Banks, Am. Prodn. and Inventory Soc. Republican. Home: 6 Palos Irvine CA 92715 Office: Douglas Aircraft Co 3855 Lakewood Blvd Long Beach CA 90846

EATON, NANCY L., librarian; b. Berkeley, Calif., May 2, 1943; d. Don Thomas and Lena Ruth (McClellan) Linton; m. Edward Arthur Eaton III, June 19, 1965 (div. 1980). AB, Stanford U., 1965; MLS, U. Tex., 1968, postgrad., 1969. Cataloger U. Tex. Library, Austin, 1968-71, head MARC unit, 1971-72, asst. to librarian, 1972-74; automation librarian SUNY, Stony Brook, 1974-76; head tech. services Atlanta Pub. Library, 1976-82; dir. libraries U. Vt., Burlington, 1982—; del. user's council, mem. exec. com. Online Computer Library Ctr., Inc., Dublin Ohio, 1980-82, 86-88, trustee, 1987—; mgr. Nat. Agricultural Text Digitalizing Project, 1986—; bd. dirs. New Eng. Library Network, 1987—. Co-author: Optical Information Systems: Implementation Issues for Libraries, 1988.; co-editor: A Cataloging Sampler, 1971, Book Selection Policies in American Libraries, 1972; contbr. articles to profl. jours. U.S. Office of Edn. post-master's fellow, 1969; Dept. Edn. Title II-C grantee, 1985, 87. Mem. ALA, Library and Info. Tech. Assn. (pres. 1984-85, bd. dirs. 1980-86), Vt. Library Assn., AAUW. Democrat. Home: 1 Potter Pl Shelburne VT 05482 Office: Univ Vt Room 113 Bailey-Howe Library Burlington VT 06506

EATON, PAULINE, artist; b. Neptune, N.J., Mar. 20, 1935; d. Paul A. and Florence Elizabeth (Rogers) Friedrich; m. Charles Adams Eaton, June 15, 1957; children—Gregory, Eric, Paul, Joy. B.A., Dickinson Coll., 1957; M.A., Northwestern U., 1958. Lic. instr., Calif. Instr., Mira Costa Coll., Oceanside, Calif., 1980-82, Idyllwild Sch. Music and Arts, Calif., 1983—; juror, demonstrator numerous art socs. Recipient award Haywood (Calif.) Area Forum for the Arts, 1986. Exhibited one-woman shows Nat. Arts Club, N.Y.C., 1977, Designs Recycled Gallery, Fullerton, Calif., 1978, 80, 84, San Diego Art Inst., 1980, Spectrum Gallery, San Diego, 1981, San Diego Jung Ctr., 1983, Marin Civic Ctr. Gallery, 1984; group shows include Am. Watercolor Soc., 1975, 77, Butler Inst. Am. Art, Youngstown, Ohio, 1977, 78, 79, 81, NAD, 1978; represented in permanent collections including Butler Inst. Am. Art, St. Mary's Coll., Md., Mercy Hosp., San Diego, Sharp Hosp., San Diego, Redlands Hosp., Riverside, 1986; work featured in books: Watercolor, The Creative Experience, 1978, Creative Seascape Painting, 1980, Painting the Spirit in Nature, 1984, Exploring Painting (Gerald Brommer); author: Crawling to the Light, An Artist in Transition, 1987. Trustee San Diego Art Inst., 1977-78, San Diego Mus. Art, 1982-83. Mem. Nat. Watercolor Soc. (exhibited traveling shows 1978, 79, 83, 85), Rocky Mountain Watermedia Soc. (Golden award 1979, Mustard Seed award 1983), Nat. Soc. Painters in Acrylic and Casein (hon.), Watercolor West (Strathmore award 1979, Purchase award 1986), Marin Arts Guild (instr. 1984—), San Diego Watercolor Soc. (pres. 1976-77, workshop dir. 1977-80), Artists Equity (v.p. San Diego 1979-81), San Diego Artists Guild (pres. 1982-83), Western Fedn. Watercolor Socs. (chmn. 1983, 3d prize 1982, Grumbacher Gold medal 1983), West Coast Watercolor Soc. (exhbns. chmn. 1983-86). Democrat. Presbyterian. Home: 10 Alta Mira Ave Kentfield CA 94904

EATON, VIRGINIA ELDRIDGE (NIA), sales executive; b. Mt. Holly, N.J., July 29, 1948; d. Howard E. and Virginia (Wills) Eldridge; m. Gilbert J. Eaton, Mar. 25, 1972. BA, Sweet Briar (Va.) Coll., 1970. Sales exec., asst. to pres. Sonex, Inc., Bethayres, Pa., 1970-72; customer relations rep. Varitype div. Am. Internat., Bala Cynwyd, Pa., 1974-76; dist. sales mgr. Computer Devices, Inc., Blue Bell (Pa.) and Nutting Lake (Mass.), 1976-83; maj. account mgr. Monroe Systems Computer Div., Inc., Willow Grove, Pa., 1983-84; ea. regional mgr. Computer Devices, Inc., Blue Bell and Nutting Lake, 1984—. V.p. Halford Civic Assn., Jeffersonville, Pa., 1981. Mem. Nat. Assn. Profl. Sales Women (sec. 1981-83, newsletter editor 1983-84, v.p. 1984-85). Republican. Episcopalian. Club: Halford Garden (pres.). Office: Computer Devices Inc 1777 Walton Rd Blue Bell PA 19422

EATON-CONLEY, DIANA JO, health and fitness facility administrator, consultant; b. Olean, N.Y., Mar. 10, 1955; d. Frank Richard and Catherine Irene (Stout) Eaton; m. Robert Michael Meyers, June 4, 1983 (div. 1985); m. Ted Byron Conley, Feb. 14, 1986. Student, Erie Community Coll., 1971-73, Fredonia U., 1974-75; diploma in clin. nutrition, Clayton U., 1982. Cert. med. asst., clin. nutritionist, phlebotomist, reflexologist, intravenous chelation technician, non-invasive vascular technician, diagnostice cons. Owner, instr. Dancing Emporium, Gowanda, N.Y., 1974-76; instr. Orlando (Fla.) Athletic and Health Club, 1976; mgr. Pres. 1st Lady Health Club, Houston, 1977; asst. adminstr. Norwell Med. Ctrs., Houston, 1977; clinic adminstr., dir. patient relations, cons., lab technician Brennan Preventive Medicine Ctr., Houston, 1977-80; v.p. Ednl. Edits. Pub. Co., Houston, 1977-80; owner, salesperson, instr. Bio-Instrumentation Spltys., San Antonio, 1980—; owner, dir. Nutrition and Home Health Care div., 1982—, N.W. Nutrition and Health Ctr., San Antonio, 1983—, Wholistic Health Opportunities and Affiliates, San Antonio and Ruidoso Downs (N.Mex.), 1986—; cons. Hearty Foods, Inc., San Antonio, 1986—, Quick-Catery, San Antonio, 1985-86; certifying instr. Vascular Diagnostic Instruments, Inc., Cherry Hill, N.J., 1979—. Author: Simple Sensible Steps, 1984, Paradise Caribe Revitalization, 1985, Paradise Caribe Vitalization, 1985; editorial bd. adv. mem. Alive Mag., 1984—. Adv. Tex. Health Freedom Council, Austin, Tex., 1981—, lobbyist, 1983-85; lectr. health/nutrition Easter Seal Orgn., San Antonio, 1985—, schs., 1984-85; radio talk show guest, San Antonio, 1982—. Recipient award N.Y. State Dept. Mental Hygiene, 1976-77; Regents scholar State of N.Y., 1973. Fellow Am. Council Applied Clun. Nutrition Found; mem. Internat. Soc. Chelations Technicians (bd. dirs., sec.. lectr. 1984—), Am. Inst. Med. Preventics, Health Freedom Council, Internat. Inst. Reflexology, Soc. Non-Invasive Vascular Technicians, Internat. Acad. Neuro-Vascular Diseases, Am. Soc. Bariatric Physicians, Nat. Assn. for Female Execs., Aircraft Owners and Pilots Assn. Home: 7254 Blanco Rd Suite 100-9 San Antonio TX 78216 Office: SW Wholistic Health Opportunities Inc 10663 W Loop 1604 North San Antonio TX 78250

EATON-TATRO, DEBORAH ARLENE, underwriter; b. Los Angeles, Jan. 7, 1956; d. William Tedrick Eaton and Martha Ellen (Hegarty) Cook; m. Eugene Roger Tatro, Sept. 6, 1980. BA, Calif. State U., Fullerton, 1981. Underwriter TransAm. Occidential Life, Los Angeles, 1982-84; chief underwriter TransAm. Assurance Co., Orange, Calif., 1985-88; pres. So. Calif. home office Los Angeles, 1988—. Mem. So. Calif. Home Office Underwriting Assn. (sec. 1986, v.p. 1987), Western Home Office Underwriters Assn., DAR. Democrat. Roman Catholic. Office: TransAm Assurance Co 1150 S Olive St Los Angeles CA 90015

EBBERS, LAURA KAY, advertising executive; b. Grand Rapids, Mich., Sept. 12, 1954; d. John Tony and Janet Elizabeth (Battjes) E. BA in English with high honors, Elmhurst (Ill.) Coll., 1976; postgrad. in advt., Northwestern U., Chgo., 1983. Account supr. HartMarx, Chgo., 1977-83; account exec. HCM/Marsteller, Chgo., 1984-85, Saffer Cravitt Freedman, Chgo., 1985-86, A. Eicoff & Co., Chgo., 1986—. Mem. Women's Advt. Club of Chgo. (dir. fin. 1985-86, chair Addy award judging com. 1986-87, Addy award 1979), Chgo. Assn. Direct Mktg. Home: 145 N Walnut Elmhurst IL 60126 Office: A Eicoff & Co 520 N Michigan Chicago IL 60611

EBEL CHANDLER, CAROLYN, newspaper publisher, manager literacy program; b. Rochester, N.Y., Nov. 1, 1936; d. Kent Dane and Emily A. (Masonic) Williams; m. William K. Ebel, Jr., June 25, 1960 (div. 1982); children—William III, Jennifer A., Bruce K.; m. Donald R. Chandler, Oct. 12, 1986. B.A., Wells Coll., 1958; M.Ed., Temple U., 1973, Ed.D., 1978. Coordinator adult ESL, Lancaster-Lebanon Intermediate Unit 13 (Pa.), 1969-72, dir. ESL, bilingual edn., 1972-80; acting exec. dir. Nat. Assn. Bilingual Edn., Washington, 1980-81; asst. prof. ESL, Georgetown U., Washington, 1983-85; with BESL/EDR, Inc., Drumore, Pa., 1979-82; mgr. literacy program Am. Newspaper Publishers Assn. Found., 1986—. Editor NABE News, 1976-82, BESL Reporter, 1975-80. Pres., Friends of Lancaster Pub. Library. Recipient Outstanding Service to Hispanic Community award Pa. State Hispanic Concerns Orgn., Harrisburg, 1976; award of merit El Centro Hispano, Lancaster, 1978. Mem. Tchrs. English to Speakers of Other Langs. (pres. Pa. affiliate 1976-77), Phi Delta Kappa. Clubs: Jr. League, Los Besol (pres. 1976-77) (Lancaster, Pa.). Home: 437 Olympia Way Great Falls VA 22066 Office: Am Newspaper Pubs Assn Found 11600 Sun Valley Dr Reston VA 22091

EBELING, ELINOR RUTH, library administrator; b. Detroit, Aug. 23, 1932; d. Vergil McKinley and Edith Athlee (Graves) Hodges; B.A., Wayne State U., 1954; M.L.S., U. Mich., 1957; hon. fellow Western Mich. U., 1967-68. Circulation/reference librarian Fordson High Sch., Dearborn, Mich., 1954-61; supr. tech. services Henry Ford Community Coll., Dearborn, 1961-67; asst. profl. library sci. Ill. State U., Normal, 1968-69; dir. Brookdale Community Coll., Lincroft, N.J., 1969—. Mem. N.J. Edn. Assn., N.J. Library Assn., ALA, Assn. Community and Regional Libraries (chmn. community jr. coll. sect. 1983-85), N.J. Library Network (officer region V), Delta Zeta, Pi Lambda Theta, Beta Phi Mu. Home: 328 Seaview Circle Neptune NJ 07753 Office: Brookdale Community Coll Newman Springs Rd Lincroft NJ 07738

EBERHART, JUDITH ELLEN, psychology educator, counselor; b. Kingsville, Tex., Nov. 14, 1944; d. Jean Forest and Reba Helena (Brogdon) E. BS, U. Oreg., 1966; MS, San Diego State U., 1973; postgrad., U.S. Internat. U., 1987—. Lic. marriage, family and child counselor, Calif.; cert. in hypnosis, Calif.; cert. career counselor. Vol. Peace Corps, Venezuela, 1966-68; recruiter Washington, 1969, adminstrv. asst., 1970; researcher, writer Consad Research Corp., Pitts., 1971; assessment officer San Diego State Found., 1973; counselor, instr. Palomar Coll., San Marcos, Calif., 1973—, dir. career ctr., 1985-87; instr. aerobics Palomar Coll., San Marcos, 1974—, Olympic Health Resort, Carlsbad, Calif., 1986—; leader, cons., trainer seminars and workshops, Carlsbad, 1975—; family counselor, psychotherapist Family Alliance, Oceanside, Calif., 1985-86; cons. adv. bd., project dir. Calif. Coll. Health Sci., National City, Calif., 1985—; commr. Calif. Assn. Community Coll., 1986—. Author (corr. course) Career Search, 1986; editor: (with others) Fit For Life, 1983; contbr. articles on health issues to profl. jours.; producer/instr. exercise TV courses. Active Save the Trees, Carlsbad, 1986. Named one of Outstanding Young Women Am., 1976; Exon Corp. grantee, 1975. Mem. Am. Assn. Counseling and Devel., Assn. Psychol. Type, Am. Assn Women in Community and Jr. Colls., Calif. Assn. Career Devel., Calif. Marriage Family Therapists, Australian/Am. Club. Home: 2050 Ave of the Trees Carlsbad CA 92008 Office: Palomar Coll West Mission San Marcos CA 92069

EBERLEY, HELEN-KAY MARIE, opera singer, classical record company executive; b. Sterling, Ill., Aug. 3, 1947; d. William Elliot and P. (Conneely) E.; m. Vincent P. Skowronski, July 15, 1972. MusB, Northwestern U., 1970, MusM, 1971. Pres. Eberley-Skowronski, Inc., Evanston, Ill., 1973—; artistic coordinator Eberley-Skowronski, Inc., 1973; founder EB-SKO Prodns., 1976, tchr.-coach, 1976; exec. dir., performance cons. E-S Mgmt., 1985; participating artist Honors Concert Northwestern U., 1970. Operatic debut Peter Grimes Lyric Opera, Chgo., 1974; starred in: Cosi Fan Tutte, Le Nozze Di Figaro, Dido and Aeneas, La Boehme, Faust, Don Giovanni, Brigadoon, others; performing artist Oglebay Opera Inst., Wheeling, W.Va., 1968, WTTW TV/PBS, Chgo., 1968, Continental Bank Concerts, Schubert, United Airlines-Schubert, Schumann, Brahms, Mendelssohn WFMT Radio, Chgo., 1982-88; producer/annotator Gentleman Gypsy, 1978, Skowronski: Strauss & Szymanowski, 1979, One Sonata Each: Franck & Szymankowski, 1982; artist/ exec. producer Separate But Equal, 1976, Opera Lady, 1978, Eberley Sings Strauss, 1980, Helen-Kay Eberley: An American Girl, 1983, Helen-Kay Eberley: Opera Lady II, 1984; performed Am. and Can. Nat. Anthems for Chgo. Cubs Baseball Team, and Chgo. Bears Football, 1977-83. Mem. Mayor's founding com. Evanston Arts Council, 1974-75; judge Ice-skating Competition Wilmette (Ill.) Park Dist., 1985-88; fin. chmn. Chgo. Youth Orchestra, 1974-77, bd. dirs. 1973-77. Recipient Creative and Performing Arts award Ind. Jr. Miss and So. Bend Jr. Miss, 1965, Louis Sundler award Northwestern U., 1966, Frederic Chramer award Northwestern U., 1967, F.K. Weyerhauser Scholar award Met. Opera, 1967, Milton J. Cross award Met. Opera Guild, 1968; prizewinner Met. Opera Nat. Auditions, Lincoln Ctr., N.Y., 1968. Mem. Am. Guild Musical Artists. Clubs: St. Mary's Acad. Alumnae Assn., Delta Gamma. Office: EB-SKO Prodns 1726 Sherman Ave Evanston IL 60201

EBERSOLE, GUYLEENE HARMON, accountant; b. Minden, La., Jan. 4, 1941; d. Guy Augustus and Anna Belle (Shinpoch) Harmon; children: Ross Harmon Florey, Rachel Florey, Jason Florey. Student Kilgore Coll., 1959-60, 74, Houston Community Coll., 1976-77; BA in Acctg. summa cum laude, U. St. Thomas, 1979, MBA, 1983. CPA, Tex., Calif. Acct., Deloitte Haskins & Sells, Houston, 1980-82; controller Oilfield Pipe & Supply Co., Houston, 1982; prin. Guyleene Harmon Ebersole, CPA, Houston, 1982-86; auditor Tex. Gen. Land Office, Austin, 1986-88; tax analyst CCH Computax, Los Angeles, 1988—; sec.-treas., dir. Sand Dollar, Inc., 1985-86; lectr. U. St. Thomas, Houston, 1984. Treas., bd. dirs. Heights Area Polit. Action Com., Houston, 1983-87; bd. dirs. North Main Redevel. Task Force, Houston, 1983; sec. Woodland Heights Civic Club, Houston, 1984. Heights coordinator Mayor Kathy Whitmire campaign, Houston, 1983; treas. Harris County Dem. Exec. Com., 1984-86; mem. parks steering com. Harris County Precinct I, 1985-86. Mem. Am. Inst. CPA's, Tex. Soc. CPA's (nat. fiscal issues com. 1983-88, acctg. and auditing com. 1984, primary key person 1983-88; Houston chpt. mgmt. adv. services com. 1984, chmn. 1986, pub.

affairs com. 1985, vice chair 1986), AAUW, Am. Contract Bridge League (cert. dir.), Harris County Women's Polit. Caucus (treas. 1985-87), Phi Theta Kappa. Democrat. Episcopalian. Home and Office: PO Box 92938 Los Angeles CA 90009-2938

EBERSOLE, MARY ELLEN FRANCES, nurse, electrologist; b. Washington, Oct. 4, 1940; d. William Ignatius and Madelina Rose (Daidone) Hayes; m. Harold Robert Ebersole, Feb. 20, 1965; children: Eileen Marie, Kathleen. Diploma with honors, Meml. Hosp. Roxborough, 1964; cert. in electrolysis, U. Md., 1976, Eastern Inst. Practical Electrolysis, 1977. Cert. Internat. Bd. Electrologists, Nat. Commn. Electrologists. Perioperative nurse Washington Hosp. Ctr., 1964-65, operating room head nurse, 1966-68, operating room coordinator, 1969-73; perioperative nurse VA Med. Ctr., Washington, 1973-76, urodynamics clinician, perioperative endourology nurse, charge nurse urology clinic, 1976—, RN orientation instr., with med. student orientation staff, 1979—; electrologist Columbia (Md.) Electrolysis, 1978-87; electrologist, pres. Exec. Electrolysis, Laurel, Md. and Columbia, 1987—; instr. Basic Cardiac Life Support Am. Heart Assn. Mem. Help for Incontinent People, Union, S.C., 1984—. Recipient Outstanding Service award Disabled Am. Vets., 1979. Mem. Am. Urologists Assn. of Allied Health Profls. of Mid-Atlantic, Urodynamic Sub Specialist Group, Am. Assn. Operating Room Nurses (cert.), Am. Electrology Assn. (chair infection control standards com. 1987), Md. Assn. Profl. Electrologists (recording sec. 1980, corr. sec. 1981), Am. Running and Fitness Assn., Nat. Assn. Female Execs. Democrat. Roman Catholic. Home: 11038 Montgomery Rd Beltsville MD 20705 Office: Exec Electrolysis Oakland Ridge Profl Ctr 9123 Old Annapolis Rd Columbia MD 21045 also: Montpelier Exec Ctr 9811 Mallard Dr Laurel MD 20708

EBITZ, ELIZABETH KELLY, lawyer; b. LaPorte, Ind., June 9, 1950; d. Joseph Monahan and Ann Mary (Barrett) Kelly; m. David MacKinnon Ebitz, Jan. 23, 1971 (div. 1981). A.B. with honors, Smith Coll., 1972; J.D. cum laude, Boston U., 1975. Bar: Maine, Mass, U.S. Supreme Ct. Law clk. Boston Legal Assistance Project, 1973-75; law clk., assoc. Law Offices of John J. Thornton, Boston, 1974-76; ptnr. Ebitz & Zurn, Northampton, Mass., 1976-79; assoc. Gross, Minsky, Mogul & Singal, Bangor, Maine, 1979-80; sole practice, pres. Elizabeth Kelly Ebitz, P.A., Bangor, 1980—. Pres. Greater Bangor Rape Crisis Bd., 1983-85; bd. dirs. Greater Bangor Area Shelter, 1985—, Maine Women's Lobby, 1986—, No. Maine Bread for the World, 1987—; Bread for the World, Maine, 2d congl. dist.; bd. advisors Bread for the World, mem. various peace, feminist and hunger orgns., Bangor, 1982—. Named Young Career Woman of Hampshire County, Nat. Bus. and Profl. Women, Northampton, 1979. Mem. ABA, Assn. Trial Lawyers Am., Sigma Xi. Democrat. Roman Catholic. Home: 111 Maple St Bangor ME 04401 Office: 15 Columbia St PO Box 641 Bangor ME 04401

EBRO, LEA LUISA, home economics and dietetics educator; b. Bacolod City, Philippines, Jan. 11, 1937; d. Leandro Sison and Elvira (Piccio) E. BS in Pharmacy, U. Philippines, 1956, BS in Home Econs., 1960; MS, Iowa State U., 1964; PhD, Ohio State U., 1977. Food adminstr. U. Ill., Champaign, 1965-67; assoc. state dir. State Sch. Food Service, Raleigh, N.C., 1967-68; asst. prof. East Carolina U., Greenville, N.C., 1968-70, SUNY, Plattsburgh, 1970-72; asst. prof. The Ohio State U., Columbus, 1972-75, grad. assoc. dean's assoc. Coll. Home Econs., 1975-77; dir. internships, assoc. prof. Coll. Home Econs., Okla. State U., Stillwater, 1978-84, prof., 1984—, interim dept. head, 1986—; instr. Iowa State U., Ames, 1964-65; lectr. Columbus (Ohio) Tech., 1975; curriculum cons. Tex. Health Ctr., Dallas, 1976; cons. Inst. Producers Services, Los Angeles, 1977. Mem. Am. Dietetic Assn., Am. Home Econs. Assn., Phi Kappa Phi, Omicron Nu. Republican. Roman Catholic. Home: 1111 Preston Dr Stillwater OK 74075 Office: Okla State U HEW 425 Stillwater OK 74075

ECHOLS, DOROTHY ELIZABETH, electrical construction company executive; b. Pauls Valley, Okla., Sept. 1, 1930; d. Luther Monroe Mayfield and Elizabeth (Ramming) Walker; m. Charles Newton Echols, Sept. 24, 1949; children: James Earl, Leslie Dwayne. Student, Okla. Community Coll. Acctg. clk. Carpenter Paper Co., Oklahoma City, 1948-49, John A. Brown, Oklahoma City, 1949-50; bookkeepr Wilson Foods, Oklahoma City, 1950-57; sec., treas. Echols Electric Inc., Moore, Okla., 1967-77, chair bd., 1977—; bd. dirs. Fiber Reclaim Inc., Oklahoma City. Del. White House Conf. on Small Bus., Washington, 1986; mem. adv. bd. SBA, 1985—. Mem. Nat. Electrical Contractors Assn., Nat. Assn. Women Bus. Owners, Internat. Exec. Women, Okla. Women Bus. Owners, Bus. Ptnrs. Inc. (state co-chair 1987), Com. of 200. Office: Echols Electric Inc 2812 N Eastern Moore OK 73160

ECHOLS, IVOR TATUM (MRS. SYLVESTER J. ECHOLS), educator, assistant dean; b. Oklahoma City, Dec. 28, 1919; d. Israel E. and Katie (Bingley) Tatum; A.B., U. Kans., 1942; postgrad. (A.R.C. scholar) U. Nebr., 1945-46; M.S. in Social Work (Nat. Urban League fellow, Porter R. Lee fellow), Columbia, 1952, postgrad. (NIMH fellow), U. So. Calif., 1961-62, D.S.W., 1968; m. Kenneth Johnston, Dec. 28, 1948 (div. June 1951); 1 dau., Kalu Helene; m. 2d, Sylvester J. Echols, June 13, 1954 (div. 1976); 1 son, Kim Arnett. Tchr. social studies high sch., Holdenville, Okla., 1942-43, Geary, Okla., 1943-45; caseworker A.R.C., Chgo., 1946-47; resident group worker, Dosoris House for Teen-Age Girls, Community Services Soc., N.Y.C., 1950-51; supr. group work Walnut Grove Center Neighborhood Clubs, Oklahoma City, 1948-51; program dir. Camp Lookout YWCA, Denver, 1951; dir. program services Presbyn. Neighborhood Services, Detroit, summer 1960, supr. group work Merrill-Palmer Inst., Detroit, 1951-70; asst. dir. Merrill-Palmer Camp, Dryden, Mich., 1951-59; prof. Sch. Social Work, U. Conn., West Hartford, 1970—, now also asst. dean; del. Inter-Univ. Consortium of Social Devel., Hong Kong, 1980; mem. Conn. adv. com. U.S. Commn. Civil Rights. Mem. Ad Hoc Com. Citizens Concerned with Equal Ednl. Opportunity, Detroit, 1964—; cons. to N.E.A. Conf. Family Camping Washington, 1959, ednl. film Scott Paper Co., Phila., 1963, 64; summer study skills project Presbyn. Ch. Bd. Nat. Missions, Knoxville, Tenn., 1965—; sec. United Neighborhood Centers Am.; pres. Protestant Community Services, Detroit, 1969-70. Recipient Educator Human Rights award UN Assn. , 1987, Sojourner Truth award Detroit chpt. Nat. Assn. Negro Bus. and Profl. Women, 1969, UN Assn. award for Edn. and Women's Rights, 1987; named Conn. Social Worker of Year, 1979. Mem. Nat. Assn. Colored Women's Clubs (participant White House Conf. on Children and Youth 1960), A.M.E. Ministers Wives, Acad. Certified Social Workers, Delta Sigma Theta. Mem. A.M.E. Ch. Home: 51 Chestnut Dr Windsor CT 06095 Office: U Conn 1800 Asylum Ave West Hartford CT 06007

ECK, ANDREA LOUISE, advertising and marketing executive; b. Easton, Pa., Oct. 31, 1962; d. Charles Anthony Bottiglieri and Almeda Louise (Eck) Migliazza. Student Northampton County Area Community Coll., Boston Ctr. for Edn., Weist Barron Acting, Walnut St Theatre Sch. Asst. mgr., salesperson Sigals Country Corner Shoe Dept., Easton, Pa., 1980; telemarketing rep. Sammons Communications, Easton, 1981; customer service rep. Christmas Club Corp., Easton, 1980-81, mgr., 1982-83, account exec., Framingham, Mass., 1984-86; self-employed advt. sales and mktg. exec., Phila., 1986-87; telemktg. rep. Phila. Drama Guild, 1986—; dir. admissions, talent recruiter John Casablancas Modeling and Career Ctr., Phila., 1988—. Reviewer theater sect. TV and Radio Reporter, 1986—, Steppin' Out TV mag. Sponsor Christian Children's Fund, Richmond, Va., 1984, 85, 86; fund-raiser Spl. Olympics, 1987. Recipient Disting. Achievement award Christmas Club Corp., 1985. Mem. Nat. Assn. Female Execs., Am. Fedn. TV and Radio Artists. Lutheran. Avocations: acting, travel, sports, aerobics. Home: 1823 E Passyunk Ave Philadelphia PA 19148

ECK, DOROTHY FRITZ, state senator; b. Sequim, Wash., Jan. 23, 1924; d. Ira Edward and Ida (Hokanson) Fritz; B.S. in Secondary Edn., Mont. State U., 1961, M.S. in Applied Sci., 1966; m. Hugo Eck, Dec. 16, 1942; children—Lauvrence, Diana. Co-mgr. archtl. and property mgmt. bus., 1955—; conf. coordinator Am. Agrl. Econs. Assn., 1967-68; state-local coordinator Office of Gov. Mont., Helena, 1972-77; mem. Mont. State Senate, 1981—; mem. Mont. Environ. Quality Council, 1981—. Bd. dirs. Methodist Youth Fellowship, 1960-64, Mont. Council for Effective Legislature, 1977-78, Rocky Mountain Environ. Council, 1982—; del., Western v.p. Mont. Constl. Conv., 1971-72; chmn. Gov.'s Task Force on Citizen Participation, 1976-77; mem. adv. com. No. Rockies Resource and Tng. Center (now No. Lights Inst.), 1979-81. Recipient Outstanding Alumna award Mont. State U., 1981. Mem. LWV (state pres. 1967-70), Common Cause, Nat. Women's Polit. Caucus. Democrat. *

ECKEBRECHT, BETTY MARIE, accountant; b. Manchester, Iowa, Jan. 13, 1958; d. James Leo and Anna Marie (Mulvehill) Broghammer; m. Steven Walter Eckebrecht, June 2, 1979. BA, U. No. Iowa, 1980. CPA, Iowa. Acctg. clk. D.D. Pyle and Co., PC, Ames, Iowa, 1980-81; acct. Dougherty and Co., PC, Ames, 1981—. Mem. Am. Inst. CPA's, Iowa Soc. CPA's, Ames C. of C. (membership com. 1984-86, chair 1987, nominating com. 1986, ambassadors com. 1986-87, accreditation fin. com. 1987, women in bus. com. 1988). Club: Altrusa of Ames (treas. 1985-87, v.p. 1987-88, pres. 1988—). Home: 1021 Top-o-Hollow Ames IA 50010 Office: Dougherty and Co PC 218 SE 16th St Ames IA 50010

ECKEL, ELAINE MARTHA, physical therapist, association chairperson; b. Phila., Feb. 4, 1941; d. Fred Jonathan and Florence Emma (Johnson) E. BS, U. Pa., 1962; MA, U. N.C., 1973. Phys. therapist Widener Sch. for Handicapped Children, Phila., 1962-64; Del. State Bd. of Health, Dover, 1964-65; physical therapist Children's Specialized Hosp., Westfield, N.J., 1965-66, Akington (Pa.) Meml. Hosp., 1966-69; chief phys. therapist Chapel Hill (N.C.) Nursing and Convalescent Ctr., 1969-71; phys. therapist Home Health Agy. of Chapel Hill, 1970-71; asst. prof. in grad. phys. therapy Duke U., Durham, N.C., 1971-86; chmn. phys. therapy assn. program Fayetteville (N.C.) Tech. Community Coll., 1986—; cons. phys. therapy assn. program, Fayetteville, 1975-76, Wake Area Health Adv. Com., Raleigh, N.C., 1983-86. Contbr. articles to profl. jours. Mem. Chapel Hill Bible Ch., 1976—; mem. appearance com. Town of Carrboro, N.C., 1981-82; mem. Friends of Old Carrboro, Carrboro, N.C., 1981—; chmn. camp com. Camp Mawavaca, Durham, 1985—. Recipient Abby Sutherland scholarship Pa. State U., 1959, 60, senatorial scholarship State of Pa., 1960-61. Mem. Am. Phys. Therapy Assn. (scholarship 1967-68, state licensure and regulation sect. sec. 1976-78, Lucy Blair service award 1984), N.C. State Examining Com. for Phys. Therapists (sec.-treas. 1973-78), N.C. Phys. Therapy Assn. (dir. 1974-78, 1985-86, pres. 1981-82, chmn. pub. relations com. 1983-84, Olive Wortman award 1987). Republican. Home: 230 Pinecrest Dr #14 Fayetteville NC 28305 Office: Fayetteville Tech Community Coll 2200 Hull St Fayetteville NC 28303

ECKENSTEIN, RUTH ANN, nurse, educator; b. Guthrie, Okla, July 20, 1951; d. Ramon Richard and Juanita Ruth (McKenzie) McNulty; m. Stephen John Terrell, July 22, 1977 (div. 1979); m. Ed Eckenstein, Dec. 31, 1986. B.S. in Health Edn., Central State U., Edmond, Okla., 1982, M.Ed. of Adult Edn., 1985; A.S. in Nursing, Okla. State U. Tech. Inst., Oklahoma City, 1976. R.N., Okla., Nebr. Staff nurse Okla. Teaching Hosp., Oklahoma City, 1976-77; dir. nurses Beatrice Manor (Nebr.), 1977-78, Good Samaritan Ctr., Wymore, Nebr., 1978-79; house supr. Logan County Health Ctr., Guthrie, Okla., 1979-82, Bapt. Med. Ctr., Oklahoma City, 1982-83; practical nurse instr. Francis Tuttle Vocat.-Tech. Ctr. Oklahoma City, 1983—; cons. Guthrie Nursing Ctr., 1979-80. Author: Team Teaching in Nursing Education, 1983; Computer Medical Terminology. Democrat. Roman Catholic. Home: 8017 NW 104th Oklahoma City OK 73132 Office: Francis Tuttle Vocat-Tech Ctr 12777 N Rockwell St Oklahoma City OK 73034

ECKERSON, NANCY FIEDLER, dietitian; b. Milw., Sept. 24, 1940; d. Lawrence Louis and Catherine Jeanne (McCarten) Fiedler; m. Raymond Grover Eckerson, July 27, 1984. BA, Rosary Coll., 1962; MS, No. Ill. U., 1979; postgrad., Gov.'s State U., 1987. Dietetic intern St. Louis U., 1963; clin. dietitian Presbyn. St. Luke's Hosp., Chgo., 1963-79; mgr. dietetics and patient food service Ingalls Meml. Hosp., Harvey, Ill., 1981—; instr. Rush U., Chgo., 1980-81, Gabriel Richard Inst., Chgo., 1980-82. Author: Quality Assurance Manual for Dietitians, 1976, A Nurse's Guide to Diabetes, 1979. religion instr. St. Bernadine's Parish, Forest Park, Ill., 1981-84. Mem. Am. Dietetic Assn. (quest subcom. 1985-87, Outstanding Service award, 1987), Ill. Dietetic Assn. (co-chair legis. 1981-83, licensure 1983-86, Outstanding Service award 1985), Chgo. Dietetic Assn., Am. Coll. Healthcare Execs., Suburban Planning Agy., South Suburban Dietetic Assn., Omnicron Nu. Club: Catholic Alumni Clubs Internat. (women's v.p., sec., regional v.p. 1972-79). Home: 2424 Heather Rd Homewood IL 60430 Office: Ingalls Meml Hosp One Ingalls Dr Harvey IL 60426

ECKERT, ARLENE GAIL, association business coordinator; b. Euclid, Ohio, July 28, 1956; d. Robert S. and Madolyn A. (King) Lough; m. Theodore Eckert III, May 14, 1983 (div. Oct. 1985). BS in Law Enforcement, U. N. Ala., 1978. Cert. social worker. Probation, parole officer Tenn. Dept. Corrections, Columbia, 1978-83; child protection service specialist II Tex. Dept. Human Services, Killeen, 1984-86; EAP bus. coordinator Associated Counseling Services, Harker Heights, Tex., 1986—. Bd. dirs. Truancy Bd. Pulaski, Tenn., 1978-84, Truancy Bd., Lawrenceburg, Tenn., 1978-84, Multidisciplinary Child Abuse Review Team, Columbia, Tenn., 1979-84. Mem. Am. Correctional Assn., Tenn. State Employees Assn., Nat. Assn. Female Execs. Lutheran. Office: Associated Counseling Services 455 E Central Texas Expressway #103 Harker Heights TX 76543

ECKHOFF, ROSALEE, nurse; b. Falls City, Nebr., Apr. 24, 1930; d. George and Blanche (Montague) Rieger; R.N., Nebr. Meth. Sch. Nursing, 1951; m. Robert Dale Eckhoff, Feb. 21, 1954; children—Dixie Dee, Monte Ray. Dir. nursing Sutherland (Nebr.) Hosp., 1952-55; head nurse med. ward Hastings (Nebr.) Regional Center, 1957-61; night supr. Good Samaritan Village, Hastings, 1962; charge nurse pediatrics Mary Lanning Hosp., Hastings, 1962-65; night supr. Broken Bow (Nebr.) Hosp., 1965-66; dir. nursing Bethel Nursing Home, Ainsworth, Nebr., 1966-67, adminstr., 1967-69; part-time staff nurse Ainsworth Hosp., 1969-70; nursing home counselor Norfolk (Nebr.) Regional Center, 1970-72; night supr. Albion (Nebr.) Boone County Hosp., 1970-75; adminstrv. dir. Mideast Nebr., Albion and Columbus Mental Health Clinic, 1975-76; dir. nursing Phelps Meml. Health Center, Holdrege, Nebr., 1976—. Mem. Nebr. Soc. Nursing Service Adminstrs. (sec.-treas.), Nebr. Mental Health Assn., Luth. Ch. Women, Dist. 4 Hosp. Assn. (dir. nurses), Am. Orgn. Nurse Execs., Nebr. Orgn. Nurse Execs. Home: 1015 West Ave Holdrege NE 68949 Office: 1220 Miller St PO Box 630 Holdrege NE 68949

ECKLEY, ALICIA KATHRYN, writer, editor, public relations specialist; b. Columbus, Ohio, Mar. 31, 1959; d. Richard McCoy and Helen Louise (Martin) E. BA in Journalism, Ohio State U., 1981. Editorial asst. Diagnostic Imaging Mag., Miller Freeman Publs., San Francisco, 1982-83, asst. editor, 1983-84; pub. affairs mgr. Squibb Corp., Princeton, N.J., 1984-87; pub. relations mgr., Diasonics, Inc., South San Francisco, Ca., 1987—. Mem. Pub. Relations Soc. Am., Nat. Assn. Female Execs. Office: 280 Utah Ave South San Francisco CA 94080

ECKLEY, GRACE ESTER, English language educator; b. Alliance, Ohio, Nov. 30, 1932; d. Clyde L. and Wilma Agnes (Hahn) Williamson; B.A., Mount Union Coll., 1955; M.A., Case Western Res. U., 1964; Ph.D., Kent State U., 1970; m. Wilton Eckley, Sept. 12, 1954; children—Douglas, Stephen, Timothy. Instr. English, Simpson Coll., Indianola, Iowa, 1965-68; prof. dept. English, Drake U., Des Moines, 1968—NEH fellow, 1984-85. Mem. AAUW. Author: Benedict Kiely, 1972; Edna O'Brien, 1974; (with Michael Begnal) Narrator and Character in Finnegans Wake, 1974; Finley Peter Dunne, 1981; Children's Lore in Finnegans Wake, 1984; contbr. articles to profl. jours. Home: 744 Chimney Creek Dr Golden CO 80401 Office: Drake U Des Moines IA 50311

ECKMAN, DONNA E., materials manager; b. Yakima, Wash., Apr. 27, 1950; d. Darold George and Jurelle (Titshaw) Vanderhoff; m. Dale Eckman (div. Sept. 1978); 1 child, Cynthia Renee. Buyer E-Systems, Greenville, Tex., 1979-82; buyer, sr. buyer, materials mgr. Sfena Corp., Grand Prairie, Tex., 1982—. Mem. Nat. Purchasing Mgrs. Assn. Office: Sfena Corp 2617 Aviation Pkwy Grand Prairie TX 75051

ECKMAN, DOROTHY MARIE, marketing professional; b. Chgo., June 10, 1947; d. John M. Pajkos and Cecelia T. (Serdel) Pajkos-Smith; m. James L. Eckman, Aug. 2, 1969 (div. Nov. 1985); children: Matthew, Michelle. BBA, Western Mich. U., 1980, MBA, 1984. Sec. Upjohn Co., Kalamazoo, 1967, staff sec., 1967-76, exec. sec., 1976-77, coordinator materials distbn., 1977-81, profl. communications adminstn. analyst, 1981-86, profl. communications ops. specialist., 1986—. Mem. Midwest Pharm. Advt. Council, (sec. 1986-87, treas. 1987-88), Pharm. Advt. Council, Am. Mktg. Assn., Nat. Assn. Female Execs. Roman Catholic. Office: Upjohn Co 7000 Portage Rd Kalamazoo MI 49001

ECKROTE, BARBARA ANNE, interior design company executive; b. Chgo., Apr. 7, 1942; d. Joseph Edward Schmidt, Jr. and Wilma Lois (Markley) Rustad; children: Jennifer Lynn Eckrote-Hernandez, John Todd, Julie Marie. BA, La. State U., 1964. Program mgr. E-Systems, Inc., Houston, 1974-78; personnel dir. Evergreen Air, Houston, 1978-80; ops. mgr. Ameron Corp., Houston, 1980-83; owner Barbara Eckrote Design, Houston, 1983—. Designer proto types El Chico Corp., Budget Rent A Car. Vol. Lunar Rendevous Festival, Clear Lake City, Tex., 1980-83. Mem. AAUW, Tex. Restaurant Assn., Houston Restaurant Assn., Tex. Assn. Interior Designers, Bay Area Mus. Build Houston, Mus. Fine Arts. Democrat. Roman Catholic. Office: PO Box 580374 Houston TX 77258

ECONOMIDES, ELAINE, lawyer; b. N.Y.C., Sept. 14, 1948; d. Basil and Anastasia (Pavlakis) E.; BA cum laude (Granite State Merit scholar, Elks Assn. scholar), U. N.H., 1970; postgrad. London Sch. Econs., 1970-71; JD, Suffolk U., 1977. Civil rights specialist GSA, Boston, 1972-73; contract negotiator Transp. Systems Center, Cambridge, Mass., 1973-78, spl. asst. to dir., 1978-79; spl. asst. to dir. Materials Transp. Bur., Washington, 1979-80, exec. officer, 1980-82; atty.-adv. RSPA, Dept. Transp., Washington, 1982-86; internat. standards rep. Office of Hazardous Materials Transp. DOT, 1986-88, dep. dir., 1988—; fed. women's program coordinator GSA, 1972-73, Transp. Systems Center, 1973-74; bd. dirs. Kendall Sq. Fed. Credit Union, 1979; admitted to Mass. bar, 1977, Fed. bar, 1978. Mem. Am. Bar Assn., ACLU, Mensa, Pi Sigma Alpha, Phi Kappa Phi, Pi Gamma Mu. Greek Orthodox. Office: US Dept Transp 400 7th St SW Washington DC 20590

ECONOMIDES, KATHLEEN DALY, health program administrator; b. Albany, N.Y., June 10, 1944; d. Daniel A. and Mary Kathleen (Rivers) Daly; m. James A. Economides, Sept. 2, 1972; children: Colleen, Mark. BA, Coll. of St. Rose, 1966. Sr. labor standards investigator N.Y. State Health Dept., Albany, 1970-78, sr. personnel adminstr., 1978-81, agy. tng., devel. specialist, 1982-84, health program adminstr., 1984—; chairperson Women's Issues Group, N.Y. State Health Dept., 1985-86. Mem. Am. Soc. Pub. Adminstrs., Capital Dist. Personnel Assn. (pres. 1986-87 recognition award 1987). Roman Catholic. Office: N Y State Health Dept Empire State Plaza Albany NY 12237

ECORD, ELIZABETH ANN, oil company executive; b. El Paso, Tex., Nov. 24, 1955; d. Bruce Bailey and Mary Louise (Schnitter) E.; m. Keith Norman Nelson, June 22, 1985. BA, U. No. Colo., 1977; MBA, U. Colo., Denver, 1987. Project cost analyst D'Appolonia Cons. Engrs., Denver, 1977-79; petroleum landman Denver, 1979-83; land rep. Grynberg Petroleum Co., Denver, 1983-85; land specialist Texaco, Inc., Denver, 1985—. Mem. Am. Assn. Petroleum Landmen, Denver Assn. Petroleum Landmen, Nat. Assn. Div. Order Analysts, Denver Assn. Div. Order Analysts. Republican. Roman Catholic. Home: PO Box 37091 Denver CO 80237 Office: Texaco Trading & Transp Inc PO Box 5568 Denver CO 80217

ECTON, DONNA R., food products company executive; b. Kansas City, Mo., May 10, 1947; d. Allen Howard and Marguerite (Page) E.; m. Victor H. Maragni, June 16, 1986; children: Mark, Gregory. BA, Wellesley Coll., 1969; MBA, Harvard U., 1971. V.p. Chem. Bank, N.Y.C., 1972-79, pres., 1981-83; v.p. Citibank, N.A., N.Y.C., 1979-81, MBA Resources, Inc., N.Y.C.; v.p. adminstrn., officer Campbell Soup Co., Camden, N.J., 1983—; chmn. Triangle Mfg. Corp. subs. Campbell Soup Co., Raleigh, N.C., 1984-87; bd. dirs. Mellon Bank Corp., Pitts., Mellon Bank N.A., Pitts., Barnes Group, Inc., Bristol, Conn., Pepperidge Farm, Norwalk, Conn. Bd. overseers Harvard U., 1984—, vis. com. sch. bus. adminstrn., 1986—; mem. Council Fgn. Relations, N.Y.C., 1987—. Named One of 80 Women to Watch in the 80's, Ms. mag., 1980, One of All Time Top 10 of Last Decade, Glamour mag., 1984, One of 50 Women to Watch, Bus. Week mag., 1987; recipient Wellesley Alumnae Achievement award, 1987. Mem. Harvard Bus. Sch. Assn. (pres. exec. council 1983-84), N.Y.C. Harvard Bus. Sch. Club (pres. 1979-80), Wellesley Coll. Nat. Alumnae Assn. (bd. dirs., 1st v.p.), Catalyst (bd. advisors 1986—). Office: Campbell Soup Co Campbell Place Camden NJ 08101

EDDISON, ELIZABETH BOLE, entrepreneur, information specialist; b. Bronxville, N.Y., June 3, 1928; d. Hamilton Biggar and Elizabeth Owsley (Boyle) Bole; m. John Corbin Eddison, Feb. 10, 1951; children: Jonathan B., Elizabeth O., Martha C. AB, Vassar Coll., 1948; MS, Simmons Coll., 1973. Pres. bd. dirs. Lahore (Pakistan)-Am. Sch., 1959-61; chmn. evaluation com. Karachi (Pakistan)-Am. Sch., 1961-63; treas. bd. dirs. La Paz Coop. Sch., Bolivia, 1963-65; v.p. Assn. Am. Fgn. Service Women, coordinator social services Urban Service Corps, Washington Pub. Schs., 1965-69; sec. bd. dirs. Colegio Nueva Granada, Bogota, Colombia, 1969-71; chmn., treas. Warner-Eddison Assocs., Inc., Cambridge, Mass., 1973—, pres., 1981-88; chmn., v.p. bus. devel. Inmagic Inc., Cambridge, 1984—; mem. steering com. State House Conf. on Small Bus., Mass., 1986—; mem. bd. advisors Info. Inst., Santa Barbara, Calif., 1984—; mem. computer applications com. Cary Meml. Library, Lexington, Mass., 1986. Compiler: Words that Mean Business, 1981; contbr. articles to profl. jours. Mem. adv. com. on internat. investment and tech. devel. U.S. Dept. State, 1980-83; mem. small bus. com. Gov.'s Bus. Adv. Council, Commonwealth of Mass., 1985—. Recipient Alumni Achievement award Simmons Coll., 1986, Disclosure Achievement award Library Mgmt. Bus. and Fin. div. Spl. Libraries Assn., 1987. Bus. Mem. Info. Industry Assn. (chair emeriti com. 1983-88, co-chair publs. com. 1984-87, chair small bus. forum 1986—, mem. steering com. mgmt. and tech. council 1987—), Assoc. Info. Mgrs. (chair publs. com. 1984-86, bd. dirs. 1984-86, Knox award 1988), Spl. Libraries Assn. (chmn. program com./library mgmt. div. 1984-85, chmn. profl. devel. com. 1987-88, chmn.-elect 1988), Am. Soc. Info. Scientists, Beta Phi Mu. Democrat. Office: Inmagic Inc 2067 Massachusetts Ave Cambridge MA 02140

EDDY, COLETTE ANN, photography studio owner; b. Sept. 14, 1950; d. William F. and Jeanne (Valeski) Trump; m. Robert K. Eddy, Aug. 21, 1976. AA, St. Petersburg (Fla.) Jr. Coll., 1970; BA, U. South Fla., 1973; MS, Nova U., 1988. Yacht caretaker The Sundowner, St. Petersburg, 1972-73; mgr. Aunt Hattie's Restaurant, St. Petersburg, 1973-79, Johnathan Jones, Inc., St. Petersburg, 1979-80; photographer, sales rep. Aerial Photos, Tampa, Fla., 1980-87; owner, photographer Aerial Innovations, Inc., Tampa, 1987—. Mem. Profl. Photographers Am., Fla. Profl. Photographers, Profl. Aerial Photographers Assn., Tampa C. of C. Republican. Home: 40 Martinique Ave Tampa FL 33606 Office: Aerial Innovations Inc 1304 Desoto Ave Suite 204 Tampa FL 33606

EDDY, DARLENE MATHIS, educator, poet; b. Elkhart, Ind., Mar. 19, 1937; d. William Eugene and Fern (Paulmer) Mathis; m. Spencer Livingston Eddy, Jr., May 23, 1964 (dec. May 1971). B.A., Goshen Coll., 1959; M.A., Rutgers U., 1961, Ph.D., 1967. Instr., lectr. Douglass Coll. and Rutgers U., 1962-64, 66-67; asst. prof. English Ball State U., Muncie, Ind., 1967-70; assoc. prof. Ball State U., 1971-75, prof., 1975—. Author: The Worlds of King Lear, 1968, Leaf Threads, Wind Rhymes, 1985, Weathering, 1988; poetry editor Forum, 1985—; contbr. articles to English Lang. Notes, Am. Lit., others; contbr. poetry to various publs. Recipient numerous research, creative teaching and creative arts grants; Woodrow Wilson Nat. fellow, 1959-62; Rutgers U. grad. honors fellow, 1964-65. Mem. Nat. Council Tchrs. of English, MLA, AAUP, Shakespeare Assn., DAR. Home: 1409 W Cardinal St Muncie IN 47303 Office: Ball State Univ 207B English Muncie IN 47303

EDDY, MELISSA JANE, professional association executive, counselor; b. Medina, Ohio, Dec. 27, 1951; d. Ernest DeRhone and Jane Anne (Lose) E.; m. Tracy Schiemenz, Jan. 17, 1981. B.A. magna cum laude, Kalamazoo Coll., 1974; M.A. with honors, Western Mich. U., 1976. Psychologist Battle Creek (Mich.) Community Mental Health Clinic, 1976-77; coordinator program services Center for Battered Women, Austin, Tex., 1978-81; pvt. practice counseling and cons., Austin, 1982—; owner women's bridal and formal-wear consignment bus., Austin, 1982-85; mem. alcohol services adv. com. Mental Health/Mental Retardation, 1980-83; mem. Austin Family Violence Diversion Network Adv. Com., 1980-84; program assoc. Tex. Council on Family Violence, Austin, 1984-87, tng. dir., 1987-88, program dir., 1988—. Bd. dirs. Dispute Resolution Ctr. of Travis County, 1983—, pres., 1984-86; campaign vol. Democratic candidates, 1980-82. Mem. Assn. Women in Psychology, Tex. Council Family Violence (dir. 1978-85), Am. Assn. for Counseling and Devel., Tex. Assn. for Counseling and Devel., Assn. for Psychol. Type (founder Austin area br.), Nat. Coalition Against Domestic Violence, Phi Beta Kappa, Alpha Lambda Delta. Research on burnout among family-violence workers, treatment programs for spouse abusers. Home: 8506B Cima Oak Ln Austin TX 78759 Office: Tex Council Family Violence 1704 W 6th St Suite 200 Austin TX 78703

EDDY, SARA LEPPER, book publishing consultant; b. Topeka, Mar. 30, 1915; d. Harold Arthur and Ferne Haun (Williams) Lepper; m. Richard Carl DeLong, Sept. 29, 1940 (div. Jan. 1949); children—John Richard DeLong (dec.), Robert Gary DeLong; m. 2d, G. Russell Eddy, Apr. 25, 1964. B.F.A., U. Kans., 1937. Asst. instr. design U. Kans., Lawrence, 1937-38; chief draftsman Western Air Lines, Burbank, Calif., 1940-45; art dir. Bert Ray Studios, Chgo., 1949-64; design prodn. mgr. Syracuse U. Press (N.Y.), 1973-85. Designer: Landmarks of Rochester and Monroe County, 1975; The Catskill Witch, 1975; Wood Structure and Identification, 1977; Tomatoes were Cheaper, 1978. Recipient Certs. of award AAUP, 1975, 78, Printing Industries of Am., 1977. Life mem. Am. Inst. Graphic Arts, Kappa Kappa Gamma, Delta Phi Delta. Republican. Congregationalist. Home: Wind Rush Farm Manlius NY 13104

EDE, JOYCE KINLAW, counselor, marketing executive; b. Lumberton, N.C., Aug. 9, 1936; d. Neil Archibald and Myrtle Carolyn (Kinlaw) Kinlaw; m. William L. Schmid, Sept. 17, 1954 (dec. Nov. 1956); 1 dau., Cheryl Ann; m. Archie L. Phillips, Jr., Nov. 11, 1960 (div. July 1973); children—Archie L. III, Michael Bartley, John Wade; m. Kenneth Russell Ede, Dec. 27, 1984. Certs. Lake Sumter Community Coll., 1976, 77, 79, Volusia Community Coll., 1977, Ocala Jr. Coll., 1979, Univ. Central, Orlando, Fla., 1980, Triton Coll., 1981. Counselor, social worker Epilepsy Assn. Central Fla.-Lake County, 1973-76; social worker Lake Sumter Community Mental Health, Med. Social Services, Leesburg, Fla., 1976-79; counselor, social worker Epilepsy Assn. Central Fla.-Lake County, 1979-81; mktg. coordinator Friendship Village, Schaumburg, Ill., 1981-84; retirement counselor Health Care Assocs., Winter Haven, Fla., 1984-85; in mktg. Cambridge Park Manor, Wheaton, Ill., 1985—; pres. Lake County Services Council, Leesburg, 1978-79; del. central Fla. Nat. Conf. on Epilepsy, Washington, 1975; mem. State Conf. on Epilepsy, Tampa, Fla., 1977-81; dir. Lake County, Epilepsy Job Tng., Tavares, Fla., 1979-81; mem., advocate Lake/Sumter County Geriatric Program, 1979; chairperson Epilepsy Bd. Fla., Tavares, 1974-75. Contbr. articles on epilepsy to profl. jours. Mem. Lake County PTA, Leesburg, 1970-76; mem. Parents Adv. Council, Lake County, Leesburg, 1977-80; mem. Parents Council, Dixie Youth Baseball League, Fruitland Park, Fla., 1980. Recipient Certs. Epilepsy Assn. Central Fla., Orlando, 1980, Kiwanis Clubs, Leesburg and Mt. Dora, Fla., 1974, Rotary Clubs, Leesburg, Mt. Dora, Groveland, Fla., 1974, Lions Clubs, Leesburg, Mt. Dora, Tavares, 1974-75. Mem. Am. Bus. Women's Assn. (hosp. chairperson 1979-80), Concerned Women for Am., Nat. Assn. Female Execs. Avocations: reading; sports; art; music; cooking; crafts; visiting library; playing piano. Home: 2324B Century Point Ln Glendale Heights IL 60139

EDELMAN, DIANE LYNN, human resource consultant,infosystems specialist; b. Chgo., Aug. 11, 1956; d. Donald R. and Harriette P. (Duncan) E. B.S. in Math., Chgo. State U., 1977. Systems analyst Zurich Am., Chgo., 1978-80; account mgr. Cyborg Systems, Chgo., 1980-83; sr. systems analyst Marsh & McLennan, Chgo., 1983; mgmt. info. systems mgr. Saxon Paint, Chgo., 1983-85; account mgr., cons. ISI, Downers Grove, Ill., 1985-86; pres. Edelman & Assocs., Ltd., Hinsdale, Ill., 1986—. Vol. Starlight Found. Mem. Micronet Computer Cons., U.S. Polo Assn., Hinsdale C. of C., Kappa Delta Pi. Episcopalian. Club: Oak Brook Polo (Ill.) (mem. ladies com., membership com.). Avocations: polo, architectural art.

EDELMAN, JUDITH HOCHBERG, architect; b. Bklyn., Sept. 16, 1923; d. Abraham and Frances (Israel) Hochberg; m. Harold Edelman, Dec. 26, 1947; children: Marc, Joshua. Student, Conn. Coll., 1940-41, NYU, 1941-42; B.Arch., Columbia U., 1946. Designer, drafter Huson Jackson, N.Y.C., 1948-58; Schermerhorn traveling fellow 1950, pvt. practice architecture, 1958-60; partner Edelman & Salzman, N.Y.C., 1960-79, Edelman Partnership (Architects), N.Y.C., 1979—; adj. prof. Sch. Architecture, City U. N.Y., 1972-76; vis. lectr. urban renewal New Sch., 1968; vis. lectr. Washington U., St. Louis, 1974, U. Oreg., 1974, Mass. Inst. Tech., 1975, City U. N.Y. Grad. Program Environ. Psychology, 1975, Pa. State U., City U. N.Y. Grad. Program Environ. Psychology, 1977, Rensselaer Poly Inst., 1977, Columbia U., 1979; First Claire Watson Forrest Meml. lectr. U. Oreg., U. Calif.-Berkeley, U. So. Calif., 1982. Major archtl. works include: Restoration of St. Mark's Ch. in the Bowery, N.Y.C., 1970-82, Two Bridges Urban Renewal Area Housing, 1970-86, Jennings Hall Sr. Citizens Housing, Bklyn., 1980, Goddard Riverside Elderly Housing and Community Ctr., N.Y.C., 1983. Recipient Bard 1st honor award City Club N.Y., 1969, Bard award of merit, 1975, 82; Residential Design award A.I.A., 1969; award for design excellence HUD, 1970; Honor award N.Y. State Assn. Architects-AIA, 1975; 1st prize Nat. Trust Historic Preservation, 1975; Honor award Nat. Trust Historic Preservation, 1983; award of merit Mcpl. Art Soc. N.Y., 1983; Pub. Service award Settlement Housing Fund, 1983. Fellow AIA (dir. N.Y. chpt., chmn. commn. archtl. edn. 1971-73, chmn. nat. task force on women in architecture 1974-75, v.p. N.Y. chpt. 1975-77, chmn. ethics com. 1975-77); mem. Alliance of Women in Architecture (founding mem., mem. steering com. 1972-74), Architects for Social Responsibility (exec. com. 1982-85), Columbia Archtl. Alumni Assn. (dir. 1968-71). Home: 13 Bank St New York NY 10014 Office: Edelman Ptnrship 434 6th Ave New York NY 10011

EDELMAN, MARIAN WRIGHT (MRS. PETER B. EDELMAN), lawyer; b. Bennettsville, S.C., June 6, 1939; d. Arthur J. and Maggie (Bowen) Wright; m. Peter B. Edelman, July 14, 1968; children: Joshua, Jonah, Ezra. Merrill scholar, univs. Paris, Geneva, 1958-59; B.A., Spelman Coll., 1960; LL.B. (J.H. Whitney fellow 1960-61), Yale U., 1963, LL.D.; LL.D., Smith Coll., 1969, Lowell Tech. U., 1975, Williams Coll., 1978, Columbia U., U. Pa., Amherst Coll., St. Joseph's Coll., Hartford, Conn.; D.H.L., Lesley Coll., 1975, Trinity Coll., Washington, Russell Sage Coll., 1978, Syracuse U., 1979, Coll. New Rochelle, 1979, Swarthmore Coll., 1980, SUNY at Old Westbury, 1981, Northeastern U., 1981, Bard Coll., 1982, U. Mass., 1983, Hunter Coll., U. So. Maine, SUNY-Albany, 1984. Bar: D.C., Miss., Mass. Staff atty. NAACP Legal Def. and Edn. Fund, Inc., N.Y.C., 1963-64; dir. NAACP Legal Def. and Edn. Fund, Inc., Jackson, Miss., 1964-68; Congl. and fed. liaison Poor People's Campaign, summer 1968; partner Washington Research Project of So. Center for Pub. Policy, 1968-73; dir. Harvard U. Center for Law and Edn., 1971-73; pres. Children's Def. Fund, 1973—. Mem. exec. com. Student Non-Violent Coordinating Com., 1961-63; mem. adv. council Martin Luther King, Jr. Meml. Library; mem. adv. bd. Hampshire Coll.; mem. Presdl. Commn. on Missing in Action, 1977, Presdl. Commn. on Internat. Yr. of Child, 1979, Presdl. Comm. on Agenda for 80's, 1980; bd. dirs. Center for Law and Social Policy, Eleanor Roosevelt Inst., Nat. Office for Rights of the Indigent, NAACP Legal Def. and Ednl. Fund; trustee, chmn. bd. Spelman Coll., Atlanta, Arts, Edn. and Ams., Carnegie Council on Children, 1972-77, Martin Luther King, Jr. Meml. Center, Nat. Council Children and TV; trustee March of Dimes, People for Am. Way, Joint Ctr. for Polit. Studies; mem. Yale U. Corp., 1971-77, German Marshall Fund Found., Aetna Found. Named an Outstanding Young Woman of Am., 1966; recipient Mademoiselle mag. award, 1965, Louise Waterman Wise award, 1970; Washington of Yr. award, 1979; Whitney M. Young award, 1979; Profl. of Yr. award Black Enterprise, 1979; Leadership award Nat. Women's Polit. Caucus, 1980; Black Womens Forum award, 1980; medal Columbia Tchrs. Coll., 1984, Barnard Coll.; Eliot award Am. Pub. Health Assn.; Hubert Humphrey Civil Rights award Leadership Council Civil Rights; John W. Gardner Leadership award of Ind. Sector; Pub. Service Achievement award Common Cause; MacArthur prize fellow, 1985. fellow U. Pa. Law Sch. (hon.); mem. Council Fgn. Relations. Address: Children's Def Fund 122 C St NW Washington DC 20001 *

EDELMAN, REVELL JUDITH, data processing executive; b. Bayonne, N.J., July 24, 1941; d. Charles and Belle (Laks) Motin; m. Martin Edelman, July 18, 1981; children: Laura Mantell, Deborah Mantell. BS in Psychology cum laude, CUNY, 1969. Systems analyst Univac div. Sperry Corp., N.Y.C., 1961-66; programmer, analyst J.C. Penney Co., N.Y.C., 1966-67; systems and programming cons. Automated Concepts, Inc., N.Y.C., 1968-72; ind. systems and programming cons. N.Y.C., 1972-76; mgr. systems and programming Citibank, NA, N.Y.C., 1976-83; v.p. data processing Columbia Savs. and Loan Assn., Fair Lawn, N.J., 1983—. Mem. Fin. Mgrs. Soc., Assn. Info. Mgrs., Mensa. Democrat. Jewish. Home: 3 Jockey Ln New City NY 10956 Office: Columbia Savs & Loan Assn 25-00 Broadway Fair Lawn NJ 07410

EDELMAN, RITA, artist; b. N.Y.C., Nov. 2, 1930; d. Arthur and Sylvia (Juskow) Goodman; m. Oscar Edelman, Mar. 7, 1954; children: Chester, Peter. Cert., Traphagen, 1951, Silvermine, 1967. Artist Conn., 1967—. One person exhibits include Pindar Gallery, N.Y.C., 1982, 84, 85, 87, Silvermine Guild, New Canaan, Conn., 1976, 81; invitational exhibits include Aldrich Mus., Ridgefield, Conn., 1981, G.E. Corp., Fairfield, Conn., 1983, Xerox Corp., Stamford, Conn., 1984, N.Y. State Mus., Albany, N.Y., 1986; permanent collection include Pepsico, Gen. Electric, Gen. Foods, Wichita (Kans.) State U., Fairfield U. Recipient Art of the Northeast U.S. Am. award, 1983, New England Exhbn. Painting and Sculpture award, Profl. Art Exhbn. award, 1978, 79. Mem. Silvermine Guild of Artists, New Haven Paint and Clay Club, Katonah Gallery. Home: 7 Manitou Ct Westport CT 06880

EDELSON, ZELDA SARAH TOLL, editor; b. Phila., Oct. 18, 1929; d. Louis David and Rose (Eisenstein) Toll; m. Marshall Edelson, Dec. 27, 1952; children—Jonathan Toll, Rebecca Jo, David Jan. B.A., U. Chgo., 1949, postgrad., 1949-52. Editor-writer Consol. Book Pubs., Chgo., 1953-56; social worker Balt. City Dept. Pub. Welfare, 1956-57; pub. relations writer Md. Dept. Employment Security, Balt., 1958-59; museum editor Yale Peabody Mus., New Haven, 1970-76, head publs., 1976—, editor mus.'s Discovery mag., 1983—; lectr. in sci. writing Yale U., 1983-84. Editor numerous publs. including: A Guide to the Age of Mammals, 1978. U. Chgo. scholar, 1947-51. Mem Council Biology Editors, Soc. Scholarly Publishing, Am. Assn. Museums (awards of distinction 1985, 86), New Eng. Conf. Museums. Office: PO Box 6666 Publications Office Yale Peabody Mus Natural History 170 Whitney Ave New Haven CT 06511

EDELSTEIN, JEAN, purchasing professional; b. Chgo., Mar. 6, 1929; d. Sam and Sadie (Cutler) Klein; divorced; children: David Allen, Raymond Lewis. Student, U. Wis., Milw. Sec. various firms, Milw., 1947-64; purchasing agt. Milw. Pub. Schs., 1964-66, sec., 1966-68; dir. corp. services/purchasing agt. Career Acad., Milw., 1968-74; buyer Kenosha (Wis.) Unified Sch. Dist. 1, 1974-81, purchasing agt., 1981—. Bd. dirs. Willow Creek Condominiums, Milw., 1979-80, pres., 1980-81; mem. citizen panel United Way, Kenosha, 1984—; mem. citizen adv. bd. social services Kenosha County, 1985-86; mem. hon. bd. Girl Scouts U.S., Kenosha County, 1985—. Mem. Nat. Assn. Pub. Purchasing, Nat. Assn. Purchasing Mgmt., Bus. Forms Mgmt. Assn. (charter mem. Milw. chpt.), Word Processing Assn. (charter mem. Milw. chpt.) Wis. Assn. Pub. Purchasing, Milw. Assn. Purchasing Mgmt. (chmn. attendance com. 1976-78, local dir. 1979-80, v.p. 1980-83, award 1984), Nat. Inst. Govtl. Purchasers. Democrat. Jewish. Office: Kenosha Unified Sch Dist 1 3600 52d St Kenosha WI 53142

EDELSTEIN, PAULA CRAVEN, entertainment company executive; b. Houston, Oct. 10, 1950; d. Moritz Virano and Judith (Berwick) Craven; m. Ronald Steven Edelstein, Dec. 27, 1981. B.A., U. Ill.-Chgo., 1974; student U. Houston, 1969-71. Pres., Adesta Prodns., Los Angeles, 1983-85; exec. asst. to v.p. Walt Disney Prodns., Los Angeles, 1985; exec. asst. to pres. Motown Prodns., Los Angeles, 1985-86; story editor RKO Pictures, 1986; pres. Adesta Fin. Group, Inc., 1987—. Author: Love Poems for Disappointed Mistresses, 1983. Mem. Women in Film, Hollywood Radio and TV Soc., Nat. Assn. for Female Execs., Am. Mgmt. Assn., Phi Theta Kappa. Democrat. Episcopalian. Avocation: horseback riding.

EDEN, LORRAINE DIANE, mortgage company executive; b. Utica, N.Y., Aug. 8, 1942; d. Frank and Wanda (Jurewicz) Lesniak; m. Ronal Dean Eden, June 28, 1969. BS, Russell Sage Coll., 1964; MS, Syracuse U., 1974. Cert. tchr., N.Y., Pa.; cert. elem.prin.; lic. real estate broker. Tchr. Whitesboro (N.Y.) Cen. Schs., 1964-69, Guilderland (N.Y.) Sch. Dist., 1969-71, Mt. Lebanon Sch. Dist., Pitts., 1971-82; sales rep. Tandy Corp., Fairfax, Va., 1982-83; sales mgr. Tandy Corp., Fairfax County, 1983-85, Falcon Microsystems, Bethesda, Md., 1985, Software Corp. Am., Herndon, Va., 1985-86; loan agt. Great Western Mortgage Co., McLean, Va., 1987—. Adv. Lockmeade Home Owner's Assn., Great Falls, Va., 1986—. Mem. Nat. Assn. Female Execs., Russell Sage Alumni Assn., Syracuse U. Alumnae Assn. Home: 1156 Riva Ridge Dr Great Falls VA 22066 Office: Gt Western Mortgage Corp 8280 Greensboro Dr Suite 310 McLean VA 22102

EDEN-FETZER, DIANNE TONI, nurse, project coordinator; b. Washington, Mar. 1, 1946; d. Lawrence Antonio Laurenzi and Eleanor Charlotte (Sparrough) Watson; m. William Earle Eden, Aug. 5, 1967 (div. 1982); 1 child, Christopher Lance; m. John Thompson Fetzer, Sept. 2, 1987. AA in Nursing, SUNY, Farmingdale, 1978. RN, N.Y., Md. Charge nurse dept. neurosurgery U. Md. Hosp., Balt., 1978-79, nurse clincian I, 1979-84, dept. nursing and neurology project coordinator Nat. Stroke Data Bank, 1984—, nursing edn. cons. dept. neurology and neurosurgery, 1984—. Fellow Stroke Council Am. Heart Assn.; mem. Am. Assn. Neurosurgical Nurses. Democrat. Roman Catholic. Home: 1303 Maywood Ave Ruxton MD 21204 Office: Univ Md Hosp 22 S Greene St Baltimore MD 21201

EDERER-SCHWARTZ, JANE, dance therapist, psychologist; b. N.Y.C., Dec. 1, 1939; d. Abel and Gertrude (Glass) Ederer. A.B., Queen's Coll., City U. N.Y., 1961; M.S.W., Columbia U., 1966, M.A., 1975. Movement therapist Day Hosp., St. Luke's Hosp., N.Y.C., 1975-79; program dir. Shellbank Jewish Center, Bklyn., 1978—; movement therapist Shaaray Tefila, N.Y.C., 1978—, Creative Arts Rehab. Center, N.Y.C., 1980—; faculty dept. dance N.Y.U., 1980-87; field work instr. Fordham U. Sch. Social Service, N.Y.C., 1987—, Hunter Coll. Sch. Social Work, 1988—; psychotherapist Nat. Inst. for Psychotherapies, N.Y.C., 1985—; pvt. practice, supr. dance therapy, psychoanalysis. Founding bd. dirs. Laban Inst. Movement Studies, N.Y.C., 1977—. Grantee, NIMH, 1964-66; cert. movement analyst Laban Inst. Movement Studies; cert. social worker, N.Y. State. Mem. Nat. Assn. Social Workers, Am. Dance Therapy Assn. (chmn. edn. N.Y. State 1980—, chmn. N.Y. State 1985—). Home: 544 E 86th St New York NY 10028 Office: 251 W 51st St New York NY

EDEY, JOHANNE LYNNE, telecommunications specialist; b. Balt., July 31, 1956; d. John Linwood and Dorothy Eleanore (Meyer) Miller; m. John Arthur Davenport, Sept. 9, 1978 (div. 1980); m. Orville Lee Edey, Apr. 25, 1987. Student, Va. Poly. Inst. and State U., 1974-78. Engring. support analyst AAI Corp., Cockeysville, Md., 1978-80; microwave engr. Western Electric Co., Cockeysville, 1980-84; telecommunications engr. No. Telecom, Balt., 1984-86; telecommunications specialist Balt. Gas & Electric Co., 1986—. Mem. Nat. Assn. Female Execs. Republican. Methodist. Home: 1800 White Hall Rd White Hall MD 21161 Office: Balt Gas and Electric Co 7152 Windsor Blvd Baltimore MD 21207

EDGAR, KATHRYN MARIE SNYDER, guidance counselor; b. Belle Fourche, S.D., Nov. 11, 1960; d. Gerald Dean Snyder and Alfreda Ann Kayras; m. John Frederick Edgar, Nov. 5, 1980; 1 child, John. AAS, Community Coll. Air Force, 1982; BS, Black Hills State Coll., 1981; MPA, U. S.D., 1983; MEd, S.D. State U., 1985. Alcoholism counselor Intercept Program, Custer, S.D., 1984-85; guidance counselor edn. services, Edwards AFB, Calif., 1985-87, Grand Forks AFB, N.D., 1987—; crisis counselor Helpline, Edwards, Calif., 1985-86. Served with USAF, 1978-84. Mem. Am. Assn. Counseling and Devel., NOW, Nat. Abortion Rights Action League, Bus. and Profl. Women-U.S.A. Democrat. Avocations: sports, fundraising for community projects. Office: Edn Services 321 CSG/DPE Grand Forks AFB ND 58205-5000

EDGAR, SUZANNE HOWZE, educational researcher; b. Washington, Dec. 17, 1942; d. Everette Clayton and Mayta Irene (Manes) Howze; m. Gerald C. Hanberry, Nov. 16, 1963 (div. 1974); children: April, Amber, Judd; m. Thomas Ray Edgar, June 16, 1984. BA, Furman U., 1964; MS, Fla. State U., 1971; PhD, U. Md., 1987. Vol. tchr. Peace Corps, Bukidnon, Philippines, 1964-65; tchr. Head Start, Rock Hill, S.C., 1966, Hampton (S.C.) County Schs., 1966-67, Wakulla County Schs., Crawfordville, Fla., 1968-70, Alexandria (Va.) City Schs., 1971-79; researcher NEA, Washington, 1979—. Mem. NOW, Am. Assn. Pub. Opinion Research, Am. Ednl. Research Assn., Spl. Interest Group for Survey Research in Edn. (sec., treas. 1987—). Office: NEA 1201 16th St NW Washington DC 20036

EDGER, ROSEMARY MITCHELL, physical therapist; b. Washington, Oct. 3, 1951; d. Anthony Albert and Helen (Rittenhouse) Mitchell; m. Jack Ray Edger, Aug. 10, 1974; children: Paul Dominic, Amanda Helene. BS in Physical Therapy, U. Md., 1975. Lic. phys. therapist, Md. Staff phys. therapist No. Va. Drs. Hosp. Corp., Arlington, 1975-77; sr. phys. therapist, dir. orthopedic surgery rotation Johns Hopkins Hosp., Balt., 1977-80; part-time phys. therapist So. Md. Hosp., Clinton, 1981, George Washington U. Med. Ctr., Washington, 1981-82; dir. indsl. back sch. Potomac Electric Power Co., Washington, 1982-83; propr., clinician Edger Therapy P.A., Greenbelt, Md., 1982—. Mem. Am. Phys. Therapy Assn. (mem. pvt. practice sect.). Republican. Roman Catholic. Club: New Carrollton Recreation (Md.). Home: 8309 Carrollton Pkwy New Carrollton MD 20784 Office: Edger Therapy PA 7525 Greenway Ctr Dr Suite 106 Greenbelt MD 20770

EDISON, HALI JEAN, economist; b. Santa Monica, Calif., May 28, 1953; d. Jack and Suzanne (Bravemen) E. BA, U. Calif., Santa Barbara, 1975; MS, London Sch. Econs., 1976, PhD, 1981. Economist Amex Bank, London, 1978; vis. lectr. U. Bergen, Norway, 1981-82; economist Fed. Res. Bd., Washington, 1982—; cons. Norwegian Cen. Bank, Oslo, 1987; lectr. U. Md., College Park, 1988. Contbr.: The ECU Market, 1987, Economic Modelling in OECD, 1988. Mem. Econometric Soc., Royal Econs. Soc., Am. Econ. Assn., Wash. Women's Outdoor. Democrat. Club: Landon Tennis (Bethesda, Md.). Office: Bd Govs Fed Res Bd Washington DC 20551

EDMANDS, SUSAN BANKS, research company executive; b. New Rochelle, N.Y., Oct. 7, 1944; d. George Dixon and Marian (Lepied) Banks; children: Whatleigh Winthrop, Benjamin Bruce II. BS, Boston U., 1969; cert., Northeastern U., Boston, 1974. Tchr. project head start Office Econ. Opportunity, Washington, 1966; English tchr. Wattana Sch., Bangkok, 1969-71; market researcher Pauline Rendell Assocs., Somerville, Mass., 1971-72; food info. specialist Find/SVP, Inc., N.Y.C., 1977-80, mgr. tech. and indsl. group, 1980—. Pres. Packer Collegiate Inst. Parents' Orgn., Brooklyn Heights, N.Y., 1987—, trustee, 1987—. Mem. Nat. Assn. Info. Mgrs., Soc. Plastics Industries, Soc. de Chimie Industrielle (mem. Am. sect.), Chem. Mktg. Research Assn. Club: Chemist's (N.Y.C.). Home: 170 Pacific St Brooklyn NY 11201 Office: Find/SVP Inc 625 Ave Americas New York NY 10011

EDMISTEN, JANE MORETZ, lawyer; b. Boone, N.C., Oct. 25, 1938; d. Ralph D. and Lola (Thompson) Moretz; B.A. with honors, U.N.C., 1960, M.A. with honors, 1962; J.D. with honors, George Washington U., 1967; 1 dau., Martha. Research analyst Georgetown U., 1962-63, Herner & Co., Washington, 1964; mil. assistance analyst USAF, Washington, 1964-66; chief, legis. reference sect. NASA, 1966-69; admitted to N.C. bar, 1967, D.C. bar, 1967, U.S. Supreme Ct. bar, 1972; faculty N.C. Central Law Sch., Durham, 1975-76; individual practice law, 1975-76; trial atty. tax div., appellate sect. U.S. Dept. Justice, Washington, 1970-74, 76-77; asst. gen. counsel HUD, 1977-79; dep. gen. counsel Merit Systems Protection Bd., 1979-81; mem. firm Moore & Foster, Washington, 1981-82; ptnr. Prokop & Edmisten, Washington, 1983-85; adj. faculty Am. U. Sch. Law, Washington, Nat. Law Ctr., George Washington U. Recipient Outstanding Adj. Faculty award Am. U., 1984. Mem. Am. Bar Assn., D.C. Bar Assn., Fed. Bar Assn. (Tom C. Clark award 1980), Kappa Beta Pi, Phi Delta Delta. Contbg. author BNA Portfolio. Office: 4400 Jenifer St NW Suite 350 Washington DC 20015

EDMISTON, NORMA, controller; b. Majagua, Cuba, Sept. 15, 1956; came to U.S., 1970; d. Joaquin Benjamin and Zenaida (Loveira) Prieto; m. Joseph Peter Edmiston, May 20, 1979; 1 child, Christine. BS summa cum laude, Fairleigh Dickinson U., 1978. CPA, N.J. Sr. auditor Peat, Marwick Mitchell & Co., Short Hills, N.J., 1978-80; sr. auditor McGraw-Hill Inc., N.Y.C., 1980-81, sr. fin. analyst, 1981-84, asst. controller, 1984-85, acquisition analyst, 1985-87, controller human resources dept., 1987—. Mem. Am. Inst. CPA's, N.J. Soc. CPA's, Am. Woman's Soc. CPA's. Republican. Roman Catholic. Home: 17 MacArthur Dr Clifton NJ 07013 Office: McGraw-Hill 1221 Ave of the Americas New York NY 10020

EDMONDS, ANNE CAREY, librarian; b. Penang, Malaysia, Dec. 19, 1924; d. William John and Nell (Carey) E. Student, U. Reading, Eng., 1942-44; B.A., Barnard Coll., 1948; M.S. in L.S, Columbia U., 1950; M.A., Johns Hopkins U., 1959; postgrad., Western Res. U., 1960-61. With War Damage Commn., London, Eng., 1944-46; children's asst. Enoch Pratt Free Library, Balt., 1948-49; reference librarian Sch. Bus. Adminstrn., CCNY, 1950-51; reference librarian, then asst. librarian readers' services Goucher Coll., Balt., 1951-60; exchange reference librarian European services library BBC, London, 1955; instr. Sch. L.S., Syracuse U., summer 1960; librarian Douglass Coll., Rutgers U., New Brunswick, N.J., 1961-64, instr., summer 1962, fall 1963; librarian Mt. Holyoke Coll., 1964—; vis. librarian U. North, Turfloop, South Africa, 1976-77; mem. library vis. com. Wheaton Coll., Norton, Mass., 1978—; Mem. South Hadley (Mass.) Bicentennial Com., 1975-76; mem. accreditation teams Middle States Assn. Colls. and Secondary Schs., 1963—, New Eng. Assn. Schs. and Colls., 1986—; bd. dirs. U.S. Book Exchange, 1973-76, 80-83; exec. com. New Eng. Library Info. Network, 1974-76, 79-85, chmn., 1982-84; mem. Adv. Commn. Historic Deerfield, 1975-81, 86—. Mem. ALA, Am. Hist. Assn., Assn. Coll. Research Libraries (pres. 1970-71, chmn. constn. and bylaws com. New Eng. chpt. 1975-76, pres. New Eng. chpt. 1983-84), AAUP, AAUW. Home: 79 Cold Hill Granby MA 01033

EDMONDS, JUDITH A., advertising executive, writer; b. San Francisco, Feb. 10, 1944; d. C.W. and Marie (Grant) E.; m. Paul E. Lower, June 15, 1963 (div. 1978); children: Scott C. Lower, Diana M. Lower. BA in Sociology, San Jose (Calif.) State U., 1965. Press sec. to Calif. Assemblyman Dennis Mangers 1976-78, freelance writer, 1978-84; assoc. editor Peninsula mag., Palo Alto, Calif., 1982-83; dir. communications ednl. software Childware Co., Menlo Park, Calif., 1983-84; owner, pres. Edmonds & Haas Advt., Palo Alto, 1984—; bd. dirs. Ronald McDonald House at Stanford U. Author: Atari Sound & Graphics, 1982; Buy a School for Your Home, 1984. Bd. dirs. Ronald McDonald House, Stanford. Mem. Bus./Profl. Advt. Assn. Office: Edmonds & Haas Advt 541 Cowper Suite A Palo Alto CA 94301

EDMONDS-GOZA, SHIRLEY EILEEN, lawyer; b. Garnett, Kans., Apr. 12, 1957; d. Thomas Franklin and Ida Mae Sarah (Moon) Edmonds; m. Kirk John Goza, Sept. 11, 1982. B.A., Pittsburg State U. (Kans.), 1979; J.D., U. Kans., 1982. Bar: Mo. 1982. Assoc. Spencer, Fane, Britt & Browne, Kansas City, Mo., 1982—. Tchr. Jr. Achievement, Kansas City, 1982-85; bd. dirs. Camping Connection; mem. Downtown Republicans, Kansas City, 1982—. Recipient Am. Jurisprudence award, 1980; Bus. and Profl. Women scholar, 1977. Mem. ABA, Kans. City Bar Assn. (chmn. publicity 1982-85), Lawyers Assn. (dir. young lawyers sect. 1984-85), Phi Alpha Delta (chairperson membership), Kappa Delta Pi (scholar 1977), Phi Kappa Phi, Omicron Delta Kappa, Lambda Sigma. Roman Catholic. Home: 8698 W 101st St Overland Park KS 66212 Office: Spencer Fane Britt & Browne 1400 Commerce Bank Bldg 1000 Walnut St Kansas City MO 63106-2140

EDMONDSON, JEANNETTE B., secretary of state; b. Muskogee, Okla., June 6, 1925; d. A. Chapman and Georgia (Shutt) Bartleson; m. J. Howard Edmondson, May 15, 1946 (dec.); children—James H. (dec.), Jeanne E. Watkins, Patricia E. Zimmer. B.A., U. Okla., 1946. Sec. of state State of Okla., Oklahoma City, 1979-87. Chmn. bd. Okla. affiliate Am. Heart Assn., 1979. Democrat. Methodist. Office: Office of Sec of State 101 State Capitol Oklahoma City OK 73105

EDWARDS, ALBERTA ROON, public relations executive; b. Landeshut, Germany, Oct. 9, 1926; d. Max H. and Karin Roon Burger; m. Roger Borgeson, 1951 (div. May 1956); m. Roger Edwards; children: Jeff, Julie, Chris. BA in Econs., Oberlin (Ohio) Coll., 1946. Asst. to treas. Savs. Bank

Life Ins. Fund, 1946-48; market research analyst Dun & Bradstreet, 1948-49; market analyst Charles Pfizer & Co., 1949-52, mgr., fgn. market research, 1952-56; with Schering Corp., Kenilworth, N.J., 1956-72, dir. mktg. info. and analysis, 1972-74, dir. mktg. adminstrv., 1974-80, staff v.p. planning and adminstrn., 1980-84, staff v.p. internat. pub. affairs, mktg. services, 1984-87, staff v.p. planning, pub. affairs, market devel., 1987-88, v.p. pub. affairs, 1988—; mem. First Am. Mktg. Del. to USSR, 1960. Contbr. articles to profl. jours. Mem. Pharm. Mfrs. Assn., Am. Mktg. Assn. (v.p. 1973-75), Internat. Mktg. Fedn. (v.p. 1972-74), Internat. Pharm. Mktg. Research Group (pres.). Office: Schering Corp 2000 Galloping Hill Rd Kenilworth NJ 07033

EDWARDS, CARLA LEE CARLIN, recreation and theme park management consultant; b. Oakland, Calif., Apr. 12, 1945; d. Clay Thomas and Eileen (Laughlin) Birdsall; m. Robert Joseph Edwards, Aug. 29, 1964 (div. 1979); children—Kent Joseph, Kelly Marie. Student San Joaquin Delta Coll., 1964-68. Announcer, K-Joy Radio Sta., Stockton, Calif., 1962-63; telephone operator San Joaquin Telephone Co. Manteca, Calif., 1963-65; co-owner Creative Touch, Manteca, 1967-70; chief communications div. Dept. Def. Tracy (Calif.), 1965-83; owner Carla Edwards Rental Properties, Manteca, 1979—; co-owner Gemini Investments, Stockton, Calif., 1981-85; owner Carla Edwards & Assocs., Santa Cruz, 1979-82, 85—; mgr. advt. Oakwood Lake, Inc., Manteca, 1981-82, gen. mgr., 1982-85; lectr., conductor workshops in field; bd. dirs. Stockton Conv. and Visitors Bur., Manteca, 1982-83. South county dir. United Cerebral Palsy, Stockton, 1981; dir. publicity Manteca Pumpkin Festival, Manteca, 1979-83; promotions dir. Muscular Distrophy, Manteca, 1982. Served with USCGR, 1976-78. Mem. San Joaquin Rental Property Owners Assn., Pacific Athletic Found., Womens Network, Delta C. of C. (dir.), Manteca C. of C., Stockton C. of C., Am. Back Soc. Republican. Roman Catholic. Clubs: Marina West Yacht, Stockton Women's Profl., Pacific Athletic Found. (Stockton). Avocations: real estate, boating, camping, theatre, white water rafting. Home: PO Box 1681 Capitola CA 95010 also: Village West Marina C-Dock Berth 43 6465 Embarcadero Stockton CA

EDWARDS, CAROL CLAY, information system specialist; b. Geneva, Ill., July 13, 1962; d. Richard Henry and Amylu (Wuthier) Clay; m. Curtis J. Edwards, Sept. 13, 1987. BS, U. Wash., 1985. Receptionist Fitzpatric Chiropractic Clinic, Issaquah, Wash., 1979-80; data processor Gt. Western Fed. Savings and Loan, Bellevue, Wash., 1980-81, Fisheries Supply Co., Seattle, 1983-84, Delta Jay Computers, Issaquah, 1983-85; coordinator ops. MCI Telecommunications, Tulsa, 1986—. Mem. LWV, Nat. Assn. Female Execs., Psi Chi. Republican. Presbyterian. Office: MCI Telecommunications 15 W 6th St Suite 2514 Tulsa OK 74119

EDWARDS, CLAUDIA ANN, real estate broker; b. Mason City, Iowa, Sept. 14, 1940; d. Eugene Frances Lillie and Lorraine Mary (Eppinger) Lillie-Manda; m. Harold Oliver Edwards, June 11, 1960 (div. May 1982); children: Laurie Ann. Gregory Stuart, Scott Christopher. BS, U. Mont., 1952. Real estate broker Valley of Calif., San Ramon, 1976-81; br. mgr. Valley of Calif., Alamo, 1981-82, Coldwell Banker, Alamo, 1982-83; real estate broker Coldwell Banker, Danville, Calif., 1983—; fin. planner WZW, St. Louis, 1983-86, Skaife and Co., Orinda, Calif., 1986—. Candidate San Ramon Valley Sch. Bd., Danville, 1976; pres. Montair PTA, Danville, 1976; mem. campaign bd. Danville Sch. Bd. Erections, 1982, Supt. of Schs. Erections Contra Costa County, Calif., 1984. Mem. AAUW, Nat. Assn. Realtors, Real Estate Securities and Syndication Inst., Inst. Fin. Planners, Calif. Assn. Realtors, Apt. Property Owners. CLubs: Blackhawk Women's, Blackhawk Niners (Danville). Home: 600 Birchwood Ct Danville CA 94526 Office: Coldwell Banker 391 Diablo Rd Danville CA 94526

EDWARDS, EDNA JANE, broadcasting company executive; b. Kenton, Ohio, Oct. 9, 1934; d. Leroy Alfred and Stella Josephine (Long) Wilcox; m. Phil Milton Edwards, Aug. 25, 1954. Student Marion Coll., 1952-54. Sec. YWCA, Lima, Ohio, 1954-55; asst. librarian Ohio Wesleyan U., Delaware, 1955-59, Kans. Wesleyan U., Salina, 1959-61; med. sec. various hosps., Ohio, Kans., 1961-64; exec. sec. Blue Ridge Broadcasting, Black Mountain, N.C., 1969-73, gen. mgr., 1973—. Producer, host radio programs Know Your Neighbor, 1974-87, Skip A Beat, 1978—, Morning Manna, 1980—. Mem. Christian Bus. and Profl. Women (chmn. 1978-80), Nat. Religious Broadcasters (bd. dirs. 1974—, sec. 1985-88, v.p. SE chpt. 1984—), Christian Writers Conf. (sec. and asst. registrar 1979), Black Mountain C. of C. Republican. Mem. Christian-Missionary Alliance. Avocations: reading; theatre; sewing; cooking. Office: Blue Ridge Broadcasting Corp Hwy 70 PO Box 158asting Corp Black Mountain NC 28711

EDWARDS, ELEANOR CECILE, comptroller; b. N.Y.C., July 23, 1940; d. Clifford Thaddeus and Lillian Louise (Taitt) Butte; m. Warren Thaddeus Edwards, Dec. 17, 1961; children: Angelique, Kelby. BBA and Acctg. summa cum laude, Mercy Coll., 1982. Supr. billing Formulette Co., Inc., Long Island City, N.Y., 1960-62; keypunch operator Temporary Agys., N.Y.C., 1963-68; tng. instr. Setab Computer Inst., N.Y.C., 1968-70; asst. office mgr. Kendrick Sytems, Inc., Elmsford, N.Y., 1970-71; office mgr. LPI Computer Corp., Millwood, N.Y., 1972-75; full charge bookkeeper Lockwood Manor Home for Adults, New Rochelle, N.Y., 1975-77; comptroller Margaret Chapman Sch., Hawthorne, N.Y., 1977—; dir. Bradhurst Ctr. Corp., Hawthorne, 1980—; cons. acct. Very Spl. Arts N.Y., 1983—. Vol. Spl. Olympics, Westchester, N.Y., 1980—, Very Spl. Arts N.Y., 1982—. Mem. Nat. Assn. Accts., Nat. Notary Assn., Delta Mu Delta, Alpha Chi. Democrat. Office: Margaret Chapman Sch 5 Bradhurst Ave Hawthorne NY 10532

EDWARDS, ELIZABETH CAROL, systems analyst; b. Towson, Md., Aug. 29, 1959; d. Daniel Martin Edwards and Nancy Dorothy (Craig) Mendoza; m. Joseph Charles Garrick, Aug. 30, 1986. AA, Anne Arundel Community Coll., 1979; BS, U. Md., 1982; MS, Johns Hopkins U., 1988; postgrad., George Washington U. From co-op employee to computer programmer software devel. sect. NASA Goddard Space Flight Ctr., Greenbelt, Md., 1980-86, software systems analyst systems devel. sect., 1986—, dir. Summer Inst. in Sci. and Tech., 1984-86, EEO counselor, 1986-87, dance coordinator MAD Prodns., 1984-86, communications coordinator MAD prodns., 1986-87, systems mgr. White Sands Ground Terminal ADP equipment, 1987—. Mem. Digital Equipment Computer Users Soc., Bus. and Profl. Women's Clubs Am., NOW, LWV. Democrat. Home: 9861 Good Luck Rd #8 Seabrook MD 20706 Office: NASA Goddard Space Flight Ctr Code 532 3 Greenbelt MD 20771

EDWARDS, INETTIE, retired teacher; b. Anderson, S.C., Nov. 2, 1917; d. Richard Henry and Gussie Louise (Datcher) Banks; m. Lylton Lorenza Edwards, Nov. 1 1947; 1 foster child, O. Marie Holman Harrell. BA, Talladega Coll., 1940; MA, Columbia U., 1946. Cert. tchr., Va. Tchr. pub. schs. Newport News, Va., 1940-78; ret. 1978. Vol. reading tchr. Newport News pub. schs., 1978—; coordinator sr. vols. in pub. schs. Ret. Sr. Vol. Program, Hampton,Va., 1982—; mem. adv. bd. vols. in pub. schs., Newport News, 1986—; vice chmn. adv. bd. Social Service, Newport News, 1987—; chmn. Newport News Bd. Elections, 1984—; mem. Parent -Tchr. Council, City Dem. Com., Women's Dem. Club. Named OUstanding Citizen, City of Newport News, 1987. Mem. NEA, Internat. Reading Assn. (founder Newport News Counci., pres. 1960-61, 66—, Celebrate Literacy award 1986). Baptist. Home: 951 12th St Newport News VA 23607-0236

EDWARDS, JANICE ANDERSON, senior disability adjudicator; b. Decatur, Ga., Aug. 11, 1954; d. Bennie Lee and Emma (Jordan) Anderson; m. Lawrence Alfonso Edwards, Sept. 11, 1955; children: Lawrence II, Janelle. Cert., Sawyer Coll. of Bus., 1973; AA, DeKalb Jr. Coll., 1977; BS, Ga. State U., 1980, MS, 1982. Sec. Equitable Life Assurance Co., Atlanta, 1974-76; sr. sec. Ga. Dept. Edn., Atlanta, 1976-80; sec. various temporary agys., Atlanta, 1980-81; sr. case worker Fulton County Family and Children Services, Atlanta, 1981-82, 84-85; disability adjudicator Ga. Dept. Human Resources, Atlanta, 1985—. Vol. rape counselor Grady Meml. Hosp., Atlanta, 1983-85. Named One of Outstanding Young Women of Am., 1984; recipient Interviewing Skills award, 1982. Mem. Mental Health Assn. of Met. Atlanta. Baptist. Home: 2116 Twin Falls Rd Decatur GA 30032

EDWARDS, JEANIE ELIZABETH, sales representative; b. Woodward, Okla., July 11, 1942. Corr. clk. Levi Strauss & Co., Amarillo, Tex., 1965-71; mgr. male placement Service Specialists, Amarillo, 1970; payroll clk. Levi Strauss & Co., Amarillo, 1971-72, personnel interviewer, 1972-73, customer service rep., 1973-75; sales rep. Levi Strauss & Co., Lubbock, Tex., 1976-79, El Paso, Tex., 1979—.

EDWARDS, KAREN DENISE, educator; b. Coventry, England, Jan. 31, 1954; d. Dennis Harvey and Eileen Theresa (Cunningham) E. BEd, Warwick U., Coventry, England, 1982; MBA, Nova U., 1986. Cert. tchr., Eng. Tchr. local sch. authority, Coventry, England, 1975-82; model, with pub. relations various co., Warwick, England, 1980-82; tchr. Pine Crest Sch., Ft. Lauderdale, Fla., 1986-87, adminstrv. asst. to Upper Sch. Prin., 1987—; cons. various co., Ft. Lauderdale, 1986-87. Recipient Duke Edinburgh award, Duke Edinburgh, London 1972. Mem. Nat. Assn. Female Exec. Roman Catholic. Home: 1121 W Cypress Dr Pompano Beach FL 33069 Office: Pine Crest Sch 1501 NE 62d St Fort Lauderdale FL 33334

EDWARDS, KATHRYN INEZ, instructional media consultant; b. Los Angeles, Aug. 26, 1947; d. Lloyd and Geraldine E. (Smith) Price; m. Gregor Quentin Edwards, June 7, 1969; 1 child, Bryan. BA in English, Calif. State U., Los Angeles, 1969, supervision credential, 1974, adminstrn. credential, 1975; MEd in Curriculum, UCLA, 1971; PhD, Claremont Grad. Sch., 1979. Tchr., Los Angles Pub. Schs., 1969-78, adv. specially funded programs, 1978-80, advisor libraries and learning-resource program, 1980-81, instructional specialist, 1981-84; cons. instructional media Los Angeles County Office of Edn., Downey, Calif., 1984—; cons. Walt Disney Prodns., Alfred Higgins Prodns., others. Author guides and curriculum kits. Recipient Resolution award Assembly mem. Gwen Moore, 1988, Cert. Commendation, Senator Diane Watson, 1988; Mabel Wilson Richards scholar, 1968, Calif. Congress Parents and Tchrs. scholar, 1968; UCLA fellow, 1968; named Outstanding Woman of Yr. Los Angeles Sentinel, 1987. Mem. Nat. Assn. Minority Polit. Women, Internat. Reading Assn. (speaker nat. conv. 1988), Los Angeles Reading Assn. (pres.), Calif. Assn. Tchrs. of English (conf. del. 1982), Assn. Supervision and Curriculum Devel., Calif. Media and Library Educators Assn., Nat. Assn. Media Women (Media Woman of Yr. 1987), Alpha Kappa Alpha. Democrat. Roman Catholic. Avocations: reading; gardening; sewing. Office: Los Angeles County Office Edn 9300 E Imperial Hwy Downey CA 90242

EDWARDS, LAURA A., rehabilitation educator; b. Portsmouth, Va., Feb. 23, 1942; d. Marvin B. and Kathryn (Aldrich) Edwards; m. Melvin Folland, Sept. 10, 1960 (dec. 1967). BA, William and Mary Coll., 1969; MS, Va. Commonwealth U., 1974. Ordained to ministry, Salvation Army, 1963. Minister Salvation Army, Williamson, W.Va., 1963-65; info. officer Commonwealth of Va. Dept. Rehab. Services, Richmond, 1969-75, coordinator tng. services, 1975-82, project mgr., 1976-79; program coordinator Pa. Coll. of Optometry, Phila., 1982-86; disting. fellow Nat. Inst. on Disability and Rehab. Research, Pa. Coll. of Optometry, Phila., 1986—. Author: (with others) Shaping the Future, 1979. Recipient spl. recognition award Va. Rehab. Assn., 1975. Mem. Nat. Rehab. Assn., Va. Rehab. Assn. (pres.-elect), Assn. for Edn. and Rehab. of Blind and Visually Impaired. Club: Toastmasters (Bluebell, Pa.) (treas. 1983-84). Home: 3120 W School House Ln J-C12 Philadelphia PA 19144

EDWARDS, LAURIE ELLEN, home-based services company executive, educator; b. San Diego, June 3, 1951; d. Donald Morgan and Doral (Erickson) Hurd; m. William E. Edwards, Dec. 5, 1981. Student Calif. Poly. State U., 1977; BA, Nat. U., San Diego, 1978; postgrad. U. Calif., San Diego, 1982-84; MS, Chapman Coll., 1986. Founder, owner La Jolla Village Secretarial Services, Calif., 1981-82; founder, owner Am. Med. Claims, La Jolla, 1981-86; pres., originator At Your Home Services, San Diego, 1984—; cons. LaJolla Light Printers, 1985—; instr. bus. Palomar Coll., Mira Costa Coll., San Diego Community Colls., 1981—; lectr. in field. Columnist University City Gazette, 1982. Mem. La Jolla Town Council, 1981-84; assoc. Indsl. Recreational Council, San Diego, 1983-85. Mem. Nat. Assn. Female Execs., Calif. Bus. Edn. Assn., ASTD, Older Womens League, Womens Internat. Ctr., Nat. U. Alumni Assn. Avocations: photography, travel, exercising. Office: At Your Home Services 10660 Scripps Ranch Blvd Suite 200 San Diego CA 92131

EDWARDS, LYDIA JUSTICE, state official; b. Carter County, Ky., July 9, 1937; d. Chead and Velva (Kinney) Justice; m. Frank B. Edwards, 1968; children: Mark, Alexandra, Margot. Student, San Francisco State U. Began career as acct, then Idaho state rep., 1982-86; treas. State of Idaho, 1987—; legis. asst. to Gov. Hickel, Alaska, 1967; conf. planner Rep. Gov.'s Assn., 1970-73; mem. Rep. Nat. Commn., 1972, del. to nat. conv., 1980. Mem. Rep. Womens Fedn. Congregationalist. Office: State Treas's Office State Capitol Bldg Rm 102 Boise ID 83720

EDWARDS, MARIE BABARE, psychologist; b. Tacoma; d. Nick and Mary (Mardesich) Babare; B.A., Stanford, 1948, M.A., 1949; m. Tilden Hampton Edwards (div.); 1 son, Tilden Hampton Edwards III. Counselor guidance center U. So. Calif., Los Angeles, 1950-52; project coordinator So. Calif. Soc. Mental Hygiene, 1952-54; pub. speaker Welfare Fedn. Los Angeles, 1953-57; field rep. Los Angeles County Assn. Mental Health, 1957-58; intern psychologist UCLA, 1958-60; pvt. practice, human relations tng., counselor tng. Mem. Calif., Am., Western, Los Angeles psychol. assns., AAAS, So. Calif. Soc. Clin. Hypnosis, Internat. Platform Assn. Author: (with Eleanor Hoover) The Challenge of Being Single, 1974, paperback edit., 1975. Office: 6100 Buckingham Pkwy Culver City CA 90230

EDWARDS, NANCY JOAN, English language educator, poet; b. Syracuse, N.Y., Aug. 22, 1941; d. Leonard Joseph and Frances (Wallace) E. Student, U. Nev., Las Vegas, 1959-60; BA, Whittier (Calif.) Coll., 1963; MA, San Jose (Calif.) State Coll., 1968; PhD, Claremont (Calif.) Grad. Sch., 1982. Cert. community coll. tchr., Calif. Prof. English Bakersfield (Calif.) Coll., 1968—, dir. stage and TV poetry edn. programs, 1974-76, dir. writer's workshop, 1979; dir. cultural programs radio sta. Pomona (Calif.) Coll., 1975-76. Author: (with R. Adam) A Poetry Reading at Yosemite, 1985; contbr. poetry to poetry and arts mags., articles to profl. jours. and popular mags. Recipient Research award of Yr., Calif. Community and Jr. Coll. Assn., 1982, Kiwanis Club Poetry and Music award; Bakersfield Coll. faculty fellow, 1985. Mem. Nat. Council Tchrs. of English (com. on composition for coll., secondary and elem. schs.), Calif. State Poetry Soc., Santa Barbara Writer's Consortium, Adminstrv. Mgmt. Soc. (v.p. 1983-84). Democrat. Office: Bakersfield Coll 1801 Panorama Dr Bakersfield CA 93305

EDWARDS, PHYLLIS ANN, cardiothoracic surgeon; b. Youngstown, Ohio, Apr. 27, 1947; d. Marcus Sumpter and Mary Agnes (Preston) E. BS in Chemistry, U. Pa., 1969; MD, Stanford U., 1975. Cert. gen. surgery. Research asst. Pa. Research Assocs., Phila., 1969-70; chem. encoder/indexer Inst. Scientific Research, Phila., 1970-71; intern/resident NYU-Bellevue Hosps., N.Y.C., 1975-77, resident, chief resident gen. surgery, 1978-81; clin. research fellow in cardiovascular medicine NYU Hosp., N.Y.C., 1977-78; clin. fellow in cardiovascular surgery Baylor Coll. Medicine, Houston, 1981-82, Tex. Heart Inst., Houston, 1982-83; commd. USN, 1983, advanced through grades to lt. cmmdr.; attending staff gen. surgeon Bethesda (Md.) Naval Hosp., 1983-84; resident in cardiovascular surgery Bethesda Naval Hosp. and Children's Hosp. Naval Med. Ctr., Washington, 1984-85; chief resident in cardiovascular surgery N.Y. Hosp.-Cornell U. Med. Ctr., N.Y.C., 1985-86; cardiothoracic surgeon San Diego Naval Hosp., 1987-88; practice medicine specializing in cardiothoracic surgery Assocs. in Cardiac Surgery, La Jolla, Calif., 1988—; instr. surgery Uniformed Services U. of the Health Scis., Bethesda, 1983-85, N.Y. Hosp.-Cornell U. Med. Ctr., N.Y.C., 1985-86, advanced trauma life support. Contbr. articles to profl. jours. Mem. AMA, ACS, Am. Coll. Chest Physicians, Nat. Assn. Female Execs., San Diego County Med. Soc., Calif. Med. Assn., N.Y. Acad. Scis., Denton A. Cooley Cardiovascular Surgery Soc. Democrat. Presbyterian. Office: Assocs In Cardiac Surgery 10666 N Torrey Pines Rd La Jolla CA 92037

EDWARDS, PHYLLIS RUTH, school system administrator; b. Needles, Calif., Nov. 7, 1944; d. Ross Allen and Ruth Margaret (Willis) E.; m. Hugh A. Patterson (div. Feb. 1979); 1 child, Ross Alexander. BA, Wheaton Coll., 1966; MEd, Boston U., 1973. Clk. Merrill Lynch, Pierce, Fenner and Smith, Boston, 1966-67; tchr. Boston Pub. Schs., 1967-71; tchr., dept. chmn. Wayland (Mass.) Pub. Schs., 1971-76; project dir. Oakland (Calif.) Pub. Schs., 1976-81; prin. Greenfield (Calif.) Union Sch. Dist., 1981-86; cons. Monterey (Calif.) Peninsula Unified Sch. Dist., 1986—; cons. Monterey County Office of Edn., Salinas, Calif., 1984—. Coordinator blood bank ARC, Greenfield, 1984-87. Mem. Internat. Reading Assn., Calif. Reading Assn., Assn. Calif. Sch. Adminstrs. Lutheran. Home: 46 Los Encinos Del Rey Oaks CA 99340 Office: Monterey Peninsula Unified Sch Dist 540 Canyon Del Rey Monterey CA 93940

EDWARDS, REBECCA SUE, foundation administrator; b. Lancaster, Ohio, Feb. 21, 1956; d. James Joseph and Geraldine Betty (Wright) Fox; m. Todd William Edwards, Oct. 7, 1978; children: Jenny Elizabeth, Tyler James. BA in Psychology and Sociology, Otterbein Coll., 1978. Exec. dir United Cerebral Palsy of Lancaster, Fairfield County, and Vicinity, Inc., 1978—. Mem. Human Resources Council, Lancaster; chmn. First Presbyn. Ch. preschool council, Lancaster, 1985-86; mem. Cen. Ohio Mental Retardation and Developmental Disabilities Planning and Adv. Council; bd. dirs. Multiple Sclerosis, Lancaster, 1980-81; active Council for Exceptional Children. Recipient Humanitarian award United Cerebral Palsy, 1985, 86, 87. Mem. Assn. of Profl. Workers for Cerebral Palsy. Club: Jr. Women's. Home: 524 E 6th Ave Lancaster OH 43130 Office: United Cerebral Palsy 681 E 6th Ave Lancaster OH 43130

EDWARDS, ROBIN MORSE, lawyer; b. Glens Falls, N.Y., Dec. 9, 1947; d. Daniel and Harriet Lois (Welpen) Morse; m. Richard Charles Edwards, Aug. 30, 1970; children: Michael Alan, Jonathan Phillip. BA, Mt. Holyoke Coll., 1969; JD, U. Calif., Berkeley, 1972. Bar: Calif. 1972. Assoc. Donahue, Gallagher, Thomas & Woods, Oakland, Calif., 1972-77, ptnr., 1977—. Mem. ABA, Calif. Bar Assn., Alameda County Bar Assn. (bd. dirs. 1978-84, v.p. 1982, pres. 1983), Entrepreneurship Inst. East Bay (bd. dirs. 1985—). Jewish. Office: Donahue Gallagher Thomas & Woods 1900 Kaiser Ctr 300 Lakeside Dr Oakland CA 94612-3570

EDWARDS, RUTH ANN WHEELER, science facility administrator, researcher; b. Pueblo, Colo., Sept. 18, 1945; d. Nathan Luzerne and Marjorie Louise (Harriss) Wheeler; m. Harry Wallace Edwards, June 8, 1966; children: William Michael, Laura Elizabeth. BA, U. Ariz., 1967; MBA, Colo. State U., 1983. Research technician Colo. State U., Ft. Collins, 1969-73, research assoc. dept. psychology, 1973—; exec. dir. Rocky Mountain Behavioral Sci. Inst., Inc., Ft. Collins, 1978—. Mem. AAAS, Am. Psychol. Assn. (student affiliate), Beta Gamma Sigma. Home: 2837 Eagle Dr Fort Collins CO 80526 Office: Rocky Mountain Behavioral Sci Inst Inc PO Box 1066 Fort Collins CO 80522

EFFINGER, KATHARINA VIOLA, hospital executive; b. Milw., June 15, 1941; d. Charles William and Eleanora (Hauer) E.; student Ft. Wayne (Ind.) Luth. Sch. Nursing, 1959-61; B.A. in Behavior Scis., Nat. Coll. Edn., Evanston, Ill., 1981. Reservation supr. Braniff Internat., 1961-69; sales rep. United Gasket Corp., 1969-70; admitting mgr. MacNeal Meml. Hosp., Berwyn, Ill., 1970-73; bus. office mgr. Lake Forest (Ill.) Hosp., 1974-77; asst. v.p. fin. Victory Meml. Hosp., Waukegan, Ill., 1978—; adv. bd. Lake County Vocat. Center. Mem. Hosp. Fin. Mgmt. Assn., Nat. Assn. Patient Accounts Mgrs. Office: 1324 N Sheridan Rd Waukegan IL 60085

EFUGHU, BEVERLY ANN ELLIS, educator, consultant; b. Chgo., Feb. 28, 1955; d. Carl and Katie (Bentte) Ellis; m. McLyn Efughu. BA in Spl. Edn., Northeastern U., 1981. Head tchr. Temple Sholom, Chgo., 1981-84; tchr. sci. Roosevelt Elem. Shc., Bellwood, Ill., 1984-86; tchr. spl. edn. Britten Elem. Sch., Westchester, Ill., 1986; tchr. learning disabilities Sunnyside Elem. Sch., Berkeley, Ill., 1986—; staff cons. Chgo. Techr.'s Ctr., 1979—. Home: 6300 N Sheridan Rd #811 Chicago IL 60660

EGAN, ANNE HAYS, consultant, minister; b. Montgomery, Ala., May 30, 1950; d. Thomas Patrick and Lorene (Whorton) E. BA, Converse Coll., 1972; MA, Fla. State U., 1973; MDiv, Princeton U., 1982. Ordained to ministry Prsbyn. ch., 1982. Caseworker ARC, Ft. Knox, Ky., 1973-74; caseworker, youth program dir. ARC, Seoul, Republic of Korea, 1975-76; sr. caseworker ARC, Ft. Bragg, N.C., 1976-77; casework supr. ARC, Cin., 1977-79; chaplain Riverside Home for the Aged, Phila., 1979-80; outreach coordinator East Side Parishes, Phila., 1980-82; asst. pastor Valley Forge Presbyn. Ch., Phila., 1982-84; cons. Nat. Presbyn. Ch., N.Y.C., Phila., 1984-85; regional cons. Devel. Dimensions, N.Y.C., 1985-87; cons., pres. Leadership Consortium, N.Y.C., 1987-88; pres. Leadership Consortium Cons. Firm, Louisville, 1988—; parish assoc. West Park Presbyn. Ch., N.Y.C., 1986—; pres. and pub. The Digest, N.Y.C. and Louisville, 1987—. Author: The Church and Social Welfare, 1985, Testing Your Organzational Health, 1987; contbng. author: Empowering Ministry in an Ageist Society, 1982; pub. newsletter The Digest, 1987. Founder, bd. dirs. Nat. Shared Housing Resource Ctr., Phila., 1981-85; chmn. bd. dirs. Interfaith Community Care Ctr., Phila., 1982-84, Human Needs Com., Phila., 1982-84; active Bread for the World, Phila., 1983—, Oxford Com., N.Y.C., 1987—; treas. Girl Scouts of Korea, Seoul, 1976. Mem. Prebyteries of N.Y. and Phila. (chmn. human needs com.), Am. Women for Econ. Devel., Am. Soc. Tng. and Devel., Nonprofit Mgmt. Assn., Soc. for Nonprofit Orgns., NOW (sec. Fayetteville, N.C. chpt. 1976-77), Nat. Assn. Female Execs., Mortar Bd. Democrat. Home and Office: Leadership Consortium 1846 Fleming Rd Louisville KY 40205

EGAN, BARBARA ELIZABETH, school system administrator; b. Cleve., Feb. 23, 1947; d. Robert Harold and Jeanette Ruth (Snyder) E.; adopted children: Linda, Quintana, Steven. BA, Miami U., Oxford, Ohio, 1968. Tchr. No. Miami Beach Jr. High Sch., North Miami Beach, Fla., 1968-71, Canton (Ohio) Pub. Schs., 1971-73; program coordinator Denver Council of Camp Fire, 1974-78; exec. dir. Redwood Empire Camp Fire, Petaluma, Calif., 1978-79; dir. fin. Camp Fire, Seattle, 1979-80, The Bush Schs., Seattle, 1980-86; mgr. bus. The Webb Schs., Claremont, Calif., 1986—; treas. PNAIS, Seattle, 1982-86; cons. in field. Editor adoption support group newsletter. Republican. Episcopalian.

EGAN, EILEEN MARY, college president, lawyer; b. Boston, Jan. 11; d. Eugene O. and Mary B. (Condon) E. A.B., Spalding U., 1956; M.A., Cath. U. Am., 1963, Ph.D. (Bd. Trustees scholar), 1966; J.D., U. Louisville, 1981. Bar: Ky. 1981. Joined Sisters of Charity of Nazareth, Roman Catholic Ch., 1944; tchr. secondary schs. Wakefield, Mass., 1956-60, Memphis, 1960-62; mem. faculty English dept. Cath. U. Am., Washington, 1963-66; chmn. dept. English, Spalding U., Louisville, 1966-67, v.p., 1968-69, pres., 1969—; prof. U. Louisville Law Sch., 1982-83; adminstrv. intern Smith Coll., Northampton, Mass., 1967-68; mem. Ky. State Commn. on Higher Edn., 1974-82, 75-77; chmn. Louisville br. Fed. Res. Bank, 1981, 84. Exec. bd. Old Ky. Home council Boy Scouts Am., 1976-87; mem. bishop's pastoral council Archdiocese of Louisville, 1975-78; mem. Louisville Com. Fgn. Relations, 1978-83; chmn. open spaces adv. com. City of Louisville, 1975-81; bd. dirs. Met. United Way, 1976-80; bd. dirs. chpt. NCCJ, 1973-84; bd. dirs. Better Bus. Bur. Greater Louisville, 1974-79, v.p., 1975-79; bd. dirs. St. Joseph Infirmary, 1979-71, trustee, 1971-76, chmn. bd. trustees, 1975-76; trustee Ky. Ind. Coll. Found., 1970—; bd. dirs. Kentuckiana Metroversity, 1972, chmn., 1982-83, exec. com., 1977—; trustee JH Systems, 1984—, Jewish Hosp., 1982—; mem. County Judge Execs. Adv. Com. on Ethics, 1986—, Ky. Exec. Adv. Bd. for the Div. of Mental Health in Corrections, 1987—; bd. dirs. Ky. Country Day Sch., 1982—. Inst. Internat. Edn. fellow, 1963; recipient Equality award Louisville Urban League, 1978, award Phi Delta Kappa, 1979; Blanche B. Ottenheimer award Louisville Jewish Community Center, 1978; Brotherhood award NCCJ, 1979; Disting. Service award Louisville chpt. Am. Jewish Com., 1987; Cultural Exchange Guest to Republic of China, 1985. Mem. Am. Assn. Higher Edn., So. Assn. Colls. and Schs., Nat. Cath. Edn. Assn. (exec. com. 1973-76), Louisville C. of C. (public edn. com. 1978-83, dir. 1981-84), English Speaking Union, AAUW, ABA, Ky. Bar Assn., Louisville Bar Assn., Am. Judicature Soc., Am. Future Soc. Democrat. Office: 851 S 4th St Louisville KY 40203

EGAN, LINDA LEE, nurse; b. Daretown, N.J., Mar. 25, 1947; d. John Joseph and Mary Elizabeth (Woodruff) Egan; A.S. in Nursing, Cumberland County Coll., 1972; B.S.N., Stockton State Coll., 1978. Cottage attendant Vineland (N.J.) State Sch., 1965-69, cottage supr., 1969-72, staff nurse, 1972-74, head nurse intensive care, 1974-75; staff nurse intensive care Cooper Med. Center, Camden, N.J., 1975-77, inservice clinician, 1977-78; dir. nursing Vineland State Sch. Hosp., 1978-79, instr. nursing inservice, 1979-82; rehab. specialist Staff Builders, San Diego, 1982-83; self-employed rehab. specialist,

1983-86; staff nurse Hemet Valley Hosp., Calif., 1986; nurse intensive care staff Tri City Med. Ctr., Oceanside, Calif., 1986-87; adminstrv. supr. Pomerado Hosp., Poway, 1987—; ICU and critical care unit nurse, 1988—; nursing care cons. (part-time) Am. Inst. for Medical Studies, 1980. Respiratory/circulatory emergency instr./multimedia first aide instr. ARC, Vineland, 1975-81. Recipient Instl. award N.J. Assn. for Retarded Children, 1969. Mem. Profl. Traveling Nurses Assn., S.Jersey Inservice Exchange, Am. Nurses Assn., N.J. Nurses Assn., Calif. Nurses Assn., Am. Assn. Critical Care Nurses, Am. Nurses Found., Century Club. Roman Catholic.

EGAN, SHIRLEY ANNE, retired nursing educator; b. Haverill, Mass.; d. Rush B. and Beatrice (Bengle) Willard. Diploma, St. Joseph's Hosp. Sch. Nursing, Nashua, N.H., 1945; B.S. in Nursing Edn., Boston U., 1949, M.S., 1954. Instr. sci. Sturdy Meml. Hosp. Sch. Nursing, Attleboro, Mass., 1949-51; instr. sci. Peter Bent Brigham Hosp. Sch. Nursing, Boston, 1951-53, ednl. dir., 1953-55, assoc. dir. Sch. Nursing, 1955-59, med. surg. coordinator, 1971-73, assoc. dir. Sch. Nursing, 1973-79, dir., 1979-85; cons. North Country Hosp., 1985-86; infection control practitioner 1986-87; nurse edn. adviser AID (formerly ICA), Karachi, Pakistan, 1959-67; prin. Coll. Nursing, Karachi, 1959-67; dir. Vis. Nurse Service, Nashua, N.H., 1967-70; cons. nursing edn. Pakistan Ministry of Health, Labour and Social Welfare, 1959-67; adviser to editor Pakistan Nursing and Health Rev., 1959-67; exec. bd. Nat. Health Edn. Com., Pakistan; WHO short-term cons. U. W.I., Jamaica, 1970-71; mem. Greater Nashua Health Planning Council. Contbr. articles to profl. publs. Bd. dirs. Matthew Thornton health Ctr., Nashua, Nashua Child Care Ctr.; vol. ombudsman N.H. Council on Aging; mem. Nashua Service League. Served as 1st lt., Army Nurse Corps., 1945-47. Mem. Trained Nurses Assn. Pakistan, Nat. League for Nursing, St. Joseph's Sch. Nursing Alumnae Assn., Boston U. Alumnae Assn., Brit. Soc. Health Edn., Cath. Daus. Am. (vice regent ct. Bishop Malloy), Statis. Study Grads. Karachi Coll. Nursing, Sigma Theta Tau. Home: Rte 1 Box 1268A Natchitoches LA 71457

EGELAND, ELIZABETH VOWELL, food products corporation executive; b. Martin, Tenn., Mar. 26, 1936; d. Vertrees and Elizabeth (Tate) Vowell; m. Elmer M.H. Nolte (div. Mar. 1976); children: Steven Martin, Stanley Vowell; m. Duane R. Egeland. AB, Memphis State U., 1956. Instr. Cobb County Mentally Retarded, Marietta, Ga., 1970-73; sales rep. Rittenbaum Bros., Atlanta, 1973-75, Nat. Labs., Montuale, N.J., 1975-77; dir. instl. sales New South Mfg. Co., Atlanta, 1978-80; nat. sales merchandiser Cornelius Co., Anoka, Minn., 1978-80; sr. nat. account mgr. Nestle Food Corp., Purchase, N.Y., 1980—. Pres. Marietta (Ga.) Council of Garden Clubs, 1968, Atlanta Kiwi Club, 1970; bd. dirs. Nat. Little League, Marietta, 1974-75. Mem. Nat. Assn. Exec. Women, Nat. Orgn. Women in Food Service Sales and Mktg. Office: Nestle Food Corp 1040 Crown Pointe Pkwy Suite 270 Atlanta GA 30338

EGELSTON, DIANE CARROLL, writer and training consultant; b. Shirley, Mass., Mar. 26, 1955; d. Robert Burnley Egelston and Rachel Louise Oliver; m. John Cutler Brorsen, Mar. 27, 1981. BA, U. Calif., Berkeley, 1977. Mgmt. assoc. Security Pacific Bank, San Francisco, 1980-81, tng. specialist, 1982-83; ops. supr. Security Pacific Bank, Oakland, Calif., 1981-82; tng. officer Wells Fargo Bank, San Francisco, 1983-85; tng. mgr. Wells Fargo Bank, Oakland, 1985—. Contbr. articles to books, popular mags. (including Ms. and Business Week's Careers). Mem. Am. Soc. for Tng. and Devel. (newsletter editor 1982-85), Calif. Writers Club, Media Alliance, Nat. Writers Club. Office: Wells Fargo Consumer Credit Div 1333 Broadway MAC 0201-031 Oakland CA 94612

EGENDORF, NORMA LUCY, advertising agency executive; b. Phila., Oct. 7, 1928; d. Louis R. and Alice J. (Petrarch) Testardi; m. Irwin A. Egendorf, Feb. 10, 1961 (div. 1980); m. Jerome Maxwell Pomerantz, Sept. 27, 1986. Student in journalism Temple U., 1950-52; Assoc., Charles Morris Price Sch. Advt. and Journalism, 1948. Advt. asst. Internat. Resistance Co., Phila., 1952-54, advt., sales promotion mgr., 1954-61; account exec. Mel Richman, Inc., Bala Cynwyd, Pa., 1961-68, v.p., acctg. supr., 1968-72; pres. The Advt. People, Inc., Bala Cynwyd, 1972—; instr. Intro. to Advt. program; lectr. in field. Contbr. numerous articles to profl. jours. Bd. dirs. Muscular Dystrophy Assn., Southeastern Pa., 1972-74, pres., 1976-88; bd. dirs. Com. of 70, Phila., 1982-88, vice chmn., 1982-84; bd. govs. Main Line YMCA, Pa., 1975-79; trustee Charles Morris Price Sch., chmn. 1982-84, com. mem. 1980—; pub. relations com. Am. Swedish Hist. Mus., 1985-86. Recipient Silver Medal award Am. Advt. Fedn., 1980, award of Merit Artist's Guild of Del. Valley, 1981, Distinguished Alunma award Charles Morris Price Sch., 1982, 3 awards of Recognition Muscular Dystrophy Assn., 1978-88. Mem. Poor Richard Club (pres. 1984-86, bd. dirs. 1980-88), Mktg. Communications Execs., Internat. (program chmn. 1982-85, bd. dirs. 1982-85), Inst. Contemporary Art (pub. relations chmn. 1980-81), Direct Mktg. Assn. (Gold Mail Box award 1968, promotion chmn. 1975-76), Phila. Club Advt. Women. Club: Germantown Cricket (Phila.) (pub. relations, promotion chmn. 1982-84). Avocations: tennis, art, sculpture, theatre. Home: 730 S American St Philadelphia PA 19147 Office: The Advt People Inc 201 N Presedential Blvd Bala Cynwyd PA 19004

EGGEBRAATEN, DORIS ALPHILD, elementary educator; b. Fortuna, N.D., Mar. 9, 1926; d. Hans Osborneson and Nellie (Nelson) Sather; m. Claude Julian Eggebraaten, June 25, 1947; children: Sonja Mae, Ronald John. Diploma, Itasca Jr. Coll., Coleraine, Minn., 1946; BEd, Sacramento (Calif.) State U., 1959. Cert. kindergarten, primary tchr., Calif. Dep. supt. Placer County Supt. Schs., Auburn, Calif., 1948-52; tchr. Rocklin (Calif.) Elem. Sch., 1952-53, Placer Hills Elem. Sch., Meadow Vista, Calif., 1954-61, Alta Vista Elem. Sch., Auburn, 1971-86; mem. kindergarten assessment com. Auburn Union Elem. Sch., 1987—. Recipient Elda Goff Annual award Auburn Union Sch. Dist., 1984-85. Mem. Calif. Tchrs. Assn., Auburn Unions Tchrs. Assn. (Dist. Service award 1986). Republican. Lutheran. Home: 208 Fulweiler Ave Auburn CA 95603

EGGERS, IDAMARIE RASMUSSEN, pharmaceutical manufacturing and research; b. Grand Rapids, Mich., Oct. 19, 1925; d. Nels Peter Victor and Karen Agnes (Feldt) Rasmussen; m. Raymond Frederick Eggers, Jr., May 29, 1955; children: Karen Elizabeth Eggers Baird, Raymond Frederick III. BS in Chemistry, U. Mich., 1945, MS, 1946. Chemist Merck & Co. Inc., Rahway, N.J., 1946-57, chem. biol. data coordinator, 1965-69, sect. head biol. data, 1969-77, mgr. biol. data, 1977-86; agt., broker Ray Eggers Agy., Rahway, 1958—. Patentee in field. Librarian Rahway Hist. Soc., 1969—, treas., 1972-84. Scholar Grand Rapids Women's Club, 1942, U. Mich. Regents, 1944-46. Mem. AAAS, Am. Chem. Soc., Metro. Women Chemists, N.Y. Acad. Sci., Rahway C. of C. Episcopalian. Club: Rahway Women's. Home and Office: 208 W Milton Ave Rahway NJ 07065

EGGERS, RENEE MARLENE, learning center coordinator; b. Ft. Worth, Feb. 8, 1956; d. Gordon M. and Ozella M. (Beebe) E. BA, Youngstown (Ohio) State U., 1978, MS in Edn., 1982, AAS, 1983, BS in Applied Sci., 1986. Tchr. Howland Christian Sch., Warren, Ohio, 1979-80; grad. asst. Youngstown (Ohio) State U., 1981-82, adj. faculty, 1982-83, adminstrv. asst. reading lab., 1983; reading instr., tutor Pa. State U., Sharon, 1983-84, lang. ctr. coordinator, 1984—. Contbr. articles to profl. jours. Recipient Pa. State U. Adv. Bd. grantee, 1984, 86. Mem. Nat. Assn. Developmental Edn., N.Y. Coll. Learning Skills Assn. Democrat. Baptist. Home: 7023 Chestnut Ridge Rd SE Hubbard OH 44425 Office: Pa State Univ Shenango Valley 147 Shenango Ave Sharon PA 16146

EGGLESTON, REBECCA HOLLAND, product manager; b. Newport News, Va., Aug. 21, 1961; d. John Marshall and Phyllis Matthews (Holland) E. BS in Indsl. Distbn., Tex. A&M U., 1983. Mgmt. trainee First Va. Banks, Arlington, 1983-84; regional mgr. Southeast Mktg., Richmond, Va., 1984; regional mgr. Fluids Research, Inc., Richmond, 1985, sales mgr., 1985-87; product mgr. ITW Devcon, Danvers, Mass., 1987—. Mem. Soc. Mfg. Engrs. Republican. Episcopalian. Home: 6206 Cohoke Pathway Ashland VA 23005

EGLESTON, GWENDOLYN WHITNELL, computer science professional; b. Mesa, Ariz., Feb. 13, 1938; d. Jerome Douglas Whitnell and Ethel (Cardon) Heldt; m. Roger Lee Egleston, Aug. 13, 1960 (div. May 1986); children: Julie, Natalie, Brian Lee. BS in Microbiology, U. Ariz., 1959; BS in Computer Sci., Beaver Coll., 1987. Jr. bacteriologist State of Ariz. Dept. Health, Phoenix, 1959-61; adminstrv. asst. Planning Data Systems, Phila., 1984-86; programmer Environ. Tectonics Corp., Southampton, Pa., 1986—. Mem. Women's Bd. Abington (Pa.) Meml. Hosp., 1984-85; past leader, council mem. Huntingdon Valley council Girl Scouts of U.S.; pres. Mothers of Meadowbrook (Pa.) Sch., 1978-79. Mem. Nat. Assn. Female Execs., Gamma Phi Beta (internat. officer). Republican. Home: 8 Rex Ave Rex Ct Unit 4 Philadelphia PA 19118 Office: Environ Tectonics Corp CountyLine Indsl Park James Way Southampton PA 19118

EHLERS, ELEANOR MAY COLLIER (MRS. FREDERICK BURTON EHLERS), civic worker; b. Klamath Falls, Oreg., Apr. 23, 1920; d. Alfred Douglas and Ethel (Foster) Collier; B.A., U. Oreg., 1941; secondary tchrs. credentials Stanford, 1942; m. Frederick Burton Ehlers, June 26, 1943; children—Frederick Douglas, Charles Collier. Tchr., Salinas Union High Sch., 1942-43; piano tchr. pvt. lessons, Klamath Falls, 1958—. Mem. Child Guidance Adv. Council, 1956-60; mem. adv. com. Boys and Girls Aid Soc., 1965-68 ; mem. Gov.'s Adv. Com. Arts and Humanities, 1966-67; bd. mem. PBS TV Sta. KSYS, 1988, Friends of Mus. U. Oreg., 1966-69, Arts in Oreg., 1966-68, Klamath County Colls. for Oreg.'s Future, 1968-70 ; co-chmn. Friends of Collier Park, Collier Park Logging Mus., 1986, 87, sec. 1988; chpt. pres. Am. Field Service, 1962-63; mem. Gov.'s Com. Governance of Community Colls., 1967; bd. dirs. Favell Mus. Western Art and Artifacts, 1971—, Community Concert Assn., 1950-80 , pres., 1966-74; established Women's Guild at Merle West Med. Ctr., 1965, trustee hosp. sec. bd. trustees, 1962-65, 76—, mem. bldg. com. 1962-67, mem. planning com., chmn. edn. and research com. hosp. bd., 1967—. Named Woman of Month, Klamath Herald News, 1965; named grant to Oreg. Endowed Fellowship Fund, AAUW, 1971; recipient greatest Service award Oreg. Tech. Inst., 1970-71, Internat. Woman of Achievement award Quota Club, 1981, U. Oreg. Pioneer award, 1981. Mem. AAUW (local pres. 1955-56), Oreg. Music Tchrs. Assn. (pres. Klamath Basin dist. 1979-81), P.E.O. (Oreg. dir. 1968-75, state pres. 1974-75, trustee internat. Continuing Edn. Fund 1977-83, chmn. 1981-83), Pi Beta Phi, Mu Phi Epsilon, Pi Lambda Theta. Presbyterian. Address: 1338 Pacific Terr Klamath Falls OR 97601

EHMAN, LINDA ANN, graphic designer; b. Toledo, Ohio, Aug. 1, 1945; d. George Peter and Regina Cecelia (Rybczynski) Domanowski; m. Bruce Butler Kellow, Mar 8, 1969 (div. July 1972); 1 child, Jennifer Lynn; m. David Howard Ehman, Feb. 23, 1974 (div. Mar. 1986); 1 child, Erin Nicole. BBA, U. Toledo, 1967, BA, 1986. Sec. Owens-Ill., Inc., Toledo, 1967-69, asst. fin. analyst, 1969-72, fin. analyst, 1972-74, asst. property tax acct., 1975-83; designer Hoeck Assocs., Toledo, 1986—. Republican. Club: Toledo Artist, O-I Art (past pres.). Home: 5078 Breezeway Toledo OH 43613 Office: Hoeck Assocs 1700 N Reynolds Rd Toledo OH 43615

EHMER, MARJY ARDUINA NICCOLL, psychologist; b. N.Y.C., Feb. 3, 1927; d. George A. and Ray (Haberman) Niccoll; B.A. cum laude, Bklyn. Coll., 1947; postgrad. N.Y. U., 1947-49; Ph.D., U. Rochester, 1959; m. Richard Ehmer, Jan. 23, 1948 (div. Sept. 1965); 1 son, George; m. 2d, Jess L. Dow, Sept. 1971. Lab. asst. Bklyn. Coll., 1946-48, instr., 1947-48; research asst. U. Rochester (N.Y.), 1948-51, Tufts Coll., Medford, Mass., 1951-54; instr. Brandeis U., Waltham, Mass., 1952; instr. U. R.I., Kingston, 1954-58, asst. prof., 1958-60; asst. prof. U. Bridgeport (Conn.), 1960-61, asso. prof., 1961-62; trainee VA Hosp., West Haven, Conn., 1962-63; asso. prof. So. Conn. State U., New Haven, 1963-69, prof., 1969-85, prof. emeritus, 1985—, dir. mental health specialization psychology dept., 1979-85; pvt. practice psychology, 1977—; asso. fellow Inst. Advanced Study in Rational Psychotherapy, N.Y.C., 1976-77. Bd. dirs., chmn. safety services com. So. Central Conn. chpt. ARC, 1979-84, also mem. exec. com. Mem. Am. Psychol. Assn., Eastern Psychol. Assn. (election com. 1958), New Eng. Psychol. Assn. (steering com. 1982-85, pres.-elect 1985, pres. 1986, past pres. 1987, steering com. 1987-89), Conn. Psychol. Assn. (co-chmn. continuing edn. com. 1977-79, editor Conn. Psychologist 1979-80), AAAS, Sigma Xi, Psi Chi. Clubs: Race Brook Country, Mount Sunapee Ski. Contbr. articles to profl. jours. Address: 497 Dogwood Rd Orange CT 06477

EHRENBERG, DARLENE BREGMAN, psychoanalyst; b. N.Y.C., Aug. 15, 1942; d. Samuel and Pauline (Gellman) Bregman; BA magna cum laude, CCNY, 1963; MS, Yale U., 1965; PhD , NYU, 1970; cert. William Alanson White Inst. Psychiatry, Psychoanalysis and Psychology, 1973; m. Bernard Ehrenberg, Nov. 25, 1970; children: Jonathan, Erica. Pvt. practice psychoanalysis and psychotherapy, N.Y.C., 1969—; tng. and supervising analyst and supr. psychotherapy William Alanson White Inst. Psychiatry, Psychoanalysis and Psychology, N.Y.C., 1977—; supr. Inst. Contemporary Psychotherapy, 1974-83; supr. psychotherapy William Alanson White Inst., 1977—; supr. Inst. for Contemporary Psychotherapy, 1974-83; clin. instr. psychiatry Albert Einstein Coll. Medicine, 1968-69; conf. presenter. Carnegie Teaching fellow CCNY, 1964, Harrison fellow NYU, 1965, NIMH tng. fellow NYU, 1970. Mem. Am. Psychol. Assn., William Alanson White Psychoanalytic Soc., Phi Beta Kappa. Asst. editor: Contemporary Psychoanalysis, 1979—, editorial bd., 1975-79; contbr. articles to profl. jours. Home and Office: 11 E 68th St New York NY 10021

EHRENKRANZ, SHIRLEY MALAKOFF, university dean, social work educator; b. N.Y.C., Nov. 9, 1920; d. Isidore and Diana Frances (Lewis) Malakoff; m. Gilbert Ehrenkranz, Mar. 29, 1946 (dec.); children—Jean, Joel, Pamela; m. Fred Kasoff, July 11, 1982. A.B., Hunter Coll., 1939; M.A., Bryn Mawr Coll., 1943; M.S.W., U. Pa., 1945; D.S.W., Columbia U., 1967. Case worker Jewish Welfare Soc., Phila., 1943-44; case supr. S.I. Social Service, N.Y., 1945-48, United Family & Children's Service, Plainfield, N.J., 1949-53; field instr. Rutgers U., 1960-62; research asst. Columbia U., N.Y.C., 1964-65; asst. prof. social work NYU, N.Y.C., 1966-68, assoc. prof. social work, 1968-73, prof. social work, 1973—; assoc. dean Sch. Social Work, NYU, N.Y.C., 1969-76, acting dean, 1976-77, dean, 1977—. Contbr. book revs., articles on social work to profl. jours. Recipient Disting. Alumna award U. Pa., 1979; NIMH grantee, 1963-64, 65. Mem. N.Y. State Assn. Deans (v.p. 1979-80, pres. 1980-81), Nat. Assn. Social Workers, Acad. Cert. Social Workers. Office: NYU Sch Social Work 3 Washington Sq N New York NY 10003

EHRENREICH, BARBARA, author; b. Butte, Mont., Aug. 26, 1941; d. Ben Howes and Isabelle (Oxley) Alexander; m. John H. Ehrenreich, Aug. 6, 1966; children: Rosa, Benjamin; m. Gary Stevenson, Dec. 10, 1983. B.A., Reed Coll., 1963; Ph.D., Rockefeller U., 1968. Editor Health Policy Adv. Ctr., N.Y.C., 1969-70; asst. prof. SUNY-Old Westbury, 1971-74; freelance writer, lectr; fellow N.Y. Inst. Humanities, N.Y.C., 1980—, Inst. Policy Studios, Washington, 1982—; editor Seven Days mag., 1974—; columnist Mother Jones mag., 1986—. Author: For Her Own Good: 150 Years of the Experts' Advice to Women, 1978, (with Deirdre English) The American Health Empire, 1970, (with John Ehrenreich) Witches, Midwives and Nurses: A History of Women Healers, 1972, (with D. English) Complaints and Disorders: The Sexual Politics of Sickness, 1973, The Hearts of Men: American Dreams and the Flight from Commitment, (with E. Hess & G. Jacobs) Re-Making Love: The Feminization of Sex, 1986, (with others) The Mean Season: The Attack on the Welfare State, 1987; contbg. editor: Ms mag., 1981—, Mother Jones mag., 1988—. Co-chmn. Democratic Socialists of Am., 1983—. Recipient Nat. Mag. award, 1980, Ford Found. award for Humanistic Perspectives on Contemporary Issues, 1981; Guggenheim fellow, 1987.

EHRLICH, AVA, television producer; b. St. Louis, Aug. 14, 1950; d. Norman and Lillian (Gellman) Ehrlich; m. Barry K. Freedman, Mar. 31, 1979; 1 child, Alexander Zev. BJ, Northwestern U., 1972, MJ, 1973; MA, Occidental Coll., 1976. Reporter, asst. mng. editor Lerner Newspapers, Chgo., 1974-75; reporter, news editor Sta. KMOX, St. Louis, 1976-79; producer Sta. WXYZ, Detroit, 1979-85; exec. producer Sta. KSDK-TV, St. Louis, 1985—; guest editor Mademoiselle mag., N.Y.C., 1971; free lance writer, coll. prof. Detroit, Chgo., St. Louis, 1974—. Trustee CORO Found., St. Louis, 1976-77, 86—; bd. dirs. Nat. Kidney Found., St. Louis, 1987. Named Outstanding Woman in Broadcasting Am. Women in Radio & TV, 1983; CORO Found. fellow in pub. affairs, 1975-76. Mem. Nat. Acad. TV Arts and Scis. (com. mem. 1986—, local Emmy award 1986), Women in Communications (sec. 1978-79), Soc. Profl. Journalists. Democrat. Jewish. Home: 7469 Teasdale Saint Louis MO 63130 Office: Sta KSDK-TV 1000 Market Saint Louis MO 63101

EHRLICH, GERALDINE ELIZABETH, food service management consultant; b. Phila., Nov. 28, 1939; d. Joseph Vincent and Agnes Barbara (Campbell) McKenna; m. S. Paul Ehrlich, Jr., June 20, 1959; children: Susan Patricia, Paula Jeanne, Jill Marie. BS, Drexel Inst. Tech., 1957—. Supervisory dietitian ARA Service Co., Phila. and San Francisco, 1959-65; dietary mgmt. cons. HEW, Washington, 1967-68; nutrition cons., hypertension research team U. Calif. Micronesia, 1970; regional sales dir. Marriott Corp., Bethesda, Md., 1976-78; dir. sales and profl. services Coll. and Health Care div. Macke Co., Cheverly, Md., 1978, gen. mgr., 1978-79; v.p. ops., div., 1979-80, pres. Health Care div., 1980-81; regional v.p. Custom Mgmt. Corp., Alexandria, Va., 1981-83, v.p. mktg., 1983-87; v.p. mktg. and healthcare sales Morrison's Custom Mgmt., Mobile, Ala., 1987—; cons. mktg. The Green House, Tokyo, 1987—; chmn. bd. Mktg. Matrix, Falls Church, Va., 1984—; bd. dirs. Ed M. Bartikowsky Inc., Kingston, Pa., Morrison Inc., Mobile. Mem. Health Systems Agy. No. Va., 1976-77; chmn. Health Care Adv. Bd. Fairfax County Va., 1973-77; vice chmn. Fairfax County Community Action Com., 1973-77; treas. Fairfax County Dem. Com., 1969-73; trustee Fairfax Hosp., 1973-77; bd. dirs. Tennis Patrons, Washington, 1984—. Mem. Internat. Women's Assn., Am. Mgmt. Assn., Nat. Assn. Female Execs., Roundtable for Women in Food Service, Soc. Mktg. Profls. Club: Internat. (Washington). Avocation: reading. Home: 6512 Lakeview Dr Falls Church VA 22041 Office: Morrison's Custom Mgmt 209 Madison St Alexandria VA 22314

EHRLICH, LESLIE SHARON, communications executive; b. Bklyn., July 30, 1952; d. Abraham and Evelyn (Kuznetz) E.; m. Lee Marc Kaswiner, Aug. 11, 1979; children: Adam Jason, Jessica Sara. BA, Hofstra U., 1973; paralegal cert., Adelphi U., 1974; MA, Montclair State U., 1977; JD, Pace U., 1981. Owner Paralegal Corp., Newark, 1975-77; supr. paralegal AT&T, N.Y.C., 1977-79, law clk. with sales dept., 1979-81; mgr. state regulatory N.Y. Telephone Co., N.Y.C., 1981-82; atty. Bell Communications Research, N.Y.C., 1983-84; mgr. contracts AT&T-IS, Morristown, N.J., 1984-86; mgr. contracts, adminstrn. and policies Timeplex, Woodcliff Lakes, N.J., 1986-87; v.p., gen. counsel M&SD, Lyndhurst, N.J., 1987-88; ptnr. Avarini and Avarini, Jersey City, 1988—; prin. Guarini & Guarini, Lyndhurst, 1988—; adj. prof. Am. Paralegal Inst., South Orange, N.J., 1982-83, Seton Hall, Newark, 1983-84. Chairperson Nat. Council Jewish Women, N.J., 1981-82, Edn./Programming, Suburban Jewish Ctr., Florham Park, N.J., 1984—; attendee Brookings Inst., Washington, 1986. Mem. ABA (vice chairperson young lawyers corp. council sect. 1984-88, pub. utility com. 1986—, student liaison antitrust com. 1979-80, Silver Key award 1979, Gold Key award 1980), N.Y. Bar Assn., N.J. Bar Assn., Exec. Women of N.J. Democrat. Jewish. Home: 8 Pheasant Way Florham Park NJ 07932 Office: M&SD Lyndhurst NJ 07071

EHRLICH, MARGARET ELIZABETH GORLEY, systems engineer, mathematics educator, consultant; b. Eatonton, Ga., Nov. 12, 1950; d. Frank Griffith and Edith Roy (Beall) Gorley; m. Jonathan Steven Ehrlich. BS in Math., U. Ga., 1972; MEd, Ga. State U., 1977, EdS, 1982, PhD, 1987; postgrad. Woodrow Wilson Coll. of Law, 1977-78. Cert. secondary tchr., Ga. Tchr. DeKalb County Bd. Edn., Decatur, Ga., 1972-83; chmn. dept. math. Columbia High Sch., Decatur, 1978-83; with product devel. Chalkboard Co., Atlanta, 1983-84; math instr. Ga. State U., Atlanta, 1983—; pres. Elise, Atlanta, 1983—; course specialist Ga. Pacific Co., Atlanta, 1984-86; systems engr. Lotus Devel. Corp., 1986—; research assoc. SUNY-Stony Brook, 1976; modeling instr. Barbizon Modeling Sch., Atlanta, 1977-81; instr. Ga. State Coll. for Kids, 1984-85; test taking cons. Communication Workers of Am., Atlanta, 1985—; tng. cons. Lotus Devel. Corp. Author: (software user manual) Micro Maestro, 1983, Music Math, 1984. Mem. editorial bd. CPA Computer Report, Atlanta, 1984-85. Active DeKalb LWV, 1980, Atlanta Preservation Soc., 1985; tchr. St. Phillips Ch. Sch., Atlanta, 1981-88; vol. Joel Chandler Harris Assn., Atlanta, 1984-87. Named STAR Tchr. DeKalb County Bd. Edn., 1979, 80, 81, Most Outstanding Tchr., Barbizon Schs. of Modeling, 1980, Colo. Outward Bound, 1985. Mem. Math. Assn. Am., Nat. Council Tchrs. Math., Ga. Council Tchrs. Math., Math. Assn. Am., Am. Soc. Tng. and Devel. Greater Atlanta, Atlanta Women's Network, DeKalb Personal Computer Instr. Assn. (pres. 1984). Democrat. Episcopalian. Club: Atlanta Track. Avocations: piano; creative crafts; aerobics; jogging; fashion modeling. Home: 5300 W Kingston Ct Atlanta GA 30342 Office: Lotus Devel Corp One Ravinia Dr Suite 1310 Atlanta GA 30346

EHRMAN, MADELINE ELIZABETH, government administrator; b. N.Y.C., July 4, 1942; d. Donald McKinley and Marie Madeleine (Brandeis) Ehrman. B.A. summa cum laude Brown U., 1964, M.A., 1965; M.Phil., Yale U., 1967. Sci. linguist U.S. Dept. State, Washington, 1969-73, regional lang. supr. U.S. Embassy, Bangkok, Thailand, 1973-75, lang. tng. supr. U.S. Dept. State, Washington, 1975-84, curriculum and tng. specialist, 1984-85, acting chmn. dept. Asian and African Langs., 1985, chmn. dept. Asian and African Langs., 1986—, acting assoc. dean Sch. Lang. Studies, 1987—. Author: The Meanings of the Modals in Present Day American English, 1966; Contemporary Cambodian, 1975; Indonesian Fast Course, 1982; Communicative Japanese Materials, 1984. Mem., ESOL/HILT Citizen's Adv. Council, Arlington County, Va., 1985—. Woodrow Wilson Found. fellow, 1964; NSF fellow, 1964-69; recipient Meritorious Honor award U.S. Dept. State, 1983. Mem. Tchrs. of English to Speakers of Other Langs., Computer Assisted Lang. Instruction Consortium, Am. Assn. Asian Studies, Assn. for Psychol. Type, Phi Beta Kappa. Avocations: reading; bicycling; gardening. Office: Fgn Service Inst 1400 Key Blvd Arlington VA 22209

EHRMANN, SUSANNA, foreign language educator; b. Detroit, Oct. 17, 1944; d. Frederick Michael and Stephanie (Fiala) Ehrmann. Student Universite Laval, summer, 1965; B.A., Antioch Coll., 1966; M.A.T., U. Chgo., 1968. Cert. tchr., Ill., Tex., Mass. Tchr. fgn. lang. U. Chgo. Lab. Schs., 1967-74, Maimonides Sch., Brookline, Mass., 1975-76, North Shore Country Day Sch., Winnetka, Ill., 1977-78, Copenhagen Internat. Jr. Sch., 1978-79, Houston Community Coll., 1979-81, 84, Kinkaid Sch., Houston, 1980-82, Alief Ind. Sch. Dist., Houston, 1982-85; pvt. instr., 1986—; free-lance researcher, 1986—; mem. North Cen. evaluating team, Chgo., Rockford, 1971; mem. M.A.T. coordinating com. on Romance langs., U. Chgo., 1971-74. Creator German Grammar Game, 1982. Reader for the blind, Chgo., 1972-74. NDEA fellow, 1966-68; Goethe Inst. grantee, summer, 1983. Mem. Am. Assn. Tchrs. of French, Am. Assn. Tchrs. of German. Jewish. Home: 6158 Cedar Creek Dr Houston TX 77057

EICHEL, GLORIA LILLIAN, guidance counselor; b. Bklyn., Apr. 13, 1914; d. Meyer and Anna Rita (Housman) Jacobs; B.A., Hunter Coll., 1936; M.S. in Guidance, Bklyn. Coll., 1969; m. Arthur Eichel, Sept. 9, 1936 (dec. Aug. 1969); children—Alan Charles, Diane Sara, Martin Alexander. Caseworker home relief div. Dept. Welfare, Bklyn., 1938-42; tchr. Bklyn. Bd. Edn., 1950-65, guidance counselor, 1965-80; supporting services-careers cons. Bur. Edn. and Vocat. Guidance N.Y.C., 1981—; ednl. cons. N.Y.C. Bd. Edn. Career Devel.--Project Access, 1985—; condr. workshops on careers at profl. convs. Active Boy Scouts Am., 1950-81. Recipient plaque for services to parents and students Parents Assn. Public Sch. 181, Bklyn., 1979; Counselor of Yr. award Community Sch. Bd. 17, Bklyn., 1980. Mem. Bklyn. Coll. Guidance Assn. (pres. 1976-79), N.Y.C. Personnel and Guidance Assn. (sec. 1976-79), Nat. Vocat. Guidance Assn. (nat. chair career poetry contest 1979-86, nat. chmn. career devel. week, 1986-87, rep. nat. conv. 1979, 80, 81), N.Y. State Personnel and Guidance Assn. (chairperson membership 1980-81, chmn. ret. counselors 1982-84), N.Y. State Vocat. Guidance Assn. (pres. 1982-84), N.Y. State Counseling Assn. (pres. area 3, 1982-84), AAUW (chairperson chpt. edn.). Contbr. articles to N.Y. State Sch. Counselors Newsletters; columnist Ret. Counselors Network, 1978-81. Home: 1410 Ave L Brooklyn NY 11230

EICHER, BONNIE CARTER, computer support representative; b. Balt., Mar. 12, 1961; d. Hollis Moore and Jane Margaret (Quince) Cornwall; m. John C. Eicher, Aug. 17, 1985. BS, La. State U., 1983. Chpt. cons. Alpha Gamma Delta, Indpls., 1984-85; computer support rep. Harris-Lanier Bus. Systems, Orlando, Fla., 1985—. Mem. Nat. Assn. Female Execs. Democrat. Roman Catholic. Home: 446 Springwood Ct Longwood FL 32750 Office: Harris-Lanier Bus Systems 370 S Northlake Blvd Suite 1000 Altamonte Springs FL 32701

EICHER, JOANNE BUBOLZ, design educator; b. Lansing, Mich., Sept. 18, 1930; d. George C. and Stella L. (Mangold) Bubolz; m. Carl K. Eicher, June 8, 1952 (div. Dec. 1974); children: Cynthia, Carolyn, Diana, Christopher P. Gannon. BA, Mich. State U., 1952, MA, 1956, PhD, 1959. Instr., asst. prof. dept. social sci. Boston U., 1957-61; asst. prof. dept. human environment and design Coll. Human Ecology, Mich. State U., 1961-69, asso. prof., 1969-72, prof., 1972-77; prof. U. Minn., 1977—, head dept. textiles and clothing, 1977-83, head dept. design, housing and apparel, 1983-87; dir. Goldstein Gallery, 1983-87; research assoc. Econ. Devel. Inst., U. Nigeria, 1963-66; cons. Time-Life, Inc., Howard U., Prentice Hall, Inc. Author: (with Mary Ellen Roach) Dress, Adornment and the Social Order, 1965, The Visible Self: Perspectives on Dress, 1973; African Dress: A Select and Annotated Bibliography of Subsaharan Countries, Vol. I, 1970; Nigerian Handcrafted Textiles, 1976; (with Erekosima and Thieme) Pelete Bite: Kalabari Cut-Thread Cloth, 1982; (with Pokornowski, Thieme and Harris) African Dress Bibliography, Vol. II, 1985. Contbr. articles to profl. jours. Research grantee Internat. Programs, Mich. State U., 1963-64, African Studies Center, 1965-66, 4-H Programs grantee Ethnic Heritage Program, 1974, research grantee Midwest U. Consortium for Internat. Affairs, 1968, 81; Ford Found. individual grantee, 1973; resident scholar Rockefeller Found. Study and Conf. Center, Bellagio, Italy, 1973; research grantee Buguma Internat. Affairs Soc., 1982, 84. Mem. Costume Soc. Am., Walker Art Ctr., Textile Mus., Mpls. Inst. Art, Am. Home Econs. Assn., Am. Sociol. Assn., Assn. Coll. Profs. Textiles and Clothing, Costume Soc. (London, Eng.), Nigerian Nat. Mus. Soc., African Studies Assn., Gamma Sigma Delta, Phi Kappa Phi, Alpha Kappa Delta, Tau Sigma, Alpha Gamma Delta. Democrat. Lutheran. Home: 2179 Folwell St Saint Paul MN 55108

EICHINGER, MARILYNNE H., science museum director. m. Martin Eichinger; 1 child, Talik. AB in Anthropolgy and Sociology magna cum laude, Boston U., 1965; MA, Mich. State U. With emergency and outpatient staff Ingham County Mental Health Ctr., 1972; pres., exec. dir. IMPRESSION 5 Sci. and Art Mus., Lansing, Mich., 1973-85; exec. dir. Oreg. Mus. Sci. and Industry, Portland, 1985—; instr. Lansing (Mich.) Community Coll., 1978; ptnr. Eyrie Studio, 1982-85; conductor numerous workshops in interactive exhibit design, adminstrn. and fund devel. for schs., orgns., profl. socs. Author: (with Jane Mack) Lexington Montessori School Survey, 1969, Manual on the Five Senses, 1974; pub. Mich. edit. Boing mag. Founder Cambridge Montessori Sch., 1964; mem. pres.'s adv. council Portland State U.; bd. dirs. Lexington Montessori Sch., 1969, Mid-Mich. South Health Systems Agy., 1978-81, Community Referral Ctr., 1981-85, Sat. WKAR-Radio, 1981-85; active Lansing "Riverfest" Lighted Boat Parade, 1980; mem. State Health Coordinating Council, 1980-82; pres.' adv. bd. Portland State U., 1987—. Recipient Diana Cert. Leadership, YWCA, 1976-77. Mem. Am. Assn. Mus., Oreg. Mus. Assn., Assn. Sci. and Tech. Ctrs. (bd. dirs. 1980-84). Club: City of Portland. Lodge: Zonta (founder, bd. dirs. East Lansing club 1978). Office: Oreg Mus of Sci & Industry 4015 SW Canyon Rd Portland OR 97221

EICHLIN, BARBARA ANNE, banker; b. Sellersville, Pa., Feb. 3, 1960; d. Richard G. and Elizabeth M. (Branigan) Kehs; m. Gary K. Price, May 5, 1979 (div. Sept. 1983); m. Jonathan W. Eichlin, Aug. 29, 1987. Asst. mgr. sales Deb Shop, Quakertown, 1976-78; clk. Bucks County Bank and Trust Co., Perkasie, Pa., 1978-79, sales rep., 1979-83, lender, 1983-84, asst. mgr., 1984-86, banking officer exec. banking dept., 1986-88; mgr., banking officer exec. banking dept. Bucks County Bank and Trust Co., Newtown, Pa., 1988—. Mem. Nat. Assn. Female Execs., C. of C. Office: Bucks County Bank and Trust Co Penns Trail Newtown PA 18940

EICKMAN, JENNIFER LYNN, conference center manager, writer, artist; b. Urbana, Ill., Nov. 7, 1946; d. Marvin A. and Emma L. (Hartrick) Smith; B.F.A., U. Ill., 1967, postgrad. in Art History, 1967-70; m. Gary Edwin Eickman, June 9, 1968. Tchr., Univ. High Sch., Urbana, 1968, Champaign (Ill.) Public Schs., 1969-70; mem. faculty U. Ill., 1968-77, Richland Coll., Decatur, Ill., 1975-77; asst. to dir. of extension in visual arts U. Ill., 1969-70, program dir. Allerton House Conf. Center, 1974—; dir. Allerton Art Inst., 1984—; bd. dirs. Monticello Design and Mfg.; pres. The Farms; guest lectr., tchr. art workshops. Mem. Pacific Tropical Bot. Gardens, Defenders of Wildlife, Nat. Trust Hist. Preservation, Internat. Platform Assn., Kappa Alpha Theta (delta chpt. corp. pres.). Staff writer Champaign-Urbana mag.; contbr. articles on art history, music, edn. and natural history. Home: Gate House Allerton Park Monticello IL 61856 Office: Allerton House Allerton Park Monticello IL 61856

EICKSTADT, KATHLEEN JOAN, financial analyst; b. Spokane, Wash., Feb. 7, 1959; d. Clifford Francis and Evelyn Beatrice (Hillstad) E. BA in Bus. Adminstrn., Ea. Wash. U., 1980, MBA, 1987. Sales assoc. Bon Marche, Spokane, 1978-81; staff acct. Rosauers, Spokane, 1981-85, fin. analyst, 1985—; cons. URM, Inc., Spokane, 1986—; researcher Mgmt. Info. Systems Inst., Spokane, 1987. Author: (jour.) Kaypro Corp., 1987. Multiple Sclerosis Found. scholar, 1977. Mem. Nat. Assn. Female Execs., MBA Soc.

EIDE, BARBY FAIRBANKS, author; b. Utica, N.Y., Aug. 26, 1938; d. Ben F. and Sally M. (Bawol) Swider; m. Leroy Michael Eide, Feb. 17, 1978. Student, City Coll. San Francisco, 1973-75. Assoc. dir. pub. relations Ford Motor Co., San Francisco, 1971-73; dir. pub. relations, ednl. programs Unity Ch., Spokane, Wash., 1975-77; nat. speaker on nonverbal communication, stress mgmt., time mgmt. 1965—; owner Barby Fairbanks Eide Profl. Prodns., Austin, Tex., 1983—; instr. Wash. State Community Coll., Spokane YWCA. Contbr. chpts. to books. Bd. dirs. City Coll. Spokane, 1977—. Mem. Am. Soc. Tng. Devel. (chmn. chpt. program 1980).

EIDE, MARLENE, county government official, law firm executive; b. Great Falls, Mont., Mar. 4, 1932; d. Howard A. and Maud (Ray) Lund; m. Donald H. Eide, Apr. 2, 1952; children: David, Don Allen, Kjersti, Jennifer. Student, U. N.D., 1949-50. Coordinator, editor, writer Williams County Hist. Soc., Williston, N.D., 1974-77; legal asst. Bjella Neff Rathert Wahl & Eiken, Williston, 1977-87, bus. mgr., 1988—; mem. Ft. Buford-Ft. Union Council, Williston, 1977-87; commr. Williams County, Williston, 1981—; mem. N.D. State Banking Bd., Bismark, 1986—. Author, editor: Wonder of Williams, 1976; also articles. Clk.-treas. Williston Twp., 1975-80; active N.W. Human Resources, 1982-88; mem. yr. of family steering com. , 1988—. Named Outstanding Woman, Williston Jaycettes, 1976; recipient appreciation cert. for service on bd. Williston Community Library, 1985. Mem. N.D. Press Women, Assn. Oil and Gas Producing Counties (v.p. 1981—), N.D. County Commrs. Assn. (exec. com. 1982, treas. 1982-87), Nat. Assn. Counties (steering com. on transp. 1987—), N.D. Assn. Counties (com. on future 1988—, transportation steering com., 1987—), Nat. Dem. County Ofcls. Lutheran. Lodges: Order Eastern Star (worthy matron 1962-63), Rainbow Girls (mother advisor 1961-63). Home: Route 1 Box 56-E Williston ND 58801 Office: Williams County Courthouse PO Box 1246 201 E Broadway Williston ND 58801

EIDT, MARY BELLAN, school system administrator; b. Vicksburg, Miss., Jan. 29, 1932; d. John Alexaner and Mary (Junkin) Bellan; m. Edward Duncan Eidt, Dec. 12, 1984. BS, Sacred Heart Coll., Grand Coteau, La., 1953; MA, Tulane U., 1961; EdD, N.E. La. U., 1979. Cert. tchr., Miss., La. Tchr. English Natchez (Miss.) Adams County Sch. Bd., 1959-66; tchr. English Concordia Parish Sch. Bd., Vidalia, La., 1966-78, supr., 1985—; tech. asst. La. State Dept. Edn., Vidalia, 1979-85; pres. Myrtle Bank Pubs., Natchez, 1981-87. Co-author: (book) The Complete Guide to Natchez. Chmn. Tacony Restoration Com., Vidalia, 1976-83; citizen rep. Vidalia Hydroelectric Plant Bldg. Com., 1988—. Mem. Internat. Reading Assn. (presenter 1985), La. Assn. Educators, Concordia Assn. Computer Edn., Natchez-Adams Assn. Educators (pres. 1961-62), Concordia Assn. Educators (pres. 1973-74), Nathcez Hist. Soc. (pres. 1985), Garden Club Am. (mem. exec. bd. 1987), Pilgrimage Garden Club Antiques Forum (chmn. 1982), Natchez Art Assn. Roman Catholic. Home: 705 N Oak St Vidalia LA 71373 Office: Concordia Parish Sch Bd 950 Vidalia LA 71373

EIFFERT, SYLVIA ANN, elementary educator; b. Eugene, Oreg., Sept. 1, 1940, d. Donald Statton and Helen Mae (Kester) Hendrickson; m. Rex Lee Eiffert, Apr. 3, 1969; children: Matthew, Heather. BA, Westmont Coll., 1963. Elem. tchr. Sch. Dist. 48, Beaverton, Oreg., 1963-68; elem. tchr. Dept. Def., Böblingen, Fed. Republic of Germany, 1968-73, Sigonella, Sicily, Italy, 1973-74, elem. tchr. Ukiah (Calif.) United Sch. Dist., 1976—. Mem. Ukiah Valley Soccer League. Mem. NEA, Calif. Tchrs. Assn, Calif. State PTA, Ukiah PTA, Ukiah Tchrs. Union. Republican. Presbyterian.

EILAND, DEANIE IVA, sales representative, counselor, writer, poet; b. Bryson City, N.C., May 25, 1938; d. James Noel and Ellen (Waldroup) Cochran; m. Royce L. Eiland, Dec. 31, 1955 (dec. Apr. 1963); children—Janice (dec.), Lynne, Sue. B.S., Bryce Bus. Coll., High Point, N.C., 1966; B.S. in Radio Tech. and Photog. Sci., Career Tng. Inst., Atlanta, 1972. Tchr. Electronic Computer Programming Inst., Atlanta, 1968-72; salesperson E.R.A. Realty, Atlanta, 1973-78; sales rep. Pitney Bowes, Atlanta, 1979-82, Dallas, 1984—; active counselor, youth orgn., Dallas. Author: Dawn Awaken, 1968; (poetry) End of the Road, 1983; Best of Sunshine, 1984. Pres. Republican fund raising group, Atlanta, 1980; mem. March Wish Found., North Tex. Food Bank, Casa de los Amigos, Storefront, Little Miracle, Brady Ctr., Boys/Girls Ctr Wayback House, Parkland Hosp. Ladies of Charity, Dallas Life Found., Salvation Army, Sr. Citizens Group, Juvenile Detention, Love for Kids, Trinity River Mission. Recipient 84 sales awards, 1979-86. Jewish. Avocations: flying; golfing; swimming; tennis. Home: 4068 Rockey Rd Dallas TX 75251

EINAN, CONNIE JEANNAE, social service administrator; b. Junction City, Kans., Oct. 28, 1946; d. Robert Dale Minard and Elsie Marie (Burge) Hughes; m. Duaine Lee Einan, July 18, 1981 (div. Jan. 1985); children: Jaennae C. Dinius, R. Andre Einan. Exec. dir. Valley Pulse Health Agy., Renton, Wash., 1970-77; provider relations specialist Blue Cross of Wash., Alaska, 1977-79; dir. planning Kadlec Med. Ctr., Richland, Wash., 1979-82; owner, cons. Einan and Shulman, Inc., Richland, 1982-85; exec. dir. Assn. for Retarded Citizens, Tri-Cities, Wash., 1985—; prof. City Coll., Bellevue, Wash., 1978-79; guest lectr. U. Wash., Seattle, Walla Walla (Wash.) Community Coll., 1976-79. Author: Certificate of Need, 1980, rev. edition, 1982. Mem. Richland City Council, 1984-86; v.p. Tri-Cities Visitors and Conf. Bur., 1984-86; chmn. Wash. State Nursing Home Adv. Council, 1983-87; commr. Valley Gen. Hosp., Renton, 1973-75. Mem. Nat. Assn. Female Execs., Nat. Conf. Execs., Planning Exec. Inst., Richland C. of C. Lodge: Soroptimists. Home: 1331 Perkins Richland WA 99352 Office: Assn for Retarded Citizens 767 Williams Blvd Richland WA 99352

EINIGER, CAROL BLUM, investment banker; b. Phila., Nov. 30, 1949; d. Bernard Michael and Bella (Karff) Blum; m. Roger William Einiger, Dec. 21, 1969; 1 child. BA, U. Pa., 1970; MBA, Columbia U., 1973. With Conde Nast Publs., N.Y.C., 1970-71, Goldman, Sachs & Co., N.Y.C., 1971-72; with 1st Boston Corp., N.Y.C., 1973—, with corp. fin. dept., 1973-79, with capital markets dept., 1979—, mng. dir., 1982—, head short-term fin. dept., 1983-88, head capital markets dept., 1985-88; vis. prof., exec.-in-residence, Columbia U., N.Y.C., 1988—. Founding chair Trustees Council Penn Women U. Pa.; assoc. trustee U. Pa., 1987—; trustee Horace Mann-Barnard Sch., 1988—; mem. Wall St. planning bd. UJA-Fedn. Honoree Women in Corp. Leadership, Catalyst, 1984. Club: Bond (N.Y.C.). Office: Columbia U Grad Sch Bus 313 Uris Hall New York NY 10027

EINODER, CAMILLE ELIZABETH, educator; b. Chgo., June 15, 1937; d. Isadore and Elizabeth T. (Czerwinski) Popowski; student Fox Bus. Coll., 1954; B.Ed. in Biology, Chgo. Tchrs. Coll., 1964; M.A. in Analytical Chemistry, Gov.'s State U., 1977; MA in Adminstrn. and Supervision, Roosevelt U., 1986; postgrad. m. Joseph X. Einoder, Aug. 5, 1978; children—Carl Frank, Mark Frank, Vivian Einoder, Joe Einoder, Tim Einoder, Sheila Einoder, Jude Einoder. Secretarial positions, Chgo., 1955-64; tchr. biology Chgo. Bd. Edn., 1964—, tchr. biology and agr., 1975-81, tchr. biology, agr. and chemistry, 1981—; human relations coordinator Morgan Park High Sch., Chgo., 1980—, tchr. biology Internat. Studies Sch., 1983—; career devel. cons. for agr. related curriculum. Bds. dirs., founding mem., author constn. Community Council, 1970—; bd. dirs., edn. cons. Neighborhood Council, 1974; rep. Chgo. Tchrs. Union, 1969. Mem. Phi Delta Kappa. Home: 10637 S Claremont St Chicago IL 60643 Office: 1744 W Pryor St Chicago IL 60643

EINREINHOFER, NANCY ANNE, art gallery director; b. Paterson, N.J., Sept. 8, 1944; d. John Edward and Nora (Niland) Gleason; m. Robert Einreinhofer, Nov. 26, 1966; 1 child, Robert. BA in Art, William Paterson Coll., 1976, BA in English, 1977, MA in Visual Arts, 1978; cert. in supervisory mgmt., Rutgers U., 1986; postgrad., Leicester U., England, 1986—. Art critic N.J. News, 1973-76; gallery curator O.K. Harris Works of Art, N.Y.C., 1978; dir. gallery William Paterson Coll., Wayne, N.J., 1979—; bd. dirs. Mus. Council of N.J., 1984—; cons. Sussex County Arts Council, N.J., 1987. Contbr. articles to profl. jours. Recipient grant Nat. Endowment for Arts, 1979, NEH, 1984-85, 87-88, N.J State Ccouncil Arts, 1984-85, 85-86, 87-88. Mem. Am. Assn. Mus., Internat. Council Mus., Mid Atlantic Assn. Mus., Assn. Coll. and U. Mus. Galleries, Mus. Council of N.J. (exec. bd. 1984-88). Home: 1 Cheyenne Trail Sparta NJ 07871 Office: William Paterson Coll Ben Shahn Galleries Wayne NJ 07470

EINSTEIN, ELIZABETH ANN, workshop leader, writer; b. Loyal, Wis., Oct. 7, 1939; d. Andrew Edward Weyer and Betty Mae (Lee) Higbie; stepchildren: Beverly, Brenda, Kurt; children: Christopher, Jeffrey. AA, Onondaga Community Coll., 1974; BA in Psychology, Mag. Journalism, Syracuse U., 1977. Free lance writer The National Observer, other pubs., 1977—; free lance stepfamily educator 1982—; speaker in field. Author: The Stepfamily: Living, Loving, Learning, 1982, New Connections: Preparing for Remarriage, 1987; co-author: Stepfamily Living, 1982, Strengthening Our Stepfamilies, 1986; corr. Human Behavior Mag., 1978-79; editor Stepfamily Bull., 1980-83; contbr. articles to profl. jours. Recipient Nat. Media Award Am. Psychol. Assn., 1978, 82, Penney-Mo. Journalism award, 1980; Middlebury Coll. fellow, 1983. Mem. Soc. Profl. Journalists, Stepfamily Assn. of Am. (founder, bd. dirs.), Parents Without Ptnrs. Home: PO Box 6760 Ithaca NY 14851

EIS, LORYANN MALVINA, educator; b. Muscatine, Iowa, Apr. 3, 1938; d. Chester N. and Anna M. (Lenz) E. AB, Augustana Coll., 1960; MEd, U. Ill., 1963; postgrad., Montclair State Coll., 1965-67, Indiana U. of Pa., 1968, U. Iowa, 1970, Western Ill. U., 1978-80. Cir. analysis engr. Automatic Electric Co., Northlake, Ill., 1960-61; math. tchr. Orion (Ill.) Community Sch. Dist., 1961-63; math. tchr., chmn. div. math. and sci. United Twp. High Sch., East Moline, Ill., 1963—; lectr. Augustana Coll., Rock Island, Ill., 1982—. Cons.: General Mathematics Textbook, 1978-79. Chmn. math. task force Edn. Service Ctr. #8, 1986-88; bd. sec. Citizens to Preserve Black Hawk Park Found., 1977—; v.p. council Salem Luth. Ch.; pres. Augustana Coll. Hist. Soc.; mem. Moline YWCA. Mem. NEA, Ill. Edn. Assn., Nat. Council Tchrs. of Math., Ill. Council Tchrs. of Math., Classroom Tchrs. Assn., Assn. Supervision and Curriculum Devel., Rock Island Scott Counties Sci. and Math. Tchrs. Assn., Women in Edn1. Adminstrn., AAUW (past state pres., regional dir. Great Lakes chpt., grantee 1975-76), Delta Kappa Gamma (state treas., internat. fin. com.), Am. Philatelic Soc., TransMiss. Philatelic Soc., Quad City Stamp Club. Republican. Home: 2037 15th St Moline IL 61265 Office: 42nd Ave and Archer Dr East Moline IL 61244

EISELE, PATRICIA O'LEARY, shopping center executive; b. Kansas City, Mo., Aug. 31, 1935; d. George Sexton and Dorothy Madeline (Stubbs) O'Leary; student Sarachon Hooley Bus. Sch., 1954-55, Rockhurst Coll., 1982-83; cert. Internat. Council Shopping Centers Mktg. Inst., 1978; m. John G. Eisele, July 16, 1955; children—Kathleen, Janice, Melissa, Patricia, John. Mktg. dir. Ward Pkwy. Center, Kansas City, Mo., 1974-79, mgr., 1979-80; mktg. counselor John Knox Village, Lee's Summit, Mo., 1981-83; gen. mgr. Leavenworth (Kans.) Plaza Shopping Ctr., 1983—; bd. dirs. local merchant's assn., 1977-80. Bd. dirs. Arthritis Found., Kansas City, Mo., 1980-82; bd. dirs., sec. Mid-Winter Art Fair Assn., Kansas City, 1980-82; chairperson Leavenworth Conv. and Visitors Bur., 1987. Recipient award Heart Assn., 1979, 80, Easter Seal Soc., 1979, Muscular Dystrophy Assn., 1978, Ararat Shrine, 1980, Boy Scouts Am., 1979, 80, Athena award. Mem. Am. Bus. Women's Assn., Leavenworth Area C. of C. (bd. dirs. 1986, 87, exec. com. 1986, 87), Women's C. of C., Chi Omega. Clubs: Altar Soc., Catholic Women's. Home: 2803 W 73d Terr Prairie Village KS 66208 Office: 3400 S 4th Trafficway Leavenworth KS 66048

EISEMANN, KATHRYN HELEN, television and film producer; b. N.Y.C., Oct. 14, 1956; d. Alexander and Sandra (Lane) E. BA, U. Hartford, 1979. Free lance photojournalist Hartford and Westport, Conn., 1978-81; head prodn. Big City Films, N.Y.C., 1982-84; free-lance coordinator films and commls. N.Y.C., 1984-86, free-lance producer TV commls., 1986—; photographer Animal Adoption Fund., N.Y., 1986—. Asst. prodn. mgr. Willy Nilly, 1986; producer, prodn. mgr. Isaac Asimov's Robots; producer, dir. promotional segments Nat. Geographic Explorer. Mem. Dirs. Guild Am. (second asst. dir. 1987). Home: 319 W 82 St New York NY 10024

EISENBERG, RUTH F., literature and communications educator, consultant; b. N.Y.C., Jan. 20, 1927; d. Samuel I. and Ida (Hollander) Berman; m. Arthur Eisenberg, Nov. 9, 1947 (div. Dec. 1963); children—Jay M., Stephen J. B.A., NYU, 1946; M.A., U. Wis., 1947. Asst. prof. Westchester Community Coll., Valhalla, N.Y., 1954-67; prof. lit. and communications Pace U., Pleasantville, N.Y., 1967—; cons. to industry. Editor: (with Carol Swidorski) Reading for Recognition, 1969; Not Quite Twenty, 1970; author: (poems) Grandmas Have Long Arms for Hugging, 1987, contbr. poetry to periodicals and mags. including I Must Explain (All Nations Poetry award 1981); developer tng. program Presentations That Work, 1984. Bd. dirs. Planned Parenthood of Westchester, 1981-83. Recipient Disting. Teaching award Pace U., 1973, 3d place award for poem Pteranodon Mag., 1983. Mem. Poetry Soc. Am., Speech Communication Assn., Nat. Council Tchrs. English, Women in Communications (chmn. Westchester 1980-82, Founders award 1982). Democrat. Jewish. Home: 90 Bryant Ave White Plains NY 10605 Office: Pace Univ Bedford Rd Pleasantville NY 10570

EISENBERG, SONJA MIRIAM, artist; b. Berlin, June 10, 1926; came to U.S., 1938, naturalized, 1947; d. Adolf and Meta Cecilie (Bettauer) Weinberger; student Queens Coll., 1943-46, Middlebury Coll., 1945; NYU, 1952-54; BA, NYU, 1954; postgrad. Nat. Acad. Sch. Fine Arts, 1961; m. Jack Eisenberg, Mar. 31, 1946; children: Ralph, Lynn, Lauren. One-woman shows: Bodley Gallery, N.Y.C., 1970, 73, 75, 80, Galerie Art du Monde, Paris, 1973, Buyways Gallery, Sarasota, Fla., 1973, 74, 75, 78, Galerie de Sfinx, Amsterdam, Netherlands, 1974, Huntsville (Ala.) Mus. Art, 1974, Anglo-Am. Art Mus., Baton Rouge, 1974, Comara Gallery, Los Angeles, 1974, Palm Spring (Calif.) Desert Mus., 1975, Fordham U., N.Y.C., 1976, Omega Inst., New Lebanon, N.Y., 1979, Am. Mus., Hayden Planetarium, N.Y.C., 1980, Avila Graphics, Ltd., 1981, YWCA, N.Y.C., 1981, Cathedral of St. John the Divine, N.Y.C., 1983, 85; group shows include: Mus. Fine Arts, St. Petersburg, Fla., 1973, Am. Watercolor Soc., 107th, 108th Exhbn., 1974, 75, Galerie Frederic Gollong, St. Paul de Vence, France, 1978, Betty Parson's Gallery, N.Y.C., 1981; represented in permanent collections: Archives Am. Art, Smithsonian Inst., Jewish Mus., N.Y.C., Fordham U. Mus., N.Y.C., Palm Springs Desert Mus., Omega Inst., Cathedral St. John the Divine; artist-in-residence Cathedral of St. John the Divine, N.Y.C., 1983-87 ("Seeing the Gospel According to St. John") with text, 41 paintings; designer WFUNA cachet for UN Water Power Conf., 1977, UN Internat. Yr. of Disabled Persons, 1981. Recipient gold medal for artistic merit Internat. Parliament for Safety and Peace, 1983, Palma D'Oro Europe, 1986. Mem. Accademia Italia delle Arti e del Lavoro (Gold medal 1981). Completed project Seeing the Gospel According to St. John (text and 41 paintings) for Cathedral of St. John, 1987. Home and Office: 1020 Park Ave New York NY 10028

EISENBRAUN, DIANNE RAE, manufacturing company executive, designer; b. Cheyenne, Wyo., July 22, 1956; d. Virtus Ray and Doris Evarene (DeJong) Meyer; m. Neal Albert Eisenbraun, Dec. 10, 1977; children: J. Gerrit, Blair Randall, Jaime Michelle. BA in Mass Communications, U. S.D., 1978. Advt. rep. Sta.'s KVRA/KVRF Radio, Vermillion, S.D., 1978-80; customer service rep. Austad's, Sioux Falls, S.D., 1980-81; mktg. asst. The Sussel Co., St. Paul, 1981-83; pres. Beautiful Bambino, Inc., Mpls., 1985—. Broadcast Media Assn. scholar, 1976. Mem. Women Entrepreneur Network, Nat. Assn. Female Execs. Republican. Mem. Assembly of God Ch.

EISENBREY, DIANE GRACE, architectural designer; b. Dover, Del., Nov. 17, 1949; d. William Howard and Grace Mary (Hufnal) E. AS, Del. Tech. & Community coll., 1969. Lic. gen. contractor, Del. Detail draftsman Richard Fox, Architects, Newark, Del., 1969-71; archtl. designer Lester Lumber & Home Ctr., St. Georges, Del., 1971-75; structural designer I.C.I., Ams., Wilmington, Del., 1975-77; archtl. designer, gen. contractor Eisenbrey Custom Designs, Gen. Contractor, Smyrna, Del., 1977—; bldg. inspector, specialist home rehab. City of Newark, Del., 1981; instr. tech. drafting Del. Tech. & Community Coll., Wilmington, 1984, Dover, 1986; instr. constrn. techniques YWCA, Wilmington, 1984. Capt. pamplet distrbn. Biden for Senator, Wilmington and Newark, 1983. Mem. Nat. Assn. for Female Execs. Democrat. Roman Catholic. Home and Office: Eisenbrey Custom Designs Box 21 1099 S DuPont Hwy Smyrna DE 19977

EISENHUTH, DIANA LEA, dental association administrator; b. Johnstown, Pa., May 23, 1950; d. Willis William and Ruth Eva Jane (Chapman) E. Grad. high sch., Elyria, Ohio. Rental agt. Westway Gardens, Elyria, 1970-71; mgr. dept. Clarkins Dept. Store, Elyria, 1971-81; mgr. Am. Dental Ctr., Brookpark, Ohio, 1981-83, The Dental Ctr. at Sears, Middleburg Heights, Ohio, 1985—. Vol. ARC, Elyria, 1968-70; leader Girl Scouts U.S., Elyria, 1969-71; counciler Camp Sunshine, Elyria, 1970-72; tutor Project Read, Elyria, 1986—. Democrat. Roman Catholic. Office: The Dental Ctr at Sears 6950 W 130th St Middleburg Heights OH 44130

EISENMAN, TRUDY FOX, dermatologist; b. Chgo., Oct. 14, 1940; d. Nathan Henry and Bernice (Greenberg) Fox; student U. Ill. at Navy Pier, Chgo., 1958-60; M.D., U. Ill., 1964; m. Theodore S. Eisenman, Aug. 19, 1962 (div. 1985); children—Lawrence, Robert. Rotating intern Milw. County Gen. Hosp., 1964-65, med. resident, 1965-66; resident in dermatology Northwestern U. Med. Sch., Chgo., 1970-73, instr., 1973—; practice medicine specializing in dermatology, Chgo., 1973—; attending dermatologist Louis A. Weiss Meml. Hosp., Chgo., 1973—. Diplomate Am. Bd. Dermatology. Fellow Am. Acad. Dermatology; mem. Chgo. Dermatol. Soc., Soc. for Investigative Dermatology, Am. Med. Women's Assn., AMA, Chgo. Med. Soc., Alpha Omega Alpha. Home: 2526 Thornwood Ave Wilmette IL 60091 Office: 4640 N Marine Dr Chicago IL 60640

EISENSTADT, KAREN MARCIA, banker; b. Bklyn., Apr. 9, 1948; d. Nathan M. and Anne (Krugman) E.; m. Cary Reich, 1985. B.A. cum laude, Bklyn. Coll., 1968; M.Regional Planning (NDEA fellow 1968-70), U. N.C., Chapel Hill, 1971. Mem. research staff Rand Corp., Santa Monica, Calif., 1970-72; with N.Y.C. Office Mgmt. and Budget, 1972-79, dep. asst. budget dir. for fin., 1977-79; asst. v.p. public fin. dept. Morgan Guaranty Trust Co., N.Y.C., 1979-82, v.p., 1982—; mem. adj. faculty New Sch., 1974, Columbia U., 1976; dir. Critical Options Mgmt. Corp., 1986. Mem. N.Y.C. Rent Guidelines Bd., 1981-86 ; bd. dirs. Citizens Housing and Planning Council, 1982. Mem. Phi Beta Kappa. Office: 23 Wall St New York NY 10015

EISENSTADT, MERRIE MADWAY, journalist; b. Phila., Apr. 25, 1957; d. Ralph K. and Bette Melba (Davis) Madway; B.J., U. Mo., Columbia, 1978; Isaac M. Wise program cert. Gratz Hebrew Coll., Phila., 1975; m. David Michael Eisenstadt, Nov. 19, 1978; children—Rachel Leah, Rebecca Karen. Editorial asst. Phila. Jewish Exponent, 1975.; research asst. WCAU-TV (CBS), Phila., On Your Side, 1977; KOMU-TV (NBC) & KBIA-FM (NPR), Columbia, Mos., 1978, reporter, Sentinel Newspapers, Montgomery and Prince George's counties, Md., 1979-80, Balt. Jewish Times, 1980-83; freelance writer, 1983—. Theme Exhbn. chmn. Balt. Jewish Am. Festival, 1981. Recipient Smolar award for excellence in N.Am. Jewish journalism, 1981. Mem. Sigma Delta Chi, Alpha Epsilon Phi (scholarship award 1976), Phi Eta Sigma, Kappa Epsilon Alpha, Omicron Delta Kappa, Kappa Tau Alpha. Jewish.

EISENSTADT, PAULINE DOREEN BAUMAN, investment company executive, state legislator; b. N.Y.C., Dec. 31, 1938; d. Morris and Anne (Lautenberg) Bauman; B.A., U. Fla., 1960; M.S. (NSF grantee), U. Ariz., 1965; postgrad. U. N.Mex.; m. Melvin M. Eisenstadt, Nov. 20, 1960; children—Todd Alan, Keith Mark. Tchr., Ariz., 1961-65, P.R., 1972-73; adminstrv. asst. Inst. Social Research U. N.Mex., 1973-74; founder, 1st exec. dir. Energy Consumers N.Mex., 1977-81; dir., host TV program Consumer Viewpoint, 1980-82; chmn. consumer affairs adv. com. Dept. Energy, 1979-80; v.p. tech. bd. Nat. Center Appropiate Tech., 1980—; pres. Eisenstadt Enterprises, investments, 1983—; mem. N.Mex. Ho. of Reps., 1985—, chairwoman majority caucus, mem. rules com. NM House; mem. exec. com. Nat. Conf. State Legislators, 1987; vice chmn. Sandoval County (N.Mex.) Democratic Party, 1981—; mem. N.Mex. Dem. State Central Com., 1981—; N.Mex. del. Dem. Nat. Platform Com., 1984, Dem. Nat. Conv., 1984; pres. Sandoval County Dem. Women's Assn., 1979-81; vice chmn. N.Mex. Dem. Platform Com., 1984—; mem. Sandoval County Redistricting Task Force, 1983-84; bd. dirs. Mediation Ctr., 1983-84; mem. Rio Rancho Ednl. Study Com., 1984—.; mem. N.Mex. First. Mem. NEA, LWV, NOW. Author: Corrales, Portrait of a Changing Village, 1980. Lodge: Kiwanis. Address: PO Box 658 Corrales NM 87048

EISENZIMMER, BETTY WENNER, insurance agent, executive; b. Twisp, Wash., July 25, 1939; d. Bren William and Julia Emogene (Salmon) Wenner; m. Erwin LeRoy Cook, June 19, 1955 (div. 1960); 1 child, Richard Jeffrey; m. Jerome Anthony Eisenzimmer, Feb. 18, 1966. Cert. in gen. ins. Ins. Inst. Am., 1981; cert. profl. ins. woman. Clk. typist MR Ins., Seattle, 1957-59; records clk. Assigned Risk Plan, Seattle, 1959-61; acct. asst. Robinson Jenner, Inc., Seattle, 1961-66; sec., acct. asst. Falkenberg & Co., Seattle, 1966-75, adminstrv. asst., 1975-77; ins. agt., corp. officer Service Ins. Inc., Seattle, 1975—; mem. adv. bd. Sch. Ins., Wash. State U. Coll. Bus., 1981—. Asst. editor Today's Ins. Woman, 1980-81. Exec. bd. Wash. chpt. Cystic Fibrosis Found., 1978-86, pres., 1983-85; mem. Wash. State Centennial Speakers' Bur., 1987—; mem. long range planning com. Cedar Cross United Meth. Ch., 1986-87, also mem. worship com., 1988. Recipient Disting. Service award Cystic Fibrosis Found., 1984; named Vol. of Yr., Wash. chpt. Cystic Fibrosis Found., 1980. Mem. Seattle C. of C., Ins. Women Puget Sound (pres. 1970-72, Ins. Woman of Yr. 1978, 81, Industry award 1984), Ins. Women's Assn. Seattle (chmn. 1992 conf., Ins. Woman of Yr. 1981), Nat. Assn. Ins. Women (nat. sec. 1976-77, regional dir. 1981-82, mem. exec. bd. 1976-77, 81-82, You Make the Difference award 1977, Regional IX Lace Speakoff winner 1983), Ind. Ins. Agts. and Brokers Wash. (edn. com. 1982-83), Ind. Ins. Agts. and Brokers King County (chmn. bylaws 1984-85), Profl. Ins. Agts. Wash. (edn. com. 1982-86, chmn. 1983-86), Wash. Ins. Council (mem. speakers bur. 1980—), Women's Bus. Exchange, Women's Profl. and Managerial Women's Network, Nat. Assn. Life Underwriters, Women Life Underwriters Conf. (nat. bd. dirs., region I dir. 1987-88), Acad. Producer Ins. Studies (fellow of acad.), Network of Exec. Women, Seattle Assn. Life Underwriters, Nat. Assn. Female Execs. Club: Toastmasters (pres. Wallingford chpt. 1986-87, ednl. v.p. 1987-88, dist. 2 area 5 gov. 1987-88, Gov.'s Honor Roll dist. 2 1987, designated able toastmaster 1987 and other awards and positions). Home: 8932 240th St SW Edmonds WA 98020 Office: Service Ins Inc 332 Securities Bldg Seattle WA 98101

EISLER, SUSAN KRAWETZ, advertising agency executive; b. N.Y.C., Aug. 18, 1946; d. Aaron and Bertha (Platt) Krawetz; m. Howard Irwin Eisler, June 8, 1980; 1 stepchild, Robin Joy, 1 adopted son, Joseph. BA, U. Pitts., 1967; MA, New Sch. for Social Research, 1971. Analyst, Marplan, Inc., N.Y.C., 1968-69; project dir. Market Facts, Inc., N.Y.C., 1969-70; assoc. research mgr. Gen. Foods, Inc., White Plains, N.Y., 1970-75, product mgr., 1975-80; research dir. Elizabeth Arden, N.Y.C., 1980-81; v.p., assoc. research dir. SSC&B: Lintas Worldwide, N.Y.C., 1981-87; sr. v.p., assoc. research dir., 1987—. Mem. Am. Mktg. Assn., Advt. Women N.Y., Advt. Research Found. (copy research council). Office: SSC&B Lintas Worldwide 1 Dag Hammarskjold Plaza New York NY 10017

EISNER, JANET MARGARET, college president; b. Boston, Oct. 10, 1940; d. Eldon and Ada (Martin) E. AB, Emmanuel Coll., 1963; MA, Boston Coll., 1969; PhD, U. Mich., 1975. Joined Sisters of Notre Dame de Namur, Roman Catholic Ch.; asst. dir. admissions Emmanuel Coll., Boston, 1966-67; dir. admissions Emmanuel Coll., 1967-71; dir. Emmanuel Coll. and City of Boston Pairings, 1976-78, asst. prof. English, 1976-78, chmn. dept., 1977-78, acting pres., 1978-79, pres., 1979—; lectr., teaching asst. U. Mich., 1971-73; mem. Mass. Bd. Regents, Mass. Bd. Regional Community Colls., until 1981. Trustee Trinity Coll. Rackham prize fellow; Ford Found. fellow. Mem. Assn. Cath. Colls. and Univs., New Eng. Enrollment Planning Council, Women's Coll. Coalition, Assn. Governing Bds., Am. Council Edn. Home: 37 Castleton St Jamaica Plain MA 02130 Office: Emmanuel Coll 400 The Fenway Boston MA 02115 •

EISNER, SUSAN PAMELA, communications executive, consultant; b. N.Y.C., Apr. 19, 1950; d. Nathaniel Julius and Frances Rochelle (Linick) E. Student Smith Coll., 1968-69; BA, Wellesley Coll., 1971; MPA, Kennedy Sch. Govt., Harvard U., 1974. Staff intern to Senator Javits, U.S. Senate, Washington, 1970; mem. staff HEW, Washington, 1971; asst. to dir. communications Dem. Nat. Com., Washington, 1972; nat. coordinator press ops. McGovern Presdl. Campaign, Washington, 1972; dir. communications Dem. Nat. Com. Telethons II and III, Washington, N.Y.C. and Los Angeles, 1973-74; creative dir. Ways and Means, Inc., Louisville, 1974; producer, writer WNET-THIRTEEN TV, N.Y.C., 1975-79, asst. dir. broadcasting, 1979-81, dir. acquisitions, scheduling and spls., 1981, dir. broadcasting, 1981-83, spl. adviser to sr. v.p., 1983; pres. Susan Eisner Assocs., N.Y.C., 1983—; dir. communications March of Dimes Birth Defects Found., N.Y., 1985-86; folk singer, Boston, 1969-71; spl. cons. to exec. dir. Nat. Urban League, 1969-71; tutor MIT, 1972. Dir. broadcasting various TV programs and mini-series including Cinema Thirteen, Classics Showcase, Star Movie, Viewer's Choice, Gala of Stars, Astaire, Hepburn, Years of Darkness, The American Worker, Black History, Celebrate Dance, Chanukah/Christmas, Disarmament, Remember the Holocaust, A Salute to Britain. Exec. producer and producer various TV spots, reports, segments including Listening To You (Nat. Assn. Ednl. Broadcasters Graphics and Design award 1978), Masterpiece Theatre Quotes Montage (Nat. Assn. Ednl. Broadcasters Graphics and Design award 1978), Haven't Stopped Dancin' Yet (Nat. Assn. Ednl. Broadcasters Graphics and Design award 1979), Window on the World (Nat. Assn. Ednl. Broadcasters Graphics and Design award 1979), Everything Beautiful At the Ballet (Nat. Assn. Ednl. Broadcasters Graphics and Design award 1979), Making Poldark--Location (Nat. Assn. Ednl. Broadcasters Graphics and Design award 1979), Work in Progress, Dance in America (Nat. Assn. Ednl. Broadcasters Graphics and Design award 1979), Cavett Conversation with Baryshnikov-Gregory, I Claudius/Poldark/Duchess of Duke Street/Upstairs-Downstairs Farewells, Masterpiece Theatre's Tenth Anniversary Party, On location--Dance in America, Summercast Live, Starfest Finale, Thirteen: The First Twenty Years; dir. communications March of Dimes for various nat. multimedia prodns. including Writer contemporary folksongs, 1969-71. Author speeches, press, and promotional materials; research on various topics. Recipient award for citizenship Am. Legion, 1965, Mayor's award for Young Citizenship, Mayor New Rochelle (N.Y.), 1965; named to Outstanding Young Women Am., U.S. Jaycees, 1981; Durant scholar, 1971; Harvard U. Kennedy Sch. adminstrn. fellow, 1971-74.

EISNER, SUSANNE GLOCK, county government official; b. Munich, Federal Republic Germany, Aug. 10, 1950; came to U.S., 1958; d. Konrad and Maria (Pfeiffer) Glock; m. Howard Eisner, Nov. 10, 1971. BA in Psychology, CCNY, 1973; MA in Psychology, George Mason U., 1979. Counselor Associated Cath. Charities, Montgomery City, Md., 1974-76; employment counselor Arlington (Va.) Pub. Schs., 1976-79; dir. Refugee Family Services, Falls Church, Va., 1979-84; bur. chief Arlington (Va.) County Bur. Labor and Tng. Services, 1984—; chairperson State Adv. Council on Refugees, Va., 1985-87. Recipient Performance/Achievement award State of Va., 1985, 86; Outstanding Adminstrv. Practice Achievement award Am. Pub. Welfare Assn., 1986. Mem. Am. Soc. Pub. Adminstrn. Home: 6415 Tone Dr Bethesda MD 20817 Office: Bur Labor and Tng Services 1801 N George Mason Dr Arlington VA 22207

EITNIER, CYNTHIA KAY, nurse; b. Lancaster, Pa., June 16, 1953; d. C. Quentin and Nancy Lee (Fisher) Martin; m. William B. Eitnier, May 24, 1986. Lic. Practical Nurse, Willow State Vocat.-Tech. Coll., 1972; Assoc. Nursing, Harrisburg Area Community Coll., 1981; B.S. in Nursing, Millersville U., 1984; postgrad. U. Ariz., 1985, U. S.C., 1986. Lic practical nurse Conestoga View, Lancaster, 1973-77, Polyclinic Med. Ctr., Harrisburg, Pa., 1977-81; R.N., 1981-85; R.N., St. Joseph Hosp., Tucson, 1985-86, mem. code team, pulmonary rehab. teams, 1985-86; nursing supr. Brian Ctr., Columbia, S.C., 1986-87, asst. dir. nursing, 1987-88; dir. nursing Rheems (Pa.) Nursing Ctr., 1988 . Mem. Nat. Assn. Female Execs., Pa. Nurses Assn. Democrat. Avocations: computers; swimming; hiking. Home: PO Box 143 Lititz PA 17543

EKLOF, SVEA CHRISTINE, professional ballet dancer; b. Los Angeles, May 31, 1951; d. Theodore Herman and Christiane (Simonpietri) E.; m. Michel Rahn, Aug. 27, 1976 (div. Jan. 1986); m. John Michael Grey, Jan. 29, 1986. Grad. high sch., Winston-Salem, N.C., 1969. Mem. corps de ballet Pa. Ballet Co., Phila., 1970-71; soloist Ballet Classico de Mex., Mexico City, 1971-73, Ballet Du Grand Theatre, Geneva, Switzerland, 1973-74, Netherlands Dance Theatre, Den Haag, The Netherlands, 1974-75; prin. dancer Ballet Du Grand Theatre, Geneva, Switzerland, 1975-76, N.C. Dance Theatre, Winston-Salem, 1976-79, Alta. Ballet Co., Edmonton, 1979-83; soloist Royal Winnipeg Ballet, Man., 1983-85; prin. dancer Royal Winnipeg Ballet Co., Man., 1985—; guest tchr. N.C. Sch. Arts, Winston-Salem, 1976-79; guest tchr. Edmonton Sch. Ballet and Alta. Ballet Sch. Ballet, 1979-83. Guest appearances include Chgo. Ballet, 1976-77, Ballet Galaxie, Taiwan, 1981, New World Ballet, Miami, Fla., 1982, West Va. Ballet, 1979-81, Edmonton Symphony Orch., 1987. Mem. Alta. Ballet Co. (adv. bd. 1986—). Office: Royal Winnipeg Ballet, 380 Graham Ave, Winnipeg, MB Canada R3C 4K2

EKMAN, LEA ANN, county official; b. Rhinelander, Wis., Nov. 9, 1946; d. S. James and Edna Marie (Ekman) Kowacz; m. Ronald David Pierce, July 30, 1970 (div. Apr. 1977); children: Erika Lynn, Lesley Ryann. BSN, Pa. State U., 1969; MPA, U. Colo., Denver, 1988. Nurse Louis A. Weiss Meml. Hosp., Chgo., 1969-70; pub. health nurse Chgo. Bd. Health, 1970-71; critical care nurse St. Anthony Hosp., Denver, 1975-76, Aurora (Colo.) Presbyn. Hosp., 1977; coordinator emergency med. services Lakewood (Colo.) Health Dept., 1977-79; dep. dir. Denver Office Emergency Preparedness, 1979-82; accounts mgr. Computer Tech. Systems, Loveland, Colo., 1983; dir., coordinator Weld County Office Emergency Mgmt., Greeley, Colo., 1984-87; emergency mgmt. specialist Fed. Emergency Mgmt. Agy., Washington, 1988; transp. safety program specialist U.S. Dept. Transp., Washington, 1988—; cons. for tng. local municipalities, 1984—; in-service instr. Platte Canyon Rescue Squad, Bailey, Colo., 1974; instr. Lakewood ARC, 1977-78; guest instr. U. Health Scis. Ctr., Denver, 1980-82. Contbr. articles to profl. jours. Recipient Cert. of Appreciation, Denver Fire Dept., 1979, Cert. of Excellence Fed. Emergency Mgmt. Agy., 1987. Mem. Weld CountyChiefs of Police Assn. (pres. 1987), Colo. Assn. Law Enforcement Trainers (v.p. 1987), Colo. Emergency Mgmt. Assn. (legis. com. 1987), Am. Soc. Pub. Adminstrs., Pa. State U. Alumni Assn., No. Colo. Weavers Guild. Republican. Episcopalian. Home: 5944 Heritage Square Dr Burke VA 22015 Office: 400 7th St SW Washington DC 20590

EKSTROM, RUTH BURT, psychologist; b. Bennington, Vt., July 2, 1931; d. Ralph Amos and Bertha Paisley (Lambert) Burt; A.B., Brown U., 1953; Ed.M., Boston U., 1956; Ed.D., Rutgers U., 1967; JD (hon.) Brown U., 1988; m. Lincoln Ekstrom, Nov. 9, 1957. Public sch. tchr., Beverly, Mass., 1953-57; sr. research asst. Ednl. Testing Service, 1957-64; vis. lectr. Rutgers U., 1958-60; dir. documentation services Ednl. Testing Service, Princeton, N.J., 1964-68, research scientist, 1968-80, sr. research scientist, 1980—. Mem. corp. (governing bd.) Brown U., 1972-88, trustee, 1972-77, fellow, 1977-88, sec. corp., 1982-88. Fellow Am. Psychol. Assn., AAAS; mem. Am. Assn. Counseling and Devel., Am. Ednl. Research Assn. (chmn. research on women and edn. 1984-85), Am. Assn. Higher Edn., Nat. Council Measurement Edn. Co-author: Education and American Youth: The Impact of the High School Experience, 1988; co-editor: Kit of Factor-Referenced Cognitive Tests, 1976; editor: Measurement, Technology and Individuality in Education, 1983; mem. editorial bd. Psychology of Women Quar., 1978-86, Jour. Counseling and Devel., 1982-85; contbr. articles to profl. jours. Home: 78 Westerly Rd Princeton NJ 08540 Office: Ednl Testing Service Princeton NJ 08541

ELAM, VERONIKA JRMTRAUD BARON, biological scientist; b. Ludwigshafen, Pfalz, Federal Republic of Germany, Dec. 9, 1943; came to U.S., 1964; d. Ludwig Von Tagnier and Rosa Baron Heinze; m. Robert J. Elam. Student, Hillsborough Community Coll., 1978. Clin. asst. Dept. Health Hillsborough County, Tampa, Fla., 1965-72; lab. technician II Tampa Branch Lab., 1972-84, biological scientist, 1984—; image cons., fashion model Evelyn Stewarts Fla. Model and Talent Agy., Tampa. Mem. Fla. Pub. Health Assn. (editorial asst.), Inter-Am. Soc. Chemotherapy. Home: Rt 1 Box 211 AA Land-O-Lakes FL 34639 Office: Tampa Beach Lab 1115 E Kennedy Blvd Tampa FL 33601

ELASARIAN, ANNA, government official; b. Waukegan, Ill., Sept. 18; d. Ohan and Siranoush (Papazian-Garabedian) E. Student, Carthage Coll., 1964, Coll. Lake County, Grayslake, Ill., 1974-76. Sec., acct. Waukegan Housing Authority, 1962-67, asst. exec. dir., 1967-77, exec. dir., 1977-85. Mem. task force com. Waukegan United Way, Lake County Community Housing Resource Bd., 1984-86; mem. bd. Lake County Community Action Project, 1977-84, sec. 1979-83; bd. dirs. Cardiac Charities Lake County, 1977-80; active Lake County Urban League, Chgo. Council on Fgn. Relations. Recipient Cert. Recognition Ill. Ho. Reps., 1984. Mem. Armenian Youth Fedn. Am. (hon.), Nat. Assn. Housing and Redevel. Ofcls. (cert. pub. housing mgr.),Am. Soc. Profl. and Exec. Women, Nat. Assn. Female Execs., Phi Theta Kappa. Episcopalian. Club: Altrusa Internat.

ELBERT, JOANNA, real estate executive; b. Chgo.; d. Joseph and Mary (Alesia) Germano; m. Phillip Myron Elbert (div. 1977); children—Kimberly, Scott, Keith, Lynn, Phillip. B.S. in Journalism, U. Ill., 1951. Personnel mgr. Adminstrv. Offices, Jewel-Osco Co., Inc., Melrose Park, Ill., 1962-67; personnel adminstr. Anocut Engring. Co., Chgo., 1967-69; pres. Joanna Elbert, Inc., real estate sales, Houston, 1978—. Active Houston Symphony League. Contbr. poetry to various quars. and anthologies including Indigo, Poetry Today, Invictus, Am. Poet, N.Am. Mentor, Driftwood East. Republican. Roman Catholic. Club: Multi-Million. Home: 201 Vanderpool Houston TX 77024 Office: Joanna Elbert Inc 1880 Dairy Ashford Suite 112 Houston TX 77077

ELBERT, LINDA, public relations executive; b. Aurora, Ill., May 29, 1960; d. Theodore Paul and Joan (Reichanbacher) E. AA, Triton Coll., 1982; BA, U. Ill., 1984. Desk asst. 1980 presdl. conv. NBC Nightly News-N.Y., N.Y.C., Detroit, 1980; desk asst. 1984 presdl. conv. NBC Nightly News-N.Y., San Francisco, Dallas, 1984; pub. relations asst. Chgo. Zool. Soc., Brookfield (Ill.), 1985-86, asst. pub. relations mgr., 1986-87, pub. relations mgr., 1987—. Contbr. articles to profl. jours. Auditor Leadership Council for Met. Open Communities, Chgo., 1983—; campaigner, clk. Paul Simon for Sen. Mem. Women in Communications, Publicity Club of Chgo., Pub. Relations Soc. Am., Am. Assn. Zool. Parks and Aquariums (assoc.). Club: Oak Park (Ill.) Cycle. Home: 1616 S 15th Ave Maywood IL 60153 Office: Brookfield Zoo Chgo Zool Soc 3300 Golf Rd Brookfield IL 60513

ELDER, ELLEN ROZANNE, editorial director, educator; b. Harrisburg, Pa.; d. B.H. and Ellen M. (Wolfe) E. AB, Western Mich. U., 1962, MA, 1964; PhD, U. Toronto, 1972. Instr. history Western Mich. U., Kalamazoo, 1968-73; dir. f Inst. Cistercian Studies at Western Mich. U., Kalamazoo, 1973—; editorial dir. Cistercian Pubs., Kalamazoo, 1973—; adj. assoc. prof. history Western Mich. U.; bd. dirs. Medieval Inst. Western Mich. U. contbr. articles to profl. jours. Mem. Episcopal Ch. (standing commn., ecumenical relations), 1980—, Anglican-Orthodox Theol. Consultation, 1981—. Anglican. Office: Cistercian Publications WMU Station Kalamazoo MI 49008

ELDER, JEAN KATHERINE, foundation administrator, educator; b. Virginia, Minn., May 30, 1941; d. Clarence Adrian and Katherine C. (Miltich) Samuelson. BS, U. Mich., 1963, AM, 1966, PhD, 1969; LHD (hon.), Davis and Elkins Coll., 1985; D in Pub. Service (hon.), Ferris State U., 1987. Tchr. 5th grade Ypsilanti (Mich.) Pub. Schs., 1963-64; tech. educable mentally retarded Quantico Marine Corps Dependent Sch., Va., 1964-65; dir. remedial reading program Iron Mountain (Mich.) Pub. Schs., 1966; research asst. U. Mich., Ann Arbor, 1966-69; asst. prof. spl. edn. Ind. U., Bloomington, 1969-71; dir. delinquency modification through edn. project Marquette (Mich.)-Alger Intermediate Sch. Dist.-Marquette County Probate Ct., 1971-72; asst. prof. edn. No. Mich. U., Marquette, 1972-76, assoc. prof., 1977-78, coordinator Title IX, 1975-76; project dir., assoc. scientist Specialist Office Three, Wis. Research and Devel. Ctr. for Cognitive Learning, U. Wis., Madison, 1976-77; assoc. prof. med. edn. Coll. Human Medicine, Mich. State U., East Lansing, 1978-82; commr. Adminstrn. of Devel. Disabilities, Washington, 1982-86; asst. sec. Office of Human Devel. Services, Washington, 1986-88; exec. dir. Make-A-Wish Found. Am., Phoenix, 1988—; cons. in field. Author: (with others) Planning Individualized Education Programs in Special Education, 1977, Pathways to Employment for Developmentally Disabled Adults, 1986; contbr. articles to profl. jours. Bd. dirs. Rehab. Internat., Am. Assn. on Mental Retardation; mem. Pres.'s Com. on Mental Retardation, 1976-79, Commn. on Presdl. Scholars, 1982-85. U.S. Office Edn. fellow, 1966-69. Fellow Am. Assn. Mental Retardation; mem. Assn. Retarded Citizens U.S., Council Exceptional Children, AAUW, Pi Lambda Theta, Phi Delta Kappa, Delta Kappa Gamma. Lutheran. Club: Zonta. Home: 8598 E Via de Dorado Scottsdale AZ 85258 Office: Make-A-Wish Found Am 2600 N Central Ave Suite 936 Phoenix AZ 85004

ELDER, RENEE-BLUMSTEIN, research and statistical consulting company executive; b. Bklyn., Apr. 1, 1957; d. Robert and Rosalie (Burak) Blumstein; m. Martin Charles Elder, June 23, 1985. BA, Queens Coll., N.Y., 1978; MA, Columbia U., 1980, MEd, 1982, MPhil, 1984, PhD, 1986. Research psychologist CCNY, 1980-85; research cons. AT&T, N.Y.C., 1986; research analyst Citibank, N.Y.C., 1986-87, research and statis. cons., 1987—; research and statis. cons. Informed Decision Services, Englewood, N.J., 1987—; edn. evaluator N.Y.C. Bd. Edn., Bklyn., 1988—, Englewood Bd. Edn., 1988—, Allendale (N.J.) Bd. Edn., 1988—. Scholar Columbia U., 1981. Mem. Am. Psychol. Assn., Am. Statis. Assn., Am. Soc. Tng. and Devel., Nat. Assn. Female Execs. Office: Informed Decision Services 51 W Hudson Ave Suite 5 Englewood NJ 07631

ELDRIDGE, MARIE DELANEY, statistician, education researcher; b. Balt., June 1, 1926; d. James Howard and Mathilda (Belz) Delaney; A.B. in Math., Coll. Notre Dame Md., 1948; Sc.M. in Biostatistics, Johns Hopkins U., 1953; m. Paul Eldridge, Apr. 3, 1961; children—Julia Delaney, Dan Pattengill. Statistician, indsl. quality control Revere Copper and Brass, Balt., 1948-49; statistician Ralph Parsons & Co., Frederick, Md., 1953-54, U.S. Govt., 1954-60; instr. U. Balt., 1958-60; supr. statistician HEW, Washington, 1960-65; with Office Statis. Programs and Standards, U.S. Postal Service, Washington, 1965-72, dep. dir., 1968-70, dir., 1970-72; dir. math. analysis div. Nat. Hwy. Traffic Safety Adminstrn., Dept. Transp., 1972-73, dir. office stats. and analysis, 1973-75; adminstr. Nat. Center Edn. Stats., Dept. Edn., Washington, 1976-84; dir. ctr. for ednl. studies Research Triangle Inst., Research Triangle Park, N.C., 1984-88; chair Durham Math. Collaborative N.C. Sch. Scis. and Math., 1987-88; cons. stats., 1988— ; mem. Edn. Commn. of States, 1976-84; mem. tech. adv. com. Calif. Assessment Program, 1978—; mem. nat. accident sample adv. com. Dept. Transp.; professorial lectr. George Washington U., 1981-84; adj. faculty Fed. Exec. Inst., 1982—. Recipient Superior Accomplishment award U.S. Postal Service, 1970; Outstanding Performance award Dept. Transp., 1975; cert. recognition HEW, 1976, 80; Presdl. Rank award, 1981. Fellow Am. Statis. Assn. (exec. council 1975-79, co-chmn. subcom. tng. statisticians for govt. 1979-81, com. fellows 1978-80); mem. Am. Edn. Research Assn., Internat. Assn. Survey Statisticians, Internat. Statis. Inst., Fed. Exec. Inst. (dir. 1982-85), Washington Statis. Soc. (pres. 1976-77), Durham Math. Council (bd. dirs. 1985-88, chmn. bd. 1987-88), Phi Delta Kappa. Democrat. Episcopalian. Office: PO Box 51789 Durham NC 27707

ELFERS, ELKE ANNEMARIE, retail executive; b. Graupen, Czechoslovakia, Sept. 8, 1944; d. W.A. and Anni Elfers. BA, Barry U., 1968; MS in Spl. Library, Cath. U., 1978. Co-owner, mgr. Children's Footwear Ctr., Burke, Va. Home: 14352 Clearview Ave Gainesville VA 22065

ELGIN, RENEE KAY, contract administrator, purchasing specialist; b. Dixon, Ill., Aug. 16, 1953; d. Robert Lyle and Evelyn Marie (McNeil) Brown; m. David J. Elgin, Aug. 19, 1972; children: Matthew David, Mitchell Robert. BS, U. Wis., Platteville, 1974. Asst. mgr. F.W. Woolworth Co., Dubuque, Iowa, 1974-76; group mgr. Zayre Corp., Dubuque, Iowa, 1976-78; clerical Cedar Rapids (Iowa) Gazette, 1979; clerical/expeditor Rockwell Internat., Cedar Rapids, 1979-81, buyer, 1981-85, subcontract adminstr., 1985-88, contract adminstr., 1988—. Active Welcome Wagon, Cedar Rapids, 1978-79, Civil New Comers, Cedar Rapids, 1978-79. Mem. Nat. Assn. Purchasing Mgmt., Am. Bus. Women's Assn. (program chmn. 1986-87, del. 1986), Nat. Assn. Female Execs., Inc., Am. Mgmt. Assn. Home: 642 Bartlett Ct NW Cedar Rapids IA 52405 Office: Rockwell Internat 440 Collins Rd NE Cedar Rapids IA 52498

ELGIN, SARAH CARLISLE ROBERTS, biology researcher and educator; b. Washington, July 16, 1945; d. Carlisle Bishop and Lorene (West) Roberts; m. Robert Lawrence Elgin, June 9, 1967; children—Benjamin Carlisle, Thomas James. B.A. in Chemistry, Pomona Coll., 1967; Ph.D. in Biochemistry, Calif. Inst. Tech., 1971. Research fellow Calif. Inst. Tech., Pasadena, 1971-73; asst. prof. biochemistry and molecular biology Harvard U., Cambridge, Mass., 1973-77, assoc. prof., 1977-81; assoc. prof. biology Washington U., St. Louis, 1981-84, prof., 1984—. Mem. editorial bd. Jour. Cell Biology, N.Y.C., 1980-82; exec. editor Nucleic Acids Research, 1983—; editorial bd. Jour. Biol. Chemistry, 1985—; contbr. papers in field. Mem. molecular biology study sect. NIH, 1986—. Research grantee NIH, 1987, 88, NSF, 1986). Fellow AAAS; mem. Am. Chem. Soc., Am. Soc. Biol. Chemists (program com. 1984), Am. Soc. Cell Biology (council 1983-85), Genetics Soc. Am. Office: Washington U Biology Dept Box 1137 Saint Louis MO 63130

ELIAS, ABIGAIL, lawyer; b. Ithaca, N.Y., June 26, 1952; d. Robert Henry and Helen (Larson) E. BA magna cum laude, Brandeis U., 1973; JD cum laude, Harvard U., 1976. Bar: N.H. 1976, D.C. 1978, Mich. 1983. Law clk. to presiding justice N.H. Supreme Ct., Concord, 1976-77; atty. region 1 Nat. Labor Relations Bd., Boston, 1977-78; atty. civil rights div. U.S. Dept. Justice, Washington, 1978-83; supervising asst. corp. counsel City Detroit, 1983-84, dep. corp. counsel, 1984—. Mem. Leadership Detroit VII, 1985-86. Mem. ABA, Mich. Bar Assn. (U.S. cts. com. 1985—), N.H. Bar Assn., Women Lawyers Assn. Mich., D.C. Bar Assn., Leadership Detroit Alumni Assn. office: City of Detroit Law Dept 1010 City-County Bldg Detroit MI 48226

ELIAS, MARY ANN, gymnastics coach; b. Methuen, Mass., July 13, 1956; d. Constantinon Dean Eliacopoulos and Virginia (Diamond) E. BS, U. Mass., 1978; MA, Adelphi U., 1979. Tchr. Cathedral Sch. St. Mary, Garden City, N.Y., 1978-79; coach Gymnastics Acad., Boston, Newton, Mass., 1979-80; tchr. Medford (Mass.) Pub. Schs., 1980-81; gymnastics coach Andover (Mass.) Sch. Ballet, 1981-83; dir., coach Sudbury (Mass.) After Sch. Programs, 1981-83; instr., coach Cumberland County Gymnastics Ctr., South Portland, Maine, 1983-85; dir. girls' program New Eng. Gym Ken-Acad. Gymnastics, Windham, N.H., 1985—; cons. fitness program Avco Corp., Waltham, Mass., 1980-81. Vol. Essex Agrl. Inst., Hawthorne, Mass., 1982, Girls Club Greater Nashua, N.H., 1983, Leominster (Mass.) Am. Softball Assn., 1986, Racket Club Concord, N.H., 1987-88. Mem. U.S. Assn., Ind. Gymnastics Clubs, U.S. Gymnastics Fedn., Nat. Assn. Women Judges. Republican. Office: New Eng Gym Ken Rt 28 Windham NH 03084

ELIAS, PATRICIA JOAN MILLER, research psychologist; b. Wis., Sept. 14, 1929; d. Rollin Francis and Rosette Ellen (Ellsworth) Miller; m. Albert Elias, Oct. 16, 1954; children: Caprice Catherine. BA, U. Calif., Berkeley, 1951, MA, 1969, PhD, 1973. dir. spl. projects Edn. Testing Service. Writer, artist Liberal Democrat. Area coordinator Am. Cancer Soc.; dir. Berkeley Mental Health fund raising. NIMH fellow. Mem. Am. Edn. Research Assn., Am. Psychol. Assn., Calif. Assn. Sch. Psychologists (chair legis. com.). Home: 820 San Luis Rd Berkeley CA 94707 Office: 1947 Center St Berkeley CA 94704

ELIAS, SARAH DAVIS, English language educator; b. Chgo., Aug. 9, 1934; d. Calvin Paul and Julia Elizabeth (Bush) D.; m. Antoine Jack Elias, Aug. 28, 1960. BA, Roosevelt U., 1957; MA, Morgan State U., 1973. Cert. tchr., Ill., Calif., Md. Elem. tchr. Chgo. Pub. Schs., 1958-62, Palo Alto (Calif.) Unified Sch. Dist., 1969-70; tchr. Balt. City Schs., 1961-69, 70—, chmn. reading dept., 1978-81, English tchr., 1982—; supervising tchr. Coppin State Coll., Balt., 1973-75; resource coordinator, tutor Johns Hopkins Tutorial Projects, Balt., 1968; social studies text cons. Harcourt, Brace, Jovanovich Pub., Balt., 1972. Mem. Mayor's Task Force on Edn., Balt., 1967-69, Mayor's Bicentennial Com., 1974-76. Am. Fedn. Tchrs.-Cornell U. fellow, 1967. Mem. Balt. Tchrs. Union (contract negotiator 1967-69), Internat. Reading Assn., Md. Council Tchrs. of English and Lang. Arts, Herbert M. Frisbey Hist. Soc., NAACP, Delta Sigma Theta. Democrat.

Baptist. Club: Chums. Home: 20 Olmsted Green Baltimore MD 21210 Office: Balt City Schs 200 E North Ave Baltimore MD 21202

ELIASOPH, ELLEN RUTH, lawyer; b. L.I., N.Y., Nov. 16, 1955; d. Eugene Leon and Beverly Sarah (Brenman) E.; m. Ira Ethan Kasoff, June 23, 1985. BA, Yale U., 1977, JD, 1982. Bar: N.Y. 1983. Assoc. Coudert Bros., Hong Kong, 1982; assoc. Paul, Weiss, Rifkind, Wharton & Garrison, N.Y.C., 1982-83, Hong Kong, 1983-84; resident atty. Paul, Weiss, Rifkind, Wharton & Garrison, Beijing, 1984-85, Shanghai, Peoples' Rep. of China, 1985-87, Tokyo, 1987—. Author: Law and Business Practice in Shanghai, 1987; contbr. articles to profl. jours. Advanced study grantee Peoples' Rep. of China, 1979-80, Fulbright Research grantee Japan, Peoples' Rep. of China, 1988. Mem. Phi Beta Kappa. Office: Paul Weiss Rifkind Wharton & Garrison 1285 Avenue of the Americas New York City NY 10019

ELIOPOULOS, CHARLOTTE, nurse; b. Balt., May 9, 1948; d. Louis Charles and Marjorie (Johns) E.; m. Angelo M. Janouris Sr. Diploma in nursing, Sinai Hosp., Balt., 1969; BS, Johns Hopkins U., 1973, MPH, 1975. Cert. in gerontol. nursing. Staff nurse Johns Hopkins Hosp., Balt., 1969-70, clin. specialist geriatrics, 1975-77; instr. Balt. City Hosps. Sch. Nursing, Balt., 1970-73; pub. health nurse Balt. City Health Dept., 1973-75; gerontol. nurseing specialist Md. Dept. Health, Balt., 1977-80; dir. nursing Levindale Geriatric Ctr. and Hosp., Balt., 1980-85; assoc. prof. Johns Hopkins Sch. Hygiene, Balt., 1981—; cons., educator Charlotte Eliopoulos & Assocs., Balt., 1985—; adj. faculty U. Md., Balt., 1982—. Author: Nursing Administration of Long Term Care, 1983, Guide to Nursing the Elderly, 1987; author, editor: Gerontological Nursing, 1987; editor: Health Assessment of Older Adult, 1983. Mem. Am. Nurses Assn. Home and Office: 11104 Glen Arm Rd Glen Arm MD 21057

ELIOT, JUDI, personnel consulting company executive; b. Phila., Apr. 9, 1946; d. Harry and Bernice (Page) Katz. Student Temple U., Media buyer, adminstrv. asst., copywriter Elkman Advt. Co., Bala Cynwyd, Pa., 1967-70; mgr., cons. C.W. Harvey Personnel, Phila., 1971-75; pres. Judi Eliot, Inc., Phila., 1976—, also cons.; leader seminars in field. Author articles. Bd. dirs. Am. Cancer Soc., Phila., 1980-83, mem. spl. events steering com., 1983-86, corp. sponsor Triathlon, 1985; fundraiser Sunshine Found., Phila., 1984-87; mem. Orgn. for Rehab. Through Tng., Phila., 1970—. Recipient Outstanding Service award Am. Cancer Soc., 1981, 82, Human Resource Profl. of Yr. award, 1986-87. Mem. Internat. Assn. for Personnel Women (bd. dirs. Phila. affiliate, dir. communications 1983, v.p. 1984-85, pres. 1985-86, past pres. philanthropic co-chmn 1986-87), Internat. Assn. for Personnel Women, Exec. Women Internat. Democrat. Jewish. Avocations: neuro-linguistics; communication theory; psychology; creative writing; travel.

ELIOT, LUCY CARTER, artist; b. N.Y.C., May 8, 1913; d. Ellsworth and Lucy Carter (Byrd) E. B.A., Vassar Coll., 1935; postgrad., Art Students League, 1935-40. tchr. painting and drawing Red Cross Bronx Vets. Hosp., N.Y.C., 1950, 51. Exhibited one-woman shows, Rochester Meml. Art Gallery, 1946, Cazenovia Coll., 1942, 47, 62, Syracuse Mus. Fine Arts, 1947, Wells Coll., 1953, Ft. Schuyler Club, Utica, N.Y., 1971, nat. shows, Pa. Acad. Fine Arts, Phila., 1946, 48, 49, 50, 52, 54, Corcoran Biennial, Washington, 1947, 51, Va. Biennial, Richmond, 1948, NAD, N.Y.C., 1971, 78, Butler Inst. Am. Art, 1965, 67, 69, 70, 72, 74, 81; represented in permanent collections: Rochester Meml. Art Gallery, Munson-Williams-Proctor Inst., also pvt. collections. Bd. dirs. Artists Tech. Research Inst., 1975-79. Recipient First prize Rochester Meml. Art Gallery, 1946; recipient Purchase prize Munson-Williams-Proctor Inst., 1949, Painting of Industry award Silvermine Guild, 1957, 1st prize in oils Cooperstown Art Assn., 1978. Mem. N.Y. Artists Equity, N.Y. Soc. Women Artists (pres. 1973-75), Audubon Artists (dir. oil 1983-85, chmn. awards 1986, 87, 88), Am. Soc. Contemporary Artists. Episcopalian. Clubs: Cazenovia (N.Y.); Cosmopolitan (N.Y.C.). Home: 131 E 66th St New York NY 10021

ELIZONDO, PATRICIA IRENE, television and film production executive; b. San Antonio, Jan. 11, 1955; d. Oscar Andres and Rosalinda (Elizondo) Elizondo. BA magna cum laude, Trinity U., 1978. Crew mem. Trinity TV Prodn. Unit, San Antonio, 1977-78; coordinator publicity and audio visual services Nat. Autonomous U. Mex., San Antonio, 1978-79; mem. prodn. crew KLRN-TV, San Antonio, 1978-79; asst. prodn. mgr. Rogers Cablesystems, San Antonio, 1979-85, spl. programs mgr., 1985-88; project dir. San Fernando TV Prodns., 1988—; mgr. pay per view ops. Producer/dir. Spanish TV series Plaza Mexico, 1982; producer, host series Cable Connections, 1984—; producer, host Cable Answers, 1987—. Recipient spl. photography award Hispanic Woman, 1980. Mem. Mortar Board (sec. 1977-78), Phi Beta Kappa. Roman Catholic. Home: 13259 Hunters View San Antonio TX 78230 Office: San Fernando TV Prodns 115 Main Plaza San Antonio TX 78205

ELJAS, EMMA REJANNE, publisher, editor; b. Paris, Aug. 7, 1946; came to U.S., 1950; m. Yves Eljas; children: Rose, Miriam. BA, CUNY, 1967, MA, 1970. Pub., owner Part Timer Newspaper, San Jose, Calif., 1979-82; co-pub., mng. editor Supercomputing Mag., Sunnyvale, Calif., 1980—. Founder, pres. Network of Women Entrepreneurs, San Jose, 1980-82. Office: Supercomputing Mag 510 S Mathilda Ave Suite 4419 Sunnyvale CA 94086

ELKHANIALY, HEKMAT ABDUL RAZEK, demographic consultant; b. Egypt, Dec. 17, 1935; came to U.S., 1961, naturalized, 1975; d. Abdul Razek Hussein and Nabiha Mursi (Kutb) E.; B. Commerce/Econs., Cairo U., 1959; Ph.D. in Sociology, U. Chgo., 1968; m. Chandra Kant Jha, Dec. 20, 1969; 1 child, Lakshmi. Mem. faculty Roosevelt U., Chgo., 1968-75, assoc. prof. sociology, 1973-75; demographic cons., Chgo., 1975—; research assoc. Population Research Ctr., U. Chgo., 1977-80; v.p. PSM Internat. Mem. Population Assn. Am., Am. Sociol. Assn., Chgo. Council Fgn. Relations. Contbr. articles to profl. jours. Home: 2800 N Lake Shore Dr Chicago IL 60657 Office: PSM Internat 446 E Ontario Suite 1000 Chicago IL 60611

ELLENBERGER, DIANE MARIE, nurse, educator; b. St. Louis, Oct. 5, 1946; d. Charles Ernst and Celeste Loraine (Neudecker) E.; R.N., Barnes Hosp., St. Louis, 1970; B.S. in Nursing St. Louis U., 1976; M.S., U. Colo., 1977. Staff nurse hosps., clin. nurse, St. Louis, 1973-76; nurse clinician, Sedalia, Mo., 1977-78; nurse clinician, educator Bothwell Hosp., Sedalia, 1977-78; clin. nurse specialist, coordinator perinatal outreach edn. Cardinal Glennon Meml. Hosp. Children, St. Louis, 1978-80; instr. McKendree Coll., Lebanon, Ill., 1980; asst. prof. Maryville Coll., St. Louis, 1982-85; nurse cons. Carr, Korein, Schlichter, Kunin and Montroy Attys. at Law, 1986—;asst. prof. nursing, Webster U., St. Louis, 1988—; owner, operator Diane Designs Needlepoint, St. Louis, 1981—. Served with Nurse Corps, USAF, 1970-72. Mem. Am. Nurses Assn., Nurses Assn. Am. Coll. Ob-Gyn, Nat. Perinatal Assn., Mo. Nurses Assn., Mo. Perinatal Assn. (v.p. 1980), Sigma Theta Tau. Mem. Divine Sci. Ch. Contbr. articles profl. jours. Office: 412 Missouri Ave East Saint Louis IL 62201

ELLENBERGER-THOMAS, MARGARET ANN, art educator; b. Waukesha, Wis., June 19, 1951; d. Melvin Michael and Elizabeth (Brewer) Thomas; 1 child, James Michael. BA in Art Edn., Beloit Coll., 1974; MA in Edn., U. Wis., Whitewater, 1981; postgrad., U. Wis., Madison, 1987. cert. elem. tchr., Wis. Tchr. Beloit Pub. Schs., 1974-87, muralist, 1985-87, art specialist gifted and talented students, 1987—; tchr. Beloit Coll.; summer tchr. Janesville (Wis.) Pub. Schs., 1985; muralist Graphics Unltd., Beloit, 1986, 87; dir., founder Summer Explorers, Saturday Explorers Beloit Coll., 1986-87, dir. Rock Prairie Showcase Festival, 1986, Beloit and Vicinity Art Show, 1983-85. Co-author: Effective Schools and Effective Teachers, 1988; contbr. chpt. to book: Teaching and Counseling Gifted and Talented Learners in Regular Classrooms. Pres. bd. dirs. YWCA, Beloit, 1987. Mem. Wis. Council for the Gifted and Talented (bd. dirs. 1984-87, v.p. 1985-86, pres. 1986-87), Wis-Gate Found. (bd. dirs. 1985-87), Future Problem Solving (bd. dirs. 1986-87), Wis. Racquetball Assn. (bd. dirs. 1986-87). Home: 3211 Canterbury Lane Janesville WI 53545

ELLER, BRENDA ANN, educator, recreational director; b. Akron, Ohio, Apr. 25, 1959; d. Paul Ray and Wanda Ann (Ammons) Miller; m. Daniel Paul Eller, Aug. 31, 1985. BA, Bob Jones U., 1981; postgrad., U. Akron, 1985. Cert. learning disabilities tchr., Ohio. Tchr. kindergarten Massillon (Ohio) Christian Sch., 1981-83, Henry Ctr. for Learning, Akron, 1984-85, Summit County Schs., Akron, 1985-86; tchr. high sch. Plain Local Schs., Canton, Ohio, 1986—; instr. evening classes Jackson Community Edn., Canton, 1986-88; exec. dir. Ohio Bapt. Acres, Massillon, 1988. Mem. AMA (aux. 1987-88) Stark County Med. Aux., Aultman Hosp. Residents Spouses Orgn. (pres. 1987-88). Republican.

ELLERIN, SUSAN MORRIS, market researcher, psychometrician; b. Riverdale, Md., May 13, 1948; d. Albert A. and Pearl Q. E.; m. Albert Janjigian, 1982; 1 child. BA, U. Pa., 1971, MS, 1972, PhD, 1976. Mem. faculty research methods and stats. Northeastern U., 1973-85, asst. prof., 1975-79, assoc. prof., 1979-85, assoc. dean arts and scis. for humanities and social scis., 1979-82; pres. STAT Resources, Brookline, Mass., 1982—; cons. in field; specialist in application of statis. and psychometric techniques to understanding market and human issues. Contbr. articles to Jour. Edn. and Psychol. Measurement, Jour. Ednl. Research, Jour. Emergency Med. Scis. Mem. Am. Mktg. Assn., Am. Psychol. Assn., Am. Ednl. Research Assn., Nat. Council Measurement in Edn., Advt. Research Found., Security Equipment Industry Assn. Office: 22 Borland St Brookline MA 02146

ELLERS, KAREN M. ELLERS, computer executive; b. Hammond, Ind., Nov. 23, 1952; d. Frank Joseph and Irene (Meduga) Malek. BS in Math, Ill. Inst. of Technology, 1973, MBA, 1980. Programer, analyst CNA Ins., Chgo., 1973-77; tech. bus. cons. Computer Task Group, Inc., Chgo., 1977-80, systems engring. mgr., 1980-85, br. mgr., 1985—. Mem. Soc. for Info. Mgmt. (sec. 1986—), Data Processing Mgmt. Assn. Office: Computer Task Group 330 E Kilbourn Suite 1090 Milwaukee WI 53202

ELLIOT, GLADYS CRISLER, oboist; b. Macon, Ga., Sept. 5, 1929; d. George Edwin and Celeste (Rhyne) Crisler; B.Mus., N.Tex. State U., Denton, 1951; m. Willard Elliot, Sept. 3, 1951 (div. June 1976). Oboist, Dallas Symphony Orch., 1951-64; Contemporary Chamber Players, U. Chgo., 1964-81, WGN Staff Orch., 1966-69; prin. oboist Lyric Opera Chgo., 1964—, Chgo. Grant Park Summer Symphony, 1966—, Orch. of Ill., 1979—; instr. DePaul U. Sch. Music, Chgo. Mem. Internat. Double Reed Soc.

ELLIOT, MAXINE KAY, management consultant; b. Manning, Alberta, Sept. 12, 1951; d. James Harold and Flora Bella (Fife) Hodgson; m. David Andrew Elliot, Nov. 2, 1973; children: Tillman James, Ginger Lee. Pres., gen. mgr. D&T Cycle Ltd., Manning, Alberta, 1970-75; pvt. practice cons. Alberta, 1975-79; fin. advisor, cons. Loc La Ronge (Saskatchewan) Indian Band, Can., 1979-80; cons. Saskatchewan Industry & Commerce, Regina, 1980-81; sr. policy analyst Dept. Cooperative Devel., Regina, 1981-83; exec. dir. Saskatchewan Assn. Friendship Ctrs., Regina, 1984; pres., gen. mgr. Mebas Consulting, Ltd., Regina, 1984—; v.p. Taycor Mgmt. Corp., Regina, 1986—, Profl. Electronics, Regina, 1987—. Commnr. Regina Police, 1982-86; mem. fire arms and ammunitions rev. Saskatchewan Police Commrs., Regina, 1983-86; pres. Saskatchewan New Dem. Women, Regina, 1985; mem. citizen's adv. com. Correction Services Can., 1984—. Home: 3225 Montague St, Regina, SK Canada S4S 1Z8

ELLIOT, SHEILA HOLLIHAN, arts company executive; b. Phila., 1946. AB in Physics, Vassar Coll., 1967; MS in Mgmt. Sci., Fairleigh Dickinson U., 1979. Creative dir. Graphics for Industry Inc., Englewood, N.J., 1967-76, v.p. fin., 1976—; sr. bus. systems analyst Thomas J. Lipton Inc., 1978—. Producer (pub. service films) American Phenomenon, 1973, Historic Preservation, 1975, Daniel Chester French 1850-1931, 1976; (presentation film) Advertising Council, 1974; contbg. editor: Condensed Computer Encyclopedia, 1968, The Artist's Magazine, 1986—; editor: Pastellagram, 1981—. Active in the arts, pub. service, films and hist. preservation; rep. to Federated Art Assns., N.J., 1977. Recipient Gold award N.Y. Internat. Film and TV Festival, 1973, Bronze award, 1974, 75, Silver award, 1977. Mem. Pastel Soc. Am. (spl. advisor to bd. 1978, bd. dirs. 1978), Soc. Illustrators, Pen and Brush Inc. (chmn. publicity 1987), Oil Pastel Assn. (exec. dir. 1983—), Nat. Trust Hist. Preservation. Office: Graphics for Industry Inc PO Box 544 Tenafly NJ 07670

ELLIOTT, CANDICE K., small business owner; b. Cedar Rapids, Iowa, Aug. 29, 1949; d. Charles H. and Eunice A. (Long) Goodrich; m. John William Jr. Elliott, Jan. 27, 1973; 1 child, Brandon Christian; 1 stepchild, John William III. BA, U. Iowa, 1971. Interior designer Dayton's, Mpls., 1971-76, Candice Interior Space Planning and Design, Guilford, Conn., 1981-87; owner, interior designer Sofa Works, King of Prussia, Pa., 1987—. Bd. dirs. The Old Capitol Restoration Com., Iowa City, 1970-76; curator Guilford Keeping Soc., 1983-88; cons. Zion Episcopal Ch., North Branford, Conn., 1985-88. Mem. Am. Soc. Interior Designers (bd. dirs. Conn. chpt., profl. mem.). Republican. Home: 13 Windsor Circle Wayne PA 19087 Office: The Sofa Works 153 S Gulph Rd King of Prussia PA 19406

ELLIOTT, DOROTHY GALE, library administrator; b. Waltham, Mass., Mar. 6, 1948; d. Robert Straight and Grace Moore (Mills) Sanborn; m. W. Mitchell Elliott, Oct. 10, 1970. BA, Wellesley Coll., 1970; M.A., U. Mo., 1977. Exec. sec. Council for Pub. Schs., Boston, 1970-72; asst. Jerry Litton for Congress, North Kansas City, Mo., 1972; exec. sec. Stephens Coll., Columbia, Mo., 1972-74; coordinator Univ. Without Walls, Stephens Coll., Columbia, Mo., 1975-76; pub. services librarian St. Joseph Pub. Library, Mo., 1977-78, dir., 1978—. Sec., Grand River Library Conf., 1982-84; bd. dirs. Mo. Libraries Film Coop., 1980-83; sec./treas. Mo. Libraries Network Bd., 1984-85; pres. N.W. Mo. Library Network Bd., 1983-85; pres. adv. council Sch. Library and Info. Sci., U. Mo., Columbia, 1985; mem. library adv. com. Mo. Coordinating Bd. for Higher Edn., 1987—, Gov.'s Adv. Council on Literacy, 1987—, Project Literacy U.S. Task Force, 1986—; mem. exec. bd. Friends of St. Joseph Pub. Library, 1982—. Editor newsletter Jr. League St. Joseph, 1985-86. Bd. dirs. Mental Health Assn. St. Joseph, 1978-81; com. mem. United Way Greater St. Joseph, 1981—, also com. Leadership, 1982— ; bd. dirs. Interfaith Community Services, 1982-85; mem. steering com. Lifelong Learning, St. Joseph, 1983—; mem. St. Joseph Area Women's Career Network, 1983—, Downtown St. Joseph, Inc., 1983-87 . Wellesley scholar, 1969; recipient Literacy St. Joseph award, 1988. Mem. ALA, Mo. Library Assn. (sec. 1983-84, chmn. legis. com. 1986-87, v.p., pres.-elect 1987-88), Pub. Library Assn. Affiliates (network com. 1988—), Beta Phi Mu. Democrat. Methodist. Clubs: Wellesley (Kansas City); Runcie (St. Joseph); St. Joseph Women's Press Club. Office: St Joseph Pub Library 10th and Felix Sts Saint Joseph MO 64501

ELLIOTT, ELIZABETH ANN, market researcher; b. Cin., Apr. 27, 1932; d. Howard E. Elliott and Kathryn E. (Forsman) Byers. B.A., Denison U., 1954. Interviewer market research dept. Procter & Gamble Co., Cin., 1954-55, field supr., 1955-58, chief field supr., 1958-60, personnel dir. and scheduler, 1960-77, tech. cons., 1977—; career adv. Denison U., 1980—; market research cons. Community Chest and other service agys., 1983—. Mem. Nat. Assn Female Execs., Delta Gamma. Republican. Presbyterian. Avocations: photography; travel; antiques; gardening; music. Home: 1326 Deliquia Dr Cincinnati OH 45230 Office: 2 Procter & Gamble Plaza Cincinnati OH 45201

ELLIOTT, GLORIA J., management consultant; b. Canonsburg, Pa., Mar. 7, 1947; d. George and Victoria (Guzik) Hadanich. B.S. with highest honors, California U. of Pa., 1969; M.S. with highest honors, Shippensburg U., 1975; nat. cert. in rehab. counseling, 1976; cert. in adminstrn. U. Wis., 1977; nat. cert. in counseling, 1985. Youth rehab. counselor Pa. Dept. Pub. Welfare, Waynesburg and Loysville, 1971-73; exec. dir. Counseling Services Ctr., Corry, Pa., 1975-78; CMHC unit dir. Mental Health Services, Roanoke, Va., 1978-80; prin., sr. cons. Elliott & Assocs., organizational and human resources devel. cons., Roanoke, 1981—; former mem. adj. faculty U. Va. Roanoke Extension, Va. Western Community Coll., Pa. State U.; mem. adj. faculty M.B.A. program Lynchburg Coll., U. Richmond, Roanoke Coll.; vice chmn. regional small bus. orgn., 1985—. Contbr. articles to profl. jours. Trainer Nat. Alliance of Bus., 1978; bd. dirs., mem. exec. com. Girl Scouts U.S.A., 1981-87, Mental Health Assn., Roanoke, 1981-84; bd. dirs. exec. com. Jr. Achievement, Roanoke, 1981—, pres. 1985-86; mem. Roanoke Centennial Com., 1982; campaign cabinet United Way, 1985, 86, 88, bd. dirs. 1987— . Named Rising Star in Va., Commonwealth mag., 1987; recipient SBA award Advocate for Women in Bus., State of Va., 1986. Mem. Am. Soc. Tng. and Devel. (dir. 1981-82, pres. 1983, chmn. 1984-85), Am. Soc. Personnel Adminstrs., Roanoke Valley C. of C. (chmn. small bus. council 1983, 86). Address: Elliott and Assocs PO Box 12386 Roanoke VA 24025

ELLIOTT, JANE RUTH MILEY, church musician; b. Abington, Pa., Jan. 15, 1950; d. Albert Milton and Naomi (Wenger) Miley; m. Richard Harold Elliott, June 11, 1977; 1 child, Jennifer Dianne. AA, Va. Intermont Coll., 1969; MusB, Wittenberg U., 1971; grad., Berliner Kirchenmusikschule, Berlin, 1975; MA in Religion, Luth. Theol. Sem., 1978. Cert. dir. music Luth. Ch. Am. Organist, choir dir. Redeemer Luth. Ch., Bristol, Tenn., 1968-69; dir. music Grosse Pointe Congl. Ch., Grosse Pointe Farms, Mich., 1971-73, Trinity Luth. Ch., Chambersburg, Pa., 1976-77; organist, choirs accompanist, dir. handbell choirs Trinity Luth. Ch., Lansdale, Pa., 1977-81; minister music Luther Meml. Luth. Ch., Blacksburg, Va., 1981-87, Christus Victor Luth. Ch., Dumfries, Va., 1988—. Co-author: Handbook for Certified Lay Professionals of Virginia Synod of Lutheran Church in America, 1984. Del. nat. conv. Luth. Ch. Am., Milw., 1986; festival coordinator Singing Children of Blacksburg, 1983-84; mem. Southeastern Pa. Synod Vocation Commn., Phila., 1979-81, council for ministry Va. Synod, Roanoke, 1982-87, profl. service mng. group, 1982-85, music dir. service of ordination, 1985. Named one of Outstanding Young Women in Am., 1983. Mem. Am. Guild Organists (dean Va. Highlands chpt. 1982-84), Assn. Luth. Ch. Musicians (charter), Choristers Guild. Home: 3994 Hidden Valley Ct Dumfries VA 22026

ELLIOTT, JANET RUTH, chemist; b. Lansing, Mich., Oct. 7, 1951; d. Jack Gresham and Verda Irene (Hendrickson) E.; m. Duncan William Brown. Aug. 27, 1977; children: Lillian Blythe, Vivian Frances. BS in Chemistry magna cum laude, U. Mich., Ann Arbor, 1973; PhD in Chemistry, Calif. Inst. Tech., 1979. Research assoc. Calif. Inst. Tech., Pasadena, 1979; instr. Evergreen Valley Coll., San Jose, Calif., 1980; asst. prof. Wellesley Coll., Mass., 1980-81; research assoc. Bioinformation Assoc., Cambridge, Mass., 1981-83; cons. in industry —, 1983; mgr. regulatory affairs Advanced Tech. Materials Inc., New Milford, Conn., 1986—, pres., 1986. Contbr. articles to profl. jours. Sci. coordinator Miller Sch., Wilton, Conn.; bd. dirs. Wahoos Swim Team, Wilton. Mem. AAAS, Am. Chem. Soc. Republican. Home: 30 Cobblestone Pl Wilton CT 06897

ELLIOTT, LEE ANN, psychologist; b. Tulsa, Jan. 22, 1923; d. John Lewis and Evelyn (Peters) Moore; m. Craig Judson Elliott (dec. Feb. 1971). B.S., Okla. State U., 1945; postgrad. UCLA, 1947-50. Part owner, Profl. Guidance Assocs., Sherman Oaks, Calif., 1961-66; mgr., dir., spokesperson Alpha Oxi Omega, North Hollywood, Calif., 1967—; vis. nurse Vis. Nurses Assn., Hollywood, Calif., 1977-78, 1978—. Mem. Republican Presdl. Task Force, U.S. Senatorial Club, 1984—. Fellow Nat. Assn. Female Execs., Smithsonian Inst.; mem. Internat. Platform Assn., Heritage Found. Avocations: dress design, writing. Home: 5251 Strohm St North Hollywood CA 91601 Office: Alpha Oxi Omega 5149 Bakman St North Hollywood CA 91601

ELLIOTT, LETHA ELAINE CRANFORD, corporate administrator; b. Memphis, Oct. 21, 1936; d. Leland H. and Letha Louise (Shofner) Cranford; m. Clinton Carson Elliott, June 21, 1968 (div. Apr. 1981); 1 child, Leland Clinton. AA, Sullins Coll., 1956; BS, Memphis State U., 1963. Dancer, actress Memphis Civic Ballet, Front St. Theatre, 1950-66; arts editor, columnist Memphis Sunday Times, 1964-65; fundraising asst. Memphis Arts Council, 1965-66; researcher, writer Wildrick & Miller Advt., N.Y.C., 1966-68; asst. adminstr. Congregation Rodeph Sholom, N.Y.C., 1972-84; adminstr. Community Ch. of N.Y., N.Y.C., 1984-87; adminstr. G.H. Avery Co. Inc., Memphis, 1987—. Choreographer (ballets) Take Care, Memphis, 1962, Paganini Variations, Memphis, 1963; editor: 84th St. Greenery Fund (newsletter), N.Y.C., 1985-87; contbr. poetry to Christian Sci. Monitor, 1985-86, articles to profl. jours. vol. Rodeph Sholom Shelter for Homeless, N.Y.C., 1984-87; active Nature Conservancy, Vermont. Mem. Nat. Assn. Ch. Bus. Adminstrs. (sec. N.Y. chpt. 1986-87), Nat. Assn. Temple Adminstrs., Nat. Assn. Female Execs., Wilderness Soc., NOW, Mensa, Alpha Psi Omega. Democrat. Jewish. Office: GH Avery Co Inc 946 Rayner St Memphis TN 38114

ELLIOTT, LINNÉA CONSTANCE, publisher; b. N.Y.C., Feb. 23, 1948; d. Samuel and Edith Anna (Peterson) Whyte, Jr.; m. Peter Thomas Elliott, Aug. 31, 1969. Ground hostess Japan Airlines, N.Y.C., 1967-68; asst. to mng. editor Southmayd Corp., Yonkers, N.Y., 1968; public relations model Seagrams Corp., N.Y.C., 1968; prodn. editor, mgr. jours., editorial dept. Pergamon Press, Elmsford, N.Y., 1968-74; assoc. pub. Appleton Century-Crofts div. Prentice-Hall, East Norwalk, Conn., 1974-84; dir. mkgt. services HP Pub. Co., N.Y.C., 1986—; cons. in field. Mem. Healthcare Businesswomen's Assn., Pharm. Advt. Council, Assn. Ind. Clin. Pubs. (treas. 1981-83, pres.-elect 1984), Nat. Assn. Female Execs. Episcopalian. Mng. editor Jour. Family Practice, 1974-83, Jour. Nat. Med. Assn., 1975-79. Home: Colonial Hill RFD #1 Mount Kisco NY 10549 Office: HP Publishing Co 10 Astor Pl New York NY 10003

ELLIOTT, PEGGY GORDON, university chancellor; b. Matewan, W.Va., May 27, 1937; d. Herbert Hunt and Mary Ann (Renfro) Gordon; m. Scott Vandling Elliott, Jr., June 17, 1961; children—Scott Vandling III, Anne Gordon. B.A., Transylvania Coll., 1959; M.A., Northwestern U., 1964; Ed.D., Ind. U., 1975. Tchr. Horace Mann High Sch., Gary, Ind., 1959-64; instr. English Ind. U. N.W., Gary, 1965-73, 1973-74, asst. prof. edn., 1975-78, assoc. prof., 1978-80, supr. secondary student teaching, 1973-74, dir. student teaching, 1975-77, dir. Office Field Experiences, 1977-78, dir. profl. devel., 1978-80, asst. to chancellor, 1981-84, acting chancellor, 1983-84, chancellor, 1984—; instr. English Am. Inst. Banking, Gary, 1969-70; profl. devel. cons. N.W. Ind. Pub. Sch. Supt.'s Assn., 1978-81; vis. prof. U. Ark., 1979-80, U. Alaska, 1982; bd. dirs. Gainer Bank and Corp. Author: Handbook for Secondary Student Teaching, 1975, 3d edit., 1977; (with C. Smith) Reading Activities for Middle and Secondary Schools: A Handbook for Teachers, 1979, Reading Instruction for Secondary Schools, 1986, How to Improve Your Scores on Reading Competency Tests, 1981; (with C. Smith and G. Ingersoll) Trends in Educational Materials: Traditionals and the New Technologies, 1983; also numerous articles. Bd. dirs. Meth. Hosp., N.W. Ind. Forum, N.W. Ind. Symphony, N.W. Ind. World Affairs Council, Boys Club N.W. Ind. Recipient numerous grants; Am. Council on Edn. fellow in acad. adminstrn. Ind. U., Bloomington, 1980-81. Mem. Assn. Tchr. Educators (nat. pres. 1984-85), Nat. Acad. Tchr. Edn. (dir. 1983—), Ind. Assn. Tchr. Educators (past pres.), North Cen. Assn. (commn. at large), Leadership Devel. Council ACE, Internat. Reading Assn., Phi Delta Kappa (Outstanding Young Educator award), Delta Kappa Gamma (Leadership/Mgmt. fellow 1980), Pi Lamda Theta, P.E.O., Chi Omega. Republican. Episcopalian. Home: 2073 Kenilworth Highlandille IN 46322 Office: Ind U NW 3400 Broadway Gary IN 46408

ELLIOTT, SHIRLEY RAE, medical technologist; b. Binghamton, N.Y., Oct. 21, 1922; d. John Rook and Carrie Marie (Keeney) Reynolds; m. Floyd Strother Elliott, Nov. 13, 1943; children: Linda Rae, Teresa Marie, Rita Kay, Susan Irene, John Roger, Katherine Claire, Floyd Strother. Student, Duke U., 1940-42; student, U. Tex., 1942-43, Sch. Med. Tech. VA Med. Ctr., 1955-56. Research technologist VA Med. Ctr., Nashville, 1956, med. technologist microbiology, chemistry, 1956-59, med. technologist, supr., 1959-66, coagulation/parasitology, technologist, 1966-72, supr. med. technology, 1972-88. Named Mother of the Yr., Gallatin Jaycettes, 1976, others. Mem. Nat. Geographic Soc., Cousteau Soc., Duke Alumni Assn., Met. Opera Guild, Am. Soc. Med. Technologists (life), Internat. Soc. Med. Technologists, Tenn. Soc. Microbiology, Am. Soc. Clin. Pathologists., Cousteau Soc., DAR. Methodist. Clubs: Nat. Commodore, Iron Dukes. Home: 1007 Bentley Cir Gallatin TN 37066 Office: 1310 24th Ave S Nashville TN 37212

ELLIOTT-LUCE, DIANNE MARIE, accountant; b. Sacramento, Calif., Mar. 18, 1951; d. Floyd Albert and Ruth Mildred (Ruble) E.; m. Michael James Luce, July 18, 1987. Student, U. So. Calif., 1969-72; AA, Yuba Coll., Marysville, Calif., 1982; postgrad., Calif. State U., Fullerton, 1984—. Loan teller 1st Valley Bank, Pittston, Pa., 1974-76; bookkeeper Sentinel Tupperware Sales, Pittston, 1976-77; store owner Wildwood Creations, South Lake Tahoe, Calif., 1977-79; restaurant owner, mgr. Vienna Inn, Marysville, Calif., 1979-80; office mgr., property mgr. Homewood Realty Inc., Yuba City, Calif., 1980-82; acct. Assocs. Transp., Yuba City, 1982; ptnr. Taylor Elliott & Co., Mission Viejo, Calif., 1983, pres., 1984—. Forum mem. Orange County Transp. Commn., Irvine, Calif., 1987; mem. human services conf. Orange County Dept. Edn., Anaheim, 1987; mem. adv. bd. Laguna Hills (Calif.) High Sch., 1987; choir mem. South Coast Community Ch.,

Irvine, 1986—. Mem. Nat. Assn. Female Execs., Am. Soc. Women Accts. (bd. dirs. 1986), Am. Mgmt. Assn., Saddleback Regional C. of C. (edn. chmn. 1986—, scholarship chmn. 1985-86, bd. dirs. scholarship found. 1987—, Cert. Appreciation 1986). Republican. Club: Le Tip (Mission Viejo)(treas. 1987—, sec. 1986-87, author newsletter 1986). Office: Taylor Elliott & Co Inc PO Box 2295 Mission Viejo CA 92690

ELLIS, BERNICE, educational planning consultant; b. Bklyn., July 14, 1934; d. Samuel and Clara (Schrier) H.; m. Seymour Scott Ellis, Feb. 7, 1954; children: Michele, Wayne. BA, Bklyn. Coll., 1956; MS, Queens Coll., 1970. Cert. fin. planner, N.Y. 1987, elem. educator, N.Y.C. Elementary tchr. L.I. Sch. Dists., Merrick, N.Y., 1956-60; tchr. reading N.Y.C. Bd. of Edn., Bklyn., 1972-73; coordinator Reading is Fundamental, Lawrence, N.Y., 1973-75; pres., founder N.Y. State Assn. for the Gifted and Talented, Valley Stream, N.Y., 1974-87; pres. Ellis Planning, Valley Stream, N.Y., 1984-87; cons. Nassau County Bd. Coop. Ednl. Services, Westbury, N.Y., 1973-74; adminstrv. intern region II U.S. Office Edn., 1977-78; adj. asst. prof. Nassau Community Coll., Garden City, N.Y., 1975—. Contbr. articles to profl. jours. Dem. Committeewoman, Nassau, N.Y., 1987; bd. dirs. Nat. Council Jewish Women Career Group, Nassau, 1987. Recipient Ednl. Professions Devel. Act fellow CUNY Inst. for Remediations Skills for Coll. Personnel, Queensborough Community Coll., 1970-73. Mem. Internat. Assn. for Fin. Planners (legislative com. 1986-87), N.Y. State Reading Assn., Adj. Faculty Assn. Nassau Community Coll., Sales Exec. Club of N.Y., L.I., N.Y. C. of C. Office: Ellis Planning 628 Golf Dr North Woodmere NY 11581

ELLIS, CYNTHIA ELAINE, insurance executive; b. Terre Haute, Ind., June 21, 1954; d. William L. and Margaret Ann (Richardson) Hoggatt; m. Joe M. Ellis, Apr. 4, 1981. BS, Ind. State U., 1976, MS, 1988. Extension agt. Purdue U. Coop. Extension Service, Bloomfield, Ind., 1976—. Bd. dirs. United Way, Linton, Ind., 1984-85, Leadership Lawrence County, Bedford, Ind., 1985-86. Mem. Nat. Assn. Extension Agts., Ind. Extension Agts. Assn. (com. chmn. 1980), Nat. Assn. Female Execs., Am. Sewing Guild, Nat. Assn. Extension Home Economists, Ind. Agricultural Leadership Program, Psi Iota Xi (treas. 1983-85). Lodge: Elks. Home: 10866 Millersburg Rd Chandler IN 47610 Office: Purdue U Coop Extension Service Rural Rt 2 Box 38A Bloomfield IN 47424

ELLIS, DENISE TAYLOR, deposit insurance company executive; b. Calif., Nov. 17, 1946; m. Billy C. Ellis, Mar. 15, 1969; 1 child. BA, U. Calif., Berkeley, 1968; MS in Bus. Adminstrn.., U. of B.C., Vancouver, Can., 1978. Fin. analyst City of Vancouver, 1978-81; research dir. Credit Union Deposit Ins. Corp., Vancouver, 1981-83, v.p. Research & Exam., 1985—; mgr. brokerage services Vancouver Stock Exchange, 1983-84; mgr. research & exam. Vancouver Stock Exchange, Vancouver, 1984-85; Mem. Vancouver Econ. Adv. Commn., 1987; bd. dirs. Fin. Execs. Inst., 1988. Fellow Vancouver Soc. Fin. Analysts; mem. Assn. Profl. Economists B.C. (pres. 1988, bd. dir. 1984-85, 2d v.p. 1985-86, 1st v.p. 1986-87), Fin. Analysts Fedn. Office: Credit Union Deposit Ins Corpof BC, 7th floor - 1380 Burrard St, Vancouver, BC Canada V6Z 2B7

ELLIS, DOROTHY TOLBERT, banker; b. Memphis, May 26, 1951; d. Roy and Dorothy (Weary) Tolbert; divorced; 1 child, Tiffany Nechelle. Student, Memphis State U., 1968-71. Records file clk. Nat. Trust Life Ins. Co., Memphis, 1971-72, jr. billing clk., 1972-74, sr. billing clk., 1974-78, asst. supr., 1978, supr. premium account, 1978-80; mgmt. trainee First Tenn. Bank, N.Am., Memphis, 1980-81, supr. II, 1981-83, ctr. mgr. I, 1983-84, ctr. mgr. II, 1984—. Advisor Jr. Achievement, 1978-79; commr. Memphis City Beautiful Commn., 1985—. Mem. Assoc. Profl. Exec. Women., Nat. Assn. Female Exec., Nat. Assn. Banking Women, NAACP. Democrat. Baptist. Office: First Tenn Bank 300 Court Memphis TN 38109

ELLIS, ERLEAN MARY, chemical company executive; b. Cornwall, N.Y., Jan. 10, 1953; d. William Thomas and Ann (Dyshuk) E. BA in Microbiology, U. South Fla., 1974; MBA, Pepperdine U., 1988. Cert. real estate agt., Calif. Sales trainee Chem. Div. Union Oil, Schaumburg, Ill., Atlanta and Chgo., 1975-77; sales rep. Chem. Div. Union Oil, Los Angeles, 1977-78, various chem. cos., Los Angeles, 1978-83; founder, pres. Orbital Chem. Corp., Los Alamitas, Calif., 1983—. Mem. AAUW (program chair, speaker), Internat. Food Technologists, Chem. Mktg. Assn., Am. Electro Plater's Soc. (bd. dirs., publicity chair 1983-84), Metal Finishers Assn. So. Calif., Park Ocean Condo Assn. (bd. dirs.). Home: 9531 Graham St Cypress CA 90630 Office: Orbital Chem Corp 3532 Katella Ave Suite 213 Los Alamitos CA 90720

ELLIS, EVA LILLIAN, artist; b. Seattle, June 4, 1920; d. Carl Martin and Hilda (Persson) Johnson; B.A., U. Wash., 1941; M.A., U. Idaho, 1950; M. in Painting (h.c.), U. delle Arti, 1983; m. Everett Lincoln Ellis, May 1, 1943; children: Karin, Kristy, Hildy, Erik. Assoc. dir. art Best & Co., Seattle, 1943; dir. Am. Art Week, Idaho, 1949-55; mem. faculty dept. art U. Idaho, 1946-48; dir., tchr. Children's Art Oreg., 1966-71; mem. faculty aux. bd. U. Wash., Seattle, 1987—; exhbns. include: Henry Gallery, U. Wash., 1941, Immanuel Gallery, N.Y.C., 1943-46, U. Mich., 1956-65, Detroit Inst. Art, 1959, Kresge Gallery, 1959-64, Portland Art Mus., 1967, Corvallis Art Center, Oreg., 1966, U. Idaho, 1946-56, U. Canterbury, N.Z., 1979, Boise Mus., 1949-55, CSA, 1972, 79, Survey of New Zealand Art, 1979, Shoreline Mus., Seattle, 1981, N.Z. Embassy, London, 1979, Karlshamn Art Soc., Sweden, 1979, Italian Acad. Art, 1982, Palos Verdes Art Ctr., calif., 1982, Aigantighe Gallery, N.Z., 1983; represented in permanent collections: U. Calif.-Berkeley, U. Wash.; guest appearances on NBC-TV, N.Y.C. Counselor Cancer Soc.; active Girl Scouts U.S.A. Recipient awards Acad. Art and Sci., 1958-66, Ann Arbor Women Painters, diploma with gold medal, Italian Acad. Art, 1980, hon. diploma fine art, 3 Nat. awards Nat. League Profl. Artists, N.Y.C.; World Culture prize, 1984; Internat. Peace award in Art, 1984; Internat. Art Promotion award, 1986, others. Fellow I.B.C. (Cambridge, Eng. chpt.); mem. Mich. Acad. Art and Sci., Nat. League Am. Pen Women, Nat. Mus. Women in Arts (charter mem.), Royal Overseas League, Fine Arts Soc. Idaho, Canterbury Soc. Art New Zealand, Copely Soc. Fine Arts (Boston), Alpha Omicron Pi. (featured in nat. mag.). Clubs: Scandinavian (pres. 1977—), Faculty Wives (pres. 1979). Address: 2603 NW 98th St Seattle WA 98117

ELLIS, GRACE CAROL, real estate executive; b. Fairview, Mo., Dec. 4, 1935; d. Leo Leslie and Grace (Allinder) Eurit; m. Leonard Eugene Ellis, Dec. 17, 1955; children—Susan Diane, Linda Jeanne, Leonard Eugene. Grad. Draughon's Bus. Sch., 1954. Real estate broker, Stillwater, Okla., 1970—; ptnr., mgr. Crestview Estates, Stillwater, 1971-85, Crestview Quick Shop and Laundry, 1971—. Republican. Baptist. Avocations: reading; gardening; traveling. Office: Crestview Quick Shop 2319 E 6th St Stillwater OK 74074

ELLIS, HELEN CHARD, writer, former health agency executive; b. East Orange, N.J., Oct. 16, 1914; d. Claude Franklin and Harriet Correll (Wallen) Chard; m. Harlan Reed Ellis, Dec. 23, 1937; children—Reed Ellis, Karen Anne Ellis Stonesifer. Student, Wooster Coll., 1931-33, U. Fla.-Gainesville, 1966-67; B.S., Simmons Coll., 1936. Part-time editorial work U. Fla.-Gainesville, 1957-70; exec. dir. Birth Defects Found., Gainesville, 1970-79; freelance writer, 1982—; instr. community edn. program Santa Fe Jr. Coll., 1984—. Compiler series of articles in Jour. of Teacher Edn., 1957-67; contbr. articles to mags. Mem., Fla. Gov.'s Alachua County Children's Commn., 1965-69, Alachua County Crime Victim Fund Rev. Com., 1979-83. Recipient March of Dimes Service award, 1982, 83, AAUW Service award, 1983, Fla. Fedn. Women's Clubs Service award, 1983. Mem. Nat. League Am. Pen Women (pres. Gainesville br. 1978-84, Fla. pres. 1986-88), Women in Communications, Fla. Freelance Writer's Assn., AAUW (past pres.), Gainesville Fine Arts Assn. (1st v.p. 1980-82). Club: Gainesville Woman's (chmn. internat. affairs 1982-83). Home: 4041 NW 12th Ave Gainesville FL 32605

ELLIS, JANE FINCKE, real estate executive; b. Newark, Aug. 27, 1956; d. Melvin R. and Estelle (Seiff) Fincke; m. Richard Lowes Ellis, Jr., June 2, 1985. B.A. in Philosophy cum laude, Yale U., 1978; M.B.A., Harvard U., 1982. Asst. treas. Chase Manhattan Bank, N.Y.C., 1978-80; corp. planner The Rockefeller Group, N.Y.C., 1982-84; dir. mktg. Rockefeller Ctr. Mgmt. Corp., 1984-86, asst. v.p. spl. projects, 1987—. Pub. mag. Center. Treas. Yale Class of 1978, chair Quarter Century Fund. Mem. Nat. Assn. Female Execs., Yale U. Alumni Assn. Club: Harvard Business School, Harvard (N.Y.C.). Avocations: running; bicycling; piano. Home: 7 Midland Gardens 5M Bronxville NY 10708 Office: Rockefeller Ctr Mgmt Corp 1230 Ave of Americas New York NY 10020

ELLIS, JANE MILES, nursing administrator, owner image consulting business; b. Louisville, Nov. 7, 1956; d. William A. and Mary Jane (Raun) Miles; m. John Robert Ellis III, Aug. 28, 1976. AS in Nursing, Western Ky. U., 1976; student, Bellarmine Coll., 1983; student in bus. adminstrn., U. Louisville, 1983—. RN; cert. emergency med. technician, Ky. Nurse Humana Hosp.-Suburban, Louisville, 1976-80; emergency dept. nurse mgr., clin. supr. Humana Hosp.-S.W., Louisville, 1980-82; emergency dept. nurse mgr., relief shift supr. Humana Hosp.-Audubon, Louisville, 1982-83, spl. projects coordinator for nursing adminstrn., 1983-84, asst. dir. nursing for nursing ops., 1985-86, asst. dir. nursing for surg. and outpatient services, 1986—; transitional care unit nurse mgr. Humana Hosp.-Univ., Louisville, 1984; nursing cons. Humana Hosp. del Pedregal, Mexico City, Humana Cen. Regional Office, Louisville, 1984-85; owner Positive Bus. Images, Louisville, 1987—; instr. Advanced Cardiac Life Support Am. Heart Assn., Louisville, 1982—. Regents scholar, 1976. Mem. Am. Nurses Assn., Ky. Nurses Assn., Nat. Assn. for Female Execs. Democrat. Methodist. Home: 7717 Nalan Dr Louisville KY 40291

ELLIS, JOANNE HAMMONDS, computer executive; b. Rome, Ga., Aug. 15, 1946; d. James Randolph and Louise (Glass) Hammonds; B.S., A.B., Jacksonville (Ala.) U., 1968; M.G.A., Ga. State U., 1979, M.P.A., 1981; 1 dau., Stephanie Louise Contrell. With GSA, 1969-82, computer systems analyst, 1985-87, dir. mgmt. services, now dir. prodn. services. Named Profl. Employee of Yr., 1979. Mem. Assn. Women in Computing, Federally Employed Women, Atlanta Assn. Fed. Execs., Nat. Assn. Female Execs., Dept. Def. Leadership Program, Beta Sigma Phi. Methodist. Home: 1143 Seabreeze Ln Gulf Breeze FL 32561 Office: Navy Regional Data Automation Ctr NAS Pensacola FL 32508

ELLIS, JUNE B., human resource consultant; b. Portland, Ind., June 17; children: Kenneth G., Reyn K. BS, Mary Washington Coll., 1942; MSW, Tulane U., 1953; PhD, Internat. U., 1977. Asst. dir. social services East La. State Hosp., Jackson, 1960-62; instr. Tulane U. Sch. Social Work, New Orleans, 1962-63, asst. prof., 1966-67; exec. dir. Family Service-Travelers Aid, Ft. Smith, Ark., 1967-71; pres. Child and Family Cons., Ft. Smith, 1971—; dir. Arkoma Transactional Analysis Inst., Ft. Smith; mem. adv. bd. Suspect Child Abuse and Neglect. Author: TA Tally, 1974, TA Talk, terms and references in transaction, 1976, BEING, 1982. Mem. Ark. Gov.'s Commn. on Status of Women, 1970-73, Ark. Gov.'s Com. Drug Abuse Prevention; mem. adv. bd. Jr. League Am.; mem. scholarship selection com. Whirlpool Corp. Mem. Internat. Transactional Analysis Assn., Am. Group Psychotherapy Assn., Am. Orthopsychiat. Assn., Acad. Cert. Social Workers, We. Ark. Mental Health Assn. (adv. bd.), Conf. for Advancement of Private Practice in Social Work. Episcopalian. Clubs: Town, Hardscrabble Country (Ft. Smith). Office: Child and Family Cons Inc 512 S 16th St PO Box 3816 Fort Smith AR 72913

ELLIS, MARILYN ANNE, executive assistant; b. Orange, Mass., Sept. 22, 1936; d. Dorila Joseph and Pauline Adelaide (Desrosiers) Duval; m. William Hemmingway Ellis, Apr. 21, 1957; 1 child, Jonathan Christopher Hemmingway. Grad. high sch., Orange. Adminstrv. asst. Dept. Navy, Washington, 1959-71, exec. sec. to asst. sec. for fin. mgmt., 1971-81, confidential staff asst. to asst. sec. for shipbuilding and logistics, 1981-84, confidential staff asst. to chief of naval material, 1984-85; exec. asst. Advanced Marine Enterprises Inc., Arlington, Va., 1985—. Mem. Citizens for a Better City, Falls Church, Va., 1986—. Mem. Navy League U.S. (bd. dirs. No. Va. council 1985—). Home: 302 Sycamore St Falls Church VA 22046 Office: Advanced Marine Enterprises Inc 1725 Jefferson Davis Hwy Arlington VA 22202

ELLIS, MARY JO, county official; b. Scottsbluff, Nebr., Nov. 13, 1928; d. Roy Edward and Hazel Belle (Parmenter) Kronberg; m. Vinton Maurice Ellis, Aug. 3, 1949; children: Martin F., Mary Ellis Shaughnessy. Dep. register of deeds Scotts Bluff County, Gering, Nebr., 1946-52, register of deeds, 1963—; asst. mgr. Fed. Land Bank, Scottsbluff, 1955-62. Sec., treas. United Way, Scottsbluff, 1974-76; v.p., bd. dirs. Foster Grandparents Assn., Scottsbluff, 1980—. Recipient Pres.' award Nebr. Assn. County Offls., 1987. Mem. Nebr. Recorders and Clks. Assn. (pres. 1971-72, 86-87), Nat. Assn. Recorders and Clks. Assn. (historian 1979—, Cert. merit 1967, 85), Panhandle County Ofcls. Assn. (pres. 1985), Scottsbluff Bus. and Profl. Women's Club (pres. 1974-75, Woman of Achievement award 1979), Scottsbluff C. of C. (chmn. women's div. 1958). Republican. Club: Twin-City Toastmistress (pres. 1968-69). Avocations: travel, flower gardening. Home: 3023 8th Ave Scottsbluff NE 69361 Office: Scotts Bluff County Adminstrv Bldg 10th St Gering NE 69341

ELLIS, MARY LOUISE, state official; b. Albert Lea, Minn., May 29, 1943; d. Stanley Orville and Neoma Lois (Guthier) Helgeson; m. Melvin Eugene Ellis, July 31, 1966; children: Christopher, Tracy. BS in Pharmacy, U. Iowa, 1966; MA in Pub. Adminstrn., Iowa State U., 1982, postgrad., 1982-83. Faculty Duquesne U., Pitts., 1977; cons. in pharmacy, Colville, Wash., 1978-79; dir. pharmacy Mt. Carmel Hosp., Colville, 1978-79; clin. pharmacist Iowa Vets. Home, Marshalltown, Iowa, 1980-81; instr. Iowa Valley Community Coll., Marshalltown, 1981-83; dir. Iowa Dept. Substance Abuse, Des Moines, 1983-86; dir. pub. health, dir. Iowa Dept. Pub. Health, Des Moines, 1986 ; chair Iowa Health Data Commn., Des Moines, 1986—; bd. dirs. Health Policy Corp. Iowa, 1986—; adj. asst. prof. U. Iowa, Iowa City, 1984—. Mem. Iowa State Bd. Health, 1981-83, v.p., 1982-83; mem. adv. council Iowa Valley Community Coll., 1983-85. Mem. Am. Pharm. Assn., Iowa Pharmacists Assn., Am. Pub. Health Assn., Iowa Pub. Health Assn. (bd. dirs.), AAUW, Alpha Xi Delta, Phi Kappa Phi, Pi Sigma Alpha. Republican. Home: 2801 Woodland Ave West Des Moines IA 50265 Office: Iowa Dept Pub Health Lucas State Office Bldg Des Moines IA 50319

ELLIS, SUSAN GOTTENBERG, psychologist; b. N.Y.C., Jan. 24, 1949; d. Sam and Sally (Hirschman) Gottenberg; B.S., Cornell U., 1970; M.A., Columbia U., 1971; M.A., Hofstra U., 1975, Ph.D., 1976; m. David Roy Ellis, July 23, 1972; children—Sharon Rachel, Dana Michelle. Instr. health edn. Nassau Community Coll., Garden City, N.Y., 1971-73; sch. psychologist public schs., Somerville, N.J., 1976-77; clin. psychologist Somerset County Community Mental Health Center, Somerville, 1976-77; sch. psychologist, Pinellas County, Fla., 1977-78; instr. St. Petersburg (Fla.) Jr. Coll., 1978; clin. psychologist, Largo, Fla., 1977—; cons. Fla. Dept. Health and Rehab. Services, Med. Center Hosp., Largo, Morton Plant Hosp., Clearwater, Fla., N.Y. State Regents scholar, 1966-71; adj. prof. Eckerd Coll. St. Petersburg, 1988. Author: Interpret Your Dreams, 1987, A Dream Primer, 1988, Make Sense of Your Dreams. Mem. Am. Psychol. Assn., Fla. Psychol. Assn., Pinellas Psychol. Assn. (treas. 1978, polit. action chmn. 1979), Kappa Delta Pi. Club: Cornell U. Suncoast (v.p. 1979-80). Home: 1904 Oakdale Ln North Clearwater FL 34624 Office: 3233 E Bay Dr Suite 100 Largo FL 34641

ELLISON, DIANE MARIE, timber company executive; b. Aberdeen, Wash., June 18, 1941; d. Russell M. and Syster (Edlund) E.; m. Thomas C. Rowe, Apr. 12, 1963 (div. 1969); children: Dawn Marie, Robert Ellison. BA in Sociology cum laude, U. Wash., 1963; teaching credential in social scis., U. Calif., Irvine, 1970; MS in Human Resource Mgmt. and Devel., Chapman Coll., 1984; cert. alcohol/drug studies, Seattle U., 1987-88. Counselor Seattle (Wash.) Detention Ctr., 1963; adolescent counselor Oakland (Calif.) YMCA, 1964; youth leader St. Andrews Ch., Newport Beach, Calif., 1971-75; tennis coach Tustin Hills Racquet Club, Tustin, Calif., 1977-80; tennis instr. Utt Currie Jr. High Sch., Tustin, 1978-80; sales and mktg. exec. Don Caster Fashions, Aberdeeen, Wash., 1980-82; prin. Ellison Timber, Aberdeen, Wash., 1982—, Ellison Truffles Corp., Aberdeen, 1984—; speaker Chapman Coll. Enterprise Inst., 1986-87. Co-author: Reach for the Sky, 1986; video producer log rolling history The Contest Logger, White Water Man, 1988. Vol. dir. Tall Ships Restoration, Aberdeen, 1986, Pacific Rim Cultural Ctr., Aberdeen, 1987; bd. govs. Evergreen State Coll., 1987—; pres., mem. steering com. Wash. State Folk Life Council, 1988—; bd. dirs. Aberdeen chpt. Am. Heart Assn., 1988—. Mem. N.Am. Truffling Soc., Pacific N.W. Writers Conf., Internat. Log Rolling Orgn., Women in Timber, Aberdeen C. of C. (bd. dirs. 1985—), U. Wash. Alumni Assn., Alumni Assn. Chapman Coll., Polson Mus., Mus. Aberdeen, Alpha Chi Omega. Republican. Lodge: Lions. Home and Office: Rt 1 Box 142 Aberdeen WA 98520

ELLISON, JOAN HELINSKI, public health director; b. Greenport, N.Y., Apr. 1, 1948; d. John Stanley and Victoria Ann (Stepnoski) H.; m. Robert Ross Ellison, May 31, 1986; children: Robert Ross Jr., Eustacia. BS in Nursing, Russell Sage Coll., 1970; MPH, U. Mich., 1973. Nurse community health Westchester County Health Dept., White Plains, N.Y., 1970-72, supervising pub. health nurse, 1973-79; dir. patient services Livingston County Health Dept., Mt. Morris, N.Y., 1979-87, pub. health dir., 1979—; bd. dirs. Finger Lakes Health Systems Agy., 1983—; adv. council Prenatal-Perinatal council N.Y. State Health Dept., 1983—; exec. com. Genesee Affiliate N.Y. Pub. Health Assn., 1981—, treas. 1981-85, pres. 1985—; chair Livingston County Emergency Med. Services Com., 1981—. Mem. Livingston County Youth Bd., 1979-84; maternal and child health adv. block grant council N.Y. State Health Dept., 1983—; co-chmn. Monroe-Livingston Maternal-Infant health action group, 1985—; mem. Health Futures for Rochester Ind. Citizens Commn., 1986—. Mem. N.Y. State Nurses Assn. (dist. 2), Am. Nurses Assn., N.Y. State Pub. Health Assn., Am. Pub. Health Assn. Office: Livingston County Health Dept Bldg 2 Murray Hill Mount Morris NY 14510

ELLISON, KATHERINE ESTHER, journalist; b. Mpls., Aug. 19, 1957; d. Ellis and Bernice June (Bender) E. BA in Internat. Relations, Stanford U., 1979. Intern reporter Washington Post, 1979, Newsweek, London, 1979-80; reporter San Jose (Calif.) Mercury, 1980—; bd. dirs. Media Alliance, San Francisco, 1986—. Co-author articles including Hidden Billions: The Draining of the Philippines, 1985 (Pulitzer prize 1986, George Polk Meml. award 1986, Investigative Reporters and Editors award 1986). Office: care San Jose Mercury News 750 Ridder Park Dr San Jose CA 95190

ELLISON, MARY-ANN ROCK, insurance company executive; b. Springfield, Vt., Apr. 27, 1956; d. Robert M. and Ann-Marie (Kearney) E. BS in Biology, So. Conn. State U., 1983. Lic. adjuster. Adjuster Paul C. Higgins, Inc., New Haven, 1982-85, Conn. Hosp. Assn., Waterbury, Conn., 1985-86; claims adminstr. J. Neale MacDonald Co., Inc., Hamden, Conn., 1986; supr. CIGNA/Ins. Co. N.Am., a unit of United Techs. Corp., Hartford, Conn., 1986-88, Chubb and Son, New Haven, 1988—. Mem. Nat. Assn. Female Execs. Office: Chubb and Son Inc PO Box 1903 Long Wharf Dr New Haven CT 06511

ELLMANN, SHEILA FRENKEL, investment co. exec.; b. Detroit, June 8, 1931; d. Joseph and Rose (Neback) Frenkel; BA in English, U. Mich., 1953; m. William M. Ellmann, Nov. 1, 1953; children: Douglas Stanley, Carol Elizabeth, Robert Lawrence. Dir. Advance Glove Mfg. Co., Detroit, 1954-78; v.p. Frome Investment Co., Detroit, 1980—. Mem. U. Mich. Alumni Assn., Nat. Trust Hist. Preservation. Home: 28000 Weymouth St Farmington Hills MI 48018

ELLNER, CAROLYN LIPTON, university dean, consultant; b. N.Y.C., Jan. 17, 1932; d. Robert Mitchell and Rose (Pearlman) Lipton; m. Richard Ellner, June 21, 1953; children—David Lipton, Alison Lipton. A.B. cum laude, Mt. Holyoke Coll., 1953; A.M., Columbia Tchrs. Coll., 1957; Ph.D. with distinction, UCLA, 1968. Tchr., prof., adminstr., N.Y. and Md., 1957-62; prof. dir. tchr. edn., assoc. dean Claremont Grad. Sch. (Calif.) 1967-82; prof., dean sch. edn. Calif. State U., Northridge, 1982—. Co-author: Schoolmaking, 1977; Studies of College Teaching (Orange County Authors award 1984), 1983. Trustee Ctr. for Early Edn., Los Angeles, 1968-71, Oakwood Sch., Los Angeles, 1972-78, Mt. Holyoke Coll., South Hadley, Mass., 1979-84; commr. Economy and Efficiency Com., Los Angeles, 1974-82, Calif. Commn. Tchr. Credentialing; bd. dirs. Found. for Effective Govt., Los Angeles, 1982, Calif. Coalition for Pub. Edn., 1985—; commr. Calif. State Commn. Tchr. Credentialing, 1987—. Ford Found. fellow, 1964-67; recipient Office of Edn. award U.S. Office of Edn., 1969-72; W. M. Keck Found. grantee, 1983. Mem. Am. Edn. Research Assn., Am. Assn. Colls. for Tchr. Edn., Assn. for Supervision and Curriculum Devel., Nat. Soc. for Study of Edn. Office: Calif State U Sch of Edn 18111 Nordhoff St Northridge CA 91330

ELLSTROM-CALDER, ANNETTE, clinical social worker; b. Duluth, Minn., Dec. 19, 1952; d. Raymond Charles Ellstrom and Ruth Elaine (Bloomquist) Larson; m. Jeffrey Ellstrom Calder, July 30, 1982. BA in Social Work, Psychology, Sociology, Concordia Coll., 1974; MSW, U. Wis., 1978. Group therapist N.D. State Indsl. Sch., 1973; social worker Fergus Falls (Minn.) State Hosp., 1974, Jackson County Dept. Social Services, Black River Falls, Wis., 1975-77; clin. social worker U. Wis. Hosp., Madison, 1979—; cons. Waupun (Wis.) Meml. Hosp., 1979-84; lectr. grad. sch. social work U. Wis., Madison, 1979—, lectr. U. Wis. med. sch., Madison, 1979-82, prin. investigator in research U. Wis. Hosp., Madison, 1985—. Editor: A Guide to Patients and Families, 1984; contbr. articles to profl. jours. Del. trustee, bd. dirs. Nat. Kidney Found., N.Y.C., 1983—, chmn. bd. dirs. Wis. chpt., Milw., 1985-87, vice chmn. 1983-85, sec. 1982-83, chmn. patient services com. 1981-82, bd. dirs. 1981—, chmn. nat. tng. and edn. com., N.Y., 1987—, mem. nat. patient services com. N.Y., 1987—; bd. dirs. Madison chpt., 1979—; mem. nat. research com. Am. Assn. Spinal Cord Injury Psychologists and Social Workers, N.Y.C., 1988. Recipient Health Advancement award Nat. Kidney Found. Wis., 1985, Vol. Yr. award Nat. Kidney Found. Wis., 1984, Vol. Service award Nat. Kidney Found. Wis., 1983, Nat. Nephrology Social Worker of Yr. Merit award Nat. Kidney Found. and Council of Nephrology Social Workers, 1987; hon. adoptee Winnebago Indian Tribe, 1978; named Outstanding Young Wisconsinite Wisc. Jaycees, 1988. Mem. Council Nephrology Social Workers (nat. v.p. 1984-86, nat. exec. com. 1984-86, Nat. Nephrology Social Worker Yr. award 1987), Nat. Assn. Social Workers, Pi Gamma Mu. Democrat. Home: 3538 Topping Rd Madison WI 53705 Office: U Wis Hosp 600 Highland Ave E5/620 Madison WI 53792

ELLSWEIG, PHYLLIS LEAH, psychotherapist, retired; b. Irvington, N.J., Apr. 19, 1927; d. Sumar and Jeanette (Geffner) Schwartz; m. Martin Richard Ellsweig, Dec. 25, 1947; children: Bruce, Steven. BS, East Stroudsburg U. (Pa.), 1947; EdM, Lehigh U., 1966, EdD, 1972. Tchr. Stroud Union High Sch., 1963-66; guidance counselor East Stroudsburg Schs., 1966-68; asst. prof. edn. East Stroudsburg U., 1968; staff psychologist, outpatient supr. Mental Health Center Carbon, Monroe and Pike Counties, Stroudsburg, 1968-80; pvt. practice in psychotherapy and clin. hypnosis Stroudsburg, 1969-87; mem. staff Pocono Hosp.; pub. speaker in field; cons. to schs., orgns. Mem. Am. Psychol. Assn., Pa. Psychol. Assn., Am. Group Psychotherapy Assn., Am. Soc. Clin. Hypnosis, Internat. Soc. Hypnosis, NOW (profl. cons. 1973—), Internat. Assn. Group Psychotherapy.

ELLWOOD-FILKINS, LEA BEATRICE, computer executive; b. Wyandotte, Mich., May 27, 1955; d. Alvin Harold and Rhoda Martha (Krahnke) Ellwood; m. John C. Filkins, July 16, 1977; 1 ward, Kim Ruth. Student, Wayne State U., 1973-74, Wayne Community Coll., 1983-87. Office and prodn. dir. Doré Inc., Detroit, 1973-75; asst. traffic dir. Sta. WDEE, Southfield, Mich., 1975-77; word processing operator Miller Canfield Paddock and Stone, Detroit, 1977-78, word processing asst. supr., 1978-80, word processing supr., 1980-82, systems coordinator, 1982-84, tng. coordinator, 1985—; dir. edn., speakers bur. Greater Metro Detroit Assn. of Info. Systems Profls., 1985-87, sec. 1986-87. Set designer The Islanders, Grosse Ile, Mich., 1985-88. Dir. Christian edn. St. James Episcopal Ch., Grosse Ile, 1984-86. Mem. Nat. Assn. Female Execs., Assn. Info. Systems Profls., Detroit Area Trainers' Assn., Detroit Inst. Arts Founders Soc. Club: West Shore Sail (mem. race com. 1988—). Office: Miller Canfield Paddock and Stone 2500 Comerica Bldg Detroit MI 48226

ELLZEY, INGEBORG CHARLOTTE, medical consultant; b. Bad Tolz, Federal Republic of Germany, May 9, 1949; came to U.S. 1955; d. Maximilian Karl and Charlotte Erna (Jaeschke) Manjura; 1 child, Karl Maximilian. B in Med. Record Adminstrn., U. Cen. Fla., Orlando, 1978; M in Pub. Adminstrn., U. Cen. Fla., 1984. Office mgr. J.V. Lara, M.D., Winter Park, Fla., 1972-86; med. cons. Med. Office Planning and Cons., Winter Park, 1978—; assoc. prof. U. Cen. Fla., Orlando, 1984-85, adj. faculty, 1982-85; adj. faculty Valencia Community Coll., Orlando, 1981-84; cons. NTS Research Corp, Durham, N.C., 1980-81. Editor newsletter Office Hours, 1986; author (tapes) Inga Ellzey Med. Mgmt. Tapes, 1987. Pres. CPR for

Citizens, Orlando, 1980-87, bd. dirs. Winter Park [illegible] 1986-87; chmn. bd. CPR for Citizens, 1987—. Named Vol. of the Yr., CPR for Citizens, 1985. Mem. Am. Soc. Pub. Adminstrn., Am. Med. Record Assn., Soc. for Study of the Presidiency, Soc. Profl. Bus. Cons., Nat. Speakers Assn., Phi Kappa Phi. Republican. Lutheran. Office: Med Office Planning & Cons PO Box 4902 Winter Park FL 32793

ELM, CAROLE ANN, quality engineer, manufacturing company executive; b. Pitts., Feb. 27, 1958; d. Elaine H. (Marsteller) E. BSChemE, Carnegie-Mellon U., 1980; MS in Psychology, U. Tenn., 1987. Process devel. engr. Arco Polymers (subs. Atlantic Richfield), Pitts., 1980-81; process mfg. engr. Celanese, Louisville, 1981-82; sr. quality process engr. Duracell USA (subs. Kraft Inc.), Cleveland, Tenn., 1983-87; mfg. tech. engr. III Rocketdyne div. Rockwell Internat., Canoga Park, Calif., 1987—. Mem. Nat. Assn. Female Execs., Am. Inst. Chem. Engrs. Republican. Home: 4404 San Blas Ave Woodland Hills CA 91364 Office: Rockwell Internat Rocketdyne Div 6633 Canoga Ave Canoga Park CA 91304

ELMAN, NATALIE MADORSKY, educational therapy administrator; b. Mt. Clemens, Mich., Dec. 12, 1939; d. Sam and Freda (Lafky) Madorsky; m. Stanley Harold Elman, Feb. 7, 1960; children: Susan Michelle, Michael Steven, Elisabeth Rose. BA summa cum laude, Newark State Coll., Union, N.J., 1970; MA, Kean Coll., Union, N.J., 1973; postgrad., Rutgers U., 1984—. Cert. tchr. Speech pathologist Cerebral Palsy Treatment Clinic, Somerville, N.J., 1970-72; tchr./handicapped Warren (N.J.) Twp. Bd. Edn., 1972-85; ednl. therapist Summit (N.J.) Ctr. for Learning, 1981—; cons. Dept. Spl. Edn. State of N.J., Trenton, 1985-86.; bd. dirs. Our House Inc. , 1981-87, pres. 1984-85, found. mem. 1987—. Author: The Resource Room Primer, 1981, Special Educators Almanac, 1984, Super Sayings-How to Teach Idioms to Kids, 1986; contbr. to Children mag., 1987, 88; panelist radio and TV shows, 1982-87. Mem. Summit Jewish Community Ctr.1970—, chairperson nursery com., 1970-73, edn. com., 1976-78, sr. citizens com., 1978-79, youth com., 1979-81, founder sr. citizens group, 1979, bd. dirs. religious program for handicapped, 1980-81; mem. planning com. Women's Resource Ctr., Summit, 1987. Mem. N.J. Assn. Learning Cons.'s, Council Exceptional Children, Assn. Children Learning Disabilities, N.J. Edn. Assn. Home: 119 Mountain Ave Summit NJ 07901 Office: Summit Ctr for Learning 7 Union Place Summit NJ 07901

ELMER, JEAN RADLEY, psychotherapist; b. Clifton Springs, N.Y., Aug. 6, 1946; d. Vaughn Ferris and Sara (Sutman) Radley; 1 child, William VII. BA, U. Maine, 1968; MSW, Boston U., 1971; postgrad., U. Wash., 1977-79. Caseworker Rensselaer County Dept. Social Services, Troy, N.Y., 1968-69, State of Hawaii, Honolulu, 1971-72, Seattle Children's Home, 1973-74; psychotherapist Divorce Lifeline, Olympia, Wash., 1977; outpatient therapist Mental Health N., Seattle, 1974-76, 78-82; pvt. practice psychotherapy Seattle, 1982—; pub. speaker KIRO-Radio sta., Seattle, 1984, Nat. Assn. Women in Constrn., Everett, Wash., 1986, Bothell (Wash.) C. of C., 1986, Civitan, Bellevue, Wash., 1985, Rotary Club, Seattle, 1985, Women Bus. Owners, Seattle, 1986. Contbr. articles to profl. pubs. Arbitrator Floating Homes Assn., Seattle, 1981. Mem. Am. Group Psychotherapy Assn., N.W. Group Psychotherapy Assn. (sec. 1983-85), Nat. Assn. Social Workers, Wash. State Soc. Clin. Social Workers, Assn. Women in Psychology, Women's Bus. Exchange, Women Bus. Owners. Democrat. Presbyterian. Club: Toastmasters. Home: 2349 Fairview Ave E Seattle WA 98102 Office: 1424 4th Ave Suite 903 Seattle WA 98101

ELMER, MARY ELIZABETH, executive recruiter; consultant; b. Utica, N.Y., Dec. 23, 1954; d. Bernard Edward and Ruth Marion (York) E.; m. Peter Julian Baskin, July 28, 1984. B.A., Siena Coll., 1977. Mktg. rep. Hartford Ins., Albany, N.Y., 1977-80, Gt. Am., Syracuse, N.Y., 1981-82; v.p., sec. Personnel Assocs., Inc., Syracuse, 1982—. Mem. Nat. Assn. Female Execs. (network dir.), Am. Soc. Profl. and Exec. Women, Nat. Assn. Woman Bus. Owners (v.p. govt. affairs Greater Syracuse chpt.), Nat. Assn. Personnel Cons. (cert. personnel cons., regent 1986—, dist. dir. 1987—), Assn. Personnel Cons. of N.Y. State, Inc., Ind. Personnel Cons. Central N.Y., Internat. Platform Assn., Siena Alumni Assn., Nat. Mus. of Women in Arts (charter). Republican. Roman Catholic. Avocations: reading, collecting antiques, refinishing furniture. Office: Personnel Assocs Inc 731 James St Courtyard Entrance Syracuse NY 13203

EL-MESSIDI, KATHY GROEHN, communications executive; b. Detroit, Jan. 23, 1946; d. Thomas Emil and Helen Margaret (Schreck); m. Adel El-Sayed Ali El-Messidi, Sept. 14, 1974; children: Lyla, Mariam. BA, U. Mich., 1967; MA, So. Oreg. Coll., 1971; PhD, U. Olka., 1976. Reporter Grosse Pointe (Mich.) News, 1966, Christian Sci. Monitor, Boston, 1967-69; writer publicity Harry & David & Jackson and Perkins Cos., Oreg., 1970-71; writer radio Sta. WNAD, Norman, Okla., 1973; instr. history U. Olka., 1972-75; writer pub. relations Houston, 1976-78; mgr. communications Bovay Engrs. Inc., Houston, 1978-80; cons. communications CRS Group Inc., Houston, 1980-81, Turner, Collie and Braden Inc., Houston; supervising editor, speech writer Exxon Prodn. Research Co., Houston, 1981-86; sr. speech writer Sandy Corp., Troy, Mich., 1986, Tenneco Inc., Houston, 1987-88. Author: Grosse Pointe, Michigan: Race Against Race (Am. Pen Women 1st pl. award for informational book), 1972, The Bargain: The Story Behind the 30-year Honeymoon of GM and the UAW, 1980. Assoc. Rice U., Houston Mem. Internat. Assn. Bus. Communicators, Women in Communications, Am. Hist. Assn., Am. Pen Women, Phi Alpha Theta. Christian Scientist. Club: Galveston Country. Home: 14502 Magic River Dr Cypress TX 77429

EL-NAJDAWI, EVA, microbiologist, researcher; b. Zliechov, Czechoslovakia, Feb. 21, 1950; came to U.S., 1982; d. Emil Škultéty and Mária (Vicenová) škultétyová; m. Mohammad Khalil El-Najdawi, Aug. 7, 1978 (div. 1980); children: Marwan, Karin. MSc, Comenius U., Bratislava, Czechoslovakia, 1973, PhD, 1976. Research asst. Inst. Virology Slovak Acad. Scis., Bratislava, Czecholslovakia, 1973-78; microbiologist Research Inst. Human Bioclimatology, Bratislava, Czecholslovakia, 1978-79, Ministry Health, Amman, Jordan, 1979-81; research asst. Sch. Dental Med. Washington U., St. Louis, 1983-85, Div. Rheumatology Dept. Internal Med. St. Louis U., 1985—. Contbr. articles to profl. jours. Home: 2536 Florent Ave Saint Louis MO 63143 Office: St Louis U Sch Med 1402 S Grand Blvd Saint Louis MO 63104

ELOMAA, ADDIE MAE, nursing instructor; b. Lincolnton, N.C., Apr. 29, 1920; d. Harry and Addie May (Hoover) Page; m. Allan Emil Elomaa, Feb. 23, 1952; children: Allan Emil Jr., John William. BS in Nursing, Emory U., 1949. RN. Instr. Emory U. Sch. Nursing, Atlanta, 1949-50; instr., staff nurse Charlotte (N.C.) Meml. Hosp., 1950-51; instr. Hudson Stuck Meml. Hosp., Ft. Yukon, Alaska, 1951-52, St. Augustine (Fla.) Tech. Ctr., 1976-87; inservice coordinator St. Augustine Geriatric Ctr, 1987—. Vol. Am. Heart Assn., Jacksonville, Fla., 1960s, March of Dimes, Jacksonville, 1960s, Cancer Crusade, Jacksonville, 1960s, local ch., Jacksonville, 1960s. Mem. Am. Nurses Assn., Fla. Nurses Assn. (pres. dist. II 1985-86), Am. Vocat. Assn. Democrat. Lutheran. Home: 258 Wisteria Rd Saint Augustine FL 32086

ELROD, MARGARET ANN, nurse, consultant; b. Fitzgerald, Ga., Dec. 13, 1919; d. Joseph Thomas and Della Ann (Booker) Hendricks; m. James William Elrod, Sept. 9, 1942 (div. 1967, dec.); children—Linda Sue, James Thomas (dec.), Robert Lee (dec.). Student Middle Ga. Coll., Cochran, 1936-37; R.N., Macon City Hosp., 1942. Pvt. duty nurse, Macon, Ga., 1942-49; dir. nurses Mitchell County Hosp., Camilla, Ga., 1953-57, Howard Hosp., Pelham, Ga., 1957-63, Rest Awhile Nursing Home, Moultrie, Ga., Jesup, Ga., 1963-67, Templeton Nursing Homes, Valdosta, Ga., 1967-78; dir. phys. health Parkwood Devel. Ctr., Valdosta, 1978-87, ret. 1987. Mem. Civic Round Table of Valdosta; bd. dirs. Long Term Care Ombudsman Adv. Bd.; vol. reader Talking Book Program, 1988; hospice vol.; bloodbank vol. Mem. Ga. State Nurses Assn. (pres. 15th dist. 1970-71, 1st v.p. 15th dist. 1988-89), Loundes County Mental Health Assn. (v.p. 1984-85, pres. 1985-86), Loundes Assn. Retarded Citizens (bd. dirs. 1983-85, service award 1983, 85-86). Democrat. Methodist. Clubs: United Spanish War Aux. (state pres. 1973-74); Pilot of Valdosta (pres. 1975-76, 77-78, 84-85). Avocation: fishing. Home: Rt 12 Box 225 Lot 10 Valdosta GA 31602

EL SAFFAR, RUTH SNODGRASS, Spanish language educator; b. N.Y.C., June 12, 1941; d. John Tabb and Ruth (Wheelwright) Snodgrass; m. Zuhair M. El Saffar, Apr. 11, 1965; children: Ali, Dena, Amir. B.A., Colo. Coll., 1962; Ph.D., Johns Hopkins U., 1966; DHL (hon.), Colo. Coll., 1987. Instr. Spanish, Johns Hopkins U., Balt., 1963-65; instr. English Univ. Coll. Baghdad, 1966-67; asst. prof. Spanish U. Md.-Baltimore County, 1967-68; asst. prof. U. Ill.-Chgo., 1968-73, assoc. prof., 1973-78, prof., 1978-83, research prof. Spanish, 1983-88; prof. Northwestern U., Evanston, Ill., 1988—; dir. summer seminar on Spanish Golden Age lit. NEH, 1979, 82. Author: Novel to Romance: A Study of Cervantes's Novelas Ejemplares, 1974, Distance and Control in Don Quixote, 1975, Cervantes's Casamiento engañoso and Coloquio de los perros, 1976, Beyond Fiction, 1984, Critical Essays on Cervantes, 1986; adv. bd. PMLA; editorial bd. Cervantes, The Comparatist, Hispanic Issues. Woodrow Wilson fellow, 1962; NEH fellow, 1970-71; Guggenheim fellow, 1975-76; Danforth assoc., 1973-79; Am. Council Learned Socs. grantee, 1978; Newberry Library fellow, 1982; U. Ill. Inst. Humanities fellow, 1985-86; sr. univ. scholar U. Ill., 1986—. Mem. MLA (exec. council 1974-78, commn. on future of the profession 1980-82, exec. com. div. on Spanish Golden Age poetry and prose 1977-82), Am. Assn. Tchrs. Spanish and Portuguese, Midwest MLA, Cervantes Soc. Am. (exec. com. 1979-82, 86—). Home: 7811 Greenfield River Forest IL 60305 Office: Univ Ill Dept Spanish Chicago IL 60680

ELSE, CAROLYN JOAN, library system administrator; b. Mpls., Jan. 31, 1934; d. Elmer Oscar and Irma Carolyn (Seibert) Wahlberg; m. Floyd Warren Else, 1962 (div. 1968); children—Stephen Alexander, Catherine Elizabeth. B.S. Stanford U., 1956; M.L.S., U. Wash., 1957. Cert. profl. librarian, Wash. Librarian Queens Borough Pub. Library, N.Y.C., 1957-59, U.S. Army Special Services, France, Germany, 1959-62; info. librarian Bennett Martin Library, Lincoln, Neb., 1962-63; br. librarian Pierce County Library, Tacoma, Wash., 1963-65, dir., 1965—. Bd. dirs. Campfire, Tacoma, 1984. Mem. South Sound Women's Network (bd. dirs.), Wash. Library Assn. (v.p. 1969-71), Pacific Northwest Library Assn. (sec. 1969-71), ALA. Club: City (Tacoma). Office: Pierce County Rural Library Dist 2356 Tacoma Ave S Tacoma WA 98402

ELSENHANS, VIRGINIA DELONG, university administrator; b. Bronxville, N.Y., Apr. 1, 1947; d. Charles Frederick and Dorothy Potter (Hobbs) Delong; m. David Williams Elsenhans, June 7, 1973 (div. 1979). BA, Elmhurst Coll., 1969; A in Applied Sci., Montgomery County Community Coll., 1976; EdM, Temple U., 1982, MBA, 1986. Cert. adult nurse practitioner, Pa. RN Temple U. Med. Ctr., Phila., 1976-80, educator community health, 1980-82, adult nurse practitioner, 1982-85; grad. asst. Sch. Bus. Adminstn. Temple U., Phila., 1985-86; adminstrv. fellw U. Mich. Hosps., Ann Arbor, 1986—; cons. Meml. Hosp., Roxborough Pa., 1982-83; rep. State Nurse Practitioner's Coalition, southeastern Pa., 1983-85; mem. adv. bd. SBI, Inc., Bala Cynwyd, Pa., 1987—. Contbr. articles to profl. jours. Mem. program com. Am. Heart Assn., Phila., 1982-84, adv. bd. Domino's House, Ann Arbor, 1987—; vice-chair dist. 1 Primary Care Clinician's and Practitioners, Phila., 1983-85; dir. Southeastern Pa. High Blood Pressure Control Program. Recipient award Am. Heart Assn., 1984. Mem. Healthcare Forum, Nat. Assn. for Female Execs. Home: 3582-2 Pheasant Run Circle Ann Arbor MI 48108 Office: U Mich Hosps N14A11 300 N Ingalls Ann Arbor MI 48109-0474

ELSNER, CARLENE W., reproductive endocrinologist; b. Columbus, Ga., Mar. 21, 1947; d. Guy Karn and Frances (Willis) Willison; m. William Elsner, Dec. 9, 1972; children: Heather Elizabeth, Ashley Melissa. BS, U. Ga., 1966; MD, Med. Coll. Ga., 1970. Diplomate Am. Bd. Ob-gyn, Am. Bd. Reproductive Endocrinology. Intern ETMH, Augusta, Ga., 1970-71; fellow reprodn. biology U. Pa., Phila., 1973-74; resident ob-gyn U. Fla., Gainesville, 1971-75; instr. dept. ob-gyn Bowman Gray Med. Sch., Winston-Salem, N.C., 1975-77; fellow reproductive endocrinology UCLA-HARBOR, Torrance, Calif., 1977-79; practice medicine specializing in reproductive endocrinology Atlanta, 1979-83, Atlanta, 1984—; cons. in-vitro fertilization Reproductive Biology Assocs., Atlanta, 1985—. Contbr. articles to profl. jours. Fellow Am. Coll. Ob-gyn; mem. Soc. Reproductive Endocrinologists (charter), Am. Fertility Soc., Atlanta Ob-gyn Soc. Office: 3895 Fairfax Ct Atlanta GA 31901 Office: 993 D Johnson Ferry Rd Atlanta GA 30342

ELSTIEN, CYNTHIA FERRARA, human resources executive; b. Chgo., Mar. 31, 1948; d. Robert Joseph and Saretta (DeSalvo) F.; m. Morris Joseph Elstien, July 24, 1980. Student No. Ill. U., 1966-69, Ins. Sch. Chgo., 1975-76. Claims examiner Lynn Ins. Group or Universal Underwriters, Des Plaines, Ill., 1966-71; sec., v.p. mfg. Stenographic Machines, Skokie, Ill., 1971—; v.p. human resources Fred S. James & Co. of Ill., Chgo., 1971—. Campaign worker for candidate for state's atty. 1972. Mem. Soc. Personnel Adminstrs. (v.p. programs Chgo. 1982-83 treas. 1983—), Soc. Human Resource Profls. Chgo. (pres. 1987, treas. 1982-83, v.p. programs 1982), Ins. Personnel Council (pres. Chgo. 1982), Internat. Platform Assn. Roman Catholic. Club: East Bank (Chgo.). Home: 327 Hambletonian Dr Oak Brook IL 60521 Office: Fred S James & Co Ill 230 W Monroe St Chicago IL 60606

ELTING, LINDA STERRETT, epidemiologist; b. Houston, Feb. 10, 1951; d. Sam L. and Mary Sue (Warrick) Sterrett; m. Phil H. Elting Jr., April 4, 1981; children: M. Kathleen, Scott P. BS in Nursing, Houston Bapt. U., 1974; MPH, U. Tex., 1981, D of Pub. Health, 1988. RN, Tex. Educator health Harris County Ctr. for the Retarded, Houston, 1974-75; staff nurse Herman Hosp., Houston, 1975-76; research project coordinator U. Tex. System Cancer Ctr., M.D. Anderson Hosp. & Tumor Inst., Houston, 1976—; educator, cons. ednl. film Pharm. Industry, 1981—; dir. research activities section infectious disease UTSCC-MDAH, Houston, 1982—, dir. program in research, mgr. infectious disease data base system, 1984—. Contbr. articles to sci. and med. jours. Youth advisor Ragnot Sailing Assn., Houston, 1985—. Mem. AAAS, Am. Assn. Med. Systems and Informatics, Assn. Practitioners in Infection Control (cert.), MUMPS User's Group, Sigma Xi. Club: Houston Yacht (youth advisor 1985—). Office: UTSCC MDAH #47 1515 Holcombe Houston TX 77030

ELVIDGE, VIVIAN PATRICIA, mus. dir.; b. Okanogan, Wash., Jan. 6, 1940; d. Floyd Kenneth and Martha Grace (Hinshaw) Byrd; A.B., Bellevue Community Coll., 1974; B.A. cum laude in Anthropology, U. Wash., 1977, M.A. cum laude in Anthropology, 1980; m. Robert Fred Elvidge, Dec. 26, 1962; 1 dau., Janice April. Vol. coordinator Marymoor Mus., Redmond, Wash., 1979, curator, 1978-80, dir., 1980—. Mem. Am. Assn. of Mus., Wash. Mus. Assn., Am. Assn. for State and Local History, Phi Beta Kappa. Methodist. Author: Redmond Historic Tour Guide, 1981; Report on Collections, Marymoor Mus.: Lace Collection, 1979, Indian Artifacts, 1978; Eastside Historic Resource Guide, 1982. Co-editor: Eastside Historic Color Book, 1985. Home: 17511 Avondale Rd Woodinville WA 98072 Office: PO Box 162 6046 W Lake Sammamish Pkwy Redmond WA 98073

ELVIG, MERRYWAYNE, real estate manager; b. Anoka, Minn., Jan. 16, 1931; d. Wayne Leroy and Erma Lou (Greenwald) Ridge; m. Donald Keith Elvig, June 15, 1955 (div. 1972); children: Amy, David. AA, Cottey Jr. Coll., 1951; BS, U. Minn., 1953. Tchr. Anoka Hennepin Sch. Dist., Anoka, 1953-56; with med. records div. East Main Clinic, Anoka, 1972-78; real estate mgr. Skurdal Properties, Anoka, 1978-79; mgr. Belma Properties, Anoka, 1986—, Bridge Ct. Bldg. Complex, Anoka, 1987—; owner, mgr. ABC Travel, Anoka, 1979—. Commr. Housing Redevel. Authority, Anoka 1978, chmn., 1984—; bd. dirs. Walker Sr. Housing Corp., Anoka, 1986—; treas. Anoka Devel. Corp., 1986—; charter and life mem. aux. Mercy Med. Ctr., Coon Rapids, Minn., 1965—, bd. dirs., 1965-71; moderator 1st Congl. Ch., Anoka, 1984-86; mem. Greehaven Study Com., Anoka. 1986—; vol. Anoka Girl Scout Council, 1963-65; chmn. Am. Cancer Drive, 1962-65. Mem. Am. Soc. Travel Agts. (bd. dirs. 1986—), Assn. Retail Travel Agts., Minn. Exec. Women in Tourism, Internat. Fedn. Women's Orgns., Anoka Landowner's Assn., Anoka Area C. of C. (pres. 1985). Republican. Clubs: Greenhaven Women's Golf (Anoka) (pres. 1987—). Lodges: Philanthropic Ednl. Orgn. Sisterhood (pres. 1966-68), Philolectian (pres. 1965-67). Home: 1933 Cressy Ave Anoka MN 55303 Office: ABC Travel 102 E Main St Anoka MN 55303

ELWELL, ELLEN C., sales training and marketing promotions executive, instructional design and marketing promotions consultant; b. Jacksonville, Fla.; d. Merrill K. and Hermine (Chalfin) Cohen; B.A., U. Mich., 1967; M.A., N.Y.U., U. Ill., 1968; m. John Lee Elwell, Feb. 10, 1968; 1 dau., Melissa Mae. Advanced mktg. support rep. IBM, Oklahoma City, 1969-73, program planner/designer sales tng. programs, Dallas, St. Louis, 1973-79; owner, operator Elwell Assos., Inc., Dallas and St. Louis, [illegible]; dir. Indpl. Catering Co., Indpls., A. Rose Prodns., Crystal Services Inc., St. Louis. Recipient Outstanding Contbn. award IBM, 1976, Notable Women of Tex. award. Mem. Am. Soc. Tng. and Devel., Am. Soc. Profl. Cons., Am. Mgmt. Assn. Author numerous corp. tng. books, 1976—. Office: 8140 Walnut Hill Ln #101 Dallas TX 75231 Office: 1231 Hanley Industrial Park Saint Louis MO 63144

ELWOOD-AKERS, VIRGINIA EDYTHE, university librarian; b. Los Angeles, Nov. 9, 1938; d. George Henry and Eileen Edythe (Kelterer) Elwood; m. Roy S. Akers, Apr. 12, 1980. B.A., UCLA, 1964; M.L.S., U. Oreg., 1972; M.A., Calif. State U.-Northridge, 1981. Editor, UCLA, 1970-71, writer, 1971-72; librarian Calif. State U., Northridge, 1972—, univ. archivist, 1972—. Author: (bibliography) Media Image of Women, 1975, Women Correspondents in Vietnam War, 1988. Mem. Soc. Calif. Archivists, Nat. Women Studies Assn., Calif. Women in Higher Edn. (chmn. 1981-82), Calif. State U. Librarians (chmn. 1984). Democrat. Episcopalian. Office: Calif State Univ-Northridge Library 18111 Nordhoff St Northridge CA 91344

ELY, MARICA MCCANN, interior designer; b. Pachuca, Mex., May 2, 1907 (parents Am. citizens); d. Warner and Mary Evans (Cook) McCann; m. Northcutt Ely, Dec. 2, 1931; children—Michael and Craig (twins), Parry Haines. B.A., U. Calif.-Berkeley, 1929; diploma Pratt Inst. of Art, N.Y.C., 1931. Free-lance interior designer, Washington and Redlands, Calif., 1931—; lectr. on flower arranging and fgn. travel, 1931—; prof. Sogetsu Ikebana Sch., Tokyo, 1972. Art editor (calendar) Nat. Capital Garden Club League, 1957-58. Pres. Kenwood Garden Club, Md.; bd. dirs. Nat. Library Blind, Washington; v.p. bd. dirs. Washington Hearing and Speech Soc., 1969; co-founder Delta Gamma Found. Pre-Sch. Blind Children, Washington. Finalist Nat. Silver Bowl Competition, Jackson-Perkins Co., 1966; garden shown on nat. tour Am. Hort. Soc., 1985. Mem. Calif. Arboretum Found., Redlands Hort. and Improvement Soc. (bd. dirs. 1982—), Yucaipa Valley Garden Club, Town and Country African Violet Soc., Hemerocallis Soc., Delta Gamma. Clubs: Redlands Country (Calif.); Washington, Chevy Chase (Washington); Berkeley Tennis (Calif.).

EMA, MIHOKO, transportation executive, translator; b. Tokyo, Mar. 29, 1939; came to U.S., 1962; d. Masashi Onoda and Shoko Ema; widowed; children: Andrew Woitschek, Odette Woitschek. Diploma in lang., Keio U., Tokyo, 1957. Certified travel counselor. Flight attendant Japan Airlines, Air France, Tokyo, Paris, 1957-61; ground hostess Military Air Transport, Wake Island, Pacific Ocean, 1962-64; pres. Travel Planners, New Orleans, 1975—. Translator: Bell of Amherst (Emily Dickinson) 1964. Mem. Inst. Cert. Travel Agents, Am. Soc. Travel Agts. Office: Travel Planners 110 Concourse One Shell Sq New Orleans LA 70139

EMANUEL, DIANE MARIE, labor relations executive; b. Mpls., Apr. 17, 1947; d. Clinton David and Muriel Ruth (Jensen) Gustafson; m. Bruce A. Bakke, June 29, 1967 (div.); 1 son, Brian Allen; m. David Harris Emanuel, Jan. 28, 1978; 1 son, Frederick Paul. Cert. profl. in human resource. Student U. Minn., 1973-77, North Tex. State U., 1978-79, 85; A.A., A.S., Tarrant County Jr. Coll., 1984. Personnel mgr. ITT Thermotech, Hopkins, Minn., 1967-77; mgr. employment and equal opportunity Fingerhut Corp., Minnetonka, Minn., 1977-78; personnel mgr. Automatic Data Processing, Dallas, 1978-79; compensation adminstr. Sky Chefs, Arlington, Tex., 1979-81, employee relations specialist, 1981-83, mgr. labor relations, 1983—; cons. Assoc. Clerical Specialist, Mpls., 1976-78. Editor: Fingerprints, 1977-78, ITT Thermotech News, 1970-77, ADP News, 1978-79. Dir. concessions Coppell Pee Wee Football Assn. (Tex.), 1983-85; den leader Coppell council Boy Scouts Am., 1982, asst. den leader Webelos, 1983; campaign chmn. City Council election campaign City of Coppell, 1983. Mem. Am. Soc. Personnel Adminstrn., Twin City Personnel Assn., Dallas Personnel Assn., Mid-Cities Personnel Assn., Nat. Assn. Female Execs. Home: 541 Rolling Hills Rd Coppell TX 75019 Office: Sky Chefs Dallas-Fort Worth Airport PO Box 619777 Dallas TX 75261

EMEK, SHARON HELENE, business consultant; b. Bklyn., Oct. 23, 1945; d. Hyman Sampson and Cynthia Gertrude (Roth) Rabinowitz; children—Aleeza Judith, Joshua Michael, Elana Yael. B.A., CCNY, 1967; M.A., Bklyn. Coll., 1970; Ed.D., Rutgers U., 1977. Dir. preliminary program for small coll. Bklyn. Coll., 1969-71, 73-74; dir. Am. Ctr. Reading Skills, Tel Aviv, 1972; asst. prof. Brookdale Community Coll., Lincroft, N.J., 1975-77, Rutgers U., New Brunswick, N.J., 1977-82; v.p. Radzik & Emek, Princeton, N.J., 1980—; speaker profl. meetings. Author (with Adam Radzik): Answers For Managers, 1986; Dealing Successfully with Key Management Issues, 1986. Contbr. articles to profl. jours. Recipient Promising Research award Nat. Council Tchrs. of English, 1978. Mem. Am. Mgmt. Assn., Am. Cons. League. Avocations: writing; reading; jogging; tennis; travel. Office: Radzik & Emek PO Box 7185 Princeton NJ 08543

EMERSON, ALICE FREY, college president; b. Durham, N.C., Oct. 26, 1931; d. Alexander Hamilton and Alice (Hubbard) Frey; divorced; children: Rebecca, Peter. A.B., Vassar Coll., 1953; Ph.D., Bryn Mawr Coll., 1964. Tchr., Newton (Mass.) High Sch., 1956-58; mem. faculty Bryn Mawr (Pa.) Coll., 1961-64; mem. faculty U. Pa., Phila., 1966-75, asst. prof. polit. sci., 1966-75, dean of women, 1966-69, dean of students, 1969-75; pres. Wheaton Coll., Norton, Mass., 1975—; dir. Bank of Boston Corp., First Nat. Bank of Boston; trustee Penn Mut. Life Ins. Co.; adv. bd. HERS Mid-America. Mem. adv. bd. Com. for Nat. Security, 1982—; bd. dirs. Corp. for Public/Pvt. Ventures, 1978-82, 86—, World Resources Inst., 1987—; pres. Sturdy Meml. Hosp., 1977—; mem. Mayor's Adv. Bd., Attleboro, Mass., 1984—; mem. Ind. Sector Research Com., 1985—; mem. adv. bd. Great Woods Ednl. Forum, 1987—. Mem. Am. Polit. Sci. Assn., AAUP, Am. Council Edn. (commn. on leadership devel. 1979-82, com. on collegiate athletics 1979—, nominating com. 1980-82), Assn. Am. Colls. (dir. 1984—), Council Fgn. Relations. Home: 28 E Main St Norton MA 02766 Office: Wheaton Coll Office of Pres Norton MA 02766

EMERSON, ANN PARKER, dietitian; b. Twin Lakes, Fla., Dec. 3, 1925; d. Charles Dendy and Gladys Agnes (Chalker) Parker; B.S., Fla. State U., 1947; M.S., U. Fla., 1968; m. Donald McGeachy Emerson, Sept. 22, 1950; children—Mary Ann, Donald McGeachy, Charles Parker, William John. Research dietitian U. Chgo., 1948-50; adminstrv. research dietitian U. Fla. Coll. Medicine, Gainesville, 1962-68, dir. dietetic edn., 1968-74, dir. dietetic internship program, 1968-75, dir. program in clin. and community dietetics, 1974-83; mem. Commn. on Dietetic Registration, 1974-77, Commn. on Accreditation, 1980-83. Pres., Gainesville chpt. Altrusa, Internat., 1977-78. VA Allied Health Manpower grantee, 1974-81; HEW Allied Health Manpower grantee, 1975-78, 78-81. Mem. Am., Fla. dietetic assns. Democrat. Roman Catholic. Club: Jr. League (Gainesville). Office: PO Box J-184 JHMHC Gainesville FL 32610

EMERSON, DOROTHY, home economist; b. Waltham, Mass.; d. Philip and M. Evelyn (Dewey) E.; grad. with honors in home econs. Framingham State Tchrs. Coll.; summer study Dartmouth Coll., Columbia U., Amherst. Tchr., Boston Public Schs., Kimball Union Acad. Urban home demonstration agt., Portsmouth, N.H.; county club agt. Sussex County, Del.; prof., asso. state 4-H Club agt. Md. Extension Service, 1923-61, now extension prof. emeritus; now cons. citizenship-leadership div. Nat. 4-H Council, also lectr. on 4-H Club work. Mem. Pen Women, Delta Kappa Gamma (hon.), Epsilon Sigma Phi (Ruby award 1975) Phi Kappa Phi. Author: Scrapbook, 1966; also articles.

EMERSON, JUDI LOEWEN, social worker; b. Los Angeles, Aug. 11, 1946; d. Wallace and Esther (Hiebert) Loewen; m. Ted Ross Emerson, May 23, 1976; children—Travis, Ashley. M. Social Work, U. Kans., 1976; B.S. summa cum laude, McPherson Coll., 1974. Cert. social worker, 1978. Social worker Topeka State Hosp., Kans., 1974-76, Kans. Children's Service League, Wichita, 1976-78; supr. State of Kans., Wichita, 1978-80; cons., edn. specialist S. Central Mental Health Ctr., El Dorado, Kans., 1980-82; cons. Rainbow Day Care, Hutchinson, Kans., 1982-84; cons., edn. coordinator Horizons Mental Health Ctr., Hutchinson, Kans., 1985—; co-chmn. edn. com. Kans. Commn. to Prevent Child Abuse, 1976-78. Treas., United Methodist Women, Nickerson, 1985; bd. dirs. Big Sisters, 1983, Arts

Council, 1983, Grant County United Way, 1976-78; mem. Hutchinson Symphony Guild, 1986—. Mem. Acad. Cert. Social Workers, Butler County Assn. to Counter Abuse (charter), PEO. Clubs: Idona Women's (pres. 1985-86), Mother's (pres. 1982-83). Avocation: tennis, piano. Home: Box 7 Nickerson KS 67561

EMERSON, NITA M., transportation company executive; b. Yuma, Colo., Dec. 25, 1947; d. Charles Allen and Wilma Mary (Rudnik) Romine; m. Carl Emerson, Oct. 7, 1967 (div. Mar. 1969). BS, Met. State Coll., 1972. Bookkeeper Mizel Devel. Corp., Denver, 1973-74; mgr. acctg. Bus. Mgmt. Assocs., Denver, 1974-76; jr. acct. Regional Transp. Dist., Denver, 1976, acct. grants, 1976-77, budget planner, 1977-80, asst. mgr. budget, 1980-83, mgr. budget, 1983—; pres. Fin. Applications, Inc., Denver, 1982—, fin. planning intern Fin. Architects, Inc., 1988—. Mem. Nat. Assn. for Neuro-Linguistic Programmers, Govt. Fin. Officer's Assn., Nat. Assn. for Female Execs. Mem. Ch. Religious Sci. Office: Regional Transp Dist 1600 Blake Denver CO 80202

EMERY, LIN, sculptor; b. N.Y.C.; d. Cornell and Jean (Weill) E.; m. Shirley Brooks Braselman, Aug. 17, 1962, 1 child, Brooks. Certificat, Sorbonne U., Paris, 1949; studies with Ossip Zadkine, Paris, 1949-50. Vis. critic architecture Tulane U., New Orleans, 1969-70; vis. artist Newcomb Sch. Art, New Orleans, 1980; lectr., vis. artist various including U. Tex., Ga. Coll., Art Acad. Cin., U. New Orleans, LaGrange Coll., 1980-86; adv. New Orleans Art com., 1987-88, Nat. Sculpture Conf.: Works by Women, Cin., 1986-87; chair studio sessions Coll. Art Assn., N.Y.C., 1979, conf. Nat. Sculpture Ctr., Lawrence, Kans., 1976. Prin. works include meml. column, fountain New Orleans Civic Ctr., 1966, 70, kinetic sculptures Lawrence Civic Ctr., 1982, fed. bldg. Houma, La., 1977, state library, Baton Rouge, 1982, various pub., corp. commns. Singapore, Chgo., Anchorage, Washington; one-woman shows include New Orleans Mus. Art, 1962, 64, Sculpture Ctr., N.Y.C., 1962, 67, Tenn. Fine Arts Ctr., Nashville, 1962, Mus. N.Mex., Santa Fe, 1966, Centennial Art Mus., Corpus Christi, Tex., 1967, Lauren Rogers Mus., Laurel, Miss., 1977, Hunter Mus., Chattanooga, 1985; solo gallery exhibits Max Hutchinson, Kouros, N.Y.C., Arthur Roger, New Orleans. Va. Ctr. Creative Art fellow, 1981; recipient mayor's award City of New Orleans, 1980, "Sweet-art" award Contemporary Arts Ctr., New Orleans, 1987; named Woman of Achievement State of La., 1984. Mem. Internat. Sculpture Ctr. (bd. dirs. 1973-79), Sculptors Guild. Democrat. Home: 7520 Dominican St New Orleans LA 70118

EMERY, MARCIA ROSE, parapsychologist; b. Phila., Mar. 19, 1937; d. David Joshua and Naomi (Carner) Rose; B.A. in Psychology, Adelphi U., Garden City, N.Y., 1958; M.S. in Clin. Psychology, CCNY, 1960; M.A. in Social Psychology, New Sch. Social Research, 1964, Ph.D., 1968; m. Gordon M. Becker, 1970 (div.); m. 2d, James D. Emery, 1982; stepchildren—Stephen, Alicia, Jamie. Research asst. Office Instl. Research, Hunter Coll., N.Y.C., 1959-62, Community Service Soc., N.Y.C., 1962-65; lectr. psychology Hunter Coll., 1965-67; assoc. prof. psychology, chmn. M.A. program in community psychology Fed. City Coll., Washington, 1968-74; ind. practice psychology and astrological counseling, Hollywood, Fla., 1981—; pres. Intuitive Mgmt. Cons. Corp.; adj. faculty Aquinas Coll., Grand Rapids; psychologist Renaissance Revitalization Center, Nassau, Bahamas, 1975; lectr., coordinator counseling Coll. Bahamas, 1976-80; condr. workshops in parapsychology throughout U.S. Author: Developing Your Intuition: A Beginner's Guide; Manage Intuitively to Improve Decision Making and Problem Solving. Grantee NIMH, 1972. Mem. Am. Psychol. Assn., Assn. Humanistic Psychology, Parapsychol. Assn., Spiritual Frontiers Fellowship, Am. Soc. Psychical Research, Am. Fedn. Astrology, Assn. Past Life Research and Therapy. Mem. Unity Ch. Address: 3512 McCoy SE Grand Rapids MI 49506

EMERY, PRISCILLA, infosystems planner; b. Bronx, N.Y., Oct. 7, 1952; d. Ismael Quintero and Aura Emma (Caban) Quintero Ravitch; m. Carmine Alfred Lanni, Oct. 7, 1973 (div. 1979); 1 child, John Victor; m. Louie Douglas Emery, Aug. 13, 1982. BA in Math., CUNY, 1974. Sr. tech. assoc. Bell Telephone Labs., Piscataway, N.J., 1974-76; analyst-programmer, tng. coordinator Blue Cross-Blue Shield of Va., Richmond, 1976-79; tng. coordinator Frito-Lay Corp., Dallas, 1979; sr. corp. systems planner Combustion Engring. Co., Stamford, Conn., 1979-85; tech. planning mgr. Primerica (formerly Am. Can Co.), Greenwich, Conn., 1985—. Contbr. articles to profl. publs. Mem. Nat. Assn. Female Execs., Four-Phase Users' Assn. (pres. N.E. region 1983-84). Democrat. Office: Primerica American Ln Greenwich CT 06836

EMERY, SUE, editor, owner bridge studio; b. Wichita County, Tex., Feb. 23, 1920; d. Billy J. and Trula V. (Mayfield) McHam; m. Horace B. Camp (div. 1958); children: Ann Camp McGrath, Connie Camp Parvin, Billy Brit; m. John Walter Emery (dec. 1972). B.A., Harding Coll., 1939. Tchr. 1939-40; with U.S. Civil Service, 1941-45; reporter Wichita Daily Times, Tex., 1945-46; independent bridge club owner-operato, freelance tournament dir., daily bull. editor; editor Am. Contract Bridge League Bridge Bull., Memphis, 1972—; staff mem. Tex. Bridge Mag., 1960's. Author, researcher: No Passing Fancy, 1977. Contbr. articles to mags. Active Womanpower for Eisenhower, 1950's, Democrats for Eisenhower, Tex., 1950's. Home: 1565 Hayne Rd Memphis TN 38119 Office: The Contract Bridge Bulletin Box 161192 Memphis TN 38186

EMILITA, MARIE BERNADETTE, advertising agency executive; b. Passic, N.J., Aug. 28, 1945; d. Chester J. and Sophia H. (Zawadzki) Lewandowski; m. Charles Peter Emilita, Dec. 19, 1970; 1 dau., Amy. B.A., Skidmore Coll., 1966. With J. Walter Thompson U.S.A., Inc., N.Y.C., 1966—, creative dir., 1979—, now sr. v.p. Home: 174 Terrace Ave Hasbrouck Heights NJ 07604 Office: J Walter Thompson USA Inc 466 Lexington Ave New York NY 10017 *

EMMEL, CAROL LYNN, infosystems specialist; b. Wausau, Wis., Apr. 23, 1958; d. Donald Le Roy and Verna Belle (Day) E. BS, Carroll Coll., 1980. Implementation specialist First Wis. Nat. Bank, Milw., 1980-84; fin. services officer M & I Data Services, Inc., Milw., 1984—. Vol. pub. broadcasting TV station auction, Milw. 1983—, Am. Lung Assn., Milw. 1982-86, Ronald McDonald House, Milw. 1985-86, Humane Animal Welfare Soc. Annual Bazaar, Waukesha, Wis., 1985—. Named one of Outstanding Young Women Am., 1983. Mem. Nat. Assn. Female Execs., Alpha Xi Delta (treas. 1982-83, v.p. 1983-85, pres. 1985-86). Republican. Lutheran. Home: 14053 W Tiffany Pl New Berlin WI 53151

EMMERICH, JO ANN, broadcasting executive; b. St. Louis, Sept. 1; d. William K. and Leora M. (Wolff) E. B.A., Catholic U. Am., 1964, M.A., 1971. Drama specialist Dept. State, Europe and Middle East, 1965-66; exec. staff Olney Theatre (Md.), 1967-68; agt. TV dept. Internat. Famous Agy., N.Y.C., 1972-75; asst. producer As the World Turns, CBS, N.Y.C., 1975-76; mgr. daytime programming ABC, N.Y.C., 1976-77, dir. daytime programming, 1977-80, v.p. daytime programs East Coast, 1980-86, v.p. daytime programs, 1986—. Mem. Am. Film Inst., Nat. Acad. TV Arts and Scis. Office: Capital Cities/ABC Inc 1330 Ave of the Americas New York NY 10019

EMMONS, CAROL ANN, mortgage banker; b. Jersey City; d. Max and Dorothy (Peters) Leuck; student El Camino Jr. Coll., Torrance, Calif., 1960-61, Dutchess Community Coll., 1974-75, D'Youville Coll., 1977-81, various courses SUNY, Buffalo, and Dale Carnegie; children—Linda, Conrad, Rodney. Mortgage adminstr., asst. br. mgr. Soc. for Savs., Hartford, Conn., 1965-75; asst. br. mgr. Reliance Equities, Inc., Poughkeepsie, N.Y., 1975-76, br. mgr., Buffalo, 1976-80, asst. v.p., 1980, pres., dir., Buffalo, 1981-83; sr. v.p. Comfed Mortgage Co., Lowell, Mass., 1983-86; v.p. Freedom Fin. Corp., Glastonbury, Conn., 1986—. Nat. Mortgage Banking Corp. Bus. adv. bd. High Sch. Students. Notary public. Mem. Mortgage Bankers Assn. Western N.Y. (pres. 1981), Conn. Mortgage Bankers Assn. (dir.), Greater Buffalo Bd. Realtors, Nat. Assn. Female Execs., Conn. Small Bus. Enterprises, Better Bus. Bur., Buffalo C. of C., Center for Women in Mgmt. of D'Youville Coll., Women for Downtown Buffalo. Office: 78 Eastern Blvd Glastonbury CT 06033

EMMONS, JUDITH CRANE, cleaning company franchise executive; b. Boston, Sept. 17, 1954; d. John Grimes and Marjorie Marie (Coughlin) E. BA, Boston Coll., 1972-76. Elem., special edn. tchr. Rogers-Pierce Children's Ctr., Arlington, Mass., 1976-81; pres. Servicemaster of North Shore Inc., Lynn, Mass., 1981—. Bd. dirs. Rogers-Pierce Children's Ctr., 1979-81, Somerville (Mass.) Council Children. Mem. Nat. Assn. Female Execs., North Shore Women Bus., Boston Coll. Alumni Assn. (alumni advisor 1980—). Roman Catholic. Home: 43 Timson St Lynn MA 01902 Office: Servicemaster of North Shore Inc PO Box 292 West Lynn MA 01905

EMMONS, LINDA NYE, state legislator; b. Ridgewood, N.J., July 8, 1937; d. Drake and Helen N. Pinkney; A.A., Centenary Coll. Women, Hackettstown, N.J., 1957; B.A., Conn. Coll., 1972; m. Richard L. Emmons, Dec. 13, 1958; children—Mark Richard, Dwight Nye. Staff asst. AT&T Co., 1957-61; self-employed accountant, 1975—; mem. Conn. Ho. of Reps. from 101st Dist., 1977—, mem. com. on revenue, bonding and fin., 1977-81, 83—, house chmn., 1985-87, mem. com. on appropriations, 1981-83, ranking mem., 1981-85, asst. minority leader for fiscal affairs; mem. Conn. Bond Commn. Mem. Madison (Conn.) Charter Commn., 1967-69, Madison Republican Town Com., 1970-77; chmn. Madison Bd. Fin., 1977-79; bd. dirs. E.C. Scranton Meml. Library, 1973—. Mem. Order Women Legislators, LWV (voters service chmn. 1968-69). Address: 111 Yankee Peddler Path Madison CT 06443

EMO, DRETHA MARY, nurse; b. Rochester, N.Y., May 28, 1943; d. George Vincent and Lelia Cecelia (Betts) E. BS in Edn., SUNY, Geneseo, 1965; MA in Geography, Ariz. State U., 1976, BS in Nursing, 1979, BS in Sociology, 1983; MS in Nursing, U. Tex., 1983. Tchr. pub. schs., various locations, 1966-69, Casa Grande Elem. Sch., Ariz., 1972-74; med. surg. nurse Scottsdale Meml. Hosp., Ariz., 1980; psychiat. nurse Samaritan Health Services, Phoenix, 1982; unit nursing supr. Austin State Hosp., Tex., 1986; cons. nursing services Healthcare Rehab. Ctr., Austin, 1986—; pres. Electric Therapeutic & Recreational Enterprises, Austin, 1986—; researcher on elderly Am. Scandinavian Found./Danish Nurses Orgn., Copenhagen, 1981; vol. Vista, Gallup, N.Mex., 1965-66. Contbr. articles to profl. jours. Served to capt. U.S. Army, 1969-72, lt. col. Res. Marshall fellow to Denmark, 1981; decorated Army Commendation medals (2). Mem. Assn. Mil. Surgeons of U.S., Res. Officers Assn., DAV, U.S. Horse Cavalry Assn., Nat. Assn. Female Execs., Am. Assn. for History of Nursing, Sierra Club, Sigma Theta Tau. Office: Eclectic Therapeutic & Recreational Enterprises PO Box 43846 Austin TX 78745

EMRICH, SAMUELLA DINGLEY, medical device company executive; b. Indpls., Aug. 1, 1933; d. Bert and Julia Catherine (Fitzsimons) Dingley; m. Carl Wallace Emrich; children: Cindy Hamn, Julie Walrath, Andrew, Lisa Hasbrouck, Jenie, Dan. BA, St. Mary of the Woods Coll., 1955. Microbiologist Eli Lilly & Co., Indpls., 1955-58; virologist Pitman-Moore subs. Dow Chem., Zionsville, Ind., 1964-70, Pitman-Moore subs. Johnson & Johnson, Washington Crossing, N.J., 1970-72; lab supr. Baxter Travenol, Mountain Home, Ark., 1973-76; lab supt. Baxter Travenol, Round Lake, Ill., 1976-77; quality assurance mgr. Am. Hosp. Supply Co., Mt. Prospect, Ill., 1977-79; dir. quality assurance Valley Lab. Inc., Boulder, Colo., 1979-81; v.p. quality assurance and regulatory affairs Staodynamics Inc., Longmont, Colo., 1981—; med. regulatory cons., 1978—. Vol. campaign leader United Way Boulder County, Colo., 1985-87. Mem. Am. Soc. Quality Control, Inst. Environ. Scis. (sr.), Assn. Bus. and Profl. Women, Nat. Assn. Female Execs. Lodge: Rotary. Office: Staodynamics Inc 1225 Florida Ave Longmont CO 80501

ENDELMAN, SHARON JEAN, librarian; b. Detroit, Apr. 11, 1948; d. Clarence Richard and Elsa Albertina (Beutler) Bice; m. Gary Edward Endelman, June 3, 1973; children: Heather Miriam (dec.), Jonathan Charles. BA in History, Kalamazoo Coll., 1970; MA in History, Brown U., 1972, PhD in History, 1976; MLS, Emory U., 1980. Teaching fellow in history Brown U., Providence, 1974-75; asst. prof. history Paine Coll., Augusta, Ga., 1976-79; asst. archivist Houston Pub. Library, 1979-80, social scis. librarian, 1980, coordinator materials selection, 1985—; serial records librarian U. Houston, 1980-82, head current jours. dept., 1982-83, head reference dept., 1983-85; research advisor Houston Women's History Project, 1985—; mem. collection devel. com. Houston Area Research Library Consortium, 1985—. Contbr. articles to profl. jours. Mem. Parents' Support Group Nat. Sudden Infant Death Syndrome Found., Houston, 1987. Recipient fellowship U.S. Dept. Def., 1971-74. Mem. ALA (standards and guidelines com. reference and adult services div. 1983-86), Serial Forum (vice chair, chair 1983-85), Assn. Research Libraries (steering com. collection analysis project at U. Houston 1983-85), Alpha Lambda Delta, Phi Beta Kappa, Beta Phi Mu. Democrat. Home: 5714 Cerritos Houston TX 77035 Office: Houston Pub Library 500 McKinney Houston TX 77002

ENDER, ELMA TERESA SALINAS, judge; b. Laredo, Tex., Aug. 11, 1953; d. Oscar D. and Elma (Lopez) Salinas; m. David Allen Ender. B in Acctg., U. Tex., 1974; postgrad., Bates Sch. Law, Mexico, 1977; JD, St. Mary's U., 1978. Bar: Tex., 1978, U.S. Dist. Ct. (so. dist.) Tex., 1979, U.S. Ct. Appeals (5th cir.) 1981, U.S. Dist. Ct. (we. dist.) Tex., 1983. Acct. Samuel Kowalsky, CPA, 1974-75; assoc. Fansler, Reese, Palacios & Alvarado, 1979-81; ptnr. Alvarado & Salinas, 1981-82, Alvarado, Salinas & Barto, 1983; judge 341st Dist. Ct., Laredo, 1983—; instr. bus. law Laredo State U., 1981-82; chmn. Webb County Juvenile Bd., 1984-86, Webb-Zapata Adult Probation Bd., 1986—, Webb County Bail Bond Bd., 1986—; faculty regional confs., mem. juvenile justice com. Tex. Ctr. for Judiciary, Inc., Austin, Tex., 1986; mem. gov.'s com Juvenile Detention Standards Task Force, Austin, 1986. Chair rules and regulation com. Webb County Dem. Party, 1980; mem. steering com. Tex. Women's Polit. Caucus, 1980; vol. United Fund, 1981, Fiesta Caceria, 1981, Borderfest, 1981-82, Heart Fair, 1982, Laredo Vol. Lawyers, Inc.; co-chair ticket dr. Laredo Philharm., 1982, chair, 1983; mem. Laredo Conv. & Visitors Bur., 1983-84, Laredo Alcoholism Treatment Ctr., 1983-84, San Martin de Porras Ch.; mem. adv. bd. Salvation Army, Laredo, 1983—; bd. dirs. Stop Child Abuse and Neglect, 1983, mem. adv. com., 1984—. Recipient recognition award Laredo Mexican-Am. C. of C., 1983; named one of Outstanding Young Women Am., 1982-85; named one of 12 outstanding women in community, Las Mujeres Orgn., 1984. Mem. ABA (taxation sect., jud. section), Tex. Bar Assn. (council "Women in the Law" sect. 1982-84, various sects.), Tex. Young Lawyers Assn. (com. on needs of Spanish-speaking persons 1979-81, chair future lawyers of Tex. com. 1980-82, legis. com. Laredo chpt. 1980-82, pres. Laredo chpt. 1981-82, bar rev. com. 1983-84), Laredo Bar Assn. (speakers com. 1979), Laredo Bus. and Profl. Women's Assn. (charter mem., v.p. 1983-84, Woman of Yr. award 1982), Laredo C. of C. (bd. dirs. 1983-84), Am. Heart Assn. (mem. Laredo div. Tex. affiliate 1981—, planned giving task force 1981-83), Las Damas de la Republica del Rio Grande (recording sec. 1981-82), Beta Sigma Phi (Lady of Yr. award Laredo chpt. 1984-85). Roman Catholic. Clubs: MAEMOC Social (hon.), Women's City (hon.). Office: 341st Dist Ct PO Box 1598 Laredo TX 78042

ENDERS, ALEXANDRA, electronics equipment executive; b. Milw., Aug. 16, 1946; d. Mark George and Elaine M. (Boivin) Snyder; m. Michael Enders, July 31, 1967 (div. Oct. 1972); children: Karen, Meredith. BS in Occupational Therapy, San Jose (Calif.) State U., 1973. Project mgr. Ctr. for Ind. Living, Berkeley, Calif., 1975-79; coordinator resource ctr. Rehab. Engring. Ctr., Children's Hosp. at Stanford, Palo Alto, Calif., 1978-83; Switzer research fellow Nat. Inst. Handicapped Research, Washington, 1984-85; program mgr. Electronic Industries Found., Washington, 1986—; mem. adv. bd. INTEX, San Antonio, 1984—, Southwest Research Inst., San Antonio, 1985—. Editor: Technology for Independent Living Source Book, 1984, Rehabilitation Technology Sourcebook, 1988; guest editor jour. Rehab. Tech. Rev., 1984-85; author jour. Archives of Phys. Medicine and Rehab., 1983; contbr. articles to prof. jours. Active Ptnrs. of the Ams. Rehab. com., San Francisco and Mexico City, 1983—, Arthritis Found. Pub. Edn. com., San Francisco, 1983, Tools for Living in the Community, Berkeley, San Francisco Bay area div. Community Health Info. Project, 1981-84, Job-Related Phys. Capacities project Ctr. for Design, Palo Alto, 1980, Let Go Life Experiences through Group Opportunity, Pacific Rehab. Hosp., Oakland, Calif., 1976-77. Mem. AAAS, Am. Congress Rehab. Medicine, Am. Occupational Therapy Assn. (registered occpuational therapist), Am. Soc. on Aging, Nat. Council on Aging, Occupational Therapy Assn. of Calif., Assn. for Advancement of Rehab. Tech., U.S.A. Toy Library Assn., World Fedn. Occupational Therapists, Phi Kappa Phi. Home: 2032 Belmont Rd NW Washington DC 20009 Office: Elec Industries Found 1901 Pennsylvania Ave NW Washington DC 20006

ENDO, SANDRA LYNN, marketing professional; b. Chgo., Oct. 4, 1955; d. Charles M. and Tomiko (Tanaka) E. BS in Edn., No. Ill. U., 1977. Cert. tchr., Ill. Supr. employee services Avon Products Inc., Morton Grove, Ill., 1977-79, supr. employment, 1979-80, supr. packaging unit, 1980-81, supr. compensation and benefits, 1981, mgr. packaging section, 1981-84, mgr. packaging, 1984—. Mem. Nat. Assn. Female Execs.

ENDOW, SHARYN ANNE, molecular genetics professor, research scientist; b. Hood River, Oreg., May 22, 1948; d. Sho Jr. and Aya (Noda) E. BA, Stanford U., 1970; MPh, Yale U., 1972, PhD, 1975. Asst. prof. Duke U., Durham, N.C., 1978-84, assoc. prof., 1984—; cons. NIEHS, Research Triangle Park, N.C., 1983-86, genetics study sect. NIH, Research Triangle Park, 1987. Author numerous papers on genetic research, 1972—. Recipient Basil O'Connor award March of Dimes Birth Defects Found., 1979-82, Research Career Devel. award NIH, 1982-87. Mem. Genetics Soc. Am., Sigma Xi. Home: 112 W Markham Ave Durham NC 27701

ENDSLEY, CAROLYN FRANCES, industrial nursing supervisor; b. Landess, Ind., Nov. 4, 1936; d. Francis Levi and Pauline Lucille (Foust) Franks; m. Rodger Malcolm Endsley, Apr. 15, 1972 (dec. 1979); 1 son, Rod Travis. R.N., Meth. Hosp.-Indpls., 1957; B.S. in Health Care Adminstrn., St. Joseph Coll., North Windham, Maine, 1986. R.N.; cert. spirometry technician, occupational health nurse, hearing conservationist. Charge nurse Marion Gen. Hosp., (Ind.), 1957-60, 67; sch. nurse Marion Coll., 1959-60; staff nurse Fisher Body, Inc., Marion, 1960-78, supr. med. dept., 1978—. Mem. Am. Occupational Health Nurses Assn., Mid Ind. Assn. Occupational Health Nurses (bd. dirs., v.p. 1979-83, pres. 1983-85), Ind. Assn. Occupational Health Nurses (com. chmn. 1983-86, bd. dirs. 1984-89, v.p. 1987-89, Nurse of Yr. award 1985), Ind. Acad. Occupational Nurses. Democrat. Club: Home Extension (treas. Fowlerton, Ind. 1978-80). Home: 4312 S Washington St Marion IN 46953 Office: Fisher Body Div GMC 2400 W 2d St Marion IN 46952

ENDYKE, DEBRA JOAN, marketing professional; b. Manchester, N.H., July 24, 1955; d. Paul Ronald and Theresa Joan (Smith) Cote; m. Michael Thomas Pidgeon, May 15, 1976 (div. Aug. 1984); m. Thomas Allen Endyke, Sept. 21, 1985. BS in Computer Sci., N.H. Coll., 1984. Mktg. specialist Bedford (N.H.) Computer Corp., 1981-84; sales and mktg. dir. electronic services program First Software Corp., Lawrence, Mass., 1984-86; account exec. Genesys Software Systems, Inc., Lawrence, 1986-87; group sales mgr. N.E. data communications div. Panasonic Co., Secaucus, N.J., 1987—; cons. data communications, ind., Derry, N.H., 1987—. Republican. Roman Catholic. Home: 77 Drew Rd Derry NH 03038 Office: 75 University Way Westwood MA 02090

ENG, ANNE CHIN, broadcast account executive; b. N.Y.C., Aug. 9, 1950; d. Fuen and Suit Fong (Mark) Eng; m. George Chin, June 28, 1978; 1 child, Lauren. A.A.S., Manhattan Community Coll., 1970; student Baruch Coll., 1972. Sales asst. AVCO Radio Sales, N.Y.C., 1972; asst., jr. media buyer R.D.R. Timebuying Services, N.Y.C., 1972-74; TV media buyer, planner Ogilvy & Mather Advt., N.Y.C., 1974-78; broadcast account exec. H.R. Television, N.Y.C., 1978-79, RKO TV Reps., N.Y.C., 1979-80, Petry TV, N.Y.C., 1980—. Avocations: Plate collecting; exercise; skiing. Office: Petry Television 3 E 54th St New York NY 10022

ENG, MABEL, film production manager; b. N.Y.C., Jan. 4, 1957; d. Michael Quon Ark and Kit Wah (Moy) E. BA in Communication Arts and Scis., Queens Coll., 1978. Sec. MCA Music, N.Y.C., 1978-79; adminstrv. asst. Panorama Records, N.Y.C., 1979-80; asst. to pres. William V. Levine Assocs., Inc., N.Y.C., 1980-81; sec. J. Walter Thompson, Inc., N.Y.C., 1981-83; program coordinator Sta. WNET-TV, N.Y.C., 1983-86; mgr. prodn. Dick Young Prodns., Ltd., N.Y.C., 1986—. Coordinator prodn. film Crack, 1987. Co-founder, mem. Agape Bapt. Ch., N.Y.C., 1985—. Democrat. Office: Dick Young Prodns Ltd 118 Riverside Dr New York NY 11426

ENG, MAMIE, librarian; b. Oceanside, N.Y., May 21, 1954; d. Yen Wah and Hong Lew (Lum) E. BA in History and Edn., Vassar Coll., 1976; MS in Library Sci., Columbia U., 1977, MA in Ednl. Psychology, 1979. Librarian adult services Henry Waldinger Meml. Library, Valley Stream, N.Y., 1979—. Mem. Am. Library Assn., N.Y. Library Assn., Nat. Librarians Assn., Nassau County Library Assn. (editor assn. newsletter 1985-88, div. pres. 1986-87), Internat. Reading Assn. (bd. dirs. Manhattan council 1985—). Office: Henry Waldinger Meml Library 60 Verona Pl Valley Stream NY 11582

ENGE, SUSAN RADOVICH, marketing executive; b. Thermopolis, Wyo., May 17, 1949; d. Kenneth Allen and Evelyn Mae (Grubbs) Radovich; m. Roby D. Enge, June 13, 1971; 1 child, K. Mark. BA cum laude, Washington U., 1971. With IBM, 1971—, administr. regional mktg. programs, 1979-81; mgr. systems engring. nat. fed. mktg. Rosslyn, Va., 1981-82; mgr. systems engring. Nat. Accounts div. Washington, 1982-83; mgr. mktg. 1984—. Home: 1104 Arctic Quill Rd Herndon VA 22070 Office: 6705 Rockledge Dr Bethesda MD 20817

ENGEBRETSON, MARY EVONE, librarian; b. Albert Lea, Minn., Apr. 9, 1947; d. Merel Harlan and Darlyne Geneva (Johnson) E.; B.A., Luther Coll., 1969; M.A., U. Denver, 1971; M.B.A., Ariz. State U., 1977. Head, bookmobile dept. Whatcom County Library, Bellingham, Wash., 1971-75; market research analyst Helene Curtis, Inc., Chgo., 1977-78; assoc. librarian U. Fla., Gainesville, 1978-85; head reference U. South Ala. Library, Mobile, 1985—. Mem. ALA, Ala. Library Assn., Spl. Library Assn. Home: 1601 Hillcrest Rd Apt 42 Mobile AL 36695 Office: U South Ala Reference Dept Mobile AL 36688

ENGEL, IVY ANNE, radiologist, educator; b. N.Y.C., Sept. 16, 1950; d. Stanley Morton and Mildred (Cassel) E.; m. Mark Edward Jacobs, June 9, 1977. B.A., Queens Coll., Flushing, N.Y., 1973; M.D., N.Y. Med. Coll., Valhalla, 1977. Diplomate Am. Bd. Diagnostic Radiology. Intern Stamford Hosp. (Conn.), 1977-78; resident in diagnostic radiology N.Y. Hosp., N.Y.C., 1978-81, fellow in radiology, 1981-82, instr. diagnostic radiology, 1982-83, asst. prof., 1983-84; asst. prof. NYU Med. Ctr., N.Y.C., 1984-85; with L.I. Diagnostic Imaging, Stony Brook, N.Y., 1986-87 ; with Little Neck (N.Y.) Radiology, 1987—. Contbr. articles to profl. jours. Mem. Radiol. Soc. N.Am., Am. Coll. Radiology, Am. Roentgen Ray Soc., N.Y. Roentgen Ray Soc., Phi Beta Kappa. Office: Little Neck Radiology 55-15 Little Neck Pkwy Little Neck NY 11363

ENGEL-ARIELI, SUSAN LEE, physician; b. Chgo., Oct. 7, 1954; d. Thaddeus S. Dziengiel and Marian L. (Carpenter) Kasper; m. Udi Arieli. BA, Northwestern U., 1975; MD, Chgo. Med. Sch., 1982. Med. technician G.D. Searle, Skokie, Ill., 1972, 73, assoc. dir., 1983-84, dir., 1984-86; research editorial asst. U. Chgo., 1974; research assoc. Loyola U., Maywood, Ill., 1977-78; mgr. Hosp. Products div. Abbott Labs, Abbott Park, Ill., 1986—; Vis. prof. Rush Presbyn.-St. Luke's Hosp., Chgo., 1985, faculty assoc., 1985; assoc. investigator, asst. prof. medicine King Drew Med. Ctr., UCLA, 1985—. Contbr. articles to profl. and scholarly jours. Bd. govs. Art Inst. of Chgo., 1985—, aux. bd., 1988—, mem. multiple benefit coms., 1984—, vice chmn. Capital Campaign, 1984-85; mem. pres. com. Landmark Preservation Council, Chgo., 1984—, chmn. multiple coms. polit. candidates, 1986; bd. dirs. Marshall unit Chgo. Boys Clubs, 1984—; mem. benefit com. Hubbard St. Dance Co. 10th Gala, 1988, Victory Garden's Theatre Annual Benefit, 1988. Internat. Coll. Surgeons fellow, 1982. Mem. AMA, Am. Coll. Physicians, Am. Fedn. for Clin. Research, So. Med. Assn., Ill. State Med. Soc., Chgo. Med. Soc., Am. Acad. Med. Dirs., Nat. Acad. Arts & Scis.

ENGELEITER, SUSAN SHANNON, state legislator; b. Milwaukee, Wis., Mar. 18, 1952; m. Gerald Engeleiter; 1 dau., Jennifer Lynn. B.S., U. Wis., 1974, J.D., 1981. Mem. Wis. Assembly, 1974-79; legis. asst. to Gov. Lee Dreyfus, 1979-80; mem. Wis. Senate, 1980—, ass. minority leader, 1982-84, minority leader, from 1984; mem. bd. dirs., St. Luke's Hosp.; mem. AAUW, Am., Wis. bar assns., Camelot Forest Civic Assn. (past pres.). Recip. award

1 of 10 best Rep. state legislators, Nat. Rep. Legis. Assn., 1986, award Wis. Assn. Future Farmers Am., 1986. Office: Wis Senate State Capitol Madison WI 53702 Other Address: 14925 Santa Maria Dr Brookfield WI 53005 *

ENGELHARDT, MARY VERONICE, educational psychologist, nun; b. Syracuse, N.Y., Mar. 29, 1912; d. Herman Joseph and Ella Marguerite (Collins) E. B.S.Ed., Cath. U., 1937, M.A., 1938, Ph.D., 1962. Joined Third Franciscan Order Roman Catholic Ch., 1929; tchr. elem. and secondary schs., 1933, 38-52; instr. edn. St. Francis Normal Sch., Syracuse, 1942-56, diocesan and community sch. supr., 1952-56; dean women, head dept. edn. and psychology Chaminade Coll. Honolulu, 1957-60; clin. instr. Child Ctr. Cath. U., Washington, 1961, supr. student teaching, 1962; instr. edn., 1961-62; head dept. edn. and psychology Maria Regina Coll., Syracuse, 1962-68, founder, dir. Reading and Speech Clinics, 1962-68; founder, dir. Franciscan Learning Ctr., Franciscan Acad., Syracuse, 1968-85; asst. mother gen. Third Franciscan Order, 1965-71, chmn. personnel bd., 1972-75, chmn. communications bd., 1972-78, also editor community newsletter. Author. Looking at God's World, Creatures in God's World, Learning More About God's World; editor: Creative Arts, 1981-83. Mem. Am. Psychol. Assn., Am. Ednl. Research Assn., Internat. Reading Assn., Nat. Soc. Poets, Nat. League Am. Pen Women (1st v.p. Central N.Y. br. 1981-83). Address: 304 E Linebaugh Ave Tampa FL 33612

ENGELHARDT, SARA LAWRENCE, organization executive; b. Phila., Aug. 23, 1943; d. Ruddick Carpenter and Barbara (Dole) Lawrence; m. Dean Lee Engelhardt, June 20, 1970; children—Barbara Elizabeth, Margaret Ann. B.A., Wellesley Coll., 1965; M.A., Tchrs. Coll., Columbia U., 1970. Staff asst. Carnegie Corp., N.Y.C., 1966-70; asst. sec. Carnegie Corp., 1972-74, assoc. sec., 1974-75, sec., 1975-87; exec. v.p. Found. Ctr., N.Y.C., 1987—. Free-lance editor and writer, Storrs, Conn., 1970-72. Bd. dirs. Nat. Charities Info. Bur., 1984—, chairperson, 1987—; trustee Found. Ctr., 1984-87. Home: 173 Riverside Dr New York NY 10024 Office: Foundation Ctr 79 Fifth Ave New York NY 10003

ENGELKING, ELLEN MELINDA, foundry pattern company executive, real estate broker; b. Columbus, Ind., May 12, 1942; d. Lowell Eugene and Marcella (Brane) E.; children: Melissa Claire Fairbanks John David Prohaska, Ellen Margaret Prohaska. Student Sullins Coll., 1961, Franklin Coll., 1961-62, Ind. U., 1963. Vice chmn., pres., chief exec. officer Engelking Patterns, Inc., Columbus, Ind., 1980—, dir., treas., chief exec. officer Engelking Properties, Inc., Columbus, 1980—; guest speaker Bus. Sch., Ind. U., Bloomington, 1985-86, Ball State U., Muncie, Ind., 1986. Campaign chmn. Am. Heart Assn., Bartholomew County, 1980-81; chmn. Mothers March of Dimes, Bartholomew County, 1967; sec. Bartholomew County Republican Party, 1976-80; bd. dirs. Found. for Youth, 1975-78, Quinco Found., 1978-79; protocol hostess Pan Am. Games X, Indpls., 1987. Mem. U.S. C. of C., Ind. C. of C., Ind. Mfg. Assn., Am. Foundrymens Soc., Internat. Platform Assn., Acad. of Model Aeronautics, Delta Delta Delta. Roman Catholic. Avocations: study and present adaptation of Shaker work ethic, remote-controlled aircrafts, literature, oil painting. Office: Engelking Patterns Inc PO Box 607 Columbus IN 47202

ENGELS, PATRICIA LOUISE, lawyer; b. Joliet, Ill., July 2, 1926; d. Fred Adolph and Loretta Mae (Fisk) B.; m. Henry William Engels, Feb. 1, 1947; children: Patrick Henry, Michael Bruce, Timothy William. BS in Edn., Olivet Nazarene Coll., 1970, MEd, 1971; JD, John Marshall Law Sch., 1979. Bar: Ill. 1979, Ind. 1979; cert. elem. and high sch. tchr., edn. adminstrn., Ill. Tchr. Bourbonnais (Ill.) and Momence (Ill.) Unit Schs., 1970-76; instr. Kankakee (Ill.) Community Coll., 1975; sole practice Ind. and Ill., 1979—. Active Lake Village (Ind.) Civic Assn., 1980—; edn. coordinator St. Augusta Ch., Lake Village, 1985—. Mem. ABA, Ind. Bar Assn., Ill. Bar Assn., Pub. Defender Bar Assn., Theta Chi Sigma, Kappa Delta Pi. Roman Catholic. Home: Rt 1 Box 448 Momence IL 60954 Office: Engels Law Office 112 Washington Lowell IN 46356

ENGELSON, DONNA HERSHISER, management consulting executive; b. Buffalo, Aug. 23, 1943; d. Robert McIntosh and Owena Mae (Swachamer) Hershiser; children from previous marriage: Christopher Dwight Broga, Jonathan Kinsman Broga; m. William Lawrence Engelson, June 14, 1977; stepchildren: William Lawrence Jr., Kristin Sue. BA, Conn. Coll., 1965. Cert. elem. tchr. Tchr. Greenwood Nursery Sch., Bklyn., 1965-66, Barrington (R.I.) Pub. Schs., 1966-67, York County Pub. Schs., Yorktown, Va., 1967-68; costumed hostess Colonial Williamsburg (Va.) Found., 1969-71; tchr. Fairfax County Pub. Schs., Alexandria, Va., 1973-84; pres. The Leadership Edge, Falls Church, Va., 1984—; Bd. dirs. Elec. Assembly Services, Alexandria, No. Va. Local Devel. Co., Fairfax. Bd. dirs. Fairfax County unit bd. dirs., 1988—. Mem. Am. Soc. Tng. and Devel., Assn. Small Research Engrng. and Tech. Firms, Va. Assn. Female Execs. (treas. 1986, sec. 1987), Alexandria C. of C., Fairfax County C. of C. (com. chair 1986—, Recruiter of Yr. 1986-87, v.p. for membership 1988—, bd. dirs. 1988—). Episcopalian. Home: 8216 Treebrooke Ln Alexandria VA 22308 Office: The Leadership Edge 5109 Leesburg Pike Suite 411 Falls Church VA 22041

ENGERRAND, DORIS DIESKOW, educator; b. Chgo., Aug. 7, 1925; d. William Jacob and Alma Willhelmina (Cords) Dieskow; B.S. in Bus. Adminstrn., N. Ga. Coll., 1958, B.S. in Elementary Edn., 1959; M. Bus. Edn., Ga. State U., 1966, Ph.D., 1970; m. Gabriel H. Engerrand, Oct. 26, 1946 (dec. June 1987); children—Steven, Kenneth, Jeannine. Tchr., dept. chmn. Lumpkin County High Sch., Dahlonega, Ga., 1960-63, 65-68; tchr., Gainesville, Ga., 1965; asst. prof. Troy (Ala.) State U., 1969-71; asst. prof. bus. Ga. Coll., Milledgeville, 1971-74, asso. prof., 1974-78, prof., 1978—, chmn. dept. bus. info. systems and communications, 1978 ; cons. Named Outstanding Tchr. Lumpkin County Pub. Schs., 1963, 66; Outstanding Educator bus. faculty Ga. Coll., 1975, Exec. of Yr. award, 1983. Fellow Am. Bus. Communication Assn. (nat. dir.1988—, v.p. S.E. 1978-80, 81-84), So. Mgmt. Assn., Nat., Ga. (Postsecondary Tchr. of Yr. award 10th dist. 1983, Postsecondary Tchr. of Yr. award 1984) bus. edn. assns., Am., Ga. (Educator of Yr. award 1984) vocat. assns., Profl. Secs. Internat., Office Systems Research Assn., Ninety-nines Internat. (chmn. N. Ga. chpt. 1975-76, named Pilot of Year N. Ga. chpt. 1973). Methodist. Contbr. articles on bus. edn. to profl. publs. Home: 1674 Pine Valley Rd Milledgeville GA 31061 Office: Ga Coll Milledgeville GA 31061

ENGHOLM, MARY KORSTAD MUELLER, art education consultant, author; b. Seattle, May 7, 1918; d. Martin and Mary Emily (Greene) Korstad; B.E., UCLA, 1940; M.Ed., St. Lawrence U., 1949; postgrad. Syracuse U., 1950-52; m. Walter Weigel, Dec. 22, 1949 (div. 1967); 1 child, Erica K. Weigel; m. 2d, Paul G. Mueller, Nov. 9, 1968 (dec. 1976); m. 3d, Glenn S. Engholm, Aug. 6, 1982. Tchr. art Riverside (Calif.) City Schs., 1944-46; art supr. Canton (N.Y.) Sch. Dist., 1946-48; asst. prof. art SUNY, Potsdam, 1948-58; art supr. Watertown (N.Y.) City Sch. Dist., 1962-67; cons., lectr. U. Nebr., Lincoln, summer 1966; art supr. Bakersfield (Calif.) City Sch. Dist., 1967-78; instr. art, continuing edn. Calif. State Coll., Bakersfield, 1971-74, 76, adj. instr., lectr., 1982-83; free-lance art cons., Bakersfield, 1978-84. Trustee Kern County Arts Council, 1976-83, Bakersfield Sister City Com., 1978-83, H. Weil Child Guidance Clinic, 1980-83, Kern County Mus. Alliance, 1978-84; pres. Kern County chpt. Young Audiences of Am., 1978-83; pres. bd. dirs. H. Weill Meml. Child Guidance Clinic, 1981-83; community adv. Jr. League Bakersfield, 1980-83; v.p. Am. Scandinavians Assn. (Monterey Bay chpt.), 1986—; bd. dirs. Lori Brock Jr. Mus., 1975-78, dir. Monterey History and Art Assn., 1986—. Mem. Nat. Art Edn. Assn., Greater Bakersfield C. of C. (Woman of Yr. women's div. 1983), Calif. Art Edn. Assn. (trustee 1979-82), Kern County Art Edn. Assn., AAUW, Calif. Tchrs. Assn., Delta Kappa Gamma. Republican. Lutheran. Author: (with Thomas and Wells) Elementary Art, 1967; Murals: Creating an Environment, 1979; contbr. articles to profl. jours.

ENGLAND, DONNA RAE, accountant; b. Fergus Falls, Minn., Jan. 7, 1959; d. Reuben W. and Lenore M. (Brekke) Lee; m. Hugh R. England. BSBA in Acctg., Mankato (Minn.) State U., 1980. CPA, Minn. Staff auditor Touche Ross & Co., St. Paul, 1980-82; acctg. officer Am. Nat. Bank and Trust Co., St. Paul, 1982-84, asst. controller, 1984-86; dir. internal audit Am. Bancorp., Inc., St. Paul, 1986—. Home: 2641 Borden Way Inver Grove Heights MN 55075 Office: Am Bancorp Inc 5th and Minnesota Sts Saint Paul MN 55101

ENGLAND, LYNNE LIPTON, lawyer, speech pathologist, audiologist; b. Youngstown, Ohio, Apr. 11, 1949; d. Sanford Y. and Sally (Kentor) Lipton; m. Richard E. England, Mar. 5, 1977. B.A., U. Mich., 1970; M.A., Temple U., 1972; J.D., Tulane U., 1981. Bar: Fla. 1981. Cert. clin. competence in speech pathology and audiology. Speech pathologist Rockland Children's Hosp. (N.Y.), 1972-74, Jefferson Parish Sch., Gretna, La., 1977-81; audiologist Rehab. Inst. Chgo., 1974-76; assoc. Trenam, Simmons, Kemker, Scharf, Barkin, Frye & O'Neill, Tampa, Fla., 1981-84; asst. U.S. atty. for Middle Dist. Fla., Tampa, 1984-87, asst. U.S. trustee, 1987—. Editor Fla. Bankruptcy Casenotes, 1983. Recipient clin. assistantship Temple U., 1972-74. Mem. Am. Speech and Hearing Assn., Fla. Bar Assn., ABA, Hillsborough County Bar Assn., Assn. Trial Lawyers Am., ALTA, Am. Bankruptcy Inst., Fed. Bar Assn., Order of Coif. Jewish. Home: 3054 Wister Circle Valrico FL 33594 Office: US Trustees Office 4921 Memorial Hwy Suite 340 Tampa FL 33634

ENGLANDER, PAULA TYO, lawyer; b. Syracuse, N.Y., Dec. 25, 1951; d. Howard James and Pauline Harriet Henderson; m. Ronald Englander, Jan. 24, 1971; children: David, Lisa. BA, SUNY, 1978; JD, Syracuse U., 1981. Bar: Colo. 1982, U.S. Dist. Ct. Colo. 1983, U.S. Ct. Appeals (10th cir.) 1983. Law clerk Kintzele & Collins, Denver, 1981-82; sole practice Denver, 1982—; cons. Orthotic and Prosthetic Assn., 1980; bd. dirs. Orthopedic Techs., Inc., Syracuse, Aurora (Colo.) Orthopedics, Inc., Gaines Brace & Limb, Inc., Lakewood, Colo. Contbr. articles to profl. jours. Asst. founding mem., asst. coordinator Export Assistance Program, 1984—. Mem. (founding) Alliance of Profl. Women, Colo. Bar Assn. (gen. and small firm sect., mem. council), ABA (legal econs. section). Home: 2055 Ivanhoe St Denver CO 80207 Office: PO Box 6936 Denver CO 80206

ENGLE, JEANNETTE CRANFILL, medical technologist; b. Davie County, N.C., July 7, 1941; d. Gurney Nathaniel and Versie Emmaline (Reavis) Cranfill; m. William Sherman Engle (div. 1970); children: Phillip William, Lisa Kaye. Diploma, Dell Sch. Med. Tech., 1960; BA, U. N.C., Asheville, 1976. Instr. Dell Sch. Med. Tech., Asheville, 1960-67; rotating technologist Meml. Mission Hosp., Asheville, 1967-68, asst. supr. hematology, 1968-71; supr. Damon Subs. Pvt. Clinic Lab., Asheville, 1971-73; chemistry technologist VA Med Ctr., Durham, N.C., 1973-74, 75-76, supr., 1974-75; asst. supr. microbiology VA Med Ctr., Salem, Va., 1976-79; supr. research Med. Service Lab., Salem, 1979—; reviewer Jour. Club, Roanoke-Salem, Va., 1980—. Author: (poem) Reflections on a Comet, 1984; contbr. numerous articles and abstracts on med. tech. to profl. jours., 1982—. Democrat. Episcopalian. Home: 5075 Northwood Dr NW Roanoke VA 24017 Office: Med Service Lab 170 Boulevard Salem VA 24153

ENGLE, SANDRA LOUISE, state agency administrator; b. Grand Haven, Mich., Aug. 5, 1949; d. J. Edward and Ethel Caroline (Westerhouse) E. AA, Muskegon Community Coll., 1969; BA in Bus. Adminstrn., Mich. State U., E. Lansing, 1971; postgrad., Mich. State U., 1984-86. Clk. and dept. mgr. Meijers Inc., Muskegon, Grand Haven, Grand Rapids, Mich., 1971-74; ins. agt. Prudential Ins. Co., Muskegon, Mich., 1974; bookkeeper Muskegon Correctional Faciltiy, Muskegon, Mich., 1974-75; bus. office mgr. Kent County Dept. of Social Services, Grand Rapids, Mich., 1975-76; budget and fin. dir. Mich. Dept. of Licensing and Regulation, Lansing, Mich., 1976-86; service area dir. Mich. Dept. of Edn., Lansing, 1987; dep. bur. dir. Mich. Dept. of Labor, Lansing, 1987-88. Mem. Humane Soc. of U.S. Clubs: Mich. Reg. Nat. Council of Corvette (Lansing) (sec. & treas. 1977-82, 84), Vintners (Lansing). Home: 3201 Continental Ave Lansing MI 48911 Office: Mich Dept of Labor 7150 Harris Dr PO Box 30015 Lansing MI 48909

ENGLEHARDT, SHEREE LEE, data processing executive; b. Toledo, Ohio, Dec. 18, 1957; d. Ford Bevard and Leora Bell (Tobey) C.; Charles Stephen Englehardt, June 25, 1988. BA in Math. and Computer Sci., Muskingum Coll., 1979; MBA, Fla. Inst. Tech., 1987. Programmer Prestolite Co., Toledo, 1979-81; programmer/analyst Fla. Power Corp., St. Petersburg, 1981-85, database analyst, 1985—. Security guard St. Petersburg Grand Prix, 1986-87; exec. advisor Jr. Achievement, St. Petersburg, 1981-84. Mem. Nat. Assn. Female Execs. Office: Fla Power Corp-B2A 3201 34th St S Saint Petersburg FL 33733

ENGLEHART, JOAN ANNE, trade association executive; b. Susquehanna, Pa., Sept. 15, 1940; d. George Louis and Muriel Elois (Washburn) Wanatt; m. Dale John Englehart, Nov. 24, 1958. AAS, Broome Community Coll., 1981; BS in Cultural Studies, Empire State Coll., 1984; postgrad., SUNY, Binghamton, 1984. Office mgr., coordinator sales Bush Transformer Corp., Endicott (N.Y.), Boston, 1959-65; mgr., cons. Snelling & Snelling, Binghamton, Endicott, 1965-71; tchr., mgr. Can. Acad., Kobe, Japan, 1971-72; adminstrv. asst. GAF Corp., Binghamton, 1973-80; owner Typewriting, Endicott, 1980-85; exec. v.p. Tioga County C. of C., Owego, N.Y., 1985-87, pres., 1988—. Mem. Broome Community Coll. Found., Binghamton, 1984-87; mem. scholarship com. Civic Club Binghamton, 1984-87; mem. Health Fair Adv. Bd., Broome and Tioga Counties, 1985—; chmn. sustaining membership com. Broome United Way, Binghamton, 1986-87. Recipient award Boy Scouts Am., 1979, Evening Student Assn., 1981, award Friends Binghamton Library, 1982, Athena award C. of C., 1986; named Woman of Achievement Broome County Status of Women Council, 1978. Mem. Assn. C. of C. Execs., Nat. Assn. Women in C. of C.'s (charter mem.), AAUW (life, pres. 1986—). Republican. Baptist. Lodge: Zonta (pres. Tioga County Area club 1985—, Women of Achievement 1985, 86, 87). Home: 4 Lancaster Dr Endicott NY 13760 Office: Tioga County C of C 188 Front St Owego NY 13827

ENGLE-SETTLES, JERI LYNN, social services consultant; b. Oklahoma City, Dec. 23, 1955; d. Jerry G. and Darlene (Woodside) Engle; m. Alwyn Cecil Settles, May 23, 1987. BS in Community Health, Pub. Safety, Sch. Health and Safety. Prevention and edn. specialist Aurora (Ill.) Drug Program, 1979-80; case worker family intervention program Grundy-Kendall Ednl. Service Program, Morris, Ill., 1980-84; asst. mgr. Wendy's Internat., Morris, 1984-85; account exec. Federated Foods, Inc., Arlington Heights, Ill., 1985-88; cons. stress mgmt., organ. devel. JES Assocs., Monroe, Mich., 1988—. Chairperson personnel policy revision com. Guardian Angel Home, Joliet, Ill., 1983-88, youth com. ARC, Morris, 1984-85; bd. dirs., cons. Operation Snowball, various No. Ill. chpts., 1980—. Named One of Outstanding Young Women of Am., 1982, 85, 86. Mem. Nat. Assn. Female Execs. Home: 10 Fernwood Ct Romeoville IL 60441 Office: JES Assocs 3105 S Grove St Monroe MI 48161

ENGLISH, ELIZABETH ANN, marketing administration executive; b. Bklyn., Jan. 15, 1955; d. Allan Joseph and Dorothy Amalia (Muoio) Magrino; m. Denis Wilfrid Bilodeau, Sept. 10, 1977 (div. June 1983); m. Edward Charles English, Nov. 14, 1984. BSBA magna cum laude, Mercy Coll., 1976; MBA, Rutgers U., 1986. Asst. buyer Abraham & Straus Dept. Store, Bklyn., 1976-77; dept. mgr. Abraham & Straus Dept. Store, Babylon, N.Y., 1977-78; buyer Hahne & Co. Dept. Store, Newark, 1978-83, Kids 'R' Us, Rochelle Park, N.J., 1983-86; asst. mgr. sales and ops. Hitachi Am., Ltd., Allendale, N.J., 1986-87; asst. mgr. nat. adminstrn. office automation products Hitachi Am. Ltd., Allendale, N.J., 1987—. Mem. Delta Mu Delta. Alpha Chi. Office: Hitachi Am Ltd 6 Pearl Ct Allendale NJ 07401

ENGLISH, ELIZABETH ANN, actress, educator; b. Bronx, N.Y., Jan. 18, 1962; d. Nicholas John and Jayne Ann (Matheson) E. BA in Theatre, Fordham U., 1984; MFA in Acting, U. Minn., 1986. Asst. instr. U. Minn., Mpls., 1985, assoc. instr., 1986; actress N.Y.C., 1986—. Appeared off-Broadway with Circle Repertory Co. in Spoon River Anthology, As Is, The Musical Comedy Murders; regional appearances include Barber of Seville, La Ronde, Much Ado About Nothing, Everyman, Riverwife's Daughters, The Music Man. U. Minn. fellow, 1984. Mem. Am. Film Industry Supporters, Actor's Equity Assn., Amnesty Internat. Democrat. Roman Catholic. Home and Office: 2894 Wellman Ave Bronx NY 10461

ENGLISH, MERLE B., newspaper reporter; b. Kingston, Jamaica; came to U.S., 1967; d. Luther and Dora (Reid) E. BS in Mass Communications, Hunter Coll., 1977; MS in Journalism, Columbia U., 1979. Sec. The Daily Gleaner, Kingston, 1961-62, reporter, 1962-67; staff writer pub. relations Xerox Corp., N.Y.C., 1968-76; reporter New York News Day, Melville, N.Y., 1981-85, Bklyn., 1985—.

ENGLISH, RUTH HILL, artist, consultant, educator; b. Andover, Mass., Feb. 7, 1904; d. Herbert Hudson and Ada Jane (Wells) Hill; grad. Abbot Acad., Andover; received pvt. instrn.; m. A. Evans Rephart, June 28, 1929; children—Susan K. (Mrs. Howard K. Simpson), Katharine K. (Mrs. Christopher R. Barnes); m. 2d, E. Schuyler English, July 4, 1959. Faculty Hampton Inst., 1924-25, Bryn Mawr Art Center (later Main Line Center of Arts), 1945-65, Wayne Art Center, 1947-49; dir. Hedgeabout Studio, Gladwyne, Pa., 1965—; lectr., art cons. throughout East, 1960-70. Past mem. womens bd. Pa. Hosp.; mem. womens bd. Babies Hosp., 1934-39. Mem. Hist. Soc. Early Am. Decoration (pres. William Penn chpt. 1950-51), Pa. Craftsmans Guild (dir. 1952-54). Republican. Episcopalian. Clubs: Acorn, Skytop (Pa.), Athenaeum. Home: 47 E Wynnewood Rd Merion PA 19066 also: Skytop PA 18357 Studio: 1124 Rose Glen Rd Gladwyne PA 19035

ENGLISH, SALLY ANN, computer executive; b. Portsmouth, N.H., May 2, 1946; d. Anthony Joseph and Sally May (Griskiewicz) Daniels; m. Robert Glenn English, Jan. 25, 1969; children: Kimberly, Melissa, Jill. BS, U. N.H., 1968, M, 1976. Med. technologist Deaconess Hosp., Boston, 1968-69; med. technologist Exeter (N.H.) Hosp., 1970-75, lab. mgr., 1975-80; asst. chief technologist data processing Emory Hosp., Atlanta, 1980-81; ednl. rep. HBO & Co., Atlanta, 1982-83, installation rep. of new tech., 1983-84; product specialist HBO & Co., 1984-85, mgr. clin. systems installation and support, 1985-86, nat. mgr. clin. services, 1986-87, nat. sales exec., 1987—. Mem. Women's Commerce Club, Nat. Assn. Profl. Saleswomen, Nat. Assn. Female Execs. Republican. Roman Catholic.

ENGLISH, ZEBORAH ANITA, public projects specialist; b. Washington, July 14, 1951; d. Zebedee English and Barbara Ann (Stevenson) English Brown. AA, Prince George's Community Coll., Largo, Md., 1974; BA, U. Md., 1978. Air traffic controller Fed. Aviation Adminstrn., Jamaica, N.Y., 1974-80; with U.S. Dept. Transp., Washington, 1980—, spl. projects coordinator, 1984—; pres. Zebb & Assocs., Marlboro, Md., 1984—; adj. instr. U. D.C., 1987—; cons. in field. Author: (handbook) FEW Public Relations, 1985. Orgn. advisor Nat. Orgn. Black Elected Legis. Women, 1984-85; commr. adv. com. Prince George's County Juvenile Ct., 1985—; founder, chmn. Elizabeth J. Miller Meml. Scholarship; officer pub. relations Martin Luther King Jr. Fed. Holiday Commn., 1987-88. Recipient 20 Yr. Service award Washington council Girl Scouts U.S., 1981; named Outstanding Young Woman Am., 1982, 85, 86. Mem. Met. Washington Women's Yellow Pages (adv. bd. 1986—), Nat. Assn. Female Execs., Nat. C. of C. for Women (chartered mem.), Fed. Employed Women Inc. (pres. 1984—, chartered mem.), Am. Soc. Assn. Execs. Democrat. Roman Catholic. Clubs: The Exec., Bus. and Profl. Women. Home: 10135 Prince Pl Apt 203 Largo MD 20772

ENGLUND, GAGE BUSH, dancer, educator; b. Birmingham, Ala., Sept. 7, 1931; d. Morris Williams and Margaret Wallace (Gagé) Bush; student Sweet Briar Coll.; student (Ford Found. scholar) Sch. Am. Ballet, 1960; m. Richard Bernard Englund, Dec. 1, 1959; children—Alixandra, Rachel Rutherford. Founder, Birmingham Civic Ballet, 1952; mem. Robert Joffrey Ballet, N.Y.C., 1957-60, soloist, 1959-60; mem. Am. Ballet Theatre, N.Y.C., 1960-63, Huntington Dance Ensemble, L.I., N.Y., 1968-69; soloist Dance Repertory Co., 1969-72; tchr. ballet, asso. chmn. Friends of Am. Ballet Theatre, N.Y.C., 1972—; rehearsal coach Am. Ballet Theatre II, 1973-85; mem. scholarship com. Am. Ballet Theatre Sch., N.Y.C., 1974—; dir. Ala. By-products Corp., 1971-77; rehearsal coach Joffrey Ballet II, 1985—. Bd. dirs. Children's Hosp. Clinic, Birmingham, 1955-57, Spoleto Festival, U.S.A., 1980-83, Ala. State Ballet, 1967——, Birmingham Civic Ballet, 1952-67; trustee Ballet Theatre Found., 1974—, v.p., 1980-81; trustee Episcopal Sch. of N.Y., 1979-83, Chapin Sch., 1982—, Animal Med. Center, N.Y.C., 1982—, Cancer Research Inst., 1984—. Recipient Silver Bowl award Birmingham Festival of Arts, 1955; named Queen of Birmingham Festival of Arts, 1957. Mem. Am. Guild Mus. Artists, Colonial Dames Ala., Jr. League N.Y.C. Episcopalian. Clubs: Lakewood Country, The Colony. Home: PO Box 469 Point Clear AL 36564

ENGLUND, LORI JEAN, financial products company executive; b. Omaha, Sept. 20, 1961; d. Earl Winston and Barbara Jean (Van Wie) McClellan; m. Leslie Donald Englund, Feb. 12, 1960; 1 child, Jessica Marie. BS, Ariz. State U., 1983. Mktg. rep. GNA, Austin, Tex., 1983-84, sr. mktg. rep., 1985-86; regional acct. exec. GNA, Austin and Long Beach, Calif., 1987; regional mktg. dir. GNA, Long Beach, 1988—. Mem. Nat. Assn. Female Execs., Fin. Inst. Mktg. Assn. Republican. Roman Catholic. Office: GNA 320 Golden Shore Ave Suite 120 Long Beach CA 90802

ENGRAM, BEVERLY LEIGH, state legislator; b. Feb. 2. Mem. Ga. Senate. Democrat. Office: Ga Senate State Capitol Atlanta GA 30334 also: PO Box 908 Fairburn GA 30213

ENGSTROM, PATRICIA MARION, infosystems specialist; b. Pitts., Aug. 20, 1951; d. William Alexander and Joan (Burley) Hill; m. Carl Roy Engstrom, Aug. 26, 1969; children: Hope Lynn, Heather Ann. Student, U. Pitts., 1968-70; BS in Bus. Adminstrn., Math., LaRoche Coll., 1976; postgrad., U. Pitts., 1987—. Programmer, analyst Mellon Bank, Pitts., 1976-79, ind. cons., 1979-81; lead programmer analyst Pitts. Nat. Bank, Pitts., 1981-82, systems programming officer, 1982-84, project mgr., 1984-85, EDP project officer, 1985-86, asst. v.p., 1986-87, v.p., 1987—; pres. Ramis Users Group of Pitts., 1984-86; chmn. Plug Info. Ctr., Pitts., 1986—. Contbr. articles to profl. jours. Mem. bd. trustees Pitts. Presbytery, 1987. Mem. Data Processing Mgrs. Assn., Nat. Assn. Female Execs., Nat. Assn. Women in Banking. Office: Pitts Nat Bank 5th and Wood Sts Pittsburgh PA 15222

ENGSTROM, SHARON HARSTED, advertising sales executive; b. Hawthorne, Calif., May 22, 1957; d. Norman Thatcher and Delores Mary (Bauler) Harsted; m. John Anthony Engstrom, Aug. 31, 1982. BA, San Diego State U., 1980. Advt. sales account exec. Dutton Industries, San Diego, 1980-81; divisional sales mgr. Advo Systems, Inc., Hayward, Calif., 1981-84; v.p. sales Mktg. Publs., Inc., Westminster, Calif., 1984—. Mem. Gamma Phi Beta (social chmn. officer 1978), Delta Upsilon. Republican. Lodge: Soroptimists, Little Sister of the Seven Stars (pres. 1977). Home: 10521 Shadyridge Dr Santa Ana CA 92705 Office: Mktg Publs Inc 7060 Garden Grove Blvd Westminster CA 92683

ENLOE, TONINA WESTON, educator; b. Greenville, N.C., Oct. 12, 1954; d. William Franklin and Nina (Baker) Weston; m. Charles Wilkerson Enloe, June 18, 1983. BS, East Carolina U., 1976, MEd, 198, 86. Tchr. Transylvania County Schs., Brevard, N.C., 1976-85, Sch. Dist. of Greenville (S.C.) County, 1985—. Co-author (student activity book) Marina Organisms in the Classroom, 1981, Coastal Ecosystems, 1981, Exlporing Kenya, 1985. Sec. Sch. Improvement Council, Greenville, 1986—. NOAA grantee, 1980, GTE grantee 1984, Alliance for Edn. grantee, 1987. Mem. NEA, Greenville County Sci. Tchrs. Assn., Greenville County Edn. Assn., Mid-Atlantic Marine Edn. Assn., Nat. Marine Edn. Assn., S.C. Sci. Tchrs. Democrat. Prebyterian. Home: 303 Strange Rd Taylors SC 29687 Office: Berea Middle Sch 151 Berea Middle Sch Rd Greenville NC 29601

ENNIS, RITA LOUISE, human resources executive; b. Louisville, May 10, 1951; d. B. Wayne and Dorothy F. (Elder) E.; m. Robert C. Vogelsang, Mar. 14, 1986. BA, Hollins Coll., 1973; postgrad., U. Louisville, 1973-74, So. Bapt. Theol. Sem., 1977-79, Johns Hopkins U., 1986—. Fed. programs coordinator Jefferson County, Louisville, 1973-75, affirmative action coordinator, 1975-81, dep. dir. personnel, 1981-86; dir. employee relations PHH Group, Hunt Valley, Md., 1986—; cons., 1979—; bd. dirs. House of Ruth spouse abuse edn. and shelter 1987—. V.p. Old Louisville Neighborhood Council, 1979-81; bd. dirs. Neighborhood Devel. Corp., 1979-81, 85—, House of Ruth, 1987-88; issues coordinator Ky. Common Cause, 1975; mem. EEO vol. council, Balt. Mem. Am. Mgmt. Assn., Am. Soc. for Personnel Adminstrn., Md. C. of C. (human relations com. 1986—). Home: 507 E 39th St Baltimore MD 21218 Office: PHH Group 11333 McCormick Rd Hunt Valley MD 21031

ENNIS, TAMARA ROSE, typographer; b. Phila., Sept. 29, 1953; d. Thomas Weber and Lynn (Evans) Roulston; m. Barry David Ennis, Feb. 21, 1979; children: Karl, Morganna. AAS in Graphic Design, Palomar Jr. Coll., 1972. Sr. typographer RW Roulston Inc., Burlington, Vt., 1964—; type dir.

Vanguard Press, Burlington Vt. News and Arts Weekly. Named Vt. State Women's 8-Ball Champion, Vt. State Assn. Pocket Billiards, 1985, 86. Mem. Nat. Assn. Female Execs. Democrat. Roman Catholic.

ENRIGHT, STEPHANIE VESELICH, financial company executive; b. Los Angeles, Mar. 24, 1929; d. Stephen P. and Violet (Guthrie) Veselich; m. Robert James Enright (dec. Sept. 1982); children: Craig James, Brent Stephen, Erin Suzanne, Kyle Stephen. BA, U. So. Calif., 1952, MS, 1975. Fin. and engring. cons. Orange County, Santa Ana, Calif., 1976-79; fin. cons. The Sim-Ehrflo Group, Newport Beach, Calif., 1979-81; pres. Enright Fin. Cons., Torrance, Calif., 1981—; fin. columnist Copley Newspapers, 1987—; adj. faculty mem., UCLA, U. So. Calif., fin. columnist Copley Daily Breeze Newspapers. Contbr. articles to profl. jours. Mem. Com. Assn. of the Peninsula, Palos Verdes, Calif., 1986; active Little Co. of Mary Hosp., Torrance. Recipient cert. Appreciation and Merit U. So. Calif. Entrepreneur Program, 1978, cert. of Appreciation Coll. Fin. Planning, 1985. Mem. Internat. Assn. Fin. Planning (bd. dirs. and officer 1982-84, Planner of Month 1984), Inst. Cert. Planners, Nat. Assn. Women Bus. Owners, Nat. Assn. Fin. Edn., Registry of Profl. Planners, Torrance C. of C. Republican. Roman Catholic. Club: Trojan Guild (Los Angeles) (bd. dirs. 1978-79). Office: Enright Fin Consultants Union Bank Tower Suite 900 21515 Hawthorne Blvd Torrance CA 90503

ENSOR, JOAN ELIZABETH, government official; b. Arlington, Va., Mar. 24, 1944; d. Leonard Joel and Doris Elizabeth (Hindman) E.; 1 child, Courtney Lynne. B.A., Westhampton Coll., 1966. Service rep. Va. Electric Power Co., Richmond and Fairfax, 1966-68; pub. health analyst Pub. Health Service, HHS, Arlington, 1968-73, program analyst Social Security, Balt. and Arlington, 1973-77, program analysis officer, 1977—. Recipient awards U.S. Govt., 1968—. Democrat. Avocations: sewing; writing; poetry. Home: 3013 Strathmeade St Falls Church VA 22042 Office: Dept Health and Human Services 3833 N Fairfax Dr Arlington VA 22203

ENTMAN, BARBARA SUE, broadcaster, writer, photographer; b. Glen Cove, N.Y., Sept. 24, 1954; d. Bernard Entman and Rose (Jacobson) Entman Pachter; B.A., U. Conn., 1976. Freelance writer/photographer, 1975—; announcer, publicity dir. Sta. WHUS-FM, Storrs, Conn., 1975-76; announcer, copywriter Sta. WKAJ-AM-FM, Saratoga Springs, N.Y., 1976-77; traffic coordinator Sta. WMHT-FM, Schenectady, 1977-79; ops. dir. Sta. WNIU-FM, Dekalb, Ill., 1980-82; ops. mgr. Sta. KUHF, Houston, 1982-86, announcer, 1987—, membership dir., 1987—; media com. Ill. Heart Assn., DeKalb, 1982, Sojourner Women's Bookstore, DeKalb, 1980-81; exhibited photographs in galleries and univs., 1970—; contbr. articles and poetry to mags. and newspapers. Newsletter editor Congregation Aytz Chayim, Houston, 1983-84; founder DeKalb Area Women's Network, 1981; bd. dirs., newsletter editor Art Resources Open to Women, 1977-79; mem. Chgo. Artists Coalition, 1981-82; mem. mems. adv. bd. Houston Women's Caucus for Arts, 1985-88, chairperson publicity, conf., 1988; del. Tex. Democratic Conv., 1984, 86. Mem. Houston Ctr. Photography, Art League of Houston, Cultural Arts Council Houston. Home: PO Box 35826 Houston TX 77235-5826

ENTREKIN, LANG MOORE, chemical executive; b. Charleston, W.Va., Feb. 16, 1943; d. Kermit Russel and Olga Adriena (Lang) Moore; m. Wayne Gaines Entrekin, Dec. 22, 1963; children: Sonya Anne, Michael Gaines. BS in Chemistry, Newberry (S.C.) Coll., 1963; MS in Textiles and Clothing, Winthrop Coll., 1980. Chemist E.I. DuPont, New Ellington, S.C., 1963; lab technician Med. U. S.C., Charleston, 1964-67; lectr. chemistry Winthrop Coll., Rock Hill, S.C., 1980-84; pres., salesperson Lang Chem. Sales, Inc., Rock Hill, 1984—. Active Rock Hill Jr. Welfare League, 1976—, York County Med. Aux., Rock Hill. Mem. Am. Chem. Soc. (treas. 1986-87), Am. Assn. Textile Chemists and Colorists, Phi Kappa Phi, Delta Zeta. Republican. Lutheran.

EPHRON, NORA, author; b. N.Y.C., May 19, 1941; d. Henry and Phoebe (Wolkind) E.; m. Dan Greenburg (div.); m. Carl Bernstein (div.); children: Jacob, Max; m. Nicholas Pileggi. B.A., Wellesley Coll., 1962. Reporter N.Y. Post, 1963-68; free-lance writer 1968—; contbg. editor, columnist Esquire mag., 1972-73, sr. editor, columnist, 1974-78; contbg. editor N.Y. mag., 1973-74. Author: Wallflower at the Orgy, 1970, Crazy Salad, 1975, Scribble Scribble, 1978, Heartburn, 1983; Screenwriter: (with Alice Arlen) Silkwood, 1983, Heartburn, 1986. Mem. Writers Guild Am., Authors Guild, P.E.N., Acad. Motion Picture Arts and Scis. Office: care Lynn Nesbit ICM 40 W 57th St New York NY 10019

EPP, MARY ELIZABETH, software engineer, consultant; b. Buffalo, Aug. 7, 1941; d. John Conrad and Gertrude Marie (Murphy) Winkelman; m. Harry Francis Epp, Aug. 31, 1963. BA in Math., D'Youville Coll., 1963; MS in Math., Xavier U., 1974, MBA in Fin., 1981, MBA in Mktg., 1987. Systems analyst Gen. Electric, Evendale, Ohio, 1965-71; techniques and ops. mgr. Palm Beach Co., Cin., 1972-73; hardware systems engr. Procter & Gamble, Cin., 1973-76; systems engr. CalComp Inc., Anaheim, Calif., 1980-84; software engr. SDRC Inc., Cin., 1984-86; project leader SAMI/Burke Mktg., Cin., 1986—; cons. Shelley & Sands, Zanesville, Ohio, 1983-85. Contbr. articles to profl. jours. Mem. Fairfield Charter Rev. Commn., 1981-83. Mem. AAUW (br. treas. 1975-79, state women's chair 1979-80, state treas. 1980-82), Assn. Computing Machinery (treas. Cin. chpt. 1987-88, prss. 1988—), Nat. Computer Graics Assn., Nat. Assn. Female Execs., Nat. Fedn. Music (Ohio fedn. music parade chair 1979-81.). Republican. Roman Catholic. Clubs: Mercy Hosp. Aux. (treas. 1978-79), Musical Arts. Avocations: bridge, skiing, music, fishing, travel. Home: 4900 Pleasant Ave Fairfield OH 45014 Office: SAMI/Burke Mktg 800 Broadway Cincinnati OH 45202

EPPERSON, OZELL MARIE, elementary educator; b. Detroit, July 30, 1931; d. Millard Sr. and Rosa (Thomas) Hudson; m. Thomas Lloyd Epperson, Dec. 28, 1981 (dec. Oct. 1985); children: Phyllis Goss, Hubert Butler Jr. BS, U. Ark., Pine Bluff, 1955; MA, Webster U., 1971. Cert. elem. tchr., Ill. Tchr. East St. Louis (Ill.) Sch. Dist. 189, 1955—. Mem. Friends of Opportunities Industrialization Ctrs., Inc. of Am. Illiteracy Program, St. Louis. Recipient Unsung Heroines award Top Ladies of Distinction, Inc., 1986. Mem. Nat. Assn. Univ. Women, Ill.-Mo. Ark. Alumni Club (pres. 1972-73), Washington Sch. PTA (sec. 1984-87), Zeta Phi Beta Sorority, Inc. (Woman of Yr. 1981). Baptist. Lodge: Order of Eastern Star (Five Point Tea Queen, Queen Elizabeth #16 br. 1985, Esther 1987—). Home: 1909 Russell East Saint Louis IL 62207

EPPERT, LORNA MAE, nursing home administrator, nurse; b. New Albin, Iowa, July 22, 1931; d. Frank Louis and Kathryn Marie (Moore) Hurley; m. Gerald Lee Eppert, Feb. 11, 1956; children—James, Steven, Mark, Lynn, Dale. B.S. in Nursing, U. Cin., 1971, M.S. in Nursing, 1974. Lic. nursing home adminstr., Ohio, Ind. Staff nurse Good Samaritan Hosp., Cin., 1957-64, evening supr., 1964-85, staff nurse, 1985-86, instr. nursing 1986-87; dir. spl. projects Miller's Merry Manor, Inc., Rushville, Ind., 1987—; instr. nursing U. Cin., 1974-78, asst. prof., 1978-81; vis. asst. prof. nursing Miami U., Hamilton, Ohio, 1985—. Served to 1st lt. USAF, 1953-56. Mem. Am. Coll. Health Care Adminstrs., Nat. League Nursing. Republican. Roman Catholic. Avocations: rafting; sewing; reading. Home: 6721 Schuster Ct Cincinnati OH 45239 Office: Millers Merry Manor Inc Hartford City IN 47348

EPPES, MAVIS, law records manager; b. Teague, Tex., Jan. 31, 1937; d. Rich and Ruth (Haynie) E. Student Sam Houston State U., 1955-58. Records mgr. Vinson & Elkins, Houston, 1959—; curriculum adv. com. records mgmt. N. Harris County Coll., 1983, 85. Recipient Records Mgmt. award The Office, 1982. Mem. Assn. Records Mgrs. and Adminstrs. (pres. 1985-86, internat. chmn. legal services industry action com. 1985-87, info. mgmt. achievement award Houston chpt. 1982, award of Achievement 1984, chpt. Mem. of Yr. 1986), Bus. Forms Mgmt. Assn., DAR, Colonial Dames, Soc. Descendants of Francis Eppes I of Va. (pres. Freestone County, Tex. chpt. 1988). Republican. Baptist. Home: 1310 Springrock Ln Houston TX 77055 Office: Vinson and Elkins 1001 Fannin 2968 First City Tower Houston TX 77002

EPPLER, CECILIA MARIA, engineer; b. Lawrence, Kans., Mar. 10, 1951; d. Jose Joaquin and Graciela Maria (Balda) Portuguez; m. Steven Jay Eppler, Feb. 7, 1976; children: Christina Michelle, James Anthony. BA in Environment Studies, U. Kans., 1974. Engring. technician Black & Veatch, Kansas City, Mo., 1974-77, J.F. Pritchard Co., Kansas City, Mo., 1977-78; sales engr. Dust Suppression Systems, Kansas City, Mo., 1978-80; application engr. Fairbanks Morse, Kansas City, Kans., 1980-82; project engr. Smith & Loveless, Inc., Lenexa, Kans., 1982—; translator, tchr. Berlitz Sch. Langs., Kansas City, Mo., 1977-80. Mem. Exec. Women Internat., Sigma Kappa. Republican. Roman Catholic. Home: 16121 W 124th Circle Olathe KS 66062

EPPLER, JUANITA ELAINE, healthcare adminstrator; b. Bartlesville, Okla., Nov. 26, 1947; d. Phillip Emmert and Betty Juanita (Swick) Pearson; m. James Edward Eppler (div.); 1 child, Michelle Leigh. BS in Nursing, U. Tulsa, 1978; MS in Nursing, Idaho State U., 1984. RN, Mo. Instr. Bartlesville (Okla.) Wesleyan Coll., 1978; staff nurse Jane Phillips Episcopal/Meml. Hosp., Bartlesville, 1974-78; office mgr., nurse E.M. Amew, M.D., Bartlesville, 1981-82; staff nurse Pocatello (Idaho) Regional Med. Ctr., 1982-83, Bannock Regional Med. Ctr., Pocatello, 1983-84; head nurse VA Hosp., Albuquerque, 1985-86; nursing care coordinator VA Hosp., Muskogee, Okla., 1986-87, utilization rev. coordinator, 1987—; grad. rep. Task Force for Devel. of Model Nurse, 1983, external program rev. Idaho State U., Pocatello, 1984. Vol. Washington County Nurses Office, Bartlesville, Okla., 1978-80. Mem. Am. Nurse Assn. (pres. 1980), Okla. Nurses Assn., (spkr. 1979),SE Idaho Assn. Nursing (speaker 1984), Sigma Theta Tau. Episcopal. Lodge: Eastern Star. Home: 1306 Patterson Muskogee OK 74403 Office: VA Hosp Honor Heights Dr Muskogee OK 74403

EPPLEY, FRANCES FIELDEN, educator, author; b. Knoxville, Tenn., July 18, 1921; d. Chester Earl and Beulah Magnolia (Wells) Fielden; m. Gordon Talmage Cougle, July 25, 1942; children—Russell Gordon Eppley, Carolyn Eppley Horseman; m. Fred Coan Eppley, Mar. 8, 1953; 1 child, Charlene Eppley Sellers. B.A. in English, Carson Newman Coll., 1942; M.A., Winthrop Coll., 1963. Tchr., East Corinth (Maine) Acad., 1942-43; tchr. pub. schs., Charlotte, N.C., 1950-53, 59-83, Greenville, S.C., 1954-56, Spartanburg, S.C., 1957-58; head start tchr., summers 1964-68. Mem. hist. com. N.C. Bapt. Conv., 1985-88. Alpha Delta Kappa grantee, 1970. Mem. NEA, N.C. Social Studies Conf., Writers Assn., Alpha Delta Kappa, Pi Kappa Delta, Alpha Psi Omega. Baptist. Author: First Baptist Church of Charlotte, North Carolina: Its Heritage, 1981; History of Flint Hill, 1983; The First Astrologer, 1983, Sammy's Song, 1984; No Show Dog, 1985; Sun Signs for Christians, 1985; Astrology and Prophecy, 1987, Our Heavenly Home, 1987, Men Like-, 1987, A Hammer in the Land, 1988, Aunt Lillian's Seafoam Candy, 1988, Women's Lib in the Bible, 1988, William Penn, 1988, Columbus Was a Christian, 1988, Horoscopes of the Presidents, 1988; (mus. drama): The Place To Be, 1982, Praise in the West, 1987; (mus. show): Songs of The People, 1983; (song): Katie, 1985, (cantata) How Come, Jesus?

EPSTEIN, BARBARA, editor; b. Boston, Aug. 30, 1929; d. H.W. and Helen (Diamond) Zimmerman; children: Jacob, Helen. B.A., Radcliffe Coll., 1949. Editor N.Y. Review of Books, N.Y.C., 1963—. Office: NY Review of Books 250 W 57th St New York NY 10019

EPSTEIN, BEE J., consultant, professional speaker; b. Tubingen, Fed. Republic Germany, July 14, 1937; came to U.S., 1940, naturalized, 1945; d. Paul and Milly (Stern) Singer; student Reed Coll., 1954-57; m. Leonard Epstein, June 14, 1959 (div. 1982); children—Bettina, Nicole, Seth. BA, U. Calif., Berkeley, 1958; MA, Goddard Coll., 1976; PhD, Internat. Coll., 1982. Bus. instr. Monterey Peninsula Coll., 1975-85; owner, mgr. Bee Epstein Assos., cons. to mgmt., Carmel, Calif., 1977—; pres. Success Tours Inc., Carmel, 1981—; founder, prin. Monterey Profl. Speakers, 1982; instr. Monterey Peninsula Coll., Golden Gate U., U. Calif., Santa Cruz, Am. Inst. Banking, Inst. Ednl. Leadership, Calif. State Fire Acad. Monterey Peninsula Coll., U. Calif., Berkeley, Foothill Coll., U. Alaska. Author: The Working Woman's Stress First Aid Handbook, How to Create Balance at Work, at Home, in Your Life; contbr. articles to newspapers and trade mags. Research grantee, 1976. Mem. Nat. Speakers' Assn., Am. Soc. Tng. and Devel., Nat. Assn. Female Execs., Peninsula Profl. Women's Network, Calif. Tchrs. Assn. Democrat. Jewish. Office: PO Box 221383 Carmel CA 93922

EPSTEIN, EILEEN RENEE, pharmacist; b. Bronx, N.Y., Sept. 15, 1951; d. Sheldon Myron and Helen Lea (Kerman) E. BS, Columbia U., 1974; MS, Arnold and Marie Schwartz Coll. Pharmacy, 1981. Lic. pharmacist N.Y., N.J., Fla. Owner New Castle Prescription Ctr., Chappaqua, N.Y., 1974-78; adminstr. pharmacy Mt. Sinai Hosp., N.Y.C., 1981-83; mgr. East Coast regional pharmacy Abbott HomeCare, Fairfield, N.J., 1983—; staff pharmacist Montefiore Hosp. and Med. Ctr., Bronx, 1976-81; presentor poster session Pediatric and Adolescent Patient Counseling, 1981. Bd. dirs. Westchestertowne Houses Condo, Yonkers, N.Y. Mem. Am. Soc. Hosp. Pharmacists, Am. Soc. for Parenteral and Enteral Nutrition, N.Y. State Council Hosp. Pharmacists (joint com. with industry 1985, chairperson midyear clin. meeting 1985, vice chairperson, 1984), N.Y.C. Soc. Hosp. Pharmacists, N.J. Soc. Hosp. Pharmacists, N.J. Pharm. Assn.; Columbia U. Pharm. Scis. Alumni Assn. (bd. dirs. 1983, 2d v.p. 1984, 1st v.p. 1985-87). Home: 27 Trenton Terr Wayne NJ 07470 Office: Abbott HomeCare 97B Fairfield Rd Fairfield NJ 07006

EPSTEIN, HELEN, writer; b. Prague, Czechoslovakia, Nov. 27, 1947; came to U.S., 1948; d. Kurt and Franci (Rabinek) E.; m. Patrick Mehr, Dec. 11, 1983; children: Daniel Kurt, Samuel Alex. BA, Hebrew U., Isreal, 1970; MSc, Columbia U., 1971. Asst. prof. N.Y.U., 1976-81, assoc. prof. journalism, 1981-87; freelance writer N.Y.C., 1968—; guest lectr., cons. coll. courses. 1985—. Author: Children of the Holocaust, 1979 (Best Books of 1979 N.Y. Times), The Companies She Keeps, 1985, Music Talks, 1987, (playwright) Here it Will Be Different, 1988; contbg. editor, Boston Review, 1985—. Recipient Clarion award Women in Communications, 1984, Holocaust award .Y. Psychol. Assn., 1984. Jewish.

EPSTEIN, JUDITH ANN, lawyer; b. Los Angeles, Dec. 23, 1942; d. Gerald Elliot and Harriet (Hirsch) Rubens; m. Joseph I. Epstein, Oct. 4, 1964; children: Mark Douglas, Laura Ann. AB, U. Calif., Berkeley, 1964; MA, U. San Francisco, 1974, JD, 1977. Bar: Calif. 1978, U.S. Dist. Ct. (no. dist.) Calif 1978, U.S. Supreme Ct. 1983, U.S. Ct. Appeals (9th cir.) 1984. With social services dept. Sutter County, Yuba City, Calif., 1964-66; bus. devel. assoc. Yuba County C. of C., Marysville, Calif., 1968-70; research clk. Calif. Supreme Ct., San Fransisco, 1977; ptnr. Crosby, Heafey, Roach & May, Oakland, Calif., 1978—; lectr. U. Calif. Grad. Sch. of Journalism in Media Law, Berkeley, 1987—; bd. dirs. Sierra Pacific Steel, Hayward, Calif. Bd. dirs., v.p. Oakland Ballet, 1980—. Recipient Pres.'s award Oakland Ballet. Mem. Calif. Women Lawyers Assn., Alameda Bar Assn. Club: Berkeley Tennis. Office: Crosby Heafey Roach & May 1999 Harrison Oakland CA 94612

EPSTEIN, SELMA, pianist; b. Bklyn.; d. Samuel and Tillie (Schneider) Schechtman; m. Joseph Epstein, May 30, 1950. Grad. Juilliard Sch., 1949. Debut as concert pianist Carnegie Hall, N.Y.C., 1942; pianist numerous concerts, recitals; recorded numerous albums and cassettes; composer piano pieces. Most recent recital: Luton, Eng., U.S. premiere of the Percy Grainger piano concerto; numerous lecture-recitals including univs. and profl. orgns. Lectr., U.S. Info. Service, Europe, Australia, Japan, Hong Kong, Okinawa, New Zealand, introducing music of U.S. 20th Century composers, women and black composers; editor: piano music by Lili Boulanger, Percy Grainger, Maria Hester, Parke and Dame Ethel Smyth; pianist for Epstein Duo; rec. artist: (album) Selma Epstein Plays Percy Grainger, Vol. 1, numerous cassettes of live performances. Grantee U.S Internat. Studies, 1960—. First American to teach full time at an Australian Conservatory, Newcastle Conservatory, 1972-75. Founder of Group Piano Studios and author of 8 group teaching manuals. Co-founder Md. Women's Symphony; founder, bd. dirs. Chromattica USA Chamber Music Group of Balt. Mem. Am. Grainger Soc. (pres.), Am. Thyroid Soc. (v.p. Md. chpt.), Internat. Congress Women in Music (bd. dirs. Mid-Atlantic region). Club: West Point Parents' (founder 1979), Md. Parents, Va. Parents. Washington Parents. Avocations: painting, gardening, reading, cooking. Home and Office: 2443 Pickwick Rd Dickeyville MD 21207

EPSTEIN, SUSAN DERMAN, public health administrator; b. N.Y.C., Apr. 9, 1948; d. Sidney C. and Sheila R. (Pollock) Derman; m. Matthew S. Epstein, May 9, 1971; children—Dale Judith, Andrew Jacob. B.A., Conn. Coll., 1970; M.Pub. Adminstrn., U. N.H., 1975. Adminstrv. asst. planning and budget N.Y.C. Health Services Adminstrn., 1970-71; sr. planner Mass. Dept. Youth Services, Boston, 1971-73; exec. dir. Newmarket Regional Health Ctr. (N.H.), 1975-76; asst. chief med. services N.H. Dept. Health and Welfare, Concord, 1976-77; program dir. United Health Systems Agy., Concord, 1977-81; dep. dir. pub. health services State of N.H., Concord, 1987; with bd. edn., Concord; cons. in field. Treas., sec. N.H. Civil Liberties Union, Concord, 1976-81; del. N.H. Democratic Conv., Manchester, 1978; chmn. med. care adv. com. N.H. Dept. Health and Welfare, 1979-81; elected Concord Sch. Bd., 1987—. Jewish. Club: West Concord Garden (treas. 1983-84).

ERB, BETTIE SUE, health care administrator; b. Bowling Green, Ky., Dec. 2, 1944; d. Raymond Claypool and Julia Evelyn (Merklin) N.; m. Allan Robert Erb, May 29, 1963 (div. July 1975); children: Kenneth Wade, Peter Travis, Ernest Robert. BS in Occupational Therapy, U. Wash., 1973. Registered Occupational Therapist. Staff therapist St. Mary Hosp., Walla Walla, Wash., 1973-75, chief occupational therapist, 1975-79, coordinator of rehab., 1979-82; dir. rehab. services St. Mary Med. Ctr., Walla Walla, 1982-84; founder, exec. dir. Three Rivers Rehab. Ctr., Richland, Wash., 1984—; bd. dirs. Northwest Assn. Rehab., Seattle, 1984-86, sec., 1986-87, Neurol. Ctr. of Richland, 1985-86, v.p., 1986-87, Lillie Rice Ctr., Walla Walla, 1984-87; cons. Green Mountain Rehab. Medicine, Bremerton, Wash., 1986-87, Walla Walla, 1987—. Mem. Am. Occupational Therapy Assn., Wash. Occupational Therapy Assn. (bd. dirs. 1974-77). Republican. Baptist. Home and Office: 633 Juniper Walla Walla WA 99362

ERB, PHYLLIS, chemical engineer; b. Milw., Aug. 7, 1941; d. Ernest Wilhelm and Mary (Anderson) Erb; B.S. in Chem. Engring., U. Wis.-Madison, 1964. Research engr. DuPont Co., Wilmington, Del., 1964-70, advt. rep. for indsl. chem., synthetic films, x-ray testing products, 1970-73; tech. rep. x-ray products, N.Y.C., 1974-77; sales mgr. Celanese Corp., Charlotte, N.C., 1977-80; advt. mgr. Ga.-Pacific Corp., Atlanta, 1980-83, dir. communications chems., 1984—. Active campaigns for gov. Del. R. Peterson and P.S. DuPont; active Young Republicans N.C.; sec. Carriage Post Condominium, N.J., 1975, 76; controller Sir Johns Hill Condominium, N.C., 1977-80; bd. dirs. Chamber Music Soc., Charlotte, 1979. Mem. Internat. Assn. Bus. Communicators, Soc. Plastics Engrs., Atlanta Women's C. of C., Am. Chem. Soc., Formaldehyde Inst. (communications com.), Chem. Mfrs. Assn. (energy task force). Home: 4 Pointe Terr Atlanta GA 30339 Office: 133 Peachtree St Atlanta GA 30303

ERBACHER, KATHRYN ANNE, writer, editor; b. Kansas City, Mo., Dec. 11, 1947; d. Philip Joseph and Thelma Lillian (Hines) E. BS in English, U. Kans., 1970; BA magna cum laude in Art, Metro State Coll., Denver, 1983. Reporter, Kansas City Star (Mo.), 1970-71; newswriter Washington U., St. Louis, 1972-76; copy editor Kansas City Star-Times (Mo.), 1976-79; editor Petro-Lewis Corp., Denver, 1979-82; assoc. Artours, Inc., Denver, 1983-84; assoc. editor arts and travel editor Denver Mag., 1984-86; freelance writer, editor, 1986—; internat. editor Gates Rubber Co., Denver, 1987—. Creative dir. TV shorts for contemporary art collection Denver Art Mus., 1983. Mem. Metro State Coll. Alumni Bd. Dirs., 1986-87, co-chair 1987 Metro State Coll. Alumni Awards Dinner, Denver; bd. govs. Metro State Coll. Found., 1986-87. Recipient award for arts writing Denver Partnership, 1986. Mem. Women in Communications (jobs chmn. Denver 1981-82). Home: 1539 Platte St Denver CO 80202

ERBE, YVONNE MARY, marketing specialist, educator; b. Wausau, Wis., Nov. 18, 1947; d. Rudolph Anton and Lucille Virginia (Andrew) Karlen; m. Drake H. Erbe, June 26, 1971; children—Daniel, Heather. B.Mus.Edn., U. Wis., Madison, 1969; postgrad. U. Wis.-Milw. Lic. music educator, Wis, Ky. Music-vocal tchr. Bayport Jr. High Sch., Greenbay, Wis., 1969-70; tchr. bassoon, oboe U. Wis.-Greenbay, 1969-70; jr. high choral dir. Kenosha Unified Schs., Wis., 1970-76; univ. supr.-edn. U. Wis.-Parkside, Kenosha, 1976-78; polit. action com. mem. Northern Hills Sch. and Onalaska Mid. Sch., 1981-89; mktg. specialist Metro Prodns., La Crosse, Wis., 1984-85; tchr. music elem., jr. high sch., LaCrosse, Wis., 1987-88, Lexington, Ky., 1988—. Parent vol. coordinator Fauver Hill Sch., 1983-84; sec. exec. bd. Great River Festival of Arts, La Crosse, 1982-83, 1st v.p. exec. bd., chmn. adult choral workshop and performance, chmn. swing choir workshop, 1983-84, pres. bd. dirs., 1984-85; pres. La Crosse Area Newcomers Club, 1982-83; tchr. Confraternity of Christian Doctrine, 1985-88, bd. dirs. La Crosse Boy Choir, 1985-88. Roman Catholic. Avocations: tennis, cross-country skiing, aerobic exercises, needlecrafts, gourmet cooking. Home: 520 16th Ave N Onalaska WI 54650

ERBISCH, CAROL SUZANNE, day care director; b. Ft. Wayne, Ind.; d. James Edwin Sr. and Susie Mae (Nutter) Doelling; m. Gerald R. Baker, June, 1962 (div. 1966); 1 child, Erin Lee; m. Jeffrey E. Baker, June, 1967 (div. 1972); 1 child, Shannon Rae; m. Gilbert Erbisch, 1985. Student, Internat. Bus. Coll., Ft. Wayne, 1961. Expeditor Wayne Fabricating, Ft. Wayne, 1971; county adminstr. Champaign (Ill.) County Bd., 1974-76; sec. WICD-TV, Champaign, 1976-77; ops. chmn. 40 Plus of Colo., Inc., Denver, 1983, v.p., 1984-85, pres., 1985-86; asst. dir. St. Anne's Extended Day Program, Denver, 1986—. Editor The Village Voice newsletter, Savoy, Ill., 1974. Chmn. Winfield Village Swimming Pool com., Savoy, 1975. Office: St Anne's Extended Day Program 2701 S York St Denver CO 80210

ERCOLINO, ELIZABETH LIND, communications engineer, quality consultant; b. Norristown, Pa., Aug. 26, 1950; d. Norman Edward and Audrey Jean (Gleckler) L.; m. Robert Bruce Ercolino, Dec. 10, 1941. Course study in art design, Phila. Coll. Art, 1966; AS in Statistics, Wharton Sch. Bus., 1977; BS in Data Communications, Rutgers U., 1983; MS in Orgnl. Design, Princeton U., 1987. Telephone operator Bell of Pa., Doylestown, 1968-71; network adminstr. Bell of Pa., Ft. Washington, 1971-77; with tng. devel. staff Bell of Pa., Phila., 1977-78, with tng. delivery staff, 1978-79, with engring. ataff, 1979-82; network design engr. N.J. Bell/Am. Bell, Parsipanny, 1982-84; with network design staff Info. Systems AT&T, Norristown, 1984-85; quality cons. Communications/Info. AT&T, Parsipanny, 1985—. Mem. Nat. Assn. Female Execs., Women in Art. Office: AT&T Rt 202/206 N Room 2C124D Bedminster NJ 07921

ERDEN, SYBIL ISOLDE, artist; b. N.Y.C., Nov. 30, 1950; d. Mark and Annelise (Stautner) E.; m. Philip M. Freund, July 7, 1970 (div. 1978). Student, Acad. of Art, San Francisco, 1970-71, San Francisco Art Inst., 1971-73. lectr. Calif. Coll. Arts and Crafts, 1978, Tempe (Ariz.) Fine Art Ctr., 1985, Collins Gallery, San Francisco, 1986, Collage Art Appreciation Group, Colorado Springs, Colo., 1987, South Park Sch. Dist., Fairplay, Colo., 1987. One-man shows include The Bush Street Gallery, San Francisco, 1977, The Top Floor Gallery, San Francisco, 1979, I-Beam, San Francisco, 1980, Diablo Valley Coll., Walnut Creek, Calif., 1980, The Stable, San Francisco, 1982, Tempe Fine Arts Ctr., 1985, Collins Gallery, San Francisco, 1986, Berkeley (Calif.) Art Ctr., 1986; exhibited in group shows at San Francisco Art Inst., 1973, The Cave, San Francisco, 1981, Alwun House, Phoenix, 1985, 87, Grand Canyon Coll., Phoenix, 1988, N.Mex. Jr. Coll., 1988, San Francisco State U., 1988; work represented in San Francisco Mus. Art, OMNI Mag., N.Y.C., Smithsonian Mus. Archive of Am. Art, Washington; executed mural office of Dr. Peter Eckman, San Francisco, 1977, HandBall Express, San Francisco, 1981. Mem. Ariz. Visionary Alternative (founder, dir. 1984-88), Am. Surrealist Initiative, Nat. Tattoo Assn. Democrat. Jewish.

ERDMAN, BARBARA, visual artist; b. N.Y.C., Jan. 30, 1936; d. Isidore and Julia (Burstein) E. Student, Chinese Inst., 1959-60; BFA, Cornell U., 1956. Visual artist Santa Fe, 1977—; pres. bd. dirs. Santa Fe Ctr. Photography, 1983; guest critic Studio Arte Centro Internat., Florence, Italy, 1986; guest lectr. Austin Coll. Sherman, Tex., 1986; mem. Oracle Conf. Polaroid Corp., nationwide, 1986—. Exhibited in numerous group shows, 1959—; one man shows include Aspen Inst., Baca, Colo., 1981, Scottsdale (Ariz.) Ctr. for the Arts, 1988. Active Santa Fe Dems., 1980—; bd. dirs. N.Mex. Right to Choose, Santa Fe, 1981-87; mem. N.Mex. Mus. Found., Aluquerque Mus. Found. Mem. Art Student's League, Soc. for

Photographic Edn. (guest lectr. 1987), Santa Fe Ctr. for Photography (pres. 1983—). Home: 2006 Conejo Dr Santa Fe NM 87501

ERDMAN, DOROTHY ANN, elementary educator, principal; b. Durango, Colo., Sept. 28, 1935; d. Robert Louis and Dorothy Alice (Booth) Frazer; m. Jimmie Roland Noe, June 14, 1954 (div.); children: David Ray, James Roland, Robert Wendler; m. Robert Ray Erdman, May 5, 1967; children: Lester Athen, Lisa Elaine. BS in Edn., No .Ariz. U., 1956; MS, Reading U. of Ariz., 1980. Cert. elem. sch. prin. 1st grade tchr. Casa Grande (Ariz.) Elem. Sch. Dist., 1956-57, La Mesa (Calif.) Elem. Sch. Dist., 1957-59; elem tchr. Santee (Calif.) Elem. Sch. Dist., 1959-69; freelance salesperson cosmetics and lingerie Calif., Ariz., 1969-74; elem. tchr. Eloy (Ariz.) Elem. Sch. Dist., 1974-82, prin., 1982—; adult edn. tchr., San Diego, 1959-60. Sec. Eloy Tchrs. Orgn., 1977-78, pres. 1978-82, bd. dirs. Casa Grande Regional Hosp., 1986—. Mem. Am. Assn. Sch. Adminstrs., Ariz. Sch. Adminstrs., Inc. (sec. 1984-85, pres. 1985-87), Nat. Assn. Elem. Sch. Prins., Ariz. AWARE. Home: 1118 N Palo Verde Eloy AZ 85231 Office: Curiel Sch Eloy Elem Sch Dist 1011 N Sunshine Blvd Eloy AZ 85231

ERDOS, RENI, public affairs consultant; b. Bronx, N.Y., Aug. 1, 1941; d. Jack and Ida (Saffer) Klein; m. Ronald Clark Erdos, Aug. 4, 1963 (div.); children: Jennifer Eden, Jordan Evan. BA in Zoology, Hunter Coll., 1962. Tchr. biology N.Y.C. Sch. Systems, 1961-68; asst. to commr. N.J. Dept. Labor and Industry, 1974-78; exec. sec. N.J. Bd. Pharmacy, 1981-82; dir. fed. legislation N.J. Hosp. Assn., Princeton, 1982-84; pres. Reni Erdos Assocs., Summit, 1984—; mem. environ. health adv. bd. Union County Freeholders, 1979-84, home health adv. bd. Union County Hospice, Elizabeth, N.J., 1984—; cons. polit. campaigns., 1972—. Chair Dem. com. City of Summit, 1972-74, 87-88; mem. N.J. Dem. State Com., 1985—. Mem. Union County Womens Polit. Caucus (founding mem.). Jewish. Home and Office: 71 Passaic Ave Summit NJ 07901

ERICH, DOROTHY BEATRICE, nurse; b. Chillicothe, Ohio, Oct. 4, 1915; d. Oliver Gustave and Daisy Mae (Orr) E.; R.N., Bethesda Hosp., 1941; B.Th., Olivet Nazarene U., 1953. Nurse, Ft. Hamilton Hosp., Hamilton, Ohio, 1953-55, Chillicothe Hosp., 1955-60; orthopedic nurse Mt. Logan Sanitorium, Chillicothe, 1960-70; nurse surgery Greenfield (Ohio) Hosp., 1970-73; nursing cons. Gospel Light Nursing Home, Kingston, Ohio, 1980-84; part-time preacher in youth work; active vol. various sr. citizen orgns.. Mem. Am. Nurses Assn. Mem. Nazarene Ch. Republican.

ERICHSEN-HUBBARD, ISABEL JANICE, educator; b. LaCrosse, Wis., June 18, 1935; d. Frank Peter August and Janice May (Grutzmacher) Erichsen; B.S. with honors, U. Wis., Madison, 1957, M.S., 1979, postgrad., 1980; m. Allan Paterson, Apr. 4, 1959; children—Janel Isabel, John Allan. Tchr., Kenosha (Wis.) Bd. Edn., 1957-60; tchr., supr. Madison (Wis.) Bd. Edn., 1968—; cooperating tchr. sr. program U. Wis. master tchr. seminars, 1978—; pvt. piano and vocal coach, 1950—; choir dir. St. Mary's Lutheran Ch., Kenosha, 1959-61; mem., soloist Madison Meth. Ch. Diocesan Choir, 1981-83, U. Wisc. Choral Union Choir. Program chair YWCA, 1961-65; chmn. UNICEF, 1960, Coop. Nursery Sch., 1960; info. chmn. Am. Cancer Soc., Dane County, 1960-68; bd. dirs. , sec. Friends of Meth. Hosp., 1986-87, also vol. escort, info. desk, chapel musician; R.S.V.P. Sch. Liaison, 1977-88; adjucator Wis. ASsn. Music Schs., 1984; vol. Am. Players Theatre, 1987—; active Methodist Women's Soc., United Ch. Women, Madison Civic Assn., U. Wis. Cooperating Mentor Program, 1987-88, Opera Buffs, Wis. Exec. Mansion Guides, Wexford Homeowners Assn. Recipient Carol award Madison Jaycette Club, 1966, 3d grand prize Wis. State Jour. Cookbook, 1971, Golden Apple award Madison Met. Sch. Dist., 1988. Mem. NEA, Wis. Music Assn. (vocal adjucator 1985—), Wis. Edn. Assn., Madison Tchrs., Inc., Lafollette Area Lang. Arts Cadre, Madison Met. Sch. Dist. Human Relations Cadre, U. Wis. Alumni Assn. (life), Sigma Alpha Iota (Sword of Honor, past pres.), Chi Omega (alumni sec. 1970-87), Pi Kappa Delta. Clubs: Cherokee Country, Jr. Golf (dir. 1974-75). Author: Reading Techniques Using the Newspapers, Magazines, 1975; Spell It Again Sam, 1978; Hidden Curriculum, 1979; contbr. to Kenosha Kindergarten Teacher's Handbook, 1958. Home: 26 E Newhaven Circle Wexford Village Madison WI 53717-1051 Office: 2421 E Johnson St Madison WI 53704

ERICKSEN, ANNA MAE, retired nursing administrator; b. Moose Jaw, Sask., Can., Nov. 1, 1919; d. Eric Andrew and Evelyn (Kyle) E.; R.N., Deaconess Hosp., Spokane, Wash., 1943. Night charge nurse Deaconess Hosp., Spokane, 1943, pvt. duty nurse, 1946, staff nurse, 1947; head nurse emergency dept., outpatient dept., Spokane Poison Center, Deaconess Hosp., 1948-57, supr., 1957-70, asst. dir., 1970-73, assoc. dir. nursing service, 1973-78, adminstrv. asst. regional outreach services, physician liaison, 1978, asst. to adminstr., dir. outreach program, coordinator continuing edn., 1978-82, dir. Spokane Poison Center, dir. physician liaison, 1979-82; dir. outreach program Physician Liaison and Reg. Poison Ctr. Deaconess Med. Ctr., 1982-87; chmn. disaster com., mem. safety com.; advisor to Wash. State Assn. Nursing Students, 1956-60; bd. dirs. Regional Emergency Med. Services Council, 1975—, 1st v.p., 1978-79, chmn., 1979—; mem. N.E. Hosp. Disaster Com., Gov.'s ad hoc com. Emergency Med. Services, Emergency Med. Ambulance Pier Com., Emergency Med. and Ambulance Review Com., Review Com. for Tng. Emergency Med. and Paramed. Technicians; bd. dirs. Nat. Poison Center Network. Mem. Spokane Health Assn.; v.p. NE Heart Assn.; recruitment nurse for ARC in Inland Empire, 1960-68; bd. dirs. Spokane Area Safety Council, 1963-67, vice chmn., 1966-67; bd. govs. Home Safety Council Wash. State, 1966-69, v.p., 1969-70; bd. dirs. NE chpt. Wash. State Heart Assn., 1966—, v.p., 1974-75; polio fund com. Spokane County Med. Soc.; chmn. adv. bd. Rape Crisis Network 1978, 1980, 1982-84; program chmn. Spokane Youth Health Council; bd. dirs. Human Tng. Services Inst., Spokane, 1974-80, sec.-treas., 1976-77; bd. dirs. ARC, 1985-87; mem. panels United Crusade; panel mem. campaign com. United Way, 1978-81; active Polio Program, 1962-69; adv. bd. Samaritan Ctr. of Inland Empire, 1981-85. Served to capt. Nurse Corps, U.S. Army, 1943-46. Named Spokane Woman of Achievement, Am. Bus. and Profl. Women, 1961, Theta Sigma Phi, 1968, Wash. State's Most Involved Nurse, 1970, Outstanding Lady of Year, Spokane, 1972; recipient Key award Inland Empire chpt. Safety Council, 1976, disting. citizen award Rotary Club of Spokane, 1982, 1st Ericksen award for emergency nursing, 1985; award of appreciation Am. Lupus Soc., 1985. Mem. Inland Empire (bd. 1956-60), Wash. State (bd. dirs. 1959-63, pres. 1960-64, chmn. careers com. 1970-72), Am. (del. 1960-62, 64), Emergency Dept. (founder Inland Empire chpt., pres. 1971, region X rep., 1970-77, asst. exec. dir. 1972, nat. pres. 1975-76, nat. bd. dirs. 1970-77) nurses assns., Spokane Greater Community Found., 1978—. Presbyterian. Clubs: Altrusa (pres. 1965-68), Epsilon Sigma Alpha (pres. Spokane chpt. 1960-62, treas. 1958-59, mem. state coms.). Home: 2311 W 16th Ave #70 Spokane WA 99204 Office: Deaconess Med Ctr-Spokane W 800 Fifth Ave PO Box 248 Spokane WA 00248

ERICKSON, DIANE QUINN, banker, lawyer; b. La Grange, Ill., Oct. 8, 1959; d. Stanley Brittian Sr. and Marilyn Agnes (Miller) Quinn; m. Russell Lee Erickson, Mar. 9, 1985. BS in Psychology, U. Ill., 1981; JD, Valparaiso U., 1984. Assoc. Dreyer, Foote, et al, Aurora, Ill., 1984-87; trust officer, atty. 1st Nat. Bank Des Plaines, Ill., 1987—. Mem. Ill. Bar Assn., DuPage County Bar Assn., N.W. Suburban Bar Assn., Chgo. Bar Assn., Nat. Assn. Female Execs., Corp. Fiduciaries Assn. Nat. Assn. Banking Women. Lutheran. Home: 148 Waxwing Ave Naperville IL 60565 Office: 1st Nat Bank Des Plaines 701 Lee St Des Plaines IL 60016-4554

ERICKSON, GAIL, lawyer; b. Pasadena, Calif., Feb. 9, 1934; d. Alfred Louis and Helen Hield (Baker) E. BA, Stanford U., 1955; JD, Harvard U., 1958. Bar: N.Y. 1959. Atty. W. R. Grace and Co., N.Y.C., 1958—, now sr. v.p., gen. counsel, sec. Mem. ABA. Democrat. Club: Harvard. Office: WR Grace and Co 1114 Ave of the Americas New York NY 10036 *

ERICKSON, JANE B., speech communications educator, consultant; b. Grosse Pointe, Mich., Apr. 7, 1945; d. Devere and Hettie Marie (Ballard) Turrell; m. Mark Kevin Erickson, Aug. 14, 1976; 1 child, Kathryn DeVere. A.A., Highland Park Community Coll., 1965; B.S., Eastern Mich. U., 1967; M.Ed., Wayne State U., 1974. Tchr. English and drama Lake Shore Schs., St. Clair Shores, Mich., 1967-69, tchr. English and debate, 1969-73, coordinator, 1973—; pvt. edn. cons., Utica, Mich., 1974—; puppeteer Mattel Toys, Sterling Heights, Mich., 1986. Vol. sr. citizens, St. Clair Shores, 1985-86. Recipient Forensic award Detroit Free Press, 1962-63; Key to City award St. Clair Shores, 1963. Mem. Nat. Indian Edn. Assn., Mich. Indian Community Edn. Assn. (sec. 1986, pres. 1987), Partnerships in Bus. (coordinator 1986—), Kappa Delta Pi, Pi Lambda Theta. Christian Scientist. Avocations: puppetry; music; reading; travel; quilting; brainstorming. Office: Lake Shore Schs 30401 Taylor Saint Clair Shores MI 48082

ERICKSON, LINDA JUANITA, advertising professional, writer; b. Cass Lake, Minn., Sept. 19, 1948; d. Lloyd Edwin Erickson and Sylvia (Carlson) Bell; m. Joseph John McGee, Nov. 25, 1969 (div. Mar. 1978); 1 child, Kristina McGee. Student, Akron (Ohio) State Coll., 1967-68. Bunny N.Y. Playboy Club, Manhattan, 1968-70; asst. bookkeeper Arista Stationery, Manhattan, 1973-74; account exec. Met. Life Ins. Co., Queens, N.Y., 1978-80; fin. cons. Bowery Savs. Bank, East Northport, N.Y., 1980-81; account exec. Nassau-Queens Publs., Jericho, N.Y., 1982-83; account exec., food critic Pennysaver of Brookhaven, Medford, N.Y., 1983-84; sales mgr., writer Long Island Nightlife mag., Deer Park, N.Y., 1984-87; owner, prin. writer The Erickson Advt. Agy., Miller Place, N.Y., 1987—; Contbr. numerous articles Dining Out. Mem. Assn. for Commerce and Industry, Mt. Sinai-Miller Place C. of C. Democrat. Lutheran. Home and Office: The Erickson Advt Agy 154 Harrison Ave Miller Place NY 11764

ERICKSON, MILDRED BRINKMEIER, university dean, educator; b. Hannibal, Mo., Sept. 8, 1913; d. Louis C. and Anna G. (Schmidt) Brinkmeier; AA, Hannibal-LaGrange Coll., 1932; BS, Northwestern U., 1934, MA, 1937; PhD, Mich. State U., 1968; m. Clifford E. Erickson, June 10, 1937; children: W. Bruce, Marilyn Kay. Tchr., Central Jr. High Sch., Hannibal, 1934-35, Sycamore (Ill.) Community High Sch., 1935-37; asst. instr. Am. thought and lang. Mich. State U., East Lansing, 1963-65, instr., 1965-68, counselor U. Coll., 1965-68, asst. prof. Am. thought and lang., 1968-71, asso. prof., 1971-75, prof., 1975-81, counselor, 1968-75, asst. dean continuing edn., 1972-75, asst. dean lifelong edn. programs, 1975-81, asst. dean and prof. emeritus, 1981—, mem. univ. com. on aging, 1974-85, univ. devel. fund com., 1979-86; cons. various bus. firms, instns., 1972—; appeared as guest various radio and TV programs, 1970—; speaker numerous community groups. Mem. Tng. Plan Adv. Task Force, Mich. Dept. Civil Service, 1979, 84—; mem. citizens budget com. East Lansing Bd. Edn., 1984-86; active Mich. Edn. Forum, 1981-83, Mich. Equal Ptnrs. in Edn., 1982-88, Mich. Arthritis Found., 1979-83, Mich. Health Adv. Council, 1981-83; mem. adv. bd. Lansing Sch. Health Project, 1977, 78; officer Band Parents, 1952-54; bd. dirs. YWCA, East Lansing, Mich., 1950-52, Lansing Women's Bur., 1978-80; bd. dirs. Mildred B. Erickson Fellowship in Support of Lifelong Edn. for Women and Men, 1974—, sec., 1974-78, mem. various coms., 1974—. Recipient Maharishi Community award, 1978, Citation of Excellence, Gov. Mich., 1978, Cert. of Recognition, YWCA, 1975; Woman of Yr. award Mich. Assn. Professions, 1980; Service to Lifelong Edn. award Mich. State U., 1980; named lifetime hon. mem. Adult and Continuing Edn. Assn. of Mich. Mem. Am. Personnel and Guidance Assn., Am. Coll. Personnel Assn., Adult Edn. Assn., Nat. Univ. Extension Assn., NEA, Soc. Study of Midwestern Lit., Mich. Women's Studies Assn., Acad. Affairs Adminstrs., Am. Assn. Higher Edn., LWV, Assn. Gen. and Liberal Studies, AAUW (state legis. com. 1981-83, state edn. com. 1983-88, state senator's edn. com. 1978—), P.E.O., Phi Mu, Sigma Alpha Iota (patroness 1971—), Phi Delta Kappa, Pi Lambda Theta (chpt. pres. 1933-35), Phi Kappa Phi (chpt. pres. 1977). Club: Zonta Internat. (Outstanding Community Service award 1981). Author: (with Francoise Murray) The Adult Female Human Being, 1975, 77, 80; contbr. articles on counseling and ednl. research to profl. jours. Home: 511 Wildwood Dr East Lansing MI 48823 Office: Mich State Univ East 7 Kellogg Ctr Lansing MI 48824

ERICKSON, NANCY SALOME, lawyer, educator; b. Orange, N.J., Sept. 26, 1945; d. George Hugh and Salome Celestia (Brennesholtz) E.; 1 child, Laura. B.A., Vassar Coll., 1967; J.D., Bklyn. Law Sch., 1973; LL.M., Yale U., 1979. Bar: N.Y. 1974. Assoc. Botein, Hays, Sklar & Herzberg, N.Y.C., 1973-75; from asst. prof. to assoc. prof. N.Y. Law Sch., N.Y.C., 1975-80; from assoc. prof. to prof. law Ohio State U. Coll. Law, Columbus, 1980-88; asst. corp. counsel N.Y.C. Law Dept., 1987—; vis. assoc. prof. law Cornell U. Law Sch., spring 1980; disting. vis. prof. Seton Hall U. Law Sch., Newark, 1986-87; asst. corp. counsel N.Y.C. Law Dept. 1987—. Editor-in-chief Bklyn. Law Sch. Law Rev., 1972-73; contbr. articles on sex discrimination, family law and constl. law to profl. jours. Mem. Soc. Study Women in Legal History (founder, coordinator 1980), Assn. Am. Law Schs. (newsletter editor sect. women in legal edn. 1978-87), Am. Soc. Legal History, Soc. Am. Law Tchrs., Met. Women Law Tchrs. Assn. N.Y.C. (a founder). Home: 619 Carroll St Brooklyn NY 11215

ERICSON, RUTH ANN, psychiatrist; b. Assaria, Kans., May 15; d. William Albert and Anna Mathilda (Almquist) E.; student So. Meth. U., 1945-47; B.S., Bethany Coll.; M.D., U. Tex., 1951. Intern, Calif. Hosp., Los Angeles, 1951-52; resident in psychiatry U. Tex. Med. Br., Galveston, 1952-55; psychiatrist Child Guidance Clinic, Dallas, 1955-63; clin. instr. Southwestern Med. Sch., Dallas, 1955-72; practice medicine specializing in psychiatry, Dallas, 1955—; cons. Dallas Intertribal Council Clinic, 1974-81, Dallas Ind. Sch. Dist., U.S. Army, Welfare Dept., Tribal Concerns, alcoholism, Adv. Bd. Intertribal Council. Fellow Am. Geriatrics Assn.; mem. So., Tex., Dallas med. assns., Am. (life), Tex., North Tex. psychiat. assns., Am. Med. Women's Assn., Dallas Area Women Psychiatrists, Alumni Assn. U. Tex. (Med. Br.), Navy League (life), Air Force Assn., Tex. (life mem.), Dallas (life mem., pres. 1972-73, 82-84) archaeol. socs., C., South Tex. Archaeol. Soc., N. Mex. Archaeol. Soc., Paleopathology Soc., Alpha Omega Alpha, Delta Psi Omega, Alpha Psi Omega, Pi Gamma Mu, Lambda Sigma, Alpha Epsilon Iota. Lutheran. Home: 4007 Shady Hill Dr Dallas TX 75229 Office: 2915 LBJ Freeway Suite 135 Dallas TX 75234

ERIKSON, PENNY LAUREN, advertising executive; b. San Francisco, Jan. 8, 1950; d. V. M. Jr. and Nadine (Palmerton) Hanks; m. Scott R. Erikson, Aug. 19, 1973 (div. May 1980); m. David Hooper, July 31, 1980. BA, U. Calif., Berkeley, 1971. Sales exec. CRM Inc., Del Mar, Calif., 1971-73; research mgr. W.H. Freeman Inc., San Francisco, 1973-76; research group head Ogilvy & Mather, N.Y.C., 1977-80; campaigns mgr. World Wildlife Fund Internat., Gland, Switzerland, 1979-80; v.p., assoc. research dir. Young & Rubicam, N.Y.C., 1980-85, sr. v.p., mgr. client services, 1985—. Office: Young & Rubicam New York 285 Madison Ave New York NY 10017

ERKER, MICHELE K., military officer; b. Carmel, Calif., Aug. 4, 1958; d. Victor Edwards and Joyce Adams (Clark) E.; m. Erich Erker, Sept. 26, 1985. BA, Mich. State U., 1980. Commd. U.S. Army, 1980, advanced through ranks to capt., 1984; platoon leader 124th maintenance battalion 2d armored div. U.S. Army, Ft. Hood, Tex., 1980-81, maintenance control officer, 1981-82; leader armament platoon/attack helicopter maintenance test pilot 5th transp. bn., 101st airborne div. U.S. Army, Ft. Campbell, Ky., 1984-85, leader repair platoon/attack helicopter maintenance test pilot, 222d aviation bn., 1985-86, adjutant personnel adminstr. HHSC, 1986—. Mem. The Whirley-Girls Inc., Army Aviation Assn. of Am., Assn. of the U.S. Army, Nat. Assn. Female Execs. Republican. Episcopalian. Home: 533 Pollard Rd Clarksville TN 37042 Office: Office of Staff Judge Advocate 101st Airborne Div Fort Campbell KY 42223

ERKKILA, BARBARA LOUISE, author, newspaper writer; b. Boston, July 11, 1918; d. John William and Adelia Parsons (Jones) Howell; student Boston U. Evening Coll., 1959; m. Onni R. Erkkila, Apr. 27, 1941 (dec. 1981); children: John W., Kathleen L., Marjorie A. Corr., Gloucester (Mass.) Daily Times, 1936-53, feature writer, 1953—, women's editor, 1967-72, community news editor, 1972-74; free-lance article writer for mags., 1953—; editor weekly mag. Essex County Newspapers, Gloucester, 1973, editorial asst., 1974-85, writer, photographer, 1970—; tchr. Russian, Ipswich (Mass.) Public Schs., evenings, 1962-63. Mem. price panel Office Price Adminstrn., 1944-46; mem. ARC nurse's aide class Addison Gilbert Hosp., Gloucester, 1942-43; mem. Gloucester Hist. Commn. 1967; formerly active Girl Scouts U.S.A.; sec. Lanesville Community Ctr., 1987—. Recipient 2d prize feature writing UPI, 1970; historian award Town of Rockport, 1978. Mem. Sandy Bay Hist. Soc., Ohio Geneal. Soc., Colo. Geneal. Soc., Del. Geneal. Soc. Republican. Congregationalist. Club: North Shore Button. Author: Hammers on Stone, 1981; Village at Lane's Cove, 1988; editor: Lane's Cove Cook Book, 1954. Home: 330 High St Gloucester MA 01930

ERKKILA, KATHLEEN LUISA, real estate professional; b. Gloucester, Mass., Mar. 17, 1947; d. Onni R. and Barbara Louise (Howell) E. BA, U Mass., 1970. Lic. real estate broker. Owner Rusty Nail Inn Inc., Sunderland, Mass., 1972-76; mgr., buyer Hadley (Mass.) Village Barn, 1972-76; prin. Kathy Stefan Real Estate Inc., Amherst, Mass., 1976—. Mem. Pioneer Valley Housing Assn., Hadley, 1983—. Named Realtor of Yr., Franklin-Hampshire Counties, 1985. Mem. Mass. Assn. Realtors (chmn. edn. 1985, deanGrad. Realtors Inst. 1985—, regional v.p. 1985—, state dir. 1983-84, comml. investment div. 1984—, regional v.p. 1986-87), Franklin-Hampshire County Bd. Realtors (pres. 1985), Translo (dir. relocation), Realtors Nat. Mktg. Inst., Nat. Assn. Realtors (cert. residential specialist, cert. real estate brokerage mgr.). Lodge: Zonta. Home: 16 Eames Ave Amherst MA 01002 Office: Kathy Stefan Real Estate Inc 462 Main St Amherst MA 01002

ERKMAN, CHRISTINE, marketing executive; b. Omaha, Dec. 29, 1952; d. Nick and Margaret (Monk) E. BA in Internat. Bus., U. Nebr., Omaha, 1986. Proofreader, paster Mut. of Omaha Ins. Co., 1971-73; sec. U. Nebr., Omaha, 1975-78; adminstrv. asst. Xerox Corp., Omaha, 1979-81; contract coordinator Cox Cable Communications, Omaha, 1981-82, Tucson, 1982; adminstrv. mgr. U.S. West Info. Systems, Inc., Omaha, 1984; v.p. Edtech, Inc. (name formerly Mktg. Advanced Process Labs.), Omaha, 1985—; advertiser The Daily Chronicle, Centralia, Wash., 1973-75; sales rep., office mgr. Katz Advt. Agy., Omaha, 1984. Regents scholar U. Nebr., 1977. Mem. Nat. Assn. of Female Execs., Fan Assn. N.Am., U. Nebr.-Omaha Alumni Assn. Republican. Presbyterian. Office: Advanced Process Labs 5084 S 135th St Suite 2 Omaha NE 68137

ERLAND, SHIRLEY, nurse; b. N.Y.C., Sept. 24, 1947; d. Endre and Sigrid (Hoiland) Erland; diploma Meth. Hosp. Sch. Nursing, 1968; B.S., Molloy Coll., 1981; M.S., Adelphia U., 1987. Critical care registered nurse. Surg. nurse Meth. Hosp., Bklyn., 1968-70; staff nurse J. B. Thomas Hosp., Peabody, Mass., 1971-73; staff nurse Mercy Hosp., Rockville Centre, N.Y., 1973-75, critical care nurse, 1975-78, staff nurse CCU, 1978-86, asst. head nurse, 1986-87, instr. staff edn., 1987—. Contbr. articles to profl. jours. Mem. Am. Assn. Critical Care Nurses, Am. Heart Assn., N.Y. State Nurses Assn., Sierra Club, Sigma Theta Tau, Phi Sigma Tau. Club: Sons of Norway. Home: 2120 Wantagh Ave Wantagh NY 11793 Office: 1000 N Village Ave Rockville Centre NY 11579

ERLANGER, ELLEN RENEE, investment banker; b. New Castle, Pa., Apr. 6, 1953; d. George Sidney Rubenson and Gloria Marion (Friedman) Rubenson Raffel; m. Thomas Nathan Erlanger, Aug. 24, 1985. BS in Journalism cum laude, Ohio U., 1975; postgrad., N.Y.U., 1980-85. Broker office leasing Met. Structures, Chgo., 1976-77, LaSalle Ptnrs. Inc., Chgo., 1978-80; asst. v.p. Chem. Bank-Real Estate, N.Y.C., 1980-81; assoc. real estate Eastdil Realty Inc., N.Y.C., 1982-83; assoc. real estate, investment banking Sonnenblick-Goldman Corp., N.Y.C., 1984-86; v.p. real estate capital mkts. Bankers Trust Co., N.Y.C., 1986—. Recipient Claudia Bernard Meml. scholarship , 1975. Mem. Young Mortgage Bankers Assn., Mortgage Bankers Assn., Young Real Estate Exec. Div. United Jewish Appeal, Women Communications Inc. (named Outstanding Member, 1975). Home: 132 Seir Hill Wilton CT 06897 Office: Bankers Trust Co 280 Park Ave 23 W New York City NY 10015

ERLANSON, DEBORAH MCFARLIN, state program administrator; b. Watertown, N.Y., Oct. 17, 1943; d. Raymond Thomas and Alberta Antoinette (Schultz) McF.; m. David Norman Erlanson, Sept. 10, 1966; 1 child, Joshua David. AA in Liberal Arts, Dutchess Community Coll., 1964; BA in Psychology, Am. Internat. Coll., 1966; MS in Edn., So. Ill. U., 1972. Occupancy tng. coordinator Decatur (Ill.) Housing Authority, 1975-76, target projects program coordinator, 1976-77, spl. services coordinator, 1977-78, asst. dir. planning, 1978-82, dir. program devel., 1982—; speaker various convs., 1978—; cons. Piatt County Housing Authority, Monticello, Ill., 1985—, Woodford Homes, Inc., Decatur, 1985-86. Mem. steering com. Near West Restoration and Preservation Soc., Decatur, 1985-86, sec. 1986; bd. dirs., parent group counselor Macon County Parents Anonymous, Decatur, 1976-80; mem. health div. Decatur Council Community Services, 1978-84. Named one of Outstanding Young Women Am., 1979. Mem. Nat. Assn. Housing and Redevel. Ofcls. (mem. nat. profl. devel. com. 1983—, vice-chmn. 1987-89, nat. task force on product devel. 1987, regional exec. bd., steering com. 1983—, regional v.p. for profl. devel. 1987-89, pres. Ill. chpt. 1984-87, exec. bd. Ill. chpt. 1983—), Ill. Assn. Housing Authorities (exec. bd. 1984-87), Decatur Women's Network Assn. (founding mem. 1982, exec. bd. dirs. 1982-85). Home: 465 W Macon St Decatur IL 62522 Office: Decatur Housing Authority 1808 E Locust St Decatur IL 62521

ERLICHSON, MIRIAM, fundraiser; b. Bronx, N.Y., July 26, 1948; d. Jack and Bess (Hyatt) E.; m. Walter Forman, Sept. 26, 1970 (div. 1975); m. Victor Petrusewicz, July 17, 1980. BA in English, CCNY, 1969; postgrad., Hunter Coll., 1970-71; MA, CCNY, 1976. Cert. secondary tchr., N.Y. Tchr. English Edicer Rodriguez Intermediate Sch. 84, Bronx, 1972-78; gen. sec. exec. staff Union Am. Hebre Congregations, N.Y.C., 1978-79; sr. sec. to dir. annual giving N.Y. Hosp.-Cornell Med. Ctr., N.Y.C., 1979-80, coordinator annual giving, 1980—. Mem. Nat. Assn. Female Execs., Jane Austen Soc. (Eng.), Phi Beta Kappa. Office: NY Hosp Cornell Med Ctr Devel Office Box 123 525 E 68th St New York NY 10021

ERNSBARGER, REBECCA FAYE, communications company administrator; b. Alvin, Tex., Sept. 9, 1949; d. Joseph Lee Mills and Bette (Stricklin) Harrell; m. Charles John Ernsbarger, Apr. 29, 1977; 1 child, Jason. Student, U. Houston, 1968-69, 86-87; Cert. in Communications, Tex. A & M, 1977, MIT, 1980. Account exec. Southwestern Bell, Houston, 1969-82; nat. account exec. AT&T, Houston, 1982-83, mgr. engring. and planning, 1983-87; dir. bus. planning and devel. System One subs. Tex. Air Corp., Houston, 1988—. Mem. Aero. Frequency Commn., Tele-Communication Assn., Nat. Assn. for Female Execs. Democrat. Roman Catholic. Office: System One Corp 2929 Allen Pwy Suite 200 Houston TX 77019

ERNST, GERALYN VINDIOLA, industrial engineer; b. Los Angeles, Aug. 26, 1961; d. Henry and Helen (Alvarran) Vindiola; m. Steven Anthony Ernst, Sept. 7, 1985. BS in Indsl. Engring., Calif. Poly. State U., 1985. Computer ops. supr. Pacific Gas & Electric Co., Avila Beach, Calif., 1985, computer ops. engr., 1985-87; indsl. engr. Marquardt Co., Van Nuys, Calif., 1987—. Vol. Spl. Olympics Com., San Luis Obispo County, Calif., 1987. Mem. Inst. Indsl. Engrs. (pres. student chpt. 1983-84), AAUW (vol. fundraisers 1986-87). Republican. Roman Catholic. Home: 25138 Marci Way Valencia CA 91355

ERNST, JANET LEE, interior designer; b. Winston-Salem, N.C., Apr. 16, 1955; d. William Lee Ernst and Marie Keith (Shouse) Snyder. BS in Home Economics, Interior Design, U. N.C., Greensboro, 1977. Instr. arts and crafts Craft Showcase, Winston-Salem, 1977-78; display design The Ltd., Inc., N.C. and S.C., 1978-79; designer ind. retail stores Winston-Salem, 1977-81; head design dept. Butler Enterprises, Inc., Winston-Salem, 1981-86; design prin. Carolina Contract Design, Winston-Salem, 1986—; pres. Triad Design Concepts, Winston-Salem and Greensboro, 1988—; cons. design and photography contract furniture mfr., Thomasville, N.C., 1986—; mentor student interns U. N.C., Greensboro, 1983, 84, 87, 88. Vol. Humane Soc., Winston-Salem, 1977-78. Mem. Inst. Bus. Designers (affiliate, edn. com. 1987), Am. Soc. Interior Designers (assoc.), Nat. Trust Hist. Preservation, Nat. Assn. Female Execs., Nat. Assn. for the Self Employed. Democrat. Moravian. Office: Carolina Contract Design/ Triad Design Concepts 8 W Third St Suite 210 Winston-Salem NC 27101

ERNST, NORA WILFORD, retired hospital administrator, gerontologist; b. Chgo., Sept. 22, 1943; d. Charles Richard and Mary Evelyn (McGarrity) Wilford; m. Marvin L. Ernst, June 15, 1963; children: Leslie, Alicia, Andrea. BS, Westmar Coll., 1965; MEd, Northeastern Okla. U., 1969; PhD, North Tex. State U., 1977. Mem. faculty U. Tex. Health Sci. Ctr., Dallas, 1978-82; dir. planning North Colo. Med. Ctr., Greeley, 1982-88; cons. Tex. Dept. Human Resources, Austin, 1978-79; research dir. S.W. Gerontol. Cons., Dallas, 1976-77; assoc. prof. U. No. Colo., Greeley, 1982-88. Author: Nursing Home Staff Development, 1982; editor: The Aged Patient, 1983. Health Resources Adminstrn. grantee, Tex. Edn. Agy. grantee, Tex. State Dept. Health grantee. Mem. Am. Hosp. Assn., Am. Gerontological Soc.

ERNSTER, SISTER JACQUELYN, College president; b. Salem, S.D., Oct. 3, 1939; d. John Ernster and Eleanor (Bie) Ingalls. B.A., Mount Marty Coll., 1965; M.A., Ind. U., 1969; Ph.D., Ohio State U., 1976. Mem. faculty Mount Marty Coll., Yankton, S.D., 1970-76, v.p. acad. affairs, 1976-83, pres., 1983—; speaker S.D. Commn. on Humanities Pub. Issues Forum, 1980-82. Corp. bd. dirs. Sisters of Sacred Heart Convent, Yankton, 1976-82; trustee Madonna Profl. Care Ctr., Lincoln, Nebr., 1977-82. Mem. editorial bd. Yankton Press and Dakotan, 1984. Bush Found. fellow, 1982-83. Mem. Am. Council on Edn. (nat. identification program 1979, nat. com. on women in higher edn. 1984—), Council for Ind. Colls., S.D. Pvt. Coll. Found., Consortium for Mid-Am. (chmn. deans 1980-81), Delta Kappa Gamma (pres. 1980-82). Club: Interchange (bd. dirs. 1985) (Yankton). Office: Mount Marty Coll 1105 W 8th Yankton SD 57078 *

ERRICKSON, BARBARA BAUER, electronic equipment company executive; b. Pitts., Apr. 5, 1944; d. Edward Ewing Bauer and Margaret J. McConnell; m. James Jay Burcham, June 30, 1966 (div. May 1972); children: James Jay II, Linda Lee; m. William Newel Errickson, Apr. 9, 1976 (div. Feb. 1987); children: David Reid, Amy Beth. BA, U. Ill., 1966; MBA, So. Meth. U., 1981. Programming trainee Allstate Ins. Co., Northbrook, Ill., 1973; programmer, team leader Motorola, Inc., Chgo., 1974-78; supr. systems Tex. Instruments, Inc., Dallas, 1978-81, product line mgr. worldwide shipping systems, 1981-83, product line mgr. shipping, inventory systems, 1983-84, mgr. mktg. info. systems, 1985, mgr. benefit systems, 1986—; dir., billing and software developer Spring Park Home Owners, Garland-Richardson, Tex., 1984—, pres. and chmn. fin., 1985, v.p. legal, 1986; active Dallas Women's Ctr., 1984—; mem. bus. adv. council So. Meth U. Bus. Adv. Program; United Way chmn. mktg. systems Tex. Instruments, 1985. Recipient Women in Leadership cert. YWCA Met. Chgo., 1977. Mem. Am. Mgmt. Assn., Am. Women in Computing (bd. dirs. 1987—), Community Assns. Inst., So. Meth. U. MBA Soc., Beta Gamma Sigma. Republican. Presbyterian. Club: Spring Park Racqette. Avocations: sailing, horseback riding, reading, oil painting. Home: 6702 Lakeshore Dr Garland TX 75042 Office: Tex Instruments Inc 6500 Chase Oaks Blvd PO Box 869305 Plano TX 75086

ERSELIUS, LYNNE LOUISE, systems analyst; b. St. Louis, Apr. 4, 1961; d. Walter G. and Marilyn (Aff) E. BSChE, U. Mo., 1983. Chemist Seven-Up Co., St. Louis, 1983-86; lab. systems analyst Marion Labs., Kansas City, Mo., 1986—. Mem. Am. Chem. Soc., Am. Inst. Chem. Engrs., Alpha Chi Sigma. Home: 10009 Walnut # 206 Kansas City MO 64114 Office: Marion Labs Inc Park A PO Box 9627 Kansas City MO 64134

ERSKINE, CORAL LONA, educator, consultant; b. Salt Lake City, Aug. 17, 1946; d. Leon Johnson and Bette Joyce (Fender) Higley; m. Stewart F. Earnest, 1965 (div. June 1966); m. Melville Cox Erskine Jr., Jan. 24, 1967; 1 child, Lael Lona. AA in Math., U. Minn., 1969; BA in Mgmt., St. Mary's Coll., 1982, MBA, 1984. Controller, treas. Eureka Resource Assn., Inc., Berkeley, Calif., 1976-84; instr. bus. St. Mary's Coll., Moraga, Calif., 1984—. Mem. Am. Mgmt. Assn., Bus. and Profl. Women Soc. (chair 1986, pres. 1987). Club: Commonwealth (San Francisco).

ERSKINE, SUSAN DOURNEY, medical company executive; b. Orange, N.J., Apr. 26, 1952; d. John J. and Patricia A. (Moreland) Dourney; m. William Norman Erskine; 1 child, Patricia Muriel. BEd, U. Miami, Coral Gables, 1974; MS, Fla. Internat. U., 1976; postgrad., Stanford U., 1976-78. Tchr. Dade County Pub. Schs., Miami, 1974-76; instr. Los Altos (Calif.) Community Coll., 1977, Stanford U., Palo Alto, Calif., 1977-78; tchr., dept. chairperson Marlborough Sch., Los Angeles, 1978-79; tchr. San Diego Job Corps Ctr., 1979-80; dir. staff devel. Centre City Hosp., San Diego, 1981-82; dir. community relations Harbor View Med. Ctr., San Diego, 1982-83; program adminstr. Western Mood and Sleep Disorder Inst., San Diego, 1983-86; v.p. ops., v.p. bd. dirs. Inter-Am. Med. Services, Inc., San Diego, 1986-87, pres., 1988—. Sec. Western Inst. Found. for Mental Health, San Diego, 1985-86, v.p., 1987. Named one of Outstanding Young Women Am., 1978. Mem. Nat. Assn. Female Execs., Women in Health Care in So. Calif., San Diego Mental Health Assn. Republican. Roman Catholic. Home: 1433 Reed Ave #1 San Diego CA 92109 Office: Inter-Am Med Services Med Services Inc 2330 First Ave #104 San Diego CA 92101

ERTLE, NANCY LOUISE, chemical company executive; b. Harvey, Ill., July 5, 1935; d. Louis Robert and Mary Loretta (O'Boyle) E. BS, U. Ariz., 1957; MBA, Northwestern U., 1968. Chemist films-packaging div. Union Carbide Corp., Chgo., 1957-75, planning mgr., 1976, dir. mktg., 1977-79, v.p. mktg., 1979-83, v.p., gen. mgr., 1983-84, pres., 1985-86; pres. Viskase Corp. (formerly Films Packaging div.), Chgo., 1986—. Mem. Inst. Food Techs., Am. Mktg. Assn., Chem. Mktg. Research Assn., Com. of 200. Office: 6733 W 65th St Chicago IL 60638

ERVIN, BETTY J(EAN), military officer, educator, psychologist; b. Savannah, Ga., Oct. 14, 1951; d. Richard and Ernestine (Mack) E. BA, Ohio State U., 1972; MA, Ea. N.Mex. U., 1978; Degree Edn. Specialist, U. N.Mex., 1981. Cert. in guidance and counseling. Authorization rep. City Nat. Bank, Columbus, Ohio, 1972-74; commd. 2d lt. U.S. Army, 1973; social worker Franklin County Welfare Dept., Columbus, 1974-76; advanced through grades to capt. Franklin County Welfare Dept., 1981; counselor Teledyne Corp., Albuquerque, 1979-83; mil. personnel officer Office Mil. Affairs, Sante Fe, 1983-84; personnel mgr. Support Personnel Mgmt., Sante Fe, 1984; asst. prof. mil. sci. Bishop Coll., Dallas, 1984—; founder, chief exec. officer Internat Enchantments, Arlington, Tex., 1987—. Chmn. Albuquerque Job Corps Ctr.; active United Way, Fort Riley, Kans. Mem. Nat. Assn. Female Execs., Res. Officers Assn., Am. Personnel and Guidance Assn. Republican. Baptist. Club: Army and Navy. Home: 2719 Golden Creek Ln #406 Arlington TX 76006

ERVIN, JANIS, communications executive; b. St. Louis, Aug. 17, 1953. BS, Washington U., St. Louis, 1977. Supr. customer service South Cen. Bell Co., New Orleans, 1978-82; mktg. support rep. N.Y. Telephone Co., N.Y.C., 1982-83, AT&T Info. Systems, N.Y.C., 1983-85; dir. telecommunications Kingsborough Community Coll., Bklyn., 1985—. Mem. IEEE, Nat. Assn. Female Execs., Assn. Coll. and Univ. Telecommunications Adminstrs. Office: Kingsborough Community Coll 2001 Oriental Blvd Brooklyn NY 11235

ERVIN-CARR, CHARLESETTA YVONNE, educator; b. Seattle, June 10, 1946; d. Charles Woodrow and Christene Rosetta (Griffin) Ervin; B.A. in Speech and English, U. Wash., 1969, M.Ed., 1971; 1 son, David Anthony Carr. Tchr. Seattle Public Schs. Dist. 1, 1971—; instr. Seattle Central Community Coll., part-time, 1977-87; instr. U. Wash., Seattle, 1979—; instr. North Seattle Community Coll., part-time, 1984—; tng. and employee devel. cons. City of Seattle, 1981—; owner, cons. Effective Communication Skills, Seattle, 1980—. Bd. dirs. Shades of Beauty, Seattle, 1979—, CAMP Cen. Area MOtivational Program, Nat. Black Child Devel. Inst. Mem. Am. Soc. Tng. and Devel., AAUW, Black Profl. Educators of Greater Puget Sound, Nat. Council Negro Women (Seattle sect.), Council on Black Am. Affairs, Women's Ednl. Network, Women's Profl. and Managerial Network, Delta Kappa Gamma. Office: PO Box 18965 Seattle WA 98118

ERWIN, ELIZABETH MAE, travel agency manager; b. Norfolk, Va., Oct. 31, 1951; d. Hal T. and Joan S. (Sandt) E. Assoc. degree, Taylor Bus. Sch., 1971; student, Temple U., 1983—. Asst. buyer shoes Ideal Shoe Co., Phila., 1971-73; retail shoe mgr. Spencer Gifts, Atlantic City, 1973-75; teller First Pa. Bank, Phila., 1976-78; accounts payable mgr. Rosenbluth Travel, Phila., 1978-83; credit and computer mgr. Parkway Travel, Inc., Phila., 1983—. Mem. Nat. Assn. Female Execs. Roman Catholic. Office: Parkway Travel Inc 37 S 16th St Philadelphia PA 19102

ESAU, KATHERINE, retired botanist, educator; b. Ekaterinoslav, Russia, Apr. 3, 1898; naturalized. Ph.D., U. Caif., 1931, LL.D. (hon.), 1966; D.Sc. (hon.), Mills Coll., 1962. Instr. botany, jr. botanist U. Calif.-Davis, 1931-37, asst. prof., asst. botanist, 1937-43, assoc. prof., assoc. botanist, 1943-49, prof., botanist, 1949-63; prof. botany U. Calif.-Santa Barbara, 1963-65, emeritus prof. botany, 1965—; Prather lectr. Harvard U., 1960. Guggenheim fellow, 1940. Fellow Am. Acad. Arts and Scis.; mem. Nat. Acad. Sci., AAAS, Swedish Royal Acad. Sci., Am. Philos. Soc., Bot. Soc. Am. (pres. 1951). Address: U Calif Dept Biol Sci Santa Barbara CA 93106

ESCALANTE, CECILIA, pharmacist; b. Caracas, Venezuela, Apr. 28, 1956; came to U.S., 1960; d. Francisco and Dafne (Ortiz) E. BS in Pharmacy, U. Md., 1981. Pharmacist Johns Hopkins Hosp., Balt., 1981-85, sr. pharmacist, 1985—. Home: 3600 Golden Eagle Dr Phoenix MD 21131

ESCALERA, KAREN WEINER, public relations company executive; b. Phila., Dec. 7, 1944; d. George Joseph and Gladys (Lieberman) Weiner; m. Alfonso G. Escalera, Sept. 8, 1978; 1 child, Kent. BA cum laude, U. Pa., 1966. Assoc. editor United Bus. Publs., N.Y.C., 1967-68; account exec. Jacobson/Wallace/Westphal, N.Y.C., 1968-69; news and feature editor Hilton Internat. Hotels, N.Y.C., 1969-74, dir. pub. relations western hemisphere, N.Y.C., 1974-79; pres. Karen Weiner Escalera Assocs., N.Y.C., 1979—. Contbr. articles to profl. jours. Recipient various firm awards. Mem. Soc. Am. Travel Writers (treas. northeast chpt. 1982-84), Pub. Relations Soc. Am., Hotel Sales and Mktg. Assn., Caribbean Tourism Assn., Caribbean Hotel Assn. Avocations: cultural activities, travel. Office: 104 5th Ave New York NY 10011

ESCALERA, LYDIA N., insurance executive; b. San Juan, P.R., Jan. 25, 1936; d. Francisco Navarro and Esperanza Ayala; m. Angel L. Escalera, Sept. 6, 1957; children: Teresita, Angel L., Alfredo L. BBA, U. P.R., 1958. Statistician Govt. P.R., San Juan, 1958-64; with Blue Cross P.R., San Juan, 1964—, mgr., 1970-71, dir. human resources and indsl. relations, 1971—. Bd. dirs. Jesus de Nazareth Coll., Carolina, P.R., 1973—, PTA, Colegio La Piedad, 1977-80, Camp Bethania, Isla Verde, 1973—; counsellor Club Pro-Cancer Hosps., Rio Piedras. Mem. Am. Soc. Personnel Adminstrn. (program dir. 1981-82, sec.-treas. 1988), Pub. Relations Mfrs. Assn., Kotten Assocs. P.R. (bd. dirs. 1980—), Execs. Assn. (pres.). Democrat. Roman Catholic. Home: 178 5th St Villamar Isla Verde PR 00913 Office: Blue Cross PR GPO Box 6068-G San Juan PR 00936

ESCHUK, MARY ELIZABETH, educational administrator; b. Daytona Beach, Fla.; d. Lloyd James and Annie (Coleman) Appleby; B.A. in English, Cleve. State U., 1969, M.Ed., 1972, Ed.S., 1979; m. Steven Eschuk, Oct. 22, 1949; children—Holly, Lauren, Steven. Tchr. English public schs., Cleve., Parma, Ohio, 1969-74; dept. head English Normandy High Sch., Parma, 1972-74; asst. prin. Hillside Jr. High Sch., Parma, 1974-76; prin. Schaaf Jr. High Sch., Parma, 1976-82, Parma High Sch., 1982—. NEH grantee, 1981; named Outstanding Educator Ohio PTA, 1981. Mem. Nat. Assn. Secondary Sch. Adminstrs., Ohio Assn. Secondary Sch. Adminstrs. (dir.), Assn. Parma Adminstrs. Co-author, lyricist musical Chicken Little; author, lyricist musicals The Butterfly that Stamped, The Cat that Walked Alone. Home: 7195 Glencairn Dr Parma OH 44134 Office: 5983 W 54th St Parma OH 44129

ESCOBAR, HILDA LOPEZ, nurse practitioner, physician assistant; b. N.Y.C., Aug. 6, 1929; d. Eladio and Josephine (Justiniano) Lopez; m. John Louis Escobar, Sept. 10, 1949; children: Linda, Michael, Jean. AAS, Nassau Community Coll., 1967; BSN, C.W. Post U., 1975. Cert. hemiodialysis nurse, 1978; adult nurse practitioner, SUNY, Upstate Med. Ctr., Syracuse, 1978. Staff nurse, South Nassau Community Hosp., Oceanside, N.Y., 1967-68; staff nurse Nassau Hosp., Mineola, N.Y., 1968-78, head nurse hemodialysis unit, 1976-78; adult nurse practitioner Community Health Program, New Hyde Park, N.Y., 1978—, nurse mgr. dept. medicine and urgent visit dept., 1986—. Mem. Am. Nurses Assn. (cert.), Am. Assn. Physician Assts. (cert. 1983), Am. Assn. Nephrology Nurses and Technicians, Phi Theta Kappa, Sigma Theta Tau (exec. bd. dirs. Alpha Omega chpt. 1988).

ESFANDIARY, MARY S., fuel science executive; b. Passaic, N.J., June 27, 1929; d. Peter J. and Veronica R. (Kida) Nieradka; m. Mohsen S. Esfandiary; children: H. Austin, Dara S. BS in Chemistry, St. John's U., 1951; postgrad., Polytechnic Inst. N.Y., 1955-56. Research chemist Picatinny Arsenal, Dover, N.J., 1951-56; supr. phys. sci. Bur. Mines, Washington, 1956-61; asst. to dir. research Nat. Iranian Oil Co., Tehran, 1961-64; lectr. U. Tehran and Aryamehr Inst. Tech., Tehran, 1961-64, 69-73; dir. internat. affairs Acad. of Scis., Tehran, 1977-79; chief geog. names br. Def. Mapping Agy., Washington, 1981-86, chief prodn. mgmt. office, 1986-87, chief support div., chief commodity inventory mgmt. div., 1987—. Contbr. papers and articles to tech. jours., 1952-78. Pres. UN Delegations Women's Club, N.Y.C., 1967-69, v.p., program dir., 1964-67; pres. Diplomatic Corps Com. for Red Cross, Bangkok, Thailand, 1974-76; v.p., bd. dirs. Found. for Blind of Thailand, Bangkok, 1973-77. Recipient Badge of Honor for Social Service, Thailand, 1975, 1st Class medal Red Cross, Thailand, 1976. Mem. AAAS, N.Y. Acad. of Scis., Mensa. Democrat. Methodist. Home: 4401 Sedgewick St NW Washington DC 20016 Office: Def Mapping Agy 6101 MacArthur Blvd Room 309 Washington DC 20315

ESH, DALIA REGINA, insurance educator, financial planner; b. Jerusalem, May 15, 1950; came to U.S., 1980; d. Jedidya Mizrahi and Orah (Debby) Mizrahi Malka; m. David Esh; children: Odelia, Roy. Cert. proficiency in English, Cambridge U., Eng., 1969; BA, Bar Ilan U., Tel Aviv, 1972, teaching cert., 1976; postgrad. U. Mo.-St. Louis, 1981-82, Washington U., St. Louis, 1983-84. CLU; chartered fin. cons. English tchr. Lady Davis Sch., Tel Aviv, 1973-80; Hebrew tchr. Epstein Acad., St. Louis, 1981-82; sales rep. Met. Ins. Co., St. Louis, 1982-85, mktg. specialist, instr., Tulsa, 1985-86, branch mgr., Carrollton, Dallas, Tex., 1986—. Originated universal life-term sales concept, 1985. Active Jewish Community Ctrs. Assn., St. Louis, 1984-85, Tulsa, 1986, Dallas, 1987—. Human resources mgmt. grantee Washington U., 1983; recipient Career Builders award Met. Ins. Co., 1982, Leader's Conf. award, 1984, Nat. Quality award, 1984, 85; named to Million Dollar Round Table, 1985. Mem. Nat. Assn. Life Underwriters, Internat. Assn. Fin. Planning, Nat. Assn. Female Execs. Jewish. Avocation: folk dancing, tennis. Office: Met Ins Co 3620 N Josey Ln Carrollton TX 75007

ESHLEMAN, CHARLENE HUMPHRIES, church association administrator; b. Richmond, Va., July 19, 1955; d. Bernard Rawles and Margaret Ruth (Durvin) Humphries; m. David Martin Eshleman, June 14, 1980. BS in Mass Communications, Va. Commonwealth U., 1977, MEd in Adult Edn., Human Resource Devel., 1988. Procedures analyst Miller and Rhodes, Richmond, 1978-81; systems mgmt. coordinator SEC Computer Co., Richmond, 1981-83; tng. coordinator Life of Va. Ins. Co., Richmond, 1984; staff devel. mgr. Fgn. Mission Bd., So. Bapt. Conv., Richmond, 1984—; star cons. Mary Kay Cosmetics, 1984—. Mem. Am. Soc. Tng. and Devel. (sec. Richmond chpt. 1988—), Assn. Psychol. Type. Baptist. Office: The Fgn Mission Bd 3806 Monument Ave Richmond VA 23230

ESPARZA, CARMEN N., accountant; b. Torreon, Mex., Nov. 8, 1961; came to U.S., 1980; d. Francisco Esparza and Petra Noyola de Esparza. Cert. English, San Bernardino Valley Coll., 1984. Lang. tutor San Bernardino (Calif.) Unified Sch. Dist., 1980-81, 83; accounts receivable supr. Anita's Mexican Foods Corp., San Bernardino, 1983—. Mem. Nat. Assn. Female Execs. Office: Anita's Mexican Foods Corp 1390 W 4th St San Bernardino CA 92411

ESPINOZA, REBECCA ANN, foundation administrator, consultant; b. Pueblo, Colo., Oct. 30, 1952; d. Charles D. and Mary Erlinda (Ortega) E. BS, U. So. Colo., 1974; MPA, North Tex. State U., Denton, 1985. Investigator for Dist. Atty., Pueblo, 1974; pvt. investigator Romar Security, Pueblo West, Colo., 1974-75; urban rehab. specialist City of Dallas, 1975-82, neighborhood rep., 1982-83, mgmt. asst., 1983-85; budget and fin. coordinator Dallas Mcpl. Ct. Judiciary, 1985-86; personnel and orgn. cons., pres. Resource Connection, Pueblo, 1986-88; exec. dir. PUeblo County ARC. Author: Guide to Basic Construction, 1983. Dir. Dallas County Rape Crisis Ctr., 1975-78, Cen. YWCA, 1982-84, Women's Coalition and Women's Issues Network, 1977-84 community chmn. rape edn., coordinator mktg. plan, 1987; mem. City of Pueblo Housing Commn., 1987, Pueblo County Comm. on Homeless, local Emergency Planning Commn. for City of Pueblo, Coalition of Human Resources. Recipient Cert. of Appreciation, City of Dallas, 1982, Cert. of Recognition, City of Dallas, 1983, Cert. of Appreciation, Goals for Dallas, 1985. Mem. Internat. City Mgmt. Assn. (assoc.), Am. Soc. Pub. Adminstrn., AAUW, Pueblo LWV, Nat. Women's Polit. Caucus. Democrat. Home: 1228 Belmont Ave Pueblo CO 81004 Office: 3821 W Pueblo Blvd Pueblo CO 81004

ESPOSITO, AMY SKLAR, lawyer; b. Bklyn., Nov. 9, 1955; d. Sidney and Rhoda (Weiner) Sklar; m. Francis Benedetto Esposito, May 4, 1985; 1 child, Melissa. BA, U. Vt., 1977; JD, Hofstra U., 1980. Bar: Fla. 1983. Assoc. Herman & Natale, Esqs., Garden City, N.Y., 1980-81, Law Offices of Gabriel Kohn, Mineola, N.Y., 1981-84; ptnr. Ostor & Sklar, Esqs., Deer Park, N.Y., 1984—. Coach mock trials Nassau County (N.Y.) High Schs., 1984-86. Mem. N.Y. State Bar Assn., Nassau-Suffolk Women's Bar Assn. (assoc., speaker on matrimonial law). Jewish. Office: Ostor & Sklar Esqs 131 Liberty St Deer Park NY 11729

ESPOSITO, BONNIE LOU, marketing professional; b. Chgo., July 20, 1947; d. Ralph Edgar and Dorothy Mae (Groh) Myers; m. Frank Merle Esposito, Aug. 15, 1969 (div. Sept. 1985); children: Mario Henry, Elizabeth Ann. BA, George Williams Coll., 1969. Caseworker Little Bros. of the Poor, Chgo., 1969-72; dir. Little Bros.-Friends of the Elderly, Mpls., 1972-78; owner Espo Inc./Mario's Ristorante, Mpls., 1978-85; mktg. mgr. City of Mpls. Energy Office, 1981—; tng. dir., facilitator The Energy Collaborative, 1987—; dir. tng. The Energy Collaborative, 1987—. Organizer Community Crime Prevention, Mpls., 1978-81. Mem. Nat. Assn. Female Execs. (bd. dirs. Monday Night Network). Office: City of Mpls Energy Office 330 City Hall Minneapolis MN 55415

ESPOSITO, DEBORAH SOULE, photographic products company official; b. Ithaca, N.Y., Sept. 11, 1950; d. Lauren M. and Maureen E. (Casterline) Soule; m. Gerard F. Esposito, Nov. 29, 1975. BA in Chemistry, Wells Coll., 1972; postgrad. Rochester Inst. Tech., 1973-74, Carnegie-Mellon U., 1980. With Eastman Kodak Co., Rochester, N.Y., 1972—, ops. mgr., 1980-82, head dept. material inspection 1982-85, program mgr. delivery of exec. tng. programs, tng. dir., 1985-87, program mgr. div. graphics imaging systems 1987—; cons. and investor real estate. Fundraiser Wells Coll., 1972—. Mem. Strong Family Assn. Am. (dir. 1982-85), Bakers Bridge Hist. Soc., Jr. League Rochester (chmn. women's issues 1985-86, chmn. Ronald McDonald House project, 1987-88, chmn. pub. relations), Landmark Soc. Western N.Y. Club: Wells (pres. 1974-76) (Rochester).

ESPOSITO, PAULETTE, manager training development; b. Stamford, Conn., Dec. 6, 1945; d. Peter and Juliette Marie (DeYulio) E. AS, Katharine Gibbs, N.Y.C., 1964; cert., Cornell U., 1983; BS, Marymount, 1985; cert., U. Mich., 1987. Sec. State Nat. Bank, Stamford, 1964; exec. sec. Gen. Time Corp., Stamford, 1966; office mgr. William Haight and Welch Advt., Greenwich, Conn., 1967; exec. asst. Combustion Engrng., Stamford, 1968; with Champion Internat. Corp., Stamford, 1976—, supr., 1978, mgr. training devel., 1986—; lectr. Katharine Gibbs Sch., 1981; cons. tchr. Stamford Pub. Schs., 1977. Bd. dirs. Am. Red Cross, Stamford, 1983; dir. Blood Program, Stamford, 1980-85; coordinator United Way Campaign, 1983-87; v.p. Stamford Police Community Council, Stamford, 1984-86. Named Young Woman of Yr., Jaycees, 1983. Mem. Am. Soc. Training and Devel., Nat. Soc. Performance and Instrn. Democrat. Roman Catholic. Club: Midday (Stamford). Office: Champion Internat Corp 1 Champion Plaza Stamford CT 06921

ESPOSITO KÖK, LISA, real estate developer, manager; b. N.Y.C., Sept. 19, 1961; d. Nicholas Joseph and Stella (Sparaccio) E.; m. George Hans Kök, Feb. 16, 1985. AB in English Lit., Italian, Cornell U., 1983. Asst. publicity mgr. Bloomingdale's, N.Y.C., 1984-86; project mgr. Am. Jubilee Liberty Weekend '86, Bklyn., 1986; asst. to pres. Maurice Sonnenberg Assoc., N.Y.C., 1986—. Mem. Fgn. Policy Orgn. (Young Profl. Group). Roman Catholic. Home: 94 Mercer St Jersey City NJ 07302

ESPY, CHRISTINE KATHERINE, nursing educator; b. Homestead, Pa., Mar. 12, 1952; d. Thaddeus and Clara Wanda (Mateuszewski) S.; m. Patrick Joseph Espy, 1975. BS in Nursing, U. Pitts., 1974. RN, Pa., Utah. Staff nurse West Penn Hosp., Pitts., 1974-77; pub. health nurse Allegheny Health Dept., Pitts., 1977-79; staff nurse Logan (Utah) Regional Hosp., 1979-80; dir. nursing Sunshine Terr. Nursing Home, Logan, 1980-82; instr. clin. and theoretical nursing Weber State Coll./Utah State U. Cooperative Nursing Program, Logan, 1982—. Chmn. membership Logan Planned Parenthood, 1984-86, sec., 1986-87; profl. educator Am. Diabetes Assn., 1986. Mem. Am. Nurses Assn., Utah Nurses Assn., Logan Bus. and Profl. Women (1st v.p. 1985-86, corr. sec. 1984-85), Bridgerland Bus. and Profl. Women (treas. 1986-87). Office: Weber State Coll Utah State Coop Nursing UMC 1205 Logan UT 84321

ESPY, RENÉ ORGAN, chiropractor; b. Flushing, N.Y., Dec. 20, 1944; d. Thomas J. Organ and Elizabeth (Wayne) Organ Wheaton. BA, Rosary Hill Coll., 1970; MA, Canisus Coll., 1974; D in Chiropractic, Tex. Chiropractic Coll., 1980. Dir. Espy Chiropractic Clinic, Guyman, Okla., 1980-81; assoc. dir. Lake Grove Chiropractic Clinic, Lake Oswego, Oreg., 1982-86; dir. Hazelfren Chiropractic Clinic, Tigard, Oreg., 1986-88; pvt. practice Chiropractic Hollywood, Calif., 1988—; chiropractor for U.S. Women's Olympic Volleyball Team, 1984. Author: The Body Beautiful, 1988; author, editor ednl. materials on immune system. Mem. Am. Chiropractic Assn., Internat. Coll. Applied Kinesiologists, Oreg. Chiropractic Physicians Assn., Aries Found. Club: City (Portland). Office: 1445 N Gardner Hollywood CA 90046

ESQUELL, MARY LOUISE, insurance company executive; b. San Antonio, May 16, 1952; d. Lee William and Victoria Bernard (Hoffman) Wilson; m. Herschell A. Esquell, July 18, 1970; children—Timothy Andrew, Melissa Diane. Student Austin Bus. Sch., 1968-69. Cert. ins. counselor, Tex. Pres. Tex. Ins. Assocs., Inc., Austin, 1983-86; ptnr. Assocs. Leasing and Fin. Services, Austin, 1985—; owner, operator Bus. Services for Profls. Computer Data Base Service, 1987—. Mem. CPCU, Ins. Women of Austin (chmn. Austin State Hosp. 1978), Fedn. Ins. Women of Tex., Ind. Agts. Tex., Ind. Agts. of Austin, Profl. Ins. Agts. of Austin, Nat. Assn. Female Execs. Republican. Baptist. Avocations: handwork; sewing; painting; swimming; boating. Home: 5210 Maulding Pass Austin TX 78749

ESQUIVEL, GISELLE BEATRIZ, psychology educator; b. Habana, Cuba, Feb. 21, 1950; came to U.S., 1961; d. Emilio Esquivel and Aurora Verdecia; M. René Cordero, June 28, 1986; 1 child, Daniel René Cordero. BA in Psychology, Rutgers U., 1972; MA in Ednl. Psychology, Montclair State Coll., 1975; D of Psychology, Yeshiva U., 1981. lic. psychologist. Sch. psychologist Paterson (N.J.) Bd. of Edn., 1972-82; pvt. practice psychology N.J., 1981—; asst. prof. Fordham U., N.Y.C., 1982—; dir. Bilingual Sch. Psychology, 1981—. Contbr. articles to profl. jours. Mem. adv. bd. Union County Mental Health, N.J., 1975-82; mem. Coalition of Advocates for Children, N.J., 1981-86. Grantee U.S. Office Edn., Nat. Inst. Mental Health, 1983-87. Mem. Am. Psychol. Assn., Nat. Assn. Sch. Psychology, N.Y. State Psychol. Assn., N.J. Psychol. Assn. Home: 106 Dellwood Rd Edison NJ 08820

ESSEX, JUDY TOWNE, hospital administrator; b. Jersey City, June 7, 1954; d. John Franklin and Margaret Ida (Miller) Towne; m. Paul Denison Essex, Aug. 7, 1976; children: Kyle Towne, Ryan Denison. BS, Davis and Elkins Coll., 1976; MPA, C.W. Post Ctr., L.I. U., 1982. Cert. tchr. health and phys. edn., N.Y. Natural resource planner Town of Denning, N.Y., 1978-80; substitute tchr. Tri Valley Cen. Sch., Grahamsville, N.Y., 1980-84; night mgr. New Age Health Farm, Neversink, N.Y., 1982-84; exec. dir. Liberty Community Coalition, N.Y., 1984-86; dir. grants and research Community Gen. Hosp., Harris, N.Y., 1986—, dir. health promotion, 1987—; exec. bd. dirs. Sullivan Diagnostic Treatment Ctr., Harris. V.p., exec. bd. dirs. Sullivan County Cares Coalition, Liberty, 1985—; mem. com. on the handicapped Town of Neversink, N.Y., 1986—; chmn. Liberty Internat. Festival and Exposition, Liberty, 1984-85; founder Parents of Challenged Children, 1987; mem. ladies aux. Neversink Fire Co. Mem. Nat. Assn. Female Execs., Am. Soc. for Healthcare Edn. and Tng., Assn. for Care Children's Health, Sullivan County C. of C. (corr. sec., exec. bd. dirs. 1985-87). Avocations: crocheting, skiing, cooking, making candy. Home: Rt 1 Box 21 Neversink NY 12765 Office: Community Gen Hosp of Sullivan County PO Box 800 Harris NY 12742

ESSIG, NANCY CLAIRE, marketing executive; b. Canton, Ohio, Oct. 4, 1939; d. Atlee L. and Bernice (Bowen) E. AB, Ohio U., 1962. Publicity asst. Charles Scribner's Sons, N.Y.C., 1962-64, Dell Pub. Co., N.Y.C., 1965-

66; publicity dir. Columbia U. Press, N.Y.C., 1966-73, sales mgr. Johns Hopkins U. Press, Balt., 1973-74, mktg. dir., 1974-83, asst. dir., mktg. dir., 1983—. Mem. Assn. Am. Univ. Presses (bd. dirs. 1981-83), Women in Scholarly Publishing (pres. 1982-83), Women's Nat. Book Assn. (pres. 1980-81), Unilibros (bd. dirs. 1981-83), Chatham Assn. (bd. dirs. 1986—, chmn. bd. dirs. 1988). Club: Johns Hopkins (Balt.). Office: Johns Hopkins U Press 701 W 40th St Baltimore MD 21211

ESTEP, M(ARGARET) FRANCES, consumer psychologist; b. Peru, Ind., Feb. 5, 1922; d. Arthur W. and Minnie (Coburn) E. B.S., Purdue U., 1945; M.A., Wayne U., 1948; postgrad. U. Mich., U. Detroit, Wayne U., 1948; Ph.D. (grad. asst.), Ohio State U., 1951. With advt. dept. Procter & Gamble Co., Cin., 1942, mfg. dept., Milan, Tenn., 1943-44; with mfg. dept. Joseph E. Seagram & Sons, Lawrenceburg, Ind., 1946; mem. research staff J.L. Hudson Co., Detroit, 1946-47; instr. and research assoc., mng. editor Indsl. Tng. Abstracts, Wayne U., Detroit, 1947-52; instr. Marygrove Coll., Detroit, 1949; psychologist, mgmt. cons. Roger Bellows & Assocs., Detroit, 1947-53; research psychologist Psychol. Research Service of Pitts., 1954; research and cons. psychologist Winkelman Bros., Detroit, 1955-56; pvt. practice psychology, Detroit, N.Y.C., 1954-57; pres. and consumer psychologist Estep and Assocs., Inc., N.Y.C., 1957—; lectr. psychology CUNY, Queens Coll., 1961-69, CUNY, Hunter Coll., 1970; lectr. Mercy Coll., Dobbs Ferry, N.Y., 1982. Lic. psychologist, N.Y. Contbr. articles to profl. jours.; Co-author textbooks on psychology. Office: 33 Gold St New York NY 10038

ESTERLINE, SHIRLEY JEANNE, lithograph company executive; b. Paulding, Ohio, June 6, 1936; d. George Gary and Catherine Genevieve (Durbin) Sontchi; m. Meredith Esterline, Apr. 1, 1956; children—Gordon Alan, Amy Jeanne. Cert. med. technologist, Elkhart U., Ind., 1956. Lab technician, Fort Wayne, Ind., 1956-57; sec. Zollner Corp., Fort Wayne, 1957-58, Magnavox Corp., Fort Wayne, 1958-61; sales coordinator Doty Lithograph Inc., Fort Wayne, 1975-77; sales mgr. Dot Line div. Dot Corp., Auburn, Ind., 1977-87, Midwest sales mgr. Falco/Sunbelt div. FL Cos., Nashville, 1987—. Recipient Top Sales award Dot Corp., 1985. Mem. Specialty Advt. Assn. Internat. (suppliers com. 1983—, cert. advt. specialist 1985—, chmn. 100 club 1983—, facilitator tng. 1985—, CAS Alumni 1985—, mgmt. awards 1984, 85, 86). Methodist. Avocations: reading; gardening. Office: 1308 Reckeweg Rd Fort Wayne IN 46804

ESTES, CARROLL LYNN, sociologist, educator; b. Fort Worth, May 30, 1938; d. Joe Ewing and Carroll (Cox) E.; A.B., Stanford U., 1959; M.A., So. Meth. U., 1961; Ph.D., U. Calif.-San Diego, 1972, D.H.L. (hon.) Russell Sage Coll., 1986; m. Philip R. Lee; 1 child, Duskie Lynn Gelfand Estes. Research asst., asst. study dir. Brandeis U. Social Welfare Research Ctr., 1962-63, research assoc., 1964-65, project dir., 1965-67, vis. lectr. Florence Heller Grad. Sch., 1964-65; research dir. Simmons Coll., 1963-64; asst. prof. social work San Diego State Coll., 1967-72; asst. prof. in residence dept. psychiatry U. Calif.-San Francisco, 1972-75, assoc. prof. dept. social and behavioral scis., 1975-79, prof. 1979—, chair dept. social and behavioral scis., from 1981, coordinator human devel. tng. program, 1974-75, dir. Aging Health Policy Research Center, 1979-85, dir. Inst. for Health and Aging, 1985—. Mem. Calif. Commn. on Aging, 1974-77; cons. U.S. Senate Spl. Com. on Aging from 1976. Recipient Matrix award Theta Sigma Phi, 1964, award for contbns. to lives of older Californians, Calif. Commn. on Aging, 1977, Helen Nahm Research award, U. Calif., San Francisco, 1986; NIMH spl. fellow for research, 1970-72. Mem. ACLU, Am. Sociol. Assn., Inst. Medicine of Nat. Acad. Scis., Assn. Gerontology in Higher Edn. (pres. 1980-81), Am. Soc. on Aging (pres. from 1982-84), Soc. Study Social Problems, Alpha Kappa Delta, Pi Beta Phi. Democrat. Author: The Decision-Makers: The Power Structure of Dallas, 1963; co-author: Protective Services for Older People, 1972; U.S. Senate Special Committee on Aging Report, Paperwork and the Older Americans Act, 1978; The Aging Enterprise, 1979; co-author: Fiscal Austerity and Aging, 1983; Long Term Care of the Elderly, 1985, Political Economy, Health and Aging, 1984, Readings in the Political Economy of Aging, 1984; contbr. articles to profl. jours. Office: U Calif Dept Social and Behavioral Scis San Francisco CA 94143

ESTES, DEBORAH A., career counselor; b. West Lebanon, N.H., Aug. 15, 1951; d. Clyde Edward and Jayne (Hartson) E. BS, Johnson (Vt.) State Coll., 1983; MS, U. Vt., 1985. Metall. technician Splitballbearing Corp., Lebanon, N.H., 1971-75; spl. edn. tchr. Norwich (Vt.) Day Care Ctr., 1976-80; adminstrv. asst. career counseling service Johnson (Vt.) State Coll., 1980-83; cross-cultural counselor Vt. Refugee Resettlement Program, Burlington, 1983-85; career counselor State of Vt. Employment and Tng. Dept., Burlington, 1985-87; chief vocational edn. and counseling in corrections State of Vt., Waterbury, 1987—; outreach worker Children at Risk, Hanover, N.H., 1980-81; adv. bd. Womens' Econ. Opportunity Program, Burlington, 1985—, Trinity Coll., Burlington. Created study tool Pursuit of Counseling, 1985. Tchr.'s aide Headstart, Lebanon, 1975-76; active Vt. Assn. Retarded Citizens, 1984—, Chittenden County Council on Families and Children, 1984—; sponsor Cambodian Assn. Refugee Resettlement, 1985—; bd. dirs. Woodside Juvenile Detention Ctr., Essex, Vt., 1986—, Adult Service Providers of Chittenden County, 1987—. Mem. Am. Assn. for Counselling and Devel., Am. Mental Health Counselors Assn., Nat. Assn. Female Execs., Interval Internat., Pub. Offender Corrections Assn., Correctional Edn. Assn., Vt. Career Counselors Assn. Democrat. Home: 701 Dorset St #4 Ashbrook South Burlington VT 05403 Office: State of Vt Dept Employment and Training Pearl St Burlington VT 05401

ESTES, ELAINE ROSE GRAHAM, librarian; b. Springfield, Mo., Nov. 24, 1931; d. James McKinley and Zelma Mae (Smith) Graham; m. John Melvin Estes, Dec. 29, 1953. B.S. in Bus. Adminstrn., Drake U., 1953, teaching cert., 1956; M.S. in L.S, U. Ill., 1960. With Public Library, Des Moines, 1956—; coordinator extension services Public Library, 1977-78, dir., 1978—; lectr. antiques, hist. architecture, libraries; mem. conservation planning com. for disaster preparedness for libraries. Author bibliographies of books on antiques; contbr. articles to profl. jours. Mem. State of Iowa Cultural Affairs Adv. Council, 1986—, Nat. Commn. on Future Drake U., 1987-88; chmn. Des Moines Mayor's Hist. Dist. Commn.; bd. dirs. Des Moines Art Ctr., 1972—; mem. bd. Friends of Library USA, 1986—; mem. nominations rev. com. Iowa State Nat. Hist. Register. Recipient recognition for outstanding working women—leadership in econ. and civic life of Greater Des Moines YWCA, 1975, Disting. Alumni award Drake U., 1979. Mem. ALA, Iowa Library Assn. (pres. 1978-79), Iowa Urban Pub. Library Assn., Library Assn. Greater Des Moines Metro Area (pres.), Iowa Soc. Preservation Hist. Landmarks (bd.dirs. 1969—). Clubs: Links, Quester's, Inc. (pres. 1982, state 2d v.p. 1984-86). Lodge: Rotary. Office: Pub Library of Des Moines 100 Locust St Des Moines IA 50308-1791

ESTES, LYNN ANGELIQUE ROE, university administrator; b. Gulfport, Miss., June 24, 1953; d. Charles Alva and Agnes (Gaddy) Roe Adams; m. James Neal Estes, Feb. 18, 1978; children: Leslie Renee, Kelley Anne. B.A., U. So. Miss., 1975, M.S., 1981. Admissions counselor U. So. Miss., Hattiesburg, 1976-78; exec. dir. Am. Cancer Soc., Gulfport, Miss., 1978-80; fin. aid-VA-admissions counselor U. So. Miss., Long Beach, 1980-84, dir. student services, 1984—; judge officers' wives scholarship program Keesler AFB, Biloxi, Miss., 1981-83; instr. fin. aid workshops Gulf Coast area high schs. (Miss.), 1982-84; instr. Miss. Assn. Student Fin. Aid Adminstrs. Workshop, Biloxi, 1982. Performer, Miss. Gulf Coast Opera Theater, 1973—; mem. spl. events com. Miss USA Pageant, Biloxi, 1981, 82; dir. Miss Gulfport Pageant, 1982; pres. Jaycee Women, Gulfport, 1983-84; judge Ocean Springs Jr. Miss Pageant, 1986. Recipient Disting. Service award United Way, Harrison County, Miss., 1982; named to Top Ten Speakers in Nation, U.S. Jaycee Women, 1982, Outstanding Sparkette in Nation, 1983. Mem. Miss. Assn. Student Fin. Aid Adminstrs. (contbg. editor newsletter 1983-84), So. Assn. Student Fin. Aid Adminstrs., Miss. Assn. Collegiate Registrars and Admissions Officers, United Daus. of Confederacy, U. So. Miss. Alumni Assn. (sec. chpt. 1985-86), Omicron Delta Kappa (v.p. 1975-76), Phi Kappa Phi, Phi Alpha Theta, Pi Gamma Mu, Alpha Sigma Alpha (pres. U. So. Miss. chpt. 1975-76, Gulf Coast chpt. 1981-83). Baptist. Office: U So Miss Gulf Park Regional Campus Long Beach MS 39560

ESTES, MARGARET TURNER, university official, educator; b. Caldwell, Kans., July 1, 1924; d. William Jennings Bryant and Margaret Violet (Kern) Turner; BA, U. Kans., 1965, MA, 1967, PhD in Sociology, 1972; m. John King Estes, Jan. 13, 1943; (dec.), children: John, Greg, David, Jennifer. Instr., U. Kans., 1965-68; asst. prof. sociology Millersville State U., Pa., 1968-70; asst. prof. anthropology/sociology Haskell Indian Coll., Lawrence, Kans., 1970-71; prof. sociology, chmn. dept. No. Ariz. U., Flagstaff, 1972-78; assoc. v.p. acad. affairs, prof. sociology Miss. State U., Starkville, 1978—. Mem. Gov. Ariz. Commn. Women, 1976, Gov. Ariz. Task Force Marriage and Family, 1976-78. Named Faculty Woman of Year, No. Ariz. U., 1973, Outstanding Adminstrv. Profl. Woman Miss. State U., 1985-86, Woman of Yr. Miss. Assn. Women in Higher Edn., 1987; Margaret Turner Estes scholarship established, 1978. Mem. Am. Assn. Higher Edn., N.Am. Assn. Summer Sessions, So. Sociol. Assn., AAAS (past dir.), Am. Sociol. Assn., Phi Kappa Phi, Phi Delta Kappa. Democrat. Congregationalist. Office: Miss State U Drawer BQ Mississippi State MS 39762

ESTEY, AUDREE, exec., cons. ballet soc.; b. Winnipeg, Man., Can., Jan. 7, 1910; d. Robert and Anna (Harrington) Phipps; student Immaculate Heart Coll., 1927-29, Ernest Belcher Ballet Sch., 1928-31, Robert Major Drama Sch., 1929-31, Koslov Ballet Sch., 1930-31; m. L. Wendell Estey, Sept. 18, 1933; children—Lawrence Mitchell, Carol.Dancer Ernest Belcher Ballet Co., Los Angeles, 1930, Fanchon and Marco Co., Los Angeles, 1930-31; actress-dancer Fox Studio, Hollywood, Calif.; 1931-32 ballet tchr. Lawrenceville and Princeton, N.J., 1938-80, Perry Mansfield Camp, Steamboat Springs Colo., summers 1949-50; head dance dept. Les Chalets Francais, Deer Isle, Maine, 1951-73; founder non-profit Princeton (N.J.) Ballet Soc., 1954, dir., cons.; founder Princeton Regional Ballet Co., 1963; founder profl. co., Princeton Ballet, 1979. Host Northeast Regional Ballet Festival-Princeton, 1968; coordinator Northeast Regional Ballet Festival-Jacob's Pillow, 1970. Apptd. by gov. N.J. State Commn. to Study Arts, 1968, trustee N.J. Sch. of the Arts, 1980. Recipient Rutgers U. award for contbn. to arts in N.J., 1982. Mem. N.E. Regional Ballet Assn. (pres., 1967-68, exec. v.p., 1968-71). Episcopalian. Choreographer over 20 ballets for children and young dancers including: Festival of the Gnomes, Pastels, Peter and the Wolf, Sleeping Beauty, Cinderella, Pied Piper, The Nutcracker (choreography for Act I currently used by Princeton Ballet), Chanson Innocente, Graduation Ball, Coppelia. Office: 262 Alexander St Princeton NJ 08540

ESTIN-KLEIN, LIBBYADA, advertising executive, medical writer; b. Newark, July 13, 1937; d. Barney and Florence B. (Tenkin) Straver; m. Harvey M. Klein, Sept. 9, 1984. Student Syracuse U., 1955-57; B.S., Columbia, 1960; R.N., Columbia-Presbyn. Med. Center, 1960; certificate N.Y. Sch. Interior Design, 1962. Med. research tech. writer, N.Y.C., 1960-62; pres. Libbyada Estin Interiors, N.Y.C., 1962-65; v.p. advt. and pub. relations Behrman/Estin Inc., N.Y.C., 1965-67; account exec., dir. pub. relations J.S. Fullerton, Inc., N.Y.C., 1967-68; med. writer L.W. Frohlich & Co., Intercon Internat. Inc., N.Y.C., 1968-69, Kallir Philips Ross Inc., N.Y.C., 1969-71; copy supr. William Douglas McAdams Inc., N.Y.C., 1971-75, Sudler & Hennessey Inc., N.Y.C., 1975-80; v.p., exec. adminstr./creative dir. Grey Med. Advt. Inc., N.Y.C., 1980-84; founder, ptnr. Estin-Sandler, Communications Inc., N.Y.C., 1984; v.p. Barnum Communications Inc., N.Y.C., 1984-86; sr. v.p. ICE Communications, Inc., Rochester, N.Y., 1986-87; pres. Estin-Klein Communications Inc., Pittsford, N. ., 1987—. Mem. Public Relations Soc. Am., Advt. Women N.Y., Am. Advt. Fedn., Am. Med. Writers Assn., Pharm. Advt. Club, Am. Nurses Assn., Allied Bd. Trade, Columbia-Presbyn. Hosp. Alumnae Assn., Columbia U. Alumnae Assn., Syracuse U. Alumnae Assn., Sigma Theta Tau, Delta Phi Epsilon. Home and Office: 289 Garnsey Rd Pittsford NY 14534

ESTLER, ELIZABETH DOWNING, military officer; b. Ames, Iowa, Dec. 30, 1955; d. James Ray and Maria Tulia (Quiros) Downing; m. Gary Lee Estler, May 21, 1983. BS, Nebr. Wesleyan U., 1975; postgrad., U. Okla. at Canal Zone, 1978-80. Commd. 2d lt. U.S. Army, 1977, advanced through grades to capt., 1981; chief All Source Intelligence Ctr., 1st Inf. Div., Ft. Riley, Kans., 1980-81, 2d brigade asst. sr. intelligence officer, phys. security crime prevention officer, 1981-82; chief Intelligence Collection Mgmt. and Dissemination Ctr., 513th M.I. Group, Ft. Monmouth, N.J., 1983-84; comdr. 174th M.I. Co., Ft. Monmouth, 1984-85; officer Intelligence Communications Security, U.S. Army Europe, Heidelberg, Fed. Republic Germany, 1985-86, officer counterintelligence/rear ops. intelligence, 1986—; mem. working women's panel Glamour mag., 1982. Editor: 201st Mil. Intelligence Bn. Newsletter, 1983-84; columnist: (newspaper) Army Materiel Command Europe News-Dispatch, 1987—. Mem. Junction City-Ft. Riley Ambassadors Program, 1981, Heidelberg Community Chorus. Mem. Assn. U.S. Army, Nat. Mil. Intelligence Assn., Nat. Assn. Female Execs. Roman Catholic. Club: Heidelberg Internat. Ski.

ESTRIN, JUDY ANN, human resources consultant; b. Los Angeles, Mar. 17, 1952; d. Sam and Dorothy (Levinson) Estrin; m. Christopher Stanley Martin, July 21, 1974 (div. Mar. 1976). BA in English, Calif. State U., Northridge, 1973; MA, George Washington U., 1987. Personnel and tng. officer First City Bank, Pasadena, Calif., 1976-79; human resource devel. cons. First Interst. Bank Calif., Los Angeles, 1979-82; sr. tng. advisor Superior Oil Co., Houston, 1982-85; sales and mktg. tng. specialist Bank Boston, 1985-86; mgr. career resource cen. Drake, Beam, Morin Inc., Houston, 1986; cons. tng. and devel. First City Bank Corp. Tex., Houston, 1986-88; mgr. career ctr. Fuchs, Cuthrell & Co. Inc., South San Francisco, Calif., 1988—. Mem. Am. Inst. Banking, Am. Soc. Tng. and Devel. Democrat. Jewish. Office: Fuchs Cuthrell & Co Inc 501 Hilltop South San Francisco CA 94080

ESTRIN, KARI (KAREN RUTH), concert producer; b. Plainfield, N.J., Nov. 5, 1954; d. Herman Albert and Pearl (Simon) E. BA with honors, Ramapo Coll. of N.J., 1976. Artist mgr., agt. Tony Rice/Rounder Records, 1981-85; founder, exec. dir. Black Sheep Concerts and Publs., Inc., Cambridge, Mass., 1980-86; tour mgr. Suzanne Vega/A&M Records, 1985; founder, cons. Palomine Mgmt., 1984—; asst. producer Nestle Folk Festival Festival Prodns., Inc., N.Y.C., 1987; Assoc. producer Gr. NE Prodns., Townsend, Mass., 1986; asst. to dir. Bershire Mountain Bluegrass Festival, Hillsdale, N.Y., 1980-81; nat. promoter Rounder Records, Cambridge, Mass., 1979; bd. dirs. Sing Out! mag. Pub., editor The Black Sheep Rev., 1982, numerous concert and festival publs.; co-producer (album) Great Acoustics, 1985. Bd. dirs. Hey, Rube Folk Music Orgn., 1983-86, Folk Arts Network, Cambridge, 1983-85, Folk Arts Ctr. of New Eng., Cambridge, 1982-84. Mem. Nat. Assn. Ind. Record Distbrs. and Mfrs. Home and Office: 315 Henry St Scotch Plains NJ 07076

ESTRIN, THELMA AUSTERN, electrical engineer; b. N.Y.C., Feb. 21, 1924; d. I. Billy and Mary (Ginsburg) Austern; m. Gerald Estrin, Dec. 21, 1941; children: Margo, Judith, Deborah. BSEE, U. Wis., Madison, 1947, MSEE, 1948, PhD, 1951. Cert. clin. engr. Research engr. UCLA Brain Research Inst., 1960-70, dir. data processing, 1970-80; prof. UCLA Sch. Engring. and Applied Sci., 1980—; dir. div. electronics, computer and systems engring. NSF, Washington, 1982-84; dir. dept. engring., asst. dean Sch. of Engring. and Applied Sci. UCLA extension, 1984; trustee Aerospace Corp., 1979-82; mem. biomed. tech. resources com. NIH, 1981-86; mem. U.S. Army Sci. Bd., 1982-83; mem. energy engring. bd. NRC, 1985—. Contbr. articles to tech. jours. Mem. Los Angeles Women in Bus. Recipient Disting. Contbn. to Engring. Edn. award NSPE, 1985, Achievement award Soc. Women Engrs. 1981, Disting. Service citation U. Wis., 1976. Fellow IEEE (bd. dirs. 1979-80, exec. v.p. 1982, recipient Centennial medal 1984, pres. Engring. in Medicine and Biology Soc. 1977), AAAS (chair-elect Engring. sect. 1987). Jewish. Home: 500 Warner Ave Los Angeles CA 90024 Office: UCLA Sch Engring and Applied Sci Boelter Hall Room 7620 Los Angeles CA 90024

ETCHESON, DENISE ELENE, architect; b. Iowa City, Iowa, May 17, 1950; d. Warren Wade and Marianne (Newgent) E.; m. Alejandro Sanchez, May 26, 1984. B.A. in Environ. Design, U. Washington, 1974, Cert. in Urban Design, 1977, M.Arch., 1977. Planner, designer Temel Muhendislik A.S., Istanbul, Turkey, 1974; project designer Astra Zarina Assocs., Seattle, 1973-74, 76-77; project designer, constrn. coordinator G.R. Bartholick Architect/Planner, Seattle, 1975, 78; project mgr. TRA Airport Cons., Seattle, 1978-84; pres. Portico Architects, Houston, 1985—; lectr. U. Wash., 1977. Mem. City of Seattle Pike Pl. Market Hist. Commn., 1975-82, vice chmn., 1977-79, chmn., 1979-81, mem. Landmarks Preservation Bd., 1976-77. Recipient U. Wash. Archtl. Found. award, 1975. Mem. Am. Planning Assn., Historic Seattle Preservation and Devel. Authority, Nat. Trust Historic Preservation, Internat. Council Monuments and Sites. Office: PO Box 60491 Houston TX 77205

ETESS, SUSAN LYNN, educational administrator; b. Syracuse, N.Y., Sept. 19, 1948; d. Abraham David and Elaine (Grossinger) Etess; B.A., Russell Sage Coll., 1970; M.A., Columbia U., 1977, postgrad.; m. Howard Lawrence Zimmerman, Dec. 17, 1979; children—Harron Etess, Andrew Etess. Tchr. social studies Dalton Sch., N.Y.C., 1971-72, coordinator for middle and lower sch. social studies, 1972-76, asst. dir. middle sch., 1975-76, dir., 1976—; project dir. Fischer-Landau Program for Gifted Children with Learning Disabilities, 1984—; adj. prof. dept. supervision and adminstrn. Bank Street Coll. Edn., 1986—. Mem. Nat. Assn. Elem. Prins., Nat. Middle Sch. Assn., Assn. Supervision and Curriculum Devel., Nat. Assn. Ind. Schs., Ind. Sch. Middle Sch. Dirs. Assn. (co-founder N.Y.C.). Home: 60 E 96th St New York NY 10028 Office: 108 E 89th St New York NY 10028

ETHAN, CAROL BAEHR, psychotherapist; b. N.Y.C., May 30, 1920; d. Irving and Sadie (Goldman) Baehr; trained Met. Inst. Psychoanalytic Studies, 1965-70; B.A. in Psychology with honors, N.Y. U., 1978; M.A. in Psychology, New Sch. Social Research, 1981; m. Sy Ethan, Mar. 18, 1955; children: Willa Capraro, Barbara Ethan. Writer, Irvington (N.J.) Herald, 1946, Walt Framer Prodns., 1949-50; tchr. Queens Coll., 1956-57; consumer psychology researcher and cons., 1950-70; staff psychotherapist Fifth Ave. Center Counseling and Psychotherapy, 1965-70; pvt. practice psychotherapy, N.Y.C., 1967—; columnist Rhinebeck Gazette-Advertiser, 1981—. Democratic committeewoman for Queens County, 1960; vol. social rehab. program Queens County Mental Health Soc., 1965-66; fellow internat. council sex edn. and parenthood Am. U. Recipient Founders Day award N.Y. U., 1978. Fellow Am. Orthopsychiat. Assn.; mem. N.Y. State Assn. Practicing Psychotherapists (cert.), Am. Mental Health Counselors Assn., Divorce Mediation Council, Am. Psychol. Assn., Internat. Acad. Behavioral Med., Counceling and Psychotherapy (clin. mem.). Address: 235 W 76th St New York NY 10023

ETHEREDGE, ZELMA VERREE, independent insurance agent; b. Houston, Sept. 6, 1935; d. Aurie J. and Hattie I. (Massey) Etheredge. BBA, U. Tex., Austin, 1958. Sec. Shell Oil Co., Houston, 1958-64; ptnr. A.J. Etheredge Co., Houston, 1964-72, owner, 1972—; bd. dirs. Houston Housing Fin. Corp., 1986—. Mem. Ind. Ins. Agts. Am., Tex. Assn. Ind. Ins. Agts., Houston Ind. Ins. Agts. Methodist. Home: 8423 Academy Houston TX 77025 Office: A J Etheredge Co 2410 Sunset Blvd Houston TX 77005

ETHIER, PATRICIA KELLEHER, insurance company executive; b. Montague, Mass., June 28, 1951; d. Edward Patterson and Mary Elizabeth (Masterson) Kelleher; A.A., Greenfield Community Coll., 1971; CLU, Am. Coll., 1986; m. Gerard R. Ethier, Aug. 3, 1973. Titlist policy title Phoenix Mut. Life Ins. Co., Greenfield, Mass., 1971-76, supr. group major med. claims, 1976-78, assoc. mgr. group claims, 1978-79, mgr. policy title, 1979-82, mgr. new products adminstrn., 1982-85, dir. ins. service systems, 1985—. Allocations chmn. Franklin County United Way, 1980-85, bd. dirs., 1980—, v.p., 1985—; mem. adv. bd. Dept. Social Services, Franklin and Hampshire Counties, 1981-86; bd. dirs. New England Learning Center Women in Transition, 1981-86; bd. dirs. Greenfield Community Coll. Found., 1986—. Fellow Life Office Mgmt. Assn. Roman Catholic. Home: 205 Fairview W Greenfield MA 01301 Office: 101 Munson St Greenfield MA 01301

ETTINGER, SHEILA JUNE, telecommunications analyst; b. Bklyn., June 2, 1938; d. Norman and Tillie (Walder) Mutterperl; m. Arnold Ettinger, Apr. 11, 1965; children: Mark, Steve, Amy. BA, Barnard Coll., 1960; postgrad., CUNY, 1961-65. Lic. sch. psychologist, Calif. Tchr. N.Y.C. Bd. Edn., 1960-65; sch. psychologist Greece (N.Y.) Cen. Schs., 1966-78; program developer City of Sunnyvale, Calif., 1979-80; sch. psychologist Cambrian Sch. Dist., San Jose, Calif., 1980-83; analyst info. systems McGraw-Hill Publs., San Mateo, Calif., 1983—. Counselor Ctr. for Living with Dying, Santa Clara, Calif., 1983; chairperson Saratoga (Calif.) Social Action Com., 1984; fine arts commr. City of Cupertino, Calif., 1987—. Jewish. Office: McGraw-Hill 951 Mariner's Island Blvd San Mateo CA 94404

ETTINGER, SUSI STEINITZ, artist; b. Berlin, July 29, 1922; came to U.S., 1939, naturalized, 1944; d. Otto and Grethe Steinitz; B.F.A. cum laude, U. Louisville, 1943; m. Manford F. Ettinger, June 2, 1944; children—Linda, Daniel. Staff lectr. Met. Mus. Art, N.Y.C., 1944-45; staff instr., dir. children's classes Springfield (Mo.) Art Mus., 1960-66; instr. and lectr. art S.W. Mo. State U., Springfield, 1964-84, ret., 1984, also former area head found. art program; one-woman shows include: Ft. Smith (Ark.) Art Mus., 1968, Sch. of Ozarks, 1972, 86, Springfield Art Mus., 1976, S.W. Mo. State U., 1980; two-artist shows, Springfield, 1974, 84; exhibited group shows in Ark., Kans., Mo., Nebr., Tenn., 1966—; represented in permanent collections: Mo. Hist. Soc., Springfield Art Mus., Harwell Art Mus., Poplar Bluff, Mo. Recipient Appreciation cert. Mo. Women in Arts, 1974. Home: 2020 Ventura Ave Springfield MO 65804

ETZEL, BARBARA COLEMAN, psychologist, educator; b. Pitts., Sept. 19, 1926; d. Walter T. and Ruth (Coleman) E. A.A., Stephens Coll., 1946; B.S. in Psychology, Denison U., 1948; M.S., U. Miami, Fla., 1950; Ph.D. in Exptl. Child Psychology, State U. Iowa, 1953. Staff psychologist Ohio State Bur. Juvenile Research, Columbus, 1953-54; asst. prof. psychology Fla. State U., Tallahassee, 1954-56; chief psychologist, child psychiatry U. Wash. Med. Sch., Seattle, 1956-61; assoc. prof. psychology Western Wash. State U., Bellingham, 1961-65, dir. grad. program in psychology, 1963-65; spl. fellow sect. early learning and devel. NIMH, Bethesda, Md., 1965-66; assoc. prof. dept. human devel. U. Kans., Lawrence, 1965-69, mem. grad. faculty, 1965—, prof. human devel., 1969—, dir. Edna A. Hill Child Devel. Lab., 1965-72, dir. Kans. Ctr. for Research in Early Childhood Edn., 1968-71, assoc. dean Office of Research Adminstrn. and Grad. Sch., 1972-74, dir. John T. Stewart Children's Ctr., 1975-85; vis. prof. Universidad Central de Venezuela, Caracas, 1981-82; cons. Manchester Sch. Presch. Program, U. Mex., Mexico City, 1973-75, George Peabody Tchrs. Coll., 1978, St. Luke's Hosp., Kansas City, Mo., 1981-83, Anne Sullivan Sch. for Handicapped Children, Lima, Peru, 1982-85. Author: (with J.M. LeBlanc and D.M. Baer) New Developments in Behavioral Research, 1977; contbr. articles to profl. jours.; mem. editorial bd. Behavior Analyst, 1979-83. Bd. dirs. Community Children's Ctr., Inc., 1968-71; trustee Ctr. for Research, Inc., U. Kans., 1975-78. Elected to U. Kans. Women's Hall of Fame, 1975; Japan Soc. Promotion for Sci. fellow, 1981. Fellow Am. Psychol. Assn. (Div. 25 Don Hake award, 1987); mem. Assn. Behavior Analysis (pres. 1987—, pres.-elect 1986-87), Soc. Research in Child Devel., Midwestern Psychol. Assn., Am. Ednl. Research Assn., AAAS, AAUP, Southwestern Soc. Research in Human Devel., Sigma Xi, Psi Chi, Pi Lambda Theta. Home: Woodsong at JB Ranch Route 1 PO Box 82-E Oskaloosa KS 66066 Office: U Kans Dept Human Devel Lawrence KS 66045

ETZLER, LOIS RUTH, systems analyst, medical technologist; b. Lancaster, Ohio, Jan. 27, 1941; d. Edward Ferdinand and Ruth Faye (Cofman) Walter; B.S. in Med. Tech., Ohio State U., 1963; postgrad. Central Mich. U.; m. Alvin Lorenz Etzler, May 4, 1963; children—Paul, Janice. Med. technologist Ohio State U. Hosp., 1962-63; blood bank technologist OB Hunter Lab., Washington, 1963-65; blood bank supr. Jewish Hosp., Louisville, 1965-66; staff technologist Greater S.E. Community Hosp., Washington, 1969-72, tech. supr., instr. Med. Tech. Sch., 1972-75, edn. coordinator Med. Tech. Sch., 1975-77, quality control supr., edn. coordinator, 1977-81, computer coordinator, quality control supr., 1981-85; programmer analyst Greater S.E. Mgmt. Co., 1985-86, sr. systems analyst, 1986—;. cons. Health Care Computer Systems, 1986. Fin. sec. Chesapeake dist. Lutheran Women's Missionary League, 1978-82, pres. zone, 1976-78, v.p. zone, 1983-85, v.p. Chesapeake Dist., 1984-88, chmn. Chesapeake dist. nominating com., 1984; pres. Women's Guild, 1st Luth. Ch., Sunderland, Md., 1984-86; del. Nat. Capitol area Luth. High Sch. Assn., 1978—. Mem. Am. Soc. Clin. Pathologists, Echo. Home: 2211 Green Valley Dr Sunderland MD 20689 Office: Dept Pathology 1310 Southern Ave Washington DC 20032

EU, MARCH KONG FONG, state official; b. Oakdale, Calif., Mar. 29, 1922; d. Yuen and Shiu (Shee) Kong; children by previous marriage—Matthew Kipling Fong, Marchesa Suyin Fong You; m. Henry Eu, July 30, 1973; stepchildren—Henry, Adeline, Yvonne, Conroy, Alaric. Student, Salinas Jr. Coll.; B.S., U. Calif.-Berkeley; M.Ed., Mills Coll., 1951; Ed.D.,

Stanford U., 1956; postgrad., Columbia U., Calif. State Coll.-Hayward; LL.D., Lincoln U., 1984. Chmn. div. dental hygiene U. Calif. Med. Center, San Francisco; dental hygienist Oakland (Calif.) Pub. Schs.; supr. dental health edn. Alameda County (Calif.) Schs.; lectr. health edn. Mills Coll., Oakland; mem. Calif. Legislature, 1966-74, chmn. select com. on agr., foods and nutrition, 1973-74; mem. com. natural resources and conservation, com. commerce and pub. utilities, select com. med. malpractice; sec. state State of Calif., 1975—, chief of protocol, 1975-83; chmn. Calif. State World Trade Commn., 1982-87; spl. cons. Bur. Intergroup Relations, Calif. Dept. Edn.; ednl., legis. cons. Sausalito (Calif.) Pub. Schs., Santa Clara County Office Edn., Jefferson Elementary Union Sch. Dist., Santa Clara High Sch. Dist., Santa Clara Elementary Sch. Dist., Live Oak Union High Sch. Dist.; mem. Alameda County Bd. Edn., 1956-66, pres., 1961-62, legis. adv., 1963. Mem. budget panel Bay Area United Fund Crusade; mem. Oakland Econ. Devel. Council; mem. tourism devel. com. Calif. Econ. Devel. Commn.; mem. citizens com. on housing Council Social Planning; mem. Calif. Interagy. Council Family Planning; edn. chmn., mem. council social planning, dir. Oakland Area Baymont Dist. Community Council; charter pres., hon. life mem. Howard Elementary Sch. PTA; charter pres. Chinese Young Ladies Soc., Oakland; mem., vice chmn. adv. com. Youth Study Centers and Ford Found. Interagy. Project, 1962-63; chmn. Alameda County Mothers' March, 1971-72; bd. councillors U. So. Calif. Sch. Dentistry, 1976; mem. exec. com. Calif. Democratic Central Com., mem. central com., 1963-70, asst. sec.; del. Dem. Nat. Conv., 1968; dir. 8th Congl. Dist. Dem. Council, 1963; v.p. Dems. of 8th Congl. Dist., 1963; dir. Key Women for Kennedy, 1963; women's vice chmn. No. Calif. Johnson for Pres., 1964; bd. dirs. Oakland YWCA, 1965. Recipient ann. award for outstanding achievement Eastbay Intercultural Fellowship, 1959; Phoebe Apperson Hearst Disting. Bay Area Woman of Yr. award; Woman of Yr. award Calif. Retail Liquor Dealers Inst., 1969; Merit citation Calif. Assn. Adult Edn. Adminstrs., 1970; Art Edn. award; Outstanding Woman award Nat. Women's Polit. Caucus, 1980; Person of Yr. award Miracle Mile Lions Club, 1980; Humanitarian award Milton Strong Hall of Fame, 1981; Outstanding Leadership award Ventura Young Dems., 1983; Woman of Achievement award Los Angeles Hadassah, 1983. Mem. Am. Dental Hygienists Assn. (pres. 1956-57), No. Calif. Dental Hygienists Assn., Oakland LWV, AAUW (area rep. in edn. Oakland br.), Calif. Tchrs. Assn., Calif. Sch. Bd. Assn., Alameda County Sch. Bd. Assn. (pres. 1965), Alameda County Mental Health Assn., So. Calif. Dental Assn. (hon.), Bus. and Profl. Women's Club, Chinese Retail Food Markets Assn. (hon.), Delta Kappa Gamma. Office: State of Calif 1230 J St Sacramento CA 95814

EUBANKS, FRANCES OLIVE DOWELL (MRS. ELI T. EUBANKS), oil company manager; b. Wellsford, Kans.; d. Frank E. and Eva (Thomas) Dowell; student U. Kans., 1945-46; B.S., Kans. State U., 1949, M.S., 1950; m. Eli T. Eubanks, Dec. 23, 1940. Teaching fellow dept. home mgmt. Kans. State Coll., Manhattan, 1949-50; instr. U. Louisville, 1950-51, U. Wash., Seattle, 1951-52; mgr. records dept. Adair Oil Co., Wichita, Kans., 1955-86. Sec. Young Democrats Club, U. Kans., 1945-46. Mem. Omicron Nu, Phi Kappa Phi. Home: Route 1 Viola KS 67149 Office: POB 2823 Wichita KS 67201

EUNPU, DEBORAH LEE, genetics counselor; b. Troy, N.Y., Mar. 24, 1952; d. Floyd F. and Sally (Loorents) E.; m. G. Taylor Tunstall, Jr., June 25, 1977. AB, Smith Coll., 1974; MS, Sarah Lawrence Coll., 1977. Diplomate Am. Bd. Med. Genetics. Sr. counselor genetics The Children's Hosp. Phila., 1977-87; dir. genetic counseling program Albert Einstein Med. Ctr., Phila., 1987—; mem. genetic disease program adv. com. State of Pa., Harrisburg, 1985—, subcom. for prevention of mental retardation, 1987—; instr. U. Pa. Sch. Medicine, 1985-87, Temple U. Sch. Medicine, 1988—. Editor: Perspectives in Genetic Counseling, 1978-83; contbr. articles to profl. jours. Bd. dirs. Women's Suburban Clinic, Paoli, Pa., 1982-86, pres., 1984-86. Mem. Am. Soc. Human Genetics, Nat. Soc. Genetic Counselors, Inc. (pres. 1985-86), Huntington Disease Soc. Am. (med. adv. bd. Del. Valley chpt. 1984—). Office: Albert Einstein Med Ctr No Div York and Tabor Rds Philadelphia PA 19141

EUSTER, JOANNE REED, librarian; b. Grants Pass, Oreg., Apr. 7, 1936; d. Robert Lewis and Mabel Louise (Jones) Reed; m. Stephen L. Gerhardt, May 14, 1977; children: Sharon L., Carol L., Lisa J. Student, Lewis and Clark Coll., 1953-56; B.A., Portland State Coll., 1965; M.Librarianship, U. Wash., 1968, M.B.A., 1977; Ph.D., U. Calif.-Berkeley, 1986. Asst. librarian Edmonds Community Coll., Lynnwood, Wash., 1968-73, dir. library-media center, 1973-77; univ. librarian Loyola U. of New Orleans, 1977-80; library dir. J. Paul Leonard Library, San Francisco State U., 1980-86; univ. librarian Rutgers U., New Brunswick, N.J., 1986—; cons. Union Ejidal, La Penita, Nayarit, Mexico, 1973; co-cons. Office of Mgmt. Studies Assn. of Research Libraries, 1979—. Author: Changing Patterns of Internal Communication in Large Academic Libraries, 1981, The Academic Library Director, Management Activities and Effectiveness, 1987; contbr. articles to profl. jours. Mem. ALA, Am. Soc. Info. Sci., N.J. Library Assn., Assn. Coll. and Research Libraries (pres. 1987-88) Library Adminstrn. and Mgmt. Assn. Office: Rutgers State Univ NJ University Libraries 169 College Ave New Brunswick NJ 08903

EUTSLER, THERESE ANNE, physical therapist; b. Jasper, Ind., Sept. 11, 1959; d. Joseph Martin and Viola Agnes (Rasche) Wagner; m. Mark Leslie Eutsler, Oct. 3, 1987. BS, Ind. U., 1982. Physicial therapist Reid Meml. Hosp., Richmond, Ind., 1982-84, Cen. Convalescent Services, Crawfordsville, Ind., 1984-85, St. Elizabeth Hosp., Lafayette, Ind., 1985-86; clinical coordinator St. Elizabeth Hosp., Lafayette, 1986—. Bd. dirs. Arthritis Found. Tippecanoe Unit, Lafayette, 1986—; del. Ind. St. Democrat Convention, Indpls., 1988. Mem. Am. Physical Therapy Assn. Orthopedic Sect. Roman Catholic. Home: 207 Main St Linden IN 47955

EVANKO, MELANIE LUCAS, banker; b. Staten Island, N.Y., Apr. 17, 1954; d. Harold Warde and Billie Arwin (Clift) Lucas; m. Robert James Evanko, Oct. 15, 1983. B.B.A., U. Ga., 1976. C.P.A., Ga. Internal auditor Trust Co. Ga., Atlanta, 1976-79, ops. officer corp. planning, 1979-81, asst. v.p. corp. tax, 1981-85; v.p. corp. tax Suntrust Bank Inc, 1985—. Co. coordinator United Way, Atlanta, 1982; team capt. High Mus. Art-Young Careers, Atlanta, 1980-83; mem. Jr. League of Atlanta. Mem. Am. Inst. Banking, Am. Inst. C.P.A.s (edn. com.), Ga. Soc. C.P.A.s (dir. exec. com.) Atlanta C. of C. (pres. com. 1982). Republican. Presbyterian. Office: Suntrust Banks Inc 25 Park Pl NE Atlanta GA 30302

EVANOFF, CAROLYN YVONNE, nuclear missile manufacturing company executive, consultant; b. Escondido, Calif., Dec. 1, 1955; d. Chester Benson and Shirly Bernice (Pederson) E.; m. Michael Kelly Morrison, Jan. 15, 1983 (div. Nov. 1984). AA, Evergreen Valley Coll., 1986; BS in Mgmt., St. Mary's U., Moraga, Calif., 1988. Police cadet Milpitas (Calif.) Police Dept., 1972-73; cashier K-Mart, Milpitas, 1973; electronic technician Raytheon Semicondr. Co., Mountain View, Calif., 1973-75; micro electronics assembler Lockheed Missiles and Space Co., Sunnyvale, Calif., 1975-77, prodn. controller, 1977-79, mfg. supr., 1979-81, product assurance supr., 1981-85, program plans specialist, 1985-86, mfg. mgr., 1986—, career counseling cons., 1979—, prodn. mgmt. cons., 1985—. Chpt. leader Young Astronauts Program, Mountain View, 1986-88. Recipient Frank G. Brewer Meml. Aerospace award CAP, Vandenberg AFB, Calif., 1987. Mem. Soc. Mfg. Engrs., Nat. Mgmt. Assn., Am. Def. Preparedness Assn., Soc. for Advancement Material and Process Engring., Calif. Tax Reduction Program, Challenger Soc., Am. Tropical Assn. Democrat. Pentecostal. Club: Lockheed Gun (Sunnyvale). Home: 3534 Shafer Dr Santa Clara CA 95051 Office: Lockheed Missiles and Space Co 1111 Lockheed Way Sunnyvale CA 94089-3504

EVANS, ALYCE DIXIE, corporate professional; b. Philipsburg, Pa., Sept. 18, 1940; d. Jerome Paul and Alyce Edith (Showers) Dugan; m. Terry Y. Evans, July 25, 1936; children: Tracy Lynn, Stacey Leigh. BS, Gwynedd-Mercy, 1960. Receptionist and various positions in constrn. field Harrisburg and Camp Hill, Pa., 1960-66; with Harrisburg Acad., Camp Hill, 1972-79; pres., chief exec. officer Testco, Inc. (material supply co.), Camp Hill, 1981—, T.I. Constrn. Co., Inc. (heavy hwy. constrn.), Camp Hill, 1986—. Patentee in field. Mem. U.S. White House Conf., 1985-86; trustee Hugh O' Brian Youth Found., 1985—. Mem/ Cen. Pa. Internat. Bus. Forum (bd. dirs. 1986—), Assn. Gen. Contractors of Am., Harrisburg C. of C. (energy bd. 1981—). Home: 318 Belaire Dr Shiremanstown PA 17011 Office: Testco Inc PO Box 3097 Camp Hill PA 17011

EVANS, CAROL ANN, computer systems programmer; b. Little Falls, N.Y., June 20, 1951; d. Harry Fred and Barbara June (Morrison) Hoffman; m. Paul Jeffrey Evans, Apr. 4, 1976 (div. Jan. 1985); 1 child, Michael Paul. Student, Coll. Lake County, 1982-84. Data processing acctg. clk. N.Y. State Facilities Devel. Corp., Albany, 1971-76; computer operator Gen. Foam Plastics, Norfolk, Va., 1976-77; computer operator, data entry C.E. Thurston Co., Norfolk, 1977-78; acctg. clk. Mobay Chem. Corp., Charleston, S.C., 1979-81; computer programmer, analyst Selective Service System, Great Lakes, Ill., 1981-83, Hdqrs. U.S. Mepcom Automation Mgmt., North Chicago, Ill., 1983-85; computer programmer, analyst Regional Automated Services Ctr., Cherry Point, NC, 1985—, Cherry Point, N.C., 1985-86. Mem. Nat. Assn. Female Execs. Lutheran. Home: PO Box 1364 Havelock NC 28532 Office: Regional Automated Services Ctr Bldg 159 Marine Corps Air Sta Cherry Point NC 28533

EVANS, CAROLYN MARGARET, court administrator; b. Camden, N.J., Jan. 19, 1946; d. Philip Louis and Margaret Caroline (Henry) Iuliucci; B.A., Rutgers U., 1968; MBA, LaSalle Univ., 1986. Probation officer Camden (N.J.) County Probation Dept., 1968-70, sr. probation officer, dir. vols., 1970-74; dir. vol. services Adminstrv. Office of Cts., Trenton, N.J., 1974-81, asst. chief jud. edn., 1981-83, chief ct. reporting services, 1983—. Mem. Nat. Assn. for Female Execs., Nat. Assn. Court Mgmt., Vols. in Cts. and Corrections Assn. of N.J. (pres. 1980-82), Nat. Assn. on Vols. in Criminal Justice (sec. 1977-79, adv. bd., chmn. com. on adult cts. and probation Nat. Guidelines Project 1980-82). Home: 921 Quaker Circle Langhorne PA 19047 Office: Justice Complex CN 988 Trenton NJ 08625

EVANS, CHARLOTTE MORTIMER, writer, communications consultant; b. Newton, N.J., Nov. 26, 1933; d. Karl Otto and Wilhelmina (Otterbach) Pfau; student Douglass Coll., 1952-54; B.S., R.N., Columbia U. Presbyn. Hosp., 1957, postgrad., 1957-59; postgrad. N.Y.U., 1959-60; M.P.A., Coll. of Notre Dame, 1979; m. John Atterbury Mortimer, Nov. 20, 1964; children—Meredith Elizabeth, Mandy Leigh; m. G. Robert Evans, Sept. 4, 1982. Spl. assignment nurse Columbia-Presbyn. Med. Center, N.Y.C., 1957-59; med. advt. copywriter Paul Klemtner & Co., N.Y.C., 1959-61, William Douglas McAdams Agy., N.Y.C., 1961-62; account exec. Arndt, Preston, Chapin, Lamb & Keen, N.Y.C., 1962-63; Rocky Mountain corr. Med. World News, Denver, 1963-64; owner Publicite, Denver; gen. mgr. Center Mktg. Assn., Palo Alto, Calif., 1964-66; freelance writer, pub. relations and mgmt. cons., Woodside, Calif., 1966-85; pres. Communications for Youth, 1979—. Mem. Palo Alto-Stanford Hosp. Aux., 1968-72; pub. relations assistance Peninsula Children's Center, Palo Alto, 1968-73, Triton Mus. Art, San Jose, Calif., 1966-70; chmn. citizens adv. com. San Mateo County Juvenile Social Services; health component Early Childhood Com., Woodside Elem. Sch. Dist.; mem. adv. com. South County Youth and Family Services Program; mem. Statewide Citizens Adv. Com. on Child Abuse and Neglect Ill. Dept. Children and Family Services, 1987—, ct.-apptd. spl. adv. Kane County steering com., 1988; bd. dirs. N.J. Jr. C. of C./UNICEF/ African Project, 1960-61; mem. San Mateo County Mental Health Adv. Bd., Friends of Woodside Library Bd, 1983-85; mem. Rep. Senatorial Inner Circle, 1982—; vol. Nat. Com. for Prevention Child Abuse and Neglect, 1987—. Home and Office: PO Box 710 Wayne IL 60184

EVANS, CHERYL ANN, insurance agent; b. Martins Ferry, Ohio, Feb. 4, 1949; d. George Roy and Beulah Virginia (Gillespie) Reppart; m. John M. Evans, Sept. 12, 1971; children: Michelle, Moriah, Justin, Christina, Amber, Angela. BS, Ohio State U., 1971, MS, 1973. Buyer Rikes Store, Dayton, Ohio, 1973-78; adminstrv. v.p. Evans Potato Co., New Carlisle, Pa., 1978-82; regional mgr. Cher-Beli, Memphis, 1982; dir. mktg. Leana Internat., Springfield, Ohio, 1983; ins. agt. McCloy Fin. Services, Columbus, Ohio, 1985—. Mem. Bus. and Profl. Women, Heib Home Economists in Bus., Mortar Bd., Kappa Alpha Theta. Republican. Presbyterian. Home: 360 Tucker Dr Worthington OH 43085

EVANS, CHERYL RUTH, administrative specialist; b. Westerly, R.I., Nov. 6, 1944; d. Calvin A. and Winifred (Stenhouse) Mitchell; divorced; 1 child, Kimberly Lynn; m. Brooks Edward Evans. AS, State Tech. Inst., Memphis, 1983. With Navy Resale Activity Memphis, Millington, Tenn., 1971—, mgr. acquisitions, 1985—. Served with USNR, 1978-87. Mem. Navy Enlisted Res. Assn., Nat. Assn. for Female Execs. Democrat. Episcopalian. Club: Bus. Profl. Womens (Millington) (pres. 1981-82). Home: PO Box 356 LaCenter KY 42056 Office: Navy Resale Activity Naval Air Station Memphis Millington TN 38054-6024

EVANS, (MARY) CLAIRE, painter, educator; b. Augusta, Ga., June 8, 1929; d. John Franklin Patrick and Mary Viola Dowling; m. Charles Lane Evans, Oct. 18, 1951; children—Joel Lane, Ellen Claire. B.A., Converse Coll., 1951; Tchr., lectr. Rocky Mountain Coll. Art and Design, Denver, 1979—. One-woman shows: Foothills Art Ctr., Golden, Colo., 1978, UMC Gallery, U. Colo., Boulder, 1979, Jack Meier Gallery, Houston, 1988; group shows include: West '82 Art and the Law, St. Paul, 1982, Joslyn Biennial, Omaha, 1984, Foothills Art Ctr., Golden, 1984, Colorado Springs Biennial, 1985, Boulder Art Ctr., 1987; represented in corp. collections including United Bank, Amoco Prodns., Petrolewis Corp., ARCO, Sohio, Am. Exploration. Studio: 2810 Wilderness Pl Suite E Boulder CO 80301

EVANS, DOROTHY ANN, court administrator, educator; b. Iowa City, Sept. 30, 1936; d. Carl L. and Olga A. (Grubio) Kinney; m. Robert P. Evans, Dec. 19, 1954 (div. June 1977); children: Joseph, Jennifer, Jeffrey. Student, U. Iowa, 1955-58; student in ct. adminstrn., Columbia Pacific U., San Rafael, Calif., 1987-88. Legal sec. R.B. Wolfe, Mt. Vernon, Iowa, 1963-70; office mgr. Golden Constrn. Co., Cedar Rapids, Iowa, 1970-71; legal asst. Kenneth C. Ellison, Tulsa, 1971-72; legal sec. Senator Walt Allen, Chickasha, Okla., 1972-73; legal asst. M.D. Wilson, Tulsa, 1973-79, office mgr., 1979-83; chief exec. officer Evans Profl. Services, Tulsa, 1983; clk. U.S. Bankruptcy Ct., Tulsa, 1983—; adj. prof. Tulsa Jr. Coll., 1984—; mem. fashion adv. bd. Sanger-Harris Dept. Stores Bankruptcy Ct., Tulsa, 1983-85, mem. bankruptcy rules com., 1987. Author: Employee's Manual, 1985, 1988, Student Handbook, 1987. Charter mem. Iowa City Community Theatre, 1955; vol. Am. Cancer Soc., Multiple Sclerosis, Iowa and Okla., 1965-83; Dem. precinct co-chair, Tulsa, 1981-83, alt. del., 1982. Mem. Nat. Conf. Bankruptcy Ct. Clks. (newsletter reporter), Fed. Ct. Clks. Assn., Nat. Assn. Female Execs. Methodist. Club: Candlewood (Tulsa). Office: US Bankruptcy Ct 4540 US Courthouse Tulsa OK 74103

EVANS, HANNAH IMOGENE, psychologist; b. Richmond, Va., Nov. 6, 1945; d. Charles and Ruth (Powell) E.; BA, U. Vt., 1967; MS, Pa. State U., 1970, PhD, 1972; MPA, U. Colo., Denver, 1981; m. Robert F. McKenzie, July 12, 1975. Clin. psychology intern, psychol. cons. II, Denver Dept. Health and Hosps., 1972-77; adj. faculty U. Colo., Denver, summer 1978; resource counselor Regional Transp. Dist., 1978-79; pvt. practice psychotherapy, Denver, 1976—. Mem. community adv. bd. Sch. Profl. Psychology, U. Denver; mem. grievance com. Colo. Supreme Ct., 1982—; staff affiliate Bethesda Hosp., 1979—; clin. assoc. sch. profl. Psychology, U. Denver. Mem. Gov.'s Front Range Task Force, 1980-81; bd. dirs. Denver Sexual Assault Council, 1974-80; founding bd. Colo. Center Women and Work, 1979-81; adv. bd. A Woman's Pl. at Rocky Mountain Hosp., 1987—; mem. Women's Forum of Colo., 1979—, selection com., 1980—; mem. Victims and Witness Assistance and Law Enforcement Bd. 2d Jud. Dist. USPHS fellow, 1968-70; named one of Faces of Colo., Colo. mag., 1976. Mem. Am. Psychol. Assn., Nat. Register of Health Service Providers in Psychology, Colo. State Bd. of Psychologist Examiners, Bd. Psychology Practice. Contbr. articles to profl. jours. and popular mags.

EVANS, HAZEL BAKER, real estate broker; b. Vanndale, Ark., Mar. 26, 1932; d. Charlie and Lillie Mae (Miller) Baker; m. Robert Liles Evans, May 2, 1952; children—Robert Baker, Jeffrey Lynn. Student Draughans Bus. Coll., Memphis, 1951. Grad., Realtors Inst., Wynne Fed. Savs. & Loan (Ark.), 1956-58, Pima Savs. & Loan, Tucson, 1958-65; mortgage loan processer Catalina Savs. Bank, Tucson, 1965-69, 1st Fed. Bank, Ft. Smith, 1969-70; real estate broker Jimmie Taylor Co., Ft. Smith, 1971-74; pres., broker Hazel Evans Real Estate, Ft. Smith, 1974-82; broker Coldwell Banker, Fort Smith, 1982—. Adv. trustee Sparks Regional Med. Ctr., 1984-86; appointed to Ft. Smith Parks Commn., 1988—. Mem. Fort Smith Bd. Realtors (realtor of yr. 1982; pres. 1983), Ft. Smith C. of C. (bd. dirs. 1978), Assn. Bus. Women Am. (pres. 1974), Women's Council Realtors (woman of yr. 1982, pres. 1977), Nat. Assn. Realtors, Ark. Assn. Realtors (cert. residential specialist, sec. 1984, state ednl. com. 1983-84, dist. v.p.). Republican. Baptist. Home: 7100 S Q St Fort Smith AR 72913 Office: Coldwell Banker Fleming Realty 2910 Rogers Ave Fort Smith AR 72901

EVANS, HEATHER H., entrepreneur, writer; b. N.Y.C., Oct. 18, 1958; d. Thomas William and Lois (Logan) E.; m. Matt Baumgardner, Dec. 20, 1986. AB cum laude, Harvard U., 1979, MBA, 1983. Analyst Morgan Stanley & Co., N.Y.C., 1979-81; pres. Heather Evans, Inc., N.Y.C., 1983-84, 1987—; v.p. Bear, Stearns & Co., Inc., N.Y.C., 1984-86; adj. prof. N.Y. U. Sch. of Bus., 1988—; bd. dirs. Lar Lubovitch Dance Co. Contbr. articles on mgmt. and working women. Recipient Outstanding Bus. Achievement award Savvy Mag., 1984. Phi Beta Kappa. Clubs: Down Town (N.Y.C.), Harvard. Office: Heather Evans Assoc 226 Jackson St Trenton NJ 08611

EVANS, JACQUELYN FAYE, publisher; b. Little Rock, Ark., Aug. 3, 1947; d. John Henry and Blanche Evon (Green) E.; 1 child, Christopher Meherwan. Student, Harvard U., 1964-66; BSBA, SUNY, Albany, 1980; postgrad., Golden Gate U. CPA, Calif., S.C. Assoc. acct. Deloitte Haskins & Sells CPAs, San Francisco, 1979-82, Friedlander & Daiker CPAs, San Francisco, 1982-83; pvt. practice acctg. San Francisco, 1983-84; controller Sheriar Press Inc., Myrtle Beach, S.C., 1984-86; pvt. practice acctg. North Myrtle Beach, S.C., 1987—; pub. Windy Hill Publs., North Myrtle Beach, 1987—; editorial cons. Avatar Found., North Myrtle Beach, 1987—, Beloved Books, Edison, N.J., 1987—. Mem. Am. Inst. CPAs (mem. com. small bus. taxation). Office: Windy Hill Publishing PO Box 2161 North Myrtle Beach SC 29598

EVANS, JANE, financial company executive; b. Hannibal, Mo., July 26, 1944; d. L. Terrell Evans and Katherine (Rosser) Pierce; m. George Sheer, June 17, 1970; 1 child, Jonathan. B.A., Vanderbilt U.; postgrad., L'Universite d'Aix Marseille. Pres. I. Miller, N.Y.C., 1970-73; v.p. internat. mktg. Genesco, N.Y.C., 1973-74; pres. Butterick Vogue Patterns, N.Y.C., 1974-77; v.p. adminstrn. and corp. devel. Fingerhut, Mpls., 1977-79; exec. v.p. fashion Gen. Mills, Inc., N.Y.C., 1979-84; pres., chief exec. officer Monet Jewelers, N.Y.C., 1984-87; gen. ptnr. Montgomery Consumer Fund, San Francisco, 1987—; dir. Equitable Life Assurance Soc., Philip Morris, N.Y.C., Catalyst, N.Y.C. Recipient award Women's Equity Action League, 1982; Entrepreneurial Woman award Women Bus. Owners N.Y.C., 1982; named Corp. Am.'s Top Woman Exec., Savvy Mag., 1983, Fin. Woman of Yr., Fin. Women's Assn., 1986; named one of Ten Most Wanted Mgrs., Fortune Mag., 1986. Mem. Young Pres. Orgn. (com. of 200), Fashion Group N.Y., Women's Forum, Fashion Inst. Tech. (bd. dirs. 1980—). Home: 350 Round Hill Rd Tiburon CA 94920 Office: Montgomery Securities 600 Montgomery St San Francisco CA 94111

EVANS, JANE COUTANT, academic administrator; b. Newburgh, N.Y., Jan. 12, 1936; d. Norman J. and Audrey Coutant; children: Duncan, Elizabeth. BA, Middlebury Coll., 1958; PhD, Yale U., 1965. Asst. prof. U. Md., College Park, 1965-69, Conn. Coll., New London, 1965-69; chmn. dept. Chinese U. Md., 1969-70; adj. assoc. prof. George Washington U., Washington, 1971-74, 77-80; pres. Mt. Vernon Coll., Washington, 1980—; bd. dirs. Council Ind. Colls., Washington, 1983-87; mem. presdl. search adv. com. Am. Assn. Colls., Washington; mem. exec. com. Consortium of Colls. and Univs., Washington. Mem. edn. com. Fed. City Council, Washington; bd. dirs. Kingsbury Ctr., Washington; mem. adv. com. Nat. Mus. Women in Arts, Washington; mem. community adv. com. Washington Jr. League, Washington. Woodrow Wilson fellow Harvard U., Cambridge, 1958-59; Ford Found. fellow Yale U., New Haven, 1961-65; Jr. Sterling fellow; Woman of Achievement award WETA, 1981. Mem. Am. Assn. Governing Bds. (adv. council of pres.'s), Women's Coll. Coalition, Pub. Leadership Edn. Network, Washington Women's Forum. Office: Mt Vernon Coll 2100 Foxhall Rd NW Washington DC 20007

EVANS, JANE G., home economist; b. Olney, Md., June 15, 1951; d. Ulysses IV and Marion Margaret (Taylor) G.; . Richard O. Evans, Feb. 28, 1981;children: Benjamin Matthew, Samuel Jeffrey. B.Sc. in Human Ecology, U. Md., 1973; M. Adminstrv. Sci., Johns Hopkins U., 1983; postgrad. in acctg. Montgomery Coll., 1983—. Tchr. home econs. Berlin (Md.) Middle Sch., 1973-75; youth program developer, Swaziland, 1975-76; vis. lectr. Md. Coop. Extension Service, 1977, 4-H and youth agt. Howard County, 1977-84; mem. faculty U. Md., 1977-84; asst. supt. 4-H foods dept. Md. State Fair, 1978-81; tchr. home econs. Jessup Correctional Inst. Women, 1972. Mem. Laytonsville Town Council, Md., 1985—. Mary Faulkner scholar, 1969; Md. Senatorial scholar, 1969; Johns Hopkins U. fellow in Orgnl. and Community Systems, 1980-81. Mem. Am. Home Econs. Assn., Md. Home Econs. Assn. (chmn. by-laws com. 1979, v.p. for programs 1980-82), Nat. Assn. 4-H Agts. (N.E. regional contact for public relations and info. com. 1981-82), Md. Assn. 4-H Agts. (chmn. nominating com. 1980-81), Md. Internat. 4-H Youth Exchange Assn., Md. 4-H All Stars, Mortar Board, Omicron Nu, Epsilon Sigma Phi. Author newsletters in field. Home: 21512 Montgomery Ave Laytonsville MD 20879

EVANS, JANET ANN, music educator; b. Muskegon, Mich., Aug. 26, 1936; d. Burt and Mildred (Gervers) Ruffner; 1 child, Eric Alan. BMus., U. Mich., 1958, MusM, 1959. Permanent secondary teaching cert., Mich. Vocal dir. South Redford (Mich.) Schs., 1959-63, orch., band and vocal dir., 1966-79; band dir. Detroit Pub. Schs., 1979—; band dir. Fine Arts Honor Bands, Detroit Pub. Schs., 1980-82, 84, 86, co-coordinator Fine Arts Festival, 1986. Author: (manual) Build Leadership NOW, 1983, Mich. NOW Policies and Guidelines, 1986; also articles. Mem. legis. liaison Older Women's League, Farmington Hills, Mich., 1981-86; del. Mich. Women's Assembly, Jackson, 1984, 86; precinct del. Mich. Dem. Party, 1984—; state chair, treas. Mich. Women's Polit. Caucus, Roseville, 1985-88. Recipient Band Scholarship award U. Mich., 1957, 58, Cert. Achievement Metro-Detroit YWCA, 1985, Cert. Spl. Recognition Detroit Pub. Schs., 1985, 88, Cert. Appreciation Mich. Dem. Party, 1986, Cert. for Outstanding Leadership Detroit Pub. Schs., 1988; named Hon. Mem. to Women Internat. League for Peace and Freedom. Member NOW (pres., N.W. Wayne County chpt., 1980-82, developer Mich. State chpt. 1982-84, adminstrv. v.p. 1984-86, Mich. Leadership award 1981, 82, Leadership plaque N.W. Wayne County 1982), ACLU (state bd. dirs. 1985—), Coalition of Labor Union Women (Metro Detroit chpt.), Mich. Women's Studies Assn., Women Band Dirs. Nat. Assn. (nat. historian 1985-87, nat. recording sec. 1988—), Am. Fedn. Tchrs., Mich. Fedn. Tchrs., Detroit Fedn. Tchrs., Mich. Sch. Band/Orch. Assn., Women in the Arts, Inc. (charter), Martha Cook Bldg. Detroit Alumnae Assn. (bd. dirs. 1968-70, 86—), Bus. and Profl. Women's Club (sec. Farmington Hills chpt. 1981-82, Leadership award pin 1982), Alpha Delta Kappa (chpt. pres. 1978-80, pres. dist. II 1980-82, Pres. award pin 1980), Tau Beta Sigma (life), Sigma Alpha Iota. Democrat. Presbyterian. Office: Clinton Sch 8145 Chalfonte Detroit MI 48238

EVANS, JOANNE MCGAUGHEY, psychiatric social worker; b. Huron, S.D., June 25, 1948; d. Kenneth Edward and Doris Adella (Hartley) McGaughey; m. Greg B. Youngman, (divorced); children: Amy, Judd, Joshua; m. Charles Wayne Evans. BA, U. Alaska, 1976; MSW, U. Okla., 1981. Nurses aide Rose of Sharon Nursing Home, Mpls., 1965-66, Violet Tchetter Nursing Home, Huron, S.D., 1967-68; counselor Booth Meml. Home, Anchorage, 1975-76; detox counselor Salvation Army, Anchorage, 1976-77, outpatient counselor, 1977-78; output therapist Northeastern Mental Health, Aberdeen, S.D., 1981-85; soical worker Care Psychiat. Ctr., Aberdeen, 1985-86; program mgr. Northeastern Mental Health, Aberdeen, 1986-87; pvt. practice psychiat. social work Aberdeen, 1985—; cons. Webster (S.D.) Child Protection, 1983—, Northeastern Mental Health, 1985-87, mem. Inter-State Child Protection, Pierre, S.D. , 1983—, Cen. High Sch. Team, Aberdeen, 1986—, Parent Support Group, Aberdeen, 1987—. Vol. Red Cross Orphanage, Bangkok, 1966-67. Mem. Nat. Assn. Social Workers, Bus. and Profl. Women, Nat. Assn. Female Execs., S.D. Chemical Dependency Assn. Democrat. Lutheran. Home: 1416 S Second St Aberdeen SD 57401

EVANS, JOANNE YOUNG, health educator; b. Oshawa, Ont., Can., Mar. 29, 1959; d. Thomas McKay and Doris Joan (Parks) Young; m. Douglas John Evans, June 20, 1981. CPHI, Ryerson Poly. Inst., Toronto, Ont.,

1980; student, Waterloo U. Cert. in pub. health inspection. Pub. health insp. Peel Regional Health Dept., Brampton, Ont., 1980-82, environ educator, 1982-85, dept. health educator, 1985—. Mem. Can. Restaurant and Food Service Assn. (cons. 1984—), Ont. Assn. Pub. Health Promotion Specialists, Ont. Pub. Health Assn., Can. Health Edn. Soc. Liberal. Office: Peel Regional Health Dept, 10 Peel Centre Dr, Brampton, ON Canada L6T 4B9

EVANS, JULIE ANN, computer sales executive; b. Suffern, N.Y., Apr. 16, 1957; d. Richard Carpenter and Antoinette Helen (Falanga) E.; m. Ronald David Frantz, July 26, 1980; 1 child, Elizabeth Evans Frantz. BA in Polit. Sci., Brown U., 1979. Asst. buyer Strawbridge & Clothier, Phila., 1979-80; dept. mgr. Bullocks, Los Angeles, 1980; design coordinator Irvine (Calif.) Co., 1981; account rep. Burroughs, Irvine, 1981-84; sales/support mgr. Burroughs now Unisys, Irvine, 1984-86; mktg. exec. Unisys, Irvine, 1986—. Contributor South Coast Reperetory Theatre, Costa Mesa, Calif., 1983—, Laguna Art Mus., Calif., 1986—. Recipient Mktg. Demonstration award Burroughs Calif. Dist., 1982, Burroughs Western Region, 1985, World Wide Legion Honor, Burroughs Corp., 1984. Mem. Associated Alumni Brown U., Women Brown U., Nat. Assn. Female Execs., Am. Prodn. Inventory Control Soc. Democrat. Roman Catholic. Office: Unisys 5 Hutton Ctr Santa Ana CA 92707

EVANS, KIM DENISE, nurse; b. Houston, Aug. 12, 1953; d. D. T. and Effie Jo (Carter) Stodghill. A in Nursing, San Jacinto Coll., 1976; BS in Nursing, U. Texas, Houston, 1987; postgrad., U. Texas, Galveston, 1987—. Pediatric ward staff nurse Ben Taub Gen. Hosp., Houston, 1976-78, pediatric ICU staff nurse, 1978-80; nurse technologist, radiotherapy M.D. Anderson Hosp., Houston, 1980-81; research nurse Children's Nutrition Research Ctr., Houston, 1981-84, head research nurse, 1984-87, research nurse supr., 1987—; immunization team mem. African Enterprise, Kampala, Uganda, East Africa, 1986; health care team mem. Health Care Ministries, Mexico City, 1987. Contbr. articles to profl. jours. active Ch. in the City, Houston, 1985—. Mem. Nat. Assn. Research Nurses Dietitians (nomination coordinator 1987-88), Nat. Assn. Female Execs., Alumni Assn. Univ. Tex., Sierra Club, Nursing Research Roundtable of Greater Houston. Home: 707 Yorkshire Houston TX 77022 Office: Children's Nutrition Research Ctr 6608 Fannin Med Towers Suite 601 Houston TX 77030

EVANS, LAVONDA DENIESE, hospital services administrator; b. Springdale, Ark., Aug. 10, 1955; d. James Edward Sr. and Edna Mae E. BS, Freed-Hardeman U., 1976. Registered laundry and linen dir.; cert. exec. housekeeper. Clk., typist Law Office of James E. Evans Sr., Springdale, 1971-73; cashier Morrison's Cafeteria, Henderson, Tenn., 1973-76; tchr. Palmetto Christian Sch., Charleston, S.C., 1977-78; clk., typist Kelly Services, Springdale, 1978-79; customer service Warner Cable, Fayetteville, Ark., 1979-81; tchr. Draughon's Sch. Bus., Tulsa, 1981-82; sec. Tulsa City (Okla.) County Health Dept., 1982-83; tchr. Am. Coll., Fayetteville, 1983-84; asst. dir. Springdale Meml. Hosp., 1983-87; mgr. laundry plant VA Hosp., Fayetteville, Ark., 1987—. Named one of Outstanding Young Woman of Am., Outstanding Young Women of Am., 1986, Pres. of Yr., Civinettes, 1975-76, Humanitarian of the Yr., Springdale Meml. Hosp., 1986. Mem. Nat. Exec. Housekeepers Assn. (pres. 1987), Nat. Assn. Institutional Linen Mgmt., Nat. Assn. Female Execs., Bus. and Profl. Women's Club. Mem. Ch. of Christ. Home: 4303 Croxdale Springdale AR 72764

EVANS, LINDA, actress; b. Hartford, Nov. 18, 1942; m. John Derek (div.); m. Stan Herman, 1976 (div.). In films: The Klansman, 1974; Avalanche Express, 1979; Tom Horn, 1980; in TV series: The Big Valley, 1965-69, Dynasty, 1980—(Emmy nominee 1983); film debut: Twilight of Honor, 1963; TV miniseries The Last Frontier, 1986. Author: Linda Evans Beauty and Exercise Book, 1983. Office: care Charter Mgmt 9000 Sunset Blvd Suite 1112 Los Angeles CA 90069 *

EVANS, LINDA ANN, educator, housing consultant; b. Waterbury, Conn., Mar. 3, 1944; d. William C. and Alice (Foust) E. BA in English, Wilberforce U., 1968; M of City Planning, Yale U., 1972; postgrad., Wesleyan U., 1988—. Program writer New Opportunities for Waterbury, 1968-69; community devel. planner Model Cities Agy., Waterbury, 1969-71; mcpl. planner Cen. Naugatuck Valley Regional Planning Agy., Waterbury, 1971-72; regional planner No. Va. Planning Dist. Commn., Falls Church, Va., 1972-76; chief housing planner Fairfax (Va.) County Housing Dept., 1976-80; cons., dir. Nat. Consumer Coop. Bank, Washington, 1980-81; v.p. Housing Support, Inc., Las Cruces, N. Mex., 1979-82; exec. dir. New Haven Housing Authority, 1982-86; instr. English State of Conn. Community Colls., Winsted, 1986—; adj. faculty Post Coll., Waterburg, Conn., 1987-88; vol. planner housing subcom. New Opportunities for Waterbury, 1987—; pres. Elm Terr. Devel. Corp., Hew Haven 1984-86; assoc. trustee mem. Pub. Housing Dir.'s Assn., Washington, 1985-86. Contbr. articles to profl. jours. Mem. Urban League, New Haven, 1987—; housing chairperson Mayor's Commn. on Poverty, New Haven, 1984; bd. dirs. Dixwell Opposes Alcoholism, New Haven, 1985-86. Recipient Outstanding Service award Mt. Zion Ch., 1984, Disting. Service award United Negro Coll. Fund, 1986. Mem. NAACP, Nat. Assn. Female Execs., Nat. Assn. Female Execs., Nat. Assn. Housing Redevel. Ofcls., Conn. Women in Planning, Alpha Kappa Alpha. Methodist. Home: 18 Center St Wolcott CT 06716 Office: No Western Community Coll Park Pl E Winsted CT 06098

EVANS, LOIS LOGAN, investment banker, former government official; b. Boston, Dec. 1, 1937; d. Harlan deBaun and Barbara (Rollins) Logan; m. Thomas W. Evans, Dec. 22, 1956; children: Heather, Logan, Paige. Student, Vassar Coll., 1954-55; BA, Barnard Coll., 1957. Alt. chief del. UN Commn. on Status Women, N.Y.C., 1972-74; bd. dirs. U.S. Commn. to UNESCO, Washington, 1974-78; pres. Acquisition Specialists, Inc., N.Y.C., 1977-81, 83-88; exec. v.p. Cambell Shea Inc., N.Y.C., 1988—; asst. chief protocol U.S. State Dept., N.Y.C., 1981-83; chmn. bd. Fed. Home Bank, N.Y.C., 1986-88, mem., 1984-88; mem. adv. bd. U.S. Export-Import Bank, 1988—, Nat. Fin. Com.. Vice chair devel. council Williams Coll., N.Y., 1979-81; co-chair Reagan-Bush Campaign, N.Y., 1984; bd. dirs. Bklyn. Jr. League, 1968-72. Mem. Women's Forum. Republican. Episcopalian. Club: Econ. of N.Y.; Barnard, River. Office: 595 Madison Ave Suite 900 New York NY 10022

EVANS, LOUISE, psychologist; b. San Antonio; d. Henry Daniel and Adela (Pariser) E.; B.S., Northwestern U., 1949; M.S. in Psychology, Purdue U., 1952, Ph.D. in Clin. Psychology, 1955; m. Thomas Ross Gambrell, Feb. 23, 1960. Intern clin. psychology Menninger Found., Topeka (Kans.) State Hosp., 1952-53, USPHS-Menninger Found. fellow clin. child psychology, 1955-56; staff psychologist Kankakee (Ill.) State Hosp., 1954; head staff psychologist child guidance clinic Kings County Hosp., Bklyn., 1957-58; dir. psychology clinic, instr. med. psychology Washington U. Sch. Medicine, 1959; clin. research cons. Episcopal City Mission, St. Louis, 1959; pvt. practice clin. psychology, 1960—; approved fellow Internat. Council Sex Edn. and Parenthood, 1984; hon. Research Bd. Advs. nat. div. Am. Biog. Inst., 1985; psychol. cons. Fullerton (Calif.) Community Hosp., 1961-81; staff cons. clin. psychology Martin Luther Hosp., Anaheim, Calif., 1963-70; lectr. clin. psychology schs. and profl. groups, 1950—; participant psychol. symposiums, 1956—; guest speaker clin. psychology civic and community orgns., 1950—. Elected to Hall of Fame, Central High Sch., Ind., 1966; recipient Service award Yuma County Head Start Program, 1972, Statue of Victory Personality of the Yr. award Centro Studi E. Ricerche Delle Nazioni, 1985; named Miss Heritage, Heritage Publs., 1965; lic. psychologist N.Y., Calif.; diplomate Clin. Psychology. Fellow Am. Psychol. Assn., Royal Soc. Health of England, Internat. Council of Psychologists (dir. 1977-79, sec. 1962-64, 73-76), AAAS, Am. Orthopsychiat. Assn., World Wide Acad. of Scholars of N.Z.; mem. AAUP, Los Angeles Soc. Clin. Psychologists (exec. bd. 1966-67), Calif. State Psychol. Assn., Los Angeles County Psychol. Assn., Orange County Psychol. Assn. (exec. bd. 1961-62), Orange County Soc. Clin. Psychologists (exec. bd. 1963-65, pres. 1964-65), Am. Public Health Assn., Rehab. Internat., Internat. Platform Assn., Am. Acad. Polit. and Social Scis., N.Y. Acad. Scis., Purdue U. Alumni Assn. (Citizenship award 1975), Am. Judicature Soc., Center for Study of Presidency, Alumni Assn. Menninger Sch. Psychiatry, Sigma Xi, Pi Sigma Pi. Contbr. articles on clin. psychology to profl. publs. Office: 905-907 W Wilshire Ave Fullerton CA 92632

EVANS, MARGARET, publishing services company executive; b. Annapolis, Md., Oct. 6, 1938; d. Frank Joseph and Margaret Mary (Ruzicka) Wanex; m. Glen Frederick Evans, Jan. 2, 1962; 1 child, Lisa Glyn. B.A., Tulane U., 1960. Systems engr. IBM Corp., Balt., 1961-62; systems supr. U.S. Naval Acad., Annapolis, Md., 1963-67; mktg. dir. Fawcett Publs., Greenwich, Conn., 1967-77; v.p., client service dir. Neodata Services, Boulder, 1977—. Mem. Am. Mgmt. Assn. (program chmn. 1978-80), Sales Exec. Club of N.Y., Fulfillment Mgmt. Assn. (bd. dirs. 1980-84, Spl. Service award 1980), Women's Direct Response Group, Direct Mktg. Club of N.Y.C. (bd. dirs. 1981-82). Democrat. Avocations: reading; writing; poetry; cooking; collecting cat artifacts. Home: 122 Cedar Heights Rd Stamford CT 06905 Office: AC Nielsen Co 1290 Ave of Americas h Floor New York NY 10104

EVANS, MARGARET A., civic worker; b. N.Y.C., Jan. 20, 1924; d. Bernard J. and Katherine (Walsh) Markey; B.A., Coll. Mt. St. Vincent, Mt. St. Vincent-on-Hudson, N.Y., 1944; evening student Columbia U.; m. John Cullen Evans, Jr., Nov. 24, 1951. Rep. N.Y. Telephone Co., 1944; personnel office Sak's 34th, N.Y.C., 1944-45, tng. supr., selling and non-selling depts., 1945-49, spl. assignment for store mgr. 1949-50; non-selling tng. supr. Gimbel Bros., 1950-51; rep. Gimbels and Sak's 34th at NCCJ Retail Group meeting, 1949-50. Instr. textile painting for ARC, Chelsea Navy Hosp., 1952-54, ARC vol., 1980—; bd. dirs. Marblehead Hosp. Aid Assn., 1954, pres., 1955-58; sec. Mass. Hosp. Assn. Council of Hosp. Auxiliaries, 1957-59, chmn. North Shore region, 1959-61, chmn.-elect, 1961-62, chmn., 1962-64; exofficio trustee Salem Hosp.; trustee Mary A. Alley Hosp., 1956-79, chmn. bd., 1974-79; mem. Welcome Wagon of Fairfield/Easton (Conn.), 1979-83; chmn. Fairfield/Easton Theater Group, Fifth Wheel Club of Fairfield, 1983-85 . Mem. Alumnae Assn. Coll. Mt. Saint Vincent, Arrangers of Marblehead (chmn. garden therapy 1967-79). Clubs: Marblehead Women's Newcomers (pres. 1953). Home: 108 Cedarwoods Ln Fairfield CT 06430

EVANS, MARTHA MACCHESNEY, educator; b. Chgo., Nov. 2, 1941; d. Luther Johnson and Harriet (MacChesney) E.; A.A., Kendall Jr. Coll., 1961; B.A., Roosevelt U., 1964; M.A., Northeastern Ill. U., 1974; cert. advanced study Nat. Coll. Edn., 1981; Ed.D., Vanderbilt U., 1986. Cert. master tchr., Ill. Tchr. lang. arts East Maine Jr. High Sch., Des Plaines, Ill., 1965-66; caseworker Cook County Dept. Public Aid, Chgo., 1966-67; tchr. English coordinated basic English program Farragut High Sch., Chgo., 1968-73, reading lab. dir., 1973-74, reading clinician Wells High Sch., Chgo., 1974-83, learning disabled tchr., 1983—; instr. continuing edn. dept. Roosevelt U., 1987—; content area reading coordinator, 1984, lead tchr. degrees of reading power, 1984-85 mem. reading clinic adv. bd. Chgo. Bd. Edn., 1976-78; part time instr. Roosevelt U., Chgo., 1987—. Chmn. membership com. 2d Unitarian Ch. Chgo., 1978-79, pres. Womans Group, 1979-80, chmn. involvement com., 1984-85 mem. adv. bd. Nat. Hydrocephalus Found., 1984—. Mem. Internat. Reading Assn. (presenter St. Louis regional conv. 1984, Minn. regional conv. 1985), Chgo. Area Reading Assn., Assn. Curriculum Devel., Assn. Children with Learning Disabilities, Phi Delta Kappa. Home: 107 E 14th St Lombard IL 60148 Office: Wells High School 936 N Ashland Ave Chicago IL 60622

EVANS, MARY JOHNSTON, corporate director; b. Shawnee, Okla., Feb. 28, 1930; d. Paul Xenophon and Helen Elizabeth (Alford) Johnston; children by previous marriage: Marcia Lee Head, Paul Johnston Head, Eric Talbott Head; m. James H. Evans, 1984. Student, Wellesley Coll., 1947-48, U. Okla., 1949. Dir. Amtrak, 1974-80, vice chmn., 1975-79; bd. dirs. Household Internat., Inc., CertainTeed Corp., The Sun Co., Inc., Baxter Internat. Inc., Delta Air Lines, Inc.; adv. bd. Morgan Stanley & Co. Pres. Jr. League Oklahoma City, 1968-69; trustee Nat. Council Crime and Delinquency, 1971-75, Presbyn. Med. Center, Oklahoma City, 1969-75, Brick Presbyn. Ch., 1985—; bd. dirs. St. Anthony Hosp., 1973-75; bd. visitors U. Pitts. Grad. Sch. Bus., 1978-85; trustee Mary Baldwin Coll., Staunton, Va., 1976-83, Carnegie Hall, 1985—. Recipient Law Day award-Liberty Bell award Oklahoma Bar Assn., 1971, Disting. Service award U. Okla., 1981; named one of Top 100 Corporate Women Bus. Week mag., 1976; named to Okla. Hall of Fame, 1978. Mem. Conf. Bd. (Sr.), Pi Beta Phi. Presbyterian (elder). Clubs: Colony, River; Maidstone (East Hampton, N.Y.). Address: 920 Fifth Ave New York NY 10021 also: Windmill Ln PO Box 488 East Hampton NY 11937

EVANS, ORINDA D., federal judge; b. Savannah, Ga., Apr. 23, 1943; d. Thomas and Virginia Elizabeth (Grieco) E.; m. Roberts O. Bennett, Apr. 12, 1975; children: Wells Cooper, Elizabeth Thomas. B.A., Duke U., 1965; J.D. with distinction, Emory U., 1968. Bar: Ga. 1968. Ptnr. Alston, Miller & Gaines, Atlanta, 1974-79; U.S. dist. judge No. Dist. Ga., Atlanta, 1979—; adj. prof. Emory U. Law Sch., 1974-77; counsel Atlanta Crime Commn., 1970-71. Mem. Atlanta Bar Assn. (dir. 1979). Democrat. Episcopalian. Home: 200 The Prado NE Atlanta GA 30309 Office: US Dist Ct 1988 US Courthouse 75 Spring St SW Atlanta GA 30303

EVANS, PAMELA ROYE, marketing executive; b. Hoisington, Kans., Aug. 25, 1957; d. John Roy and Sarah Mace (Alder) E. BS in Bus., U. Kans., 1980. Sales rep. Home & Automotive Products div. Union Carbide Corp., Seattle, 1981; dist. sales mgr. Syracuse, N.Y., 1981-82; mktg. assoc. Danbury, Conn., 1982-84, assoc. product mgr., 1984; asst. product mgr. Grocery Products div. Ralston Purina, St. Louis, 1984-85, product mgr., 1985-86; product mgr. Eveready Battery Co. subs. Ralston Purina, St. Louis, 1986—. Home: 946 Golf Course Dr Saint Louis MO 63132 Office: Ralston Purina Co Checkerboard Sq Saint Louis MO 63164

EVANS, PAULINE (DAVIDSON), physicist, educator; b. Bklyn., Mar. 24, 1922, d. John A. and Hannah (Brandt) Davidson; B.A., Hofstra Coll., 1942; postgrad. N.Y. U., 1943, 46-47, Cornell U., 1946, Syracuse U., 1947-50; m. Melbourne Griffith Evans, Sept. 6, 1950; children—Lynn Janet Evans Hannemann, Brian Griffith. Jr. physicist Signal Corps Ground Signal Service, Eatontown, N.J., 1942-43; physicist Kellex Corp. (Manhattan Project), N.Y.C., 1944; faculty dept. physics Queens Coll., N.Y.C., 1944-47; teaching asst. Syracuse U., 1947-50; instr. Wheaton Coll., Norton, Mass., 1952; physicist Nat. Bur. Standards, Washington, 1954-55; instr. physics U. Ala., 1955, U. N.Mex., 1955, 57-58; staff mem. Sandia Corp., Albuquerque, 1956-57; physicist Naval Nuclear Ordnance Evaluation Unit, Kirtland AFB, N.Mex., 1958-60; programmer Teaching Machines, Inc., Albuquerque, 1961; mem. faculty dept. physics Coll. St. Joseph on the Rio Grande (name changed to U. Albuquerque 1966), 1961—, assoc. prof., 1965—, chmn. dept., 1961—. Mem. Am. Phys. Soc., Am. Assn. Physics Tchrs., Fedn. Am. Scientists, AAUP, Sigma Pi Sigma, Sigma Delta Epsilon. Patentee in field. Home: 730 Loma Alta Ct NW Albuquerque NM 87105 Office: U of Albuquerque Dept Physics Albuquerque NM 87140

EVANS, RONDA, health facility administrator; b. Laytonville, Calif., July 14, 1949; d. Ray E. and Ruth (Onstot) E.; divorced; 1 child, Nickole Megan. BA in Psychology, Calif. State U., Los Angeles, 1981. Cert. nursing home adminstr., Calif. Mgr. mktg. So. Calif. Presbyn. Homes, Glendale, Calif., 1979-85; pvt. practice cons. Evans Options, Sun Valley, Calif., 1985-87; adminstr. ARA Living Ctrs., Pico Rivera, Calif., 1987—. Mem. Calif. Assn. Health Care Facilities, Calif. Found. on Employment and Disability (treas. 1985, chair 1986-88), Nat. Assn. Female Execs.

EVANS, ROSALEEN MALOOLY, voice educator, pianist; b. El Paso; d. Elias and Mamie (Coury) Malooly; 1 child, John Anthony. MusM, Colo. Coll., 1945; postgrad., U. So. Calif., 1949; grad. theatre study, London; continuing edn. classes, U. Md., Tulane U., Hofstra U., U. Bridgeport, So. Meth. U. Vocal coach Miss Teen Pageant-U.S.A.; previously supper club performer Beverly Hills, Calif.; performance coach, voice and musical theatre coach El Paso, 1945—. Named Woman of Yr. in Music El Paso Herald-Post. Mem. Nat. Soc. Arts and Letters, Mu Phi Epsilon. Office: 814 N Walnut El Paso TX 79903

EVANS, SARAH FRANCES HINTON, nurse; b. Athens, Clark County, Ga., July 19, 1924; d. Charles Jackson and Bessie Marie (Hickman) Hinton; R.N., Macon Hosp. Sch. Nursing, 1945; B.S. in Nursing, Med. Coll. Ga., 1975; m. Omer Fountain, Oct. 9, 1948 (div. 1964); children—Anita Francine, Sarah Alice; m. John Duggan Evans, Feb. 14, 1969 (dec. Apr. 1971). Night supr. Ware County Hosp., Waycross, Ga., 1946-47; staff nurse nursery and obstetrics Mercy Hosp., Macon, Ga., 1947-48; staff nurse obstetrics Macon (Ga.) Hosp., 1952-54, 55-56, head nurse colored labor and delivery, 1956-64, obstet. staff nurse, 1964-65; head nurse newborn nursery Med. Center Central Ga., Macon, 1965-74, infection control nurse, 1974—; mem. Ga. Bd. Nursing, 1977-80. Mem. Am. Nurses Assn. (del. from Ga. 1976, 78), Assn. Practitioners in Infection Control (cert.), Ga. Heart Assn., Ga. Public Health Assn., Sixth Dist. Ga. Nurses Assn., Med. Center Central Ga. Alumnae, Med. Coll. Ga. Alumnae Assn. Baptist. Home: 6375 Houston Rd Macon GA 31206 Office: Med Ctr Cen GA Box 6000 Macon GA 31208

EVANS, SHERLI, public relations executive; b. Orlando, Fla.; d. Harold William and Marjorie (Foster) E.; m. Erwin Goldman, Jan. 3, 1955 (div. June 1988); children: Adam, Audrey. AB, UCLA, 1964, MA, 1968. Pub. relations cons. Los Angeles, 1976-83, N.Y.C., 1983—. Author: Mary McCarthy: A Bibliography, 1968; author TV scripts, 1970-76; contbr. articles to bus. and art publs. Mem. Writers Guild (co-pres. women's group 1971), Nat. Womens Polit. Caucus. Democrat. Roman Catholic. Home and Office: 141 Wooster St #7C New York NY 10012

EVANS, SUSAN ANN, lawyer; b. Washington, Aug. 31, 1954; d. Robert David and Clara Mae (Messick) E.; m. Robert Stevens Greenlief, Dec. 26, 1980 (div. Oct. 1983); m. Ralph Nicholas Boccarosse, May 27, 1986; 1 child, Caroline Morgan Boccarosse. BA, U. Va., 1976; JD, U. Richmond, 1979. Bar: Va. 1979, U.S. Ct. Appeals (4th cir.) 1979, D.C. 1982, U.S. Dist. Ct. D.C. 1982. Law clk. to presiding justice Va. Cir. Ct. (19th cir.), Fairfax, 1979-80; assoc. Siciliano, Ellis, Dyer & Boccarosse, Fairfax, 1980-85, ptnr., 1986—; atty. Va. Med. Malpractice Panel Rev., 1984—. Mem. Fairfax Bar Assn. (chmn. CLE membership com.), No. Va. Def. Lawyers Assn. (treas. 1983-85, v.p. 1985-86, pres. 1987-88), Va. Assn. Def. Attys. Baptist. Home: 11561 Southington Ln Herndon VA 22070 Office: Siciliano Ellis Dyer and Boccarosse 10521 Judicial Dr #300 Fairfax VA 22030

EVANS, SUZANNE MARIE, medicinal chemist; b. Hartford, Conn., Oct. 29, 1953; d. George Thomas and Frances Mary (Clew) E. BS magna cum laude, Fairfield U., 1975; MS, Purdue U., 1977; cert. in mgmt., Elmhurst Coll., 1982; postgrad., U. Ill., 1985—. Teaching and research asst. Purdue U., West Lafayette, Ind., 1975-77; chemist medicinal chemistry dept. G.D. Searle & Co., Skokie, Ill., 1978-81, chemist research and devel., 1981-82, data base coordinator, 1982-83, biomecular structure analyst, 1983-85; sr. computational chemist Chemlab, Inc., Lake Forst, Ill., 1985-88; computational chemistry educator, cons. The BOC Group, Inc., Providence, 1986-88; sr. scientist Tech. Ctr., Providence, 1988—; teaching asst. U. Ill., Chgo., 1985-87; cons. computational chemist Intersoft, Inc., Lake Forest, 1985-88; speaker in field. Author: Opiates, 1986, Process of First Eurepean Seminar on Computer-Aided Molecular Design, 1984; contbr. articles to profl. jours.; patentee in field. Career educator Nat. Sci. Found., 1980, Lincoln Jr. High Sch., Skokie, 1980-82, Elk Grove Village (Ill.) High Sch., 1984. Fellow U. Ill., 1987&. Mem. Am. Chem Soc. (lectr. Milw. sect. 1985, Analytical Chemistry award 1974). Office: The BOC Group Inc Tech Ctr 100 Mountain Ave Murray Hill Providence NJ 07974

EVANS, VERA FRAZIER, food service executive, caterer; b. Dermott, Ark., Mar. 11, 1935; d. Leon W. and Alberta (Hall) Frazier; divorced, 1974; 1 dau., Kim Denise Azadiani. Cert. Loop Coll., Chgo., 1965, 1977; cert. Saga Mgmt. Sch., Kalamazoo, 1980. Food service worker Michael Reese Hosp., Chgo., 1953-56, food service supr., 1959-63, cost control analyst, 1963-64, food service mgr., 1964—. Co-chmn. Michael Reese Hosp. and Martin Luther King Scholarship Com., 1971, treas., 1974; bd. dirs. Michael L. Reese Hosp. Fed. Credit Union, 1979. Mem. Dietary Mgrs. Assn. (treas. 1976-78, pres.-elect 1985-86, pres. 1986-87). Methodist. Avocations; collector African sculpture and pressed glass. Home: 9356 S King Dr Chicago IL 60619

EVANS, VICTORIA A., environmental company executive; b. Louisville, June 19, 1950; d. Frank William and Kathryn Cecilia (Finn) Evans; m. Douglas Alan Latimer, Feb. 14, 1982. Student Bowling Green U., 1968-71; B.S. in Natural Resources, U. Mich., 1972, M.S. in Natural Resources, 1976. Environ. planner Gilbert-Commonwealth Assoc., Jackson, Mich., 1974-76; environ. rev. officer Dept. Interior, Washington, 1976-78; bur. chief Wis. Pub. Service Commn., Madison, 1978-79; visibility program mgr. Nat. Park Service, Washington, 1979-82; environ. cons. Gaia Assocs., Sausalito, Calif., 1982—. Author numerous papers in field. Bd. dirs. Lucas Valley Home Owners Assn., San Rafael, 1984, v.p., 1985-86, pres., 1986—; bd. dirs. Marin Citizens for Energy Planning, San Rafael, 1984, v.p., 1986, pres. 1987—; bd. dirs. environ. forum, Larkspur, Calif., 1984, Marin Conservation League, 1984—. Recipient Spl. Achievement award Nat. Park Service, 1980. Mem. Women Energy Assn. (bd. dirs. 1984-87), Air Pollution Control Assn., TE-5 Visibility Com., Pacific Energy and Resources Ctr. Democrat. Avocations: cross-country skiing, gardening, natural history. Home: 1268 Idylberry Rd San Rafael CA 94903 Office: Gaia Assocs Fort Cronkhite Bldg 1055 Sausalito CA 94965

EVANS, ZOE ANDES, microbiologist; b. Knoxville, Tenn., Mar 5, 1934; d. James Osborn and Esther Marie (Crawford) Andes; BS, Coll. of William and Mary, 1955; MS, U. Tenn., 1972; PhD (NIH trainee), Med. Coll. Va., 1977; m. James Montgomery Evans, Sept. 26, 1956; children—Janet Marie, Karen Hungerford. Microbiologist, Bapt. Meml. Hosp., Memphis, 1956-58, 68-70; research asst. Vanderbilt U., Nashville, 1966-68; instr., asst. dir. clin. microbiology U. Va. Sch. Medicine, Charlottesville, 1972-75; asst. prof. U. Ala., Huntsville, 1977-81; assoc. prof., chmn. dept. med. tech. U. Tex. Southwestern Med. Ctr., Dallas, 1981-83, assoc. prof., chmn. dept. med. lab. scis., 1983—; cons. microbiology, 1977—. specialist in pub. health, med. lab. microbiology Am. Acad. Microbiology; adv. bd. med. lab. tech. Dallas Community Coll. Dist., 1984—. Mem. AAAS, Am. Soc. Allied Health Professions, Am. Soc. for Microbiology, Southeastern Immunology Conf., Southwestern Assn. Clin. Microbiology, Ala. Acad. Sci., Am. Soc. Clin. Pathologists, Reticuloendothelial Soc., Am. Soc. Med. Tech., Bus. and Profl. Women's Assn., Bus. and Profl. Women of Dallas Inc. (bd. dirs. 1987—), Phi Kappa Phi, Sigma Xi. Presbyterian. Contbr. papers, abstracts in field to profl. lit. Office: U Tex Southwestern Med Ctr Dallas TX 75235

EVANS-RUBIN, ILENE, fundraising executive; b. N.Y.C., Oct. 3, 1948; d. Arnold Mortimer and Marilyn (Diamond) R. BFA, Phila. Coll. Art, 1970; MSW, Temple U., 1980. Asst. dir. Yoke Crest, Inc., Harrisburg, Pa., 1972-73; contract rep. Gov.'s Council on Drug and Alcohol Abuse, Harrisburg, 1974-75; ptnr., art dir. Rubin and Evans Design Studio, Phila., 1975-77; dir. devel. Gaudenzia, Inc., Phila., 1977-80; grant officer Dept. Health City of N.Y., 1980-84; dir. devel. Smithsonian Instn./Archives Am. Art, N.Y.C., 1984-86; pub. health analyst Ctrs. for Disease Control, Atlanta, 1987—. Mem. Nat. Soc. Fund Raising Execs. Democrat. Jewish.

EVDOKIMOVA, EVA, ballerina; b. Geneva, Switzerland, Dec. 1, 1948; m. Michael Gregori, 1982. Student, Munich State Opera Ballet Sch., Royal Ballet Sch., London; studied privately with Maria Fay (London), Vera Volkova (Copenhagen), Natalia Dudinskaya (Leningrad). Debut Royal Danish Ballet, Copenhagen, 1966; Prima Ballerina Assoluta, Deutsche Oper Berlin, 1969—; frequent guest artist with numerous major ballet cos. worldwide including London Festival Ballet, Am. Ballet Theatre, Paris Opera Ballet, La Scala, Kirov Ballet, Tokyo Ballet, Teatro Colon, Nat. Ballet of Can., and all other nat. ballet cos.; most frequent ptnr. of Rudolf Nureyev, 1971—; premiered roles in all Rudolf Nureyev's classical ballet prodns.; repertoire of more than 85 roles includes Swan Lake, Giselle, La Sylphide, Sleeping Beauty, Romeo and Juliet, Don Quixote, La Bayadere, Onegin, Raymonda; created roles in ballets including: Aspects (by Frank Schaufuss), Cinderella, The Idiot (both by Valery Panov), Sphinx (by Glen Tetley), Tristan and Isolde (by Loyce Houlton), Unicorn (by John Neumeier), Medea, A Family Portrait (both by Birgit Cullberg), Carmencita (by Patrice Montagnon), Transfigured Night, Child Harold (both by Hans Spörli), Undine (by Tom Schilling); film appearances include The Nutcracker, La Sylphide, Cinderella, A Family Portrait, The Romantic Era, Invitation to the Dance, Portrait of Eva Evdokimova. Recipient Diploma, Internat. Ballet Competition, Moscow, 1969; winner Gold medal Varna Internat. Ballet competition, 1970; awarded title Prima Ballerina, Berlin Senate, 1973; first fgn. mem. Royal Danish Ballet, first Am. and Westerner to win any internat. ballet competition, first Am. to perform with Kirov Ballet, 1976, first Am. to perform in Peking after the Cultural Revolution, 1978, first and only Am. dancer with portrait in permanent collection, Mus. Drama and Dance, Leningrad, first Am. ballerina to perform as guest artist,

Great Theatre, Warsaw, 1988. Office: care Gregori Prodns PO Box 279 FDR Sta New York NY 10150-0279 also: Deutsche Oper Berlin, 1000 Berlin (West) 10 Germany

EVELETH, KATHERINE LUCKE, electronic company administrator; b. Rio de Janeiro, Dec. 3, 1962; (parents Am. citizens); d. George Stimson and Phyllis Ann (Bennett) E. BS in Biomed. Engring., Math., Vanderbilt U., 1984. Bus. planner Electronic Data Systems, Bethesda, Md., 1985—; vol. Suburban Hosp., Bethesda, 1987. Mem. Nat. Assn. Female Execs., Assn. Women in Computing (v.p. pub. 1986—). Home: 10648 Sawdust Circle Rockville MD 20850 Office: Electronic Data Systems 6430 Rockledge Dr Bethesda MD 20817

EVENSON, KATHERINE ANN, manufacturing executive; b. Montreal, Que., Can., Mar. 4, 1951; came to U.S., 1954; d. Michael John and Helen Katherine (Reynolds) Minahan; m. Eric Walter Evenson, Dec. 1, 1984. Student, Skidmore U., 1988—. Mgr. investment properties Rohema Realty, Inc., Englewood Cliffs, N.J., 1976-81; buyer Brisco Mfg., Elizabeth, N.J., 1977-81; asst. to v.p. Fisher Bros. Steel Corp., Englewood, N.J., 1981-82, product mgr., 1984—; mgr. mktg. Laurel Steel Products, Ltd., Burlington, Ont., Can., 1983-84; free-lance corr. local newspapers. Regent's scholar N.Y. State, 1968,. Mem. Nat. Assn. Female Execs., Assn. Women in the Metal Industries. Republican. Roman Catholic. Office: Fisher Bros Steel Corp Nordhoff Pl Englewood NJ 07631

EVERETT, MARY ELIZABETH, retirement home administrator; b. Okmulgee, Okla., June 3, 1929; d. Frederick Joseph and Harriet Lucille (Daratt) E.; m. Thomas Henry Everett, May 29, 1951; children: Deborah Maciolek, Thomas Stephen. BA, Salem Coll., 1951. Pres. Greater Balt. Med. Ctr. Aux., 1981-83, chmn. geriatrics; pres. Md. Assn. Hosp. Aux., Balt., 1984-86, seminar planner; pres. bd. mgrs. Wesley Home, Balt., 1986—, trustee; lectr. in field. Leader Girl Scouts U.S.A., Towson, Md.; bd. dirs. Towson Meth. Ch. Mem. Md. Assn. Hosp. Aux. (bd. dirs.). Republican. Clubs: Three Arts, Salem (Balt.) (bd. dirs.). ,. Home: 4 Candlelight Ct Lutherville MD 21093 Office: Wesley Home 2211 W Rogers Ave Baltimore MD 21209

EVERHART, DOROTHY ELIZABETH, social work administrator; b. Hanover, Pa., Aug. 23, 1951; d. Dean Baker and Muriel Rebecca (Heckler) E. BA, Lycoming Coll., 1973; M in Divinity, Boston U., 1976; cert. pub. administrn., Marywood Coll., 1984; postgrad., Temple U., 1986—. Pastor Knoxville-Austinburg Parish, 1976-78; caseworker protective services Tioga County Agy. for Children, Wellsboro, Pa., 1978-79, caseworker service planning, 1979-80, supr. protective services, 1980-81, unit supr. children's services, 1981-85; dir. family services Tioga County Human Services Agy., Wellsboro, 1985—; part-time instr. Williamsport Area Community Coll., Wellsboro, 1985—. Bd. mem. Wellsboro Community Concert Assn., 1978—; flute, piccolo player Wellsboro Town Band, 1978—; mem. policy bd. Victim/Witness Program, Wellsboro, 1986—. Mem. NOW (pres. Tioga County chpt. 1977-79, 83, 87), Nat. Assn. Social Workers. Democrat. Presbyterian. Home: 86 Walnut St Wellsboro PA 16901 Office: Tioga County Human Services Agy PO Box 766 Wellsboro PA 16901

EVERIDGE, FOXENE LAMBERT, company executive, real estate broker; b. Troy, Ala., Dec. 4, 1939; d. R. Fox and Edith (Bragg) Lambert; m. Jerry F. Everidge, Dec. 23, 1957; children: J. Stanley, Steven F., Stuart L. Grad. high sch., Marianne, Fla. Owner Greater Charleston Trading Post, Goose Creek, S.C., 1971-72; sec. ERA O'Shaughnessy Realty, N. Charleston, S.C., 1973-74, adminstrv. asst. to pres., 1974-79; regional coordinator ERA of the Carolinas, Charleston, S.C., 1979-81; sales assoc. ERA O'Shaughnessy Realty, N. Charleston, 1981-84, broker, mgr., 1984—; pres. Carolina Boilers/COMAR Industries, Charleston, S.C., 1982-88; chmn. bd. COMAR Industries Inc., Charleston, S.C., 1988—. Mem. Greater Charleston Bd. Realtors, Trident C. of C. Lodge: Order Eastern Star. Home: 10 Venice Ave Hanahan SC 29418 Office: COMAR Industries Inc 2718 Azalea Dr Charleston SC 29418

EVERINGHAM, JOYCE DUBERT, library administrator; b. Hornell, N.Y., May 14, 1929; d. John Griniliffe and Genie Mae (Herda) Dubert; m. Neil Gilbert Everingham, Sept. 17, 1955; 1 child, N. Mark. B.A., SUNY-Albany; M.L.S., SUNY-Geneseo, postgrad. Librarian, East Pembroke Sch., N.Y., City Sch. Dist., Williamsport, Pa.; coordinator libraries Westhill Schs., Syracuse, N.Y.; dir. pilot project Sch. Library System Syracuse City Schs., 1979-82, supr. libraries, 1969-82; exec. dir. Western N.Y. Library Resources Council, Buffalo, 1983—; mem. N.Y. Hist. Documents Inventory State Com. Mem. ALA, N.Y. Library Assn., Western N.Y. Hosp. Library Assn., Mid-Atlantic Records & Archives, Pub. Library Sect. N.Y. Library Assn., N.Y. Documentary Heritage (steering com. 1987—), Western N.Y. Ry. Hist. Soc. Avocations: music, basketball, sports, camping, crafts. Office: Western New York Library Resources Council Lafayette Square Buffalo NY 14203

EVERITT, ALICE LUBIN, labor arbitrator, academic dean; b. Washington, Dec. 13, 1936; d. Isador and Alice (Berliner) Lubin; B.A., Columbia U., 1968, J.D., 1971. Assoc. firm Amen, Weisman & Butler, N.Y.C., 1971-78; spl. asst. to dir. Fed. Mediation and Conciliation Service, Washington, 1978-81; editor Dept. Labor publ., 1979, pvt. practice labor arbitration, Washington, N.Y.C., 1981—; dean admissions Hofstra U. Sch. Law 1985—; mem. various nat. mediation and arbitration panels including U.S. Steel and United Steelworkers of Am. Mem. Am. Arbitration Assn., Soc. Profls. Dispute Resolution, Indsl. Relations Research Assn., Civil War Roundtable of Washington, N.Y.C. Home: Georgica Rd PO Box 293 East Hampton NY 11937 Office: Hofstra U Sch Law 116 Law Hempstead NY 11550

EVERSON, DIANE LOUISE, publishing executive; b. Edgerton, Wis., Mar. 27, 1953; d. Harland Everett and Helen Viola (Oliver) E. BS, Carroll Coll., 1975. Advt. mgr. Edgerton (Wis.) Reporter, 1976—; pres. Silk Screen Customs, 1981—. Pub. Directions mag., 1981—. Trustee Carroll Coll., 1987—. Democrat. Lutheran. Home: 114 Kellogg Rd Edgerton WI 53534 Office: Directions Pub 21 N Henry Edgerton WI 53534

EVERT, CHRISTINE MARIE (CHRIS EVERT), professional tennis player; b. Ft. Lauderdale, Fla., Dec. 21, 1954; d. James and Colette Evert; m. John Lloyd, Apr. 17, 1979 (div.); m. Andy Mill, July 30, 1988. Amateur tennis player until Dec. 1972, profl. tennis player, 1972—. Recipient Lebair Sportsmanship trophy, 1971; named Female Athlete of Yr. AP, 1974, 75, 77, 80; Athlete of Yr. Sports Illustrated, 1976; Greatest Woman Athlete of Last 25 Years Women's Sports Found., 1985. Mem. U.S. Lawn Tennis Assn. (Top Women's Singles Player award 1974), Nat. Honor Soc. Address: care Internat Mgmt Group 1 Erieview Plaza Cleveland OH 44114 also: Polo Club of Boca Raton 5400 Champion Blvd Boca Raton FL 33496 *

EVERTON, MARTA VE, ophthalmologist; b. Luling, Tex., Nov. 12, 1926; d. T.W. and Nora E. (Eckols) O'Leavy; B.A., Hardin-Simmons U., 1945; M.A., Stanford U., 1947; M.D., Baylor U., 1955; postgrad. N.Y.U.-Bellevue Hosp., 1956-57; m. Robert K. Graham, Oct. 15, 1960; children—Marcia, Christie, Leslie Fox. Intern, Meth. Hosp., Houston, 1955-56; resident in ophthalmology Baylor Affiliated Hosps., Houston, 1957-59; clin. instr. ophthalmology Baylor U., 1959-60; asst. clin. prof. ophthalmology Loma Linda U., 1962-73; practice medicine specializing in ophthalmology, Houston, 1959-60, Pasadena, Calif., 1961-74, Escondido, Calif., 1974—. Mem. AMA, Am. Acad. Ophthalmology, Am. Med. Women's Assn., Alpha Omega Alpha. Home: 3024 Sycamore Ln Escondido CA 92025 Office: 810 E Ohio Ave Escondido CA 92025

EVERTS, SANDRA LYNNE, college administrator; b. Milw., July 11, 1955; d. Neal Anson (dec.) and Gladys May (Neubauer) Timple; m. Mark Anthony Everts, Aug. 10, 1978. BS in Mktg., U. Wis., La Crosse, 1977. Adminstrv. asst. Milw. Sch. of Engring., 1977-79, mgr. profl. programs, 1980-82, dir. continuing edn., 1982—; exec. dir. Engrs. and Scientists of Milw., Inc., 1986—. Editor monthly news publ. Milw. Engring., 1986. Com. mem. Internat. Sci. and Engring. Fair, Milw., 1980-81, Goals 2000 for Greater Milw., 1984-85. Mem. Am. Soc. Engring. Edn., Learning Resource Network. Lutheran. Home: 11004 W Langlade St Milwaukee WI 53225 Office: Milw Sch Engring 1025 N Milwaukee St PO Box 644 Milwaukee WI 53201-0644

EVILSIZER, MARJORIE JOAN, speech language pathologist; b. N.Y.C., Aug. 10, 1961; m. Randall Joseph Evilsizer. Speech lang. pathologist, Dewey County Cooperative, Vici, Okla., 1985-87, Putnam City Sch., Oklahoma City, 1987—. Cert. clinical competence, elem. sch. tchr., Okla. Recipient Headstart Service award Wilshire Headstart Ctr., 1982, Human Service award United Way. Mem. Am. Speech Lang. Hearing Assn., Nat. Assn. Female Execs.

EWEN, MARY ELLEN M., horticulturalist, retailer; b. Brookline, Mass., Dec. 19, 1949; d. Gerald M. and Mary Louise (Kolling) M.; m. Frederick G. Ewen, Oct. 25, 1981. AAS, Boston Bus. Sch., 1971. Office mgr. Philip S. White, M.D., Boston, 1970-77; owner, mgr. The Grower's Market Corp., Cambridge, Mass., 1977—. Democrat. Roman Catholic. Home: 18 Muster Ct Lexington MA 02173 Office: The Grower's Market Corp 889 Memorial Dr Cambridge MA 02138

EWEN, PAULA ROBEY, transportation executive; b. La Plata, Md., Sept. 9, 1955; d. Kentzing Carver and Peggy Ruth (Smallwood) R.; m. Wayne Bruce Ewen, June 26, 1973. BS, U. Md., 1984; postgrad., USC, 1986. Computer technician Naval Ordnance Sta., Indian Head, Md., 1974-76; computer analyst Rehab Group, Inc., Arlington, Va., 1976-77, Murry's Steaks, Inc., Forestville, Md., 1977-78; computer specialist Exec. Office of the Pres., Washington, 1978-81; computer specialist Dept. of Transp., Washington, 1981—, spl. asst., 1984—. Mem. Assn. Female Execs., Charles County Bus. and Profl. Orgn. Home: Rt 1 Box 30 Port Tobacco MD 20677 Office: Dept Transp 400 Seventh St SW Washington DC 20590

EWERS, DEBORAH A., nurse; b. Berea, Ohio, Sept. 27, 1953; d. Robert A. and Helen L. (Cimperman) E. BS in Nursing, St. John's Coll., Cleve., 1978. RN, Ohio; cert. in basic life support. Staff nurse U. Hosps. Cleve., 1978-79, advanced clin. nurse, 1979-80, head nurse, 1981—; staff nurse research ctr. Brigham Women's Hosp., Boston, 1980-81; mem. sci. and tech. issues com. AIDS Commn. Greater Cleve. Violinist Lorain County Civic Orch. Mem. Ohio Nurse Assn., Greater Cleve. Nurses Assn., Nat. Assn. Female Execs., DAR, Delta Zeta. Office: U Hosps Cleve University Circle Cleveland OH 44106

EWING, MARY ARNOLD, lawyer; b. Shreveport, La., Feb. 21, 1948; d. George and Christine (Cocek) Hengy; m. Robert Craig Ewing, Aug. 30, 1981; 1 child, Kyle Ross. BA, U. Colo., 1972; JD, U. Denver, 1975. Bar: Colo. 1975, U.S. Supreme Ct. 1979. Assoc. Johnson & Mahoney, Denver, 1975-80; ptnr. Branney, Hillyard, Ewing & Barnes, Englewood, Colo., 1980-85, Bucholtz, Bull & Ewing, Denver, 1985—; asst. prof. law U. Denver, 1977-78, part time prof. 1978—; mem. faculty Nat. Inst. Trial Advocacy, 1984-87; instr. nat. session 1984, 85, 87, Nat. Bd. Trial Advocacy, regional session, 1984, 85, 86, 87. Chmn. Denver County Task Force, 1976-77; treas. Cen. Com. 1st Congl. Dist., 1976-77; v.p. Young Rep. League Denver, 1975, pres. 1976; mem. govt. relations com. Jr. Symphony Guild, 1978—. Mem. ABA, Colo. Bar Assn. (ethics com.), Denver Bar Assn. (vice chmn. new lawyers assistance com. 1977), Colo. Women's Bar Assn., Internat. Platform Assn., Mountain States Combined Tng. Assn., Rocky Mountain Dressage Soc. (sec. High Plains chpt. 1979-80), Assn. Trial Lawyers Am., Colo. Trial Lawyers Assn. (bd. govs., chmn. interprofl. com. 1980, dir. 1981—), Am. Arbitration Assn., Am. Trakehner Assn., Rocky Mountain Trakehner Assn. (v.p. 1987), U. Denver Coll. Law Alumni Council, Kappa Beta Pi (pres. 1977-78). Club: Toastmasters; Arapahoe Hunt; Greenwood Athletic. Home: Nonesuch Farm 816 W Quarry Rd Littleton CO 80124 Office: Bucholtz Bull & Ewing 1666 S University Blvd Denver CO 80210

EWING-TAYLOR, JACQUELINE MARIE, human resources executive; b. Elkton, Md., Feb. 7, 1953; d. Harvey Wilson and Hilda Mae (Somers) Ewing; m. Danny Lee Taylor, Dec. 27, 1983. Student, U. Miami, Coral Gables, Fla., 1971-72, Centre Coll., 1973-75, U. Nev., 1980—. Sales person Raleigh's, Washington, 1972-75, asst. mgr., 1975-76; mgr. pro shop Congl. County Club, Bethesda, Md., 1976-78; mgr. sales Macy's, Reno, 1978-79; trainee Nev. Nat. Bank, Reno, 1979-80, tng. specialist, 1980-81, personnel asst., 1981-84, compensation and benefits officer, 1984-86, asst. v.p., asst. personnel mgr., 1986—; instr. Truckee Meadows Community Coll., Reno, 1981—; lectr. U. Nev., Reno, 1982—; personnel cons. for various employers, Nev., 1985—; bd. dirs. Nev. Health Systems. Advisor Jr. Achievement, Reno, 1980-83; bd. dirs. ACLU, Reno, 1984-87; personnel com. chmn. Planned Parenthood, Reno, 1984-86; fundraising chmn. Planned Parenthood of Nev., Reno, 1985; vice chmn., bd. dirs. Adolescent Care and Treatment, Reno. Mem. Nat. Assn. Bank Women (fundraising com. 1984-85), Am. Compensation Assn., Am. Inst. Banking (speaking award 1982), No. Nev. Personnel Assn. Republican. Club: Toastmasters (ednl. v.p. 1979, pres. 1980-81, Toastmaster of Yr. 1981, 83). Home: 4640 Canyon Dr Reno NV 89509 Office: Nev Nat Bank 2597 Mill St Reno NV 89502

EXLINE, DORICE, real estate executive, consultant; b. Chgo., Nov. 7, 1960; d. Daniel Leroy and Dolores Theresa (Badon) E. Student, Moraine Valley Community Coll., 1978-80; BA, DePaul U., 1982. Lic. real estate broker, Ill. Asst. to pres. Oak Lawn (Ill.) News Agy., 1978-80; recruiter Moraine Valley Community Coll., Palos Hills, Ill., 1981-84; sr. sales rep. Lincoln Tech. Inst., Oak Lawn, 1984-85; sales mgr. Ctr. for Robotic Tech., Chgo., 1985-86; realtor Century 21 R.M. Post, Chgo., 1985-86, Wm. C. Groebe and Co., Oak Lawn, 1986-87; pres. Exline and Assoc., Inc., Oak Lawn, 1987—. Mem. Nat. Orgn. for Women, Chgo., 1979—, Nat. Abortion Rights Action League, Chgo., 1984—; pub. relations Common Cause, Chgo., 1984-87. Mem. Women's Council Realtors, Nat. Assn. Female Execs. Club: Sierra. Office: Exline & Assoc Inc. Real Estate Cons 9515 S Cook Oak Lawn IL 60453

EXUM, FRANCES BELL, foreign language educator; b. Birmingham, Ala., May 11, 1940; d. Frank Kinney and Frances Henrietta (Bell) E.; BA in Spanish cum laude, Fla. State U., 1962, MA in Spanish, 1963, PhD in Spanish, 1970. Instr. Spanish, N.C. Wesleyan Coll., 1963-65, Greensboro Coll., 1965-67; asst. prof. Spanish, Winthrop Coll., 1970-73, assoc. prof., 1973-77, prof., 1977—. Mem. MLA, South Atlantic MLA (exec.com. 1986-88, Spanish I sec. 1984, nominating com. 1986-88), Assn. Internat. de Hispanistas, Am. Assn. Tchrs. Spanish and Portuguese (pres. S.C. chpt. 1979-80), Cervantes Soc. Am., Soc. Spanish and Portuguese Hist. Studies, AAUP (pres. chpt. 1976-77), Renaissance Soc. Am., Phi Beta Kappa, Phi Kappa Phi (pres. chpt. 1984-85), Pi Beta Phi. Author: The Metamorphosis of Lope de Vega's King Pedro, 1974; editor: Essays on Comedy and the Gracioso in Plays by Agustín Moreto; contbr. articles and book revs. to profl. pubs. Home: 3757 Harwick Place Charlotte NC 28211 Office: Winthrop Coll Dept Modern & Classical Langs Rock Hill SC 29733

EYE, CAROLYN ANN, academic administrator; b. Tiverton, Eng., Oct. 30, 1944; came to U.S., 1947; d. Louis Leroy and Louise Caroline (Williams) Sanders; 1 child, Daniel Eric. BA, Coe Coll., 1969; MA, U. Iowa, 1978. Tchr. Anamosa (Iowa) Schs., 1969-81; prin. Gretna (Nebr.) Schs., 1982—. Mem. Nat. Assn. Elem. Sch. Principals, Am. Bus. Womens Assn. (pres. 1986-87, Bus. Woman of Yr. 1986), AAUW, Nat. Assn. Women Adminstrs., Phi Delta Kappa, Delta Kappa Gamma. Democrat. Episcopalian. Office: Gretna Pub Schs 801 South St Gretna NE 68028

EYRE, PAMELA CATHERINE, army officer; b. Chgo., Nov. 3, 1948; d. Francis Thomas and Jane (Burd) E.; m. Burke Owen Buntz, Jan. 10, 1986. B.A., Central State U. Okla., 1972; M.P.A., U. Okla., 1976. Commd. 2d lt. U.S. Army, 1973, advanced through grades to maj., 1986; test and evaluation officer Fort Gordon, Ga., 1982-85, research and devel. coordinator Pentagon, Washington, 1985-88, with army gen. staff, 1988— . Fellow Armed Forces Communications Electronics Assn. Avocation: foxhunting. Home: 5011 Larno Dr Alexandria VA 22310

EZELL, ANNETTE SCHRAM, educator, university administrator; b. West Frankfort, Ill., June 19, 1940; d. Woodrow C. and Rosa (Franich) Schram; BS in Nursing, U. Nev., 1962, MS in Physiology, 1967, postgrad., 1969; EdD in Pub. Adminstrn., Brigham Young U., 1977; children: Michael L., Rona Maria. Staff nurse Washoe Med. Center, Reno, 1962; teaching asst. U. Nev., Reno, 1962-63, instr., 1963-64, 1965-67, asst. prof., 1967-71; curriculum specialist U. Nev. Med. Sch., 1971-72, project mgr. Fed. Grant Intercampus Nursing Edn. Project, 1969-71, assoc. prof., curriculum specialist rural nurse practitioner program, 1971-73, staff assoc. Mountain States Regional Med. Program, 1974-75; cons. Nev. Dept. Edn., 1975-77; asst. dean acad. affairs U. Utah, Salt Lake City, 1977-80; acting Dean, 1981, dir., prof. doctoral program Edn. Adminstrn.; prof., dept. head Coll. Human Development, Pa. State U., 1982-85; dean Coll. Profl. Studies, prof. bus. adminstrn. U. So. Colo., Pueblo, 1985-87; asst. to pres. Towson State U., Balt., 1987—; cons. higher edn., TV edn., research methology; adviser to various research, polit. and ednl. bds. Mem. Am. Ednl. Research Assn., AAAS, Am. Acad. Arts and Scis., AAUP, Am. Council on Edn., Am. Assn. Higher Edn., Soc. for Coll. & Univ. Planning, Decision Scis. Inst., Sigma Xi, Phi Kappa Phi, Delta Kappa Gamma. Home: 2515 Boston St #1006 Baltimore MD 21224 Office: Towson State U Towson MD 21204

EZRATTY, ROBERTA S., management consultant; b. N.Y.C., Dec. 10, 1935; d. Ralph and Julia (Desind) Small; m. Harry A. Ezratty, Mar. 10, 1957 (div. 1981); children: Laurie, Michelle. BA, Hunter Coll., 1957. Cert. graphologist. Mktg. mgr., cons. Cable TV of San Juan, P.R., 1981-87; pres. Creative Innovations, Glendale, Ariz., 1980—; cons. Citibank N.A., San Juan, 1980-82; graphologist various attys., groups, N.Y., P.R., 1972—; speaker Kiwanis, San Juan, 1983-87; lectr. various schs., radio-TV programs; bd. dirs. Dynamic Resources Group, Glendale, 1987—. Author-editor: 800 Toll Free From P.R. and V.I.'s, 1982; contbr. lead articles leisure guide Tourist Book, 1979-83. Mem. Am. Assn. Univ. Women, Women Cable TV, Assn. Sales Mktg. Execs. Club: Overseas Press. Home and Office: Creative Innovations 5329 W Beryl Ave Glendale AZ 85302

EZZARD, MARTHA MCELVEEN, state senator, lawyer; b. Atlanta, Nov. 8, 1938; d. George Davant and Gladys Caroline (Lewis) McElveen; A.B. in Journalism, U. Ga., 1960; M.A., U. Mo., 1968; J.D., U. Denver, 1982; m. John A. Ezzard, Dec. 27, 1960; children—Shelly Lynne, Lisa Annette, John A. With Atlanta Jour., 1959-60, Sta. WSB-TV, Atlanta, 1960; tchr. Littleton (Colo.) High Sch., 1961-62; with Sta. KOMU-TV, Columbia, Mo., 1965-68; gov.'s press aide, 1973-75; polit. columnist Rocky Mountain Jour., Denver, 1976-77; mem. Colo. Ho. of Reps. from 37th Dist., 1978-80, Colo. Senate from 26th Dist., 1980-87; assoc. Davis, Graham & Stubbs, Denver; lectr. environ. law Denver U.; bd. dirs. United Bank Littleton. Bd. dirs. Women's Found.; candidate U.S. Ho. of Reps., 1986. Named Outstanding Rep. Legislator, 1986, Best Legis., Westword Newspaper, 1986, Englewood Bus. and Profl. Woman of Yr., 1986; recipient Rocky Mountain Womens Inst. award, 1987. Mem. ABA (continuing legal edn. lectr.), Colo. Bar Assn., Denver Bar Assn., Women's Forum. Episcopalian. Clubs: Oxford. Office: Colo Senate State Capitol Denver CO 80203 also: 370 17th St Denver CO 80201

FAANES-NYREN, CARI JONELLE, credit union executive; b. Rice Lake, Wis., Aug. 22, 1962; d. Alton Curtis and Phyllis Elva (Beranek) Faanes; m. Kenneth Floyd Nyren, May 1, 1987. Student, U. Wis., Stevens Point, 1977, U. Wis. Ctr., Barron County, 1979-80. Bridal cons. Gramac's, Rice Lake, 1981-83; bookkeeper Rice Lake Credit Union, 1983-85, collections mgr., 1985—; sec. Chippewa Valley chpt. Credit Unions, 1987-88; appointed to Credit Union Bd. Rev., 1988. Chmn. membership Wis. Young Reps., 1985; vice chmn. 3d Congl. Dist. Reps., 1986-87, youth rep.; chmn. Barron County Reps., 1987—; active Citizens Adv. Bd., Rice Lake, 1986—, sec. 1987. Mem. Chippewa Valley Chpt. Credit Unions. Episcopalian. Home: 328 Hatten Ave Rice Lake WI 54868 Office: Rice Lake Credit Union 1421 S Main St Rice Lake WI 54868

FAATZ, JEANNE RYAN, state legislator; b. Cumberland, Md., July 30, 1941; d. Charles Keith and Myrtle Elizabeth (McIntyre) Ryan; B.S., U. Ill., 1962; postgrad. (Gates fellow) Harvard U. Program Sr. Execs. in state and local Govt., 1984; M.A., U. Colo.-Denver, 1985. children—Kristin, Susan. Tchr., English and speech, Ill. and Colo., 1963-67; sec. to majority leader Colo. Senate, 1976-78; mem. Colo. Ho. Reps. from Dist. 1, 1978—, chmn. edn. com., mem. judiciary com.; coll. instr. Metro State Coll., Regis Coll., 1985. Past pres. Harvey Park (Colo.) Homeowners Assn., Southwest Denver YWCA Adult Edn. Club; Southwest met. coordinator UN Children's Fund, 1969-74; mem. citizens adv. council Ft. Logan Mental Health Center; bd. mgrs. Southwest Denver YMCA; bd. dirs. Southwest Denver Community Health Services. Mem. Bear Creek Republican Women's Club. Home: 2903 S Quitman St Denver CO 80236 Office: State Capitol Denver CO 80203

FABACHER, DIANE HAINS, psychiatric social worker; b. Baton Rouge, June 9, 1941; d. James Hubert and Frances (Gremillion) H.; m. Edward B. Fabacher, Jr., Feb. 9, 1963 (div. Feb. 1980); children: Edward B. III, Todd, Scott, Stacy, Julie. BS in Social Counseling, Our Lady of Holy Cross Coll., 1984; MSW, Tulane U., 1984. Adolescent, women's place social worker Greenbriar Hosp., Covington, La., 1968-88; dir. YWCA Parent Aide Program, New Orleans, 1985-86; pvt. practice Covington, 1988—. Mem. Nat. Assn. Social Workers, Northshore Social Workers Assn., La. Soc. Clin. Social Workers, Nat. Assn. Female Execs., NOW. Republican. Home: 516 Woodridge Blvd Mandeville LA 70448 Office: Greenbriar Hosp Greenbriar Blvd PO Box 1836 Covington LA 70434

FABBRI, ANNE R., art museum administrator; b. Norristown, Pa.; d. Remo and Anne Wilde (Butterworth) F.; A.B. cum laude, Radcliffe Coll.; M.A. in Art History, Bryn Mawr Coll., 1971; m. Joseph Henry Butera (div.); children—Virginia, Remo, Jay. Art lectr. Villanova U., Pa., 1971-73, Drexel U., Phila., 1974-76; art critic, art editor The Drummer, Phila., 1976-79; art critic The Bulletin, Phila., 1978-80; dir. Alfred O. Deshong Mus., Widener U., Chester, Pa., 1980-82, The Noyes Mus., Oceanville, N.J., 1982—; vis NEH fellow U. Calif.-Berkeley, 1979, Princeton U., 1980. Mem. Am. Assn. Museums, Artists Equity Assn., Coll. Art Assn., Internat. Assn. Art Critics. Home: One Independence Pl 305 6th St and Locust Walk Philadelphia PA 19106 Office: The Noyes Museum Lily Lake Rd Oceanville NJ 08231

FABER, CAROL ANTOINETTE, petroleum company executive; b. Terre Haute, Ind., Dec. 26, 1937; d. Fred Malooley and Regina Carolyn (Collins) Breiner; m. Daniel Keith Faber, Sept. 14, 1963; children: John Craig Lund, Jeffrey Scott Lund, Lisa Anne Lund. Student, Valencia Jr. Coll., Orlando, Fla., 1979-80, Seminole Jr. Coll., 1980. Dental asst. Dr. McCormick, Indpls., 1955-57; office mgr. for various dentists Orlando, 1961-70, pvt. practice in interior design, 1978-81; gen. office worker Aero Petroleum, Inc., Orlando, 1981-82; field supr. Aero Petroleum, Inc., Bowling Green, Ky., 1982-84; pres., founder Cheyenne Petroleum, Inc., Bowling Green, 1984—; bd. dirs. Corvette World Hdqrs., Bowling Green. Active Selective Service Bd., Orlando, 1983—. Mem. Ky. Ind. Petroleum Producers Assn. (exec. bd. 1986-87), Ky. Oil and Gas Assn., Nat. Assn. Female Execs., Bowling Green C. of C., Landmark Assn., Friends of Arts-Capital Arts Ctr., Phi Theta Kappa. Republican. Episcopalian. Office: Cheyenne Petroleum Inc 1712 Rollingwood Way Bowling Green KY 42101

FABER, SANDRA MOORE, astronomer, educator; b. Boston, Dec. 28, 1944; d. Donald Edwin and Elizabeth Mackenzie (Borwick) Moore; m. Andrew L. Faber, June 9, 1967; children: Robin, Holly. B.A., Swarthmore Coll., 1966, D.Sc. (hon.), 1986; Ph.D., Harvard U., 1972. Asst. prof., astronomer Lick Obs., U. Calif.-Santa Cruz, 1972-77, assoc. prof., astronomer, 1977-79, prof., astronomer, 1979—; mem. NSF astronomy adv. panel; vis. prof. Princeton U., 1978, U. Hawaii, 1983, Ariz. State U., 1985; Phillips visitor Haverford Coll., 1982; mem. Nat. Acad. Astronomy Survey Panel, 1979-81; chmn. vis. com. Space Telescope Sci. Inst., 1983-84;. Assoc. editor: Astrophys. Jour. Letters; editorial bd.: Ann. Revs. Astronomy and Astrophysics, 1982-87; contbr. articles to profl. jours. Trustee Carnegie Instn., Washington, 1985—. Recipient Bart J. Bok prize Harvard U., 1978; NSF fellow, 1966-71; Woodrow Wilson fellow, 1966-71; Alfred P. Sloan fellow, 1977-81; listed among 100 best Am. scientists under 40, Sci. Digest, 1984; Tetelman fellow, Yale U., 1987. Mem. Am. Astron. Soc. (councilor 1982-84, Dannie Heineman prize 1986), Internat. Astron. Union, Nat. Acad. Scis., Phi Beta Kappa, Sigma Xi. Office: Lick Obs U Calif Santa Cruz CA 95060

FABRAY, NANETTE, actress; b. San Diego, Oct. 27, 1920; d. Raoul Bernard and Lillian (McGovern) Fabares; m. David Tebet, Oct. 26, 1947 (div. July 1951); m. Ranald MacDougall, 1957 (dec. Dec. 1973); 1 son,

Jamie. Student, Los Angeles City Coll.; D.H.L. (hon.), Gallaudet Coll., 1970; D.F.A. (hon.), Md. Coll., 1972. Appeared as actress in: Broadway shows Let's Face It, 1941, Meet the People, 1940, By Jupiter, 1943, Bloomer Girl, 1944, High Button Shoes, 1947, Arms and the Girls, 1950, Love Life, 1948, Make A Wish, 1951, Mr. President, 1962, Jackpot, 1973, No Hard Feelings, 1973, Applause, 1973-74, Plaza Suite, 1973-74, The Secret Affairs of Mildred Wild, 1977; co-star (with Sid Caesar) on Caesar's Hour, CBS-TV, 1954-56; star: TV series Yes, Yes Nanette, 1961-62; spls. Happy Birthday & Goodby, 1974, George M!, 1970; motion pictures include Private Lives of Elizabeth and Essex, 1939, The Bandwagon, 1952, The Happy Ending, 1969, A Child is Born, 1940, Cockeyed Cowboys of Calico County, 1970, That's Entertainment, Part 2, 1976, Harper Valley PTA; TV appearances include: One Day at a Time, CBS-TV. Trustee Eugene O'Neill Meml. Found., Nat. Theatre of Deaf; bd. dirs., v.p. Nat. Assn. Hearing and Speech Agys.; bd. dirs. Pres.'s Nat. Adv. Com. on Edn. Deaf, Pres.'s Com. on Employment Handicapped, Muses of Calif. Mus. Found.; mem. Nat. Council on Handicapped, 1982—. Recipient two Donaldson awards for High Button Shoes, 1947, Tony award for Love Life, 1949, Emmy award as best comedienne, 1955, 56, best supporting performer Caesar's Hour, 1955, Eleanor Roosevelt Humanitarian award, 1964, Human Relations award Anti-Defamation League, 1969, 1st ann. Cogswell award Gallaudet Coll., 1970, Pres.'s Distinguished Service award, 1970; named Woman of Year Radio and TV Editors, 1963, Woman of Year Jewish War Vets. Am., 1969. Office: care Writers & Artists Agy 11726 San Vicente Blvd Suite 300 Los Angeles CA 90049 *

FACKLER, SANDRA LEE, genealogist; b. Greenfield, Ohio, July 4, 1949; d. Albert Reed and Annalee (Howe) F. Student, So. State Community Coll., 1979-80, Sinclair Community Coll., 1980-81. Pvt. practice genealogy Washington Court House, Ohio, 1976—. Editor: History Fayette County, Ohio, 1984; author: The Fayette County Chronicle, vols. I and II; columnist The Family Tree, 1983-84, 86—. Mem. Council of Ohio Genealogists (editor newsletter 1986—), Council of Geneal. Columnists, Fayette County Geneal. Soc. (co-founder, exec. sec. 1981—, editor newsletter 1981—), Ohio Geneal. Soc., Ross County Geneal. Soc., Jackson County Geneal. Soc., Greene County Geneal. Soc. Home: 703 Park Dr Washington Court House OH 43160 Office: PO Box 119 Washington Court House OH 43160

FACTOR, ELLEN LEE, publishing company executive; b. Boston, Feb. 7, 1945; d. Martin and Natalie (Green) Weiner. Student Boston U. Sch. Edn., 1967-68; B.S. in Bus. Edn., U. Mich., 1969; postgrad. in edn. NYU, 1973-74; M.B.A. in Mktg., Fordham U., 1983. Circulation mgr. McGraw Hill Publs. Co., N.Y.C., 1973-76, mgr. distbn. research McGraw Hill Info. Systems Co., 1976-80, distbn. mgr., 1980-85, mgr. market adminstrn., 1985-87, dir. mkt. adminstrn., 1988—. Cons. Arts and Bus. Council, N.Y.C., 1979-80, 84—. Bd. dirs. Fairmont Tenant's Corp., 1986—. Office: McGraw Hill Info Systems Co 1221 Ave of Americas New York NY 10020

FADER, SHIRLEY SLOAN, writer; b. Paterson, N.J.; d. Samuel Louis and Miriam (Marcus) Sloan; m. Seymour J. Fader; children: Susan Deborah, Steven Micah Kimchi. BS, MS, U. Pa. Writer, journalist, author, Paramus, N.J., 1956—; writer People and You, jobmanship columns Family Weekly, 1971-81, contbg. writer, 1977-81; columnist, writer How To Get More From Your Job column, contbg. editor Glamour mag., 1978-81; columnist, writer Start Here column Working Woman mag., 1980-87, contbg. editor, 1982—; writer Women Getting Ahead column Ladies' Home Jour., 1981—, Work Strategies column Working Mother mag., 1987—, How Would You Handle It? column New Idea mag., Australia, 1986—; contbg. editor Working Mother, 1988; coordinator ann. writers' seminar Bergen Community Coll., 1973-75. Author: The Princess Who Grew Down, 1968, From Kitchen to Career, 1977, Jobmanship, 1978, Successfully Ever After: A Young Woman's Guide to Career Happiness, 1982: contbr. articles to numerous nat. mags. Mem. Authors Guild, Am. Soc. Journalists and Authors (nat. v.p. 1976-77, nat. exec. council 1976-78, 83-86), Nat. Press Club. Address: 377 McKinley Blvd Paramus NJ 07652

FAGAN, BETTY MAHON, financial executive; b. Jackson, Tenn., Apr. 25, 1932; d. Robert Perry and Claire (Rogers) Mahon; B.A. cum laude, Vanderbilt U., 1953; m. Arthur Lawrence Fagan, Jr., Dec. 27, 1962; children—Perry Lawrence, Mark Malone, Anthony Rogers. Jr. analyst Smith Barney & Co., N.Y.C., 1960-65; v.p., sr. analyst White, Weld & Co., Inc., N.Y.C., 1972-78, Merrill Lynch, N.Y.C., 1978-80, First Boston Corp., N.Y.C., 1980-82; portfolio strategist Ford Found., N.Y.C., 1982—. Past trustee, chmn. fin. com. Greenfield Hill Congregational Ch.; bd. dirs., chmn. fin. com. YWCA of N.Y.; bd. dirs., mem. investment com. United Ch. Found. Mem. Fin. Women's Assn., Fin. Analysts Fedn., N.Y. Soc. Security Analysts. Club: Cosmopolitan (past gov., chmn. fin. com.) (N.Y.C.).

FAGERBURG, JOAN E., university administrator; b. Normal, Ill., Nov. 27, 1939. BA, MacMurray Coll., 1961; MS in Edn., Purdue U., 1962, PhD, 1967. Resident dir. Ill. State U., Normal, 1962-65; asst. dean of students, internat. student advisor No. Ariz. U., Flagstaff, 1967—. Vol. Mus. No. Ariz., Flagstaff. Named Faculty Woman of the Yr. Assoc. Women Students of No. Ariz. U., 1976-77; awarded a trip to Republic China by Minister of Edn. of Taiwan, 1981; Fulbright scholar, Fed. Republic Germany, 1988. Mem. NOW, Nat. Assn. of Women Deans, Adminstrs., and Counselors (research com. 1981-83), Ariz. Assn. Women Deans, Adminstrs., and Counselors, Nat. Assn. Fgn. Student Affairs. Office: No Ariz U PO Box 4095 Flagstaff AZ 86011

FAGERSTEN, BARBARA JEANNE, special education educator; b. San Francisco, Feb. 29, 1924; d. Ernest Mauritz and Louise (Hopkins) F.; m. Harold Gurish, Feb. 7, 1950 (div. 1970); children: Michael, Matthew, Jonathon. BA, San Francisco State U., 1951; MS, Dominican U., 1973, degree in spl. edn., 1975. Personnel sec. Arabian Am. Oil Co., San Francisco, 1944-45; union sec. Jeweler's Union, San Francisco, 1946-48; med. sec. Mt. Zion Hosp., San Francisco, 1949-50; spl. edn. tchr. Marin Office Edn., San Rafael, Calif., 1967—; bd. dirs. DeWitt Learning Ctr., San Rafael, 1969. bd. dirs. Marin Tchrs. Credit Union, San Rafael, 1978—, Marinwood Community Services, San Rafael, 1986—; commr. Parks and Recreation Marinwood, San Rafael, 1983-86. Mem. Calif. Assn. Neurol. Handicapped Children (trustee 1966-74). Democrat. Home: 272 Blackstone Dr San Rafael CA 94903 Office: Marin Office Edn 1111 Las Gallinas San Rafael CA 94903

FAGIN, CLAIRE MINTZER, educational administrator; b. N.Y.C., Nov. 25, 1926; d. Harry and Mae (Slatin) Mintzer; m. Samuel Fagin, Feb. 17, 1952; children: Joshua, Charles. B.S., Wagner Coll., 1948; M.A., Tchrs. Coll. Columbia, 1951; Ph.D., N.Y. U., 1964; D.Sc. (hon.), Lycoming Coll., 1983; D. Sc. (hon.), Cedar Crest Coll., 1987, U. Rochester, 1987. Staff nurse Sea View Hosp., Staten Island, N.Y., 1947, clin. instr., 1947-48; clin. instr. Bellevue Hosp., N.Y.C., 1948-50; psychiat. nurse cons. Nat. League for Nursing, N.Y.C., 1951-52; asst. chief psychiat. nursing service clin. ctr. NIH, 1953-54, supr., 1955; research project coordinator dept. psychiatry Children's Hosp., Washington, 1956; instr. psychiat.-mental health nursing NYU, N.Y.C., 1956-58, asst. prof., 1964-67, dir. grad. programs in psychiat. mental health nursing, 1965-69, assoc. prof., 1967-69; chmn. nursing dept., prof. Herbert H. Lehman Coll., CUNY, N.Y.C., 1969-77; dir. Health Professions Inst., Montefiore Hosp. and Med. Ctr., 1975-77; Margaret Bond Simon dean sch. of nursing U. Pa., Phila., 1977—; mem. task force Joint Commn. Mental Health of Children, 1966-69; gov.'s com. on children N.Y. State, 1971-75; pres. Council on Deans of Nursing, Sr. Colls. and Univs. N.Y. State, 1974-76; cons. to many pub. and private univs. and health care agys.; cons. Pan Am. Health Nursing, Washington, 1972-74, NIMH, HEW, 1974-76, NIMH, 1979, 83; mem. expert adv. panel on nursing WHO, 1974—; mem.-at-large Nat. Bd. Med. Examiners, 1980-83; dir. Provident Mut. Ins. Co., 1977—, audit com., 1978—, chmn., 1985—, exec. com., 1986—; mem. nat. adv. mental health council NIMH, 1983-88; speaker profl. convs., radio and TV; bd. dirs. Daltex Corp., 1984—, compensation com. Contbr. articles to profl. publs. Recipient achievement award Wagner Coll., 1956, achievement award Wagner Coll. Sch. Nursing, 1973, achievement award Tchrs. Coll., 1975, disting. alumna award N.Y. U., 1979, Founders award Sigma Theta Tau, 1981, NIMH fellow, 1950-51, 60-64; Am. Nurses Found. disting. scholar, 1984. Mem. Inst. of Medicine, Nat. Acad. Scis. (governing council 1981-83), Am. Acad. Nursing (governing council 1976-78), Am. Orthopsychiat. Assn. (bd. dirs. 1972-75, exec. com. of bd. 1973-75, pres. 1985-86), Coll. Physicians Phila. Office: U Pa Nursing Edn Bldg Philadelphia PA 19104

FAGNANI, MICHELE ANN, production supervisor; b. San Francisco, July 15, 1945; d. Melvin ANthony and Ann (Garetti) F.; m. Ronnie Dale Harrison, Jan. 27, 1962 (div. 1967); children: Tamera Ann, Troy James. Student, San Mateo (Calif.) Bus. Coll., 1964, John Roberts Powers Coll., 1968. Draftsman Ampex, Redwood City, Calif., 1965-68, Numetrics, Palo Alto, Calif., 1968-70; electronic assembler WEstvalley Engring., Palo Alto, 1970-72; prodn. control planner Fairchild, San Jose, Calif., 1972-78; prodn. supr. Intel, Sunnyvale, Calif., 1978-80; prodn. mgr. Robinton Product, Inc., Sunnyvale, 1980-83; % Optical Coating Labs., Santa Rosa, Calif., 1983-85, Weightronics, Santa Rosa, 1986—; landlord rentals, San Jose and Santa Rosa, 1978; rancher, Santa Rosa, 1982-85. Democrat. Roman Catholic. Home: 9339 Hwy 116 Forestville CA 95436 Office: Weightronics 2320 Airport Blvd Santa Rosa CA 95402

FAHR, LINDA MEYERS, radiologist; b. N.Y.C., Sept. 20, 1942; d. Paul Tabor and Jessie V. (Jones) Meyers; B.A., Barnard Coll., 1964; M.D., U. Iowa, 1968; m. James Dwight Watson, Mar. 29, 1980; children—John Pearson Fahr, Bruce Tabor Fahr. Resident in radiology U. Iowa, Iowa City, 1971-74; staff radiologist VA Hosp., Houston, 1974-77, chief dept. radiology, 1977-79; chief radiologist MacGregor Med. Assocs., Houston, 1980-84, Loma Linda Radiology Group Inc., 1984—, asst. prof. Loma Linda (Calif.) U. Med. Ctr., 1987—; clin. asst. prof. Baylor Coll. Medicine, Houston, 1974-79. Mem. Am. Assn. Women Radiologists (pres. 1983, past pres. 1984), Am. Coll. Radiology, Radiol. Soc. N.Am., Calif. Radiol. Soc., San Bernadino County Med. Assn., Women's Profl. Assn. (exec. bd. 1984), Calif. Med. Assn., Inland Radiol. Soc. Office: Loma Linda U Med Ctr 11234 Anderson Loma Linda CA 92354

FAHRENKAMP, BETTYE M., state legislator; b. Wilder, Tenn.; m. Gilbert H. Fahrenkamp, 1952 (dec.). B.S., U. Tenn., 1949; M.A., U. Alaska, 1962. Formerly sch. music tchr.; mem. Alaska Senate, 1978—. Served with WAC, 1944-46. Chmn. dist. Democratic com., 1968-72; nat. Dem. committeewoman, 1972-78. Office: Office of the State Senate State Capitol Juneau AK 99811 *

FAHY, NANCY LEE, food products executive; b. Schenectady, N.Y., Aug. 15, 1946; d. Christopher Mark and Frances (Lee) F.; m. Steven Neil Wohl, June 8, 1945 (div. Apr. 1978). BS cum laude cum laude, Miami (Ohio) U., 1968. Educator Palatine (Ill.) Pub. Schs., 1968-70, Glencoe (Ill.) Pub. Schs., 1970-78; sales rep. Keebler Co., Elmhurst, Ill., 1978-80, dist. mgr., 1980-82, account mgr., 1982-83, zone mgr., 1983-85, account mgr., 1985—. Vol. Lincoln Park Zool. Soc., Chgo., 1975-78. Mem. Food Products Club, Merchandising Execs. Club (bd. dirs. 1984-85), Grocery Mfgs. Sales Execs. Club (bd. dirs. 1984-85, asst. sec. 1987—), Phi Beta Kappa. Office: Keebler Co 1001 Entry Dr Bensenville IL 60106

FAIBISOFF, SYLVIA G., library school director. BA in History, Hunter Coll., 1941; BLS, Case Western Res. U., 1942, MLS, 1968, PhD in Library Sci., 1975. Documents librarian Cornell U. Library, Ithaca, N.Y., 1956-61, serials dept. head, 1961-68; instr. Syracuse (N.Y.) U., 1968-69, research fellow, 1972-73; exec. dir. South Cen. Research Library, Ithaca, 1968-75; asst. prof. library sci. U. Ill., Champaign, 1975-76; assoc. prof., co-dir. library U. Ariz., Tucson, 1976-78; assoc. prof., dept. chair No. Ill. U., DeKalb, 1978-82; prof., dir. Sch. of Library and Info. Studies U. Okla., Norman, 1982—. Editor: (monograph series) Computer & Information Science series, 1985—; co-editor: Changing Times: Changing Libraries, 1976, Bibliography of Newspapers in 14 New York Counties, 1978; contbr. numerous articles to profl. jours. Recipient Nat. Merit award Nat. Assn. State & Local Historians, 1979, Outstanding Service to Librarians award South Cen. Research Libraries Council, 1987; Fulbright fellow, Yugoslavia, 1983. Mem. ALA, Am. Soc. for Info. Sci. (pres. Okla. chpt. 1987-88), Okla. Library Assn. (planning com. 1987-88). Office: Univ of Okla Sch of Library & Info Studies 401 W Brooks Norman OK 73019

FAIKS, JAN OGOZALEK, state senator, real estate developer; b. Hempstead, N.Y., Nov. 17, 1945; d. Edmund Frank and Anna Marie (Chupella) Ogozalek. B.A., Florida State U., 1967. Tchr. Anchorage Sch. Dist., 1968-76, counselor, 1976-78; owner, mgr. Green Connection, Anchorage, 1978-81; mem. Alaska State Senate, Juneau, 1982—, pres. Author: Llama Training-Who's In Charge, 1981. Editor course devel. in career math., 1976. Bd. dirs. People Against State Income Tax, 1979—, Common Sense for Alaska, bd. dirs. Common Sense for Alaska, 1980—, research chmn., v.p., 1980-82; bd. dirs. Anchorage Symphony, 1984, Alaska Spl. Olympics; Recipient First Lady vol. award Gov. of Alaska, 1981; President's award Common Sense for Alaska, 1981; named Outstanding Secondary Tchr., Anchorage Sch. Dist., 1977. Mem. Nat. Council State Legislators, Anchorage C. of C. (bd. dirs. 1981-86, legis. chmn. 1980-82), Gen. Fedn. Women's Club (legis chmn. 1979-82), Anchorage Symphony Women's League (pres. 1980-81), Anchorage C. of C. (bd. dirs. 1987—, exec. com. 1981-82), Phi Beta Phi (pres. 1974-76). Republican. Presbyterian.Avocations: backpacking, fishing, llamas.

FAILINGER, DIANNE MARIE, personnel executive; b. Frostburg, Md., Nov. 27, 1958; d. Kermit Belvin and Thelma Josephine Failinger. B.S., Frostburg State Coll., 1980. Intern guidance counseling Braddock Jr. High, Cumberland, Md., 1980; field supr. Western Md. Consortium, Cumberland, 1980; residential services specialist Friends Aware, Cumberland, 1977-81; equal opportunity officer Allegany County Human Resources Devel. Commn., Inc., Cumberland, 1980-82, personnel officer, 1982-84; personnel adminstr. Precise Metals and Plastics, Inc., Cumberland, 1984-86; personnel specialist Meml. Hosp. and Med. Ctr., Cumberland, 1987—; v.p. Crystal Towers, Inc., Frostburg, 1987—. Bd. dirs. Community Housing Resources, Cumberland, 1982-84; program advisor Coop. Extension Service, Cumberland, 1983-86; human rights advisor Archway Sta., Cumberland, 1983—; chmn. pub. relations Gov.'s Youth Adv. Council, Balt., 1978-82; mem. Allegany County Children's Council, Cumberland, 1979-83; mem. ch. council St. Paul's Luth. Ch., Frostburg, 1984-86; sec. Frostburg Tourism Adv. Council, 1986—; mem. Cumberland Choral Soc. Recipient Letter of Appreciation/Commendation, Gov. Md., 1982; mem. community council March of Dimes, 1987—. Mem. Frostburg Bus. and Profl. Assn. (treas. local chpt. 1984-86, v.p. local chpt. 1987-88), NOW (treas. local chpt., v.p. 1987—), Delta Omicron, Psi Chi. Republican. Lutheran. Home: 109 W Main St Frostburg MD 21532 Office: Memorial Hosp & Med Ctr Inc 600 Memorial Ave Cumberland MD 21502

FAIN, DEBORAH LEE, sales consultant; b. Tucson, Oct. 14, 1949; d. Roy Albert and Fawn Thelma (Hudson) Echeverria; m. David Lyons Fain, Nov. 16, 1968; children: Zoë Celeste, Asa Lyons. Student. U. Ariz., 1967-68, Santa Barbara Coll., 1970-71. Field support rep. Savin Bus. Machines, Denver, 1974-76, Lanier Bus. Products, Denver, 1976-78; mgr. nat. support Lanier Bus. Products, Atlanta, 1978-83; exec. v.p., founder Samna Corp., Atlanta, 1983-85; pres., founder MSK Corp., Atlanta, 1985-87; cons., founder, pres., chief exec. officer Fain, Greer & Hixson, Atlanta, 1987—, also bd. dirs.; bd. dirs. Echeverria Corp. Republican. Roman Catholic.

FAIR, SHARON DAVIS, broadcast executive; b. Dayton, Ohio, July 31, 1956; d. Prince and Alice Juanita (Rockhold) Davis; m. Dale Samuel Fair, July 14, 1954; 1 child, Dale II. BA, U. Dayton, 1978. Prodn. technician Sta. WHIO-TV, Dayton, 1978; broadcast trainee Sta. WDTN-TV, Dayton, 1978-79, continuity clk., 1979, asst. community services dir., 1979-82, community services dir., 1982-86, community and human resources dir., 1986—; bd. dirs. Womanline, Inc. Vol. United Negro Coll. Fund, West Area YMCA/YWCA, mem. communications com.; mem. mayor's task force on housing alternative for the elderly, City of Dayton, So. Christian Leadership Conf., Dayton, Dayton/Montgomery County Scholarhsip com., Youth Opportunities Task Force, Montgomery County Teen Pregnancy/Parenting Coalition; bd. dirs. Emergency Resource Bank, Dayton Urban League, Dayton Contemporary Dance Co., Turk Logan Sch. of Broadcasting, Dayton Pub. Schs. Media Adv. Bd., nat. bd. dirs. AIM for the Handicapped. Named one of Outstanding Young Women of Am., 1982. Mem. Am. Women in Radio and TV (bd. dirs.), Ohio Assn. Broadcasters, Internat. Assn. Bus. Communications, Dayton Area C. of C. Democrat. Office: WDTN-TV 4595 S Dixie Ave Dayton OH 45439

FAIRBANKS, CAROLINE LESLIE, material science consultant; b. Los Angeles, Nov. 16, 1944; d. Pedro Alexander and Katherine (Gutjahr) Arrendondo; m. Howell Beach Fairbanks, Sept. 11, 1977; 1 child, Katherine Leslie. BA in Zoology, Chemistry, U. Minn., 1968. Scientist Control Data Corp., Mpls., 1969-74; project engr. Magnetic Peripherals, Mpls., 1974-78, mgr. media tech., 1979-84, mgr. plated media pilot plant, 1984-85, cons. in materials sci., 1986-87, mgr. thinfilm, head mfr., 1988—. Mem. Soc. Plastics Engrs. (past pres., bd. dirs.), Minn. Women's Network, NOW. Home: 201 McBoal Saint Paul MN 55102 Office: 7801 Computer Ave Minneapolis MN 55435

FAIRBANKS, MARY JOANNE, educational administrator; b. Massena, N.Y., Dec. 21, 1939; d. James William and Inez (Cappiello) Phillips; Assoc. in Bus. Adminstrn., Central City Bus. Inst., Syracuse, N.Y. 1959; A.S. in Accounting LaSalle Extension U., 1974; student in mgmt., Syracuse U., 1974—. Sec. elec. and computer engring. dept. Syracuse U., 1959-65, asst. to adminstrv. asst., 1965-72, publs. mgr. Assembly on U. Governance, 1970-72, coordinator computer confs., 1972-81, adminstr. short course Air Force intrasystem analysis program, 1974-78, supervisory asst. to chmn. dept. elec. and computer engring. and mgr. Air Force Post-Doctoral Program, Rome Air Devel. Center, 1972-78, adminstrv. asst. to chmn. dept. indsl. engring. and ops. research 1978-82, dir. Engring. Coop. Edn. program, 1982—; mgr. electromagnetic compatibility analysis techniques advancement program, 1978-82; coordinator workshops on computer architecture, 1977-79; ofcl. stenographer 1985 Project, USMC, 1963; mem. computer scoring team XIII Olympic Winter Games, Lake Placid, N.Y., 1980; Alpine ofcl. U.S. Ski Assn., 1980—; mem. Syracuse U. Career Planning and Placement Council. Pres. LWV Met. Syracuse, 1981-83, voters service dir. N.Y. State, 1983-87, publs. editor LWV of N.Y. State, 1987—, 2d v.p. N.Y. State, 1986. Mgr., editor publs. Onondaga County Bicentennial Quilt, 1976; editor 7 elec. engring. textbooks, 1960-78; author: The Road to the Voting Booth, 2 vols., 1986; co-author: Career Portfolio for Volunteers, 1980, Patterns of Government in Onondaga County, 1981; contbr. articles to profl. jours. Mem. Am. Soc. Engring. Edn. (chair membership coop. edn. div. 1988—), Coop. Edn. Assn., Ohio Coop. Edn. Assn., N.Y. State Coop. and Experiential Edn. Assn., Middle Atlantic Placement Assn., Nat. Commn. for Coop. Edn. Home: 140 Edgehill Rd Syracuse NY 13224 Office: Syracuse U 359 Link Hall Syracuse NY 13210

FAIRCLOUGH, ELLEN LOUKS, Can. politician, mem. Privy Council; b. Hamilton, Ont., Can., Jan. 28, 1905; d. Norman Ellsworth and Nellie Bell (Louks) Cook; student schs. Hamilton, Ont.; LL.D., McMaster U., 1975; m. David Henry Gordon Fairclough, Jan. 28, 1931; 1 son, Howard Gordon. Founder, prin. acctg. practice, 1935-57; mem. Ho. of Commons Can., 1950-63, sec. of state, 1957-58, minister citizenship and immigration, 1958-62, mem. Privy Council, 1957—, postmaster gen., 1962-63; adv. mem. Can. del. to UN, 1950; del. to Conf. of Parliamentarians from NATO Countries, Paris, 1955; ambassador extraordinary to Argentina for presdl. inauguration, 1958; apptd. sec. Hamilton Trust & Savs. Corp., 1963-77 (amalgamated with Can. Permanent Trust); past chmn. Hamilton Hydro Electric Commn., 1974-86 Past v.p. Young Conservatives Ont.; alderman Hamilton City Council, 1946-50, controller, 1950; bd. dirs. Can. Council Christians and Jews; patron Huguenot Soc., United Empire Loyalists' Assn., Hamilton br. Can.; hon. treas. dir. Chedoke-McMaster Hosps. Found., 1977—, exec. dir. 1983-86. Decorated officer Order of Can.; govt. bldg. named in her honor, 1982. Fellow Chartered Accts.; mem. Gen. Accts. Assn. Can. (life), United Empire Loyalist Assn. (dominion sec. 1935-40), Imperial Order Daus. of Empire (officer provincial and nat. chpts. 1935-48), Hamilton C. of C. Anglican. Lodge: Zonta (pres., Hamilton 1940-42). Club: Hamilton; Albany (Toronto).

FAIRLEE, CAROL H., actuary; b. Saratoga, N.Y., July 11, 1944; d. Arthur Hamann and Jean (Stephens) Vigars; m. Raymond M. Fairlee, July 1970 (div. 1976); children: Jason, Eric. BA, SUNY, Albany, 1966, postgrad., 1966-67. Cert. math. and Russian tchr. Credit asst. W.T. Grant Co., Albany, 1962-66; tchr. jr. high Sch. 12, Troy, N.Y., 1967-68; night mgr. Redwood Lanes, Albany, 1968-69; chairperson Math. dept. Acad. of Holy Names, Albany, 1969-79; actuary, dept. mgr. N.Y. State Tchrs. Retirement System, Albany, 1979—. Cellist Little Falls (N.Y.) Symphony Orch., 1962-70, Schenectady Symphony Orch., 1970-72, Music Co. Orch., 1987—; mgr. North Colonie Elem. Basketball League, Latham, N.Y., 1984-85; mgr., asst. player agt. Latham Little League, 1979-86. Mem. Adirondack Actuaries Club (v.p. meeting adminstrn. 1986-87), Kappa Mu Epsilon. Roman Catholic. Home: 9C Rolling Ridge Apts Latham NY 12110

FAIRWEATHER, PAMELA GENE, sales executive; b. Houston, Feb. 19, 1945; d. Kenneth Everett and Norma Gene (Evans) F.; Piere Gene Lumpkin, Oct. 10, 1963 (div. Dec. 1982); children: Peyton Bruce, Laura Ann. Student, Independence Jr. Coll., 1978-79. Spl. services rep. Braniff Internat., Houston, 1965-72; owner, tchr. Danceland Studios, Fredonia, Independence, Parsons, Kans., 1972-77; adminstrv. asst. St. Margaret's Mercy Hosp., Fredonia, 1977-80; sales rep. Gencom Communications, Tampa, Fla., 1980-81; sales rep. Motorola Communications, Tampa, 1981-86, dist. mgr., 1986-88; with mktg. dept. The Cellular Store, 1988—. Fellow Nat. Assn. Female Execs., Nat. Assn. Profl. Saleswomen. Home: 131 Garland Circle Palm Harbor FL 33536

FAISON, DELORES, government accountant; b. Atlanta, Aug. 28, 1945; d. Harry and Ella Maud (Hunter) Campbell; 1 child, Harold Ernest Campbell. Student CUNY, Helene Fuld Sch. Nursing, N.Y.C., U. Ariz.; grad. with high honors, Pima Coll., 1984; postgrad., Columbia Pacific U., 1987—. In various positions U.S. Govt., N.Y.C., 1965-74; health unit coordinator Polyclinic Med. Ctr., Harrisburg, Pa., 1978-81, St. Joseph's Hosp., Tucson, 1981-86; acctg. technician Agrl. Research Service, Dept. Agr., Tucson, 1984—; v.p. Tucson Employees Benefit Assn., 1984-85. Recipient Woman On The Move award YWCA, Tucson, 1985. Mem. Nat. Assn. Health Unit Coordinators, Nat. Assn. Female Execs., Federally Employed Women, Fed. Women's Program (alt. rep.), Phi Theta Kappa. Democrat. Baptist. Club: Federally Employed Women (com. chairperson 1985—) (Tucson). Avocations: writing; singing; public speaking.

FAISON, DELPHINE ANN, personnel coordinator; b. Fairbanks, Alaska, Nov. 5, 1945; d. Harry Bernard and Ruth Eleanor (Avey) Palmer; m. Dennis Michael Faison, May 18, 1985. BA in English, U. Hawaii, 1969. Lien supr. Oreg. Dept. Welfare, Salem, 1970-71, welfare worker, 1971-72, adminstrv. supr., 1972-73; procedures analyst Spokane (Wash.) Sch. Dist. #81, 1974-76; personnel asst. Fidelity Mut. Savs., Spokane, 1976-78; personnel adminstr. Gifford-Hill & Co., Spokane, 1978-81; personnel supr. Snohomish County Pub. Utility Dist., Everett, Wash., 1981-83; affirmative action coordinator Wash. Water Power Co., Spokane, 1983—; instr. Inst. Extended Learning Spokane Community Coll., 1986—; EEO cons. J.M. Glasc, Spokane, 1986—. Advisor Jr. Achievers, Spokane, 1980-81; founder, chmn. Inland Empire Affirmative Action Coalition, Spokane, 1984-85; commr. Spokane City Civil Service Commn., Spokane, 1987—; apptd. to Gov.'s Affirmative Action Policy Com., 1988—. Recipient Meritorious Achievement award Edison Electric Inst., 1987. Mem. Pacific NW Personnel Mgmt. (assoc. dir., superior merit 1987), Am. Soc. Personnel Adminstrn. (pres., achievement award for creative excellence 1986), Am. Assn. Affirmative Action (Wash. state rep. 1987). Lodge: Eagles. Office: The Washington Water Power Co E 1411 Mission PO Box 3727 Spokane WA 99202

FAISON, LOIS PARKER, marketing executive; b. Chgo., Oct. 25, 1929; d. Ross I. and Lois B. (Harger) Parker; m. Edmund Winston J. Faison; children: Charles, Dorothy, Barbara. BA, U. Hawaii, 1971, MA, 1973. Pres. Lois Faison Research, Honolulu, 1968-73, East West Research Design, Kailua, Hawaii, 1973—; exec. v.p. Scandata Hawaii Inc.; ptnr. Adwatch Hawaii Inc. Editor: Hawaii Advt. Agy. Directory, 1985-88, Mktg. Sci. Jour.; contbr. articles on mktg. to profl. jours. Mem. Am. Mktg. Assn., Small Bus. Hawaii, Pacific and Asia Affairs Council, Soc. Corp. Planners, Am. Acad. Advt., Women in Communications (bd. dirs.), Hawaii C. of C., Japan-Am. Soc. Lodge: Soroptimist (bd. dirs.). Office: 735 Bishop St Suite 235 Honolulu HI 96813

FAJARDO, KATHARINE LYNN, public relations executive, former mining company executive, actress; b. Akron, Ohio, Mar. 19, 1951; d. Edwin Murray and Diane (Zabiegalski) H.; B.A., Johns Hopkins U., 1973; M.B.A., U. Calif.-Irvine, 1987. Dir. pub. affairs council Electronic Industries Assn.,

Washington, 1974-75; pension cons. Proskauer, Rose, Goetz & Mendelsohn, N.Y.C., 1976-77; sr. mktg. cons. The Equitable Life Assurance Soc., N.Y.C., 1977-78; dir. advt., assoc. dir. public affairs St. Joe Minerals Corp., N.Y.C., 1979-82, mgr. communications projects, 1982-83; computer cons., 1984-86; client services mgr. Burson-Marstellar, N.Y.C., 1988—; actress, 1983—; leading roles include Goodbye Charlie, Picnic, Witness for the Prosecution. Recipient Nicholson award, 1980, 81; named Best Supporting Actress, Orange County, Calif., 1983. Mem. Am. Mgmt. Assn., Pub. Relations Soc. Am. Home: 16 Forest Hill Rd West Norwalk CT 06850

FAJARDO, TERESA ANA GUZMAN, transportation company executive; b. Boyaca, Columbia, Dec. 1, 1938; d. Elias Campo Novoa and Luisa Maria Uzcategui; m. Guillermo Alfredo Guzman, Aug. 23, 1958 (div. Oct. 1978); children: Jose, Cristina, Liliana, Rodrigo. BS in Bus. Adminstrn., Universidad Nacional, Bogota, Colombia, 1957. Ocean export mgr. Fla. Internat. Forwarding, Miami, 1969-74; pres., owner Olympic Internat. Freight Forwarders, Miami, 1974—. Republican. Roman Catholic. Home: 11550 SW 97th St Miami FL 33172 Office: Olympic Internat Freight Forwarders 7300 NW 56th St Miami FL 33166

FAKES, BONNIE MARIE, English language educator; b. Murfreesboro, Tenn., Oct. 2, 1945; d. George W. and Marie (Turner) DeHoff; m. Ray Travis Fakes, Oct. 2, 1971; children: Travis Ray, Laura Marie, Paul Tray, Matthew Turner, Bonnie Beth. BA summa cum laude, Magic Valley Christian Coll., 1964; MA, Mid. Tenn. State U., 1965, postgrad., 1975-76; postgrad., Peabody Coll., 1966. Cert. tchr., Tenn. Med. sec. Murfreesboro (Tenn.) Med. Clinic, 1964-65; history tchr. David Lipscomb High Sch., Nashville, 1965-66; entertainer Dept. Def., Vietnam and Thailand, 1967; pubs. asst. DeHoff Pubs., Murfreesboro, 1967; admissions counselor Cumberland U., Lebanon, Tenn., 1967-73; English tchr. Lebanon High Sch., 1973—; space ambassador Nat. Aero. and Space Adminstrn., Washington, 1985—, finalist Tenn. Tchr. in Space, 1985; lectr. U.S. Space Found., Colorado Springs, Colo., 1987; cons. in field, 1985-87. Author: The District Governor in Action; editor: Teacher in Space Cookbook, 1986; contbr. articles to profl. jours. Active various state and local campaigns. Mem. NEA, Tenn. Edn. Assn. (Service citation 1986), Wilson County Edn. Assn., Nat. Council Tchrs. of English, Tenn. Council Tchrs. of English, Nat. Fedn. Bus. and Profl. Women (pres. Murfreesboro 1975), DAR. Democrat. Mem. Ch. Christ. Home: Rt 4 Box 375 Cairo Bend Rd Lebanon TN 37087

FALCO, JOANN, independent fundraising consultant, educator; b. N.Y.C., Aug. 9, 1953; d. Joseph J. and Mary J. Falco. BA summa cum laude in English, Barry Coll., 1974, MA, 1976; EdD., U. Miami, 1987. Asst. dir. Fla. Pub. Interest Research Group, U. Miami, Fla., 1976-79, adminstrv. aide to asst. v.p. devel., 1980-81; prof. English Dade Community Coll., 1985—; ind. devel. cons., Washington and Miami, 1981—.

FALCO, MARIA JOSEPHINE, political scientist, academic administrator; b. Wildwood, N.J., July 7, 1932; d. John J. and Mafalda M. (Barbieri) F. A.B., Immaculata (Pa.) Coll., 1954; Fulbright scholar, U. Florence, Italy, 1954-55; M.A., Fordham U., 1958; Ph.D., Bryn Mawr (Pa.) Coll., 1963; postdoctoral research fellow, Yale, 1965-66; NSF grantee, U. Mich., summer 1968. Instr., asst. prof. history and polit. sci. Immaculata Coll., Pa., 1957-63; asst. prof. polit. sci. Washington Coll., Chestertown, Md., 1963-64; research asst. Genevieve Blatt; candidate for U.S. Senator from Genevieve Blatt, Pa., 1964-65; asst. prof., assoc. prof. polit. sci. Le Moyne Coll., Syracuse, N.Y., 1966-73; chmn. polit. sci. dept. Le Moyne Coll., 1967-73; prof. polit. sci. Stockton State Coll., Pomona, N.J., 1973-76; chmn. social and behavioral scis. faculty U. Tulsa, 1976-79; dean Coll. Arts and Scis., Loyola U., New Orleans, 1979-85; prof. polit. sci. Loyola U., New Orleans, 1985-86; v.p. acad. affairs DePauw U., Greencastle, Ind., 1986-88, prof. polit. sci., 1988—. Author: Truth and Meaning in Political Science: An Introduction to Political Inquiry, 1973, Bigotry!: Ethnic, Machine and Sexual Politics in a Senatorial Election, 1980; editor: Through the Looking-Glass: Epistemology and the Conduct of Political Inquiry: An Anthology, 1979; Feminism and Epistemology: Approaches to Research in Women and Politics, 1987; also articles.; cons. editor: Political Parties and the Civic Action Groups. Pres. Syracuse chpt. New Democratic Coalition, 1970-71. Named Outstanding Educator in U.S., 1975; Faculty fellow in state and local politics Nat. Center for Edn. in Politics, 1964. Mem. Womens Caucus Polit. Sci. (pres. 1976), Am. Polit. Sci. Assn. (mem. Benjamin Evans Lippincott award com. 1976, chmn. sect. program com. 1975, mem. com. acad. freedom and profl. ethics), Midwestern Polit. Sci. Assn. (mem. com. status of women), Northeastern Polit. Sci. Assn., SW Polit. Sci. Assn. (outstanding conv. paper com.), AAUP (v.p. LeMoyne chpt. 1971-72), Founds. Polit. Theory Group, Common Cause. Roman Catholic. Home: 801 Shadowlawn Ave Greencastle IN 46135 Office: DePauw U Asbury Hall Greencastle IN 46135

FALCON, KAREN GAY, designer, linens manufacturer; b. N.Y.C., Jan. 31, 1949; d. Joseph Albert Falcon and Olcay Kent. AA, Pierce Coll., 1970; BA, Calif. State U., Los Angeles, 1972. Sales mgr. Animan Designs, Los Angeles, 1972-76; pres. Kare-Free, Los Angeles, 1976-79; founder, chief exec. officer Hollywood Nights, Inc., Los Angeles, 1979-87; gen. mgr. Dresher Linens/Hollywood Nights div. Dresher, Inc., 1987—; cons. European mktg. Magma Heimtex, Friesenheim, Fed. Republic Germany, 1985—; seminar speaker SBA, Los Angeles, 1982—. Sponsor Soc. for Prevention Cruelty to Animals, Los Angeles, since 1980—. Mem. Nat. Bath, Bed and Linen Assn., Waterbed Mfrs. Assn. (speaker 1977—, best trade show exhibit awards 1981, 83, 84, 85, 86), Nichiren Shoshu Am. Democrat. Avocations: travel, music. Office: Hollywood Nights Inc 1930 E 15th St Los Angeles CA 90021

FALCONE, NOLA MADDOX, financial company executive; b. Augusta, Ga., July 8, 1939; d. Louia Vernon and Geneva Elizabeth (Fox) Maddox; m. Charles Anthony Falcone, Dec. 6, 1968; 1 child, Charles Maddox. B.A., Duke U., 1961; M.B.A., U. Pa., 1966. Security analyst, portfolio mgr. pension and personal trust dept. Chase Manhattan Bank, N.Y.C., 1961-63, 66-70; investment officer personal trust dept. Chase Manhattan Bank, 1968-70; portfolio mgr. Lieber & Co., 1974-75; br. mgr., registered rep. Lieber & Co., Arlington, Va., 1978-79; portfolio mgr. Lieber & Co., Harrison, N.Y., 1979-80; ptnr. Lieber & Co., 1981—; pres. Evergreen Total Return Fund, Inc., Lieber & Co., 1985—; dir. Saxon Woods Asset Mgmt. Corp., Harrison. Mem. fin. com. Jr. League, Scarsdale, N.Y., 1972-75; trustee 1st Bapt. Ch. of White Plains, N.Y., 1973-74; numerous additional vol. activities. Mem. Fin. Analysts Soc. Democrat.

FALCONER, HANNAH JEAN, librarian; b. Collinsville, Ill., Nov. 15, 1933; d. Thomas Charles Sr. and Fannie Lula (Askew) Lott; m. Raymond N. Falconer, June 12, 1960; children: Leona Alisa Falconer Franklin, Carolyn Anita Falconer Brown, Maria Elizabeth. BA, Wilberforce U., 1955; MS, So. Ill. U., 1976. Cert. secondary tchr., media specialist. Tchr. English Lovejoy (Ill.) High Sch., 1956-68; tchr. English East St. Louis (Ill.) Sr. High Sch., 1968-71, asst. librarian, 1971-76, librarian, 1976—. Tchr. catechism St. Joseph Ch., East St. Louis, 1985—, treas. aux., 1982-84, sec., 1984-86, pres., 1986—. Mem. Am. Fedn. Tchrs., Ill. Assn. Black Vocat. Educators, NAACP, Alpha Kappa Alpha (25 yrs. service award 1984). African Methodist Episcopal Zion. Home: 402 Gray Blvd East Saint Louis IL 62205

FALK, ALMA MARTHA, retired educator; b. Chgo., Apr. 18, 1910; d. Henry and Alma (Wolowski) Weihofen; cert. Chgo. Tchrs. Coll., 1932; B.A., George Washington U., 1937, M.A., 1957; postgrad. Howard U.; m. James E. Curry, Apr. 28, 1934 (dec. Aug. 1972); 1 dau., Aileen Curry-Cloonan; m. 2d, Byron A. Falk, Nov. 22, 1966 (dec. Mar. 1984). Tchr., Hull House, Chgo., 1930-32; social worker Ill. Relief Commn., 1932-35; tchr. elem. sch., Chgo., 1937-38, 46-47; office mgr. law firms in P.R. and Washington, 1948-53; elem. tchr. Jr. Village Sch., Washington, 1953-57; reading coordinator Washington Public Schs., 1957-72; instr. George Washington Reading Clinic, 1957-66; pres. Greater Washington Reading Council, 1966-67. Vol. asst. CD Milk Sta. Program, San Juan, P.R., 1942-46; instr. Urban Service Corps. of Vols., 1952-56; bd. dirs. Internat. Student House, Washington, 1980—; mem. Nat. Capitol Area Retiree Council, 1987—. Recipient citation White House Conf. on Children, 1962. Mem. AAUW (chmn. edn. com. Washington br. 1959-61, dir. 1976-80), Nat. Mil. Wives, Internat. Reading Assn., Am. Fedn. Tchrs., Women's Internat. League for Peace and Freedom, Washington Tchrs. Union (rep. reading specialists 1968-70), Am. Humanist Assn., UN Assn., Internat. Platform Assn., Phi Delta Gamma. Clubs: George Washington U. (charter), Army and Navy (Washington). Avocations: published and recorded lyricist and song writer. Home: 922 24th St NW Washington DC 20037

FALK, BARBARA ANN, financial analyst b. Eugene, Oreg., Feb. 1, 1944; d. Everett Henry and Phyllis Ruth (Wetgen) F.; student So. Oreg. State Coll., 1962-63; A.S., Lane Community Coll., 1971. Accounts receivable bookkeeper Junction City Implement Co. (Oreg.), 1963-64, Eugene Farmers' Co-op, 1964-65; bookkeeper Chef Francisco, Inc., Eugene, 1978-79, sr. acct., 1979, acctg. supr., 1980-84, corp. fin. analyst, 1984—. Mem. acctg. adv. com. Lane Community Coll., 1982—, chmn., 1983-85. Mem. Nat. Assn. Female Execs., Nat. Assn. Accts. (dir. chpt. 1971-79, pres. chpt. 1979-80, nat. dir. 1981-83. Pacific N.W. council prin. 1983-84, Eugene-Springfield chpt. Most Valuable Mem. 1979, 82), Eugene-Springfield Credit Assocs. (dir. 1978-82), Am. Mgmt. Soc. Republican. Baptist. Home: 140 Tatum Ln Eugene OR 97404

FALK, ELIZABETH MOXLEY, opera and theatre producer; b. Memphis, Sept. 21, 1942; d. Warren Luke and Elizabeth Ann (Beshears) Moxley; m. Lee H. Falk, Dec. 31, 1976. Dir. mktg. Chesebrough-Pond's Internat., N.Y.C. and Beirut, 1961-65; account exec. Lintas Advt., Durban, Republic South Africa, 1965-67; mgr. mktg. Revlon Inc., N.Y.C., 1969-72; account supr. BBDO Advt. Inc., N.Y.C., 1972-75; dir. new product devel. Alexandra de Markoff, N.Y.C., 1975-79; producer Concert Opera Manhattan, N.Y.C., 1986—; producer, stage mgr., co. mgr. Vineyard Opera Theatre, N.Y.C., 1986—; assoc. producer New Artists Coalition, N.Y.C., 1986—; ind. producer Elizabth Moxley Falk Presents, N.Y.C., 1987—; cons. casting Met. Opera; artistic cons. New Artists Coalition, Vineyard Theatre, Newport (R.I.) Music Festival; chmn. project Am. Landmark Festivals at Carnegie Hall, N.Y.C., 1988; v.p. Provincetown Acad. Living Arts, Turo, Mass.; adv. bd. Castle Hill Sch. Arts, Truro, Mass., Northwood Inst., Mich. and Tex. Author: The Evil Within, 1980, Mirror Images, 1981; playwright: Goldsmith's Last Rites, 1983, White Tie and Veils, 1984. Advisor Cranston for Senate, Calif., 1980, 86, Badillo for Congress, N.Y.C., 1972, 74. Mem. Women's Project Am. Place Theatre, Nat. Assn. Female Execs., Mystery Writers Am., Found. Extension-Devel. Am. Profl. Theatre, Alliance Resident Theatres, Cen. Opera Services. Democrat. Home and Office: 7 W 81st St #12C New York NY 10024

FALK, JUSTINA CHEN, advertising executive; b. Taipei, Republic of China, May 30, 1951; came to U.S., 1976; d. Liang Yih and Helen Y.Y. (Lee) Chen; m. Edward Falk. BBA in Acctg., Nat. Chengchi U., Taipei, 1973; M in Profl. Acctg., U. Tex., 1978. CPA, Tex. Systems analyst Ministry Fin., Taipei, 1973-76; auditor, cons. Price Waterhouse & Co., Houston, 1978-80; cons. CEXEC, Inc. for Dept. Energy, Houston, 1980-81; fin. analyst Hydril Co., Houston, 1981-82; asst. city controller City of Houston, 1982; pres. Graphics and Advt. Agy., Houston, 1983—; owner Gift World, Baytown, Tex., 1986—; Mem. U.S. Dept. Commerce's Nat. Adv. Bd. of Minority Bus. Devel. Agy. Publ., mng. editor mag. Asian Panorama, 1983-86; contbg. writer Issues Mag., 1981-86. Founder, 1st pres. Tex. Asian Rep. Caucus, 1985-86; exec. bd. dirs. Tex. Fedn. Rep. Women, 1985-86. Recipient Small Bus. award Houston Minority Bus. Devel. Agy., Houston, 1985. Mem. Tex. Soc. CPA's, Issues Research and Ednl. Found. (bd. dirs. 1981—). Methodist. Office: Graphics and Advt Agy 2600 SW Freeway Suite 1001 Houston TX 77098

FALK, MIRI, urban planner; b. Tel Aviv, Israel, Dec. 11, 1947; came to U.S., 1975, naturalized, 1983; d. Nachman and Devora (Fineberg) Bar-Shalom; m. Yeshayahu Arie Falk, Apr. 10, 1975; children—Tomer Menachem, Idan Dor. B.S. in Civil Engring., Technion Inst., Israel, 1974; M.Urban Planning, NYU, 1981. Profl. engr., Israel. Engr., Urban Planning Dept., Tel Aviv, 1973-75; asst. traffic mgr. Govt. Israel, N.Y.C., 1976-81; fin., planning coordinator Ivy Hill Park Corp., N.Y.C., 1982—. Served with Israeli Army, 1966-68. Mem. Israel Architects and Engrs., Nat. Assn. Female Execs., Am. Planning Assn. Avocations: painting, art, music.

FALK, WENDY MARILYN, industrial engineer; b. Bronx, N.Y., May 28, 1959; d. Max and Felicia (Eisenbaum) Gruber; m. Jay S. Falk. B in Indsl. Engring. Gen. Motors Inst., 1982; postgrad. Poly. U., Bklyn. From indsl. engr. to sr. indsl. engr. Gen. Motors Co., Tarrytown, N.Y., 1982—. N.Y. State Regents scholar Gen. Motors Inst., Flint, Mich., 1977-82. Mem. Am. Prodn. and Inventory Control Soc. (local pres. 1985-86, nat. Silver Circle award 1984), Am. Inst. Indsl. Engrs. (local bd. dirs. 1985-86), Soc. Mfg. Engrs., Soc. Women Engrs., Nat. Assn. Female Execs., Alpha Pi Mu. Jewish. Avocations: reading, travel, needlework. Home: PO Box 889 Natick MA 01760 Office: CPC Div Gen Motors Corp 199 Beekman Ave N Tarrytown NY 10591

FALKE, BETTY LOUISE NEWMAN, accountant; b. Llano, Tex., Dec. 1, 1946; d. Travis Alger and Edith Lucile (Tate) Newman; m. Vernon George Mangold (div. July 1981); 1 child, Ian Keith; m. Joseph Renford Falke, Jan. 24, 1987; 1 child, Samantha May. Student, San Antonio Jr. Coll.; BBA, U. Tex., San Antonio, 1985. Data claims analyst Blue Cross/Blue Shield, San Antonio, 1980-82; regional sec., acct. BioMed. Applications, San Antonio, 1982-83; with acctg. dept. Comprehensive Bus. Services, Boerne, Tex., 1983-85; acct. Cadwalladder Ins. Agy., San Antonio, 1986, Data Processing Support, Inc., San Antonio, 1987—, Archive Retrieval Systems, Inc., San Antonio, 1987—; pvt. practice acctg. San Antonio, 1987—. Vol. San Antonio Metro. Ministries, 1987—, Boy Scouts of Am., San Antonio, 1978—; mem. Am. Luth. Women, San Antonio, 1972—. Recipient scholarship Women in Bus., 1983. Mem. Nat. Assn. Accts., Leon Springs Merchants Assn. Republican. Lodge: Hermann Sons. Home and Office: 25403 Brewer Dr San Antonio TX 78257

FALKENBERG, MARY ANN THERESA, realtor; b. Chgo., Dec. 8, 1931; d. Joseph and Catherine (Bausch) Haselsteiner; student Barat Coll., 1953; m. Charles V. Falkenberg, Jr., Apr. 9, 1955; children—Catherine, Grace Ann, Susan Marie, Charles V., Robert, Thomas, Martin, Mary, Elizabeth, Joseph. Tchr. piano, 1946-73; organist St. Thomas of Villanova Ch., 1960—, choir dir., 1960—; sales staff Quinlan & Tyson, Realtors, Inc., Palatine, Ill., 1970-77; pres., co-owner, broker, mgr. Assos. Realty Corp., Palatine, 1978—. Named Palatine Woman of Yr., Suburban Press Found., 1962; cert. home protection cons. Mem. Women in Mgmt., Am. Mgmt. Assn., Ill. Assn. Realtors (life mem. two million dollar club, mem. three million dollar club), Nat. Assn. Realtors (accredited profl. residential appraiser, cert. real property appraiser), Nat. Assn. Female Execs., N.W. Suburban Bd. Realtors (edn. com. 1977-78, non-resident com. 1982, broker-lawyer com. 1986-88, grievance com. 1988), MAP (bd. dirs. 1986-88, sec. 1988), Women in Sales, Barat Coll. Alumni Assn. Club: Women's. Republican. Roman Catholic. Home: 517 Warwick St Palatine IL 60067 Office: 240 E Northwest Hwy Palatine IL 60067

FALKSEN, SUZANNE CATHERINE MARGARET, data processing executive; b. N.Y.C., Nov. 3, 1947; d. Catherine (Depke) Marsh; m. James Allen Falksen, Mar. 16, 1967 (div. June 1979). AB, Vassar Coll., 1968. Registered land surveyor. Faculty Boston Coll., Chestnut Hill, Mass., 1969-70; pres. Earth Umbra, Nashua, N.H., 1972-74; survey party chief City of Phoenix, Ariz., 1976-77; applications systems mgr. Engring. Automation, Chandler, Ariz., 1977-80; data processing mgr. Estimatic Corp., Englewood, Colo., 1981-82; mgr. pipeling mapping MSM Cons., Denver, 1982; exec. v.p. Applied Engring. Assocs., Las Cruces, N.Mex., 1983—; systems mgr. Contel Spacecom, Las Cruces, 1982—. Republican. Mormon. Office: Contel Spacecom PO Box 235 Las Cruces NM 88004

FALLCREEK, STEPHANIE JEAN, state agency administrator; b. Springfield, Mo., May 6, 1950; d. Martha Jean (Barton) Wertz; m. Jerry R. Tillman, 1987; 1 child, Christopher. AB in History, U. Okla., 1972; MSW in Social Welfare, U. Calif., Berkeley, 1974, DSW in Social Welfare, 1984. Dir. Inst. for Geron. Research and Edn., N.Mex. State U., Las Cruces, 1983-87, N.Mex. State Agy. on Aging, 1987—; pres. Fallcreek & Assocs., Santa Fe, 1982—; sr. assoc. Age Wave Inc., Emeryville, Calif., 1985-87; cons. various hosps. and health care orgns.; speaker confs. and trade shows; guest radio and TV programs on aging. Author: (with others) A Healthy Old Age: A Sourcebook for Health Promotion with Older Adults, Health Promotion and Aging: Strategies for Action, Health Promotion and Aging: A National Resource of Selected Programs; also articles and book chpts. Danforth fellow, 1972-78. Mem. Geron. Soc. Am., Am. Soc. on Aging, Nat. Council on the Aging, Soc. for Values in Higher Edn., Nat. Assn. Social Workers, AAUW (corp. rep.). Home: Rt 5 Box 3606 Santa Fe NM 87501

FALLER, JUNE, asset management executive; b. Cin., June 2, 1940; d. Michael John and Viola M. (Bauman) Fries; m. James J. Faller, Aug. 18, 1936; children: Stephen J., Gary T., Michael C. Lic. real estate, ins., security agt. Real estate sales agt. Schneider Realtor, Cin., 1961-79; pres. Fair Acres Devel. Corp., Cin., 1979-82; regional v.p. A.L. Williams Co., Cin., 1982—. Pres. St. Ignatius Parish Council, Cin., 1975-80. Roman Catholic. Club: Women Art (Cin.). Home: 4249 W Fork Rd Cincinnati OH 45247 Office: Faller Williams & Assocs 5201 Northbend Rd Cincinnati OH 45247

FALLER, SUSAN GROGAN, lawyer; b. Cin., Mar. 1, 1950; d. William M. and Jane (Eagen) Grogan; m. Kenneth R. Faller, June 8, 1973; children—Susan Elisabeth, Maura Christine, Julie Kathleen. B.A., U. Cin., 1972; J.D., U. Mich., 1975. Bar: Ohio 1975, U.S. Dist. Ct. (so. dist.) Ohio 1975, U.S. Ct. Appeals (6th cir.) 1982, U.S. Ct. Claims 1982, U.S. Supreme Ct. 1982, U.S. Tax Ct. 1984. Assoc. Frost & Jacobs, Cin., 1975-82, ptnr. 1982—; v.p. exec. com. Women Entrepreneurs' Conf., Cin., 1984—. Assoc. editor Mich. Law Rev., 1974-75; contbg. author: LDRC 50-State Survey of Media Libel and Privacy Law, 1982—. V.p. Summit Alumni Council, Cin., 1982-85, bd. dirs. 1983-85; trustee Newman Found., Cin., 1980-86, Catholic Social Service, Cin., 1984—, nominating com., 1985—, chmn., 1986-88. Mem. Fed. Bar Assn., ABA, Ohio Bar Assn., Cin. Bar Assn. (various coms.), Assn. Profl. Women, Greater Cin. Women Lawyer's Assn., U. Cin. Alumni Assn., U. Mich. Alumni Assn., Mortar Bd., Phi Beta Kappa, Theta Phi Alpha. Roman Catholic. Clubs: Leland Yacht (Mich.); Lawyers, College, Clifton Meadows (Cin.). Home: 5 Belsaw Pl Cincinnati OH 45220 Office: Frost & Jacobs 2500 Central Trust Ctr 201 E 5th St Cincinnati OH 45202

FALLIN, BARBARA MOORE, personnel director; b. Paducah, Ky., Nov. 12, 1939; d. James Perry Moore and Margaret Arminta (Winn) Kastner; m. Jon Ball, Jan. 21, 1961 (div. July 1963); m. Ralph Daniel Fallin, May 23, 1965; children: Wade, Cathi, Cindy Pergrim, Danielle. Student, Fla. Christian Coll., 1957-58. Exec. asst. to controller The Borden Co., Tampa, Fla., 1958-65; mktg. asst. Martin-Marietta Corp., Shalimar, Fla., 1965-71; asst. to pres. Browning-Marine, Ft. Walton Beach, Fla., 1973; personnel coordinator Keltec Fla., Shalimar, 1974-78; personnel mgr. Metric Systems Corp., Ft. Walton Beach, 1979-87, personnel dir., 1987—; Mem. Job Service Employer Com., Ft. Walton Beach, 1985—; mem. adv. bd. Bay Area Vocat.-Tech. Ctr., Ft. Walton Beach, 1988—. First mistress Krewe of Bowlegs, Ft. Walton Beach, 1983-84, first lady to cap'n Billy Bowlegs XXXII, 1986-87. Mem. Am. Soc. Personnel Adminstrn., Emerald Coast Personnel Mgmt. Assn. (pres. 1986-88, bd. dirs. 1988—). Republican. Methodist. Club: Mardi Gras (Ft. Walton Beach). Office: Metric Systems Corp 645 Anchors St Fort Walton Beach FL 32548

FALLON, JANICE ANN, insurance underwriter; b. Jersey City, N.J., Sept. 13, 1949; d. John Frederick and Regina Teresa (Russell) F.; divorced; children—Benjamin James, Michael Joseph. File clk., gen. clk. Chubb Group Ins. Cos., N.Y.C., 1967-70, policy typist, 1970-71, asst. underwriter, 1972-76, underwriter mandated bus., 1976-77, retro-dividend analyst, 1977-80, spl. risk underwriter, 1980—. Mem. Nat. Assn. Female Execs. Democrat. Roman Catholic. Home: 2600 Kennedy Blvd Jersey City NJ 07306 Office: 15 Mountain View Rd Warren NJ 07060

FALLON, KRISTINE K., architect, computer applications consultant; b. Bklyn., Jan. 28, 1949; d. William Peter and Kathleen L. (O'Connell) F. BS, Georgetown U., 1970; MArch, Va. Poly. Inst. and State U., 1977. Architect Skidmore, Owings & Merrill, Chgo., 1977-80, computer prodn. mgr., 1981-82, assoc., 1982-84, mgr. Chgo. Computer Group, 1983-84; dir. computer graphics A. Epstein and Sons Internat., Inc., Chgo., 1984, v.p., 1985-86; pres. Computer Tech. Mgmt., Inc. subs. A. Epstein and Sons Internat., Inc., Chgo., 1986—; coordinator design confs. Designing for Electronic Offices, 1984, 85; lectr. in field. Exhibitor Chicago Women in Architecture Progress and Evolution 1974-84 Chgo. Hist. Soc., 1984; editorial bd. A/E Systems Report, 1987. Advisor Archtl. Tech. Adv. Com. Triton Coll, River Grove, Ill., 1985—; industry sponsor Chgo. Consortium Colls. and Univs. Vocat. Instr. Practicum, 1986. Mem. AIA (Chgo. chpt. bd. dirs. 1985-89, v.p. 1985-87, del. Ill. council 1987-89), Chgo. Women in Architecture (pres. 1980-82, v.p. 1982-84). Office: Computer Tech Mgmt Inc 600 W Fulton St Chicago IL 60606

FALLS, KATHLEENE JOYCE, photographer; b. Detroit, July 3, 1949; d. Edgar John and Acelia Olive (Young) Haley; m. Donald David Falls, June 15, 1974; children: Daniel John, David James. Student, Oakland Community Coll., 1969-73, Winona Sch. Profl. Photography, 1973-80. Printer Guardian Photo, Novi, Mich., 1967-69; printer, supr. quality control N.Am. Photo, Livonia, Mich., 1969-76; free lance photographer Livonia, 1969-76; owner, pres. Kathy Falls, Inc., Carleton, Mich., 1976—; instr. Monroe County Community Coll. Continuing Edn., 1981-83; nat. artisan judge Congl. High Sch. Art Competition, 1985—; owner Picture Perfect, Carleton, 1987. Author: Emergency Print Retouching for Photographers; contbr. articles to profl. jours. Represented in spl. categories in the Nat. Loan Collection, Profl. Photographers Am., 1980, 81, 83, 87; represented in permanent collections Monroe County Hist. Mus., Archives Notre Dame. Catechist St. Patrick's Ch., Carleton, 1984-87; active Big Bros. and Big Sisters, Monroe, 1986-87; corr. sec. Monroe Women's Ctr, 1986—. Recipient numerous awards granted by profl. photographic orgns. Mem. Detroit Profl. Photographers Assn. (bd. dirs. 1987—, artisan chmn. 1981-82, Best of Show award 1981, 83), Profl. Photographers Mich. (artisian chairperson 1982-83, Best of Show award 1976, 81, Artist of Yr. 1980), Profl. Photographers Am. (cert. profl. photog. specialist), Am. Photographic Artisans Guild (council mem., bd. dirs. 1987—), Monroe County Fine Arts Council, Monroe C. of C. (chmn. council women bus. owners), Nat. Orgn. Women Bus. Owners, Nat. Assn. Female Execs. Democrat. Roman Catholic. Club: Monroe Camera. Home and Office: 14554 Grafton Carleton MI 48117

FALLS, WALDTRAUT MARGRETE GOETZE, medical librarian; b. N.Y.C., June 28, 1941; d. Otto Paul and Anna Irma (Zander) Goetze; A.B., State U. N.Y. at Albany, 1963, M.A. (scholar), 1964; M.S., Columbia U., 1967; m. John Allen Falls, Jr.; children—John Francis, Michael Gregory. Asst. advt. librarian Curtis Pub. Co., N.Y.C., 1964-65; library asso. N.Y. U. Commerce Library, N.Y.C., 1965-67; librarian, instr. N.Y.C. Community Coll., Bklyn., 1967-69, 70, 73-75; med. librarian Victory Meml. Hosp., Bklyn., 1975-87, clin. librarian, U. Medicine and Dentistry N.J., Newark, 1987—. Mem. ALA, Med. Library Assn., Bklyn., Queens and S.I. Health Scis. Librarians, N.Y. Library Club (life). Home: 328 78th St Brooklyn NY 11209 Office: Univ Hosp Rm 346 UMDNJ 20 12th Ave Newark NJ 07103

FAMIGLIETTI, LISA, speech language pathologist; b. Ft. Bragg, N.C., July 14, 1954; d. Carmen Anthony Famiglietti and Edna M. (Wheatly) Hunt; m. Arthur Quincy Lyon, Aug. 27, 1976 (div. 1981); m. Robert N. Snider Jr., Dec. 3, 1983. BA, Tex. Tech. U., 1975, MS, 1977. Dir. audiol. services Austin (Tex.) State Sch., Tex. Dept. Mental Health and Mental Retardation, 1979-83, clin. dir. speech-lang. services, 1983-87; owner, gen. practitioner Cen. Tex. Audiology and Speech Pathology Services, Austin, 1983—; pres. Live Oak Rehab. Services, Inc., Austin, 1987—. Mem. Am. Speech Lang. Hearing Assn. (mem. task force 1986), Tex. Speech Lang. Hearing Assn. (councillor 1986—, chmn. task force 1983-85), S.W. Apasiology Soc., Phi Kappa Phi, Alpha Lambda Delta. Home: 10810 River Terr Austin TX 78733 Office: Cen Tex Audiology and Speech Pathology Services 3839 Bee Cave Suite 145 Austin TX 78746

FANAROFF, SHERI VAN GREENBY, lawyer; b. N.Y.C., May 10, 1955; d. Stanley Harold and Betty Dorothy (Segal) Van Greenby; m. Paul Albert Fanaroff, May 23, 1982, 1 child, Seth David. Student, U. Geneva, 1974-75; AB, Brown U., 1976; JD with honors, U. N.C., 1979. Bar: N.Y. 1980, N.J. 1984. Assoc. Seward and Kissel, N.Y.C., 1979-84, Corbin Silverman and Sanseverino, N.Y.C., 1984-88; asst. gen. counsel Fred S. James & Co., Inc., N.Y.C., 1988—; Contbr. articles to profl. jours. Mem. ABA, Nat. Assn. Female Execs., Order of Coif. Jewish. Office: Fred S James & Co Inc 1285 Ave of Americas New York NY 10019

FANCHER, HELEN IRENE, former state legislator, rancher, lobbyist; b. Seattle, Mar. 1, 1931; d. Robert Warren and Mary Caroline (Foy) Walker; student U. Wash., 1948, Eastern Wash. U., 1949-50; m. John T. Fancher, Aug. 14, 1950; children—Scott, Donald, Nancy Connelly. Profl. musician, Seattle, Spokane, Wash., 1947; sec.-treas., dir. Pilot Wheel Ranch, Inc., Tonasket, Wash., Three Toed Feedlot, Inc., Quincy, Wash., 1971—; mem. Tri-County Law and Justice Commn., 1970, Okanogan County Planning Commn., 1974; mem. Wash. Ho. of Reps., 1976-82, asst. majority leader, 1981-82. Precinct committeeman Republican party; dir. Agr.-Forestry Leadership Found., 1982; pres. Okanogan County Cow Belles, 1972-73; v.p. Wash. State Cow Belles, 1975-76; mem. Wash. State Timber Tax Adv. Com. mem. Quincy City Planning Commn. and Bd. Appeals; mem. Quincy City Council, 1985-87; mem. Grant County Clean Air Bd., 1985—, chmn.; sec.-treas. Golden Valley Water Assn. Named Hon. State Farmer, Future Farmers Am., 1982. Mem. Nat. Cow Belles and Cattlemen's Assn., Musicians Union, Am. Legis. Exchange Council, Quincy C. of C. (bd. dirs. 1984); Mu Phi Epsilon. Home: 1020 Rd S NW Quincy WA 98848

FANG, ANNA J. H., public relations executive; b. Hong Kong, June 16, 1955; d. Sheng Chung and Cynthia W.M. (Li) F. BA, U. Calif., Santa Cruz, 1984, MA, 1986. News asst. Sta. KLRT-FM, Lake Tahoe, Calif., 1976-82; communications dir. publs., pub. relations Santa Cruz C. of C., 1986—; dir., publicist Arakunen Gallery, Florence, Ore., 1976-82. Co-mgr. Willamette People's Food Co-Op, Eugene, 1976-82; area coordinator Santa Cruz Leads Club, 1986—. Mem. Nat. Assn. Rising Communicators, Pub. Relations Roundtable, Assn. for Asian Studies, Monterey Bay Internat. Trade Assn. (pub. relations dir. 1987). Home: 301 Doris Ave Aptos CA 95003 Office: Santa Cruz Area C of C 105 Cooper St Suite 243 Santa Cruz CA 95060

FANN, GAIL LEE, business educator; b. Hutchinson, Kans., July 31, 1953; d. James L. and Sylvia M. (Bassler) F.; m. Kenneth D. Abbott, Mar. 21, 1978 (div. Aug. 1984). BS magna cum laude, No. Ariz. State U., 1976; MEd, Ariz. State U., 1979, EdD, 1986. Tchr., dept. chair Bradshaw Mountain High Sch., Dewey, Ariz., 1977-80; instr. Yavapai Coll., Prescott, Ariz., 1980-82; pres., tng. dir. Info Ctr., Inc., Prescott, 1982-84; dir. Visions of the Future, Phoenix, 1984-85; faculty assoc. Ariz. State U., Tempe, 1985-86, asst. prof. bus., 1986—; cons. Ray Ryan & Assocs., Scottsdale, Ariz., 1984-86. Co-author 13 instructional packages in office automation and communications, 1981—; contbr. articles and papers to prof. jours. Mem. Internat. Council Small Bus., World Future Soc., Assn. Bus. Communication, Nat. Bus. Edn. Assn., Ariz. Bus. Edn. Assn. (pres. 1983-84, mem. exec. bd. 1978-85). Club: Twilight Toastmasters (Tempe) (sec. 1987—). Office: Ariz State U Tempe AZ 85287

FANNIN, MARIANNE BENJAMIN, banker; b. Providence, Ky., May 28, 1933; d. Oliver kerney and Gwendolyn (Kemp) Benjamin; m. Thomas Newton Fannin, Aug. 28, 1953; children: Mary Todd, Tamara Fannin Knappenberger. AA, Stephens Coll., 1953; student, Ariz. State U., 1973. Research analyst M.R. West Mktg. Research, Phoenix, 1973-81; prin., ptnr. Western Diversified, Phoenix, 1977—; v.p. Fannin Ins., Inc., Phoenix, 1984—; chair Republic Nat. Bank Ariz., Phoenix, 1985—. Active Rep. campaigns, Ariz., 1955—; co-chair Citizens Trans. Com., Phoenix, 1979; chair-elect Maricopa Community Colls. Found. Bd., Phoenix, 1987; bd. dirs. Phoenix Indsl. Devel. Authority, Phoenix, 1982—; mem. women's aux. Goodwill Industries, St. Joseph Hosp. Episcopalian. Home: 77 E Missouri Phoenix AZ 85012 Office: Rep Nat Bank 2020 North Cen Phoenix AZ 85004

FANNING, KATHERINE WOODRUFF, editor; b. Chgo., Oct. 18, 1927; d. Frederick William and Katherine Bower (Miller) Woodruff; m. Marshall Field, Jr., May 12, 1950 (div. 1963); children: Frederick Woodruff, Katherine Woodruff, Barbara Woodruff; m. Lawrence S. Fanning, 1966 (dec. 1971); m. Amos Mathews, Jan. 6, 1984. B.A., Smith Coll., 1949; LL.D. (hon.), Colby Coll., 1979; Litt. D. (hon.), Pine Manor Jr. Coll., 1984; L.H.D. (hon.), Northeastern U., 1984. With Anchorage Daily News, from 1965, editor, pub., 1972-83; editor The Christian Science Monitor, 1983—. Mem. Anchorage Urban Beautification Commn., 1968-71, Alaska Ednl. Broadcasting Commn., 1971-75; dir. Alaska Repertory Theater, 1975-81; pres. Greater Anchorage Community Chest, 1973-74. Recipient Elijah Parish Lovejoy award Colby Coll., 1979; Smith Coll. medal, 1980; Mo. medal of Honor, U. Mo. Journalism award, 1980. Mem. Am. Soc. Newspaper Editors (dir., v.p. 1986), Sigma Delta Chi. Office: The Christian Sci Monitor One Norway St Boston MA 02115 *

FANNING, KAY EILENE, retail cosmetics company executive; b. Springfield, Ohio, Sept. 4, 1942; d. Wilbur J. and Ethel Waddle; B.S., Wittenberg U., 1964; student U. Dayton, summer 1965, Bowling Green U., summer 1966; m. Robert H. Fanning, Feb. 1, 1964; children—Leann Kay, (Robert) Shane, Aaron Carter. Tchr., Shawnee High Sch., Springfield, Ohio, 1964-67; tchr. Clark Tech. Coll., 1967-70; beauty cons. Fashion Two Twenty Cosmetics, Springfield, 1969-70, assoc. dir., 1970-78, dir., 1978, regional mgr. Cher-Beli Creations, Inc., Memphis, 1981-82, v.p., 1982-83; pres. Leana Internat., Inc., 1983—, zone v.p. Contempe Fashions, Kansas City, 1987—. Mem. Clark County Bd. Edn., 1974—, v.p., 1978, pres., 1979; mem. Springfield-Clark County Joint Vocat. Sch. Bd. Edn., 1979—, v.p., 1981-82, 88, pres., 1982—; mem. Clark County Republican Women. Mem. Nat. Assn. Female Execs., Springfield Area C. of C., Alpha Delta Pi. Republican. Baptist. Address: 364 W Jackson Rd Springfield OH 45502

FANSLER, ANNE H., sales executive; b. Knoxville, Tenn., July 21, 1951; d. Alexander Jones and Mary Belle (Lothrap) Harkness; m. David S. Egerton, Apr. 21, 1972 (div. 1979); children: David, Mary. Student, Agnes Scott Coll., Decatur, Ga., 1969-71, U. Tenn., 1971-73. Mktg., advt. mgr. Volunteer Realty, Knoxville, 1975-77; adminstrv. asst. nat. sales Creative Displays, Knoxville, 1977-81; salesperson WEZK Radio, Knoxville, 1981-86, sales mgr., 1988—; sales and mktg. mgr. Cellular One, Knoxville, 1986-87; cons. nat. outdoor advt., Berkline Corp., Morristown, Tenn., 1978-81, U. Tenn., Knoxville C. of C.; speaker nat. convs. Contbr. articles to profl. jours. Bd. dirs. Knoxville Polit. Action Com., 1983—, Knoxville Arts Council, 1981-83, Knoxville Beautification Bd., 1978-83; com. mem. Dogwood Arts Festival, 1982—, United Way, 1977-81. Mem. Ad Club (bd. dirs. 1978-81). Republican. Presbyterian. Home: 538 Broame Rd Knoxville TN 37909 Office: WEZK 825 Central Knoxville TN 37919

FANTACI, MARY KATHRYN, publishing company executive; b. Rochester, N.Y., June 2, 1962; d. Arthur Raymond and Margaret Ann (Lutz) F. BA in English, Holy Cross, 1984; MBA, Suffolk U., 1985-88. Customer service rep. Bank New Eng., Boston, 1984-85; fin. asst. Boston Found., 1985, jr. acct., 1985-86; bus. mgr. Blackwell Sci. Publications, Boston, 1986—. Democrat. Roman Catholic. Office: Blackwell Sci Publs 3 Cambridge Ctr Cambridge MA 02142

FANTON, DOLORES PFRENGLE, pharmacist; b. Rochester, N.Y., June 15, 1952; d. Gerald Charles and Mildred David Pfrengle; m. Kenneth Roy Fanton, Oct. 30, 1982. Degree, Eastman Sch. Music, 1970; BS in Pharmaceutics, SUNY, Buffalo, 1976, BS in Pharmacy, 1976; MBA, U. Rochester, 1981. Registered pharmacist, N.Y. Hosp. pharmacist, supr. Surg. Supply, Rochester, N.Y., 1976-82; engr. solutions Bausch and Lomb, Rochester, N.Y., 1983; pharmacist N.Y. St. Govt., Rochester, 1985—; cons. physicians, Rochester, 1976—.

FANUS, PAULINE RIFE, librarian; b. New Oxford, Pa., Feb. 14, 1925; d. Maurice Diehl and Bernice Edna (Gable) Rife; m. William Edward Fanus, June 20, 1944; children: Irene Weaver, Larry William, Daniel Diehl. BS, Pa. State U., 1945; MLS, Villanova U., 1961; postgrad., Temple U., 1986—. Periodical librarian Tex. Coll. Arts Industries, Kingville, 1945; tchr. nursery sch. Studio Sch., Wayne, Pa., 1953-55; librarian circulation, reference Franklin Inst., Phila., 1963-66; asst. librarian Ursinus Coll., Collegeville, Pa., 1966; catalog librarian, instr. Eastern Coll., St. Davids, Pa., 1967-71; head librarian Agnes Irwin Sch., Rosemont, Pa., 1971—. Book reviewer The Book Report. Mem. AAUP (chpt. sec. Eastern Coll. 1979-71), Pa. Library Assn. Home: Country Club Rd Phoenixville PA 19460 Office: Agnes Irwin Sch PO Box 407 Rosemont PA 19010

FARACE-EPLEY, DIANA MARIA, educator, human relations counselor; b. Bklyn., Jan. 2, 1948; d. Nicholas Vincent and Catherine (Mauro) F.; m. James Pascal Epley, Jr., July 29, 1973. A.A.S., Suffolk County Community Coll., 1968; B.A. in Psychology summa cum laude, St. Leo Coll., 1976; M.A. in Human Relations, Webster U., 1984. Figure cons. Barbara-Wayne Figure Salon, N.Y.C., 1970-71; evening mgr. Nu-Dimensions Figure Salon, N.Y.C., 1971-72; adminstrv. asst. to dir. sales/mktg. Hazletine Corp., Greenlawn, N.Y., 1972-73; faculty City Colls. of Chgo., Zaragoza, Spain, 1973-74, Stratford Women's Coll., Tampa, Fla., 1974; ops. mgr. Stanton & Assocs. Constrn., 1976-78; officer Richard's Auto Grooming, Inc., 1978-79; faculty Florence-Darlington TEC, Florence, S.C., 1979-81, St. Anne's Cath. Elem. Sch., 1982; tutor, tchr., counselor Darlington Acad. (S.C.), 1982; area dir. office occupations Preston Coll. Tech. and Bus. Careers, Columbia, S.C., 1983-84; owner, mental health counselor PMS Research and Peripheral Treatment Clinic, 1985; ednl. resource adviser Davis-Monthan AFB Learning Ctr., Cochise Coll., Sierra Vista, Ariz., 1986—; br. safety monitor 377th CSG Housing Supply (USAF) Ramstein, Fed. Republic Germany, 1987—. Exhibited paintings Sumter Gallery Art, 1983. Benefactor, St. LeBre Missionary for Indians in Utah, 1983-84, Christian Appalachian Project in Ky., 1984—; mem. Florence-Darlington Tech. Coll. Ednl. Found., 1981—. Mem. Secretarial Guild Am., S.C. Ednl. Tchrs. Assn., Sumter Artists Guild, Smithsonian Assocs. Roman Catholic. other: PO Box 6635 APO NY 09012

FARAH, CYNTHIA WEBER, photographer, publisher; b. Long Island, N.Y., June 2, 1949; d. Andrew John and Aria Emma (Jelnikova) Weber; m. James Clifton Farah, Jan. 12, 1974; children—Elise, Alexa. B.A. in Communications, Stanford U., 1971. Prodn. staff Sta. KDBC-TV, El Paso, Tex., 1971-73; v.p. Sanders Co. Advt., El Paso, 1973-74, film critic El Paso Times, 1972-77; free lance photographer, El Paso, 1974—; pres. CM Pub., El Paso, 1981—. Photographer, co-author: Country Music: A Look at the Men Who've Made It, 1982; author: Literature and Landscape: Writers of the Southwest, 1988. Bd. dirs. N. Mex. State U. Mus. Adv. Bd., Las Cruces, 1982—; dir., vice-chmn. Shelter for Battered Women, El Paso, 1982; active Jr. League, 1977—, C. of C. Leadership El Paso Program, 1983-84; mem. El Paso County Hist. Comm., 1984—, vice chmn., 1986, 87, El Paso County Hist. Alliance (v. chmn. 1986—); trustee El Paso Community Found., 1984—; adv. bd. El Paso Arts Resources dept. Recipient Clara Barton Medallion ARC, 1979. Mem. Tex. Profl. Photographers Assn., Stanford U. Alumni Assn. Episcopalian.

FARB, RUTH ANN, banker; b. Long Branch, N.J., Jan. 4, 1939; d. Louis H. and Toba (Vallens) F. BA, Douglass Coll., 1960; postgrad., Rutgers U., 1972-74, Stanford U., 1986. Various positions Fed. Res. Bank, Chgo., 1960-74, asst. v.p., 1974-79, v.p., 1979-86; v.p., chief fin. officer Lakeside Bank, Chgo., 1986—; instr. Stonier Grad. Sch. Banking, New Brunswick, N.J., 1975-77; Am. Inst. Banking, Chgo., 1976-78, 87. Bd. dirs. Sr. Ctrs. of Met. Chgo., 1985—, Jr. Achievement of Met. Chgo., 1985—. Mem. Chgo. Network (bd. dirs. 1984-86), Chgo. Fin. Exchange (bd. dirs. 1979-85, pres. 1983), Robert Morris Assn. (bd. dirs. 1985—). Club: Bankers of Chgo. Lodge: Rotary. Office: Lakeside Bank 141 W Jackson Blvd Chicago IL 60604

FARBER, THERESE ANN, adult education administrator; b. Canton, Ohio, May 20, 1930; d. Fred Paul and Mary Alice (Munter) Jacobs; m. Conrad Myers Farber, Aug. 18, 1973; children: Conrad Joseph, Mary Beth. BS in Edn., St. John Coll., 1960; MA in Ednl. Adminstrn., U. Notre Dame, 1966; postgrad. courses, various u. Tchr. elem. various schs. systems, 1949—; elem. demonstration tchr. Cleve. Diocese, 1955-57, cons. music, 1958-60; cons. arts Va., 1961; cons. spelling bee 1961; prin. elem. Youngstown Diocesan Schs., 1964-70; system-wide dept. chmn. Massillon City (Ohio) Schs., 1976-80; instr. math. Lorn Andrews Jr. High Sch., Massillon, 1980—; dir. adult basic edn. Adult Learning Ctr., Massillon, 1980—; cons. area prins. Youngstown, 1968-70, supr. curriculum com. Youngstown, 1964-70; prin. summer enrichment classes McKinley Mus. Author of sch. annual, 1977-80; bd. dirs. sch. newspaper, 1974-80, dir. transition plan: "Walk Out Proudly", 1979-80. Vol. Literary adult basic edn., Massillon, 1982—, Salvation Army; participant Taft Inst. Kent State U., 1981; active St. Clement Altar and Rosary Soc., St. Peter Guild. Scholar Taft Inst., 1978, 82, 85, Freedom Found., Valley Forge, Pa., 1980, 81, 84-87; recipient spelling Rep. award Youngstown Diocese, 1963, Longevity award Adult Basic Edn. Ohio, 1984, Outstanding Elem. Tchr., Nat. Pub., 1975; named sch. annual Dedicatee, E.A. Jones Jr. High Sch., Massillon. Mem. Ohio Educator's Assn. (vol. 1983-84, sch. rep. 1976-80), Massillon Edn. Assn. (sch. rep.), Assn. Support and Devel. curriculum, Ohio Assn. Adult Edn., Notre Dame Alumni Assn., Notre Dame Acad. Guild and Alumni. Club: Massillon Booster. Home: 8472 Bender SW Navarre OH 44662 Office: Adult Learning Ctr 22 Federal St NE Massillon OH 44646

FARENTHOLD, FRANCES TARLTON, lawyer; b. Corpus Christi, Tex., Oct. 2, 1926; d. Benjamin Dudley and Catherine (Bluntzer) Tarlton; AB, Vassar Coll., 1946; JD, U. Tex., 1949; LLD, Hood Coll., 1973, Boston U., 1973, Regis Coll., 1976, Lake Erie Coll., 1979, Elmira Coll., 1981, Coll. of Santa Fe, 1985; children—Dudley Tarlton, George Edward, Emilie, James Dougherty, Vincent Bluntzer (dec.). Bar: Tex. 1949. Mem. Tex. Ho. of Reps., 1968-72; dir. legal aide Nueces County, 1965-67; asst. prof. law Tex. So. U., Houston; pres. Wells Coll., Aurora, N.Y., 1976-80. Mem. Human Relations Com., Corpus Christi, 1963-68, Corpus Christi Citizen's Com. Community Improvement, 1966-68; mem. Tex. adv. com. to U.S. Commn. on Civil Rights, 1968-76; mem. nat. adv. council ACLU; mem. Orgn. for Preservation Unblemished Shoreline, 1964—; Democratic candidate for Gov. of Tex., 1972; del. Dem. Nat. Conv., 1972, 1st woman nominated to be candidate v.p. U.S., 1972; nat. co-chmn. Citizens to Elect McGovern-Shriver, 1972; chmn. Nat. Women's Polit. Caucus, 1973-75; trustee Vassar Coll., 1975-83; bd. dirs. Texans for a Bilateral Nuclear Weapons Freeze, 1983-84, Fund for Constl. Govt., Ctr. for Devel. Policy, 1983—, Mexican Am. Legal Def. and Ednl. Fund, 1980-83; chmn. Inst. for Policy Studies, 1986—. Recipient Lyndon B. Johnson Woman of Year award, 1973. Mem. State Bar Tex. Office: 1203 Central Bank Bldg 2100 Travis Houston TX 77002

FARINA, ANA BEATRIZ, electronics sales executive; b. Guayaquil, Ecuador, May 16, 1950; came to U.S., 1962; d. Luis A. and Luz Aurora (Rodriguez) Moreira; m. Manuel Jose Farina, Dec. 15, 1979; children: Kevin, Mark. AA, Latin-Am. Inst., 1971. Adminstr. asst. M&T Chem. Inc., N.Y.C., 1971-75; mgr. sales Singer Products Co., N.Y.C., 1975-78; v.p. Argil Internat. Ltd., N.Y.C., 1978-83; pres. KMA Enterprises Inc., Bklyn., 1983—. Mem. Nat. Assn. Female Execs. Roman Catholic.

FARINA, KATHERINE LYNN, information specialist; b. Stamford, Conn., Apr. 20, 1955; d. Frank Gilbert and Katherine Rosella (Wilder) F. BA, Manhattanville Coll., 1977. Mgr. customer service Polycast Tech. Corp., Stamford, 1977-81; researcher Disclosure Inc., N.Y.C., 1981-83; sr. research analyst FIND/SVP, N.Y.C., 1983—. Mem. Societé de Chimie Industrielle, Chem. Mktg. Research Assn., Chemist Club N.Y. Democrat. Roman Catholic. Office: FIND/SVP Info Clearing House 625 Ave Americas New York NY 10011

FARINA, WENDY DIANE, marketing consultant; b. Newark, Jan. 22, 1959; d. Mario Gerard and Lois (Wachman) F. Student, U. London, 1980, Marymount Coll., 1980; BS, U. Ariz., 1981; postgrad., Baruch Coll. CUNY, 1987—. Dept. head, planner Lerner Stores Corp., N.Y.C., 1981-83; class analyst, merchandiser Lane Bryant, Inc. (ltd. corp.), N.Y.C., 1983-84; mgmt. cons. Bell & Co., Inc., Milw., Denver, Balt., Ark., 1984-86, Peat Marwick Main & Co., N.Y.C., 1986—; founder, owner Farina's Favorites, N.Y.C., 1983—. Mem. Nat. Retail Mchts. Assn., Met. Retail Fin. Execs. Assn., Electronic Banking Econs. Soc., Nat. Assn. Female Execs. Home: 425 W 22nd St New York NY 10011 Office: Peat Marwick Main & Co 345 Park Ave New York NY 10154

FARINELLI, JEAN L., public relations firm executive; b. Phila., July 26, 1946; d. Albert J. and Edith M. (Falini) F. B.A., Am. U., Washington, 1968; M.A., Ohio State U., Columbus, 1969. Asst. pub. relations dir. Dow Jones & Co., Inc., N.Y.C., 1969-71; account exec. Carl Byoir & Assocs., Inc., N.Y.C., 1972-74, v.p., 1974-80, sr. v.p., 1980-82; pres. Tracy-Locke/BBDO Pub. Relations, Dallas, 1982-87; pres. Creamer Dickson Basford, Inc., N.Y.C., 1987-88, pres., chief exec. officer, 1988—. Recipient PR CaseBook, PR Reporter, N.H., 1984; Silver Spur, Tex. Pub. Relations Assn., Dallas, 1985. Mem. Pub. Relations Soc. Am. (Silver Anvil award 1980, 81, 85, Excalibur award Houston chpt. 1985, chmn. Counselor's Acad. 1986 Silver Anvil awards, chmn. 1989 Spring Conf. Counselors Acad.), Internat. Assn. Bus. Communicators (Gold Quill award 1985), Women in Communications, Women Execs. in Pub. Relations, Nat. Investor Relations Inst. Clubs: Nat. Arts (N.Y.C.). Home: 333 E 56th St New York NY 10022 Office: Creamer Dickson Basford 1633 Broadway New York NY 10019

FARINHOLT, (MARY) KATHARINE WOLTZ (MRS. WILLIAM WORTHAM FARINHOLT), writer, educational consultant; b. Chapel Hill, N.C., Feb. 5, 1912; d. Albert Edgar and Daisy (Mackie) Woltz; B.A. with honors, Agnes Scott Coll., 1933; M.Ed., Emory U., 1964; m. Holcombe Tucker Green, Oct. 16, 1934; children—Caroline Tucker, Holcombe Tucker; m. 2d, William Wortham Farinholt, July 18, 1959; 1 stepson, Lewis Sharp. Tchr. English, Belmont (N.C.) High Sch., 1933-34; tchr. English, Westminster Schs., Atlanta, 1958-59, 64-74, prin. Girls' Jr. High Sch., 1964-74; now cons. Author: Alexander's Daughter, 1984, Aquarius Child, Book of Verse, 1987. Pres. Atlanta council Girl Scouts U.S.A., 1953, bd. dirs., 1950-53; pres. Child Service Assn. Atlanta, 1956-58; mem. exec. bd. Atlanta Music Club, 1951-59; hon. bd dirs. Met. Atlanta Child Service and Family Counseling Center, 1975—; trustee Agnes Scott Coll., 1944-45, Appleton Ch. Home, Macon, Ga., 1962-65; patron High Mus. Art. Named One of 10 Leading Ladies of Atlanta, 1975; recipient Outstanding Alumna award Agnes Scott Coll., 1983; collection named in her honor Emory U.; Katharine Woltz Farinholt Scholarship established her honor Agnes Scott Coll., 1983. Mem. Nat. (jr. high sect. chmn. 1969-70, mem. exec. bd. 1969-70, editorial bd. jour. 1972-74, adv. com. 1975, treas. 1975-77, citation 1982), Ga. assns. women deans, adminstrs. and counselors, Ga. Assn. Middle Sch. Prins. (sec.), Mortar Bd. (nat. treas. 1945-47, fellowship chair 1950-52), Nat. Assn for Women Deans and Counselors, Nat. Soc. Colonial Dames Am. (bd. mgrs. Ga. 1985-87), Atlanta Opera Guild, Friends of Decorative Arts, Atlanta Bot. Gardens, Atlanta Hist. Soc., Dixie Council Authors and Journalists, Village Writers Group, Agnes Scott Coll. Alumnae Assn. (pres. 1944-45, bd. dirs. 1983-85, citation 1975), AAUW, Phi Beta Kappa, Delta Kappa Gamma. Episcopalian (pres. women's group). Club: Wayside Garden, Piedmont Driving, Tuesday Bridge, Thursday Book. Address: 3462 Paces Pl NW Atlanta GA 30327

FARKAS, GLENDA LAMMERS, management analyst; b. Mobile, Ala., Nov. 10, 1959; d. John Dillard and Geraldine (Johnson) Lammers; m. Joel Randall Farkas, Mar. 23, 1985. BA in Acctg., Birmingham-So. Coll., 1981. Auditor U.S. Army Yuma (Ariz.) Proving Ground, 1981-84, mgmt. analyst, 1984—. Mem. Am. Bus. Women's Assn. (v.p. 1986—, Woman of Yr. 1987), Assn. U.S. Army, Am. Soc. Mil. Comptrollers (v.p. 1986-87), Internat. Assn. Quality Circles, Yuma County C. of C. Democrat. Methodist. Home: 2490 Yowell Ct #10 Yuma AZ 85364

FARLEY, DONNA OETJEN, health adminstrator; b. Westfield, N.J., Sept. 28, 1943; d. Donald V. and Grace S. Oetjen; m. David P. Farley, Apr. 29, 1967 (div. June 1978); children: Kristina Lynn, William David. BA, Coe Coll., 1965; MPH, U. Ill., Chgo., 1975, MS, 1976. Tech. asst. Ill. Pollution Control Bd., Chgo., 1976-77; assoc. dir. Suburban HSA, Oak Park, Ill., 1977-80; exec. dir. Dental Assisting Nat. Bd., Chgo., 1980-83; v.p. Alexian Bros. Med. Ctr., Elk Grove Village, Ill., 1983-85; sr. v.p. Ancilla Systems, Inc., Elk Grove Village, 1985-87; pres. PKR Assocs., Inc., Elk Grove Village, 1987—; trustee, past. chmn. Alexian Bros. Med. Ctr., 1973-82; past. chmn. Elk Grove Health Bd., 1970-76. Bd. dirs. Girl Scouts USA Council, Elk Grove, 1980-82, United Way of Elk Grove 1984—. Named Citizen of Month Voice Newspaper, 1977. Mem. Soc. Hosp. Planning and Mktg., Am. Pub. Health Assn., Greater O'Hare Assn. of Industry and Commerce (bd. dirs. 1983-85), Elk Grove Jaycees (Citizen of Yr. 1972). Home & Office: 700 D Bordeaux Ct Elk Grove Village IL 60007

FARLEY, FRANCES, state legislator; b. Grand Forks, N.D.; m. Eugene W. Farley, 1946. BS, U. N.D., 1944; MS, NYU, 1945. Mem. Utah State Senate. Del. Dem. Nat. Convention, 1972. Address: 1418 Federal Way Salt Lake City UT 84120 *

FARLEY, JENNIE TIFFANY TOWLE, industrial and labor relations educator; b. Fanwood, N.J., Nov. 2, 1932; d. Howard Albert and Dorothy Jane (Van Wagner) Towle; m. Donald Thorn Farley Jr., June 16, 1956; children—Claire Hamlin, Anne Tiffany, Peter Towle. BA, Cornell U., 1954, MS, 1969, PhD, 1970. Mem. editorial staff Mademoiselle and Seventeen mags., N.Y.C., 1954-56; freelance writer, Eng., Sweden, Peru, 1956-67; lectr., research assoc., adj. asst. prof. Cornell U., Ithaca, N.Y., 1970-72, dir. women's studies, 1972-76, asst. prof. Sch. Indsl. and Labor Relations, 1976-82, assoc. prof., 1982—, exec. bd. dirs. women's studies program, 1970—; vis. prof. Ctr. for Women Scholars and Research on Women Uppsala U., Sweden, 1985-86; trustee Cornell U., 1988—. Author: Affirmative Action and the Woman Worker, 1979, Academic Women and Employment Discrimination, 1982; editor: Sex Discrimination in Higher Education, 1982, The Woman in Management, 1983, Women Workers in Fifteen Countries, 1985. Bd. dirs. Nat. Women's Hall of Fame, Seneca Falls, N.Y., 1986—. Recipient Corinne Galvin award Tompkins County Human Rights Commn., 1987. Mem. AAUP, Ithaca AAUW (pres. 1980-82), Grad. Women in Sci., Sociologists for Women in Soc., Tompkins County NOW. Club: Cornell Women's of Tompkins County. Home: 711 Triphammer Rd Ithaca NY 14850 Office: Sch Indsl and Labor Relations Cornell U Ithaca NY 14853

FARLEY, LINDA NELL, chemical company executive; b. Charleston, W.Va., Nov. 24, 1941; d. Frederick Paul and Frances Eloise (Hale) Farley. Student, Eastern Mont. Coll. of Edn., 1959-60, W.Va. State Coll., 1959-60. Instr. gymnastics Lawrence Frankel Inst., Charleston, 1960-61; sec. Union Carbide Corp., Institute, W.Va., 1961-73, office services supr., 1973-81, mgmt. devel. assoc., 1981—, also sr. office supr., public relations adminstr., non-exempt tng. adminstrn., 1981-87; adminstrv. mgr. Anesthesia dept., Bowman Gray Sch. of Medicine Wake Forest U., 1987—. Mem. Nat. Assn. Female Execs., Am. Soc. Tng. and Devel. Club; Altrusa (corr. sec. 1976-77) (Charleston). Office: 300 S Hawthorne Rd Winston-Salem NC 27103

FARLEY, MARIAN DIEDRE, librarian; b. Manhasset, N.Y., Mar. 1, 1955; d. John Joseph and Rita Sarah (Johnston) Farley. B.A., St. Bonaventure U., 1977; M.L.S., SUNY-Albany, 1978. Librarian-instr. Iona Coll., New Rochelle, N.Y., 1980-82; head circulation dept. U. Lowell (Mass.), 1982-83; library dir. Analytic Scis. Corp., Reading, Mass., 1983—. Mem. ALA, Spl. Libraries Assn., Route 128 Librarians, New Eng. On-Line Users Group. Democrat. Roman Catholic. Home: 6 Newcastle Dr #12 Nashua NH 03060 Office: Analytic Scis Corp 55 Walkers Brook Dr Reading MA 01867

FARLEY, PEGGY ANN, finance company executive; b. Phila., Mar. 12, 1947; d. Harry E. and Ruth (Lloyd) F.; m. W. Reid McIntyre, Dec. 31, 1985. AB, Barnard Coll., 1970; MA with high honors, Columbia U., 1972. Admissions officer Barnard Coll., N.Y.C., 1973-76; adminstr. Citibank NA, Athens, Greece, 1976-77; cons. Organization Resources Counselors, N.Y.C., 1977-78; sr. assoc. Morgan Stanley and Co., Inc., N.Y.C., 1978-84; sr. v.p., chief operating officer AMAS Securities, Inc., N.Y.C., 1984—, also bd. dirs.; bd. dirs. AMAS Group, London. Author: The Place Of The Yankee And Euro Bond Markets In A Financing Program For The People's Republic of China, 1982. Mem. Asia Soc., China Inst., Columbia U. Seminar on China-U.S. Bus. Republican. Presbyterian. Club: Metrpolitan (N.Y.C.). Home: Box 1 RD 6 Branchville NJ 07826 Office: AMAS Securities Inc 520 Madison Ave New York NY 10022

FARLOW, LYNNE ANN, military officer; b. Lima, Ohio, Apr. 22, 1960; d. Thomas Eugene and Ann (Lowry) Coe; m. Michael James Farlow, Apr. 27, 1985. BS, U.S. Naval Acad., 1982; MBA, Marymount U., 1987. Commd. USN, 1982; asst. for nat. security affairs Office of the Chief of Naval Ops., Washington, 1982-85; officer in charge support activity detachment Office of the Chief of Naval Ops., Ft. Ritchie, Md., 1985—. Mem. AAUW, Assn. MBA Execs., Nat. Assn. Female Execs., U.S. Jaycees. Republican. Methodist.

FARMER, ALLENE VALERIE, information specialist, government executive; b. Washington, Sept. 23, 1958; d. Thomas Jonathan and Allena V.

(Joyner) F. Student, Richmond Coll., London, 1980; B.A., Clark Coll., 1980; grad. cert. U. Oxford, Eng., 1981; M.L.S., U. Md., 1986. Library asst. NUS Corp., Gaithersburg, Md., 1981-82; cataloger Library of Congress, Washington, 1982-84, copyright specialist, 1984-85; congl. fellow Ho. of Reps. Com. on D.C., Washington, 1985—; English tutor, writer Natural Motion, Washington, 1983-84; intern, archivist Howard U., Washington, 1985. Compiler; Single Mother's Resource Directory, 1984. Compiler, editor: Policy Research, 1985. Author booklet: D.C. Statehood Issue, 1986. Mem. U. Md. College Park Black Women's council, College Park, Md., 1984; vol. Congl. Black Caucus Found., Washington, 1985. Recipient Fgn. Study award Am. Inst. for Fgn. Study, 1981; Congl. Black Caucus fellow, 1985. Mem. Library of Congress Profls. Assn., ALA, Daniel A.P. Murray Afro-Am. Culture Assn. of Library of Congress, NAACP, Delta Sigma Theta (tutor 1986). Avocations: travel; writing; dance; drama; tennis. Home: 8504 Barron St Takoma Park MD 20912 Office: Congress of US Ho of Reps Com on DC 2135 Rayburn House Washington DC 20515

FARMER, CATHERINE ARMBRUSTER, public relations executive; b. Omaha, Jan. 12, 1948; d. Joseph Francis and Helen Jane (Grommesch) Armbruster; m. Samuel Carter Farmer, IV, May 9, 1981; children: Catherine Carter, Joseph Powell. Student St. Mary's of Notre Dame, 1966-69; B.A., U. Mo., 1971. News dir. Sta. KSOO, Sioux Falls, S.D., 1971-73; talk show producer, hostess Sta. WLYH-TV, Lancaster, Pa., 1973-74, Sta. WBNG-TV, Binghamton, N.Y., 1974-75; dir. pub. relations Pa. Dutch Visitors Bur., Lancaster, 1976-77; owner Cathy Farmer Pub. Relations, Lancaster, 1978-86; corp. v.p., dir. pub. relations div. Kelly Michener, 1986—; instr. writing Pa. State U.-Middletown, 1978; guest lectr. Millersville State U., Lancaster, 1978-79. Office: Kelly Michener Advt 416 W Marion St Lancaster PA 17603

FARMER, DOROTHA F., administrative associate; b. New Bloomfield, Mo., Nov. 8, 1942; d. James B. and Bertha E. (Vaughan) Gray; student U. Mo., 1971—; m. John C. Farmer, Sept. 2, 1961; stepchildren—John C. (dec.), Michael A. Clinic sec. Ellis Fischel State Cancer Hosp., Columbia, Mo., 1961-64; sec. to dir. Mo. Div. Employment Security, Columbia, 1965-66; departmental sec., dept. indsl. engring. U. Mo., Columbia, 1966-71, office mgr. bioengring./advanced automation program, 1974-78, adminstrv. asso., radiology computer research center, Mid-Am. Bone Diagnostic Center, 1978-83, adminstrv. assoc. radiol. scis. research, 1983—; cons. NIH, 1980-82. Mem. Bus. and Profl. Women, Mo. Farmers Assn., Women's Progressive Farmers Assn. Roman Catholic. Contbr. articles to profl. jours. Home: RR 1 Clark MO 65243 Office: U Mo 410 Lewis Hall Columbia MO 65211

FARMER, ELAINE F., state legislator; b. New Castle, Pa., Mar. 14, 1937; d. John R. and Pearle (McLure) Frazier; m. Sterling N. Farmer, Aug. 22, 1959; children: Heather, Drew. BBA, Case Western Reserve U., 1958, MEd, 1964. Employment supr. Stouffer Corp., Cleve., 1958-60; tchr. Lakewood Schs., Cleve., 1960-64; subs. tchr. North Allegheny Schs., Pitts., 1972-77; agt. Howard Hanna Real Estate Services, Pitts., 1977-86, mgr., 1983-86; elected mem. Ho. of Reps., Harrisburg, Pa., 1986—. Councilman Town of McCandless, Pa., 1980-86; trustee Northland Library, Pitts., 1980-85; liaison Planning Commn., McCandless, 1984-86. Mem. Nat. Order Women Legislators, Am. Legis. Exchange Council, North Hills C. of C., Airport C. of C., Nat. Assn. Realtors, Pa. Assn. Realtors, Greater Pitts. Bd. Realtors. Republican. Presbyterian. Office: House of Reps Box 178 Harrisburg PA 15237

FARMER, HELEN SWEENEY, psychologist; b. Ottawa, Can., Dec. 23, 1929; d. Henry Bertrum and Mabel Sarah (Switzer) Sweeney; m. James A. Farmer, Jan. 25, 1955; children: James Sweeney, David Sargent, Paul Alexander. BA, Queens U., Can., 1952; BD, Union Theol. Sem., 1955; MA, Columbia U., 1969; PhD, UCLA, 1972. Dir. evaluation services INSGROUP, Long Beach, Calif., 1971-74; asst. prof. counseling psychology U. Ill., Urbana, 1974-81, assoc. prof., 1981-87, prof., 1987—. Author: (with Tom Backer) New Career Options for Women: Counselor's Sourcebook, 1977, New Career Options for Women: A Woman's Guide, 1977; contbr. articles to profl. jours. Queens U. scholar, 1949, Can. govt., 1949-52; grantee Nat. Inst. Edn., 1974, 76, 78. Fellow Am. Psychol. Assn. (div. sec. 1984-87); mem. Am. Ednl. and Research Assn. (div. v.p. 1984-86), Am. Assn. Counseling and Devel. Home: 2204 S Staley Rd Champaign IL 61821 Office: U Ill Sch Edn Dept Ednl Psychology Champaign IL 61820

FARMER, JANENE ELIZABETH, artist, educator; b. Albuquerque, Oct. 16, 1946; d. Charles John Watt and Regina M. (Brown) Kruger; m. Michael Hugh Bolton, Apr. 1965 (div.); m. Frank Urban Farmer, May, 1972 (div.). B.A. in Art, San Diego State U., 1969. Owner, operator Iron Walrus Pottery, 1972-79; designer ceramic and fabric murals, Coronado, Calif., 1979-82; executed commns. for clients in U.S.A., Can., Japan and Mex.; pvt. tchr. pottery; mem. faculty U. Calif.-San Diego; substitute tchr. Calif. community colls.; designer fabric murals and bldg. interiors, Coronado and La Jolla, Calif., 1982—; tchr. Blessed Sacrament Sch., San Diego, 1982-85, San Diego Unified Sch. Dist., 1985-87. Mem. Coronado Arts and Humanities Council; resident artist U. Calif.-San Diego. Recipient grant Calif. Arts Council, 1980-81; U. San Diego grad. fellow dept. edn., 1984. Mem. Am. Soc. Interior Designers (affiliate). Roman Catholic. Home: 4435 Nobel Dr #35 San Diego CA 92122

FARMER, MARY MARGARET WILSON, medical technologist; b. Asheville, N.C., July 5, 1933; d. Roeby Bryant and Flossie Aurora (Montieth) Wilson; B.S., Wake Forest Coll., 1954; B.S. in Med. Tech., Bowman Gray Sch. Med. Tech., 1954; m. Gary Clayton Farmer, Apr. 28, 1962; children—Mary Elizabeth, Melissa Margaret. Med. technologist Aston Park Hosp., Asheville, 1954-56, Occupational Health Services, Asheville, 1956-58; med. technologist, asst. lab. supr. Meml. Mission Hosp., Asheville, 1958-62; med. technologist, lab. dir. Joseph E. Seagram & Co., N.Y.C., 1962-65; dir. blood collections and phlebotomy Richmond (Va.) Met. Blood Bank, 1974-77; lab. mgr., med. technologist Thoms Rehab. Hosp., Asheville, 1980—; lab. dir. Thoms Rehab. Hosp.; sec./treas. Assos. for Human Devel., Asheville. Chmn. fund raising Biltmore PTA, Asheville, 1978-79, chmn. membership, 1979-80; v.p. Valley Springs PTA, Skyland, N.C., 1980-81, pres., 1981-82; mem. Roberson dist. Buncombe County (N.C.) Schs. Adv. Council, 1981-82; mem. outreach, youth and worship commns. All Souls Episc. Ch., co-dir. acolyte program; v.p. Women of Gen. Theol. Sem., 1963-64. Recipient Citizenship award United Daus. of Confederacy. Mem. Am. Soc. Med. Technologists, Am. Soc. Clin. Pathologists (med. technologist), AAUW, N.Am. Benefit Assn., Western N.C. Lab. Mgrs. Assn., Clin. Lab. Mgmt. Assn., Episcopal Church Women, Beta Sigma Phi (pres. Beta Tau chpt. 1961-62). Democrat. Clubs: Mahjong, Bridge. Home: 8 Busbee Rd Asheville NC 28803 Office: 1 Rotary Dr Asheville NC 28803

FARMER, SUSAN LAWSON, broadcasting executive, former secretary of state; b. Boston, May 29, 1942; d. Ralph and Margaret (Tyng) Lawson; m. Malcolm Farmer, III, Apr. 6, 1968; children: Heidi Benson, Stephanie Lawson. Student, Garland Jr. Coll., 1960-61, Brown U., 1961-62. Mem. Providence Home Rule Charter Commn., 1979-80; sec. of state State of R.I., Providence, 1983-87; chief exec. officer, gen. mgr. WSBE-TV, Providence, 1987—; spl. advocate R.I. Family Ct., 1978—; mem. nat. voting standards panel Fed. Election Commn. co-chmn. Nat. Voter Edn. Project; mem. electoral coll., 1984; chmn. Gov.'s Com. on Ethics in Govt., 1985-86; mem. teaching facility and adv. panel Internat. Ctr. on Election Law and Adminstrn.; mem. natl. edn. adv. com. Pub. Broadcasting System, 1987—; trustee Eastern Ednl. TV Network, 1987—. Bd. dirs. Justice Resources Corp., Marathon House, Inc., R.I. Council Alcoholism, R.I. Hist. Soc.; mem. Mayor's Task Force on Child Abuse, R.I. Film Commn.; v.p. Miriam Hosp. Found.; mem. adv. com. Women in Polit. and Govtl. Careers Program, U. R.I., 1985—; mem. adv. bd. Com. for Study of Am. Electorate-Ford Found. Project-Efficacy in State Voting Laws, 1986; mem. Commn. to Study Length of Election Progress, 1985—; steering com. Nat. Fund for America's Future, Project Vote R.I. Mem. R.I. Women's Polit. Caucus (Woman of Yr. award 1980), Bus. and Profl. Women (Woman of Yr. 1984), LWV, Common Cause, Save the Bay, Women for a Non-nuclear Future, Providence Preservation Soc., Orgn. State Broadcasting Execs. Republican. Home: 147 Lloyd Ave Providence RI 02906 Office: WSBE-TV 24 Mason St Providence RI 02903

FARNHAM, ROSANNE VLANDIS, beer company field sales manager; b. Iowa City, Apr. 9, 1960; d. John William and Katherine (Cheston) V.; m. Jeffrey Alan Farnham, Oct. 18, 1987. BA, U. Conn., 1982. Camp counselor Camp Akiba, Reeders, Pa., 1979; waitress The Tavern, Nantucket, Mass., 1980; spl. events coordinator Hartford Distbrs. Inc., Manchester, Conn., 1981-83; project mktg. team Anheuser-Busch Inc., St. Louis, 1983-85; field sales mgr. Anheuser-Busch Inc., Pearl River, N.Y., 1985—. Recipient Ella T. Grasso award U. Conn. Alumni Assn., 1982; scholarship Advt. Club of Greater Hartford, 1981. Mem. U. Conn. Alumni Assn. (Albany chpt. coordinator). Greek Orthodox. Office: Anheuser-Busch Inc One Blue Hill Plaza Pearl River NY 10965

FARQUHAR, KAREN LEE, business forms company executive, consultant; b. Warwick, N.Y., May 27, 1958; d. Wesley Thomas and Margaret Anne (Storms) Kervatt; m. David W. Farquhar, July 17, 1982; 1 child, Lauren Nichole. Assoc. Sci., Roger Williams Coll., 1978, B.S. cum laude, 1980. Office mgr. Price-Rite Printing Co., Dover, N.J., summer 1975-76; cons. SBA, Bristol, R.I., 1978-80; account exec. P.M. Press Inc., Dallas, 1980—, sales trainer, 1984-85; v.p. KDF Bus. Forms Inc., Dallas, Tex., 1984—. Printer, Tex. Aux. Charity Auction Orgn., Dallas, 1985, Crescent Gala, Dallas, 1986. Recipient various awards Clampitt Paper Co., Dallas, 1982, P.M. Press Inc., 1983-86, 87, Mead Paper Co., 1985. Mem. Printing Industry in Am., Internat. Assn. Bus. Communicators, Nat. Bus. Forms Assn. Republican. Baptist. Avocations: piano; aerobics. Home: 429 Dillard Ln Coppell TX 75019

FARQUHAR, KIMBERLY ANNE, senior implementation specialist; b. Weymouth, Mass., Aug. 29, 1962; d. George William Farquhar and Sanra Louise (Frye) Taylor. A in Fin., Bentley Coll., 1985; cert. in benefit plans, Northeastern U., 1980-84. Dividend auditor Boston Fin., Quincy, Mass., 1982-84; trust acct. Putnam Inservco, Boston, 1984-85; sr. participant acct. State St. Bank & Trust, Quincy, 1985-87, participant record keeping analyst, 1987-88; sr. implementation specialist KPMG Peat Marwick, Boston, 1988—. Counselor Dove, Quincy; fund raiser Walk for Hunger, Boston, 1986-87. Home: 25 Block St Abington MA 02351 Office: KPMG Peat Marwick One Boston Pl Boston MA 02108

FARR, BEVERLY AGNES, shoe manufacturing company official; b. Middleboro, Mass., Dec. 6, 1928; d. George Sampson and Bertha Josephine (Duffany) Barney; m. Stanley Thomas Farr, May 30, 1949 (dec. Mar. 1987); 1 child, Paul Thomas. A.A., Arlington Acad. Music, 1947. Prodn. clk. W.L. Douglas Shoe Co., Brockton, Mass., 1948-49; customer service rep. Commonwealth Shoe, Whitman, Mass., 1950-51; schedule and prodn. dept. Knapp Shoe Co., Brockton, 1951-53; asst. to office mgr. Givren Shoe Co., Rockland, Mass., 1953-54, Porter Shoe Co., Milford, Mass., 1954-57; purchasing mgr., leather buyer Foot-Joy, Inc., Brockton, 1957—, dir. purchasing, 1988—. Com. mem. Conservation Commn., Halifax, Mass., 1979. Mem. Nat. Assn. Female Execs. Republican. Club: Boot & Shoe (first woman on com.). Avocations: aerobics, silk flower arranging, flower gardening. Home: 27 Cedar Ln PO Box 493 Halifax MA 02338 Office: Foot-Joy Inc 144 Field St Brockton MA 02403

FARR, JEAN GATLING, educator; b. Ahoskie, N.C., Mar. 18, 1933; d. John Deans and Louise (Ruffin) Gatling; m. Everett L. Farr Jr., Aug. 8, 1952; children: Carolyn, Everett L. III, Eleanor Farr Jarosz. BA, James Madison U., 1953; postgrad., U. Va., 1953-55, Pa. State U., 1963-65; MS, Temple U., 1969. Cert. tchr., Va., Del., Pa. Tchr. Charlottesville (Va.) City Schs., 1954-55; prin. Southampton County Schs., Courtland, Va., 1955-59; tchr. Caesar Rodney Schs., Camden, Del., 1960-62, Centennial Schs., Warminster, Pa., 1962-71; tchr., cons. Bucks County Intermediate Unit, Doylestown, Pa., 1971-76; tech. asst. gifted programs Pa. Dept. Edn., Harrisburg, 1976-82; headmistress The Crefeld Sch., Phila., 1982-86; supr. gifted Phila. City Schs., 1986—; auditor Pa. Dept. Edn., 1982—. Author: (with others) Parents' Guide to Gifted Programs, 1972, Guidelines for Planning and Operating Programs for the Gifted, 1986; contbr. articles to profl. jours. Mem. Centennial Sch. Bd., Warminster, 1972-78. Recipient Educator of Yr. award Pa. Assn. Gifted Edn., 1978. Mem. Delta Kappa Gamma, Zeta Tau Alpha. Democrat. Baptist. Club: North Hills (Pa.) Country. Office: Phila City Schs Stevens Adminstrn Bldg 13th and Spring Garden Sts Philadelphia PA 19123

FARR, M. PAIGE, construction company executive; b. Carlisle, Pa., Sept. 26, 1945; d. Harold Monroe and Jane Arthur Eugenia (Kean) LeBell; m. Joseph Farr, May 18, 1984. BA in Psychology summa cum laude, Mercy Coll., Dobbs Ferry, N.Y., 1983. Bookkeeping asst. Trumid Constrn. Co. Inc., Yonkers, N.Y., 1970-72, office mgr., 1972-76, corp. sec., 1976-79; v.p. JayVal Contracting Corp., Tarrytown and Peekskill, N.Y., 1979-83, Farr-Guarino Contracting Corp., White Plains, N.Y., 1983—; pres. Farr Crest Excavating Corp., East White Plains, N.Y., 1987—. Mem. Catskill Center. Mem. Contractors Assn. Westchester, Putnam and Dutchess Counties. Democrat. Office: Farr-Guarino Contracting Corp 128 Fulton St White Plains NY 10606

FARR, PATRICIA HUDAK, librarian; b. Youngstown, Ohio, Mar. 10, 1945; d. Frank Francis and Anna Frances (Tylka) Hudak; m. William Howard Farr, Aug. 28, 1971; children: Jennifer Anne, William Patrick. BA, Youngstown State U., 1970; MLS, U. Md., 1980. Children's librarian Pub. Library Youngstown and Mahoning (Ohio), 1970-71; asst. Fla. State U. Library, Tallahassee, 1971-73; research asst. John Hopkins U. Sch. Hygiene and Pub. Health, Balt., 1974-76; asst. Mary Washington Coll. Library, Fredericksburg, Va., 1976-79; children's librarian Cen. Rappahannock Regional Library, Fredericksburg, 1980-84, young adult services coordinator, 1984—. Revision editor HEW pub. Thesaurus of Health Edn. Terminology, 1976; compiler Health Edn. Monographs, 1974-76. Youngstown State U. scholar, 1963-64; R.V. Lowery Meml. scholar, 1979-80. Mem. ALA, Va. Library Assn. Democrat. Episcopalian. Club: Rappahannock Twirlers Square Dance. Home: 618 Kings Hwy Fredericksburg VA 22405 Office: Cen Rappahannock Regional Library 1201 Caroline St Fredericksburg VA 22401

FARRAH, PEGGY ANN, educator; b. Everson, Pa., Aug. 26, 1945; d. George Jacob and Abla (Nassar) F. BS in Social Scis., Ind. U. of Pa., 1966, MA in History, 1969; ArtsD in History, Carnegie-Mellon U., 1982; cert. adminstrn., U. Pitts., 1988. Secondary tchr. Hempfield Area Sch. Dist., Greensburg, Pa., 1966-83, instrnl. leader, 1983-86; coordinator staff devel. and testing Greensburg Salem Sch. Dist., 1986—; ednl. cons., 1983—. contbr. articles to Carnegie-Mellon Mag., Pitts. Press, 1985. Mem. Assn. for Supervision and Curriculum Devel., Assn. of Secondary Sch. Prin., Staff Devel. Council, Pa. Assn. Sch. Adminstrs. Democrat. Eastern Orthodox. Home: 119 Canyon Ct Latrobe PA 15650 Office: Greensburg Salem Sch Dist 11 Park St Greensburg PA 15601

FARRAR, ELAINE WILLARDSON, artist; b. Los Angeles, Feb. 27, 1929; d. Eldon and Gladys Elsie (Larsen) Willardson; BA, Ariz. State U., 1967, MA, 1969, now doctoral candidate; children:Steve, Mark, Gregory, Leslie Jean, Monty, Susan. Tchr., Camelback Desert Sch., Paradise Valley, Ariz., 1966-69; mem. faculty Yavapai Coll., Prescott, Ariz., 1970—, chmn. dept. art, 1973-78, instr. art in watercolor and oil and acrylic painting, intaglio, relief and monoprints, 1971—; one-man shows include: R.P. Moffat's, Scottsdale, Ariz., 1969, Art Center, Battle Creek, Mich., 1969, The Woodpeddler, Costa Mesa, Calif., 1979; group show Prescott (Ariz.) Fine Arts Assn., 1982, 84, 86, N.Y. Nat. Am. Watercolorists, 1982; Ariz. State U. Women Images Now, 1986, 87; works rep. local and state exhibits; supt. fine arts dept. County Fair; com. mem., hanging chmn. Scholastic Art Awards. Mem. Mountain Artists Guild (past pres.), Nat. League Am. Pen Women (Prescott br.), NEA, Ariz. Edn. Assn., Nat. Art Edn. Assn., Ariz. Coll. and Univ. Faculty Assn., AAUW, Verde Valley Art Assn., Ariz. Women's Caucus for Art, Kappa Delta Pi, Phi Delta Kappa. Republican. Mormon. Home: 635 Copper Basin Rd Prescott AZ 86303 Office: Yavapai Coll Art Dept 1100 E Sheldon Rd Prescott AZ 86301

FARRAR, MARCIA G., municipal center foundation executive; b. Phila., Nov. 1, 1941; d. Leon L. and Sylvia (Silcoff) Rhinehart; m. Wayne H. Farrar, Dec. 26, 1959; children: Crystal L., David A. BA, U. Mass., 1979. Program dir. People Bridge Action, Athol, Mass., 1976-79; exec. dir. Piedmont Neighborhood Ctr., Worcester, Mass., 1979-82; alumni dir. Cen. New Eng. Coll., Worcester, 1982-83; exec. dir. Martin Luther King Ctr., Newport, R.I., 1983—. V.p. Office for Children, Gardner, Mass., 1977-79; chairperson Worcester Neighborhood Assn., 1977-79; vice chairperson Worcester Tchr. Corps, 1977-79; mem. This is Worcester task force, 1977-79; active Dem. gubernatorial campaign, Newport, 1985—. Methodist. Home: 45 Malbone Rd Newport RI 02840 Office: Martin Luther King Ctr 20 W Broadway Newport RI 02840

FARRAR, PAULINE ELIZABETH, accountant, real estate broker; b. Madison, Wis., July 2, 1928; d. William Charles and Mary Anna (Killalley) Selmer; m. James Walter Byers, Aug. 15, 1950 (dec. June 1972); children: Marvin Lee, Marjorie Sue; m. Robert Bascom Farrar, Apr. 14, 1974; stepchildren: Katrinka Jo Farrar Sandahl, Jon Randle Farrar. Student, U. Wis., 1946-49, U. Houston, 1956-57. Acct. Sterling Hogan, Houston, 1951-54, Lester Prokop, Houston, 1959-64, Holland Mortgage Co., Houston, 1964-68, Jetero Bldg Corp., Houston, 1968-71; real estate assoc. Mills Paulea Realtors, Houston, 1976-80, ERA, Nelson & Assocs., Missouri City, Tex., 1980-81; owner, broker Property-Wise Realty, Sugar Land, Tex., 1981—; tax assesor, collector Sequoia Utility Dist., Houston, 1969-71. Leader Girl Scouts U.S.A., Houston, 1962-72; organizer, coordinator ladies program Stafford (Tex.) Ch. of Christ, 1978-81. Mem. Tex. Assn. Realtors (bd. dirs. 1986-87), Cert. Real Estate Brokers (v.p. Tex. chpt., sec.-treas.), Ft. Bend County Bd. Realtors (pres. 1987—), Women's Council of Realtors (founding chmn. Ft. Bend/SW Houston chpt. 1986, pres. 1988), Nat. Realtors Inst. (cert. residential specialist, cert. real estate broker, grad. realtors inst., LTG). Office: Property-Wise Realty 6730 Hwy 6 Sugar Land TX 77478

FARRELL, BARBARA LOU, nursing consultant, resort owner; b. Bklyn., May 16, 1935; d. Edwin Linwood and Ada Louise (Bundrick) F. AA, Green Mountain Coll., 1955; BS, Columbia U., 1958, MA, 1966. Nursing supr., instr. Columbia-Presbyn. Hosp. Emergency Services, N.Y.C., 1958-62; commd. 2d lt. USAF, 1962, advanced through ranks to lt. col., resigned, 1976; asst. chief nurse for ambulatory care VA Med. Ctr., San Francisco, 1976-80, assoc. chief nursing services, 1980-83; pres. Timberhill Ranch Ltd., Timbercove, Calif., 1983—; cons. to surgeon gen. Aerospace Nursing, 1973-76; from med. augmentee to chmn. dept. nursing David GrantUSAF Med. Ctr., Travis AFB, 1976—. Adv. Redwood Coast Med. Service, Stewart Point, Calif., 1983-85. Served to col. USAF Res., 1980—. Fellow Aerospace Med. Assn. (assocs., pres. flight nurses sect. 1975-76); mem. Am. Nurses Assn. Mem. Reformed Ch. Am. Home and Office: Timberhill Ranch 35755 Hauber Bridge Rd Timbercove Cazadero CA 95421

FARRELL, EILEEN MARIE, nurse, administrator; b. N.Y.C., Oct. 8, 1950; d. William James and Ann Marie (Hogan) F. BS in Nursing, Columbia U., 1972, MPH, 1986. Cert. emergency nurse. Staff nurse Vanderbilt Clinic, Columbia Presbyn. Med. Ctr., N.Y.C., 1972-74, sr. supr. evenings Emergency Services, Vanderbilt Clinic, 1974-77, sr. supr. days, 1978-80, adminstrv. nurse clinician emergency services, 1980-86, tng. coordinator info. systems div. nursing, 1986—, nursing liaison ambulatory care, 1982; preceptor, cons. Edna McConnell Clark and Columbia U. Sch. Nursing, 1978-86, preceptor ambulatory care Columbia U. Sch. Pub. Health, 1980-82; tchr. seminars in field. Mem. Emergency Nurses Assn., N.Y. State Nurse's Assn., Am. Pub. Health Assn., Nat. Assn. Female Execs., Columbia U. Presbyn. Hosp. Alumnae Assn. Office: Columbia Presbyn Med Ctr Cen Nursing Office 622 W 168th St New York NY 10032

FARRELL, JUNE MARTINICK, public relations executive; b. New Brunswick, N.J., June 30, 1940; d. Ivan and Mary (Tomkovich) M.; B.S. in Journalism, Ohio U., 1962; M.S. in Public Relations, Am. U., Washington, 1977; m. Duncan G. Farrell, July 31, 1971. Public relations asst. Corning Glass Works, N.Y.C., 1963-65; assoc. beauty editor Good Housekeeping mag., N.Y.C., 1966; public relations specialist Gt. Am. Ins. Co., N.Y.C., 1967-68; assoc. editor Ea. Airlines, N.Y.C., 1968-82, regional public relations mgr., Washington, 1976-82; public relations dir. Nat. Captioning Inst., Falls Church, Va., 1982-83; dir. media relations Marriott Corp., 1984—; adj. instr. Montgomery County Community Coll., also mem. hotel/tourism adv. bd., 1980—; staff cons. Office of Public Liaison, White House, 1981-82. Creator, condr. spl. career awareness program for inner city youth, Washington, 1979-80; mem. public relations com. Jr. Achievement, 1979; motivational counselor for youth Nat. Alliance of Businessmen, 1979; bd. dirs. Am. Travel Mktg. Services; trustee Nat. Hosp. Orthopedics and Rehab., 1984—. Mem. Soc. Am. Travel Writers (mem. pub. relations com.), Am. Soc. Travel Agts., Travel Industry Assn. Am. (nat. conf. planning com., pub. relations com.), Women in Communication, Phi Mu. Republican. Clubs: Zonta, Internat. Aviation. Home: 6630 Lybrook Ct Bethesda MD 20817 Office: Marriott Corp One Marriott Dr Bethesda MD 20817

FARRELL, NAOMI, editor, correspondent, nurse researcher; b. Glasgow, Scotland, Apr. 21, 1941; came to Can., 1949, USA, 1963; d. Louis and Minnie (Przestrzeleniec) F. AAS with honors, CUNY, 1970; BSN, Hunter Coll., 1973; UN studies cert., L.I. U., 1978, MS in Social Sci. and Internat. Affairs, 1979. RN. TV performer Can., 1959-63; adminstr. Health Ins. Plan, N.Y.C., 1964-65; nurse, researcher Cornell Med. Ctr., N.Y.C., 1977-80; assoc. editor Al Hoda, New Lebanese Am. Jour., N.Y.C., 1979—; UN corr., freelance writer Globe and Mail of Can., 1980—; cons. Internat. Med. Tourism, 1985. Author numerous articles and poems for newspapers and mags. Mem. internat. adv. bd. Symphony for UN, 1986. Research paper on world hunger accepted by UN Research and Tng. Library and used in Presdl. Commn. on World Hunger, Washington, 1979. Mem. UN. Corrs. Assn. (assoc. editor 1985—), Soc. Writers of UN (v.p. 1985-86), Fgn. Press Assn., UN Assn. (citation for position paper 1978), Soc. Internat. Devel., N.Y. Acad. Scis., Am. Nurses Assn. Home: 321 E 48th St New York NY 10017

FARRELL, PATRICIA ANN, psychologist, educator; b. N.Y.C., Mar. 11, 1945; d. Joseph Alexander and Pauline (Loth) F.; BA, Queens Coll., 1976; MA, N.Y. U., 1978, postgrad., 1980—. Assoc. editor Pubs. Weekly Mag., N.Y.C., 1968-72; editor Bestsellers Mag., N.Y.C., 1972-73; assoc. editor King Features Syndicate, N.Y.C., 1973-78; staff psychologist, intake coordinator Mid-Bergen Community Mental Health Ctr., Paramus, N.J., 1978-84; instr. Bergen Community Coll., Paramus, 1978-88; cons. Family Counseling Service of Ridgewood, N.J., 1984; clin. psychology intern Marlboro Psychiat. Hosp., N.J., 1984-85, staff psychologist, 1985-87; research analyst Mt. Sinai Sch. of Medicine, 1987—; cons. Intensive Weight Loss Program, Cath. Med. Ctr. Bklyn. and Queens; guest radio shows Sta. WWDJ, Hackensack, N.J. Mem. Bergen County Task Force on Crimes Against Children, Bergen County Task Force on Alcoholism and Drunken Driving, 1984. Recipient Social Scis. award Queens Coll., 1976. Mem. AAAS, Am. Psychol. Assn. (assoc.), N.J. Psychol. Assn. (assoc.), Eastern Psychol. Assn. (assoc.). Contbr. articles to Writer's Digest, Real World, newspapers. Avocations: fitness, racquetball. Office: The Mount Sinai Sch of Med Dept of Psychiatry 130 W Kingsbridge Rd Bronx NY 10468

FARRELL, SUZANNE, ballerina; b. Cin.; d. Robert Ficker and Donna (Von Holle) Holly; m. Paul Mejia, Feb. 21, 1969. Studies with Marian LaCour, Cin. Conservatory Music; LHD, Georgetown U., 1984, Fordham U., 1987. hon. lectr. dance U. Cin.; mem. faculty Sch. Am. Ballet. With N.Y. City Ballet, 1961-69, 75—, became featured dancer, 1962, prin. dancer, 1965-69; appeared in film version Midsummer Night's Dream; Bejart Ballet of 20th Century, Brussels, 1971-75; created roles in other ballets Ah, Vous Dirais Je, Maman?, Juliet in Romeo and Juliet; The Young Girl in Rose in Nijinsky . . . Clown of God, 1971, Bolero, The Rite of Spring; Laura in I Trionfi; N.Y.C. Ballet in New Ravel Festival, Tzigane, In G Major, 1976; featured in TV show: Balanchine Dance in Am., Parts I-IV. Recipient Merit award Mademoiselle mag., 1965, Dance mag. award, 1976, award of honor for arts and culture N.Y.C., 1979, Spirit Achievement award Albert Einstein Coll. Medicine, 1980, Emmy award, 1985, Golden Plate award Am. Acad. of Achievement, 1987. Office: NYC Ballet Lincoln Ctr State Theater New York NY 10023

FARRELL-DONALDSON, MARIE DELOIS, municipal official; b. Detroit, Aug. 10, 1947; d. Herman and Lorine (Carter) Morgan; m. Joseph C. Farrell, July 18, 1970 (div. 1974); 1 child, Piper; m. Clinton Lavonne Donaldson, Nov. 29, 1975; 1 child, Christia. BS, Wayne State U., 1969; cert. in govt., Harvard U., 1982. CPA, Mich. Acct. Iceman, Johnson and Hoffman, Ann Arbor, Mich., 1969-71; comptroller Model Neighborhood Devel., Detroit, 1972-74; pvt. practice acctg. Detroit, 1974-75; auditor gen. City of Detroit, 1975-84, ombudsman, 1984—. Treas. Mich. Metro Girl Scouts Am., 1984—, United Community Services, Detroit, 1985—; pres.

Detroit chpt. Nat. Council Alcoholism, 1979-85. Named Michiganian Yr. Detroit News, 1982, Outstanding Young Working Woman Glamour Mag., 1985, Outstanding Alumni Wayne State U., 1985. Mem. Nat. Assn. Black Accts. (bd. dirs.), Nat. Council Govt. Accts. (bd. dirs. 1979-82), Women's Econ. Club (pres. 1987—), Mich. Assn. CPA's (bd. dirs. 1985—), Alpha Kappa Alpha. Methodist. Office: City Detroit Office Ombudsman 114 City-County Bldg Detroit MI 48226

FARRELL-LOGAN, VIVIAN, actress; b. N.Y.C.; m. Harvey Lewis, Aug. 5, 1979 (dec. Aug. 1980); m. Tracy Harrison Logan, June 3, 1984. BS in Edn., Syracuse U.; MA in Theatre, NYU. Tchr. elem. sch. Levittown (N.Y.) Schs., 1965-75; tchr. workshops Coll. of Cape Breton, N.S., Can., 1977-79. Actress: (stage) Gateway Playhouse, Bellport, N.Y., Playhouse 3200, Richmond, Va., Bartke's Dinner Theatre, Tampa, Fla., (film) Impulse; narrator for Nutcracker, Eglevsky Ballet Co. with L.I. Symphony Orch., Nassau Coliseum, Uniondale, N.Y., 1978-79; appeared as The Musical Storyteller, Lincoln Ctr., N.Y.C., Carnegie Recital Hall, N.Y.C., various libraries and schs., N.Y. area; performer, writer (album) The Musical Storyteller, 1978; author: (children's book) Robert's Tall Friend: A Story of the Fire Island Lighthouse, Island-Metro Publs., Inc., 1987. Grantee Nassau County (N.Y.) Office of Cultural Devel., 1986-88, grantee N.Y. State Council on the Arts, 1988. Mem. Actors Equity Assn., Screen Actors Guild, AFTRA, Twelfth Night Club, Ninety-Nines, Alpha Psi Omega, Zeta Phi Eta. Office: PO Box 734 Lindenhurst NY 11757

FARRENKOPF, JOAN HELEN, restorationist, artist; b. Massillon, Ohio, Aug. 7, 1953; d. Robert and Elizabeth F. Student, London Coll. Printing, 1974; B.F.A., Syracuse U., 1975. Pres., Farrenkopf Designs, Syracuse, N.Y., 1976—; tchr. Everson Mus. Art, 1972, Marshall U., 1975, Cortland Arts Council, 1979. Restored old Victorian houses that became nat. hist. dist., 1979. One woman shows include Canton Cultural Ctr., 1974, Lowe Art Ctr., 1974, Syracuse U., 1974, Massillon Mus., 1973, Marshall U., 1979, Canton Art Inst., 1979, Everson Mus., 1979. Recipient Pat Earle award Preservation League of Central N.Y., 1981; scholar London Coll. Printing, 1974. Mem. Tully Hist. Soc. (trustee), Landmarks Soc. Central N.Y. (exec. bd.), Nat. Trust Historic Preservation, N.E. Hawley Devel. Assn. (bd. dirs.), Nat. and Profl. Women (N.Y. State Young Careerist award 1982). Home: 209 Green St Syracuse NY 13203 Office: 1100 Malden Rd Syracuse NY 13211

FARRER, CLAIRE ANNE RAFFERTY, anthropologist, educator; b. N.Y.C., Dec. 26, 1936; d. Francis Michael and Clara Anna (Guerra) Rafferty; 1 child, Suzanne Claire. BA in Anthropology, U. Calif., Berkeley, 1970; MA in Anthropology, U. Tex., 1974, PhD in Anthropology, 1977. Various positions 1953-73; fellow Whitney M. Young Jr. Meml. Found., N.Y.C., 1974-75; arts specialist, grant adminstr. Nat. Endowment for Arts, Washington, 1976-77; Weatherhead resident fellow Sch. Am. Research, Santa Fe, 1977-78; asst. prof. anthropology U. Ill., Urbana, 1978-85; assoc. prof., coordinator applied anthropology Calif. State U., Chico, 1985—; cons. in field, 1974—; mem. film and video adv. panel Ill. Arts Council; mem. Ill Humanities Council, 1980-82. Co-founder, co-editor Folklore Women's Communication, 1972; editor spl. issue Jour. Am. Folklore, 1975, 1st rev. edit., 1986; co-editor: Forms of Play of Native North Americans, 1979. Active various civic orgns. Recipient 10 awards, fellowships and grants. Fellow Am. Anthrop. Assn., Soc. for Applied Anthropology, Assn. Anthrop. Study of Play; mem. Am. Ethnol. Soc., Am. Folklore Soc., Am. Soc. Ethnohistory. Mem. Soc. of Friends. Office: Calif State U Dept Anthropology Butte 311 Chico CA 95929-0400

FARRER-MESCHAN, RACHEL (MRS. ISADORE MESCHAN), physician; b. Sydney, Australia, May 21, 1915; came to U.S., 1946, naturalized, 1950; d. John H. and Gertrude (Powell) Farrer; m. Isadore Meschan, Sept. 3, 1943; children—David, Jane Meschan Foy, Rosalind Meschan Weir, Joyce Meschan Robinson. MB, BS, U. Melbourne (Australia), 1940; MD, Wake Forest U., 1957. Intern Royal Melbourne (Australia) Hosp., 1942; resident Women's Hosp., Melbourne, 1942-43, Bowman-Gray Sch. Medicine, Wake Forest U., Winston-Salem, N.C., 1957-73, asst. clin. prof. dept. ob-gyn, 1973—. Co-author (with I. Meschan): Atlas of Radiographic Anatomy, 1951, rev., 1959; Roentgen Signs in Clinic Diagnosis, 1956; Synopsis of Roentgen Signs, 1962; Roentgen Signs in Clinical Practice, 1966; Radiographic Positioning and Related Anatomy, 1968; Analysis of Roentgen Signs in General Radiology, 1973; Roentgen Signs in Diagnostic Imaging, Vol. III, 1986, Vol. IV, 1987. Home: 305 Weatherfield Ln Kernersville NC 27284

FARRIGAN, JULIA ANN, educator; b. Albany, N.Y., July 19, 1943; d. Charles Gerald and Julia Tryon (Shepherd) F. B.S., in Elem. Edn., SUNY Coll. at Plattsburgh, 1965; M.S. in Curriculum Planning and Devel., SUNY-Albany and U. Manchester (Eng.), 1973; postgrad. in adminstrv. services Calif. State U.-Fresno, 1976-78. With, Monroe-Woodbury Central Sch. Dist., Monroe, N.Y., 1965—, dist. coordinator gifted programs 1979—; tchr. The Pine Tree Sch., Monroe. Mem. NEA, Assn. Supervision and Curriculum Devel., N.Y. Acad. Sci., Mid-Huson Educators Gifted and Talented, Advocacy for Gifted and Talented Edn. N.Y. (state officer, editor state newsletter), DAR (William McIntosh chpt.), Delta Kappa Gamma (state asst. treas.). Democrat. Methodist. Contbr. articles in field to profl. jours. Office: Pine Tree Sch Pine Tree Rd Monroe NY 10950

FARRINGTON, HELEN AGNES, utility company executive; b. Queens, N.Y., Dec. 1, 1945; d. Joseph Christopher and Therese Marie (Breazzano) F. A.S., Interboro Inst., N.Y.C., 1965; A.A., Ohio State U., 1983, B.S. in Human Resource Mgmt., 1986. Mgmt. cert. U. Mich., 1980. With Ohio Power div. Am. Electric Power Co., Newark, Ohio, 1979-87; mgr. human resources Citizens Utilities Co., Stamford, Conn., 1987—. Mem. Am. Mgmt. Assn., Am. Soc. for Personnel Adminstrn., Am. Soc. Profl. Female Execs., Nat. Assn. Female Execs., Licking County C. of C. Home: 97 Richards Ave Apt B-4 Norwalk CT 06850

FARRIS, ANN, lawyer; b. Albuquerque, Jan. 12, 1954; d. Marshall Elmer and Joan (Taul) F. BA, U. N.Mex., 1976, JD, 1980. Bar: N.Mex., U.S. Dist. Ct., U.S. Ct. Appeals (10th cir.). Asst. dist. atty. Office Dist. Atty., Farmington, N.Mex., 1981; sole practice Albuquerque, 1982—. Active Albuquerque Civic Chorus. Mem. ABA, Albuquerque Bar Assn. Democrat. Presbyterian. Office: Barrister Hall Law Offices 407 7th St NW Albuquerque NM 87102

FARRIS, ELAINE ELIZABETH, computer executive; b. Lowell, Mass., Sept. 3, 1953; d. Fred Joseph and Doris Blanche (Dube) F. BA, Emmanuel Coll., 1975. Mktg. adminstrn. Computervision Corp., Bedford, Mass., 1976-78, mktg. communications, 1978-81; mgr. market adminstrn. Telesis Systems Corp., Chelmsford, Mass., 1981-84, new product program mgr., 1984-85, mgr. sales adminstrn., 1985-86, mgr. prodn., 1986-87; program mgr. Apollo Computer, Chelmsford, 1987-88, OEM sales specialist, 1988—. Office: Apollo Computer Co 330 Billerca Rd Chelmsford MA 01824

FARRIS, VERA KING, college president. BA in Biology magna cum laude, Tuskegee Inst., 1959; MS in Zoology, U. Mass., 1962, PhD in Zoology/Parasitology, 1965; LHD (hon.), Marymount Manhattan Coll., 1985; LLD (hon.), Monmouth Coll., West Long Branch, N.J., 1987; DSc honoris causa, Johnson and Wales Coll., 1988. Pres. Stockton State Coll., Pomona, N.J., 1983—; research assoc. U. Mich., Ann Arbor, 1965-66, instr. zoology and parasitology, 1967-68; instr. biology SUNY, Stony Brook, 1968-70, asst. prof. pathology and biology, 1970-72, assoc. prof., 1972-73, asst. to v.p. for acad. affairs, 1969-70, dean spl. programs, 1970-72; assoc. prof. biol. scis. SUNY, Brockport, 1973-77, prof., 1977-80, asst. v.p. acad. affairs, 1973, assoc. v.p. acad. affairs, 1974-77, chairperson dept. women's studies, 1975, acting dean liberal studies, 1976, acting dean social programs, 1977, acting v.p. acad. affairs, 1977-79, vice provost acad. affairs, 1979-80; prof. Kean Coll. N.J., Union, 1980-83; pres., prof. Stockton State Coll., Pomona, N.J., 1983—; pro; speaker at schs., profl. assn., colls.; bd. dirs. Elizabethtown Gass Corp. Contbr. articles to profl. jours. Mem. adv. bd. Children's TV Workshop, N.Y.C., 1979—, Woodson Found., 1986—; apptd. to Gov.'s Commn. for Adv. Council on Holocaust Edn. in N.J., 1982—, Martin Luther King, Jr. Commemorative Commn. N.J., 1984—; mem. N.J. State Bd. Examiners, 1984—, student assistance bd. N.J. Dept. Higher Edn., 1984—; 1st vice chair N.J. Pub. Broadcasting Authority, 1984—; founding mem. Gov.'s Award Acad., 1986—; mem. commn. on minorities in higher edn. Am. Council on Edn., 1987—, bd. dirs., 1988. Recipient Meritorious Service award Brockport Students, 1980, award N.J. unit Nat. Assn. Negro Bus. and Profl. Women's Clubs, Inc., 1982, award of merit Kean Coll. Student Govt., 1982, Black History award City of Atlantic City, 1984, Kappa Alpha Psi award, 1984, award Nat. Black Women's Assn., 1984, Achievement in Edn. award NAACP, 1984, award Nat. Assn. for Equal Opportunity in Higher Edn., 1984, Presdl. citation, 1984, Service Award of Yr. Alpha Theta Lambda chpt. Alpha Phi Alpha, 1985, award Upsilon Alpha chpt. Omega Psi Phi, 1985, Humanitarian award Chapel of 4 Chaplains, 1985, Woman of Yr. award Holly Shores Girl Scouts, 1985, Disting. Community Service award Anti-Defamation League of Atlantic City B'nai B'rith, 1985, N.J. Women of Achievement award N.J. State Fedn. Women's Clubs and Douglass Coll.- Rutgers U., 1985, 86, recognition award Council of Black Faculty and Staff/Stockton State Coll., 1986, award Zulu chpt. Lambda Sigma Upsilon, 1986, cert. of appreciation B'nai B'rith, 1986, award Nat. Assn. Black Women in Higher Edn., 1986, Brotherhood/Sisterhood award South Jersey chpt. NCCJ, 1986, Educator of Yr. award Black Atlantic City Pub. Co., 1987, hon. citation Fellowship of Chs. Atlantic City, 1987, Golden Trefoil award Del. Valley council Girl Scouts U.S., 1987, People of Yr. award Galloway Twp. Edn. Found., 1988, Women's History Month award Bloomfield (N.J.) Coll. 1988; named a hon. citizen of Atlanta, 1984; named Role Model Sun Newspaper, 1988; honored as 1st Woman Coll. Pres. of N.J. by N.J. Coll. and Univ. Coalition on Women's Edn., 1983. Mem. Am. Assn. State Colls. and Univs. (com. on undergrad. edn. 1984—), Mid. States Assn. Colls. and Schs. (trustee 1982—). Home: 300 Shore Rd Linwood NJ 08221 Office: Stockton State Coll Office of the Pres Pomona NJ 08240

FARROW, MIA VILLIERS, actress; b. Los Angeles, Feb. 9, 1945; d. John Villiers and Maureen Paula (O'Sullivan) F.; m. Andre Previn, Sept. 10, 1970 (div. Feb. 1979); children: Matthew Phineas and Sascha Villiers (twins), Lark Song, Fletcher Farrow, Summer Song, Gigi Soon Mi, Misha, Satchel. Student pub., pvt. schs. Actress appearing in TV and films. Debut in The Importance of Being Earnest, N.Y.C., 1964; starred in TV series Peyton Place; films include Hurricane, Rosemary's Baby, See No Evil, 1971, The Public Eye, 1972, The Great Gatsby, Peter Pan, A Wedding, 1978, Death on the Nile, A Midsummer Night's Sex Comedy, Zelig, The Purple Rose of Cairo, 1985, Broadway Danny Rose, Hannah and her Sisters, 1986, September, 1987, Radio Days, 1987; appeared in stage plays Romantic Comedy, Mary Rose, The Three Sisters, The House of Bernarda Alba, Ivanov; joined Royal Shakespeare Co., London, 1974. Recipient Golden Globe award, 1967; Best Actress award French Acad., 1969; Rio de Janeiro Film Festival award, 1969; Italian Academy award, 1970. Address: care Lionel Larner Ltd 850 7th Ave New York NY 10019 *

FARWELL, MARGARET JOHN, medical foundation/medical center executive; b. Chgo., Sept. 8, 1947; d. John Howland and Carol (Bowers) F. Student U. Exeter, Devon, Eng., 1968; BA, Baker U., 1969; postgrad. U. Kans., 1974-76. Jr. account exec. Biddle Advt. Agy., Kansas City, Mo., 1970-72; admissions officer Baker U., Baldwin, Kans., 1972-74, Benedictine Coll., Atchison, Kans., 1974-76; asst. dir. devel. Rush-Presbyn.-St. Luke's Med. Ctr., Chgo., 1978-81; devel. assoc. Mus. Sci. and Industry, Chgo., 1981-83; exec. v.p./dir. fund devel. Columbus-Cuneo-Cabrini Med. Found./Med. Ctr., Chgo., 1984-87; program speaker Chgo. Planned Giving Officers Roundtable, 1984, 86. Bd. dirs., sec. women's bd. Travelers and Immigrants Aid, Chgo., 1982—. Mem. Nat. Soc. Fundraising Execs. (membership com. Chgo. chpt. 1981-83, cert. com. 1982-83, co-chmn. nat. conf. com. 1985-86), Nat. Assn. Hosp. Devel. (regional conf. speaker Chgo. 1984), Nat. Cath. Devel. Conf., 1200 Club of Ill. (bd. dirs. Chgo. chpt. 1983-85). Republican. Episcopalian. Office: Columbus-Cuneo-Cabrini Med Found 676 N St Clair Suite 1900 Chicago IL 60611

FARWELL, SIGRID OLAFSON, consulting company executive; b. Ithaca, N.Y., June 4, 1933; d. Peter and Harriette (Smith) O.; B.A., Cornell U., 1955; tchr. cert. U. Colo., 1972, M.A., 1978; m. Theodore Austin Farwell, Jr., July 11, 1954; children—Karin, Peter, Eric Edward. Owner, tchr. Farwell Ballet Sch., Littleton, N.H., 1960-68; inservice coordinator nine sch. dists. Northwest Colo., 1974-75; head theatre dept. Platt Jr. High Sch., Boulder, Colo., 1976-79, Fairview High Sch., Boulder, 1979-80; pres. Sigrid Farwell & Assos., Inc., Boulder, 1980—, BDF Reflections, Inc., 1982-84. Founder Evergreen Jr. Theatre, 1970, Storybook Players, 1973; mem. Council Arts and Humanities, Steamboat Springs, 1973-75; vol. horseback riding and skiing programs Fitzsimmons Army Hosp. Amputee programs, 1970-73. Recipient Internat. Yr. of Child award for service and dedication, Family Acad. Internat. Children's Center, Stravanger, Norway and San Francisco, 1979. Mem. Internat. Platform Assn., Am. Soc. Group Psychotherapy and Psychodrama, Rocky Mountain SEN, Pub. play The Child of Fear, 1978. Home and Office: 7363 Cortez Ln Boulder CO 80303

FASANO, CLARA, sculptor; b. Castellaneta, Italy, Dec. 14, 1900; emigrated to U.S., 1907, naturalized, 1939; d. Pasquale and Julia (de Feudis) F.; m. Jean de Marco, July 8, 1936. Student, Cooper Union Art Inst., Art Students League, N.Y.C., 1917-21, Julien Academie and Colarossi Academie, Paris, 1924-26; scholar, Rome, Italy, 1922-24. Tchr. sculpture adult edn. Bd. Edn., N.Y., 1948-58; tchr. Manhattanville Coll. Exhibited at, Salon d'Automne, Paris, 1925; worked in own studio, exhibited in, Rome, 1926-32; exhibited in numerous shows, including, Worlds Fair, N.Y.C., 1939, Whitney Museum, NAD, Pa. Acad., Art Inst. Chgo., Met. Mus. Art, Am.-Brit. Center N.Y.C., Ferragil, Buckholz galleries; works represented in permanent collections at, Met. Mus. Art, N.Y.C., Manhattanville Coll. Sacred Heart, Purchase, N.Y., Norfolk Mus. Arts and Scis., Smithsonian Instn., Washington, Syracuse U., also pvt. collections, U.S., abroad; important works include series of twelve portraits in bronze, the last being of His Excellency Giuseppe Cataldi, pres. Corte dei Conti of Italy. Grantee, recipient citation Nat. Inst. Arts and Letters, 1952; recipient medal of Honor with citation Am. Artists Mag., Audubon Annual Exhbn., 1956, hon. mention Archtl. League N.Y., Gold Medals Exhbn., 1956, Daniel Chester French medal NAD, 1965, Peter Caesar Alberti award Italian Execs. Am. Inc., 1967, Dessie Greer award for sculpture NAD, 1968, 2d pl. sculpture competitions for entrance Supreme Ct. of Bklyn., for fountain sculpture for lobby 100 Church St. bldg., N.Y.C., sculpture commn. for relief Middleport (Ohio) Post Office U.S. Treasury Dept. competition for Apex Bldg. in Washington. Academician NAD; Fellow Nat. Sculpture Soc. (hon. mention 1956); mem. Audubon Artists (M. Grumbacher prize 1954), Sculptors Guild, Nat. Assn. Women Artists (Anonymous prize 1945, Marcia Brady Tucker prize 1950, medal of Honor for sculpture 63d ann. exhbn. 1955). Subject of articles, works reproduced in Am. Artist mag., Nat. Sculpture Rev., also books Sculpture in Modern America, Contemporary American Sculpture, The Materials and Methods of Sculpture. Office: 1083 Fifth Ave New York NY 10028

FASBENDER, CLEMENTINE MARIE, medical center training administrator; b. N.Y.C., Apr. 2, 1936; d. William Lawrence and Clementine E. (Makray) Scully; children: William D., Edward J., Bart C. BA in English and Edn., St. John's U., Jamaica, N.Y., 1957; MS, CUNY, 1979. Editor, copywriter U.S. Life Ins. Co., N.Y.C., 1958-61; office mgr. Mount & Rilling, Bklyn., 1961-76; legal asst. Previte, Glasser & Farber, Jackson Heights, N.Y., 1976-77; adminstr., researcher N.Y. State Assembly, N.Y.C., 1977-79; tng. dir. Lincoln Med. and Mental Health Ctr., Bronx, N.Y., 1980—; program dir. Forest Hills (N.Y.) Adult Edn. System, 1980—; tchr. ESL, N.Y.C., 1971-80; pvt. practice cons., Jackson Heights, 1985—. Editor Capsule newsletter, Lincoln Med. Ctr., 1980—. Mem. AAUW, Am. Soc. for Health Edn. Trainers, Assn. Hosp. Personnel Adminstrs., Council Tng. Dirs. (sec. 1982-84, vice chair 1985-86), Mensa (dir. vols. Greater N.Y. area, bd. dirs.). Roman Catholic. Home: 33-11 82d St Jackson Heights NY 11372 Office: Lincoln Med and Mental Health 234 E 149th St Bronx NY 10451

FASCIA, DOMENICA MARY, medical technologist; b. Mechanicsville, N.Y.; d. Anthony and Assunta (Dinardo) F.; B.S., Calif. State U., Los Angeles, 1970, M.A., 1974. Chief med. technologist St. Mary's Hosp., Troy, N.Y., 1951-56, Santa Teresita Hosp., Duarte, Calif., 1956—. Registered sanitarian; profl. entomologist; hazard control mgr. Mem. Am. Soc. Clin. Pathologists, Am. Registry Profl. Etomologists, Internat. Soc. Clin. Lab. Tech., Calif. Assn. Med. Tech., Am. Soc. Microbiology, Am. Assn. Blood Banks, Assn. of Practitioners in Infection Control, Healthcare Safety Profls., Am. Philatelic Soc. Democrat. Roman Catholic. Clubs: Am. Contract Bridge League, Federated Women's Am. Address: 403 N Grand Ave Monrovia CA 91016

FASS, BARBARA, city official. Mayor, Stockton, Calif., 1985—. Address: Office of Mayor 425 N El Dorado St Stockton CA 95202 *

FAUBEL, NANCY CAROLINE, business executive; b. Rochester, N.Y., July 10, 1958; d. Robert S. and Elisabeth (Torrey) F. BS, Alfred U., 1979; MBA, U. Rochester, 1983. Cert. flight instr., comml. pilot; lic. real estate agt.; notary pub. Engr. I, Babcock & Wilcox, Augusta, Ga., 1979-80, sales engr., Phila., 1980-82; v.p. Precision Equipment Services, Rochester, 1983-86; pres. Valley Aviation, Eastern W.Va. Regional Airport, 1986—; pres., owner Baron's Restaurant, Eastern W.Va. Regional Airport, 1986—. Del., 19th Ward Community Assn., Rochester, 1986; capt. CAP, 1985—. Mem. Nat. Assn. Female Execs., Rochester Pilots Assn., Rochester Real Estate Bd., Martinsburg-Berkeley C. of C. (aviation com.). Republican. Lodge: Kiwanis (bd. dirs. S. Berkeley, W.Va.). Avocations: flying, carpentry, art. Home: Rt 4 Box 431-C Martinsburg WV 25401 Office: Valley Aviation W Va Regional Airport Martinsburg WV 25401

FAUDE, DIANE ELAINE, state official; b. Medford, Wis., May 13, 1950; d. Harley Herbert and Iris Elaine (Ogle) F.; 1 child, Diana Lynn. Grad. high sch., Owen, Wis. With Manpower, Milw., 1968-69; claims adjuster ITT Life Ins. Corp. subs. ITT Corp., Thorp, Wis., 1970-75; stenographer Alaska State Bldg. Authority, Anchorage, 1975-77, sec., 1977-80, adminstrv. asst., 1980-85, adminstrv. officer, 1985-86, budget officer, 1986—. Home: 4831 Loretta Ln Anchorage AK 99507 Office: Alaska State Bldg Authority 624 W Internat Airport Rd Anchorage AK 99518

FAUL, JUNE PATRICIA, education specialist; b. Detroit; d. John William and Shirley Olive (Block) Lynch; m. George Johnson Faul, Dec. 22, 1949; children: Robert Michael, Alison. Student, Coll. Sequoias, 1942-44, UCLA, 1947; BA, U. Calif., Berkeley, 1952. Cert. elem. tchr., Calif. Tchr. Tulare County (Calif.) Schs., 1945-46, Tulare City Schs., 1946-48, Visalia (Calif.) City Schs., 1948-49, Richmond (Calif.) City Schs., 1951-52, Pacific Grove (Calif.) Sch. Dist., 1965-85; designated English teaching specialist State of Calif., 1969—; lectr. Calif. State U., Fresno, 1969, U. Calif., Santa Cruz, 1970. Active human relations commn. City of Richmond, 1962-64; mem. adv. bd. Family Resource Ctr.; founding mem., 1st pres. Monterey (Calif.) Peninsula Child Abuse Prevention Council, 1974; hon. life mem. Calif. PTA; bd. dirs. Carmel Cultural Commn., 1964-67, Harrison Meml. Library, Carmel, Calif., 1978-84; mem., chmn. bd. Monterey Peninsula Airport Dist., 1980—. Mem. Union Concerned Scientists, Nat. Orgn. to Insure Sound Controlled Environment, Friends of Hopkins Marine Station (founder, bd. dirs.) Carmel Heritage (founder, bd. dirs.), Monterey NAACP (life), Monterey Mus. Art (life), Monterey Symphony Guild (life). Democrat. Avocation: writing. Home: PO Box 4365 Carmel CA 93921

FAULKENBERRY, JEAN MITCHELL, educator; b. Ranger, Tex., Dec. 20, 1926; d. John Rufus and Annie (Adams) Mitchell; m. Thomas R. Faulkenberry, July 8, 1949; children: Joyce, Ray, Thomas Dale, Richard Lance, Roanld Gene. AS, Midland Coll., 1979. Student services dir. Ft. Stockton (Tex.) Ind. Sch. Dist., 1959—. Author: The Gavel is Yours, 1985, Efficient School Secretary, 1986; mag. editor The Tex. Sec., 1973-74, Nat. Edn. Sec., 1979-81; contbr. articles to profl. jours. Mem. steering com. Clements for Gov., Tex., 1982, gov. com., 1986—; mem. Lone Star Lobsters, Tex., 1983—. Mem. Nat. Assn. Ednl. Office Personnel (past pres., cons. 1960—), Am. Assn. Sch. Adminstrs., Tex. Ednl. Secs. Assn. (pres. 1978-79, cons. 1960—), Tex. Assn. Sch. Adminstrs., Assn. Tex. Profl. Educators, Pecos County Ednl. Sec.-Aides (pres. 1972, 84, Sec. of Yr. 1984, 88). Baptist. Lodges: Order Ea. Star (worthy matron 1968, 78), Social Order Beauceant. Home: Box 613 Fort Stockton TX 79735 Office: Ft Stockton Ind Sch Dist Fort Stockton TX 79735

FAULKNER, GWEN, English instructor; b. Perry, Fla., Aug. 14, 1947; d. Thomas Jefferson and Sara Helen (Cone) F. AA, North Fla. Jr. Coll., 1968; BA, Fla. State U., 1969, MA, 1971. Instr. English Taylor County High Sch., Perry, 1972-80; instr. English North Fla. Jr. Coll., Madison, 1981—, dir. theatre, 1982—; pub. realtions officer Taylor Sch. Dist., Perry, 1975-77; co-owner, photographer Bob's Photos, Perry, 1974-81. editorialist Taco Times, 1971-74. Coordinator queen's pageant Fla. Forest Festival, Perry, 1973-77, chair parade com., 1975; area rep. Gator Boosters, Inc., Gainesville, 1985-87. Mem. NEA, Nat. Council Tchrs. of English, Fla. Council Tchrs. of English (1986 Honor award 1986), Fla. Assn. Community Colls. (Outstanding Theatre Arts Program 1987), Fla. Theatre Conf., Delta Kappa Gamma. Democrat. Baptist. Home: 1209 N Quincy St Perry FL 32347 Office: North Fla Jr Coll 1000 Turner Davis Dr Madison FL 32340

FAUNCE, SARAH CUSHING, museum curator; b. Tulsa, Aug. 19, 1929; d. George Jr. and Helen Pauline (Colwell) F. B.A., Wellesley Coll., 1951; M.A., Washington U., St. Louis, 1959; postgrad., Columbia U., 1960-63. Tchr. history Hartridge Sch., Plainfield, N.J., 1954-56; tchr. art Mary C. Wheeler Sch., Providence, 1958-59; instr. art history Barnard Coll., N.Y.C., 1962-64; sec. adv. council art history Columbia U., 1963-70, registrar, curator, 1965-70; curator paintings and sculpture Bklyn. Mus., 1970—; exhbn. cons. Jewish Mus., N.Y.C., 1968-70; adv. bd. Skowhegan Sch. Painting and Sculpture, N.Y.C., 1978—; adv. council art history dept. Columbia U., 1970—. Exhbn. catalog author: Anne Ryan Collages, 1974, Carl Larsson, 1982; author, editor: Belgian Art 1880-1914, 1980; editor: Northern Light: Realism and Symbolism in Scandinavian Painting 1880-1910, 1982. Travel grantee Columbia U., 1963. Mem. Coll. Art Assn., Victorian Soc., Am. Assn. Mus., Phi Beta Kappa. Democrat. Episcopalian. Home: 28 E 92d St New York NY 10128 Office: The Bklyn Mus Eastern Pkwy New York NY 11238

FAUR, YVONNE CONSTANCE, microbiologist; b. Romania, Sept. 11, 1916; came to U.S., 1963, naturalized, 1968; d. Alexander S. and Clara I. (Abra) Ardan; M.D., U. Bucharest, 1940; m. Aurel Sebastian Faur, Nov. 20, 1943. Chief microbiology lab. Cantacuzino State Inst., Bucharest, 1948-62; research scientist immunohematology dept. N.Y.U., 1963-66; cons. microbiologist Bur. Labs., N.Y. State Dept. Health, 1966-73, sr. research scientist, 1973—, lectr. microbiology, 1967—. Recipient Sci. Paper award Am. Public Health Assn., 1979. Fellow Am. Acad. Microbiology; mem. Am. Soc. Microbiology. Author manual, 60 papers in field. Patentee medium for pathogenic neisseria. Office: 455 1st Ave New York NY 10016

FAUSETT, PATRICIA LEE, electronics company executive; b. Washington, Feb. 8, 1944; d. Gerald LeRoy and Bernice Kennedy; B.S., Purdue U., 1965; M.B.A. Golden Gate U., 1983; m. Richard Orlin Fausett, Sept. 15, 1979; children—Stephen Johnson, Jr., Michael Lee Johnson. Tchr., Franklin Sch., Burlingame, Calif., Peter Hoy Sch., Lombard, Ill., 1966-71; acct. Hewlett-Packard, Palo Alto, Calif., 1978-81, buyer, 1981-84, corp. materials contract mgr., 1984-87, sr. contract mgr., 1987—. Treas., Almond Sch. PTA, Los Altos, Calif., 1978-79. Mem. AAUW, Alpha Chi Omega, Alpha Delta Kappa. Democrat. Roman Catholic. Office: 3000 Hanover St Palo Alto CA 94303

FAUST, ANNE SONIA, lawyer; b. Honolulu, Aug. 27, 1936; d. Alfred and Geneva Dora (Barnett) F. B.A., U. Hawaii, 1960; cert. Coro Found. Internship in Pub. Affairs, 1961; J.D., Harvard U., 1964. Bar: Hawaii, 1964. Dep. corp. counsel City and County of Honolulu, 1964-66; asst. researcher Legislative Reference Bur., Honolulu, 1966-69; assoc. counsel Legal Aid Soc., Honolulu, 1969-70; dep. atty. gen. State of Hawaii, Honolulu, 1970-72; atty., exec. officer Hawaii Pub. Employment Relations Bd., Honolulu, 1972-80; 1st dep. corp. counsel County of Maui, Wailuku, Hawaii, 1980-81; chief antitrust div. Dep. Atty. Gen., State of Hawaii, Honolulu, 1981-86; chief regulatory Hawaiian Homelands Hawaii Housing Authority Div. Dept. Atty. Gen. State of Hawaii, 1986—; ex-officio mem. Gov.'s Com. Status of Women, Hawaii, 1971-72; mem. Hawaii Bd. Bar Examiners, 1975-79. Mem. ABA (membership chmn. Hawaii 1965), Phi Beta Kappa, Phi Kappa Phi. Mem. Ch. of Christ. Club: Obedience Tng. of Hawaii (Honolulu) (treas. 1982-87). Home: 47-415 Kapehe St Kaneohe HI 96744 Office: Dept Atty Gen State Capital 4th Floor Honolulu HI 96813

FAUST, MARGARET SILER, psychology educator; b. Tientsin, China, Feb. 22, 1926; came to U.S., 1928; d. Charles Arthur and Marion Louise (Pierce) Siler; m. William Langdon Faust, Aug. 26, 1950; children—Katherine, Ann, Marion. B.A., Pomona Coll., 1948; M.A., Stanford U., 1951, Ph.D., 1957. Lic. psychologist, Calif. From asst. prof. to prof. Scripps Coll., Claremont, Calif., 1960-70, prof. psychology, 1970—. Author: Somatic Development of Adolescent Girls, 1977; contbr. articles to profl. jours. Bur. for Edn. of Handicapped Postdoctoral fellow UCLA, 1980; Grant Found. grantee, 1970-72. Mem. Am. Psychol. Assn., Soc. for Research in Child Devel., Sigma Xi. Office: Scripps Coll Psychology Dept Claremont CA 91711

FAUST, NAOMI FLOWE, educator, poet; b. Salisbury, N.C.; d. Christopher Leroy and Ada Luella (Graham) Flowe; A.B., Bennett Coll.; M.A., U. Mich., 1945; Ph.D., N.Y. U., 1963; m. Roy Malcolm Faust, Aug. 16, 1948. Elem. tchr. Public Schs. Gaffney (S.C.); tchr. English, French, phys. edn. Atkins High Sch., Winston-Salem; instr. English, Bennett Coll. and So. U., Scotlandville, La., 1944-46; prof. English, Morgan State Coll., Balt., 1946-48; tchr. English, Greensboro (N.C.) Public Schs., 1948-51, N.Y.C. Public Schs., 1954-63; prof. edn. Queens Coll. of City U. N.Y., Flushing, 1964-82; lectr. in field; writer, lectr., poetry readings, 1982—. Named Tchr.-Author of 1979, Tchr.-Writer; cert. of Merit for poem Cooper Hill Writers Conf., 1970; Achievement award L.I. br. AAUW, 1985. Mem. AAUP, Nat. Council Tchrs. English, Nat. Women's Book Assn., World Poetry Soc. Intercontinental, N.Y. Poetry Forum, NAACP, United Negro Coll. Fund, Alpha Kappa Alpha, Alpha Kappa Mu, Alpha Epsilon. Author: Discipline and the Classroom Teacher, 1977; (poetry) Speaking in Verse, 1974; All Beautiful Things, 1983; contbr. poetry to jours. Home: 112-01 175th St Jamaica NY 11433

FAUSTO-STERLING, ANNE, educator; b. N.Y.C., July 30, 1944; d. Philip and Dorothy Ruth (Dannenberg) Sterling; B.A., U. Wis., 1965; Ph.D., Brown U., 1970; m. Nelson Fausto, Dec. 3, 1966. Asst. prof. Brown U., Providence, 1971-76, asso. prof. biology, 1976-86, prof. biology, 1986—; NSF grant reviewer devel. biology. Mellon fellow Wellesley Center for Research on Women, 1980-81; fellow Pembroke Center Research and Teaching on Women, 1982-83. Mem. AAAS, Soc. Developmental Biology, History of Sci. Soc., Nat. Women's Studies Assn., Internat. Soc. Developmental Biology. Contbr. articles to publs. sci. and women's studies. Office: Box G Brown Univ Providence RI 02912

FAVREAU, SUSAN DEBRA, management consultant; b. Cleve., Dec. 15, 1955; d. Donald Francis and Helen Patricia (Rafferty) F. Cert., N.Y. State Police Acad., 1974; student, Hudson Valley Community Coll., 1983-85, Cornell U., 1984, SUNY, 1984—. Communications specialist N.Y. State Police, Loudonville, 1974-87; communications specialist div. hdqrs., 1987—; mgmt. cons., sec.-treas., dir. Don Favreau Assocs., Inc., Clifton Park, N.Y., 1983-86, v.p., 1986—; adj. faculty Internat. Assn. Chiefs of Police; NYSPIN coordinator FBI/Nat. Crime Info. Ctr. cert. program, 1983. Author: Teamwork in the Telecommunication Center, 1986, One More Time: How to be a Mature and Successful Telecommunications Manager, 1987; also NYSPIN cert. manuals. Recipient Dirs. commendation N.Y. State Police Acad., 1977, commendation N.Y. State Police, 1978, Supt.'s commendation N.Y. State Police, 1986. Mem. Nat. Assn. Female Execs., N.Y. State Civil Service Assn., Emergency Communicators' Profl. Assn. (mem. adv. bd.), Colonie Police Benevolent Assn. (hon.), Assoc. Pub. Safety Communications Officers (planning commn. mem. Atlantic chpt. 1986, registration chair annual NE conf. 1986), N.Y. State Troopers Police Benevolent Assn. (hon.), Nat. Bus. Women Am., Internat. Assn. Chiefs Police, Am. Horse Shows Assn. Republican. Roman Catholic. Avocations: equestrienne, target shooting, reading, sewing. Home: 4D Hollandale Apts Clifton Park NY 12065 Office: Hdqrs NY State Police State Office Bldg Campus Albany NY 12226

FAWELL, BEVERLY, state legislator; b. Oak Park, Ill., Sept. 17, 1930. BA, Elmhurst Coll.; postgrad., No. Ill. U. Mem. Ill. Ho. Reps., 1981-83, Ill. Senate, 1983—. Republican. Office: 2 S 630 Arboretum Glen Ellyn IL 60137 *

FAY, DARCY HUNT, international training and organizational development consultant, educator; b. Cleve.; d. Horace Byron Jr. and Bette (Berne) Fay; m. Paul L. Bundick. BA in Polit. Sci., Boston Coll., 1970; M. in Internat. Adminstrn., Sch. for Internat. Tng., Brattleboro, Vt., 1979; postgrad. Fielding Inst. Cert. in intercultural tng. Tchr. Internat. Sch. Tokyo (Japan), 1971-74, Am. Sch. of Barcelona (Spain), 1974-75; dir. African/Am. Educators program AAUW Ednl. Found., Washington, 1977-81; cons. Internat. Soc. for Intercultural Edn., Tng. and Research, Washington, 1982-84; cons. Delphi Research Assocs., Washington, 1984-85, World Bank, Washington, 1984-85; pvt. practice cons., Washington, 1986—. Contbr. articles to profl. jours. Recipient Japanese Flower Arrangement award Sogetsu Sch., Tokyo, 1974. Mem. Asia Soc., Assn. for Women in Devel., Capital Press Women, Internat. Soc. Intercultural Edn., Tng. and Research (1984 conf. steering com., program com., chmn. conf. publs. com.), Nat. Assn. Female Execs., Am. Soc. Tng. and Devel., Assn. for Women in Devel., NOW, Soc. for Internat. Devel./Women in Devel., Nat. Mus. Women in Arts (charter), OD Network. Home: 4545 Connecticut Ave NW #635 Washington DC 20008

FAY, SISTER MAUREEN A., college administrator. BA in English magna cum laude, Siena Heights Coll., 1960; MA in English, U. Detroit, 1966; PhD, U. Chgo., 1976. Tchr. English, speech, moderator student newspaper, student council St. Paul High Sch., Groose Point, Mich., 1960-64; chairperson English dept., dir. student dramatics, moderator student publs. Dominican High Sch., Detroit, 1964-69; co-dir. Cath. student ctr. Adrian (Mich.) Coll., 1969-71; instr. English Siena Heights Coll., Adrian, 1969-71; evaluators inst. criminal justice execs. U. Chgo., 1971-73; instr. English U. Ill., Chgo., 1971-74; dir. evaluation sch. new learning DePaul U., Chgo., 1974-75; fellow in acad. adminstrn. Saint Xavier Coll., Chgo., 1975-76, dean. grad. studies, 1979-83, dean continuing edn., 1976-83; asst. prof. No. Ill. U., Dekalb, 1980-83; pres. Mercy Coll. Detroit, 1983—; v.p. VAUT Corp. bd. dirs. four inner city high schs., Archdiocese Chgo.; mem. exec. com. Assn. Mercy Colls.; adv. com. Adult Learning Services, The Coll. Bd., Met. Affairs Corp. of Detorit and SE Mich., cons. Nat. Assn. for Religious Women, 1974-75, North Cen. Assn. Colls. and Schs., evaluator commn. on higher edn.; trustee Rosary Coll., River Forest, Ill.; mem. div. bd. Mercy Hosps. and Health Services of Detroit; bd. dirs. Nat. Bank of Detroit. Asst. editor: (book rev.): Adult Education, A Journal of Research and Theory, 1971-74. Steering com. Metro Detroit GIVES; exec. com., edn. task force Detroit Strategic Planning com., 1987; trustee Mich. Opera Theatre; bd. dirs. Greater Detroit Interfaith Round Table Nat. Conf. Christians and Jews, Inc., The Detroit Symphony. Mem. Am. Assn. Higher Edn., North Cen. Assn. (cons., evaluator commn. on higher edn.), Nat. Assn. Ind. Colls. and Univs., Assn. Ind. Colls. and Univs. of Mich. (exec. com.), Am. Assn. Cath. Colls. and Univs., AAUW, Pi Lambda Theta. Office: Mercy Coll Detroit Office of the Pres 8200 W Outer Dr Detroit MI 48219

FAY, NANCY ELIZABETH, nurse; b. Fulton, N.Y., May 10, 1943; d. Harold and Jean (Junker) Sant; m. Ronald George Fay, July 30, 1966; step children: Rory Patrick, Ronald George Jr. R.N., Genesee Hosp., Rochester, N.Y., 1964. Cert. nurse practitioner; cert. physician's asst., cert. diabetes educator. N.Y. Head maternity nurse St. Luke's Hosp., Utica, N.Y., 1975-78, diabetes clinician, 1978-82, co-dir. diabetes out-patient clinic, 1980-82; nurse practitioner, physician's asst. Slocum Dickson Med. Group, Utica, 1982—. Recipient Extra Mile award St. Luke's Hosp., 1979, Outstanding Citizenship award Am. Legion, Utica, 1982; Diabetes research grantee Diabetes Project, Ctr. Disease Control Utica, 1980-82, 21st Ann. Scroll award Cen. N.Y. Acad. Medicine, . Mem. Am. Diabetes Assn. (pres. Utica chpt. 1983—, Outstanding Vol. of Yr. 1978, bd. dirs. N.Y. State affiliate 1983—, 1st v.p. 1986-87, Program award 1985-86, profl. edn. chmn. 1983—, chair patient and pub. edn. Upstate Affiliate, 1987—, 1st v.p., 1988-89, applicant nat. com. patient and pub. and profl. edn. 1988-89, pres.-elect N.Y. State Affiliate 1988-89), Am. Acad. Physician's Assts., Am. Assn. Diabetes Educators, Womens Health and Edn. Referral Service St. Luke's Hosp. (bd. dirs. 1987—). Republican. Methodist. Avocations: doll collecting, dancing, poetry, bike riding. Home: Valley Rd Oriskany NY 13424 Office: Slocum Dickson Med Group 430 Court St Utica NY 13502

FAY, TONI GEORGETTE, public affairs administrator; b. N.Y.C., Apr. 25, 1947; d. George E. and Allie C. (Smith) Fay. B.A., Duquesne U., Pitts., 1968; M.S.W. (NIMH fellow 1970-72), U. Pitts., 1972, M.Ed., 1973; cert. Yale U. Drug Dependence Inst., 1973. Caseworker, N.Y.C. Dept. Welfare, 1968-70; regional commr. Gov. Pa. Council Drugs and Alcohol, 1973-76; dir. social services Pitts. Drug Abuse Ctr., 1972-73; dir. planning and devel. Nat. Council Negro Women, 1977-79; exec. v.p. D. Parke Gibson Assocs., 1979-82; mgr. community relations Time Inc., N.Y.C., 1982-83, dir. corporate community relations and affirmative action, 1983—; dir. corp. community relations, 1984. Bd. dirs. N.Y.C. Pvt. Industry Council; v.p. Nat. Coalition of 100 Black Women; v.p., bd. dirs. Mary McLeod Bethune Mus. and Archives, Washington, Girls Scout U.S.A. Council of Greater N.Y., Protestant Welfare Fedn. N.Y., Coro Found.; mem. Bus. Urban Issues Council of Conf. Bd. Named Woman of Yr., Pitts. YWCA, 1975; recipient Twin award YWCA of USA, 1987; named one 100 Top Women in Bus., Dollars and Sense Mag., 1986. Mem. Exec. Leadership Council, Alpha Kappa Alpha. Office: Time Life Bldg Rockefeller Ctr New York NY 10020

FAYEN, EMILY GALLUP, systems analyst, administrator; b. Newton, N.J., Feb. 9, 1941; d. Winslow S. and Esther (Hoagland) Gallup; m. Rick Fayen, Feb. 17, 1973 (div. 1982). BS in Math. and Physics, U. Md.; M of Pub. Adminstrn. in Info. Sci., Am. U. With Documentation, Inc., Bethesda, Md., 1963-65; tech. document analyst Naval Ship Research and Devel., Carderock, Md., 1965-68; ops. research analyst FDA, Washington, 1968; sr. systems analyst Computer Scis. Corp., Falls Church, Va., 1968-73; cons. U.S. Govt., 1972-76; sr. engr. Creare, Inc., Hanover, N.H., 1973-74; reference librarian Fiske Free Library, Claremont, N.H., 1976-77; programmer, analyst Norris Cotton Cancer Ctr.-Dartmouth Coll., Hanover, 1977-79; dir. library automation Dartmouth Coll., 1979-84; asst. dir. libraries U. Pa., Phila., 1984—; lectr. USIA AMPART, Europe, 1987. Contbr. articles to profl. jours. Mem. Assn. Computing Machinery, Am. Soc. Info. Sci. (chair Spl. Interest Group/Tech. Info. Soc. 1982-83, chair Spl.Interest Group/Users Online Interaction 1983-84), Am. Library Assn., Nat. Acad. Scis. (NRC task force to Indonesia 1986-87). Home: 2509 Waverly St Philadelphia PA 19146 Office: U Pa Library 3420 Walnut St Philadelphia PA 19104

FAZZINI, GEORGIA CAROL, small business owner; b. Chicago Heights, Ill., Feb. 17, 1946; d. George and Corella A.T. (Roggeveen) Tjemmes; m. Dan Fazzini, Dec. 31, 1964; 1 child, Daniel Edward. Student, Ill. State U., Normal, 1963-64, Nat. Beauty Coll., 1979. Sec. Marshall Erdman & Assoc., Madison, Wis., 1972-73, U. Wis., Madison, 1973-74, 1974; sec. Waukegan (Ill.) Devel. Ctr., 1974-75; br. adminstr. Universal Bus. Machines, Boise, Idaho, 1982-83; owner Substitute Sec. Typing Service, Boise, 1983-87, Revisions Resume Writing Service, Tulsa, 1987—; cons. Nat. Multiple Sclerosis Soc., Boise, 1982-86, Placed Co. Employment Agy., Boise, 1983-85; instr. resumes Boise Schs./Dept. of Community Edn., 1986-87. Author: (poem) Unrequited Love, 1986. Pres. News Neighbors League, Canton, Ohio, 1978-79; vice chmn., bd. dirs., sec. Nat. Multiple Sclerosis Soc. (Idaho chpt.), Boise, 1982-86; guest speaker Miss Teen Pageant, Boise, 1983-84; lobbyist Boise Secretarial Services, 1985-86. Recipient Rose of Month award New Neighbors League, 1979, Patient Achievement award Nat. Multiple Sclerosis Soc., 1983. Home: 3803 E 99th Pl Tulsa OK 74137 Office: Sub Sec Typing Service 4477 Emerald Suite C130 Boise ID 83706

FEAGLER, VIRGINIA MILLER, institutional researcher; b. Princeton, Ind., Mar. 25, 1940; d. Warren Hamilton and Helen (Smith) Miller; children: Troy A., Eric C. BA in History, Ind. U., 1963, MS in Edn., 1966; MA in Librarianship, U. Denver, 1976. Library asst. Ind. U. Biology Library, Bloomington, 1963-65; serials librarian Washington U. Sch. Medicine Library, St. Louis, 1966-68; serials librarian, dir. Philsom Network Washington U. Sch. Medicine Library, 1970-73; adminstrv. asst. Colo. commn. on Higher Edn., Denver, 1974-77; asst. dir. instl. analysis Colo. State U. Office Budgets and Planning, Ft. Collins, 1977-78; assoc. dir. Colo. State U. Office Budgets and Planning, 1978-84, dir. instl. analysis, 1984-87; asst. to dean for budgeting, planning Colo. State U. Coll. Applied Human Scis., 1987—; participant Acad. Mgmt. Inst., Denver, 1986-87; lectr. in field. Contbr. articles to profl. jours. Agy. liaison United Way, Ft. Collins, 1985-87. MLA scholar, 1973-74. Mem. Assn. for Instl. Research, Colo. Assn. PLanners and Instl. research, Rocky Mt. Assn. for Instl. research, Colo. Women in Higher Edn. Adminstrn., Am. Assn. of Collegiate Registrars & Admissions Officers. Unitarian. Home: 1213 Village Ln Fort Collins CO 80521 Office: Colo State U Deans Office Coll Applied Human Scis Fort Collins CO 80523

FEAGLES, GAIL WINTER, lawyer; b. Warrenton, Mo., Dec. 11, 1951; d. Henry George and Evelyn May (Schulze) Winter; m. Prentiss Eric Feagles, Aug. 9, 1975; children: Eric, Amy. A.B. in French, B.S. in Edn., U. Mo., 1972; J.D., Duke U., 1976. Bar: Va. 1976. Assoc., Hazel, Beckhorn & Hanes, Fairfax, Va., 1976-82, ptnr., 1983—; ptnr. Hazel, THomas, Fiske, Beckhorn and Hanes. Bd. dirs. Wesley Housing Devel. Corp., Alexandria, Va., 1983—; v.p., bd. dirs. Wesley Property Mgmt. Corp., 1987—; chmn. Community Outreach Devel., 1984-87; active Fairfax United Methodist Ch., 1978-85, St. Matthew's United Meth. Ch., 1985—; Mem. ABA, Fairfax County Bar Assn. (mem. library com. 1979-82, mem. com. 1979-81, sec. real estate sect. 1982-84, chmn. 1984-87, vice chmn. 1987—, mem. fee arbitration com. 1983—), Phi Beta Kappa.Named One of Va.'s Outstanding Women Attys. Va. Women Atty.'s Assn. Office: Hazel Beckhorn & Hanes PO Box 547 Fairfax VA 22030

FEALEY, MARY LINDA, personnel director; b. Ancon, Republic Panama, Feb. 4, 1951; d. Fred Ethan and Marion (Orr) Wells; m. Guy Michael Fealey, June 19, 1971; children: Guy Ethan, Jamie Laurayan. AAS, Canal Zone Coll., Balboa, Republic Panama, 1971. Sec. USAF, Howard AFB, Canal Zone, Republic Panama, 1969-79, personnel specialist, 1979-80; personnel specialist USAF, Phoenix, 1980-83; personnel specialist USN, Whidbey Island, Oak Harbor, Wash., 1984-86, dep. personnel officer, 1986—; cons. Working Women, Oak Harbor, 1984-87; mem. Puget Sound Compensation Soc., Oak Harbor, 1987—. Republican. Unitarian. Office: Civilian Personnel Dept Bldg 110 NAS Whidbey Island Oak Harbor WA 98278-2300

FEARS, MARSHA ANETTE, corporate professional, accountant; b. Akron, Ohio, Sept. 8, 1945; d. Garfield Jr. and Freda Lee (Hill) F.; 1 child, S. Lamont. BS, U. Akron, 1978. CPA, Ohio. Sec. Goodyear Aerospace, Akron, 1968-73; acctg. clk. Goodyear Tire & Rubber Co., Akron, 1973-76, jr. acct., 1976-78, acct., 1978-83, sr. acct., 1983-86, sect. mgr., 1986—. Counselor Jr. Acmhievement, Akron, 1972. Mem. Ohio Soc. CPAs. Democrat. Baptist. Office: Goodyear Tire & Rubber Co 1144 E Market St Akron OH 44305

FEATHERMAN, SANDRA, educator; b. Phila., Apr. 14, 1934; d. Albert N. and Rebe (Burd) Green; B.A., U. Pa., 1955, M.A., 1978, Ph.D., 1978; m. Bernard Featherman, Mar. 29, 1958; children—Andrew Charles, John James. Asst. prof. dept. polit. sci. Temple U., Phila., 1978-84, assoc. prof., 1984—, chmn. grad. program, 1982-84, dir. MPA program, 1984-85. Mem. Sch. Bd. Nominating Panel, Phila., 1969-71, 79-81; bd. dirs. Citizens Com. Public Edn. in Phila., 1977—, pres., 1979-81; pres. Pa. Fcdn. Community Coll., faculty senate Temple U., 1985-86, dir. Ctr. for Pub. Policy, 1986—, asst. to pres., 1986—; trustees, 1974-75; trustee Community Coll. Phila., 1970—, chmn. bd. trustees, 1984-86; life trustee Samuel Fels Found.; bd. dirs. United Way S.E. Pa., 1977—, United Way Pa., 1981-84, Concerto Soloists of Phila., 1978-81; mem. commn. jud. selection and evaluation Phila. Bar Assn., 1979-81; nat. bd. dirs. Girls Clubs Am., 1971-74, pres., Phila., 1971-73; mem. Pa. Council on Arts, 1979-83; dir. Women and Founds. Corp. Philanthropy, 1986—; mem. nat. bd. dirs. Women and Founds.-Corp. Philanthropy, 1986—; v.p. Jewish Community Relations Council, 1982—, bd. dirs. 1986—; speaker Commonwealth of Pa. Humanities Council, 1988. Recipient Brooks Graves award Pa. Polit. Sci. Assn., 1982, City of Phila. Community Service award, 1984, Louise Waterman Wise award Am. Jewish Congress, 1988. Mem. Am. Planning Assn., Am. Polit. Sci. Assn., Am. Soc. Public Adminstrn., AAUW (dir. Phila. chpt. 1975-78, 80—, pres. 1984—, chair internat. fellowships panel 1987—, nat. chair ednl. found. program Internat. Fellows Panel 1988—, Outstanding Woman award 1986). Author: Jews, Black and Ethnics, 1979; also articles. Home: 2100 Spruce St Philadelphia PA 19103 Office: Temple U Broad and Montgomery Sts Philadelphia PA 19122

FECHTEL, ALICIA MARIE, insurance executive, lawyer; b. Dallas, Nov. 30, 1946; d. Joseph Charles and Hazel Louise (Rustin) F.; m. Richard George Pfeil, May 15, 1967 (div. May 1971); children—Lisa Ann, Alison Louise. B.A., Mercer U., Macon, Ga., 1973; J.D., So. Meth. U., 1976. Bar: Tex. 1977. Staff atty. Lone Star Life Ins. Co., Dallas, 1977-79, asst. gen. counsel, 1979-82, dir., 1983—; v.p., gen. counsel, sec. Kmart Ins. Services, Inc., Dallas, 1982—; dir. Tex. Life, Accident & Health Guaranty Fund, KM Ins. Co., Dallas, Lone Star Life Ins. Co.; mem. adv. coms. Nat. Assn. Ins. Commrs., 1983—. Founder Woman's Crisis Ctr., Macon, 1973; mem. Women Meeting Women, Dallas, 1981. Mem. ABA, Tex. Bar Assn., Women Lawyers Assn. Roman Catholic.

FEDELE, SUSAN MARIE, banker; b. Bklyn., Mar. 21, 1949; d. John Joseph and Carmela Clare (Porcelli) F. Student, Fordham U., 1975-78. Typist Mfrs. Hanover Trust, N.Y.C., 1967-71, clk., 1971-74; personnel adminstr. Phila. Internat. Bank, N.Y.C., 1974-76, supr., 1976-78, mgr., 1978-80, asst. treas., 1980-81, asst. v.p., 1982-85, v.p., 1985—; mem. com. Council on Internat. Banking, N.Y.C. Mem. Nat. Assn. of Female Execs. Democrat. Roman Catholic. Office: Phila Internat Bank 55 Broad St New York NY 10004-2550

FEDELLE, ESTELLE, artist; b. Chgo.; d. John and Julia (Porebski) Szymanski. Student, Am. Acad., 1944-47, Northwestern U., 1949-51, Inst. Design, Art Inst. Chgo.; also pvt. study. Exhibited in 52 one-person shows including Wheaton (Ill.) Pub. Library, Libertyville (Ill.) Art League; exhibited in group shows Visual Arts Ctr., Chgo., Chgo. Pub. Library, Ill. State Fair, Grand Cen. Gallery, N.Y.C., numerous others; portraitist; pvt. art tchr., 1950—; dir. Fedelle Art Studio, Chgo.; newspaper columnist Art and You, 1974—. Author: How to Begin Painting for Fun, 1964; contbg. author: Fun Book on Painting, How to Paint from your Color Slides. Recipient 82 awards for painting including Margaret R. Dingle award, 1953; Cert. of Merit Disting. Service in Art, 1967. Mem. Oak Park Art League, Nat. League Am. Pen Women, Park Ridge, Mcpl. Art League (bd. dirs.), Regent Art League, Am. Portrait Soc., Am. Soc. Artists, Internat. Fine Arts Guild. Home: 1500 S Cumberland St Park Ridge IL 60068 Office: Fedelle Studio 6219 Northwest Hwy Chicago IL 60631

FEDMAN, KATHLEEN RENAE, director of sales and marketing; b. Omaha, Nov. 11, 1956; d. Benjamin and Virginia Mae (Kelly) F. BS, U. Nebr., 1980. Dir. pub. relations Ariz. Downs, Phoenix, 1980-81; asst. dir. mktg., dir. group sales AK-SAR-BEN, Omaha, 1981-83; dir. sales and mktg. The Residence Inn, Omaha, 1983—; bd. dirs. Hotel Sales Mgmt. Assn. Internat., Omaha, 1986—; mem. Tourism Bd. com., Omaha, 1984—. Vol. cancer and leukemia socs., Omaha, 1985—. Recipient Bronze Key Jaycees, Omaha, 1985. Mem. Jr. League of Omaha, Hotel Sales Mgmt. (bd. dirs. 1986—). Democrat. Roman Catholic. Home: 6148 Pinkney Omaha NE 68104

FEDOROFF, NINA VSEVOLOD, research scientist, consultant; b. Cleve., Apr. 9, 1942; d. Vsevolod N. and Olga S. (Snegireff) Stacy; m. T. Patrick Gaganidze, June 18, 1966 (div. 1978); children—Natasha, Kyr. B.S., Syracuse U., 1966; Ph.D., Rockefeller U., 1972. Asst. Mgr. translation bur. Biol. Abstracts, Phila., 1962-63; flutist Syracuse Symphony Orch., N.Y., 1964-66; acting asst. prof. U. Calif., Los Angeles, 1972-74; postdoctoral fellow UCLA and Carnegie Instn. Washington, Los Angeles and Balt., 1974-78; staff scientist Carnegie Instn. of Washington, Balt., 1978—; prof. dept. biology Johns Hopkins U.; mem. devel. biology panel NSF, Washington, 1979-80, sci. adv. panel Office of Tech. Assessment, Congress, Washington, 1979-80, recombinant DNA adv. com. NIH, Bethesda, Md., 1980-84; mem. commn. on life scis., basic biology bd. NRC, Nat. Acad. Sci., Washington, 1984—. Contbr. articles to profl. jours., chpts. to books. Editor Gene, 1981-84; editor, bd. of rev. editors Science, 1985—. Grantee NSF and U.S. Dept. Agr., 1979-84, NIH, 1984—. Mem. AAAS, Phi Beta Kappa (vis. scholar 1984-85), Sigma Xi. Avocations: chamber music; hiking; skiing. Office: Carnegie Inst of Washington Dept Embryology 115 W University Pkwy Baltimore MD 21210

FEE, ELIZABETH, history educator, researcher, consultant; b. Belfast, No. Ireland; d. John A.T. and Deirdre Fee. MA, Princeton U., 1971, Cambridge (Eng.) U., 1975; PhD, Princeton U., 1978. Teaching asst. Princeton (N.J.) U., 1971-72; instr. SUNY, Binghampton, 1972-74; archivist Johns Hopkins U., Balt., 1974-78, assoc. prof. Sch. Hygiene and Pub. Health, 1974—; cons. Princeton U., 1984. Author: Disease and Discovery, 1987; editor: Women and Health, 1983, (with Dan Fox) AIDS: The Burdens of History, 1988; contbr. articles to profl. jours.; editorial cons. Internat. Jour. Health Services. Fulbright travel grantee, 1971, Scholar Exchange program grantee, 1983, research grantee Rockefeller Archives Ctr., 1984, 85, NSF, NEH; nat. fellow W.K. KEllogg Found., 1984-87. Mem. History of Sci. Soc., Am. Assn. History of Medicine, Am. Pub. Health Assn. Office: Johns Hopkins Sch Hygiene 624 N Broadway Baltimore MD 21205

FEE, FRANCES CLARK, human resources specialist; b. New Brunswick, N.J., Aug. 3, 1942; d. Matthew James and Kathryn Elizabeth (Emens) F. BSBA, Caldwell Coll., 1986. Sec. Hercules, Inc., Rocky Hill, N.J., 1961-62, IBM Corp., Dayton, N.J., 1962-65, Merck & Co., Inc., Rahway, N.J., 1965-69; exec. sec. Ohrbach's, Inc., N.Y.C., 1969-71, Spiral Metal Co., South Amboy, N.J., 1971, Pilot Woodworking Co., Inc., Moonachie, N.J., 1971; exec. sec. BASF Wyandotte Corp., Parsippany, N.J., 1971-74, coordinator EEO programs, 1974-77, supr. mgmt. edn. programs, 1977-79, compensation analyst, 1979-81; supr. human resources BASF Wyandotte Corp. (name now BASF Corp.), Geismar, La., 1981—. Bd. dirs. Am. Heart Assn. Baton Rouge Chpt., 1986—. Roman Catholic. Club: Montclair Operetta (life). Home: 15414 Springwood Ave Baton Rouge LA 70817 Office: BASF Corp Chem Div River Rd Geismar LA 70734

FEE, SORENA, naval officer; b. Chgo., Oct. 1, 1962; d. George Edward Fee Jr. and Marilyn Lee (Smith) Murphy. BA, Sophie Newcomb Coll., 1984. Commd. ensign USN, 1984, advanced through grades to lt., 1986-1984; watch officer Barber's Point Naval Facility USN, Hawaii, 1984-85; watch officer COMOCEANSYSPAC Pearl Harbor, 1985-86, officer intelligence, spl. projects COMOCEANSYSPAC, 1986-88; lectr. EEO Navy workshops, Les Amis du Vin. Mem. Hawaii Women's Officers Assn.

FEELEY, KATHLEEN, college president, English language educator; b. Balt., Jan. 7, 1929; d. Jerome Lawrence and Theresa (Tasker) F. B.A. in English, Coll. Notre Dame of Md.; M.A. in English, Villanova U.; Ph.D. in English, Rutgers U.; student, Claremont U. Ctr. Inst. for Study of Change. Joined Sch. Sisters of Notre Dame, Roman Cath. Ch. Am. Council on Edn. intern in acad. adminstrn. to 1971; pres. Coll. Notre Dame of Md., Balt., 1971—; asst. prof. English, then assoc. prof., then prof. Coll. Notre Dame of Md.; dir. Balt. Gas and Electric Co., Md. Econ. Devel Corp.; trustee St. Vincent Coll., Latrobe, Pa., Marian House, Notre Dame Preparatory Sch.; lectured at St. John Coll., Santa Fe, Ga. State Coll., Longwood Coll., Wheaton Coll., Fairfield U.; lectr. colls., univs., Japan, 1981. Author: Flannery O'Connor: Voice of the Peacock; contbr. articles to profl. jours. Named Woman of Yr., Jewish Nat. Fund Women's Aux., 1975, Good Will Ambassador in Israel, Am.-Israel Soc., 1976; recipient Woman of Yr. award Md. Colonial Soc., 1976, J. Jefferson Miller award Greater Balt. Com., 1979, Andrew White medal Loyola Coll., Balt., 1981, Hannah G. Solomon award Nat. Council Jewish Women, 1987, Jimmie Schwartz Found. medallion, 1987. Mem. Council on Fgn. Affairs (bd. dirs.), Assn. Catholic Colls. and Univs. (trustee). Home: Caroline House 4701 N Charles St Baltimore MD 21210 Office: Coll Notre Dame of Md 4701 N Charles St Baltimore MD 21210 *

FEELEY, SHARON DENISE, marketing and management consultant; b. Chgo., Sept. 17, 1949; d. Darrell Ford and Florence Marsha (Gregorek) F. Student, SUNY, 1987—. Coll. mgr. Sara Beattie Secretarial Coll., Hong Kong, 1976-77; bus. mgr. Transplex Inc., Oak Park, Ill., 1977-79, gen. mgr., 1981-84; trade officer Far East State of Ill., Hong Kong, 1979-81; purchase agt., contract sales aide Honeywell Inc., Bensenville, Ill., 1984-86; now internat. bus. mktg. and mgmt. cons. Lake Zurich, Ill., 1986—. Editor: Tai Chi Classics, 1978. Mem. Asian Women's Mgmt. Assn. (vice chmn., founding mem. 1979-81), Mensa Club. Lodge: Rosicrucians. Home: 1183 Betty Dr Lake Zurich IL 60047

FEENEY, ANDREA CHARLTON, lawyer; b. San Francisco, June 8, 1955; d. Francis Joseph and Phyllis Dorothy (Mutch) Charlton; m. Thomas Joseph Feeney, Sept. 10, 1983; 1 child, Joseph Edward; B.A. English, Stanford U., 1977; J.D., U. Pacific, Mc George Sch. Law, 1980. Bar: Calif. 1980. Environ. policy analyst Nat. Commn. on Air Quality, Washington, 1980-81; Pacific Gas & Elec. Co., San Franciso, 1981, legis. rep., energy conservation trainee, adminstr. legis. services, 1982, adminstr. state issues, 1983, adminstr. fed. issues, 1985—. Bd. dirs. Monterey Heights Homes Assn., 1985-86, San Francisco Performing Arts Services, 1987—. Recipient writing and speech awards U. Pacific McGeorge Sch. Law, 1979; mem. Internat. Law Moot Ct. Honors Bd., 1979-80; recipient regional award Jessup Internat. Law Moot Ct., 1979. Mem. Fed. Energy Bar Assn., State Bar Calif., U. Pacific Student Bar Assn. (bd. govs., v.p., budget dir.), Jr. League San Francisco. Democrat. Roman Catholic. Clubs: Jr. League of San Francisco, Spinsters of San Francisco (charity chmn. 1981-82, mem. adv. bd. 1982-83). Office: Pacific Gas & Elec Co 77 Beale St San Francisco CA 94106

FEENEY, RITA ANNE, food industry executive; b. Portland, Maine, Nov. 20, 1952; d. Leo J. and Mildred (DeSantis) Thiboutot; m. Daniel Joseph Feeney, Apr. 3, 1976; children: Danielle, Michelle. Student, Hudson Coll., 1980, Andover Coll., %. Sec. Casco Bank, Portland, Maine, 1970-73, Pierce, Atwood, Sribner, Allen & McKusick, Portland, 1973-75; office supr. Honeywell, Portland, 1975-77; customer service mgr. Port Cycle Foods, Rockland, Maine, 1981-82, product sales mgr., 1982-84, regional sales mgr., 1984-87, nat. sales mgr., 1987—. Republican. Roman Catholic. Home: 77 Highland Ave Gardiner ME 04345 Office: Port Cycle Foods Inc 43 Pelham Indsl Park Greer SC 29651-8505

FEHAN, KATHRYN HELEN, management professional; b. Kenmore, N.Y., Apr. 21, 1961; d. Richard John and Barabara Jean (Guilfoyle) F. Mktg. specialist N.Y. State Credit Union League, Inc., Albany, 1983-85, conversion specialist Western N.Y. Terr., 1983-86, conversion specialist State of N.Y., 1986-87, product mgr., devel. specialist, 1987-88, EFT mgr., 1988—. Republican. Roman Catholic. Home: 60 Teneyck Ave Albany NY 12209 Office: NY State Credit Union League Inc 2 Wall St Box 15021 Albany NY 12212-5021

FEHER, PATRI, artist, designer, photoartist; b. Bridgeport, Conn., July 27, 1952; d. Dezso and Anne Cecile (Borsody) F. Grad. high sch., Fairfield, Conn. With Wise Eye PhotoGraphics, Fairfield, Conn., 1976-80; instr. Westport (Conn.) Recreational Dept., 1985; photographer, designer PhotoFashion, Fairfield, 1980-87; ptnr. Einstein's, N.Y.C., 1985-87; photo cons. Brookfield Craft Ctr., South Norwalk, Conn., 1986, contbg. artisan. Author: Cyanotype, 1981, Adventures in Blueprinting, 1983; exhibited at Fashion Inst. of Tech., 1986. Mem. Nat. Orgn. Homebased Bus. Women, Entrepreneurial Women's Network, Women's Econ. Devel. Democrat. Roman Catholic. Home: 27 Churchill St Fairfield CT 06430 Office: KoKoMo/PhotoFashion 29 Churchill St Fairfield CT 06430

FEHL, PATRICIA KATHERINE, educator; b. Cin., May 29, 1927; d. Norman and Gertrude (Morris) F.; A.B. cum laude, DePauw U., 1949; M.S., Ind. U., 1955, Ed.D., 1966. Tchr., Crawfordsville Schs., Ind., 1950-52; critic tchr., lab. sch., coll. methods instr. Ind. U., Bloomington, 1952-62; assoc. prof. health, phys. edn. and recreation U. Cin., 1962-73; prof., chmn. dept. gen. program Sch. Phys. Edn., W.Va. U., Morgantown, 1973—. Kennedy Found. grantee, 1966. Fellow Am. Sch. Health Assn.; mem. Am. Alliance for Health, Phys. Edn., Recreation and Dance (honor award 1986, v.p. recreation 1973-75, chmn. nominating com. 1985, 88), Midwest Dist. AAHPERD (historian, 1974-78, pres. 1978-80, Pres.'s award 1976, Honor award 1983, meritorious award 1986. parliamentarian 1973, 76, 87, 88), Ohio Assn. Health, Phys. Edn. and Recreation (v.p., chmn. div. girls and women's sports 1970-72, meritorious award 1973), W.Va. Assn. Health, Phys. Edn. and Recreation (v.p. recreation 1975; Honor award 1978, Ray O. Duncan award 1987), W.Va. Recreation and Parks Assn. (bd. dirs. 1978-81, treas. 1983, pres. 1982-84; profl. cert. 1980), Ohio Parks and Recreation Assn. (pres. 1972; Meritorious award 1974), Midwest Assn. Phys. Edn. for Coll. Women (governing bd.), Nat. Recreation and Park Assn., Phi Delta Kappa, Pi Lambda Theta, Delta Kappa Gamma. Contbr. articles to jours.; contbr. to Ohio Secondary Girls Phys. Edn. Curriculum Guide. Address: 1336 Cherry Ln Morgantown WV 26505

FEHRENBACH, ALICE R. O'SULLIVAN, psychologist; b. Denver, Nov. 14, 1910; d. John Alexander and Gertrude (Gaffney) McTammany; A.B., Barnard Coll., 1931; M.A., U. Denver, 1944, Ph.D., 1955; m. Frank O'Sullivan, July 6, 1940 (dec. Feb. 1941); m. 2d, Carl E. Fehrenbach, June 8, 1953 (dec. 1961). Tchr., Denver public schs., 1935-47, psychologist, 1948-68; pvt. practice psychology, Denver, 1948—; prof. psychology Regis Coll., 1968-76, prof. emeritus, 1976—, faculty lectr., 1972, acting dir. counseling service, 1971-73, dir. counseling services, 1974-76; staff Mt. Airy Psychiat. Ctr., 1976—; vis. lectr. U. Nev., Stanford U.; guest appearances radio, TV series, Denver; mem. interregional bd. Am. Bd. Profl. Psychology, 1978-83; mem. Colo. Bd. Psychologist Examiners. Bd. dirs. Camp Fire Girls, 1949-55. Recipient Alumnae Recognition award Barnard Coll., 1975; Dir.'s award Regis Coll., 1975; Outstanding Social Action award Colo. Mental Health Assn., 1975; Disting. Service award Am. Bd. Profl. Psychologists, 1983, 86; Cert. recognition Meritorious and Dedicated Service Am. Bd. Profl. Psychologists, 1986. Diplomate in sch. psychology Am. Bd. Profl. Psychologists. Fellow Am. Psychol. Assn. (Champus peer rev. bd. 1985-87); mem. Colo. Psychol. Assn. (dir.; pres. 1973-74; Disting. Service award 1969, Disting. Past Pres. award 1984), Rocky Mountain Psychol. Assn. (exec. bd., Disting. Service award 1982, Cert. recognition disting. contbn. to div. clin. psychology 1986), English-Speaking Union, Assn. Specialized Services (pres. 1953-54), Denver Mental Health Assn. (profl. adv. bd.), Columbia U. Women's Club Colo. (founder 1948, pres. 1948-50), Denver Women's Press Club, Women's Forum Colo., Delta Kappa Gamma. Lodge: Zonta. Author personality test; contbr. articles to profl. jours. Office: 3232 S Josephine St Denver CO 80210

FEIDER, CAROL WARD, principal; b. Kansas City, Mo., Sept. 21, 1944; d. James Edward and Eunice Marie (Atwell) Ward.; divorced; children: Sarah Carolyn, Nancy Aileen. BA, Drake U., 1965; postgrad., Ohio State U., 1968; MA, Cen. Mich. U., 1978. Reading tchr. Welch Jr. High Sch., Ames, Iowa, 1965-68; English tchr. Jefferson Intermediate Sch., Midland, Mich., 1976-79, asst. prin., 1984-87; adminstrv. asst. Cen. Intermediate Sch., Midland, 1979-84; prin. Northeast Intermediate Sch., Midland, 1987—. Adv. bd. Grace A. Dow Pub. Library, Midland, 1981—, pres. adv. bd., 1985-87; bd. dirs. Midland County Sch. Employee's Credit Union, 1983-86. Mem. Mich. Assn. Secondary Sch. Prins., Mich. Assn. Middle Sch. Educators, Phi Beta Kappa. Home: 1208 Scott St Midland MI 48640 Office: NE Intermediate Sch 1305 E Sugnet Midland MI 48640

FEIG, BARBARA KRANE, educator, author; b. Mitchell, S.D., Nov. 8, 1937; d. Peter Abraham and Sally (Gorchow) Krane; m. Jerome Feig, June 8, 1963; children: Patricia Lynn, Lizabeth Ann. Student, Washington U., St. Louis, 1955-58; BE, Nat. Coll. Edn., 1960; postgrad., Northeastern Ill. U. Tchr. various schs., 1960-68, Anshe Emet Day Sch., Chgo., 1982—, Sacred Heart, Chgo., 1982—, New City Day Sch., Chgo., 1983—; pres. J.B. Pal & Co., Inc., Chgo., 1975—; bd. dirs. Barclee Cosmetics, Inc., Chgo., Media Merchandising, Chgo. Author: Now You're Cooking: A Guide to Cooking For Boys and Girls, 1975, The Parents' Guide to Weight Control For Children, 1980; developer ednl. toy, 1985. Mem. womens bd. Francis Parker Sch., Chgo., 1972—; trustee Chgo. Inst. for Psychoanalysis, 1975—; bd. dirs. Juvenile Diabetes Found., Chgo., 1976—. Mem. Women of the Professions and Trades, Jewish Fedn. Home: 904 Castlewood Terr Chicago IL 60640

FEIGEL, CELESTE LOUISE, financial services administrator; b. Los Angeles, May 16, 1952; d. Emery John and Helen Louise (Bradbury) W.; m. Robert Richardson Feigel, Apr. 11, 1971 (div. 1973). BBA, Western State U., Doniphan, Mo., 1987. Credit mgr. accounts receivable Gensler-Lee Diamonds, Santa Barbara, Calif., 1973-74, Terry Hinge and Hardware, Van Nuys, Calif., 1975-78; credit mgr., fin. analyst Peanut Butter Fashions, Chatsworth, Calif., 1978-82; personnel mgr. Charter Mgmt. Co., Beverly Hills, Calif., 1982-83; co-owner, v.p. Noreen Jenney Communicates, Beverly Hills, 1983-85; credit mgr., fin. analyst Cen. Diagnostic Lab., Tarzana, Calif., 1985—; cons. Results Now, Inc., Tarzana, 1986-87. Mem. Nat. Assn. Credit Mgmt., Credit Mgrs. Assn. So. Calif., Credit Ednl. Found., Nat. Assn. Female Execs., Nat. Humane Ednl. Found. Republican. Roman Catholic.

FEIGIN, BARBARA SOMMER, advertising executive; b. Berlin, Germany, Nov. 16, 1937; came to U.S., 1940, naturalized, 1949; d. Eric Daniel and Charlotte Martha (Demmer) Sommer; m. James Feigin, Sept. 17, 1961; children: Michael, Peter, Daniel. BA in Polit. Sci., Whitman Coll., 1959; cert. of Bus. Adminstrn., Harvard-Radcliffe Program Bus. Adminstrn., 1960. Mktg. research asst. Richardson-Vick Co., Wilton, Conn., 1960-61; market research analyst SCM Corp., N.Y.C., 1961-62; group research supr. Benton & Bowles, Inc., N.Y.C., 1963-67; assoc. research dir. Marplan Research Co., N.Y.C., 1968-69; exec. v.p. research and mktg. services Grey Advt. Inc., N.Y.C., 1969—, mem. agy. policy council; bd. dirs. VF Corp. Author articles in field. Vice chmn., bd. overseers Whitman Coll.; bd. advisors grad. degree program in mktg. U. Ga. Recipient Women Achievers award YWCA, 1987. Mem. Advt. Research Found. (bd. dirs. 1987), Am. Assn. Advt. Agys. (research com.), Market Research Council, Agy. Research Dirs. Council, Communications Research Council. Home: 535 E 86th St New York NY 10028 Office: Grey Advt Inc 777 3rd Ave New York NY 10017

FEIGON, JUDITH TOVA, physician, educator; b. Galveston, Tex., Dec. 2, 1947; d. Louis and Ethel (Goldberg) Feigon; m. Nathan C. Goldman. AB, Barnard Coll., Columbia U., 1970; postgrad. in sci., Rice U. and U. Houston, 1970-71; MD, U. Tex.-San Antonio, 1976. Diplomate Am. Bd. Ophthalmology. Intern, Mt. Auburn Hosp., Cambridge, Mass. Intern and clin. teaching fellow, Harvard U. Med. Sch., 1976-77; resident in ophthalmology, Baylor Coll. Medicine, Houston, 1977-80, fellow in retina, 1980-82, clin. instr., 1982—; asst. prof. ophthalmology U. Tex. Med. Br., Galveston, 1982-85, clin. asst. prof., 1985—; practice medicine specializing in ophthalmology, vitreoretinal diseases and surgery, Houston, 1983—; physician advisor to Houston br. Tex. Soc. to Prevent Blindness; mem. staff Methodist, St. Lukes/Tex. Children's, John Sealy, Park Plaza. Mem. AMA, Am. Acad. Ophthalmology, Tex. Med. Assn., Harris County Med. Soc., U. Tex.-San Antonio Alumni Assn., Harvard Med. Sch. Assoc. Alumni Assn., Vitreous Soc.. Contbr. articles to profl. publs. Office: 6410 Fannin Suite 404 Houston TX 77030

FEIL, NAOMI WEIL, script writer, gerontologist; b. Munich, Germany, July 22, 1932; came to U.S., 1937, naturalized, 1944; d. Julius and Helen (Kahn) Weil; m. Edward Feil, Dec. 29, 1963; children: Edward G., Kenneth J.; children by previous marriage: Victoria, Beth. Student Oberlin Coll., 1950-51, Western Res. U., 1950-51; BS cum laude, Columbia U., 1954, MSW, 1956. Dir. group work William Hodson Ctr., 1960-62, Bird S. Coler Hosp., Welfare Island, N.Y., 1962-63, Montefiore Home for Aged, 1963-80; script writer, actress documentary films Edward Feil Prodns., 1963—; exec. dir. Validation Tng. Inst., Inc., 1983; cons. Case Western Res. U., also adj. field instr.; workshop leader; group worker, cons. Amasa Stone. Author: Validation: The Feil Method, 1982, Resolution: The Final Life Task, 1985, also books on gerontology, documentary films; films include: Where Life Still Means Living, 1965, The Inner World of Aphasia, 1967, Looking for Yesterday: 100 Years to Live, 1981 (various internat. awards); contbr. articles to Gerontology mag., Humanistic Jour., Pilgrimmage mag. Recipient award for Human Relations in Pub. Service, Cleve., 1974, Cine award for Documentary Films, 1965, 68, 82, Disting. Service award Assn. Ohio Philanthropic Homes and Housing for Aging, 1986. Mem. Nat. Assn. Social Workers, Transpersonal Psychology Assn., Humanistic Psychology Assn., Univ. Film Assn., Gerontology Assn. Democrat. Jewish. Founder validation theory for restoring dignity to the aged. Home: 21987 Byron Rd Cleveland OH 44122 Office: 4614 Prospect Ave Cleveland OH 44103

FEILD, RACHEL NANNEY, printing company executive; b. Spindale, N.C., Nov. 11, 1927; d. Roy and Cora Lillian (Beam) Nanney; B.S., Queens Coll., Charlotte, N.C., 1947; m. George Feild, Jr., May 26, 1951 (div. 1957); children—John Anthony, Kathryn Elizabeth. With Aerospace Industries Assn. Am., Inc., Washington, 1956-69, com. exec. procurement and finance, 1961-69; part-owner, sec.-treas. Taylor Printing Co., Inc., Hyattsville, Md., 1969—. Mem. Nat. Assn. Female Execs., Episcopalian. Office: 5206 46th Ave Hyattsville MD 20781

FEIN, LEAH GOLD (MRS. ALFRED G. FEIN), psychologist; b. Minsk, Russia; d. Jacob Lyon and Sarah Freda (Meltzer) Gold; B.S., Albertus Magnus Coll., 1939; M.A., Yale U., 1942, Ph.D. (Marion Talbot fellow), 1944; m. Alfred Gustave Fein, June 10, 1944; 1 son, Ira Hirsh. Health educator New Haven Schs., 1930-43; instr. psychology Carleton Coll., 1944-45; research asso. Conn. Interracial Commn., 1946; chief psychologist Seattle Psychiat. Clinic, 1947-48; prof. U. Bridgeport, 1946-47, 52-58; ind. clin. practice, specializing in clin., child consultation, Seattle, 1948-52, Stamford, Conn., 1952-67, N.Y.C., 1967-81, West Palm Beach, Fla., 1982-87, Stamford, Conn., 1987—; clin. cons. Conn. Commn. on Alcoholism Clinic, 1952-64; research asso. Soc. for Investigation Human Ecology; therapist Norwalk Psychiat. Clinic, 1952-64; cons. Child Edn. Found., 1953-56; dir. research Sch. Nursing Norwalk Hosp., 1961-64; dir. clin. services cerebral palsy and mental retardation, Waterbury, Conn., 1964-65; assoc. prof. Quinnipiac Coll., Hamden, Conn., 1965-66; cons., instr., med. staff N.Y. Hosp.-Cornell Med. Center, White Plains, 1966-67; dir. psychology Psychiat. Treatment Center, N.Y., 1967-68; research asso. Roosevelt Hosp. Child Psychiatry, 1968-69; supr., cons. research psychologist Bur. Child Guidance, N.Y.C. Board Edn., 1969-72; faculty Greenwich Inst. Psychoanalytic Studies, 1971-79; sr. research scientist Postgrad. Center for Mental Health, N.Y.C., 1980-82; mem. program com. Internat. Congress Social Psychiatry, 1974; research cons. N.Y.C. Mayor's Vol. Action Com., Human Resources Adminstrn., N.Y.C. Study of Delinquency and Study Abused and Neglected Children; cons., inservice trainer Center Group Counseling, Boca Raton, Fla., 1982-84; manuscript reviewer Perceptual Motor Skills. Diplomate clin. psychology Am. Bd. Profl. Psychology. Fellow Soc. Personality Assessment, Am. Psychol. Assn. (council of reps. div. 42, 1983-86), Am. Acad. Psychotherapists, Internat. Council Psychologists (v.p. 1961-62, 71-73, pres. 1973-75), Am. Orthopsychiat. Assn., N.Y. Acad. Sci.; mem. Nat. Assn. Gifted (v.p. 1961-62), Internat. Council Women Psychologists (chmn. profl. relations among psychologists), Psychologists in Pvt. Practice (treas. 1972-78), Am. Psychol. Assn. (sec. div. psychotherapy 1966-69; council of reps. 1982-86), N.Y. State Psychol. Assn., Fla. Psychol Assn., Am. Assn. Group Psychotherapy and Psychodrama (council 1973-75), World Fedn. Mental Health, Nat. Council Jewish Women, Hadassah. Club: Yale (N.Y.C.). Author: The Three Dimensional Personality Test—Reliability, Validity and Clinical Implications, 1960; The Changing School Scene: Challenge to Psychology, 1974; editor Jour. Internat. Understanding, vol. 9-10, 1974; Jour. Psychology Div. Am. Friends Hebrew U.; guest editor Jour. Clin. Child Psychology, 1975; cons. editor Jour. Psychotherapy in Pvt. Practice; others; contbr. Jour. Clin. Psychology, other profl. jours. Address: Newburry Common 1450 Washington Blvd Apt N 706 Stamford CT 06902

FEIN, LINDA ANN, nurse anesthetist, consultant; b. Cin., Dec. 10, 1949; d. Joseph and Elizabeth P. (Kannady) Stofle; m. Thomas Paul Fein, Dec. 11, 1971. Nursing diploma, Miami Valley Hosp. Sch. Nursing, Dayton, Ohio, 1971, Wright State U., Dayton, 1969; postgrad. U. Cin. Med. Ctr., 1978. Nursing asst. Miami Valley Hosp., Dayton, 1969-71; staff nurse operating room Cin. Children's Hosp. and Med. Ctr., 1971, 73, Peninsula Hosp., Burlingame, Calif., 1972-73; staff nurse operating room and emergency room Doctors Hosp., San Diego, 1972; staff nurse emergency room Ohio State U. Hosps., Columbus, 1973-75, head nurse operating room, 1975-76; staff nurse anesthetist Bethesda Hosps., Cin., 1978-86; staff nurse anesthetist Mercy Hosp. of Fairfield, Cin., 1986—; childbirth educator psychoprophylactic method, 1975—; critical care nursing cons. Med. Communicators & Assocs., Salt Lake City, 1985—; co-owner Exec. Shops, Cin., 1982-85; speaker in field. Mem. search com. Cin. Gen. Hosp. Sch. of Anesthesia for Nurses, 1981-82; bd. dirs. YWCA, 1988—. Recipient Recognition of Profl. Excellence, First Nurse Anesthesia Faculty Assocs., 1982. Mem. Miami Valley Hosp. Sch. of Nursing Alumni Assn., Cin. Gen. Hosp. Sch. Anesthesia for Nurses Alumni Assn., Nurse Anesthetists of Greater Cin., Ohio Assn. Nurse Anesthetists, Am. Assn. Nurse Anesthetists, Am. Assn. Operating Room Nurses, Am. Assn. Critical Care Nurses, Nat. Registry of Cert. Nurses in Advanced Practice, Nat. Assn. Female Execs., Altrusa Internat. (officer 1985—). Republican. Methodist. Lodge: Eastern Star. Avocations: antiques; gourmet cooking; African violets; roses; swimming; skiing; writing, traveling. Home: 650 History Bridge Ln Hamilton OH 45013 Office: Med Communicators and Assocs 3760 S Highland Dr Suite 252 Salt Lake City UT 84106

FEIN, SYLVIA, author, painter; b. Milw., Nov. 20, 1919; d. Alfred E. and Elizabeth (Routt) F.; B.S., U. Wis., Madison, 1942; M.A., U. Calif., Berkeley, 1951; m. William K. Scheuber, May 30, 1942; 1 dau., Heidi. One-woman exhbns. include: U. Wis. Meml. Union Gallery, 1942, Milw. Art Inst., 1942, Perls Galleries, N.Y.C., 1946, Feingarten Galleries, San Francisco, 1957, 59, Carmel, Calif., 1959, N.Y.C., 1961, Sagittarius Gallery, N.Y.C., 1958, St. Mary's Coll., Moraga, Calif., 1960, Kunstkabinett, Frankfurt, W.Ger., 1960, Mills Coll. Art Gallery, Oakland, Calif., 1962, Ruthermore Galleries, Oakland, 1962, Maxwell Galleries, San Francisco, 1963, Nicole of Berkeley (Calif.), 1965, Bresler Galleries, Milw., 1966, Oshkosh (Wis.) Pub. Mus., 1967; numerous group exhbns., 1941—, latest being 5th Winter invitational Calif. Palace Legion of Honor, 1964, Art of Landscape, San Francisco Art Inst. travelling exhibit, 1964-65, Three Painters, St. Mary's Coll., 1964, Magic and Fantastic Art, Walnut Creek (Calif.) Library, 1968; author: Heidi's Horse, 1976; owner, pub. Exelrod Press, 1975—; chmn. Archtl. Rev. Comm., Pleasant Hill, Calif., 1975. Home: 341 Strand Ave Pleasant Hill CA 94523 Office: PO Box 2303 Pleasant Hill CA 94523

FEINBERG, BARBARA, interior designer; b. N.Y.C., Oct. 23, 1941; d. Alexander and Eunice (Michael) Youngerman; m. Ira David Feinberg, Aug. 1964 (div. 1968). B.F.A., Boston U., 1963. Jr. designer Hans Krieks Assocs., Boston, 1963-66; prin. Barbara Feinberg Design, Boston, 1966-71, Miami, 1971-74; designer Designs for Interiors & Unigram, Inc., N.Y.C., 1974-77; pvt. practice interior designing, N.Y.C., 1977-79; owner Feinberg Orsini Assocs., N.Y.C., 1979-85, Feinberg Assocs., 1985—. Office: 30 E 23d St New York NY 10010

FEINBERG, ELEANOR KEMLER, psychotherapist; b. Winthrop, Mass., July 26, 1938; d. Mathew and Ann Kemler; m. Walter Feinberg, June 21, 1964; children: Deborah Lee, Jill Suzanne. BA, Boston U., 1960; MEd, State Coll. at Boston, 1963; PhD, U. Ill., 1974. Registered psychologist, Ill. Lectr. U. Ill., Champaign, 1974-79; psychotherapist Champaign County Mental Health Ctr., 1979-83, part-time psychotherapist, 1985-87; pvt. practice psychotherapy Champaign, 1983—; adj. prof. U. Ill., 1986—; workshop leader Ctr. for Health Info., 1982—; guest speaker on psychol. issues area orgns., radio and TV programs, 1983—; part-time psychotherapist Champaign County Mental Health Ctr., 1985-87—. Author: (monograph with Walter Feinberg) The Invisible and Lost Community of Work and Education, 1979; local radio and TV guest. Mem. Am. Psychol. Assn., Ill. Psychol. Assn. Club: Executive of Champaign County. Home and Office: 1704 Henry St Champaign IL 61821

FEINBERG, GLENDA JOYCE, restaurant chain executive; b. Louisville, Feb. 8, 1948; d. Harold and Winnie Esther (McIntosh) F.; divorced; 1 child, Anthony John. Student, Purdue U., 1967-68, Ind. U., 1977-79. Cert. in restaurant and personnel mgmt. Beverage mgr. Don Ce Sar Beach Hotel, St. Petersburg Beach, Fla., 1979-80; catering dir. Best Western-Skyway Inn, St. Petersburg, Fla., 1980-83; gen. mgr. Village, Inc., St. Petersburg Beach, 1983-86; banquet mgr. Tradewinds Resort Hotel, St. Petersburg Beach, 1986-87; exec. mgr. Ponderosa, Inc., Clearwater, Fla., 1987—. Democrat. Office: Ponderosa Inc 1101 Cleveland St Clearwater FL 34615

FEINBERG, LYNN K., marketing professional; b. Jersey City, June 22, 1960; d. Raymond Matthew and Wilma (Lieb) F. BA in English and Music, Rutgers U., 1982. Media asst. J. Walter Thompson, N.Y.C., 1982-84; researcher CBS Mags., N.Y.C., 1984-85; cons. prodn. Chase Manhattan Bank, N.Y.C., 1985—. Mem. Nat. Assn. Female Execs., Assn. Graphic Arts (award 1987), Internat. Assn. Bus. Communicators. Home: 66 Wyckoff St New Brunswick NJ 08901 Office: Chase Manhattan Bank 140 Broadway 25th New York NY 10081

FEINBERG, RUTH KUBERSKY, counselor; b. Bklyn., Oct. 31, 1938; d. Abraham F. and Lillian S. (Kleidman) Kubersky; m. Arnold Bernard Feinberg, Jan. 22, 1972; children: Marcia Smith, Marilyn Weiss, Cathy Feinberg Weiss, Carla Feinberg Ashton, Martha. BA, Bklyn. Coll., 1959; MA, Case-Western U., 1972; PhD, Kent State U., 1984. Cert. counselor. Tchr. Shaker Heights (Ohio) High Sch., 1970-72; dir. vol. services Nat. Council Jewish Women, Cleve., 1974-79; pvt. practice cons. Indpls., 1979-81; exec. v.p., counselor, cons. Futures Unltd., Inc., Indpls., 1981—. vol. exec. Internat. Exec. Service Corps, Santo Domingo, Dominican Rep., Sept.-Nov. 1986; bd. dirs., pub. affairs chair Planned Parenthood, Indpls., 1986—; program chair Dialogue Today, Indpls., 1985-87; bd. dirs. Jewish Community Relations Council, 1985. Mem. Am. Assn. Counseling & Devel., Adult Devel. and Aging div. Am. Assn. Counseling & Devel. Home: 6901 N Pennsylvania Indianapolis IN 46220 Office: Futures Unltd 1295 W 86th St Indianapolis IN 46260

FEINER, ARLENE MARIE, librarian, researcher, consultant; b. Spring Green, Wis., Mar. 23, 1937; d. Herman Joseph and Cecelia Margaret (Meixelsperger) F. B.A. in History, Alverno Coll., 1959; M.A. in Library Sci., Rosary Coll., 1971; M.A. in Orgnl. Devel., Loyola U., Chgo., 1985. Gen. office worker USIA, Washington, 1959-60; adminstrv. sec. Nat. Council Cath. Women, Washington, 1960-62; asst. librarian Munich campus, U. Md., Fed. Republic Germany, 1962-64; preliminary cataloger, 1st editor MARC Pilot Project, Library of Congress, Washington, 1965-67; head librarian Acad. of the Holy Cross, Kensington, Md., 1967-70, Jesuit Sch. of Theology Library, Chgo., 1971-79, coordinator serial activities; women's studies bibliographer, Loyola U., Chgo., 1979-86; tech. services, collection devel. coordinator DuPage Library System, 1986—. Editor: (bibliography) Current Serials, 1980-85. Compiler: (bibliography) Guide to Women's Studies Sources, 1985. Contbr. articles to profl. jours. Bd. dirs. Women's World Ctr., Chgo., 1985—. Assn. of Theol. Schs. in U.S. and Can. grantee, 1976. Mem. Chgo. Area Women's Studies Assn., ALA, several library coms., Chgo. Area Women's Studies Assn., Nat. Assn. Female Execs. Roman Catholic. Avocations: poetry; hiking; music. Home: 336 W Wellington Ave Apt 2102 Chicago IL 60657

FEINGOLD, MARIE, publishing executive; b. New York, May 18, 1919; d. Seymour A. and Edna (Weiss) Goodman; m. S. Norman Feingold, Mar. 24, 1947; children: Elizabeth Anne, Margaret Ellen, Deborah Carol, Marilyn Nancy. BA, Coll. of William and Mary, 1939; postgrad., Columbia U., 1939-40; MA Advanced Grad. Specialist, U. Md., 1968. Cert. rehab. counselor. Researcher, security analyst J.S. Bache and Co., N.Y.C., 1941-43; researcher, editor N.W. Levin, N.Y.C., 1943-46; researcher, security analyst Cowan and Co., N.Y.C., 1946-47; pres. Bellman Pub. Co., Bethesda, Md., 1952—; rehab. counselor D.C. Dept. Rehab., Washington, 1966-83; mem. Com. on Rehab. Counselor Cert., Washington, 1975-79. Author, editor: Scholarships Fellowships and Loans, 8 vols., 1949-87. Mem. Womens Nat. Book Assn., Ednl. Press Assn. (Washington chpt.), Washington Book Pub. Assn., Women in Communications, Phi Beta Kappa. Home: 9707 Singleton Dr Bethesda MD 20817 Office: Bellman Pub Co PO Box 34937 Bethesda MD 20817

FEINGOLD (GOODMAN), MARILYN N., financial analyst; b. Boston; d. S. Norman and Marie (Goodman) F. BA magna cum laude, U. Pitts.; postgrad., UCLA, 1976; student, U. Wash., 1976. Arts liaison to White House Office for Presdl. messages on Arts Related Matters Nat. Endowment for the Arts, Washington, 1978-82, writer, 1978-82, music program specialist, 1982-83, coordinator of regional reps. program, 1983-84, coordinator for grants and info. mgmt., 1984-86; sr. cons. Nutri-Metics Internat., Washington, 1984—; founder Feingolf Artist Mgmt., Washington, 1985—; program analyst Fin. Mgmt. Service, Washington, 1986; guest lectr. Yale U. Grad. Sch. of Music, New Haven, 1985; script cons. New Playwright's Theatre of Washington, 1977-79, co-chmn. fundraising; cons. for research Pub. TV Sta. WETA, Washington, 1977. Co-author: 88 Ways to Get The Job and Career of Your Choice, 1987. Music therapist psychiat. hosps. and nursing homes for the aged, Pitts. Mem. Nat. Assn. Profl. Saleswomen (assoc), U. Pitts. Alumni Assn. Home: 2939 Van Ness St NW Washington DC 20008

FEINN, BARBARA ANN, economist; b. Waterbury, Conn., Feb. 16, 1925; d. David Harris and Dora (Brandvein) F. A.B. magna cum laude, Smith

Coll., 1946; M.A. (univ. scholar), Yale U., 1947, Ph.D. (univ. fellow), 1952; cert. Oxford (Eng.) U., 1949. Research economist First Nat. City Bank, N.Y.C., 1953-54; assoc. economist Office Messrs. Rockefeller, N.Y.C., 1954-61; asst. to dir. N.Y. State Office for Regional Devel., N.Y.C., 1961-62; cons. economist Nelson A. Rockefeller, N.Y.C., 1963-64; pvt. cons., 1965-68; sr. council economist N.Y. State Council Econ. Advisers, N.Y.C., 1969-72; chief economist Office S.C. Gov., Columbia, 1972—, mem. bd. econ. advisors, 1976—, sec. bd. econ. advisors, 1986—; adj. prof. bus. adminstrn. U. S.C., Columbia, 1972-74. Ofcl. participant White House Conf. on Balanced Nat. Growth and Econ. Devel., 1978; del. meetings on nat. balanced growth Nat. Govs. Assn., Leesburg, Va., 1977; mem. S.C. Gov.'s Task Force on the Economy, 1980—; mem. productivity measurement com. S.C. Council on Productivity, 1981—. Dir. Smith Coll. Alumnae Fund Program, N.Y.C., 1965-66, mem. spl. gifts com., 1971; del. assembly Assn. Yale Alumni, 1983-86. Recipient Wilbur Lucius Cross medal Yale U., 1987. Mem. Am. Econ. Assn., Nat. Assn. Bus. Econs., Soc. Govt. Economists, Downtown Economists Luncheon Group, Western Econ. Assn., N.Y. Assn. Bus. Economists, Atlanta Econ. Club, Carolinas Econ. Assn., Phi Beta Kappa. Clubs: Yale (N.Y.C. and cen. S.C.); Summit, Wildewood (Columbia, S.C.); Sea Pines (Hilton Head Island, S.C.); Smith Coll. (Columbia). Contbr. articles to profl. jours. Home: 50 Mallet Hill Ct Columbia SC 29223 Office: Gov's Office Columbia SC 29201

FEINSTEIN, CONNIE IDELE, account executive; b. Salt Lake City, June 4, 1953; d. Herman Nathan and Muriel (Berenter) F. Student, Bellevue (Wash.) Coll., Shoreline North Seattle Coll. Supr. sales reps. McGraw Hill, Kent, Wash., 1977-82; account mgr. Memorex, Anaheim, Calif., 1982—. Republican. Jewish. Office: Memorex Corp 1661 N Raymond Anaheim CA 92801

FEINSTEIN, DIANNE, former mayor; b. San Francisco, June 22, 1933; d. Leon and Betty (Rosenburg) Goldman; m. Bertram Feinstein, Nov. 11, 1962 (dec.); 1 child, Katherine Anne; m. Richard C. Blum, Jan. 20, 1980. B.S., Stanford U., 1955; LLB (hon.), Golden Gate U., 1977; D Pub. Adminstrn. (hon.), U. Manila, 1981; D Pub. Service (hon.), U. Santa Clara, 1981; JD (hon.), Antioch U., 1983, Mills Coll., 1985; PhD in Humane Letters (hon.), U. San Francisco. Intern in pub. affairs Coro Found., San Francisco, 1955-56; asst. to Calif. Indsl. Welfare Commn., Los Angeles, also San Francisco, 1956-57; mem., vice-chmn. Calif. Women's Bd. Terms and Parole, Los Angeles, also San Francisco, 1962-66; chmn. San Francisco City and County Adv. Com. for Adult Detention, San Francisco, 1967-69; supr. City and County of San Francisco, 1970-78; mayor of San Francisco 1978-88; pres. San Francisco City and County Bd. Suprs., 1970-72, 74-76, 78; mem. Mayor's Com. on Crime, 1967-69; chair Urban Econ. Policy Com., 1981-87; chair Task Force on AIDS, 1983-87; bd. govs. Bay Area Council, 1972—; mem. Bay Conservation and Devel. Commn., 1973-78; bd. dirs., Bank of Calif. Chmn. bd. regents Lone Mountain Coll., 1972-75. Recipient Women of Achievement award Bus. and Profl. Women's Clubs of San Francisco, 1970, Disting. Woman award San Francisco Examiner, 1970, CORO Found. award, 1979, Scopus award Am. Friends Hebrew U., Jerusalem, 1981, Brotherhood/Sisterhood award Nat. Conf. of Christians and Jews, 1986, Comdr.'s award U.S. Army, 1986, French Legion of Honor award Pres. Mitterand, 1984, Disting. Service award, USN; named Team Number One Mayor All-Pro City Mgmt. Team City and State Mag., 1987. Office: 909 Montgomery St San Francisco CA 94133

FEIR, DOROTHY JEAN, entomologist, physiologist, educator; b. St. Louis, Jan. 29, 1929; d. Alex R. and Lillian (Smith) F. B.S., U. Mich., 1950; M.S., U. Wyo., 1956; Ph.D., U. Wis., 1960. Instr. biology U. Buffalo, 1960-61; mem. faculty St. Louis U., 1961—, prof. biology, 1967—; mem. tropical medicine and parasitology study sect. NIH, 1980-84. Editor Environ. Entomology, 1977-84. Mem. Entomol. Soc. Am. (pres. elect 1988), AAAS, Am. Physiol. Soc., N.Y. Acad. Sci., Mo. Acad. Sci. (v.p. 1987-88), Sigma Xi, Internat. Soc. Devel. and Comparative Immunology. Office: St Louis U Biology Dept Saint Louis MO 63103

FEIRSTEIN, JANICE, real estate executive; b. Binchester, Eng., Dec. 3, 1942; came to U.S., 1967; d. Edward Mons and Mary (Watson) Walmsley; m. Laurence Feirstein, Aug. 27, 1967; 1 child, Douglas. Grad. in bus., Christison U., Spennymoor, Eng., 1961; grad. in mgmt., Inst. Fin. Edn., Ft. Lauderdale, Fla., 1980. Mgr. gift and gourmet cookware store, Lauderhill, Fla., 1977-78; exec. asst. Werbel Roth Sec., Ft. Lauderdale, Fla., 1978-79; from teller to new accounts rep. to asst. br. mgr. to br. mgr. Broward Fed. Savs. and Loan, Ft. Lauderdale, 1979—; v.p., resort mgr. Broward Ocean View Properties, Inc., Ft. Lauderdale, 1982—; bd. dirs. Inst. Fin. Edn., 1981-83; mem. fin. com. Am. Resort and Recreational Devel. Assn., 1986. Vol. Gen. Hosp., Plantation, Fla., 1977-78; mem. adv. com. Broward County Sch. Bd., 1982; active Coop. Bus. Edn., Broward County, 1980-81, Nat. Adoption Ctr., 1986, Outreach Broward, 1986. Mem. Nat. Assn. for Female Execs., Light House Cove Condominium II Assn. (bd. dirs., v.p., sec. 1983—), Light House Cove Condominium IV Assn. (bd. dirs., v.p., sec. 1985—), Light House Cove Condominium Community Assn. (bd. dirs., v.p., sec. 1983—), Ft. Lauderdale C. of C., Pompano Beach C. of C. Office: Broward Ocean View Properties Inc 1406 N Ocean Blvd Pompano Beach FL 33062

FEIST-FITE, BERNADETTE, health and food specialist, travel consultant; b. Linton, N.D., Sept. 28, 1945; d. John K. and Cecilia (Nagel) F.; B.S. in Dietetics, U. N.D., Grand Forks, 1967; M.S. in Edn., Troy (Ala.) State U., 1973; Ed.D. U. So. Calif.; m. William H. Fite. Commd. officer USAF, 1965, advanced through grades to maj., 1986—; prof. health and fitness Nat. Def. U., Ft. McNair, Washington; speaker, lectr.; instr. USAF dietetic internship. Mgr. coffee house Unitarian Ch., 1972-74; mem. Alexandria Little Theatre, 1977-78. Decorated Air Force Commendation medal, Dept. Def. Meritorious Service medal. Mem. Soc. Internat. Edn., Tng. and Research, Am. Dietetic Assn., Internat. Food Service Execs. Assn., VFW, Assn. Mil. Surgeons U.S., Exec. Female, Air Force Assn., Soc. Nutrition Edn., Dietitians in Bus. and Industry, Sports and Cardiovascular Nutritionists, Am. Soc. Profl. and Exec. Women. Roman Catholic. Club: Andrews Officers. Home: PO Box 4-816 5904 Mount Eagle Dr Alexandria VA 22303 Office: NDU-A-ED Health Fitness Fort McNair DC 20319-6000

FEIT, EVELYN BARBARA, security analyst; b. N.Y.C., Oct. 6, 1932; d. Henry and Cecilia (Klapper) Weinrich; m. Theodore Feit, Oct. 24, 1954; children—Helen, Sheila, Norman. A.B., Barnard Coll., 1953. Chartered fin. analyst. Bond analyst Dun & Bradstreet, N.Y.C., 1953-54; statistician Brookings Instn., Washington, 1954-55; statistician, editor Wiesenberger Fin. Services, N.Y.C., 1972-73; pension fund performance analyst Wertheim & Co., N.Y.C., 1973-76; security analyst, v.p. Kidder, Peabody & Co., N.Y.C., 1976—. Contbr. articles to profl. jours. Pres., PTA, Hunter Coll. High Sch., N.Y.C., 1971. Mem. Investment Tech. Assn., Fin. Women's Assn., N.Y. Soc. Security Analysts. Jewish. Office: Kidder Peabody & Co Inc 10 Hanover Sq New York NY 10005

FELCHLIN, MARY KATHLEEN CONROY, financial executive; b. Cleve., Feb. 16, 1951; d. Ernest J. and Margaret Jane Conroy; B.A., U. Calif., Berkeley, 1973; M.B.A., U. So. Calif., 1977. Adminstrv. asst. Mason McDuffie Investment Co., Berkeley, 1974-75; mortage mktg. staff Gibraltar Savs. & Loan, Beverly Hills, summer 1976; account officer Wells Fargo Bank, Los Angeles, 1977-79; sr. account officer Citicorp Real Estate, Inc., Los Angeles, 1979-80, asst. v.p., 1981-82, v.p., 1982—; v.p. Citicorp Real Estate Capital, 1985—. Wittenberg fellow, 1975-76; Commerce Assos. fellow, 1976-77. Mem. Am. Mgmt. Assn. Home: 8960 Wonderland Ave Los Angeles CA 90046

FELDHAMER, THELMA LEAH, architect; b. Bklyn., May 10, 1925; d. Frank and Anna Pearl (Shapiro) Sitzer; m. Carl Feldhamer, Aug. 27, 1950; children: Randi Judith Wathen, Mark David. BArch, Cooper Union for Advancement Sci. and Arts, 1978. Registered architect, Colo. Prin. Thelma Feldhamer, P.C., AIA Architect, Denver, 1980—. Active Pres. Council of Denver; pres.-elect to Colo. State Drafting Tech. Com. State Bd. Community Colls. and Occupational Edn., City and County of Denver Dept. Pub. Works Affirmative Action Office and Goals com. Maj., personnel officer Colo. Wing, CAP, Lowry AFB, 1979—. Mem. AIA, Women in Architecture (Denver chpt.), Bus. and Profl. Women's Club, Denver, Inc. (pres. 1974-76), Denver C. of C. Democrat. Jewish. Club: Altrusa (2d v.p., bd. dirs. Denver 1984). Lodge: El Mejdel Temple, Daus. of Nile. Office: Feldhamer & Assocs PC 3650 S Yosemite St Suite 205 Denver CO 80237

FELDMAN, BEATRICE, social worker; b. N.Y.C., Feb. 21, 1930; d. Leon S. and Sarah (Goldin) Shapiro; m. Daniel W. Feldman, Apr. 6, 1952; children: Robert Adam, Joshua Charles. BA, U. Mich., 1951; MS, Columbia U., 1955. Licensed ind. social worker, ACSW. Caseworker N.J. St. Bd. Child Welfare, Newark, 1951-53, Children's Services, Cleve., 1955-58, Jewish Family Service, Cleve., 1958-59; social worker research VA Hosp., Cleve., 1962; intake worker Youth Service, Cleve., 1962-63; social worker psychiat. Sagamore Hills (Ohio) Childrens Psychiat. Hosp., 1965-71; therapist child Jones Home, Cleve., 1972-74; dir. social work St. John Hosp., Cleve., 1974-86; pres. B. Feldman and Assocs., Beachwood, Ohio, 1986—; cons. Hosp. Home Health Cleve. 1986-87; trustee, bd. dirs. Crisis Intervention Team Mental Health Services 1974, trustee, cons., 1987—. Mgr. Johnson President Office, Shaker Heights, Ohio 1964. Mem. Nat. Assn. Social Workers, Acad. Cert. Social Workers, N.E. Ohio Chpt. Soc. Hosp. Social Worker Dirs. (pres. 1978-79), Am. Soc. Aging, Nat. Assn. Pvt. Geriatric Care Mgrs., Ohio Soc. Clin. Social Work. Jewish. Home and Office: 23213 Fairmount Blvd Beachwood OH 44122

FELDMAN, BELLA TABAK, scupltor, educator; b. N.Y.C., Mar. 1, 1940; d. Abraham and Tesse (Rahs) Tabak; m. Leonard Feldman; children: Nina, Ethan. BA, Queens Coll., 1961; MA, Calif. State U., San Jose, 1972. Lectr. Makerere U. Sch. Fine Arts, Kampala, Uganda, 1968-70, Santa Rosa (Calif.) Jr. Coll., 1972-75; asst. prof. Calif. Coll. Arts and Crafts, Oakland, 1975-79, grad. dir., 1975-79, prof. sculpture, 1982—, chair dept. sculpture, 1987—; guest lectr. Chgo. Art Inst., 1986, U. Hawaii. Group Shows include Space Gallery, Los Angeles, 1987, Tangents traveling show; one woman shows include Artemsia Gallery, Chgo., 1987, Miller/Brown Gallery, San Francisco, 1987. Fellow Nat. Endowment Arts, 1986. Mem. Women's Caucus for Arts, Artists Equity. Democrat. Jewish. Home: 12 Summit Ln Berkeley CA 94708 Office: Calif Coll Arts and Crafts Broadway at Coll Ave Oakland CA 94618

FELDMAN, JUDITH ELLEN, banker; b. N.Y.C., Apr. 7, 1945; d. Carl Benjamin and Florence Siskind m. Melvyn J. Feldman, Aug. 18, 1968; 1 son, Jonathan. BA, Vassar Coll., 1966; MS, Stevens Inst. Tech., 1969. Mem. tech. staff Bell Telephone Labs., Holmdel, N.J., 1966-69; with Morgan Guaranty Trust Co. N.Y., N.Y.C., 1969-84, v.p. fin. analysis, 1969-84; v.p., head securities industry div. First Nat. Bank Chgo., N.Y.C., 1984—. Pres. 353 W. 29th St. Housing Corp., 1982-84; mem. nat. devel. council Stevens Inst. Tech. Office: 153 W 51th St New York NY 10019

FELDON, JOAN SORGE, marketing researcher; b. Evanston, Ill., July 18, 1932; d. Clarence Christopher and Jane (Back) Sorge; m. Richard A. Feldon, June 11, 1954; children—Jill Allison, Richard Alden, Reed Andrew. B.S., Northwestern U., 1954. Mktg. asst., project dir. Action Data, Inc., Cin., 1976-77, project dir. client services, 1977-80, v.p., 1980-82; pres. The Answer Group, Cin., 1982—. Vice-pres. Terrace Park Community Theatre, 1959—; mem. Cin. Music Theatre, 1960—; actor Playhouse in the Park, Cin., Edgecliff Theatre, Cin.; pres. Playhouse Prompters, Cin. Mem. Actors Equity, Am. Mktg. Assn. (sec. 1982-83, hospitality chmn. 1981-82), Mktg. Research Assn., Inc., Internat. Visitors Assn. Republican. Episcopalian. Clubs: Internat. of Frankfort (Ger.) (bd. dirs.); Terrace Park Country (Ohio). Avocations: tennis; golf; community theatre. Home: 3765 Chimney Hill Dr Cincinnati OH 45241 Office: The Answer Group 11161 Kenwood Rd Cincinnati OH 45242

FELDSTEIN, LISA ZOLA, art dealer, consultant; b. Santa Monica, Calif., Dec. 9, 1958; d. Donald James and Dorothy Naomi (Kahn) Zola; m. Alan H. Feldstein, Oct. 19, 1980; 1 child, Sasha Leigh. BA in History, UCLA, 1980; MBA, Pepperdine U., 1986. Theater, community service mgr. Los Angeles Trade-Tech. Coll., 1980; corp. art dir. Louis Newman Galleries, Beverly Hills, Calif., 1980-84; dir., v.p. Toluca Lake Galleries, Burbank, Calif., 1984-86; owner Zola Fine Art, Los Angeles, 1986—; speaker, panelist Art Expo N.Y. and Art Expo Dallas, N.Y.C., 1983; project art cons. Litton Industries, Beverly Hills, 1984—, Union Bank, Los Angeles, 1986—. Contbr. articles to mag. Canvasser Dem. Party, Los Angeles, 1972; mem. Campaign for Econ. Democracy, Los Angeles, 1986—; bd. dirs., founding mem. Royce 2-7, UCLA, 1986—; coordinator Santa Monica Arts Council Movin' on th Mall, 1984. Carnation Found. scholar, 1985, 86. Mem. Amnesty Internat., Nat. Assn. Female Execs., Alpha Epsilon Phi. Democrat. Jewish. Office: 8730 W Third St Los Angeles CA 90048

FELICIANO, GLORIA, human resources executive; b. N.Y.C., July 10, 1946; d. Armando and Carmen (Lespier) F. B.B.A., Bernard Baruch Coll., 1982. Legal sec. to adminstrv. asst. in personnel Richardson-Vicks, Westport, Conn., 1967-75; mgr. adminstrv. services Internat. Basic Economy Corp., N.Y.C., 1975-79; personnel dir. Toyomenka (America) Inc., N.Y.C., 1979-84; v.p. human resources PolyGram Records, Inc., N.Y.C., 1985—. Mem. Am. Soc. Personnel Adminstrn., Am. Mgmt. Assn. Republican. Roman Catholic.

FELLENSTEIN, CORA ELLEN MULLIKIN, credit union executive; b. Edwardsville, Ill., June 2, 1930; d. Russell K. and Elberta Mable (Rheude) Mullikin; m. Charles Frederick Fellenstein, Feb. 24, 1951; children—Keith David, Kimberly Diane. Student Community Coll., 1980-83. Cert. consumer credit exec. Teller, loan officer, office mgr. Credit Union of Johnson County, Mission, Kans., 1976-84, 1st v.p., supr. lending, collections and Mastercard depts., 1984-86, exec. v.p., 1987—. Author: Moore Family History, 1987. Precinct committeewoman Johnson County Republicans, Olathe, Kans., 1976—; vol. Cerebral Palsy, 1957-66, Olathe Community Hosp., 1976—, Shawnee Mission Med. Ctr., 1986— . Mem. Internat. Credit Assn., Kans. Credit Assn., Credit Women Internat. (dir. 1983—), Nat. Assn. Female Execs., DAR (treas. 1976-86), Daus. Am. Colonists (treas. 1976-86), Beta Sigma Phi. Republican. Mem. Christian Ch. Club: Friends of Historic Mahaffie Farmstead (Olathe), Soroptimist Internat. Avocations: genealogy, philately, numismatics, camping. Home: 2000 Arrowhead Dr Olathe KS 66062 Office: Credit Union Johnson County 6025 Lamar St Mission KS 66202

FELLER, SHERYL JANET, management consultant; b. Winnipeg, Man., Can., Dec. 13, 1950; d. George Arthur and Olga (Andersen) Nichols; m. Barry Feller, June 22, 1974; children—Jamie George, Lindsay Janet. Diploma dental hygiene U. Man., 1970, BA, 1974, MBA, 1981. Demonstrator, Sch. Dental Hygiene U. Man., Winnipeg, 1971-73, lectr., 1973-75, asst. prof., 1975-78, acting dir., 1976-78, asst. prof. Faculty Dentistry, 1981; pres., owner SJB Mgmt. Cons., Stonewall, Man., 1982—; dental hygiene clin. practice, Winnipeg, 1970-81. Bd. dirs. Stonewall Children's Ctr., 1982-85. Vol. Centre Winnipeg, 1983-86. Isbister scholar Govt. Man., 1968. Mem. Can. Dental Hygienists Assn. (chmn. long-range planning com. 1983—), Man. Dental Hygienists Assn, Mgmt. Cons. Assn. Man., Inst. Cert. Mgmt. Cons. of Man. (exec. council 1985—), Man. Soc. Tng. and Devel., Winnipeg Women's Network, U. Man. Alumni Assn. (bd. dirs. 1984—); Avocation: horses. Office: SJB Mgmt Cons, Box 287, Sanford, MB Canada R0G 2J0

FELLERS, RHONDA GAY, lawyer; b. Gainesville, Tex., July 20, 1955; d. James Norman and Gaytha Ann (Sanders) F.; m. Bruce C. Hinton, Oct. 15, 1981 (div. Oct. 1985). BA, U. Tex., 1977, JD, 1980; LLM in Taxation, U. Denver, 1987. Bar: Tex. 1981, Colo. 1981, U.S. Dist. Ct. (no. dist.) Tex. 1982, U.S. Dist. Ct. Colo. 1985, U.S. Tax Ct. 1985, U.S. Ct. Appeals (5th cir.) 1986. Assoc. Walters & Assocs., Lubbock, Tex., 1981-83; gen. counsel Security Nat. Bank, Lubbock, 1983; assoc. Melvin Coffee & Assocs., P.C., Denver, 1984-85, 87—; sole practice Lubbock, 1983-87. Mem. ABA, Tex. Bar Assn., Colo. Bar Assn., Denver Bar Assn., Colo. Women's Bar Assn. Office: 2121 S Oneida Suite 336 Denver CO 80224

FELLIN, OCTAVIA ANTOINETTE, librarian; b. Santa Monica, Calif.; d. Otto P. and Librada (Montoya) F.; student U. N.Mex., 1937-39; B.A., U. Denver, 1941; B.A. in L.S., Rosary Coll., 1942. Asst. librarian, instr. library sci. St. Mary-of-Woods Coll., Terre Haute, Ind., 1942-44; librarian U.S. Army, Bruns Gen. Hosp., Santa Fe, 1944-46, Gallup (N.Mex.) Public Library, 1947—; post librarian Camp McQuaide, Calif., 1947; free lance writer mags., newspapers, 1950—; library cons.; N.Mex. del. White House Pre-Conf. on Libraries and Info. Services, 1978; dir. Nat. Library Week for N.Mex., 1959. Vice-pres., publicity dir. Gallup Community Concerts Assn., 1957-78, 85—; organizer Gt. Decision Discussion groups, 1963-85; mem. Gallup St. Naming Com., 1958-59, Aging Com., 1964-68; chmn. Gallup Mus. Indian Arts and Crafts, 1964-78; mem. publicity com. Gallup Inter-Tribal Indian Ceremonial Assn., 1966-68; mem. Gov's. Com. 100 on Aging, 1967-70; N.Mex. Humanities Council, 1979; mem. U. N.Mex.-Gallup Campus Community Edn. Adv. Council, 1981-82; N.Mex. organizing chmn. McKinley Hosp. Aux., pres., 1983; mem. N.Mex. Library Adv. Council, 1971-75, vice chmn., 1974-75; chmn. adv. com. Gallup Sr. Citizens, 1971-73; mem. steering com. Gallup Diocese Bicentennial, 1975-78, chmn. hist. com., 1975; chmn. Trick or Treat for UNICEF, Gallup, 1972-77; chmn. pledge campaign Rancho del Nino San Huberto, Empalme, Mexico; bd. dirs. Gallup Opera Guild, 1970-74; bd. dirs., sec., organizer Gallup Area Arts Council, 1970-78; mem. N.Mex. Humanities Council, 1979, Gallup Centennial Com., 1980-81; mem. Cathedral Parish Council, 1980-83, v.p., 1981. Recipient Dorothy Canfield Fisher $1,000 Library award, 1961; Outstanding Community Service award for mus. service Gallup C. of C., 1969, 70, Outstanding Citizen award, 1974, Benemerenti medal Pope Paul VI, 1977, Celebrate Literary award Gallup Internat. Reading Assn., 1983-84. Mem. ALA, N.Mex. Library Assn. (v.p., sec., chmn. hist. materials com. 1964-66, salary and tenure com., nat. coordinator N.Mex. legislative com., chmn. com. to extend library services 1969-73, Librarian of Yr. award 1975, chmn. local and regional history roundtable 1978, Community Achievement award 1983), AAUW (v.p., co-organizer Gallup br., N.Mex. nominating com. 1967—, chmn. fellowships and centennial fund Gallup br., chmn. com. on women), Plateau Scis. Soc., N.Mex. Folklore Soc. (v.p. 1964-65, pres. 1965-66), N.Mex. Hist. Soc. (dir. 1979—), Gallup Hist. Soc., Gallup Film Soc. (co-organizer, v.p. 1950-58), LWV (v.p. 1953-56), NAACP, Gallup C. of C. (organizing chmn. women's div. 1972, v.p. 1972-73), N.Mex. Women's Polit. Caucus, N.Mex. Mcpl. League (pres. librarian's div. 1979—), Dictionary Soc. N. Am., Alpha Delta Kappa (hon.). Roman Catholic (Cathedral Guild, Confraternity Christian Doctrine Bd. 1962-64, Cursillo in Christianity Movement, mem. of U.S. Cath. Bishop's Adv. Council 1969-74; corr. sec. Latin Am. Mission Program 1972-75, sec. Diocese of Gallup Pastoral Council 1972-73, corr. sec. liturgical commn. Diocese of Gallup 1977);chmn. Artists Coop., 1985—; mem. N.Mex. Diamond Jubilee/U.S. Constitution Bicentennial Gallup Com., 1986—. Author: Yahweh the Voice that Beautifies the Land. Home: 513 E Mesa Ave Gallup NM 87301 Office: 115 W Hill St Gallup NM 87301

FELLOWS, RUTH ARLENE, income maintenance supervisor; b. Morganfield, Ky., June 15, 1936; d. James Nathan and Emma Mae (Briscoe) Farmer; m. Larry Eugene Fellows, Nov. 19, 1954 (div. May 1976); children: Laretta, Larry, Jr., Jerome; remarried, Mar. 25, 1986. Cert., Lockyears Bus. Inst., Evansville, Ind., 1955, H & R Block Tax Inst., St. Louis, 1979. Preparer tax, clk. Anderson Bookkeeping Service, Evansville, 1954-56; with Stevenson Realty Inc., Evansville, 1957-59; clk.-typist Div. Family Services, St. Louis, 1962-65, caseworker, 1965-72, case analyst, 1972-73, supr. income maintenance, 1973—. Mem. Antioch Bapt. Ch., 1977—, mem. gospel choir, 1978—. Mem. Sallye Flagg Missionary Circle (sec. 1986—), Am. Bridge Assn., Beta Mu Theta (sec., treas. 1986). Democrat. Club: Paragon Bridge. Lodges: Liberty, Order Eastern Star. Home: 5517 Gilmore Saint Louis MO 63120

FELSTED, CARLA MARTINDELL, librarian; b. Barksdale Field, La., June 21, 1947; d. David Aldenderfer Martindell and Dorthe (Hetland) Horton; m. Robert Earl Luna, Aug. 24, 1968, (div. 1972); m. Hugh Herbert Felsted, Nov. 2, 1974. BA in English, So. Meth. U., 1968, MA in History, 1974; MLS, Tex. Woman's U., 1978. Cert. secondary tchr., Tex.; cert. learning resources specialist, Tex. Tchr. Bishop Lynch High Sch., Dallas, 1968-72, Lake Highlands Jr. High Sch., Richardson, Tex., 1973-75; instr. Richland Coll., Richardson, Tex., 1973-76; library asst. So. Meth. U., Dallas, 1977-78; librarian Tracy-Locke Advt., Dallas, 1978-79; corp. librarian Am. Airlines, Inc., Euless, Tex., 1979-84; research librarian McKinsey & Co., Dallas, 1984-85; reference librarian St. Edward's U., Austin, Tex., 1985—; ptnr. Southwind Info. Services and Southwind Bed/ Breakfast, Wimberley, Tex., 1984—. Editor, compiler: Youth and Alcohol Abuse, 1986. Mem. adv. bd. Sch. Library and Info. Scis. Tex. Woman's U., Denton, 1982-84; mem. curriculum com. Wimberley Ind. Sch. Dist., 1986; bd. dirs. Hays-Caldwell Council on Alcohol and Drug Abuse, San Marcos, Tex., 1986—. St. Edward's U. grantee, 1986; So. Meth. U., 1972. Mem. ALA, Tex. Library Assn. (dist. program com., membership com. 1986—), Wimberley C. of C. (bd. dirs. 1987—). Lutheran. Home: Rt 2 Box 15 Wimberley TX 78676

FELTMAN, LOIS JEAN, marketing professional; b. Alma, Mich., Dec. 2, 1944; d. Lawrence Wilson and Alice Belle (parker) Townsend; m. Jerome Lee Feltman, Dec. 11, 1965 (div. Feb. 1984); children: Tina, Tony, Todd, Tyrone. Sales coordinator Champion Bldg. Products, Gaylord, Mich., 1977-79; prodn. control mgr. Midwest Metallurgical Lab., Marshall, Mich., 1982—. Hostess home tour, Hist. Soc., Marshall, 1982, 83, 84; den mother Cub Scouts Boy Scouts Am., Gaylord, 1977, 78. Mem. Nat. Assn. Female Execs., Profl. Secs. Internat. (treas. 1985-87). Republican. Methodist. Home: 412 Locust Marshall MI 49068 Office: Midwest Metall Lab 15290 15 Mile Rd Marshall MI 49068

FELTON, ELAINE LOUISE, veterinarian; b. Warsaw, N.Y., Jan. 4, 1955; d. Howard William Felton and Mary Lou (Fister) Gregg. BS, Cornell U., 1976; DVM, N.Y. State Coll. Vet. Medicine, 1979. Staff veterinarian Batavia (N.Y.) Animal Hosp., 1979-82; asst. med. dir. Humane Soc. N.Y., N.Y.C., 1982—. Mem. Am. Vet. Med. Assn., Am. Animal Hosp. Assn., N.Y. State Vet. Med. Soc., N.Y.C. Vet. Med. Soc. Presbyterian. Office: Humane Soc NY 306 E 59th St New York NY 10022

FELTON, JUDITH R., psychoanalyst, educator; b. Phila., Aug. 21, 1942; d. Martin and Laura (Goldman) Kirshenbaum; AB in Govt., Wheaton (Mass.) Coll., 1963; MSW, Rutgers U., 1966, PhD, Rutgers U. Grad. Sch. Arts and Scis., 1983; grad. N.Y. Center for Psychoanalytic Tng., 1978; m. Stephen Felton, Feb. 8, 1966; 1 dau., Jane Jennifer. Clin. social worker VA, Newark, 1967; psychotherapist Santa Barbara (Calif.) Mental Health Services, 1967-69; supr. Santa Barbara Counselling Center, 1967-69; pvt. practice psychoanalysis, 1969—; psychoanalyst, therapist Fifth Ave. Center for Psychotherapy, N.Y.C., 1969-72; instr. Marymount Manhattan Coll., 1971; psychotherapy supr. clin. faculty, dept. psychiatry Rutgers U. Med. Sch., New Brunswick, N.J., 1972-75, teaching asst. Grad. Sch. Social Work, 1974-76; vis. lectr. Bryn Mawr Coll. Sch. Social Work and Social Research, 1980; mem. faculty N.Y. Center for Psychoanalytic Tng., 1980—, N.J. Inst. Psychoanalysis and Psychotherapy, 1982—. Bd. dirs. N.Y. Ctr. for Psychoanalytic Tng., Inst. for Psychoanalysis and Psychotherapy N.J., 1986—. NIMH fellow, 1965; diplomate Am. Bd. Psychotherapy. Recipient Disting. Faculty award Atlantic County Psychoanalytic Soc., 1987. Fellow N.J. Soc. for Clin. Social Work; mem. Nat. Assn. Soc.ial Workers, Conf. Psychoanalytic Psychotherapists, Nat. Assn. for Advancement Psychoanalysis, Groves Conf. on Family, Acad. Cert. Social Workers, Soc. for Psychoanalytic Tng. (bd. dirs. 1983—, dir. social sci. program 1983-86), AAUP, Am. Psychol. Assn. Mem. editorial bd. jour. Current Issues in Psychoanalytic Practice, 1983—; contbr. articles to profl. jours. Home and office: 159 Valley Rd Princeton NJ 08540

FEND, EILEEN, personnel service owner; b. Salt Lake City, Oct. 29, 1927; d. Mark and Louise (Irvine) Warburton; m. Jack Hartman, Oct. 28, 1958 (dec. 1968); children: Pamela Greene, Teri Gervais, Mark Hartman; m. Helmut Fend, June 21, 1975. Student, Utah State U., 1945-49, U. So. Calif., 1985. Purchasing agt. Futurecraft Corp., City of Industry, Calif., 1959-64; dir. Vivian Woodard, Panorama City, Calif., 1964-75; pres., owner On Call Personnel, Manhattan Beach, Calif., 1978—; chmn. bd. dirs. Hour Gang Personnel, Orange County, Calif., 1982—; cons. and lectr. in field. Coordinator, Duologue Vendor Com.; mem. roundtable Calif. State U., Dominguez Hills South Bay Bus. Roundtable; bd. dirs. Women in Mgmt. Career Opportunity Liaison; scholarship bd. Bank of Am., Redondo Beach, El Segundo Rotary Club. Mem. Internat. Assn. Personnel Women (hostess nat. mid-winter bd. meetings), Personnel and Indsl. Relations Assn., Bus. Mgmt. Assn., Women in Mgmt. (1st v.p. 1988—, C. of C. (Calif.), Nat. Assn. Women Bus. Owners (pub. affairs com.), Calif. Assn. Personnel Consultants (temprary services sect.), South Bay Mktg. Network (v.p.). Club: Leads (coordinator 1987). Avocation: skiing. Office: On Call Personnel 505 N Sepulveda Manhattan Beach CA 90277

FENNELL, MARYLOUISE, community relations executive; b. Bridgeport, Conn., July 3, 1939; d. Joseph M. and Elizabeth (Higby) F. BA, Diocesan Sisters Coll., West Hartford, Conn., 1961; MEd, U. Hartford, 1972, cert. advanced grad. study in counselor edn., 1973; EdD, Boston U., 1976. Jr. high sch. tchr., 1961-71; draft counselor U. Hartford, Conn., 1971-72; clin. prof., 1971-74; mem. adj. faculty St. Joseph Coll., West Hartford, 1972-76, assoc. prof., 1976-82, cert. officer, 1976-77, coordinator tchr. edn., 1976-78, chmn. edn. div., 1979-80, founding mem., dir. Counseling Inst., 1976-82, chmn. counselor edn. dept., 1976-82, dir. Inst. in Ministry, 1979-82, asst. dean grad. sch., 1980-82; teaching fellow, mem. adj. faculty Boston U., 1974-76; practice psychotherapy and counseling West Hartford Counseling Service, 1976-82; pres. Carlow Coll., Pitts., 1982-88; sr. v.p. corporate and community relations, Gateway Group, Pitts., 1988—; part-time vocat. edn. counselor House of Good Shepherd, Hartford, 1970; part-time guidance counselor Mt. St. Joseph Acad., West Hartford, 1972; vis. prof. religious studies Assumption Coll., Worcester, Mass., 1981-82. Bd. dirs. Family Study Ctr., Inc., 1977-82, Pitts. Chamber Music Soc., 1983—, Penn's S.W. Assn., 1983—, Mom's House, 1983—; trustee Pitts. Symphony, 1984—, Gaelic Soc. Am., 1983-88; chmn. bd. dirs., v.p. Family Study Ctr. Conn., Inc., 1978-82; ednl. cons., bd. dirs. Manchester Counseling Ctr., 1976-82; mem. adv. bd. pastoral care dept. St. Mary Home, West Hartford, 1980-82; mem. Archdiocesan com. on Status of Women, Hartford, 1980-82; mem. senate Sisters of Mercy of Conn., 1980-82; mem. community relations com. Pa. council Girl Scouts U.S.A., 1982—; mem. citizens sponsoring com. Allegheny Conf., 1982—; pvt. industry cons. CETA, Pitts., 1982-87. Recipient Outstanding Service award Pitts. Black Catholics, 1983, Leadership award Pitts. YWCA, 1984, others. Mem. Pa. Assn. Colls. and Univs., Commn. Ind. Colls. and Univs., Pa. Elected Women's Assn., Assn. Tchr. Educators, Assn. Counselor Edn. and Supervision, Am. Personnel and Guidance Assn., North Atlantic Regional Assn. Counselor Edn. and Supervision, Conn. Personnel and Guidance Assn. (bd. dirs., membership chmn. 1978-79, exec. bd. 1977-82), Am. Assn. Pastoral Counselors, Conn. Assn. Pastoral Counselors (exec. bd.), Am. Mental Health Counselors Assn. Office: The Gateway Group Inc One Gateway Ctr Pittsburgh PA 15222

FENNELL, REBEKAH SUE, association executive; b. Marlette, Mich., Apr. 25, 1955; d. Alfred Conrad and Lavonne Marie (Koenecke) F.; m. Thomas Patrick Dowdall, Oct. 14, 1984. BA, Mich. State U., 1980; cert. exec. development program, U. Md., 1988. Exec. asst. Nat. Orgn. for Women, Washington, 1980-81; supr. telemktg. Pub. Interest Communications, Falls Church, Va., 1981-82; research asst. Nat. Assn. Criminal Justice Planners, Washington, 1981-86, asst. dir. for adminstrn., 1986—. Vol. coordinator Arlington County Spl. Olympics, Va., 1982-83; vol. dir. No. Va. Spl. Olympics, Arlington, 1983-84, chmn. personnel com., v.p. area council, 1984-85, chmn. adv. com., 1985-86, dir. games adminstr., 1986; counselor Schumacher Clin., Planned Parenthood Metro. Washington, 1987—. Named one of Outstanding Young Women of Am., 1984; recipient Vol. of Yr. honorable mention Va. Spl. Olympics, 1984-85. Mem. Am. Soc. Assn. Execs., Nat. Assn. Female Execs., NOW, Greater Washington Soc. Assn. Execs. Office: Nat Assn Criminal Justice Planners 1511 K St Suite 445 Washington DC 20005

FENNELL ROBBINS, SALLY, free-lance writer, promotional consultant; b. Greensburg, Pa., Feb. 17, 1950; d. Clifford Seanor and Charlotte Louise (Hoffman) Fennell; B.S. in Journalism, Ohio U., 1972 cum laude; M.A. in Journalism, magna cum laude, Marshall U., 1974; cert. in writing for TV Ctr. Media Arts, 1986. Intern, reporter Tribune-Rev., Greensburg, Pa., 1972; prodn. asst. Harper's Bazaar, N.Y.C., 1972; reporter UPI, Birmingham, Ala., 1972-73; reporter, dept. editor HFD-Retailing Home Furnishings, Fairchild Pubs., N.Y.C., 1975-77; account exec. supr., client service mgr., v.p. Burson-Marsteller, N.Y.C., 1977-83; group mgr., v.p. pub. relations div. Ketchum Communications, 1983-84; grad. teaching asst. Sch. Journalism/Reporting, Marshall U., Huntington, W.Va., 1973-74. Recipient Lasher award Ohio U. Sch. Journalism, 1972. Mem. Soc. Profl. Journalists/Sigma Delta Chi, Am. Mgmt. Assn., Assn. Edn. in Journalism and Mass Communication, Pub. Relations Soc. Am. Home and Office: 237 East 20th St New York NY 10003

FENNER, FREDA D'SOUZA, marketing executive; b. Madras, India, Nov. 1, 1957; came to U.S., 1973; d. John Mathew and Lucy (D'Cunha) D'Souza; m. Steven John Fenner, June 17, 1978. BA, U. Detroit, 1978. News editor Contractor Pub. Co., Detroit, 1978-81; pub. relations specialist SEMTA, Detroit, 1981-83; acct. exec. Anthony M. Franco, Inc., Detroit, 1983-86; exec. dir. Yes 150 Found., Mich., 1986—; prin. Fenner Communications Co., Detroit, 1988—; v.p. Nat. Investor Relations Inst. Detroit, 1986-87; bd. dirs. Internat. Assn. Bus. Communicators, 1984-86; chmn. bd. dirs. PRSA, 1985-86. Contbr. articles to profl. jours. Active various fundraising drives; mem. pres. cabinet U. Detroit, 1984—, Founder's Soc., Detroit Inst. Arts, 1985—; chmn. publicity com.Concerned Citizens for the Arts, 1985. Recipient Tower award U. Mich., 1985. Mem. Women in Communications, Nat. Assn. Fundraising Execs., Mich. Assn. Fundraising Execs., India League of Am. (bd. dirs., membership chmn.1987), U. Detroit Nat. Alumni Bd. (bd. dirs. 1980—). Roman Catholic. Clubs: Indian Village Garden (Detroit), India Bridge (Mich.), Historical Soc. (Bluewater chpt.). Home: 1073 Iroquois Ave Detroit MI 48214 Office: Yes 150 Found 100 E Big Beaver Rd Troy MI 48214

FENSTERSTOCK, JOYCE NARINS, investment banker; b. N.Y.C., Dec. 30, 1948; d. Charles S. and Frances D. (Kross) Narins; BA in Psychology, Wellesley Coll., 1970; MBA, Harvard U., 1973; m. Blair C. Fensterstock; children: Michael Bayard, Evan Steele, Laurel Sage. Assoc. corp. fin. Warburg Paribas Becker Inc., Chgo., 1974-75, Goldman, Sachs & Co., N.Y.C., 1973-78; sr. v.p. corp. fin., mng. dir. Paine Webber Inc., N.Y.C., 1978—. Mem. Fin. Women's Assn. Club: Harvard (N.Y.C.). Home: 120 E 75th St New York NY 10021 Office: 1285 Ave of Americas New York NY 10019

FENTON, ELLEN-SUE, broadcasting company administrator; b. N.Y.C., May 21, 1948; d. Roland Russell and Millie Sylvia (Perlman) F. Student, Nassau Community Coll., 1967-68; BA, Northeastern U., 1970. Personnel asst. Nat. Can Corp., Maspeth, N.Y., 1970-73; customer relations rep. Eastern Express, inc., Maspeth, 1973-76; dir. personnel and tng. Ednl. Broadcasting Corp., N.Y.C., 1976-82, dir. corp. adminstrn., 1983—; dir. personnel and adminstrn. Cable Health Network, N.Y.C., 1982-83; dir. and fin. chair Booth St. Owners Corp., Forest Hills, N.Y., 1986—. Named one of Outstanding Young Women Am. Mem. Am. Mgmt. Assn., Risk and Ins. Mgmt. Soc., Inc., Pub. Telecommunications Fin. Mgrs. Assn. (dir., chair human resources council 1986—). Democrat. Office: Ednl Broadcasting Corp 356 W 58th St New York NY 10019

FENTON, LOIS (CLAIRE) SLOAN, executive attire consultant and speaker; b. Pitts., May 3, 1929; d. Samuel Abraham and Katherine Janet (Sugerman) Sloan; m. Malcolm Fenton (div. Oct. 1973); children: Kirk, Gregg, Scott, Matthew. BS, Carnegie Mellon U., 1946-50; postgrad., U. Pitts., 1950-53. Tchr. Pitts. Pub. Sch., 1950-53; lectr. Company's Coming, Mamaroneck, N.Y., 1968-77; lctr., cons. Exec. Wardrobe Engring., Mamaroneck, N.Y., 1977—. Author: Dress for Excellence, 1986. Democrat. Jewish. Club: Mamaroneck Garden (pres. 1966-68, program chmn. 1964-66). Office: Exec Wardrobe Engring 721 Shore Acres Dr Mamaroneck NY 10543

FENTON, PAULA BLANCHE, lawyer; b. N.Y.C., Apr. 29, 1947; d. Robert and Janet (Munk) F. BA with honors, U. Pa., 1969; JD, Columbia U., 1972. Assoc. Reavis & McGrath, N.Y.C., 1972-77; sr. clk. to presiding justice N.Y. State Supreme Ct., N.Y.C., 1977-79; ptnr. Fine, Tofel, Saxl, Berleson & Barandes, N.Y.C., 1979-83; counsel, dir. spl. events Am. Ballet Theatre, N.Y.C., 1983-87; sr. atty. Radio City Music Hall Prodns., Inc., N.Y.C., 1987—; arbitrator Am. Arbitration Assn., N.Y.C., 1979—; chmn. secondary sch. com. U. Pa., N.Y.C., 1981-84; cons. Aspen Camp for the Deaf, Colo., 1986. Bd. dirs. New Leadership Israel Bonds, 1980-82, San Diego Performances, 1987—. Recipient Award of Merit Israel Bonds, 1981. Democrat. Jewish. Office: Radio City Music Hall Prodns Inc 1260 Ave of the Americas New York NY 10020

FENWICK, MILLICENT HAMMOND, retired diplomat, former congresswoman; b. N.Y.C., Feb. 25, 1910; d. Ogden Haggerty and Mary Picton (Stevens) Hammond; children: Mary Fenwick Reckford, Hugh. Student, Columbia Extension Sch., New Sch. for Social Research. Assoc. editor Conde Nast Publs., N.Y.C., 1938-50; mem. N.J. Gen. Assembly, 1970-73; dir. div. consumer affairs N.J. Dept. Law and Pub. Safety, 1973-74; mem. 94th-97th Congresses from N.J. 5th Dist., 1975-83; U.S. amb. UN Food and Agr. Orgn., 1983-87. Author: Vogue's Book of Etiquette, 1948, Speaking Up, 1982. Vice chmn. N.J. advisory com. to U.S. Commn. on Civil Rights, 1958-72; mem. Bernardsville (N.J.) Bd. Edn., 1938-41; mem Bernardsville Borough Council, 1958-64. Republican. Home: Mendham Rd Bernardsville NJ 07924

FERENCE, PATRICIA SUSAN, nurse; b. N.Y.C., Nov. 19, 1950; d. Edward Joseph Ference and Ann Carol (Fox) Gray. RN, Misericordia Hosp. Sch. Nursing, Bronx, N.Y., 1974. Nurse Montefiore Hosp., Bronx, 1974-77, North Shore Univ. Hosp., Manhasset, N.Y., 1977—. Mem. Am. Nurses Assn., N.Y. State Nurses Assn. Home and Office: 219-46 93d Ave Queens NY 11428

FERENCSIK, JOANNE MARIE, training consultant; b. Phila., Sept. 22, 1959; d. John Joseph and Helen (Dezwol) F. BS in Physics, Georgetown U., 1981; MBA, U. Houston, 1986. Research asst. Applied Sci Tech., Arlington, Va., 1980-81; physicist Phila. Electric Co., 1981-82; tech. trainer Ford Aerospace, Houston, 1982-85; tng. cons. Shared Med. Systems, Malvern, Pa., 1987—. Recipient Leadership award U. Houston, 1986. Mem. Nat. Assn. Female Execs., Am. Soc. Tng. and Devel., MBA Assn. (pres., founder 1986, Leadership award 1986), Sigma Iota Epsilon. Home: 25 Flintlock Ln Wayne PA 19087 Office: Shared Med Systems 51 Valley Stream Pkwy Malvern PA 19355

FERENS, MARCELLA (MRS. JOSEPH J. FERENS), educator, business executive; b. Pitts.; d. Ignatius and Marcella (Buzas) Slevinskas; student Greensburg Bus. Coll., 1934-35, Maison Frederic Cosmetology, 1936, Kree Inst. Electrolysis, N.Y., 1952; B.S., U. Pitts., 1957; postgrad. Mid-Western U., 1962; M.Ed., Duquesne U., 1964; m. Joseph J. Ferens, Nov. 27, 1937; children—Joseph Ferens, James. Cosmetologist and electrologist, Manor and Darragh, Pa., 1937—; research in hair regrowth, Darragh, 1954—; tchr. cosmetology Uniontown (Pa.) Vocat. High, 1954-55; tchr. algebra, reading and drama dir. Harold Jr. High Sch., Greensburg, Pa., 1958—; pres. Marcella Ferens Inc.; treas. Schumacher Labs. Inc., Darragh. Insp., Chem. Corps, Dept. Army, N.Y., 1951. Mem. Nat. Council Tchrs. Math., Nat., Pa. edn. assns. Patentee in field. Home: Box 84 Daragh PA 15625

FERETIC, EILEEN SUSAN, editor; b. N.Y.C., Aug. 31, 1949; d. Joseph Anthony and Eileen Helen (Sohl) F. B.A., Fordham U., 1971. Editor Manpower Edn. Inst., N.Y.C., 1970-72, UTP div. Hearst Bus. Communications, L.I., N.Y., 1972—, Corporate Systems mag., 1975-80, Office Products News, 1972-82, Today's Office, 1982—; also editorial dir. Office Group, 1978—; industry rep. U.S. Dept. Commerce, 1980, 83; mem. Pres.'s Pvt. Sector Survey on Cost Control/Office Automation Task Force, 1982. Co-author textbook on adminstrv. procedures in electronic office, 1979. Recipient N.Y. Daily News award journalism, 1970; Long Island Press Club Writing award. Mem. Am. Soc. Bus. Press Editors Assn. (writing award). Home: 115 Rita Dr East Meadow NY 11554 Office: Today's Office 645 Stewart Ave Garden City NY 11530

FERGUS, PATRICIA MARGUERITA, educator emeritus, writer, editor; b. Mpls., Oct. 26, 1918; d. Golden Maughan and Mary Adella (Smith) F.; B.S., U. Minn., 1939, M.A., 1941, Ph.D., 1960. Various personnel and editing positions with U.S. Govt., 1943-59; mem. faculty U. Minn., 1964-79, asst. prof. English, 1972-79, coordinator writing program conf. on writing, 1975, dir. writing centre, 1975-77; prof. English and writing, dir. writing ctr., assoc. dean Coll., Mt. St. Mary's Coll., Emmitsburg, Md., 1979-81; dir. writing seminars Mack Truck, Inc., Hagerstown, Md., 1979-81; writer, 1964—; editorial asst. to pres. Met. State U., St. Paul, 1984-85; speaker in field; cons. in field; dir. 510 Groveland Assocs.; bus. mgr. Eitel Hosp. Gift Shop; mem. St. Olaf Ch. Choir, St. Olaf Parish Adv. Bd. Recipient Outstanding Contbn. award U. Minn. Twin Cities Student Assembly, 1975; Horace T. Morse-Amoco Found. award, 1976; Ednl. Devel. grantee U. Minn., 1975-76; Mt. St. Mary's Coll. grantee, 1980; 3d prize vocal-choral category Nat. Music Composition Contest, Nat. League Am. Pen Women, 1986; speaker and Bronze Medalist, 13th Internat. Biographical Congress. Mem. Internat. Biog. Centre Assn., Am. Biog. Inst. (hon. research adv. bd.dep. gov.), Am. Biog. Research Assn., AAUW, Nat. (regional judge writing awards program 1974, 76-77, state coordinator 1977-79) Minn. (chmn. career and job opportunities com., mem. spl. com. on tchr. licensure, sec. legis. com.) councils tchrs. English, Nat. League Am. Pen Women (pres. Minn. br.), World Lit. Acad., Mpls. Poetry Soc. (pres.; 1st prize Haiku contest 1984, 3d prize poetry contest 1986, 1st prize poetry contest 1987, 3d prize poetry contest 1988), League Minn. Poets, Midwest Fedn. Chaparral Poets (2d prize poetry contest 1987, 3d prize poetry contest 1988), AAUP, Pi Lambda Theta. Roman Catholic. Author: Spelling Improvement, 4th edit., 1983; contbr. to Minn. English Jour., Downtown Cath. Voice, Mpls., Mountaineer Briefing; contbr. poems Minn. English Jour., Mpls. Muse, The Moccasin, Heartsong, North-star Gold, The PoetryLetter. Home and Office: 1770 Bryant Ave S #410 Minneapolis MN 55403

FERGUSON, ALICE LEE, mortgage company executive; b. Stoneham, Mass., Sept. 29, 1955; d. Donald and Alice (Hughes) Crooker; m. Dana A. Lunden, June 4, 1976 (div. 1981); 1 child, Katie Beth; m. Kenneth R. LeBaron, July 31, 1982 (div. 1986); 1 child, Alexander Colin; m. Oliver B. Ferguson, June 19, 1987. Student, Plymouth St. Coll., 1973-76, BS, 1988; student, Merrimack Valley Coll., 1976-84, 88—. Head teller, sr. fin. counselor Numerica Savs. Bank, Manchester, N.H., 1980-84; loan originator Nat. Mortgage Co., Bedford, N.H., 1985—; instrs. program Fred Villaris Studios of Self Def., Manchester, 1987—. Mem. N.H. Repertory Theatre, Manchester, 1970-71, Elect Warren Rudman com., Manchester, 1978-79, Plymouth Players, 1973-76. Mem. Nat. Assn. Female Execs., Salem N.H. Bd. Realtors, Londonderry, N.H. Womens Club, N.H. Soc. for Psychic Research, Delta Zeta. Home: PO Box 2769 Chesapeake VA 23320 Office: Nat Mortgage Co 10 Corporate Dr Bedford NH 03102

FERGUSON, ANN JO, quality assurance specialist; b. Coldwater, Mich., Aug. 21, 1952; d. Marion D. and Pauline Elizabeth (Smith) Kentner; children from previous marriage: Matthew Paul Keeslar, Nathan Leon Keeslar; m. Gary Steven Ferguson, Jan. 31, 1978; 1 child, Katie Ann. Chem. technician U. N.C., Chapel Hill, 1973-75; lab. technician Geo-Test, Inc., Monroe, Mich., 1976-77; asst. lab. supr. Bowser-Morner, Inc., Toledo, 1977-79; sr. lab. technician Prestolite Battery div. Allied Corp., Toledo, 1979-81, asst. engr., 1981-83, quality assurance engr., 1983-85; mgr. quality Mather Seal div. Fed. Mogul, Milan, Mich., 1986; dir. quality assurance and tng. Sharon Mfg., Lambertville, Mich., 1986—; cons. ptnr. S.P.C. Tng., Toledo, 1985—. Mem. Am. Soc. for Quality Control (cert.; co-chair edn. com. 1987-88). Republican. Roman Catholic. Home: 5306 Westcroft Dr Sylvania OH 43560 Office: Sharon Mfg Co 7325 Douglas Rd Lambertville MI 48144

FERGUSON, DEE ANN, academic director; b. Columbus, Ohio, July 13, 1947; d. Walter Lewis and Rachel Dixon (Stone) Lucas; m. David Elton Ferguson (dec. June 1969); 1 child, Patrick Antonio. B cum laude, Ohio State U., 1966; MBA, U. Exeter, Eng., 1975. Mng. dir. Lori of London, Internat. London, 1973-80; bus. mgr., cons. Los Angeles, 1978-80; adminstr. Gussi Watches, Los Angeles, 1979-82; dir. facilities Marlborough Sch., Los Angeles, 1983—; mem. steering com. Earthquake Preparedness Marlborough Sch., 1984—. Inventor roll-r-shoe, load stabelizer, chem. formulae. Mem. Assn. Phys. Plant Admistrs. of Colls. and Univs., Am. Inst. Plant Engrs. (treas.-elect 1988, bd. dirs.). Roman Catholic. Home: 1147 N Wilcox Pl Los Angeles CA 90038 Office: Marlborough Sch 250 S Rossmore Ave Los Angeles CA 90004

FERGUSON, JUDITH KENNERLY, public utility executive; b. Mooresville, N.C., Mar. 2, 1947; d. Glenn Carson Kennerly and Wilma Ruth (Johnson) Kennerly Thompson; m. George Robert Holbrook, Dec. 4, 1966 (div. May 1977); 1 child, Kevin Holbrook; m. John Martin Ferguson, Dec. 17, 1977. Grad. high sch., Mooresville, N.C., 1965. Sec. Aetna Life and Casualty, Charlotte, N.C., 1965-66, Am. Credit Corp., Charlotte, 1966-67; data processor Burlington Industries, Mooresville, 1967-70, sec., 1973-75; head cashier N.G. Speir, Inc., Charlotte, 1970-73; document control supr. Duke Power Co., Charlotte, N.C., 1975—. Mem. Assn. Info. and Image Mgmt., Nuclear Info. and Records Mgmt. Assn. (chairperson program planning com., 1983-87, regulations com., 1987—), Nat. Assn. Female Execs. Republican. Presbyterian. Office: Duke Power Co PO Box 33189 Charlotte NC 28242

FERGUSON, KAYE IRENE, fundraiser, marketing professional; b. Lansing, Mich., Jan. 20, 1939; d. Alfred Richard and Iris Francis (Kast) Collins; m. Stanley M. Ferguson, June 21, 1958 (div. 1985); children: Kelley Ann, Carrie Jane, Stanley M. BA, Mich. State U., 1958; postgrad., Memphis State U., 1974-75. Freelance writer Detroit, 1958-68; educator Met. Soc. for Blind, Detroit, 1968-69; media buyer, copy writer John R. Chapman Co., Royal Oak, Mich., 1969-71; talk show host Sta. KERO-TV, Bakersfield, Calif., 1971-74; creative dir. Lanigan, Inc., Memphis, 1974-75, Merritt Mosby Advt. Agy., Memphis, 1975-80; v.p., creative dir. Myers/Ferguson Assocs., Memphis, 1980-85; dir. tourism City of Memphis Conv. and Visitors Bur., Memphis, 1985-86; assoc. dir. Meth. Hosps. Found., Memphis, 1986-88; v.p. devel. Luth. Social Services of Mich., 1988—; regional dir. State Tenn. Dept. Tourism, Memphis, 1986-87; profl. soprano soloist, various events, 1958—. Bd. dirs. Memphis Symphony Chorus, 1983-85, Am. Lung Assn., 1983-86; bd. dirs., past pres. Alliance for Blind and Visually Impaired, Memphis, 1985-88; mem. adminstrv. bd. Germantown United Meth. Ch., 1983-88, also music dir. 1980-88. Recipient Outstanding Vol. award March of Dimes, Bakersfield, 1974, Outstanding Service award Am. Lung Assn., 1984. Mem. Memphis Advt. Fedn. (chmn. various coms. 1982-86), Nat. Assn. Female Execs., Am. Women in Radio and TV (sec. 1972-73), Nat. Assn. Hosp. Devel., Nat. Soc. Fund Raising Execs., Meth. Fellowship of Musicians (sec.-treas. 1986-87), Delta Delta Delta. Republican. Club: PEO. Office: Lutheran Social Services of Michigan 8131 E Jefferson Ave Detroit MI 48214

FERGUSON, MARY ROSALIE, utilities company executive; b. Indpls., Jan. 1, 1939; d. Francis John and Catherine Marie (Osterman) Schmidt; m. Kenneth H. Ferguson, Jr. (div. July 1969); 1 child, Kimberlie Marie. Student in English, Butler U., 1957-73; student in mgmt., Ind. U. Purdue U. at Indpls., 1982—. Staff supr. mktg. Ind. Bell. Telephone Co., Indpls., 1967-72, evaluator assessment ctr., 1972-73, accounts mgr. mktg., 1973-82, specialist bus. services, 1982, mgr. spl. services, 1982—; cons. mgmt., Indpls., 1986—. Mem. exec. com. 2d Quadrennial Internat. Violin Competition of Indpls., 1986; performance site chairperson Pan Am. Music Festival of Champions, Indpls., 1987; bd. dirs. Cathedral Arts, Inc., Indpls., 1987, Fine Arts Soc., Inc., Indpls., 1987; bd. dirs. Indpls. Opera, 1988. Named Nat. Am. Businesswoman Yr. Am. Businesswomen's Assn., 1973. Mem. Women's Bus. Initiative, Inc., The Network of Women in Bus., Inc. (charter mem. Exec. Club 1985-87, pres., bd. dirs. 1981-85, chair exec. club 1988, Networker of Yr., 1984), Telephone Pioneers Am. Republican. Roman Catholic. Club: Business (Indpls.) (pres. 1983). Office: Ind Bell Telephone Co Inc 220 N Meridian Room 795 Indianapolis IN 46250

FERGUSON, SANDRA MAREA, educational consultant; b. N.Y.C., Dec. 18, 1946; d. Edward Augustus and Oletha Gertrude (Higgs) F. B.S.Ed., St. John's U., 1968; M.S. Ed., Fordham U., 1977. Primary tchr. Bd. Edn. N.Y.C., 1967-69; adult educator Manpower Inc., N.Y.C., 1969-70; reading instr. Youth Devel., Inc., N.Y.C., 1970-71; ednl. cons. Scott Foresman & Co., Oakland, N.J., 1971—. Mem. Internat. Reading Assn., Nat. Council Tchrs. English, N.Y. State Reading Assn., Nat. Geog. Soc., Delta Sigma Theta. Democrat. Roman Catholic. Clubs: N.Y. Bot. Gardens, Camera. Home: 700 Columbus Ave New York NY 10025 Office: Scott Foresman & Co 99 Bauer Dr Oakland NJ 07436

FERGUSON, SUSAN KATHARINE STOVER, nurse; b. Warsaw, Ind., Mar. 11, 1944; d. Robert Eugene and Barbara Louise (Swaney) S.; m. Philip Charles Ferguson, May 29, 1942; children: Scott Duane, Shawn Alaine, Erin Kirsten. Diploma in nursing, Meth. Hosp., 1966; BA in Psychology, Purdue U., 1988. Staff nurse, health hazard appraiser Meth. Hosp. of Ind., Indpls., 1966-68; staff nurse USPHS, Bethel, Alaska, 1968-70; instr. childbirth preparation Wabash, Ind., 1975-83; nurse Family Physicians Associated, Wabash, 1976-83; research asst. Purdue U., West Lafayette, Indiana, 1986-88; staff nurse Charter Beacon Hosp., Ft. Wayne, Ind., 1988—. Bd. dirs. Hoosiers for Safety Belts, Indpls., 1987—, Ind. Med. Pol. Action Com., Indpls., 1986-87; coordinator, founder Safe Start Infant Safety Seat Loan Program, Wabash, 1981-87; participant in leadership devel. com. Wabash County C. of C., 1983; workshop leader Wabash County Hosp. Stop Smoking Program, 1982-83. Mem. Ind. Child Passenger Safety Assn. (pres. 1985-87), Ind. State Med. Assn. Aux. (chmn. program workbook 1982-86), Am. Nurses Assn., Nat. Passenger Safety Assn., Am. Psychol. Assn. (student affiliate), Wabash County Med. Soc. Aux. (pres. 1981-83). Republican. Home: 2611 Neptune's Crossing Fort Wayne IN 46815 Office: Ind Child Passenger Safety Assn PO Box 40815 Indianapolis IN 46240

FERGUSON, SYBIL, franchise business executive; b. Barnwell, Alta., Can., Feb. 7, 1934; came to U.S., 1938, naturalized, 1976; d. Alva John and Xarissa (Merkley) Clarke; m. Roger N. Ferguson, July 10, 1952; children: Debra Kay, Michael David, Wade Clarke, Lois Christine, Julie Xarissa. Student public schs. Founder Diet Ctr. Inc., Rexburg, Idaho, 1970—; bd. dirs. Am. Health Products, Diet Ctr. Counselor Tng., Ferguson's Pharm. Labs., Diet Ctr. Shipping and Receiving Co., Diet Ctr. Print Shop, Audio Visual Studio, Sybils, Inc., Ferguson & Assocs., Golden Eagle Ranches. Author: The Diet Center Program, Lose Weight Fast and Keep It Off Forever, 1983, Diet Center Cookbook. Charter mem. women's aux. Madison Meml. Hosp., Rexburg; founding sponsor Children's Miracle Network Telethon; bd. advisors Exchange, Working Mother's Network; mem. nat. adv. council Brigham Young U., Salt Lake City, Ricks Coll., Boise State U.; mem. Rexburg Civic Assn. Recipient Bus. Leader of Yr. award Ricks Coll., 1980; named Great Figure of Franchising, 1987, to Community Leaders Am., one of Top 60 Women Entrepreneurs, Saavy mag. Mem. Internat. Franchise Assn., Am. Entrepreneur Assn., Rexburg C. of C. (program dir. 1976), Com. of 200 (founder). Mormon. Lodge: Soroptimists (v.p. Rexburg chpt. 1975, award 1979). Office: Diet Center Inc 220 S 2d St W Rexburg ID 83440

FERGUSON, VERBENA SHOULTZ, educator; b. Phila., July 23, 1936; d. Otis and Octavia V. (Tooks) Shoultz; 1 child, Daryll M. BS, State Tchrs. Coll., Cheyney, Pa., 1955; MEd, Antioch Grad. Sch., 1975; PhD, Union for Experimenting Colls. and Univ., Cin., 1979. Classroom tchr. Bd. Pub. Edn., Phila., 1958-64, reading cons., ednl. improvement program for disadvantaged, 1964-68, reading specialist, achievement for individual devel. program in middle and jr. high sch., 1977—; dir. tutoring program for Spanish-speaking students Jefferson Sch., 1968-71; pres., exec. dir. Ferguson Tutorial Services, Phila., 1980—. Pub.: How-to Reading Program for Young Children. Recipient Higgins Sci. award Chapel of Four Chaplains, 1970, merit cert. in reading/lang. arts Ednl. Improvement Program; NDEA grantee, 1968-69. Mem. Internat. Reading Assn., Assn. for Supervision and Curriculum Devel., Council for Basic Edn., Phila. Fedn. Tchrs., Delta Sigma Theta. Democrat. Episcopalian. Designer reading program for deaf. Home: 6550 N Gratz St Philadelphia PA 19126 Office: 1015 Chestnut St Suite 926 Philadelphia PA 19107

FERGUSON-PELL, MARGARET ALICE, health science facility press and public relations officer; b. New Haven, Aug. 14, 1951; d. Franklin Eldridge and Virginia Boardman (Porter) F.; m. Martin William Ferguson-Pell, Dec. 29, 1973. BA in English summa cum laude, Wheaton Coll., 1973. Antiquarian book specialist John Smith & Son, Glasgow, Scotland, 1974-76; book editor Heatherbank Press, Milngavie, Scotland, 1977-78; press officer Scottish Opera Theatre Royal, Glasgow, 1978-82; pub. relations and devel. officer Helen Hayes Hosp., West Haverstraw, N.Y., 1982—. Pub. relations officer Rockland County Disaster Preparedness Team, Rockland, N.Y., 1983—; trustee Chappaqua (N.Y.) Library, 1985—; bd. dirs. Am. Friends of Scottish Opera, N.Y., 1982—, Westchester Ind. Living Ctr., White Plains, N.Y., 1988—. Mem. N.Y. State Head Injury Assn. (bd. dirs. Southern region, Recognition award 1986), Nat. Union Journalists, Rockland Devel. Group, Phi Beta Kappa. Office: Helen Hayes Hosp Rt 9W Haverstraw NY 10993

FERGUSSON, FRANCES DALY, college president, educator; b. Boston, Oct. 3, 1944; d. Francis Joseph and Alice (Storrow) Daly. B.A., Wellesley Coll., 1965; M.A., Harvard U., 1966, Ph.D., 1973. Teaching fellow Harvard U., Cambridge, Mass., 1966-68; asst. prof. Newton Coll., Mass., 1969-75; assoc. prof. U. Mass., Boston, 1974-82, asst. chancellor, 1980-82; provost, prof. Bucknell U., Lewisburg, Pa., 1982-86; pres. Vassar Coll., Poughkeepsie, N.Y., 1986—. Trustee Mayo Found., 1988—; bd. dirs. Soc. Archtl. Historians. Recipient Founder's award Soc. Archtl. Historians, 1973. Office: Vassar Coll Raymond Ave Poughkeepsie NY 12601

FERLAND, DARLENE FRANCES, management consultant; b. Pawtucket, R.I., Feb. 11, 1954; d. Stephen William and Frances Grace (Masterson) Regula; m. Edward Oscar Ferland. AS in Criminal Justice, Salve Regina Coll., 1975, BA in History and Polit. Sci., 1976, MA in History, 1980, postgrad. Dir. Barbizon Sch. R.I., Providence, 1979-82, Barbizon Agy. R.I., Providence, 1980-81; tchr. Bay View Acad., Riverside, R.I., 1982-84; v.p. Edward Ferland Constrn. Co., Pawtucket, R.I., 1983—; pres. Enterprising Images Inc., Pawtucket, 1985—; guest lectr. Providence Coll., 1980—. Active Am. Heart Assn. Mem. Bay View Alumnae Assn. (pres. 1981-84, Outstanding Alumna award 1983), Arrive Alive Am. (nat. bd. 1986—), Salve Regina Alumni Assn. (pres. 1986), AAUW (Providence chpt. pres. v.p. 1983-86, legis. chair 1982-83). Democrat. Roman Catholic. Home and Office: 225 Greeslitt Ave Pawtucket RI 02861

FERN, CAROLE L., lawyer; b. Freeport, N.Y., Sept. 2, 1958; m. Tariq Rafique. BA, Johns Hopkins U., 1979; JD, Harvard U., 1983. Bar: N.Y. 1983, Calif. 1987. Assoc. Shearman & Sterling, N.Y.C., 1987—. Mem. ABA, N.Y.C. Bar Assn., Phi Beta Kappa. Democrat. Unitarian. Office: Shearman & Sterling Citicorp Ctr 153 E 53d St New York NY 10022

FERNANDES-SALLING, LEHUA, lawyer, state senator; b. Lihue, Hawaii, Dec. 6, 1949; d. William Ernest Braga and Evelyn (Ohai) Fernandes; m. Michael Ray Salling, Aug. 14, 1971. B.S., Colo. State U.; J.D., Cleveland Marshall Coll. Law. Assoc. Fernandes Salling & Salling, Kapaa Kauai, Hawaii, 1976—; mem. Hawaii Senate, 1982—. Address: 1250 Kuhio Hwy B-308 Kapaa HI 96746 *

FERNANDEZ, ISABEL LIDIA, college administrator; b. Miami, Fla., Jan. 23, 1964; d. Rafael Juvencio and Lidia Rafaela (Morin) Fernandez. BBA, Fla. Internat. U., Miami, 1984. Personnel cons. Miami, 1984—; asst. dir. human resources Turnberry Isle Yacht & Country Club, Miami, 1985-87; dir. personnel Sheraton River House, Miami, 1987-88; coordinator hospitality mgmt. programs Miami-Dade Community Coll., 1988—. Editor newspaper The Sunblazer, 1983-84; contbr. articles to profl. jours. Named Employee of the Month, Coconut Grove Hotel, Miami, 1985. Mem. Nat. Assn. Female Execs., Am. Hotel and Motel Assn. (pres. gretate Miami chpt.). Republican. Lutheran. Club: Young Reps. (pub. relations com.). Home: 201 NW 60 Ave Miami FL 33126

FERNANDEZ, LINDA FLAWN, entrepreneur, social worker; b. Tampa, Fla., Sept. 14, 1943; d. Frank and Rose (D'Amico) F.; 1 child, Marci. B.S., U. South Fla., 1965; M.S., U. Nev., 1976. Social worker Hillsborough County, Tampa, Fla., 1965-67; parole officer adult div. Fla. Parole Commn., Tampa, 1967-69; dir. social services Sunrise Hosp., Las Vegas, Nev., 1969-78; ind. real estate investor, Fla. and Nev., 1965—; pres. Las Vegas Color Separations, Inc., 1978—, Las Vegas Typesetting, Inc., 1983—; LMR Enterprises, Inc., Las Vegas, 1984—; sec.-treas. Sierra Color Graphics, Inc., Las Vegas, 1983—; v.p., sec. Western Greeting Inc., Las Vegas, 1988— . Founder, organizer Human Relations, pet mascots for elderly; team ofcl. girls' softball, 1985 . Recipient numerous awards Ad Club Fedn. Mem. Las Vegas C. of C. (congl. com.) Women's Las Vegas C. of C., Ad Club Fedn., Citizens for Pvt. Enterprise, U.S. C. of C. Avocations: tennis; water skiing. Office: 3351 S Highland Dr Suite 210 Las Vegas NV 89109

FERNANDEZ, MORAIMA, accountant; b. Sagua La Grande, Cuba, Feb. 24, 1951; came to U.S., 1967; d. Camilo M. and Maria Z. (Diaz) F. AA, Miami Dade Community Coll.; student, Fla. Internat. U. With accounts payable dept. Green Giant Co., Miami, 1973-75; bookkeeper Atico Mortgage Investors, Miami, 1975-76; comptroller Heavy Duty Parts, Inc., Miami, 1976-78, Equipment Leasing, Inc., Miami, 1978-80; pres. Alphacounts, Inc., Miami, 1980—. Commr. Dade County Commn. on the Status of Women; mem. com. Small and Minority bus. Adv. Council. Recipient Appreciation awards, IRS, Fla. Assn. Ind. Accts., Dade County Pub. Schs., Dade County Elections Dept., Dade County Reps. Mem. Nat. Soc. Pub. Accts., Fla. Assn. Ind. Accts. (v.p., Appreciation award), Internat. Assn. for Fin. Planning, Latin-Bus. and Profl. Women's Club, Am. Soc. Notaries. Republican. Roman Catholic. Office: Alphacounts Inc 2355 Salzedo St Suite 309 Coral Gables FL 33134

FERNANDEZ-ARRONDO, MARIA DEL CARMEN, educator; b. Guines, Cuba, Mar. 26, 1931; came to U.S., 1960; d. Guillermo and Amada (Mendiandua) Fernandez-Arrondo; m. Santiago J. Fernandez-Pichs, Jan. 16, 1954; children: Santiago Sam Fernandez, Julio G. Fernandez. BA, U. Havana, 1953, Pacific U., Oregon, 1965; MA, Pacific U., 1969. Cert. Spanish/polit. sci. tchr., Calif. Tchr. Indio (Calif.) High Sch., 1965-88, Palm Desert (Calif.) High Sch., 1988—; chmn. Fgn. Lang. dept. Indio High Sch., 1977-82; advisor Spanish Honor Soc., 1970—. Co-author: The Tutor System, Books 1 and 2, 1976 (patentee), The New Spanish System, 1969. Named Outstanding Teacher Indio High Sch., 1980, Teacher of the Month Indio High Sch. Student Body, 1986. Mem. Calif. Tchrs. Assn., NEA, Am. Assn. Tchrs. of Spanish and Portugese, Desert Sands Tchrs. Assn., Delta Kappa Gamma. Republican. Roman Catholic.

FERNÁNDEZ HERNÁNDEZ, NIVIA AURORA, nutrition and dietetics educator; b. San Juan, P.R., Feb. 26, 1955; d. Manuel and Aurora (Hernández) F.; m. Fernando Ramírez Muñiz, June 22, 1973; children: Jennifer, Nilza, Ramírez Fernández. BS magna cum laude, U. P.R., 1975; MS, Emory U., 1979. Prof. U. P.R. Sch. Home Econs., Food, and Nutrition Area, Río Piedras, 1979—; cons. Commonwealth of P.R. Dept. Edn., Sch. Lunch Program, Hato Rey, 1980-84. Contbr. articles to profl. jours. Pres. San Juan Young Mother's Program of Am. Mothers, Inc., 1984-86. Recipient Mary Eggings medallion American Mothers, Inc., 1985. Mem. Coll. Nutritionists and Dietitians of P.R. (pres.-elect 1985-86, pres. 1986-87), Am. Dietetic Assn. (pres.-elect P.R. chpt. 1981-82, pres. P.R. chpt. 1982-83, Recognized Young Dietitian of Yr. 1982). Home: Doce de Octubre St #416 El Vedado Hato Rey PR 00918

FERNÁNDEZ OLMOS, MARGARITE, educator, writer; b. N.Y.C., Feb. 24, 1949; d. Peter and Virginia (Ortiz) F.; m. Enrique R. Olmos, Mar. 23, 1973, 1 child, Gabriela. BA, Montclair State Coll., 1970; MA, NYU in Spain, 1972; PhD, NYU, 1979. Adj. lectr. NYU, 1972-76, Fordham U., N.Y.C., 1975-76, Hostos Community Coll., Bronx, N.Y., 1973-76; instr. CUNY, Bklyn., 1976-81, asst. prof., 1981-83, assoc. prof., 1984—; vis. fellow in Romance Langs. Princeton (N.J.) U., 1986-87. Author: La Cuentistica de Juan Bosch, 1982; (with others): Contemporary Women Authors of Latin America: Introductory Essays and New Translations, 1983; contbr. articles to profl. jours. Fellow Ford Found. 1970-75, 1985-86, Penfield 1977; recipient research award Profl. Staff Congress-CUNY 1986-87, 88—. Mem. N.Am. PEN, Modern Lang. Assn., Nat. Assn. Tchrs. Spanish and Portuguese, Puerto Rican Policy Network. Home: 105 Mimosa Ln Staten Island NY 10312 Office: Bklyn Coll Dept Modern Languages Bedford Ave and Ave H Brooklyn NY 11210

FERNSTROM, MEREDITH MITCHUM, financial services company executive, public responsibility professional; b. Rutherfordton, N.C., July 26, 1946; d. Lee Wallace and Ellie (Saine) Mitchum; m. John Richard Fernstrom, Dec. 28, 1968. B.S., U. N.C.-Greensboro, 1968; M.S., U. Md., 1972. Tchr. home econs. Prince Georges County pub. schs., Md., 1968-72; assoc. dir. market research H.J. Kaufman Advt., Washington, 1972-74; dir. consumer edn. Washington Consumer Affairs Office, 1974-76; dir. consumer affairs U.S. Dept. Commerce, Washington, 1976-80; v.p. consumer affairs Am. Express Co., N.Y.C., 1980-82, sr. v.p.-pub. responsibility, 1982—; former mem. consumer adv. council Fed. Res. System, Washington; bd. dirs. Nat. Consumers League, Washington, 1982—, N.Y. Met. Better Bus. Bur., N.Y.C., 1983—, Internat. Credit Assn., 1984—. Mem. policy bd. Jour. Retail Banking; contbr. articles to profl. jours. Bd. dirs. Womens' Forum N.Y., 1987—; commr. Nat. Commn. Working Women, 1987—. Recipient Consumer Edn. award Nat. Found. Consumer Credit Fedn., 1981, Disting. Woman award Northwood Inst., 1985, Matrix award N.Y. Women in Communications, Inc., 1986. Mem. Soc. Consumer Affairs Profls. (pres. 1985), Advt. Women N.Y. (Advt. Woman of Yr. award 1987), Fin. Women's Assn., Women's Econ. Roundtable, Am. Home Econs. Assn. Office: Am Express Co Am Express Tower World Fin Ctr New York NY 10285-4725

FERRANTE, OLIVIA ANN, educator; b. Revere, Mass., Nov. 9, 1948; d. Guy and Mary Carmella (Prizio) F. BA, Regis Coll., 1970; MEd, Boston Coll., 1971, postgrad., 1977-81; postgrad., Middlebury Coll., 1977-81, Lesley Coll., 1982. Cert. history tchr., tchr. of blind. Chmn. Braille dept. Nat. Braille Press, Boston, 1971-74; tchr. visually impaired Revere Sch. Dept., 1974—; cons. Revere PTA, 1984—. Contbr. articles to profl. jours. Vol. Morgan Meml., Boston, 1983—; mem. Revere Com. for Handicapped Affairs, 1985—, Everett (Mass.) Chorus, 1974-76; soloist Revere Music Makers, 1977-79. Mem. NEA, Mass. Tchrs. Assn., Revere Tchrs. Assn., Nat. Space Soc. Democrat. Roman Catholic. Home: 115 Reservoir Ave Revere MA 02151 Office: Revere High Sch Spl Needs Dept 101 School St Revere MA 02151

FERRARA, RUTH REIORDAN, association executive; b. Ducktown, Tenn., Nov. 8, 1924; d. Robert Harrison and Lillian (Fralix) Reiordan; student public schs.; grad. Jones Bus. Coll.; m. Joseph James Ferrara, Oct. 10, 1946; children—James Michael, John Richard. Machinist, Jacksonville (Fla.) Naval Air Sta., 1942-44; with Greyhound Bus Co., Jacksonville, 1944-45; head cashier womens apparel Mangels Ladies Wear, Jacksonville, 1945-46; owner, operator restaurant, Jacksonville, 1946-47, Copperhill, Tenn., 1946-48; bookkeeper Henley & Beckwith, Inc., Jacksonville, 1949-50; mem. purchasing dept. Am. Hardware Corp., New Britain, Conn., 1948-49; sec.-mgr. Greater Jacksonville Fair Assn., 1966-69, dir., 1959-69, exec. sec., 1965-70; pres. Fla. Fedn. Fairs and Livestock Shows, 1969-70, also dir. public relations; exec. sec. Fla. Fedn. Fairs, 1970-85, S.C. State Fair, Greenville, 1972-77; exec. sec., mgr. North Fla. Fair, Tallahassee, 1977—. Mem. Fla. Council for Aged, 1966-70; mem. aging com. Community Planning Council, 1966-70. Bd. dirs. Jacksonville Fair, 1959-68, State and Provincial Assn. Fairs, 1976—; sec. Venetia Boys Club, 1958-62; bd. advisers Cathedral Towers, 1966-70. Democrat. Methodist. Clubs: Jacksonville Garden (dir. 1960-68), Order Eastern Star, Venetia Manor Garden Circle (pres. 1960-62). Office: 441 Paul Russell Rd Tallahassee FL 32301

FERRARA-HAZELL, CATHERINE LUCILLE, computer scientist; b. Bronx, Nov. 9, 1951; d. Basil Garnett Hazell and Catherine Lena Ferrara. BS in Computer Sci., Russell Sage Coll., 1986. Credit and collections corr. Kimball Systems, Farmingdale, N.Y., 1972-74; counselor, client advocate Victims Info. Bur., Hauppauge, N.Y., 1974-76; painting contractor Rainbow Women Painters, Albany, N.Y., 1976-80; bus. mgr. Caribbean Rendezvous, East Setauket, N.Y., 1980-82; acad. computer services mgr. Russell Sage Coll., Troy, N.Y., 1983—, computer workshop instr., 1986—. Author: (poetry) Love Song to the Warriors, 2 vols., 1976; (cassette) Kisses and Revolution, 1987. Co-founder Albany Women Against Rape, 1979. Mem. NOW (co-chairperson rape task force 1973-75, pres. Huntington chpt. 1975—). Office: NY State Div of Budget The Capitol Room 145-M Albany NY 12224

FERRARINI, ELIZABETH MARY, writer; b. Cambridge, Mass., Sept. 8, 1948; d. Bruno and Alessandrina (Iannuzzi) F. BS in Journalism magna cum laude, Suffolk U., 1982; M in Communications, Simmons Coll., 1988. Owner Infomania, Boston, 1979-86; cons. editor Leading Edge World Trade, Needham, Mass., 1986—; tchr. Northeastern U., Boston, 1985—. Author: Confessions of an Infomaniac 1984, Infomania: The Guide to Essential Electronic Services, 1985; filmmaker Horn Pond Commissions, 1986; contbr. articles to mags. Fellow Assn. Women in Computing, Boston Computer Soc., Internat. Assn. Bus. Communicators. Democrat. Roman Catholic.

FERRARO, GERALDINE ANNE, lawyer, former congresswoman; b. Newburgh, N.Y., Aug. 26, 1935; d. Dominick and Antonetta L. (Corrieri) F.; m. John Zaccaro, 1960; children: Donna, John, Laura. B.A., Marymount Manhattan Coll., 1956; J.D., Fordham U., 1960; postgrad., N.Y. U. Law Sch., 1978; hon. degree, Marymount Manhattan Coll., 1982, NYU Sch. Law, 1984, Hunter Coll., 1985. Bar: N.Y. 1961, U.S. Supreme Ct. 1978. Individual practice law N.Y.C., 1961-74; asst. dist. atty. Queens County, N.Y., 1974-78; chief spl. victims bur. 1977-78; mem. 96th-98th Congresses from 9th N.Y. Dist.; sec. House Democratic Caucus; fellow Harvard Inst. of Politics, Cambridge, MA, 1988. Author: Ferraro, My Story, 1985. Chmn. Dem. Platform Com., 1984. Mem. Queens County Bar Assn., Queens County Women's Bar Assn. (past pres.), Nat. Dem. Inst. for Internat. Affairs (bd. dirs.), Council Fgn. Relations. Roman Catholic. Office: 218 Lafayette St New York NY 10012

FERRARO, HELEN THERESA, lawyer; b. Savannah, Ga., June 10, 1956. BS in Criminal Justice summa cum laude, Armstrong State Coll., 1978; JD magna cum laude, U. Ga., 1981. Bar: Ga., 1981. Ptnr. Smith Gambrell & Russell (formerly Smith, Cohen, Ringel, Kohler & Martin), Atlanta, 1981—. Mem. Young Careers of High Mus. of Arts, Atlanta, 1987. Mem. ABA, Ga. State Bar, Atlanta Bar Assn. Lodge: Order of the Coif. Office: Smith Gambrell & Russell 3333 Peachtree Rd NE Suite 1800 East Tower Atlanta GA 30326

FERRARO-NEITZEL, KIM ANN, account executive; b. Racine, Wis., Apr. 21, 1956; d. Matthew T. and Jean Carol (Becker) Ferraro; m. Mark Richard Neitzel, Mar. 8, 1986. Systems cons. ITT, Milw., 1981-83, United Techs., Milw., 1983-85, No. Telecom, Milw., 1985-86; sales mgr. Mid Plains Communication Systems, Milw., 1986; account exec. Wis. Bell Communications, Brookfield, 1986—. Mem. Nat. Assn. Female Execs. Republican. Lutheran.

FERREE, MYRA MARX, sociologist, educator; b. Morristown, N.J., Oct. 10, 1949; d. Irwin F. and Marguerite (Sosnoski) Marx; m. G. Donald Ferree. Student, U. Hamburg, Fed. Republic Germany, 1969-70; BA, Bryn Mawr (Pa.) Coll., 1971; PhD, Harvard U., 1976. Sr. research assoc. Boston Coll., 1975-76; asst. prof. sociology U. Conn., Storrs, 1976-81, assoc. prof., 1981-87, prof., 1987—, dir. Women's Studies Program, 1985-87; guest prof. J.W. Goethe U., Frankfurt, Fed. Republic Germany, 1985; cons. editor Allen and Unwin Pubs., Winchester, Mass., 1984—. Author: (with Beth Hess) Controversy and Coalition: The New Feminist Movement, 1985 (Choice Best Book, 1985); co-editor Analyzing Gender, 1987; assoc. editor Gender and Society, 1986—, The Sociological Quarterly, 1985—, Contemporary Sociology, 1980-83. German Acad. Exchange Service Research fellow, 1982-85; named Outstanding Conn. Woman in Edn. UN/USA Assn., 1988. Mem. Am. Sociol. Assn. (chair sex and gender sect. 1985-86, com. on nominations 1986-88, com. on coms. 1984-86), Eastern Sociol. Soc. (chair com. on women 1977-79), Soc. for Study of Social Problems (program com. 1984), Sociologists for Women in Society. Episcopalian. Office: Univ Conn Dept Sociology U-68 Storrs CT 06268

FERREIRA, AUDREY LEE BLISS, community worker; b. Palo Alto, Calif., Apr. 4, 1931; d. Paul Randolph and Lucile (Hartman) Bliss; student Humboldt State Coll., Arcata, Calif., 1948-49, Willamette U., Salem, Oreg., 1949-52; m. John Gordon Selby, Feb. 10, 1952; children—Clinton, Katherine, Janet, Barbara; m. Charles E. Ferreira, Dec. 27, 1982. Chmn., Young Audiences of Bay Area, 1974-75; del. Young Audiences Council Calif., 1974-75; chmn. vol. program Oakland (Calif.) pub. schs., 1975-76, vol. music performances, 1969-80; pres. Montclair PTA, 1969-71, dir. 28th Dist., 1973-75, v.p. 28th Dist., 1975-76, pres. 28th Dist., 1976-78; v.p. Oakland Unit Ch. Women United, 1975; news editor Oakland Girl Scout Assn., 1968-70, area chmn., leader, 1966-74; city sect. chmn. Am. Cancer Soc., 1970-75; bd. dirs. Vol. Bur. Alameda County, 1974-78; mem; commn. discipline, attendence and sch. safety Oakland pub. schs., 1974-78; deacon Presbyn. Ch., 1977—; mem. Republican State Central Com. Calif., 1973-74; bd. dirs. Marcus A. Foster Ednl. Inst., 1978-81; bd. mgrs. Calif. Congress Parents and Tchrs., 1978-81; legis. adv. Calif. PTA, 1979-81; mem. com. credentials Calif. Commn. on Tchr. Credentialing, 1979-84; pres. Georgetown Divide Health Care Aux., 1983-85; v.p. Georgetown Divide Rep. Women Federated, 1986; co-dir. ARC Disaster Services, Georgetown Divide, 1985—. Recipient Marcus Foster grant for elementary sch. museum, 1971, Order Golden Sword, Am. Cancer Soc., 1974, 75; named hon. life mem. Calif. PTA, recipient Continuing Service award, 1976. Mem. United Presbyn. Women, Nat. Fedn. Rep. Women, Am. Needlepoint Guild, Embroiderers Guild Am., Nat. Standards Council Am. Embroiderers, P.E.O., Pi Beta Phi, Theta Alpha Phi. Address: PO Box 573 Garden Valley CA 95633

FERREIRA, CAROLYN DAY, title company executive; b. Toledo, Mar. 1, 1936; d. Vincent Trafford Day and Edith Jemima (Fraser) Portman; children: Thompson Day, Douglas Fraser, Kimberly Adair; m. Mervyn M. Ferreira, June 17, 1979. BS, UCLA, 1958. Residential sales Emmette Gatewood, Realtor, Los Gatos, Calif., 1974-78; residential sales Ticor Title Ins., San Jose, Calif., 1978-82, mgr. adminstrv. services, 1982-84; spl. project sales Ticor Title Ins., Redwood City, Calif., 1984-85; sales mgr. Transamerica Title Ins., San Jose, 1985-86; v.p., mgr. N.Am. Title Co., San Jose, 1986-87. Mem. Women's Council of Realtors (com. chmn. 1984, bd. dirs. 1986—, Affiliate of Yr. 1984).

FERRELL, ANNA BELLE, retail/wholesale company executive; b. Piggott, Ark., Mar. 15, 1927; d. Thomas J. and Nora (Griffin) Johnson; m. William A. Harder, Sept. 20, 1949 (dec. Nov. 1967); m. James R. Ferrell, Feb. 23, 1969; 1 dau., Nora. Corr. student U. Mo.-Columbia 1949-52; student Memphis State U., 1983. Credit mgr. Sears Roebuck & Co., Caruthersville, Mo., 1953-59; bookkeeper Bain Motor Co., Hayti, Mo., 1959-62; purchasing asst. E.L. Bruce Hardwoods, Memphis, 1963-69; v.p., ops. mgr. Choctaw Scale & Electronics Co., Memphis, 1969-87, pres., 1987—. Vol. investigator Mo. Dept. Human Services, 1947-62; foster mother Boys Town, 1977-82. Mem. Nat. Scalemen's Assn. (sec. 1969-83), Nat. Fedn. Small Bus. Republican. Methodist. Lodge: Rebekah (state pres.). Home: 5184 Warfield Dr Memphis TN 38117 Office: 1805 Bartlett Rd Memphis TN 38134

FERRELL, RUTH MORRIS (MRS. FRANK M. FERRELL), lawyer; b. Portsmouth, Va., Apr. 29, 1928; d. Francis Hubert and Ruth (Whitehead) Morris; B.A., Agnes Scott Coll., 1949; M.A., Emory U., 1952; J.D., U. Pa., 1960; m. Frank M. Ferrell, Apr. 7, 1958. Bar: Del. 1960, U.S. Supreme Ct. Practiced in Wilmington, Del., 1960—; law clk. judges Del. State Cts., 1961-62; dep. atty. gen. Del., 1963-70; head civil div. Del. Atty. Gen's Office, 1967-70; state solicitor of Del., 1969-70; asst. regional atty. Phila. Regional Litigation Center, U.S. EEO Commn., 1973; mem. Gov.'s Commn. on Status Women, 1963-68; mem. European adv. council U.S. Dept. State, 1971-72. Pres., Women's Republican Club Wilmington, 1965-67. Recipient award for outstanding pub. service Rep. Nat. Com. N.E. Regional Women's Conf., 1967. Mem. ABA (mem. council local govt. sect.), Del. Bar Assn., Fed. Bar Assn., Assn. Trial Lawyers Am.; Supreme Ct. Hist. Soc., Christina Bus. and Profl. Women's Club (pres.), Mortar Bd., Phi Beta Kappa. Presbyterian. Contbr. articles to profl. publs. Home: 17 Cragmere Rd Wilmington DE 19809 Office: PO Box 9551 Wilmington DE 19809

FERRELL, SHARON LEGG, financial executive; b. Pearisburg, Va., Nov. 20, 1951; d. Basil Ray and Mary Elizabeth (Auer) Legg; m. Thomas Edward Ferrell, June 15, 1974; children: Laura E., Jennifer Leigh. BBA in Acctg., Marshall U., 1973, MBA in Fin., 1978; attended, U. N.C., Chapel Hill, 1985. CPA, Ohio, N.C. Staff acct. Deloitte Haskins & Sells, Cin., 1973-75, John C. Muse Co., Sanford, N.C., 1977-80; regional auditor United Mine Workers Health and Retirement Fund, Logan, W.Va., 1976-77; treas. Maxway Corp., Sanford, 1982—, v.p., chief fin. officer, 1986-87, sr. v.p., chief fin. officer, 1987—; sr. v.p., chief fin. officer Danners Inc., 1987—. Mem. Am. Inst. CPA's, Carolinas Cash Mgmt. Assn. (v.p. 1985-86, pres. 1986-87). Republican. Presbyterian. Home: 45 Lost Tree Rd Pinehurst NC 28374 Office: Maxway Corp 800 E Main St Sanford NC 27330

FERRERI, JOANNE M., financial analyst. BS in Applied Math., Polytechnic Inst. N.Y., 1978; MBA, Pace U., 1982. Project leader AT&T Western Electric, Newark, N.J., 1978-80; systems analyst AT&T Western Electric, N.Y.C., 1980-85; systems analyst AT&T Western Electric, Berkeley Heights, N.J., 1985-87, fin. and strategic analyst, 1987—. Mem. Soc. Women Engrs., Nat. Assn. Female Execs.

FERRI, KAREN LYNN, lawyer, food company executive; b. McKeesport, Pa., Aug. 15, 1956; d. Edward James and Carole Elizabeth (Petterson) Ferri. B.A., Duquesne U., 1977, J.D., 1981. Bar: Pa. 1981, U.S. Dist. Ct. (we. dist.) Pa. 1981, U.S. Supreme Ct. 1986. Law clk. Weiler & Dolfi, Pitts., 1980-81, assoc., 1981-84; of counsel Stokes, Lurie & Cole, Pitts., 1984—, sole practice, Murraysville, 1984—; weekend mgr. Ferri Supermarkets Inc., Murraysville, Pa., 1977—; atty. Ferri Enterprises, 1981—. Bd. dirs. Crisis Ctr. North, Pitts.; Recipient Sr. Leaders award Duquesne U., 1977, Am. Jurisprudence award Joint Pubs. Total Client-Service Library Pitts., 1978-79. Mem. Allegheny County Bar Assn. (vol. indigent divorce program, high sch. edn. program, family law sect.), Pa. Bar Assn. (family law sect.), Amnesty Internat., Greepeace, Internat. Platform Assn., Westmoreland County Bar Assn., ABA., Duquesne U. Alumni Assn. Roman Catholic. Clubs: AMAA Investment, Young Republicans, Variety (Pitts.), Pitts. Scuba. Home: Chatham Ctrer Chatham Tower Unit 3C Pittsburgh PA 15219 Office: Stokes Lurie & Cole 2100 Law and Fin Bldg Pittsburgh PA 15219

FERRICK, JOAN ALICE, commercial artist; b. Providence, Sept. 21, 1960; d. Joseph Frank and Edna Beatrice (LaPlante) S.; m. Michael Mark Ferrick, Dec. 31, 1987; 1 child, Sarah Michele. Cert., R.I. Coll., 1980; student, R.I. Sch. Design, 1981-82, Community Coll. R.I., 1984. Apprentice Hanover Advt., Providence, 1980, mgr., 1980-83; photo stylist Klitzner Industries, Providence, 1983-84, Direct Press/Modern Litho, Greenville, R.I., 1985-86; free-lance comml. artist JoanArt Services, Providence, 1987—. Coordinator Day Care Focus Outreach Ctr., Providence, 1988—. Democrat. Roman Catholic.

FERRIER, LORETTA JEAN, psychotherapist; b. Paris, Tex., Feb. 5, 1937; d. Robert Syme and Virginia (Smith) F.; m. Howard B. Franklin, Sept. 1971 (div. 1980). BA in Psychology, Antioch W. West, 1975; PhD in Psychology, Inst. Transpersonal Psychology, 1979. Ordained to ministry Ch. of Tzoddi, 1978. Adminstrv. asst. dept. sociology and anthropology San Jose (Calif.) State U., 1963-65; adminstrv. asst. dept. exobiology Stanford U., Palo Alto, Calif., 1965-67; adminstr., researcher Elmwood, Calif., 1969-70; founder, dir. Soc. Overweight Studies, San Jose, 1974-79; prin. Loretta Ferrier, A Corp., Novato, Calif., 1985—; lectr. human potential workshops, 1973—; guest speaker TV and radio; pub. relations Human Potential Movement, Calif., 1974-79; coordinator workshops, 1976—; founder Concresence-Networking, San Francisco, 1981-82; advisor to Calif. bd. dirs. Bus. Execs. for Nat. Security, 1987—; bd. dirs. Karma Triyana Dharmachakra Ctr., Woodstock, N.Y. Author: A Transpersonal Approach to the Successful Femal Entrepreneur, 1980; author, editor Dialogue, 1986, Wings, 1987; contbr. articles to Scene mag., Nuvo mag., other mags., 1980-82. Mem. forming com. Hunger Project, San Francisco, 1977-78; mem. Commn. on Juvenile Justice and Delinquency Prevention, State of Calif., 1982; advisor Ark Found., Ark Communication Inst., Lafayette, Calif., 1987—. Fellow Am. Assn. Counselors, No. Calif. Soc. Clin. Hypnosis, Profl. Women's Network; mem. Nat. Speakers Assn. Home and Office: 24 Boulevard Terr Novato CA 94947

FERRIGNO, HELEN FRANCES, librarian, musician, educator; b. Trenton, N.J., Aug. 25, 1937; d. Joseph John and Frances (Leniart) Klidzia; m. Maurice Ferrigno, Oct. 3, 1964; children—Lisa, Nina. Student Hartt Coll. Music, Hartford, Conn., 1962-64; B.A., Rivier Coll., Nashua, N.H., 1977-80; M.L.S., Simmons Coll., 1982. Pvt. music tchr., Conn. and N.H., 1965—; free-lance flutist and piccoloist, 1974—; co-owner/mgr. Ancus Books, Nashua, 1974—; cataloger/info. cons./systems analyst Digital Equipment Corp., Merrimack, N.H., 1984—; librarian Daniel Webster Coll., Nashua, 1982-84, chmn. lecture series, 1982-83; flutist Nashua Symphony Orch., 1975-77. Mem. parents adv. bd. New Eng. Conservatory Prep. Sch., Boston, 1981-82; vol. Am. Heart Assn. Mem. ALA, Assn. Coll. and Research Libraries, Library and Info. Tech. Assn., New Eng. Library Assn., Beta Phi Mu. Roman Catholic. Home: 76 Manchester St Nashua NH 03060

FERRIS, EVELYN SCOTT, lawyer; b. Detroit, d. Ross Ansel and Irene Mabel (Bowser) Nafus; m. Roy Shorey Ferris, May 21, 1969 (div. Sept. 1982); children—Judith Ilene, Roy Sidney, Lorene Marjorie. J.D., Willamette

U., 1961. Bar: Oreg. 1962, Fed. Dist. Ct. 1962. Law clk. Oreg. Tax Ct., Salem, 1961-62; dep. dist. atty. Marion County, Salem, 1962-65; judge Mcpl. Ct., Stayton, Oreg., 1965-76; ptnr. Brand, Lee, Ferris & Embick, Salem, 1965-82; chmn. Oreg. Workers' Compensation Bd., Salem, 1982—. Bd. dirs. Friends of Deepwood, Salem, 1979-82, Salem City Club, 1972-75; bd. dirs. Marion County Civil Service Commn., 1970-75; com. mem. Polk County Hist. Commn., Dallas, Oreg., 1976-79; mem. Oreg. legis. com. Bus. Climate, 1967-69, Govs. Task Force on Liability, 1986. Recipient Outstanding Hist. Restoration of Comml. Property award Marion County Hist. Soc., 1982. Mem. Oreg. Mcpl. Judges Assn. (pres. 1967-69), Altrusa, Internat., Mary Leonard Law Soc., Western Assn. Workers Compensation Bds. (pres. 1987—). Phi Delta Delta. Republican. Episcopalian. Club: Capitol (Salem) (pres. 1977-79). Home: 747 Church St SE Salem OR 97301 Office: Oreg Workers' Compensn Bd 480 Church St SE Salem OR 97310

FERRO, JACQUELINE ANN, compensation professional; b. Wareham, Mass., Sept. 12, 1960; d. William Joseph and Janet Elaine (Garofalo) F. BS in Pub. Adminstrn., Bentley Coll., 1982; MS in Pub. Adminstrn., Suffolk U., 1984. Personnel asst. Harvard Community Health Plan, Boston, 1982-84; staff assoc., intern Fed. Service Impasses Panel, Washington, 1984; personnel asst. Safety Ins. Co., Boston, 1984-85; compensation coordinator St. Joseph Hosp. and Trauma Ctr., Nashua, N.H., 1985—. Bd. dirs. Nashua Area Girls Club, 1987. Mem. Nat. Assn. Female Execs., Am. Soc. Pub. Adminstrn., Am. Soc. Healthcare Human Resources Adminstrn., Internat. Assn. Personnel Women, Am. Compensation Assn. Office: St Joseph Hosp and Trauma Ctr 172 Kinsely St Nashua NH 03061

FERRO-NYALKA, RUTH RUDYS, librarian; b. Chgo., June 2, 1930; d. Joseph F. and Anna (Serbenta) Rudys; B.A., U. Chgo., 1950; M.A. in Library Sci., Rosary Coll., 1972; children—Keith A. Krisciunas, Kevin L. Krisciunas, Kenneth M. Krisciunas; stepchildren—Anita L. Abbate, Vincent A. Abbate; m. Frank Ferro-Nyalka; stepchildren—Eleanor, Christine, Sylvia, André, Annette Ferro-Nyalka. Tchr. elem. sch. Westmont, Ill., 1961-63; librarian Dist. 105 public schs., La Grange, Ill., 1972—, tchr. program for gifted children, 1979-81, 82-85, coordinator gifted program, 1981-82. Mem. ALA, Ill. Library Assn., NEA, Ill. Edn. Assn., Dist. 105 Tchrs. Assn. (pres. 1983-85), AAUW. Roman Catholic. Home: 5800 Doe Circle Westmont IL 60559 Office: 1001 Spring Ave LaGrange IL 60525

FERRY, DIANE LOUISE, educator; b. Ligonier, Pa., Apr. 24, 1947; d. William Glenn and Marjorie (Houpt) F.; m. David C. White, Nov. 25, 1983; children—William Austin David, Megan Elizabeth. BA cum laude, Gettysburg Coll., 1969; M.B.A., Shippensburg State Coll., 1974; Ph.D., Wharton Sch., U. Pa., 1978. Computer systems analyst Dept. Army, Chambersburg, Pa., 1970-74; research asso. U. Pa., Phila., 1975-78; instr. Temple U., Phila., 1977-78; assoc. prof. dept. bus. adminstrn. U. Del., Newark, 1979—; cons. Urban Inst., Washington. Mem. Nat. Acad. Mgmt., Assn. for Computing Machinery, Phi Beta Kappa (treas. Alpha chpt. of Del.). Author: (with A.H. VandeVen) Measuring and Assessing Organizations, 1980. Office: U Delaware Dept Bus Adminstrn Newark DE 19716

FERRY, JOAN EVANS, school counselor; b. Summit, N.J., Aug. 20, 1941; d. John Stiger and Margaret Darling (Evans) F. BS, U. Pa., 1964; EdM, Temple U., 1967; postgrad., Villanova U., 1981. Cert. elem. sch. tchr., elem. sch. coulselor. Indsl. photographer Bucksco Mfg. Co., Inc., Quakertown, Pa., 1958-59; math. and German tutor St. Lawrence U., Canton, N.Y., 1959-61; research asst. U. Pa., Phila., 1963; tchr. elem. sch. Pennridge Schs., Perkasie, Pa., 1964-74, 75-77, elem. sch. counselor, 1981—; pvt. practice counselor Perkasie, 1981—; tutor Math, German St. Lawrence U., Canton, N.Y., 1959-61; supervisory tchr. East Stroudsburg U., Pennridge Schs., 1971-74; research asst. U. Pa., Phila., 1963; mem. acad. coms. for Pennridge Schs.; adj. faculty Bucks County Community Coll., 1983—; instr. Am. Inst. Banking, 1982—; notary pub., 1986—; mcpl. auditor, 1984—; cons. in field. Author (with others) Life-Time Sports for the College Student: A Behavioral Objective Approach, 1971, 3d rev. edit. 1978, Elementary Social Studies as a Learning System, 1976. Vol. elem. sch. counselor Perkasie, 1979-81; mem. Hilltown Civic Assn., 1965-70; exec. com. chairperson Hilltown Parent Tchr. Orgn., 1965-73; mem., soloist Good Shepherd Episcop. Ch. Choir, Hilltown, 1964-77. Grantee NSF, Washington, 1972-73, Philanthropic Edn. Orgn., Doylestown, Pa., 1982; recipient Judith Netzky Meml. Fellowship award B'nai B'rith, Phila., 1979 Durning scholar Delta Delta Delta, Arlington, Tex., 1981, Am. Mgmt. Assns. scholar, N.Y.C., 1982; named to Internat. Tennis Hall of Fame. Mem. NEA, Pa. State Edn. Assn. (polit. action com. for edn., chair Pennridge Schs. 1986—, del leadership conf. 1987), Pennridge Edn. Assn. (faculty rep 1986-88, exec. council 1986—, negotiations resource com. 1987—), Am. Inst. Banking (chairperson 1987), U.S. Tennis Assn. (hon. life), Pa. and Middle States Tennis Assn., U.S. Profl. Tennis Registry, Nat. Ski Patrol System, Pa. Elected Women's Assn., Bucks County Assn. of Twp. Ofcls., Nat. Assn. Female Execs., Pa. Sch. Counselors Assn., Pa. Assn. Notaries, Am. Soc. Notaries, AAUW, Internat. Fedn. of Univ. Women, Kappa Delta Pi. Episcopalian. Clubs: Mediterranean, Nockamixon Boat, Peace Valley Yacht. Home: 834 Rickert Rd Perkasie PA 18944 Office: Pennridge Schs Fifth St Perkasie PA 18944

FERRY, ROBERTA JOANNE, medical office manager; b. Chgo., Oct. 3, 1961; d. Dale Alfred and Karen Jean (Chute) Schneider; m. James Eugene Ferry, June 26, 1982. Student pub. schs., Huntington Beach, Calif. With Sears Roebuck & Co., Westminster, Calif., 1977-78, Nordstrom, Costa Mesa, Calif., 1978; sec. Warner Village Lab., Fountain Valley, Calif., 1978-80; office mgr. Orange Coast Urology, Huntington Beach, Calif., 1980—. Vol., Spl. Olympics, Los Angeles, 1976-78; mem. council Luth. Ch. Resurrection, Huntington Beach, 1985—, cons., tchr., 1984—. Mem. Nat. Assn. Female Execs., Med. Group Mgmt. Assn. Democrat. Avocations: skiing, aerobics, camping; needlework. Office: Orange Coast Urology 17742 Beach Blvd #200 Huntington Beach CA 92647

FERSHTMAN, JULIE ILENE, lawyer; b. Detroit, Apr. 3, 1961; d. Sidney and Judith Joyce (Stoll) F. Student, Mich. State U., 1979-81; BA in Philosophy and Polit. Sci., Emory U., 1983, JD, 1986. Bar: Mich. 1986. Summer assoc. Kitch, Saurbier et al, Detroit, 1985; assoc. Miller, Canfield, Paddock and Stone, Detroit, 1986—. Mem. Mich. Women's Hist. Ctr. and Hall Fame, Dem. Nat. Com. Mem. ABA, Am. Trial Lawyers Assn., Common Cause, Women Lawyers Assn. Mich., Mich. Women's Hist. Ctr. and Hall of Fame, Nat. Mus. Women and Arts, NOW, Soc. Coll. Journalists, Planned Parenthood, Phi Alpha Delta, Omicron Delta Kappa, Phi Sigma Tau, Pi Sigma Alpha. Democrat. Home: 31700 Briarcliff Franklin MI 48025 Office: Miller Canfield Paddock & Stone 2500 Comerica Bldg Detroit MI 48226

FERTEL, KATY ALTMAN, magazine editor; b. Phila., Apr. 2, 1960; d. Ashley J. and Sandra (Kimmelman) Altman; m. Craig A. Fertel, Oct. 8, 1983. BS in Art, Northeastern U., Boston, 1982. Asst., dir. hotel and restaurant advt., Gourmet mag., N.Y.C., 1982-84, editorial asst., 1984-85, editor, 1985—. Contbg. editor Long Beach Island Arts Found. Cookbook, 1977. Mem. N.Y. Women's Culinary Alliance. Home: 245 E 93d St Apt 9F New York NY 10128

FESLER, ELIZABETH, educator, psychologist; b. Youngstown, Ohio, Nov. 5, 1930; d. Raymond and Mary (Theodore) Cosetti; B.S., Kent State U., 1952, M.S., 1961, Ph.D., 1974; m. July 8, 1953; children—Kim. Tchr., Buchtel High Sch., Perkins Jr. High Sch., 1952-62; counselor, Akron, Ohio, 1962-70; psychologist Akron Public Schs., 1970-76, coordinator spl. needs, 1976-78, dir. spl. edn., 1978-80, prin. Goodrich Jr. High Sch., 1978-80, dir. spl. edn., 1980—. Pres., Support Inc., suicide prevention; bd. dirs., chmn. edn. div. Planned Parenthood Assn.; v.p. bd. dirs. Mental Health Assn.; mem. women's aux. bd. Summit County Juvenile Ct.; mem. Children's Transitionals Services Bd. Kent State U. scholar; community advisor Jr. League. Mem. Am. Assn. Psychologists, Ohio Assn. Psychologists, Akron Assn. Psychologists, Am. Assn. Secondary Sch. Prins., Ohio Assn. Secondary Sch. Prins., Akron Assn. Secondary Sch. Prins., Nat. Assn. Sch. Psychologists, Alpha Xi Delta. Home: 65 N Wheaton Rd Akron OH 44313 Office: 65 Steiner Ave Akron OH 44301

FESTE, KAREN ANN, political science educator; b. Mpls., Jan. 4, 1944; d. Chris and Ruth T. (Vold) F. m. Roger A. Hanson, Sept. 23, 1966; 1 child, Kristina Feste-Hanson. BA, Concordia Coll., Moorhead, Minn., 1965; MA, U. Minn., 1969, PhD, 1973. Asst. prof. U. Denver, 1972-77, assoc. prof. internat. studies, 1977—; sr. researcher Caci, Inc., Washington, 1980; vis. prof. USAF Acad., Colorado Springs, Colo., 1981, 84, Brigham Young U., Provo, Utah, 1983; cons. Govt. Egypt, Cairo, 1978-83, Govt. Thailand, Bangkok, 1984; mem. Denver com. Council on Fgn. Relations, 1981—. Author: The Arab-Israeli Conflict, 1978; editor Monograph Series, 1978—. Fulbright vis. prof. Vienna, Austria, 1986-87; grantee Pew Meml. Trust, Phila., 1986—, Ford Found., 1986—. Mem. Am. Polit. Sci. Assn., Internat. Studies Assn., Am. Profs. Peace in Middle East, Am. Scandinavian Found. Democrat. Office: U Denver Grad Sch Internat Studies Denver CO 80208

FETRIDGE, BONNIE-JEAN CLARK (MRS. WILLIAM HARRISON FETRIDGE), civic worker; b. Chgo., Feb. 3, 1915; d. Sheldon and Bonnie (Carrington) Clark; student Girls Latin Sch., Chgo., The Masters Sch., Dobbs Ferry, N.Y., Finch Coll., N.Y.C.; m. William Harrison Fetridge, June 27, 1941; children—Blakely (Mrs. Harvey H. Bundy III), Clark Worthington. Bd. dirs. region VII com. Girl Scouts U.S.A., 1939-43, mem. nat. program com., 1966-69, mem. nat. adv. council, 1972-85, mem. internat. commr.'s adv. panel, 1973-76, mem. Nat. Juliette Low Birthplace Com., 1966-69, region IV selections com., 1968-70; bd. dirs. Girl Scouts Chgo., 1936-51, 59-69, sec., 1936-38, v.p., 1946-49, 61-65, chmn. Juliette Low world friendship com., 1959-67, 71-72; mem. Friends of Our Cabana Com. World Assn. Girl Guides and Girl Scouts, Cuernavaca, Mexico, 1969—, vice chmn., 1982-87; founding mem., pres. Olave Baden-Powell Soc. of World Assn. Girl Guides and Girl Scouts, London, 1984—; asst. sec. Dartnell Corp., Chgo., 1981—; bd. dirs. Jr. League of Chgo., 1937-40, Vis. Nurse Assn. of Chgo., 1951-58, 61-63, asst. treas., 1962-63; women's bd. dirs. Children's Meml. Hosp., 1946-50. Staff aide, ARC and Motor Corps, World War II. Vice pres. Latin Sch. Parents Council, 1952-54; bd. dirs. Latin Sch. Alumni Assn. 1964-69, Fidelitas Soc., 1979; women's bd. U.S.O., 1965-75, treas., 1969-71, v.p., 1971-73; women's service bd. Chgo. Area council Boy Scouts Am., 1964-70, mem.-at-large Nat. council, 1973-76, mem. nat. Exploring com., 1973-76; governing mem. Anti-Cruelty Soc. of Chgo. . Recipient Citation of Merit Sta. WAIT, Chgo., 1971; Baden-Powell fellow World Scout Found., Geneva, 1983. Mem. Nat. Soc. Colonial Dames Am. (Ill. bd. mgrs. 1962-65, 69-76, 78-82, v.p. 1970-72, corr. sec. 1978-80, 1st v.p. 1980-84, state chmn. geneal. info. services com. 1972-76, hist. activities com. 1979-83, mus. house com. 1980-83, house gov. 1981-82), Youth for Understanding (couriers bicentennial project), English-Speaking Union, Chgo. Dobbs Alumnae Assn. (past pres.), Nat. Soc. DAR, Chgo. Geneal. Soc., Conn. Soc. Genealogists, New Eng. Historic Geneal. Soc., N.Y. Geneal. and Biog. Soc., Newberry Library Assos., Chgo. Hist. Soc. Guild. Republican. Episcopalian. Clubs: Casino, Saddle and Cycle, The Racquet of Chgo. Home: 2430 Lakeview Ave Chicago IL 60614

FETSKE, RUTH BETTY, advertising agency executive; b. Rahway, N.J., Sept. 24, 1922; d. Plato Settle and Mitzie (Mihalovics) Bumgarner; student public and pvt. schs., Rahway, N.J., N.Y.C.; m. William A. Fetske, Jan. 29, 1944. Editorial asst. Woman's Home Companion mag., N.Y.C., 1941-44; photog. stylist Anton Bruehl Studios, N.Y.C., 1944-45; fashion copywriter West-Marquis Advt. Agy., Los Angeles, 1945-46; copywriter Lerner Shops, N.Y.C., 1946-47; copywriter, account exec. Dorland Internat. Advt. Agy., N.Y.C., 1947-48; advt. mgr. Marcus Breier Sons, Inc., men's outerwear, N.Y.C., 1951-53; account exec. Lester Harrison Advt. Agy., N.Y.C., 1953-60, Mervin & Jesse Levine Advt. Agy., N.Y.C., 1960-68; pres., owner Ruth B. Fetske Assos., Inc., N.Y.C. and Conn., 1969-85. Mem. Fashion Group, Inc., Nat. Assn. Female Execs., Conn. Valley Tourism Commn. (bd. dirs. 1987-92). Contbg. writer/photographer to profl. publs. Office: PO Box 248 Cobalt CT 06414

FETTE, MARY PATRICIA, nurse; b. Waseca, Minn., Apr. 1, 1956; d. William Carl and Phyllis Barbara (Lynch) Poehler; m. Jeffrey Lynn Fette, Sept. 16, 1978. Assoc. in Nursing, Austin (Minn.) Community Coll., 1978. R.N., Minn.; cert. med.-surg. nurse, emergency nurse, Staff nurse Lakeshore Nursing Home, Waseca, 1974-75, nursing supr., 1975-77; head nurse Meml. Hosp., Waseca, 1977—; transport nurse Neste Ambulance, 1983—. Vol. ARC, 1978—. Mem. Am. Nurses Assn., Minn. Nurses Assn., Critical Care Nursing Assn., Emergency Nurses Assn. Roman Catholic. Home: 409 14th Ave NW Waseca MN 56093 Office: Meml Hospital 100 5th Ave NW Waseca MN 56093

FETTER, CAROLYN MARIE, pharmaceutical company executive; b. Bklyn., Jan. 13, 1952; d. Edward H. and Teresa A. (Maloney) F.; m. N. Jay Diener, Sept. 16, 1978. B.A., St. John's U., 1973; M.B.A., Rutgers U., 1985. Owner, Family & Friends Rec. Co., Bklyn., 1974-76; media planner Benton & Bowles Advt., N.Y.C., 1976-77; product mgr. Block Drug Co., Jersey City, 1977-81; sr. product mgr. Sterling Drug Co., N.Y.C., 1981-82; dir. acquisitions and new product devel. Johnson & Johnson Dental Care Co., New Brunswick, N.J., 1982—. Mem. Nat. Assn. Female Execs. Avocation: microcomputers. Office: Johnson & Johnson Co JH-315 501 George St New Brunswick NJ 08903

FETTER, ELIZABETH ANN, management consultant; b. Philipsburg, Pa., Aug. 26, 1958; d. John David and Mary Joan (Larson) F. BA in Philosophy and Rhetoric, Pa. State U., 1980; MS in Indsl. Adminstrn., Carnegie Mellon U., 1982. Fin. analyst Chevron Corp., San Francisco, 1982-86, banking ops. supr., 1986-87; mgmt. cons. Marakon Assocs., San Francisco, 1987—; adj. lectr. Golden Gate U., San Francisco, 1983—. Bd. dirs., fin. com., treas. YWCA of San Francisco, 1986—. Mem. Pa. State U. Alumni Assn., Phi Kappa Phi (pres. 1977-78). Clubs: San Francisco Waltz, Art Deco Soc. Home: 2335 Larkin St #4 San Francisco CA 94109 Office: Marakon Assocs 444 Market St San Francisco CA 94104

FETTERHOFF, BARBARA GILLAM, office administrator; b. Bryn Mawr, Pa., Mar. 17, 1929; d. Neal F. and Helen (Olson) Gillam; m. Ira L. Fetterhoff, May 28, 1955; children—Hans, Heidi. B.A., U. Del., 1951. Med. Sec. Smith Kline, Phila., 1951-55, Johns Hopkins U., Balt., 1955-56, Springfield St. Hosp., Sykesville, Md., 1957-59, Dr. John T. King, Balt., 1963-78; office mgr., med. sec. Ira L. Fetterhoff, M.D., Hagerstown, Md., 1980—. Author: Women's Resource Booklet, 1987; compiler Outstanding Women of Washington County, Md., 1979, 84; editor, project dir. Reaching the Public: Publicity Guide for Community Groups in Tri-State Area, 1983. Local/state officer LWV, 1981—; mem. Md. Gov.'s Adv. Com. on Reapportionment and Redistricting, 1981; Md. Adminstrv. Bd. Election Laws, 1983-87. Recipient citation for work on title IX, Gov. Md., 1984. Mem. AAUW (br. pres. 1975, 83, v.p. state membership 1980-82, assn. nominating com. 1981-83, v.p. state program 1985-88, meritorious award 1984), Commn. Women Washington County (v.p. 1988—), Alpha Iota, Phi Kappa Phi. Republican. Episcopalian. Office: 1610 Oak Hill Ave Hagerstown MD 21740-2929

FETTERMAN, CAROLE L., public relations coordinator, producer, writer; b. Buffalo, Jan. 7, 1953; d. Harry William Fetterman and Jean Audrey (Solters) Dailey. Cert. Pub. Relations and Advt., SUNY-Buffalo, 1981, A.A., 1982; B.A., State Univ. Coll.-Buffalo, 1983. Producer Sta. WGR-TV, Buffalo, 1981-83, assignment editor/writer, 1981-82, news writer, researcher Sta. WGR, 1982; comml. continuity coordinator Sta. WGRZ-TV, Buffalo, 1983-85; pub. affairs producer: Open Rap, Inquiry, 1981-83; broadcast publicity coordinator Curtains Up, 1985. Publicity coordinator Friends of Philharm. MUNY Tennis Tournament, 1985. Nat. Acad. TV Arts and Scis. Republican. Roman Catholic. Home: 78 Fairfield Ave Lancaster NY 14086

FETTERMAN, NELMA IRENE, home economist; b. Starbuck, Man., Can., Feb. 21, 1938; d. Laude and Hesper Orpha (Olsen) F.; B.Ed., U. Alta., 1965; M.A., Mich. State U., 1968; Ph.D., Ohio State U., 1977. Elem. sch. tchr., Domain, Man., Can., 1958-60; jr. high sch. English tchr., Lethbridge, Alta., Can., 1960-62; high sch. tchr., Nanton, Alta., 1965-66; jr. high sch. home econs. tchr., Edmonton, Alta., 1966-67; assoc. prof. home econs. U. Alta., Edmonton, 1968-87, prof. 1987—. Contbr. articles to profl. jours. Mary A. Clarke scholar, 1974-75; Marion K. Piper internat. fellow, 1975-76. Mem. Am. Home Econs. Assn., Assn. Coll. Profs. Textiles and Clothing, Am. Soc. Info. Sci., Can. Home Econs. Assn., Alta. Home Econs. Assn. Mem. United Ch. Can. Home: 247 Surrey Gardens, Edmonton, AB Canada T5T 1Z3 Office: U Alta, 223 B Home Econs Bldg, Edmonton, AB Canada T6G 2M8

FETTERS, JOAN FRANCES, child care center administrator, educator; b. South Sioux City, Nebr., Apr. 4, 1939; d. Elmer David and Rose Viola (Leuenhagen) Owen; m. Harold Lee Fetters, June 9, 1958; children—Ricky Lee, Troy Dow, Mark Owen. B.A., U. No. Colo., 1960; postgrad. Mesa Coll., 1975. Tchr. pub. schs., Los Angeles, Oakland and Woodland, Calif., 1960-67, Ft. Collins, Colo., 1967-70, Crow Indian Reservation, Pryor, Mont., 1971-72; owner, mgr. Children's Workshops, Ft. Collins, 1983—, Learning Tree Children's Ctrs., Grand Junction, Colo., 1975—. Mem. Mesa County Dirs. Orgn. (pres. 1978-79), Larimer County Assn. for Edn. of Young Children, Nat. Assn. for Edn. of Young Children. Avocations: piano; reading; biking. Home: 3206 Norwood Ct Fort Collins CO 80525 Office: Children's Workshops 635 S Grant Fort Collins CO 80521

FETTWEIS, YVONNE CACHÉ, archivist; b. Los Angeles, Nov. 28, 1935; d. Boyd Eugene and Georgette Louisa (Tilmann) Adams; m. Rolland Phillip Fettweis, July 22, 1967; children: Maurice C.B. II, Michele-Yvonne (Mrs. Paul E. Cenzer); m. Maurice Lee Caché, Jan. 8, 1955 (div. 1962). B.A., Wagner Coll., 1954; postgrad Am. U., 1973, Bentley Coll., 1981. Legal sec., asst. Judge, Davis & Stern, and Orfinger & Tindall, Daytona Beach, Fla., 1961-66; head recording sect., bd. dirs. First Ch. Christ, Scientist, Boston, 1969-71, research assoc., 1971-72, adminstrv. archivist, 1972-78, sr. assoc. archivist, 1979-84, records adminstr., 1984—. Exec. sec. Volusia County Goldwater campaign, Daytona Beach, 1964. Mem. Soc. Am. Archivists, Automated Records and Techniques Task Force, Am. Mgmt. Assn., New Eng. Archivists, Assn. Records Mgrs. and Adminstrs. (bd. dirs. 1983—), Assn. Col. and Research Librarians, Bay State Hist. League. Republican. Christian Scientist. Lodges: Order Eastern Star, Order Rainbow (bd. dirs. 1972-77). Home: 42 Edgell Dr Framingham MA 01701 Office: 1st Ch Christian Sci Christian Sci Ctr 175 Huntington Ave Boston MA 02115

FETZ, MARGOT, management consultant; b. Evanston, Ill., Nov. 10, 1935; d. Wesley and Mary (Slater) Hardenbergh; m. James Lawrence Talbot, Nov. 15, 1957 (div. Dec. 1981); children: Katrin, Gretchen, Susan. AB, U. Calif., Berkeley, 1958; MBA, Seattle U., 1986. Cert. systems profl. Dept. mgr. U. Mont. Library, Missoula, 1973-76; exec. asst. Soc. Photo-optical Instrumentation Engrs., Bellingham, Wash., 1977-78; cons. The Organizer, various cities, Wash., 1979-81; analyst Wash. Mut. Savs. Bank, Seattle, 1981-82; info. systems analyst Alpac Corp., Seattle, 1982-85; prin. Focus Cons., Seattle, 1985—. Author: Archival Inventory Washington State Department Civil Defense, 1979; (bibliography) Bibliography of Sir Douglas Mawson, 1958; contbr. articles to profl. jours. Chmn. County Parks Feasibility Com., Missoula, 1973-74; vice chmn. drafting com. Missoula Local Govt. Study Commn., 1974-76; bd. dirs. Musica Viva Internat., Bellingham, 1979-81. Recipient Wall Street Jour. award, 1985. Mem. Assn. Records Mgrs. and Adminstrs. (v.p. publicity 1982-83), Assn. Systems Mgt. (chmn. awards 1984—, chmn. membership com. 1985-86, sec. 1986—), Office System Research Assn., Nat. Assn. Female Execs., Women's Network, Seattle U. MBA Assn., Greater Seattle C. of C. Club: City (Seattle).

FEUER, BARBARA APRIL, association executive; b. N.Y.C., Apr. 19, 1949; d. George Phillip and Norma June (Wolin) F. B.A., Am. U., 1971; cert. de la Langue Francaise, Sorbonne, Paris, 1970; M.S. with honors, U. LaVerne, 1979, M in Human Resource Devel., Am. U., Washington, 1988. French, Pub. Schs., Washington, 1973-75; program coordinator YMCA Human Devel. Ctr., San Diego, 1976-80; tng. specialist Assn. Flight Attendants, Washington, 1980-82, dir., 1982—; instr. U. Md., 1985—; instr. ESL, positive parenting San Diego Community Colls., 1976-79; psychol. asst. San Diego Family Inst., 1978-80. Contbr. articles to profl. publs. Mem. Task Force on Women and Alcoholism, Washington, 1981-83, N. Am. Commn. on Women, 1983-84; cons. human resource devel. Named one of Outstanding Young Women Am., 1983. Mem. Assn. Labor Mgmt. Adminstrs. and Cons. on Alcoholism (chpt. v.p. 1981- 82, chpt. pres. 1982-83, bd. dirs.), Am. Soc. Tng. and Devel. Office: Assn Flight Attendants 1625 Massachusetts Ave NW Washington DC 20036

FEUERHELM, JILL ANN, media specialist, educational software designer; b. Pasadena, Calif., May 7, 1948; d. Robert Warren and Jane Mary (Bode) Feuerhelm; m. Thomas Glenn Layton, May 23, 1980. A.A., Pasadena City Coll., 1968; B.S. in Edn., No. Ariz. U., 1971. Cert. tchr., Ariz. Tchr. Tolleson Sch. Dist., Ariz., 1973-75; Title I coordinator Kilbuck Sch., Kuskokwim Sch. Dist., Bethel, Alaska, 1975-79; microcomputer specialist, children's librarian Eugene Pub. Library, Oreg., 1983-85; software designer The 22d Ave Wordshop, Eugene, 1982-85, Cinderella, Seuss and Mother Goose, 1987, prodn. mgr., 1983-85; pres. TJ, Inc., 1985—. Designer computer software The Hinky Pinky Game, 1983, Rebus Writer, 1986. Mem. ALA, Pacific Northwest Library Assn., Oreg. Library Assn., Oreg. Ednl. Media Assn., Eugene Software Council. Office: 1430 Willamette Suite 236 Eugene OR 97401

FEUSSNER, ELLEN PATRICIA, sales executive; b. Summit, N.J., Mar. 17, 1951; d. Frank Smith and Carolyn Marie (Williams) F. BS, Radford U., 1973. Cert. quality edn. systems instr. Sales rep. Indirecto, Inc., Linwood, N.J., 1975-76; regional mgr. Indirecto, Inc., Long Beach, Calif., 1976-77; sales rep. Johnson & Johnson, Los Angeles, 1977-79, A-V Sci. Aids, Inc., Phila., 1979-81; sales rep., trainer Codman & Shurtleff, Inc., Phila., 1981-84, div. mgr., 1984-86; mgr. sales tng. Codman & Shurtleff, Inc., Randolph, Mass., 1987, product dir., 1988—. Bd. Trustees Tara Ct. Condominium Assn. Mem. Rep. Task Force. Republican. Roman Catholic. Office: Codman & Shurtleff Inc Randolph Indsl Park Pacella Park Dr Randolph MA 02368

FEW, MELINDA MULLINIKS, stock brokerage company executive; b. Memphis, Oct. 13, 1938; d. Robert Curlee and Hallie Agnas (Marshall) Mulliniks; m. Robert Pierce Few, Jan. 13, 1962 ; 1 son, Marshall Read. Student, Memphis State U., 1956-58, v.p. Henderson, Few & Co., Atlanta, 1963-67; broker Robinson-Humphrey Co., Inc., Jacksonville, Fla., 1978-81; v.p. Blackstock & Co., Inc., Jacksonville, 1981-85; broker Johnson, Lane, Space, Smith & Co., Inc., 1985—; sec.-treas., dir. Nat. Health Care Systems, Denticare, Inc. Active Ponte Vedra Woman's Club (bd. dirs., past pres.). Republican. Presbyterian. Home: 215 Pablo Rd Ponte Vedra Beach FL 32082 Office: Johnson Lane Space Smith & Co Inc Jacksonville FL 32202-4435

FEY, CAROL ANN, lawyer; b. Cin., Mar. 28, 1954; d. Richard Edward and Betty Jane Mildred (Luckhardt) F. BA, Miami U., Oxford, Ohio, 1976; JD, Ohio State U., 1984. Bar: Ohio 1985, U.S. Dist. Ct. (no. and so. dists.) Ohio, 1985, U.S. Ct. Appeals (6th cir.) 1986. Examiner Cin. Met. Housing Authority, 1976-77; project adminstr. Mid-Ohio Regional Planning Commn., Columbus, 1977-82; asst. atty. gen. State of Ohio, Columbus, 1985; staff atty. to justice Clifford F. Brown Ohio Supreme Ct., Columbus, 1985-86; assoc. Mowers, Cope & Kizer Co., Legal P.A., Columbus, 1986—. Mem. ABA, Ohio Bar Assn., Columbus Bar Assn., Nat. Assn. Women Lawyers, Women Lawyers of Franklin County, Columbus Career Women (pres. 1987—), Order of Coif. Office: Mowers Cope & Kizer Co Legal PA 3600 Olentangy River Rd Columbus OH 43214

FEY, TERESA ANN, advertising executive; b. San Antonio, May 27, 1939; d. Bartholomew John and Mary Ellen (Routzen) Krizek. Mgr. nat. traffic Sta. KONO-TV (now KSAT-TV), San Antonio, 1957-67; office mgr. Frazer-Wiggins, Collins and Lewis, San Antonio, 1967-68; dir. radio-TV Wyatt Advt., San Antonio, 1968-70; v.p. media Brooks, Johnson, Zaumer Advt., San Antonio, 1970-81, McCann-Erickson Regional Mktg., Houston, 1981—. Mem. Am. Women Radio and TV (pres. S. A. chpt. 1977). Office: McCann-Erickson Regional Mktg 1320 Post Oak Blvd #2050 Houston TX 77056

FIALKOFF, CHERYL NAGEL, physician; b. N.Y.C., June 8, 1955; d. David and Doris (Barnett) Nagel; m. Richard Jay Fialkoff, June 8, 1986. BA, Cornell U., 1977; MS, Sarah Lawrence Coll., 1979; MD, Albert Einstein Coll. Medicine, 1986. Genetic counselor St. Mary's Hosp. for Children, Queens, N.Y., 1979-82; intern in internal medicine Montefiore Hosp. Ctr., Bronx, N.Y., 1986-87; resident in dermatology Hosp. of U. Ill., Chgo., 1987—. Contbr. articles to sci. jours. Mem. AMA, Phi Kappa Phi, Phi Beta Kappa, Alpha Omega Alpha. Office: U Ill Coll Medicine E Dept Derm Room 376 808 S Wood St Chicago IL 60612

FIALLO, ARMIDA, medical company executive; b. Los Angeles, Nov. 4, 1947; d. Reyes Kastruita and Giovanni Frances; divorced; 1 child, Kimberly. AA, East Los Angeles Coll., 1973; BA, Univesidad de Mexico, 1979. Pres. Neo Ipno Inc., Temple City, Calif., 1970-86; mgr. ALH Chiropratic Office, Alhambra, Calif., 1986—; cons. med. billing hosps. and med. offices, Los Angeles, 1980—. Democrat. Roman Catholic. Address: 824 S 1st St Alhambra CA 91801

FICK, ANN MARIE, medical practice executive, controller; b. Kokomo, Ind., June 1, 1957; d. Jack Lewis and Mildred Faith (Monger) Graber; m. Brian Fick, Dec. 27, 1979; 1 child, Michelle Brionne. Student, Boise State U., 1975-77; BBA, Kans. State U., 1979. CPA, N.Mex. Staff acct. Denham, Pineda & Co., Albuquerque, 1980-81; sr. staff acct. Neff & Co., Albuquerque, 1981-86; controller, v.p. Slade Enterprises, Inc., Albuquerque, 1986-88; controller Radiology Assocs. of Albuquerque, PA, 1988—. Bd. dirs. Meals on Wheels of Albuquerque, 1985—. Mem. Am. Soc. Women Accts. (pres. 1986-87, pres.-elect 1985-86, v.p. 1984-85, bd. dirs. 1982-84, 87-88). Republican. Presbyterian. Club: Pilot of Albuquerque.

FICKES, MARITA CLARK, accountant; b. Chappell, Nebr., Mar. 22, 1946; d. Irven Frank and Birdie Mae (Williams) Clark; m. Allen Horton Zimmer, June 11, 1966 (div. Nov. 1973); m. Mark Blaine Fickes, Jr., June 8, 1974; children: Matthew Clark, Morriah Lynn. B.S., U. Nebr., 1969, postgrad., 1977-78. CPA, Nebr., Colo. Tchr., Neligh pub. schs., Nebr., 1969-71, Elgin pub. schs., Nebr., 1971-72; salesperson Sears Roebuck Co./Gold Key Realty, Lincoln, 1972-74; mgmt. trainee Gen. Electric Co., Hendersonville, N.C., 1978-79; staff acct. Fred A. Lockwood & Co., CPA's, Gering, Nebr., 1979-81; prin. M.C. Fickes, CPA, Chappell, 1981-86; mgr. acctg. dept. Colo. Med. Cons.'s, Inc., Denver, 1986-87. Sec. bd. dirs. Chappell Area Med. Services, 1981-86 , Sidney Meml. Hosp., Nebr., 1985-86 ; mem. Rural Health Manpower Commn., Nebr., 1984-86 , Nebr. Health Planning Com. Mem. Am. Inst. CPA's, Nebr. Soc. CPA's, Colo. Soc. CPA's, Am. Morgan Horse Assn., Phi Upsilon Omicron, Omicron Nu. Avocations: gardening; equitation; music. Home: 770 E Old Stone Dr Highlands Ranch CO 80126 Office: Colo Med Cons 501 S Cherry St #700 Denver CO 80222

FICULA, TERESA, psychologist; b. Perth Amboy, N.J., Aug. 30, 1957; d. Alex and Lorraine (Lorentzen) Vollmann; m. John Ficula, Aug. 11, 1979; 1 child, Robert. BS, U. Fla., 1979; MS in Clin. Psychology, E. Washington U., Cheney, 1981; MS in Sch. Psychology, E. Washington U., 1981; PhD, U. Utah, 1987. Psychologist Psychol. and Ednl. Services, Tamarac, Fla., 1985-87, Crossroads Schs., Davie, Fla., 1987—; research cons. Primary Children's Med. Ctr., Salt Lake City, 1983-85; lectr. U. Utah, Salt Lake City, 1983-85; co-dir. Neuropsychol. Eval. & Services, Boca Raton, 1987—. Author: School Phobic and Delinquent Adolescents, 1987; (with others) Psychology of Adolescence, 1983, Handbook of Prevention, 1986; contbr. articles to profl. jours. Mem. Nat. Head Injury Found., Nat. Aphasia Assn. NIMH grantee, 1981-83; Mariner Eccles fellow U. Utah, 1984-86. Mem. Am. Assn. Female Execs., Exec. Women of Coral Springs, Am. Psychol. Assn. (assoc.). Democrat. Roman Catholic. Home: 4020 nw 113 Ave Coral Springs FL 33065

FIEDLER, BOBBI, political commentator, former Congresswoman; b. Santa Monica, Calif., Apr. 22, 1937; m. Paul Clarke; children—Lisa, Randy. Student, Santa Monica City Coll., Santa Monica Tech. Sch.; LL.D. (hon.), West Coast Coll. Law, 1979. Owner, mgr. 2 pharmacies; mem. Los Angeles Bd. Edn., 1977; co-founder BUSTOP antibusing orgn.; mem. 97th-99th Congresses from 21st Dist. Calif.; political comentator KABC-TV, Los Angeles, 1986—. Bd. dirs. Com. Investigating Valley Ind. City/County; mem. sponsors bd. B'nai B'rith Youth Orgn.; mem. Republican Women's Federated. Mem. Bus. and Profl. Women's Assn., Navy League, Hadassah. Republican.

FIEDLER, CYNTHIA MARIE, nurse; b. Exeter, N.H., Aug. 31, 1957; d. David Charles Carr and Joan Elizabeth (Taylor) Carr Bruno; m. Dana Albert Fiedler. BS in Nursing, Fitchburg (Mass.) State Coll., 1979. RN, Fla., Calif., Mass. Staff, charge nurse Cardinal Cushing Hosp., Brockton, Mass., 1979-83, Santa Monica (Calif.) Med. Ctr., 1983-84; staff nurse Hosp. Staffing Services, Fort Lauderdale, Fla., 1984, Staff Builders, Boston, 1984—; staff, charge nurse Faulkner Hosp., Jamaica Plain, Mass., 1988. Recipient Nat. Cancer Soc. award, Fitchburg, Mass., 1979. Campaigner Walpole, Mass. town elections. Unitarian. Home: 465 Maple St Mansfield MA 02048

FIELD, CHARLOTTE, retired association executive; b. Seattle, June 9, 1915; d. Charles Henry and Evelyn Maude (Westcott) F.; B.A., U. Wash., 1936. Fashion coordinator Bon Marche Dept. Store, Seattle, 1940-41, display coordinator, 1941-44, asst. merchandising mgr., 1944-45, asst. rep., N.Y.C., 1945-46; asst. dir. publicity Lord & Taylor Dept. Store, N.Y.C., 1946-47; merchandising coordinator, design cons., asst. to pres. Gump's Dept. Store, San Francisco, 1949-50; account exec. Abbott Kimball Agy., San Francisco, 1951-54; dir. nat. food publicity Wash. State Apple Commn., Seattle, 1957-75. Mem. Am. Women in Radio and TV (pres. Evergreen chpt. 1966-67), Nat. Edn. Found. (rep. Am. Women in Radio and TV 1967-68), Elec. Women's Round Table. Club: Wash. Athletic. Home: 319-101 SE #313 Bellevue WA 98004

FIELD, JULIA ALLEN, futurist, conceptual planner; b. Boston, Jan. 5, 1940; d. Howard Locke and Julia Wright (Field) Allen. B.A. cum laude, Harvard U. 1960, postgrad. Grad Sch. Design, 1964-65; postgrad. Pius XII Grad. Sch., Florence, Italy, 1961; postgrad. Walden U. Inst. for Advanced Studies, 1982—. Cons. to archtl. and environ. firms, 1964-69; cons. Forestry Dept. of Simla (India), 1968-69; founder, v.p. Black Grove, Inc., Miami, Fla., 1970-80; founder, pres. Amazonia 2000, Bogotá, Colombia, 1971—; leader Task Force Amazonia 2000, DAINCO, 1977-78; pres. Acad. Arts and Scis. of the Ams., Miami, Fla., 1979—; mem. presdl. adv. com. on tech. devel. Group of Yr. 2000, Colombia, 1971-74; mem. man and biosphere com. UNESCO, Colombia, 1972-78; mem. task force on colonization Report to Pres. Colombia, 1972; cons. So. Unified Command, Republic of Colombia 1981—; hon. nat. insp. resources and environment Republic of Colombia, 1982—; bd. visitors Duke U. Primate Ctr., 1979—; prin. speaker various seminars, congresses. Mem. City of Miami Bicentennial Com., 1975-76; coordinator Community of Man Task Force, Miami, 1975-76; mem. Blueprint for Miami 2000, 1982—; participant Only One Earth Forum UN Environ. Program/Rene Dubos Ctr., N.Y.C., 1987. Author: Amazonia 2000, 1978, Amazonia as a World Model, 1972. Advisor Tech. Update, 1985-86. Fellow Royal Geog. Soc. (London); mem. World Future Soc., Interna.t Assn. Hydrogen Energy, UN Assn. U.S., Planetary Citizens, Am. Farmland Trust, ACLU, Soc. Colombiana de Ecologia.

FIELD, KAREN ANN, real estate broker; b. New Haven, Conn., Jan. 27, 1936; d. Abraham Terry and Ida (Smith) Rogovin; m. Barry S. Crown, June 29, 1954 (div. 1969); children: Laurie Jayne, Donna Lynn, Bruce Alan, Bradley David; m. 2d Michael Lehmann Field, Aug. 10, 1969 (div. 1977). Student Vassar Coll., 1953-54, Harrington Inst. Interior Design, 1973-74, Roosevelt U., 1987—. Owner Karen Field Interiors, Chgo., 1970-86, Karen Field & Assocs., Chgo., 1980-81; now dir. sales La Thomus Realty Group div. La Thomus & Co., Chgo., 1988—; pres., ptnr. Field Pels & Assocs., Chgo., 1981-86. Mem. women's council Camp Henry Horner, Chgo., 1960; bd. dirs., treas. Winnetka Pub. Sch. Nursery (Ill.), 1961-63; mem. exec. com. woman's bd. U. Chgo. Cancer Research Found., 1965-66, pres. jr. aux., 1960-66; bd. dirs., sec. United Charities, Chgo., 1966-68, Victory Gardens Theatre, Chgo., 1979; co-founder, pres. Re-Entry Ctr., Wilmette, Ill., 1978-80; mem. br. Parental Stress Services, Chgo., 1981—. Recipient Servian award Jr. Aux. of U. Chgo. Cancer Research Found., 1966, Margarite Wolf award Women's Bd., U. Chgo. Cancer Research Found., 1967. Mem. Chgo. Real Estate Bd., North Side Real Estate Bd. Condex, Chgo. Council Fgn. Relations, English Speaking Union (jr. bd. 1958-59). Office: La Thomus and Co 15 E Superior Chicago IL 60614

FIELD, NANCY HAYDEN, biology educator; b. Manitowoc, Wis., Mar. 15, 1941. BS, U. Wis., 1963; MS, S.D. State U., 1971. Cert. tchr. Gen. sci. tchr. Madison (Wis.) Sch. System, 1963-64; research asst. Animal Behavior Lab. Pa. State U., 1964-63; spl. edn. tchr. Penns Valley High Sch., Center Hall, Pa., 1966-68; research asst. Wildlife dept. S.D. State U., Brookings, 1968-70; field research aid Coll. Forestry U. Wash., Seattle, 1973; sub. tchr. Bellevue, Issaquah (Wash.) Sch. Systems, 1978-81; biology instr. Bellevue Community Coll., 1979-84, Oreg. State U., Corvallis, 1985-87, Western Oreg. State Coll., Monmouth, 1987—; organizer First Earth Day. S.D. State U., 1970. Author: Discovery Book for the Seattle Aquarium, 1979, Discovering Mt. Rainier, 1980, Discovering New Volcanoes, 1980, Discovering the Princess Marguerite, 1982, Discovering Slamon, 1984, Discovering Marine Mammals, 1987. Leader Girl Scouts of Am., Bellevue, Wash., 1972-82; den mother BoyScouts Am., Corvallis, 1984-86. Mem. The Wildlife Soc. (environtl. action com. 1974-75, sec. Wash. chpt. 1972-74), NW Assn. for Environtl. Studies (scholarship com., 1984—), N.Am. Assn. for Envrintl. Edn., Moclips Cetological Soc., NW Assn. of Book Publishers, Sigma Epsilon Sigma, Gamma Sigma Delta. Home: 5800 SW West Hills Rd Corvallis OR 97333

FIELD, SALLY, actress; b. Pasadena, Calif., Nov. 6, 1946; divorced; children: Peter, Eli; m. Alan Greisman, Dec. 1984, 1 son, Samuel. Student, Actor's Studio, 1973-75. Starred in TV series Gidget, 1965, The Flying Nun, 1967-69, The Girl With Something Extra, 1973; film appearances include The Way West, 1967, Stay Hungry, 1976, Heroes, 1977, Smokey and the Bandit, 1977, Hooper, 1978, The End, 1978, Norma Rae, 1979 (Cannes Film Festival Best Actress award 1979, Acad. award 1980), Beyond the Poseidon Adventure, 1979, Smokey and the Bandit II, 1980, Back Roads, 1981, Absence of Malice, 1981, Kiss Me Goodbye, 1982, Places in the Heart, 1984 (Acad. award for best actress 1984), Murphy's Romance (also exec. producer), 1985, Surrender, 1987, Punchline, 1987; TV movies include Maybe I'll Come Home In the Spring, 1971, Marriage: Year One, 1971, Home for the Holidays, 1972, Bridges, 1976, Sybil, 1976 (Emmy award 1977). Office: care Creative Artists Agy 1888 Century Park E Suite 1400 Los Angeles CA 90067 *

FIELDER, JUDY PARSONS, nurse; b. Columbia, S.C., Nov. 25, 1947; d. Charles Henry and Frances (Buttler) P.; m. Dennis Lee Fielder, Apr. 8, 1972 (div. June 1983); children: Keri Selden, Sara Ruth. BSN, Salve Regina Coll., 1970; M in Nursing, Emory U., 1987. RN, Ga., R.I. Staff Navy Regional Med. Ctr., San Diego, 1970-75; childbirth educator Childbirth Edn. Assn., San Diego, 1975-77, Orange Park, Fla., 1977-79; staff nurse Shallowford Community Hosp., Atlanta, 1984-87; nurse practitioner Butler & Gross Ob/Gyn P.C., Atlanta, 1987—. Pres. Four Seasons Civic Assn., Atlanta, 1980-82. Served to lt. USNR, 1970-75. Mem. Am. Nurses Assn., Nurses Assn. Am. Coll. Ob/Gyn (cert. nurse practitioner), Internat. Childbirth Edn. Assn., Am. Acad. Nurse Practitioners, Sigma Theta Tau. Home: 8110 Winged Foot Dr Atlanta GA 30338 Office: Butler & Gross Ob/Gyn PC 5675 Peachtree-Dunwoody Rd NE Atlanta GA 30342

FIELDS, BESSIE MARIE WILLIAMS, educator; b. Pasco, Wash., Sept. 14, 1940; d. Joe and Velma (Johnson) W.; m. Frederick Marshall Fields, Aug. 16, 1957 (div. Jan. 1973); children: Greta Marie, John Duane. BS, Portland State U., 1971, MS, 1981; EdD, Nova U., 1988. Cert. counseling and devel.; cert. tchr., Ore. Counselor, instr. Portland (Ore.) State U., 1971-83; instr. Portland Community Coll., 1975-81, Marylhurst (Ore.) Coll., 1981-82; counselor Anchorage (Alaska) Community Coll., 1983-87; assoc. prof. U. Alaska, Anchorage, 1987—; cons.Frd. Govt., 1970-73. Mem. NAACP, Urban League. Recipient Community Leaders award Ednl. Bd. Am., 1976-77, Positive Community Contributions award City of Portland, 1977. Mem. Am. Assn. Counseling and Devel., Alpha Kappa Alpha. Republican. Methodist. Lodges: Toastmaster Internat., AKA. Office: Univ Alaska 2533 Providence Ave Anchorage AK 99508

FIELDS, DAISY BRESLEY, human resource development consultant; b. Bklyn.; student Hunter Coll., 1932-35, Am. U., 1949-53; m. Victor Fields, Aug. 2, 1936; 1 dau., Barbara Fields Ochsman. Personnel officer USAF Base, Norfolk, Va., 1942-45; asst. personnel officer Dept. Agr., Phila., 1945-47; asst. dir. personnel Smithsonian Instn., Washington, 1954-60; chief spl. programs NASA, Washington, 1960-67; spl. asst. Fed. Women's Program, VA, Washington, 1967-70; sr. program asso. Nat. Civil Service League, 1971-72; cons. Equal Employment Opportunity/Affirmative Action, 1972-75, 78 ; exec. dir. Federally Employed Women, Washington, 1975-77; pres. Fields Assocs., Silver Spring, Md., 1978—; exec. dir. The Women's Inst., Am. U.; instr. Mt. Vernon Coll., 1979-80, Am. U., 1982. Chmn., Montgomery County (Md.) Personnel Bd., 1972-78; chmn. legis. com. Comm. for Women in Public Adminstrn., 1976-79; commr. Md. Commn. for Women, 1973-77; commr. Montgomery County Commn. for Women, 1979-82; pres. Clearinghouse on Women's Issues (editor newsletter); v.p. Women's Inst. (mng. editor newsletter). Recipient award UN Assn. U.S.A., 1980. Mem. Nat. Assn. Female Execs., Nat. Council Career Women, Women's Equity Action League (pres. Md. 1972-74; award 1978), Federally Employed Women (pres. 1969-71, editor newsletter 1972-77, recipient award 1974, 78), Nat. Press Club, Am. News Women's Club Internat. Women's Writing Guild, Washington Ind. Writers;, Capital Press Women, Fedn. Orgns. Profl. Women (exec. council 1976-77, 80-82), Nat. Assn. Women Bus. Owners. Author: A Woman's Guide to Moving Up in Business and Government, 1983; contbr. articles to profl. jours. Home and Office: 13905 N Gate Dr Silver Spring MD 20906

FIELDS, DEBORAH JEAN, systems analyst; b. Santa Monica, Calif., Sept. 5, 1953; d. Conrad Herman and Amy Jean (Poppe) K.; m. Gary Edward Ball, Nov. 1, 1980 (div. Oct. 1986); m. Lloyd George Fields, Jr., Feb. 20, 1988. BS in Physics and Math. cum laude, U. Utah, 1976. Assoc. engr. Aeronutronics Div. Ford Aerospace, Newport Beach, Calif., 1976-78; engr. Spectra Research Systems, Irvine, Calif., 1978-79; sr. engr. Sparta, Inc., Laguna Hills, Calif., 1980-85, program mgr., 1985— . Contbr. research reports to tech. jours. Patron Center 500 for the Performing Arts, Costa Mesa, Calif., 1986. Mem. Am. Business Women's Soc., Am. Astronautical Soc. Republican. Office: Sparta Inc 23041 de la Carlota Suite 400 Laguna Hills CA 92653-1507

FIELDS, FREDRICA HASTINGS, designer, craftsman; b. Phila., Jan. 10, 1912; d. Theodore Mitchell and Carolyn Corlies (Baily) Hastings; student Wellesley Coll., 1930-32, Art Students League, 1933; m. Kenneth E. Fields, July 10, 1934; children—David Edward (dec.), Luellen, Stephen Francis. Designer craftsman in stained glass, 1948—; exhibited in one man show Artists Mart, Washington, 1955, First Presbyn. Ch., Stamford, Conn., 1976, Concordia Coll., Bronxville, N.Y., 1982, Greenwich (Conn.) YWCA, 1982; exhibited in group shows Nat. Soc. Arts and Letters, Washington, 1951, Smithsonian Instn., 1951, 53, 54, 57, 58, Corcoran Gallery Art, 1955, 56, Nat. Conf. on Religious Architecture, N.Y.C., 1967, Washington, 1970, Greenwich (Conn.) Art Soc. Ann. Exhbns., 1968-78, Stamford (Conn.) Art Soc., 1972, Danbury (Conn.) Public Library, 1974, Stained Glass Internat., N.Y.C., 1982; represented in permanent installations at Washington Cathedral, Marie Cole Auditorium, Greenwich Library, YWCA, Greenwich, Assn. for Research and Enlightenment Meditation/Prayer Center, Virginia Beach, Va., Conn. Hospice Inc., Branford, Concordia Coll., Bronxville, N.Y., many pvt. collections; tchr. classes in stained glass, Washington, 1950, YWCA, Greenwich, 1966, at studio, 1968-71. Recipient awards in stained glass Corcoran Gallery Art, 1955, 56, B.F. Drakenfeld award 6th Internat. Exhbn. of Ceramic Arts, Nat. Collections Fine Arts, Smithsonian Instn., 1957. Mem. Stained Glass Assn. Am., Greenwich Art Soc. Address: 561 Lake Ave Greenwich CT 06830

FIELDS, GAYLE J., vocational administrator; b. Jenkins, Ky., Aug. 13, 1943; d. Roland and Leona (Osborne) Jones; m. Harrison R. Fields, Sept. 2, 1961; children: Brad, Tricia, Scott, Jimmy. AB, U. Ky., 1964; MA, Ea. Ky. U., 1971. Sec. Gen. Telephone Co., Lexington, Ky., 1965-66, Jonabell Farm, Lexington, 1966-67, Manpower Services, Columbia, S.C., 1967-68; tchr. Fairfield County Bd. Edn., Winnsboro, S.C., 1968-69; sec. Clark County Bd. Edn., Winchester, Ky., 1969-70, Ea. Ky. U., Richmond, 1972-74; tchr. Monroe County Bd. Edn., Bloomington, Ind., 1974-75; sec. Mellott and Adams CPA, Hazard, Ky., 1975-76; tchr. Hazard SVTS, 1976-87; vocat. adminstr. Vocat. Edn. Region 12, Hazard, Ky., 1987—; sec. Regional Adv. Council, region 12, Hazard, 1987-88. Mem. Am. Vocat. Assn., Ky. Vocat. Assn. (sec. 1984-86), Ky. Bus. Edn. Assn., Upper Ky. River Vocat. Assn. (pres. 1980-81, 82-83), Beta Sigma Phi. Democrat. Episcopalian.

FIELDS, JANE KOLBER, hospital administrator; b. Buffalo, Apr. 9, 1952; d. Joseph Charles and Irene Mary (Kencik) Kolber; m. Lyle A. Fields, May 1, 1977; children: Jake, Casey. BS in Nursing, U. Rochester, 1974; MS Boston U., 1976. Community health nurse Monroe County Dept. Health, Rochester, N.Y., 1974-75; home care coordinator Montefiore Hosp., Bronx, N.Y., 1976-78; home care adminstr. Nyack Hosp., N.Y., 1978-85, v.p. community health services, 1985—. Sec. bd. dirs. Am. Cancer Soc., Rockland County unit, Nyack, 1983-85. Mem. Nat. Assn. Home Care, Home Care Assn. N.Y. State (bd. dirs. 1985—, 2d v.p. 1988-89), N.Y. State Pub. Health Assn., Sigma Theta Tau. Democrat. Roman Catholic. Avocations: tennis, skiing. Home: PO Box 7034 Ardsley on Hudson NY 10503 Office: Nyack Hosp North Midland Ave Nyack NY 10960

FIELDS, JOAN R., chemical company executive; b. N.Y.C., Jan. 18, 1930; d. Albert and Etta (Levy) Ross; B.S., Adelphi U., 1951; cert. early childhood edn. Ann Reno Inst., 1951; children—Larry M., Paul B. Tchr., Woodward Sch., Bklyn., 1951-52, Syosset Sch. Dist., 1959-65; corp. sec. Albatross U.S.A. Inc., Long Island City, N.Y., 1966-69, pres., chmn. bd., 1969—; chmn. bd., pres. Etro Realty Corp., 1969—, Apparel Innovations Inc., 1978—; pres. J.R.F. Properties Inc., 1980—. Mem. young profl. com. United Jewish Appeal; mem. Sutton Pl. Synagogue. Mem. N.Y. Assn. Women Bus. Owners, Internat. Platform Assn., Queens C. of C. (city affairs com.), Phi Sigma Sigma. Clubs: B'nai B'rith, Excelsior. Home: 303 E 57th St New York NY 10022 Office: 36-41 36th St Long Island City NY 11106

FIELDS, KARLA JO, accountant; b. Fayette, Ala., Jan. 27, 1959; d. Bobby Frank and Dorothy (O'Dell) F. AS, Faulkner State Jr. Coll., 1979; BS, Troy (Ala.) State U., 1981, postgrad. in bus., 1983—. Staff acct. Troy State U., 1981-82; comptroller Baldwin County Commn., Bay Minette, Ala., 1982-86; sr. acct. Wood, Robertson & Assocs., Bay Minette, 1986—. Mem. vocat. adv. com. Faulkner State Jr. Coll., Bay Minette, 1983—, chair, 1986—; bd. dirs. Baldwin County Rural Transp. System, Bay Minette, 1985-86, Baldwin County Agy. on Aging, 1985-86; mem. Baldwin County Transp. Bd., 1986. Mem. Nat. Assn. Female Execs., Circle K, Phi Theta Kappa, Phi Beta Lambda. Mem. Christian Ch. Home: 23175 Pecan St Robertsdale AL 36567 Office: Woods Robertson & Assocs PO Box 699 Bay Minette AL 36507

FIELDS, MARTHA JACOBS, state official, educational adminstrator; b. Greensboro, Ala., Jan. 26, 1940; d. Homer Lee and Lois (Newell) Jacobs; m. John Pope Fields, July 12, 1980; 1 child, Leigh Bolt. B.S., Troy U.; M.Ed., Auburn U., also postgrad. Counselor, psychologist Henry County Pub. Schs., Hendland, Ala., 1970-71, local dir. spl. edn., Abbeville, Ala., 1971-72; local dir. spl. edn. Montgomery County Pub. Schs., Montgomery, Ala., 1972-76; staff specialist Md. Dept. Edn., Balt., 1976-77, dir. div. spl. edn., 1977-79, asst. state supt., 1979-87, asst. deputy state supt., 1987—; instr. Auburn U., Montgomery, 1973-76; mem. Md. Gov.'s Adv. Com. Coordinating Services to Handicapped, 1979—; chmn., mem. State Coordinating Com. for Services to Handicapped, Balt., 1979-87; mem. Gov.'s Task Force on Spl. Edn. Funding, Gov.s Interagy. Coordinating Com. Infants and Toddlers. Named Educator of Yr., Girl Scouts Central Md., 1981; Woman Mgr. of Yr., State of Md., 1983. Mem. Council for Exceptional Children, Nat. Assn. State Dirs. Spl. Edn. (pres.-elect 1983-84, pres. 1984-85), Council Adminstrs. Spl. Edn. (legis. chair 1982-84). Democrat. Baptist. Office: Md Dept Edn 200 W Baltimore St Baltimore MD 21201

FIELDS, RONA MARCIA, psychologist; b. Chgo., Oct. 27, 1934; d. William Samuel and Kate Darcy (Goldman) Katz; BA, Lake Forest Coll., 1953; MS, U. Ill., 1955; MA, Loyola U., Chgo., 1964; PhD, U. So. Calif., 1970; m. Armond Fields, June 9, 1953 (div. 1967); children—Louis Marc, Sean Steven, Cathy Nikema, Miriam Star. Community psychologist Chgo. Bd. Health, 1963-64; psychologist NDEA program Monrovia (Calif.) Guidance Ctr., 1964-67; asst. prof. psychology Pasadena (Calif.) City Coll., 1966-69; prof. human devel. Calif. State U., Los Angeles, 1967-72, Pacific Oaks Coll., Pasadena, 1969-71; vis. prof. edn. Calif. State U., Northridge, 1971-72; assoc. prof. sociology Clark U., Worcester, Mass., 1972-76; founding mem., bd. dirs. Sozialwissenschaftliches Inst. fur Katastrophen und Umfallforschung, Kiel, W.Ger.; assoc. Transnat. Family Research Inst., Bethesda, Md.; pres. Assocs. in Community Health and Devel.; free-lance journalist. Co-chmn. campaign Betty McCann for Va. State Legislature, 1979; sec. Alexandria (Va.) Mayor's Com. for Handicapped, 1980-82; bd. dirs. Nat. Capitol YMCA, 1982-85; v.p. Alexandria YMCA, 1982-84, pres., 1984, Woman of Yr., 1983; candidate for sheriff, Alexandria, Va., 1984; mem. Amnesty Internat. Med. Commn., 1973-75. Recipient Phila. Mayor's award for Outstanding Service in Human Rights, 1978; named Disting. Alumna Lake Forest Coll., 1978, Outstanding Alumna, 1983. Fellow Peace Research Inst. of Oslo; mem. Am. Psychol. Assn. (task force status of women 1970-73, bd. social and ethical responsibility 1971-73), Am. Sociol. Assn., Internat. Studies Assn., Sociologists for Women in Soc., Soc. Psychol. Study of Social Issues, Gaelic League (exec. com. 1985-86), Irish Am. Cultural Inst., Psychologists for Social Action (nat. coordinator 1969-72), So. Calif. Peace Action Council (leadership collective 1969-72), Assn. Women in Psychology. Author: Society on the Run, 1973; The Armed Forces Movement and the Portuguese Revolution, 1978; Society Under Siege, 1976; Northern Ireland, 1979; The Future of Women, 1985; contbr. articles to profl. jours., chpts. to books. Home and Office: 222 E Del Ray Ave Alexandria VA 22301

FIELDS, SHELIA RHONDA (SHELIA RHONDA CLINE), dietitian; b. Welch, W.Va., Aug. 27, 1953; d. Orville and Amanda (Mingo) Cline; m. Dallan Fields, Sept. 22, 1974 (div. July 1981). BS Dietetics, Marshall U., 1974, MA foods and nutrition, 1984. Registered dietitian. Nutritionist Huntington State Hosp., Huntington, W.Va., 1976-87; cons. dietitian Cabell County, Huntington, 1987—; cons. dietitian Cabell County, Huntington, and Ceredo, W.Va., 1987—; lectr. in field. Mem. Am. Dietetic Assn., Am. Soc. Hosp. Food Service Adminstrs., W.Va., Ohio, Ky. Dist. Dietetic Assn. (nominating com. 1986-87, chmn. older Am. health fair 1981), W.Va. Pub. Employees Assn., Kappa Omicron phi Alumni Assn. (pres. 1987—). Home: 6225 Highland Dr Huntington WV 25705

FIELO, MURIEL BRYANT, space engineer, interior designer; b. Bklyn., Dec. 11, 1921; d. Harry and Minnie (Dick) Bryant; student CCNY, evenings 1938-41, Rutgers U., evenings 1965-69; cert. N.Y. Sch. Interior Design, 1970; m. Julius Fielo, June 17; 1 son, Michael Kenneth. Gen. mgr. Fidelity Discount Corp., Irvington, N.J., adv. supr. Lincoln Loan Co., Essex County, N.J., 1941-49; interior designer Alex Fielo Interior Decorators, Newark, part-time 1942-49, prin., 1949-69, owner, 1969—; designer, cons. space engr. MUDGE Interior Design Studios, East Orange, N.J., 1969—. Essex County freeholder clk. Bd. Freeholders, part-time 1972-76; commr. East Orange Bus. Devel. Authority, 1977-86; mem. U.S. adv. council SBA-Region II, 1980-81; active LWV, 1950-55; organizer, 1st pres. South Orange chpt. Women's Am. ORT, 1952-54, mem. nat. speakers bur., 1952-65, parliamentarian No. N.J. council, 1955-65; pres. Amity chpt. B'nai B'rith, Newark, 1946-48, v.p. No. N.J. council, 1948-49, various nat. and state positions, 1948-80; mem. nat. com. on sect. fund raising Nat. Council Jewish Women, 1979-81, nat. tour. chmn., 1979-81; trustee community services council Oranges and Maplewood, United Way of Essex and West Hudson, 1981-83; bd. dirs. East Orange Central Ave. Mall Assn., 1979-83, chmn. new voter registration drive East Orange 2d Ward, 1955—, entire city, 1969; pres. East Orange Democratic Club, 1957-58, campaign coordinator for Dem. mayoral candidate, 1969, calendar coordinator Essex County Dem. party, 1970-76; mem. N.J. Bipartisan Coalition for Women's Appts., 1981—. Named Outstanding Entrepreneur of 1984, N.J. Gov., Outstanding Orgn. Pres., Kean Coll. Profl. Women's Assn., 1985, Wonder Woman of 1986, Bus. Jour. of N.J., One of 8 Women to Watch in 1987 Jersey Woman Mag., 1987; also recipient various awards for civic service. Mem. Internat. Soc. Interior Designers (dir. 1981-85), Nat. Home Fashions League (N.J. membership chmn. N.Y. chpt. 1981-82), Interior Design Soc., N.J. Assn. Women Bus. Owners (state bd. 1979-82), Women Entrepreneurs N.J. (pres. 1981-85, chief exec. officer 1987—), N.J. Home Furnishings Assn. (bd. dirs. 1981-84, 86—), Constrn. Specifications Inst., N.J. Soc. AIA (profl. affiliate), Guild Designer Woodworkers, Women Bus. Ownership Ednl. Coalition (N.J. State pres. 1985-87, chief exec. officer 1987—, mem. steering com. interior designers for licensing in N.Y. 1985—), East Orange C. of C. (dir. 1977—, v.p. 1981-85), Bus. and Profl. Women's Club of Oranges (dir. 1958-66). Jewish. Mem. adv. panel Interior Design Mag., 1977—. Office: MUDGE Interior Design Studio 185 S Clinton St East Orange NJ 07018

FIELSTRA, HELEN ADAMS (MRS. CLARENCE FIELSTRA), education educator; b. Elkhorn, W.Va., Feb. 26, 1921; d. Fred Russell and Clara Sue (Williams) Adams; m. Edmond T. Dooley, Jr., Nov. 15, 1941 (div.

1948); 1 dau., Dereth Dooley Pendleton, m. Clarence Fielstra, Jan. 1, 1956. A.B., UCLA, 1950; M.A., Stanford U., 1954, Ed.D., 1967. Tchr. Santa Monica (Calif.) Unified Sch. Dist., 1947-50; elem. coordinator San Diego County Schs., 1950-52; lectr. edn. Stanford U., 1953-54, UCLA, 1957-58; gen. elementary supr. Burbank (Calif.) Unified Sch. Dist., 1954-56, Beverly Hills (Calif.) Unified Sch. Dist., 1959-61; asst. prof. edn. Calif. State U., Northridge, 1961-67; asso. prof. Calif. State U., 1967-70, prof., 1970—; sec.-treas., editor Fielstra Publs., Inc., Pacific Palisades, Calif.; sec.-treas. Hadco, Inc., Los Angeles.; Tng. coordinator Office Econ. Opportunity Tng. and Devel. Center, 1965-66; cons., speaker curriculum devel. and instructional supervision, 1952—; prin. investigator U.S. Office Edn. Project Tchr. Edn. for Disadvantaged, 1968-70; dir. interdisciplinary social sci. projects NSF, 1972-83; dir. Western Regional Center Edn. Devel. Center, 1974-76; chief cons. early childhood edn. Listener Corp. Author: (with L.G. Thomas, A. Coladarci, Lucien Kinney) Perspective on Teaching, 1961, (with Clarence Fielstra) Africa With Focus on Nigeria, 1963, Relationship Between Selected Factors and Pupil Success in Elementary School Foreign Languages Classes; also various monographs, curriculum guides, 2 ednl. films. Trustee, mem. exec. com. Calif. State U. Found., Northridge, 1970-72. Recipient Disting. Prof. award Calif. State Univ. and Coll. System, 1969, certificate of service Asso. Students Calif. State U., Northridge, 1970. Mem. Nat. Soc. for Study Edn., Am. Ednl. Research Assn., Nat. Council Social Studies (mem. publs. bd. 1970-72), Calif. Tchrs. Assn. (life), NEA (life), Congress of Faculty Assns. (founder), Assn. Supervision and Curriculum Devel., Stanford U. Alumni Assn., Calif. Assn. Supervision and Curriculum Devel. (chmn. state com. on supervision in structure public edn.), Calif. Council on Edn., AAUP, Calif. Higher Edn. Assn. (dir. 1970-74, pres. 1973-74), Calif. Coll. and U. Faculty Assn. (pres. chpt. 1969-70, state pres. 1972-73), Delta Zeta, Pi Lambda Theta, Delta Kappa Gamma (pres. Beta Eta chpt. 1960-62). Democrat. Clubs: Stanford (Los Angeles County); Palisadian Woman's. Home: 14177 Sunset Blvd Pacific Palisades CA 90272 Office: Calif State U Northridge CA 91330

FIGGE, CHARLENE ELIZABETH, religious organization administrator; b. Ste. Genevieve, Mo., Apr. 16, 1948; d. William Henry and Frieda Christina (Bauman) F. B in Music Edn., Fontbonne Coll., 1970; MS, U. Dayton, 1979. Joined Sisters of Divine Providence, Roman Cath. Ch., 1965; cert. elem. vocal and instrumental tchr. Tchr. Mary Queen of Universe Sch., St. Louis, 1970-71, Mt. Providence Boys; Sch., St. Louis, 1971-75, 1978-81; tchr. St. John's Sch., Imperial, Mo., 1975-76, St. Pius X Sch., Shreveport, La., 1976-78, Ascension Sch., St. Louis, 1981-85; justice coordinator, dir. devel., asst. provincial Sisters of Divine Providence, St. Louis, 1985—. Mem. Religious Involved in Social Concerns, St. Louis, 1985—, World Peace Com., St. Louis, 1985—, Interfaith Com. on Latin Am., St. Louis, 1985-87, Midwest Coalition on Responsible Investment, St. Louis, 1985—, Nat. Cath. Devel. Conf., 1985—. Mem. Nat. Soc. Fund Raising Execs. Democrat. Office: Sisters Divine Providence 8351 Florissant Rd Saint Louis MO 63121

FIGNAR, ROSEMARY CASEY, management consultant; b. Pottsville, Pa., July 6, 1945; d. Joseph Edward and Marie (Burns) Casey; m. Eugene Michael Fignar, June 15, 1968. BS in Home Econs. Edn., Coll. Misericordia, Dallas, Pa., 1967; postgrad., U. Puget Sound, Robert Morris Coll. Tchr. in Home Econs. Pitts. Bd. Edn., 1968-70; dietician Kaufmann's Dept. Store, Pitts., 1971-73; consumer and pub. affairs Beecham Products, Pitts., 1974-79; mgr. consumer affairs Pepsi-Cola Bottling Group, Purchase, N.Y., 1979-81; pvt. practice in human resources mktg. cons. Old Greenwich, Conn., 1982—; arbitrator Better Bus. Bur. Mem. exec. bd. United Way, Greenwich, Conn. Mem. Women in Mgmt. (bd. dirs.), Am. Soc. Tng. and Devel., Issues Mgmt. Assn., Soc. Consumer Affairs Profls. Address: 21 West End Ave Old Greenwich CT 06870

FIGUEROA, MARIANA YVETTE, information systems administrator; b. N.Y.C., Nov. 5, 1952; d. Angel Antonio Figueroa and Petra (Rodriquez) Rivera. BA, Fordham U., 1974. Adminstrv. asst. Montefiore Hosp., N.Y.C., 1975-80; adminstrv. asst. GTE Telenet Communications, N.Y.C., 1980-81, electronic mail specialist, 1981-82; assoc. systems engr. Paramus, N.J., 1982-83, systems engr., 1983-84, dist. systems engring. mgr., 1985; installation mgr. Walsh, Greenwood Info. Systems, N.Y.C., 1986; mgr. sales support Contel Fin. Systems, Greenwich, Conn., 1987—. Mem. Nat. Assn. Female Execs. Democrat. Roman Catholic. Home: 17A Adler Pl New York NY 10475 Office: Contel Fin Systems 600 Steamboat Rd Greenwich CT 06830

FIGURELLI, JENNIFER CONSTANCE, psychologist; b. Jersey City, May 11, 1945; d. Francesco Antonio and Jean (Bigler) F.; B.S., St. Lawrence U., 1966; M.A., U. S.C., 1970; Ph.D., Fordham U., 1977; postgrad. U. Calgary, Jersey City State Coll. Research psychologist Alta. (Can.) Mental Hosp., Ponoka, 1967; psychol. research asst. U. Calgary (Alta.), 1968-69; psychologist Columbia (S.C.) Public Schs., 1969-70; psychologist Jersey City Public Schs., 1970-82, dir. bur. spl. services, 1982—; asst. prof. psychology St. Peter's Coll., Jersey City, 1970—. Mem. S.C. State Com. on Legalization Abortion, 1970. Mem. NEA, N.J., Jersey City edn. assns., Nat. Assn. Sch. Psychologists (chmn. ad hoc com. 1972-73), Am., N.J., Inter-Am., Southeastern psychol. assns., Internat. Assn. Applied Psychology, N.J. Assn. Sch. Psychologists, Soc. Research in Child Devel., Am. Ednl. Research Assn. Editorial bd. Sch. Psychology Digest. Office: 241 Erie St Jersey City NJ 07306

FILCHOCK, ETHEL, educator, poet. BS in Edn., Kent State U. Tchr. Cleve. Pub. Schs. Author: Voices in Poetics: Vol. 1, 1985 (Merit award); composer: Praise God, The Lord is Coming. Chmn. sch. United Way, 1985-86. Recipient Cert. of Achievement N.Y. Profl./Amateur Song Jubilee, 1986. Mem. Nat. Assn. Female Execs., Am. Fedn. Tchrs. Roman Catholic. Club: Akron Manuscript.

FILER, ELIZABETH ANN, psychotherapist; b. N.Y.C., Oct. 16, 1923; d. Edwin and Edith Louise (Levy) Filer. B.S., Columbia U., 1944, M.A., 1945, M.S., 1954. Cert. bd. clin. social worker. Asst. tchr. to asst. dir. Mallay Nursery Sch., Bklyn., 1943-52; tchr., guidance staff N.Y. Sch. for Nursery Years, 1954-60; liaison social worker The Reece Sch., N.Y.C., 1954-60; cons. to schs. in N.Y.C., 1960-71; ednl. cons./therapist Ednl. Inst. for Learning and Research, N.Y.C., 1961-65; clin. social worker, psychotherapist in pvt. practice, N.Y.C., 1971—; cons. in field. Bd. dirs. Recreation Room and Settlement, N.Y.C., 1962-73. Recipient Founders Day award and Bicentennial medal Columbia U., 1954. Mem. Nat. Assn. Social Workers, N.Y. State Soc. Clin. Social Work Psychotherapists, Nat. Inst. for Clin. Social Work Advancement, Soc. for Psychoanalytic Psychotherapy, World Fedn. for Mental Health. Avocations: swimming; sports; opera; reading; needlepoint; travel. Home: 240 E 79th St New York NY 10021

FILICE, MARY GERARDA, brokerage firm executive, media production company owner; b. Chgo., Oct. 2, 1952; d. James Vincent and Virginia (Aimone) F. BA, Loyola U., Chgo., 1974; MA, Columbia Coll., Chgo., 1984. Surveillance supr. Chgo. Bd. Options Exchange, 1975-78; mgr. trading dept. European Options Exchange, Amsterdam, The Netherlands, 1978-80; pvt. practice bus. cons. Chgo., 1980-82; owner, producer, director, writer Filice Prodns., Chgo., 1982—; v.p. Keeley Investment Corp., Chgo., 1982—, Keeley Asset Mgmt. Corp., Chgo., 1987—. Producer, dir., writer: (film) Our Father, 1984 (Cert. Merit, Chgo. Internat. Film Festival 1984, 1st Place dramatic category Midwest regional award 12th Ann. Student Acad. Awards 1985, Hon. Mention, Cinestud 85 Internat. Student Film Festival 1985); producer, dir., co-writer: (film) No Place Like Home, 1986 (1st Place, Great Lakes Film Festival 1986, Hon. Mention, Festival of Ill. Film and Video Makers 1987, Festival des Femmes, Creteil, France, 1987). Ill. Art Council fellow, 1985, 86, Ctr. for New TV fellow, 1985. Mem. Regional Investment Brokers Services, Assn. Ind. Video and Filmmakers, Women in the Dirs. Chair (bd. dirs. 1986-87, v.p. 1988). Club: Mid-Town Tennis (Chgo.). Office: Keeley Investment Corp 401 S LaSalle St #1201 Chicago IL 60605

FILIPPONE, ELLA FINGER, organization executive; b. Kearny, N.J., Feb. 2, 1935; d. Ferdinand and Eliese R. Finger; grad. Katharine Gibbs Sch., 1954; B.A., U. Beverly Hills (Calif.), 1980, Ph.D., 1982; m. Joseph J. Filippone, Mar. 3, 1962; children—Joseph John, Thomas Carl, Andrew Daryl, Frederick Lewis. With Va.-Carolina Chem. Corp., 1954-56, Moulin Prodns., 1956, Schuster Woolens, Inc., 1957; with Stricker Research Assocs., Inc., 1957-63, v.p., partner, 1960-63; chmn., Passaic River Coalition, Basking Ridge, N.J., 1970-75, exec. adminstr., 1975—; sec. Passaic Valley Ground Water Protection Com., 1980—. Recipient award of merit EPA, 1975, cert. achievement Dept. Interior, 1980; German Marshall Fund grantee, 1982, Japan-U.S. Freindship Com. grantee, 1988. Mem. AAAS, Fedn. Water Pollution Control Fedn., Am. Water Resources Assn., Am. Econ. Assn., Acad. Polit. Sci. Lutheran. Editor Goals and Strategies, 1973—. Home: 25 Holmesbrook Rd Basking Ridge NJ 07920 Office: Passaic River Coalition 246 Madisonville Rd Basking Ridge NJ 07920

FILLEY, DOROTHY MCCRACKEN, museum consultant, antique costume restorer; b. St. Augustine, Fla., Mar. 22, 1915; d. Fred Wellman and Rozella May (Leith) McCracken; m. Marcus Lucius Filley IV, Sept. 11, 1937; children—Leith Child Filley Colen, Linda Derrick Filley Laguerre. BS in Fine Arts, Skidmore Coll. 1936; MA in Museology, SUNY-Oneonta, 1974. Founder, dir. Rensselaer County Jr. Mus., Troy, N.Y., 1954-59; exhibits cons. to N.Y. State historian N.Y. State Edn. Dept., Albany, 1956-57; mus. cons. Hist. Soc., Saratoga Springs, N.Y.-Park Casino, 1971-74; curator, coordinator Rockefeller Empire State Mall Art Collection, Albany, 1978-80; curator exhibits and collections Albany Inst. History and Art, 1974-81, mus. cons., 1981—; mem. N.Y. State Council on the Arts Mus. Adv. Bd., N.Y.C., 1974-75; cons. compiling history Town of Colonie, Newtonville, N.Y., 1975; mem. adv. bd. Shaker Heritage Soc., Albany, 1981—; cons. textiles and comstumes Albany Inst. History and Art, 1983—; cons. Troy Savs. Bank Collection of bank presidents, 1988; spl. research cons. History of SUNY Univ. Plaza Bldg., 1986. Author: Recapturing Wisdom's Valley, 1975. Mem. Cooperstown Grad. Assn., Jr. League Troy (pres. 1950-51). Republican. Club: Country of Troy. Avocations: gardening, tennis, swimming, wildlife preservation. Home: Box 245 RD 3 Troy NY 12180 Office: Albany Inst History and Art 125 Washington Ave Albany NY 12210

FILLIS-WALLS, MARION KAY, accountant; b. Ilford, Essex, Eng., July 21, 1956; d. Edward John and Joan Eileen (Gatfield) Fillis; m. Miron Vislocky, May 2, 1980 (div. June 1984); m. Erich Muller Walls, July 21, 1984 (div. Jan. 1988). Student, Royal Soc. Arts, Eng. Adminstr. UN, N.Y.C., 1978-81; adminstrv. asst. Carl Zeiss, Inc., Thornwood, N.Y., 1981-84; acct. IBM Corp., Houston, 1984-87; account exec. TexCom, Inc., Houston, 1987—. Mem. County C. of C. Republican. Anglican. Home: 712A Country Pl Dr Houston TX 77079

FILZEN, CHRISTINE MARIE, photographer; b. New Ulm, Minn., Mar. 8, 1955; d. Joseph P. and Eleanor R. (Janni) F. A.S., St. Cloud State U., 1978, B.A., 1979; postgrad. U. Minn., 1987-88. Photo asst. St. Cloud (Minn.) State U., 1976-79; photo processor Brown Photo Co., Mpls., 1978-79; photo tech. Sta. KSTP-TV, Mpls., 1979-81; sr. photographer U. Minn.-Mpls., 1981-84; color insp. Brown Photo Co., Mpls., 1984-85; mdse. technician Donaldsons, 1985-88 ; photo lab mgr., U. Minn. Dept. Journalism, 1988—; freelance photographer, reporter, 1975-79; judge Minn. Edn. Assn. Sch. Bell Awards, 1977; producer sports video tapes, 1982-84; judge Southwestern Minn. Regional Sci. Fair, 1985-86. Active Youth Minn.; mem. Assn. Retarded Citizens, v.p., 1971-73. Mem. Sigma Delta Chi (v.p. 1977-78), Minn. Press Club, Women in Communications, Nat. Press Photographers Assn., Communicators Plus. Democrat. Roman Catholic. Office: U Minnesota Dept of Journalism Photo Lab 111 Murphy Hall 206 Church St SE Minneapolis MN 55455

FINBERG, BARBARA DENNING, foundation executive; b. Pueblo, Colo., Feb. 26, 1929; d. Rufus Raymond and Velma Aileen (Hopper) Denning; m. Alan R. Finberg, June 21, 1953. B.A., Stanford U., 1949; M.A., Am. U. of Beirut, Lebanon, 1951. Intern U.S. Dept. State, Washington, 1949-50, fgn. affairs officer, Tech Coop. Adminstrn., 1952-53; program specialist, area chief Inst. Internat. Edn., N.Y.C., 1953-59; editorial assoc., program officer Carnegie Corp. N.Y., N.Y.C., 1959-80, v.p. program, 1980-88, exec. v.p., 1988—; program advisor A.L. Mailman Family Found. Mem. adv. council N.C. Central U. Sch. Library Sci., Durham, 1973-86; trustee Stanford U., 1976-86, v.p. bd. dirs., 1982-85; mem. accreditation com. Assn. Am. Law Schs., 1986—; adv. com. The Henry A. Murray Research Ctr. for the Study of Lives, Radcliffe Coll., 1986—; trustee N.Y. Found., 1979—, vice chmn. bd. dirs., 1983-85, chmn., 1985—. Rotary Found. fellow, 1950-51. Mem. Am. Ednl. Research Assn., Soc. for Research in Child Devel., Council on Fgn. Relations. Club: Cosmopolitan of N.Y. Home: 165 E 72d St Apt 19L New York NY 10021 Office: Carnegie Corp NY 437 Madison Ave New York NY 10022

FINCH, CAROLYN-BOGART, speech and language pathologist, lecturer; b. Mineola, N.Y., June 24, 1938; d. Harold Edwin and Ruth (Waring) Bogart; m. Gordon M. Finch (div. Oct. 1982); children: David Harold, Martha Louise; m. Donald Hall Hulme; children: Wendy Harriet Hulme, Allison Elizabeth Hulme. BS, Elmira Coll., 1965; MS, Western Conn. State U., 1972; postgrad., Nova U., 1982. Cert. speech and lang. pathologist, early childhood edn., elem. edn. Speech therapist Elmira (N.Y.) City Schs., 1963-65; supervision therapist Speech and Hearing Clinic, Elmira Coll., 1966-67; speech therapist Greenshire Residential Sch., Cheshire, Conn., 1968-69; speech pathologist Danbury (Conn.) City Schs., 1970-73; owner, dir. Peter Piper Sch. and Learning ctr., Brookfield Center, Conn., 1973-88, Speech Pathology Assocs., Danbury, 1974-87; mem. adj. faculty Western Conn. State U., Danbury, 1974-86, prof., 1986-87; bus. broker R. Lember Assocs., Danbury, 1987—; bd. dirs. Liberty Nat. Bank, Danbury; freelance lectr., 1986-87, R. Zemper Assocs., 1987-88; pres., nat. speaker Bogart Communications, Inc., Danbury; account exec. V.R. Bus. Brokers. Author: (multisensory articulation program) Portraits of Sounds, 1969, (book and posters) Survival Sign System, 1982, Universal Handtalk, 1988. Dem. nominee Danbury Town Com., 1985; mem. adv. com. Fairfield County 4-H. Recipient Mayoral Proclamation for Survival Sign System, City of Danbury, 1986. Mem. Conn. Speech and Hearing Assn., Am. Assn. Univ. Profs., Nat. Assn. Female Execs., Quota Club of Candlewood Valley (v.p. 1983-86, pres. 1986-87). Home and Office: Bogart Communications 51 Cedar Dr Danbury CT 06811

FINCH, DIANE SHIELDS, district merchandising manager; b. Detroit, Aug. 25, 1947; d. Earl Arthur and Carrie (Steele) Shields; m. Glenn A. Finch III, Oct. 5, 1968; 1 child, Jennifer Lynn. AA, U. Houston, 1969; student, U. St. Thomas, 1970-73, Rice U., 1980. Apt. mgr. Moonmist Manor, Houston, 1972-75; sales merchandiser Mattel Toys, Houston, 1975-77; sales merchandiser Plough Sales, Houston, 1977-79, ter. mgr., 1979-80, area mdse. mgr., 1980-84, dist. sales mgr., 1984-86; dist. mdse. mgr. Schering Plough Consumer Ops., Houston, 1986—. Area chmn. Assn. Community TV, Houston, 1985-87; mem. Friends of Ronald McDonald House; mem. Citizens Animal Protection. Mem. Nat. Assn. Female Execs., Am. Mgmt. Assn., Tex. Exec. Women, Houston Fedn. Profl. Women. Home: 10203 Huntington View Dr Houston TX 77099 Office: Schering Plough Consumer Ops PO Box 424 3030 Jackson Ave Memphis TN 38151

FINCH, LINDA MARTIN, architect; b. Phila., Apr. 30, 1948; d. Thomas Vernon and Roma Northcutt (Morgan) F.; B.Arch. with honors, U. Fla., 1971. Registered architect, Fla., Tex.; cert. Nat. Council Archtl. Registration Bds. Project architect Oscar Vagi & Assos., Ft. Lauderdale, Fla., 1978-79; prin. Linda Finch, Architect, Ft. Lauderdale, 1978-81; dir. design Michael A. Shiff & Assos., Ft. Lauderdale, 1980—; works include: Margate Mcpl. Complex, Lauderhill Mcpl. Complex, rural housing rehab. No. Fla. county, Lauderdale Lakes Recreation Ctr., Ft. Lauderdale Country Club, Markham Park Phase I, Markham Park Native Animal Habitat, Royal Palm Park, Mission Lake, Wolf Park, Fire Station Park, Lighthouse Point Mcpl. Complex, Coral Springs Library, Lauderhill Library, Lauderdale Lakes Library, Oakland Park Community Ctr., Lauderhill Community Ctr., North Lauderdale Community Ctr., 30-story mixed use bldg., Ft. Lauderdale, numerous others; gov.'s appointee to Fla. Bd. Architecture. Advisor Greater Victoria Park Civic Assn.; mem. Nat. Sex Equity Demonstration Project, Broward County Bd. Zoning and Code Enforcement, Rural Housing Rehab. Adv. Project, Hist. Preservation Bd. for Broward County, Greater Victoria Park Civic Assn. Recipient design award for hdqrs. bldg. Internat. Union Operating Engrs., 1981, design award for Coral Springs br. Broward County Library, 1983, for Lauderhill Mcpl. Complex, 1984, for Royal Palm Park, Oakland Park, 1985. Mem. AIA (treas., v.p., pres. Broward County chpt.; mem. Women's task group liaison) Assn. Women in Architecture, Union Internationale des Femmes Architects, Nat. Assn. Female Execs. Democrat. Research on modern European architecture. Office: 2701 W Oakland Park Blvd Suite 300 Oakland Park FL 33311

FINCHER, MARGARET ANN, educator; b. Harrodsburg, Ky., June 2, 1934; d. Henry Alexander and Minnie Bee (White) Cathey; B.S. in Bus. Edn., Auburn U., 1955; M.Ed., U. New Orleans, 1978; m. Willie John Fincher, Jr., Apr. 1, 1955; children—John Richard, Joseph Michael, Judy Darlene, James Andrew. Bookkeeper, Markle's Drug Store, Auburn, Ala., 1952-54; asst. to dir. Auburn U. Library, 1955; elem. tchr., Birmingham, Ala., 1958-64; bus. edn. tchr. Abramson High Sch., New Orleans, 1964—; owner, mgr. craft shop Fanci Krafts, New Orleans, 1977-78; asst. supr. Shaklee Corp., 1979-85. Supr. adult Bible tng. dept. Word of Faith Temple, 1982, cons. library devel., 1982, tchr., 1975-80, deaconess, 1983—; bd. dirs. Lamb Day Care Center, 1979-81; sustaining mem. Meth. Hosp. Aux., 1967—; adv./sponsor Christian Life on Campus Club. Recipient Am. Legion citation of appreciation, 1981; Future Bus. Leaders Am., award of Appreciation, 1976. Mem. ALA, Donna Villa Improvement Assn., Metro. Ednl. Media Orgn., Ch. and Synagogue Library Assn., So. Bus. Edn. Assn., Nat. Bus. Edn. Assn., La. Assn. Bus. Edn., La. Library Assn., La. Vocat. Assn., United Tchrs. New Orleans, Policemen's Assn. New Orleans (hon.), Phi Delta Kappa. Republican. Mem. Christian Ch. Office: 5552 Read Blvd New Orleans LA 70127

FINCHER, SANDRA JEAN, financial company executive; b. Evanston, Ill., Aug. 4, 1937; d. Kenneth E. and Alice Elizabeth (McNiel) Whitlock; m. Charles E. Fincher, June 7, 1979. Student, Ft. Dodge Jr. Coll., 1955-56. Agy. sec. Life Investors Ins. Co. of Am., Cedar Rapids, Iowa, 1964-74; regional office mgr. Life Investors Ins. Co. of Am., Dallas, 1974-78; personnel coordinator Target, Dallas, 1978-79; adminstrv. mgr. CIGNA Individual Fin. Services, Cherry Hill, N.J., 1979—. Editor: monthly company publ. Mem. Nat. Assn. Female Execs. Democrat. Home: 344 Cleveland Ave West Berlin NJ 08091 Office: CIGNA Individual Fin Services 1800 Chapel Ave W Suite 300 Cherry Hill NJ 08002 other: CIGNA Individual Fin Services 220 Lake Dr E Cherry Hill NJ 08002

FINDLEN, MARY ANTOINETTE, marketing executive; b. Waverly, N.Y., Jan. 1, 1939; d. Joseph Raymond and Clara Rosalinda (Saccucci) Campagna; m. James Peter Findlen; children: Paula Elisabeth, Leslie Avery. BA, Cornell U., 1962; MBA, Pace U., 1974. Exec. asst. John Carl Warnecke & Assocs., Washington, 1963-65; adminstrv. asst. Nash Engring. Co., Silver Springs, Md., 1968-72; asst. to gen. mgr. Euster Assocs., Armonk, N.Y., 1972-75; market research analyst Parsons Brinckerhoff, N.Y.C., 1975-77, mktg. analyst, planner, 1977-78, coordinator, corp. planning, 1978-79, mgr. mktg. services, 1979-82; cons. The Coxe Group, Phila., 1982; mktg. dir. Edwards and Kelcey, Inc., Livingston, N.J., 1982—. Assoc. editor A/E Marketing Journal, Newington, Conn., 1982-83, contbg. editor, 1983—. Asst. scout leader Girl Scouts Am., Katonah, N.Y. chpt., 1974-75; telephone canvasser Democratic Party, Greenbelt, Md., 1968-72. Mem. Soc. Mktg. Profl. Services (chmn. N.Y. membership com. 1980-84, award jury 1982, 86), Am. Mktg. Assn., Delta Mu Delta. Office: Edwards and Kelcey Inc 70 S Orange Ave Livingston NJ 07039

FINDLEY, MARY BAKER, violinist; b. Norfolk, Va., May 9, 1943; d. Henry Givens and Virginia Marie (Bredenfoerder) Baker; m. David Francis Findley, Mar. 3, 1966. MusB, U. Cin., 1965, MusM, 1966, DMA, 1974; student Staatlich Hochschule Musik, Frankfurt/Main, Fed. Republic Germany, 1966-68. Pvt. studio, Cin., 1972-75, Tulsa, 1976-80; adj. asst. prof. violin Oral Roberts U., Tulsa, 1976-80; Arts Council Okla. artist-in-residence, 1977-81; concertmaster, soloist, founding mem., bd. dirs. Tulsa Little Symphony Orch., 1978-80; founder Tulsa Chamber Music Festival, 1980; founding mem. Washington Music Ensemble, 1981—; concert soloist and recitalist; pvt. studio tchr., Washington, 1981—; instr. violin George Washington U. and Levine Sch. Music (both Washington), 1981—; founder All-Okla. String Symposium, 1977, Summer Serenades, 1986; concert master, soloist, bd. dirs. Amadeus Chamber Orch., 1984—. Mem. Am. String Tchrs. Assn., Music Educators Nat. Conf., Nat. Sch. Orch. Assn., Music Tchrs. Nat. Assn., Mortar Board, Suzuki Assn. Ams., Coll. Music Soc., Sigma Alpha Iota (Performance award 1972). Office: George Washington U Music Dept Washington DC 20052

FINE, FAY BLAIR, social worker; b. Dvinsk, Latvia, Feb. 10, 1920; d. Morris L. and Pauline (Kleinstine) Blair; m. Julius L. Fine, Nov. 18, 1945; children—Sandra Fine Thurm, Jeffrey. Community relations assoc. Jewish Community Fedn., Cleve., 1964-73; asst. prof., asst. dir. continuing edn. Case Western Res. U., Cleve., 1974-77; adminstr. staff devel. dept. Summit County Children's Services Bd., Akron, Ohio, 1978—; adj. instr. Northeast Ohio Univ. Coll. Medicine; adj. prof. Sch. Applied Social Scis., Case Western Res. U. Pres. alumni bd. Sch. Applied Social Scis., Case Western Res. U., mem. bd. overseers, 1986, numerous coms.; mem. Ohio Gov.'s Com. Sexual Abuse Tng., 1985—. Scholar Tulane U. Mem. Nat. Assn. Social Workers, Ohio Assn. Child Care Worker Tng., Ohio Child Welfare Tng. Bd., numerous civic assns. Council on Continuing Edn. Unit, Acad. Cert. Social Workers, Pentelicus. Democrat. Jewish. Office: Summit County Children's Services Bd 264 S Arlington St Akron OH 44306

FINE, JO RENÉE, audio-visual production executive; b. Norfolk, Va., June 19, 1943; d. Ruby Arthur and Tillie Fern (Goldman) F.; B.A., Smith Coll., 1965; M.A., N.Y.U., 1968, Ph.D., 1973; m. Edward Trieber, Apr. 12, 1981; 1 child, Jessica Fine Trieber. Probation officer N.Y.C. Office Probation, 1966; research asst. N.Y.U., N.Y.C., 1966-68, asso. research scientist Inst. Developmental Studies, 1968-73, research scientist, 1973-77, adj. asst. prof. dept. ednl. psychology, 1973-76; program analyst N.Y. State Dept. Mental Hygiene, N.Y.C., 1977-78; pvt. practice psychotherapy, N.Y.C., 1978-81; pres. CVM Prodns., Inc., N.Y.C., 1978—; cons. to bds. edn., N.Y.C., also greater met. area, 1973—. Mem. Am. Psychol. Assn., Pharm. Advt. Council, Nat. Assn. Women Bus. Owners, Am. Jewish Com.,Am. Soc. for Tng. and Devel., Advt. Women of N.Y. Co-author: The Synagogues of New York's Lower East Side, 1978. Home: 55 W 16th St New York NY 10011 Office: 13 E 16th St New York NY 10003

FINE, VIVIAN, composer, retired educator; b. Chgo., Sept. 28, 1913; d. David and Rose (Finder) F.; privately ed.; m. Benjamin Karp, Apr. 5, 1935; children—Margaret, Nina. Faculty, N.Y. U., 1945-48, Julliard Sch. Music, 1948, State U. N.Y. at Potsdam, 1951, Conn. Coll. Sch. Dance, 1963; music dir. B. deRothschild Found., 1954-60; faculty music div. Bennington (Vt.) Coll., 1964-87. Recipient award Am. Acad. and Inst. Arts and Letters, 1979; Rockefeller Found. grantee, 1964; Ford Found. grantee, 1969; Nat. Endowment of Arts grantee, 1974; Woolley Fund grantee, 1973; Martha Baird Rockefeller Fund for Music grantee, 1981; Guggenheim fellow, 1980; Koussevitsky Found. grantee, 1984. Mem. ASCAP, Inst. of Am. Acad./Inst. Arts and Letters. Composer: Race of Life, 1937, Suite for Piano, 1940, Four Elizabethan Songs, 1943, The Great Wall of China, 1947, A Guide to the Life Expentancy of a Rose, 1956, String Quartet, 1957, Concertante for Piano and Orch., 1944, Sonata for Violin and Piano, 1952, Alcestis, 1960, Quintet for Trumpet, Harp and String Trio, 1967, Paean for Brass Ensemble and Female Chorus, 1969, Two Neruda Poems, 1971, Concerto for Piano, Strings and Percussion, 1972, Teisho, 1975, The Women in the Garden, 1977, Romantic Ode, 1976, Brass Quartet, 1977, Momenti, 1978, Missa Brevis, 1972, Sonnets for Baritone and Orch., 1976, Drama for Orch., 1982, Poetic Fires, 1984, Ode to Purcell, 1984, Song for St. Cecilia's Day, 1985, Sonata for Cello and Piano, 1986, Dancing Winds, 1987; commd. by Elizabeth Sprague Coolidge Found., San Francisco Symphony.

FINELLI, SUSAN CATHERINE, legal administrator; b. N.Y.C., Oct. 30, 1950; d. Alfons B. and Celia I. (Barberio) Paske; m. John J. Finelli, Apr. 7, 1973. BA, NYU, 1978. Legal sec. Lord Day & Lord, N.Y.C., 1969-73, Miller & Summit, N.Y.C., 1973-78; paralegal Rogers Hoge & Hills, N.Y.C., 1978-81; legal adminstrn. Katz, Robinson Brog & Seymour, P.C., N.Y.C., 1981-83; dir. fin. and adminstrn. Kay Collyer & Boose, N.Y.C., 1984—; mem. faculty NYU, PLI speaker; pres., Hammarskjold Cons., Inc. Contbr. articles to law jours. Mem. Assn. Legal Adminstrs. (sec. exec. com. 1984—, pres. 1984-86), N.Y. State Bar Assn. (com. law office econs. and mgmt.), Nat. Female Exec. Assn., Internat. Platform Assn. Democrat. Roman Catholic. Club: N.Y. Health and Racquet. Office: Kay Collyer & Boose One Dag Hammarskjold Pl New York NY 10017

FINGERMAN, SUE WHITSELL, toxicologist; b. Earlington, Ky., May 4, 1932; d. John Frank and Pauline Arden (Long) Whitsell; m. MIlton Fingerman, Mar. 31, 1958; children: Stephen Whitsell, David Clay. BA, Transylvania Coll., 1955; MS, Tulane U., 1959, PhD, 1975. Instr. biology Xavier U., New Orleans, 1969-71; research asst. in biology Tulane U., New Orleans, 1972-75, research assoc., 1975-77, 78-80, research assoc. in biology and chemistry, 1977-78; environ. toxicologist Okla. State U., Stillwater, 1980-81; biolog. cons. New Orleans, 1980—; vis. asst. prof. Tulane U., New Orleans, 1984; research asst. in biology Marine Biolog. Lab., Woods Hole, Mass., summers 1970-73. Asst. editor Copeia, New Orleans, 1956-58, Tulane Studies in Zoology, 1957-58; contbr. numerous articles to profl. jours. Mem. Soc. Environ. Toxicology, Am. Soc. Zoologists (edn. com. 1978-79), Sigma Xi. Democrat. Methodist. Home and Office: 1730 Broadway New Orleans LA 70118

FINIZZI, MARGUERITE H(ELENE), educator; b. Allentown, Pa., Nov. 16, 1934; d. John Michael and Margaret Mary (Havrilla) Martin; BS in Secondary Edn., Kutztown State Coll., 1956; MA in English, Lehigh U., 1973; m. Joseph Anthony Finizzi, Nov. 19, 1954. Tchr. English, Harrison-Morton Jr. High Sch., Allentown, 1956-64, Louis E. Dieruff High Sch., Allentown, 1964-76, Allen High Sch., Allentown, 1976—; adviser pubs. Allen HighSch., 1978—, Quill and Scroll chpt., 1978, intramural bowling, 1985-88; instr. to develop. drug edn. competency for tchrs., Pa. dept. edn. Student Assistance Program and Intervention Team Tng., 1987; mem. in-service council Allentown Sch. Dist., 1987—; welfare chmn. AWTC, 1987—; discussion leader for jr. classes Jewish Day Sch., 1969-71; v.p. Fearless Ladies Bowling League, 1986-87; judge numerous acad. contests, Tchr. Expectations and Student Achievement, 1987, coordinator implementation, 1988; lectr., speaker in field; seminar discussion leader Council of Youth, 1980; adviser Student Newspaper Adv. Program. Pres. Lehigh County (Pa.) Coordinating Council, 1967-71; mem. steering com. Allentown Sch. Dist., 1984. Recipient Meritorious award Kutztown State Coll., 1956; Newspaper Fund fellow, 1981; Commonwealth Partnerships fellow for lit. Inst. Secondary Tchrs., 1985. Mem. NEA, AAUW, Nat. Council Tchrs. English (co-chmn. conf. 1985, bd. judges 1987), Pa. Council Tchrs. English (bd. judges, 1987), Pa. State Edn. Assn. (editor eastern region constn.), Allentown Edn. Assn. (social chairperson 1964-79, exec. sec. 1964-69), Allentown Women Tchrs. Club (editor constn. and by-laws, welfare chmn. 1986-88), Lehigh U. Alumni, Kutztown U. Alumni (pres. Lehigh County 1969-72), Columbia Sch. Press Assn. (bd. judges, 1987, adviser Reflector Sci. newsletter, 1979-80), Pa. Sch. Press Assn. Home: 3025 Pearl Ave Allentown PA 18103

FINK, DIANA, insurance consultant; b. St. Petersburg, Fla., Aug. 4, 1955; d. Harold W. and Deloras (Muller) Knight; m. Bernard James Fink; 1 child Bernard Joseph. Student, St. Petersburg Jr. Coll. Dep. commr. in-charge Fla. State Ins. Commr's. Office, 1972-84; office mgr. Wallace, Welch and Willlingham, St. Petersburg, 1984-88, v.p., 1988—; instr. State of Fla. property and casualty qualification licensing courses. Vol. March Dimes, 1984-85; mem. Suncoast Cathedral Ch., St. Petersburg, Missionette leader, fouder-leader Sonlight Puppeteers; tchr. Fire Safety Edn., St. Petersburg Fire Dept.; child abuse counselor, student motivator, tutor, Pinellas County Sch. Mem. Ins. Women St. Petersburg (various coms.), Nat. Assn. Ins. Women (pres. 1986-87, chmn. pub. relations com. 1985-86, other coms.), Nat. Assn. Female Exec., Ind. Insurors Greater St. Petersburg, Cert. Profl. Ins. Women (cert.), Cert. Ins. Counselors (cert.). Democrat. Mem. Assemblies God.

FINK, HEIDI MARIE, banker; b. Woodruff, Wis., Aug. 7, 1963; d. Gerald Duane and Sylvia Marie (Meckelholt) Bettin; m. Michael W. Fink, Mar. 24, 1984. Student, Nicolet Coll., 1984—. Clk. ins. Lakeland Med. Assn., Woodruff, 1981-84; loan officer Valley Nat. Bank, Woodruff, 1984—. Mem. Lakeland Area Jaycees (treas. 1986—). Roman Catholic. Home: 8826 French Ln Woodruff WI 54568

FINK, JENNIE CONNIE, leasing company executive; b. Phila., Aug. 9, 1926; d. Matthew and Angelina (DePaul) Rossi; m. Eugene Andrew Fink, Nov. 23, 1968 (dec.); 1 child, Mark Matthew. Student, Levitan Bus. Sch. Corr. Sears, Roebuck & Co., Phila., 1944-59; sec. Tony DePaul & Son, Phila., 1959-61; exec. sec. White Motor Co., Phila., 1963-65, Midvale Heppenstall, Phila., 1965-68; sec./treas. Transp. Leasing Systems Inc., North Wales, Pa., 1972-79; pres. Transp. Leasing Systems Inc., North Wales, 1979—. Mem. Pvt. Carrier Conf., Pa. Motor Truck Assn., U.S. C. of C., Horsham C. of C. Republican. Roman Catholic. Home: 1832 Webster Ln Amber PA 19002 Office: Transp Leasing Systems Inc English Village Profl Ctr Rts 309 and 63 North Wales PA 19454

FINK, LINDA MARIE, pathologist; b. Loma Linda, Calif., Jan. 20, 1959; d. Ivan Leon and Elizabeth Campos (Costa) Reeve; m. David Bruce Fink, Feb. 21, 1949; 1 child, Aaron David. Student, U. So. Calif., 1988. Office asst. Dr. Reeve & Burlison, Sierra Madre, Calif., 1974-80; microbiology asst. U. Calif., Riverside, 1978; microbiology tech. Loma Linda U., 1976-79, cardiology tech., 1978-79; cardiology tech. St. Lukes Hosp., Pasadena, Calif., 1979-80; with cardiology section Meth. Hosp. of So. Calif., Arcadia, 1980-81; tumor registry, pathology coordinator pathology dept. Foothill Presbyn. Hosp., Glendora, Calif., 1981-84, 86—. Democrat. Office: Foothill Presbyn Hosp 250 S Grand Ave Glendora CA 91740

FINK, LOIS MARIE, art historian; b. Michigan City, Ind., Dec. 30, 1927; d. George Edward and Marie Helen (Hensz) F. B.A., Capital U., 1951; M.A., U. Chgo., 1955, Ph.D., 1970; H.H.D. (hon.), Capital U., 1982. Instr. Lenoir Rhyne Coll., Hickory, N.C., 1955-56; instr. Midland Coll., Fremont, Nebr., 1956-58; asst. prof. Roosevelt U., Chgo., 1958-70; curator Nat. Mus. of Am. Art, Smithsonian Instn., Washington, 1970—; adv. com. Washington area Archives Am. Art, 1979—. Co-author: Academy: The Academic Tradition in American Art, 1975; contbg. author: Elizabeth Nourse: A Salon Career, 1983; contbr. articles to profl. jours. Fellow The Soc. for the Arts, Religion, and Contemporary Culture; mem. Coll. Art Assn., Am. Studies Assn. Office: Nat Mus of Am Art Smithsonian Instn Washington DC 20560

FINK, ROSALIND SUE, lawyer, university administrator; b. Cleve., May 24, 1946; d. Sanford and Bess (Tiktin) F.; m. Robert Cannel Herz, Feb. 4, 1979; 1 child, Zachary Robert. AB, Barnard Coll., 1968; JD, Yale U., 1972. Bar: N.Y. 1973, U.S. Dist. Ct. (so. dist.) N.Y., 1973, U.S. Ct. Appeals (2d cir.) 1975, U.S. Supreme Ct., 1977. Assoc. Proskauer Rose Goetz & Mendelsohn, N.Y.C., 1972-74, Dretzin & Kauff, P.C., N.Y.C., 1974-75; asst. atty. gen. N.Y. State Dept. Law, N.Y.C., 1975-80; dir. Office Equal Opportunity and Affirmative Action, Columbia U., N.Y.C., 1980—. Exec. bd. Barnard Coll. Women's Ctr., N.Y.C., 1980-84; staff Am. Council Edn. Task Force on Affirmative Action, Washington, 1981-83. Mem. N.Y. County Lawyers' Assn. (bd. dirs. 1982-88, spl. com. programs and pub. issues 1985—, com. women's rights 1973—, chair 1981-84, house com. 1983—, civil rights com. 1987-88, word processing com. 1982-84), Assn. Bar City of N.Y. (civil rights com. 1980-83, edn. com. 1985-88—), Nat. Assn. Coll. and Univ. Attys. (vice chmn. affirmative action and nondiscrimination section 1983-84, chmn. 1984—, honors and awards com. 1987-88, program com. 1985-86). Democrat. Jewish. Office: Columbia U 305 Low Meml Library 116th St and Broadway New York NY 10027

FINK, VALERIE ANN, home economics educator; b. Chgo., Feb. 13, 1954; d. Joseph Michael and Elsie (Daghi) F. BA, Rosary Coll., 1976; MS, No. Ill. U., 1983, postgrad. Rosary Coll. Grad. Sch. Fine Arts, Florence, Italy, 1984, Iowa State U., 1986, Auburn U., 1986. Sales, gen. office Jamie Lynn Bridals, Chgo., 1976-77, Galzier Corp., Chgo., 1977-78; with Stone & Adler Advt., Chgo., 1978-79; substitute tchr. various high schs., Cook County, Ill., 1979; retail salesperson I. Magnin, Oak Brook, Ill., part-time, 1985-86; tchr., dept. chmn. Westchester Dist. 92 1/2, Ill., 1980—. Author cognitive skills test: Home Economics Basic Skills Indicator, 1982. Docent Chgo. Archtl. Found., 1981-85. Mem. Westchester Edn. Assn. (treas.), Am. Home Econs. Assn., Ill. Home Econs. Assn., Omicron Nu. Roman Catholic. Avocations: travel, golf, sewing, cooking, local theater guild prodns. Office: Westchester Middle Sch 1620 Norfolk Westchester IL 60153

FINKELSTEIN, ANITA JO, lawyer; b. Cleve., Jan. 2, 1957; d. Denis and Helen (Graber) Fabian; m. Ben Finkelstein, Mar. 20, 1983. BA in Econs. and Bus. Adminstrn., Wittenberg U., 1979; JD, Yale U., 1982. Bar: D.C. 1982; CPA, Ill. Assoc. Shaw, Pittman, Potts & Trowbridge, Washington, 1982—. Home: 4434 Garrison St NW Washington DC 20016 Office: Shaw Pittman Potts & Trowbridge 2300 N St NW Washington DC 20037

FINKELSTEIN, GAIL FREDRICA ILLMAN, chemist; b. Mt. Vernon, N.Y., Aug. 6, 1949; d. Isadore and Charlotte Rhoda (Stengel) Illman; m. Jacob Noah Finkelstein, Aug. 22, 1971; children: David Brian, Ilana Caryl. BA in Chemistry, Carnegie-Mellon U., 1971; MS in Biol. Materials, Northwestern U., 1976. Sr. environ. chemist Rochester (N.Y.) Products div. Gen. Motors Corp., 1979—; cons. County-Wide Fire Dept., Monroe County, N.Y., 1982—, Indsl. Mgmt. Council, Rochester, 1983—; bd. dirs. Chem. Hazard Info. Team, Rochester, Ctr. for Environ. Info. Contbr. articles to profl. jours.; co-developer chem. response system, 1979. Pres. Highland-Grove Homeowners Assn., Brighton, N.Y., 1984—; advisor Monroe County Dept. Planning, 1985—; bd. dirs. Rochester Area Hillel Found., 1986—; mem. Monroe County Local Emergency Planning Com., 1987—. Recipient Recognition award Rochester Safety Council, 1984. Mem. Acad. Hazardous Materials Mgmt. (diplomate), Acad. Hazard Control Mgmt. (diplomate). Democrat. Jewish. Home: 74 Westerloe Ave Rochester NY 14620 Office: Rochester Products div Gen Motors Corp 25 Franklin St Rochester NY 14692

FINKELSTEIN, HONORA MOORE, writer, editor, consultant; b. Midwest, Wyo., July 18, 1941; d. Stanley and Gladys Beatrice (Parker) Moore; m. Thomas Norton Lynch, May 16, 1964 (div. Feb. 1980); children: Aileen Marie, Kathleen Bernadette, Bridget Colleen; m. Jay Laurence Finkelstein, Mar. 15, 1980; 1 child, Michael Marcus. BA in English, Rice U., 1963; MA in English, U. Tex., 1970; PhD in English, U. Houston, 1976; grad. pub. course, Rice U., 1977. Teaching fellow U. Houston, 1971-76; publs. editor Ctr. Mgmt. Studies Johnson Space Ctr., 1974-75; asst. prof. Houston Bapt. U., 1975-79; instr. U. Tex., El Paso, 1979-80; owner, operator Communications Unltd., Houston and El Paso, 1976-80, Communications, Ink, Reston, Va., 1980—; editor lifestyle sect. Times Newspaper, Arundel Orgn., No. Va., 1987—; workshop dir. Internat. Women's Writing Guild, N.Y., 1986—; freelance cons. Conoco Oil Co., Aliviance Drug Abuse Clinic, Xebec Corp., Creative Wellness Programs, Houston, El Paso, Washington, 1976—. Author: A Very Short Guide to Style, 1975; co-author: Car Buyer Beware, 1977, Beautiful Skin, 1985; contbr. numerous papers, articles, presentations and revs. to profl jours. Participant RESULTS Lobby, No. Va., 1987. Served with USN, 1963-64. Grantee Nat. Soc. Arts & Letters, 1970; named Faculty Woman of Yr. Assn. Women Students Houston Bapt. U., 1979; recipient 1st place award for best presentation of a spl. holiday, 2nd place award for best lifestyle section Suburban Newspapers of Am. Assn., 1987, 1st place award Va. Press Assn., 1988. Mem. Internat. Women's Writing Guild, Nat. League Am. Pen Women, No. Va. Writers' Network, Grad. English Soc. (pres. 1974-75), Phi Kappa Phi. Home: 12202 Nutmeg Ln Reston VA 22091 Office: Times Newspapers 405 Glenn Dr Sterling VA 22170

FINKENKELLER, KAREN MARIA ZANG, marketing professional; b. St. Louis, Dec. 21, 1941; d. Charles R. and Mary Etta (Shoults) Zang; m. Donald Joseph Finkenkeller, Oct. 15, 1960; children: Lisa Michelle, Mark Donald, Donald-Jeffrey Terence. Student, Lindenwood Coll., St. Charles, Mo., 1980-82, 87—. Sr. customer rep. Xerox Corp., St. Louis, 1965-73; sales rep. Exec. Cons., Clayton, Mo., 1973; dir. admissions Hickey Bus. Sch., St. Louis, 1973-76; owner retail-wholesale bus., St. Louis, 1976-78; territorial mgr. Robert Morris Coll., Carthage, Ill., 1978-82; rep. ITT Tech. Inst., St. Louis, 1982-83, sales supr., 1983-85, mktg. and sales mgr., 1985—; area mktg. and sales mgr. ITT Ednl. Services, St. Louis and Kansas City, 1987—. Mem. Nat. Assn. Female Execs. Republican. Roman Catholic. Home: #3 Old Mill Rd Troy IL 62294 Office: ITT Tech Inst 3750 Lindell Blvd Saint Louis MO 63108

FINLAY, AUDREY JOY, educator, naturalist; b. Davidson, Sask., Can., Sept. 18, 1932; d. Leonard Noel and Vilhemine Marie (Rossander) Barton; m. James Campbell Finlay, June 18, 1955; children: Barton Brett, Warren Hugh, Rhonda Marie. BA, U. Man., 1954; profl. diploma in edn., U. Alta., 1974, MEd, 1978. Social worker Children's Aid, Brandon, Man., 1954-55; foster home worker Social Services Province of Sask., Regina, 1955-56, City of Edmonton, Alta., 1956-59; naturalist City of Edmonton, 1965-74; tchr., cons., adminstr. Edmonton Pub. Bd., 1974—; cons. edn., interpretation numerous projects, 1965—. Author: Winter Here and Now, 1982; co-author: Alberta Parks, 1987; contbr. articles to profl. jours. Chmn., chief exec. officer Wildlife '87: Canadian Centennial Wildlife Conservation, 1985-87. Named Ms. Chatelaine, Chatelaine Mag., 1975. Fellow Alta. Tchrs. Assn., Environ. Outdoor Council (founder, 1st pres., disting.); mem. Canadian Nature Fedn. (v.p. 1984—), Edmonton Natural History Soc. (Lonan Goulden award 1980), Am. Nature Study Soc. (bd. dirs. 1984—), N.Am. Environ. Edn. Assn. (bd. dirs. 1983—), Fedn. Alta. Naturalists (bd. dirs. 1970s). Home and Office: Box 8644 Station L, Edmonton, AB Canada T6C 4J4

FINLAY, CHERYL SCHRATZ, academic program director; b. Pitts., Apr. 12, 1954; d. Walter Alfred and Helen Anne (Budnick) Schratz; m. Kevin Robert Finlay, Aug. 26, 1978. BA, Thiel Coll., 1976; MEd, Duquesne U., 1977; PhD, U. Pitts., 1986. Dir. career planning and placement Point Park Coll., Pitts., 1978-84; dir. career programs, ctr. profl. devel. Chatham Coll., Pitts., 1984-87, exec. dir. ctr. profl. devel., 1987—. Mem. Nat. Assn. Female Execs., AAUW, Am. Soc. Tng. and Devel., Nat. Assn. Women Deans, Adminstrs., and Counselors, Coll. Placement Council, Exec. Women's Council, Mid-Atlantic Placement Assn., Pa. Assn. Women Deans, Adminstrs., and Counselors, Pa. Counseling Assn., Pa. Coll. and Personnel Assn., Thiel Coll. Alumni Assn. (bd. dirs.). Republican. Lutheran. Home: 623 Whitney Ave Pittsburgh PA 15221 Office: Chatham Coll Woodland Rd Pittsburgh PA 15232

FINLEY, ANN MARIE, marketing executive; b. Milw., Mar. 29, 1962; d. Richard Donald and Helen Margaret (Sullivan) F. BA, Georgetown U., 1984. Regional mgr. Aims Media, Van Nuys, Calif., 1984-85; mktg. specialist Nat. Archives, Washington, 1985; dir. govt. mktg. Encyc. Britannica Films, Chgo., 1986-87; mktg. dir. The Exec. TV Workshop, Washington, 1987—; editorial cons. Am. Enterprise Inst., Washington, 1984—. Mem. Women in Communications, Am. League of Lobbyists, Women in Advt. and Mktg., Am. Women in Radio and TV. Home: 1510 N 12th St Apt 303 Arlington VA 22209

FINN, BARBARA JUNE, nurse, educator; b. Evansville, Ind., Dec. 18, 1938; d. Roscoe F. and Doris J. (Lehmann) Norris; diploma Protestant Deaconess Hosp. Sch. Nursing, 1959; student U. Evansville, 1956-57, St. Petersburg Jr. Coll., 1968, U. South Fla., 1976-78; 1 dau., Melissa Ann. Nurse physician's office, Clearwater, Fla., 1959-63; gen. med. nurse Morton F. Plant Hosp., Clearwater, 1963-66; nurse physician's office, Clearwater, 1966-68; head nurse emergency dept. Clearwater Community Hosp., 1968-72; adminstrv. coordinator to emergency physicians, Clearwater, 1972-76; chairperson emergency med. tech. program St. Petersburg (Fla.) Jr. Coll., 1976—; cons. to Fla. Dept. Edn., 1980-81, Tampa Bay Med. Center (Fla.), 1974-75; chmn. edn. com. Tampa Bay Regional Health Planning Council, 1979-80. Mem. Pinellas County Emergency Med. Services Adv. Council, vice-chmn., 1979-80, chmn. edn. and tng. com., 1981-82, chmn. subcom. C.P.R., 1982; mem. adv. council Fla. Gulf Health Systems Agy., 1981-82; instr.-trainer Am. Heart Assn., 1978—; sec. bd. dirs. Pinellas County Tchrs. Credit Union, 1984—, chmn. 1987-88; mem. Clearwater Community Chorus, Pinellas Advanced Life Support, 1987—. Mem. Fla. Nurses Assn. (dir. 1968-70, v.p. 1968-69), Nat. Assn. Emergency Med. Technicians and Paramedics, Fla. Emergency Med. Technician Assn., Emergency Med. Service Educators Fla. (rec. sec. 1982-83). Democrat. Presbyterian. Home: 1316 S Evergreen Dr Clearwater FL 34616 Office: PO Box 13489 Saint Petersburg FL 33733

FINN, JOAN LOCKWOOD, writer, public relations executive, educator; b. Plainfield, N.J., June 6, 1929; d. William Albert and Ada Louise (Dayton) F.; BA in Am. History, Harvard U., 1951; MA, Columbia U., 1979, EdM, 1981, EdD, 1984. Copywriter, J.C. Penney Co., Inc., 1957-58; jr. account exec. Dudley-Anderson-Yutzey, 1958-61; account exec. Theodore R. Sills & Co., 1961-63, Ted Bates & Co., 1963-67; account supr. Henderson & Roll, 1967-69; dir. press relations Motion Picture Assn. Am., N.Y.C., 1969-73; communications specialist Coopers & Lybrand, N.Y.C., 1973-78, Urban Acad. for Mgmt., Inc., N.Y.C., 1978-82, Am. Inst. CPAs, N.Y.C., 1982-84; dir. pub. relations KMG Main Hurdman, N.Y.C., 1984-87; account mgr. Hill, Holliday, Connors & Cosmopulos, N.Y.C., 1987—; instr. communications skills Mgmt. Inst. NYU, 1987—, Grad Schs. Bus. and Pub. Adminstrn., 1987—. Mem. Pub. Relations Soc. Am. (accredited). Democrat. Presbyterian. Club: Harvard (N.Y.C.). Author: Heritage of Evil, 1968; Kiss More, or How to Get Across in Writing, 1977; librettist: (operetta) Chicken Little, 1973; editor Diet Ann., 1973; Diet Yearbook, 1973; contbr. articles to Motor Boating, Ideal Romances, Am. Mercury, Jack O'Dwyer's Newsletter, New Ideas for Figure and Diet, Modern Maturity, Public Relations Jour. Home: 17 W 54th St New York NY 10019 Office: Hill Holliday Connors & Cosmopulos 885 3d Ave New York NY 10022-4802

FINN, RUTH ANGELL, town clerk-treasurer; b. Randolph, Vt., July 19, 1935; d. Philip Alvin and Alice Marion (Amee) Angell; m. Richard Murley Finn, June 18, 1960; children—Charles Philip, Carolyn Ruth. B.S., Simmons Coll., 1957; postgrad. N.E. Law Sch., 1958; grad. Vt. Real Estate Commn., 1972—. Intern, U.S. Dept. Budget, Washington, 1957; adminstrv. asst. John Marsh Agy., Barre, Vt., 1960-61; paralegal Angell & Angell, Randolph, Vt., 1968-84; clk.-treas. Town of Barre, 1984—. Co-chmn. ARC Blood Bank, Barre, 1966-70. Mem. Internat. Inst. Mcpl. Clks., Vt. Town Clks. Assn., AAUW (pres. 1965-67), DAR (state officer 1983—). Club: Simmons. Lodge: Order Eastern Star. Avocations: music (piano and organ); skiing; genealogical history, tennis, golf. Home: 23 Windy Wood Rd Barre VT 05641 Office: Town of Barre Municipal Bldg Websterville VT 05678

FINN, TONI JEAN, education program director; b. Castine, Maine, Oct. 18, 1951; d. Mark Francis Sawyer and Jean Ada (Witham) Wight; m. Don William Finn, Dec. 18, 1970; children: Kelly William, Leslie Diane. BS in Acctg., Ark. State U., 1977. Sec., bookkeeper Finn's Trailer Sales, Abilene, Tex., 1972-74; office mgr. Robert J. Martin, DDS, Fayetteville, Ark., 1977-78; rate clk. Standard Register Co., Fayetteville, Ark., 1978-80; adminstrv. asst. Mason, Warner and Co., Lubbock, Tex., 1980-85; assoc. dir. Ctr. for Profl. Devel., Lubbock, Tex., 1985—. Served with USN, 1969-71. Mem. Am. Bus. Women's Assn., Am. Soc. Tng. and Devel., Assn. Sch. Bus. Ofcls. Mem. Ch. of Christ. Home: 4406 88 Place Lubbock TX 79424 Office: Ctr for Profl Devel PO Box 4550 Lubbock TX 79409

FINNEGAN, LANNETTA KAYE, financial analyst; b. Havre de Grace, Md., Feb. 26, 1956; d. Wilbur Jesse and Joan Belle (Martin) Hildebrand. BA, U. Md.-Balt., 1976; M in City and Regional Planning, Cath. U. Am., 1981. Cons., Peat Marwick Mitchell, Washington, 1974-81; transp. analyst Mass Transit Adminstrn., Balt., 1981-83, spl. asst. to dir. fin., 1983-85, mgr. fin. analysis, 1985-86; dir. strategic planning Md. Port Adminstrn., 1986-88; mgr. planning, 1988—. Mem. Smithsonian Resident Assoc. Program, 1977—; lector, eucharistic minister St. Joseph's Catholic Ch., Odenton, Md., 1979-83. Mem. Am. Mgmt. Assn., Am. Planning Assn., Am. Inst. Cert. Planners, Women's Transp. Seminar (pres. 1983-84; award 1984), U. Md. Alumni Assn. Home: 301 Warren Ave Apt 409 Baltimore MD 21230 Office: Md Port Adminstrn World Trade Ctr Baltimore MD 21202

FINNERTY, EILEEN, personnel director; b. Waushara, Wis., Jan. 5, 1928; d. Clifford J. and Hazel (Baitinger) F. BA, U. Wis., 1950, sr. profl. in human resources. Personnel and tng. rep. Gimbels-Midwest, Milw., 1950-58, mgr. personnel br. store, 1958-66, asst. personnel dir., 1966-76, dir. wage and benefits, 1976-78; dir. personnel T.A. Chapman Co., Milw., 1978-80, St. Norbert Coll., De Pere, Wis., 1980—; personnel cons. pvt. practice and vol., De Pere, 1980—; speaker St. Norbert Coll., De Pere, 1980—. Mem. NE Wis. Personnel Assn. (sec., treas. 1981-83), Coll. and Univ. Personnel Assn., Am. Soc. Personnel Adminstrs., Mgmt. Women. Democrat. Roman Catholic. Office: St Norbert Coll De Pere WI 54115

FINNERTY, LOUISE HOPPE, government official; b. Alexandria, Va., Jan. 19, 1949; d. William G. and Ruth A. (Ehren) Hoppe; m. John D. Finnerty, May 21, 1988. B.A., Va. Commonwealth U., 1971; postgrad., Am. U., 1972-73. Staff asst. to Dr. Henry Kissinger Nat. Security Council, Washington, 1971-73; adminstrv. asst. Nat. Petroleum Council, Washington, 1973-75; profl. staff mem. Senate Armed Service Com., Washington, 1976-81; spl. asst. Office Legis. Affairs, Dept. State, Washington, 1981-84, dep. asst. sec. of state, 1984-88; mgr. govt. affairs Pepsi Co., Inc., Purchase, N.Y., 1988—. Republican. Lutheran. Home: 330 E 75th St 30B New York NY 10021 Office: PepsiCo Inc Purchase NY 10577

FINNEY, JOAN MARIE MCINROY, state official; b. Topeka, Feb. 12, 1925; d. Leonard L. and Mary M. (Sands) McInroy; m. Spencer W. Finney, Jr., July 24, 1957; children: Sally, Dick, Mary. B.A., Washburn U., 1974. Mem. staff U.S. Senator Frank Carlson, Topeka and Washington, 1953-69; commr. elections Shawnee County, Kans., 1970-72; adminstrv. asst. to mayor of Topeka 1973-74; treas. State of Kans., Topeka, 1974—. Bd. dirs. Hayden High Sch. Alumni Assn., Washburn Alumni Assn., Kans. Community Service orgns., St. Francis Hosp. and Med. Ctr. Aux., Mended Hearts Inc. Mem. Nat. Assn. State Auditors (pres. 1987—), Comptrollers and Treas. , Nat. Assn. State Treas., Nat. Unclaimed Property Assn., Kans. Fedn. Women's Democratic Clubs, Reinisch Rose Garden Soc., Santa Fe Railroad Ret. Employers Club, Am. Legion Aux., Sigma Alpha Iota. Catholic. Office: Office State Treas 700 Harrison Topeka KS 66601 *

FINNIGAN, SHEILA ELIZABETH, artist; b. Cleve., Nov. 27, 1940; d. John Michael and Betty (Friedberg) F.; m. James H. Feldman, July 27, 1969; children: Maureen, Abigail. BA, Ohio State U., 1963; MS, UCLA, 1968; BFA, Coll. Arts and Crafts, 1972. Artist, Chgo., 1973-88; represented by ARC Gallery, Chgo., 1987—. One-woman shows include ARC Gallery, Chgo., 1988, Noyes Cultural Art Ctr., Evanston, Ill., 1988; exhibited in group shows at Oak Park (Ill.) Art League Ann. Show, 1986, NAB Gallery, 1986, Evanston & Vicinity 7th Ann. Juried Art Exhbn., 1986, Artemesia Gallery, 1986, ARC Gallery, 1986, Skokie (Ill.) Fine Arts Commn. Ann. Show, 1986, 87, Countryside (Ill.) Art Ctr., 1987, 88, 89 (1st prize), Suburban Fine Arts Ctr., 1987 (award of excellence ann. show 1987), Esther Saks Gallery, 1987, State of Ill. Art Gallery, 1988, Limelight, Chgo., 1988, ARC at Chgo. Internat. Art Exposition, 1988; two-person show Ohio State U., Newark campus, 1988; work featured on Sta. WGN-TV, Chgo., 1988; work appeared in Chicago Tribune mag., 1988. Mem. Nat. Acad. Recording Arts and Scis. Club: Chgo. Press. Studio: 999 Green Bay Rd Glencoe IL 60022

FINORE, DIANE, sales executive; b. Abington, Pa., Aug. 11, 1950; d. Carmen George and Anna B. (Signore) F. AS, Tobe Coburn Sch., 1972; BA, Temple U., 1974; MA, NYU, 1984. Dir. spl. events Mus. Am. Folk Art, N.Y.C., 1982-85; pub. rep. Taxi Pub. Inc., N.Y.C., 1986-87; dir. sales SALES, Inc., N.Y.C., 1987—. Roman Catholic. Office: Sales Inc 699 Madison Ave New York NY 10021

FIOCK, SHARI LEE, design entrepreneur, researcher; b. Weed, Calif., Oct. 25, 1941; d. Webster Bruce and Olevia May (Pruett) F.; m. June 6, 1966 (div. 1974); children—Webster Clinton Pfingsten, Sterling Curtis. Cert. Art Instrn. Sch., Mpls., 1964; pvt. student, Lic. health, life and disability, Calif. Copywriter Darron Assocs., Eugene, Oreg., 1964-66; staff artist Oreg. Holidays, Springfield, 1966-69, part-time 1971; co-owner, designer Artre Enterprises, Eugene, 1969-74; design entrepreneur Shari & Assocs., Yreka, Calif., 1974— (retained as cons., devel. sec., chief fin. officer Cascade World Four Season Resort, Siskiyou County, Calif., 1980-86); cons., pres. Reunions, Family, Yreka, 1984—. Designer 5 ton chain saw sculpture, Oreg. Beaver, 1967; illustrator: Holiday Fun Book, 1978; creator Klamath Nat. Forest Interpretive Mus., 1979—. Author, illustrator Calling All Descendants, 1986. Residential capt. United Way, Eugene, 1972; researcher Beaver Ofcl. State Animal, Eugene, 1965-71; counselor Boy Scouts, 1983—. Mem. Nat. Assn. Interpreters, Nat. Mus. of Women in the Arts, Nat. Writers Club (founder, pres. Siskiyou chpt., past v.p. State of Jefferson chpt.). Avocations: family activities; outdoor recreation; travel; theater; music. Home and Office: 406 Walter's Ln Yreka CA 96097

FIONDELLA, JUNE LEA BELL, public utility executive; b. Meriden, Conn., May 24, 1941; d. Joseph Doran and Mildred (Hourigan) Bell; m. Louis Andrew Fiondella, Sept. 2, 1963; children—Kim Lisa, Tracy Lea. B.S. in Bus. Mgmt. cum laude, Post Coll., 1983. With Northeast Utilities,

Hartford, Conn., 1959—, mgr. communications services, 1976-80, mgr. communications and adv. services, 1980-83, mgr. communications services and spl. projects, 1983—; chmn. Electric Council N.E. Pub. Info. Com., 1982. Recpient Pres.'s Circle of Distinction for acad. excellence, Post Coll., 1982. Mem. Women in Communications (asst. treas. 1987-88, bd. dirs. 1988-89), Pub. Relations Soc. Am., Internat. Assn. Bus. Communicators, Nuclear Energy Women, Pub. Utilities Communicators Assn. (pres. 1986, regional chmn. New Eng. 1983, Maple Leaf award 1984, dir.-at-large, 1988), Advt. Club Greater Hartford, Conn. Assn. Bus. Communicators, Hartford Woman's Network, Nat. Assn. Female Execs. Democrat. Roman Catholic. Home: 1414 Meriden Ave Southington CT 06489 Office: NE Utilities Box 270 Hartford CT 06141

FIORATTI, HELEN COSTANTINO, designer, antique dealer; b. N.Y.C., Mar. 16, 1931; d. Arturo and Ruth (Teschner) Costantino; B.S., Parsons Sch. Design; m. Nereo Fioratti, Nov. 19, 1963; 1 dau., Arianna. Jewelry, furniture designer; pres. L'Antiquaire and the Connoisseur, Inc., N.Y.C. Exhibited in one-woman shows. Mem. F.W. Richmond Found. (bd. dirs.). Republican. Author: How to Know French Antiques. Home: 555 Park Ave New York NY 10021 Office: 36 E 73d St New York NY 10021

FIORAVANTI, NANCY ELEANOR, banker; b. Gloucester, Mass., Apr. 10, 1935; d. Richard Joseph and Evelyn Grace (Souza) Fioravanti; grad. high sch. Various positions and depts. Bank of New Eng.-North Shore (formerly Cape Ann Bank and Trust Co., successor to Gloucester Safe Deposit & Trust Co.), Gloucester, 1953—, with trust dept., 1959-86, asst. trust officer, 1970-84, trust officer, 1984-86; trust officer Cape Ann Savs. Bank, 1986—. Treas. art adv. com. Gloucester Lyceum and Sawyer Free Library. Mem. Nat. Assn. Bank Women, Bus. and Profl. Women's Club. Home: PO Box 1638 Gloucester MA 01930 Office: 109 Main St Gloucester MA 01930

FIORE, JOAN DE WOLFE, civic leader; b. Detroit, July 15, 1924; d. Richard Perrien and Rachel Elizabeth De Wolfe; m. Pasquale Peter Fiore, Nov. 25, 1949; children—Richard, Jill. Grad. Kingswood Girls Sch., Cranbrook, Mich.; student UCLA. Vice pres. Fitness with Finesse, Inc., Houston; regent, Princeton chpt. DAR, 1974-77, Seimes microfilm chmn., Washington, 1977—; state regent N.J., Nat. Soc. Magna Charta Dames; mem. Assn. of Descs. of Knights of the Garter, Gen. Soc. Mayflower Descs., Elder William Brewster Soc., First Colony of Mayflower Descs., Plantagenet Kings of Eng. Soc., Sovereign Colonial Soc. Americans of Royal Descent, Richard 3d Soc., Nat. Soc. Colonial Dames of XVII Century, Japan Soc. Vol. chmn. Med. Ctr., Princeton, N.J., 1960-77; Natural History Mus., N.Y.C., Nat. Trust Historic Preservation; Princeton Hist. Soc., Friends of Vielles Maisons Fracaises Inc. Republican. Quaker. Home: 18 Sturgis Rd Kendall Park NJ 08824

FIORE, MARY, magazine editor. Former editor Photoplay mag.; mng. editor Good Housekeeping mag. Office: Good Housekeeping 959 8th Ave New York NY 10019 *

FIORE-BARTA, JACQUELINE ANN, retail clothing company administrator; b. Chgo., Jan. 30, 1961; d. John Anthony and Giovanna (Interlandi) Fiore; m. William James Barta, Sept. 28, 1985. BS, Ill. State U., 1983. Asst. store mgr. The Closet, Normal, Ill., 1981-83, Kohl's Dept. Stores, Indpls., 1983-84; coordinator, developer regional tng. programs Mainstreet, Bannockburn, Ill., 1984—. Mem. Nat. Assn. Female Execs., Kappa Omicron Phi. Roman Catholic. Office: Mainstreet 2345 N Waukegan Rd Bannockburn IL 60015

FIORELLA, BEVERLY JEAN, medical technologist; b. Owensboro, Ky., Oct. 29, 1930; d. Gabriel and Agnes Loretta (Kurz) F.; B.S., Webster Coll./St. Louis U., 1952; M.A., Central Mich. U., 1976. Chief microbiology and blood bank St. Mary's Hosp., Kansas City, Mo., 1956-67; instr., asst. prof. med. lab. scis. dept. Coll. Assoc. Health Professions, U. Ill., Chgo., 1967-74, assoc. prof., 1974-80, prof., 1980—, assoc. head dept. med. lab. scis., 1977—, grad. program coordinator, 1977-81; mem. adv. panel on health ins. Subcom. Health of Com. on Ways and Means, Ho. of Reps., 1975-80; cons. lab. improvement sect. immunohematology divs. labs. Dept. Public Health State of Ill., 1975-85; cons. editor Clin. Lab. Scis., 1987—. Named Med. Technologist of Yr., Mo. Soc. Med. Technologists, 1967. Mem. Am. Soc. Med. Tech. (pres. 1976-77), Am. Assn. Blood Banks, Ill. Med. Tech. Assn. (exec. sec. 1987—, named Ill. Med. Technologist of Yr. 1976), Chgo. Soc. Med. Technologists (treas., dir. 1969-70), Chicagoland Blood Bank Soc. (v.p. 1975-76), Acad. Clin. Lab. Physicians and Scientists, Am. Soc. Allied Health Professions, Internat. Soc. Blood Transfusion, Alpha Mu Tau. Mem. bd. editors Med. Tech.- A Series, 1970-74. Office: U Ill Chgo Dept Med Lab Scis M/C 518 808 S Wood St Chicago IL 60612

FIORI, PAMELA, editor; b. Newark, Feb. 26, 1944; d. Edward A. and Rita Marie (Rascati) F.; m. Colton Givner. B.A. cum laude, Jersey City State Coll., 1966. Tchr. English Gov. Livingston High Sch., Berkeley Heights, N.J., 1966-67; assoc. editor Holiday Mag., N.Y.C., 1968-71; assoc. editor Travel & Leisure Mag., N.Y.C., 1971-74, sr. editor, 1974-75, editor-in-chief, 1975-80; editor-in-chief, exec. v.p. Am. Express Pub. Corp. (Travel & Leisure/Food & Wine), 1980—. Contbr. articles to periodicals; columnist: Window Seat, 1976—. Named an Outstanding Young Woman of Am., 1976. Mem. Am. Soc. Mag. Editors, N.Y. Travel Writers. Home: 345 East 57th St New York NY 10022 Office: Travel & Leisure 1120 Ave of Americas New York NY 10036

FIORITO, FAYE LYNN, communications executive; b. Heilbron, Fed. Republic of West Germany, June 8, 1959; d. Donald and Janice Lorraine (Bower) F. BA, Muhlenberg Coll., 1981; degree in mktg., Nat. U., 1985. Adminstrv. asst. to staff dir. Fed. Reserve Bd., Washington, 1983-84; sales rep. Computerland Corp., San Diego, 1985-86; account exec. U.S. Sprint Communications, San Diego, 1986—. Fund raiser Multiple Sclerosis Soc., San Diego, 1985-86; active Big Sister Orgn., San Diego, 1986-87. Mem. Nat. Assn. of Profl. Saleswomen (treas. 1985-86), Winners Circle. Republican. Unitarian. Club: Toastmasters. Home: 12213 Carmel Vista Rd #236 San Diego CA 92130 Office: US Sprint Communications 2650 Camino del Rion San Diego CA 92108

FIPPINGER, GRACE J., telecommunications company executive; b. N.Y.C., Nov. 24, 1927; d. Fred Herman and Johanna Rose (Tesio) F. B.A., St. Lawrence U., 1948; LL.D. (hon.), Marymount Manhattan Coll., 1980; D.Comml. Sci. (hon.), Molloy Coll., 1982. Dist. mgr. N.Y. Telephone Co., South Nassau, 1957-65; div. mgr. N.Y. Telephone Co., 1965-71; gen. comml. mgr. N.Y. Telephone Co., Queens, 1971—, Bklyn., 1973—; v.p., sec., treas. N.Y. Telephone Co., 1974-84; v.p., treas., sec. NYNEX Corp., N.Y.C., 1984—; mem. Manhattan East adv. bd. Mfrs. Hanover Trust Co.; bd. dirs. Conn. Mut. Life Ins., Gulf & Western Industries, Inc., Apple Bank for Savs., Bear Stearns Co., Pfizer, Inc. Former mem. State Manpower Adv. Council; former mem. Gov.'s Econ. Devel. Adv. Council; past bd. dirs. Consumer Credit Counseling Service Greater N.Y., 1972—; hon. bd. dirs. Am. Cancer Soc., 1974—, YMCA Greater N.Y., 1975—; former dir. A.R.C., L.I., Nassau County Health and Welfare Council; trustee Citizens Budget Commn., 1974—; former dir. exec. bd. Nassau County Fedn. Republican Women. Named Woman of Year, Bus. and Profl. Women Nassau County, 1969, Woman of Achievement, Flatbush Bus. and Profl. Women's Assn., 1974, Woman of Year, Soroptimist Club Nassau County; hon. mem. Soroptimist Club Central Nassau, 1974; recipient John Peter Zenger award Nassau County Press Assn., 1975, Outstanding Bus. Women of 1977 award Marymount Manhattan Coll., 1978; honoree Catalyst Inc., 1977, Women's Equity Action League, 1978, Republican Women in Bus. and Industry, Cath. Med. Ctr. Bklyn./Queens, 1983, Girl Scouts, 1984, Clark Garden, Long Island, 1985. Mem. Am. Mgmt. Assn. (former trustee and mem. exec. com.), Nat. Assn. Corp. Treas., Fin. Execs. Inst., Am. Soc. Corp. Secs., Am. Soc. Corp. Treas. Inc., Fin. Womens Assn. N.Y., N.Y. Chamber Commerce and Industry (chmn. mems. council 1977-79), L.I. Assn., Ladies Profl. Golf Assn. (hon.). Clubs: St. Lawrence of L.I. (N.Y.C.), Columbus, Board Room (N.Y.C.). Home: 131 Terrace Ct Woodbury NY 11797 Office: Nynex Corp 335 Madison Ave New York NY 10017

FIREBAUGH, FRANCILLE MALOCH, university official; b. El Dorado, Ark., July 15, 1933; d. Delton Verdis and Dorothy Lucille (Measeles) Maloch, B.S., U. Ark., 1955, M.S., U. Tenn., 1956, Ph.D., Cornell U., 1962; m. John David Firebaugh, Dec. 28, 1970. Instr., U. Tex., Austin, 1956-58, asst. prof. home econs. Ohio State U., Columbus, 1962-65, asso. prof., 1965-69, prof., 1969-88, dir. Sch. Home Econs., 1973-82, acting v.p. agrl. adminstrn., exec. dean of agr., home econs., natural resources, 1982-83, assoc. provost Office Acad. Affairs, 1983-84, vice provost for internat. affairs, 1984-88; dean coll. human ecology Cornell U., Ithaca, N.Y., 1988—; mem. joint com. on agrl. research and devel. Bd. Internat. Food and Agr., 1982-87. Author: Home Management: Context and Concepts, 1975, Family Resource Management, 1981, 88. Bd. dirs. Columbus Council on World Affairs, 1987-88; moderator First Baptist Ch., 1981-83, 88. Mem. Nat. Council Family Relations, AAAS, Am. Home Econs. Found. (bd. dirs. 1987-89), Am. Home Econs. Assn., Ohio Home Econs. Assn., Ohio State U. Faculty Club (pres. 1988), Assn. Women in Devel. (sec. 1988—), Sigma Xi, Sigma Delta Epsilon, Omicron Nu, Phi Upsilon Omicron, Gamma Sigma Delta, Phi Kappa Phi, Epsilon Sigma Phi. Clubs: Torch, Columbus Met. after Oct. 1 Office: Cornell U Coll Human Ecology Office of the Dean Martha Van Rennsalaer Hall Ithaca NY 14853

FIRESTEIN, CECILY BARTH, artist; b. N.Y.C., Apr. 25, 1933; d. Sidney Monte and Esther (Schwartz) Barth; m. Stephen Kern Firestein; children: Conrad Elliot, Lesley Adam. BA, Adelphi U., 1953; MA, NYU, 1955, cert. in advanced study, 1958; cert., N.Y. Sch. of Interior Design, 1964. Cert. elem. tchr., N.Y. Art tchr., cons. Union Free Schs. Dist. #24, Valley Stream, N.Y., 1953-60; printmaker Phoenix Gallery, Valley Stream, 1962—; interior designer Firestein Interiors, Valley Stream, 1964—; tchr. Parson's Sch. Design, N.Y.C., 1982, The New Sch., N.Y.C., 1979, 80, South St. Seaport Mus., N.Y.C., 1981, Cooper Hewitt Mus., N.Y.C., 1980, Mus. of the City of N.Y., 1978; art critic Art Speak, N.Y.C., 1983—; cons. Miami (Fla.) Preservation League, 1980, Tarrytown (N.Y.) Hist. Soc., 1979. Author: Rubbing Craft, 1977; artist, printmaker rep. in collections Cin. Mus. of Art, 1986, New York Pub. Library, 1987, Yale U. Art Gallery Mus., 1988; one-woman exhibitions (20) at galleries and mus., 1962—. Blockwatcher N.Y.C. Police Dept., 1987. Recipient Artist-in-residence award Bronx Mus. of History, Grant award N.Y. State Council on the Arts, 1974. Mem. Art Students League (life), Phoenix (exec. sec. 1987—), Kappa Delta Pi, Pi Lambda Theta. Democrat. Jewish.

FIRESTONE, ESTHER VIOLET, counselor; b. Xilitla, San Luis, Mex., Dec. 15, 1950; d. Ezequiel and Ruth May (Tijerina) Cepeda; m. Ronald Lee Firestone, Dec. 27, 1969; children: LeMel, Homer. AA in Social Sci., Pasadena City Coll., 1982; BA in Social Sci., Thomas Edison Jr. Coll., 1985; MA in Psychology, Nat. U., 1986. Vocat. nurse various hosps., Glendale, Calif., 1971-74; missionary nurse Ch. of God, Bolivia, 1974-78; nurse acute care unit various hosps., Riverside, Calif., 1978-79; office mgr., physiotherapist Firestone Chiropractic Clinic, Riverside and Yucca Valley, Calif., 1979—; exec. dir. Vacation Samaritans, Yucca Valley, 1984-85; psychotherapist Morongo Mental Health, Yucca Valley, 1986—; conv. speaker numerous chs. and orgns., 1974—; tchr. Bible study groups, Bolivia, U.S., 1974—. Leadership scholar Nat. U., 1986. Mem. Calif. Assn. Marriage and Family Therapists. Republican. Lodge: Soroptomist. Home: 57610 Crestview Dr Yucca Valley CA 92284

FIRMIN, ROXANE HAEFELE, teleproductions company executive; b. Wayne, Mich., Jan. 21, 1949; d. Leslie Poss and Jane (Gregory) Haefele; m. Roger L. Cheney, Oct. 2, 1971 (div. Apr. 1980); children: Derek John, Rebecca Lee Leslie, Jessica Sunshine; m. Alfred J. Firmin, Dec. 26, 1983; 1 child, John Gregory. Student, U. Ariz., 1967-71, U. Iowa, 1980-81, Wayne State U., 1981-82. Actress, concession mgr. Arena Fair Summer Theater, Wooster, Ohio, 1965-67; actress Jam Handy, Detroit, 1967, Tucson, Ariz., 1970; producer Sunrise TV Prodns., Dearborn, Mich., 1980-81, Henry Ford Hosp., Detroit, 1982; pres. Roxy Teleprodns. Inc., Dearborn, 1983—; dir., pres. Carousel Theatre, Indianol, Iowa, 1980; cons. United Parcel Service, Livonia, Mich., 1985, The Austin Co., Cleve., 1985, Pacific Marine Research, Seattle, 1986, St. Mary Hosp., Livonia, 1986. Producer (video tng. programs) State of Mich., 1983, Leaseway Transp. Co., 1986, Heublein Inc., 1987; (med. programs) Henry Ford Hosp., 1982-83. Sec. Spiritual Assembly of Bahai's of Chicago Heights, Ill., 1971-75, Warren County, Iowa, 1976-77; mem. Dist. Teaching Com., No. Ill., 1973. Mem. Internat. TV Assn., Detroit Producers Assn., Nat. Assn. Female Execs. Office: Roxy Teleprodns Inc 29108 Ford Rd Garden City MI 48135

FIRSTENBERG, JEAN, film institute executive; b. N.Y.C., Mar. 13, 1936; d. Eugene and Sylvia (Moses) Picker; m. Paul Firstenberg, Aug. 9, 1956 (div. July 1980); children—Debra, Douglas. BS summa cum laude, Boston U., 1958. Asst. producer Altman Prodns., Washington, 1965-66; media advisor J. Walter Thompson, N.Y.C., 1969-72; asst. for spl. projects Princeton U., N.J., 1972-74, dir. publs., 1974-76; program officer Markle Found., N.Y.C., 1976-80; dir. Am. Film Inst., Los Angeles and Washington, 1980—; Mem. com. Los Angeles Task Force on Arts; nat. adv. bd. Peabody Broadcasting Awards. Trustee Boston U.; mem. adv. bd. Will Rogers Inst., N.Y.C., Big Sisters of Los Angeles; bd. dirs. Variety Club of Calif., Los Angeles. Recipient Alumni award for disting. service to profession Boston U., 1982; seminar and prodn. chairs at directing workshop for women named in her honor Am. Film Inst., 1986. Mem. Women in Film (Los Angeles and Washington), Trusteeship for Betterment of Women, Acad. Motion Picture Arts and Scis. Office: Am Film Inst 2021 N Western Ave PO Box 27999 Los Angeles CA 90027

FISCH, EDITH L., lawyer; b. N.Y.C., Mar. 3, 1923; d. Hyman and Clara L. Fisch; m. Steven Ludwig Werner, Dec. 14, 1963 (dec.). B.A., Bklyn. Coll., 1945; LL.B., Columbia U., 1948, LL.M., 1949, J.Sc.D., 1950. Bar: N.Y. 1948, U.S. Supreme Ct. 1957. Grad. asst. Columbia U. Law Sch., N.Y.C., 1948, fellow in law, 1949-50, assoc. firm Conrad & Smith, N.Y.C., 1951-57; pvt. practice, N.Y.C., 1957-62, 65—; asst. prof. law N.Y. Law Sch., 1963-65; counsel firm Brodsky, Lenett & Altman, N.Y.C., 1973-75; pres. Lond Publs., 1958—; ednl. dir. Found. for Continuing Legal Edn., 1964—; editor N.Y.C. Charter and Adminstrv. Code, 1965—; presenter lectures, seminars and courses for profl. groups. Author: The Cy Pres Doctrine in the U.S., 1950; (with others) State Laws on the Employment of Women, 1953; Lawyers in Industry, 1956; Fisch on New York Evidence, 1959, 2d edit. 1977; (with others) Charities and Charitable Foundations, 1974; contbr. numerous articles to legal publs. County committeewoman 7th Dist. N.Y. Dem. party, 1949-52; bd. dirs., treas. nat. women's com. Brandeis U., 1964-68. Mem. N.Y. Women's Bar Assn. (pres. 1970-71, bd. dirs. 1971-73, adv. council 1974—), Nat. Assn. Women Lawyers, Assn. Bar City N.Y., Bklyn. Coll. Lawyers Group (rec. sec. 1961-63, bd. govs. 1963-65), Am. Arbitration Assn. (nat. panelist), Acad. Polit. Sci., AAUW, Alumni Assn. Columbia U., Bklyn. Coll. Alumni Assn. Home: 250 W 94th St New York NY 10025 Office: Call Hollow Rd Pomona NY 10970

FISCHBARG, ZULEMA F., physician, pediatric educator; b. Buenos Aires, Mar. 22, 1937; came to U.S., 1962; d. Naun and Esther (Pollner) Fridman; m. Jorge Fischbarg; children: Gabriel Julian, Victor Ernesto. MD, U. Buenos Aires, 1960. Pediatric intern Children's Hosp., Louisville, 1962-63, resident in pediatrics, 1963, chief resident in pediatrics, 1964; fellow hematology Michael Reese Med. Ctr., Chgo., 1964-66, Presbyn. St. Lukes Hosp., Chgo., 1966-67; fellow pediatric hematology Children's Meml. Hosp., Chgo., 1967-68; asst. clin. pediatrician U. Chgo., 1968-69; instr. in pediatrics Cornell U. Med. Sch., N.Y.C., 1970-72, asst. prof. in pediatrics, 1972-76, assoc. prof. pediatrics, 1978—; assoc. attending pediatrician N.Y. Hosp., 1979—; assoc. attending in pediatrics St. John's Hosp./Cath. Med. Ctr., N.Y.C.; instr. in medicine Ill. U., Chgo., 1967-68; asst. attending pediatrician, N.Y. Hosp., N.Y.C., 1972-76. Fellow Am. Acad. of Pediatrics, Queens Pediatric Soc.; mem. N.Y. Acad. of Medicine, N.Y. Soc. for the Study of Blood. Democrat. Jewish. Home: 175 E 62d St 6D New York NY 10021 Office: 37-51 72d St Jackson Heights NY 11372

FISCHER, ASMA QURESHI, pediatric neurologist; b. Pakistan, Apr. 8, 1950; came to U.S., 1975; d. Muhammad Siddique and Mahmudah Qureshi; M.B., B.S., U. Karachi, 1973; m. Paul Mehdi Fischer, Dec. 30, 1977. Resident in pediatrics Waterbury (Conn.) Regional Hosp.-U. Conn., 1975-77, Brookdale Hosp. Med. Center, Bklyn., 1977-78; fellow in pediatric neurology Bowman-Gray Med. Sch., Winston-Salem, N.C., 1978-81; instr. pediatric neurology U. Nebr.-Creighton U. med. schs., Omaha, from 1981; now faculty dept. neurology Med. Coll. Ga., Augusta. cons. in field. Mem. Am. Acad. Neurology, Child Neurology Soc., Assn. Pakistan Physicians, Internat. Assn. Child Neurology, Nat. Assn. Female Execs. Muslim. Author papers in field. Office: Med Coll Ga Dept Neurology Augusta GA 30907

FISCHER, CATHERINE PATRICIA, librarian; b. Rayne, La., Sept. 24, 1947; d. Alexandre and Nola (Granger) Hoffpauir; m. Lance J. Fischer; children: Jason, Rachel. BS in Library Sci., Gallaudet U., 1972, MS in Ednl. Tech., 1984. Library technician Model Secondary Sch. for the Deaf, Washington, 1971-72, asst. Learning Resources Ctr., 1972-81, sr. asst., 1981-84, librarian, acting supr., 1984-87; lectr. in field. Mem. ALA, Md. Ednl. Media Orgn., Assn. for Ednl. Communicators Tech., Am. Assn. of Deaf and Blind. Office: Model Secondary Sch for Deaf 800 Florida Ave NE Washington DC 20002

FISCHER, DALE SUSAN, lawyer; b. East Orange, N.J., Oct. 17, 1951; d. Edward L. and Audrey (Tenner) F. BA magna cum laude, U. So. Fla., 1977; JD, Harvard U., 1980; student Dickinson Coll., 1969-70. Bar: Calif. 1980. Ptnr. law firm Kindel & Anderson, Los Angeles, 1980—; lawyer in classroom Constl. Rights Found., 1981—. Mem. ABA, Los Angeles County Bar Assn. Home: 3695 Hampton Rd Pasadena CA 91107 Office: Kindel and Anderson 555 S Flower Los Angeles CA 90071

FISCHER, FRIEDA SCHEIBLE, social services administrator; b. Devine, Tex., Mar. 10, 1947; d. Arthur Milton and Vergie May (Clark) Scheible; m. Arthur A. Fischer, (dec.); stepchildren: Albert, Virginia. BA in Sociology, Ark. Tech. U., 1970; M in Rehab. Counseling, Ark. State U., Jonesboro, 1973; postgrad., U. Ark., Fayetteville, Little Rock, 1979—. Cert. rehab. counselor, Ark. Rehab. tchr., social worker Services for Blind and Visually Impaired, Forrest City, Ark., 1970-73; vocat. rehab. counselor Services for Blind and Visually Impaired, Pine Bluff, Ark., 1973-76; mental retardation aide Sesame Sch., Monticello, Ark., 1978-80, tchr. spl. edn., 1980-81; instr. Human Devel. Ctr., State of Ark., Warren, 1981-84, program coordinator, 1984—; Mem. Internal-Agy. Grievance Com. State of Ark. Dept. Human Services, Little Rock, 1987—. Asst. to coordinator Spl. Olympics, Monticello, 1979-80, co-area coordinator, 1980-82; treas. Drew County Hist. Soc., 1984-85; vol. Drew County Literacy Council, 1987—. Mem. AAUW, Assn. Retarded Citizens, S.E. Ark. Geneal. Soc., Nat. Rehab. Counselors Assn. (sec./treas. SW region 1975-76), Nat. Assn. Female Execs., Bradley County Assn. Retarded Citizfens, Drew County Geneal. Soc. Presbyterian. Home: 816 N Chester Monticello AR 71655

FISCHER, JEANNE MORGAN, educator; b. Woodstock, Ill., May 14, 1946; d. William Douglas and Marie Mary (Miller) Morgan; divorced; 1 child, Drew James; m. Donald Lee Fischer, Aug. 8, 1987. B of Edn., U. Wis., Whitewater, 1968, Master of Ednl. Profl. Devel. in Human Relations, 1979. Elem. tchr. Beloit (Wis.) Pub. Schs., 1968—; tchr. edn. methods Beloit Coll., 1984—. Author, illustrator: Shoplifting is for the Birds, 1977. Bd. mem., clk., Sch. Dist. Beloit Turner, Wis., 1984—. Recipient Outstanding Community Service award Woman's div. Greater Beloit Assn. of Commerce, 1977, Cert. Leadership, YWCA, 1985, 87. Mem. NEA, Wis. Edn. Assn., Beloit Edn. Assn., Phi Kappa Phi, Delta Kappa Gamma (sec., past pres. local chpt. 1973—, sec. state chpt. 1985—). Republican. Mem. Ch. of Christ. Club: Beloit Jr. Women's (Beloit, 1st dist. jr. dir.). Home: 849 Morning Glory Ln Beloit WI 53511 Office: Beloit Pub Schs 910 Townline Ave Beloit WI 53511

FISCHER, JUDITH EILEEN, educational consultant, career development; b. Westbrook, Maine, Mar. 9, 1949; d. Roland Emmett Jr. and Ruth Etta (Fenderson) Luffsey; m. James Michael Plageman, May 23, 1970 (div. Apr. 11, 1975); 1 child, Michael Trever Plageman; m. Larry Ray Fischer, June 2, 1978; children: Erin Boyer, Lindsey Elizabeth, Kevin Luffsey. Student, Chowan Jr. Coll., Murfreesboro, N.C., 1966; BS, Longwood Coll., Farmville, Va., 1970; EdM, U. Richmond, 1988. Cert. bus. instr., Va. Sec. to dist. mgr. Phillips Petroleum Co., Richmond, 1970-72; instr., placement dir. The Pan-Am. Sch., Richmond, 1975-81; ednl. cons., dean Inst. Bus. and Tech., Richmond, 1982-83; dean Sch. Exec. Secs., Richmond, 1982-83; evaluation specialist Council Noncollegiate Continuing Edn., Richmond, 1987—; part-time instr. The Collegiate Schs., Richmond, St. Catherine's Sch., Richmond, 1980-81; adj. prof. John Typer Community Coll., Richmond, 1982-83; acad. dean Commonwealth Coll., Richmond, 1987—; chmn. adv. com. Henrico Tech. Edn., 1988—. Mem. adv. com. Henrico County Lay, Richmond, 1978-80; recorder Regional Vocat. Adv. Council, 1987—; bd. dirs. Dumbarton Elem. Sch. PTA, Richmond, 1978-80; chmn. occupational adv. bd. Va. Commonwealth U., 1983—. Mem. Va. Assn. Pvt. Career Schs. (exec. dir. 1985-87, newsletter editor 1985-87), Va. C. of C. Roman Catholic.

FISCHER, MARGARET ELEANOR, psychologist, educator; b. Newark; d. John T. and Mary (Worden) F.; B.S. cum laude in Psychology, Seton Hall U., 1958; postgrad. U. Paris, 1958, Carl G. Jung Inst., Switzerland, 1958-59, NYU, 1959-60, U. Md., 1960-63; M.A. magna cum laude in Ednl. Psychology, San Diego State U., 1966; postgrad. (NDEA grantee), U. Alaska, 1965; Ph.D. cum laude in Psychology, U. Wash., 1970. Lic. pilot, comml. helicopter, fixed wing. Resident counselor Children's Center, N.Y.C., 1959-60; tchr. Am. Dependents' Schs., Okinawa, Germany, Turkey, France, 1960-64; tchr. English as fgn. lang. Jean Giraudoux Lycée, Chateauroux, France, 1963-64; tchr. English and French, Sweetwater Sch. Dist., Chula Vista, Calif., 1964-66; asst. to editor Rev. of Ednl. Research Jour., Seattle, 1967-68; psychologist vocat. rehab. program Edmonds Sch. Dist., Lynnwood, Wash., 1968-70, Charles Denny Youth Center, Everett, Wash., 1969-71; instr. psychology Seattle Community Coll., 1971; asst. prof. dept. social scis., humanities and edn. Purdue U., Lafayette, Ind., 1971-72; lang. evaluation specialist Def. Lang. Inst., Monterey, Calif., 1972; research psychologist U. Calif., San Francisco, 1972; asst. prof. psychology U. Calif., Santa Cruz, 1973, Mass. State Colls., 1973-76; pvt. practice psychology, Mass., 1976-78; psychologist N.Y. State Dept. Mental Hygiene, 1978, Alaska div. mental health Harborview Devel. Center, Valdez, 1978-79; psychologist Alaska Psychiat. Inst., Anchorage, 1979—; personnel officer Civil Air Patrol, Alaska, 1987—; mem. Alaska State Bd. Psychologists and Psychol. Assocs. Examiners, 1986—. Ambassador to Mauritius Anchorage organizing com. 1994 Winter Olympics, 1988—. Recipient internat. travel award Purdue U., 1972, scholarly support award Mass. State Coll., 1974, 75, 76; lic. psychologist, Alaska. Mem. Am. Psychol. Assn., Internat. Council Psychologists (area chmn. Alaska 1979-80), Interam. Soc. Psychologists, DAR, Mensa. Contbr. articles to psychol. jours. Home: 7935 Hillside Dr Anchorage AK 99516 Office: Alaska Psychiat Inst 2900 Providence Dr Anchorage AK 99508

FISCHLER, BARBARA BRAND, librarian; b. Pitts., May 24, 1930; d. Carl Frederick and Emma Georgia (Piltz) Brand; m. Drake Anthony Fischler, June 3, 1961; 1 child, Owen Wesley. AB cum laude, Wilson Coll., Chambersburg, Pa., 1952; MM with distinction, Ind. U., 1954, AMLS, 1964. Asst. reference librarian Ind. U., Bloomington, 1958-61, asst. librarian undergrad. library, 1961-63, acting librarian, 1963; circulation librarian Ind. U.-Purdue U., Indpls., 1970-76, pub. services librarian Univ. Library, sci., engring. and tech. unit, 1976-81, acting dir. univ. libraries, 1981-82, dir. univ. libraries, 1982—; vis. and assoc. prof. (part-time) Sch. Library and Info. Sci., Ind. U., Bloomington, 1972—, counselor/coordinator, Indpls., 1974-82; resource aide adv. com. Ind. Voc. Tech. Coll., Indpls., 1974-86; adv. com. Area Library Services Authority, Indpls., 1976-79; mem. core com., chmn. program com. Ind. Gov.'s Conf. on Libraries and Info. Services, Indpls., 1976-78; mem. Ind. State Library Adv. Council, 1985—; cons. in field. Contbr. articles to profl. jours. Fund raiser Indpls. Mus. Art, 1971, Am. Cancer Soc., Indpls., 1975; vol. tchr. St. Thomas Aquinas Sch., Indpls., 1974-75; fund raiser Am. Heart Assn., Indpls., 1985; bd. dirs., treas. Historic Amusement Found., Inc., Indpls., 1984—, bd. advisors N.Am. Wildlife Park Found., Inc., Battle Ground, Ind., 1985—. Recipient Outstanding Service award Cen. Ind. Area Library Service Authority, 1979; Outstanding Librarian award Ind. Library/Ind. Library Trustee Assn., 1988. Mem. ALA, Ind. State Library Adv. Council, Midwest Fedn. Library Assns. (chmn. local arrangements for conf. 1986-87, sec. 1987—, bd. dirs. 1987—), Ind. Library Assn. (chmn. coll. and univ. div. 1977-78, chmn. library edn. div. 1981-82, treas. 1984-86), German Shepherd Dog Club of Cen. Ind. (pres. 1978-79, treas. 1988—), Wabash Valley German Shepherd Dog Club (pres. 1982-83), Cen. Ind. Kennel Club (bd. dirs. 1984-86), Pi Kappa Lambda, Beta Phi Mu. Republican. Presbyterian. Home: 4255 Cooper Rd Indianapolis IN 46208 Office: Ind-Purdue U 815 W Michigan St Indianapolis IN 46202

FISCHLER, PAMELA FRAN, advertising agency executive; b. Bklyn., Sept. 25, 1951; s. Martin Lee and Gilda Augusta (Gerber) G.; m. Burton Fischler, July 3, 1973. Student Stephens Coll., 1969-71; BA, Hofstra U., 1973. New acct. exec. Unique Security Agy., Great Neck, N.Y., 1973-75; career counselor, acct. exec. Dartmouth Cons., N.Y.C., 1975; acct. liaison MGA, Inc., Advt., Great Neck, N.Y., 1975-76, v.p. pub. relations and media, 1977-80, exec. v.p., 1980—. Bd. dirs. Soc. of Friends of Touro synagogue, Newport, R.I. Democrat. Jewish. Home: Grants Corner North Salem NY 10560 Office: MGA Plaza Westbury NY 11590

FISCHLER, SHIRLEY BALTER, lawyer; b. Bklyn., Oct. 9, 1926; d. David and Rose (Shapiro) Balter; m. Abraham Saul Fischler, Apr. 9, 1949; children—Bruce Evan, Michael Alan, Lori Faye. B.A., Bklyn. Coll., 1947, M.A., 1951; J.D., Nova U., Ft. Lauderdale, Fla., 1977. Tchr., N.Y.C. Bd. Edn., 1948-50, Richmond (Calif.) Pub. Schs., 1965-66; assoc. firm Panza & Maurer, Ft. Lauderdale, 1977—; pro bono atty. Broward Lawyers Care, 1982-86. Bd. govs. Nova. U. Law Ctr., 1982—; mem. Commn. on Status of Women, Broward County, Fla., 1982-87, vice chair, 1983-84. Mem. ABA, Fla. Bar Assn., Broward County Bar Assn., Fla. Assn. Women Lawyers. Home: 5000 Taylor St Hollywood FL 33021 Office: Panza & Maurer 3081 E Comml Blvd Fort Lauderdale FL 33308

FISCHMAN, MYRNA LEAH, accountant, educator; b. N.Y.C.; d. Isidore and Sally (Goldstein) F. BS., Coll. City N.Y., 1960, M.S., 1964; Ph.D., NYU 1976. Asst. to controller Sam Goody, Inc., N.Y.C.; tchr. accounting Central Comml. High Sch., N.Y.C., 1960-63, William Cullen Bryant High Sch., Queens, N.Y., 1963-66, vocat. adviser, 1963-66; instr. acctg. Borough of Manhattan Community Coll., N.Y.C., 1966-69; self employed acct., N.Y.C., 1960—; chief acct. investigator rackets, Office Queens Dist. Atty., 1969-70, community relations coordinator, 1970-71; adj. prof. L.I. U., 1970-79, prof. acctg. taxation and law, 1979—, coordinator grad. capstone courses, 1982—, dir. Sch. Professional Accountancy Bklyn. campus, 1984—; dir. Faculty Acctg. Taxation and Law Bklyn. campus, 1986—. Research cons. pre-tech. program Bd. Edn., City N.Y.; acct.-adviser Inst. for Advancement of Criminal Justice; acct.-cons. Coalition Devel. Corp., Interracial Council for Bus. Opportunities; treas. Breakfree Inc., Lower East Side Prep. Sch.; mem. edn. task force Am. Jewish Com., 1972—; mem. steering com., youth div. N.Y. Dem. County Com., 1967-68, del. to Nat. Conv., Young Dems. Am., 1967, rep. assigned to women's activities com., 1967; mem. Chancellor Com. Against Discrimination in Edn., 1976—; chmn. supervisory com. Fed. Credit Union #1532, N.Y.C., 1983—; mem. legis. adv. bd. N.Y. State Assemblyman Denis Butler, 1979—; chmn. consumer council Astoria Med. Center, 1980—; mem. subcom. on bus. edn. to the econ. devel. and mktg. com. Bklyn. C. of C., 1984—. Recipient award for meritorious service Community Service Soc., 1969; C.P.A., N.Y. Mem. Jewish Guild for Blind, Jewish Braille Inst., Friends Am. Ballet Theatre, Friends Met. Mus. Art, Community Welfare Com., Assn. Govt. Accts. (bd. dirs. N.Y. chpt. 1984—, dir. research and manuscripts 1985—), Am. Acctg. Assn., Nat., Eastern (co-chmn. ann. meeting 1967) bus. edn. assns., Nat., Eastern (chmn. ann. meeting, 1968) bus. tchrs. assns., Internat. Soc. Bus. Edn., Grad. Students Orgn. NYU (treas. 1971-73, v.p. 1973-74), NEA, AAUP, Doctorate Assn. N.Y. Educators (v.p. 1975—), Am. Assn. Jr. Colls., Young Alumni Assn. ; chmn. supervisory com. Fed. Credit Union #1532, N.Y.C., 1983—; Coll. (mem. council), Emanu-El League Congregation Emanu-El, N.Y. (chmn. community services com. 1967-68), Nat. Assn. Accts. (bd. dirs. N.Y. chpt. 1985—, dir. profl. devel. 1986-87, dir. pub. relations 1987-88), Tax Inst. L.I. U. (dir. Bklyn. chpt. 1984—), Delta Pi Epsilon (treas. 1976). Jewish. Democrat. Club: Women's City (N.Y.C.). Developed new bus. machine course and curriculum Borough Manhattan Bus. Community Coll. Home: PO Box 6241 Astoria NY 11106 Office: L I U Zeckendorf Campus Brooklyn NY 11201

FISH, HELEN THERESE, teacher, author; b. Mpls., Mar. 17, 1944; d. John Howard and Helen Therese (Ochs) Berg; m. Ronald Bruce Fish, Oct. 13, 1967; children: Eric James, Angela Diane, Christine Ann. BS, U. Minn., Mpls., 1966; postgrad., U. Minn., Mankato, 1969-70, U. Wis., Whitewater, 1970-72; MEd, Brenau Coll., 1986; postgrad., U. Ga., 1986—. Cert. elem. tchr., Minn., Wis., Ill., Kans., Ga. Kindergarten tchr. Lincoln Hills Sch., Mpls., 1966-68; tchr. 1st grade Hoover Sch., Mankato, 1969-70; kindergarten tchr. Todd Sch., Beloit, Wis., 1970-73; tchr. presch., K-1 Wilson Sch., Janesville, Wis., 1973-75; tchr. gifted and reading specialist (remedial) Lakewood Sch., Park Forest, Ill., 1975-77; tchr. kindergarten, 1st and 3d grades Sibley Sch., Albert Lea, Minn., 1977-82; tchr. kindergarten Most Pure Heart Sch., Topeka, 1982-84, Enota Sch., Gainesville, Ga., 1985—; cons. and field test tchr. Research and Devel. Ctr. U. Wis., Madison, 1970-79; demonstration tchr. Internat. Reading Assn. Conv., New Orleans, 1975. Author: Starting Out Well: Approaches for Parents in Exercise and Nutrition; editor Y's Menettes. Sec., treas. PTA, Mpls, Mankato, Albert Lea, Beloit, Janesville, Park Forest, Topeka, Gainesville; leader Girl Scouts U.S., Blue Birds, Topeka; softball coach, Gainesville. Named one of Outstanding Tchrs. Am., 1972. Mem. Ga. Edn. Assn., Pi Lamda Theta (Honorary Teaching Soc. award). Republican. Roman Catholic. Home: 3650 Brown Well Ct Gainesville GA 30501 Office: Enota Sch Enota Ave W Gainesville GA 30501

FISH, LILIAN MANN, lawyer; b. Methuen, Mass., Sept. 6, 1901; d. Samuel Eleazer and Ella Agnes (Hobbs) Mann; m. Charles Melvin Fish, Dec. 25, 1923 (div. 1933). Student U. So. Calif., 1930's-40's; J.D. magna cum laude, Southwestern U., 1932. Bar: Calif. 1932, U.S. Dist. Ct. (so. dist.) Calif. 1932, U.S. Ct. Appeals (9th cir.) 1934, U.S. Supreme Ct. 1936. Sec. Lloyd S. Nix, Atty., San Pedro, Calif., 1926-29, Los Angeles, 1931-32; sec. Office of City Prosecutor (Lloyd S. Nix), Los Angeles, 1929-30, Victor R. Hansen, atty., Los Angeles, 1930-31; assoc. Lloyd S. Nix, Los Angeles, 1932-44, Price, Postel & Parma, Santa Barbara, Calif., 1949-71; sole practice, Los Angeles, 1944—, Santa Barbara, 1971—; editor Ancestors West quar., 1979—. Vice pres. Los Angeles County Young Republicans, 1939-40; bd. dirs. Santa Barbara Trust Hist. Preservation, pres., 1975, also sec.; bd. dirs. Santa Barbara County Geneal. Soc., 1978—, also editor, hon. life mem.; bd. dirs. Santa Barbara Hist. Soc., 1971-76, chmn. library com., 1978-83; pres. Santa Barbara Bus. and Profl. Women, 1955-56, Nat. Bus. and Profl. Women, Los Angeles, 1945-46; registrar Mission Canyon chpt. DAR, Santa Barbara, 1965-80, 85—(Roll of Honor cert. 1978). Recipient Cert. of Recognition for service Calif. Senate, 1980; Cert. of Service, Bicentennial Com., City of Santa Barbara, 1975-77; named Woman of Yr., Mar Vista Bus. and Profl. Women's Assn., 1979. Mem. ABA, State Bar Calif. (mem. probate estate planning sect.) Santa Barbara County Bar Assn. (del. state bar convs. 1950s), Women Lawyers Club Los Angeles (pres. 1940-41), Soc. Genealogists (London), Phi Delta Delta. Republican. Mem. United Ch. of Christ. Home: 2546 Murrell Rd Santa Barbara CA 93109

FISH, SUSAN LYN, sales engineer; b. Pittsfield, Mass., Nov. 6, 1952; d. Frank Ward and Arolyn Francis (Hawkes) F. AA in Liberal Studies, Berkshire Community Coll., 1972; BS in Mgmt., Bentley Coll., 1974; AA in Machine and Tool Design, Springfield Tech. Community Coll., 1982. From mgr. to dist. mgr. Fayva Shoes, Canton, Mass., 1974-79; mgmt. cons. Alexander Proudfoot, Chgo., 1979; drafter, detailer, computer aided designer Stone & Webster Engring., Boston, 1982-83, Engring. Design Assocs., Foxboro, Mass., 1983-84; tng. rep., application engr. VIA Systems, Chelmsford, Mass., 1984-87; sales engr. Automated Images, Woburn, Mass., 1987—. Office: Automated Images 500 W Cummings Park Woburn MA 01801

FISHBONE, MARIE LYNN, marketing specialist; b. Norwich, Conn., May 22, 1959; d. Morris Abraham and Jean Joyce (Banas) F. Student, R.I. Sch. Design, 1977-78; BA, Conn. Coll., 1982; MBA, Northeastern U., 1986. Tchr. learning disabilities Preston (Conn.) Bd. Edn., 1982-84; adminstrv. mktg. asst. Burroughs Corp., Roseland, N.J., 1985; adminstr., research asst. Northeastern U., Boston, 1986; cons. mktg. Norwich, Conn., 1986—; mktg. asst. Chelsea Groton Savs. Bank, Norwich, 1987—; sec. child devel. adv. bd. Conn. Coll., 1980-81; cons. Preston Edn. Gifted and Talented, 1987. Instr., coach YMCA, Norwich, 1982—; instr. ARC, New London, Conn., 1983—; vol. St. Catherine of Siena Parish, Preston, 1980-85; bd. dirs. St. Catherine Folk Choir, Preston, 1979-83, Norwich Rose Arts Festival, 1988—, Nashantucket Land Trust, 1983-86. Conn. state scholar, 1977-81. Mem. Nat. Assn. Female Execs. Democrat. Roman Catholic. Home: RFD 6 18 Burdick Rd Preston CT 06360

FISHER, AGNES, beauty products company manager; b. Richmond, Ind., Nov. 17, 1943; d. George Washington and Ruth (Craig) Barker; m. Melvin K. Fisher, Oct. 20, 1961 (div. 1988); children: Lisa Fisher Eldridge, Linda. Sec., office mgr. Rice's Monuments, Richmond, 1973-76; sales rep. Avon Products, Inc., Cin., 1977-79, dist. sales mgr., 1979—, leadership trainer, 1981, div. panel mem., 1985-86. Recipient Circle of Excellence award Avon Products, Inc., 1981, Activity Leadership award, 1985, 86. Mem. Nat. Assn. Female Execs. Republican. Club: Nettle Creek Steppers (v.p. 1973, pres. 1974, treas. 1976, 80, sec. 1981) (Hagerstown, Ind.). Avocations: reading, traveling. Home: 501 Colonial Dr New Castle IN 47362 Office: Avon Products Inc 175 Progress Pl Cincinnati OH 45214

FISHER, ANITA JEANNE, educator; b. Atlanta, Oct. 22, 1937; d. Paul Benjamin and Cora Ozella (Wadsworth) Chappelear; m. Kirby Lynn Fisher, Aug. 6, 1983; 1 child by previous marriage, Tracy Ann. BA, Bob Jones U., 1959; postgrad. Stetson U., 1961, U. Fla., 1963; M.A.T., Rollins Coll., 1969; Ph.D. in Am. Lit., Fla. State U., 1975; postgrad. Writing Inst., U. Cen. Fla., 1978, NEH Inst., 1979. Cert. English, gifted and adminstn. supr. Chmn. basic learning improvement program, secondary sch. Orange County, Orlando, Fla., 1964-65; chmn. composition Winter Park High Sch., Fla., 1978-80; chmn. English depts. Orange County Pub. Schs., Fla., 1962-71; reading tchr. Woodland Hall Acad., Reading Research Inst. Found., Tallahassee, 1976; instr. edn., journalism, reading, Spanish, thesis writing Bapt. Bible Coll., Springfield, Mo., 1976-77; prof. English, SW Mo. State U., Springfield, 1980-84, instr. continuing edn., courses in music and creative writing, 1981-82, editor LAD Leaf; tchr. English County Schs., Fla., 1984—, gifted students, 1986—. Contbr. writings to publs. in field, papers to nat. profl. confs. Vol. Greene County Action Com., 1977, Heart Fund, 1982. Writing Program fellow U. Cen. Fla., 1978. Mem. Fla. Council Tchrs. of English, MLA, Nat. Council Tchrs. of English, Volusia County Council Tchrs. of English, Voice of Youth Advocates (book reviewer), Kappa Delta Pi. Republican. Presbyterian.

FISHER, ANN, business executive, lawyer; b. N.Y.C., Apr. 5, 1939; d. William Parker and Dorothy Howe (Douglas) Fisher; m. William J. Danaher, Feb. 22, 1958 (div. 1963); children—Dorothy Lynn Danaher, Jo Ann Danaher Chitty. M.B.A., U. Miami, 1976, J.D., 1981. Bar: Fla. 1981. Sales promotion mgr. Aristar Mgmt. Corp., Miami, 1965-71, dir. instl. sales Terner's of Miami Corp., Miami, 1971-80; assoc. Stinson, Lyons et al, Miami, 1981-83; co-owner Now Courier, Inc., Hialeah, Fla., 1983-84; pres. Cannon & Fisher Corp., 1984-86; prin. Ann Fisher, P.A., 1986—; owner Corp. Records, Inc., 1986—. Mem. Nat. Assn. Women Bus. Owners (com. chmn., v.p. Greater Miami chpt. 1984, sec., bd. dirs.), Fla. Bar Assn., Fla. Assn. Women Lawyers, Dade County Bar Assn., Coral Gables Bar Assn. (bd. dirs.), U. of Miami Sch. of Bus. Alumni Assn. (bd. dirs.), Beta Gamma Sigma. Republican. Club: Entrepreneurial of South Fla. (sec., bd. dirs.). Lodge: Rotary. Home: 1514 Zuleta Ave Coral Gables FL 33146

FISHER, ANNA LEE, physician, astronaut; b. St. Albans, N.Y., Aug. 24, 1949; m. William Frederick Fisher; 1 child, Kristin Anne. B.S. in Chemistry, UCLA, 1971, M.D., 1976; MS in Chemistry, 1987. Physician, 1976-78; astronaut NASA, Johnson Space Ctr., 1978—, mission specialist STS, 51-A, 1984. Office: NASA Johnson Space Ctr Astronaut Office Houston TX 77058

FISHER, BARBARA ALDEN MOLNAR, writer, editor; b. Hamilton, Ohio, May 30, 1942; d. George William and Marion Shepard (Drew) Molnar; m. Thomas Graham Fisher, June 2, 1963; children: Anne Corwin, Thomas Molnar. BA, Ind. U., 1964, MA, 1968. Library dir. Rensselaer Pub. Library (Ind.), 1965-68; tchr. pvt. sch., Remington, Ind., 1969-70; reporter Rensselaer Republican, 1972-74; owner, mgr. Barbara's Plants, Remington, 1975-76; freelance writer, Remington, 1979—; mng. dir. Jasper County Council on Aging, 1979-81; editor Remington Press, 1981-83; advt. dir., contbg. editor Lafayette Bus. Digest, 1984; owner Wordswork, 1985-86; dir. advt., asst. editor The Purdue Alumnus, 1985-88; adult services librarian Plainfield Pub. Library, 1988—. Contbr. numerous articles to newspapers and mags. Bd. advisors Planned Parenthood of Jasper County, Rensselaer, 1974-78; mem. Jasper County Welfare Bd., Jasper County Mental Health Assn., 1968-78; sec. Remington Park Bd., 1981-86. Recipient Vanguard award Greater Lafayette Women in Communication, 1984. Democrat. Presbyterian. Address: 933 Harding St Plainfield IN 46168

FISHER, CAROL ANNE, property management company executive; b. Dallas, Apr. 23, 1954; d. Austin and Bernice Claire (Berndt) Bonner; m. Henry R. Smith (div. 1976); 1 child, Paul Timothy. Student, Hardin-Simmons U., 1972. Exec. recruiter G. McKinnerney & Assocs., Dallas, 1978-79, Odell & Assocs., Dallas, 1979-80; with comml. leasing dept. GLA & Assocs., Dallas, 1981; dir. comml. leasing Comml. Investors, Dallas, 1982-83; ptnr. Baty-Fisher Assocs., Dallas, 1983; dir. personnel Dalcor Property Mgmt. Inc., Dallas, 1985—; speaker in field. Author, editor newsletter Insite, 1987-88. Vol. Wednesday's Child Golf Tournament, Dallas, 1988. Mem. Tex. Bus. Council (charter), Dallas Personnel Assn. Republican. Office: Dalcor Property Mgmt 2911 Turtle Creek Suite 900 Dallas TX 75219

FISHER, CELIA BURG, psychologist. d. Norman H. and Helen Elenor (Berken) Burg; m. Gary Stephen Fisher; two children. BS, Cornell U., 1970, MA in Psychology, 1975; PhD in Expl. Psychology, New Sch. Social Research, 1978. Licensed psychologist. Instr. LaGuardia Comm. Coll., 1975-77, Barnard Coll., N.Y.C., 1976-78; adj. prof. Grad. Faculty New Sch. for Social Research, N.Y.C., 1982, Columbia U., N.Y.C., 1982; research assoc. Princeton (N.J.) U., 1978-79; asst. prof. Fordham U., N.Y.C., 1979-85, assoc. prof., 1985—; dir. grad. program devel. psychology, Fordham U., 1985—; mem. N.Y. State Bd. for Psychology, 1987—. Contbr. articles to profl. jours. Recipient fellowship Nat. Research Service, 1979, grant NIMH, 1982-83. Mem. Am. Psychol. Assn., Soc. Research in Child Devel., Ea. Psychol. Assn., Nat. Council on Family Relations, Nat. Resource Council, Soc. Research in Adolescence, Hasting Ctr. Inst. Soc., Ethics and Life Scis. Office: Fordham Univ Dept Psychology Bronx NY 10458

FISHER, CONSUELO C. (CONNIE), communications executive, writer, editor; b. Oakland, Calif., Dec. 30, 1933; d. George Thomas and Laura (Koski) Carmona; m. Russell Craig Fisher, June 4, 1967; children—Laura Elizabeth Slay, Landrum Bilyeu, Belinda Marie, Nadine Gerry. Student, Sch. Journalism, Mexico City Coll., 1952-55. Reporter-columnist El Excelsior & The News, Mexico City. 1949-54; travel agt. Redwood Travel Advisors & GTS Travel, San Rafael, Calif., 1962-72; dir. community relations Vitam Ctr. Inc, Norwalk, Conn., 1973-75; owner, dir. Connie Fisher Communications, Wilton, Conn., 1975-78; writer The Hour, Norwalk, 1978-80; pub. affairs coordinator Continental Telephone of Tex., Dallas, 1980-83; mgr. mktg. communications publs. No. Telecom Inc., Richardson, Tex., 1983-86; mgr. mktg. communications Ericsson Network Systems, Richardson, 1986—; press liason Conn. senatorial candidate, Wilton, 1974; pub. relations dir., v.p. Wilton Playshop, 1974-80. Contbr. articles to profl. jours. Parish directory editor, eucharistic minister All Saints Cath. Ch., Dallas. Mem. Am. Sch. Alumni Assn. Mexico City (Bronze Quill award 1982, 83, 84, 85, 86), Internat. Assn. Bus. Communicators (Coty award 1984). Club: Dallas Press (Katy award 1984, Matrix award 1985, Gold Ring award 1985). Home: 6533 Clearhaven Circle Dallas TX 75248

FISHER, EVALYN JEAN, interior designer; b. Roswell, N.Mex., Aug. 27, 1943; d. Newel Edward and Genevieve (Kester) Porter; m. Robert Earl Fisher, Apr. 3, 1966. BA in Art and Design, Calif. State U., Los Angeles, 1968. Cert. tchr., Calif.; cert. interior and environ., designer, Calif. Art instr. pub. schs. Baldwin Park and Rialto, Calif., 1969-74; visual arts specialist pub. schs. Riverside, Calif., 1975-79; assoc. designer Maryanne Levine Interior Designs, Los Angeles, 1982-85; prin. Evalyn Fisher, ASID & Assocs., Redlands, Calif., 1985—; adj. instr. U. Calif., Riverside, Fashion Inst. Design and Merchandising, Los Angeles and Santa Ana, Calif., 1985—. Recipient numerous design awards from area hist. socs. and civic groups. Mem. Am. Soc. Interior Designers (cert., chmn. significant interiors survey com. 1987—, chmn. com. 1987—), Nat. Trust Hist. Preservation (design assoc.). Democrat. Office: Evalyn Fisher ASID & Assocs 300 E State St Suite 503 Redlands CA 92373

FISHER, FLORENCE ANNA, assn. exec., author, lectr.; b. Bklyn., May 28, 1928; d. Frederick I. and Florence (Goldstein) Fisher; student pub. schs., Phila.; m. Stanley Eigenfeld, Dec. 20, 1953; 1 son, Glenn Mark Love. Founder, pres. The Alma Soc., Inc. (Adoptees' Liberty Movement Assn.), N.Y.C., 1971—; mem. Mabon Policy Advisory Council Odyssey Inst., Inc., N.Y.C., 1977-78; author: (autobiography) The Search for Anna Fisher, 1973. Office: PO Box 154 Washington Bridge Station New York NY 10033

FISHER, (MARY) JEWEL TANNER, former construction company executive; b. Port Lavaca, Tex., Oct. 31, 1918; d. Thomas M. and Minnie Frances (Dunks) Tanner; grad. Tex. Lutheran Coll., 1937; m. King Fisher, Aug. 13, 1937; children—Ann Fisher Boyd, Linda Fisher LaQuay. Sec. treas. King Fisher Marine Service, Inc., Port Lavaca, 1959-82; dir., cons. King Fisher Marine Service; artist. Trustee Champ Traylor Hosp., 1976-81, Golden Crescent Council Govts., 1980-81. Lic. pvt. pilot. Mem. DAR (regent Guadalupe Victoria chpt. 1986-88), Daus. Republic Tex., 99's, Internat. Orgn. Women Pilots. Home: Box 166 Port Lavaca TX 77979 Office: Box 108 Port Lavaca TX 77979

FISHER, JOANN YVONNE, military professional; b. Washington, Mar. 8, 1947; m. Robert Lawrence Dickens, Jan. 19, 1976; 3 children. Student, Merritt Jr. Coll., 1970, Laney Jr. Coll., 1970-71, John F. Kennedy U., 1980-84. With U.S. Civil Service Commn., Washington, 1967-68, Naval Sta. Treasure Island, San Francisco, 1968-69, State Dept. Pub. Health, Berkeley, Calif., 1972-73, Bechtel Corp., San Francisco, 1973-76, Brown and Root, San Francisco, 1976; enlisted USNR, 1976, advanced through grades to petty officer 1st class, 1985. Sec. Adv. Neighbor Commn., Washington, adv. neighborhood city commr. Bolling AFB. Address: Bolling AFB 249 Burwell St Washington DC 20032

FISHER, JOHANNA MARIE, real estate legal represenative; b. Breitengussbach, Fed. Republic Germany; came to U.S., 1972; d. Manning June and Kunigunda (Fürsel) Kunigunda June; m. Herman Fisher, June 5, 1981; children: Johann, Ursula, Sabine, Herman III (stepson). B in Legal Studies cum laude, SUNY, Buffalo, 1982. cert. Legal Asst. Adminstrv. asst. def. dept. Seiman's Electronics, Fed. Republic Germany, 1976-78; credit counselor Goldome Savs. Bank, Buffalo, 1983-85; with Pack, Hartman, Ball & Huckabone, Buffalo, 1985-86. Writer poetry, short stories. Mem. Nat. Assn. Female Execs. Lodge: Order Eastern Star.

FISHER, JUDITH ANN, state disability official; b. Oklahoma City, Feb. 18, 1947; d. Raymond Earl and Paula Ione (Goodwin) F. BA, Tex. Tech U., 1969, MA, 1973. Adjudicator Disability Determination Unit State of N.M., Albuquerque, 1973-74, quality assurance supr., 1974-80, asst. adminstr., 1980—; mem. regional policy com. Social Security Adminstrn., Dallas, 1977-79; guest speaker Social Security Mgmt. Forum, Denver, 1983. Vol. VISTA, 1972, Victim-Offender Mediation Program, Albuquerque. Recipient Alumni Award Tex. Tech U.; named Outstanding Adjudicator N.Mex. Assn. Disability Examiners, 1980. Mem. Phi Kappa Phi. Republican. Baptist. Home: 3808 Valerie Pl NE Albuquerque NM 87111 Office: NMex Disability Determination Unit 3301 Juan Tabo NE Albuquerque NM 87111

FISHER, KATHRYN MARIE, aerospace facilities planner; b. Helena, Mont., Jan. 21, 1958; d. William Joseph and Joyce Elizabeth (Dewey) Hrouda; m. John Dennis Fisher, Aug. 27, 1983; 1 child, Eric. . B.S. in Bus. Adminstrn., U. No. Colo., 1980. Assoc. engr. Martin Marietta Aerospace, Denver, 1980-81, layout specialist, 1981-83, sr. layout specialist, 1983, acting chief facilities layout, 1983, chief facilities planning, 1983—; acting mgr. Facilities Control, Denver, 1986-87. Democrat. Methodist. Home: 6969 S Sheridan Blvd Littleton CO 80123 Office: Martin Marietta Denver Aerospace PO Box 179 Denver CO 80201

FISHER, LETITIA CATHERINE, marketing educator, educational consultant; b. Mineola, N.Y., Apr. 25, 1932; d. Thomas Joseph and Letitia Catherine (Hanley) F. B.S., U. New Haven, 1966; M.S., U. Bridgeport, 1968, cert. in advanced studies, 1974; M.P.A., NYU, 1982. Cert. distributive edn. tchr./coordinator, N.Y., Conn.; cert. intermediate adminstr., supr., Conn. Distributive edn. coordinator West Haven High Sch. (Conn.), 1967-69; asst. mgr. employee benefits R.H. Macy & Co., N.Y.C., 1969-73; merchandising specialist Bloomingdale's, New Rochelle, N.Y., 1973-74; job placement/mktg. instr. Bd. Coop. Ednl. Services, North Westchester Tech. Ctr., Yorktown Heights, N.Y., 1974-76; assoc. prof., chmn. bus. dept. Elizabeth Seton Coll., Yonkers, N.Y., 1976-83; asst. prof., curriculum chmn. retail bus. mgmt. SUNY at Westchester Community Coll., Valhalla, 1983—; reviewer texts, simulations McGraw-Hill Book Co., N.Y.C., 1979, 83, Macmillan Pubs., N.Y.C., 1987; reviewer computer simulations Prentice-Hall, Inc., Englewood Cliffs., N.J., 1983. Author: Strategic Marketing Plan for Human Services Personnel, 1987 (Nat. Assn. Counties award for Westchester County 1987). Vol. Am. Cancer Soc., N.Y.C., 1955-64; campus rep. United Way of Westchester, Yonkers, N.Y., 1978-79. Recipient scholastic award J. C. Penney & Co., 1956, citation Am. Cancer Soc., 1957, Citizens Adv. Transp. award City of Yorktown (N.Y.), 1976, Service to Youth award Kinney Corp., 1982; Nat. Assn. of Counties award, 1987, Outstanding Leadership and Service award Assn. of Mktg. Educators, 1987; grantee Sears Found., 1968-69. Mem. Assn. Mktg. Educators (v.p. 1982-83, pres. 1983-85, Leadership award 1987), Distributive Edn. Clubs Am. (cert. appreciation 1979, recognition service 1983, county-state adviser 1983), Mktg. and Distributive Edn. Assn. (life), Am. Mktg. Assn. Home: 126 Church St Apt 5-C New Rochelle NY 10805 Office: SUNY Westchester Community Coll 75 Grasslands Rd Valhalla NY 10595

FISHER, MARCIA ANN, legal admininstrator; b. Geneva, Ill., Feb. 28, 1957; d. Robert L. and Beverly J. (Hopp) F. Student, Moser Bus. Sch., 1975; student, U. Ill., 1975-76; BS, U. Iowa, 1978, BS in Indsl. Relations, 1980. Paralegal Rate, Nolan, Moen & Parsons, Iowa City, 1980-82, legal adminstr., 1982—. Appointed Iowa State Foster Care Review Bd., 1987; del. Citizen Ambassador Program to People's Republic of China, 1988. Rotary scholar, 1975. Mem. Nat. Assn. Legal Adminstrs., Iowa Assn. Legal Adminstrs., Iowa Assn. Legal Assts. (treas. 1984).

FISHER, MILDRED LUCILLE, retired nurse; b. Briggs, Tex., Feb. 12, 1919; d. Hubert W. and Zula (Stewart) Hall; m. Gordon Williams, Sept. 26, 1936 (div. 1979); children—Barbara, Marilyn Williams Stone. Student, Tex. Woman's U., U. Houston. Lic. R.N., Tex. Pvt. office nurse Dr. Alan Lambert, Houston, 1955-56, 57-60, Dr. Victor Zima, Houston, 1956-57; nurse Galena Park Schs. (Tex.), 1960-73, Sam Houston Hosp., Houston, 1973-77, Gen. Post Office, Houston, 1978-79, Leander Schs. (Tex.), 1979-85. Campaign worker Senator Lloyd Doggett, Austin, Tex., 1981-83. Democrat. Methodist. Club: Byliners. Home: 1617 Cimarron 12F Portland TX 78374

FISHER, NANCY, screenwriter, producer, director; b. N.Y.C., Oct. 21, 1941; d. Seymour and Tema Fisher; m. Peter David Wild, Aug. 25, 1973; 1 child, Sarah Olivia. B.A., Barnard Coll., 1962. Prodn. supr. CBS, N.Y.C., 1964-66; owner, mgr. Serendipity Talent Agy., N.Y.C., 1966-68; writer, producer Grey Advt., N.Y.C., 1968-70; creative group head Benton & Bowles Advt., London, 1970-74, McCann Erickson Advt., N.Y.C., 1974-75; creative dir. Norman, Craig & Kummel Advt., N.Y.C., 1975-78; pres. Nancy Fisher Inc., Weston, Conn., 1978—; pres. Creative Programming, Inc., N.Y.C., 1981—. Creator, writer, producer TV series Womanwatch, 1982—, Celebrity Chefs, 1983—; numerous home video cassettes including Look Mom, I'm Fishing (Parents Choice award 1987), The Annapolis Book of Seamanship Video Series, The Christmas Carol Video, Video Dog, Video Cat, Video Baby. Recipient 5 broadcast awards Network Documentary Series, 1982-84. Mem. Dirs. Guild of Am., Am. Women in Radio and TV. Club: Wings (N.Y.C.) Office: Creative Programming 30 E 60th St New York NY 10022

FISHER, NAOMI YASUDA, banker; b. Kanazawa, Japan, Oct. 14, 1952; d. Naohisa and Yoshiko (Fujimaki) Yasuda; m. Arnold Stanley Fisher, June 20, 1976; 1 child, Jeffrey Akira. BA, UCLA, 1975, MA, 1980; BA, Hiroshima (Japan) U., 1980. Loan adminstr. The Sumitomo Bank of Calif., Los Angeles, 1976-77, Security Pacific Nat. Bank, Los Angeles, 1978-79; loan officer The Fuji Bank, Ltd., Los Angeles, 1981-83, asst. v.p., 1983-84, v.p., 1985—. Scholar Japan Scholarship Soc., 1971-74, Ministry of Edn. of Japan, 1974-75. Mem. Japan-Am. Soc. of So. Calif., Japan Bus. Assn. of So.

Calif., Nat. Assn Female Execs. Office: The Fuji Bank Ltd 333 S Grand Ave Los Angeles CA 90071

FISHER, PEG JEAN, marketing and training consultant; b. Kenosha, Wis., Oct. 15, 1940; d. Edwin and Lucille (Grimm) Reuter; B.S., U. Wis., Milw., 1964, M.S., 1969. Curriculum officer Nat. Assn. Housing and Redevel. Ofcls., Washington, 1971-72; dir. tng. and mgmt. devel. N. Am. ops. Manpower Temporary Services, Milw., 1973-76; cons., trainer Manpower Temporary Services, Milw. also Universal Tng. Systems Co., Northbrook, Ill., 1976-77; gen. mgr. Universal Tng. Systems, 1977-80; pres. Peg Fisher & Assos., Racine, Wis., 1980—; internat. mktg. cons. CREACTIVE, internat. cons. and mktg. firm, Belgium, 1981-86; profl. assoc., mem. adv. bd. communication program U. Wis., Parkside, 1982—; instr. Mgmt. Inst. U. Wis., Madison. Sec., Preservation-Racine Inc., 1981-82; chmn. Starving Artists Outdoor Art Fair, Racine Art Guild, 1981; mem. Humane Soc. Animal Shelter. Author: Successful Telemarketing, 1985; Telemarketing Excellence, 1985, Planning Your Telephone Sales Operation; contbg. editor Supply House Times, Elec. Distbr., Indsl. Distbn., Modern Distbn. Mgmt., Telemktg. mags., Agy. Sales, others; mem. bd. editorial advisers Teleprofl. mag. Mem. Inst. Mgmt. Cons., Profl. Dimensions. Home: 1201 S Wisconsin Ave Racine WI 53403

FISHER, REBECCA A. B., designer, consultant; b. Omer, Mich., Sept. 29, 1950; d. A. Phillip and G. J. (Fox) Brandenmuehl; m. R. Fisher (div. 1969). BA in Art Edn., W. Mich. U., 1975. Free-lance designer, illustrator N.Y.C.; art dir. Curtin & Pease div. Penton IPC Pub., Clearwater, Fla., 1977-84; prin. R. Fisher, Clearwater, 1984—. Cons. Big Bros. and Big Sisters, Clearwater. Recipient (for advt. programs) Addy award, Gold Mail Box award. Mem. Graphic Designers Guild, Am. Bus. Women Palm Harbor (treas.). Office: 2280 US 19 N Suite 233A Clearwater FL 33575

FISHER, ROBERTA LANE, lawyer; b. Cleve., Apr. 11, 1952; d. James Edward and Betty Jayne (Bucy) Lane; m. Fredrick Lee Fisher, Sept. 16, 1972; children: Jamie Elizabeth, John Fredrick, Jennifer Katherine. BA in Linguistics with distinction summa cum laude, Ohio State U., 1973; JD, Harvard U., 1976. Bar: Ohio 1976. Assoc. Squire, Sanders & Dempsey, Cleve. and Columbus, Ohio, 1976-85; ptnr. Squire, Sanders & Dempsey, Columbus, 1985—. Mem. ABA, Ohio Bar Assn., Columbus Bar Assn., Nat. Assn. Bond Lawyers, Bond Atty.'s Workshop (steering com.). Home: 6711 Elmers Ct Worthington OH 43085 Office: Squire Sanders & Dempsey 155 E Broad St Bancoho Nat Plaza Columbus OH 43215

FISHER, ROBIN LEEANN, manufacturing company executive; b. Latrobe, Pa., Oct. 12, 1955; d. Raymond William and Shirley Ann (Jones) Boring. BA in Polit. Sci., Ind. U. Pa., 1977. Insp. product assurance Westinghouse Electric Corp., Blairsville, Pa., 1978-81, mgr., tng. product coordinator, 1983-84; 1st line supr. product assurance, 1984—. Mem. Nat. Assn. Female Execs., Westinghouse Foreman's Assn., Smithsonian Instn. Assocs., Ind. U. Pa. Alumni Assn., Nat. Arbor Day Found. Democrat. Roman Catholic. Home: RD 3 Box 437 Blairsville PA 15717 Office: Westinghouse Electric Corp Specialty Metals Plant RD 4 Box 333 Blairsville PA 15717

FISHER, ROSALIND ANITA, personnel executive; b. Jackson, Tenn., Feb. 5, 1956; d. Hartwell E. and Gwendolyn C. (Meriweather) F. BS in Psychology, Cen. Mo. State U., 1978; MS in Community Devel., So. Ill. U., 1986. Tchr. Kansas City (Mo.) Sch. Dist., 1980-82; adminstrv. asst. Urban Affairs dept. City of Kansas City, 1982, specialist Human Relations dept., 1982-85, vol. mediator, 1985—; employee relations and tng. mgr. Personnel and Risk Mgmt. dept. U. Nebr., Lincoln, 1985-87; asst. dir. personnel services dept. Kans. State U., Manhattan, 1988—; instr. div. continuing studies U. Nebr., Lincoln, 1987—; cons. Chancellor's Commn. on Sexual Harassment, Lincoln, 1987—; speaker women's issues. cons., trainer Stop Violence Coalition, Kansas City, 1984-85; arbitrator Cornhusker Better Bus. Bur., Lincoln, 1985-87; bd. dirs. YWCA, Lincoln, 1986-87. Recipient Appreciation award Stop Violence Coalition, 1984. Fellow Coll. and Univ. Personnel Assn., Am. Soc. for Tng. and Devel., Univ. Assn. for Adminstrv. Devel. (exec. com., chair profl. devel. 1986-87), Nat. Assn. Negro Bus. and Profl. Women (Outstanding Vol. of Yr. award 1985), Women of Color Task Force (chair 1986-87). Democrat. Baptist. Home: 724 Ridgewood Dr Manhattan KS 66502

FISHER, SUSAN GROSSMAN, banker; b. N.Y.C., July 27, 1946; d. Bernard and Leah Irene (Gordon) Grossman; B.A. in Math., U. Wis., 1967; M.A., Columbia U., 1968, M.B.A., 1976; m. Yale L. Fisher, June 17, 1968; children—Douglas Carl, Robin Leah. Asst. trust officer Mfrs. Hanover Trust Co., N.Y.C., 1971-73, asst. v.p., 1973-76, v.p. trust div., 1977-79; v.p. Wells Rich Greene, Inc., N.Y.C., 1979-80; v.p., dir. mktg. met. div. Chem. Bank, N.Y.C., 1980-82, v.p., dist. head worldwide pvt. banking div., 1982-83; sr. v.p. Marine Midland Bank, N.Y.C., 1983-85; sr. v.p. Mfrs. & Traders Trust Co., 1985—; dir. Veeco Instruments, Inc., 1983-86. Mem. leadership devel. group for execs. Brandeis U., 1974—. Dir. Emanuel Midtown YM-YWHA, YWCA of City of N.Y., 1979-82, Dance Notation Bur., United Neighborhood Houses N.Y., women's bd. Jewish Guild for Blind, Nat. Choral Council, Council Mcpl. Performance, 1980-86, Friends of the Theater Collection, Mus. of City of N.Y., WNYC Found.; mem. Manhatten Community Bd. #5, 198-82; nat. chmn. Rep. Nat. Com. Nat. Women's Coalition; gov. Space Commerce Roundtable Found., Ctr. for Study of the Presidency, Nat. Adv. Council. Mem. Inst. Quantitative Research in Fin. (dir. 1975-79), N.Y. State Bankers Assn. (com. communications policy 1981-83), Fin. Women's Assn. N.Y. (dir. fin. 1979-82, pres. 1980-81), Women's Forum (dir.), Investment Tech. Symposium (dir. 1974-78), Council Mcpl. Performance (dir. 1980-86), N.Y. Chamber Commerce and Industry, Communications Industry Council (steering com.), Bank Aminstrn. Inst. (trust and fin. prods. commn. 1983-86), Columbia Grad. Sch. Bus. Alumni Assn. (dir. 1981—, pres., 1985-87), Beta Gamma Sigma. Club: Econ. (N.Y.C.). Office: Mfrs & Traders Trust Co 654 Madison Ave New York NY 10021

FISHER, WENDY ASTLEY-BELL, marketing professional; b. London, Jan. 23, 1944; d. Leonard Astley and Rita (Duis) Astley-Bell; m. Richard Van. Mell, Mar. 21, 1970 (div. May 1980); m. Lester Emil Fisher, Jan. 23, 1981. Student, U. Alberta, 1963; BA honors, Northwestern U., 1965; student, U. Chgo., 1965-66. Artist various agys., Chgo., 1966-70; freelance artist various advt. agys., Chgo., 1970-76; dir. special projects Lincoln Park Zool. Soc., Chgo., 1976-81; pres. Mailworks Inc., Chgo., 1981—; Lectr. numerous bus. confs., 1982—. Co-author: The First Hundred Years, 1975. Bd. mgrs. Visiting Nurses Assn., 1980-84; mem. adv. council Theatre Sch. DePaul U., 1984-86; mem. women's bd. dirs. Lincoln Park Zool. Soc., 1981-84. Mem. Econ. Club Chgo., Women Direct Response, Nat. Assn. Women Bus. Owners, Am. Assn. Zool. Parks and Aquariums, Nat. Soc. Fund Raising Execs. Chgo. chpt. (bd. dirs., 1981-86, co-chair internat. conf. 1986, co-chair midwest fund raising 1987), Women Communications (bd. dirs. 1981-82) (named outstanding woman entrepreneur Chgo. chpt. 1983), Chgo. Assn. Direct Mktg. (bd. dirs. 1982-86), Jr. League Chgo. (bd. mgrs. 1970-73). Home: 3180 N Lake Shore Dr Chicago IL 60657 Office: Mailworks Inc 230 N Michigan Ave Chicago IL 60601

FISHER-DICKENS, JOANN YVONNE, naval petty officer; b. Washington, Mar. 8, 1947; d. Warren G.H. and Irene (Warren) Fisher; m. Robert Lawrence Dickens, Jan. 19, 1976 (div. 1978); children: Phyllis Ann Fisher, Ericka Lynn Fisher, Donald Steven Fisher. Student Merrit Jr. Coll., Oakland, Calif., 1970, Laney Jr. Coll., Oakland, 1970-71, J.F.K. U., Orinda, Calif., 1980-84. Enlisted U.S. Navy Res., 1976, active duty, 1978—, petty officer 1st class, 1982; with adminstrv. dept. Navy Recruiting Exhibit Ctr., Washington, 1985-86; elected Adv. Neighborhood Commr. Bolling AFB, 1986-88. Democrat. Methodist. Home: 249 Burwell St Bolling AFB Washington DC 20332 Office: Navy Recruiting Exhibit Ctr Washington Navy Yard Washington DC 20374

FISHMAN, HELENE BETH, social worker; b. Portchester, N.Y., Oct. 23, 1937; d. Henry William and Hortense (Baumblatt) Sandground; B.A., Mt. Holyoke Coll., 1959; M.S. in Social Work, Columbia U., 1961; m. Bernard Fishman, Feb. 14, 1959; children—Kara Jo, Charles Lee. Psychiat. social worker Children's Village, Dobbs Ferry, N.Y., 1961, 1965-66; asst. dir. Afro-Am. Cultural Found., White Plains, N.Y., 1968-78; mental health technician tchr., White Plains, 1970-71; cons. social worker, Hartsdale, N.Y., 1978—; cons. edn./research Oceanic Soc., Stamford, Conn., 1985-86. Chmn. cottage program Greenburgh Dist. 7; active PTA. Mem. Assn. for Children with Learning Disabilities (chmn. dist. 7). Jewish. Home: 6 Old Farm Ln Hartsdale NY 10530

FISHMAN, LINDA KAY, social worker; b. Youngstown, Ohio, Feb. 8, 1939; d. Samuel Richard and Syd Ruth (Hoffman) Zoss; m. Lawrence Shelden Fishman, June 12, 1960 (div. 1975); 1 child, Julie Ann. BA magna cum laude, U. Mich., 1960, MSW, 1961. Clin. social worker VA Hosp., Los Angeles, 1963-65; social work cons. USPHS, Washington, 1965-67; exec. sec. Health Planning div. USPHS, N.Y.C., 1968; social work cons. Jarrett Assocs., Van Nuys, Calif., 1975-84; dir. social services and planning Nat. In Home Health Services, Van Nuys, 1984-87; dir. planning Nat. In-Home Health Services, Van Nuys, 1987—; dir. case mgmt. SCAN Health Plan, Long Beach, Calif. Recipient Dirs. Commendation, VA Ctr., 1965. Fellow Soc. Clin. Social Workers; mem. Nat. Assn. Social Workers (cert., Home Health Task Force, 1986—), Am. Pub. Health Assn., Nat. Conf. Social Welfare, Home Health Social Workers (chmn. 1986-87), Phi Beta Kappa, Phi Kappa Phi. Home: 248 S Detroit St Los Angeles CA 90036 Office: SCAN Health Plan 521 E 4th St Long Beach CA 90802

FISHMAN, MADELINE DOTTI, management consulting company executive, consultant; b. Chgo., Oct. 7, 1942; d. Martin and Anne (Sweet) Binder; m. Norton Lee Fishman, Apr. 7, 1963; children: Mark Nathan, Marla Susan. BEd, Nat. Coll. Edn., 1964, MS, 1972. Tchr., Rochester Schs. (Minn.), 1963-64, Orange County Schs., Orlando, Fla., 1967-68; reading cons. Palatine Schs. (Ill.), 1972-73; instr. Parent Effective Tng., Wilmette, Ill., 1974-76, tchr. Effectiveness Tng., 1974-76; pres. Profls. Diversified, Wilmette, Ill., 1976—; remedial and enrichment reading tchr. Waukegan (Ill.) Pub. Schs., 1986; mgmt. cons. World Wide Diamonds Assn., Schaumburg, Ill., 1979—, Artistic Color, Dallas, 1983-87; Pearl direct distbr. Amway Corp., Ada, Mich., 1976—; co-owner Lasting Impressions, 1988—. Author: Organic Gardening, 1975, The Go-Getters Planner, 1986. Leader, Camp Fire Girls, Evanston, Ill., 1963, 75. Recipient Ednl. Scholarship, Nat. Coll. Edn., 1971. Mem. Kappa Delta Pi. Jewish.

FISK, JEAN A., child development clinic administrator; b. Aberdeen, S.D., June 11, 1946; d. Darwin A. and Ardith (Severance) F.; m. Giles Banks Lidell, II, Dec. 28, 1985; 1 stepson, Giles Banks III. B.S., U. Wis., Oshkosh, 1972; M.S.Ed., U. Wis., Whitewater, 1974; postgrad. Nat. Coll. Edn., Evanston, Ill., 1975, No. Colo. U., 1979. Supr., N.W. Spl. Edn. Dist., Freeport, Ill., 1972-73; cons. Racine County Spl. Edn., Union Grove, Wis., 1973-74; instr. Nat. Coll. Edn., 1974-77; founder, exec. dir. Chgo. Clinic for Child Devel., 1976—; in-service dir., cons. to schs. Recipient Title VI-D fellowship award, 1972. Mem. Assn. for Children with Learning Disabilities, Exec. Female Assn., Council for Adminstrs. in Spl. Edn., Hyde Park Businessmen's Assn., Council for Exceptional Children. Christian. Club: Zonta. Author: EmH-SLD????, 1972; Handbook for Parents of Children with Learning Disabilities, 1973; Nonsense Syllables as an Aide to Teaching Reading, 1973. Office: 1525 E 53d St Chicago IL 60615

FISK, SHERRY ELAINE, manufacturing company executive; b. Dallas, Sept. 21, 1948; d. Robert Joseph Grisham and Alma Nadine (Grey) Bell; m. Neal Paul Fisk, Dec. 28, 1979; 1 child, Aubrey Nadine. BA, UCLA, 1970. Loan officer Security Nat. Bank, Denver, 1971-74; v.p. Rocky Mountain Hardware, Denver, 1974-79; pres. Best Tool Co., Hico, Tex., 1979—. Mem. Nat. Assn. Female Execs., Rep. Nat. Com., Nat. Firearms Assn. Office: Best Tool Co 421 Pecan Hico TX 76457

FISZER-SZAFARZ, BERTA (BERTA SAFARS), research scientist; b. Wilno, Poland, Feb. 1, 1928; m. David Szafarz; children—Martine, Michel. M.S., U. Buenos Aires, 1955, Ph.D., 1956. Lab. chief Cancer Inst. Villejuif, France, 1961-67; vis. scientist Nat. Cancer Inst., Bethesda, Md., 1967-68; lab. chief Institut Curie, Orsay, France, 1969—; vis. scientist Inst. Applied Biochemistry, Mitake, Gifu, Japan, 1986. Contbr. articles to profl. jours. Mem. European Assn. Cancer Research, Am. Assn. Cancer Research (corres. mem.), European Cell Biology Orgn., French Soc. Cell Biology.

FITCH, MARY KILLEEN, human resources specialist; b. Carroll, Iowa, July 15, 1949; d. Michael Francis and Mildred (Pauley) Killeen; m. David Paul Fitch, July 3, 1971. BS, Iowa State U., 1971, MS, 1975; postgrad. U. Minn., 1982—. Personnel adminstr. Control Data Corp., Roseville, Minn., 1976-77; sr. compensation analyst/employee relations rep. Honeywell, Inc., Mpls., 1977-80; human resource mgr./compensation and benefits mgr. No. Telecom, Inc., Minnetonka, Minn., 1980-82; adj. instr., teaching asst. Lakewood Community Coll./U. Minn., Mpls., 1982-84; compensation cons. Gen. Mills, Wayzata, Minn., 1984-85; mgr. compensation Northwestern Nat. Life Ins., Mpls., 1985-87; prin. compensation specialist Comml. Bldgs. Group, Honeywell, Inc., Mpls., 1987—; cons. exec. compensation Honeywell Inc., Mpls., 1984; cons. human resources Les Kraus & Assocs., Edina, Minn., 1984; pres. Personnel Mgmt. Services of Twin Cities, St. Paul, 1983—. Author: (with Paul Muchinsky) Organization Behavior and Human Performance, 1975; (with John Fossum) Personnel Psychology, 1985. Chmn., bd. dirs. Kathadin, United Way Agy., Mpls., 1985—; curriculum com. U. Minn., 1983-84. George Catt Iowa State U. scholar, 1970. Mem. Am. Soc. Personnel Adminstrn., Twin Cities Personnel Assn. (program chmn. 1978-81, benefits council 1987—), Indsl. Relations Research Assn., AAUW, Am. Psychol. Assn., Acad. Mgmt., Am. Compensation Assn., Psi Chi, Phi Kappa Phi. Avocations: dressage, karate. Home: 1188 90th St E Inver Grove Heights MN 55075 Office: Honeywell Inc Comml Bldgs Group Honeywell Plaza Minneapolis MN 55408

FITCH, RACHEL, nurse; b. Deering, Mo., July 27, 1933; d. Allen Edward and Rosie Leola (Jones) Farr; R.N., St. Vincent Hosp., 1954; student Little Rock U., 1965-67; B.S., St. Louis U., 1974, M.S., 1976, Ph.D., 1983; m. Coy Dean Fitch, Mar. 31, 1956; children—Julia Anne, Jaquelyn Kay. Psychiat. staff nurse VA Ft. Root Hosp., North Little Rock, Ark., 1954-57; surg.-med. staff nurse St. Vincent Infirmary, Little Rock, 1957-65; acute care nurse Georgetown U. Hosp., Washington, 1968-69; public health nurse to adminstr. South office Vis. Nurse Assn. Greater St. Louis, 1970-73; cons. in edn. St. Louis City Health Dept., 1977-80; research specialist Sen. John C. Danforth, St. Louis, 1980; owner RFF Assocs., 1983-86; project dir. study of infant mortality in city of St. Louis, 1978. Mem. community health edn. com. Am. Heart Assn., 1977—; bd. dir. League of Women Voters of Mo., 1984—, editor newspaper, 1984-87, dir. social policy, 1987—; bd. dirs. St. Louis Met. Med. Soc. Aux., St. Louis Univ. Hosp. Aux. Mem. Am. Public Health Assn., Acad. Polit. Sci., Sigma Theta Tau.

FITE, DIANA LYNN, physician; b. Amarillo, Tex., Apr. 10, 1953; d. John Victor and Sylvia Mae (Hancock) Ellis; m. Ronald Patrick Patton, Dec. 15, 1977; children—Tracy Patton, Anna Patton, Arthur Patton, Elizabeth Patton, Alexandria Patton. B.S., West Tex. State U., 1975; M.D., U. Tex., 1978. Diplomate Am. Bd. Emergency Medicine. Intern, Hermann Hosp., Houston, 1978-79, resident, 1979; dir. gynecology clinic U. Houston, 1980-81; emergency physician Sam Houston Hosp., Houston, 1979-83; emergency room physician Spring Branch Hosp., Houston, 1983—; owner Gyncare-Pedicare: A Clinic for Women and Children, Houston, 1981-87, Audio Prophiles, Inc., Houston, 1983—, Advanced Med. Arts, Houston, 1987—; dir. Cyfair Vol. Fire Dept., Houston, 1984—; med. dir. Village Fire Dept., Houston, 1985—, Jersey Village Fire Dept., 1985—, West Lake Fire Dept., 1986—. Mem. Am. Coll. Emergency Physicians, Harris County Med. Soc., Tex. Med. Assn. (alt. del. 1986, 87), Nat. Assn. EMS Physician Dirs., Western Br. Med. Soc. (v.p. 1987—, pres.-elect 1988—), Houston Soc. Emergency Medicine (pres.-elect 1988—). Republican. Episcopalian. Office: Advanced Med Arts 4536 Hwy 6 N Houston TX 77084

FITERMAN, JUDITH MARILYN, television producer; b. Louisville, Ky., June 29, 1944; d. Maurice Melvin and Regina Grace (Baer) F. BA, U. Md., 1967. Editor, producer Sta. WUSA-TV, Washington, 1970—. Recipient 2 Emmy awards, 1985, Peabody award U. Ga., 1984, Dupont award Columbia U., N.Y.C., 1985, James E. Scripps award Evening News Assn., Detroit, 1985, Nat. Press Club award, Washington, 1985. Mem. Nat. Assn. TV Arts and Scis. Home: 4014 Jeffry St Wheaton MD 20906 Office: 40th and Brandywine St NW Washington DC 20016

FITTERER, BARBARA TROMBLEY, clergywoman; m. John A. Fitterer, Dec. 23, 1977. A.B. in English, magna cum laude, U. Rochester, 1966, M.A. in English Lit., 1967; M.Div. magna cum laude, Wesley Theol. Sem., 1979; postgrad. Princeton Theol. Sem., 1983-84; PhD., Theol. Union, Berkley, 1988. Ordained deacon Episcopal Ch., 1979, ordained priest, 1979. Tchr. English, Pittsford High Sch., N.Y., 1967-68; instr. English, U. Rochester, N.Y., 1967-68; editor, nat. cons. Houghton Mifflin Pub. Co., 1968-75, mgr. Washington office, 1976-79; Presidential fellow President's Exec. Exchange Program, Washington, 1975-76; curate Parish of St. John the Evangelist, Hingham, Mass., 1979-80; co-dir. Bishop's staff Episcopal Diocese Calif., 1980-83; assoc. rector St. Stephen's Episcopal Ch., Belvedere, Calif., 1983-84, St. John's Episcopal Ch., Ross, Calif., 1984-86; dir. ecumenical ministry First Baptist Ch. Washington, 1976-78; liturgist U.S. Naval Chapel, Washington, 1977-79; clin. pastoral edn. assoc. Sibley Hosp., Washington, 1978; offered opening prayers U.S. Ho. of Reps. and U.S. Senate, 1982, 83, 85, 87 (first ordained woman to do so). Mem. trustees council U. Rochester, 1975-85; elected standing com. SYNOD, Diocese of Calif., 1983, 84. Served with Chaplain's Res. Corps, USN, 1978-80. Named to Outstanding Young Women Am.; Reading fellow Coll. Preachers, Washington, 1983. Mem. Am. Bus. Women's Assn. (hon.), Rockefeller Found. (Bellagio 1987). Office: St. John's Episcopal Ch PO Box 5202 Larkspur Standing Sta Larkspur CA 94939-5202 Mailing Address: Box 534 Ross CA 94957

FITZGERALD, ALICE MARIE, nurse; b. Eldora, Iowa, Sept. 11, 1925; d. Sam and Hazel (Dunn) Newby; m. Robert C. Fitzgerald, Sept. 14, 1946; 1 child, Vicki Lee Schuck. BS in Health and Arts, Coll. St. Francis, 1982. Head nurse Mercy Hosp., Marshalltown, Iowa, 1946-48; office nurse physician's office, Garwin, Iowa, 1948-50; pvt. duty nurse local hosps., Marshalltown, 1950-65; head nurse Iowa Vets. Home, Marshalltown, 1966-67, nurse supr. I, 1967-80, nurse supr. II (nursing clin. coordinator), 1980—. Mem. Pres. Eisenhower's People to People Internat. Orgn.; mem. steering com. Cen. Iowans for Handicapped, 1967, treas. 1967—. Am. Nurses Assn. (cert.), Iowa Nurses Assn., Assn. Rehab. Nurses (Iowa chpt. pres. 1978-80, 86—). Republican. Mem. Ch. of the Brethren. Home: 2039 190th St Marshalltown IA 50158 Office: Iowa Vets Home 13th & Summit Marshalltown IA 50158

FITZGERALD, CAROL J., foundation administrator; b. Chgo., July 2, 1950; d. Lucien W. and Dian (Gorgas) F.; m. Douglas Paul Becknell, Jul. 10, 1971; 1 child, Rachel Fitzgerald Becknell. BS in Edn., No. Ill. U., 1973; MA, Ill. State U., 1976. Tchr. Prophetstown (Ill.) High Sch., 1976-77; dir. program Sterling-Rock Falls YWCA, Ill., 1977-80; county coordinator Highland Coll. CETA, Freeport, Ill., 1980-81; tchr. Sauk Valley Coll., Dixon, Ill., 1981-82; coordinator region N. Cen. Ill. Council Govts., Princeton, 1982-83; exec. asst. Sterling C. of C., 1985; exec. dir. Sterling-Rock Falls YWCA, 1985—. Dir. Lincoln Land Chpt. ARC, 1986—; sec. Sterling-Rock Falls Ministerial Assn., 1986—; steering com. mem. Daily Bread Food Co-op, 1980—; treas. Rock Valley Nuclear Freeze Coalition, 1982. Mem. Sauk Valley NOW (pres. 1978, 81), Nat. Assn. YWCA Exec. Dirs., Nat. Assn. Female Exec. Unitarian. Office: YWCA 412 First Ave Sterling IL 61081

FITZGERALD, ELLA, singer; b. Newport News, Va., Apr. 25, 1918; m. Ray Brown (div. 1953); 1 son, Ray. Began singing with Chick Webb Orch., 1934-39; tours throughout U.S., Japan, Europe; with Jazz at the Philharmonic troupe, 1948-57; rec. artist for Decca, 1936-55, Verve, from 1956, now Pablo Records; appeared in motion picture Pete Kelly's Blues, 1955; nightclub appearances include Sahara Hotel, Caesar's Palace, both Las Vegas, Fairmont Hotel, San Francisco, Ronnie Scott's Club, London; appeared on TV in spls. with Frank Sinatra; also on All Star Swing Festival, 1972, concert with Boston Pops, 1972; later with more than 40 symphony orchs. throughout U.S.; records include At Duke's Place, 1966, Best, 1967, Clap Hands, 1961, Cote d' Azur, (with Ellington), 1967, Ella, Ella Fitzgerald; In Hamburg, 1965, Mack the Knife, Ella in Berlin, 1960, Sunshine of Your Love, Things Ain't What They Used to Be, Tribute to Porter, 1965, Whisper Not, 1966, Watch What Happens, 1972, Take Love Easy, 1975, Ella in London, 1975, Lady Time, 1978, A Perfect Match (with Count Basie), 1979, A Tisket a Tasket, 1985, Montreux Ella, numerous others. Recipient 8 Grammy awards, numerous popularity awards from Down Beat mag., Metronome mag., Musicians Poll, JAY Award Poll; named number 1 female singer 16th Internat. Jazz Critics Poll, 1968, Am. Music award, 1978; recipient Kennedy Center honor, 1979, Grammy award as best female jazz vocalist, 1981, 84; recipient Nat. Medal of the Arts, 1987. Address: care Norman Granz 451 N Canon Dr Beverly Hills CA 90210 *

FITZGERALD, JANET ANNE, college president; b. Woodside, N.Y., Sept. 4, 1935; d. Robert W. and Lillian H. (Shannon) F. B.A. magna cum laude, St. John's U., 1965, M.A., 1967, Ph.D., 1971. Joined Sisters of St. Dominic of Amityville, Roman Catholic Ch., 1953; NSF postdoctoral fellow Cath. U. Am., summer 1971; prof. philosophy Molloy Coll., Rockville Centre, N.Y., 1969—; pres. Molloy Coll., 1972—; chmn. L.I. Regional Adv. Council on Higher Edn., 1981-84, trustee, 1985—; trustee Commn. on Ind. Colls. and Univs., Fellowship of Cath. Scholars, 1977—, v.p., 1977-80; Roman Cath. Ch. rep. to Nat. Congress Ch.-Related Colls. and Univs., 1979; trustee Cath. Charities, Diocese of Rockville Centre, 1979-82. Author: Alfred North Whitehead's Early Philosophy of Space and Time, 1979. Mem. bd. advisors Sem. of Immaculate Conception, 1975-80; mem. adv. bd. pre-theology program Dunwoodie Sem., Archdiocese of N.Y. Mem. Am. Cath. Philos. Assn. (spl. commn. on status of women in philos. profession). Office: Molloy Coll 1000 Hempstead Ave Rockville Centre NY 11570

FITZGERALD, JANICE S., public relations executive, academic administrator; b. Poughkeepsie, N.Y., Nov. 2, 1948; d. Lloyd Raymond and Emily Mae (Anderson) Spinner. BA magna cum laude, U. Pa., Cheyney, 1972, MEd, 1973; MA, Villanova U., 1980; postgrad., Carnegie Mellon U., 1979. Prof. U. Pa., Cheyney, 1972-74, dir. pub. relations, 1974-83; dir. pub. relations Pa. State System of Higher Edn., Harrisburg, 1983—, exec. assoc. to chancellor, dir. communications, 1985—; reader Nat. Edn. Assn.; pres. Correct Correspondence; free lance writer. Vol. radio reader, Tri-County Assn. of Blind, Suburban Guild, Community Gen. Osteo. Hosp. Named one of Outstanding Women in Am., 1981, named Alumnus of Yr. Nat. Assn. Equal Opportunity, 1985; recipient award Chapel of Four Chaplains, 1982, Valedictory and Alumni Key award Cheyney U. Pa., 1972. Mem. Coll. and U. Pub. Relations Assn. of Pa., Pub. Relations Soc. of Am., Edn. Writers Assn. Office: Office of Chancellor 301 Market St Harrisburg PA 17108

FITZGERALD, JOYCE LUCILLE, biologist, coal company official; b. Coshocton, Ohio, Mar. 9, 1947; d. Earl Lester and Doris Lucille (Lapp) F.; B.S. in Edn. and Biol. Scis., Ohio U., 1970, postgrad., 1971; postgrad. Ohio State U., 1972. Instr. biol. sci. Zanesville (Ohio) Public Schs., 1970-72; adminstrv. asst. Ohio Dept. Natural Resources, Columbus, 1972-73; adminstrv. dir. Boys, Inc., Columbus, 1973-74; biologist Skelly & Loy, Cons. Engrs., Harrisburg, Pa., 1975-76; adminstrv. chief Ohio EPA, Columbus, 1976-78; mgr. environ. affairs Ind. div. Peabody Coal Co., Evansville, 1978-86; mgr. corp. environ. affairs Peabody Coal Co., Henderson, Ky., 1986—. Mem. Ind. CAP (2d lt.), Evansville; bd. dirs. A Network of Evansville Women, 1988. Recipient Ind. Environ. Achievement award Izaak Walton League Ind., 1987, Community Devel. award Warrick County C. of C., 1988; named Ohio Wildlife Conservationist of Yr., 1977; cert. wastewater operator, Ind.; cert. biologist U.S. Fish and Wildlife Service; lic. pvt. pilot FAA. Mem. Ind. Wildlife Soc., Ind. Water Resources Assn., Nat. Wildlife Fedn., Ind. Coal Inst., Women in Mining Inc. (officer), Ind. Sportsman Alliance.

FITZGERALD, JUNE GILL, trade association executive; b. Coconut Grove, Fla., Oct. 16, 1925; d. Alan Lawson and Chadsey Rebecca (Edwards) Gill; m. Frank S. Fitzgerald, June 29, 1950; children—April Ann Fitzgerald Pena Marsden, Kathryn Ruth Fitzgerald Pachuta. Student U. Miami, 1947. Meetings mgr. Archtl. Aluminum Mfrs. Assn., 1966-74; exec. asst. Pan Am. World Airways, Miami, Fla., 1942-57; exec. sec. Noise Control Products and Material Assn., Chgo., 1976-82; pres. Fitzgerald Corp., Chgo., 1971—. Mem. Am. Soc. Assn. Execs., Chgo. Soc. Assn. Execs., Inst. Assn. Mgmt. Cos., Garage Door Council (exec. sec. 1982—), Nat. Assn. Garage Door Mfrs. (exec. sec. 1974—), Screen Mfrs. Assn. (exec. sec. 1974—), Broadcast Advt. Club (exec. dir. and sec. 1974—), Am. Assn. Ret. Persons, Nat. Assn. for Female Execs. Home: 3950 Lake Shore Dr Apt 502A Chicago IL 60613

Address: 1140 NW 199th St North Miami Beach FL 33169 Office: Fitzgerald Corp 655 655 Irving Park Rd Chicago IL 60613

FITZGERALD, LAURINE E., university dean, educator; b. New London, Wis., Aug. 24, 1930; d. Thomas F. and Laurine (Branchflower) F. B.S., Northwestern U., 1952, M.A., 1953; Ph.D., Mich. State U., 1959. Instr. English, dir. devel. reading lab., head resident-dir. Wis. State Coll., Whitewater, 1953-55; area dir. residence and counseling Ind. U., 1955-57; teaching grad. asst. guidance and counseling, then instr., counselor Mich. State U., East Lansing, 1957-59; asst. prof. psychology and edn., assoc. dean students U. Denver, 1959-62; asst. prof. counseling psychology, staff counselor for Carnegie Found. project U. Minn., 1962-63; asst. dean, asst prof. Mich. State U., 1963-70, assoc. dean students. prof. adminstrn. and higher edn., dir. div. edn. and research, 1970-74; dean Grad. Sch., prof. counselor edn., dir. N.E. Wis. Coop. Regional Grad. Ctr. U. Wis.-Oshkosh, 1974-85; dean/dir. Ohio State U.-Mansfield, 1986-87, prof. edn. policy and leadership, 1985—; vis. lectr. U. Okla., Norman, 1961; vis. prof. Oreg. State U., 1977; cons. in field. Author numerous articles in field; co-author monographs, texts. Adv. bd. Mansfield Gen. Hosp., 1986—; bd. dirs. Renaissance Theatre, 1986— ; exec. council Ohio Consortium on Tng. and Planning, 1985-87; bd. dirs. New Beginnings, 1986—, v.p., 1987—. Recipient Higher Edn. Rocky Mountain council Girl Scouts U.S.A., 1961, Evelyn Hosmer U. Denver, 1962; Elin Wagner Found. fellow, 1963-64; named Old Master Purdue Univ., 1979. Mem. Am. Psychol. Assn., Mich. Psychol. Assn., Am. Personnel and Guidance Assn., Am. Coll. Personnel Assn. (sec. 1965-67, exec. bd. 1968-70, chmn. women's task force 1970-71, editor jour. 1976-82, disting. scholar award 1985, sr. scholars 1985—, chmn. scholars 1986-87), Assn. Counselor Edn. and Supervision, Am. Assn. Higher Edn., Nat. Assn. Women Deans, Adminstrs. and Counselors (pres. 1980), AAUP (chpt. treas. 1955-56), NEA, Mich. Assn. Women Deans, Adminstrs. and Counselors (pres. 1967-69), Ohio Assn. Women Deans, Adminstrs. and Counselors, Mich. Coll. Personnel Assn., Wis. Coll. Personnel Assn., Midwest Assn. Grad. Schs. (pres. 1980-82), Intercollegiate Assn. Women Students (editorial bd., nat. adviser), AAUW, Women's Equity Action League (past pres. Mich., nat. sec.-treas. legal and edn. def. fund), Bus. and Profl. Women's Club (chpt. pres. 1980, state officer 1981, Lena Lake Forest fellow 1966-67, named Most Disting. Women in Edn., Mich. 1973), Wis. Soc. for Higher Edn. (Achievement award 1985), Mortar Bd., Altrusa Internat., Beta Beta Beta, Psi Chi, Alpha Lambda Delta, Delta Kappa Gamma. Clubs: Zonta (pres. Lansing club, chmn. internat. status of women com. 1960-85), Altrusa Internat. Home: 1430 Royal Oak Dr Mansfield OH 44906 Office: Ohio State U 301 Ramseyer 29 W Woodruff Ave Columbus OH 43210

FITZGERALD, PATRICIA ANN, motivational and management consultant; b. Dallas, Sept. 16, 1937; d. Thomas O'Neil and Minerva Hannah (Gililland) Anderson; student Sawyer Bus. Coll., 1955, Phoenix City Coll., 1960-66, Brigham Young U., Hawaii, 1979, U. Calif.-Irvine, 1979, UCLA, 1979-80; m. Gerald William Fitzgerald, Mar. 6, 1976; children by previous marriage—Vicki Lee Jones Duncan, Gregg Ronald Jones, Randall Thomas Jones, Lori Lynn Jones. Service rep. So. Calif. Gas Co., 1956-60, Ariz. Public Service, 1961; sales rep. Shaw Walker Co., 1967-68; sales mgr. Selective Office Service, 1968-69; communications cons., mktg. mgr. Pacific Telephone Co., Orange, Calif., 1970-80; pres. Fitzgerald & Assocs., Anaheim Hills, Calif. and Denver, 1979—; cons. in field. Recipient awards of appreciation Personnel and Indsl. Relations Assn., Brooks Coll., Pacific Telephone. Mem. Am. Soc. Tng. and Devel. (appreciation award), Am. Mktg. Assn., Women in Mgmt. (appreciation award), Internat. Platform Assn., Nat. Speakers Assn., Relief Soc. Republican. Mormon. Contbr. articles to bus. mags. and newspapers, Long Beach and Los Angeles; various appearances ednl. TV, Orange County. Home and Office: 4 Shetland Ct Highlands Ranch CO 80126

FITZGERALD, SARA JEAN, journalist; b. Flint, Mich., Aug. 22, 1951; d. Glen Ray and Mary Louise (Ellis) F.; B.A., U. Mich., 1973; m. Walter W. Wurfel, Aug. 30, 1975; 1 son, Stephen Fitzgerald. Reporter, copy editor St. Petersburg Times, 1973-75; asso. editor Nat. Jour. mag., Washington, 1975-79; CompuServe editor, asst. city editor, editor fed. report page Washington Post, 1979—, assoc. editor nat. weekly edition. Recipient Mark of Excellence award Sigma Delta Chi, 1973. Mem. Women in Communications, Inc., Phi Beta Kappa. Office: 1150 15th St NW Washington DC 20071

FITZGERALD-REDDY, KATHLEEN APRIL, environmental research manager; b. Jamaica, N.Y., Apr. 6, 1955; d. Leo Thomas and Florence Ann (Kehoe) Fitzgerald; m. James M. Metcalfe, Jan. 17, 1981 (div. May 1982); m. John Morley Reddy, Feb. 15, 1985; 1 child, Kathleen Elizabeth. Student, U. N.H., 1973-78. Profl. model Barbizon Agy., Boston, 1974-76, Hart Agy., Boston, 1976-78; announcer Sta. WBBX Kressman Broadcasting Co., Portsmouth, N.H., 1978-80, Sta. WOKQ The Fuller-Jeffrey Group, Dover, N.H., 1980-85; environ. analyst Briggs Assocs, Inc., Rockland, Mass., 1985-86; mgr. environ. research Briggs Assocs, Inc., Rockland, 1986—. Recipient Graniteer award Ad Club of N.H., 1979, Achievement Cert. in Hazardous Waste Regulations Lion Tech., 1986. Mem. Soc. for the Preservation of New Eng. Antiquities, Hampton Hist. Soc. Democrat. Roman Catholic. Home: 15 Blake Ln Hampton NH 03842 Office: Briggs Assocs Inc 400 Hingham St Rockland MA 02370

FITZGIBBONS, CAROL ANNE, public relations executive; b. Phoenix, Dec. 15, 1947; d. Richard Bedell and Evelyn Edith (Sadler) Kidwell; m. R. Michael Fitzgibbons, May 19, 1974. BS, Ariz. State U., 1970, MS, 1973. Tchr. Radcliffe Hall, Anaheim, Calif., 1974-75; revenue coordinator Harbor Regional Ctr., Torrance, Calif., 1975-76, community program developer, 1976-78, acting dir. community affairs, 1978; dir. community affairs San Diego Imperial Counties Devel. Services, Inc., 1978-86; dir. Friends of Hanidcapped Children, 1987—. Recipient Accomodation Senator Jim Ellis, 1986. Mem. Am. Acad. Mental Deficiency. Republican. Methodist. Club: PEO (pres. 1984-86, sec. 1982-84). Home: 449 G Ave Coronado CA 92118

FITZNER, YVONNE, graphic designer, singer, songwriter; b. Bussum, Holland, Oct. 22, 1942; d. Adi and Eva (Kloot) F. Student, Sch. Visual Arts, 1961-65, 75-76. Trainee, draftsperson Big G Press, N.Y.C., 1960-62; sole staff artist Audio Visual Sch. Service, N.Y.C., 1962-64; staff artist, designer Basic Systems, Inc., N.Y.C., 1964-67; freelance designer, prodn. artist Cato Johnson Assocs., N.Y.C., 1970-78; freelance designer/prodn. artist various cos., N.J., N.Y.C., 1978—. Contbr. articles to music jours.; producer (film) "Play On Words", 1976. Entertainer John V. Lindsay Mayoral Reelection Campaign, N.Y.C., 1969; vol. artist, fundraiser Howard Samuels Gubernatiorial Campaign, 1974, Ramsey Clark Senatorial Campaign, 1976. Recipient Cert. of Design Excellence, Lettergraphics Internat., Inc., 1971, poster illustration award, Art Dirs. Club N.J., 1974, Cert. of Excellence, Communication Collaborative, Inc., 1977. Mem. The Songwriters Guild, ASCAP, Graphic Artists Guild, Type Dirs. Club. Home and Office: 231 E 76th St New York NY 10021

FITZPATRICK, DONNA R., government official; b. Washington, May 9, 1948; B.A., Am. U., 1972; J.D., George Washington U., 1980. Legal asst. O'Connor & Hannan, 1976-80, assoc., 1980-83; sole practice, also cons. to Dept. Energy, 1983-84; prin. dep. asst. sec. for conservation and renewable energy Dept. Energy, Washington, 1984-85, asst. sec., 1985—. Office: Dept of Energy Conservation & Renewable Energy 1000 Independence Ave SW Washington DC 20585

FITZPATRICK, M. LOUISE, nursing educator; b. South River, N.J., May 24, 1942; d. John Francis and Bettina (Galassi) F. Diploma in nursing, Johns Hopkins U., 1963; BSN, Cath. U. Am., 1966; MA, Columbia U., 1968, MEd, 1969, EdD, 1972; cert., Harvard U., 1985. Former assoc. prof., dept. nursing edn. Tchrs. Coll., Columbia U., N.Y.C.; dean, prof. Villanova U. Coll. Nursing, Villanova, Pa., 1978—; cons. Middle States Assn., Phila., U. So. Calif.; cons., reviewer USPHS; bd. dirs. Nurses Ednl. Funds Inc., N.Y.C. Author: The National Organization for Public Nursing, Development of a Practice Field, 1975; editor: Present Realities/Future Imperatives, 1977, Historical Studies in Nursing, 1978, Nursing in Society: A Historical Perspective, 1983; also 21 articles in profl. jours. Fellow, WHO, Copenhagen, 1975, Am. Acad. Nursing, 1978; recipient Disting. Alumni award Columbia U. Tchrs. Coll., N.Y.C., 1983, Columbia U., 1983. Mem. Am. Nurses Assn. (past chmn. cabinet on nursing edn.), Am. Assn. Colls. Nursing. Democrat. Roman Catholic. Office: Villanova Univ Coll of Nursing Villanova PA 19085

FITZPATRICK, MARY THERESE, psychologist, educator; b. Bklyn.; d. John and Elizabeth Fitzpatrick; Ph.D., Fordham U., 1966. Tchr., counselor high sch. Diocese of Bklyn., 1957-59; jr. high counselor, tchr. Diocese of N.Y., 1961-64; prof. Molloy Coll., Rockville Centre, N.Y.,1964, also chmn. dept.; cons. in field. Recipient Disting. Service medal Molloy Coll. Mem. Am. Psychol. Assn., Eastern Psychol. Assn., Internat. Transactional Analysis Assn., Fordham Counseling Assn., Assn. Advancement Higher Edn., Nassau County Psychol. Assn., Phi Delta Kappa. Author: Getting to Know Me, 1967; Understanding Death, 1976. Office: Molloy Coll Rockville Centre NY 11570

FITZPATRICK, MYRTIE CONSTANCE JACKSON, educational administrator; b. Tyler, Tex., Nov. 28, 1934; d. Flemmie Alonzo and Lillie Jane (Burnley) Jackson; m. David Oakley Fitzpatrick, May 25, 1958; children—Sabrina Rochelle Fitzpatrick Jackson, Deenean Yolanda. BS, Tex. Coll., 1954; reading specialist cert. Calif. State U.-San Jose, 1959; MS, Calif. State U.-Hayward, 1974; PhD, U. Santa Barbara, Calif. Operator/supr. Pacific Telephone-AT&T, Redwood City, Calif., 1959-62; tchr. Ravenswood Sch. Dist., Palo Alto, Calif., 1962-69, resource tchr., 1969-70, follow-through dir. U.S. Office of Edn., 1970-81, prin., 1981—; dir. My-Dae Creations, Menlo Park, Calif. Mem. Menlo Park Bicentennial Com., 1976, City Council Election Com., 1968, Homeowners Improvement Assn., Menlo Park. Recipient profl. awards. Mem. Calif. Tchrs. Assn., Ravenswood Tchrs. Assn. (sec.), Assn. Calif. Sch. Adminstrs., NEA, AAUW, Alpha Kappa Alpha, Beta Kappa Chi. Democrat. Mem. Ch. of Christ. Home: 1307 Windermere Ave Menlo Park CA 94025

FITZPATRICK, NANCY HECHT, corporation executive; b. East Orange, N.J., Dec. 29, 1942; d. Ira Youngwood and Bettie Jane (Van Cleave) Hecht; student Upsala Coll., 1960-62, New Sch. Social Research, 1962-64, Johns Hopkins U. (summer) 1987; m. Alan Rush Fitzpatrick, Dec. 15, 1973. Copy trainee Am. Home mag., N.Y.C., 1962-64, asst. copy editor, 1964-68; v.p. Creative Communications Assos., Newark, 1968-70; sr. editor Family Circle mag., N.Y.C., 1970-77; corp. sec., v.p. mktg. Alternative Telecommunications Corp., N.Y.C., 1977—. Mem. N.Y. Women in Communications (screening com. Matrix Awards 1977), NOW, Nat. Abortion Rights Action League, Empire Women in Telecommunications (pres.), LWV, Nat. Fedn. Bus. and Profl. Women's Clubs, Eastern Bedford Environ. Assn. (treas.) Editor various publs.

FITZPATRICK, RUTH LERMAN, government agency director; b. Louisville, July 28, 1932; d. Sam and Rose Lee (Bein) Lerman; m. Joseph Lloveras Fitzpatrick, July 8, 1958; children: Josephine, Michael, Tamara. BA, Barnard Coll., 1954; MS in Edn., Bank Street Coll., N.Y.C. Adminstrv. asst. Pub. Edn. Assn., N.Y.C., 1960-61; kindergarten tchr. Columbus (Ohio) Pub. Schs., 1961-62, Yellow Springs (Ohio) Schs., 1961-62; student tchr. supr. Ohio State U., Columbus, 1963-69; dir. Miami County Head Start, Troy, Ohio, 1973-74; student tchr. supr. U. Ky., Lexington, 1974-78, dir. lab. experiences and tchr. cert., 1981-84; early childhood specialist Ky. Dept. Human Resources, Frankfort, 1978-81, dir. instnl. resources, 1984—; cons. Fitzpatrick and Nelli, Lexington, 1981—. Mem. nat. task force Bus. and Profl. Women, 1985. Named Woman of Yr., Bus. and Profl. Women, 1984. Mem. Nat. Assn. Edn. of Young Children, So. Assn. Children Under Six (program com. Bluegrass chpt.), Ky. Assn. Tchr. Educators, Bluegrass Bus. and Profl. Women's Club, Profl. Women Forum. Democrat. Home: 547 N. Broadway Lexington KY 40508 Office: Ky Dept Edn 1727 Capital Plaza Tower Frankfort KY 40601

FITZSIMMONS, KATHLEEN MARION, consumer affairs executive; b. Bklyn., June 13; d. James W. and Helena A. (Ritter) F.; B.S., U. Dayton, 1968; M.S., Purdue U., 1971. Supr., Practical Evaluations Lab., Colgate-Palmolive, Piscataway, N.J., 1971-73, supr. consumer relations, N.Y.C., 1973-77, mgr. consumer affairs, 1978-85; dir. consumer affairs Richardson-Vicks, USA., Wilton, Conn., 1985—. Vol. Bellevue Hosp., N.Y. Hosp., vol. arbitrator N.Y. Better Bus. Bur., 1984—; mem. Girl Scouts SW Conn. Council, 1988—. Recipient Silver Trivet award Stokely Van Camp, 1968, TWIN Tribute to Women in Industry, YWCA, 1981. Mem. Soap and Detergent Assn. (chmn. consumer affairs com. 1981-83), Home Economists in Bus. (chmn. N.Y.C. 1980-81), Soc. Consumer Affairs Profls., Am. Home Econs. Assn., Women in Mgmt. Office: Ten Westport Rd Wilton CT 06897

FITZSIMONS, SHARON RUSSELL, logistics executive; b. Toronto, Ont., Can., June 25, 1945; d. Leslie Alfred and Winifred Marjorie (Williston) Russell; m. John Henry Fitzsimons, Jan. 4, 1969; children: Luke Edward, Michael Russell. BA, U. So. Calif., 1968; MA, Calif. State U., 1971; MS in Bus. Adminstrn., U. Calif., Irvine, 1978. Mgr. research William Pereira Assocs., Newport Beach, Calif., 1970-71; asst. mgr. interior design Concept Environment Inc. subs. Ford Motor Co., Orange County, Calif., 1971-72; v.p. Urban Interface Group, Orange County, 1972-74; cons. in field, 1975-76; mgr. strategic planning Mission Viejo Co., Orange County, 1976-80; mgr. fin. Philip Morris Internat., N.Y.C., 1980-82, asst. treas., 1982-84, dir. U.S. export logistics and customer service, 1987—; logistics exec. Philip Morris Ltd., Melbourne, Australia, 1984-86. Office: c/o Philip Morris Internat 120 Park Ave New York NY 10017

FIX, NANCY R., chemical products sales executive; b. Batavia, N.Y., May 7, 1948; d. E. William Jr. and Theresa Mae (Maloney) Rideout; m. John E. Fix, Sept. 6, 1969 (div. 1973); 1 child, Amy Catherine. BA in Anthropology, Syracuse U., 1970. Sales rep. Ayerst Labs., Syracuse, N.Y., 1979-81, Wyeth Labs., Syracuse, 1974-79, 1981-83, spl. nutritional sales rep., 1983-84, dist. sales mgr., 1984—.

FIX-ROMLOW, JEANNE KAY, hair care products company executive; b. Madison, Wis., June 29, 1947; d. Glen H. and Violet M. (Bohnsack) Fix; m. Paul James Romlow, July 24, 1947. Student, Madison Area Tech. Sch., 1966. Mgr. Fashion Fabrics, Madison, 1973-74; dir. promotion Livesey Enterprises, Madison, 1976-77; sales assoc. First Realty Group, Madison, 1977-79; territory mgr. Aerial Beauty and Barber Supply, Madison, 1979-83; regional dir. John Paul Mitchell Systems, Chatsworth, Calif., 1983-85, v.p., 1985—. Home: 12 Oak Grove Dr Madison WI 53717 Office: John Paul Mitchell Systems 20801 Nordhoff St Chatsworth CA 91311

FLACK, DORA DUTSON, writer, performing artist, lecturer; b. Kimberly, Idaho, July 9, 1919; d. Alonzo Edmund and Iona (James) Dutson; student Brigham Young U., U. Utah, Utah State U.; m. A. LeGrand Flack, Jan. 7, 1946; children—Marc Douglas, Lane LeGrand, Kent Dutson, Marlane, Karen, Marie. Exec. sec. Utah State Nat. Bank, Salt Lake City, 1938-46; author: (with Vernice G. Rosenvall and Mabel H. Miller) Wheat for Man...Why and How, 1952; England's First Mormon Convert, 1957; (with Louise Nielson) Dutson Family History, 1957; What About Christmas?, 1971; Fun with Fruit Preservation, 1972; (with others) The Joy of Being a Woman, 1972; (with Lula P. Betenson) Butch Cassidy, My Brother, 1975; Dry and Save, 1976 (U.S. Info. Service selection for Internat. Book Fair, Cairo, 1978); (with Janice T. Dixon) Preserving Your Past, 1977; Christmas Magic, 1977; Testimony in Bronze, 1980; (with Karla C. Erickson) Gifts Only You Can Give, 1984; Bread Baking Made Easy, 1984; (with others) Flood Fighters, 1984; contbr. numerous articles, stories to hist., religious and homemaking mags.; performing artist western U.S.; TV and radio appearances; mem. lit. panel Utah Arts Council, 1979-81; mem. faculty Brigham Young U. Edn. Week, 1976-83; mem. faculty World Conf. on Records, Salt Lake City, 1980. Mem. Utah Gov.'s Com. on Employment Handicapped, 1975-81. Recipient numerous state and nat. writing awards, including Utah State Inst. Fine Arts, 1969, 73-75, 77, 80, 84. Mem. League Utah Writers (Writer of Yr. award 1982), Nat. League Am. Pen Women, Daus. Utah Pioneers. Republican. Mormon. Club: Soroptimists. Home and Office: 448 E 775 N Bountiful UT 84010

FLACK, ROBERTA, singer; b. Black Mountain, N.C., Feb. 10, 1939; d. Laron and Irene F.; m. Stephen Novosel, 1966 (div. 1972). B.A. in Music Edn., 1958. Tchr. music and English lit. pub. schs. Farmville, N.C., Washington, 1959-67; rec. artist Atlantic Records, 1968—. Star ABC TV spl. The First Time Ever, 1973; composer: (with Jesse Jackson and Joel Dorn) Go Up, Moses; albums include: First Take, 1969, Chapter Two, 1970, Quiet Fire, 1971, Killing Me Softly, 1973, Feel Like Makin' Love, 1975, Blue Lights In The Basement, 1977, Roberta Flack, 1978, The Best of Roberta Flack, 1981, I'm The One, 1982, Born To Love, 1983, Hits and History, 1984, Roberta Flack, 1985; writer TV theme song Valerie. Recipient Gold Record for The First Time Ever I Saw Your Face, 1972; Grammy awards for best record (The First Time Ever I Saw Your Face), 1972, (Killing Me Softly With His Song), 1973, best pop vocal duo (Where Is The Love), 1972, best female pop vocal (Killing Me Softly With His Song), 1973; winner Downbeat's reader poll as best female vocalist, 1971-73; City of Washington celebrated Roberta Flack Human Kindness Day, 1972. Mem. Sigma Delta Chi. Office: care Atlantic Records 75 Rockefeller Plaza New York NY 10019 *

FLADELAND, BETTY, historian, emerita educator; b. Grygla, Minn., Jan. 18, 1919; d. Arne O. and Bertha (Nygaard) F. B.S., Duluth State Coll., 1940; M.A., U. Minn., 1944; Ph.D. (Rackham fellow), U. Mich., 1952. Mem. faculty Wells Coll., Aurora, N.Y., 1952-55, Central Mich. U., 1956-59, Central Mo. State Coll., 1959-62; mem. faculty So. Ill. U., Carbondale, 1962—; prof. history So. Ill. U., 1968—, disting. prof., 1985, disting. prof. emerita, 1986—; vis. prof. U. Ill., summer 1966. Author: James Gillespie Birney: Slaveholder to Abolitionist, 1955, Men and Brothers: Anglo-American Antislavery Cooperation, 1972, Abolitionists and Working Class Problems in the Age of Industrialization, 1984, also articles. Recipient Anisfield-Wolf award in race relations, 1972, Queen award, 1984; grantee Am. Philos. Soc., 1963, 75, Lilly Found., 1962; NEH teaching grantee, 1984. Mem. Am. Hist. Assn., So. Hist. Assn. (exec. council), Orgn. Am. Historians (exec. bd.), Assn. Study Afro-Am. Life and History, Norwegian-Am. Hist. Soc., Soc. Historians Early Am. Republic (adv. bd., bd. editors, pres.), ACLU, NAACP, Phi Beta Kappa, Phi Kappa Phi. Home: Rt 2 Box 620 Carbondale IL 62901 Office: So Ill Univ Dept of History Carbondale IL 62901

FLADMARK, SHEILA GWEN, business executive; b. Colorado Springs, Oct. 9, 1957; d. Lorentz Walter and Edith (Hunter) F. BAS, U. Fla., 1978. Engr., McDonnell Douglas Aircraft, Long Beach, Calif., 1978-80; sales rep. Evans & Sutherland, Irvine, Calif., 1980-82, Apollo Computer Co., Schaumburg, Ill., 1982-83; mgr. software integration Orcatech, Schaumburg, 1983-84; account mgr. Mentor Graphics, Schaumburg, 1984-85; sr. account mgr. Ridge Computer, Schaumburg, 1986—; pres. Concepts in Achievement, Melbourne, Fla., 1986—. Mem. Nat. Internat. Platform Assn. (bd. dirs.), Fla. Spacecoast Council for Internat. Visitors, South Brevard Women's Networking Orgn. Lutheran. Avocations: scuba diving, dancing, piano, travel, racquetball. Home: 909 Bluewater Dr Indian Harbour Beach FL 32937

FLAESGARTEN, GRACE LUDMILA, personnel director, educator, consultant; b. Cleve., Feb. 18, 1932; d. Raymond Ratliff and Estelle (Ostasiuk) Tachuk; m. Charles Paul Flaesgarten, Feb. 23, 1958; children: Gregory J., Sue Ann Flaesgarten Clark. BA, Capital U. Office mgr., adminstr. personnel Coopers & Lybrand, Cleve., 1970-76; personnel mgr. Med. Mut., Cleve., 1976-80; cons. in field, Cleve., 1980-82; dir. personnel CSX Beckett Aviation, Cleve., 1982-84; instr. in field, Cleve., 1984-86; exec. dir. personnel Lafayette Telemobile Corp., Valley View, Ohio, 1986—. Treas. Boy Scouts Am., Cleve., 1967-77. Named one of Outstanding Vols., Boy Scouts Am., Businesswoman of Yr. Mem. Am. Bus. Women's Assn. (pres. 1973-74), Am. Soc. Personnel Adminstrs. (com. chairperson 1980-81), Saferiders Assn. Am. (exec. dir. 1986—). Home: 10232 Unity Ave Cleveland OH 44111

FLAGG, DONNA MAE, nurse; b. Jamestown, N.Y., July 27, 1946; d. Angelo James and Jennie Rosalind (Allette) Cuoco; m. Paul Michael Flagg, Dec. 8, 1979; 1 child, Nikki Lynn. AAS in Nursing, Jamestown U., 1970. RN, N.Y. Staff nurse WCA Hosp., Jamestown, 1970-76; staff nurse Jamestown Presbyn. Home, 1978, nursing supr., 1978-80, dir. nursing, 1980-86, acting adminstr., 1983-84; RN coordinator Vis. Nurses Chautauqua County, Jamestown, 1986—. Mem. Chautauqua County Profls. Democrat. Roman Catholic. Home: 623 Palmer St Jamestown NY 14701 Office: Vis Nurses Chautauqua County 336 E 5th St Jamestown NY 14701

FLAHERTY, GERLINDE M. (LYNN), electronic information systems company official; b. Stuttgart, Fed. Republic Germany, Feb. 19, 1942; came to U.S., 1959; d. Wilhelm and Frida (Lorenz) Klenk; m. Gerard Eugene Flaherty, June 9, 1962; children—Curt P., Wayne T. Ed., Germany. With Honeywell Corp., 1959—, word processing coordinator, Ft. Washington, Pa., 1977-83, sr. systems rep. Honeywell Bull Inc., Bala Cynwyd, Pa., 1983—. Mem. Assn. Info. Systems Profls. (pres. Ft. Washington chpt. 1982-86), Am. Bus. Women's Assn. (v.p. membership 1984, pres. 1987-88, Woman of Yr. 1983), Nat. Assn. Female Execs. Home: 1194 Emma Ln Warminster PA 18974 Office: Honeywell Bull Inc 121 Presidential Blvd Bala Cynwyd PA 19004

FLAHERTY, MARIE GLORIA, comparative literature educator; b. Kearny, N.J., May 30, 1938. B.A., Rutgers U., 1959; M.A., Johns Hopkins U., 1960, Ph.D., 1965. Asst. prof. German, Northwestern U., 1964-71; assoc. prof. German and chmn. dept. Bryn Mawr Coll., 1971-84; prof. Humanities Inst., U. Ill.-Chgo.; mem. faculty Aston Magna Acad. Mem. Am. Soc. 18th Century Studies (pres. 1987-88), Am. Lessing Soc., Renaissance Soc. Am., Am. Musicol. Soc., MLA. Author: Opera in the Development of German Critical Thought; Contbr. articles to profl. jours. Address: Humanities Inst U Ill Box 4348 MC189 Chicago IL 60680

FLAMMANG, SUSANN, author, publisher; b. Kenosha, Wis., June 2, 1950; d. Leslie James and Beatrice (Woodward) Flammang Sampe. Pres., The Family of God, Las Vegas, 1984—, World Harvest, 1985—, pub., editor The Family of God Newsletter, Poets for Africa, 1986—; exec. dir. World Harvest, 1985—; producer, broadcaster Heart-to-Heart, Sta. KUNV TV, Las Vegas. Author of 30 books, numerous works of poetry. Recipient numerous poetry awards including Calif. Fedn. of Poets award, 1983, Humanitarian award Clark County, 1986, Woman of Achievement award, 1987, Gov's Art award, 1985, 86. Mem. Internat. Women's Writing Guild, Internat. PEN Assn., Acad. Am. Poets. Office: The Family of God/World Harvest PO Box 19571 Las Vegas NV 89132

FLANAGAN, ANITA MARIE, environmental administrator, consultant; b. South Charleston, W.Va., Sept. 25, 1940; d. Henry August and Mary Margaret (Hodge) Thormahlen; m. Shaun Michael Flanagan; children: Michael Lawrance, Sheilah Mary Catherine. AB, Northeastern U., 1963; BS, Southeastern Mass. U., 1977; Environ. Health mgmt. degree, Harvard U., 1983. Planning cons. Town of Duxbury (Mass.), 1983; mgr. Pub. Participation Program Mass. Dept. Environ. Mgmt., Boston, 1984-86; community relations dir. Clean Harbors Inc., Braintree, Mass., 1986-88; hazardous waste coordinator, mem. oil spill response team Town of Duxbury, 1980-85. Mem. Am. Pub. Health Assn., Soc. for Risk Analysis, Am. Chem. Soc. (health and safety sect.), Nat. Assn. Environ. Profls. Club: Harvard Old Colony.

FLANAGAN, DEBORAH MARY, lawyer; b. Hackensack, N.J., Sept. 17, 1956; d. Joseph Francis and Mary Agnes (Fitzsimmons) F.; m. Glen H. Koch, Aug. 27, 1983. BA summa cum laude, Fordham U., 1978, JD, 1981; LLM taxation, NYU, 1987. Bar: N.Y. 1982 and U.S. Dist. Ct. 1988. Sr. tax atty. McGraw-Hill Inc., N.Y.C., 1981—; sec., v.p. Internat. Archtl. Found. Inc., N.Y.C., 1982—; v.p. MHFSCO, Ltd. subs. McGraw-Hill, Inc., N.Y.C., 1984—. Mem. ABA, N.Y. State Bar Assn., Assn. of Bar of City of N.Y., N.Y. County Lawyers Assn., Fordham U. Law Alumni Assn. Home: 114 Harrison Ave Hasbrouck Heights NJ 07604 Office: McGraw-Hill Inc 1221 Ave of Americas New York NY 10020

FLANAGAN, JOSEPHINE RITA, sales executive; b. Hollywood, Calif., Mar. 19, 1955; d. Joseph and Gloria Ann (DeGirolamo) Picarro; m. Francis L. Flanagan, May 29, 1982. AA in Acctg., Ocean County Coll., Toms River, N.J., 1975; BS in Acctg. and Mktg., Rider Coll., Lawrenceville, N.J., 1977; MS in Mgmt., Stevens Inst. Tech., Hoboken, N.J., 1987; postgrad., NYU, 1987—. Acct. C. Itoh, Inc., N.Y.C., 1977-79; account exec. NCR Corp., N.Y.C., 1979-82; sr. account rep. Wang Labs., Inc., Rutherford, N.J., 1982—. Mem. Women's Exec. Network, Am. Mgmt. Assn., Exec. Women, East Hanover Flower Club. Democrat. Roman Catholic. Club: East

Hanover Flower. Lodge: Rotary. Home: 14 Nina Dr East Hanover NY 07936

FLANAGAN, JUDITH ANN, entertainment specialist; b. Lubbock, Tex., Apr. 28, 1950; d. James Joseph and Jean (Breckenridge) F. BS in Edn., Memphis State U., 1972. Area supr. Walt Disney World Parade, Orlando, Fla., 1972-81; parade dir. Gatlinburg (Tenn.) C. of C., 1981-85; prodn. mgr. The 1982 World's Fair, Knoxville, 1982; cons. Judy Flanagan Prodns./Spl. Events, Gatlinburg, 1982—, Miss U.S.A. Pageant, Knoxville, 1983; prodn. coordinator Nashville Network, 1983; account exec. Park Vista Hotel, Gatlinburg, 1986-87; prdn. mgr. The 1984 World's Fair Parades/Spl. Events, New Orleans; dir. sales The River Ter. Resort, Gatlinburg, 1985-86; scheduler show and rides project Universal Studios, Universal City, Calif. Recipient Gatlinburg Homecoming award, 1986. Mem. Tenn. Soc. Assn. Execs., Nat. Assn. Female Execs., Hotel/Motel Assn. Democrat. Roman Catholic. Home: 511 E Magnolia St Kissimmee FL 32743

FLANAGAN, PATRICIA ANN, sales professional; b. Syracuse, N.Y., Nov. 15, 1950; d. Nathan Schwartz and Nina (Collette) Pynes; m. Martin Joseph Flanagan, June 3, 1972 (div. 1981); 1 child, Kierstin. Student, Onondaga Community Coll., 1987—. Cert. emergency med. tech., N.Y. Asst. mgr. Pepper Auto Sales, Syracuse, 1969-70; mem. office staff Gen. Accident Ins. Co., Syracuse, 1970-72, Dominick Falcone Ins. Co., Syracuse, 1972-74; mgr. Soo-Lin Restaurant, Dewitt, N.Y., 1974-75; bookkeeper Soo-Lin Restaurant, Dewitt, 1975-81; sales mgr. Data Handling Products, Ltd., Syracuse, 1981—; partner Candlewick, Truxton, N.Y., 1987; gen. mgr. Soo-Lin Restaurant Inc., 1987—; tchr. canine obedience Coop. Edn. Services, Syracuse. Mem. Am. Kennel Club (bred fourth place skye terrier in nat. competition, 1985), Potomac Skye Terrier Club, Md. Home: 6514 Truxton-Tully Rd Tully NY 13159 Office: Soo-Lin Restaurant Erie Blvd E De Witt NY 13214

FLANAGAN, SHARON ELAYNE, foundation administrator; b. Ennis, Tex., Sept. 28, 1953; d. James Douglas Sr. and Ruth (Nelson) Mooring; m. Lewis Barrett Flanagan Jr., June 14, 1980; 1 child, Lewis Barrett III. BS in Psychology, Southern Meth. U., 1975, M of Pub. Adminstrn., 1977. Adminstrv. asst. Dallas Office of Human Devel., 1976-77, program specialist, 1977-80; aux. ops. mgr. M.L. King Ctr., Dallas, 1980-82, adminstrv. asst. property mgmt., 1982-84, with fin. dept., 1984-85; exec. dir. Dallas Bethlehem Ctr., 1985—. Zale Found. fellow, 1976; recipient Extra Mile award Dallas Council Boy Scouts Am., 1986. Mem. Delta Sigma Theta. Democrat. Methodist. Office: Dallas Bethlehem Center 4410 Leland Ave Dallas TX 75215

FLANNAGAN, LINDA DIANA, real estate consultant; b. Beechgrove, Ind., May 16, 1949; d. Joseph William and Norma Ethel (Ryker) F.; 1 child, Teresa Christine. BS, Calif. State U., Fullerton, 1972. Lic. ins. agt., Calif.; lic. real estate agt., Calif. Chmn. bd. dirs. The Flannagan Co., Belmont, Calif., 1972—. Vol. 100-mile bike/walk for coastal devel., 1975; developer Neighbor Tenn Ctr., 1976; co-founder Singles Against Cancer, West Los Angeles, Calif., 1981-85. Mem. Bldg. Owners and Mgrs. Assn. Internat., Community Redevel. Agy., ICSC, Internat. Fedn. Agrl. Producers, Nat. Assn. Securities Dealers. Club: Studio 20 (Los Angeles). Home and Office: 400 Davey Glen Rd #4826 Belmont CA 94002

FLANNIGAN, GAIL ELIZABETH, hotel marketing and tourism executive, consultant; b. Staten Island, N.Y., Dec. 15, 1946; d. Charles Joseph and Winifred Mae (Kinder) F.; m. Terence William Rufer, Sept. 18, 1982. B.A., Georgian Ct. Coll., 1968; postgrad. U. Maine, 1968, Fairleigh Dickinson U., 1970-73; diploma Sch. Hotel Mgmt. NYU, 1977. Tchr. John F. Kennedy Meml. High Sch., Iselin, N.J., 1968-69, Saddle River Country Day Sch., N.J., 1968-73; research asst. to author Gay Talese, N.Y.C., 1973-77; account exec. Hyatt Hotels, N.Y.C., 1977-79; mktg. rep. Monaco Tourist Office, N.Y.C., 1979-80; dir. sales and mktg. Gulf and Western Hotels, N.Y.C., 1980-85; pres. Gail Flannigan Assocs., N.Y.C., 1985—; pres. nat. meeting planners orgn. TWR Inc., N.Y.C., 1985—. Author poetry in mags. Community lectr., high sch. speaker on alcoholism, N.Y.C., 1980—. French govt. grantee, U. Maine, 1968. Mem. Nat. Assn. Female Execs. (networking program 1981-82), Meeting Planners Internat., Soc. Incentive Travel Execs., N.Y. Soc. Assn. Execs., Phi Sigma Epsilon. Republican. Roman Catholic. Avocations: Writing; skiing; running. Office: Gail Flannigan Assocs 163 E 36th St New York NY 10016

FLECHNER, ROBERTA FAY, graphic designer; b. N.Y.C., June 7, 1949; d. Abraham Julius and Evelyn (Medwin) F. B.A., CCNY, 1970; M.A., NYU, 1972; cert. Printing Industries Met. N.Y., N.Y.C., 1974, 75, 79. Researcher, asst. editor Arno Press, N.Y.C., 1970-73; free-lance editor Random House, N.Y.C., 1973-74, graphic designer/compositor coll. dept., 1984—; graphic designer Core Communications in Health, N.Y.C., 1974-76; prodn. mgr. Heights-Inwood News, N.Y.C., 1976-77; art dir., graphic designer Jour. Advt. Research, N.Y.C., 1976-81; prin., graphic designer/compositor Roberta Flechner Graphics, N.Y.C., 1976—; graphic designer/compositor W. W. Norton & Co., Inc., 1977—; mech. artist Fawcett, N.Y.C., 1979-80; graphic designer Avon Internat., N.Y.C., 1982; art dir., compositor, layout artist Source: Notes in the History of Art, N.Y.C., 1982—; graphic designer John Wiley & Sons, Inc., N.Y.C., 1985. Designer stationery, 1979 (Art Direction mag., Creativity-cert. distinction 1979). Art dir. enviroNews, N.Y. State Atty. Gen.'s Environ. Protection Bur., N.Y.C., 1977-78. Mem. Graphic Artists Guild, NOW, Women's Nat. Book Assn. (cons.), Nat. Assn. Female Execs., Women's Caucus for Art, Am. Inst. Graphic Arts, CCNY Alumni, NYU Alumni. Office: 106-15 Queens Blvd Forest Hills NY 11375

FLECK, JOANNE ELIZABETH TUHKANEN, medical facility specialist; b. Duluth, Minn., Nov. 19, 1939; d. Toivo and Kathryn (Dolliver) Tukhanen; m. Marvin Charles Fleck, 1959; children: Kathryn Sarah Kockler, Toivo Paul, Tammy Ray Smith. Cert. lic. practical nurse, Miller Sch. Nursing, St. Paul, 1959; diploma in emergency med. tng., Area Vocat. Tng. Inst., St. Cloud, Minn., 1977; AA in Mental Health/Social Work, Coll. of St. Benedict, 1981. With nursing dept. Vets. ADMX Med. Ctr., St. Cloud, 1974-79, with med. adminstrv. service, 1979-84, with occupational therapy sect., 1984-86, EEO cons., 1986—, with occupational therapy sect., 1984-86, patient adv.and rep., 1986—. Active Girl Scouts U.S., U.S. and Italy, 1966-74; pres. Noncommd. Officers' Wives Club, Italy, 1974. Named Non-Commd. Officer Wife of Yr. NCOWC, 1973.; recipient spl. recognition award Commr. Minn. Dept. Vet. Affairs, 1988. Mem. Nat. Assn. for Female Execs., St. Cloud Symphony (bd. dirs.), Am. Hosp. Assn. for Patient Reps., St. Cloud C. of C. (legis. and sartell divs.), Quality Assurance Profls. of Minn. (mem. editorial bd.). Home: PO Box 322 Sartell MN 56377 Office: Vets ADMX Med Ctr Saint Cloud MN 56301

FLECK, MARIANN BERNICE, health scientist; b. San Francisco, June 19, 1922; d. Erwin and Grace B. (Fisher) Kahl; m. Jennings McDaniel, June 1946; m. Jack Donald Fleck, Mar. 28, 1980; children: Gary, Eugene. B of Vocat. Edn., Calif. State U., 1965, BA, 1965, MA, 1968; PhD, U. Santa Barbara, 1975. Prof. life sci. div., adminstr. Fullerton (Calif.) Coll., 1960-75; profl. adminstr. Cypress (Calif.) Coll., 1975-80, prof. emeritus, 1980—; dir., owner Profl. Services Assn. Counseling, Santa Ana, Calif., 1977-80, Hypnosis Ctr., La Mirada, Calif., 1975-80; producer Dr. Mariann Health Program, Sta. KJON, Boonville, Ark., 1980-85; dir. Jack Fleck Golf and Health Acad., Magazine, Ark., 1980—; cons. and lectr. in field. Mem. Am. Guild Hypnotherapists, Am. Personnel and Guidance Assn., Calif. Personnel and Guidance Assn., Am. Running and Fitness Assn. (profl. mem.), Hypnotherapists Speakers Platform. Republican. Presbyterian. Home: Route 1 Box 15A Magazine AR 72943 Office: H&P Internat Magazine AR 72943

FLEEMAN, MARY GRACE, lawyer, librarian; b. Morgantown, W.Va., Aug. 24, 1947; d. George Ellis and Mary Jane (Stackpole) Moore; m. Keith Patrick Fleeman, Oct. 25, 1980. B.S., Allegheny Coll., 1969; M.S. in L.S., U. N.C., 1971; M.S.M., Frostburg State Coll., 1979; J.D. with highest honors, George Washington U., 1985. Library fellow U. N.C., Chapel Hill, 1970-71; asst. exchange and gift librarian U.S. Geol. Survey, Reston, Va., 1971-73, serials cataloger, 1973-74; cataloger Frostburg State Coll. (Md.), 1974-79; serials cataloger U. Okla., Norman, 1979-80; head cataloger George Washington U. Law Library, Washington, 1980-85; atty. Arnold & Porter, Washington, 1985—. Mem. ABA, Md. State Bar Assn., D.C. Bar Assn., Am. Assn. Law Libraries, Law Librarians Soc. of Washington, Order of Coif. Beta Phi Mu; Alpha Xi Delta. Home: 4023 McColl St Rockville MD 20853 Office: Arnold & Porter 1200 New Hampshire Ave NW Washington DC 20036

FLEET, JHERI CHASTAIN, writer; b. Oklahoma City, May 10, 1940; d. Joe and Geraldine Frances (MacCabe) Chastain; m. John James Fleet II, Mar. 18, 1960 (div. Oct. 1976); children: John James III, Joe Chastain II, Geraldine Frances III. Student, William Woods Coll., 1958-59; BJ, U. Okla., 1961. Owner, pres. Lemon-Twist, Dallas, 1974-76, Jheri Fleet, Inc., Midland, Tex., 1977-79; dir. pub. relations Theatre Tulsa, 1979-80; freelance writer, photojournalist Tulsa and Midland, Tex., 1981-86; hist. writer Gen. Telephone Co., San Angelo, Tex., 1986-88; instr. Tulsa Jr. Coll., 1982-84, Odessa Coll., 1984-86, U. Tex., 1988. Author: Child's Guide to Dallas, 1968, Child's Guide to Tulsa, 1980, Child's Guide to Permian Basin, 1985, History of General Telephone of the Southwest, 1988; appeared in commls. and films including HeartBreak Hotel, 1988; contbr. numerous articles to profl. jours. and popular mags. Mem. Authors League, Authors Guild, Women in Communications, Soc. Profl. Journalists, Nat. Fedn. Press Women, Austin Writers League (exec. dir. 1988—), Okla. Writers Fedn., Internal Women's Writers Guild, Tulsa Nightwriters (v.p. 1980-84), Tex. Nightwriters (founder, pres. 1984-86). Republican.

FLEISCHER, BARBARA JANE, organizational psychologist, consultant, researcher; b. N.Y.C., July 10, 1948; d. Francis Joseph and Dolores (Pietri) F. A.B. cum laude, St. Louis U., 1970, M.S., 1975, Ph.D., 1978. Lic. in indsl. and organizational psychology, La. Evaluation cons. Change in Liberal Edn., Washington, 1974-75; evaluation coordinator St. Louis CETA office, 1975-76; dir. research services U. So. Miss. Sch. Nursing, Hattiesburg, 1976-78; organizational cons. S. Miss. Home Health, Hattiesburg, 1979-80; staff psychologist Wellness Inst., New Orleans, 1981-84; dir. tng. Associated Catholic Charities, New Orleans, 1980-86, dir.tng., Loyola U. Inst. for Ministry, 1986— ; cons. New Orleans, 1980—. Contbr. articles to profl. jours. Grantee Nat. Ret. Tchrs. Assn.-Am. Assn. Ret. Persons Andrus Found., 1977, German Protestant Orphan Asylum, 1984. Mem. Am. Psychol. Assn., Am. Assn. Tng. Dirs. Roman Catholic. Avocations: music, church service, tennis. Office: Loyola U Inst for Ministry 6363 St Charles Ave New Orleans LA 70118

FLEISCHHACKER, SUSAN ELLEN KATHRYN ANNE, marketing executive, computer systems designer; b. Iowa City, June 7, 1952; d. Rudolph Joseph Fleischhacker and Margaret Ellen Gardner. ALB cum laude, Harvard U., 1985. Systems engr. Electronic Data Systems, Dallas, 1975-77; systems analyst Textron, Tehran, Iran, 1977-79; sr. systems analyst Am. Can Co., Greenwich, Conn., 1979-81; cash mgmt. Chem. Bank, N.Y.C., 1981-83; ops. mgr. Mecinite, Stamford, Conn., 1983; sr. v.p. mktg., CD Pub. Co., Mecinite, N.Y.C., 1984—. Bd. dirs. Urban League of Southwestern Fairfield County, Stamford, 1983—; pres. Urban League Guild, 1984; founder Greenwich Exec. Roundtable, 1980, pres., 1980-82. Republican. Roman Catholic.

FLEISCHMAN, BARBARA GREENBERG, public relations consultant; b. Detroit, Mar. 20, 1924; d. Samuel J. and Theresa (Keil) Greenberg; BA, U. Mich., 1944; m. Lawrence A. Fleischman, Dec. 18, 1948; children: Rebecca, Arthur, Martha. Tchr., Detroit Public Schs., 1944-45, psychoanalyst's sec., Detroit, 1947-49; sec. Greenberg Ins. Agy., Detroit, 1947-49; customer/public relations cons. Kennedy Galleries, N.Y.C., 1976—. Bd. dirs. Detroit Artists Market, 1958-66; mem. women's com. Detroit Inst. Arts, 1957-66, founder, pres. vol. com., 1961-66; bd. dirs. Friends of Channel 13, 1968-80, pres., N.Y.C., 1975-79, chmn. auction, 1975, trustee, 1975-84; pres. Friends of N.Y. Pub. Library, 1979—, trustee, 1980—, v.p. bd., 1987—; trustee The Acting Co., 1986—, pres. 1988—; governing bd. Off the Record Luncheons, Fgn. Policy Assn., 1978-85; assoc. producer Channel 13 Auction, 1978-80. Club: Cosmopolitan. Office: care Kennedy Galleries Inc 40 W 57th St New York NY 10019

FLEISHER, JERRILYN, financial consultant; b. Phila., May 7, 1952; d. Earl D. and Bette (Romisher) F.; m. Steven M. Bierman, May 28, 1978; 1 child, Emily Larissa. B.A., Dickinson Coll., 1973; M.B.A., Wharton Sch., U. Pa., 1975. Promotion analyst Gillette Co., Boston, 1975-77; product mgr. Chesebrough Ponds Co., Greenwich, Conn., 1977-80, Loreal Co., N.Y.C., 1980-81; account exec. Futterman Orgn., N.Y.C., 1981-83; fin. cons. Shearson Lehman Bros., Greenwich, 1983—. Mem. Internat. Platform Assn., Phi Beta Kappa. Home: 12 Martin Dale N Greenwich CT 06830 Office: Shearson Lehman Bros 2 Greenwich Plaza Greenwich CT 06830

FLEISHER, NORMA JEAN, accountant; b. Grand Island, Nebr., Oct. 21, 1926; d. Duward Arthur Bodenhamer andMyrtle May (Bouchard) Fricke; m. Niles H. Searls, May 8, 1945 (div. 1954); children: Nancy Kail, Janet Davis; m. Emmett C. Fleisher, Oct. 19, 1957 (dec. July 1981); children: Laura, William. CPA, Nebr. Bookkeeper various firms, Lincoln, Nebr., 1952-61; staff acct. Dana F. Cole & Co., Lincoln, Nebr., 1961-72; controller Sunflower Beef Packers, Inc., York, Nebr., 1972-80; pvt. practice tax acctg. Seward and Lincoln, Nebr., 1972—; sr. acct. tax Lincoln (Nebr.) Telecommunications Co., 1980—. Contbr. tax articles to prof. jours. Fin., calling/caring com. Grace United Meth. Ch., 1984—; active Boosalis for Gov., Nebr., 1986; mem. bd. Camp Fire, Lincoln, 1986—. Mem. Am. Inst. CPA's, Nebr. Soc. CPA's (chmn. com. 1968-69, 1983), Assn. Better Mgmt. (treas.), Lincoln C. of C. (com. mem.), Lincoln Women's C. of C. (chmn.). Home: 261 Sycamore Dr Lincoln NE 68510 Office: Lincoln Telecommunications Co 1440 M St Lincoln NE 68510

FLEMING, ALICE CAREW MULCAHEY (MRS. THOMAS J. FLEMING), author; b. New Haven, Dec. 21, 1928; d. Albert Leo and Agnes (Foley) Mulcahey ; m. Thomas J. Fleming, Jan. 19, 1951; children—Alice, Thomas, David, Richard. AB, Trinity Coll., 1950; MA, Columbia Coll., 1951. Bd. dirs. N.Y. chpt. Medic Alert Found. Internat., United Hosp. Fund of N.Y. Recipient Nat. Media award Family Service Assn. Am., 1973, Alumni Achievement award Trinity Coll., 1979. Mem. PEN, Authors Guild. Author: The Key to New York, 1960, Wheels, 1960, A Son of Liberty, 1961, Doctors in Petticoats, 1964, Great Women Teachers, 1965, The Senator from Maine: Margaret Chase Smith, 1969, Alice Freeman Palmer: Pioneer College President, 1970, Reporters At War, 1970, General's Lady, 1971, Highways into History, 1971, Pioneers in Print, 1971, Ida Tarbell, The First of the Muckrakers, 1971, Nine Months, 1972, Psychiatry, What's it All About?, 1972, The Moviemakers, 1973, Trials that Made Headlines, 1974, Contraception, Abortion, Pregnancy, 1974, New on the Beat, 1975, Alcohol: The Delightful Poison, 1975, Something for Nothing, 1978, The Mysteries of ESP, 1980, What to Say When You Don't Know What to Say, 1982, The King of Prussia and a Peanut Butter Sandwich, 1988; editor: Hosannah the Home Run!, 1972, America Is Not All Traffic Lights, 1976; contbr. articles to mags. Address: 315 E 72d St New York NY 10021

FLEMING, ALICE MAY, psychiatrist; b. Boston; d. Michael J. and Julia M. (Penney) F.; B.A., Radcliffe Coll., 1933; Ed.M., Harvard U., 1938; M.D., Boston U. Sch. Medicine, 1950. Intern, St. Vincent Hosp., N.Y.C., 1950-51; resident Boston State Hosp., 1951-52, Univ. Hosp., 1952-53, Putnam Children's Center, 1953-55, Judge Baker Guidance Center, 1955-81; pvt. practice, dir. Boston unit Judge Baker Pilot Tng. Program in Delinquency, 1956-61; dir. Cape Cod Child Guidance Clinic, Barnstable, Mass., 1954-65; dir. Boston Juvenile Ct. Clinic, 1965-81; mem. staff Children's Hosp. Med. Center and Judge Baker Guidance Center, Boston, 1955-81; mem. faculty Harvard Med. Sch., Boston, 1955—, vis. lectr. psychiatry, 1981—; pvt. practice specializing in child psychiatry, Boston, 1953—; cons. psychiatrist May Sch. for Autistic Children, Chatham, Mass., 1957-78, Kennebec Mental Health Clinic, 1964-77; mem. corp. Boston Children's Services, 1981—; mem. staff Children's Hosp. and Med. Center. Served to lt. (j.g.) USNR, 1943-46. Recipient Marsalin award, 1966; Judge John F. Perkins award Boston Juvenile Ct., 1982; Harvard Chair award, 1984. Mem. AMA, New Eng. Council Child Psychiatry, Am. Psychiat. Assn., Mass. Med. Soc., Mass. Med. Soc., Barnstable Med. Soc. Home: Box 353 East Wareham MA 02538 Office: 295 Longwood Ave Boston MA 02115

FLEMING, BARBARA JEAN, physician; b. Lorain, Ohio, May 31, 1945; d. Samuel and Eleanore Grace (Marks) Herman; children: Kevin S., Kathryn E. BA, Boston U., 1969, MD, 1969. Diplomate Am. Bd. Internal Medicine. Intern San Francisco Gen. Hosp., 1969-70; resident specializing in internal medicine Mt. Sinai Hosp., Cleve., 1970-71; resident specializing in internal medicine Univ. Hosps., Cleve., 1972-74, NIH endocrine fellow, 1974-75, with VA Med. Ctr., Cleve., 1975—, staff physician, 1975—, chief sect., 1976-82, assoc. chief of staff, 1982—; asst. prof. medicine Case Western Res. U., Cleve., 1976—; lectr. Cuyahoga Community Coll., Cleve., 1980—. Bd. trustees Diabetes Assn. Greater Cleve., 1977—; governing bd. Cleve. Health Care for Homeless Project, 1987—; vol. Shaker Heights (Ohio) Schs., 1979—; active Health Care for Indigent Com., Fedn. for Community Planning, Cleve., Am. Diabetes Assn. Recipient State Vets. award Am. Legion, 1982, Service award DAV, 1985. Mem. ACP, Soc. for Gen. Internal Medicine. Jewish. Office: VA Med Ctr 10701 East Blvd Cleveland OH 44106

FLEMING, (BEVERLY) JEANNE, psychologist; b. Chattanooga, Apr. 3, 1949; d. Delbert and Gladys Marie (Hicks) Swanson; B.S., U. Fla., 1971; M.S. in Marriage and Family Counseling, Loma Linda (Calif.) U., 1975; Ph.D., U.S. Internat. U., San Diego, 1979; m. John Richard Fleming, Sept. 6, 1973; 1 son, Jason. Ind. practice marriage-family counseling, Calif., 1975-78; custody investigator Cowlitz County (Wash.) Family Ct., 1979-81; psychology resident Dean V. Harris & Assocs., Vancouver and Longview, Wash., 1981-82; pvt. practice psychology, Vancouver, 1982-84, Longview, Wash., 1983—; mem. family life com. Oreg. conf. Seventh-day Adventists; bd. dirs. Children's Home Soc. Wash.; cons. in field. Mem. Am. Psychol. Assn., Am. Assn. Marriage and Family Therapists, Western Psychol. Assn., Wash. Psychol. Assn. (exec. bd. 1981-83), S.W. Wash. Assn. Psychologist (sec.-treas. 1981-82). Author articles in field. Office: 783 Commerce Suite 200 Longview WA 98632

FLEMING, JULIA ANN, symphony orchestra director; b. Florence, Ala., June 26, 1947; d. Julius Davis and Margaret Montgomery (Grubb) F. MusB with distinction, Rhodes Coll., 1969; MusM, Ind. U., 1972, postgrad., 1973-75. Coordinator residence life Ind. U., Bloomington, 1972-75; asst. dir. Memphis Arts Council, 1975; dir. devel. and info. Tenn. Arts Commn., Nashville, 1975-77; assoc. dir. Affiliate Artist, Inc., N.Y., 1977-82; dir. devel. San Antonio Festival, 1982; assoc. dir. B.T.G. Mgmt., N.Y., 1983-84; dir. devel. N.J. Symphony Orch., Newark, 1984—; mem. major instns. La. Arts Council, Baton Rouge, 1986; chairperson fellowship panel S.C. Arts Commn., Columbia, 1984. Mem. N.Y.C. Jr. League, 1985— (mgr. arts mgmt. adv. com. 1987); bd. advisors Solisti N.Y. Chamber Orch., N.Y., 1986—, Fonda Dance Forum, N.Y., 1984—. Mem. Nat. Soc. Fundraising Execs. (bd. dirs. N.J. chpt. 1986—), Am. Symphony Orch. League (chair regional orch. devel. dirs. 1986-87). Office: NJ Symphony Orch 213 Washington St Newark NJ 07101

FLEMING, KATHLEEN ADAIR, chemist; b. Glendale, Calif., Apr. 7, 1944; d. Charles MacGregor and Kathleen Adair (Sanders) Brown; m. Thomas Michael Fleming, Jan. 28, 1984; children: Iolana Adair Carver, Matthew Charles. B.A., Coll. Notre Dame, Belmont, Calif., 1977; postgrad. U. Calif.-Davis, 1977-79. Chemist, Hunt Products Co., Inc., Dallas, 1979—; Mem. Am. Chem. Soc., Soc. Cosmetic Chemists. Republican. Presbyterian. Home: 1944 Oak Bluff Dr Carrollton TX 75007 Office: Hunt Products Co Inc 8321 Carpenter Freeway Dallas TX 75247

FLEMING, NANCY POE, municipal official; b. Grimesland, N.C., Mar. 20, 1934; d. Thomas Poe and Nannie Esther (Wiliford) F. BA, U. N.C., 1955; MSW, U. Conn., 1960. Photographer Am. Photographic Co., Washington, 1955-56; psychiat. aide Inst. of Living, Hartford, 1956; social worker City of Hartford, 1956-60, child welfare worker, 1960-63, social service supr., 1963-72, dir. casework, 1972-79, dir. dept. elderly services, 1979—; cons. Conn. Labor Mobility Project, Hartford, 1966-67; dir. Housing Now, Inc., Hartford, 1974-75; bd. dirs. Project Find, Hartford, 1973-79; tree farmer, Bolton, Conn., 1976—. Mem. Salvation Army Shelter Task Force, 1970, Coop. Housing Task Force, Hartford, 1972. Recipient Outstanding Pub. Employee award Hartford Area Jaycees, 1976. Mem. Am. Assn. Retired Persons, Am. Forestry Assn. Home: PO Box 9486 Hop River Rd Bolton CT 06043 Office: Dept Elderly Services 10 Columbus Blvd Hartford CT 06103

FLEMING, RHONDA, actress, singer, humanitarian; b. Los Angeles; d. Harold Cheverton and Effie (Graham) Louis; m. Ted Mann; 1 child, Kent Lane. Student, pub. and pvt. schs., Los Angeles, Beverly Hills. Appeared in 40 motion pictures, including Spellbound, 1945, Spiral Staircase, 1945, A Connecticut Yankee in King Arthur's Court, 1949, The Great Lover, 1949, The Eagle and the Hawk, 1950, Last Outpost, 1951, Hong Kong, 1952, Tropic Zone, 1953, Tennessee's Partner, 1955, Gunfight at OK Corral, 1956, Home Before Dark, 1958, Pony Express, 1953, The Nude Bomb, 1980; Broadway debut in The Women, 1973; appeared in musical plays, including The Boyfriend, 1975, Marriage Go Round, 1960, Bell, Book and Candle, 1963, Kismet, 1976; sang Gershwin concert in; 10-week tour, 1963; starred in Las Vegas, Nev., 1959, one-woman concert at Hollywood Bowl, 1960, numerous guest appearances on TV series and talk shows including MacMillen and Wife, Love Boat; TV movies include The Last Hours Before Morning, 1975; NBC's Legends of the Screen, 1980, Metromedia Spl. Road to Hollywood, 1983, Wildest West Show of the Stars, 1986. Bd. dirs. World Opportunities, Internat. Olive Crest Treatment Ctrs. for Abused Children; Assoc. mem. Freedoms Found. at Valley Forge, Pepperdine U.; founding mem. Los Angeles Music Ctr., J.D.F. Found. for Alzheimer's Disease; mem. Childnelp USA, Music Ctr.'s Blue Ribbon 400, ARCS, Los Angeles Philanthropic Fedn. Inc.; supporter of animal rights and wildlife protection groups. Recipient award NCCJ, Gold Angel award Religion in Media, Woman of the World award Childhelp, USA, Eve award Mannequins of the Assistance League, 1986; Named Woman of Year City of Hope. Mem. Achievement Rewards for Coll. Scientists, United Cerebral Palsy/Spastic Found., Child Help (Woman of World award), Animal and Wildlife Protection Inst. Am., Los Angeles Philanthropic Assn.

FLEMING, SIDNEY HOWELL, psychiatrist, educator; b. Lubbock, Tex., May 22, 1938; d. McKinley and Wilna Adrian (Simer) Howell; B.A., Agnes Scott Coll., Decatur, Ga., 1959; M.D., Emory U., 1964; m. J.D. Fleming, Jr., June 28, 1960; 1 dau., Julie Adrianne. Intern, Emory U./Va. Hosp., Atlanta, 1964-65, resident in psychiatry, 1965-68; mem. faculty Emory U. Med. Sch., 1968—, assoc. prof. psychiatry, 1979—, chmn. Pres.'s Commn. on Status of Women, 1984-85. Grantee NIMH, 1969-71; diplomate Am. Bd. Psychiatry and Neurology. Mem. Am. Psychiat. Assn. (editorial bd. on curriculum on psychiatry of women and men 1979-81, com. on women 1985), AMA, Assn. Acad. Psychiatrists, Ga. Psychiat. Assn., Med. Assn. Ga. Republican. Club: Druid Hills. Address: 2238 Hill Park Ct Decatur GA 30033

FLEMING, VIRGINIA HESSE, client service manager; b. Redondo Beach, Calif., Jan. 24, 1959; d. Frederick William Hesse and Betty (Brunson) Bathgate; m. Patrick Edward Fleming, Sept., 1987. BS in Bus. Adminstrn., Calif. State U., Northridge, 1982. Horse trainer Pacific Horse Ctr., Sacramento, 1976-79; asst. restaurant mgr. Carl's Jr. Restaurant, Agoura, Calif., 1979-80; adminstrv. acct. specialist IBM, Burbank, Calif., 1980-82; sr. cons. Arthur Anderson & Co., Costa Mesa, Calif., 1982-85; client service rep. J.D. Edwards & Co., San Francisco, 1985—; treas. Bay Area Women's Leadership Group, San Francisco, 1986—. Presenter Profl. Presenters Program, San Francisco, 1986—; vol. World Peace Group, San Francisco, 1986—. Mem. Nat. Assn. Female Execs., Nat. Assn. Profl. Women, U.S. Equestrian Team, Aircraft Owners Assn., Nat. Orgn. Women, Delta Sigma Pi. Mem. Religious Science Ch.

FLEMMING, MARILYN REDINGER, educator; b. Brockport, N.Y., Apr. 7, 1940; d. Harold and Winifred (Bateman) Redinger; m. Frederick L. Flemming, Mar. 7, 1942 (div. 1966); 1 child, Eric. BS, SUNY, Brockport, 1961; MS, Westminster Coll., 1963; C.A.S., SUNY, Brockport, 1984. Cert. elem. tchr., Pa., N.Y.; cert. sec. tchr., N.Y. Tchr. Grove City (Pa.) Schs., 1961-63, Edgewood Schs., Pitts., 1963-64, Pitts. City Schs., 1964-65, Crafton-Carnegie Schs., Pitts., 1965-66, Brockport Schs., 1966-69, 1970—. Mem. Brockport Tchrs. Assn. (union rep. 1985-87, chmn. conf. com. 1986-87, 25 yr. pin 1986, bldg. rep. 1985-87), N.Y. State United Tchrs., Alumni Assn. Republican. Lutheran. Club: Carnegie Tech. Wives (pres. 1964). Home: 4 Ogee Trail Brockport NY 14420 Office: Brockport Schs Hartshore Blvd Brockport NY 14420

FLENER, ANDREA KAREN, rehabilitation counselor; b. Glasgow, Ky., Oct. 16, 1956; d. Bobby Ross and Sue (Wilson) F. BA in Psychology, U. Ky., 1977, M in Rehab. Counseling, 1987. Specialist child support enforcement Ky. Dept. Human Resources, Frankfort, 1977-79; rehab. counselor Office Vocat. Rehab. div. Ky. Dept. Edn., Louisville, 1979-81; prin. rehab. counselor Madisonville, 1981-83; chief rehab. counselor Ky. Workers' Compensation Bd., Frankfort, 1983—; Cert. rehab. counselor. Mem. Am. Assn. Counseling Devel., Ky. Assn. State Employees. Methodist.

FLESCHNER, MARCIA HARRIET, marketing executive, personnel consultant; b. Bklyn., Mar. 31, 1947; d. Max and Bettina (Koerner) F.; m. Arthur Mace Teicher, Nov. 23, 1974; 1 son, Craig Morgan. B.A., CUNY, 1967. Sr. vice pres. market research, placement dir. Smith's 5th Ave Agy., Inc., N.Y.C., 1965—. Mem. Am. Mktg. Assn. (2d v.p. 1987-88, dir. N.Y.C. chpt. 1973-87 , cert. 1975, 82), Nat. Assn. Personnel Cons., Advt. Women N.Y., Assn. Personnel Cons. N.Y. (dir. 1979-80). Club: Castaways Yacht (New Rochelle, N.Y.). Office: Smith's 5th Ave Agy Inc 17 E 45th St New York NY 10017

FLESHMAN, LINDA EILENE SCALF, communications and marketing executive; b. Oklahoma City, Sept. 17, 1950; d. James Truman and Dortcha Virginia (Stiles) Scalf; children: Leatha Michele, Misty Dawn. AA, Tarrant County Jr. Coll., 1977; BA, North Tex. State U., 1979. Copywriter, Advt., Graphics & Mktg., Ft. Worth, 1978-80; editor Ft. Worth mag. Ft. Worth C. of C., 1980-81; mktg. prodn. coordinator City of Fort Worth, 1981-83; dir. pub. relations Circle T council Girl Scouts U.S.A., Ft. Worth, 1983-85; mgr. corp. tng. Am. Airlines Direct Mktg., 1984-87; dir. corp. communications LeasPak Internat., 1987—. Mem. Internat. Bus. Communicators, Am. Women in Radio and TV, Women in Communication. Democrat. Roman Catholic. Home: PO Box 14807 Fort Worth TX 76117 Office: LeasPak Internat 2120 LeasPak Pkwy Bedford TX 76021

FLETCHER, HON. BETTY B., judge; b. Tacoma, Mar. 29, 1923. B.A., Stanford U., 1943; LL.B., U. Wash., 1956. Bar: Wash. 1956. Former mem. firm Preston, Thorgrimson, Ellis, Holman & Fletcher, Seattle, 1956-1979; judge U.S. Circuit Ct. for 9th Circuit, Seattle., 1979—. Mem. ABA, Wash. Bar Assn., Order of Coif, Phi Beta Kappa. Office: US Ct of Appeals 1010 5th Ave Seattle WA 98104

FLETCHER, CATHY ANN, auditor; b. Barnesville, Ga., Aug. 23, 1949; d. John James and Dorothy Lee (Banks) Fletcher; 1 child, Lisa Faye. Student, Ohio State U., 1969-70; AS, Mass. Bay Community Coll., 1982; BS, Northeastern U., Boston, 1984. Mail clk. Fed. Reserve Bank, Boston, 1971-72; office mgr. Breckenridge Sportswear, Boston, 1973-74; asst. dir. Whittier Street Health Ctr., Boston, 1974-81; sec. to dir. Northeastern U., 1981-84; auditor Def. Contract Audit Agy., Burlington, Mass., 1984—; sec., bd. dirs. Boston Tenant Policy Council, 1977-79. Author: Softball Team Book, 1975. V.p., bd. dirs. Bromley Health Tenant Mgmt. Corp., Jamaica Plain, Mass., 1976—; mem. fund-raising com. Com. to Elect Jessie Jackson Pres., Boston, 1984; apptd. fed. women program coordinator State of Mass., 1988. Mem. AAUW, Nat. Assn. Female Execs., Nat. Tenants Orgn., NAACP, Sigma Epsilon Rho. Club: Hawkettes Social (pres., mem. profl. council). Lodge: Elks. Avocations: reading, swimming, cooking, walking, travel. Office: Def Contract Audit Agy 2 Wayside Rd Burlington MA 01803

FLETCHER, ELIZABETH ANN, insurance company executive; b. Yuba City, Calif., Aug. 9, 1945; d. Walter Merle and Alice Irene (Snyder) Russell; m. Dean L. Fletcher; children: Melinda M., Christine L., Dean R. Student, Chico State Coll., 1963-64. Engring. aid Pacific Tel. and Tel., San Jose, Calif., 1968-72; mini-course program dir. San Jose Unified Sch. Dist., Calif., 1974-76; treas. Mission Counties Ins. Agy. Inc., San Jose, Calif., 1977—; lectr. San Jose City Coll., 1985. Contbr. column and photographs (hon. mention, 1985) to local newspaper. Speaker marriage encounter and engaged encounter, No. Calif., 1979-82; dir. Senior Garden project, San Jose, 1981. Mem. Profl. Ins. Agts. Democrat. Roman Catholic.

FLETCHER, LOUISE, actress; b. Birmingham, Ala., 1936; d. Robert Capers F. B.S., N.C. State U.; student acting with Jeff Corey. Films include Thieves Like Us, 1974, Russian Roulette, 1975, One Flew Over the Cuckoo's Nest, 1975 (Acad. award Best Actress), Exorcist II: The Heretic, 1977, Natural Enemies, 1979, The Lucky Star, 1980, Once Upon a Time in America, 1982, Brainstorm, 1983, Firestarter, 1983, Strange Invaders, 1983, Invaders From Mars, 1986, The Boy Who Could Fly, 1986; appeared in TV show Maverick. Office: care William Morris Agy 151 El Camino Beverly Hills CA 90212 *

FLETCHER, MARJORIE AMOS, librarian; b. Easton, Pa., July 10, 1923; d. Alexander Robert and Margaret Ashton (Arnold) Amos; A.B., Bryn Mawr Coll., 1946; m. Charles Mann Fletcher, May 14, 1949; children—Robert Amos, Elizabeth Ashton, Anne Kennard. Asst. to dir. research, then research asst. to pres. Pa. Mut. Life Ins. Co., 1946-49; officer A.R. Amos Co., Phila., 1949-66; part-time tchr., 1965-68; librarian Am. Coll., Bryn Mawr, Pa., 1968-77, archivist, 1973—, dir. oral history collection, 1975—, lectr. on archives, 1975—, asst. prof. edn., 1973—, dir. archives and oral history, 1977—. Recipient awards Phila. Flower Show, 1965—. Mem. Spl. Libraries Assn. (pres. Phila. 1977-78), Soc. Am. Archivists (chairperson oral history sect. 1981-87), Oral History Assn., Hist. Soc. Pa., U.S. Pony Club, D.A.R., Nat. Soc. Colonial Dames in Commonwealth of Pa. Republican. Presbyterian. Clubs: Phila. Skating; Davis Creek Yacht; Bridlewild Pony (sponsor), Bridlewild Trails (Gladwyne). Author articles in field. Home: 1135 Norsam Rd Gladwyne PA 19035 Office: Am Coll Bryn Mawr PA 19010

FLETCHER, MARY LEE, business exec.; b. Farnborough, Eng.; d. Dugald Angus and Mary Lee (Thurman) F.; B.A., Pembroke Coll., Brown U., 1951. Ops. officer C.I.A., Washington, 1951-53; exec. trainee Gimbels, N.Y.C., 1953-54; head researcher Ed Byron TV Prodns., N.Y.C., 1954; copywriter Benton & Bowles, Inc., N.Y.C., 1955-63; creative dir. Alberto-Culver Co., Melrose Park, Ill., 1964-66; v.p. advt. and publicity Christian Dior Perfumes, N.Y.C., 1967-71; v.p. Christian Dior-N.Y., N.Y.C., 1972-78, exec. v.p., dir., 1978-85; cons. Fletcher & Co., N.Y.C., 1985—. Home: 12 Beekman Pl New York NY 10022 Office: 885 3d Ave New York NY 10022-4082

FLETCHER, RAMONA NEAL, textile company supervisor; b. Danville, Va., Aug. 12, 1943; d. J. Edward and Mattie Sue (Guill) Neal; student Danville Community Coll., 1980—; m. Floyd Fletcher, Jr., Sept. 27, 1980; 1 stepson, James Christopher; 1 dau., Deborah. Office cashier G.C. Murphy Co., 1964-70; sec. to supt. yarn dyeing Dan River, Inc., Danville, 1970-80, dyeing supr., 1980—. Chmn. safety com. and waste com. March of Dimes, 1975-80; active Spl. Olympics, 1978. Named ambassador City of Danville, 1982-83. Mem. Am. Bus. Women's Assn., Tobacco Textile Mus., Internat. Platform Assn., Am. Film Inst., Beta Sigma Phi. Republican. Baptist. Home: 130 D2 Navajo Ct Danville VA 24540 Office: Dan River Inc W Main St Danville VA 24541

FLETCHER, SHERRY LYN, elementary school principal; b. Ashland, Kans., Dec. 29, 1947; d. James Thomas Fletcher and Maxine (Lane) Cecil; m. Baxter Barnard Brown, Nov. 1, 1982. BA in Edn., N.Mex. State U., 1968, MA in Edn., 1975, endorsement in ednl. adminstrn., endorsement in early childhood, 1984; Montessori cert., St. Nicholas Tng. Cen., London, 1976. Elem. tchr. pub. schs. pub. schs., Las Cruces, N.Mex., 1969-75; dir., founder Montessori Unltd., Las Cruces, 1976; tchr. Truth or Consequences (N.Mex.) Pub. Schs., 1983-85, elem. prin., 1983—; cons. McGraw Hill Pub. Support Writing Assessment Project, others 1981—; mem. steering com. State Bd. Edn., Santa Fe, 1985-86, mem. adv. com. early childhood, 1985-86, revision of state spl. edn. regulations, 1988. Mem. Elephant Butte/Caballo Leaseholders' Assn. (sec. 1985—), N.Mex. Assn. for the Edn. Young Children, Assn. Supervision and Curriculum Devel., Assn. Sch. Adminstrs. Republican. Home: Star Route N Box B Truth or Consequences NM 87901 Office: Truth or Consequences Schs Box 952 Truth or Consequences NM 87901

FLETCHER, WENDY SCOTT, educator; b. White Plains, N.Y., Dec. 13, 1945; d. Cyril Scott and Olga Noreen (Brigg) F.; m. Richard Morse Low, Mar. 13, 1982; children: Heather Morse, Sarah Wendy. B.A., U. South Fla., 1968; postgrad. UCLA, 1972-74. Tutor autistic children Child Guidance Center, Tampa, Fla., 1968-69; art tchr. Summer Gifted Program, U. South Fla., Tampa, 1968; tchr. Hillsborough County, Fla., 1968-69, Sydney (Australia) Ch. of Eng. Girls Grammar Sch., 1970; tchr. remedial reading Garvey Jr. High Sch., Rosemead, Calif., 1971-72; Title I math specialist Garvey Sch. Dist., Rosemead, Calif., 1972-75; tchr. Lexington (Mass.) Pub. Schs., 1976—. Club: New Eng. Aquarium Dive. Author and illustrator: My Ancestors Are From Australia and Canada, 1975.

FLETSCHER, KAY MARTIN, property inspectors; b. Manzanola, Colo., Apr. 25, 1935; d. Charles Frederick and Hattie (Kerr) Martin; m. Theodore Franklin Fletscher, Dec. 30, 1955; children: Martin A., Theodore E., Katyn Blust, Amy K. Student, San Jose (Calif.) State U., 1953-55. Sec., asst. Med. Offices, San Jose and Santa Cruz, Calif., 1957-80; salesperson Century 21-Era Real Estate Ctr., Scotts Valley, Calif., 1980-84; bus. devel. Ticor Title-Redding Title, Santa Cruz, 1984-87; owner, bus. mgr. Fletscher Property Inspectors, Scotts Valley, 1987—. Chair Old West Casino Night, Santa Cruz, 1986, 88, WCR Benefit Fashion Show, Santa Cruz, 1987, Am. Women's Voluntary Services, San Jose, 1957-71; community leader Ben Lomond 4H (Calif.), 1972-82. Recipient Silver Clover award Santa Cruz County 4H, 1972. Mem. Santa Cruz Bd. Realtors (Affiliate of Yr. award 1986, producer, writer of entertainment for award ceremony 1985-87), Santa Cruz Women's Council of Realtors Calif. Scholastic Fedn. (life), Delta Epsilon Kappa, Beta Sigma Phi (named Woman of Yr., 1983-84, pres.). Democrat. Office: Fletscher Property Inspectors 4113 Scotts Valley Rd Scotts Valley CA 95066

FLIEGELMAN, AVRA LEAH, editor; b. Hartford, Conn., Mar. 5; d. Irving and Rose (Bason) F.; student public schs. With publicity dept. Columbia Pictures Corp., N.Y.C., 1949; with Asso. Artists Prodns., and successor UA-TV, N.Y.C., 1955-58; with Broadcast Info. Bur. , N.Y.C., 1958—, editor-in-chief, 1969—, exec. v.p., 1979—. Mem. Am. Women in Radio and TV. Democrat. Jewish. Home: 174 Dix Hills Rd Huntington Station NY 11746 Office: 19 W 44th St New York NY 10036

FLINK, JANE DUNCAN, public relations exective, publisher; b. Atlanta, Feb. 17, 1929; d. James Archibald and Frances (Watkins) Duncan; m. Richard Albert Flink, Nov. 20, 1954; children: Jennifer, Elizabeth, Caroline, Charles Albert, James Duncan. Student Carleton Coll., 1948-49, U. Mo., 1967, Columbia (Mo.) Coll., 1974-75. Reporter, Tri-Town News, Greendale, Wis., 1958-61; reporter, photographer, feature writer, editor Cen. Mo. Rural and Farm Life mag., Centralia (Mo.) Fireside Guard, 1973-78, asst. editor, 1982-83; editor Bus. Briefs, MFA Oil Co., Columbia, Mo., 1977; editor Lifestyles, Kingdom Daily News, Fulton, Mo., 1978-82; assoc. editor Mo. Ruralist, Columbia, 1983-85; dir. external relations Winston Churchill Meml. and Library, Westminster Coll., Fulton, Mo., 1985—; owner, pub. Boone County Jour., Ashland, Mo. Rep. committeewoman Ward I, Centralia, 1972, 74, 76; mem. exec. bd. Friends of Churchill Meml., Fulton; mem. Boone County Commn. on Child Abuse, 1978-81. Recipient numerous editorial awards. Mem. Nat. Fedn. Press Women (nat. achievement award 1982), Mo. Press Women (dist. v.p. 1978-79, v.p. 1985-87, chmn. honors, awards 1979-81, Woman of Achievement award 1988), Mo. Mus. Assocs., Mo. Press Assn., PEO, Sigma Delta Chi, Centralia C. of C. (bd. dirs. 1983-86—), Mo. Travel Council, English Speaking Union, Royal Oak Found., Centralia Hist. Soc. Club: Centralia Country. Home: The Clearing Route 4 Centralia MO 65240 Office: Winston Churchill Meml and Library Westminster Coll Fulton MO 65251

FLINT, SUSAN LOUISE, public relations executive; b. Culver City, Calif., Feb. 1, 1947; d. Otto Antone and Genevieve Florence (Lindsay) Grunwald; m. Virgil Eugene Flint, Dec. 6, 1975. BA in Journalism, Pepperdine U., 1967. Pub. relations asst. Hollywood Presbyn. Hosp., Los Angeles, 1968; editor-in-chief So. Calif. Bus., Los Angeles, 1968-70; pub. relations mgr. Avco Community Developers, Inc., San Diego, 1972-75; editor-in-chief The Breeze, Carlsbad, Calif., 1975-76; pres., cons. Susan Flint Advt. & Pub. Relations, Yuma, Ariz., 1978-84; community relations dir. San Diego Hospice Corp., 1984-85; community resources dir. Youth Devel., Inc., San Diego, 1985-86; cons. Susan Flint Advt. & Pub. Relations, Palm Springs, Calif., 1986-87; pub. relations dir. Palm Springs Desert Mus., 1987—. Bd. dirs. Easter Seal Soc. Ariz., Yuma, 1982-84; council mem. Desert Trail Council Boy Scouts, Yuma, 1983-84; vol. Home Run Hotline, San Diego, 1985—. Recipient Community Service award Desert Council Boy Scouts Am., 1984. Mem. Women in Communications (past bd. dirs.), Nat. Assn. Female Execs., Nat. Fedn. Press Women, San Diego Press Club, Beta Sigma Phi. Republican. Home: 28-850 Avenida Condesa Cathedral City CA 92234 Office: Palm Springs Desert Mus 101 Museum Dr Palm Springs CA 92262

FLINT-SHAW, LYNN MARIE, speech and language pathologist; b. New Orleans, Aug. 31, 1954; d. Eddie Nicholas and Lena Mary (Hernandez) Flint; m. Rufus Shaw, Jr., Oct. 1, 1983. B.S. with honors, Xavier U., 1975; M.C.D. in Communication Disorders, La. State U. Med. Ctr., 1977. Speech-lang. pathologist Callier Ctr., U. Tex.-Dallas, 1977-79; speech-lang. pathologist, cons., Dallas, 1979-85; cons. Head Start Program, Dallas, 1979-85. Bd. dirs. Women of Arts, Dallas, 1982, Dallas Ballet, 1983-84; v.p. United Cerebral Palsy, Dallas, 1981-82, bd. dirs. 1980-86; bd. dirs. ASHA Minority Ethnic Com., Washington, 1983—, chmn. com., 1986-87; cons. speech pathologist Plano Gen. Hosp. (Tex.), 1981, 82, 83. Recipient Cert. of Appreciation Head Start Program, Dallas, 1981; award Ctr. Inner City Studies, Ill., 1981. Mem. Am. Speech-Lang.-Hearing Assn., Nat. Black Assn. Speech, Lang. and Hearing (recruitment chair 1980-86), Tex. Speech and Hearing Assn., Dallas Assn. Speech Pathologists and Audiologists, Organized Associated Speech-Lang. Pathologists and Audiologists (pres. 1987). Roman Catholic. Home: 6616 Braddock Pl Dallas TX 75232 Office: 7557 Rambler Rd Suite 750 Dallas TX 75231

FLISI, CLAUDIA BETH, public relations company administrator; b. Rahway, N.J., Aug. 13, 1947; d. Irving Joseph and Sylvia Vivian (Olenick) Engelman; m. Fernado Luigi Flisi, May 5, 1972; children: Maximilian Arthur, Alexander Joseph. BA with distinction, Mt. Holyoke Coll., 1970; MA, Johns Hopkins U., Washington, 1972; cert. in pub. relations, UCLA, 1976; postgrad., U. Warwick, Coventry, Eng., 1977-78. Free-lance writer Atlanta, 1972-75; rep. corp. communications Whittaker Corp., Los Angeles, 1975-77; mgr. internal communications Am. Express, N.Y.C., 1978-80; coordinator mktg. services Towers, Perrin, Forstere, Crosby, N.Y.C., 1981-82; account supr., mgr. advt. services Burson-Marsteller, N.Y.C., 1983-86; account dir. J. Walter Thompson Italia S.P.A., Milan, 1986—; speaker various groups including NYU, 1986, Advt. Council, 1985, Bocconi U., Fiera di Milano, CESMA Mgmt. Inst., IABC Internat. Conf., 1987. Contbr. various articles to mags., newspapers; contbg. author: Love and Money, 1985. Mem. steering com. Sch. Advanced Internat. Studies, Johns Hopkins U., 1983-86, World Affairs Council Los Angeles, 1975-77, Atlanta Council Internat. Visitors, 1974-75; bd. dirs. Consumer Affairs Ft. Lee, N.J., 1983-85. Mem. Internat. Assn. Bus. Communicators (v.p. 1982-83, bd. govs., 1984-86), Profl. Women's Assn. Milan. Unitarian.

FLOCKE, JENELLE LOUISE, military public affairs specialist; b. Bellville, Tex., July 3, 1949; d. Calvin Joe and Rose Army (Grubb) Mikeska; m. Robert Alfred Flocke, Oct. 5, 1968; 1 child, Catherine Rose. Student Blinn Coll., George Mason U. Bn. sec. 1st Bn., 68th Armored Div., Baumholder, Fed. Republic Germany, 1978-79; info. asst. Soldier's Mag., Alexandria, Va., 1980-81; sec., stenographer warrant officer div. U.S. Army, Alexandria, 1981-83; sec., adminstrv. asst. OASA (M&RA) Dept. Army, Pentagon, Washington, 1984-85, pub. affairs specialist, 1986—; congl. fellow Caucus for Women's Issues, Washington, 1985-86; sec. Army Fed. Women's Program, Pentagon, 1984-87. Instr. CPR, Alexandria, 1982-86; troop leader Girl Scouts U.S.A. Troop 1685, Springfield, 1980-84, Troop 00553, Baumholder, 1977-78; chmn. bd. dirs. Timbers Community, Springfield, Va., 1986-88, Women in Def., Inc., 1986—. Recipient Outstanding Performance awards Dept. Army, 1979-85, Spl. Service award Combined Fed. Campaign, 1985. Mem. Nat. Assn. Female Execs., Federally Employed Women, Women in Def., Phi Beta Lambda (state sec. 1967-68). Lutheran. Club: Konza Klub (Brenham, Tex.). Avocations: horseback riding, reading, camping, dancing, cooking. Home: 8812 Winding Hollow Way Springfield VA 22152 Office: Congl Caucus for Women's Issues 2471 Rayburn House Off ice Bldg Washington DC 20515

FLOM, JULIA MITTLE, civic worker; b. Bowman, S.C., Aug. 2, 1906; d. Edward Nathan and Minnie Josephine (Jackson) Mittle; m. Samuel Louis Flom (dec.); children—Joann Flom Greenberg, Edward L., Mary Sue Flom Rothenberg. Student Randolph-Macon Women's Coll., 1924-26, So. Sem., Buena Vista, Va., 1923. Bd. dirs. Univ. Community Hosp., Tampa, Fla., 1982—, Hillsborough Mental Health Assn., Tampa, 1965—, Vis. Nurses, Tampa, 1970-84, Temple Schaarai Zedek Sisterhood, Tampa, 1927—; chmn. bldg. com. Suncoast council Girl Scouts U.S.A., 1930-60; founding mem. U. South Fla., 1956—, pres.'s council, 1984-85; mem. Salvation Army, Easter Seal Guild, 1970—; Fla. Orch. and Guild, 1968—; bd. fellows U. Tampa, 1983—; mem. Jewish Welfare and Community Ctr.; mem. Council Jewish Women; founding mem., council Tampa Bay Performing Arts, 1984; mem. Tampa Mus. Patrons; mem. adv. bd. U. Tampa.; mem. bd. Community Hosp. Found., Tampa Gen. Hosp.; charter mem. St. Joseph Council Jewish Women. Democrat. Established scholarship U. Tampa Nursing Sch., engring. endowment scholarship U. So. Fla. Recipient Order of Elephant award Lowry Pk. Zool. Soc., Deans Soc. for Excellence award U. So. Fla. Lodge: Hadassah. Avocations: golf; painting. Address: 2403 Ardson Pl Apt 501B Tampa FL 33629

FLOOD, (HULDA) GAY, magazine editor; b. Plainfield, N.J., Aug. 14, 1935; d. William Edward and Lucy (Dycker) F.; B.A., Smith Coll., 1957. Picture dept. Sports Illustrated, Time Inc., N.Y.C. 1957-58, letters dept., 1958-59, reporter, 1959-60, writer-reporter, 1960-71, asso. editor, 1971-85, sr. editor, 1985—. Life mem. Alumnae Assn. Smith Coll., Inc., Smith Students Aid Soc., Inc. Mem. Reformed Ch. Club: Smith Coll. (N.Y.C.). Home: 103 Gedney St Apt 4B Nyack NY 10960 Office: Sports Illustrated Time & Life Bldg Rockefeller Center New York NY 10020

FLOOD, JOAN MOORE, corporate librarian; b. Hampton, Va., Oct. 10, 1941; d. Harold W. and Estalena (Fancher) M.; B.Mus., North Tex. State U., 1963, postgrad., 1977; postgrad. So. Meth. U., 1967-68, Tex. Women's U., 1978-79, U. Dallas, 1985-86; 1 dau. by former marriage, Angelique. Bar: Tex. Clk. Criminal Dist. Ct. Number 2, Dallas County, Tex., 1972-75; reins. librarian Scor Reins. Co., Dallas, 1975-80, Assocs. Ins. Group, 1980-83; corp./securities legal asst. Akin, Gump, Strauss, Hauer & Feld, 1983—. Mem. ABA, Spl. Libraries Assn., Am. Assn. Law Librarians, Tex. Libraries Assn., S.W. Libraries Assn., Dallas County Library Assn., Dallas Assn. Legal Assts., ABA, State Bar Tex. (charter mem. legal assts. div.), Dallas Assn. Law Librarians, other orgns. Republican. Episcopalian. Home: PO Box 1763 Dallas TX 75221

FLORA, JOANNE M., communications executive; b. Newark, Jan. 6, 1949; d. Angelo R. and Mary A. (Norton) Flora; BA in Communication Arts, Fordham U., 1970. Asst. to dir. advt. and pub. relations subsidiary Continental Ins. Cos., N.Y.C., 1970-71, pub. relations asst. parent co. N.Y.C., 1971, asso. editor publs. div., 1971-73, editor, 1973-74, mgr., 1974-76; fin. editor Morgan Stanley & Co., Inc., N.Y.C., 1976-79; communications officer human resources div. Chem. Bank, N.Y.C., 1979-80, communications mgr. div., 1980-84; v.p. corp. communication J.P. Morgan (name formerly Morgan Guaranty Trust Co. N.Y.), N.Y.C., 1984—. Home: 2600 Kennedy Blvd Jersey City NJ 07306 Office: JP Morgan 20 Pine St New York NY 10015

FLORCZYK-MATT, SANDRA, personnel executive; b. Syracuse, N.Y., Oct. 29, 1955; d. Alexander Stephen and Josephine (Iorio) Florczyk; m. Louis C. Matt, Jr., Nov. 1, 1980. B.A., Syracuse U., 1977; M.B.A., Nova U., 1984. Adminstr. law office Robbins, Gaynor & Bronstein, P.A., St. Petersburg, Fla., 1981—. Co-editor Community Link, 1976. Mem. Am.soc. Personnel Adminstrs., Assn. Legal Adminstrs. Republican. Roman Catholic. Avocations: art; tennis; traveling; golf. Home: PO Box 707 Mango FL 33550 Office: Robbins Gaynor & Bronstein PA 150 2d Ave N Suite 1700 Saint Petersburg FL 33701

FLOREK, CAROL REGINA, nurse, lawyer; b. Chgo., Mar. 28, 1944; d. Edward John and Isabelle Mary (Jarzyna) F. BS in Nursing, No. Ill. U., 1966; MS in Nursing, Calif. State U., 1971; JD, U. West Los Angeles, 1988. RN. Nurse Critical Care Services, Los Angeles, 1977—. Mem. Los Angeles World Affairs Council; vol. Am. Heart Assn., Los Angeles. Ill. State scholar, 1962-66; Educated Profl. Devel. Assn. fellow, 1971. Mem. Am. Assn. Critical Care Nurses. Democrat.

FLORENCE, VERENA MAGDALENA, legal administrator; b. Interlaken, Switzerland, Nov. 4, 1946; came to U.S., 1967; d. Paul Robert and Marie (Raess) Demuth; m. Kenneth James Florence, Dec. 10, 1967. BA, U. Calif., Berkeley, 1974; MS, UCLA, 1979, PhD, 1982. Research scientist Procter & Gamble, Cin., 1983; adminstr. Swerdlow & Florence, Beverly Hills, Calif., 1984—. Contbr. articles to profl. jours. Democrat. Home: 1063 Stradella Rd Los Angeles CA 90077 Office: Swerdlow & Florence 9401 Wilshire Blvd Suite 828 Beverly Hills CA 90212

FLORES, MARGARITA FRANCES, banker; b. Washington, Aug. 21, 1959; d. Jose Francisco and Margarita (Fernández-Mattei) F. BS in Biology, U. P.R., 1981; BBA in Mgmt., Fla. Atlantic U., 1986. Computer operator Bosch, Inc., Delray Beach, Fla., 1984; teller City Fed. Savs. Bank, Boca Raton, Fla., 1984-85, rep. new accounts, 1985-86, asst. ops., 1986-87; adminstrv. asst. C&S Nat. Bank S.C., Columbia, 1987—; tutor computer langs., Boca Raton, 1981-86. Mem. Boca Raton Mus. Mem. Assn. MBA Execs., Nat. Assn. for Exec. Women, Am. Bankers Assn. Republican. Roman Catholic. Home: 3200 Fernandina Rd #107F Columbia SC 29210

FLORES, ROBIN ANN, social worker, administrator; b. Allentown, Pa., Oct. 6, 1949; d. Norman Henry and Ann May (Huff) Flores. B.S. in Edn., Kutztown U., 1971; M.S. in Adminstrn., U. Scranton, 1983. Caseworker gerontology Lehigh County Area Agy. for Aging, Allentown, Pa., 1973-75, info. referral outreach coordinator, 1975-78, supr. community services, 1979—; lectr. on aging process, Lehigh County, Pa., 1978—; utilization community resources, Lehigh County, 1978—. Mem. adv. bd. Community Action Com. of Lehigh Valley, 1979-82, Elder Well, 1987—; Pa. del. White House Conf. on Aging, Hershey, Pa., 1981; bd. dirs. Vis. Nurse Assn. of Lehigh County, 1982—, Women Inc., 1983-87; adv. bd. Homecare, Inc., 1982—, Geriatric Edn. Modules, Allentown Osteo. Hosp., 1979; mem. profl. adv. com. Lehigh Valley Hospice, 1984—; mem. utilization and rev. bd. Vis. Nurse Assn., 1979—; consumer rep. Pa. Power and Light Co., Nat. Assn. Female Execs., Lehigh County, Pa., 1978—; co-chmn. Human Services Tng. Coop., 1975-81. Mem. Allentown Art Mus., Old Allentown Preservation Assn., Quota Internat. Home: 237 N Lumber St Allentown PA 18102 Office: Lehigh County Area Agy on Aging 523 Hamilton St Allentown PA 18101

FLORESTANO, PATRICIA SHERER, university administrator; b. Washington, Mar. 15, 1936; d. Wilbur L. and Virginia M. (Moriconi) F.; B.A. in Am. Civilization, U. Md., 1958, M.A. in Govt. and Politics, 1970, Ph.D. in Pub. Adminstrn. and Am. Govt., 1974; m. Thomas Florestano, Nov. 29, 1959; children—Leslie C., Thomas. Research staff State Legis. Commn. on Intergovt. Coop., 1972-75, State Gov.'s Commn. on Functions of Govt., 1973-75; staff asst. to pres. Md. Senate, 1975-78; asst. prof. Inst. Urban Studies, U. Md., College Park, 1974-79, dir. Inst. Govtl. Service, 1979-85, v.p. govtl. relations, 1985—; cons. cdnl. evaluation, mgmt. and survey research. Lector St. Elizabeth Ann Seton Ch., 1970—; dir. Crofton (Md.) Gymnastics Program, 1972-74; vice chmn. Anne Arundel County (Md.) Commn. on Women, 1975; mem. Anne Arundel County Schs. Adv. Forum, 1975-76, chmn. nominations com., 1976-78. Recipient Outstanding Teaching award Students Assn. of U. Md., 1979. Mem. Am. Soc. Pub. Adminstrn. (pres. 1983-84, conf. fellow), Am. Polit. Sci. Assn., So. Polit. Sci. Assn., Urban Affairs Assn. (past chmn. governing bd.), So. Consortium Univ., Pub. Service Orgns. (former editor). Democrat. Roman Catholic. Author: (with other) The States and Metropolitan Areas, 1981; Attitudes of Special Interest Groups and the Public on Chesapeake Bay Areas, 1980; also articles. Home: 1516 Farlow Ave Crofton MD 21114 Office: Cen Adminstrn 3300 Metzerott Rd Adelphi MD 20783

FLORIAN, MARIANNA BOLOGNESI, civic leader; b. Chgo.; d. Giulio and Rose (Garibaldi) Bolognesi; B.A. cum laude, Barat Coll., 1940; postgrad. Moser Bus. Sch., 1941-42; m. Paul A. Florian III, June 4, 1949; children—Paul, Marina, Peter, Mark. Asst. credit mgr. Stella Cheese Co., Chgo., 1942-45; With ARC ETO Clubmobile Unit, 1945-47; mgr. Passavant

Hosp. Gift Shop, 1947-49; pres., Jr. League Chgo. Inc., 1957-59; pres. woman's bd. Passavant Hosp., 1966-68; bd. dirs. Northwestern Meml. Hosp., 1974-81, mem. exec. com., 1974-79; pres. Women's Assn., Chgo. Symphony Orch., 1974-77, founder WFMT radio marathon, 1976; chmn. Guild Chgo. Hist. Soc., 1981-84, trustee Chgo. Hist. Soc., 1981-84; trustee Orchestral Assn., 1977—, v.p. 1978-82, vice chmn. 1982-86, mem. exec. com. 1978-87; mem. women's bd. Northwestern U.; mem. vis. com. dept. music U. Chgo., 1980—; mem. bd. Antiquarian Soc. Art Inst. Chgo., 1986—. Recipient Citizen Fellowship, Inst. Medicine Chgo., 1975. Clubs: Friday (pres. 1972-74), Contemporary; Winnetka Garden.

FLORIO, MARYANNE J., statistician, educational administrator; b. Queens, N.Y., Sept. 28, 1940; d. Edgar Vincent and Helen Louise (Schultze) Spaeth; m. James J. Florio, June 25, 1960 (div. 1985); children: Christopher, Gregory, Catherine. BS summa cum laude, Trenton State Coll., 1979; MEd, Temple U., 1981, postgrad., 1982—. Cert. biofeedback therapist, tchr., N.J. Research and evaluation asst. Woodhaven Ctr., Phila., 1981-82; statis. and computer cons., program asst. Systems & Computer Tech. Corp., Phila., 1982-83; biofeedback therapist Ctr. for Creative Devel., Ardmore, Pa., 1984-85; computer scientist stats. research N.J. Dept. Health, Trenton, 1985-87; evaluation coordinator N.J. Dept. Edn., Trenton, 1987—; pvt. design and computing cons., 1983—; trainer computer and statis. software, N.J., Pa., 1984—, Camden County Comm. on Women, 1985—. Chmn. long-range planning, bd. dirs., 1st v.p. Camden County council Girl Scouts U.S., 1975—. Elks Club scholar, 1958, Systems and Computer Tech. Corp. scholar, 1982; Temple U. grad. fellow, 1984. Mem. Am. Edn. Research Assn., Biofeedback Soc. Am., Biofeedback and Behavioral Med. Soc. Pa. Home: 290 Evergreen Rd Barrington NJ 08007

FLORSHEIM, NEENA BETH, counselor, educational consultant; b. Milw., July 30, 1952; d. Roy Henry and Rosalie (Kaiman) Nirenberg; m. Richard S. Florsheim, Mar. 2, 1949; children: Ali, David, Rebecca. BS in Mgmt., Cardinal Stritch Coll., 1984; MS in Edni. Psychology, U. Wis., Milw., 1986; postgrad., Marquette U. Counselor Jewish Family and Children's Service, Milw., 1981—; acad. counselor Cardinal Stritch Coll., Milw., 1985-86, educator, 1985—; pres., owner Achievement Assocs., Ltd., Milw., 1986—; instr. St. Francis Coll. Bd. dirs. Orgn. for Rehab. thru Tng., Milw., 1973—, PTA, Milw., 1983—. Mem. Am. Assn. for Counseling and Devel., Wis. Assn. for Counseling and Devel., Assn. for Humanistic Edn. and Devel., Nat. Career Devel. Assn., Nat. Employment Counselors Assn. Office: Achievement Assocs Ltd 6270 N Port Washington Rd Milwaukee WI 53217

FLORY, TERESE MARIE, agricultural organization administrator; b. Paterson, N.J., Sept. 15, 1954; d. Eugene Miles and Mary Louise (Zambon) F. BS, Ramapo Coll., Mahwah, N.J., 1976; MS, Ind. U., 1978. Waterfront dir., outdoor edn. instr. Camp Speers Eljabar YMCA, Dingmans Ferry, Pa., 1976-77, outdoor edn. dir., program dir., 1980, assoc. dir., 1980-82; outdoor edn. instr. Ridgewood (N.J.) Sch. System, 1977, 79, asst. dir. outdoor edn., 1979, outdoor edn. cons., 1983-84; asst. dir. Camp Piomingo YMCA, Louisville, 1978; outdoor edn. dir. Ho Ho Kus (N.J.) Sch. System, 1979; environ. edn. coordinator Youth Conservation Corps, McGuire AFB, N.J., 1979; outdoor edn. cons. Camp Bernie YMCA, Port Murray, N.J., 1983-84, Rutgers U., New Brunswick, N.J., 1983-84; 4H agt. Hunterdon County, Flemington, N.J., 1984—. Author: The Line and the Dot, 1982, numerous country music songs. V.p. Hunterdon County conservation recreation council Round Valley Youth Ctr., Lebanon, N.J., 1985-87; vol. Morales Park Com., Flemington, 1985-87; mem. music ministry Immaculate Conception Cath. Ch., Annandale, N.J., 1983-85. Recipient Appreciation award Jr. Leaders Assn., 1985. Mem. Nat. Assn. Extension 4H Agts. (chair Nat. Camping Task Force 1986-87), N.J. Assn. 4H Agts. (treas. 1986—, Outstanding Service award 1985), Am. Assn. Univ. Profs., Camp Speers Eljabar YMCA Alumni Assn. (musical performer, vol. 1980-82, 84-87). Home: 1307 Normandy Ct Flemington NJ 08822 Office: 4-H 4 Gauntt Place Flemington NJ 08822

FLOWERS, JUANZETTA SHEW, nursing educator; b. Gadsden, Ala., Aug. 8, 1941; d. Shelly Jerome and Pluma Lee (Odom) Shew; m. Charles Ely Flowers, Jr., Sept. 25, 1972. B.S.N., U. Ala., 1966; M.A., U. Ala.-Birmingham, 1978, M.S.N., 1983, D.S.N., 1985. Pub. health nurse, Birmingham, Ala., 1966-68; sch. nurse, New Ulm, Germany, 1970; instr. U. Ala. Sch. Medicine-Birmingham, 1974-78, assoc. prof. dept. ob-gyn, 1978—, asst. prof. Sch. Nursing, 1985—. Pres., Birmingham Humane Soc., 1975-77, Found. for Women's Health in Ala., 1988—. Mem. AAUW, Am. Nurses Assn., Soc. Sci. Study Sex, Orgn. Obstetric, Gynecologic & Neonatal Nurses (chmn. Ala. sect. 1977-81), Nat. League Nursing, Am. Assn. Sex Educators, Counselors and Therapists, Sigma Theta Tau, Phi Kappa Phi. Home: 3757 Rockhill Rd Birmingham AL 35223 Office: Univ Ala Sch Nursing UAB Station Birmingham AL 35294

FLOWERS, JUDITH ANN, advertising executive; b. Oxford, Miss., Feb. 21, 1944; d. Woodrow Coleman and Ola Marie (Harding) Haynes; m. Sayles L. Brown Jr., Apr. 20, 1963 (div. Apr. 1974); children: Sayles L. III, Gregory A., Matthew C., Stephen W.; m. Taylor Graydon Flowers Jr., Apr. 27, 1979. Grad. high sch., Clarksdale, Miss. Office mgr. The KBH Corp., Clarksdale, 1964-69; office mgr., estimator Willis & Ellis Constrn., Clarksdale, 1969-75; with advt. prodn. Farm Press Pub., Clarksdale, 1975-79, advt. mgr., 1979-86, dir. advt. services, 1986—. Counselor youth ct. County Youth Ct., Clarksdale, 1985—. Mem. Bus. and Profl. Women (corr. sec. 1987-88, 2d v.p. 1988—), Agri-Women Am., Nat. Assn. Female Execs., Nat. Agri Mktg. Assn., Clarksdale C. of C. (mem. agri bus. commn.), So. Garden History Soc. Republican. Baptist. Home: Box 3126 Dublin MS 38739 Office: Farm Press Pub Intersection Hwy 61 & 6 Clarksdale MS 38614

FLOWERS, MARIAN WILLIAMS, educator; b. Houston, Dec. 5, 1933; d. Isaac Leon and Clara Louise (Petrie) Williams; m. Roosevelt Flowers, Dec. 27, 1969. B.S. in Phys. Edn. and Health, Tex. So. U., 1955, M.S. in Phys. Edn. and Health, 1959. Tchr. high sch., Houston, 1955-70; tchr. Crenshaw High Sch., Los Angeles, 1970—. Recreational dir. summer program City Parks and Recreation, Houston, 1955-65; docent March of Dimes, Los Angeles, 1982. Recipient plaque Girls Athletic Assn., 1979; Crenshaw-Dorsey Community Salute award Push for Excellence, 1977; named Outstanding Basketball and Softball Coach, Girls' Athletic Assn., 1975, 76, 78, Coach of Yr. for championship team Los Angeles Unified Sch. Dist., 1985. Mem. NAACP, Alpha Kappa Alpha (chmn. com.). Office: Crenshaw High Sch 5010 11th Ave Los Angeles CA 90043

FLOWERS, MAXINE ROGERS, psychiat. social worker; b. South Pittsburg, Tenn., Jan. 7, 1935; d. Omer Leighton and Mamie Gertrude (Parker) Rogers; A.B., Birmingham So. Coll., 1956; M.S., Columbia U., 1964; postgrad. Menninger Found., 1965; m. John Baxton Flowers, III, Oct. 4, 1969; 1 son, Bryan. Child welfare worker Dept. Public Welfare, Nashville, 1956-59; caseworker Children's Home Soc., Miami, Fla., 1959-63; caseworker Menninger Found. Children's Service, 1965-69; supr. adult services Pitt County Mental Health Center, 1969-71; staff social worker div. child psychiatry Duke U. Med. Center, Durham, N.C., 1971—, chief social worker div. child psychiatry, 1976-88 ; chief social worker community Guidance Clinic, 1976-88; cons. day care centers; bd. dirs. Durham Nurses Assn., Family Counseling Services Durham; mem. profl. adv. com. Mental Health Assn. Trustee, Hist. Preservation Soc. Durham; mem. Assn. Preservation of Eno Valley, Mus. Life and Sci. Mem. Acad. Cert. Social Workers, Nat. Assn. Social Workers, N.C. Soc. Clin. Social Work (ethics chmn.), N.C. Soc. Colonial Dames Am. (chmn. hist. activities com., mem. Durham-Orange com.). Democrat. Methodist. Home: 128 Pinecrest Rd Durham NC 27705 Office: Duke U Med Ctr Trent and Elba Sts Durham NC 27705

FLOWERS, TERESA JO, advertising and marketing specialist, model; b. Smithfield, N.C., Aug. 24, 1961; d. Joel Pias and Carolyn Faye (Cotton) F. Profl. modeling student, John Robert Powers, 1980-81; AA in Fashion Design and Illustration, Bauder Fashion Coll., 1981; Diploma in Comml. Art and Advt., Art Inst. of Atlanta, 1983; postgrad. in Bus. Mktg. and Internat. Studies, Oglethorpe U., 1987—. Mktg. asst. Barkley Office Systems, Atlanta, 1981; mktg. cons., comml. artist Wilkins Advt., Atlanta, 1981—; advt. and mktg. specialist MCI Telecommunications, Atlanta, 1984-87; pub. relations and mktg. exec. Bianca Internat. div. R.L. White Communications, 1987—; mktg. cons. Mt. Paran Ch.-TV Ministry, Atlanta, 1987—, fashion design photography model. Appeared in: (films) For Ladies Only, Six Pack, Cannonball Run; numerous print and runway modeling assignments. Vol. publicity com. Ga. Spl. Olympics, 1986—, Nat. Crusade Against Drug Abuse and Crime, 1987; mem. High Mus. of Art-Young Careers; judge Miss N.C., Miss Sun Queen, Miss Atlanta-county pageants. Named Miss So. Smile, 1979, 81, Miss. N.C. Hemisphere, 1979, 81, Model of Yr. 1979, 81, finalist Miss Ga.-U.S.A., 1983. Mem. Women in Communications, Inc., Women's C. of C., Women's Commerce Club, Nat. Assn. Female Execs. (bd. dirs. Atlanta chpt. 1986—). Republican. Mem. Ch. of God. Club: Toastmasters. Home: 2850 Delk Rd Marietta GA 30080 Office: PO Box 550029 Atlanta GA 30355-2529

FLOWERS, VIRGINIA ANNE, state educational administrator; b. Dothan, Ala., Aug. 29, 1928; d. Kyrie Neal and Annie Laurie (Stewart) F. B.A. (State of Fla. scholar), Fla. State U., 1949; M.Ed., Auburn (Ala.) U., 1958; Ed.D. (Delta Kappa Gamma scholar, teaching asst.), Duke U., 1963. Elem. and secondary sch. tchr., adminstr. Dothan and Dalton, Ga., 1949-61; asst. prof., then prof. edn., head dept. Columbia (S.C.) Coll., 1963-68, assoc. dean, then dean, 1969-72; prof. edn. Va. Commonwealth U., 1968-69; assoc. dean, asst. provost, acting dean, vice provost Trinity Coll. Arts and Scis., Duke U., 1972-74, prof. edn., chmn. dept., asst. provost ednl. program devel., 1974-80; dean Sch. Edn., Ga. So. Coll., Statesboro, 1980-85; asst. vice chancellor Univ. System of Ga., Atlanta, 1985-88, vice chancellor, 1988—; bd. dirs., exec. com. Am. Assn. Colls. Tchr. Edn., 1979-84, pres., 1983-84; bd. dirs., exec. com. Learning Inst. N.C., 1976-80. Co-author: Law and Pupil Control, 1964, Readings in Survival in Today's Society, 2 vols, 1978; editorial bd.: Jour. Tchr. Edn, 1980-82, Ednl. Gerontology, 1979—; contbr. articles to profl. jours. Adv. trustee Queens Coll., Charlotte, N.C., 1976-78; vice chmn. continuing commn. study black colls. related to United Methodist Ch., 1973-76. Recipient Star Tchrs. award Dalton. Mem. So. Assn. Colls. and Schs. (commn. on colls.), Am. Ednl. Research Assn., Nat. Orgn. Legal Problems in Edn., Am. Assn. Higher Edn., NEA, AAUP, Assn. Study Higher Edn., Am. Assn. Colls. Tchr. Edn. (pres. 1983), Kappa Delta Pi, Phi Delta Kappa. Home: 619 N Superior Ave Decatur GA 30033 Office: Univ System of Ga Bd Regents 244 Washington St SW Atlanta GA 30334

FLOYD, BILLIE JEAN, state legislator, educator; b. Ada, Okla., Dec. 24, 1929; m. Ben C. Floyd; 2 daus. Asst. prof. East Central U.; mem. Okla. Senate from Dist. 13, 1985—. Active Federated Democratic Women's Club. Mem. AAHPER, Bus. and Profl. Women. Mem. Christian Ch. Home: Rt 7 Box 238 Ada OK 74820 Office: Okla State Capitol Bldg Oklahoma City OK 73105 Other: Rt 7 Box 238 Ada OK 74820

FLOYD, BRENDA CAROL, optometrist; b. Sacramento, Calif., Jan. 8, 1955; d. Louis Carrell and Catherine Louise (Hawkins) F.; m. Richard Joseph Brochetti, June 22, 1985. A.A. summa cum laude, Gaston Coll., 1973; B. in Chemistry summa cum laude, U. N.C.-Charlotte, 1975; B.S. in Physiol. Optics cum laude, U. Ala.-Birmingham, 1979, O.D. cum laude, 1981. Lic. optometrist, Tex. Research asst. U. Ala., Birmingham, 1977-79, researcher, 1980-81; optometrist Optical Clinic, Dallas, 1981-85; pvt. practice optometry, Lewisville, Tex., 1985—; clinician, intern Diabetes Hosp., Birmingham, 1980-81, Ctr. Devel. and Learning Disorders, Birmingham, 1980-81. Columnist eye care Lewisville Daily Leader. Sustaining mem. Republican Nat. Com., 1983—. Mem. Tex. Assn. Optometrists, Am. Optometric Found., Women in Optometry, Gamma Beta Phi. Baptist. Avocation: piano compositions. Home: 3745 Casa Del Sol Dallas TX 75228 Office: 724 W Main St Suite 200 Lewisville TX 75067

FLOYD, GAIL M., international sales administrator; b. Columbia, S.C., Nov. 21, 1953; d. Louie B. Muse and Mildred Kathleen Henderson; m. Trammell Thomas Floyd, Jan. 4, 1952; 1 child, Krista Michelle. Student, Dalton Jr. Coll., 1975-76. Customer service rep. Westpoint Pepperell Inc., Dalton, Ga., 1971-75, export coordinator internat. sales, 1976-82, credit mgr. internat., 1982-83, adminstrv. coordinator, 1983-87; v.p. mktg. Regent International Ltd., Chatsworth, Ga., 1987—; bd. dirs. World Trade Council, Chattanooga, Tenn. Counsellor Jr. Achievement, Dalton, 1982-83; advisor, solicitor United Way, Dalton, 1983-85. Mem. Nat. Assn. Female Execs. Democrat. Pentecostal.

FLOYD, JANE BIGGERSTAFF, nurse, educator; b. Rutherfordton, N.C., Feb. 15, 1943; d. James Garland and Katie (Earley) Biggerstaff; BS in Nursing, Lenoir Rhyne Coll., Hickory, N.C., 1965; MA in Nursing (HEW grantee), Emory U., Atlanta, 1967; m. John G. Floyd, June 18, 1967; children: Kelly Jane, John Robert II. Instr., Lenoir Rhyne Coll., Hickory, N.C., 1966, 67-71, Druid City Hosp., Tuscaloosa, Ala., 1972-75; asst. prof. Samford U., Birmingham, 1977-79; asst. prof. U. South Fla., Tampa, 1980-86, Calhoun Coll., Decatur, Ala., 1986—; cons. Sch. Bd. Hillsborough County (Fla.), Women's Hosp. Mem. adv. bd. Crippled Children's Assn.; chmn. public edn. Am. Heart Assn.; active Girl Scouts U.S.A.; chmn. bd. Wee World Day Sch.; bd. cons. Childbirth Edn. Assn. Mem. Am. Nurses Assn., Nurses Assn. Am. Coll. Obstetricians and Gynecologists, Sigma Theta Tau, Zeta Tau Alpha. Baptist. Clubs: U. South Fla. Women's. Home: 5741 Whiteway Dr Tannahill Circle SE Huntsville AL 35802 Office: Calhoun Coll Decatur AL 35802

FLOYD, MADGE BLACK, minister, church administrator; b. Atlanta, Sept. 23, 1935; d. William Howard and Nena Madge (Estes) Black; m. Carl M. Floyd Jr., June 14, 1958 (div. May 1981); children: Christine Elizabeth, Carl M. III. AB, Emory U., 1958; MDiv, Pitts. Theol. Sem., 1969; D in Ministry, Boston U., 1978. Ordained to ministry United Meth. Ch. Pastor 1st United Meth. Ch., Greensburg, Pa., 1971-72, Castle Shannon United Meth. Ch., Pitts., 1973-79; exec. dir. TOGETHER Program, United Meth. Ch., Pitts., 1979-84; supt. Pitts. dist. United Meth Ch., 1984—; stewardship assoc. Gen. Bd. Discipline, United Meth. Ch., Nashville, 1979—, bd. dirs. Gen. Bd. Pensions, Evanston, Ill., 1984—; mem. commn. stewardship Nat. Council Chs., N.Y.C., 1979-84. Fellow Order of St. Luke. Democrat. Office: United Meth Ch Pitts Dist 600 Fox Dr Pittsburgh PA 15237

FLOYD-TENIYA, KATHLEEN, business services executive; b. Berwyn, Ill., June 23, 1953; d. David James and Phyllis L. (Lyons) Floyd; m. Robert Don Teniya, June 20, 1982; one child: James David. Cert. credit and fin. analyst, lic. realtor, Ill. Indsl. specialist Technicon Instrument Corp., Elmhurst, Ill., 1971-74, service contract adminstr., 1974-76; asst. to pres. Elmed, Inc., Addison, Ill., 1976-77; credit rep. mgr. Memorex Corp., Lombard, Ill., 1977-79; nat. sales rep. Midcontinent Adjustment Co., Glenview, Ill., 1979-83, asst. v.p. sales, 1983-86; pres., chief exec. officer, (Inteletek) Innovative Telemktg. Techniques Inc., Itasca, Ill., 1986—. Newspaper editor, publicity chmn. Dupage County chpt. Young Ams. for Freedom, 1969-70, pres., 1970-71; mem. Teenage Republican Orgn., 1968-71. Mem. Nat. Assn. Female Execs. Lutheran. Clubs: Lombard Women's Rep., Ill. Fedn. Rep. Women. Home: 263 Evergreen Ln Bloomingdale IL 60108 Office: (Inteletek) Innovative Telemktg Techniques Inc PO Box 0163 Itasca IL 60143

FLUKE, LYLA SCHRAM, publisher, educator; b. Maddock, N.D.; d. Olaf John and Anne Marie (Rodberg) Schram; m. John M. Fluke, June 5, 1937; children: Virginia Fluke Gabelein, John M. Jr., David Lynd. BS in Zoology and Physiology, U. Wash., Seattle, 1934, diploma teaching, 1935. High sch. tchr., 1935-37; tutor Seattle schs., 1974-75; pub. Portage Quar. mag., Hist. Soc. Seattle and King County, 1980—. Author articles on histroy. Founder N.W. chpt. Myasthenia Gravis Found., 1953, pres., 60-63; obtained N.W. artifacts for destroyer tender Puget Sound, 1966; mem. Seattle Mayor's Com. for Seattle Beautiful, 1968-69; sponsor Seattle World's Fair, 1962; charter mem. Seattle Youth Symphony Aux., 1974; bd. dirs. Cascade Symphony, Salvation Army, 1985-87; mem. U.S. Congl. Adv. Bd.; benefactor U. Wash., 1982—, nat. chmn. ann. giving campaign, 1983-84; benefactor Stanford U., 1984; mem. condr.'s club Seattle Symphony, 1978—. Fellow Seattle Pacific U., 1972—. Mem. Wash. Trust for Hist. Preservation, Nat. Trust for Hist. Preservation, N.W. Ornamental Hort. Soc. (life, hon.), Smithsonian Assocs., Nat. Assn. Parliamentarians (charter mem., pres. N.W. unit 1961), Wash. Parliamentarians Assn. (charter), IEEE Aux. (chpt. charter mem., past pres.), Seattle C. of C. (women's div.), Seattle Symphony Women's Assn. (life, sec. 1982-84, pres. 1985-87), Hist. Soc. Seattle and King County (exec. com. 1975-78, pres. women's mus. league 1975-78, pres. Moritz Thomsen Guild of Hist. Soc., 1978-80, 84-87), Highlands Orthopedic Guild (life), Wash. State Hist. Soc, Antiquarian Soc. (v.p. 1986-88), Stanford Assocs., Sterling Circle (pres. 1988—). Republican. Lutheran. Clubs: Women's U., Rainier, Seattle Golf, Seattle Tennis, U. Wash. Pres.'s. Address: 1206 NW Culbertson Dr Seattle WA 98177

FLUKER, BRENDA ANN, lawyer; b. Demopolis, Ala., Mar. 3, 1952; d. Clinton and Pandora E. (Essex) F.; 1 child, Brandy Fluker Oakley. BS, Ala. A&M U., 1972; JD, Tulane U., 1978. Bar: Mass. 1979, U.S. Supreme Ct. 1984. Underwriter Liberty Mut. Ins. Co., Boston, 1972-74, filing analyst, 1974-75, counsel, 1979—; of counsel Rosa Parks Day Care Ctr., Roxbury, Mass., 1979—. Active Urban League Eastern Mass., Boston, 1984-85. Mem. ABA, Nat. Bar Assn. (regional dir. bd. govs. 1981-82, 1986-87), Mass. Bar Assn. (corp. counsel com. 1980), Mass. Black Lawyers Assn. (sec. 1981-83, exec. com. 1981-83, 85-86, v.p. 1988-89), Mass. Black Women Attys. Assn. (exec. com. 1980-82). Democrat. Baptist. Office: Liberty Mut Ins Co 175 Berkeley St PO Box 140 Boston MA 02117

FLUMENBAUM, JUDITH ADLER, foundation administrator; b. Bamberg, Federal Republic of Germany, Jan. 23, 1947; came to U.S., 1955; d. Ted Adler and Rose (Fand) Ross; m. Bill Flumenbaum, 1969 (div. 1970). BA, UCLA, 1968; grad. cert. in edn., U. Calif., Berkeley, 1969. Pub. sch. tchr. Los Angeles and Vallejo, Calif., 1969-70, 72-74; dir. child care Westside Jewish Community Ctr., Los Angeles, 1974-75; dir. univ. program United Jewish Appeal, N.Y.C., 1975-83, dir. staff devel., 1983-85, dir. bus. and profl. women's council, 1985—. Exec. producer: (film) Encounter Israel, 1976; project dir.: United Jewish Appeals Book of Songs and Blessings, 1982. Mem. bd. govs. Lincoln Square Synagogue, N.Y.C., 1986—. Recipient Louis Kraft award, 1980, William Haber award B'nai Brith Hillel, 1982. Mem. Assn. Jewish Community Orgns. Personnel (past regional chair), Conf. Jewish Communal Service, Nat. Assn. Female Execs. Office: United Jewish Appeal 99 Park Ave Suite 300 New York City NY 10016

FLUOR, MARJORIE LETHA WADE, author; b. Christiansburg, Va., May 6, 1926; d. Hubert Dodd and Ida (Sowers) Wade; m. John Simon Fluor, Aug. 17, 1956 (dec. Sept. 1974); m. Thurman Moore, July 27, 1979. Author: (geneal. book) Birth and Death Records Floyd County, Virginia, 1980; co-author: (with Michael Evlanoff) Alfred Nobel The Loneliest Millionaire, 1969. Chmn. vols. ARC, 1960-62; mem. adv. bd. Children's Hosp., Orange County, 1965-68; bd. dirs. Orange County Symphony Assn., 1964-69, Orange County Community Chest, 1962-66, Salvation Army, 1963-68, YWCA, 1963-68, Girl Scouts U.S., 1977—, World Affairs Council Orange County, 1975—, mem. exec. bd. Holmes Research Ctr., Los Angeles, 1975—; spl. rep. Calif. Bicentennial Celebration Commn., 1967-69; trustee United Ch. Religious Sci., 1980-85. Recipient Headliner award Orange County Press County, 1966, Heart to God, Hand to Man award Salvation Army, 1968, Disneyland Community Service Program award, 1967, Practitioner Emeritus Recognition award Golden Circle Ch. of Religious Sci., 1988. Mem. DAR (past regent, state asst. chaplain), Freedoms Found. (life), Assistance League, Federated Rep. Women, Philanthropic Ednl. Orgn., Les Dames de Champagne (chmn. 1970-74). Club: Pro Am. (Santa Ana). Lodge: Order Eastern Star. Home: 1920 Heliotrope Dr Santa Ana CA 92706

FLY, CELIA PATTERSON, research company executive; b. Direct, Tex., Aug. 15, 1928; d. Martin and Laura (Hollingshead) Patterson; B.S., Tex. Tech. U., 1951; m. A.B. Fly, July 6, 1947; children—Charles Bruce, Gerald Wayne. Adminstrv. dietitian St. Anthony's Hosp., Amarillo, Tex., 1955-57, Calif. Hosp., Los Angeles, 1957-59; office mgr. Hydro-Jet Service, Inc., Hydro-Torq Pump Co., Amarillo, 1959—; also dir.; dir., sec. treas. Marine Metals Inc., Fly Enterprises, Inc., Aero-Span, Inc., Amarillo; controller Aero-Span Research Ltd., Hi-Plains Minerals Ltd., Amarillo, 1980—; sec., treas., office mgr. Tuff-N-Lite Inc., 1980—. Mem. Aircraft Owners and Pilots Assn., The Ninety-Nines. Republican. Inventor vapor suppression solar collector film system. Home: 136 Bayrock Circle PO Box 30400 Amarillo TX 79120 Office: 500 W Farmers Ave Box 30400 Amarillo TX 79120

FLYNN, ANNETTE THERESA, infosystems specialist; b. Miami, Fla., July 10, 1953; d. William Lowry and Ann Theresa (Karnafel) F. AA in Pre-Computer Systems, Miami-Dade Community Coll., 1973; BS in Computer Sci., Fla. Internat. U., 1975. Computer programer, analyst City of Miami Beach, Fla., 1975-79; project mgr. Burroughs Corp., Miami, Fla., 1979-84; sr. project mgr. Ericsson Info. Systems, Miami, 1984-87; sr. project adminstr. ISC Systems Corp., Miami, 1987—. Mem. Phi Theta Kappa. Democrat. Roman Catholic. Home and Office: 7845 W Meridian St Miramar FL 33023

FLYNN, ELIZABETH ANNE, advertising and public relations company executive; b. Washington, Aug. 21, 1951; d. John William and Elizabeth Goodwin (Mahoney) F. A.A., Montgomery Coll., Rockville, Md., 1972; B.S. in Journalism, U. Md., 1976; postgrad. San Diego State U., 1976. Writer, researcher, Sea World, Inc., San Diego, 1977-79; sr. writer Lane & Huff Advt., San Diego, 1979-80; account exec. Kaufman, Lansky, Baker Advt., San Diego, 1980-82; mng. dir. Excelsior Enterprises, Beverly Hills, Calif., 1983-84; sr. account exec. Berkhemer & Kline, Inc., Los Angeles, 1985; pres. Flynn Advt. & Pub. Relations, Los Angeles, 1985—; cons. Coca-Cola Bottling Co. Los Angeles, 1982-84. Bd. dirs. Friends of Reconstructive Surgery, Beverly Hills, 1983—. Recipient Cert. of Distinction, Art Direction Mag., 1982. Mem. Nat. Assn. Female Execs., Beverly Hills C. of C., Republican. Roman Catholic. Avocations: screenwriting; short stories; painting; horseback riding. Office: Flynn Advt & Pub Relations 1440 Reeves St Suite 104 Los Angeles CA 90035

FLYNN, JUDITH ANNE, public relations executive; b. Hartford, Conn.; d. Jere J. and Helen P. (Kelly) F. B.A., U. Pa., 1959; M.A., Trinity Coll., Hartford, 1963. Pub. health edn. cons. Conn. Dept. Health, Hartford, 1962-64; assoc. editor Macmillan Co., N.Y.C., 1964-66; staff publicist Pub. Relations Soc. Am., N.Y.C., 1966-68; asst. v.p. pub. relations Bankers Trust Co., N.Y.C., 1968-75, asst. v.p., pub. relations Marine Midland Bank, N.Y.C., 1978-80; nat. dir. pub. relations Arthur Young & Co., N.Y.C., 1980-83; owner, dir. Flynn Communications Group, N.Y.C., 1983—. Bd. dirs. Brownstone Revival Commn., N.Y.C., 1984. Mem. New Eng. Soc. (N.Y.C.), Pub. Relations Soc. Am., Am. Women Entrepreneurs Nat. Assn. Female Execs. Club: Princeton (N.Y.C.). Home and office: 153 E 57th St New York NY 10022

FLYNN, JUDITH C., business exec.; b. Wichita Falls, Tex., Nov. 27, 1945; d. W.H. and Teena H. Chittum; B.A. (with hons.), Grove City (Pa.) Coll., 1966; M.A.T. (teaching fellow 1967), Brown U., 1967; MBA U. South Fla., 1987; m. Harold F. Flynn, Jr.; children—Harold F., III, Peter Craig, Alison J. Tchr., Franklin (N.H.) High Sch., 1967-68; internat. advt. coordinator Franklin Mint, Franklin Center, Pa., 1969-72; fin. mgr. Fire Service Agy., Annapolis, Md., 1972-74; asst. to comptroller Alcoa Marine Corp., Washington, 1974-76; v.p. fin., dir. Martel Labs., Inc., Balt., 1977-80, exec. v.p., 1982—; pres., dir. Martel Lab. Services, St. Petersburg, Fla., 1982-87; dir. Leartek Corp., 1977-80, Chgo. Aerial Survey, Inc., Des Plaines, Ill., 1982—; exec. v.p., dir. Geonex Corp., St. Petersburg, Fla., 1986—; pres., dir. ENR Group, 1987—; pres., chmn. Bd. Verde, Inc., Watsonville, Ca., 1987—; v.p., chmn. Bd. Delta Aerial Survey, Inc., Denver, 1987—; dir., chmn. ITECh, Anchorage, 1987—; bd. dirs. Unified Personnel Bd. of Pinellas County, 1985—; mem. campus adv. bd. U. South Fla., 1986—, exec. council, bus. and industry employment and devel. council of Pinellas County, 1984—. Mem. Engring. Soc. Balt., Nat. Assn. Female Execs., Internat. Oceanographic Found., Nat. Assn. Women Bus. Owners, Com. of 200 (nat. sec. 1984), Assn. Women Govt. Contractors, Beta Gamma Sigma, Phi Kappa Phi, Sigma Iota Epsilon. Republican. Episcopalian. Office: Geonex Corp 301 4th St N Saint Petersburg FL 33701

FLYNN, JUDITH E., educator; b. St. Louis, Aug. 16, 1944; d. Warren Campbell and Ruth (Tobin) F. BS, Tex. Wesleyan Coll., 1967. Cert. tchr., Tex. Tchr. Arlington (Tex.) Ind. Sch. Dist., 1967—; chairperson communications com. Arlington Schs., 1986-87, mem. policy com. sick leave bank, 1986—. Active Big Bros./Big Sisters, Inc., 1976; editor local Rep. newsletter; mem. PTA. Named Tchr. of the Yr. Duff Elem. Sch. faculty and PTA, 1972-73. Mem. Assn. Tex. Profl. Educators, PTA. Baptist. Home: 3612 San Rafael Arlington TX 76013

FLYNN, MARIE COSGROVE, portfolio manager; b. Honolulu, Jan. 1, 1945; d. John Aloysius and Emeline Frances (Cael) Cosgrove; B.A., Trinity Coll., 1966; student U. Fribourg (Switzerland), 1964-65; m. John Thomas Flynn, Jr., June 3, 1968; children—Jamie Marie, Jacqueline Elizabeth. Mgmt. trainee, analyst U.S. Govt., Washington, 1967-70; coordinator nat. reading council F.X. Doherty Assos., N.Y.C., 1970-71; security analyst Corinthian Capital Co., N.Y.C., 1971-73; portfolio mgr. Clark Mgmt. Co., Inc., N.Y.C., 1973-78; v.p., sr. portfolio mgr. Lexington Mgmt. Corp., Saddle Brook, N.J., 1978—. Mem. Fin. Analysts Fedn., Inst. Chartered Fin. Analysts, Fin. Women's Assn., N.Y. Soc. Security Analysts, Bus. and Profl. Women's Club. Home: 70 Evergreen Dr Berkeley Heights NJ 07922 Office: Park 80 W Plaza II PO Box 1515 Saddle Brook NJ 07662

FLYNN, PRISCILLA JANE, newspaper publishing executive; b. Providence, Dec. 17, 1948; d. Ernest Howard and Mabel Jane (Burke) Gardiner; m. Martin Joseph Flynn, Oct. 15, 1966; children: Bryan Patrick, Martin Brett. A in Bus., Community Coll. of R.I., 1986. From office clk. to fin. dir. Wilson Pub. Co., Wakefield, R.I., 1970—. Mem. New Eng. Press Assn., R.I. State Fedn. Bus. and Profl. Women (2d v.p. 1987—), Chariho Bus. and Profl. Women (pres. 1984-86). Republican. Roman Catholic. Home: 4975 South County Trail Wakefield RI 02813 Office: Wilson Pub Co 187 Main St Wakefield RI 02880

FOCH, NINA, actress, educator; b. Leyden, Netherlands, Apr. 20, 1924; came to U.S. 1927; d. Dirk and Consuelo (Flowerton) F.; m. James Lipton, June 6, 1954; m. Dennis de Brito, Nov. 27, 1959; 1 child, Dirk de Brito; m. Michael Dewell, Oct. 31, 1967. Grad., Lincoln Sch., 1939; studies with Stella Adler. adj. prof. drama U. So. Calif., 1966-68, 78-80, adj. prof. film 1987—; artist-in-residence U. N.C., 1966, Ohio State U., 1967, Calif. Inst. Tech., 1969-70; mem. sr. faculty Am. Film Inst., 1966-68, 74-77; founder, tchr. Nina Foch Studio, Hollywood, Calif., 1973—; founder, actress Los Angeles Theatre Group, 1960-65; bd. dirs. Nat. Repertory Theatre, 1967-75; creative cons. to dirs., writers, producers of all mediums. Appeared in motion pictures Nine Girls, 1944, Return of the Vampire, 1944, Shadows in the Night, 1944, Cry of the Werewolf, 1944, Escape in the Fog, 1945, A Song to Remember, 1945, My Name Is Julia Ross, 1945, I Love a Mystery, 1945, Johnny O'Clock, 1947, The Guilt of Janet Ames, 1947, The Dark Past, 1948, The Undercover Man, 1949, Johnny Allegro, 1949, An American in Paris, 1951, Scaramouche, 1952, Young Man with Ideas, 1952, Sombrero, 1953, Fast Company, 1953, Executive Suite, 1954 (Oscar award nominee), Four Guns to the Border, 1954, You're Never Too Young, 1955, Illegal, 1955, The Ten Commandments, 1956, Three Brave Men, 1957, Cash McCall, 1959, Spartacus, 1960, Such Good Friends, 1971, Salty, 1973, Mahogany, 1976, Jennifer, 1978, Rich and Famous, 1981; appeared in Broadway plays including John Loves Mary, 1947, Twelfth Night, 1949, A Phoenix Too Frequent, 1950, King Lear, 1950, Second String, 1960; appeared with Am. Shakespeare Festival in Taming of the Shrew, Measure for Measure, 1956, San Francisco Ballet and Opera in The Seven Deadly Sins, 1966; also many regional theater appearances including Seattle Repertory Theatre (All Over, 1972 and The Seagull, 1973); actress on TV, 1947—, including Playhouse 90, Studio One, Pulitzer Playhouse, Playwrights 56, Producers Showcase, Lou Grant (Emmy nominee 1980), Mike Hammer; series star: Shadow Chasers, 1985, War and Remembrance, 1986; many other series, network spls. and TV films; TV panelist and guest on The Dinah Shore Show, Merve Griffin Show, The Today Show, Dick Cavett, The Tonight Show; TV moderator: Let's Take Sides, 1957-59; assoc. dir. (film) The Diary of Ann Frank, 1959; dir. (nat. tour and on-Broadway) Tonight at 8:30, 1966-67; assoc. producer re-opening of Ford's Theatre, Washington, 1968. Hon. chmn. Los Angeles chpt. Am. Cancer Soc., 1970. Recipient Film Daily award, 1949, 53. Mem. Acad. Motion Pictures Arts and Scis. (co-chmn. exec. com. fgn. film award, exec. com. student film award, com. mem. spl. projects), Hollywood Acad. TV Arts and Scis. (gov. 1976-77). Office: PO Box 1884 Beverly Hills CA 90213

FODOR, DOROTHY ANN, educational therapist; b. Whiting, Ind., May 23, 1931; d. Martin Peter and Eleanor (Birmer) Kauchak; m. Louis Fodor, Apr. 19, 1952; children: Jane M. Butke, Janet F. Walton, Elizabeth, Karen. BS in Edn., Elmhurst Coll., 1968; MEd, Nat. Coll. Edn., 1984. Cert. tchr. Tchr. Notre Dame Sch., Clarendon Hills, Ill., 1968-84, Triton Coll., River Grove, Ill., 1984; edn. therapist Chgo. Area Rehab. and Edn. Services, Calumet City, Ill., 1984-85; edn. therapist, program case mgr. New Medico Rehab. Services Chgo., Downers Grove, Ill., 1985—. Roman Catholic. Clubs: Clarendon Women's, Notre Dame Women's. Office: Rehab Services Chgo 1307 Butterfield Suite 412 Downers Grove IL 60515

FOEGE, ROSE ANN S., human resources professional; b. Bklyn., Aug. 22, 1941; d. Thomas Edward and Catherine Mary (Demarsico) Scudiero; m. William Henry Foege, Apr. 19, 1975. BA, Queens Coll., 1973; MS cum laude, Iona Coll., 1981. Cert. Am. Registry Radiologic Technologists. X-ray technician St. Clare's Hosp., N.Y.C., 1956-61; supr. x-ray N.Y. Internat. Longshoremen's Assn. Med. Ctr., N.Y.C., 1960-67, Life Extension Inst., N.Y.C., 1967-73; radiologic technologist Exxon Corp., N.Y.C., 1973-81, coordinator systems and records, 1981-86; sr. human resources specialist Exxon Cen. Services div. Exxon Corp., Florham Park, N.J., 1986—. Vol. Wykagyl Neighborhood Assn., New Rochelle, N.Y. Mem. Am. Soc. Personnel Adminstrs., Am. Mgmt. Assn., Am. Acad. Med. Adminstrs., Am. Soc. Radiologic Technologists, Nat. Assn. Female Execs., Mensa, Iona Coll. Alumni Assn. Home: 149 Wykagyl Terr New Rochelle NY 10804 Office: Exxon 180 Park Ave Florham Park NJ 07932

FOERSTER, KATHRYN STUEVER, home economist; b. Yale, Mich., Nov. 20, 1954; d. Alfred Charles and Doris Estella (Brennan) Stuever; m. Michael Terrance Eagan, Aug. 30, 1975 (div. Jan. 1979); m. Mark Regan Foerster, July 4, 1981; 1 child, Elizabeth Stuever. BS, Mich. State U., 1976, MA, 1981. Instr. Alpena (Mich.) Community Coll., 1977-78; home economist, Coop. Extension Service Harrisville, Mich., 1976-78, Coldwater, Mich., 1978-82, Marshall, Mich., 1982—; trainer Elder Services, Foster Grandparents, Extension Homemakers, others, various locations Mich., 1976—; bd. dirs. Nutrition Council, Battle Creek, Mich., 1983—, Head Start, Battle Creek, 1986—. Author (booklet) Leadership Roles Among Women, 1981; columnist (weekly) Family Focus appearing in 6 newspapers, 1976—; developer packaged program Positive Parenting, 1980, Cooking for Happy Hearts, 1986. Exec. dir. Ad Hoc, Marshall, 1983—. Named one of Outstanding Young Women Am., 1979-83, Outstanding Young Careerist, Bus. & Profl. Women, Coldwater, Mich., 1980. Mem. Nat. Assn. Extension Home Economists (com. chair 1985-86), Mich. Assn. Extension Home Economists (pres. 1988—), Am. Home Econs. Assn. (cert.), Mich. Home Econs. Assn. (coms. 1976—), Battle Creek Home Econs. Assn. (pres., sec 1983-87), NOW (pres. Coldwater 1979-80), AAUW (officer Marshall and Coldwater), Omicron Nu, Phi Kappa Phi. Lutheran (chair social ministry). Lodge: Altrusa (charter v.p. Coldwater 1981-82). Office: Coop Extension Service 315 W Green St Marshall MI 49068

FOGARTY, ELIZABETH RUMMANS, retired librarian, researcher; b. Portsmouth, Ohio, Nov. 1, 1916; d. George Rummans and Mattie Belle (Shaver) Jordan; m. Joseph Christopher Fogarty, Oct. 6, 1945 (dec. Jan. 1977); children—Patricia C., Michelle., Josephine S. B.A. magna cum laude, Ohio Wesleyan U., 1938; M.L.S., U. Ill., 1939. Post librarian U.S. Army, Camp Atterbury, Ind., 1942-45; organizer of library Legis. Auditor's Calif. Capitol Office, Sacramento. 1952-53; med. research librarian U.S. Army Med. Ctr., Ryukyu Islands, Japan, 1967-70, U.S. Army Hosp., Ft. Polk, La., 1970-72; librarian pub. services McAllen Pub. Library, Tex., 1974-76. Researcher for Calif. state legislators and physicians. Chmn. council on ministries, mem. adminstrv. bd. St. Mark United Meth. Ch., McAllen, 1975—; Germany country commr. North Atlantic Girl Scout Bd. Europe, 1961-63. Mem. AAUW (pres. McAllen br. 1977-81, dir. internat. relations Tex. state div. bd. 1981-84, conductor internat. relations workshops at Tex. state and nat. convs. 1981—, Outstanding Woman of yr. award 1980), DAR (regent Sam Maverick chpt. 1983-85), Colonial Dames 17th Century (pres. Capt. Thomas Jefferson chpt. 1985—, Tex. state bd. 1985—, v.p. 1987—), United Daus. Confederacy (treas. Palo Alto chpt. 1982-84), ALA, LWV, Mortar Board, U.S. Daus. 1812, The Jamestowne Soc., Internat. Platform Assn., Nat. Soc. Daus. Am. Colonists, Phi Beta Kappa, Delta Delta Delta, Delta Sigma Rho, Phi Sigma Alpha. Methodist. Home: 405 Vermont St McAllen TX 78503

FOGARTY, LINDA CRAIG, marketing professional; b. Oswego, N.Y., Oct. 20, 1957; d. Edward Carroll and Diane Irene (Fastenau) C.; m. Paul Thomas Fogarty, June 14, 1980 (div. June 1986); children: Edward Franklin, Charles Thomas. BS, Cornell U., 1979. Asst. dir., pub. relations mgr. Day Care and Child Devel. Council Tompkins County, Ithaca, N.Y., 1979-80; asst. media buyer McKinney, Silver & Rockett, Raleigh, N.C., 1980-81; media dir. Swanson, Rollheiser, Holland, Lincoln, Nebr., 1981-83; dir. Beaver Brook Child Care Ctr., Austin, Tex., 1983-84; pvt. practice media cons. Austin, 1984-85; mgr. mktg. communications Coburn Optical Industries, Inc., Tulsa, 1986—; cons. Grot, Inc., Denton, Tex., 1984—. Editor newsletter Child Devel. News, 1978-80. Recruiter Cornell Admissions Ambassador Network-Secondary Schs., Tulsa, 1986—. Mem. AAUW, The Am. Women in Radio and TV, Nat. Assn. Female Execs., Friends of Tulsa Zoo, Cornell U. Alumni Assn. Republican. Roman Catholic. Home: 419 W Quanah Pl Broken Arrow OK 74011 Office: Coburn Optical Industries 4606 S Garnett Pl Suite 200 Tulsa OK 74146

FOGEL, ADELAIDE FORST, lawyer; b. N.Y.C., July 26, 1915; d. Leon and Antoinette (Hahn) Forst; B.A., Washington Sq. Coll., 1936; LL.B., N.Y. U., 1939; m. David Fogel, June 2, 1940; children—Ann Fogel Vivell, Susan Lee Fogel Lloyd. Admitted to N.Y. State bar; individual practice law, N.Y.C., 1940—. Patron N.Y. Philharmonic; trustee Temple Israel, N.Y.C., past pres. Sisterhood. Mem. Met. Mus. Art, Mus. Natural History, N.Y. U. Law Alumni Assn.

FOGEL, KATE Z(ERBE), marketing executive; b. Irvington, N.J., Dec. 4, 1953; d. Frank James and Catherine Marie (Fitgerald) Senters; m. Les Fogel, Sept. 28, 1984. BS in bus. adminstrn., Wake Forest U., 1975. Registered Ins. Inst. Am. Mgr., telemarketing Colonial Penn Group Inc., Phila., 1975-81; v.p., mktg. Allied Consumer Services Inc., Cherry Hill, N.J., 1981-83; v.p. mktg., prin. Am. Homestead Inc., Mt. Laurel, N.J., 1983-86, Affiliated Health Care Inc., Mt. Laurel, N.J., 1986—; cons. Arthur D. Little Corp., Princeton, N.J., 1986—. Lectr. N.Y. State Assembly, Older Women's League of Pa. on private sector alternatives to elderly housing problems, 1985. Tutor, pub. relations expert Coalition for Literacy, Princeton, N.J., 1987. Mem. Direct Mktg. Assn., Nat. Steering Com. STAR Mgmt. Info. System, Nat. Assn. Female Execs. Republican. Home: 700 Stephen Dr Princeton NJ 08540 Office: Affiliated Health Care Inc 210 Carnegie Ctr Ste 103 Princeton NJ 08540

FOGEL, MARJORIE, advertising/public relations executive; b. Port Chester, N.Y., Dec. 14, 1931; d. Maurice and Betty Schneider; student Pembroke Coll. of Brown U., 1949-50, N.Y.U., 1951-52, 78; m. Harold V. Fogel, June 12, 1954; children—Jonathan, Glenn. Prodn. asst., then prodn. mgr., copywriter, editor Jack Danowitz Advt., Inc., N.Y.C., 1951-56; community/public relations coordinator Planned Communities, Inc., Rye, N.Y., Washington, 1975-76; free-lance public relations, 1977; exec. dir. Energy Resources Devel. Inst., also exec. dir. Apt. Owners Adv. Council, White Plains, N.Y., 1978-79; founder, prin. Marje Fogel Communications, Rye Brook, N.Y., 1980—; founder, pres. Marjac Enterprises, producer Condo Showcase. Vol. ARC, 1955-59, United Hosp., 1968-77; mem. Westchester County Democratic Com., 1972-81; mem. exec. com. Port Chester-Town of Rye Voter Registration Dr., 1972-76; coordinator fund-raising, community relations Mental Health Assn. Westchester County, 1975; mem. steering com. Port Chester-Town of Rye Bicentennial, 1975-76; bd. dirs. Port Chester-Town of Rye Community Action Program, 1976-77; publicity coordinator Dem. candidates, 1975-77; mem. Rye Town Planning Bd., 1980-82, Village of Rye Brook Planning Bd., 1982-86. Recipient ARC service award; United Hosp. service award; Westchester Mental Health Vol. Service award. Mem. Advt. Club. Westchester, Am. Advt. Fedn. Address: 201 Country Ridge Dr Rye Brook NY 10573

FOGLE, JOE ANN, film editor; b. Norfolk, Va., July 2, 1945; d. Silbert and Marie (Miller) Freshman; m. Daniel Richard Fogle, Dec. 24, 1968 (div. Jan. 1976); children: Dena Rachel, Dara Rani. Student, U. Utah. Comml. asst. Filmex West, Los Angeles, 1965-68; post-prodn. coordinator M.T.M. Enterprises, Los Angeles, 1976, film editor, 1976-84; film editor Twentieth Century-Fox Film Corp., Los Angeles, 1985, Amblin Entertainment, Los Angeles, 1985-87; free-lance editor 1987—. Editor Three O'Clock High, 1987. Nominee for Emmy award Outstanding Editing for a Series, Single Camera Prodn., 1986, 87. Mem. Acad. TV Arts and Scis.

FOGLESONG, SUSAN LYN, insurance agent; b. Southwest City, Mo., July 7, 1948; d. Joseph August and Violet Aline (Wilfong) Minges; m. Marion David Foglesong, June 17, 1972 (div. Nov. 1974); 1 child, Violet Susanna Beasley. Med. Asst., Kansas City Bus. Coll., 1971. Med. asst., Midwest Orthopedic Group, Kansas City, Mo., 1971-72; med. transcriber Lakeside Osteopathic Hosp., Kansas City, Mo., 1974-76; new bus. coordinator ESCO Life Cons., Kansas City, Mo., 1977-82; adminstrv. asst. group rep. Bankers Life & Casualty Co., Kansas City, Mo., 1982-84; services coordinator Assn. Services Internat., Overland Park, Kans., 1985; sales service asst. U.S. Life Ins., Overland Park, Kans., 1985-87; Am. United Life Ins., 1987—, office mgr. Columnist, Cub Communicator, 1984—. Regional coordinator, state rep. Concerned United Birthparents, 1984—, state rep., legis. reporter, 1980—; editor, legis. dir., liaison coordinator, corresponding sec. Kansas City Adult Adoptees, 1982—; key chairperson A.L.A.R.M.; legis. dir. Am. Adoption Congress Region VI, 1983—, alternate dir. and registered agt., regional dir., 1988—; 1st v.p. PTA, 1988—. Mem. Kansas City Life Underwriters, Life Ins. Co. Office Mgmt., Nat. Assn. Female Execs. Republican. Mem. Unity Church. Avocations: quilting; gardening; sewing; crafts; writing children's stories. Office: Am United Life Ins Co 6407 W 64th Suite 307 Overland Park KS 66202

FOG-TOOPS, JENNIFER JANE, psychologist; b. Toronto, Ont., Can., May 14, 1949; came to U.S., 1952, naturalized, 1967; d. Hans Thomas and Edna Jeanmarie (Harrington) Fog; m. Gary C. Toops, Jan. 27, 1984. BA, Ashland Coll., 1971; MA, U. Miss., 1973, PhD, 1979. Lic. psychologist, Calif. Mental health coordinator Head Start program Marshall (Miss.) and Lafayette (Miss.) Counties, 1975-76; staff psychologist Region 2 Mental Health Ctr., Oxford, Miss., 1977-80; dir. The Inter-Community Alternatives Network, Pasadena, Calif., 1980-84; staff psychologist dept. psychiatry Kaiser Permanente, W. Covina, Calif., 1984—; part-time dir. psychol. svcs. The Creative Counseling Ctr., Hollywood, Calif., 1983-84; psychol. cons. Health Svcs. Ctr., Mt. San Antonio Coll., Walnut, Calif., 1983—; instr. dept. psychology Ind. U./Purdue U., indpls., 1976-77; practicum supr. psychology dept. U. Miss., 1980; field placement supr. psychology dept. Occidental Coll., Eagle Rock, Calif., 1980-81; practicum and internship supr. Fuller Grad. Sch. Psychology, Pasadena, 1980-84; pvt. practice clin. psychology, Pasadena, 1982-83, W. Covine, 1985, Covina, 1988—; lectr. in field. Contbr. articles to profl. jours. Elder, Knox Presbyn. Ch., Pasadena. NIMH fellow, 1975-76; U. Miss. fellow, 1972-79; U.S. Dept. Labor Manpower fellow, 1972-74; recipient Commendation for Outstanding Community Svc., Calif. State Assembly, 1983, Outstanding Achievement award, Nat. Assn. Counties, 1984. Mem. Am. Psychol. Assn., Calif. Psychol. Assn., Los Angeles Psychol. Assn., Pasadena Area Psychol. Assn., We. Psychol. Assn. Democrat. Presbyterian. Office: Kaiser Permanente Dept Psychiatry 1539 Garvey Ave N West Covina CA 91790

FOLEY, DONNA BRESLAWSKI, manufacturing engineer; b. Brockport, N.Y., Dec. 2, 1958; d. Daniel and Nancy Lee Breslawski; m. Kirk Andrew Foley, June 2, 1984. AAS in Drafting and Design, SUNY at Morrisville, 1979; BTech in Mech. Design Tech., SUNY at Utica, 1981. Asst. engr. Utica Screw Products, Inc. (N.Y.), 1980-81, engr., 1981-82; mfg. engr., mgr. quality control O.P. Held, Inc., Utica, 1982-87; sales engr. Davenport Machine Tool, Rochester, N.Y., 1987—. Mem. Nat. Screw Machine Products Assn., Soc. Mfg. Engrs., Indsl. Engring. Soc. Home: 1179 Earl's Dr Victor NY 14564 Office: 167 Ames St Rochester NY 14601

FOLEY, EILEEN MARY, history, social studies teacher; b. Greenwich, Conn., June 7, 1954; d. Joseph William and Mary Carol (Modugno) Gagon; m. William Charles Foley, July 11, 1980; 1 child, Gareth Charles. BA, U. Conn., 1976; MA, West Conn. u., 1983. Cert. tchr., Conn. Tchr. history Joel Barlow High Sch., Redding, Ct., 1982-87, Ridgefield (Conn.) High Sch., 1982—; advisor Joel Barlow Student Council, 1980-82, Ridgefield Class of 1986, 1982-86. Creator: (writing program) Thinking and Writing in the Social Studies, 1986-87. Active Danbury Preservation Trust, Conn., 1982—. Mem. Nat. Edn. Assn., Conn. Edn. Assn., Ridgefield Edn. Assn., Nat. Council for the Social Studies. Democrat. Roman Catholic. Home: 16 Park Ave Danbury CT 06810 Office: Ridgefield High Sch 700 N Salen Rd Ridgfield CT 06877

FOLEY, KATHLEEN A., advertising agency executive; b. Fresh Meadows, N.Y., Oct. 15, 1952; d. Thomas and Audrey Foley; grad. Marymount Coll., 1974; student Inst. European Studies, Vienna, Austria, 1973-74; grad. Mgmt. Program, Smith Coll., 1985. With Ogilvy & Mather, Inc., N.Y.C., 1974—, account exec., 1981-82, account supr., 1982-87, v.p., 1983—, mgmt. supr., 1987—. Class rep. Marymount Coll. Alumnae Assn., 1974—. Roman Catholic. Club: Racquet of East Hampton. Office: 2 E 48th St New York NY 10017

FOLEY, LISA ANN, computer company professional; b. Natick, Mass., Sept. 23, 1960. BA in Sociology and Human Resources Mgmt., Boston Coll., 1982; postgrad., Babson Coll., 1985—. Lic. real estate broker. Corp. staffing specialist Prime Computer Inc., Natick, 1983—. Recipient Prime Excellence award Prime Computer Inc., 1984. Mem. Am. Mgmt. Assn., New Eng. Human Resources Assn., Phi Beta Kappa, Alpha Kappa Delta.

FOLEY, LYNN M., sales professional; b. Green Bay, Wis., Oct. 24, 1962; d. Harold J. and Marie A. (Wrobelewski) F. BSBA, U. Wis., Stevens Point, 1985. Profl. sales rep. Pfizer Labs., Moline, 1985—. Vol. Arthritis Found., Davenport, Peoria, 1985—, Rock Island County (Ill.) Humane Soc., 1987, Elderhealth Cottage Hosp., Galesburg, Ill., 1987. Named one of Outstanding Young Women Am., 1985. Mem. Nat. Assn. Female Execs., Quad City Pharm. Soc. Roman Catholic. Club: Young Profls. (Quad Cities).

FOLEY, MARY MIX, architectural writer, editor; b. Muncie, Ind., Oct. 14, 1918; d. Charles Melvin and Margaret Louisa (Tracy) Mix; m. Justin John Foley, June 4, 1949; 1 son, Stephen Prescott. B.A., Syracuse U., 1940; postgrad. Columbia U., 1944-45. Asst. editor McCall's Mag., N.Y.C., 1940-43; assoc. editor Archtl. Forum, N.Y.C., 1943-49; exec. staff mem. pub. relations AIA, Washington, 1949-54; author: The American House, 1980; (with Albert Christ-Janer) Modern Church Architecture, 1969; (with others) Housing Choices and Housing Constraints, 1960, Building, U.S.A., 1955; contbr. articles to newspapers and mags.; author brochures. Mem. Soc. Archtl. Historians, Nat. Trust for Historic Preservation.

FOLEY, SUSAN MARY, public relations executive; b. Boston, May 3, 1960; d. Francis L. and Nancy M. (Kelleher) F. BA, Simmons Coll., 1982. Sales mgr. exec. mgmt. tng. program Abraham & Straus, Bklyn., 1982-83; acct. exec. Arnold and Co., Boston, 1983-85; sr. acct. exec. Clarke & Co., Boston, 1985-86, mgr., 1986; v.p. Clarke & Co., N.Y.C., 1986-87, sr. v.p., 1987—. Mem. Manhattan Soc., Pub. Relations Soc. Am., Simmons Coll. Alumni Assn. (v.p.). Home: 230 W 55th St Apt 2911 New York NY 10019 Office: Clarke & Co 500 Fifth Ave 24th Floor New York NY 10110

FOLK, SHARON LYNN, printing company executive; b. Bellefontaine, Ohio, June 13, 1945; d. Emerson Dewey and Berdena Isabelle (Brown) F.; A.A. in Liberal Arts, Sacred Heart Coll., 1965, L.H.D. (hon.), 1985; A.B. in Econs. and Bus. Adminstrn., Belmont Abbey Coll., 1968. Exec. v.p. Nat. Bus. Forms, Inc., Greeneville, Tenn., 1968-73; sec., treas. Nat. Forms Co., Inc., Gastonia, N.C., 1969-73, chairperson, bd. dirs., pres., 1973—, SF Enterprises, Inc., Greeneville, 1987—, Andrew Johnson Golf Club, Inc., Greeneville, 1987—; mem. bus. adv. com. Bus. Ptnrs., Inc., Washington, 1987—; bd. dirs. Andrew Johnson Bank, Greeneville, chairperson employee relations com., Internat. Bus. Forms Industries, Arlington, Va., 1978-83. Mem. fin. com. YMCA, Greeneville, 1977-78, bd. dirs., 1977-80; bd. dirs. United Way, 1980-85, Greeneville, Takoma Hosp. Found., Greeneville, 1987—; mem. presdl. steering com. U.S. Senator Howard Baker, 1979-80; mem. Republican Presdl. Task Force, 1981—; life mem. Rep. Nat. Com., 1981—; mem. Rep. Senatorial Inner Circle, Washington, 1984—; vice-chmn. parish council Notre Dame Cath. Ch., Greeneville, 1984-85, chmn., 1985-87; founding mem. Com. 200, Chgo., 1981—, vice chmn., membership chmn. Southeast region, 1983-84, bd. dirs. 1984-85, v.p., bd. dirs., 1985-86; mem. bd. advisors Belmont Abbey Coll., 1984—, trustee, 1986-89; trustee Sacred Heart Coll., Belmont, N.C., 1985—; 2d lt. CAP, 1984—; maj. Civilian Guard, Middleboro, Ky., 1986—; oblate Order of St. Benedict, Our Lady Help of Christians Abbey, Belmont, 1967—. 1st lt. Search and Rescue Pilot Civil Air Patrol, Aux. USAF, Maxwell Air Force Base, Ala., 1984—. Mem. Nat. Bus. Forms Assn., Forms Mfrs. Credit Interchange, Am. Mgmt. Assn., Tenn. Bus. Roundtable (bd. dirs. 1986), Belmont Abbey Alumni Coll. Assn. (bd. dirs. 1986—), U.S. Tennis Assn. (life), Airplane Owners and Pilots Assn. Avocations: tennis, airplane pilot, photography, golf, reading, music. Home: 1131 Hixon Ave Greeneville TN 37743 Office: Nat Bus Forms Co Inc 100 Pennsylvania Ave Greeneville TN 37743

FOLK, SYLVIA DWIGHT, marketing specialist; b. Charleston, S.C., Apr. 17, 1956; d. Francis Marion III and Sylvia Jo (Brogdon) Dwight; m. Tony Herman Folk, Aug. 5, 1978; children: Daniel Dwight, Rachel Elizabeth. BA, Coll. of Charleston, 1978, postgrad., 1984; postgrad., The Citadel, 1979-82. Med. transcriptionist Charleston West Internal Medicine, 1978-79; personnel asst. The News & Courier/ The Evening Post, Charleston, 1979-80, pub. relations asst., 1980-83, circulation route supr., 1983; adminstrv. asst. honors program Coll. of Charleston, 1983-84; mktg. specialist USAF Morale, Welfare & Recreation Div., Charleston AFB, 1984—. Editor (newsletter) Lifestyle; contbr. articles to AFB publ. Mem. communications bd. Trident United Way. Mem. Advt. Fedn. Charleston, Pub. Relations Soc. Am. Episcopalian. Home: 1417 Lenavar Dr West Charleston SC 29407 Office: Morale Welfare and Recreation Div 437 ABG/SSPA Charleston AFB SC 29404-5225

FOLLANSBEE, DOROTHY L. (DOROTHY L. LELAND), publisher; b. St. Louis, Mar. 24, 1911; d. Robert Leathan and Minnie Cowden (Yowell) Lund; grad. Sarah Lawrence Coll., 1931; m. Austin Porter Leland, Apr. 24, 1935 (dec. 1975); children—Mary Talbot Leland MacCarthy, Austin Porter Jr. (dec.), Irene Austin Leland Barzantny; m. 2d, Robert Kerr Follansbee, Oct. 20, 1979. Pres., Station List Publ. Co., St. Louis, 1975—; dir. Downtown St. Louis Inc. Hon. chmn. Old Post Office Landmark Com., 1975—; bd. dirs. Services Bur. St. Louis, 1943, pres., 1951; bd. dirs. Robert E. Lee Meml. Assn.; mem. St. Louis County Parks and Recreation Dept., 1969; bd. dirs. Stratford Hall, Va., 1953—, pres., 1967-70, treas., 1970—; bd. dirs. Historic Bldgs. Commn. St. Louis County, 1959-85, Mo. Hist. Soc., 1960-77, Mo. Mansion Preservation Com., 1975-80, Chatillon DeMenil House, 1977-79. Recipient Landmarks award Landmarks Assn. St. Louis, 1974; Pub. Service award GSA, 1978; Crowneshield award Nat. Trust for Hist Preservation, 1979. Mem. Colonial Dames Am., Daughter of the Cin. Episcopalian. Clubs: St. Louis Country, Fox Chapel Golf, Princeton of N.Y., St. Louis Jr. League. Home: 35 Pointer Ln St Louis MO 63124 Home: 1001 River Oaks Dr Pittsburgh PA 15215 Office: 1221 Locust St Saint Louis MO 63101

FOLLANSBEE, NANCY DAMON, investment management executive; b. Rochester, N.Y., Dec. 1, 1958; d. Winthrop Damon and Carolyn (Allen) Follansbee. B.A., William Smith Coll., 1980. Corp. sec., mgr. mktg. services Grace Capital Inc., N.Y.C., 1980-84; corp. sec. Dirs. Capital Inc., N.Y.C., 1982-84, Dirs. Mgmt. Corp., N.Y.C., 1983-84; mktg. rep. Gardner and Preston Moss, Inc., Boston, 1985—; guest lectr. Am. Mgmt. Assn., N.Y.C., 1983. Tutor Vol. Services for Children, N.Y.C., 1982-84; corr. Prison Action Group, Rochester, 1980. Mem. Jr. League Boston, Assn. Investment Mgmt., Internat. Found. Employee Benefit Plans, No-Load Mut. Fund Assn. Republican. Presbyterian. Home: 9A Oak Square Ave Madison NJ 02135 Office: Gardner and Preston Moss Inc One Winthrop Square Boston MA 02110

FOLLENDORE, JOAN STEARNS, writing consultant, writer; b. Mpls., Jan. 29, 1936; d. Stanley Rolfe and Alice Mae (Kolstad) Stearns; m. William Austin Rosenblum, June 6, 1956 (div. 1965); children: Bruce Stanley, Camille Rosenblum Burks; m. Lee L. Follendore, Oct. 28 1966 (div. 1980); m. Herschel Katchen, Feb. 14, 1988. Student, UCLA, Westwood, 1953-55, U. Calif., Berkeley, 1955. Owner, mgr. Joan's Sample Shop, Sherman Oaks, Calif., 1955-57; distbr. Holiday Magic Cosmetics, Malibu, Calif., 1966-68; dir. devel. Palisades Prep. Schs., Pacific Palisades, Calif., 1981-84; writing cons., Los Angeles, 1983—; instr. writing Pierce Coll., Tarzana, Calif., 1980 82, West Los Angeles Coll., 1982-87, Santa Monica Coll., 1982-87, UCLA, 1987. Author: You Can Learn Metric Easily, 1976, From our Immigrants with Love, 1977; author syndicated column Here Comes Metric, 1974-75; contbr. numerous articles to mags. and newspapers. Active Children's Home Soc. Auxs., local PTA's, Lutheran ch. groups; Rep. precinct chmn., La-Canada, Calif., 1960; local chmn. Goldwater for pres., LaCanada and Flintridge, 1964; mem. Calif. State Rep. Cen. Com., 1964-66; mem. campaign staff Jud Leetham for Calif. Atty. Gen., Redondo Beach, Calif., 1965-66. Mem. Friends of Marina del Ray (Calif.) Library (bd. dirs. 1987-88), Book Publicists of So. Calif. (moderator 1986). Clubs: Marina City (Marina del Ray), Westlake Yacht (Westlake Village, Calif.), Braemar Country (Woodland Hills, Calif.). Office: 13376 Washington Blvd Suite 5 Los Angeles CA 90066

FOLLIS, NANCY LOUISE, consulting company executive; b. Hamden, Conn., Sept. 12, 1957; d. Louis and Rose-Marie (Piccolo) F. BS cum laude, Ithaca Coll., 1979; EdM, Harvard U., 1984. Dir. Medi-Health Systems, Inc., Woburn, Mass., 1979-80; mgr. Woman's World Health Spa, Burlington, Mass., 1980-82; health promotion coordinator Corp. Health Strategies, Boston, 1983-84; dir. mktg. Corp. Health Mgmt. Network, N.Y.C., 1984-85; sr. account exec. Total Health HMO, Elmhurst, N.Y., 1985-86; pres., cons. Health Mgmt. Cons., N.Y.C., 1986—; asst. Beth Israel Hosp., Boston, 1984; vol. Roxbury Multi-Service Ctr., Boston, 1984. Vol. Help Line Telephone Services, Marble Collegiate Ch., N.Y.C., 1987, shift supr. 1988, vol. Am. Heart Assn., Lawerence, Mass., 1982. Mem. Assn. Fitness in Bus., Assn. Tng. and Devel., Nat. Assn. Female Execs., Am. Women for Econ. Devel., Phi Kappa Phi. Club: Toastmasters (ednl. v.p. 1986-87). Lodge: Rotary (sportsmanship award 1974). Home: 396 Third St #10 Brooklyn NY 11215 Office: Health Mgmt Cons 305 Madison Ave Suite 411 New York NY 10165

FOLLMAN, DOROTHY MAJOR, therapist; b. Colden, N.Y., Nov. 7, 1932; d. Francis Emri and V. Blanche (Feedham) Major; m. Roy John Follman, Nov. 26, 1954; children: John J., Mark J., Curtis J., Thomas J. BS in Recreation Edn. magna cum laude, SUNY, Cortland, 1954; MEd, SUNY, Buffalo, 1979. Cert. therapeutic recreation specialist. Asst. dir. health edn. YWCA, Niagara Falls, N.Y., 1954-55; instn. tchr. N.Y. State Dept. Corrections, Albion, 1968-70, N.Y. State Narcotic Addiction Control Commn., Albion, 1970-71, Medina, 1971-73; sr. recreation therapist N.Y. State Drug Abuse Control Commn., Medina, 1973-76, N.Y. State Office of Mental Health, Rochester, 1976-77; head recreation therapist Buffalo, 1977—; instr. Medaille Coll., Buffalo, 1983-84, mem. adv. bd. 1982-87; bd. dirs. Metcalf Endowment Fund, Cortland, 1981-87. Mem. adv. bd. SUNY, Brockport, 1986—; choir dir. United Meth. Ch., Kenyonville, N.Y., 1965-75, United Meth. Ch., 1980—; honoree 36th Ann. Cortland Coll. Recreation Conf., 1986. Named Woman of Yr. Friends of Buffalo Psychiatric Ctr., 1986. Mem. Nat. Therapeutic Recreation Soc., N.Y. State Recreation and Parks Soc., Inc. (exec. bd. 1985—, disting. service 1985, profl. service 1987), Niagara Frontier Recreation and Parks Soc. (exec. bd. 1983-86, awards chmn. 1983-86, award for excellence 1987), SUNY-Cortland Alumni Adv. Bd. Office: Buffalo Psychiatric Ctr 400 Forest Ave Buffalo NY 14213

FOLSOM, RODDELLE BRANTLEY, librarian; b. Washington County, Ga., Mar. 8, 1925; d. Roger Tennyson and Evona (Smith) Brantley; m. Elton Brown Folsom, May 30, 1946; 1 child, Kathryn Yvonne. Student South Ga. Coll., 1941-42, 43-44; BS in Edn., U. Ga., 1955; MLS, Fla. State U., 1973. Tchr. elem. and high schs., Ga., 1944-51; extension librarian S. Ga. Regional Library, Valdosta, 1952-71, acting dir., 1971-73, dir., 1973—. Bd. dirs. Valdosta Girl's Club, 1977-79, sec., 1978-79, bd. dirs. and pres. adult edn. dept. Valdosta chpt., 1982-83. Mem. AAUW (editor newsletter 1975), Southeastern Library Assn., Ga. Library Assn., Lowndes Adult Edn. Assn. (pres. 1977-78), Valdosta and Lowndes County Library Assn. (pres. 1981-82), So. Ga. Associated Libraries, Tri-State Library Assn. Democrat. Baptist. Clubs: Wymoduasis (1st v.p. 1982-84, pres. 1984—), Quota (1st v.p. 1978-79, pres. 1979-80, governing bd. women's bldg. 1984—). Home: 1110 Dellwood Dr Valdosta GA 31602 Office: 300 Woodrow Wilson Dr Valdosta GA 31602

FOLSOM, WYNELLE STOUGH, retired wood products manufacturing executive; b. Bankston, Ala., July 19, 1924; d. Richard Carey and Ora Beatrice (Fowler) Stough; m. Eugene Bragg Folsom, Sept. 3, 1944; children—Don Wayne, Dana L. Student U. Ala., Livingston U., 1962-63, Draughan Bus. Coll., Montgomery, Ala., 1941-42, Alexander State Coll., Alexander City, Ala., 1967-68, Chilton Vocat. & Tech. Sch., Clanton, Ala., 1969-70. Sec., Ala. Power Co., Birmingham, 1942-44; med. librarian Santa Rosa Hosp., San Antonio, 1944-46; payroll clk. Dow Chem. Co., Freeport, Tex., 1946-48; with audit dept. Sears, Roebuck & Co., Selma, Ala., 1956-66; sec.-treas. Oakline Chair Co., Inc., Selma, 1967-83, pres., 1983-86. Chmn. publicity Cahaba Regional Library (Friends of the Library), Clanton, Ala., 1979; mem. Selma-Dallas County Historic Preservation Soc., 1982-87. Mem. Selma C. of C. Republican. Mem. Ch. of Christ. Clubs: Hemorcallis Garden (pres. 1979), Woman's Study (chmn. publicity 1967-69). Avocations: needlework, fishing, reading, painting, gardening. Home: 200 Chris Circle Selma AL 36701 Office: Oakline Chair Co Inc 3003 Citizens Parkway PO Box 871 Selma AL 36701

FONDA, JANE, actress; b. N.Y.C., Dec. 21, 1937; d. Henry and Frances (Seymour) F.; m. Roger Vadim (div.); 1 child, Vanessa; m. Tom Hayden, Jan. 20, 1973; 1 child, Troy. Student, Vassar Coll. Appeared on Broadway stage in There Was A Little Girl, 1960, The Fun Couple, 1962; appeared in Actor's Studio prodn. Strange Interlude, 1963; appeared in films Tall Story, 1960, A Walk on the Wild Side, 1962, Period of Adjustment, 1962, Sunday in New York, 1963, In the Cool of the Day, 1963, The Love Cage, 1963, La Ronde, 1964, Cat Ballou, 1965, The Chase, 1966, Any Wednesday, 1966, The Game Is Over, 1967, Hurry Sundown, 1967, Barefoot in the Park, 1967, Barbarella, 1968, Spirits of the Dead, 1969, They Shoot Horses, Don't They?, 1969, Klute, 1970 (Acad. award for best actress), Steelyard Blues, 1973, A Doll's House, 1973, The Blue Bird, 1976, Fun With Dick and Jane, 1976, Julia, 1977, also producer Coming Home, 1978 (Acad. award best actress), California Suite, 1978, Comes a Horseman, 1978, also producer The China Syndrome, 1979, Electric Horseman, 1979, Nine to Five, 1980, On Golden Pond, 1981, Rollover, 1981, The Dollmaker (Emmy award best actress), ABC-TV, 1984, Agnes of God, 1985, The Morning After, 1986 (Oscar nomination best actress); author: Jane Fonda's Workout Book, 1981, Women Coming of Age, 1984, Jane Fonda's New Workout & Weight-Loss Program, 1986, Jane Fonda Workout Video (top grossing video of all time), 5 additional videos. Recipient Golden Apple prize for female star of yr. Hollywood Women's Press Club, 1977, Golden Globe award, 1978; rated No. 1 heroine of young Ams., U.S. News Roper Poll., 1985, 4th most admired woman in Am., Ladies Home Jour. Roper Poll, 1985. Office: care Fonda Films PO Box 491355 Los Angeles CA 90049

FONDREN, DORIS GRAY, lawyer; b. College Park, Ga., Jan. 6, 1930; d. Otha Pope and Mattie Ardell (Lamb) G.; divorced. Student, W. Ga. Coll., 1949; LLB, Jackson Sch. of Law, 1963; postgrad., U. Tex., 1963-65, Our Lady of the Lake Coll., 1965-66. Bar: Miss. 1963, Ga. 1975. Sole practice Marietta, Ga., 1975—. Mem. Ga. State Bar Assn., Miss. Bar Assn., Atlanta Bar Assn., Cobb Bar Assn. Office: 585 Barnett Bank Bldg Suite 585 Marietta GA 30060

FONG, JANA REE, landscape architect; b. Oakland, Calif., Apr. 22, 1955; d. Lyman Kay and Marie (Chang) F. Degree in Gen. Design and Engring., Cabrillo Jr. Coll., Aptos, Calif., 1975; BS in Landscape Architecture, Calif. State Poly. U., 1979. Draftsman Peridian Group, Irvine, Calif., 1977-79; landscape designer Hawaii Design Assocs., Honolulu, 1979-80; designer, planner Belt, Collins & Assocs., Honolulu, 1980-81; landscape designer Media Five Ltd., Honolulu, 1981-82, dept. head, landscape architect, 1984-87; prin., toy designer Jana Fong & Co., Seattle, 1982-83, landscape architect, 1983-84; sr. landscape designer Earth Enterprises, Seattle, 1982-84; landscape architect Tongg, Clarke & Mechler, Honolulu, 1987—. Author: History of Hawaiian Landscapes; designer toys, games for children and adults. Mem. Am. Soc. Landscape Architects (sec. Honolulu chpt. 1981-82, pres. 1987-88, chmn. hist. preservation com. 1987-88, legis. affairs com. 1987-88, mem. mayor's beautification com.), Associated Chinese Univ. Women. Home: 1020 Aoloa Pl #402B Kailua HI 96734

FONTAINE, BARBARA ALICE, lawyer, educator; b. Woonsocket, R.I., Dec. 8, 1935; d. John Nelson and Alice Claire (Hackett) F. AB in Chemistry, Brown U., 1959; MA in Library Sci., Wesleyan U., 1970; JD, Pace U., 1981. Bar: R.I. 1982, U.S. Supreme Ct. 1987. Tchr. chemistry and physics Lincoln Sch., Providence, 1960-62; vol. U.S. Peace Corps, Ethiopia, 1962-64; tchr. chemistry and physics, head dept. chemistry and physcis Bellingham (Mass.) High Sch., 1964-69; tchr. chemistry and physics Ardsley (N.Y.) High Sch., 1969-81; lectr. math. Community Coll. of R.I., Lincoln, 1983-84; sole practice, Wakefield, R.I., 1982-85, 87—; cons., spl. asst. atty. gen. State of R.I., 1985-87; mem. Conservation Law Found., Providence, 1982-85. V.p. Cath. Alumni Club, N.Y.C., 1977-79; rep. Ardsley Tchrs.' Union, 1974-77; mem. Project Persona, Providence, 1982—; sec. Snug Harbor-East Matunuck Civic Assn., 1983—; bd. dirs. South County Community Action, 1983—, Heritage Playhouse, 1984-85. NSF fellow, 1966-68; recipient cert. of honor Westinghouse Ednl. Found., 1974, 78, Tchr. award Sci. Tchrs. of N.Y. State, 1973. Mem. R.I. Bar Assn., R.I. Trial Lawyers Assn., R.I. Law Inst., Mensa (pres. R.I. chpt. 1982-84), Lawyers in Mensa, Audubon Soc. Democrat. Roman Catholic. Club: R.I. Civic Chorale. Home: 801 Succotash Rd Wakefield RI 02879 Office: 72 Pine St Providence RI 02903

FONTAINE, REBECCA STUART, financial planning analyst; b. Gallup, N.Mex., May 7, 1954; d. Arthur Lester and DeAva (Cato) Stuart; m. Robert A. Fontaine, Apr. 11, 1980; 1 child, Eric. BA, N.Mex. State U., 1975; MSW, U. Calif., Berkeley, 1977, cert. in personal fin. planning, 1987. Cert. dollarplan instr. Probation officer U.S. Govt. Probation and Parole Bds., Oakland, Calif., 1977-81, dir. fin. responsibility program, 1981-85; fin. planner D/A Fin. Group, Orinda, Calif., 1985-86; personal fin. planning analyst The Permanente Med. Group, Inc., Oakland, 1986—; instr. dollarplan Nat. Ctr. for Fin. Edn., San Francisco, 1985—; cons. Fontaine, Faria and Assocs., San Ramon, Calif., 1985—. Instr. CPR Am. Heart Assn., Concord, Calif., 1980—; active variety community programs including Planned Parenthood, Voter Registration, N.Mex. Women's Caucus, Dona Ana County (N.Mex.) Rape Crisis Ctr. and Las Cruces (N.Mex.) Juvenile Probation Dept., 1972-75. Scholar NIMH, U. Calif., Berkeley, 1975-77, City Panhellenic, 1973. Mem. Internat. Assn. Fin. Planning, Bus. and Profl. Women's Assn. (legis. com. Bay Valley dist. 1983, Young Careerist award 1982, 86). Democrat. Roman Catholic. Club: Newcomers (San Ramon). Office: The Permanente Med Group 1924 Broadway Oakland CA 94612

FONTANA, BARBARA JEAN, legislative analyst, nutritionist; b. Chgo., Sept. 9, 1946; d. Robert Alfred and Virginia (Hartmann) Lubker; children—Brent, Ryan. B.S., Cornell U., 1968; M.A., San Francisco State U., 1974; Ph.D., U. Md.-College Park, 1983. Dietitian, Yale U., 1968-71; food service tng. Fremont Schs. (Calif.), 1973-77; research nutritionist Georgetown U., 1977-78; nutrition edn. chief food programs U.S. Dept. Agr., Washington, 1978-80, nutritionist Extension Service, 1980-81, exec. sec. Nat. Agrl. Research and Extension Users Adv. Bd., 1981-84; staff dir. agr. Nat. Govs. Assn., 1984—; lectr., advisor San Francisco State U., 1976-77. Office: Nat Govs Assn Hall of States 444 N Capitol St Washington DC 20001

FONTS, PATRICIA DIANNE, educator; b. Chgo.; d. Alfred Allen Crisler and Ida Lee (Brown) Crisler Thorpe; m. Brigido Castillo Fonts, III, June 24, 1973 (div.); 1 child, Brigido Castillo IV. B.S. in Edn., Chgo. State U., 1975; postgrad. Roosevelt U. Tchr. pub. schs., Chgo., 1975-80, Archdiocese of Chgo., 1985—; tng. specialist Mayor's Office of Employment Tng., 1980-84; tax preparer H&R Block, Inc., 1987-88, Fonts and Fonts Inc. 1987—. Leader Girl Scouts U.S.; tutor in program for young adults. Mem. Nat. Cath. Edn. Assn., NEA, Nat. Assn. Female Execs., Nat. Bus. Edn. Assn. Exec. Females, Alpha Kappa Alpha. Avocations: horticulture, cooking, music.

FOOR, SHIRLEY JEAN, publisher, writer; b. Northville, Mich., Mar. 1, 1938; d. Royal Clarence and Dorothe Sara (Kent) Snow; m. Benjamin Charles Foor, Aug. 24, 1956 (div. Sept. 1981); children—Laurie Foor Meyer, Sharon, Timothy, Daniel, Jonathan. Student Black Hawk Coll., Moline, Ill., 1971-76, Manatee Jr. Coll., Bradenton, Fla., 1978-79, U. South Fla., Tampa, 1984-87. Feature writer The Daily Dispatch, Moline, Ill., 1971-72, reporter, 1972-73, asst. state editor, 1973-76; asst. city editor The Bradenton (Fla.) Herald, 1976-77, city editor, 1977-80, mng. editor, 1980-85; editor, The Islander, Anna Maria, Fla., 1985-86; editor The Bradenton Press, 1986-87. Bd. dirs. pres. Manatee County Girls Club, Inc., Bradenton, 1980-85; mem. Manatee County LWV, Bradenton, 1981; organizer, mem. Manatee County Women's Network, Bradenton, 1980—; bd. dirs. Manatee Artificial Kidney and Disease Prevention Ctr., Bradenton, 1981-82. Named Chpt. Woman of Yr., Am. Bus. Women's Assn., 1978. Mem. Nat. League Am. Pen Women, Nat. Fedn. Press Women (merit award, editorial writing 1984), Fla. Freelance writers Assn., Fla. Press Women (merit award, editorial writing 1984), Fla. Soc. Newspaper Editors, Am. Bus. Women's Assn. (charter pres. 1977-78). Democrat. Roman Catholic. Office: 1304 67th St NW Bradenton FL 34209

FOOTE, BARBARA AUSTIN, civic foundation executive; b. Seattle, Mar 26, 1918; d. Edwin Charles and Marion (Roberts) A.; m. Robert Lake Foote, June 14, 1941; children: Markell Foote Kaiser, Marion Roberts, Helen Foote Schloerb. AB, Vassar Coll., 1940. Tchr. Shady Hill Sch., Cambridge, Mass., 1942-43, Madeira Sch., Greenway, Va., North Shore Country Day Sch., Winnetka, Ill., 1960-71; mem. exec. com. Chgo. Community Trust, 1970-85, chmn. exec. com., 1978-85; bd. dirs. Harris Bank, Glencoe and Northbrook, Ill., Glencoe Nat. Bank, The New Eng. (name formerly New Eng. Mut. Life Ins. Co.), Boston. Author book of verse, 1948. Pres. Jr. League Chgo., 1947-49, Assn. Jr. Leagues Am., 1954-56, Glencoe Bd. Edn., 1957-63; trustee Vassar Coll., 1966-74. Mem. Vassar Alumni Assn. (nat. pres. 1975-78), Phi Beta Kappa. Congregationalist. Clubs: Fortnightly of Chgo.; Cosmopolitan (N.Y.C.). Home: 587 Longwood Ave Glencoe IL 60022

FOOTE, DOROTHY GARGIS, publishing company executive; b. Sheffield, Ala., Jan. 27, 1942; d. Tracy E. and Mary Helen (Cox) Gargis; m. A. Edward Foote, Mar. 15, 1960; children: Anthony E., Kevin A., Michele. Student, U. So. Miss., 1966-67; AS in Nursing, NW Coll., 1985; BS in Nursing, U. N. Ala., Florence, 1987; postgrad., U. Ala., Huntsville, 1987—. Lic. nurse, Ala. Real estate agt. McWaters Realty, Athens, Ga., 1977-79; acctg. clk. U. Ga., Athens, 1979-81; nursing supr. Eliza Coffee Hosp., Florence, 1985—; v.p. Thornwood Books, Florence, 1980—. Editor newsletter Dames Digest, 1970. Pres. Band Boosters, Athens, 1976. Mem. Am. Nursing Assn., Ala. State Nurses Assn., Phi Theta Kappa, Beta Sigma Phi(pres. 1976-77, sec. 1987—). Home: 222 Shirley Dr Florence AL 35630

FOOTE, EVELYN PATRICIA, military officer; b. Durham, N.C., May 19, 1930; d. Henry Alexander and Evelyn Sevena (Womack) F. BA summa cum laude, Wake Forest U., 1953; student, U.S. Army Command & Gen. Staff Coll., Leavenworth, Kans., 1971-72, U.S. Army War Coll., Carlisle, Pa., 1976-77; MS in Govt. and Pub. Affairs, Shippensburg State U., 1977; student, U. Va. Sch. Bus. Adminstrn., 1980. Enlisted U.S. Army, 1960, advanced through grades to brig. gen., 1986; platoon officer WAC U.S. Army, Ft. McClellan, Ala., 1960-61; officer selection officer 6th recruitingdist U.S. Army, Portland, Oreg., 1961-64; comdr. WAC U.S. Army Engr. Brigade, Ft. Belvoir, Va., 1964-66; student Adj. Gen. Officer Advanced Course, Ft. Benjamin Harrison, Ind., 1966; exec. officer, chief adminstrv. div., info. office U.S. Army, Vietnam, 1967; exec. officer, office personnel ops. WAC, Washington, 1968-71, plans and programs officer, 1972-74; personnel mgmt. officer U.S. Army Forces Command, Ft. McPherson, Ga., 1974-76; comdr. 2d basic tng. bn. U.S. Army Tng. Brigade and Military Police Sch., Ft. McClellan, Ala., 1977-79; faculty mem. U.S. Army War Coll., 1979-82; student Fgn. Service Inst., Dept. of State, Washington, 1982-83; comdr. 42d Mil. Police Group, Mannheim, Fed. Republic of Germany, 1983-85; spl. asst. to comdg. gen. 32d Army Air Def. Command Hdqrs., Darmstadt, Fed. Republic of Germany, 1985-86; dep., insp. gen. for inspections Hdqrs. Dept. of the Army, Washington, 1986-88; dep. comdg. gen. Mil. Dist. Washington, comdr. Ft. Belvoir, Va., 1988—; lectr. various Army groups. Contbr. articles to military jours. Decorated Legion of Merit with oak leaf Cluster, German Cross of Service, lst class; recipient Bronze Star medal, Meritorious Service medal with two oak leaf clusters, Disting. Service award Wake Forest U., 1987. Mem. Assn. U.S. Army, Bus. & Profl. Women U.S.A., Exec. Women in Govt., Federally Employed Women, WAC Vets. Assn. Democrat. Lutheran. Office: DCG/Mil Dist Washington Office Comdr General Fort Belvoir VA 22060

FOOTE, FRANCES CATHERINE, association executive; b. Chgo., Apr. 3, 1935; d. Peter and Ellen Gertrude (Quinn) F. BS in Edn., Cardinal Stritch Coll., 1957; MS in Edn., Ill. State U., 1966. Cert. tchr., Ill. Tchr. Sch. Dist. 123, Oaklawn, Ill., 1959-84; asst. prin. Sch. Dist. 123, Oaklawn, 1971-80; pres. Am. Now Inc., St. Petersburg, Fla., 1985—; instr. Geography Workshops for tchrs., 1967-70, Use of Newspaper in Classroom Workshops, 1973-75; co-chairperson Social Studies Curriculum Revision. Officer PTA, Oak Lawn, Ill., 1973-76; mem. Rep. Nat. Com., Washington, Maximo Moorings Civic Assn., St. Petersburg. Mem. Am. Fedn. Tchrs. Roman Catholic. Home and Office: 280 126th Ave Apt #203 Saint Petersburg FL 33711

FOOTE, VICTORIA MARGARET, counselor; b. Indian Town Gap, Pa., June 14, 1952; d. Charles Joseph Fries and Marie Emma (Farren) Brockelbank; m. Thomas Erwin Foote, Nov. 16, 1982; 1 child, Aaron Brandon. BA, Colo. State U., 1977; MA, U. No. Colo., 1980. Cert. tchr., Colo., Alaska; cert. substance abuse counselor. Asst. dir. Phillips Alcoholism Treatment Ctr., Bethel, Alaska, 1977-79; cons. Alcoholism and Drug Misuse Edn. Cons. and Trainers, Anchorage, 1979-87; distance learning coordinator Rochester (N.Y) Inst. Tech. Coll. Continuing Edn., 1987—; adj. instr. Kuskokwin Community Coll., Bethel, 1977-85; resident counselor Our House Inc., Greeley, Colo., 1979-80; regional trainer Yukon-Kuskokwin Health Corp., Bethel, 1980-81; asst. gen. mgr. Bethel Broadcasting Inc., 1981-86; co-founder Pub. TV Network Alaska, 1982-86. Chmn. alcoholism bd. Phillips Alcoholism and Drugs., Bethel, 1986; bd. dirs. Parks and Recreation, Bethel, 1984-85. Mem. Tundra Women's Coalition (organiser 1977, chmn. 1980-83), Nat. Assn. Female Execs., Nat. Assn. Alcoholism Counselors, Rochester Women's Network. Home: 48 Arvine Heights Rochester NY 14611

FORAKER-THOMPSON, JANE, criminology educator, researcher; b. Alhambra, Calif., Oct. 23, 1937; d. Field and Margaret Hall (Foraker) Thompson; m. Laurence E. Lynn, Aug. 24, 1958; m. Edwin W. Stockly, July 22, 1979; children—Stephen, Daniel, Diana, Julia Suzanne. Student U. N.Mex., 1955-56; BA, U. Calif.-Berkeley, 1959, MA, 1965; PhD, Stanford U., 1985; postgrad. U. Leiden (Netherlands), summer 1973. A founder, active Stanford/Soledad Teaching Project, 1971-74; criminal justice specialist Bernalillo County Mental Health Ctr., Albuquerque, 1974-75; chief planner N.Mex. State Police, Santa Fe, 1975-78; project mgr. N.Mex. restitution project N.Mex. Criminal Justice Dept., Santa Fe, 1978-80; pres. Analysis, Innovation, Devel., Inc., human services cons., Santa Fe, 1980-81; asst. prof. criminal justice Boise State U., 1981-86, assoc. prof., 1986—; mem. N.Mex. Task Force on Victims of Sex Crimes, 1974-81, pres., 1978-80; chairwoman N.Mex. Gov.'s Task Force on Family Policy, 1979-80; first pres., chairwoman bd. Alternatives, Inc., treatment program for offenders, 1974-75; mem. ABA Jail Incapacitation and Prisons Com., 1982-83; mem. planning com. workshop leader N.W. Regional New Call to Peacemaking Conf., 1983; mem. N.Mex. Council Community Mental Health Services, 1974-81, mem. exec. com., 1979-80; mem. adv. bd. Albuquerque Rape Crisis Ctr., 1974-75; mem. adv. bd. N.Mex. Bar Assn. Community Corrections, 1975; pres. Citizens for Prison Change, Inc., N.Mex., 1980-81; clk. Santa Fe Religious Soc. Friends, 1976-78, N. Mex. quar. meetings, 1978-80, clk. Boise Valley Worship Group, 1982-83; mem. peace and justice com. Idaho Diocese Episcopal Ch., 1983—; mem. Ada County Citizens for Peace (Idaho); bd. dirs. Boise Stepping Stone Ministries Halfway House for Offenders, 1987—, Idaho Conservation League, 1986—; mem. community mediation conciliation program, 1986—; mem., past pres. Banguard, 1984—; mem. Fgn. Relations Council, Idaho Natural Resources Legal Found. Canadian govt. grantee, 1986. Mem. Western Assn. Sociologists and Anthropologists (pres. 1986-87), U.S. and Can. Acad. Soc., Am. Polit. Sci. Assn., Am. Soc. Pub. Adminstrn., ABA, Nat. Orgn. Victim Assistance, Acad. Criminal Justice Scis., Am. Soc. Criminology, Internat. Soc. Law Enforcement and Criminal Justice Instrs., Idaho Mediation Assn. (bd. dirs. 1986—), C. of C. (com. on state and fed. legislation), Snake River Alliance. Contbr. articles to profl. jours. Office: Boise State U Dept Anthropology Sociology and Criminal Justice Boise ID 83725

FORBES, CYNTHIA ANN, small business owner, marketing educator; b. Richmond, Calif., Dec. 27, 1951; d. James Martin and Mary Jane (Clafferty) Forbes; m. Larry Charles Osofsky, Mar. 20, 1970 (div. 1980); 1 child, Anna; m. William Charles Ham, Aug. 30, 1986. BA, U. Calif., 1977; MS, Golden Gate U., 1981. Research asst. U. Calif., Berkeley, 1975-77, Chevron Research, Richmond, 1977-79; specialist dealer affairs Chevron USA, San Francisco, 1979-80, sales rep., San Fafael, Calif., 1981-84, adminstrv. supr., San Ramon, Calif.; 1984-85, advt. mgr. Chevron Chem. Co., San Francisco, 1986—; assoc. prof. Golden Gate U., San Francisco, 1981—. Vol., lectr. child abuse prevention. Mem. Contra Costra Women's Network, Nat. Agrimarketers Assn. Democrat. Jewish. Avocations: mountaineering, bicycling. Home: 83 Acacia Dr Orinda CA 94563 Office: Golden Gate Univ 1536 Mission St San Francisco CA 94105

FORBES, PHYLLIS ROSSITER, public agency administrator; b. Jacksonville, Fla., Mar. 11, 1944; d. Ernest Jr. and Eleanor May (Henry) Rossiter; 1 child, Jessica Ann. AB, Stanford U., 1965; MA, U. Ariz., 1967, PhD, 1972. Research asst. Tucson Pub. Schs., 1967-68; tchr. German lang. Palo Verde High Sch., Tucson, 1968-70; asst. to provost U. N.H., Durham, 1972-74, asst. to pres., 1974-80, asst. dir. phys. plant, 1980-81, dir. adminstrv. services, 1981-85; div. chief mgmt. services Arlington (Va.) County Govt., 1985—; cons. Am. Dental Hygienists, Manchester, N.H., 1980, N.H. Dept. Personnel, Concord, 1980-81, New London (N.H.) Hosp., 1984-85. Contbr. articles to profl. jours. Mem. ad hoc commn. on goals Oyster River Schs., Durham, 1978; mem. Coalition for Fair Sch. Fin., Durham, 1979-80; bd. dirs. Seacoast Alliance for Transp., N.H., 1983-84. Mem. Assn. for Psychol. Type, Assn. Phys. Plant Adminstrs., Organizational Devel. Network, AAUW. Home: 2548B S Arlington Mill Dr Arlington VA 22206

FORD, AGNES, insurance executive; b. Bklyn., Jan. 16, 1948; d. Edward and Anna (Anger) F.; 1 child, James. B.A., Bklyn. Coll., 1971. Cert. in ocean marine ins. Tchr., N.Y.C. Bd. Edn., 1971-72; asst. yacht underwriter Home Ins. Co., N.Y.C., 1972-75; offshore drilling rig underwriter All Am. Marine Slip, N.Y.C., 1975-78; reinsurance underwriter Am. Internat. Underwriters, N.Y.C., 1978-86; statis. mgr. Lancer Ins. Co., N.Y.C., 1986—. Chairperson Cub Scout pack Greater N.Y. council Boy Scouts Am., Bklyn., 1977-81, mem. com., 1981-84. Mem. Bklyn. Coll. Alumni Assn., Coll. Ins. Alumni Assn., Am. Marine Ins. Forum. Democrat. Roman Catholic. Avocations: dancing; camping; reading. Home: 2418 E 22d St Brooklyn NY 11235 Office: Lancer Ins Co 55 John St New York NY 10038

FORD, ALLA TCHIKOFF, book dealer; b. Romny, USSR, Apr. 2, 1910; d. Valentine Vasilievish and Mary (Rusin) T.; m. Robert Graham Ford (dec. 1985); children: Barbara Ford Morris, Janice Campbell. Student, Hunter Coll., 1928-29; professeurs a'l stranger, Sarbonne U., Paris, 1929-31; student, U. Polit. Sci., 1931-32, Sci. Mind, 1960-67. Rare book dealer N.Y., Fla., 1957—; owner Ford Press Co., Fla., 1958. Author: Musical Fantasies of L. Frank Baum, 1958, Joys of Collecting Children's Books, 1969, UFO's in Oz, 1980; also pub. of miniature and large books. Mem. Am. Assn. Retired Persons, Internat. Miniature Soc., Miniature Book Soc., Book Source Monthly. Democrat. Religious Science. Club: Three Sherlock Holmes. Home and Office: 114 S Palmway Lake Worth FL 33460

FORD, ANN SUTER, health care consultant, planner, educator, nurse; b. Mineola, N.Y., Oct. 31, 1943; d. Robert M. and Jennette (Van Derzee) Suter; m. W. Scott Ford, 1964; children—Tracey, Karin. R.N., White Plains Hosp. Sch. Nursing (N.Y.), 1964; B.S.N. with high distinction, U. Ky., 1967; M.S. in Health Planning, Fla. State U., 1971, Ph.D., 1975. Nurse, U. Ky. Med. Ctr., 1964-65, Tallahassee Meml. Hosp., 1968-69; guest lectr. health planning dept. urban and regional planning Fla. State U., Tallahassee, 1973-76, health planner and research assoc., 1974-76, vis. asst. prof., 1976-77, asst. prof. and dir. health planning splty., 1977-83, assoc. prof., 1982-83; health care analyst and policy cons., 1983-86; med., health program analyst Aging and Adult Services for State of Fla., 1986—; coordinator Fla. Alzheimer's Disease Initiative, 1986—; bd. dirs. Fla. Lung Assn.; mem. exec. com. human services and social planning tech. dept. Am. Inst. Planners, 1977-78. Author: The Physician's Assistant: A National and Local Analysis, 1975; contbr.

numerous articles on health edn. and health planning to profl. jours.; contbr. chpts. to books; author research reports. USPHS grantee, 1965-67; HEW grantee, 1978; Univ. fellow Fla. State U., 1971-72; recipient Am. Inst. Planners' Student award, 1975. Mem. Am. Planning Assn. (charter mem. human services and social planning tech. dept. 1976—, chmn. health planning session Oct. 1978, 79, health policy liaison 1979-83, author assn. health policy statement), Am. Health Planning Assn., Phi Kappa Phi. Address: 2602 Cline St Tallahassee FL 32312

FORD, BETTY (ELIZABETH) BLOOMER, wife of former President of United State; b. Chgo., Apr. 8, 1918; d. William Stephenson and Hortence (Neahr) Bloomer; m. Gerald R. Ford (38th Pres. U.S.), Oct. 15, 1948; children: Michael Gerald, John Gardner, Steven Meigs, Susan Elizabeth. Student, Sch. Dance Bennington Coll., 1936, 37; LL.D. hon., U. Mich., 1976. Dancer Martha Graham Concert Group, N.Y.C., 1939-41; model John Powers Agy., N.Y.C., 1939-41; fashion dir. Herpolsheimer's Dept. Store, Grand Rapids, Mich., 1943-48; dance instr. Grand Rapids, 1932-48; pres., bd. dirs. The Betty Ford Ctr., Rancho Mirage, Calif. Author: autobiography The Times of My Life, 1979. Bd. dirs. Nat. Arthritis Found. (hon.); formerly active Cub Scouts Am.; program chmn. Alexandria (Va.) Cancer Fund Drive; chmn. Heart Subday, Washington Heart Assn., 1974; pres. ARC Senate Wives Club; supporter Nat. Endowment Arts; mem. Nat. Commn. Observance Internat. Women's Year, 1977; bd. dirs. League Republican Women, D.C.; trustee Eisenhower Med. Ctr., Rancho Mirage; advisory bd. Rosalind Russell Med. Research Fund; hon. chmn. Palm Springs Desert Mus.; nat. trustee Nat. Symphony Orch.; trustee Nursing Home Advisory and Research Council Inc.; mem. Golden Circle Patrons Ctr. Theatre Performing Arts; bd. dirs. The Lambs, Libertyville, Ill. Episcopalian (tchr. Sunday sch. 1961-64). Home: Rancho Mirage CA 92270 *

FORD, CAROL MARIE, engineer; b. St. Paul, Nov. 15, 1956; d. Roland Beverly and Rosemarie (Noren) F. BS in Math. and BS in Physics, U. Minn., 1978, BEE, 1982. Engr. Boeing, Seattle, 1979, Honeywell, Mpls., 1979—. Office: Honeywell 2600 Ridgeway Pkwy Minneapolis MN 55440

FORD, CATHY ZOE, dentist; b. Knoxville, Tenn., June 2, 1953; d. Lester Smith and Velma (Dyer) Ford; m. James Tate McClung, Jr., June 17, 1978; children: Lindsay Hunter, Megan Ford McClung. BA, U. Tenn., 1974; DDS, La. State U., 1979. Med. rep. Arnar-Stone Labs., New Orleans, 1974-75; gen. practice dentistry, Rocky Mount, Va., 1980—; cons. Eldercare, Rocky Mount, 1982-84. Vol. Jr. League of Roanoke Valley, Va., 1982—. Recipient Achievement in Oral Surgery award La. Soc. Oral and Maxillofacial Surgeons, 1977-79, Am. Assn. Oral and Maxillofacial Surgeons award in oral surgery, 1979. Mem. Alpha Lambda Delta. Republican. Presbyterian. Avocations: golf, tennis. Home: 5119 Elk Hill Dr Roanoke VA 24014 Office: 40 West 630-B W Franklin St Rocky Mount VA 24151

FORD, CHARLOETTE LUCILLE, small business owner; b. Las Aminas, Colo., Nov. 9, 1938; d. Elvin Eldredge and Mildred Irene (McCammond) Martin; m. Jerry Ford, Dec. 22, 1958 (dec. Dec. 1987); children: Tamala, Kamala. Grad. high sch., Spearman, Tex., 1957. Sec. Dorothymae's Trunks, Spearman, 1974-76; owner Charlotte Ford Trunks, Spearman, 1977-88. Author (pub.) Trunk Talk vol. 1-5, 1980-82. Mem. Rep. Nat. Com., 1985-88. Mem. Nat. Assn. Female Execs. Baptist. Home: 1116 S Townsend Box 1033 Spearman TX 79081 Office: Charlotte Ford Trunks 313 Main Box 536 Spearman TX 79081

FORD, DAWN SHEELER, consumer and public affairs executive; b. Balt., Dec. 15, 1944; d. Norman C. and Betty A. (Larsh) Sheeler; m. Richard Ford, June 1, 1969; 1 son, Christopher Norman. B.S., U. Md., 1966. Staff assoc. pub. relations hdqrs. Chesapeake and Potomac Telephone Co., 1968; asst. chief info. office Land Between the Lakes, TVA, Ky., 1969-73, chief info. office Land Between the Lakes, TVA, 1973-76, info. officer TVA, Knoxville, 1976-78, adminstrv. asst. to chmn. bd., 1978, chief citizen action office, 1978-84; pres. Consumer Awareness Mgmt., 1984—. Chmn. pilot campaign United Way, 1987; bd. dirs. Knoxville LWV, 1978. Recipient Best Ann. Report award Internat. Assn. Broadcast Communicators, 1977. Mem. Pub. Relations Soc. Am. (pres., dir. vol. chpt.; Pub. Relations Practitioner of Yr. 1982), Issues Mgmt. Assn., Exec. Women's Assn., Knoxville C. of C. (chmn. diplomat 1987-88, bd. dirs. 1988—), Federally Employed Women (co-chmn. regional tng. conf. 1977—), Beta Sigma Phi (Woman of Yr. 1974), Pi Beta Phi (province pres., 1982-86). Office: PO Box 30121 Knoxville TN 37930

FORD, ELLEN HODSON, composer; b. Lincoln, Ill., Feb. 1, 1913; d. Albert and Mary (Fairclough) Hodson; m. John Joseph Janov, May 10, 1933 (dec. Sept. 1948); children: Alberta, Patricia, Jacqueline, David; m. James Gregory Ford, June 13, 1964. Studies with Avelyn Kerr, Paul Sasstavitich, Chgo., 1940-48. Pvt. practice organ teaching Chgo., 1948-63; pub. Gabbriel Music Co., Taylorville, Ill., 1984. Composer, pub. 70 compositions, 1976-87. Recipient Cert. Recognition Josephine Oblinger, 1984; recognized by Queen Elizabeth II, also the Queen Mother of Eng. for compositions submitted. Mem. ASCAP, Am. Women's Composers Orgn., Music Arts Club. Republican. Episcopalian. Club: Women's (Taylorville). Lodge: Order Ea. Star. Home and Office: 421 W Franklin St Taylorville IL 62568

FORD, E(MMA) JANE, public relations executive; b. Anderson, Ind., Mar. 25, 1918; d. Kenneth E. and Emma (Thomas) Griffith. BGS, Ind. U.-Purdue U. at Indianapolis, 1982. Advt. dir. Farm Bur. Ins., Indpls., 1956-73; pub. relations dir. Brulin & Co., Indpls., 1973-76; pub. info. dir. Ind. Arts Commn., Indpls., 1976-79, Indpls. Art League, Indpls., 1982-84; ret. 1984—; talent coordinator, moderator Indy Internat. Cable TV, Indpls.; vice chmn. Service Corps of Retired Execs. Author: (play) An Evening With Zane Gray, 1985. Named Ad Woman of Yr. Ad Club of Ind., 1961. Mem. Women in Communications (sec.), Woman's Press Club of Ind. (sec.), Pub. Relations Soc. of Am., AAUW (assoc. editor). Republican. Episcopal.

FORD, KATHLEEN, artist, designer, writer; b. San Francisco, Mar. 3, 1932; d. Edward Francis and Mary Catherine (Donnelly) Dowd; student San Francisco Coll. for Women. 1950-53; B.A. in Design, Salinger Sch. Design, San Francisco, 1954. Head designer swimwear Gantner of Calif., San Francisco, 1954-55; asst. designer Jantzen, Inc., Seattle, 1955-56; owner, mgr. Kathleen Dowd Boutique, Sausalito, Calif., 1956-62; designer Constructions For Sound and Video, objects for manufacture, 1976—; author: The Three-Cornered House, 1968; The End (film); Last And 1/2 (film); author, designer American Point 50 (film); author screenplays The Rocker and Sweetheart, Key Grip, Kicked Out!, Bel Air Bump!; authored kits for making miniature prodns.; dir. The Loyola Internat. Art Consortium. Mem. Contemporary Authors, Writers Guild of Am. Home: 425 Castenada Ave San Francisco CA 94116

FORD, LEE ELLEN, scientist, educator, lawyer; b. Auburn, Ind., June 16, 1917; d. Arthur W. and Geneva (Muhn) Ford; B.A., Wittenberg Coll., 1947; M.S., U. Minn., 1949; Ph.D., Iowa State Coll., 1952; J.D., U. Notre Dame, 1972. CPA auditing, 1934-44; assoc. prof. biology Gustavus Adolphus Coll., 1950-51, Anderson (Ind.) Coll., 1952-55; vis. prof. biology U. Alta. (Can.), Calgary, 1955-56; asso. prof. biology Pacific Luth. U., Parkland, Wash., 1956-62; prof. biology and cytogenetics Miss. State Coll. for Women, 1962-64; chief cytogeneticist Pacific N.W. Research Found., Seattle, 1964-65; dir. Canine Genetics Cons. Service, Parkland, 1963-69. Sponsor Companion Collies for the Adult, Jr. Blind, 1955-65; dir. Genetics Research Lab., Butler, Ind., 1955-75, cons. cytogenetics, 1969-75; legis. cons., 1970-79; dir. chromosome lab. Inst. Basic Research in Mental Retardation, S.I., 1968-69; exec. dir. Legis. Bur. U. Notre Dame Law Sch., also editor New Dimensions in Legislation, 1969-72; editor Butler Record Herald, 1972-76; bd. dirs. Ind. Interreligious Com. on Human Equality, 1976-80; exec. asst. to Gov. Otis R. Bowen, Ind., 1973-75; dir. Ind. Commn. on Status Women, 1973-74; bd. dirs. Ind. Council Chs.; editor Ford Assos. pubs., 1972-86; mem. Pres.'s Adv. Council on Drug Abuse, 1976-77. Admitted to Ind. bar, 1972. Adult counselor Girl Scouts U.S.A., 1934-40; bd. dirs. Ind. Task Force Women's Health, 1976-80; mem. exec. bd., bd. dirs. Ind.-Ky. Synod Lutheran Ch., 1972-78; bd. dirs., mem. council St. Marks Lutheran Ch., Butler, 1970-76; mem. social services personnel bd.; mem. DeKalb County (Ind.) Sheriff's Merit Bd., 1983-87; founder, dir., pres. Ind. Caucus for Animal Legislation and Leadership, 1984-87. Mem. or ex-mem. AAUW, AAAS, Genetics Soc. Am., Am. Human Genetics Soc., Am. Genetic Assn., Am. Inst. Biol. Scis., Am. Soc. Zoologists, La., Miss., Ind., Iowa acads. sci., Bot. Soc. Am., Ecol. Soc. Am., Am. (dir.), Ind. (dir.), DeKalb County (dir.) bar assns., Humane Soc. U.S. (dir. 1970-88), DeKalb County Humane Soc. (founder, dir. 1970-86), Ind. Fedn. Humane Socs. (dir. 1970-84), Nat. Assn. Women Lawyers (dir.), Bus. and Profl. Women's Club, Nat. Assn. Republican Women (dir.), Women's Equity Action League (dir.), Assn. So. Biologists, Phi Kappa Phi. Club: Altrusa. Editor: Breeder's Jour., 1958-63; numerous vols. on dog genetics and breeding, guide dogs for the blind. Contbr. over 2000 sci. and popular publs. on cytogenetics, dog breeding and legal topics; contbr. Am. Kennel Club Gazette, 1970-81, also others. Researcher in field. Home and Office: 824 E 7th St Auburn IN 46706

FORD, LORETTA C., nurse, educator, university dean emeritus; b. N.Y.C., Dec. 28, 1920; d. Joseph F. and Nellie A. (Williams) Pfingstel; R.N., Middlesex Gen. Hosp., New Brunswick, N.J., 1941; B.S. in Nursing, U. Colo., 1949, M.S., 1951, Ed.D., 1961; D.Sc. (hon.), Ohio State Med Coll.; m. William J. Ford, May 2, 1947; 1 dau., Valerie. Staff nurse New Brunswick Vis. Nurse Service, 1941-42; supr., dir. Boulder County (Colo.) Health Dept., 1947-58; asst. prof., then prof. U. Colo. Sch. Nursing, 1960-72; dean Sch. Nursing, dir. nursing, prof. U. Rochester (N.Y.), 1972-86; vis. prof. U. Fla., summer 1968, U. Wash., Seattle, 1974; mem. educators adv. panel GAO; dir. Security Trust Co., Rochester, Rochester Telephone Co.; internat. cons. in field. Bd. dirs. Threshold Alte. Youth Services, Easter Seal Soc., ARC, Monroe Community Hosp. Served with Nurse Corps, USAAF, 1942-46. Named Colo. Nurse of Year; recipient N.Y. State Gov.'s award for women in sci., medicine and nursing. Fellow Am. Acad. Nursing; mem. Nat. League Nursing (fellowship, Linda Richards award), Am. Coll. Health Assn. (Boynton award), Am. Nurses Assn., Am. Public Health Assn., Inst. Medicine. Author articles in field, chpts. in books. Office: 601 Elmwood Ave Box HWH Rochester NY 14642

FORD, LUCILLE GARBER, economist, educator, college dean and official; b. Ashland, Ohio, Dec. 31, 1921; d. Ora Myers and Edna Lucille (Armstrong) Garber; m. Laurence Wesley Ford, Sept. 1, 1946; children: Karen Elizabeth, JoAnn Christine. A.A., Stephens Coll., 1942; B.S. in Commerce, Northwestern U., 1944, M.B.A., 1944; Ph.D. in Econs., Case Western Res. U., 1967. Cert. fin. planner. Instr. Allegheny Coll., Meadville, Pa., 1945-46, U. Ala., Tuscaloosa, 1946-47; personnel dir., asst. sec. A.L. Garber Co., Ashland, Ohio, 1947-67; prof., chmn. dept. econs. Ashland Coll., 1970-75, dir. Gill Ctr. for Econ. Edn., 1975-86, v.p., dean Sch. Bus., Adminstrn. and Econs., 1980-86, v.p. acad. affairs, 1986—; commr. North Cen. Assn. Colls. and Schs.; bd. dirs. Nat. City Bank, Nat. City Corp., Ohio Edison, A. Schulman Co., Shelby Ins. Co.; lectr. in field. Author University Economics—Guide for Education Majors, 1979; Economics: Learning and Instruction, 1981; contbr. articles to profl. jours. Candidate for lt. gov. of Ohio, 1978; trustee Stephens Coll., 1977-80; elder Presbyterian Ch.; bd. dirs. Presbyn. Found., 1982-88; active ARC. Recipient outstanding alumni award Stephens Coll., 1977; recipient outstanding prof. award Ashland Coll., 1971, 75. Mem. Am. Econs. Assn., Nat. Indsl. Research Soc., Am. Artitration Assn. (profl. arbitrator), Assn. Pvt. Enterprise Edn. (pres. 1983-84), North Cen. Assn. Colls. & Schs. (commr.), Omicron Delta Epsilon, Alpha Delta Kappa. Republican. Home: 1717 Upland Dr Ashland OH 44805 Office: Ashland Coll Ashland OH 44805

FORD, MAUREEN MORRISSEY, civic worker; b. St. Joseph, Mo., July 1, 1936; d. Albert Joseph and Rosemary Kathryne (FitzSimons) Morrissey; student U. N.Mex., 1953-54, U. Bridgeport (Conn.), 1966-68; BS, Fairfield U., 1986, postgrad. in Applied Ethics, 1986—; m. James Henry Lee Ford, Jr., Feb. 12, 1954; children: Kathryne Elizabeth, Maryellen, James Henry Lee III, William Charles, Maureen Lee. Charity and sch. vol., 1959—; fundraiser for community causes, mus., agys., 1964—; active presdl. campaign Barry Goldwater, 1963-64, congressional campaign Senator Lowell Weiker, 1968; pre-sch. tchr. Nature Ctr. Environ. Activities, 1966-68, trustee, v.p. bd. dirs., 1968-75; assoc. program in applied ethics, Fairfield U., 1986—; v.p. Women's League, 1966-70; mem. exec. com. Republican Women's Club, Westport, 1967-68; leader, trainer Troops on Fgn. Soil br. Girl Scouts USA, Caracas, Venezuela, 1971-72; founding trustee, treas. Kara Mus., Norwalk, Conn.; mem. adv. council Fairfield County (Conn.) for spl. edn. Staples High Sch.; bd. dirs. CLASP; mem. exec. com. Group Home Search; cons., facilitator life planning workshops Merideth Assocs., Westport; mem. 1st selectmen's com. on recycling, 1974-75; bd. dirs. PTA, 1976-79; mem. YWCA of Bridgeport Com. of 100 and Task Force; v.p. bd. dirs. YWCA, 1980-87, pres., 1984-85; v.p. Conf. Women's Orgns., Bridgeport; founding mem. Concerned Women Colleagues of Bridgeport; pres. Jr. League Eastern Fairfield County, Inc., 1977-78; v.p., sec. J.H.L.F. Inc., Westport. Mem. Assn. Jr. League Am., Westport Tennis Assn. Roman Catholic. Home: 299 Sturges Hwy Westport CT 06880

FORD, PATRICIA, interior designer; b. Warsaw, N.Y., Feb. 17, 1947; d. Homer James and Ellen Louise (Dixon) F.; B.A. cum laude in Fine Arts, UCLA, 1969, M.A. in Fine Arts, 1971. Designer, Herb Rosenthal & Assos., Los Angeles, 1973; sr. designer Charles Kratka Planning and Design, Los Angeles, 1973-75; partner The Ford Wilson Partnership, Los Angeles, 1975-78; pres. Ford Design Group Inc., Los Angeles, 1978-82; dir. interior design Bobrow Thomas & Assocs., architects, Los Angeles, 1982-84; ptnr. Kaneko Ford Design, Los Angeles, 1985—; specialist in health care, interior design and graphics, pediatrics emphasis Shriners Hosps., U. Va., UCLA, U.S. Navy; cons. to Los Angeles Olympic Organizing Com., 1984—. Mem citizens adv. council Los Angeles Olympics of 1984, 1980—; mem. Los Angeles Hdqrs. City Assn. 1980—. Mem. Assn. Women in Architecture (v.p.), Am. Soc. Interior Designers, AIA, Town Hall. Episcopalian. Contbr. articles to profl. jours. Office: Kaneko Ford Design 2200 Michigan Ave Santa Monica CA 90404

FORD, ROSEMARY LAWLESS, advertising executive; b. N.Y.C., June 11, 1944; d. Eugene Edward and Vera (McNamara) Ford; m. Jan Preston Wilkison, May 25, 1968 (div. Nov. 1980); children: Elizabeth Ford, Holly Vogt; m. Roy L. Markum, Sept. 12, 1987. AA, Marymount U., 1964. Copywriter Howard Marks Advt. subs. NCK Orgn., N.Y.C., 1965-66; promotion dir. Sta. WIXY Radio, Cleve., 1966-67; asst. dir. advt. and promotion Sta. WKYC subs. NBC Radio, Cleve., 1967-68; coordinator publicity The Higbee Co., Cleve., 1969-71; v.p. Ogilvy & Mather Spl. Markets, Houston, 1979-85; pres. Ford Advt. and Pub. Relations, Houston, 1985—; served on lawyers com. on advt. State Bar Tex. Mem. women's council Cleve. Mus. Art; active Jr. League Houston, Guild of Houston Mus. Fine Arts. Mem. Am. Mktg. Assn. (profl.), Houston Advt. Fedn., Pub. Relations Soc. Am. Presbyterian. Club: The Print (Cleve. Mus. Art), The Houstonian. Office: Ford Advt and Pub Relations 17 S Briar Hollow Garden Suite Houston TX 77027

FORD, RUTH, actress; b. Brookhaven, Miss.; d. Charles and Gertrude (Cato) F.; m. Zachary Scott, July 6, 1952; 1 dau., by previous marriage. B.A., U. Miss., M.A. Actress (first appearence) play, Ivoryton Playhouse, Conn., 1937, Ways and Means, Ivoryton Playhouse, Conn., 1937; Orson Welle's Mercury Theatre Co., 1938, Cyrano de Bergerac, 1946, No Exit, 1947, Hamlet, 1949, Macbeth, The Failures, A Phoenix Too Frequent, Six Characters in Search of an Author, (debut) Requiem for a Nun, Royal Ct., London, 1957, Lovey, 1965, Dinner at Eight, 1966, The Ninety-Day Mistress, 1967, The Grass Harp, 1971, Madame de Sade, 1972, A Breeze from the Gulf, 1973, The Charlatan, 1974, The Seagull, 1977, The Aspern Papers, 1978, Harold and Maude, 1980, The Visit, 1983; (first appearence) film. 1941, Wilson, Dragonwyck, Keys of the Kingdom, Act One, Play It As It Lays, Too Scared to Scream. Mem. AFTRA, Screen Actors Guild, Actors Equity. Democrat. Address: 1 W 72d St New York NY 10023

FORDHAM, PATRICIA KAY, state agency administrator; b. Salt Lake City, May 29, 1938; d. William O. Birk and Eleanore (Erskine) Birk Murphy; m. Lawrence L. Bell, Mar. 25, 1956 (div. June 1960); children: Sherri Lee Bell, Dana LaMont Bell; m. Allen Ronald Fordham, Nov. 18, 1976. BS, U. Utah, 1980, MEd, 1984. Tchr. Jordan dist. Alta High Sch., Sandy, Utah, 1980-84; instr. U. Utah, Salt Lake City, 1984-85; dir. competency testing Utah State Office Edn., Salt Lake City, 1985—. Author: Accounting, 1986. Elected bd. dirs. Iron Blosam Owner's Assn., Snowbird, Utah, 1986—; leader Weight Watchers, Salt Lake City, 1976—. Mem. Nat. Bus. Edn. Assn., Utah Bus. Edn. Assn., Utah Vocat. Assn., Delta Pi Epsilon (pres. 1987—). Republican. Mormon. Home: 1045 E 5600 S Salt Lake City UT 84121 Office: Utah State Office Edn Competency Testing PO Box 30808 Salt Lake City UT 84130

FORD-WALKER, CONNIE JEAN, nurse; b. Frankfort, Ky., Nov. 2, 1948; d. Artist Edwin and Cornellia Isola (Riddle) Ford; m. William Benjamin Walker, Jr., Dec. 27, 1970 (div. 1985). Assoc. in Nursing, St. Petersburg Jr. Coll., 1967; B.S. in Nursing, U. So. Fla., 1981; MBA, Nova U., 1988. R.N., Fla. Staff nurse Palms of Pasadena Hosp., St. Petersburg, Fla., 1976-78, clin. instr. edn., 1981-82, dir. surg. nursing, 1982-83, project coordinator internat. nursing course, 1983-84, dir. nursing resources, 1984-85; asst. dir. operating room Meml. Hosp., Sarasota, Fla., 1985-86; cons. VHA Cons. Services, Tampa, 1987—; instr. basic operating room nursing State Vocat. Coll., St. Petersburg, 1979-82. Mem. Assn. Operating Room Nursing (bd. dirs., chmn. nat. cert. bd. 1982-83), Am. Nurses Assn. (bd. dirs.), Nat. League for Nurses, Beta Sigma Phi. Republican. Mem. Christian Ch. (Disciples of Christ). Club: St. Petersburg Yacht. Avocations: sailing, cooking, reading, piano. Home: 1545 49th St N Saint Petersburg FL 33710

FOREHAND, JENNIE MEADOR, state legislator; b. Nashville, Dec. 17, 1935; d. James T. and Estelle (Woodall) Meador; student Woman's Coll. of U. N.C., Greensboro, 1954-56; B.S. in Indsl. Relations, U. N.C., Chapel Hill, 1958; m. William E. Forehand, Jr., July 19, 1958; children—Mary Virginia, John Bentley. Reporter, Charlotte (N.C.) News, 1954-56; probation counselor Juvenile Ct., Charlotte, 1958; tchr. Anne Arundel County (Md.), 1958-60; statis. analyst NIH, Bethesda, Md., 1961-62; edn. research project evaluator Montgomery County (Md.) Bd. Edn., 1973-74; interior designer, owner Antiques and Interiors, Rockville, Md., 1971—; mem. Md. Ho. of Dels., 1978—; mem. appropriations com., joint capital budget com., health and environ. subcom., Md. com. on Physical Fitness, Bd. Md. State Games; co-chair Gov's. Task Force on Sr. Citizen Ctrs.; adv. bd. First Women's Bank of Md. Planning bd. Montgomery County Health Systems Agy., chmn. edn. and community involvement; past chmn. Rockville Civic Improvement Adv. Commn.; consumer rep. Rockville Econ. Devel. Council; mem. Montgomery County Bd. of Edn. Med. Adv. Com.; mem. Md. Community Mental Health Adv. Bd.; pres. local civic assn.; bd. dirs. Mid-Md. Lung Assn., Montgomery County Hist. Soc.; bd. dirs. local sch. PTA; adv. bd. Mont. Hospice Soc., mem. Peerless Rockville Hist. Preservation, Ltd., Questers. Mem. Women's Caucus of Md. Gen. Assembly, AAUW, Nat. Order Women Legislators, Md. Assn. Elected Women, Women's Polit. Caucus. Democrat. Methodist. Office: 224B House Office Bldg State House Annapolis MD 21401

FOREMAN, CAROL LEE TUCKER, business executive; b. Little Rock, May 3, 1938; d. James Guy and Willie Maude (White) Tucker; A.A., William Woods Coll., Fulton, Mo., 1958; A.B., Washington U., St. Louis, 1960; postgrad. Am. U.; LL.D. (hon.), William Woods Coll., Fulton, Mo., 1976; m. Jay Howell Foreman, June 13, 1964; children—Guy Tucker, Rachel Marian. Research asst. Com. on Govt. Ops., U.S. Senate, 1961; assoc. Fed. Counsel Assocs., 1961-63; instr. Am. govt. William Woods Coll., Fulton, 1963-64; exec. asst. to Rep. James Roosevelt, 1964; dir. research and publs. Democratic Nat. Com., 1965-66; Congressional liaison aide HUD, 1967-69; chief info. liaison Center for Family Planning Program Devel., Planned Parenthood-World Population, 1969-71; dir. policy coordination Commn. on Population and Am. Future, 1971-72; exec. dir. Citizens Com. on Population and Am. Future, 1972-73, Paul Douglas Consumer Research Center, 1973-77, Consumer Fedn. Am., 1973-77; asst. sec. food and consumer services Dept. Agr., Washington, 1977-81; pres. Foreman & Co., 1981-86, ptnr. Foreman & Heidepriem, 1986—; exec. dir. Ctr. for Women Policy Studies, 1983-84; mem. Interdeptl. Task Force on Women; mem. D.C. Commn. on Status Women, 1973-74; dir. Consumer's Union, 1982-83, Food Research and Action Ctr., 1983—; dir. Commodity Credit Corp., 1977-81, Nat. Consumer Coop. Bank, 1979-81; vice-chmn. Center Nat. Policy, 1982-84, dir., 1981—; trustee Washington U., St. Louis, 1987—. Recipient Disting. Alumni award Washington U., 1979. Mem. Women's Equity Action League (past pres. local chpt.), Nat. Planning Assn. (dir. 1985—), Women's Nat. Dem. Club, Pi Beta Phi. Presbyterian. Home: 5408 Trent Ct Chevy Chase MD 20015 Office: Foreman & Heideprim 1751 "N" St NW Suite 301 Washington DC 20036

FOREMAN, CHRISTINE HAIRSTON, medical director, diagnostic technologist; b. Martinsville, Va.; d. Willis Isiah and Roxie (Helms) Hairston; m. Henry Foreman Jr.; 1 child, Clifton Charles Roderick. Student, CCNY, 1949-51, Mandell Med. Asst. Sch., 1951-52, Bronx Community Coll., 1969-70, NYU Med. Sch., 1978. Cert. in EEG, N.Y. Electroencephalography technologist Bronx Mcpl. Hosp. Ctr., 1957, Albert Einstein Coll. Medicine, Bronx, 1961-63; supr. EEG Bronx Mcpl. Hosp. Ctr., 1968-78, dir. EEG, 1978—; lectr. in field. Rep., Bronx Block Assn., 1985. Recipient Stephenson Meml. award Ea. Soc., 1973. Mem. Met. EEG Soc. (treas. 1978—), Nat. Assn. Negro Bus. and Profl. Women (Profl. award 1988), Nat. Council Negro Women (Bethune Achievement award 1987-88). Roman Catholic. Home: 3522 DeReimer Ave Bronx NY 10466 Office: Bronx Mcpl Hosp Ctr Detp Electroencephalography 2E-16 Bronx NY 10461

FOREMAN, HELEN CLEARY, mayor; b. Jacksonville, Ill., July 8, 1904; d. Edward Purcell and Minnie Marie (Wait) C.; m. Orville N. Foreman, June 8, 1927 (dec.); children: Margaret, Constance, Edward. AB, Ill. Coll., 1925; AM, U. Ill., 1929; LLD (hon.), Ill. Coll., 1979; D of Pub. Adminstrn. (hon.), MacMurray Coll., 1987. Tchr. Dixon (Ill.) High Sch., 1925-27; instr. U. Ill., Champaign, 1928; alderman City of Jacksonville, 1973-84, mayor, 1984—. Mem. Rep. Women's Club, Jacksonville, 1932— (pres. 1932); nat. bd. dirs. League of Women Voters, 1951-56. Mem. Ill. Mcpl. League (v.p. 1987—), Cen. Ill. Mayor's Assn. (treas. 1986-87, v.p. 1987—), Catholic Daughters of Am. Roman Catholic. Home: 1313 Mound Ave Jacksonville IL 62650 Office: City of Jacksonville 200 W Douglas Jacksonville IL 62650

FOREMAN, NANCY JEAN, interior designer; b. Balt., Feb. 21, 1949; d. Ernst and Julia (Rosenthal) Guggenheim; m. Jeff Foreman, Apr. 1, 1978. BS, U. Md., 1970. Interior designer Lucas Design Group, Balt., 1972-76; space planner Md. Casualty Co., Balt., 1976-77; interior designer Michael Asner & Assocs., Balt., 1977-78; pres. Nancy Foreman Design, Timonium, Md., 1978—. Fundraiser Kennedy Inst. for Handicapped Children, Balt., 1986; mem. Greater Balt. Com., 1985—; bd. dirs. Grant-A-Wish Found., 1988—. Mem. Am. Soc. Interior Designers (bd. dirs. 1987—), Comml. Real Estate Women, Bldg. Office Mgrs. Assn., Nat. Assn. Indsl. Office Parks, Balt. County C. of C. Office: 16 Greenmeadow Dr Timunium MD 21093

FORER, MARGERY PATRICIA, greeting card company executive; b. N.Y.C., Mar. 17, 1922; d. David and Hattie Bregman; m. David Forer, Dec. 17, 1948; children: David Brett, Katherine Ellen. BS, Skidmore Coll., 1943. Asst. testing dept. Manhattan Project, Columbia U., 1943-44; fashion reporter Women's Wear Daily, 1944-47; 1st fashion editor Footwear News, 1947-49; co-founder Brett-Forer Greetings, N.Y.C., 1949, since sec.-treas.; also fashion coordinator, stylist-designer Brett-Forer; mem. adv. bd. greeting card com. UNICEF; speaker, cons. in field. Mem. Greeting Card Assn. (pres. 1982). Office: 790 Madison Ave New York NY 10021

FOREST, DORIS ELIZABETH, publishing executive; b. N.Y.C., Jan. 12, 1936; d. Norman Ellis and Winifred Elizabeth (Smith) Riley; m. Andre Forest; 1 child, Jacqueline Elizabeth. Student, N.Y. U., 1954-56, The Fashion Inst. of Tech., The New Sch. Asst. to pres. S. Augstein & Co., Inc., 1956-61; buyer for evening salon Lord & Taylor, 1962-64; exec. asst. to dir. adminstrn. Council on Fgn. Relations, N.Y.C., 1965-70, bus. mgr., 1970-74, asst. v.p., 1974-78; v.p., dir. adminstrn. Council on Fgn. Relations, Inc., N.Y.C., 1978-87; bus. mgr. Fgn. Affairs Mag., N.Y.C., 1970-74, assoc. pub., 1974-78, pub., 1978-87; publs. and adminstrn. dir. Parlimentarians Global Action, 1987—. Mem. Fgn. Policy Assn., Leadership Network Advt. Group (past chmn.), Mag. Pubs. Assn. (dep. chmn. internat. advt. com.), Personnel Council (co-founder, mem. steering com.). Democrat. Roman Catholic. Clubs: Liberty (mem. exec. com. 1984—). Office: Parliamentarians Global Action 211 E 43d St New York NY 10017

FOREST, KAY FRANCES, city administrator; b. Belleville, Ill., Nov. 30, 1948; d. Arthur H. and Marian (Hartnagel) Kastel; m. Alan John Forest; 1 child, Stacy Ann. BS, Western Ill. U., 1970; MBA, Keller Grad. Sch. Mgmt., Chgo., 1987. Asst. dir. of recreation Glenview (Ill.) Park Dist.,

1970-73; exec. dir. Ill. Park and Recreation Assn., Palatine, Ill., 1973—; trustee Ill. Park and Recreation Found., 1975-82; mem. Gov.s Task Force on Ams.Outdoors, Springfield, 1986—. Mem. Am. Soc. Assn. Execs., Nat. Recreation and Park Assn. (council chmn. 1982—), Nat. Youth Sport Coaches Assn. (state dir. Ill. chpt. 1986—), Ill. Conservation, Recreation and Park Found. (sec., treas. 1982—), Chgo. Soc. Assn. Execs. Home: 25962 N Oak Hills Rd Barrington IL 60010 Office: Ill Park and Recreation Assn 262 E Palatine Rd Palatine IL 60067

FORESTER, JEAN MARTHA BROUILLETTE, educator, librarian; b. Port Barre, La., Sept. 7, 1934; d. Joseph Walter and Thelma (Brown) Brouillette; B.S., La. State U., 1955; M.A. (Carnegie fellow 1955-56), George Peabody Coll. Tchrs., 1956; m. James Lawrence Forester, June 2, 1957; children—Jean Martha, James Lawrence. Librarian Howell Elementary Sch., Springhill, La., 1956-58; asst. post librarian Fort Chaffee, Ark., 1958; command librarian Orleans Area Command, U.S. Army, Orleans, France, 1958-59; acquisitions librarian Northwestern State U., Natchitoches, La., 1960; serials librarian La. State U., New Orleans, 1960-66; mem. faculty La. State U., Eunice, 1966-85, asst. librarian, 1972-85, assoc. librarian, 1985-87, acting librarian, 1987-88, dir. libraries, 1988—; asst. prof., 1972-85, faculty senator, 1978-80, 85-86. Active Eunice Assn. Retarded Children. Mem. La. Library Assn. (sect. sec. 1971-72, coordinator serials interest group 1984-85), UDC, Delta Kappa Gamma (chpt. parliamentarian 1972-74, rec. sec. 1984-86), Alpha Beta Alpha, Phi Gamma Mu, Phi Mu. Democrat. Baptist. Mem. Order Eastern Star. Co-author: Robertson's Bill of Fare. Contbr. articles to profl. jours. Home: PO Box 304 Eunice LA 70535 Office: La State U Eunice LeDaux Library PO Box 1129 Eunice LA 70535

FORESTIERI, MARY CATHERINE, speech communication educator; b. Benton Harbor, Mich., July 13, 1940; d. Sebastian and Marjorie May (Hill) F. BA, Western Mich. U., 1962; MFA, U. Oreg., 1969. Adminstrv. asst. Gen. Motors Acceptance Corp., N.Y.C., 1962-63; girl Friday J. Walter Thompson, N.Y.C., 1964; adminstrv. asst. Kesselman Advt., N.Y.C., 1964; sales asst. H.R. TV Sales, N.Y.C., 1965; substitute tchr. Benton Harbor (Mich.) Pub. Schs., 1965-67; teaching asst. U. Oreg., Eugene, 1967-69; faculty speech dept. Lane Community Coll., Eugene, 1969—; pvt. cons., Eugene, Salem, Oreg., 1982—. Contbr. articles to profl. jours. Mem. Speech Communication Assn. (community coll. nominating com. 1986-87), Western Speech Communication Assn., Internat. Listening Assn. (founding mem.). Democrat. Roman Catholic. Home: 3067 Whitbeck Blvd Eugene OR 97405 Office: Lane Community Coll 4000 E 30th Ave Eugene OR 97405

FORGASCH, SUSAN BARBARA, microcomputer technology consultant; b. Bronx, Oct. 14, 1957; d. Morris David and Rosalind (Feldman) F.; m. Robert Jeffrey Lopatkin, July 20, 1986. BA summa cum laude, Queens Coll., 1978. CPA, N.Y., chartered fin. planner. Sr. auditor Ernst & Whinney, N.Y.C., 1978-80; quality assurance analyst Coopers & Lybrand, N.Y.C., 1980-81, quality assurance supr., 1981-83, product mgr., tax software devel., 1983-87, microcomputer audit services mgr., 1987—; faculty continuing edn. dept. Queens Coll., 1985-86, mem. alumni adv. bd., 1987. Mem. Am. Inst. CPA's, N.Y. Soc. of CPA's. Democrat. Jewish. Home: 83-35 139 St Briarwood NY 11435 Office: Coopers & Lybrand 1251 Ave of the Americas New York NY 10020

FORGIONE, STEPHANIE JULIA, real estate management executive; b. Jamaica, N.Y., Dec. 11, 1942; d. Louis and Julia (Zawoluk) Majore; m. Joseph Edward Cox, Sept. 7, 1963 (div. Dec. 1975); 1 child, Debra Ann; m. Louis Victor Forgione, Dec. 28, 1980; stepchildren—Cheryl, Jay, JoAnn, Anthony. Student Jamaica Vocat. Sch. Sales recorder Rueben H. Donnelley, N.Y.C., 1960-62; sec. Durkee Famous Foods, Jamaica, N.Y., 1962-64; adminstrv. asst. Am. Home Products, N.Y.C., 1964-67; bookkeeper W.T. Grant Co., Riverhead, N.Y., 1967-69; sec. Scheinberg, Wolfet al, Riverhead, 1969-70; bookkeeper Hall Huntley, Middle Island, N.Y., 1970-73; asst. v.p. Bayport Assocs., 1973—. Democrat. Roman Catholic. Avocations: boating; bowling; antiques. Home: 601 Terrace Rd Bayport NY 11705 Office: Bayport Assocs 100 Terrace Rd Bayport NY 11705

FORGY, LEAH JANE, advertising agency executive; b. Tallahassee, Apr. 8, 1959; d. Joseph Valentine and Janette Telford (Smith) F. BA in Illustration, U. Houston, 1981. Mgr. cost control Goodwin, Dannenbaum, Littman and Wingfield, Inc., Houston, 1981-85; asst. creative dir. AdPlex, Inc., Houston, 1985-87; mgr. print traffic Taylor Brown and Barnhill, Houston, 1987—. Republican. Presbyterian. Clubs: Ad-2 Fedn., Art Dirs. (Houston). Home: 2214 Turtle Creek Missouri City TX 77459 Office: Taylor Brown and Barnhill 4544 Post Oak Pl #264 Houston TX 77027

FORIS-MILLER, CAROLYN M., histotechnologist; b. N.Y.C., Mar. 13, 1937; d. John Stephen and Caroline Bernice (Banoff) Foris; M. Herbert J. Miller. A.A., Thomas A. Edison Coll., 1979. Technician dept. Hosps. of City of NY., 1959-68; instr. histology Allen Sch. for Med. Tech.; supr. histology Wycoff Heights Hosp., 1968-70; mgr. tissue pathology lab. Metpath, Inc., Teterboro N.J., 1970-84; coordinator anatomic pathology services Woodhull Med. and Mental Health Ctr., Bklyn., 1985-86. Coordinator legis. adv. bd. dirs. for chmn. health for N.Y. State, 1974-75; moderator of community discussion sessions on drug abuse, 1973; bd. govs. Mid Queens Regular Democratic Orgn., 1965-75, sec., v.p., also campaign coordinator for candidates of this orgn., editor newsletter. Recipient certs. Merit and Appreciation, N.Y. State Assemblymen. Mem. Nat. Soc. for Histotech. (charter mem. pub. relations com.), N.Y. Soc. for Histotech. (charter mem., co-editor newsletter 1975-76, editor 1984-85, chmn. membership com.), N.J. Soc. for Histotech. (charter mem.), Am. Soc. Clin. Pathology (assoc. and affiliate member). Roman Catholic.

FORKAN, PATRICIA ANN, association executive; b. N.Y.C., June 13, 1944; d. Robert James and Elaine May (Van Horn) F.; BA in Polit. Sci., Pa. State U., 1966; postgrad. Am. U., 1968-69; m. Robert Eugene Eisenbud, Apr. 16, 1977. Manpower analyst Dept. Labor, Washington, 1967-69; nat. coordinator Fund for Animals, N.Y.C., 1970-76; v.p. program and communications Humane Soc. of U.S., Washington, 1976-86, sr. v.p. 1987—; mem. U.S. del. Internat. Whaling Commn., 1978, Re-negotiation of Conv. for Regulation of Whaling, 1978, U.S. del. North Pacific Fur Seal Commn., 1985; mem. U.S. Public Adv. Com. to Law of the Sea, 1978-83; treas. Council for Ocean Law; advisor, contbr. weekly TV show Living with Animals; advisor Animal Polit. Action Com. Contbr. articles to environ. and animal welfare publs. Co-host weekly radio show, 1986-87. Office: Humane Soc of US 2100 L St Washington DC 20037

FORMAN, ELLEN SARI, entertainment services executive; b. Bklyn., Mar. 27, 1950; d. Philip and Molly (Morhaim) F. BS, Boston U., 1972; MA, NYU, 1975; MS, L.I. U., 1979; PhD, Fla. Inst. Tech., 1987. Cert. alcoholism counselor. Dance therapist St. Vincents Hosp., N.Y.C., 1974-78; dir. therapeutic activities Ferncliff Manor for Retarded, Yonkers, N.Y., 1978-81, clin. services dir., 1981-82; coordinator summer vacation program Bronx Devel. Services, N.Y.C., 1980-82, coordinator leisure program, 1982-85, edn. program specialist, 1985-86; chief exec. officer Creative Arts Enterprises, Inc., N.Y.C., 1982—; pvt. practice psychotherapy N.Y.C., 1985—. Author newsletter Workshops and Courses, 1975-76; co-editor: (booklet) Educational Opportunities, 1979; producer dance therapy tng. video, 1976; contbr. articles to profl. jours. Trainer Spl. Olympics, Bronx, 1983-86. Mem. Am. Dance Therapy Assn., N.Y. Fedn. Alcoholism Counselors, Am. Psychol. Assn., Nat. Assn. Female Execs. Democrat. Jewish. Home: 300 Mercer St #33-H New York NY 10003 Office: Creative Arts Enterprises Inc 80 8th Ave #1806 New York NY 10011

FORMAN, JEANNE LEACH, piano and voice educator; b. Los Angeles, Mar. 3, 1916; d. Rowland E. and Charlotte F. (Van Wickle) Leach; student U. Redlands, 1934-36, UCLA, 1937; m. Edward S. Forman, July 28, 1945; children—Bonnie Jeanne (Mrs. James Field Ottinger), Karen Lynn (Mrs. Patrick Maginnis), Wendy K. Forman (Mrs. Michael Bolduc). Pvt. tchr. piano, Pasadena, Calif., 1945-52, Tucson, 1952-58, Sunnyvale, Calif., 1958-75, Santa Barbara, Calif., 1976—; owner, dir. Jeanne Forman Studios, Sunnyvale; owner/dir. Jeanne Forman Enterprises (Music to Write By), 1982—; owner J. Forman Advt. Agy.; propr. Jeanne Forman Advt. and Enterprises; writer Los Angeles Times, 1978-80; columnist The Galeria Santa Barbara News Press, 1978—; publicity writer Music Tchrs. Assn.; tchr. of blind Santa Clara County Assistance League; lectr. on blind techniques, rapport in communications; freelance writer; gen. edn. staff Brooks Inst. Photography, Santa Barbara guest appearances There is a Way, Sta. KHJ-TV, Los Angeles. Composer (music) I Love to Hear the Bells, 1986. Active Santa Clara Assistance League. Mem. Calif. Assn. Profl. Music Tchrs., Music Tchrs. Nat. Assn., Compositions performed by U. Calif., Santa Barbara, 1971. Author: Security, 1984; Secret of the Pig, 1984. Home: 1119 Alameda Padre Serra Santa Barbara CA 93105

FORMAN, LESLIE ANN, data processing executive; b. Detroit, Apr. 15, 1954; d. Donald Adam Forman and Rebecca Mabel (Mayer) Lundy. BS, U. Bristol (Eng.), 1975; MS, U. Mich., 1977, Pace U., 1984. Mem. tech. staff AT&T Bell Labs., Holmdel, N.J., 1977-80; dept. head AT&T Bell Labs., Whippany, N.J., 1985—; dist. mgr. AT&T, Basking Ridge, N.J., 1980-85. Active Morristown Jr. League, Morristown, N.J., 1985—. Mem. Am. Mgmt. Assn., Am. Assn. Ind. Investors, Nat. Assn. Female Execs., Planning Forum. Office: AT &T Bell Labs 1 Whippany Rd Rm 3A348 Whippany NJ 07981

FORMAN, LINDA EILEEN, retail exec.; b. N.Y.C., Oct. 16, 1946; d. Sol and Thelma (Schoenfeld) F.; student Control Data Inst., 1970; m. Jery Doyle Williams, Dec. 20, 1980. Asst. advt. dir. Dunham's, Trenton, NJ., 1967-69; writer Desmond's, Los Angeles, 1970; prodn. supr. May Co., Los Angeles, 1970-72; prodn. mgr. Bullocks, Los Angeles, 1972-78; creative dir. Gore Graphics, Los Angeles, 1978-79; v.p. John A. Brown, Oklahoma City, 1979-81; v.p. Harris', San Bernardino, Calif., 1981—. Office: 300 North E St San Bernardino CA 92416

FORMAN, MARILYN, transportation executive, consultant; b. N.Y.C., Sept. 18, 1935; d. Sam Resnick and Henrietta (Zuckerman) Resnick; m. Sanford Forman; children: Suzanne, Jody. BS, Foundling Hosp., 1953. Pediatric nurse N.Y. Hosp., N.Y.C., 1953-55; travel cons. Audro, Gentry, Roses Internat., Los Angeles, 1973-86; transp. exec. FSM Transp. Assoc., Redondo Beach, Calif., 1978—; exec. Alliance Air Freight Co., Long Beach, Calif., 1985—, Marilyn Forman Travel Assocs., Redondo Beach, 1986—, Alliance Travel Services, Redondo Beach, 1987—. Mem. Am. Soc. Travel Agts., Pacific Area Travel Agts. Democrat. Jewish. Home: 496 Palos Verdes Blvd Redondo Beach CA 90277

FORMAN, MAXINE MATTY, retail executive; b. Newark, N.J., Jan. 11, 1943; d. Meyer and Beatrice (Sher) F.; m. Peter George Stone (div.). BA, N.Y.U., 1964. Asst. buyer, exec. trainer Bloomingdale's, N.Y.C., 1964-66; assoc. buyer robes and dayware Macy's, N.Y.C., 1966-67; buyer intimate apparel Adam's Purchasing, N.Y.C., 1967-69, Gus Mayer Stores, N.Y.C., 1969-73; sales rep. merchandising Hoechst Fibers/Maker-Trevira, N.Y.C., 1973-77; merchandiser Russ Togs, Inc., N.Y.C., 1977-87, sr. v.p. merchandising and design, 1987—; guest lectr. F.I.T., N.Y.C., Coca Cola U.S.A., Interstate Bank, Tex., various fashion groups. Mem. Bus. and Profl. Women (exec. com. 1978—), Fashion Group. Home: 249 E 48th St New york NY 10017

FORMAN, PAULA, advertising agency executive. Exec. v.p. Saatchi & Saatchi DFS Compton, N.Y.C. Office: Saatchi & Saatchi DFS Compton 375 Hudson St New York NY 10014 *

FORNELL, MARTHA STEINMETZ, educator, artist; b. Galveston, Tex., Dec. 19, 1920; d. Joseph Duncan and Martha Lillian (McRee) Steinmetz; m. Earl Wesley Fornell, Sept. 20, 1947 (dec. Mar. 1969). B.Mus. cum laude, U. Tex., 1943; postgrad. U. Houston, 1953-56, Lamar U., 1957-60. Music cons., fgn. program editor Voice of America, USIA, N.Y.C., 1944-46; advt. cons. fed. agys., San Antonio, 1946-47; tchr. music secondary schs., Houston, 1953-56; tchr. art Beaumont (Tex.) Ind. Sch. Dist., 1956-79; collages exhibited Galerie Paula Insel, N.Y.C., 1974-84, Ponce, P.R., 1976-79, 82, 84. Recipient Circuit awards Tex. Fine Arts Assn., 1962-64, Invitational awards, 1964-65. Mem. Tex. Fine Arts Assn., Mu Phi Epsilon. Contbr. articles to Am.-German Rev. Address: 2303 Evalon Ave Beaumont TX 77702

FORNEY, MARY ANN, family medicine educator, substance abuse researcher; b. Havrede Grace, Md., Dec. 14, 1948; d. Albert Frank and Frances Anna (Indrychova) Kotras; m. Paul David Forney, June 4, 1971; children: Sean Christopher, Scott David, Jennifer Lynn. BS, Salisbury (Md.) State Coll., 1970; EdM, Augusta (Ga.) Coll., 1980; PhD, U. S.C., 1983. Cert. elem. tchr., Ga. Tchr. pub. schs. Bel Air, Md., 1970-75; grad. asst. Augusta Coll., 1979; instr. Paine Coll., Augusta, 1982-83, acting chair, dir. edn., 1983-84; asst. prof. Med. Coll. Ga., Augusta, 1984—; adj. prof. Ga. So. Coll., Statesboro, 1986—; personnel chmn. Augusta Open Door Kindergarten, 1985-86, also bd. dirs. Contbr. articles on health and substance abuse to med. jours. Area capt. Mothers March of Dimes, Augusta, 1984-85. Research grantee Nat. Inst. on Alcohol Abuse and Alcoholism, 1986—. Mem. Am. Ednl. Research Assn., Ea. Ednl. Research Assn., Northeastern Ednl. Research Assn., Phi Kappa Phi, Phi Delta Kappa. Democrat. Roman Catholic. Home: 123 Stone Mill Dr Martinez GA 30907 Office: Med Coll Ga 1120 15th St Augusta GA 30912

FORNEY, VIRGINIA SUE, educational counselor; b. Little Rock, Sept. 15, 1925; d. Robert Millard and Susan Amanda (Ward) Tate; m. J.D. Mullen, Jr., Oct. 13, 1945 (div. 1966); children—Michael Dunn, Patricia Sue; m. Bill E. Forney, Apr. 29, 1967. Student Tex. State Coll. for Women, 1943-46; B.F.A., U. Okla., 1948; postgrad. Benedictine Heights Coll., Tulsa, 1957-58; M.Teaching Arts, Tulsa U., 1969; postgrad. Okla. State U., intermittently, 1969—. Cert. secondary tchr., sch. counselor, vis. sch. counselor, Okla. With Sta. WNAD, U. Okla., 1947-49; tchr. lang. arts Tulsa Bd. Edn., 1959-73; women's counselor Tulsa YWCA, 1980; vis. sch. counselor Tulsa County Supt. of Schs. Office, 1980—. Mem. budget com. United Way Greater Tulsa, 1980-86, edn. com. Planned Parenthood Greater Tulsa, 1980-86; mem. Tulsa County adv. council Okla. State U., 1983—; chairperson Tulsa Coalition for Parenting Edn., 1983-84; chairperson problems of youth study Tulsa Met. C. of C., 1984-85; mem. gen. bd. March of Dimes Greater Tulsa, 1985. Mem. Am. Assn. for Counseling and Devel., Internat. Assn. Pupil Personnel Workers (state bd. dirs. 1982-86), Okla. Assn. Family Resource Programs (regional v.p. 1982-86, state pres. 1986-87), Program Internat. Ednl. Exchange (community coordinator for Tulsa 1986—), LWV Okla. (chairperson juvenile justice study 1976-77). Democrat. Unitarian. Avocation: piano.

FORONDA, ELENA ISABEL, educator; b. N.Y.C., Jan. 15, 1947; d. Severino Deliso and LaVerne (Ibanez) F.; BS in Music, Hunter Coll., City U. N.Y., 1969, MA in Music Edn., 1971. Tchr. vocal music N.Y.C. Public Sch. System, 1970—; asst. dir. tchr. placement Hunter Coll., City U. N.Y., summers 1971-72; examination asst. N.Y.C. Pub. Sch. System Bd. Examiners, 1987—. Sponsor children in Philippines and El Salvador, World Vision Internat.; del. Asian Am. Women's Caucus, 1977 mem. Hunter Coll. choirs, 1968-69, 71. Dist. winner Nat. Piano Playing Auditions, 1965; recipient N.Y. State permanent cert. Dept. Edn., 1971. Mem. Music Educators Nat. Conf., N.Y. State Sch. Music Assn., Amateur Chamber Players (Vienna, Va.), Internat. Platform Assn. Democrat. Episcopalian.

FORREST, DEBORAH ANN, professional and professional career counselor, clinical researcher; b. Maryville, Tenn., Feb. 24, 1950; d. Lowell Bedford and Mary Frances (Bird) F. Diploma in nursing, St. Mary's Nursing Sch., 1971; BS in Nursing, Ga. State U., 1976; MS in Nursing, Pa. State U., 1978. RN, Ga., Tenn. Staff nurse operating room DeKalb Gen. Hosp., Atlanta, 1971-72; asst. operating room supr. Henrietta Egleston Children Hosp., Atlanta, 1972-76; operating room coordinator Tulane U. Med. Ctr., New Orleans, 1978-79; assoc. operating room dir. Meth. Hosp.-Cen., Memphis, 1979-80; pres. Forrest Cons. Co., Atlanta, 1980—. Contbr. articles to profl. jours. Fellow Am. Soc. for Laser Medicine and Surgery; mem. Am. Mktg. Assn., Assn. of Operating Room Nurses (pres. local chpt. 1984-85), Am. Cancer Soc., Endometriosis Assn., Pa. State Alumni Assn., Am. Bus. Women's Assn., Nat. Assn. Female Execs. Office: Forrest Cons Co PO Box 720025 Atlanta GA 30358-2025

FORREST, MARION PATRICIA, marketing entrepreneur; b. Flushing, N.Y., Oct. 15, 1935; d. William and Beatrice (Giordano) Jones; m. John Fletcher, Jan. 19, 1952 (div. Jan. 1958); 1 child, John; m. Theodore Forrest, April 23, 1966 (div. 1970); children: Diane. Student, Pierce Jr. Coll., 1967-69. Model various TV and photo print, San Diego, 1961-62; mktg. Beverly Hills, Calif., 1972-74; real estate sales Jack Heller Realty, Beverly Hills, Calif., 1977-81; owner, pres. The Beverly Hills Estate, 1982-84; owner Forrest Prodns., Beverly Hills, 1982-84. Producer: film The Butterfly Garden, 1972, Culturally Speaking, 1986; originator, pub. audio tapes Culturally Speaking. Vol. social worker for Los Angeles homeless. Mem. Publisher's Mktg. Assn. Home: 9925 Robbins #5 Beverly Hills CA 90212

FORREST, NOVA EARLINE, analyst, secretary; b. McMinnville, Tenn., Aug. 9, 1949; d. Earl James Rigsby and Mamie Noveline (Snipes) Hankins; m. Ralph Arvine Smith Jr., Dec. 9, 1967 (div. 1980); children: Mary Louise Smith, Ralph Arvine Smith III, Stuart Franklin Smith; m. Thomas Eugene Forrest, Aug. 14, 1982. Grad. high sch., Indpls. Acctg. clk., sec. Ind. Bell Telephone Co., Indpls., 1969-71; sec. Diversified Mgmt. Corp., Indpls., 1972-73; personnel staff, credit bookkeeper, sec. Peachtree Fabrics, Inc., Indpls., 1975-82, computer operator, corp. sec., 1982; exec. sec. sales and mktg. Health Systems Alternatives, San Pedro, Calif., 1983, Processing Mgmt. Systems, Phoenix, 1983-85; exec. sec. fin., analyst Mercy Care Plan, Phoenix, 1985—. Sunday sch. tchr. North Hills Ch. of God, Phoenix, 1987—. Mem. Nat. Assn. Female Execs. Republican. Mem. Ch. of God.

FORREST, VICTORIA KAUFMAN, talent and management consultant, photojournalist; b. N.Y.C., Mar. 23, 1944; d. Michael David and Elizabeth Sarah (Levy) Kaufman; m. David Mortimer Forrest, Apr. 30, 1936; 1 child, Heather Elizabeth. BS, 1964. Writer, freelance photographer Atlanta, 1964-68; talent and mgmt. cons. Forrest and Co., Dunwoody, Ga., 1968—. Columnist, photojournalist Forsyth Daily News, Tenn Free Press, Dean Image, 1987—. Bd. dirs. scholarship fund com. Shallowford Hosp., Dunwoody, 1982-85. Republica. Jewish. Home: 2396 Ledgewood Dr Dunwoody GA 30338

FORREST, VIRGINIA OGDEN RANSON, civic leader; b. Balt., June 24, 1896; d. Henry Warfield and Nannie Deaver (Cooper) Ranson; ed. Calvert Sch., Arundell Sch.; m. Frederick Beasley Williamson, Jr., July 4, 1917 (dec. July 1957); children: Virginia Williamson Hutton, Beverley Williamson Magill, Frederick Beasley Williamson III; m. 2d, Wilbur Studley Forrest, Apr. 20, 1960 (dec. Mar. 1977). Dir., Goodall Rubber Co., hon. dir., 1973—. Pres. Jr. League, Elizabeth, N.J., 1924-26, hon. mem., 1944; mem. hostess com. Franklin Inst., Phila., 1941; mem. N.J. Recreation Soc., Elizabeth, 1934-35, rep. N.J. to nat. conv., Chgo., 1935; chmn. New Hope (Pa.) chpt. A.R.C., 1939-43, head flood disaster chpt., 1955, chmn. home service, 1943-45; hon. v.p. New Hope Art Assocs., 1940; mem. adv. com. Jonathan Dickinson State Park, Martin County, Fla., 1970—; organizer adviser Bucks County Conservation Alliance, Martin County Conservation Alliance, 1966-74; bd. dirs. Honey Hollow Watershed Assn., 1969—, Soc. Prevention Cruelty Children Family Welfare Bd., Elizabeth, 1928, YWCA, Elizabeth, 1928, Abington (Pa.) Meml. Hosp. Women's Bd., 1941, Vis. Nurse Assn., New Hope, 1941-49; bd. dirs., 2d v.p. Garden Club, Stuart, Fla., 1951-60; trustee Egnolf Day Nursery, Elizabeth, 1923-36; trustee Holmquist Sch. for Girls, New Hope, Martin County Pub. Library, Stuart, 1958-61; bd. dirs. Free Pub. Library Elizabeth, 1926-39, sec., 1927-36; bd. dirs. Keep Fla. Beautiful Com.; mem. founders bd. Transylvania U., Lexington, Ky., 1979. Recipient award Fla. Fedn. Garden Clubs, 1961, Gov.'s gold medal conservation award (1st woman recipient), 1961, Gov. Kirk's Conservation award, 1970, conservation award U.S. Dept. Interior, 1979, Women of Achievement Del. Valley Girl Scouts, 1987; honoree Martin County Audubon Soc., 1976; named hon. Ky. Col., 1978. Mem. Fla. (recipient award 1960, chmn. Bald Eagle project 1959—, mem. wild life com., 1959—, v.p. 1962-69, hon. v.p. 1970—), Martin County (dir. 1957-78, dir. emeritus, 1978—, chmn. exec. com. 1973-74), Bucks County (dir., adviser, citation for conservation, 1972) Audubon socs., New Hope Hist. Soc. (dir. 1959-60, 67—), Fla. Fedn. Garden Clubs (hon. life), Colonial Dames N.J., Woman Fly Fishers Am. Clubs: Mt. Vernon (Balt.); Hartwood (Monticello, N.Y.); Martin County Anglers (dir. 1966—); L.I. (Eastport, N.Y.). Home: Pennswood Village D105 Newtown PA 18940

FORRESTER, LESLEY (PHYLLIS), college program administrator; b. Toronto, Can., Dec. 27, 1945; d. Victor Graham and Phyllis Isabel (Hamilton) Robb; m. Stephen Wells Forrester, Aug. 11, 1967 (div. 1978). Hon. BA in Anthropology, U. Toronto, 1967, MSW, 1971. Social worker Sir James Whitney Sch., Belleville, Ont., 1971-73, Trenton (Ont.) Family and Children's Ctr., 1973-74; coordinator, social worker Quinte Alt. Sch., Belleville, 1976-78; human relations tchr. Loyalist Coll., Belleville, 1980-81, mgr. breakthrough program, 1986, equal opportunity advisor, 1983-87; community worker Otherways, Inc., Belleville, 1978-81; pvt. practice social work Belleville 1978-81; vice-chairperson, liason com. Save the Youth Now Group, Millhaven Penitentiary, Belleville, 1979-81; mem. Hastings County Counsellors Assn., Belleville, 1976-78. V.p., founding mem. Human Ecology Found., Quinte, 1987; founding mem. Women's Network, Belleville, 1978, Big Brothers and Sisters, Trenton, 1978, bd. dirs., 1977-79; treas. Planned Parenthood, Belleville, 1971-76. Mem. Colls. Adv. Com. on Affirmative Action (Eastern region rep. 1987). Home: 10 Patterson St Apt 11, Belleville CAN K8N 1S9 Office: Loyalist Coll, PO Box 4200, Wallbridge-Loyalist Rd, Belleville CAN K8N 5B9

FORRESTER, VICTORIA WADSWORTH, librarian, author-illustrator; b. Pasadena, Calif., Mar. 18, 1940; d. Victor and Leslie (Wadsworth) Parkin; m. Alan Harry Forrester, June 14, 1960; 1 child, Chad. BA, UCLA, 1961, MLS, 1963, MA, 1970. Reference librarian Santa Monica (Calif.) Library, 1963-66, children's librarian, 1969-71; head librarian St. Mark's Sch., San Rafael, Calif., 1980—; author-illustrator; Bears and Theirs, 1982, Oddward, 1982, The Touch Said Hello, 1982, The Magnificent Moo, 1983, Words to Keep Against the Night, 1983, A Latch Against the Wind, 1985; author: The Candlemaker and other Tales, 1984, Poor Gabriella, 1986; contbr. More Surprises, 1987. Home: One Owlswood Dr Larkspur CA 94939

FORST, JUDITH DORIS, mezzo soprano; b. New Westminster, B.C., Can., Nov. 7, 1943; d. Gordon Stanley and Euna Jessie (Thompson) Lumb; m. Graham Nicol Forst, May 30, 1964; children: Noel Graham, Paula Judith. Mus.B., U. B.C., Vancouver, 1965. featured lectr. U. B.C., U. Mont. Debut with Seattle Opera Co., 1967; debut with Met. Opera, 1968-74, guest artist, 1977; guest artist appearances throughout U.S. including San Francisco, New Orleans, Ft. Worth, Santa Fe and Seattle opera cos., N.Y.C. Opera, Opera Soc. Washington, Can. Opera Co., Toronto, Ont., Miami Opera Co., Vancouver Opera Assn., Edmonton Opera Assn., Winnipeg Opera Assn., Calgary Opera Assn., Montreal Symphony, Vancouver Symphony., Balt. Opera Co., Nat. Arts Ctr., Ottawa, Ont., Can., appeared in performance for Queen Elizabeth, Vancouver, 1983; European debut Orchestre de la Radio-Diffusion Française, Paris, 1985, Bayersiche Staatsoper, Munich, 1987. Named Canadian Woman of Year, 1978; named Walter and Ida Olsen Young Am. Artist of Yr. Miami Opera Assn., 1980; Disting. Alumnus award U. B.C., 1986. Mem. Actors Equity, Am. Guild Musical Artists, Assn. Canadian TV Radio Artists, Vancouver Symphony Soc. (bd. dirs.). Office: care Columbia Artists Mgmt 165 W 57th St New York NY 10019

FORSYTHE, MARY MACCORNACK, state legislator; b. Whitehall, Wis., May 23, 1920; d. Robert Lee and Gladys Fry MacCornack; B.Mus., St. Olaf Coll., 1942; m. Robert A. Forsythe, July 18, 1942; children—Robert A., Polly Forsythe Johnson, Jean Forsythe Peterson, Ann Forsythe Smith, Joan. Tchr., Viroqua, Wis., 1942-43, Whitehall, Wis., 1944-46; mem. Minn. Ho. of Reps., St. Paul, 1972—, chmn. appropriations com., 1985-86. Mem. Guthrie Theater Found., 1973-80; mem. Minn. Commn. on Econ. Status of Women, 1976-79, Minn. News Council, 1979-86; trustee Fairview Riverside Hosp., 1980-86, Fairview-Southdale Hosp., 1986—; mem. exec. com. Seat Belt Coalition, Gov.'s Residence Adv. Task Force, Fairview Corp. Bd.; mem. Gov.'s Adv. Task Force on Women and Corrections, 1979-87. Recipient Disting. Alumna award St. Olaf Coll., 1974; Dr. I. Michael Kuhn award Nat. Hemophilia Found., 1978; Outstanding Woman of Edina Bicentennial award, 1978; Community Service award Edina Optimists, 1982. Mem. Nat. Conf. State Legislators (vice chmn. human resources com. 1977-78). Republican. Lutheran. Home: 5308 Brookview Ave Edina MN 55424 Office: State Office Bldg Saint Paul MN 55155

FORSYTHE, PATRICIA HAYS, foundation executive; b. Curtis, Ark.; d. John Chambers and Flora Jane (Eby) Hays; m. Kurt G. Pahl, Dec. 15, 1962 (div. Dec. 1980); children: Thomas Walter, Susan Clara; m. Robert E. Forsythe, June 20, 1981; 1 child, Nathaniel Ryan. BA, Calif. State U., Los Angeles, 1974; MSLS, U. So. Calif., 1976. Asst. to dir. devel. office The Assocs., Calif. Inst. Tech., Pasadena, 1978-81; exec. dir. Iowa City Pub. Library Found., 1982—. Mem. LWV (editor 1985-87), Eastern Iowa Nat. Soc. for Fund Raising Execs. (pres. 1988), Am. Library Assn., Iowa City C. of C. Congregationalist. Club: Hancher Guild (Iowa City) (audience devel. 1981-85, pres. 1985-86). Home: 1806 E Court St Iowa City IA 52240 Office: Iowa City Pub Library Found 123 S Linn Iowa City IA 52240

FORT, CATHERINE FOARD, organizational development consultant; b. Orange, N.J., July 29, 1927; d. Henry Gilbert Foard and Catherine (Williams) Blackwell;m. James Frazier Fort, Sept. 30, 1950; children: James Frazier Jr., Keith Douglas, Catherine Williams Johnston. Student, St. Mary's Jr. Coll., 1944-45, U. Ga., 1945-47; BGS, George Washington U., 1978; MA in Applied Behavioral Sci., Whitworth Coll., 1983. Workshop instr. George Washington U., Washington, 1974-80; ind. cons. nationwide, 1970—; liason staff Intermet Sem., Washington, 1973-77; organizational cons. Congressional Clearinghouse on the Future, Washington, 1978-81; dir. Parish Intern Program Episcopal Diocese of Washington, 1978-82; coordinator Profl. Devel. Program Mid-Atlantic Assn. for Tng. and Consulting, Washington, 1976—, network cons., 1970—; network cons. The Alban Inst., Inc., Washington, 1977—, also bd. dirs., 1987—. Contbr. articles to various newsletters and periodicals, 1978—. Pres., League of Women Voters, Alexandria, Va., 1955-56; v.p., PTA of George Mason Sch., Alexandria, Va., 1962-63; del., Dem. State Conv. Lee Dist., Fairfax County, Va., 1981, 88; sr. warden, Immanuel-Episc.-Ch.-on-the-Hill, Alexandria, Va., 1984-85; mem. steering com., Assn. for Creative Change within Religious and Social Systems 1977-80, profl. devel. recognition com., 1980-84, recipient profl. recognition, 1978. Mem. Cert. Cons. Internat. (cert. 1985, profl. reviewer), Soc. Mayflower Descendants (N.C.). Home and Office: 5950 Wilton Road Alexandria VA 22310

FORT, MILDRED ANN, public health agency administrator; b. St. Louis, Jan. 18, 1951; d. Kermit and Helen Marie (Hughes) F. Student, So. Ill. U., 1969-72; AS in Gen. Sci., State Community Coll., East St. Louis, Ill., 1972; BA in Biol. Sci., Sangamon State U., Springfield, Ill., 1974, MA in Health Service Adminstrn., 1978. Research intern Ill. Dept. Pub. Health, Springfield, 1976-78, pub. health rep., 1978; project area coordinator Ill. Dept. Pub. Health, Edwardsville, 1979-85, also regional cons., 1983-85; program coordinator Ill. Dept. Pub. Health, Springfield, 1985—, Research in Human Devel., Springfield, 1978; mem. adv. bd. Madison (Ill.) County Urban League Family Planning, 1980—, St. Louis Lead Poisoning Prevention Council, 1980-86; cons. Infant Mortality Reduction Initiative, East St. Louis, 1986—, Metro-East Health Care Rights Coalition, East St. Louis, 1986—. Chairperson adminstrv. council Aldersgate Community United Meth. Ch., East St Louis, 1985—; bd. dirs. United Meth. Children's Home, Mt. Vernon, Ill., 1986—, Ethnic Minority Local Ch., Mt. Vernon, 1984—. Mem. Am. Pub. Health Assn., Ill. Pub. Health Assn., Ill. Assn. Maternal and Child Health.

FORTI, CORINNE ANN, corporate communications executive; b. N.Y.C., July 26, 1941; d. Wilbur Walter and Sylvia Joan (Charap) Bastian; B.A., CUNY, 1963; m. Joseph Donald Forti, Aug. 18, 1962 (dec.); 1 dau., Raina. Adminstrv. asst. Ednl. Broadcasting Corp., 1963-65; adminstrv. asst. W.R. Grace & Co., N.Y.C., 1965-67, pub. relations rep., 1967-70, mgr. info. services, 1970-79, dir. info. services, 1980-86, dir. info. and advt., 1986-87; pres. Bastian-Forti Communications, 1988—; lectr. photography and graphics Am. Mgmt. Assn. Bd. dirs. YM/YWCA Day Care, Inc. Named to Acad. Women Achievers, YWCA, 1979; recipient citation award in communications Nat. Council of Women, 1979. Mem. Am. Women in Radio and TV, Chem. Mfrs. Assn., Am. Mgmt. Assn., Women Execs. in Pub. Relations (bd. dirs.). Republican. Roman Catholic. Home: 1246 Calle Yucca Thousand Oaks CA 91360

FORTIN, ANITA BUCSAY, sales professional; b. Allentown, Pa., Sept. 19, 1960; d. Zoltan Andrew and Viola Katherine (Durko) Bucsay; m. Brian Mark Fortin, June 16, 1984. BSChemE, U. Lowell, 1983. Sales engr. Alpha Industries, Woburn, Mass., 1983-84; sales rep. Wright Line, Inc., Worcester, Mass., 1984, account rep., 1985, design specialist, 1986, account mgr., 1987-88, sr. account mgr., 1988; owner, pres. SkinFitness Ltd., Hudson, Mass., 1987—. Mem. Nat. Assn. Female Execs. Home: 425 Main St #4A Hudson MA 01749

FORTIN, DENISE ANNE, personnel assistant; b. Pawtucket, R.I., June 22, 1952; d. Raymond Lawrence and Eunice Virginia (Halde) F. Gen. office clk. Attleboro Dye and Finishing, Seekonk, Mass., 1968-70; accounts receivalbe clk. Adams Drug, Pawtucket, 1970-71; gen. account clk. Kaufman and Miller, Pawtucket, 1971-74; accounts receivable, payroll clk. Tower Iron Works, Seekonk, 1974-75, exec. sec., 1975-78; bookkeeper Atlas Boiler Works, East Providence, R.I., 1978-80; personnel sec. Hersey Products, Dedham, Mass., 1980-84; personnel asst. Butler Automatic, Inc., Canton, Mass., 1984-88, Scandinavian Design Corp. Hdqrs., Canton, Mass., 1988—. Mem. Dem. Town Com., Seekonk, 1971; trustee Seekonk Libraries, 1971. Roman Catholic. Home: 1300 Worcester Rd Framingham MA 01701 Office: Scandinavian Design Corp Hdqrs Human Resources Dept Canton MA 02021

FORTUNE, JANET ELLIS, banker; b. Toledo, Ohio, July 16, 1945; d. Robert Michael and Ruth (Gray) Ellis; m. Philip L. Fortune, June 10, 1967; children: Molly Lynne, Philip L. BEd, Ohio U., 1966; JD, Emory U., 1980. Bar: Ga. 1981. Tchr. Mich. Pub. Schs., Bedford, 1966-70; v.p., trust officer First Nat. Bank of Atlanta, 1981—. Mem. Ga. Bar Assn., Ga. Bankers Assn. (legis. com. 1986-87). Presbyterian. Office: First Nat Bank of Atlanta 2 Peachtree St Atlanta GA 30302

FORWARD, DOROTHY ELIZABETH, legal assistant; b. Medford, Mass., Oct. 12, 1919; d. Roy Clifford and Julia (Lane) Hurd; student UCLA, 1964; m. Winston W. Forward, Sept. 29, 1942. Sec. nat. dir. fund raising ARC, Washington, 1943-46; legal sec. William W. Waters, Esq., Los Angeles, 1953-56; office mgr. Winston W. Forward, Ins. Adjuster, Arcadia, Calif., 1956-64; legal asst. John M. Podlech, Esq., Pasadena, 1964-79; dir. Calif. Probate Insts., Arcadia, 1970—; ind. probate legal asst., 1979—; condr. workshops in probate procedures, 1969—. Recipient ARC Meritorious Service award, 1945; named Legal Sec. of Yr., Pasadena Legal Secs. Assn., 1974, 75, 77; Freedom Through Edn. award, Pasadena Legal Secs. Assn., 1975. Mem. Nat. Assn. Legal Secs., Legal Secs. Inc., Calif. Legal Secs. Assn. (parliamentarian 1982-84), Pasadena Legal Secs. Assn. (pres. 1976-78), Los Angeles County Forum of Legal Secs. (chmn. 1978-80), Nat. Assn. Legal Assts. (charter). Contbg. author: Calif. Legal Secretary's Handbook, 1984, 85. Office: PO Box 311 Arcadia CA 91006

FOSGATE HEGGLI, JULIE DENISE, marketing executive; b. El Paso, Tex., Feb. 17, 1954; d. Orville Edward and Patricia (Ward) Fosgate; m. Bjarne Heggli, June 20, 1980; children: Elise Mai, Kristin April. BA in Broadcasting, U. So. Calif., 1976, MA in Journalism, 1978. On-bd. editor Royal Viking Line, San Francisco, 1978-80; editor Stentor, Trondheim, Norway, 1981; staff Grunion Gazette, Long Beach, Calif., 1981; news editor Nine Network Australia, Los Angeles, 1981-82; editor South Coast Metro News, Costa Mesa, Calif., 1981-82; v.p. The Newport Group, Newport Beach, Calif., 1982-85; exec. editor Orange County This Month, Newport Beach, 1985; exec. dir. mktg. Gen. Group Cos., Harbor City, Calif., 1985-87; sr. v.p. mktg. Automax Corp., Los Angeles, 1987—. Mem. Nat. Assn. Female Execs., Phi Beta Kappa. Home: 225 Glendora Ave Long Beach CA 90803 Office: Automax Corp 11040 Santa Monica Blvd Los Angeles CA 90025

FOSHAY, MAXINE VALENTINE SHOTTLAND, civic worker, public relations executive; b. N.Y.C., Feb. 14, 1921; d. Maximillian Stanford and Violet Gertrude (Turner) Shottland; m. Robert Lethbridge Foshay, Mar. 16, 1956. B.A., Royal Acad. Dramatic Arts (London), 1943. Field rep. Am. Cancer Soc., N.Y.C., 1967-68; dir. fund raising and pub. relations Preventive Medicine Inst., Strang Clinic 1969-71; dir. fund raising and pub. relations Fedn. Handicapped, N.Y.C., 1971-72; exec. dir. Irvington House, 1972-73; chmn. group affiliates Meml. Sloan Kettering, 1960-66; v.p. Meml. Sloan Kettering Soc., 1966-67; vol. Meml. Sloan Kettering Cancer Soc., 1956-77; prin. Maxine V. Foshay and Assocs., 1977—; bd. dirs. Elder Craftsman, N.Y.C.; dir. devel. Children's Asthmatic Found. N.Y. Mem. Daus. Brit. Empire State N.Y. (1st v.p. 1986-87, statewide pres. 1987-88, Medal Brit. Empire Her Majesty's Honours List 1987).

FOSLER, GAIL D., economist, government official; b. Los Angeles Dec. 7, 1947; d. Richard E. and Helen Elizabeth (O'Gorman) Deschner. A.B. in Econs. U. So. Calif., 1969; M.B.A. in Fin., NYU, 1972. Research analyst Chgo. Dept. Human Resources, 1970-72; research assoc. I.C.F., Inc., 1972-74; asst. v.p., economist Manufacturers Hanover, 1974-78; chief economist Senate Budget Com., Washington, 1981—, dir. and chief economist Sen. Budget Com., 1986—. Address: Senate Budget Com SD-633 Washington DC 20510

FOSNOT, CATHERINE TWOMEY, education educator; b. Norwich, Conn., Aug. 22, 1947; d. Gerald Francis and Eileen (Rathbun) Twomey; m. John Douglas Fosnot, June 7, 1969 (div. 1982); children: Damien, Joshua. Tchr. Roscoe (N.Y.) Cen., 1969-70, Harrison Elem., Hamilton, Ohio, 1970-71, Village South Elem., Centerville, 1973-73; tchr., administr. Albany (N.Y.) Area Open Sch., 1973-75; instr. dept. edn. Van den Berg Learning Ctr. SUNY, New Paltz, 1975-78; head tchr. dept. early childhood edn. univ. lab. day sch. U. Mass., Amherst, 1978-79, dir. student tng. sch. edn., 1979-83; asst. prof. dept. edn. So. Conn. State U., New Haven, 1983—; Cons. Summermath ELM project, Mt. Holyoke Coll., 1986—, Larchmont (N.Y.) Schs., 1987, Hyde Park (N.Y.) Elem. Schs., 1985—, Madison (Conn.) Pub. Schs., 1984—, Sch. Dists. Lawrence, New Brunswick, So. Brunswick, West Windsor-Plainsboro, N.J., 1978, Flying Goose Nursery, Peekskill, NY., 1978, Albany Area Open Sch., 1976. Editor: The Constructivist, 1985—. Ednl. Communications and Tech./Eric Young Scholar, 1984. Mem. Nat. Assn. for the Edn. Young Children, Jean Plaget Soc. (reviewer 12th annual symposium 1982), Assn. for Constructivist Teaching (pres. 1985—), Assn. Ednl. Communications and Tech. (reviewer 1987, bd. dirs. Research and Theory Div., reviewer of Young Researcher award, 1986,87). Home: Old Post Rd Worthington MA 01098 Office: So Conn U Dept Edn 148 Davis Hall New Haven CT 06515

FOSSELL, JUDITH ANN, educator; b. Eldora, Iowa, June 1, 1942; d. Harold Martin and Julia Ann (Wasson) Dubberke; m. Leon Robert Fossell, July 30, 1977. BA, U. North Iowa, 1960, MA, 1988; postgrad., Drake U., 1973-76. Tchr. Waterloo Community Schs., Iowa, 1964—; acting prin. Irving Elem. Sch., 1988—, Roosevelt Elem Sch., Waterloo, 1985. Commr. Waterloo Cablevision Commn., 1982 ; bd. dirs., pres. Big Brother/Big Sister, Black Hawk County, Iowa, 1978-84; bd. dirs. ISEA Credit Union, 1982-86, Area 7 M.S. League, 1974-76; steering com. candidates Dem. Party, Black Hawk County, 1980-86; task force mem. F.I.N.E. Research ad hoc com., Iowa, 1986; pres. Hawkeye UniServ Unit, Waterloo, 1975-76. Named Young Educator of Yr., Waterloo, 1973; Charles F. Martin award, Iowa State Edn. Assn., 1980. Mem. Iowa Edn. Assn. (dir.), NEA, Waterloo Edn. Assn. (pres. and bd.), Grant PTA, Urban Edn. Assn. (pres. 1973-74). Democrat. Lutheran. Office: Waterloo Community Schs 1223 Mobile St Waterloo IA 50103

FOSTER, ALICIA JOHNSON, accountant; b. Balt., Oct. 29, 1939; d. Lynnwood and Rosie (Mickey) Johnson; m. Harry Young, 1959 (div. 1968); children: Kirk, Dina Marie, Michael; m. Ronald Foster, Feb. 1, 1969 (div. Dec. 1978). BS in Acctg., Morgan State U., 1978; MS in Fin., U. Balt., 1981. CPA, Md. Acct. Morgan State U., Balt., 1978-79, instr., 1979-85; auditor Alexander Grant & Co., CPA, Balt., 1979-81, audit sr., 1981-82; audit mgr. Taylor, Williams & Assocs., CPA, Balt., 1982-83; audit ptnr. Abrams, Foster, Nole & Williams, CPA, Balt., 1983—; treas. bd. dirs. N. Cen. Balt. Health Corp., Balt., 1981-85; presenter various seminars. Nat. Assn. Black Accts. (treas. 1985-87), Md. Assn. CPA'a (vol. services com. 1982-84, small bus. com. 1986—), Greater Balt. Com. Democrat. Baptist. Home: 3304 Kenjac Rd Baltimore MD 21207 Office: Abrams Foster Nole & Williams Village of Cross Keys The Quadrangle Suite 272B Baltimore MD 21210

FOSTER, BARBARA ANNE, motion picture producer, screenplay writer; b. Cin., Jan. 22, 1955; d. Walter Norman and Rhea Mae (Baumann) F. BS in Communication Arts, Xavier U., Cin., 1977. With positive assembly MGM Labs, Los Angeles, 1977; edit. asst. Burbank (Calif.) Editorial, 1978; film insp. Four Star Internat., Beverly Hills, Calif., 1979-80; owner Horizan Unlimited Prodn. Co., Burbank, Calif., 1980; pres. Sunburst Pictures Inc., Los Angeles, 1981—. Producer film Lady Lightning, 1988. Mem. Antique Auto Club Am., Plymouth 4th Cylinder Club.

FOSTER, BETTY LOUISE, educator; b. Lincoln, Nebr., Nov. 12, 1943; d. Burt Willis and Elizabeth Julia Hunt. B.S. in Elem. Edn., U. Nebr., 1965, postgrad. in Elem. Edn. Reading; postgrad. in Elem. Edn. and Reading, Kearney State Coll., endorsement in teaching reading; m. Gary A. Foster; children: Ann Louise, Geofrey Algot; foster children: Matt Urbauer, Don Simmons, Ronda Real. Tchr. reading departmentalized grades 5-6 South Sioux City (Nebr.) Schs., 1967-69, supplemental reading tchr. Title I, 1970-71; supplemental reading tchr. Title I Grand Island (Nebr.) Schs., 1971—. Organizer, tchr. Head Start in South Sioux City Community Center and Chs., 1968-69; active Girl Scouts U.S.A., 1970—; v.p. Neighborhood Taskforce, Inc., 1980-82; pres. S. Locust/Barr Neighborhood Assn., 1980-81; mem. Mayor's Taskforce for Tornado Recovery, 1980-81; v.p. YWCA Grand Island, 1983; organizer Grand Island Women's Network, 1984; local rep., hodt family North Atlantic Cultural Exchange League, 1987, Grand Island Internat. Visitors Program, 1987; coach elem. level Olympics of the Mind, 1986-88, Oddyessy of the Mind, 1987-88. Mem. Nat., Nebr., Grand Island Edn. Assns., Internat. (sec. Central Council 1974—), Nebr., State reading assns., PTA of Children with Learning Disabilities, AAUW (pres. Grand Island br. 1979-80, state v.p. 1981-82, state topic chmn. 1980-81), Nebr. Coalition of Women, LWV, Assn. of Nebr. Art Clubs (chmn. state conv. 1987, sec. 1987—), Assn. of Nebr. (chmn. of conv. 1987), Grand Island Art Club (pres. 1985-86), Alpha Delta Kappa, Sigma Kappa. Developed self correcting games. Certified in elementary edn., kindergarten-6th grade, Nebr., Iowa; specialist in diagnosis and remediation of reading problems with learning disabilities problems, gifted children; cert. foster home, Nebr. Home: 1311 S Lincoln St Grand Island NE 68801 Office: 1314 W 7th St Grand Island NE 68801

FOSTER, CAROLINE ROBINSON, personnel director; b. Mobile, Ala., Oct. 2, 1937; s. Lucius Waite and Vassar Austill (Bowling) Robinson; m. Edward Eugene Foster, May 23, 1964; children—Robin Caroline, Edward Eugene. Student, Troy State U., 1956-57; B.S. in Bus. Adminstrn., U. S. Ala., 1983. Sec., Pacific Fin. Corp., Yuma, Ariz., 1957-58; sec. Univ. Hosp., Mobile, 1962-64; sec. to dir., asst. dir. social service, 1966-68; asst. to pres., dir. personnal Goodwill Industries, Inc., Mobile, 1968-79; exec. asst. Mobile County Commr. Jeff Mims, Mobile County Commn., 1979; regional recruitor ARC Blood Service, Ga., Fla. and Ala., 1979; regional personnel mgr. Retail Consumer Services, Inc./Citicorp., 1980; job developer U. South Ala. Work Search Project, 1980—; exec. sec., asst. to minister Chicksasw United Methodist Ch., 1983—; chmn. program com. Personnel and Indsl. Relations Conf., Ala. Continuing Edn., 1977, conf. chmn., 1978; speaker in field. Mem. exec. com. Mobile County Republicans; regional rep. ARC, 1979; area rep. Am. Intercultrual Student Exchange; team leader bus. div. United Fund, 1981; area rep. Am. Scandinavian Student Exchange Program, 1980-81. Mem. Internat. Mgmt. Council (del. to USSR, Council-YMCA mgr. exchange program, named Key Person 1977), Am. Soc. Personnel Adminstrs. (dist. dir. 1979-80, mem. leadership tng. com. 1979-80, mem. coll. relations com. 1981—, mem. vocat. edn. com. 1983-84), Women in Mgmt., Mobile Personnel Assn. (bd. dirs. 1972-74, sec.-treas. 1975-76, v.p. 1976-77, pres. 1977-78). Baptist. Club: Gayfers Career Women. Home: 5778 Honor St Mobile AL 36608

FOSTER, CATHERINE RIERSON, metal components manufacturing company executive; b. Balt., Mar. 14, 1935; d. William Harman and Ella Fredericka (Magsamen) Rierson; m. Morgan Lawrence Foster, Nov. 17, 1957; children: Diana Kay, Susan Ann, Morgan Lawrence, Heather Lynne. Student Balt. City Coll., 1955, Johns Hopkins U., 1956-57, Glendale Coll., 1962-63. Sec., Martin Co., Balt., 1956-57, adminstrv. sec., 1957-58; v.p., corp. sec. Fostermation, Inc., Meadville, Pa., 1971—, also dir.; mem. adv. com. Vocat./Tech. Sch., Meadville, 1982-86. Pres. La Crescents, La Crescenta, Calif., 1962; active City Hosp. Aux., Meadville, 1969-86; active Republican Women's Workshop, Glendale, Calif., 1966-68, Com. to Elect Ronald Reagan, Glendale, 1967; bd. dirs. YMCA, Meadville, 1988—, also chmn. fin. com., 1988—. Mem. Nat. Assn. Female Execs., Daus. Am. Revolution. Lutheran. Lodge: Order Eastern Star. Avocations: genealogy, European history, bridge. Home: 1121 Lakemont Dr Meadville PA 16335 Office: Fostermation Inc 200 Valleyview Dr Meadville PA 16335

FOSTER, EILEEN ANNETTE, TV producer; b. La Chappelle, St. Mesmin, Loiret, France, Dec. 9, 1962; came to U.S., 1964; d. James Kinch III and Barbara Nan (Yarrington) F. Student, Houston Bapt. U., Houston Community Coll., 1985. Receptionist Sta. KPKC-TV, Houston, 1982, intern news, 1982-83, producer TV news, 1982—, assoc. news producer, 1983-85, producer weekly sports program, 1984-85, producer news conf., 1984—, reporter community affairs program, 1984, field producer live remotes; guest lectr. Rafael Landivar U., Guatemala City, 1986-87. Movie extra Urban Cowboy, 1979. Tutor Adult Illiteracy Program Houston Community Coll., 1986. Mem. Soc. Profl. Journalists, Nat. Assn. Female Execs., Amnesty Internat. Office: Sta KPRC-TV 8181 SW Freeway Houston TX 77074

FOSTER, ELAINE ELIZABETH, art educator; b. Lawrence, Mass., Jan. 13, 1934; d. Ernest Webster and Elizabeth Josephine (Dubuc) F. Cert., Sch. of the Worcester Art Mus., 1955; BA, Clark U., 1957, MA, 1961; profl. diploma, Columbia U., 1965, EdD, 1970. Supr. art Auburn (Mass.) Elem. Schs., 1957-59; tchr. art Auburn Pub. Jr. High Sch., 1959-61, Auburn Pub. High Sch., 1961-65; from asst. prof. to prof. art Jersey City State Coll., 1966—. Author: Collage Film Guide, Crayon Film Guide, 1966, A Great School of Fine Arts in N.Y.C.: A Study of the Development of Art at Columbia University (1860-1914), 1970; lectr. The Brain and Art, 1975—; group shows include 25 exhbns. in N.E. Mem. Nat. Art Edn. Assn., Univ. Council for Art Edn. (pres. 1980-82), Am. Assn. Univ. Profs. (pres. local chpt. 1978-80), Soc. N.Am. Goldsmiths, Am. Craft Council, Dromenon/The Possible Soc. in N.Y. Avc.

FOSTER, FERN ALLEN (MERONEY), sex counselor, administrator, consultant; b. Ranger, Tex., Sept. 19, 1921; d. Jess and Grace (Bradley) Meroney; m. Austin Foster; children—Gayanne, Stuart, Ann, William, David. A.A., Ranger Coll., 1941; B.A., Newport U., 1981. Cert. social worker, Tex. Sex counselor Marriage Counseling Assocs., Fort Worth, 1964-69, The Edna Gladney Home, Fort Worth, 1971-83; psychotherapist VA Hosp. and Clinic, New Orleans, 1969-71; sex counselor Fort Worth Counseling Ctr., 1971-84, dir., 1984—; fellow in human sexuality Tex. Sch. of Profl. Psychology, Fort Worth, 1985—; cons. human sexuality Blackwell Counseling Ctr., Fort Worth, 1985—. Mem. Am. Assn. Sex Educators, Counselors and Therapists (cert.), Sex Info. and Edn. Council of U.S., Nat. Council on Adoption, Am. Assn. Counseling and Devel., Am. Mental Health Counselors Assn. Club: Century II (Fort Worth). Home: 166 Victorian Dr Fort Worth TX 76134 Office: Fort Worth Counseling Ctr PO Box 6242 Fort Worth TX 76115

FOSTER, FLORENCE PEREY, educational administrator; b. Hollis, N.Y., Jan. 26, 1924; d. John Francis and Florence Louise (Spilbor) Perey; B.S. in Foods and Nutrition, Beaver Coll., 1946; M.A. in Early Childhood Edn., Kean Coll. N.J., 1964; postgrad. Bank Street Coll. Edn., 1965, Rider Coll., 1968, Glassboro State Coll., 1972, Trenton State Coll., 1979; m. Gerald R. Foster, July 27, 1943; 1 son, Brian Gerald. Social worker Dept. Public Welfare, Long Island, N.Y., 1947-48; nutritionist Beechnut Co., N.Y.C., 1948-49; head tchr. Wesley Hall, Westfield, N.J., 1958-62; dir. Bound Brook (N.J.) Coop., 1962-63; head tchr. Pickwick Nursery East Orange, N.J., 1963-64; edn. dir. Child Service Assn., Newark, 1964-66; asst. in early childhood N.J. State Dept. Edn., Trenton, 1966-68, coordinator fed. early children programs, 1968-69, dir. early childhood and state follow through coordinator, 1969-70, dir. early childhood edn., 1971-72; asso. dir. Follow Through and Head Start Bank Street Coll. Edn., N.Y.C., 1970-71; dir. Bainbridge Nursery Sch. and Crosswicks (N.J.) Country Day Sch., 1972-73; N.J. head start regional tng. officer Region 2 Office Child Devel., HEW, Rider Coll., Lawrence, N.J., 1973-75; exec. dir. Egenolf Day Nursery Assn., Elizabeth, N.J., 1975-77; N.J. Head Start Regional tng. officer, Region 2 Adminstrn. for Children, Youth and Families, Dept. Health and Human Services, Rutgers U., New Brunswick, N.J., 1977-78; dir. child devel. assoc., head start supplementary tng. program dept. elem. early childhood and reading Trenton State Coll., 1978—. NDEA fellow for Early Childhood Adminstrs., 1965. Mem. Nat. Assn. Edn. Young Children, Organization Mondiali pour l'Education Prescolaire, N.J. Assn. Edn. Young Children (edn. and research chmn. 1962-84, chpt. pres. 1968-70), Assn. Childhood Edn. Internat. Congregationalist. Editor Young World, 1962-84; contbr. articles to profl. jours. Home: 810 Harding St Westfield NJ 07090 Office: Trenton State Coll Dept Elem Early Childhood and Readiness Tng Hillwood Lakes CN 550 Trenton NJ 08625

FOSTER, GOLDA MARIE, publishing and marketing consultant; b. San Angelo, Tex., Apr. 22, 1948; d. Horace Martin and Golda Marie (Triplett) F. Student, Angelo State U., 1969. News reporter San Angelo Standard-Times, 1966-67; fashion illustrator Hemphill-Wells, San Angelo, 1968-71; recreational vehicle sales mgr. Jim Bass Ford, San Angelo, 1972-74; mag. editor Anchor Pub. Co., San Angelo, 1974-75; city mgr. Nat. Car Rental, San Angelo and Abilene, Tex., 1975-82; adminstr. KNA Oilfield Services, Inc., Kenai, Alaska, 1983-84; prodn. mgr. Womack-Kleypas-Gette Advt., San Angelo, 1985-86; owner Hist. Mktg. & Resources, San Angelo, 1986—; owner Foster Pubs. Group, San Angelo, 1987—; bd. dirs. Tricom Assn. Advt. Fedn., San Angelo. Editor: Tom Green County History, 1987-88, Founders & Settlers of Heart of Texas, 1987-88; designer brochures. Rep. precinct chair Taylor County, Abilene, 1982; pres. Confederate Air Force Cols. Ladies, Abilene, 1981-82; friend Ft. Concho Mus., San Angelo Mus. Fine Arts; mem. Abilene Centennial Com., 1981; sec., chair pubs. Tom Green County Hist. Commn., San Angelo, 1986—; bd. dirs. Downtown San Angelo Assn., 1987—, Tom Green County Hist. Preservation League, 1987—. Mem. Tex. State Hist. Assn., Tex. Hist. Found., Bus. and Profl. Women's Club, West Tex. Hist. Assn., Tom Green County Hist. Soc., San Angelo Geneal. and Hist. Soc., United Daughters of Confederacy, Colonial Dames 17th Century (sec. 1984—). Episcopalian. Lodge: Kiwanis. Home: 1115 N Van Buren San Angelo TX 76901 Office: Hist Mktg & Resources 221 N Main San Angelo TX 76903

FOSTER, HELEN LAURA, geologist; b. Adrian, Mich., Dec. 15, 1919; d. Stanley Allen and Alice Mary (Osborn) F. BS, U. Mich., 1941, MS, 1943, PhD, 1946. Registered profl. geologist, Calif. Tchr. Blissfield (Mich.) High Sch., 1941-42; instr. geology Wellesley (Mass.) Coll., 1946-48; instr. field geology U. Mich. Field Camp, Jackson, Wyo., 1947; geologist U.S. Geol. Survey, Tokyo, 1948-55, Ishigaki-shima, Tokyo (Japan) and Washington, 1955-65, Menlo Park (Calif.) and Alaska, 1965—. Contbr. articles to profl. jours. Recipient Outstanding Achievement award U. Mich., 1976, Meritorious Service award U.S. Dept. Interior, 1984. Fellow AAAS, Geol. Soc. Am. (various com. memberships); mem. Am. Geophys. Union, Am. Assn. Petroleum Geologists, Penisula Geol. Soc. (v.p. 1977-78), U. Mich. Alumni Assn. (corr. sec.), Eagle Hist. Soc. Club: Sierra. Home: 270 O'Keefe St Apt. H Palo Alto CA 94303 Office: US Geol Survey 345 Middlefield Rd Menlo Park CA 94025

FOSTER, JOYCE ANN, auditor; b. Louisiana, Mo., Dec. 8, 1942; d. Ralph Pendleton and Sybil (Creech) Norton; m. Gilbert Lee Foster, May 14, 1965 (div. 1972); children: Tina Louise, Terry Lee. AS in Bus. Mgmt., Internat. Corr. Sch. Sec. Sverdrup Corp., St. Louis, 1960-73, document coordinator, 1973-81, contract adminstr., 1981-86, mgr. operational audits, 1986—. Mem. Inst. Internal Auditors, Nat. Assn. Female Execs. Republican. Methodist. Office: Sverdrup Corp 801 N 11th St Saint Louis MO 63101

FOSTER, LAURA, lawyer; b. Lubbock, Tex., Mar. 12, 1957; d. Arthur James and Ada Wre (Handlin) F.; m. James Lowe Nuckolls, Dec. 22, 1984. BA with honors, U. Tex., 1978; JD, So. Meth. U., 1984. Bar: Tex. 1984, U.S. Dist. Ct. (no. dist.) Tex., 1986. Trust administr. Tex. Commerce Bank, Austin, 1979-81; assoc. Glast, Ungerman et al, Dallas, 1984-85, Wilford & Ragir, Dallas, 1985-87; ptnr. Wilkerson and Foster, Dallas, 1988—. Editor law rev. So. Meth. U., 1983. Mem. Dallas Bar Assn. (Pro Bono Achievement award 1986, Meritorious Service award 1987), Dallas Assn. Young Lawyers (homeowner's rights com., legal aid com. 1986—),. Office: Wilkerson and Foster 2622 Commerce Dallas TX 75226

FOSTER, MARGERY SOMERS, educator; b. Boston, Mar. 27, 1914; d. L. Brent and Grace (Butler) F.; B.A., Wellesley Coll., 1934; Ph.D., Radcliffe Coll., 1958; Litt.D., Russell Sage Coll., 1968. Asst. to actuary New Eng. Mut. Life Ins. Co., 1934-43; dep. comptroller and dir. devel. Wellesley Coll., 1946-54; lectr. econs. Harvard U. Sch. Bus. Adminstrn., 1956-58; lectr. econs., sec. coll. Mt. Holyoke Coll., 1958-64; prof. econs., dean coll. Hollins Coll., 1964-67; prof. econs., dean coll. Douglass Coll. of Rutgers U., 1967-75. Univ. prof. econs. Rutgers, 1975-80, prof. emeritus, 1980—; past dir. Prudential Ins. Co., Pub. Service Electric & Gas Co., N.J., 1973-75. Mem. commn. on tests Coll. Entrance Exam. Bd., 1966-70, trustee, 1969-72; mem. commn. on instl. affairs Assn. Am. Colls., 1971-74; mem. Harvard U. overseer's vis. com. for Warren Center in Am. History, 1973-79; trustee Middle States Assn. Colls. and Schs., 1973-79, Island Inst. Served to lt. Women's Res., USNR, 1943-46. Mem. Am. Econ. Assn., Econ. History Assn., Econ. History Soc. Clubs: Appalachian Mountain, Cosmopolitan, Univ. Women's Club. Author: Out of Smalle Beginnings, An Economic History of Harvard College in the Puritan Period, 1962. Spl. research on Am. colonial econ. history, history of edn., pub. fin. Address: Box 60 Francestown NH 03043

FOSTER, MARTHA TYAHLA, educational administrator; b. Coaldale, Pa., Apr. 22, 1955; d. Stephen and Frances (Solomon) Tyahla; m. David Marion Foster, Jan. 3, 1981. B.A., U. Va., 1977, M.Ed., 1981, Ed.S., 1981. Legis. asst. U.S. Ho. of Reps., Washington, 1977-79; asst. dean summer session U. Va., Charlottesville, 1981; program cons. campus activities U. Houston, 1981; coordinator student affairs Capitol Inst. Tech., Kensington, Md., 1982-83, asst. dean students, Laurel, Md., 1983-84, assoc. dean students, 1984-86, dean students, 1986-87; bd. dirs. Curry Sch. Edn. Found. U. Va. Mem. Arlington County Commn. on Status of Women. Named Woman of Yr. Bus. and Profl. Women's Club, Vienna, Va., 1986 . Mem. Am. Coll. Personnel Assn., Am. Assn. Counseling and Devel., Acad. Advisers of the Potomac and Chesapeake Area, Am. Soc. Tng. and Devel. (met. D.C. chpt.), Va. Counselors Assn. Methodist. Lodge: Order of Eastern Star (worthy matron 1988-89).

FOSTER, MARY CHRISTINE, motion picture, television executive; b. Los Angeles, Mar. 19, 1943; d. Ernest Albert and Mary Ada (Quilici) F.; m. Paul Hunter, July 26, 1982. BA, Immaculate Heart Coll., Los Angeles, 1967; M of Journalism in TV News Documentary, UCLA, 1968. Dir. research and devel. Metromedia Producers Corp., Los Angeles, 1968-71; dir. devel. and prodn. services Wolper Prodns., Los Angeles, 1971-76; mgr. film programs NBC-TV, Burbank, Calif., 1976-77; v.p. movies and mini series Columbia Pictures TV, Burbank, 1977-81, v.p. series programs, 1981; v.p. program devel. Group W. Prodns., Los Angeles, 1981-87; pres. div. motion pictures and TV Walsh Communications Group, Inc., Los Angeles, 1987; v.p. TV The Agency, Los Angeles, 1988—; instr. communications UCLA, 1987; lectr. in field, 1970—. Creator (TV Series) Sullivan, 1985, Auntie Mom, 1986. Bd. dirs. Immaculate Heart High Sch., Los Angeles, 1980—; mem. exec. com. Humanitas Awards, Human Family Inst., 1985—, Los Angeles Roman Cath. Archdiosesan Communications Commn., Los Angeles, 1986—. Mem. Women in Film (bd. dirs. 1974-78), Nat. Acad. TV Arts and Scis. Democrat. Home: 2367 W Silver Lake Dr Los Angeles CA 90039 Office: The Agency 10351 Santa Monica Blvd Suite 211 Los Angeles CA 90025

FOSTER, MARY FRAZER (LECRON), anthropologist; b. Des Moines, Feb. 1, 1914; d. James and Helen (Cowles) LeCron; B.A., Northwestern U., 1936; Ph.D., U. Calif., Berkeley, 1965; m. George McClelland Foster, Jan. 6, 1938; children—Jeremy, Melissa Foster Bowerman. Research asso. dept. anthropology U. Calif., Berkeley, 1955-57, 75—; lectr. in anthropology Calif. State U., Hayward, 1966-75; mem. faculty Fromm Inst. Lifelong Learning, U. San Francisco, 1980. Fellow Am. Anthropol. Assn.; mem. Linguistic Soc. Am., Internat. Linguistic Assn., Southwestern Anthrop. Assn., AAAS, Soc. Woman Geographers. Democrat. Author: (with George M. Foster) Sierra Popoluca Speech, 1948; The Tarascan Language, 1969; editor: (with Stanley H. Brandes) Symbol As Sense: New Approaches to the Analysis of Meaning, 1980, (with Robert A. Rubinstein) Peace and War=Cross-Cultural Perspectives, 1986. Home: 790 San Luis Rd Berkeley CA 94707

FOSTER, MARY SUE, small business owner; b. Rolla, Mo., Feb. 24, 1944; d. Samuel Franklin and Dolly Doris (Callahan) F.; m. Michael Dietrich Loehr, Dec. 18, 1965 (div. 1976); children: Kimberley Anne, Eric Michael; m. Mark Richard Birnbaum, June 4, 1981. BS in Edn., S.E. Mo. State, 1966; MEd, U. North Tex., 1972. Tchr. high schs., Ohio, Minn. and Tex., 1966-74; dir. career info. Women's Ctr. Dallas, 1974-76; prin. Foster & Wood, Dallas, 1976—, Goodmove Inc., Dallas, 1981—. Author: Move It!, 1984. Fundraiser Breakthrough Found., San Francisco, 1984—; bd. dirs. Girls Clubs Dallas, 1978-80, Women's Ctr. Dallas, 1977-79, Dallas Youth at Risk, 1986—. Mem. Bus. Exchange, Dallas (pres. 1984-86). Office: Goodmove Inc PO Box 835337 Richardson TX 75083

FOSTER, ROYCE PORTER, general contracting company executive; b. Wilkes County, Dec. 12, 1928; d. Lee Roy and Vassie Beatrice (Byrd) Porter; m. Roy George Foster, June 20, 1953; children—Karen Elizabeth, Melanie Ann, John Andrew. Student Draughon's Bus. Coll., 1945-46. Cert. ceramics tchr. Clk.-typist Coble Dairies, Wilkesboro, N.C., 1946-47; bookkeeper Lineberry Foundry, North Wilkesboro, N.C., 1947-53; bookkeeper Nat. Meml. Park, Falls Church, Va., 1953; bookkeeper T.A. Talley & Son, Richmond, Va., 1955-56; bookkeeper Q.M. Tomlinson, Inc., Roanoke, Va., 1965-82, exec. v.p., 1982—. Mem. adv. bd. Va. Western Community Coll., Roanoke, 1980-81. Mem. Nat. Assn. Women in Constrn. (pres. 1979-81), Am. Bus. Women's Assn., Am. Mgmt. Assn., Nat. Assn. Female Execs. Democrat. Presbyterian. Office: QM Tomlinson Inc 2001 Centre Ave NW Roanoke VA 24022

FOSTER, RUTH IRENE, educator; b. Adair County, Iowa, Mar. 6, 1916; d. Clyde Manson and Rachel Virginia (Martin) Archer; B.S., Drake U., 1954, M.S., 1962; postgrad. U. Iowa, 1969, U. So. Calif., 1970; m. David R. Foster, June 30, 1938. Tchr. rural sch. Adair County (Iowa), 1934-38, Polk County Schs. (Iowa), 1942-54; tchr. Des Moines Pub. Schs., 1954-85, mem. adv. council staff devel., 1978; supr. elem. student tchrs. Coll. Edn., Iowa State U., 1986—. Mem. Cadre-Tchrs., Cen. Dist. Iowa State Edn., 1971-72; mem. teaching triad Classroom Tchr. Conf., U. Okla., summer 1969; mem. edn. and cert. com. Iowa Dept. Public Instrn., 1970-75; mem. Nat. Council Accreditation of Tchr. Tng. Edn., 1980-87; mem. Iowa Profl. Teaching Practices Commn., 1971-76; mem. teaching staff, models of teaching Nat. Tchr. Corps Inst., U. Richmond (Va.), summer 1975; regional coordinator Nat. Survey for Preservice Preparation Tchrs., Nat. Center for Ednl. Stats., Stanford U., 1975-76; mem. vis. team Nat. Council for Accreditation Tchr. Edn., 1970-87; mem. Project Profile taskforce Coll. Edn. Iowa State U., 1982—, mem. adv. com., 1984-86; mem. adv. com. div. edn. Grandview Coll., Des Moines, 1985—. Republican precinct committeewoman, 1967-69. Recipient Living Meml. scholarship, Delta Kappa Gamma, 1970; Charles Martin State Edn. award, 1981-82; Ruth Foster award for outstanding service to teaching profession named in her honor, 1985. Mem. Women's C. of C. (profl.), NEA (del. constl. conv. 1971-72), Des Moines Edn. Assn. (parliamentarian 1972-74), Am. Bus. Women Club, Iowa Edn. Assn. (dist. pres. 1966-68, rep. World Conf. Orgns. Teaching Profession 1972, mem. instrnl. profl. devel. council 1972-74, 77—), Iowa Instrnl. Profl. Devel., Nat. (sec. 1967-69), Iowa (pres. 1970-72) assns. classroom tchrs., Des Moines Edn. Assn. (1st v.p. 1966-68, chmn. instrnl. profl. devel. com. 1978-85), AAUW, Phi Delta Kappa, Kappa Kappa Iota (v.p. state chpt. 1974-75, pres. state cen. council presidents 1975-76, state pres. 1976-77, nat. exec. com. 1984-85, v.p. nat. com. 1987—, chmn. nat. conv. 1978, post III nat. exec. com. 1979-81), Delta Kappa Gamma Epsilon. Republican. Mem. Christian Ch. Mem. Order Eastern Star, Daus. of Nile. Home: 1004 McKinley Des Moines IA 50315

FOSTER, SALLY MARIE, contracts manager, consultant; b. Washington, Apr. 21, 1954; d. Eric Foster and Vera (Prevette) Foster Rollo. B.A., U. Md., 1976; J.D., Wake Forest U., 1980. Law intern Office Chief Counsel, FAA, Washington, 1980-81; contracts adminstr. Brit. Aerospace, Inc., Herndon, Va., 1981-83; contracts specialist JWK Internat. Corp., Arlington, Va., 1983; dir. contracts, legal systems, staff legal cons. systems internat. div. Computer Scis. Corp., Fairfax, Va., 1983-85; contracts mgr. Electronic Data Systems Ltd., London, 1985-87; contracts mgr. Electronic Data Systems Corp., Washington, 1987—; sr. mem. CAP, Maxwell AFB, Ala., 1979-87 ; sr. contracts negotiator EDS, Gout Systems Corp., 1987—; bd. dirs. Venture Clinic, Inc. Recipient First Honors, Dorothy Shaw Leadership award Alpha Delta Pi, 1976. Mem. Nat. Contracts Mgmt. Assn., Nat. Assn. Female Execs., Phi Alpha Delta, Phi Alpha Theta. Democrat. Methodist. Club: Nat. Capitol Rottweiler. Lodge: Women of Moose. Home: 7203 Sewell Ave Falls Church VA 22046 Office: Electronic Data Systems Govt Systems Group 6430 Rockledge Dr Bethesda MD 20817

FOSTER, SHEILA SMINK, media supervisor, small business owner; b. Balt., Dec. 12, 1939; d. George Cadwalder Smink and Agnes Beth (Clark) Swearer; m. Jay Royce Brinsfield, May 14, 1960 (div. Aug. 1964); m. Stephen Paul Foster, Aug. 7, 1964 (div. June 1972); 1 child, Mark Patrick. AA in Chemistry, U. Del., 1964, BA in Chemistry and Journalism, 1979. Lab technician Johns Hopkins Hosp., Balt., 1958-60: physical tester E.I. duPont deNemours and Co., Inc., Wilmington, Del., 1960, indsl. x-ray technician, 1960-65, research technician, 1965-72, tech. writer, 1972-75, media coordinator, 1975-77, media supr., 1977—. Mem. Citizens Coalition for Justice, Wilmington, 1985-86. Mem. Wilmington Women in Bus., Sierra Club (vice chair Del. chpt. 1985-86, treas. 1983-85). Democrat. Methodist. Club: Kirkwood Fitness (Wilmington). Home: 209 W 16th St Wilmington DE 19802 Office: EI duPont deNemours & Co Inc 10th and Market Sts EAD NA-214- Wilmington DE 19898

FOSTER, SUSAN CHANDLER, management consultant; b. Montgomery, Ala., Sept. 21, 1949; d. Horace Leonard and Mary Charles (Howell) Chandler; m. George E. Shirley, Dec. 1, 1967 (div. 1978); 1 child, Scott. BS, Troy State U., 1978; MS, U. So. Calif., Los Angeles, 1983. Chief force devel. Hdqrs. 60th Ordnance Group, Zweibrucken, Fed. Republic Germany, 1981-84; staff asst. Sec. of Army, Arlington, Va., 1984-85; program analyst Dep. Chief of Staff Logistics, Arlington, 1985-86; dept. mgr. CACI, Inc., Arlington, 1986—. U.S. Army Legis fellow, 1987. Office: CACI Inc 1837 Jeff Davis Hwy Suite 100 Arlington VA 22203

FOSTER, VIRGINIA HIGHLEYMAN, nonprofit association executive; b. Kansas City, Mo., Apr. 15, 1935; d. Wilbur Beck and Virginia Josephine (Ledterman) Highleyman; m. Daniel Lee Foster (div. 1984); children: Kenneth Lee, Steven Harp. BA, Oakland State U., 1957; MA, Lindenwood Coll., St. Charles, Mo., 1978. Dist. dir. Girls Scouts U.S.A., Chgo., 1957-62; dir. devel. ARC, Fairfax, Va., 1975-77; exec. dir. YWCA, Fairfax, 1977-79; nat. asst. exec. dir WICS Inc., Washington, 1979-84; dir. fin. Nat. Dem. Inst. for Internat. Affairs, Washington, 1984-87; pres., exec. dir. Va. Spl. Olympics Inc., Richmond, Va., 1987—; cons. V.H. Foster Assocs., Washington, 1974—; adj. trainer Nat. Ctr. for Vol. Action, Washington, 1976-79. Chmn. bd. Hannah Harrison Career Sch., Washinton, 1984-86; pres. YWCA, Fairfax, 1972-74, Mansfield, Ohio, 1961-62, bd. trustees, 1961-62, bd. dirs., Washington, 1974-75; bd. dirs. ARC, Fairfax, 1972-75. Recipient Orenda award YMCA-YWCA, 1968. Mem. Am. Soc. Assn. Execs., Nat. Am. Soc. Assn. Execs., Nat. Assn. Spl. Olympics Profls. Democrat. Episcopalian. Home: 4962 Sabra Ln Annandale VA 22003 Office: Virginia Special Olympics Inc 530 E Main St Richmond VA 32319

FOSTER-NOBEL, CAROL ANN, physician; b. Torrance, Calif., July 5, 1955; d. Duane Ray and Loretta Margaret (Hill) F. B.A. in Biology, Point Loma Coll., 1977; M.D., U. Calif.-San Diego, 1981. Resident in gen. surgery U. Calif.-San Diego Med. Ctr., 1981-82, resident in head and neck surgery, 1982-83; staff physician emergency medicine Rees Stealy Med. Group, San Diego, 1983-84; adj. prof. Point Loma Coll. Sch. Nursing, 1985-87; v.p. G.L. Nobel MD, Inc, 1987—. Mackenzie Found. scholar, 1978-80; Country Friends of U. Calif.-San Diego, scholar, 1978-79; Ruth B. White Meml. Fund scholar, 1979-80. Mem. AMA, Phi Delta Lambda. Home: PO Box 3166 Rancho Santa Fe CA 92067 Office: 3023 Bunker Hill Suite 103A San Diego CA 92109

FOTI, MARGARET MAI, education consultant; b. Hoboken, N.J., Mar. 6, 1938; d. Angelo Julius and Margaret (Egan) Mai; m. Henry Carl Koenig, June 25, 1960 (div. May 1981); children: Mai Anne, Jo Ellen; m. Anthony Philip Foti, Aug. 1987. EdB, Jersey City State U., 1959; Ms in Edn., Psychology, Rutger su., 1973; cert. learning cons., Kean Coll., 1986. Tchr. Ridgefield (N.J.) Bd. Edn., 1960-61; tchr. sci., math. and reading St Bartholomews Sch., Scotch Plains, N.J., 1971-77; tchr. program math. underachievers South Plainfield (N.J.) Bd. Edn., 1977-78; tchr. handicapped Plainfield (N.J.) Bd. Edn., 1981-86; learning cons. Union County Vocat. Tech. Sch., Scotch Plains, N.J., 1986—. Vol. Spl. Olympics, Plainfield, 1987. Mem. Orgn. Learning Cons. Roman Catholic. Club: Suburban (Scotch Plains). Home: 270 Pompano Rd Love Ladies NJ 08008

FOTINOS, KATHERINE, educator; b. San Francisco, Apr. 12, 1926; d. Christ Anastasios and Ageliki George (Pilarinos) F. B.A., San Francisco State Coll., 1948; M.A., Stanford U., 1955. Life diploma tchr. Calif. Tchr. Excelsior Sch., San Francisco, 1948-53, Ridgepoint III, San Francisco, 1953-54, Jedediah Smith Sch., San Francisco, 1954-55; head tchr. Washington Irving Sch., San Francisco, 1955-60, Jean Parker Sch., San Francisco, 1960—; curriculum designer 1951—; cons. Calif. Geog. Alliance. Co-author: Curriculum Guide for Language Arts, Curriculum Guide for Music, Curriculum Guide for Social Studies and Science (all for grades K-6 in San Francisco Unified Sch. Dist.). Designer Deaf Scrabball, 1981. Vol. Assn. for Deaf and Blind, 1980—; docent Calif. Hist. Soc., Sonoma; festival decoration chmn. Greek Orthodox Ch., Solono County 1982; vol. Sonoma Rep. Com., 1982; U.S. senatorial candidate campaign chmn. Sonoma County, 1986; scholarship chmn. Northern Div. Calif. Fedn. Rep. Women, 1987-88. Mem. AAUW, Calif. PTA (hon. life), Calif. Tchrs. Assn., Stanford Edn. Club (sec. 1972-74), Sonoma Valley Chorale, Sonoma County Ballet Guild, Am. Chorale Dirs. Assn., Sonoma Valley Rep. Women (charter mem.), Nat. Fedn. Rep. Women (fed. regent), Alpha Delta Kappa (life; pres. 1962-64). Clubs: Jack Anderson, Etude Music (scholarship chmn.). Lodge: Daus. Penelope (v.p. 1974-76). Avocations: travel, archaeology, dance, art, gardening. Home: 150 El Portola Dr Sonoma CA 95476

FOUCH, STEPHANIE SAUNDERS, advertising executive; b. Yonkers, N.Y., Apr. 22, 1947; d. Stephan L. and Rosetta J. (Arvonio) Saunders; BA Vassar Coll., 1968; m. Gregory G. Fouch, Mar. 6, 1976; 1 child, Charlotte Michaux. Asst. account exec. Chirurg & Cairns, Inc., N.Y.C., 1968-70; account exec. Benton & Bowles, Inc., N.Y.C., 1971-75; pub. cons., N.Y.C. and Washington, 1975-77; v.p. Weitzman, Dym & Assos., Inc., Washington, 1978-82; v.p., client services dir. Abramson Assos., Washington, 1982-83; v.p., Rosenthal, Greene & Campbell, Inc., Washington, 1985-87; sr. v.p., acct. mgmt. dir., Soghigian & Macuga, Inc., Washington, 1987—; advt.and mktg. cons., 1983—; speaker, adv. in field. Bd. dirs. Henry St. Settlement, N.Y.C., 1971-73. Recipient Merit award United Fund Greater N.Y., 1972. Mem. Am. Advt. Fedn., Washington Media Mgmt. Network, Advt. Club Washington. Clubs: Bethesda Country; Vassar (dir. N.Y.C. 1972-74). Office: 1101 30th ST NW Washington DC 20007

FOUCHEK, PAULA TROTT, marketing professional; b. Ennis, Tex., June 19, 1951; d. Jack Starnes and Bennie Jo (Bozeman) Trott; m. Kip Richard; 1 child, Shea Daniel. BS in English and Speech, East Tex. State U., 1973. Sec. Pearcy/Christon Realtors, Dallas, 1973-74; tchr. Irving (Tex.) High Sch., 1974-77; rep. mktg. Metroplex Paper and Supply div. Motford, Inc., Dallas, 1977-79; cons. sales tng. Xerox Learning Systems, Dallas, 1978; coordinator pub. relations TexaSweet Citrus Advt., McAllen, Tex., 1980-84; exec. dir. Tex. Fresh Promotional Bd., Harlingen, 1984—. Mem. United Fresh Fruit and Vegetable Assn. (mem. fresh approach com. 1984—), Produce Mktg. Assn. (mem. nutrition task force 1984-87), Can. Fruit Wholesalers Assn., Fresh Produce Council. Republican. Methodist. Office: Tex Fresh Promotional Bd 6912 W Expressway 83 Harlingen TX 78552-3701

FOUGHT, SHERYL KRISTINE, environmental engineer, educator; b. Washington, Mo., Oct. 17, 1949; d. James Paul and Alice Marie (Kasper) McSpadden; m. Randy Bruce Stucki, Nov. 23, 1968 (div. 1973); children: Randy Bruce, Sherylynne Sue; m. Larry Donald Fought, July 31, 1980 (div. 1982); 1 ch, Erin Marie. BS, N.Mex. State U., 1976, postgrad., 1977-79. Tchr. N.Mex. State U., Las Cruces, 1977-78; hydrologist U.S. Dept. Interior, Las Cruces, 1978-81; environ. sci. U.S. EPA, Dallas, 1981-84; hazardous waste inspector Ariz. Dept. Health Service, Phoenix, 1984-85; environ. engr., technician Yuma Proving Ground U.S. Army, 1985-87, chief phys. scientist environment div., 1987—. Co-author: The Ghost Town Marcia, 1975, tng. manuals. Served with USMC, 1958-60. Recipient Environ. Quality award and Army Environ. Quality award, U.S. Army, 1986. Mem. Nat. Assn. Female Execs., Nat. Environ. Tng. Assn., Federally Employed Women, Fed. Women Engrs. and Scientists, The Wildlife Soc., ir Pollution Control. Assn., DOD-Excellent Installations. Democrat. Home: PO Box 3063 YPG Yuma Proving Ground Yuma AZ 85365-9102 Office: US Army Yuma Proving Ground Attn: STEYP-ES Yuma AZ 85365-9102

FOURCARD, INEZ GAREY, foundation executive; b. Bklyn., Sept. 26, 1930; d. George W. and Frances E. (MacDonald) Garey; student Pratt Inst., 1946-48; B.F.A., McNeese State U., 1963; m. Waldren Arthur Fourcard, Aug. 7, 1948; children—Chrystal Frances, Sharon Lynn, Waldren Arthur, Andrea Renee, David Marquard, Anita Lynn. Exhibited in numerous one man shows throughout U.S., also in Eng., France and Spain; mem. gifted and talented sect. of Spl. Edn. State of La., 1971-73; mem. adv. council Child Centered/Parent Tutored Kindergarden Program, 1974—; mem. La. Task Force for Community Edn., 1974-75; v.p. La. Assn. for Sickle Cell Anemia, 1974—; named best statewide vol.; mem. Calcasieu Parish Bicentennial Com., 1974—; exec. dir. Southwestern Sickle Cell Anemia Found., Lake Charles, La., 1973—; bd. dirs. World Sickle Cell Anemia Found.; del. to Dem. Nat. Convs., 1980, 84. Named Hon. Citizen of Fort Worth, 1977; recipient Award of Merit, Human Relations Council of Lake Charles Deanery, award for services to sickle cell disease Sigma Gamma Rho, award for community service Phi Beta Sigma. Democrat. Roman Catholic. Important works include The Widow in pvt. collection Bertrand Russell Peace Found., London. Home: 1414 St John St Lake Charles LA 70601 Office: PO Box 3254 118 Enterprise Blvd Lake Charles LA 70601

FOURNIER, ALMA FANTON, nurse; b. Fairfax, Vt., July 24, 1939; d. Hubert Ralph and Elizabeth (Meunier) Fanton; m. Leo C. Fournier, Mar. 3, 1962 (dec. Nov. 1986); children: Christopher Charles, Michael Alan, Paul Lloyd. BS, U. So. Maine, 1983. Asst. dir. nursing Houlton (Maine) Regional Hosp., 1985-87, acting dir. nursing, 1987-88, dir. nursing, 1988—; pres. bd. dirs. Aroostook Alcohol and Drug Abuse Prevention Council, 1985-87. Pres. Maine Affiliate Am. Heart Assn., So. Aroostook div., 1988—. Recipient Outstanding Service award Aroostook Alcohol and Drug Abuse Council, 1986. Mem. Nat. League Nursing, Am. Orgn. Nurse Execs., Orgn. Maine Nurse Execs. Republican. Roman Catholic. Home: 48 River St Houlton ME 04730 Office: Houlton Regional Hosp 20 Hartford St Houlton ME 04730

FOURROUX, MARGARITA, electronics company executive; b. LaFeria, Tex., Dec. 18, 1950; d. Isidro and Elida (Trevino) Garcia; m. Melvin R. Fourroux, June 5, 1978; children: Josie, Matthew. Assoc. in Bus., Belleville Area Coll., Ill., 1986. Adminstrv. asst. Alpha Enterprises, Honolulu, 1978-81; purchasing agt. Poly Disc Systems, Torrance, Calif., 1981-83; purchasing mgr. Indicator Controls, Gardena, Calif., 1984-85, Hickey Mitchell Ins., St. Louis, 1985-87; sr. buyer Pulse Electronics, Rockville, Md., 1987—. Mem. Am. Purchasing Soc., Adminstrv. Mgmt. Soc., Nat. Assn. Purchasing Mgmt., Nat. Assn. Female Execs. Roman Catholic. Avocations: oil painting, reading, drawing. Office: Pulse Electronics 5706 Frederick Ave Rockville MD 20852

FOUSHEE, GERALDINE GEORGE, municipal county government official, detective; b. Newark, Aug. 14, 1947; d. Clarence Milton and Anna Mae (Smith) George; m. Joseph Edward Foushee, Aug. 14, 1966; children: Chere Michele, Kyle Edward. AS in Edn. magna cum laude, Essex County Coll., 1976; BA in Polit. Sci. magna cum laude, Rutgers U., 1981. Cert. tchr., N.J. Computer keypunch operator Continental Ins. Co., Newark, 1965-66; computer verification operator Blue Cross/Blue Shield of N.J., Newark, 1966; tech. asst., adminstrv. asst., acting coordinator learning resource ctr. Essex County Coll., Newark, 1968-79; investigator field claims, adjustor Hartford Ins. Group, Randolph, N.J., 1979-81; police officer Newark Police Dept., 1981-84; detective fugitive warrant squad Sheriff's Office Essex County, Newark, 1984-86; exec. sec. Alcoholic Beverage Control Bd. City of Newark, 1986—; spl. instr. Newark Police Acad., 1986—. Mem. adv. bd. Div. of Youth and Family Services, Newark, 1986—. Recipient Merit award State of N.J. Tng. Commn., 1981, Law Enforcemnt award City of Newark Mayor James Sharpe, 1986, Service award Lions Club, Hillside, N.J.; named Police Officer of Month, Woman of Yr., Grace Reformed Bapt. Ch., 1987. Mem. Internat. Assn. Women Police (Cert. of Merit award 1984), Nat. Orgn. Black Law Enforcement Execs., Nat. Black Alcoholism Council, North N.J. Women in Police, Nat. Council Negro Women (Woman of Yr. 1987), Nat. Black Police Assn., Safety Officers Coalition, Essex County Coll. Alumni Assn., Baton's Inc. (chairwoman com. 1986-87), Fraternal Order Police (bd. dirs. 1982-84, Police Officer of Month 1982), Bronze Shields, Inc. (fin. sec 1982-86, Police award 1981, Achievement award 1987), Alpha Sigma Lambda. Democrat. Office: Alcoholic Beverage Control City Hall Annex 31 Green St Newark NJ 07102

FOUST, BOBBIE, newspaper and magazine editor; b. Calvert City, Ky., Apr. 30, 1934; d. Clarence Lee and Hilda Mae (Barnhart) Freeman; m. Ray Foust Jr., Oct. 7, 1950; children: Donna Foust Townsend, Jackie Foust Bader, Terrie Foust White, Dennis. Student, Murray (Ky.) State U., 1986—. Reporter, photographer Calvert (Calvert City, Ky.) News, 1968-72, Tribune-Courier, Benton, Ky., 1972-77; reporter, photographer Tribune-Courier and Leisure Scene, Benton, Ky., 1980—, editor, 1980-87; editor Marshall Messenger, Benton, 1977-79; editor, dir., owner Photo/News/Promotions, Calvert, 1987—. Recipient Blue Ribbon Nat. Newspaper Found., 1985. Mem. Ky. Press Women Inc. (pres. 1983), Ky. Press Assn. (dir., award 1986), W. Ky. Press Assn. (pres. 1983), Bus. and Profl. Women (Woman of Achievement 1987), Nat. Assn. Female Execs. Democrat. Baptist. Home: Rt 2 Box 47B Calvert City KY 42029 Office: Photo News Promotions 802 Hickory St Calvert City KY 42029

FOUST, JUDITH MARY, librarian; b. Detroit, Oct. 2, 1947; d. Charles E. and Mary Jane (Voletti) Muneio; m. Thomas N. Foust, Aug. 26, 1969; children: Karen Marie, Adrea Michelle. BS in Math., Nazareth Coll., 1968; MLS, Wayne State U., 1969; M in Pub. Adminstrn., Pa. State U., 1979. Librarian Detroit Pub. Library, 1968-70; law librarian Pa. State Library, Harrisburg, 1971-78, state law librarian, 1978-81, coordinator tech. services, 1981-82, dir. library devel., 1982—. Author Intro to Legal Research, 1978, Library Logo...Guide, 1986. Vol. WITF Auction, Harrisburg, 1987; tchr. marriage preparation, Harrisburg, 1987. Mem. ALA (pub. com. 1986—). Roman Catholic. Home: 5909 Clover Rd Harrisburg PA 17112 Office: State Library of Pa PO Box 1601 Harrisburg PA 17105

FOUTS, ELIZABETH BROWNE, psychologist, metals company executive; b. New Orleans, July 5, 1927; d. Donovan Clarence and Mathilde Elizabeth (Hanna) B.; m. James Fremont Fouts, June 19, 1948; children—Elizabeth, Donovan, Alan, James. BA, Tulane U., 1948; MS, N.E. La. U., 1973, postgrad., 1984. Cert. sch. psychologist, La.; cert. reality therapist, La. Instr. spl. ed., psychol. cons. N.E. La. U., Monroe, 1971-73; sch. psychologist Ouachita Parish Schs., Monroe, 1973-87; sec.-treas Fremont Corp., Monroe, 1967—, Auric Metals Corp., Salt Lake City, 1975—. Bd. dirs. Assn. for Retarded Citizens, Monroe, 1982—, treas., 1984, pres., 1987; mem. exec. bd. Episcopal Diocese of Western La., 1983—. Named Outstanding Sch. Psychologist State of La., 1987. Mem. Nat. Assn. Sch. Psychologists, Council for Exceptional Children, La. Sch. Psychologists Assn. (pres. 1979-80, Outstanding Woman Sch. Psychologist 1984). Avocations: biking; skiing; swimming. Home: PO Box 7070 Monroe LA 71211 Office: Ouachita Parish Sch Bd 100 Bry St Monroe LA 71201

FOWKE, EDITH MARGARET FULTON, author, emeritus English language educator; b. Lumsden, Sask., Can., Apr. 30, 1913; d. William Marshall and Margaret (Fyffe) Fulton; m. Franklin George Fowke, Oct. 1, 1938. Student, Regina Coll., 1929-31; B.A. with high honors in English and History, U. Sask., 1933, M.A. in English, 1938; LL.D. (hon.), Brock U., 1974, U. Regina, 1985; D.Litt., Trent U., 1975, York U., 1982. Editor Western Tchr., Saskatoon, Sask., 1937-45; assoc. editor Mag. Digest, Toronto, Ont., 1945-50; freelance writer CBC Radio, 1950-71; assoc. prof. English, York U., Downsview, Ont., 1971-77; prof. York U., 1977-83, prof. emeritus, 1983—. Author: Folk Songs of Canada, 1954, Folk Songs of Quebec, 1957, Songs of Work and Freedom, 1960, Canada's Story in Song, 1960, Traditional Singers and Songs from Ontario, 1965, More Folk Songs of Canada, 1967, Lumbering Songs from the Northern Woods, 1970, Sally Go

Round the Sun, 1969, Penguin Book of Canadian Folk Songs, 1974, Folklore of Canada, 1976, Ring Around the Moon, 1977, Folktales of French Canada, 1979, Sea Songs and Ballads from Nineteenth Century Nova Scotia, 1981, Singing Our History, 1985, Tales Told in Canada, 1986, Red Rover, Red Rover: Children's Games Played in Canada, 1988; editor: Songs and Sayings of an Ulster Childhood by Alice Kane, 1983, Can. Folk Music Jour., 1973—; co-editor: Bibliography of Canadian Folklore in English, 1982, Explorations in Canadian Folklore, 1985. Decorated Order Can. Fellow Am. Folklore Soc., Royal Soc. of Can.; mem. Writer's Union Can., English Folk Dance and Song Soc., Assn. Can. Univ. Tchrs. English, Can. Assn. Univ. Tchrs., Can. Folk Music Soc. (exec. com.), Folklore Studies Assn. Can., Writers' Union Can., Mensa. Home: 5 Notley Pl, Toronto, ON Canada M4B 2M7 Office: Winters Coll, 4700 Keele St, Downsview, ON Canada M3J 1P3

FOWLER, ANNE VICTORIA, personnel company executive; b. Denver, Feb. 12, 1945; d. Nicholas John and Estelle (Sullivan) F. MS in Human Resource Mgmt., Am. U., 1988. V.p. Midland Ins. Co., N.Y.C., 1971-85; asst. v.p. E.W. Blanch Co., N.Y.C., 1985-86; owner, mgr. Norrell Services, Inc., Shrewsbury, N.J., 1987—. Mem. Internat. Assn. Personnel Women (membership chmn. Monmouth County 1988—), Shrewsbury Bus. Council-Greater Red Bank C. of C. (membership chmn. 1988—). Home: 150 Manor Dr Red Bank NJ 07701 Office: Norrell Services Inc One N Revmont Dr Shrewsbury NJ 07702

FOWLER, ARDEN STEPHANIE, choral director; b. N.Y.C., May 24, 1930; d. Arthur Simon and Lenore Irene (Strouse) Bender; m. Milton Fowler, Aug. 6, 1951; children: Stacey Alison, Crispin Laird. Student, Traphagen Sch., 1947-49; BA, Marymount Coll., Tarrytown, N.Y., 1976; MusM, U. So. Fla., 1978. Designer Rubeson's Sportswear, N.Y.C., 1949-51; free-lance designer Dobb's Ferry, N.Y., 1952-72; organist/choir dir. Children's Village, Dobb's Ferry, 1972-74; music specialist Highland Nursery Sch., Chappaqua, N.Y., 1972-76; music therapist Cedar Manor Nursing Home, Ossining, N.Y., 1974-76; founder, pres. Gloria Musicae Chamber Chorus, Sarasota, Fla., 1979-85, mng. dir., 1985—; soloist various chs., choruses, N.Y. and Fla., 1953—; faculty vocal music St. Boniface Conservatory, Sarasota, 1979-81; music critic Sarasota Herald Tribune, 1986—. Mem. Nat. Assn. Tchrs. Singing, Assn. Profl. Vocal Ensembles, Sarasota County Arts Council, Sigma Alpha Iota, Phi Kappa Phi. Democrat. Episcopal. Home: 4244 Marina Ct Cortez FL 34215 Office: Gloria Musicae Inc PO Box 2616 Sarasota FL 34230

FOWLER, AUSTINE BROWN, educational association administrator, professor; b. Washington, Apr. 6, 1936; d. Amos Cummings Brown and Marian (Woody) Stephens; m. Milton Otis Fowler Sr., June 18, 1959; 1 child, Milton Otis Jr. BS, D.C. Tchrs. Coll., 1960; Ma in Edn., George Washington U., 1969, EdS, 1972. Sales clk. Crosby's Shoe Store, Washington, 1957-60; tchr. Washington D.C. Pub. Schs., 1960-70, dir. head start, 1970-77, dir. health services, 1978-79, edn. supr., 1985—; edn. specialist U.S. Dept. HHS, Washington, 1979-80; social sci. research analyst U.S. Dept. HHS, 1980-82; mgmt. analyst Nat. Archives, Capitol Heights, Md., 1983-85; trainer nat. head start Ppogram, Washington, Md. and Pa., 1970-77; guest lectr. MAT program Trinity Coll., Washington, 1975-80; mem. 19th St. Bapt. Lab. Sch. Bd., Washington, 1987—, Dept. Labor Day Care Bd., Washington, 1985-87; adj. prof. U. D.C., 1976—. Mem. exec. com. Nat. Capitol Area chpt. March of Dimes-Birth Defects Found., also vice chair exec. com., 1985-87, Birth Defects Found., 1987—, chmn. exec. com. 1987—; bd. dirs. D.C. Assn. Retarded Citizens, 1982-84; trustee St. Paul Bapt. Ch., D.C., 1984—; bus. mgr. LeDroit Park Reunion Com., Washington, 1983-85, chairperson 1985—. Fellow NSF, Rockefeller Found. Mem. Nat. Assn. for Edn. of Young Children, Assn. for Curriculum Devel., Washington Assn. for Edn. of Young Children (mem.-at-large), Delta Sigma Theta, Phi Delta Kappa, Phi Lambda Theta, Phi Delta Kappa. Democrat. Baptist. Club: Circle #1 Missionary Soc. Home: 4530 Fort Totten Dr NE #412 Washington DC 20011

FOWLER, BETTY JANMAE, dance company director, editor; b. Chgo., May 23, 1925; d. Harry and Mary (Jacques) Markin; student Art Inst., Chgo., 1937-39, Stratton Bus. Coll., Chgo., 1942-43, Columbia U., 1945-47; B.A., Eastern Wash. U., 1984; 1 dau., Sherry Mareth Connors. Mem. public relations dept. Girl Scouts U.S.A., N.Y.C., 1961-63; adminstrv. asst. to editor-in-chief Scholastic Mags., N.Y.C., 1963-68; adminstrv. dir. Leonard Fowler Dancers, Fowler Sch. Classical Ballet, Inc., N.Y.C., 1959-78, tchr. ballet, 1959-61; editor Bulletin, Kiwanis weekly publ., Spokane, Wash., 1978-82, also adminstrv. sec. Kiwanis Club; instr. Spokane Falls Community Coll., 1978. Cert. metabolic technician Internat. Health Inst. Address: W 5615 Lyons Ct Spokane WA 99208

FOWLER, CAROL HELEN, software consultant; b. Parma, Ohio, July 29, 1954; d. Adelbert C. and Gloria Carol (Larsen) F. BS in Edn., Slippery Rock (Pa.) State U., 1975. Tchr. Fayette County Schs., Fayetteville, W.Va., 1975-76, Shaler Area Sch. Dist., Glenshaw, Pa., 1976-80; support rep. Diacon Systems, Cleve., 1980-81; supr. services Columbus, Ohio, 1981-82; mgr. conversion Pro-Computer Systems, Columbus, 1982-83; specialist bus. accounts Digital Equipment Corp., Columbus, 1983-87; cons. software licensing Stow, Mass., 1987—. Office: Digital Equipment Corp 129 Parker St Maynard MA 01754

FOWLER, CINDA PFENNIG, convention service company executive; b. Indpls., Sept. 25, 1942; d. John Richard and Ila Wayne (Reynolds) Pfennig; m. William Clifford Fowler, Dec. 21, 1965; children: Julia Irene, Mallory Leigh. BS in Edn., Ind. U., 1964. Tchr., Washington Twp., Indpls., 1964-66; owner, operator Presenting Atlanta, Inc., Ga., 1973—. Mem. Atlanta Jr. League, 1974—; mem., fund raiser Salvation Army, Atlanta; bd. dirs. Am. Cancer Soc., Atlanta; bd. dirs. Ga. Amateur Athletics Assn. Mem. Hotel Sales Mktg. Assn., Atlanta Conv. and Visitors Bur. (treas. 1980—), Meeting Planners Internat., Am. Soc. Assn. Execs., Profl. Conv. Mgrs. Assn. Republican. Methodist. Lodge: Kiwanis. Avocation: travel. Office: Presenting Atlanta Inc 110 E Andrews Dr NW Atlanta GA 30305

FOWLER, ELAINE DANIELSON, educator; b. Concordia, Kans., Oct. 25, 1938; d. Clarence Frederick and Blanche Vendla (Magnus) Danielson; B.S., Kans. State U., 1960; M.S., U. Kans., 1964; Ph.D., U. Tex., Austin, 1969; m. Donald Fowler, Aug. 25, 1968; children—James, Thomas. Tchr. pub. schs., Topeka, 1960-63, Center Sch. Dist., Kansas City, Mo., 1964-66; teaching asst. U. Tex., Austin, 1966-69, asst. prof., 1969-75, assoc. prof. 1975—; cons. Pullman-Kellogg Project, Algeria, Africa, 1978. Vice pres. Austin Assn. Retarded Citizens, 1980-82. Mem. Nat. Council Tchrs. English, Internat. Reading Assn., Delta Kappa Gamma, Phi Kappa Phi, Phi Delta Kappa, Phi Lambda Theta. Methodist. Author: Banner English Series, 1981; contbr. articles to profl. jours. Home: 4801 Crestway Dr Austin TX 78731 Office: U Tex EDB 406 Austin TX 78712

FOWLER, HARRIET WHITTEMORE, art museum curator; b. Geneva, N.Y., Apr. 6, 1946. B.A., Cornell U., 1977, Ph.D., 1981; student Smith Coll., 1964-67. Interim dir. U. Ky. Art Mus., Lexington, 1982, curator, 1981—. Author (exhbn. catalogue) New Deal Art; WPA Works at the Univ. of Ky., 1985. Mem. Hist. Properties Adv. Commn. of Ky., 1985-88. Recipient Frances Sampson Fine Arts prize Cornell U., 1977. Mem. Phi Kappa Phi. Home: 110 Broadway Versailles KY 40383 Office: Univ Ky Art Mus Rose and Euclid Sts Lexington KY 40506

FOWLER, KATHLEEN ANNE, advertising executive; b. Alliquippa, Pa., Aug. 10, 1962; d. Roy Kenston and Theresa Bernadine (Kovach) F.; m. Stephen Robert Wright, Aug. 27, 1983 (div. Nov. 1985); 1 child, Matthew. BA, Indiana U., Pa., 1983. Advt. sales executive Pennysaver Publs. of Pa., Pitts., 1983—. Mem. Nat. Assn. Female Execs., Alpha Sigma Alpha (Alpha Gamma chpt.). Republican. Presbyterian. Home: 5621 Curry Rd Pittsburgh PA 15236 Office: Pennysaver Publs of Pa 511 Rodi Rd Penn Hills PA 15236

FOWLER, LINDA MCKEEVER, hospital administrator, management educator; b. Greensburg, Pa., Aug. 7, 1948; d. Clay and Florence Elizabeth (Smith) McK.; m. Timothy L. Fowler, Sept. 13, 1969 (div. July 1985). Nursing diploma, Presbyn. U. Hosp., Pitts., 1969; BS in Nursing, U. Pitts., 1976, M in Nursing Adminstrn., 1980; DPub Adminstrn., Nova U., 1985. Supr., head nurse Presbyn. Univ. Hosp., Pitts., 1969-76; mem. faculty Western Pa. Hosp. Sch. Nursing, Pitts., 1976-79; acute care coordinator Mercy Hosp., Miami, 1980-81; asst. adminstr. nursing North Shore Med. Ctr., Miami, 1981-84, v.p. patient care, 1984-88, Golden Glades Regional Med. Ctr., Miami, 1988—; mem. adj. faculty Barry U., Miami, 1984—, Broward Community Coll., Ft. Lauderdale, 1984—, Nova U., 1986—; cons. Strategic Health Devel. Inc., Miami Shores, Fla., 1986—. Dept. HEW trainee, 1976, 79-80. Mem. Am. Orgn. Nurse Execs. (legis. com. 1988—), Fla. Orgn. Nurse Execs. (bd. dirs. 1986—), South Fla. Nurse Adminstrs. Assn. (sec. 1983-84, bd. dirs. 1984-86), U. Pitts. Alumni Assn., Presbyn. U. Alumni Assn., Nat. Assn. Female Execs., Sigma Theta Tau. Lutheran. Club: Ft. Lauderdale Dog (bd. dirs. 1981-82, 83-85, v.p. 1982-83). Home: 1040 SW 110th Terr Davie FL 33324 Office: Golden Glades Regional Med Ctr 17300 NW 7th Ave Miami FL 33169

FOWLER, NANCY CROWLEY, government economist; b. Newton, Mass., Aug. 8, 1922; d. Ralph Elmer and Margaret Bright (Tinkham) Crowley; m. Gordon Robert Fowler, Sept. 11, 1949; children—Gordon R., Nancy P., Betty Kainani, Diane Kuulei. A.B. cum laude, Radcliffe Coll., 1943; Grad. Cert., Harvard-Radcliffe Mgmt. Tng. Program, 1946; postgrad. U. Hawaii, 1971-76. Econ. research analyst Dept. Planning & Econ. Devel., Honolulu, 1963-69; assoc. chief research Regional Med. Program, Honolulu, 1969-70; economist V and VI, Dept. Planning and Econ. Devel., Honolulu, 1970-78, chief policy analysis br., 1978-85, tech. info. services officer, 1985—; staff rep. State Energy Functional Plan Adv. Com., Honolulu, 1983—, Hawaii Integrated Energy Assessment, 1978-81. Contbr. articles to profl. jours. Com. mem. Kailua Com. to Re-elect Mayor Eileen Anderson, 1984. Recipient Employee of Yr. award Dept. Planning and Econ. Devel., Honolulu, 1977, others. Mem. Hawaii Econs. Assn. (various offices). Democrat. Clubs: Radcliffe of Hawaii, Propeller of Port of Honolulu (pres.). Avocations: gardening; surfing. Home: 203 Aumoe Rd Kailua HI 96734

FOWLER, TERRI (MARIE THERESE), artist; b. Decatur, Ga., Sept. 26, 1949; d. John Francis and Marjorie (Benson) Herndon; m. John Charles Fowler, July 29, 1972; children: Courtney Marie, Douglas Edwin. Studied with Carolyn Wyeth, Wyeth Sch. Art, 1972. speaker to arts groups, schools. One-woman shows include Hampden Sydney Coll., 1973, Longwood Coll., 1976, C&S Bank Camden, S.C., 1979, Benfield Gallery, 1985-87; exhibited in cen. chpt. Va. Mus., 1973 (recipient award 1973), Colonial Williamsburg, 1974-77, Md. St. House, Md. St. Senate, 1983-85; works selected by Am. Heart Assn. for Holiday Card Series, 1986-87, commnd. Prince Edward County Bicentennial Com., 1976; exhibited in many nat. and internat. pvt. collections. Active with Girl Scouts Am. cen. Md. Mem. Balt. Watercolor Soc., Md. Fedn. Art. Anapolis Watercolor Club., San Diego Watercolor Soc., U.S. Naval Acad. Womens Club and Garden Club. Home: 123 Groh Ln Annapolis MD 21403

FOX, ALICE BARBARA, psychotherapist; b. N.Y.C.; d. Herman and Ann (Klaw) F. BS, NYU, 1970; MSW, Hunter Coll., 1979. Drug therapist Bernstein Inst., N.Y.C., 1971-77; family therapist Bershire Farms for Boys, L.I., 1977-78, Ackerman Inst., N.Y.C., 1978-79; pvt. practice psychotherapy N.Y.C., 1979—; counselor The Door, N.Y.C., 1970-71; therapist, cons. N.Y. Mental Health Inst., L.I., 1986—. Fellow World Orgn. Social Psychiatrists, Nat. Assn. Social Workers. Address: 135 W 82d St New York City NY 10024 also: 333 W 57th St Suite 103 New York NY 10019

FOX, ANDREA NANCY, advertising executive; b. Phila., Nov. 29, 1949; d. Leonard Martin Fox Sr. and Nola Shirley (Greenberg) Silverman. BS in Edn., Syracuse U., 1971. Cert. elem. tchr., N.Y. Media coordinator Altman, Stoller, Weiss, N.Y.C., 1971-72; from asst. media buyer to v.p., assoc. media dir. J. Walter Thompson Co., Atlanta, 1972-88, v.p., media dir., 1988—; media buyer, planner Weltin Advt., Atlanta, 1974-78, Tucker Wayne & Co., Atlanta, 1978-80. Named One of the South's 10 Best and Brightest Advt. Week mag., 1985, Media Planner Woman of Yr. Am. Women in Radio and TV, 1986. Mem. Atlanta Media Planners Assn. (treas. 1982-83), U.S. Tennis Assn., Atlanta Lawn and Tennis Assn. Clubs: Atlanta Ad, Atlanta Sporting. Office: J Walter Thompson Co 950 E Paces Ferry Rd NE Atlanta GA 30326

FOX, ANNETTE JOY, marketing specialist; b. Pacific Grove, Calif., Mar. 8, 1951; d. Kenneth Fredrick and Emma Margaret (Courtney) Brosi; children: Amber Leigh, Heather Leigh; m. Frederick William Fox, Dec. 15, 1985. BA, Ind. U., 1977; MBA, Amber U., 1987. Tax investigator Ind. Dept. Revenue, Indpls., 1971-73; service rep. Ind. Bell, Indpls., 1973-81, Southwestern Bell, Dallas, 1981-83; account specialist AT&T Info. Systems, Dallas, 1983-84; account exec. Executone, Dallas, 1984-85; coordinator mktg. Contel, Dallas, 1985-88; product mgr. Contel, Merrifield, Va., 1988—. Troop leader Girl Scouts Am., Richardson, Tex., 1985—; coach Richardson Soccer Assn., 1984-85. Mem. Am. Mktg. Assn., U.S. Telephone Assn., Nat. Assn. Female Execs. Club: Toastmasters. Home: 15801 Palmer Ln Haymarket VA 22069 Office: Contel PO Box 401 Merrifield VA 22116

FOX, CHRISTEEN BEHLER, banker; b. Miami, Fla., May 27, 1955; d. Charles Franklin and Harna C. (Ink) Behler; m. Frederick William Fox Jr., mar. 8, 1980 (div. Nov. 1986). BMusic Edn., Fla. State U., 1976. Cert. in music edn. K-12, Fla. Tchr. Dade County Pub. Schs., Miami, 1977-79; adminstrv. asst. real estate lending Am. Savs. and Loan, Miami, 1980-81, Brickellbanc Savs. & Loan, Miami, 1982-83; adminstrv./exec. asst. lending Capital Bank, Miami, 1983-85; exec. asst. lending Royal Palm Savs. & Loan, West Palm Beach, Fla., 1985-86; officer residential real estate loan Sun Bank of St. Lucie County, Ft. Pierce, Fla., 1986-87; officer real estate loan Fla. Fed. Savs. & Loan Assn., Ft. Pierce, 1987; tchr. St. Lucie County Pub. Schs., 1987—. Mem. Assn. Profl. Mortgage Women, Am. Businesswomens Assn., Nat. Assn. Female Execs., Treasure Coast Opera Soc., Fla. State U. Alumni Assn. (nat. adv. bd. 1982-84). Republican. Baptist. Home: 4j902 Myrtle Dr Fort Pierce FL 34982 Office: St Lucie County Sch Bd 3909 Delaware Ave Windmill Point Elem Fort Pierce FL 34950

FOX, CONNIE PATRICIA, writer; b. Chgo., Feb. 12, 1932; d. Hugh Bernard and Helen Marie (Mangan) F.; m. Lucio Ungaro de Zavallos, June 5, 1957 (div. 1970); children—Hugh, Cecilia, Marcella; m. Nono Woodyne Grimes, Oct. 3, 1970; children—Margaret, Alexandra, Christopher. B.S., Loyola U., Chgo., 1954, M.A., 1955; Ph.D., U. Ill., 1958. Author: (poetry) Blood Cocoon, 1980, The Dream of the Black Topaze Chamber, 1984, Babishka, 1985, Schreckliche Engel, 1985, Oma, 1985, Nachthymnen, 1986, The Dram Of The Black Topaze Chamber, 1987. Contbr. poetry and fiction to Telephone, Invisible City, Thirteenth Moon, Mockersatz, Big Scream, others. Spl. issue of Corona mag. devoted to Connie Fox, 1985. Mem. Com. Small Mag. Editors and Publishers. Home: 526 Forest St East Lansing MI 48823

FOX, JOAN MICHELLE, advertising executive; b. N.Y.C., Jan. 31, 1947; d. Walter Bernard and Doris (Rachelson) Strauss; m. Martin Leonard Fox, Jan. 8, 1978; children: Wendy Robyn, Jessica Randi. Assoc. in Bus. and Fin., CCNY, 1964, BA in Spl. Edn./Econs., 1966. Tchr. spl. edn. N.Y.C. Sch. System, 1967-69; controller Beaumont-Bennett Advt., N.Y.C., 1969-72; bus. mgr. Radio Sales div. Metromedia, N.Y.C., 1972-74; asst. treas. Einstein Assocs. Inc., N.Y.C., 1974-77; from controller to sr. v.p. fin. planning and adminstrn. Ogilvy & Mather U.S., N.Y.C., 1977—. Mem. ASCAP, Assn. Advt. Fin. Mgrs., Corp. East Mgrs., Assn. N.Y. Treas. and Fin. Mgrs. Assn., Advt. Women of N.Y., Women's Econs. Round Table, Am. Mgmt. Assn. Office: Ogilvy & Mather 2 E 48th St New York NY 10017

FOX, JOAN PHYLLIS, environmental engineer; b. Rockledge, Fla., July 16, 1945; d. John A. and Nonie L. (Knutson) Fox. BS in Physics with high honors, U. Fla., 1971; PhD in Civil Engring., U. Calif., Berkeley, 1980. Engr. Bechtel, Inc., San Francisco, 1971-76; dir. program and prin. investigator Lawrence Berkeley Lab., 1977-81; prin. engr., pres. Fox Cons., Berkeley, 1981—; guest lectr. dept. conservation and resource studies U. Calif., Berkeley, 1980-84. Contbr. articles on oil shale, hazardous waste, water quality control and water resources in San Francisco Bay area to profl. publs. Grantee Dept. Energy, 1976-81, EPA, 1978-81. Mem. Am. Geophys. Union, Nat. Resources Def. Council, Am. Chem. Soc., ASTM, Water Pollution Control Fedn., Nat. Acad. Scis. (past mem. com. on surface mining and reclamation, mem. subcom. on QA/QC of com. irrigation-induced water quality problems 1986—), AAAS, Audubon Soc., Phi Beta Kappa, Sigma Pi Sigma. Office: 2530 Etna St Berkeley CA 94704

FOX, JOYCE PINN, banker; b. New Haven, Conn., Feb. 3, 1931; d. Samuel Harold and Sylvia Ruth (Seligson) Pinn; m. Robert Jay Fox, Nov. 6, 1949; children: Judith Fox Javelly, Ian Joseph. BA, Queens Coll., 1964; MS, Hunter Coll., 1972. Urban affairs assoc. Chase Manhattan Bank, N.Y.C., 1972-74, global credit dept., 1974-75, work out officer, 1975-81, internat. dept., 1981-83; loan quality control Am. Express Bank, N.Y.C., 1983-86, sr. v.p. global restructure and recovery, 1986-88; sr. v.p. LDC Bank, N.Y.C., 1988—; bd. govs. Robert Morris Assocs., N.Y.C. Mem. Fin. Women's Assn., Phi Beta Kappa. Office: Am Express Bank American Express Tower World Financial Ctr New York NY 10285-2150

FOX, JUDITH HOOS, curator; b. Oakland, Calif., June 13, 1949; d. Sidney Samuels and Ida (Russakoff) Hoos; m. Charles Franklin Fox; 1 child, Jocelyn. BA, Bryn Mawr (Pa.) Coll., 1971; MA, U. Minn., 1974. Curatorial intern Walker Art Ctr., Mpls., 1973-75; exhibitions curator Inst. Contemporary Art, Boston, 1975-76; asst. dir. Wellesley (Mass.) Coll. Mus., 1977-82; curator Mus. of Art, R.I. Sch. Design, Providence, 1982-84; ind. curator Boston, 1984—; cons. Mus. of Fine Arts, Boston, 1985-86, Fine Arts Planning Group, Boston, 1985, 87-88. Mem. Am. Assn. Mus., Coll. Art Assn., Art Table. Home and Office: 21 Myrtle St Jamaica Plain MA 02130

FOX, JULIE MARIE, educational company executive; b. Freemont, Ohio, May 30, 1962; d. Thomas Leo and Susan Jane (Gibson) F. Student, Metro State Coll., 1982, St. Petersburg (Fla.) Jr. Coll., 1986; BS, Ohio U., 1987. Intern Sagamore Inst., Raquet Lake, N.Y., 1980; instrl. aide Clear Creek County Cours and Schs., Idaho Springs, Colo., 1980-82; varsity soccer, jr. varsity volleyball coach Jefferson County Schs., Denver, 1980-84; pub. relations cons. Omni Worldwide Corp., Clearwater, Fla., 1984-86; writer, pub. speaker Omni Prevention Edn. Network, Clearwater, Fla., 1984—; writer, editor, cons., speaker Quest Internat., Columbus, Ohio, 1980—. Co-author: Alive & In Person wellness manual, 1984, Facilitation, 1984, Always a Winner, Healthy Competition, 1986, Check it Out, Saying NO for Young People, 1986, Canned Confidence, 1988, The Confident Leader, 1988. Mem. Nat. Assn. Women, Nat. Assn. Female Execs. Office: Quest Internat PO Box 566 Granville OH 43023

FOX, KELLY DIANE, assistant buyer; b. Brockton, Mass., Sept. 9, 1959; d. James H. and Betty Jane (Calloway) F.; m. Alan David Goldberg, July 6, 1985; 1 child, Andrew Jason. B.A., Allegheny Coll., 1980; postgrad. in Bus. Adminstrn., Suffolk U., 1983-84; student Temple U., London, 1978, Syracuse U., London, 1979. Asst. mgr. Casual Male, Braintree, Mass., 1980, Hit or Miss, Braintree, 1981-82; merchandiser Foxmoor, West Bridgewater, Mass., 1982; distbr. Hill's Dept. Stores, Canton, Mass., 1982-85; asst. buyer BJ's Wholesale Club, Natick, Mass., 1985—; cheerleading coach Avon High Sch., Mass., 1982-83. Mem. Nat. Assn. Female Execs. Methodist. Avocations: dance; exercise; cooking; art galleries.

FOX, MARILYN MURPHY, lawyer; b. Elizabeth, N.J., May 13, 1942; d. Thomas Patrick and Florence Ann (Weickhardt) Murphy; m. John James Williams, July 25, 1964; children—Patrick, Kathryn; m. John R. Fox, 1987. B.S., U. Kans., 1964; M.L.S., Emporia State Coll., 1974; J.D., U. Mo. at Kansas City, 1979. Bar: Kans. 1979, Ariz. 1984. Tchr., Shawnee Mission (Kans.) Sch. Dist., 1964-66, Virginia Beach, Va., 1967-68, Newport, R.I., 1969-70; librarian Center Sch. Dist., Kansas City, Mo., 1973-75; partner Williams & Oberhelman, Mission, Kans., 1979-84; Kans. counsel Buck, Bohm, & Stein, P.C., 1983-84; assoc. Brown & Herrick, Mesa, Ariz., 1984—. Bd. dirs. Kans. Legal Services of Olathe, 1981-84. NDEA fellow, 1965. Mem. ABA, State Bar Ariz., East Valley Bar Assn., Maricopa County Bar Assn., Kans. Bar Assn., Kans. Trial Lawyers Assn., Kansas City Bar Assn., Johnson County Bar Assn. (bench-bar com. domestic relations 1981—), Mid-Am. Family Mediation Assn. (pres. 1985-86). Republican. Home: 3735 E Ahwatukee Dr Phoenix AZ 85004 Office: Brown & Herrick 1745 E Alma School Mesa AZ 85004

FOX, MARY MASELLI, psychologist; b. Chgo. BA, Carleton Coll., 1964; PhD, Duke U., 1970. Cert. clin. psychologist, N.Y. With Marin County Mental Health Services, San Rafael, Calif., 1970-71; dir. Adult Mental Health Services of Gaston County, Gastonia, N.C., 1971-72; co-founder Family Therapy Services, Gastonia, 1972-73; asst. prof. psychiatry U. Rochester (N.Y.) Sch. Medicine, 1979-84, dir. psychotherapy and group relations program, 1979-84, clin. asst. prof. psychiatry, 1984-87, clin. assoc. prof. psychiatry, 1987—. Contbr. articles to profl. jours. Co-chmn. Agate Gifted Edn. Study Group, Brighton, N.Y., 1985—; local rep. Am. Field Service, Brighton, 1986—; bd. dirs. Rochester Chamber Orchestra, 1987. Mem. Am. Psychol. Assn., Am. Assn. Higher Edn., Nat. Assn. Women Deans, Adminstrs. and Counselors. Office: 1513 South Ave Rochester NY 14620

FOX, MURIEL, public relations executive; b. Newark, Feb. 3, 1928; d. M. Morris and Anne L. (Rubenstein) F.; m. Shepard G. Aronson, July 1, 1955; children: Eric R., Lisa S. Student, Rollins Coll., 1944-46; B.A. summa cum laude, Barnard Coll., 1948. Art critic, bridal editor Miami (Fla.) News, 1946; reporter U.P.I., 1946-48; polit. speechwriter, publicist 1949-50; with Carl Byoir & Assos., N.Y.C., 1950-86; TV-radio writer Carl Byoir & Assos., 1950-52, dir. TV-radio dept., 1952-57, v.p., 1956-74, group v.p., 1974-76, exec. v.p., 1977-85; pres. subs. MediaCom Communications Tng., 1975-85, By/Media Inc., 1981-85; sr. cons. Hill & Knowlton, Inc., 1986—; dir. Harleysville Ins. Co., Rorer Group Inc.; Co-chmn. Vice Presdl. Task Force on Women, 1968; mem. steering com. Women's Forum, 1974-79, pres., 1976-78; mem. Women's Econ. Adv. Com., N.Y.C., 1974-78; mem. nat. adv. com. Nat. Women's Polit. Caucus; mem. nat. adv. bd. Women Today, Ethnic Woman. Bd. dirs. N.Y. Diabetes Assn., 1956-66; bd. dirs. Holy Land Conservation Fund, United Way of Tri-State, Internat. Rescue Com., 1977-84; v.p. Rockland Ctr. for the Arts, 1985—. Named one of 100 Top Corp. Women Bus. Week mag., 1976; recipient Matrix award Women in Communications, 1977, Bus. Leader of Year award ADA, 1979; Disting. Alumna award Barnard Coll., 1985; Eleanor Roosevelt Leadership award, 1985. Mem. Am. Women in Radio and TV (dir. 1959-61, chmn. nat. publicity com. 1955-57, chmn. nat. pub. relations com. 1957-59, Achievement award 1983), NOW (founder, v.p. 1967-70, chmn. bd. 1971-73, chmn. nat. adv. com. 1973-74, bd. dirs. Legal Def. and Edn. Fund 1974—, v.p. Fund 1977-78, pres. 1978-81, chmn. bd. 1981—), Am. Arbitration Assn. (bd. dirs. 1983—). Home and Office: 66 Hickory Hill Rd Tappan NY 10983

FOX, NANCY JAMES, company administrator; b. St. James, Minn., May 20, 1950; d. Latimer B. and Amy Pearl (Halverson) James; m. Jeffrey Michael Fox, Nov. 30, 1974; 1 child, Joshua James. B.A., Macalester Coll., 1972; postgrad. Hochschule fuer Musik, Frankfurt, West Ger., Wolfgang Goethe U., Frankfurt, Shenandoah Coll. Tchr. Jugendmusikschule, Frankfurt, 1971-74; paralegal Kuykendall, Costello & Hanes, Winchester, Va., 1976-77; sec. VDO Instruments, Inc., Winchester, 1978-79, credit mgr., 1979-81, br. mgr., 1982-85, regional sales mgr., 1985-87; nat. sales mgr. Jaeger-LeCoultre SA, Inc., 1988—. Recipient Janet Wallace Music award Macalester Coll., 1970. Mem. Nat. Assn. Female Execs., Am. Assn. Individual Investors. Office: VDO Instrument Inc PO Box 2897 Winchester VA 22601

FOX, PAULA (MRS. MARTIN GREENBERG), author; b. N.Y.C., Apr. 22, 1923; d. Paul Hervey and Elsie (de Sola) F.; m. Richard Sigerson (div. 1954); children: Adam, Gabriel; m. Martin Greenberg, June 9, 1962. Student, Columbia U. Condr. writing Seminars U. Pa. Author: 16 children's books, including How Many Miles to Babylon, 1966, Portrait of Ivan, 1968, Blowfish Live in the Sea, 1970; (novels) Poor George, 1967; Desperate Characters, 1970, The Western Coast, 1972, The Slave Dancer, 1974 (John Newbery medal), The Widow's Children, 1976, The Little Swineherd and Other Tales, 1978, A Place Apart, 1983 (Am. Book award), A Servant's Tale, 1984, One-Eyed Cat, 1985 (Newbery honor book 1985). Guggenheim fellow, 1972; Recipient Arts and Letters award Nat. Inst. Arts and Letters, 1972, Hans Christian Andersen medal, 1978; Recipient fiction citation Brandeis U., 1984. Mem. P.E.N., Authors League.

FOX, RENÉE CLAIRE, sociology educator; b. N.Y.C., Feb. 15, 1928; d. Paul Fred and Henrietta (Gold) F. A.B. summa cum laude, Smith Coll., 1949, L.H.D., 1975; Ph.D., Harvard U., 1954; M.A. (hon.), U. Pa., 1971; Sc.D. (hon.), Med. Coll. Pa., 1974, St. Joseph's Coll., Phila., 1978; D. honoris causa, Katholieke U., Belgium, 1978. Research asst. Bur. Applied

Social Research, Columbia U., 1953-55, research assoc., 1955-58; lectr. dept. sociology Barnard Coll., 1955-58, asst. prof., 1958-64, assoc. prof., 1964-66; lectr. sociology Harvard U., 1967-69; research fellow Center Internat. Affairs, 1967-68, research assoc. program tech. and soc., 1968-71; prof. sociology, psychiatry and medicine U. Pa., Phila., 1969—, Annenberg prof. social scis., 1978—, chmn. dept. sociology, 1972-78; Sci. adviser Centre de Recherches Sociologiques, Kinshasa, Congo, 1963-67; vis. prof. sociology U. Officielle du Congo, Lubumbashi, 1965; vis. prof. Sir George Williams U., Montreal, Que., Can., summer 1968; Phi Beta Kappa vis. scholar, 1973-75; dir. humanities seminar med. practitioners Nat. Endowment Humanities, 1975-76; maitre de cours U. Liége, Belgium, 1976-77; vis. prof. Katholieke U., Leuven, Belgium, 1976-77; Wm. Allen Neilson prof. Smith Coll., Mass., 1980; mem. bd. clin. scholars program Robert Wood Johnson Found., 1974-80; mem. Pres.'s Commn. on Study of Ethical Problems in Medicine, Biomed. and Behavioral Research, 1979-81; dir. human qualities of medicine program James Picker Found., 1980-83; Fal Golden Kass lectr. Harvard U. Sch. Medicine and Radcliffe Coll., 1983. Author: Experiment Perilous, 1959, (with Willy DeCraemer) The Emerging Physician, 1968, (with Judith P. Swazey) The Courage to Fail: Essays in Medical Sociology, 1979, 2d edit., 1988, L'Incertitude Medicale, 1988; assoc. editor: Am. Sociol. Rev, 1963-66, Social Sci. and Medicine; mem. editorial com.: Ann. Rev. Sociology, 1975-79; assoc. editor Jour. Health and Social Behavior, 1985-87; mem. editorial adv. bd.: Tech. in Soc, Science, 1982-83; editorial bd.: Bibliography of Bioethics, 1979—, Culture, Medicine and Psychiatry, 1980-86, Jour. of AMA, 1981—; contbr. articles to profl. jours. Bd. dirs. medicine in Public Interest, 1979—; mem. tech. bd. Milbank Meml. Fund, 1979-85; mem. overseers com. to visit univ. health services Harvard Coll., 1979-86; trustee Russell Sage Found., 1981-87. Recipient E. Harris Harbison Gifted Teaching award Danforth Found., 1970; Radcliffe Grad. Soc. medal Wilson Ctr., 1977; Wilson Ctr., Smithsonian Instn. fellow, 1987-88, Guggenheim fellow, 1962. Fellow African Studies Assn., AAAS (dir. 1977-80, chmn. sect. K 1986-87), Am. Sociol. Assn. (council 1970-73, 79-81, v.p. 1980-81), Am. Acad. Arts and Scis., Inst. Medicine (Nat. Acad. Scis., council 1979-82), Inst. Soc., Ethics and Life Scis. (founder, gov.); mem. AAUP, AAUW, Assn. Am. Med. Colls., Social Sci. Research Council (v.p., dir.), Eastern Sociol. Soc. (pres. 1976-77), N.Y. Acad. Scis., Soc. Sci. Study Religion, Inst. Intercultural Studies (asst. sec. 1969-78, sec. 1978-81, v.p. 1987—), Am. Bd. Med. Specialists, Phi Beta Kappa (senate 1982-87). Home: 135 S 19 St Philadelphia PA 19103

FOX, ROBERTA FULTON, lawyer, state legislator; b. Phila., Nov. 25, 1943; d. Robert Fulton and Irmgard F.; B.A., U. Fla., 1964, J.D., 1967; m. Mike Gold; 1 stepdau., Shari Anna Gold. Admitted to Fla. bar, 1968; mem. Govt. Research Council, Miami-Dade C. of C., 1964-65; staff Goldin & Jones, Gainesville, Fla., 1968; atty. Migrant Legal Services, Miami, 1968-69, Legal Services Greater Miami, 1970-72; pvt. practice law, Coral Gables, Fla., 1972-80; partner firm Gold & Fox, P.A., from 1972; mem. Fla. Ho. Reps., 1976-82; mem. Fla. Senate, 1982-86 ; mem. Gov.'s Commn. on Marriage and the Family Unit, 1974-76; chairperson Dade County Women's Polit. Caucus, 1971-74; Women's Action Center, Inc.; chairperson sex-biased discrimination com. of minority affairs com. Democratic Issues Conv., 1976-78. Mem. affirmative action agy. adv. bd., treas. Transition, Inc.; mem. council, bd. dirs. Planned Parenthood of S. Fla.; bd. dirs. NOW Legal Def. and Edn. Fund.; hon. bd. dirs. Girls Clubs Greater Miami. Recipient Outstanding State Legislator award, 1979; Gov.'s award for Art, 1980. Mem. Bus. and Profl. Women, Fla. Women Lawyers Assn., Fla. Bar Assn., Voters Inc., Coral Gables C. of C., Nat. Women's Polit. Caucus, Fla. Women's Polit. Caucus, Dade County Women's Polit. Caucus, LWV, AAUW, Citizens League, Inc., ACLU, Panel of Am. Women, Common Cause, U. Fla. Law Center Assn., Zero Population Growth. Office: 7700 N Kendall Dr Suite 612 Miami FL 33156

FOX, RUTH INABU, health planner, economist; b. Salt Lake City, Oct. 4, 1918; d. Masataro and Mitsuye (Kushigami) Inabu Kushiue; m. Jack Jay Fox, June 13, 1939; children: Dolores Fox Emspak, John Reed. BA, U. Colo., 1940, MA, 1946. Research assoc. U. Colo., Boulder, 1946-49; dir. Office Devel. Evaluation and Research, Westchester County, White Plains, N.Y., 1967-69; dir. div. health planning and research Westchester County, White Plains, N.Y., 1969-74, asst. commr. health planning and program devel., 1974-79, program dir. regional emergency med. services system, 1974-79; emergency med. services cons. Westchester County, Valhalla, N.Y., 1979-86; asst. prof. community and preventive medicine N.Y. Med. Coll., Valhalla, 1970—. Del., adv. com to county execs. Stop Drinking and Driving Program, 1981—; v.p. Women of Westchester, 1980—, Nat. Women's Polit. Caucus, Westchester, 1982-84, Westchester Health Action Coalition, 1986—; bd. dirs. Cage Teen Ctr., 1962—, Westchester County Mental Health Assn., 1968-83; pres. White Plains Council Community Services, 1979-84; Dist. leader Democratic Party White Plains, 1960-64; mem. N.Y. State Health Care Campaign-Citizen Action, 1987—; pres. Westchester Coalition Permanent Housing for Low and Middle Income People, 1987—; mem. Rainbow Coalition, 1986—, Coalition for Nat. Health Care System, 1986—; voter service chmn. LWV, White Plains, 1956-58. Recipient Disting. Service award Commn. Human Rights White Plains, 1984. Fellow Inst. Trauma and Emergency Care; mem. Am. Pub. Health Assn., Westchester County Assocs., Hudson Valley Regional Emergency Med. Services Council (del.), Older Womens League, Gray Panthers, Advocacy League for Mentally Ill., N.Y. State Communities Aid Assn. Avocations: reading, travel. Home and Office: 424 S Lexington Ave White Plains NY 10606

FOX, SHIRLEY MAY, artist; b. Rose City, Mich., Sept. 22, 1933; d. Earl Ren and Crystal Beatrice (Bartels) F.; m. Robert Marvin Turner, Dec. 15, 1951 (div. July 1975); children: Robert Lee, August Christopher, Crystal Allene; m. John Walter White, Oct. 25, 1981 (div. Oct. 1983). B of Visual Arts, Ga. State U., 1976. Owner Shirley Fox Studios and Galleries, Atlanta, 1977—. Mem. Intown Bus. Assn. (bd. dirs. 1984-87), Midtown Bus. Assn., Profl. Picture Framers Assn. (pres. Atlanta chpt. 1982-84, bd. dirs. nat. 1984-86), Internat. Soc. Appraisers (assoc.), Am. Soc. Interior Designers (assoc.). Lutheran. Club: Zonta (Atlanta). Office: Shirley Fox Studios and Galleries 1586-90 Piedmont Ave Atlanta GA 30324

FOX, VIRGINIA GAINES, public broadcasting executive; b. Campbellsville, Ky., Apr. 30, 1939; d. Harold Durrett and Kathryn (Arnold) Gaines; m. Victor Fox, Dec. 27, 1963. B.A. in Edn., Morehead State U., 1961; M.S.L.S., U. Ky., 1969. Cert. tchr., librarian, Ky. Tchr. Franklin County Schs., Frankfort, Ky., 1961-62, Mason County Schs., Maysville, Ky., 1962-63, Whiteland Elem. Sch., Ind., 1963-64; tchr., librarian Fayette County Schs., Lexington, Ky., 1964-68; utilization specialist Ky. Ednl. TV, Lexington, 1968-69, asst. dir. edn. for evaluation, 1969-70, exec. asst. to exec. dir., 1970-71, dir. edn., 1971-74, dir. edn. and programming, 1974-75, dep. exec. dir., 1974-80; pres., chief exec. officer So. Ednl. Communications Assn., Columbia, S.C., 1980—; mem. nat. adv. com. Children's TV Workshop, N.Y.C., 1979—, Teleconnect Database Mktg. Co., Cedar Rapids, Iowa, informal sci. edn. panel NSF, Washington, 1986—; dir. Editorial Integrity Project, Columbia, 1984—. Exec. producer TV programs: Just One Day, 1979 (Eudora Welty award 1980), Vectoria, 1978 (Corp. for Pub. Broadcasting award 1979), GED. Named Woman of Yr. in Edn., Lexington Bus. and Profl. Women's Club, 1971-72. Mem. Am. Soc. Assn. Execs., Nat. Assn. Ednl. Broadcasters, ALA, Assn. for Ednl. Communications and Tech. (Edgar Dale award region V 1975), Wildlife Action. Episcopalian. Avocations: reading; golf; piano; running. Home: PO Box 5416 Columbia SC 29250 Office: Southern Ednl Communications PO Box 5008 Columbia SC 29250

FOXEN, LYNNE ANNE, insurance company executive; b. Teaneck, N.J., Mar. 8, 1950; d. Joseph Patrick and Yolanda A. (Franchini) F. BS, St. Peter's Coll., 1980. Asst. treas. arms div. Ashford Holding Corp., N.Y.C., 1975-77, fin. planning mgr. MIC div., 1977-82, asst. v.p., 1982-84; dir. Empire Blue Cross Blue Shield, N.Y.C., 1984—. Mem. Assn. Women in Prodn., Assn. Female Execs. Home: 147 Magnolia Ave Tenafly NJ 07670

FOXMAN, LORETTA DOROTHY, human resource consultant; b. Los Angeles, Sept. 4, 1939; d. Frederick and Helen (Goldberg) F.; m. Walter L. Polsky, Aug. 9, 1964; children—Michael William, Susan Jennifer. B.A., Calif. State U.-Los Angeles, 1963; M.A., Columbia U., 1964. Tchr., Culver City Unified Sch. Dist. (Calif.), 1964-68; asst. dir. St. Christopher Acad., Westfield, N.J., 1971-75; curriculum cons. Middlesex Community Coll. Daycare Ctr., Edison, N.J., 1973, Lakeview Montessori Acad., Summit, N.J., 1975; instr. Northwestern U., Evanston, Ill., 1982—; prin. Jack Dill Assocs., Chgo., 1976-81; exec. v.p. CAMBRIDGE Human Resource Group, Inc., Chgo., 1981—. Chmn. various coms. LWV, Cranford, N.J. and Glencoe, Ill., 1971—; mem. Ad Hoc Rent Control Com., 1973; chair adv. bd. Northwestern U. Program on Women, 1982—. Author: Resumes That Work: How to Sell Yourself on Paper, 1984; contbg. editor Personnel Jour.; contbr. several articles to profl. jours. Mem. AAUW, Am. Soc. Human Resource Profls. (Woman of Achievement award), Women in Mgmt. Office: Cambridge Human Resource Group Inc 2 N Riverside Suite 2200 Chicago IL 60606

FOXWORTHY, LISA PAIGE, accountant; b. Williamsport, Ind., Feb. 12, 1963; d. Earl Ward and Carolyn Faith (Turpin) F. BS in Acctg., Ind. U., 1985, postgrad., 1987—. CPA, cert. managerial acct. Product inspector Frito-lay Inc., Frankfort, Ind., 1982-83; acct. Lacy Diversified Industries, Indpls., 1985-87; mgr. reports and analysis Firstmark Fin. Corp., Indpls., 1987; securities analyst Indpls. Life Ins. Co., 1987—. Mem. Ind. CPA Soc., Nat. Assn. Female Execs., 500 Festival Assocs., Indpls. Mus. Art, Ind. ALumni Club. Office: Indpls Life Ins Co PO Box 1230 Indianapolis IN 46206

FOY, DEBORAH SANFORD, social worker; b. Monroe, La., Feb. 17, 1954; d. Fred Darden Sanford and Gladys (Schoen) Thompson; m. Gary Dee Foy, May 9, 1981. BA in Sociology and Social Work, S.W. Tex. State U., 1975. Cert. social worker. Social worker Dept. Human Services State of Tex., Austin, 1976-81; program coordinator Day Care Assn. of Ft. Worth and Tarrant County, 1982-84; disability examiner Disability Determination div. Tex. Rehab. Commn., Austin, 1984—; cons. Social Studies, Austin and Travis County, Tex. 1984. Vol. Hotline to Help, San Marcos, Tex., 1975-78, Big Bro.-Big Sister program, Austin, 1978-80; treas. Sandybrook Neighborhood Assn., Ft. Worth, 1981-83; chairperson County Community Resources, Lockhart, Tex., 1977-79. Mem. Nat. Assn. Social Workers, Nat. Assn. Disability Examiners, Tex. Assn. Disability Examiners, Milwood Neighborhood Assn. Home: 4522 Sidereal Dr Austin TX 78727-5105

FOY, DENISE COLLEEN, information systems company executive; b. Detroit, Jan. 22, 1960; d. James Edward and Frances Maria (Fava) Foy. BS in Edn., Wayne State U., 1982, MEd, 1983. Inventory coordinator Cert. Collateral Corp., Chgo., 1983-84, database ops. mgr., 1984-85, v.p. database ops., 1985-88; v.p. ops. Original Research II, div. Cert. Collateral Corp., Chgo., 1988—; lectr. in field. Mem. Nat. Assn. Female Execs. Lodge: Rotary.

FRACKMAN, NOEL, art critic; b. N.Y.C., May 27, 1930; d. Walter David and Celeste (Barman) Stern; m. Richard Benoit Frackman, July 2, 1950; 1 dau., Noel Dru. Student Mt. Holyoke Coll., 1948-50; BA, Sarah Lawrence Coll., 1952, MS, 1953; postgrad. Columbia U., 1964-67; MA, Inst. Fine Arts, NYU, 1976, PhD, 1987. Art critic Scarsdale Inquirer (N.Y.), 1962-67, Patent Trader, Mt. Kisco, N.Y., 1962-71; assoc. Arts Mag., N.Y.C., 1968—; lectr. Aldrich Mus. Contemporary Art, Ridgefield, Conn., 1967-75, Gallery Passport Ltd., N.Y.C., 1968—; curator of edn. Storm King Art Ctr., Mountainville, N.Y., 1973-75. Author (catalogue) John Storrs, Whitney Mus. of Am. Art, 1986; contbr. articles and/or revs. to various mags. including: Arts Mag., Harper's Bazaar, Feminist Art Jour., Art Voices. Sarah Williston scholar, 1948-50; recipient 1st prize, coll. publs. contest Mademoiselle mag., 1961. Mem. Internat. Assn. Art Critics, Art Table Inc., Coll. Art Assn. Home: 3 Hadden Rd Scarsdale NY 10583

FRADKIN, MINDY SUE, fashion stylist, costume designer; b. Balt., June 3, 1955; d. Robert Bernard Fradkin and Dorothy (Wolfe) Hight. Student, Art Ctr., Los Angeles, 1979-81; AA with honors, Art Ctr. Coll. of Design, Los Angeles, 1983. Freelance asst. stylist, Los Angeles, 1982-83, N.Y.C., 1983-84; stylist, prodn. coordinator Cailor Resnick Studio, N.Y.C., 1984; freelance fashion stylist and costume designer for print and film, N.Y.C., 1985—. Appeared on TV in World of Photography. Active Big Sisters. Mem. Nat. Assn. Broadcast Employees and Technicians, Assn. Stylists and Coordinators (sec. 1984-85), Stylists and Allied Services (bd. dirs. 1985-86). Democrat. Jewish. Avocations: writing, opera, classical and jazz music, reading, films. Office: 313 W 75th St 4B New York NY 10023

FRAGUERO, KAREN LEE, banker; b. Sonora, Calif., Nov. 10, 1963; d. Laurence Raymond and Clara Catherine (Anderson) F. Student, Columbia (Calif.) Coll., 1983, 87—. Asst. v.p., mgr. Sentinel Savs. & Loan Assn., Sonora, 1982—. Coach Sonora High Sch. Basketball Spiritleaders, 1987. Mem. Nat. Assn. Female Execs., Oakdale (Calif.) C. of C. Roman Catholic. Home: 9642 Fraguero Rd Sonora CA 95370 Office: Sentinel Savs & Loans Assn 1449 E F St Oakdale CA 95361

FRAHM, SUE ADELE, university administrator; b. Beatrice, Nebr., Jan. 16, 1941; d. Berwin Richard and Kathryn Mary (Burroughs) Shaffer; m. Larry Dean Frahm, Aug. 17, 1963; children—Jeffrey Michael, Kristi Anne. B.A., Nebr. Wesleyan U., 1962; M.S., U. Nebr.-Lincoln, 1978. Instr. Southeast Community Coll., Lincoln, 1972-77, project asst. Ctr. on Aging, 1977-78, aging coordinator, 1978-79, asst. coordinator adult edn., 1979-80; dir. alumni Nebr. Wesleyan U., Lincoln, 1981—; trainer Minn. Couples Communication Program, Mpls., 1977-82. Pres., 1st v.p. YWCA, Lincoln, 1978-85; bd. dirs. Lincoln council Camp Fire, 1975-78, Lincoln Ctr. for Srs., 1970-76; co-pres. Community Adv. Council, Lincoln, 1985-86. Mem. Adult Continuing Edn. of Nebr., Omicron Nu. Avocations: jogging, reading, backpacking. Home: 8033 Sanborn Dr Lincoln NE 68505 Office: Nebr Wesleyan U 50th and St Paul Sts Lincoln NE 68504

FRAIR, BETTY BOLLBACK EVANS, public relations officer, educator; b. Bklyn., May 28, 1927; d. Anthony J. and Elizabeth (Balzer) Bollback; m. C. Hans Evans, June 10, 1961 (dec. July 1977); m. Wayne Frair, May 2, 1987. B.R.E., Nyack Coll., 1949; M.A., NYU, 1951; postgrad. Northwestern U., 1953, Columbia U., 1952-57. Audiologist Manhattan Eye, Ear, Nose and Throat Hosp., N.Y.C., 1949-54; tchr. Lexington Sch. for Deaf, N.Y.C., 1954-59; supervising Deaf, Phila., 1960-68; prin. Middle Sch., Pa. Sch. for Deaf, 1968-71; asst. prof. spl. edn. Pa. State U., University Park, 1962-71; specialist in deaf edn. Chester County Child Devel. Ctr., Coatesville, 1971-78; assoc. dean students King's Coll., Briarcliff Manor, N.Y., 1978-86, instr. speech, 1978-79, dir. dept. continuing edn., 1980-86, cons. study skills ctr., 1982-86, dir. pub relations, 1986—; cons. Nat. Com. Library Standards for Schs. for Deaf, N.Y., 1965-66; lectr., speaker civic, religious and profl. groups. Active Chester County Health and Welfare Assn., 1962; social dir. Word of Life Summer Confs., N.Y., 1955-60; corp. mem. Lancaster Sch. of Bible, 1973; v.p. Living Word Radio Ministry Internat., 1974-77; summer seminar coordinator Camp of Woods, Speculator, N.Y., 1978—; hon. mem. program agy. United Presbyn. Ch. U.S.A., 1977—. Recipient Outstanding Service award Coatesville Area Council PTA. Mem. Coatesville Hosp. Aux., Conv. Am. Instrs. for Deaf, Presbyn. Women's Assn. (pres. 1976-77), Delta Kappa Gamma. Republican. Address: Kings Coll Briarcliff Manor NY 10510

FRALEY, RUTH ANN, librarian; b. Peekskill, N.Y., Oct. 16, 1942; d. Joseph Edward and Cora Marie (McEachern) Salerno; B.A., SUNY, Albany, 1964, M.S. in L.S., 1966; M.B.A., Union Coll. Schenectady, 1981; m. James M. Fraley, Sept. 26, 1964; children—Christine, Melissa, Heather. Library media specialist Schenectady Public Schs., part-time 1966-72; reference librarian, then head tech. services Library Resources Center, Schenectady County Community Coll., 1972-79, chmn. adv. com., 1981—; head Hawley Library, SUNY, Albany, 1979-81, head Grad. Library Public Affairs and Policy, 1981-86; chief librarian N.Y. State Ct. System, 1986—. Recipient SUNY Chancellor's award for Excellence, 1979. Mem. ALA (chmn. publ. award jury resources and tech. services div. 1982-84, chmn. circulation stats. com. library adminstrn. mgmt. div. 1982—, chmn. stats. sect. 1985-86), Am. Assn. Law Librarians, N.Y. Library Assn. (pres. 1986, past pres. resources and tech. services sect.), Hudson-Mohawk Library Assn., Upstate N.Y. Labor History Assn., Albany Women's Forum. Roman Catholic. Author, editor in field. Home: 29 Roslyn Dr Ballston Lake NY 12019 Office: Office of Ct Adminstr Agy Bldg 4 10th floor Empire Sta te Plaza Albany NY 12223

FRAME, ANNE PARSONS, civic worker; b. Berkeley, Calif., Jan. 3, 1904; d. Reginald Hascall and Maude (Bemis) Parsons; A.B., Mills Coll., 1924; postgrad. Columbia, 1924-25; m. Frederic D. Tootell, Apr. 3, 1926 (div. July 1935); children—Geoffrey H., Natalie (Mrs. Oliver); m. Jasper Ewing Brady, July 31, 1935; (dec. Dec. 1941); 1 son, Hugh Parsons; m. Howard Andres Frame, Mar. 29, 1948. Dir. Parsons, Hart & Co., Seattle, Hillcrest Orchard Co., Seattle. Mem. bd. mgmt. Palo Alto br. A.R.C., 1955-61; trustee Children's Hosp. & Med. Ctr., Seattle, 1942-48; bd. dirs. Children's Health Council, Palo Alto, Calif., 1953-63, 64-76, pres., 1954-58; sponsor Nat. Recreation Assn., 1942-66, trustee, 1948-66; sponsor Nat. Recreation and Park Assn., 1966—, trustee, 1966-73; trustee Nat. Recreation Found., 1964—; 1st v.p. Children's Hosp. at Stanford Sr. Aux., 1965-85, bd. dirs. Hosp., 1962-72; former mem. adv. com. Holbrook-Palmer Park; trustee Mills Coll., 1952-62; bd. dirs. Holbrook-Palmer Recreation Park Found., 1968-86; bd. govs. San Francisco Symphony Assn., 1949-79; mem. Atherton (Calif.) Park and Recreation Commn., 1968-81. Mem. LWV, Bowne House Hist. Soc., San Mateo County, Seattle, Chgo., Calif. hist. socs., Calif. Heritage Council, San Francisco Mus. Art, Seattle Art Mus., Museum Soc., Nat. Trust for Historic Preservation, Nat. Soc. Colonial Dames Am. Episcopalian. Clubs: Sunset, Tennis (Seattle); Woodside-Atherton Garden (dir. 1966-68); Francisca (San Francisco).

FRAME, DOROTHY ELIZABETH, public relations executive; b. Bklyn.; d. Edward Francis and Edna Sophie (Groef) Feltmann; m. Manson Frame, Mar. 24, 1956 (div. 1978); 1 child, Manson Andrew. Student, Hofstra U., 1952-58, SUNY, Plattsburg, 1983, Hofstra U., 1984. Assoc. editor Sperry Rand, Great Neck, N.Y., 1955-58, editor, 1958-61; mng. editor Salvo Mag., Inc., L.I., 1964-67; dir. pub. info. North Shore Schs., Sea Cliff, N.Y., 1967-78; dir. communications Ednl. Mgmt. Inst., Glen Cove, N.Y., 1978-81; pres. Dorothy E. Frame Assocs., Inc., Glen Head, N.Y., 1981—; Bd. dirs. Ed. Com., Inc., Farmingdale, N.Y.; cons. spl. events N.Y. div. Gimbels, N.Y.C., 1975-85. Contbr. articles to profl. jours. Bd. dirs. Robert Constant Scholarship Fund, Glen Head, N.Y., 1984—. Mem. Nat. Sch. Pub. Relations Assn. (publs. awards of excellence, 1978, 82, 83), N.Y. State Sch. Pub. Relations Assn. (award of excellence 1985, spl. purpose publs. 1986), Nat. Bus. and Profl. Women's Club. Club: Research and Investment of L.I. (pres. 1987—). Home and Office: 5 Cross Ln Glen Head NY 11545

FRAME, JEAN GROETZ, educator, consultant; b. Medina, Ohio, July 18, 1951; d. Edward Joseph and Gwendolyn Mae (Lindley) G.; m. Carl Ralph Frame, Dec. 10, 1983. B.S., U. Akron, 1973, postgrad., 1973-83. Elem. tchr. Medina City Schs., Ohio, 1973—; cons. staff devel. team Medina Schs., 1982—; staff cons. Medina Drug Prevention Program, 1982—; dir. summer sch. age program Nurtury Presch., Medina, 1980-81; writer of reading and sci. goals and curricula, 1986. Composer of musical scores, 1972, 73. Jennings Found. scholar Kent State U., 1984-85. Mem. AAUW, Medina City Tchrs. Assn. (bldg. rep.) Medina City Staff Devel. Team, Kappa Delta Pi. Avocations: biking, travel, teaching piano, reading, gardening. Home: 7007 Buffham Rd Seville OH 44273 Office: Garfield Elem Sch 234 S Broadway St Medina OH 44256

FRANCA, CELIA, director, choreographer, dancer, narrator; b. London, Eng., June 25, 1921; m. James Morton, Dec. 7, 1960. Student, Guildhall Sch. Music, Royal Acad. Dancing; LL.D., U. Windsor, 1959, Mt. Allison U., 1966, U. Toronto, 1974, Dalhousie U., 1976, York U., 1976, Trent U., Peterborough, Ont., Can., 1977, McGill U., 1986; D.C.L., Bishop's U., 1967; D.Litt., Guelph U., 1976. Mem. jury 5th Internat. Ballet Competition, Varna, Bulgaria, 1970, 2d Internat. Ballet Competition, Moscow, 1973. Debut: corps de ballet Mars, The Planets (Tudor), Mercury Theatre, London, 1936; soloist, Ballet Rambert, London, 1936-38, leading dramatic dancer, Ballet Rambert, 1938-39, guest artist, Ballet Rambert, 1950, dancer, Ballet des Trois Arts, London, 1939, Arts Theatre Ballet, London, 1940, Internat. Ballet, London, 1941, leading dramatic dancer, Sadler's Wells Ballet, 1941-46, guest artist, choreographer, Sadler's Wells Theatre Ballet, London, 1946-47, dancer, tchr., Ballets Jooss, Eng., 1947, ballet mistress, leading dancer, Met. Ballet, London, 1947-49, dancer, Ballet Workshop, London, 1949-51, founder, artistic dir., Nat. Ballet Can., Toronto, 1951-74, a prin. dancer, Nat. Ballet Can., 1951-59, co-founder, Nat. Ballet Sch., Toronto, 1959—; prin. roles include Black Queen in Swan Lake; title roles in Lady from the Sea; choreographer: ballets, including Midas, London, 1939, Cancion, London, 1942, Khadra, London, 1946, Dance of Salome, BBC-TV, 1949, The Eve of St. Agnes, BBC-TV, 1950, Afternoon of a Faun, Toronto, 1952, Le Pommier, Toronto, 1952, Casse-Noisette, 1955, Princess Aurora, 1960, The Nutcracker, 1964, Cinderella, 1968, numerous others for CBC, Can. Opera Co.; author: The National Ballet of Canada: A Celebration, 1978. Bd. dirs. Can. Council; hon. patron Osteoporosis Soc. Can., Nat. Breast Screening Study. Decorated Order of Can.; recipient Key to City of Washington, 1955; Woman of Year award B'nai B'rith, 1958; award for outstanding contbn. to arts Toronto Telegram, 1965; Centennial medal, 1967; Hadassah award of merit, 1967; Molson award, 1974; award Internat. Soc. Performing Arts Adminstrs., 1979; twice visited China at invitation of Chinese govt. to teach; in Beijing mounted full-length Coppelia, 1980; honored as one of founders of Can.'s major ballet cos. at Alta. Ballet Co.'s 15th anniversary, 1981; recipient Can. Dance award, 1984; Gold Card IATSE local 58, 1984; diplôme d'honneur Can. Conf. Arts, 1986, Woman Yr. award St. George's Soc. Toronto, 1987, Order of Ont., 1987. Office: 250 Clemow Ave, Ottawa, ON Canada K1S 2B6

FRANCHIK, CAROL ANN, law firm administrative manager; b. Chgo., Jan. 5, 1939; d. Florian J. and Mildred E. (Backofen) Ostrowski; student Morton Coll., 1964; 1 son, Mark William. Legal sec. Hajek & Hucek, Cicero, Ill., 1956-58, Kirkland & Ellis, Chgo., 1958-59, 63-67; exec. sec. DeSoto Chem. Coatings, Chgo., 1961-63; adminstrv. mgr. Wildman, Harrold, Allen & Dixon, Chgo., 1967-79; v.p., controller Duff & Phelps, Inc., Chgo., 1979-83; adminstrv. mgr. Siegan, Barbakoff, Gomberg, Gordon & Elden, Ltd., Chgo., 1984; dir. fin. and adminstrn. Holleb & Coff, Chgo., 1984—; pres. Law Officers Mgrs. Assn., Chgo., 1976. Mem. adv. bd. Prairie State Coll., 1978-79; exec. bd. Fullersburg Homeowners Assn., 1980-81. Mem. ABA, Assn. Legal Adminstrs. Nat. Fedn. Bus. and Profl. Women's Clubs, Inc. Office: 55 E Monroe Chicago IL 60603

FRANCHINI, ROXANNE, banker; b. N.Y.C., Mar. 20, 1951; d. Tullio and Jean (Brady) F. Ed. Emerson Coll., Ricker Coll., New Sch. Social Research. With Princess Marcella Borghese div. Revlon, N.Y.C., 1972-73; stewardess TWA Airlines, 1973-74; asst. to pres. N.Y. Shipping Assn., N.Y.C., 1974-79; benefits mgr. Kidde, Inc., 1979-83; 2d v.p. pension trust fin. services Chase Manhattan Bank, N.A., N.Y.C., 1983-85, v.p. mgr. global securities, 1985—; coordinator community fund raising campaigns. Mem. Nat. Assn. Female Execs., Am. Mgmt. Assn., AAUW, Internat. Founds. Employee Benefits, Internat. Ops. Assn., S.W. Pension Conf., Nat. Investment Co. Service Assn. Office: 1211 Ave of the Americas New York NY 10036

FRANCIS, CAROLYN RAE, educator, musician, author; b. Seattle, July 25, 1940; d. James Douglas and Bessie Caroline (Smith) F; m. Barclay Underwood Stuart, July 5, 1971. BA in Edn., U. Wash., 1962. Cert. tchr., Wash. Tchr. Highline Pub. Schs., Seattle, 1962-64; musician Olympic Hotel, Seattle, 1962-72; 1st violin Cascade Symphony Orch., 1965-78; tchr. Bellevue (Wash.) Pub. Schs., 1965—; pres. Innovative Learning Designs, Mercer Island, Wash., 1984—; instr. string instruments; speaker inservice workshops convs. music educators, London, Vancouver, B.C., Can., Indpls., Seattle, N.Y.C., Los Angeles, Sacramento, Chgo., Balt., San Antonio, Fresno, Calif., Lexington, Ky. Author-pub.: Music Reading and Theory Skills, Levels 1, 2, 1986, Level 3, 1984; contbr. articles to profl. jours., 1984—. Bellevue Schs. Found. grantee, 1985-86, 1986-87. Mem. Am. String Tchrs. Assn., Music Educators' Nat. Conf., Nat. Assn. Music Tchrs., NEA, Nat. String Orch. Assn.

FRANCIS, DAWN ELIZABETH, chemist, scientist; b. Detroit, Mar. 19, 1924; d. Herbert Frank and Nana Dolores (Ross) Watson; m. Roderick Douglas Francis, Mar. 12, 1955; 1 child, Darryl Thomas. BS in Chemistry, Wayne State U., 1949, MS in Inorganic Chemistry, 1963, PhD in Inorganic Chemistry, 1968. Acad. dean Shaw Coll., Detroit, 1971-72; founder, pres. Drake Inst. Scis., Detroit, 1972-74; founder Francis Labs., Detroit, 1969—; devel. pure and natural organic fertilizer, 1986; synthesized active component, 1987. Mem. Delta Sigma Theta. Office: 400 Renaissance Ctr Suite 500 Detroit MI 48243

FRANCIS, MARLENE JOAN, university administrator; b. Battle Creek, Mich., July 15, 1936; d. Richard Bates and Bertha Estelle (Winger) Crandell; m. Arthur Batchelor Francis, Aug. 14, 1982. BA in English, Kalamazoo

Coll., 1958; MA in English, U. Akron, 1965; PhD in Edn., U. Mich., 1984. Instr. English U. Akron, Ohio, 1965-79, asst. to dean, 1975-79; asst. to dean U. Mich., Ann Arbor, 1982—; bd. trustees exec. com. Kalamazoo Coll.; officer Ohio Bd. United Ministries in Higher Edn., Columbus, 1977-79. Mem. Am. Assn. Higher Edn., Assn. for Study of Higher Edn. (nominating com.), Mich. Assn. Women Deans and Adminstrs., Nat. Council Tchrs. English, Conf. Coll. Composition and Communication. Baptist. Home: 2440 Adare Rd Ann Arbor MI 48104 Office: U Mich Sch Edn Ann Arbor MI 48109

FRANCIS, NANCY MARGARET, data processing supervisor; b. Hamilton, Ont., Can., Nov. 16, 1952; d. Harold Frederick and Margaret Lynch (Fenwick) Peters; m. Garry Robert Francis. Aug. 21, 1976; children: Sean Michael, Brian Patrick, Kevin James. Computer operator Can. Centre for Inland Waters, Burlington, 1973, coding clk., 1974; data control, scheduling clk. McMaster U. Med. Centre, Hamilton, 1974-78; data control supr. McMaster U. Med. Ctr., St. Joseph's Hosp., Hamilton, 1978-82; programmer analyst St. Joseph's Hosp., Hamilton, 1982-86, supr. data processing services, 1986—. Office: St Josephs Hosp, 50 Charlton Ave E, Hamilton ON, CAN L8N4A6

FRANCISCO, ANNA B., travel agency owner; b. Waterbury, Conn., Nov. 22, 1933; d. Izauro and Amalia (DosSantos) Branco; m. Sebastian V. Francisco, May 31, 1954; children: Philip M., David P. Sales person Worth's, Waterbury, Conn., 1950-51; travel agt. Madeline Roberts Travel Agy., Waterbury, 1951-54, travel agy. mgr., 1954-60, travel agy. mgr., owner, 1960—. Mem. Am. Soc. Travel Agts., Am. Bus. Women's Assn. (past pres., Woman of Yr.). Club: Quota (1st v.p. Waterbury chpt.). Office: Madeline Roberts Travel Agy Inc 95 N Main St Waterbury CT 06702

FRANCK, IRENE MARY, author; b. Albany, N.Y., Mar. 14, 1941; d. Otto Charles and Pauline (Zuk) Franck; m. David M. Brownstone, Jan. 20, 1969; m. Lawrence E. Samuels, June 1961 (div. Mar. 1964). B.A., Harpur Coll. SUNY-Binghamton, 1962. Tchr. English, Susquehanna Valley Central Sch., Conklin, N.Y., 1962-63; writer Switchmen's Union N.Am., Conklin, 1962-67; office mgr. L.W. Hayes Real Estate & Ins., Binghamton, 1963-65, also folksinger, The Gate; chief operator N.Y. Telephone Co., Albany, 1965-67; tchr. English, Jefferson (N.Y.) Central Sch., 1967-68, Robert Louis Stevenson Sch., N.Y.C., 1968-70; editor John Wiley & Sons, N.Y.C., 1970-79; prin. The Hudson Group, Inc., Pleasantville, N.Y., 1979-87, pres., 1980-82; v.p., treas. Temeraire Enterprises, Chappaqua, N.Y., 1980—. Author: Island of Hope, Island of Tears: The Great Migration Through Ellis Island to America, 1979, The VNR Dictionary of Business and Finance, 1980, The VNR Real Estate Dictionary, 1981, The VNR Investor's Dictionary, 1981, The Dictionary of Publishing, 1982, The Sales Professional's Advisor, 1983, The Manager's Advisor, 1983, The Self-Publishing Handbook, 1985, The Silk Road: A History, 1986, ten vols. in the 15-vol. Work Throughout History series--Builders, 1986, Communicators, 1986, Financiers and Traders, 1986, Leaders and Lawyers, 1986, Artista and Artisans, 1987, Clothiers, 1987, Harversters, 1987, Helpers and Aides, 1987, Scientists and Technologists, 1988, Warriors and Adventurers, 1988, The AMA Handbook of Key Management Forms, 1987, Great Historic Places of America, 1987, one vol. in the America's Ethnic Heritage series: The Scandinavian-American Heritage, 1988; editor Film Rev. Digest quar., 1975-77; editor The 1985 Science Calendar and the 1986 Science Calendar. Mem. Authors Guild, Orgn. Am. Historians, Oral History Assn., Am. Hist. Assn.

FRANCK, JANE PAUL, library administrator; b. Akron, Ohio, Jan. 11, 1921; d. Francis O. and Irene A. (Neumann) Paul; m. Wolf Franck, Sept. 4, 1953 (dec. 1966); children: Irene Cecily, Julie Louise. BA cum laude, Hofstra U., 1942; BS in Library Service, Columbia U., 1943, MA with honors, 1949; postgrad., CUNY, 1968-74. Music librarian Columbia U., N.Y.C., 1943-49; archivist, spl. collections librarian CCNY, N.Y.C., 1960-68; librarian, adminstrv. officer Ford Found., N.Y.C., 1968-77; dir. Milbank Meml. Library, Tchrs. Coll., Columbia U., N.Y.C., 1977—; adj. lectr. Pratt Inst. Library Sch., Bklyn., 1963-68; founder, chmn. Consortium Found. Libraries, 1970-74; mem. Queens Coll. Adv. Com. on Post Masters Program for Library Dept., 1975—; mem. adminstrv. services com. N.Y. Met. Reference and Research Library Agy., 1973-77; mem. evaluation com. Conn. Dept. Higher Edn., 1984-85; mem. renovation of Milbank Meml. Library, 1979—; mem. search com. for pres., v.p., dean acad. affairs and v.p. for fin. and adminstrn. Tchrs. Coll., 1983-85; mem. com. for revision of 1970 UNESCO Standard for Libraries, 1976; cons. libraries in U.S., Iran, Italy, Pakistan, Spain, Fed. Republic Germany, Thailand, Singapore, Peoples Republic of China. Editor CircumSpice, 1965-68, Milbank Matters; contbr. articles to profl. jours. Mem. women's coordinating com., Ford Found., 1976-77; mem. Nat. Trust for Hist. Preservation, various consumer and civic groups. William Mason scholar Columbia U., N.Y.C., 1947-49. Mem. ALA (rep. to U.S. mission to UN 1978-85, internat. com. 1978-81, chmn. internat. relations round table 1977-79, edn. and behavioral scis. nominating com. 1979, standards com. 1978-82, adv. bd. for accreditation St. John's Univ. 1975, various other coms.) Am. Musicological Soc., Internat. Fedn. Library Assn. (library theory and research com. 1976-84, statistics and standards com. 1971-81), Music Library Assn. (archivist 1967-79), Soc. Am. Archivists, LWV. Democrat. Mem. United Ch. of Christ. Home: 25 Underhill Rd Ossining NY 10562 Office: Columbia U Tchrs Coll Milbank Meml Library 525 W 120th St New York NY 10027

FRANCKE, GLORIA NIEMEYER, pharmacist, editor, publisher; b. Dillsboro, Ind., Apr. 28, 1922; d. Albert B. and Fannie K. (Libbert) Niemeyer; m. Donald Eugene Francke, Apr. 15, 1956. BS in Pharmacy, Purdue U., 1942; PharmD, U. Cin., 1971; postgrad. U. Mich., 1945; PharmD (hon.) Purdue U., 1988—. Pharmacist, Dillsboro Drug Store, 1943-44; instr. Sch. Pharmacy, Purdue U., Lafayette, Ind., 1943; asst. to chief pharmacist U. Mich. Hosp., Ann Arbor, 1944-46; assoc. editor Am. Jour. Hosp. Pharmacy, Washington, 1944-64; asst. dir. Div. Hosp. Pharmacy of Am. Pharm. Assn., Washington, 1946-56; exec. sec. Am. Soc. Hosp. Pharmacists, Ann Arbor, 1949-60; acting dir. dept. communications, Washington, 1963-64; drug lit. specialist Nat. Library Medicine, Bethesda, Md., 1965-67; clin. pharmacy teaching coordinator VA Hosp., Cin., 1967-71; asst. clin. prof. clin. pharmacy Coll. Pharmacy, U. Cin., 1967-71; chief program evaluation br. Alcohol and Drug Dependence Service, VA, Central Office, Washington, 1971-75; dir. Pharmacy Intelligence Ctr., Am. Pharm. Assn., Washington, 1975-85; mem. Roche Hosp. Pharmacy Adv. Bd., 1971-74; judge for ann. Lunsford Richardson Pharmacy awards, 1963, 64; mem. com. standards for drug abuse treatment and rehab. programs Joint Commn. Accreditation of Hosps., 1974-75. Author: (with D. E. Francke, C. J. Latiolais and N.F. H. Ho) Mirror to Hospital Pharmacy, 1964. Contbr. articles on hosp. pharmacy and clin. pharmacy to profl. jours. Recipient H.A.K. Whitney award Mich. Soc. Hosp. Pharmacists, 1953, Disting. Alumnus award Purdue U. Sch. of Pharmacy, 1985, Remington Honor medal, 1987; also various commendations. Mem. Am. Pub. Health Assn., Internat. Pharm. Fedn., Am. Inst. History of Pharmacy (exec. sec. 1966-78), Tex. Soc. Hosp. Pharmacists (hon.), Am. Pharm. Assn. (hon. chmn. 1986), Am. Soc. Hosp. Pharmacists, Drug Info. Assn., Kappa Epsilon, Rho Chi. Presbyterian. Home and Office: 3900 Cathedral Ave NW #403-A Washington DC 20016

FRANCO, ANNEMARIE WOLETZ, editor; b. Somerville, N.J., Sept. 18, 1933; d. Frederick Franz and Bertha (Laugginger) Woletz; m. Frederick Nicholas Franco. Student, Wood Coll. of Bus. Editorial asst. Internat. Musician, then assoc. editor, 1965—. Mem. Internat. Labor Communications Assn., Labor Press Council Met. N.Y. Republican. Presbyterian. Home: Mt Pleasant Village 50-2A Morris Plains NJ 07950 Office: Internat Musician 1501 Broadway Suite 600 New York NY 10036

FRANCO, JANET ANN, investment management company executive; b. Cleve., Dec. 10, 1954; d. Gerald J. and Nancy (McKinley) Clarke; m. Thomas C. Franco, Aug. 14, 1976; children: Patrick Lanigan, Nicholas Taylor. BA, Smith Coll., 1976. Analyst fin. Internat. Paper, N.Y.C., 1977-80, mgr. investor relations, 1980-82; securities analyst and portfolio mgr. Capital Research, N.Y.C., 1982-85, v.p., 1985—, mgr. research, 1988—. Fulbright scholar, 1976, 77. Mem. Fin. Analyst Fedn. (forest products splinter group, constrn. and bldg. materials splinter group), Phi Beta Kappa. Democrat. Roman Catholic. Office: Capital Research 280 Park Ave New York NY 10017

FRANCOIS, DENISE JOANNE, administrative assistant; b. Port of Spain, Trinidad, West Indies, Dec. 19, 1961; came to U.S., 1967.; d. Ethelbert Alpheus and Margaret Octavia (Nixon) F. BA, Boston Coll., 1983; MA in Polit. Sci., Villanova U., 1986. Adminstrv. asst. Morgan Stanley & Co., N.Y.C., 1986-88; cert. paralegal NYU, 1988—. Youth advisor Grace Episcopal Ch., Linden, N.J. Mem. AAUW, Common Heritage Inst., Polit. Sci. Assn., Boston Coll. Club, Pi Sigma Alpha. Office: Morgan Stanley & Co Inc 1251 Ave of Americas New York NY 10020

FRANCOS, ALEXIS, educator; b. Lancaster, Pa., July 7, 1949; d. Charles George and Esther Helen (Gannes) F. BS in Edn., Millersville (Pa.) U., 1972; secondary cert. in French, Millersville State Coll., 1976; MLS, U. Pitts., 1980. Substitute tchr. Sch. Dist. Lancaster, 1972-79, 82-86, tchr. adult basic edn., gen. edn. diploma program, 1986—; reference librarian Point Park Coll., Pitts., 1980-82; library asst. Bur. of the Mines U.S. Dept. Interior, Pitts., summer 1980; info. specialist ISC Techs., Inc., Lancaster, summer 1984; substitute tchr. Hempfield Sch. Dist. (Landisville, Pa.), Ephrata (Pa.) Area Sch. Dist., Columbia (Pa.) Sch. Dist., 1983-86; tutor Millersville U., 1972-73, Lancaster area, 1986—. Mem. Am. Library Assn., Pa. Library Assn., Nat. Hist. Preservation Trust, Am. Assn. Univ. Women, Musical Arts Soc. Lancaster, Pa. Republican. Eastern Orthodox. Club: Pilot (Lancaster) (chaplain 1984-85). Home: 600 N School Ln Lancaster PA 17603 Office: Adult Enrichment Ctr 500 E Strawberry St Lancaster PA 17602

FRANK, BEATRICE SILVERSTEIN, lawyer, educator; b. Rochester, N.Y., July 24, 1928; d. Joseph Eliot and Margaret Lois (Goldberg) Silverstein; m. Lloyd Frank, Dec. 26, 1954; children: Margaret, Frederick. BA, Sarah Lawrence Coll., 1950; JD, Cornell U., 1953. Bar: N.Y. Assoc. Telsey Lowenthal Rothenberg and Mason, N.Y.C., 1953-58; assoc. dir. Consumer Help Ctr. local N.Y.C. TV, 1973-78, dir. Consumer Help Ctr., 1978; dir. Consumer Protection Clinic Sch. Law NYU, 1978—, clin. assoc. prof. law. Chairprson Roosevelt Hosp. Community Bd., N.Y.C., 1973-76; mem. Mayor's Com. on Judiciary, N.Y.C., 1983. Mem. Assn. of Bar of City N.Y. (chairperson com. medicine and law 1985—, mem. spl. com. drugs and law 1986), Assn. Am. Law Schs. (exec. com. sect. clin. legal edn.), AAUP. Democrat. Jewish. Home: 25 Central Park W 17Q New York NY 10023 Office: NYU Sch Law 40 Washington Square S New York NY 10012

FRANK, EDITH SINAIKO, civic worker; b. Madison, Wis., July 16, 1902; d. Isaac and Sarah (Goldberg) Sinaiko; B.A., U. Wis., 1924, postgrad., 1963-66; grad. Wheeler Sch. Music, 1922, Cosmopolitan Sch. Music, 1926-42; m. David S. Frank, June 24, 1924 (dec. 1962); 1 dau., Suzanne Frank Freund. Pres., Toledo Friends of Library, 1949; pres. N.W. Ohio Fedn. Music Clubs, 1950; bd. dirs. Madison Friends of Library, 1973; mem. bd. Toledo Symphony Orch., 1951; mem. women's com. Chgo. Symphony, 1951; mem. bd. Met. Housing and Planning Council Chgo.; pres. women's council City Renewal, Chgo.; mem. bd. Madison Civic Center Commn., 1973-82; mem. bd. Found. for Arts, 1974—; bd. curators Aux. State Hist. Soc. Wis., 1976, pres. aux., 1974-76; mem. U. Wis. Bascom Hill Soc. Recipient Service award Municipal Defense Council, Charleston, W.Va., 1945, Outstanding Citizen award Toledo Newspaper Guild, 1951, Page I Citizenship award Madison Newspaper Guild, 1976, award Rotary Club, 1976. Mem. Women in Communications (pres. Madison chpt. 1966), Madison Press Club (sec. 1969-70), Wis. Acad. Scis., Arts and Letters, LWV (past state bd. dirs., past pres. Toledo), Theta Sigma Phi. Clubs: Arts (Chgo.); University (Madison, Wis.). Home: Plymouth Harbor Apt 710 700 John Ringling Blvd Sarasota FL 34236

FRANK, ELLEN, lawyer; b. Bklyn., Nov. 24, 1957; d. Leon and Gladys (Reznik) Frank. B.S., Bklyn. Coll., 1979; J.D., Boston Coll., 1982. Bar: N.Y. 1983, Mass. 1983. Fiscal analyst HUD, N.Y.C., summer, 1979; assoc. F. Strafaci, Bklyn., 1982-83; assoc. firm F. Lee Bailey and Aaron J. Broder, N.Y.C., 1984; sole practice law, N.Y.C., 1984—, tchr., coach mock trial team High Sch. Graphic Communication Arts, N.Y.C., 1985-87. Moderator Conf. on Legal Rights of Battered Women, N.Y.C., 1983; sec. 61st Civilian Patrol, Bklyn., 1979; mem. King's Hwy. Devel. Corp., Bklyn., 1982—. Recipient Alumni Assn. award Boston Coll., 1980. Recipient House Sense award Housing, Preservation and Devel., 1986, 87. Mem. ABA, N.Y. Women's Bar Assn. (matrimonial law, internat. law coms.), N.Y. State Trial Lawyers Assn., New York County Lawyers Assn. (law, youth and citizenship com.), Phi Alpha Delta (publicity dir. Boston 1981-82). Democrat.

FRANK, HILDA RHEA KAPLAN, dancer; b. Houston, Dec. 30, 1939; d. Sam and Bertha (Grevsky) Kaplan; m. Robert Stuart Frank, Feb. 28, 1960; children—Karen Denise Frank Hurwitz, Daniel Steven, Nancy Alyson. Student Newcomb, Coll., New Orleans, 1957-59, U. Houston, 1959-60, Butler U., 1960. Dance tchr. Joy Alexander Sch. Dance, Houston, 1955-57, Jane Browning Sch. Dance, Houston, 1965-69, Rudy Jenkins, Sch. Ballet, Houston, 1968-69, Xperience Gymnastic Team, Houston, 1972-75; dance tchr. Jewish Community Ctr., Houston, 1975-80, dance com. chmn., 1978—, bd. dirs., 1987—; dance panelist Cultural Arts Council Houston, 1980-85, 1988—; sec.-treas. Discovery Dance Group, Houston, 1981-84, pres., 1984-85; trustee Houston Dance Coalition, 1985-87. Choreographer: To Live Another Summer, 1980; Jewish Fairy Tale, 1974; My Son, The President, 1981; dir., choreographer Emanu El Israeli Dancers, Houston, 1973—. Recipient scholarship Jacob's Pillow Dance Festival, Lee, Mass., 1959; named Vol. of Yr., Jewish Community Ctr., Houston, 1985. Mem. Houston Dance Coalition (trustee 1985—), Cultural Arts Council Houston. Jewish. Clubs: Hadassah, Sisterhood of Emanu El (Houston) (Israeli dance dir. 1973—). Home: 1 Woods Edge Ln Houston TX 77024

FRANK, PATRICIA ANNE, state senator; b. Cleve., Nov. 12, 1929; d. Paul Conrad and Mildred Patricia (Roane) Collier; m. Richard H. Frank; children: Stacy Frank Straley, Hillary Frank Weber, Courtney. BBA in Fin. and Taxation, U. Fla., Gainesville, 1951; postgrad. Georgetown U. Law Sch., 1951-52. Bus. economist anti-trust div. Dept. Justice, Washington, 1951-53; mem. staff U.S. Congressman John R. Foley, 1959-60; mem. Fla.Ho. of Reps. from 67th Dist., 1976-78; mem. Fla. State Senate from 23d Dist., 1978—; spl. U.S. ambassador to independence celebration, St. Vincent's Island, 1979; mem. judiciary civil, econ., community and consumer affairs, adminstrv. procedures, personnel, retirement and collective bargaining coms., 1986-88; chmn. econ., community and consumer affairs, 1984-86; chmn. edn. com. 1980-84. Mem. Tampa Bay Com. Fgn. Relations, Fla. Council on Asian Affairs, 1986—, Georgetown U. Bd. Regents, 1986—; vice chmn. assessment policy com. Nat. Assessment Ednl. Progress, 1981-83, chmn., 1983—; mem. task forces Hillsborough County Juvenile Delinquency, 1984-85, Joint Exec. and Legis. for Tchr. Quality Improvement, 1982, Fla. Juvenile Justice and Delinquency Prevention, 1982-85; mem. So. Regional Edn. Bd., 1979-90; vice chmn. Legis. Adv. Council (SREB), 1986-87, chmn., 1987-88; chmn. Hillsborough County Legis. Delegation, 1982-83; mem. Sch. Bd. of Hillsborough County, 1972-76. Recipient 1983 award Fla. Fedn. Bus. and Profl. Women's Clubs, Inc., Human Rights award City of Tampa, 1984; named Prominent Personality, Fla. League of Cities, 1985, Citizen of Yr., Tampa Bay Unit Nat. Assn. Social Workers; numerous other awards from municipalities, orgns., and civic groups. Home: 825 1/2 Bayshore Blvd Tampa FL 33606 Office: 312 Senate Office Bldg Tallahassee FL 32301 also: 300 South Hyde Park Ave Tampa FL 33606-2234

FRANK, PAULA FELDMAN, business executive; b. Tulsa; d. Maurice M. and Sarah (Bergman) Feldman; B.S., Northwestern U., 1954; m. Gordon D. Frank, Dec. 15, 1955; children—Cynthia Jan, Margaret Jill. Directed, wrote and appeared in TV films for Nat. Safety Council, Chgo., 1954-55; appeared in TV commls., 1955-56; asst. prodn. mgr. Kling Films, Chgo., 1956; now pres. Gaston Ave. Optical Inc., Dallas. Social chmn. Baylor Hosp. Vol. Corp., Dallas, 1962—; asst. dir. Des Plaines (Ill.) Theater Guild, 1956-57, Pearl Chappell Playhouse, Dallas, 1962-63, Dallas Theater Center, 1964. Mem. Hockaday Alumni Assn., Idle Wives Book Rev. Club (treas.), Tau Gamma Epsilon, Phi Beta, Sigma Delta Tau. Home: 7123 Currin Dr Dallas TX 75230

FRANK, ROBYN CLAIRE, librarian; b. Washington, July 28, 1945; d. Vincent Leonard and Ann Elizabeth (Richards) Gingerich; m. Luther Kyle Baugham, Dec. 16, 1966 (div. 1970); m. 2d, Stephen Earl Frank, Mar. 22, 1975; children—Evelyn, Ingrid. B.S., U. Md., 1967; M.L.S., 1972. Research asst. Research Info. Ctr., Pub. Schs. D.C., 1967-69; asst. project dir. U.S. Office Edn., Ednl. Reference Ctr., Am. Soc. Info. Sci., Washington, 1971-73; tech. info. specialist Food and Nutrition Ctr., U.S. Dept. Agr., Beltsville, Md., 1978-78, dir., acting dep. adminstr. food and nutrition info., 1978-83, chief food, nutrition and human ecology Nat. Agrl. Library, 1983-87 , head info. ctrs. br., 1987—; mem. young exec. com., 1976. Editor: Directory of Food and Nutrition Information Services and Resources, 1984. Recipient John Cotton Dana Library Pub. Relations award, 1986. Mem. Am. Soc. Info. Sci. (chmn. info. services to edn. 1979-80), Spl. Libraries Assn. (sec. food agr. and nutrition div. 1984-85, chair food, agr. and nutrition div. 1987-88), Soc. Nutrition Edn., Assocs. of Nat. Agrl. Library, Alpha Chi Omega. Lutheran. Lodge: Vasa Order. Office: Nat Agrl Library Info Ctrs Br Room 304 Beltsville MD 20705

FRANK, RUBY MERINDA, employment agency executive; b. McClusky, N.D., June 28, 1920; d. John J. and Olise (Stromme) Hanson; student coll., Mankato, Minn., also Aurora (Ill.) Coll.; m. Robert G. Frank, Jan. 14, 1944 (dec. 1973); children—Gary Frank, Craig. Exec. sec., office mgr. Nat. Container Corp., Chgo., 1943-50; owner, pres. Frank's Employment, Inc., St. Charles, Ill., 1957—; bd. dirs. St. Charles Savs. & Loan Assn., Sta. WFXW-FM, Geneva. Sec. bd. trustees Delnor Hosp., St. Charles, 1959-78, chmn. bd., 1985—, also life mem. Women's aux.; vice chmn. Kane County (Ill.) Republican Com., 1968-77; pres. Women's Rep. Club, 1969-77; local bd. Am. Cancer Soc.; adv. council Dellora A. Norris Cultural Arts Center; bd. govs. Luth. Social Service Baker Hotel (sec. 1987, vice chmn. 1988); adv. bd. Aurora U., 1988—; chmn. bd. Delnor Hosp.; co-vice chmn. Delnor Community Health System. Recipient Exec. of Yr. award Fox Valley PSI; Charlemagne award for community service, 1982; bd. dirs. Aurora Found. Mem. St. Charles C. of C. (pres., bd. dirs. 1976-82, ambassador), Kane-DuPage Personnel Assn. (v.p. 1971—), Nat., Ill. employment assns., Ill. Assn. Personnel Cons. (dir.), Women in Mgmt. Lutheran. Clubs: St. Charles Country; Execs. of Chgo. Contbr. weekly broadcast Sta. WGSB, 1970-80, WFXW weekly interview program. Home: 534 Longmeadow Circle Saint Charles IL 60174 Office: Arcada Theater Bldg 5 1st Ave Saint Charles IL 60174

FRANK, SANDRA KAYE, mathematics educator; b. Springfield Twp., Mich., June 11, 1941; d. Virgil Euleas and Dorothy Arliene (Wells) Noble; m. Joseph Frederic Frank, Aug. 1, 1970; 1 child, Joseph Lindbergh. B.A., Central Mich. U., 1963; M.A., U. Mont., 1967. Tchr. math. Dearborn Pub. Sch., Mich., 1963—, Edsel Ford High Sch., 1978—. Mem. Mich. Council Tchrs. Math., Mich. Assn. Computer Users and Learners, Nat. Council Teachers of Math., Math. Assn. Am. Clubs: Mich. Flyers, Ninety-Nines. Home: 21222 Audette St Dearborn MI 48124

FRANKEL, ELLEN, magazine editor; b. Boston, Mar. 26, 1938; d. Archie and Frances (Tocman) Sudhalter; m. Hyman Frankel, Oct. 1, 1965; children: Elizabeth Gennis, Shepherd Gelber, Dylan Yarne. Student, Syracuse U., 1955-57. Account exec. The Siesel Co., N.Y.C., 1975-77; design editor 1001 Decorating Ideas, N.Y.C., 1977-81; assoc. decorating editor Woman's Day, N.Y.C., 1981-83; editor home furnishings sect. McCall's mag., N.Y.C., 1983-86; editor in chief 1001 Home Ideas, N.Y.C., 1986—; judge Daphne Awards-The Hardwood Inst., N.Y.C., 1985-87, Casual Furniture Awards, Chgo., 1986-87. Recipient Editorial Excellence award Dallas Market Ctr., 1984; named to Writer's Hall of Fame So. Furniture Market Ctr., 1985. Mem. Am. Soc. Mag. Editors, Nat. Home Fashions League (bd. dirs. 1984-85). Office: 1001 Home Ideas 3 Park Ave New York NY 10016

FRANKEL, JUDITH JENNIFER MARIASHA, clinical psychologist; b. Bklyn., May 25, 1947; d. Simon and Tamara (Wien) F.; m. Anthony R. D'Augelli, Sept. 1, 1968 (div. 1985); children: Jennifer Hadley, Rebecca Lindsey. BA, New Coll. at Hofstra U., 1968; MA, U. Conn., 1971, PhD, 1972. Lic. psychologist, Pa. Research psychologist Family Consultation Ctr., Roslyn, N.Y., 1968, Conn. State Dept. Mental Health, Hartford, 1969-71; staff intern VA Hosp., West Haven, Conn., 1971-72; asst. prof., dir. program devel. and evaluation Addiction Prevention Lab. Pa. State U., State College, 1972-80; pvt. practice psychology State College, 1976—; psychol. cons. PYRAMID Orgn., Walnut Creek, Calif., 1975-78, N.Y. Dept. Mental Health, 1976, Alaska Dept. Mental Health, 1976, Nat. Inst. Alcohol Abuse Prevention, Nat. Inst. Drug Abuse Prevention, Nat. Youth Alternatives Program, 1975-79; pres. Mental Health Profls., State College, 1978-80. Author: Decisions Are Possible, 1975, Communication and Parenting Skills, 1976, Helping Others, 1980; contbr. articles to profl. jours. Campaigner Stein for Rep., 1982, Wachob for Congress, 1984; community action chair Congregation Brit Shalom, State College, 1985-87, ednl. liaison coordinator, 1985-87. USPHS fellow, U. Conn., 1969-71. Mem. Am. Psychol. Assn., Eastern Psychol. Assn., Cen. Pa. Psychol. Assn., Phi Beta Kappa, Phi Kappa Phi. Democrat. Jewish.

FRANKEL, LINDA DAIGNAULT, economic development administrator; b. Springfield, Mass., Aug. 12, 1945; d. Alfred Philip and Jeane (Lacine) Daignault; m. James Melton Howell, Sept. 24, 1983. BA, Wellesley Coll., 1967; MA in Teaching, Brown U., 1969. Sr. copy editor Wall St. Transcript, N.Y.C., 1970-74; dir. econ. devel. program New Eng. Regional Commn., Boston, 1974-75; spl. asst. to sr. v.p., fin. U. Mass. System, Boston, 1975-76; pres. Council for Econ. Action, Inc., Boston, 1976—, dir., 1980—; cons. urban affairs Bank of Boston, 1978—. Fundraiser, French Library, Boston, 1981; bd. dirs. New Eng. Congl. Inst., Washington, 1980—. Mem. Council Urban Econ. Devel., Wellesley Coll. Alumni Assn. Episcopalian. Home: 73 Beacon St Boston MA 02108 Office: Council Econ Action Inc 17th Floor 100 Federal St Boston MA 02110

FRANKEL, LOIS ELAINE, philosophy educator; b. Los Angeles, Feb. 20, 1956; d. Alvin Lawrence and Margaret Alice (Davis) Frankel. BA in Philosophy, Loyola Marymount U., 1976; PhD, U. Calif., Berkeley, 1980. Vis. asst. prof. SUNY, Binghamton, 1980-81, Washington U., St. Louis, 1981-82; asst. prof. Ohio State U., Columbus, 1982-86, U. Colo., Colorado Springs, 1986—. Contbr. articles to profl. jours. Mem. Am. Philos. Assn., Soc. Women in Philosophy, Leibniz Soc. of Am. Office: U Colo Dept Philosophy Box 7150 Colorado Springs CO 80933

FRANKEL, RACHEL HELFAND, publishing company consultant; b. Phila., Mar. 21, 1956; d. William Hirsch and Audrey (Real) Helfand; m. William Balter Frankel, Apr. 4, 1982. BA, Swarthmore Coll., 1978. Ops. coordinator Wildenstein & Co., N.Y.C., 1978-81; ops. mgr. Thoroughbred Equity Co., Inc., Elmont, N.Y., 1981-83; productivity cons. McGraw-Hill, Inc., N.Y.C., 1983-84, systems planning cons., 1984-87; productivity and orgnl. mgmt. cons. Coopers and Lybrand, N.Y.C., 1987—. Home: 35 W 9th St New York NY 10011

FRANKENTHALER, HELEN, painter; b. N.Y.C., Dec. 12, 1928; d. Alfred and Martha (Lowenstein) F.; m. Robert Motherwell, Apr. 6, 1958 (div.). B.A., Bennington Coll., 1949; L.H.D., Skidmore Coll., 1969; D.F.A., Smith Coll., 1973, Moore Coll. Art, 1974, Bard Coll., 1976, N.Y. U., 1979; D.Art, Radcliffe Coll., 1978, Amherst Coll., 1979. tchr., lectr. Yale U., 1966, 67, 70, Hunter Coll., 1970, Princeton U., 1971, Cooper Union, N.Y.C., 1972, Washington U. Sch. Fine Arts, 1972, Skidmore Coll., 1973, Swathmore Coll., 1974, Drew U., 1975, Harvard, 1976, Radcliffe Coll., 1976, Bard Coll., 1977, Detroit Inst. Arts, 1977, also N.Y. U., U. Pa., Sch. Visual Arts, Goucher Coll., Wash. U., Yale Grad. Sch., U. Ariz., 1978, Graphic Arts Council N.Y., 1979, Harvard U., 1980, Phila. Coll., 1980, Williams Coll., 1980, Yale U., 1981, Brandeis U., 1982, U. of Hartford, 1983, Syracuse U., 1985; U.S. rep. Venice Biennale, 1966. One-woman shows include, Tibor de Nagy Gallery, N.Y.C., 1951-58, Andre Emmerich Gallery, N.Y.C., 1959-73, 75, 77, 78, 79, 81, 82, 83, 84, 86, 87, Jewish Mus., N.Y., 1960, Everett Ellin Gallery, Los Angeles, 1961, Galerie Lawrence, Paris, 1961, 63, Bennington Coll., 1962, 78, Galleria dell'Ariete, Milan, 1962, Kasmin Gallery, London, 1964, David Mirvish Gallery, Toronto, 1965, 71, 73, 75, Gertrude Kasle Gallery, Detroit, 1967, Nicholas Wilder Gallery, Los Angeles, 1967, Andre Emmerich Gallery, Zurich, 1974, 80, Swathmore (Pa.) Coll., 1974, Solomon R. Guggenheim Mus., N.Y.C., 1975, Corcoran Gallery Art, Washington, 1975, Seattle Art Mus., 1975, Mus. Fine Arts, Houston, 1975, Ace Gallery, Vancouver, B.C., Can., 1975, Rosa Esman Gallery, N.Y.C., 1975, 3d Internat. Contemporary Art Fair, Paris, 1976, 81, retrospective Whitney Mus. Am. Art, 1969, Whitechapel Gallery, London, Eng., 1969, Kongress-Halle, Berlin, Kunstverein, Hannover, 1969, Heath Gallery, Atlanta, 1971, Galerie Godard Lefort, Montreal, 1971, Fendrick Gallery, Washington, 1972, 79, John Berggruen Gallery, San Francisco, 1972, 79, 82, Portland (Oreg.) Art

Mus., 1972, Waddington Galleries II, London, 1973, 74, Janie C. Lee Gallery, Dallas, 1973, Houston, 1975, 76, 78, 80, 82, Met. Mus. Art, N.Y.C., 1973, Gallery Diane Gilson, Seattle, 1976, Greenberg Gallery, St. Louis, 1977, Galerie Wentzel, Hamburg, Germany, 1977, Jacksonville (Fla.) Art Mus., 1977-78, Knoedler Gallery, London, 1978, 81, 83, USIA exhbn., 1978-79, Atkins Mus. Fine Art, William Rockhill Nelson Gallery Art, Kansas City, Mo., 1978, 80, numerous others; exhibited in group shows including, Whitney Mus., 1958, 71, 75-79, 82, Carnegie Internat., Pitts., 1955, 58, 61, 64, Columbus Gallery Fine Arts, 1960, Guggenheim Mus., 1961, 76, 80, 82, Seattle World's Fair, 1962, Art Inst. Chgo., 1963, 69, 72, 76, 77, 82, 83, San Francisco Mus. Art, 1963, 68, Krannert Mus., U. Ill., 1959, 63, 65, 67, 80, Washington Gallery Modern Art, 1963, Pa. Acad. Fine Arts, 1963, 68, 76, N.Y. World's Fair, 1964, Am. Fedn. Arts Circulating Exhbn., 1964, U. Austin Art Mus., 1964, Rose Art Mus. Circulating Exhbn., 1964, Detroit Inst. Arts, 1965, 67, 73, 77, U. Mich. Mus. Art, 1965, Md. Inst., 1966, Norfolk Mus. Arts and Scis., 1966, Venice Biennale, 1966, Smithsonian Instn., 1966, Expo '67, Montreal, 1967, Washington Gallery Modern Art, 1967, Ga. Mus. Art, Athens, 1967, U. Okla. Mus. Art, Norman, 1968, Philbrook Art Center, Tulsa, 1968, Cin. Mus., 1968, U. Calif. at San Diego, 1968, Mus. Modern Art, N.Y.C., 1969, 75, 76, 80, 82, Met. Mus., N.Y.C., 1969-70, 76, 79, 81, Va. Mus., Richmond, 1970, 74, Balt. Mus. Art, 1970, 76, Boston U., 1970, Boston Mus. Fine Arts, 1972, 82, Des Moines Art Center, 1973, Mus. Fine Arts, Houston, 1974, 82, Smith Coll. Mus. Art, Northampton, Mass., 1974, El Instituto de Cultura Puertorriquena, San Juan, 1974, Basil (Switzerland) Art Fair, 1974, 76, Finch Coll. Mus. Art, N.Y.C., 1974, S.I. Mus., 1975, Denver Art Mus., 1975, Visual Arts Mus., N.Y.C., 1975, 76, Mus. Modern Art, Belgrade Yugoslavia, 1976, Galleria d'Arts Moderna, Rome, 1976, Grey Art Gallery, N.Y.C., 1976-78, 81, Bklyn Mus., 1976-77, 82, Edmonton Art Gallery, Alta., Can., 1977, 78, Albright-Knox Mus., Buffalo, 1978, Fogg Art Mus., Harvard U., 1978, 83, Nat. Gallery Art, Washington, 1981, St. Louis Art Mus., 1982, Phoenix Art Mus., 1980; represented in permanent collections, Met. Mus. Art; exhibited in group shows including, Chrysler Mus., Norfolk, Va., 1976; represented in permanent collections, Bklyn. Mus.; exhibited in group shows including, Everson Mus., Syracuse, N.Y., 1976, 79; represented in permanent collections, Solomon R. Guggenheim Mus.; exhibited in group shows including, Art Gallery of Ont., Toronto, 1979; exhibited in group shows including: Hirshorn Mus. and Sculpture Garden, Washington, 1980; Tate Gallery, London, 1981, Walker Art Ctr., Mpls., 1981, numerous others; represented in permanent collections: NYU, Mus. Modern Art, Albright-Knox Art Gallery, Buffalo, Whitney Mus., N.Y.C., U. Mich., High Mus., Atlanta, Milw. Art Inst., Wadsworth Atheneum, Hartford, Newark Mus., Yale U. Art Gallery, U. Nebr. Art Gallery, Carnegie Inst., Pitts., Detroit Inst. Art, Balt. Mus. Art, Univ. Mus., Berkeley, Calif., Bennington (Vt.) Coll., Art Inst. Chgo., Cin. Art Mus., Cleve. Mus. Art, Columbus Gallery Fine Arts, Honolulu Acad. Arts, Contemporary Arts Assn., Houston, Pasadena Art Mus., William Rockhill Nelson Gallery Art, Mus. Fine Arts, Kansas City, Mo., City Art Mus., St. Louis, Mus. Art, R.I. Sch. Design, Providence, San Francisco Mus. Art, Everson Mus., Syracuse, N.Y., Smithsonian Instn., Walker Art Inst., Mpls., Washington Gallery Modern Art, Wichita Art Mus., Brown Gallery Art, Nat. Gallery Victoria, Melbourne, Australia, Australian Nat. Gallery, Canberra, Victoria and Albert Mus., London, Eng., Tokyo Mus., Ulster Mus., Belfast, No. Ireland, Elvehjem Art Center, U. Wis., Israel Mus.-Instituto Nacional de Bellas Artes, Phila. Mus. Art, Phoenix Art Mus., Corcoran Gallery Art, Boston Mus. Fine Arts, Springfield (Mass.) Mus. Fine Arts, Witte Mus., San Antonio, Abbott Hall Art Gallery, Kendal, Eng., Mus. Contemporary Art, Nagaoka, Japan, Guggenheim Mus., N.Y.C., 1984, others. Trustee Bennington Coll., 1967—. Fellow Calhoun Coll., Yale U., 1968—; Recipient 1st prize for painting Paris Biennale, 1959; Gold medal Pa. Acad. Fine Arts, 1968; Great Ladies award Fordham U., Thomas Moore Coll., 1969; Spirit of Achievement award Albert Einstein Coll. Medicine, 1970; Gold medal Commune of Catania, III Biennale della Grafica d'Arte, Florence, Italy, 1972; Garrett award 70th Am. Exhbn., Art Inst. Chgo., 1972; Creative Arts award Nat. Women's div. Am. Jewish Congress, 1974; Art and Humanities award Yale Women's Forum, 1976; Extraordinary Woman of Achievement award NCCJ, 1978; Alumni award Bennington Coll., 1979. Mem. Nat. Inst. Arts and Letters. Office: care Andre Emmerich 41 E 57th St New York NY 10022

FRANKL, JEANNE SILVER, association executive; A.B. in Lit. summa cum laude, Brown U., 1952; LL.B., Yale U., 1955; m. Kenneth R. Frankl; 1 dau., Kathryn. Admitted to Conn. bar, 1955, N.Y. bar, 1956; law sec. to Hon. Edmund L. Palmieri, 1955-56; atty. Port of N.Y. Authority, 1956-60; assoc. firm Rosenman Colin Kaye Petschek Freund & Emil, N.Y.C., 1960-67; chief of program planning, office of edn. liaison, City Human Resources Adminstrn., 1967-69; spl. asst. to dep. adminstr. N.Y.C. Human Resources Adminstrn., 1969-70; asst. dir. Community Sch. System Project, N.Y. Lawyers Com. for Civil Rights under Law, 1970, dir., 1970-73; counsel and law project dir. Public Edn. Assn., N.Y.C., 1973-80, exec. dir., 1980—; lectr. Rutgers U. Law Sch. Edn. Law Seminar, 1972-73. Mem. Assn. of Bar City of N.Y., Phi Beta Kappa. Home: 45 Christopher St New York NY 10014 Office: Pub Edn Assn 39 W 32d St New York NY 10001

FRANKLIN, BARBARA HACKMAN, educator, corporate director, management consultant; b. Lancaster, Pa., Mar. 19, 1940; d. Arthur A. and Mayme M. (Haller) Hackman; m. Wallace Barnes, Nov. 29, 1986. BA with distinction, Pa. State U., 1962; MBA, Harvard U., 1964; DS. (hon.), Bryant Coll., 1973. Mgr. environ. analysis Singer Co., N.Y.C., 1964-68; asst. v.p. Citibank, N.Y.C., 1969-71; mem. White House staff, Washington, 1971-73; commr., vice chmn. U.S. Consumer Product Safety Commn., Washington, 1973-79; sr. fellow, dir. govt. and bus. program Wharton Sch., U. Pa., Phila. and Washington, 1979—; pres., chief exec. officer Franklin Assocs., Washington, 1984—; adviser to comptroller gen. U.S., 1984—; bd. dirs. Aetna Life and Casualty Co., Dow Chem. Co., Westinghouse Electric Corp., Black & Decker Corp., Automatic Data Processing, Inc., Nordstrom, Inc. Trustee, Pa. State U.; mem. Pres.'s Adv. Com. Trade Negotiations, 1982-86; bd. visitors Def. Systems Mgmt. Coll.; services policy adv. com. of U.S. Trade Representatives. Recipient Disting. Alumni award Pa. State U., 1972, Catalyst Award for Corp. Leadership, 1981, Excellence in Mgmt. award Simmons Coll., 1981, ann. award Am. Assn. Poison Control Ctrs., 1979, cert. appreciation, Am. Acad. Pediatrics, 1978, Award for Corp. Social Responsibility, CUNY, 1988. Fellow Nat. Assn. Corp. Dirs.; mem. Am. Inst. CPA's (bd. dirs.), Women's Forum Washington, Nat. Women's Econ. Alliance Found. (bd. govs., Dir.'s Choice award 1987), Nat. Women's Forum. Republican. Lutheran. Club: F Street (Washington); Econ. of N.Y. Contbr. articles to publs. Avocations: exercise, skiing, sailing. Office: Franklin Assocs 1320 19th St NW #400 Washington DC 20036 Office: U Pa Wharton Sch Bus 115 Vance Hall Philadelphia PA 19104

FRANKLIN, BEVERLY JEAN, artist; b. Los Angeles, Dec. 2, 1922; d. Harvey Franklin and Marian Ida (Cox) Keyse; student Baylor U., Waco, Tex., 1958-59; m. Charles Francis Franklin, Oct. 27, 1946; children: Christine Marie Franklin Carlin, Peter Charles, Kathleen Anne Franklin Watton. One-woman shows include La Jolla (Calif.) Art Assn., 1975, 76, Knowles Gallery, La Jolla, 1978, 80, 82, 84, 86, 88. Mem. La Jolla Art Assn. (dir. 1973-76), San Diego Watercolor Soc. (dir. 1976-77), Nat. League Am. Pen Women (pres. La Jolla br. 1985-87), Los Angeles Art Assn. Address: 7205 Via Capri La Jolla CA 92037

FRANKLIN, LYNN IRENE, marketing executive; b. Pitts., Feb. 11, 1955; d. W. Phillip and Dolores Marie (Bahler) S.; m. Jon Daniel Franklin, May 20, 1988. BA in Writing magna cum laude, U. Pitts., 1977. Dir. publications, editor Davis & Elkins (W. Va.) Coll., 1977-79; dir. pub. info., editor Hood Coll., Frederick, Md., 1979-81; mgr. internal communications, editor The Nature Conservancy, Arlington, Va., 1981-85; editor, internal communications Suburban Bank, Bethesda, Md., 1985-86; mktg. officer Sovran Fin. Corp., Balt., 1986-88, writer, 1988—. reporter (newspaper) The Pitts. Press., 1977, editor (mag.) Forward, 1977-79 (newspaper) The Suburbanite, 1985-86, (newsletter) Profile 1979-81, On the Land, 1981-85. Mem. Internat. Assn. Bus. Communicators, Sigma Delta Chi. Democrat.

FRANKLIN, MARGARET LAVONA BARNUM (MRS. C. BENJAMIN FRANKLIN), civic leader; b. Caldwell, Kans., June 19, 1905; d. LeGrand Husted and Elva (Biddinger) Barnum; B.A., Washburn U., 1952; student Iowa State Tchrs. Coll., 1923-25, U. Iowa, 1937-38; m. C. Benjamin Franklin, Jan. 20, 1940 (dec. 1983); children—Margaret Lee (Mrs. Michael J. Felso), Benjamin Barnum. Tchr. pub. schs., Union, Iowa, 1925-27, Kearney, Nebr., 1927-28, Marshalltown, Iowa, 1928-40; advance rep. Chautauqua, summers 1926-30. Mem. Citizens Adv. Com., 1965-69; mem. Stormont-Vail Regional Ctr. Hosp. Aux.; bd. dirs. Topeka Pub. Library Found., 1984—. Recipient Waldo B. Heywood award Topeka Civic Theatre, 1967; named Outstanding Alpha Delta Pi Mother of Kans., 1971; Topeka Public Library award, 1977. Mem. DAR (state chmn. Museum 1968-71), AAUW (mem. 50 yrs.), Gemini Group of Topeka, Topeka Geneal. Soc., Topeka Art Guild, Topeka Civic Symphony Soc. (dir. 1952-57, Service Honor citation 1960), Doll Collectors Am., Marshalltown Community Theatre (pres. 1938-40), Topeka Pub. Library Bd. (trustee 1961-70, treas., 1962-65, chmn. 1965-67), Shawnee County Hist. Soc. (dir. 1963-75, sec. 1964-66), Nat. Multiple Sclerosis Soc. (dir. Kans. chpt. 1963-66), Stevengraph Collectors Assn., Friends of Topeka Public Library (dir. 1970-79, Disting. Service award 1980), P.E.O. (pres. chpt. 1956-57, coop. bd. pres. 1964-65, chpt. honoree 1969), Native Sons and Daus. Kans. (life), Topeka Stamp Club, Alpha Beta Gamma, Nonoso. Republican. Mem. Christian Ch. Clubs: Western Sorosis (pres. 1960-61), Minerva (2d v.p. 1984-85), Woman's (1st v.p. 1952-54), Knife and Fork.

FRANKLIN, MARY CHRISTINE, health sciences facility administrator; b. Madisonville, Ky., Jan. 10, 1950; d. Charles Ewing and Genevieve Frances (Boehman) Johnson; m. Anthony Franklin, Mar. 22, 1969 (div. Apr. 1979); children: Christina Raquel, Jhan Paul. BA, U. Evansville, 1987. Supr. housekeeping Welborn Hosp., Evansville, Ind., 1975-80; dir. environ. services and safety Gibson Gen. Hosp., Princeton, Ind., 1980-82, St. Mary's Med. Ctr., Evansville, 1982-86; dir. housekeeping and interior decorating services Deaconess Hosp., Evansville, 1986—; coordinator Nat. Exec. Housekeeper's Assn. cert. program U. Evansville, 1980—; speaker in field. Contbr. articles to profl. jours. Mem. activities com. Evansville PTA, 1980-83; active Easter Seals, Evansville, 1982, March of Dimes, Evansville, 1985; mem. Evansville Polit. Action Com., 1982—; mem. Dem. precinct com., Evansville, 1978-80. Mem. Nat. Exec. Housekeeper's Assn. (pres. Evansville chpt. 1981-83, midwest dist. 2d vice gov. 1984-86, nat. bd. dirs. 1986—, Outstanding Mem. 1983), Nat. Assn. Female Execs., Am. Bus. Women's Assn., Am. Laundry and Linen Coll. Alumni Assn. (Achievement award 1984). Baptist. Club: Bowling League (Evansville) (v.p. 1984-86). Lodge: Order of Eastern Star. Home: 513 Jackson Ave Evansville IN 47713 Office: Deaconess Hosp 600 Mary St Evansville IN 47710

FRANKLIN, SHERYL J., information services executive; b. Buffalo, June 25, 1954; d. W. Eugene and Shirley M. (Shults) F. Student, Bapt. Bible Coll., 1971-72, U. Scranton, 1974-76, Camden County Coll., Blackwood, N.J., 1979-80. Personnel clk. Met. Life Ins. Co., Clarks Summit, Pa., 1973-75, programmer, 1976-77; sr. programmer/analyst First Pa. Bank, Phila., 1977-81; cons. AGS Info. Services (formerly SDA), Phila., 1981, account supr., 1981-82, tech. mgr., 1983-84, account exec., 1984, br. mgr., 1984-87, v.p., 1987—. Mem. Data Processing Mgmt. Assn., Network of Women in Computer Tech. Republican. Mem. Dutch Reformed Ch. Office: AGS Info Services Inc 275 S 19th St Suite 1500 Philadelphia PA 19103

FRANKMANN, CAROL ANN, dietitian; b. Chanute, Kans., Jan. 29, 1942; d. Sammy Cleo and Estella May (Wood) Barnhart; m. Clinton Stephen Frankmann, Nov. 18, 1967; 1 child, Stephen Clinton. BS, Kans. State U., 1964; MS, Tex. Woman's U., 1982. Lic. dietitian, Tex. Research dietitian Meth. Hosp., Baylor Coll. Medicine, Houston, 1966-68; nutrition cons. Tex. Gulf Bakers Council, Houston, 1968-70; research dietitian U. Tex. M.D. Anderson Hosp., Houston, 1971-78, supr., 1978-81, assoc. dir. nutrition and food service, 1981—; bd. dirs. Tex. Dietetic Assn. Found., Austin, Tex., 1984-86; adj. instr. Univ. Tex. Sch. Allied Health, 1986—. Mem. South Tex. Dietetic Assn. (pres. 1973-74, assembly rep. 1984-85), Tex. Dietetic Assn. (diet therapy chmn. 1977-79, nominating com. chmn. 1979-80, bylaws chmn. 1982-83), Am. Dietetic Assn., Am. Soc. Parenteral and Enteral Nutrition, Omicron Nu, Phi Upsilon Omicron, Alpha Chi Omega. Republican. Baptist. Office: U Tex MD Anderson Cancer Ctr 1515 Holcombe Blvd Houston TX 77030

FRANKS, NANCI BERNICE, food products executive; b. Enid, Okla., Dec. 1, 1951; d. Donald E. and Barbara Ruth (Fronterhouse) Nichelson; m. Rick Franks (div. 1979); 1 child, James. Student, U. Santa Barbara, 1970-72, Calif. State U., 1974. Mgr. sales Liquid Paper Corp., Dallas, 1979-80; office mgr., paralegal Steinberg Demoff, Beverly Hills, Calif., 1973-78; account exec. Roth Young Personnel Services, Westwood, Calif., 1978-79; chief exec. officer Natural Food Products, Manhattan Beach, Calif., 1980—. Home: 3133 The Strand Hermosa Beach CA 90254 Office: Natural Food Products 300 Manhattan Beach Blvd #207 Manhattan Beach CA 90266

FRANKS, SUSAN, stockbroker; b. Bkln., July 5, 1952; d. Leonard and Lena (Finz) F. BA cum laude, Bklyn. Coll., 1974. Stockbroker Oppenheimer & Co., N.Y.C., 1979-81, Thomson McKinnon Securities, N.Y.C., 1981-82, L.F. Rothschild, Unterberg, Towbin, N.Y.C., 1982-84, Moore & Schley, N.Y.C., 1984—. Vol. N.Y. Shelter for Homeless, N.Y.C.. Mem. Stockbrokers Soc. Republican. Office: Moore & Schley 45 Broadway New York NY 10006

FRANKS, VIOLET, psychologist; b. N.Y.C., July 20, 1926; d. Joseph and Sarah (Chomsky) Greenberg; m. Cyril Maurice Franks, Mar. 29, 1952; children: Steven, Sharon. BS, Queens Coll., 1947; MA, U. Minn., 1950; PhD, U. London, 1959. Pvt. practice psychologist Princeton, N.J., 1970—; dir. psychology Carrier Found., Belle Mead, N.J., 1980—; pvt. practice psychologist Princeton Ctr. for Psychotherapy, 1984—; adj. prof. Rutgers U., New Brunswick, N.J., 1980—. Editor: Women and Therapy, 1974, Gender and Disordered Behavior, 1979, Stereotyping of Women, 1983. Fellow Am. Psychol. Assn.; mem. Clin. Psychology of Women (treas.), N.J. State Bd. Psychol. Examiners (vice chmn. 1975-80). Home: 315 Prospect Ave Princeton NJ 08540

FRANKSON-KENDRICK, SARAH JANE, publisher; b. Bradford, Pa., Sept. 24, 1949; d. Sophronus Ahimus and Elizabeth Jane (Sears) McCutcheon; m. James Michael Kendrick, Jr., May 22, 1982. Customer service rep. Laros Printing/Osceola Graphics, Bethlehem, Pa., 1972-73; assoc. editor Babcox Publs., Akron, Ohio, 1973-74; assoc. editor Bill Communications, Akron, 1974-75, sr. editor, 1975-77, editor-in chief, 1977-81; assoc. pub. Chilton Co./ABC Pub., Chgo., 1981-83, pub., 1983—. Recipient Automotive Replacement Edn. award Northwood Inst., 1983, award for young leadership and excellence Automotive Hall of Fame, 1984. Mem. Automotive Parts and Accessories Assn. (bd. dirs., chmn. forward planning com., mem. market research com.), Internat. Assn. Bus. Communicators, Am. Mgmt. Assn., Women in Communications, 500 Automotive Execs. Club (bd. dirs., pres.). Republican. Club: Knollwood Country (Lake Forest, Ill.). Office: Chilton Co/ABC Publishing 100 S Wacker Dr Chicago IL 60606

FRANN, MARY, actress; b. St. Louis, Feb. 27. Studies at Northwestern U. Formerly staff mem. KSDK-TV, St. Louis, later with ABC, Chgo.; various appearances Chgo. theaters; in Story Theatre, Los Angeles, N.Y.C., other theatre appearances Los Angeles; TV series: Newhart, 1982—, My Friend Tony, 1969, Days of Our Lives, Return to Peyton Place, King's Crossing, 1982, Mike Hammer, 1987; motion pictures for TV: Portrait of an Escort, Gidget's Summer Reunion, Eight is Enough, A Family Reunion; hostess Miss USA pageant, 1986, 87, Miss Universe pageant, 1986, 87; commentator Tournament of Roses Parade, 1985-87. Office: care William Morris Agency 151 El Camino Beverly Hills CA 90212

FRANTA, ROSALYN, food company executive; b. Wilmington, Del., Aug. 29, 1951; d. William Alfred and Virginia Louise (Ellis) F. BS in Voc. Home Econs. Edn., Purdue U., 1972, MS in Foods and Nutrition, 1974. Registered dietitian. Home economist Kellogg Co., Battle Creek, Mich., 1974-75, nutrition and consumer specialist, 1975-77, mgr. advt. to children, 1977-79, corp. adminstrv. asst., 1979, dir. nutrition, 1979-82, dir. nutrition and analytical services, 1982, v.p. nutrition and chemistry, 1983, v.p. quality and nutrition, 1983-87, v.p., asst. to chmn., 1987—; chmn. tech. com. Grocery Mfrs. Am., Washington, 1985-87, mem. tech. com. planning group 1982—; trustee Internat. Life Scis. Inst., Washington, 1982—; v.p. Internat. Life Scis. Inst. Nutrition Found., Washington, 1985—, mem. exec. com. 1985—. Contbr. articles on food sci. and nutrition to profl. jours. Recipient Ada Decker Malott Meml. scholarship, Purdue U., 1970. Mem. Inst. Food Technologists, Am. Dietetic Assn., Phi Kappa Phi, Gamma Sigma Delta, Omicron Nu, Alpha Omicron Pi (mem. Phi Upsilon chpt.). Republican. Lutheran. Office: Kellogg Co One Kellogg Sq Battle Creek MI 49016

FRANTZ, GERALDINE C., insurance agent; b. Calera, Okla., Jan. 27, 1937; d. Haskell Adelbert and Mabel Rebecca (Skaggs) Castleberry; m. Wayne L. Frantz, June 8, 1958; children: Cheryln Sue, Carma Lee. BS in Bus. Edn., Southeastern (Okla.) State Coll., 1954; MS in Bus. Edn., Kans. State Tchrs. Coll., 1964. Pvt. sec. Nat. Coop. Refinery Assn., McPherson, Kans., 1959-61; tchr. Pub. Schs., Iowa, Mo., Kans., Nebr., Okla., 1957-58, 61-71; tchr. bus. Colorado Springs Pub. Schs., 1971-72, coop. office edn. coordinator, 1972-85; agt., broker Prin. Fin. Group Des Moines, Iowa, Colorado Springs, 1985—, Denver, 1988—. Mem. Nat. Assn. Life Underwriters, Colorado Springs Assn. Life Underwriters, Exec. Women Internat. (publs. reporter, mem. philantropy com.), Nat. Assn. Female Execs. (mem. chmn., long-range planning com.). Republican. Methodist. Home: 2832 Country Club Cir Colorado Springs CO 80909 Office: Prin Financial Group 7555 E Hampden Suite 104 Denver CO 80231

FRANTZ, MARY ALISON, archaeologist, photographer; b. Duluth, Minn., Sept. 27, 1903; d. Alfred J. and Mary Katherine (Gibson) F. B.A., Smith Coll., 1924; postgrad. Am. Acad. Rome, 1924-25, Am. Sch. Class. Studies, Athens, Greece, 1929-30; Ph.D., Columbia U., 1937; postgrad. (fellow) Dumbarton Oaks Research Library, Washington, 1941. Reader, Index of Christian Art, Princeton U., 1927-29; mem. staff Agora Excavations, Am. Sch. Classical Studies, Athens, 1933-40, 49-66, research fellow, 1967—; mem. Inst. Advanced Study, Princeton, N.J., 1976-77; polit. analyst OSS, Washington, 1942-45; cultural attache U.S. Embassy, Athens, 1947-49. Decorated Order of Benevolence (Greece), 1956. Mem. Am. Philos. Soc., Archaeol. Inst. Am., Medieaval Acad. Am., German Archaeol. Inst. Author: The Church of the Holy Apostles, 1971, (with others) Olympia, 1967, (with Martin Robertson) The Parthenon Frieze, 1975, (with John Travlos) The Athenian Agora, Vol. XXIV, Late Antiquity: A.D. 267-700, 1988; assoc. editor Allied Mission to Observe the Greek Elections, 1946; contbr. photographs to archaeol. books, jours., articles to profl. jours. Address: 27 Haslet Ave Princeton NY 08540

FRANTZVE, JERRI LYN, industrial psychologist, management consultant; b. Huntington Beach, Calif., Sept. 9, 1942; d. Rolland and Marjorie Cleone (Ferrin) Weiland; m. Kenneth Wayne Himsel, Oct. 22, 1965 (div. Feb. 1975); 1 child, Deborrah Marie. Student, Purdue U., 1964-68; BA in Psychology and History, Marian Coll., 1969; MS in Organizational Psychology, George Williams Coll., 1976; PhD in Indsl. and Organizational Psychology, U. Ga., 1979. Case worker Marion County Welfare Dept., Indpls., 1970-71; mkgt. research analyst Quaker Oats Co., Barrington, Ill., 1971-75; mgmt. cons. J.L. Frantzve & Assocs., Ponca City, Okla., 1978—; asst. prof. sch. of mgmt. SUNY, Binghamton, N.Y., 1979-83; personnel research advisor Conoco, Inc., Ponca City, 1983-84, personnel research coordinator, 1984, personnel research and acad. affairs coordinator, 1984-86, welfare benefits dir., 1986—; instrn. cons. USAF, Rome, N.Y., 1979-83; dir. Israel Overseers Research Program, Ginozar, Israel, 1982, Japanese Overseas Research Program, Tokyo, 1983. Author: Behaving in Organizations: Tales from the Trenches, 1983, Guide to Behavior in Organizations, 1983; contbr. articles to profl. jours. Bd. dirs. Broome County Alcoholism Clinic, Binghamton, N.Y., 1980-83, dir. Broome County Mental Health Clinic, Binghamton, 1981-83; del. Dem. Caucus, Okla., 1985. Mem. Am. Psychol. Assn. (com. on women in psychology 1986—), Acad. of Mgmt. (placement dir. 1982), Am. Soc. for Personnel Adminstrn., Soc. for Personality and Social Psychology, Assn. for Women in Psychology, AAUW, Delta Sigma Pi. Home: 420 Drake Dr Ponca City OK 74604 Office: Conoco Inc PO Box 1267 Ponca City OK 74603

FRANZ, HOLLY GAIL, healthcare executive; b. Catskill, N.Y., Aug. 9, 1955; d. Charles John and Rosalie Jane (Legacy) F. BS in Nursing, SUNY, Plattsburgh, 1977. Camp nurse Boy Scouts Am., Woronoco, Mass., summer 1977; staff nurse New Eng. Med. Ctr., Boston, 1978-83; organ donation coordinator New Eng. Organ Bank, Boston, 1983-86, dir. organ donation div., 1986—; mem. Mass. Dept. Pub. Health Task Force, 1986, 87; co-investigator grant proposal by Nat. Transp. Act., 1986. Contbr. articles to profl. jours. Vol. ARC, Boston, 1977-78. Mem. N.Am. Transplant Coordinators Orgn. (co-chmn. membership com.), Am. Council on Transplantation, Am. Assn. Critical Care Nurses, Am. Soc. Profl. and Exec. Women, United Network of Organ Sharing (profl. edn. com. 1988, procurement and distbn. com. 1988), Sigma Theta Tau. Office: New Eng Organ Bank 138 Harvard St Brookline MA 02146

FRANZ, JUDY ROSENBAUM, physics educator; b. Chgo., May 3, 1938; d. Eugene Joseph and Ruth (Comroe) R.; m. Frank Andrew Franz, July 11, 1959; 1 child, Eric Douglas. A.B., Cornell U., 1959; M.S., U. Ill., 1961, Ph.D., 1965. Research physicist IBM Research Lab., Zurich, Switzerland, 1965-67; asst. prof. Ind. U., Bloomington, 1968-74, assoc. prof., 1974-79, prof. physics, 1979-87, assoc. dean Coll., 1980-82; prof. physics W. Va. U., 1987—; vis. prof. Tech. U. Munich, W.Ger., 1978-79, Cornell U., Ithaca, N.Y., 1985-86. Contbr. articles to profl. jours. Mem. materials research adv. com. NSF, 1986—. Recipient Disting. Teaching award Ind. U., 1978; von Humboldt Found. research fellow, 1978-79; research grantee Research Corp., 1972-73, NSF, 1973-81, NATO, 1980-83. Fellow Am. Phys. Soc. (councilor 1984—, chmn. edn. com. 1983-85, exec. com. 1985), AAAS; mem. Assn. Women in Sci. (councilor 1981-83), Am. Assn. Physics Tchrs., AAUP, Phi Beta Kappa, Sigma Xi (pres. local chpt. 1981-82). Avocations: tennis; gardening. Office: W Va Univ Dept Physics Morgantown WV 26506

FRANZ, LYDIA MILLICENT TRUC, real estate executive; b. Chgo., Jan. 11, 1924; d. Walter and Lydia (Kralovec) Truc; Mus.B., Ill. Wesleyan U., 1944; Mus.M., Northwestern U., 1949; m. Robert Franz, Aug. 27, 1952 (dec. Aug. 1983). Tchr. music pub. schs., Muskegon, Mich., 1947-48; mktg. research analyst Grant Advt. Agy., Chgo., 1949; mktg. research asst. Buchen Co., Chgo., 1949-52; asst. to dir. mktg. research Sherman Marquette Advt. Co., Chgo., 1952; asst. to pres., dir. media and research Andover Advt. Agy., 1952-55; salesman Boehmer & Hedlund, realty, Barrington, Ill., 1960-63; pres. Century-21-Country Squire, Inc., Barrington, 1963—; dir. Clyde Fed. Savs. & Loan Assn., 1984—. Recipient Disting. Alumni award Ill. Wesleyan U., 1988. Mem. real estate adv. com. William Rainey Harper Coll., Palatine, Ill., 1971—, Office of Real Estate Research, U. Ill., Champaign. Served with WAC, 1944-46. Mem. Women in Real Estate (pres. 1966-67), Barrington Bd. Realtors (pres. 1968-69), Ill. Assn. Realtors (dir. 1972-75, 81—, gov. Realtor's Inst. of Ill. 1972-78, exec. com. 1977—, pres. 1984, Realtor of Yr. 1988), Nat. Assn. Realtors (dir. 1982—), Realtors Nat. Mktg. Inst. (bd. govs. 1979, regional gov. 1980), Barrington C. of C. (pres. 1974, dir. 1972-75, 84—, Merit award 1985), Barrington Bus. and Profl. Women's Club, Mensa, Sigma Alpha Iota. Republican. Home: 408 E Hillside Ave Barrington IL 60010 Office: 209 Park Ave Barrington IL 60010

FRANZ, NANCY KAY, 4-H agent; b. Milw., Dec. 24, 1958; d. Bruce Edwin and Jessie Mary (Hooper) F. BS, Northland Coll., 1981; MEd, U. Wis., 1985. Dir. backpacking Milw. Girl Scout Council Camps, 1975-78; coordinator youth conservation corps. U.S. Forest Service, Washburn, Wis., 1978-81; youth agent Douglas County Univ. Ext. 4-H, Superior, Wis., 1981-87, Bayfield County Univ. ext. 4-H, Washburn, Wis., 1987—; chair natural sci. youth devel. com. Wis. Youth Devel., Madison, 1984-87. Author, editor County 4-H Newsletter, 1981-87; author Camp Staff Handbook, 1984. Trainer No. Pine Girl Scout Council, Duluth, Minn., 1979-87; vol. U.S. Forest Service, Washburn, 1981-87; liturgist Messiah Lutheran Ch., Washburn, 1983-87, edn. com. 1987—; bd. dirs. Head of the Lakes Fair, Superior, 1982-86; judge county fair Wis. Dept. Agriculture, Madison, 1982-87. Mem. Nat. Assn. 4-H Agents, Wis. Assn. of 4-H Agents (treas. 1983-85, Outstanding Program Development 1983, Scholar 1983, Outstanding Youth Program 1984), Nature Study Soc. (author jour. 1985-86), Superior Youth Bd., Wis. Assn. Environtl. Educators, Women Outdoors, Women Support,. Office: Washburn County Extension Courthouse Washburn WI 54891

FRANZHEIM, BARBARA, restoration company executive, fine arts consultant; b. Newark, Feb. 7, 1939; m. Kenneth Franzheim, II, Apr. 15, 1966 (div. 1973); children—Pamela Franzheim Tower, Sabrina, Melita; m. 2d, Daniel Dror, Sept. 27, 1974 (div. 1985); 1 son, Daniel. B.A., Montclair Coll., 1962; postgrad., NYU, 1962, Fordham U., 1965-66; M.E., Seton Hall U., 1964. Tchr. English, N.J., 1962-64; with editorial dept. McGraw-Hill,

N.Y.C., 1965; with Batten Barton Durstine & Osborn, N.Y.C., 1965; various positions fashion industry, N.Y.C., 1965-66; with U.S. Fgn. Service, South Pacific, N.Z., Tonga, Fiji, Samoa, 1969-72; owner Hist. Restoration Co., Tex. and N.Y.C., 1976—; chief exec. officer Three Sources Corp., Houston, 1976—. Restorations include: Cabin, Xalapa Farm, Paris, Ky., 1969, U.S. Embassy Resindece, Lowerhutt, New Zealand, 1981, 1412 North Blvd., Houston, 1975, Inness Hall, Lexington, Ky., 1975, Gardenside, Southhampton, 1979, La Favorita, Palm Beach, Fla., 1984, 635 Park Ave., N.Y.C., 1985; contbg. author Bluegrass mag. Advisor Town of Versailles Main St. Assn.; bd. dirs. Tex. Children's Hosp., Houston, 1967-68, Tex. Mental Health Assn., Houston, 1968-69, Contemporary Arts Mus., Houston, 1976-80, Houston Symphony, 1981-82, Houston Grand Opera, 1975-85. Mem. U.S. Simmental Cattle Assn. (breeder). Republican. Roman Catholic. Clubs: Houston, Houstonian, University (Houston). Home: 160 Wells Rd Palm Beach FL 33480 Address: Bellefleur Farm Clifton Pike Versailles KY 40383 Office: Historic Restoration Co 5 Chamberlain Ave Warren NJ 07060

FRASCA, JENNIFER TERESE, insurance agent, broker; b. Riverside, Calif., Sept. 14, 1960; d. Stanley John and Irene Mary (Saso) F. BA in Health and Safety Studies with high honors, Calif. State U., Los Angeles, 1980. Tchr. life sci. Rowland (Calif.) Unified Sch. Dist., 1981-82; mgr. sales Jack LaLanne's European Health Spas, Downey, Calif., 1981-82; ins. agt. Mut. of Omaha and Ind. Ins. Sales, Long Beach, Calif., 1982—; owner, gen. ptnr. Farrell and Frasca Ins. Services, Huntington Beach, Calif., 1987—. Republican. Roman Catholic. Home: 8455 Basin Huntington Beach CA 92646

FRASER, GAIL ROBIN, computer programmer; b. White Plains, N.Y., Nov. 8, 1954; d. Waymon Woodrow and Mary Lucile (Royce) F. AA, Colby Coll., 1974; BA, Skidmore Coll., 1976; MBA, U. Conn., 1985. Sr. account rep. Sperry Univac Co., Valley Forge, Pa., 1978-80; mgr. mgmt. info. services tng. Eastern Airlines, Miami, Fla., 1980-81; sr. data base analyst Pitney-Bowes Co., Stamford, Conn., 1981-85; adminstr. data base aerospace bus. group Gen. Electric Co., Burlington, Vt., 1985-87; program mgr., corp. info. tech. Gen. Electric Co., Bridgeport, Conn., 1987—; owner, mgr. Eqelleous-Demand Morgans, Shelburne, Vt., 1986-87, Base Design, Shelton, Conn., 1988—. Republican. Episcopalian. Office: Gen Electric Co Corp CIT Tech Bldg 28DE 1285 Boston Ave Bridgeport CT 06601

FRASER, LEILA, banker; b. Chgo., May 26, 1942; d. Paul and Emily (Dzierzyck) Hucko; 1 child, Alec. AB in Polit. Sci. with high distinction, U. Ill., 1964, MA, 1966, PhD, 1971. Teaching asst. Carleton U., Ottawa, Ont., Can., 1967-68; lectr. polit. sci. U. Ky., Lexington, 1970, asst. dir., then acting dir. Office Internat. Programs, 1970-72; staff assoc., then asst. to vice chancellor U. Wis., Milw., 1972-76, asst. vice chancellor, 1976-77, asst. to chancellor, 1977; chief adminstr. to mayor City of Milw., 1977-82; sr. v.p. Banc One Wis. Corp., Milw., 1982—. Contbr. articles to profl. jours. Bd. dirs. United Performing Arts Fund, Milw. Forum; mem. adv. com. on women and minorities Office Wis. Commr. Securities, 1976-80; mem. Gov.'s Commn. Wis. Strategic Devel., 1983-85; bd. dirs. Milw. Exposition, Conv. Ctr. and Arena, 1978-82; bd. dirs., chmn. mktg. com. Milw. County Research Park Bd., 1987—, United Performing Arts Fund, 1987—; bd. dirs., exec. com. treas. Milw. Symphony Orch., 1979— , World Festivals Inc., 1982—, Milw. Urban League, 1984—; mem. corp. bd. adv. com. Milw. Sch. Engrng., 1983—; bd. dirs., past pres. Milw. Council Alcoholism, 1979-84; bd. dirs., chmn. mktg. div. United Way Greater Milw., 1987—, mem. campaign cabinet, 1986-87; mem. adv. council Robert M. LaFollette Inst. Pub. Affairs U. Wis., Madison, 1984—; mem. adv. bd. dept. bus. Cardinal Stritch Coll.; bd. dirs. exec. com. Forward Wis., 1985—; U. Wis., Milw. Found., 1986-87; mem. U. Ill. Bus. Adv. Council, 1987—; mem. Am. Council on Edn. Nat. Commn. on Higher Edn. Issues, 1981-83; active Bus. against Drunk Drivers; telethon co-chmn. United Cerebral Palsy of Southeastern Wis., 1987-88; U.S. rep. 20th Gen. Conf. of UNESCO, Paris, 1978. Recipient Outstanding Achievement award 4th Dist. Wis. Fedn. Women's Clubs, 1978, YWCA of Greater Milw., 1986; fellow Am. Council Edn., 1976-77. Mem. Am. Bankers Assn. (edn.l. policy and devel. council 1983-86), Assn. Bank Holding Cos. (govt. relations com. 1983—), Bank Mktg. Assn., Phi Beta Kappa, Phi Delta Kappa. Office: Marine Corp 111 E Wisconsin Ave Milwaukee WI 53202

FRASER, LUCILLE, banker; b. Bronx, N.Y., Sept. 3, 1964; d. James and Irma (Perrone) Barbookles; m. Michael John Fraser, June 19, 1988. Cashier Jamesway Corp., Monroe, N.Y., 1984-85; specialized account teller Key Bank Corp., Chester, N.Y., 1985; teller Norstar Bank Corp., Middletown, N.Y., 1985-86, Cornwall-on-Hudson, N.Y., 1986—; head teller Fleer/Norstar Corp., Amsterdam, N.Y., 1988—. Mem. Am. Banking Inst. (profl. cert., Bronze star 1986, Gold star 1987). Roman Catholic. Home: PO Box 378 Tribes Hill NY 12177

FRASER, RENEE WHITE, advertising agency executive; b. Columbus, Ohio, June 15, 1952; d. William Burval and Ruth Ann (Stuber) White; m. Scott Cameron Fraser, Dec. 10, 1978; children: Caneel, Skye. BA, U. So. Calif., 1973, MA, 1975, PhD, 1981. Sr. assoc. PLOG Research, Reseda, Calif., 1977-79; v.p. Leiberman Research, Century City, Calif., 1979-80; research dir., v.p. Young & Rubicam, Los Angeles, 1980-84; sr. v.p., dir. strategic planning and research Bozell Jacobs Kenyon & Eckhardt, Los Angeles, 1984—; bd. dirs. Vols of Am., Los Angeles, Sharon Clark & Assocs., Los Angeles. Author: Behavioral and Psycho-cultural Factors in Planning Health Care Systems, 1978, Environmental Health Issues in Developing Health Care Systems in Third World Countries, 1978. Recipient Disting. speaker award Direct Mktg. Assn., 1985, Disting. speaker award U. So. Calif. Sch. Bus., 1986. Mem. Am. Mktg. Assn., Am. Psychol. Assn., Sigma Chi. Home: 10758 National Blvd Los Angeles CA 90064 Office: Bozell Jacobs Kenyon & Eckhardt 12121 Wilshire Blvd Los Angeles CA 90025

FRASSANITO, ADRIENNE ANNE, educator; b. Queens, N.Y., July 29, 1950; d. Salvatore Anthony and Mary (Aiello) F. BFA, C. W. Post Coll., 1973, MS in Music Edn., 1975; postgrad., Bklyn. Coll., 1983-85; cert., Memphis State U., 1984. Cert. Orff-Schulwerk tchr. levels 1, 2, 3, master class. Tchr. music Smithtown (N.Y.) Pub. Schs., 1973-74, Garden City (N.Y.) Pub. Schs., 1974—; clinician various sch. dists., 1984—. dir. music Ch. of the Holy Spirit, New Hyde Park, N.Y., 1978—. Mem. Music Educators Nat. Conf., Nassau Music Educators Assn., L.I. Orff-Schulwerk Assn. (exec. bd., pres. 1985-87). Republican. Roman Catholic. Office: Garden City Pub Schs Stratford Ave and Weyford Terr Garden City NY 11530

FRATANTONI, KATHLEEN MARGARET, accountant; b. Phila., Jan. 31, 1959; d. Robert John and Louise (Lily) Risse; m. Ronald Michael, Sept., 1984. BS, Cabrini Coll., Radnor, Pa., 1981; MS, Widener U., 1984. CPA, Pa. Tax acct. Glickman, Berkovitz, Levinson & Weiner, Elkins Park, Pa., 1983—. Mem. Am. Inst. CPA's, Pa. Inst. CPA's, Am. Women's Soc. CPA's. Office: Glickman Berkovitz Levinson & Weiner One Breyer Office Park Suite 200 Elkins Park PA 19117

FRAUSTO, MARÍA CHRISTINA, educator; b. San Jose, Calif., Dec. 25, 1952; d. Carlos and Hortencia (Pasillas) F. BA, U. of the Pacific, 1975; postgrad., Calif. State U., San Jose, 1975—. Cert. elem. and secondary tchr., Calif. Tchr. kindergarten, 1st grade bilingual edn. San Jose Unified Sch. Dist., 1975-81; bilingual resource tchr. Santee Sch., Franklin-McKinley Sch. Dist., San Jose, 1981-85; tchr. 1st grade bilingual edn. McKinley Sch., San Jose, 1985—; master tchr. for student tchrs. San Jose State U., 1985—; presenter workshops on bilingual edn. and teaching ESL. Grantee East Valley Ednl. Found., San Jose, 1987. Mem. Calif. Assn. Bilingual Edn. (chair fundraising 1982-84). Democrat. Roman Catholic. Club: McKinley Track (San Jose). Home: 2339 Ravine Dr San Jose CA 95133 Office: Franklin McKinley Sch Dist 2072 Lucretia Ave San Jose CA 95122

FRAVEL, ELIZABETH WHITMORE, accountant; b. Hagerstown, Md., Oct. 17, 1951; d. John W. and Dorothy E. (McCullough) Whitmore; m. Benjamin H. Fravel, May 28, 1971; children: Christine E., John W. BBA, Bridgewater Coll., 1973. CPA. Jr. staff acct. Rockingham Meml. Hosp., Harrisonburg, Va., 1973-75; mgr. customer service Pentamation Enterprises Inc., Sparks, Md., 1975-83; sr. acct. Good Samaritan Hosp., Balt., 1983-84; pvt. practice acctg. Balt., 1984-86, Annapolis, Md., 1986-87; staff acct. Hammond & Heim Chartered Accts., Annapolis, Md., 1987—. Treas. Belmont Condominium Assn., Balt., 1983-85. Mem. Am. Inst. CPA's, Md. Assn. CPA's, Healthcare Fin. Mgmt. Assn. (advanced).

FRAY, NANCY BETH, management consultant; b. Washington, Dec. 7, 1951; d. Charles Thomas Fray and Mary Elizabeth (Biggs) Corwin. BS in Stats., Colo. State U., 1973. Statistician First Security Datacorp, Denver, 1974-75; systems analyst Air Products Chems., Allentown, Pa., 1976-80, Shared Med. Systems, King of Prussia, Pa., 1980-81; mgr. Peat Marwick, N.Y.C., 1982-87; cons. Eastbourne Cons. Group, N.Y.C., 1987—. Mem. Data Processing Mgmt. Assn. (bd. dirs. 1985-87), Assn. Info. Systems Profls., Adminstrv. Mgmt. Soc., Wo/Men in Telecommunications. Office: Eastbourne Cons Group 305 Madison Ave New York NY 10165

FRAZER, MARILEE HELEN, pathologist; b. Wilmington, Del., Nov. 20, 1953; d. August Henry and Christine (Hoover) F. BA in Biol. Scis., U. Del., 1975; MD, Jefferson Med. Coll., 1978. Diplomate Am. Bd. Anatomic Pathology, Am. Bd. Forensic Pathology. Dep. coroner Cuyahoga County Coroner's Office, Cleve., 1983-84; asst. med. examiner Wayne County Med. Examiner's Office, Detroit, 1984—. Fellow Am. Coll. Pathology; mem. Nat. Assn. Med. Examiners, Am. Acad. Forensic Scis. Office: Wayne County Med Examiners Office 400 E Lafayette Detroit MI 48226

FRAZER, WENDY, nurse, physician assistant; b. Steubenville, Ohio, June 3, 1943; d. Richard William and Mary Elizabeth (Sliday) F. RN, Beaver Valley Gen. Hosp., New Brighton, Pa., 1964; AAS, Cuyahoga Community Coll., 1983. RN, Ohio, Pa. Pediatrics nurse Cleve. Clinic Found., 1962-65; asst. head nurse Cardiovascular Lab., 1965-73; surg. nurse clinician cardiothoracic surgery Cleve. Clinic Found., 1978-86, nurse clinician gen. thoracic surgery, 1986—; admissions officer Lakewood Hosp., 1984-85; instr. cardiovascular tech. program Cuyahoga Community Coll., Cleve., 1987, clin. preceptor surg. asst. program, 1984-87; mem. steering com. Master's Group of Phoenix Ctr., 1986-88; physician asst. membership com. Alumnus Assn., 1986. Assoc. founder, counselor Inst. Creative Living, 1976-80. Mem. Nat. Acad. Physician Assts., Nat. Assn. Cardiovascular Physician Assts., Ohio Assn. Physician Assts., Cleve. Zool. Soc., Cleve. Mus. Art, Nat. Geog. Soc., Smithsonian Soc. Republican. Baptist. Office: Cleve Clinic Found 9500 Euclid Ave Cleveland OH 44106

FRAZIER, GENEVIEVE LAVERNE, lawyer; b. Warren, Ohio, Sept. 2, 1953; d. George Donald and Gladys Emma (Cooper) F. A.A., Dalton (Ga.) Jr. Coll., 1972; B.S. magna cum laude, U. Ga., 1974; J.D., Emory U., 1980. Bar: Ga. 1981. Ty. sales mgr. Wyeth Labs., Chattanooga, 1974-78; law clk. Dekalb Jud. Circuit, Atlanta, 1980-81; asst. dist. atty. Gwinnett Jud. Circuit, Ga., 1981-83; assoc. Chambers, Mabry, Mc Clelland & Brooks, Atlanta, 1984—; tchr. Gwinnett County and Mcpl. Police Depts., 1981-84, Gwinnett County Pub. Schs., 1981-84. Com. chmn. Gwinnett County LWV, 1982-83, treas., 1984; state v.p. Young Republicans, 1977-78; mem. Nat. Audubon Soc., 1982-84. P.W. Fattig Entomology scholar, 1973; Emory Acad. scholar, 1979; Dalton Jr. Coll. acad. scholar, 1971. Mem. Ga. Bar Assn., ABA, Atlanta Bar Assn., Gwinnett County Bar Assn., Phi Kappa Phi, Gamma Sigma Delta. Methodist. Club: Bus. and Profl. Women's of Gwinnett County (dir., Young Careerist). Home: 115 Michigan Ave Decatur GA 30030 Office: Chambers Mabry Mc Clelland & Brooks 2200 Century Center Pkwy 825 Atlanta GA 30345

FREDERICH, KATHY W., social worker; b. Ashland, Ky., Apr. 19, 1953; d. James Greeley and Jo Ann (Sparks) Walker; divorced; m. Harry Donald Frederich, Sept. 5, 1987; stepchild, David Scott. BA with distinction, U. Ky., 1978. Tng. supr. Blue Grass Assn. for Retarded Citizens, Lexington, Ky., 1971-75, Bur. Vocational Rehab., Lexington, 1976-77; social worker Ky. Dept. for Social Services, Lexington, 1978-79, field office supr., 1979-85; social work program specialist cen. office Ky. Dept. for Social Services, Frankfort, Ky., 1985—; instr. Ky. Sheriff's Acad. Lexington Fayette Div. of Police, 1981—, Ky. Dept. for Social Services, Richmond, Ky., 1987—; cons., trainer for field staff, Ky., 1983—. Recipient Outstanding Service award Lexington Fayette div. of Police, 1984, Ky. Sheriff's Acad. tribute, 1986,87, 88, Outstanding Kentuckian award Gov. Martha Layne Collins, 1987, Outstanding Youn Am. Women award ; Named Ky. Col. Gov. Martha Collins, 1985. Mem. Ky. Domestic Violence Assn. Democrat.

FREDERICK, ARLENE MAE WILLGING, nurse, educator; b. Passaic, N.J., Oct. 29, 1942; s. Arthur William and Mae Frances (Randazzo) Willging; m. Robert Arthur Frederick, June 19, 1965; children: Robert Arthur, Elyse, Dawn, Kristen. BSN, Georgetown U., 1964; MSN, U. Tex., San Antonio, 1973; EdD, U. S.C., 1980. Project dir. S.C. Nurses Assn., Columbia, 1974-76; instr. Incarnate Word Coll., San Antonio, 1973-74; instr. Columbia Assn. Prepared Childbirth, 1974—; instr. Midlands Tech. Coll., Columbia, 1981-83; pres. Profl. Health Edn. Cons., Columbia, 1980—; nurse clinician Richland Meml. Hosp., Columbia, 1983-85; nursing edn. dir. William S. Hall Psychiat. Inst., Columbia, 1986-88. Author: (with others) Are You Ready? A Guide for Prepared Childbirth, 1976, 2d edit., 1983, Expanding Horizons in Childbirth Education, 1985, Childbirth Education: Practice, Research and Theory, 1988. Chmn. edn. com. S.C. Bd. Examiners Nursing Home Adminstrs., 1981—; mem. S.C. Maternal Child Health Adv. Com., 1983—, chair, 1985—. Served to 1st lt. AUS, 1962-66. Mem. S.C. Nurses Assn. (chmn. council on edn., 1980-84), Central Midland Dist. Nurses Assn. (pres. 1985-87), Am. Nurses Assn., Am. Soc. Psychoprophlaxis Obstetrics (edn. cons. 1974—), Nurses Assn. of Am. Coll. Ob-Gyn., Sigma Theta Tau. Office: Profl Health Edn Cons PO Box 210372 Columbia SC 29221

FREDERICK, CYNDIE LOUISE, banker; b. McAllen, Tex., Mar. 14, 1961; d. John Robert and Doris Ann (Nauer) Bacak; m. David Charles Frederick, July 24, 1981; children: Ryan David, Brandon Robert. Student, Austin Community Coll., 1985. Service mgr. H.E. Butt Grocery, Austin, Tex., 1977-82; br. mgr. Tex. Fed. Savs., Austin, 1982-83, human resources specialist, 1983-85; br. mgr. Bright Banc Savs. Assn., Austin, 1985-86, retail banking officer, 1986-87, asst. v.p., 1988—. Vol. March of Dimes, Austin, 1983—, United Way, 1985, Tex. Spl. Olympics, 1988, Make-A-Wish Found., 1988—; mem. Texans Civil Justice, 1987—. Mem. Nat. Assn. Female Execs., Eanes Bus. & Profl. Assn., Inst. Fin. Edn., (bd. dirs.), Austin Bd. of Realtors (affiliate), Cedar Park (Tex.) C. of C. Republican. Roman Catholic. Home: 9905 Talleyran Dr Austin TX 78750 Office: Bright Banc Savs Assn 13928 Research Blvd Austin TX 78750

FREDERICK, ELIZABETH ANN, social worker; b. Ossining, N.Y., Dec. 29, 1954; d. Anthony and Helen Jane (Garrison) F. AA, Dutchess County Community Coll., Poughkeepsie, N.Y., 1975; BA in Psychology, Marist Coll., Poughkeepsie, 1978, cert. legal asst., 1979; postgrad., SUNY, New Paltz, 1981-83; MSW, SUNY, Albany, 1985. Psychology intern Hudson River Psychiat. Ctr., Poughkeepsie, 1978; legal intern Dutchess County Pub. Defenders Office, 1978; intake counselor Women's Ctr. SUNY, New Paltz, 1980-81; intern social work Rehab. Support Services, Albany, 1983-84; aging service specialist Sr. Service Ctrs. of Albany Area, Inc., 1985—. V.p. fin. NOW, N.Y., 1980, pres. Dutchess County chpt., 1980, pres. Albany chpt., 1983; mem. Mid-Hudson Coalition for Free Choice, Poughkeepsie, 1976; del. NOW N.Y. State. Mem. Nat. Assn. Social Workers, Capital Dist. Assn. Providers of Aging Services, Nat. Assn. for Female Execs., Nat. Council Sr. Citizens, Older Women's League (steering com., maintenance com.). Democrat. Club: Women's Bldg. (Albany). Office: Sr Service Ctrs of Albany Area Inc 25 Delaware Ave Albany NY 12210

FREDERICK, MARIJANE, human resources professional; b. Bklyn., Dec. 10, 1953; d. William Paul and Helen (Stepien) F.; m. Sewell Fletcher Hipps Jr., Sept. 8, 1979; 1 child, Matthew Frederick Hipps. BA in Secondary English Edn. summa cum laude, SUNY, Albany, 1975. Field supr. Nat. Opinion Research Ctr. Rand Corp., Fitchburg, Masss., 1975-76; field rep. Glen Slaughter and Assocs. Rand Corp., Fitchburg, Mass., 1976-77; systems and procedures specialist Nat. Rural Electric Coop. Assn., Washington, 1977-79, personnel specialist, 1979-81; personnel dir. Palmetto Electric Coop. Inc., Hilton Head Island, S.C., 1981—. Mem. Sigma Tau Beta. Office: Palmetto Electric Coop Inc PO Box 1218 111 Mathews Dr Hilton Head Island SC 29925

FREDERICK, NANCY, government official; b. Lakewood, Ohio, Aug. 23, 1932; d. Howard Peter and Marian Bissell (Slater) F.; B.A., U. Colo., 1955; postgrad., George Washington U., 1962-63, U.S. Dept. Agr., 1964-65, Fgn. Service Inst., 1968; m. Francis Liell Wenger. Reporter/photographer, city editor Robinson (Ill.) Daily News, 1956-61; area reporter UPI, 1956-61; spl. asst. to Congressman Peter Mack, Washington, 1961-62; with AID, 1962—, info. officer/photographer, 1962-65, editor Front Lines, 1966-68, program analyst devel. planning offices Latin Am. and Africa Burs., 1968-69, asst. desk officer Nigeria Relief and Rehab., 5 Central African countries, also Sahelian Drought Emergency Unit, 1969-74, human resources devel. officer Central/West African Affairs, 1972-74, planning asst. to coordinator Women in Devel. AID, 1974-77, program analyst to dep. dir. Am. Schs. and Hosps. Abroad, 1978—; mem. AID Women's Adv. Com., 1973-75; AID adviser, U.S., del. UN World Conf. Internat. Women's Yr., Mexico City, 1975; U.S. del. UN Conf. Status of Women, Geneva, Switzerland, OAS Inter. Am. Conf. for Women, 1976; asst. founding spl. offices for women devel. activities, Peace Corps, WHO, FAO, World Bank; agy. speaker, panelist various confs., 1975-77. Trustee Chesapeake Environ. Protection Assn., editor Chesapeake Environ. Protection Assn. Quar., 1979—. Recipient five awards Fed. Editors Assn., 1966-69, various awards and citations AID, cert. Nat. Council of Negro Women, 1975. Author, co-author plans and papers in field. Home: Route 1 Box 170 West River MD 20778 Office: FVA/ASHA AID Washington DC 20523

FREDERICK, PAULINE, broadcast news analyst; b. Gallitzin, Pa.; d. Matthew Phillip and Susan (Stanley) F.; m. Charles Robbins. A.B., Am. U., Washington, also A.M.; numerous hon. degrees. State Dept. corr. U.S. Daily; radio editorial asst. H.R. Baukhage, Blue Network and ABC; free-lance Western Newspaper Union, N.Am. Newspaper Alliance; also news commentator ABC, 1946-53; news corr. NBC, 1953-74; also UN corr. ABC, NBC; radio anchor Dem. and Rep. Convs. NBC, 1956; internat. affairs analyst Nat. Public Radio; moderator 2d debate Pres. Ford-Gov. Carter, Oct. 6, 1976. Trustee Am. U.; mem. council Save the Children, UN Assn. U.S.A. Recipient Headliner award Theta Sigma Phi, Alfred I duPont award, George Foster Peabody award for contbn. to internat. understanding, Golden Mike award for outstanding woman in radio-TV McCall's; Paul White award for contbn. to broadcast journalism Radio and TV News Dirs. Assn.; voted radio's woman of the year Radio-TV Daily poll; U. Mo. Sch. Journalism medal; spl. citation for UN coverage Nat. Fedn. Women's Clubs; East-West Center award; Journalism Achievment award U. So. Calif.; 1st Pa. Journalism Achievment award; Carr Van Anda award Ohio U. Sch. Journalism; named to N.Y. Profl. Journalists Soc. Hall of Fame. Fellow Soc. Profl. Journalists; mem. UN Corrs. Assn. (pres.), Assn. Radio and Television Analysts, Council on Fgn. Relations.

FREDERICK, VIRGINIA FIESTER, state legislator; b. Rock Island, Ill., Dec. 24, 1916; d. John Henry and Myrtle (Montgomery) Heise; B.A., U. Iowa, 1938; postgrad. Lake Forest Coll., 1942-43; m. C. Donnan Fiester (dec. 1975); children—Sheryl Fiester Ross, Alan R., James D.; m. 2d Kenneth Jacob Frederick, 1978. Free-lance fashion designer, Lake Forest, Ill., 1952-78; pres. Mid Am. China Exchange, Kenilworth, Ill., 1978-81; mem. Ill. Ho. of Reps., Springfield, 1979—. Alderman, first ward Lake Forest, 1974-78; del. World Food Conf., Rome, 1974. mem. Ill. Commn. on Status of Women subcom. pensions and employment, 1976-79; co-chmn. Conf. Women Legislators, 1982-85. Named Chgo. Area Woman of Achievement, Internat. Orgn. Women Execs., 1978. Recipient Lottie Holman O'Neal award, 1980, Jane Addams award, 1982. Mem. LWV (local pres. 1958-60, state dir. 1969-75, mem. nat. com. 1975-76), AAUW (local pres. 1968-70, state pres. 1975-77, state dir. 1963-69, mem. nat. commns. 1967-69), UN Assn. (dir.), Chgo. Assn. Commerce and Industry (dir.). Methodist. Address: 1540 Greenleaf Ave Lake Forest IL 60045

FREDERICK-MAIRS, T(HYRA) JULIE, alcohol agency official; b. Islip, N.Y., Jan. 4, 1941; d. Manuel and Thyra C. (Thorsen) Cajiao; B.A., Adelphi U., 1961; M.S.W., U. So. Calif., 1972. Social worker Los Angeles County Dept. Social Services, 1966-67, social work supr., 1967-70; planning cons. Los Angeles County Dept. Social Services and Los Angeles County Chief Adminstr.'s Office, 1972-76; dep. to supr. 4th Dist., Los Angeles County, 1976-80; asst. dir. Los Angeles County Office Alcohol Programs, 1980—. Mem. or past mem. Los Angeles Child Sexual Abuse Project, Commn. for Sex Equity, Los Angeles Unified Sch. Dist., Harbor Police Community Adv. Council, Los Angeles; mem. San Pedro and Peninsula Family Stress Task Force, Los Angeles; mem. ops. com. Interagy. Council on Child Abuse and Neglect; bd. dirs. Marshall High Sch. PTA, Los Angeles; adv. com. UCLA Alcohol Research Center; mem. Westside Child Trauma Council. U. So. Calif. fellow, 1988. Mem. Los Amigos de la Humanidad, Women in Health Adminstrn., Alpha Epsilon Delta, Beta Beta Beta. Clubs: Bus. and Profl. Women's, Soroptimists (pres. Los Angeles County 1987-88, dir. Found. of Los Angeles, 1986-88), Cath. Maritime (dir.). Author: (with others) Youth Program Planning, 1975.

FREDERIKSEN, KATHLEEN ANN, data systems executive; b. Pontiac, Mich., May 27, 1961; d. John Henry and Patricia June (Monte) F. A in Bus. Adminstrn., Oakland Community Coll., 1985. Adminstrv. sec. D'Arcy-MacManus and Masius Advt., 1979-81; bus. systems analyst, adminstrv. sec. pub. relations and advt. Burson-Marsteller/Young and Rubicam, Chgo. and Detroit, 1981-84; systems cons. Rainbow Computers, Troy, Mich., 1984-86, Heath/Zenith Computers, Farmington Hills, Mich., 1986-87; pres. Sharpcopy, Southfield, Mich., 1987—; speaker in field Oakland U., Rochester, Mich., 1987. Mem. Nat. Assn. Female Execs., Soc. Tng. and Devel., Southfield C. of C. Democrat. Roman Catholic. Club: Toastmasters (Southfield) (2 Best Speaker awards 1987, adminstrv. v.p. 1987). Home: 2716 Colonial Way Bloomfield Hills MI 48013

FREDINE, ANNE BOYCE, library director; b. Waterbury, Conn., Nov. 1, 1944; d. Jay and Mabel L. (Cobb) B.; m. Richard Earle Fredine, Apr. 27, 1968. BA in Anthropology, Wheaton Coll., 1966; MS in Library Sci., U. Minn., 1974. Cataloger, head librarian Medtronic, Inc., Mpls., 1971-75; dir. Nashua (Iowa) Pub. Library, 1976-84; cons. librarian Northeastern Iowa Regional Library, Waterloo, 1984-86; dir. Moorhead (Minn.) Library, Lake Agassiz Regional Library, 1986—; mem. task force Regional Library System, State Library of Iowa, Des Moines, 1982-84; com. mem. standards com. Iowa Library Assn., Des Moines, 1984-86. Author: Libraries and Communities, 1985. Mem. community study City of Nashua, 1983; bd. dirs. Moorhead Cable Access TV, 1986—. Mem. ALA, Minn. Library Assn., Moorhead Area C. of C. (mem. task force 1986—). Republican. Mem. Evangelical Free Ch. Office: Lake Agassiz Regional Library 118 S 5th St PO Box 900 Moorhead MN 56560

FREDRICK, SUSAN WALKER, tax company manager; b. Painesville, Ohio, Nov. 17, 1948; d. Floyd Clayton and Margaret (Merkel) Walker; m. Stephan Douglas Fredrick, Oct. 20, 1973. BS, Mt. Union Coll., Alliance, Ohio, 1970; MS, U. Conn., 1973. Research asst. Boyce Thompson Inst., Yonkers, N.Y., 1971-74; dir. quality control Lawley, Matusky, Skelly, Tappan, N.Y., 1974-75; field supr. Ecological Analysts, Middletown, N.Y., 1975-76; scientist Pandullo Quirk Assocs., Wayne, N.J., 1976-78; editor Biosis. Info. Service, Phila., 1978-80; tax preparer H&R Block, Inc., King of Prussia, Pa., 1978-80, dist. mgr., 1980—; guest lectr. Temple U., 1981-86. Mem. Am. Mgmt. Assn., Nat. Assn. Female Execs., Nat. Assn. Enrolled Agents. Club: Keystone Divers (West Chester, Pa.). Lodge: Soroptimists. Office: H&R Block Inc King of Prussia Plaza Q2A King of Prussia PA 19406

FREE, ANN COTTRELL, writer; b. Richmond, Va.; d. Emmett Drewry and Emily (Blake) Cottrell; grad. Collegiate Sch. for Girls, Richmond, 1934; student Richmond div. Coll. William and Mary, 1934-36; A.B., Barnard Coll., Columbia, 1938; m. James Stillman Free, Feb. 24, 1950; 1 dau., Elissa. Reporter Richmond Times Dispatch, 1938-40; Washington corr., Newsweek, 1940-41, Chgo. Sun, 1941-43, N.Y. Herald Tribune, 1943-46; pub. information dir. UNRRA China Mission, Shanghai, 1946-47; corr. Middle and Nr. East and Europe, 1947-48; writer-photographer Marshall Plan, Washington and Western Europe, 1949-50; contbr. editor Between the Species; contbr. newspapers and mags.; Washington editor EnviroSouth Quar., 1977-82. Mem. Friends of the Rachel Carson Nat. Wildlife Refuge (hon. founding mem.); chmn. Mrs. Roosevelt's Press Conf. Assn., 1943; cons. expert Rachel Carson Council; chmn. Vieguez Puerto Rico Animal Emergency Fund;

coordinator Albert Schweitzer Summer Fellows Program. Recipient Dodd Mead-Boys' Life Writing award, 1963, Albert Schweitzer medal, Animal Welfare Inst., 1963, Jr. Book award certificate Boys Clubs of Am., 1964; Humanitarian of Yr. awards Washington Animal Rescue League, 1971, Montgomery County Humane Soc., 1971, Washington Humane Soc., 1983, News Writing award Dog Writers Assn. Am., 1975, 78, Rachel Carson Legacy award, 1987; recognition Dept. Interior, 1969. Mem. Soc. Woman Geographers. Club: Washington Press, Am. Newswomen's (bd. dirs.). Author: Forever the Wild Mare, 1963; Animals, Nature and Albert Schweitzer, 1982, No Room, Save in the Heart, 1987. Home: 4700 Jamestown Rd Bethesda MD 20816

FREE, HELEN M., chemist, consultant; b. Pitts., Feb. 20, 1923; d. James Summerville and Daisy (Piper) Murray; m. Alfred H. Free, Oct. 18, 1947; children—Eric, Penny, Kurt, Jake, Bonnie, Nina. B.A. in Chemistry, Coll. of Wooster, Ohio, 1944; M.A. in Clin. Lab. Mgmt., Central Mich. U. Cert. clin. chemist Nat. Registry Clin. Chemists. Chemist Miles Labs., Elkhart, Ind., 1944-78, dir. mktg. services research products div., 1978-82, chemist, mgr., cons. Ames div. Miles Labs., 1982—; adj. instr. Ind. U., South Bend, 1975—. Author: (with others) Urodynamics and Urinalysis in Clinical Laboratory Practice, 1972, 76. Contbr. articles to profl. jours. Patentee in field. Women's chmn. Centennial of Elkhart, 1958. Recipient Disting. Alumni award Coll. of Wooster, 1980. Fellow AAAS, Am. Inst. Chemists (co-recipient Chicago award 1967); mem. Am. Chem. Soc. (bd. dirs., chmn. women chemists com. internat. action com., grants and awards com., profl. and member relations com., nominating com., council policy pub. affairs and budget, Service award local chpt. 1981, councilor; Garvan medal 1980, co-recipient Mosher award, 1983), Am. Assn. for Clin. Chemistry (council, bd. dirs., nominating com. and pub. relations com., nat. membership chmn., profl. affairs coordinator, pres.), Am. Soc., Med. Tech. (chmn. assembly; Achievement award 1976), Iota Sigma Pi (hon.). Presbyterian. Lodge: Altrusa (pres. 1982-83, bd. dirs.). Home: 3752 E Jackson Blvd Elkhart IN 46516 Office: Miles Inc Diagnostics Div PO Box 70 Elkhart IN 46515

FREED, MARILYNNE MAUD, manufacturing company executive; b. Youngstown, Ohio, Sept. 18, 1949; d. Warren P. and Phyllis I. (Avery) F.; m. William E. Pastor, May 20, 1978; children: Will A., Daniel E. B.S., Case Res. U., 1971. Acctg. mgr. TV and radio Sta. WFMJ, Youngstown, 1971-72; bus. mgr. Sta. WFLD-TV, Chgo., 1972-74; v.p., treas. Youngstown Steel and Alloy Corp., Canfield, Ohio, 1974-82; pres. Life-Time Truck Products Inc., Youngstown, 1982—. Choir dir. Ohltown United Meth. Ch., Youngstown, 1982—, bd. dirs., 1983—, chmn. fin. com. 1985—. Mem. Family Bus. Assn. N.E. Ohio (charter; bd. dirs., v.p. 1978-80) Pvt. Industry Council Mahoning County (chmn. 1980-83), Youngstown C. of C. (legis. com. 1982—). Republican. Office: 4300 Simon Rd PO Box 3346 Youngstown OH 44512

FREEDMAN, ANNE BELLER, public speaking and marketing consultant; b. Gardner, Mass., June 22, 1949; d. Gabriel Philip Freedman and Natalie Engler (Beller) Lyons; m. Edward A. Fischer, May 20, 1979; 1 child, Lynne Heather. BSJ U. Fla., 1971. Staff writer Coral Gables Times, Miami, 1972-73; reporter Miami News, 1973-74; assoc. editor Miami Phoenix, 1974-75; freelance writer, Miami, 1975-80; corr. Advt. Age, Miami, 1977-81; pres. Exec. S.O.S., Inc., Miami, 1980—. Contbr. articles to profl. jours. Bd. dirs. Miami/Bogota-Calé Sister Cities Program, 1983-85. Mem. South Miami/Kendall C. of C. (editor monthly newsletter 1980-83, dir., 1982-85, chmn. bus. com. 1985-88, editor ann. directory and buyer's guide 1986-87, Presdl. award 1983), Nat. Assn. Women Bus. Owners (chair public relations 1981, dir. tng. and devel. 1987—, dir. corp. ptnrs. 1988—), Coral Gables C. of C., Kendall Bus. and Profl. Assn. Clubs: Toastmasters (pres. 1984), Kendall Bus. and Profl. Women. Home: 6721 SW 113th Pl Miami FL 33173 Office: 11410 N Kendall Dr Suite 207 Miami FL 33176

FREEDMAN, AUDREY WILLOCK, labor economist; b. Cleve., Nov. 25, 1929; d. Sylvester Rhodes and Hilda Louise (Reiber) Willock; m. Monroe H. Freedman, Sept. 24, 1950; children—Alice, Sarah, Caleb, Judah. B.A. in Econs., Wellesley Coll., 1951. Labor economist Communications Workers Am., AFL-CIO, Washington, 1958-60; economist Bur. Labor Stats., Washington, 1961-67, Manpower Adminstrn., 1967-71; mem. policy staff Cost of Living Council, liaison U.S. Pay Bd., Washington, 1971-72; sr. cons. Orgn. Resources Counselors, N.Y.C., 1973-75; sr. research assoc. Conf. Bd., N.Y.C., 1976-85, exec. dir. Human Resources Program group, 1985; exec. dir. Human Resources Program Group, The Conf. Bd., N.Y.C., 1985—; mem. bus. research adv. council, price and indsl. relations subcoms. U.S. Bur. Labor Stats.; mem. econs. bd. U.S. Dept. Agr. Grad. Sch., 1972-75; mem. adv. bd. Columbia U. Bus. Sch., Syracuse U. Author: Security Bargains Reconsidered, 1978; Managing Labor Relations, 1979; Industry Response to Health Risk, 1981; The New Look in Wage Policy and Employee Relations, 1985; contbr. articles to profl. jours. Recipient Disting. Service award U.S. Dept. Labor, 1967, Presdl. citation, 1972. Mem. Am. Fedn. Govt. Employees (v.p. local chpt. 1965-68, chmn. civil rights com. 1964-69), Am. Econ. Assn., Indsl. Relations Research Assn., Am. Statis. Assn. Jewish.

FREEDMAN, BETSY, management consultant; b. Springfield, Mass., Aug. 16, 1942; d. Herman and Marcia (Glickman) F.; m. Seymour Goldfond, Oct. 10, 1980; m. Neil Solomon, June 27, 1967 (div. May 1977); children—Leslie, Amy. A.S., Endicott Coll., 1962. Cons., Tamblyn & Brown, N.Y.C., 1962-67; exec. dir. East Mid Manhattan C. of C., N.Y.C., 1974-78; exec. v.p. Lawson Assocs., N.Y.C., 1978—. Cons., Orr Shalom Village, Jerusalem, 1980—, bd. dirs., 1982-83. Pres., Nat. Council Jewish Women, Monmouth County, N.J., 1972-73, recipient Outstanding Community work award, 1970. Republican. Jewish. Home: 80 East End Ave New York NY 10028 Office: Douglas M Lawson Assocs 545 Madison Ave 7th Floor New York NY 10022

FREEDMAN, ESTELLE BRENDA, historian, educator; b. Harrisburg, Pa., July 2, 1947; d. Theodore Henry and Martha Harriet (Pincus) F. BA in History, Barnard Coll., 1969; MA in History, Columbia U., 1972, PhD in History, 1976. Instr. Princeton U. (N.J.), 1974-76; asst. prof. Stanford U., Calif., 1976-83, assoc. prof. history, 1983—; assoc. editor: Signs: Jour. of Women in Culture and Society, 1980-85; mem. Coordinating Com. on Women in Hist. Profession. Author: Their Sisters' Keepers, 1981 (Hamilton manuscript prize 1978), (with others) Intimate Matters: A History of Sexuality in America, 1988; assoc. editor: Victorian Women, 1981 (Sierra prize 1982); editor The Lesbian Issue, 1985; contbr. articles to publs. Hon. dissertation fellow Woodrow Wilson Found., 1974-75; ind. study fellow NEH, 1982-83; AAUW Founders fellow, 1985-86; Stanford Humanities Ctr. fellow, 1985-86; recipient Dean's award for Disting. Teaching, Stanford U., 1978, Dinkelspiel award for outstanding service to undergrad. edn., 1981. Mem. Orgn. Am. Historians, Am. Hist. Assn., Nat. Women's Studies Assn. Jewish. Office: Stanford U Dept History Stanford CA 94305

FREEDMAN, JUDITH GREENBERG, senator, importer; b. Bridgeport, Conn., Mar. 11, 1939; d. Samuel Howard and Dorothy (Hoffman) G.; m. Samuel Sumner, Dec. 24, 1964; 1 child, Martha Ann. Student, Boston U., 1957-58, U. Mich., 1958-59; BS, So. Conn. State U., 1961, MS, 1972. Tchr. Hollywood (Fla.) Pub. Schs., 1961-62, White Plains (N.Y.) Pub. Schs., 1962-64, Wilton (Conn.) Pub. Schs., 1964-66; tutor Weston (Conn.) Pub. Schs., 1966-72, 1977-80, tchr., 1982-84; owner Judith's Fancy, Wesport, Conn., 1984—; state senator from Conn. 1987—. Pres., v.p. Rep. Women's Assn., 1976-80; pres. Rep. Women of Westport, 1976-79; mem. Bd. Edn., Westport, 1983-87. Jewish. Home: 17 Crawford Rd Westport CT 06880 Office: Human Services Com LOB 2200 Hartford CT 06106

FREEDMAN, MARION GLICKMAN, counsellor; b. N.Y.C., Feb. 3, 1922; d. Edward and Minnie (Tokarsky) Glickman; m. Bernard M. Freedman, Nov. 29, 1941; children: Rochelle Freedman Hassen, Diane Freedman Slatz. BS, NYU, 1942, MA in Secondary Edn., 1964, MA in Guidance, 1967, postgrad., 1975-77. BS NYU, 1942, MA in Secondary Edn., 1967; tchr. high sch., guidance counselor Bushwick High Sch., Bklyn., 1965-74; guidance counselor James Monroe High Sch., Bronx, N.Y., 1974-76, 77—; career counselor Walton High Sch., Bronx, 1976-77. Mem. Am. Personnel Assn. and Guidance Assn., N.Y. State Personnel and Guidance Assn., N.Y.C. Personnel and Guidance Assn., Nat. Bd. Cert. Counselors, NYU Alumni Assn., Delta Pi Epsilon. Jewish. Home: 6556 174th St Flushing NY 11365 Office: 1300 Boynton Ave Bronx NY 10472

FREEDMAN, PHYLLIS B., civic worker; b. N.Y.C., Jan. 10, 1928; d. Irving and Pauline D. (Janowitz) Blonder; m. Jack I. Freedman, Jan. 19, 1947; children—Douglas S. Freedman, Robyn Freedman Spizman. Student Syracuse U. Pres., Brandeis U. Nat. Women's Commn., Atlanta, 1958-60, nat. v.p., 1970-73; sec. Atlanta Jewish Community Ctr., Atlanta, 1960-62; life mem. Atlanta Jewish Fedn., 1988—, sec., asst. treas., 1970-75 , pres. yr. round women's div., 1960-62; mem. nat. bd. Women's div. United Jewish Appeal, N.Y.C., 1960-62, 81-82, nat. chair Women's div. Council of Jewish Fedn., N.Y.C., 1981-83; co-chair Israel Expo, Atlanta Jewish Com. Ctr., 1985; bd. dirs. Council Jewish Fedns., 1981—, Brandeis U. Nat. Women's Commn. (hon.); pres. Jewish Family Service, 1980-82. Recipient Pres.'s Council award Brandeis U., 1976, Disting. Service award B'nai Brith, 1983. Democrat. Jewish. Home: 1470 Wesley Pkwy NW Atlanta GA 30327

FREEDMAN, SANDRA WARSHAW, mayor; b. Newark, Sept. 21, 1944; m. Michael J. Freedman; 3 children. BA in Govt., U. Miami, 1965. Mem. Tampa (Fla.) City Council, 1974—, chmn., 1983-86; mayor City of Tampa, 1987—. Bd. dirs. Jewish Community Ctr., 1974-75, Boys and Girls Clubs Greater Tampa, Hillsborough Coalition for Health, Tampa Community Concert Assn.; mem. sports adv. bd. Hillsborough Community Coll., 1975-76; sec. Downtown Devel. Authority, 1977-78; bd. dirs., v.p. Fla. Gulf Coast Symphony, 1979-80; vice chmn. Met. Planning Orgn., 1981-82; corp. mem. Neighborhood Housing Service; bd. fellows U. Tampa; mem. steering com. Hillsborough County Council of Govt.'s Constituency for Children; mem. exec. bd. Tampa/Hillsborough Young Adult Forum; chmn. bd. trustees Berkeley Prep. Sch.; trustee Tampa Bay Performing Arts Ctr., Inc., Tampa Mus.; mem. ethics com. Meml. Hosp.; mem. Tampa Preservation, Inc., Tampa/Hillsborough County Youth Council, Davis Islands Civic Assn., Tampa Hist. Soc., Met. Ministries Adv. Bd., Rodeph Sholom Synagogue, Sword of Hope Guild of Am. Cancer Soc., Friends of the Arts. Recipient Spessard L. Holland Meml. award Tampa Bay Com. for Good Govt., 1975-76, Human Rights award City of Tampa, 1980, award Soroptimist Internat. Tampa, 1981, Status of Women award Zonta of Tampa II, 1986, Woman of Achievement award Bus. & Profl. Women; named to Who's Who and Why of Successful Fla. Women, 1984. Mem. Hillsborough County Bar Aux., Greater Tampa C. of C., C. of C. Com. of 100 (exec. com.), Fla. League of Cities (bd. dirs.), Tampa Urban League, Nat. Council Jewish Women, U. Miami Alumni Assn., Athena Soc., Hadassah. Office: Office of the Mayor 306 E Jackson St Tampa FL 33602

FREEHLING, DEBORAH JUNE, physician; b. Milw., Jan. 3, 1955; d. Frank Eugene and Betty June (Barfknecht) F. BS, U. Ill., 1977; MD, U. Ill., Chgo., 1981. Intern, then resident U. Calif. Davis Med. Ctr., Sacramento, 1981-83; resident in ear, nose and throat, otolaryngology Mass. Eye and Ear Infirmary, Boston, 1983-86; career physician, lectr. Kaiser Found. Hosp., Santa Clara, Calif., 1986—; instr. med. students Harvard Med. Sch. Mass Eye and Ear Infirmary, 1984-85, teaching asst. dissection course, 1985-86; discussant New Eng. Jour. Medicine, Boston, 1985-86. Contbr. articles to profl. jours. Tchr. Sunday sch. Menlo Park (Calif.) Presbyn. Ch., 1986—. Alpha Lambda Delta fellow, 1976. Fellow Am. Acad. Otolaryngology, Head and Neck Surgery (diplomate 1987); mem. Am. Acad. Facial Plastics and Reconstructive Surgery, Am. Acad. Otolaryngologic Allergy, Peninsula Ear, Nose and Throat Soc. Club: Decathlon (Santa Clara). Home: 250 S Balsamina Way Portola Valley CA 94025 Office: Kaiser Found Hosp 900 Kiely Blvd Santa Clara CA 95051

FREELAND, CLAIRE ANN BENNETT, psychologist; b. Washington, July 28, 1955; d. Lawrence H. and Devora M. (Spintman) Bennett; m. Howard S. Freeland, June 18, 1978; children: Rachel M., David S. BA, Johns Hopkins U., 1976; MA, Ind. U., 1978; PhD, U. Md., 1981. Lic. clin. psychologist. Instr. Sch. Medicine U. Md., Balt., 1981-84; psychologist Hearing and Speech Agy., Balt., 1981—. Contbr. articles to profl. jours. Mem. Am. Psychol. Assn., Soc. Research in Child Devel., Soc. Pediatric Psychology. Office: Hearing and Speech Agy 2220 Saint Paul St Baltimore MD 21218

FREELAND, FRANCES JEANNETTE, alcoholism treatment center executive; b. Danville, Ill., Apr. 11, 1938; d. John Terrence and Marie Amber (Iliff) F.; B.S. in Nursing, Coll. Mt. St. Joseph, Cin., 1960; M.S. in Extension Edn., Purdue U., Indpls., 1978, postgrad. in health adminstrn. Staff nurse in premature and critical care nursery Good Samaritan Hosp., Cin., 1960-61; joined Carmelite order, Roman Catholic Ch., 1961, with Carmelite Contemplative Community, Indpls., 1961-71; staff nurse VA Hosp., Indpsl., 1971-72; med./surg. staff nurse St. Francis Hosp., Beech Grove, Ind., 1972-74; dir. alcoholism detoxification unit Salvation Army, Indpls., 1974-79, program dir. Salvation Army Adult Rehab. Center, 1979-85; administrv. asst. Salvation Army Harbor Light Ctr., 1985—; tchr. alcoholism therapy; mem. Ind. Substance Abuse Task Force; v.p. Ind. Free Standing Addiction Agys. Coalition. Bd. dirs., mem. exec. bd. First Step Inc., half-way house for women, Indpls. Recipient award of appreciation Koala Center, Lebanon, Ind., 1978, Salvation Army Territorial Nurse Yr. award, 1984. Mem. Ind. Nurses Soc. on Alcoholism, Nat. Nurses Soc. on Alcoholism (planning com. 1982 Forum). Democrat. Home: 1365 N Dearborn St Indianapolis IN 46201 Office: 925 N Delaware St Indianapolis IN 46202

FREELAND, SANDRA TUCKER, federal agency administrator; b. Starkville, Miss., July 22, 1948; d. John Earl and Hazel Ruth (Ballinger) Tucker; m. Charles Alan Freeland, May 9, 1981. BA cum laude, Millsaps Coll., Jackson, Miss., 1969. Agt. IRS, Atlanta, 1969-82, appeals officer, 1982-85, staff asst. to RDA, 1985-86, asst. RDA, 1986—. Pres. Tucker, Ga. Edinburgh Estates Civic Club, 1983. Recipient Nat. Meth. scholarship, Millsaps Coll., 1966-69, Acad. Leadership scholarship, Millsaps Coll., 1966-69, Wall St. Jour. award, 1969. Democrat. Protestant. Club: Univ. Yacht. Office: IRS 275 Peachtree St Room 625 Atlanta GA 30043

FREEMAN, ANNE HOBSON, writer, English language educator; b. Richmond, Va., Mar. 19, 1934; d. Joseph Reid Anderson and Mary Douthat (Marshall) Hobson; m. George Clemon Freeman, Jr., Dec. 6, 1958; children: Anne Colston McEvoy, George Clemon, Joseph Reid Anderson. A.B., Bryn Mawr Coll., 1956; postgrad. London U., 1956-57; M.A., U. Va., 1973. Fiction writer, 1956—; reporter Internat. News Service, Eastern Europe, 1957; editor Va. Mus. Fine Arts, Richmond, 1959-63; lectr. English, U. Va., Charlottesville, 1973—; chmn. adv. com. Bryn Mawr Bull., Pa., 1978-81; firm historian Hunton & Williams, Richmond, 1984-88. Contbr. stories to various mags., anthologies, lit. jours. Mem. Richmond Area Democratic Woman's Club, 1968—; bd. dirs. Va. Hist. Soc., Va. Commn. for Humanities and Pub. Policy, Nat. Council Friends of Kennedy Ctr., Washington, 1983-85, Mus. of Confederacy, Richmond. Fulbright scholar, 1956-57; Va. Ctr. for Creative Arts fellow, 1981-83, 85. Episcopalian. Clubs: Va. Writers, Country of Va., Woman's (Richmond). Home: 10 Paxton Rd Richmond VA 23226 Office: U Va Dept English Wilson Hall Charlottesville VA 22903

FREEMAN, ANTOINETTE ROSEFELDT, lawyer; b. Atlantic City, Oct. 7, 1937; d. Bernard Paul and Fannie (Levin) Rosefeldt; m. Alan Richard Freeman, June 22, 1958 (div. Apr. 1979); children—Barry David, Robin Lisa. BA, Rutgers U., 1972; JD, Ind. U., 1975; LLM, Temple U., 1979. Bar: Pa. 1975, U.S. Dist. Ct. (ea. dist.) Pa. 1976, U.S. Ct. Appeals (3d cir.) 1982. Substitute tchr. Washington Twp. Sch. Dist., Indpls., 1972; dep. prosecutor intern Marion County Prosecutor, Indpls., 1974-75; asst. dist. atty. City of Phila., 1975-76; mgr. EEO, Wyeth Labs., Radnor, Pa., 1976-80, SmithKline & French Labs., Phila., 1980-82; atty. SmithKline Beckman Corp., Phila., 1982—; arbitrator Am. Arbitration Assn., 1976—. Counsel Regional Interests Developing Efficient Transp., 1983-85; adv. bd. Family Service Phila., 1980-81, Greater Phila. C. of C., 1983; pres. Croskey Ct. Condominium Assn., 1983-87; bd. dirs. Logan Sq. Neighborhood Assn., 1983—, pres., 1985-87; v.p., sec. Friends of Logan Sq. Found., counsel Hapoel Games USA; chairperson Ctr. City Coalition for Quality of Life; atty. Vol. Lawyers fot the Arts, Phila., 1985—. Mem. ABA, Pa. Bar Assn., Phila. Bar Assn., Merit Employers Council (1st v.p. 1978-79), Phila. Women's Network, Phila. Lawyers Club, Phila. Vol. Lawyers for Arts. Democrat. Jewish. Office: Smith Kline Beckman Corp One Franklin Plaza Philadelphia PA 19101

FREEMAN, ARLEEN ELYNNE, real estate professional; b. Oct. 17, 1942; d. Sussie (Schwartz) F. BS, U. Ill., 1963. Cert. real estate broker, Calif. Pres. Freeman Enterprises, San Diego, 1977—; broker Freeman Realty, San Diego, 1977—, GAM Properties, San Diego, 1982—; Pres. bd. dirs. Franciscan, San Diego. Appeared with comedy group Material Witless, 1986. Renovator several bldgs. Mem. San Diego Apt. Assn., San Diego Bd. Realtors. Office: Freeman Realty 8390 Miramar Pl Suite 3 San Diego CA 92121

FREEMAN, DIANNE MENDOZA, association executive; b. Laredo, Tex., Aug. 12, 1947; d. Luis Felipe Sr. and Alicia Juanita (Puentes) Mendoza; 1 child, Dina Rochelle Uribe. BA, Our Lady of Lake U., San Antonio, 1968; MEd, Our Lady of Lake U., 1975; MA, Incarnate Word Coll., 1973; PhD, U. Tex., Austin, 1982. Tchr. Laredo Ind. Sch. Dist., 1968-73; test instrument specialist Edgewood Ind. Sch. Dist., San Antonio, 1973-76; research assoc., proj. coordinator SW Edn. Devel. Lab., Austin, 1976-77; assoc. coordinator office student affairs Austin Ind. Sch. Dist., 1977-79; vis. instr. Laredo State U., 1979-82; title VII migrant supr. Laredo Ind. Sch. Dist., 1982-83; dir. devel., pub. relations Mercy Regional Med. Ctr., Laredo, 1983-86; exec. v.p. Laredo C. of C., 1986—. Mem. United Way of Laredo, 1982— (past pres.), Princess Pocahontas Council, Laredo, 1982— (1st v.p.), George Washington's Birthday Celebration Assn., Laredo, 1982—, Auxiliary to Mercy Regional Med. Ctr., Laredo, 1982—, Leadership Tex., Austin, 1984—; bd. dirs. Leadership Laredo, 1986—; bd. dirs., exec. com. United Way of Tex., 1986—. Named One of Outstanding Young Women of Am., 1977. Democrat. Roman Catholic. Club: Women's City (Laredo). Home: 511 Surrey Laredo TX 78041 Office: Laredo C of C PO Box 790 Laredo TX 78042-0790

FREEMAN, DONNA COOK, small business owner; b. Waldron, Ark., Apr. 18, 1937; d. Oliver Raymond and Lura Edna (Doyle) Cook; m. Clarence Lee Freeman, Jan. 24, 1954; children: Scott, Kevin, Steven, Melissa, Melinda. Student, Humphrey's Bus. Coll., Tracy, Calif., U. So. Calif., Bodega Bay (Calif.) Sch., 1973-75. Staff dept. aquaculture U. Calif. Bodega Marine Lab., 1976-77; real estate assoc., 1978-82; ptnr. Freeman's Union 76 Service, Bodega Bay, 1983—; co-owner fishing vessel Noyo Belle, 1981-84. Vice chmn. Shoreline Trust Ednl. Program Services, 1981—; bd. dirs. Bodega Bay Area Rescue, 1973-74; chmn. Bodega Bay Fisherman's Festival, 1973-74, 83; alt. mem. Dem. Cen. Com., 1982; mem. local bd. SSS, 1982—; chmn. Spud Point Adv. Bd., 1985—; bd. dirs. Sonoma County Fair, 1985—, Coastal Fisheries Found., 1986—; Sonoma County (Calif.) grand juror; 1983-84; mgr. polit. campaign, 1984. Mem. Bodega Bay Fisherman's Aux., Bodega Bay C. of C. (pres. 1979-81, bd. dirs. 1982-86), Bodega Bay Community Assn., Bodega Bay Grange. Home: 1409 Hwy One Bodega Bay CA 94923

FREEMAN, ELIZABETH ANNE, publishing executive; b. Summit, N.J., June 30, 1958; d. Richard Everett and Virginia (Fogel) F. AB, Middlebury Coll., 1980; cert., Pushkin Inst., Moscow, 1978. Mng. editor Welt Internat. Corp., Washington, 1980-81; prodn. editor, promotions coordinator, editor Sage Publs., Inc., Beverly Hills, Calif., 1981-85; editor Allen & Unwin, Inc., Winchester, Mass., 1985—. Mem. Nat. Assn. Female Execs., Bookbuilders Boston, Acad. Mgmt., Am. Assn. Advancement Slavic Studies, Am. Psychol. Assn. (div. 35), Phi Beta Kappa. Home: 260 Massachusetts Ave Arlington MA 02174 Office: Allen & Unwin Inc 8 Winchester Pl Winchester MA 01890

FREEMAN, EVELYN G., government official; b. Dayton, Tenn., Oct. 2, 1934; d. Charles Lee and Beulah Elizabeth (Swafford) Gentry; B.S., Tenn. Tech. U., 1968; postgrad. U. Tenn., 1970-72; Middle Tenn. State U., 1969-75; m. James R. Freeman, May 19, 1984; children by previous marriage—Thomas Lee Henderson (dec.), Yvonne Elizabeth Ownby. Legal sec. U.S. Atty. for Eastern Dist. Tenn., Dept. Justice, Chattanooga, 1963-66; with TVA, 1966-69, staff records officer, micrographics specialist, Chattanooga, 1975-83, mgr. micrographics dept. Dept. HUD, 1983-85, U.S. Dept. Commerce, 1985-86, 88—, VA Adminstrn. 1986-88; mktg. and mgmt. dept. head Walker County Tech. Sch., Lafayette, Ga., 1969-70; office occupations instr. State Area Vo-Tech. Sch., Chattanooga, 1970-72; instr. Edmondson Coll., Chattanooga, 1972-74; workshop instr. Chattanooga Area Literacy Movement Tchrs., 1978-83; notary pub., State of Tenn., 1962-83. Sec., Fed. Employed Women, 1976; vol. First Offender program, Chattanooga, 1972-74. Mem. Assn. of Records Mgrs. and Adminstrs. (chpt. pres. 1979-80, program chmn. 1980-81), Nat. Micrographics Assn. (pres. Tenn. Valley chpt. 1982-83), Chattanooga Paralegal Assn., Chattanooga Engrs. Club (pub. dir. for regional sci. and engring. fair 1976-79), Freedoms Found. Am., Assn. Info. and Image Mgmt. (sec. Nat. Capitol chpt. 1984-85), Assn. Records Mgmt. (Greater Washington chpt.), Fed. Govt. Micrographics Council. Democrat. Baptist. Clubs: Atlanta Skylarks Flying, Daisy Jr. Women's (pres. 1959-60). Home: 6471 Gildar St Alexandria VA 22310 Office: 1921 Jefferson Davis Hwy Crystal Mall 2 Arlington VA 22202

FREEMAN, FLORENCE ELEANOR, lawyer; b. Cambridge, Mass., Feb. 25, 1921; s. Elbern and Olive Blanche (Rice) F.; AB, Wellesley Coll., 1942; JD, U. Pa., 1945. Bar: Del. 1947, U.S. Dist. Ct. Del. 1948, U.S. Ct. Appeals (3d cir.) 1950, Mass. 1954, U.S. Dist. Ct. Mass. 1960. Assoc., Lynch & Hermann, Wilmington, Del., 1946-53; sole practice, Weston, Mass., 1954-69; ptnr. Freeman & Conceison, Weston, 1970-83, Freeman & White, Weston, 1984—; town counsel Town of Weston, 1968-86, spl. counsel, 1986—. Author: (play) Portrait of a Prince, 1965. Pres. Weston LWV, 1960-62, Weston Drama Workshop, 1963-71; mem. bd. selectmen Town of Weston, 1964-68; sec., trustee So. New Eng. Conf. United Meth. Ch., Boston, 1971-74, chancellor, 1976-86 ; bd. visitors Boston U. Sch. Theology, 1978—; chmn. bd. advisors Anna Howard Shaw Ctr.; mem. council fin. and adminstrn. United Meth. Ch., Chgo., 1980-88, alt. jud. council, 1980—, chmn. legal responsibilities com. 1980-88. Mem. ABA, Bar Assn. Club: Footlight (Boston) (pres. 1962-64); Wellesley Coll. Office: Freeman & White 483 Boston Post Rd Weston MA 02193

FREEMAN, JANET ELIZABETH, aerospace engineer; b. Tacoma, Apr. 13, 1956; d. Robert Mark and Ethel Viola (Cox) F. SB in Mech. Engring., MIT, 1978; MS in Aeronautics, Calif. Inst. Tech., 1984, Engrs.' degree in Aero., 1986. Design engr. Metal Marine Pilot, Inc., Tacoma, 1978-81; mem. tech. staff Hughes Aircraft Co. Space and Communications Group, El Segundo, Calif., 1981-86, project engr., 1986-87, sr. project engr., 1987; sr. specialist engr. Boeing Aerospace Co., Seattle, 1987—. Patentee in field. Mem. AIAA, Soc. Women Engrs. (sr.), Los Angeles Urban Math./Sci. Collaborative (assoc.). Club: Toastmasters (local officer 1982, 83, 86, CTM award 1984). Office: The Boeing Co PO Box 3999 Seattle WA 98124

FREEMAN, JOYCE MARY, fast food company executive; b. Arlington, S.D., Dec. 5, 1932; d. Milo Andrew and Orpha Laurinda (Austad) Peterson; m. Meredith N. Freeman, Oct. 23, 1971; stepchildren—James Michael, Judith Ann; children—Mary Ann, Connie Jane, Keith Milo, Dawn Joy. Student N.W. Coll. Commerce, 1951, Dakota State Coll., 1969-71; B.S. summa cum laude, Black Hills State Coll., 1977; postgrad. W.Va., Coll., 1977—. Data processor, payroll, mail and supply clk., sec. Buckingham Transp. Co., Rapid City, S.D., 1951-53; night supr. at nursing home, Arlington, S.D., 1966-67; supr., Dakota State Coll. Alumni Assn. and coordinator Karl E. Mundt Library, Dakota State Coll., Madison, S.D., 1967-71; mgr. fed. program budget Temple U., Phila., 1971; substitute tchr. Mercer County Pub. Schs. (W.Va.), 1977-81; owner, mgr. Taco Hut, Princeton, W.Va., 1978—, Marion, Va., 1980-83, Wytheville, Va., 1981—, Wardrobes Unltd. Princeton, W.Va., 1982—. Mem. AAUW, Nat. Fedn. Ind. Bus., Princeton C. of C., Kappa Delta Pi. Methodist. Home and Office: PO Box 609 Athens WV 24712

FREEMAN, JUNE BIBER, arts writer; b. Newark, July 10, 1928; d. Irving and Hilda (Zuckerman) Biber; m. Edmond W. Freeman III, May 31, 1926; children: Andrew, Gretchen, David, Eric. PhB, U. Chgo., 1947, BS, 1949, postgrad. Cert. Psychol. examiner, Ark. Psychologist Jeff County Mental Health Ctr., Pine Bluff, Ark., 1964-65; dir. state services Ark. Arts Ctr., Little Rock, 1975-80; dir. Ark. Artists Registry U. Ark. at Little Rock, 1982-83; writer, columnist Pine Bluff (Ark.) Comml., 1985—. Mem. Govs. Commn. on Status of Women, Ark., 1970, Ark. Art Council, 1984—, UAPB Devel. Council, Pine Bluff, 1981—; pres. Pine Bluff Sister Cities, 1984—. Mem. Ark. Psychol. Assn., Am. Assn. Mus. Democrat. Home and Office: 9 Southern Pines Dr Pine Bluff AR 71603

FREEMAN, PATRICIA ELIZABETH, library and education specialist; b. El Dorado, Ark., Nov. 30, 1924; d. Herbert A. and M. Elizabeth (Pryor) Harper; m. Jack Freeman, June 15, 1949; 3 children. B.A., Centenary Coll.,

1943; postgrad. Fine Arts Ctr., 1942-46, Art Students League, 1944-45; B.S.L.S., La. State U., 1946; postgrad. Calif. State U., 1959-61, U. N.Mex., 1964-74; Ed.S., Peabody Coll., Vanderbilt U., 1975. Librarian, U. Calif.-Berkeley, 1946-47, U.S. Air Force, Barksdale AFB, 1948-49, Albuquerque Pub. Schs., 1964-67; ind. sch. library media ctr. cons., 1967—. Painter lithographer; one-person show La. State Exhibit Bldg., 1948; author: Pathfinder: An Operational Guide for the School Librarian, 1975; compiler, editor: Elizabeth Pryor Harper's Twenty-One Southern Families, 1985. Mem. task force Goals for Dallas-Environ., 1977-82; pres. Friends of Sch. Libraries, Dallas, 1979-83. Honoree AAUW Ednl. Found., 1979; vol. award for outstanding service Dallas Ind. Sch. Dist., 1978; AAUW Pub. Service grantee 1980. Mem. ALA, AAUW (dir. Dallas 1976-82, Albuquerque 1983-85), LWV (sec. Dallas 1982-83, editor Albuquerque 1984—), Nat. Trust Historic Preservation, Friends of Albuquerque Pub. Library, N.Mex. Symphony Guild, Alpha Xi Delta. Home: 3016 Santa Clara SE Albuquerque NM 87106

FREEMAN, SARA CELESTE, banker; b. Tulsa, Mar. 24, 1948; d. Walter F. and Helen (Smith) F.; BA, St. Louis U., 1970, MA, 1974. Teller, Webster Groves Trust Co., St. Louis, 1970-73; grad. asst. St. Louis U., summer 1973, adminstrv. asst. Mental Health Inst., 1973-74; with Bank of Okla., N.A., Tulsa, 1974-82, asst. v.p., 1978-82, v.p., mgr. secured lending adminstrn. dept., 1979-82; v.p., mgr. credit and collateral ops. RepublicBank 1st Nat. Midland (Tex.), 1982-83, div. mgr. credit adminstrn., 1983—; part-time instr. Tulsa Jr. Coll.; instr. banking courses, 1985, 86; guest speaker. Bd. dirs. Am. Heart Assn., 1985-86; mem. personnel com., chmn. fair com. St. Ann's Parish. Mem. Nat. Assn. Bank Women, Phi Alpha Theta. Author manuals. Office: PO Box 1599 Midland TX 79702

FREEMAN, TINA, photographer, studio executive, consultant; b. New Orleans, May 5, 1951; d. Richard W. and Montine (McDaniel) F.; m. Philip M. Woollam, May 31, 1979. B.F.A. in Photography, Art Ctr. Coll. Design, Los Angeles, 1972; student history of photography, Helmut Gernsheim (France), 1978, 79, Beaumont Newhall, Carmel, Calif., 1981. Freelance photographer, Los Angeles, 1972-74; owner, mgr. Tina Freeman Photography, New Orleans, 1974-82, Freeman-Anacker Gallery, New Orleans, 1975-77; curator photography New Orleans Mus. Art, 1977-82, cons. curator, 1982-85; pres. Decatur Studio, New Orleans, 1982—; lectr. Free U., New Orleans, 1980. Mem. admissions com. Met. Leadership Forum, New Orleans, 1981-85, 87—; mem. mayor's task force Iberville Cemeteries Area, 1981-82; bd. dirs. Gallier House Mus., New Orleans, 1974-77, Traveler's Aid, New Orleans, 1974-77, Ella West Freeman Found., 1977—, New Orleans Philharm. Symphony Soc., 1978-82, La. Council for Music and Performing Arts, 1980—, Met. Area Com., 1982—, Save Our Cemeteries, New Orleans, 1982-84; bd. dirs. Contemporary Arts Ctr., 1984-86, 87—, v.p., 1985-86; bd. dirs. Planned Parenthood of La., 1984—, sec., 1984-85. Mem. Am. Soc. for Mag. Photographers, Soc. for Photog. Edn. Solo shows include: Cuningham-Ward Gallery, N.Y.C., 1977, Galerie Simonne Stern, New Orleans, 1978, 80, 83, Betty Cuningham Gallery, N.Y.C., 1981, Newcomb Art Gallery, Tulane U., New Orleans, 1983; group shows include: Cuningham-Ward Gallery, 1978, Contemporary Arts Ctr., New Orleans, 1979, Nat. Arts Club, N.Y.C., 1979, Galerie Simonne Stern, 1979-85, Los Angeles Art Assn. Gallery, 1982, Witkin Gallery, 1987. Editor: Diverse Images, 1979; The Photographs of Mother St. Croix, 1982; Leslie Gill: A Classical Approach to Photography, 1983; contbr. articles to Arts Quar., 1978-83.

FREIBURGER, OPAL ARLENE, nursing educator; b. Allen County, Ind., Apr. 10, 1932; d. James M. and Esther L. (Winters) Reed; m. Edgar J. Freiburger, May 1, 1954; children: Anthony J., Connie T., Mark A. AD in Nursing, Purdue U., Ft. Wayne, Ind., 1972, BS in Nursing, 1977; MA in Nursing, Ball State U., 1982; EdD, Internat. Grad. Sch., St. Louis, 1988. Staff nurse Caylor-Nickel Hosp., Bluffton, Ind., 1972-74, charge nurse, 1974-78, house supr., 1977-79, clin. instr., 1979-84; instr. staff edn./profl. devel. The Luth. Hosp. Ft. Wayne Inc., 1984—. Instr. CPR Am. Heart Assn., Ft. Wayne, 1979—, trainer, 1985—; mem. planning com., symposium Allen County Cancer Soc., Ft. Wayne, 1986-88. Mem. Ind. State Nurses' Assn. (com. on approval 1982-84, chairperson 1984-86, dist. bd. dirs. 1983-87), Ind. Soc. for Healthcare Edn. and Tng., Sigma Theta Tau. Office: The Luth Hosp Ft Wayne 3024 Fairfield Ave Fort Wayne IN 46807

FREID, LAURA GOTTESMAN, publisher, editor; b. N.Y.C., May 16, 1952; d. Herman Louis and Nina (Edelson) F.; m. Sherman Teichman, June 16, 1974 (div. 1981); m. David Gottesman, Nov. 28, 1985. Lang. cert., U. Sorbonne, Paris, 1970; student, Skidmore Coll.; BA, Washington U., St. Louis, 1975. Researcher, cons. Dell Pub. Graphics Design, N.Y.C., Cambridge, Mass., 1970, 74-75; editor Boston U. Today, 1976-78, dir. pubs., 1978-81; asst. v.p. Boston U., Brookline, 1981—; editor in chief Bostonia mag., Brookline, 1978—, pub., editor, 1986—. Editor: Cooking By Degrees, 1981. Mem. adv. bd. Am. Council on Edn., Washington, 1986—, N.E. Council on Higher Edn., Boston, 1986—; advisor Assn. Internat. Students. Recipient Editorial Excellence award Council for Advancement and Support of Higher Edn., Washington, 1978-87, Periodical Writing award, 1987; named one of Top 10 Mag. Editors Newsweek mag., 1983, 84, 85, 87, 88. Mem. Council for Support and Advancement of Edn. (trustee 1984-86, Sibley Soc. 1984), Am. Soc. Mag. Editors, Mag. Pubs. Assn., Boston C. of C. Club: Boston Ad. Office: Bostonia Mag 10 Lenox St Brookline MA 02146

FREIER, SUSAN MARCIE, music educator, violinist; b. Bklyn., Dec. 13, 1953; d. George David and Ruth (Hollenberg) F.; m. Benjamin A. Miller, May 24, 1981; children: Sarah, Rachel. B.S. in Biology, Stanford U., 1975, B.A. in Music, 1975; M.A., 1976; Mus.M., Eastman Sch. Music, 1980. Asst. prof. violin Ind. U., South Bend, 1980—; in residence Garth Newel Music Camp, summers 1985—, Downeast Music Camp, Maine, summers 1984, 85, Grand Teton Music Festival, Wyo., summers 1980-84, Somerset Music Festival, 1987; vis. resident string quartet Tex. Christian U., Ft. Worth, 1985-87 pedagogue Ft. Worth Suzuki Inst., summer 1986, 87, Chgo. Suzuki Inst., summer 1987; mem. Chester String Quartet, 1978—; coach, South Bend Youth Symphony, 1980—, master classes Oberlin Conservatory, Cleve. Inst. Music, 1988. Winner top awards in quartet competitions, Munich, Germany, Portsmouth, Eng., Chgo. Mem. Chamber Music Am., Am. String Tchr's Assn. Avocations: hiking; jogging. Office: Ind U Dept Music 1700 Michawaka Ave South Bend IN 46634

FREIR, PAMELA, advertising company executive; b. Halifax, N.S., Can., Dec. 3, 1940; d. Mervyn George and Frances Eleanor (Jackman) Smith; m. D. Noel Freir (dec. 1971); children: Gregory James, Jonathan; m. Christopher John Bayliss; children: Bridget, Barnaby, Catherine, Clara. BA, U. Western Ont., 1961. Writer Sears Roebuck Corp., Toronto, Ont., 1972-74, Kert Advt., Ltd., Toronto, Ont., 1974-75, Ogilvy & Mather Direct, Ltd., Toronto, 1975-78, Vickers & Benson, Ltd., Toronto, 1978-79; creative dir. Ogilvy & Mather, Ltd., Toronto, 1979-83; sr. v.p., creative dir. Saatchi & Saatchi, Compton Hayhurst, Ltd., Toronto, 1983—. Mem. Assn. Agy. Creative Dirs. Home: 68 Pricefield Rd, Toronto, ON Canada M4W 1Z9 Office: Saatchi & Saatchi Compton, Hayhurst Ltd, 55 Eglinton Ave E, Toronto, ON Canada M4P 1G9

FREITAG, EILEEN MARGARET, health services adminstrator; b. N.Y.C., Dec. 22, 1949; d. Fred H. and Lilly (Toch) F. Ba in Psychology, Russell Sage Coll., 1972; MBAin Health Care Mgmt., Boston U., 1982. Blood donor recruiter New Eng. Deaconess Hosp., Boston, 1972-74; unit mgr. Vis. Nurses Assn. Boston, 1974-77, coordinator unit mgrs., 1977-82, dir. admissions, 1982-85, exec. dir., 1985—; bd. dirs. Health Action Forum Greater Boston, 1985-87, Mass. Assn. Community Health Agencies, 1986—, Vis. Nurses's Assn. Mass., 1984—. Mem. Mass. Pub. Health Assn., Am. Pub. Health Assn., Women in Health CAre Mgmt., Am. Mktg. Assn. Home: 47 Oakland St Brighton MA 02135 Office: Vis Nurse Assn Boston 100 Boylston St Boston MA 02116

FREITAS, BEATRICE B(OTTY), opera theater artistic director, musician, educator; b. Youngstown, Ohio, Aug. 28, 1938; d. John and Pauline (Esterhay) Botty; m. Lewis P. Freitas, Nov. 30, 1963; children—Roslyn K., John B. B.A., Oberlin Coll., 1958; M.Mus., Boston U., 1959; spl. student Juilliard Sch. Music, 1959-62. Artistic dir. Hawaii Opera Theatre, Honolulu; pianist, organist, harpsichordist, tchr. Recipient Outstanding Achievement in Area of Arts award YMCA, 1983.

FREIWALD, JOYCE GROSS, company executive; b. Fulton, Mo., June 22, 1944; d. Fred Alfred and Susan (Kist) Gross; B.S. in Math. (scholar), U. N.Mex., 1966; postgrad. in math. and physics, 1967-68, M.Arch. (scholar), 1976; m. David Allen Freiwald, Apr. 3, 1976; children—Wesley, Todd, Christopher. Mathematician, Air Force Weapons Lab., Albuquerque, 1963-65, Sandia Nat. Lab., Albuquerque, 1966-69; owner, mgr. Costello Cons. Co., Albuquerque, 1970-72; scientist Sci. Applications, Inc., Albuquerque, 1973-75; pres. Phoenix Forth, Inc., Albuquerque, 1975-76; mem. staff Los Alamos Nat. Lab., 1976-81; Republican staff dir. U.S. Ho. Reps. Com. on Sci. and Tech., Washington, 1981-86; mgr. bus. devel. Ga. Techs., San Diego, 1986—. Candidate for Albuquerque City Commn., 1970, N.Mex. Senate, 1971; chairwoman N.Mex. Equal Rights Legis. Com., 1972, Citizen's Coalition for Land Use Planning, 1975; former mem. various state and county bds. and commns. Mem. Assn. Women in Sci., N.Mex. Women in Sci., Am. Nuclear Soc., Am. Astron. Soc., Women in Aerospace, AAUW, AAAS, Nat. Assn. Female Execs., Phi Kappa Pi, Kappa Mu Epsilon, Alpha Delta Pi. Republican. Contbr. numerous articles on energy, environ. and tech. issues to profl. jours. Home: 10574 Livewood Way San Diego CA 92131 Office: PO Box 85608 San Diego CA 92138-5608

FRELICH, PHYLLIS, actress; b. Devils Lake, N.D., Feb. 29, 1944; d. Phillip and Esther (Dockter) F.; m. Robert Steinberg, May 17, 1968; children: Reuben, Joshua. B.S. in L.S, Gallaudet Coll., 1967. Acting tchr. Nat. Theater of the Deaf, Waterford, Conn., 1977-79, 83, R.I. Sch. for Deaf, Providence, 1977-78, U. R.I., North Kingston, 1978. Appeared in numerous stage plays, 1965—; latest being Woyzeck, all with Nat. Theatre of the Deaf, 1979, Songs from Milkwood, Broadway, Children of a Lesser God, Broadway, 1980, Poets from the Inside, N.Y.C., Public Theater, 1980, Night of 100 Stars, 1982, The Debutante Ball, 1984; dir. Gin Game, N.Y. Deaf Theatre. Recipient Humanitarian award Gallaudet Coll., 1980; Rough Rider award State of N.D., 1981; California's Year of Handicapped award, 1980; Critic's Circle award, 1980; Tony award best actress for Children of a Lesser God, 1980. Mem. Actors Equity Assn., Nat. Assn. Deaf. Office: care Artist Group Ltd 1930 Century Park West Suite 303 Los Angeles CA 90067 *

FRELS, LOIS MARIAN PARNELL (MRS. CALVIN EDWIN FRELS), educator; b. Geneseo, Ill., Nov. 20, 1929; d. Floyd Vinton and Mary Jane (Davis) Parnell; R.N., Moline (Ill.) Pub. Hosp., 1950; student pub. Health U. Minn., Loyola U., Chgo., 1951-54; B.N.S., Augustana Coll., Rock Island, Ill., 1959; M.A., U. Iowa, 1964, diploma for testing, Marianne Frostic Ctr. Ednl. Therapy, Los Angeles, 1969; Ph.D., U. Minn., 1977; m. Calvin Edwin Frels, Oct. 28, 1950; children—Mark Edwin, Arlan James. Sch. nurse East Moline Elem. Schs., 1951-54; pub. health work East Moline Vis. Nurses Assn., 1955-57; sch. nurse, project dir., nurse cons. United Twp. High Sch., East Moline, 1957-67; instr. psychology Blackhawk Jr. Coll., Moline, part time 1966-68; tchr., dir. gifted program Silvis (Ill.) Elem. Schs., 1968; counselor Pleasant Valley (Ia.) High Sch., 1969-70; asst. prof. Marycrest Coll., Davenport, Iowa, 1970-73; chmn. nursing div. Iowa Wesleyan Coll., Mt. Pleasant, 1973-76; dir. div. nursing Bradley U., Peoria, Ill., 1976-88. Sec., East Moline Community Resource Council, 1965-67; mem. Riverdale Unit 100 Bd. Edn., Port Byron, Ill., 1964-67, 68-73; chmn. Rock Island County Fact Finding Com. White House Conf. Children and Youth, 1970, Ill. Com. of Nurse Examiners, 1982—; organizer Little White House Conf. Children and Youth, Rock Island County, 1969; del. Nat. White House Conf. on Children and Youth, 1970; 2d v.p. Rock Island Country Welfare Council, 1968-70; mem. adv. bd. Ill. Dept. Pub. Health, 1987—; mem. Bylaws com. Nat. Council State Bds. of Nursing, 1986-88. Bd. dirs. Opportunity Mentally Handicapped. Ill. Dept. Pub. Recipient Mergen award Bradley U. Instrn. grantee Western Ill. U., 1968; Nurse traineeship grantee, 1973. Fellow Am. Sch. Health Assn. (chmn. sch. nurse study com. 1973-77, disting. service award 1978; chmn. sch. nurse subcom. 1984-86), mem. Nat. League Nursing (Disting. Service award 1987), Iowa Citizens League for Nursing (pres. 1975-77), Am., Ill. nurses assns., Am. Edn. Research Assn., Am., Ill. public health assns., Ill. Sch. Health Assn. (pres.-elect 1988, mem. Ill. task force on rural health 1988—, chmn. legis. resolutions com. 1986), Nat. League Nursing (sec. Midland regional assembly 1979—), Ill. League Nursing (pres. 1983-86), Royal Soc. Health (London, Eng.), Am. Assn. Colls. Nursing, Phi Kappa Phi, Sigma Theta Tau, Pi Lambda Theta. Editorial bd. Jour. Sch. Health. Home: 25329 1st Ave N Hillsdale IL 61257

FREMONT-SMITH, MARION R., lawyer; b. Boston, Oct. 29, 1926; d. Max and Frances (Davis) Ritvo; m. Joseph Miller, Sept. 12, 1948 (div.); m. 2d, Paul Fremont-Smith, July 6, 1961; children by previous marriage—Beth Miller Hanson, Keith Lane Miller, E. Bradley Miller. B.A. with high honors, Wellesley (Mass.) Coll., 1948; LL.B. cum laude, Boston U., 1951. Bar: Mass. 1951, U.S. Supreme Ct. 1979. Instr. dept. polit. sci. Wellesley Coll., 1958-59; asst. atty. gen. Commonwealth Mass., Boston, 1961-62; project dir. Russell Sage Found., Boston, 1963-65; assoc. Choate, Hall & Stewart, Boston, 1964-71, ptnr., 1971—; dir. Fed. Tax Inst. New Eng., Ind. Sector, Washington. Trustee Carnegie Endowment for Internat. Peace, Washington. Fellow Am. Bar Found., Am. Coll. Probate Counsel, Am. Coll. Tax Counsel, Acad. Estate and Trust Law; mem. ABA (chmn. com. on exempt orgns. tax sect.), Council on Fgn. Relations. Author: Foundations and Government: State and Federal Law and Supervision, 1965, Philanthropy and the Business Corporation, 1972; contbr. articles to profl. jours. Office: Choate Hall & Stewart 53 State St 35th Floor Exchange Pl Boston MA 02109

FRENCH, BRENDA CAROLYN, computer company executive; b. Newburyport, Mass., May 16, 1940; d. Arthur Charles and Emily Lancey (Reid) Browne; m. Richard Enright French, Feb. 17, 1968; 1 son, Richard Enright. B.A. cum laude, U.N.H., 1961; M.B.A., Simmons Coll., 1977. With Digital Equipment Corp., Maynard, Mass., 1977—, material mgr., 1979-80, strategic planning mgr., 1980-83, order fulfillment mgr. 1983—. Adviser urban renewal project Hist. Commn., Newburyport, 1973-75; mgr. continuing edn. Newburyport YMCA, 1964-75. Mem. Simmons Alumni Assn. Unitarian. Office: Digital Equipment Corp Digital Dr Westminster MA 01473

FRENCH, JEANA TURNER, health and social services agency executive; b. Tallahassee, Fla., Feb. 22, 1947; d. Cleveland Adelbert and Myra Alice (Hartsfield) Turner; B.S., Fla. State U., 1967, M.S., 1970, Ph.D., 1972; m. John H. French, Jr., Dec. 27, 1966. Tchr. 2d grade Leon County Sch. System, Tallahassee, 1967-69, tchr. Head Start program, 1968; instr. early childhood edn. Fla. State U., Tallahassee, 1969-71, program coordinator, academic advisor, 1971-72, asst. prof., 1974-78; mental health program analyst Fla. Dept. Health and Rehab. Services, 1978-79, tng. mgr., 1979-81, dir. staff devel. and tng., 1981-86; pvt. practice cons., Tallahassee, 1986—; curriculum specialist Wakulla County, Crawfordville, Fla., 1972-73; dir. evaluation and research Choctaw Reservation Project, Philadelphia, Miss., 1973-74; cons. Cherokee (N.C.) Reservation Evaluation and Research Project, 1973-74; cons. Metcor, Inc., Washington, 1973-74; mem. 25th anniversary commemoration com. Fla. State U., 1972; mem. Fla. Democratic Credentials Com., 1972; instr. Fla. Dem. Polit. Leadership Schs., 1974; mem. adv. bd. Sch. Social Work, Fla. State U., 1981—; mem. steering com. Ctr. for Pub. Affairs and Govt. Services, 1985—; mem. Leon County (Fla.) Dem. Com., 1979-81; del. Fla. Dem. Primary Conv., 1984. Mem. Fla. State U. Coll. Edn. Alumni Assn. (dir. 1976-78, 85—), Nat. Assn. Edn. of Young Children, Fla. Assn. Children Under Six, Nat. Council Social Studies, Assn. Childhood Edn., Am. Soc. Tng. and Devel., Internat. Reading Assn., Fla. State U. Alumni Assn. (dir. 1984—), Phi Kappa Phi, Kappa Delta Pi, Phi Delta Kappa, Alpha Gamma Delta. Democrat. Methodist. Contbr. bibliography, research papers in field. Home and Office: 1206 Sarasota Dr Tallahassee FL 32301

FRENCH, JOYCE NORTON, educational administrator; b. Buffalo, Dec. 9, 1929; d. Thomas Lowell and Verna (Cutler) Norton; B.A., Wellesley Coll., 1951; M.S., U. Bridgeport, 1967; Ph.D., Columbia U., 1976; m. Donald Frank French, June 11, 1951; children—Susan Linda French Falk, Richard Norton. Tchr., Greenwich (Conn.) Pub. Schs., 1965-70; head lower and middle schs. Greenwich Country Day Sch., 1970-76; dir. tchr. edn. Manhattanville Coll., Purchase, N.Y., 1977-85; dir. Literacy Ctr. Tchrs. Coll., Columbia U., 1988—; adj. prof. Manhattanville Coll., 1987—; vis. prof. Tchrs. Coll. Columbia U., 1980-81; fellow Research Inst. for Study of Learning Disabilities, 1978-80; sch. cons. Mem. Am. Psychol. Assn., Internat. Reading Assn., N.Y. Acad. Scis., Internat. Platform Assn., Sigma Xi. Contbr. articles to profl. jours.; author books on high sch. reading, adult literacy and SAT English preparation; speaker profl. orgns. Home: 185 Shore Rd Old Greenwich CT 06870 Office: Columbia U Tchrs Coll New York NY 10022

FRENCH, STEPHANIE TAYLOR, arts administrator; b. Newark; d. William Taylor and Connie V. French; B.A., Wellesley Coll., 1972; M.B.A., Harvard U., 1978; m. Amory Houghton, III, Sept. 8, 1979; 1 dau., Christina French Houghton. Traffic mgr. Radio Sta. KFRC, 1973-74; dir. European Gallery, San Francisco, 1974-75; acct. exec. Young & Rubican, N.Y.C., 1978-79; acct. supr. Rives Smith Baldwin & Carlberg, Houston, 1980-81; mgr. cultural affairs and spl. programs Philip Morris Cos. Inc., N.Y.C., 1981-86, dir., cultural and contributions programs, 1986— ; free-lance on-air talent and prodn. San Francisco and Oakland cable TV stas., 1973-76. Bd. dirs. Twyla Tharp Dance Co., Art Table, Am. Fedn. of Arts, Am. Council on Arts; co-chmn. producers council Bklyn. Acad. Music, Dance Theatre Workshop; co-chmn. Assocs. of Babies' Hosp., Columbia Presbyn. Med. Ctr. Clubs: Harvard Bus. Sch., Wellesley. Home: 161 E 90th St Apt 2C New York NY 10128 Office: Philip Morris Cos Inc 120 Park Ave New York NY 10017

FRENGUT, RENEE HIRSCH, psychologist, marketing research executive; b. N.Y.C., May 14, 1945; d. Erich F. and Eleanore F. (Kaplan) Hirsch; B.A., CCNY, 1966; M.A., Yeshiva U., 1968, Ph.D. (NIMH fellow), 1977. Instr. (part-time) dept. psychology N.Y. Inst. Tech., N.Y.C., 1968-69; clin. intern N.Y. State Psychiat. Inst., Columbia U. Coll. Physicians and Surgeons, 1969-70; staff psychologist Westchester County Community Mental Health Bd., 1970-71; staff psychologist Abbott House for Children, Irvington, N.Y., 1971-72, supr. exptl. therapeutic group homes, 1971-72; mem. faculty dept. psychology Montgomery Coll., Rockville, Md., 1972-74; staff psychologist Potomac Found. for Mental Health, Rockville, Md., 1973-75; pvt. practice clin. psychology, 1974-77; research cons. social research div. NBC, N.Y.C., 1976; qualitative media research cons. R.H. Bruskin Assocs., New Brunswick, N.J., 1976; lectr. (part-time) psychology Mercy Coll., Dobbs Ferry, N.Y., 1976-78; research group head The Nowland Orgn., Greenwich, Conn., 1977-78; pres. Qualitative Decisions Center, Inc., N.Y.C., 1978-84, Market Insights, Inc., Bronxville, N.Y., 1984—. Cert. psychologist. Mem. Am. Psychol. Assn., Am. Mktg. Assn. Office: 270 Bronxville Rd Bronxville NY 10708

FRESCH, MARIE BETH, court reporter; b. Norwalk, Ohio, Jan. 16, 1957; d. Ralph Roy and Vonda Mae (Brunkhorst) Spiegel; m. James R. Fresch, Aug. 5, 1978. AS in Bus., Tiffin U., 1977; cert. in ct. reporting, Acad. Ct. Reporting, 1979. Registered profl. reporter, Ohio. Ofcl. reporter Seneca County Common Pleas Ct., Tiffin, Ohio, 1979-80; owner, operator Marie B. Fresch & Assocs., Norwalk, 1980—. Mem. Nat. Shorthand Reporters Assn., Ohio Shorthand Reporters Assn. (student promotions and pub. relations coms. 1986—), Baron Users Group (cert. reporter computer support group), NOW (sec. Port Clinton chpt. 1984-86, treas. 1986-87), Am. Legion Aux., Kappa Delta Kappa. Democrat. Methodist. Lodge: Order of Eastern Star (esther 1979-81). Home and Office: 47 Warren Dr Norwalk OH 44857

FRESCOLN, KATHARINE PITMAN, emeritus history educator; b. Swarthmore, Pa., May 9, 1917; d. John Himes and Katharine Elsie (Anders) Pitman; m. Joseph Wright Frescoln, Jan. 6, 1942. A.B., Wittenberg U., 1965; M.A., W.Va. U., 1966, Ph.D., 1971. Social studies tchr. sch. Parsons, W.Va., 1963-65; instr., asst. prof., assoc. prof. history Shepherd Coll., Shepherdstown, W.Va., 1967-75, prof., 1975-85, prof. emeritus, 1985—. Contbr. articles to profl. jours. Samuel Sprecker scholar, 1959. Mem. Am. Hist. Assn., Am. Assn. for Advancement Slavic Studies, N.Am. Conf. on Brit. Studies, MidAtlantic Conf. on Brit. Studies, DAR, Phi Alpha Theta (Internat. councillor 1980-82). Home: Heatherfield PO Box 683 Shepherdstown WV 25443

FRESKOS, ROSEMARY, journalist, editor, publisher, correspondent; b. Chgo., Aug. 24, 1934; d. Ralph and Rosalia (Armendariz) Diaz; m. John M. Freskos, Nov. 13, 1955; children—John, Elena. Student U. Calif.-Berkeley, 1952, Chgo. Art Inst., 1953-54, Cleve. Inst. Art, 1969-72, Kent State U., 1972-73. Cert. travel agt. Sec. various companies, Chgo., 1953-61; ski instr. The Ski Haus, Cleve., 1969-73; tchr. enameling Valley Art Ctr., Chagrin Falls, Ohio, 1973-74; travel agt. Chagrin Station, Chagrin Falls, 1974-75; free-lance writer Sun Newspapers, Cleve., 1973-76; pres., editor Ski Sun, Inc. Publs., Chagrin Falls, 1978-86; midwest corr. The Ski Industry Letter, 1983—; contbr. Ski Magazine, 1979—, Ski Bus. Tabloid, 1983-86, various ski trade jours., 1973—; West U.S. editor FODORS Ski Resorts Guide, 1988, editor, pub. Annual Directory Ohio Ski Clubs, 1979-86. Mem. U.S. Ski Writers Assn. (pres. 1985-86), So. Calif. Ski Writers Assn., Rocky Mountain Ski Media Assn., Midwest Ski Writers Assn. (pres. 1978-81), Nat. Sportscasters and Sports Writers Assn., Assn. Internat. de la Presse Sportive, Chagrin Valley Art Assn. (First prize enameling 1977), Aircraft Owners and Pilots Assn. Roman Catholic. Avocations: skiing; traveling, golf; tennis, art. Home and Office: PO Box 90586 San Diego CA 92109

FREUND, CAROL MARGUERITE, clinical psychologist; b. Queens, N.Y., Feb. 15, 1957; d. Charles George and Doris Marguerite (Egeland) F. BA, SUNY, Geneseo, 1978; PhD, U. Nebr., 1985. Lic. expert parachutist. Clin. psychologist, asst. unit dir. South Beach Psychiat. Ctr., Staten Island, N.Y., 1985-88; clin. psychologist Forsyth-Stokes Mental Health Ctr., Winston-Salem, N.C., 1988—. NIMH fellow, 1979-83; recipient Gold Wings award, 12 Hour Free Fall award. Mem. Am. Psychol. Assn. , Assn. Women in Psychology, North Am. Personal Construct Psychology Network, Nat. Assn. Women's Studies, U.S. Parachute Assn. Home: 825 Scenic View Dr Atlanta GA 30339 Office: 2700 Reynolda Rd #703 Winston-Salem NC 27106

FREUND, ROYLE LAUNCEY, investment and manufacturing executive; b. Milw., June 14, 1930; d. Leroy and Anne (Edelman) Michel; m. Michael Freund; children—Kim Glaser Selbert, Leslie Glaser Kanner. With Revell, Inc., Venice, Calif., 1958-82, pres., chief exec. officer, 1970-79, chairwoman bd., 1972-79, vice chairwoman bd., 1979-82; pres. R&M Investment Co.; v.p. RMC Holding Co.; owner Royle Art Ltd. Video-tape participant UCLA mgmt. course, 1974. Mem. Toy Mfrs. Assn. (dir. 1975), Hobby Industry Assn. Am. (dir. 1974-75, sec. 1975, exec. com. 1975), Young Pres. Orgn. (exec. com. 1976-77), young Pres. Orgn.-Grads. (bd. dirs.), World Bus. Council. Office: 1341 Ocean Ave Suite 371 Santa Monica CA 90401

FREY, AUDREY ETHEL, publishing company executive; b. India, Feb. 27, 1926; came to U.S., 1948, naturalized, 1953; d. Louis Percival and Marguerita Isabel (D'Silva) Spencer; m. Eric Konstantin Frey, Jan. 21, 1961. SC honors degree, Cambridge (Eng.) U., 1942; student, Govt. Sch. Art, 1942-47, Art Students League, 1949-50, 51-52. With McGraw-Hill Pub. Co., N.Y.C., 1950—, prodn. mgr. Coal Age, also Engrng. and Mining Jour., 1955-66, mgr. bus. Internat. Mgmt., 1966-69, U.S. mgr. mktg. services Internat. Mgmt. Network of Publs., 1969-76, mgr. service ops. Internat. Group of Publs., 1976-82, dir. U.S. internat. publs., 1983-84, mgr. pub. relations services and mktg. communications, 1984—; speaker internat. mag. communications; panel mem. bus. seminars. Contbr. articles to profl. jours. Mem. Mus. Natural History, Nat. Wildlife Fedn., Art Students League. Recipient 3 first awards Printing Industries Met. N.Y. Home: 2860 Bailey Ave Apt Box 106 New York NY 10463 Office: 1221 Ave of Americas New York NY 10020

FREY, JUDY WHITTER, state official; b. Jacksonville, Fla., June 3, 1950; d. Thomas Lytle and Cleo (Crews) Whitter; m. Robert Andrew Frey, Aug. 1, 1981. B.A. in History, Jacksonville U., 1972, M.B.A., 1985; postgrad. U. No. Fla., 1982—. Social worker State of Fla., Jacksonville, 1972-78, social rehab. services counselor II, 1978-82, supr., 1982-87, human services program analyst, 1987—; spl. agt. Naval Investigative Service Dept. Navy, 1978. Active March of Dimes Fund Drive, Jacksonville; vol. ofcl. Jacksonville Track Club. Mem. Jacksonville U. Alumni Bd. Govs. (pres. 1983-84), Jacksonville Alumnae Panhellenic Assn. (bd. dirs. 1972-76, 77-78, 81—), Zeta Tau Alpha (Zeta Day chmn. 1983; Key Woman 1982-88). Club: Civitan. Baptist. Home: 7419 Clinton St Jacksonville FL 32208 Office: 5920 Arlington Expressway Jacksonville FL 32211

FREY, LINDA SUE, history educator; b. Toledo, Feb. 21, 1947; d. Henry H. and Dolores A. (Saionz) F. B.S. in Edn. summa cum laude, Ohio State

U., 1967, B.A. summa cum laude, 1967, M.A., 1968, Ph.D., 1971. Asst. prof. U. Mont., Missoula, 1971-76, assoc. prof., 1976-82, prof., 1982—, chmn. history dept., 1983-86. Author: A Question of Empire, 1983; Frederick I, 1984; co-compiler: Women in Western European Tradition, 1983, vol. 2, 1984, supplement, 1986, Societies in Upheaval, 1987. NEH grantee, 1977-78; Am. Council Learned Socs. grantee, 1981; faculty intern U.S. Office Edn., 1980. Mem. Am. Hist. Assn., Conf. on Slavic and East European History, Am. Assn. for Study of Hungary History (exec. com. 1982-84). Home: 100 Hillview Way Missoula MT 59803 Office: Univ Mont Dept History Missoula MT 59812

FREY, NORMA CLAIRE, psychiatric social worker; b. Buffalo, Apr. 15, 1929; d. Severn Michael and Antoinette (Langlois) Frey. B.A., Ursuline Coll., New Orleans, 1950; grad. Tulane U., Sch. Social Work, 1954; M.S.W., McGill U., Montreal, Que., Can., 1960. Cert. social worker, advanced clin. practitioner, Tex. Welfare visitor La. State Dept., Gretna, 1951-53; child welfare worker, dept. pub. welfare, Alexandria, La., 1954-56; case worker U. Tex. Med. br., Galveston, 1956-59; psychiat. social worker Tex. Research Inst. Mental Scis., Houston, 1960-85, ret.; pvt. cons. adv. council Adult Mental Health, Mental Retardation Authority, Houston, 1982—, chmn. com. to study homeless mentally ill, 1982-86, chmn. com. to study goals of continuity of care; v.p., founding mem. Tex. chpt. Alliance Mental Recovery, Houston, 1980-86; adj. faculty U. Houston Sch. Social Work, 1972-86; bd. dirs. Houston/Harris County Coalition for Homeless. Recipient Honor Merit award adj. faculty, U. Houston, 1978—; Honor Merit award, Tulane U. Alumnae, 1974. Fellow Am. Orthopsychiat. Assn.; mem. Nat. Assn. Social Workers, Acad. Cert. Social Workers, Mental Health Assn., Mental Health Assn. of Harris County Continuity of Care Consortium. Republican. Roman Catholic. Club: Houston Grand Opera Guild.

FREY, SHARON PATRICE, real estate development executive; b. Levenworth, Kans., Jan. 22, 1947; d. Edward Antone and Thelma Lucille (Earl) F.; m. Douglas K. McPherson, July 20, 1932 (div. May 1987). Student, Kans. State Tchrs. Coll., 1966-69, Am. Inst. Banking, 1970. Investment banking City Nat. Bank, Kansas City, Mo., 1969-71; comml. real estate sales various cos., Phoenix, 1971-74; comml. real estate mgmt. and sales Hermosa Realty Corp., Phoenix, 1974-82, Merrill Lynch Comml. Real Estate, Phoenix, 1982-85; salesperson comml. real estate Merrill Lynch Comml. Real Estate (subs. L.J. Hooker Internat.), Dallas, 1985—; instr. Inst. Real Estate Mgmt., Chgo., 1983—, pres. Greater Phoenix chpt., 1985; mem. Merrill Lynch Comml. Real Estate Nat. Producer Council, Stamford, Conn., 1984-85; pres. Cert. Comml. Investment Mems. Phoenix chpt., 1981; councillor Comml. Investment Real Estate Council, 1985—. Contbr. articles to profl. jours.; mem. editorial bd. Comml. Ivestment Jour., 1982—, Jour. Property Mgmt., 1986—. Mem. Comml. Real Estate Women, Omega Tau Rho. Democrat. Roman Catholic. Office: LJ Hooker Internat 2000 One Galleria Tower 13325 Noel Rd Dallas TX 75240

FREYER, ELLEN JACOBS, film producer; b. Los Angeles, Nov. 7, 1940; d. Lewis and Lillian (Wilentz) Jacobs; m. Stuart Freyer, July 30, 1961 (div. 1978); children—Daniel Benjamin, Adam Stephen. Student Brandeis U., 1957-59; B.A. in Art History, Barnard Coll., 1961; M.A. in Cinema Studies, NYU, 1971. Asst. film editor freelance, N.Y.C., 1972-76; adj. lectr. St. Peter's Coll., Jersey City, 1972-75, Hunter Coll., N.Y.C., 1980-83, Syracuse U., 1987; freelance producer, writer, N.Y.C., 1976-83; project mgr. TeleCulture, Inc., N.Y.C., 1982-83; asst. project mgr. Wonderworks/PBS, N.Y.C., 1983-84, prodn. supr., 1984—; juror, guest speaker on children's TV, programmer film festivals colls. and univs., N.Y., 1972-87; U.S. cons. Internat. Film Festival, Hebrew U. Jerusalem Cinemateque, 1986-87; cons. Notable Am. Women, Cambridge, Mass., 1978. Author: Adapting Children's Books for Television: The Lion and the Unicorn, 1987; producer, dir.: Marathon Woman, Miki Gorman, 1981, Girls' Sports: On The Right Track, 1976. Founding mem. Washington Square Day Care Center, N.Y.C., 1973; founding dir. After School Art Workshops, N.Y.C., 1974. Grantee Women's Fund-Joint Found. Support, 1978, Hoso-Bunka Found. Japan, 1979, N.Y. State Council Arts, 1979, Mitsubishi Internat., 1980, NEH, 1981; recipient Cine Golden Eagle award, Blue Ribbon Am. Film Festival, N.Y. Film Festival. Mem. N.Y. Women in Film, Nat. Acad. TV Arts and Scis. Home: 112 W 15th St New York NY 10011

FREYTAG, SHARON NELSON, lawyer; b. Larned, Kans., May 11, 1943; d. John Seldon and Ruth Marie (Herbel) Nelson; m. Thomas Lee Freytag, June 18, 1966; children: Kurt David, Hillary Lee. BS with highest distinction, U. Kans., Lawrence, 1965; MA, U. Mich., 1966; JD cum laude, So. Meth. U., 1981. Bar: Tex. 1981, U.S. Dist. Ct. (no. dist.) Tex. 1981, U.S. Ct. Appeals (5th cir.) 1982. Tchr. English, Gaithersburg (Md.) High Sch., 1966-70; instr. English, Eastfield Coll., 1974-78; law clk. U.S. Dist. Ct. for No. Dist. Tex., 1981-82, U.S. Ct. Appeals for 5th Circuit, 1982; assoc. in litigation Haynes and Boone, Dallas, 1983—, vis. prof. law Southern Meth. U., 1985 86. Editor in chief Southwestern Law Jour., 1980-81; contbr. articles to law jours. Mem. ABA, Tex. Bar Assn., Dallas Bar Assn., Dallas Mus. Art, Dallas Shakespeare Soc., Order of Coif, Barristers, Phi Delta Phi, Phi Beta Kappa. Lutheran. Office: Haynes & Boone 3100 First Republic Plaza Dallas TX 75202

FRICKE, CAROL B., artist, educator; b. Booneville, Mo., July 17, 1945; d. Louis Raymond and Carolyn (Kessler) Borelli; m. Richard J. Fricke, June 17, 1967; children: Laura Jeanne, Richard Louis, Amanda Carolyn. BS, Cornell U., 1967; MAT, Manhattanville Coll., 1986. Cert. art educator, N.Y., Conn. Art tchr. New Canaan (Conn.) Country Sch.; artist Ridgefield, Conn.; dir. 14th Nat. Print Exhibition Silvermine Guild Ctr. for the Arts, New Canaan, 1983; chair membership com. Art Place Gallery, Southport, Conn. Exhibited in Katonah (N.Y.) Gallery, 1977, 80, 86, Silvermine Guild Ctr. for the Arts, New Canaan, 1978, 81 (Art of Northeast award 1981), Art Place Gallery, 1987, New Cannan Art Exhibition (award 1978, 82), Nat. Artist's Alliance, New Haven, 1978, Nat. Assn. Women Artists Exhibition, 1979, Stamford Mus., 1981, 83, 85, Vineyard Gallery, 1982, Hermine Merel Smith Gallery, Edgartown, Mass., 1984, 85. Bd. dirs. Ridgefield Library, Ridgefield Community Kindergarten, Caudatowa Garden Club; tchr. St. Mary's Parish. Grantee Conn. Commn. on the Arts, 1979. Mem. Women's Caucus for Art, Silvermine Guild of Artists (mem. steering com.), Nat. Assn. Women Artists, Artists Assn. of Nantucket, Nat. Art Edn. Assn., Conn. Art Edn. Assn., Conn. Art Educators Assn., LWV. Democrat. Roman Catholic. Office: New Canaan Country Sch Box 997 New Canaan CT 06877

FRIDAY, SUSAN MARQUIS, dancer; b. Denton, Tex., May 20, 1947; d. Robert Lincoln and Corrine Marie (Zimmerly) Marquis; m. Alan Lee Allen, June 1, 1965 (div. Mar. 1983); children: Kimberly Kay, Stuart Jade; m. Bill Friday, Jan. 2, 1984. Student, Texas Woman's U. Instr. dance Liz Gallego Sch. Dance, Denton, 1979-83, Jacqueline Meyer Sch. Dance, Farmers Branch, Tex., 1982-83; owner, operator Marquis La Petite Dancers, Denton, 1984—; instr. dance Denton Ballet Acad., 1984-88; artistic dir. Gibson Sch. Dance, Denton, 1986-87; soloist Denton Civic Ballet, 1984—. Assoc. Denton Benefit League, 1987—. Recipient Josh award Denton Community Theatre, 1985. Mem. SW Regional Ballet Assn., Alpha Chi, Phi Kappa Phi. Republican. Presbyterian. Club: Arts Guild. Home: 3108 Old Orchard Ln Denton TX 76201 Office: PO Box 743 Denton TX 76201

FRIDLEY, SAUNDRA LYNN, internal audit manager; b. Columbus, Ohio, June 14, 1948; d. Jerry Dean and Esther Eliza (Bluhm) Fridley. BS, Franklin U., 1976; MBA, Golden Gate U., 1980. Accounts receivable supr. Internat. Harvester, Columbus, Ohio, San Leandro, Calif., 1972-80; sr. internal auditor Western Union, San Francisco, 1980; internal auditor II, County of Santa Clara, San Jose, Calif., 1980-82; sr. internal auditor Tymshare, Inc., Cupertino, Calif., 1982-84, div. controller, 1984; internal audit mgr. VWR Scientific, Brisbane, Calif., 1984-88, audit dir., 1988—. Mem. Friends of the Vineyards. Mem. Internal Auditors Speakers Bur., Inst. Internal Auditors (pres., founder Tri-Valley chpt.), Internal Auditor's Internat. Seminar Com., Nat. Assn. Female Execs. Avocations: woodworking; gardening; golfing. Home: 862 Bellflower St Livermore CA 94550 Office: VWR Scientific 3745 Bayshore Blvd Brisbane CA 94005

FRIE, DIANA JOAN, healthcare executive; b. Hamilton, Ohio, May 10, 1949; d. Charles Herman and Ilona (Imamura) F. BA, DePauw U., 1971; MA, U. Mich., 1975; PhD, U. Toledo, 1983. Cert. emergency med. technician. Substitute tchr. Toledo Pub. Schs., 1971-72; phys. dir. Middletown (Ohio) Area YMCA, 1972-74; instr. Miami U., Oxford, Ohio, 1975-82; program designer Toledo Hosp., 1982-84, health edn. services coordinator, 1984-85; exec. dir. Toledo Community Hosp. Oncology Program, 1985—; part-time instr. U. Toledo, 1987; health edn. cons. Toledo Hosp., St. Vincent Med. Ctr., Toledo, 1985—. Author: Instructors Manual for Health: The Science of Human Adaptation, 1986. Chmn. health and safety services ARC, Toledo, 1982—; instr., trainer Am. Heart Assn., Toledo, 1982—; bd. dirs. Am. Cancer Soc., Toledo, 1986—. Adminstrv. fellow Miami U., 1980-81; grantee Nat. Cancer Inst., 1987—. Mem. Am. Alliance for Health, Phys. Edn., Recreation and Dance. Office: Toledo Community Hosp Oncology Program 3314 Collingwood Blvd Toledo OH 43610

FRIED, HELEN JANE, university administrator; b. Yonkers, N.Y., July 12, 1944; d. Sydney Arnold and Sara (Rapapport) F. BA, SUNY, Binghamton, 1966; MA in Edn., Syracuse U., 1968; postgrad., U. Conn., 1972-75; PhD, Union Grad. Sch., 1977. Hall dir. Trenton (N.J.) State Coll., 1968-70, coordinator off-campus housing, 1970-71; tchr. high sch. English Pioneer Valley Regional Sch., Northfield, Mass., 1971-72; coordinator staff tng. resdl. life U. Conn., Storrs, 1974-85; dir. resdl. life U. Hartford, 1985-88, dir. resdl. edn., 1988—. Mem. editorial bd. Jour. of Coll. and Student Personnel, 1983—. Mem. Am. Coll. Personnel Assn. (chair com. on women 1985—, exec. council 1987—), Conn. Coll. Personnel Assn. (pres. 1982-83), Conn. Women in Higher Edn. Adminstrn. (program com. 1986—). Office: U Hartford Office of Resdl Life West Hartford CT 06117

FRIED, N(ANCY) ELIZABETH, compensation consultant; b. Cleve., Apr. 11, 1948; d. Herbert and Frieda (Jacobs) F. BS, Ohio State U., 1970, MA, 1975, PhD, 1978. Tchr. Ohio Youth Commn., Columbus, 1970-71, Columbus Pub. Schs., 1972-74; adj. prof. Franklin U., Columbus, 1980-86; adminstrv. services analyst Nationwide Ins. Cos., Columbus, 1977-79, compensation analyst, 1979-80, sr. compensation analyst, 1980-81, compensation mgr., 1981-83; prin. cons. N.E. Fried and Assocs., Columbus, 1983—; chairperson Property Casualty Insurers Survey Group, New Orleans, 1981-82; adv. com. mem. Nat. Assn. Ind. Insurers Joint Survey, Chgo., 1982-83; faculty Am. Compensation Assn., Scottsdale, Ariz., 1983—; leader continuing mgmt. edn. seminars Lehigh U., Bethlehem, Pa., 1983-84, U. Okla., 1984. Author: Independent Research in Compensation, 1985; co-author: Proofreading Communications, 1983; contbr. articles to profl. jours. mem. adv. com. Council Exceptional Children, Washington, 1978, Southwestern Pub. Sch., Grove City, Ohio, 1978-80; chmn. adv. com. Ft. Hayes Career Ctr., Columbus, 1977-81. Edn. Profls. Devel. Act fellow State of Ohio, 1975-76; Grantee Nat. Def. Ohio State Univ., 1967-70, Columbus Pub. Schs., 1971. Mem. Am. Compensation Assn. (cert.), Am. Soc. Personnel Adminstrs., Women's Bus. Bd., Dublin Women in Bus. and Professions. Clubs: Women Investing Today (founder 1981, pres. 1982), Capital. Home and Office: 5590 Dumfries Ct West Dublin OH 43017-9426

FRIED, RONNEE, marketing research company executive; b. N.Y.C., Dec. 16, 1947; d. Phillip Frank Fried and Gloria Edith (Pfeffer) Sandow. B.A., George Washington U., 1969. Field dir. AHF Mktg. Research, N.Y.C., 1969-73; project dir. Decisions Ctr. Inc., N.Y.C., 1973-76, Ogilvy & Mather Advt., N.Y.C., 1977; assoc. group mgr. Data Devel. Corp., N.Y.C., 1977-81; ptnr., exec. v.p. Brown Koff & Fried Inc., N.Y.C., 1981—; dir. Wats Interviewing Network Inc., Rutherford, N.J. Mem. speakers bur. Greater N.Y. Conf. Soviet Jewry, 1979—. Mem. Am. Mktg. Assn. (Effie Awards Judging co-chmn. 1982, membership com. 1981, Recognition award 1982), Advt. Women N.Y. Jewish. Club: Tarrytown Group. Avocations: 1948 Chrysler New Yorker. Home: One Fifth Ave New York NY 10003 Office: Brown Koff & Fried Inc 14 W 23d St New York NY 10010

FRIEDAN, BETTY, author, feminist leader; b. Peoria, Ill., Feb. 4, 1921; d. Harry and Miriam (Horwitz) Goldstein; m. Carl Friedan, June 1947 (div. May 1969); children—Daniel, Jonathan, Emily. AB summa cum laude, Smith Coll., 1942, LHD, 1975; LHD, SUNY, Stony Brook, 1985, Cooper Union, 1987. Research fellow U. Calif. at Berkeley, 1943; lectr. feminism univs., women's groups, bus. and profl. groups in U.S. and Europe; founder N.O.W., 1st pres., 1966-70, chairwoman adv. com., 1970-72, mem. bd. dirs. legal def. and edn. fund; organizer Nat. Women's Polit. Caucas, 1971, Internat. Feminist Congress, 1973, First Women's Bank, 1973, Econ. Think Tank for Women, 1974; v.p. Nat. Assn. Repeal Abortion Laws, 1970-73; Disting. vis. prof. sch. journalism and studies of women and men in soc., U. So. Calif., 1987; vis. prof. sociology Temple U., 1972, Queens Coll., 1975; vis. lectr., fellow Yale, 1974; lectr. New Sch. Social Research, N.Y.C., 1971; sr. research assoc. Ctr. Social Scis., Columbia U., N.Y.C., 1979-81; bd. dirs. NOW Legal Defense and Education fund; co-chmn. Nat. Comms. Women's Equality. Author: The Feminine Mystique, 1963, It Changed My Life: Writings on the Women's Movement, 1976, The Second Stage, 1982, new edit., 1986; mem. editorial bd. Present Tense mag.; contbg. editor McCall's mag, 1971-74; contbr. Atlantic Monthly; contbr. articles to New York Times, Cosmopolitan, Saturday Rev., Family Circle, Good Housekeeping, and others. Mem. exec. com. Am. Jewish Congress, co-chair nat. commn. women's equality, 1984-85; mem. nat. bd. Girl Scouts USA, 1976 82; mem. N.Y. County Democratic Com. Recipient Humanist of Yr. award, 1975; Inst. Politics fellow Kennedy Sch. Govt., Harvard U., 1982, Mort Weisinger award for outstanding mag. journalism Am. Soc. Journalists and Authors, 1979; named Author of Yr. Am. Soc. Journalists and Authors, 1982; Research fellow Ctr. Population Studies, Harvard U., 1982-83, Chubb fellow Yale U., 1985, Andrus Ctr. Gerontology fellow U. So. Calif., 1986. Mem. AFTRA, Author's Guild, Soc. Mag. Writers, Am. Soc. Journalists and Authors (Mort Weisinger award 1979, Author of Yr. 1982), Assn. Humanistic Psychology, Am. Sociology Assn., Gerontol. Soc. Am., Coffee House, Phi Beta Kappa. Address: 1 Lincoln Pl #40K New York NY 10023

FRIEDBERG, REBECCA DAVID, public relations executive; b. Alexandria, Va., Apr. 3, 1962; d. Arthur William and Charlotte Elizabeth (Antesberger) F. BA in Journalism and Polit. Sci., Ind. U., 1984. Sportswriter U.S. Olympic Tng. , div. Miller High Life News Bur., Colorado Springs, Colo., 1984; adminstrv. asst. U.S. Soccer Fedn., Colorado Springs, 1984; communications asst. Aluminum Assn., Washington, 1985-86; account exec. Pub. Relations Aids, Washington, 1985-86; v.p. MediaDirect, Washington, 1987—; chmn. pub. affairs Tast of South, Inc., Washington, 1987—; with directory of experts Broadcast Interview Source, 1987—. Co-author, editor Colorado Springs Today, 1984; editor Star Spangled Beer, 1987. Mem. Beethoven Soc. of Washington, Washington Opera Soc. Republican. Roman Catholic. Club: Occoquan (Va.) Boat (coxswain rowing team). Office: Media Direct 1625 Eye St NW Washington DC 20006

FRIEDEL, LYNN KAPEGHIAN, computer company executive; b. Phila., Nov. 16, 1949; d. Edward and Ellen Brown (Wardrop) Kapeghian; m. Seymour A. Friedel, Mar. 17, 1985; 1 child, Joshua Edward. BA summa cum laude, U. N.H., 1982; MBA, Plymouth State Coll., 1984. Pres., owner LKC Communications, Inc., Merrimack, N.H., 1976-83; v.p. fin. and adminstrn. Itran Corp., Manchester, N.H., 1983-86, Termiflex Corp., Merrimack, 1986—. Office: Termiflex Corp 316 Daniel Webster Hwy Merrimack NH 03054

FRIEDENBERG, KAREN ROSEN, real estate associate; b. Savannah, Ga., May 3, 1949; d. Emanuel F. and Thelma Z. (Reed) Rosen; 1 child, Jodi. B.S. in Mass Communications, Emerson Coll., 1971; student U. N.C., summer 1968, Harvard U., summer 1967, U. Ga., 1967-69. Exec. trainee Jordan Marsh, Boston, 1974-76; broadcast dir. Rich's, Atlanta, 1976-78; mktg. dir. Northlake Mall, Atlanta, 1978-80, Lenox Square, Atlanta, 1980-82; retail leasing assoc. Trammell Crow Co., Atlanta, 1982-85, Kern & Co., Atlanta, 1985-86, Retail Properties Group, 1986—. Bd. dirs. Atlanta Women's Network, Feminist Action Alliance, Atlanta, Atlanta chpt. Nat. Council Jewish Women; patron High Mus. Art, Ctr. for Puppetry Art; mem. Ga. Women's Polit. Caucus. Mem. Comml. Real Estate Women, Atlanta Advt. Club, Women's Commerce Club. Republican. Jewish. Lodge: Hadassah (Atlanta). Avocations: aerobics; bicycling; hiking; rafting. Home: Four Pendleton Pl Atlanta GA 30342 Office: Retail Properties Group 6075 Roswell Rd Suite 210 Atlanta GA 30328

FRIEDLAND, BERNICE UDELLE, psychologist, educator; b. Akron, Ohio, June 18, 1935; d. Hymen H. and Ida S.; B.Sc., Ohio State U., 1956; M.Ed., Frostburg State Coll., 1969; Ed.D., W.Va. U., 1972; children by previous marriage—Holli, David Michael. Asso. prof. psychology Coppin State Coll., 1972-80; adj. prof. Bowie State Coll., Loyola Coll.; pvt. practice psychology, Balt., 1976—; psychologist Spring Grove State Hosp., Balt., 1978-83; chief psychology and psychiat. services Md. Correctional Instn. for Women, 1983—; bd. dirs. Blind Industries and Services of Md.; bd. advisors rehab. div. Balt. Goodwill Industries, 1979-83; cons., inservice trainer ednl. and vocat. rehab. agys. Bd. dirs. Alfred Adler Inst., Washington, 1984—. Mem. Am. Personnel and Guidance Assn., Am. Psychol. Assn., Nat. Rehab. Assn., N.Am. Soc. Adlerian Psychology. Author: (with W. McKelvie) Career Goal Counseling, 1978; editor Individual Psychologist, 1976-80; mem. editorial bd. Jour. Rehab., 1979-80; contbr. articles to profl. publs. Home: 6819 Cherokee Dr Baltimore MD 21209 Office: 101 W Read St Baltimore MD 21201

FRIEDLAND, MARY-ELLEN, public relations professional; b. Rutland, Vt., July 8, 1958; d. Bernard and Louise (Maynard) Huntoon; m. David Marshall Friedland, Mar. 7, 1987. BA, Duquesne U., 1980. Community relations project coordinator Cen. Vt. Pub. Service, Rutland, 1981-87; coordinator Nat. Orgn. Partnership Program, Nat. Orgn. on Disability, Washington, 1987-88; writer Rockport Inst., Washington, 1988—. Bd. mem. Jr. Achievement, Citizen's Advocacy Group, Area Agy. Aging.

FRIEDLANDER, PATRICIA ANN, publishing executive; b. Chgo., May 9, 1944; d. James Farrell and Therese Mary (Pfeiler) Crotty; m. Daniel B. Friedlander, July 3, 1971 (div. Apr. 1978); children: Michael Derek, David Colin. BA, Cardinal Stritch Coll., 1966; MA, U. Wis., Milw., 1968; postgrad., U. Chgo., 1968-69, U. London, 1968—. Instr. U. Wis., Milw., 1966-68, Chgo. State U., 1968-71, Argo Community High Sch., Summit, Ill., 1971-73, Park Dist., Park Forest South, Ill., 1973-77; counselor Will County Mental Health Clinic, Park Forest South, 1977-78; sales rep. Prentice-Hall, Inc., Englewood Cliffs, N.J., 1978-84; nat. sales mgr. Dow Jones-Irwin, Homewood, Ill., 1984-87; dir. mktg. Nat. Textbook Co., Lincolnwood, Ill., 1987—; dir. Printer's Row Bookfair, Chgo., 1985. V.p. Townhome Assn., Park Forest South, 1978; den mother Cub Scouts Am., Park Forest South, 1981-84. Mem. Am. Book Travelers, Midwest Book Travelers (pres. 1983-87), Chgo. Book Clinic, Lincoln Park Zool. Assn. (life). Home: 2320 W Farwell Chicago IL 60645 Office: Nat Textbook Co 4255 W Touhy Ave Lincolnwood IL 60646

FRIEDMAN, BARBARA GLATT, clinical mental health counselor; b. Newark, May 13, 1937; d. Ben Harry and Sadie (Gudis) Glatt; m. Bernard Friedman, June 11, 1955 (dec.); children: Barry Jay, Ronnie Mark, Mitchell Ira. BA, Edison State Coll., 1979; postgrad., Trenton State Coll., 1979-80; MS, U. Pa., 1982; PhD S.W. Univ., 1988. Cert. counselor, clin. hypnotherapist, mental health counselor, N.J. Counselor Am. Youth Crisis Ctr., Oberursel, Fed. Republic of Germany, 1972-74; career counselor Vol. Employment Service Team, Camden County, N.J., 1977-79; counselor Glassboro (N.J.) State Coll. Counseling Ctr., also cons.; pvt. practice psychology, Cherry Hill, N.J., 1980—; tchr. adult edn., 1982—; assoc. Ednl. Info. Resource Ctr., Sewell, N.J., 1987—; cons., psychol. counselor Together, Inc., Glassboro, 1983—; dir.-founder Alts. in Direction, 1983; workshop facilitator; guest lectr. in field. Mem. Parents' Campaign for Handicapped Children and Youth; bd. dirs. Frankfurt (Fed. Republic of Germany) Am. Jewish Community Chapel, 1969-72. Recipient cert. of recognition, Oberursel, 1973, presdl. cert. of honor Camden County Coll., 1978. Mem. Nat. Bd. Cert. Counselors, Am. Assn. Counseling and Devel., Am. Mental Health Counselors Assn. (holistic counseling spl. interest network), N.J. Mental Health Counselors Assn., Nat. Acad. Cert. Clin. Mental Health Counselors (cert.), Am. Guild Hypnotherapists (registered), N.J. Mental Health Counselors Assn., N.J. Profl. Counselors Assn., N.J. Career Devel. Assn., Arthritis Found., Cherry Hill C. of C. (chmn. edn. com. 1984-88, mem. speakers bur. 1985—, cert. of recognition 1985), N.J. Career Devel. Assn., Small Bus. Council, N.J. Assn. Women Bus. Owners. Home: 16 Dartmouth Rd Cherry Hill NJ 08034

FRIEDMAN, COLLETTE SWEET, kitchen and interior designer; b. Los Angeles, Feb. 25, 1933; d. Maurice Paul and Ilona M. (Feld) Albert; student Los Angeles Valley Coll., 1961-63; student Calif. State U., Northridge, 1964, Pierce Coll., 1965-67, UCLA, 1968-70; children—Scott D., Brian C., Victoria A., Valaree L., Collette. Lic. gen. contrator. Interior designer, North Hollywood, Calif., 1962-76; owner/designer Better Homes and Kitchens, Westlake Village, Calif., 1976—. Recipient award Bank of America, 1951. Mem. Nat. Kitchen and Bath Assn. (sec. So. Calif. chpt. 1979-82), Conejo Assn. Profl. Interior Designers, Am. Bus. Woman's Assn. (charter), Nat. Assn. Women in Constrn., Westlake Village C. of C., Conejo Valley C. of C., Zonta Internat. Office: 31121 Via Colinas 1004 Westlake Village CA 91362

FRIEDMAN, DORIS TOLTZ, lawyer; b. Chelsea, Mass., Dec. 16, 1932; d. Harry H. and Frances (Wilner-Wyzanski) Toltz; m. Samuel Joseph Friedman, Aug. 28, 1955; children: Ruth Lynn, Laura Beth, Jill Ann. BA, Tufts U., 1954; LLB, Boston U., 1957. Bar: Mass. 1957, N.Y. 1971, U.S. Supreme Ct. 1975. Sole practice Boston, 1957-71, Tarrytown, N.Y., 1971-82, atty. in charge Legal Aid Soc. Westchester, White Plains, N.Y., 1977-84; sr. ptnr. Friedman and Schnabel, White Plains, 1982—; sole practice White Plains, 1971—, pvt. family mediator, 1981—; arbitrator Am. Arbitration Assn., N.Y., 1982—; bd. dirs. N.Y. Women's Bar Assn., Westchester County, 1982-85, N.Y. State Council Div. Mediators, N.Y., 1984—, pres. 1987. Contbr. various articles to profl. jours. Chmn. Community Opportunity Ctr. Tarrytowns Inc., 1963—; justice Village of Tarrytown, 1982-85, 1987—. Mem. Acad. Family Mediators, N.Y. State Bar Assn., N.Y. Women's Bar Assn., Westchester Bar Assn. Democrat. Jewish. Home: 39 Cottontail Ln Irvington NY 10533 Office: Friedman and Schnabel 10 Mitchell Pl White Plains NY 10601

FRIEDMAN, ELIZABETH ANN, educational administrator; b. N.Y.C., June 6, 1948; d. Aaron and Florence (Giatas) Zicherman; m. Paul Lawrence Friedman, May 25, 1975. BA cum laude, U. Pitts., 1970. Mgmt. analyst U.S. Dept. Commerce, 1970-73; tng. systems analyst Inst. Law and Social Research, Washington, 1973-78; dir. curriculum devel. and adminstrn. D.C. Bar (Unified), 1978-81; mgr. edn. programs Assn. Trial Lawyers Am., Washington, 1981-82; exec. dir. Inst. Profl. and Exec. Devel., Washington, 1982—; mem. community adv. council WETA Pub. TV/Radio. Home: 3042 P St NW Washington DC 20007 Office: Inst Profl and Exec Devel 2300 M St NW Suite 260 Washington DC 20037

FRIEDMAN, ESTELLE YUDKIN, librarian; b. Bklyn., June 20, 1927; d. Isidore and Josephine (Kreditor) Yudkin; m. Izchak Friedman, Jan. 28, 1951; children—Jonathan, Wilma. B.A., Bklyn. Coll., 1947; M.L.S., Pratt Inst., 1969. Librarian, N.Y. Pub. Library, N.Y.C., 1969-72, sr. librarian, 1972-80, sr. br. librarian, 1980-83, supervising br. librarian, 1983—. Mem. ALA, N.Y. Library Assn. Home: 600 W 239th St Riverdale NY 10463 Office: NY Pub Library Fifth Ave and 42d St New York NY 10018

FRIEDMAN, FRANCES, public relations firm executive; b. N.Y.C., Apr. 8, 1928; d. Aaron and Bertha (Itzkowitz) Fallick; m. Clifford Jerome Friedman, June 17, 1950; children—Kenneth Lee, Jeffrey Bennett. B.B.A., CCNY, 1948. Dir. pub. relations Melia Internat., Madrid, N.Y.C., 1971-73; sr. v.p. Lobsenz-Stevens, N.Y.C., 1973-75; exec. v.p. Howard Rubenstein Assocs., N.Y.C., 1975-83; pres., prin. Frances Friedman Assocs., N.Y.C., 1983-84; pres., chmn. bd. dirs. Greycom, Inc., N.Y.C., 1984—. Bd. dirs. ACRMD-Retarded Children, N.Y.C., 1983-85, City Coll. Fund, N.Y.C., 1970-79; mem. adv. bd. League for Parent Edn., N.Y.C., 1961-65; editor South Shore Democratic newletter, North Bellmore, N.Y., 1958-61, press sec. N.Y. State Assembly candidate, 1965, N.Y. State Congl. candidate, 1968; officer Manhasset Dem. Club, N.Y., 1965-69; mem. adv. com. N.Y.C. Council candidate, 1985. Mem. Pub. Relations Soc. Am., Women in Communications, City Club N.Y. Democrat. Jewish. Home: 860 Fifth Ave New York NY 10021 Office: Greycom Inc Pub Rel 777 3d Ave New York NY 10017

FRIEDMAN, HELEN RUTH, psychologist, educator; b. Rome, N.Y., Dec. 30, 1951; d. Henry and Cecilia (Osipowitz) F. BS in Psychology cum laude, St. Lawrence U., Canton, N.Y., 1973; MS, Memphis State U., 1976, PhD, 1980. Cert. psychologist, Mo. Research asst. Correctional Research and Evaluation Ctr., Memphis, 1977-78; psychology intern Malcolm Bliss Mental Health Ctr., St. Louis, 1978-79; clin. psychologist St. Louis State Hosp., 1980-84; child sexual abuse treatment team mem. Child Guidance Ctr. Washington U. Sch. Medicine, St. Louis, 1983-84; pvt. practice clin.

psychology St. Louis, 1981—; asst. prof. dept. interdisciplinary studies Fontbonne Coll., St. Louis, 1984—; mem. Children's Mental Health Services Council, 1980-84, Mental Health Players; lectr. on mental health issues. Mem. Am. Psychol. Assn., Mo. Psychol. Assn. (mem. profl. standards rev. com., mem. ad hoc com. on impaired psychologists, 1984-86), St. Louis Psychol. Assn. (sec. 1981-83, pres. 1984-85), Mental Health Assn. St. Louis (bd. dirs., mem. speakers bur.), Internat. Soc. for Study Multiple Personality and DissociationStates, Soc. for Sci. Study Sex, Phi Beta Kappa, Psi Chi. Jewish. Home and Office: 542 Donne Ave Saint Louis MO 63130

FRIEDMAN, LESLIE J., scriptwriter, businesswoman, author; b. N.Y.C., Oct. 12, 1948; d. Henry and Bernice A. Friedman; BA, U. Cin., 1970; MS, U. Ky., 1972. Children's librarian, then br. librarian trainee Pub. Library Cin. and Hamilton County, 1970-73; art librarian U. Ga., 1974-77; freelance lectr. women's media image, 1975—; producer: Mr. Whipple Groupies: Looking at Women's Advt. Image; Womanhood: A Pornographic Vision; author: Sex Role Stereotyping in the Mass Media, An Annotated Bibliography, 1977; owner Clarity Writing Service; v.p. JES Search Firm, Inc. Data Processing Recruitment, Atlanta, 1983—. Mem. advisory bd. Atlanta Vocat. Counseling Center, Atlanta Council Battered Women, Leadership Buckhead. 100 K Club honoree, 1985-87. Mem. Women's Inst. Freedom Press, Women in Film, Art Libraries Soc. N.Am. (past regional pres.), Nat. Assn. Personnel Cons. Home: 47 St Claire Ln Atlanta GA 30324 Office: 3379 Peachtree Rd Suite 550 Atlanta GA 30326

FRIEDMAN, MARIA ANDRE, public relations executive; b. Jackson, Mich., June 12, 1950; d. Robert Andre and Mary MacLean (Thompson) Hoving; m. Stanley N. Friedman, July 22, 1973; children—Alexandra, Adam. B.A. cum laude, U. Md., 1972, M.A., 1980; postgrad., Nova U., 1987—. Writer, U.S. Bur. Mines, Washington, 1973-78; head writer Nat. Ctr. for Health Service Research and Health Care Tech. Assessment, DHHS, Rockville, Md., 1978-85, chief publs. and info. br., 1986—; pres. Medi-Systems, Inc., Silver Spring, Md., 1980—; v.p. Metro Med. Assocs., Silver Spring, 1982—, MediSystems Fin. Services, 1984—. Mem. Nat. Assn. Govt. Communicators, Pub. Relations Soc. Am., NOW. Home: 12535 Heurich Rd Silver Spring MD 20902 Office: Nat Ctr for Health Services Research and Health Care T ech Assessment 18-12 Parklawn Bldg Rockville MD 20857

FRIEDMAN, MARNA WENDY, marketing consultant; b. Pequannock, N.J., Jan. 13, 1959; d. Harold and Marcia Ruth (Nyman) F. Student, Fairleigh Dickinson U., 1977-78; BS, C.W. Post Coll., Greenvale, N.Y., 1981; MA, New Sch. Social Research, N.Y.C., 1986. Mgr. sales Macy's Dept. Store, N.Y.C., 1981-82; traffic coordinator Direct Mktg. Agy., Stamford, Conn., 1982-83; prodn. coordinator The N.Y. Community Trust, N.Y.C., 1983-86; mktg. cons. MWF, Ewing, N.J., 1986—; asst. prof. Mercer County Community Coll., West Windsor, N.J. ; v.p., bd. dirs. Prescriptive Promotions, Ewing, 1984—; pres., bd. dirs. Baby Basket Co., Ltd., Ewing, 1986—; cons. Friedman Enterprises, Ewing, 1978—, Ferraioli, Wesdyk & Freifeld, Prompton Lakes, N.J., 1984-85, Helene Fuld Med. Ctr., Trenton, N.J., 1988—. Pub. info. officer Fedn. Protestant Welfare Agys., Inc., N.Y.C., 1987—; mem. com. Morris County Dem., Montville, 1983-84; mem. Nat. Dem. Com., Washington, 1983—. Mem. Women in Communications (edn. com.), Internat. Communications Assn., Nat. Acad. TV Arts & Scis., Broadcasting Edn. Assn., Am. Mktg. Assn., Am. Women Entrepreneurs. Jewish. Avocations: music, travel, gourmet cooking, calligraphy. Home: 1 cromwell Ct West Trenton NJ 08628 Office: 3 Ronit Dr Ewing NJ 08628

FRIEDMAN, MERYL A. ROSEN, lawyer; b. Washington, Apr. 4, 1949; d. Sidney A. and Florence T. (Schwarzman) Rosen; m. Richard S. Friedman, Nov. 4, 1979; 1 child, L. E. Friedman. Student, U. Lancaster (Eng.), 1969-70; BA, Case Western Reserve U., 1971; JD, Villanova U., 1983, postgrad., 1983-87. Bar: Pa. 1983, U.S. Supreme Ct. 1988. Legal asst. corp. matters communications Satellite Corp., Washington, 1972-78; legal asst. Planning Research Corp., Washington, 1978-79; law clk. Dilworth, Paxson, Kalish & Kauffman, Phila., 1979-80, 81; tax research Grad. Tax Program Villanova (Pa.) U., 1982-83; atty. Needle, Feldman & Herman, Phila., 1983-85; sole practice West Chester, Pa., 1985—. Contbr. articles to profl. jours. Mem. exec. com. Chester County Dem. Party, 1981—, dist. leader, 1981—, campaign chmn. 1984. Herman Mitchell Schwartz award Villanova U., 1983. Mem. ABA, Pa. Bar Assn., Phila. Bar Assn., Chester County Bar Assn. Jewish. Club: Democratic Women's(West Chester). Lodge: Kesher Israel Sisterhood. Office: 225 N Church St West Chester PA 19355

FRIEDMAN, NANCY JO, public relations executive; b. Manhasset, N.Y., Mar. 4, 1956; d. Lee J. and Natalie (Scharlin) F. BA, Antioch Coll., 1977. Adminstrv. asst. Travel & Leisure Mag., N.Y.C., 1979-80; dir. pub. relations Dominican Tourist Info. Ctr., N.Y.C., 1980-83; acct. supr. Jessica Dee Communications, N.Y.C., 1983-85; v.p. pub. relations Rubell/Schrager, N.Y.C., 1985-87; pres. Nancy J. Friedman Pub. Relations, N.Y.C., 1987—. Mem. Soc. Am. Travel Writers. Office: 252 E 61st St #2A S New York NY 10021

FRIEDMAN, S. LILA, librarian; b. Bklyn., Sept. 25, 1926; d. Ephraim Eliezer and Naomi (Weisdorff) Ritter; m. S. Lester Friedman, Jan. 25, 1946; children—Matthew, Joel, Amy. B.A., Bklyn. Coll., 1948; M.L.S., L.I. U., 1975. Cert. library media specialist, secondary sch. tchr. library, N.Y. Librarian, Hunter Coll. High Sch., N.Y.C., 1973-74, Hawthorne (N.Y.) Cedar Knolls Sch., 1976, Samuel Tilden High Sch., Bklyn., 1978-79, Bellerose Jewish Ctr., Floral Park, N.Y., 1980—, dir. library, 1980—; librarian Katharine Gibbs Sch., Huntington, N.Y., 1984—. Area chmn. Queens United Cerebral Palsy, 1969, 71. Recipient 25th Anniversary award State of Israel Bonds, 1975, Youth Services award B'nai B'rith, 1983. Mem. ALA, Assn. Jewish Libraries, L.I. Assn. Jewish Libraries (charter mem.), Am. Assn. Sch. Librarians. Jewish. Home: 80 49 252d St Bellerose NY 11426 Office: Bellerose Jewish Ctr 254 04 Union Turnpike Floral Floral Park NY 11004

FRIEDMAN, SUE TYLER, foundation executive, technical publications company executive; b. Nürnberg, Fed. Republic Germany, Feb. 28, 1925; came to U.S., 1938; d. William and Ann (Federlein) Tyler; m. Gerald Manfred Friedman, June 27, 1948; children—Judith Fay Friedman Rosen, Sharon Mira Friedman Azaria, Devora Paula Friedman Zweibach, Eva Jane Friedman Scholle, Wendy Tamar Friedman Spanier. R.N., Beth Israel Sch. Nursing, 1941-43. Exec. dir. Ventures and Publs. of Gerald M. Friedman, 1964—; owner Tyler Publications, Watervliet and Troy, N.Y., 1978—; treas. Northeastern Sci. Found., Inc., Troy, 1979—; treas. Gerry Exploration, Inc., Troy, N.Y., 1982—; office mgr. Rensselaer Ctr. Applied Geology, Troy, 1983—. Pres. Pioneer Women/Na'amat, Tulsa, 1961-64, treas., Jerusalem, Israel, 1964, pres., Albany, N.Y., 1968-70; bd. dirs. Temple Beth-El, 1965—, dir. Hebrew Sch., 1965-80. Sue Tyler Friedman medal for distinction in history of geology created in her honor, Geol. Soc. London, 1988. Jewish. Avocation: world travel. Home: 32 24th St Troy NY 12180 Office: Rensselaer Ctr Applied Geology 15 3d St Box 746 Troy NY 12181

FRIEDMAN, SUSAN LYNN BELL, public relations specialist; b. Lafayette, Ind., May 23, 1953; d. Virgil Atwood and Jean Loree (Wiggins) B.; m. Frank H. Friedman, July 31, 1976; 1 child, Alex Charles. B.A., Purdue U., 1975; M.S., Ind. State U., 1981. Asst. dir. pub. relations Vincennes U. Jr. Coll., Ind., 1977-83; dir. Knox County C. of C., Vincennes, 1983-84; writer/editor VSE Corp., Alexandria, Va., 1984-85; asst. to pres. Am. Assn. Community and Jr. Colls., Washington, 1985-87; owner/pres. SBF Promotions, 1987—; mgr., program developer Community Based Children's Services, 1988—, cons., 1982-84; mem. Tech. Coll. of the Lowcountry (S.C.) Found. Bd. dirs., 1987—; Knox County chpt. Am. Heart Assn., 1982-84; mem. exec. bd. Leadership Vincennes, 1982-84; Hoosier scholar, 1971, 72; pres. Annandale BPW, 1987-88, bd. dirs. Beaufort-Jasper Comprehensive Health Services, Inc. Mem. Am. Assn. Women in Community and Jr. Colls. (nat. liaison 1985-87), LWV (chpt. v.p. 1982-84). Democrat. Home: 41 Wade Hampton Dr Beaufort SC 29902

FRIEDMANN, EMILY MACCARO, accountant, company executive; b. N.Y.C., Nov. 9, 1949; d. William Anthony and Katherine Gladys (Butzgy) Maccaro; m. James Bernard Friedmann, Nov. 11, 1978; children—Katherine, Margaret. B.S., Syracuse U., 1971. Cost acct. Automatic Connectors, Commack, N.Y., 1971-76; sr. cost analyst Standard Brands, N.Y.C., 1976-77; asst. controller So. Calif. Carton, Gardena, 1977-79; mgr. fin. planning Dynachem Corp., Tustin, Calif., 1979-84; mgr. cost acctg. Targeted Coverage Inc., Pomona, Calif. Republican. Roman Catholic. Home: 716 Big Falls Dr Diamond Bar CA 91765 Office: 533 W Foothill Blvd Glendora CA 91740

FRIEDRICH, MARGRET COHEN, guidance counselor; b. Balt., June 4, 1947; d. Joseph Cohen and Judith (Kline) Cohen Roisman; m. Jay Joseph Friedrich, May 16, 1971; children—David Benjamin, Marc Adam, Samantha Lauren. B.Ed., U. Miami-Fla., 1969, M.Ed., 1970. Cert. alcoholism and addiction counselor. Grad. asst. U. Miami, Coral Gables, Fla., 1969-70; tchr. Balt. Bd. Edn., 1970; guidance counselor Ridgewood Bd. Edn., N.J., 1970—; student assistance counselor, 1986—, chmn. student assistance com., 1986—; alcoholism counselor Bergen County Dept. Health, Paramus, N.J., 1981-82; in-service tchr. Ridgewood Bd. Edn., 1983, supr., coordinator peer counseling program high sch., 1979—; with Assn. Mental Health and Counseling of No. N.J., 1985—; cons. N.J. Student Assistance Program, student asst. cons. N.J. Dept. Edn., chmn. student asst. com. Author tech. papers. Exec. bd. Hadassah, Ridgewood-Glen Rock, N.J., 1971—; youth leadership com. United Jewish Appeal, Bergen County, 1974-75; sec. Bergen County Youth Com. Substance Abuse, Paramus, 1980—, conf. coordinating com., 1983; treas. Ridgewood Coalition Substance Use and Abuse, 1983-84; co-chmn. fundraiser, treas. United Parents/Safe Homes, Ridgewood, 1984; lectr./educator Passaic County Juvenile Conf. Com., Paterson, N.J., 1984. Reisman scholar, 1969; U. Miami teaching asst., 1970, recipient Recognition award, 1968. Mem. N.J. Assn. Alcoholism Counselors, Nat. Assn. Suicidology, N.J. Edn. Assn., Ridgewood Edn. Assn., Bergen County Edn. Assn., N.J. Task Force on Women and Alcohol, N.J. Personnel and Guidance Assn., Sigma Delta Tau. (exec. bd. 1965-69). Democrat. Jewish. Office: Ridgewood High Sch Ridgewood NJ 07451

FRIEDRICH, ROSE MARIE, travel agency executive; b. Chgo., May 17, 1941; d. Theodore A. and Ann Bernadine (Coppoth) Dlugosz; m. Gerhard K. Friedrich, Apr. 18, 1964; 1 child, Alan C. Student, Roosevelt U., 1986—. Cert. travel agt. Travel cons. Chgo. Motor Club, 1959, Drake Travel, Chgo., 1960-65; mgr. 1st Nat. Travel, Arlington Heights, Ill., 1969-71, Total Travel, Palatine, Ill., 1971-76; owner, mgr. Travel Bug Ltd., Lake Zurich, Ill., 1977—; advisor Coll. Lake County, Grayslake, Ill., 1985—. Author: (books) Travel Career Textbook, 1980, Guide to Tour Organizing, 1984, Build Profits Through Group Travel, 1984, Independent Travel Agent, 1986. Mem. Inst. Cert. Travel Cons. (chmn. edn. forum 1981-84, appreciation award 1984), Soc. Travel and Tourism Educators, State of Ill. Council Vocat. Edn. (mem. Career Guidance Consortium, Appreciation award 1986), Lake Zurich C. of C. (pres. 1984-85). Republican. Roman Catholic. Home: 407 E Knob Hill Dr Arlington Heights IL 60004 Office: Travel Bug Ltd 15 S Old Rand Rd Lake Zurich IL 60047

FRIEND, CYNTHIA M., chemist, educator; b. Hastings, Nebr., Mar. 16, 1955; d. Matthew Charles and Elise Germaine Friend; children: Ayse K., Kurt Y. BS, U. Calif., Davis, 1977; PhD, U. Calif., Berkeley, 1981. Postdoctoral assoc. Stanford (Calif.) U., 1981-82; asst. prof. Harvard U., Cambridge, Mass., 1982-86; assoc. prof. Harvard U., Cambridge, 1986—; research collaborator NSLS/Brookhaven Nat. Labs., Cambridge. Recipient Presdl. Young Investigator award NSF, 1985. Mem. Am. Phys. Soc., Am. Chem. Soc., Am. Vacuum Soc. Office: Harvard Univ 12 Oxford St Cambridge MA 02138

FRIEND, MIRIAM RUTH, personnel company executive; b. Scranton, Pa., May 19, 1925; d. Benjamin and Etta (Weiss) Loewy; m. Sidney Friend, Aug. 27, 1950. BA, Syracuse U., 1947; cert., Inst. Pub. Welfare Tng. Cornell U., 1950. Social worker Child Placement div. N.Y. State Dept. Welfare, Binghamton and Ithaca, 1948-52; v.p. Office Help Temps., Yonkers, N.Y., 1954-83; pres. Friend & Friend Personnel Agy., Yonkers, N.Y., 1985—. Mem. Eliz Seton Coll. Adv. Council; pres. Pvt. Industry Council, Yonkers, 1981-82, Yonkers Gen. Hosp. Aux., 1983-84, Big Bros./Big Sisters, Yonkers, 1978-80; bd. dirs. Salvation Army, Yonkers, 1977—; publicity chmn. Sen. John E. Flynn Salute, 1986; chmn. breakfast com. Yonkers C. of C., 1978; chmn. Work Opportunities Referral for Kids; chmn.; bd. mem. Community Planning Council; trustee Yonkers Gen. Hosp., 1978—. Recipient Disting. Service award United Way, 1983, Community Service award Yonkers Council of Chs., 1984, Woman in Bus. award YWCA, 1986; named Pioneer of Industry Ind. Office Services, Hilton Head, S.C., 1984. Mem. Assn. Bus. Profl. Women, Psi Chi. Clubs: Racquet, Amackassin (Yonkers). Lodge: Soroptimists (pres. 1970-72), Rotary. Home: 11 Abbey Pl Yonkers NY 10701 Office: Friend & Friend Personnel Agy 480 N Broadway Yonkers NY 10701

FRIEND, SHARLEE BRUCHA FRIEDMAN, retired social worker; b. Chelm, Poland, Jan. 18, 1920; came to U.S., 1921; d. Abe Joseph and Minnie (Shtainman) Friedman; m. Leonard N. Friend, June 7, 1942 (dec.); children—Harold, Geraldine, David Lee, Francine, Barbara. MS, Sam Houston State U., Huntsville, Tex., 1974; MSW, U. Houston, 1977. Cert. social worker. Caseworker, Dept. Pub. Welfare, Houston, 1963-76; social worker Harris County Children's Protective Service, Houston, 1976-85; cons. Women's Success Devel. Ctr., Houston, 1977-80. Tchr. Beth Yeshurun Synagogue, Houston, 1953-64; bd. dirs. Jewish War Veterans Shrine, Washington, 1980-86; mem. nat. exec. bd., pres. Nat. Ladies Aux. Jewish War Veterans, 1985-86; charter mem., chmn. legis. com. Jewish Community Ctr., Braeswood-SW, Tex., 1988—. Mem. Am. Assn. Ret. Persons. Democrat. Lodges: B'nai B'rith Women (chpt. pres. 1961-63, council pres. 1964-65, state pres. 1966-67), Hanna Senesch Hadassah (pres. 1975-76).

FRIER, SHARON BOATWRIGHT, music educator, pianist; b. Valdosta, Ga., Feb. 24, 1942; d. Clifford Eugene and Margaret Louise (Shaw) B.; divorced; children: Laurie Lancaster Swift, John Kevin Lancaster; m. Archie A. Frier. AB in Music, Valdosta State Coll., 1963; MA in Edn., Ea. Ky. U., 1973; cert. Yamaha Music Schs. Am., 1976. Instr. Cumberland Coll., Williamsburg, Ky., 1971-75; dir. music 1st Bapt. Ch., Williamsburg, 1973-75; owner, dir. Music Lab., Valdosta, Ga., 1976-85; instr. music Valdosta State Coll., 1977-85, Troy State U., Moody AFB, 1984-87; pianist Lee St. Bapt. Ch., Valdosta, 1984-87; nurse specialist music Park Ave. Bapt. Sch., Titusville, Fla., 1987—; owner Frier Enterprises, 1987—; lit. meet adjudicator Southeastern Assn. Ind. Schs., 1982, 84. Named to Outstanding Young Women Am., U.S. Jaycees, 1974. Mem. Music Tchrs. Nat. Assn., Ga. Music Tchrs. Assn. (cert., v.p. publicity and editor newsletter 1981-82), South Ga. Music Tchrs. Assn. (pres. 1978-79), Sigma Alpha Chi, Alpha Chi. Democrat. Avocations: sewing, gardening. Home: PO Box 6061 Titusville GA 32782

FRIES, HELEN SERGEANT HAYNES, civic leader; b. Atlanta; d. Harwood Syme and Alice (Hobson) Haynes; student Coll. William and Mary, 1935-38; m. Stuart G. Fries, May 5, 1938. Bd. mem. Community Ballet Assn., Huntsville, Ala., 1968—; mem. nat. nurses aid com. ARC, 1958-59; dir. ARC Aero Club, Eng., 1943-44; supr. ARC Clubmobile, Europe, 1944-46; mem. women's com. Nat. Symphony Orch., Washington, 1959—, chmn. residential fund drive for apts., 1959; bd. dirs. Madison County Republican Club, 1969-70; mem. nat. council Women's Nat. Rep. Club N.Y., 1963—, chmn. hospitality com., 1963-65; bd. mem. League Rep. Women, 1952-61; patron mem., vol. docent Huntsville Mus. Art; vol. docent Weeden House, Twickenham Hist. Preservation Dist. Assn., Inc., Huntsville. Recipient cert. of merit 84th Div., U.S. Army, 1945. Mem. Nat. Soc. Colonial Dames Am., Daus. Am. Colonists, DAR, Nat. Trust Hist. Preservation, Va., Nat., Valley Forge (Pa.), Eastern Shore Va., Huntsville-Madison County hist. socs., Assn. Preservation Va. Antiquities, Greensboro Soc. Preservation, Tenn. Valley Geneal. Soc., Friends of Ala. Archives, AIM, Nat. Soc. Lit. and Arts, English Speaking Union, Turkish-Am. Assn. Clubs: Army-Navy, Washington, Capitol Hill, Army-Navy Country (Washington); Garden (Redstone Arsenal), Redstone (Ala.) Yacht; Huntsville Country, Heritage (Huntsville, Ala.). Home: 409 Zandale Dr Huntsville AL 35801

FRIES, MAUREEN HOLMBERG, English literature educator; b. Buffalo, July 14, 1931; d. Howard Henry and Margaret Teresa (Wiley) Holmberg; children—Jeb Stuart, Howard Gordon, John Pelham, Sheila Maureen. A.B. magna cum laude, D'Youville Coll., 1952; M.A., Cornell U., 1953; Ph.D., SUNY-Buffalo, 1969. Advt. copywriter Eastman Advt. Co., Ithaca, N.Y., 1953-54, Coe Advt. Co., Syracuse, N.Y., 1954; free-lance journalist, Buffalo, 1964-69; teaching fellow SUNY-Buffalo, 1965-69; asst. prof. N.Y. State U. Coll. at Fredonia, 1969-73, assoc. prof., 1973-77, prof. medieval Brit. lit., 1977—; lectr. and cons. in field; participant, chmn. numerous confs. Contbr. articles to profl. jours., chpts. to books; Mem. editorial bds. Avalon to Camelot, 1984—, Interpretations, 1984—. Reader various publs. Recipient Chancellor's award for Excellence in Teaching, 1977, Callista Jones award, 1982; named to Kasling Meml. lectureship State U. of N.Y. Coll. at Fredonia, 1985; NEH fellow, 1975-76; grantee State Univ. of N.Y. Faculty Research awards, 72, 73, 79, 80, Am. Philos. Soc., summer 1978, Am. Council Learned Socs. travel grant, summer 1978, NEH, 1979; Fulbright Research and Lecturing award, sr. professorship Universitat Regensburg, Fed. Republic Germany, Apr.-July 1984, other awards, grants, fellowships. Mem. Am. Classical League, Internat. Assn. Univ. Profs. of English Internat. Courtly Lit. Soc., Medieval Acad. of Am., MLA (chairperson Arthurian Discussion Group ann. meeting Houston 1980, N.Y.C. 1981, mem. exec. com. 1978-82, organizer, chairperson other ann. meetings northeastern and southeastern chpts.), Société Internationale Arthurienne. Democrat. Roman Catholic. Office: New York State Univ Coll at Fredonia 254 Fenton Hall Fredonia NY 14063

FRIMML, JAYMEE JO, chiropractor, nurse; b. Watertown, S.D., Oct. 18, 1949; d. Rodney Elsworth and Marie Ruth (Musta) Dale; m. Steven James Frimml, July 1, 1984; 1 child, Richard Mark. AS in Nursing, So. Coll., Collegedale, Tenn., 1970; student U. Ariz., 1979-81; D. Chiropractic, Palmer Coll. Chiropractic, Davenport, Iowa, 1985. Registered nurse, Tenn., Tex., Okla., Mich., Ariz., Iowa, Idaho. Emergency room nurse Madison Hosp., Tenn., 1970-71; nursing supr. Wilson N. Jones Hosp., Sherman, Tex., 1972-74; neonatal nurse specialist Lansing Gen. Hosp., Mich., 1974-78; clin. nurse leader, pediatrics Tucson Med. Ctr., 1978-81, pulmonary nurse specialist, 1981-82; chiropractor Cramer Chiropractice Clinic, Boise, Idaho, 1986; owner, operator Chiropractic Ctr., 1986—. Contbr. biweekly articles Idaho Press Tribune. Bd. dirs. Seventh-day Adventist Better Living Com., Caldwell, Idaho, 1986. Mem. Am. Chiropractice Assn., Internat. Chiropractic Assn., Council on Roentgenology, Idaho Assn. Chiropractice Physicians (mem. polit. action com.), Nampa C. of C., Sigma Phi Chi (legis. com.). Seventh-day Adventist. Lodge: Soroptimists. Home: 3613 Juanita Way Nampa ID 83651 Office: Chiropractic Ctr 228 Holly St Nampa ID 83651

FRIST, JANE ELIZABETH, real estate agent; b. Richmond, Va., Jan. 26, 1935; d. Chester and Lois Elizabeth Frist; m. Arnold Cornelius Harms (div. 1978); children: Jane Alden, John David, Robert Dale. BA, Agnes Scott Coll., 1956; postgrad., Princeton Theol. Sem., 1956-59; Cert. Elem. Edn., U. Denver, 1968. Tchr. Madison Nursery Sch., 1964-67, Univ. Park Elem., Denver, 1967-73; sub. tchr. Denver Pub. Schs., 1973-78; real estate agt. Russ Wehner Realty, Denver, 1977-78, Moore and Co., Denver, 1978-80, ReMax Real Estate, Denver, 1980-82, Merrill Lynch Realty, Orlando, Fla., 1982—; judge Parade of Homes, Orlando, 1985—. Illustrator: (book) No Wings in the Manse, 1955; illustrator, writer of stories, poetry mag. Aurora, 1952-56. Elder Montview Presbyn. Ch., Denver, 1976-79, 1st Presbyn. Ch. Orlando, Fla., 1986—. Mem. Orlando-Winter Park Bd. of Realtors, Merrill Lynch 3 Million Leading Edge Soc. Republican. Club: Orlando Country. Home: 2824 Waymeyer Dr Orlando FL 32812 Office: Merrill Lynch Realty 211 E Colonial Dr Orlando FL 32801

FRITTS, KAREN IRWIN, mortgage company manager; b. Parsons, Kans., Nov. 30, 1946; d. Ralph Edward and Bernice Irene (Murray) Irwin; m. William E. Fritts Jr., Apr. 24, 1965; 1 child, Timothy Matthew. Grad. high sch., Topeka, 1964. Proof operator SW State Bank and Tr., Topeka, 1964-68, Cen. Nat. Bank, Junction City, Kans., 1966; ops. mgr. Lauterbach Realty, Inc., Topeka, 1969-77; sr. mortgage lending officer People's Fedl. Savs. and Loan, Topeka, 1977-82; counselor System 3, A Trust, Topeka, 1982-85; br. mgr. First Union Home Equity Corp., Topeka, 1985—. Active Topeka PTA, 1978-80; campaign vol. Slattery for Congress, Topeka, 1982. Mem. Women' s Council Realtors (treas. 1987), Topeka Home Builders Assn., Topeka Profl. Remodelers Council (v. chmn. 1986—). Democrat. Episcopalian. Home: 5740 SW Fairlawn Rd Topeka KS 66619 Office: First Union Home Equity Corp 2930 S Wanamaker Dr Topeka KS 66614

FRITZ, BARBARA HUGHES, lawyer; b. Rusk County, Tex., Feb. 11, 1928; d. Charles Allen and O'Dell (Harris) Hughes; m. Richard J. Fritz, June 14, 1952; children—Catherine, Maranda. B.B.A., U. Houston, 1974, J.D., 1977. Bar: Tex. 1977; cert. family law Tex. Bd. Legal Specialization. Product mgr. Johns-Manville Sales Corp., Houston, 1956-66; creative dir. copy Madison Advt., Inc., Louisville, 1968-71; store mgr. Spalding Services, Inc., Louisville, 1971-73; ptnr. Fritz & Fritz, Victoria, Tex., 1977-87; ct. master 4th Adminstrv. Jud. Dist. Tex., 1987—. Mem. Tex. Bar Assn., Assn. Trial Lawyers Am., Order Barons, Phi Kappa Phi. Address: PO Box 4626 Victoria TX 77903

FRITZ, ETHEL MAE HENDRICKSON, writer; b. Gibbon, Nebr., Feb. 4, 1925; d. Walter Earl and Alice Hazel (Mickish) Hendrickson; BS, Iowa State U., 1949; m. C. Wayne Fritz, Feb. 25, 1950; children—Linda Sue, Krista Jane. Dist. home economist Internat. Harvester Co., Des Moines, 1949-50; writer Wallace's Farmer mag., Des Moines, 1960-64; free-lance writer, 1960—. Chmn. Ariz. Council Flower Show Judges, 1983-85. Accredited master flower show judge. Mem. Women in Communications (pres. Phoenix profl. chpt.; nat. task force com. 1980—), Am. Soc. Profl. and Exec. Women, Am. Home Econs. Assn., SW Writers' Conf., Ariz. Authors Assn., Phi Upsilon Omicron, Kappa Delta. Republican. Methodist. Club: PEO. Author: The Story of an Amana Winemaker, 1984, Prairie Kitchen Sampler, 1988.

FRITZ, FORREST MAE, state official; b. Fulton, Ohio, Aug. 21, 1929; d. Clarence Robert and Anna Ella (Liggett) Skinner; m. Jerrold Eli Fritz, Aug. 20, 1954; children—Frederic Allen, Jeri Anne, Teri Anne. Student pub. schs., Cardington, Ohio. Sec. Hydraulic Press Mfg., Mt. Gilead, Ohio, 1947-53, Waring Enterprises, Delaware Water Gap, Pa., 1953-55; sec. Office Employment Security, Stroudsburg, Pa., 1962-69, claims interviewer, 1969, unemployment compensation supr., 1969—. Mem. Am. Mgmt. Assn., Bus. and Profl. Women of Stroudsburg (newsletter editor 1983-84, treas. 1984-85, 2d v.p. 1985-86). Republican. Methodist. Home: 181 Analomink St East Stroudsburg PA 18301 Office: Office Employment Security 730 Phillips St Stroudsburg PA 18360

FRITZ, JEAN GUTTERY, writer; b. Hankow, People's Republic China, Nov. 16, 1915; d. Arthur Minton and Myrtle (Chaney) Guttery; m. Michael Fritz, Nov. 1, 1941; children: David, Andrea. BA, Wheaton Coll., Norton, Mass., 1937, LittD (hon.), 1987; LittD (hon.), Washington and Jefferson Coll., 1982. Author: Fish Head, 1954, The Late Spring, 1957, The Animals of Doctor Schweitzer, 1958, The Cabin Faced West, 1958, How to Read a Rabbit, 1958, Brady, 1960, I, Adam, 1963, Magic to Burn, 1964, Early Thunder, 1967, George Washington's Breakfast, 1969, Cast for a Revolution, 1972, And Then What Happened, Paul Revere?, 1973, Why Don't You Get a Horse, Sam Adams?, 1974, Where Was Patrick Henry on the 29th of May?, 1975, Who's that Stepping on Plymouth Rock?, 1975, Will You Sign Here, John Hancock?, 1976, The Secret Diary of Jeb and Abigail, 1976, What's the Big Idea, Ben Franklin?, 1976, Can't You Make Them Behave, King George?, 1977, Brendon the Navigator, 1979, Stonewall, 1979, Where Do You Think You're Going, Christopher Columbus?, 1980, The Man Who Loved Books, 1981, Traitor: The Case of Benedict Arnold, 1981, The Good Giants and the Bad Pukwudgies, 1981, Homesick: My Own Story, 1982 (Am. Book award 1983, Child Study Book award 1983, Honor Book, Newberry Medal Book 1983), China Homecoming, 1985, The Double Life of Pocahontas, 1983 (Boston Globe/Horn Book award 1984), Make Way for Sam Houston, 1986 (Western Writers award 1987), Shh! We're Writing the Constitution, 1987. Recipient Christopher award Cath. Library Assn., 1982, Regina Medal Cath. Library Assn., 1985, Laura Ingalls Wilder award ALA, 1986. Home: 50 Bellewood Ave Dobbs Ferry NY 10522

FRITZ, JOANNE LEE (JONI), association executive; b. Bklyn., May 5, 1936; d. Theodore Roosevelt and Josephine (Chandler) L.; m. John D. Allen Jr., June 16, 1956 (div. Jan. 1970); children: John D. III, Cynthia Allen de Ramos, Victoria Lee Burnett; m. Nicholas Fritz Jr., July 4, 1970. Student, Cornell U., 1954-56; BA in Sociology with distinction, George Washington U., 1971. Tchr. Enon Elem. Sch., Chester, Va., 1958-59; med. records analyst Fairax (Va.) Hosp., 1962-66; med. asst. Drs. Apter and Morrissey Ltd., 1966-72; assoc. dir. Nat. Assn. Pvt. Residential Resources, Falls Church, Va., 1972-76, exec. dir., 1976—; panelist Office Human Devel. HHS,

1980-83; speaker pvt. residential services nat. and state confs.; sec. Consortium for Citizens with Devel. Disabilities, 1974-82, chmn. housing task force, 1983-85, chmn. staff wage and hour task force, 1986—; mem. steering com. Forum on Long Term Care, Washington, 1979—; bd. dirs. Accreditation Council for Services to Mentally Retarded and other Developmentally Disabled Persons, 1979-80; mem. adv. panels various orgns. Author, editor, Links, 1976—. Trustee Commn. on Accreditation of Rehab. Facilities, 1984—. Mem. Am. Assn. Mental Retardation, Assn. Retarded Citizens, Nat. Head Injury Found., Nat. Assn. Women Execs. Office: Nat Assn Pvt Residential Facilities Mentally Handicapped 6400 H 7 Corners Pl Falls Church VA 22044

FRITZ, WENDY LEE, human resources, personnel administrator; b. Milw., Mar. 5, 1961; d. Robert Dean and Sheila Kay (Hodgson) Schmidt; m. Thomas Joseph Fritz, Aug. 13, 1983. BA in English, U. Wis., Milw., 1983. Documentation specialist Aardvark Pub./McGraw-Hill, Milw., 1984, personnel adminstr., 1984-86; corp. personnel mgr. Roadrunner Freight Systems, Milw., 1986-88; sr. employment rep. Fleet Mortgage Corp., Milw., 1988—. Mem. Am. Soc. Personnel Adminstrs., Internat. Assn. Personnel Women (bd. dirs.), Personnel-Indsl. Relations Assn. Wis. (various coms.), Nat. Assn. Female Execs. Home: 726 Sherman Way West Bend WI 53095 Office: Roadrunner Freight Systems 2040 W Oklahoma Milwaukee WI 53215

FRITZE, ELIZABETH BLACKMAN, writer, consultant; b. Woodbury, N.J., Oct. 24, 1934; d. Hilmar A. and Elizabeth (Smith) F. BA, Randolph-Macon Woman's Coll., Lynchburg, Va., 1957; MEd, U. Va., 1971. Cert. tchr., guidance counselor. Tchr., counselor pub. schs., Del., Pa. and N.J., 1957-73; supr. Pitney Bowes, Stamford, Ct., 1973-78; sr. tech. writer Exxon Office Systems, Florham Park, N.J., 1978-80; cons. Gen. Electric Info. Services, Piscataway, N.J., 1981-82; ind. cons. Budd Lake, N.J., 1982—; panel speaker Pratt Computer Graphics Conf., N.Y., 1987. Mem. Nat. Assn. Female Execs. Office: 100 U S Hwy 46 Suite 56-A Budd Lake NJ 07828

FRITZE, SHEILA KAY, librarian; b. Belleville, Ill., Oct. 31, 1949; d. Orel Emil and Louise Elizabeth (Zimmerman) Boos; m. James Ronald Fritze, June 17, 1972; children: Elizabeth Ann, Julia Louise. AA, Belleville Area Coll., 1969; BS, U. Ill., 1971, MS, 1972. Librarian, Wellington Community Sch. Dist. (Ill.), 1972-74, Crescent City Pub. Library, 1975-82, Eagle Valley Elem. Sch. (Colo.), 1983—. Pres. Eagle Valley Elem. sch. PTA, 1987-88; Sunday sch. supt. 1st Luth. Ch. of Gypsum, Colo., 1986—. Named Dist. Clubwoman of Yr., 8th Dist. Ill. Jr. Woman's Club, 1980. Mem. Colo. Ednl. Media Assn., Friends of the Library, Beta Phi Mu, Kappa Delta Phi. Republican. Lutheran. Clubs: Eagle Dandelion (pres. 1985-86), Crescent City Jr. Women's (sec. 1979-81). Home: 0400 Camino Dorado PO Box 985 Eagle CO 81631 Office: Eagle Valley Elem Sch PO Box 780 Eagle CO 81631

FRIZZELL, LUCILLE BRIDGERS, librarian; b. Yazoo City, Miss., Dec. 17, 1925; d. Thomas Alfred Bridgers and Maie Hollingsworth; m. Byron Waters Frizzell, July 24, 1952; children: Peter Graham, David Edward, Mark Dillard. BS, East Tenn. State U., 1977, MS, 1980. Cert. secondary tchr., Tenn. Sec. U.S. Steel Corp., 1946-53; librarian Steed Coll., Johnson City, 1980-82, Bristol Coll., Johnson City, 1982-84, Draughons Jr. Coll., Johnson City, 1984—. Charter mem. Washington County Hist. Soc., 1987—. Mem. Tenn. Library Assn., Boone Tree Library Assn. (v.p. 1986-87), Tenn. Audio-Visual Assn., Tri-Cities Area Health Scis. Library Consortium, DAR (treas. Johnson City chpt. 1959-60), Nat. Soc. So. Dames (v.p. East Tenn. chpt. 1986-88), Watauga Assn. Genealogists (charter mem.). Republican. Baptist. Club: Monday (Johnson City). Home: 1111 Southwest Ave Johnson City TN 37604 Office: Draughons Jr Coll 2220 College Dr Johnson City TN 37602

FRIZZI, VIRGINIA AGNES, college official, writer; b. Pitts., Nov. 20, 1953; d. Joseph Nicholas and Virginia Lourdes (Sheehan) Frizzi, Sr. B.A., Point Park Coll., 1975, M.A., 1984; postgrad. U. Pitts., 1977-81. Freelance writer, Pitts., 1975—; dir. media relations and pub. relations Point Park Coll., Pitts., 1976—; book reviewer Pitts. Press, 1981—. Contbr. articles and revs. to publs. including S.C. Monitor, Seventeen mag. Mem. pub. relations com. Am. Cancer Soc. of Western Pa., Pitts. Planned Parenthood. Mem. Women in Communications (pres. Pitts. 1982-83, Matrix award 1983), Soc. Profl. Journalists (treas. Pitts. 1977—, rep. to Pitts. Press Club Golden Quill competition com. 1981-82, 85-88, nat. freedom of info. and profl. chpt. devel. com. 1983—, asst. dir. for Western Pa.), Pitts. Press Club, Women's Press Club Pitts., Nat. Fedn. Press Women. Home: 1715 Chislett St Pittsburgh PA 15206 Office: Office of Media Relations Point Park Coll 201 Wood St Pittsburgh PA 15222

FROEHLICH, EDNA BORG, psychologist,educator; b. Union City, N.J., July 28, 1918; d. Adolph Franz and Anna Lena (Frese) Borg; m. Paul Edward Froehlich, June 27, 1944; children: Pauline, Kathleen, Linda. BA cum laude, Montclair (N.J.) State Coll., 1939; MA in Psychology, Columbia U., 1956, EdD in Psychology, 1970. Lic. psychologist, N.J. Tchr. high sch. N.J., 1939-60; instr. psychology Fairleigh Dickinson U., Teaneck, N.J., 1959-60; reading cons., sch. psychologist Palisades Park (N.J.) Pub. Schs., 1962-69; clin. psychologist Columbia-Presbyn. Med. Ctr., N.Y.C., summer 1966; instr. psychology Bergen Community Coll., Paramus, N.J., 1970-71; sch. psychologist Glen Rock (N.J.) Pub. Schs., 1970-72, dir. spl. services, 1972-84; pvt. practice psychology Tenafly, N.J., 1973—; speaker, cons. schs. and orgns. N.J., 1970—; coordinator Spl. Edn. Adv. Bd. for Region IV, Bergen County, N.J., 1975-76, 78-79. Author memory designs test. Hon. v.p. Glen Rock Spl. Edn. PTA, 1972-84. Mem. Am. Psychol. Assn., N.J. Psychol. Assn. (emeritus), N.J. Assn. Sch. Psychologists (life), N.J. Acad. Psychology (Psychologists Recognition award 1985), Glen Rock Adminstrs. Assn. (pres. 1979-80), Bergen County Assn. Lic. Psychologists, Bergen County Assn. Sch. Psychologists (pres. 1972-73). Home and Office: 208 Engle St Tenafly NJ 07670

FROHMAN, CAROLE JOAN, interior designer, appraiser; b. Bklyn., July 22, 1930; d. Arthur and Shirley R. (Kaplan) Frohman; m. Harvey Wiener, May 22, 1955 (div. June 1964); 1 child, Byron. B.S. in Elem. Edn., Barnard Coll., 1950; postgrad. Ohio State U., 1957-58; student Frank LaForge, Estelle Liebling, William Herman, Alberto Digoristiaga. Child prodigy, performing most of maj. concert halls of world; apprentice Ruby Ross Wood-Billy Baldwin Interior Design Co., 1949-51, assoc. designer, 1951-53; now pres. Carole Frohman Interior Design, North Miami, Fla.; dir. design, Swissco Corp., 1988. Fund raiser Dem. party, Boston, 1946; entertainer USO, 1943-45, VA Hosp., Miami, Fla., 1972-75. Contbg. author, co-editor cook book to raise funds for ARC. Juilliard Prep. Sch. scholar, 1941; named Most Talented Newcomer Am. Motion Pictures, 1946. Mem. Nat. Home Fashions League (v.p. program com. 1982-85), Am. Soc. Interior Design, Profl. Antique Dealers Assn., Internat. Soc. Interior Design, Nat. Acad. Theater Arts and Scis., NOW, SAG, AGVA, AFTRA. Democrat. Avocation: voice coaching. Home: 11960 NE 19th Dr #15 North Miami FL 33181 Office: Carole Frohman Interior Design 11960 NE 19th Dr #15 No 11960 NE 19th Dr #15 N Miami FL 33181

FROMER, MARGOT JOAN, writer; b. N.Y.C., Aug. 30, 1939; d. Maurice Mordechai and Beatrice Constance (Neuman) F. BS, Boston U., 1961; MA, Columbia U., 1964, MEd, 1967; doctoral student in philosophy, Georgetown U., 1980-81. Asst. prof. Rutgers U., Camden, N.J., 1974-78, U. Del., Newark, 1978-80; pres. Fromer Writing and Editing Service, Silver Spring, Md., 1980-87; co-pub., sr. editor Phillips-Neuman Co., Bethesda, Md.; feature writer Emergency Dept. News, N.Y.C., 1981-82; adj. prof. Am. Univ., Washington, 1983; cons. Resource Applications, Balt., 1982-84; contbg. editor The Washington Blade, 1983-84; contbr. newsletter of Am. Inst. Cancer Research, Falls Ch., Va., 1983—; lectr. in healthcare field; appearances on TV and Radio; mgr. 12 credit course for 13 faculty mems. and 9 health agys., U. Del. Author: Community Health Care and the Nursing Process, 1979, 2d edit. 1983, Ethical Issues in Health Care, (Book of Yr. award Am. Jour. Nursing), 1981, Ethical Issues in Sexuality and Reproduction, (Book of Yr. award Am. Jour. Nursing), 1983, (with Frances G. Conn) How to Quit Smoking in 30 Days---Without Cracking Up, 1982, "Instructors Guide" for Fundamentals of Nursing, 1983, AIDS: Acquired Immune Deficiency Syndrome, 1983, Menopause, 1985, Osteoporosis, 1986; author numerous articles for newspapers, profl. jours., pamphlets, reference books, others; sr. editor and co-pub. Phillips-Neuman Co., Bethesda, Md.; editor (monograph) Ethical Issues in Health Administrn., Assn. Univ. Programs in Health Adminstrn., (final report) Financing Grad. Medical Edn., Arthur Young Co. and HHS; manuscript reviewer C.V. Mosby Co., Appleton-Century-Crofts, Pubs., Resource Applications, Inc., Addison-Wesley Pub. Co. NEH grantee, 1979, C.V. Mosby grantee, 1980. Mem. ACLU, Am. Soc. Journalists and Authors, Lit. Friends of D.C. Library (exec. com. 1985—, sec. 1986—), NOW, Nat. Women's Health Network, Authors Guild, Washington Ind. Writers, Women and Health Roundtable. Democrat. Jewish.

FROMM, ERIKA (MRS. PAUL FROMM), clinical psychologist; b. Frankfurt, Germany, Dec. 23, 1910; came to U.S., 1938, naturalized, 1944; d. Siegfried and Clementine (Stern) Oppenheimer; m. Paul Fromm, July 20, 1938; 1 child, Joan (Mrs. Greenstone). Ph.D. magna cum laude, U. Frankfurt, 1933; postgrad. child care program, Chgo. Inst. for Psychoanalysis, 1949-51. Diplomate: Am. Bd. Examiners in Profl. Psychology, Am. Bd. Examiners Clin. Hypnosis. Chief psychologist Apeldoorn State Hosp., Holland, 1935-38; chief psychologist Francis W. Parker Sch., 1944-51; supervising psychologist Inst. for Juvenile Research, 1951-53; asst. prof. to assoc. prof. Northwestern U. Med. Sch., 1954-61; prof. U. Chgo., 1961-76, prof. emeritus, 1976—. Author: (with L.D. Hartman) Intelligence-A Dynamic Approach; (with Thomas M. French) Dream Interpretation: A New Approach, 1964, 2d edit., 1986; (with Ronald E. Shor) Hypnosis: Developments in Research and New Perspectives, 1972, 2d edit., 1979; (with Daniel P. Brown) Hypnotherapy and Hypnoanalysis, 1986; (with Daniel Brown) Hypnosis and Behavioral Medicine, 1987; also numerous articles in profl. jours.; mem. editorial bd. Jour. Clin. and Exptl. Psychopathology, 1951-59; clin. editor: Internat. Jour. Clin. and Exptl. Hypnosis, 1968—; assoc. editor Bull. Brit. Soc. Exptl. and Clin. Hypnosis, 1982—; mem. bd. cons. editors Psychoanalytic Psychology, 1982-88; mem. adv. bd. editors Imagination, Cognition and Personality: Sci. study of Consciousness, 1981—. Numerous scientific awards. Fellow Am. Psychol. Assn. (pres. div. 30 1972-73, Psychoanalysis award 1985), Am. Orthopsychiat. Assn. (dir. 1961-63), AAAS, Soc. Clin. Exptl. Hypnosis (sec. 1965-67,v.p. 1971-75, pres. 1975-77, Best Research Paper award 1965, Arthur Shapiro award 1973, Best Clin. Paper award 1986, Best Book Pub. in the Field of Hypnosis award 1987); mem. Am. Bd. Psychol. Hypnosis (pres. 1971-74), Ill. Psychol. Assn. (council 1951-53, 55-57, bd. examiners 1959-62, v.p. bd. examiners 1960-61), Soc. Projective Techniques, Am. Bd. Examiners in Psychol. Hypnosis (Morton Price award 1970), Nat. Acad. Practice in Psychology (Disting. Practitioner in Psychology 1982), Sigma Xi. Home: 5715 S Kenwood Ave Chicago IL 60637 Office: U Chgo Dept Behavioral Scis Chicago IL 60637

FROMMELT, KATHERINE HELEN MURRAY, nurse; b. Lancaster, Wis., Sept. 7, 1947; d. William Roy and Ivanelle Patricia (Key) Murray; m. David John Frommelt, Jan. 25, 1969; children—Sean J., Jennifer L., Bridget A., Molly K. and Meghan C. (twins). R.N., Mercy Med. Ctr. Sch. Nursing, 1968; B.S.N., U. Dubuque, 1983, postgrad., 1984—. Staff nurse for psychol. mental health U. Wis. Hosp., Madison, 1968-69; instr. Sch. Nursing, Mercy Med. Ctr., Dubuque, Iowa, 1969-70, inservice edn. dir., 1969-70; nursing vol. instr., coordinator Hospice of Dubuque, 1982—, bd. dirs., 1983—, chairperson, 1986—; nurse of hope Iowa div. Am. Cancer Soc., 1983—; occupational health program dir. Frommelt Industries, Dubuque, 1985—. Bd. dirs., mem. pub. relations and legis. action com. Mercy Med. Ctr., Dubuque, 1983—; mem. St. Joseph's Sch. Bd. Edn., Dubuque, 1984—, pres., 1985—. Recipient Vol. Health Service award Iowa Med. Soc. Aux., 1985, Outstanding Vol. award Am. Cancer Soc., 1985, Mercy Med. Ctr. Disting. Alumni award, 1986. Mem. Sigma Theta Tau. Roman Catholic. Clubs: Iowa State Mothers of Twins (state rep. 1982-83); Dubuqueland Mothers of Twins (pres. 1980-82, adv. bd. 1983—), Sertoma (Service to Mankind award Dubuque 1984). Home: 995 Prince Phillip Dr Dubuque IA 52001

FRONK, RHONDA BETH, accountant; b. Liberal, Kans., Sept. 8, 1956; d. Ronald Solomon and Margaret Belle (Williams) F. BA in Edn. magna cum laude, Oral Roberts U., 1979. Trust officer First Nat. Bank, Liberal, 1978-79; tchr. Tyrone (Okla.) Pub. Schs., 1979-80; staff acct. Leming and Thomas, CPA's, Tulsa, 1981-85, Sparks & Chancey, CPA's, Fort Smith, Ark., 1985-87; asst. controller Kennedy & Noel Devel., Phoenix, Ariz., 1987; internal auditor North Phoenix Bapt. Ch., 1987—. Contbr. articles to local newspapers and nat. publs., 1984-87. Exec. dir. Big Bros./Big Sisters, Inc., Liberal, 1980; activities chmn. 1st United Meth. Singles Club, L.I.V.E. Singles Club, Fort Smith, 1982-87; lighting supr. Theatre Tulsa, 1984-85; vol. ch. youth worker, 1987—. Mem. Gospel Music Assn., U.S. Golf Assn. Republican. Baptist. Home: 15402 N 28th St Suite 129 Phoenix AZ 85032 Office: N Phoenix Bapt Ch 5757 N Central Ave Phoenix AZ 85012

FRONTIERE-ROSENBLUM, GEORGIA, professional football team executive; m. Carroll Rosenblum, July 7, 1966 (dec.); children: Dale Carroll, Lucia; m. Dominic Frontiere. Pres. Los Angeles Rams, NFL, 1979—. Bd. dirs. Los Angeles Boys and Girls Club, Los Angeles Orphanage Guild, Los Angeles Blind Youth Found. Named Headliner of Yr., Los Angeles Press Club, 1981. Office: Los Angeles Rams 2327 W Lincoln Ave Anaheim CA 92801 *

FRONVILLE, CLAIRE LOUISE, museum administrator, consultant; b. Seattle, Apr. 17, 1956; d. Ralph Jean-Marie and Louise Mary (Heidenreich) F.; m. Gerard Nicholas Giovaniello, Oct. 4, 1981. BA, Wellesley Coll., 1978; MBA, Georgetown U., 1984. Legis. researcher Congressman Les AuCoin, Washington, 1978-79, Com. on Merchant Marine and Fisheries U.S. House of Reps., Washington, 1979-82; mgmt. intern GTE Corp., Washington, 1983; pvt. practive mktg. cons. Washington, 1984; assoc. dir. for communications Smithsonian Instn. Traveling Exhbn. Service, Washington, 1984-86, assoc. dir., 1987—; career cons. Georgetown U. Sch. of Bus., Washington, 1984—. Named Durant Scholar Wellesley Coll., 1978. Mem. Am. Assn. Mus., Phi Beta Kappa. Democrat. Office: Smithsonian Instn 1100 Jefferson Dr SW Room 3146 Washington DC 20560

FROOKS, DOROTHY, lawyer, author; b. Saugerties, N.Y.; d. Reginald and Rosita (Siberez) F.; LL.B., Hamilton Coll., 1918, LL.M., 1919; spl. courses Harvard U., N.Y. U., St. Lawrence U., U. N.C. Law Sch., Tulane U., Duquesne U.; Ps.D., Nat. Inst. Psychology, 1946; student Indsl. Coll. Armed Forces, 1953. Admitted to N.Y. State bar, 1920, U.S. Customs Ct., 1932, U.S. Supreme Ct., 1934, Fed. bar P.R., 1925, Alaska bar, 1935, Calif. bar, 1926, La. bar, 1929, U.S. Ct. Claims, 1950, U.S. Ct. Mil. Appeals, 1954, Hawaii bar, 1958, C.Z. bar, 1959; atty. Salvation Army, N.Y.C., 1920-21; organizer Poor Man's Ct., 1921; atty. for com. U.S. Coast Guard, 1939-40; counsel N.Y. State Bd. Edn., 1940-41; owner, editor Public Service Record, N.Y.C., 1920-21; pub. Murray Hill News, Oyster Bay News, 1916-19; columnist N.Y. Evening World, 1929-32; del. 1st Inter-Am. Bar Conf., Havana, 1921, Internat. Law Conf., Oxford, Eng., 1932, Atty. Gen.'s Crime Congress, Washington, 1934, Gov.'s Crime Conf., Albany, 1935; candidate for Congress-at-large State N.Y., 1934; nat. judge adv. Vets. of World War I, Inc., 1969; arbitrator Small Claims Ct., 1970—. Served as chief yeoman U.S. Navy in charge woman enrollments and recruiting, World War I; served in Judge Adv. Office, U.S. Army, World War II. Recipient medal for patriotic service by Woodrow Wilson, 1918. Mem. Nat. Assn. Woman Lawyers (organizer, pres. 1921-22, chmn. mil. and naval law com. 1946), Nat. Aero. Assn., Am. Judicature Assn., Wis. Archaeol. Soc., Am. Bar Assn., N.Y. State Bar Assn., Westchester County Bar Assn., Inter-Am. Bar, Women of Greater N.Y. (pres.), Murray Hill Assn. (pres.), Iota Tau Tau, Epsilon Eta Phi. Presbyterian. Clubs: Westchester Jr. League, Eastern Star, Peekskill Country (dir.). Author: The American Heart, 1919; Civilization, 1922; Criminal Obscenity, 1923; Chronology of the Catholic Church; Loves Law, 1927; Wills and Estates, 1929; All in Love, 1932; Over the Heads of Congress, 1935; Portia on Horseback, 1943; The Olympic Torch, 1946; Girls Get Their Men, 1947; How to Use the Small Claims Court, 1979; Wills, 1981; Lady Lawyer, 1975; Labor Courts-Outlaw Strikes, 1984; Poisoned with Power, 1986. Office: Route 6 Lake Mohegan Peekskill NY 10547 Law Office: 237 Madison Ave New York NY 10016

FROST, CAROL SHIRLEY, manufacturing company executive; b. Boston, Oct. 1, 1929; d. Charles J. and Agnes R. (Carroll) Popp; student Boston schs.; m. Donald Frost, Oct. 15, 1949 (dec.); children—Donald, Lorraine, Charles, Linda; m. 2d John M. Marenghi, Oct. 3, 1982. Pres., owner Klarmann Rulings, Inc., Waltham, Mass., 1960-76, Manchester and Litchfield, N.H., 1976—. Mem. Soc. Photog. Scientists and Engrs. Office: Bancroft Hwy Route 3A Litchfield NH 03108

FROST, FELICIA DODEE, brokerage firm executive; b. Oklahoma City, Oct. 19, 1956; d. Carl S. Frost and Mikki (Matheny) Marcus. Student So. Meth. U., 1974-76. Gen. mgr. Keystone Readers Service, Dallas, 1976-80; adminstrv. mgr then asst. v.p. Merrill Lynch Pierce Fenner and Smith, Dallas, 1980—. Pub. Frost Reading and Math Program, 1979. Mem. Dallas Securities Dealers Assn., Nat. Assn. Securities Dealers (gen. securities prin., mcpl. securities rulemaking bd. prin., registered options prin.), Alpha Lambda Delta. Republican. Mem. Unity Ch. of Christianity. Home: 5590 Spring Valley St Unit C 207 Dallas TX 75240 Office: Merrill Lynch Pierce Fenner and Smith 2000 Premier Place 5910 N Central Expressway Dallas TX 75206

FROST, ROSE KOBEL, library executive; b. Saginaw, Mich., Jan. 20, 1950; d. Philip Raymond and Angeline Alice (Brink) Grybowski; m. Lawrence J. Frost, Jan. 23, 1988. AA, Delta Coll., 1969; BA, Mich. State U., 1971; MA, U. S. Fla., 1977. Cert. permanent profl. librarian, Mich. Library aide, librarian Orlando Pub. Library, Fla., 1973-78; sales rep. Baker & Taylor, Momence, Ill., 1978-81; pub. relations officer Saginaw Pub. Library, 1981-83; librarian Delta Coll., University Center, Mich., 1983-85; supr. user services Grace Dow Library, Midland, Mich., 1985-88; exec. dir. Presque Isle County Library, Rogers City, Mich., 1988—; chmn. Video Cassettes in Pub. Libraries Conf., 1986. Chmn. networking YWCA, Bay City, Mich., 1985; trustee Carrollton (Mich.) Pub. Schs., 1985-88. Mem. ALA, Mich. Library Assn. (pub. relations com. 1981-84, chmn. intellectual freedom com. 1985-87, presenter Best of Show awards 1984, panel mem. conf. 1984), AAUW (newsletter editor 1983-84). Clubs: Welcome Aboard; Bay City Networking (chmn. 1985). Avocations: classical music, theater, travel, swimming, reading.

FRUEAUF, MARY LOUIS, insurance company executive; b. Biddeford, Maine, Apr. 16, 1945; d. Edward Francis and Mary Louise (Gallagher) Byrnes; m. Alezander Frueauf, June 18, 1966; children: Lara Louise, Christopher George. BE, Wheelock Coll., 1966; cert., Perdue Mgmt. Inst., 1987. Tchr. Los Angeles City Schs., 1966-67; career cons. Alco Tech., Torrance, Calif., 1967; entertainment and women's editor Gardena (Calif.) Valley News, 1967-79; regional dir. of N.H., Maine, and Vt. Colonial Life and Accident Ins. Co., Columbia, S.C., 1976—. Mem. Nat. Assn. Life Underwriters, Nat. Assn. Female Execs. Home: 57 Maidstone Dr Merrimack NH 03054 Office: Colonial Life and Accident Ins Co 10 Northern Blvd Amherst NH 03031

FRUHMANN, KAREN ANNE, laboratory administrator; b. Orange, N.J.; d. Robert Whitin and Anna (Harvey) Mullin; B.A. magna cum laude in Psychology and Biology, William Paterson Coll., 1974; cert. med. tech. St. Mary's Hosp., 1975; M.S. summa cum laude in Med. Tech., Fairleigh Dickinson U., 1977; postgrad. Southeastern U., 1982-85. Cert. bioanalyst, clin. lab. dir. Am. Bd. Bioanalysis. Biochemistry technologist Raritan Valley Hosp., Greenbrook N.J., 1975-76; asst. supr. enzymology, tech. writer quality assurance, diagnostic researcher, chemistry adminstr. Warner Lambert Gen. Diagnostics, Morris Plains, N.J., 1976-78; dir. lab. services Kessler Inst. for Rehab. W. Orange, N.J., 1979—. Mem. Am. Soc. Clin. Pathologists (affiliate mem.), N.Y. Acad. Scis., Am. Soc. Med. Tech., N.J. Soc. Med. Tech., Assn. for Women in Sci., Nat. Certification Agy. (clin. lab. scientist), Alpha Mu Tau. Presbyterian. Contbr. articles on hematology to profl. jours. Office: Kessler Inst 1199 Pleasant Valley Way West Orange NJ 07052

FRUITT, LISA JAN, corporate communications director; b. Boston, Jan. 13, 1958; d. Paul N. and Myrna L (Shufro) F. BA with high honors, Brandeis U., 1979; MS, Boston U., 1983. Visitor services asst. John F. Kennedy Library, Boston, 1979-80, pub. relations coordinator, 1980-81; cons. pub. relations The Beacon Cos., Boston, 1983-84; dir. communications Beacon Hotel Corp., Boston, 1984—; bd. dirs. Friends of John F. Kennedy Library, Boston, 1983—. Office: Beacon Hotel Corp 30 Rowes Wharf Boston MA 02110

FRUMBERG, GLORIA, marketing executive; b. N.Y.C., Mar. 26, 1927; d. Joseph Morris and Ruth Sarah (Berlinger) Grossman; student public schs.; m. Ira Herbert Frumberg, May 15, 1949; children—Lawrence Lee, Charles Iver. Sec. public relations mfg. co., 1946-49; asst. advt. and promotions dir. mfg. corp., 1949-51; dist. mgr. World Book Ency., 1962-70; nat. mktg. mgr. Ency. Brit., Atlantic Beach, N.Y., 1970—. Pink Lady vol. Long Beach (N.Y.) Meml. Hosp., 1961-63; former pres. South Shore chpt. Kidney Found. N.Y. Mem. Women's Direct Response Group (pres. N.Y. chpt. 1980-81), Direct Mktg. Assn., Direct Mktg. Club of N.Y. Office: PO Box 57 Atlantic Beach NY 11509

FRUTH, BERYL ROSE, physician; b. Carey, Ohio, Mar. 27, 1952; d. Oscar W. and Alice (Arnett) Fruth. BA in Chemistry magna cum laude, Asbury Coll., 1973; MD, Ohio State U., 1977. Diplomate Am. Acad. Family Practice. Intern Grant Hosp., Columbus, Ohio, 1977-78, resident, 1978-79, chief resident, 1979-80; practice medicine specializing in family practice, Columbus, 1980—; asst. dir. family practice residency Grant Hosp., 1980-81; med. dir. Columbus Dispatch, St. Anthony Breast Evaluation Ctr., 1986—; lectr. Columbus Cancer Clinic, 1984. Contbr. Ohio State U. Med. Sch. Learning Module in Alcoholism, 1983-84. Named Alumna of Yr., Vanlue Sch., Ohio. Fellow Am. Acad. Family Physicians; mem. AMA, Am. Med. Women's Assn. Home: 206 Eastmoor Blvd Columbus OH 43209 Office: 20 Governors Pl Columbus OH 43203

FRY, BARBARA ANN, government official; b. St. Charles, Ill., Nov. 10, 1937; d. Robert Nicholas and Marianne Eloise (Earhart) Wilford; B.S., U. Ill., 1959; M.B.A., Roosevelt U., 1976; m. Ronnie Darrel Fry, June 15, 1974; children—Kim Buskirk, Gena Buskirk. Budget analyst, then budget officer Navy Electronics Supply Office, Great Lakes, Ill., 1962-73; regional budget officer IRS, Chgo., 1973-75, Atlanta, 1975-76, regional fiscal mgmt. officer, 1976-83, regional mgmt. analysis officer, 1983—; former mem. adv. com. EEO. Past treas. Loch Lomond Property Owners Assn., PTA. Served with USAF, 1959-61. Mem. AAUW (past treas.), Fed. Employees Credit Union (past mem. credit com., mem. supervisory com.), Federally Employed Women (past co-chmn. Inter-Agy. Council, past pres. Atlanta chpt., past legis. chmn.), Nat. Assn. Female Execs., Atlanta Assn. Fed. Execs. (past treas.), Decatur Bus. and Profl. Women (past pres., past. v.p., past treas.) U. Ill Alumni of Atlanta (treas. 1984-87), Sigma Kappa Alumnae of Atlanta (treas. 1987-87). Lodge: Zonta (pres. 1988—, past v.p., past sec., past bd. dirs.). Home: 1511 Montevallo Circle Decatur GA 30033 Office: 275 Peachtree St NE Atlanta GA 30043

FRY, NENAH ELINOR, college president; b. Chgo., Nov. 5, 1933; d. August Jether and Gladys Alberta (Bobcock) F. B.A., Lawrence U., 1955, LL.D., 1984; M.A., Yale U., 1957, Ph.D., 1964; D.Litt., Wilson Coll., 1980. Instr. Lawrence Coll., Appleton, Wis., 1959-61; asst. prof., then assoc. prof. history Wilson Coll., Chambersburg, Pa., 1963-75; dean of coll. Wells Coll., Aurora, N.Y., 1975-83; pres. Sweet Briar Coll., Va., 1983—; evaluator Middle States Assn., Phila., 1970—; trustee Lawrence U. Bd. dirs. Lynchburg Fine Arts Ctr., Pres.'s Com., NCAA. Woodrow Wilson fellow, 1955. Mem. Am. Hist. Assn., Soc. for French History, Berkshire Conf. Women Historians, Phi Beta Kappa (assoc.). Office: Sweet Briar Coll Office of the Pres Sweet Briar VA 24595

FRYE, DELLA MAE, portrait artist; b. Roanoke, Va., Feb. 16, 1926; d. Henry Vetchel and Helen Lavinia Theradosia (Eardley) Pearcy; m. James Frederick Frye, Nov. 1, 1944; children: Linda Jeanne Frye Chaikin, James Marvin, David Scott. Student, Hope Coll., 1968, Grand Valley State Coll., 1969-71. Asst. med. records librarian Bapt. Hosp., Little Rock, 1944; receptionist, sec. Stephens Coll., Columbia, Mo., 1945-46; art tchr. Jenison (Mich.) Christian Sch., 1965-67, pvt. classes, 1964-74; realtor 1978-80; with Diversified Fin., 1979-82; portrait artist 1967—; cons. World Traders, Grand Rapids, Mich., 1986—. Author various poems; exhbns. include Salon Des Nations (cert. honor), 1984, Ann Arbor (Mich.) Art Guild, Kalamazoo Artists, Internat. Art Gallery, Hawaii, La Mandragore Gallery Internationale D'Art Contemporain. Pres. mother's club Jenison Christian Sch.,

1965-66; treas. Band Boosters, Jenison, 1966. Recipient awards for nat. contests in portrait painting. Republican. Baptist. Home: 7677 Steele Ave Jenison MI 49428 Mailing Address: PO Box 2484 Grand Rapids MI 49501

FRYE, HELEN JACKSON, federal judge; b. Klamath Falls, Oreg., Dec. 10, 1930; d. Earl and Elizabeth (Kirkpatrick) Jackson; m. William Frye, Sept. 7, 1952; children: Eric, Karen, Heidi; m. Perry Holloman, July 10, 1980. B.A. in English; B.A. with honors, U. Oreg., 1953, M.A., 1960, J.D., 1966. Bar: Oreg. 1966. Public sch. tchr. Oreg., 1956-63; pvt. practice Eugene, 1966-71; circuit ct. judge State of Oreg., 1971-80; U.S. dist judge Dist. Oreg. Portland, 1980—. Office: US Dist Ct 118 US Courthouse 620 SW Main St Portland OR 97205

FRYE, JUDITH ELEEN MINOR (MRS. VERNON LESTER FRYE), editor; b. Seattle; d. George Edward and Eleen G. (Hartelius) Minor; student U. Cal. at Los Angeles, evenings 1947-48, U. So. Calif., 1948-53; m. Vernon Lester Frye, Apr. 1, 1954. Accountant, office mgr. Colony Wholesale Liquor, Culver City, Calif., 1947-48; credit mgr. Western Distbg. Co., Culver City, 1948-53; partner in restaurants, Palm Springs, Los Angeles, 1948, partner in date ranch, La Quinta, Calif., 1949-53; partner, owner Imperial Printing, Huntington Beach, Calif., 1955—; editor New Era Laundry and Cleaning Lines, Huntington Beach, 1962—; registered lobbyist, Calif., 1975-84. Mem. Laundry and Cleaning Allied Trades Assn., Laundry and Dry Cleaning Suppliers Assn., Calif. Coin-op Assn. (exec. dir. 1975-84), Cooperation award 1971, Dedicated Service award 1976), Nat. Automatic Laundry and Cleaning Council (Leadership award 1972), Women in Laundry/Drycleaning (past pres.; Outstanding Service award 1977), Printing Industries Assn., Master Printers Am., Nat. Assn. Printers and Lithographers, Huntington Beach C. of C. Office: 22031 Bushard St Huntington Beach CA 92646

FRYE, MELISSA WOODARD, health science administrator; b. Raleigh, N.C., June 12, 1950; d. Moses Washington and Evelyn A. (Lewis) Woodard; m. Gaither Clyde Frye, Nov. 13, 1977 (div. July 1984). BS in History, East Carolina U., 1972. Examiner N.C. Disability Determination Services, Raleigh, 1972-74, examiner II, 1974-75, supr. I, 1975-80, supr. II, 1980-86, med. adminstr., 1986—. Mem. Nat. Assn. Disability Examiners (v.p. 1978-79, bd. dirs. 1979-80, pres. 1980-81), Nat. Assn. Female Execs., Phi Alpha Theta (local pres. 1972), Gamma Theta Upsilon, Phi Kappa Phi. Democrat. Methodist. Office: Disability Determination Services Dept Human Resources PO Box 243 Raleigh NC 26702

FRYZ, BETTY FARINA, educator; b. Pitts., Mar. 29, 1930; d. Frank Joseph and Theresa (Pagliaro) Farina; m. Joseph Michael Fryz Sr., Aug. 6, 1955; children: Joseph Michael Jr., Deborah Lynn. BS in Music Edn., Ind. U., 1951; postgrad., Carnegie-Mellon U., 1953. Tchr. music elem. sch., jr. and sr. high schs. Moon Area Sch. Dist., Coraopolis, Pa., 1951—, choral dir., tchr. piano, 1987—, head humanities dept., 1987—; pvt. practice piano tchr., Pa., 1960-80; cons. music Prentice-Hall, Pa., 1971-73; chmn. jr. high music curriculum com. Dist. 1, Pa., 1984-86. Mem. Mid. States Evaluating Com.; bd. dirs. Am. Youth Symphony and Chorus. Named one of Outstanding Secondary Educators of Am., 1974. Mem. NEA, AAUW, Music Educators Nat. Conf. (chairperson 1987—), Pa. Music Educators Assn., Pi Kappa Sigma (pres. 1949-51). Roman Catholic. Office: Moon Area Sch Dist 1407 Beers School Rd Coraopolis PA 15108

FUCCI, LINDA DEAN, banker; b. Roanoke, Ala., July 2, 1947; d. Alton Hershall and Irma Nell (Trimble) Dean; AS, So. Union State Jr. Coll., Opelika, Ala., 1967; spl. courses Am. Inst. Banking, Am. Inst. Real Estate, Auburn U., Air U., Lanett, Ala.; grad. sch. banking, La. State U., 1986. m. Bob Fucci, Aug. 1981; children: Allen, Debbie, Nicky, Mark. With Bank of East Ala., Opelika, 1968-72; adminstrv. asst. Auburn (Ala.) Nat. Bank, 1972-80, asst. v.p., 1980-82, v.p., 1982-84, v.p., cashier, chief fin. officer, 1984—; sec.-treas. Auburn Nat. Bancorporation, 1985—; recruiter, pilot Air Trans, Auburn, 1979-81. Treas. Lee County Heart Assn., 1979-81; crusade chmn. Lee County Cancer Soc., 1980, pres., 1980; mem. Ala. Bankers Found. (mgmt. com.), Auburn Heritage Soc. Cert. flight instr. Mem. Nat. Assn. Bank Women, Am. Heart Assn., Am. Inst. Banking (pres. East Ala. chpt. 1981, state com. 1982-84, instr. 1983—), Aircraft Owners and Pilots Assn., Ala. Bankers Assn. (funds mgmt. com. 1984—, vice chmn. 1988). Pilots Lobby. Roman Catholic. Home: PO Box 592 Auburn AL 36830 Office: PO Box 711 Auburn AL 36830

FUCHS, ANNE SUTHERLAND, magazine publisher; b. Volta Redonda, Brazil, Apr. 19, 1947; d. Paul Warner and Evelyn Coffman; m. James E. Fuchs, Feb. 6, 1982. Student, Sorbonne, Paris, 1967-68, Western Coll. for Women, Oxford, Ohio, 1966-67; B.A., NYU, 1969. Vice pres., pub. Woman's Day Spl. Interest Mags.-CBS Mags., N.Y.C., 1980-82; vice pres., pub. Cuisine Mag., CBS Mags., N.Y.C., 1982-84; vice pres., pub. Women's Day mag. DCI Communications, Inc., N.Y.C., 1985—. Chmn. women's bd. Madison Sq. Boys and Girls Club, N.Y.C.; mem. Com. 200, USIA; bd. dirs. N.Y.C. Partnership, N.Y.C. Partnership Found. Mem. Fin. Women's Assn. N.Y., N.Y. Jr. League, Advt. Women of N.Y., Women in Communications, Women's Forum, Com. of 200, Fin. Women's Assn. N.Y. Club: Economic (N.Y.C.). Office: Woman's Day Mag 1515 Broadway New York NY 10036

FUCHS, ELINOR, theater critic, playwright; b. Cleve., Jan. 23, 1933; d. Joseph Fuchs and Lillian Kessler; m. Michael Oakes Finkelstein, May 3, 1962 (div. 1984); children—Claire Oakes Finkelstein, Katherine Eban Finkelstein. B.A. summa cum laude, Radcliffe Coll., 1955; M.A., Hunter Coll., 1975; M.Phil., CUNY Grad. Ctr., 1976. Research dir. Sextant Prodns.-ABC, N.Y.C., 1960-61; producer-writer Channel 13/WNET, N.Y.C., 1962-63; adj. lectr. SUNY-Stony Brook, 1975, 82; lit. mgr.-dramaturg Chelsea Theater Ctr., N.Y.C., 1978-79; staff theater critic Soho News, N.Y.C., 1979-82; contbg. critic Village Voice, N.Y.C., 1982—; dramaturg Women's Interart Theatre, N.Y.C., 1984-85; cons. Nat. Endowment for Arts, Washington, 1982-83; mem. Plays-in-Process selection com. Theatre Communications Group, N.Y.C., 1983-84. Author play/book: (with Joyce Antler) Year One of the Empire (produced Odyssey Theatre, Los Angeles 1980, Drama-Logue Critic's award in playwriting 1980), 1973; contbr. numerous articles to periodicals, including Am. Theatre, Comparative Drama, Art and Cinema, Theatre Communications, Vogue, Drama Rev., Performing Arts Jour.; co-editor spl. issues on Am. Theatre Alternatives théâ trales, Brussels, Nos. 9 and 10; editor: Plays of the Holocaust, an International Anthology, 1987. Vice pres. Performing Artists for Nuclear Disarmament, N.Y.C., 1983-84. Scholar Swedish Inst., Stockholm, 1981; fellow MacDowell Colony, Peterborough, N.H., 1982; Rockefeller fellow, 1984-85; fellow Bunting Inst., Radcliffe Coll., 1985-86; vis. prof. Emory U., 1987, sr. lectr., 1988—. Mem. Dramatists' Guild, League Profl. Theatre Women, Assn. Theater in Higher Edn., Modern Lang. Assn., Phi Beta Kappa. Democrat.

FUCHS, MARY ALLISON, hotel company executive; b. Detroit, Feb. 10, 1926; d. Lloyd H. and Mary (Peek) Allison; m. Arthur B. Fuchs, Oct. 31, 1948; 1 child, Gregory A. Student U. So. Calif.-Los Angeles. Asst. controller Anderson-Dunham, Los Angeles, 1947-56; paymaster Frontier Hotel, Las Vegas, 1956-57; asst. controller Tropicana Hotel, Las Vegas, 1957-73; paymaster MGM Grand Hotel, Las Vegas, 1973—, v.p., dir. Employees Credit Union, 1983—. Named Boss of Yr., Am. Bus. Women's Assn., 1985. Mem. Internat. Assn. Hospitality Accts. (Las Vegas chpt.; sec. 1981, treas. 1982, v.p. 1983, pres. 1984, chmn. bd. dirs. 1985, awards 1981, 84). Avocations: travel; reading. Office: Bally's Grand Inc 3645 Las Vega Blvd S Las Vegas NV 89109

FUCHSLUGER, DONNA JEAN, lawyer; b. Balt., Feb. 14, 1952; d. John Henry and Thelma Jean (Hammel) F.; stepmother, Mary Patricia (Dunn) F. BA, Wake Forest U., 1974; MLA, John Hopkins U., 1978; JD, Catholic U., 1984. Bar: Md. 1985, D.C. 1986, U.S. Ct. Appeals (3d, 4th, 5th, 6th, 7th, 8th, 9th, 10th and 11th cirs.) 1986. Real estate specialist Army Corps of Engrs., Balt., 1974-79, Washington, 1979-86; trial atty. HHS, Balt., 1986—. Bd. govs. St. Thomas More Soc., Balt., 1987—; vol. CONTACT, Balt., 1978-79, Second House Counseling Ctr., Riverdale, Md.; contbr. Covenant House, N.Y.C., 1985—; patron Walters Art Gallery, Balt., 1986—. Recipient Outstanding Support award USAF, 1978, Outstanding Service award USN, 1978; Carswell Scholar Wake Forest U., 1970-74. Mem. ABA, Md. Bar Assn., MENSA, Handel Choir. Democrat. Roman Catholic. Office: HHS Office Gen Counsel Baltimore MD 21235

FUENTES, MARTHA AYERS, playwright; b. Ashland, Ala., Dec. 21, 1923; d. William Henry and Elizabeth (Dye) Ayers; B.A. in English (Ione Lester creative writing award), U. South Fla., 1969; m. Manuel Solomon Fuentes, Apr. 11, 1943. Author plays: The Rebel, 1970; Mama Don't Make Me Go To College, My Head Hurts, 1963; Two Characters in Search of An Agreement, 1970; author fiction: A Cherry Blossom for Miss Chrysanthemum. contbr. articles to local, regional and nat. newspapers, feature articles to nat. mags.; author TV plays and feature articles for children and young adults; lectr., instr. workshops on drama, writing for TV. Recipient George Sergel drama award U. Chgo., 1969. Mem. Southeastern Theatre Assn., The Alliance of Resident Theatres, Authors Guild, Dramatists Guild, Soc. Children's Book Writers, Romance Writers Am., Southeastern Writers Assn., AAUW, United Daus. Confederacy. Roman Catholic. Club: U. South Fla. Alumni. Avocation: reading, animal rights, environmental protection, theater, travel. Home and Office: 102 3d St Belleair Beach FL 34635

FUGATE, VIRGINIA KIMBROUGH, sales professional; b. Birmingham, Ala., July 31, 1940; d. George Willis and Sarah Margaret (Postelle) F.; m. Neil Peter Clarke, May 21, 1970 (div. Mar. 1973). B in Music Edn., Fla. State U., 1962. Trainee draftsman Broward County Tax Assessor's Office, Fla., 1963; from systems engr. to adv. mktg. rep. IBM, 1963-70, 78-82; programmer, analyst 1st Nat. Bank Atlanta, 1970-71; program adminstr. Ins. Systems Am., Inc., 1971-72; sr. systems analyst Trusco Data Systems/Trust Co. Bank Ga., 1972-73; from systems engr. to mktg. rep. Data 100 Corp., 1973-78; sr. sales rep. Datapoint Corp., N.Y.C., 1982-84, 85—; account exec. Wang Labs., 1984-85. Backstage tour guide Met. Opera Guild, N.Y.C., 1982—, dir. vols., 1985—. Mem. DAR, Sigma Kappa (sec. 1960-61). Republican. Presbyterian. Home: 400 E 71st St 10V New York NY 10021

FUGELBERG, NANCY JEAN, educator; b. Tarentum, Pa., Mar. 6, 1947; d. Stanley and Mary (Struhar) Homer; m. Darrell Marvin Fugelberg, Aug. 27, 1977. Cert. master piano classes and music lit. Mozarteum, Salzburg, Austria, 1968; B.Music Edn., Mount Union Coll., 1969; postgrad. Kent State U., 1976. Music tchr. Alliance Sch. Dist., Ohio, 1969-70, Minerva Sch. Dist., Ohio, 1970—; ch. organist First Imamnuel United Ch. of Christ, Alliance, Ohio, 1969-85. Pianist for musicals Carnation Players, Alliance, 1969-72. Recipient award for working with handicapped children Minerva Sch. Dist., 1981; Alumni Service award Mu Phi Epsilon, 1983, 84; named One of Outstanding Young Women Am., 1981. Mem. Music Educators Nat. Conf., Minerva Tchrs. Assn., NEA, Mu Phi Epsilon (chpt. v.p. 1980-82, pres. 1982-84). Democrat. United Ch. of Christ. Avocations: plants, traveling. Address: 345 S Rockhill Ave Alliance OH 44601

FUGLIE, KAREN MARGARET, foundation administrator; b. Riverside, Calif., Apr. 9, 1942; d. Chester Norrdin and Margaret (Stewart) F. BA, U. Calif., Riverside, 1964; MA in French, U. Wis., 1966, PhD in French, 1972. Instr. French Marquette U., Milw., 1968-70, U. Wis. Parkside, Kenosha, 1970-72; program officer NEH, Washington, 1972—. Bd. dirs. Capitol Hill Arts Workshop, Washington, 1983-85. Fellow Woodrow Wilson Found., 1964-65. Office: NEH Div Fellowships Washington DC 20506

FUHRMAN, SUSAN DONAHUE, exercise physiologist; b. Milw., Nov. 26, 1959; d. James Jerome and Gloria Grace (Kingsley) Donahue; m. Gregg Alan Fuhrman, June 6, 1987. BS in Nursing, U. Wis., Eau Claire, 1982; MS in Human Kinetics, U. Wis., Milw., 1988. Cert. exercise specialist Am. Coll. Sports Medicine. Staff nurse Mt. Sinai Med. Ctr., Milw., 1982-84; cardiovascular intensive care nurse St. Luke's Hosp., Milw., 1984-87, instr. cardiopulmonary resuscitation, 1984—, instr. first aid, 1985—, cardiac rehab. nurse, exercise physiologist, 1986-88; cardiac rehab. coordinator St. Joseph's Hosp., Milw., 1988—; Research asst., health care dir. U. Wis., Milw., 1986-88; guest lectr. U. Wis., 1987; continuing edn. instr. U. Wis., Milw., 1987-88; presenter St. Luke's Family Practice, Milw., 1987. first aid coordinator Multiple Sclerosis Bike Tour, 1986. Mem. Women's Sports Found., Am. Coll. Sports Medicine, Am. Alliance of Health, Physical Edn., Recreation and Dance, Am. Assn. Cardiovascular and Pulmonary Rehab. (charter), Am. Nurses Assn. (charter), Am. Heart Assn. Office: St Joseph's Hosp Cardiac Rehab 5000 W Chambers St Milwaukee WI 53210

FUJIWARA, ELIZABETH JUBIN, lawyer, social worker; b. New Orleans, Dec. 20, 1945; d. Otha Ernest and Yvette Marie (Jubin) Barron; m. Ronald Toshio Fujiwara, Jan. 7, 1978; children: Jean Paul Jubin Toshiro, Maria Sachiko, Cathleen Sumiko Yonahara. Student, U. Tex., Irving, 1963-64; BA in Sociology, Loyola U., New Orleans, 1967; MSW, U. Hawaii, 1971, JD, 1983. Exec. dir. ACLU of Hawaii, Honolulu, 1975-77; specialist in equal edn. opportunity Dept. Edn., Honolulu, 1978; asst. dir. Inst. Productive Behavior, Honolulu, 1978-80; faculty research asst. William S. Richardson Sch. Law, U. Hawaii, Honolulu, 1981; law clk. to presiding justice Intermediate Ct. Appeals Hawaii, Honolulu, 1984-86; sole practice Honolulu, 1986-87; ptnr. Fujiwara & Fujiwara, Attys. At Law, Honolulu, 1988—. Editor-in-chief Handbook Women's Legal Rights in Hawaii, 1988. Active Hawaii Women's Polit. Action League, 1983-88, Ad Hoc Com. Abortion Rights, 1977-79; organizer Coalition Against Capital Punishment, 1976-78; Peace Corps trainee in Puerto Rico and Guatemala, 1968. Named one of Outstanding Young Women of Yr. State Commn. on Status of Women, 1976, Outstanding Hawaii Woman Lawyer of Yr., 1988. Mem. ABA, Hawaii Bar Assn., Assn. Trial Lawyers Am., Hawaii Women Lawyers (co-chair pay equity com. 1985-87, spouse abuse and women prisoners legal penal project 1985-88, mem. legis. com. 1985-87, bd. dirs.), Clark Hatch Health Club, Women's Support Group, Kappa Beta Gamma. Democrat. Buddhist. Office: Cen Pacific Plaza 220 S King St Suite 1501 Honolulu HI 96813

FUKUSHIMA, BARBARA NAOMI, accountant; b. Honolulu, Apr. 5, 1948; d. Harry Kazuo and Misayo (Kawasaki) Murakoshi; B.A. with high honors, U. Hawaii, 1970; postgrad. Oreg. State U., 1971, 73, U. Oreg., 1972; m. Dennis Hiroshi Fukushima, Mar. 23, ı974; 1 son, Dennis Hiroshi Jr. Intern, Coopers & Lybrand, Honolulu, 1974; auditor Haskins & Sells, Kahului, Hawaii, 1974-77; pres. Book Doors, Inc., Pukalani, 1977—; pres. Barbara N. Fukushima C.P.A., Inc., Wailuku. 1979—; sec. treas. Target Pest Control, Inc., Wailuku, 1979—; internal auditor, acct. Maui Land & Pineapple Co., Inc., Kahului, 1977-80; auditor Hyatt Regency Maui, Kaanapali, 1980-81; ptnr. D & B Internat., Pukalani, 1980—; instr. Maui Community Coll., Kahului, 1982-85; fin. cons. Merrill Lynch, Pierce, Fenner & Smith, Inc., 1986—. Recipient Phi Beta Kappa Book award, 1969. Mem. Am. Inst. C.P.A.s, Hawaii Soc. C.P.A.s, Nat. Assn. Accts., Hawaii Assn. Public Accts., Bus. and Profl. Women's Club. Tenrikyo. Home: 200 Aliiolani St Pukalani HI 96768 Office: 270 Hookahi St Suite 210 Wailuku HI 96793

FULCHER, LYNDA ROSIER, civic leader; b. Augusta, Ga., Aug. 23, 1949; d. Sylvester Louis Sr. and Gladys Mildred (Toole) Rosier; m. Garry Pilcher Fulcher Sr., Jan. 19, 1968; children: Garry P. Jr., Theresa Lynn. Student, Augusta Tech., 1984, U. Ga., Macon, 1985, U. Ga., Augusta, 1987. Society editor The Richmond County Times, Augusta, 1983—; pub. relations rep. Richmond County Homemakers Council, 1982, 83, 84, 85, 86. Contbr. articles to profl. jours. Mem. adv. bd. Richmond Council PTA, Augusta, 1984-86, Richmond County Extension, Augusta, 1983-85, Richmond County Recreation, Augusta, 1985—; vol. March of Dimes, Augusta, 1983—, Jeff Maxwell Library, Augusta, 1982—; state chmn. Ga. Homemakers Council, Athens, 1987; chair Democrat chpt. Recipient Ga. Homemaker award, Ga. Homemaker Council, 1984; named Vol. of Yr., Richmond County 4-H Club, 1984. Mem. Ga. Twins Assn., 4-H Vol. Leaders Assn. (v.p. 1985—), DAR. Methodist. Clubs: South Augusta Woman's (pres. 1987—), Happy 55, Augusta Photography (mem. chair 1985), Exchange Fair (chair, 1983-86). Office: The Richmond County Times 3111 Peach Orchard Rd Augusta GA 30906

FULCOMER, VIRGINIA ANN, psychologist; b. Greeley, Minn., Oct. 11, 1916; d. Louis John and Viola Florence (Sybrant) Rohlf; m. Charles Frederick Fulcomer, Sept. 1, 1938; children: Judith Fulcomer Willour, Mark Charles, Cheryl Fulcomer Kriska. BA, UCLA, 1956; MS in Edn., Westminster Coll., 1959; PhD, Case Western Res. U., 1963. Lic. psychologist, Ohio. Psychologist Child Guidance Ctr., Youngstown, Ohio, 1962-69, dir., 1964-69; dir. Child and Adult Mental Health Ctr., Youngtown, 1971-77; pvt. practice psychology Youngstown, 1969-71, 77—, Scioto Paint Mental Health Ctr., Chillicothe, Ohio, 1984-87. Mack fellow Westminster Coll., New Wilmington, 1960. Mem. Am. Psychol. Assn., Ohio Psychol. Assn., Psi Chi, Kappa Delta Pi. Republican. Presbyterian. Home: 708 3d St Waverly OH 45690

FULENWIDER, CLAIRE KNOCHE, utility company executive; b. Balt., Apr. 16, 1942; d. Fred Edward and K. Ethel (Broening) F.; m. H. Gerard Knoche (div. 1979); children: Nathan, Nadine. BS in Polit. Sci., Hood Coll., 1964; MS in Ednl. Psychology, Western Md. Coll., 1968; MA in Polit. Sci., U. Wis., 1976, PhD in Polit. Sci., 1978. Dir. energy policy studies Ctr. for Pub. Policy State Wis., Madison, 1978-81; lectr., dir. research dept. Polit. Sci. and Women's Studies U. Wis., Madison, 1981-82; mgr. energy utilization Madison Gas and Electric Co., 1982-86, dir. market and energy utilization, 1986—; Author: Feminism in American Politics, 1981; contbr. articles to scholarly jours. Trustee Hood Coll., Frederick, Md., 1971-82; bd. dirs. Young Women's Christian Assn., 1986-88. Mem. New Harvest Found. (bd. dirs. 1985—). Democrat. Office: Madison Gas and Electic Co PO Box 1231 Madison WI 53701

FULLER, BETTY WASHINGTON LEWIS WORKS, non-profit organization administrator, deacon; b. North Conway, N.H., Feb. 1, 1951; d. David Albert and Lucy Robb (Winston) Works; m. Frank Earl Fuller III, May 18, 1974; 1 child, Mary Austin. AB, Sweet Briar (Va.) Coll., 1972; MDiv, Va. Theol. Seminary, 1975. Ordained deacon Episc. Ch., 1975. Cons. Resource Ctr. for Small Chs., Luling, Tex., 1978-82; pres. Seedlings, Inc., San Marcos, Tex., 1982—; asst. to rector St. Mark's Episcopal Ch., San Marcos, 1983—; chaplain San Marcos Treatment Ctr., 1981-82. Trustee North Conway Inst., Boston, 1976—; mem. Jr. Service League, San Marcos. Home: 10 Tanglewood San Marcos TX 78666 Office: Seedlings Inc PO Box 1062 San Marcos TX 78667

FULLER, CECILIA, biotechnology company executive; b. N.Y.C., July 26, 1937; d. Cecil and Elizabeth (Williams) Randall; m. George Fuller, Mar. 12, 1955; children—Joi Denise, Steven George. B.A. in Psychology, SUNY-Old Westbury, 1976; M. in Orgn. Devel., U. San Francisco, 1986. Exec. dir. Freeport Econ. Oppuntunity Commn., N.Y., 1972-78; regional personnel coordinator Trans World Airlines, 1978-81; employee relations specialist SmithKline, Burlingame, Calif., 1981-84; mgr. human resources Becton Dickinson, Mountain View, Calif., 1984—; cons. in field. Mem. Am. Soc. Personnel Adminstrs., No. Calif. Human Resource Council, Calif. Assn. Affirmative Action Officers, PABPA, AMA, ACA. Avocation: fitness. Office: Becton Dickinson 2375 Garcia Ave Mountain View CA 94043

FULLER, DIANA L., lawyer; b. Morgantown, W.Va., Nov. 16, 1952; d. William Fleming and Amelia Marie (Lattanzi) F.; m. Robert Deeb Batey, July 21, 1979. B.S., W.Va. U., 1972, J.D., 1977. Bar: W.Va. 1977, U.S. Dist. Ct. (so. dist.) W.Va. 1977, Fla. 1978, U.S. Dist. Ct. (no., mid. and so. dists.) Fla., U.S. Ct. Appeals (5th and 11th cirs.). Law clk., ct. crier to chief judge U.S. Dist. Ct. (mid. dist.) Fla., Tampa, 1977-79, arbitrator arbitration program; ptnr. Fowler, White, Gillen, Boggs, Villareal & Banker, P.A., Tampa, 1983-85; ptnr. Smith & Fuller, P.A., Tampa, 1985—; lectr. in area of constrn. law. Contbr. articles to profl. jours. Mem. ABA (del. gen. assembly young lawyers div. 1984), Am. Judicature Soc., Fed. Bar Assn., Hillsborough County Bar Assn., W.Va. Trial Lawyers Assn., Greater Tampa C. of C., Phi Alpha Delta. Home: 2418 W Palm Dr Tampa FL 33629 Office: 201 E Kennedy Blvd Suite 201 Tampa FL 33602

FULLER, JANICE CAROL, nurse; b. Detroit, Jan. 22, 1942; d. James Edward and Marjorie Ann (Brumitt) Smith; div.; children: Colleen, Lana, James, John. Degree in Practical Nursing, E.C. Goodwin Tech. Coll.-New Britain Gen. Hosp., 1969; diploma in Nursing, Tunxis Community Coll., 1981; student in familty therapy porgram, U. Conn., 1983-84; student, Mid State Sch. Family Therapy, 1984-85. RN Conn.; cert. psychiat. and mental health nursing A.N.A. Lic. practical nurse Geri-Care, Farmington, Conn., 1969-71; staff nurse for pvt. physician, New Britain, Conn., 1971-75, NCCB, Bristol, Conn., 1975-81; supr. nursing NCCB, Bristol, 1981-84, Elmcrest Psychiat. Inst., Portland, Conn., 1984-86; exec. dir. Coping Ctr., Middletown, Conn., 1986—; lectr. on drugs and family violence various pub. schs. Mem. exec. bd. New Haven chpt. Am. Heart Assn., 1986; bd. dirs. sexual assault crisis service Middlesex County, 1987-88, Nat. Orgn. Victim Assistance, 1988, Am. Heart Assn. Middlesex County, 1986-88. Mem. Am. Nurses Assn., Nat. Assn. Female Execs. Home: Middletown CT 06457 Office: Coping Ctr 770 Saybrook Rd Middletown CT 06457

FULLER, JEAN MEREDITH, metal processing executive; b. Fresno, Calif., May 11, 1947; d. Edwin Earnest and Marjorie Louise (Hendrickson) Schober; m. Ross Anthony Gray, June 30, 1972 (div. Mar. 1981); m. David Neil Fuller, Dec. 3, 1983. BA in Home Econs., Calif. State U., Fresno, 1971, MS in Home Econs., 1972. Asst. prof. U. Nev.-Reno, 1972-78, assoc. prof., 1978-83; estimator, bus. mgr. Nev. Sheet Metal, Reno, 1983—. Contbr. articles to reviews and profl. jours. Mem. Clark County Community Debt Counsel, Las Vegas, 1975-79, Rep. Cen. Com., Las Vegas, 1976. Recipient 1st Place Newsletter award Standard Brands, Western Region, 1981; Gen. Foods Media grantee, 1980. Mem. Women in Constrn. (sec. 1986-87), Nat. Assn. Female Execs., Phi Kappa Phi. Office: Nev Sheet Metal 2101 Timber Way Reno NV 89511

FULLER, KAREN ANN, health service administrator; b. Buffalo, Feb. 7, 1947; d. F. Robert and Phyllis (Townsend) Kirsch; divorced; children: Ray D. Fuller, Dean Alan Fuller. Assoc. in Applied Sci. in Nursing, Niagara County Community Coll., 1973; BS in Nursing, D'Youville Coll., 1975; MS, Southwest U., 1985, PhD, 1986. RN, N.Y., Fla.; lic. practical nurse, N.Y.; cert. adult home adminstr., N.Y. Nurse's aide Mt. View Hosp., Lockport, N.Y., 1969-73; staff nurse in-charge Lockport Meml. Hosp., 1973-75; dir. nursing Newfane (N.Y.) Health Facility, 1976-78, Erie County Home & Infirmary, Alden, N.Y., 1978-79; dir. health care Manpower, Inc., Buffalo, 1979-82; dir. nursing Beechwood Residence & Nursing Home, Getzville, N.Y., 1982-84, St. Francis Hosp., Buffalo, 1984-86; adminstr. Bassett Manor, West Side Manor Wegman Cos., Williamsville and Liverpool, N.Y., 1987—; cons. in field. Author: The Ambulatory Surgery Experience, 1986. Mem. Occupational Adv. Council, Liverpool, 1987—. Fed. grantee, D'Youville Coll., 1975; Lilla Hooper Meml. scholar, 1974-75. Mem. Nat. Assn. Female Execs. Republican. Presbyterian. Home: 26 Bob-O-Link Ln Lockport NY 14094 Office: Bassett Manor 245 Bassett Rd Williamsville NY 14221

FULLER, MARGARET VIRGINIA, nurse; b. Wynne, Ark., Dec. 28, 1948; d. Earnest B. and Irene (Robinson) Fowlkes; m. John Luther Fuller, Dec. 12, 1969; children: Johnny, Mary Virginia. Diploma, Meth. Hosp. Sch. of Nursing, Memphis, 1969. RN. Head nurse of diagnostic neurology Meth. Hosp., Memphis, 1975-77, head of patient mgmt. system, instr., 1977-81, coordinator of nursing info. system, 1981-85; mgr. patient care system Healthcare Internat., Austin, Tex., 1985—; speaker in field. Mem. Am. Nurses Assn., Tex. Nurses Assn., Tenn. Nurses Assn. Republican. Baptist. Home: 11521 Chancellroy Austin TX 78759 Office: Healthcare Internat 9737 Great Hills Trail Austin TX 78759

FULLER, NELL BENTON, medical librarian; b. Rock Hill, S.C., Apr. 6, 1917; d. James Newton and Annie Clementine (Bolling) Benton; A.B., U. N.C., Greensboro, 1940; M.S. in L.S., U. N.C., Chapel Hill, 1968; m. Henry Shepard Fuller, Dec. 15, 1962 (dec.). High sch. tchr., Stony Point, N.C., 1940-43; asst. librarian Bowman Gray Med. Sch., Wake Forest U., Winston-Salem, N.C., 1944-45, librarian, 1945-62; mem. faculty and staff Claude Moore Health Scis. Library, U. Va. Med. Center, Charlottesville, 1966-84, asst. prof., 1970-75, assoc. prof., 1975-84, head tech. services, 1970-84. Democrat. Presbyterian. Home: 1 Amberhill Ct Greensboro NC 27405

FULLER, RENEE NUNI, psychologist, educational publisher; b. Mannheim, Fed. Republic Germany, Apr. 14, 1929; came to U.S., 1938; d. Eric Woldemar and Fridel Gronau (Henning) Stoetzner; widowed. Student, Swarthmore (Pa.) Coll., 1947-49; BA, Hunter Coll., 1951; MA, Columbia U., 1953; PhD, NYU, 1963. Research scientist Letchworth Village N.Y. State Dept. Mental Hygiene, Thiells, 1961-67; project dir. Staten Island (N.Y.) Soc. Mental Health, 1967-68; chief psychol. services Rosewood Hosp. Ctr., Owings Mills, Md., 1968-75; pres. Ball-Stick-Bird Publs. Inc., Stony Brook, N.Y., 1975—. Author: In Search of the IQ Correlatin, 1977, (reading series) Ball-Stick-Bird; contbr. articles to profl. jours. Recipient Disting. Achievement award Fairleigh-Dickinson U., N.J., 1979. Fellow: Am. Psychopathol. Assn.; mem. Am. Psychol. Assn., Behavior Genetics Assn., Am. Ednl. Research Assn. Office: Ball-Stick-Bird Publs Inc PO Box 592 Stony Brook NY 11790

FULLER, SHARON S., insurance agent; b. Hagerstown, Md., Sept. 6, 1946; d. Gerald Browning and Lillian Dorathy (Lane) Smith. Student schs. Hagerstown. Cert. ins. agt., Fla.; lic. ins. rep., mgr. With Washington Adventist Hosp., Takoma Park, Md., 1968-79; word processing coordinator Fla. Hosp., Orlando, 1979-84; info. systems adminstr. Broad & Cassel, Miami, Fla., 1984-85; ins. agt., Orlando, 1985—; owner, gen. mgr. Fuller Agy., 1987—. Contbr. articles to profl. publ. Active Competency Evaluation Com. Orange County Pub. Schs., Orlando, 1984-85. Mem. Assn. Info. Systems Profls. (v.p. 1985). Seventh-day Adventist. Avocations: reading; travel. Home: 8712 Gopher Ln Orlando FL 32829 Office: Fuller Agy PO Box 720356 Orlando FL 32822

FULLER, SHERRILYNNE, health science library director; b. Mishawaka, Ind., Dec. 18, 1945; d. Ellsworth Franklin and Dollie May (Kollar) Badman; m. David Richard Fuller, Sept. 5, 1981; 1 child, Heather Lynne. BA in Biolgy, Ind. U., 1967, MLS, 1968; PhD, U. So. Calif., 1984. Analyst info. UCLA, 1972-74; head reference services Norris Med. Library UCLA, 1974-76; librarian pub. services Norris Med. Library U. So. Calif., 1976-78, assoc. dir., 1978-84; lctr. Norris Med. Library UCLA, 1982-84; asst. prof. Sch. Med. U. Minn., Mpls., 1984-88; dir. Bio-Med. Library U. Minn., Mpls., 1984-88, Health Sci. Library and Info. Ctr. U. Wash., Seattle, 1988—. Author: Schema Theory in the Representation and Analysis of Text, 1984. Mem. Med. Library Assn. (bd. dirs. 1986—, chair fin. com. 1987—), Minn. Council Health Sci. Libraries (chair 1986-87), Am. Library Assn., Assn. Computing Machinery, Soc. Clin. Trial. Office: U Wash Health Sci Library and Info Ctr SB-55 Seattle WA 98195

FULLER, SUE, artist; b. Pitts.; d. Samuel Leslie and Carrie (Cassedy) F. B.A., Carnegie Inst. Tech., 1936; M.A., Columbia U., 1939. Producer: movies String Composition, 1970, 74; one-woman shows include Bertha Schaefer Gallery, McNay Art Inst., San Antonio, Norfolk Mus. Currier Gallery, Corcoran Gallery, Smithsonian Instn., others; exhibited in group shows including Aldrich Mus., Corcoran Gallery, Phila. Mus., Mus. Modern Art, Whitney Mus., Bklyn. Mus., Brit. Mus., London, others; represented in permanent collections Addison Gallery Am. Art, Larry Aldrich Mus., Chgo. Art Inst., Des Moines Art Ctr., Ford Found., Met. Mus., Guggenheim Mus., Whitney Mus. Am. Art, Tate Gallery London, Brit. Mus. London, Library of Congress, others; commd. works include Unitarian Ch. All Souls, N.Y.C., 1980, Tobin Library, McNay Art Mus., San Antonio, 1984. Recipient Alumni Merit award Carnegie Mellon U., 1974, CAA/WCA Nat. Honor award, 1986; Louis Comfort Tiffany fellow, 1948; Guggenheim fellow, 1949; Nat. Inst. Arts and Letters grantee, 1950; Eliot Pratt Found. fellow, 1966-68; Mark Rothko Found. grantee, 1973; U. Cin. Nat. Sculpture Conf.: Works by Women honoree, 1987. Home: PO Box 1580 Southampton NY 11969

FULLERTON, BETTY JANE, computer services consultant; b. Los Angeles, Mar. 29, 1925; d. Melvin and Louise Katherine (Kuntz) Woldstad; B.A. cum laude, U. So. Calif., 1946, postgrad. in Asiatic studies, 1946-47; registered cert systems professional; m. Hal Bradford Fullerton, Jr., Sept. 7, 1944 (dec. 1974); children—Hal, Frances, Lorraine, Charlotte (dec.), Scott, Kent (dec.), Rhonda. Corp. sec. and dir. Kern Drilling Co. Internat., Ltd., Whittier, Calif., 1963-66, United Drilling Services, Inc., Whittier, 1964-75; local advt. rep. The Christian Science Monitor, 1967-70; staff asst. Brown & Root, Inc., Houston, 1975-77, office mgr. personnel tng. and devel. dept., 1977-78, industry rep. computer services div., 1978-82; systems analyst/engring. software adminstrv. mgr. AAA Tech., 1983-87. Dist. precinct chmn. Republican Central Com. of Los Angeles County, 1960-64; mem. Republican State Central Com. of Calif., 1962-64; bd. dirs. Whittier area council Girl Scouts U.S., 1962-64, v.p. personnel, 1962-63; v.p. youth activities Freedom Found., Valley Forge women's div., Los Angeles County, 1964-66; bd. dirs. 1st Ch. of Christ, Scientist, Whittier, 1971-73; bd. dirs. Family YMCA, East Whittier, Calif., 1973-75; 1st reader 9th Ch. of Christ, Scientist, Houston, 1976-79, chmn. bd. trustees, 1979-83. Named Republican Woman of Yr., Whittier, 1972. Mem. Am. Soc. Tng. and Devel., Assn. Systems Mgmt., Project Mgmt. Inst. Engrs. Council of Houston (dir. tech. careers com.), Assn. of Inst. for Cert. Computer Profls. Home: 5103 243 Ave NE Redmond WA 98053

FULLERTON, CHARRON ELIZABETH, business official; b. New Rochelle, N.Y., July 14, 1946; d. John Sudall and Lucille Josephine (Phillips) Fullerton. B.A., Fordham U. Editor-in-chief Pelham Sun (N.Y.), 1968-77; asst. editor MONY, N.Y.C., 1977-79, communication specialist, 1979-81, customer communications mgr., 1981-85, dir. internal and customer communications, 1985-87, dir. creative services, 1987—; freelance editor, N.Y.C., 1972—. Recipient Bicentennial award Pelham Bicentennial Com. (N.Y.), 1976. Fellow Life Mgmt. Assn. (bd. exam. reviewers 1983—), Life Advertisers Assn., Soc. Consumer Affairs Profls., Fin. Advt. Mktg. Assn., Women in Communications (Outstanding Mem. award 1984). Democrat. Roman Catholic. Home: 312 W 88th St New York NY 10024

FULLERTON, DIANE CAROLINE, property management company executive; b. Mpls., Feb. 6, 1943; d. Carl and Mildred (Christensen) Hansen; student U. Minn.; children—Scott Anthony, Kristen Marie. Asst. to pres. Nat. Car Rental, Mpls.; asst. controller Imperial Oil Co., Los Angeles; profl. model and instr., Los Angeles; regional mgr. Alta Property Mgmt., 1978-80; exec. v.p. Mercury Property Mgmt., Irvine, Calif., 1980-85, pres., 1985—; also cons. Mem. Community Assn. Insts., Bldg. Industry Assn. (frequent keynote speaker), Calif. Assn. Subdiv. Cons. (frequent speaker). Author and exec. producer of video Your Homeowner Association - Make It Work for You. Republican. Office: 96 Corporate Pk Suite 300 Irvine CA 92714

FULLERTON, DOROTHY MALLAN, modeling agency executive; b. Ancon, C.Z., May 6, 1938; d. Daniel Harrington and Dorothy (Heintzelman) Mallan; m. Geoge Latimer Fullerton, May 31, 1957 (div. 1979); children—Daphne, Stuart, Nicholas. Student Women's Christian Coll., Madras, India, 1956, Corcoran Art Sch., 1960; Cours de Civilization certificate, Sorbonne, Paris, 1971, Ecole du Louvre, 1972. Antique dealer, Paris, 1970-73, antique sales rep., Heritage Place, San Francisco, 1979-81; fashion model Model Mgmt., Ford, N.Y., Brebner, San Francisco, 1980-85, talent dir., model mgmt., San Francisco, 1983-85, Grimmé Agy, San Francisco, 1987. One man shows include Rehobeth Art League, Del., 1965, Boston Visual Artists, Union, Mass., 1976, Artist Co-op, 1984, Castlebury Gallery, Arlington, Tex.; group shows include: Leahy Hosp., Boston, 1976, Chez Henri, Warren, Vt., 1977, Artist Co-op of San Francisco, 1980-85; represented in permanent collections: Schueler, Boston, Latham, France, Frapier, France, McNally, Zena Jones, Ruth Assawa, Bea Kribs, San Francisco; also pvt. collections. Mem. Artist Cooperative Gallery (mem. bd.), San Francisco Women Artist Gallery, Artist Cooperative Gallery (pres. 1982), Jr. League San Francisco, Nat. Mus. Women in Arts. Republican. Episcopalian. Avocations: music; fishing; hiking; traveling. Home: 145 Connecticut San Francisco CA 94107 Office: Model Mgmt 1400 Castro St San Francisco CA 94114

FULLERTON, GAIL JACKSON, university president; b. Lincoln, Nebr., Apr. 29, 1927; d. Earl Warren and Gladys Bernice (Marshall) Jackson; m. Stanley James Fullerton, Mar. 27, 1967; children by previous marriage—Gregory Snell Putney, Cynde Gail Putney. B.A., U. Nebr., 1949, M.A., 1950; Ph.D., U. Oreg., 1954. Lectr. sociology Drake U., Des Moines, 1955-57; asst. prof. sociology Fla. State U., Tallahassee, 1957-60; asst. prof. sociology San Jose (Calif.) State U., 1963-67, asso. prof., 1968-71, prof., 1972—, dean grad. studies and research, 1972-76, exec. v.p. univ., 1976-78, pres., 1978—; bd. dirs. EUDUCOM, Assoc. Western Univs., Inc., 1980—; mem. sr. accrediting commn. Western Assn. Schs. and Colls., 1982—, chmn., 1985-86. Author: Survival in Marriage, 2d edit, 1977, (with Snell Putney) Normal Neurosis: The Adjusted American, 2d edit, 1966. Carnegie fellow, 1950-51, 52-53; Doherty Found. fellow, 1951-52. Mem. Am. Sociol. Assn., AAAS, Western Coll. Assn. (exec. com., past pres.), Nat. Collegiate Athletic Assn. (pres.'s commn.), San Jose C. of C. (bd. dirs.), Phi Beta Kappa. Home: 97 E St James St #58 San Jose CA 95112 Office: San Jose State U Office of the Pres Washington Sq San Jose CA 95192

FULLING, KATHARINE PAINTER, educator, writer; b. Dodge City, Kans., Aug. 6; d. William George and Carrie (Lopp) Painter; B.A., Northwestern U., 1945; M.A., Columbia U., 1947; postgrad. Vassar Coll., 1948, San Marcos U., Lima, Peru, 1948-49, (fellow) Inst. Internat. Edn., U. Madrid, Spain, 1952-53; m. Virgil H. Fulling, Sept. 24, 1948. Asst. dir. Casa Panamericana, Mills Coll., 1944; asst. to dir. Fine Arts Dept., Columbia U., N.Y.C., 1945-47; tchr. public schs. Port Washington, L.I., N.Y., 1953-55; lectr. Global Edn., UN, N.Y.C., 1953-56; public relations dir. Nat. League Am. Pen Women, Washington, 1958-60; Non-Govtl. Orgns. rep. United Women of the Ams., UN, N.Y.C., 1959-62; lectr. Asia and Africa Halls, Smithsonian Inst., Washington, 1965-69; lectr. Folger Shakespeare Library, Washington, 1969-73; art reviewer Wyo., Denver Art Mus., 1974—; mem. nat. adv. bd. for Bob Dole's Presdl. campaign, 1988—, Nat. Trust for Historic Preservation, Washington, 1987—; charter mem. Nat. Mus. Women in Arts, 1987—. Mem. Wyo. Council for Humanities, 1979-80; bd. dirs. Am. Security Council, Washington. Mem. Asia Soc., Inter-Am. Center, AAUW, Nat. League Am. Pen Women (Woman of Achievement award 1973), LWV (pres. 1967-69), Nat. Mus. Women in the Arts (charter), Buffalo Bill Hist. Mus., Mark Twain Soc. (hon. mem.), Sigma Alpha Iota, Kappa Delta. Club: National Press (Washington). Author: The Cradle of American Art, 1948; Mantillas and Silver Spurs, 1952; contbr., columnist numerous jours. and mags. Address: 1295 Race St Apt 312 Denver CO 80206

FULLMER, LOIS MARIE, recreation center executive; b. Grandview, Iowa, Nov. 28, 1931; d. Charles and Margaret (Coder) Howell; student State U. Iowa, 1955-56, Mason City (Iowa) Jr. Coll., 1956-57; m. Edward E. Fullmer, Feb. 24, 1956; children—Sara, Jay Edward. Mgr. farm, 1956-64; sales rep. Russell Stover Candies, 1966-70; buyer Disneyland, Anaheim, Calif., 1970-79; buyer retail mdse. div. Walt Disney Co., Burbank, Calif., 1979—. Served with WAVES, 1951-52. Office: 500 S Buena Vista Burbank CA 91521

FULRATH, IRENE, corporate executive; b. N.Y.C., Nov. 15, 1945; d. Logan and Grace (Sheehy) F. B.A., Wheaton Coll., Ill., 1967. Media exec. Doyle Dane Bernbach, N.Y.C., 1967-72; acct. exec., retail sales mgr. Sta. WABC, N.Y.C., 1972-84; acct. exec. Sta. WABC-TV, N.Y.C., 1984-86; corp. sales mgr., Am. Express Co., 1987—. Mem. Fin. Advt. and Mktg. Assn. (bd. dirs. 1981-84, sec. 1984-85, v.p. 1985-86, pres 1986-87). Republican. Presbyterian. Avocation: travel. Home: 150 E 56th St New York NY 10022 Office: Am Express Co 100 Church St New York NY 10007

FULTON, JOYCE ROSALIE, banker; b. Ware, Mass., Jan. 21, 1938; d. Joseph E. and Rose A. (Regin) Rabschnuk; student Clark U., U. Mass.; grad. Williams Coll. Sch. of Banking, 1971; m. Harlan W. Fulton, June 15, 1958; children—Catherine Joy, Margaret Beth. With Ware Trust Co. (Mass.), 1960—, v.p., 1973-75, exec. v.p., 1975-77, pres., 1977-86, regional pres., 1986-87, chmn. bd., 1980—; exec. v.p. Country Bank for Savs., 1987—. Bd. dirs. Mary Lane Hosp., Gilbertville (Mass.) Library Assn.; trustee New Eng. Sch. Banking at Williams Coll. Mem. Nat. Assn. Bank Women, Mass. Bankers Assn. (dir.), Bank Adminstrn. Inst. (pres. Western Mass. chpt., state dir. 1980-82, dist. dir.), Quaboag Valley C. of C. (pres.). Office: Ware Trust Co 73 Main St Ware MA 01082

FULTON-BEREAL, ARLENE R., construction and maintenance company executive; b. Phila., Nov. 6, 1946; d. Moses and Ruth Fulton. Student Entrepreneurial Devel. Tng. Ctr., Phila., 1970, Antioch U., 1978-80, Temple U., 1977-78. Cert. gen. contractor, Phila., Pa. Mentor supr. pub. relations Juvenile Justice, Phila., 1975-77; Southeast Pa. dir. Project J.O.E.Y., Commonwealth of Pa. Dept. Children & Youth, Phila., 1978-80; chief exec. officer, pres. Bereal Constrn. and Maintenance Co., Inc., Phila., 1980—; mem. Pa. Dept. Transp. Cert. Appeals Bd., 1986—; apptd. Mayor's Small Bus. Adv. Council, 1987. Author alternative to prison youth program, 1977. Bd. dirs. Pa. Dem. Inst., Phila., 1985; chmn. youth dept. Chs. of God in Christ, Eastern Jurisdiction of Pa., Phila., 1978—. Recipient Humanitarian award Chapel of Four Chaplains, 1978. Mem. Nat. Assn. Minority Contractors, Coalition Minority Contractors (bd. dirs. 1983—), Nat. Assn. Negro Bus. and Profl. Women, Am. Women's Heritage Soc. (bd. dirs., chairwoman constrn.), Nat. Polit. Congress Black Women (bd. dirs., officer 1985), Nat. Assn. Women in Constrn. (legis. awareness chmn. 1983-84). Democrat. Mem. Pentecostal Ch. Avocations: reading, music, creative writing. Office: Bereal Constrn and Maintenance Co Inc 401 N Broad St Suite 300 Philadelphia PA 19108

FULWEILER, PATRICIA PLATT, civic worker; b. N.Y.C., Mar. 19, 1923; d. Haviland Hull and Marie-Louise (Fearey) Platt; A.B. cum laude, Bryn Mawr Coll., 1945; M.B.A., Columbia U., 1950; m. Spencer Biddle Fulweiler, Oct. 5, 1946; children—Marie-Louise Fulweiler Allen, Pamela Spencer, Hull Platt, Spencer Biddle. Jr. copywriter, asst. account exec. Dorland Internat. Pettingell & Fenton, N.Y.C., 1945-46; statistician, fin. staff treas.'s office Gen. Motors Corp., N.Y.C., 1950-52; asst. account mgr. investment dept. Fiduciary Trust Co., N.Y.C., 1953-61; bd. dirs. Chapin Brearley Exchange, Inc., N.Y.C., 1964-74, treas., 1966-71, pres., 1971-73; bd. dirs. Knickerbocker Greys, 1965—, treas., 1970-75; bd. dirs., treas. City Gardens Club, N.Y.C., 1974-79, chmn. ways and means com., 1974-81; bd. dirs. Nat. Soc. Colonial Dames State N.Y., 1973-82, asst. treas., 1973-82; mem. fin. com. Alumnae Assn. Bryn Mawr Coll., 1970-76; bd. dirs. Daus. of Cin., 1974-81, scholarship adminstr., 1976-81; pres. Ladies Christian Union, 1982-87, chmn. fin. com., 1987—; rec. sec. Women's Assn. St. James Ch., N.Y.C., 1972-75, co-chmn. Spring Festival, 1974-75, chmn., 1975-76, treas., 1976-81, mem. Altar Guild, 1975—treas. Churchwomen's League for Patriotic Service, 1982-86; mem. scholarship com. Youth Found., 1981—; membership chmn. Huguenot Soc. Am., registrar, 1986—. Mem. Soc. Sponsors of U.S. Navy, Colonial Dames Am. (bd. dirs. 1987—), Nat. Soc. Colonial Dames. Republican. Clubs: Colony, Thursday Evening, Wilson Point Beach Assn.. Daughters of the Cin. Ch. Home: 158 E 83d St New York NY 10028

FUNDORA, RAQUEL (FERNÁNDEZ), poet, writer; b. Bolondró n, Cuba, May 19, 1924; came to U.S., 1959; d. Gerardo Francisco and Carolina (Ferná ndez) Fundora; m. Roberto Rodrí guez de Aragó n, Sept. 14, 1951; children: Pepí n, Lianne, Raquel Aurora. Grad. in Bus. Adminstrn., Immaculada Sch., Havana, Cuba, 1948. Collections of poems include: Nostalgia Inconsolable, 1973, El Canto del Viento, 1983; contbr. poetry to lit. mags., 1970-84. Recipient Diploma of Honor Lincoln-Marti, HEW, 1973; Juan J. Remos, Cruzada Educativa Cubana, 1975; Cert. of Appreciation City of Miami, 1976, Miami Cuban Lions Club, 1980. Mem. Cí rculo de Cultura Panamericano (pres. Miami chpt. 1982-85, chmn. cultural congress U. Miami 1983-85), Grupo Artí stico Literario Abril, Poets and Writers, Latin C. of C. of U.S.A. (founder, 1st dir. Camacol Library 1980). Roman Catholic. Club: Big Five (Miami, Fla.). Home and Office: 935 SW 24th Rd Miami FL 33129

FUNK, ELLA FRANCES, genealogist, author; b. Domino, Ky., Apr. 7, 1921; d. Roy William and Edna Rene (Cummins) Roach; B.Liberal Studies, Mary Washington Coll., Fredericksburg, Va., 1982; m. Eugene Boyd Funk, June 20, 1942; children: Susan Teresa, Eugene Boyd. Exec. sec. Lang. Labs., Inc., Bethesda, Md., 1969-70; office mgr. legal firm Donovan Leisure Newton & Irvine, Washington, 1970-76; genealogist, hist. researcher, writer, 1976—; vol. Assn. Preservation Va. Antiquities. Named Exec. of Week, Sta. WGMS, Washington, June 1975. Life mem. Nat. Geneal. Soc.; mem. Hist. Fredericksburg Found., DAR, Alpha Phi Sigma, Sigma Phi Gamma. Mem. Christian Ch. (Disciples of Christ). Club: Woman's (Fredericksburg, Va.). Lodge: Order Eastern Star. Author: Cummins Ancient, Cummins New, vol. 1, 1978, vol. 2, 1980, Joseph Funk, a biography, 1984, Benjamin's Way, 1988. Address: Box 557 Low Locust Grove VA 22508

FUNK, JOAN GAIL, materials engineer; b. Richmond Heights, Mo., Aug. 27, 1960; d. Earl Jay and Romona Jean (Pickett) F. BS in Engring. Sci. and Mechanics, Tenn. Technol. U., 1983; M in Materials Sci., U. Va., 1987. Materials research engr. Langley Research Ctr. NASA, Hampton, Va., 1983—. Active crisis hotline Contact Peninsula, Inc., Newport News, Va., 1984—; vol. tutor Peninsula Literacy Council, Inc., Hampton, 1987—. Mem. Am. Soc. for Composites, Soc. for Advancement Material and Process Engring., Nat. Assn. for Female Execs., Nat. Fedn. Bus. and Profl. Women's Clubs, Va. Fedn. Bus. and Profl. Women's Clubs, Va. Peninsula Bus. and Profl. Women's Clubs (2d v.p. 1985-86, pres.-elect 1986-87). Office: NASA Langley Research Ctr Mail Stop 188B Hampton VA 23665-5225

FUNK, JOYCE ANNE, minister; b. Jacksonville, Ill., Mar. 2, 1952; d. Floyd William and Virginia Lorraine (Lackey) F. BA, Eureka Coll., 1974; M of Divinity, Yale U., 1977. Ordained to ministry Christian Ch. (Disciples of Christ). Assoc. minister West Haven (Conn.) Bapt. Ch., 1975-77, Union Baptist Ch., Mystic, Conn., 1977-79; pastor Woodward (Iowa) Christian Ch., 1979-81; assoc. regional minister Christian Ch. in the Upper Midwest, Iowa, Minn., N.D., S.D., 1979-81, Christian Ch. in Oreg., Portland, 1981—; mem. exec. com. Ecumenical Ptnrship. (nat. bd.), 1986—; bd. dirs. Ecumenical Ministries of Oreg., Portland, 1987—; rep. Consultation on United and Uniting Chs., Potsdam, Fed. Republic of Germany, 1987. Contbr. articles to denominational publs. bd. chair Groton-Stonington Youth Services, Groton, Conn., 1978-79; mem. Portland City Club, 1986—; elder Lynchwood Christian Ch. Named Outstanding Young Career Woman Bus. and Profl. Women, 1979, Outstanding Young Alumna Eureka Coll., 1984. Mem. Ecumenical Ministries of Oreg., Council on Christian Unity, Internat. Christian Women's Fellowship, Nat. Assn. Female Execs., Internat. Assn. Women Ministers (sec. 1981). Democrat. Club: YWCA. Lodge: Order Eastern Star. Office: Christian Ch Oreg 0245 SW Bancroft Suite F Portland OR 97201

FUNKE, JULIE A., graphics brokerage executive; b. Indpls., May 3, 1950; d. Paul R. and Rosetta A. (Freeman) Wheeler; m. William R. Funke, Jan. 25, 1969 (div. 1976); 1 son, Brian Dean; m. Benjamin H. Wolfenberger, Apr. 25, 1981 (dec. 1987). Student Ind. U. Exec. sec. City of Bloomington (Ind.), 1973-75; customer service rep. Herff Jones, Indpls., 1975-76; rep. trainee Maury Boyd & Assocs., 1976-77, customer service rep., 1977-82, v.p., 1983—. Mem. Women in Communications, Am. Soc. Assn. Execs., Coll. Fraternity Editors Assn., Profl. Fraternity Assn. (dir. 1982-86), Gamma Phi Beta (internat. officer 1985-87). Republican. Home: 8141 Castle Cove Rd Indianapolis IN 46256 Office: Maury Boyd & Assocs Inc 5783 Park Plaza Ct Indianapolis IN 46220

FUNKE, ODELIA CATHARINE, political scientist, analyst; b. Washington, Sept. 30, 1947; d. Frederick Anton and Teresa Wilhemina (Dietrich) F. B.A. cum laude, Catholic U. Am., 1969; M.A., U. Va., 1971, Ph.D. in Polit. Theory and Govt., 1974. Asst. prof. U. Mo.-Kansas City, 1973-79; cons EPA, Washington, 1980-81, social sci. research analyst, 1981-83, br. chief, 1983—; cons. for project on genetic research U.S. Office Tech. Assessment, Washington, spring 1980; asst. prof. George Washington U., Washington, spring 1982, fall 1983; postdoctoral fellow Johns Hopkins U., 1977. Contbr. revs., articles to profl. publs. Recipient Spl. Achievement awards EPA, 1982, 84, 87, Bronze medals, 1985, 87, Outstanding Performance awards, 1984-86, Fed. Exec. Inst., 1987; Thomas Jefferson fellow, 1970-71; NDEA grantee, 1971; Dupont grantee, 1971-72; U. Va. fellow, 1972-73; NEH summer seminar grantee, 1977. Fellow Royal Geog. Soc.; mem. Assn. for Politics and the Life Scis. (council, editorial bd.), Fed. Exec. Inst. Alumni Assn., Am. Polit. Sci. Assn., Lychnos Soc., Order Ky. Cols., Phi Beta Kappa, Pi Gamma Mu. Roman Catholic. Office: EPA 401 M St SW Washington DC 20460

FUNKEY, MARY ANN, retail executive, realtor; b. Evergreen Park, Ill., Nov. 7, 1955; d. William Anthony and Virginia Mary (Gavin); m. Corey Donovan, Oct. 1, 1978. BA in Communication Arts, Loyola U., Chgo. Store mgr. Joy's Clock Shop, Chgo., 1981—, Brooks Clothing, North Riverside, Ill., 1981—, Jean Nicole, Chgo., 1981—, Allison's, Chgo., 1981—; dist. mgr. Gateway Apparel, St. Louis, Mo., 1985—; trainer mgmt. of human resources-retail supervisory, 1986—; pvt. practice fashion cons.; modern dance instr. various Chgo. studios. Mem. women's adv. council Misericordia Home for Retarded Children, Chgo., 1986—; trustee Queen of Peace High Sch., Oak Lawn, Ill., 1987. Mem. Council Cath. Women. Democrat. Roman Catholic. Home: 14521 Mustang Dr Lockport IL 60441 Office: Gateway Apparel 128 Ogden Ave Downers Grove IL 60515

FURGASON, KIMBERELY ANNE, U.S. Army officer; b. Milw., Aug. 30, 1958; d. Richard Leo Furgason and Gwendolyn Dorothy (Dick) Wedor. Student U. Nev.-Reno, 1976-78; BS, U. Pacific, 1980. Commd. 2d lt., U.S. Army, 1980, advanced through grades to capt., 1984; installation club officer U.S. Army, Ft. Ritchie, Md., 1984-85, asst. area club mgr., Kaiserslautern, Fed. Republic Germany, 1980-84. Mem. U.S. Republican Nat. Com. Mem. Club Mgrs. Assn. Am., Nat. Assn. Female Execs. Presbyterian. Lodge: Internat. Order of Rainbow. Avocations: cross-stitch, gourmet cooking and baking, sailing. Home: 5900 Watercrest Dr Fayetteville NC 28304

FURGIUELE, MARGERY WOOD, educator; b. Munden, Va., Sept. 28, 1919; d. Thomas Jarvis and Helen Godfrey (Ward) Wood; B.S., Mary Washington Coll., 1941; postgrad. U. Ala., 1967-68, Catholic U. Am., 1974-76, 80; m. Albert William Furgiuele, June 19, 1943; children—Martha Jane Furgiuele MacDonald, Harriet Randolph. Advt. and reservations sec. Hilton's Vacation Hide-A Way, Moodus, Conn., 1940; sec. TVA, Knoxville, 1941-43; adminstrv. asst., ct. reporter Moody AFB, Valdosta, Ga., 1943-44; tchr. bus. Edenton (N.C.) High Sch., 1944-45, tchr. bus., coordinator Culpeper (Va.) County High Sch., 1958-82; ret., 1982; tchr. Piedment Tech. Edn. Center, 1970—. Co-leader Future Bus. Leaders Am., Culpeper, mem. state bd., 1979-82; state advisor 1978-79, Va. Bus. Edn. Assn. Com. chmn., 1978-79. Certified geneal. record Searcher. Mem. Nat., Va. bus. edn. assns., Am., Va. vocat. assns., Smithsonian Assos. Club: Country (Culpeper). Home: 1630 Stonybrook Ln Culpeper VA 22701

FURNESS, BETTY, broadcast journalist, consumer adviser, actress; b. N.Y.C., Jan. 3, 1916; d. George Choate and Florence (Sturtevant) F.; m. John Waldo Green, Nov. 27, 1937 (div. Aug. 1943); 1 dau., Barbara Sturtevant; m. Hugh B. Ernst, Jr., Jan. 3, 1945 (dec. Apr. 1950); m. Leslie Midgley, Aug. 15, 1967. Student, Brearly Sch., N.Y.C., Bennett Sch., Millbrook, N.Y.; LL.D. (hon.), Iowa Wesleyan Coll., 1968, Pratt Inst., Bklyn., 1978, Marymount Coll., 1983; D.C.L. (hon.), Pace U., 1973, Marymount Coll. Manhattan, 1976. Movie actress, 1932-37; appeared: stage plays Doughgirls; commls. for, Westinghouse Corp., 1949-60; appeared on, CBS-radio in, Dimension of a Woman's World, Ask Betty Furness, 1961-67; spl. asst. to, Pres. U.S., for consumer affairs, 1967-69; chmn., Pres.'s Com. Consumer Interests, 1967-69; columnist: McCall Mag, 1969-70, 72; chmn., exec. dir., N.Y. State Consumer Protection Bd., 1970-71, commr., N.Y. Dept. Consumer Affairs, 1973, now with, NBC News, N.Y.C., Bd. dirs., Consumers Union, 1969—, Common Cause, 1971-75. Office: NBC News 30 Rockefeller Plaza New York NY 10112

FURR, KYMBERLY RENEE, dance studio owner; b. Iredall City, N.C., Nov. 30, 1956; d. Garry Martin Furr and Helen Irene (Hare) Beaver. Grad. high sch., Kannapolis, N.C. Owner Kymberly's Sch. Dance, Kannapolis, 1977—, dir. dance camp, 1988—. Attended convs. Hoctor Dance Caravan, N.J., 1979—. Den mother Boy Scouts Am., Kannapolis, 1972-77; youth group leader Blackwelder Park Ch., Kappapolis, 1987; mem. com. C.H.I.C.K.E.N. Club (drug program); mem. Baptist Young Women, 1987. Recipient Appreciation award St. David's Luth. Ch., 1974; named one of Outstanding Young Women Am., 1985. Mem. Profl. Dance Tchrs., Old Courthouse Theatre (sponsor), Kannapolis C. of C. Democrat. Clubs: Optimists (recipient Friend Youth award, 1987), Mt. Pleasant Swim (mgr. 1982—). Home: 511 E 12th St Kannapolis NC 28081 Office: Kymberly's Sch Dance 529 N Rose Ave Kannapolis NC 28081

FURST, CARYN MELODY, public relations counselor; b. N.Y.C., Aug. 15, 1949; d. S. Robert and Ann (Bruder) F. B.S., Cornell U., 1971. Asst. editor Madison Ave. mag., N.Y.C., 1971-73; assoc. editor Parade mag., 1973-74; features editor Women's Life mag., N.Y.C., 1974; v.p. The Softness Group, Inc., N.Y.C., 1974-78; sr. v.p., account group dir. Carl Byoir & Assocs., Inc., N.Y.C., 1978-86; group v.p. Burson-Marsteller, N.Y.C., 1986—. Recipient Thoth award Washington chpt. Public Relations Soc. Am., 1980; Silver Anvil, Public Relations Soc. Am., 1981, 82, 83. Home: 36 E 36th St New York NY 10016

FURST, DIANE MARIE, personnel executive; b. Chgo., Mar. 16, 1953; d. William Gene and Ann (Palladino) Bunn; m. Thomas Lawrence Furst, Aug. 18, 1973. BBA, Coll. Boca Raton, 1987; student, Nova U., Broward Community Coll. Mgr. human resources Nichols Homeshield Inc., Hollywood, Fla., 1977-80; mgr. employee relations Mitel Corp., Baca Raton, 1980-84; pres. Crystal Clean Systems Inc., Parkland, Fla., 1984-85; mgr. personnel

Coca Cola Corp., Hollywood, 1985; dir. human resources Arvida, Boca Raton, 1985-86; mgr. compensation Alamo Rent-a-Car, Boca Raton, 1986; cons. human resource mgmt. D.M. Furst & Assocs., Boca Raton, 1988—. Mem. BNA's Personnel Policies Forum, Am. Personnel Assn., Nat. Assn. Female Execs., Parkland's Women's (editor newsletter). Democrat. Roman Catholic. Clubs: Toastmasters (v.p. 1983-84), Gold Coast Sailing., Coconut Grove Sailing. Home: 6344 NW Terr Parkland FL 33067

FURST, MARIAN JUDITH, geologist; b. Chgo., Jan. 12, 1950. B.A. in Chemistry, Reed Coll., 1972; S.M. in Inorganic Chemistry, U. Chgo., 1973; Ph.D. in Geochemistry, Calif. Inst. Tech., 1979. Geologist, mem. profl. staff Schlumberger-Doll Research, Ridgefield, Conn., 1979-82; well log analyst and chief geologist Schlumberger Well Services, Houston and Dallas, 1982-84, geologist U.S.A.-East, Dallas, 1984-85, U.S.A.-Land, 1985-86, stratigraphic analyst RPI Internat., Inc., Boulder, Colo., 1987—. Contbr. articles to profl. publs. Mem. Am. Assn. Petroleum Geologists, Soc. Profl. Well Log Analysts, Assn. Women Geoscientists, AAAS, Dallas Geol. Soc., Sigma Xi. Avocations: masters swimming, track. Office: RPI Internat Inc 2845 Wilderness Pl Boulder CO 80301

FURSTMAN, SHIRLEY ELSIE DADDOW, advertising executive; b. Butler, N.J., Jan. 26, 1930; d. Richard and Eva M. (Kitchell) Daddow; grad. high sch.; m. Russell A. Bailey, Oct. 1, 1950 (div. Oct. 1967); m. 2d, William B. Furstman, Dec. 24, 1977. Asst. corporate sec. Hydrospace Tech., West Caldwell, N.J., 1960-62; sec. to pres. R.J. Dick Co., Totowa, N.J., 1962-63, Microlab, Livingston, N.J., 1963; asst. corporate sec. Astrosystems Internat., West Caldwell, N.J., 1963-65; corporate sec. Internat. Controls Corp., Fairfield, N.J., 1965-73; sec. to pres. Global Financial Co., Nassau, Bahamas, 1974-75; office mgr. Internat. Barter, Nassau, 1975-76; sec. to pres., corp. sec. Haas Chem. Co., Taylor, Pa., 1976-77; asst. to pres., pub. Am. Home mag., N.Y.C., 1977-78; office mgr. Gilbert, Whitney & Johns, Inc., Whippany, N.J., 1979—. Home: 11A Foxwood Morris Plains NJ 07950

FUSCO, JACQUELINE TECCE, systems consultant; b. N.Y.C., Apr. 23, 1956; d. Sam L. and Lee M. (Malandri) Tecce; m. William Fusco, Apr. 7, 1984; 1 child, Samantha Nicole. BA in Pychology St. Francis Coll., Bklyn., 1978, AAS in Bus Adminstrn., 1978. Teller Chem. Bank, N.Y.C., 1975-78; asst. dir. lease adminstrn. Brooks Fashion Stores, N.Y.C., 1979-81; coordinator info. services Richard Kove Assocs., N.Y.C., 1981-86; v.p. Bilco Mech. Corp., Port Washington, N.Y., 1985—; pres., systems cons. J.T.F. Word Processing, 1988—; . Mem. Anti-Vivisection Soc., 1978—, Save Our Strays, Bklyn., 1978—; vol. Rusk Inst., N.Y.C., 1982; mem. Citizens to Replace LILCO, 1985—. Mem. Nat. Assn. Female Execs., Ill. Mgmt. and Exec. Search Cons., Paret Resource Ctr., Psi Chi, Chi Beta Phi. Republican. Roman Catholic. Home: 8 Guilford Rd Port Washington NY 11050 Office: Bilco Mechanical Corp Port Washington NY 11050

FUSEK, JACQUELINE JANE, school psychologist; b. N.J., Aug. 9, 1935; d. Alexander Julius and Mary (Gebrian) Witulski; m. Emil John Fusek, Aug. 7, 1971. BA in Secondary and Elem. Edn., Montclair (N.J.) State Coll., 1958; MA in Counseling, Fairfield (Conn.) U., 1962, advanced profl. cert. sch. psychology, 1967; cert. sch. adminstrn., U. Conn., 1975. Tchr. Bethel (Conn.) pub. schs., 1958-63; elem. counselor Danbury (Conn.) pub. schs., 1963-66; counselor, sch. psychologist Ridgefield (Conn.) pub. schs., 1966-68, Westport (Conn.) pub. schs., 1966-78; pvt. and parochial schs. Westport (Conn.) pub. schs., Westport, 1978—; pvt. practice sch. psychology, counseling Ctr. Human Devel., Westport, 1980—; pres. Fairfield Personnel and Guidance Assn., 1971; bd. dirs. New England Personnel Guidance Assn., 1973; psychologist Headstart Program, Bethel, summer 1969; leader workshops and confs., keynote speaker in field. Author papers and reports in field. Bd. dirs. Danbury Assn. Advance Handicapped and Retarded, 1965, Danbury Music Ctr., 1980—; violinist Danbury Symphony Orch., 1958—. Mem. Am. Assn. Counseling and Devel., Conn. Assn. Counseling and Devel. (chair govt. relations com. 1982), Am. Mental Health Couselors Assn., Am. Sch. Counselors Assn., Conn. Sch. Counselors Assn. (pres. 1972, chair interprofl. relations 1982-84, Service award 1973), NEA, Conn. Edn. Assn., Westport Edn. Assn., Nat. Assn. Edn. Young Children, Conn. Assn. Sch. Psychologists (cert. profl. devel. 1984), N.E. Coalition Ednl. Leaders, Nat. Bd. Cert. Counselors. Roman Catholic. Office: 30 Wooster Heights Danbury CT 06810

FUSILLO, ANNE M(ARIE), travel agency executive, consultant; b. Lansford, Pa., Sept. 12, 1921; d. Stephen Andrew and Mary Helen (Repko) Oracko; m. Frank Fusillo, June 28, 1947; children—Marianne, Merrie Beth. Student TV prodn. Columbia Coll., Chgo., 1960-62, Central Pa. Bus. Coll., 1941-42; also workshops on ins., bus. mgmt. and travel. Sec./supr. Bur. Vital Stats., Harrisburg, Pa., 1939-41; exec. sec. War Dept., Berwick, Pa., 1941-43, N.Y.C., 1943-45, Washington, 1945-47; exec. sec. Gary Diocesan and Pub. Schs. (Ind.), 1958-62, assoc. editor Gary Diocesan Publ., 1962-66; editor Fraternally Yours, First Catholic Slovak Ladies Assn., Beachwood, Ohio, 1966-80; travel cons., ptnr. Tour Desk One, Inc., Wheaton, Ill., 1979—. Editor, designer brochures, ann. report. Mem. press and pub. relations coms. United Fund, Gary, 1965-73; pres., sec.-treas Press and Pub. Relations sect. Nat. Frat. Congress Am., Chgo., 1968-77; pres. Ind. Frat. Congress, Indpls., 1974-75; pres. N.W. Ind. Visiting Nurse Assn., Hammond, 1965-69, editor newsletter, 1973-75; leader Girl Scouts U.S.A., 1957-60, 65-67; pres. Gary Diocesan Council Cath. Women, 1968-69; sec. N.W. Ind. Cath. Youth Orgn., 1963-74; pres. woman's aux. bd. Mundelein Coll., Chgo.,1967-70; organizer Leisure Club 55 at St. Michael's Parish, Wheaton, 1987; tchr. cooking Wheaton Sch. Dist. Adult Edn., 1981-83; vol. Marianjoy Rehab. Hosp., Wheaton, 1981-83. Recipient Pro Deo et Juventute award, Cath. Youth Orgn., 1968. Mem. Cath. Press Assn., Pacific Area Travel Agts., Assn. Retail Travel Agts. Republican. Clubs: Gary Women's, Marianjoy Rehab. Hosp. Aux. Office: Tour Desk One Inc 404 S Main St Wheaton IL 60187

FUSILLO, LISA ANN, dance educator; b. Washington, Jan. 11, 1951; d. Matthew Henry and Alice Elbert (Zeigler) Fusillo. Student Butler U., 1969-72; teaching cert. Royal Ballet Sch., 1975; BS, George Washington U., 1976; MA, Tex. Womans U., 1978, PhD, 1982. M. Robert Forshay Smith Jr., June 19, 1982. Dancer, Butler Ballet, Indpls., 1969-72; mus. asst. Royal Ballet, London, 1973-75; dancer Liz Lerman Group, Washington, 1975-76; teaching asst. Tex. Womans U., Denton, 1976-77, mem. adj. faculty, 1978, 81; choreographic asst. Leonide Massine, W. Ger., London, Paris, San Francisco, N.Y., 1976-78; instr. Skidmore Coll., Saratoga Springs, N.Y., 1978-80; asst. prof. ballet Tex. Christian U., Ft. Worth, 1981-85, assoc. prof., 1985— ; artistic cons., guest choreographer Chattanooga Civic Ballet, 1984; master tchr., artistic cons. San Angelo Civic Ballet, 1985; free lance choreographer, master tchr. in U.S. and Europe; artistic dir. Contemporary Dance Co., 1986; dance researcher EARTHWATCH Found., Okinawa, Japan, 1985; mem. faculty Am. Dance Festival, 1987; guest artist, choreographer Nat. Inst. Arts, Cloud Gate Contemporary Dance Theater, Taipei, Taiwan, Republic of China, 1987. Fulbright scholar, 1987-88. Mem. AAHPER, Imperial Soc. Tchrs. Dancing, Royal Acad. Dancing, AAUP, Sigma Alpha Iota, Alpha Chi, Pi Lambda Theta, Chi Tau Epsilon. Office: Tex Christian U Dept Ballet and Modern Dance Box 32889 Fort Worth TX 76129

FUTCH, BARBARA JEAN, production and planning specialist; b. Meadville, Pa., Oct. 17, 1950; d. Edgar Eugene and Lillian Mae (Rupp) Treharne; m. Michael Futch, July 13, 1974. BS in Edn., Indiana U. of Pa., 1972; postgrad., Johns Hopkins U., 1973-74. Packaging specialist Tobyhanna (Pa.) Army Depot, 1981-85, mgmt. analyst, 1985-87, chief of prodn., planning and control, 1987—. Methodist. Club: Pocono Mt. Kennel (Stroudsburg, Pa.) (bd. dirs. 1986). Home: Rd #7 Box 7552 Stroudsburg PA 18360 Office: Tobyhanna Army Depot Supply Directorate SDSTO-SS Tobyhanna PA 18466

FUTRELL, IVA MACDONALD, law librarian; b. New Orleans, Nov. 15, 1942; d. Frank Whitmore and Yvonne (Trapolin) Macdonald; m. John William Futrell, Aug. 13, 1966; children: Sarah Y., Daniel B. BA, Tulane U., 1963, LLB, 1966; MLS, U. Ala., 1974. Bar: La., 1966. Law clk. La. Civil Dist. Ct., New Orleans, 1967-71; librarian U. Ga., Athens, 1976-79; environ. librarian Environ. Law Inst., Washington, 1980-86; law librarian Hunton & Williams, Washington, 1986—. Mem. Law Librarians Soc. D.C., Am. Assn. Law Libraries, Spl. Libraries Assn. Office: Hunton & William 2000 Pennsylvania Ave NW Suite 9000 Washington DC 20006

FUTRELL, MARY ALICE HATWOOD, association executive; b. Alta Vista, Va., May 24, 1940; d. Josephine Austin; m. Donald Lee Futrell. B.A., Va. State U., 1962; M.A., George Washington U., 1968; postgrad., U. Md., U. Va., Va. Poly Inst. and State U.; DHL (hon.), Va. State U., George Washington U., 1984, Spellman Coll., 1986, Cen. State U., 1987; DEd, Eastern Mich. U., 1987; hon. doctorates, U. Lowell, Adrian Coll. Bus. edn. tchr. Parker-Gray High Sch., Alexandria, Va., 1963-65; bus. edn. tchr., dept. chmn. George Washington High Sch., 1965-80; pres. NEA, Washington, 1983—; mem. adv. com. on tchr. cert. State of Va., 1977-82, adv. com. to U.S. Commn. on Civil Rights, 1978; mem. Gov.'s Com. on Edn. of Handicapped, 1977; state rep. to Edn. Commn. of States, 1982; mem. Carnegie Found.'s Nat. Panel on Study of Am. High Sch., Carnegie Forum on Edn. and Economy, task force on teaching as profession; mem. edn. adv. council Met. Life Ins. Co.; trustee Joint Council on Econ. Edn.; mem. study commn. on Global Perspectives in Edn.; mem. Va.-Israel Commn., Nat. Select Com. on Edn. Black Youth; mem. Nat. Bd. for Profl. Teaching Standards; chairperson edn. com. Nat. Council for Accreditation Tchr. Edn.; mem. task force on educationally disadvantaged Com. for Econ. Devel. Mem. editorial bd. ProEdn. mag.; bd. advisers Esquire Register, 1985. Mem. women's council Democratic Nat. Com., Dem. Labor Council; former pres. ER-America, nat. chairperson; mem. U.S. Nat. Commn. to UNESCO; mem. adv. council Internat. Labor Rights Edn. and Research Fund; mem. Nat. Dem. Inst. for Internat. Affairs, Nat. Labor Com. for Democrary and Human Rights; bd. advisers Project VOTE; mem. Martin Luther King Jr. Fed. Holiday Commn.; trustee Nat. History Day; bd. dirs. U.S. Com. for UNICEF, Nat. Found. for Improvement Edn., Citizen-Labor Energy Coalition. Recipient Human Rights award NCCJ, 1976, cert. of appreciation UN Assn., 1980, Disting. Service medal, Columbia Univ., 1987, Schull award Ams. for Dem. Action, Pres.'s award NAACP, numerous others; named Outstanding Black Bus. and Profl. Person, Ebony mag., 1984, One of 100 Top Women in Am., Ladies Home Jour. mag., 1984, One of 12 Women of Yr., Ms. mag., 1985, One of Top 100 Blacks in Am., Ebony mag., 1985-87; Ford Found. and Nat. Com. on U.S.-China Relations grantee, 1981. Mem. NEA (bd. dirs. 1978-80, task force on sch. vols. 1977-78, head human relations com. to 1980, sec.-treas. 1980-83) (Creative Leadership in Women's Rights award 1982), Edn. Assn. Alexandria (pres. 1973-75), Va. Edn. Assn. (pres. 1976-78) (Fitz Turner Human Rights award 1976), World Confedn. Orgns. of Teaching Profession (exec. com., 1985—, chmn. women's caucus, 1984—, women's concerns com., chmn. fin. commn., 1986-87), Am. Assn. Colls. Tchr. Edn., Am. Assn. State Colls. and Univs., People for The Am. Way (adv. council). Office: NEA 1201 16th St NW Washington DC 20036

FUTTER, ELLEN VICTORIA, college president; b. N.Y.C., Sept. 21, 1949; d. Victor and Joan Babette (Feinberg) F.; m. John A. Shutkin, Aug. 25, 1974; children—Anne Victoria, Elizabeth Jane. Student, U. Wis., 1967-69; AB magna cum laude, Barnard Coll., 1971; JD, Columbia U., 1974, LLD (hon.); LLD (hon.), Hamilton Coll., NYU; DHL (hon.), Amherst Coll. Bar: N.Y. 1975. Assoc. Milbank, Tweed, Hadley & McCloy, N.Y.C., 1974-80; acting pres. Barnard Coll., N.Y.C., 1980-81, pres., 1981—, also trustee; bd. dirs. Fed. Res. Bank of N.Y, Mut. Benefit Life. Mem. Helsinki Watch; trustee Ednl. Testing Service; friend N.Y.C. Commn. on Status of Women; bd. dirs. Regional Plan Assn., Milbank Meml. Fund, Legal Aid Soc., Consortium on Financing Higher Edn., The Am. Assembly. Recipient Spirit of Achievement award Albert Einstein Coll. Medicine Yeshiva U., Abram L. Sachar award Brandeis U., Elizabeth Cutter Morrow award YWCA. Mem. ABA, N.Y. State Bar Assn., Assn. Bar City of N.Y., Nat. Inst. Social Scis., Council Fgn. Relations, Am. Assn. for Higher Edn. (bd. dirs.), Phi Beta Kappa. Club: Cosmopolitan. Office: Barnard Coll 3009 Broadway New York NY 10027

FYFE, JANET HUNTER, library educator, historian; b. Blantyre, Scotland, Apr. 29, 1929; came to Can., 1963; d. James Stanley and Jean (Burleigh) F. M.A., U. Edinburgh, 1950; Ph.D., U. Guelph, 1977. Cert. ALA, 1956. Br. librarian Borough of Heston and Isleworth, Hounslow, Eng., 1956-58; sr. asst. librarian U. St. Andrews, Scotland, 1958-63; reference librarian U. Sask., Regina, Can., 1963-65, head dept. bibliography and book selection, Saskatoon, 1965-70; assoc. prof. Sch. Library and Info. Sci., U. Western Ont., London, 1970-81, prof., 1981—, mem. univ. senate, 1981-86, exec. com. faculty assn., 1982-84, chmn. status of women com., 1982-84; bd. mem. Internat. Inst. for Garibaldian Studies, Sarasota, Fla., 1982. Author, editor: Autobiography of John McAdam, 1980; author: Directory of Special Collections in Canadian Libraries, 1968; History Journals and Serials: An Analytical Guide, 1986; contbr. hist. articles to jours.; editor: Sask. Library, Saskatoon, 1966-70. Vis. research fellow Inst. for Advanced Studies in Humanities, U. Edinburgh, 1979; research grantee Social Scis. and Humanities Research Council Can., 1979, 83, 84. Fellow Library Assn.; mem. Sask. Library Assn. (councillor 1964-66), Saskatoon Library Assn. (pres. 1969-70), various hist. and library assns. Club: Internat. Toastmistress (pres. London 1982-83). Home: 432 Oak Park Dr, London, ON Canada N6H 3N4 Office: Univ Western Ont, Sch Library & Info Sci, London, ON Canada N6G 1H1

GAARDER, MARIE, speech pathologist; b. New Britain, Conn., July 19, 1935; d. Nicholas and Clara (Sangeloty) Sarris; B.S., U. Ill., 1957; postgrad. U. Md., 1962-63, Our Lady of Lake U. Grad. Sch. Social Work, San Antonio, 1976-77; m. Kenneth R. Gaarder, Dec. 8, 1962; children—Jason, Galen. Founder speech therapy program Flossmoor (Ill.) Sch. Dist. 161, 1957-59; speech pathologist Prince George's County (Md.) Bd. Edn., 1959-65, Sidwell Friend's Sch., Washington, 1966-67, St. Maurice Sch. for Learning Disabilities, Potomac, Md., 1968-69; pvt. practice speech therapy, Chevy Chase, Md., 1967—; adminstrv. officer Gaarder Med. Corp., Chevy Chase, 1977—. Pres., Prince George's chpt. Council for Exceptional Children, 1963-64; mem. Florence Crittenton Circle, 1966-69, Hospitality and Info. Service for Diplomats, 1967—; chmn. activities com. Jr. Teens, 1979-80; chmn. publicity YWCA Internat. Fair, 1977-79, chmn. entertainment, 1983, chmn. 1987-88; mem. internat. com. Woman's Nat. Democratic Club; co-chmn. Adv. Com. for Quality Integrated Edn. in Montgomery County, 1977-78; bd. dirs. D.C. br. YWCA, 1981-82, Washington Ctr. Music Therapy Clinic, Cath. U. Am., 1983—, The Samaritans of Washington, 1984—; chmn. Career Day, Nat. Symphony Ednl. Activities, 1981—; chmn. oral history 65th Birthday Town of Chevy Chase; chmn. Mid-Atlantic regional adv. bd. Am. Found. for the Blind, 1984-85. Recipient cert. of appreciation Opera Guild San Antonio, 1977. Mem. Am. Speech, Lang. and Hearing Assn. (advanced cert.), Md. Speech, Lang. and Hearing Assn., Internat. Assn. Logopedics and Phoniatrics, World Affairs Council of Washington, Zeta Phi Eta. Greek Orthodox. Club: Capitol Speakers (sec. chpt. III 1983-84) (Washington). Contbg. author: San Antonio Cookbook II, 1976. Home and Office: 4221 Oakridge Ln Chevy Chase MD 20815

GABBAY, SARAH G., marriage and family therapist; b. Greensboro, N.C., Sept. 18, 1951; d. Meir S. and Florence E. (Ritchie) G. BA, U. N.C., Greensboro, 1974, MEd, 1985, postgrad., 1985—. Pvt. practice acctg. Greensboro, 1974-85; gen. acct. U. N.C., Greensboro, 1978-84; practice therapy specializing in marriage and family counseling Greensboro, 1984—; cons. Rape Ctr. Greensboro, 1980-81, therapist, 1975-81, staff coordinator, 1978-81; therapist Greensboro Urban Ministry, 1985-87. Mem. Am. Assn. Marriage and Family Therapists (clin., bd. dirs. Guilford County 1986-87), Nat. Council on Family Relations, Family Life Council, Nat. Assn. Female Execs., NOW, Omicron Nu. Democrat. Jewish. Home: 320 S Chapman St Greensboro NC 27403-1614 Office: 912 N Elm St Suite 208 Greensboro NC 27401

GABER, TINA MERRI, public relations specialist, counselor; b. Phila., Mar. 24, 1951; d. David and Iva (Bandes) G. B.A., U. Fla., 1974; M.Ed., U. Miami, 1976. Tchr. spl. edn. Dade County Pub. Sch. System, Miami, 1977; counselor dept. univ. family services U. Miami Med. Sch., 1977-80; counselor Fla. State Employment Service, Miami, 1980-85; dir. pub. relations Carriage House/Carriage Club, Miami Beach, Fla., 1985; dir. pub. relations Diabetes Research Inst., U. Miami Sch. Medicine, 1985; spl. projects coordinator Royal Palm Hotel, Miami Beach, Fla., 1985-86; asst. mgr. Royal Palm Hotel, Miami Beach, 1986—. Mem. City of Miami Beach Adv. Bd. on Juvenile Problems, 1983-84; mem. City of Miami Beach Adv. Bd. on Recreational Ctrs. and Park Facilities, 1984—; mem. Debbie School Mailman Ctr. for child devel. U. Miami, 1985—; mem. grant com. Community Com. for Devel. Handicaps, 1985; mem. Bass Mus. of Art, 1984—, Friend of the Library, 1983—, Ctr. for the Fine Arts, 1985—, mem. S. Fla. Art Ctr., 1985—; trustee Ronald McDonald House of South Fla., Miami, 1984—(vol. coordinator, 1985, editor newsletter, 1985—), bd. dirs. Historic Mgmt. Corp., 1986—. Mem. Greater Miami C. of C., Dade County Mental Health Assn., Dade County Assn. Retarded Citizens, Fla. Personnel and Guidance Assn., Benjamin Franklin Soc., Gt. Miami Jewish Fedn., Dade County Fed. Revenue Sharing, U. Miami Alumni Assn., Miami Beach Jaycee Women (pres. 1983-84). Avocations: sculpture, needlepoint, art, gardening.

GABLE, MARTHA ANNE, educator; b. Phila.; d. James F. and Stella (Gingrich) G. BE, Ind. U., 1942; MEd, Temple U., 1935. Tchr., Phila. Pub. Schs., 1926-41, asst. dir. phys. and health edn., Phila., 1942-48, asst. dir. sch. and community relations, 1948-55, dir. radio-TV edn., 1955-68; editor Am. Assn. Sch. Adminstrs., Washington, 1968-73, cons. Editechnology, 1973—; mem. Pa. Gov.'s Adv. Commn. on Edn., 1956-58, White House Conf. on Edn., 1955; cons. Joint Council Ednl. TV, Washington; chmn. adv. com. Pa. Ednl. TV, 1960-68; del. Internat. Conf. Ednl. TV, London, 1954. Judge, Olympic Games, London, 1948, Helsinki, 1952, Melbourne, 1956, Rome, 1960, Tokyo, 1964; bd. dirs. Phila. Home and Sch. Council, 1950-68; v.p. Women for Greater Phila. Named Disting. Dau. of Pa.; recipient Pres.'s award Phila. C. of C., Silver Medal award Phila. Club Advt. Women, Trustee Service award Pop Warner Little League, Service award Mus. Council Phil. and Del. Valley; named to Pa. Sports Hall of Fame. Mem. Phila. Pub. Relations Assn. (Hall of Fame), Am. Women in Radio and TV, NEA, Pub. Relations Soc. Am., TV-Radio Advt. Club, AAUW, Am. Assn. Sch. Adminstrs., Phila. Mus. Art, Women in Communications, Am. Newswomen's Club. Presbyterian. Club: Cosmopolitan, Nat. Press. Home: 2601 Parkway Philadelphia PA 19130

GABLER, MARILYN ANN, free-lance writer; b. Ft. Worth, May 8, 1954; d. Wayne Conway and Sarah Katherine (Powell) Rose; m. William Havard Gabler, Oct. 30, 1982. BA in Journalism, U. Tex., Arlington, 1976; postgrad., Tex. Christian U., 1986—. Tech. writer Gen. Dynamics Corp., Ft. Worth, 1979-82, engrng. writer, 1982-83, sr. analyst, 1983-84, tech. pubs. editor, 1984-86; fashions cons. Mary McCauley, Inc., Ft. Worth, 1987-88; freelance writer TandyCrafts, Ft. Worth, 1979. Contbr. articles to retail publs. State del. Tex. Dem. Party, 1978. Mem. Toastmasters. Episcopalian. Home and Office: 7053 Misty Meadow S Fort Worth TX 76133

GABRIA, JOANNE BAKAITIS, information processing systems equipment company executive; b. Washington, Pa., Jan. 16, 1945; d. Vincent William and Mary Jo (Cario) Bakaitis. BA in English, U. Dayton, 1965, MA in Mktg. Communications, 1973, MBA, 1979. Advt. writer Dancer-Fitzgerald-Sample, Dayton, Ohio, 1969-72; advt. coordinator Monarch Marking Systems, Dayton, 1972-73; product tech. editor Frigidaire div. GM, Dayton, 1973-77; dir. tech. communications Mead Tech. Lab., Dayton, 1977-79; publs. mgr. NCR Corp., Dayton, 1979-81, internat. product mgr., 1981-86, mgr. internat. market analysis, 1986-87, mgr. Internat. Market Research, 1987—. bd. dirs. Contact-Dayton, 1984-85. Author: Microwave Cooking in 3 Speeds, 1976, Communications Standards, 1978, Retail Operations, 1982; editor: Ivy Jour., 1980-82. Chair numerous coms. St. Leonard Community, Centerville, Ohio, 1978—; telephone vol. Contact-Dayton Crisis Intervention, 1982-86; big sister Big Bros./Big Sisters, Dayton, 1985-86; bd. dirs. Miami Valley chtp. Nat. Kidney Found. of Ohio, 1987—. Recipient Disting. Achievement award Contact-Dayton, 1985, Outstanding Service award Miami Valley chpt. Nat. Kidney Found. of Ohio, 1988. Mem. Nat. Assn. Female Execs., Dayton Soc. Natural History, Marianist Affiliates (co-chmn. 1981-86). Democrat. Roman Catholic. Avocations: gardening, nature, classical music. Home: 7807 Graceland St Dayton OH 45459 Office: NCR Corp World Hdqrs-2 1700 S Patterson Blvd Dayton OH 45479

GABRIEL, BARBARA JAMIESON, educator; b. Pasadena, Calif., Jan. 21, 1929; d. Hamer Hershal and Hazel (Kendall) Jamieson; m. Albert Lawrence Gabriel, June 28, 1947; children—Sam Winston, Bryn Patricia Petersen. B.A. magna cum laude, Calif. State U.-Long Beach, 1971, M.A. in Ednl. Adminstrn., 1982. Cert. tchr., sch. adminstr., Calif. Bilingual tchr. Parkview Sch., 1973-78, minimum essential tchr., 1978-80; instructional materials specialist Mountain View Sch. Dist., El Monte, Calif., 1980—, bilingual program cons., 1985—; dir. Title VII project, 1988-89. Mem. State Book Rev. Com., 1979, Four Dist. Task Force, 1979; sec. El Monte/So. El Monte Coordinating Council; mem. 1989 Cabe Conf. Planning Com.; supporting mem. Aero-Space Mus., Globe Theatre. Mem. Internat. Reading Assn., Assn. Supervision and Curriculum Devel., Nat. Council Tchrs. English, San Diego Zool. Soc., Long Beach Art Mus., Audubon Soc., Phi Kappa Phi, Kappa Delta Pi, Phi Delta Kappa. Clubs: Alamitos Bay Yacht, (Long Beach, Calif.). Office: 2850 N Mountain View Rd El Monte CA 91732

GABRIEL, GAIL VIRGINIA, marketing professional; b. San Francisco, Sept. 6, 1946; d. Albert Leon and Virginia Einnet (Woods) Lavaysse; m. Lyman Jee, Nov. 3, 1973 (div.); m. Jerry Ronald Gabriel, Oct. 11, 1980; 1 child, Alene Michelle. Adminstrv. asst., assoc. Rockrise Odermatt Mountjoy Assocs., San Francisco, 1968-79; mktg. dir., assoc. Robinson Mills & Williams, San Francisco, 1979-87; lectr. in field. Author (with others) Architectural Secretaries Handbook, 1975. Mem. bldg. com. St. Perpetua's Ch., Lafayette, Calif., 1986. Mem. Archtl. Secs. Assn. (No. Calif. chpt. pres. 1973-74, nat. edn. chair 1974-75, nat. pres. elect 1975-76, nat. pres. 1976-77, nat. dir. 1977-78), Soc. Mktg. Profl. Services (pres. San Francisco chpt. 1986-87). Republican. Roman Catholic. Home and Office: Gabriel Consulting 1069 Serrano Ct Lafayette CA 94549

GADINSKY, APRIL DEANNE, management consultant; b. N.Y.C., Apr. 12, 1963; d. Martin and Dorothy (Vitucci) G. BS in Systems Analysis, U. Miami, 1984, MBA, 1985, MS, 1987. Mgmt. cons. Deloitte Haskins and Sells, Miami, Fla., 1985-86; mgmt. services cons. Fla. Power and Light, Miami, 1986—; info. systems researcher U. Miami, Coral Cables, Fla., 1982-84, mgmt. sci. grad. asst., 1985; cons. Eastern Airlines, Miami, 1985, Fontainebleau Hilton Hotel, Miami Beach, Fla., 1987. Mem. Am. Cancer Soc., Miami, 1986. Mem. IEEE, Data Processing Mgmt. Assn. (v.p. student br. 1982-84), Assn. Systems Mgmt., Nat. Assn. Female Execs., Inst. Mgmt. Scis., Ops. Research Soc. Am., Am. Bus. Women's Assn. Home: 10220 SW 87 St Miami FL 33173

GADOMSKI, EVELYN, sales professional; b. Oranienburg, Fed. Republic Germany, Feb. 26, 1934; came to U.S., 1956; d. Rudi and Irmgard (Friszewsky) Hempler; m. John Anthony Gadomski, Dec. 6, 1954 (dec. Dec. 1976); children: Karin Ann, Susan Rose (dec.), Mark Steven. Student, Cedar Crest Coll., 1977-78, Muhlenberg Coll., 1982-83. Sec. Gaismeier, Ulm, Fed. Republic Germany, 1952-53; waitress U.S. Army, Ulm, 1953-54; sec. Harvey Hubbell Inc., Bridgeport, Conn., 1973-74, sales trainee, 1974-75, field salesperson, 1975-79, sr. salesperson, 1979—. Chairperson inner city ministry, St. Paul's Luth. Ch., Allentown, Pa., 1985—. Lodge: Soroptimists. Home: 26 S Jefferson St Allentown PA 18102 Office: Hubbell Inc State St and Bostwick Ave Bridgeport CT 06605

GADSBY, BARBARA ANN, financial planner, consultant; b. Springfield, Mass., Dec. 24, 1945; d. Edward F. and Margaret E. (Price) Corcoran; m. Thomas F. Tiedgen, Apr. 27, 1968 (div. June 1975); m. G. Lawrence Gadsby Jr., May 5, 1978. AA, Vt. Coll., Montpelier, 1965. CLU; chartered fin. cons. Adminstrv. asst. Mass. Mut. Life Co., Springfield and Hartford, Conn., 1965-75; office mgr. Am. Nat. Life Ins. Co., Springfield, 1976; traveling trainee Conn. Gen. Life Ins. Co., Bloomfield, 1976; sales rep. Conn. Gen. Life Ins. Co., Springfield, 1976-77; dir. mktg. NN Life Ins. Services, Johnson, R.I., 1978-80; sales rep. New Eng. Mut. Life Co., Providence, 1980-82; pvt. practice fin. planner Southeastern New Eng. Fin. Group, Newport, R.I., 1982—; pres. Heritage Prodns., Ltd., Newport, R.I., 1988—; cons. Northwestern Mut. Life Ins. Co., Providence, 1986-87. Bd. dirs. YWCA of Greater R.I. Mem. Am. Soc. of CLU's and Chartered Fin. Cons. (v.p. edn. 1986—), R.I. Life Underwriters (pub. relations chair), Newport County Women's Network (co-founder), R.I. Women's Career Network. Republican. Episcopalian. Home: 33 Bonniefield Dr Tiverton RI 02878 Office: Southeastern New Eng Fin Group 1341 W Main Rd Middleport RI 02840

GAERTNER DORADO, MARIANNE, lawyer; b. Neptune, N.J., May 18, 1956; d. Wolfgang W. and Marianne L. (Weber) Gaertner; m. Richard Manuel Dorado, Oct. 1, 1982. BA, Yale U., 1978; JD, U. Mich., 1981. Bar: N.Y. 1982. Adminstrv. asst. W.W. Gaertner Research, Inc., Norwalk, Conn., 1972-79; assoc. Shearman & Sterling, N.Y.C., 1981—; dir. W.W. Gaertner Research, Inc., 1981—. Contbr. articles to profl. jours.; editor U. Mich. Jour. Law Reform, 1980-81. Externship Office Legal Advisor U.S.

Dept. State, 1980. Mem. ABA. Republican. Roman Catholic. Club: Yale. Home: 111 E 30th St New York NY 10016 Office: Shearman & Sterling 599 Lexington Ave New York NY 10022

GAETANO, JOYCE ANN, chemical engineer; b. Pitts., Apr. 4, 1956; d. Samuel S. and Elizabeth A. (Brandy) G. BS in Chem. Engring., U. Pitts., 1978. Engr. research div. Westinghouse Corp., Pitts., 1978; tech. product rep. Mobay Corp. subs. Bayer Corp., Pitts., 1979-81, product mgr., 1981-83, tech. mktg. specialist, 1983-85, project mgr., 1985—. Contbr. articles to profl. jours. Mem. Western Pa. Soc. Engrs., Soc. Automotive Engrs., Soc. Plastics Industry (chmn. polyurethane com. 1979—). Home: 1439 Hidden Timber Manor Pittsburgh PA 15220 Office: Mobay Corp Mobay Rd Pittsburgh PA 15205

GAFFNEY, DOROTHEA FINNEN, retired federal employee, book company executive; b. Paterson, N.J., Aug. 19, 1918; d. Charles Christopher and Mary (Mitchell) Finnen; m. Harold R. Gaffney, Aug. 25, 1951; 1 child, Hale R. Student, Am. U., 1949-51. Asst. chief supply br. spl. services, U.S. Army, 1945-51; procurement officer Quartermaster Corp., U.S. Army, 1951-55; purchasing and contracting officer U.S. Air Force, 1956-59, U.S. Coast Guard, 1959-69; chief procurement br. 3d dist. U.S. Coast Guard, 1969-75; v.p. Am. Overseas Book Co., Norwood, N.J. 1975—. Recipient Silver medal for meritorious achievement U.S. Sec. Transp., 1974. Roman Catholic. Club: Garden Club (pres. 1980-84). Home: 22 Lambeth Ln Lakehurst NJ 08733

GAGE, NANCY ELIZABETH, accountant, college administrator, educator; b. Chgo., Aug. 22, 1947; d. Winfred Paul and Anne Ellen (Osbon) Rankhorn; m. Walter Howard Crane, June 14, 1969 (div. June 1977); 1 child, Patrick; m. James Lewis Gage, June 10, 1977 (div. Oct. 15, 1981); 1 child, Laura Anne. B.S., Ill. Inst. Tech., 1969; postgrad. Winona State U., 1978-80, U. Minn., 1981-82. Cert. tchr. math., Wash., Mich., Ill. Tchr. math. St. Bede Acad., Eau Claire, Wis., 1977; accounts specialist U. Minn., Mpls., 1981, asst. adminstr., 1981-82, assoc. adminstr., 1982-83; grants acct. Coll. of DuPage, Glen Ellyn, Ill., 1984, cash disbursements mgr., 1984-87, chief acct., 1987—; chmn. supervisory com. Fed. Credit Union, 1985-86, mem. project team payroll/personnel systems implementation, 1985-87; mem. project team gen. ledger system implementation,, 1987—. Contbg. author math. curriculum, 1972. Media contact coordinator Common Cause, Manistique, Mich., 1975-76; bd. dirs. pres. Manistique Coop. Nursery Sch., 1974-75; mem. Bicentennial program com. Manistique Jr. Women's Group, Manistique, 1975-76, Chgo. Tchrs. Against the Vietnam War, 1969. Recipient Coll. of DuPage Outstanding Service award, 1987-88; State of Ill. fellow, 1970; Ill. Inst. Tech. scholar, 1964. Mem. Nat. Assn. Female Execs., Coll. of DuPage Classified Personnel Assn., Am. Soc. Profl. and Exec. Women, Kappa Phi Delta (treas. 1967-68). Democrat. Unitarian. Club: Manistique Extension Homemakers (treas. 1974-76). Avocations: tapestries; embroidery; singing; gardening; camping; reading. Home: 1571 Fairway Dr Apt 101 Naperville IL 60540 Office: Coll of DuPage Fin Office 22d St at Lambert Rd Glen Ellyn IL 60137

GAGNÉ, GEORGETTE MARIE, computer company executive; b. New London, Conn., Apr. 1, 1950; d. Armand Joseph and Yvette Alice (Capistran) G.; m. Stephen John Cordeiro, May 22, 1982. BA, U. Mass., Boston, 1972. Phototypographer South Middlesex News, Framingham, Mass., 1973-74, advt. rep., 1974-76; proofreader Digital Equipment Corp., Maynard, Mass., 1976-78, assoc. tech. editor, 1978-81; tech. editor Digital Equipment Corp., Shrewsbury, Mass., 1981-83, sr. tech. editor, 1983-86; publishing unit mgr. Digital Equipment Corp., Marlboro, Mass., 1986—. Recipient 12 editing awards Soc. Tech. Communications. Mem. Nat. Assn. Female Execs., Humane Soc. (distbn. chairperson Framingham chpt.). Club: Middlesex Striders. Home: 65 Pearl St Holliston MA 01746 Office: Digital Equipment Corp MR02-2/D14 1 Iron Way Marlboro MA 01752

GAGNON, EDITH MORRISON, ballerina, singer, actress; b. Chgo., Apr. 8; grad. Chalif Sch. Dancing, N.Y.C.; student Northwestern U.; voice student Forest Lamont of Chgo. Opera Co.; grad. Chalif Sch. of N.Y.; trained with Ivan Tarasoff; m. Alfred Gagnon, Feb. 3, 1977; children by previous marriage—Joyce, Morton. Premiere ballerina Pavley and Oukrainsky Russian Ballet of Chgo., performer with Chgo., Met., Ravinia Opera Cos.; appeared Birthday of Infanta, Greenwich Follies, The Five O'Clock Girl; founder, dir., instr. Sch. of Dance, St. Louis; singer in concert, Carnegie Hall; commentator radio programs Women on the Home Front, Sta. KSD, St. Louis, and CD program Sta. WEW, St. Louis U.; voice coach, producer, performer benefit performances, St. Louis, San Francisco area. Pres. Pets Unlimited, San Francisco; bd. dirs. Artists Embassy. Mem. Pacific Musical Soc. (v.p. San Francisco), Equity Guild. Clubs: Burlingame Country; International Embassy, Francisca

GAGNON, LYNNE MARIE, nurse; b. Presque Isle, Maine, Aug. 1, 1951; d. Guilford Monroe and Caroline (Folger) Smith; m. Daniel Gale Gagnon, Dec. 29, 1971; children—Amber, Dawn, Beth. Nursing diploma Mercy Hosp. Sch. of Nursing, Portland, Maine, 1972; student St. Joseph's Coll., North Windham, Maine, 1969-72, U. Maine-Orono, 1980-84; BSN SUNY-Albany, 1987. Registered nurse, Maine; cert. emergency nurse. Staff nurse St. Agnes Hosp., Balt., 1972-73, Hartford Hosp., Conn., 1973-74; staff nurse, charge nurse A.R. Gould Meml. Hosp., Presque Isle, Maine, 1974-77; staff nurse I, emergency dept. Eastern Maine Med. Ctr., Bangor, Maine, 1979-82, staff developer, 1982—; mem. Gov.'s Adv. Bd. to Emergency Med. Services, 1983-86, chmn., 1985-86, 86-88; chmn. 11th and 14th Ann. New Eng. Symposium on Emergency Nursing, 1985. Bd. dirs. Orono Vol. Rescue Service, 1985—, v.p. 1987, pres. 1988; mem. Maine Seat Belt Coalition, 1986. Mem. Am. Nurses Assn., Maine State Nurses Assn., Emergency Dept. Nurses Assn. (chpt. pres. 1979-81), Nat. Emergency Nurses Assn. (bd. dirs. 1988—), Maine Emergency Nurses Assn. (pres. 1984, 85-86), Nat. Bd. Cert. for Emergency Nurses. Democrat. Roman Catholic. Avocations: cross-country skiing; sewing; reading. Home: RFD 5 Box 260 Bangor ME 04401 Office: Ea Maine Med Ctr Edn and Tng Ctr 489 State St Bangor ME 04401

GAGNON, YVONNE, public relations specialist; b. Old Town, Maine, Feb. 3, 1946; d. Louis and Florence (Sirois) Gagnon. B.A., Albertus Magnus Coll., 1968; postgrad. Fgn. Service Inst., 1975, NYU. Tchr., Peace Corps, Fiji Islands, 1969-71, Colchester/W. Hartford, Conn., Woburn, Mass., 1968, 72-74; manpower tng. and planning advisor Pacific Arch. & Engrs., Jakarta, Indonesia, 1975-77; owner, dir. Transcultural Research Internat., W. Newton, Mass., 1977-80; pub. affairs mgr. Freeport Indonesia, N.Y.C., 1980-85; pub. relations mgr. Nynex Internat., White Plains, N.Y., 1986—. Producer film documentary: Mining Challenge, 1981. Mem. Pub. Relations Soc. Am. Office: NYNEX Internat 4 W Red Oak Ln White Plains NY 10604

GAILEY, SUSAN COIA, psychologist; b. Phila., Apr. 6, 1954; d. Alfred Theodore and Caroline Susan (Dimeo) Coia; m. Ronald Hugh Gailey, Oct. 22, 1977; children: Alycia Susan, Brian Ronald. BA in Psychology, LaSalle Coll., 1976; MEd in Sch. Psychology, Temple U., 1979; MA in Social Psychology, U. Houston, 1985; PhD in Social Psychology, Pacific Western U., 1986. Intern sch. psychology Community Mental Health Mental Retardation Clinic, Phila., 1978-79; sch. psychologist Hatboro-Horsham Sch. Dist., Horsham, Pa., 1979, Montgomery County Intermediate Unit, Norristown, Pa., 1979, Trenton (N.J.) Pub. Schs., 1979-81; research asst. U. Houston and Tex. Inst., Houston, 1981-83; assoc. psychologist St. Louis Devel. Disabilities Treatment Ctrs., 1986—; cons. behavioral systems analysis Systems Ctr., U. Houston, 1983; mem. adv. council Am. Inst. Cancer Research. Vol. psychiat. ward Hahnemann Hosp., Phila., 1975; mem. Christian edn. com. St. Timothy's Episcopal Ch., 1988—. Home: 432 Madewood Ln Chesterfield MO 63017 Office: St Louis Devel Disabilities Treatment Ctrs 1438 S Grand Saint Louis MO 63104

GAILLARD, MARY KATHARINE, physics educator; b. New Brunswick, N.J., Apr. 1, 1939; d. Philip Lee and Marion Catharine (Wiedemayer) Ralph; children: Alain, Dominique, Bruno. BA, Hollins (Va.) Coll., 1960; MA, Columbia U., 1961; Dr du Troiseme Cycle, U. Paris, Orsay, France, 1964, Dr-es-Sciences d'Etat, 1968. With Centre National de Recherche Scientifique, Orsay and Annecy-le-Vieux, France, 1964-84; maitre de recherches Centre National de Recherche Scientifique, Orsay, 1973-80; maitre de recherches Centre National de Recherche Scientifique, Annecy-le-Vieux, 1979-80, dir. research, 1980-84; prof. physics U. Calif., Berkeley, 1981—; Morris Loeb lectr. Harvard U., Cambridge, Mass., 1980; Chancellor's Disting. lectr., U. Calif., Berkeley, 1981; Warner-Lambert lectr. U. Mich., Ann Arbor, 1984; vis. scientist Fermi Nat. Accelerator Lab., Batavia, Ill., 1973-74, Inst. for Advanced Studies, Santa Barbara, Calif., 1984; group leader L.A.P.P., Theory Group, France, 1979-81, Theory Physics div. LBL, Berkeley, 1985-87; sci. dir. Les Houches (France) Summer Sch., 1981; cons., mem. adv. panels U.S. Dept. Energy, Washington, and various nat. labs. Co-editor: Weak Interactions, 1977, Gauge Theories in High Energy Physics, 1983; author or co-author 120 articles, papers to profl jours., books, conf. proceedings. Recipient Thibaux prize U. Lyons (France) Acad. Art & Sci., 1977. Fellow Am. Phys. Soc. (mem. various coms., chair com. on women); mem. Assn. Women in Sci., AAAS. Office: U Calif Dept Physics Berkeley CA 94720

GAINER, LEILA JOSEPHINE, trade association executive; b. Balt., Dec. 4, 1948; d. Theodore Leo and Leila Lee (Harrison) Dworkowski; m. Robert Michael Gainer, Aug. 21, 1971. BA in English, Frostburg State Coll., 1970. Editor labor law reports Commerce Clearing House, Inc., Washington, 1970-75, reporter, editor in community devel., edn., 1975-77; editor Washington Report Nat. Assn. Regional Councils, Washington, 1977-78, lobbyist, 1978-83, dir. fed. relations, communications, research, 1983-86; dir. nat. affairs Am. Soc. Tng. Devel., Alexandria, Va., 1986—. Mem. Coalition Adult Edn. Assns. (bd. dirs.), Am. League Lobbyists, Am. Soc. Assn. Execs., Nat. Tech. Edn. Coalition (steering com.), Nat. Assn. Female Execs. Office: Am Soc Tng Devel 1630 Duke St Alexandria VA 22313

GAINES, KATHLYN ANNE, nursing specialist; b. Florence, Colo., Dec. 20, 1934; d. William Cody Gaines and Estelle May (Smith) Rizk. B.S. in Nursing, Syracuse U., 1962; M.Nursing, U. Fla., 1969; D.S. in Nursing, U. Ala., 1981. R.N. Rehab. coordinator Ohio State U., Columbus, 1965-67; asst. prof. Western Carolina U., Cullowhee, 1969-73; clinician Duke U./ Highland Hosp., Asheville, N.C., 1973-75; mental health coordinator Vis. Nurses Assn., Cleve., 1980-81; chmn. nursing div. Carson-Newman Coll., Jefferson City, Tenn., 1982-86; clin. nurse specialist Lakeshore Mental health Inst., Knoxville, 1986—; rehab. nursing cons. Ohio Dept. Health, Columbus, 1965-67, Orthopedic Hosp., Asheville, 1970-72; mental health nursing cons. Smokey Mountains Mental Health Ctr., Cullowhee, 1970-72, Highland Hosp., Asheville, 1970-72; mem. adv. council Your Home Vis. Nurse, Knoxville, 1982—. Mem. Friends of the Library, Jefferson City, 1982—. Mem. Am. Nurses Assn., Am. Orthopsychiatric Assn., Inc., Assn. Rehab. Nurses, Nat. League for Nurses, Council Psychiat. Mental Health Nurses, AAUW, LWV, Sigma Theta Tau, Omicron Delta Kappa, Beta Sigma Phi. Episcopalian. Club: Les Amies (Jefferson City). Avocations: crocheting; reading; flower gardening; jigsaw puzzles. Home: 806 S Branner #31 Jefferson City TN 37760 Office: Lakeshore Mental Health Inst 5908 Lyons View Dr Knoxville TN 37760

GAINES, PAMELA GAYE, corporate credit executive; b. Chgo., July 20, 1960; d. William J. and JoAnn (Stone) Helm; 1 child, Erica K. Diploma in Programming Computers for Bus., Devry Inst. Tech. Clerk Oakbrook Marriott Hotel, Ill., 1981-82, credit supr., 1982-84; supr. Marriott Downtown Hotel Corp., Chgo., 1984-85; credit mgr. Executive House Hotel, Chgo., 1985—; corp. credit mgr. Mgmt. Group, Inc., Chgo., 1986—. Recipient Employee of Month award Marriott Oakbrook Hotel, 1983; Predsl. Honor Soc. Devry Inst. Tech., 1984. Assoc. mem. Chgo. Hotel and Motel Assn. (meeting hostess 1985-87, v.p. 1987), Chgo. Hotel Motel Credit Mgrs. Assn. (pres. 1988), Nat. Credit Mgrs. Assn. (assoc., legis. com. mem. 1988-89). Office: Ambassador West Hotel 1300 N State Pkwy Chicago IL 60610

GAISER, SHARON DARLENE, financial planner; b. Hazel Park, Mich., Nov. 9, 1945; d. Phillip Nelson and Mary Louise (Metcalf) Jourdan; m. Richard Eric Gaiser, June 3, 1967 (div. 1982); m. Ronald Revere Yerman, Aug. 3, 1984; children: Jason Richard, Jon Eric. Student Cen. Mich. U. Sec., D.P. Bros., Advt., Detroit, 1964-65, Gen. Motors, Warren, Mich., 1965-69; customer service rep. Consumers Power, Pontiac, Mich., 1977-79; sales engr. Infinity, Inc., Southfield, Mich., 1980—, pres. rep. div., 1985—; fin. planning and services rep. Waddell & Reed Fin. Services, 1987—. Creative participant Bi-centennial Floatable Boatable Community Affairs 1976 (award). Pres. Rochester Newcomers Club, Rochester Hills, 1978-79, PTA Peace Lutheran Sch., Utica, Mich., 1978-79; mem. Beautification Commn., Sterling Heights, Mich., 1972-73, Hist. Commn., Rochester Hills, 1976-77. Recipient sales awards, Pro Log Corp. and Infinity, Inc., 1982, 83, 84. Home: 400 Willow Grove Rochester Hills MI 48063 Office: Infinity Inc 3310 Auburn Rd Auburn Heights MI 48057

GAISER, SHEILA MARIE, travel consultant; b. Elizabeth City, N.C., Nov. 17, 1944; d. Cyrus Newton and Ethel Marie (Herbig) G.; m. Curtis W. Bryan, May 5, 1967 (div. 1973); children—Richard M., Steven M. Student Tex. Tech U., 1962-64; B.S., North Tex. State U., 1966, postgrad., 1976-81. Tchr. Irving Ind. Sch. Dist. (Tex.), 1966-71; bookkeeper Arthur Andersen & Co., Dallas, 1972-75; staff acct. Bosco Fastening Service Ctr., Dallas, 1975-80; mgr. compliance dept. Maguire Oil Co., Dallas, 1980-86; tax consultant, Santa Fe Minerals, Inc., 1986-87; travel cons. Airport Travel Inc., 1987—; co-chmn. KERA-TV, Dallas, 1977, mem., 1976—; active PTA, Farmers Branch, Tex., 1975—. Mem. AAUW (legis. com., chmn. Farmers br./Carrollton 1984-85, v.p. 1985-86, pres. 1986-88, interbr. council rep. 1986-88), Nat. Accts. Assn., Nat. Assn. Female Execs., Phi Chi Theta. Mem. Christian Ch. Office: Airport Travel Inc 4455 LBJ Freeway Suite 115 Dallas TX 75244

GAISSER, JULIA HAIG, classical educator; b. Cripple Creek, Colo., Jan. 12, 1941; s. Henry Wolseley and Gertrude Alice (Lent) Haig; m. Thomas Korff Gaisser, Dec. 29, 1964; 1 son, Thomas Wolseley. A.B., Brown U., 1962; A.M., Harvard U., 1966; Ph.D., U. Edinburgh (Scotland), 1966. Asst. prof. Newton Coll. (Mass.), 1966-69, Swarthmore Coll., (Pa.), 1970-72, Bklyn. Coll., 1973-75; assoc. prof. dept. Latin Bryn Mawr Coll. (Pa.), 1975-84, prof., 1984—, editor Bryn Mawr Latin Commentaries, 1983—. Mem. Mid-East selection com. Marshall Scholarships, Washington, 1975—, chmn., 1984—; mem. mng. com. Intercollegiate Ctr. for Classical Studies in Rome, Stanford, Calif., 1984—, chmn. 1988—. Marshall scholar, U. Edinburgh, 1962-64; NEH summer stipend, 1977; research grantee Am. Philosophical Soc., 1980; ACLS Travel grant, 1985; NEH sr. fellow, 1985-86. Mem. Am. Philological Assn. (dir. 1985—), Renaissance Soc. Am., Internat. Neo-Latin Soc. Office: Bryn Mawr Coll Dept Latin Bryn Mawr PA 19010

GAL, HILLARY GENE, infosystems specialist; b. Austin, Tex., Feb. 1, 1952; d. Martin and Jean Marion (Genebach) G.; m. Rustin Allan Billingsly, Dec. 15, 1978 (div. 1981); m. William Kiley, Nov. 3, 1984. B in Music, Fla. State U., 1973, MFA, 1976. Asst. dir. dance 92d St YMHA, N.Y.C., 1978-82; freelance dance notation N.Y.C., 1980-82; asst. v.p. systems Drexel Burnham Lambert, N.Y.C., 1983—; mem. computer com. Dance Notation Bur., N.Y.C., 1986—. Bd. dirs. Laban Inst. for Movement Studies, N.Y.C., 1987, Dance Edn. Found., Westchester, 1982. Office: Drexel Burnham Lambert Inc 25 Broadway New York NY 10004

GALANE, IRMA ADELE BERESTON, electronic engineer; b. Balt., Aug. 23, 1921; d. Dr. Arthur and Sarah (Hillman) Bereston; B.A., Goucher Coll., 1940; postgrad. Johns Hopkins, 1940-42, Mass. Inst. Tech., 1943, George Washington U., 1945, 65, 73, 77, 79, U. Md., 1958, Army Mgmt. Sch., 1964; 1 dau., Suzanne Felice Galane Duvall. Physicist, Naval Ordnance Lab., 1942-43; electronic engr. Navy Bur. Ships, 1943-49, Army Office Chief Signal Officer, 1949-51, Navy Bur. Aeros., 1951-56, Air Research and Devel. Command, USAF, 1956-57, FCC, 1957-60, NASA, 1960-62; supervisory electronic engr. USCG Hdqrs., 1962-64; sci. specialist engring. scis. Library of Congress, 1964-65; project engr. Advanced Aerial Fire Support System, Army Materiel Command, 1965-66; engr. Naval Air Systems Command, 1966-71; electronic engr. Spectrum Mgmt. Task Force, FCC, 1971-76, sr. research engr. FCC, 1976—; Judge nat. capitol awards for engrs. and architects, 1975. Registered profl. engr., D.C. Mem. IEEE (sr.), Am. Inst. Aeros. and Astronautics, Nat. Soc. Profl. Engrs. (chmn. publs. com. 1959-60, co-chmn. civil def. com. 1965, spl. asst. to pres. 1965), Soc. Women Engrs. (sr. mem.; nat. membership chmn. 1952, nat. dir. 1953, mem. nat. scholarship com. 1958), Armed Forces Communications and Electronics Assn., Fedn. Profl. Assn., Am. Ordnance Assn., Johns Hopkins Alumni Assn., AAAS, U.S. Naval Inst., Marine Tech. Soc., Internat. Platform Assn., Smithsonian Inst. (assoc.), Mensa. Editor: The Met. Washington Profl. Engr., 1958-60. Home: 4201 Cathedral Ave NW Washington DC 20016

GALANTE, JANE HOHFELD, pianist, music historian; b. San Francisco, Feb. 14, 1924; d. Edward and Lillian (Devendorf) Hohfeld; A.B., Vassar Coll., 1944; M.A., U. Calif.-Berkeley, 1949; m. Clement Galante, Dec. 26, 1956; children—Edward Elio, John Clement. Instr., U. Calif., Berkeley, 1948-52, Mills Coll., Oakland, Calif., 1950-52; music editor Berkeley, A Jour. of Modern Culture, 1944-52; founder, dir. Composer's Forum of San Francisco, 1946-56; concert pianist German tours for USIS, 1952-54; Young Audience Concerts, San Francisco, 1963-70; now mem. Lyra Chamber Music Ensemble; trustee Morrison Chamber Music Center at San Francisco State U., ; hon. trustee San Francisco Conservatory of Music, 1970—. Transl.: Darius Milhaud (Paul Collaer). Decorated chevalier de l'ordre des arts et des lettres. Mem. Am. Fedn. of Musicians, Women Musicians Club of San Francisco, Chamber Music Am.

GALANTE, MARY THERESE, nurse; b. Albany, N.Y., Nov. 25, 1956; d. Thomas Joseph and Anne Therese (Davis) Dunvar; m. Nicholas Thomas Galante, III, June 10, 1978; children—Elizabeth Nolan, Nicholas Thomas, Katharine Carey, James Davis. B.S. in Nursing, Catholic U. Am., 1978. Nurse pvt. office, Washington, 1975-77; nurse acute CCU, St. Peter Hosp., Albany, N.Y., 1979-80, registered profl. nurse Tri-Cities Nursing Registry, Albany, 1982—, patient care coordinator, 1983—. Vol., mem. fundraising com. Am. Cancer Soc., 1979—, Leukemia Soc., 1978—, M.S. Assn., 1983—; sec., chmn. Jr. League Provisional Com., Troy, N.Y., 1983-85, chmn. ways and means com., 1986-87, mem. ednl. policy and long-range planning com. Emma Willard Children's Sch., 1985-86, bd. dirs., 1984-87, active mem. Jr. League of Albany, 1987—. Author: Hold the Fort, 1984. Mem. Am. Nursing Assn., Nat. League Nursing. Democrat. Roman Catholic. Home: 10 Loudon Heights N Loudonville NY 12211

GALBRAITH, NORMA LUCILLE, investment counseling firm executive; b. Nelta, Tex., Nov. 9, 1938; d. Dennis Wayne and Pauline (Neal) Shrode; m. Lawrence C. Galbraith III, Aug. 23, 1957 (div. Apr. 1980); children—Sherri Lynn Galbraith Morgan, Lawrence C. IV. Student Eastfield Coll., 1977, Amber U., 1980—. Bookkeeper, H.E. Vaughan-Cotton, Dallas, 1966-70; sec., bookkeeper Dallas Christian Sch., Mesquite, Tex., 1970-75; sr. sec. Bonanza Internat., Dallas, 1975-77; trust portfolio asst. Mercantile Bank, Dallas, 1977-80; controller MSecurities Corp., Dallas, 1981-87, asst. v.p., 1987—. Sec. Dallas Christian Sch. PTA, Mesquite, Tex., 1971. Mem. Nat. Assn. Female Execs. Mem. Ch. of Christ. Home: 9423 Gonzales Dr Dallas TX 75227 Office: MSecurities Corp 1717 Main St Dallas TX 75201

GALBRAITH, RUTH LEGG, retired university dean, home economist; b. Lecompte, La., Nov. 5, 1923; d. Byron S. and Dora Ruth (Lindley) Legg; m. Harry W. Galbraith, June 16, 1950; 1 son, Allan Legg. B.S., Purdue U., 1945, Ph.D., 1950. Chemist E.I. duPont de Nemours, Waynesboro, Va., 1945-46; textile chemist Gen. Electric Co., Bridgeport, Conn., 1946-47; teaching asst. Purdue U., 1947-48, research fellow, 1948-50; prof. textiles and clothing U. Tenn., Knoxville, 1950-55; asso. prof. U. Ill., Urbana, 1956-64; prof. U. Ill., 1964-70, chmn. textiles and clothing div., 1962-70; prof., head consumer affairs dept. Auburn (Ala.) U., 1970-73; dean Sch. Home Econs., head home econs. research, 1973-85; mem. task force on quality of living Dept. Agr., 1967-68; mem. nat. adv. com. Flammable Fabrics Act, 1971-73; mem. U.S. Dept. Agr. Com. of Nine, 1981-83, chmn., 1983. Mem. editorial bd.: Research Jour. Home Econs., 1973-77, chmn. policy bd., 1978-80; contbr. articles to profl. jours. Recipient Disting. Alumni award Purdue U., 1970. Fellow Am. Inst. Chemists; mem. Am. Home Econs. Assn. (chmn. agy. mem. unit 1975-76, chmn. research sect. 1978-80, Outstanding Home Economist award 1984), Ala. Home Econs. Assn. (pres. 1983-84), Am. Assn. Textile Chemists and Colorists, Am. Chem. Soc., ASTM (3d v.p. com. D-13 textiles 1975-79), Assn. Adminstrs. Home Econs., Nat. Council Adminstrs. Home Econs., AAUW, Sigma Xi, Omicron Nu, Phi Kappa Phi, Delta Kappa Gamma. Home: 368 Singleton St Auburn AL 36830

GALE, MARLA, clinical social worker; b. Uniontown, Pa., July 20; d. Saul and Sarah (Lisowitz) Krongold; m. Edward Gale, June 12, 1954; children: Jeffrey, Wendy, Lori. AB magna cum laude, U. Miami, 1970; MSW, Barry Coll., 1972. Diplomate in clin. social work. Research social worker VA Hosp., Miami, Fla., 1971; caseworker Jewish Family Service Broward County, Hollywood, Fla., 1971-81, supr. profl. staff, 1981—; mem. clin. faculty Barry U., Miami Shores, Fla.; parent effectiveness instr.; real estate investor and developer; pres. Gold Coast Convenient Food Marts. Mem. Nat. Assn. Social Workers, Acad. Cert. Social Workers, Common Cause, Project Newborn, Met. Mus., Animal Protection Soc., Diabetes Research Inst. Democrat. Jewish. Office: 4517 Hollywood Blvd Hollywood FL 33021

GALE, SHIRLEY MCCLARD, travel agency executive, child psychologist; b. Clearlake, S.D., Jan. 19, 1931; d. George Marvin and Lillian Deloris (Beck) McClard; m. Kenneth Stanley Gale, Aug. 25, 1951; children: Kenneth, Lyndy, Kathy, David. AB, Friends U., 1952; MA, N.Mex. State U., 1967; EdS, Ea. N.Mex. U., 1978. Cert. tchr., sch. psychologist. Tchr. elems. schs. in Kans., Ariz., Va., N.Mex., 1952-67, counselor, ednl. diagnostician Portales (N.Mex.) Schs., 1967-84, coordinator spl. edn., 1980-84; pres. Internat. Tours of Tucson, 1984—; chair N.Mex. State Testing Commn., 1980-84; mem. N.Mex. State Commn. Spl. Edn., 1976-80; chair N.Mex. State Commn. Foster Care, 1982-84. Editor Travel Trivia, 1984—. Sec. Altrusa Internat., 1978-84, LWV, 1966-80. Mem. Am. Bus. Women's Assn., Am. Soc. Travel Agts., Pacific Area Travel Assn., Cruise Lines Internat. Assn., Tucson Met. C. of C., NEA (life), AAUW (v.p. 1966-68), Resources for Women, Delta Kappa Gamma (pres. 1982-84), P.E.O. Avocations: music, sports. Home: 3150 N Avenida Del Conejo Tucson AZ 85749 Office: Internat Tours Tucson 7650 E Broadway Suite 207 Tucson AZ 85710

GALER, MARY JANE, state legislator, librarian; b. Port Arthur, Tex., June 30, 1924; d. Harry F. and Clara Williams (Graham) Perkins; B.S.L.S., Carnegie Inst. Tech., 1947; B.A. in Edn., U. Pitts., 1945; m. Robert Fulton Galer, Nov. 7, 1951; children—Frank Fulton, Barbara Jean, Robin Robson. Librarian, U.S. Army, Korea, Japan and Calif., 1948-52, Ft. Benning, Ga., 1960-65, Mobile (Ala.) Public Library, 1966; asso. prof. library sci. Columbus (Ga.) Coll., 1967-76; mem. Ga. Ho. of Reps., 1977—; dir. library services Troy State U. at Ft. Benning, 1986—. Co-founder, bd. dirs. Contact Teleministries, 1978-82; bd. dirs. Columbus Symphony, 1979-86, 87—; mem. Ga. Democratic Com.; del. Dem. Nat. Conv., 1980, 88; adv. com. project Nat. Women's Edn. Fund, 1982-83. Recipient Columbus Public Service award, 1975, Women Helping Women award Soroptimist Internat., 1975, Maxine Goldstein freedom award Democratic Women, 1984, others. Mem. LWV, DAR, Ga. Library Assn., AAUW (pres. 1975-79), Nat. Conf. State Legislatures (co-chmn. women's network 1982-83, exec. com. 1984-87), Defense Adv. Com. Women in the Service, 1988—, Phi Delta Kappa, Alpha Delta Kappa. Presbyterian. Club: Soroptimist (public affairs chmn. 1977, dir. 1978). Indexer: (with others) microfilm collection Herstory; author: Women and State Pensions; Legislative Guide to Issues of Equity.

GALICIAN, MARY-LOU, broadcasting educator; b. New Bedford, Mass., Apr. 5, 1946; d. Benn and Evelyn Nancy (Scott) G. BA magna cum laude, L.I. U., 1966; MS, Syracuse U., 1969; EdD, Memphis State U., 1978. Writer, N.Y. corr. Standard Times, New Bedford, 1961-66; producer, dir., talk show host Sta. WCMU-TV, Mt. Pleasant, Mich., 1967-70, dir. programming, 1968-70; v.p., dir. Evelyn-Nancy Cosmetiques, Inc., New Bedford, 1970-73; nat. advt. mgr. Maybelline Co./Schering-Plough, Memphis, 1973-75; pres., creator FUN-dynamics!, Memphis, Little Rock, Phoenix, 1976—; prof. journalism Memphis State U., 1978-80; nat. mktg. mgr. Fedn. Am. Hosps., Little Rock and Washington, 1980-82; prof. broadcasting Ariz. State U., Tempe, 1983—; motivation, communication cons. various nat. pub. and pvt. orgns., 1966—; speaker, performer nat. convs. and co., 1966—; mem. broadcast services subcom. FCC Industry Adv. Com., Grand Rapids, Mich., 1967-70; mem. adv. bd. Cen. Mich. Ednl. Resources Council, Mich., 1967-70; anchor nat. TV fund drives, 1984—. Author: Medical Education and the Physician-Patient Relationship, 1978, The Dr. Galician Prescription for Healthy Media Relations, 1980; writer, producer No Miracles Here, 1967, Witch is it?, 1969-70, Saturday's Child: 20 Years of Network TV Children's Programs, 1969; editor: The Coming Victory, 1980; radio hostess To Broadway with Love, 1967, TV hostess Interview with Mary-Lou Galician, 1967-70; scriptwriter, songwriter, presenter FUN-dynamics! The FUN-damentals of DYNAMIC Living, 1976—; writer, performer FUN-dynamics! FUN-notes, 1982; contbr. articles to profl. publs. Charter mem. Symphony League of Cape Cod, Mass., 1972-73; adviser Boy

Scout Explorer Post, Cape Cod, 1972-73; mem. exec. bd. Tenn.-Ark.-Miss. Girl Scouts U.S., Memphis, 1973-75; patron Memphis Ballet Co., 1974-75; mem. steering com. Make Today Count, Memphis, 1976; Health Systems Agy. Council mem. MidSouth Med. Ctr. Council, Memphis, 1976-78; chair campaign kick-off Valley of the Sun United Way, Phoenix, 1987; co-chair Ariz. State U. United Way Campaign, 1988-90. Recipient Cert. Achievement, S.W. Edn. Council for Journalism, 1985, 86, 87, Walter Cronkite Sch. Service award, 1988; named Mich.'s Woman of Yr., Outstanding Ams. Found., 1969; Conolly Coll. scholar L.I. U., 1963-66; grantee Ariz. State U., 1984, 85, 87; Syracuse U. fellow, 1966-67. Mem. AAUW (bd. dirs. Mich. and Mass. chpts. 1967-73), Am. Advt. Fedn. (pyramid awards com. 1980), Am. Women in Radio and TV (com. chair Tenn. chpt. 1979), Ariz. State U. Faculty Women's Assn., Assn. Edn. in Journalism and Mass Communication, Broadcast Edn. Assn. (promotion com. 1985, leadership challenge com. 1988—), Pub. Relations Soc. Am. (faculty adviser Ariz. State U. 1983-84), Sales and Mktg. Execs. Internat. (com. chair Ark. chpt. 1981-83), Women in Communications Inc. (founding faculty adviser Cen. Mich. U. 1969-70, Memphis State U. 1979-80, Ariz. State U. 1985—, bd. dirs. Phoenix Profl. chpt., 1985—, mem. Nat. bd. dirs. and v.p. Far West region, 1987—, nat. editorial bd. 1987—, Outstanding Adv. award 1985-86), Zeta Tau Alpha (gen. faculty adviser 1968-70, membership adviser 1974-75). Club: Univ. of Ariz. State U. Home: 614 E Diamond Dr Tempe AZ 85283 Office: Ariz State U Walter Cronkite Sch Journalism Tempe AZ 85287-1305

GALINDO, ERNESTINE, manufacturing executive; b. Plugerville, Tex., Jan. 23, 1931; d. Eliseo Barrera and Rita (Ortegon) Guajardo; m. Thomas Galindo II, Feb. 20, 1955; children—Thomas Eliseo III, Guillermo Eloy. Prodn. staff El Fenix, Austin, Tex., 1960-73; pres. El Galindo, Inc., Austin, 1973—. Recipient Businesswoman of Yr. award Mex. Am. C. of C., 1983. Home: 2911 Bowman Austin TX 78703 Office: El Galindo Inc 1601 E 6th St Austin TX 78702

GALKIN, FLORENCE, social worker; b. N.Y.C., Dec. 27, 1925; d. Victor and Sadie (Sobel) Greenwald; BA, Hunter Coll., 1946; MSW, U. Pa., 1951; advanced cert. Columbia U., 1961, postgrad., NIMH fellow, 1962-64; m. Bernard Galkin, Dec. 18, 1948; children: Judith, William Seth. Caseworker, Jewish Child Care Assn., N.Y.C., 1951-57; field instr. community orgn. Birds Coler Hosp., 1968; ombudsman program Community Council Greater N.Y., 1978—; research assoc. Center Policy Research, 1980—; exec. dir. Community Action and Resources for the Elderly, 1976—; nat. v.p.Am. Jewish Congress, 1986—. Bd. dirs. Nat. Coalition for Nursing Home Reform, 1978-79. Mem. Nat. Assn. Social Workers. Jewish. Author: People and Nursing Homes, 1977; (with others) Neighborhood Information Center: A Study and Some Proposals, 1966; (with Hochbaum) The New York State Patient Advocacy Program, Patients and Their Complaints, 1978, Discharge Planning: No Deposit, No Return, 1982, Medicaid Patients Need Not Apply, 1987. Home: 400 E 56th St New York NY 10022 Office: Am Jewish Congress 15 E 84th St New York NY 10028

GALL, ADRIENNE LYNN, managing editor; b. Long Branch, N.J., Jan. 25, 1960; d. Robert Conrad and Anna May (Critchfield) Gall. B.A., Hood Coll., Md., 1982. Editorial asst. Polo Mag., Fleet St. Corp., Gaithersburg, Md., 1982-83; assoc. editor Nat. Solid Wastes Mgmt. Assn., Washington, 1983-86; mng. editor Am. Soc. Tng. & Devel., Alexandria, Va., 1986—. Mem. Nat. Assn. Female Execs., Smithsonian Assocs. Democrat. Avocations: equestrienne; historic preservation; environmental conservation. Office: Am Soc Tng & Devel 1630 Duke St Box 1443 Alexandria VA 22313

GALL, ELIZABETH BENSON, dating service executive; b. Williamson, W.Va., June 11, 1944; d. Thomas Jefferson Bluebaum (stepfather) and Ollie Mae (Moore) Bluebaum Walker; 1 stepchild, Charles B. Walker; 1 child, Thomas Ethan. Ptnr., dir. Chicagoland Register, dating service, Chgo., 1974-84; cooking instr. Elizabeth Benson Internat. Cooking Lessons, 1978-84; owner Ethnic Party People Catering, 1981—, Phone-A-Friend Dating Service, Chgo., 1984—. Home and Office: 6314 N Troy St Chicago IL 60659

GALL, LENORE ROSALIE, educational administrator; b. Bklyn., Aug. 9, 1943; d. George W. Gall and Olive Rosalie (Weekes) Gall Bryant. AAS, NYU, 1970, cert. tng. and devel., 1975, BS in Mgmt., 1973, MA in Counselor Edn., 1977; EdM and EdD, Columbia U., 1988. Various positions Ford Found., N.Y.C., 1967-75; dep. dir. career devel. Grad. Sch. Bus., NYU, N.Y.C., 1976-79; dir. career devel. Pace Lubin Sch. Bus., N.Y.C., 1979-82; dir. career devel. Sch. Mgmt., Yale U., New Haven, 1982-85; asst. to assoc. provost Bklyn. Coll., 1985-88, asst. to provost, 1988—; adj. lectr. LaGuardia Community Coll., L.I. City, N.Y., 1981—, Sch. Continuing Edn. NYU, 1983-84; dir., sec. devel. workshop Coll. Placement Services, Bethlehem, Pa., 1978-81. Bd. dirs. Langston Hughes Community Library, Corona, N.Y., 1975-83, 86—, chair, 1975-79, 82-83, 2d v.p., 1986, 1st v.p., 1987-88, chair awards com. Dollars for Scholars, Corona, 1976—. Mem. Assn. Black Women in Higher Edn. (exec. bd., membership chair, pres.-elect 1988), Am. Assn. Univ. Adminstrs., Nat. Assn. Univ. Women (chaplain 1987-88, 2d v.p. 1988), AAUW, Nat. Assn. Women Deans and Adminstrs., Black Faculty and Staff Assn. Bklyn. Coll. (1st vice-chair 1986-87, chair 1987-88), New Haven C. of C. (chmn. women bus. and industry conf. 1984), Nat. Council Negro Women Inc. (1st v.p. North Queens sect. 1986—), Phi Delta Kappa, Kappa Delta Pi. Mem. A.M.E. Ch. Office: CUNY Bklyn Coll 3137 Boylan Hall Bedford Ave and Ave H Brooklyn NY 11210

GALLAGHER, ANNE PORTER, business executive; b. Coral Gables, Fla., Mar. 16, 1950; d. William Moring and Anne (Jewett) Porter; m. Matthew Philip Gallagher, Jr., July 31, 1976; children: Jacqueline Anne, Kevin Sharkey. B.A. in Edn., Stetson U., 1972. Tchr. elem. schs., Atlanta, 1972-74; sales rep. Xerox Corp., Atlanta, 1974-76, Fed. Systems, Rosslyn, Va., 1976-81; sales rep. No. Telecom Inc. Fed. Systems, Vienna, Va., 1981-84, account exec., 1984-85, sales dir., 1985—. Mem. Nat. Assn. Female Execs., Pi Beta Phi. Episcopalian. Avocations: skiing, aerobics, needlepoint. Home: 4052 Seminary Rd Alexandria VA 22304 Office: No Telecom Fed Systems Inc 8614 Westwood Center Dr Vienna VA 22180

GALLAGHER, CATHY LOUISE, health care consultant; b. Detroit, Jan. 21, 1948; d. Norman James and Vera Pearl (Prott) G. BA, Adrian (Mich.) Coll., 1970; MA, Mich. State U., 1980. Home service advisor Consumer Power Co., Muskegon, Mich., 1970-72; home economist, info. specialist, media cons. coop. extension service Mich. State U., East Lansing, 1972-81; sales rep. John Hancock Mut. Ins. Co., Southfield, Mich., 1981-82, Surgikos subs. Johnson & Johnson Co., Toledo, 1982-84, NDM Corp., Milw., 1984-85; profl. services cons. HPI Health Care Services, Inc., Milw., 1985-86; sr. cons. HPI Health Care Services, Inc., Milw. and Atlanta, 1986—; speaker in field. Mem. Nat. Speakers Assn., Wis. Profl. Speakers Assn. Home: 9102 North 75th St Apt 3-B Milwaukee WI 53223-2056 Office: HPI Health Care Services 1080 Holcomb Bridge Rd Suite 200 Roswell GA 30076

GALLAGHER, DOLORES ELIZABETH, psychologist; b. N.Y.C., Aug. 7, 1944; d. Joseph and Elizabeth (Goehringer) Ruebeck; B.S., Fordham U., 1965; M.A., Duquesne U., 1967; Ph.D. (NIMH fellow), U. So. Calif., 1979; m. William J. Gallagher, Aug. 27, 1966 (dec. 1979); m. 2d, Larry W. Thompson, Dec. 12, 1981. Rehab. psychologist Fedn. Handicapped, N.Y.C., 1965-72; staff psychologist Altoona (Pa.) Hosp. Community Mental Health Center, 1972-74; clin. psychologist Los Angeles County Occupational Health Services, 1975-77; intern Neuropsychiat. Inst. of UCLA, 1977-78; staff psychologist Adult Counseling Center, Andrus Gerontology Center, U. So. Calif., 1978-79, acting dir., 1980-81; adj. asst. prof. psychology U. So. Calif., 1978-80; co-dir. interdisciplinary team tng. program in geriatrics Palo Alto VA Med. Center, 1981-83, asst. dir. edn. and evaluation, 1983-85; assoc. dir. edn. and program evaluation Geriatric Research Edn. and Clin. Ctr., Palo Alto VA Med. Ctr., 1985—; pvt. practice Cognitive Therapy Assocs., Los Altos, Calif.; lectr. Stanford U. Sch. Medicine; clin. asst. prof. dept. psychiatry, instr. program in human biology, 1983—; research cons. aging projects in Los Angeles and San Francisco Bay areas. Trustee, Suicide Prevention and Crisis Center San Mateo County, 1981—; cons. Los Angeles County Suicide Prevention Center, 1981—. Recipient grants Nat. Inst. Aging, NIMH; lic. psychologist, Calif.; cert. Nat. Register Health Service Providers in Psychology. Mem. Am. Psychol. Assn., Soc. Psychotherapy Research, Gerontol. Soc. Am., Calif. Council Gerontology and Geriatrics, Sierra Club. Democrat. Mem. Self-Realization Fellowship. Author: (with others) Depression in the Elderly: A Behavioral Treatment Manual, 1981; (with Larry Thompson) Treatment of Late-Life Depression; contbr. articles profl. jours. Home: 2049 Fallen Leaf Ln Los Altos CA 94022 Office: Geriatric Research Edn and Clin Center 182B Palo Alto VA Medical Center 3801 Miranda Ave Palo Alto CA 94304 Other: Cognitive Therapy Assocs 745 Distel Dr Suite F Los Altos CA 94022

GALLAGHER, DONA LEE, vocational educator; b. Chgo., Dec. 2, 1935; d. Starr Reynolds and Sarah Lillard (Newton) Dickson; m. James Lawrence Gallagher, June 9, 1956; children: Theresa, Timothy, Thomas, Tina. BA, U. Guam, 1970; postgrad., Tex. A&M U., 1971, Stephen F. Austin U., 1971, North Tex. U., 1972. cert. tchr., tex. Various clerical postions Tex., 1955-70; tchr. career devel. Jefferson Jr. Sch., Beeville, Tex., 1970-71; edn. cons. San Antonio Independant Schs., 1971-73; vocat. educator Gatesville (Tex.) Jr. High Sch., 1973—; instr. Cen. Tex. Coll., Killeen, 1986—; cons. on workshops, curriculum Tex. Edn. Agy., 1973—; facilitator permanent diaconate program Diocese of Austin, Gatesville, 1979—. Alt. del. Rep. State Convention, Gatesville, 1980, chair precinct, Gatesville, 1980-86; dir. religious edn., organist Our Lady of Lourdes Catholic Ch., Gatesville, 1983—. Mem. Tex. Vocat. Guidance Assn., Tex. Computer Edn. Assn., Sisters of Charity of Nazareth Assoc. Home: 202 Mulberry PO Box 665 Gatesville TX 76528-0665

GALLAGHER, ELEANOR, financial institution administrator; b. Paterson, N.J., Dec. 14, 1936; d. Stephen and Vera Francis (Stagg) Margiel; married, 1959; children: Margaret, Patricia. Asst. treas. North Jersey Fed. Credit Union, Totowa, N.J., 1972-84, v.p., 1984—. Mem. Passaic Valley C. of C. (2d v.p. 1984-85, 1st v.p. 1985-87, pres. 1987—). Roman Catholic.

GALLAGHER, IDELLA JANE SMITH (MRS. DONALD A. GALLAGHER), foundation executive, author; b. Union City, N.J., Jan. 1, 1917; d. Fred J. and Louise (Stewart) S.; Ph.B., Marquette U., 1941, M.A., 1943, Ph.D., 1963; postgrad. U. Louvain, Belgium, U. Paris; m. Donald A. Gallagher, June 29, 1938; children—Paul B., Maria Noel. Lectr. philosophy Marquette U., 1943-52, 54-56; instr. philosophy Alverno Coll., Milw., 1956-58; asst. prof. philosophy Villanova U., 1958-62; asst. prof. philosophy Boston Coll., 1962-68, asso. prof., 1968-69; assoc. prof. philosophy U. Ottawa, 1969-71, prof., 1971-73; projects adminstr. DeRance Found., Milw., 1973-80, v.p., 1981—; vis. prof. philosophy Niagara U., 1976-81. Mem. Sudbury (Mass.) Com. for Human Rights, 1963-69; trustee Mt. Senario Coll., Ladysmith, Wis., 1976-86. Recipient Sword and Shield award St. Louis U., Baguio City, Philippines, 1975. Mem. Metaphys. Soc. Am., Am. Cath. Philos. Assn. (exec. council 1967-69), Am. Soc. Aesthetics, Assn. Realistic Philosophy, AAUP, Brit. Soc. Aesthetics, Canadian Philos. Assn., Canadian Assn. U. Tchrs., Phi Alpha Theta, Phi Delta Gamma. Author: (with D. A. Gallagher) The Achievement of Jacques and Raissa Maritain, 1962; The Education of Man, 1962; (with D. A. Gallagher) A Maritain Reader, 1966; (with D.A. Gallagher) St. Augustine—The Catholic and Manichaean Ways of Life, 1966. Morality in Evolution: The Moral Philosophy of Henri Bergson, 1970. Gen. editor: Christian Culture and Philosophy Series, Bruce Pub. Co., 1965-68. Contbr. to New Cath. Ency., also articles to profl. jours. Home: 7714 W Wisconsin Ave Wauwatosa WI 53213 Office: DeRance Found 7700 W Bluemound Rd Milwaukee WI 53213

GALLAGHER, LINDY ALLYN, banker; b. Kalamazoo, Sept. 27, 1954; d. Karl P. Joslow and Audrey S. Phillips; m. Thomas J. Gallagher, Nov. 29, 1975; 1 child, James Allyn Buckley. BS, U. Pa., 1975; MBA, Columbia U., 1982. Faculty, researcher U. Pa., Phila., 1976-80; corp. banking officer Bank of Montreal, N.Y.C., 1982-84; v.p. Citibank NA, N.Y.C., 1984—; treas. 957 Lexington Corp., 1981-87, also bd. dirs. Editor Columbia Jour. World Bus., 1980-82. Active N.Y.C. Women's Nat. Rep. Club, 1986—, New Canaan, (Conn.) Newcomers Club, 1986—. Republican. Episcopalian. Clubs: Doubles (N.Y.C.), Columbia. Office: Citibank NA 153 E 53d St New York NY 10043

GALLAGHER, MARY PATRICIA, food services executive; b. Ewa, Hawaii, Dec. 14, 1958; d. Edward Francis and Carmen Marie (Martin) G. BA in Econs. and Communications, Marymount Coll., Tarrytown, N.Y., 1980; MBA, U. Phoenix, Costa Mesa, Calif., 1985. Mgr. food service Saga Corp., N.Y., Fla. and Calif., 1978-82; dir. catering Barnabey's Hotel, Manhattan Beach, Calif., 1982-83, cons., 1984-85; mgr. interior Dobbs Internat. Airline Services, Los Angeles, 1983-84; dir. catering Crown Plaza Hotel, Los Angeles, 1985-86; dir. corp. food service Am. Sr. Inns, Irvine, Calif., 1986-87; dir. ops. Sr. Living Systems, Encino, Calif., 1987—. Mem. Chefs de Cuisine Assn., Nat. Assn. Catering Execs., Nat. Assn. Female Exec.s., Calif. Poly. Hospitality Soc. Republican. Roman Catholic. Home: 8738 Delgany Ave #309 Playa del Rey CA 90293

GALLAGHER, NANCY ELIZABETH, tax consultant, business executive; b. Ontario, Oreg., June 27, 1950; d. Martin Patrick Gallagher and Dorothy Ann (Bush) Turner; children—Susan Elizabeth, Sean Michael. Student U. Oreg., 1968-72. Lic. tax cons., notary pub. Bar mgr., Lamar's, Eugene, Oreg., 1972-73; tax preparer H & R Block, Eugene, Oreg., 1973-77; ptnr. Gallagher, Raven & Assocs., Eugene, 1977-81, Gallagher & Assocs., Eugene, 1988—; instr. Am. Inst. Taxation, Vancouver, Wash., 1984-85. Chairperson Aslan House Counseling Ctr., Eugene, 1976—; mem. external adv. bd. Lane Community Coll. Bus. Ctr. Mem. Internat. Assn. Fin. Planners, Assn. Tax Cons. (v.p. 1981-82, Disting. Service award 1979), Eugene Bus. Women (v.p.), Alliance for Career Advancement. Democrat. Home: 4560 Larkwood St Eugene OR 97405 Office: Gallagher Raven Assocs 1745 Coburg Rd Suite 2 Eugene OR 97401-4957

GALLAGHER, RITA J., real estate company executive. Comml. real estate broker, Ariz. Sch. Real Estate, 1983; Comml. appraiser, Lincoln Ctr., Phoenix, 1986. Lic. real estate broker, appraiser, Ariz. Real estate broker Century 21, Tempe, Ariz., 1976-79; comml. broker Realty Advisers, Tempe, 1979-83; v.p., designated broker Martorico div. Taurean Real Estate Group, Mesa, Ariz., 1984-86; broker, agt. Farwest Holdings, Internat., B.C., Can., 1980—; project mgr. Thayer Estates, Mesa, 1982-85, Friendly Cove, Mesa, 1982-85, Forest Knoll, Mesa, 1985—. Recipient Million Dollar award Bd. Realtors, 1983, Multi-Million Dollar award, 1984, 85, Prestigious Internat. award Farwest Holdings, 1985; named Top Ten Realtor Mesa-Chandler-Tempe Bd. Realtors, 1986. Mem. Nat. Assn. Realtors, Mesa-Chandler-Tempe Realtors, Women Networking (dir. 1983-86), Nat. Assn. Female Execs., Mesa C. of C., Soroptimist Internat. Avocations: golf, tennis, reading. Home: 2718 S Rogers St Mesa AZ 85202 Office: Martorico Div Taurean Real Estate Group 1745 S Alma School Mesa AZ 85202

GALLAGHER-ASHBY, ANN JESSICA, tranportation executive, researcher; b. Jersey City, Apr. 9, 1962; d. James Leo and Dorothy Patricia (Maietta) G.; M. Theodore Michael Ashby, June 20, 1987. Student, Upsala Coll., 1980-82; cert. in paralegal studies, Montclair State Coll., student, 1985—. Traffic coordinator VIHO Trucking Inc., Hillside, N.J., 1980-85; dist. mgr. Bergen Record, Hackensack, N.J., 1985; legal asst. Samuel Weiner Esq., North Haledon, N.J., 1986; dir. project Oasis Cons. Inc., N.Y.C., 1986—. Mem. Nat. Assn. Female Execs., Phi Alpha Delta, Omicron Delta Epsilon. Home: 45 Linden Ave Elmwood Park NJ 07407

GALLAHER, CYNTHIA LEE, editor, publisher; b. Chgo., Jan. 16, 1953; d. Gilbert Patrick Gallaher and Evelyn Marion (Bryg) Hamm; m. Carlos J. Cumpian, Sept. 8, 1984; 1 child, Julian Xavier Cumpian. BA, U. Ill., Chgo., 1974. Mng. editor Salome Mag., Chgo., 1976-79; tchr. in creative writing PACE Inst., Chgo., 1981-83; publisher, editor Before the Rapture Press, Chgo., 1978—; dir. Movimiento Artistico Chicano, Chgo., 1983—; readings coordinator Galeria Quique Poetry Reading Series, Chgo., 1983—. Editor: Amphora Full of Light, 1985; contbr. articles to profl. jours. Mem. Ill. Writers, Inc. Democrat. Mennonite. Office: Before the Rapture Press PO Box A3604 Chicago IL 60690

GALLANT, SANDRA KIRKHAM, psychologist; b. Dallas, July 15, 1933; d. Eugene Raley and Anita Bernice (Brandenburg) Kirkham; A.B., Hollins Coll., 1954; M.S., Va. Commonwealth U., 1956; m. Wade Miller Gallant, Jr., Sept. 15, 1979. Psychologist aide Lynchburg Tng. Sch. and Hosp., 1954-56, Rehab. Center of Rapides Parrish, 1956; clin. psychologist Bowman Gray Sch. Medicine, Wake Forest U., 1956-64, staff psychologist, acting dir. reading, speech and psychology center, 1962-64; staff psychologist Reading Speech and Psychology Center, part-time 1964-74; sch. psychologist Winston-Salem/Forsyth County Schs., part-time, 1974-75; clin. psychologist Child Guidance Clinic, Winston-Salem, N.C., 1975-82; ptnr. Triad Psychol. Assocs., 1982—; cons. to various community orgns. and agys. Bd. dirs. Family Services, 1964-66; bd. dirs. Little Theatre, 1963-66, pres., 1964-65; trustee to exec. com. Arts Council, 1965-68, v.p., 1967-68; bd. dirs. Mental Health Assn. Forsyth County, 1971-77, 79-85, pres., 1974-75; bd. dirs. Mental Health Assn. N.C., 1975-82, sec., 1977-79, v.p., 1979-81. Named Vol. of Yr., Mental Health Assn. Forsyth County, 1976; co-recipient Forsyth Mental Health Bell award, 1981. Mem. Am. Psychol. Assn., N.C. Psychol. Assn. Episcopalian. Home: 2534 Warwick Rd Winston-Salem NC 27104 Office: Triad Psychol Assocs 840 W 4th St Winston-Salem NC 27101

GALLERY, SHARON MENDELSON, publications and marketing professional; b. Buffalo, June 21, 1953; d. Robert Philip and Anajeane (Brady) Mendelson; m. Philip Daly Gallery, Nov. 28, 1981; children: Matthew Robert, Nathaniel Philip, Victoria Louise, Emily Chapin. BA in Studio Art, Sweet Briar (Va.) Coll., 1975; publs. specialist cert., George Washington U., 1977, MBA in Mktg., 1981. Publs. asst. Am. Soc. Indsl. Security, Washington, 1975-76; asst. publs. mgr. Am. Soc. Indsl. Security, Arlington, Va., 1976, publs. mgr., 1976-79, dir. publs., 1979-85; cons., pres. Gallery Communications & Mktg., Augusta, W.Va., 1985—. Editor: Security Management, 1984, Physical Security, 1986, Computer Security, 1987, Substance Abuse In The Workplace, 1987-88, Current Topics in Security Management, 1988; contbr. articles to profl. jours. Mem. alumnae mag. com. Sweet Briar Coll., 1986-88; bd. dirs. Literacy Vols. Hampshire County, W.Va., 1987-88. Mem. Soc. Nat. Assn. Publs. (v.p. D.C. chpt. 1984-85, pres. 1985-86, chmn. mktg. commn. 1986-87), Nat. Assn. Female Execs., Assn. Mktg. Roundtable, Wash. Edl. Press Assn., Kaypro Users Group (D.C. chpt.). Roman Catholic. Home and Office: State Rt 1 Box 139-A Augusta WV 26704

GALLICE, SONDRA JUPIN (MRS. GARDNER RUSSELL BROWN), personnel executive; b. Urbana, Ill.; d. Earl Cranston and Laura Lorraine (Rose) Jupin; B.S., Lindenwood Coll., 1958; M.B.A., Loyola Coll., 1982; m. Gardner Russell Brown, Jan. 12, 1980; 1 son, Thomas Alan Gillice. Div. tng. supr. Liberty Mut. Ins. Co., Chgo., N.Y.C., 1958-68; personnel officer N.Y. Citibank, 1968-70, 1st Nat. Bank of Chgo., 1970-72; mgr. human resources Potomac Electric Power Co., Washington, 1973-81; dir. personnel U.S. Synthetic Fuels Corp., Washington, 1981-86, v.p. human resources, Guest Services, Inc., 1987—. Mem. industry adv. bd. Behrand Coll., Pa. State U.; v.p. Guest Services, Inc. Mem. Edison Electric Inst. (chmn. tng. and mgmt. devel. com.), AAUW (pres. Falls Church br. 1976-78), Am. Soc. Tng. and Devel., Washington Nat. Restaurant Assn., Am. Soc. Personnel Adminstrs., Washington Personnel Assn., Greater Met. Washington Bd. Trade. Republican. Clubs: Soroptimists (pres. Washington chpt. 1979-80), DAR, Army Navy Country, Soc. Magna Charta Dames. Club: Edgartown (Mass.) Yacht, Country Club Culpeper, Inc. Home: 1101 S Arlington Ridge Rd #1112 Arlington VA 22202 Office: 3055 Prosperity Ave Fairfax VA 22031-2290

GALLINOT, RUTH MAXINE, educational consultant, educator; b. Carlinville, Ill., Feb. 16, 1925; d. Martin Mike and Augusta (Kumpus) G. BS, Roosevelt U., Chgo., 1971, MA with honors, 1974; PhD, Union for Experimenting Colls. and Univs., Cin., 1978. Adminstrv. asst., exec. sec. Karoll's Inc., Chgo., 1952-66; asst. dean Cen. YMCA Community Coll., Chgo., 1966-81, dir. life planning inst., 1979-80; pres. Gallinot & Assocs., Chgo. and St. Louis, 1980—; mem. task force Office Sr. Citizens and Handicapped, City of Chgo., 1971-79; mem. criteria and guidelines com. Council on Continuing Edn. Unit, 1983-86, survey and research com., 1984-86; mem. nat. adv. council bus. edn. div. Am. Vocat. Assn., 1980-84, sec., 1982-84. Developer leisure time adult edn. time series for elderly Uptown model cities area dept. human resources City of Chgo., 1970; host show Sta. WGCI-FM, Chgo., 1975-81; editor: Certified Professional Secretaries Review, 1983; contbr. articles to profl. jours. Chmn. Commn. Status of Women in State of Ill., 1963-68; del. White House Conf. on Equal Pay, 1963, White House Conf. on Civil Rights, 1965, City of Chgo. White House Conf. on Info. and Library, 1976, State of Ill. White House Conf. Info. Services and Library Services, 1977; life mem. Mus. Lithuanian Culture, Chgo., 1973—; pub. mem. Fgn. Service Selection Bd. U.S. Dept. State, 1984; bd. dirs. Luths. for Chgo., 1978-83, also founding member; member adv. edn. com. Chgo. Commn. Human Relations, 1968-75, Task Force Office Sr. Citizens and Handicapped City of Chgo., 1975-79. Recipient Leadership in Civic, Cultural and Econ. Life of the City award YWCA, Chgo., 1972, Achievement in Field Edn. award Operation P.U.S.H., Chgo., 1975. Mem. Profl. Secs. Internat. (pres. 1961, 62, ednl. cons. 1980-84), Edn. Network Older Adults (v.p., sec. 1979-86), Nat. Assn. Parliamentarians (Ill. chpt., Chgo. chpt.), Literacy Council Chgo. (bd. dirs. 1979-86). Club: Zonta of Chgo. (treas. 1965-66). Home and Office: Gallinot & Assocs 11161 Estrada Dr #9 Spanish Lake Saint Louis MO 63138

GALLIONE, PATRICIA ARDEN, small business owner; b. Paintsville, Ky., Feb. 5, 1943; d. Eugene V. and Garnett M. (Necessary) Ward; m. Robert J. Gallione, Oct. 18, 1962; 1 child, Richard Kevin. Student, Mayo Coll., Paintsville, 1961. Sec. U.S. Dept. Labor, Washington, 1961-62; office mgr. G&J Investigations, Hackensack, N.J., 1962-64; ptnr. Gallione Detective Agy., Hackensack, 1964-74, pres., 1974—. Mem. Nat. Assn. Chiefs Police, Nat. Assn. Legal Investigators, Pvt. Detective Assn. N.J. (membership chair 1982-85, exec. v.p. 1985—, cert. of appreciation 1985), World Assn. Detectives, Nat. Council Investigation & Security, Am. Law Enforcement Assocs., Crime Clinic of N.J. and N.Y., Am. Fedn. Police, Nat. Assn. Female Execs. Club: 200 of Morris. Office: 286 Terrace Ave Hasbrouck Heights NJ 07604

GALLO, JOYCE A. CALDERONE, organization administrator; b. Buffalo, Aug. 28, 1928; d. Wesley Floyd and Florence Mae (Plugh) Bigelow; m. John Kreitner, Dec. 31, 1946 (div. 1966); children: David, James, Pamela, Deborah; m. Francis Jerome Gallo, Feb. 15, 1985. Student, SUNY, Buffalo, 1946, 64, 67, Edison Community Coll., 1974-77, Parsons Sch. Design, 1985. Teller dept. loans Marine Midland Bank, Buffalo, 1964-73; supr. dept. loans 1st Nat. Bank, Naples, Fla., 1973-74; supr. loans, credit, new accounts Barnett Bank, Naples, 1974-79; with McFadden-Sprowls Inc., Naples, 1979-81; bookkeeper, receptionist C.A. Murphy Law Offices, Naples, 1981-83; adminstrv. asst. 1st Regency Internat. Devel., Naples, 1983-85; dir. sales Vanderbilt Inn on the Gulf, Naples, 1985-86; coordinator vols. LUVS for Youth Haven, Naples, 1986—, also bd. dirs. Co-chmn. United Fund Dr., Naples, 1980; sec., rep. Erie County Bd. LWV, Buffalo, 1964; del. Fla. Women's Conf., Orlando, 1977. Mem. Am. Bus. Women's Assn. (past pres. Naples br., del. nat. conv., named Woman Yr. 1979), Nat. Assn. Female Execs. Republican. Roman Catholic. Club: Pilot. Home: 106 Warwick Hills Dr Naples FL 33962

GALLO, MARY ELLEN, wholesale beverage distribution company executive; b. Allentown, Pa., May 2, 1957; d. Frank and Elizabeth Eugenia (Clark) Banko; m. Vincent James Gallo, Jr., Aug. 28, 1982; 1 child, Anthony James. BS, Purdue U., 1979, BA, 1980. Sec. Banko Beverage Co., Allentown, 1980-82, pres., 1982—. Bd. dirs. Bethlehem Musikfest Assn., Pa., 1983—, mktg. co-chmn., 1985—, chmn. food vendor com., 1986—; bd. dirs. Cities in Schs., Lehigh Valley, 1985—, treas., 1987-88. Named Outstanding Young Citizen Bethlehem Jaycees, 1987. Mem. Bethlehem Area C. of C. (bd. dirs. 1985—), Nat. Beer Wholesalers Assn., Malt Beverage Distbrs. Assn., Pa. Beer Wholesalers Assn. Democrat. Roman Catholic. Avocations: eucharistic ministry, music, dancing, needlework. Home: 2201 Meadow Ln Dr Easton PA 18042 Office: Banko Beverage Co 2124 Hanover Ave Allentown PA 18103

GALLO, VIVIAN PAULA, insurance company executive; b. N.Y.C., Mar. 17, 1946; d. Lazarus Fidelio and Rosalie (Magro) G. BA, CCNY, 1967. CLU. Claims examiner bur. disability determinations Dept. Social Services, State of N.Y., N.Y.C., 1967-68; claims adjuster C.N.A. Ins., N.Y.C., 1968-70; claim approver Guardian Life Ins. Co., N.Y.C., 1970-73, sr. claim approver, 1973-76, chief health claim approver, 1976-79, system analyst health claims, 1979-81; bus. analyst/cons. Computer Horizons Corp., N.Y.C., 1981-83; systems analyst Home Life Ins. Co., N.Y.C., 1983-84; cons. Bus. Intelligence Services, N.Y.C., 1984-85; adminstrv. assoc. mgr. spl. projects and tng., mgr. core customer service tng. Empire Blue Cross and Blue Shield, N.Y.C., 1985—; asst. chmn. Ea. Claim Conf., N.Y.C., 1979, 81, mem. program com., 1980. Asst. publs. AWC Newsletters, 1985-87. Mem. Assn. Women in Computing (mem.-at-large exec. bd. 1984-87), Am. Soc. CLU's. Home: 215 W 95th St New York NY 10025 Office: Empire Blue Cross and Blue Shield 622 3d Ave New York NY 10017

GALLOWAY, ERNESTINE ROYAL, religious administrator; b. Newark, May 7, 1928; d. Seymour Page Galloway and Ethel (Bishop) Bigham. BA, NYU, 1957, MA, 1960; MA, NYU, 1969, EdD, 1981. Dir. edn. Concord Baptist Ch., Bklyn., 1956-60; social worker Westminster Neighborhood Assn., Los Angeles, 1962-64; field coordinator Newark Pre-Sch. Council, 1965-67, social service coordinator, 1967-69; N.Y. regional dir. Student YWCA, N.Y.C., 1970-72, co-dir., 1972-74; instr. Seton Hall U., South Orange, N.J., 1976-78; mgr. Nat. Ministries/Am. Bapt. Chs. in the U.S.A., Valley Forge, Pa., 1978—. Fellow Am. Anthropology Assn., Soc. for Intercultural Edn., Tng., and Research. Baptist. Home: 25 Warman St Montclair NJ 07042 Office: Nat Ministries/ABUSCA PO Box 851 Valley Forge PA 19482-0851

GALLOWAY, LOIS, education and personal development counselor; b. Orangeburg, S.C., Feb. 28, 1941; d. Fairy Dykes and Bernice (Glover) Brown; children: Donna Patton, Darryl W., Gary W.; m. Carl Wesley I Galloway, Apr. 10, 1982; 1 child, Carl Wesley II. AA, Mira Costa Coll., 1973; BA in Psychology, U. San Diego, 1975, MA in Counseling, 1976. Counselor Mira Costa Coll., Oceanside, Calif., 1975-80; owner, figure cons. Venus De Milo, Livermore and San Pablo, Calif., 1980-83; pvt. counselor employment, cons. sales San Francisco, 1983; coordinator, counselor Palomar Coll., San Marcos, Calif., 1983—, lectr. single parenting program, 1983; lectr. single parenting Oceanside, 1975-78. Mem. NAACP, Negro Bus. and Profl. Women, Am. Women in Jr. Community Coll. Democrat. Baptist. Lodge: Order Eastern Star (Marshall of West).

GALLOWAY, PHYLLIS HYACINTH, English language educator; b. Savla-Mar, West Indies, Sept. 13, 1935; d. Timothy Augustus and Mary M Sevina (Monteith) Brooks; m. Lloyd George Galloway, Dec. 19, 1959; children: Michelle Ann, Christopher George. Cert. of edn., Shortwood Tchrs. Coll., 1956; BA, Howard U., 1965, MA, 1966, MS, 1985. Elem. sch. tchr. Ministry of Edn., Jamaica, 1957-60; lectr. Shortwood Tchrs. Coll., Jamaica, 1960-62, 69-76; instr. Howard U., Washington, 1966-69, 76—; mgr. Jamaica Dance Group, Washington, 1963-69; writing cons. Jamaica Telephone Co., Kingston, Jamaica, 1965-66; early childhood program asst. Peace Corps. of Jamaica, 1965-66; gen. mgr. Traditions Pub. Co., Washington, 1987—. Author: Mechanis 6 Conventions in Formal Writing, 1985, Anancy and Brer Goat, 1986, Anancy and Bird Cherry Island, 1986, Anancy and Chiefs Daughter, 1986; editor Trinity Newsletter, 1984—, Jour. of Knowledge Engrs., 1988—; producer (TV program) Honoring the Common Slave, 1987, The Adventures of Anancy, 1987. Fellow Nation's Capitol Writing Project, 1985. Mem. Nat. Council of Tchrs. of English, Nat. Assn. for Female Execs., Assn. for Supervision and Curriculum Devel., Coll. Lang. Assn., Schs. Industry Council. African Methodist Episcopal Zion. Home: 8830 Piney Branch Rd Apt #411 Silver Spring MD 20903 Office: Howard U Grad Expository Writing Sixth St NW Washington DC 20056

GALLUCCI-SPEEDY, KIM ALICIA, lawyer; b. Orange, N.J., Sept. 18, 1961; d. Ralph Joseph Jr. and Evelyn (Landrud) Gallucci; m. Timothy Del Speedy, Aug. 16, 1986. BS in Mgmt., Montclair (N.J.) State Coll., 1983; JD cum laude, N.Y. Law Sch., 1987. Assoc. Pelavin, Pelavin and Powers, PC, Flint, Mich., 1987—. Mem. ABA, Women Lawyers Assn Mich., N.Y. Law Sch. Alumni Assn. Office: Pelavin Pelavin and Powers PC Phoenix Bldg Suite 200 Flint MI 48502

GALLUP, JANET LOUISE, business official; b. Rochester, N.Y., Aug. 11, 1951; d. John Joseph and Mildred Monica (O'Keefe) VerHulst; m. Robert Hicks Gallup, June 26, 1982 (div. Nov. 1985); 1 son, Jason Hicks. B.A., Hofstra U., 1973; M.A. (grad. asst.), Calif. State U.-Long Beach., 1979. Asst. trader E.F. Hutton, N.Y.C., 1973-75, Los Angeles, 1975, instr. Calif. State U.-Long Beach, 1978-79; fin. analyst Rockwell Internat., Seal Beach, Calif., 1979-85, coordinator mgmt. and exec. devel. and succession planning, 1985—. Vol. Cedar House Ctr.-Child Abuse, Long Beach, 1976. Democrat. Roman Catholic. Office: Rockwell Internat 2600 Westminster Blvd Seal Beach CA 90740

GALLUPS, VIVIAN LYLAY BESS, federal agency administrator; b. Vicksburg, Miss., Jan. 14, 1954; d. Vann Foster and Lylay Vivian (Stanley) Bess; m. Ordice Alton Gallups, Jr., July 12, 1975. BA, Birmingham So. Coll., 1975, MA in Mgmt., 1985; MA in Edn., U. Ala., Birmingham, 1975. Counselor Columbia (S.C.) Coll., 1975-76; case mgr. S.C. Dept. Social Services, Lexington, 1976; benefit authorizer, payment determination specialist then recovery reviewer Social Security Adminstrn., Birmingham, 1977-85; contract adminstr. U.S. Dept. Def., Birmingham, 1985—. Hospice vol. Bapt. Med. Ctr.-Montclair, Birmingham, 1982; trustee, treas. Resurrection House, Birmingham, 1984-85; vol. counselor Cathedral Ch. of Advent, Birmingham, 1987. Mem. Nat. Contract Mgmt. Assn. (chpt. sec. 1987), Am. Assn. Counseling and Guidance, Assn. Religious and Value Issues in Counseling, Federally Employed Women, Nat. Cathedral Assn., Ala. Zool. Soc. Episcopalian. Home: 566 12th Ct PO Box 126 Pleasant Grove AL 35127-0126 Office: US Dept Def Def Logistics Agy 2121 8th Ave N Suite 104 Birmingham AL 35203

GALT, ELIZABETH ANNE, investment company executive; b. New Haven, Aug. 18, 1952; d. William Egleston and Alfreda (Sill) G.; m. John Arthur Hirsch, Nov. 2, 1981. B.A., Bennington Coll., 1975. Sales exec. Bear, Stearns & Co., N.Y.C., 1979-81; dir. mktg. The Leuthold Group, N.Y.C., 1981-84; v.p. Abel, Noser & Co., N.Y.C., 1984-85; investment policy com., dir. mktg. Sloate, Weisman, Murray & Co., Inc., N.Y.C., 1985-87; owner E. Galt Ltd., N.Y.C., 1987—. Pres., bd. dirs., mem. exec. com. City Harvest, N.Y.C., 1986-87. Mem. Am. Investment Mgmt. Sales Execs., Fin. Women's Assn., Plan Sponsors & Money Mgrs. Club: Cosmopolitan. Avocations: tennis; skiing; photography.. Home: 414 Round Hill Rd Greenwich CT 06831 Office: 420 E 54th St New York NY 10022

GALVACH, PATRICIA SWELGIN, safety products company executive, consultant; b. Wilkes Barre, Pa., May 25, 1944; d. Herman G. and Jennie Theresa (Malkoski) Swelgin; m. James Joseph Galvach, Oct. 6, 1962 (div.); children—James, Theresa. B.S., Kean Coll., 1980; M.B.A., Montclair State Coll., 1983. Acctg. clk. N.J. Bell Telephone Co., Elizabeth, 1961-63; mem. office staff Bettman Nut Co., Rahway, N.J., 1970-73; accounts payable supr. Wing Co., Linden N.J., 1973-76; asst. controller Falcon Safety Products, Mountainside, N.J., 1976-80; dir. acctg. Boyle Midway Internat., N.Y.C., 1980-81; controller Falcon Safety Products, Inc., Mountainside, 1981—. Advisor Understanding Am. Bus. Project, N.J. Bus. and Industry Assn., Hillside, N.J., 1981, Westfield Day Care Ctr., 1980-82; chmn. Woodbridge council Boy Scouts Am. (N.J.), 1973-77; bd. dirs. North Princeton (N.J.) Devel. Ctr. Mem. Alpha Kappa Psi, Omicron Delta Epsilon. Office: Falcon Safety Products Inc 1065 Bristol Rd Mountainside NJ 07092

GALVIN, MARYANNE, psychologist, educator; b. Worcester, Mass., Mar. 6, 1954; d. Stephen F. and Bernadette M. (McGinn) Galvin; B.S., Wheelock Coll., 1976; M.Ed. (Mass. Fedn. of Women's Clubs fellow), U. Mass., Amherst, 1978, Ed.D., 1980. Psychologist, Wellesley (Mass.) Public Sch., 1980-81, U. Mass. Med. Sch., Worcester, 1980-81; asst. prof. U. N.H., Durham, 1981-82; pvt. practice psychology, Durham, 1981-83, Boston, 1984—; clin. dir. sch. consultation program Tufts New Eng. Med. Ctr., Boston, 1982—; research psychologist Tufts Sch. Medicine, 1986—; asst. prof. Harvard Med. Sch., 1988—; psychologist McLean Hosp., Boston, 1988—; cons. McBer and Co., Boston. Recipient of commendation UN, 1975; NSF grantee, 1985. Mem. Internat. Council Psychologists, Am. Bd. Profl. Psychologists, Am. Psychol. Assn., Mass. Assn. for the Advancement of Individual Potential, Mass. Psychol. Assn., Physicians for Social Responsibility. Roman Catholic. Club: New Eng. Masters Competitive Swim. Contbr. articles on psychology to profl. jours. Home: 199 Mass. Ave #205 Boston MA 02115 Office: 82 Marlboro St Boston MA 02116

GALVIN, PATRICIA ROSSI, lawyer; b. Detroit, June 26, 1941; d. Ernerst Francis and Christine (Zaffina) Rossi; m. John Patrick Galvin, June 19, 1970; children: Jennifer, Julie, John Patrick. AB in English, U. Detroit, 1963; MA in English, U. Mich., 1969; JD, U. Detroit, 1970. Bar: Mich. Tchr. English Grosse Pointe (Mich.) Bd. Edn., 1963-67; staff atty. Neighborhood Legal Services, Detroit, 1970-71; asst. prosecuting atty. Wayne County, Mich., 1971-76; sole practice Grosse Pointe, 1976—. Bd. dirs. Wayne County Cath. Social Services, Detroit, 1973—; trustee Village Council of Grosse Pointe Shores, 1980—. Mem. Detroit Bar Assn., ABA, Am. Trial Lawyers Assn., State Bar Mich. (rep. assy. 1979-83), Women Lawyers Mich., U. Detroit Law Alumni (pres. bd. 1988), League Women Voters. Home: 888 Lake Shore Grosse Pointe MI 48236 Office: 21002 Mack Ave Grosse Pointe MI 48236

GAMBLE, ARLENE MARIE, librarian; b. Houston, Feb. 19, 1947; d. Randolph Bernard, Sr., and Antionette (Navy) Jacobs; B.A.L.S., Univ. Without Walls, Internat. Hispanic U., 1979; m. Casanova Gamble, May 10, 1968; children—Troy L'Keith, K'Lah Treniece. Supr., Res. Reading Facility, Rice U., Houston, 1969-77; mgr. tech. services Am. Productivity Center, Houston, 1977—; now fashion designer, prin. Beautiful U Boutique, Houston. Mem. Spl. Libraries Assn., Houston On-Line Users. Office: Beautiful U Boutique PO Box 25202 Houston TX 77265

GAMBRELL, LUCK FLANDERS, corporate executive; b. Augusta, Ga., Jan. 17, 1930; d. William Henry and Mattie Moring (Mitchell) Flanders; m. David Henry Gambrell, Oct. 16, 1953; children: Luck Davidson, David Henry, Alice Kathleen, Mary Latimer. BA, Duke U., 1950; diplome d'etudes françaises L'Institut de Touraine, Tours, France, 1951. Chmn. bd. LFG Co., 1960—. Mem. State Bd. Pub. Safety, 1981—; bd. dirs. Atlanta Symphony Orch., 1982-85; mem. Chpt. Nat. Cathedral, Washington, 1981-85; mem. World Service Council YWCA, 1965—, council Presbytery Greater Atlanta, 1988; elder Presbyterian Ch.; trustee Student Aid Found., Atlanta, 1975—; mem. Bd. Councilors The Carter Ctr., Emory U. Mem. Atlanta Jr. League, Alpha Delta Pi.

GAMBRELL, SARAH BELK, retail executive; b. Charlotte, N.C., Apr. 12, 1918; d. William Henry and Mary (Irwin) Belk; B.A., Sweet Briar Coll., 1939, D. Humanities, Erskine Coll., 1970, U. N.C.-Asheville, 1986; m. Charles Glenn Gambrell; 1 dau., Sarah Belk. pres., v.p., dir. Belk Stores, various locations, 1947—, pres. 32 stores. Trustee Princeton (N.J.) Theol. Sem., Johnson C. Smith U., Charlotte, N.C., Warren Wilson Coll., Swannanoa, N.C.; trustee nat. bd. YWCA; bd. dirs. Parkinson's Disease Found.; bd. dirs. Opera Carolina, Charlotte, Planned Parenthood, Charlotte, YWCA, Charlotte; hon. trustee Cancer Research Inst., N.Y.C.; hon. bd. dirs. YWCA, N.Y.C., Mem. Fashion Group, Inc., Jr. League N.Y.C., Nat. Soc. Colonial Dames, DAR. Home: 300 Cherokee Rd Charlotte NC 28207 Office: PO Box 31788 Charlotte NC 28231 also: 111 W 40th St New York NY 10018

GAMIN, JULIE ANN, educational author; b. Tampa, Fla., July 8, 1945; d. Elton and Mary Elizabeth (Turnbull) G. BA, SUNY, Potsdam, 1967; postgrad., U. So. Miss., 1970-71; EdM, Reading Specialist, SUNY, Buffalo, 1977. Tchr. English and reading, pub. schs., also Children's Psychiat. Ctr., N.Y. and Tex., 1969-77; itinerant resource tchr. Dallas Ind. Sch. Dist., 1977-78; dir. Better Reading Through Parents, Dallas, 1978—; staff writer Leonard's Learning Circus (Learning Prodns., Inc.), Dallas, 1979—. Author: Revised Better Reading through Parents Program, 1980, Program for Spanish-Speaking Parents, 1980, Program for Non-Reading Parents, 1980, Family Puppet Shows, Leonard's Learning Circus, 1980. Del. local and state Dem. presdl. convs. Fellow U. So. Miss., 1970-71; U.S. ESAA grantee, 1978-79, 79-80. Mem. Nat. Council Tchrs. English, Internat. Reading Assn., ALA, Nat. Conf. Parent Involvement, Nat. Com. Citizens in Edn., Nat. PTA. Office: 1303 Reynoldston Ln Dallas TX 75232

GAMMELL, GLORIA RUFFNER, sales executive; b. St. Louis, June 19, 1948; d. Robert Nelson and Antonia Ruffner; m. Doyle M. Gammell, Dec. 11, 1973. AA in Art, Harbor Coll., Harbor City, Calif., 1969; BA in Sociology, Calif. State U., Long Beach, 1971. Cert. fin. planner. Bus. analyst Dun & Bradstreet Inc., Los Angeles, 1971-81; rep. sales Van Nuys, Calif., 1981-86; v.p., sec. bd. dirs. Gammell Industries, Paramount, Calif., 1986—. Mem. Anne Banning Assistance League, Hollywood, Calif., 1981-82; counselor YWCA, San Pedro, Calif., 1983-84; fundraiser YMCA, San Pedro, 1984-85; mem. womens adv. com. Calif. State Assembly, 1984-86. Recipient Best in the West Presdl. Citation, 1981-86. Home: 991 Channel St San Pedro CA 90731

GAMMETER, MARCIA, communications executive; b. Fremont, Mich., June 18, 1951; d. Harry J. and Drucilla (Zwahlen) Nash; m. Hermann Gammeter. BA in Communications, Bowling Green State U., 1975. Pub. relations mgr. Detroit C. of C., Detroit, 1978-80; pub. relations, mktg. mgr. Atlanta Symphony Orch., 1980-81; account supr., pub. relations Cargill Wilson & Acree, Inc. Advt., Atlanta, 1981-84; v.p. corp. communications Cotton States Ins. Cos., Atlanta, 1984—. bd. dirs. Boy Scouts of Am., Atlanta; mem. first v.p. DeKalb Council for the Arts, Atlanta; organizer Rep. Nat. Conv., Detroit, 1980. Recipient Boy Scouts Service award. Mem. Ga. Exec. Womens Network (pres.-elect), Internat. Assn. Bus. Communicators, Atlanta Women's Commerce Club, Am. Mktg. Assn., Atlanta Zool. Soc. Republican. Mormon. Office: Cotton States Ins Co 244 Perimeter Ctr Pkwy Atlanta GA 30346

GAMMON, JUANITA LAVERNE, artist, educator; b. McLeansboro, Ill.; d. Lloyd W. and Grace F. (Munsell) G. BFA, U. Ill., MFA. Head communications career program Parkland Coll., Champaign, Ill., 1967—; free lance illustrator, copywriter; lectr.; art show judge, condr. workshops; former dir. Corn Country Graphics. Exhibited at Nat. Acad. Design, N.Y.C., U. Ill., Parkland Coll., others; represented in numerous collections; editor coll. mag. Intercom. Bd. dirs. East Cen. Ill Cultural Affairs Consortium, 1973; advisor art acquisitions com. Parkland Found; supr. Champaign County Art Show, 1973—. Mem. NEA, Ill. Art Edn. Assn., Assn. Jr. Colls., Ill. Hist. Soc., U. Ill. Alumni Assn., Art Alumni Assn. Club: Champaign-Urbana Advt.-Art. Home: 711 W Healey St Champaign IL 61820

GANDY, JOYCE ANN, business administrator, former dance educator; b. Picher, Okla., Feb. 2, 1937; d. Sheppard Levi and Naydeen Maxine (Phillips) G.; m. Bernard Diamond, Aug. 2, 1985. A.A., Parsons Jr. Coll., 1957; dance student of Thalia Mara, Gertrude Edwards Jory, Yurik Lazowsky, Robert Joffrey, Luigi, Frank Wagner. Cert. Cecchetti Council Am. Owner, tchr. Joyce's Dance Studio, Parsons, Kans., 1953-66; gen. sec. Nat. Acad. Ballet and Theatre Arts, N.Y.C., 1966-72; sec., adminstrv. asst. to office, convs. mgr. Am. Inst. Steel Constrn., N.Y.C., 1973-79, office mgr., Chgo., 1979-80, personnel adminstr., Chgo., 1980-81; bus. adminstr. Bernard Diamond, D.D.S., P.A., Edison, N.J., 1983—. Recipient various dance grants, 1949-66, Scholarship awards, Parsons Jr. Coll., 1954, 55, 57. Mem. Nat. Assn. Female Execs. Mem. Ch. of Christ. Avocations: drawing, music, dance, gardening. Office: Bernard Diamond DDS PA 42 Parsonage Rd Edison NJ 08837

GANE, JANET, design educator, news reporter; b. North Tonawanda, N.Y., May 12, 1953; d. Francis Peter and Renalda (Straccamore) G. AAS, Niagara County Coll., 1971-73; BS in Art Edn., SUNY, Buffalo, 1974, postgrad., 1974-75, EdD, 1976-84; MS in Art Edn., Purdue U., 1976. Tchr., dept. chair Interior Design Niagary U., Niagary Falls, N.Y., 1976-83; dir. creative service Sta. WJYE-FM, Buffalo, 1977-80; news reporter and weather anchor Sta. WGRZ-TV, Buffalo, 1980-82; dir. community service, pub. relations Healy, Schualte & Comstock Advt., Buffalo, 1980-81; dir. pub. relations Faller, Klenk & Quinlan, Inc., Buffalo, 1981-82; with new programming, and research prodn. depts. Cable Time, Inc., Buffalo, 1981-83; pres. entertainment div. Ten Unltd., Buffalo, 1983-84; pres. Janet Gore & Assocs., Venice, Calif., 1984—; pres., recording artist Thorfinn Records, Buffalo, 1981-84; creative dir. mktg. and promotion, Miramax Films, N.Y.C., 1982-83; dir. concert promotion and advt., Harvey & Corky Prodns., Buffalo, 1982-83; asst. exec. dir. Melody Fair Theatre, North Tonawanda, 1982-83, assoc. dir., 1981-82; creative producer, recording artist, Rainbow Records, Buffalo; advt. mktg. dir. Fur Mary, Jesi, Italy, 1982-84; guest lectr. SUNY, Buffalo, Amherst, 1983, Rochester Inst. Technology, 1982, 83, Niagary County Community Coll., Sanborn, 1979, Rochester City Schs., 1978-79. Author: An Exemplary Curriculum for Interior Design Education, 1984; prodn. asst. art film The Natural, Last Embrace; one woman shows include: Koinonia Cafe and Gallery, Buffalo, 1983-84, Spring Arts Festival, Buffalo, 1977; paintings exhibited at Jerel Gallery, Snyder, N.Y., 1974-84, North Tonawanda Pub. Library, 1976-83, Clarence Ctr. Emporium, Clarence Center, N.Y., 1981-83, Albright-Knox Art Gallery, 1980-81, The Mark Twain Ann. Art Festival, Elmira, N.Y., 1977, Magic Theatre Gallery, West Lafayette, Ind., 1975, Purdue U., West Lafayette, 1975, Gallery 229 and Uptown Hall Gallery SUNY, Buffalo, 1973-75, Gallery 1 Niagary County Community Coll., Sanborn, N.Y., 1971-73; speaker in field. Mem. Albright-Knox Art Gallery, Buffalo, Los Angeles County Mus. of Art, Laguna Beach Mus. of Art. Recipient Courier Express Advt. award, 1980, Buffalo News Advt. award, 1980, Outstanding Tchr. award N.Y. State Art Tchrs. Assn., 1984. Mem. AFTRA, Screen Actors Guild, Women in Communications, Inc., Graphic Artist Guild, Am. Film Inst., Am. Soc. of Interior Designers, Am. Vocat. Assn., N.Y. State United Tchrs. Assn., Acad. Motion Pictures and Scis., Omicron Tau Theta. Club: Advt. (Los Angeles). Office: Film Adv Bd 7080 Hollywood Blvd #312 Hollywood CA 90028

GANESH, CHERIE MARGARET, real estate project manager; b. Memphis, Jan. 17, 1950; d. Terrence Billy and Mary Margaret (Hanna) Miller; m. Robert W. Proctor, Aug. 5, 1971 (div. May 1981); m. Nagraj Ganesh, June 25, 1983. Student, Memphis State U., 1967-71; MusB, U. Ariz., 1972; grad., Inst. Fin. Edn., Chgo., 1980; postgrad., U. San Diego, 1987—. Constrn. disbursement processor Keystone Savs., Westminster, Calif., 1977-79, Home Fed. Savs., Santa Ana, Calif., 1979-80; project coordinator Home Capital Devel. Group, San Diego, 1980-86; broker, v.p. Sumukham Corp. (owned by Nagraj & Cherie), San Diego, 1984—; mgr. asset Homevest Real Estate Securities, San Diego, 1986-87; project mgr. Home Capital Devel. Group, San Diego, 1987—; bd. dirs. Community Assns. Inst., San Diego, 1983—, pres. 1987—; edn. com. Homebuilders Council BIA, San Diego, 1986—. Mem. Nat. Assoc. Female Execs., South San Diego Bay Cities Bd. Realtors. Republican. Office: Home Capital Devel Group 5300 NW 33d Ave Suite 205 Fort Lauderdale FL 33309

GANEY, SUSAN CHARLINE, market research company executive, consultant; b. Buffalo, Mar. 10, 1944; d. Charles Bronson and Margaret Mary (Hewitt) Wall; m. M. James Ganey, Nov. 5, 1966; children—Christine, Charles. Student SUNY-Fredonia, 1962-63; Erie Community Coll., 1987—; innkeeper cert. Holiday Inn Tng. Sch., Memphis, 1963. Asst. innkeeper Holiday Inn, Hamburg, N.Y., 1963-66; owner, operator Goody Two Sue's, Hamburg, 1966-76; comptroller Niagara Frontier Mktg. Research Inc., Hamburg, 1976-88; owner, cons. firm CMG Enterprises, Hamburg, 1984—, Bus. Aid, Inc., 1987—. Troop leader Buffalo and Erie County council Girl Scouts U.S., 1976-78, field dir., 1978-80; pres., treas. Lakeshore Investment Club, Hamburg, 1979-85; campaign mgr., treas., town clk.'s office campaign, Hamburg, 1978, 83; ruling elder Wayside Presbyterian Ch., 1983-89, pres. women's assn., 1984-86. Mem. Buffalo Bus. and Profl. Women's Club (sec. 1977). Nat. Assn. Female Execs. Republican. Club: Wanakah Country (pres. women's assn. 1972) (Hamburg). Lodge: Kiwanis. Home and Office: CMG Enterprises 4944 Kennison Pkwy Hamburg NY 10475

GANGEY, CAROL KALLINIKI, information processing executive; b. Los Angeles, Sept. 23, 1946; d. Victor and Doris Mary (Bastian) Adams; m. Stephen Wayne Gangey, Feb. 8, 1981. AA, Los Angeles City Coll., 1966; BA, UCLA, 1968. Lic. ins. agt., Calif. Exec. sec. UCLA, 1970, coordinator programs, 1970-81; adminstrv. asst. Calif. State U., Northridge, 1981-83; owner, pres. Pacific Processing Services, Camarillo, Calif., 1983—; life, disability agt. Kansas City Life Ins. Co., Camarilio, 1985—. Bd. dirs. Camarillo Community Theatre, 1986-87; mem. Camarillo July 4th Com., 1986, 87, Camarillo Women's Day Com., 1987, speaker, 1988. Recipient Proclamation of Mayor, City of Camarillo, 1986. Mem. Am. Bus. Women's Assn. (chpt. pres. 1986-87, extension award 1985, Chpt. Woman of Yr. award 1986), Ventura County Profl. Women's Network, AAUW, Nat. Assn. Female Execs. (network dir. 1985-86, dir. pub. relations 1988—), Camarillo C. of C. Club: Trade Unltd. (bd. dirs. 1985-86). Office: Pacific Processing Services 355 N Lantana Suite 803 Camarillo CA 93010

GANGI, RAYNA MARIE, telecommunications company executive; b. Jamestown, N.Y., Mar. 20, 1950; d. Alfred C. and Ruby (Ball) G. BA in Am. Studies, SUNY, Buffalo. Computer engr. IBM Corp., Buffalo, 1971-76; computer specialist SUNY, Buffalo, 1976-83; site engr. Timeplex, Inc., N.J., 1984-85; v.p. data communications Clarity Research, Inc., Buffalo, 1985—; cons. WSC, SUNY-Buffalo, 1971-80, ASK-WOMEN, Buffalo, 1987—; pres. Housestory, Inc., Buffalo, 1983—. Editor: Women in Work Force, 1920-85; contbr. articles to profl. jours. Pres. Main-Jewett Tenants Assn., 1982, Auburn Block Assn., Buffalo, 1986. Served as lance cpl. USMC, 1968-71. Mem. Internat. Assn. Computer Cosn., Internat. Assn. Fin. Planning, Nat. Assn. Female Execs., SUNY-Buffalo Alumni Assn. (senator profl. staff com. 1985-87), Phi Beta Kappa. Democrat. Office: IDS/AMEX (CRI) 3407 Delaware Ave Buffalo NY 14217

GANGLE, SANDRA SMITH, lawyer; b. Brockton, Mass., Jan. 11, 1943; d. Milton and Irene M. (Powers) S.; m. Eugene M. Gangle, Dec. 21, 1968; children—Melanie Jean, Jonathan Rocco. BA, Coll. New Rochelle, 1964; MA, U. Oreg.; JD, Willamette U., 1980. Bar: Oreg. 1980. Instr. French, Oreg. State U., Corvallis, 1968-71, Willamette U., Salem, Oreg., 1971-74; instr. ESL, Chemeketa Community Coll., Salem, 1975-79; labor arbitrator Salem, 1980—; mem. Oreg., Idaho, Wash., Mont. Arbitration Panels; sole practice Salem, 1980-86; ptnr. Depenbrock, Gangle & Naucler, 1986—; clin. prof. Portland State U., 1981-84; cons. State Oreg., 1981. Contbr. articles to profl. jours. Land-use chmn. Faye Wright Neighborhood Assn., Salem, 1983-84; mem. Civil Service Commn., Marion County Fire Dist., Salem, 1983—; mem. U.S. Postal Service Expedited Arbitration Panel, 1984—; mem. Salem Neighbor-to-Neighbor Panel; mem. panel Fed. Mediation and Conciliation Service, 1986—. NDEA fellow, 1967. Mem. Am. Arbitration Assn. (arbitrator), Soc. Profls. in Dispute Resolution, ABA, Oreg. Trial Lawyers Assn., Marion County Bar Assn., Oreg. Assn. Adminstrv. Law Judges. Office: Depenbrock Gangle & Naucler 831 Lancaster Dr NE Suite 209 Salem OR 97301

GANN, CAROLE BRANNON, small business owner; b. Atlanta, Apr. 26, 1958; d. Lester Travis and Ruby Jean (Mouchet) Brannon; m. Richard Gann, Nov. 28, 1981 (div. May 1984); 1 child, Jennifer Jean; 1 child, David Eddie Jackson Jr. Student, Reinhart Coll., 1975-76, Kennasaw Coll., 1978-80, Barbazon, 1980. Adminstr. Munich Am., Atlanta, 1977-78; adminstr. dir. Sunspace Corp., Atlanta, 1979-80; credit dir. Fin. One, Marietta, Ga., 1982-83; owner Carole's Party Shop, St. Simons Island, Ga., 1985-87. Contbr. articles to jours. Lutheran. Office: Carole's Party Shop 238 Retreat Village Saint Simons Island GA 31522

GANN, JEAN POPE, insurance agency executive, fine arts appraiser; b. Winfield, Ala., Dec. 5, 1917; d. Garvin and Clara (Couch) Pope; m. John Henry Gann, Apr. 6, 1935; children—John Garvin, W. Gerald, Jean Gann Nelson. Student U. Howard Coll., 1949-52, U. Ala., 1964-68, Montevallo, Ala., 1983-84, Samford U., 1983-85. Lic. ins. agt.; cert. appraiser fine arts and antiques. Owner, mgr. Sylacauga Ins. Agy., Ala., 1952—; instr., trainer Sylacauga High Sch., 1960—; co-chmn. Citywide Sales Clinic, Sylacauga C. of C., 1972. Contbr. articles to profl. jours. Mem. Birmingham (Ala.) Mus. Art, 1979—; exec. bd. dirs. United Givers Fund, Sylacauga, 1978-81; charter mem. Sylacauga Mus. and Arts Ctr., 1982—; v.p. Sylacauga High Sch. PTA, 1961-62; chmn. edn. Am. Cancer Soc., South Talladega County, Ala., 1953-61; mem. Ala. Women's Polit. Caucus, 1978—; mem. Nat. Democratic Com., Ala. Dem. Com., Ala. Citizens for ERA; tchr. adult Bible class 1st Bapt. Ch., 1945—, mem. long range planning com., 1950-58; chmn. com. that established Ave. of Flags in Sylacauga, 1972; pres. Bapt. Women's Orgn., 1964-65, 76-80; chmn. prayer breakfast Nat. Bus. Women's Week, 1979-85. Named Woman of Achievement, Sylacauga Bus. and Profl. Women's Club, 1976, Sylacauga Woman of Yr., Sylacauga Exchange Club, 1961; recipient cert. in Christian tng. Howard Coll., Samford U., 1983; cert. of recognition 1st Bapt. Ch., 1985. Mem. Soc. Fine Arts U. Ala., Ala. Ind. Ins. Agts. (legis. com. 1978-79, 84-85), Nat. Assn. Ind. Ins. Agts., Ala. Fedn. Bus. and Profl. Women's (dist. chmn. for young careerists 1972-73, legis. chmn. Sylacauga chpt. 1983—, pres. 1962, 62, 73), Sylacauga Bus. & Profl. Women's Club (legis. chmn. 1980-87), U.S.A. Young Careers (chmn. 1987-88, internat. chmn. 1988), Nat. Trust for Hist. Preservation, Sylacauga C. of C. (mem. com. 1952—), Sylacauga Antique Group, League of Women voters, Alpha Lambda Delta. Club: Coosa Valley Country (charter mem.). Avocations: antique buff-collector; historical sites and buildings. Home: 300 W Bay St Sylacauga AL 35150 Office: Sylacauga Ins Agy PO Box 598 Sylacauga AL 35150

GANN, JO RITA, social services administrator; b. Talihina, Okla., June 2, 1940; d. Herbert and Juanita Rita (Fields) G. BS, Okla. Bapt. U., 1962; M Theatre Arts, Portland State U., 1970. Tchr. Oklahoma City Pub. Schs., 1962-64; teen dir., dir. health edn. YWCA, Oklahoma City, 1964-67; camp dir., teen dir. YWCA, Portland, Oreg., 1967-72; asst. dir., program coordinator YWCA, Flint, Mich., 1972-75; exec. dir. YWCA, Salem, Oreg.,

1975—; chair N.W. regional staff YWCA, Portland, 1983; chief exec. officer bus. panel Oregonian's Pub. Co. Co-author: A New Look at Supervision, 1980. Del. UN Conf. for Non-Govtl. Orgns.; internat. study del. on world econ. interdependence to Ghana, Africa; speaker Global Concerns, Salem and Portland, 1981—; mem. pres.'s council Salem Summerfest, 1985, 86. Mem. Exec. Dirs. YWCA of U.S., Nat. Orgn. Female Execs. Democrat. Christian Scientist. Office: YWCA 768 State St Salem OR 97301

GANNETT, MARYE DECKER, government agency official; b. Union, Iowa, May 12, 1928; d. Bert George and Gertrude Grace (Haugen) D.; m. Ellis Wells Hubbard, Mar. 18, 1950 (dec. 1960); children—David Wells, Steven Ellis; m. Arthur Chauncey Gannett, Apr. 4, 1970. B.A., U. Minn., 1949; M.S., George Washington U., 1973. Cert. data processing computer programmer. Asst. editor U. Minn. Press, Mpls., 1948-50; English instr. Tng. Inst., Tokyo, 1954-57; sec., treas. Weissberg-Bros. Realty, Arlington, Va., 1958-67; computer specialist U.S. Gen. Services Adminstrn., Washington, 1968-75; mgr. U.S. Immigration and Naturalization Service, Washington, 1975-83, U.S. Dept. Def., Fort Meade, Md., 1983—. Author: Best Loved Poets, 1982. Sec. Prince Georges Hosp. Citizens Adv. Bd., Hyattsville, 1974-77. Mem. Nat. Speakers Assn., Bus. and Profl. Women, Assn. Computing Machinery (cert.), Assn. Systems Mgmt. (cert.), Data Processing Mgmt. Assn. (cert.), Toastmasters Internat. (dist. editor 1983-85, Disting. Toastmaster, 1983, Top 10 award 1984, Dist. and regionalSpeech Champion 1987-88), Nat. Speakers Assn. Avocations: vol. scouts and senior citizens. Home: 6800 Baltimore Ave Univ Park Hyattsville MD 20782

GANNON, SISTER ANN IDA, philosophy educator, former college president; b. Chgo., 1915; d. George and Hanna (Murphy) G. A.B., Clarke Coll., 1941; A.M., Loyola U., Chgo., 1948, LL.D., 1970; Ph.D., St. Louis U., 1952; Litt.D., DePaul U., 1972; L.H.D., Lincoln Coll., 1965, Columbia Coll., 1969, Luther Coll., 1969, Marycrest Coll., 1972, Ursuline Coll., 1972, Spertus Coll. Judaica, 1974, Holy Cross Coll., 1974, Rosary Coll., 1975, St. Ambrose Coll., 1975, St. Leo Coll., 1976, Mt. St. Joseph Coll., 1976, Stritch Coll., 1976, Stonehill Coll., 1976, Elmhurst Coll., 1977, Manchester Coll., 1977, Marymount Coll., 1977, Governor's State U., 1979, Seattle U., 1981, St. Michael's Coll., 1984, Nazareth Coll., 1985, Holy Family Coll., 1986, Keller Grad. Sch. Mgmt. Mem. Sisters of Charity, B.V.M.; tchr. English St. Mary's High Sch., Chgo., 1941-47; residence, study abroad 1951; chmn. philosophy dept. Mundelein Coll., 1951-57, pres., 1957-75, mem. faculty philosophy dept., 1973-85, emeritus faculty, 1987—, archivist, 1986—. Contbr. articles philos. jours. Mem. Adv. Bd. Sec. Navy, 1975-80, Chgo. Police Bd., 1979—; bd. dirs. Am. Council on Edn., 1971-75, chmn., 1973-74; nat. bd. dirs. Girl Scouts U.S.A., 1966-74, nat. adv. bd., 1976-85 ; trustee St. Louis U., 1974-87, Ursuline Coll., Cath. Theol. Union, 1983—, DeVry Inc., 1987—; bd. dirs. Newberry Library, 1976—, WTTW Pub. TV, 1976—, Parkside Human Services Corp., 1983—. Recipient Laetare medal, 1975; LaSallian award, 1975; Aquinas award, 1976; Chgo. Assn. Commerce and Industry award, 1976; Hesburgh award, 1982. Mem. Am. Cath. Philos. Assn. (exec. council 1953-56), Assn. Am. Colls. (dir. 1965—, chmn. 1969-70), Religious Edn. Assn. Am. (pres. 1973, chmn. bd. 1975-78), N. Central Assn. (commn. on colls. and univs. 1971-78, chmn. exec. bd. 1975-77, dir.), Assn. Governing Bds. Colls. and Univs. (dir. 1979—). Address: 6363 Sheridan Rd Chicago IL 60660

GANNON, ANNE DURNEY, banker; b. Bethlehem, Pa., May 15, 1952; d. Joseph J. and Barbara J. (Graveline) Durney; 1 child, Christopher P. Gannon. B.A. in Polit. Sci. and History, Rosemont Coll., 1974; postgrad. in bus. adminstrn. Temple U., 1974-77, Stonier Grad. Sch. Banking, Rutgers U., 1977-80; m. Joseph H. Gannon, Oct. 11, 1980. Mut. fund adminstr. Provident Nat. Bank, Phila., 1974-76, mgr. fed. funds dept., 1976—, head Eurodollar trader Nassau br., 1980-86, div. head, facilities mgmt., 1986—. Mem. Greater Phila. Money Marketeers, Rosemont Coll. Alumnae Assn. (dir. and treas. 1978-80). Republican. Roman Catholic. Club: Cynwyd (Pa.). Home: 4 Meredith Rd Green Hill Farms PA 19151 Office: Provident Nat Bank Broad and Chestnut Sts Philadelphia PA 19101

GANNUSCIO, SUSAN BAKER, surety company executive; b. Jackson, Tenn., Jan. 16, 1955; d. Fred William Jr. and Kathryn Rose (Thomas) Baker; m. E. Ray Putnam, Dec. 27, 1974 (div. Aug. 1983); m. Mark Stephen Gannuscio, Aug. 24, 1985. Student, Jackson State Community Coll., 1973-75, Union U., 1975-76. With Fireman's Fund Ins. Co., Nashville, 1977—, surety exec. underwriter, 1986-88; surety underwriting/mktg. mgr. Fireman's Fund Ins. Co., San Francisco, 1988—. Mem. allocations com. United Way Nashville, 1983-84. Mem. Constrn. Fin. Mgmt. Assn. (bd. dirs.), Surety Assn. Tenn. (legis. chmn. 1984, v.p. 1986-87, pres. 1988), Nat. Assn. Female Execs. Republican. Methodist. Home: 89 Heather Ave #12 San Francisco CA 94118 Office: Fireman's Fund Ins Co One Market Plaza Spear St Tower San Francisco CA 94105

GANS, MARION LOIS, public relations executive; b. Paterson, NJ; d. Joseph George and Hattie (Alexander) Edelman; m. Irwin Gans; children: Edward M., Julie E., Robert F. BS cum laude, Syracuse U.; MA, Fairfield U., 1973. Tchr. Stamford (Conn.) High Sch.; dir. pub. relations BiCultural Day Sch., Stamford, 1972-78; owner Marion Gans Communications, Stamford, 1978-82; pres. Gans Pub. Relations, Inc., Stamford, 1982—; cons. Cahill Assocs., Westport, Conn., 1984—. Contbr. articles to mags., newspapers. Press sec. Dem. mayoral candidate, Stamford, 1977; com. mem. Voluntary Action Council, Stamford, 1984; bd. dirs. Stamford Land Conservation Trust; v.p. Jr. Achievement Southwestern Conn. Recipient 13 awards for pub. relations and writing. Mem. Southwestern Area Commerce and Industry Assn., Women in Mgmt. (bd. dirs. 1984—), Stamford Symphony Soc. Democrat. Jewish. Office: Gans Pub Relations 126 Woodside Green Suite 2C Stamford CT 06905

GANTZ, NANCY ROLLINS, nurse; b. Buffalo Center, Iowa, Mar. 7, 1949; d. Troy Gaylord and Mary (Emerson) Rollins; diploma in Nursing, Good Samaritan Hosp. and Med. Center, Portland, Oreg., 1973; BSBA, City Univ., 1986; MBA, Kennedy-Western U., 1987; m. Aug. 1981. Nurse ICU, Good Samaritan Hosp., 1973-75; charge nurse Crestview Convalescent Hosp., Portland, 1975; dir. nursing services Roderick Enterprises, Inc., Portland, 1976-78, Holgate Center, Portland, 1978-80; nursing cons. in field of adminstrn., 1980-84; coordinator CCU; mgr. ICU/CCU Tuality Community Hosp., Hillsboro, Oreg., 1984-86; head nurse intensive care unit, cardiac surgery unit, Good Samaritan Hosp. & Med. Ctr., Portland, 1986-88, nurse mgr. critical care units, 1988—; mem. task force Oreg. State Health Div. Rules and Regulations Revision for Long Term Health Facilities and Hosps., 1978-79. Mem. Am. Nurses Assn. (cert.), Oreg. Nurses Assn., Nat. League Nursing, Am. Assn. Critical Care Nurses (regional cons., pres. elect greater Portland chpt. 1985-86, pres. 1986-87), Am. Heart Assn., Oreg. Heart Assn., Geriatric Nurses Assn. Oreg. (founder, charter pres.), Clackamus Assn. Retarded Citizens. Adventist. Home: 2670 NW Eastway Ct Beaverton OR 97006

GANZ, MARY KEOHAN, lawyer; b. Weymouth, Mass., Nov. 17, 1954; d. Francis Lawrence and Margaret (Quinn) Keohan; m. Alan H. Ganz, Sept. 7, 1980. B.A. magna cum laude, Emmanuel Coll., 1976; J.D., Suffolk U., 1979. Bar: Mass., N.H., U.S. Dist. Ct. Mass.; lic. real estate, cert. tchr., notary pub., Mass.; justice of peace, notary pub., N.H. Law clk., sec. Pullman & Weitzen, Boston, 1977-78; law clk. Law Office Alan H. Segal, Braintree, Mass., 1978-79; law clk., assoc. Law Office Michael J. Yerandi, Braintree, 1979-81; sole practice, Seabrook, N.H., 1981—; trustee U.S. Savs. Bank Am., Seabrook, 1982-84; dir. U.S. Savings Bank Am., 1988—. Active Seacoast Community Women, Hampton, N.H., 1983—; Network of Emmanuel Women, 1983—. Mem. ABA, Mass. Bar Assn., N.H. Bar Assn., Rockingham County Bar Assn., Mass. Women Lawyers, Seabrook Bus. and Profl. Assn. (dir. 1983—, pres. 1986-88), Kappa Gamma Pi, Phi Delta Phi. Roman Catholic. Office: Seabrook Profl Bldg PO Box 238 549 Lafayette Rd Seabrook NH 03874

GAPEN, DELORES KAYE, librarian, educator; b. Mitchell, S.D., July 1, 1943; d. Lester S. and Lena F. G. B.A., U. Wash., 1970, M.L.S., 1971. Gen. cataloger Coll. William and Mary, Williamsburg, Va., 1971-72; instr., asst. head Quick Editing Ohio State U., Columbus, 1972-74; head Ohio State U., 1974-77; asst. dir. tech. services Iowa State U., Ames, 1977-81; dean, prof. univ. libraries U. Ala., University, 1981-84; dir. gen. library system U. Wis., Madison, 1984—; exec. com. Council U. Wis. Libraries, 1985-87; cons. Northeast Mo. State U., 1980, Assn. Research Libraries task force on bibliog. control, 1981, Pa. State U., 1982, Conn. Coll., 1982; vice chmn. exec. com. of bd. trustees U. Wis. Online Computer Library Ctr., Madison, 1984-86, also mem. research libraries adv. com. (chair task force on Future of Research Library Coop. in Changing Techs. Environment, 1986, chmn. com. short cataloging records, 1983-84); cons. Bryn Mawr Coll. Online System Planning, 1983, Council Library Resources Edn. Task Force on Future of Library Sch. Edn., 1983, Tex. A&I U. reaffirmation team cons. for So. Assn. Colls. and Schs., 1984, Dickinson Coll. Library Autocat System, 1987; chair Assn. of Research Libraries Task Force for Govt. Info. in Electronic Form, 1986-87; mem. Assn. of Research Libraries Task Force on Scholarly Communication, 1983-87. Contbr. articles to profl. pubs. Mem. AAUP, ALA, Southeastern Library Assn., Ala. Library Assn., Assn. Research Libraries (chmn. task force govt. info. in electronic form 1986-87, bd. dirs. 1987-90), Bus. and Profl. Women's Assn., Beta Phi Mu, Alpha Lamba Delta. Democrat. Roman Catholic. Home: 702 Seneca Pl Madison WI 53711 Office: Meml Library 728 State St Madison WI 53706

GAPPA, WANDA BETH, geriatric activities director; b. Port Washington, Wis., Apr. 24, 1962; d. Franklin Delano and Carol Ruth (Krueger) Runkel; m. Mitchell Lee Gappa, Mar. 28, 1987. AA in Occupational Therapy, Milw. Area Tech. Coll., 1982. Occupational therapist asst. Sheboygan (Wis.) Meml. Hosp., 1982-84; dir. Adult Community Learning Ctr., Mequon, Wis., 1984-88; resident mgr. Friendship Manor, Plover, 1988—. Lutheran.

GARAM, MARTHA JANE, editor; b. Cleve., Aug. 8, 1947; d. William Bertram and Yetta Lillian (Shaftel) Webber; children: Jennifer Barbara, Michelle Debra. AB in Edn., U. Mich., 1969; MA in English, NYU, 1970. Cert. secondary sch. tchr., N.Y. Tchr. English George W. Hewlett High Sch., N.Y., 1971-74; project asst. Am. Council on Teaching Fgn. Langs., Hastings-on-Hudson, N.Y., 1982-83; freelance reporter The Enterprise, Hastings-on-Hudson, 1982-83, copy editor, 1983-84, editor-in-chief, 1983-88; sr. editor Housewares Executive, N.Y.C., 1988—; editor newsletter Parent-Tchr.-Student Assn., Hastings Pub. Schs., 1981-82. Mem. Hastings Creative Arts Council, 1981—. Recipient cert. of merit N.Y. State Sch. Bds. Assn., 1986, award County Bd. of Legislators, 1988. Mem. N.Y. Press Assn., Nat. Assn. for Female Execs. Office: Housewares Executive 475 Fifth Ave 609 New York NY 10017

GARAZI, IDA SHWARTZ, artist, interior designer; b. Havana, Cuba, Aug. 21, 1936; came to U.S., 1959; d. Moris and Pola (Levin) Shwartz; children: Susana, Diana; m. Phillip Albert Winter, Sept. 4, 1985. Cert. in Interior Design, Am. U., Havana, 1959; AA, Miami Dade Jr. Coll., 1976; student, Fla. Internat. U. Textile color coordinator David and Dash Interior Design, Miami, Fla., 1962-64; cons. in interior design Saul Siegal Fabrics, Miami, 1964-66; asst. dir. sales Jordan Marsh Art Gallery, Miami, 1971-76; interior designer Red Tag Furniture, Miami, 1977-87; mem. coop. gallery South Fla. Art Gallery, Miami Beach, Fla., 1985—. One-woman shows include Menorah Temple, Miami, 1979, Bacardi Art Gallery, Miami, 1980, South Fla. Art Gallery, Miami, 1986, Louis Flower and Art Gallery, Bay Harbor, Fla., 1987; group exhbns. include Fla. Internat. U., Miami, 1984, 85, Barbara Gillman Gallery, Miami, 1985, North Miami Met. Mus., 1985; featured work pub. South Fla. Home and Garden Mag., 1987. Art dir. Interam. chpt. Hadassah, Miami, 1981. Mem. Women's Caucus for Art, Miami Watercolor Soc., Allied Arts, Phi Pheta Kappa. Jewish. Home: 1261 99th St Bay Harbor Islands FL 33154

GARBÁTY, MARIE LOUISE, art collector and patron; b. Berlin, Ger., Mar. 9, 1910; widowed. Patron, Met. Opera, N.Y.C. Opera; patron, hon. mem. Allentown (Pa.) Art Mus.; mem. N.Y.C. Opera Guild; fellow in perpetuity Met. Mus. Art; life fellow Mus. Fine Arts, Boston; internat. centennial patron Mus. Fine Arts, Boston; benefactor, life mem. Chrysler Mus., Norfolk, Va.; assoc. mem. Solomon Guggenheim Mus., N.Y.C., cofounder Am. Shakespeare Festival Theater, Stratford, Conn.; friend N.Y.C. Library; mem. Am. Fedn. Art, China Inst. Am. Inc., N.Y.C., Asia Soc., N.Y.C., Art Mus., Palm Beach, Fla.; donations numerous museums, libraries, profl. socs., including Met. Mus. Art, N.Y.C., U. Wash., Cooper Union Mus., Boston U. Library, Calif. State Coll. Library, Fullerton, Yale U. Library, Hoover Library, Stanford U., Library of Congress, Art Inst., Chgo., Carnegie Inst. Art, others.

GARBER, BARBARA JEAN, educator; b. Colorado Springs, Oct. 31, 1927; d. Clarence Albert and Mattie Ethel (Buchanan) Ebbert; m. Harry Daniel Garber Jr., Apr. 12, 1957; children: Douglas Ray, Teri Ann Garber Langston, Gigi Ann Garber Skipper. BA, Stetson U., 1978, MEd, 1986. Cert. tchr., Fla. Adminstrv. asst. legal office Eglin Air Force Base, Fla., 1952-57; tchr. Enterprise (Fla.) Elementary Sch., 1978-88, Deltona (Fla.) Middle Sch., 1988—; producer Enterprising Enterprise, 1985; co-chair sch. wide econ. project Old Country Fair, 1986, All American Day, 1987. Mem. Dem. Exec. Com., Volusia County, Fla., 1984-85. Mem. NEA, Volusia Educators Assn., Fla. Tchrs. Assn., Alpha Delta Kappa, Kappa Delta Pi. Democrat. Methodist. Home: 445 N Clara Ave Deland FL 32720 Office: Enterprise Elementary Sch 211 Main St Enterprise FL 32725

GARBER, CHARNA JANICE, wholesale shoe company executive; b. Lynn, Mass., Apr. 21, 1937; d. Saul William and Lena (Kline) Chalek; m. William Garber, Oct. 11, 1956; children—Holly Jeske, Ellise Garber. Student, U. N.H., 1960, 61, 62, Am. Inst. Banking, Lynn, Mass., 1954, 55. Mgr. customer services The Rochester Banks (N.H.), 1964-66; bus. mgr. computer dept. MIT, 1973-78; line builder, fashion coordinator Cole-Haan Footwear, 1978-80; sales rep. Internor Trade, N.Y.C., 1980-82; pres. C. G. Assocs. Inc., N.Y.C., 1982—; sec.-treas., owner N.E. Fashion Shoe Show, N.Y.C., 1976—; pres. d'Rossana Shoes. Bd. dirs. Dollars for Scholars, Mass., N.H., 1960-66. Mem. 210 Assn., Boot and Shoe Travelers Assn., Nat. Shoe Travelers Assn., Footwear and Accessories Council, NOW. Democrat. Jewish. Club: Hadassah. Home: 201 E 87th St Suite 21J New York NY 10128 Office: D'Rossana Co 12 W 57th St Room 801 New York NY 10019

GARBER, JUDITH ANN, health care services executive; b. Ville Platte, La., Dec. 6, 1949; d. Gordon Lee and Hazel (Pitre) Dardeau; m. Melvin Paul Garber, June 10, 1972; children—Raegan Dyane, Dustin Paul. B.S. in Nursing, U. Southwestern La., 1972. Head nurse Rehab. Ctr., Ithaca, N.Y., 1973-74; charge nurse County Hosp., Ames, Iowa, 1975-76; nurse cons. pvt. industry, Tacoma, 1980-83; unit mgr. med. rev. Health Care Cost Containment, Orlando, Fla., 1983-86; pres. Cost Containment Cons., Altamonte Springs, Fla., 1986—. Speaker nat. edn. conf. Self-Insurance Inst. Am., San Francisco, 1985. Mem. Nat. Assn. Female Execs., Fla. Utilization Rev. Assn., Fla. Occupational Health Nurses Assn., Self-Insurance Inst. Am., Central Fla. Claims Assn. (bd. dirs., pres.). Republican. Roman Catholic. Club: Seminole Soccer (Longwood, Fla.). Office: PO Box 915155 Longwood FL 32791-5155

GARCIA, CHERYL DEE, marketing professional; b. Ainsworth, Nebr., Mar. 24, 1957; d. Harlan Lloyd and Joyce Leona (Sanden) Carlson; m. Michael Raymond Garcia, May 24, 1980. BA in Journalism, N.Mex. State U., 1979. Exec. sec. 1st Interstate Bank, Albuquerque, 1980-82; sales acct. exec. Sta. KRKE, Albuquerque, 1982-83, Radio Station KKOB, Albuquerque, 1983—; v.p. Albuquerque Bus. Assocs., 1986—. Mem. Better Bus. Bur. (vol. arbitrator 1986—). Republican. Lodge: Kiwanis. Home: 14501 Oakwood Pl NE Albuquerque NM 87123 Office: KKOB-AM 77 Broadcast Plaza SW Albuquerque NM 87103

GARCIA, CONCEPCIÓN NICOLASA, elementary educator, researcher, writer; b. Cienfuegos, Cuba, Aug. 17, 1939; came to U.S., 1962; d. Rodolfo and Juana Joaquina (Ferre) G. Student, U. Havana, Cuba, 1959-61; B in Edn., U. Miami, 1967, MEd, 1972, postgrad., 1981—. Cert. tchr., assoc. master tchr., Fla. Tchr. Dade County Bd. Pub. Instrn., Miami, 1967-72, reading specialist, 1972-73, adminstrv. asst., 1973-76, tchr., 1976—; researcher Archivo General de Indias, Sevilla, Spain, summers 1978, 79, 80; intern Dade County Hist. Assn., 1978. Contbr. articles to Revista Ideal mag., 1975-81, Anuario Iglesia Católica, 1976-80; author booklets Guadalupe Press, 1976-78. Bd. dirs. Allapattah YMCA, Miami, 1970-76; vol. Mother Teresa's Shelter for Homeless, Miami, 1981-86. Mem. United Tchrs. of Dade County, Cath. Tchrs. Guild (pres. 1977-78), Phi Delta Kappa. Democrat. Roman Catholic. Office: Sunset Elem Sch 5120 SW 72nd St Miami FL 33143

GARCIA, ELLIE, entrepreneur, consultant; b. N.Y.C., Jan. 4, 1960; d. Jose and Blanca E. (Quiles) G.; m. Rafael Velazquez, Oct. 12, 1975 (div. Sept. 1985); 1 child, Rafael Velazquez II. AA, Interamerican U., Bayamon, P.R., 1982. Adminstrv. asst. The Atlantic Orgn., San Juan, P.R., 1980-82; office mgr. Bernard Marko & Assocs., Miami, Fla., 1983-86; media and traffic dir. Advt. Assoc., Miami, 1986; owner Specialized Office Services, Miami, 1986—; cons. mktg. Unicom Plus Corp., Miami, 1987—; cons. mgmt. Ives Dairy Mini Bay, Miami, 1987—, Ralph Choeff Architect and Start-to-Finish Gen. Contractors, Miami, 1987. Mem. Am. Film Inst., Nat. Assn. Female Execs., Alpha Delta Sigma. Roman Catholic.

GARCIA, JOSEFINA MARGARITA, dancer, nurse, educator; b. Mascota, Jalisco, Mex., May 2, 1906; came to U.S., 1923, naturalized, 1944; d. Manuel Garcia Perez and Margarita (Garcia) Flores; diploma Nat. Coll., Kansas City, Mo., 1933; tchrs. cert. State Tchrs. Coll., Queretaro, Mex., 1935; R.N., Bethany Hosp. Sch. Nursing, 1939; diploma in psychiat. nursing Inst. of Living, Hartford, Conn., 1941; B.S., Tchrs. Coll., Columbia U., 1943, M.A. in Health and Phys. Edn., 1945; Ph.D. in Dance and Related Arts, Tex. Woman's U., 1958. Elem. tchr. Meth. Normal Sch., Puebla, Mex., 1934-36; dir. religious edn., nurse, coordinator phys. edn. George O. Robinson Sch., San Juan, P.R., 1939-40; psychiat. nurse psychiat. div. N.Y. Okla. White Plains, 1941-43; tchr. health Poly. Inst., San German, P.R., 1943-44; charge corrective gymnastics Hosp. for Spl. Surgery, N.Y.C., 1944-45; nurse Bellevue Hosp., N.Y.C., 1945-50; tchr., performer La Meri's Ethnologic Center, N.Y.C., 1945-47; lectr., dancer Pearl Buck's East and West Assn., 1947-49; artist, tchr., nurse Jacob's Pillow U. of Dance, Lee, Mass., summers 1949-55; pvt. duty nurse Harkness Pavillion, N.Y.C., 1952-55; supr. psychiat. div. Parkland Meml. Hosp., Dallas, 1956-58; grad. asst. in dance Tex. Woman's U., Denton, 1956-58; chmn. health, phys. edn. and recreation dept. Okla. Coll. for Women, Chickasha, 1958-63 (on leave), instr., 1934-36, 39-40, prof., 1963-64; vis. prof. edn. Miami U., Coral Gables, Fla., 1963-64; dir. dance in dept. health and phys. edn., prof. phys. edn. Madison Coll., Harrisonburg, Va., 1964-67; tchr. English as secondary lang., bilingual edn. N.Y.C. Bd. Edn.; part-time staff Grady Meml. Hosp., Chickasha, 1962-63; numerous dance recitals and workshops, 1940—; tchr. Mexican and Latin Am. dance Tina Ramirez Dance Studio, N.Y.C.; cons. Sacred Dance Guild; choreographer on Mexican themes Alliance Latin Am. Arts, summers 1973-74; artist-in-residence Spelman Coll., Atlanta, 1978-79; relief night nurse, prof. geriatric health and exercises Williams Residence, N.Y.C. Vol., Channel 13 Public TV; founder Center for Internat. Security Studies; mem. Am. Security Council; bd. govs. N.Y. chpt. Arthritis Found. Fellow AAHPER; mem. Am., Okla., N.Y. State (dir.) nurses assns., Nat., So., Va. assns. phys. edn. coll. women, ANTA, Okla. Edn. Assn., Va. Assn. Health, Phys. Edn. and Recreation (chmn. 1962-63), AAUW, Chickasha Bus. and Profl. Women's Club (past chmn. internat. relations com.), Nat. Dance Tchrs. Guild, Nat. Council Arts in Edn., Mus. Natural History, Dance Notation Bur., Internat. Platform Assn., Pan Am. Women's Assn. (dir. 1967—, v.p.), Dance Film Library Assn. (dir. 1967—), Film Soc. (dir.), Profl. Dance Tchrs. Assn., Nat. Council Sr. Citizens, Met. Opera Guild, Cooper-Hewitt Mus., Nat. Geog. Soc., N.Y. YWCA, Kappa Delta Pi, Phi Sigma Iota. Contbr. articles on dance to profl. publs., Groliers Ency., Richards Ency. Home: 720 West End Ave Suite 821 New York NY 10025

GARCIA, KATHERINE LEE, comptroller, accountant; b. Portland, Oreg., Nov. 4, 1950; d. Gerald Eugene and Delores Lois (Erickson) Moe; m. Buddy Jesus Garcia; Nov. 19, 1977; children: Kevin, Brett, Rodd. BS cum laude, U. Nevada, 1976. CPA, Idaho, Nev. Retail clk. Raleys, Food King, Reno, 1968-76; sr. acct. Pieretti, Wilson and McNulty, Reno, 1976-78, Deloitte Haskins and Sells, Boise, Idaho, 1979-81; sr. acct. Washoe County, Reno, 1981-83, chief deputy comptroller, 1983—. Treas., bd. dirs. Friends of 4 (pub. TV), Boise, 1979-81. Recipient Cert. of Excellence in Fin. Reporting, Nat. Council Govt. Accts., 1982—. Mem. Am. Inst. CPA's (state and local govt. com. 1987-88), Nev. Soc. CPA's (state and local govt. com. 1987-88), Govt. Fin. Officer's Assn., Nev. Govt. Fin. Officer's Assn. Republican. Home: 655 W Joy Lake Rd Reno NV 89511 Office: Washoe County PO Box 11130 Reno NV 89520

GARCIA, LAURA CATHERINE, utilities executive; b. Hollywood, Fla., Mar. 11, 1957; d. Thomas Tubens and Felicia (Acebal) G. BSEE, U. Miami, 1979. With Fla. Power and Light Co., Miami, 1980—, constrn. services mgr., 1988—. Counselor Soc. Abused Children, Kendall, Fla., 1985-86; instr. Jr. Achievement, Miami, 1986-87, Adult Illiterate, 1987. Early admission scholar U. Miami, 1975. Mem. Leadership Miami Assn., Greater Miami C. of C. Republican. Roman Catholic. Club: Hurricane. Home: 933 NE 199th St 205 North Miami FL 33179 Office: Fla Power & Light Co 4200 W Flagler St Miami FL 33134

GARCIA, ROBERTA, sales executive, financial manager; b. Weslaco, Tex., Apr. 14, 1958; d. Antonio and Maria Elva (Salinas) Ramirez; m. Jorge Alberto Garcia (div.); children: Bobby Jo, Jorge Alberto Jr. Grad. high sch., Weslaco, Tex. Sales mgr. Ed Payne Motors, Inc., Weslaco, 1977-82, fin. mgr., 1982—. Pres. Parent-Tchrs. Orgn., Weslaco, 1982, v.p., 1983. Mem. Nat. Assn. of Female Execs., Dodge Sales Mgrs. Soc. Democrat. Roman Catholic. Home: 2327 Camelot Dr Weslaco TX 78596 Office: Ed Payne Motors Inc 727 E Hwy 83 Weslaco TX 78596

GARCIA-BAHNE, BETTY, social work educator; b. Pomona, Calif., Sept. 27, 1943; d. Charles Trujillo and Mary Louise (Garcia) Garcia. BS in Social Sci., Calif. State Poly. U., Pomona, 1965; MSW, San Diego State U., 1966-68; PhD in Social Psychology, Boston U., 1985. Lic. clin. social worker. Psychiat. social worker Calif. State Dept. Social Welfare, Santa Ana, 1968-70; clin. social worker U. Calif.-San Diego Psychol. Services, La Jolla, 1970-77; teaching fellow psychology dept. Boston U., 1977-84; clin. social worker Family Service of Greater Boston, 1983-88; asst. prof. Simmons Coll. Sch. Social Work, Boston, 1986—; co-investigator research project NIMH, 1974-76; field instr. San Diego State U. Sch. Social Work, 1971-77; cons. Mass. State div. Forensic Mental Health, Boston, 1986—. NIMH grantee, 1980-81. Mem. Am. Psychol. Assn., Nat. Hispanic Psychol. Assn. (v.p. Mass. chpt. 1986-87), Nat. Assn. Social Workers. Office: Simmons Coll Sch Social Work 51 Commonwealth Ave Boston MA 02116

GARCIA COLL, CYNTHIA, psychology educator; b. San Juan, P.R., June 10, 1953; d. Juan Garcia Esteves and Maria T. Coll; m. Barry M. Lester, May 30, 1982; children: Nataniel, Andres. BA in Psychology, Biology, U. P.R., 1974; MA in Devel. Psychology, U. Fla., 1977; PhD in Personality Psychology, Harvard U., 1981. Asst. prof. pediatrics, adj. asst. prof. psychology Brown U., Providence, 1981—; asst. prof. pediatrics U. P.R. Med. Sch., Rio Piedras, 1985—; co-investigator Ford Found., 1985—, March of Dimes Found., 1987—; prin. investigator Maternal and Child Health, 1988—. Mem. editorial bd. Child Devel. mag., 1987—, Infant Behavior and Devel., 1988—. Bd. dirs. United Way Southeastern New Eng., Providence, 1987—; mem. com. for minority participation Soc. for Research in Child Devel., 1987—; mem. com. for child devel., research,and pub. policy Nat. Acad. Scis., 1987—. Office: Women and Infants Hosp Brown U Program in Medicine 101Dudley St Providence RI 02905

GARCIA-OLIVER, MAGDALENA BARBARA, industrial engineer; b. N.Y.C., Mar. 4, 1963; d. Angel J. and Maria Magdalena (Oliver) Garcia. AA, Miami-Dade Community Coll., 1983; BS in Indsl. Engring., U. Miami, 1985. Data analyst, clk. Fla. Power & Light, Miami, 1985-86; analyst procedures Kislak Mortgage Corp., Miami, 1986-87, analyst methods, 1987; analyst Procedures Devel. Unit City of Miami, 1987—. Mem. Inst. Indsl. Engrs. (sec. 1984-85), Soc. Women Engrs., Nat. Assn. for Female Execs., Fla. Engring. Soc., U. Miami Alumni Assn. Republican. Roman Catholic. Home: 4426 SW 132 Pl Miami FL 33175-3927 Office: City of Miami Office Indsl Engring 3006 Aviation Ave Miami FL 33133

GARDELLA, ELIZABETH, association executive; b. Long Branch, N.J., Mar. 23, 1951; d. John Anthony and Marilyn (Lennon) G.; m. David Gilamn, Aug. 20, 1983. BA, Boston U., 1974; MA, U. Md., 1979; cert. mgmt., Columbia U., 1985. Program assoc. coll. engring. U. Md., College Park, 1979-81; dir. planning and devel. Alliance Resident Theaters, N.Y.C., 1981-85; program planning cons. Playwrights Horizins Theater, N.Y.C., 1981-85; exec. dir. Nat. Dance Inst., N.Y.C., 1985—. Office: Nat Dance Inst 599 Broadway New York NY 10012

GARDINE, JUANITA CONSTANTIA FORBES, educator; b. St. Croix, V.I., Aug. 6, 1912; d. Alphonso Sebastian and Petrina (Actien) Forbes; B.A., Hunter Coll., 1934; M.A., Columbia U., 1940; postgrad. U. Chgo., 1949, NYU, 1960-66, Cheyney Coll., 1967; M.Ed., U. Ill.-Chgo., 1986; m. Cyprian A. Gardine, Apr. 23, 1942; children—Cyprian A., Vicki Maria Camilla, Letitia Theresa, Richard Whittington. Tchr. elementary schs., 1934-35; tchr. math. high sch., 1935-41, 48-49; acting asst. high sch. prin., 1941; jr. high sch. prin., 1941-47; substitute tchr. English, math., physics, Montclair, N.J., 1947-48; asst. supt. edn., 1949-55; assoc. dean Community Colls., supr. elem. schs., 1955-57; high sch. prin., 1957-58; supr. ednl. stats., 1958-62; social worker Dept. Welfare, 1962-63; prin. Christiansted (St. Croix) Pub. Grammar Sch., 1963-74; tchr. math. evening session extension classes Cath. U. P.R., 1960-61; asst. dir. and tutor St. Croix Tutorial Sch., 1974-82; part-time instr. math. Coll. V.I., 1974-75, 80-81. Past sec. bd. dirs. St. Croix Fed. chpt. ARC; mem. bd., chmn. supervisory com. St. Croix Fed. Credit Union; past sec. St. Croix Sch. Health Com., Girl Scout Com., Fredericksted Hosp. Aux.; past mem. and pres. St. Croix (V.I.) Mental Health Assn. Pres., Tchrs. Assn., 1940, Municipal Employees Assn., 1942. Sch. named in her honor, 1974; honoree P.R. Friendship Day Com., 1979, St. John's Ch., 1981. Mem. Am. Statis. Assn., NAESP, V.I. Fedn. Bus. and Profl. Women's Clubs (past sec.), Episcopal Ch. Women of V.I. (past chmn. world affairs com.), Christiansted Bus. and Profl. Women's Club (past pres.; Woman of Year 1966), Daus. King (sec.), Christiansted Bus. and Profl. Club (past parliamentarian, past pres.). Episcopalian (past pres. women's group). Home: 142 Whim Estate Frederiksted Saint Croix VI 00840 Mailing address: Box 1505 Christiansted Saint Croix VI 00820

GARDIS, GILDA J., quality analyst; b. Jersey City, Jan. 16, 1944; d. William Patrick and Gilda Esther (Weber) Cornett; m. David Richard Gardis, Oct. 8, 1966 (div. 1981). Student, Oceanside-Carlsbad Jr. Coll., Santa Monica City Coll. Prin. typist clk. UCLA, 1966-69, adminstrv. asst., 1969-73, acctg. asst., 1973-75, mgmt. services officer, UCLA, 1975-79; mgmt. services officer U. Calif., San Diego, La Jolla, 1979-85; quality analyst Teledyne Kinetics, Solana Beach, Calif., 1986—; part-time sales rep. Mervyn's, Oceanside, Calif., 1986—. Active Oceanside High Sch. Booster Club, 1980-83. Recipient Tiffany award Manpower, Inc., Carlsbad, Calif., 1985. Mem. Am. Mgmt. Assn. (assoc.), Nat. Assn. Female Execs., Network Exec. Women, Teledyne Kinetics Recreation Assn. (sec. 1987, chairperson 1988). Roman Catholic. Avocations: tennis, bicycling, art, bowling. Home: 3559 Guava Way Oceanside CA 92054 Office: Teledyne Kinetics 410 S Cedros Solana Beach CA 92075 Mailing Address: PO Box 1401 Oceanside CA 92054

GARDNER, ANNE LANCASTER, lawyer; b. Corpus Christi, Tex., Aug. 19, 1942; d. Jack Quinn and DeWitte (Benton) Lancaster; BA, U. Tex., 1964, LLB, 1966; 1 child, Travis Gregory. Admitted to Tex. bar, 1966; asst. dir. continuing legal edn. State Bar Tex., 1966-67; law clk. to U.S. Dist. Ct. judge, 1967-71; ptnr. Simon, Peebles, Haskell, Gardner & Betty, Ft. Worth, 1971-85, McLean, Sanders, Price, Mead & Ellis, P.C., Ft. Worth, 1985-88, Shannon, Gracey, Ratliff & Miller, Ft. Worth, 1988—. Fellow Tex. Bar Found. (life); mem. Am., Ft. Worth-Tarrant County (dir., v.p.) bar assns., State Bar Tex., Tex. Assn. Def. Counsel (bd. dirs.), U. Tex. Law Sch. Assn. (dir.), Tex. Assn. Def. Counsel (bd. dirs.), Kappa Beta Pi, Delta Zeta. Editor legal jours. Office: Shannon, Gracey, Ratliff & Miller 2200 First City Bank Tower Fort Worth TX 76102

GARDNER, LAURENE, social worker; b. Kinston, N.C., Dec. 27, 1957; d. Willie James and Hilda Grace (Gooding) G.; divorced. B in Social Work, East Carolina U., 1980; MSW, U. N.C., 1981. Social worker Caswell Ctr., Kinston, 1981-84, Dobb's Sch., Kinston, 1984—; adj. prof. East Caroline U., Greenville, 1984—. Bd. dirs., vol. Big Bros./Big Sisters Kinston/Lenoir County, 1987—; vol. Hospice Program Kinston/Lenoir County, 1987—. Named one of Outstanding Young Women Am., 1984, 87. Mem. Nat. Assn. Social Workers, Acad. Cert. Social Workers, N.C. Juvenile Services Assn., NAACP, Delta Sigma Theta (Kinston alumnae chpt.). Democrat. Methodist. Home: 1116 Harper Dr PO Box 2378 Kinston NC 28501

GARDNER, LYNN SULLIVAN, public relations executive; b. N.Y.C., Sept. 30, 1957; d. John Joseph and Christina Mary (Broderick) Sullivan; m. Randy Alan Gardner, Oct. 9, 1982. B.A., Boston Coll., 1978; postgrad. New Sch. Social Research, N.Y.C., 1985. Assoc. producer Miss Universe, Inc., N.Y.C., 1979-81, Time-Life Video, N.Y.C., 1981; script supr. RG Prodns./NBC., N.Y.C. and Los Angeles, 1981-83; agt. Elite Model Mgmt., N.Y.C., 1983-84; v.p. pub. relations The Solomon Orgn., N.Y.C., 1983—. Admission counselor Boston Coll., N.Y.C., 1979—; activist Am. Soc. Prevention Cruelty Animals, N.J., 1982—, North Shore Animal League, N.J., 1982—; foster parent Christian Children's Fund, Zambia, Africa, 1983—, Covenant House of Internat. Platform Soc.; Mem. Nat. Assn. Female Execs., Media Network, Am. Women in Radio and Television, Am. Film Inst., Internat. Platform Soc., Nat. Mus. Women in Arts, ASPCA, Boston Coll. Alumni Club. Democrat. Roman Catholic. Avocations: collecting crystal cats, acting, children's theatre, reading, traveling. Home: 35 Clark St #4-D Brooklyn Heights NY 11201 Office: The Solomon Orgn 18 E 48th St New York NY 10017

GARDNER, MARIA EVRARD, pharmacist; b. Allentown, Pa., June 20, 1949; d. August E. and Helen Evrard; B.S. in Pharmacy, Phila. Coll. Pharmacy, 1972. Pharm.D., 1974; m. Lee Allan Gardner, July 5, 1975; children—Anne Christine, Megan Marie. Intern, Thomas Jefferson U. Hosp., 1972-73, resident in pharmacy, 1973-74, clin. pharmacist med. service, 1974-76, primary care pharmacist, 1974-76; adj. clin. instr. Phila. Coll. Pharmacy and Sci., 1974-76; outpatient clin. pharmacist Tucson VA Hosp., 1976-78; clin. pharmacist Tucson Gen. Hosp., 1978-85, Project AgeWell, 1986—; assoc. prof. pharmacy practice U. Ariz., Tucson, 1977—; research assoc. U. Ariz. Coll. Medicine. Mem. Am. Pharm. Assn., Am. Soc. Hosp. Pharmacists, So. Ariz. Soc. Hosp. Pharmacists (dir. 1979-80, sec. 1977-78), Am. Soc. Cons. Pharmacists, Ariz. Council Hosp. Pharmacists, Am. Assn. Colls. Pharmacy, Rho Chi. Republican. Roman Catholic. Contbr. articles on pharmacology to profl. pubs. Home: 1432 N Sarnoff Dr Tucson AZ 85715 Office: U Arizona Coll Pharmacy Tucson AZ 85721

GARDNER, MARJORIE HYER, science administrator; b. Logan, Utah, Apr. 25, 1923; d. Saul Edward and Gladys Ledingham (Christiansen) Hyer; B.S., Utah State U., 1946, Ph.D. (hon.), 1975; M.A., Ohio State U., 1958, Ph.D., 1960; cert. Ednl. Mgmt. Inst., Harvard U., 1975; m. Paul Leon Gardner, June 6, 1947; children—Pamela Jean, Mary Elizabeth. Tchr. sci., journalism and English high schs., Utah, Nev., Ohio, 1947-56; instr. Ohio State U., Columbus, 1957-60; asst. exec. dir. Nat. Sci. Tchrs. Assn., 1961-64; vis. prof. Australia, India, Yugoslavia, Nigeria, Thailand, Peoples Republic of China, 1965-82; assoc. dean, dir. Bur. Ednl. Research and Field Service, College Park, Md., 1975-76; dir. Sci. Teaching Center, U. Md., College Park, 1976-77, prof. chemistry, 1964-84; dir. Lawrence Hall Sci., U. Calif.-Berkeley, 1984—; div. dir. NSF, 1979-81; cons. UNESCO, 1970—; NSF grantee, 1964—; recipient Catalyst medal Chem. Mfrs. Assn., 1980, Nyholm medal Royal Soc. Can., 1987, U.S.U. Centennial award, 1987, ACS Chemical Edn. award, 1988. Fellow AAAS (council), Am. Inst. Chemistry; mem. Am. Chem. Soc., Chemistry Assn. Md. (pres.), Internat. Union of Pure and Applied Chemistry (exec. com.), Internat. Orgn. Chemistry in Devel. (edn. panel), Assn. Edn. of Tchrs. of Sci., Nat. Assn. Research in Sci. Teaching, Nat. Sci. Tchrs. Assn., Am. Assn. Higher Edn., Soc. Coll. Sci. Tchrs. (pres.), Fulbright Alumni Assn. (pres., dir.), Phi Delta Kappa, Phi Kappa Phi. Author: Chemistry in the Space Age, 1965; editor: Theory in Action, 1964, Vistas of Sci. Series, 1961-63; Investigating the Earth, 1968, Interdisciplinary Approaches to Chemistry, 1973, 1978-79; Under Roof, Dome and Sky, 1974, Toward Continuous Professional Development: Designs and Directions, 1976; contbr. articles in on chemistry and sci. edn. to profl. jours. Home: 517 Vista Height Rd Richmond CA 94805 Office: U Calif Lawrence Hall of Sci Centannial Dr Berkeley CA 94720

GARDNER, MARY BERTHA HOEFT CHADWICK, retired postmaster, small business owner; b. Vernal, Utah, June 13, 1914; d. Edward and Hazel (Burgess) Hoeft; B.S. in Elem. Edn., Utah State U., 1950; m. Rulon Chadwick, Sept. 3, 1935 (div. July 1949); children—Mary Jo Chadwick Wight, Adriana Chadwick Forsgren; m. Leon D. Gardner, July 14, 1951 (dec. May 1974). Bookkeeper, Model Dairy, 1935-49; Weber Central Dairy, 1949-51, Bishops Storehouse, 1950-51; sch. tchr., Ogden, Utah, 1950-51; clk. Post Office, Honeyville, Utah, 1956-72, postmaster, 1972-81; owner Country Store/RV Campground, Mantua, Utah. Pres., Relief Soc. Ch. Jesus Ch. of Latter-day Saints, mem. stake bd. relief soc., mem. stake bd. Sunday sch., mem. stake bd. mut. improvement assn. orgn., stake spl. interest leader 1982-86; mem. Utah State Women's Legis. Council, 1983-85. Mem. Nat. League Postmasters (exec. v.p. state br., editor newsletter), Nat. Assn. Postmasters, AAUW (treas.), Daus. Utah Pioneers, Bus. and Profl. Women's Club (treas. Brigham City, treas. treas. No. Dist. 1984-85, Logan 1985-86). Home: 8440 N Hwy 69 Honeyville UT 84314

GARDNER, MEREDITH LEE, communication executive; b. Providence, Nov. 25, 1941; d. Leo and Gertrude Gloria (Ketover) Gleklen; m. Daniel Ezra Mahni, May 28, 1971 (div. 1980). A.A., Colby Sawyer Coll., New London, N.H., 1961; B.A., NYU, 1963; M.A. in Devel. Psychology, Columbia U., 1965. Dir. Office Student Activities, Hunter Coll., N.Y.C., 1965-66; dir. Internat. Office, Boston Coll., Chestnut Hill, Mass., 1966-72; dir. ret. sr. vol. program Commonwealth of Mass., Boston, 1972-74, dir. Office Citizen Participation, 1974-76; research assoc. Hadley Lockwood, N.Y.C., 1976-78; assoc. Gilbert Tweed Assocs., N.Y.C., 1978-80; sr. assoc. MBA Mgmt., Inc., 1980-81; pres. Too Young To Retire, N.Y.C., 1981-87; v.p. sales Halliday/Herrmann and Maverick, 1987—; cons. sales tng., motivational speaker, 1981-87. Author: My Friend Frank, 1985. Republican. Jewish. Club: Toastmasters (cert., sgt. at arms N.Y. club). Avocations: sailing; bicycling; flea market hunting; dancing; talking with older people. Home: 321 W 78th St New York NY 10024

GARDNER, NANCY HAZARD, small business owner; b. Washington, Feb. 17, 1949; d. Everette Browning and Vera Kathryn (Rushworth) G. BS, U. Md., 1972. Trainer Equitable Trust Bank, Balt., 1970-74; program analyst U. Md., College Park, 1974-77; adminstr. Nat. Acad. Scis., Washington, 1977-80; office mgr. Ctr. for Population Options, Washington, 1980-81; comptroller Carltech Assocs., Inc., Columbia, Md., 1981-83; fin. dir. Helschien Health Ctr., Columbia, 1983-84; pres. Sensitive Systems, Inc., Savage, Md., 1982—; chmn. bd. dirs. Sensitive Systems, Inc., Balti. Mem. Nat. Assn. Female Execs. Office: Sensitive Systems Inc 2914 O'Donnell St Baltimore MD 21224

GARDNER, NANCY STEWART, sales executive; b. Chgo., Oct. 26, 1957; d. John Stewart and Carolyn Jean (Kurt) G. BA in Internat. Bus., Carthage Coll., Kenosha, Wis., 1982. Ski instr., race coach Wilmot Mt. (Wis.), Inc., 1979—; leader div. clinic Profl. Ski Instrs. of Am., Milw., 1986-88; asst. dir. Ski Sch., Wilmot Mt., 1980-82; regional mgr. Carrol Corp., Chez Chocolat, Arlington Heights, Ill., 1983-84; ter. mgr. Unitog Bus. Cothing, Kansas City, Mo., 1985—. Mem. Profl. Ski Instrs. of Am., Internat. Ski Instrs. Fedn., Chgo. Met. Ski Council, Alpha Kappa Psi. Republican. Office: Unitog Bus Clothing 101 W 11th St Kansas City MO 64141

GARDNER, NATALIE NELLIE JAGLOM, advertising agency executive; b. Cernauti, Rumania; came to U.S., 1939, naturalized, 1946; b. Abraham and Nadia (Shoenberg) Jaglom; student Ohio State U., 1943, N.Y. U., 1944, U. Calif., Berkeley, 1945; m. Ralph David Gardner, Apr. 9, 1952; children—Ralph David, John Jaglom (dec.), Peter Jaglom, James Jaglom. Dir. Ralph D. Gardner Advt., N.Y.C., 1955—; pres. Gardner Internat., Inc., 1981—; dir. N.Y. Commodities Corp., Overseas Barters, Inc. Vol., ARC, 1944; hosp. vol. Am. Women's Vol. Services, 1944-45; active UN Host Family Program. Home: 135 Central Park W New York NY 10023 Office: 888 7th Ave 34th Floor New York NY 10106

GARDNER, ROSE MARIE, make-up artist, stock broker; b. Chgo., Apr. 8, 1926; d. Timothy Joseph and Mildred (Rokas) Mahoney; m. Sully King Kokavec (div. 1955); 1 child, Kevin King; m. Charles Keith Gardner (dec. 1985); children: Karen Ann, Karla Jean. Student, Drake U., 1944-45, Depaul U., Chgo., 1945-46. Registered profl. make-up artist. Apprentice Syd Simons Studios, Chgo., 1947-52; freelance artist various studios including NBC, CBS, Sarra Studios, Chgo., 1955-64, Carter and Bush Campaign, 1972-76; staff mem. NBC, N.Y.C., 1964-72; freelance artist, stock broker Graystone Nash Investment Co., N.Y.C., 1982—. Recipient 3 Emmy nominations, 1968-84. Mem. Make-up Artist Union (sec. local 849 1952-60, v.p. local 798 1980-82), Nat. Acad. Arts & Sci. (bd. govs. 1976-77). Democrat. Home. 280 Crocker Pl Haworth NJ 07641

GARDNER, SHIRLEY MAE, software company executive; b. Chgo., Mar. 7, 1932; d. Ross Edward and Viola (Schwartz) Blake; m. William Rex Gardner, June 9, 1973. AA in Bus. Adminstrn., North Park Coll., 1952; BS in Bus. Adminstrn., U. Ill., Chgo., 1954. Print prodn. coordinator Poole Bros., Chgo., 1954-60; graphic arts coordinator Combined Ins. Co., Chgo., 1960-65; asst. print shop supr. Standard Rate & Data Service, Skokie, Ill., 1965-70; supr. art, typesetting Schiele Graphics, Chgo., 1970-73; print prodn. operator Regensteiner Corp., Chgo., 1973-75; purchasing agt. Morongo Unified Sch. Dist., Twenty-Nine Palms, Calif., 1975-78, Soc. for Visual Edn. div. Singer Inc., Chgo., 1980-84; dir. purchasing Mindscape, Inc., Northbrook, Ill., 1984-88; founder, owner Eagle Bindery Inc., Lincolnwood, Ill., 1988—. Chmn. bd. dirs. United Cerebral Palsy, Lincolnwood, Ill. Mem. Printing Industry of Ill., Nat. Assn. Female Execs., VFW Aux., Phi Pi Omega. Roman Catholic. Home: 8924 Robin Dr Des Plaines IL 60016

GARDNER, TRUDI YORK, lawyer, insurance company executive; b. Portland, Oreg., Mar. 19, 1947; d. Harry and Martha (Gevurtz) York; m. Alan Joel Gardner, Dec. 19, 1971; children: Jordan Casey, Andrew Ryan. BA, UCLA, 1969; MS, Portland State U., 1971; postgrad. N.Y. Law Sch., 1975-76; JD Lewis and Clark Law Sch., 1977. Bar: Washington 1978, U.S. Dist. Ct. (we. dist.) Wash. 1979; cert. tchr. Calif., Oreg. Law clk. U.S. Atty.'s Office (so. dist.) N.Y.C., 1976, to law firm, Portland, Oreg., 1977; fin. relations specialist Puget Sound Power & Light Co., Bellevue, Wash., 1978-79; asst. atty. gen. Dept. Labor and Industries, State of Wash., Seattle, 1979-80; sole practice, Bellevue, 1980-81; regional atty. for Mont., Idaho, Wash., Oreg, Utah and Wyo., Ins. Corp. of Am., Houston, 1981—, regional v.p., 1984-87; curriculum cons. Portland (Oreg.) Pub. Schs., 1972. Assoc. editor: Multnomah Lawyer, Multnomah County Bar Assn., Portland, 1973. Contbr. articles, cover stories to Sunday supplement of The Oregonian, radio scripts for Am. Heritage Assn. to Sta. KWJJ; contbr. short stories to mags. Mem. King County United Way Conf. Panel for Developmentally Disabled, Seattle, 1978-79. Mem. Wash. State Bar Assn. (pub. relations com. 1978-81), Seattle-King County Bar Assn., Portland City Club, Seattle Mcpl. League, Pi Sigma Alpha, Pi Lambda Theta. Clubs: Women's Univ.; Bellevue Athletic. Home and Office: 2921 130th Pl NE Bellevue WA 98005

GAREFFA, SHIRLEY A., advertising executive; b. Detroit, Sept. 10, 1951; d. Henry J. and Gertrude (Miczulski) Superson; m. Peter M. Gareffa, Aug. 19, 1972; 1 child, Jennifer Ann. Student in computer sci., Macomb County (Mich.) Community Coll., 1971-73; cert., N.Y. Media Decisions Sch., 1979. Mgr. computer ops. City Bldg. Maintenance, Inc., Detroit, 1974; acct. clerk Simons-Michelson Co., Detroit, 1974-75, asst. mgr. acctg. dept., 1975-77; media buyer Simons Michelson Zieve, Inc., Troy, Mich., 1977-78, mgr. media dept., 1978-82; founder, pres. Profl. Media Services, Ltd., St. Clair Shores, Mich., 1982-85; co-founder, v.p. media devel. Ethnic Flair Ltd., Southfield, Mich., 1985—; small bus. cons., 1982—; field rep., Outdoor Services, Inc., Chgo., 1982—; lectr. various adv. groups., 1986—. Bd. dirs. Fathers for Equal Rights, Southfield, 1983-84; mem. sounding bd. Detroit Symphony Orch., 1984—. Mem. Nat. Assn. Female Execs., AdCraft Club Detroit, NAACP. Club: St. Clair Shores Country. Home: 22702 Clairwood Saint Clair Shores MI 48080 Office: Ethnic Flair Ltd 18444 W Ten Mile Rd Suite 104 Southfield MI 48080

GAREY, PATRICIA MARTIN, artist; b. State College, Miss., Nov. 11, 1932; d. Verey G. Martin and Eva Myrtle Jones; m. Donald L. Garey, Aug. 1, 1953; children: Deborah Anne, Elizabeth Laird. BS in Costume Design, Tex. Women's Univ., 1953; MFA, Tex. Tech. U., 1973. Prodn. mgr. Cox Advt. Agy., Roswell, N.M., 1958-63; art instr. Coll. of Southwest, Hobbs, N.M., 1967-69, 72-73; artist-in-residence N. Mex. Arts Commn., Santa Fe and Hobbs, 1974-76; studio artist Hobbs, 1976—. One-woman shows include N. Mex. Jr. Coll., Hobbs, 1969, Coll. of SW, 1974, 79, Sangre de Cristo Arts Ctr., Pueblo, 1979, U. Tex. of Permian Basin, Odessa, 1980, N.Mex. Jr. Coll.; represented at Beverly Gordon Gallery, Dallas, Sylvia Ullman Am. Crafts, Cleve., Design Today, Lubbock Tex.; work exhibited at Roswell Mus. Art, Southeastern N. Mex. Small Painting Exhibit (2d pl., 1966), Llano Estacado Art Exhbn. 1967 (Hon. Mention Oil Painting), 68 (2d pl. Graphics), 69 (Hon. Mention Graphics, 2d pl. Sculpture, 2d pl. Acrylics), 75 (1st pl. Ceramics), 76 (1st pl. Drawing, 2d pl. Painting), Americas Gallery, Taos, 1974, Blair Gallery, Santa Fe, 1974, Mus. Fine Arts, Santa Fe, 1976, Tex. Tech. U., 1977, Little Rock Art Ctr., Ark., 1978, Hills Gallery, Santa Fe, 1979, Dallas Mus. Fine Art, 1987, Beaux Arts Ball Art Auction, 1988; represented in collections Beverly Gordon Gallery, Dallas, Von Grabil Gallery, The Borgata, Scottsdale, Ariz. Bd. dirs. Southwest Symphony, Hobbs, 1986—. Mem. Delta Phi Delta, Chi Omega. Democrat. Methodist. Home and Studio: 315 E Alto Hobbs NM 88240

GAREY, RUTH ARLENE, personnel executive; b. Duluth, Minn., Mar. 28, 1930; d. Kenneth I. Disbennetté and Mae Hazel (Sandman) Peterson; m. Robert H. McCormick, Aug. 27, 1950; children: Michael, Patrick, Kathleen. BA, Portland Community Coll., 1952. Dir. women's banking Citizen's Bank, Lake Oswego, Oreg., 1967-69; from mktg. officer to assoc. v.p. Oreg. Bank, Portland, 1969-87; v.p. personnel Oreg. Bank div. Security Pacific, Portland, 1987; pres. Personnel Specialty Services/McCormick Enterprises, Portland, 1987—. Mem. Am. Soc. Personnel Dirs., Pacific NW Personnel Dirs., Nat. Assn. Bank Women (bd. dirs. 1977-85), Portland C. of C. Republican. Presbyterian. Club: Mazamas (Portland). Home and Office: 8234 SW Capitol Hwy Portland OR 97219

GARFIELD, CAROL FLETCHER, computer manufacturer executive; b. Cambridge, Mass., Sept. 8, 1959; d. John P. and Nora (McMaster) Fletcher; m. Stephen B. Garfield. Student, Northeastern U., 1982. Customer services rep. Burroughs UNISYS, Woburn, Mass., 1980-86; customer services br. mgr. New Eng. UNISYS, Woburn, Mass., 1986—. Office: UNISYS 400 Unicorn Park Dr Woburn MA 01801

GARFIELD, JOAN BARBARA, mathematics and statistics educator; b. Milw., May 4, 1950; d. Sol L. and Amy L. (Nusbaum) G.; m. Michael G. Luxenberg, Aug. 17, 1980; children—Harlan Ross and Rebecca Ellen (twins). Student, U. Chgo., 1968; B.S., U. Wis., 1972; M.A., U. Minn., 1978, Ph.D., 1981. Asst. prof. math./stats. The Gen. Coll., U. Minn., Mpls., 1981—, coordinator research and evaluation, 1984-87; created various tables on evaluations of coll. retention programs, 1979-82, 85. Mem. Am. Statis. Assn., Am. Assn. Higher Edn., Am. Ednl. Research Assn., Internat. Assn. for Statis. Computing, Internat. Study Group on Learning Probability and Stats. (sec. 1987—). Jewish. Club: Mpls. Twins Topics (research chmn. 1984—). Avocations: violin, viola. Office: U Minn Gen Coll Div Sci Bus Math 216 Pillsbury Ave SE 106 Nicholson Hall Minneapolis MN 55455

GARFINKEL, FRAN SYLVIA, financial planner; b. Bronx, Jan. 21, 1959; d. Sol and Louise Marion (Goldberg) G. BS in Recreation, Calif. State U., 1981. Adminstr. Recreation and Parks Dept., 1981-84, Calif. State Northridge Alumni Assn., 1984-86; fin. planner IDS/Am. Express, Glendale, Calif., 1986—. Bd. dirs. Calif. State U. Northridge Student Union, 1983-85; mem. Calif. State U. Alumni Council, Long Beach, Calif., 1984-86. Named one of Outstanding Young Women in Am., 1981, 84; recipient Outstanding Contbds., Calif. State U. Northridge. Student Union, 1985. Mem. Bus. and Profl. Women (chmn. ways and means com. Verdugo Hills chpt. 1987, chmn. Young Careerist Verdugo Hills chpt. 1988—), Nat. Assn. Female Execs. (network dir. 1987—), Calif. State U. Northridge Associated Students (hon. life mem.). Democrat. Jewish. Office: IDS Fin Services 100 W Broadway Suite 100 Glendale CA 91210

GARGANO, FRANCINE ANN, lawyer; b. Plainfield, N.J., Feb. 10, 1957; d. Rosalie Janice (Ferrin) Gargano. B.A., Seton Hall U., 1980; J.D. cum laude, Detroit Coll. of Law, 1983. Bar: N.J. 1983, U.S. Supreme Ct, 1986. Sole practice, South Plainfield, N.J., 1983—; dir. YWCA Legal Clinic, Plainfield, 1983—; Union County coordinator Haitian Pro Bono Projects, ABA, Plainfield, 1983—; research asst. prof. Detroit Coll. Law, Detroit, 1980-83. Trustee Plainfield Area YWCA, 1983-84; bd. dirs. Haifian Advancement Assn., Elizabeth, N.J., 1983-84; mem. N. Plainfield Bd. Adjustment. Recipient Internat. Legal Scholar award Detroit Coll. Law Internat. Law Soc., 1980-82, Jessup Internat. Law Competition award, 1982; H. Rakol Scholarship award Detroit Bar Assn., 1982. Mem. ABA, Union County Bar Assn., N.J. Bar Assn., Plainfield Bar Assn., Am. Immigration Lawyers Assn., Detroit Coll. Law Internat. Law Soc. (pres. 1980-82). Democrat. Roman Catholic. Office: 113 Watchung Ave North Plainfield NJ 07060

GARIBALDI, MARIE LOUISE, state supreme court justice; b. Jersey City, Nov. 26, 1934; d. Louis J. and Marie (Servente) G. BA, Conn. Coll., 1956; LLB, Columbia U., 1959; LLM in Tax. Law, NYU, 1963; LLD, Drew U., 1983, St. Peter's Coll., Jersey City, 1983. Atty. Office of Regional Counsel, IRS, N.Y.C., 1960-66; assoc. McCarter & English, Newark, 1966-69; ptnr. Riker, Danzig, Scherer & Hyland, Newark, 1969-82; assoc. justice N.J. Supreme Court, Newark, 1982—. Contbr. articles to profl. jours. Trustee St. Peter's Coll.; co-chmn. Thomas Kean's campaign for Gov. of N.J., 1981, mem. transition team, 1981; mem. Gov. Byrne's Commn. on Dept. of Commerce, 1981. Recipient Disting. Alumni award NYU Law Alumni of N.J., 1982; recipient Disting. Alumni award Columbia U., 1982. Fellow Am. Bar Found.; mem. N.J. Bar Assn. (pres. 1982), Columbia U. Sch. Law Alumni Assn. (bd. dirs.). Home: 34 Kingswood Rd Weehawken NJ 07087 Office: 583 Newark Ave Jersey City NJ 07306

GARITY, JOAN PATRICIA, nurse, educator; b. Quincy, Mass., Apr. 29, 1944; d. Philip Francis and Virginia (Corcoran) Garity. B.S., Boston Coll., 1966; M.Ed., Northeastern U., 1971; Ed.D., Boston U., 1985. R.N., Mass. Vol. nursing clinic Mt. St. Joseph Acad., Mandeville, Jamaica, W.I., 1966-67; staff nurse Boston City Hosp., 1967-68; staff nurse Quincy City Hosp., Mass., 1968; dir. inservice edn. Quincy City Hosp., 1968-70, staff nurse recovery room, 1970-71; staff devel. specialist, dept. nursing, Mass. Gen. Hosp., Boston, 1971—, coordinator mgmt. edn., 1980-85, coordinator of student clin. placement, staff devel. services,1985— ; cons., lectr. in field; mem. adv. bd. Regis Coll. Sch. of Nursing, Weston, 1986—. Contbr. articles to profl. jours. Co-chmn. Gov.'s Adv. Council on Continuing Edn. for Nurses, Boston, 1986-87; del. to Europe People to People, 1988. Am. Orgn. Nurse Execs. scholar Am. Nurses Found., 1984. Mem. Am. Nurses Assn., Mass. Nurses Assn. (mem. Council on Continuing Edn. 1980-81, co-chair Commn. on Continuing Edn. 1982-83, Cabinet on Continuing Edn. 1984, Nursing Practice award 1985), Boston Coll. Alumni Assn. (Excellence in Sci. award 1988), Sigma Theta Tau, Pi Lambda Theta, Alpha Gamma. Democrat. Roman Catholic. Avocations: novels, museums, art, concerts, traveling. Home: 9 Tingley Rd East Braintree MA 02184 Office: Mass Gen Hosp Fruit St Boston MA 02114

GARITY, YVONNE DOLL, military officer; b. Frankfurt, Fed. Republic of Germany, Apr. 26, 1959; d. John Martin and Doris (Muser) Doll; m. Rudolph Edwin Garity, Dec. 12, 1942; 1 child, Erin; 1 stepchild, Kathy. BS, U.S. Mil. Acad., 1981; MS, U.S.C., 1987. Commd. 2d lt. U.S. Army, 1981, advanced through grades to capt., 1984; physical security officer 101st Ordnance Bn., Heilbronn, Fed. Republic of Germany, 1981-85; co. comdr. U.S. Disciplinary Barracks Mil. Police Bn., Leavenworth, Kans., 1985-86; classification officer U.S. Disciplinary Barracks Mil. Police Bn., Leavenworth, 1986-87, Mil. Police Bn. S-3 Hdqrs., Leavenworth, 1988—. Decorated Army Commendation medal U.S. Army, 1985, Army Achievement medal, 1984, 86. Roman Catholic.

GARLAND, JOAN BRUDER, psychologist, social worker; b. Cleve., Sept. 30, 1931; d. Henry Ignatius and Mary (Maher) Bruder; A.B., Mt. Holyoke Coll., 1952; postgrad. Wellesley Coll., 1952-53, U. Sao Paulo (Brazil), 1965-66; M.S., Sarah Lawrence Coll., 1974; M.S. in Social Work, Columbia U., 1977, PhD in Psychology Union for Experimenting Colls. and Univs., 1986; Diplomate Clin. Social Work. m. Paul Griffith Garland, Aug. 28, 1954; children—Bonnie (dec.), Patrick, John, Cathryn. Grad. asst., chemistry dept. Wellesley (Mass.) Coll., 1952-53; chemist Polaroid Corp., Cambridge, Mass., 1953-54, 55-56; CAPES research fellow U. Sao Paulo, 1954-55; clin. instr. retardation N.Y. Med. Coll., Valhalla, 1978-80; social worker, psychiat. day treatment program Jewish Child Care Assn., Pleasantville (N.Y.) Cottage Sch., 1980; family research investigator Albert Einstein Coll. Medicine, Bronx, N.Y., 1982-86; Founder, v.p. Crime Victims Assistance Agy., Inc., 1981-83. Treas. council Girl Scouts, Sao Paulo, 1965-67; bd. dirs. PTA, 1972-73; bd. deacons Scarsdale (N.Y.) Congregational Ch., 1975; patient rep. White Plains (N.Y.) Med. Center, 1977. Cert. in family therapy, Center for

Family Learning, Phila. Child Guidance Ctr.; cert. ind. social worker, N.Y. State, Conn. Fellow Soc. Clin. Social Work Psychotherapists, Am. Orthopsychiat. Assn.; mem. Nat. Assn. Social Workers, Acad. Cert. Social Workers, AAUP, Nat. Soc. Genetic Counselors, N.Y. Acad. Scis. Clubs: Mt. Holyoke, Wellesley (Fairfield County). Home: 139 Old Church Rd Greenwich CT 06830

GARLAND, SARA G., government relations consultant; b. New Rockford, N.D., May 1, 1946; d. John A. and Annabelle (Stephenson) G.; B.A., U. N.D., 1968, M.A., 1972; m. Kim E. Uhl, Aug. 10, 1979; children—Stephanie Garland, Joshua Edward, Jonathan Stewart. Reporter, Sta. KXJB-TV, Fargo, N.D., 1968-69; instr. speech, U. N.D., 1969-72; asst. dir. public affairs Corp. Public Broadcasting, 1972-76; legis. asst. to Rep. Margaret Heckler, 1976-77, to Sen. Quentin Burdick, 1977-85; asst. Senate Appropriations Com. Washington Coordinator, fundraiser, Harriett Woods for Senate Campaign, 1985-86; polit. cons. 1987—. Bd. dirs. Peacepac Council for a Livable World; mem. D.C. Adv. Neighborhood commr. Mem. Capitol Hill Women's Polit. Caucus. Presbyterian. Home and Office: 137 13th St NE Washington DC 20002

GARLAND, SYLVIA DILLOF, lawyer; b. N.Y.C., June 4, 1919; d. Morris and Frieda (Gassner) Dillof; m. Albert Garland, May 4, 1942; children—Margaret Garland Clunie, Paul B. B.A., Bklyn. Coll., 1939; J.D. cum laude, N.Y. Law Sch., 1960. Bar: N.Y., 1960, U.S. Ct. Appeals (2d cir.), 1965, U.S. Ct. Claims, 1965, U.S. Supreme Ct., 1967, U.S. Customs Ct., 1972, U.S. Ct. Appeals (5th cir.), 1979. Assoc. firm Borden, Skidell, Fleck and Steindler, Jamaica, N.Y., 1960-61, Fields, Zimmerman, Skodnick & Segall, Jamaica, 1961-65, Marshall, Brater, Greene, Allison & Tucker, N.Y.C., 1965-68; law sec. to N.Y. Supreme Ct. justice, Suffolk County, 1968-70; ptnr. firm Hofheimer, Gartlir, Gottlieb & Gross, N.Y.C., 1970—; asst. adj. prof. N.Y. Law Sch., 1974-79; mem. com. on character and fitness N.Y. State Supreme Ct., 1st Jud. Dept., 1985—. Author: Workman's Compensation, 1957; Wills, 1959; Labor Law, 1962; contbg. author: Guardians and Custodians, 1970; editor-in-chief Law Rev. Jour., N.Y. Law Forum, 1959-60 (service award 1960); contbr. article to mag. Trustee N.Y. Law Sch., 1979—; pres. Oakland chpt. B'nai B'rith, Bayside, N.Y., 1955-57. Recipient Disting. Alumnus award, N.Y. Law Sch., 1978. Mem. ABA (litigation sect.), N.Y. State Bar Assn., Queen's County Bar Assn. (sec. civil practice 1960-79), N.Y. Law Sch. Alumni Assn. (pres. 1976-77), N.Y. Law Forum Alumni Assn. (pres. 1963-65). Jewish. Home: 425 E 58th St New York NY 10022

GARLICK, NANCY BUCKINGHAM, clarinetist, conductor; b. White Plains, N.Y., Feb. 1, 1946; d. Robert and Betty (Bonnar) Buckingham; B.S., SUNY, Potsdam, 1968; M.M., Manhattan Sch. Music, 1970; postgrad. Ecoles Americaines des Beaux Arts, Fontainebleau, 1973, Tanglewood, 1974; m. D. Stevens Garlick, Aug. 30, 1980. Clarinetist Am. Wind Symphony, 1969, Opera Orch. of N.Y., 1970, Nat. Orch. Assn., 1970, New Haven Symphony, 1971-75, Waterbury Symphony, 1974, Lakeside Symphony, 1976-81, Shenandoah Valley Music Festival of Am. Symphony Orch. League, 1977-78, Mo. Symphony Soc. Performing Arts Ctr., 1979, Am. Inst. Mus. Studies Orch., Graz, Austria, 1983; music dir. Wooster (Ohio) Symphony Orch., 1977-83; assoc. prof. music Coll. Wooster, 1975-85; clarinetist Wooster Trio, 1980-83; music dir. Youth Orch. Charlottesville/Albemarle, 1986-87; mem. founder Albemarle Ensemble, 1987—, Ash Lawn Opera Co., 1986; lectr. clarinet U. Va., 1985—; prin. clarinetist Charlottesville Symphony, 1985—; N.Y. debut Wooster Trio, 1981; soloist Boston Pops Orch., in Weber's Concertino, New Haven Coloseum, 1973. Westchester Music Tchrs. Assn. grantee, 1964; Coll. Wooster Faculty grantee, 1977; recipient Nat. Orch. Assn. Accomplishment award, 1970. Mem. Internat. Clarinet Soc., Coll. Music Soc. Home: 1829 Brandywine Dr Charlottesville VA 22901 Office: U Va Dept Music Old Cabell Hall Charlottesville VA 22903

GARMAN, NANCY JOAN, information science consultant; b. Indpls., Oct. 4, 1946; d. Kenneth Antles and Marian (Henley) Goodwell; m. John T. Garman, Mar. 28, 1970; children: Jeanne Marie, James Henley. BA, Coll. Wooster, 1968; MS in Library Sci., Columbia U., 1969. Bus. reference librarian Northwestern U., Evanston, Ill., 1969-70; engring. librarian Avco Ordnance div. Avco Corp., Richmond, Ind., 1970; asst. med. librarian Colo. State Hosp., Pueblo, 1971-72; reference librarian Krannert Grad. Sch. Mgmt. Purdue U., West Lafayette, Ind., 1982-85; owner Info-Find Info. Services, Covington, Ky., 1985—. Editor DATABASE mag., 1986—; editor book rev. column ONLINE and DATABASE mags., 1985-86, contbr. numerous articles, 1985—. Elder Cen. Presbyn. Ch., Lafayette, Ind., 1985-86, other ch. activities; pres. Newcomers Club, Lafayette, 1980-81. Mem. ALA, Spl. Libraries Assn., Am. Assn. Info. Sci. Presbyterian. Home and Office: Info-Find 14 Princeton Ave Fort Mitchell KY 41017

GARMAN, TERESA AGNES, state legislator; b. Ft. Dodge, Iowa, Aug. 29, 1937; d. John Clement and Barbara Marie (Korsa) Lennon; m. Merle A. Garman, Aug. 5, 1961; children: Laura Ann Garman Hansen, Rachel Irene, Robert Sylvester, Sarah Teresa. Grad. high sch., Ft. Dodge. With employee relations dept. 3M Co., Ames, Iowa, 1974-86; mem. Iowa Ho. of Reps., Ames, 1986—. Mem. Am. Bus. Women's Assn., Rep. Farm Policy Council, Story County Rep. Women (campaign chair 4th Dist.), Friends of Mamie Eisenhower. Roman Catholic. Clubs: Boone Women's, Story County Porkettes, Farm Bur. Home: Rural Rt 2 Ames IA 50010 Office: State Capitol Des Moines IA 50319

GARMIZE, SHARON MARIE, artist, small business owner; b. Plymouth, Pa., Feb. 12, 1950; d. Michael and Josephine (Kovalick) Berish; m. Richard M. Garmize, Apr. 4, 1970 (div. Aug. 1982). Student, Pa. State U., 1967-69. Buyer Allied Stores div. Pomeroys Inc., Wilkes Barre, Pa., 1970-75, div. sales mgr., 1975-77; pres., owner SMG Sales Corp., Wilkes Barre, 1975-82; designer, owner Sharon Garmize Needlepoint Designs, Moutaintop, Pa., 1977—. Specialist in needlework miniatures with more than 50 pub. designs, 1981—; works displayed in group shows Monaco and London Chpts. of Am. Needlepoint Guild (best of show), 1982. Selected as one of subjects in book Masters in Miniature, 12 Artists at Work, by Anne Day Smith. Fellow Internat. Guild Miniature Artisans (trustee 1981-83); mem. Nat. Assn. Miniature Enthusiasts (Acad. of Honor 1988), Am. Crafts Council. Democrat. Roman Catholic. Home and Office: 27 Yorktown Rd Mountaintop PA 18707

GARNER, CARRIE LEE, guidance counselor; b. Nashville, Jan. 21, 1938; d. Maxwell and Rosie (Haynes) Hyde; widowed March 1982. BS in Social Studies, Tenn. State U., 1956; MS in Guidance and Counseling, Ind. U., 1961; postgrad., NYU, 1968. Cert. couunselor; registered practicing counselor. Counselor Arturus Sch., Ft. Richardson, Alaska, 1962-65, Anne Chestnutt High Sch., Fayetteville, N.C., 1966-68, Reid Ross High Sch., Fayetteville, 1968-84; secondary guidance counselor, cons. State of N.C., 1984—. Bd. dirs. Pines Carolina Council Girl Scouts Am., 1985—; active Coll. Heights Presbyn. Ch. Recipient Ella Stephens Barrett Leadership award, 1988. Am. Assn. for Counseling and Devel. (chairperson human rights, awards com., govt. relations com. 1985—, mem. various coms., programs), Am. Sch. Counselor Assn., Nat. Vocat. Assn., N.C. Assn. for Counseling and Devel. (pres., chairperson pub. relations com., govt. relations com., regional liaison network and registry liaison), N.C. Assn. for Religious and Value Issues and Counseling, N.C. Assn. for Specialists in Group Work, N.C. Mental Health Assn., N.C. Assn. for Humanistic Edn. and Devel., N.C. Assn. for Religious and Value Issues and Counseling, Phi Delta Kappa, Alpha Kappa Alpha. Home: 3401 Cranbrook Dr Fayetteville NC 28301

GARNER, GIROLAMA THOMASINA, educational administrator, educator; b. Muskegon, Mich., Sept, 15, 1923; d. John and Martha Ann (Thomas) Funaro; student Muskegon Jr. Coll., 1941; B.A., Western Mich. U., 1944, M.A. in Counseling and Guidance, 1958; Ed.D., U. Ariz., 1973; m. Charles Donald Garner, Sept. 16, 1944 (dec.); 1 dau., Linda Jeannette Garner Blake. Elem. tchr., Muskegon and Tucson, 1947-77; counselor Erickson Elem. Sch., Tucson, 1978-79; prin. Hudlow Elem. Sch., Tucson, 1979-87, adj. prof. U. Ariz., 1973—, Tucson Pima Community Coll., 1981—, Prescott Coll., 1986—; mem. Ariz. Com. Tchr. Evaluation and Cert., 1976-78; del. NEA convs. Active ARC, Crippled Children's Soc., UNESCO, DAV Aux., Rincon Renegades; bd. dirs. Hudlow Community Sch., 1973-76. Recipient Apple award for teaching excellence Pima Community Coll., 1982. Mem. Nat. Assn. Sci. Tchrs., Tucson Edn. Assn., Ariz. Edn. Assn., NEA, Assn. Supervision and Curriculum Devel., AAUW, Tucson Adminstrs., Pima County Retired Tchrs., Delta Kappa Gamma, Kappa Rho Sigma, Kappa Delta Pi. Democrat. Christian Scientist. Home: 6922 E Baker St Tucson AZ 85710 Office: 502 N Caribe St Tucson AZ 85710

GARNER, JO ANN STARKEY, educator; b. Ft. Hamilton, N.Y., Dec. 25, 1934; d. Joseph Wheeler and Irene Dorothy (Vogt) Starkey; m. James Gayle Garner, Mar. 2, 1957; children: Mary Vivian Pine, Margaret Susan Gillis, Kathryn Lynn. BA in History, Govt., Law, U. Tex., Austin, 1956; post-grad., Trinity U., 1973. Cert. deaf edn. and elem. tchr., Tex. Kindergarden tchr. Platenstrasse Internat. Sch., Frankfort, Federal Republic of Germany, 1964-66; tchr. of deaf Sunshine Cottage Sch. for Deaf, San Antonio, 1966—; speech cons. Trinity U., 1978, cooperating tchr., 1978—. Mem. Tex. Alexander Graham Bell Assn. (charter), San Antonio Geneal. and Hist. Soc., The Bright Shawl, Rep. Nat. Com., Sunshine Sch. for Deaf (supporting mem.), German-Texan Heritage Soc., Alpha Delta Pi. Republican. Episcopalian. Home: 2027 Edgehill Dr San Antonio TX 78209 Office: Sunshine Cottage Sch for Deaf 103 Tuleta San Antonio TX 78209

GARNER, OLLIE BELLE, contracting company executive; b. Waynesburg, Ky., Feb. 6, 1928; d. Rufus D. and Nettie B. (Hubble) Stonecypher; Rogers Bus. Coll., Somerset, Ky., 1947; m. Leo M. Garner, May 26, 1947. Sec., Pulaski County (Ky.) Extension Office, Somerset, 1948-50; bookkeeper W.C. Brass & Assos., Indpls., 1951-62; sec., bookkeeper Acme Constrn. Co., Indpls., 1963-65; sec., v.p., dir., co-owner J & O Contractors, Inc., Indpls., 1965—. Mem. Early Am. Soc., Marion County Art League, Nat. Assn. Women Bus. Owners, Network of Women in Bus., Nat. Assn. Women in Constrn., Internat. Platform Assn., Indpls. Mus. Art, YWCA. Club: Economic. Home: 7515 W Mooresville Rd Camby IN 46113 Office: 3906 W Washington St Indianapolis IN 46241

GARNER, SHARON BUSH, accountant; b. DeFuniak, Fla., Dec. 25, 1956; d. Willard Pat Bush and Aria (Woodham) West; m. Howard Edward Garner, July 12, 1974; children: Lori Suzanne, John Vincent. AA, Chipola Jr. Coll., 1975; BA in Acctg., U. Fla., 1977. Retail acctg. mgr. Fleming Foods Corp., Geneva, Ala., 1978; staff acct. Coats & McCullar, Bonifay, Fla., 1979-81; pvt. practice acctg. Bonifay, 1981—. Bd. dirs. Children's Ch. and First Bapt. Ch., Bonifay, 1985-87. Mem. C.of C. Democrat. Baptist. Office: 116 N Waukesha St Bonifay FL 32425

GAROOGIAN, RHODA, librarian; b. Bronx, N.Y.; d. David and Rose (Fried) Lillian; m. Andrew Garoogian, Feb. 19, 1954; children: David, Neill. BA, Bklyn. Coll., 1961, MA, 1970; MLS, Pratt Inst., 1971, postgrad., 1974. Reference librarian Medgar Evers Coll., Bklyn., 1976; asst. dean Grad. Sch. Library and Info. Sci. Pratt Inst., Bklyn., 1977-85; mgr. tgn. and documentation H.U. Wilson Co., Bronx, 1985-86, dir. Wilsonline info. systems, 1986—. Author: Child Care Issues, 1977, Careers for Librarians, 1985; editor Software Rev., 1980-81; contbr. articles to profl. jours. Recipient Fannie L. Simone award Spl. Librarians Assn., 1988. Mem. ALA, Am. Soc. Info. Sci. Office: H U Wilson Co 950 University Ave Bronx NY 10245

GARR, TERI, actress; b. Lakewood, Ohio, 1952. Appeared in films including: The Conversation, 1974, Young Frankenstein, 1974, Won Ton Ton, The Dog Who Saved Hollywood, 1976, Oh God!, 1977, Close Encounters of the Third Kind, 1977, Mr. Mike's Mondo Video, 1979, The Black Stallion, 1979, Tootsie, 1982, One From the Heart, 1982, The Sting II, 1983, The Black Stallion Returns, 1983, Mr. Mom, 1983, Firstborn, 1984, After Hours, 1985, Miracles, 1986; TV movies include Doctor Franken, 1980, Prime Suspect, 1982, The Winter of Our Discontent, 1983, To Catch a King, 1984, Intimate Strangers, 1986, Pack of Lies, 1987, Teri Garr in FlapJack Floozie, 1988; regular on TV series The Sonny and Cher Comedy Review, 1974; other TV appearances include Law and Order, 1976, Fresno. Office: care Bill Treusch Assocs 853 7th Ave Apt 9A New York NY 10019 *

GARRETSON, CINDY L., foundation administrator; b. Denver, July 21, 1952; d. Robert William and Betty Lou (Edmonson) G.; 1 child, Michelle Lea. BBA, U. Neb., Omaha, 1979. Instr. Wayne Community Coll., Goldsboro, N.C., Cen. Valley Ctr. for Migrant and Seasonal Farmworkers, Merced, Calif.; founder, dir. Children of Am. found., Merced, 1983—; instr. Defense Plus program, Merced, 1983—. Author: FINGERPRINTS: They're not just kids play, 1986. Mem. Nat. Ctr. Missing and Exploited Children, Washington, Merced County Child Abuse Coordinating Com., Merced County Children's Services Network, Calif. Child Abuse Services. Named Most Dedicated Vol. Merced County, 1986. Office: Children of America Box 133 Merced CA 95341

GARRETT, CAROL ANN, speech and language pathologist; b. Danville, Va., June 24, 1940; d. James Claude Swanson and Hilma May (Hall) G.; A.A., Averett Coll., 1960; B.S. magna cum laude, Miss. U. for Women, 1962; M.Ed., U. Va., 1966. Speech-lang. pathologist Lynchburg (Va.) Public Schs., 1962—; pvt. practice speech-lang. pathology Lynchburg, 1963—; cons. in field. Mem. Am. Speech-Lang.-Hearing Assn. (com. on disorders of central auditory processing 1986, nat. elections com. 1988—), Speech and Hearing Assn. Va., Central Va. Speech-Lang.-Hearing Assn. (chmn. 1984-85), AAUW (life), Spl. Edn. Adv. Com. Lynchburg Public Schs., Beta Sigma Phi (life, pres. Lynchburg council 1964-65, pres. chpt. 1965-66, 68-71, 73-75, Girl of Yr. award 1969-71, 73-75), Methodist. Home: 723 Custer Dr Lynchburg VA 24502 Office: Lynchburg Public Schs 10th and Court Sts Lynchburg VA 24504

GARRETT, ECHO MONTGOMERY, magazine editor; b. Nashville, May 8, 1960; d. Bobby LaRoy and Sonja Carol (Cox) Montgomery; m. Kevin Newton Garrett, Apr. 3, 1982. BS in Journalism, Auburn U., 1982. Adminstr. copyright House of Gold Music, Nashville, 1982-83; editorial asst. McCall's mag., N.Y.C., 1983-84, asst. editor, 1984-85; asst. editor Venture mag., N.Y.C., 1985-86, assoc. editor, 1986—; free-lance writer. Chmn. Front Page Awards Dinner Dance, 1988. Mem. Newswomen's Club N.Y.C. (treas. 1986—), Investigative Reporters & Editors, Auburn Alumni. Republican. Mem. Ch. of Christ. Office: Venture Mag 521 Fifth Ave 15th Floor New York NY 10175

GARRETT, GLORIA SUSAN, social services professional; b. Tampa, Fla., Nov. 30, 1951; d. Howard Leon and Marie Leonora (Garcia) G.; m. Michael Thomas McClain, May 16, 1973; 1 child, Molly Kathleen Garrett McClain. Student, Agnes Scott Coll., 1969-71, U. South Fla., 1971-72; BA, Ga. State U., 1977, MEd, 1979. Sr. caseworker DeKalb County Dept. Family and Children Services, Decatur, Ga., 1979-80, 82-84; prin. caseworker DeKalb Councy Dept. Family and Children Services, Decatur, Ga., 1980-82, 84-85, casework supr., 1985-86; sr. casework supr., claims mgr. DeKalb County Dept. Family and Children Services, Decatur, Ga., 1986—. Mem. Am. Pub. Welfare Assn., Ga. County Welfare Assn. Office: DeKalb County Dept Family & Children Services 1 W Court Sq Decatur GA 30030

GARRETT, HELEN MARIE, state senator; b. Paducah, Ky.; d. John Frank and Helen Eunice (Bean) Rickman; m. John Thomas Garrett, 1952 (dec.); children—Tom, Carol. Mem. Ky. Senate, majority whip. Democrat. Office: Ky Senate State Capitol Frankfurt KY 40601 *

GARRETT, MARGO PAIGE, pianist, music educator; b. Raleigh, N.C., July 25, 1949; d. Laurie William and Elizabeth (Snipes) G.; m. Charles D. Kavalovski, June 4, 1987. MusB, N.C. Sch. Arts, 1971; MusM, Manhattan Sch. Music, 1974. Faculty N.C. Sch. Arts, Winston-Salem, 1971-72, Sarah Lawrence Coll., Bronxville, N.Y., 1974-83, Manhattan Sch. Music, N.Y.C., 1974-83, Tanglewood Music Ctr., Lenox, Mass., 1979—; asst. prof. Aaron Copland Sch. Music div. Queens Coll., Flushing, N.Y., 1985-86; faculty The Juilliard Sch., N.Y.C., 1985—, coordinator accompanying dept., 1986—; pvt. practice teaching, N.Y.C., 1974—; guest artist univs., 1974—; guest lectr. Westminster Choir Coll., Princeton, N.J., 1983-85; faculty, co-dir. accompanying dept. New Eng. Conservatory, Boston, 1986—. Pianist, accompanist numerous concerts; recordings on various labels. Office: The Juilliard Sch Lincoln Ctr New York NY 10023

GARRETT, MARY JANE, computer scientist, educator; b. Mt. Clemens, Mich., Nov. 28, 1942; d. Andrew Vincent and Irma Clara (Ahlers) Tesner; divorced; children: Patrick Walter, Paula Jean. BA in Math and Edn., Wayne State U., 1963, MEd in Math Edn., 1965. Cert. data processor, computer programmer, systems profl. Tchr. Grant Jr. High, East Detroit, Mich., 1963-65, Matanuska Borough Schs., Wasilla, Alaska, 1965-67, Imlay City (Mich.) Pub. Schs., 1967-68; mgr. Gold Bar (Wash.) Store and Service Sta., 1971-72; research programmer, analyst Universal Electric, Owosso, Mich., 1979-80; programmer, analyst City of Flint (Mich.), 1980, 83, 85; vocat. data processing, account computing Shiawassee County Ind. Sch. Dist., Corunna, Mich., 1980—; part-time tchr. Mott Community Coll., Flint, 1975-81, Lansing Community Coll., Owosso br., Mich., 1981—; supr. data processing programs Owosso Lincoln Sch. Learning Ctr., 1983—; computer coordinator Shiawassee County Ind. Sch. Dist., Corunna, 1986—. Contbr. articles to profl. jours. Leader Boy Scouts Am., Flint, 1976-79 (merit badge counselor 1985—), Girl Scouts Am., Flushing, Mich., 1977-80; tchr. jr. ch. Flushing United Meth. Ch., 1986—. Mem. Data Processing Mgmt. Assn., Mid Mich. Assn. Computer Machinery, Internat. Council Computers in Edn., Nat. Bus. Educators Assn., Internat. Inst. Forecasters, Phi Kappa Phi. Club: Ednl. and Recreation Computer (librarian 1983-86). Office: Shiawassee County Ind Sch Dist 202 N Brady Corunna MI 48817

GARRETT, NANCY ROBERTS, editor; b. Terre Haute, Ind., Dec. 5, 1954; d. Jack Richford and Anne Marie (Dennison) Roberts; m. William H. Garrett Jr., Jan. 2, 1978 (div. Sept. 1986). BS in Journalism cum laude, Ind. State U., 1977. Sports reporter Terre Haute Tribune-Star, 1975-76; sports reporter Paris (Ill.) Daily Beacon-News, 1977-80, reporter, photographer, 1981-85, mng. editor, 1985—; editor Marshall (Ill.) Independent, 1980-81; corr. Sta. WTWO-TV, Terre Haute, 1978—; media adviser State Sen. Harry Woodyard, Chrisman, Ill., 1983—; advt. cons. Rep. William Black, Danville, Ill., 1986—. Author, editor Series Clark County Park Dist., 1980-81 (2d pl. award Ill. Press Assn.). Deacon Paris Presbyn. Ch., 1982, Elder, 1985—; mgr. Paris Youth Ctr., 1981-86; pres. Edgar County Young Rep., Paris, 1987—; dir. Community Concert Assn.. Mem. Assn. Soc. Profl. Journalists, Sigma Delta Chi. Presbyterian. Home: 704 E Court Apt 7 Paris IL 61944 Office: Paris Daily Beacon-News North Main St Paris IL 61944

GARRETT, PAMELA DENISE, educator; b. Los Angeles, Nov. 2, 1954; d. Travis and Bette Jean (Perkins) G. B.A. in Child Devel. Calif. State U.-Los Angeles, 1976; A.A. in Psychology, West Los Angeles Coll., 1974. Tchrs. credential, Calif. Tchr.'s aide Los Angeles Unified Sch. Dist., 1975-76, tchr. Children's Ctr., 1977-79; tchr. Marcus Garvey Pre-Sch., Los Angeles, 1976-77; tchr. Compton Unified Sch. Dist. (Calif.), 1979—, Stephen C. Foster Elem. Sch., 1981-87, George Washington Carver Elem. Sch. 1987—; cons. Mary Kay Cosmetics, Inc., 1975—; asst. dir., mem. bd. Creative Learning Inst., Compton, Calif., 1983—; travel cons. L.A. By Pam, sight seeing tours. Mem. Nat. Council Negro Women, Calif. Tchrs. Assn., Internat. Platform Assn., Research Council of Scripps Clinic and Research Found., Nat. Assn. Female Entrepreneurs, Tau Gamma Delta, Phi Delta Kappa. Democrat. Baptist. Home: 847 E 116th Pl Los Angeles CA 90059

GARRINGER, JAYNE ANN, computer services professional; b. Dunnville, Ont., Can., Mar. 23, 1956; d. Ronald William and Anna Isabelle (Bilger) G. Degree in data processing, Fanshawe Coll., London, Ont., 1983, Degree in info. systems, 1984. Various positions Can. Imperial Bank, Alta. and Sask., 1977-83; savs. officer Royal Trust, Alts., Ont., 1978-79; programmer-analyst Chil-Con Products Ltd., Brantford, Ont., 1984; mgr. computer services Tri-ad Graphic Communications, Inc., Toronto, 1984-88; cons. micro computer bus. solutions Advent Info. Resources Ltd., Toronto, 1988—. Jr. Achievement leader, London, 1982-83. Mem. Can. Info. Processing Soc. Lutheran. Office: Advent Info Resources Ltd, 4174 Dundas St West, Suite 300, Toronto, ON Canada M8X 1X4

GARRISON, BRENDA JOYCE, travel agency owner; b. New Britain, Conn., Feb. 4, 1943; d. James and Justina (Fernandez) Tella; m. Wayne Garrison, Nov. 1, 1975. Student, Hartford Airline Personnel Sch., 1961-62, U. Conn., 1966, Tunxis community Coll., 1975. Supr. Allstate Ins., West Hartford, Conn., 1962-63; ins. cons. W.L. Hatch Co., New Britain, 1963-64; sales rep. Am. Mut. Ins. co., Wethersfield, Conn., 1964-69; asst. sec. Hartford (Conn.) Ins. Group, 1969-85; exec. v.p. Uniglobe Passport Travel Inc., Windsor, Conn., 1985—, also bd. dirs. Mem. Assn. Entrepreneurial Women, Windsor C. of C., Conn. Animal Welfare League. Roman Catholic. Office: Uniglobe Passport Travel 200 High St Windsor CT 06095

GARRISON, SARA KATHERINE, government agency administrator, banker; b. Seattle, Apr. 7, 1951; d. William L. and Mary M. (Higginson) G.; m. Timothy Bever; children: Zachary, Margaret. BS, U. Wis., 1973; MS in Psychology, Tulane U., 1974, PhD in Psychology, 1976. Adj. tchr. Hunter Coll. CUNY, 1976-77; mem. staff Fed. Res. Bank of San Francisco, 1977-79, mgr., 1979-80, officer, 1980-82, v.p., 1982-84, sr. v.p., 1984—. Office: Fed Reserve Bank PO Box 7702 San Francisco CA 94120

GARRISON, SUSAN ELODIE, hospital administrator; b. San Rafael, Calif., Jan. 11, 1946; d. Dwight Collum and Laura Eloise (Frazier) Birch. BA, U. Calif., Berkeley, 1968, M in Pub. Health, 1975. Planner and research cons. Bay Area Social Planning Council, Oakland, Calif., 1968-72; asst. adminstr. Kaiser Found. Hosps., West Los Angeles, Calif., 1975-76, adminstr., 1977-79; adminstr. Kaiser-Permanente Med. Ctr., Anaheim, Calif., 1979-85, Kaiser Found. Hosp., Fontana, Calif., 1985—. Named Emerging Leader Assn. Western Hosps., 1986. Mem. Am. Coll. Healthcare Execs., So. Calif. Hosp. Assn. (com. chmn.), Calif. Hosp. Assn. Office: Kaiser Found Hosp 9961 Sierra Ave Fontana CA 92335

GARRISON, WANDA BROWN, paper manufacturing company employee; b. Madison County, N.C., Sept. 16, 1936; d. Roy Lee Brown and Zella Arizona (Miller) Brown Hannah; m. Charles Mitchell Garrison, July 9, 1955; children—Roy Lee, Marsha Joan; 1 step-son, Charles Mitchell, Jr. Student air-line hostess Weaver Airlines, St. Louis, 1954-55; student Haywood Tech. Coll., Clyde, N.C., 1967-68; student IBM, Asheville, N.C., 1977; student in data processing Agy. Record Control, Atlanta, 1978. Operator Day Co., Waynesville, N.C., 1954-57; driver Haywood County Schs., Waynesville, 1970-71; operator Am. Enka, N.C., 1972-75; bookkeeper L. N. Davis Ins. Co., Waynesville, 1975-80; stock preparation Champion Internat., Canton, N.C., 1980—. Sec./treas. James Chapel Baptist Ch., Haywood County, N.C., 1965-77; pres. Fire Dept. Aux., Crabtree, N.C., 1973—; pres. Women Mission Union, Crabtree Bapt. Ch., Haywood County, 1977-80; v.p. Gideon Aux., Haywood County, 1982-84, pres., 1984-87; state aux. follow-up rep., 1984-87, state zone leader, 1987-88. Recipient Life Saving plaque Lion's Club, Waynesville, 1972. Mem. AFL-CIO. Democrat. Home: Hwy 209 Route 1 Box 230A Clyde NC 28721

GARRO, BARBARA, risk management consultant; b. Camden, N.J., Feb. 3, 1943; d. Dominic and Mildred Barbara (Homiak) G.; m. James Edward Stephano, Nov. 28, 1964 (div. 1975); children: Victoria Lynne, Karen Marie. CPCU; lic. property/casualty cons. N.Y., N.H., Vt. Sales, mktg. asst. Publickers Distillers Products, Inc., Phila., 1961-62; paralegal LaBrum & Doak/ Rawle & Henderson/Miller, Pincus & Greenberg, Phila., 1962-67; bus. owner Retail Sundries Store, Phila., 1972-78; free-lance writer 1979—; tax cons. Safeguard Scientifics, Inc., King of Prussia, Pa., 1980; corp. ins. adminstr. Safeguard Scientifics, Inc., King of Prussia, 1980-85; dir. risk mgmt. Comcast Corp., Bala Cynayd, Pa., 1985-87; dir. risk mgmt. services UK&W Tech. Resources, Ltd., Albany, N.Y., 1987—; pres. Garro Enterprises, Albany, N.Y., 1987—. Columnist (newspaper column) Corp Talk, 1986—; contbr. articles to profl. jours. Adv. bd. Upper Merion CATV, King of Prussia, Pa., 1987. Mem. Nat. Speakers Assn. (bd. dirs. Albany chpt. 1987—), CPCU Soc. (I-Day com. 1985-86), Women in Cable, Nat. Assn. Female Execs. Republican. Roman Catholic. Club: Toastmasters (Troy, N.Y.). Home: 32 B Coachman Sq Clifton Park NY 12065 Office: Urbach Kahn & Werlin 66 State St Albany NY 12207

GARROTT, IDAMAE T., state legislator; b. Washington, Dec. 24, 1916; A.B., Western Md. Coll., 1936, L.L.D. (hon.); married; 2 children. Mem. Md. Ho. of Dels., 1979-87, mem. ways and means com., joint com. on energy. Mem. Md. State Senate, 1987—, econ. and environ. affairs com., joing com. on fed. relations. Mem. Montgomery County Council, 1966-74, chmn. planning com., 1970-74, pres., 1971; bd. dirs. Washington Met. Area Transit Authority, 1972-74; bd. dirs. Washington Suburban Transit Commn., 1971-74, chmn., 1972; bd. dirs. Met. Washington Council Govts., pres., 1974, chmn. land use com., 1969-74; bd. dirs. Solid Waste Mgmt. Agy. Met. Washington, 1969-74; pres. Montgomery County LWV, 1963-66,

Montgomery County Humane Soc., 1976-77; bd. dirs. Wheaton Rescue Squad, 1982-84. Recipient John Dewey award, 1982; Humanitarian award Montgomery County Humane Soc., 1983; Cert. Appreciation, Montgomery County Edn. Assn., 1984, Horn Book award, 1985, Thomas B. Cook award, 1987, Md. Assn. of Deaf award, 1987. Author: Paying Our Way, Maryland State Taxes and You, 1958. Office: 221 Lowe Bldg Annapolis MD 21401

GARRY, JACQUELYNN LEE, holding corporation executive; b. Salem, N.J., Mar. 11, 1957; d. Henry Edward Klingler and Josephine Sarah (Poulson) Parker. Student, Delcastle Vocat. Tech. Inst., 1975; AA, AS, Fort Steilacoom Community Coll., AS in Bus., AS in Broadcasting; student, L.H. Bates Vocat. Tech. Inst., 1979-80. Mgr. inventory control, pub. relations McDonalds of Wilmington, Del., 1974-77; sales account rep. Rainbow of Tacoma/Auburn, Wash., 1977-80; mgmt. trainee Agy. Rent-A-Car, Wash., 1980; sales mgr. Puget (Wash.) Mobilex Inc., 1980-82; planning specialist Bus. Ins. Assocs., 1982, Target Ins. Bus. Service, 1982-84; chief exec. officer Just Like Gold, Inc., San Diego, 1983—. Dir. TV including The Music Hour, Meet the Candidates; co-dir. film The Great Am. Masacare; producer TV The Fashinable Female, (co-producer) Condomania; author newspaper columns The Fashionable Female, 1984-85. Served with USAF, 1974-77. Mem. Ch. Religious Sci.

GARSIDE, MARLENE ELIZABETH, advertising executive; b. Newark, Dec. 1, 1933; d. Abraham and Shirley (Janow) Carnow; B.S. in Commerce and Fin., Bucknell U., 1955; m. Stanley Kramer, Aug. 7, 1955 (dec. 1967); children—Deborah Frances, Elizabeth Anne; m. Martin Lutman, Aug. 27, 1969 (dec. 1981); m. Michael J. Weinstein, Apr. 9, 1983 (dec. 1984); m. Normand Garside, Apr. 5, 1986. Asst. research dir. Modern Materials Handling Co., Boston, 1955-57; econ. analyst, project adminstr. United Research Co., Cambridge, Mass., 1957-58; free lance tech. writer, econ. analyst, 1958-66; asst. mgr. survey planning and market research IBM, White Plains, N.Y., 1967-69; mgr. research services McKinsey & Co., Cleve., 1969-72; former v.p., dir. Am. Custom Homes, former dir. Liberty Builders, Inc., Cleve.; owner, v.p., dir. Am. Custom Builders Inc., Cape Coral, Fla., 1978—; ptnr., dir. Star Realty Inc., Cape Coral, 1980—; account exec. Media Graphics, Inc., Naples, Fla., 1984; advt. mgr. Fox Electronics, Ft. Myers, Fla., 1984-86; v.p. Langdon Advt., Ft. Myers, 1987-88; asst. mgr. facility State of Fla. Dept. Health and Rehabilitative Services, Ft. Meyers, 1988—. Mem. Econ. and Indsl. Devel. Task Force, City of Cape Coral, 1979. Mem. Nat. Assn. Homebuilders, Bldg. Industry Assn., Constrn. Industry Assn., Nat. Bd. Realtors. Home: 1482 Sautern Dr Fort Myers FL 33919 Office: State of Fla Dept Health Rehab Services 6719 Winkler Ave Fort Myers FL 33919

GARWOOD, BARBARA ANN, psychologist, educator; b. Cleve., Jan. 7, 1936; d. Bradford Earl and Hazel Elizabeth (Obrock) Garwood; B.S. John Carroll U., 1963; M.A., Case-Western Res. U., 1968; Ph.D., Kent State U., 1973. Tchr., sr. high sch. English, Euclid (Ohio) Pub. Schs., 1966-68; cons. sch. psychologist Mayfield (Ohio) City Schs., 1973-76; sch. psychologist Cleve. City Schs., 1968-72; assoc. staff Richmond Heights Gen. Hosp.; pvt. practice psychology, Mentor, Ohio; prof. psychology Lakeland Community Coll., Mentor; mem. Ohio Bd. Psychology, 1976-81, pres., 1980-81. Mem. Lakeland Faculty Assn. (pres. 1980-81), Cleve. Psychol. Assn. (v.p. 1974-75), Ohio Sch. Psychologists Assn. (pres. 1976-77). Club: Pavilion Skating. Contbr. articles to profl. jours. Home: 6361 Candlewood Ct Mentor OH 44060 Office: 9853 Johnnycake Ridge Rd Mentor OH 44060

GARY, SHARON DELIGHT, psychological examiner; b. Decatur, Tex., June 14, 1951; d. Dorthea (Somerville) Gary; B.S. with honors in Psychology, State Coll. Ark. (name changed to U. Central Ark.), 1973; M.S. in Clin. Psychology, Memphis State U., 1975, postgrad. in clin. psychology, 1975-76. Liaison worker Foster Home and Group Home programs N.E. Community Mental Health Center, Memphis, 1975-76; psychol. examiner, asst. dir. Hutt Psychol. Group, Memphis, 1976-79; cons. psychol. examiner Sequoyah Center, Tenn. Psychiat. Hosp. and Inst., Memphis, 1976-77; coordinator, instr. foster care program Center for Govt. Tng., U. Tenn., Memphis, 1978—; owner, psychol. examiner Psychol. Services of Memphis, 1979—; cons. St. Peter Home for Children, 1982-84, Holston's Meth. Children's Home, 1983—; active workshops, seminars on learning disabilities child devel.; mem. Women's Resource Center, 1977-82, Multidisciplinary Child Abuse Rev. Team, 1979—, active Region IX Child Abuse Rev. Team, 1979—, active NOW march for ERA; mem. Tenn. Juvenile Justice Commn., 1985—, mem. grant rev. com. Juvenile Justice Commn., 1986—, acting chmn. grant rev. com., 1987— ; participant in lobbying for Ark. Assn. Children with Learning Disabilities; head panel on psychol. effects of being in foster care Juvenile Ct. Judges Ann. Conf., Tenn., 1980; resource person for adoptive families. Recipient Ark. Traveler cert., 1978, cert. of appreciation Tenn. Foster Care Assn., 1979, cert. of appreciation Boys Town, 1984. Mem. Am. Psychol. Assn., Tenn. Area Psychol. Assn. (bd. dirs. 1987-88), Memphis Psychol. Assn., Nat. Rehab. Assn., Assn. for Children with Learning Disabilities, Council on Adoptable Children, Psi Chi. Bd. dirs., sec. Unity Christ Ch., 1987—. Clubs: Exec. Women Memphis (charter mem., sec. 1978-81), Zonta (pres. 1985-86) (Memphis). Author: Parenting Happy Children: Coping with Destructive Behavior, 1985. Contbr. chpt. to Juvenile Court Review Board Manual. Home: 3163 Highmeadow Dr Memphis TN 38128 Office: Psychol Services Memphis 1835 Union Ave E Suite 215 Memphis TN 38104

GARZA, JANET KAY, librarian; b. Columbus, Ohio, Jan. 7, 1940; d. Floyd Edwin and Ruth Ozette (Cotterman) Weir; m. Stanley Robert Zurek, June 8, 1984 (div. Nov. 1985); children: Terri Lynn, Cindy Kae; m. Jorge Ramiro Garza, Dec. 27, 1987. BA in History, Ohio State U., 1977; MLS, U. Denver, 1981. Dir. Woodstock Country Sch., South Woodstock, Vt., 1977-78, Reading (Vt.) Pub. Library, 1978-79; assoc. dir. Windsor (Vt.) Pub. Library, 1979; asst. law librarian U. Wyo., Laramie, 1981-84; assoc. dir. pub. services Cen. Ariz. Coll., Coolidge, 1984—, treas. faculty senate, 1987—. Mem. com. End Illiteracy in Western Pinal County, Casa Grande, Ariz., 1987. Grantee Ariz. Humanities Council, 1986-87. Mem. AAUW (chair women's issues Casa Grande and Ariz. 1987—, first v.p. programs 1987—), Am. Assn. Women in Community and Jr. Colls., Am. Assn. Law Librarians, Beta Phi Mu. Democrat. Presbyterian. Office: Cen Ariz Coll Woodruff at Overfield Coolidge AZ 85228

GARZARELLI, ELAINE MARIE, economist; b. Phila., Oct. 13, 1951; d. Ralph J. and Ida M. (Pierantozzi) G.; B.S., Drexel U., 1973, M.B.A., 1977; doctoral candidate NYU, 1980. with A.G. Becker, N.Y.C., from 1973, v.p., economist, 1975-84, mng. dir., 1984; exec. v.p. Shearson Lehman Bros., 1984—; lectr. in field. Named Businesswoman of Yr. Fortune Mag., 1987. Mem. Nat. Assn. Bus. Economists, Women's Fin. Assn., Am. Statis. Assn., Women's Bond Assn. Developer Sector Analysis, econometric model for predicting industry profits and stock price movements. Home: 280 Butler Rd Springfield PA 19064 Office: Shearson Lehman Hutton Inc World Fin Ctr Tower C New York NY 10285

GASKILL, LISA SHARIDAN, mechanical engineer; b. Cheyenne, Wyo., Apr. 27, 1960; d. John Franklin and Marcia Mae (Schoening) G. BSME, Colo. State U., 1983; MBA in Mktg., U. Denver, 1988. Cert. engr.-in-tng. Design mech. engr. Johnson & Johnson Ultrasound, Englewood, Colo., 1983-84; design mech. engr. Honeywell Inc., Littleton, Colo., 1984-85, quality engr., 1985—. Inventor in field. Republican. Presbyterian. Office: Honeywell Inc 4800 E Dry Creek Rd MS 101 Littleton CO 80112

GASKO, HELEN CAPELINI, quality consultant; b. Mt. Vernon, N.Y., Feb. 28, 1964; d. John and Helen Mary (Budzinski) Capelini; m. Robert M. Gasko, Feb. 1, 1964. AAS, Westchester Community Coll., 1962; BS, Mercy Coll., 1973; MBA, Fordham U., 1982. Lab. technician Union Carbide Corp., Tarrytown, N.Y., 1962-77; tech. specialist N.Y.C., 1977-79, market analyst, 1979-81, market mgr., 1981-84; mgr. quality tng. Danbury, Conn., 1984—. Bd. dirs. Condominium Bd., Bethel, Conn., 1981—. Mem. Am. Soc. Quality Control, Am. Soc. Tng. and Devel., Soc. of Plastics Engr. Republican. Home: 39 Hudson Glen Bethel CT 06801 Office: Union Carbide Corp 39 Old Ridgebury Rd Danbury CT 06817

GASPARD, BRENDA R. BARFIELD, university official; b. Cabool, Mo., Aug. 11, 1956; d. Arnold Barto and Ruby Rose (Britzman) Barfield; m. L. Missildine, July 13, 1976 (div. Apr. 1979); 1 child, Hunter; m. Herff L. Moore, Jr., July 1, 1983 (div. 1987); children: Terri, Christopher, Kimberley; m. Jacques Gaspard, 1988; children: Scott, Chantal. BBA, East Tex. State U., 1983; postgrad. St. John Fisher Coll., 1984. Office mgr. Barfield Distbrs., New Boston, Tex., 1975-83; br. mgr. Manpower Temp. Services, Rochester, N.Y., 1984-85; acct. Div. Continuing Edn., U. Central Ark., Conway, 1985-87, Indsl. Developers Ark., 1985-87; acct. Acadian, Inc., Texarkana, Ark., 1988—; ptnr. Bowie County Distbg. Co., 1988; dir. Barfield Distbg. Co. Editor-in-chief profl. newsletter Continuing Edn. Horizons, 1986. Mem. U. Central Ark. Staff Assn., Bus. and Profl. Women. Avocations: reading, cross-stitching, ceramics. Office: Univ Central Ark Div Continuing Edn Conway AR 72032

GASPER, JO ANN, government official; b. Providence, Sept. 25, 1946; d. Joseph Siegleman and Jeanne Van Matre Shoaf; m. Louis Clement Gasper, Sept. 21, 1974; children: Stephen Gregory, Jeanne Marie, Monica Elizabeth, Michelle Bernadette (dec.), Phyllis Anastasia, Clare Genevieve. B.A., U. Dallas, 1967, M.B.A., 1969. Adminstrv. asst. U. Dallas, 1964-68; asst. dir. adminstrn. Britian Convalescent Ctr., Irving, Tex., 1964-68; pres. Medicare Ctrs., Inc., Dallas, 1968-69; bus. mgr., treas. U. Plano, Tex., 1969-72; ins. agt. John Hancock Ins. Co., Dallas, 1972-73; systems analyst Tex. Instrument, Richardson, 1973-75; pvt. practice acctg., bus. cons. McLean, Va., 1976-81; editor, pub. Congl. News for Women and the Family, McLean, Va., 1978-81, Register Report, McLean, Va., 1980-81; dep. asst. sec. for social services policy HHS, Washington, 1981-85; exec. dir. White House Conf. on Families, HHS, Washington, 1982-85; dep. asst. sec. for population affairs HHS, Washington, 1985-87; policy advisor to under sec. U.S. Dept. Edn., Washington, 1987-88. Co-chmn. St. John's Refugee Resettlement Commn., Va., 1977; bd. dirs., treas. Council Inter-Am. Security, Washington, 1978-80; active Fairfax County Citizens Coalition for Quality Child Care, Va., 1979-80; del. White House Conf. on Families, Va., 1979-80; active Franklin Area Citizens Neighborhood Watch, McLean, Va.; mem. U.S. adv. Inter-Am. Commn. on Women, OAS, 1982-85; U.S. del. XVI Pan Am. Child Congress, Washington, 1984; mem. nat. family policy adv. bd. Reagan/Bush Campaign, 1980. Recipient Eagle Forum award, 1979, Wanderer Found. award, 1980, Bronze medal HHS, 1982; named Outstanding Conservative Woman, Conservative Digest, 1980, 81. Mem. Exec. Women in Gov. (treas. 1985, sec. 1986). Roman Catholic. Home: 6235 Park Rd McLean VA 22101 Office: US Dept Edn 300 Maryland Ave SW Washington DC 20202

GASPERONI, ELLEN JEAN LIAS (MRS. EMIL GASPERONI), interior designer; b. Rural Valley, Pa.; d. Dale S. and Ruth (Harris) Lias; student Youngstown U., 1952-54, John Carroll U., 1953-54, Westminster Coll., 1951-52; grad. Am. Inst. Banking; m. Emil Gasperoni, May 28, 1955; children—Sam, Emil, Jean Ellen. Mem. Coeurde Coeur Heart Assn., Orlando Opera Guild, Orlando Symphony Guild. Mem. Jr. Bus. Women's Club (dir. 1962-64). Presbyterian. Clubs: Sweetwater Country (owner, pres.) (Longwood, Fla.); Lake Toxaway Golf and Country (N.C.). Home: 1126 Brownshine Ct Longwood FL 32779

GASS, GERTRUDE ZEMON, psychologist, researcher; b. Detroit; d. David Solomon and Mary (Goldman) Zemon; m. H. Harvey Gass, June 19, 1938; children: Susan, Roger. BA, U. Mich., 1937, MSW, 1943, PhD, 1957. Lic. clin. psychologist, Mich. Mem. faculty Merrill-Palmer Inst., Detroit, 1958-69, lectr., 1967; mem. faculty Advanced Behavioral Sci. Ctr., Grosse Pointe, Mich., 1969-72; pvt. practice clin. psychology Birmingham, Mich., 1972—; adj. prof. psychology U. Detroit, 1969-75; cons. Continuum Ctr. Oakland U., Rochester, Mich., 1961-77, Traveler's Aid, Detroit, 1959-75; pres. Shapero Sch. Nursing, Detroit, 1967-72, cons. 1958-78; psychol. cons. Physician's Ins. Co. of Mich., 1988—. Mem. Adv. Com Sch. Needs, 1954-56; trustee Sinai Hosp. Detroit, 1972—; bd. dirs. Tribute Fund United Community Services, 1955-67. Fellow Am. Assn. Marriage-Family; mem. Am. Orthopsychiatric Assn. (v.p. 1975-76), Psychologists Task Force (v.p. 1977-84), Mich. Inter-Profl. Assn. (pres. 1976-78), Mich. Assn. Marriage Counselors (1979-80), Mental Health Adv. Service, Blue Cross and Blue Shield of Mich., Phi Kappa Phi, Pi Lambda Theta. Office: 30200 Telegraph Rd Birmingham MI 48010

GASTEYER, CARLIN EVANS (MRS. HARRY A. GASTEYER), cultural center administrator; b. Jackson, Mich., Mar. 30, 1917; d. Frank Howard and Marian (Spencer) Evans; student Barnard Coll., 1934-35; B.A., CUNY, 1983; m. Harry A. Gasteyer, Jan. 8, 1944; 1 dau., Nancy Catherine. Clk., First Nat. City Bank, 1939-42; statistician Bell Telephone Labs., 1942-45; dir. asst. S.I. Mus., 1956-61; bus. mgr. Mus. of the City of N.Y., 1961-63; mus. adminstr., 1963-66; asst. dir. Monmouth (N.J.) Mus., 1966-67, Mus. of City of N.Y., 1967-70; vice dir. adminstrn. Bklyn. Mus., 1970-74; dir. planning Snug Harbor Cultural Center, S.I., N.Y., 1975-79; cable TV Cons., 1980—; adj. lectr. mus. studies Coll. S.I. CUNY, 1985—. Active Girl Scouts. Co-founder, pres. Jr. Mus. Guild, S.I. Mus., 1956-58. Mem. N.Y.C. Local Sch. Bd. 54, 1960-61. Mem. Am. Assn. Mus., Mus. Council of N.Y.C. Club: Cosmopolitan. Home: 50 Fort Pl Staten Island NY 10301

GASTON, CAROLE ROACH, advertising executive; b. Ft. Worth, Sept. 17, 1947; d. Dewey Revero and Margarette Bille (Parker) Roach; divorced; children: Kimberly Kathryn, Joseph Mark. BA in English, Miss. U. for Women, 1972. Real estate assoc. West Realty, Columbus, Miss., 1974-76; mktg. asst. Ericson and Assocs., Nashville, 1982-83; acct. exec. Brumfield-Gallagher, Nashville, 1983—. Chmn. Mid. Tenn. Women for Reagan, Nashville, 1984—; mem. fin. com. Presdl. Inaugural, Washington, 1985; mem. communications div. Rep. Nat. Conv., Dallas, 1984; mem. budget com. Harriman, Tenn., 1981, personnel com., 1981; bd. dirs. Women's Missionary Union, Harriman, 1980, Bapt. Young Women, Harriman, 1980. Office: Brumfield-Gallagher 3401 West End Ave Nashville TN 37203

GASTON, CHERYL P., public relations consultant; b. Ottumwa, Iowa, Aug. 31, 1944; d. Nat and Lois A. (Jorgenson) Press; m. Neil A. Gaston, June 28, 1964; children: Jeffrey A., Drew D. BS in English Edn., Trenton (N.J.) State Coll., 1967, MEd in English Edn., 1975. Accredited in pub. relations, Pub. Relations Soc. Am. Tchr. Ewing High Sch., Trenton, 1967-69; pub. info. dir. Trenton State Coll., 1975-78, mem. adj. faculty, 1975-76; pub. info. dir. N.J. Pub. Broadcasting Authority, Trenton, 1978-80; owner, pres. Cheryl Gaston Assocs., Rosemont, N.J., 1980-83, Gaston & Madden Assocs., Inc., Flemington, N.J., 1983—. Author (newsletter) PRTIPS, 1986—. Mem. Del. Twp. Bd. Edn., Sergeantsville, N.J., 1982-85; bd. dirs. Ctr. for Ednl. Advancement, Flemington, 1986—. Mem. Hunterdon County C. of C. (bd. dirs. 1986—). Office: Gaston & Madden Assocs Inc 62 Pennsylvania Ave Flemington NJ 08822

GASTON, REBECCA LEE, medical sales specialist; b. Johnstown, Pa., June 5, 1952; d. Willard Calvin and Wanda Caroline (Varner) G.; m. James Allen Conner, July 23, 1976 (div. 1977). Student, Miami Valley Hosp. Sch. Radiol. Tech., Dayton, Ohio, 1970-72; A in Applied Sci. cum laude, Sinclair Coll., 1979. Instr. Miami Valley Hosp. Sch. Radiology, Dayton, 1972-79; supr. cardiovascular lab. Grandview Hosp., Dayton, 1979-84; physicians asst. Dr. James Laws, Dayton, 1982-84; med. sales specialist Honeywell Med. Corp., Balt., 1984-86, Med. Graphics Corp., Balt., 1986—; cons. Cardiopulmonary Rehab., Balt., 1984. Mem. Am. Soc. Radiol. Tech., Nat. Soc. Cardiopulmonary Tech., Dayton Soc. Cardiopulmonary Tech. (chairperson program com. 1978), Greater Dayton Med. Imaging Soc. (pres. 1983), Washington Soc. Cardiopulmonary Technologists, Nat. Aquarium Assn., NOW.

GATES, BARBARA LYNN, school administrator, educator; b. Billings, Mont., May 13, 1954; d. Joseph Isacc and Ima Evelyn (Daugherty) G. B.S. in Elementary Edn., Eastern Mont. Coll., 1976. Cert. tchr., Mont. Tchr., Union Sch., Lindsay, Mont., 1976-79, Greycliff Sch., Mont., 1979-80; supr. Alliance Christian Sch., Lewistown, Mont., 1981-83, prin., supr., 1983-86; prin., supr. Paradise Christian Acad., Lewistown, Mont., 1986—.

GATES, DEANNA L., insurance/pension fund executive; b. Omaha, Oct. 28, 1948; d. Robert C. and Kathryn L. (Adams) Gates; m. Robert E. Matthews, Jan. 3, 1970 (div.); m. 2d, Alan J. Sorem, Oct. 26, 1980. B.A., Wayne State Coll., 1971; M.B.A., Fordham U., 1981. Sec. Ark. Presbytery, Little Rock, 1975-76, United Presbyn. Ch., N.Y.C., 1976-77; adminstrv. asst. United Presbyn. Ch. hdqrs., N.Y.C., 1977-79; budget adminstr. United Brands Co., N.Y.C., 1979-82, treasury analyst, 1982-84; sr. investment analyst Amalgamated Life Ins. Cos., N.Y.C., 1984-85. Chairperson Planning Com., N.Y.C. Presbytery, 1984; elder Broadway Presbyn. Ch., 1985-88. Mem. N.Y. Cash Mgrs. Assn. (group leader 1983). Democrat. Home: 70 LaSalle St Apt 13G New York NY 10027

GATES, DOROTHY LOUISE, educator; b. National City, Calif., Feb. 21, 1926; d. Harold Roger and Bertha Marjorie (Lippold) Gates; B.A., U. Calif., Santa Barbara, 1949; M.A., U. Hawaii, 1963, Ph.D., 1975; postdoctoral student U. Uppsala (Sweden), 1976, Bedford Coll., London, 1978, Cuban Ministry of Justice, 1979, Cambridge U., Eng., 1986. Dept. probation officer, Riverside County, Calif., 1950-54, 55-61; dir. La Morada, probation facility, Santa Barbara County, 1963-65; prof. sociology San Bernardino Valley Coll. (Calif.), 1965-87, prof. emeritus, 1987—; part-time tchr. criminology U. Redlands (Calif.), 1975—; chmn. Riverside County Juvenile Justice and Delinquency Prevention Commn., 1971—. Pres. Women's Equity Action League, Hawaii, 1972; mem. adv. group Riverside County Justice System, 1982. bd. dirs. San Bernardino County Mental Health Assn., Cooper Burkhart House, Riverside; mem. adv. council Ret. Sr. Vol. Program, San Bernardino; academic pres. San Bernardino Valley Coll., 1986. Recipient Cert. of Recognition, Riverside YWCA; named Citizen of Achievement, San Bernardino LWV, 1985; NEH fellow U. Va., 1977; named Outstanding Prof. San Bernardino Valley Coll., 1987. Mem. Western Gerontology Assn., Am. Soc. Criminology, Calif. Probation, Parole and Correctional Assn. (award 1969), LWV. Lodge: Kiwanis. Address: 4665 Braemar Pl #212 Riverside CA 92501

GATES, JACQUIE KATHERINE, financial consultant; b. Birmingham, Ala., Apr. 11, 1938; d. John Warren and Inez (Pillar) Kirk; m. Charles James Gates, June 6, 1955 (div. Aug. 1970); 1 child, Katherine Ann. Mgr. Chgo. Health Clubs, LaGrange, Ill., 1966-69; cons. Johnson Printers, Downers Grove, Ill., 1970-79; pres. Delegates Inc., Bensenville, Ill., 1980—; pres. Art/Temps, 1985—; owner, cons. fin. services Key Concepts, Bensenville, 1987—. Pub., editor: The GraphiConnection, 1983; host: (weekly live cable show) In Focus, 1986-87. Town chair Am. Cancer Assn., Palatine, Ill., 1979-80; commr. Bensenville Cable Services; apptd. to state com. The Ill. Connection, 1987-88. Recipient of numerous awards Ill. Fine Arts, 1975-78. Mem. Nat. Fedn. Bus. and Profl. Women's Orgn. (pres. 1983-84, Ill. State Networking chmn. 1988-89), Breakfast Forum (founder 1982). Office: Delegates Inc Suite 200 W Devon Suite 10 Bensenville IL 60106

GATES, MADI, interior designer; b. Salix, Iowa, Aug. 13, 1938; d. Ralph Fredrick Madison and Joyce Elaine (Rugger) King; m. James Roland Gates, Dec. 30, 1962; children: Kirsten Ann. BS in Nursing Edn., U. Minn., 1963; student interior design program, Calif. Poly. State U., 1983. Staff nurse Winnebago (Nebr.) Indian Reservation, 1959-60; intensive care nurse U. Minn. Hosp., Mpls., 1960-63; head nurse Sierra Vista Hosp., San Luis Obispo, Calif., 1963-64, "float" nurse, 1966-80; owner, designer Madi Gates Interiors, San Luis Obispo, Calif., 1983—. Mem./seamstress Altar Guild St. Stephen's Episc. Ch., San Luis Obispo, 1968-80; mem. Children's Home Soc., San Luis Obispo, 1971—; chmn. Achievement House Workshop for the Disabled, San Luis Obispo, 1980-81, bd. dirs.; pres. Rep. Women, San Luis Obispo, 1969-70. Recipient scholarship Sioux City (Iowa) Med. Aux., 1956-59; named Nurse of Yr., U. Minn., 1962. Mem. Cen. Coast Interior Designers, Am. Soc. Interior Designers (assoc., cert. masters level), San Luis Obispo C. of C. Clubs: Ninety-nines (San Luis Obispo) (treas. 1979-80), Pharmacy Aux. (pres. 1963-64). Home and Office: 125 Serrano Heights San Luis Obispo CA 93401

GATES, MARTINA MARIE, food products company executive; b. Mpls., Mar. 19, 1957; d. John Thomas and Colette Clara (Luetmer) G. BSBA in Mktg. Mgmt. cum laude, Coll. St. Thomas, 1984, MBA in Mktg., 1987. Tchrs. asst. Mpls. Area Vocat. Tech. Inst., Mpls., 1978-79; sec., regional sales mgr. Internat. Multifoods, Mpls., 1979, sec. bakery mix, mktg. mgr., 1979-80, sec., v.p. sales and new bus. devel., 1980, customer service rep. regional accounts, 1980-81, customer service rep. nat. accounts, 1981-82, credit coordinator indsl. foods div., 1982-85, asst. credit mgr. consumer foods div., 1985, advt./sales promotion mgr. indsl. foods div., 1985-86, asst. credit mgr. fast food and restaurant div., 1986-87, dir. devel. USA and Can. franchise area, 1987—. Vol. seamstress Guthrie Theater Costume Shop, Mpls., 1975—; alumni mem. New Coll. Student Adv. Council St. Thomas, St. Paul, 1984—; vol. Mpls. Aquatennial, 1987. Mem. Omicron Delta Epsilon.

GATES-VIVOLI, LISA, small business owner; b. Washington, July 7, 1955; d. Chester Robert and Peggy Jean (Dalton) Gates; m. Sergio Vivoli, Nov. 3, 1978 (div. Nov. 1, 1984); m. Mitchell Cohen, Sept. 21, 1987. AA, Fleming Coll., Florence, Italy, 1974. Dir. The Am. Sch. in Switzerland, Lugana, 1974-80; counter person Gelateria Vivoli E Caffé, Florence, 1978-80; costumer, choreographer, scene designer English Theatre of Florence, 1978; tchr. Dance Sch. Theatre, Florence, 1978-81; sec., treas. Vivoli Da Firenze, Inc., Los Angeles, 1981-82; event coordinator Calif. Catering Co., Beverly Hills, Calif., 1983; chef, sales rep. St. Germain To Go, West Hollywood, Calif., 1984; chef, cons. Posh Affair Catering Co., Los Angeles, 1984-87; owner, chef, party planner Lisa Gates-Vivoli Catering, Los Angeles, 1985—. Mem. Mus. Contemporary Art, Los Angeles, Los Angeles County Mus. Art, Los Angeles Theatre Ctr., NOW, Los Angeles, Music Ctr. Unified Fund. Recipient Outstanding Achievement in Art award Bank of Am., Miraleste, Calif., 1972. Mem. Am. Inst. Wine and Food, Da Camera Soc. (patron), Roundtable for Women in Foodservice, Nat. Assn. Female Execs. Democrat. Home and Office: 825 Bedford St #202 Los Angeles CA 90035

GATEWOOD, ALTHEA NEYSA, civic association administrator, consultant; b. Washington, Aug. 12, 1951; d. Alvie Jessie and Geneva Lois (Robinson) Lacewell; divorced; children: Arnisha Nichole, Ariel Nathan. Student, Fed. City Coll., 1969-71, Upward Mobility Coll., 1971-72, U. D.C., 1980, Gallaudet Coll., Washington, 1980. Adminstrv. asst. D.C. Dept. Health and Human Services, Washington, 1978-81; adminstr., conf. coordinator Nat. Assn. Neighborhoods, Washington, 1984—; tech. dir., chief audio technician TV Broadcast/FEC, Washington, 1982—; pres. A&G Assocs., 1983—. Author: The World and Poetry, 1974, God's Words, 1976. Mem. Nat. Assn. for Female Execs. Office: Nat Assn Neighborhoods 1651 Fuller St NW Washington DC 20009

GATEWOOD, TELA LYNNE, lawyer; b. Cedar Rapids, Iowa, Mar. 23; d. Chester Russell and Cecilia Mae (McFarland) Weber; m. R.E. Gatewood, Mar. 18, 1982. B.A. with distinction, Cornell Coll., Mt. Vernon, Iowa, 1970; J.D. with distinction, U. Iowa, 1972. Bar: Iowa 1973, Calif. 1974, U.S. Supreme Ct. 1984. Instr., LaVerne Coll., Pt. Mugu, Calif., 1973; asst. city atty. City of Des Moines, 1973-78; sr. trial atty. and supervisory atty. EEOC, Dallas, also Phila., 1978—, acting regional atty., Dallas Dist., 1987—. Bd. dirs. Day Care Inc., Des Moines, 1975-78, sec., 1977, pres., 1978. Recipient Performance award EEOC, 1982, 84. Mem. ABA, Fed. Bar Assn., U.S. Supreme Ct. Bar Assn., Nat. Assn. Female Execs., AAUW. Office: EEOC 8303 Elmbrook Dr Dallas TX 75247

GATHERS, PATRICIA KATHLEEN, accountant; b. Johnstown, Pa., July 23, 1964; d. James Richard Jr. and Patricia Elizabeth (O'Connor) Chynoweth; m. Gerald Floyd Gathers, Dec. 24, 1985. Degree, LaSalle U., 1986. CPA. Office clk. Somerset (Pa.) County Treas.'s Office, 1983; accts. payable clk. Blue Ribbon Services, Phila., 1984; intern Arthur Andersen & Co., Phila., 1985; staff acct. Brazina & Co., Bala Cynwyd, Pa., 1985-86, Arthur Andersen & Co., Phila., 1986—. Vol. Muscular Distrophy Assn., Davidsville, Pa., 1973, Vol. Income Tax Assistance, Phila., 1983. Mem. Am. Inst. CPA's, Nat. Assn. Female Execs., Nat. League Postmasters (sec.-treas. Pa. chpt. 1982-83), Alpha Epsilon. Democrat. Roman Catholic. Home: 400 Presidential Blvd Philadelphia PA 19131 Office: Arthur Andersen & Co 5 Penn Ctr Philadelphia PA 19103

GATRELL, KIM ANN, human resource systems consultant; b. Dnaville, Ill., July 22, 1958; d. Bille Francis Gatrell and Shirley Ann (Long) Simmons. Student acctg., fin. and math., Ohio State U., 1976-79, 79-80; AAS in electronics, Columbus Tech. Inst., 1983. Teller, teller supr., payroll supr. Bank One, Columbus, Ohio, 1976-80, human resources sytems supr., specialist, 1982-83; credit card processing adminstr., sales coordicator Fin. Inst. Services, Inc., Nashville, 1983-85; human resource systems cons. Maven Corp., Columbus, 1985—. Serves as comdr. Fla. N.G. Mem. Am. Payroll Assn., Nat. Assn. Exec. Females, Aircraft Owners and Pilots Assn. Republican. Episcopalian. Home: 1288 NE 150th St North Miami FL 33161 Office: Maven Corp 3700 Corporate Dr Suite 112 Columbus OH 43229

GATSOS, ELAINE MARY, lawyer; b. Allentown, Pa., July 19, 1955; d. Stephen Louis and Zoe Ann (Bozion) G. B.A., Purdue U., 1977; J.D., Nova U., 1980. Assoc., Titone & Roarke, P.A., Lauderhill, Fla., 1980-82, Stuart & Walker P.A., Fort Lauderdale, Fla., 1982-87; sole practice, 1987—; asst. city atty. City of Coconut Creek, Fla., 1982-87, City of Boca Raton, Fla., 1988—. Pres., Young Democrats of Broward County (Fla.), 1982-85; parliamentarian Fla. Young Democrats, 1984; bd. mem. Council of Pres. of Democratic Clubs, Broward County, Fla., 1984. Named Grad. of Yr., Phi Delta Phi, 1980. Mem. ABA, Nat. Assn. Women Lawyers, Broward County Bar Assn., Broward County Women Lawyers Assn. Democrat. Greek Orthodox. Office: 1499 W Palmetto RD Suite 412 Boca Raton FL 33486

GATTI, ROSA MARIE, television network executive; b. Phila., June 27, 1950; d. William Jules and Ruth Marie (Hahn) G. BA in French, Villanova U., 1972. Sports info. dir. Villanova (Pa.) U., 1974-76, Brown U., Providence, 1976-80; dir. communications ESPN, Bristol, Conn., 1980-81, v.p. communications, 1981—. Mem. Women in Cable, Internat. Radio and TV Soc., Football Writers, Cable TV Advt. and Mktg., Cable TV Pub. Affairs Assn. Office: ESPN ESPN Plaza Bristol CT 06010

GATTO, BARBARA ANNE, educator; b. Pitts., Sept. 26, 1949; d. Gloria Jane (Intrieri) Lechner; m. Frank J. Gatto, June 9, 1973. BS in Edn., Edinboro U., 1971; postgrad., Pa. State U., 1976, Westminster Coll., 1978. Sub. tchr. various towns, Pa., 1971-72; tchr. Kiski Area Sch. Dist., Vandergrift, Pa., 1972—. Vice chair Westmoreland County Drug and Alcohol Exec. Comm., 1980-86, chair, 1983-85; mem. Alleghany Valley Mental Health/Mental Retardation Adv. Bd., 1983-84, vice chair, 1985-86, chair, 1986-88; chairperson Instrnl. and Profl. Devel. Council Southwestern Region PSEA. Mem. NEA, Pa. Edn. Assn. (women's caucus, woemn's leadership trainer, 1983—, speaker alcohol and drug abuse for Dept. Edn. 1984—, Southwestern region exec. bd. 1985—, pres.-elect 1985-87, state del. to NEA 1987, 88), Kiski Area Edn. Assn. (spl. services chair 1975-85, sec. 1978-81, chair instrnl. profl. devel. 1985—), Westmoreland Edn. Council (sec. 1983-85, pres. elect 1985-87, pres. 1987—), Math. Council of Western Pa. (treas. 1985-87), Pa. Suprs. of Math., Pa. Council Math. Tchrs., Nat. Assn. Female Execs. Republican. Roman Catholic. Club: Wallbangers Racquet. Lodge: Elks. Home: 433 Franklin Ave Vandergrift PA 15690

GATYAS, NANCY CAROL, education educator; b. Green Bay, Wis., Aug. 27, 1933; d. Bernard Charles and Leonora Petra (Jorgensen) Sleger; m. Frank Gatyas, Nov. 4, 1950; children: Frank, Kenton. Grad., Sheboygan County Tchrs. Coll., 1971; BA, Lakeland Coll., 1979; MA in Reading, Cardinal Stritch Coll., 1983. Cert. tchr., cert. reading specialist, Wis. Tchr. elem. schs. Plymouth, 1970-84; instr. speed reading U. Wis., Sheboyhan, Wis., 1984; reading specialist Riverview Middle Sch., Plymouth, 1982-84, Middleton-Cross Plains Schs., Wis., 1984—. Chmn. Plymouth Conservation Drives, 1974-81; active Dept. Agr. Mem. Wis. State Reading Assn. Republican. Lutheran. Clubs: Monroe Woman's, (program chmn. 1987, pres. 1988), Plymouth Woman's (pres. 1970-72), Sheboygan County Woman's (pres. 1972-74). Home: 2618 22nd Ave Monroe WI 53566

GATZA, MARIE, psychotherapist; b. Cheektowaga, N.Y., May 10, 1934; d. Edward Francis and Mary Josephine (Sobus) Slominski; m. James Gatza, July 31, 1954 (div. June 1982); children: Mark, Edward, Lee Ann, Mary Beth, Paul. BA in Psychology, U. Buffalo, 1954; MS in Social Work, U. Tex., 1961; D in Social Work, U. Pa., 1975. Caseworker Erie County Welfare Dept., Buffalo, 1954-56; intake worker Travis County Welfare Dept., Houston, 1957-58; social worker Family Services, Austin, Tex., 1960-61; psychiat. social worker Austin Community Guidance Clinic, 1961-62; supr. adoption dept. Chester County Children's Services, West Chester, Pa., 1964-71; dir. tng. Catholic Social Services, Phila., 1973-81; pres. Inst. for Christian Healing, Narberth, Pa., 1981-85; pvt. practice psychotherapy Malvern, Pa., 1985—; instr. social work practice U. Pa., 1972-73; lectr. in field, 1976—. Assoc. editor Jour. of Christian Healing; contbr. articles to profl. jours. Bd. dirs. St. Francis Country House, Darby, Pa., 1982—. Mem. Acad. Cert. Social Workers, Nat. Assn. Social Workers, Nat. Conference of Catholic Charities (program com. 1977-80), Assn. Christian Therapists (bd. dirs. 1979-85), Council on Social Work Edn. (program com. 1979-80). Democrat. Roman Catholic. Home and Office: 7 Clover Lane Malvern PA 19355

GAUCK, RITA JO, elementary school educator; b. Greensburg, Ind., Nov. 4, 1952; d. Walter Henry and Betty Lou (Bickel) G. BA, U. Evansville, 1974; MS, Purdue U., 1978. Cert. elem. tchr., Ind. Tchr. first grade Valparaiso (Ind.) Community Schs., 1974—; Chmn. Cooks Corners Sch. poetry program, Valparaiso, 1986; facilitator Cooks Corners Sch. bldg. base team, 1982-85. Editor Happy Mother's Day Cookbook, 1974-87, First Writes, 1976-78, 81-84. Active Ind. United Meth. Children's Home Aux., Lebanon, 1985—; founder Roasters and Toasters Support Group, Hemlock Haven, Ind., 1986-87, also pres. Mem. NEA, Ind. State Tchrs. Assn., Valparaiso Tchrs. Assn. (bldg. rep. 1979-80), Internat. Reading Assn., U. Evansville Alumni Assn., Purdue North Cen. Alumni Assn., Psi Iota Xi. Methodist. Office: Cooks Corners Sch 358 Bullseye Lake Rd Valparaiso IN 46383

GAUDIO, MAXINE DIANE, biofeedback therapist, stress management consultant; b. Stamford, Conn., Oct. 7, 1939; d. Robert Fridolin and Doris (Altstadter) Goodman; m. Arthur Sebastian Gaudio, Oct. 7, 1962; 1 child, Dante Sebastian. Relaxation therapist The Biofeedback Clinic, New Canaan, Conn., 1970-73; chief EEG technologist St. Barnabas, Bronx, N.Y., 1973-75; biofeedback therapist Biofeedback Clinic, Stamford, Conn. and Winston-Salem, N.C., 1973—; clin. dir. Biofeedback Unltd. N.C., 1979—; clin. dir. Creative Mind Systems, Stamford, Conn., 1980—; tech. advisor Creative Mind Systems N.C., 1980-83; indsl. cons. major corps. U.S.A., 1976—; writer, creator stress video Hartley Prodns., Old Greenwich, Conn., 1984—; writer, creator, narrator Robert Gross Assocs., Stamford, Conn., 1984. Author, narrator video: Stress, 1984, Your Secret Energy Source, 1984; writer, dir. audio/visual package Captain Mind; creator, producer Stress and Relaxation, 1986-87; author, narrator book and tapes: Creative Union, 1980; author: Land Within the Shadow, 1980. Exec. dir. Friends of Children, Darien, Conn., 1985-87; bd. dirs. cons. Childhope, N.Y.C., 1987—. Mem. Am. Fedn. Press Women, Am. Soc. EEG Technologists, Am. Assn. Advancement Tension Control, Biofeedback Soc. Am., Biofeedback Soc. N.C., Internat. Platform Assn. Avocations: swimming; fencing; flying; metaphysics; astrology; piano. Club: Conn. Press. Home: 3 Hackett Circle Apt 2 Stamford CT 06905

GAUGER, MICHELE ROBERTA, photographer, studio administrator; b. Elkhorn, Wis., Feb. 28, 1949; d. Robert F. and Christiane J. (Guiffaut) Marszalek; m. Richard C. Gauger, May 3, 1969. Student U. Wis., Superior, 1967-69, U. Wis., Whitewater, 1978-80, Winona Sch. Profl. Photography-Chgo., 1984-87. Wedding photographer Fossum Studio, Elkhorn, 1973-78; owner Photography by Michele, Whitewater, 1978-81; pres., photographer, mgr., Michele Inc. of Wis., Whitewater, 1981—, Foxes Reg., 1987—; speaker Wedding Photographers Internat. Conv., Las Vegas, Nev., 1986, Tenn. Profl. Photographers Assn., Nashville, 1987, Twin Cities Profl. Photographers, Mpls., 1987; lectr. Supra Color Seminar, Mpls., 1987, San Francisco Profl. Photographers Assn., 1988, Monterey Profl. Photographers Assn. Contbr. articles to profl. jours.; works exhibited Chinese Nat. Gallery, Beijing. Mem. Nat. Arbor Found., Nebr., 1984—. Recipient 1st place Wedding Photography award Internat. Wedding Photography, 1983, 84, 87, 88 (two awards), 2nd place award, 1985, Grand award, 1988. Mem. Profl. Photographers Am. (Natl. Loan Collectional 1984), Exhibited Chinese Nat. Gallery, Beijing, China, Wis. Profl. Photographer Assn., Wedding Photographer Internat., Whitewater C. of C. Republican. Roman Catholic. Avocations: world travel, big game hunting, horseback riding, cooking. Home: Gauger Rd Rt 2 Whitewater WI 53190 Office: Michele Inc Rt Rt 2 Whitewater Lake Whitewater WI 53190

GAUGHAN, PEARL MARY, former public health nurse, consultant; b. Reading, Pa., Apr. 9, 1921; d. Raymond Bucher and Lillian May (Fields) Fichthorn; m. Michael J. Gaughan, Jr., Feb. 14, 1946 (dec. 1985); children—Michael J., Patricia Ann. R.N., Reading Hosp. Sch. Nursing, 1943; student UCLA, 1965-83, U. So. Calif., 1965-83, Calif. State U.-San Bernardino, 1965—. Pvt. duty nurse, Reading, Pa., 1943-45; charge nurse U.S. Army Hosp., Richmond, Va., 1945-47; pvt. duty nurse, Roswell, N.M., 1947-48; charge nurse U.S. Indian Hosp., Winslow, Ariz., 1948-51; pvt. duty nurse, San Bernardino, Calif., 1951-62; asst. dir. Vis. Nurse Assn., San Bernardino, Calif., 1963-70; pub. health nurse San Bernardino County Health Dept., 1970-83; now ret.; student nurse cons. Calif. State U., others, 1965—. Author: Home Nursing Care Procedure, 1974. Instr. San Bernardino chpt. ARC, 1957-59; sec. Am. Lung Assn., 1975-86, bd. dirs., 1987—; chmn. children and youth commn. Calif. dept. Am. Legion, 1983-87, vice chmn., 1988—; chmn. stroke com. Am. Heart Assn., 1977—; pres. Arrowhead Republican Women, 1958; active Boy Scouts Am., Girl Scouts U.S.A., 1955-67; comdr. Am. Legion Post 14, San Bernardino, Calif., 1974. Served as lt. Army Nurse Corps, 1945-47. Named Citizen of Yr. San Bernardino LWV, 1986. Mem. Calif. Nurses Assn., So. Calif. Pub. Health Assn., Hosp. Discharge Planners Assn., Am. Assn. Continuity of Care, Bus. and Profl. Women of San Bernardino (committeewoman), Reading Hosp. Alumni Assn., Am. Nurses Assn., Nat. Orgn. World War Nurses, Internat. Platform Assn. Republican. Roman Catholic. Lodge: Elks Wives Orgn. (sec. 1960-63). Home: 2870 Serrano Rd San Bernardino CA 92405

GAULDING, JULIA MILLER, marketing executive; b. Richmond, Va., Dec. 27, 1954; d. Ellison Parks Gaulding Jr. and Nelda Rose (Suites) Jernigan. B.A., U. South Fla., 1978; M.Internat. Bus., Fla. Internat. U., 1984; hon. degree in internat. trade Cambridge (Eng.) U., 1980, in internat. instns. U. Geneva, 1976. Mktg. adminstr. Miami Dept. Trade and Commerce (Fla.), 1980-81, Deloitte Haskins & Sells, Miami, 1981-84; pres. JMG Strategies, Miami, 1984-86; v.p. Julia M. Gaulding and Ptnrs., Inc., 1986—; dir. E.P. Supe Gaulding Import & Export, Inc., Miami. Team capt. March of Dimes Walkathon, Miami, 1982; mem. Com. of 100, Miami's for Me, 1982. Mem. Internat. Ctr. of Fla. (Pallot award 1978-84), Am. Advt. Assn., Am. Mktg. Assn., Pub. Relations Soc. of Am., South Dade C. of C. Methodist. Office: Julia M Gaulding & Ptnrs Inc 8331 NW 66th St Miami FL 33166

GAULKE, MARY FLORENCE, library administrator; b. Johnson City, Tenn., Sept. 24, 1923; d. Gustus Thomas and Mary Belle (Bennett) Erickson; m. James Wymond Crowley, Dec. 1, 1939; 1 son, Grady Gaulke (name legally changed); m. 2d, Bud Gaulke, Sept. 1, 1945 (dec. Jan. 1978); m. 3d, Richard Lewis McNaughton, Mar. 21, 1983. B.S. in Home Econs., Oreg. State U., 1963; M.S. in L.S., U. Oreg., 1968, Ph.D. in Spl. Edn., 1970. Cert. standard personnel supr., standard handicapped learner, Oreg. Head dept. home econs. Riddle Sch. Dist. (Oreg.), 1963-66; library cons. Douglas County Intermediate Edn. Dist., Roseburg, Oreg., 1966-67; head resident, head counselor Prometheus Project, So. Oreg. Coll., Ashland, summers 1966-68; supr. librarians Medford Sch. Dist. (Oreg.), 1970-73; instr. in psychology So. Oreg. Coll., Ashland, 1970-73; library supr. Roseburg Sch. Dist., 1974—; resident psychologist Black Oaks Boys Sch., Medford, 1970-75; mem. Oreg. Gov.'s Council on Libraries, 1979. Author: Vo-Ed Course for Junior High, 1965; Library Handbook, 1967; Instructions for Preparation of Cards For All Materials Cataloged for Libraries, 1971; Handbook for Training Library Aides, 1972. Coordinator Laubach Lit. Workshops for High Sch. Tutors, Medford, 1972. Mem. So. Oreg. Library Fedn. (sec. 1971-73), ALA, Oreg. Library Assn., Pacific N.W. Library Assn., Delta Kappa Gamma (pres. 1980-82), Phi Delta Kappa (historian, research rep.). Republican. Methodist. Clubs: Lodge: Order Eastern Star (worthy matron 1956-57). Home: 1625 Days Creek Rd Days Creek OR 97429 Office: Roseburg Pub Schs 1419 Valley View Dr Roseburg OR 97470

GAUNT, SANDRA LEE, dietitian; b. Chgo., Oct. 1, 1946; d. George A. and Beatrice Gaunt; divorced; children: Chandra, Karn. BS in Dietetics and Instl. Mgmt., U. Wis., 1969. Adminstrv. dietitian Luth Hosp., LaCrosse, Wis., 1970-73; cons. State of Wis., Madison, 1973-76, specialist procurement, 1976-81; dir. dietetic services SunHealth, Charlotte, N.C., 1981-85; dist. mgr. ARA, Hunt Valley, Md., 1985-87, Morrison's Custom Mgmt. Services, Mobile, Ala., 1987—. Mem. Am. Dietetic Assn., Fla. Dietetic Assn., Dietitians in Bus. and Industry (sec. 1986-87). Republican. Methodist. Office: Morrison's Custom Mgmt 4721 Morrison Dr Mobile AL 36625

GAUNTT, HOLLY CHRISTINE, insurance executive; b. Camden, N.J., June 4, 1945; d. George Roller and Rubie Peacock (Morgan) G. BA, Elmhurst Coll., 1968. Claims supr. Hartford Ins. Co., St. Charles, Ill., 1970-77; worker's compensation claims supr. Reliance Ins. Co., Rolling Meadows, Ill., 1977-80; head office workers compensation supr. Zurich-Am. Ins. Co., Schaumburg, Ill., 1980-83; sr. claims examiner Argonaut Ins., Chgo., 1983-85; owner Holly C. Gauntt, Schaumburg, 1985-87; pres. Holly C. Gauntt Ltd., Schaumburg, 1987—. Officer Del Lago II Condominium Assn., Schaumburg, 1987. Mem. Am. Soc. Hosp. Risk Mgmt., Ill. Assn. Quality Assurance Profls. Office: Holly C Gauntt Ltd 455 Verde Dr Schaumburg IL 60173

GAUSMAN, EDITH MARIE, retired foundation executive; b. N.Y.C., Jan. 17, 1919; d. George and Eliza (Heuermann) G. Fiduciary acct. Sage Gray Todd & Sims, N.Y.C., 1950-64; asst. v.p. Scudder, Stevens & Clark, N.Y.C., 1964-72; asst. treas. Commonwealth Fund, N.Y.C., 1972-75; treas. Commonwealth Fund, 1975-81. Vice pres. bd. trustees Riverside Ch., N.Y.C., 1976-78; bd. dirs. Westside Ecumenical Ministry to the Elderly, Inc., 1979-84. Mem. Bus. and Profl. Women's Club. Home: 11 Riverside Dr New York NY 10023

GAUTHIER, LINDA KATHERINE, aerospace and electronics company executive; b. N.Y.C., Oct. 4, 1947; d. Norman Leonard and Catherine (Layer) G.; student Pan Am. Art Sch., 1966-69, Dutchess Community Coll., 1980—. Clk., Samberg Bros., Maspeth, N.Y., 1964; statis. clk. N.Y. Telephone Co., Bklyn., 1964-65; sec. Govt. Employees Ins. Co., 1965-66; adminstrv. asst. Rheingold Breweries, Bklyn., 1966-69; partner ARTvertising Agy., N.Y.C., 1969-71; reprographic services mgr. Singer Co., Stamford, Conn., 1971-85, reprographic services mgr., 1985—. Mem. Union Vale Park Commn., 1977-78, Union Vale Bicentennial Com., 1975-76; chmn. publicity Union Vale Republican Club, 1977-78. Recipient citation of appreciation Am. Legion, 1967; award of merit Union Vale Bicentennial Com., 1976, cert. of merit Dutchess Community Coll.; Mgmt. award The Singer Co., 1983. Mem. Bus. Forms Mgmt. Assn. (sec. N.Y. chpt.), Mgmt. Books Inst., Nat. Assn. Female Execs., Am. Soc. Exec. Women, Exec. Program. Roman Catholic. Club: All Sport Fitness and Racquetball. Office: Singer Co 8 Stamford Forum Stamford CT 06904

GAUTT, SANDRA WHAYNE, educator; b. Chgo., Nov. 12, 1943; d. Thaddeus Alonzo and Alyce Louise Whayne; B.Ed. cum laude, U. Mo., Columbia, 1964, M.Ed., 1966, Ph.D., 1975; m. Prentice Gautt, June 5, 1971. Tchr., Woodhaven Learning Center, Columbia, 1966-68; supr. Hosp. Sch., U. Mo., Columbia, 1968-69; tchr. supr. Spl. Sch. Dist., St. Louis County, Mo., 1969-71; instr. dept. spl. edn. U. Mo., 1971-76, asst. prof., 1977-81, assoc. prof., 1981—; cons., field reader spl. edn. program Div. Innovation and Devel. and Div. Personnel Preparation, U.S. Dept. Edn., U.S. Dept. Edn. grantee, 1978-85; ACE fellow in acad. adminstrn., 1984-85. Mem. Council for Exceptional Children, Pi Lambda Theta, Phi Delta Kappa, Kappa Delta Pi, Alpha Kappa Alpha. Office: Dept Spl Edn U MO 351 Townsend Hall Columbia MO 65211

GAVIN, VIDA REGINA, educational administrator; b. Birstonas, Lithuania, Aug. 12, 1941; d. Jurgis and Elena (Ciurlionis) Strazdas; came to U.S., 1948, naturalized, 1959; B.S., Northeastern U., 1968, M.Ed., 1973, EdD, 1986; m. Charles F. Gavin, June 26, 1965; 1 son, David. Dept. head, coordinator spl. services and reading Public Schs. Dedham (Mass.), 1971-81; dir. spl. services, reading Scituate (Mass.) Public Schs., 1981—. Named Outstanding Secondary Educator of Am., Mass., 1974. Mem. Internat. Reading Assn., Council Exceptional Children, Assn. Supervision and Curriculum Devel., Adminstrs. Spl. Edn., New Eng. Coalition Ednl. Leaders, Mass. Reading Assn., Mass. Assn. Children with Learning Disabilities, Phi Delta Kappa, Delta Kappa Gamma. Roman Catholic. Avocations: music, reading, drama, sailing. Home: 141 Forest St PO Box B Norwell MA 02061 Office: Scituate Pub Schs 606 Chief Justice Cushing Hwy Scituate MA 02066

GAVINS-BOLDS, BEATRICE BRENDA, government financial management specialist; b. Bklyn., Nov. 3, 1946; d. John Edward and Ellree (Williams) Gavins. B.S., CUNY, 1975. Adminstrv. asst. OEO, N.Y.C., 1967-73; adminstrv. asst. Social Security Adminstrn., HEW, N.Y.C., 1973-74, auditor, 1974-75, exec. asst. Office Child Support Enforcement, 1977-79, Health Care Financing Adminstrn., 1979-80, fin. mgmt. specialist Office Family Support Adminstrn., 1980—. Recipient Exemplary Employee award Social Security Adminstrn., N.Y.C., 1974; Spl. Achievement award Health Care Financing Adminstrn., N.Y.C., 1979; Disting. Performance cert. Office Civil Rights, N.Y.C., 1980, cert. appreciation U.S. Dept Defense. Mem. Federally Employed Women (chpt. pres. 1979-82, regional mgr. 1982-85, nat. v.p. for tng. 1985-876, by-laws chair 1987-88, Disting. Service award 1982), Coalition 100 Black Women, Nat. Assn. Female Execs. Avocations: tennis; skiing; bridge; backgammon. Home: 144 Lincoln Pl Brooklyn NY 11217

GAWEHN, DOROTHY JEANNE, retail sales company executive; b. Omaha, Jan. 20, 1931; d. Robert Floyd and Margaret Marie (Sitzman) Sealock; m. Kenneth Emil Gawehn, Apr. 17, 1951 (div. Jan. 1985); children—Marilyn Gawehn Jeffries, Kenneth M., Eric M., Celeste Gawehn-Yates. Grad. high sch., Omaha, Nebr. Systems technician Nat. Welding Co., Richmond, Calif., 1926-63; lead data entry operator United Grocers Co., Fresno, Calif., 1964-68, data processing mgr., 1968-72, computer operator shift supr., Oakland, Calif., 1972-76, documentation specialist, 1976-82; mgr. adminstrv. systems Baddour, Inc., Memphis, 1983—. Reader for the blind Sta. WTTL, Memphis, 1983—; vol. worker Crisis and Suicide Intervention, Memphis, 1985—, Docent for Ramesses exhibit, 1987. Recipient Key to Memphis. Mem. Internat. Tng. In Communication (club del. 1985-86), Data Processing Mgmt. Assn (Performance award 1973, Yosemite chpt.), Assn. Computing Machinery (sec., newsletter editor 1985—), Mensa. Republican. Roman Catholic. Avocations: backpacking; reading; writing; travel; hiking. Home: 6644 Elkgate Rd Memphis TN 38115 Office: Baddour Inc 4300 Getwell Rd Memphis TN 38118

GAY, ALICE FELTS, advertising company executive; b. Atlanta, Oct. 3, 1949; d. Thomas Gordon and Jane (Copas) F.; 1 child, Kimberly Creed. AB in Psychology, U. Ga., 1971, ABJ in Journalism, 1971, MEd in Mental Retardation, 1973. Tchr. spl. edn. Commerce (Ga.) City Schs., 1972-73; community relations specialist Ga. Retardation Ctr., Athens, 1978-80; dir. pub. relations St. Mary's Hosp., Athens, 1980-83; account exec. The Adsmith, Athens, 1983-86; co-owner advt. agy. And Assocs., Athens, 1986—; cons. pub. relations Athens Regional Library, 1986—. Author, dir. (videotape) The Spirit of Athens, 1984 (Grand award 1984); contbr. articles to mags and profl. jours. Crusade chmn. United Cerebral Palsy of Ga., Athens, 1976, Am. Cancer Soc., Athens, 1976, pub. edn. chmn., 1978, bd. dirs. 1978-85; bd. dirs. Jr. League of Athens, 1986—; pres. Athens Jr. Woman's Club, 1978; pres.-elect. Jr. League Athens, 1988—. Recipient Gold Archie award, Athens AdClub, 1983, 84; Award of Merit, So. Indsl. Devel. Council, 1984, Video Communications award, Atlanta Chpt. Internat. TV Assn., 1984; named one of Outstanding Young Women of Am., 1978, 79, 82, 84, 87. Mem. Ga. Fedn. of Women's Clubs (chmn. state edn. dept. 1980-82, chmn. state. edn. jr. conf. 1978-80), Delta Gamma. Baptist. Lodge: Order of the Eastern Star. Home and Office: 260 Skyline Pkwy Athens GA 30606

GAY, BESSIE JEAN, computer software manager; b. Atlanta, Oct. 8, 1952; d. James W. and Lena (Sinkfield) Gay. Student Ga. State U., 1974. Supr. C & S Nat. Bank, Atlanta, 1970-74; systems engr. EDS, Dallas, 1975-77; mng. product cons. ISA, Atlanta, 1978-81; customer service mgr. Dyer, Wells & Assocs., Atlanta, 1981—. Chmn. Cascade United Meth. Ch. Evangelism Com., Atlanta, 1981-84; pres. Cascade United Meth. Ch. Singles Ministry, Atlanta, 1984-86; mem. Big Sister Program, Atlanta, 1982. Mem. Am. Bus. Women Assn. (membership chmn. 1978-79), Southern Snow Seekers Ski Club. Office: Dyer Wells & Assocs 2251 Lake Park Dr Smyrna GA 30080

GAY, BONNIE LEWIS, lawyer; b. Newton Grove, N.C., Jan. 20, 1942; d. Clarence Henry and Patricia Lucile (Brock) Lewis; m. William Jan Gay, Mar. 10, 1962 (div. 1976); 1 child, Heather Laurie. BA, Am. U., 1962, LLB, 1964. Bar: Va. 1964, D.C. 1966, N.J. 1978, U.S. Supreme Ct., 1972. Law clk. U.S. Dist. Ct. D.C., 1964-66; sole practice, McLean, Va., 1966-68; project dir. Computer Retrieval Systems, Bethesda, Md., 1968-70; atty. opinion sect. office gen. counsel Dept. Treasury, Washington, 1970-73, tech. asst. to asst. gen. counsel, 1974-77; legal counsel Bur. Engraving and Printing, Washington, 1977-80; of counsel office chief counsel Office Revenue Sharing, Washington, 1980-84; asst. dir. Legal Edn. Inst., Dept. Justice, Washington, 1984—; mem. faculty U. Md., 1980—. Contbr. articles to profl. jours.; editorial bd. Fed. Bar News and Jour., 1986—. Bd. dirs., legal counsel Treasury Hist. Assn., 1973-76, 79-80, 81-83, 85—; sec. Cleveland Terr. Owners Assn., 1981-82; mem. Treasury Women's Adv. Com., 1974-76; trustee Universalist Nat. Meml. Ch., 1969-75, chmn. music, 1969-71, chmn. fin., 1971-75; bd. dirs. Treasury Dept. Fedn. Credit Union, 1975-77; mem. Dean's Adv. Council Washington Coll. Law, 1982-85. Mem. ABA (corp. and banking subcom., adminstr. law, vice chmn., continuing legal edn. com. 1988—), Fed. Bar Assn. (treas. D.C. chpt. 1982-83, bd. dirs. 1980—, rec. sec. 1983-84, corr. sec. 1984-85, 2d v.p. 1985-86, 1st v.p. 1986-87, pres. elect 1987-88), D.C. Bar Assn. (sec. medico-legal com. 1973-75, mem. continuing legal edn. com. 1986—), Va. State Bar, Women's Bar Assn. D.C., Kappa Beta Pi (province pres. 1972-74). Home: 7008 Benjamin St McLean VA 22101 Office: Legal Edn Inst 1875 Conn Ave NW Room 1034 Washington DC 20530

GAY, CLAUDINE MOSS, physician; b. Alma, Ga., Nov. 30, 1915; d. Fred and Rosa (Mercer) Moss; B.S., Coll. William and Mary, 1935; M.D., U. Va., 1939; m. Lendall C. Gay, June 29, 1940 (dec. 1971); children—Gordon B., Spencer B.; m. J. Marion Bryant, 1974 (dec. 1986). Intern, Gallinger Mcpl. Hosp., Washington; practice medicine specializing in family practice, Washington, 1940—; mem. staff, exec. bd. Sibley Meml. and Capitol Hill Hosp., Washington; mem. Pres.'s Council on Malpractice, 1965; mem. health adv. commn. HEW, 1971-78; U.S. del. Med. Women's Internat. Congress, 5 times; del. Pres.'s Workshop on Non-Govtl. Orgn. Trustee Moss Charity Trust Fund, 1966—; adv. bd. Med. Coll. Pa., 1977; mem. president's council Coll. William and Mary. Recipient Capitol Hill Community Achievement award, 1986. Fellow Am. Acad. Family Practice (del. 1971-81; alt. del. to ho. dels. 1964-71); mem. Assn. Med. Women Internat. (del. 1966-72, councillor 1978-84), Royal Acad. Medicine, Pan Am. Med. Soc., D.C. Acad. Gen. Practice (pres.), Am. Med. Women's Assn. (councilor orgn. and mgmt. 1972-73, v.p. 1974, nat. pres. 1977, Blackwell medal 1988), D.C. Med. Women's Assn. (pres.), AMA, D.C. Med. Soc. (dir., exec. bd., past v.p., mem. nominating com. 1970, 81, relative value study com. 1970-72, constn. and constn. bylaws com., sec. family practice sect. 1966, 69, 78), DAR. Clubs: Women's Roundtable for Health Issues, Washington Forum (pres. 1987-88), Zonta (dir.). Home: 5030 Loughboro Rd NW Washington DC 20016 Office: 403 E Capitol St SE Washington DC 20003

GAY, ELIZABETH DERSHUCK, artist; b. Phila., Nov. 27, 1927; d. John Raymond and Marguerite Sloane (Bright) Dershuck; B.A., Sweet Briar Coll., 1949; postgrad. Nat. Acad. Fine Arts, N.Y.C., 1957-58; m. Frank Lipscomb Gay, Jan. 8, 1955; children—Frank, Jack, Rutherford. One-woman shows include: Little Gallery, Katonah, N.Y., 1975, Mamaroneck Artists Guild, 1977, Hazleton (Pa.) Art League, Cassandra Gallery, White Plains, 1980, Sweet Briar Coll., Benedict Gallery, 1984; group shows include: Beaux Arts Finale, 1975, Westlake Gallery, White Plains, 1976, Lever House, 1977, Union Carbide, 1977, Knickerbocker Artists, 1976, 77, 79, 80-81, Nat. Arts Club, 1977, 79, New Eng. Exhbn. at Silvermine, 1977, Hudson Valley Arts Assn., 1975, 77, 79, Salmagundi Club, 1978, 81, NAD, 1980, Bergen County Mus. (N.J.), 1983, Westchester Community Coll., 1984; traveling exhbns. Nat. Assn. Women Artists, 1980-82; instr. Watercolor North Castle Adult Edn., 1974-77; instr., mem. adv. bd. Pelham Art Center, 1979—; mem. Artists Equity Assn. N.Y., Knickerbocker Artists N.Y., Mamaroneck Artists Guild, Nat. Assn. Women Artists, Catherine Lorillard Wolfe Art Club N.Y. Republican. Clubs: Whippoorwill, Green Acres Garden. Home: 37 Round Hill Rd Armonk NY 10504

GAY, ELIZABETH KIRK, library director; b. Lexington, Ky., Oct. 25, 1946; d. John Breckenridge and Susan Weakley (Lytle) G. BA, Vanderbilt U., 1968; MLS, U. Calif., Berkeley, 1969; MBA, UCLA, 1982. Sr. librarian, librarian Los Angeles Pub. Library, 1969-76, subject dept. mgr., 1976-79, asst. cen. library dir., 1979-84, cen. library dir., 1984—. Mem. Calif. Mus. Found., 1984—. Mem. ALA (mem. steering com. cen. library discussion group 1984-85, mem. Am. Assn. Pubs./Resources and Tech. Services Com. 1984—), Calif. Library Assn. Democrat. Presbyterian. Home: 800 W First

St #806 Los Angeles CA 90012 Office: Los Angeles Pub Library 630 W 5th St Los Angeles CA 90071

GAY, GRETCHEN M., nurse, administrator; b. Burlington, Kans., May 7, 1930; d. Donald Melvin and Millie Jane (Mattox) Remer; A.A. in Nursing, Johnson County Community Coll., 1973; student parapsychology under Joaquin Cunanan, Manila, 1978. Student, then grad. nurse Olathe Community Hosp. (Kans.), 1972-73; night supr. VA Hosp., Leavenworth, Kans., 1973-77; asst. dir. nursing Mid Continent Psychiat. Hosp., Olathe, 1978-84; supr. Western Mo. Mental Health Ctr., Kansas City, 1984—; dir. nursing Troost Nursing Home, 1980—; owner cons. firm Endless Horizons; co-writer grant and co-founder 1st Level Six Treatment Ctr. of Kans. for Wayward Children, Olathe, 1979; an organizer Nurse Adv. Tng. Program, Chgo., 1977. Lic. nursing home adminstr.; R.N. Mem. Metasci. Found., Soc. for Improvement Human Functioning, Mo. League for Nursing, Am. Holistic Nurses Assn., Martin Psychiat. Research Found., Brain Mind. Mem. Unity Ch. Home: 811 Layton Dr Olathe KS 66061 Office: Western Mo Mental Health Ctr 600 E 22d St Kansas City MO 64108

GAY, MARILYN FANELLI MARTIN, television producer, talk show hostess; b. San Francisco, July 16, 1925; d. Louis and Gertrude (Dondero) Fanelli; m. William Thomas Martin, Jan. 11, 1953 (div. 1956); m. Mel Raymond Gay, May 3, 1963. Student U. Calif.-Berkeley, 1943-46, U. Oreg., 1946. Producer, hostess, writer TV show In God We Trust, Protestant Ch. Fedn., on Sta. KTLA, Los Angeles, 1954-55, A Woman's World TV talk show on NBC TV outlet sta., Las Vegas, 1956, radio show Party with the Stars, Los Angeles, 1958; writer Passing Parade Films, ABC-TV, 1958, Telephone Time; producer, hostess, writer The Marilyn Gay Show, Group W Cable, Valley Cable, Cox Cable, Century Cable, King Cable, Cablevision, Simmons Cable, 1982—. Dir. spl. features, coordinator radio and TV, Invest in America Campaign, 1957. Contbg. feature writer Los Angeles Times, 1957. Recipient award DAR, 1943, Commemorative medal of Honor Hallmark, 1985. Mem. Nat. Fedn. Press Women, Calif. Press Women, Writers Guild Am.-West (founding), Alpha Delta Pi. Mem. Ch. of Religious Science. Address: 1990 Ginger St #101 Oxnard CA 93030

GAYLOR, DIANE MARIE, psychiatric social worker; b. Cleve., June 10, 1938; d. Albert Francis and Helen Catherine (Pietrazk) G. Student, Kent State U., 1956-60; BA in Sociology with honors, LaVerne U., 1967, MA in Teaching English, 1974; MSW, U. Iowa, 1979. Diplomate in clin. social work, Am. Acad. Cert. Social Workers; lic. social worker, Iowa. Tchr. elem. schs. Cleve. Pub. Schs., 1958-64; tchr. elem. schs. Chino (Calif.) Pub. Schs., 1967-68, 70-76, reading specialist, 1968-70, reading specialist upper elem. grades, 1970-76; social worker, chem. dependency unit Cherokee (Iowa) Mental Health Inst., 1977-78, social worker, children's unit, 1978-79; psychiat. social worker Keith Barnett, Psychiatrist, Sioux City, Iowa, 1979—. Mem. NEA, Nat. Assn. Social Workers, Acad. Cert. Social Workers, Iowa Mental Health Assn., Am. Bd. Examiners in Social Work. Home: 2021 Indian Hills Sioux City IA 51104 Office: PO Box 2018 Sioux City IA 51104

GAYLORD, CLARICE ELAINE, government official; b. Los Angeles, Apr. 14, 1943; d. Clarence and Wilma Mae (Fisher) Armstrong; m. Thaddeus Johnson Gaylord,Aug. 26, 1970; children: Travis Jared, Altoria Denise. BA in Zoology, UCLA, 1965; MS in Zoology, Howard U., 1967, PhD in Zoology, 1971. Lab. instr. zoology dept. Howard U., Washington, 1965-68, zoology instr., 1968-69, research asst., 1969-71; program adminstr. immunology/epidemiology NIH, Nat. Cancer Inst., Bethesda, Md., 1972-76; chief breast cancer virus sect. NIH, Nat. Cancer Inst., Bethesda, 1976-78; exec. sec. pathbiochemistry sect. NIH Div. Research Grants, Bethesda, 1980-84; dir. research grants program EPA, Washington, 1984—, mem. sr. exec. service, 1988—; mem. adv. bd. Coll. Arts and Scis., N.C. Cen. U., Raleigh, 1987—; mem. adv. council Nat. Inst. Environ. Health Scis., 1984-87. Mem. Framework for Managerial Excellence, Washington, 1985-87, Fed. Women's Program, Washington, 1985-87; vice chmn. EEO adv. group Nat. Cancer Inst., Bethesda, Md., 1974-80; leader jr. troop Girl Scouts U.S.A., Ft. Washington, Md., 1981-83. Mem. Minority Women in Sci., Women in Sci. and Engring., Nat. Assn. Female Execs., Sigma Xi, Betra Kappa Chi, Delta Sigma Theta. Democrat. Baprtist. Home: 605 Camelot Way Fort Washington MD 20744 Office: US EPA 401 M St SW Washington DC 20460

GAYLORD, NELLIE WOLFE, retired educational administrator; b. Luthersville, Ga., Aug. 20, 1922; d. John Thomas and Madie (Jones) Wolfe; B.A. (scholar), Clark Coll., 1943; M.S. (scholar), Atlanta U., 1950; postgrad. Temple U., U. Pa.; m. Clyde Felton Gaylord, Jr., Aug. 2, 1953; 1 son, Clyde Felton III. Tchr., Atlanta Pub. Schs., 1944-46; tchr. Sch. Dist. Phila., 1946-69, tchr. on spl. assignment, 1969-70, adminstrv. asst. to dist. supt., 1970-72, vice prin., 1972-75, prin. secondary sch., 1975-86; guest lectr. West Chester State Coll., Pa. State U. Vice chmn. Moorestown (N.J.) Zoning Bd. of Adjustment, 1981, chmn., 1982; vice chmn. Moorestown Shadetree Adv. Com., 1976, chmn., 1977; merit badge counselor Boy Scouts Am., 1974-87; mem. Citizens Adv. Com. on Drug Abuse, 1970; bd. dirs. West End Community Center, Moorestown, N.J., pres. 1973; membership solicitor YMCA; vestryman Episcopal Ch. Recipient Meritorious Service award United Negro Coll. Fund, 1958; service award Cancer Crusade, 1969; NSF grantee, 1963-66. Mem. Phila. Assn. Sch. Adminstrs., Black Women Ednl. Alliance, Assn. for Supervision and Curriculum Devel., Phila. Clark Coll. Alumni, Alpha Kappa Alpha (N. Atlanta regional dir., past chpt. pres.). Republican. Clubs: Links (eastern area chmn. internat. trends and services 1983-87), The Ems (Moorestown). Home: 405 Glen Ave Moorestown NJ 08057 Office: Sulzberger 48th and Fairmont Ave Philadelphia PA 19139

GAYNOR, LEAH, radio public relations writer, broadcaster; b. Irvington, N.J.; d. Jack and Sophia Kamish; A.A., Miami Dade Community Coll., 1970; B.A., Fla. Internat. U., 1975, postgrad., 1975—; m. Robert Merrill, Mar. 27, 1954 (div.); children—Michael David, Lisa Heidi, Tracy Lynn. Owner, operator Lee Gaynor Assos., pub. relations, Miami, Fla., 1970-72; exec. dir. Ft. Lauderdale (Fla.) Jaycees, 1970-71; host interview program Sta. WGMA, Hollywood, Fla., 1971-73, stas. WWOK and WIGL-FM, Fla., 1973-79; occupational specialist Lindsey Hopkins Edn. Ctr. Dade County Pub. Schs., publicity-pub. relations, Miami, 1971—, broadcaster talk show sta. WEDR-FM; host, producer weekly half-hour pub. service talk program, The Leah Gaynor Show, 1985—. Citizens Adv. Com. Career and Vocat. Edn., 1973—; mem. adv. com. North Miami Beach High Sch., 1977-79; communications com. Council Continuing Edn. Women Miami, 1972-79; mem. publicity Com. Ctr. Fine Arts, Mus. Sci. Mem. Women in Communications, Am. Women in Radio and TV (dir. publicity Goldcoast chpt. 1974-76), Internat. Assn. Bus. Communicators, Pub. Relations Soc. Am., Alliance Career Edn. (publicity chmn.), Nat. Schs. Pub. Relations Assn., Women's C. of C. So. Fla. Democrat. Home: 1255 NE 171 Terr North Miami Beach FL 33162 Office: 750 NW 20th St Miami Fl 33127

GAYNOR, MAGDALEN, lawyer; b. Nashville, Feb. 27, 1953; d. James William and Marion (Patterson) Gaynor. B.A., Simmons Coll., 1975; J.D., Fordham U., 1978. Bar: N.Y. 1979, Fla. 1979, U.S. Supreme Ct. 1979. Assoc. firm Buchman Buchman & O'Brien, N.Y.C., 1979-86, Baer Marks & Upham, N.Y.C., 1986-88; sole practice, White Plains, N.Y., 1988—. Mem. ABA, N.Y. State Bar Assn., Estate Planning Council of N.Y.C. Clubs: Westchester Country (Rye, N.Y.); Liberty (N.Y.C.). Office: 34 S Broadway New York NY 10601

GAYNOR, SUZANNE MARIE, health care executive; b. Phila., Jan. 10, 1941; d. Howard Aloyousis and Irene Marie (Dunn) Gaynor; m. John Michael Hayes, May 26, 1962 (div. 1982); children—Marguerite, Jennifer, Christopher. Diploma in nursing Fitzgerald-Mercy Sch. Nursing, 1961; B.S., Marymount U. Va., 1977, M.B.A., 1981; postgrad. U. Mich., 1987—. R.N., Pa., Va. Service coordinator Upjohn Health Care, Washington, 1972-74, tng. coordinator, 1974-75; health intern U.S. Senate, Washington, 1977; health analyst Am. Blood Commn., Arlington, Va., 1977-79, dir. regionalization program, 1979-83, cons., 1983; dir. regional services Greater N.Y. Blood Program, N.Y.C., 1983—; mem. interagy. tech. com. Working Group on Blood Resources and Blood Substitutes, Dept. Health and Human Services, 1981-83; mem. subcom. on blood supply and blood services Com. on Pub. Health, N.Y. Acad. Medicine, 1984—; mem. Blood Bank Task Force Region II, Regional Comprehensive Hemophilia Treatment Ctrs. Contbr. articles to profl. jours. Discussion leader Jr. Great Books, Arlington, Va., 1974-75. Recipient Plaque for Recognition of Service, Am. Blood Commn., 1983; PEW fellow U. Mich. Grad. Sch. Pub. Health, 1986—. Mem. Am. Assn. Blood Banks (dist. adv. group), Council Community Blood Ctrs. (membership com.), Nat. Assn. Female Execs., LWV (bd. dirs. 1973-76), NOW, Delta Sigma Epsilon. Democrat. Roman Catholic. Office: N Y Blood Ctr 310 E 67th St New York NY 10021

GAZES, MICHELLE CZERNER, sales executive; b. Oceanside, N.Y., Nov. 24, 1953; d. Alfred S. and Ingeborg Rose (Israelski) Czerner. BA, George Washington U., 1975. Account exec. Sta. WMAL ABC Broadcasting Corp., Washington, 1975-76, Co-op mgr., 1976-79; gen. sales mgr. Sta. BELO Broadcast Corp., Dallas, 1980-82; sales mgr. Sta. KNBN-TV, Dallas, 1982-83; account exec. Sta. KDFW-TV Times Mirror Corp., Dallas, 1982-83, nat. sales mgr., 1983-84; Gen. sales mgr. Sta. KDFI-TV 27 Dallas Media Investors, 1984—. Bd. dirs. Dallas Diabetes Assn., 1982-84; aid to Sen. LLoyd Bentsen, Washington, 1974-76; vol. Foster Child Advocate Services, Dallas, 1984; mem. People for the Am. Way, Am. Jewish Congress. Mem. Am. Women Radio and TV (v.p. 1985-86, pres. 1986-87), Advt. Broadcast Execs. Tex. Democrat. Jewish. Office: Sta KDFI-TV 27 433 Regal Row Dallas TX 75247

GAZLAY, KRISTIN COLLINS, communications executive; b. Frankfurt, Fed. Republic Germany, Sept. 23, 1958; (parents Am. citizens); d. John Collins and Carolyn Knox G. BA, So. Meth. U., 1980, BFA, 1980. Corr. AP, San Antonio, 1983-84; news editor AP, Dallas, 1984, asst. bur. chief, 1985-87, bur. chief, 1987—. Office: AP 1101 W 2d St Little Rock AR 72201

GEANOULES, FRANCES CARMELA, cosmetics and pharmaceutical company executive; b. N.Y.C., July 14, 1945; d. Nicholas and Mary Josephine (Lombardo) Oliveri; m. Anthony Peter Geanoules, Oct. 8, 1967; children—Anthony Peter, Maria Claire. Sec., Equitable Life Assurance Soc., N.Y.C., 1963-64; wage and salary asst. Revlon, Inc., N.Y.C., 1965-68, compensation analyst, 1969-75, mgr. compensation, 1976-83, dir. compensation planning and adminstrn., 1984-85, dir. compensation planning and benefits adminstrn., 1986—. Mem. Am. Soc. Personnel Adminstrs., Am. Compensation Assn. Republican. Roman Catholic. Office: Revlon Inc 2147 Route 27 Edison NJ 08818

GEANURACOS, ELSIE DA SILVA, foreign language educator; b. Bklyn., Dec. 29, 1922; d. John and Maria (Nascimento) Da Silva; m. George James Geanuracos, Jan. 28, 1945; children: Constance, Patricia, James, Joan, John. BA, Hunter Coll., 1944; student Columbia U., 1944-47. 1st tchr. Portuguese lang. N.Y.C. Sch. System, 1945-50, Spanish tchr., 1945-50; prof. Spanish U. Bridgeport, Conn., 1969, 72, 73, Housatonic Community Coll., Bridgeport, 1970; founder, adviser Portuguese Scholarship Program, U. Bridgeport, 1973—, sec. Halsey Internat. Scholarship Program, 1974, mem. bd. advisers, instr. Spanish, Womens' Inst. U. Bridgeport; tutor Tutoring Ctr. Bridgeport. Com. mem. Womens' Aux. to Fairfield County Med. Assn., Am. Cancer Soc. Bridgeport chpt.; translator Bridgeport Hosp. Aux.; mem. bd. assoc. U. Bridgeport; mem. Bklyn. Hist. Soc., Bklyn.; mem. Greater Bridgeport Symphony Guild. Recipient citation for community service Am. Cancer Soc. Bridgeport chpt.; citation as an internationalist UN Assn., 1975; 10-yr. service plaque Portuguese Scholar Ship Program of HISP, 1983. Mem. AAUW (treas. Fairfield chpt.), UN Assn., Judeo-Christian Women's Assn. (mistress of ceremonies first awards luncheon 1974), Alpha Delta Pi. Avocations: swimming, reading, drapery making, knitting, traveling. Home: 102 Lu Manor Dr Fairfield CT 06432

GEARY, MARY JO, computer software company executive; b. Argyle, Minn., July 14, 1958; d. Frank Gabrial and Louise Francis (Marynik) Yutrzenka; m. Charles Vetter Geary, May 1, 1982. BS, St. Cloud (Minn.) State U., 1980. Sales rep. Xerox Corp., Mpls., 1981, Lesher-Leighton Printing, Mpls., 1982-83; account mgr. Hagen Systems, Inc., Mpls., 1983-86, cons., 1985-87, supr., 1986—. Roman Catholic. Office: Hagen Systems Inc 6438 City West Pkwy Minneapolis MN 55344

GEBBIE, KRISTINE MOORE, state official; b. Sioux City, Iowa, June 26, 1943; d. Thomas Carson and Gladys Irene (Stewart) Moore; m. Neil Gebbie; children: Anna, Sharon, Eric. BSN, St. Olaf Coll., 1965; MSN, UCLA, 1968. Project dir. USPHS tng. grant, St. Louis, 1972-77; coordinator nursing St. Louis U., 1974-76, asst. dir. nursing, 1976-78, clin. prof., 1977-78; adminstr. Oreg. Health Div., Portland, 1978—; assoc. prof. Oreg. Health Scis. U. Portland, 1980—; mem. Presdl. Commn. on Human Imunodeficiency Virus Epidemic, 1987—. Author: (with Deloughery and Neuman) Consultation and Community Organization, 1971, (with Deloughery) Political Dynamics: Impact on Nurses, 1975; (with Scheer) Creative Teaching in Clinical Nursing, 1976. Bd. dirs. Luth. Family Services Oreg. and S.W. Wash., 1979-84; bd. dirs. Oreg. Psychoanalytic Found., 1983-87. Recipient Disting. Alumna award St. Olaf Coll., 1979. Mem. Assn. State and Territorial Health Ofcls., 1988 (pres. 1984-85, exec. com. 1980-87, McCormick award 1988), Am. Pub. Health Assn., Hastings Ctr., N.Am. Nursing Diagnosis Assn. (treas. 1983-87), Oreg. Pub. Health Assn., Am. Soc. Pub. Adminstrn. (adminstrn. award II 1983). Club: City of Portland. Office: Oregon State Health Div 1400 SW 5th St Portland OR 97207

GEBO, EMMA MARIE JOKI, academic administrator, education instructor; b. Billings, Mont., Jan. 1, 1945; d. Waino August and Vera H. (Luoma) Joki; m. David Ray Gebo, Sept. 12, 1964; children: Lorri D., Paul A., Robyn J. BS in Home Econs., Mont. State U., 1966; MEd, U. Mont., 1971; postgrad., Colo. State U., 1986—. Cert. secondary tchr., Idaho. Substitute tchr. various cities, Idaho, Mont., 1967-74; adult instr. Fashion Fabrics, Pocatello, Idaho, 1975-76; clothing instr., tchr. edn. Idaho State U., Pocatello, 1975-80, dept. chmn., tchr. edn., 1980—. Editor: Idaho Adult Living/Teen Living, 1986, Idaho Cooperative Vocational Education, 1984, 86, Curriculum Guides for Home Economics, 1987. Named Outstanding Young Women of Am., 1978-81, Pocatello Disting. Young Woman, Jayceettes, 1981; Am. Vocat. Assn. fellow, Ellen S. Richards fellow, 1987. Mem. Idaho Home Econs. Assn. (pres. 1983-85, disting. home economist 1985), Home Econs. Edn. Assn. (publs. bd. 1986, 87), Nat. Assn. Tchr. Educators Vocat. Home Econs. (newsletter editor 1986), Am. Home Econs. Assn. (by-laws com. 1983-85), Am. Vocat. Assn., Nat. Future Homemakers Am. (tchr. task force 1984-88, hon. mem. Idaho chpt.). Methodist. Home: 2409 S Fairway Pocatello ID 83201 Office: Idaho State U Home Econs Vocat Tchr Edn Campus Box 8081 Pocatello ID 83209

GEDDES, JANE, professional golfer; b. E. Northport, N.Y., Feb. 5, 1960; d. Gerard George and Helen Evelyn (Zielinski) G. Student, Fla. State U., 1978-82. Profl. golfer 1983—. Champion U.S. Women's Open, 1986; named Most Improved Golfer, Golf Digest, 1986. Roman Catholic.

GEDDES, LANELLE EVELYN, nurse, physiologist; b. Houston, Sept. 15, 1935; d. Carl Otto and Evelyn Bertha (Frank) Nerger; B.S.N., U. Houston, 1957, Ph.D. (fellow), 1970; m. Leslie Alexander Geddes, Aug. 3, 1962. Staff nurse Houston Ind. Sch. Dist., 1957-62; instr. to asst. prof. physiology Baylor U. Coll. Medicine, 1972-75; asst. prof. nursing Tex. Women's U., 1972-75; prof., head Sch. Nursing, Purdue U., 1975—. Recipient teaching awards. Mem. Am. Nurses Assn., Nat. League Nursing, Am. Assn. Critical-Care Nurses, AAAS, N.Y. Acad. Scis., Phi Kappa Phi, Sigma Theta Tau, Iota Sigma Pi. Lutheran. Contbr. articles sci. jours., chpts. in books. Office: Purdue Univ West Sch Nursing Lafayette IN 47907

GEDDES, SUSAN, infosystems specialist; b. Stoneham, Mass., Apr. 29, 1927; d. James Gardner and Katherine (Artz) G. BA, Tufts U., 1949. Programmer Lockheed Missile & Space, Sunnyvale, Calif., 1956-64; analyst Macy's, San Francisco, 1964-65; systems analyst Stanford (Calif.) U., 1965-69, Library of Congress, Washington, 1969-70; computer specialist Nat. Library Medicine, Bethesda, Md., 1970—. Mem. Am. Soc. Info. Sci. (chair spl. interest group on library automation 1973-74, pres. Potomac Valley chpt. 1976-77). Home: 10919 Deborah Dr Potomac MD 20854

GEDNEY-THACHER, ANNE LOUISE, production company executive; b. White Plains, N.Y., Aug. 29, 1956; d. Gerald Shields and Patricia Anne (McGrath) Gedney; m. Christopher Webb Thacher, July 12, 1980. AA, Sacramento City Coll., 1977-78; student, U. Calif., Davis, 1978-79. Asst. prod. mgr. EUE/ Screen Gems, N.Y.C., 1980-83; freelance producer, dir. N.Y., 1983-87; v.p. MetaFive, N.Y.C., 1987—. Mem. Dirs. Guild of Am. Roman Catholic. Home: 273 Vandelinda Ave Teaneck NJ 07666 Office: MetaFive Inc 30 W 26th St New York NY 10010

GEE, IRENE, food stylist; b. N.Y.C., Aug. 17, 1950; d. Jimmy Set and Lin Fung (Ng) G.; B.A., Hunter Coll., 1971; M.S. in Family and Consumer Studies, Lehman Coll., 1974, M.S. in Guidance and Counseling, 1978; m. Oct. 17, 1981. Tchr., Olinville Jr. High Sch., Bronx, N.Y., 1971-75, Lehman Coll., Bronx, 1975-77, Harry Eiseman Jr. High Sch., Bklyn., 1978-80; food stylist, recipe developer Ladies Home Jour., 1977-78; food stylist, recipe developer Woman's Day Mag., 1979—, home economist, 1980—; owner, operator Irene's Catering, 1984—; food coordinator Evander Childs High Sch.; food cons. Corn Products Corp., 1978—; food stylist Nabisco, 1978, also Perdue Co.; reciper writer, judger natural food contsts Scholastic Mag.; judge nat. contests Choices mag.; developer recipe booklets various cos. including Progresso and Fla. Mushrooms; cons. food cos. and publs.; comml. model Mauna Loa Macadamia Nuts, Lewis & Neale; recipe developer Lipton Co. Contbr. articles to Forecast and Choices mags. Mem. Am. Home Econs. Assn., Home Economists in Bus., Am. Counseling Assn., Omicron Nu. Contbr. articles Woman's World mag.

GEE, JENNIFER, lawyer; b. San Francisco, Apr. 6, 1949; d. Bing Lai Won and Shuk Fong (Yee) Gee; m. Melvin Buck Sher Lee, Sept. 1, 1974; children—Michael David, Eric Robert, Katherine Anne. B.A. with honors U. Calif-Berkeley, 1971, J.D., 1974. Bar: Calif. 1974. Trial atty. EEOC, San Francisco, 1974-82; hearing officer Calif. New Motor Vehicle Bd., Sacramento, 1981—; adminstrv. judge U.S. Merit Systems Protection Bd., San Francisco, 1982—. Mem. Museum Soc., Chinese for Affirmative Action, both San Francisco, Action on Smoking, Health, Washington. John Woodman Ayer fellow U. Calif., 1974. Mem. ABA, Bar Assn. San Francisco, Asian Am. Bar Assn., Nat. Assn. Women Judges. Democrat. Clubs: Commonwealth (San Francisco), Prythanean Alumni (Berkeley) Office: US Merit Systems Protect Bd 525 Market St 28th Floor San Francisco CA 94105

GEERDES, MARY ELIZABETH, nurse, military officer; b. Albuquerque, Nov. 6, 1947; d. Joseph John and Grace Garnet (Gladwin) Boyle; m. Franklin Geerdes, Oct. 12, 1985; children: David, Eric. BSN, U. N.Mex., 1969, MA in Edn., 1971. RN. Staff nurse Presbyn. Hosp., Albuquerque, 1969-71; commd. lt. (j.g.) USN, 1971, advanced through grades to lt. comdr.; clin. instr. Naval Hosp., Camp Pendleton, Calif., 1971-73, charge nurse, 1975-78; instr. Naval Sch. Health Scis., San Diego, 1973-75; charge nurse Naval Hosp., Okinawa, Japan, 1978-80; officer div. emergency nursing Naval Hosp., Long Beach, Calif., 1983-86; officer div. emergency nursing Naval Hosp., San Diego, 1980-83, clin. cons. emergency nursing, 1986—; instr. advanced cardiac life support, 1983—. Mem. Assn. Mil. Surgeons, Emergency Nurses Assn. (instr. trauma nurse care course 1987—), Undersea/Hyperbaric Med. Soc., Nat. Assn. Female Execs., Profl. Assn. Diving Instrs (emeritus). Republican. Roman Catholic. Office: Naval Hosp STAF #560 San Diego CA 92134

GEFFEN, BETTY ADA, theatrical personal manager; b. Lachine, Que., Can., May 12, 1911; came to U.S., 1942, naturalized, 1945; d. Joseph and Minnie (Illievitz) Gottheil; student public schs., Montreal, Que.; m. Jacob N. Geffen, Dec. 23, 1944; 1 dau., JoAnn Merle. Sec., Saul Cohen/Trustee in Bankruptcy, Montreal, 1926-28, Maxwell Cummings Real Estate, 1928-30, Monroe Abbey, Atty., 1930-31; with Tic-Toc, Stanley Grill and Chez Maurice, Montreal, 1931-41; sec. H.L. Green, N.Y.C., 1941-44; pvt. personal mgr., casting cons., N.Y.C., 1950—; cons. Consab Assos. Corp., N.Y.C., 1966—. Trustee Israel Cancer Research Fund.; vol. Floating Hosp. Mem. Nat. Acad. TV Arts and Scis., Women of the Motion Picture Industry, Motion Picture Pioneers, Internat. Platform Assn., The Nat. Mus. Women in the Arts (charter). Democrat. Clubs: Variety Women N.Y. (v.p. 1977-81, pres. 1982-86, chmn. bd. 1986—), Brandeis U. Home and Office: 17 W 71st St Apt 7-A New York NY 10023

GEFFNER, DONNA SUE, speech pathologist, audiologist, educator; b. N.Y.C.; d. Louis and Sally (Weiner) G.; B.A. magna cum laude, Bklyn. Coll., 1967; M.A., N.Y. U., 1968, Ph.D. (NDEA fellow), 1970, postgrad. student Advanced Inst. Analytic Psychotherapy, 1973-75. Asst. prof. Lehman Coll., 1971-76; asso. prof. dept. speech St. John's U., 1976-81, prof., 1982—, dir. Speech and Hearing Center, 1976—, chmn. dept. speech communication scis. and theater, 1983—, developer M.A. program in speech pathology and audiology; pvt. practice, 1980—; cons. to corp. execs.; TV producer and hostess NBC, 1977-78, CBS, 1978-79. Emmy nominee for Outstanding Instrnl. Program, 1978; recipient award Pres.'s Com. on Employment of Handicapped, Pres's. medal for Outstanding Faculty Achievement St. Johns U., 1987; N.Y. State Edn. Dept. grantee, 1976-78; City U. N.Y. Research Found. grantee, 1972. Fellow Am. Speech, Lang. and Hearing Assn. (legis. councillor 1978-87); mem. N.Y. State Speech and Hearing Assn. (pres. 1978-80), Audiology Study Group N.Y., Contbr. articles to profl. jours. and textbooks; issue editor Jour. Topics in Lang. Disorders, 1980; editor ASHA monograph, 1987. Office: Saint John's Univ Speech and Hearing Ctr Grand Central Pkwy Jamaica NY 11439

GEHRES, SISTER RUTH, academic administrator; b. Evansville, Ind., Apr. 4, 1933; d. Fay Alvin and Floretta Marie (Snyder) G. BA in English, Brescia Coll., 1962; PhD in English, St. Louis U., 1968. Elem. tchr. St. Joseph Sch., Nebraska City, Nebr., 1954-57; elem. prin. Our Lady of Mercy Sch., Hodgenville, Ky., 1957-58; jr. high sch. tchr. Sts. Joseph and Paul Sch., Owensboro, Ky., 1958-62; prof. English Brescia Coll., Owensboro, 1967—, chairperson Humanities Div. and English dept., 1969-77, alumni dir., 1977-79, pres., 1986—; tchr. English Gymnasium der Ursulinen, Straubing, Fed. Republic Germany, 1984-85. Bd. dirs. Jr. Achievement, Owensboro, 1986—, Leadership Owensboro, 1986—; bd. dirs and sec. Ky. Ind. Coll. Fund, Louisville, 1986—. Mem. MLA, Nat. Assn. Ind. Colls. and Univs., Assn. Cath. Colls. and Univs., Council Ind. Ky. Colls. and Univs., C. of C. Office: Brescia Coll 717 Frederica St Owensboro KY 42301

GEHRING, MARY ELLEN, group operations executive; b. Ishpeming, Mich., May 4, 1953; d. Llewellyn J. and Colleen E. (Parviainen) Pope; m. David C. Gehring, Apr. 3, 1983 (div.); 1 child, Mark Anthony. Student, North Mich. U., 1971-73. Lic. optician. Optician, dept. mgr. Cole Vision Corp., Columbus, Ohio, 1977-82, 85-87; groupn ops. mgr. Cole Vision Corp., Milw., 1982-85, Atlanta, 1987—. Mem. Am. Bd. Opticianry. Republican. Lutheran. Club: Atlanta Ski-Hi. Home and Office: 3109 Calumet Circle Kennesaw GA 30144

GEHRKE, KAREN MARIE, accountant; b. Gaylord, Minn., Apr. 12, 1940; d. Stanley Henry and Frieda Marie (Hammel) Ostermann; m. Orville Raymond Gehrke, Oct. 21, 1961; children: Kimberly, Karla, Kent. Grad. high sch., Gaylord, 1958. Inspector Fingerhut Mfg., Gaylord, 1959-60; rewinder 3M, Hutchinson, Minn., 1960-61; packer 3M, Hutchinson, 1971-72; sec. Boehmke Ins. Agy., Gaylord, 1961-63, Law Office of H.A. Knobel, Gaylord, 1964-68; teller First State Fed. Savs. and Loan, Hutchinson, 1969; sec. Wally's Tire Shop, Hutchinson, 1970, Lyle R. Jensen, CPA, Hutchinson, 1974-84; owner Jensen Acctg., Hutchinson, 1984—. Mem. Nat. Assn. Female Execs., Nat. Soc. Pub. Accts., Minn. Assn. Pub. Accts., Hutchinson Area C. of C. Office: Jensen Acctg Box 513 Hutchinson MN 55350

GEIGER, CONSTANCE JANE, nutrition educator, consultant; b. Pitts., June 8, 1953; d. Richard Raymond and Geraldine (Kadavy) G.; m. Dan L. Chichester, May 2, 1981. BS in Foods, Nutrition, U. N.C., 1975; MS in Med. Dietetics, Ohio State U., 1978; PhD in Nutrition, Food Scis., Utah State U., 1988. Registered dietitian. Dietition Kingsdale Gynecologic Assn., Columbus, 1977-78; nutritionist, research assoc. AMA, Chgo., 1978-81; research assoc Nutrition and Food scis. Utah State U., Logan, 1983-84, instr. clin., 1984; assoc. instr. Div. Foods and Nutrition U. Utah, Salt Lake City, 1981-85, asst. prof., dir. grad. prog., 1985-86, asst. prof., dir. div., 1986—; cons. med. affairs NutraSweet Co., Skokie, Ill. 1985—. Contbr. articles to profl. jours. Bd. dirs. Community Services Council, Salt Lake City, 1986—. Mem. Utah Dietetic Assn. (pres. 1986-87, leg. com. 1986—, various com.), Am. Dietetic Assn., Am Soc. Parenteral and Enteral Nutrition, Soc. Nutrition Today, Inst. Food Technologists, Chgo. Dietetic Assn., Chgo. Nutrition Assn., Utah Nutrition Council, Columbus Dietetic Assn., Richmond Dietetic Assn., Jr. League Salt Lake City, Omlicron Nu. Home: 3698 Gilroy Rd Salt

Lake City UT 84109 Office: U Utah Div Foods and Nutrition HPR-N-239 Salt Lake City UT 84109

GEIGER, VIRGINIA RALPH, sales representative; b. Indpls., Mar. 21, 1941; d. William Morris and Mary Louise (Mikels) Ralph; m. John Carroll Geiger, May 18, 1985; 1 child from previous marriage, Andrea Lane Bayliff. AA in Police Sci., Gaston Coll., 1977; BS in Home Econs., Winthrop Coll., 1983. Instr. adult edn. sewing Western Peidmont Community Coll., Morganton, N.C., 1968-70; mgr. fabric store Leslie Fay, Inc., Lincolnton, N.C., 1972-73; designers asst. Hillside House Interiors, Lincolnton, 1972-73; office worker Owen Steel Co., Gastonia, N.C., 1973-74; police officer Gastonia Police Dept., 1975-80; inside steel sales Steel & Pipe Supply, Omaha, 1981; self-employed drapery fabricator Indpls., 1984; sales rep. Roger Popp, Inc., Indpls., 1985, Robert Allen Fabrics, Mansfield, Mass., 1985—. Mem. Am. Soc. Interior Designers (industry found.).

GEISENDORFER, ESTHER LILLIAN, nurse; b. Ferryville, Wis., May 18, 1927; d. Peter C. and Christie G. (Quamme) Walker; student U. Wis.-LaCrosse, 1944-45; R.N., Fairview Hosp. Sch. Nursing, Mpls., 1948; m. James V. Geisendorfer, Sept. 23, 1949; children—Jane, Karen, Lois. Staff nurse Worthington (Minn.) Clinic, 1948-50; pvt. duty nurse, Sioux Falls, S.D., 1950-51; obstet. nurse Fairview Hosp., Mpls., 1951-53; staff nurse St. Anthony Hosp., Rock Island, Ill., 1953-54; obstet. nurse Fairview Hosp., Mpls., 1954-58, post anesthesia recovery nurse, 1958-62, emergency room nurse, 1962-66, obstet. nurse, 1966-68, head nurse obstetrics, 1968-76; staff devel. instr., clinician, Bellin Meml. Hosp., Green Bay, Wis., 1976—; instr. in prenatal and Lamaze classes Ob-Gyn Assocs. of Green Bay Ltd. Mem. Wis. Assn. Perinatal Care, Nordfjord Laget in Am., Wis. Nurses Assn. (Disting. Service award 1981), Nurses Assn. Am. Coll. Obstetrics and Gynecology (cert., founder Northeast Wis. chpt.), Wis. Acad. Scis., Arts and Letters, Nat. Perinatal Assn., Wis. Perinatal Assn. Lutheran. Home: 1001 Shawano Ave Green Bay WI 54303 Office: 744 S Webster Ave Green Bay WI 54301

GEISLER, ROSEMARY P., computer dealer/lessor company executive; b. Chgo., Apr. 5, 1947; d. James Vincent and Raffaella Mary (DeSeno) Pastorello; student Triton Coll., 1970-72; B.A., DePaul U., 1981; m. Ervin R. Geisler, Aug. 17, 1968. Asst. market analyst Evans Products Co., Rolling Meadows, Ill., 1970-76; office services mgr., asst. market analyst Comdisco, Inc., Rosemont, Ill., 1976-78, asst. mktg. product mgr., 1978-80, dir. dealer relations, 1980-81, mktg. product mgr., market maker, 1981-83, asst. v.p., 1983-85, v.p., 1985, sr. v.p. mktg. div., 1985—. Mem. Des Plaines (Ill.) Youth Commn. Mem. DePaul U. Alumni Assn. Home: 85 Brinker Rd Barrington Hills IL 60010 Office: Comdisco Inc 6400 Shafer Ct Rosemont IL 60018

GEISSERT, KATY, mayor; b. Wash., 1926; m. Bill Geissert; children: Bill Jr., Jack, Holly, Doug, Ann. BA in Journalism, Stanford U., 1948. Mem. Torrance (Calif.) City Council, 1974-86; mayor City of Torrance, 1986—; mem. Gov.'s Infrastructure Rev. Task Force, Calif. Past chmn. Torrance Park & Recreation Commn.; past mem. fin. adv. com. Torrance Sch.; past chmn. adv. bd. Calif. State U., Dominguez Hills, Torrance Salvation Army; mem. bond steering com. Torrance Library, 1967; chmn. local park bond issue steering com., 1971, Los Angeles County Sanitation Dist. Bd.; community cons. South Bay Harbor Vol. Bur.; mem. adv. bd. Torrance YWCA; bd. dirs. Switzer Ctr., region III United Way, Torrance LWV; mem. city selection com. Los Angeles County. Recipient PTA Hon. Service award, Woman of Distinction award Soroptimists, Community Service award Riviera Homeowners Assn., spl. citation Nat. Recreation & Park Assn.; named Disting. Citizen of Yr. Torrance Area C. of C., 1973, Woman of Yr. YWCA, Woman of Achievement award Redondo Marina Bus. & Profl. Women's Club. Mem. U.S. Conf. Mayors, League Calif. Cities (del., cities transp. com.), Calif. Elected Women's Assn. (bd. dirs.). Office: Office of the Mayor 3031 Torrance Blvd Torrance CA 90503

GEIST, ANDREA LEE, sales representative; b. Alexandria, Va., Dec. 30, 1958; d. Thomas Geist and Sondra Lee (Villella) Whitlow. BA, Tex. Tech U., 1980. Rep. Am. Sci. Products, Grand Praire, Tex., 1980—. Mem. Nat. Asssn. Female Execs., Inst. Environ. Sci. (sec. 1986—), Alpha Chi Omega. Republicatn. Home: 21604 Mount Laurel Dr Lago Vista TX 78645

GEITHMAN, PATRICIA JARZYNSKI, health care facility executive; b. Toledo, Sept. 11, 1947; d. Leo Paul and Christine (Fuz) Jarzynski; m. David Alan Geithman, Dec. 27, 1968 (div.); children: Brett Wyle, Keira Johanna. BBA, Cleve. State U., 1976, MBA, 1981. Instr. Dyke Coll., Cleve., 1981-85, Cleve. State U., 1985; dir. mktg. Grace Hosp., Cleve., 1985-86; dir. mktg. and devel. St. John Hosp., Cleve., 1986—; bd. dirs. Cudell Improvement, Inc., Cleve., Educated Childbirth, Cleve. (pres., v.p., 1978-80); v.p. Bay Village Nursery Sch. Mem. Am. Mktg. Assn., Acad. Health Services Mktg., Bay Villlage Jr. Women (pres. and v.p. 1983-85), Sales and Mktg. Execs. Republican. Roman Catholic. Club: Press (Cleve.). Home: 399 Tanglewood Ln Bay Village OH 44140 Office: St John Hosp 7911 Detroit Ave Cleveland OH 44102

GEIZHALS, JUDITH SUSAN, psychologist; b. N.Y.C., Nov. 2, 1949; d. Harold Gustav and Charlotte (Rothowitz) Rotkin; m. Benjamin Geizhals, Sept. 1, 1973; children: Charles, Emily. BA in Art History, NYU, 1971; MS in Occupational Therapy, Columbia U., 1973; MA in Psychology, Hofstra U., 1977, PhD in Clin. and Sch. Psychology, 1980. Lic. psychologist, occupational therapist. Occupational therpaist Albert Einstein Coll. Medicine, N.Y.C., 1973-74; dir. day ctr. Riverdale Mental Health Clinic, N.Y.C., 1974-76; pvt. practice occupational therapy Riverdale and Port Washington, 1974-81; psychologist Port Washington (N.Y.) Sch. Dist., 1980-81, South Shore Ctr. Psychology, Merrick, N.Y., 1980-82; pvt. practive psychology Port Washington, 1982—; lectr. Parent Resource Ctr., Port Washington, 1982-84, Parent and Child Edn., Manhasset, N.Y., 1983-85. Mem. Residents for a More Beautiful Port Washington, 1985—, Friends of Library, Port Washington, 1983—, Friends of the Arts, Locust Valley, N.Y., 1984—. Mem. Am. Psychol. Assn., Nassau County Psychol. Assn. Democrat. Jewish.

GELBER, LINDA CECILE, lawyer, banker; b. Hackensack, N.J., Oct. 30, 1950; d. Melvin W. and Beverly E. (Gilman) Gelber. B.A., Ind. U., 1972, M.B.A., 1974, J.D., 1978; cert. fin. services counselor, Am. Bankers Assn. National Grad. Trust Sch., 1983. Bar: Ind. 1978, U.S. Dist. Ct. (so. dist.) Ind. 1978, U.S. Supreme Ct. 1983. Program analyst Indiana Legis. Services Agy., Indpls., 1978-80; v.p., trust officer First National Bank, Kokomo, Ind., 1980-85, asst. v.p. Mchts. Nat. Bank, Indianapolis, 1985-87, Midlantic Nat. Bank, Edison, N.J., 1987—; part-time instr. Indiana U., Kokomo, 1981-82, Ball State U., Muncie, Ind., 1979-80. Bd. dirs. United Way, Kokomo, 1983-85, div. chmn. fund raising campaign, 1983. Mem. ABA, Am. Inst. Banking (v.p. 1983-85), Estate Planning Council Indpls., Howard County (Ind.) Bar Assn. (sec.-treas. 1981), Indiana State Bar Assn., Indpls. Bar Assn., Cen. Ind. Corp. Fiduciaries Assn. Club: Altrusa (Kokomo). Office: Midlantic Nat Bank 1 Engle St Englewood NJ 07631

GELBURD, DIANE ELIZABETH, archeologist; b. N.Y.C., Sept. 28, 1952; d. Irving and Margaret Beryl (Thorbes) G.; m. Stephen Robert Potter, June 22, 1980. B.A., George Washington U., 1974, M.A., 1978; PhD Am. U., 1988. Teaching fellow George Washington U., 1975-77; archeologist/anthropologist Smithsonian Instn./George Washington U., Dobe/Botswana, 1976; archeologist Bur. Reclamation, Washington, 1977; archeologist Nat. Park Service, Washington, 1977-79, assoc. anthropologist, 1979-80; nat. cultural resources specialist Soil Conservation Service, Washington, 1980-88, asst. dir. econ. and social scis. div., 1988—. Contbr. articles to profl. jours. CPR instr. ARC, Arlington, Va., 1983-86. Recipient Achievement award Bur. Reclamation, Washington, 1977; Cert. of Appreciation, Soil Conservation Service, 1984; Disting. Service award USDA, 1986; Spl. Commendation award Soil Conservation Soc. Am., 1986; Recognition award Soil Conservation Service, 1986, Cert. of Merit, 1987; Am. U. fellow 1986-87. Mem. Am. Soc. Conservation Archeology (exec. com. 1988—), Am. Anthrop. Assn., Am. Women in Space, George Wright Soc. (local chpt. treas. 1982), Soil and Water Conservation Soc. (vice chmn. human resources div. 1985-86, chmn. 1986-87, local chpt. sec. 1984, v.p. 1985, pres. 1987), Soc. Am. Archeology (exec. com. fed. archaeology 1979-84), Phi Kappa Phi. Lutheran. Office: US Dept Agr Soil Conservation Services PO Box 2890 Washington DC 20013

GELEHRTER, ANN GORRIS, educational specialist; b. Cleve., Aug. 2, 1949; d. William Eugene and Marian (Stropko) Gorris; m. George Ludwig Gelehrter, June 30, 1972; children: Thomas Aaron, David Andrew. BA, Georgian Ct. Coll., 1971; MEd, John Carroll U., 1986. Cert. specialist in learning disabled, behavior disordered and gifted and talented, Ohio. Tchr. Gesu Sch., University Heights, Ohio, 1971-80; ednl. specialist, office dir. Townsend Learning Ctr., Cleveland Heights, Ohio, 1986-88; reading specialist Hathaway Brown Sch., Shaker Heights, Ohio, 1988—. Editor: (book) Rave Reviews, 1983. Founder Children's Mus., Cleve., 1985-86; exec. bd. dirs. The Cleve. Play House, 1982—. Mem. Ohio Assn. for Gifted Children, Consortium Ohio Coordinators for the Gifted. Democrat. Roman Catholic. Home: 2733 Leighton Rd Shaker Heights OH 44120 Office: Townsend Learning Ctr 2460 Fairmount Blvd Cleveland Heights OH 44106

GELGUR-CORWIN, DONNA, cosmetics executive, writer; b. Los Angeles, Dec. 9, 1949; d. Sidney David and Lorraine (Muller) Gelgur; m. Stanley J. Corwin, Aug. 27, 1983; 1 child, Alexandra Lane. BA in English and Drama, U. Ariz., 1972; MFA, UCLA, 1976. Cert. tchr., Calif. Studio tchr., rep. labor law Internat. Alliance Theatre and Stage Employees, Los Angeles, 1974-81; freelance journalist Los Angeles, 1978—, freelance screenwriter, 1980—; co-owner, pres. Wellington Labs., Inc., Culver City, Calif., 1986—; cons. script, book adaptation Norman Lear Co., Los Angeles, 1986. Screenwriter numerous scripts; contbr. more than 150 articles to mags., profl. jours. Chairwoman exec. com. Neil Bogart Cancer Found. for Children, Los Angeles, 1987-88; mem. contemporary art council Los Angeles County Mus., 1987—; mem. Cystic Fibrosis Found., Los Angeles, 1981—, Cedars Sinai Women's Guild, Los Angeles, 1984—, United Jewish Women, Los Angeles, 1987. Mem. Women In Film, Screen Actors Guild, Writers Guild Am.

GELLER, ESTHER (BAILEY GELLER), artist; b. Boston, Oct. 26, 1921; d. Harry and Fannie (Geller) G.; m. Harold Shapero, Sept. 21, 1945; 1 child, Hannah. Diploma, Sch. Boston Mus. Fine Arts, 1943. Tchr. Boston Mus. Sch., 1943, Boris Mirski Sch., 1945-49; art cons. Leonard Morse Hosp., Natick, Mass. One-woman shows Boris Mirski Art Gallery, Boston, 1945-47, 49, 52, 61, Addison Gallery Am. Art, Children's Art Centre, Andover, Mass., 1953-55, Mayo Gallery, Provincetown, Mass., 1958, Marion (Mass.) Art Centre, 1966, St. Mark's Sch., Southboro, Mass., 1969, Decenter Gallery, Copenhagen, 1969, Regis Coll., Weston, Mass., 1970, Am. Acad. Gallery, Rome, (1971), Newton (Mass.) Library, 1973, Newton Art Centre, 1978, Artworks of Wayne, Providence, 1979, Stonehill Coll., Easton, Mass., 1986; group shows include San Francisco Mus., Va. Mus. Art, Chgo. Art Inst., Worcester Art Mus., U. Ill., Smith Coll., Inst. Contemporary Art, DeCordova Mus., USIA traveling show, USIS circulating exhbn., Far East, Boston Mus., pastel show Regis Coll., 1984. Cabot fellow, 1949; Studios Am. Acad. fellow, 1949-50, 70-71, 75; MacDowell Colony-Yaddo fellow, 1945, 67, 69. Mem. Boston Visual Arts Union, Arts Wayland Assn. Home: 9 Russell Circle Natick MA 01760 Office: Loker Studios 47 Loker St Wayland MA 01778

GELLER, JANICE GRACE, nurse; b. Auburn, Ga., Feb. 25, 1938; d. Erby Ralph and Jewell Grace (Maughon) Clack; student LaGrange Coll., 1955-57; B.S.N., Emory U., 1960; M.Sc., Rutgers U., 1962; m. Joseph Jerome Geller, Dec. 23, 1973; 1 dau., Elizabeth Joanne. Psychiat. staff nurse dept. psychiatry Emory U., Atlanta, 1960; nurse educator Ill. State Psychiat. Inst., Chgo., 1961; clin. specialist in mental retardation nursing Northville, Mich., 1962; faculty Rutgers U. Coll. Nursing, Newark, 1962-63, U. Mich. Coll. Nursing, Ann Arbor, 1963-64, Rutgers U. Advanced Program in Psychiat. Nursing, 1964-66, Teheran Coll. for Women, Iran, 1967-69; clin. specialist psychiat. nursing Roosevelt Hosp., N.Y.C., 1969-70; faculty, guest lectr. Columbia U., N.Y.C., 1969-70; supr. Dept. Psychiat. Nursing, Mt. Sinai Hosp., N.Y.C., 1970-72; pvt. practice psychotherapy, N.Y.C., 1972-77, Ridgewood, N.J., 1977—; faculty, curriculum coordinator in psychiat. nursing William Alanson White Inst. Psychiatry, Psychoanalysis and Psychology, N.Y.C., 1974-84; mem. U.S. del. of Community and Mental Health Nurses to People's Republic of China, 1983. Recipient 10th Anniversary award Outstanding Clin. Specialist in psychiat.-mental health nursing in N.J., Soc. Cert. Clin. Specialists, 1982. Fed. Govt. grantee as career tchr. in psychiat. nursing, Rutgers U., 1962-63; cert. psychiat. nurse and clin. specialist, N.J., N.Y. Mem. Am. Nurses Assn. (various certs.), N.J. State Nurses Assn., Soc. Cert. Clin. Specialists in Psychiat. Nursing, Council Specialists in Psychiat. Mental Health Nursing, Am. Group Psychotherapy Assn., Am. Assn. Mental Deficiency, World Fedn. Mental Health, AAAS, Friends of the Hermitage, LWV, Soc. of Valley Hosp. of Ridgewood, AMA Aux., Bergen County Med. Soc. Aux., Sigma Theta Tau. Club: Coll. Contbr. articles to profl. jours.; editorial bd. Perspectives in Psychiatric Care, 1971-74, 78-84; author: (with Anita Marie Werner) Instruments for Study of Nurse-Patient Interaction, 1964. Address: 159 Fairmount Rd Ridgewood NJ 07450

GELLER, LINDA BERGER, software development corporation executive, financial executive; b. Bklyn., June 10, 1944; d. Nathan and Sylvia (Dombush) Berger; m. Richard Morton Geller, Sept. 4, 1966; children: Lisa, Deborah, Naomi. Student N.Y. U., 1962-64, New Sch. Social Research, 1964-65; BS, SUNY-Old Westbury, 1977; MA, N.Y. Inst. Tech., 1983; cert. advanced bus. mgmt. SUNY. Cert. tchr. N.Y. Bus. mgr. Tri-Tech., West Babylon, N.Y., 1967-72, treas., chief fin. officer, 1972-81, dir., 1981—; pres., chief exec. officer Am. Software Devel. Corp., West Babylon, 1981—; dir. Babylon Blueprint, Tri-Tech. Chairperson Long Island Div. Israel Bonds, Hicksville, N.Y., 1984; v.p. Oyster Bay Jewish Ctr., N.Y., 1980; trustee Wantagh Jewish Ctr., N.Y., 1970-76; chairperson Parents Assn. Solomon Schechter, Jericho, N.Y., 1976-80. Ednl. grantee L.I. Regional Edn. Ctr. Econ. Devel., 1985. Mem. Women Econ. Devels. L.I. (bd. dirs. 1988—), Nat. Assn. Women Bus. Owners (founder Long Island chpt. 1985, officer 1985-88). Republican. Avocations: skiing, music, choir member. Office: Am Software Devel Corp 11 Farmingdale Rd West Babylon NY 11704

GELLER, MARCIA LYNN, advertising executive; b. Paterson, N.J., Jan. 6, 1961; d. Leslie Melvin and Phyllis Eileen (Fisher) G. BA in Communications cum laude, U. Pa., 1983. Asst. media planner Wunderman, Ricotta & Kline, N.Y.C., 1984-85, media planner, 1985-86; sr. media planner McCann Direct, N.Y.C., 1986, media supr, 1986—. Active Vol. Services for Children, N.Y.C., 1986—. Office: McCann Direct 485 Lexington Ave New York NY 10017

GELLER, MARGARET JOAN, astrophysicist; b. Ithaca, N.Y., Dec. 8, 1947; d. Seymour and Sarah (Levine) Geller. A.B., U. Calif.-Berkeley, 1970; M.A., Princeton U., 1972, Ph.D., 1975. Research fellow Center for Astrophysics, Cambridge, Mass., 1974-78; research assoc. Harvard Coll. Obs., Cambridge, 1978-80; sr. vis. fellow Inst. of Astronomy, Cambridge, Eng., 1978-82; asst. prof. Harvard U., 1980-83; astrophysicist Smithsonian Astrophys. Obs., Cambridge, 1983—. Contbr. articles to profl. jours. NSF fellow, 1970-73. Mem. Am. Astron. Soc. (councillor), Assoc. Univs. for Research in Astronomy (dir-at-large), AAAS, Internat. Astron. Union. Office: Ctr for Astrophysics 60 Garden St Cambridge MA 02138

GELLERT, GEORGIA MARRS, public relations executive; b. Denver, Oct. 8, 1917; d. William Middelton and Blanche (Boak) Marrs; student U. Denver, 1936-37; m. Winfield Turrell Barber, Jan. 18, 1941 (dec. May 1948); m. 2d, Nathan Henry Gellert, Mar. 12, 1954 (dec. Nov. 1959); m. 3d, James Kedzie Penfield, May 19, 1978. Soc. editor Denver Post, 1937-41; tech. writer, editor Consol. Vultee Aircraft, USN Radio and Sound Lab., San Diego, 1944-46; mgr. box office Central City Opera House Assn., Denver, 1948; soc. editor Denver Post, 1949-51; publicity dir. N.A.M., San Francisco, 1951-54; asst. exhibits dir. Seattle Worlds Fair, 1960-62; pub. relations dir. Seattle Center, 1962-64; free lance pub. relations, Seattle, 1964—; dir. Pacific Search Press, 1977-87. Trustee Seattle Symphony Orch., 1960—, sec. bd., 1964-65, v.p., mem. exec. com., 1973-76, 79-83; dir. Allied Arts of Seattle, 1960—, treas., 1966-68; dir. Pottery N.W., Seattle, 1966-68; trustee Seattle Childrens Home, 1954-61, pres., 1959-61; trustee Gov's. Mansion Found., 1972-88, mem. exec. com., 1975-80; trustee Seattle Ctr. Found., 1984—. Mem. Women in Communications, English-Speaking Union (dir. Seattle br. 1976—), Pi Beta Phi. Episcopalian. Clubs: Denver Womans Press, Seattle Tennis, Washington Athletic. Home: 1232 38th Ave E Seattle WA 98112 Office: 1232 38th Ave E Seattle WA 98112

GELMAN, ELAINE EDITH, nurse; b. Bklyn., Feb. 16, 1927; d. Michael Levi and Shirley (Drezner) Rodkinson; m. David Graham Gelman, Apr. 6, 1952; children: Eric, Andrew, Amy. BS, CUNY, Queens, 1946; RN, NYU, 1948. Cert. pediatric nurse practitioner, N.Y., 1977. Operating room staff, supr. Queens Gen. Hosp., Bellevue, Beth-El Hosp., N.Y.C., 1948-61; labor and delivery room staff, supr. Georgetown Hosp., Washington, 1962-66; pub. health nurse N.Y.C. Dept. Pub. Health, 1966-72; pediatric nurse practitioner child and youth program Roosevelt Hosp., N.Y.C., 1972-82; pvt. practice N.Y.C., 1982—. Mem. Dem. County Com., N.Y.C., 1984—. Fellow Nat. Assn. Pediatric Nurses Practitioners (legis. chmn. 1986-88), Coalition of Nurse Practitioners, Inc. (pres. 1984-85, 87-88). Jewish. Home: 229 W 78th St New York NY 10024 Office: Pediatric Practice 241 Central Park West New York NY 10024

GELNZINSKI, MARY FRANCES, educational adminstrator; b. Winona, Minn., July 20, 1934; d. Frank Dominic and Frances Hattie (Weir) G. BA, Coll. of St. Teresa, 1962; postgrad., U. Rennes, France, 1963, U. Wis., 1967-72; MA, Cath. U., 1981. Tchr. secondary schs., coll., Minn., Wis., 1958-72; research assoc. Nat. Cath. Edn. Assoc., Washington, 1972-79; program dir. Council of Ind. Colls., Washington, 1979—, cons., 1981—. Recipient NDEA fellowship U.S. Dept. Edn., 1962, 63, 64; named Outstanding Alumna Coll. St. Teresa, 1986. Mem. Women Adminstrs. in Higher Edn. (steering com. 1983-85), Nat. Assn. Female Execs., Am. Assn. Higher Edn. Office: Council Ind Colls One Dupont Circle Suite 320 Washington DC 20036

GELORMINO, JOAN ANN, educator; b. Torrington, Conn., Jan. 3, 1939; d. Erminio and Jennie Rose Gelormino; B.S., Western Conn. State Coll., Danbury, 1960; M.S., U. Hartford, 1966; Ed.D., Nova U., Ft. Lauderdale, Fla., 1975. Tchr., Conn., 1960-68, tchr., dir., resource tchr. Early Childhood Learning Center, adj. faculty U. Hartford, 1969-71; dir. Early Childhood Program Univ. Sch., Nova U., 1971—, assoc. dir. Sch. Center, 1973—; cons. Early Childhood Program, Waterbury, West Hartford, Farmington, Conn., Long Beach, N.Y., Half Hollow, N.Y., Merrick, N.Y., Learning Inst. N.C.; cons. migrant edn., Fla. Seminole Pre-Sch. Programs, Broward County, Fla., 1970-75; bd. dirs., v.p. United Way Child Care Centers, Broward County, 1975—, pres., 1976-78. Mem. Broward County Environ. Control Bd., 1979-80; pres. Kids in Distress, 1987-88. Mem. Nat. Assn. for Edn. Young Children, Assn. for Childhood Edn. Internat., Soc. for Research Child Devel., Fla. Assn. for Children Under Six (conf. chmn. Hollywood 1980) Author: Pre-Number and Mathematic Skill Sequence With Activities, 1969; Constructing Games for Early Childhood Classrooms, 1974; Transactional Analysis For Parents and Teachers of Young Children, 1975. Home: 9800 SW 4th St Fort Lauderdale FL 33324 Office: 7500 SW 36th St Fort Lauderdale FL 33314

GELSINGER-BROWN, LINDA MAE, cardiac data systems research specialist; b. Robesonia, Pa., Jan. 8, 1950; d. Clarence Daniel and Esther (Forry) Gelsinger; m. Richard A. Brown, Aug. 12, 1973. A, Pa. Jr. Coll. of Med. Arts, 1969; student, Ea. Coll., St. Davids, Pa., 1969-70; BA in Social Studies and Biology, St. Joseph's U., Phila., 1975. Supr. cardivascular research lab. Lankenau Hosp., Phila., 1970-76; sales rep. Med. Monitors, Inc., Wyncote, Pa., 1976-77, Data Med., Inc., Wynnewood, Pa., 1977-81; systems specialist Cardiac Data Corp., Inc., Bloomfield, Conn., 1980-81; mktg. rep. Cardio Data Systems, Haddonfield, N.J., 1981-82, nat. sales mgr., 1982-86, sr. research specialist, 1987-88; sr. clin. scientist Wyeth-Ayerst Research, Radnor, Pa., 1988—. Singer Kol Simcha Choral, Phila., 1973—, Sweet Adelines Barbershop chorus, 1974. Mem. Am. Soc. Profl. and Exec. Women, Am. Mgmt. Assn., Am. Mktg. Assn., Assocs. Clin. Pharmacology, Nat. Assn. Female Execs., Sigma Eta Chi. Republican. Jewish. Home: Box 1036 RD #2 Robesonia PA 19551 Office: Wyeth-Ayerst Research 145 King of Prussia Rd Radnor PA 19087

GELSINON, ELIZABETH SIMONE, account executive; b. Bklyn., Mar. 3, 1956; d. Angelo Anthony and Josephine (Masiello) Simone; m. John Edward Gelsinon, Apr. 22, 1983; 1 child, Jessica Kate. BS, Quinnipiac Coll., 1977. Credit analyst Dun & Bradstreet, N.Y.C., 1978-79, mgr. clerical systems, 1979-81, mgr. new product devel., 1981-83; mktg. support mgr. Dun & Bradstreet, Murray Hill, N.J., 1983-84; account rep. Dun & Bradstreet, N.Y.C., 1984-87, sr. account rep., 1987; systems analyst Dun & Bradstreet Info. Systems, Berkeley Heights, N.J., 1987—. Office: Dun & Bradstreet 100 Locust Ave Berkeley Heights NJ 07922

GEMMEL, MELISSA OAKES, data processing executive; b. Corning, N.Y., Oct. 26, 1951; d. Robert Lee and A. Betty (Bronson) Oakes; m. Stephen G. Gemmel, Nov. 20, 1982; children: Darius, Marlea. BA in Math., Keuka Coll., 1977. System analyst Tenneco Gas Co., Houston, 1977-80; cons. engr. Corning (N.Y.) Glass Works, 1980-81; sr. systems analyst Scientific Calculations, Fishers, N.Y., 1981-84; sr. sales engr. Hartman Material Handling, Victor, N.Y., 1984-85; pres., chief exec. officer Spectrum Software Systems, Stanley, N.Y., 1985—; adj. faculty Corning Community Coll., 1980-81. Vice chair Citizens Responsible Waste Mgmt., Geneva, N.Y. 1987; mem. N.Y. St. Pub. Info. Research Group, N.Y.C. 1987. Mem. Rochester C. of C. Democrat. Mem. Soc. Friends. Office: Spectrum Software Systems Inc 4496 Old Mill Rd Stanley NY 14561

GENCARELLI, JANE B., state legislator; b. Fall River, Mass., Apr. 28, 1929; d. Clement Stanley and Jane (Malone) Bradshaw; m. Francis Gencarelli, 1953; children: David, Ann Gencarelli Cruso, Lisa Jane, Francesca Gencarelli Wish. Grad. New Eng. Conservatory of Music, Boston. Tchr. music Town of Westerly, 1956-76, Southeastern Mass. U., 1967-75; vice chmn. Westerly Sch. Com., 1981-83; mem. R.I. State Senate from Dist. 26, 1983—. Named Woman of Yr., Profl. Women's Club, 1983, Outstanding Profl. Woman, AAUW, 1985. Mem. Mu Phi Epsilon. Club: New England Conservatory. Roman Catholic. Republican. Office: State Senate Office State Capitol Providence RI 02903 Address: 18 Timothy Dr Westerly RI 02891

GENGENBACH, MARIANNE S., chiropractic educator; b. West Chester, Pa., Oct. 24, 1956; d. Siegfried K. and Helga (Hunger) Schmidt-Gengenbach. BA cum laude, Washington U., St. Louis, 1978; D of Chiropractic Medicine, Logan Coll. Chiropractic, 1983. Diplomate Nat. Bd. Chiropractic Examiners; cert. chiropractic sports physician, 1987. Clinic dir. Logan Coll. Chiropractic, Chesterfield, Mo., 1983-85, instr. pediatrics, 1983—, instr. athletic injuries, 1984—, module edn. coordinator, 1984-85, postgrad. instr., 1986, dir. clin. edn., 1986—; gen. practice chiropractic medicine, St. Louis, 1983—. Mem. Am. Chiropractic Assn. (council on sports injuries and physical fitness, mem. Acad. Chiropractic Sports Physicians 1986, pres. 1988, cert.), Found. for Chiropractic Edn. and Research, Women's Sports Found., Mo. State Chiropractic Assn., Logan Coll. Alumni Assn. Democrat. Mem. Ethical Soc. Avocations: soccer; running. Office: Logan Coll Chiropractic 1851 Schoettler Rd Chesterfield MO 63006-1065

GENIUS, JEANNETTE MORSE (MRS. HUGH FERGUSON MCKEAN), artist; b. Chgo.; d. Richard Millard and Elizabeth (Morse) G.; m. Hugh Ferguson McKean, June 28, 1945. Student, Dana Hall, 1926-27, Pine Manor, 1927-28, 28-29; DFA, Rollins Coll., 1962. Pres. Winter Park (Fla.) Land Co., 1930—; owner, mgr. Ctr. St. Gallery, Winter Park, 1947—; mem. adminstrv. bd. Winter Park office Sun Bank, N.A.; dir. Morse Mus. Am. Art. One-woman shows include Maitland (Fla.) Research Studio, 1951, Contemporary Arts Gallery, N.Y.C., 1953, 56, 64, Pen and Brush Club, N.Y.C., 1959, Morse Mus. Am. Art, Winter Park, 1968, Fla. Fedn. Art, DeBary, 1970, Art Ctr., Daytona Beach, Fla., 1971, Longboat Key (Fla.) Art Ctr., 1974, James Hunt Barker Galleries, Palm Beach, Fla., 1975-78, Fla. So. Coll., 1975; exhibited in group shows at Allied Artists Am., N.Y., Norton Gallery, Palm Beach, Currier Gallery, Manchester, N.H., Delgado Mus., New Orleans, Contemporary Arts Gallery, Butler Art Inst., Youngstown, Ohio, Pioneer Gallery, Stockton, Calif., Am. Embassy Gallery, Athens, Greece, Kunst Mus., Berne, Switzerland, Royal Scottish Acad. Galleries, Edinburgh, Royal Birmingham So. Artists, Eng., Museo des Bellas Arts, Argentine, U. Cen. Fla., Orlando, 1976, Copley Soc., Boston, 1979, many others; represented in permanent collections at Ga. Mus. Art, Columbus Mus. Arts and Crafts, many pvt. collections. Trustee emeritus Rollins Coll.; mem. Jr. League, N.Y.C. Decorated Order of Hosp. St. John of Jerusalem; recipient 2d prize Soc. Four Arts, 1950, Algernon Sydney Sullivan medallion, 1954, Cervantes medal Hispanic Inst. Fla., 1952, Citation of Merit Holiday Mag., 1968, Fla. Gov.'s award for Arts, 1975, John Young award, 1979; Outstanding Citizen of Yr. award Winter Park C. of C., 1987; numerous other awards. Mem. Am. Soc. Interior Designers, Nat. Assn. Women Artists (hon. v.p.), Fla. Fedn. Arts (1st prize award 1948), Fla. Artists Group, N.H. Art Assn., Nat. Arts Club, Artists Equity, Pen and Brush Club (2d prize award 1953, 1st prize award 1959, 3d prize award 1962). Clubs: Women's Athletic (Chgo.), Women's (Winter Park), Rosalind (Orlando), Cosmopolitan (N.Y.C.), Wonalancet (N.H.). Address: PO Box 40 Winter Park FL 32790

GENOVA, DIANE MELISANO, lawyer; b. Yonkers, N.Y., Aug. 8, 1948; d. Joseph Louis and Ines (Fiumana) Melisano; m. Clyde Barry Schechter, Dec. 29, 1968 (div. Aug. 1981); m. Joseph Steven Genova, Jan. 15, 1983; 1 child, Anthony Robert. AB, Barnard Coll., 1970; postgrad. Harvard U., 1970-71; J.D., Columbia U., 1975. Assoc., Milbank, Tweed, Hadley & McCloy, N.Y.C., 1975-80, Tung, Drabkin & Boynton, N.Y.C., 1980-81; v.p., asst. resident counsel Morgan Guaranty Trust Co. N.Y., N.Y.C., 1981—. Harlan Fiske Stone scholar, 1972-75. Mem. Assn. Bar City N.Y., N.Y. State Bar Assn., ABA. Roman Catholic. Club: Montauk (Bklyn.). Office: Morgan Guaranty Trust Co 23 Wall St New York NY 10015

GENOVESE, ROSE, hotel executive; b. Queens, N.Y., Oct. 7, 1960; d. Paul Robert and Marlene Marie (Zampardi) G. AA in Applied Sci., Nassau Community Coll., Garden City, N.Y., 1980. Sales adminstr. Grand Hyatt, N.Y.C., 1980-83, sales mgr., 1983-85; dir. sales Halloran House, N.Y.C., 1985-88, dir. sales and mktg., 1988—. Mem. Hotel Sales and Mktg. Assn. (bd. dirs.). Office: Halloran House 525 Lexington Ave New York NY 10017

GENS, HELEN DIANE, software company executive; b. Boston, May 15, 1934; d. Julius and Sarah Leah (Lipman) Pransky; m. Richard H. Gens, June 10, 1952; children: William E., Sara Gens Birenbaum, Julie Gens Rich, James A., Cory J., Noah B. Cert. paralegal, Mt. Ida Jr. Coll., 1980. Treas., dir. Med. Services Corp. Am., Newton, Mass., 1963-71; pres., med. cons. Medicons, Inc., Boston, 1971-77; exec. v.p. Consulteo, Inc., Newton, 1977-83; pres. Substantive Software, Inc., Manchester, N.H., 1983-85, HDG Software, Inc., Sherborn, Mass., 1985—; cons. Concord Healthcare Corp., Nashville, 1986-87, Integrated Health Services, Cockeysville, Md., 1986-87. Author, editor (software) Legal Ease, 1986, Legal Ease Real Estate, 1986, Legal Ease Corporate, 1986. Mem. town meeting Town of Sherborn, 1983—. Mem. Nat. Office Products Assn., Artificial Intelligence Assn., Nat. Assn. for Female Execs. Republican. Jewish. Home and Office: 381 Old Jail Ln Barnstable MA 02630

GENTILIN, KAREN EILEEN, advertising professional; b. Kew Gardens, N.Y., Aug. 5, 1963; d. Garth and Mary L. (Vaughan) G. BA, Adelphi U., 1983-85. Mgr. Village Luggage, Rockville Center, N.Y., 1980-85; acct. group asst. J.P. Lohman Comml. Real Estate Advt., N.Y.C., 1985-86; real estate salesperson H.K. Benjamin Realty, Woodside, N.Y., 1985-86; acct. coordinator Young & Rubicam, N.Y.C., 1986—. Mem. Nat. Assn. Female Execs., Delta Mu Delta. Office: Young & Rubicam 285 Madison Ave New York NY 10017

GENTLE, CARLA ALLEGRA, human resources manager, consultant; b. Colorado Springs, Colo., Feb. 27, 1955; d. John Edward and Rebecca (Lijavetsky) Gentle. B.A., Western State Coll., 1977; postgrad. U. Colo., 1979-81. Personnel asst. Occidental Fire and Casualty, Englewood, Colo., 1980-81; sr. employment specialist Petroleum Info. Corp., Littleton, Colo., 1981-85; human resources generalist Davis Graham & Stubbs, Denver, 1985-86; human resources mgr. St. Paul Cos., Aurora, Colo., 1987—; pvt. practice cons., Denver, 1983—. Vice chmn. Young Republicans, Jefferson County, Colo., 1983; mem. Rep. Women's Task Force, 1983; performing mem. Diane Page Jazz Dancers, 1985—. Western State Coll. athletic scholar, 1976. Mem. Colo. Soc. Personnel Adminstrs., Am. Soc. Personnel Adminstrs., Internat. Assn. Personnel Women, Women's Edn. Service Assn. Republican. Home: 6550 E Mississippi #7 Denver CO 80224 Office: 12250 E Iliff #400 Aurora CO 80014

GENTLEMAN, JULIA B., state senator; b. Des Moines, Aug. 24, 1931; d. John and Marguerite Brooks; B.S., Northwestern U., 1953; m. Gregor Gentleman, 1954; children: Karen L., Marcia M., Katherine B., J. Brooks, MacGregor III. Formerly mem. Iowa Ho. of Reps., 1975-78; mem Iowa Senate, 1979—. Republican. Office: Iowa State House Des Moines IA 50319 *

GENTRY, JILL JONES, dentist; b. Logansport, Ind., Sept. 30, 1953; d. W. Max and Patricia Maxine (Harner) Jones; m. Philip Arthur Gentry, July 24, 1982; 1 child, Peter Daniel. BS, Purdue U., 1975, MS, 1977; DDS, Ind. Sch. Dentistry, 1982. Acad. advisor Purdue U., West Lafayette, Ind., 1976-78; gen. practice dentistry VA Hosp., Indpls., 1983—; staff dentist Millers Merry Manor Nursing Home, Logansport, 1983-86. Mem. Y-Bd., Cass County Family YMCA, Logansport, 1985; mem. adminstrn. bd., trustee 1st United Meth. Ch., Logansport, 1984—. Mem. ADA, Am. Gen. Dentistry, Ind. Dental Assn., Kappa Kappa Kappa. Republican. Home: 3011 Greenhills Dr Logansport IN 46947 Office: 1107 E Broadway PO Box 76 Logansport IN 46947

GENTRY, KATHRYN JENNIFER, property management executive; b. Vancouver, British Columbia, Can., July 13, 1950; d. Carl P. and Joan Mary (Davenport) Johnson; m. G. Allen Gentry, Sept. 18, 1971 (div. 1984); 1 child, Michael. B in Edn., U. British Columbia, 1972. Elem. tchr. West Vancouver Sch. Dist., British Columbia, 1972-74, Abbotsford Sch. Dist., British Columbia, 1974-76; real estate agt. Colonial Realty, Ferndale, Wash., 1978; resident mgr. Trupp-McGinty Realty, St. Simons Island, Ga., 1983-85, vacation rental mgr., 1985-86; v.p. mktg. THE Mgmt. Co., St. Simons Island, 1986-87; v.p, gen. mgr. THE Mgmt. Co., St. Simons Island, Ga., 1987—, The Mng. Broker, St. Simons Island, 1987—; mng. broker The Mgmt. Co., St. Simons Island, Ga., 1987—. Mem. Ga. Hosp. and Tourism Assn. (vice chmn. local chpt. St. Simons Island 1987-88), Women's Council of Realtors, Colonial Coast Travel Assn. (chmn. Pride Campaign 1986, v.p. representing Glynn County 1987—), Brunswick, Glynn County Tourist and Conv. Council, Walmar Grove Homeowners Assn. (pres. 1985-87, treas. 1987—). Episcopalian. Office: The Management Co 196 Retreat Village PO Box 1 Saint Simons Is GA 31522

GENTRY, WANDA MARKHAM, automotive executive; b. Franklin, Ky., Oct. 7, 1939; d. Thomas Harris and Edith Nell (Dinwiddie) Markham; student Bowling Green Bus. U., 1957-58; m. William Henry Gentry, Dec. 30, 1961; children—Jonathan Markham, Laura Leigh. Sec. to gen. mgr. N.H. Granite State Ins. Co., Jacksonville, Fla., 1958-60; sec. Ky. State Hwy. Dept., 1960-63; sec. to dir. of nurses East Ridge Community Hosp., Chattanooga, 1974, adminstrv. asst., 1974-76; adminstrv. asst. to pres. and chmn. bd. Tenn. Natural Resources Inc., and Nashville Gas Co., 1976-86; exec. asst. Beaman Automotive Group, 1986—. Mem. Exec. Women Internat. (dir. Nashville chpt. 1978-82), Dream Makers. Republican. Baptist. Club: Cumberland. Home: 4502 Franklin Rd Nashville TN 37204 Office: 814 Church St Nashville TN 37203

GENYK, RUTH BEL, psychotherapist; b. Los Angeles, Apr. 5, 1955; d. John Douglas Bel and Ella Adiline (Lips) Medeiros; m. Carl J. Hattermann, June 11, 1977 (div. Dec. 1979); m. Edward A. Genyk, Aug. 8, 1983; children: Steven, Timothy, Devlon, Suzanne. Student, U. Copenhagen, 1975; BA, BSW, Whittier Coll., 1977; MA, U. Detroit, 1979; MSW, U. Mich., 1987. Social worker, community liaison Family Service, Whittier, Calif., 1976-77; social worker Children's Group Home, Detroit, 1977, Family Group Homes, Ann Arbor, Mich., 1977; probation officer Dept. Corrections, Detroit, 1978-86, cons., 1977-79; psychotherapist, cons., liaison Cath. Social Services, Jackson, Mich., 1986—. Mem. Jr. League. Mem. Am. Corrections Assn., Mich. Corrections Assn., Nat. Assn. Social Workers. Democrat. Roman Catholic. Office: Wildwood Franchise 505 Wildwood Jackson MI 49201

GENZEL, RHONA, English langauge educator; b. N.Y.C., Feb. 15, 1943; d. Raymond and Gertrude (Prussak) Beldegreen; m. George Genzel, Nov. 19, 1942; children: Robert, Brette. BA, CUNY, 1964; postgrad., NYU, 1964-68; MA, Syracuse U., 1988. Cert. English tchr., N.Y.; cert. Russian tchr., N.Y. Tchr. N.Y.C. Bd. Edn., 1964-68; trainer Xerox Corp. Webster, N.Y., 1969-74; educator Rochester (N.Y.) City Sch. Dist., 1974-79; instr. Rochester Inst. Technology, 1979-81, supr. ESL program, asst. prof., 1982-84, dir. ESL, assoc. prof., 1985-88, prof., 1988—, chair English Lang. Ctr., 1986—; asst. prof. U. Rochester, 1978; pres. Protocol Internat., 1985—. Author: Culturally Speaking, 1986. Coordinator of Dem. campaigns, Rochester, 1980-82. Mem. AAUW (Woman of Yr. Achievement award 1987), N.Y. State Tchrs. of English to Speakers of Other Language (chair 1986—, asst. chair 1985-86), Rochester Inst. Technology Women's Network (pres. 1986-88), Soc. for Interculutral Edn. and Tng. Resources, Nat. Assn. Fgn. Student Affairs, N.Y. State Assn. Fgn. Language Tchrs. Democrat. Office: Rochester Inst Technology One Lomb Meml Dr Rochester NY 14623-0887

GEOGHEGAN, PATRICIA, lawyer; b. Bayonne, N.J., Sept. 9, 1947; d. Frank and Rita (Mihok) G. BA, Mich. State U., 1969; MA, Yale U., 1972, JD, 1974; LLM, NYU, 1982. Bar: N.Y. 1975. Assoc. Cravath, Swaine & Moore, N.Y.C., 1974-82, ptnr., 1982—. Mem. ABA, N.Y. State Bar Assn., Assn. of Bar of City of N.Y. Office: Cravath Swaine & Moore One Chase Manhattan Plaza New York NY 10005

GEO-KARIS, ADELINE JAY, state legislator; b. Tegeas, Greece, Mar. 29, 1918; student Northwestern U., Mt. Holyoke Coll.; LLB, DePaul U. Admitted to Ill. bar; founder Adeline J. Geo-Karis and Assos., Zion, Ill.; former mcpl., legis. atty. Mundelein, Ill., Vernon Hills, Ill., Libertyville (Ill.) Twp., Long Grove (Ill.) Sch. Dist.; justice of peace; former asst. state's atty.; mem. Ill. Ho. of Reps., 1973-79; mem. Ill. Senate, 1979—, minority spokeswoman jud. com. Served to lt. comdr. USNR.; comdr. Res. ret. Recipient Americanism medal DAR; named Woman of Yr. Daus. of Penelope, Outstanding Legislator Ill. Fedn. Ind. Colls. and Univs., 1975-78, Legis. award Ill. Assn. Park Dists., 1976. Sponsor Guilty but Mentally Ill Law. Office: 2610 Sheridan Rd Suite 217 Zion IL 60099 *

GEONIE, PAULA RUBIN, crime prevention association executive; b. Bklyn., Apr. 17, 1951; d. Samuel and Rhoda (Jablowitz) Rubin; children—Michael, Evan; m. Robert Geonie. Student Hofstra U. Pres., founder Let's Increase and Insure Security in our Neighborhoods, Inc., New Hyde Park, N.Y., 1982—; co-founder L.I. Crime Victims Services Task Force, Garden City, N.Y., 1986. Co-author: Playing It Safe, 1985. Chmn. health and safety Roslyn Country Club Civic Assn., Roslyn Heights, N.Y., 1982—. Recipient Pres.'s Vol. Action award for Pub. Safety, Nat. Vol. and Action Coms., Washington, 1986, Eleanor Rossevelt award, N.Y. State, 1987; Merit award Nat. Assn. Chiefs of Police, 1986, Div. Criminal Justice Services, 1987; Nat. Crime Prevention award, 1987. Mem. Nat. Orgn. for Victim's Assistance, Internat. Soc. Crime Prevention Practioners, Families Aware of Childhood Traumas, L.I. Assn. Crime Prevention Officers, Families Aware of Childhood Traumas. Avocations: drawing; painting; photography; tennis. Office: Liaison Inc Herricks Community Ctr 999 Herricks Rd New Hyde Park NY 11040

GEORGE, DEBRA ANNE, accountant; b. Coral Gables, Fla., Dec. 2, 1958; d. William George (stepfather) and Mildred Elizabeth (Wells) Preston. AA, Daytona Beach (Fla.) Community Coll., 1977; BS in Acctg., Fla. So. Coll., 1980. CPA, Fla. Sr. staff acct. Geller, Ragans, James, Oppenheimer & Creel, CPA's, Orlando, Fla., 1980-83; controller Br. Properties, Inc., Ocala, Fla., 1983-88; acctg. supr. Disney Devel. Co., Orlando, Fla., 1988—. Bd. dirs., treas., mem. various coms. Marion County United Way, Ocala, 1984-88. Named Outstanding Young Woman of Am., 1985. Mem. Am. Inst. CPA's, Fla. Inst. CPA's (local chpt. treas. 1985-86, state bd. govs. 1986—, v.p. 1986-87, pres. 1987-88), Altrusa (treas. Ocala club 1986-87), Phi Chi Theta, Kappa Delta. Democrat. Baptist. Home: 3437 Bocage Dr #517 Orlando FL 32812 Office: Disney Devel Co 8801 Vistana Centre Dr Suite 200 Orlando FL 32821

GEORGE, IDA RUSH, management consultant; b. Columbia, S.C., Apr. 17, 1942; d. Paul Daniel and Ida Evelina (Dasher) Rush; m. Samuel Asbury George, Apr. 1, 1961; children: Lisa Renee, Liles Courtney. BA, U. S.C., 1964. Tchr. Lexington County Sch. Dist. #5, Irmo, 1964-67, 68-73, Lexington (S.C.) County Sch. Dist. #1, 1975-79; tng. specialist S.C. Nat. Bank, Columbia, 1979-82; pres. Organizational Devel., Inc., Montgomery, Ala., 1982—; cons. ACTION, Washington, 1986—, U. Ala., Birmingham, 1986—, Ala. Dept. Edn., Montgomery, 1986—, Ala. Office of Voluntary Citizen Participation, Montgomery, 1983—. Author: Beyond Promises, 1983, You Can Teach Others, 1985. Mem. adv. council Ala. Assembly on Volunteerism, 1985—; com. chairperson United Way Community Council, Montgomery, 1986—; bd. dirs. Landmarks Found, Montgomery, 1984—. Mem. Am. Soc. Tng. and Devel. (v.p. 1983—, past bd. dirs.), Assn. Voluntary Action Scholars, Assn. for Vol. Adminstrn., Vol. Nat. Ctr. (assoc.). Episcopalian. Office: Organizational Devel Inc 3552 Carter Hill Rd Montgomery AL 36111

GEORGE, JOYCE JACKSON, judge; b. Akron, Ohio, May 4, 1936; d. Ray and Verna (Popadich) Jackson; children: Michael Eliot, Michelle Renè. BA, U. Akron, 1962, JD, 1966; postgrad. Nat. Jud. Coll., Reno, 1976, NYU Sch. Law, 1983; LLM, U. Va., 1986; postgrad. U. Va., 1987—. Bar: Ohio 1966, U.S. Dist. Ct. (no. dist.) Ohio 1966, U.S. Ct. Appeals (6th cir.) 1968, U.S. Supreme Ct. 1968. Tchr. Akron Bd. Edn., 1962-66; asst. dir. law City of Akron, 1966-69, pub. utilities advisor, 1969-70, asst. dir. law, 1970-73; sole practice, Akron, 1973-76; referee Akron Mcpl. Ct., 1975, judge, 1976-83; judge 9th Dist. Ct. Appeals, Akron, 1983—; tchr., lectr. Ohio Jud. Coll., Nat. Jud. Coll.; Author: Judicial Opinion Writing Handbook, 1981, 2d edit, 1986; contbr. articles to profl. publs. Recipient Outstanding Woman of Yr. award Akron Bus. and Profl. Women's Club, 1982; Alumni Honor award U. Akron, 1983; named Woman of Yr. in politics and govt. Summit County, Ohio, 1983. Mem. Akron Bar Assn. (lawyers assistance com.), Ohio Bar Assn., Ohio Jud. Conf. and Ohio Jud. Coll. (chair revision project Resource Manual for Judges), Ohio Legal Ctr. Inst., ABA (victims com., criminal justice div.). Office: 9th Dist Ct Appeals 161 S High St Akron OH 44308

GEORGE, LYNELLE EUNICE, purchasing manager; b. Los Angeles, Apr. 13, 1946; children—Kelli Rhondelyn, Damon Scott, Corey Bernard. A.A., W. Los Angeles Coll., 1982; B.A., Calif. State U. Dominguez Hills-Carson, 1985, M in Pub. Adminstrn., 1988; cert. risk mgmt. and ins., 1986. Adminstrv. asst. Los Angeles County/MLK-Drew Med. Ctr., 1978-80; procurement mgr. Los Angeles County/Harbor-UCLA Med. Ctr., Torrance, 1980-82, Los Angeles County/Pub. Health Programs, Los Angeles, 1982-84; fixed asset coordinator Harbor-UCLA Med. Ctr., 1984; procurement specialist Los Angeles County/U. So. Calif. Med. Ctr., Los Angeles, 1984-86; dir. purchasing Los Angeles County Health Services Adminstrns. Pub. Health Programs, 1986—. Corr. fin. sec. Assistance League of Stovall Found., Los Angeles, 1985-86, chmn. escort com., 1984-85, pres., 1988; mem. Los Angeles Pub. Health Programs safety com., 1982-84, forms rev. com., 1982-84, supply com., 1982-84, others; Mem. Nat. Assn. Female Execs. Democrat. Avocations: travel, writing.

GEORGE, MARY SHANNON, state senator; b. Seattle, May 27, 1916; d. William Day and Agnes (Lovejoy) Shannon; B.A. cum laude, U. Wash., 1937; postgrad. U. Mich., 1937, Columbia U., 1938; m. Flave Joseph George; children—Flave Joseph, Karen Van Hook, Christy, Shannon Lowrey. Prodn. asst., asst. news editor Pathe News, N.Y.C., 1938-42; mem. fgn. editions staff Readers Digest, Pleasantville, N.Y., 1942-46; columnist Caracas (Venezuela) Daily Jour., 1953-60; councilwoman City and County of Honolulu, 1969-74; senator State of Hawaii, 1974—, asst. minority leader, 1978-80, minority policy leader, 1983-84, minority floor leader, 1987, minority leader, 1987—, chmn. transp. com., 1981-82; mem. Nat. Air Quality Adv. Bd., 1974-75, Intergovtl. Policy Ady. Com. Trade, 1988—, White House Conf. Drug FreeAm., 1988—. Vice chmn. 1st Hawaii Ethics Commn., 1968; mem. budget com. Aloha United Fund, 1970; co-founder Citizens Com. on Constl. Conv., 1968; vice-chmn. platform com. Republican Nat. Conv., 1976, co-chmn., 1980; bd. dirs. Hawaii Planned Parenthood, 1970-72, 79-86, Hawaii Med. Services Assn., 1972-86; mem. adv. bd. Hawaii chpt. Mothers Against Drunk Driving, 1984—. Recipient Jewish Men's Club Brotherhood award, 1974; Outstanding Legislator of Yr. award Nat. Rep. Legislators Assn., 1985; named Woman of Yr., Honolulu Press Club, 1969, Hawaii Fedn. Bus. and Profl. Women, 1970; Citizen of Yr., Hawaii Fed. Exec. Bd., 1973, 76. Mem. LWV (pres. Honolulu 1966-68), Mensa, Phi Beta Kappa, Kappa Alpha Theta. Episcopalian. Author: A Is for Abrazo, 1961. Home: 782-G N Kalaheo Ave Kailua HI 96734 Office: Hawaii State Capitol Honolulu HI 96813

GEORGE-PERRY, SHARON JUANITA, management consultant; b. Modesto, Calif., Sept. 21, 1938; d. H. Edward and Beatrice C. (Wright) Melin; m. John L. George, Apr. 27, 1956 (div. 1974); children: Terri A., Tami L., Timothy J., Tobin E.; m. William E. Perry Jr., Apr. 19, 1980. MBA in Mgmt., 1984. Cert. elem. edn., Calif., elem., secondary counseling, Tex. Tchr. elem. Hayward (Calif) Unified Sch. Dist., 1965-73; tchr. diagnostics, group therapist Tex. Youth Council, Brownwood, 1974-75; assoc. dir. New Directions Psychiat. Half Way House, Abilene, Tex., 1975-77; exec. dir. Mental Health Assn., Abilene, 1977-78, San Francisco, 1979-84; assoc. ptnr. Perry Assoc. Mgmt. Cons., San Francisco, 1983—; exec. dir., cons. Vision of Am. At Peace, Berkeley, Calif., 1984, Oakes Childrens Ctr., San Francisco, 1985—; mktg. dir. Mental Health Providers of Calif., 1988—; vis. lectr. McMurry Coll., Abilene, 1976-78; cons. Dyess AFB, Abilene, 1976-78, Abilene Youth Ctr., 1976-78; speaker in field, 1979—. Chair Commn. on Status of Women of Marin County, Calif., 1985—; mem. adv. com. Displaced Homemaker Project, Sacramento, 1985—; founder, exec. dir. Children's Mental Health Policy Bd., 1984—; pres. Artisans Gallery, Mill Valley, Calif., 1984—. Grantee Fed. Dept. Justice, Brownwood, 1975, pvt. community founds., Calif., 1979-87. Mem. Council of Calif. Mental Health Contractors, Am. Soc. Profl. Exec. Women, Nat. Assn. Female Execs., Children's Mental Health Policy Bd. (1984—). Avocations: travel, gourmet cooking, hiking, public speaking. Home and Office: 317 Morning Sun Ave Mill Valley CA 94941

GEORGESON, ELISABETH ANN, insurance agency executive; b. Seattle, May 28, 1955; d. Sverre Johannes and Mary Elizabeth (Foster) Ludvigsen; m. John Georgeson, Jan. 17, 1950. Technician Indsl. Indemnity, Pasadena, Calif., 1973-76, McKay Wright & Co., Arcadia, Calif., 1976-78; mktg. David Stephens & Co., South Pasadena, Calif., 1978-81; office mgr. El Camino Ins. Agy., Vista, Calif., 1981-86, v.p., 1986—. Mem. Chartered Property Casualty Underwriters, Cert. Profl. Ins. Women, Ins. Ednl. Assn. (instr. 1986-87). Office: El Camino Ins Agy 1365 W Vista Way Vista CA 92083

GEORGOPOULOS, MARIA, architect; b. Moussata, Cefalonia, Greece, Apr. 2, 1949; came to U.S., 1973; d. Vassilios and Joulia Georgopoulos; m. Demetrios Georgopoulos (div. 1974). BArch, Nat. Poly. Sch. Greece, Athens, 1972; MS, Columbia U., 1976. Registered architect, N.Y., Greece. Project mgr. Architects Design Group, N.Y.C., 1976-79, Griswold, Heckel & Kelly, N.Y.C., 1979-80; project dir. Lehman Bros., Kuhn Loeb Inc., N.Y.C., 1980-85; v.p. L.F. Rothschild Inc., N.Y.C., 1985—. Mem. AIA, Am. Women Entrepreneurs, Greek Inst. Architects. Greek Orthodox. Club: Douglaston (N.Y.). Home: 14 Melrose Ln Douglaston NY 11363 Office: L F Rothschild Inc 222 Broadway New York NY 10038

GERAGHTY, LAURA LEE MARIE, state official, consultant; b. St. Paul, Sept. 5, 1944; d. John Charles and Leona Ann (Fahley) G.; m. Richard A. Beens, Aug. 9, 1974; 1 child, Jennifer Lois Beens. BA, Coll. St. Catherine, 1966. Social worker Ramsey County Welfare Dept., St. Paul, 1966-70, vol. coordinator, 1970-75; dir. Minn. Office on Vol. Services, Dept. Adminstrn., St. Paul, 1975—; co-chair Vols. for Minn., 1982-84; mem. community faculty Met. State U., St. Paul, 1980—; chmn. adv. com. MA in Orgnl. Leadership Coll. of St. Catherine, St. Paul, 1985—; mem. Action's Nat. Steering Com., Washington, 1980-81; mem. Human Resources Com. of Pres. Task Force on Pvt. Sector Initiatives, Washington, 1982-83. Chmn., Consumer Action Now, St. Paul, 1971-72; bd. dirs. Coalition to Advocate Pub. Utility Responsibility, Minn., 1972-73; mem. Metro Rate Authority, St. Paul, 1973. Recipient Woman of Achievement award West Suburban C. of C., Mpls., 1983, Good Neighbor award WCCO Ladies, 1983; Pres. Vol. Action award Pres. Reagan, Washington, 1984; Outstanding Achievement award for govt./community devel. St. Paul YWCA, 1985. Mem. Assn. for Vol. Adminstrn. (pres. 1983-85), Minn. Assn. Vol. Dirs., Corp. Volunteerism Council, Coll. of St. Catherine Alumnae Assn. (v.p. 1988—). Roman Catholic. Office: Minn Office on Vol Services Dept Adminstrn 500 Rice St Saint Paul MN 55155

GERARD, BARBARA, educator, visual artist; b. N.Y.C., Apr. 21, 1943; d. Arthur and Edith (Perrone) De Bernarda; BS, NYU, 1963, MA, 1966, postgrad., 1972; profl. diploma, City Coll. of CUNY, 1975; postgrad. Columbia U., 1977-79; m. Marvin Hartenstein, Sept. 18, 1976; 1 son by previous marriage, David Gerard. Graphic designer C. A. Parshall Advt. Agy., N.Y.C., 1962; art tchr. Herman Ridder Jr. High Sch., N.Y.C., 1963-65; free lance designer Sam Muggeo Advt. Inc., N.Y.C., 1965-67; art chmn. Herman Ridder Jr. High Sch., 1967-70; program counselor recruitment and tng. of Spanish-speaking tchrs., N.Y.C. Bd. Edn., 1970-72, program coordinator bilingual pupil services Ctr. for Bilingual Edn., 1972-75, dir. bilingual tchr.-intern program, 1975-79, dir. Ctr. for Dissemination, 1979-81; owner, v.p. George Gerard Assocs., Inc., Port Washington, N.Y., 1981-83; cons. Yeshiva U., Pace U., 1973, Aspiria of N.Y., 1974, Children's TV Workshop - Sesame St., 1975; adj. lectr. CCNY, 1973-74, N.Y.U., 1974-75, Coll. New Rochelle, 1974-75; cons., participant WNBC-TV, 1970, 75, 79; project dir. N.Y.C. Bd. Edn., 1983—. One woman shows: Lincoln Inst. Gallery, N.Y., 1968, Henry Hicks Gallery, Bklyn., 1976, Second Story Spring St. Gallery, N.Y., 1976, Viridian Gallery, N.Y., 1977, 79; exhibited in group shows Loeb Student Center Gallery, N.Y.C., 1962, 63, Riverdale Community Gallery, N.Y., 1965, Environment Gallery, N.Y.C., 1969, Metamorphosis, N.Y., 1970, Concepts II, N.Y.C., 1971, Union Carbide, N.Y., 1972, Lever House, 1973, Westchester Arts Soc., White Plains, N.Y., 1973, Gillary Gallery, Jericho, L.I., 1974, Manhattan Savs. Bank, 1976, Bklyn. Acad. Music, 1976, Pvt. Viewings/The Erlichs, The Colins, 1976, Gallery 91, Bklyn., 1976, Henry Hicks Gallery, Bklyn., 1975, 76, 77, Lincoln Center, Avery Fisher Hall N.Y., 1976, Second Story Spring St. Gallery, 1976, Bergdorf Goodman, White Plains, 1976, First Women's Bank, 1976, 80, Viridian Gallery, 1976, 77, 80, Womanart Gallery, 1976, Norman Kramer Gallery, Danbury, Conn., 1976, Mfrs. Hanover Bank, N.Y., 1977, Guild Hall Mus., East Hampton, N.Y., 1977, 80, Union of Maine Artists, Portland, 1977, Northeastern U., Boston, 1978, Vered Internat. Gallery, East Hampton, 1978, Women in the Arts Gallery, 1979, Rensselaer Inst., Troy, 1979, Marie Pellicone Gallery, 1981, N.Y. Tech. Coll., 1982, Guild Hall Mus., 1983, 84, Gov. of N.Y.-World Trade Ctr., 1985, Marte Previti Gallery, 1986, South Street Gallery, Guild Hall Mus., 1987; represented in permanent collections Mus. Contemporary Crafts, N.Y.C., BBD&O Advt., Inc., N.Y.C.; also pvt. collections. Chmn., Pres.' Task Force on Bilingual Edn., 1972; v.p. Viridian Gallery, 1976-77; bd. dirs. Nat. Assn. Italian-Am. Dirs., 1982; v.p. Italian Bilingual Bicultural Educators Assn., 1982. HEW/Fed. Govt. ESEA Title VII grantee, 1975-79; recipient Nat. Scene Award for Achievement in Arts and Culture, 1979. Mem. NEA, Nat. Assn. Bilingual Edn., N.Y. State Assn. Bilingual Edn., Council Supervisory Adminstrs., NOW, Am. Council for Arts, Coalition of Women Artists Orgn., Assn. of Artist-Run Galleries, Women in the Arts, Advt. Women N.Y., Women Bus. Owners of N.Y. Contbr. articles to profl. jours. Home: 30 Waterside Plaza Apt 29F New York NY 10012 Office: 131 Livingston St Brooklyn NY 11201

GERARD, JEAN BROWARD SHEVLIN, ambassador, lawyer; b. Portland, Oreg., Mar. 9, 1938; d. Edwin Leonard and Ella (Broward) Shevlin; m. James Watson Gerard, June 20, 1959 (dec. 1987); children: James W., Harriet C. AB, Vassar Coll., 1959; JD, Fordham U., 1977; LLD (hon.), U. S.C., 1983. Bar: N.Y. 1978, Fla. 1978, D.C. 1979, U.S. Dist. Ct. (ea. and so. dists.) N.Y. 1978. Atty. Cadawalader, Wickersham & Taft, N.Y.C., 1977-81; ambassador, permanent rep. of U.S. to UNESCO, Paris, 1981-85; U.S. ambassador to Luxembourg, 1985—. Editor: Fordham Internat. Law Forum, 1977. Bd. govs. Women's Nat. Rep. Club, 1967-73, 74-80, pres., 1971-73; hon. del. Rep. Nat. Conv., N.Y.C., 1972; alt. del. 18th Congl. Dist. N.Y., N.Y.C., 1980. Recipient SAR medal, 1970, medal of honor VFW, 1982. Mem. N.Y. County Lawyers Assn., Assn. Bar City of N.Y. Presbyterian. Clubs: Colony; City Midday (N.Y.C.); Capitol Hill (D.C.); Cercle de l'Union Interallièe (Paris); Cercle Munster (Luxembourg). Office: US Ambassador to Luxembourg care US State Dept Washington DC 20520 also: 22 blvd Emmanuel Servais, 2535 Luxembourg Luxembourg

GERARD-SHARP, MONICA FLEUR, communications executive; b. London, Oct. 4, 1951; came to U.S., 1975; d. John Hugh Gerard-Sharp and

Doreen May (Kearney) Dewhurst; m. Ali Edward Wambold, Nov. 21, 1981. BA in Philosophy and Lit. with honors, U. Warwick, Eng., 1973; MBA in Fin., Mktg. and Internat. Bus., Columbia U., 1980. Editor Inst. Chem. Engrs., London, 1973-74; sub-editor TV Times Ltd., London, 1974-75; press officer, editor UN, N.Y.C., 1975-78; bus. mgr. Time-Life Video Time Inc., N.Y.C., 1980-81, mgr. fin. analysis Time-Life Films, 1981, v.p. T.V.I.S., 1982-83, dir. strategy and devel. video group, 1984-85, asst. treas., officer, 1985-87; assoc. pub. Fairchild Pubs., Capital Cities/ABC, N.Y.C., 1987—; cons. UN Bus. Council, N.Y.C., 1979; bd. rep. U.S.A. Network, N.Y.C., 1983-85; bd. dirs. Maga-Link, Communications Bridge. Editor: Everyone's United Nations, 1977; contbg. editor Asia Pacific Forum, 1976-77; contbr. articles to profl. jours. and mags., 1973-78. Bd. dirs. 151-161 Owners Corp., N.Y.C., 1984-85. Bronfman fellow, 1979-80. Mem. Nat. Acad. Cable Programming, Am. Film Inst., Beta Gamma Sigma. Roman Catholic. Home: 161 W 86th St New York NY 10024 Office: Fairchild Pubs 7 E 12th St New York NY 10003

GERBER, ANN JADE, editor, columnist, author; b. Chgo., Sept. 17, 1930; d. Benjamin James and Henrietta (Rabin) G.; m. Bernard James Kaplan, Apr. 23, 1966; children—Jeffrey, Blair. Student Wright Jr. Coll., Northwestern U., Mundelin U. Reporter, Lerner Newspapers, Chgo., 1945-46, assoc. editor, 1946-58, editor, 1958-87; society columnist Chgo. Sun-Times, 1987—; pub. relations cons. Harlem-Irving Shopping Ctr., Chgo., 1955-56. Author: Chicago's Classiest Cuisine, 1983; Chicago's Sweet Tooth, 1985. Named Woman of Yr., Variety Club Women of Ill., 1982; recipient Editorial Excellence award Lerner Newspapers, 1982, hon. mention for columns, Ill. Press Assn., 1983. Jewish. Home: 5036 Fairview Ln Skokie IL 60077 Office: Chgo Sun-Times 401 N Wabash Ave Chicago IL 60611

GERBER, HADASSA, advertising agency executive; b. N.Y.C., Mar. 15, 1952; d. Benjamin and Rosalyn (Pollack) G. BBA, Bernard Baruch Coll., 1973; postgrad., Pratt Inst., 1973-74, 75-77. Media planner Ted Bates & Co., N.Y.C., 1972-74; asst. media dir. Grey Advt. Inc., N.Y.C., 1975-78; v.p., asst. media dir. BBDO, N.Y.C., 1978-80; sr. v.p., dir. media info. and new technologies McCann-Erickson Inc., N.Y.C., 1982-85; sr. v.p., dir. media planning Wells Rich Greene Inc, N.Y.C., 1987—; lectr., instr. Bernard Baruch, Coll., 1979-80, Parson Sch. Design, 1980—, NYU, 1982. Mem. Videotex Industry Assn. (dir. 1982-84, new tech. com. 1982-86), Am. Assn. Advt. Agys. (new tech. com. 1982-85).

GERBERDING, JOAN ELIZABETH, broadcasting company executive; b. Rockville Center, N.Y., July 29, 1949; d. Henry William and Edith Louise (Perry) G. Student West Chester State U., 1967-69. Asst. pub. relations dir. Conn. Heart Assn., Hartford, 1970-71; publs. editor Hartford Steam Boiler Ins. Co., 1971-72; asst. account exec. Wilson Haight & Welch, Inc., Hartford, 1972; copywriter Internat. Silver Co., Meriden, Conn., 1973-74; acct. exec. WCOD FM, Hyannis, Mass., 1975-76, gen. sales mgr., 1976-79, v.p., gen. sales mgr., 1979-80; sales devel. mgr. Nassau Broadcasting Co., WHWH AM/WPST FM, Princeton, N.J., 1980-82, gen. sales mgr., 1982-83, v.p. sales, 1983-85, corp. v.p., 1985—; cons. Woman's Newspaper of Princeton, 1984—; lectr., cons. Am. women in radio and TV, 1980—; lectr. Princeton YWCA/Women programs, Princeton, 1984—. Recipient YWCA TWIN award, Princeton, 1984. Mem. Am. Women in Radio and TV, N.J. Broadcasters Assn., Am. Bus. Assn., Inc., Princeton Bus. Assn., Radio Advt. Bur. Democrat. Episcopalian. Avocations: writing, music, running. Home: 3 Sunrise Ave Hopewell NJ 08525

GERBI, SUSAN ALEXANDRA, biology educator; b. N.Y.C.; Mar. 13, 1944; d. Claudio and Jeanette Lena (Klein) Gerbi; m. James Terrell McIlwain, Apr. 10, 1976. BA, Barnard Coll., 1965; MPhil, Yale U., 1968, PhD, 1970. NATO and Jane Coffin Childs Fund fellow Max-Planck Institut fur Biologie, Tubingen, Fed. Republic Germany, 1970-72; asst. prof. biology Brown U., Providence, 1972-77, assoc. prof., 1977-82, prof., 1982—, dir. grad. program in molecular and cell biology, 1982-87, asst. dir. grad. program in molecular biology, cell biology and biochemistry, 1987—; vis. assoc. prof. Duke U., Durham, N.C., 1981-82; mem. genetics research grants rev. panel NSF, 1979-80; mem. genetic basis of disease com. NIH, 1980-84. Contbr. articles to profl. jours. Dist. commr. Palmer River Pony Club, 1973-75. N.Y. State Regents scholar, 1965; NIH fellow, 1970; NIH research grantee, 1974—, research career devel. grantee, 1975-80. Mem. Am. Soc. for Cell Biology (program chair 1986, council mem. 1988—), Soc. for Devel. Biology, Genetics Soc., Sigma Xi (nat. lectr.). Office: Brown U Biomedical Div Providence RI 02912

GERDS, GRETCHEN DOROTHEA, publishing executive; b. Nutley, N.J., Feb. 26, 1924; d. Fritz and Margareta (Plank) G. LittB, Rutgers U., 1946. Reporter, feature writer Herald News, Passaic and Clifton, N.J., 1946-50; dir. pub. relations Am. Nurses' Assn., N.Y.C., 1950-54; feature editor Am. Jour. Nursing, N.Y.C., 1956-62, mng. editor, 1962-82; v.p., editorial dir. Am. Jour. Nursing Co., N.Y.C., 1982—. Author: Steve and the Burro's Secret; contbr. articles to profl. jours. Mem. Am. Mgmt. Assn., Sigma Delta Chi. Office: Am Jour of Nursing 555 W 57th St New York NY 10019

GEREAU, MARY C., consultant; b. Winterset, Iowa, Oct. 10, 1916; d. David Joseph and Sarah Rose (Stack) Condon; B.A., U. Iowa, 1939, M.A., 1941; student Mt. Mercy Jr. Coll., 1935-37; m. Gerald Robert Gereau, Jan. 14, 1961. Program dir. ARC, India, 1943-45; dean of students Eastern Mont. Coll., 1946-48; supt. pub. instrn. state of Mont., 1948-56; sr. legis. cons. NEA, 1957-73; dir. legislation Nat. Treasury Employees Union, 1973-76; legis. asst. to Senator Melcher, Mont., 1976-86. Mem. Council Chief State Sch. Officers (dir. 1953-56, pres. 1956), Rural Edn. Assn. (exec. bd. 1953-56), Nat. Women's Party (v.p. 1984—), Equal Rights Ratification Council (nat. chmn.), NEA. Named Conservationist of Yr., Mont. Conservation Council, 1952; recipient Disting. Service award VFW, 1951; Disting. Service award, Chief State Sch. Officers, 1956. Club: U.S. Congress Burro (pres. 1983-84). Contbr. articles on state govt., edn. to profl. jours. Office: 400 Madison Suite 401 Alexandria VA 22314

GEREMIA, FRANCES ELLEN, real estate professional; b. Meriden, Conn., Feb. 5, 1943; d. Joseph and Mary Ellen (Barillaro) Passarelli; m. Peter Richard Geremia, Sept. 29, 1962; children: Peter Phillip, Gina Marie. Student, Vocat. Tech. Coll., 1983, U. N.H., Durham and Portsmouth, 1985, 87. Cert. realtor, Mass.; grad. realtors inst. Free-lance artist Rye, N.H., 1976-80; v.p. sec. Damart Thermaware, Portsmouth, 1980-81; mgr. materials Hampshire Controls Corp., Portsmouth, 1981-83, Genesis Physics Corp., Portsmouth, 1983-85; broker real estate ERA McCoy Profls., Exeter, N.H., 1986—, dir. relocation, 1987—. Vol. Rep. Party, Partsmouth, 1980. Recipient award Tom Hopkins Seminar, 1986. Mem. Am. Prodn. and Inventory Control Soc. (v.p. publicity 1984-85, v.p. membership 1985-86), Nat. Assn. Realtors, Nat. Assn. Purchasing Mgrs. Roman Catholic. Club: Toastmasters (Portsmouth)(2 best speaker awards 1987). Home: 571 Brackett Rd Rye NH 03870 Office: ERA McCoy Profls 140 Epping Rd Exeter NH 03833

GERHARDT, ROSARIO A., materials scientist; b. Lima, Peru, May 20, 1953; d. Jacob K. and Tarcila (La Cruz) G.; m. Michael Paul Anderson, Sept. 27, 1980; children: Heidi Margaret, Kathleen Elizabeth. BA, Carroll Coll., 1976; MS, Columbia U., 1979, D Engring. Sci., 1983. Teaching asst. Columbia U., N.Y.C., 1978-79, grad. asst., 1979-83, research assoc., 1983-84; postdoctoral fellow Rutgers U., Piscataway, N.J., 1984-86, asst. research prof., 1986—; cons. in field. Contbr. articles to profl. jours. Mem. Am. Ceramic Soc., Am. Phys. Soc., N.Y. Acad. Sci., Electron Microscopy Soc. Am., Materials Research Soc., Sigma Xi. Roman Catholic. Club: Materials Sci. N.Y. (sec. 1988). Home: 92 Long Hill Rd Gillette NJ 07933

GERHART, DOROTHY EVELYN, insurance executive, real estate professional; b. Monett, Mo., Apr. 20, 1932; d. Manford Thomas and Norma Grace (Barrett) Ethridge; m. Robert H. Gerhart, Apr. 11, 1952 (div. Dec. 1969); children: Sandra Gerhart Kreamer, Richard A., Diane Gerhart Lacey. Grad. high sch., Tucson; student, U. Ariz., 1950-53. Owner Gerhart Ins., Tucson, 1967-70; agt. Mahoney-O'Donnell Agy., Tucson, 1970-73, Gerhart & Mendelsoh Ins., Tucson, 1973-78; agt., mgr. personal lines dept. Tucson Realty and Trust, 1978-83; ins. agt. San Xavier Ins. Agy., Tucson, 1983-85; v.p., sec., agt. Gerhart & Moore Ins., Inc., Tucson, 1985—. Vol. Palo Verde Psychiat. Hosp. Mem. Ind. Ins. Agts. Tucson (bd. dirs. 1973, 74, v.p. 1975, pres. 1976, First Woman Pres.), Fed. Home Life Ins. Co. (Pres.'s Club award 1986), Altrusa Club of Tucson (bd. dirs. 1984, membership chmn. 1985, fund raising chmn. 1986). Republican. Baptist. Mailing Address: PO Box 13421 Tucson AZ 85732 Office: Gerhart & Moore Ins Inc 310 S Williams Blvd Suite 170 Tucson AZ 85711

GERHART, GLENNA LEE, pharmacist; b. Houston, June 11, 1954; d. Henry Edwin and Gloria Mae (Mrnustik) G. BS in Pharmacy, U. Houston, 1977. Registered pharmacist, Tex. Staff pharmacist Meml. City Med. Ctr., Houston, 1977-84, asst. dir. pharmacy, 1984—. Mem. Am. Soc. Hosp. Pharmacists, Tex. Pharm. Assn., Harris County Pharm. Assn., U. Houston Alumni Orgn. (life), Kappa Epsilon. Republican. Methodist. Clubs: Houston Cat, Nat. Cougar. Lodge: Slavonic Benevolent Order of Tex. Home: 19811 Cardiff Park Ln Houston TX 77094 Office: Meml City Med Ctr 920 Frostwood Houston TX 77024

GERISCH, MARY ELISE, lawyer; b. Detroit, Apr. 21, 1950; d. Robert Albert and Betty Vivian (Gee) G.; m. John Francis Soghigian, Sept. 17, 1976; children: Ben Robert Soghigian, John Steven Soghigian. B.A., Briarcliff Coll., 1972; postgrad. U. Detroit Bus. Sch., 1972-73; J.D., Detroit Coll. Law, 1977. Bar: Mich. 1981, N.Y. 1987. Student atty. supr. Legal Aid, Detroit, 1974-76; assoc. Willford, Hanson & Pemberton, Gladwin, Mich., 1977-78; ptnr. Schneider, Handlon & Gerisch, Midland, Mich., 1978-82, Gerisch & Bourne, P.C., Midland, 1982-86; adj. instr. Northwood Inst. Bd. dirs. Harbor House, Midland, 1984-85, Family/Children's Services, Midland, 1983-86, Ctr. Against Sex Assault, Midland, 1982-85, Fathers for Equal Rights, Southfield, Mich., 1983—, Women's Council Realtors, Midland, 1981-83; Cub Scout pack commdr. Boy Scouts Am., Greenwich, Conn., 1986—. Mem. N.Y. State Bar Assn., Am. Soc. Women Accts., Sanford C. of C. (Mich.), Midland C. of C., Nat. Assn. Women Accts., Women Lawyers Assn. (sec./treas. 1982—), Am. Trial Lawyers Assn., Mich. Bar Assn., ABA (fed. practice com. 1982—), Young Bus. Peoples Assn., Delta Theta Phi. Episcopalian. Club: Exec. 100. Home: 20 Bishop Dr S Greenwich CT 06830

GERLOCK, RHEDA S., optometrist; b. Lamar, Colo., Aug. 25, 1959; d. Dave and Lydia (Weimer) G. Student, Adams State Coll., 1977-78, Colo. State U., 1978-80; OD, So. Calif. Coll. of Optometry, 1984. Optometrist Dr. Robert Larson, Lamar, 1984-85, Vision Care Specialists, PC, Aurora, Colo., 1985—; vol. glaucoma screenings Nat. Soc. to Prevent Blindness, 1985—; clin. investigator various contact lens mfrs., 1985—. Mem. Jr. Symphony League, Denver. Mem. Am. Optometric Assn., Colo. Optometric Assn. (legis. com.), Omega Delta, Alpha Chi Omega. Office: Vision Care Specialists 1550 S Potomac Suite 155 Aurora CO 80012

GERLOTT, ELEANOR LLOYD, librarian; b. Lebanon, Pa., Sept. 13, 1955; d. Arthur Wesley and Christine Evelyn (Plasterer) Lloyd; m. Karl Thomas Gerlott, May 17, 1986. BS in Edn., Shippensburg (Pa.) U., 1977; MS in Lib. Sci., Drexel U., 1981. Library systems specialist Sci. Press, Inc., Ephrata, Pa., 1981-82; law librarian County of Lancaster, Pa., 1982—; cons. Armstrong World Industries, Lancaster, Pa., 1986-87; instr.'s asst. Pa. State U., Lancaster, 1987—. Mem. Am. Assn. Law Libraries, Pa. Library Assn., Lancaster County Library Assn. (treas. 1981—). Republican. Home: PO Box 173 Lititz PA 17543 Office: Lancaster County Law Library 50 N Duke St Lancaster PA 17602

GERMAN, JOAN ALICE WOLFE, author; b. Phila., Feb. 9, 1933; d. Merrill Pierce Wolfe and Jeanette (Anderson) Evans; m. Donald Robert German, Sept. 4, 1954 (dec.); 1 child, Donald Robert. Student Temple U., 1951-54. Adminstrv. asst. dept. pub. relations Vertol Aircraft Corp., Morton, Pa., 1954-58; freelance writer, 1964—. Author: What Am I?, 1979, Guess What?, 1979, The Money Book, 1981; (with D.R. German) Passkeys, 1967, Dividends, 1969, The Bank Teller's Handbook, 1970, rev. edit., 1981, Successful Job Hunting for Executives, 1974, Bank Employee's Marketing Handbook, 1975, Tested Techniques in Bank Marketing, vol. 1, 1977, vol. 2, 1979, Make Your Own Convenience Foods, 1979, How to Find a Job When Jobs Are Hard to Find, 1981, The Bank Employee's Security Handbook, 1982, Checklists for Profitability, 1983, The Only Money Book for the Middle Class, 1983, Money A to Z: A Consumer's Guide to the Language of Personal Finance, 1984; Ninety Days to Financial Fitness, 1986. co-editor Branch Banker's Report, 1968-88; editor Bank Teller's Report, 1969—; contbg. editor Bank Mktg. Report, 1967-86; contbr. to Banker's mag., Brides, Compass, Consumers Digest, Cosmopolitan, Dynamic Years, Easy Living, Money Maker, Nat. Enquirer, Tables, Woman's Day, poetry jours. Founder, dir. Community Craft Ctr., Hopkinton, Mass., 1968-69; bd. dirs. Berkshire Mental Health Assn. Pittsfield, Mass., 1981-82; chmn. bd. The Learning Connection, Pittsfield, Mass., 1987—. Mem. Nat. League Am. Pen Women (br. pres. 1974-76, pres. Mass. 1976-78), Am. Soc. Journalists and Authors (dir.-at-large 1979-81, chmn. Berkshire Hills chpt. 1983—), Authors Guild, Boston Authors Club, Berkshire Poets Workshop (founder), Phi Gamma Nu. Unitarian. Office: 1008 West Mountain Rd Cheshire MA 01225

GERMANY-BALLINTYN, RHONDA, management consultant; b. Ypsilanti, Mich., Aug. 22, 1956; d. Mack and Rose Mary (Mollette) Germany; m. Nicolaas Johann Ballintyn, May 29, 1982. BSChemE, U. Mich., 1979; MBA, U. Conn., Danbury, 1988. Various positions Union Carbide Corp., Chgo. and Hackensack, N.J., 1979-84; mktg. mgr., internat. lic. mgr. Union Carbide Corp., Danbury, 1984-85; dir. mktg. Medallic Art Co., Danbury, 1985-86; mgmt. cons. Chem Systems Inc., Tarrytown, N.Y., 1986-88, Booz-Allen and Hamilton, N.Y.C., 1988—. Mem. Am. Inst. Chem. Engrs., Soc. Plastics Industry, Soc. Plastics Engrs., Assn. Female Execs., Internat. Packaging Conf. Home: 2 Partridge Ln PO Box 7 New Fairfield CT 06812

GERNSBACHER, HELEN RUTH, food service equipment distributing company executive; b. Dallas, July 14, 1917; d. Robert and Sarah (Lynn) Stern; m. Harold Gernsbacher, Sr., Jan. 4, 1942 (dec. Aug. 1981); children—Sandra Gernsbacher O'Connor, Karen Gernsbacher Becker, Harold. Student U. Tex., 1933-36. Ptnr., Gernsbacher's, Fort Worth, 1946-82; pres. Gernsbacher's, Inc., Fort Worth, 1982—. Mem. Food Equipment Distbrs. Assn., Tex. Restaurant Assn. Democrat. Jewish. Avocations: books; antiques; travel. Home: 2916 Harlanwood Dr Fort Worth TX 76109 Office: PO Box 9090 Fort Worth TX 76107

GERONEMUS, DIANN FOX, social work consultant; b. Chgo., July 4, 1947; d. Herbert J. and Edith (Robbins) Fox; B.A. with high honors, Mich. State U., 1969; M.S.W., U. Ill., 1971; 1 dau., Heather Eileen. Lic. clin. social worker, marriage and family therapist, Fla. Social worker neurology, neurosurgery and medicine Hosp. of Albert Einstein Coll. Medicine, 1971-74; prin. social worker ob-gyn and newborn infant service Rush-Presbyn.-St. Luke's Med. Center, Chgo., 1974-75; social worker neurology, adminstr. Multiple Sclerosis Treatment Center, St. Barnabas Hosp., Bronx, N.Y., 1975-77, socio-med. researcher (Nat. Multiple Sclerosis Soc. grantee), dept. neurology and psychiatry, 1977-79, dir. social service, 1979-80; field work instr. Fordham U. Grad. Sch. Social Service, 1979-80; preceptor, social work program Fla. Atlantic U., Fla. Internat. U.; mem. edn. com., med. adv. bd., program com. Nat. Multiple Sclerosis Soc., 1980-83, area service com., 1983-86; pvt. practice psychotherapy; social work cons.; cons. in gerontology, rehab. and supervision. Mem. Acad. Cert. Social Workers, Nat. Assn. Social Workers (diplomate), Registered Clin. Soc. Hosp. Social Work Dirs., Am. Orthopsychiat. Assn. Jewish. Contbr. articles to profl. jours. Home: 833 NW 81st Way Plantation FL 33324

GEROWIN, MINA, finance company executive. d. Charles and Frieda G. BA, Smith Coll., Northampton, Mass., 1973; JD, U. Va. Law Sch., 1976; MBA, Harvard Bus. Sch., 1980. Bar: N.Y. 1976. Broker trainee Shearson Hammill, Basel, Switzerland, 1971, 72; assoc. Nestlé SA, Vevey, Switzerland, 1976, 77, BrownWood et al, N.Y.C., 1977-78; cons. McKinsey & Co., London, 1979-80; banker Lazard Freres & Co., N.Y.C., 1980-86, Dean Witter Reynolds, N.Y.C., 1986—. Bd. dirs. Am. Ballet Theater, N.Y.C., 1983—. Baker Scholar Harvard Bus. Sch., Boston, 1980. Mem. N.Y. State Bar. Clubs: Smith, Harvard Bus. Sch. (N.Y.C.). Office: Dean Witter Reynolds 2 World Trade Ctr New York NY 10021

GERRING, CHERYL BUTLER, school librarian; b. Oceanside, Calif., May 15, 1949; d. Arthur Norris and Dorothy Louise (Raab) Butler; m. Alan Irwin Gerring, Oct. 15, 1978; children: Charlene Louise, Michael Norris. B.A., Towson State U., 1971; M.L.S., U. Md., 1974. Tchr. English, Show Hill Middle Sch. (Md.), 1971-73; library media specialist Samuel Ogle Jr. High Sch., Bowie, Md., 1975-78; in-service program devel. specialist Prince George's Pub. Schs., Upper Marlboro, Md., 1978-79; library media specialist Benjamin Tasker Middle Sch., Bowie, 1979—; presenter Prevocat. Workshop, Upper Marlboro, 1977, Md. Middle Sch. Conf., Bowie, 1983; cons. Library Theater, Washington, 1979-81. Co-author: pamphlet/booklet Career Resource Center, 1977, Volunteer Handbook, 1978, Integrating Library Media Skills into the English Curriculum (guide), 1983, Integrating Library Media Skills into the Social Studies Curriculum (guide), 1984. Oneg shabbat chmn. Jewish Community Ctr. Prince George's County, Greenbelt, 1979, librarian, 1980-83. Named Outstanding Young Educator, Bowie/Crofton Jr. C. of C., 1977, Outstanding Educator, Prince George's County, Upper Marlboro, 1983, Outstanding Tchr. City of Bowie, 1986. Mem. Md. Ednl. Media Orgn. (treas. 1985-87), Ednl. Media Assn. Prince George's County (sec. 1981-82, Appreciation award 1980), Md. Middle Sch. Assn., Beta Phi Mu. Democrat. Office: Benjamin Tasker Mid Sch 4901 Collington Rd Bowie MD 20715

GERRINGER-BUSENBARK, ELIZABETH JACQUELINE, systems analyst, consultant; b. Edmund, Wis., Jan. 7, 1934; d. Clyde Elroy and Evangeline Matilda Knapp; student Madison Bus. Coll., 1952, San Francisco State Coll., 1953-54, Vivian Rich Sch. Fashion Design, 1955, Dale Carnegie Sch., 1956, Murray Sch. Modern Dance, 1956, Biscayne Acad. Music, 1957, Los Angeles City Coll., 1960-62, Santa Monica (Calif.) Jr. Coll., 1963; Hastings Coll. of Law, 1973, Wharton Sch., U.Pa., 1977, London Art Coll., 1979; Ph.D., 1979; m. Roe Devon Gerringer-Busenbark, Sept. 30, 1968 (dec. Dec. 1972). Actress, Actors Workshop San Francisco, 1959, 65, Theatre of Arts Beverly Hills (Calif.), 1963, also radio; cons, and systems analyst for banks and pub. accounting agys.; artist, singer, songwriter, playwright, dress designer. Pres., tchr. Environ Improvement, Originals by Elizabeth, Dometrik's, JIT-MAP, San Francisco, 1973—; ordained ministerUnitarian Ch., 1978. Author: New Highways, 1967; Happening - Impact-Mald, 1971; Seven Day Rainbow, 1972; Zachary's Adversaries, 1974; Fifteen from Wisconsin, 1977; Bart's White Elephant, 1978; Skid Row Minister, 1978; Points in Time, 1979; Special Appointment, A Clown in Town, 1979; Happenings, 1980, Votes from the Closet, 1984, Wait for Me, 1984, The Stairway, 1984, The River is a Rock, 1985, Happenings Revisted, 1986, Comparative Religion in the United States, 1986, Lumber in the Skies, 1986, The Fifth Season, 1987, Summer Thoughts, 1987; mem. Unitarian Soc. (steering com. explorations in worship). Club: Toastmasters. Address: PO Box 1640 7th and Mission Station San Francisco CA 94101

GERRISH, CATHERINE RUGGLES, food company executive; b. Winona, Minn., July 10, 1911; d. Clyde O. and Frances (Holmes) Ruggles; A.B., Radcliffe Coll., 1932, A.M., 1934; Ph.D., Harvard U., 1937; m. Hollis G. Gerrish, Sept. 10, 1946. Research asst. Harvard U., 1937-39; instr., asst. prof. econs. U. Ill., 1939-42; with Bur. Budget, Exec. Office President, 1943-45; assoc. prof. U. Ill., 1946; asst. editor Quar. Jour. Econs., 1951-69; treas., v.p. Squirrel Brand Co., Cambridge, Mass., 1966—. Mem. Am. Econ. Assn., Nat. Tax Assn. Home: 207 Grove St Cambridge MA 02138 Office: 17 Boardman St Cambridge MA 02139

GERSCHBACHER, CORINE MARIE, computer and electronics manufacturing company executive; b. Whittier, Calif., Mar. 8, 1961; d. Frank Joseph Gerschbacher and Shirley Ann Stahl. BA in Mktg., Whittier Coll., 1983. Acctg. analyst Health Valley Foods, Montebello, Calif., 1982-84; mktg. coordinator Bland Contracting Co., Whittier, 1984-85; project mktg. specialist research and devel., Taxan Corp., City of Industry, Calif., 1985-87; hi-tech industry analyst Creative Micro Systems Group, Whittier, 1987—; cons. computer systems, Whittier, 1985-87; lectr. Computer Trading Post, Glendale, Calif., 1987—. Editorial corr., writer The Computer Inputer mag., 1987—; contbg. ariter PC Mag.; contbg. editor Computer Graphics World mag., reader rev. bd., 1986-87; prodn. corr. Nat. TV programming The Computer Show, 1986—; photo journalist, reporter, computer pub. realtions advisor. Milo Hunt Merit scholar Whittier Coll., 1980-83; recipient cert. of appreciation Pi Sigma Epsilon, 1986. Mem. MBA Assn. (local activities dir. 1983-84), Calif. Scholarship Fedn. (life), Alpha Pi Delta. Home: 11611 Broadway Apt A Whittier CA 90601 Office: Creative Micro Systems Group 11611-A Broadway Whittier CA 90601

GERSH-NEŠIC, BETH SUSAN, art historian; b. Toledo, Sept. 28, 1952; d. David and Mildred (Gerst) Gersh; m. Dušan Nešic, May 1, 1987; 1 stepchild, Mladen. BA, SUNY, Binghamton, 1974, MA, 1977; M in Philosophy, CCNY, 1986, postgrad., 1986—. Asst. to the dir. Grey Art Gallery, N.Y.C., 1985—; instr. art history NYU, 1985—. Office: Grey Art Gallery 33 Washington Pl New York NY 10003

GERSHON, ANNE ANGEN, physician, medical researcher; b. Pa., Aug. 30, 1938; d. Willard Ferguson and Elda (Yarborough) Angen; m. Michael D. Gershon, June 10, 1961; children: Perry, Timothy, Dana. AB, Smith Coll., 1960; MD, Cornell U., 1964. Intern N.Y. Hosp., N.Y.C., 1964-65, resident, 1966-68; from instr., asst. prof. to assoc. to prof. pediatrics NYU Med. Ctr., N.Y.C., 1970-86; prof., chief div. infectious disease in pediatrics Columbia U., N.Y.C., 1986—; mem. adv. com. on immunization practice, USPHS, Atlanta, 1982-86. Author: (with others) Infectious Diseases of Children, 1986. NIH grantee; named NIH fellow, Oxford, Eng., 1965-66. Mem. Soc. for Pediatric Research (mem. exec. council 1979-80), Pediatric Infectious Disease Soc., Infectious Disease Soc. Am., Am. Soc. for Microbiology (found. lectr. 1987), Am. Soc. for Clin. Investigation. Home: 176 E 93d St New York NY 10128 Office: Columbia U Dept Pediatrics Coll of Physicians and Surgeons 650 W 168th St New York NY 10032

GERSKE, JANET FAY, lawyer; b. Chgo., Nov. 14, 1950; d. Bernard G. Gerske and L. Fay (Knight) Capron; m. James P. Chapman, Dec. 5, 1982. B.S., Northwestern U., 1971; J.D., U. Mich., 1978. Bar: Ill. 1978, U.S. Dist. Ct. (no. dist.) Ill. 1978. Sole practice, Chgo., 1978-80, 84—; assoc. Jerome H. Torshen Ltd., Chgo., 1980-84. Chpt. chmn. Ind. Voters Ill./Ind. Precinct Orgn., Chgo., 1982-84 ; co-chmn. Ill. Women's Agenda Com., 1985-88 . Mem. ABA, Assn. Trial Lawyers Am., Ill. Trial Lawyers Assn., Women's Bar Assn. Ill. (co-chmn. rights of women com. 1985-86), Chgo. Bar Assn. (co-chmn. legal status of women com. young lawyers sect.), Nat. Assn. Social Security Claimants' Rep., Ill. State Bar Assn. Democrat. Home: 850 W Oakdale Ave Chicago IL 60657 Office: 39 S LaSalle St Chicago IL 60603

GERSONI-EDELMAN, DIANE CLAIRE, author, editor; b. Bklyn., Apr. 16, 1947; d. James Arthur and Edna Bernice (Krinski) Gersoni; B.A. cum laude, Vassar Coll., 1967; m. James Neil Edelman, Oct. 5, 1975; children—Michael Lawrence, Sara Anne. Asst. editor, then asso. editor Sch. Library Jour. Book Rev., 1968-72; free lance writer, 1972-74, 77—; writer, editor Scholastic Mags., Inc., N.Y.C., 1974-77; author: Sexism and Youth, 1974; Work-Wise: Learning About the World of Work from Books, 1980; cons., speaker in field. Club: Vassar (N.Y.C.). Contbr. articles, book revs. to anthologies, newspapers, mags. Home: care Edelman 301 E 78th St New York NY 10021

GERSOVITZ, SARAH VALERIE, painter, printmaker, playwright; b. Montreal, Que., Can., Sept. 5, 1920; d. Solomon and Eva (Gampel) Gamer; student MacDonald Coll., Montreal Mus. Fine Arts, Ecole des Arts Appliques; diploma communication arts, M.A., Concordia U.; m. Benjamin Gersovitz, June 22, 1944; children—Mark, Julia, Jeremy. Tchr. painting and drawing Bronfman Centre, Montreal, 1972—; one-woman shows include Montreal Mus. Fine Arts, 1962, 65, Art Gallery Greater Victoria, 1966, U. Alta., 1968, Burnaby Art Gallery, 1969, Art Gallery Hamilton, 1969, Mt. St. Vincent U., 1971, Coll. St. Louis, 1972, Inst. Cultural Peruano, Lima, 1973, Confedn. Art Gallery, 1976, St. Mary's U., 1976, U. Sherbrooke, 1979, 83, Peter Whyte Gallery, 1982, London Regional Art Gallery, 1982, Holland Coll., 1982, Stewart Hall Art Gallery, 1984, U. Kaiserslautern (W.Ger.), 1984, others; represented in permanent collections Library of Congress, N.Y. Pub. Library, Nat. Gallery South Australia, Inst. Cultural Peruano, Lima, Am. Embassy, Ottawa, House of Humour and Satire, Gabrovo, Bulgaria, Israel Mus., Jerusalem, numerous Can. mus., univs. and embassies including Nat. Gallery Can., Montreal Mus. Fine Arts, Le Musée du Québec, Le Musée d'Art Contemporain; group exhbns. include 3d Internat. Play Group Exhbn., N.Y.C., 1973, Internat. Triennial, Grenchen, Switzerland, 1961, V, VI and X Internat. Biennial, Ibiza, Spain, 1972, 74, 82, II and III Internat. Biennial, Norway, 1974, 76, III and IV Internat. Biennial, Frechen,

Germany, 1974, 76, 1st Internat. Bienal, Segovia, Spain, 1974, III Biennial Graphic, Cali, Colombia, 1976, 11th and 13th Biennale, Lljublana, Yugoslavia, 1975, 1979, ann. exhbn. NAD, N.Y.C., 1975, 11th Bienale Internat. d'Art de Menton, France, 1976, contemporary miniature Exhbn., U. Mich., 1977, XVIII and XXI Premio Internat. de Dibujo, Barcelona, 1979, 82, XV Internat. Bienal de São Paulo (Brazil), 1979, Bienal des Grabado, Maracaibo, Venezuela, 1977, Premio Internat. per l'Incisione, Biella, Italy, 1980, Internat. Biennale des Arts Grafiques, Brno, Czechoslovakia, 1980, 84, 1st and 2d Internat. Miniature Print Exhbn., Seoul, 1980, 82, Wesleyan Internat. Exhbn. Prints and Drawings, Macon, Ga., 1980, Salón Nacional de Grabado, Lima, Peru, 1981, Exhbn. Que. Graphics, Hong Kong, 1982, VI Biennale Internat. de Gabrovo, 1983; 4th Internat. Print Biennale, Seoul, Korea, 1983, VI Bienal Internat. de Arte, Valparaiso, Chile, 1983, 85, 3d Miniprint Internat., Cadaques, Spain, 1983, Internat. Print Exhibit, Taipei, Taiwan, 1984, 86; numerous others U.S. and abroad. Recipient 1st prize Seagram Fine Arts Expn., 1968; Graphic Art prize Winnipeg Art Gallery Bienial, 1962; Anaconda award Can. Soc. Painters-Etchers, 1963, 67; 1st prize Concours Graphique, U. Sherbrooke, 1977; purchase award Mus. de Que., 1966, Nat. Gallery South Australia, 1967, Dawson Coll., 1974, Thomas More Inst., 1977, Law Faculty U. Sherbrooke, 1979; hon. mention Miniature Painters, Sculptors, and Engravers, Washington, 1976; 1st prize and 2 gold medals Nat. Playwriting Competition, Ottawa, 1982, hon. mention awards, 1979, 80, 83; Travel award House of Humour and Satire, 1985; semi-finalist, Drury Coll. for The Artist, 1987; finalist design for Eh, Harry?, Jacksonville U., 1987, West Coast Ensemble, Lons Angeles for The Artist, 1987, The Studio and the Winding Stairs, 1987; finalist designation for Nighty-Night and the Artist, 1985; winner Country Playhouse, Houston for The Winding Stairs, 1985; contender for honors nat. playwriting competition for Food for Thought, 1985. Mem. Royal Can. Acad. Arts (council 1981-82), Societe des Graveurs du Que., Dramatists Guild. Address: 5173 Mayfair Ave, Montreal, PQ Canada H4V 2E8

GERST, ELIZABETH CARLSEN (MRS. PAUL H. GERST), university dean, researcher, educator; b. N.Y.C., June 10, 1929; d. Rolf and Gudrun (Wiborg) Carlsen; A.B. magna cum laude, Mt. Holyoke Coll., 1951; Ph.D., U. Pa., 1957; m. Paul H. Gerst, Aug. 3, 1957; children—Steven Richard, Jeffrey Carlton, Andrew Leigh. Instr. physiology Grad. Sch. Medicine, U. Pa., 1955-57, Cornell U. Med. Coll., N.Y.C., 1957-58; instr. Columbia Coll. Physicians and Surgeons, N.Y.C., 1959-61, asst. prof., 1961—, dir. Center Continuing Edn. in Health Scis., 1978-87, asst. dean continuing edn., 1984-87, dir. Office Med. Edn., N.Y. Acad. Med., 1987—; Authors: (with others) The Lung, Clinical Physiology and Pulmonary Function Tests, 1955, rev. edit., 1962. Pres. Citizen's Ednl. Council Tenafly, 1972-73; vice chmn. Tenafly Environ. Commn., 1972-77; mem. Citizens Long-Range Planning Com., Tenafly Bd. Edn., 1973-77, chmn. supt. search, edn., tchr. hiring, personnel coms.; vice chmn. Tenafly Environ. Commn., 1972-77; trustee Tenafly Nature Center, 1972-80; bd. dirs., chmn. environ. quality Tenafly LWV, 1971-78; v.p. Bergen County LWV, 1973-75. Porter fellow Am. Physiol. Soc., 1956-57. Mem. Middle States Assn. Colls. and Schs. (team Commn. on higher edn., 1984—), Soc. Med. Coll. Dirs. of Continuing Med. Edn., Am. Physiol. Soc. (task force Women in Physiology 1973-75), N.Y. County Med. Soc. (com. on continuing med. edn. 1978—), Physiol. Soc. Phila., Harvey Soc., Biophys. Soc., Alliance Continuing Med. Edn., N.Y. Acad. Scis., AAAS, Phi Beta Kappa, Sigma Xi, Sigma Delta Epsilon. Unitarian. Home: 141 Tekening Dr Tenafly NJ 07670 Office: Office of Med Edn NY Acad of Med 2 E 103rd St New York NY 10029

GERTZ, NANCY ELLEN, health policy consultant; b. Providence, R.I., July 29, 1957; d. Julius and Sandra (Yuffee) G.; m. Michael Louis Cohen, Sept. 21, 1985. BA, Clark U., 1979; MS, U. Wash., 1981; postgrad., Boston U., 1986—. Health educator U. Mass. Med. Sch., Worcester, 1978-79; dir. health promotion Puget Sound Health Systems Agy., Seattle, 1979-83; pres. Nancy E. Gertz & Assocs., N.Y.C., 1983-84; bus. mgr., dir. health promotion The Equitable Co., N.Y.C., 1984-86; health policy cons. Boston, 1986—; researcher Nat. Health Service, London, 1978; cons. Nat. Cancer Inst., 1983, Fed. Bur. Health Professions, 1984, Alexander & Alexander, Inc., N.Y.C., 1983-84, Health Policy Inst., Boston U., 1987. Pew Health Policy fellow, Boston U., 1986. Mem. Am. Pub. Health Assn., Nat. Assn. Female Execs., Assn. for Health Services Research, Soc. Prospective Medicine (dir. 1985-88). Home: 10 Allston St Newtonville MA 02160

GESS, ELAINE MARGRET FISCHER, office service executive; b. Fargo, N.D., Aug. 24; d. Frederick George and Zulu Lodema (Barton) Fischer; m. David Leroy Gess, July 9, 1953; children: Richard, Glenn, Pamela, Charles, Diane, Cheryl, John. BS in Mktg., Met. State Coll., Denver, 1985. Sales assoc. Allen Assocs., Denver, 1985-87; account mgr. TAD Temporary Service, Denver, 1987-88; account temporary TAD Temporary Service, Golden, Colo., 1988—. Mem. Am. Mktg. Assn., Lakewood C. of C. Home: 621 S Taft St Lakewood CO 80228

GESSERT, AUTUMN ROBERTA, telecommunications administrator; b. Milw., Nov. 25, 1958; d. Sherman Albert and Nancy Ann (Darnold) G.; divorced; 1 child, Phillip Patrick. Student, Marquette U., 1982-83, Nat. Ctr. Degree Studies. Telex operator Aqua-Chem, Inc., Milw., 1981-82, translator French, 1982-83, project coordinator, 1983-85, coordinator telecommunications, 1985-86; mgr. telecommunications Mark Travel Corp., Milw., 1986-87; instr. computer networks and literacy U.S. Fed. Govt., Yuma, Ariz., 1987—. Served as pfc. U.S. Army, 1977-78. Mem. Wis. Telecommunications Assn., Nat. Assn. for Female Execs. Republican. Lutheran. Office: Info Systems Command Attn: ASNC-TYU-I Yuma Proving Ground Yuma AZ 85365

GESSERT, LISE LYNNE, finance company executive; b. Milw., Apr. 24, 1954; d. Edmund Kurt and Lynne Carol (McCoy) Rieger; m. Robert Joseph Gessert, June 17, 1978; children: Justin Michael, Jamie Lynne. BA in Chemistry, Carthage Coll., 1975; MBA in Finance, Marquette U., 1984. Lab. technician Indsl. Bio-Test, Decatur, Ill., 1976-77, asst. group leader, 1977-78; lab. technician A.F. Staley Mfg. Co., Decatur, 1978-81; sr. account exec. Emjay Corp., Milw., 1985-86; asst. v.p. The Milw. Co., 1986—. Advisor Jr. Achievement, Milw., 1987. Mem. Investment Mgmt. Cons. Assn. Inc. Office: The Milw Co 790 N Milwaukee St Milwaukee WI 53202

GESSNER, BETH WILIAMS, education program director; b. Plainview, Tex., Oct. 24, 1930; d. Paul Issac and Mary Helen (Nealy) Williams; m. Dave J. Gessner, June 14, 1925; children: David, Suzanne, Mark, Robin. BS, Bob Jones U., 1951; MEd, Fla. Atlantic U., 1969; EdD, Nova U., 1987. Tchr. St. Lucie County Sch. System, Ft. Pierce, Fla., 1965-80, primary edn. specialist, 1980-83, presch. cons., 1983-84, cons. Fla. diagnostic and learning resources system, 1984-85, coordinator, 1985—; adj. prof. Fla. Atlantic U., Boca Raton, Nova U., Ft. Lauderdale, Fla., Indian River Community Coll., Ft. Pierce; cons. Fla. Sch. Vols., Fla. Assn. Children with Learning Disabilities. Author: Lifestyle Learning Activities, 1979; contbr. articles to mags. Cons. Parent Edn. Network Fla., St. Lucie County, 1986—; dir. Parent to Parent Support Group, St. Lucie County, 1986—; mem. Gov.'s Child Advocacy, St. Lucie County, 1984—. Named Tchr. Yr., St. Lucie County Sch. Bd., 1974. Mem. Fla. Adminstrn. Suprs. Assn., Nat. Assn. for Edn. of Young Children, Council for Exceptional Children, LWV. Home: 697 NE Horizen Ln Port Saint Lucie FL 33452 Office: Fla Diagnostic and Learning Resources System 532 N 13th St Fort Pierce FL 33450

GESUMARIA, DONNA BEATRICE, pharmacist; b. Newark, July 22, 1955; d. Cosmo Lincoln and Nancy (Cassese) Rossi; m. Robert Hugh Gesumaria, Feb. 4, 1978; 1 child, Robert Cosmo, 1987. BA in Biology and Chemistry, Kean Coll. N.J., 1977; BS in Pharmacy, U. Colo., 1986. Lic. pharmacist, Colo. Research scientist dept. biochemistry and drug metabolism Hoffman-La Roche, Inc., Nutley, N.J., 1977-78, research scientist dept. toxicology, 1978-80; research scientist dept. toxicology Rohm & Haas Co., Spring House, Pa., 1981-82; pharmacy intern, pharmacist Drug Systems Pharmacy, Commerce City, Colo., 1986; pharmacist Don's Prescription Shop, Inc., Wheatridge, Colo., 1986—. Mem. Golden (Colo.) Landmarks Assn. Mem. Am. Pharm. Assn., Colo. Pharm. Assn., Nat. Assn. Retail Druggists, Rho Chi (sec. 1985-86), Lambda Alpha Sigma.

GETTINGER, MIRIAM ELLEN, nurse, educator; b. Jersey, N.J., June 23; d. Charles LeRoy and Esther (Hersh) King; m. Kenneth Harold Gettinger, Nov. 28, 1953; children: Randy Craig, Neal Cory. AA in Sci. (honors student), Dutchess Coll., 1970; vocat. certs. SUNY-Oswego, 1972, 73, Utica Rome Sch., 1975, 76, 77, NYU, 1978, Cornell U., 1983; grad. Labor Studies Program, Cornell U., 1985. Cert. tchr. Office mgr., Croton, N.Y., 1953-57; operating room technician Peekskill Hosp. (N.Y.), 1962-64; operating room nurse Butterfield Hosp., Cold Spring, N.Y., 1970-71, emergency room nurse, 1970-71; pvt. care infant nurse, Bklyn., 1971—; indsl. nurse Indian Pt. Atomic Energy Plant, Verplank, N.Y., 1971—; tchr. Bd. of Coop. Ednl. Services, Yorktown Heights, N.Y., 1971—, chmn. com. sch. pub. relations, 1981—; cons. Marr's Extended Care Facility, Mohegan, N.Y., 1982—; pres., owner Masako Mimi Japanese Restaurant, N.Y.C., 1988—; mem. adv. council Cornell U. Sch. Indsl. and Labor Relations; mem. Assemblyman William Ryan's adv. bd. Com. leader Boy Scouts Am., Peekskill, 1961-63; advisor state senator Mary Goodhue, Albany, N.Y., 1980—, state assemblyman George Pataki; del. N.Y. tchrs. Retirement System, Albany, 1983; mem. geriatrics West County Mental Health Bd., White Plains, 1981-82; vol. Israel Def. Force, 1986-87; pres. PTO; leader Youth Group. Mem. N.Y. State United Tchrs. Union (v.p., negotiator local 1978-82), N.Y. Tchrs. Retirement, N.Y. State Nurses Assn., United Staff Assn. (v.p. 1978-82). Independent Republican. Jewish. Home: 8 Foxhill Rd Peekskill NY 10566 Office: Bd of Coop Edn Services Pinesbridge Rd Yorktown Heights NY 10598

GETTLE, JUDY ANN, YWCA official; b. Lebanon, Pa., May 19, 1946; d. Warren George and Julia Harriet (Kreiger) G.; B.A. in Psychology, Lebanon Valley Coll., 1968; M.Ed. in Counselor Edn., Slippery Rock (Pa.) State Coll., 1973; Ph.D. in Counselor Edn., U. Pitts., 1985. Tchr., North Allegheny Sch. Dist., Pitts., 1968-73; coordinator adolescent and children's services No. Communities Mental Health/Mental Retardation, Pitts., 1974-80; dir. counseling and women's services YWCA Greater Pitts., 1980—; ind. counselor, 1975—. Grantee Henry Frick Found. Mem. Am. Assn. Counseling and Devel., Assn. Counselor Edn. and Supervision, Nat. Acad. Cert. Clin. Mental Health Counselors, Am. Mental Health Counselors Assn., Assn. for Psychol. Type, Pitts. Feminist Therapists, Psi Chi. Home: 158 S Linwood Ave Pittsburgh PA 15205 Office: YWCA 4th and Wood Sts Pittsburgh PA 15222

GETTY, CAROL PAVILACK, government official; b. Wilmington, Del., Apr. 9, 1938; d. Frank Clifton McGrew and Maxine (Remaly) Fogarty; m. Lawrence Lee Pavilack, Aug. 18, 1960 (div. 1980); children—Douglas Brooks, Joann Clements; m. James John Getty, May 8, 1985. B.A., Wellesley Coll., 1960; M.S. in Criminal Justice, Ariz. State U., 1978; postgrad. Phoenix Coll., 1974, U. Oreg., 1975. Tchr. math. Beaver County Day Sch., Chestnut Hill, Mass., 1960-62; engring. aide Air Research, Phoenix, 1960-63; computer analyst Motorola, Phoenix, 1963; tchr. math. Phoenix County Day Sch., 1964-69; mem. Ariz. Bd. Pardons and Paroles, Phoenix, 1978-83; commr. U.S. Parole Commn., Washington, 1983—; tech. adviser Maricopa County Alts. to Incarceration Commn., 1980-83. Chmn. Annual Reports, Ariz. Bd. Pardons and Paroles, 1979, 80, 81, co-chmn. Rule Book, 1980. Treas., asst. treas., sec., impact community action, admissions & fin. Jr. League Phoenix, 1970-80; docent, treas. Phoenix Art Mus. League, 1968-79; vice chmn. Criminal Justice Adv. Com., Phoenix, 1973-78. Mem. Exec. Women in Govt., Nat. Fedn. Republican Women, Am. Correctional Assn., Am. Paroling Authority, Womens C. of C. Republican. Unitarian. Clubs: Soroptimist International; Wellesley (Kansas City, Mo.). Home: 7709 NW Westside Dr Kansas City MO 64152 Office: US Parole Commn Dept of Justice 10920 Ambassador Dr Kansas City MO 64153

GETTY, JUDITH LEE, public relations professional; b. Altoona, Pa., Mar. 17, 1945; d. Charles Henry and Leda May (Helsel) Hoffman; divorced; children: James Francis, Charles Lloyd, Amy Ruth. BS in Early Childhood Edn., Towson State U., 1976; postgrad., Wesleyan U., Middleton, Conn., 1982-83. Cert. tchr., Pa., Conn. Tchr., adminstr. East Haddam (Conn.) Sch. Dist., 1979-83; supr. retail advt. graphic arts dept. The Day Pub. Co., New London, Conn., 1983-84, mgr. community relations and promotions, 1984—. Mem. adv. bd. Ret. Sr. Vol. Program, Southeastern Conn., 1984—, adv. com. Southeastern Employment Edn. Collaborative, New London, 1984—; v.p. Am. Cancer Soc. Southeastern Conn. div. Recipient First Place Newspaper in Edn. Promotion award, Internat. Newspaper Mktg., 1986, 1987, Robert A. Macklin Meml. In Depth award, Hickey-Mitchell's 26th Ann. Internat. Newspaper Carrier contest, 1986. Mem. LWV, Internat. Assn. Bus. Communicators, Nat. Assn. Female Execs., Women in Communication, New London County Women's Network, Pub. Relations Network, Southeastern Conn. C. of C., Norwich Area C. of C. Office: The Day Pub Co 47 Eugene O'Neill Dr New London CT 06320

GETZ, AMELIA MARLANE, security manager; b. Marion, Ind., Feb. 7, 1948; d. William Frederick and Jane Ann (Currens) G. Cert., U. Strangers, Perugia, Italy, 1965; BS, Purdue U., 1970; MA, Ball State U., 1983. Dep. office Howard County Sheriff Dept., Kokomo, Ind., 1971-72, matron, 1972-73, dep. sheriff, patrol officer, 1973-74, spl. agt. special investigations, 1974-76; sgt. security Chrysler Transmission and Casting, Kokomo, 1976-78, 81-82, mgr. security, 1985—; exec. devel. program Chrysler Transmission, Kokomo, 1978-81, fin. analyst, 1982-85. Advisor Jr. Achievement, Kokomo, 1984; allocations officer Howard County United Way, Kokomo, 1985—. Mem. Nat. Mgmt. Assn. (treas. 1979-84, v.p. 1985—). Baptist. Home: 1518 S Armstrong Kokomo IN 46902 Office: Chrysler Transmission 2401 S Reed Rd Kokomo IN 46902

GETZ, ILSE (ILSE DANES), painter, sculptor; b. Nuremberg, Ger., Oct. 24, 1917; d. Abraham and Pauline (Mann) Bechhold; student Art Students League, N.Y.C.; student of George Grosz, Morris Kantor; m. Gibson A. Danes, June 29, 1964. Exhibited in more than 40 one-woman shows in U.S., France, Germany, Italy, Can.; works in museums and pvt. collections; dir. Bertha Schaefer Gallery, 1952-56; asst. to Leo Castelli, N.Y.C., 1957-58; dir. Downstairs: World House Gallery, 1958-59; tchr. Positano Art Workshop, Italy, summers 1956, 58; designed backdrop/set Ionesco's The Killer, 1960. Yaddo Found. fellow, 1959. Home: Irvin Ln Newtown CT 06470

GETZENDANNER, SUSAN, lawyer, federal court judge; b. Chgo., July 24, 1939; d. William B. and Carole S. (Muehling) O'Meara; children—Alexandra, Paul. B.B.A., Loyola U., 1966, J.D., 1966. Bar: Ill. bar 1966. Law clk. to presiding justice U.S. Dist. Ct., 1966-68; assoc. Mayer, Brown & Platt, Chgo., 1968-74, ptnr., 1974-80; judge U.S. Dist. Ct., Chgo., 1980-87; ptnr. Skadden, Arps, Slate, Meagher & Flom, Chgo., 1987—. Recipient medal of excellence Loyola U. Law Alumni Assn., 1981. Mem. ABA, Chgo. Council Lawyers. Office: Skadden Arps Slate Meagher & Flom 333 W Wacker Dr Chicago IL 60606

GEUL, KATHERINE FRASHER, legal association administrator; b. Pasadena, Calif., Dec. 10, 1951; d. Wallace Goodman Frasher and Margaret Elaine (Lackey) Dillon; m. Roy Eduard Geul, Aug. 13, 1978; children: Ryan, Brandon, Tyler. BA, U. Nev., 1973; grad., N.H. State Police Acad., Concord, 1974; MS, Calif. State U., Long Beach, 1978. Counselor Suicide Prevention and Crisis Call Ctr., Reno, 1972-73; police officer Concord Police Dept., 1973-74; legal sec. Terence J. Mix, Redondo Beach, Calif., 1974-76; litigation research legal sec. Barrette, Stearns, Collins, Torrance, Calif., 1976-77; exec. dir. Los Angeles Trial Lawyers Assn., 1977—. Named one of Outstanding Young Women Am., 1976; recipient Presdl. award Calif. Trial Lawyers Assn., 1983, Presdl. Award of Merit, Assn. Trial Lawyers Am., 1984. Mem. Nat. Assn. Trial Lawyer Execs. (v.p. 1981-82, pres. 1983-84), Am. Soc. Assn. Execs., So. Calif. Soc. Assn. Execs. Democrat. Home: 7517 Alpine Way Tujunga CA 91042 Office: Los Angeles Trial Lawyers Assn 2140 W Olympic Blvd #324 Los Angeles CA 90006

GEWELBER, RHONA WEINBERG, dairy feed company executive; b. Lynwood, Calif., Apr. 23, 1953; d. Bob and Marcha (Wallin) Weinberg; m. Ytzkak Gewelber, Mar. 27, 1977; children: Hali Morrisa, Civon Leah. BA in Religion and Philosophy, Stephens Coll., 1975; student, Oxford U., Eng., 1973-74. Mgr., buyer Golden Boutique, Honolulu, 1975-76; exec. sec. Zellerbach Paper Co., Los Angeles, 1976-78; adminstrv. asst. Coast Grain Co., Norwalk, Calif., 1978-80; v.p. mktg. Coast Grain Co., Ontario and Corcoran, Calif., Phoenix, 1980—, also bd. dirs.; mem. agrl. adv. council U. Calif., Riverside, 1986—. V.p. Ida Mayer Cummings Aux. of Jewish Homes for the Aging, 1979—. Recipient Vol. of Yr. award Ida Mayer Cummings Aux., Los Angeles, 1982. Mem. Calif. Grain and Feed Assn., Nat. Family Bus. Assn., Women in Family Owned Bus., Calif. Women for Agr., Calif. Agrl. Found., Hanford & Tulare (Calif.) Women's Trade Clubs, Chino Valley C. of C., Calif. Hwy. Patrol 11-99 Found. Republican. Home: 15510 Olive Branch Dr La Mirada CA 90638 Office: Coast Grain Co 3333 E Airport Dr Ontario CA 91761

GEWIRTZ, GERRY, editor; b. N.Y.C., Dec. 22, 1920; d. Max and Minnie (Weiss) G.; m. Eugene W. Friedman, Nov. 11, 1945; children: John Henry, Robert James. B.A., Vassar Coll., 1941. Editor Package Store Mgmt., 1942-44, Jewelry Mag., 1945-53; freelance editor promotion dept. McCall's Mag., Esquire, 1953-56; free-lance fashion and gifts editor Jewelers Circular Keystone, N.Y.C., 1955-71; editor, pub. The Fashionables, 1971-74, The Forecast, 1974—, Nat. Jeweler, Ann. Fashion Guide, 1976-80; editor, assoc. pub. Exec. Jeweler, 1980-83; editor The Gerry Gewirtz Report, N.Y.C., 1983—, The Fashion Source (formerly Internat. Fashion Index), N.Y.C., 1984—. Mem. exec. com. Inner City Council of Cardinal Cooke, N.Y.; chairperson women's task force United Jewish Appeal Fedn.; former bd. govs. Israel Bonds; former trustee Israel Cancer Research Fund, Central Synagogue; bd. dirs. Double Image Theater; former pres. women's aux. Brandeis U. Honored guest Am. Jewish Com., 1978; Israel Cancer Research Fund, 1978-81; recipient Disting. Community Service award Brandeis U., 1987; named to Jewellry Hall Fame, 1988. Mem. N.Y. Fashion Group, Nat. Home Fashions League, Women's Jewelry Assn. (pres. 1983-87 , named editor who has contbd. most to jewelry industry 1984), Phi Delta Epsilon. Clubs: N.Y., Vassar, Overseas Press. Home: 45 Sutton Pl S New York NY 10022 Office: Gerry Gerwitz Report 310 Madison Ave Suite 824 New York NY 10017

GEYER, GEORGIE ANNE, syndicated columnist, educator, author; b. Chgo., Apr. 2, 1935; d. Robert George and Georgie Hazel (Gervens) G. B.S., Northwestern U., 1956; postgrad. (Fulbright scholar), U. Vienna, Austria, 1956-57; Litt. D. (hon.), Lake Forest Coll., (Ill.), 1980. Reporter Southtown Economist, Chgo., 1958; soc. reporter Chgo. Daily News, 1959-60, gen. assignment reporter, 1960-64, Latin Am. corr., 1964-67, roving fgn. corr. and columnist, 1967-75; syndicated columnist Los Angeles Times Syndicate, 1975-80; columnist Universal Press Syndicate, 1980—; Lyle M. Spencer prof. journalism Syracuse U., 1976; steering com. Aspen Inst. Latin Am. Governance Project, 1981-82; convenor Iran Com. for Dem. Action and Human Rights; regular panelist TV news program Washington Week in Rev.; commentator on the BBC; regular panelist Voice of America; regular questioner Meet the Press; sent by Internat. Communication Agy. on 3 worldwide speaking tours on Am. journalism: Nigeria, Zambia, Tanzania and Somalia, 1979, Philippines and Indonesia, 1981, Iceland, Norway, Belgium and Portugal, 1982; panelist Presdl. Debates, Oct., 1984; rep. Fulbright scholar program 40th anniversary, New Zealand, 1987. Author: The New Latins, 1970, The New 100 Years War, 1972, The Young Russians, 1976; (autobiography) Buying the Night Flight, 1983; The First War We Can Drive To, 1988, Fidel!, 1988. Active Orgn. for S.W. Community Chgo., 1960-64; trustee Am. U., Washington, 1981—. Recipient 1st prize Am. Newspaper Guild, 1962; 2d prize Ill. Press Editors Assn., 1962; award for best writing on Latin Am. Overseas Press Club, 1966; Merit award Northwestern U., 1968; Nat. Headliner award Theta Sigma Phi, 1968; Maria Moors Cabot award Columbia U., 1970; Hannah Solomon award Nat. Council Jewish Women, 1973; Ill. Spl. Events Commn. Woman's award, 1975; Northwestern U. Alumnae award, 1981; Woodrow Wilson fellow Rollins Coll., Winter Park, Fla., 1982; Disting. fellow Mortar Bd. Nat. Sr. Honor Soc., Am. U., 1982. Mem. Mortar Bd., Women in Communications, Chgo. Council on Fgn. Relations (dir.), Inst. Internat. Edn. (dir.), Midland Authors, Internat. Inst. Strategic Studies, Internat. Soc. Polit. Psychology, Women's Inst. for Freedom of Press, Internat. Press Inst., Sigma Delta Chi. Home and Office: The Plaza 800 25th St NW Washington DC 20037

GEZELMAN, REGINA MARY JUNE, insurance company manager; b. Bridgeport, Conn., Oct. 24, 1952; d. Samuel Benedicto and Antoinette (Morena) June; m. Ralph Lee Gezelman, III; 1 child, Michael Andrew. B.A. in Journalism, U. Bridgeport, 1974. Supr. cashiers King Cole Stores, Bridgeport, Conn., 1970-76; dept. sec. U. Bridgeport, 1975-76; exec. sec. Glendinning Assocs., Westport, Conn., 1976-77; adminstrv. asst. Meredith Assoc., Westport, 1977-79; asst. to pres. Hiland Assocs., Westport, 1979; exec. mgr. Ponderosa Inc., Southington, Conn., 1979-85; fin. sec. Covenant Ins. Co., Hartford, Conn., 1985-87, supr. cash mgmt., 1987-88, supr. commercial services unit, 1988—. Roman Catholic. Home: 2 Woodside Ct Burlington CT 06013 Office: Covenant Ins Co 95 Woodland St Hartford CT 06105

GHAHREMANI, JOANNE SUE, communications specialist, federal agency official; b. Balt., Mar. 25, 1950; d. Alfred I. and Lorraine M. (Galumbeck) Aaronson; m. Manucher H. Ghahremani, Aug. 31, 1980. BS in Physics, U. Denver, 1971; postgrad., U. Md., 1986—. Instr. English Imperial Iranian Air Force, Tehran, Iran, 1971-72; systems engr., programmer Singer Link, Binghampton, N.Y., 1975-76; sales rep. Am. Telecommunications Corp., College Park, Md., 1977-79, Telephone Corp. Am., Beltsville, Md., 1979-84; communications mgmt. specialist Telecommunications Dept. U.S. GSA, Washington, 1984; telecommunications specialist Nat. Weather Service, Silver Spring, Md., 1985—. Author: The Humanistic Approach to Sales, 1983; editor (manual) Nat. Weather Service Telecommunications Gateway, 1986. Key person GSA United Way, 1985; high sch. tutor Gen. Services Adminstrn., 1985. Mem. Telecommunications Mgmt. of the Capitol Area. Republican. Jewish. Office: Nat Weather Service 8060 13th St Silver Spring MD 20910

GHEZZI, GRACE BARANELLO, accountant; b. Syracuse, N.Y., May 26, 1955; d. Pasquale J. and Barbara J. (Scrimale) Baranello; m. Reno Ghezzi, Jr., Oct. 7, 1978; children: Lisa, Nicholas. Student, Powelson Bus. Inst., 1973-74; BS in Acctg. magna cum laude, Le Moyne Coll., 1977. CPA, N.Y. Staff acct. Deloitte, Haskins & Sells, Syracuse, 1977-79, Cherry Hill, N.J., 1979; corp. auditor McGraw-Hill Co., Hightstown, N.J., 1979-80; pvt. practice acctg. Herkimer, N.Y., 1980-84, Syracuse, 1984-87; ptnr. Peters, Ghezzi & Kawa, Syracuse, 1987—. chair fin. com. St. Charles Borromeo Ch., Syracuse, 1986-88. Mem. Am. Inst. CPA's, N.Y. State Soc. of CPA's. Republican. Roman Catholic. Home: 600 Bronson Rd Syracuse NY 13219 Office: 614 N Salina St Syracuse NY 13208

GHILERI, SIRLEEN JEAN, programmer analyst; b. Southgate, Calif., Mar. 7, 1943; d. Sirl and Dorothy Jean (Kaylor) Myhand; m. Richard Alan Wilson, Apr. 10, 1960 (div. 1972); children—Richard Alan Jr., Michael Dale; m. Norman Phillip Ghileri, Mar. 12, 1973. A.A., Golden West Jr. Coll., 1970. Peace Corps, vol., Ethiopia, 1971; eligibility worker Santa Cruz Co., Calif., 1972-76; rancher Ghigleri Ranch, San Juan Bautista, Calif., 1976-82; applications programmer Madic Corp., Santa Clara, Calif., 1983-85; sr. programmer analyst Skyway Systems, Santa Cruz, 1985—. Foreman Santa Cruz County Grand Jury, 1977-78. Mem. Prime Users Group, Mensa, Santa Cruz Bonsai Kai, Saturday Morning Quilting Ladies (founder). Avocations: bonsai, quilting, investing.

GHILONI, CLAIRE TERESE, state agency program administrator; b. Boston, July 4, 1955; d. John Anthony and Theresa Mary (Dini) G. BS, Bridgewater (Mass.) State Coll., 1977. Cert. elem. and spl. edn. tchr., Mass. Coordinator edn., house mgr. Hegner Ctr., Medford, Mass., 1977-81; program dir. East Middlesex Assn. for Retarded Citizens/East Middlesex Industries, Stoneham, Mass., 1981-85; dir. statewide supported work Bay State Skills Corp./Mass. Rehab. Commn., Boston, 1985—; cons. Scott Meyer, MSW, Boston, 1986—. Office: Mass Rehab Commn 20 Park Plaza Room 337 Boston MA 02116

GHIRALDINI, JOAN, financial executive; b. Bklyn., Mar. 31, 1951; d. Robert and Anne (Centineo) G.; B.A., Smith Coll., 1972; M.B.A., U. Pa., 1975. Intern, N.Y.C. Econ. Devel. Adminstrn., 1971; econ. specialist Western Electric Co., N.Y.C., 1975-76; sr. fin. analyst Internat. Paper Co., N.Y.C., 1976-78, mgr. strategic planning, 1978-81; dir. fin. planning Executone Inc., Jericho, N.Y., 1981-82, dir. strategic bus. planning, 1982-83; dir. corporate analysis Equitable Life Assurance, N.Y.C., 1983-84; asst. v.p. First Boston Corp., N.Y.C., 1985—. Mem. Am. Fin. Assn., N.Am. Soc. for Corp. Planning, Fin. Women's Assn. N.Y. Clubs: Wharton Bus. Sch. (past v.p.), Smith Coll. N.Y. (bd. dirs.). Home: 155 E 38th St New York NY 10016 Office: First Boston Corp 5 World Trade Center New York NY 10048

GHNASSIA, JILL DIX, English language educator; b. Harrisburg, Pa., Oct. 19, 1947; d. Robert Clough and Sara Elizabeth (Hottenstein) Dix; m. Maurice Jean-Henri Ghnassia, Dec. 18, 1980. AB cum laude, Bucknell U., 1969; MA, Duke U., 1972, PhD, 1983. Asst. prof. English U. Hartford, Conn., 1985—; adj. prof. N.C. Wesleyan Coll., Rocky Mount, N.C., 1983-85; reviewer cons. MacMillan Pub. Co., N.Y.C., 1986—. Scholar Duke U., 1972-74, fellow, 1974-76. Mem. MLA, South Atlantic Modern Languages Assn., NE Modern Languages Assn., Nat. Council Tchrs. of English, NE Assn. Tchrs. of English, Conn. Council of Tchrs. of English, NE Victorian Studies Assn., Am. Assn. Univ. Women, Phi Beta Kappa (treas. Greater Hartford chpt.), Kappa Delta Pi, Alpha Lamda Delta (sr. award). Democrat. Lutheran. Home: PO Box 1069 New Hartford CT 06057 Office: U Hartford Coll Basic Studies 200 Bloomfield Ave West Hartford CT 06117

GIAMBRONE, JUDY MARIE, product design engineer; b. Rochester, N.Y., Jan. 1, 1958; d. Raymond Samuel and Mary Annette (Colotti) G. BS in Chem. Engring., Clarkson U., 1980; BA in Chemistry, St. John Fisher Coll., 1980; postgrad., Rochester Inst. Tech., 1984. Devel. engring. Reversal Products div. Eastman, Rochester, N.Y., 1981-84; design coordinator laser printers health scis. div. Eastman Kodak, 1984-88, supr. laser printer systems Health Scis. div., 1988—. Office: Eastman Kodak Co C Plant B-8 2d Fl Rochester NY 14650

GIANINNO, SUSAN MCMANAMA, research psychologist, advertising agency executive; b. Boston, Dec. 25, 1948; d. John Carroll and Barbara (Frances) Magner; m. Lawrence John Gianinno, June 7, 1970; 1 dau., Alexandra Christin. B.A. in English Lit. and Psychology cum laude, Boston Coll., 1970; M.A. in Ednl. Psychology, Northwestern U., 1973; postgrad. in behavioral scis., U. Chgo. Psychiat. asst. Quinn Psychiat., Pavilion St Elizabeth's Hosp., Brighton, Mass., 1967-70; research assoc. com. human devel., dept behavioral scis. U. Chgo., 1973-79; resident adv. U. Chgo. Housing Systems, from 1979; research assoc., then research supr. Needham, Harper and Steers Advt. Inc., Chgo., 1979-80; dir. spl. projects Needham, Harper and Steers Advt. Inc., Chgo., Il, from 1981; now exec. v.p., dir. research services Young & Rubicam N.Y. Contbr. papers, reports to profl. jours. Univ. scholar U. Chgo., 1975-77. Mem. Am. Psychol. Assn., Assn. Consumer Research, Nat. Council Family Relations, Am. Mktg. Assn., Midwest Assn. Pub. Opinion Research, Mass. Tchrs. Assn. Home: 5454 South Shore Dr Chicago IL 60615 Office: Young & Rubicam NY 285 Madison Ave New York NY 10017 *

GIANNETTASSIO, ANGELA RITA, insurance company executive; b. Phila.; d. Harry Ericor Enrico and Tomasina (D'Urso) G. BBA magna cum laude, Temple U., 1977, MBA in Fin., 1983. Lic. real estate broker, Pa. and N.J. Mgr. real estate Prudential Ins. Co., Phila., 1960—. Mem. GEAR neighborhood Assn. Mem. Building Owners and Mgrs. Assn., Clear Air Soc., Beta Gamma Signa. Club: St. Monica's Bowling. Home: 2132 Shunk St Philadelphia PA 19145

GIANOLA, PATTI LEE, nursing educator; b. Worcester, Mass., Sept. 10, 1954; d. Harold Raymond and Edna Maude (Williamson) Thompson; m. James Howard Morse, Sept. 18, 1976 (div. June 1979); m. Peter Joseph Gianola, June 20, 1981; 1 son, Andrew Thompson. A.A., Quinsigamond Community Coll., 1976; B.S.N., Worcester State Coll., 1982. Gerontology nurse Westboro Nursing Home (Mass.), 1976-77; med.-surg. nurse Framingham Union Hosp. (Mass.), 1977-78, ICU nurse, 1978-81; instr. nursing sci. Central Maine Med. Ctr., Lewiston, 1982-83; instr. nursing edn. St. Mary's Gen. Hosp., Lewiston, 1983-87; with Androscoggin Cardiology Assocs., Auburn, Maine, 1987—; nurse vol. ARC Blood Mobile, Framingham, 1978-80; instr. basic life support Am. Heart Assn., Lewiston, 1983. Mem. Am. Assn. Critical Care Nurses. Democrat. Methodist. Lodge: Order of Rainbow Girls. Office: St Mary's Gen Hosp 45 Golder St Lewiston ME 04240

GIANTURCO, PAOLA, advertising executive; b. Urbana, Ill., July 22, 1939; d. Cesare and Verna Bertha (Daily) Gianturco; B.A., Stanford U., 1961; postgrad. U. So. Calif., 1971; 1 child, Scott Sangster. Pub. relations dir. Joseph Magnin, San Francisco, 1961-67; pub. relations dir., account exec. Hall & Levine Advt. Agy., Los Angeles, 1968-73, v.p., account supr., 1973-76, sr. v.p., 1977-82; v.p. Dancer Fitzgerald Sample, 1982-87, v.p. mgmt. supr. Saatchi and Saatchi DFS, Inc., 1987—. Past bd. dirs. The Country Schs., Mem. Women in Communications, Stanford Profl. Women (past mem. bd. dirs.), Women in Communications, Internat. Assn. Bus. Communicators, Bus. and Profl. Advt. Assn. Home: 30 Cecily Ln Mill Valley CA 94941 Office: Saatchi & Saatchi DFS Corp Communications Group 1010 Battery St PO Box 7166 San Francisco CA 94120

GIASOLLI, ROSE MARIE ANTOINETTE LEVATO, real estate company executive; b. Chgo., Mar. 14, 1939; d. Rosario A. and Carmella (D'Ambrose) Levato; student Chgo. Sch. Music, 1957, Santa Monica City Coll., 1960, South West Coll., 1965, student U. Hawaii, 1970, El Paso Community Coll., 1977-79; cert. U. Tex., 1975; grad. Real Estate Inst., 1979; m. Mero V. Giasolli, Aug. 10, 1957; children—Vincent S., Michael J., Anthony R., Robert M. Real estate sales agt. PDC Realty, El Paso, Tex., 1975-77; real estate broker DeWitt & Rearick Inc., El Paso, 1977-79; partner and prin. broker White-Giasolli-Hary Inc., El Paso, 1979-80, dir., 1980—; partner, pres. Remax West, El Paso, 1981—. Active performing mem. Ballet Folklorica, El Paso, 1978-85, support mem., 1985—; founder Ladies Mission Group, Kwajalein Island, Marshall Islands, 1968, pres., 1968-70; bd. dirs. Family Outreach, Shelter for Battered Women; 1st Woman pres. Investment Property Exchangors 1985-86, 86-87; chmn. si se puede dozen El Paso Civic Group. Cert. residential specialist. Mem. Tex. Assn. Realtors (profl. standards com.), Nat. Assn. Realtors, El Paso Bd. Realtors (chmn. Make Am Better program), Women's Council of Realtors (founder El Paso chpt. 1979, pres. 1979-81), Internat. Real Estate Fedn., El Paso C. of C., Soc. Arts and Letters. Clubs: Amici Italian (founder, pres. 1977-78), Tex. A&M Mothers (pres. 1979-80). Office: 250 Thunderbird El Paso TX 79912

GIBB, LISA JO CHRISTENSON, speech-language pathologist; b. Moline, Ill., Dec. 17, 1961; d. Richard Alan and Joanne Allen (Atkinson) Christenson; m. Ronald Scott, Feb. 14, 1987. BS, U. Wis., Stevens Point, 1984, MS, 1986. Cert. speech-lang. pathologist, myofunctional therapist in neuromuscular facilitation and neurodevel. therapy. Speech-lang. pathology clin. fellow Med. Ctr., Princeton, N.J., 1987-88, speech-lang. pathologist, 1988—, care staff orientator, inservice presentor, 1987-88, supr. stroke/aphasia support group, 1988—. Contbr. articles in field to profl. jours. Mem. Am. Speech-Lang.-Hearing Assn., Myofunctional Therapy Assn. Am., N.J. Speech and Hearing Assn. (com. for ann. state conv.). Republican. Club: Jr. League (Delaware Valley). Home: 110 Lowell Ct Apt 2 Princeton NJ 08540 Office: Med Ctr Princeton 79 Bayard Ln Princeton NJ 08540

GIBBAS, DORIS BERTHE, federal agency administrator; b. Fall River, Mass., Aug. 12, 1929; d. Adelard Edward and Eva Rose (Aubut) Berube; children: Clair, John, Mark. Postmaster U.S. Postal Service, Center Strafford, N.H., 1983-85, Rollinsford, N.H., 1985—. Chair voter registration Rollingsford, Am. Red Cross, Dover, N.H., 1986-87. Mem. Nat. Assn. Postmasters, Post Office Women, Nat. Assn. Exec. Women., Am. Legion Aux. Roman Catholic. Club: Gold Star Wives.

GIBBENS, CAROLBETH, librarian; b. Pueblo, Colo., May 1, 1944; d. Meril Sidney and Madge (Slade) G. BA, Ft. Lewis Coll., 1965; MLS, U. So. Calif., 1967. Cert. tchr., Calif. Circulation librarian U. Calif., Santa Barbara, 1967-70, reference librarian, 1970—, instr., 1973—, interlibrary loan librarian, 1986-87, coordinator data services, 1986—; instr. library sci. dept. U. So. Calif., Los Angeles, 1976-78. Editor: Student Political Awareness, 1971. Bd. dirs. Univ. and State Employees Credit Union, Goleta, Calif., 1980—. Mem. Calif. Assn. Research Libraries, Calif. Clearinghouse on Library Instn. Home: PO Box 14628 UCSB Santa Barbara CA 93107 Office: U Calif Santa Barbara Reference Dept Library Santa Barbara CA 93107

GIBBES, PAMELA SHIRLEY, communications executive, consultant; b. Greenville, S.C., Aug. 17, 1952; d. Leland Hugh and Laura Virginia (Mullikin) Shirley; m. William Ravenel Gibbes, Aug. 12, 1972 (div. Oct. 1986); 1 child, Garland Virginia. BA with honors, U. S.C., 1973. Prof. history Pepperdine U., Philippines, 1974-76; rep. sales The Burroughs Corp., Jacksonville, Fla., 1976-78, mgr. sales, 1978-82; exec. dir. Rosen, M.D. & Assocs., Jacksonville, 1982-84; dir. corp. devel. Reynolds, Smith & Hills, Jacksonville, 1984-86; mgr. ops. AT&T, Jacksonville, 1986—; apptd. mem. Gov.'s Bus. Adv. Council, 1984—, S.E. U.S. Adv. Bd. for Improvements in Edn.; cons. bus., Jacksonville, 1982—, U. North Fla., Jacksonville, 1982—, Fla. Community Coll., Jacksonville, 1982—; lectr. in field. V.p. Selva Marina Community Assn., Jacksonville, 1984-86; elder Palms Presbyn. Ch., Jacksonville, 1983—; apptd. mem. Leadership Jacksonville, 1985-86. Mem. Jacksonville C. of C. (various bus. coms.), Selva Marina C. of C., Phi Beta Kappa, Phi Sigma Tau. Republican. Club: Jacksonville Ski. Home: 1885 N Sherry Dr Atlantic Beach FL 32233 Office: AT&T 8000 Baymeadows Way Jacksonville FL 32216

GIBBONS, BARBARA, author, columnist, cooking educator; b. Newark. Writer nat. syndicated column The Slim Gourmet, United Features Syndicate, 1971—; organizer, instr. low-calories cooking classes, 1968—; guest on radio and TV programs including Today and Good Morning, America. Author: The Slim Gourmet Cookbook (Tastemaster award), 1976; The International Slim Gormet Cookbook (Tastemaster award), 1978; Family Circle Creative Low Calorie Cooking; The Consumer Guide Diet Cookbook; The Diet Watchers Cookbook; The Year-Round Turkey Cookbook, 1979; Lean Cuisine, 1979; The Light and Easy Cookbook, 1980; Calories Don't Count, 1980; Salads for All Seasons, 1982; Slim Gourmet Sweets and Treats, 1982, The Thirty-Five Plus Diet for Women, 1987 (New York Times Bestseller List). Mem. Am. Soc. Journalists and Authors, Authors Guild, Nat. Fedn. Press Women. Clubs: Newswomen's (N.Y.C.), Travel Journalists Guild. Address: 15 Wayland Dr Verona NJ 07044

GIBBONS, CECILIA, nurse, hospital administrator; b. Salem, Mass., June 8, 1936; d. James and Beatrice (Gilhooly) G. Diploma, St. Elizabeth's Hosp., 1957; BS in Nursing, U. Tenn., 1981; MS in Nursing, U. Ala., 1983. RN. Staff RN VA Med. Ctr., West Roxbury, Mass., 1959-69, asst. chief nursing service, 1984-85; supr. operating room VA Med. Ctr., Nashville, 1977-81; supr. nursing home VA Med. Ctr., Syracuse, N.Y., 1983-84; chief nursing service VA Med. Ctr., Sioux Falls, S.D., 1985—; head nurse operating room Faulkner Hosp., Boston, 1969-77. Grantee VA, 1981. Mem. Am. Nurses Assn., Orgn. Nurse Execs., Sigma Theta Tau. Office: VA Med Ctr 2501 W 22d St Sioux Falls SD 57101

GIBBONS, JULIA SMITH, judge; b. Pulaski, Tenn., Dec. 23, 1950; d. John Floyd and Julia Jackson (Abernathy) Smith; m. William Lockhart Gibbons, Aug. 11, 1973; children: Rebecca Carey, William Lockhart Jr. B.A., Vanderbilt U., 1972; J.D., U. Va., 1975. Bar: Tenn. 1975. Law clk. to judge U.S. Ct. Appeals, 1975-76; assoc. Farris, Hancock, Gilman, Branan, Lanier & Hellen, Memphis, 1976-79; legal advisor Gov. Lamar Alexander, Nashville, 1979-81; judge 15th Jud. Cir., Memphis, 1981-83, U.S. Dist. Ct. (we. dist.) Tenn., Memphis, 1983—. Fellow Am. Bar Found.; mem. ABA, Tenn. Bar Assn., Memphis and Shelby County Bar Assn., Nat. Assn. Women Judges, Am. Judicature Soc., Phi Beta Kappa, Order of Coif. Presbyterian. Office: US Dist Ct 1157 Fed Bldg 167 N Main St Memphis TN 38103

GIBBONS, SHEILA MARIE, aerospace company executive; b. N.Y.C., Mar. 31, 1931; d. Joseph Vincent and Edna Marie (McCarthy) MacAvoy; children: Laura Cecile Burns, Philip Damian, Sally Honora Mc Mahon. BA in Art, Queens Coll., CUNY, 1952; JD, St. John's U., 1976. Bar: N.Y. 1977, Calif. 1977. Assoc. Carnahan & Freeman, Woodland Hills, Calif., 1977; asst. sec. Northrop Corp., Los Angeles, 1978-80, sec., 1980-83, v.p., sec., 1983—. Honoree Tribute to Women in Internat. Industry, Nat. Bd. YWCA, Houston, 1983. Mem. ABA, Los Angeles Bar Assn. (subcom. fed. securities law), Am. Soc. Corp. Secs. (bd. dirs. 1985-88, pres. Los Angeles chpt. 1984-88, adv. com. 1981-88, securities law com. 1981-84, ad hoc com. on tender offers 1984-85, securities industry com. 1985—), Am.-Irish Hist. Soc. Office: Northrop Corp 1840 Century Park E Los Angeles CA 90067

GIBBS, ANN, chemist; b. Corpus Christi, Tex., May 19, 1941; d. Frank James and Elizabeth Ann (Setzer) G.; student Tulane U., 1958-59; BA, U. Tex., Austin, 1961; MS, U. Ark., 1964. Research asst. Inst. Marine Sci., U. Tex., 1960-62; chemist DuPont Co., Savannah River plant, Aiken, S.C., 1966—; mem. ad hoc com. NDA instrumentation U.S. Dept. Energy, 1980-82. AEC fellow, 1962-65. Mem. ASTM (chair C26, 12 1988—), AAAS, Am. Chem. Soc. (chmn. Savannah River sect. 1980, alt. councilor Savannah River sect. 1985—), Am. Phys. Soc., Am. Nuclear Soc. (sec. Savannah River sect. 1986-87), Inst. Nuclear Materials Mgmt (exec. bd. Savannah River sect. 1983-86). Presbyterian. Research in nuclear spectroscopy and nondestructive instrumentation. Home: PO Box 6624 North Augusta SC 29841 Office: Bldg 221-10H Savannah River Plant Aiken SC 29808

GIBBS, JEWELLE TAYLOR, clinical psychologist; b. Stratford, Conn., Nov. 4, 1933; d. Julian Augustus and Margaret Pauline (Morris) Taylor; A.B. cum laude, Radcliffe Coll., 1955; postgrad. Harvard-Radcliffe Program in Bus. Adminstrn., 1959; M.S.W., U. Calif., Berkeley, 1970, Ph.D., 1980; m. James Lowell Gibbs, Jr., Aug. 25, 1956; children—Geoffrey Taylor, Lowell Dabney. Jr. mgmt. asst. U.S. Dept. Labor, Washington, 1955-56; market research coordinator Pillsbury Co., Mpls., 1959-61; clin. social worker Stanford (Calif.) U. Student Health Service, 1970-74, 78-79, research assoc. dept. psychiatry, 1971-73; asst. prof. Sch. Social Welfare U. Calif., Berkeley, 1979-83, acting assoc. prof., 1983-86, assoc. prof., 1986—, mem. exec. com. Sch. of Social Welfare, 1987—, chmn. task force on safety, 1986-88; pvt. practice as clin. psycho-therapist, 1983—; fellow Bunting Inst., Radcliffe Coll., spring, 1985. Bd. regents U. Santa Clara (Calif.), 1980-84; mem. Minn. State Commn. on Status of Women, 1963-65; co-chairperson Minn. Women's Com. for Civil Rights, 1963-65. NIMH fellow, 1979; Soroptimist Internat. grantee, 1978-79. Fellow Am. Orthopsychiat. Assn. (bd. dirs. 1985-86); mem. Am. Psychol. Assn., Nat. Assn. Social Workers, Internat. women's Forum (San Francisco chpt.), Western Psychol. Assn., Am. Assn. Sociology (McCormick award 1987). Democrat. Mem. editorial bd. Am. Jour. Orthopsychiatry, 1980-84; bd. publs. Nat. Assn. Social Workers, 1980-82; contbr. chpts. to books, articles to profl. jours. Office: Haviland Hall Sch Social Welfare U Calif Berkeley CA 94720

GIBBS, JUNE NESBITT, state senator; b. Newton, Mass., June 13, 1922; d. Samuel Frederick and Lulu (Glazier) Nesbitt; m. Donald T. Gibbs, Dec. 8, 1945; 1 child, Elizabeth. BA in Math., Wellesley Coll., 1943; MA in Math., Boston U., 1947; postgrad., U. R.I., 1981-84. Mem. Republican Nat. Com. from, R.I., 1969-80; sec. Republican Nat. Com., 1977-80; mem. R.I. State Senate, 1985—; mem. def. adv. com. Women in Services, 1970-72, vice chmn., 1972. Mem. Middletown Town Council, 1974-80, 82-84, pres., 1978-80. Served to lt. (J.G.) USNR, 1943-46. Home: 163 Riverview Ave Middletown RI 02840 Office: Minority Office Statehouse Room 120 Providence RI 02903

GIBBS, MARY BRAMLETT, banker; b. Corona, Calif., Sept. 18, 1953; d. Kenneth Frank and Kathy Lee (Hill) Harris; m. Charles Merrill Gibbs, 1987; student U. Md., 1974-77, Southwestern Grad. Sch. Banking. Bookkeeper, First State Bank & Trust, Houston, 1972; successively teller, sec., relief supr., mgr., br. mgr. Peoples Nat. Bank of Md., Suitland, 1972-77; with Post Oak Bank, Houston, 1977-82, asst. v.p. ops. mgmt., 1980-82; v.p. comml. loan ops. First City Nat. Bank Houston, 1982—. Bd. dirs., life mem. Big Sisters-Big Bros. of Houston; mediator Neighborhood Justice Ctr., 1981; mem. Christ Ch. Cath.; bd. dirs. Tex. So. U. Found. Named Outstanding Young Houstonian, 1985, Woman on the Move, 1987. Mem. Nat. Assn. Bank Women, NOW, Houston C. of C. (chair leadership Houston policy council). Contbr. articles to profl. jours. Office: 1001 Main St B-13 Houston TX 77001

GIBBY, MABEL ENID KUNCE, psychologist; b. St. Louis, Mar. 30, 1926; d. Ralph Waldo and Mabel Enid (Warren) Kunce; student Washington U., St. Louis, 1943-44, postgrad., 1955-56; B.A., Park Coll., 1945; M.A., McCormick Theol. Sem., 1947; postgrad. Columbia U., 1948, U. Kansas City, 1949, George Washington U., 1953; M.Ed., U. Mo., 1951, Ed.D., 1952; m. John Francis Gibby, Aug. 27, 1948; children—Janet Marie (Mrs. Kim Williams), Harold Steven, Helen Elizabeth, Diane Louise, John Andrew, Keith Sherridan, Daniel Jay. Dir. religious edn. Westport Presbyn. Ch. Kansas City, Mo., 1947-49; tchr. elementary schs., Kansas City, 1949-50; high sch. counselor Arlington (Va.) Pub. Schs., 1952-54; counselor adult counseling services Washington U., 1955-56; counseling psychologist Coral Gables (Fla.) VA Hosp., 1956—; counseling psychologist Miami (Fla.) VA Hosp., 1956—, chief counseling psychology sect., 1982-86; psychologist State of Fla., Miami, 1987—; coordinator vocat. rehab. sect. psychology service, 1986—, psychologist Office Disability Determination Fla. Hdqrs., 1987—. Sec. bd. dirs. Fla. Vocat. Rehab. Found. Recipient Meritorious Service citation Fla. C. of C., 1965, President's Com. on Employment of Handicapped, 1965; commendation for meritorious service Com. on Employment of Physically Handicapped Dade County, 1965, 81, named outstanding rehab. profl., 1966, 81; named Profl. Fed. Employee of Year, Greater Miami Fed. Exec. Council, 1966; Outstanding Fed. Service award Greater Miami Fed. Exec. Council, 1966; Fed. Woman's award U.S. Civil Service Commn., 1968, Community Headliner award Theta Sigma Phi, 1968, Outstanding Alumni award Park Coll., 1968, Freedom award The Chosen Few, Korean War Vets. Assn., 1986; certificate of appreciation Bur. Customs, U.S. Treasury Dept., 1969, Fla. Dept. Health and Rehab. Services, 1970. Mem. Am., Dade County (past sec.) psychol. assns., Nat., Fla. (past dir. Dade County chpt.) rehab. assns., Nat. Rehab. Counseling Assn. (past sec.). Patentee in field. Home: 10260 SW 56th St Miami FL 33165

GIBLETT, ELOISE ROSALIE, hematology educator; b. Tacoma, Wash., Jan. 17, 1921; d. William Richard and Rose (Godfrey) G. B.S., U. Wash., 1942, M.S., 1947, M.D. with honors, 1951. Mem. faculty U. Wash. Sch. Medicine, 1957—, research prof., 1967-87, emeritus research prof., 1987—; asso. dir., head immunogenetics Puget Sound Blood Center, 1955-79, exec. dir., 1979-87, emeritus exec. dir., 1987—; former mem. several research coms. NIH. Author: Genetic Markers in Human Blood, 1969; Editorial bd. numerous jours. including Blood, Am. Jour. Human Genetics, Transfusion, Vox Sanguinis; Contbr. over 190 articles to profl. jours. Recipient fellowships, grants, Emily Cooley, Karl Landsteiner, Philip Levine and Alexander Wiener immunohematology awards, distinguished alumna award U. Wash. Sch. Med., 1987. Fellow AAAS; Mem. Nat. Acad. Scis., Am. Soc. Human Genetics (pres. 1973), Am. Soc. Hematology, Am. Assn. Immunologists, Brit. Soc. Immunology, Internat. Soc. Hematologists, Am. Fedn. Clin. Research, Western Assn. Physicians, Assn. Am. Physicians, Sigma Xi, Alpha Omega Alpha. Home: 6533 53d St NE Seattle WA 98115 Office: Puget Sound Blood Ctr Terry and Madison Sts Seattle WA 98104

GIBSON, ALTHEA, professional tennis player, golfer, state official; b. Silver, S.C., Aug. 25, 1927; d. Daniel and Annie B. (Washington) G.; m. William A. Darben, Oct. 17, 1965; m. Sydney Llewellyn, Apr. 11, 1983. B.S., Fla. A&M Coll., 1953; D. Pub. Service (hon.), Monmouth Coll., 1980; LittD (hon.), U. N.C., Wilmington, 1987. Amateur tennis player in U.S., Europe and S.Am., 1941-58; asst. instr. dept. health and phys. edn. Lincoln U., Jefferson City, Mo., 1953-55; made profl. tennis tour with Harlem Globetrotters, 1959; community relations rep. Ward Baking Co., 1959; joined Ladies Profl. Golf Assn. as profl. golfer, 1963; apptd. to N.Y. State Recreation Council, 1964; staff mem. Essex County Park Commn., Newark, 1970; recreation supr. Essex County Park Commn., 1970-71; dir. tennis programs, profl. Valley View Racquet Club, Northvale, N.J., 1972; tennis pro Morven 1973—; athletic commr. State of N.J., 1975—; recreation mgr. City of East Orange, N.J., 1980; mem. N.J. State Athletic Control Bd., 1986. Appeared in: movie in The Horse Soldiers, 1958; author: I Always Wanted to Be Somebody, 1958. Named Woman Athlete of Yr. AP Poll, 1957-58; named to Lawn Tennis Hall of Fame and Tennis Mus., 1971; named to Black Athletes Hall of Fame, 1974; named to S.C. Hall of Fame, 1983; named to Fla. Sports Hall of Fame, 1984. Mem. Alpha Kappa Alpha. Home: PO Box 768 East Orange NJ 07019

GIBSON, CHARLENE KREIGER, business counselor; b. Chillicothe, Ohio, Aug. 2, 1935; d. Leslie Bryan and Ruth (Miller) Kreiger; m. Edwin Marvin Gibson, May 3, 1953; children: Cindy Anne, Cathleen June. AS, U. Indpls., 1980; BS, Ind. U., 1984. Dental materials research sec. Ind. U. Sch. Dentistry, Indpls., 1952-65; sec. sales Blue Ribbon Realty, Indpls., 1965-68; owner, operator J.C.'s Secretarial Service, Indpls., 1968-75; legal asst. James L. Powell Atty. at Law, PC, Indpls., 1975-80; tax litigation legal asst. Bayh, Tabbert & Capehart Law Firm, Indpls., 1980-82; probate and estate acct. legal asst. Gerald L. Cowan, Lawyer, Indpls., 1982-84; owner Gen. Bus. Services, Cicero, Ind., 1985—. Asst. campaign organizer Nels Acherson for Fifth Dist. U.S. Congress, Noblesville, Ind., 1980; candidate Dem. precinct com., Cicero, 1980; active Found. for Christian Living Bible Club, Pawling, N.Y. Mem. Nat. Assn. Legal Assts. (dist. dir. Tulsa, Indpls. 1976-80), Ind. Legal Assts. (pres. 1978-80, treas. 1980-82). Mem. Disciples of Christ Ch. Home: 32 Forest Bay Ln Cicero IN 46034 Office: Gen Bus Services 240 S Range Line Rd Carmel IN 46032

GIBSON, ELEANOR BEATRICE, artist, library consultant; b. London, Mar. 8, 1905; d. Harry Hepburn and Anne Elizabeth (White) G.; brought to U.S., 1905, derivative citizenship, 1914; grad. Loomis-Chaffee Sch., 1923; A.B., Cornell U., 1928; student St. Joseph Coll., West Hartford, 1937-38; M.S. in Library Sci., Syracuse U., 1957. With Aetna Life & Casualty Co., Hartford, Conn., 1928-42, librarian research div., 1933-42; librarian Logan Lewis Library, Carrier Corp. Research Center, Syracuse, N.Y., 1947-67, spl. adviser, 1967-70; tech. supr. computerized union catalogue project Conn. State Library, Hartford, 1968-71; now artist, library cons. Served from 1st lt. (WAAC) WAC, AUS, 1942-46; capt., 1950-51. Recipient Honors award Spl. Libraries Assn., 1968, named to Hall of Fame. Mem. Spl. Libraries Assn. (pres. Western N.Y. 1959-60; nat. chmn. metals materials div. 1961-62), Conn. Acad. Fine Arts (sustaining mem.), West Hartford Art League (hon. life), Alumni Assn. Syracuse U. Sch. Library and Info. Sci. (pres. 1967-68), Loomis-Chaffee Fifty Plusers, Friends of Fidelco Guide Dog Found., Nat. Mus. Women in Arts (charter mem.), Conn. Law Enforcement Found., Wadsworth Atheneum, New Britain Mus. of Am. Art, Am. Legion, Assn. on Am. Indian Affairs, Pi Lambda Sigma (pres. 1958-59), Beta Phi Mu (local pres. 1959-60). Episcopalian. Editor: Guide to Metallurgical Information, 1965; contbr. articles to profl. jours. Home: 23 Fernridge Rd West Hartford CT 06107-1425 Studio: White Studio Leighton Hill Rd Newbury VT 05051

GIBSON, ELEANOR JACK (MRS. JAMES J. GIBSON), psychology educator; b. Peoria, Ill., Dec. 7, 1910; d. William A. and Isabel (Grier) Jack; m. James J. Gibson, Sept. 17, 1932; children: James J., Jean Grier. B.A., Smith Coll., 1931, M.A., 1933, D.Sc., 1972; Ph.D., Yale U., 1938; D.Sc., Rutgers U., 1973, Trinity Coll., 1982, Bates Coll., 1985; L.H.D. (hon.), SUNY-Albany, 1984; DSc, U. S.C., 1987. Asst., instr., asst. prof. Smith Coll., 1931-49; research assoc. psychology Cornell U., Ithaca, N.Y., 1949-66; prof. Cornell U., 1972—, Susan Linn Sage prof. psychology, 1972—; fellow Inst. for Advanced Study, Princeton, 1959-60, Inst. for Advanced Study in Behavioral Scis., Stanford, Calif., 1963-64; vis. prof. Mass. Inst. Tech., 1973, Inst. Child Devel., U. Minn., 1980; vis. disting. prof. U. Calif., Davis, 1978; vis. scientist Salk Inst., La Jolla, Calif., 1979; vis. prof. U. Pa., 1984; Montgomery fellow Dartmouth Coll., 1986; Woodruff vis. prof. psychology, Emory U., 1988. Author: Principles of Perceptual Learning and Development, 1967 (Century award), (with H. Levin) The Psychology of Reading, 1975. Recipient Wilbur Cross medal Yale U., 1973; Howard Crosby Warren medal, 1977; medal for disting. service Tchrs. Coll., Columbia U., 1983; Guggenheim fellow, 1972-73. Fellow AAAS (div. chairperson 1983), Am. Psychol. Assn. (Distinguished Scientist award 1968, G. Stanley Hall award 1970, pres. div. 3 1977, Gold medal award 1986); mem. Eastern Psychol. Assn. (pres. 1968), Soc. Exptl. Psychologists, Nat. Acad. Edn., Psychonomic Soc., Soc. Research in Child Devel. (Disting. Sci. Contbn. award 1981), Nat. Acad. Sci., Am. Acad. Arts and Scis., Brit. Psychol. Soc. (hon.), N.Y. Acad. Scis. (hon.), Italian Soc. Research in Child Devel. (hon.), Phi Beta Kappa, Sigma Xi. Home: RD1 Box 265A Middlebury VT 05753

GIBSON, ELISABETH JANE, principal; b. Salina, Kans., Apr. 28, 1937; d. Cloyce Wesley and Margaret Mae (Yost) Kasson; m. William Douglas Miles, Jr., Aug. 20, 1959; m. Harry Benton Gibson, Jr., July 1, 1970. A.B., Colo. State Coll., 1954-57; M.A. (fellow), San Francisco State Coll., 1967-68; Ed.D., U. No. Colo., 1978; postgrad. U. Denver, 1982. Cert. tchr., prin., Colo. Tchr. elem. schs., Santa Paula, Calif., 1957-58, Salina, Kans., 1958-63, Goose Bay, Labrador, 1963-64, Jefferson County, Colo., 1965-66, Topeka, 1966-67; diagnostic tchr. Cen. Kans. Diagnostic Remedial Edn. Ctr., Salina, 1968-70; instr. Loretto Heights Coll., Denver, 1970-72; co-owner Ednl. Cons. Enterprises, Inc., Greeley, Colo., 1974-77; resource coordinator Region VIII Resource Access Project Head Start Mile High Consortium, Denver, 1976-77; exec. dir. Colo. Fedn. Council Exceptional Children, Denver, 1976-77;

asst. prof. Met. State Coll., Denver, 1979; dir. spl. edn. Northeast Colo. Bd. Coop. Edn. Services, Haxtun, Colo., 1979-82; prin. elem. jr. high sch., Elizabeth, Colo., 1982-84; prin., spl. projects coordinator Summit County Schs., Frisco, Colo., 1985—; prin. Frisco Elem. Sch., 1985—; cons. Colo. Dept. Edn., 1984-85; cons. Colo. Dept. Edn., 1984-85, Montana Dept. Edn., 1978-79, Love Pub. Co., 1976-78, Colo. Dept. Inst., 1974-75; pres. Found. Exceptional Children, 1980-81; pres. bd. dirs. Northeast Colo. Services Handicapped, 1981-82; bd. dirs. Dept. Ednl. Specialists, Colo. Assn. Sch. Execs., 1982-84; mem. Colo. Title IV Adv. Council, 1980-82; mem. Mellon Found. grant steering com. Colo. Dept. Edn., 1984-85. Mem. Colo. Dept Edn. Data Acquisition Reporting and Utilization Com., 1983, Denver City County Commn. for Disabled, 1978-81; chmn. regional edn. com. 1970 White House Conf. Children and Youth; bd. dirs. Advocates for Victims of Assault, 1986—; mem. adv. bd. Alpine Counseling Ctr., 1986—; mem. placement alternatives commn. Dept. of Social Services, 1986—; mem. adv. com. Colo. North Cen. Assn. Recipient Ann. Service award Colo. Fedn. Council Exceptional Children, 1981. Mem. Colo. Assn. Retarded Citizens, Assn. Supervision Curriculum Devel., Nat. Assn. Elem. Sch. Prins., Kappa Delta Pi, Pi Lambda Theta, Phi Delta Kappa. Republican. Methodist. Club: Order Eastern Star. Author: (with H. Padzensky) Goal Guide: A minicourse in writing goals and behavioral objectives for special education, 1975; (with H. Padzensky and S. Sporn) Assaying Student Behavior: A minicourse in student assessment techniques, 1974. Contbr. articles to profl. jours. Home: 2443 S Colorado Blvd Denver CO 80222 Office: Frisco Elem Sch PO Box 7 Frisco CO 80443

GIBSON, JUDITH ANN, English language educator; b. Salem, Ill., Mar. 1, 1947; d. Charles Francis and Sarah Jane (Gough) Laughlin; m. Gregory Allen Gibson, Aug. 8, 1981. AA, Brevard Jr. Coll., Cocoa, Fla., 1968; BS, Ind. U., 1971; MS, Marantha Coll., Watertown, Wis., 1981. Cert. tchr. Ind., Wis., Fla. Tchr. Indpls. Pub. Schs., 1971-74, Santa Rosa Christian Sch., Milton, Fla., 1974-76; instr. Maranatha Coll., Watertown, Wis., 1976-81; tchr. Bapt. Acad., Indpls., 1981-83, Colonial Christian Sch., Indpls., 1983-85; adminstrv. asst. Dept. Edn. Tchr. Quality sect., Indpls., 1985—; co-chairperson Ind. Tchr. of Yr. Com., 1986—; mem. Internal Functional Com. for Internship Porgram Ind.; cons. in field. Mem. Nat. Fed. Rep. Women, Indpls., 1984, Indpls. Symphonic Choir, 1982-85, Indpls. Opera Co., 1986—; co-founder WBRI Radio Chorale Co., 1983. Recipient Brotherhood/Service award Ashdot Pres. Ashdot Yaakov Ichud, Israel Kibbutz, 1978. Republican. Presbyterian. Home: 4544 Glastonbury Ct #76 Indianapolis IN 46237

GIBSON, LAURA NORMAN, personnel director; b. Cleve., May 16, 1956; d. George R. and Coral L. (Hendrickson) Norman. BS in Bus., Fla. So. Coll., 1978; MBA, Fla. Atlantic U., 1981. Auditor trainee 1st Nat. Bank Palm Beach, Fla., 1978-79; adminstrv. asst. personnel dept. APC Energy Group, Palm Beach, Fla., 1979-80; adminstrv. asst. Peat, Marwick, Mitchell & Co., Washington, 1980-81; dir. personnel Jason Soda Systems, Inc., South Windsor, Conn., 1982-86, Brennan Coll. Service, Inc., Springfield, Mass., 1986—. Coordinator Cleve. Red Cross Bloodmobile, 1974; vol. Clev. and Lakeland, Fla. Red Cross, 1975-77, Palm Beach Big Brother/Big Sister program, 1980; campaign capt. Springfield (Mass.) United Way, 1987. Mem. Am. Soc. Personnel Adminstrs., Am. Compensation Assn., Kappa Delta Pi, Omnicron Delta Kappa, Phi Xi Theta (treas., outstanding bus. woman member, 1978). Office: Brennan Coll Service 45 Island Pond Rd Springfield MA 01118

GIBSON, MARTHA ALTHOUSE, savings and loan association executive; b. Orangeburg, S.C., Apr. 6, 1943; d. Woodrow Elie and Pearl (Wall) Rudd; student Patricia Stevens Finishing Coll., 1962, U. N.C., 1965, Foot Hill Coll., 1972; 1 dau., Robin Marie Althouse; m. Marvin McCall Gibson, 1982. With Chevy Chase Savs. Bank, Md., 1972-83 v.p., controller, 1977-83; sec.-treas. Glade Drive Devel. Co., North Ode Street Devel. Co., 1981-83; exec. v.p. Kingsley Savs. Assn., Gaithersburg, Md., 1983-84; asst. sec. Manor Investment Co. Mem. Fin. Mgrs. Soc. Savs. Instns. (editor chpt. newsletters. chmn. chpt. coms., nat. award of excellence 1977-78, treas. 1981-82, sec. 1982-83, v.p. 1983-84), Nat. Savs. and Loan League, Md. Savs. and Loan League, Women's Network, Republican. Clubs: Jr. Women's, Innerwheel of Greater Washington, Capital Speakers. Editor Inner Wheel Newsletter, 1984-85. Home: 9000 Clewerwall Dr Bethesda MD 20817

GIBSON, NANCY GREENLEAF, traffic engineer; b. Saginaw, Mich.; d. David Scott and Hazel Virginia (Atwood) Greenleaf; m. Thomas H. Gibson, Jr., June 18, 1983. BS in Engring., U. Mich., 1982. Acting transp. dir. Bi-State Met. Planning Commn., Rock Island, Ill., 1984-85; transp. engr. SE Mich. Council of Govts., Detroit, 1985-86; traffic engr. City of Ann Arbor, Mich., 1986—. Office: City of Ann Arbor 100 N Fifth Ave Ann Arbor MI 48107

GIBSON, PATRICIA ANN, library administrator; b. Joplin, Mo., Nov. 14, 1942; d. Arrell Morgan and Dorothy (Deitz) G. BA in English, U. Okla., 1963, MLS, 1966, PhD in Edn., 1977. English tchr. Norman (Okla.) Pub. Schs., 1963-65; pub. services librarian U. Okla. Health Scis. Ctr., Oklahoma City, 1966-68, serials librarian, 1971-72, dir. media prodn., 1972-77; coordinator library services Okla. Regional Med. Program, 1968-70; head reference dept. Wichita State U., 1978-80; mgr. library devel. DataPhase Systems, Inc., Kansas City, Mo., 1980-82; v.p. info. systems, library dir. Family Health Found. Am., Kansas City, 1982—; cons. Am. Coll. Cardiology Library, 1986-87. Contbr. articles to profl. jours. Chmn. regional screening com. Am. Field Service, Kansas City, 1987. Kellogg Found. grantee, 1987-88. Mem. Med. Library Assn. (cert., chmn.-elect library research sect. 1988), Kansas City Met. Library Network (pres. 1986, sec. 1987—). Democrat. Presbyterian. Office: Family Health Found Am 8880 Ward Pkwy PO Box 8418 Kansas City MO 64114-0418

GIBSON, ROXANNE HOLLY, management consultant; b. Salina, Kans., Sept. 8, 1960; d. John Richard and Freida (Kleeman) Depe; m. G. Carl Gibson Jr., Feb. 7, 1981. BA in Journalism, U. Okla., 1982. Tech. writer TG&Y Stores, Co., Oklahoma City, 1982-84; mgmt. cons. R.H. Gibson & Assocs., Lawton, Okla., 1984—; cons. in field. Author, editor: (newsletter) Personnel Mgmt. News, 1984—, Opportunity Update, 1986—, Jr. League News, 1987—. Bd. dirs. Miss U. of Okla. Scholarship, Norman, 1984—, Am. Cancer Soc., Lawton, 1985—, Lawton Jr. League, 1986—; speaker Project Plus Literacy, Lawton, 1986—; food drive chmn. Lawton Food Bank, 1988. Mem. Bus. and Profl. Women (1st v.p. 1987—, Young Careerist 1986), Okla. Women Bus. Owners, H.H. Herbert Sch. Journalism Alumni Assn. Democrat. Lutheran. Home: 1405 Keystone Lawton OK 73505 Office: RH Gibson & Assocs PO Box 7111 Lawton OK 73506

GIBSON, RUTH LYNN, counselor, writer; b. Chgo., May 25, 1937; d. Eric Ebastad and Ruth Elsie (Erickson) Flesvig; m. Dennis Lee Gibson, June 18, 1960; children: Steven, David, Scott. BS, Wheaton (Ill.) Coll., 1959. Teaching Waysata (Minn.) Sch. System, 1972-75; dir. Wheaton Counseling Assocs., 1980—; alumni assn. worker Wheaton Coll., 1972-75; counseler, writer, speaker Wheaton Counseling Assocs., 1975—. Author: Chipped Dishes, Zippers, and Prayer, 1977; booklets: Memory Sampler, 1986, Say Yes, 1986. Sec. West Suburban Evangelical Fellowship, Wheaton, 1987—. Home: 1213 E Wakeman Wheaton IL 60187 Office: Wheaton Counseling Assocs 1616 E Roosevelt Rd Wheaton IL 60187

GIBSON, SAMANTHA LIVINGSTON, sales representative; b. Mesa, Ariz., Dec. 9, 1941; d. Burr and Gwendolyn (Porter) Webb; student No. Ariz. U., Flagstaff, 1961, Coll. San Mateo, Calif., 1969, U. Ariz., Tucson, 1977; m. David Kent Gibson, June 2, 1981; children by previous marriage—Laurence, Donald and Danielle Livingston. Public relations ofcl. Sahara Tahoe Hotel, Stateline, Nev., 1969-71; with South Lake Tahoe C. of C., 1972-75; mgr. Winslow (Ariz.) C. of C., 1975-76; preventive maintenance analyst S.W. Forest Industries, Snowflake, Ariz., 1976-82, Brown & Root, 1985, Weyerhauser Paper Mill, Vallient, Okla., 1986; cons. troubleshooting mech. problems through vibration analysis. Mem. Snowflake Planning and Zoning Commn., 1977-78. Mem. Paper Industry Mgmt. Assn., Ariz. Assn. Indsl. Devel. (dir. 1975-76), Indsl. Devel. Endeavor Assn. (dir. 1975-76), Snowflake-Taylor C. of C. Republican. Research on trending in vibration analysis, analyzing mech. problems in rotating equipment. Home: PO Box 997 Snowflake AZ 85937 Office: Country Club at Fairway Snowflake AZ 85937

GIBSON, SUSAN BETH, sales professional; b. Cleve., Sept. 27, 1950; d. William John Szucs and Doris Caroline (Miller) Szucs-Oliveri; m. James D. Gibson, June 17, 1972 (div. Oct. 1978); 1 child, Brian William. BS of Edn., Bowling Green (Ohio) State U., 1972; postgrad., Columbia Pacific U. Tchr. Chgo., Detroit and Los Angeles, 1972-76; pub. devel. rep. Davis Mktg., Kansas City, Kans., 1979-80; territory sales mgr. B.G. Maintenance Mgmt., Kansas City, 1980-81; med. sales rep. Winthrop Labs., N.Y.C., 1982-83; pharm. sales rep. Reid Rowell, Inc., Marietta, Ga., 1983—. Tchr., pastoral leader St. Michael The Archangel, Clearwater, Fla., 1986. Mem. Nat. Assn. Female Execs., Philippine Am. Med. Assn., Beta Sigma Phi. Republican. Roman Catholic. Home: 318 Mae Ct Palm Harbor FL 34683

GIBSON, VERNA KAYE, retail company executive; b. Charleston, W.Va., June 22, 1942; d. Carl W. and Virginia E. (Meyers) LeMasters; m. James E. Gibson, Apr. 28, 1962; children: Kelly, Elizabeth. Grad. with honors in fashion mktg. and retailing, Marshall U., Huntington, W.Va., 1962. Buyer, mdse. mgr. Smart Shops, Huntington, W.Va., 1965-71; trainee to asst. buyer Limited Stores, Inc., Columbus, Ohio, 1971-72, assoc. buyer to buyer, 1972-77, div. mdse. mgr., 1977-79, v.p. sportswear, 1979-82, exec. v.p. gen., mdse. mgr., 1982-85; pres. Limited Stores, Inc., Columbus, 1985—; bd. dirs. Midland Mutual Life Ins. Co., Columbus, J. Duffy's, Columbus; dir. Fed. Res. Bd., Cleve. Recipient Harry L. Wexner award Limited Stores, Inc., 1983, Disting. Alumni award Marshall U. Alumni Assn., 1986; named Merchandiser of Yr., Apparel Merchandising, 1986. Office: Limited Stores Inc PO Box 16528 Columbus OH 43216

GIBSON, VIRGINIA LEE, lawyer; b. Independence, Mo., Mar. 5, 1946. BA, U. Calif., Berkeley, 1972; JD, U. Calif., San Francisco, 1977. Bar: Calif. 1981. Assoc. Pillsbury, Madison & Sutro, San Francisco, 1980-83; ptnr. Chickering & Gregory, San Francisco, 1983-85, Baker & McKenzie, San Francisco, 1985—. Mem. ABA (employee benefits subcom. tax sect.), Calif. Bar Assn. (exec. com. tax sect. 1985—), San Francisco Bar Assn. (internat. and comparative law taxation sects.), Western Pension Conf. (chmn. program com. 1986—), Internat. Found. Employee Benefit Plans. Office: Baker & McKenzie 2 Embarcadero Ctr Suite 2400 San Francisco CA 94111

GIBSON-GEE, JOYCE ANN, county official; b. Murray, Ky., Feb. 27, 1955; d. E.D. and V. Maude (Parker) Winchester; m. Richard Gee; children: Joshua Darrell, Alecia Brooke. Cert. water distbn. operator, cert. wastewater operator, cert. landfill operator, Ky. Supr. utility ops. Water and Wastewater div., City of Murray Pub. Works and Utilities, 1974-86; mgr. Hardin County Water Dist. 1, Radcliff, Ky., 1986—; bd. dirs. Ky. Water Well Cert. Bd., 1986-88. Mem. Nat. Assn. Female Execs., Am. Water Works Assn., Ky. Water and Wastewater Ops. Assn., Ky.-Tenn. Water Pollution Control Fedn. Democrat. Baptist. Home: PO Box 1147 Radcliff KY 40160

GIDDENS, ZELMA KIRK, broadcasting executive; b. Lafayette, Ala.; d. James William and Eunice (Rice) Kirk; grad. So. Union Jr. Coll., 1932; student Auburn U., 1934-35; m. Kenneth R. Giddens, May 19, 1934; children—Annsley Giddens Green, Therese Giddens Greer, Sara Kay. With Sta. WKRG-AM, 1947-55; with Sta. WKRG-AM-FM-TV, Mobile, Ala., 1955—, pres., 1969—. Founder, Mus. for Women's Art, Washington; trustee, Nat. Symphony. Mem. Smithsonian Assos., Mobile C. of C., Nat. Gallery Art Circle, Friends of Kennedy Ctr., Nat. Press Club, Am. Newspaper Women's Assn. Home: 2555 N Delwood Dr Mobile AL 36606 Office: 555 Broadcast Dr Mobile AL 36616

GIDDINGS, LUCILLE CASSELL, nurse; b. Port Chester, N.Y., Jan. 30, 1947; d. Curtis Emmitt and Rose (Lucente) Cassell; R.N., St. Clare's Hosp., N.Y.C., 1969; B.A., Coll. Mt. St. Vincent, Bronx, N.Y., 1979; M.P.A., NYU, 1982; m. William Alfred Giddings, Apr. 2, 1977. Staff nurse hosps. in N.Y. State, 1969-71; elem. sch. nurse Port Chester-Rye Town Bd. Edn., 1971-82; dir. interdepartmental services Our Lady of Mercy Hosp. Med. Center, Bronx, N.Y., 1982-83, dir. admissions, 1984-86, asst. adminstr., 1986-87; v.p. med. support services, 1987—; health services mgmt. cons. New Dimensions in Leadership, Inc., 1983-84; chmn. Port Chester br. ARC, 1978. Recipient Rev. Mother Jean Marie award, 1969. Mem. Am. Hosp. Assn., Am. Soc. Public Adminstrn.,NYU Alumni Assn., Coll. Mt. St. Vincent Alumni Assn. Home: 56 Hastings Ave Croton-on-Hudson NY 10520 Office: 600 E 233d St Bronx NY 10466

GIDDINGS-DARSOW, DARA JANEL, marketing professional; b. Wichita, Kans., Dec. 21, 1957; d. Nelson Paul and Dorothy Louise (Kennedy) Giddings; m. Neal Rolen Darsow, Feb. 11, 1984. AA, Maplewoods Community Coll., Gladstone, Mo., 1979. Systems planner Hallmark Cards Inc., Kansas City, Mo., 1977-78, systematic analyst, 1978-79, telemarketing rep., 1979-81; assoc. account rep. Hallmark Mktg. Corp., Kansas City, Mo., 1981-82, account rep., 1982-83, account mgr., 1983-85; sales rep. various independent contracts, Tacoma, 1985-86; mktg. mgr. Express Personnel Services, Tacoma, 1986—. Vol. Planned Parenthood, Tacoma, 1983; mem. LWV. Mem. Tacoma Execs. Assn., Sales & Mktg. Execs. Internat., Pierce County C. of C., Fed. Way C. of C. Democrat. Methodist. Club: Leads (Tacoma South chpt.). Home: 3512 12th Ave NW Gig Harbor WA 98335 Office: Express Personnel Services 2000 Tacoma Mall Office Bldg 351 Tacoma WA 98409

GIDEON, MARIANNE ELIZABETH, administrative assistant, salesperson; b. Waynesburg, Pa., Feb. 17, 1949; d. George and Rose (Vignovich) Prodan; m. Nelson Kerr Gideon, Oct. 7, 1977. AA in Sci and Bus., Robert Morris Coll., 1969. Part time sec. Robert J. Bushee & Assoc., Pitts., 1967, 68, 69; legal sec. A.J. Marion, Waynesburg, Pa., 1969-70; med. sec. Centerville Clinics, Inc., Carmichaels, Pa., 1970-79, adminstrv. sec., 1979-87; dir. Primary Care Satellites, Carmichaels, 1987—. Active Greene Acad. of Arts, Carmichaels, 1986—. Mem. Nat. Assn. Female Execs., U.S. Ski Team Assn. (assoc.), Carmichaels C. of C. Democrat. Roman Catholic. Office: Centerville Clinics Inc RD #1 Box 144A Fredericktown PA 15333

GIDEON, MIRIAM, composer; b. Greeley, Colo., Oct. 23, 1906; d. Abram and Henrietta (Shoninger) G.; m. Frederic Ewen, 1949. B.A., Boston U., 1926; M.A., Columbia, 1946; D.Sacred Music, Jewish Theol. Sem., 1970. Music faculty Bklyn. Coll., 1944-54, Coll. City N.Y., 1947-55, Cantors Inst., Jewish Theol. Sem., 1955—, Manhattan Sch. Music, N.Y.C., 1967—; vis. prof. music City Coll., CUNY, 1971-76, prof. emeritus, 1976—. Composer: opera Fortunato; for orch. Symphonia Brevis, Lyric Piece for Strings; 2 cantatas, 2 sacred services in Hebrew; 18 cycles for solo voice and instrumental ensemble; works for solo voice and piano; instrumental sonatas and suites; recs. orchestral and chamber works by Westminster Records, CRI, New World Records, Desto Records, Serenus Records; works performed in Europe, Far East, U.S. and S.Am. by Internat. Soc. Contemporary Music, League Composers, London, Prague, Tokyo, Zurich symphony orchs. Recipient Bloch prize for choral work, 1948; Nat. Fedn. Music Clubs and A.S.C.A.P. award for symphonic music, 1969; Nat. Endowment of Arts grantee, 1974; commd. Library of Congress, 1979. Mem. Am. Acad. Arts and Letters, Am. Composers Alliance (bd. govs.), Internat. Soc. Contemporary Music (gov.). Home: 410 Central Park W New York NY 10025

GIEDT, JOYCE MARIE, management executive; b. Aberdeen, S.D., Sept. 19, 1949; d. William C. and LaVerne L. (Wagemann) G. BA, Sioux Falls Coll., 1972. Tng. specialist CENEX, Inver Grove Heights, Minn., 1973-85; mgr. tng. Lend Lease Co. subs. Nat. Car Rental Co., Mpls., 1985-88; mgr. mktg. Lend Lease Trucks Inc., Mpls., 1988—. Mem. Am. Soc. for Tng. and Devel., Nat. Assn. Female Execs. Office: 7700 France Ave S Minneapolis MN 55435

GIER, KATHLEEN AGATHA, social services director; b. Kansas City, Aug. 21, 1923; d. August Karl and Margaret Mary (Heilman) Hummel; m. John Joseph Gier, Oct. 9, 1948; children: Margaret, Joseph, Amy. Prin. Acme Brass and Machine Works, Kansas City, 1940-86. Pres. Kansas City PTA, 1964-66, Kansas City Band Parent Club, 1966-68, Kansas City Warmth and Light Coalition, 1984-85, Kansas City Parish Workers Assn.; sec. Kansas City Emergency Assistance Coalition, 1977-84; troop leader Kansas City Girl Scouts U.S., 1965-69; bd. dirs. Kansas City Mid-Am. Assistance Coalition, 1985—, Co-operative Social Services, 1972—. Recipient St. Anne award Kansas City Diocesan Office of Scouting, 1968. Mem. Mo. Assn. for Social Welfare, 1976—. Roman Catholic. Home: 1457 E 76th Ter Kansas City MO 64131

GIERLASINSKI, KATHY LYNN, accountant; b. Chewelah, Wash., May 21, 1951; d. John Edward and Margaret Irene (Seefeldt) Rail; m. Norman Joseph Gierlasinski, May 23, 1987. BBA, Gonzaga U., 1984. Legal sec. Redbook Pub. Co., N.Y.C., 1974-75, Howard Michaelson, Esquire, Spokane, Wash., 1975-76; sec. Burns Internat. Security Services, Spokane, 1977-79; sec. to controller Gonzaga U., Spokane, 1979-81, acctg. asst., 1981-82; staff acct. Martin, Holland & Petersen, CPA's, Yakima, Wash., 1984-87; sr. staff acct. Strader Hallet & Co., P.S., Bellevue, Wash., 1988—; treas. White Pass Ski Patrol, Nat. Ski Patrol Systems, Wash., 1987—; editor Mt. Spokane Ski Patrol (chmn. audit com.), 1983-84. Mem. Am. Soc. Women Accts. (editor 1987). Republican. Lutheran. Home: 8248 126th Ave Apt C301 Kirkland WA 98033 Office: Strader Hallett & Co PS 2750 Northup Way Suite 400 Bellevue WA 98004

GIES, CAROL J., public relations and marketing executive; b. Detroit, Jan. 20, 1947; m. Craig M. Gies, Mar. 31, 1966. BS, Wayne State U., 1971, MA, 1972; MBA, Mich. State U., 1985. Pub. relations dir. Met. Detroit Conv. and Visitors Bur., 1973-78, v.p. civic affairs, 1979; exec. dir. host com. Rep. Nat. Conv., 1980; exec. dir. Mich. Host Com. for Super Bowl XVI, 1982; sr. v.p. Anthony M. Franco, Inc., Detroit, 1982-87; v.p. Ketchum Pub. Relations, Chgo., 1987-88; dir. pub. relations Bloomingdale's, Chgo., 1988—; ptnr. Root Photographers, Inc., Chgo., 1987—; instr. MBA program Cen. Mich. U. Recipient Gold Quill, Internat. Assn. Bus. Communicators, 1975; Mich. Embassy of Tourism award; named Woman of Wayne Headliner, 1980. Mem. Pub. Relations Soc. of Am. (Nat. Silver Anvil award, 3 dist. awards). Office: Root Photographers Inc 1131 W Sheridan Rd Chicago IL 60660 also: Ketchum Pub Relations 142 E Ontario Chicago IL 60611

GIESSLER, EMILY SWEARINGEN, educational sales representative; b. Fort Wayne, Ind., Oct. 19, 1940; d. Milton Park and Sarah Lucile (Engle) Swearingen; B.A., Tex. Christian U., 1962; M.A., St. Francis Coll., 1966; children by previous marriage—James Hugh Engle, Melinda Sue Engle. Dir. edn. Am. Cancer Soc., Fort Worth, 1963; tchr. North Adams Community Sch., Decatur, Ind., 1963-79; sr. sales dir. Mary Kay Cosmetics Co., Decatur, Ind., 1978-86; sales rep. Nystrom Co., 1986—. Treas. 1st United Meth. Ch., Decatur, lay speaker. Mem. Nat. Assn. Female Execs., Internat. Platform Assn., Tri Kappa. Republican. Address: 3501 Renzel Blvd #122 Fort Worth TX 76116

GIFFIN, MARGARET ETHEL (PEGGY), management consultant; b. Cleve., Aug. 27, 1949; d. Arch Kenneth and Jeanne (Eggleton) G. BA in Psychology, U. Pacific, Stockton, Calif., 1971; MA in Psychology, Calif. State U., Long Beach, 1973; PhD in Quantitative Psychology, U. So. Calif., 1984. Psychometrist Auto Club So. Calif., Los Angeles, 1973-74; cons. Psychol. Services, Inc., Glendale, Calif., 1975-76, mgr., 1977-78, dir., 1979—; researcher Social Sci. Research Inst., U. So. Calif., Los Angeles, 1981; mem. tech. adv. com. on testing Calif. Fair Employment and Housing Commn., 1974—, mem. steering com., 1978—. Mem. Internat. Personnel Mgmt. Assn. Assessment Council, Am. Psychol. Assn., Western Psychol. Assn., Personnel Testing Council So. Calif. (pres. 1980, exec. dir. 1982, 88, bd. dirs. 1980—). Club: Athletic (Los Angeles). Home: 330 S Westmoreland Ave Los Angeles CA 90020 Office: 100 W Broadway #1100 Glendale CA 91210

GIFFORD, GAYLE LYNN, non-profit development organization manager/director; b. Hartford, Conn., Dec. 15, 1953; d. Russell William Gifford and Elsie (George) Forster; m. Jonathan Walker Howard, June 18, 1983; 1 child, Emma G. AB magna cum laude, Clark U., 1975. Claims rep. Social Security Adminstrn., Providence, 1976-83; dir. sponsor relations Foster Parents Plan, Warwick, R.I., 1983—; mem. devel. edn. com. InterAction, Washington, 1986—. Mem., coordinator Amnesty Internat. U.S.A., Providence, 1976—; founder, bd. dirs. R.I. Mobilization for Survival, 1977-82, Women for Non-Nuclear Future, Providence, 1980—, pres. edn. fund, 1988—; bd. dirs. Am. Friends Service Com., Providence, 1977-82. Mem. Internat. Assn. Bus. Communicators (Award of Excellence, 1984), Soc. Internat. Devel., Soc. Intercultural Tng., Edn. and Research, Nat. Assn. Female Execs., Phi Beta Kappa. Democrat. Office: Foster Parents Plan 155 Plan Way Warwick RI 02886

GIFFUNI, CATHE, writer; b. N.Y.C., July 18, 1949; d. Joseph Vincent and Flora (Baldini) G. BA in Art History, Hollins Coll., 1970; postgrad., Columbia U., 1971-72. Author: Bessie Head: A Bibliography, 1986, A Bibliography of Louise Arner Boyd, 1986, Joseph O'Neill: A Bibliography, 1987, Annie Smith Peck: A Bibliography, 1987. Home: 240 E 27th Apt 20K New York NY 10016

GIKAS, CAROL SOMMERFELDT, museum director; b. St. Louis; m. Ken Gikas. Student, U. Mo., 1968-70; BA in Studio Art, U. Ark., Little Rock, 1973; MA, U. Tex., 1977; postgrad. Mus. Mgmt. Inst., U. Calif., summer 1981. Asst. mus. registrar Ark. Arts Ctr., Little Rock, 1972-74; assoc. curator Leeds Gallery, U. Tex., Austin, 1977-80; exec. dir. La. Arts and Sci. Ctr., Baton Rouge, 1980—; mem. grants adv. panel So. Arts Fedn., 1981, Arts & Humanities Council Greater Baton Rouge, 1982, 83, div. arts La. State Arts Council, 1981, 85; mem. adv. bd. U.S.S. Kidd/La. Naval Mus., Baton Rouge, 1981, 84, La. Dept. Edn., 1981; state rep. to council S.E. Mus. Conf., 1984, 85. Sec. Gov.'s commn. for Anniversary of La. State Capitol, 1981, 82; active Baton Rouge C. of C. Goals Conf., 1984, 85, Leadership Greater Baton Rouge, C. of C., 1985, 86; trustee ARC, 1986—; mem. Mayor's Commn. for Bicentennial of U.S. Constn. Mem. Am. Assn. Mus., Art Mus. Assn. (regional rep. 1983—). Office: La Arts & Sci Ctr Inc PO Box 3373 Baton Rouge LA 70821

GIL, LOURDES, writer, editor; b. Havana, Cuba, Dec. 14, 1952; came to U.S., 1961; d. Ernesto and Concepcion (de la Campa) Valdes-Munoz; m. Ariel Antonio Rodriguez, Nov. 20, 1983; 1 child, Gabriel. Cert., U. Madrid, 1973; BA, Fordham U., 1974; MA, NYU, 1978. Translator The Dispatch, Union City, N.J., 1974-75; editor Romanica NYU, 1975-83; translating editor King Features Syndicate, N.Y.C., 1977-84; pres. Giralt Pubs., North Bergen, N.J., 1985—. Author: (poetry) Neumas, 1977, Vencido Fuego Especie, 1983; editor lit. jour. Lyra, 1986. Cintas lit. fellow, 1979; recipient poetry awards Ateneo de Barcelona, Venezuela, 1982, Chilean Writers Soc., N.Y.C., 1984, Royal Biennal Poetry, Belgium, 1984. Mem. Internat. Women Writers Guild, Poets and Writers, Acad. Am. Poets, Poetry Soc. Am., Assn. Hispanic Arts, Bensalem Assn. Women Writers, Emporium Writers Artists (v.p. 1977-78), Heredia Lit. Guild (pres. 1978-81), Am. Soc., Inst. Latin Am. Writerrs, Inst. Ibero-Am. Studies, Conservatory of Am. Letters. Roman Catholic. Home: 317 77th St North Bergen NJ 07047 Office: Giralt Pubs Inc PO Box 450 Times Sq Sta New York NY 10108

GILBERT, CAROL LYNN, librarian, educator; b. Chico, Calif., Sept. 19, 1951; d. Richard Perry and Emma L. (Knecht) Timmons. BA with honors, Calif. State U., Sacramento, 1978, postgrad., 1978-81; MLS with honors, San Jose State U., 1983. Book repairer Calif. State U., Sacramento, 1979, library asst., 1979-80, reference asst., 1980-82, asst. librarian, 1983-85; collection devel. librarian Solano County, Fairfield, Calif., 1983-84; field services librarian Braille and Talking Book Library, Calif. State Library, 1984-87; conversion project librarian Calif. State Library Automation Office, 1987—; pres. Library Staff Assn., Calif. State U., Sacramento, 1979-80, library staff ombudsman, 1980-81, rep. staff acad. senate library subcom., 1981-82, chair state library orientation com., 1986-88. Compiler: Index to the Chicano Library Serials Set on Microfilm, 1982; Art History: A Selected Bibliography, 1983; book reviewer Lector, 1983-85; contbr. articles to profl. jours. Library staff rep. Calif. State Employees Assn., Sacramento, 1980. Mem. ALA, Calif. State Library Assn. (com. 1986-87). Office: Calif State Library 600 Broadway Sacramento CA 95818

GILBERT, DIANA ZAJA, word processing, purchasing executive; b. Hammond, Ind., Mar. 18, 1955; d. Clifford Frances and Corinthy Lucille (Kerr) Zaja; m. David Ellis Gilbert, Dec. 6, 1975; 1 son, Kyle Ellis. BA, Purdue U., 1979. Receptionist, ABA, Chgo., 1973-75, sec. word processing, 1975-78, supr. word processing, 1978-81, dir. word processing, 1981-86, dir. word processing and purchasing, 1986—; council mem. client and adv. Norrell Temporary Service, Chgo., 1984; speaker, cons. Cahner's Exposition

Group, 1983-84. Contbr. articles to profl. jours. Vol. women's bd. No. Ind. Arts Assn., Munster, 1982—. Democrat. Home: 8620 Greenwood St Munster IN 46321 Office: ABA 750 N Lake Shore Dr Chicago IL 60611

GILBERT, DIANE CHRISTINE, research administrator; b. Springfield, Mass., Apr. 10, 1945; d. Theodor Geisel and Dorothy Jean (Preston) Wallace; m. Richard Barry Gilbert, June 27, 1970. AB in Govt., Bates Coll., 1967; postgrad. in managerial acctg. MIT, 1967. Mgmt. intern NASA Electronics Research Center, Cambridge, Mass., 1967-68, adminstrv. officer, 1968-70; exec. asst. endocrine unit Mass. Gen. Hosp., Boston, 1972-81, asst. to chief medicine, 1981-87; spl. asst. planning and analysis Office Research Tech. Affairs, Mass. Gen. Hosp. and Div. Research Affairs The Gen. Hosp. Corp., 1987—; pvt. fin. mgr. Windham, N.H., 1979-86; Nat. Council of Univ. Research Adminstrs., 1986—; co-coordinator Mass. Com. for NIH Centennial, 1986-88. Active local community affairs. Republican. Office: Mass Gen Hosp Div of Research Affairs Fruit St Boston MA 02114

GILBERT, JOAN SCHOPPE, production manager; b. Barton, Vt., Aug. 11, 1943; d. Rolfe Weston and Dorothy Lena (Spencer) S. BA magna cum laude, U. Mass., 1965. Cert. tchr. Tchr. high sch. Gorham (Maine) Schs., 1965-66; tchr. Sherwood Hall Sch., Mansfield, Eng., 1966-67; tchr. middle sch. Meden Sch., Warsop, Eng., 1967-68; dept. head high sch. Goffstown (N.H.) Schs., 1968-82; dir. circulation T.H.E. Jour., Acton, Mass., 1982-83; prodn. mgr. The Robb Report, Acton, 1983-87, prodn. dir., 1988—; prdn. mgr. Londy Swardlick Mackey, Portland, Maine, 1987-88; Mem. Women in Prodn., N.H. Assn. of Tchrs. of English (bd. dirs.), Phi Beta Kappa.

GILBERT, JOAN STULMAN, petroleum company executive; b. N.Y.C., May 10, 1934; student Conn. Coll. for Women, 1951-53; m. Phil E. Gilbert, Jr., Oct. 6, 1968; children—Linda Cooper, Dana, Patricia. Br. coordinator Vol. Service Bur., Westchester, N.Y., 1970-72; public relations dir. Westchester Lighthouse, 1972-76; exec. dir. Westchester Heart Assn., 1976-77; community relations mgr. Texaco Inc., White Plains, N.Y., 1977—. Bd. dirs. Lend-A-Hand, Coll. Careers, Teatown Lake Reservation, New Orchestra of Westchester, Westchester Coalition, Youth Counseling League, United Way of Westchester, Pvt. Industry Council, former trustee Westchester Council for the Arts, Choate-Rosemary Hall. Mem. Met. Transit Authority (insp. gen. mgmt. adv. bd.), Pub. Relations Soc. Am. (chpt. pres. 1977), Advt. Club (dir.), Women in Communications, Sales and Mktg. Execs. Westchester (former dir.). Westchester County Assn. Home: The Croft Spring Valley Rd Ossining NY 10562 Office: 2000 Westchester Ave White Plains NY 10650

GILBERT, JUDITH ARLENE, lawyer; b. Los Angeles, Jan. 9, 1946; d. Beril B. and Dorothy Marilyn (Stern) Gilbert; student U. Calif.-Berkeley, 1963-64; AB in Econs. magna cum laude, UCLA, 1967; JD, Harvard U., 1970; m. Joel Philip Schiff; children: Lauren Michelle, Jared Daniel. Bar: Calif. 1971. Assoc. Rosenfeld, Meyer & Susman, 1970-72, Quittner, Stutman, Treister & Glatt, Los Angeles, 1972-74, Abeles & Markowitz, and predecessor, Beverly Hills, Calif., 1974-76; sr. counsel legal dept., credit advice-N.Am. Div. Sect. Bank of Am. Nat. Trust & Savs Assn., 1977-88, sr. counsel legal dept. Denton, Hall, Burgin & Warrens, 1988—; judge protem Mcpl. and Small Claims Ct. mem. arbitration panel Los Angeles Superior Ct.; planning com. ann. meeting State Bar Calif., 1986-87, also host com. ann. meeting , 1987; bd. dirs. Pub. Counsel, 1986—. Mem. Los Angeles County Com. Human Resources; active Girl Scouts U.S.A., Cystic Fibrosis, City of Hope. Mem. ABA (litigation and banking, corp. & comml. sects., comml. transactions litigation com., creditor's rights litigation com., others), Calif. State Bar Conf. (resolutions com. of state bar, 1988—,del. 1974—, vice chair com. living wills and right to die 1977, com. on rights and obligations of unmarried cohabitators 1978-80, and legal separation 1980-81), Los Angeles Bar Assn. (bd. trustees 1984-85, comml. law and bankruptcy, taxation and copyroght sects. steering com., co-chair fund raising sub-com. 1986), Beverly Hills Bar Assn. (ex-officio mem. bd. govs., exec. com. pres. 1985-86, 86-87, del. to state bar conf. of dels. 1973—, vice chair, 1980, chair, 1982, 1986—, atty. fee disputes panel, numerous other positions), Calif. Women Lawyers Assn., Women Lawyers Assn. Los Angeles, Fin. Lawyers Conf., Comml. Law League Am., Fed. Bar Assn., Thespians, Collegian Singers, Brick Muller Soc., UCLA Alumni Assn. (adv. bd., mem. scholarship bd.), Tower and Flame, Phi Beta Kappa, Gamma Delta Epsilon, Pi Gamma Mu, Omega Delta Epsilon, Phi Chi Theta, Delta Phi Epsilon. Clubs: Merchants, Sutherland (sec.-treas. 1968-69). Office: 2121 Ave of the Stars 22nd Floor Fox Plaza Los Angeles CA 90067

GILBERT, JUDITH M., community relations executive; b. Miami, Fla., Dec. 2, 1934; d. Stanley C. and Martha (Scheinberg) Myers; children: Robert, Carolyn, Mark. Student, U. N.C., 1952-53; BA, U. Fla., 1956. Project coordinator Miami Beach Redevel. Agy., Miami Beach, Fla., 1977-78, dir. community services, 1978-79; dir. victim/witness services Office of State's Atty., 11th Judicial Cir. of Fla., Dade County, Miami, 1980; exec. dir. S.E. region Am. Jewish Congress, Miami, 1980-83; assoc. dir. community relations Greater Miami Jewish Fedn., Miami, 1983—. Bd. dirs. Stanley C. Myers Community Health Ctr. Inc., Miami Beach, 1988—, Dade-Monroe Mental Health Bd., 1982-84, High Sch. in Israel, Miami, 1978-80; mem. Fla. Ednl. Equity Act Adv. Group, Dade County Schs., 1986-88; pres. Nat. Council Jewish Women, Miami, 1974-77; v.p. So. Dist. Nat. Council Jewish Women, 1976-77. Recipient Vol. Activist award Germaine Monteil, 1972, Hannah G. Solomon award Nat. Council Jewish Women, 1978. Mem. AAUW, Nat. Community Relations Dirs. Assn., Human Relations Profls. of Greater Miami, Alpha Epsilon Phi. Office: Greater Miami Jewish Fedn 4200 Biscayne Blvd Miami FL 33137

GILBERT, KIM EILEEN, lawyer; b. Berkeley, Calif., June 20, 1947; d. Charles R. and Elvyna J. (Waller) G. B.A., U. Calif.-Davis, 1967; M.A., Rutgers U., 1969; J.D., U. Pacific, 1974. Bar: Calif. 1974, U.S. Dist. Ct. (ea. and cen. dists.) Calif. 1974, U.S. Supreme Court 1979. Legis. asst. Calif. State Legislature, Sacramento 1967-68; prin. research cons. Eagleton Inst. Politics, New Brunswick, N.J., 1969; econ. budget analyst Calif. State Dept. Fin., Sacramento, 1970-72; govtl. program analyst Calif. State Dept. Health, Sacramento, 1973; asst. to v.p. and gen. counsel HMO Internat., Los Angeles, 1973-74; sole practice, Beverly Hills, Calif., 1974—; judge pro tem Superior Ct., Los Angeles, 1980—, Mcpl. and Small Claims Ct., 1980—. House analyst desk Am. Broadcasting Co., N.Y.C., 1968; campaign staff Citizens for Unruh Com., Sacramento, 1970; Sacramento County com. Common Cause, Sacramento, 1972-73. Calif. State scholar, 1964, Eagleton fellow, Rutgers U., 1968. Mem. Los Angeles County Bar Assn., Beverly Hills Bar Assn., Los Angeles Trial Lawyers Assn., Women Lawyers Assn. of Los Angeles, Westside Women Lawyers Assn., San Fernando Valley Women Lawyers Assn., ABA, ACLU. Democrat. Roman Catholic. Office: 9100 Wilshire Blvd Suite 501 E Tower Beverly Hills CA 90212-3408

GILBERT, LUCIA ALBINO, psychology educator; b. Bklyn., July 27, 1941; d. William V. and Carmelina (Cutro) Albino; m. John Carl Gilbert, Dec. 18, 1965; 1 child, Melissa Carlotta. B.A., Wells Coll., 1963; M.S., Yale U., 1964; Ph.D., U. Tex., 1974. Lic. psychologist, Tex. Supr. research info. G.S. Gilmore Research Lab., New Haven, 1964-67; tchr. St. Stephen Sch., Austin, Tex., 1967-69; asst. prof. Iowa State U., Ames, 1974-76; asst. prof. U. Tex., Austin, 1976-81, assoc. prof., 1981-86, prof., 1986—. Author: Men in Dual Career Families, 1985, Sharing It All: the Rewards and Struggles of Two-Career Families, 1988; editor spl. issue Parenting, Dual Career Families. Recipient Excellence in Teaching award U. Tex., 1981-86. Fellow Am. Psychol. Assn. (rep. council 1980-83, 86-89); mem. Assn. Women in Psychology, Tex. Psychol. Assn. Avocations: swimming; progressive country music; ecology. Home: 4402 Balcones Dr Austin TX 78731 Office: U Tex Austin TX 78712

GILBERT, MYRNA JEAN, anthropologist; b. Boulder, Colo; d. Albert L. and Elizabeth (Goggin) Hall; B.A., Ariz. State U., 1957, M.A. in English, 1964; M.A. in Anthropology, U. Calif., Santa Barbara, 1974, Ph.D., 1980; m. Richard Leon Gilbert, Mar. 24, 1956 (dec. 1979); 1 dau., Lisa Anne. Research asso. Social Process Research Inst., U. Calif., Santa Barbara, 1974-76, Spanish Speaking Mental Health Research Inst., UCLA, 1976-78, scholar in Hispanic alcohol studies, 1984—; research project dir. Centro Familiar de Santa Barbara, 1978-81; program officer founds. and corp. relations Direct Relief Internat., Santa Barbara, 1981-84; research cons. Calif. Office Alcohol and Drug Programs, Sacramento, 1976-77, Calif. Commn. on Alcoholism for Spanish Speaking, Sacramento, 1978, Nat. Inst. on Drug Abuse, 1985—; researcher kinship networks in Mex., 1973-74. Bd. dirs. Zona Seca, 1984—, Santa Barbara Family Care Center, 1972-75, 82-84, Santa Barbara Mus. Art, 1970-72; mem. nat. adv. bd. Womens Alcoholism Prevention Project Women's Action Alliance; chmn., organizer on alcohol related issues U.S./Mex. Conf., 1987. NIMH grantee, 1978-81, 82-84; Nat. Inst. Alcohol and Alcohol Abuse grantee, 1982-84, 86, 87; Office Child Devel. grantee, 1976-78. Mem. Am. Anthrop. Assn., Soc. for Med. Anthropology, Nat. Assn. Practicing Anthropologists (governing council 1987), Soc. Applied Anthropology, Santa Barbara Mus. Art (pres. docent council 1970-72). Contbr. articles on research in Hispanic communities, families and substance abuse to profl. jours. Home: 5254 Calle Morelia Santa Barbara CA 93111 Office: UCLA Spanish Speaking Mental Health Research Ctr Los Angeles CA 90024

GILBERT, NANCI ELAINE, real estate developer, small business owner; b. Honolulu, Jan. 10, 1943; d. James Carl and Josephine (Sullivan) G. Student, Coll. Marin, 1978, U. So. Calif., 1981; AS in Radio, TV, Endicott Coll., 1963. Lic. gen. contractor. Owner, broker Russian River (Calif.) Resort Properties, 1981-83; pres., owner Crystal Bay (Nev.) Holding Co., 1983-87; developer, owner RRR Properties, Roseville, Calif., 1983-87; ptnr. Valley Investment Properties, Roseville, Calif., 1987—. Mem. Smithsonian Assn., Nat. Geog. Soc. Mem. Nat. Assn. Females Execs., Sacramento Women's Network, Women Bus. Sonoma County, Bay Area Career Women, Comml. Brokers Assn. Sacramento (cert., Million Dollar Club 1981, Multi-million Dollar Club 1981-84), Sierra Club. Republican. Episcopal. Clubs: Alpine Explorers (Nevada County, Calif.) (pres. 1984-87); Adventurers (Placer County, Calif.) (pres. 1985-87). Office: RRR Properties PO Box 2283 Roseville CA 95746

GILBERT, NANCY JEAN, personnel director; b. St. Charles, Ill., Nov. 3, 1957; d. Baron G. and Carol J. (Griffith) Schaub; m. Sherwin R. Gilbert, Nov. 1, 1980; children: Nicole C., Gregory S. B in Bus., Western Ill. U., 1980. Personnel asst. WER Indsl. div. Emerson Electric, Chgo., 1980-82; personnel mgr. Capital Cities/ABC, Inc., Lombard, Ill., 1982-86, asst. dir. personnel, Mar. 1986 to Oct. 1986, dir. personnel, 1986—. Mem. Am. Soc. Personnel Adminstrs., Personnel Assn. DuPage County. Office: ABC Pub Agrl Group 580 Waters Edge Lombard IL 60148

GILBERT, NANCY LOUISE, librarian; b. Norfolk, Va., Nov. 3, 1938; d. Oscar Linwood Jr. and Mary Margaret (Nicholls) G. BA, Greensboro Coll., 1961; MLS, U. North Carolina, 1968. Librarian Va. Beach (Va.) Pub. Library, 1968, U.S. Army, Worms, Crailsheim and Mannheim, Fed. Republic Germany, 1968-74, Pentagon Library, Washington, 1974-80, U.S. Army Mil. History Inst., Carlisle Barracks, Pa., 1980—. Mem. ALA, Spl. Libraries Assn., Mid-Atlantic Region Archives Conf. Home: 1404 Bradley Dr #B-314 Carlisle PA 17013

GILBERT, RACHEL SHAW, state legislator, real estate broker; b. Ottawa, Kans.; d. Herbert M. and L.C. Ferris (Pile) Shaw; B.A., U. Nebr., 1956; M.A., Coll. of Idaho, 1969; children—Cheryl Allison Gilbert Brady, Kimberly Lynn. Sch. tchr., Nebr., 1952-57; broker Walker & Co. Real Estate, Boise, Idaho, 1969-71; broker-owner Gilbert & Assocs. Realtors, Boise, 1972-82; mem. Idaho Ho. of Reps., 1980-83, Idaho Senate, 1984—. Bd. dirs. United Way, Boise, 1963-68, Boise Philharm. Orch., 1966-68; chmn. Idaho Legis. Dist. 15, 1980. Mem. Nat. Assn. Realtors (dir. 1980-86), Idaho Assn. Realtors (dir. 1978-80), Idaho Assn. Commerce and Industry (dir.), Boise C. of C. (v.p. 1979). Republican. Home: 1111 Marshall St Boise ID 83706 Office: 1487 N Cole St Boise ID 83704 *

GILBOE, CATHERINE MARY, state agency administrator; b. Troy, N.Y., Jan. 19, 1955; d. Theodore Thomas and Eleanor Madeline (Johnson) G. BA, Russell Sage Coll., 1977; MA, cert. advanced grad. studies, Assumption Coll., 1979. Vocat. evaluator Albany (N.Y.) County Assn. of Retarded, 1977-78, dir. rehab. services, 1978-80, acting exec. dir., 1980-82, dir. community residences, 1983-85; program mgr. U.C.P. Ctr. for the Disabled, Albany, 1982-85; asst. advocate N.Y. State Office of Advocate for the Disabled, Albany, 1985-88; project coordinator, dir. info. referral N.Y. State Office of Advocate for the Disabled, 1988—; cons. computer tng., Waterford, N.Y., 1987—. Vol. Girl Scouts U.S., Waterford, 1987, McDonald House, Albany, 1982. Democrat. Roman Catholic. Home: 28 Linda Ln Waterford NY 12188 Office: NY State Office Advocate of Disabled 1 Empire State Plaza Albany NY 12223

GILBREATH, FREIDA CAROL, data processing executive; b. Huntsville, Ala., Oct. 26, 1949; d. Murray and Edna Merle (Smith) Dixon; m. Robert Keith Gilbreath, May 4, 1969; children: Scott McKinley, Emily Luanne. Student, N.E. Jr. Coll., Rainsville, Ala., 1967-69. Salesperson Dunnavant's Dept. Store, Huntsville, 1968-69, Pensacola (Fla.) Mill Supply Co., 1970-71; with Arkay Trucking Co., Guntersville, Ala., 1971-72, Creswell Indsl. Supply, Guntersville, 1972; computer operator Guntersville Hosp., 1972-77, Housing Devel. Co., Huntsville, 1977-79, Fort Payne (Ala.) Med. Ctr., 1979-84, Centre (Ala.) Med. Ctr., 1982-84; programmer-analyst Bapt. Med. Ctr., Birmingham, Ala., 1984—. Mem. Data Processing Mgmt. Assn., Nat. Assn. Female Execs. Methodist. Office: Bapt Med Ctr 3201 4th Ave S Birmingham AL 35222

GILCHRIST, ANNE MARIE, computer scientist; b. Augusta, Ga., Apr. 23, 1960; d. Albert Waller and Agnes Marie (Gallaher) G.; 1 child Joanna Christine. BS in Info. and Computer Sci., Ga. Inst. Tech., 1982. Sr. software analyst Intergraph, Huntsville, Ala., 1982-84; research scientist Ga. Tech Research Inst., Atanta, 1984—. Mem. Assn. for Computing Machinery, Computer Soc. of IEEE. Home: 2417 Woodacres Rd NE Atlanta GA 30345 Office: Ga Tech GTRI/SEL/DSD Atlanta GA 30332

GILCHRIST, ELLEN LOUISE, writer; b. Vicksburg, Miss., Feb. 20, 1935; d. William Garth and Aurora (Alford) G.; children—Marshall Peteet Walker, Jr., Garth Gilchrist Walker, Pierre Gautier Walker. B.A. in Philosophy, Millsaps Coll., 1967; postgrad., U. Ark., 1976. Freelance writer, journalist; commentator, morning edit. of news Nat. Pub. Radio, Washington, 1984, 85. Author: The Land Surveyor's Daughter, 1979, In The Land of Dreamy Dreams, 1981, The Annunciation (Book of Month Club alternate in U.S. and Sweden), 1983, Victory Over Japan (Am. Book award 1984), 1984, Drunk With Love, 1986, Falling Through Space, 1987; contbr. short stories, poems to lit. publs. Recipient Poetry award U. Ark., 1976; Craft in Poetry award N.Y. Quar., 1978; Fiction award The Prairie Schooner, 1981; Poetry award Miss. Arts Festival, 1968; Saxifrage award, 1983; Fiction award Miss. Acad. Arts and Sci., 1982, 85; J. William Fulbright prize U. Ark., 1985; Lit. award Miss. Inst. Arts and Letters, 1985; 2 Pushcart prizes; grantee NEA, 1979. Mem. Author's Guild.

GILCHRIST, JAN SPIVEY, artist, educator; b. Chgo., Feb. 15, 1949; d. Charles and Arthric (Jones) Spivey; m. Arthur Van Johnson, Aug. 1, 1970 (div. Aug. 1980); 1 child, Ronké Diarra; m. Kelvin Keith Gilchrist, Sept. 5, 1983; 1 child, William Kelvin. Student, Hartwick Coll., 1985; BS in Art Edn., Ea. Ill. U., 1973; MA in Painting, U. No. Iowa, 1979. Tchr. Chgo. Bd. Edn., Chgo., 1973-75; art tchr. Dist. 147, Harvey (Ill.) Schs., 1976-79, Cambridge (Mass.) Sch. Dept., 1980-81, Joliet (Ill.) Pub. Schs., 1982-83; freelance artist Glenwood, Ill., 1983—; illustrator for Putnam Pub., N.Y.C., Ill. State Dept. Represented in permanent collections Isabelle Neal Gallery, Evanston Art Ctr. Co-op Gallery; commns. include Ea. Ill. U., 1974, State of Ill. Families With A Future campaign, 1986-87, Putnam Pub. to illustrate Children of Long Ago, 1987, Nathaniel Talking by Eloise Greenfield, 1988, series books on AIDS for children, parents, tchrs., clergy and Dr.s for State of Ill., 1987; juried full mem. Ward-Nasse Gallery, N.Y.C., Prism Gallery, Evanston, Ill. Recipient Purchase awards Dusable Mus., Chgo., 1983-85; Purchase award Varied Treasures, Ill. Benedictine Coll., Lisle, Ill., 1985. Mem. Ill. Artisans Shop, Art. Inst. Chgo. Sales and Rental Gallery, Chgo. Artists Coalition, Ward-Nasse Gallery N.Y.C., Phi Delta Kappa. Democrat. Home: 304 Ingleside Glenwood IL 60425 Office: Evanston Art Coop Gallery 2603 Sheridan Rd Evanston IL 60202

GILDEA, JOYCE ASHER, publishing executive, consultant; b. Balt., Aug. 24, 1945; d. William Edward and Annie Birdsal (Conley) Asher; m. Francis X. Gildea, Oct. 4, 1969. BA, Hood Coll., 1966. Intelligence analyst Nat. Security Agy., Ft. Meade, Md., 1966-69; pub. relations cons. Balt. and Washington, 1968-70; sr. communications cons. Towers, Perrin, Forster & Crosby, Phila. and N.Y.C., 1970-81; v.p. Human Resources Network, Phila., 1981-82; pres. The Editorial Office/JAG Inc., Radnor, Pa., 1982—; exec. editor Communications and Mgmt., N.Y.C., 1971-81; mng. editor Health Cost Mgmt. Jour., Phila., 1983—; editor The Options Jour., Cheyenne, Wyo., 1987—. Co-author: Corporate Economic Education Programs, 1979, Handbook of Business Problem-Solving, 1981, Case Studies in Organizational Communications, 1981; contbr. articles to profl. jours. Speechwriter, editor Dem. Party, Washington, 1968-70. Recipient Gold Quill award Internat. Assn. Bus. Communicators, 1975, 77, 82, Silver Anvil award Pub. Relations Soc. Am. Office: The Editorial Office 825 Hollow Rd Radnor PA 19087

GIL DEL REAL, MARÍA TERESA, epidemiologist; b. Cucuta, Colombia, Jan. 5, 1941; came to U.S., 1962, naturalized, 1969; d. Antonio E. and Rosa (Calvo) Gil del R.; Asso., Bogotá Bus. Coll., 1961; B.A. in Anthropology, Rutgers U., 1979; M. in Pub. Health, Epidemiology, Columbia U., 1986; m. John R. Romano, Oct. 10, 1964; children—Christina M., John Alexander. Freelance translator, simultaneous interpreter, 1977-79; bilingual editor Princeton Internat. Translations, Princeton Junction, N.J., 1979-80; research asst. Robert Wood Johnson Found., Princeton, 1980-83; researcher U. Madrid, 1983-1984; analyst N.J. State Dept. Health, Trenton, 1985—; cons. internat. pub. health. Mem. Am. Biog. Inst. Research Assn., Phila. Epidemiol. Soc., Epidemiologic Research Assn., Soc. Epidemiol. Research, Alpha Sigma Lambda. Home: 76 Princeton Ave Rocky Hill NJ 08553 Office: NJ Dept Health div of Epidemiology & Disease Control Cancer Epidemiology Program Trenton NJ 08625

GILDEN, NINA BETH, media and historical consultant, television producer; b. St. Louis, May 27, 1957; d. Louis and Joanne Audrey (Bamberger) G.; m. Ormond Albert Seavey; 1 child, Aaron Louis. Cert., Institut Ste. Andre, Tournai, Belgium, 1975; B.A., Washington U., St. Louis, 1978; Dir. polit. action com. Coalition for New Fgn. and Mil. Policy, Washington, 1978; mil advisor Hon. Patricia Schroeder, U.S. Congress, Washington, 1979-80; spl. cons. women's affairs U.S. Dept. Def., Washington, 1980; pres. Nina Gilden Assocs., Washington, 1981—; historian, dir. oral history project COMSAT Corp., 1985-88; video-historian Nat. Air and Space Mus., Smithsonian Instn., Washington, 1987-88; cons. Congresswomen's Caucus, U.S. Congress, 1979-80, Coalition on Women in Def., Washington, 1979-80. Producer TV show Jack Anderson Confidential, 1982, The Lawmakers, PBS-TV, 1984. Author articles on def. spending and strategic arms, 1979. Univ. fellow George Washington U., 1985-87. Office mgr. McGovern for Pres., St. Louis, 1972; organizer United Farm Workers Union, St. Louis, 1973; vol. coordinator Morris Udall for Pres., St. Louis, 1976. Recipient Am. Youth Found. award Danforth Found., 1974; Am. Field Service scholar, 1974-75. Mem. Orgn. of Am. Historians, Phi Delta Gamma. Democrat. Jewish. Office: Nina Gilden Assocs 7214 Spruce Ave Takoma Park MD 20912

GILE, MARY STUART, educational executive; b. Montreal, Que., Can., Mar. 24, 1936; d. William Gillies and Hazel Irene (Stuart) Sinclair; m. Robert Hall Gile, Mar. 29, 1974; children—D. Christopher, Julia Mary, John, Robertson Sinclair. B.Sc., McGill U., 1957; M.Ed., U. N.H., 1971; Ed.D., Vanderbilt U., 1982. Specialist phys. edn. Protestant Sch. Bd. Greater Montreal, 1957-64, kindergarten tchr. White Mountains Sch. Bd., Littleton, N.H., 1965-67; dir. Open Door Kindergarten, Salem, N.H., 1967-69; coordinator State Follow Through, State of N.H., 1969-80, N.H. Right to Read, 1973-74, U.S. Sec.'s Initiative in Excellence chpt. 1 Edn. Consol. and Improvement Act, 1983-84; sr. cons. edn. N.H. State Dept. Edn., Concord, 1969-85; v.p. edn. and devel. Acad. Applied Sci., Concord, 1985—; state dept. staff assoc. to U. N.H., Durham, 1970-74; mem. Gov.'s Task Force on Sexual Harassment, Concord, 1981-83; chair N.H. Trust Fund for Prevention of Child Abuse and Neglect, 1986, Commr.'s Com. on Alt. Work Schedules, Concord, 1982-84 ; commr.'s rep. State Day Care Adv. Com., Concord, 1984-85. Contbr. articles to profl. jours. Pres., Concord Parents and Children, 1977-82; chmn. Citizens Adv. Bd. to Community Devel., 1978-82; bd. govs. Merrimack County United Way, 1983-88; pres. N.H. Assn. for Mental Health, 1984-86. Recipient Appreciation cert. Maine Dept. Edn., 1984, cert. outstanding achievement N.H. State Bd. Edn., 1985, Imperial Oil Ltd. scholar, 1953; U. N.H. early childhood fellow, 1969. Mem. N.H. Assn. for Edn. Young Children. Phi Delta Kappa. Congregationalist. Avocations: skiing; music; theatre; hiking.

GILES, JUDITH MARGARET, communication educator; b. Sonora, Calif., Nov. 20, 1939; d. James Wilson and Phyllis Sue (Stafford) G. BA, Calif. State U., 1982; MA, CBN U., Virginia Beach, Va., 1986; A. Ministry, Christ for the Nations, Dallas, 1974. Real estate broker Mason McDuffie, Berkeley, Calif., 1975-77, Taylor Realty, Sonora, Calif., 1978-82; adminstr., instr. Christ for the People, Pleasant Hill, Calif., 1975-77, Mt. Zion Ministries, Concord, Calif., 1977-88; instr. Calif. Assn. Realtors, Sacramento, 1980-82; adminstrv. asst., instr. Air Force Chaplaincy, Washington, 1983-84; asst. media/press coordinator Nat. Religious Broadcasters, Washington, 1983-86; grad. teaching asst. Christian Broadcasting Network U., Virginia Beach, Va., 1984-86; instr. Global Outreach Bible Inst., Modesto, Calif., 1987—; real estate broker Re/Max Real Estate Cen., Modesto, Calif., 1987—; lectr. in field; communications cons.; radio commentator. Author: A Historical Overview of the Women's Movement In America, 1986; producer/dir. TV documentary: The United Jewish Fedn., 1985, What's in a Name, 1985, Chiropractic Lutheran Council, 1984. Mgr. pub. relations dir. South Lake Tahoe Community Choir, 1971. Named Assoc. of Yr., Recruiter of Yr. Century 21, 1987. Mem. Calif. Assn. Realtors, Nat. Assn. Realtors. Republican. Club: Women's. Lodges: Order Eastern Star, Rainbow Girls. Home: 2020 Chetenne Way #250 Modesto CA 95356

GILES, LYNDA FERN, social worker; b. Detroit, May 18, 1943; d. Samuel and Shirley (Finkelstein) S.; m. David Reuven Schenk, Sept. 5, 1965 (div. July 1975); children: Jared, Jamie; m. Conrad Leslie Giles, Nov. 26, 1978. BA, U. Mich., 1965; MSW, Wayne State U., 1977; predoctoral student, U. Mich. Cert. social worker, clin. social worker. Clinical social worker Counseling Assocs. Inc., Southfield, Mich., 1977—. Mem. com. identity and affiliation Jewish Welfare Fedn., Detroit, 1985—, mem. com. on univ. relations, 1987—, com. on edn., 1987—. Mem. Nat. Assn. Social Workers, Counseling Assocs. (chmn. Southfield gifted and talented program 1979-81), Mich. Soc. Clin. Social Workers. Democrat. Club: Franklin Country. Home: 6300 Westmoor Birmingham MI 48010 Office: Counseling Assocs Inc 25835 Southfield Rd Southfield MI 48075

GILES, TINA MARIE, accountant; b. Pineville, La., Oct. 1, 1962; d. Billy Ray and Lois Marie (Lasyone) G. BS, La. Coll., 1984. CPA, La. Acct. Ditto Apparel Calif., Inc., Colfax, La., 1984-87, Brian Clinic, Alexandria, La., 1987—. Mem. Am. Inst. CPA's, Am. Women's Soc. CPA's, La. Soc. CPA's, Nat. Assn. Female Execs. Democrat. Baptist. Home: PO Box 213 Bentley LA 71407 Office: Brian Clinic 201 4th St Alexandria LA 71301

GILFEATHER-DYER, JANICE MARY, nurse; b. Medford, Mass., Apr. 29, 1938; d. George William and Dorothy Frances (Vasconcellos) G.; m. Ernest Wilson Dyer; stepchildren Andrea, Ned. RN. Home: 18 Christo Dr Hilton Head Island SC 29928

GILFILLAN, MARY LOUISE, systems analyst, real estate associate; b. Charleston, S.C., Nov. 2, 1931; d. Leon William and Wilhelmina A. (Mack) Aiken; divorced; 1 child, Deborah Yvonne. BA, Queens Coll., 1985. Keypunch operator Met. Life Ins., N.Y.C., 1955-56, capt. calculating, 1957-59, supr. keypunch, 1960-63, correspondent, 1963-65, policy examiner, 1965-70, claims approver, 1970-80, sr. approver, 1980-84, systems analyst, 1985-87, analyst bus. systems, 1987—. Home: 204-09 115th Ave Saint Albans NY 11412

GILFORD, ROSE MALETZ, travel agency executive, lawyer; b. Boston, July 18, 1920; d. Morris and Fannie (Priceman) Maletz; m. Warren S. Gilford, Nov. 26, 1944; 1 dau., Sarah Gilford Wolfe. Student Queens U., Ont., Can., 1938-40; J.D., Boston U. Sch. Law, 1943. Bar: Mass. 1943, D.C. 1945; Cert. travel agt. Law clk. Supreme Court Mass., Boston, 1943-44; editor Mass. Law Jour., Boston, 1945-47; legal counselor for students Boston U., 1947-59; founder, pres., chief exec. officer Chestnut Hill Travel Inc., Mass., 1955—; forum chmn. Inst. Cert. Travel Agts., Wellesley, Mass., 1981-

82; mem. adv. bd. Pan Am. Airways, Boston, 1983—; mem. nat. adv. bd. Sonesta Internat. Hotels, Boston, 1982—; mem. adv. bd. Travel Edn. Ctr., Cambridge, Mass., 1981—. Assoc. editor in chief Boston U. Law Rev., 1942-43. Bd. dirs. Brookline Taxpayers Assn., Mass., 1965-67; govt. chmn. League of Women Voters-Mass., 1941-51; chmn. United Fund of Brookline, 1965-66; town meeting mem. Town of Brookline, 1945-67. Mem. Inst. Cert. Travel Agents, Am. Soc. Travel Agents, Mass. Assn. Women Lawyers. Clubs: Boston Yacht (Marblehead); University (Boston), Sloane (London). Avocations: antiques, history, museums, gardens. Home: 135 Perkins St Jamaica Plain MA 02130 Office: Chestnut Hill Travel Inc 1210 Boylston St Brookline MA 02167

GILFOYLE, NATHALIE PRESTON, lawyer; b. Lynchburg, Va., May 4, 1949; d. Robert Edmund and Dorothea Henry (Ward) Gilfoyle; m. Christopher Y.W. Ma, Sept. 9, 1978; children—Olivia Otey, Rohan James. B.A., Hollins Coll., Roanoke, Va., 1971; J.D., U. Va., Charlottesville, 1974. Bar: Mass. 1974, D.C. 1977. Staff counsel Rate Setting Commn., Boston, 1974-76; ptnr. Peabody, Lambert & Meyers, Washington, 1976-84; ptnr. McDermott, Will and Emery, 1984—; bd. dirs. Washington Lawyers Com. Civil Rights Under Law, Washington, 1982—; participating counsel Vol. Lawyers for Arts, Boston, 1974-76, Washington, 1978—. Bd. dirs. ACLU Nat. Capital Area, Washington, 1980-83, Filmore Early Learning Ctr., 1977-81. Mem. ABA, D.C. Bar Assn., Mass. Bar Assn., Women's Bar Assn. Episcopalian. Office: McDermott Will & Emery 1850 K St NW Washington DC 20006

GILFOYLE, PHYLLIS J., human resources executive; b. Boston; d. J. Mark and Doris Jeanette (McGowan) Sherwood; children: Jennifer Greco, Nancy White, Sandra Kutchins, Richard, Mark. BA, U. Chgo., MA, MLS, PhD. Chief librarian Bd. Library Dirs., Country Club Hills, Ill., 1964-71; librarian Blue Cross-Blue Shield, Chgo., 1971-76; mgr. regional personnel Marsh & McLennan, Inc., Chgo., 1976-79; asst. v.p. compensation and benefits Marsh & McLennan, Inc., N.Y.C., 1979-85; sr. v.p. human resources FPC Assocs., Chgo., 1985—, The Midland Fin. Cos., Chgo., 1986—; cons. Forty Plus, Chgo., 1985—, Female Small Bus. Owners, Chgo., 1985—, Ind. Labor Attorneys, Chgo., 1985—, Bus. and Profl. Assn., 1986—. Contbr. articles to profl. jours. Mem. Bd. Edn. Dist. 160, Ill., 1968-71; bd. dirs. Suburban Library System, Ill., 1966-72, Forty Plus, Chgo., 1987—. Recipient State Civic Leader State of Ill., 1970. Mem. Am. Compensation Assn., Am. Soc. Personnel Adminstrs., Soc. Human Resource Profls. (policy and practice com. 1987—), Ill. Library Assn. (Freedom of Speech and Press award 1971), Bus. and Profl. Women of Chgo. (chair network 1987—), Nat. Assn. Female Execs., LWV (chair library unit 1986—). Mem. Soc. of Friends. Home: 1642 E 56th St Apt 517 Chicago IL 60637

GILHOOLEY, CATHERINE PATRICIA, social worker; b. Orange, N.J.; d. Patrick J. and Bridget T. (Farley) G. BS, Seton Hall U., 1953; MSW, Fordham U., 1973. Diplomate clin. social work. Supr. N.J. Bell Telephone Co., Newark, 1946-69; social worker N.J. Div. Youth and Family Services, Elizabeth, 1969-71; asst. chief Drug Dependence Treatment Ctr., VA Med. Ctr., East Orange, N.J., 1973—. Mem. Nat. Assn. Social Workers, Acad. Cert. Social Workers, Nat. Assn. Social Workers Register of Clin. Social Workers, Seton Hall U. Alumni Assn., Fordham U. Alumni Assn. Home: 154 Freeman Ave East Orange NJ 07018 Office: VA Med Ctr Tremont Ave East Orange NJ 07018

GILKES, CHERYL LOUISE TOWNSEND, sociologist, educator, minister; b. Boston, Nov. 2, 1947; d. Murray Luke, Jr., and Evelyn Annette (Reid) Townsend. BA, Northeastern U., Boston, also MA, PhD; MDiv, Boston U., 1988. Lectr. Univ. Coll. Northeastern U., 1973-78; instr. sociology Boston State Coll., 1974-78, U. Mass., 1976; asst. prof. sociology Boston U., 1978-87; John D. and Catherine T. MacArthur asst. prof. black studies and sociology, Colby Coll., Waterville, Maine, 1987—; vis. lectr. Tufts U., 1974; research assoc., vis. lectr. sociology of religion Harvard U. Div. Sch., 1981-82; vis. lectr. Afro-Am. studies Simmons Coll.; faculty fellow Bunting Inst., Radcliffe Coll., 1982-84. Contbr. articles and revs. to profl. jours. and chpts. to books. Sec. Cambridge Civic Unity Com., 1978-87; mem. adv. com. Schlessinger Library, Racliffe Coll., 1984-86; pres. Cambridge Black Cultural and Hist. Assn., 1978-87; parliamentarian, asst. dean congress Christian Edn. United Bapt. Conv., Mass., R.I. and N.H., 1986—; assoc. minister Union Bapt. Ch., Cambridge, Mass., 1982—. Nat. Fellowships Fund dissertation fellow, 1977-78, Socialization Tng. fellow Northeastern U., 1970-73. Mem. Am. Sociol. Assn. (Spivak dissertation fellow 1977-78), Eastern Sociol. Soc., Mass. Sociol. Assn., Soc. Study of Social Problems, Assn. Humanist Sociology, Am. Acad. Religion, Soc. Study of Symbolic Interaction, Assn. Black Sociologists, Sociologists Women in Soc., Soc. Sci. Study of Religion, Soc. Study Black Religion, Urban League of Eastern Mass., Phi Kappa Phi, Delta Sigma Theta. Office: Colby Coll Dept Sociology Waterville ME 04901

GILKES, MARTHA JANE WATKINS, government consultant, scuba diving educator, underwater photographer, photojournalist; b. Aberdeen, Miss., Jan. 28, 1953; d. Robert McCluney and Martha Evelyn (Rye) Watkins; m. David Anthony Gilkes, June 1, 1981. B.A., Miss. State U., 1974, M.A., 1975. Served with U.S. Peace Corps, Grenada, 1975-77; cons. disaster relief Am. embassy, Barbados and Antigua, West Indies, 1977-88; free-lance scuba diving instr., 1979-88; owner, operator Fanta-Sea Island Divers, Antiqua, 1988; Contbr. articles to mags. Photographer underwater postcards. Pres. Eastern Caribbean Safe Diving Assn., Barbados, 1984-88, Barbuda/Antigua Diving Club, Antigua, 1984-85. Mem. Alpha Zeta, Phi Mu. Republican. Baptist. Address: Dorchester House, Half Moon Bay Antigua also: PO Box 4680 Charlotte Amalie Saint Thomas VI 00801

GILL, BERTHENIA LOIS, state government official; b. Conway, Ark., Oct. 12, 1936; m. Alvin Gill; children: Wannette, Fred, Maria. AA, Shorter Coll., 1976; BA, Philander Smith Coll., 1978. Coordinator, counselor Cen. Mo. Devel. Corp., Appleton City, 1970-71, equal opportunity officer, 1971-77; teller Twin City/First Nat. Bank, Conway and Little Rock, 1973-78; crime prevention specialist Cen. Little Rock 1978-80; paralegal Cen. Ark. Legal Services, Little Rock, 1981-82; edn. and tng. specialist Minority Bus. Ark. Indsl. Devel., Little Rock, 1982-84, asst. dir., 1984—; state minority bus. liaison Ark. Indsl. Devel. Commn., 1987—; organizer Minority Bus. Network, 1987; substitute tchr. Little Rock Schs., 1977-78; part-time instr. history Nat. Bapt. Conv. U.S., throughout Ark., 1982—; mem. Nat. Bus. Task Force/Nat. Bus. Alliance, Washington, 1985-86; TV host Black Access, Little Rock, 1986—. Girls' camp counselor Ark. Young Citizens, 1964-69; vol. probation officer Little Rock Cts., 1979-80; coordinator Youth Leadership Conf., Conway, 1987; bd. dirs., pub. relations Sickle Cell Research Little Rock; appointed to Gov.'s Youth 2000 Task Force, 1988; chair publicity com. Ark. Land and Farm Devel. Corp., 1988—. Recipient Outstanding Services award Philander Smith Coll., 1988. Mem. AAUW (pub. relations chair Little Rock br. 1980-85, membership chair 1988—), Nat. Council Negro Women, Assn. Ark. Entrepreneurs (charter), Philander Smith Coll. Alumni Assn. (pres. 1985-87, Disting. Alumni 1986). Baptist. Home: PO Box 21 Mayflower AR 72106

GILL, CAROLE O'BRIEN, family therapist; b. Providence, R.I., Apr. 7, 1946; d. Charles Warren and Angelina (Carcieri) O'Brien; m. Frank Ralston Gill, Oct. 17, 1964, (div. 1975); children: Michael Patrick, Peter Ralston. BA in Edn., U. R.I., 1978, BA in Psychology, 1984, MS in Marriage and Family Therapy, 1986. Cert. tchr., marriage and family therapist. Tchr. East Greenwich Sch. System, R.I., 1978-79; counselor U. R.I., Providence, 1984; clin. asst., therapist Family Therapy Clinic, Kingston, R.I., 1984-86, family therapist, East Greenwich, 1985-87, Ptnrs. in Psychotherapy, East Greenwich, 1986—, Children's Friend and Service, 1988—; pvt. practice, Bay View Counseling, 1988—; vol. Hotline/Sympatico, Wakefield, R.I., 1984; coordinator Women's Connection U. R.I., 1984; co-facilitator women's abuse group Women's Resource Ctr., Wakefield, R.I., 1985-86. Mem. Friends of East Greenwich Pub. Library, 1981—. Mem. R.I. Chpt. Nat. Com. for Prevention of Child Abuse, Nat. Council on Family Relations, Am. Assn. Female Execs., R.I. Marriage and Family Assn. (v.p. 1988—, pres. student assoc. orgn. 1987-88), Am. Assn. Marriage and Family Therapists, Am. Psychol. Assn., New Eng. Psychol., Am. Assn. Marriage and Family Therapy, Assn. Avocations: archeology, anthropology, photography, needlework, music. Office: Children's Friend and Service 2 Richmond St Providence RI 02903

GILL, EVALYN PIERPOINT, editor, publisher; b. Boulder, Colo.; d. Walter Lawrence and Lou Octavia Pierpoint; student Lindenwood Coll., B.A., U. Colo.; postgrad. U. Nebr., U. Alaska, M.A., Central Mich. U., 1968; m. John Glanville Gill, Nov. 10, 1943; children—Susan Pierpoint, Mary Louise Glanville. Lectr. humanities Saginaw Valley State Coll., University Center, Mich., 1968-72; mem. English faculty U. N.C., Greensboro, 1973-74; editor Internat. Poetry Rev., Greensboro, 1975—; pres. TransVerse Press, Greensboro, 1981—. Bd. dirs. Eastern Music Festival, Greensboro, 1981—, Greensboro Symphony, 1982—, Greensboro Opera Co., 1982—, Weatherspoon Assn.; chmn. O. Henry Festival, 1985. Mem. Am. Lit. Translators Assn., MLA, N.C. Poetry Soc., Phi Beta Kappa. Author: Poetry By French Women 1930-1980, 1980, Dialogue, 1985, Southeast of Here: Northwest of Now, 1986; contbr. poetry to numerous mags. Home: 1501 Kirkpatrick St Greensboro NC 27408 Office: PO Box 2047 Greensboro NC 27402

GILL, JANE ROBERTS, clinical social worker; b. Boston, Dec. 6, 1923; d. Penfield Hitchcock and Cecilia (Washburn) Roberts; student Wellesley Coll., 1941-43; B.A., Boston U., 1954, M.S.W., 1956; m. Peter Lawrence Gill, Dec. 24, 1943 (div. 1973); children—Jonathan Penfield, Dorcas Pearson, Nicholas Brinton, Timothy Roberts. Diplomate Clin. Social Work. Social worker Beth Israel Hosp., Boston, 1956-57, South End Family Program, Boston, 1957-58, Margaret Gifford Sch., Cambridge, Mass., 1963-65; Adams House Psychiat. Clinic, Boston, 1967-76; supr. sr. clin. social work, coodinator outpatient clinic, Faulkner Hosp., Boston, 1975-87, staff mem. The John R. Graham Headache Ctr., 1987—; pvt. practice social work, Brookline, 1970—; clin. instr. Simmons Coll. Sch. of Social Work, 1971-79. Mem. social service com. Am. Heart Assn., 1979—; program chmn. Mass. Mental Health Center, 1969-71; bd. dirs. Rutland Corner House, 1982—; mem. Democratic Town Com., Newton-Wellesley, 1959-64. Lic. ind. clin. social worker. Mem. Register Clin. Social Workers, Acad. Psychosomatic Medicine, Internat. Headache Soc., Peacham Hist. Assn. of Vt., Putney Sch. Alumni Assn. Contbr. papers to profl. meetings. Office: 318 Allandale Rd Chestnut Hill MA 02167 also: Faulkner Hosp Center St at Allandale Rd Boston MA 02130

GILL, MARGARET GASKINS, lawyer; b. St. Louis, Mar. 2, 1940; d. Richard Williams and Margaret (Cambage) Gaskins; m. Stephen Paschall Gill, Dec. 21, 1961; children: Elizabeth, Richard. BA, Wellesley Coll., 1962; JD, U. Calif., Berkeley, 1965. Bar: Calif. 1966. Assoc. Pillsbury, Madison & Sutro, San Francisco, 1966-73, ptnr., 1973—, mem. mgmt. com., 1984—, chair assoc. review com., 1988—; referee Calif. State Bar Ct., 1979-82. Mem. steering com. Trinity Episcopal Ch., Menlo Park, Calif., 1980-82, com. to revise constitution, Diocese Calif., 1981-82; trustee St. Luke's Hosp. Found., San Francisco, 1983—; mem. adv. council Ch. Div. Sch. of the Pacific, 1986. Fellow Am. Bar Found.; mem. ABA (spl. com. on corps., spl. com. bus. law sect.), Calif. Bar Assn. (corp. com. 1982-85, chairperson 1985, exec. com. 1985, vice chairperson 1987-88, chair nominating com. bus. law sect. 1988), San Francisco Bar Assn. Republican. Episcopalian. Office: Pillsbury Madison & Sutro 235 Montgomery St San Francisco CA 94104 also: Pillsbury Madison & Sutro 225 Bush St San Francisco CA 94104

GILL, MARY MARGARET, speech educator; b. Milbank, S.D., Dec. 14, 1956; d. Ray Edwin and Margaret Irene (Steltz) G. BA, S.D. State U., 1979, MA, 1982. Grad. teaching asst. S.D. State U., Brookings, 1979-80, technician data control, 1980-83; dir. forensics U. N.D., Grand Forks, 1983—. Contbr. articles to profl. jours., 1986—. Mem. Am. Forensic Assn., Speech Communication Assn., N.D. Intercollegiate Speech League (exec. sec. 1985, 87), Cross Exam. Debate Assn. (nat. council 1986—), Delta Sigma Rho (Tau Kappa Alpha chpt.), Pi Kappa Delta. Democrat. Methodist. Home: 2021 S 17th St Apt 315 Grand Forks ND 58201 Office: U ND Sch Communication Grand Forks ND 58202

GILL, PATRICIA JANE, human resource executive; b. Mt. Vernon, N.Y., Jan. 20, 1950; d. J. Morgan and Magdalina (Manganiello) G. BA in History, St. Mary's Coll., 1971; MA in Counseling, NYU, 1973; MBA in Mktg., Fordham U., 1979. Tchr., counselor Mt. Vernon Bd. Edn., 1970-74; tng. mgr. St. Luke's Hosp., N.Y.C, 1974-78; dir. personnel Bernard Hodes Advt., N.Y.C., 1978-80; mgr. mgmt. programs group Devel. Dimensions Internat., Pitts., 1980-82; v.p. Swan Cons., N.Y.C., 1982-83; nat. sales mgr. Reader's Digest, Pleasantville, N.Y., 1983-84; owner Alexis-Gill Assocs., White Plains, N.Y., 1982—; cons. in field. Author: Roleplaying, 1979. Worker Project Hope, New Rochelle, N.Y., 1986—. Mem. Am. Soc. Tng. and Devel. (pres. 1988), Soc. of Systems Quality (bd. dirs. 1987—), Nat. Speakers Assn. Roman Catholic. Office: Alexis-Gill Assocs 50 Main St Suite 1000 White Plains NY 10606

GILL, RACHEL BEVERLY, physician assistant; b. Winter Garden, Fla., Oct. 27, 1959; d. Marvin Henry and Erma (Gray) Osborne; m. Raymond George Gill, May 12, 1959; 1 child, Mary Deanna. BS in Biology and Chemistry, Trevecca Nazarene Coll., 1980, BS, 1983. Allergy technician Dr. Thomas Guy Pennington, Nashville, 1979-82; cert. physician's asst. Ft. Worth Pediatric Surg. Assn., 1984, Dr. Jacques R. Caldwell, Gainsville, Fla., 1985—; cons. Arthritus Found., Gainsville, 1985. Choir Univ. Ch. of the Nazarene, Gainsville, 1985-87. Mem. Am. Acad. Physicians' Assts., Am. Mgmt. Assn., Nat. Assn. of Female Execs., Fla. Acad. of Physicians' Assts., Med. Mgmt. Democrat. Home: 5584 Manfields Jacksonville FL 32207 Office: Dr Arnold Graham Smith MD, PA 4237 Salisbury Rd Jacksonville FL 32216

GILL, REBECCA, engineering manager; b. Brownsboro, Tex., Sept. 17, 1944; d. Milton and Dona Mildred (Magee) La Losh; m. Peter Mohammed Sharma, Sept. 1, 1965 (div.); m. James Fredrick Gill, Mar. 9, 1985; children: Erin, Melissa, Ben. BS in Physics, U. Mich., 1965; MBA, Calif. State U., Northridge, 1980. Tchr., Derby, Kans., 1966; weight analyst Beech Aircraft, Wichita, Kans., 1966; weight engr. Ewing Tech. Design, assigned Boeing-Vertol, Phila., 1966-67, Bell Aerosystems, Buffalo, 1967; design specialist Lockheed-Calif. Co., Burbank, 1968-79; sr. staff engr. Hughes Aircraft Missile Systems, Canoga Park, Calif., 1979-82, project mgr. AMRAAM spl. test and tng. equipment, 1982-85, project mgr. GBU-15 guidance sect., Navy IR Maverick Missile, Tucson, 1985—; sec. Nat. Cinema Corp. Com. chmn. Orgn. for Rehab. through Tng., 1971-75; speaker ednl. and civic groups. Pres. Briarcliffe East Homeowners Assn. Recipient Lockheed award of achievement, 1977. Mem. Soc. Allied Weight Engrs. (dir., sr. v.p., chmn. pub. relations com.), Aerospace Elec. Soc. (dir.), Nat. Assn. Female Execs, Hughes Mgmt. Club (bd. dirs., chmn. spl. events, chmn. programs). Republican. Club: Tucson Racquet. Office: Hughes Aircraft Missile Systems Bldg 805 MS L5A Tucson AZ 85734

GILL, SANDRA LEE, health care executive; b. Mt. Clemens, Mich., June 23, 1948; d. Richard Sullivan and Evelyn (Sherrill) G.; m. Andre Louis Delbecq, July 1, 1977. BA cum laude, Mich. State U., 1970, MA magna cum laude, 1974; postgrad. in mgmt. and orgn. theory, U. Wis., 1977-79; postgrad. in orgn. and mgmt. systems, Fielding Inst., Santa Barbara, Calif., 1982—. Tchr. deaf-blind program Mich. Sch. for the Blind, 1969-72; coordinator services for deaf-blind children Mich. Dept. Edn., 1972-77; coordinator Ctr. for Evaluation Research, Tng. and Devel. U. Wis., Madison, 1978-79; orgnl. devel. specialist Kaiser-Permanente Med. Care Program of No. Calif., 1980-81; orgnl. devel. coordinator O'Connor Hosp., San Francisco, 1981-82; pres. Performance Mgmt. Resources Inc., Santa Clara, Calif., 1982—; instr. Coll. Profl. Studies U. San Francisco, 1979—; faculty mem. Estes Park Inst. for Med. Leadership, Englewood, Colo., Am. Acad. Med. Dirs., Tampa, Fla. Contbr. articles to profl. jours. Mem. Am. Assn. Healthcare Cons. (assoc.), Kappa Delta Pi, Omicron Nu, Phi Kappa Phi. Roman Catholic. Office: Performance Mgmt Resources Inc 999 Oakmont Plaza Dr Suite 600 Westmont IL 60559-5504

GILL, YVONNE T., principal; b. Houston, Oct. 7, 1937; d. Eugene Ashley Thigpen and Clela A. (Mooney) Eaves. BS in Edn., U. Houston, 1965, MEd, 1971, postgrad., 1971-72. Tchr. Lakewood Elementary Sch., Houston, 1965-75, prin., 1977—; asst. prin. W. E. Rogers Elementary Sch., Houston, 1973-75; supr. North Forest Sch. Dist., Houston, 1975-77. Chmn. Whitmire for Re-election Campaign, 1986-86; vol. Ctr. Attitudinal Healing, 1985—. Named Oustanding Elementary Tchr., Outstanding Elementary Tchrs. Am., 1973. Mem. Tex. Elem. Prins. and Suprs. Assn. (dist. 4 treas. 1984-85, 86-87, v.p. 1987, pres.-elect 1988), Nat. Assn. Elem. Sch. Prins., Greater Houston Reading Council, Tex. PTA, Assn. Supervision and Curriculum Devel. Democrat. Unitarian. Office: Lakewood Elem Sch 8800 Grandriver Houston TX 77078

GILLEN, ADRIENNE KOSCIUSKO, librarian, researcher; b. Northampton, Mass., Jan. 7, 1947; d. Mitchell Fred and Gloria Theresa (Maynard) K.; m. William A. Gillen, May 24, 1986. BA, U. Mass., 1969. Library asst. Hotchkiss Sch., Lakeville, Conn., 1971-72; grants mgr. Conn. Planning Com. on Adminstrn., Hartford, 1972-73; researcher Dept. Youth Service, Bridgeport, Conn., 1974-75, White House, Washington, 1976; librarian Rep. Nat. Com., Washington, 1977-79; librarian U.S. Senate, Rep. Policy Com., Washington, 1979-82; library dir. White House, Washington, 1982—; exec. adv. com. mem. Fedlink Library of Congress. Republican. Roman Catholic. Office: Exec Office of Pres Library and Info Services Div Rm 308 OEOB Washington DC 20503

GILLENWATER, ANNE RIDINGS, maintenance planner; b. Detroit, Apr. 23, 1936; d. James Clarence and Mary Sue (Hughes) Ridings; B.S. in Bus. Adminstrn., U. Tenn., Knoxville, 1971, also postgrad. With Aluminum Co. Am., Alcoa, Tenn., 1962—, various secretarial positions, 1962-71, adminstrv. analyst, 1971-73, indsl. engr., 1973-75, systems analyst, 1975-76, systems design engr., 1976-80, maintenance planner, 1980—. Adviser Alcoa Jr. Achievement; chmn. plant savs. bond campaign, 1972; mem. Tenn. Commn. on Women, 1974-81, chmn., 1975, 80, 81; bd. dirs. Laurel Lake Youth Camp, treas., 1977—; co-sponsor White House Conf. on Domestic and Econ. Affairs, 1975; bd. dirs. Blount County Girls Club, 1980—. F.T. Bonham scholar, 1953-54. Cert. profl. sec. Mem. Am. Inst. Indsl. Engrs., Soc. Women Engrs. (sec., 1976, SE student activities coordinator, 1977-79, pres. Knoxville, 1979, nat. chmn. new student sects., 1979-80, dir., 1981), Am. Soc. Tng. and Devel. (pres. 1981 region 4 conf. chair 1984, dir. 1986-87), Tenn. Valley Personnel Assn. (TIPC chmn., 1981, treas. 1982, pres.-elect 1983, pres. 1984, rep. 1986-87), Nat. Secs. Assn. (pres. 1972-74), AAUW, Smoky Mountain Passion Play Guild. Republican. Baptist. Clubs: Knoxville Club LeConte, Delta Zeta. Speaker workshops, seminars, confs.; instr. human relations and adminstrn. Home: Route 5 Box 200 24 Fairoaks Dr Maryville TN 37801 Office: PO Box 9158 N-40 Alcoa TN 37701

GILLEO, SANDRA V., educator; b. Somerville, N.J., May 8, 1944; d. Sam B. and Frances (Green) Hammer; m. Robert James Gilleo (div. Dec. 1981); children: Robert T.I., Felise V. BA, Trenton (N.J.) State Coll., 1967; MA, Newark State Coll., 1971. Cert. tchr., N.J., Pa. Tchr. elem. Franklin Twp. Sch. Dist., Quakertown, N.J., 1966-67, Bricktown (N.J.) Twp. Sch. Dist., 1967-69; reading specialist Lawrence Twp. Sch. Dist., Lawrenceville, N.J., 1969-72; tchr. elem. New Hope-Solebury (Pa.) Sch. Dist., 1972—. Librarian Village Library of Wrightstown, Pa., 1972—; vol. John B. Anderson presdl. campaign, Bucks County, Pa., 1980; mem. Second Monday adv. com. for women, Doylestown, Pa., 1982-84. Served with USNR from 1965-71. Mem. Franklin Twp. Edn. Assn., Brick Edn. Assn., Lawrenceville Edn. Assn., New Hope-Solebury Edn. Assn., Sierra Club. Jewish. Club: Honey Hollow W.A. Home: 2650 Windy Bush Rd Newtown PA 18940 Office: New Hope-Solebury Elem Sch N Sugan Rd Solebury PA 18963

GILLER, RUTH EDNA, business association executive; b. Hampstead, London, Eng., Nov. 5, 1929; came to U.S., 1952; d. George and Judith (Gunzburg) Bradlaw; m. Marshall Giller, Jan. 27, 1952; children: Paul Bradlaw, Sara. Student London U., 1946-50. Mgr., Children's Zoo Festival of Britain, 1950-52; mgr. Better Bus. div. Cape Kennedy Area C. of C., 1967-72; mgr. Trade Practice div. Better Bus. Bur., Eastern Pa., Phila., 1972-78; exec. dir. Better Bus. Bur. Western Mich., Grand Rapids, 1979—. Mem. Scottish Israelite Soc., Soc. Consumer Affairs Profls., West Mich. Women Execs., Women in Communications. Democrat. Jewish. Club: Torch. Office: Better Bus Bur Western Mich 620 Trust Bldg Grand Rapids MI 49503

GILLESPIE, BETTY RUE, accountant; b. Harrison, Ark., Dec. 15, 1942; d. Rue F. and Lucille (Roberts) Stokes; m. Robert L. Gillespie, Aug. 7, 1964; children: Cynthia, Kelly. BS in Edn., U. Cen. Ark., 1963, MS in Edn., 1967. Cert. tchr., Ark., CPA, Ark. Tchr. Danville (Ark.) High Sch., Ark., 1963-83; acct. Betty R. Gillespie, CPA, Harrison, Ark., 1983—; instr. U. Cen. Ark., Conway, 1978;. Treas., Pianist Bruno (Ark.) Bapt. Ch., 1984—; leader Girl Scouts Am., Danville, 1976. Mem. Ozark Region Chpt. CPA's (sec., treas. 1986, v.p. 1987, pres. 1988), Bus. Profl. Women (speaker 1987, sec. 1976), Music Club (treas. 1978). Home: Rt 1 Box 235 Everton AR 72633 Office: 1114 Hwy 62-65B N Harrison AR 72601

GILLESPIE, (MARGARET) JEAN, educator, researcher; b. Winnipeg, Man., Can., Jan. 13, 1927; d. Gordon Stanley and Ethel Mary (Matchett) Thornton; m. Gordon Neil Gillespie, Sept. 17, 1949; children: Catharine, Victoria, James, Peter. BA in Physiology and Biochemistry, U. Toronto, 1948, MA, 1949; PhD, U. Alberta, 1984. Research assoc. Banting Inst., U. Toronto, Ont., Canada, 1948-50; research asst. Trent U., Peterborough, Ont., Canada, 1965-68; lab. instr. U. Alberta, Edmonton, Alta, Canada, 1968-72; asst. prof. Faculty Rehab. Med. U. of Alta., Edmonton, Can., 1975-87, Dept. Pharmacology U. Alta., Edmonton, Can., 1988—; asst. prof. dept. pharmacol. U. Alberta, 1988—. Contbr. articles to profl. jours. Mem. Soc. Neurosci., Can. Neurosci. Assn., Can. Physiol. Soc., Exec. Acad. Women's Assn. Club: Derrick Golf and Winter. Home: 11607 44A Ave, Edmonton, AB Canada TGJ 1A2 Office: U Alta, Dept Pharmacology, 9-70 Med Sci Bldg, Edmonton, AB Canada T6G 2H7

GILLESPIE, MAUREEN ELIZABETH, telecommunications company public relations executive; b. Queens, N.Y., Sept. 10, 1945; d. John Francis and Ruth Irene (Bertschy) Hogan; children: Lauren Beth Alles, Kirsten Leigh Alles. Student, Queens Coll., 1962-65, 70-72, Hunter Coll., 1977-79, NYU, 1976-77. Writer N.Y. Telephone Co., N.Y.C., 1979-83, pub. relations mgr. product publicity and cultural advt., 1983-84, mgr. customer info., editor HELLO bill insert, 1984-87; pub. relations mgr. NYNEX Corp., 1987—; freelance editor mags. and newspapers. Lobbyist various edn. orgns., 1977; founder, chmn. Clermont Tenants Assn., N.Y.C., 1976-81; campaign aide various state legislators, 1976-80. Recipient Andy award Advt. Club N.Y., 1984. Mem. Women in Communications, N.Y. Press Club, N.Y.C. Commn. Status of Women.

GILLESPIE, NELLIE REDD, academic administrator; b. Brookhaven, Miss.; d. Zelmer Morris and Willie (Woods) Redd; divorced; 1 child, David Lauren. BS in Acctg., U. So. Miss., 1958; postgrad., Nat. Assn. Coll. Univs. Bus. Officer's Inst. Sr. auditor Fla. State U., Tallahassee, 1968-74, controller, 1974-76, asst. v.p. adminstrv. affairs, 1976-78, assoc. dir. student fin. affairs, 1978-82; adminstr. dept. revenue State of Fla., Tallahassee, 1982-83; dir. fin., adminstrn. City of Altamonte Spring, Fla., 1983-84; internal auditor Jackson (Miss.) State U., 1984—. Vol. Graham/Mixson gov. campaign, inaugural com., 1983, Ray Mabus gov. campaign, 1987; Gov.'s appointee Miss. Bd. Health and Human Services, 1988-92; div. leader United Way, Cancer Fund drives; mem. Leon High Sch. Choral Parent Assn., dist. adv. council Leon County Sch. Bd.; bd. dirs. Ctr. for Creative Employment. Mem. Assn. Coll. Univ. Auditors, Nat. Assn. Coll. Univ. Bus. Officers (so. chpt.), Am. Mgmt. Assn., Nat. Assn. Female Execs., Inst. Internal Auditors, AAUW (v.p. 1967—), Nat. Assn. Bds. Pharmacy (gov.'s com. Fla. bd. 1979-83), Am. Assn. Computer Profls. (audit com. dist. III), Fla. LWV, U. So. Miss. Alumni Assn., Tallahassee Ins. Women's Assn. (charter, treas. 1960-65), Sigma Sigma Sigma. Democrat. Mem. Ch. Christ. Club: Pilots (Anchor Club sponsor). Lodge: Civitan.

GILLETT, SUE JACKSON, medical facility administrator; b. Chgo., Oct. 19, 1945; d. Robert Freeman and Mary Martha (Charles) Jackson; m. Robert L. Gillett, Oct. 18, 1973 (div. Dec. 1979). BA, So. Ill. U., 1966; postgrad., U. S. Fla., 1967-69. Adminstr. Midtown Med. Lab., Sarasota, Fla., 1972—; pres., owner Medscan Cardiac Lab., Sarasota, 1974—; adminstr. Midtown Radiology, Sarasota, 1985—. Republican. Episcopalian. Office: Midtown Med Lab 1217 East Ave S Sarasota FL 34239

GILLETTE, ETHEL MORROW, columnist; b. Oelwein, Iowa, Nov. 27, 1921; d. Charles Henry and Myrne Sarah (Law) Morrow; student Coe Coll., 1939-41; BA, Upper Iowa U., 1959; MA, Western State Coll., 1969; m. Roman A. Gillette, May 6, 1944; children: Melody Ann, Richard Alan, William Robert. Stenographer, Penick & Ford, Cedar Rapids, Iowa, 1941-43,

FBI, Washington, 1943-44; tchr. Fayette (Iowa) High Sch., 1959-60, Jordan Jr. High Sch., Mpls., 1960-64, Montrose (Colo.) High Sch., 1964-68; family living, religion editor The News-Record, Gillette, Wyo., 1977-79, columnist Distaff Side, 1979-84. Mem. Western Writers Am. (assoc.), Nat. Writers Club. Contbr. articles to various mags. Home: 1804 E Locust St Montrose CO 81401

GILLETTE, FRANKIE JACOBS, savings and loan executive; b. Norfolk, Va., Apr. 1, 1925; d. Frank Walter and Natalie (Taylor) Jacobs; m. Maxwell Claude Gillette, June 19, 1976. BS, Hampton U., 1946; MSW, Howard U., 1948. Lic. clin. social worker; cert. jr. coll. tchr., life. Youth dir. YWCA, Passaic, N.J., 1948-50; dir. program Ada S. McKinley Community Ctr., Chgo., 1950-53; program dir. Sophie Wright Settlement, Detroit, 1953-64; dir. Concerted Services Project, Pittsburg, Calif., 1964-66, Job Corps Staff Devel., U. Calif., Berkeley, 1966-69; spl. program coordinator U.S. Community Services Adminstrn., San Francisco, 1969-83; pres. G & G Enterprises, San Francisco, 1985—; bd. dirs. Time Savs. and Loan Assn., San Francisco, 1980—, chmn. bd. dirs. 1986—. Mem. Nat. Assn. Negro Bus. and Profl. Women's Clubs (pres. 1983-87). Office: The Nat Assoc of Negro Bus & Profl Womens Club Inc 1806 New Hampshire Ave NW Washington DC 20009

GILLETTE, JOYCE LYNNE, nursing educator; b. Youngstown, Ohio, Oct. 8, 1948; d. Frederick T. Gillette and Eleanor (Kulow) G. BS in Nursing, U. Rochester, 1973; MA, Kent State U., 1980; postgrad. in nursing, Calif. State U., Los Angeles, 1986—. RN. Charge nurse, supr. Shaker Med. Ctr., Cleve., 1973-74; pub. health nurse Cuyahoga County Bd. Health, Cleve., 1974-77; charge nurse Met. Gen. Hosp., Cleve., 1977-78; occupational health nurse Ohio Crankshaft, Cleve., 1978-80; asst. dir. edn. St. Francis Med. Ctr., Lynwood, Calif., 1980-83; nurse educator Daniel Freeman Hosp., Inglewood, Calif., 1983-86; clin. instr., acting dir. edn. Anaheim (Calif.) Meml. Hosp., 1986-88; med./surg. nurse educator UCI Med. Ctr., Orange, Calif., 1988—; program dir. Am. Heart Assn., Akron, Ohio, 1978, instr. CPR, Orange County, Calif., 1981—. Editor: CEN Rev. Manual, 1984. Mem. outreach com. St. Joseph's Episc. Ch., Buena Park, Calif., 1984—. Office: UCI Med Ctr 101 The City Dr Orange CA 90803

GILLETTE, SUSAN DOWNS, advertising executive; b. Phila., Mar. 4, 1950; d. George Woodrow and Ruth (McFarland) Downs; m. Raymond Gene Gillette, Oct. 6, 1979; children: Margaret Anne, Lindsay Ray. BA, No. Ill. U., 1972. Advt. asst. Wescom Inc., Downers Grove, Ill., 1972-73; copywriter Steven Walters Advt., Chgo., 1973-75; dir. creative services DDB Needham Worldwide, Chgo., 1975—. Active Acquired Immune Deficiency Syndrome pub. info. com. Chgo. Dept. Pub. Health; tchr. local Sunday Sch. Recipient Gold Lion award Cannes Film Festival, 1978, Silver Lion award, 1987, Vol. award Am. Cancer Soc., 1986; named Creative Dir. of Yr., Ad Week mag., 1986. Clubs: Women's Ad, Chgo. Ad. Office: DDB Needham Chicago 303 E Wacker Dr Chicago IL 60601

GILLEY, NANCY DEAN, data processing executive; b. Ft. Worth, Mar. 6, 1942; d. Harvey Lee and Minnie Lee (Jones) Elrod; m. Eddie Baker Gilley, Aug. 24, 1959; 1 son, Rockie Dean. B.S. in Computer Sci., North Tex. State U., 1971; B.S. in Computer Sci., Tex. Inst. Tech., 1971-73; B.S. in Bus. Mgmt., Electronic Computer Programming Inst., Dallas, 1977. Asst. data processing mgr. SMC Corp., Dallas, 1970-73; data processing mgr. H.P. Foley Co., Dallas, 1973-78; v.p. data processing Ft. Worth Pipe Co., 1978-81; dir. mgmt. info. systems Ryan Cos., Arlington, Tex., 1981-85, dir. membership Tex. Soc. C.P.A.s, Dallas, 1985—; pres. Gilley & Assocs. D.P. cons. and researcher, Ft. Worth, 1980—; advisor Nat. Edn. Ctr., Dallas, Tex. Inst. Vol. Stars for Children, Arlington, 1984-85. Mem. Exec. Bus. Women Am., Am. Execs. in Constrn., DFW System 38 Users Group (founding pres.), West Tex. System 38 Users Group (founding), DFW/System 34-36 Users Group (founding), mem. common TCPA Staff PC Users Group (cons., and programming. Office: Gilley & Assocs 5816 Meyers Rd Arlington TX 76017

GILLIAM, JULIANNE KEMPER, video tape producer; b. Kansas City, Mo., May 11, 1927; d. James Madison and Gladys Woods (Grissom) Kemper; m. William Sutherland Beckett, 1948; 1 child, Deirdre Beckett; m. Digby Gallas, 1958 (div. 1965); children: Marina, Evan; m. Gardner Burnett Gilliam, Oct. 18, 1975. Founder, owner, pres. Magnus Films, 1983—. Exec. producer film Anna, starring Sally Kirkland and Paulina Porizkova, 1986. Recipient Lillian Gish award Women in Film Soc., 1987. Home: 2416 34th St Santa Monica CA 90405 Office: 225 Santa Monica Blvd Suite 511 Santa Monica CA 90401

GILLIAM, LYNDA FAYE, telecommunications consultant; b. Cleve., Oct. 30, 1949; d. Warren and Vernice Octavia (White) G.; 1 child, Raven Vernice. BA in Bus., Kent (Ohio) State U., 1971; AA in Communications, Massey Inst., 1973. Ops. mgr. Tel Inc. Communications, Los Angeles, 1974-77; asst. office mgr. BBDO/West Advt., Los Angeles, 1977-80; project coordinator AM West Telephone Co., Los Angeles, 1980-82, Com Systems, Inc., Los Angeles, 1982-84; sales mgr. Dencom Systems, Inc., Los Angeles, 1984-85; free-lance telecommunications cons. Los Angeles, 1985—; trainer, cons. AT&T Phone Co., Los Angeles, 1985-87. Vol. career guidance cons. Los Angeles Youth Guidance; counselor Young Dems., Los Angeles, 1985. Mem. Nat. Assn. Female Execs., Summit Orgn. Roman Catholic. Home and Office: Gilliam and Assocs 4532 W 16th Pl Los Angeles CA 90019

GILLIAM, MARY, travel executive; b. Pampa, Tex., Apr. 18, 1928; d. Roy and Hylda O. (Bertrand) Brown; divorced; 1 child, Terry K. AA, Amarillo (Tex.) Bus. Coll., 1949. Flight attendant Braniff Internat. Airways, Dallas, 1950-53; from reservation agt. to mgr. passenger sales Trans-World Airlines, various locations, 1953-81; exec. v.p. Lakewood (Colo.) Travel, 1981; mgmt. cons. Bank One Travel, Columbus, Ohio, 1981-82; pres. Icaria Travel, Inc., Tucson, Ariz., 1986—, Intensive Trainers Inst., Tucson, 1983—; examining team Council for Noncollegiate Continuing Edn. Mem. Tucson Better Bus. Bur., 1983—, Ariz. Rep. Com., 1978—. Recipient Award of Excellence Trans-World Airlines, N.Y.C., 1972, Pres.' Hall of Fame award, 1973. Mem. Am. Soc. Travel Agts. (scholarship chmn., nat. schs. com., Industry Service award 1980), Inst. Cert. Travel Agts., Pacific Asia Travel Assn., Women in Travel, Soc. Travel and Tourism Educators. Republican. Methodist. Office: Intensive Trainers Inst 2700 W Broadway Tucson AZ 85745

GILLIAM, PAULA HUTTER, transportation company executive; b. N.Y.C.; d. Irving and Edna Phyllis (Manes) Hutter; m. Stanley Spencer Rolnick (div. 1959); children: Jeffry Hutter Gilliam, Pamela Sara Bielory; m. Peter Gilliam, 1981. AA, Centenary Coll. Pres. Paula Rolnick Sales, N.Y.C., 1963-74; mdse. mgr. Kirby Block Internat., N.Y.C., 1974-78; pres. P.M.G. Internat. Ltd, N.Y.C., 1981—; dir. corp. sales Rical Air Express, Inc., N.Y.C., Rical Ocean Forwarding, N.Y.C., Theatre Off Park, ptnr. The Goldon Unicorn Restaurants. Producer (Broadway show) Stardust, 1987; exec. producer (plays) Long Days Journey Into the Night, 1988, Ah Wilderness. V.p. Murray Hill Com., 1982—, chmn. block party, 1983—; bd. advisors 132 E 35th St., N.Y.C., 1984-86; vol. aide June Eisland Council Women, Riverdale, N.Y., 1979—; bd. dirs. Theater Off Park, 1983—. Mem. Women in INternat. Traffic. Democrat. Clubs: Women's Traffic, Met. Traffic. Home and Office: 132 E 35th St New York NY 10016

GILLIARD, DEBORA J., educator; b. Portland, Oreg., Jan. 20, 1956; d. Billy E. and Charlotte E. (Cramer) Wickham; m. Gary L. Gilliard, Sept. 3, 1977. BS, U. N. Colo., 1978; MBA, U. Colo., Denver, 1986. CPA, Colo.; arbitrator Better Bus. Bur. Tax supr. Franchise Acctg. Systems, Inc., Denver, 1978-81; office mgr. Nat. Home Nursing Service, Bella Vista, Ark., 1981-82; acct. Tyson Foods, Inc., Springdale, Ark., 1982-83, United Bank of Denver, Denver, 1983-85; research asst. U. Colo., Denver, 1986; instr. Community Coll. of Aurora, Aurora, Colo., 1986—, Met. State Coll., Denver, 1987—; mem. textbook selection com. Community Coll. of Aurora, 1987. Cert. arbitrator Better Bus. Bur.; trustee Colo. Bus. and Profl. Women's Found., Inc. Mem. Bus. and Profl. Women's Club Inc. (1st v.p. 1987—), Cherry Creek Jaycees. Republican.

GILLIARD, JUDY ANN, sales professional; b. Ventura, Calif., Aug. 21, 1946; d. Sam Albert and Betty (Hardacre) G. A in Hotel and Restaurant Mgmt., Santa Barbara (Calif.) Community Coll., 1974. Supr. dining room Santa Barbara Biltmore, 1972-73; supr. food service, instr. dining room ops. Santa Barbara Community Coll., 1972-73; cons. J. Gilliard & Co., Santa Barbara, 1973-74; exec. mgr. Head of the Wolf Restaurant, Palm Springs, Calif., 1974-76; salesperson Indio (Calif.) Daily News, 1976-77; sales cons. Jurgensons Restaurant, Palm Springs, 1977-79; account exec. Sta. KPSI-FM, Palm Springs, 1978-84, gen. sales mgr., 1984-88, v.p., gen. mgr., 1988—. Co-author: The Guiltless Gourmet, 1983. Home: 696 North Hermosa Palm Springs CA 92262

GILLICE, SONDRA JUPIN, personnel executive; b. Champaign, Ill.; d. Earl Cranston and Laura Lorraine (Rose) Jupin; 1 child by previous marriage, Thomas Alan Gillice; m. Gardner Russell Brown, Jan. 12, 1980. BS, Lindenwood Coll., 1958; MBA, Loyola Coll., 1982. Div. tng. supr. Liberty Mutual Ins. Co., N.Y.C., 1958-68; personnel officer Citibank, N.Y.C., 1968-70, First Nat. Bank Chgo., 1970-73; mgr. human resources Potomac Electric Power Co., Washington, 1973-81; dir. personnel U.S. Synthetic Fuels Corp., Washington, 1981-86; v.p. human resources Guest Services, Inc., Fairfax, Va., 1986—; chmn. tng. and mgmt. devel. com. Edison Electric Inst., 1979-80, chmn. exec. and mgmt. program, 1980-81; mem. adv. com. Pa. State U., Behrend Coll. Mem. Am. Soc. Personnel Adminstrs., Washington Personnel Assn. (sec. 1975-76), Internat. Platform Assn., Washington Bd. Trade, Nat. Restaurant Assn. Washington. Episcopalian. Club: Army Navy Country, Edgartown (Mass.) Yacht. Lodges: DAR, Soroptomist (pres. Washington club 1979-80, Golden Gavel award 1980), Kiwanis. Home: 1101 S Arlington Ridge Rd #1112 Arlington VA 22202 Office: 3055 Prosperity Ave Fairfax VA 22231-2290

GILLILAND, TARA ALICIA, small business owner; b. San Francisco, Nov. 18, 1941; d. William Augustine McAuliffe and Dorothy Jean (Von Alven) McAuliffe Vallee; m. Jack Edward Bankhead (dec. Mar. 1967); m. Lewis Lovell Gilliland. BS, La. State U., 1963. Asst. buyer Kreegers, New Orleans, 1963-64; mgr. Unit Design Inc., Baton Rouge, 1965-84, owner, pres., 1984—; owner, v.p. Tax Advisors, Baton Rouge, 1982—. Del. to White House Conf. Small Bus., Washington, 1986. Mem. Am. Subcontractors Assn. La. (pres. 1986-88), Am. Subcontractors Assn. Baton Rouge (pres. 1987—) (recipient outstanding chpt. service award, 1985), La. Assn. Enrolled Agts. (sec. 1986-87), Baton Rouge C. of C. (mem. nat. affairs council), La. Coalition Small Bus. Republican. Roman Catholic. Office: Unit Design Inc 210 Terrace Baton Rouge LA 70802

GILLIO, CAROLYN IRENE, psychotherapist; b. Wells, Minn., Jan. 1, 1931; d. William Frederick and Antonia Willemina (Augst) Moll; m. Cesar Padilla, June 28, 1953 (div. 1967); children: Paula, Mark, Julie; m. Frank Gillio, May 24, 1969. BA, Gustavus-Adolphus Coll., 1952; postgrad., U. Chgo., 1952-53; MSW, U. Calif., Berkeley, 1955. Psychotherapist Agnews St. Hosp., San Jose, Calif., 1955-56; supr. San Jose Family Services, 1956-68; Psychotherapist Mid-Peninsula Psychotherapy Clinic, Sunnyvale, Calif., 1968-76; pvt. practice psychotherapy Sunnyvale, 1976—; adj. instr. U. Calif.-Santa Cruz Extension, Sunnyvale, 1979-80; cons. Santa Clara County (Calif.) Mental Health, 1975-78, other orgns. in field. Mem. Cen. Core Comprehensive Mental Health Planning Commn., Santa Clara, Calif., 1965-67; chmn. Sunnyvale Coordinating Council, 1968; bd. dirs. No. County Social Planning Council, Santa Clara, 1968-69. Recipient Disting. Service award Santa Clara County Family Service, 1968; named Disting. Woman on Mid-Peninsula, Girls Club of the Mid-Peninsula, 1973. Fellow Nat. Assn. Social Workers (bd. dirs. 1970-71), Soc. Clin. Social Workers (legis. com. 1975-77), Soc. Clin. Social Work (bd. dirs. 1977-81); mem. AAUW, Alphas. Home and Office: 869 Cumberland Dr Sunnyvale CA 94087

GILLIS, CHRISTINE DIEST-LORGION, financial planner, stockbroker; b. San Francisco; d. Evert Jan and Christine Helen (Radcliffe) Diest-Lorgion; B.S., U. Calif., Berkeley; M.S., U. So. Calif.; children—Barbara Gillis Pieper, Suzanne Gillis Seymour (twins). Cert. fin. planner. Account exec. Winslow, Cohu & Stetson, N.Y.C., 1962-63, Paine Webber, N.Y.C., 1964-65; sr. investment exec. Shearson Hammill, Beverly Hills, Calif., 1966-72; cert. fin. planner, 2nd v.p. Shearson Lehman Hutton, Glendale, Calif., 1972—. Cert. fin. planner. Mem. Inst. Cert. Fin. Planners, Town Hall of Calif. (life, corp. sec. 1974-75, dir., gov. 1976-80), Women Stockbrokers Assn. (founding pres. N.Y.C. 1963), Women of Wall Street West (pres. 1979-84), Navy League (life; dir.), Assistance League Pasadena, AAUW (life; trustee Ednl. Found.), Bus. and Profl. Women, Phi Chi Theta (life). Episcopalian. Clubs: U. So. Calif. Town and Gown (life). Home: 959 Regent Park Dr La Canada Flintridge CA 91011 Office: 225 W Broadway Glendale CA 91204

GILLISS, BARBARA ELLEN, educational company executive, educator, travel executive; b. Lewiston, Idaho, June 18, 1938; d. Albert Arnold Anderson and Dorothy Maude (Desso) Nobach; m. Harvey Eugene Keating, June 18, 1960 (div. Dec. 1976); children: Brian Elliot, Kimberly Ellen; m. Charles Maxwell Gilliss, Mar. 25, 1979. BS in Edn., West Oreg. State Coll., 1960; MEd, Adminstrn., U. Hawaii, 1972; postgrad., U. San Diego. Cert. tchr., supr., Hawaii, Oreg., Calif. Tchr. Parkrose Sch. Dist., Portland, Oreg., 1962-63, North Vancouver (B.C., Can.) Sch. Dist., 1964-66; adminstrv. asst., dissemination specialist Hawaii State Dept. Edn., U. Hawaii Curriculum Research & Devel. Group, Honolulu, 1967-77; curriculum coordinator, tchr. supr. Windward Dist. Hawaii State Dept. Edn., Kaneohe, 1978-82; resident instr. UCLA, Los Angeles, 1980; instr. Mt. San Jacinto (Calif.) Coll., 1982—; owner Automotive Service Ctr., Hemet, Calif., 1984-85; part-owner Uniglobe Butterfield Travel, Rancho Californ, Calif, 1987—; pres. Ednl. Materials Unltd., Rancho Californ, 1980—; cons. bilingual edn. Hawaii State Dept., 1981-83; comptroller, ops. mgr. C.M. Gilliss Investments and Real Estate, Honolulu, Rancho California, 1979—. Contbr. articles to profl. jours. Mem., com. chair Homeowner's Assn., Rancho California, 1985—. Recipient Leadership award Hahaione PTA, 1975. Mem. Western Oreg. Coll. Alumni Assn., Am. Assn. of U. Women, Nat. Assn. Female Execs. Democrat.

GILLMAN, SANDRA RABINOVITCH, advertising company executive; b. Montreal, Jan. 1, 1944; came to U.S., 1970; d. Benjamin Rabinovitch and Sadie (Zelman) Zibelman; m. David Gillman, Dec. 20, 1964 (div. 1980); 1 child, Bradley Carl. AA, Sir George Williams U., Montreal, Can., 1967. Asst. buyer Steinberg's Ltd., Montreal, 1961-67; buyer Sir George Williams U., Montreal, 1967-70; sales rep. George Stuart, Inc., Orlando, Fla., 1979-81, Advanced Bus. Products, Orlando, 1981-82; sales promotion coordinator Geiger/Marquis' Splty. Advt. Co., Winter Park, Fla., 1983—. Recipient Disting. Sales award Sales and Mktg. Execs., 1981, Silver Pyramid award, 1984; named Salesperson of Yr. Purchasing Mgmt. Assn., Orlando, 1985. Mem. Exec. Women Internat., Nat. Assn. Female Execs., Fla. Pub. Relations Assn., Orlando C. of C. Office: Geiger/Marquis' Splty Advt 340 N Maitland Ave Maitland FL 32750

GILLMOR, KAREN LAKO, strategic planner; b. Cleve., Jan. 29, 1948; d. William M. and Charlotte (Sheldon) Lako; m. Paul E. Gillmor, Dec. 10, 1983; children—Linda D., Julie E. B.A. cum laude, Mich. State U., 1969; M.A., Ohio State U., 1970, Ph.D., 1981. Asst. to v.p. Ohio State U., Columbus, 1972-77, spl. asst. dean law, 1979-81; asst. to pres. Ind. Central U., Indpls., 1977-78; research asst. Burke Mktg. Research, Indpls., 1978-79; v.p. pub. affairs Huntington Nat. Bank, Columbus, 1981-82; fin. cons. Ohio Rep. Fin. Com., Columbus, 1982-83; chief mgmt. planning and research Indsl. Commn. Ohio, Columbus, 1983-86; mgr. physician relations Univ. Hosps., Columbus, 1987—; legis. liaison Huntington Bancshares, Ohio, Ohio State U., Columbus. Bd. dirs. Womens' Rep. Club Ohio, McMaster Inst., Nat. Adv. Com. Women's Health. Grantee Andrew W. Mellon Found. 1978, Carnegie Corp. 1978. Mem. Women in Mainstream, Women's Roundtable, Ohio Fedn. Republican Women, Am. Assn. Counseling and Devel., Am. Assn. Higher Edn., Council Advancement and Support Edn., DAR, Phi Delta Kappa. Methodist. Clubs: Capital, University (Columbus), Ohio State U. Faculty. Office: Univ Hosps 410 W Tenth Ave Columbus OH 43210

GILLOM, THELMA JEAN, computer operator; b. Chattanooga, Oct. 12, 1958; d. Robert Lewis and Rosa Mae (Felton) G.; 1 child, Ca' Trecha Bridgette Butts. AS in Computer Tech., Chattanooga State Tech. Community Coll., 1985; student, Tusculum Coll., 1988—. Sec. Am. Nat. Bank, Chattanooga, Tenn., 1976-79; exec. sec. Bank Am., Los Angeles, 1979-81; word processor TVA, Chattanooga, 1981-83, computer operator, 1983—. Mem. U.S. and Tenn. Jaycees, 1982—; chpt. mgmt. v.p. Greater Brainerd (Tenn.) Area Jaycees, 1985-86, chpt. dir., 1986-87. Mem. Federally Employed Women. Home: 914 Woodmore Terr Chattanooga TN 37411 Office: TVA 124 Edney Bldg Chattanooga TN 37401

GILLUM, ELSIE FELTS (JUDY), engineering company executive; b. Jacksonville, Fla., June 16, 1930; d. Ethelbert Hayward and Elsie Maybeth (Gregory) Felts; m. Don Edwyn Massey, July 22, 1957 (div. Apr. 1966); m. Jimmie Corbett Gillum, June 30, 1968. Assoc. Sci., Hillsborough Community Coll., 1984. Cert. profl. sec. Sec., Rosenblum's, Jacksonville, Fla., 1948-50; exec. sec. Gibbs Corp., Jacksonville, 1950-60, Ryder Truck Lines, Jacksonville, 1960-62; asst. corp. sec. Greiner Engring. Scis., Inc., Tampa, Fla., 1962—. Mem. Profl. Secs. Internat. (pres. City Ctr. chpt. 1985-86, Sec. of Yr. 1985-86, Fla. div. Sec. of Yr. 1986-87), Exec. Women Internat. (sec. 1984), Nat. Assn. Female Execs., League Women Voters, Greater Brandon C. of C., Greater Tampa C. of C. Democrat. Roman Catholic. Avocations: needlework; reading; gardening. Home: Route 1 Box 574 Dover FL 33527 Office: Greiner Engring Scis Inc PO Box 23646 5601 Mariner St Tampa FL 33630

GILMAN, BARBARA DIANE, real estate manager; b. Tacoma, Wash., Apr. 27, 1954; d. Richard Arthur and B. Janet (Settle) G. BA, U. So. Calif., 1977; JD, Loyola U., Los Angeles, 1980. Bar: Calif. 1981. Law clk. to justice Calif. Ct. Appeals, Los Angeles, 1980-81; assoc. in law firms, San Francisco, 1981-83; escrow officer San Francisco, 1983-85, DHL, 1985—. Exec. editor Loyola of Los Angeles Internat. and Comparative Law Jour., 1979-80. Mem. State Bar Assn. Calif., Jr. League San Francisco. Office: DHL Airways Inc 333 Twin Dolphin Dr Redwood City CA 94065

GILMAN, ESTHER, artist, illustrator, set designer; b. Cleve., Aug. 13, 1925; d. Joseph and Bertha (Tenenbaum) Morgenstern; m. Richard M. Gilman, Sept. 1, 1949 (div. 1964); 1 son; Nicholas Alexander. B.S. in Design, U. Mich., 1961; M.A., NYU, 1981. Stage designer The Open Theater La Mama, N.Y.C., 1964-68; freelance illustrator, N.Y.C., 1964—; dir. Designers Workshop, N.Y.C., 1971—; visual cons. The Open Theater, 1964-68; bd. dirs., cons. The Feminist Press, Old Westbury, L.I., 1970-75; one person exhbn. U. Wis., Madison, 1987; one woman shows at Razor Gallery, N.Y., 1978, Washington Sq. E. Gallery, N.Y.C., 1981, Americana in Soho, 1981, Salle Polyvalente, St. Amand Montrond, France, 1983, Symposium on Women in Arts , U. Wis., 1987, Jewish Community Ctr., 1988; exhibited in group shows at Mus. Modern Art Young Printmakers, N.Y.C., 1956, Riverside Mus., N.Y.C., 1962, Nat. Acad. N.Y., 1965, Am. Water Color Soc., 1966; Illustrator books: Little Girl and Her Mother, 1964; Nothing But a Dog, 1972 Little Boat, 1974; I've Considered My Days, 1964; designer stage sets: Viet Rock, 1966; Keep Tightly Closed, 1966; It's Almost Like Being, 1964, Miss Nefertitti Regrets, 1965. Recipient medal of honor for watercolor, Painters and Sculptors Soc. N.J., 1958; first prize Robert Boardman award Painter Soc. N.J., 1956; Am. Inst. Graphic Art award, 1970. Fellow Va. Ctr. for Creative Arts, Cummington Community for the Arts; mem. Art Students League N.Y. Address: 160 Riverside Dr New York NY 10024

GILMAN, MARGARET VIRGINIA, magazine publisher; b. New Brunswick, N.J., Oct. 15, 1939; d. Arthur Gilman and Helen (Stockheimer) Essink; m. Stephen Joseph De Luca, May 25, 1979. B.A., Beaver Coll., 1961. Copy editor McCall's Needlework & Crafts, N.Y.C., 1967, sr. editor, 1974-76, mng. editor, 1976-79, editor, 1979-84, editor-in-chief, pub., 1984, pub., editorial dir., v.p., 1985—. Mem. Fashion Group, Inc., Am. Soc. Mag. Editors, Women in Communication. Office: McCall's Needlework & Crafts 825 7th Ave New York NY 10019

GILMAN, ROBERTA RIGHTER, French educator; b. New London, Ohio, Sept. 6, 1951; d. Roderic Elliott and Elsie Mae (Earl) Righter; m. Bradley Morris Gilman, Aug. 5, 1978; children: Douglas Righter, Caitlin Elise. BA, Kalamazoo (Mich.) Coll., 1974; cert. pratique, L'Universite de Caen, France, 1973, U. Sorbonne, France, 1975; MA, Oakland U., 1984. Cert. secondary tchr., Mich.; lic. real estate broker, Mich. French tchr. Detroit Country Day Sch., Birmingham, Mich., 1974-78; French and Eng. tchr. Chandler Sch., Pasadena, Calif., 1979-80; asst. head Bloomfield U. Sch., Birmingham, 1981-85; French tchr. Troy (Mich.) Pub. Schs., 1985—, chaiperson fgn. lang. dept., 1987—. Mem. Beverly Hills (Mich.) Parks and Recreation Bd. Grantee Oakland U., 1981. Mem. Nat. Edn. Assn., Mich. Edn. Assn., Troy Edn. Assn., Oakland Fgn. Lang. Tchrs. Assn., DAR. Republican. Episcopalian. Clubs: Village Womens, Beverly Hills Swim and Tennis (Beverly Hills). Home: 32286 Verona Circle Birmingham MI 48009 Office: Troy Pub Schs 2222 E Long Lake Troy MI 48089

GILMORE, JUDY MARY, banker; b. Manchester, N.H., Feb. 1, 1947; d. Richard James and Lumina Mary (Provencher) Straw; m. Gerald Lee Gilmore; children Richard W., Paul J. Student, Mt. St. Mary, Hooksett, N.H., Am. Inst. Banking, Manchester, N.H. Clk. Amoskeog Bank, Manchester, N.H., 1973-79; supr., bookkeeping Amoskeog Bank, Manchester, 1979-81, mgr. research, 1981-83, asst. cashier, 1983-84, asst. v.p., 1984-85, v.p. ops., 1985-86; v.p., user service Amoskeog Info. Services, Manchester, 1986-87; v.p. branch adminstr. Amoskeog Bank, Manchester, 1987—. Chmn. Ashland, N.H. Sch. Bd., 1986, vice chmn., 1987; mem. fin. com. St. Agnes Ch., Ashland, 1985-86, budget com. Ashland Sch., 1981-83. Mem. Bank Adminstrn. Inst. Republican. Roman Catholic. Home: 17 Riverside Dr Ashland NH 03217 Office: Amoskeas Info Services Inc 286 Commercial St PO Box 6060 Manchester NH 03108-6060

GILMORE, JUNE ELLEN, psychologist; b. Middletown, Ohio, Oct. 22, 1927; d. Linley Lawrence and Elizabeth Kathleen (Barker) Wetzel; m. John Lester Gilmore, July 6, 1945; children: John Lester Jr., Michael Edward. BS, Miami U., Oxford, 1961; MS, Miami U., 1964. Lic. psychologist, Ohio. Intern in psychology Hamilton (Ohio) City Schs., 1963-64; psychologist Talawanda, Shiloh, Trenton Schs., Butler County, Ohio, 1964-66, Franklin (Ohio) City Schs., 1966-72, Wapakoneta (Ohio) City Schs., 1972-76, Cin. City Schs., 1978-86; pvt. practice psychology 1975—; planner, evaluator Warren/Clinton Counties Mental Health Bd., Ohio, 1986—. Co-author: Summer Children-Ready or not for School, 1986. Sec. Tri County Drug Council, Lima, Ohio, 1974; chmn. Auglaize County Social Services, Wapakoneta, Ohio, 1973-75. Mem. Ohio Sch. Psychologists Assn. (exec. bd. 1982-86), Southwestern Ohio Sch. Psychologist Assn. (pres.), Southwest Council Exceptional Children (Pres.), Nat. Assn. Sch. Psychologists, Ohio Psychol. Assn., Butler County 648 Mental Health Bd. (bd. dirs. 1978-86, pres. 1983-84). Republican. United Methodist. Home and Office: 6120 Michael Rd Middletown OH 45042

GILMORE, KYNNA LYNNETTE, public relations professional; b. Big Spring, Tex., Nov. 1, 1956; d. William Kenneth and Elizabeth Rose (Hildreth) G. BA, Tex. Tech U., 1979; M in Religious Edn., Golden Gate Bapt. Theol. Sem., 1981. Assoc. dir. pub. info. Calif. Bapt. Coll., Riverside, 1982, dir. pub. info., 1982-84; dir. pub. relations U. Mary Hardin-Baylor, Belton, Tex., 1984-88; adminstr. staffing/EEO Tex. Instruments, Temple, 1988—. Publicity chairperson Golden Gate Missions Conf., Mill Valley, Calif., 1981, Redlands (Calif.) Easter Pageant, 1984; publs. chairperson Bill Glass Crusade for Christ, Belton, 1987; mem. Bell County Sesquicentennial com., 1985-86. Mem. Tex. Bapt. Pub. Relations Assn. (sec. 1986, pres.-elect 1987), Bell County Communications Profls. Assn. (1st v.p. 1986, pres. 1987), Bapt. Pub. Relations Assn., Alpha Chi Omega. Republican. Baptist. Office: Tex Instruments PO Box 6102 MS 3209 Temple TX 76502

GILMORE, MARJORIE HAVENS, lawyer, civic worker; b. N.Y.C., Aug. 16, 1918; d. William Westerfield and Elsie (Medl) Havens; A.B., Hunter Coll., 1938; J.D., Columbia, 1941; m. Hugh Redland Gilmore, May 8, 1942; children—Douglas Hugh, Anne Charlotte Gilmore Decker, Joan Louise. Admitted to N.Y. State bar, 1941, Va. bar, 1968; research asst. N.Y. Law Revision Commn., 1941-42; assoc. firm Spence, Windels, Walser, Hotchkiss & Angell, N.Y.C., 1942, Chadbourne, Wallace, Parke & Whiteside, N.Y.C., 1942-43; atty. U.S. Army, Washington, 1948-53. Sec., Thomas Jefferson Jr. High Sch. PTA, 1956-58; parliamentarian Wakefield High Sch. PTA, 1959-60, chmn. citizenship com., 1960-61; publicity chmn. Patrick Henry Sch. PTA, sec., 1964-65; parliamentarian Nottingham PTA, 1966-69; mem. extracurricular activities com. Arlington County Sch. Bd.; area chmn. fund drive Cancer Soc., 1955-56; active Girl Scouts U.S.A., 1963-70; mem. '41 com. Columbia Law Sch. Fund. Recipient Constl. Law award Hunter Coll., 1938. Mem. Arlington Fedn. Women's Clubs (rec. sec. 1979-80), No. Dist. Va. Fedn. Women's Clubs (chmn. legis. com. 1986-88, chmn. pub. affairs No.

dist. 1988—), Columbia Law Sch. Alumni Assn., Alpha Sigma Rho. Presbyn. Club: Williamsburg Woman's of Arlington (corr. sec. 1970-72, 1st v.p. 1972-74, pres. 1974-76, chmn. communications 1981-82, chmn. legis. com. 1982-86). Home: 3020 N Nottingham St Arlington VA 22207

GILMORE, SUSAN ASTRID LYTLE, speech and language pathologist; b. Phila., July 12, 1942; d. Ford Bertrand and Astrid Elizabeth (Hammerstrom) Lytle; m. Stuart Irby Gilmore, June 6, 1970 (div. Dec. 1981); 1 child, Ford Lytle. BA, U. Pacific, 1964, MA, 1965; PhD, Ohio U., 1968. Cert. pub. sch. adminstr., elem. tchr., speech-lang. pathologist, Calif. Asst. prof. spl. edn., speech-lang. pathology La. State U., Baton Rouge, 1968-76, assoc. prof., 1976-79; supr. spl. edn. Sacramento City Unified Sch. Dist., 1979—, acting adminstrv. specialist Spl. Edn. Dept., 1988—; cons. State Dept Health, Baton Rouge, 1970-75, State Dept. Hosps., Baton Rouge, 1973-75; instr. U. Pacific, Stockton, Calif., 1979, ind. examiner Sacramento City Unified Sch. Dist., 1979; acting adminstrv. specialist Spl. Edn. Dept. Sacremento City Unified Sch. Dist., 1988—. Editor: (asst.) Lang., Speech and Hearing Services in Schs., 1983—; contbr. articles to profl. jours. Vestry mem. Trinity Episcopal Cathedral Ch., Sacramento, 1983-85, altar guild mem. 1980—; bd. dirs. Friends of People With Chronic Mental Illness, Sacramento, 1983-85. Mem. Assn. Calif. Sch. Adminstrs., Am. Speech-Lang.-Hearing Assn., Calif. Speech-Lang.-Hearing Assn. (cert. of appreciations 1985—), Council for Exceptional Children (sec.), Am. Assn. Mental Deficiency, Kappa Alpha Theta (pres. 1961-62), Phi Delta Kappa. Republican. Home: 6333 Driftwood St Sacramento CA 95831 Office: Sacramento City Unified Sch Dist 4701 Joaquin Way Sacramento CA 95822

GILSON, JAMIE MARIE, writer; b. Beardstown, Ill., July 4, 1933; d. James Noyce and Sallie Anna (Wilkinson) Chisam; B.S. with honors in Speech, Northwestern U., 1955; m. Jerome Gilson, June 19, 1955; children—Tom, Matthew, Anne. Tchr., Thacker Jr. High Sch., Des Plaines, Ill., 1955-56; writer for ednl. radio, TV and film, producer div. radio and TV, Chgo. Public Schs., 1956-59; continuity dir. Sta. WFMT, Chgo., 1959-63; writer column and articles Chgo. Mag., 1977-87; author children's books, including: Harvey, the Beer Can King (Merit award Friends Am. Writers 1979), 1978; Dial Leroi Rupert, D.J., 1979; Do Bananas Chew Gum (Carl Sandburg award Friends Chgo. Public Library 1981, Charlie May Simon award; Arkansas child-voted prize 1983), 1980; Can't Catch Me, I'm the Gingerbread Man, 1981; Thirteen Ways to Sink a Sub, 1982 (Okla. Sequoyah award 1985, Young Reader's Choice award Pacific Northwest Library Assn. 1985, N. Mex. Land of Enhancement award, 1986; Fla. Sunshine State Young Readers award, 1987; Ohio Buckeye Youg Readers award, 1987); 4B Goes Wild, 1983; Hello, My Name is Scrambled Eggs, 1985, Hobie Hanson, You're Weird, 1987; tchr. creative writing 6th grade students, 1974—; lectr. on writing. Mem. Soc. Midland Authors, Children's Reading Round Table, Soc. Children's Book Writers.

GILSON, JUNE ELIZABETH, lawyer; b. Wilmington, Del., June 19, 1955; d. James William and Adele (Bukowski) Gilson; m. Arthur Thomas Donato, Jr., May 7, 1983. B.A. in Polit. Sci., U. Del., 1977; J.D., Del. Law Sch., 1980. Bar: Pa. 1980. Jud. clk. Judge Domenic D. Jerome, County of Del., Media, Pa., 1981-84; atty. Sereni & Lunardi, Broomall, Pa., 1983-84, German, Gallagher and Murtagh, Phila., 1984—; atty. Legal Clinic of Eugene Malady, Upper Darby, Pa., 1980-81. Recipient Am. Jurisprudence award Del. Law Sch., 1980. Mem. ABA, Pa. Bar Assn., Phila. County Bar Assn., Pi Sigma Alpha. Republican. Roman Catholic. Home: 204 Poplar Ave Wayne PA 19087 Office: German Gallagher & Murtagh 1818 Market St Suite 3100 Philadelphia PA 19103

GIMBEL, JUDITH ANNE, small business owner; b. Seattle, Sept. 18, 1936; arrived in Canada, 1964; d. Clostin Allen and Dorothy Mae (Gepford) Carl; m. Howard Vance Gimbel, May 27, 1956; children: Karen, Roger, Janette, Glenn, Keith. BS in Health Sci., Atlantic Union Coll., 1979; MPH, Loma Linda U., 1979. Exec. sec. Walla Walla Coll., College Place, Wash., 1955-56, So. Pacific Pipelines, Colton, Calif., 1956-58; exec. dir. Gimbel Eye Ctr., Calgary, Alta., Can., 1982-87, chmn bd., 1987—; founder, dir., chair Gimbel Eye Found., 1984—. Active PRIDE Can., Saskatoon, Sask., PRIDE Lacombe (Alta.). Mem. Am. Coll. Healthcare Mktg., Am. Soc. Ophthalmic Adminstrs., Med. Group Mgmt. Assn., Kids of Western Can. Progressive Conservative. Adventist. Office: Gimbel Eye Ctr, 450 4935-40 Ave NW, Calgary, AB Canada T3A 2N1

GINADER, BARBARA MALIA, investment banker; b. Scranton, Pa., Sept. 6, 1956; d. George William and Eleanore Ann (Malia) G. BA in English and Polit. Sci., Cedar Crest Coll., 1978; MBA, Harvard U., 1982. Asst. v.p. First Nat. Bank Boston, 1982-85; v.p. Bear, Stearns & Co., Inc., N.Y.C., 1985—. Bd. trustees Cedar Crest Coll. Episcopalian. Office: Bear Stearns & Co Inc 245 Park Ave New York NY 10167

GINALSKI, JUNE JOYCE IRENE HOUGLUND, management systems company executive; b. Kimberley, B.C., Can., May 6, 1938; came to U.S., 1961, naturalized, 1972; d. Charles A. and Elsie Joyce (Hartley) Hougland; m. William Ginalski, Nov. 28, 1969 (div. June 1988); stepchildren: Mark, Kevin. AS, Victoria Coll., 1958; BS, U. B.C., 1959; PhD, Oreg. State U., 1963; postgrad. Harvard U., 1976; HHD, U. Metaphysics. Dir. computing lab. Oreg. State U., 1961-66; cons. Gen. Electric Co., 1966-71; mgr. research and devel. Ramada Inns, Inc., Phoenix, 1972-73; asst. v.p. First Nat. Bank-Western Bancorp. Corp., Phoenix, 1973-78; v.p. planning Gt. Western Bank & Trust Co., Phoenix, 1978-80; asso. Continental Mgmt. Systems, 1980-82; managing partner, Am. Computing Co., 1982—. Mem. Nat. Assn. Bank Women (past dir.), Assn. for Research and Enlightenment, Futurist Soc. Democrat. Religious Scientist. Clubs: Harvard; Ariz. Yacht. Home: 5501 E Calle Tuberia Phoenix AZ 85018 Office: Am Computing Co 845 N 3d Ave Phoenix AZ 85003

GINGERICH, FLORINE ROSE, lawyer; b. Lowville, N.Y., Nov. 25, 1951; d. Beryl J. and Marion A. (Jantzi) G. BA in History, Goshen Coll., 1973; JD, U. Mich., 1976. Bar: Wash. 1976, U.S. Dist. Ct. (we. dist.) Wash. 1976. Assoc. Davis, Wright & Jones, Seattle, 1976-83; v.p., corp. counsel Seattle Trust and Svgs., 1983-85, v.p., sec., corp. counsel, 1985-87; assoc. Hiscock and Barclay, Seattle, 1987—. Mem. planning and allocations conf. panel United Way of King-Seattle County, 1979-82; bd. dirs. Consumer Credit Counseling Services of Seattle, 1982-83, Friends of Youth, Renton, Wash., 1986—, v.p., 1988—. Mem. ABA, Wash. State Bar Assn., Seattle-King County Bar Assn. Clubs: Seattle, Columbia Tower (Seattle). Office: Hiscock and Barclay 1000 2d Ave 37th Floor Seattle WA 98104

GINIGER, EDITH, business school executive; b. N.Y.C., July 24, 1934; d. Meyer and Molly (Rosenblatt) Kirschner; m. Ivan H. Giniger, Apr. 11, 1954; children: Martin, Jeffrey, Robert. Grad. high sch., N.Y.C., 1952; diploma in secretarial scis., Associated Bus. Careers, Highland Park, N.J., 1976. Cert. sch. dir., word processing instr. Buyer Interstate Dept. Stores, N.Y.C., 1953-54; successively sec., admissions dir., placement dir. Associated Bus. Careers, Highland Park, N.J., 1976—; owner, sch. dir., v.p. Inst. Bus. Careers, Highland Park, 1984—; counselor Inst. Bus. Careers; govt. contract liaison Middlesex County Employment & Tng. Commn., New Brunswick, N.J., 1980-86, Union County Employment & Tng. Commn., Elizabeth, N.J., 1985-86. v.p., fundraiser Metuchen-Edison Soccer Club, N.J., 1978-82; bd. dirs. Cen. N.J. Jewish Home for Aged, Somerset, N.J., 1981-83. Mem. Am. Bus. Woman's Assn. (bd. dirs. 1982), N.J. Bus. Educators Assn., Pvt. Career Schs. Assn. (conv., workshop com., 1985), N.J. Coll. Personnel Assn., Raritan Valley C. of C. Democrat. Jewish. Home: 2 Opatut Ct Edison NJ 08817 Office: Inst Bus Careers 1131 Raritan Ave Highland Park NJ 08904

GINSBERG, ELIZABETH, artist, educator; b. N.Y.C., 1942. B.F.A., R.I. Sch. Design, 1964. Instr., R.I. Sch. Design, Providence, 1970-71; assoc. prof. Moore Coll. Art, Phila., 1971-86; mem. faculty Parson Sch. Design, N.Y.C., 1976-77; lectr. Kyoto Fujikawa Coll. Art, (Japan), U. Utah, Salt Lake City, R.I. Sch. Design; dir. travel/study program to Japan, Moore Coll. of Art, 1973; one-person shows: Chuo Gallery, Tokyo, 1965, Salt Lake Art Ctr., 1973, Susan Caldwell Gallery, N.Y.C., 1976, U.S. Courthouse, N.Y.C., 1981, Marsha Mateyka Gallery, Washington, 1982, 88, Mus. of Hudson Highlands, Cornwall-on-Hudson, N.Y., 1985, John Nichols, N.Y.C., 1985, Kinokoniga Gallery, Tokyo, 1988; group shows include: Kaigado Gallery, Tokyo, 1965, Fischman-Weiner Gallery, Phila., 1967, Providence Art Club, 1971, Del. Art Mus., Wilmington, 141 Prince St. Gallery, N.Y.C., 1974, Tweed Mus., Duluth, Minn., 1972, Henri Gallery, Washington, 1973, Moore Coll. of Art Gallery, Phila., Henri Gallery, 1974, Marion Locks Gallery, Phila., Harcus, Krakow, Rosen and Sonnabend Gallery, Boston, 1975, Del. Art Mus., 1976, Henri Gallery, 1976, Susan Caldwell Gallery, Pratt Manhattan Ctr., N.Y.C., Moore Coll. of Art Gallery, 1977, U.S. Courthouse, N.Y.C., Sebastian-Moore Gallery, Denver, Sargent Gallery, Eastern Ill., U., Charleston, Moore Coll. of Art Gallery, 1980, Judith Christian Gallery, N.Y.C., 1981, Ericson Gallery, N.Y.C., Heydt-Bair Gallery, Santa Fe, Marsha Mateyka Gallery, Washington, Lubbock Arts Festival (Tex.), Gallery 429 West Broadway, Okayama, Japan, 1983, Marsha Mateyka Gallery, Washington, 1984, Fuji Gallery, Tokyo, 1985, Conlon-Grenfell Gallery, San Diego, 1985, McNay Art Mus., San Antonio, 1986, Woods-Gerry Gallery, R.I. Sch. Design, 1986, Mayor's Office, Phila., 1986, Mus. of the Hudson Highlands, Cornwall-on-Hudson, N.Y., 1986, Arts for Living Ctr., Henry Street Settlement, N.Y.C., 1986, numerous others; represented in permanent collections: Chase Manhattan Bank, N.A., N.Y.C., Gallery Point, Tokyo, Union Carbide Corp., N.Y.C., First Nat. City Bank, N.Y.C., European-Am. Bank, N.Y.C., U.S. Steel Corp., N.Y.C., Am. Fedn. Savs., Orlando, Fla., First Options of Chgo., Port Authority of N.Y., Chuo Koron Sha Corp., Tokyo, Security Pacific Nat. Bank, Carmichal, Calif., Davis, Polk, and Wardwell, N.Y.C., A.P.F., N.Y.C., Cigna Collection, Phila. Carnegie grantee, 1963-64; Textron fellow, 1965; commd. work Parsippany Plaza Corp. Ctr., N.J., 1985. Moore Coll. of Art Faculty Research grantee, 1982. Office: 5 Great Jones St New York NY 10012

GINSBERG, MARILYN KAPLAN, publisher; b. N.Y.C., Aug. 9, 1952; d. Samuel H. and Anne (Kuntz) Kaplan; m. Michael I. Ginsberg, Oct. 5, 1980. B.A., Queens Coll., CUNY, 1973; M.S., SUNY-Albany, 1974. Asst. to pub. World Press Rev., N.Y.C., 1976-77, circulation dir., 1977-82, assoc. pub., 1982-84, pub., 1984—. Mem. Direct Mktg. Club of N.Y. Office: World Press Review 200 Madison Ave New York NY 10016

GINSBURG, ESTELLE, artist; b. St. Louis. Student, U. Mo., Bklyn. Mus. Art Sch., Cornell U. Art lectr., tchr. Five Towns Music and Art Found., N.Y., Hewlett-Woodmere Sch. Dist., North Shore Community Arts Ctr., N.Y., Nassau Office Cultural Devel. in Sch. Program. One-woman shows include Cen. Hall Gallery, N.Y., Brentanos Gallery, N.Y., Town Hall Showcase, N.Y., Post Coll., N.Y., Port Washington Library, N.Y., Peninsual Pub. Library, N.Y., Nassau Library Systems, N.Y., Fine Arts Mus. Nassau County, N.Y.; exhibited in group shows at Hofstra U., N.Y., L.I. U., N.Y., N.Y. State Pavillion, Norfolk (Va.) Mus. Art, J. Walter Thompson Co., N.Y., Heckscher Mus., N.Y., Fordham U., N.Y., Nat. Acad., N.Y., Audobon Soc., N.Y., N.Y. Inst. Tech., Grad. Ctr. CUNY, Ball State U., Plaza Gallery, Rochester, N.Y., Royal Acad., Stockholm, Fontana Gallery, Pa., R.A.A. Gallery, N.Y.C., Cen. Art Gallery, N.Y., Brentanos Gallery, N.Y., Rhoda Ochs Gallery, N.Y., Art Resources, Ltd., N.Y., Isis Gallery, N.Y., Nancy Stien Gallery, N.Y.C.; represented in permanent collections C.W. Post Coll., N.Y., U. Mass., Amherst, Far Gallery, N.Y.C., Avnet Gallery, N.Y., Tasca Gallery, N.Y.C., North Shore Arts Gallery, N.Y., Artium Gallery, N.Y., Lenid Gallery, N.Y., Off Broadway Gallery, N.Y., Kessler Gallery, Provincetown, Mass.; represented in pvt. and pub. collections throughout U.S., Europe and South Am. Recipient Mixed Media award Heckscher Mus., N.Y., Five Towns Music and Art Found., N.Y., Port Washington Library Exhbn., N.Y., Sculpture award North Shore Juried Art Exhbn. Home and Office: 370 Longacre Ave Woodmere NY 11598

GINSBURG, RUTH BADER, federal judge; b. Bklyn., Mar. 15, 1933; d. Nathan and Celia (Amster) Bader; m. Martin David Ginsburg, June 23, 1954; children: Jane Carol, James Steven. AB, Cornell U., 1954; postgrad., Harvard Law Sch., 1956-58; LLB Kent scholar, Columbia Law Sch., 1959; LLD (hon.), Lund (Sweden) U., 1969, Am. U., 1981, Vt. Law Sch., 1984, Georgetown U., 1985, DePaul U., 1985, Bklyn. Law Sch., 1987; DHL (hon.), Hebrew Union Coll., 1988. Bar: N.Y. 1954, D.C. 1975, U.S. Supreme Ct. 1967. Law sec. to judge U.S. Dist. Ct. (So. Dist. N.Y.), 1959-61; research assoc. Columbia Law Sch., N.Y.C., 1961-62; assoc. dir. project internat. procedure Columbia Law Sch., 1962-63; asst. prof. Rutgers U. Sch. Law, Newark, 1963-66; assoc. prof. Rutgers U. Sch. Law, 1966-69, prof., 1969-72; prof. Columbia U. Sch. Law, N.Y.C., 1972-80; U.S. Circuit judge U.S. Ct. Appeals, D.C. Circuit, Washington, 1980—; Phi Beta Kappa vis. scholar, 1973-74; fellow Center for Advanced Study in Behavioral Scis., Stanford, Calif., 1977-78; lectr. Salzburg Seminar, Austria, 1984; gen counsel and bd. dirs. Am. Bar Found., 1979—, exec. com., 1981—, sec., 1987—. Author: (with Anders Bruzelius) Civil Procedure in Sweden, 1965, Swedish Code of Judicial Procedure, 1968, (with others) Sex-Based Discrimination, 1974, supplement, 1978; contbr. numerous articles to legal jours.; vol. editor: Business Regulation in the Common Market Nations, vol. 1, 1969. Mem. ABA, Am. Law Inst. (council mem. 1978—), Council on Fgn. Relations., Am. Acad. Arts and Scis. Office: US Ct of Appeals US Courthouse 3rd & Constitution Ave NW Washington DC 20001

GINTER, SALLY ANN, chemical company executive; b. Kalamazoo, Mich., Dec. 2, 1944; d. Hubert Clayton and Dorothy Lucille (McCallum) Pettengill; m. Ronald Francis Cornier, June 11, 1966 (div. Apr. 1973); 1 child, Nicole Lynn; m. Thomas O'Neal Ginter, Sept. 1, 1973; 1 child, Mark Allan. BA in Chemistry, Albion Coll., 1967. Chemist Dow Chem. Co., Midland, Mich., 1967-72, research chemist, 1972-75, sr. research chemist, 1975-78, research specialist, 1978-82, research leader, 1982-84, devel. assoc., 1984-86, mgr. tech. service and devel., 1986-87, devel. mgr. New Ventures Commercialization, 1987—; treas. Brominated Flame Retardant Industry Panel, Lancaster, Pa., 1986-87; adv. Nat. Acad. Fire Scis., Salt Lake City, 1986-87. Contbr. articles to profl. jours., 1971-84; holder numerous patents. Mem. Nat. Tax Limitation Com., Washington, 1980, Huepac, Midland, 1987. Mem. Fire Retardants Chem. Assn. (treas., bd. dirs. 1984-87), Soc. Plastics Industry, Phi Beta Kappa, Alpha Lambda Delta, Alpha Xi Delta. Republican. Methodist. Office: Dow Chem Co 2020 WHDC Midland MI 48674

GIOMI, THELMA ANNE, clinical psychologist; b. Albuquerque, Feb. 26, 1947; d. James E. and Esma Anne (Snyder) G. BA cum laude, U. N.Mex., 1969, MA, 1972, PhD, 1974. Diplomate Am. Bd. Psychotherapy. Psychometrician Albuquerque Pub. Schs., 1969-70; intern Pitts. Child Guidance, 1974-75; clin. psychologist U. N.Mex., Albuquerque, 1975-81; pvt. practice clin. psychologist Albuquerque, 1981—; dir. Psychology Internship Program, U. N.Mex., 1979-81; adj. asst. prof. psychology, U. N.Mex., 1980, clin. assoc. Nat. Sci. Found. grantee, 1968. Mem. AAAS, Am. Psychol. Assn., N.Mex. Psychol. Assn., Nat. Register of Health Care Providers, Southwest Writers Workshop, Albuquerque Conservation Assn., Phi Beta Kappa, Phi Kappa Phi. Club: Rio Grande Writers Assn. (Albuquerque). Office: 406 San Mateo Blvd NE Suite 8B Albuquerque NM 87108

GIORDAN, JUDITH CYNTHIA, chemical executive, researcher; b. Jersey City, June 24, 1953; d. Samuel Joseph and Edith Linda (Thor) G. BS, Rutgers U., 1975; PhD, U. Md., 1980. From scientist to sr. scientist to program coordinator Polaroid Corp., Waltham, Mass., 1982-87; tech. supr. to sr. tech. supr. Alcoa Corp., Alcoa Ctr., Pa., 1987—. Patentee in field; contbr. articles to profl. jours. George H. Cook fellow Rutgers U., 1975, Gillette Research fellow, 1980, Alexander von Humboldt fellow, 1980-81; NSF grantee, 1983—. Mem. Am. Chem. Soc., Am. Ceramics Soc., Alpha Zeta, Alpha Tau Alpha (sec. 1974-75). Jewish. Office: Alcoa Corp Alcoa Tech Ctr Alcoa Center PA 15069

GIORDANO, LYNNE CATHERINE ANDREWS, insurance company executive; b. Bklyn., Nov. 15, 1932; d. Noel and Sally Madalyn (Caccioppie) Andrews; m. Francis Luke Giordano, Aug. 30, 1965 (div. Feb. 1970). Student, Coll. of Ins., N.Y.C., 1953. Gen. clk. Home Ins. Co., N.Y.C., 1948-50, automobile technician, 1950-53, automobile underwriter, 1953-63, agy. analyst, 1963-66; account servicer Frank B. Hall & Co. N.Y., Inc., N.Y.C., 1966-70, 72-76, asst. v.p., 1976-86, v.p., 1986—; multi-line underwriter Greater N.Y. Mut., N.Y.C., 1970-72. Mem. Nat. Assn. Ins. Women N.Y.C. (v.p. 1979-81, pres. 1981-83, legis. chmn. 1983-84), Am. Legion Aux. (v.p. Kings County 1966-69, pres. 1969-70, chairperson child welfare com., chairperson community service com., chairperson VA com.; pres. Mellett Bros. , v.p., sec., treas.; mem. Bill Brown chpt.), Freedoms Found. Republican. Roman Catholic. Home: 2050 E 18th St Brooklyn NY 11229

GIORDANO, PATRICIA SCHOPPE, interior decorator; b. Houston, Aug. 29, 1947; d. Conrad Joseph and Ellen Patricia (Condon) Schoppe; m. Natale Joseph Giordano, Apr. 17, 1971; children: Keith Joseph, Michael David, Ryan Peter. Student, U. Houston, 1965-67, NYU, 1969. Prin. Patricia S. Giordano Interiors, Ridgefield, Conn., 1975—; pub. speaker various floral design and horticulture workshops. Bd. dirs. Family and Children's Aid, Inc., Danbury, Conn., 1976-79, program review com., nominating com., 1978, head pub. relations, 1978-79, pres. aux., 1976-79; v.p. Twin Ridge Homeowners' Assn., Ridgefield, Conn., 1978-79, chmn., founder area beautification, 1978. Recipient award of Excellence Fed. Garden Clubs Conn., 1984, Tricolor award Nat. Council State Garden Clubs, 1984, Aboreal award Nat. Council State Garden Clubs, 1984, Hort. Excellence award Nat. Council State Garden Clubs, 1984. Mem. Allied Bd. Trade, Caudatowa Garden Club (v.p. 1987-88). Republican. Roman Catholic. Club: Caudatowa Garden (v.p. 1987).

GIORGI, ELSIE AGNES, physician; b. N.Y.C., Mar. 8, 1911; d. Anacleto and Maria (Maserati) G. B.A., Hunter Col., 1931; M.D., Columbia U., 1949. Diplomate Am. Bd. Internal Medicine. Intern Cornell 2d med. div., Bellevue Hosp., N.Y.C., 1949-50; asst. resident in medicine Cornell div. Cornell 2d med. div., Bellevue Hosp., 1950-52, chief resident in medicine, 1952-53, chief gen. med. clinics, 1953-59, assoc. attending physician, 1953-62; practice medicine specializing in internal medicine Bellevue Hosp., 1953-61, Los Angeles, 1962—; psychiat. trainee Cedars of Lebanon Hosp., Los Angeles, 1961-62, assoc. attending physician, 1962—; dir. div. home care and extended care, Cedars-Sinai Med. Ctr., Los Angeles, 1962-66; chief adolescent clinic, med. dir. clinics Mt. Sinai Hosp., Los Angeles, 1962-66, assoc. attending physician dept. medicine, 1962-69, attending physician, 1970—; med. dir., coordinator U. So. Calif. Family Neighborhood Health Services Ctr. for Watts, 1966-67; attending physician Los Angeles County Hosp., U. So. Calif. Med. Ctr., 1966-71; assoc. mem. dept. internal medicine Orange County Med. Ctr., Calif., 1969—, dir. ambulatory care services, 1969-72; staff St. John's Hosp., Santa Monica, Calif., 1970—; asst. prof. clin. medicine, attending sr. physician internal medicine Cornell U. Med. Coll., 1957-62; asst. prof. clin. medicine UCLA, 1962-66, guest lectr. Sch. Social Welfare, 1964—, assoc. clin. prof. medicine and community medicine Sch. Medicine, 1972—, PRIMEX, 1972-73; asst. prof. medicine Sch. Medicine, U. So. Calif., 1966-69, adj. prof. medicine, community medicine, family medicine Coll. Medicine, U. Calif., Irvine, 1969-72; cons. Martin E. Segal Co., 1969—, VA Hosp., Long Beach, Calif., 1972—, Washington, 1972—; cons. health care sect. Social Security Adminstrn., Balt., Los Angeles County Health Dept., Calif. Council for Health Plan Alternatives, Burlingame, Regional Med. Care Program, 1971-73, Tb and Health Assn. of Los Angeles; mem. nat. adv. bd. Nat. Council Sr. Citizens, Washington; mem. adv. com. USPHS, Calif. Dept. Pub. Health; mem. med. adv. com. Vis. Nurse Assn., Los Angeles, 1976; mem. adv. bd. Life Extension Inst., N.Y.C.; mem. edn. com. Am. Cancer Soc., San Francisco; cons. ednl. films. Author sect. in textbook; contbr. articles to profl. publs. Active Town Hall, Los Angeles; vol., bd. dirs. South Central Child Care Ctrs. for South Central Los Angeles; mem. nat. adv. bd. for legal research and services for elderly Nat. Council Sr. Citizens; mem. UCI-21 project com. U. Calif. Recipient Achievement award AAUW, 1968, Better Life award Am. Nursing Home Assn., 1974, lifetime commitment award Watts Health Found., 1987; named to Hall of Fame, Hunter Coll. Alumni Assn., 1976. Mem. AMA, New York County Med. Assn., Calif. Med. Assn., Los Angeles County Med. Assn., Los Angeles County Soc. Internists, Am. Pub. Health Assn. (med. care sect.), Gerontol. Soc., Western Gerontology Assn., Comprehensive Health Planning Assn., Nat. Acad. Scis., Inst. Medicine. Home: 153 S Lasky Dr Suite 3 Beverly Hills CA 90212

GIOSEFFI, DANIELA, poet, author, educator; b. Orange, N.J., Feb. 12, 1941; d. Daniel Donato and Josephine (Buzevska) G.; m. Richard J. Kearney, Sept. 7, 1965 (div.); 1 child, Thea D.; m. Lionel B. Luttinger, June 6, 1986. B.A., Montclair State Coll., 1963; M.F.A., Catholic U. of America, 1966. Cons., poet N.Y. Poets-in-the-Schs., Inc., N.Y.C., 1972-85; freelance writer, lectr. at numerous univs. throughout U.S. and Europe, 1977—; prof. speech and Communication Arts, St. Francis Coll., Pace U., 1981—, Bklyn. Coll., 1981—; novels include: The Great American Belly, 1977, 4th edit., 1979; collection of poems: Eggs in the Lake, 1979; non-fiction: Earth Dancing; Mother Nature's Oldest Rite, 1981; Women on War and Survival: Global Voices for the Nuclear Age, 1988; contbr. poetry and fiction to numerous periodicals and anthologies; performer stage presentations of work throughout U.S. and Europe; plays produced Off-Off-Broadway include The Golden Daffodil Dwarf, Care of the Body, The Sea Hag in the Cave of Sleep, N.Y.C., 1988. Pres. Bklyn. Citizens for Sane Nuclear Policy; exec. bd. Writers and Pubs. Alliance for Nuclear Disarmament, 1978—. Grantee N.Y. State Council on Arts, 1972, 77 ; recipient Poetry/Fiction award Creative Artists' Pub. Service Program, N.Y.C., 1971. Mem. PEN Am. Ctr., Actors' Equity Assn., Acad. Am. Poets, Nat. Book Critics Circle, PEN Women's Com. Address: Earth Celebrations PO Box 197 Brooklyn Heights NY 11202

GIOVALE, GINGER GORE, personnel professional; b. Salt Lake City, Oct. 12, 1943; d. Wilbert Lee and Genevieve (Walton) Gore; m. John Peter Giovale, June 20, 1965; children: Peter, Danny, Mike, Mark. BS in Math., Westminster Coll., Salt Lake City, 1965. With personnel dept. W.L. Gore & Assocs., Flagstaff, Ariz., 1976-84; bd. dirs. W.L. Gore & Assocs., Newark, Del., 1977—. Trustee Westminster Coll., 1977—; parent advisor Flagstaff Pub. Schs., 1982—. Office: WL Gore & Assocs 1505 N Fourth St Flagstaff AZ 86001

GIOVANNI, NIKKI, poet; b. Knoxville, Tenn., June 7, 1943; d. Jones and Yolande Cornelia (Watson) G.; 1 son, Thomas Watson. BA with History in honors, Fisk U., 1967; postgrad. in social work, U. Pa., 1967; LHD (hon.), Wilberforce U., 1972, Worcester U., 1972; DLitt (hon.), Ripon U., 1974, Smith Coll., 1975, Coll. Mt. St. Joseph on Ohio, 1983. Founder Nixtom Ltd., 1970; asst. prof. black studies Queens Coll., CCNY, 1968; assoc. prof. English Rutgers U., 1968-72; prof. creative writing Coll. Mt. St. Joseph on the Ohio, 1985; vis. prof. English Ohio State U., 1984. Poet, writer, lectr.; author: Black Feeling, Black Talk, 1968, Black Judgement, 1969, Re-Creation, 1970, Broadside Poem of Angela Yvonne Davis, 1970, Night Comes Softly, 1970, Spin a Soft Black Song, 1971, Gemini, 1971, My House, 1972, A Dialogue: James Baldwin and Nikki Giovanni, 1973, Ego Tripping and Other Poems for Young Readers, 1973, A Poetic Equation: Conversations Between Nikki Giovanni and Margaret Walker, 1974, The Women and the Men, 1975, Vacationtime, 1980, Those Who Ride the Night Winds, 1983; rec. artist: (album) Truth Is On Its Way, 1972, others; TV appearances include: Soul!, Nat. Ednl. TV network, numerous talk shows including the Tonight Show; participant Soul at the Center, Lincoln Center Performing Arts, N.Y.C., 1972. Vol. worker Nat. Council Negro Women, now life mem. Recipient Mademoiselle mag. award outstanding achievement, 1971, Omega Psi Phi award, others; Ford Found. grantee, 1967. *

GIOVANNIELLO, MARGARET MONTGOMERY TORR, judge, lawyer; b. Terre Haute, Ind., May 23, 1927; d. Raymond Osborne and Luella B. (Montgomery) Torr; m. Joseph Louis Giovanniello, June 10, 1951; children—Rocco, Raymond, Joseph, Earle. B.A., U. Wis., 1949; J.D., Bklyn. Law Sch., 1956. Bar: N.Y. 1957, U.S. Dist. Ct. (so. and ea. dists.) N.Y. 1962, U.S. Ct. Appeals (2d cir.) 1975, U.S. Supreme Ct. 1978. Atty. Giovanniello & Giovanniello, Bklyn., Cedarhurst, N.Y., 1957—; adminstrv. law judge N.Y. State Unemployment Ins. Appeals Bd., N.Y.C., 1977—; bd. dirs. Community Action for Legal Services, N.Y.C.; N.Y. Network of Bar Leaders, 86—. U. Wis. scholar, 1945-46. Mem. ABA, N.Y. State Bar Assn., Kings County Criminal Bar. Protestant Lawyers Assn., N.Y. Women's Bar Assn., Nassau Suffolk Women's Bar (treas. 1982-83, bd. dirs., corr. sec.), Bklyn. Bar Assn. (bd. dirs. 1982—, ethics com. 1978—), Bklyn. Women's Bar Assn. (pres. 1982-84), Nat. Assn. Adminstrv. Law Judges (pres. 1986-87, pres.-elect 1985-86, v.p. 1984-85), Nat Conf. Adminstrv. Law Judges, N.Y. State Adminstrv. Law Judges (pres. 1984-85), Bklyn. Law Sch. Alumni Assn. Democrat. Roman Catholic. Clubs: Bklyn., Town t. Roman Catholic. Clubs: Bklyn., Town Hall. Home: 718's President St Brooklyn NY 11215 Office: N Y State Unemployment Ins Appeals Bd 1 Main St Brooklyn NY 11201

GIOVE, BARBARA ANN JEAN, photographer; b. Bklyn., Aug. 6, 1954; d. Salvatore Thomas and Theresa Ann (Vitale) G.; student York Coll., 1972-73, Queens Coll., 1973-74. Freelance photographer, Jamaica Estates, N.Y.,

1956—. Mem. Internat. Photography Soc., Photog. Soc. Am., Nat. Found. Ileitis and Colitis, Cousteau Soc., Animal Protection Inst., Nat. Audubon Soc., Am. Soc. Prevention of Cruelty to Animals, Fund for Animals, Nat. Wildlife Soc., The Statue of Liberty and Illis Island Found., Greenpeace. Democrat. Roman Catholic. Home and Office: 182 04 80th Dr Jamaica Estates NY 11432

GIRARD, DEBORAH ANN, screenwriter; b. N.Y.C., Apr. 29, 1954; d. George Peter Arthur and Anastasia Rose (Bukauchis) G; m. Philip James Bosi. BA cum laude, Hunter Coll., 1976. Assoc. producer Smith/Greenland Advt., N.Y.C., 1978-79, Sta. WOR-TV, N.Y.C., 1979-80; writer Warner-Amex, N.Y.C., 1981, Young & Rubicam Advt., N.Y.C., 1982; assoc. producer, writer Sta. WCBS-TV subs. CBS-TV News, N.Y.C., 1982-84; assoc. producer CBS-TV News, Los Angeles, 1984-85; writer Simon & Schuster Software, N.Y.C., 1986, The Travel Channel, N.Y.C., 1987—; writer screenplay Ailes Communications Inc., N.Y.C., 1987-88. Assoc. producer: Best TV Commercials :30, 1979 (Andy award 1979); writer: (variety series) Livewire, 1981 (Best Children's Cable Program award 1981). Mem. Internat. TV Assn. Republican. Roman Catholic.

GIRARD, ELISA MICHELE, graphic artist; b. Paterson, N.J., May 3, 1953; d. Theodore Alsdorf and Estelle Ellen (Farley) Girard; m. Thomas Joseph Hernandez, Oct. 8, 1983. B.F.A., St. Mary's Coll., Notre Dame, Ind., 1975. Art asst. Tech. Pub. Co. div. Dun & Bradstreet Corp., Barrington, Ill., 1975-79; staff artist, 1979-81, art dir. for Power Engring. Mag. and Electric Light & Power mag., 1981-86; art dir. Plant Engring. mag., 1987; asst. graphics coordinator Tech. Publ. Co., 1986-87; dir. art and prodn. Applied Tech. Publs., Inc., 1987—; propr., chief exec. officer EMG Entepnses, Barrington, 1978—. Mem. Nat. Humane Soc., Am. Soc. for the Prevention of Cruelty to Animals, St. Mary's Alumni Assn. Democrat. Roman Catholic. Office: Applied Tech Publs Inc 1300 S Grove Ave Suite 205 Barrington IL 60014

GIRARD, NETTABELL, lawyer; b. Riverton, Wyo., Feb. 24, 1938; d. George and Arranetta (Bell) Girard. Student, Idaho State U., 1957-58; B.S., U. Wyo., 1959, LL.B., 1961. Bar: Wyo. 1961, U.S. Supreme Ct. 1969, D.C. 1969. Practiced in Riverton, 1963-69; atty.-adviser on gen. counsel's staff HUD; assigned Office Interstate Land Sales Registration, Washington, 1969-70; sect. chief interstate land sales Office Gen. Counsel, 1970-73; ptnr. Larson & Larson, Riverton, 1973-85; sole practice Riverton, 1985—; guest lectr. at high schs.; condr. seminar on law for layman Riverton br. A.A.U.W., 1965; condr. course on women and law; lectr. equal rights, job discrimination, land use planning. Editor: Wyoming Clubwoman, 1966-68; bd. editors Wyo. Law Jour, 1959-61; writer Obiter Dictum column Women Lawyers Jour; also articles in legal jours. Chmn. fund drive Wind River chpt. ARC, 1965; chmn. Citizens Com. for Better Hosp. Improvement., 1965; chmn. sub-com. on polit., legal rights and responsibilities Gov.'s Commn. on Status Women, 1965-69, adv. mem., 1973—; rep. Nat. Conf. Govs. Commn., Washington, 1966; local chmn. Law Day, 1966, 67; mem. state bd. Wyo. Girl Scouts U.S.A., sec., 1974—, mem. nat. bd., 1978-81; state vol. adviser Nat. Found., March of Dimes, 1967-69; legal counsel Wyo. Women's Conf., 1977; pres. Riverton Civic League, 1987-88. Recipient Spl. Achievement award HUD, 1972, Disting. Leadership award Girl Scouts U.S.A., 1973, Franklin D. Roosevelt award Wyo. chpt. March of Dimes, 1985, Thanks Badge award Girl Scout Council, 1987; named outstanding woman Wonder Woman and Girl Scouts U.S.A., 1982. Mem. Wyo., Fremont County, D.C. bar assns., Women's Bar Assn. for D.C., Internat. Fedn. Women Lawyers, Am. Judicature Soc., Am. Trial Lawyers Assn., Nat. Assn. Women Lawyers (del. Wyo., nat. sec. 1969-70, v.p. 1970-71, pres. 1972-73), AAUW (br. pres.), Wyo. Fedn. Women Clubs (state editor, pres. elect 1968-69, treas. 1974-76), Progressive Women's Club, Kappa Delta, Delta Kappa Gamma (hon. mem. state chpt.). Club: Riverton Chautauqua (pres. 1965-67). Home: 224 W Sunset St PO Box 687 Riverton WY 82501 Office: 513 E Main St Riverton WY 82501

GIRDEN, LISA JAN, family and marriage therapist; b. Stamford, Conn., Aug. 28, 1959; d. Eugene Lawrence and Charlene Margot (Tobin) Girden. BA, Bucknell U., 1981; MS, U. Pa., 1982, 84. Cert. in marriage and family therapy. Tchr., Internat. Sch. Paris, 1980-81; mental health worker Ctr. for Autistic Children, Phila., 1983; asst. dir., acting dir. Old Pine Community Ctr., Phila., 1984-85; counselor Inst. for Learning, Phila., 1985—; pvt. practice psychology, family therapy, Phila., 1986—, Rittenhouse Counseling Assocs., Phila., 1985-86; dir. aftersch. program Old Pine Community Ctr., Phila., 1985—; psychologist Downs Syndrome children Cooke Found., 1987—. Mem. Am. Psychol. Assn., Assn. Humanistic Psychology, Am. Assn. Counseling and Devel. Avocations: skiing, horseback riding, needlepoint, gourmet cooking, travel.

GIROD, JUDY, interior design firm executive; b. Alexandria, La., Aug. 24, 1948; d. John James and Lily (McKnight) Capdevielle; m. Jerold S. Girod, Aug. 22, 1970. B.F.A. in Interior Design, La. State U., 1971. Interior designer Bowles Inc., 1970-72; interior designer, mgr. dept. Clyde W. Smith Co., 1972-75; interior designer Blitch Architects, 1975-78; owner, pres. Judy Girod Interior Design Inc. (now Girodesign), New Orleans, 1978—. Contbr. series on interior design to Gambit Mag. Bd. dirs. Coliseum Sq. Assn., 1980-86, St. Charles Ave. Bus. Assn., 1982; co-pres. Magazine St. Bus. Assn., 1984, Fashion Group of New Orleans Council, 1986, treas., 1988—; bd. dirs. Crescent House Home for Battered Women, 1985-89. Mem. La. State U. Alumni Assn. (dir. Greater New Orleans Met. chpt. 1979-80), Am. Soc. Interior Designers (pres. La. dist. chpt. 1982-83, nat. bd. dirs. 1985, tri-state bd. dirs. 1986—, apptd. by gov. La. State Bd. Examiners for Interior Designs 1985—), Inst. Bus. Designers, Delta Zeta. Republican. Roman Catholic. Clubs: Spring Fiesta, Fashion Group, Preservation Resource Ctr. Avocation: fencing. Home: 1402 Magazine St New Orleans LA 70130 Office: 1943 Magazine St New Orleans LA 70130

GIRONE, JOAN CHRISTINE CRUSE, county official; b. Kingston, Ont., Can., Aug. 30, 1927; naturalized U.S. citizen; d. Arthur William and Helen Wilson Cruse; m. Joseph Michael Girone, June 26, 1954; children: Susan, Richard, William. Buyer, Franklin Simon, Inc., N.Y.C., 1946-54; supr. Midlothian dist. Chesterfield County (Va.) Bd. Suprs., 1976-88, vice chmn., 1976-82; Founding mem. Capitol Area Agy. on Aging, 1973—; commr., chmn. Richmond (Va.) Regional Planning Dist. Commn., 1976-88; chmn. community edn. adv. com. Va. Bd. of Edn., 1972-79; mem. Va. Gov.'s Adv. Bd. on Aging, 1980-82; chmn. Richmond Met. Transp. Planning Orgn., 1981-88; bd. visitors Va. State U., 1980-84; chmn. Chesterfield County Com. to elect John Warner and Paul Trible to U.S. Senate, 1979, 82, 84; Chesterfield chmn. Marshall Coleman for Gov., 1981—; chmn. Women for Reagan-Bush, 1984; state chmn. Va. Fedn. Rep. Women, 1985, mem. candidate recruitment com., 1985; mem. Central Va. River Basin com., 1985; evaluation task force United Way of Greater Richmond, 1985; bd. dirs. Maymont Found., 1982—, YMCA Greater Richmond, ARC Va. Capital chpt., Family and Children's Services, 1988. Recipient Good Govt. award Richmond First Club, 1985. Mem. Va. Assn. Counties (exec. bd. 1982-87). Club: Huguenot Republican Woman's (Rep. Woman of Yr. 1983). Home: 2609 Dovershire Rd Bon Air VA 23235

GIROUARD, PEGGY JO FULCHER, ballet educator; b. Corpus Christi, Tex., Oct. 25, 1933; d. J.B. and Zora Alice (Jackson) Fulcher; m. Richard Ernest Girouard, Apr. 16, 1954 (div. Mar. 1963); children—Jo Linne, Richard Ernest. B.S. in Elem. Edn., U. Houston, 1970. Ballet Instr. Emmamae Horn Studio, Houston, 1951-81; owner, dir. Allegro Acad. Dance, Houston, 1981—; adminstrv. asst. Sugar Creek Homes Assn., Sugar Land, Tex., from 1979; artistic dir. Allegro Ballet Houston, from 1976. Choreographer (with Glenda W. Brown) Masquerade Suite, 1983, Sebelius Suite, 1983, Shannan, 1984, Papa Shamus, 1986, Silhouettes, 1987. Mem. Cultural Arts Council Houston. Recipient Stream award 1986. Mem. Dance Masters Am. (dir. 1977-80), S.W. Regional Ballet Assn. (chmn. craft of choreography 1983—, coordinator to nat. assn. 1983—), Regional Dance Am. (mem. ad hoc com.), West Meml. Houston C. of C., Am. Bus. Women's Assn. Democrat. Home: 9925 Warwana St Houston TX 77080

GIROUX, MARIE ELISABETH, nail care company administrator; b. Brisbane, Queensland, Australia, Apr. 7, 1952; came to U.S., 1960; d. Max Oscar and Elisabeth E. (Backlund) Sikstrom; m. Lance Giroux, Feb. 27, 1984; children: Peter, Cari, Nicholas. Student, Spokane Falls Community Coll., 1970-72. Flight attendant United Airlines, 1972—; sr. sales coordinator Am. Natural Nail Care Co., Novato, Calif., 1985—. Mem. Nat. Assn. Female Execs., San Francisco Vis. and Conv. Bur., Nat. Assn. Profl. Saleswomen.

GIRTH, MARJORIE LOUISA, lawyer, educator; b. Trenton, N.J., Apr. 21, 1939; d. Harold Brookman and Marjorie Mathilda (Simonson) G. A.B., Mt. Holyoke Coll., 1959; LL.B., Harvard U., 1962. Bar: N.J. 1963, N.Y. 1976, U.S. Supreme Ct. 1969. Pvt. practice Trenton, 1963-65; research assoc. Brookings Instn., 1965-70; assoc. prof. law SUNY Law Sch., Buffalo, 1971-79; prof. SUNY Law Sch., 1979—; assoc. dean U. Va. Law Sch., 1986-87; vis. prof. U. Va. Law Sch., 1979-80. Author: Poor People's Lawyers, 1976, Bankruptcy Options for the Consumer Debtor, 1981, (co-author) Bankruptcy: Problem, Process, Reform, 1971. Bd. dirs. Buffalo and Erie County YWCA, 1972-76, Buffalo Unitarian-Universalist Ch., 1981-84; mem. commn. on peace, justice and human rights Internat. Assn. Religious Freedom, 1976-79; chmn. Erie County Task Force on Status of Women, 1985-87. Mem. ABA (council, bus. law sect. 1985—, consumer bankruptcy com. 1978—, chmn. consumer bankruptcy com. 1983-86), Assn. Am. Law Schs. (com. on acad. freedom and tenure 1987—), N.Y. Bar Assn. (chmn. banking, corp. bus. law sect. 1986-87, mem. exec. com. 1980—, bankruptcy law com., 1978—, chmn. bankruptcy law com. 1980-82), Erie County Bar Assn., N.Y. Women's Bar Assn., Mt. Holyoke Alumnae Assn. (Centennial award 1972). Office: SUNY North Campus O'Brian Hall Buffalo NY 14260

GISH, LILLIAN, actress; b. Springfield, Ohio; d. James Lee and Mary (Robinson) Gishi. AFD, Rollins Coll.; HHD, Mt. Holyoke Coll.; DFA (hon.), Bowling Green State U., 1976, Middlebury Coll. Debut on stage at 5; appeared in films including Birth of a Nation, Hearts of the World, Broken Blossoms, Way Down East, Orphans of the Storm, Scarlet Letter, Annie Laurie, The Wind, The Enemy, Night of the Hunter, Duel in the Sun, Portrait of Jennie, The Unforgiven, 1960, Follow Me Boys, 1966, The Comedians, 1967, La Boheme, A Wedding, 1978, Thin Ice (TV), 1980, Hambone and Hillie, 1984, Sweet Liberty, 1986, The Whales of August, 1987 (Nat. Bd. Rev. Film Award Best Actress 1987); movies made in Italy include The White Sister, Romola; appeared in plays including Crime and Punishment, 1948, Miss Mabel (title role), 1950, The Curious Savage, 1950, A Trip to Bountiful, Portrait of a Madonna, The Wreck of the 5:25, The Family Reunion (Pulitzer prize), All the Way Home, 1960-61, Romeo and Juliet (role of nurse), 1965, Anya, 1966, I Never Sang for My Father, 1967-68, Too True To Be Good, 1963, A Passage to India, 1963, Uncle Vanya, 1973, A Musical Jubilee, 1975, also TV plays including Twin Detectives, 1976, Sparrow, 1977, Hobson's Choice, 1983; appeared in TV series The Love Boat; toured Europe, Russia, U.S. as lectr. on art films, 1969, 71-73; Royal Command appearance, Queen Elizabeth the Queen Mother, 1980; author: The Movies, Mr. Griffith and Me, 1969, Dorothy and Lillian Gish, 1973, An Actor's Life for Me, 1987. Recipient hon. Acad. Award, 1971, Handel medallion City of N.Y., 1973, Kennedy Center honors City of N.Y., 1982, Life Achievement award Am. Film Inst., 1984. Address: 430 E 57th St New York NY 10022

GIST, SHEILA M., travel agency executive; b. N.Y.C., June 28, 1962; d. Woodrow and Eunice (Mims) Gist. Student, NYU, 1980-82, Queens Coll., 1983-85. Cashier, mgr. Uncle Woody's Deli, Hollis, N.Y., 1976-82; office mgr. City Marshal, Bklyn., 1980-82; sec. credit life I.M. Oberman Assoc., N.Y.C., 1982; pres., mgr. IGT Travel, Hollis, 1983—; cons. 369th Vet. Assn., N.Y.C., 1984-85, Pepsi-Cola USA, Somers, N.Y., 1983—. Mem. Am. Soc. Travel Agts., Assn. Retail Travel Agts., Nat. Assn. Female Execs. Democrat. Home: 83-19 141st St #303 Briarwood NY 11435-1621 Office: IGT Travel 197-17 Hillside Ave Hollis NY 11423

GIST, SUZANNE, educator, consultant; b. Effingham, Ill., Sept. 18, 1958; d. Albert Neal and Nancy Carolyn (Drake) G. Student, N. Tex. State U., 1977-79, Tex. Woman's U., 1979; BS in Nursing, U. Tex., Arlington, 1979-81; postgrad., Marymount U., 1987—. RN; cert. diabetes educator. Staff nurse Irving (Tex.) Community Hosp., 1981-82, charge nurse, 1982, nurse ICU, 1982-83; diabetes edn. cons. Becton Dickinson, Rochelle Park, N.J., 1983-85; E. coast mgr. Franklin Lakes, N.J., 1985—; instr. CPR AHA, Irving, Tex., 1982-83; recruiter Irving Community Hosp., 1981-83. Mem. Am. Diabetes Assn., Juvenile Diabetes Assn., Am. Assn. Diabetes Educators, Nat. Assn. Female Execs., Delta Zeta. Republican. Home: 4632 D S 28th Rd Arlington VA 22206 Office: Becton Dickinson 1 Becton Dr Franklin Lakes NJ 07417

GIST-WILLIAMS, CHERYL LYNN, computer consultant; b. Chgo., Apr. 1, 1956; d. Horace Llewellyn and Geraldine (Taylor) Gist; m. Bruce R. Williams, Aug. 2, 1980; 1 child, Candace Asha. BA, Barat Coll., 1977; MBA, Roosevelt U., 1979. Budget analyst City of Chgo., 1978-80; fin. analyst Xerox Corp., Des Plaines, Ill., 1980-84; mgr. micro-computer ctr. Montgomery Ward Co., Chgo., 1984-85; tech. staff rep. United Airlines/Covia Corp., Rosemont, Ill., 1986—; cons. in field. Organizer Ill. Shore council Girl Scouts U.S.A., Evanston, Ill., 1982. Mem. Ill. Realtor Assn., Nat. Assn. Realtors. Office: Covia Corp 9700 W Higgins Rd Rosemont IL 60018

GITHENS, PENNY BUFFIE, health care consultant; b. Wilmington, Ohio, Nov. 12, 1949; d. Paul Robert and Aileen (Smith) G.; m. Edward Frederick Buffie, Sept. 9, 1978. BS, Purdue U., 1972; MS, Ind. U., 1981; student, The Wharton Sch., 1983-85. Tchr. of chemistry, physics Peace Corps, Kenya, 1972-74; tchr. of chemistry, math. Milford Acad., Conn., 1978-79; research assoc. Yale Sch. Med., New Haven, Conn., 1979-82; asst. dir. U. Pa., Lauder Inst., Phila., 1983-85; healthcare cons. Fulton, Longshore & Assocs., Haverford, Pa., 1986-87; research assoc. health policy ctr. Vanderbilt Inst. Pub. Policy Studies Vanderbilt U., Nashville, 1987—. Co-author (with others) of articles in epidemiological jours. NDEA fellow, Ind. U., 1977-78. Mem. Del. Valley Health Care Mktg. Consortium, Nat. Assn. Female Execs. Home: 1308 Creek View Ct Nashville TN 37221 Office: Vanderbilt U Box 1503-Station B Nashville TN 37235

GITNER, DEANNE, writer; b. Lyons, N.Y., Jan. 8, 1944; d. Myron and Mary (Kurland) Gebell; m. Gerald L. Gitner, June 24, 1968; children: Daniel Mark, Seth Michael. AB, Cornell U., 1966. Cert. English tchr. Tchr. English Gates (N.Y.) Chili Cen. Sch., 1966-68, Wantagh (N.Y.) Jr. and Sr. High Sch., 1968-70, J. Weiner Sch., Houston, 1980-81; writer Bellaire Texan, Houston, 1980; rep. sales McDougal Littel & Co., Chgo., 1981-83; writer Millburn Short Hills Ind., New Providence, N.J., 1987—. Contbr. articles to profl. publs. Mem. Nat. Council Jewish Women (v.p. Houston sect. 1976-79, pres. 1980-81, Vol. award, v.p. Essex County, N.J. sect. 1983-88). Office: PO Box 336 Short Hills NJ 07078

GITT-EDWARDS, PATRICIA E., communications executive; b. N.Y.C., Mar. 8, 1941; d. Michael A. and Cornelia K. (Cunn) Gitt; B.S. in Home Econs., U. Vt., 1962; M.B.A. in Mktg., Fordham U., 1980; m. Lee A. Edwards, Nov. 1, 1981. Acct. exec. The Rowland Co., Inc., 1968-71; account exec. Hill & Knowlton, Inc., N.Y.C., 1973-75; mgr. communications Life Savers, Inc., N.Y.C., 1976-80; owner, mgr. Patricia Gitt Co., N.Y.C., 1980—. Mem. Women in Radio and TV (tres. N.Y.C. chpt. 1981-83, chpt. pres. 1984-86). Office: 305 E 24th St New York NY 10010

GITTLER, CAROL SPEAR, real estate broker; b. Chgo., Aug. 13, 1940; d. Louis L. and Esther (Katz) Spear; B.A., Roosevelt U., Chgo., 1978; m. Marvin Gittler, July 9, 1960; children—Michelle, Caryn, Susan, Mandy, Debra. Engaged in real estate, 1975—; real estate researcher U. Chgo., 1976-77; sec. Forus Investment Corp., Chgo., 1978—; pres. C.A.T.S. Realty, Chgo., 1980—; prin Heritage Realty Group, Chgo., 1986—. Cons. to Rep. Carol Braun, 1978—. Mem. Nat. Assn. Realtors, Hyde Park Hist. Soc., Franklin Honor Soc. Jewish. Home: 5458 Hyde Park Blvd Chicago IL 60615 Office: Heritage Realty Group 5120 Hyde Park Chicago IL 60615 Office: 120 W Madison St Chicago IL 60602

GITTMAN, BETTY, education administrator; b. N.Y.C., Mar. 15, 1945; d. Kallman and Rebecca (Santcroos) G.; m. Ira Loeb, Aug. 5, 1965 (div. 1977); children: Stephen Loeb, Leslie Loeb, Sherry Loeb; m. Victor Arnel, Mar. 5, 1981. BS, NYU, 1966; MS, CUNY, 1969; PhD, Hofstra U., 1979, cert. advanced study, 1987. Cert. ednl. adminstr., N.Y. Tchr. N.Y.C. Bd. Edn., Kew Gardens, 1966-68; instr. New Sch. for Social Research, N.Y.C., 1980-81; tech. adminstr. Bd. Coop. Ednl. Services of Nassau County, Westbury, N.Y., 1984, dir. program devel., evaluation cons., 1981-86, adminstr. 1987—; adj. prof. C.W. Post Campus L.I. U., Brookville, N.Y., 1987. Hofstra U. Doctoral fellow, 1976. Mem. Am. Ednl. Research Assn., Northeastern Ednl. Research Assn., Am. Psychol. Assn., N.Y. Acad. Sci., Nat. Council Adminstrv. Women in Edn., Nat. Council on Measurement in Edn., Mensa (research dir. Greater N.Y. children's com. 1984-85), Kappa Delta Pi. Democrat. Jewish. Office: Bd Coop Ednl Services of Nassau County Office Instn Planning and Research Valentines and The Plain Rd Westbury NY 11590

GIURGIU, ALEXANDRA MARIA, business executive, industrial engineer; b. N.Y.C., Mar. 28, 1958; d. Mircea Anthony and Lucia (Badescu) G.; m. Alessandro A. Piol. B.S., Sch. Engring. and Applied Sci. Columbia U., 1979, M.S., 1983. Registered engr. N.Y. Sr. officer for project fin. and adminstrn. Chemtex, Inc., N.Y.C., 1979-84; dir. internat. ops. Intersoft Corp. (doing bus. as Lifeboat Assocs.), N.Y.C., 1984; dir. strategy and corporate devel. Ing. C. Olivetti & C.S.p.A., N.Y.C., 1986—; freelance writer Defis mag., Paris, 1983—. Home: 7000 Blvd East Guttenberg NJ 07093 Office: Olivetti 535 Madison Ave 19th Fl New York NY 10022

GIVAN, PRISCILLA WHITE, marketing consultant; b. Greenwich, Conn., July 21, 1942; d. John Hazen and Mary Tefft (Schwarz) White; m. Curtis Varney Givan, June 22, 1963 (div. Feb. 1981); children: Amy Gwendolyn, Curtis Varney Jr. AA, Lasell Jr. Coll., 1962; BA in English, U. R.I., 1986. Pres., owner Pearson Travel Corp., Providence, R.I., 1974-80; mgr. product Taco Inc., Cranston, R.I., 1980-83, dir. mktg. services, 1983-84; mgr. UNIPAS div. Taco, Cranston, R.I., 1984-85; cons. mktg. & Mgmt. Priscilla White Givan and Assoc., Barrington, R.I., 1985—; lectr. Brown U. 1986, R.I. Sec. St. Women Bus. 1986. Vestry mem. St. Johns Epis. Ch., 1985—; mem. human resource com. R.I. Technology Council. Mem. Jr. League Providence (bd. dirs. 1975-79), Barrington YMCA (bd. dir. 1973-76), Advt. Club (bd. dirs.), Woman's Network (bd. dirs. 1986—), Providence C. of C., Narragansett Bay Yachting Assn (chmn. jr. sailing orgn. 1974-78), Nat. Assn. Female Execs. Republican.. Episcopalian. Home: 5 Anchorage Way Barrington RI 02806 Office: Priscilla White Givan and Assoc 5 Anchorage Way Barrington RI 02806

GIVEN, ELAINE FORTNEY, librarian; b. Reading, Pa., Sept. 17, 1937; d. Stanley M. and Marie Daisy (Tomlinson) Fortney; m. William Todd Given, Nov. 17, 1962; 1 son, Scott William. B.S., Kutztown Coll., 1959; M.S., Villanova U., 1978. Librarian, Spring Grove Sch. Dist. (Pa.), 1959-60, Palmyra High Sch., Pa., 1960-62, Souderton Area Sch. Dist. (Pa.), 1969—, Franconia Sch., 1983—. Mem. ALA, Pa. Sch. Librarians Assn., Pa. Edn. Assn., NEA. Office: Souderton Area Sch Dist 366 Harleysville Pike Souderton PA 18964

GIVENS, JANET EATON, author; b. N.Y.C., July 5, 1932; d. Irving Daniel and Matilda (Schmelzle) E.; m. Richard Ayres Givens, Aug. 24, 1957; children—Susan Ruth, Jane Lucile. B.A., Queens Coll., 1953; M.A., Columbia U., 1955. Lic. tchr., N.Y. Tchr. pub. elem. schs., Silver Spring, Md., 1953-55, Mamaroneck, N.Y., 1955-59; supr. prospective tchrs., part-time lectr. Queens Coll., N.Y.C., 1959-68. Author: The Migrating Birds, 1964; Something Wonderful Happened, 1982; Just Two Wings, 1984; contbg. author: Tensions Our Children Live With, 1959. V.p. PTA, Pub. Sch. 219, Queens, N.Y., 1972-73, del. to United Parents Assn., 1971-72, editor PS 219 News, 1971-73. Home: 147-11 68th Rd Flushing NY 11367

GIVENS, JEAN FRANCES, stockbroker; b. Rochester, N.Y., Jan. 15, 1948; d. Miles Parker and Mary Imogene (Morgan) G. BS, Lynchburg Coll., 1969; PhD, U. Minn., 1974; cert. fin. planning, Reagan Sch. of Advanced Mgmt., 1982. Virologist Roswell Park Meml. Inst., Buffalo, 1973-76; application specialist Millipore Corp., Bedford, Mass., 1976-78; applications scientist Nuclepore Corp., Pleasanton, Calif., 1978-79; account exec. Merril Lynch, Lexington, Ky., 1979-85, fin. cons., 1985—; ptnr. Matrix Fin. and Devel., Lexington, 1985—. Bd. dirs. Modern Dance/Ky., Lexington, 1983, treas., 1984, pres. 1985; speaker adv. forum Midway (Ky.) Coll., 1982, adv. council Alternatives for Women, Lexington, 1985—; mem. People to People Forum, Lexington, 1983. Mem. Profl. Women's Forum (founder). Home: 1344 Strawberry Ln Lexington KY 40502 Office: Merrill Lynch PO Box 220 Lexington KY 40584

GJOLAJ, GJELINA, advertising executive; b. Gruda, Yugoslavia, Mar. 25, 1962; came to U.S., 1969; naturalized, 1987; d. Leka and Mare (Linadi) G. ABA, Detroit Coll. Bus., 1983, BBA magna cum laude, 1985. Office adminstr., bulletin editor Ch. of the Resurrection, Detroit, 1981-83; legal asst. Honigman Miller Schwartz and Cohn, Detroit, 1984-86; account exec. Profl. Mktg. and Advt., Southfield, Mich., 1986—; vol. career cons., Met. Detroit, 1985. Recipient medal of merit Congressman Dennis Hertel, 1981. Mem. Direct Mktg. Assn. Detroit, Adcraft Club Detroit, Women's Advt. Club, Detroit Circulation Council, Am. Mktg. Assn., Nat. Assn. Female Execs., Albanian/Am. Cultural Orgn., Phi Beta Kappa. Office: Profl Mktg and Advt 21415 Civic Ctr Dr Suite 300 Southfield MI 48076

GLACEL, BARBARA PATE, educator, management consultant; b. Balt., Sept. 15, 1948; d. Jason Thomas Pate and Sarah Virginia (Forwood) Wetter; m. Robert Allan Glacel, Dec. 21, 1969; children—Jennifer Warren, Sarah Allane, Ashley Virginia. A.B., Coll. William and Mary, 1970; M.A., U. Okla., 1973, Ph.D., 1978. Tchr. Harford County (Md.) Schs., 1970-71; tchr. Dept. Def. Schs., W.Ger., 1971-73; ednl. counselor U.S. Army, W.Ger., 1973-74; lectr. U. Md., W.Ger., 1973-74; adj. prof. Suffolk U., Boston, 1975-77, C.W. Post Ctr., L.I. U., John Jay Coll. Criminal Justice, N.Y.C., 1979-80, St. Thomas Aquinas Coll., N.Y.C., 1981; acad. adviser Central Mich. U. 1981-82; adj. prof. St. Mary's Coll., Leavenworth, Kans., 1981, Anchorage Community Coll., 1982; asst. prof. U. Alaska-Anchorage, 1983-85; mgmt. cons. Barbara Glacel & Assocs., Anchorage, 1980—; gen. mgr. mgmt. programs Hay Systems Inc., Washington, 1986-88; founder and prin. Pace Cons. Group, Burke, Va., 1988—; ptnr. Pracel Prints, Williamsburg, Va., 1981-85; sr. mgmt. tng. specialist ARCO Alaska, Inc., 1984-85; 2d v.p. Chesapeake Broadcasting Corp. Md.; guest lectr. U.S. Mil. Acad. Chmn. 172d Inf. Brigade Family Council; mem. U.S. Army Sci. Bd., 1986—. Recipient Comdr.'s award for pub. service U.S. Dept. Army, 1984. AAUW grantee, 1977-78. Mem. Am. Soc. Tng. and Devel. (bd. dirs. Anchorage chpt.), Am. Psychol. Assn., Am. Soc. Pub. Adminstrn., Am. Polit. Sci. Assn. Pi Sigma Alpha. Author: Regional Transit Authorities, 1983; (with others) 1000 Army Families, 1983. Home: 5617 Tilia Ct Burke VA 22015 Office: Pace Cons Group Burke VA 22015

GLAD, JOAN BOURNE, clinical psychologist, educator; b. Salt Lake City, Apr. 24, 1918; d. E. LeRoy and Ethel G. (Rogers) Bourne; m. Donald D. Glad, Sept. 10, 1938 (dec. 1980); children—Dawn JoAnne, Toni Ann, Sue Ellen, Roger Bruce. B.A., UCLA, 1953; M.A., U. Utah, 1960, Ph.D., 1965. Chief psychologist Utah State Dept. Health, Salt Lake City, 1955-65; dir., adminstr. Child and Family Guidance Clinic, Salt Lake City, 1965-68; dir. parent edn. Children's Hosp. Orange County, 1968-75; adminstr. Family Learning Ctr., Santa Ana-Tustin Community Hosp., Santa Ana, Calif., 1975-77; dir. Glad & Assocs., Tustin, Calif., 1977—; instr. Grad. Sch., Chapman Coll., Orange, Calif., 1970-73; cons. Calif. Assn. Neurologically Handicapped Children, Orange, 1970-77; lectr. self esteem Fullerton (Calif.) Coll., 1980-82. Author: Reading Unlimited, 1965. Mem. Assn. Holistic Health (a founder San Diego), Assn. Mormon Counselors and Psychotherapists, Calif. Assn. Neurologically Handicapped Children. Republican. Mem. Ch. of Jesus Christ of Latter-day Saints. Office: Glad & Assocs 1500 E Katella Suite M Orange CA 92667

GLADSTONE, JOYCE ANN, insurance agent; b. Bigstone, Va., Aug. 18, 1942; d. William R. and Mary A. (Hensley) Bailey; children: Tammy L., Michelle R.; m. George H. Rouse, Sept. 15, 1979. BS, East Tenn. State U., 1965; MS, Boston U., 1976; cert. advanced grad. studies, Va. Tech. U., 1982. Cert. tchr., Va. Tchr. Army Edn. Ctr., Ft. Sill, Okla., 1965-66, Ft. Carson, Colo., 1967-69, Penns Grove (N.J.) Pub. Sch., 1966-67; salesperson Salad Master Corp., Dallas, 1971-72; prin. U.S. Dependent Schs., Pisa, Italy, 1972-76; supr. alt. edn. Donald J. Howard Vocat. Sch., Winchester, Va., 1976-79; instr. Va. Tech. U., Blackburg, 1979-84; agt. State Farm Ins. Co., Vienna, Va., 1984—. Leader 4-H, Va., 1979-88; sec. Outstanding Virginian Day Com., Warrington, 1980-82; organizer No. Va. 4-H Ambassadors, 1981-86;

chmn. Smithsonian Spring Celebration, 1982. Mem. Nat. Assn. Female Execs., AAUW, Va. Assn. 4-H Adult Leaders (speaker 1983), State Farm Millionaires Club, State Farm Legion of Honor, Am. Bus. Women, Phi Delta Kappa (program v.p. 1979-84, v.p. membership com., pres., nat. del., dist. del., speaker 1983, Pres.' award 1983). Office: State Farm Ins Co 374 Maple Ave E Suite 200 Vienna VA 22180

GLAESSMANN, DORIS ANN, county official; b. Northampton, Pa., Feb. 18, 1940; d. Frank G. and Theresa (Fischl) Zwikl; m. Edward Glaessmann, Sept. 1, 1962; children: Edward Jr., Robert F. Grad. high sch., Northampton, 1958. Sec., bookkeeper John F. Moore Agy., Inc., Allentown, Pa., 1958-64; ct. clk. Criminal div. Clk. of Cts. Office, Allentown, 1968-69, asst. dep. clk., 1969-76, chief dep. clk., 1976-82; clk. of cts. Criminal and Civil divs. County of Lehigh, Allentown, 1982—. Den mother, sec. Cub Scout Pack 140, Allentown, 1973—; mem., past bd. dirs. Quota Club Allentown, 1983—; mem. council St. Peter's Evang. Luth. Ch., Allentown, 1984—. Mem. Nat. Assn. County Recorders and Clks., Internat. Assn. Clks., Recorders, Election Officials and Treas., Pa. Prothonotaries and Clks. Assn. (2d v.p.), Pa. Elected Women's Assn. (past treas., past pres. Lehigh Valley Chpt.). Democrat. Home: 945 E Lynnwood St Allentown PA 18103-5250 Office: County of Lehigh 455 Hamilton St PO Box 1548 Allentown PA 18105-1548

GLANTZ, GINA, consultant; b. N.Y.C., Apr. 3, 1943; d. Nathan L. and Lillian (Rosenbaum) Stritzler; m. Ronald A. Glantz, Oct. 17, 1968; children—Amy Samantha, Peter Samuel. B.A., U. Calif.-Berkeley, 1965. Chief of staff County Exec. Peter Shapiro, County of Essex, N.J., 1978-82; owner, mgr. Gina Glantz Cons., Springfield, N.J., 1982-83; sr. cons. Mondale for Pres., Washington, 1984; nat. field dir. Mondale/Ferraro, Inc., Washington, 1984; ptnr. Martin & Glantz, San Francisco, 1985—. Chmn. nat. edn. and tng. council Democratic Nat. Com., Washington, 1981-84. Home: 96 Ave Del Norte San Anselmo CA 94960 Office: Martin & Glantz 1840 Van Ness San Francisco CA 94109

GLASER, JOY ALODIA, real estate broker; b. Manila, Jan. 12, 1947; d. Amadeo B. and Carmen (Austria) Barrios; m. Otto Glaser; children: Nancy, Michael. Dist. sec. Southland Corp., Baton Rouge, 1983-85; real estate broker William Hart Realty, Baton Rouge, 1985-87; bus. brokerage specialist Am.'s Bus. Specialist, Baton Rouge, 1986-88; pres., real estate broker La. Property Rentals and Sales, Inc., 1988—; realtor Hart Realty, Baton Rouge, 1985—; tax cons., Baton Rouge, 1985—; asset mgmt. cons. United Liberty Life Ins., Baton Rouge, 1986—. Home: 404 Pebblebrook Dr Baton Rouge LA 70815

GLASER, RUTH BONNIE, psychologist; b. Tenafly, N.J., May 11, 1937; d. John H. and Ruth Louise (Ferris) T.; divorced; children: Louise Ferris, William Thompson. BA, U. Calif., Berkeley, 1971, MA, 1975, PhD, 1976. Licensed psychologist. Pvt. practice psychologist Berkeley, 1976—, U. Calif., Berkeley, 1976—; bd. dirs., dean of students San Francisco Postgrad. Inst. Psychoanalytic Psychotherapy, 1985—; faculty Children's Hosp., San Francisco, 1980—; evaluator Western Assn. Schs. and Colls., Oakland, Calif., 1981—. Fellow NIMH, 1972-75. Mem. Am. Psychol. Assn., Am. Orthopsychol. Assn., Kappa Mu Epsilon. Home: 1140 Grizzly Peak Blvd Berkeley CA 94708 Office: 268 Arlington Ave Kensington CA 94707

GLASPIE, APRIL CATHERINE, diplomat; b. Vancouver, B.C., Can., Apr. 26, 1942. BA, Mills Coll., 1963; MA, Johns Hopkins U., 1965. With Foreign Service U.S. Dept. of State, 1966—; polit. officer U.S. Embassy, Cairo, 1973-77; asst. to Asst. Sec. State for Near Ea., S. Asian Affairs Washington, 1977-78; polit. officer U.S. Embassy, London, 1978-80, U.S. Mission to UN, N.Y.C., 1980-81; dir. lang. inst. U.S. Embassy, Tunis, Tunisia, 1981-83; polit. officer, dep. chief of mission U.S. Embassy, Damascus, Syria, 1983-85; dir., Office of Jordan, Lebanon, and Syrian Affairs U.S. Dept. of State, Washington, 1985-87; ambassador to Iraq 1987—. Address: U S Ambassador to Iraq care State Dept Washington DC 20520 *

GLASS, ANNETTE CECILE, staff development coordinator; b. Oakland, Calif., May 7, 1953; d. Edward John and Margaret Ann (Criss) Green; 1 child, K. Oscar. Staff devel. coordinator Gillingwater Mgmt., Austin, Tex., 1979—; speaker, tchr. in field. Author: (book) The Battle, 1981, newspaper column, Joyfully Yours, 1983-84. Mem. Women's Aglow Fellow (v.p. 1986-87). Republican.

GLASS, BARBARA BELL, banker; b. Tulsa, Feb. 7, 1944; d. James Martin and Betty Lee (Johnson) Bell; m. William Albert Kidwell, Aug. 27, 1966 (div. 1977); children—Holly Lee, William Christopher; m. Ronald Roy Glass, Mar. 20, 1981. B.S., Okla. State U., 1966; M.A., U. Okla., 1979. Cert. profl. in human resources. Grad. asst. U. Okla., Norman, 1978-79, research asst., 1979-80; mgmt. trainee Fourth Nat. Bank, Tulsa, 1980-81, asst. cashier, 1981-82, asst. v.p., 1982-83, v.p., 1983—, v.p. and trust officer, 1987. Mem. profl. women's adv. bd. Tulsa Jr. Coll., 1982-83; trustee Patti Johnson Wilson Found.; mem. adv. bd. U. Tulsa Mgmt. Devel. Ctr.; bd. dirs. YWCA, Tulsa. Mem. Am. Soc. Tng. and Devel., Am. Soc. Personnel Adminstrs., Tulsa Employee Benefits Group, Tulsa Equal Employment Opportunity Coordinators Assn. Democrat. Unitarian Universalist. Home: 3612 S Braden Pl Tulsa OK 74135

GLASS, CAROLYN BENNION, specialty advertising company executive; b. Jacksonville, Fla., Mar. 13, 1946; d. Thomas Raymond and Vivian Pauline (Thomas) Bennion; m. Theodore C. Glass, Jan. 23, 1965 (div. 1983); children: Lorilee, T. Scott, Michael C. Grad. high sch., Jacksonville. Sec. Jacksonville (Fla.) Splty. Advt. Co., 1975-80, sales rep., 1980-82, v.p., 1982-83, exec. v.p., 1983—. Mem. Jacksonville Advt. Fedn., Riverside Avondale Preservation Soc. Democrat. Baptist. Office: Jacksonville Splty Advt Co 6030 Arlington Expressway Jacksonville FL 32211

GLASS, SHERYL ANN, software consultant; b. Norfolk, Va., July 8, 1957; d. Thomas Frederick and Barbara Ann (Barbee) Dawson; m. Dean Howard McGorrill, May 7, 1977 (div. May 1984); m. John Richard Glass, Jan. 24, 1985; children: Eric Dean Glass, Jessica Leigh Glass. Student, Wheaton Coll., 1974-76, Framingham State, 1982-84. Programmer/ analyst Digital Equipment Corp., Marlboro, Mass., 1978-79; cons. Community Data Services, Manchester, Mass., 1979-87. Mem. Am. Indian Sci. and Engring Soc., Am. Med. Writers Assn. Mormon. Office: Community Data Services PO Box 1463 Manchester MA 01944

GLASSER, EVE ISABELLE, program director; b. N.Y.C., Oct. 24, 1941; d. Louis and Frances (Cohen) Kirschner; m. Martin J. Glasser; children: Elizabeth Anne, Geoffrey Hugh. BA, Hunter Coll., N.Y.C., 1963; postgrad., Hofstra U., 1983—. Editor Levittown (N.Y.) Tribune, 1972-78, Wantagh (N.Y.)/Seaford Citizen, 1979-82; freelance writer N.Y. Times, N.Y.C., 1976-82; editor-in-chief, writer Hofstra U., Hempstead, N.Y., 1982-83, asst. dean student services, 1983-86; coordinator pub. relations, sports promotion Hofstra U., Hempstead, 1987—; dir. univ. relations Adelphi U., Garden City, N.Y., 1986-87; mem. Levittown Bd. Edn., 1979-82, pres., 1981-82; mem. adv. council Literacy Vols. Am., Garden City; rep. L.I. Coalition for Fair Broadcasting, N.Y.C., 1985-87. Contbr. articles to profl. jours. Com. mem. Nassau Rep. Club. Recipient Nat. Best Heart award Am. Heart Assn., 1977, Spl. Edn. award for outstanding service to children, 1980. Mem. Pub. Relations Soc. Am., L.I. Communicators Assn. Jewish. Home: 826 Brent Dr Wantagh NY 11793 Office: Hofstra U Hempstead NY 11550

GLASSMAN, CAROLINE DUBY, state justice; b. Baker, Oreg., Sept. 13, 1924; d. Charles Ferdinand and Caroline Marie (Colton) Duby; m. Harry Paul Glassman, May 21, 1953; 1 son, Max Avon. LLB summa cum laude, Williamette U., 1944. Bar: Oreg. 1944, Calif. 1952, Maine 1969. Atty. Title Ins. & Trust Co., Salem, Oreg., 1944-46; assoc. Belli, Aske & Pinney, San Francisco, 1952-58; ptnr. Glassman, Beagle & Ridge, Portland, Maine, from 1978; judge Maine Supreme Ct., Portland; lectr. Sch. Law, U. Maine, 1967-68, 80. Author: Legal Status of Homemakers in State of Maine, 1977. Mem. ABA, Oreg. Bar Assn., Calif. Bar Assn., Maine Bar Assn., Maine Trial Law Assn. Roman Catholic. Home: 56 Thomas St Portland ME 04102 Office: Maine Supreme Ct 142 Federal St Portland ME 04112-0368 *

GLASS-RIDGLEY, DEBORAH A(NNE), graphic artist; b. Cin., Aug. 29, 1955; d. James Douglas and John Rae (Meyers) G.; m. Robert D. Ridgley. Student in design communiastions, Art Acad. Cin., 1974-78, Aix-en-Provence, France, 1976; BS, U. Cin., 1978. Graphic designer Sta. WCET-TV 48, Cin., 1978-81; art dir. Am. Med. Systems, Cin., 1982-84; owner, creative dir. Cin., 1984—; advt. mgr. Hillebrand Nursing Ctr., Cin., 1984—. Designer posters (awards 1978, 82, 87). Recipient T-Cup award Johnston Paper, Cin., 1987. Mem. Cin. Assn. Profl. Saleswomen, Art Acad. Alumni, Cin. Art Mus. Republican. Roman Catholic. Home: 8326 Wetherfield Ln Cincinnati OH 45236

GLAZE, LYNN FERGUSON, development consultant; b. Oakland, Calif., May 24, 1933; d. Kenneth Loveland and Constance May (Pedder) Ferguson; m. Harry Smith Glaze, Jr., July 3, 1957; children—Catherine, Charles Richard. B.A., Stanford U., 1955, M.A., 1966. Devel. dir. Greenwich Acad., Conn., 1982-84; devel. cons. Del. Learning Ctr., Brandywine Mus., Opera Del., Ctr. for Creative Arts, 1984-87; dir. devel. Am. Lung Assn. Del., Wilmington, 1987—. Pres. Darien-Norwalk YWCA, Conn., 1973-76; sec. Darien Republican Town com., Darien, 1974-79; dist. chmn. Darien Rep. Meeting, 1974-76; vestry St. Luke's Ch., Darien, 1979-82; justice of the peace, Darien, 1981-84; bd. dirs. Episc. Ch. Home, 1987; mem. Gov.'s Small Bus. Council, 1987; mem. Del. Rep. State Com., 1987—. Coro Found. fellow 1981. Mem. Nat. Soc. Fund Raising Execs. (Brandywine chpt.).

GLEASON, DEBORA RAE, research analyst; b. Canton, Ohio, Mar. 9, 1957; d. William Waymon and Mary Joan (Huffman) Fisher; m. David Gleason, June 20, 1980. BS in Agr., W.Va. U., 1979; postgrad., Cameron U., 1986—. Tech. editor Vinnell Corp., Lawton, Okla., 1982-85; research analyst LB&M Assocs., Lawton, 1985—. Author field manual on Pershing II; editor numerous mil. manuals. Served with U.S. Army, 1979-82, now capt. res. Mem. Res. Officers Assn. (life), Tau Beta Sigma (pres. Delta Beta chpt. 1977-78). Democrat. Roman Catholic. Home: PO Box 246 Medicine Park OK 73557 Office: LB&M Assocs 111 "C" Ave Suite 200 Lawton OK 73501

GLEASON, JEAN WILBUR, lawyer; b. St. Louis, Oct. 31, 1943; d. Ray Lyman and Martha (Bugbee) W.; m. Gerald Kermit Gleason, Aug. 28, 1966 (div. 1987); children—C. Blake, Peter Wilbur. B.A., Wellesley Coll., 1965; LL.B. cum laude, Harvard U., 1968. Bar: Calif. 1969, D.C. 1978. Assoc. Brobeck, Phleger & Harrison, San Francisco, 1969-72; spl. counsel to dir. div. corp. fin. SEC, 1972-76, assoc. dir. div. investment mgmt., 1976-78; of counsel Fulbright & Jaworski, Washington, 1978-80; ptnr. Fulbright & Jaworski, 1980—. Mem. ABA (chmn. subcom. on securities and banks, bus. sect.), D.C. Bar Assn. (chmn. steering com. bus. sect.), Fed. Bar Assn. (exec. council, securities com.), Am. Bar Retirement Assn. (bd. dirs.), Phi Beta Kappa. Home: 3411 Woodley Rd NW Washington DC 20016 Office: Fulbright & Jaworski 1150 Connecticut Ave NW Washington DC 20036

GLEGHORN, NANCY JANE, accountant; b. Memphis, Dec. 7, 1943; d. James R. and Mary A. (Hurst) Heflin; divorced; children: Robert S. Pelley, Tracy L. Pelley; m. Gordon A. Gleghorn. BBA, U. Okla., 1972. Internal auditor Hart Indsl. Supply Co., Oklahoma City, 1972-73, Internat. Environ. Mfg. Co., Oklahoma City, 1973; pres. Nancy J. Pelley, Inc., Moore, Okla., 1975—; speaker in field. Mem. adv. com. Moore-Norman (Okla.) Vo-Tech. Ctr., 1975-79, South Oklahoma City Jr. Coll., 1976-79. Mem. Am. Inst. CPA's, Okla. Soc. CPA's, Am. Women Soc. CPA's, Enlisted Assn. N.G. U.S. (treas. 1986—), Okla. Air N.G. Non-Commd. Officer Assn. (treas. 1984—), N.G. Assn. Okla., Nat. Assn. for Female Execs. Club: Toastmasters (Oklahoma City). Office: 526 SW 4th Moore OK 73160

GLEICH, CAROL SUE, health professions education executive; b. Kewanee, Ill., Jan. 18, 1935; d. Carl and Edna (Krause) Gleich; A.B., U. Iowa, 1958, M.S., 1967, Ph.D., 1972. Program dir. med. tech. program, asst. prof. dept. pathology U. Iowa, Iowa City, 1972-77; health manpower edn. officer Bur. Health Professions, Health Resources and Services Adminstrn., HHS, Rockville, Md., from 1977, now allied health cons. to Egypt; dir. Geriatric Edn. Ctrs. of PHS; adj. assoc. prof. U. Md. Sch. Medicine; mem. Iowa Health Manpower Com., 1976—; cons. U. Wis. System Acad. Affairs, 1976; panelist and participant workshops. Cert. clin. chemistry technologist, Nat. Registry Clin. Chemistry. Mem. Am. Soc. Allied Health Professions, Nat. Council for Internat. Health, Am. Soc. Clin. Pathologists (assoc.; cert. med. technologist; sec. ASCP Bd. Registry, 1975-77), Am. Soc. Med. Tech., D.C. Soc. Med. Tech. (Outstanding Med. Technologist of Yr. 1975), Beta Beta Beta, Alpha Mu Tau. Assoc. editor Am. Jour. Med. Tech., 1974-83, Jour. Allied Health, 1982-85; contbr. articles to profl. publs., papers to confs. Home: 14800 Rocking Spring Dr Rockville MD 20853 Office: Parklawn Bldg Room 4C-16 5600 Fishers Ln Rockville MD 20857

GLEITER, SYLVIA KAY, state agency administrator; b. Roseau, Minn., Mar. 26, 1942; d. Herman N. and Ella M. (Efshen) Fadness; m. Vernon W. Gleiter, Mar. 14, 1964; children: Kelly, Gina, Daniel. BE, U. Wis., Whitewater, 1970. Customer service rep. Wis. Dept. Transp., Madison, 1971-76, supr., 1976-83, tng. officer, 1983—. Founder Horn of Plenty Food Pantry, Rio, Wis., 1983—; planner, coordinator Sr. Citizen Activities, Rio, 1986—. Am. Bus. Women's Assn. Lutheran.

GLEN, BEVERLY RUTH, social service director; b. Windsor, Ont., Can., Sept. 20, 1940; d. Walter Arno and Eugenie Edith (Weinmann) Hensel; m. Todd Veazie Glen, Apr. 14, 1963 (div. 1983); children: Sean Tracy, Erin Colleen. BA, Middlebury Coll., 1962. Career counselor Yale U., New Haven, 1963-65; publicist, costume designer Fullerton (Calif.) Coll., 1973-83; adminstrv. asst. YWCA of North Orange County, Fullerton, 1983-85, exec. dir., 1985—; cons. Fullerton Coll. Dept. Theatre Arts, 1983—, Regional Theater Co., Fullerton, 1983—. Pres. Fullerton Coll. Faculty Wives, 1967-69; v.p. Fullerton Community Nursery, 1968-70, PTA Fullerton, 1971-73; judge F.C. High Sch. Theatre Festival, Fullerton, 1981—; v.p., bd. dirs. Regional Theatre Co., 1988-89; treas. So. Calif. Council YWCA. Mem. Nat. Assn. YWCA Exec. Dirs., So. Calif. Council YWCAs, Nat. Assn. Female Execs., United Way Chief Exec. Officer Roundtable. Democrat. Episcopalian. Lodge: Soroptimists Internat. Office: YWCA North Orange County 321 N Pomona Ave Fullerton CA 92632

GLENN, CLAUDIA RAE, sales executive; b. Covington, Ky., Aug. 25, 1953; d. Gail Barnett and Lorraine Adele (Issac) G. Student, No. Ky. U., 1974, 84. Computer operator Manual Arts Furniture, Cin., 1972-74; legal sec. Mechley & Mechley, Cin., 1974; sec. Pillsbury Co., Ft. Mitchell, Ky., 1974-76; mgr. data processing Scallan Supply, Cin., 1976-78; legal sec. Keating Muething & Klekamp, Cin., 1978-84; sales rep. Seibert Office Equipment, Newport, Ky., 1985; rep. sales Multi-Disc Computer, Newport, 1985-86, Oxford Chems., Atlanta, 1986—. Bd. dirs. Villages of Beechgrove, Independence, Ky., also mem. fin. com. Democrat. Methodist. Home: 4251-3 Berrywood Dr Independence KY 41051 Office: Oxford Chems Atlanta GA 30366

GLENN, DIANE JOHNSON, educator, consultant; b. Dunkirk, N.Y., July 12, 1942; d. Rexford Donald and Rosemary (Goggin) Johnson; divorced; 1 child, Rosemary. BS in Edn., Medaille Coll., 1968; MS in Edn., SUNY, Buffalo, 1971; EdD in Edn., Memphis State U., 1975. Tchr. Diocese Buffalo, 1963-68, Akron (N.Y.) Cen., 1968-71; elem. counselor Keystone Cen. Schs., Lock Haven, Pa., 1971-73; teaching asst. Memphis State U., 1973-75; coordinator counseling U. Tenn. Ctr. Health Scis., Memphis, 1975-76; coordinator human service program Herkimer (N.Y.) County Community Coll., 1976-78; dir. guidance Liverpool (N.Y.) Cen. Schs., 1978—; cons. U.S. Dept. Edn., Washington, 1986, N.Y. St. Edn. Dept., Albany, 1987. Contbr. articles to profl. jours. Bd. dirs. YMCA; mem. Onondaga City Task Force Persons Need Supervision, 1982-82, Syracuse, 1982-83, Sch. Agy. Linkage Com., 1983-84; exec. com. Herkimer County Council Soc. Concern, 1976-78. Scholar Fed. Republic Germany, 1986. Mem. N.Y. State Assn. Counseling Devel. (hon. life, pres. 1985-86, v.p. profl. relations 1980-81), Onondaga City Counselors Assn. (pres. 1978-80), Sch. Adminstrs. Assn., Am. Assn. Counseling Devel. Office: Liverpool Cen Schs 800 Fourth St Liverpool NY 13088

GLENN, JUDY CAROLE, nurse, naval officer; b. Birmingham, Ala., July 2, 1946; d. Talmadge William and Maude Elizabeth (Steading) G.; diploma in nursing Univ. Hosp., Birmingham, 1967; BSN, Samford U., 1975; MSN in Cardiovascular Nursing, U. Ala., Birmingham, 1978; postgrad. Calif. Coast U. Staff nurse Univ. Hosp., 1967-68; charge nurse CCU, Lloyd Noland Found., Fairfield, Ala., 1968-70; charge nurse Bessemer (Ala.) Carraway Med. Center, 1970-75, unit coordinator, 1975-76, cardiovascular clin. specialist, 1978-80; commd. lt. USNR, 1979; asst. charge nurse intermediate intensive care Naval Regional Med. Center, San Diego, 1981-83, staff nurse, charge nurse med. ward Naval Hosp., Long Beach, Calif., 1983-85; promoted to lt. comdr., 1984; chief nurse clin. investigation Naval Med. Research Unit 3, Cairo, 1985—; instr. CPR, corpsman cardiology course; mem. regional area CPR com. Ala. Heart Assn., 1979-80, CPR regional course coordinator, 1977-78. Camp nurse Assembly of God Ch., Montgomery, Ala., 1968, 77, 78; lectr. WHO/EMRO AIDS Tng. Workshop, Cairo, 1986-88. Recipient citation Ala. Heart Fund, 1975; USPHS Title II trainee, 1977-78. Mem. Am. Nurses Assn., Am. Heart Assn. (council on cardiovascular nursing), Am. Assn. Critical Care Nursing (tech. assistance panel 1978-79). Republican. Office: Naval Med Research Unit 3 Cairo FPO New York NY 09527

GLENN, KATHYRN IRENE, infosystems specialist; b. Santa Ana, Calif., May 13, 1952; d. Kenneth Elmer Glenn and Irene Mae (Jones) Cross. Key punch operator Master Computer, Indio, Calif., 1970-75; data input specialist Valley Meml. Hosp., Indio, 1975-77; key punch operator Indio Community Hosp., 1977-81; ops. staff Eisenhower Med. Ctr., Rancho Mirage, Calif., 1981-84; data processing mgr. John F. Kennedy Meml. Hosp., Indio, 1984—. Mem. Nat. Assn. Female Execs. Office: John F Kennedy Meml Hosp 47111 Monroe St Indio CA 92201

GLENN, LETSY JANE MUIR, banker; b. Houston, June 18, 1945; d. Samuel Ewing Bailey and Juanita Jean (Ohlman) M.; m. Steven Glenn, June 8, 1968 (div. Jan. 1973). BA in Econs., U. Denver, 1967; postgrad., U. Colo., Denver, 1974. From teller to mktg. dir. Colo. Fed. Savs. & Loan, Denver, 1967-76; mktg. dir. Golden (Co.) Savs., 1976-78; research analyst The Newport Group, Irvine, Calif., 1978-79; mgr. mktg. Hemet (Calif.) Savs. & Loan, 1979-82, br. adminstr., 1983—; instr. Arapahoe Community Coll., Denver, 1974, U. Calif., Riverside, 1986. Editor: Hemet United Way, 1985, 87. Chmn. Mayor's Com. for Arts, Riverside, 1979-81; dir. U. Calif. Fin. Edn. Bd., Riverside, 1986. Named Woman of Recognition, Riverside YWCA, 1986. Mem. Nat. Assn. Female Execs., Hemet C. of C., Riverside C. of C., Kappa Delta. Democrat. Episcopalian. Office: Hemet Fed Savs & Loan 445 E Florida Hemet CA 92343

GLENN, MARTHA ANN (MARTI), psychotherapist, educator; b. Brunswick, Ga., Sept. 11, 1946; d. Daniel Jackson and Eula Anne (Glenn) Pippin; m. Kenneth Earl Bruer; children: Tanis Anne, Richard Clark. AA, Hinds Jr. Coll., 1966; BA, U. Fla., 1975, M of Health Sci., 1976, PhD, 1982. Tchr. Vicksburg (Miss.) City Sch. Dist., 1969-72; instr. Santa Fe Community Coll., Gainesville, Fla., 1974-76, 80-82; dir. The Growing Ctr., College Station, Tex., 1976-79; adminstr., therapist Gestalt Inst., Gainesville, 1979-82; dean of students, prof. The Human Relations Inst., Santa Barbara, Calif., 1982—; pvt. practice psychotherapist Santa Barbara, 1982—. Fellow Mott Found., 1980. Mem. Assn. Humanistic Psychology, Am. Soc. for Tng. and Devel., Inst. Noetic Sci. Methodist. Office: Human Relations Inst 5200 Hollister Ave Santa Barbara CA 93111

GLENNON, DIANNE MARIE, infosystems specialist; b. Weymouth, Mass., Apr. 11, 1953; d. Paul William and Anna Mary (Carrara) G. BS in Civil Engring., MIT, 1976, MS in Mgmt., 1985. Civil engr. C. E. Maguire, Waltham, Mass., 1976-77, Bryant Assocs., Boston, 1977-80; sales engr. Boston Edison, 1980-83; microcomputer coordinator Citibank Internat., Miami, 1985-87; relationship mgr. Citicorp Real Estate Inc., Miami, 1988—. Fellow Am. Assn. Univ. Women, 1984. Home: 5005 Collins Ave #525 Miami Beach FL 33130

GLESS, SHARON, actress; b. Los Angeles. Student, Gonzaga U. Appeared in TV series Faraday and Company, 1973, Switch!, 1975-78, Turnabout, 1979, House Calls, 1981-82; star TV series Cagney and Lacey, 1982—(Emmy nomination 1983); appeared in TV miniseries The Immigrants, 1978, The Last Convertible, 1979; numerous other guest appearances in TV series; TV movies include All My Daughters, 1972, My Darling Daughters' Anniversary, 1973, Richie Brockelman: The Missing 24th Hours, 1976, The Islander, 1978, Crash, 1978, Hardhat and Legs, 1980, The Miracle of Kathy Miller, 1981, Letting Go, 1985; motion pictures include The Star Chamber, 1983. Recipient Emmy Award, 1986, 87 for best actress in a drama series (Cagney and Lacey). Office: care Creative Artists Agy Inc 1888 Century Park E Suite 1400 Los Angeles CA 90067

GLESSNER, DEBORAH IRENE, elementary education media specialist; b. Harrisburg, Pa., July 27, 1948; d. Clarence Francis and Dorothy Harriet (Zinszer) G. BS in Edn. and Library Sci., Shippensburg State U., 1970, MS in Communication, 1976. Librarian intermediate sch. Council Rock Sch. Dist., Richboro, Pa., 1970-77, elem. sch. librarian, media specialist, 1978—. Pres. Bucks County Services for Deaf and Hearing Impaired, Levittown, Pa., 1982-84, editor newsletter, 1980-84, bd. dirs., 1980-85. Recipient Qualified Rider award U.S. Dressage Fedn., 1987. Mem. Council Rock Sch. Dist. Edn. Assn., Pa. State Edn. Assn., Nat. Edn. Assn., Bucks County Sch. Librarians Assn., Pa. Sch. Librarians Assn., Eastern States Dressage and Combined Tng. Assn. (organizer ann. show 1985-86), Pi Delta Epsilon. Democrat. Presbyterian. Home: 77 Bustleton Pike Churchville PA 18966

GLICK, BETTY JANE, accountant; b. Carlisle, Pa., Sept. 15, 1935; d. Benjamin Burns and Margaret Irene (Brinkerhoff) Bailey; student pub. schs., Carlisle; m. Carl Samuel Glick, Jr., Sept. 4, 1953; children: Elizabeth Rose, Carl Samuel III (dec.), John Robert, William Joseph. Sec., Bedford Shoe Co. div. G.R. Kinney Co., Carlisle, 1953-54, bookkeeper, 1956-57, lacer pre-fit room, 1959; acct. M.G. Riley, C.P.A., Kenai, Alaska, 1966-82. Program chmn. Kenai PTA, 1968-69, pres., 1969-70; mem. Kenai Planning & Zoning Adv. Com., 1974-76, chmn., 1976; mem. Kenai City Council, 1976-83, vice mayor, 1979-82; mem. Kenai Peninsula Borough Assembly, 1982—, v.p., 1984-85, pres., 1985-86, 87; parliamentarian Kenai Peninsula Borough Planning and Zoning Com., 1976-77, vice chmn., 1977-81, chmn., 1981-82; workshop speaker Kenai Peninsula Community Coll., 1984-86. Treas., Jr. Achievement, Kenai, 1978-81, chmn., 1981-82, community co-ordinator, 1983-85; bd. dirs. Jr. Achievement Alaska, 1982-85; bd. dirs. Cook Inlet Council on Alcohol and Drug Abuse, 1983-85; chmn. steering com. for sheltered workshop/residential care facility for handicapped People Count, Inc., 1983-86; pres. Kenai Peninsula Caucus, Inc., 1986—. Named Citizen of Month, Kenai C. of C., 1977. Mem. Alaska Mcpl. League (dir. 1980—, 2d v.p. 1981-82, 1st v.p. 1982-83, pres. 1983-84), Nat. League Cities (small cities adv. council 1983-84), Nat. Assn. Counties (bd. dirs. western interstate region 1984-87, mem. pub. lands steering com. interstate region 1987—), Billiken Bus. and Profl. Women's Club (named Woman of Yr. 1978), LWV (parliamentarian Alaska ann. meeting 1983). Club: Cen. Peninsula Rep. Women's.

GLICK, CYNTHIA SUSAN, lawyer; b. Sturgis, Mich., Aug. 6, 1950; d. Elmer Joseph and Ruth Edna (McCally) G. A.B., Ind. U., 1972; J.D., Ind. U.-Inpls., 1978. Bar: Ind. 1978, U.S. Dist. Ct. (so. dist.) Ind. 1978, U.S. Dist. Ct. (no. dist.) Ind. 1981. Adminstrv. asst. Gov. Otis R. Bowen, Ind., 1973-76; law clk. Ind. Ct. Appeals, 1976-79; dep. pros. atty. 35th Jud. Cir., LaGrange County, Ind., 1980-82, pros. atty., 1983—. Campaign aide Ind. Rep. State Cen. Com., Indpls., 1972-73. Named Hon. Speaker, Ind. Ho. of Reps., 1972, Sagamore of the Wabash, Gov. Ind., 1974. Fellow Ind. Bar Found.; mem. ABA, Am. Judicature Soc., Ind. State Bar Assn., LaGrange County Bar Assn. (pres. 1983-86), DAR, Delta Zeta. Republican. Methodist. Lodge: Eastern Star. Home: 113 W Spring St LaGrange IN 46761 Office: Office of Prosecuting Atty LaGrange County Ct House LaGrange IN 46761

GLICK, DEBORAH KAREN, marketing professional; b. Liberty, N.J., Oct. 12, 1954; d. Stanley and Grete Bettina (Mueller) G.; m. Richard Dale Kirschner, Mar. 7, 1987. BS, SUNY, Albany, 1975; MBA, Columbia U., 1980; JD, N.Y. Law Sch., 1987. From sales mgr. to assoc. mdse. mgr. Macy's New York, N.Y.C., 1976-79; from mktg. assoc. to sr. prodn. mgr. Pfizer Inc., N.Y.C., 1980-86, group product mgr., 1986-88; dir. mktg. Schein Pharm. Inc., 1988—. Mem. Murray Hill com. N.Y.C. Mem. Healthcare Bus. Women's Assn., Advt. Women of N.Y., Am. Mktg. Assn., Am. Women's Econ. Devel. Corp. Democrat. Jewish. Home: 120 E 34th St Apt 16F New York NY 10016

GLICK, DEBORAH KELLY, accountant; b. Waterbury, Conn., Sept. 9, 1953; d. John Francis and Jeanne Doris (Weaving) Kelly; m. William Martin Glick Jr., June 30, 1973 (div. Oct. 1977); children: Kimberly, William III. BS, Post Coll., Waterbury, 1982. CPA, Conn. Staff acct. DeAngelis Lombardi & Kelly CPA's, Waterbury, 1981-82, John J. Baldelli, CPA, Naugatuck, Conn., 1982-84; ptnr. Baldelli Glick & Co. CPA's, Naugatuck, 1984—. Mem. Am. Inst. CPA's, Conn. Soc. CPA's, Nat. Soc. Pub. Accts., Nat. Soc. Exec. Females. Democrat. Roman Catholic. Office: Baldelli Glick & Co CPAs 35 Porter Ave Naugatuck CT 06770

GLICK, JUDITH MYRA, medical illustrator; b. Elizabeth, N.J., Oct. 3, 1947; d. Isadore and Doris (Schwartz) G. BS in Art Edn., Ohio State U., 1970; BS in Med. Art, Med. Coll. Ga., 1972, MS in Med. Art, 1973. Med. illustrator Ednl. Media Support Ctr., Boston, 1973-75; free-lance med. illustrator N.Y.C., 1975—. Mem. Soc. Illustrators, Assn. Med. Illustrators. Democrat. Jewish. Club: Pharm. Advt. Home and Office: 301 E 79th St 26-C New York NY 10021

GLICK, MARY, accountant; b. Cambridge, Mass., June 21, 1951; d. Jackand Evelyn (Sherer) D.; m. Mark Glick, Sept. 1, 1973; children—Herman, Jason. B.S., Boston U., 1973, M.B.A., 1974. C.P.A., N.Y. Supervising acct. Ernst & Whinney, N.Y.C., 1974-79; lectr. acctg. Marymount Manhattan Coll., N.Y.C., 1977; asst. prof. acctg. C.W. Post Center L.I. U., Greenvale, N.Y., 1979-80, Hofstra U., Hempstead, N.Y., 1980—; pvt. practice acctg., Roslyn, N.Y., 1979—. Mem. Am. Inst. C.P.A.s, N.Y. State Soc. C.P.A.s, Am. Womens Soc. C.P.A.s, Mensa.

GLICK, RUTH BURTNICK, author, lecturer; b. Lexington, Ky., Apr. 27, 1942; d. Lester Leon and Beverly (Miller) Burtnick; m. Norman Stanley Glick, June 30, 1963; children: Elissa, Ethan. BA, George Washington U., 1964; MA, U. Md., 1967. Author, 1973—; bd. dirs. Columbia Literary Assocs., Ellicott City, Md., 1981—; lectr. S.W. Writers Conf., Houston, 1984, Nebr. Writers' Guild, Omaha, 1985, Bouchercon, Balt., 1986, Triangle Romance and Fiction Writers' Conf., Raleigh, 1988. Author: (with Nancy Baggett) Dollhouse Furniture You Can Make, 1977, Dollhouse Lamps and Chandeliers, 1979, Soups On, 1985; (with Eileen Buckholtz, Carolyn Males and Louise Titchener) Love Is Elected, 1982 (named one of best romances 1982), Southern Persuasion, 1983; (with Titchener) In the Arms of Love, 1983 (Romance best seller list), Brian's Captive, 1983 (Romance best seller list), Reluctant Merger, 1983 (Romance best seller list), Summer Wine, 1984, Beginners Luck, 1984, Mistaken Image, 1985, Hopelessly Devoted, 1985, Summer Stars, 1985, Stolen Passion, 1986, Indiscreet, 1988; (with Baggett and Gloria Kaufer Greene) Don't Tell 'Em It's Good for 'em, 1984, Eat Your Vegetables!, 1985; (with Buckholtz) End of Illusion, 1984, Space Attack, 1984, Mission of the Secret Spy Squad, 1984, Mindbenders, 1984, Doomstalker, 1985, Captain Kid and the Pirates, 1985, The Cats of Castle Mountain, 1985, Logical Choice, 1986, Great Expectations, 1987, A Place in Your Heart, 1988, Saber Dance, 1988, Postmark, 1988; (Peregrine Connection series) Talons of the Falcon, 1986, Flight of the Raven, 1986, In Search of the Dove, 1986 (Lifetime Achievement award for Romantic series 1987); (not collaboration) Dollhouse Kitchen and Dining Room Accessories, 1979, Invasion of the Blue Lights, 1982, More Than Promises, 1985, The Closer We Get, 1988, also others; contbr. articles to profl. jours. U. Md. Am. studies fellow, 1964-65; recipient Lifetime Achivement award for romantic suspense series, 1987. Mem. Wash. Ind. Writers, Author's Guild, Romance Writers of Am. (lectr. Detroit 1984, Atlanta 1985, Dallas 1987), Wash. Romance Writers, Internat. Platform Assn.

GLICK-COLQUITT, KAREN LYNNE, college administrator; b. Bucyrus, Ohio, Sept. 2; d. Phillip Dole and Bernice Grace (Shasteen) Glick; B.S.J., Bowling Green State U., 1967, M.A., 1979; m. Michael Colquitt; children—M. Todd, K. Christine. Editor, Bowling Green (Ohio) State U., 1972-74; account exec. Howard E. Mitchell, Jr., Advt., Findlay, Ohio, 1974-77; asst. to dir. Student Devel. Program, Bowling Green State U., 1977-79; dir. pub. info. Bluffton (Ohio) Coll., 1980-83; asst. to v.p. for instl. advancement Findlay (Ohio) Coll., 1983-85; assoc. dir. devel. Bluffton Coll., 1985—. Mem.Council Advancement and Support of Edn., Internat. Assn. Bus. Communicators. Episcopalian. Club: Bowling Green U. Press (charter mem. 1983). Office: Bluffton Coll Bluffton OH 45817

GLICKENHAUS, SARAH BRODY, speech therapist; b. Mpls., Mar. 8, 1919; d. Morris and Ethel (Silin) Brody; B.S., U. Minn., 1940, M.S., 1945; m. Seth Morton Glickenhaus, Oct. 23, 1944; children—James Morris, Nancy Pier. Speech therapist, Davison Sch. Speech Correction, Atlanta, 1940-42; speech pathologist U. Minn., Mpls., 1945-46; speech therapist Queens Coll., N.Y.C., 1946-48; speech therapist VA, N.Y.C., 1949-50; pvt. practice, New Rochelle, N.Y., 1950-71; speech therapist Abbott Sch. United Free Sch. Dist. 13, Irvinton, N.Y., 1971—; tutor learning disabled children New Rochelle Public Schs., 1968-71. Mem. Am. Speech Hearing And Lang. Assn., N.Y. State Speech and Hearing Assn., Westchester Speech and Hearing Assn., AAAS. Club: Harvard (N.Y.C.). Jewish. Home and Office: 100 Dorchester Rd Scarsdale NY 10583

GLICKLICH, LUCILLE BARASH, physician, child psychiatrist; b. Fond du Lac, Wis., Jan. 10, 1926; d. Peter and Freda (Pevnick) Barash; m. Marvin Glicklich, Sept. 12, 1948 (div. Apr. 1983); children—Daniel, Anne, Peter, Lynn, Barry; m. John A. Rosenberg, Aug. 12, 1984. B.A., U. Wis.-Madison, 1947, M.D., 1950. Diplomate Am. Bd. Pediatrics, Am. Bd. Psychiatry and Neurology, Am. Bd. Child Psychiatry. Intern, Youngstown Hosp. Assn., Ohio, 1950-51; resident in pediatrics Milw. Children's Hosp., 1951-53, practice medicine specializing in psychiatry Marquette Med. Sch. Associated, Wis., 1967-69; child psychiatry fellow Marquette and Milw. Childrens Hosp., 1969-71; med. dir. children's div. Curative Workshop, Milw., 1959-63, Easter Seals Child Devel. program, 1963-67; chief med. cons. Milw. Pub. Schs., 1964-67; asst. prof. pediatrics Med. Coll. U. Wis., Milw., 1965-85, assoc. clin. prof., 1985—, asst. prof. psychiatry, 1971-85; dir. liaison psychiatry Milw. Children's Hosp., 1975-85; dir. Child-Family Psychiatry Program, assoc. prof., vice chmn. dept. psychiatry U. Wis. Med. Sch., Milw. Clin. Campus, 1985—; hosp. staff appointments Milw. Children's Hosp., Milw. Psychiatric Hosp., Milw. County Med. Comples, Mt. Sinai Med. Ctr.; lectr. various colls. and univs.; cons. in field. Contbr. articles to profl. publs. Active mem. N'Shei group, Jewish Parenting, Communication for the 80's; Jewish Fedn. Women's div., Milw. Childrens Hosp. Jr. Aux. Target M.D. program U. Wis., Milw., 1981, congl. Emmanuel Yom Hashoah, 1982, Milw. Neonatal Nursing Consortium, Marquette U. panel Survivors of Holocaust, 1984; bd. dir. Milw. Bd. of Jewish Edn. Bd., 1971-78, pres. 1974-76, Milw. Jewish Fedn., 1977—; bd. trustees Congl. Beth Israel, 1975-77, youth commn. 1971-77; mem. Kesher Jewish Woman's network; mem. task force on teen pregnancies Planned Parenthood, 1984. Fellow Am. Acad. Child Psychiatry, Am. Psychiat. Assn., Am. Acad. Pediatrics (Wis. Br.); mem. Am. Soc. Adolescent Psychiatry, Wis. Council Adolescent and Child Psychiatry (sec. 1981-82, pres.-elect 1982-83, pres. 1983-85), Am. Orthopsychiatric Assn., Milw. Pediatric Soc., Soc. Adolescent Medicine, AMA, Wis. State Med. Soc. (del. 1978—, bd. dirs. 1985—, reference com. 1982—), Milw. County Med. Soc. (sec. treas. 1981, pres.-elect 1984, pres. 1985), Am. Med. Women's Assn. (Southeastern Wis. chpt. vice-dir. 1977-79), Women in Medicine in Wis. (bd. dirs. 1979-82, pres. 1979-80), Wis. Council Child and Adolescent Psychiatry (pres. 1984-86). Avocations: travel; bicycling; racquetball; walking; reading. Home: 3431 N Lake Dr Milwaukee WI 53211 office: Mt Sinai Med Ctr 950 N 12th St PO Box 342 Milwaukee WI 53201

GLICKMAN, LAURA LEE, lawyer; b. Bklyn., Apr. 26, 1946; d. Daniel Bernard and Miriam K. (Friedman) Glickman; A.B. with honors, UCLA, 1967, J.D., 1970; m. James D. Leewong, Feb. 18, 1979; children—Andrea Jane, Hilary Anne. Bar: Calif. U.S. Supreme Ct., U.S. Ct. Appeals, U.S. Dist. Ct. Practiced in Pacoima, Calif., 1971-72, Los Angeles, 1972—; staff atty. San Fernando Valley Neighborhood Legal Services, Inc., Pacoima, 1971-72, directing atty., 1972; clin. supervising atty. Legal Aid Found. Los Angeles, 1972-74; adj. clin. prof. Loyola U. Sch. Law, Los Angeles, 1972-74. Chmn. young profl. leadership group Jewish Fedn. Council Greater Los Angeles, 1977-78, also mem. community relations com., 1978, leadership devel. com., 1978; referee bd. retirement Los Angeles County Employees Retirement Assn., 1975—. Recipient Bancroft-Whitney award, 1968, Appellate Advocacy award UCLA Law Sch., 1970. Mem. State Bar Calif., Los Angeles County Bar Assn., Women Lawyers Assn. Los Angeles, UCLA Law Alumni Assn. (dean's counsel), Calif. Women Lawyers Assn. Office: 911 Wilshire Blvd Suite 1070 Los Angeles CA 90017

GLINER, GAIL STECKEL, educator; b. Los Angeles, Mar. 13, 1944; d. Morris Leo Steckel and Lucille (Yellin) Caplan; m. Jeffrey Alan Gliner, June 19, 1966; children: Keith, Melissa. BA, U. Calif., 1965; MA, Bowling Green (Ohio) State U., 1968; PhD, U. Calif., 1980. Cert. secondary tchr. Calif. Research asst. in statistics Rand Research Corp., Santa Monica, Calif., 1965; tchr. in math. Findlay (Ohio) High Sch., 1966-67; instr. in math. Bowling Green (Ohio) State U., 1968-71; tchr. in math., sci. Bishop High Sch., Santa Barbara, Calif., 1972-74; statistician Applied Magnetics Corp., Santa Barbara, Calif., 1974-75; math instr. U. Calif. Student Spl. Services, Santa Barbara, Calif., 1975-77; lectr. U. Calif., Santa Barbara, Calif., 1978-81; statistical analyst Colo. State U., Ft. Collins, 1981-82; assoc. prof. Met. State Coll., Denver, 1982—; teaching asst. Bowling Green State U., 1967-68; instr. Santa Barbara City Coll., 1975-77; research asst. U. Calif. Santa Barbara, 1979-80, postgrad. research assoc., 1980. Contbr. articles to profl. jours. Mem. Math. Assn. Am., Am. Statis. Assn., Nat. Council Tchrs. of Math., Am. Ednl. Research Assn., Sch. Sci. and Math., Kappa Mu Epsilon. Office: Met State Coll 1006 Eleventh St Denver CO 80204

GLOGAU, LILLIAN FLATOW FLETCHER, educational adminstrator; b. N.Y.C., Feb. 15, 1925; d. Henry and Diana (Heller) Flatow; m. Jerome N. Glogau, Nov. 20, 1963; children: Jordan, Laurence, Alexander. BA cum laude, Bklyn. Coll., 1946; MA, Columbia U., 1949; EdD, CUNY, 1969. Tchr. N.Y.C. Sch. System, 1946-49; tchr. Plainview (N.Y.) Schs., 1959-61, adminstr., 1961-66; prin. Spring Valley (N.Y.) Schs., 1966-87; sole cons. Lillian Glogau Assocs., Ltd., Nanuet, N.J., 1987—; pres. Pragmatix Corp., S. Orange, N.J., lectr., cons. in field. Author: Nongraded Primary, 1967, You and N.Y. City, 1970, Let's See, 1971, The Elementary School Media Center, 1972; contbr. articles to profl. jours. Recipient Founders Day award CUNY, 1970, award of excellence County of Rockland, 1986, cert. appreciation 22nd Congl. Dist. N.Y., 1986, cert. achievement Town of Ramapo, 1986, cert. merit N.Y. State Senate 38th Dist., 1986, cert. appreciation House of Reps. Congress, Washington. Mem. PTA (life), Am. Assn. Sch. Adminstrs. (recipient cert. merit 1986), Am. Soc. Curriculum Devel., N.Y. State Sch. Adminstrs. Assn., Kappa Delta Pi, Pi Lambda Theta. Home: 19B Winthrop Rd Jamesburg NJ 08831

GLOGOWSKI, PATRICIA CAROL, real estate company executive; b. Rahway, N.J., Dec. 22, 1942; d. Bernard Anthony and Helen (Sisco) Duff; m. John Peter Glogowski, Dec. 2, 1961 (div. Feb. 1976); children: John J., Michael D. Student, Drake's Bus. Coll., 1962, Kean Coll., 1975. Lic. broker, N.J. Freelance real estate saleswoman/broker Kenilworth, N.J., 1971-77; owner, mgr., broker Happy Homes Realty, Kenilworth, 1977-83; broker, Union county dir. Berg Realtors, Clark, N.J., 1983-85; dist. mgr. Berg Realtors/ First Metro Comml., Clark, 1985-86; broker, comml. and investment mgr. Berg Realtors/ First Metro Comml., South Plainfield, N.J., 1985-86; owner, mgr., broker Glowgowski Realty, Inc., Kenilworth, 1986—. Active Boy Scouts Am., 1975-78. Recipient Realtor of Yr. award, 1983, Real Estate award of Merit Suburban News, 1986. Mem. N.J. Assn. Realtors (polit actions com 1986-88, Made Am. Better award 1980, 83, Pres.'s Excellence award 1987), Greater Eastern Union County Bd Realtors (1st v.p. 1985-86, pres. 1986-87, congl. coordinator 1987-88, Outstanding Leadership award 1980). Club: Plainfield Ski (sec. 1983-84). Home: 29 Tisbury Ct Scotch Plains NJ 07076 Office: 342 E Westfield Ave Roselle Park NJ 07204

GLOSHEN, DONNA RAE, educational business manager; b. Omaha, Aug. 3, 1938; d. Joseph Paul and Lucille Brown Millen; m. James Milton Gloshen, Apr. 16, 1966; children: Linda Marie, Sandra Kay, Cheryl Lynn. BSBA, U. Nebr., Omaha, 1983; MBA, U. Nebr., Lincoln, 1985. Acct. Siouxland Dressed Beef, Fargo, N.D., 1960-66; corp. acct., office mgr. Western Med. Enterprises, Hayward, Calif., 1969-72; gen. acctg. mgr. Acurex Corp., Sunnyvale, Calif., 1972-74; bus. mgr. Ednl. Service Unit #3, Omaha, 1974—; bd. trustees Nebr. Liquid Asset Fund Plus. Bd. dirs. Candlewood Homeowners Assn., 1974-79, treas. 1974-77, pres. 1979; active United Way, Jr. Achievement, Girl Scouts Am. Mem. Assn. Sch. Bus. Officials Internat. (dir. 1983-86, v.p. 1987, pres. elect 1988), Nebr. Assn. Sch. Bus. Officials (pres. elect 1981, pres. 1982), Nebr. Council Sch. Adminstrs. (bd. mem 1981-83, chmn. 1982). Club: Nebr. Balloon (pres. 1980). Home: 4725 S 184 Plaza Omaha NE 68135 Office: Ednl Service Unit #3 4224 S 133 St Omaha NE 68137

GLOSSER, ELIZABETH BARBARA, recruitment corporation executive; b. Plymouth, Pa., June 25, 1939; d. Charles B. and Elizabeth (Ruddy) G.; B.A., Coll. Misericorida, Dallas, Pa., 1961; M.Ed. (NDEA fellow), Rutgers U., 1965; M.B.A., Fairleigh Dickinson U., 1978. Tchr., Neptune High Sch., N.J., 1961-64; counselor, Westwood, N.J., 1965-69; tchr., River Dell, N.J., 1969-71; mgr. sales adminstrn. Xerox Corp., 1972-73, cons., 1971-72, product mgr., 1972, sales mgr., 1973-79; asst. prof. bus. and econs. Marymount Coll., Tarrytown, N.Y., also pres. Women at Work, 1979-81; mng. dir. The Exec. Exchange, Englewood Cliffs, N.J., 1981—; sec.-treas. Exec. Registry, Hackensack, N.J., 1983—; pres. Exec. Alternatives, Manasquan, N.J., 1986—. Fund raiser Multiple Sclerosis Soc., Am. Cancer Soc.; pres. Bergen County Friends of R.S.V.P., also trustee. Roman Catholic. Author: Moments Matter, 1977. Home: 17 Lincoln Ave Avon By The Sea NJ 07717 Office: 560 Sylvan Ave Englewood Cliffs NJ 07632

GLOVER, KAREN MARIE, engineer; b. Randolph, Nebr., July 15, 1955; d. Robert E. and Helen (Marano) R.; children: Robert, Denise. BS in Engring., U. Nebr., Omaha, 1979. Tech. rep. Xerox Corp., Omaha, 1977-79; distbn. engr. Northwestern Bell, Omaha, 1979-81, regulatory engr., 1981-82, market supervisor, 1982-86, product evaluation, telecommunications equipment inspector, 1987, network planning engr., 1987—. Mentor Vision of Hope, Omaha, 1987—. Mem. NOW, U.S. West Women (pub. relations mgr. 1987—), Soc. Women Engrs. Office: Northwestern Bell 1314 DOTM Room 920 Omaha NE 68102

GLOVER, LAURICE WHITE, psychoanalyst, musician; b. Los Angeles, Oct. 15, 1930; d. Lawrence Francis and Alice Violet (King) White; B.A., Occidental Coll., 1951; M.S. in Social Work, Columbia U., 1956; cert. in psychoanalysis and psychotherapy Postgrad. Ctr. Mental Health, N.Y.C., 1971, cert. in supervision of psychoanalysis, 1975; student pipe organ Norman Wright, Robert Owen, Virgil Fox; m. Norman James Glover, Aug. 18, 1956 (div. 1963), remarried, 1983; stepchildren—Valerie Scott, Norman James, Susan Charlotte, John Thomas. Pvt. practice psychoanalysis, N.Y.C., 1968—; faculty and sr. supr. psychoanalysis Postgrad. Ctr. Mental Health, N.Y.C., 1976—, asst. dean of tng., 1982—, tng. analyst, 1985—; asst. clin. prof. psychiatry Albert Einstein Coll. Medicine, Yeshiva, U., N.Y.C., 1975—; adj. asst. prof. psychology Bronx Community Coll., 1974; tng. analyst Nat. Psychol. Assn. for Psychoanalysis, 1974-76; psychoanalysis faculty Nat. Inst. Psychotherapies, 1978—; faculty, sr. supr. psychoanalysis, tng. analyst Tng. Inst. Mental Health Practitioners, 1979-84. Organist, choir dir. Throggs' Neck Lutheran Ch., Bronx, N.Y., 1964-67; jazz organist Hotel Barbizon for Women, 1965-66; organist, choir dir. 4th Ave. Meth. Ch., Bklyn., 1967—74. Mem. Soc. Clin. Social Workers, Nat. Assn. Social Workers, Am. Group Psychotherapy Assn., Am. Guild Organists, Am. Theatre Organists Soc., Am. Fedn. Musicians. Contbr. articles to profl. publs. Office: 271 Central Park W New York NY 10024

GLOVER, MARY KATHRYN, auditor; b. Amarillo, Tex., July 20, 1957; d. James Thomas and Ruby Fay (Upton) Croxson; m. Thomas Edwin Glover, May 14, 1975; Derek Hamilton, Alexander Hamilton. Student, N.M. State U., 1981-82. Acctg. tech. Fin. Mgt. Br. APO, N.Y.C., 1978-80; full charge bookkeeper J&J Investments, Ltd, Alamogordo, N.M., 1981-83; income auditor Sheraton Anchorage (Alaska), 1984—. Participant Walk for Mankind, Wichita, Kans., 1972-73; vol. Multiple Sclerosis Soc., Anchorage, 1985; mem. Ladies Retreat Com., Anchorage, 1986-87; donor Blood Bank of Alaska, Anchorage, 1985—; Sunday Sch. helper Ch. of Christ, Anchorage, 1985-87. Republican. Home: 4660 Reka #D23 Anchorage AK 99508 Office: Sheraton Anchorage 401 E 6th Ave Anchorage AK 99501

GLOVER, PEGGY DORIS, library director; b. Vancouver, Wash., Oct. 5, 1931; d. Verne and Doris (Hodge) Neal; m. Richard G., Jan. 2, 1960. BA in English, Pomona Coll., 1953; MLS, Carnegie Inst. Tech., Pitts., 1954. Librarian Enoch Pratt Free Library, Balt., 1954-56; base librarian U.S. Air Force, Eng., Fed. Republic Germany, 1956-60; librarian I and II Free Library, Phila., 1960-61, head community services, 1965-70, coordinator, 1970-85, dep. dir., 1985—; head librarian tech. data div. Def. Indsl. Supply Ctr., Phila., 1961-65. Author: Library Services for the Woman in the Middle, 1985; contbr. articles to profl. jours. Mem. Am. Library Assn., Pa. Library Assn. Democrat. Office: The Free Library of Phila Logan Square Philadelphia PA 19103

GLOVER, RITA ANNE, communications consultant; b. Manhattan, Kans., Nov. 11, 1951; d. Gordon Wakeman and Margaret Evelyn (Oehrle) G.; m. Charles Edward Peterson, Mar. 23, 1973 (div. Oct. 1982). B of Music, Wichita State U., 1973. Adminstrv. asst. MIT Genetic Toxicology Lab., Cambridge, Mass., 1976-79; exec. sec. MIT Science, Tech. and Society Program, Cambridge, 1979-81; trainer, tech. writer Racal-Redac, Inc., Westford, Mass., 1983-85; tech. writer Cullinet Inc., Westwood, Mass., 1985-86; exec. dir. Music for People, Litchfield, Conn., 1986; communications cons. Atex, Inc., Bedford, Mass., 1986-87; sr. tech. writer SILC Techs., Burlington, Mass., 1988—; bd. dirs. Music for People Found., Litchfield, 1986-87. Democrat.

GLOVIAK-FERRY, KRISTIN, designer; b. Chgo., May 31, 1949; d. John James and Rose Elizabeth (Greglak) Gloviak; m. Stephen Robertson Ferry, Feb. 12, 1983; children: John Anthony Ferry, Chloé Elizabeth Ferry. BFA, Kans. City Art Inst., 1971. Designer Source, Inc., Chgo., 1972-75; dir. art Woman Mag., Chgo., 1975-76, Foote, Cone & Belding, Chgo., 1977-78; pres. research and devel. Glo Apparel Inc., Los Angeles, 1980—; Gloviak Apparel designer label Lou Falcone Design, Inc., Los Angeles, 1979-84; computer apparel input operator Barco of Calif., Gardena, 1981-82; computer operator Cole of Calif., Los Angeles, 1984-86; instr. apparel design Los Angeles Trade Tech. Coll., 1986—; founder, pres. Glo Apparel, Inc.; vis. artist, lectr. Kansas City (Mo.) Art Inst., 1981. Designer: Chgo. '75 Exhibit, 1975, R.I. Coll., 1976, Art Dirs. Club of Los Angeles, 1981; inventor automatic measurement applied to apparel fit. Home: 12324 Allin St Culver City CA 90230

GLOWACKI, JO ELAINE, retail executive, consultant; b. Toledo, Nov. 3, 1948; d. David Lloyd George and Hazel Olive (Kidd) Swartzlander; m. David Paul Glowacki, May 27, 1967; 1 child, Jason David. BA in Bus., Siena Heights Coll., 1986. Teller Sylvania (Ohio) Bank, 1966-67; clk. Social Security Adminstrn., Toledo, 1967-70; v.p. Glow Industries Inc., Toledo, 1974—; bus. specialist Glowacki, Everhardt & Assocs., Toledo, 1987—; instr. Penta County Adult Edn., Perrysburg, Ohio, 1984-86; mem. adv. bd. div. bus. Lourdes Coll., Sylvania, 1986-87. Bd. dirs. Toledo ARC, 1986-87. Named Women's Bus. Advocate, SBA, 1986; Carl Perkins grantee, 1986. Mem. Am. Soc. Tng. and Devel., Nat. Assn. Women Bus. Owners, Toledo Area Small Bus. Assn. (bd. dirs. 1986-87), Toledo Area C. of C. Democrat. Lodge: Zonta. Office: Glowacki Everhardt & Assocs 245 N Huron #818 Toledo OH 43604

GLOWITZ, CHARLINE SILVIA, educational management consultant; b. N.Y.C., Oct. 8, 1951; d. Solomon Jacob and Claire Sara (Liker) G. Qualified dir. N.Y. State Edn. Dept. Human resources adminstr. Tech. Career Insts. (formerly RCA Insts.), N.Y.C., 1974-79; exec. dir. N.Y. State Assn. of Career Schs., N.Y.C., 1979-86; pvt. practice ednl. mgmt. consulting, N.Y.C., 1986—. Recipient Outstanding Achievement award N.Y. State Assn. Career Schs., 1985. Mem. Am. Soc. Assn. Execs., N.Y. Soc. Assn. Execs., Nat. Assn. Female Execs., N.Y.C. C. of C., Alpha Beta Kappa. Home: 175 W 87th St New York NY 10024

GLUCK, DORIS HEFFER, mathematics educator; b. June 15, 1938; m. Herman R. Gluck; children: Mark, Roberta. BA in Math., NYU, 1959; postgrad. in math., U. Pa., 1969-70; MA in Math., Temple U., Phila., 1971. Cert. elem. tchr., secondary math. tchr., elem. supr. Tchr. math. East Brunswick (N.J.) Sch. Dist., 1959-60, Haverford (Pa.) Sch. Dist., 1966-67; lower sch. math. coordinator The Agnes Irwin Sch., Rosemont, Pa., 1973-76; secondary math. tchr. Overbrook Sch. for the Blind, Phila., 1976-77; elem. tchr. Radnor Twp. Sch. Dist., Wayne, Pa., 1977-84, chpt. 1 math. specialist, 1984—, instr. computer inservice program, 1984-85, chair math. curriculum com., 1984-86; instr. pre-freshman program U. Pa., Phila., August, 1982-85; instr. Delaware County Intermediate Unit, 1987; lectr. in field. Mem. NEA, Nat. Council Tchrs. Math., Pa. Council Tchrs. Math., Assn. Tchrs. Math. in Phila. and Vicinity, Radnor Township Edn. Assn. (chair class size com. 1982-83, bldg. rep. 1982-84, mem. instrn. and profession devel. com. 1978—, scholarship com. 1986—), Assn. for Supervision and Curriculum Devel., Phi Delta Kappa. Office: Radnor Twp Sch Dist 681 S Wayne Ave Wayne PA 19087

GLÜCK, LOUISE ELISABETH, poet; b. N.Y.C., Apr. 22, 1943; d. Daniel and Beatrice (Grosby) G.; m. Charles Hertz (div.); 1 child, Noah Benjamin; m. John Dranow, 1977. Student, Sarah Lawrence Coll., 1962, Columbia U., 1963-65. Vis. poet Goddard Coll., U. N.C., U. Va., U. Iowa; Elliston prof. U. Cin., 1978; vis. faculty Columbia U., 1979; faculty M.F.A. program Goddard Coll., also Warren Wilson Coll., Swannanoa, N.C.; Holloway lectr. U. Calif., Berkeley, 1982; vis. prof. U. Calif.-Davis, 1983; Scott prof. poetry Williams Coll., 1983, faculty, 1984—; Regents prof. UCLA, 1985-87. Author: Firstborn, 1968, The House On Marshland, 1975, Descending Figure, 1980, The Triumph of Achilles, 1985. Recipient Lit. award Am. Acad. and Inst. Arts and Letters, 1981, Nat. Book Critics Circle award in poetry, 1985, Melville Cane award Poetry Soc. Am., 1986, Sara Teasdale Meml. prize Wellesley Coll., 1986; grantee Rockefeller Found., NEA, 1969-70, 79-80, 88—, Guggenheim Found., 1975-76, 87-88.

GLUECK, SYLVIA BLUMENFELD, writer; b. Tulsa, Dec. 23, 1925; d. Maurice and Sina (Turk) Blumenfeld; m. Norton Shushan Glueck, June 15, 1947; children: Nancy Eisen, Milton Glueck. BJ, U. Mo., Columbia, 1949. Publicity dir. Sta. WDSU, New Orleans, 1946-47; advt. copywriter Swiftway Direct Mail, New Orleans, 1961; freelance writer and author New Orleans and San Antonio, 1965—. Author mag. articles and newspaper features, 1984-85, (Golden Pro award 1986). Mem. Women in Communication, Austin Writers Guild, San Antonio Writers Guild (publicity chmn.), Alamo Writers, San Antonio Profl. Writers Group, Mensa, Am. Assn. Univ. Women. Home and Office: 309 W Magnolia #1 San Antonio TX 78212

GLYNN (MASTERSON), CARLIN, actress; b. Cleve., Feb. 19, 1940; d. Guillford Cresse and Lois Carlin Wilks) G.; m. Peter Masterson, Dec. 29, 1960; children: Carlin Alexandra, Mary Stuart, Peter C.B. Student Sophie Newcomb Coll., 1957-58. Appeared in broadway plays Best Little Whorehouse in Texas, 1978-82 (Tony award best featured actress mus.); appeared in off-broadway plays Winter Play, 1983, Alterations, 1984, Outside WACO, 1985, starring role Pal Joey, Goodman Theater, Chgo., 1988; films include Sixteen Candles, 1984, Three Days of the Condor, 1974, Continental Divide, 1980, The Trip to Bountiful, 1985, Blood Red, 1987; actress, resource dir. Sundance Inst., 1983-85; numerous appearances on T.V. including Mr. President; Founder, exec. dir. Citizens Action Fund, N.Y.C., 1974-75; bd. dirs. Consumer Action NOW, N.Y.C., 1970-80. Recipient Theatre World award, 1978, Lawrence Olivier award, 1981. Mem. Actors Studio, Screens Actors Guild, Actors Equity Assn., AFTRA. Episcopalian.

GLYSH, ELIZABETH ANN, management consultant; b. St. Petersburg, Fla., May 10, 1937; d. Robert Jurey Ingles and Mildred Marcella Whitaker. BA, Alverno Coll., 1958; MA, U. Oreg., 1967, PhD, 1972. Tchr. Bergan High Sch., Fremont, Nebr., 1961-64; with Alverno Coll., Milwaukee, 1964-74; dir. community services Sch. Sisters of St. Francis, Milwaukee, 1974-77; tchr. Alvernia High Sch., Chgo., 1958-61, prin., 1977-79; dir. Glysh and Assocs., Chgo., 1979—; bd. dirs. LaFarge Lifelong Learning Inst., Milwaukee, 1975-77, Womanspace, Rockford, Ill., 1977-79; trustee Alverno Coll., Milwaukee, 1970-74. Author, editor of numerous tech. writings, 1970-79. Grantee Nat. Sci. Found., 1960-70, Ford Found., 1973, Higher Edn. Act Title I, 1970-74, HEW Pub. Health Service, 1970-75. Mem. Alverno Alumni Assn. (pres. 1976-77), Sch. Sisters of St. Francis. Roman Catholic. Office: Glysh & Assocs PO Box 25730 Chicago IL 60625

GNADT, JOAN THERESE HARNEY, cardiologist, educator; b. Milw., July 20, 1949; d. Thomas Holland and Rose Caroline (Kriege) Harney; m.

Gregory James Gnadt, June 25, 1971; children: Geoffrey James, Victoria Rose. Student, Marquette U., 1967-68; BS in Zoology, U. Wis., Milw., 1971; MD, Med. Coll. Wis., 1976. Intern Martinez (Calif.) VA Med. Ctr., 1977-78, resident in internal medicine, 1978-80, fellow in cardiology, 1980-82, staff in cardiology, 1982, acting asst. chief cardiology, 1982-87, dir. geriatrics/gerontology; asst. clin. prof. medicine U. Calif., Davis, 1982-87. Fellow Am. Coll. Cardiology, ACP; mem. Gerontologic Soc. Am., Am. Med. Women's Assn. Roman Catholic. Home: 2617 N Wahl Ave Milwaukee WI 53211 Office: 1218 W Kilbourn Ave Suite 207 Milwaukee WI 53233

GNIADEK, CHERYL LYNN, financial accountant; b. Chgo., Feb. 21, 1947; d. Theodore Edward and Elsie Amelia (Grasmick) Whiffen; m. Richard Lawrence Gniadek, Nov. 15, 1969 (dec. Feb. 1979). BSBA, Ill. State U., 1969. Prodn. sec. Universal Tng. Systems, Lincolnwood, Ill., 1969-71; exec. sec. Alliance Am. Insurers, Chgo., 1971-78; temp. sec. Kelly Services, Grand Rapids, Mich., 1978-79; sec. Honeywell, Inc., Grand Rapids, 1979-80, sales corr., 1980-81; adminstr. customer quality Honeywell, Inc., Ft. Washington, 1981-84; rep. customer service Honeywell, Inc., Valley Forge, Pa., 1984-88; fin. acct. 1987—. Mem. Am. Bus. Women's Assn. (New Directions Charter chpt., pres. 1986, Woman of Yr. 1985), Instrument Soc. Am. (treas. edn. com. Phila. sect.), Nat. Assn. Female Execs. Democrat. Roman Catholic. Home: 857 Thoreau Ct Warminster PA 18974 Office: Honeywell Inc 1100 Virginia Dr Fort Washington PA 19034

GNOZZO, NANCY ANN, sales executive; b. Buffalo, Sept. 29, 1945; d. George and Lucille Mary (Lorenzo) Miserantino; m. Joseph Daniel Gnozzo, May 28, 1966 (div.); children: Jamie, Steven. BS, SUNY, Buffalo, 1967. Tchr. Bd. Coop. Ednl. Services, Umsville, N.Y., 1971-72; dir. Barbizon Sch. Modeling Services, Buffalo, 1978-80; account exec. Sta. WPhD, Buffalo, 1980-82; account exec., regional mgr. Sta. WHTT, Buffalo, 1982—; voice talent coordinator free lance, Buffalo, 1978-88. Mem. Am. Women in Radio and TV, Nat. Assn. Female Execs. Office: Sta WHTT Buffalo Hilton Hotel Church and Terrace Sts Buffalo NY 14202

GO, SIAN TJING, hematologist; b. Amsterdam, Netherlands, Sept. 6, 1950; came to U.S., 1966, naturalized, 1971; d. Gam Ping and Olga Martha (Oostveen) Go. B.S. with honors in Biophysics, U. Calif.-Berkeley, 1972; M.D., U. Calif.-Davis, 1976; postdoctoral scholar, intern, resident in med. oncology, U. Calif.-San Francisco, 1977-78; honor baccalaureate U. Calif.-Berkeley, 1970-72. Resident in internal medicine N.Y. Infirmary-Beekman Hosp., 1980-81, Rockefeller U. Hosp. & Clinic, N.Y.C., 1981-83; hematology-oncology fellow Meml. Sloan-Kettering Cancer Ctr., 1981-83; fellow Am. Cancer Soc.; staff attending physician Rockefeller U., N.Y.C., 1981-83; biochemistry-hematology fellow Harvard U., Cambridge, 1983—, Brigham Hosp., 1984-87, Mass. Gen. Hosp., Boston, 1984-87; clin. instr. in medicine U. Calif.-San Francisco, 1978-80. Editor: Chinese Character Dictionary, 1984. Mem. Nora Lam Evang. Ministries. Mem. Am. Soc. Internal Medicine. Home: 105 Charles St Suite 410 Boston MA 02114 Office: 23 Edward T Sullivan Rd #3 Cambridge MA 02138

GOBAR, GAIL TAMARA, nurse; b. Bronx, N.Y., Nov. 4, 1940; d. Jack Arthur and Anne (Schussler) Ossin; m. Seymour Gobar, June 11, 1936; children: Bonnie Deborah, Tammy Dana. RN, N.y. Med. Coll. and Flower and Fifth Ave. Hosp., 1961; EdD (hon.), Rhyme U., Buffalo, 1985. Head nurse of cardiology Flower and Fifth Ave. Hosp., N.Y.C., 1961-62; head nurse, supr. Jersey Shore Med. Ctr., Neptune, N.J., 1962-65; surg. asst. Dr. M. Levbarg DDS, Bricktown, N.J., 1978-80; adminstr. for handicapped programming Family YMCA's of Ocean County, Lakewood, N.Y., 1981-87; also bd. dirs. Family YMCA's of Ocean County; freelance writer Penfield, N.Y., 1987—; part-time nurse Jersey Shore Med. Ctr., Neptune, 1967-70; part-time staff nurse Medictr. of Am., Lakewood, 1968-70; govs. appointe Juvenile Alcohol Prevention Adv. Bd., Ocean County, 1982-84. Contbr. articles to local weekly newspaper, Ocean County, 1978-81. Mem. Lakewood Bd. Edn., Ocean County Bd. of Elections, 1978-83; pres. coordinator Parents Against Forced Busing, Lakewood, 1972-75; troop leader Ocean County Girl Scouts, Lakewood, 1972-77; coordinator Pop Warner Girls Activities, Lakewood, 1975-80. Recipient Ocean County Girl Scouts Hidden Heroine award, 1976, Assistance to Handicapped award N.J. Dept. of Human Services, 1984. Mem. N.J. SCh. Bds. Assn. Republican. Jewish. Lodge: Rotary (recipient Speakers award 1985) (Lakewood). Clubs: Sisterhood Ahavat, Shalom (bd. dirs. Lakewood chpt. 1964-70).

GOCKLEY, BARBARA JEAN, materials manager; b. Pittsburgh, July 26, 1951; d. William Ervin and Dorothy Marie (Wolf) Cain; m. William Lee Gockley, Mar. 29, 1975; children: Ervin Cain, Marianne Cain, William Cain, Malinda Cain. Student, Ind. U. Pa., 1969-71, Thomas Edison State Coll., 1986—. Cert. Prodn. Inventory Mgmt., Purchasing Mgmt. Asst. materials mgr. Redman Mobile Homes, Ephrata, Pa., 1972-75; mgr. inventory control Gym-Kin, Inc., Reading, Pa., 1975-77; supr. prodn./inventory control Wyomissing Converting, Reading, 1979-82; mgr. prodn./inventory control Dorma Door Controls, Inc., Reamstown, Pa., 1982-85, project mgr., 1985-86; materials mgr. Powder Coatings Group div. Morton Thiokol, Reading, 1986—; dir. programs Congress for Progress Inc., 1984-88, vice chmn., 1988—; instr. Berks campus Pa. State U., Reading, 1985-86. Dir. Reinholds (Pa.) PTA, 1978-81; bd. dirs. Cocalico Sch. Bd., Denver, Pa., 1985—. Recipient Internat. Vol. Service award Am. Prodn. and Inventory Control Soc., 1986. Mem. Am. Prodn. and Inventory Control Soc. (treas. Schuylkill Valley chpt. 1981-82, pres. 1982-84, dir. membership Region IX, 1985-86, asst. v.p. 1987, v.p. 1988), Nat. Assn. Purchasing Mgrs., Assn. Mfg. Excellence, Nat. Assn. Female Execs., Am. Bus. Women's Assn., Soc. Mfg. Engrs. Republican. Presbyterian. Club: Mothers of Twins (nominating chmn. 1977-78) (Lancaster, Pa.). Office: Morton Thiokol Powder Coatings Group PO Box 15640 Reading PA 19612

GOCKLEY, GRETCHEN BLAUGHER, chemical engineer; b. Pitts., Feb. 3, 1955; d. Donald Edwin and Rita Christina (Walters) Blaugher; m. James Milton Gockley, Aug. 5, 1978; 1 child, Allison Ann. BA, Washington and Jefferson Coll., 1977; MS, Carnegie-Mellon U., 1979. Research engr. Westinghouse Research and Devel. Ctr., Pitts., 1978-82; engr. Westinghouse Steam Generator Tech. Div., Pitts., 1982-86; sr. engr. Westinghouse Service Tech., Pitts., 1985-88; sr. project engr. Westinghouse Nuclear Services Div., Pitts., 1988—. Contbr. chpt. to On-Line Process Control, 1981. Trustee Washington (Pa.) and Jefferson Coll., 1988—. Mem. Am. Chem. Soc., Am. Inst. Chem. Engrs., Washington and Jefferson Coll. Allegheny Alumni Assn. (sec. Pitts. chpt. 1986—). Republican. Presbyterian. Club: Pitts. Athletic. Office: Westinghouse Nuclear Services 2400 Mosside Bldg Monroeville PA 15146

GODDESS, LYNN BARBARA, real estate broker; b. N.Y.C., Mar. 3, 1942; d. Eugene Daniel and Hazel Cecile (Kinzler) G.; divorced. BS, Columbia U., 1963, postgrad., 1964-66. Sec. coordinator John M. Burns Assembly Campaign, N.Y.C., 1963; dir. spl. events, projects Kenneth B. Keating Senatorial Campaign, N.Y.C., 1964; dist. dir. fund raising Muscular Dystrophy Assn. Am. Inc., N.Y.C., 1965-66; exec. acct. fund raising, pub. relations Victor Weingarten Co., N.Y.C., 1966-67, Oram Group (formerly Harold L. Oram Inc.), N.Y.C., 1967-70; dir. devel. City Ctr. Music Drama Inc., N.Y.C., 1970; sales person Whitbread-Nolan, N.Y.C., 1971-73; from asst. v.p. to sr. v.p. Cross and Brown Co., N.Y.C., 1973-1985; sr. v.p. Cushman and Wakefield Inc., N.Y.C., 1985—. Trustee Young Adults. Mem. Nat. Soc. Fund Raisers, Assn. Fund Dirs., Real Estate Bd. N.Y. (named Most Ingenious Broker Yr. 1975). Office: Cushman and Wakefield Inc 1166 Ave Americas New York NY 10036

GODEK, KAREN DENISE, aerospace engineer; b. Tokyo, Dec. 21, 1956; (parents Am. citizens); BS in Aerospace Engring., U. Tex., 1978; MS in Systems Engring., U. Houston, 1985. Sr. engr. Lockheed Engr. and Mgmt. Services, Houston, 1978-86; aerospace engr. NASA/Johnson Space Ctr., Houston, 1986—. Vol. Clear Lake Emergency Med. Corps, Houston, 1979—. Recipient Youth Appreciation award Dallas Optimist Club, 1972. Mem. AIAA (sr., treas. Houston sect. 1983-84, vice-chmn. 1984-85, chmn. 1986-87), Alpha Chi, Tau Beta Pi, Sigma Gamma Tau. Office: NASA/Johnson Space Ctr Houston TX 77058

GODFREY, KAREN LYNN, accountant; b. Chgo., Apr. 16, 1954; d. Donald Edward and Sophia Susan G.; m. Richard Alan Israel. BS, U. Ill., 1976. CPA, Ill., Calif. Acct. Commonwealth Edison, Chgo., 1976; supring. sr. Peat Marwick Mitchell and Co., Chgo., 1977-80; external reporting mgr. Oakland, Calif., 1980-84; mgr. acctg. Micropro Internat. Corp., San Rafael, Calif., 1984-86, controller, 1986—. Mem. Calif. Soc. CPA's. Office: Micropro Internat Corp 33 San Pablo San Rafael CA 94903

GODFREY, KIM MCALISTER, retail executive; b. Woodruff, S.C., Dec. 30, 1958; d. James Calhoun and Nancy (Caldwell) McAlister; m. Robert James Godfrey; 1 child, Lindsey Paige. BA in Elem. Edn., U. S.C., 1982, MBA, 1983—. Cert. tchr., S.C. Adminstrv. asst. Dr. G.R. Shanbhag and Assocs., Woodruff, 1977-78; sales rep. Reimer's Dept. Store, Woodruff, 1978-80; tchr. Spartanburg County Sch. Dist., Woodruff, 1981-82; pres., owner Godfrey Carpets, Inc., Woodruff, 1983—. Mem. decorating com. First Bapt. Ch., Woodruff, 1984-87, music com.; chair bd. dirs. Small Towns Program, Woodruff, 1987—; Rep. cand. for Spartanburg County Council, 1987; mem. S.C. Reps.; chmn. Nat. Bus. Women's Week, 1984. Mem. Nat. Assn. Female Execs., Nat. Fedn. Ind. Bus., Greater Woodruff Area C. of C. (pub. speaker, bd. dirs. 1985-87, pres. 1986), Bus. and Profl. Women (v.p. 1985). Republican. Baptist. Club: Woodruff Jr. Women's. Home: 1404 Marsh Cove Ct Ponte Vedra Beach FL 32082 Office: Godfrey Carpets Inc 107 N Main St Woodruff SC 29388

GODFREY, MARY ROSE, business owner, financial planner; b. Medford, Mass., Nov. 27, 1942; d. Francis R. and Rose (Cuneo) Dittami; A.B., Regis Coll., Mass., 1964; m. William K. Godfrey, Oct. 15, 1966; children—Angela, James, Thomas. Auditor, IRS, Boston, 1964-67, group supr., 1968-69, field agt., 1969-70, instr., 1966-70; tax accountant, Holliston, Mass., 1970-73; treas. New Eng. Adv. Group, Inc., Newton, Mass., 1974-81, also dir.; pres., owner Suburban Airport Transit, 1981-84; owner, gen. mgr. Priority Express, 1983—; v.p., owner Manathon Lines, Framingham, Mass., 1984—; sales rep. Dallamora Realtors, 1988—. Mem. Sherborn Republican Town Com., Sherborn Yacht Club Race Com. Mut. Benefit Agts. Assn. (treas. 1977-79, dir.), Boston Life Underwriters; bd. dirs. Big Brother/Big Sister, 1986-87; assessor 1st Parish Unitarian Universalist Ch., Framingham. Club: Pres.'s. Home: 194 Maple St Sherborn MA 01770 Office: 196 Fountain St Framingham MA 01701

GODFREY, NEALE, banker. Pres. First Women's Bank of N.Y. Office: First Women's Bank of NY Office of the Pres 111 E 57th St New York NY 10022 *

GODFREY, SUSAN LYNN, advertising agency executive; b. Mt. Holly, N.J., Dec. 7, 1962; d. Edward Lancaster and Dorothy Evelyn (Marmon) G. BA, U. Del., 1984; MA, Glassboro State Coll., 1987. Assoc. producer ITS Corp., Marlton, N.J., 1985-87; pres. Imagicians, Medford, N.J., 1987—; cons. pub. relations various banks and bus., N.J., Pa., 1986—. Asst. producer, dir. tng. video The Big Picture, 1986; writer, producer video program Public Relations-The Strongest Link, 1987; audio engr. tng. video Keeping Health Care Healthy, 1986. Mem. Nat. Assn. Female Execs., Internat. TV Assn., Pub. Relations Soc. Am., Alpha Chi Omega (rush chmn. 1983-84, exec. bd. 1983-84, pres. 1983-84), Phi Alpha Theta (treas. 1983-84). Republican. Roman Catholic. Home: 1142 Mt Laurel-Hainesport Rd Mount Laurel NJ 08054 Office: Imagicians Robinson Rd Taunton Lake Medford NJ 08055

GODFREY, SUSAN REUTERSHAN, defense contractor administrator; b. Southampton, N.Y., Sept. 5, 1953; d. Robert Gordon and Ann Patricia (Cronin) Reutershan; m. James B. Godfrey, Apr. 24, 1982 (div. 1986). BS, Skidmore Coll., 1975; MBA, Fla. Inst. Tech., 1983. Budget analyst Grumman Aerospace Corp., Bethpage, N.Y., 1975-76, program planner, 1976-79; budget planner Stuart, Fla., 1979-81, 1981-82; adminstr. research ctr. United Technologies Inc., West Palm Beach, Fla., 1982-86, sr. adminstr., 1986-87, sr. adminstr. optical systems div., 1988%. Mem. Am. Bus. Women's Assn. (pres. Orchid chpt. 1986-87, Sailfish chpt. 1985), Nat. Wildlife Fedn., Skidmore Alumni Assn., Skidmore Club Southeast Fla. Republican. Roman Catholic. Home: PO Box 1315 Stuart FL 34995 Office: United Technologies Optical systems Inc PO Box 109660 West Palm Beach FL 33410

GODWIN, CAROL HENDERSON, property company executive; b. Charleston, W.Va., Sept. 25, 1945; d. NIcholas Robert Henderson and Mary Alice (Martin) Tighe; m. James H. Godwin Sr., Oct. 6, 1978; children: Kimerley Anne Hager, Mary Elizabeth Hager. BS magna cum laude, U. Charleston, 1967. Acct. Hager Diesel Service, Tampa, Fla., 1968-78; with residential sales Hillsborough Homes, Tampa, 1978-80; with Lincoln Property Co., Tampa, 1980—, mgr. regional property, 1986-87, v.p., 1987—. Author: Patty Pelican, 1976. Bd. dirs. Tampa Apt. Assn., 1987—. Democrat. Methodist. Clubs: Circle T Saddle (Tampa) (sec. 1986); Temple Terrace Woman's (Fla.) (treas. 1976, v.p. 1977). Office: Lincoln Property Co 2901 W Busch Blvd Tampa FL 33618

GODWIN, JANICE RIVERO, clergywoman; b. N.Y.C., Sept. 24, 1953; d. Angel Vincent and Laura Choate (Quinn) Rivero; m. J. Badger Godwin, Nov. 19, 1977; children: Kristen, Ryan. BS, Coll. William and Mary, 1975; MDiv, Wesley Theol. Sem., 1980. Ordained to ministry Meth. Ch., 1981. Pastor Cedar Grove United Meth. Ch., Winchester, Va., 1980-81, Arcola (Va.)-Ryan United Meth. Ch., 1981-84, Messiah United Meth. Ch., Springfield, Va., 1984—. Mem. Va. Conf. Bd. Ordained Ministers. Office: Messiah United Meth Ch 6215 Rolling Rd Springfield VA 22152

GODWIN, SARA, writer; b. St. Louis, Feb. 18, 1944; d. Robert Franklin II and Annabelle (Palkes) G.; married, 1961 (div. 1977); children: Jane, Josh. BA, Calif. State U., 1967; grad., UCLA, 1968-70, U. Calif., Berkeley, 1970-71, W.I. Inst. Fairleigh Dickinson U., St. Croix, V.I., 1971-72; MA, Dominican Coll., 1974. Writer, editor Standard Oil of Calif., San Francisco, 1975-77, Gannett Corp., San Rafael, Calif., 1977-79; sr. writer Shaklee Corp., San Francisco, 1979—. Contbr. cover stories and feature articles to numerous U.S. and fgn. mags.; featured in radio show "Ask the Gardener" on KFRC, San Francisco, 1980-81. Recipient 1st prize Calif. Press Women, for travel writing, 1982, corp. communications, 1983, personal column, 1984. Fellow Royal Hort. Soc.; mem. Am. Mgmt. Assn., Pacific Area Travel Assn., U. Calif. Alumni Assn. Clubs: Commonwealth (San Francisco). Home: PO Box 1503 Ross CA 94957

GODZAC, SUSAN JEAN, optometrist; b. Syracuse, N.Y., Oct. 1, 1951; d. William John and Claire Jeanette (Ladouceur) G.; m. Andrew Michael Prischak, Mar 13, 1952; children: Amanda Beth, Rachael Marie. BA, SUNY, Oswego, 1973; BS, Pa. Coll. Optometry, 1976, OD, 1978. Assoc. optometrist Erie, Pa., 1978—. Recipient Irving Borish award Pa. Coll. Optometry, 1978. Mem. Am. Optometric Assn. Office: 4600 Buffalo Rd Erie PA 16510

GOEBEL, MARISTELLA, clinical psychologist, educator; b. Racine, Wis., Sept. 10, 1915; d. James Nicholas and Henrietta Marie (Rademacher) Goebel. BS, Edgewood Coll., 1944; MA, Cath. U. Am., 1946, PhD, 1966; cert. in biofeedback, BCIA, 1978. Diplomate Am. Bd. Clin. Biofeedback. Mem. Dominican Sisters; tchr. English Cathedral High Sch., Sioux Falls, S.D., 1946-47, Heart of Mary High Sch., Mobile, Ala., 1947-49; assoc. prof. edn. Rosary Coll., River Forest, Ill., 1949-61, prof. psychology, 1966—; clin. psychologist Hines VA Hosp., Ill., 1970—; cons. Sinsinawa Dominican Sisters, Wis., 1966—. Author, editor tchr. guides Southwestern Curriculum Com., vols. Kindergarten-grade 8. Mem. editorial bd., assoc. editor Clin. Biofeedback and Health, Am. Assn. Biofeedback Clinics, Des Plaines, 1980—. Contbr. numerous articles to profl. jours. Mem. task force ch. related project Chgo. Heart Assn., 1979—, NHLBI Hypertension Investigation Pooled Project, 1982—, Citizens Ambassador Del. to China, 1987. Recipient NIH awards, 1962-33, 65-66, 82-84, Outstanding Achievement in Psychol. Research, Ill. Psychol. Assn., 1982; Performance award Hines VA Hosp., 1983. Clin. fellow Am. Assn. Biofeedback Clinicians, Des Plaines, Ill., 1983. Mem. AAAS, Am. Psychol. Assn., Soc. Clin. and Exptl. Hypnosis, Biofeedback Soc. Am., Soc. Behavioral Medicine. Avocations: gardening, knitting, bicycling. Home: 7900 W Division River Forest IL 60305 Office: Hines VA Hosp Hines IL 60141

GOELL, ABBY JANE, painter, appraiser; b. N.Y.C.; d. Stanley Mendel and Anne (Bellin) Wershof; B.A., Syracuse U., 1949; cert. N.Y. Sch. Interior Design, 1958; M.F.A., Columbia U., 1965; postgrad. Attingham Park, Shropshire, Eng., summer 1963, Pratt Graphic Art Center, 1966; 1 son, Mark Jordan. One-woman show: Automation House, N.Y.C., 1973; group shows include: Lumley-Cazalet, London, 1976; AAAL, 1977, Childe Hassam Purchase Exhbn., N.Y.C., 1977, U.S. Dept. State, Havana, Cuba, 1979, Sculpture Center, N.Y.C., 1981, Silvermine Ann., 1981, 82, TAGA Pratt Graphic Exhbn., Caracas, 1982; represented in permanent collections: Chase Manhattan Bank, Mus. Modern Art, N.Y.C., Atlantic Richfield Oil Co., Yale U., Sloane-Kettering Meml. Center, N.Y.C., Grafisches Kabinet, Munich, W.Ger., Neuberger Mus., Purchase, N.Y., Print Room, N.Y. Pub. Library, Smith Coll. Art. Mus., Northampton, Mass.; co-pub. Arcadia Press, N.Y.C., 1980—; tchr. Hunter Coll., 1967, Lab. Inst. Merchandising, 1967-70. Yaddo fellow, 1968; Va. Center for Creative Arts fellow, 1981. Mem. Am. Soc. Appraisers (sr.), Women's Caucus for Art, Victorian Soc. in Am., Nat. Trust Historic Preservation, Art Students League of N.Y. (life). Democrat. Club: Coffee House. Editor: English Silver 1675-1825, 1980; bibliography The Artists Book, 1988. Home and office: 37 Washington Square W New York NY 10011

GOEPFERICH, MICHELE MARGARET, communications company executive; b. Detroit, Sept. 8, 1955; d. James Patrick and Margaret Adele (Jones) Murphy; m. Robert Goepferich, Feb. 15, 1975 (div. 1978); 1 child, Adrian Mathias. AA, Suffolk Community Coll., Selden, N.Y., 1976; studied theatre K.D. Studios, Dallas, 1981-83. Underwriter Foremost Ins. Co., Dallas, 1979-81; office mgr. Group Benefits Services Co., Dallas, 1981-82; asst. advt. dir., mgr. tradeshows Compucon, Inc., Richardson, Tex., 1982-84; sales rep. Wang Labs., Dallas, 1984-87, Voice-Com, Inc., Dallas, 1987—. Contbr. Am. Poetry Anthology, 1985; performer Running Image Modern Dance Co., Dallas, 1982-84. Mem. North Dallas C. of C. (several coms.), Nat. Assn. Female Execs. (dir. local network Dallas), Nat. Writers Assn., Stage Club of Dallas. Democrat. Roman Catholic. Home: 438 Melrose Dr Richardson TX 75080

GOERING, JANEAL FAYE, mathematics educator; b. Newton, Kans., Dec. 14, 1962; d. Verne Maynard and Ruth Ella (Entz) G. Student, Grace Coll. of Bible, Omaha, 1981-82; BA in Math., Tabor Coll., 1985. Cert. secondary tchr., Okla. Math. tchr. Okla. Bible Acad., Enid, 1985—. Mennonite.

GOERING, JUDITH ANN, military officer; b. Ashland, Ohio, Aug. 29, 1951; d. Raymond Albert and Marion Louise (Smith) G. BA, Heidelberg Coll., Tiffin, Ohio, 1974; postgrad. in edn., So. Ill. U., 1986—. Cert. tchr., N.Y. Tchr. jr. high sch. Greece Cen. Schs., Rochester, N.Y., 1974-79, tchr. high sch., 1979-81; enlisted USAF, 1981, commd. 2d lt., 1982, advanced through grades to capt., 1986; chief morale, welfare and recreation div. USAF, Scott AFB, Ill., 1982-87, Loring AFB, Maine, 1988—; dir. camp Seven Lakes Council, Girl Scouts U.S., Geneva, N.Y., summers 1973-80; lectr. on mil. recreation, 1986—. Mem. Air Force Assn., Am. Alliance for Health, Phys. Edn., Recreation and Dance, Nat. Recreation and Park Assn., Women's Sports Found., NOW, Girl Scouts Am. (life). Office: USAF 42 CSG/SS Loring AFB ME 04751

GOETTLICH RIEMANN, WILHELMINA MARIA ANNA, scientist, chemist; b. Jaworow, Poland, June 25, 1934; came to U.S., 1965; d. Jan Stanislaw Goettlich and Kazimiera Henryka (Smielowska) Goettlich-Glazewska; m. Stanislaw Alexander Salomon, Mar. 28, 1958 (div. Nov. 1964); m. Hans Peter Yerndorff Storm Riemann, Aug. 28, 1965. BS in Food Chemistry, Warsaw Agrl. U., Poland, 1954, MS in Food Chemistry, 1957; PhD in Chemistry, Gdansk (Poland) Poly. U., 1977. Research asst. Dairy Research Inst., Warsaw, 1957-62; asst. prof. Meat Research Inst., Warsaw, 1961-65; staff research assoc. U. Calif., Davis, 1966-83, researcher, 1986-87; chief coordinator Comecon Meat Research Inst., Warsaw, 1962-65; cons. Polish Patent Commn., Warsaw, 1963-65; lectr. U. Calif., Davis, 1974-75, Meat Research Inst., Warsaw, 1965. Contbr. articles to profl. jours.; patentee in field. Mem. Am. Dairy Sci. Assn., Inst. Food Technologists, Am. Fedn. Tchrs., Sigma Xi. Lodge: Soroptomists.

GOETZ, BETTY BARRETT, health physicist; b. Atlanta, Jan. 8, 1943; d. Vose Matthew and Fay (Howard) Barrett; m. Charles David Goetz, Mar. 25, 1972; children: Lisa Fay, Gayle Catherine. BA, Emory U., 1963, M in Med. Sci, 1972; BS, U. Ga., 1965. Tchr. jr. high sci. City of Decatur (Ga.) Bd. of Edn., 1965-66; tech. specialist, radiology Emory U. Sch. of Medicine, Atlanta, 1967-72, sr. assoc. allied health professions, 1977-82, health physicist, 1973—, sr. assoc. community health, 1983—; cons. in field. Contbr. articles and papers to profl. jours. Mem. Decatur, Ga. Edn. Adv. com., 1987, St. Thomas More Parent's Club, Decatur, 1980—, St. Thomas More Bd. of Edn., 1981-85. Mem. Health Physics Soc. (sec. Atlanta chpt. 1976-79), SE Chpt. Am. Assn. of Physicists in Medicine, Ga. Assn. Radio Physicists, SE U. Radiation Safety Officers. Republican. Methodist. Home: 3661 Canadian Way Tucker GA 30084 Office: Emory U Memorial Bldg 469 Woodruff Atlanta GA 30322

GOFF, CHRISTINE EASTER, nursing home administrator; b. Monticello, Ky., Apr. 8, 1939; d. Thomas Haden and Pernia Jane (Bridgeman) Dishman; m. Edward Bybee Jr., Dec. 8, 1956 (div. Feb. 1976); children: Linda, Patricia, Donna, Douglas; m. Gale Brooks Goff, Oct. 1, 1977. Grad. high sch., Monticello. Adminstr., dir. activity Dishman Nursing Home, Monticello, 1970—. Republican. Baptist. Club: Monticello Women's. Lodge: Order of Eastern Star. Home: Box 217 Michigan Monticello KY 42633 Office: Monticello KY 42633

GOFORTH, LYDIA GELDMEIER, retired educator, property manager; b. Riesel, Tex., Dec. 24, 1915; d. Fred C. and Katherine (Kohen) Geldmeier; m. J. Morris Goforth, Aug. 18, 1940 (dec. 1970); children: James M., Katherine A. Masser. BA, Baylor U., 1938; MA, U. Tex., 1954, postgrad., 1960-72. Tchr. English Comfort (Tex.) Ind. Sch. Dist., 1938-40, 45-57; tchr. English San Antonio Ind. Sch. Dist., 1957-61, counselor, 1961-63, supr. English, 1963-70, tchr. English, 1980-82; dir. adult edn. Tex. Edn. Agy., Austin, 1974-79; dir. curriculum Fredericksburg (Tex.) Ind. Sch. Dist., 1970-74; instr. English San Antonio Coll., 1957-82; property mgr. Goforth Properties, San Antonio, 1982—; cons. Random House Pub. Co. Mem. Tex. Council English Tchrs. (past v.p., past pres.). Republican. Methodist. Home: 714 E Olmos San Antonio TX 78212 Office: 7400 Louis Pasteur San Antonio TX 78229

GOGATE, SHASHI ANAND, physician; b. Indore, India, July 9, 1938; d. Kashinath M. and Manorama R.; M.B.B.S., M.G.M. Med. Coll., 1962; M.S., Ohio State U., 1969; m. Anand B. Gogate, June 20, 1962; children—Sangita, Soniya, Sanjay. Instr., research asso. Ohio State U., 1970-73, asst. prof. pathology, 1973-75, asst. clin. prof., 1975-87;assoc. clin. prof. 1987—; dir. lab. Columbus Pathology Lab., 1975-79; chief pathologist Lancaster-Fairfield Community Hosp., 1976—; pres. S.A. Gogate M.D., Inc., 1978—. Mem. adv. bd. Internat. Mediation Soc., Columbus. Fellow Coll. Am. Pathologists, Am. Soc. Clin. Pathologists; mem. AMA, Ohio Med. Assn., Franklin County Med. Soc., Fairfield County Med. Soc., Internat. Acad. Pathology, Republican. Hindu. Contbr. articles to profl. jours. Home: 6112 Sedgwick Rd Worthington OH 43085 Office: Lancaster Fairfield Community Hosp 401 N Ewing St Lancaster OH 43130

GOGGIN, MARGARET KNOX, librarian, educator; b. Nyack, N.Y., Feb. 24, 1919; d. Henry Julian and Eleanor (Green) Knox; m. John Mann Goggin, Nov. 22, 1962. A.B., Maryville Coll., 1940; B.S., Peabody Coll., 1942; M.S., U. Ill., 1948, Ph.D., 1957. Tchr., librarian Flintville (Tenn.) High Sch., 1940-42; reference asst. Joint U. Library, Nashville, 1942-43; acting reference librarian Joint U. Library, 1943-45; vis. instr. Peabody Library Sch., Nashville, 1943-45; readers adviser Youngstown (Ohio) Pub. Library, 1945-46; bibliographer, reference librarian Office Tech. Services Dept. Commerce, Washington, 1946-47; reference asst. U. Ill., 1948-49; asst. to dir. U. Fla. Libraries, asst. prof. library sci., 1949-50, head dept. reference and bibliography, asso. prof. library sci., 1950-62; asst. dir. U. Fla. Libraries (Readers Services), asso. prof. library sci., 1965-66, asst. dir. libraries, prof. library sci., 1966, acting dir. libraries, 1967-68; dean Grad. Sch. Librarianship, U. Denver, 1968-79, prof., 1979-84, prof. emeritus, 1984—; vis. lectr. U. Okla. Library Sch., summer 1959, Emory U. Sch. Librarianship, 1965; dir.

Satellite Library Info. Network, 1974-76; prin. investigator Telefax Library Info. Network, 1978-79; cons. U.S. Office Edn. div. Library Programs, 1968-69, Aims Community Coll., Greeley, Colo., 1973, Wash. State Library, 1978-79, Loretto Heights Coll., Denver, 1981; co-owner Book Seminars, Inc., 1986—; interim dir. Collection Mgmt., Emory U., 1986-88. Haitian research, Haiti and Paris on Rockefeller Found. grants, 1958, 61-62; Fulbright grantee, 1972; OAS grantee for multi-nat. library edn. program, 1974-75. Mem. ALA (past div. pres.), Colo. Library Assn. (dir. 1978-79), Mountain Plains Library Assn. (dir. 1978-79), Assn. For Library and Info. Sci. Edn. (pres. 1977), Nat. League Am. Pen Women, Delta Kappa Gamma, Beta Phi Mu (past dir.). Club: Altrusa (bd. dirs. Denver 1974-76, 80-82, pres. 1983-84). Home and Office: 4024 NW 15th St Gainesville FL 32605

GOGICK, KATHLEEN CHRISTINE, magazine editor; b. N.J., Aug. 3, 1945; d. Joseph John and Emeline (Radwin) Wadowski; m. Robert Joseph Gogick, Feb. 24, 1968; 1 son, Jonathan. B.S., Fairleigh Dickinson U., Rutherford, N.J., 1967. Asst. beauty and fiction editor Cosmopolitan mag., N.Y.C., 1967-68; mdsg. and publicity coordinator Co-ed mag., N.Y.C., 1968-69; creative services coordinator Estee Lauder, Inc., N.Y.C., 1969-71; asso. beauty and health editor Town and Country mag., N.Y.C., 1971-75; editor-in-chief Co-ed mag., 1976-80; editorial dir. home econs. div. Scholastic Inc., 1981-86; pres., pub. Corp. Mags. Inc., 1986—. Mem. Women's Econ. Roundtable, Advt. Women N.Y., Women in Communications. Club: University. Home: 41 E Hartshorn Dr Short Hills NJ 07078 Office: 56 Main St Millburn NJ 07041

GOGOLA, DENISE R., computer analyst; b. Lowell, Mass., Aug. 10, 1960; d. Joseph A. and Rita V. (Belanger) Bastien; m. Leonard J. Gogola, Jan. 1, 1985. Student, Pasco-Hernando Community Coll., 1984—. Telecommunications operator service adminstrn. Wang Labs., Inc., Burlington, Mass., 1978-79; with mktg. adminstrn. div. Wang Labs., Inc., Tampa, Fla., 1979-81; top instr. Tandy Corp./Radio Shack, Clearwater, Fla., 1982-83; traveling instr. Tandy Corp./Radio Shack, Clearwater and St. Petersburg, Fla., 1983-84; customer support rep. Tandy Corp./Radio Shack, Tampa, Fla., 1984; pres. VAR Enterprising Computer Facts, Inc., New Port Richey, Fla., 1985—; instr. Pasco-Hernando Community Coll., New Port Richey, 1985—; part time instr. Tandy Corp./Radio Shack, Clearwater, 1982; temp. computer operator Peoneer Western Critikon, Great Am. Temp. Services, Paradyne St. Anthony's Hosp., Tampa and Largo, Fla., 1982; designer Sunny Fla. Dairy, Tampa, 1982. Mem. Leads Club, New Port Richey, 1986, Civic Jasmine Acres, 1985—. Mem. Calusa-Bus. Profl. Women. Democrat. Roman Catholic. Home and Office: 1304 N Driftwood Dr New Port Richey FL 33552

GOGOLIN, MARILYN TOMPKINS, educational administrator, language pathologist; b. Pomona, Calif., Feb. 25, 1946; d. Roy Merle and Dorothy (Davidson) Tompkins; m. Robert Elton Gogolin, Mar. 29, 1969. BA, U. LaVerne, Calif., 1967; MA, U. Redlands, Calif., 1968; postgrad., U. Washington, 1968-69; MS, Calif. State U., Fullerton, 1976. Cert. clin. speech pathologist; cert. teaching and sch. adminstrn. Speech/lang. pathologist Rehab. Hosp., Pomona, 1969-71; diagnostic tchr. Los Angeles County Office of Edn., Downey, Calif., 1971-72, program specialist, 1972-75, cons. lang., 1975-76, cons. orgns. and mgmt., 1976-79, asst. to supt., 1979—; cons. lang. sch. dists., Calif., 1975-79; cons. orgn. and mgmt. and profl. assns., Calif., 1976—; exec. dir. Los Angeles County Sch. Trustees Assn., 1979—. Founding patron Desert chpt. Kidney Found., Palm Desert, Calif., 1985. Doctoral fellow U. Washington, 1968; named One of Outstanding Young Women Am., 1977. Mem. Am. Mgmt. Assn., Am. Speech/Hearing Assn., Calif. Speech/Hearing Assn., Am. Edn. Research Assn. Baptist. Home: 15 Sweetwater Irvine CA 92715 Office: Los Angeles County Office Edn 9300 E Imperial Hwy Downey CA 90242

GOINS, RHONDA DELISA, communications executive; b. Shreveport, La., Sept. 7, 1958; d. Willie Theodore and Mattye Lucille (Ewell) G.; m. Gary Steven Hamilton, June 25, 1983 (div. Sept. 1985). BA in Communications cum laude, Calif. State U., Long Beach, 1980; postgrad., Loyola Marymount U., Los Angeles, 1983-85. Adminstr. prodn. engrng. Hughes Aircraft Co., El Segundo, Calif., 1981-83, adminstr. bus. ops. and adminstrn., 1984-85, sr. adminstr. div. 79 adminstrn., 1985-86, sr. adminstr. div. 79 adminstrn. and tng., 1987-88, sr. analyst material processing ops., 1988—. Editor: (newsletters) Prodn. Engring., 1981-83, Product Line Press, 1983-84, Total Quality Observer, 1985, Tactical Material Ops. Outlook, 1987—; contbg. editor: (newsletter) People and Progress, 1984; prodn. film coordinator: Making The Grade, 1986. Vol. Youth Motivation Task Force, Los Angeles, 1982—. Recipient cert. of Achievement YWCA, 1987. Mem. Internat. Assn. Bus. Communicators, Inter-group Women's Forum, NAACP, Hughes Black Profl. Forum, Delta Sigma Theta (life). Avocations: travel, fishing, camping, collecting antique jewelry boxes, reading. Home: 1127 Elderglen Ln Harbor City CA 90710 Office: Hughes Aircraft Co PO Box 902 El Segundo CA 90245

GOLA, SANDRA VALENTINA, graphic designer, educator; b. Passaic, N.J., Mar. 10, 1955; d. Henry Andrew and Ann (Skripak) G. B.F.A., Pratt Inst., 1978. Asst., Brodsky Graphics, N.Y.C., 1980-82; art dir. Cycles Peugeot, Carlstadt, N.J., 1982-83; owner, pres. Skylight Graphics, Hackensack, N.J., 1983—; instr. Art Ctr. of No. N.J., New Milford, 1983-85, Parsons Sch. of Design, N.Y.C., 1985-86. Designer: Challenge tire tube packaging (Creativity award 1983), Johnson & Jonnson Ultrasound sales kit (Art Dir. Club of N.J. award 1985), KLM stationery (Creativity award 1984), Letraset Sales Portfolio (DESI award 1987, Creativity award 1987). Mem. Art Dir.'s Club of N.J., Nat. Assn. Female Execs., Mensa. Avocations: bicycling, aerobics, nautilus, skiing. Home: 466 Boulevard Garfield NJ 07026 Office: Skylight Graphics 166 Main St Hackensack NJ 07601

GOLD, ANNE, educator; b. N.Y.C., Nov. 23, 1949; d. Louis Walter and Marjorie Ann G. BA, George Washington U., 1971; MA, Manhattanville Coll., 1980; profl. diploma in ednl. adminstrn., Fordham U., 1983. Cert. tchr., adminstr., N.Y. Tchr. music Shelter Rock Jr. High Sch., Albertson, N.Y., 1974-76, Eastchester (N.Y.) High Sch., 1979-80, Hommocks Sch., Larchmont, N.Y., 1980-81; music specialist Mt. Vernon (N.Y.) Pub. Schs., 1982-83, adminstrv. intern., 1982-83; dir. music and art Webster (N.Y.) Cen. Schs., 1983-86; asst. prin. Henry H. Wells Middle Sch., Brewster, N.Y., 1986—; cons. to music educators, 1983—. Chairperson Webster Cultural Arts Assn., 1983-85. Mem. Music Educators Nat. Conf., Am. choral Dirs. Assn., Nat. Art Educators Assn., N.Y. State Middle Sch. Assn., Assn. Supervision and Curriculum Devel., Webster Music Edn. Assn. (chair 1983-85). Home: Box 561 Bedford Hills NY 10507 Office: Wells Middle Sch Route 312 Brewster NY 10509

GOLD, LYNN ANNE, educator, consultant; b. Madison, Wis., May 26, 1945; d. Arthur John and Jean Marie (Colligan) Knabel; m. Richard Frank Gold, June 6, 1966 (div. May 1979). BA, Purdue U., 1967; MS, U. Bridgeport, 1974. Cert. tchr., Ind., Washington, Conn., N.Y. Tchr. Attica Pub. Schs. (Ind.), 1967-68, Richland Pub. Schs. (Wash.), 1968-69, Marymount Secondary Sch., Tarrytown, N.Y., 1969-70, Lakeland Pub. Schs., Shrub Oak, N.Y., 1970-73, Rye City Pub. Schs. (N.Y.), 1973-81, Norwalk Community Coll. (Conn.), 1982-83, East Meadow Pub. Schs., L.I., N.Y., 1986-87, Clyde (N.Y.) Savannah Pub. Schs., Pawling (N.Y.) Cen. Schs., 1987—; cons. Silver Assocs., Springdale, Conn., 1979—; cons., lectr. Darien Pub. Schs. (Conn.), 1983; guest speaker Conn. Assn. for Gifted, Farmington, 1983; advanced trainer Structure of the Intellect, 1987. Author health care column, 1983, 86—; assoc. editor Jour. Holistic Medicine, 1984-85. Conn. state coordinator Internat. Legion of Intelligence, Golden, Colo., 1983—; press coordinator Rep. mayoral candidate, Stamford, Conn., 1985. Mem. Am. Soc. Tng. and Devel., Assn. for Gifted, Assn. Productivity Specialists, Conn. Assn. Gifted Children, Flower Essence Soc., Huxley Inst., Nat. Assn. Gifted Children, Nat. Health Fedn., Soc. Accelerative Learning and Teaching, Purdue Alumni Assn., Mensa, Intertel (coordinator Conn. chpt.). Republican. Roman Catholic. Clubs: Rochester Curling, Nutmeg Curling (Darien). Office: Silver Assocs PO Box 4728 Springdale CT 06907

GOLD, SHIRLEY JEANNE, state legislator, labor relations specialist; b. N.Y.C., Oct. 2, 1925; d. Louis and Gussie (Lefkowitz) Diamondstein; BA in Music, Hunter Coll., 1945; MA in Behavioral Sci. (Crown-Zellerbach Corp. scholar), Reed Coll., 1962; m. David E. Gold, June 22, 1947; children: Andrew, Dana. Tchr., Portland (Oreg.) Public Schs., 1954-68; pres. Portland Fedn. Tchrs., Am. Fedn. Tchrs./AFL-CIO, 1965-72, pres. Oreg. Fedn. Tchrs., 1972-77; cons. labor relations to univs., coll., Portland, 1977-80; mem. Oreg. Ho. of Reps., Salem, 1980—, majority leader, 1985—, chmn. legis. rules, ops. and reform, human resources com., 1983-84, revenue com., 1987—, policy and priorities, com. of edn., commn. of states, 1987—, campaign fin. reform com., 1987—; mem. Oreg. Tchr. Tenure Rev. Bd., 1965-72; mem. Nat. Multi-State Consortium, 1974; mem. Speak Out Oreg. com. to White House and Congress, 1978; mem. Oreg. Task Force on Tax Reform; AFL-CIO scholar George Meany Inst., 3 times, 1976-77; commr. Edn. Commn. of States; mem. Oreg. Commn. on Women. Chairperson precinct com., conv. del. Oreg. Democratic Party, 1960-80, dist. leader, chairperson edn. com., 1978-80; charter mem., mem. exec. bd., v.p. Oreg. Council for Cts., 1977-80. Named to Hunter Coll. Hall of Fame, 1985, Citizen of Yr., 1985. Mem. Hunter Coll. Alumni Assn., Reed Coll. Alumni Assn., Pacific N.W. Labor History Assn., Portland Fedn. Tchrs., Oreg. Fedn. Tchrs., Oreg. Fedn. Dem. Women, Oreg. Coalition for Nat. Health Security, Oreg. Women's Polit. Caucus, Com. on Drug Abuse, Northwest Oreg. Health System, ACLU, Coalition Labor Union Women. Jewish. Contbr. articles on labor relations to Willamette Week newspaper, 1977-80; editor Oreg. Tchr. newspaper, 1970-72. Office: H295 State Capitol Salem OR 97310

GOLDAPER, GABRIELE GAY, clothing executive, consultant; b. Amsterdam, The Netherlands, May 4, 1937; came to U.S., 1949; d. Richard and Gertrud (Sinzheimer) Mainzer; married, 1957; children: Carolyn, Julie, Nancy. BA in Econs., Barnard Coll., 1959; BS in Edn., U. Cin., 1960; postgrad., Xavier U., 1962. V.p. planning, systems and material control High Tide Swimwear div. Warnaco, Los Angeles, 1974-79; v.p., customer support cons. Silton AMS, Los Angeles, 1979-80; exec. v.p., ptnr. Prisma Corp., Los Angeles, 1980-84; exec. v.p. Mindstar Prods., Los Angeles, 1984-85; gen. mgr. Cherry Lane, Los Angeles, 1985-86; dir. inventory mgmt. Barco Uniforms, Los Angeles, 1986; mgmt. cons. to clothing industry Santa Monica, Calif., 1986—; instr. Calif. State U., 1978-79, UCLA Grad. Bus. Mgmt. Sch., 1979-86, Fashion Inst. Design and Merchandising, 1985—; chmn. data processing com. Calif. Fashion Creators, 1980; mediator Los Angeles County Bar Assn.; cons. Exec. Service Corps; lectr. various colls. Author: A Results Oriented Approach to Manufacturing Planning, 1978, Small Company View of the Computer, 1979; also articles. Elected mem. Commn. on Status Women, 1985—. Mem. Apparel Mfrs. Assn. (mgmt. systems com. 1978-80), Calif. Apparel Industries Assn. (exec. com., bd. dirs. 1980), Am. Arbitration Assn. Home: 37 Village Pkwy Santa Monica CA 90405

GOLDBERG, ALICE SUSAN, advertising agency executive; b. New Britain, Conn., Mar. 5, 1932; d. Zundie A. and Sally (Hoffman) Finkelstein; m. Irwin Ulysses Goldberg, June 3, 1956. BA, Barnard Coll., 1953. Research analyst Biow Co., N.Y.C., 1953-56; project dir. Benton & Bowles, Inc., N.Y.C., 1956-60, market research supr., 1960-68, v.p., assoc. research dir., 1968-74, sr. v.p., research mgr., 1974-83, sr. v.p., research dir., 1983-86; sr. v.p., exec. dir. research and planning D'Arcy, Masius, Benton & Bowles, N.Y.C., 1986—, chmn. research council, 1986—; chmn. profit-sharing com. Benton & Bowles, Inc., N.Y.C., 1976—. Mem. Am. Mktg. Assn. (bd. dirs., pres. 1986-87), Market Research Council, Copy Research Council. Home: 450 E 63d St New York NY 10021 Office: D'Arcy Masius Benton & Bowles 909 3d Ave New York NY 10022 *

GOLDBERG, BARBARA ANN, human relations education specialist; b. Opa-Locka, Fla., Apr. 10, 1952; d. Leon Goldberg and Bessie Love (Francis) Mannheimer; children: Tosha, Cinnamon, Jeaneé. AA in Edn., Miami Dade Jr. Coll., 1972; AS in Social Services, Community Coll. of the Air Force, Maxwell AFB, Ala., 1982. Enlisted USAF, 1978, advanced through grades to staff sgt.; served as air craft maintenance specialist Abilene, Tex., 1978-82; equal opportunity and treatment/human relations specialist Ft. Walton Beach, Fla., 1982-84; program dir. equal opportunity and treatment/human relations Hanscom AFB, Mass., 1985-87, non-commd. officer-in-charge equal opportunity and treatment/human relations, 1987—; instr. human relations, cons. Hanscom AFB, Eglin AFB, 1983—. Chairperson Fed. Women's Week Celebration, Hanscom AFB, 1986, Attic Furniture Assistance Program, Hanscom AFB, 1986-87; coach Youth Soccer, Youth T-Ball, Hanscom AFB, 1987. Mem. Federally Employed Women. Jewish. Office: 3245 ABG/SLE Hanscom AFB MA 01731-5000

GOLDBERG, BARBARA SUE, educational administrator, counselor, clinical social worker; b. Bklyn., June 26, 1947; d. Norman Leonard Goldberg and Ray (Greenberg) Green. B.A. in English, L.I.U., 1967, M.S. in Guidance and Counseling, 1970; M.S.W., Hunter Sch. Social Work, 1973; MS in Ednl. Adminstrn., Baruch Coll., CCNY, 1987, Adler Inst. Cert. tchr., sch. social worker, counselor, asst. prin. adminstr. N.Y. Tchr. English, Eastern Dist. High Sch., N.Y.C., 1967-72, dean of girls, 1970-72, supportive service counselor, 1977-80, coll.-bound counselor, 1973-76; caseworker Addiction Research and Treatment Corp., N.Y.C., 1972-73, group therapist, 1973; supportive service counselor Sarah J. Hale High Sch., N.Y.C., 1980-85; asst. project coordinator coll.-bound program, N.Y.C. Bd. Edn., 1985-86; asst. prin. spl. edn. Washington Irving High Sch., 1987—, support service counselor, 1988. Contbr. editor guidance manuals. Mem. Register Clin. Social Workers, Acad. Cert. Social Workers, N.Y.C. Personnel and Guidance Assn., N.Am. Soc. Adlerian Psychologists, Phi Delta Kappa. Avocations: skiing; travel; camping; modern dance. Home: 200 E 28th St New York NY 10016

GOLDBERG, BONNIE HOPE, educator; b. Louisville, Aug. 31, 1952; d. Samuel and Gertrude (Yussman) G. AA, Lincoln (Ill.) Jr. Coll., 1972; BS, George Peabody Coll., 1975; MEd, Tenn. State U., 1986. Cert spl. edn. tchr. Spl edn. tchr. Arnett Elem. Sch., Erlanger, Tenn., 1977-79, Walton Ferry Elem. Sch., Hendersonville, Tenn., 1984-86, Vena Stuart Elem. Sch., Gallatin, Tenn., 1979-84, 86—. Mem. Tenn. Edn. Assn. Democrat. Jewish. Home: 910 Laura St Gallatin TN 37066

GOLDBERG, CAROL RABB, retail chain executive; b. Newton, Mass., Mar. 25, 1931; d. Sidney Rabinovitz and Esther Vera (Cohn) Rabb; m. Avram J. Goldberg, June 18, 1950; children: Deborah, Joshua. B.A. magna cum laude in Sociology, Jackson Coll. Tufts U., 1955; postgrad., Harvard U. Bus. Sch., 1969. Fashion model Hart Agy.; free-lance fashion coordinato; trousseau coordinator Joseph Magnin, San Francisco, until 1958; with The Stop & Shop Cos., Inc., Boston, 1958—, market mgr. North New Eng. Region, Bradlees div., 1971, v.p., gen. mgr. Boston Supermarket div., 1972-77, sr. v.p., 1979-82, exec. v.p., chief operating officer, 1982-85, pres., chief operating officer, dir., 1986—; pres. Stop & Shop Mfg. Co., Boston, 1977-79; chief exec. officer Bradlees, Boston, 1988—; trustee, dir. Putnam Fund Groups; bd. dirs. The Cowles Media Co. Mem. Bus. Adv. Council Carnegie-Mellon U.; bd. regents higher edn. com. Mass.; mem. nat. adv. com. Ctr. Pub. Service Tufts U.; mem. bd. visitors sch. medicine Boston U.; mem. bd. overseers Sta. WGBH-TV Edn. Found.; bd. dirs. J.F. Kennedy Library Found.; mem. corp. Mass. Gen. Hosp.; bd. dirs. Harvard U. Bus. Sch. Assn., Greater Boston Arts Fund; mem. Babson Coll. Found., Boston Mcpl. Research Bur. Recipient Pride award Simmons Coll., 1977, Alumni Achievement award Harvard U. Bus. Sch., 1986, Simmons Coll. Grad. Sch. Mgmt. award for Excellence in Mgmt., 1987; named Advt. Woman of Yr. Boston, 1967. Clubs: Comml., Mchts. (Boston). Office: Stop & Shop Cos Inc PO Box 369 Boston MA 02101

GOLDBERG, GERALDINE ELIZABETH, biokinesiologist; b. Neptune, N.J., Mar. 22, 1939; d. Albert Voorhees and Katherine Irene (Mulholland) McCormick; B.S. cum laude, East Stroudsburg U., 1967; M.A. in Psychology, Fairleigh Dickinson U., 1971; m. Arthur Goldberg, July 1, 1961. Staff clin. psychologist Youth Devel. Clinic, Newark, 1971-75; psychotherapist in clin. psychology Mental Health Cons. Center, N.Y.C., 1975—; human resources specialist AGE Corp., Livingston, N.J., 1979—, sec. bd. dirs., 1977—, v.p., 1980—. Mem. N.J. Assn. Profl. Psychologists (past pres.), Am. Psychol. Assn. (asso.), N.J. Psychol. Assn. (asso.).

GOLDBERG, HONEY LYNN, lawyer; b. Bklyn., Mar. 18, 1957; d. Marvin and Gloria (Smerling) G. AB, Brown U., 1979; JD, Harvard U., 1982. Bar: Ill. 1982, U.S. Tax Ct. Assoc. Maver, Brown and Platt, Chgo., 1982-84; atty. Abbott Labs., North Chicago, Ill., 1984-86, sr. atty., 1986—. Mem. ABA, Chgo. Council on Fgn. Relations.

GOLDBERG, JODI LYNN, nurse; b. Hartford, Conn., Jan. 12, 1961; d. Lazarus and Selma (Rome) G. BS in Nursing, U. Miami, 1983. RN. Student nurse VA Hosp., West Haven, Conn., 1982, Miami, Fla., 1982-83; lic. practical nurse Coral Gables (FLa.) Hosp., 1983; RN in neurosurgery George Washington Hosp., Washington, 1984-86; nurse evaluator, markerter New Medico Assocs., Lynn, Mass., 1986—. Mem. Assn. Rehab. Nurses, Nat. Assn. Female Execs., Continuity Care Assn., No. Va. Head Injury Found., Md. Head Injury Found., D.C. Head Injury Found. Home and Office: 9925 Lake Landing Rd Gaithersburg MD 20879

GOLDBERG, LEE WINICKI, furniture co. exec.; b. Laredo, Tex., Nov. 20, 1932; d. Frank and Goldie (Ostrowiak) Winicki; student San Diego State U., 1951-52; m. Frank M. Goldberg, Aug. 17, 1952; children—Susan Arlene, Edward Lewis, Anne Carri. With United Furniture Co., Inc., San Diego, 1953-83, corp. sec., dir., 1963-83, dir. environ. interiors, 1970-83; founder Drexel-Heritage store Edwards Interiors, subs. United Furniture, 1975; founding ptnr., v.p. FLJB Corp., 1976—, founding ptnr., sec. treas., Sea Fin., Inc., 1980, founding ptnr., First Nat. Bank San Diego, 1982. Den mother Boy Scouts Am., San Diego, 1965; vol. Am. Cancer Soc., San Diego, 1964-69; chmn. jr. matrons United Jewish Fedn., San Diego, 1958; del. So. Pacific Coast region Hadassah Conv., 1960, pres. Galilee group San Diego chpt., 1960-61; supporter Marc Chagall Nat. Mus., Nice, France, Smithsonian Instn., Los Angeles County Mus., La Jolla (Calif.) Mus. Contemporary Art, San Diego Mus. Art. Recipient Hadassah Service award San Diego chpt., 1958-59. Democrat. Jewish.

GOLDBERG, MARILYN, trade show executive; b. Chgo., Nov. 18, 1946; d. Sol and Reva (Weinhouse) Greenberg; m. Louis Goldberg; children: Michele, Stephanie. BBA, U. Wis., 1967. Asst. v.p. ops. Revere Sportswear Co., Chgo., 1968-70, exec. v.p. ops., 1970-71; v.p. ops. Tradeshow Exhibit Corp., Hoffman Estates, Ill., 1985—. Mem. Schaumburg Atheletic Assn., Roselle, Jaycees, Strays Halfway House. Home: 995 Gannon Dr Hoffman Estates IL 60194 Office: Tradeshow Exhibit Corp 2500 W Higgins Rd Hoffman Estates IL 60195

GOLDBERG, NORMA LORRAINE, public welfare administrator; b. South Bend, Ind., May 6, 1929; d. James Albert and Minnie Sylvia (Kaplan) Seamon; m. Albert Goldberg, Apr. 19, 1959 (dec. Dec. 1976); children—Lisa Ann, Paul Ephraim. B.S., Ind. U.-Bloomington, 1950; postgrad. Sch. Social Work, Ind. U.-Indpls., 1950-52. Sch. social worker Indpls. Pub. Schs., 1951-53; with Marion County Dept. Pub. Welfare, Indpls., 1953-66, 71-73, asst. dir., 1961-64, dir., 1964-66, intake supr., 1971-73; asst. dir. Ind. Dept. Pub. Welfare, Indpls., 1973-79, dir., 1979-87, regional adminstr., rep. Family Support Adminstrn., Dallas, 1987—; mem. steering com. Whitehouse Conf. on Children and Youth, Indpls., 1982-83; mem. program com. Gov.'s Conf. on Children and Youth, Indpls., 1982-83. Founder Welfare Service League, Indpls., 1968, pres., 1968-71, mem., 1968—. Mem. steering com. Indpls. sect. Nat. Council Jewish Women, 1982-87; mem. steering com. Guardian ad Litem Project; mem. Republican Round Table, Indpls., 1983—; city chmn. adult bd. B'nai B'rith Youth Orgn., 1985-86. Recipient Gov.'s Voluntary Action Program Community Service award Gov. of Ind., 1980. Mem. Assn. Women Execs., Dallas Council World Affairs, Dallas Women's Found., Ind. Conf. on Social Concerns (state coordinator 1963-64), Network of Women in Bus., Indpls. Council of Women (program chmn. 1968-71). Club: The 500, Inc. Lodge: Order Eastern Star. Office: Family Support Adminstrn 1200 Main Tower Suite 1700 Dallas TX 75202

GOLDBERG, PAULA BURSZTYN, pharmacologist; b. Siedlce, Poland, Jan. 9, 1938; came to U.S., 1951; d. Hersz and Henia (Wodonos) B.; divorced; children: Philip Leon, Judith Margaret. Student, CCNY, 1961, Bklyn. Coll., 1967; BS in Pharmacy, Columbia U., 1962; PhD in Pharmacology, SUNY, Bklyn., 1968. Instr. Med. Coll. Pa., Phila., 1973-75, research asst. prof., 1975-76, asst. prof., 1976-83, assoc. prof., 1983-85; assoc. sr. investigator Smith Kline & French Labs., Phila., 1985-86, sr. investigator, 1986—; vis. prof. U. Costa Rica Faculty Pharmacy, 1969; cons. Nat. Inst. on Aging, 1977-85, GKS, Inc., 1979; columnist Geriatric Nursing, 1979; adj. prof. Drexel U., Phila., 1976-77; postdoctoral fellow Med. Coll. of Pa., Phila., 1972-73; vis. assoc. prof., 1985—. Editor CRC Handbook Pharmacology on Aging; mem. editorial bd. J. Cardiovascular Pharmacology, 1984—; contbr. articles to prof. jours. Guest presentor Sta. KQED TV Program Nat. Ednl. TV; bd. dirs. Solomon Schechter Day Sch., Phila, 1980-85; bd. dirs., dir. adult edn. Adath Zion Congregation, Phia., 1980-86. Fellow Am. Heart Assn., 1973-74; recipient J.C. Olshansky Gold Medal award, Columbia U., L. Leiterman Gold Meda award, 1962. Fellow Gerontol. Soc. Am.; mem. Am. Soc. Pharmacol. and Exptl.Therapeutics, N.Y. Acad. Scis., Assn. Women in Sci. (Phila. chpt. v.p. 1988—), Soc. for Exptl. Biology and Medicine, Sigma Xi. Home: 805 Kendrick St Philadelphia PA 19111 Office: Smith Kline and French Labs PO Box 1539 King of Prussia PA 19406-0939

GOLDBERG, STEPHANIE BENSON, editor, lawyer; b. Chgo., May 10, 1951; d. Harry and Bernice (Benson) G. BA, U. Ill., 1972; JD, DePaul U., 1985. Bar: Ill. 1987. Free-lance writer 1972-78; asst. editor Apt. Life, Des Moines, 1978-79; research asst. Keck, Mahin & Cate, Chgo., 1980-81, Lord, Bissell & Brook, Chgo., 1981-85; asst. editor ABA Jour., Chgo., 1986—. Contbr. articles to law publs. Democrat. Jewish. Home: 600 S Dearborn Chicago IL 60605 Office: ABA Journal 750 N Lake Shore Dr Chicago IL 60611

GOLDBERG, SUSAN SOLOMON, cultural organization administrator; b. N.Y.C., Mar. 18, 1944; d. Elias and Minnie (Barnett) Solomon; m. Eric A. Goldberg, Mar. 27, 1966; children—Evan, Jessica, Joanna. B.A., Harpur Coll. SUNY-Binghamton, 1965; M.S., Columbia U., 1966. Librarian N.Y. Pub. Library, 1966-67, br. librarian, 1967-68; reference librarian Bklyn. Pub. Library, 1971-72; reference librarian Finkelstein Meml. Library, Spring Valley, N.Y., 1975-76; coordinator adult services Tucson Pub. Library, 1977-80, dep. dir., 1980-87; mng. dir. Ariz. Theatre Co., Tucson, 1987— ; mem. adj. faculty Pima Community Coll., Tucson, 1978, U. Ariz., Tucson, 1978-79. Contbg. author: Critical Issues Conference 8, 1979; Public Librarianship, 1982; Reorganization in the Public Library, 1984. Vice pres. Cultural Alliance of Tucson, 1981-82; chmn. arts and culture com. Tucson Tomorrow, 1982-87; mem. Ariz. Commn. on Arts, Phoenix, 1983-87. Mem. ALA, Pub. Library Assn. (pres.), Library Adminstrn. and Mgmt. Assn., Ariz. Library Assn., NOW (pres. Rockland County br. 1974-76). Home: 5450 E 6th St Tucson AZ 85711 Office: Arizona Theatre Co PO Box 1631 Tucson AZ 85702

GOLDBERG, WHOOPI, actress; b. N.Y.C., Nov. 13, 1955; d. Robert and Emma (Harris) Johnson; m. David Claessen; 1 child, Alexandrea Martin. Mem. San Diego Repetory Theatre, 1975-80, Blake St. Hawkeyes, Berkeley, Calif., 1980-84. Appeared in one-person show Whoopi Goldberg on Broadway, 1984-85; films include The Color Purple, 1985, Jumping Jack Flash, 1986, Burglar, 1986, Telephone, 1987, Fatal Beauty, 1987. Address: care Creative Artists Agy Inc 1888 Century Park E Suite 1400 Los Angeles CA 90067

GOLDBERGER, BLANCHE RUBIN, sculptor, jeweler; b. N.Y.C., Feb. 2, 1914; d. David and Sarah (Israel) Rubin; m. Emanuel Goldberger, June 28, 1942; children—Richard N., Ary Louis. B.A., Hunter Coll., N.Y.C., 1934; M.A., Columbia U., 1936; Certificat d'Etudes, Sorbonne, Paris, 1936; postgrad. Westchester Arts Workshop Sculpture and Jewelry, White Plains, 1961-70, Silvermine Coll. Arts, 1962, Nat. Acad. Arts, N.Y.C., 1968. Tchr. French and Hebrew, N.Y.C. High Sch. System, Scarsdale Jr. and Sr. High Schs. One-woman shows include: Bloomingdale's, Eastchester, N.Y., 1975, Scarsdale Pub. Library, N.Y., 1976, Temple Israel, White Plains, N.Y., 1975, Greenwich Art Barn, Conn., 1972 Westlake Gallery, White Plains, N.Y., 1981; exhibited in group shows at Hudson River Mus., Yonkers, N.Y., 1978, Silvermine-New Eng. Ann., Silvermine, Conn., 1979; represented in permanent collection at Scarsdale High Sch. Library, N.Y.; also pvt. collections. Recipient award Beaux Arts of Westchester, White Plains, N.Y., 1967, First Prize, White Plains Art Show. Mem. Nat. Assn. Women Artists, Nat. Assn. Tchrs. French, Scarsdale Art Assn. (bd. dirs.; first prizes for sculpture). Jewish. Avocations: lecturing on sculpture, reading contemporary lit. in Hebrew, the violin, classical music concerts.

GOLDBERGER, NORMA MILLER, medical facility administrator; b. Toronto, Ont., Can., Dec. 25, 1945; came to U.S., 1967; d. Alec and Faye (Shapiro) Miller; m. Stephen Goldberger, Sept. 14, 1945; children: David, Joshua, Jessica. BA, U. Toronto, 1966, MA, 1967; student, U. Mich., 1968-69; postgrad., Boston Coll., 1969-70. Pres. Akron (Ohio) Women's Clinic, 1976—. Bd. dirs. Christian and Jewish Relations Com., Canton, Ohio, 1986—, Temple Israel Religious Sch., Canton, 1985—; mem. North Canton Player's Guild, 1986—. Mem. Nat. Abortion Fedn., Nat. Abortion Rights League, NOW, ACLU, Union of Soviet Jews. Office: Akron Women's Clinic 513 W Market St Akron OH 44303

GOLD-BIKIN, LYNNE Z., lawyer; b. N.Y.C., Apr. 23, 1938; d. Herbert Benjamin Zapoleon and Muriel Claire (Wimpheimer) Sarnoff; m. Roy E. Gold, Aug. 20, 1956 (div. July 1976); children—Russell, Sheryl, Lisa, Michael; m. Martin H. Feldman, June 28, 1987. B.A. summa cum laude, Albright Coll., 1969-73; J.D., Villanova Law Sch., 1973-76. Bar: Pa. 1976, U.S. Dist. Ct. (ea. dist.) Pa. 1976, U.S. Supreme Ct. 1979. Assoc. Pechner, Dorfman, Wolffe, Rounick & Cabot, Norristown, Pa., 1976-81; ptnr. Olin, Neil, Frock & Gold-Bikin, Norristown, 1981-82; pres. Gold-Bikin Devlin & Assocs., Norristown, 1982—. Author: Pennsylvania Marital Agreements, 1984; contbg. editor, Fairshare Mag., 1987—; course planner for 12 manuals on continuing legal edn., 1978—. Mem. Albright Coll. Pres.'s Council, Reading, Pa., 1982—. Fellow Am. Acad. Matrimonial Lawyers; mem. ABA (family law sect. council mem. 1981—), Pa. Bar Assn. (family law sect. council mem. 1980—), Montgomery County Bar Assn. (chmn. family law com. 1984-86). Home: 307 Hughes Rd King of Prussia PA 19406 Office: Gold-Bikin Devlin & Assocs 512 Dekalb St Norristown PA 19401

GOLDBLATT, EILEEN MICHELLE WITZMAN, program director; b. N.Y.C., Mar. 30, 1946; d. Ben and Sylvia (Schoenfield) Witzman; m. Myron Everett Goldblatt Jr., Mar. 22, 1970; children: Tracy Ellen, David Laurence. BS, Russell Sage Coll., 1967; MS, Bank Street Coll, 1980. Tchr., tchr. trainer N.Y.C. Bd. Edn., 1967-73, adminstr. mus. and cultural programs, 1984—; ednl. cons. Cooper-Hewitt Mus., N.Y.C., 1979-80; dir. mus., collaborative sch. programs Mus. Collaborative, Inc., N.Y.C., 1981-84; bd. dirs. Cultural Instn. Network, N.Y.C. Author: (workbook) Electroworks, 1980, (exhbn. guide) Smithsonian: A Treasure Hunt, 1979, (curriculum) The Ancient Egyptians, 1980; creator Cultural Institution Network Menu, 1984, 85, 86. Mem. exec. bd. N.Y.C. Art Tchrs. Assn., 1984—. Mem. Am. Assn. Mus., Internat. Council Mus. (com.), Nat. Art Edn. Assn., N.Y.C. Mus. Educators Roundtable, N.Y.C. Art Tchrs. Assn. Club: The Women's City, Inc. (N.Y.C.). Office: N Y C Bd Edn 131 Livingston St Room 412 Brooklyn NY 11201

GOLDBLATT, KATHLEEN BOYLE, nursing educator; b. Youngstown, Ohio, May 2, 1941; d. Edward Bernard and Mary Stewart (Woodard) Boyle; m. Edward L. Goldblatt, May 29, 1962 (div. 1981); children: Jill M., Dana L., Angela L., Edith D. BSN, U. Ala., 1965; MSN, Case Western Res., Cleve., 1969. Registered Nurse. Clin. asst. U. Ala., Tuscaloosa, 1965-66; instr. U. Ala., Birmingham, 1971-74, asst. prof., 1975-77, assoc. prof. grad. faculty, 1977-79, prof., chmn. MSN degree program, 1979-81; teaching asst. U. N.C., Chapel Hill, 1966-67; prof., dean U. Mo. Sch. of Nursing, Kansas City, 1981—; cons. Shanghai 2d Med. U., 1987; bd. dirs. Truman Med. Ctr., Inc., Edgar Snow Meml. Found. Editor: (ednl. pub.) NAACOG Update Series, vol. II, 1984, 85; writer video instrl. programs, 1974; Contbr. articles to profl. jours. Mem. Civiettes; bd. dirs. U. Mo. at Kansas City Friends of the Library, 1984—, Brookwood Forest PTA, 1972-80. Ala. State Nurses Assn. scholar, 1963, 64, 65; Children's Bur. dept. HEW grantee, 1967, 68, 69; named one of Outstanding Young Women of Am., 1974. Mem. Am. Nurses Assn. Instl., Nat. Osteoporosis Adv. Council, Council for Grad. Edn. in Adminstrn. in Nursing (chairperson 1986—), Nurses Assn. Am. (edn. coordinator dist. VII). Roman Catholic. Home: 4300 W 112th St Leawood KS 66211 Office: U Mo Kansas City 2220 Holmes St Kansas City MO 64108

GOLDEEN, DOROTHY ANN, art gallery executive; b. San Francisco, Nov. 12, 1948; m. Scott Morgan, Oct. 1986. BA, U. Calif., 1972. With Hansen, Fuller & Goldeen, San Francisco, 1972-78; prin. Fuller & Goldeen, San Francisco, 1978-86; pres. Dorothy Goldeen Gallery, Santa Monica, Calif., 1986—; presenter numerous seminars in field; adv. mem. Celebration of Bay Area Art, KQED-TV Art Auction, 1985. Host Maynard Dixon Retrospective, KQED-TV, 1975; contbr. articles to profl. jours. and essays to exhibition catalogs. Mem. founders circle, planning com. Jewish Community Mus., 1965. Mem. Santa Monica Art Dealers Assn. (v.p.), San Francisco Art Dealers Assn. (bd. dirs. 1979-80), Art Dealers Assn. Am., Soc. for the Encouragement of Contemporary Art, Profl. Orgn. Women in the Arts. Home and Office: 1547 9th St Santa Monica CA 90401

GOLDEN, CAROLE ANN, immunologist, microbiologist; b. Los Angeles, Sept. 23, 1942; d. Floyd Winfred and Betty Lee (Cantland) G. AB, Okla. Coll. Liberal Arts, 1963; MS in Microbiology, Miami U., Oxford, Ohio, 1969, PhD in Immunology, 1973. Research asst. prof. medicine U. Utah Med. Sch., Salt Lake City, 1973-79; sr. scientist Utah Biomed. Test Lab., Salt Lake City, 1976-82; v.p., sci. dir. Microbiol. Research Corp., Bountiful, Utah, 1978-87; v.p. research and devel. Environ. Diagnostics, Inc., Burlington, N.C., 1987—. Contbr. articles to profl. jours. Recipient citation Tech. Commn., 1983. Mem. AAAS, Am. Soc. Microbiology, N.Y. Acad. Sci., Reticuloendothelial Soc., Soc. Analytical Cytology, Am. Mensa, Am. Tissue Culture Assn. Republican. Home: 2 White Oak Elon College NC 27244 Office: Environ Diagnostics Inc 2990 Anthony Rd PO Box 908 Burlington NC 27215

GOLDEN, CONSTANCE JEAN, aerospace executive; b. Highland Park, Ill., June 8, 1939; d. Herman William and Chrystle O'Linda Leuer; BS in Math, Physics, Beloit Coll. summa cum laude, 1961; AM in Math., Harvard, 1962; PhD in Math., Stanford U., 1966, MS in Ops. research Engring., 1970; m. Charles Joseph Golden, June 13, 1962; 1 dau., Kerri Lynn. Scientist/engr. research and devel. div. Lockheed Missiles & Space Co., Sunnyvale, Calif., 1962-68, sr. scientist/engr. Palo Alto research labs., 1968-74, mgr. planning requirements and mgmt. control, missile systems div., Sunnyvale, 1975-78; program mgr. manned space ops. studies Ford Aerospace, Palo Alto, 1978-79, corp. strategy mgr., Detroit, 1980-81, mgr. mission ops. and tech. devel., Sunnyvale, Calif., 1982-84, mgr. adv. programs, 1984—; mem. comml. satellite survivability task force. Nat. Security Telecommunications Adv. Com., 1982-84; mem. Nat. Def. Exec. Res.-Fed. Emergency Mgmt. Agy.; mem. adv. council for sci. and math. Mills Coll., 1976-80. NSF fellow, 1961-62; recipient Tribute to Women in Industry award, 1985-86; named Disting. Woman of Yr. Lockheed, 1976. Mem. AIAA (space systems tech. panel 1982-83), Armed Forces Communications and Electronic Assn. (sect. dir. 1979-80), Am. Astronautical Soc. (chmn. San Francisco Bay Area sect. 1984), Soc. Women Engrs. (fellow 1982, past pres. San Francisco Bay Area sect., past nat. scholarship chmn.), Jr. Achievement, Phi Beta Kappa (award 1960-61). Club: Toastmasters (past pres., ATM). Contbg. author: Second Careers for Women, 1975. Office: Ford Aerospace 1260 Crossman Ave Sunnyvale CA 94089

GOLDEN, LAURA LORETTA, educator; b. Lexington, Ky., June 11, 1940; d. Hubert Anthony and Caroline Garrard (Holt) G.; B.S., Fla. State U., 1964; M.Ed., Ga. Coll., 1971. Instr., Fla. State U., Tallahassee, 1964-70, Middle Ga. Coll., Cochran, 1971-73; asst. prof. Ga. Coll., Milledgeville, 1973-75; asst. prof., co-dir. athletics head coach women's basketball Colo. Coll., Colorado Springs, 1975-81; asst. prof. phys. edn., head coach womens basketball Central Mich. U., Mount Pleasant, 1981-84; head coach women's basketball U. Ill., Champaign, 1984—. Mem. Mich. Basketball Coaches Assn., Womens Nat. Basketball Coaches Assn. Office: Armory Bldg 505 E Armory Dr Champaign IL 61820 *

GOLDEN, LIBBY, artist; b. N.Y.C.; d. Simon and Anna (Guskoff) Siegel; m. Alfred Golden. Diploma in Arts, Cooper Union Art Sch., 1932; postgrad., Hunter Coll., 1934-36, NYU, 1937. One-woman shows include Seligmann Galleries, N.Y.C., Arwin Galleries, Detroit, De Boicourt Gallery, Birmingham, Mich., Chapman Gallery, Toledo, Gallery Three, Boston, Scottsdale (Ariz.) Ctr. for the Arts, 1982, Phila. Mus. Art; exhibited in group shows at Met. Mus. Art, N.Y.C., Associated Am. Artists, N.Y.C., Boston Mus. Art, Nat. Acad. Art (Prize award), Seattle Art Mus., Phila. Mus. Art (Purchase award 1962), Colorprint, U.S.A. (Prize award 1964), Mich. Painters and Printmakers (Prize award 1960), Butler Inst. Art, Bklyn. Mus.; represented in permanent collections Detroit Inst. Arts, Grand Rapids (Mich.) Art Mus., Flint (Mich.) Inst. Art, Colby Coll. Art Mus., Art Mus. Richmond, Matthews Ctr., Scottsdale Ctr. for the Arts, U.S. State Dept., AMA, Mich. Blue Shield, Owens-Ill. Print Collection, Nat. Bank Detroit, Chrysler Corp., Fed. Mogul Corp., The Clarke Collection, London, Temple Beth El, Denver and Birmingham, The Temple, Sylvania, Ohio, St. Vincents Med. Ctr., Toledo, Blain Clinic, numerous others; represented in numerous pvt. collections; commd. oil painting Ctr. for Beethoven Studies, San Jose (Calif.) U., 1986. Home and Office: 7527 N del Norte Dr Scottsdale AZ 85258

GOLDEN, MARLENE PATRICIA, accountant, controller; b. Palisades Park, N.J., Sept. 21, 1955; d. Irwin Arthur and Louise (Gomez) Forman; m. Daniel Eugene Golden, May 6, 1984. BS, Montclair State Coll., 1977; postgrad., Fairleigh Dickinson U., 1981-83. Cashier, bookkeeper Atlantic & Pacific Tea Co., Palisades Park, 1972-76; gen. acct. Pub. Service Electric & Gas, Newark, 1976-77; asst. to controller Am. Leprosy Missions, Inc., Bloomfield, N.J., 1977-80, dir. data processing, 1980-83, controller, 1983—; cons. acct. McCarthy Landscapes, Palisades Park, 1980-81, Abbey Chiropractic Ctr., Bogota, N.J., 1984—. Mem. Assn. Female Execs., Christian Ministries Mgmt. Assn., Montclair State Coll. Alumni Assn., Phi Chi Theta Alumni Assn., Phi CHi Theta Undergrad. Alumni Assn. Roman Catholic. Home: 262 W Madison Ave Dumont NJ 07628 Office: ALM One Broadway Elmwood Park NJ 07407

GOLDEN, NANCY FELICE, sales professional; b. Long Beach, N.Y., Mar. 26, 1950; d. Romie James and Lucille Eleanor (Mehler) Rice. BA in Secondary Edn., Hofstra U., 1971. Dept. mgr., asst. buyer Forest Distributors Co., Garden City, N.Y., 1971-73; buyer Times Square Stores Inc., Bklyn., 1973-77, Caldor Inc., Norwalk, Conn., 1977-79, Lechmere Inc., Woburn, Mass., 1979-80; prin., pres. N. Golden Assocs., Malden, Mass., 1980—; ptnr. Tausey/Golden Sales Assocs., Salem, Mass., 1986—. Editor The New Englander newsletter, 1984-85, 87; copyrighted composer, lyricist, 1986—. Vol. Mondale/Ferraro campaign, 1984, United Way of Boston, 1987. Mem. Housewares Club New Eng. (pres., chmn. bd. dirs. 1985—). Democrat. Jewish. Office: Tausey/Golden Sales Assocs 710 Turnpike St Stoughton MA 02072

GOLDEN, RENATA MICHELE, photographer, journalist; b. Chgo., Nov. 3, 1952; d. Michael Frances and Eileen Rose (Foley) G. Student, U. N.Mex., 1974-76; BA, Ariz. State U., 1978. Photojournalist The Mesa (Ariz.) Tribune, 1978-80; research asst. Mus. for Contemporary Art, Chgo., 1981; darkroom printer for Olympics AP, Los Angeles, 1984; instr. photography City of Phoenix, 1983-87; owner, photographer Renata Golden Photography, Phoenix, 1980—. One-woman photography exhibitions Phoenix Pub. Library, 1984, Austin Gallery, Scottsdale, Ariz., 1987; author, photographer articles and pictures for numerous publs. including Scottsdale Progress, USA Today, U.S. News and World Report, Christian Science Monitor, N.Y. Photo Dist. News. Office: 1222 E Edgemont Phoenix AZ 85006

GOLDEN, TERESA VITAGLIANO, business official; b. Mt. Vernon, N.Y., June 5, 1955; d. Vincent Jack and Audrey Mildred (Fabini) Vitagliano; B.A. in Econs., Coll. Mt. St. Vincent, 1975; M.B.A. in Corp. Fin., Pace U., 1979; m. George Patrick Golden, Jan. 3, 1976; children—Helen Marie, George Christopher. Accounts receivable mgr. ITEL Corp., White Plains, N.Y., 1975-78; fin. systems cons. Sci. Timesharing Corp., White Plains, 1978-79; systems analyst IBM, Poughkeepsie, N.Y., 1979-80, graphics mktg. rep., 1980-82, programming planner, 1982-83, mgr. graphics market support, White Plains, 1983-85, bus. planner, Armonk, N.Y., 1985-87; forecasting mgr., White Plains, 1987—. Republican. Roman Catholic. Home: 33 Flower Rd Hopewell Junction NY 12533 Office: IBM 44 S Broadway White Plains NY 10601

GOLDFARB, MINDY SUSAN, accountant; b. Bronx, June 15, 1962; d. Nat and Sheila Phillis (Geselov) G. BBA in Pub. Acctg., Pace U., 1984. CPA, N.Y. Acct. tax dept. Oppenhein, Appel, Dixon and Co., N.Y.C., 1984-87, Deloitte, Haskins and Sells, Hackensack, N.J., 1987—. Mem. Am. Inst. CPA's, N.Y. State Soc. CPA's. Democrat. Jewish. Office: Deloitte Haskins & Sells 411 Hackensack Ave Hackensack NJ 07601

GOLDFEDER, FERN GAIL, executive recruiter; b. Bronxville, N.Y., Feb. 12, 1955; d. Herbert Ken and Lorene (Shum) G. BS in Communications, Emerson Coll., 1977, MS in Speech, 1978. Polit. reporter, reporter/producer Devel. Issues program Sta. WTBS-FM, Boston, 1975-78; dir. communications Misericordia Hosp. Med. Ctr., Bronx, N.Y., 1978-80; pres. Fern Gail Goldfeder Communications and Mktg., Inc., Yonkers, N.Y., 1980-83; sr. account mgr. Sales Cons., Inc., Hawthorne, N.Y., 1983—. Contbr. articles Forbes mag., Wall Street Jour., Christian Sci. Monitor, N.Y. Daily News. Recipient awards Lions Club, Bronx, 1978-80, Women In Sales, Eastchester, N.Y., 1986. Republican. Home: 1 Remsen Rd #3K Yonkers NY 10710

GOLDHABER, GERTRUDE SCHARFF, physicist; b. Mannheim, Fed. Republic of Germany, July 14, 1911; came to U.S., 1939, naturalized, 1944; d. Otto and Nelly (Steinharter) Scharff; m. Maurice Goldhaber, May 24, 1939; children: Alfred Scharff, Michael Henry. Student, univs. Freiburg, Zurich, Berlin; Ph.D., U. Munich, 1935. Research assoc. Imperial Coll., London, Eng., 1935-39; research physicist U. Ill., 1939-48, asst. prof., 1948-50; assoc. physicist Brookhaven Nat. Lab., Upton, N.Y., 1950-58; physicist Brookhaven Nat. Lab., 1958-62, sr. physicist, 1962—; cons. nuclear data group NRC, Nat. Acad. Scis., AEC Labs. ACDA, 1974-77; adj. prof. Cornell U., 1980-82, Johns Hopkins U., 1983-86; Phi Beta Kappa vis. scholar, 1984-85. Mem. editorial com. Ann. Rev. Nuclear Sci, 1973-77; N. Am. rep. bd. editors Jour. Physics G (Europhysics Jour.), 1978-80. Trustee-at-large Univ. Research Assn. governing Fermi Nat. Accelerator Lab., 1972-77; ednl. adv. com. N.Y. Acad. Scis., 1982—; Nat. Adv. Com. on Pre-Coll. Material Devel., 1984-88. Fellow Am. Phys. Soc. (council 1979-82, chmn. panel on improvement pre-coll. physics literacy 1979-82, chmn. audit com. 1980, mem. com. on profl. opportunities 1979-81, com. on history of physics, exec. com. 1983-84), AAAS (mem.-at-large sect. B physics com. 1986—); mem. Nat. Acad. Scis. (mem. report rev. com. 1973-81, mem. acad. forum adv. com. 1974-81, mem. com. on edn. and employment of women in sci. and engring. 1978-83, commn. on human rights 1984-87), Sigma Xi. Home: 91 S Gillette Ave Bayport NY 11705 Office: Brookhaven Nat Lab 510A Upton NY 11973

GOLDICH, MARY PATRICIA, health care administrator; b. Orillia, Ontario, Can., Mar. 8, 1953; d. Albert Crockett and Patricia Irene (Dennis) McIsaac; m. Geoffrey Shaw Goldich, May 26, 1979; 1 child, Meredith McIsaac. BA with honors, U. Western Ontario, 1975; MS in Health Edn., U. Ill., 1977. Instr. dept. health edn. Eastern Ill. U., Charleston, 1977-79; survey report analyst Joint Commn. on Accreditation of Hosps., Chgo., 1980-81; quality assurance coordinator Mt. Sinai Hosp., Chgo., 1981-82; dir. quality assessment/utilization St. Joseph Hosp. and Health Care Ctr., Chgo., 1982—. Mem. Ill. Assn. Quality Assurance Profls. Roman Catholic. Home: 3107 N Kenmore Chicago IL 60657 Office: St Joseph Hosp & Health Care Ctr 2900 N Lake Shore Dr Chicago IL 60657

GOLDMAN, ARLENE LESLIE, office supply company executive, troubleshooter; b. Paterson, N.J., July 7, 1956; d. Jacob and Bertha (Deck) G.; student Am. U., 1974. Asst. store mgr., asst. buyer Latt's Country Squire, Washington, 1976-77; ops. mgr. Complement, Washington, 1977-78; with Bidermann Industries, 1978-83, prodn. mgr. Jean-Paul Germain div., N.Y.C., 1979-80, dir. ops., 1980-81, v.p., 1981-83; nat. sales mgr. Ralph Lauren div., 1984-86; ind. cons., 1986; dir. ops. Summit Office Supply, N.Y.C., 1986—. Mem. Friend Whitney Mus., Met. Mus. Art (sustaining mem.), ORT. Home: 23 E 10th St Apt 608 New York NY 10003 Office: Summit Office Supply Co 303 W 10th St New York NY 10014

GOLDMAN, BARBARA DEREN, film producer, interior decorator; b. Bridgeport, Conn., Dec. 22, 1949; m. James Goldman, Oct. 25, 1975. BS, U. Bridgeport, 1971. Pres. Barbara Deren Assocs., N.Y.C., 1975—, Raoulfilm Inc., N.Y.C., 1979—. Co-author: Where to Eat in America, 1987.

GOLDMAN, ELAINE, executive search firm executive; b. Detroit, July 26, 1944. BSJ, Northwestern U., 1968; cert., L'Institute Catholique, 1972; MS, Ind. U., 1974. Reporter Sta. WHAS-TV, Louisville, Ky., 1974-76; prof. mass communications Va. Commonwealth U., 1974-76; mgr. Pub. Relations Inst., 1977-78; ptnr. Goldman Scott & Assocs., 1978-80; prin. Jones Goldman & Co., 1981; exec. v.p. Haley, Kiss & Dowd, 1981-84; pres. The Goldman Group Inc., 1984—. Mem. Internat. Assn. Bus. Communicators, Pub. Relations Soc. of Am. Office: The Goldman Group Inc 149 Madison Ave Suite 205 New York NY 10016

GOLDMAN, GAIL MEURICE, arts administrator; b. Jamestown, N.Y., Jan. 31, 1953; d. Simon and Meurice Henrietta (Finer) G. BFA, Syracuse U., 1976. Program officer Nat. Endowment for the Arts, Washington, 1977-82, regional site evaluator, 1985—; dir. individual artist programs Colo. Council on the Arts and Humanities, Denver, 1982—; cons. pub. art various cities, 1982—. Contbr. articles to profl. jour.; artist, designer pub. sculpture City of Denver, 1984. Juror Commn. on Cultural Affairs, Denver, 1985—. Mem. Soc. N. Am. Goldsmiths, Am. Crafts Council, Washington Guild Goldsmiths (pres. 1980-82), Colo. Lawyers for the Arts, Colo. Artist Craftsmen. Democrat. Jewish. Office: Colo Council Arts & Humanities 770 Pennsylvania St Denver CO 80203

GOLDMAN, JANET PARKER, business administrator; b. Brookline, Mass., June 9, 1958; s. Robert Alan and Lucy (Thimann) P. BA, Cornell U., 1980. Lic. real estate. Sales rep. McGraw-Hill Co., Boston, 1981-82; office mgr. Chestnut Hill (Mass.) Psych. Assn., 1982-85; dir. adminstrv. services The Parker Acad., Sudbury, Mass., 1985—; profl. devel. specialist The Parker Acad., Sudbury, 1985—. Producer, host children's TV show Adams-Russell Cable, Acton, 1987—. Vol. tchr. English as a 2d Language Cornell U., Ithaca, N.Y., 1980-81; story reader Children's Reading Program, Acton Sch., 1985—. Named one of Outstanding Young Women of Am., 1980. Mem. Am. Soc. Profl. and Exec. Women. Office: The Parker Acad 248 Concord Rd Sudbury MA 01776

GOLDMAN, JILL MINKOFF, pharmaceutical company information systems executive; b. Kansas City, Mo., July 12, 1953; d. Julius Burt and Eloise Joy (Shlensky) Minkoff; m. Barry Charles Goldman, Jan. 30, 1982; children—Joshua Scott, Elise Lynn. Certificat D'Assiduite, Université de Grenoble (France), 1968; B.A., Pomona Coll., 1974. Mktg. rep. IBM, Riverside, Calif., 1974-77, San Francisco, 1978-79; dir. store systems Neiman Marcus, Dallas, 1979-81; dir. end-user computing services. Marion Labs., Kansas City, Mo., 1982—. Sch. pres. ARC, Kansas City, Mo., 1966-67; v.p. chpt. B'nai B'rith Girls, Kansas City, 1968-69. Mem. Menorah Hosp. Aux., Nat. Council Jewish Women, Share, Inc., Guide Internat. Corp. Club: Toastmasters. Home: 5406 State Line Mission Hills KS 66208 Office: Marion Labs Inc 9300 Ward Pkwy Kansas City MO 64114

GOLDMAN, JOAN, lawyer, social worker; b. St. Louis, Mar. 4, 1938; d. Morris Albert and Regina (Aron) Greenberg; m. Michael Robert Goldman, Aug. 19, 1961 (div.); children: Tamara Ruth Goldman Sher, Joshua Charles, Abigail Helaine. BA, U. Ill., 1960; MSW, Loyola U., Chgo., 1982, JD, 1982. Bar: Ill. 1982; cert. social worker, Ill. Sole practice, Chgo., 1982-87; assoc. Borovsky, Ehrlicht & Kronenberg, 1987—; vis. lectr. Loyola U. Sch. Social Work, Chgo. Mem. Chgo. Bar Assn., Ill. State Bar Assn., ABA, Nat. Assn. Social Workers, Mortar Board. Jewish. Home: 247 Franklin Rd Glencoe IL 60022

GOLDMAN, KATHRYN LOUISE, organizational consultant; b. N.Y.C., Mar. 15, 1946; d. George Samuel and Jeanne Gordon (Rosenbluth) G. BA magna cum laude, Goucher Coll., 1967; cert. in critical langs., Princeton U., 1967; M in Philosophy, Columbia U., 1973, PhD, 1980. Lic. clin. sociologist, Tex. Researcher Internat. Research and Exchanges Bd., N.Y.C., 1973; profl. counselor Austin (Tex.) Community Coll., 1975-78, chair human devel. div., 1978-84; pvt. practice organizational cons. Carmel, Calif., 1980-88; orgnl. devel. cons. Exxon Chemicals, Linden, N.J., 1988—; prof. mgmt. Monterey (Calif.) Inst. Internat. Studies, 1984—, Naval Postgrad. Sch., Monterey, 1984. Contbr. articles to profl. jours. Bd. dirs. Neighborhood Assn., Peninsula Concerned Neighbors, Pacific Grove, Calif., 1985. Fulbright fellow, 1967-78, Univ. fellow, 1970-73. Mem. Acad. Mgmt., Sociol. Practice Assn. Office: Exxon Chems PO Box 536 Linden NJ 07036

GOLDMAN, LAURA NAN, physician; b. Long Branch, N.J., Apr. 1, 1953; d. Max Isaac and Evelyn (Frumkin) G.; m. Scott D. Haas, May 3, 1986. BS cum laude, Franklin Marshall Coll., 1975; MD, Rutgers U., 1979. Resident in family practice Brown U., Pawtucket, R.I., 1979-82; family physician Manet Community Health Ctr., Quincy, Mass., 1982-84; med. dir. New Eng. Health Assocs., Boston, 1984—; clin. instr. Tufts Med. Sch., Boston, 1984—. Mem. Com. for Health Rights in Cen. Am., 1982-87. Mem. Am. Med. Women's Assn., Physicians for A Nat. Health Policy, Physicians for Social Responsibility, Phi Beta Kappa. Office: New Eng Health Assocs 77 Summer St Boston MA 02139

GOLDMAN, MYRA FRANCES, physical education educator; b. N.Y.C., Feb. 11, 1935; d. Harry G. BS, U. Maine, 1957; MS, Pa. State U., 1962; PhD, NYU, 1972; AS, Endicott Coll., 1987. Tchr. New Milford (Conn.) Pub. Schs., 1957-59; grad. asst. Pa. State U., University Park, 1959-60; tchr. Bellefonte (Pa.) Pub. Schs., 1960-61; instr. Douglass Coll. Rutgers U., New Brunswick, N.J., 1961-65; tchr. New Rochelle (N.Y.) Pub. Schs., 1965-67; grad. asst. NYU, 1967-69; from asst. to assoc. prof. phys. edn. U. Mass., Boston, 1969-79, prof., 1979—. Co-author: Dimensions of Physical Education, 1969, Humanistic Physical Education, 1972. Mem. Youth Commn., Hamilton, Mass., 1979-85. Mem. Am. Alliance for Health, Phys. Edn., Recreation and Dance (numerous offices ea. dist. assn. 1957—, Presdl. medallion 1978, 86, Honor award 1982), Mass. Alliance for Health, Phys. Edn., Recreation and Dance (numerous offices 1969—), Pi Beta Phi, Pi Lambda Theta. Office: U Mass Boston Harbor Campus Sci Ctr Boston MA 02125

GOLDMAN, PAMELA, broadcasting professional; b. N.Y.C., Sept. 2, 1961; d. Daniel B. and Shirley (Dworsh) G. BA in Polit. Sci., SUNY, Binghamton, 1984. Sales account exec. Sportset Inc., Massapequa, N.Y., 1984-86, mgr. sales, 1986, dir. sales, mktg, promotions, 1986-87; page NBC TV, Manhattan, N.Y., 1988—; pres., owner Under Constrn., Locust Valley, N.Y. 1987—. Mem. Nat. Assn. Broadcasters, Pi Sigma Alpha. Home: 23 Fountain Ln Jericho NY 11753

GOLDMAN, PATRICIA ANN, govt. ofcl.; b. Newton, N.J., Mar. 22, 1942; d. Jacob Joseph and Miriam Louise (Cassiday) G.; B.A. in Econs., Goucher Coll., 1964; m. Charles E. Goodell, July 1, 1978. Research asst. Joint Econ. Com. of Congress, 1964-65; legis. asst. ad hoc subcom. on war on poverty, edn. and labor com. U.S. Ho. of Reps., 1965-66; research cons. U.S. C. of C., 1966, dir. manpower and poverty programs, 1967-71; legis. counsel Nat. League Cities, also U.S. Conf. of Mayors, 1971-72; exec. dir. The House Wednesday Group, U.S. Ho. of Reps., 1972-79; mem. Nat. Transp. Safety Bd., Washington, 1979-88, vice chmn., 1982-88; sr. v.p. US Air, Arlington, Va., 1988—; vis. prof. Woodrow Wilson Nat. Fellowship Program; lectr. Brookings Instn. Program for Sr. Govt. Execs. Chmn. bd. trustees Goucher Coll.; former treas. Nat. Women's Edn. Fund; former mem. adv. bd. Nat. Women's Polit. Caucus, also past chmn. Republican Women's Task Force; former chair governing bd. Ripon Soc. Fellow Kennedy Inst. Politics, Harvard U., 1978. Named Woman of Yr., Women's Transp. Seminar, 1982. Office: US Air Group 1911 Jefferson Davis Hwy Arlington VA 22202

GOLDMAN, RACHEL BOK, civic volunteer; b. Phila., Mar. 28, 1937; d. W. Curtis and Nellie Lee (Holt) Bok; m. James Nelson Kise, Dec. 20, 1958 (div. May 1974); children: Jefferson B, C. Curtis; m. Allen S. Goldman, Nov. 28, 1981; stepchildren: Jonathan, Benjamin Allen, Adam Louis. Student, Sweet Briar (Va.) Coll., 1955-57; BA in Art History, U. Pa., 1977. Bd. dirs. Arts Exchange mag., 1977-79, chmn. bd. dirs., 1977-79. Mem. collector's circle Pa. Acad. Fine Arts, 1983-85, exhbn. selection com. Morris Gallery, 1979-82; mem. Rittenhouse Sq. Women's Com. Pa. Orchestra, 1979-85; mem. Indian com. Pa. Yearly Meeting, 1971-75; mem. ladies' com. Powel House, 1965-69; co-founder Friends of Curtis Inst. Music, 1982—, chmn. 1982-85; bd. dirs. Mary Louis Curtis Bok Found., 1982—, The Curtis Inst. Music, 1982—, The Buten Mus., 1982-84, Brady Cancer Research Inst.

1983—, Settlement Music Sch., 1984-87, The Phila. Award, 1970—, Elfreth's Alley Assn., 1962-65, sec. 1963-65; bd. dirs. The Am. Found., 1955-83, sec.-treas., 1980-83; bd. dirs. The Community Sch. of Phila., 1971-74, chmn. bd. dirs., co-founder, adminstr.; bd. dirs. Women in Transition, 1973-78, div. counselor, 1974-76; bd. dirs. Friends of Phila. Mus. Art, 1977-83, sec., 1979-81, program chmn., 1981-82, co-chmn., 1982-83; bd. dirs. Samuel Yellin Found., 1977—, co-founder, sec., 1977-84. Democrat. Clubs: Camden Yacht (Maine), Cosmopolitan of Phila. (house com. 1981-84).

GOLDMAN, SHERYL ANN, educational administrator; b. Pitts., Dec. 16, 1948; d. Albert W. and Marion (Schmidt) G. Student, Carnegie Mellon U., 1966-68; BS in Biology, U. Pitts., 1970, MS in Microbiology, 1976; MS in Music Theory, Duquesne U., 1985, postgrad., 1985-86. Research technician various cos., 1969-76; lectr. Penn. State U., McKeesport, 1975; teaching asst. U. Pitts., 1975-76; tchr. Our Lady Mercy Acad., Monroeville, Pa., 1976-77; instr. Community Coll. of Allegheny County, Pitts., 1977-82, 1986-87; conductor parish choir Mother Good Counsel Ch., Pitts., 1982; dir. music Concord Presbyn. Ch., Pitts., 1986-87; asst. tutorial coordinator Learning Skills Program Duquesne U., Pitts., 1978—. Mem. choir Rodef Shalom Synagogue, 1960-64, First United Meth. Ch. Pitts., 1976-83. Mem. Am. Soc. Microbiology, Beta Beta Beta. Democrat. Jewish. Office: Duquesne U Learning Skills Program 312 Administrn Bldg Pittsburgh PA 15282

GOLDSCHMID, MARY TAIT, economist, consultant; b. Oxford, Ohio, July 15, 1947; d. Joseph Charles and Elizabeth Colville (Tait) Seibert; m. Harvey Jerome Goldschmid, Dec. 21, 1973; children: Charles Maxwell, Paul MacNeil, Joseph Tait. Student, London Sch. Econs., 1968; BA, Smith Coll., 1969; MBA, Columbia U., 1973, PhD, 1975. Security analyst Argus Research, N.Y.C., 1969-70; economist Chase Manhattan Bank, N.Y.C., 1970-71, Exxon Corp., N.Y.C., 1974-86, Goldschmid P.C., N.Y.C., 1986—. Contbr. articles to profl. jours. Trustee Riverdale Country Sch., Bronx, 1986—, pres. Parents Assn. 1986-87. Mem. Am. Econs. Assn., Women's Fin. Assn., Internat. Assn. Energy Economists, Nat. Assn. Bus. Economists. Clubs: Cosmopolitan, Riverdale Yacht. Home: 691 W 247th Bronx NY 10471

GOLDSMITH, KATHLEEN MAWHINNEY, accountant; b. Bklyn., July 16, 1957; d. James R. and Carmela (Ditria) Mawhinney; m. Marc Bruce Goldsmith, Oct. 7, 1979; 1 child, James Ryan. BS, Alfred U., 1979; MBA, U. Conn., 1986. CPA, Conn. Acct., Price Waterhouse, Stamford, Conn., 1979-83; controller OCE Bus. Systems Inc., Stamford, 1983—. Adv., Jr. Achievement, 1980-81. Named Outstanding Young Women of Am. Mem. Am. Inst. CPAs, Conn. Soc. CPAs, Phi Kappa Phi, Delta Mu Delta. Home: 24 Lampost Dr West Redding CT 06896 Office: OCE Inc 1351 Washington Blvd Stamford CT 06902

GOLDSMITH, MELISSA KAY, television executive; b. N.Y.C., June 18, 1958; d. Nat and Ruth Bernice (Wells) G.; m. Lawrence Howard Stone, June 14, 1987. Student, Union Coll., 1976-78; BA, Brown U., 1979-81. Ind. producer, dir. Sta. WNET, N.Y.C., 1981-83; assoc. producer, devel. exec. Smith-Tomlin Prodns., N.Y.C., 1983-84; v.p., assoc. dir. program devel. Batten, Barton, Durstine and Osborn, N.Y.C., 1984—. Producer, dir. (documentary) Banana Kelly, 1982 (local emmy award 1983). Bd. dirs. Banana Kelly Community, Bronx, N.Y., 1981-83, Improvement Assn. Nat. Endowment for the Humanities grantee, 1980. Democrat. Jewish. Office: Batten Barton Durstine & Osborn 1285 Avenue of the Americas New York NY 10019

GOLDSMITH, SUSAN LEE, marketing executive; b. N.Y.C., May 8, 1955; d. Arthur Austin Jr. and Carolyn Evelyn (Milford) G.; m. K. B. McKellop, 1987. Student, U. Munich, Fed. Republic Germany, 1976; BA in English, German, Skidmore Coll., 1977. Jr. supr. MBI Inc., Norwalk, Conn., 1978-80, sr. supr., 1980-84, group supr., 1984-86, mgr. customer service, accts., 1986-87, ops. mgr., 1987—. Tutor trainer Literacy Vols., Norwalk, 1981-85; vol. UN Club of Fairfield, Norwalk, 1984. Mem. AAUW, Nat. Assn. Female Execs.

GOLDSTEIN, BONNIE JOY, private investigator; b. St. Paul, June 19, 1949; d. Howard E. Goldstein and Marisse (Butwin) Holland; m. James Thomas Grady, Mar. 31, 1985; children: Rachel, Nathan Howard. Student, U. Minn., 1967. Ptnr. Hanrahan & Mintz, Washington, 1979-81; prin. Goldstein & Assoc., Washington, 1981-82; investigator Rogovin Huge & Lenzer, Washington, 1982-84; ptnr. Goldstein & Denton, Washington, 1984—. Contbr. articles to profl. jours. Office: Goldstein & Denton 3000 Connecticut Ave NW Washington DC 20008

GOLDSTEIN, CHARLOTTE L(IPSON), marketing professional, public relations executive; b. Boston, Aug. 1, 1929; d. George Lipson and Frances (Feldstein) L.; m. Norman R. Goldstein, Sept. 15, 1948; children—Sue, David, Julie. Student Mary Brooks Coll., 1945-47. Pres. Engineered Inspection System, Robbinsville, N.J., 1970—. Contbr. articles to profl. jours. Bd. dirs. Congregation Beth Chaim, 1977-82, Sunday Sch. tchr., 1952-69, adult edn. com., mem. bd. continuing edn., caring coms.; charter mem. West Windsor Library Commn., 1981-85; mem. West Windsor Twp. Commn. on Aging. Mem. Middlesex County (N.J.) Bd. Realtors (assoc.), Mercer County Bd. Realtors, Hunterdon County Bd. Realtors, So. Monmouth County Bd. Realtors, Somerset County Bd. Realtors, Burlington County Bd. Realtors, Pa.-Bucks County C. of C. Princeton C. of C., Mercer C of C. Republican. Jewish. Clubs: Hadassah (pres. 1952-53), B'nai B'rith (bd. dirs. 1968-70). Avocations: china painting, cooking, traveling, bridge, reading. Home: 10 Jeffrey Ln Princeton Junction NJ 08550 Office: Engineered Inspection System Inc 1200 Route 130 Robbinsville NJ 08691

GOLDSTEIN, DEBRA EDELSON, lawyer; b. Stamford, Conn., Oct. 5, 1950; d. A. Herbert and Sylvia (Gordon) Edelson; m. Jeffrey S. Goldstein, Aug. 11, 1974; children—Jennifer Alyss, Lisa Nicole. B.A., Wellesley Coll., 1972; J.D., Georgetown U., 1975. Bar: N.Y. 1976. Atty., Ogilvy & Mather Advt., N.Y.C., 1975-79, v.p., atty., 1979-86, sr. v.p., assoc. gen. counsel, 1986—. Mem. Lawyers Pro-Choice, Planned Parenthood, N.Y.C., 1982—. Mem. Am. Assn. Advt. Agys. (legal affairs com. 1985—, chmn. 1988—), Am. Corp. Counsel Assn., Women in Law Depts., N.Y. State Bar Assn. (exec. com. corp. counsel sect. 1982—, sec. corp. counsel sect. 1984, pub. relations com. 1983—). Democrat. Jewish. Office: Ogilvy & Mather Advt 2 E 48th St New York NY 10017

GOLDSTEIN, DEBRA HOLLY, lawyer; b. Newark, Mar. 11, 1953; d. Aaron and Erica (Schreier) Green; m. Joel Ray Goldstein, Aug. 14, 1983; children: Stephen Michael, Jennifer Ann. BA, U. Mich., 1973; JD, Emory U., 1977. Bar: Ga. 1977, Mich. 1978, D.C. 1978, Ala. 1984. Tax analyst atty. Gen. Motors Corp., Detroit, 1977-78; trial atty. U.S. Dept. Labor, Birmingham, Ala., 1978—. Chairperson Women's Coordinating Bur., Birmingham, 1983-85; active United Way, Birmingham, 1983, 87, Temple Beth-El Adult Edn., 1985-86, program chmn. Sisterhood, 1987-88; scholarship chairperson Nat. Council Jewish Women, 1986; steering com. Birmingham Bus. and Profl. Women Fedn., 1987-88. Mem. ABA, Ga. Bar Assn., D.C. Bar Assn., Mich. Bar Assn., Birmingham Bar Assn. (law day com.), Ala. Bar Assn. Jewish. Lodges: B'nai B'rith Women (chairperson S.E. region 1984-86, counselor 1986-88, recipient Women's Humanitarian award 1983), Zonta (v.p. 1983-84), Hadassah (local bd. dirs. 1979-83). Office: US Dept Labor Office of Solicitor Suite 201 2015 2d Ave N Birmingham AL 35203

GOLDSTEIN, HANNAH, real estate developer, business consultant; b. N.Y.C., Apr. 6, 1934; d. William and Cecil (Rock) Rosenblatt; A.A., U. Fla., 1953; B.S. in Bus. Adminstrn., N.Y. U., 1955; children—Joyce Dara, Mitchell Bruce, Stephen Elliott, Russell Jay. Self-employed, N.Y.C., 1954-65; with Equitable Life Assurance Soc., N.Y.C., 1962-65; with Creative Programs and Paul Breiff Assocs., N.Y.C., 1965-70; mem. N.Y. Mercantile Exchange and Nat. Stock Exchange, 1967-70; pres. J. Pierre Internat., N.Y.C., 1968-73, Discovery Internat. Ltd., Scottsdale, Ariz., 1972—, Goldwest Internat. Ltd., Scottsdale, 1980—; v.p. Southwest Ice Products, Inc., Scottsdale, 1984—, Mobile Ice Corp., Scottsdale, 1984—; bus. cons. Closeburn Horse Farm, 1983-85. Bd. dirs. Friends of Channel 8, Tempe, 1977—; mem. econ. devel. com. Scottsdale Town Enrichment Program, 1981-82; Democratic Precinct committeewoman, 1980—; State Dem. Committeewoman, 1981—; bd. dirs. Treatment Alts. for Street Crimes, Phoenix, 1983—, Phoenix Little Theatre; mem. econ. devel. com. Animal Welfare League, others. Mem. English Speaking Union, Ariz. World Trade Assn., Nat. Assn. Cable TV, Nat. Assn. TV Programming Execs., Am. Statis. Assn., Am. Mgmt. Assn., Nat. Acad. TV Arts and Scis., Alumni Assn. N.Y.U. Sch. Commerce, Beta Gamma Sigma. Clubs: N.Y. Univ.; Nucleus (Phoenix). Home: 8132 E Valley View Rd Scottsdale AZ 85253

GOLDSTEIN, JOYCE ESERSKY, restaurant owner; b. Bklyn., July 17, 1935; d. Gerry Lewis and Jeanne (Salata) Esersky; m. Marc Evan Goldstein, Sept. 15, 1957 (div. Aug. 1972); children: Evan Matthew, Karen Anne, Rachel Laura. BA, Smith Coll., 1956; MFA, Yale U., 1959. Painter San Francisco, 1961-65, cooking tchr., 1965-71; tchr., dir. Calif. St. Cooking Sch., San Francisco, 1971-76; tchr. U. Calif., Berkeley, 1976-83; chef, mgr. Chez Panisse Cafe, Berkeley, 1981-83; chef, owner Sq. One Restaurant, San Francisco, 1984—. Author: Feedback, 1977; columnist Bon Appetit mag., 1982—, San Francisco Chronicle, 1986—. Named one of Top 25 Am. Cooks, Cooks mag., 1985. Mem. San Francisco Food Soc., Am. Inst. Food and Wine (bd. dirs. No. Calif. chpt. 1985-87). Jewish. Office: Square One Restaurant 190 Pacific Ave Mall San Francisco CA 94111

GOLDSTEIN, MARCIA LANDWEBER, lawyer; b. Bklyn., Aug. 7, 1952; d. Jacob and Sarah Ann (Danovitz) Landweber; m. Mark Lewis Goldstein, June 3, 1973. AB, Cornell U., 1973, JD, 1975. Bar: N.Y. 1976, U.S. Dist. Ct. (so. and ea. dists.) N.Y., U.S. Ct. Appeals)2d and 9th cirs.). Assoc. Weil, Gotshal & Manges, N.Y.C., 1975-83, ptnr., 1983—; visiting lectr. Yale U. Mem. ABA (com. on creditors' rights, corp. counsel com.), Assn. of Bar of City of N.Y. (bankruptcy and reorgn. com.), Practicing Law Inst. (panel 1985, 86). Office: Weil Gotshal & Manges 767 Fifth Ave New York NY 10153

GOLDSTEIN, MARCI-ANN F., health care executive, psychologist; b. Phila., Feb. 2, 1951; d. Howard M. Goldstein and Alayne (Abrams) Plotnick. B.S., Drexel U., 1972; M.A., Villanova U., 1974; Ed.D., Temple U., 1979. Research assoc. Pa. Hosp., Phila., 1972-73; dir. career counseling Delaware County Community Coll., Media, Pa., 1973-75; research assoc., dept. adminstr. adult edn. Temple U., Phila., 1976-79; dir. adult/continuing edn. Baruch Coll., N.Y.C., 1980-81; dir. tng. Am. Woman's Econ. Devel. Corp., N.Y.C., 1981-83; v.p. Med. Directions, N.Y.C., 1983-84; sr v.p. The Corson Group, 1984-85, Richards Cons., Ltd., N.Y.C., 1986—; mem. N.Y. Bus. Group on Health, 1983—; nat. bd. dirs. Roundtable for Women in Food Service, N.Y.C., 1981—; instr. Pa. State U.-Abington, 1976-79. Appointed mem. N.Y.C. Commn. Status of Women, 1981—. Recipient Outstanding Sr. award Drexel U., 1972, Key and Triangle award, 1972. Mem. Nat. Assn. Female Execs. (nat. adv. bd.), Key and Triangle Soc. (pres.). Jewish. Home: 10 Waterside Plaza #37H New York NY 10010 Office: Richards Cons 366 Madison Ave New York NY 10017

GOLDSTEIN, MARSHA FEDER, tour company executive; b. Chgo., July 7, 1945; d. Charles S. and Geraldine (Shulman) Feder; m. Michael Warren Goldstein, Dec. 26, 1966; 1 child, Paul Goldstein. B.A., Roosevelt U., Chgo., 1967. Tchr. art Chgo. Pub. Schs., 1967-68; free-lance artist, Chgo., 1968-71; tchr. architecture Brandeis U., Northfield, Ill., 1974-80; tour guide My Kind of Town Tours, Highland Park, Ill., 1975-79, owner, 1979—; art cons. Randall Pub. Co., Inc., 1984—. Editor: Highland Park by Foot or Frame, 1980. Contbr. to book in field. Commr. Highland Park Landpark Commn.; charter mem. Nat. Mus. Women in the Arts. Recipient Cert. of Completion, Chgo. Arch. Found., 1975; Cert. of Appreciation, Machinery Dealers Nat. Assn., 1982. Mem. Nat. Assn. Women Bus. Owners (corp. resource com.), Women's Exec. Network, Chgo. Assn. Commerce & Industry, Chgo. Conv. and Tourism Bd., Chgo. Soc. Assn. Execs., Milw. Conv. and Tourism Bd., No. Ill. Tourism Council. Republican. Jewish. Club: Brandeis U. Nat. Women (bd. dirs., v.p. 1977-84). Home: 266 Aspen Ln Highland Park IL 60035 Office: My Kind of Town Tours PO Box 924 Ravinia Sta Highland Park IL 60035

GOLDSTEIN, MYRNA, journalist; b. Rochester, N.Y., Aug. 5, 1948; d. R. Earl and Evelyn (Cohen) G. BS in Journalism, Northwestern U., 1970. Market editor, reporter Fairchild Publ. Inc., N.Y.C., 1971-73; feature writer Gannett Co., Rochester, N.Y., 1974-76; editorial writer, columnist Gannett Co., Rochester, 1976-81; freelance journalist, photographer Venice, Milan, Rome, 1981-85; writer feature Cannett Co., White Plains, N.Y., 1986—; instr. Italian Manhattan Community Coll., 1985-87, Elizabeth Seton Coll., 1987-88. Reporter several articles (nominee Pulitzer Prize 1980). Supporter Am. Field Service, N.Y.C. 1985—. Nominated for Pulitzer Prize, 1980. Mem. Soc. Profl. Journalists, Hadassah (life), Sierra Club, Zionist Orgn. Am. Home: 35 W 96th St New York NY 10025 Office: Gannett Newspapers Lifestyles Dept Corp Park II 1 Gannett Dr White Plains NY 10604

GOLDSTEIN, SANDRA, consumer products importing company executive, designer and importer; b. Chgo., Dec. 7; d. Jack Julius and Esther Judith (Glickman) Gilbert; student U. Wis., U. Ill.; m. Seymour Leo Goldstein, Aug. 12, 1951; 1 child, Jennie S. Co-founder, sr. v.p., sales mgr. Jennie G. Sales Co., Inc., Lincolnwood, Ill., 1961—. Bd. dirs. Ill. Found. Dentistry for Handicapped. Mem. Nat. Assn. Convenience Stores, Nat. Oil Jobbers Assn., Ill. Petroleum Assn., Tex. Oil Marketers Assn., Intermountain Oil Jobbers Assn., Wis. Oil Jobbers Assn., Ind. Oil Jobbers Assn., Mich. Oil Jobbers Assn., Mo. Oil Jobbers Assn., Iowa Oil Jobbers Assn. Clubs: Carleton (Chgo.), Springs Country (Rancho Mirage, Calif.). Home: The Springs 23 Cornell Rancho Mirage CA 92270 Office: Jennie G Sales Co 3770 W Pratt Ave Lincolnwood IL 60645

GOLDSTON, LINDA LEEBOV (MRS. EDWARD M. GOLDSTON), lawyer; b. Pitts., Aug. 17, 1942; d. Mike and Florence (Labovitz) Leebov; A.B., U. Pitts., 1964; student U. Seven Seas, fall 1963; J.D., U. Pitts., 1967; m. Edward M. Goldston, Apr. 12, 1969; children—Joseph Leebov, Samuel Morris. Admitted to Pa. bar, 1968; shareholder Baskin, Flaherty, Elliott and Mannino, P.C., Pitts., 1968-88; pres. Wittlin, Goldston & Caputo, P.C., Pitts., 1988— . Past pres. Temple Sinai. Mem. Am., Pa., Allegheny County bar assns., Nat. Assn. Women Lawyers, Nat. Council Jewish Women, Women's Am. O.R.T., Ladies Hosp. Aid Soc., Ladies Aux. Jewish Home for Aged. Lodges: B'nai B'rith, Hadassah. Home: 1309 Beechwood Blvd Pittsburgh PA 15217 Office: Wittlin Goldston & Caputo PC 1010 One Oxford Ctr Pittsburgh PA 15219

GOLDWYN, JUDITH S., civic worker; b. N.Y.C., Apr. 1, 1940; d. Raymond B. and Rosetta (Van Gelder) Schlessel; B.A., N.Y.U., 1962; M.A., L.I.U., 1973; m. Ronald M. Goldwyn, Aug. 20, 1961; children—Ira D., Laura-Jill. Tchr., Gt. Neck, N.Y., 1972-77; pub. relations dir., owner The Word Factory, Gt. Neck, 1977-86; exec. dir. Ronald McDonald House L.I., 1986—. V.p. pub. relations Gt. Neck United Community Fund, 1983-86, dir., 1983—; producer United Community Players, 1986—. Mem. Gt. Neck Village Bus. Assn. (pres.), Gt. Neck C. of C. (dir.). Office: Ronald McDonald House LI 267-07 76th Ave New Hyde Park NY 11042

GOLFIS, ANITA JANE, food products executive; b. Hibbing, Minn., Oct. 13, 1942; d. Richard H. and Valeria (Valeri) Carlson; m. Arthur R. Golfis, June 30, 1962; children: Christopher, Michelle. Student, Hibbing Jr. Coll., 1960-61, Roosevelt U., 1983-86. Sales person OHM Electronics, Palatine, Ill., 1975-76; cost acct. AM Bruning div., Schaumburg, Ill., 1976-77; sales service rep. Allied Corp., Schaumburg, 1977-79; sales rep. Amoco Corp., Schaumburg, 1979-84, Nat. Can. Co., Chgo., 1984-87; pres. Assoc. Brokerage, Elgin, Ill., 1987—. Home and Office: 9N799 Beckman Trail Elgin IL 60123

GOLICZ, PEGGY LOUISE, real estate appraiser; b. Washington, May 21, 1946; d. Ernest P. and Alicia A. (Peter) Erickson; student Wash. State U., Pullman, 1968; m. Lawrence J. Golicz, Aug. 3, 1968; children—Eric John, Karl Peter, Mark Joseph. Various secretarial and adminstrv. asst. positions, 1968-74; engaged in real estate, 1974—; broker, v.p. property mgmt., dir. Total Realty, Inc., Madison, 1978—; v.p. Am. Appraisal & Feasibility Corp., Madison, 1978—, also dir.; cons. in field. Mem. Nat. Center Housing Mgmt., Am. Inst. Real Estate Appraisers (candidate), Nat. Assn. Realtors, Greater Madison Bd. Realtors, Nat. Assn. Female Execs., Westmoreland Youth Hockey Assn., Alpha Phi. Club: Order Eastern Star. Author papers in field. Home: 1619 Elderwood Circle Middleton WI 53562 Office: 6506 Schroder Rd Madison WI 53711

GOLIN, SHARON DENISE, lawyer; b. Phila., Feb. 10, 1957; d. Albert and Lucille (Ostrow) G. AA, U. Miami, Coral Gables, Fla., 1976; BS in Chemistry, U. Fla., 1978; JD, Stetson U., 1982. Legal clk. Rohlfing, Smith & Coates, Honolulu, 1984-85; assoc. atty. Oliver, Lee, Cuskaden, Ogawa & Lau, Honolulu, 1985-87; corp. counsel Bur. Med. Econs., Ltd., Honolulu, 1987—. Mem. ABA, Hawaii Bar Assn., Hawaii Women Lawyers. Jewish. Office: Bur Med Econs Ltd 111 N King St #309 Honolulu HI 96817

GOLL, DAWN MARIE, small business owner; b. Robbinsville, N.C., July 24, 1960; d. Robert Dale and Dawn Grey (Postell) Hamilton; m. Gregory John Goll, Feb. 14, 1986; 1 child, Ashley Madeline. Student, Mich. State U., 1984, Eastern Mich. U., 1987—. Cert. illeracy tchr., 1988. Employment cons. Washentaw County, Ann Arbor, Mich., 1982—; prin. Klassic Resume Service, Whitmore Lake, Mich., 1986—; liaison Washentaw Community Coll., Ann Arbor, 1984—, WorkSkills Corp., Ann Arbor, 1985—, Yorkwood Ctrs., Ypsilanti, Mich., 1986—, Cleary Coll., Ypsilanti, 1986—. Program coordinator Mich. Youth Core, 1987; program activist Washtenaw County Illiteracy Program, Ypsilanti, 1987; program monitor Summer Youth Employment and Tng. Program, Ypsilanti, 1986-87. Mem. Nat. Assn Female Execs. (exec. com. 1986—), Midnight Muscle Auto Club. Home: 855 W Eight Mile Rd Box 291 Whitmore Lake MI 48189

GOLLIS, ELAINE SANDRA, nurse; b. Fall River, Mass., Mar. 30, 1938; d. Harold and Esther (Packer) G.; m. Pasquale Margiotta, May 16, 1968 (div. Oct. 1986); children: Ellen, Mark. Nurse, Worcester City Hosp., 1959; student, Post Coll., 1986—. Dir. nursing Hebrew Home and Hosp., Hartford, Conn., 1963-68, Jewish Home for Aged, San Francisco, 1968; clin. supr. Hebrew Home and Hosp., Hartford, 1971-81, coordinator patient care, 1981-82; clinic coordinator ambulatory care Hebrew Home and Hosp., Hartfield, 1982-84, ombudsman, 1984, acting dir. nursing, 1984-85, asst. dir. nursing, 1985—; clinical assoc. Dept. Restorative Dentistry Sch. Dental Med. U. Conn., Farmington, 1986—, geriodontic seminarian, 1986—. Mem. Conn. Orgn. Nurse Execs., Am. Nurses Assn. (cert. nurse adminstr.). Jewish. Office: Hebrew Home and Hosp 615 Tower Ave Hartford CT 06112

GOLLNICK, REBECCA LEWIS, communications manager; b. Frankfurt, W. Germany, Sept. 10, 1957; d. Herbert Bruce and Marie (Losey) Lewis; m. Clayton Robert Gollnick, Oct. 22, 1983. B.B.A., U. Tex.-Austin, 1979. With Yaring's Austin, Tex., 1973-78; account exec. AT&T Long Lines, Houston, 1979-83; nat. account mgr. AT&T Communications, Houston, 1983-86, sales mgr. 1987—. Mem. allocations panel United Way, Houston, 1981-86; advisor Jr. Achievement, Houston, 1980. Mem. U. Tex. Ex-Students Assn., Alpha Phi Alumnae. Roman Catholic. Office: AT&T 333 Clay St 17th Floor Houston TX 77002

GOLOMB, LYNNE ROOTH, educational psychologist; b. Chgo., Sept. 2, 1945; d. Eli and Florence (Goodman) Rooth; B.A., U. Pitts., 1966, M.S., 1968; Ed.D., Loyola U., 1980; m. Harvey Golomb, Dec. 28, 1965; children—Adam Simon, Sara Rooth. Grad. asst. Arsenal Family Childrens Center, Pitts., 1967-68; tchr., therapist League Sch., Boston, 1968-69; tchr., developer infant day care program Dept. Labor Nat. Capitol Area Day Care, Washington, 1969-71; cons. Programs for Handicapped, Chgo., 1974-78; pvt. practice ednl. psychology, Chgo., 1978—; psychologist Lakeview Learning Ctr., Chgo. Assn. Retarded Citizns Early Intervention Program; adj. prof. Loyola U., Chgo., 1981—. NIMH fellow, 1966. Mem. Am. Psychol. Assn., Nat. Assn. Edn. Young Children, Council Exceptional Children, Ill. Sch. Psychologists Assn. Home and Office: 5412 S Blackstone Ave Chicago IL 60615

GOLTZ, SUSAN ACKERMAN, lawyer; b. Newark, Dec. 12, 1946; d. Morris and Ruth (Abend) Ackerman; 1 dau., Amanda Lauren. Student Beaver Coll., Glenside, Pa., 1964-66, City of London Coll., Eng., 1966-67; B.A., U. Mich., 1968, postgrad., 1968-69; J.D., NYU, 1971. Bar: N.Y. 1971, D.C. 1978. Asst. dist. atty. Bronx County, N.Y., 1971-74; legal officer U.S. Supreme Ct., Washington, 1974-78; assoc. Chapman, Duff & Paul, Washington, 1978-79; ptnr. DiSalle & Staudinger, Washington, 1979—; mem. adv. bd. Bur. Prosecution and Def. Service, State of N.Y., 1979; conferee Nat. Conf. Causes of Popular Dissatisfaction with Adminstrn. of Justice, St. Paul, 1976. Mem. ABA, Nat. Women's Law Ctr. Network, NYU Law Alumni Assn. Home: 2472 Belmont Rd NW Washington DC 20008 Office: 1825 Eye St NW Washington DC 20006

GOLUB, SHARON BRAMSON, psychologist, educator; b. N.Y.C., Mar. 25, 1937; m. Leon M. Golub, June 1, 1958; children: Lawrence E., David B. Diploma, Mt. Sinai Hosp. Sch. Nursing, 1957; BS, Columbia U., 1959, MA, 1966; PhD, Fordham U., 1974. Head nurse Mt. Sinai Hosp., N.Y.C., 1957-59; contbg. editor RN Mag., Oradell, N.J., 1967-74; asst. prof. psychology Coll. New Rochelle, N.Y., 1974-79, assoc. prof., 1979-86, prof., 1986—, dir. women's studies, 1978-79, chmn. dept. psychology, 1979-82, asst. prof. psychology, 1986—; pvt. practice individual and group psychotherapy Harrison, N.Y., 1976—; adj. prof. psychiatry N.Y. Med. Coll., Valhalla, 1980—. Editor: Menarche (Assn. Women in Psychology Disting. Pub. award 1984, Am. Jour. Nursing Book of Yr. award 1984), 1983, Lifting the Curse of Menstruation, 1983, Health Care of the Female Adolescent, 1984, Health Needs of Women as They Age, 1985, (with Rita Jackaway Freedman) Psychology of Women: Resources for a Core Curriculum, 1987; editor: Women and Health, 1982-86, mem. editorial bd., 1986—; contbr. articles to profl. jours., chpts. to books. Grantee Nat. Library Medicine, 1983-84; NIH research fellow, 1971-74. Fellow Am. Psychol. Assn. (chmn. task force on teaching psychology of women 1980-83), Soc. for Menstrual Cycle Research (pres. 1981-83, bd. dirs. 1981—), Assn. Women in Psychology, Am. Assn. Sex Educators, Counselors and Therapists, Ea. Psychol. Assn., Phi Beta Kappa, Sigma Xi, Psi Chi. Office: Coll New Rochelle Dept Psychology New Rochelle NY 10801

GOMAN, CYNTHIA MARIE, federal agency administrator; b. Omaha, Nebr., Mar. 31, 1957; d. Joseph Edward and Caroline Maxine (Schalk) Miller; m. Thomas Leonard Goman, Jan. 2, 1951; children: Thomas, Marie, Timothy. Student, U. Nebr. Supr. U.S. Postal Service, Omaha, 1981-83, personnel asst., 1981-86, programs coordinator, 1986—. Mem. ladie's guild St. Joan of Arc, Omaha, 1982-87. Mem. Federally Employed WOmen (programs coordinator 1985-87). Roman Catholic. Club: Toastmasters. Office: US Postal Service 1124 Pacific St Omaha NE 68108-9431

GOMEZ, ALICE RUTH, nurse; b. Kansas City, Mo., Jan. 7, 1945; d. Thomas Sinclair Evilsizer Jr. and Katherine Louise (Roach) Maxwell; m. Edward Raymond Gomez, Aug. 10, 1963 (div. June 1974); children: Gregory, Marie. AA in Nursing, U. Albuquerque, 1970. RN, cert. nurse practitioner, NAACOG. Nurse St. Joseph Hosp., Albuquerque, 1970-72, Surg. Assocs., Albuquerque, 1972-73; nurse U. N.Mex. Hosp., Albuquerque, 1974-75, head nurse, 1975-76; coordinator perinatal unit Sch. Med. U. N.Mex., Albuquerque, 1976-84; nurse practitioner Panhandle Planned Parenthood, Amarillo, Tex., 1986—. Treas. Tex. Tech-Amarillo Allies, 1986—. Recipient scholarship Alpha Zeta, 1985. Mem. Alpha Chi. Republican. Home: PO Box 40-5 Rt 8 #5A Amarillo TX 79118

GÓMEZ, MIRENE IRUNE, educator; b. Palma Soriano, Oriente, Cuba, Jan. 22, 1938; came to U.S., 1968; d. José Miguel and Irma De La Luz (Reyes) G. Grad., Oriente's Normal Sch. for Tchrs., 1958, French Alliance, 1965, John Reed Sch. of Langs., 1965, U. Bridgeport, 1965, Abraham Lincoln Sch. of Langs., 1978. Cert. elementary, secondary, Spanish tchr., Conn. Prof. French French Alliance Mex., Mexico City, 1967-68; instr. art Hall Neighborhood House, Bridgeport, Conn., 1969-71; asst. tchr. Bridgeport Bd. of Edn., 1971-74, tchr., 1974—; tchr. English, Spanish Adult Edn., Bridgeport, 1969-72, 75-76, 82-84; prin., instr. summers Pvt. Industry Council Youth Program, Bridgeport, 1982-86. Abstractionist surrealist painter, toothpick sculptress; exhibitions include 1st Baptist Ch., Bridgeport, 1970, Bridgeport Assn. for Bilingual Bicultural Edn., Lafayette Plaza, 1977, Bridgeport Pub. Library, 1984, Andrew Warde Meml. High Sch., Fairfield, Conn., 1985, Spanish Literary Soc. Southern Conn., Alumni Conf. Ctr., New Haven, Conn., 1985, The New Reality: Hispanic Artists in Conn. at Housatonic Community Coll., Bridgeport, 1987. Sec. Mayor's Adv. Council on Minority Affairs, Bridgeport, 1981-83, Cuban Patriotic Council, Bridgeport, 1982-83; vice chmn. Bd. Commrs. Housing Sites Devel. Agys., Bridgeport, 1981-85; chmn. Bd. of Commrs. Urban Homesteading Program, Bridgeport, 1983-85; coordinator 4th Ann. Women's Congress, Hartford, Conn., 1985; bd. commrs. Conn. Aging Dept., 1984-86. Home: 15 Wakeley St Shelton CT 06484 Office: Mimi Gómez Wet Backs PO Box 2234 Bridgeport CT 06608

GOMEZ, VIKKI LYNNE, educator; b. Gainesville, Fla., Sept. 17, 1949; d. Hubert Ellsworth and Clara Maxine (Wimberly) Ridaught; m. Glenn George Gomez, Dec. 18, 1971; children: Kristin Emily, Tyler Alexander. B of Mus. Edn., Fla. State U., 1971; MEd, Fla. Atlantic U., 1976. Tchr. Broward Sch. Bd., Ft. Lauderdale, Fla., 1971-78, 82—; clinic adjudicator Broward County Band Clinic, Ft. Lauderdale, 1971-78. Active Girl Scouts U.S., Miramar, 1985—. Republican. Methodist. Home: 7650 Granada Blvd Miramar FL 33023

GOMEZ-CARRION, YVONNE, physician; b. Bklyn., Feb. 6, 1957; d. William and Josephine (Aitcheson) Carrion. B.A., Princeton U., 1979; M.D., Columbia U., 1983. Intern, then resident in ob-gyn Columbia Presbyn. Med. Ctr.-Sloan Hosp. Women and Children, 1983—; chief residen ob-gyn. Columbia Prebyn. Hosp., N.Y.C.; dir. Roxbury (amss.) Comprehensive Community Health Ctr.; mem. attending staff Beth Israel Hosp.; ob-gyn instr., cons. Pre-Med. Research/Edn. Program, N.Y.C., 1979—. Mem. Coll. Ob-gyn. Democrat. Roman Catholic. Office: Roxbury Comprehensive Community Health Ctr 435 Warren St Roxbury MA 02119

GONCE-CARTWRIGHT, NOREEN CALLIHAN, investment executive; b. Los Angeles, May 3, 1937; d. Fred Horace and Lyla (Lee) Callihan; m. Sherman Bret Gonce, May 3, 1955 (div. Dec. 1974); children: Sara Lyn, Laura Lee, Peter Bret, Elizabeth Ellen; m. Farnandeze Salvester Cartwright, Jan. 15, 1982. Grad. high sch., Las Vegas, Nev., 1955. Sec. Fed. Res. Bank, Portland, Oreg., 1977-78; office mgr. City Housing Devel., Portland, 1978-80, Function Form, Inc., Portland, 1980-81; mgr. inventory control Biamp Systems, Portland, 1981; asst. purchasing agt. Rogers Cablesystems, Portland, 1982, producer TV, hostess, 1982-84; asst. br. mgr. Univ. Securities, Portland, 1982-84; registered prin. FSC Securities, Portland, 1984-86; owner, chief exec. officer Gonce Investment Adv., Portland, 1985—; registered prin. Integrated Resources, Portland, 1986—. Columnist newspaper, 1965-72 (Best Column award 1968); contbr. articles to newspapers and mags. Bd. dirs. Frontier Girl Scout Council, Las Vegas, 1969, Clark County Humane Soc., Las Vegas, 1973; pres. Clark County Dem. Women, Las Vegas, 1972. Named Outstanding Mem. award Silver State Kennel Club, 1970. Mem. Internat. Assn. for Fin. Planners (cert.). Home: 28611 Chapman Rd Scappoose OR 97056

GONCHAR, ROSALIE JAMES, wholesale food company executive; b. Savannah, Ga., Sept. 9, 1927; d. Thomas Patterson James and Catherine Mae (Crider) Roberts James; m. Gershon Alexander Gonchar, Dec. 27, 1952 (dec. Jan. 14, 1988). With IBM-code sect. Nat. Security Agy., Washington, 1943-45; computer operator So. States Iron-Roofing Co., Savannah, 1948-53; owner, pres. Gonchar Produce Co., Savannah, 1955—. Mem. United Fresh Fruit and Vegetable Assn. Democrat. Jewish. Lodges: B'nai B'rith, Hadassah. Avocation: artist. Office: Gonchar Produce Co Inc US Hwy 80 Garden City GA 31408

GONCHER, SUSAN ELLEN, computer software executive; b. Herrin, Ill., Nov. 3, 1950; d. John and Doris Elaine (Cook) Grozik; m. Donald John Goncher, Oct. 20, 1973; children: Andrew Joseph, Katrina Elise. BS, So. Ill. U., 1972; MS, Nat. Coll. Edn., 1981. Tchr. English, Bloomingdale Sch. Dist., Ill., 1973-74; personnel asst. Chgo. Pneumatic Tool Co., Bensenville, Ill., 1974-75; exec. asst. Bus. Appraisal Co., Oak Brook, Ill., 1975-76, System Devel. Corp., Oak Brook, 1976-77; office services mgr. Advanced System Applications, Inc., Bloomingdale, Ill., 1977-80, mgr. personnel adminstrn., 1980-84; with CA Bus. Ptnrs., Bloomingdale, Ill., 1986-87; owner, pres., Statice Gro, West Chicago, Ill., 1987—. Contbr. articles to profl. jours. Ill. State scholar, 1968. Mem. Am. Soc. Personnel Adminstrn., Am. Mgmt. Assn., Alpha Omicron Pi. Russian Orthodox. Home: 1704 Jeanette Ave Saint Charles IL 60174 Office: Statice Gro PO Box 25 West Chicago IL 60174

GONNELLA, NINA CELESTE, pharmaceutical researcher; b. Phila., Dec. 22, 1953; d. Anthony and Antoinette E. Gonnella. BA, Temple U., 1975; PhD, U. Pa., 1979; postdoctoral, Calif. Inst. Tech., 1979-81, Columbia U., 1981-83; research assoc., Yale U., 1984. Sr. research scientist CIBA Geigy Pharm. Co., Summit, N.J., 1983—. Contbr. articles to profl. jours. NSF fellow, 1976-79. Mem. Am. Chem. Soc., Phi Lambda Upsilon. Office: CIBA GEIGY 556 Morris Ave Summit NJ 07901

GONOS, STEPHANIE SUZANNE, engineer, scientist; b. McKeesport, Pa., Nov. 13, 1956; d. Stephen Albert Gonos and Nellie (Theresa) Pobojeski. BA in Psychology, Calif. U. of Pa., 1977; MS in Info. Sci., U. Pitts., 1983. Data processing research asst. U. Pitts., 1978-83; assoc. programmer IBM Corp., Gaithersburg, Md., 1983-85; sr. assoc. engr. IBM Corp., Gaithersburg, 1985—. Service unit mgr. Girl Scouts Am., 1986—. Republican. Roman Catholic. Office: IBM Corp 18100 Frederick Pike Gaithersburg MD 20879

GONSALVES, STEPHANIE ANN, lawyer; b. Honolulu, Oct. 11, 1955; d. Stephen and Josephine (Rivera) G. B.S. cum laude, U. San Francisco, 1977; J.D., Stanford U., 1981. Bar: Hawaii 1981. Atty., Cades Schutte, Fleming & Wright, Honolulu, 1981—. Bd. dirs. Big Bros./Big Sisters of Honolulu, 1981—, sec., 1984-85, pres., 1987 . Mem. ABA, Hawaii State Bar Assn., Hawaii Women Lawyers (dir. 1984-87, treas. 1985-87), Hawaii Women Lawyers Found. (bd. dirs. 1984-87), Alpha Sigma Nu. Democrat. Roman Catholic. Office: Cades Schutte Fleming & Wright 1000 Bishop St Honolulu HI 96813

GONYA, PATRICE YEAGER, insurance company official; b. Bremen, Ga., Aug. 17, 1951; d. Forest William and Madge Moore (Cain) Yeager; B.S., U. Mo., Columbia, 1972, M.B.A., 1978; m. David E. Gonya. CPCU; CLU. Devel. trainee State Farm Ins. Co., Columbia, 1972-73, jr. acct., 1973-74, acct., 1974-77, asst. acctg. mgr., Springfield, Pa., 1977-79, acctg. supt., 1979-83, acctg. mgr., Rohnert Park, Calif., 1983-86, mgmt. asst., 1986-87, asst. div. mgr., 1987—. Vol. drives Heart Fund, 1975, 76; office co-chmn. United Way, 1979, chmn., 1980, mem. campaign effectiveness council, 1982. Mem. Nat. Assn. Accts., Nat. Assn. Female Execs., Sonoma County Transp. Com. Office: 6400 State Farm Dr Rohnert Park CA 94926

GONZALES, LUCILLE CONTRERAS, educational administrator; b. Colton. Calif., Nov. 30, 1937; d. Antonio Colunga and Ramona (Arroyo) Contreras; AA, San Bernardino Valley Coll., 1958; BA, U. Calif., Santa Barbara, 1960; MA, Claremont Grad. Sch., 1969; m. Enrique Gonzales, Aug. 27, 1960; children: Leticia Maria, Cecilia Maria. With Chino (Calif.) Public Schs., 1960-85, bilingual classroom tchr., 1970-74, bilingual coordinator, 1974-76, coordinator consol. application-intergroup relations, 1976-78, supr. spl. projects, 1978, adminstr. spl. projects, 1978-82, dir. spl. projects, 1982-85; dir. state and fed. programs Pomona Pub. Schs., Calif., 1985—; trainer State Dept. Edn. for Program Quality Review Trainers and Reviewers for Elem., Middle Grades, and Reviewers for Secondary in Edn.; mem. State Supts. Regional Adv. Hispanic Council, State Supts. Middle Grade Task Force, advisory com. on gifted edn., State Dept's. Middle Grades Program Quality Criteria Task Force, State's Supt. Adv. Com. on Gifted Edn. Mem. Migrant Regional Exec. Bd.; mem. Bilingual Dirs. Task Force. Mem. Nat. Assn. Female Execs., San Bernardino County Assn. Compensatory Edn. Dirs. (pres., v.p.), P.E.O., Assn. Secondary Spl. Projects, Assn. Calif. Sch. Adminstrs., Calif. Assn. of Adminstrs. of State and Fed. Ednl. Programs, Nat. Assn. Fed. Ednl. Program Adminstrs., Am. Assn. Sch. Adminstrs., Assn. State and Fed. Adminstrs. of Programs, Los Angeles County Bilingual Dirs., Large Urban Dirs., Assn. Large Urban Dirs., Pi Lambda Theta, Delta Kappa Gamma, Phi Delta Kappa. Lodge: Soroptimist. Home: 4955 Tyler St Chino CA 91710 Office: 800 S Garey Pomona CA 91716

GONZALEZ, CELIA MARIA, affirmative action administrator, researcher; b. N.Y.C., Apr. 13, 1945; d. Charles Ralph and Epifania (Olivieri) G.; children: Richard, Anthony. AA with honors, Sullivan County Community Coll., Loch Sheldrake, N.Y., 1975; BA in Psychology, Mt. St. Mary Coll., Newburgh, N.Y., 1978; cert. in employment and tng. adminstn., U. Buffalo, 1976; cert. in exec. devel., Ctr. for Women in Govt., Albany, N.Y., 1984. Employment and tng. adminstr. Orange County, Newburgh, N.Y., 1975-78; spl. academic program coordinator Marist Coll., Poughkeepsie, N.Y., 1980-82; dir. affirmative action N.Y. State Office Mental Health, Albany, 1982-86; assoc. N.Y. State Gov.'s Office Employee Relations, Albany, 1986—. chmn. disability com. of N.Y. State Affirmative Action Council, Albany, 1986—; mem. Orange County Econ. Devel. Commn., Goshen, N.Y., 1982, Orange County Human Rights Commn., Goshen, 1983, Centro Civico cultural orgn., Albany, 1986, NE Council on AIDS, Albany, 1986. Mem. Holding Our Own Women's Found. (bd. dirs. 1987—, pres. bd. dirs. 1988—), Nat. Assn. Puerto Rican Women. Democrat. Roman Catholic. Home: 34 Hungerford Rd Albany NY 12203 Office: Gov's Office of Employee Relations Agy Bldg#2 Empire State Plaza Albany NY 12223

GONZALEZ, DIANE KATHRYN, social worker; b. Cin., Aug. 20, 1947; d. Joseph Curtis and Kathryn Mary (Diskin) Gonzalez; B.A. in Social Work, U. Dayton, 1969; A.M. in Social Work, U. Chgo., 1973; m. Thomas Connolley Leibig, July 5, 1974; 1 dau., Abigail. Social worker Hamilton County Welfare Dept., Cin., 1969-71; social worker obstetrics dept. and prenatal clinic social service dept. St. Francis Hosp., Evanston, Ill., 1973-78; rap group leader Teen Scene, Planned Parenthood Assn., Chgo., part-time, 1979-80; social worker Chgo. Comprehensive Care Center, 1980—; chmn. adv. com. Evanston Continuing Edn. Center, 1978-80. Mem. landmark dist. com. Old Town Triangle, 1983— (chmn. 1987—); gen. co-chmn. Old Town Art Fair, 1984-85, gen. chmn. 1986-87. Mem. Nat. Assn. Social Workers (cert.), Acad. Cert. Soc. Workers. Roman Catholic. Home: 218 W Menomonee St Chicago IL 60614

GONZALEZ, KIMBERLY REGINA, controller; b. Walnut Creek, Calif., Nov. 5, 1964; d. Earl Glenn and Marilynn Mae (Roberts) K.; m. George Gonzalez, May 30, 1987. BS in Internat. Bus. summa cum laude, Woodbury U., 1986. Controller Charisma Missions Inc., Los Angeles, 1985—, dir., treas., 1986—. Mem. Am. Soc. Profl. and Exec. Women, Nat. Assn. Female Exec., Am. Mgmt. Assn. Republican. Roman Catholic. Home: 629 Ave A Redondo Beach CA 90277 Office: Charisma in Missions Inc 1059 S Gage Ave Los Angeles CA 90023

GONZALEZ, MARIA ESTHER, educator; b. Tegucigalpa, Honduras, Aug. 29, 1938; came to U.S., 1955; d. Ernesto Absalon and Eudoxia (Salgado) Castillo; m. Domingo Gonzalez, June 15, 1958; children: Dominick, Marissa, Wilfredo, Adonis. AA, Touro Coll., 1979, BA, 1981. Drug prevention coordinator Bklyn. Pub. Schs., 1969-70, drug specialist instr., 1970-80, instr. substance abuse prevention, specialist, 1980-86, substance abuse prevention/intervention specialist, 1986—. Past pres. PTA Bklyn. Dist. 32 Sch Bd., mem., 1980-84; coordinator Nydia Velazques polit. campaign, Bklyn., 1985-86; mem. Latin Council for Latin Am. Advancement. Recipient Puerto Rican of Yr. award Bklyn. Bd. Edn., 1978, Sch. Bd. Election award, N.Y.C. Bd. Edn., 1980-83, La Prensa Puertorriqueña award Puerto Rican Press, Inc., 1984, 15 Yr. Service award N.Y. Div. Substance Abuse, 1987. Mem. Assn. Puerto Rican Women, E. Harlem Parents Against Drugs, Bklyn. Voters Club, Nat. Assn. Female Execs., Say No To Drugs Club, Puerto Rican Tchrs. Educators. Home: 75 Grant Ave Brooklyn NY 11208 Office: Sch Community New Tommorrow 176 E 115th St New York NY 11224

GONZALEZ, MARIA VILLAR, educator; b. Madrid, May 17, 1951; came to U.S., 1966; d. Manuel and Maria del Carmen (Martinez) Villar; m. Jose Felix Gonzalez, Aug. 25, 1974; children: Alejandro Jose, Kristy Marie. BA, Jersey City State Coll., 1974; postgrad., Nicholls State U., 1977-81, La. State U., 1985. Cert.tchr. Spanish, French, Gen. Sci., N.J., La., Fla. Tchr. English as Second Lang. Ascul, Bilbao, Spain, 1974-76; tchr. French, Spanish, Gen. Sci. Morgan City (La.) High Sch., 1976-85; tchr. J.B. Maitland Elem. Sch., Morgan City, 1986; ednl. tng. ctr. coordinator Nat. Puerto Rican Forum, Miami, Fla., 1986-87; tchr. Spanish as 2d lang. Coral Reef Elem. Sch., 1987—; counselor Nat. Puerto Rican Forum; freshmen, hispanic students advisor Morgan City High Sch., 1976-85. Mem. Profl. Educators La., United Tchrs. Dade. Republican. Roman Catholic. Club: Newcomers and Friends of Laredo. Home: 1733 SW 100th Ave Miami FL 33165 Office: Coral Reef Elem 7955 SW 152 St Miami FL 33157

GONZALEZ, MIRIAM, minorities professional; b. Mayaquez, P.R., Feb. 5, 1947; d. Alberto Gonzalez and Monserrate Rios; children: Anibal, Alberto, Rivera. BA, We. Mich. U., 1970. Spanish-Am. specialist Calhaun Community Action Agy., Battle creek, Mich., 1969-74; exec. dir. planning Govt. of Mayaquez, 1974-76; personnel service mgr. Digital Equipment Corp., San German, P.R., 1976-79, product mgr., 1979-81, personnel mgr., 1981-84; pub. relations mgr. Digital Equipment Corp., Mayaquez, 1984-85; mgr. minority edn. and women's program Digital Equipment Corp., Concord, Mass., 1985—. Developer grants comprehensive employment and tng. act, 1974-75. Pres. Hospitality Commn. First Productivity Conf. of Ams., San Juan, 1985; organizer Hispanic Heritage Week, Mass., 1986. Recipient Outstanding Vol. Service award Calhoun Head Start, Battle Creek, Mich., 1974, Sec. Housing, Washington, 1972, Service award Hispanic Leadership Group, 1987. Mem. Nat. Assn. Minority Engr. Dirs., Nat. Action Council Minorities in Engring., Spanish Am. Assn., Hispanic Leadership Group, Nat. Assn. Female Execs. Home: 110 Brook St Framingham MA 01701 Office: Digital Equipment Corp 150 Coulter Dr CF02-1/K75 Concord MA 01742

GONZÀLEZ, NORMA, management consultant; b. Havana, Cuba, Nov. 9, 1945; came to U.S., 1962; d. Carlos Agustin and Rosa Maria (Rivero) Cruz; m. Albert Gonzàlez, July 3, 1965 (div. 1981); children: Albert Jr., Daniel; m. Bruce Beckman, May 26, 1983. B in Econs. and Psychology, Rutgers U., 1981, MBA, 1981-82. Customer relations mgr. Taggart Internat., East Brunswick, N.J., 1978-80; program devel. Middlesex County Community Coll., New Brunswick, N.J., 1980-84; tng. and devel. mgr. Anne Arundel County, Utilities, Glen Burnie, Md., 1984—; officer Md. Adv. Council for Environ. Tng., 1985—. Author, designer mgmt. system programs, 1984—; contbr. articles to profl. jours. Co-founder Middlesex County Area chpt. Grey Panthers, 1979. Recipient Managerial Excellence award Nat. Assn. Counties, 1986; High Performance Recognition award Anne Arundel County, Md., 1987. Fellow Water Pollution Control Fedn.; mem. Water and Waste Assn. (trustee 1985-87, Trainer of Yr. 1987), Am. Soc. for Tng. and Devel., Nat. Environ. Tng. Assn., Nat. Assn. Counties (Tng. Managerial Excellence award 1986). Republican. Methodist. Office: Anne Arundel County 7409 Baltimore and Annapolis Blvd Glen Burnie MD 21061

GONZLIK, PAMELA JOAN, cable television performer; b. N.Y.C., Apr. 20, 1948; d. John Martin and Regina (Cohen) Gonzlik; secretarial diploma, A.O.S. acctg. degree, Taylor Bus. Inst., 1975; student in acctg. Pace U., 1975. Stock records clk. G. A. Saxton & Co., N.Y.C., 1970-71; sec., bookkeeper Acme Quilting Co., Inc., N.Y.C., 1971-73; acct., sec., office mgr. Alwyn Ptnrs., N.Y.C., 1975-77; treas. Independence Plaza Tenants Orgn. and Rent Strike Com., 1977-78; sec. Atalanta Corp., N.Y.C., 1978-80, exec. sec., adminstv. asst. splty. foods div., 1986-87; adminstrv. asst.; office mgr. Sandy Soroush Designs, Inc., N.Y.C., 1987-88; legal sec. City of N.Y. Law Dept., 1980-86; polit. action vol. Mondale for Pres. campaign; cable TV vol., producer, host, performer Musical Interludes cable TV show Exptl. TV Coop., Inc., N.Y.C., 1978-82; performer cabaret showcase Dangerfield's, 1984; performer passenger talent shows aboard Cunard Countess, 1985-86, Queen Elizabeth II, 1986-88; vol., adminstrv. asst. ETC Studios, 1978-82; developer cable TV game shows. Mem. Nat. Wildlife Fedn., Nat. Carousel Assn., Channel 13, and Channel 21 Pub. Broadcasting Service, WNYC-Pub. Radio,, NOW, Phi Chi Theta (rec. sec. Gamma Xi chpt. 1976-77). Home: 40 Harrison St Apt 38E New York NY 10013

GOOCH, PATRICIA CAROLYN, cytogeneticist; b. Michie, Tenn., Mar. 28, 1935; d. James Lide and Mary Frances (Hyneman) G. BS, U. Tenn., Knoxville, 1957. Tchr. sci. Knoxville City Sch. System, 1957-58; biologist Oak Ridge Nat. Lab., 1958-70, 73—; research assoc. Grad. Sch. Biomed. Sci., U. Tex., Houston, 1970; sr. research analyst Northrop Corp., NASA-Johnson Space Ctr., Houston, 1970-72; organizing com. sci. confs. Contbr. articles to profl. jours. Named Outstanding Tenn. Woman, U. Tenn. Panhellenic Assn., 1974, one of Outstanding Young Women of Am., 1968. Mem. Anderson County Dem. Women's Club (membership chmn. 1985-86). Mem. AAAS, Am. Genetic Assn., Genetics Soc. Am., Environ. Mutagen Soc., U. Tenn. Alumni Assn. (chpt. treas. 1980-81, chpt. sec. 1981-82, chpt. v.p. 1982-83, chpt. pres. 1983-84, nat. bd. govs. 1984-87), Oak Ridge Panhellenic Assn. (benefit chmn. 1961), Delta Gamma Alumni Assn. (pres. Knoxville Area 1959-61, 67-69), Sigma Xi (chpt. admissions com. 1977-79). Mem. Ch. of Christ. Club: Big Orange (sec. 1978-80, 82-84). Home: 226 Tusculum Dr Oak Ridge TN 37830 Office: Oak Ridge Nat Lab Biology Div PO Box Y Oak Ridge TN 37830

GOOD, ANNE LEEPER (MRS. JOHN CARTER GOOD), civic worker; b. Jackson, Tenn., Nov. 10, 1923; d. Robert Allen and Ola (Crittenden) Leeper; A.B., B.S. cum laude, Lambuth Coll., 1944; m. John Carter Good, Oct. 28, 1945; children—John Robert, Carter Crittenden, William Allen. Co-chmn. Introduction to Washington com. The Hospitality and Info. Service, 1968-71, treas., 1971-75, v.p., 1975-77, pres., 1977-79, chmn. fin. com., 1983-85, exec. com., 1985-86; trustee Meridian House Internat., 1977-79, counselor, 1980—; membership chmn. Spanish Portuguese Study Group, 1968-69, v.p., 1969-70, pres., 1970-71; mem. ladies' bd. House of Mercy, 1970—, treas., 1972-74, trustee, treas., 1986—. Bd. dirs. D.C. br. Nat. Capitol Area YWCA, 1971-78, 79-85, rec. sec., 1974, treas., 1974-76, 81-85; com. Hannah Harrison Career Sch., 1971-78, 79—, chmn., 1976-77, chmn. investment com., 1985-86; bd. dirs. Nat. Capital Area YWCA, 1973-79, fin. com., 1978—; bd. dirs. Rosemount Infant Day Care Ctr., 1972-82, v.p., 1974-76; bd. dirs. Washington chpt. Achievement Rewards for Coll. Scientists, 1971-72. Clubs: St. Albans School Mothers (pres. Washington 1964-65), Air Force Officers Wives (mem. bd. Washington 1959-61).

GOOD, BARBARA KATHLEEN, research company executive; b. Jasper, Ala., Aug. 18, 1954; d. William Hershel and Lois Lorene (Bolin) Raines. BS, U. Ala., Birmingham, 1976; MBA, Ala. A&M, 1979. Cost analyst GTE-Automatic Electric, Huntsville, Ala., 1977-79, Sci. Applications, Inc., Huntsville, 1979-80, Raytheon Co., Huntsville, 1980-81; sr. cost analyst Teledyne Brown Engring., Huntsville, 1981-83; dir. cost analysis div. Applied Research, Inc., Huntsville, 1983-88, v.p. resource and requirements directorate, 1988%. Mem. Space System Cost Analysis, Am. Def. Preparedness Assn., Inst. of Cost Analysis, Nat. Estimating Soc. Republican. Baptist. Home: 4985 Seven Pines Circle Huntsville AL 35805 Office: Applied Research Inc 5025 Bradford Blvd Huntsville AL 35805

GOOD, LINDA LOU, educator; b. Zanesville, Ohio, May 30, 1941; d. John Robert and Alice Laura (Fulkerson) Moore; B.S. in Elem. Edn., Ohio U., 1964; m. Larry Alvin Good, Jan. 11, 1964; children—Jason (dec.), Alicia and Tricia (twins), Amy Jo. Tchr., West Muskingum Sch. Dist., 1962-64; 1st grade tchr., Bellevue, Ohio, 1964-68, 2d grade tchr., Zanesville Sch. System, 1970—; head tchr. Munson Sch., Zanesville. Co-chmn. Zane Trace Commemoration; pres. Munson-Garfield Schs. PTA; mem. Trinity Presbyn. Ch. Mem. NEA, Ohio Edn. Assn., Zanesville Edn. Assn., Eastern Ohio Tchrs. Assn. Methodist.

GOOD, MARY LOWE (MRS. BILLY JEWEL GOOD), business executive, chemist; b. Grapevine, Tex., June 20, 1931; d. John W. and Winnie (Mercer) Lowe; m. Billy Jewel Good, May 17, 1952; children: Billy, James. B.S., Ark. State Tchrs. Coll., 1950; M.S., U. Ark., 1953, Ph.D., 1955, LL.D. (hon.), 1979; D.Sc. (hon.), U. Ill., Chgo., 1983, Clarkson U., 1984, Ea. Mich. U., 1986, Duke U., 1987. Instr. Ark. State Tchrs. Coll., Conway, summer 1949; instr. La. State U., Baton Rouge, 1954-56; asst. prof. La. State U., 1956-58; asso. prof. La. State U., New Orleans, 1958-63; prof. La. State U., 1963-80; Boyd prof. materials sci., div. engring. research La. State U., Baton Rouge, 1979-80; v.p., dir. research UOP, Inc., Des Plaines, Ill., 1980-84; pres. Signal Research Ctr. Inc., 1985—; pres. engineered materials research div. Allied-Signal Inc., Des Plaines, Ill., 1986—; chmn. Pres.'s Com. for Nat. Medal Sci., 1979-82; mem. Nat. Sci. Bd., 1980—; adv. bd. NSF chemistry section, 1972-76, com. medicinal chemistry NIH, 1972-76, Office of USAF Research, 1974-78, chemist div. Brookhaven and Oak Ridge Nat. Labs., 1973-83, chemical tech. div. ORNL, catalysis program Lawrence-Berkeley Lab., coll. engring. La. State U. Contbr. articles to profl. jours. Bd. dirs. Oak Ridge Assoc. Univs., Industrial Research Inst.; trustee Renssalaer Polytech. Inst.; adv. bd. Mayor Byrne's Chgo. Task Force High Tech. Devel. Recipient Agnes Faye Morgan research award, 1969; Distinguished Alumni citation U. Ark., 1973; Scientist of Yr. award Indsl. R & D Mag., 1982; AEC tng. grantee, 1967; NSF internat. travel grantee, 1968; NSF research grantee, 1969-80. Fellow AAAS, Am. Inst. Chemistry (Gold medal 1983), Chem. Soc. London; mem. Am. Chem. Soc. (1st woman dir. 1971-74, regional dir. 1972-80, chmn. bd. 1978, 80, pres. 1987, Garvan medal 1973, Herty medal 1975, award Fla. sect. 1979), Internat. Union Pure and Applied Chmistry (pres. inorganic div. 1980-85), Nat. Acad. Engring., Phi Beta Kappa, Sigma Xi, Iota Sigma Pi (regional dir. 1967—, hon. mem. 1983). Club: Zonta (past pres. New Orleans club, chmn. dist. status of women com. and nominating com., chmn. internat. Amelia Earhart scholarship com.). Home: 295 Park Dr Palatine IL 60067 Office: Signal Research Ctr Inc 50 E Algonquin Rd Des Plaines IL 60017

GOOD, SUSAN PAULINE, banker; b. Sanger, Calif., Aug. 17, 1953, d. Alfred Anton and Elsbeth (Grimm) Good; AA, Reedley Coll., 1973; BA summa cum laude, Calif. State U., Fresno, 1975. Advt. asst. Bell Pub. Relations Agy., Fresno, Calif., 1976-77; account exec. Meeker Advt., Fresno, Calif., 1977-78; dir. advt. Coast Savs. and Loan, Fresno, Calif., 1978-81, asst. v.p., br. promotions mgr., br. mgr., 1981-84, br. mgr., 1984—. Mem. mktg. com. U.S. League Savs. Assn., 1980-81; chmn. Fresno City-County Commn. on Status Women, 1979; chmn. Fresno County Dem. Cen. Com., 1985-86; pres. Calif. State U. Fresno Alumni Assn., 1981; regional dir. Calif. Dem. Party; pres. Leadership Fresno Alumni Exec. Bd., 1987; mem. Charter Leadership Fresno Class, 1985; parliamentarian Jr. League of Fresno. Recipient cert. of achievement Inst. Fin. Edn., 1982, Silver medal Am. Advt. Fedn., 1982. Mem. Fresno Advt. Fedn. (pres. 1982), Inst. Fin. Edn., C. of C. (past chmn. ambassadors, Calif. State U. Fresno Alumni). Roman Catholic.

GOODALE, TONI KRISSEL, development consultant; b. N.Y.C., May 26, 1941; d. Walter DuPont and Ricka Krissel; A.B. cum laude, Smith Coll., 1963; student U. Geneva, 1962-63; postgrad. Hunter Coll., 1964-65; m. James Campbell Goodale, May 3, 1964; children—Timothy Fuller, Ashley Krissel, Clayton A. (Ward). Congl. intern Senator Keating, U.S. Senate, Washington, 1963; broadcast analyst FCC, Washington, 1963-64; adminstrv. asst., dir. grant research dept. Ford Found., N.Y.C., 1964-67, cons. public edn. dept., 1968-69; N.Y. rep. Smith Coll., N.Y.C., 1975-78, asst. dir. devel., 1978-79; pres. Goodale Assocs., N.Y.C., 1979—; vis. com. continuing edn. New Sch. Social Research; lectr., writer in field; mem. bd. advs. First Women's Bank. Mem. alumnae fund com. Smith Coll., v.p. class, chmn. 25th reunion; trustee, alumnae fund chmn., mem. alumnae council, bd. dirs. Brearley Sch.; mem. exec. com. Parents' Assn., St. Bernard's Sch.; mem. benefit com. N.Y. Philharmonic; trustee, bd. govs. Churchill Sch.; trustee N.Y. Inst. Child Devel.; mem. women's div. Legal Aid Soc.; mem. N.Y. com. Joffrey Ballet; mem. benefit com. Grosvenor House; vice chmn. N.Y.C. Opera Benefit; mem. com. sch. Am. Ballet.; mem. vis. com. for continuing edn. New Sch. for Social Research. Mem. Am. Council Arts (vice-chmn. bd., exec. com., chmn. nat. patrons commn., chair long range planning com.), Am. Assn. Fund-Raising Counsel (bd. dirs.trust for philanthropy), Nat. Assn. Fund Raising Execs. (dir.), Brearley Sch. Alumnae Assn., Smith Coll. Alumnae Assn. Clubs: Cosmopolitan, Smith, Washington, Seventh Regiment Armory, Doubles Internat. Office: 3 W 51st St New York NY 10019

GOODALIS, KRISTIN DEE FURLONG, food products manager; b. Champaign, Ill., May 5, 1961; d. Austin James and Carol Jean (Osterman) Furlong; m. Thomas Edwin Goodalis, Oct. 19, 1985. BS, U. Ill., 1983. Sales rep. beverage div. Procter and Gamble, Oak Brook, Ill., 1983-85, sales rep. food div., 1985, dist. field rep food div., 1986, unit mgr. retail food div., 1986—. Republican. Presbyterian. Office: Procter and Gamble 814 Commerce Dr Oak Brook IL 60521

GOODE, LOVETT DAVIS, insurance company executive, consultant; b. N.Y.C., Dec. 26, 1958; d. Dudley Anthony and Ivy Joy Davis; m. Darrell C. Goode, Feb. 14, 1982; 1 child, Lyle Scott. Personnel mgr. State Mutual Life of Am., Beverly Hills, Calif., 1980—; mktg. cons. Marsh & McLennan, Los Angeles, 1982—. Internship, Aid to Rep. Bunte Mass. State House, Boston,

1978, affirmative action dir. for State of Mass., 1979. Recipient citation for Exceptional Community Service, State of Mass., 1979. Mem. Nat. Assn. Female Execs., Nat. Assn. Securities Dealers (lic. rep.). Democrat. Methodist. Home: 85 N Holliston #8 Pasadena CA 91106

GOODEN, BARBARA ANN, credit union executive; b. Waycross, Ga., July 14, 1946; d. James William and Juanita Christine (Davis) G. A.A. in Psychology, A.A. in Bus. Adminstrn., A.A. in Edn., Waycross Jr. Coll.; grad. Sch. Fin. Counseling, Fla. State U., 1986; student Cert. Credit Union Execs. Cert. consumer credit executive; lic. real estate salesman, Ga. With Eli Witt Co., Tampa, Fla., 1968-80, credit union rep., 1974-80; credit card coordinator 1st R.R. Community Fed. Credit Union F/K/A Waycross Seaboard System Fed. Credit Union, 1980-84, collection coordinator, 1984—; owner Craftmasters, 1987—. Contbr. articles on consumer credit to Waycross Jour. Herald, 1985. Women's rep. Southeast Area Employment and Tng. Council, Waycross, 1972-80. Mem. Waycross Credit Women (pres. 1984-85), Soc. Cert. Consumer Credit Execs., Ga. Soc. Credit Union Loan and Collection Coordinators (charter), League Credit Unions. Baptist. Club: Okefenokee Bus. and Profl. Women's (v.p. 1972-74). Avocations: reading, cake decorating, floral art, crafts, cooking. Home and Office: 513 Riverside Dr Waycross GA 31501 Office: 1st RR Community Fed Credit Union F/K/A Waycross Seaboard System PO Box 1256 Waycross GA 31502

GOODENOUGH, URSULA WILTSHIRE, cell biologist, researcher, educator; b. Queens Village, N.Y., Mar. 16, 1943; d. Erwin Ramsdell Goodenough and Evelyn (Wiltshire) Pitcher; m. Robert Paul Levine, Aug. 10, 1969 (div. 1980); children—Jason, Mathea; m. John Edward Heuser, July 29, 1980; children—Jessica, Thomas, James. Student Radcliffe Coll., 1960-61; B.A., Barnard Coll., N.Y.C., 1963; M.A., Columbia U., 1965; Ph.D., Harvard U., 1969. Asst. prof. biology Harvard U., 1971-76, assoc. prof., 1976-78; assoc. prof. Washington U., St. Louis, 1978-81, prof., 1981—; mem. study sect. NIH, Bethesda, Md., 1977-81. Author: Genetics, 1974, 3d edit., 1984; contbr. articles to profl. jours. Grantee NIH, NSF. Mem. Am. Soc. Cell Biology (assoc. editor jour. 1978-81). Democrat. Office: Washington U Dept Biology Saint Louis MO 63130

GOODEY, ILA MARIE, psychologist; b. Logan, Utah, Feb. 1, 1948; d. Vernal P. and Leona Marie (Williams) Goodey. BA with honors in English and Sociology, U. Utah, 1976; Grad. Cert. Criminology, U. Utah, 1976, MS in Counseling Psychology, 1984, PhD in Psychology, 1985. Speech writer for dean of students U. Utah, Salt Lake City, 1980—, psychologist Univ. Counseling Ctr., 1984—; cons. Dept. Social Services, State of Utah, Salt Lake City, 1983—; pvt. practice psychology Consult West, Salt Lake City, 1985-86; pub. relations coordinator Univ. Counseling Ctr., 1985—; cons. Aids Project, U. Utah, 1985—; pvt. practice psychology, Inscapes Inst., Salt Lake City, 1987—; writer civic news Salt Lake City Corp., 1980—. Author book: Love for All Seasons, 1971; play: Validation, 1979; musical drama: One Step, 1984. Contbr. articles to profl. jours. Chmn. policy bd. Dept. State Social Service, Salt Lake City, 1986—; campaign writer Utah Dem. Party, 1985. Recipient Creative Achievement award Utah Poetry Soc., 1974, English SAC, U. Utah, 1978. Mem. Am. Psychol. Assn., Utah Psychol. Assn., AAUW, Internat. Platform Assn., Mortar Board, Am. Soc. Clin. Hypnosis, Utah Soc. Clin. Hypnosis, Soc. Psychol. Study Social Issues, League of Women Voters, Phi Beta Kappa, Phi Kappa Phi, Alpha Lambda Delta. Mormon. Clubs: Mormon Theol. Symposium, Utah Poetry Assn. Avocations: theatrical activities, creative writing, travel, political activities. Office: U Utah Univ Counseling Ctr 450 SSB Salt Lake City UT 84112 also: Inscapes Inst 34 S 600 E Salt Lake City UT 84102

GOODFELLOW, JOAN BENNETT, building trade executive; b. Williamsport, Pa., Nov. 6, 1928; d. Kenneth Victor and Martha Emily (Covert) Bennett; m. John Goodfellow, May 30, 1955 (div. 1974); 1 child, John Charles, II. Student Ithaca Coll. Gen. mgr. Bennett Chem. Co., Hagaman, N.Y., 1948-65, Halifax Tile & Floor, Ormond Beach, Fla., 1967-70; office mgr. Service Paint & Glass, Daytona Beach, Fla., 1967; owner, pres. Halifax Tile & Floor Covering, Inc., Ormond Beach, 1970—; v.p. New Era, Inc., Ormond Beach, 1982—. Fellow Nat. Assn. Women in Construction (charter mem.), Nat. Assn. Home Builders Inc., Internat. Pilot Club, Inc., (internat. affairs dir.). Avocations: Golf; travel. Home: 2926 Anchor Dr Ormond Beach FL 32074 Office: Halifax Tile & Floor Covering Inc 275 Kenilworth Ave Ormond Beach FL 32074

GOODFELLOW, ROBIN IRENE, surgeon; b. Xenia, Ohio, Apr. 14, 1945; d. Willis Douglas and Irene Linna (Kirkland) G. B.A. summa cum laude, Western Res. U., Cleve., 1967; M.D. cum laude, Harvard U., 1971. Diplomate Am. Bd. Surgery. Intern, resident Peter Bent Brigham Hosp., Boston, 1971-76; staff surgeon Boston U., 1976-80, asst. prof. surgery, 1977-80; practice medicine specializing in surgery, Jonesboro, La., 1980-81, Albion, Mich., 1984-87, Coldwater, Mich., 1987—. Bd. overseers Case Western Res. U., 1977-82. Fellow AAUW, 1970; mem. AMA, Phi Beta Kappa. Republican. Methodist.

GOODHART, KAREN STEPHAN, sales executive; b. Bklyn., Jan. 14, 1947; d. Frank Herman and Bernadette (Brady) S.; m. James Stanley Goodhart, June 7, 1969 (div. Jan. 1983); children: Kristen Stephanie, Erika Lee. BA, Alvernia Coll., 1969. Elem. tchr. Schuylkill Valley Sch., Leesport, Pa., 1969-78; mgr. sales Radio Shack, Reading, Pa., 1978-84, The Computer Source, Reading, 1984; buyer Boscov's, Reading, 1985-86; with sales dept. Info. Mgmt., Blue Bell, Pa., 1986; mgr. sales Bio-Med Pa., Inc., Allentown, 1986-87, v.p. sales, 1987-88; v.p. sales Med. Disposal Services, Inc., Reading, 1988. Mem. Nat. Solid Waste Mgmt. Assn., Am. Soc. Health Care, Nat. Exec. Housekeeping, Assn. Practitioners Infection Control. Democrat. Roman Catholic. Office: Med Disposal Services Inc 1420 Clarion St Reading PA 19601

GOODHUE, MARY BRIER, lawyer, state senator; b. London; d. Ernest and Marion H. (Hawks) Brier; naturalized, 1942; B.A., Vassar Coll., 1942; LL.B., U. Mich., 1944; m. Francis A. Goodhue, Jr., May 15, 1948; 1 son, Francis A., III. Admitted to N.Y. State bar, 1945; asso. firm Root, Clark, Buckner & Ballantine, N.Y.C., 1945-48; asst. counsel N.Y. State Crime Commn., 1951-53, Moreland Commn., 1953-54; mem. firm Goodhue Banks Arons & Pickett and predecessors, Mt. Kisco, 1955—; mem. N.Y. State Assembly from 93d Dist., 1975-78, N.Y. State Senate, 1979—. Trustee, Presbyn. Hosp., N.Y.C., Westchester Mental Health Assn.; N.Y. del. Nat. Women's Conf., Houston, 1977. Mem. ABA, West Bas Assn., No. Westchester Bar Assn. Office: 126 Barker St Mount Kisco NY 10549 also: McLain St Mount Kisco NY 10549

GOODING, BARBARA JEAN, marketing professional, consultant; b. Phila., Dec. 25, 1941; d. Campbell Russell and Winifred Muriel (Long) Pittsinger; m. John Norman Sutton, Nov. 24, 1960 (div. Feb. 1969); children: Jacqueline, Rosanne; m. Thomas Michael Gooding, Jan. 1, 1983. Cert., C.M. Price Sch. Journalism, 1959-60; student, Montgomery City Coll., 1975-78, Widener U., 1978-81, No. Va. Community Coll., 1983-85. Dir. mktg. planning Pine Run Community, Doylestown, Pa., 1974-77; dir. sales Chad Co., Chadds Ford, Pa., 1977; account exec. Continental Am. Life, Wilmington, Del., 1978-82; mgr. direct mail Applied Mktg./Membership Services, McLean, Va., 1982-85; dir. mktg. RKI Group Plans, Chantilly, Va., 1985—; cons. Life Care Retirement Communities; freelance writer. Mem. Women's Direct Response Group (pres. 1986-88, v.p. 1985-86), Direct Mktg. Assn. Washington, Nat. Assn. Female Execs., Washington Postal Customers Council. Home: 206 W Maple Ave Sterling VA 22170 Office: RKI Group Plans 14325 Willard Rd Chantilly VA 22021

GOODKIN, DEBORAH GAY, internal management consultant; b. Oceanside, N.Y., Dec. 8, 1951; d. Harold and Rose (Mostkoff) G.; m. Glenn Richard; 1 child, Samuel Goodkin Richard. B.A., Syracuse U., 1972; M. Urban Planning, NYU, 1977. Planner, Nassau-Suffolk Planning, Hauppauge, N.Y., 1972; asst. to treas. Nat. Assn. Savs. Banks, N.Y.C., 1973; planning aide Dept. City Planning, N.Y.C., 1973-79; planner, real property mgr. N.Y.C. Bd. Edn., 1979-81, dir. Capital Budget Bur., 1981-85; supervising mgmt. engr. Port Authority N.Y. & N.J., 1985—; cons. C Corp., Los Angeles, 1983—. Security cons. Democratic Nat. Com., N.Y.C., 1980. Recipient C.F.O. Award of Excellence, 1987. Mem. Women in Govt. (guest lectr. 1983), Syracuse U. Alumni Assn., NYU Alumni Assn. Author: (zoning law) Bay Ridge Zoning Dist., 1978. Artist: Show of Selected Works, Sireuil, France, 1983. Office: Port Authority One World Trade Ctr New York NY 10048

GOODMAN, ANNE BAKER, art consultant; b. Bklyn., Oct. 15, 1928; d. Benjamin and Bessie (Cutler) Baker; m. David Goodman, Nov. 27, 1947 (div. 1978); children: Mark, Henry, Lori. Student, Inst. Fashion Tech., N.Y.C., 1946-47, Silvermine Coll. Art, 1965-66, Art Students' League, N.Y.C., 1975-77. Tchr. sculpture Weston, Conn., 1966; color coordinator Century 21, Miami, Fla., 1967-69; buyer, mgr. mus. shop Mus. of City of N.Y., 1970-72; art cons. Anne Goodman Art Cons., Los Angeles, 1977—; speaker profl. meetings. Office: 4337 Marina City Dr #739 Marina del Rey CA 90292

GOODMAN, CAREN ANDREA, advertising executive; b. Asheville, N.C., May 13, 1962; d. Bernard Paul Goodman and Ellen Ann (Silver) Gladding. BA in Journalism, U. N.C., 1984. Media planner, buyer, acct. exec. Van Laan & Assocs., Cary, N.C., 1984-85; acct. exec. Price McNabb Advt., Raleigh, N.C., 1985, Ketchum Communications, Phila., 1986—; v.p. media div. Jencarrob, Inc., Asheville, 1986—; cons., media buyer N.C. Assn. Educators, Raleigh, 1986—. Co-chair Addy Awards, 1986—. Mem. Triangle Advt. Fedn. Republican. Jewish. Home: 101-B4 Choptank Ct Cary NC 27511

GOODMAN, ELLEN HOLTZ, journalist; b. Newton, Mass., Apr. 11, 1941; d. Jackson Jacob and Edith (Weinstein) Holtz; m. Robert Levey; 1 dau., Katherine Anne. B.A. cum laude, Radcliffe Coll., 1963; hon. degrees, Mt. Holyoke Coll., Amherst Coll., U. Pa., U. N.H. Researcher, reporter Newsweek Mag., 1963-65; feature writer Detroit Free Press, 1965-67; feature writer columnist Boston Globe, 1967-74, assoc. editor, 1986—; syndicated columnist Washington Post Writers Group, 1976—; radio commentator Spectrum, CBS, 1978-80, NBC, 1979-80; commentator NBC Today Show, 1979-81. Author: Close to Home, 1979, Turning Points, 1979, At Large, 1981, Keeping in Touch, 1985. Trustee Radcliff Coll. Named New Eng. Newspaper Woman of Year New Eng. Press Assn., 1968; recipient Catherine O'Brien award Stanley Home Products, 1971, Media award Mass. Commn. Status Women, 1974, Columnist of Year award New Eng. Women's Press Assn., 1975, Pulitzer Prize for Commentary, 1980, prize for column writing Am. Soc. Newspaper Editors, 1980; Nieman fellow Harvard U., 1974. Office: Boston Globe Boston MA 02102

GOODMAN, GAIL BUSMAN, small business owner; b. N.Y.C., Feb. 8, 1953; d. Irving Laurence and Harriet (Topol) Busman. BS, Tufts U., 1975. Staff occupational therapist St. Joseph's Hosp., Yonkers, N.Y., 1975-77; sr. occupational therapist N.Y. Hosp., White Plains, 1977-79; chief occupational therapist Phelps Hosp., Tarrytown, N.Y., 1979-80; occupational therapy cons. Elmwood Manor Nursing Home, Nanuet, N.Y., 1982-83; dir. dealer ops. Facelifters, Bklyn., 1981-83; dir. franchising, asst. v.p. tng., research and devel., Facelifters Home Systems, Inc., Bklyn., Chgo., 1983-86; pres. Visual Impact, Suffern, N.Y., 1987—; guest speaker Columbia U., N.Y.C., 1977, 78, 79, 82. Mem. Westchester Assn. Women Bus. Owners, Women In Sales (bd. dirs.), Democrat. Jewish. Avocations: reading, movies, needlepoint, antique refinishing.

GOODMAN, GERTRUDE AMELIA, civic worker; b. El Paso, Tex., Oct. 24, 1924; d. Karl Perry and Helen Sylvia (Pinkiert) G. BA, Mills Coll., 1945. Chmn. El Paso chpt. Tex. Social Welfare Assn., 1963-65, bd. dirs., 1965-70; exec. dir. Pan-Am. Round Table El Paso, 1970-71, sec., 1973-74, Tex. part bd. dirs., 1966—; founder, 1st chmn. El Paso Mus. Art Members Guild, 1966-68; bd. dirs. Mus. Art Assn., 1962-69, also v.p.; chmn., dir. El Paso C. of C. Woman's Dept., 1976-77; pres. bd. dirs. El Paso Pub. Library, 1978-80; pres. El Paso County Hist. Soc., 1981-82, bd. dirs., 1986-87; mem. planning div. El Paso United Way, 1953—, chmn. agy. relations com., 1985—; hon. dir. El Paso Cancer Treatment Ctr., 1976—; bd. dirs. El Paso Sesquicentennial, 1986. Recipient Hall of Honor award El Paso County Hist. Soc., Nat. Human Relations award NCCJ, 1981, numerous awards for civic vol. work. Home: 905 E Cincinnati Ave El Paso TX 79902

GOODMAN, VALERIE DAWSON, psychiatric social worker; b. Bluefield, W.Va., Feb. 2, 1948; d. Francis Carl and Lesly (Collett) Dawson; m. David William Goodman, June 9, 1985; 1 child, Amanda Lynn. BS, W.Va. U., 1970, MS, 1972; M in Social Work, U. Md., 1980. Lic. social worker. Social worker Md. Children's Aide Family Services Soc., Balt., 1972-78; social worker III Montgomery County Dept. Social Services, Rockville, Md., 1980-81; clin. social worker Johns Hopkins Hosp., Balt., 1981-83, sr. social worker, 1981-88; pvt. practice Balt., 1986—; supr. Johns Hopkins Hosp., 1983-86, chair Brogden com., 1984-85. Speaker in field. Mem. Kappa Delta. Home: 64 Hamlet Dr Owings Mills MD 21117

GOODMAN, VIOLET LOWERY, realtor, investment counselor; b. Konawa, Okla., Sept. 10, 1913; d. Harvey Adell and Ruth Izora (Collins) Lowery; m. Orville C. Goodman, Dec. 24, 1934; children—Bruce Lowery, Alan Dale. Student in Bus., U. Okla., 1935-39; student in Nursing, Milw. Vocat.-Tech. U., 1943-47. Grad. Realtors Inst. Instr., Beauty Culture, Milw., 1940-47, Motor and Armature Repair, Norman, Okla., 1948-55; apt. mgr., Norman, 1970-75; real estate salesperson Acad. Realty, Inc., Norman, 1962—; instr. comml. and real estate investments, Okla. Real Estate Inst., 1970-74; counselor creative financing. Author instructor's manual: Commercial Real Estate, 1970. Mem. Nat. Assn. Realtors, Okla. Assn. Realtors (edn. com. 1970-76, dean of edn. 1972, state dir. 1968-76), Norman Bd. Realtors (pres. 1973, Realtor of Yr. 1972, Spl. Recognition award 1979), Realtor Nat. Mktg. Inst. (chmn. membership com. 1972-74), Norman C. of C., Bus. and Profl. Women (pres. 1968). Democrat. Presbyterian. Lodges: Order Eastern Star, White Shrine. Club: Altrusa. Home: 4321 24th Ave NW Norman OK 73069 Office: Acad Realty Inc 419 W Gray St Norman OK 73069

GOODMAN, YETTA M., educator; b. Cleve., Mar. 10, 1931; d. William and Dora (Shapiro) Trachtman; B.A. in History, Los Angeles State Coll., 1952, M.A. in Elem. Edn., 1956; Ed.D. in Curriculum Devel., Wayne State U., 1967; m. Kenneth S. Goodman, 1952; children—Debra, Karen Goodman Castro, Wendy Hood. Elem. and secondary tchr., public schs., Los Angeles, 1952-63; supr. pre-service teaching experiences Wayne State U., 1963-67; asst. to prof. U. Mich., Dearborn, 1967-75; prof. edn., co-dir. program in lang. and literacy U. Ariz., 1975—; speaker, cons. ednl. issues. Active in orgns. concerned with children's rights. Recipient Faculty Recognition award Tucson Trade Bur., 1978, Outstanding Tchr. Educator of Reading award Internat. Reading Assn., 1983. Mem. Nat. Council Tchrs. English (bd. dirs. 1976—, pres. 1978-79), Center Expansion of Lang. and Thinking (bd. dirs. 1972—, pres. 1976-79), Internat. Reading Assn. (chairperson and active mem. various coms. 1962—), Assn. Supervision and Curriculum Devel., Am. Ednl. Research Assn., Assn. Childhood Edn. Internat. Jewish. Author books, including: (with C. Burke and B. Sherman) Reading Strategies: Focus on Comprehension, 1981; (with D. Watson and C. Burke) Reading Miscue Inventory: Alternate Procedures, 1986; contbr. numerous articles, chpts. to profl. publs.; also audio tapes scripts video, films. Home: 5649 E 10th St Tucson AZ 85711 Office: U Ariz Coll Edn Program in Lang & Literacy Tucson AZ 85721

GOODREAU, LOU ANN, secondary educator; b. Herkimer, N.Y., Nov. 27, 1955; m. L. Thomas Goodreau, July 4, 1986. AAA, Herkimer County Community Coll., 1975; BS in Bus. Edn., SUNY, Albany, 1977, MS, 1980. Tchr. bus. Cairo-Durham Cen. Sch., Cairo, N.Y., 1977-82, Poland (N.Y.) Cen. Sch., 1982—; instr. adult edn. Herkimer County Community Coll., 1984—; advisor Poland Cen. Sch. Store, 1982—. Mem. Bus. Tchrs. Assn. N.Y., Poland Tchrs. Assn., Delta Pi Epsilon. Presbyterian. Home: 21 Meadowbrook Dr New Hartford NY 13413

GOODRICH, GLORIA JEAN, federal agency administrator; b. Lima, Ohio, Feb. 21, 1934; d. Orville John and Lila Mae (Rigel) Mortimer; m. Merlin Virgil Goodrich, June 6, 1953; children: Sandra Kay, Gregory Lynn, Geoffrey Virgil. Student, Owosso Coll., 1952-55, 67-68, Muskegon (Mich.) Community Coll., 1971-73. Cert. legal asst. Estimator E.H. Sheldon & co., Muskegon, 1975-77; dep. clk. U.S. Fed. Ct., Tucson, 1977-81, supr., 1982—. Tchr. ch. sch., Ohio, Mich., Ariz., 1950—; leader Boy Scouts Am. and Girl Scouts U.S., Mich., 1966-71; mem. Tucson Clean and Beautiful. Mem. Ariz. Assn. for Ct. Mgmt., Tucson Assn. Legal Assts., Nat. Assn. for Female Execs. Avocations: walking, reading, sewing, teaching, needlework.

GOODSELL, JOAN WALDRON, librarian; b. Bridgeport, Conn., May 19, 1949; d. Frederic and Elinor (Engels) G. BA, U. Conn., 1971; MS, Drexel U., 1973. Librarian Laventhal, Kreckstein, Horwath & Horwath, Phila., 1978; catalog librarian Inter-Am. U., San German, P.R., 1974-78; cataloger, art librarian Info. Ctr. J. Walter Thompson Co., N.Y.C., P.R., 1978-83, collection devel. librarian creative library, 1983-85, asst. mgr. creative library, 1985—. Sustaining mem. Am. Shakespeare Theater Guild, Stratford, Conn., 1980—. Mem. ALA (Library and Info. Tech. Assn. 1984—, Library Adminstrn. and Mgmt. Assn., small libraries publs. series com.), Spl. Libraries Assn. (chmn. mus. arts and humanities group 1983-84), Assn. N.Y.C. Ballet Guild, Phi Beta Kappa. Episcopalian. Home: 65-60 Booth St 5L Rego Park NY 11674 Office: J Walter Thompson Co Creative Library 466 Lexington Ave New York NY 10017

GOODSON, CAROLE EDITH MCKISSOCK, technology educator; b. Des Moine, Dec. 31, 1946; d. William Thompson and Edith (Johnson) McKissock; m. Robert Wayne Peterson, July 1978; 1 son, David Shelby Peterson. B.S., U. Houston, 1968, M.Ed., 1971, Ed.D., 1975. Tchr., Spring Branch Ind. Sch. Dist., Houston, 1968-69; mem. faculty Coll. Tech., U. Houston, 1972—, instr., 1972-75, asst. prof., coll. counselor, 1975-78, assoc. prof., coll. counselor, 1978-81, assoc. prof., chmn. related courses tech., 1981—, assoc. dean, assoc. prof. tech. math., 1982—. Author: (with S.L. Miertschin) Technical Mathematics With Applications, 1983, 2d edit., 1986; Technical Mathematics with Calculus, 1985; Technical Algebra with Applications, 1985; contbr. articles to publs. Recipient Dow Outstanding Young Faculty award Am. Soc. Engring. Edn., 1982. Mem. Am. Soc. Engring. Edn. (vice chmn. 1985-86, chmn. 1987—, sec.-treas. div. 1982-84, regional chair 1982-83), Nat. Council Tchrs. of Math., Math. Assn. Am., Phi Kappa Phi (chpt. pres. 1985), Tex. Assn. of Sch. of Engring. Tech. (sec. 1986—). Presbyterian. Office: U Houston Coll Tech 361-T2 University Park Houston TX 77004

GOODSON, PATRICIA RANDOLPH, concert pianist, educator; b. Newport News, Va., Aug. 26, 1954; d. George Royden and Evelyn Patricia Dodge (Andrew) G. BA, Duke U., 1976; MM in Piano Performance, Peabody Conservatory Music, 1980. Lectr. piano Hood Coll., Frederick, Md., 1977-80; freelance pianist N.Y.C., 1980-81; mgr. creative services Gen. Computer Co., Cambridge, Mass., 1981-84, account exec. Rizzo, Simons, Cohn, Boston, 1985-87. Composer video game music and sound effects. Mem. Chamber Music Am., Bibliotheque Francaise, Boston Mus. Fine Arts. Home and Office: 1519 8th St Charlestown MA 02129

GOODSON, SHANNON LORAYN, behavioral scientist, consultant; b. Beaumont, Tex., May 26, 1952; d. James Ernest and Lorayn (Miller) G. BS in Psychology, Lamar U., 1974, MS in Psychology, 1977. Mgmt. asst. Southwestern Life, Dallas, 1978-79; co-founder, exec. v.p. Behavioral Scis. REsearch Press, Inc., Dallas, 1979—. Author: (with others) Psychology of Call Reluctance, 1986; contbr. articles to profl. jours. Mem. SE Psychol. Assn. Office: Behavioral Sciences Research Press 2695 Villa Creek Dr Suite 100 Dallas TX 75234

GOODSPEED, BARBARA, artist; b. Gardner, Mass., Sept. 1, 1919; d. George Daniel and Bernice (Lucas) G. Diploma Stoneleigh Coll., 1939, Famous Artist Schs., Westport, Conn., 1955. Free-lance photographer, N.Y.C., 1941-52, Christmas card designer, Sherman, Conn., 1952-69, oil and watercolor, fine arts artist, Sherman, 1969—. Illustrator: Forever Flowers, 1979. Recipient Merit award Sheffield Art League, 1979, 81, 83, others; named Artist of Yr., Art League of Harlem Valley, 1981. Fellow Am. Artists Profl. League (John Dole Meml. award); mem. Salmagundi Club, Hudson Valley Art Assn., Acad. Artists, Nat League Am. Pen Women, Kent Art Assn., Inc. (press. 1970-72, 80-83, 85—, medal of Merit 1979), Berkshire Watercolor Soc. (co-founder, sec. 1984—), Housatonic Art League (v.p., bd. dirs. 1977-83). Avocations: camping; crafts. Home and Studio: Holiday Point Rd PO Box 406 Sherman CT 06784

GOODSTONE, ERICA MAE, sex counselor, health and physical education educator; b. N.Y.C., Apr. 16, 1946; d. Morris Goodstone and Muriel (Carnel) Goodstone Schaeffer. B.A., Queens Coll., 1966; M.A., N.Y. U., 1970, Ph.D., 1983. Cert. elem. and high sch. educator, N.Y.; lic. mental health and sex counselor. Primary tchr. Pub. Sch. 219, Queens, N.Y., 1966-67; exec. sec. Gotham Rec. Co., N.Y.C., 1967; tchr. 4th grade Pub. Sch. 106K, Bklyn., 1967-68; tchr. phys. edn., Women's tennis varsity coach, women's gymnastics varsity coach, Bayside High Sch., Queens, 1969-74; assoc. prof. health and phys. edn. Fashion Inst. Tech., N.Y.C., 1974—; women's athletic dir., women's varsity tennis coach Fashion Inst. Tech., N.Y.C., 1974-82. adj. lectr. Kingsborough Community Coll., Bklyn., 1971-73, Manhattan Community Coll., 1983-85; pvt. practice sexual counseling, mind/body therapy. Mem. AAHPERD, AAUW, Nat. Council Internat. Health, Soc. Sci. Study Sex, Am. Assn. Sex Educators, Counselors and Therapists, Soc. Sex Therapy and Research, Am. Shiatsu Assn., Rubenstein Synergy Assn., Am. Assn. Counseling and Devel., Am. Mental Health Counselor Assn., N.Y. State Soc. Med. Massage Therapists, Alliance Massage Therapists, N.Y. State Assn. Two Yr. Colls. Democrat. Jewish. Contbr. articles to mags. Home: 180 1/2 E 64th St New York NY 10021 Office: Fashion Inst Tech 227 W 27 St New York NY 10001-5992

GOODWIN, ELIZABETH TANNER, dentist, researcher; b. Biddeford, Maine, May 15, 1957; d. Charles Victor and Shirley (Mewer) Tanner; m. Kurt Joseph Goodwin, July 5, 1980; children: Sarah Joy, Megan Elizabeth. BA in Zoology and BS in Chem. Engring., U. Maine, 1979; DMD, Tufts U., 1982. Researcher USPHS/Tufts U., Boston, 1979-82; gen. practice dentistry USPHS, Unalhaven, Maine, 1982-85; researcher USPHS, Boston, 1985—; dentist Dr. Norman Rogers, Methven, Mass., 1986—; research task team Pub. Health Service, Boston, 1986—; educator dentistry Mass. Edn. Dept., Georgetown, Mass., 1986—. Organizer Hotline: Rape, Suicide, Drugs, Alcohol, Orono, 1977-79, Adopt-a-Grandparent, Groveland, Mass., 1985—; pres. Health Council, Vinalhaven, 1983, 84-85; mem., sec. Mothers Against Drunk Driving, Georgetown, 1985—; mem. Mothers Against Nuclear War, Boston, 1986—. Mem. ADA, Am. Acad. Gen. Dentists, Acad. of Women Dentists (Woman Dentist of Yr. 1983-85), Mass. Dental Soc. of Merrimac Valley, Phi Beta Kappa, Phi Kappa Phi. Presbyterian. Club: Young Profls. with Children (Georgetown) (sec. 1985-86, pres. 1986—0. Lodge: Order of Eastern Star (Worthy Assoc. Matron 1983-85). Home: PO Box 193 Groveland MA 01834

GOODWIN, JEAN MCCLUNG, psychiatrist; b. Pueblo, Colo., Mar. 28, 1946; d. Paul Stanley and Geraldine (Smart) McClung; m. James Simeon Goodwin, Aug. 8, 1970; children: Laura (dec.), Amanda Harding Goodwin, Robert Caleb, Paul Joshua, Elizabeth Cronin Goodwin. BA in Anthropology summa cum laude, Radcliffe Coll., 1967; MD, Harvard U., 1971; MPH, UCLA, 1972. Diplomate Am. Bd. Psychiatry and Neurology, Am. Bd. Forensic Psychiatry. Resident in psychiatry Gerogetown U. Hosp., 1972-74, U. N.Mex. Medicine, 1974-76; asst. dir., dir. psychiatric residents tng. U. N.Mex., 1979-85; prof., dir. joint academic program Med. Coll. Wis., Milw. County Mental Health Complex, 1985—; from inst. to assoc. prof. dept. psychiatry U. N.Mex. Sch. Medicine, 1976-85; cons. protective services Dept. Human Services, N.Mex., 1976-84; lectr. profl. groups. Author: (book) Effects of Hight Altitude on Human Birth, 1969, Sexual Abuse: Incest Victims and their Families, 1982; editorial bd. Jour. Psychosocial Stress, 1985—; contbr. numerous articles on child abuse to profl. jours. Chmn. work group on child sexual abuse Surgeon Gen.'s Violence and Pub. Health, Leesburg, Va., 1985. Recipient Saville Prize in Family Planning, UCLA Sch. Pub. Health, 1972; Nat. Cen. Child Abuse and Neglect grantee, 1979-82, Nat. Inst. Aging grantee, 1980-85. Fellow Am. Psychiat. Assn. (dist. br. treas., sec. N.Mex. br. 1980-82, exhibits subcom. 1985—), Internat. Soc. Study Multiple Personality Dissociative Disorders (child abuse liason com. 1984), Am. Profl. Soc. Sexual Abuse Children (bd. dirs. 1986), Am. Med. Women's Assn. (state dir. 1978-80),. Democrat. Roman Catholic. Home: 4015 N Lake Dr Milwaukee WI 53211 Office: Milw County Mental Health Complex 9455 Watertown Plank Rd Milwaukee WI 53226

GOODWIN, KATIE MAXINE-AGIN, disability management services executive; b. Cleve., Feb. 26, 1952; d. Jerome and Cecile Sarah (Gray) Agin;

D.S., Ohio State U., 1975. Occupational therapist Ga. Retardation Center, Atlanta, 1975-76; rehab. specialist Internat. Rehab. Assocs., Atlanta, 1976-78, account rep., 1978-79, Midwest regional mktg. mgr., Chgo., 1979-80, dist. sales mgr., Detroit, 1980-82, sales tng. tchr., 1979-84; mem. rehab. counseling adv. com. Mich. State U., 1982-85; rehab. cons. ConServ Co., Southfield, 1986—. Mem. Ga. Self-Insured Assn. (com. rep. 1978-79), So. Assn. Workers Compensation Adminstrn., Mich. Assn. Rehab. Profls. (membership chmn. 1981-82), Mich. Rehab. Assn. (chmn.), Am. Occupational Therapy Assn., Nat. Rehab. Assn., Detroit Adjusters Assn., Nat. Assn. Profl. Saleswomen (Mich. publicity com.), NOW. Home: 26100 W 12 Mile Rd #234 Southfield MI 48034

GOODWIN, OCTAVIA DARLENE, insurance administrator; b. Balt., Oct. 18, 1959; d. Joseph and Daisy (Wilson) G. BA, St. Mary's U., 1981, cert. paralegal, 1984. Sec. theology dept. So. Meth. U., San Antonio, 1977-81; typist ACTION, Washington, 1981; sr. claims examiner Postmasters Benefit Plan, Alexandria, Va., 1981-82, tech. reviewer, 1982-84, asst. supr., 1984—; supr. prodn. Mut. Omaha, Rockville, Md., 1987—. counselor juvenile delinquents, San Antonio, 1979-80, Tex. Youth Council, San Antonio, 1980-81; sec. Chateauneuf Homeowners Assn., Alexandria, 1983-84. Mem. Nat. Assn. for Female Execs. Democrat. Baptist. Home: 4215 Buckman Rd Alexandria VA 22309 Office: Mut of Omaha 2094 Gathers Rd Rockville MD 20850

GOODWIN, SHARON, nurse, psychiatric consultant, therapist; b. N.Y.C., Oct. 19, 1944; d. Orland and Grace (Doonan) G. R.N., St. Louis City Hosp., 1965; Psychiat. Assoc., Mo. Inst. Psychiatry, St. Louis, 1971. Staff nurse St. Louis City Hosp., 1965-66, head nurse isolation, 1966-67, head nurse psychiatry, 1966-68, community psychiatry developer, 1967-81; dir. nursing Fairground Nursing Home, St. Louis, 1970-71; asst. dir. med. program Community Placement Program, St. Louis, 1972-79; asst. dir., med. advisor Places for People, St. Louis, 1979-82; dir. outpatient alcoholism treatment program, St. Joseph Hosp., Houston, 1982-87, private practice Houston, 1987—; chemical dependency counselor U. Houston, 1985-87; community psychiatry cons. Mo. Mental Health Div., St. Louis, 1979-82; community psychiatry trainer U. Mo. Social Work, St. Louis, 1981-82; bd. dirs., clin. advisor The Gathering Place Rehab Ctr.; founder, dir. The Recovery Collective; founder Women in New Growth Sobriety. Presenter Washington U. Social Services Dept., St. Louis, 1976-81. Mem. Internat. Assn. Psychosocial Rehab. Centers (presenter 1977). Home: 5501 Valerie Houston TX 77081

GOOGINS, SONYA FORBES, banker; b. New Haven, Nov. 9, 1936; d. Edward and Madeline Forbes; m. Robert Reville Googins, June 21, 1958; children: Shawn W. and Glen. R. BE, U. Conn., 1958; postgrad., Dartmouth Inst., 1978. Tchr. Manchester (Conn.) High Sch., 1958-61, Creative Nursery Sch., Glastonbury, Conn.; pres. Colonial Printing Co., Glastonbury, 1971-76; sales mgr. Glastonbury Stationers, 1977-81; br. mgr., lending officer to bank officer Conn. Nat. Bank, Hartford, 1982—. Mayor Town of Glastonbury, 1983-85, 87-89; council mem. and majority leader Town Council, 1979—; active Econ. Devel. Commission, Youth Services Commn., League Women Voters, Rep. Town Coms.; active policy bd. Capitol Region Council Govts., Hartford, 1983-85, 87-89, treas., 1987—. Recipient Outstanding Service award Friends of Glastonbury Youth, 1985. Mem. Glastonbury Bus. and Profl. Women (past pres. and founder, Woman of Yr. 1986), Glastonbury C. of C. (bd. dirs. 1975-80), Hartford Women's Network. Roman Catholic. Club: Glastonbury Jr. Woman's (past pres.). Home: 74 Forest Ln Glastonbury CT 06033 Office: Conn Nat Bank 777 Main St Hartford CT 06103

GOORVITCH, NORMA RUTH, accountant; b. N.Y.C., Jan. 14, 1944; d. Irving and Gertrude (Greenberg) Rubenstein; m. David Goorvitch, June 3, 1966; children: Stephen, Laura. BA, U. Mich., 1964; MA, U. Calif., Berkeley, 1966; BS, San Jose State U., 1981. Estimator Dalmo Victor, Belmont, Calif., 1981-84; contract acct., computer div. Rolm Mil-Spec, San Jose, Calif., 1984; sr. cost acct. Zilog, Inc., Campbell, Calif., 1984-86; govt. compliance supr. EIMAC div. Varian Assocs., San Carlos, Calif., 1986—. Vol. Community Friends, Santa Clara, Calif., 1975-76. Mem. Beta Gamma Sigma, Alpha Lamda Delta.

GOOTEE, JANE MARIE, lawyer; b. Jasper, Ind., July 5, 1953; d. Thomas H. and Anne M. (Dreifke) G. BA, Ind. U., 1974; JD cum laude, St. Louis U., 1977. Bar: Ind. 1977, Mo. 1978, Mich. 1980, Ohio 1983, U.S. Dist. Ct. (so. dist.) Ind. 1977, U.S. Dist. Ct. (ea. dist.) Mich. 1980, U.S. Ct. Appeals (7th cir.) 1978, U.S. Supreme Ct. 1980, U.S. Ct. Appeals (6th cir.) 1982, U.S. Ct. Appeals (4th cir.) 1986. Dep. atty. gen. Ind., Indpls., 1977-79; corp. atty. Dow Chem. Co., Midland, Mich., 1979-81, ea. div. counsel, 1981-84, sr. atty., 1984-86, Mich. div. counsel, 1986—; mem. issue mgmt. team Dow Chem. Groundwater, 1986-87; adv. com. Nat. Chamber Litigation Ctr. Environ. Law, 1985—; mem. Great Lakes Community Coll. Adv. Bd., 1987—; chair Dow Epidemiology Instl. Rev. Bd., 1984—; pro-bono def. Midland Cir. Ct., 1980-81; adj. prof. Saginaw Valley State Coll., University Center, Mich., 1979-80. Bd. dirs. Big Sisters Midland, 1979-81, 84-86, Big Bros./Big Sisters Midland, 1986—, also pres., 1988—; exec. bd. Boy Scouts Am. Lake Huron Area Council, 1988—. Mem. ABA, Mo. Bar, Mich. Bar Assn., Bar Assn. Greater Cleve. (corp. sec. gov.'s com. 1983), Assn. Trial Lawyers Am. Republican. Roman Catholic. Home: 1412 Brentwood Dr Midland MI 48640 Office: Dow Chem Legal Dept Michigan Div 47 Bldg Midland MI 48667

GOOTGELD, MARLA, electronics executive; b. Racine, Wis., July 8, 1954; d. Erwin Howard and Betty Jane (Gorsuch) Jacobi; m. Gary Lynn Gootgeld, Sept. 9, 1956; children: Shannon Marie, Jessica Ann. AS in Bus., West Valley Coll., 1974; BSBA, San Jose (Calif.) State U., 1976. Assoc. buyer Nat. Semiconductor, Sunnyvale, Calif., 1979-80; buyer NCR Micrographics, Mountain View, Calif., 1980-82; sr. buyer Calif. Microwave, Inc., Sunnyvale, 1982-87; purchasing supr. XMR, Inc., Santa Clara, Calif., 1987—. Home: 3188 Cyrus Ave San Jose CA 95124 Office: XMR Inc 5403 Betsy Ross Dr Santa Clara CA 95054

GOPLEN, DONNELLE, counselor; b. Loco, Okla., Nov. 5, 1936; d. Allen R. and Dorothy R. (Carmichael) Bean; B.A. with honors, U. N.Mex., 1974, M.A., 1977; postgrad. Family Therapy Inst., 1981-82; m. Bruce C. Goplen, Sept. 26, 1969; children—Stephen Harvey, Donald Harvey. State welfare worker State Welfare Agy., N.Mex., 1975-77; counseling intern Presbyn. Hosp., Albuquerque, 1977; social worker State of N.Mex., 1977-78; vol. mental health aide Prince William County (Va.) Community Mental Health Center, 1978-79, coordinator Social Activity Center; program coordinator family services comprehensive support program Community Services Bd. of Prince William County. Mem. AAUW, Nat. Cert. Counselors. Home: 18414 Cedar Dr Triangle VA 22172 Office: Prince William Community Services Bd 234 S Fraley Blvd Dumfries VA 22026

GORALL, KIMBERLY ANN, computer company executive, consultant; b. Rochester, N.Y., Feb. 5, 1957; d. Donald James and Constance Jean (Croft) G. BA in Geol. Scis., U. Buffalo, 1980. Curatorial asst. Pinch Mineralogical Mus., Rochester, 1980; asst. mineralogist Dr. David H. Garske, Bisbee, Ariz., 1981; tech. analyst Burroughs Corp., Rochester, 1981-86; provider/MIS liaison Rochester Area Health Maintenance Orgn., 1986—; pres., founder Croft Enterprises Ltd., Inc., Rochester, 1988—. Co-author: (with others) Monteregian Treasures: The Minerals of Mont Saint-Hilaire, Quebec, 1988; editor-in-chief mag. Citron, 1973-75 (Best in N.Y. 1975). Pres. geol. soc. U. Buffalo, 1978-79; chmn. Cub Scouts Am. Gates, N.Y., 1987-88. Regents scholar, 1975. Mem. Nat. Assn. Female Execs., Cen. N.Y. Communications Assn., Gemological Inst. Am., Rochester Acad. Scis., Soc. Tech. Communication, Internat. Gem Mineral and Fossil Soc. Democrat. Roman Catholic. Home: 1412 Elmwood Ave Rochester NY 14620 Office: Croft Enterprises Ltd PO Box 40490 Rochester NY 14604

GORDEN, MARSHA, industrial chemist, international development consultant; b. Glen Cove, N.Y., Apr. 17, 1933; d. David George and Jeanne (Bernstein) Cohen; m. Morton Gorden, Dec. 19, 1954; children: Nicole, Lisa. BA in Chemistry, Conn. Coll., 1954; student, Universite de Paris, 1955-56; EdM in Sci. Edn., Boston U., 1957; MA in Chemistry, Wellesley Coll., 1968. Research chemist Pfizer Inc., Bklyn., 1954; tchr. chemistry, physics Westwood Mass. High Sch., 1957-58; chemistry tchr. Weston Mass. High Sch., 1962-64; teaching asst. Wellesley Mass. Coll., 1964-66; chemistry researcher U. Pa., Phila., 1966-68; instr. Internat. Sch. Am., 1968-69; co-founder, environ. chemist Devel. Sciences Inc., Sagamore, Mass., 1970-78, materials mgr., 1979-84, v. p., 1984—; cons. energy services and equipment, 1985—; speaker Radcliffe Coll. summer program sci., Cambridge, 1983—. Co-editor: Environ. Mgmt. Sci. Politics, 1972. Advisor summer program Cape Cod YMCA, 1971-75. Scholar NSF, 1964-66. Mem. Am. Chem. Soc., Am. Inst. Chem. Engrs. Home: 11 Shaw Rd RFD 1 East Sandwich MA 02537 Office: Devel Sciences Inc 39 Pleasant St PO Box 444 Sagamore MA 02561

GORDON, CAROL HANCOCK JOHNSON, telephone company manager; b. Flushing, N.Y., Mar. 21, 1947; d. Carl and Ophelia Lucille (Balkcom) Hancock; B.A., Radford U., 1969; postgrad. Brenau Coll., 1983—; m. A.J. Gordon III, Sept. 1986; 1 dau., Heather Lynn Johnson. Service rep. Ohio Bell Telephone Co., Cleve., 1969-72, S. Central Bell, Birmingham, Ala., 1972-77; service rep. So. Bell, Atlanta, 1977-79, mgr. Phone Ctr. Store, Atlanta, 1979-81; asst. mgr. Residence Service Ctr., Decatur, Ga., 1981-82, asst. mgr. residence staff, Atlanta, 1982-84, asst. staff mgr. hdqrs., Atlanta, 1984-86; asst. staff mgr. mktg. support BellSouth Services, 1986-88, staff mgr., 1988—. Active United Way. Republican. Presbyterian. Home: 3937 Cedar Circle Tucker GA 30084 Office: 675 W Peachtree St NE Atlanta GA 30375

GORDON, CAROLYN ELAINE, home economist; b. New Castle, Ind., July 24, 1946; d. Forest Eugene and Leora Kathleen (Hensly) Lawrence; m. Don Bill Gordon, June 10, 1967 (div. 1972); children: Charles William, Christa Lynn. BS, Purdue U., 1971; MBA, U. Indpls., 1981. Extension home economist Purdue U. Extension Service, Brownstown, Ind., 1972-83; extension home economist, county extension dir. Purdue U. Extension Service, Brownstown, 1983—; TV hostess Cablenews 2, Seymour, Ind., 1983-87. Bd. dirs. Leadership Jackson County, Seymour, Ind., 1986—; chmn. program com. Coalition on Literacy, Seymour, 1986—. Recipient award for disting. service Nat. Assn. Extension Home Econs. Mem. Ind. Extension Agts. Assn., Ind. Assn. Extension Home Economists, Nat. Assn. Extension Home Economists, Community Devel. Soc. Methodist. Lodge: Order of Eastern Star. Office: Purdue Extension Jackson County PO Box O Brownstone IN 47274

GORDON, CATHERINE YURCHENCO, information scientist; b. Cooperstown, N.Y., Apr. 19, 1950; d. John A. and Mary Catherine (Cumberland) Yurchenco; m. Thomas R. McLean, July 13, 1968 (div. 1976); 1 child, Stewart John; m. Joseph A. Gordon, Oct. 1976. Student, West Chester State U., 1968-69; BA, Immaculata Coll., 1972; MLS, Villanova U., 1975. Tchr. spec. edn. Chester County (Pa.) Intermediate Unit, 1973-75; law librarian Stradley, Ronan, Stevens and Young, Phila., 1975-77; client liason and mktg. rep. Mead Data Cen., Boston, 1977-83; asst. product mgr. Mead Data Cen., Dayton, 1983-84; sr. product analyst Dialog Info. Services, Palo Alto, Calif., 1984-86; product mgr. Dialog Info. Services, Palo Alto, 1986—. Presbyterian. Office: Dialog Info Systems 3460 Hillview Ave Palo Alto CA 94304

GORDON, CINDY RENÉE, retail executive; b. Fla., Dec. 31, 1955; d. Bobby Jack and Elissa Marlene (Scogin) Young; m. Charles Marvin Gordon, Mar. 12, 1983; children: Charles Marvin Jr., Andrew Young. BS in Zoology, U. Mich., 1978. Telecommunications analyst Malone & Hyde, Memphis, 1983-86, telecommunications mgr., 1986-87, dir. telecommunications, 1987—. Mem. Internat. Communication Assn., Telecommunication/Tenn., Alpha Gamma Delta.

GORDON, DARLENE ESTELLE, law officer; b. Fairbury, Ill., May 5, 1947; d. John R. and Una E. (Schmidt) G.; child, John C. Student, Faith Bapt. Bible Coll., Ankenny, Iowa, 1968-71, Joliet Jr. Coll., 1975-78. Sec. Honeggers & Co., Inc., Fairbury, Ill., 1965-66; clk, keypunch operator Caterpillar Tractor Co., Joliet, Ill., 1966-70; key punch operator Central Nat. Bank, Des Moines, 1971; sec. Will County Sheriff's Police, Joliet, 1971-74; dep. sheriff Will County Sheriff, Joliet, 1974—. Vol. Crisis Line, Joliet, Ill., 1984-86; den leader Cub Scouts Am., Lockport, Ill. council, 1984-86; leader Awana Bible club, Joliet, 1984-85. Mem. Ill. Crime Prevention Assn. (v.p. 1985-86), Internat. Assn. Crime Prevention Practitioners, Nat. Assn. Female Execs., Am. Fed. State, County and Mcpl. Employees, Fraternal Order of Police. Republican. Baptist. Home: 520 Parkview Ln #5 Lockport IL 60441

GORDON, ELISABETH CARLTON, personnel director; b. Evanston, Ill.; d. Richard Cleghorn Overton and Cornelia (Smythe) Nordstrom; m. John Scott Gordon, Jan. 29, 1966 (div. 1986); children: Adnrea, Bruce, Tim. BA, Oberlin Coll., 1966. Personnel staffing specialist U.S. Office of Personnel Mgmt., Washington, 1966-69, program analyst, 1969-72; chief staffing div. U.S. Office of Personnel Mgmt., Boston, 1972-87, area mgr., 1987—; cons. Denning Mobile Robotics, Woburn, Mass., 1985—. Mem. citizen's rev. com. United Way, Mass. Bay, 1980-86, allocations coordinating com. 1987—. Mem. Am. Soc. Profl. and Exec. Women, Fed. Employed Women (v.p. 1978, pres. 1979), Am. Soc. Pub. Adminstrs. Home: 12 Arbella Dr Beverly MA 01915

GORDON, GWENDOLYN ANNIE ELIZABETH, nursing manager; b. Ballymena, North Dreland, Aug. 6, 1944; d. William and Margaretta Jane (Martin) G. B in Adminstrn., Can. Sch. Mgmt., Toronto, 1987; student in Nursing, U. Lethbridge. Charge nurse Royal Victoria Hosp., Belfast, North Dreland, 1969-75; nurse Calgary (Alta.) Gen. Hosp., 1975, asst. head nurse, 1975-79, head nurse, 1979-80, unit nursing supr., 1980-82, coordinator, 1982—; cons. Peter Lougheed Hosp., Calgary, 1987. Vol. United Way Campaign, Calgary, 1986, Olympic Winter Games, 1987, Calgary Olympic Devel. Assn. Mem. Alta. Assn. Registered Nurses, South Cen. Operating Room Nurses Assn. (pres. 1987), Am. Operating Room Nurse, Hospice Calgary Soc. Presbyterian. Club: Beddington Community (Calgary). Home: 109 Berwick Dr NW, Calgary, AB Canada T3K 1C6

GORDON, JANE ELLEN, epidemiologist; b. N.Y.C., Aug. 12, 1946; d. William M. and Myrna Rebecca (Raymond) G.; 1 child, Jenifer Gordon Friedman. BS, CUNY, 1967; MS, Tulane U., 1970; PhD, U. N.C., 1979. Research technician NYU Med. Ctr., 1968-69; research assoc. Tulane U., New Orleans, 1971-73; research asst. Internat. Fertility Research Program, Chapel Hill, N.C., 1973-74; research asst. prof. Sch. Medicine, Yale U., New Haven, 1979-82; epidemiologist Nat. Inst. for Occupational Safety and Health, Cin., 1982-84; research dir. Greater Cin. Occupational Health Ctr., 1984-85; clin. assoc. prof. Oreg. Health Scis. U., Portland, 1987—; asst. state epidemiologist Oreg. State Health Div., Portland, 1986—; temporary advisor World Health Orgn., Geneva, Switzerland, 1982; dir. Oreg. State Injury Registry, Portland, 1986—; chmn. Oregon Clandestine Drug Lab. Com., 1987—. Contbr. articles to profl. jours. Served as lt. USPHS, 1982-84. Fellow U.S. Pub. Health Service, 1969-70. Mem. Am. Coll. Epidemiology, Soc. Occupational and Environ. Health, Am. Pub. Health Assn., Assn. Women in Sci., Soc. Epidemiologic Research, Sierra Club, Amnesty Internat. Club: City of Portland. Office: Oreg State Health Div 1400 SW 5th Ave Portland OR 97201

GORDON, JANINE M., advertising agency executive; b. N.Y.C., Oct. 2, 1946; d. Moses Fortune and Emma (Leo) Mager. B.A., U. Pa., 1968. Asst. buyer Bloomingdale's, N.Y.C., 1968-69; fashion credits editor Harper's Bazaar, N.Y.C., 1969-72; asso. dir. pub. relations Cotton, Inc., N.Y.C., 1972-73; press officer Harrods Ltd., London, 1973-74; project mgr. J.C. Penney Co., Inc., N.Y.C., 1974-75; dir. pub. relations Bozell, Jacobs, Kenyon & Eckhardt, Inc., N.Y.C., 1975-77; exec. v.p. corp. communications Saatchi & Saatchi Compton Inc., D.F.S., 1977—. Mem. Advt. Women N.Y., Public Relations Soc. Am., Pub. Club London. Club: Cosmopolitan. Home: 162 E 80th St New York NY 10021 Office: Saatchi & Saatchi DFS Compton Inc 375 Hudson St New York NY 10014

GORDON, JOAN I., lawyer; b. N.Y.C., Nov. 1, 1945; d. Morris and Dora (Mittman) G. A.B., Vassar Coll., 1967; M.A., Brown U., 1969; J.D., Am. U., 1974. Bar: Md. 1974, D.C. 1975, U.S. Dist. Ct. 1976, U.S. Supreme Ct. 1978, N.Y. 1981. Intern, N.Y. State Pub. Adminstrn., Albany, 1969-70; adminstrv. asst. to asst. commr. N.Y. State Health Dept., Albany, 1970-71; staff counsel Washington Suburban San. Commn., Hyattsville, Md., 1975-80; legal counsel and govt. affairs officer Montgomery Community Coll., Rockville, Md., 1980-84, gen. counsel, 1984—; research cons. Inst. Studies in Justice and Soc. Behavior, Am. U. Law Sch., Washington, 1974. Contbr.: Maryland Criminal Jury Instructions and Commentary, 1975. Mem. prospective students com. Vassar Coll., Washington, 1975-83; Democratic precinct vice-chmn. Montgomery County, 1976-82; mem. archtl. control com. Redland Crossing Homeowners Assn., Derwood, Md., 1982-84, bd. dirs., 1984—, pres. bd. dirs., 1986-87. v.p. 1987-88. Recipient Am. Jurisprudence award, 1972, 73. Mem. Nat. Assn. Women Lawyers (legis. com. 1976, council of dels. 1977-83), D.C. Bar Assn. Md. Bar Assn. Women's Bar Assn. Md., Montgomery County Bar Assn., Women's Bar Assn. Montgomery County, Nat. Assn. Coll. and Univ. Attys. (vice chmn. continuing legal edn. com. 1986, com. on nat. office 1985-87, bd. dirs. 1987—), Am. Corporate Counsel Assn. Jewish. Home: 15909 Yukon Ln Derwood MD 20855 Office: Montgomery Community Coll 900 Hungerford Dr Rockville MD 20850

GORDON, JOAN MAY, communication analyst, career exploration specialist; b. Lancaster, Ohio, Nov. 24, 1946; d. George Leo and Esther May (George) G.; m. James J. Thimmes, Aug. 22, 1970 (div. Nov. 1975). BS in Edn., Capital U., 1969; cert. in profl. edn., Ohio State U., 1975, MA in Communication, 1980, postgrad., 1983—. Cert. tchr., Ohio. Tchr. Upper Arlington Schs., Columbus, Ohio, 1968-80, career edn. program specialist, 1980-81, career edn. exploration analyst, 1982—; communications cons. Ohio Bar Assn., Mich. Bar Assn., Ohio and Mich. ednl. adminstrs., radio and TV broadcast studios, Ohio State U., Capital U., local bus. Co-host Upper Arlington Today TV Show, 1981-83; contbr. articles to profl. jours. Sec. adv. commn. Columbus Area Cable TV. Mem. Internat. Communications Assn., Internat. Assn. Bus. Communicators, Assn. Supervision and Curriculum Devel., Assn. Ednl. Communications and Technology, Am. Assn. Career Edn., Upper Arlington Edn. Assn. (v.p. 1974-75), Capital U. Alumnae Assn., World Future Soc., Pi Lambda Theta, Phi Delta Kappa. Republican. Home: 662 S Grant Ave Columbus OH 43206 Office: Upper Arlington City Sch Dist 1950 Mallway Columbus OH 43221

GORDON, JUDITH RUTH, courseware development company executive; b. Bklyn., July 24, 1939; d. William and Goldie Freda (Levy) G. B.S. cum laude, Pa. State U., 1961; M.S.W., Columbia U., 1963; J.D., Golden Gate U., 1971. Cert. community coll. tchr. Group worker Jewish Child Care Assn., N.Y.C., 1963-64; sr. child welfare worker San Francisco Dept. Social Services, 1965-67, child welfare supr., 1968-76; sales trainer Century 21 Office, San Jose, Calif., 1977-80; v.p. courseware devel. Pinnacle Courseware, Inc., San Jose, 1982—. Founder Bay Area Big Sisters, Inc., 1967; vol. Good Samaritan Hosp., San Jose, 1977-82; vol. English as a Second Lang. instr.; arbitrator Better Bus. Bur., San Jose, 1985—; vol. various profl. and little theater groups, Bay Area, 1966—; co-founder Placement Suprs. Assn., No. Calif., 1975. Mem. Nat. Soc. Performance and Instrn., Coordinators of Data Processing Edn. (assoc.), Nat. Assn. Realtors, Calif. Assn. Realtors, Alpha Nu, Psi Chi. Democrat. Jewish. Avocations: hiking; photography; writing poetry; racquetball; collecting science fiction books. Home: 1465 Luning Dr San Jose CA 95118 Office: Pinnacle Courseware Inc 841 Blossom Hill Rd Suite 215 San Jose CA 95123

GORDON, JULIA WEBER, artist; b. Athenia, N.J., Dec. 29, 1911; d. John and Pearl (Dobos) Weber; m. Philip Gordon, Nov. 24, 1954 (dec. Oct. 11, 1983). BA in Psychology, Douglass Coll., 1933; MA in Edn., Columbia U., 1940; EdD in Human Devel., U. Md., 1952; LHD (hon.), Rutgers U., 1966. Tchr. Warren County, N.J., 1933-40; demonstration tchr. Kellogg Found., Mt. Pleasant, Mich., 1937; supr. rural elem. schs. Warren County, 1940-48; asst. prof. edn. U. Md., College Park, 1948-51; creator, dir. Office of Child and Youth Study N.J. State Dept. of Edn., Trenton, 1957-68; founder, prof., dir. Ctr. for Human Devel. Fairleigh Dickinson U., Rutherford, N.J., 1968-71; artist Princeton, N.J., 1972—; cons. Office of Health, Edn. and Welfare, Washington, 1969, Operation Follow Through, Washington, 1967, div. elem. edn., 1962. Author: My Country School Diary, 1946, 1971; contbr. articles to profl. jours. Mem. Assn. for Childhood Edn. Internat., NEA, N.J. Edn. Assn., Assn. for Humanistic Psychology, Princeton Art Assn. (trustee 1987—), Assn. for Sch. Psychologists (3d Annual award 1970), Phi Beta Kappa. Home: 117 Crestview Dr Princeton NJ 08540

GORDON, JUNE, psychology educator, consultant; b. Oshkosh, Wis., June 17, 1929; d. Felix and Harriet (Fero) Staerkel; m. Donald Emmanuel Gordon, Feb. 6, 1951; children—Bonita, Judy, Teresa, Thomas, Alexander, Philip. B.S., Rollins Coll., 1971, M.Ed., 1974; Ed.S., U. Fla., 1976; Ed.D., Fla. State U., 1979; advanced study Jung Inst., Switzerland, 1982, U. Wis., 1984; imagery tng., London, 1985. Cert. sch. psychologist, Fla.; lic. mental health counselor. Free lance artist, Calif., Fla., Wis., Ala., 1958-74; coordinator women's program Seminole Community Coll., Sanford, Fla., 1974-84; adj. prof. psychology Rollins Coll. and Seminole Community Coll., Winter Park, Fla., 1974—; pvt. practice counseling mental health service Sanford, 1984—; bd. dirs. Project Wedge, Central Fla. Ednl. Consortium for Women, Orlando; cons. in field. Artist: painting Mother; Mother, The CIA is Coming (Wis. Blue Ribbon 1967), The Skaters (Merit award, Oviedo, Fla. 1985); author: (with others) Divorce, 1977; Legal Rights, 1979; contbr. articles to profl. jours. Founder Cen. Fla. Commn. on Status of Women, 1975; pres. Seminole County Mental Health Ctr., Inc., Fla., 1980-81; bd. dirs. Met. Alcohol Council, Orlando, 1981-83, Citrus council Girl Scouts U.S., 1984—; committeewoman Democratic Exec. Com. of Seminole County, 1981-84; gov.'s appointee East Cen. Fla. Regional Planning Council, 1983-86. Recipient Fannie Lou Hamers Human Rights award NOW, 1980. Mem. AAUW (pres. 1983-85, bd. dirs. Fla. state div. 1986-88), Nat. Wellness Assn., Jung Soc. North Fla., Fla. Assn. Community Colls., Future Soc. Avocations: all artistic and creative activities, designing, traveling, gardening. Home: 309 Idyllwilde Dr Sanford FL 32771

GORDON, LENORE DORIS, microbiology educator; b. Shenandoah, Pa., Nov. 23, 1931; d. Daniel and Betty (Mainker) G.; B.S. cum laude, Fairleigh Dickinson U., 1955; M.A. in Edn., Health Care, Central Mich. U., 1977. Microbiologist, Babies Hosp., Columbia U., N.Y.C., 1955-59, Belinson Hosp., Petah Tikva, Israel, 1960-72; head microbiology sect. Barnert Meml. Hosp., Paterson, N.J., 1972-75; instr. infection control U. Medicine and Dentistry N.J., Newark, 1977—; participant profl. confs. Mem. Am. Soc. Microbiology, Assn. Practitioners in Infection Comtrol, Am. Soc. Med. Tech., Central Mich. U. Alumni Assn. Home: 215 Passaic Ave Apt 5-J Passaic NJ 07055

GORDON, MARY CATHERINE, author; b. L.I., N.Y., Dec. 8, 1949; d. David and Anna (Gagliano) G.; m. James Brain, 1974; m. Arthur Cash, 1979; children—Anna Gordon, David Dess Gordon. BA, Barnard Coll., 1971; MA, Syracuse U., 1973. Tchr. English Dutchess Community Coll., Poughkeepsie, N.Y., 1974-78, Amherst (Mass.) Coll. Novels include Final Payments, 1978, The Company of Women, 1981, Men and Angels, 1985; (short stories) Temporary Shelter, 1987. Recipient Kafka prize for Fiction, 1979, 82. Roman Catholic. Address: care Random House Inc Publicity Dept 201 E 50th St New York NY 10022 •

GORDON, MARYLU TRACEWELL, lawyer, political scientist; b. Kansas City, Mo., Oct. 28, 1935; d. Arthur Nelson and Helen Louise (Boone) Tracewell; m. James Dell Gordon, Sept. 11, 1963; children—Kevin Dell, Kent Tracewell, Tracy Helen, Kelly Claire. Student Lindenwood Coll., St. Charles, Mo., 1953-54, Washington U., St. Louis, 1963; B.A., Okla. U., 1965, M.A., 1966, postgrad., 1967-69; J.D., Oklahoma City U., 1975. Bar: Okla. 1975, U.S. Dist. Ct. (we. dist.) Okla. 1975, U.S. Ct. Appeals (10th cir.) 1976, U.S. Tax Ct. 1976. Instr. polit. sci. No. Okla. Coll., Tonkowa, 1966-67; tchr. history Moore (Okla.) High Sch., 1967-68; asst. prof. polit. sci. Oklahoma City U., 1969-75; asst. city atty., Oklahoma City, 1977-82; ptnr. Gordon & Gordon, Oklahoma City, 1982—; law clk. U.S. Dist. Ct. (we. dist.) Okla.; guest lectr. U. S.C., 1975, Cen. State U., Edmond, Okla., 1975, Taft Inst., Oklahoma City, 1972-76. Contbr. to Justice in America, 1973. Bd. dirs. New World Sch., 1972; pres. bd. dirs. Youth Services of Oklahoma County, 1984; mem. ACLU, NOW; resource person, lectr. Okla. Humanities Council, 1973-79. OEO grantee, 1971. Mem. ABA, Oklahoma County Bar Assn., Okla. Bar Assn., Pi Sigma Alpha. Club: Gourmet of Oklahoma City (chef). Home: 2825 NW Grand Blvd Oklahoma City OK 73116

GORDON, PAMELA ANN, pharmaceutical company executive, cytotechnologist; b. Bklyn., Feb. 17, 1953; d. Norman Anthony and Louise

Regina (Cooper) G.; student Barry Coll., 1971-74; Cytotechnologist, U. Miami, 1975; B.B.A., Fla. Atlantic U., 1980. Staff cytotechnologist, instr. U. Miami (Fla.) Med. Sch., 1975-77; chief cytotechnologist Diagnostic Lab., North Palm Beach, Fla., 1977-78; sales rep. Glaxo Inc., N.C., 1981-85, dist. mgr., Kansas City, Mo., 1985—; didactic and microscopic instr. U. Miami Sch. Cytotechnology, 1975-77. Mem. Am. Soc. Cytology, Am. Soc. Clin. Pathologists, Fla. Soc. Cytology, So. Assn. Cytotechnologists, Nat. Assn. Female Execs. Delta Sigma Pi. Home: 9933 Edelweiss Circle Shawnee Mission KS 66203

GORDON, RITA SIMON, civic leader, former nurse, educator; b. Frederick, Md., Feb. 1, 1929; d. Jacob and Anna (Stein) Simon; m. Paul Perry Gordon, July 2, 1948; children—Stuart Yael, Hugh Ellis, Myla. R.N., Frederick Meml. Hosp., 1949. R.N., Md. Surg. staff nurse Prince Georges Gen. Hosp., 1949-50; pediatric staff nurse (part-time) Frederick Meml. Hosp., 1950-54; surg. office nurse, 1960-62; nurse blood program ARC 1954-83. Author: (with Paul P. Gordon) Textbook History of Frederick County. 1975. Mem. Frederick County Bd. Edn., 1975-85, pres., 1979-80, 83-84; mem. exec. com. Md. Assn. Bd. Edn., Annapolis, 1978-85, pres., 1983-84; bd. assocs. Hood Coll., Frederick, 1985—; mem. Md. Task Force on Ednl. Funding, Annapolis, 1983-84, Md. Values Edn. Com., Annapolis, 1979-83, Fed. Relations Network, Nat. Sch. Bd. Assn., 1978-82; bd. dirs. Community Commons, Frederick, 1983-85; area field rep. Am. Field Service, Frederick, 1970-75; assoc., mem. adv. com. Vocat. Tech. Edn., publicity com. 1973 Snow Ball, Frederick Meml. Hosp. Aux.; past bd. dirs., v.p. Beth Sholom, 1982-83, historian, past pres. Beth Sholom Sisterhood; past bd. dirs. Nat. Council Jewish Women, Frederick; vol. aide Frederick Waverly Elem. Sch.; officer, chmn. fund raising North Market St. Sch.; active Girl Scouts U.S.A.; past pres., v.p. Frederick Improvement Found. Editor, Town Crier. Named Woman of Yr., Bus. and Profl. Woman's Club, 1975; Frederick's Outstanding Woman, Internat. Woman's Yr., 1975. Mem. Frederick Sect. Nat. Council Jewish Women (pres. 1986-88), C. of C. (Planned Growth-2000 com.), Md. Hist. Soc., Internat. Graphoanalysis Soc., Md. Jewish Hist. Soc., Frederick County Hist. Soc. Clubs: Woman's Civic (Frederick); Rotary Inner Wheel (Gaithersburg, Md.) (v.p. 1975). Avocation: hist. research. Home: 202 Meadowdale Ln Frederick MD 21701

GORDON, THELMA STONE, audio-visual specialist, librarian; b. Boston; children: Emily, Richard, Daryl. BA, U. Bridgeport, 1969; MLS, So. Conn. State U., 1972; postgrad., Sacred Heart U., 1984. Freelance artist Newton, Mass. and Tampa, Fla., 1955-65; exec. sec., bd mem. Associated Women Investors, Tampa, 1959-62; substitute art tchr., libararian Westport (Conn.) Bd. Edn., 1962-65; library asst. U. Bridgeport, Conn., 1964-65; art and music librarian Westport (Conn.) Pub. Library, 1967-82, head audio-visual services, 1982—; chmn. picture div. Spl. Libraries Assn., 1977-78, bd. dirs., 1980; chmn. adult services sect. Conn. Library Assn., 1974; state rep. Art Libraries Assn. of N.Am., 1975. Contbg. author: Handbook of Picture Librarianship, 1981; contbr. chpts. to books, articles to mags., profl. newsletters. Bd. dirs. Friends of Music, Fairfield County, 1985—; mem. Westport-Weston Arts Council, 1982—, Fairfield County, Mus. Modern Art, N.Y.C., 1984—. Mem. ALA, Home Cinema Soc., Edn. Film Library Assn., Spl. Libraries Assn. (chmn. picture div. 1977-78), Conn. Library Assn. (chmn. adult services sect. 1974), Art Libraries Assn. (panelist at nat. conf. 1977), N.Y.C. Mus. Modern Art. Home: 32 Lincoln St Westport CT 06880 Office: Westport Pub Library Arnold Bernhard Plaza Westport CT 06880

GORDON, VERONA CHRISTOFFERSON, nursing educator; b. Waubun, Minn., Oct. 3, 1923; d. Gunder and Clara (Sorenson) Christofferson; m. A.H. Gordon, May 17, 1947 (dec. 1982); children—Candace, Elizabeth, Christine, Susan, Robert. B.S. in Nursing Edn., U. Minn., Mpls., 1955, M.S. in Psychiatric Nursing, 1970, Ph.D. in Higher Edn., 1976. Psychiat. charge nurse VA Hosp., Mpls., 1966-67; instr. pediatrics Swedish Hosp. Sch. Nursing, Mpls., 1967-71; assoc. prof. psychiat. nursing Gustavus Adolphus Coll., St. Peter, Minn., 1971-78; prof. psychiat. nursing U. Minn., Mpls., 1978—. Author research studies and health care manuals. Trustee Met. Med. Ctr., Mpls., 1977—. Recipient edn. scholarship Finnish Ministry Edn., Helsinki, 1983, Edgar M. Clarkson award Gustavus Adolphus Coll., 1976, named Woman of Achievement, Minn. LWV, 1979. Mem. Royal Coll. Nursing Research London, Am. Nurses Assn., Minn. Nurses Assn. (mem. polit. bd. 1980-85, commn. on edn. 1981-83, named Nurse of Yr. 1985), Sigma Theta Tau, Sigma Xi, Phi Lambda Theta, Phi Delta Kappa. Democrat. Lutheran. Office: Univ Minn Sch Nursing 6-101 Health Scis Unit F 308 Harvard St SE Minneapolis MN 55455

GORE, CATHERINE ANN, social worker; b. Mullens, W.Va., Feb. 2, 1937; d. Bernard Joseph and Agnes Cecilia (Spradling) G.; BA, Thomas More Coll., 1968; MSW, Ohio State U., 1971, MA in Pub. Adminstrn., 1983; PhD in Social Work, 1986. Caseworker, Cath. Charities, Cin., 1967-69, 71-72; psychiat. social worker Mcpl. Ct. Psychiat. Clinic, Cin., 1973; instr. psychiat. social work, social work supr., Ct. Psychiat. Ctr., U. Cin., 1974-77, asst. prof. psychiat. social work, coordinator consultation services, 1978-80, grad. research and teaching assoc. Ohio State U., Columbus, 1981-85; cons. Hamilton County Welfare Dept.; instr. No. Ky. U. Mem. Nat. Assn. Social Workers, Acad. Cert. Social Workers. Democrat. Roman Catholic. Home: 1545 Northview Ave Cincinnati OH 45223

GORELICK, JUDY LYNNE, software sales executive; b. N.Y.C., Jan. 26, 1957; d. Herbert A. and Betty (Sharfstein) G.; m. Bruce Kaminstein, Apr. 8, 1957; 1 child, Lea. BBA, U. Mich., 1978; MBA in Mktg., NYU, 1982. Sales rep. NCR Corp., N.Y.C., 1978-81; nat. mktg. mgr. D & B Computing Services, N.Y.C., 1982-87; sales mgr. Oracle Corp., N.Y.C., 1988—. Vol. Foster Parents Plan, N.Y.C., 1987. Mem. NYU Grad. Sch. Bus. Alumni Assn. Home: 165 Duane St New York City NY 10013

GORELICK, MOLLY CHERNOW, psychologist, educator; b. N.Y.C., Sept. 17, 1920; d. Morris and Jean (Zabraun) Chernow; m. Leon Gorelick, Apr. 12, 1941; children: Walter, Peter. AB, UCLA, 1948, MA, 1955, EdD, 1962. Tchr., counselor Los Angeles City Bd. Edn., 1948-61; instr. Exceptional Children's Found., Los Angeles, 1963-70, chief guidance services, 1963-70; prof. Calif. State U., Northridge, 1970—; research project dir. Vocat. Rehab. Adminstrn. HEW, Los Angeles, 1964-66, project dir., 1971-75; owner, dir. Hi-Ho Day Camp, 1950-57; cons. Riverside County Schs., 1962-70, Kennedy Child Study Ctr., 1975-79; researcher Preschool Integration of Children with Handicaps, 1971-75. Co-author: Rescue series, 5 vols., 1967-68; contbr. articles to profl. jours. Mem. adv. bd. UCLA Sch. Social Welfare, Calif. State Regional Diagnostic Ctr. Children's Hosp., Mirman Sch. Gifted Children, Calif. Ednl. Ctr., Friendship Day Camp. Mem. Am. Western Psychol. Assn., NEA, Council Exceptional Children, Am. Assn. Mental Deficiency, Phi Beta Kappa, Pi Lambda Theta, Pi Gamma Mu. Home: 600 N June St Los Angeles CA 90004 Office: Calif State U Northridge CA 91324

GOREN, JUDITH ANN, psychologist; b. Detroit, Apr. 5, 1933; d. Herman and Evelyn (Apple) Wise; m. Robert Goren, Dec. 20, 1953; children: Gary, Steven, Nancy. BA, Wayne State U., 1954, MEd, 1972; PhD, Union Grad. Sch., 1983. Lic. psychologist, Mich. Tchr. secondary edn. Detroit Pub. Schs., 1954-56; tchr. elem. edn. USAF schs., Etain AFB, France, 1956-57; instr. adult edn. U. Detroit, 1973-77; psychotherapist Samalona Clinic, Birmingham, Mich., 1975-85; clin. psychologist Southfield, Mich., 1985—. Author: Coming Alive, 1975; contbr. poetry to jours., anthologies. Mem. Am. Psychol. Assn., Mich. Psychol. Assn.

GORENA, MINERVA, educator; b. Edinburg, Tex., Mar. 30, 1943; d. Humberto and Eva (Benavides) Gorena; BA, Pan Am. Coll., 1963; MEd, U. Tex., Austin, 1975. Tchr., Hidalgo County Common Sch. Dist., Runn, Tex., 1963-64, Mission (Tex.) Ind. Sch. Dist., 1964-67, Pharr-San Juan-Alamo Ind. Sch. Dist., Pharr, Tex., 1967-69; counselor Out-of-Sch. Neighborhood Youth Corps, assoc. City County Econ. Devel. Corp., Edinburg, Tex., 1969-70; materials specialist Title VII Bilingual Edn. Program, Region XIII Edn. Service Ctr., Austin, Tex., 1970-74; cons. div. bilingual edn. Tex. Edn. Agy., Austin, 1974-77; mgr. user services Nat. Clearinghouse for Bilingual Edn./Inter-Am. Research Assocs., Inc., Rosslyn, Va., 1978-81, assoc. dir., 1981-86, exec. assoc. 1978-86; research assoc., coordinator ednl. personnel tng. program George Washington Univ., Washington, 1987—. NDEA fellow, 1967. Mem. Austin Area Assn. for Bilingual Edn. (sec. 1975-76), Nat. Assn. for Bilingual Edn. (del. 1979), Tex. State Tchrs. Assn. (Region XIII chpt. pres. 1973-74), Nat. Assn. Female Execs., Va. Assn. Bilingual Edn., Va. Assn. Hispanic Am. Dems., Nat. Assn. Latino Elected Ofcls., Nat. Council Hispanic Women (newsletter editor 1986-87),George Washington U. Higher Edn. Assn. (pres. 1988—), YMCA, Phi Delta Kappa. Roman Catholic. Editor: Information and Materials to Teach the Cultural Heritage of the Mexican American, 1972, Resources in Bilingual Education: A Preliminary Guide to Government Agency Programs of Interest to Minority Language Groups, 1979; Sources of Materials for Minority Languages: A Preliminary List, 1979. Home: 2805 S Columbus St Arlington VA 22206 Office: George Washington U Funger Hall #214 2201 G St NW Washington DC 20052

GORG, JANET TAIT, media buyer, account coordinator; b. St. Louis, Jan. 9, 1956; d. Wesley Ernest Bernard and Jane Cora (Tait) G. B.A., Bloomsburg State U., 1978; student Marshall U., 1978-79. Draftsman, Henkels & McCoy, Blue Bell, Pa., 1978-79; grad. asst. Marshall U., 1978-79; dir. mktg. Community Fed. Savs. & Loan, Blue Bell, Pa., 1979-81; media buyer Dalaba, Leonard & Pease, Inc., Bala Cynwyd, Pa., 1982-84, media buyer/account coordinator, 1984-86; media buyer, account coordinator Leonard, Blavat & Connery, Inc., 1986—. Episcopalian. Home: 224 Forrest Ave Ambler PA 19002 Office: Leonard Blavat & Connery Inc 610 W Germantown Pike Suite 421 Plymouth Meeting PA 19462

GORHAM, LINDA JOANNE, financal planning company executive; b. Boston, June 25, 1951; d. Joseph Leo and Rose (Avila) G. AS, Northeastern U., 1975, BS, 1976; MBA, Babson Coll., 1978. Various positions Stop & Shop Co. Inc., Boston, 1974-83; sr. analyst Capital Fin. Planning, Needham, Mass., 1983-85; fin. cons. United Resources, Needham, 1985-86; mng. dir. Mingolelli Fin. Services, Framingham, Mass., 1986—; v.p. Mingolelli & Assocs., Framingham, 1986-88; with Lyons Planning Group, Waltham, Mass., 1988—; adj. faculty Northeastern U., 1988—. Mem. Inst. Cert. Fin. Planners, Am. Soc. Profl. and Exec. Women, Nat. Assn. Female Execs., Babson Coll. Women Alumni in Bus., Babson Women Investors Club, Babson Mentor Program (chairwoman 1986—), Babson Women in Bus., Sigma Epsilon Rho. Office: Lyons Planning Group Ltd 51 Sawyer Rd Waltham MA 02154

GORLIN, CATHY ELLEN, lawyer; b. Shields Twp., Ill., July 25, 1953; d. Robert James and Marilyn (Alpern) G.; m. Marshall Howard Tanick, Feb. 20, 1982; 1 child, Lauren Gorlin. B.A. magna cum laude, Wesleyan U., 1975; J.D., U. Minn., 1978. Bar: Minn. 1978. Law clk. Minn. Atty. Gen.'s Office, St. Paul, summer 1976, Mpls. and Bloomington City Atty.'s Office, 1977-78; assoc. Mullin, Weinberg & Daly, Mpls., 1978; law clk. to judges Hennepin County Family Ct., Mpls., 1979-80, temp. referee, summer 1980; assoc. Larkin, Hoffman, Daly & Lindgren, Ltd., Mpls., 1980-84; ptnr. Best & Flanagan, 1984—; chairperson family law dept.; sec. Hennepin Lawyer Mag., 1983-85; chmn. Minn. Women Lawyers Appointments Com., Mpls., 1983—; mem. Supreme Ct. Task Force on Gender Fairness in the Cts., 1987; Supreme Ct. Legal Cert. Bd., 1986—. Contbr. articles to legal publs.; guest appearances radio. Advance person Vice-Pres. Mondale, 1979, vol. various polit. candidates; del. 3d dist. conv., Minn., 1980-84. Named Atty. of Month, Larkin, Hoffman, Daly & Lindgren, Ltd., 1983. Mem. ABA, Minn. Bar Assn. (chmn. 1985-86), Hennepin County Bar Assn. (rep. to child support task force 1982, chmn. exec. com. family law sect., chmn. sect. 1982-84), Minn. Trial Lawyers Assn., Jewish Bus. and Profl. Women's Group (dir., support group coordinator), Minn. Women's Network (dir.), Jewish Family and Children Service Counseling Com., West Suburban C. of C. Democrat. Jewish. Home: 1230 Angelo Dr Golden Valley MN 55422 Office: Best & Flanagan 3500 IDS Tower Minneapolis MN 55402

GORMAN, ELIZABETH E., comptroller, educator; b. Jacksonville, Tex., Sept. 9, 1926; d. Robert Fielden an Leona (McLain) McBride; m. Walter Gorman, April, 15, 1946 (dec. Dec. 1978); children: Mary E. Gorman Hawkins, Judith D. AA, St. Louis Community Coll., 1978. Asst. to dept. mgr. Gen. Am. Life, St. Louis, 1964-76; lab. instr. St. Louis Community Coll., 1976-78, tchr. continuing edn., 1980—; bookkeeper Hal's Interiors, St. Louis, 1978, Form's Mfg. Inc., St. Louis, 1978-81; comptroller Printing Industries St. Louis Inc., 1981—; asst. treas., v.p. Galic Credit Union, St. Louis, 1968-76. Fin. sec. Bethesda Luth. Ch., Pine Lawn, Mo., 1979-82, chmn. social ministry com., 1984—. Home: 5816 Tholozan Saint Louis MO 63109 Office: Printing Industries St Louis Inc 321 N Spring Saint Louis MO 63108

GORMAN, LILLIAN R., banker, industrial psychologist; b. N.Y.C., July 4, 1953; d. Helmuth H. and Ida A. (Malitsch) Degen; BA in Psychology, Lehman Coll., CUNY, 1975; MA in Indsl. Psychology, Case Western Res. U., 1978, PhD in Indsl. Psychology, 1979; MBA in Corp. Fin., U. So. Calif., 1986; m. Mark R. Gorman, Oct. 23, 1976. Econ. benefits asst. Girl Scouts U.S.A., N.Y.C., 1971-75; psychologist personnel research services, Personnel Research & Devel. Corp., Cleve., 1975-79, staff cons., 1977-78; mgr. personnel research First Interstate Bank, Los Angeles, 1979-82, v.p., mgr. human resource planning and devel., 1982-85; v.p., mgr. human resource planning and exec. devel. First Interstate Bancorp, Los Angeles, 1985-86; sr. v.p., human resources dir. First Interstate Bank, Los Angeles, 1986—, also bd. dirs.; cons. psychology; bd. dirs. Human Interaction Research Inst., First Interstate Systems, Inc. Chmn. bd. dirs. INROADS/Los Angeles, 1986—; bd. dirs. Los Angeles Entrepreneurship Acad. Mem. Am. Psychol. Assn., Am. Soc. Personnel Adminstrs., Personnel Testing Council So. Calif., Human Resource Planning Soc., Phi Beta Kappa. Lutheran. Home: 1332 Allenford Ave Los Angeles CA 90049

GORMAN, LINDA KORN, psychologist; b. Phila., June 1, 1953; d. Samuel and Muriel (Grass) Korn; B.A., Dickinson Coll., 1975; M.A., Temple U., 1978, Ph.D., 1980. Cert. sch. psychologist, N.J., Pa.; lic. psychologist, Pa. Clinic asst. Psychol. Services Ctr., Temple U., 1976-77, clinic supr., teaching asst., 1978-80; clin. psychology intern Norristown State Hosp., Pa., 1977-78; psychologist Program of Aux. Services for Students, non-pub. schs., Bala Cynwyd, Pa., 1980-83; psychologist St. Gabriel's Hall, Phoenixville, Pa., 1981, Phoenixville Psychol. Assocs., 1982-83, Hampton Psychol. Ctr., Huntingdon Valley, Pa., 1983; asst. dir. dept. psychology, dir. psychology internship program Eastern State Sch. and Hosp., Trevose, Pa., 1983—; pvt. clin. practice, Plymouth Valley, Pa., 1985—. Mem. Am. Psychol. Assn., Eastern Psychol. Assn., Pa. Psychol. Assn., Phila. Soc. Clin. Psychologists, Assn. Advancement Psychology, AAUW (lectr. 1982), Mensa, Dickinson Coll. Alumnae, Temple U. Alumnae, Phi Beta Kappa Alumnae, Pi Beta Phi Alumnae, Psi Chi, Alpha Psi Omega. Home: 777 West Germantown Pike #619 Plymouth Meeting PA 19462 Office: 3740 Lincoln Hwy Trevose PA 19047

GORMAN, MARCIE SOTHERN, franchise executive; b. N.Y.C., Feb. 25, 1949; d. Jerry R. and Carole Edith (Frendel) Sothern; m. N. Scott Gorman, June 14, 1969 (div.); children—Michael Stephen, Mark Jason. A.A., U. Fla., 1968; B.S., Memphis State U., 1970. Tchr., Memphis City Sch. System, 1970-73; tng. dir. Weight Watchers of Palm Beach County and Weight Watchers So. Ala., Inc., West Palm Beach, Fla., 1973—, area dir., then pres., 1977—; pres. Markel Ads, Inc. Cubmaster Troop 130. Hon. lt. col. a.d.c. Ala. Militia. Mem. Women' Am. ORT (program chmn. 1975), Optometric Soc. (sec. 1973), Weight Watchers Franchise Assn. (chair mktg. com., mem. advt./mktg. council, chairperson region IV bd. dirs.), Nat. Orgn. Women, Exec. Women of the Palm Beaches, Am. Bus. Women's Assn., Nat. Assn. Female Execs. Lodge: Zonta. Home: 429 N Country Club Dr Atlantis FL 33462 Office: 7597 Lake Worth Rd Lake Worth FL 33467

GORMAN, PATRICIA JANE, editor; b. Oak Ridge, Feb. 28, 1950; d. Joseph Francis and Ruth (Kommedahl) G.; m. Adrian Thomas Higgins, Apr. 22, 1978; 1 child, Mary Catherine. BJ, U. Mo., 1972. Feature writer, copyeditor Northamptonshire Evening Telegraph, Eng., 1972-76; asst. editor Am. Tchr. Am. Fedn. Tchrs., AFL-CIO, Washington, 1976-78, 79-82, mng. editor Am. Educator, 1978-83, dir. editorial dept., from 1982, now editor Am. Tchr.; mem. delegation of labor editors to Israel, AFL-CIO, Washington, 1983. Author TV study guides for tchrs., 1979-83. Mem. Internat. Labor Communications Assn. Democrat. Roman Catholic. Office: Am Fedn Tchrs 555 New Jersey Ave NW Washington DC 20001

GORMAN, WILMA AURORA, commercial development chemist; b. Chgo., Dec. 27, 1955; d. Jose and Guillermina (Pagan) Figueroa; m. Ralph Raulli, Sept., 1978 (div. Sept. 1980); m. Mark Bestic Gorman, Aug. 10, 1985. BS in Chemistry, Northeastern Ill. U., 1977. Synthesis chemist Stepan Co., Northfield, Ill., 1977-79, detergent chemist, 1979-85, comml. devel. chemist, 1985—. Contbr. articles to profl. jours. Mem. Am. Chem. Soc., Chem. Specialities Mfrs. Assn. Democrat. Roman Catholic. Home: 4953 N Kenneth Chicago IL 60630 Office: Stepan Co 200 Frontage Rd Northfield IL 60093

GORTON, LAURIE ANN, editor; b. Buffalo, Nov. 26, 1949; d. James Wallace and Doris Ida (Torke) G.; B.A. in Journalism cum laude, U. Wis., Madison, 1971. Asso. editor Cooking for Profit, Madison, 1971-74; editor, pub. dir. Baking Industry, Putman Pub. Co., Chgo., 1974-83; editor Bakers Digests 1983—, Baking & Snack Systems (formerly Baking Equipment), 1983—, Baking Buyer, 1984—; assoc. editor Milling and Baking News, Sosland Pub. Co., 1983—. Mem. Inst. Food Technologists, Am. Assn. Cereal Chemists, Am. Soc. Bakery Engrs., Phi Beta Kappa, Sigma Delta Chi. Christian Scientist. Office: Sosland Pub Co 9000 W 67th St Merrian KS 66202

GOSE, GRACE SMITH, wholesale lumber company executive; b. Burke's Garden, Va., Oct. 14, 1909; d. Tilden Hendricks and Margaret (Wynn) Short; m. Lionel Charles Smith, Oct. 30, 1927 (dec. Sept. 1956); children—Lionet Elizabeth and Hilah Mae (twins); m. John Paul Gose, Mar. 28, 1959. B.S. in Biology, Concord Coll., Athens, W.Va., 1954, B.S. in Vocat. Home Econs., 1956; lifetime cert. W.Va. U., 1976. Cert. tchr., W.Va. Elem. tchr., pub. schs., Sommers County, W.Va., 1954-61; supt. women's prison, Penoe Spring, W.Va., 1961-65; high sch. tchr., pub. schs., Raleigh County, W.Va., 1965-68, 70-79; owner, operator L. C. Smith Mine Timbers, Jumping Branch, W.Va., 1979—; active in real estate, Jumping Branch, 1945—. Mem. Internat. Assn. Chiefs of Police (life), Nat. Ret. Tchrs. Assn. Democrat. Methodist. Lodge: Order Eastern Star. Avocations: selling real estate; travel in U.S. and Canada. Home and Office: PO Box 81 Jumping Branch WV 25969

GOSS, DONNA RICHARDSON, English language educator; b. Florence, Ala., July 6, 1953; d. Bradley and Lillian Evelyn (Wilson) Richardson; m. Terry Lee Goss, May 25, 1974; children: Amy Suzanne, William Marshall. BS with honors, U. North Ala., 1975; student, North West Jr. Coll., 1986. Educator lang. arts Colbert County Bd. Edn., Tuscumbia, Ala., 1975—; chmn. philosophy and goals, lang. arts, major ednl. priorities coms. Leighton (Ala.)Middle Sch. Curriculum, 1982—. Missions tchr. Calvary Bapt. Ch., Tuscumbia, 1985. Mem. Am. Edn. Assn., NEA, Colbert County Educators Assn., Nat. English Tchrs. Democrat. Baptist. Lodge: Order Eastern Star (sentinel Killen chpt. 1971-72, officer 1972—). Home: 609 Pickwick St Sheffield AL 35660 Office: Colbert County Bd Edn Box 309 Leighton AL 35646

GOSS, DOROTHY ANN, home economics educator; b. Fulton County, Ind., Sept. 21, 1937; d. Herschel Edward and Helen Irene (Messinger) G. BS, Purdue U., 1959; MS, U. Ill., 1965; PhD, Cornell U., 1984. Cert. home economist. Tch. home econs. Lapaz (Ind.) Sch., 1959-61, Clay High Sch., South Bend, Ind., 1961-64; extension specialist U. Ill., Urbana, 1965-75, U. Minn., St. Paul, 1979-85, Okla. State U., Stillwater, 1985—. Mem. Am. Home Econs. Assn. (sect. vice chair 1987—), Okla. Home Econs. Assn. (sect. sec. 1986—), Nat. Council Family Relations, Assn. Fin. Counseling and Planning Edn., LWV (bd. dirs. Stillwater chpt. 1986—), AAUW, Nat. Audubon Soc., Omicron Nu, Epsilon Sigma Phi (Disting. Service award 1985). Office: Okla State U Home Econs Coop Extension 338 Home Economics W Stillwater OK 74078

GOSS, GEORGIA BULMAN, translator; b. N.Y.C., Dec. 1, 1939; d. James Cornelius and Marian Bright (McLaughlin) Bulman; m. Douglas Keith Goss, Dec. 21, 1957; children—Kristin Anne, David. B.A., U. Mich., 1961. Librarian, High Altitude Obs., Boulder, Colo., 1963-64, U.S. Bur. Standards, Boulder, 1964-65; cons. editor Spanish lang. pilots' tng. manual, 1981-82; freelance translator, Englewood, Colo., 1982—. Mem. Internat. Trade Assn. Colo., Phi Sigma Iota. Republican. Episcopalian. Home and Office: 5091 S Boston St Englewood CO 80111

GOSS, PATRICIA BELLAMY, missiles and space company official; b. Montreal, Que., Can., May 21, 1944; d. Clifford J. and May Glenn (Black) Bellamy; naturalized, 1966; A.B., UCLA, 1966, M.A., 1967; Ph.D., N.Y. U., 1978; children—Jennifer Suzanne, Geoffrey Bellamy. Lectr., dir. forensics UCLA, 1967-73; asst. prof. Lehman Coll., City U. N.Y., 1973-79; mgmt. cons. Lockheed Missiles and Space Co., Sunnyvale, Calif., 1980—. Named Debate Coach of Yr., Georgetown U., 1971; recipient H.A. Wichelns award for outstanding article in Free Speech Yearbook, Speech Communication Assn., 1975. Mem. Speech Communication Assn. Democrat. Office: Lockheed Missiles and Space Co 1111 Lockheed Way 057/90 B 580 Sunnyvale CA 94086

GOSS, RITA JEAN, psychologist; b. Wichita, Kans., Feb. 16, 1952; d. Miles Smith and Esther Lorene (Brooks) G.; m. Allan Dale Schrag, Dec. 29, 1973; 1 child, Leah. BA in Psychology summa cum laude, Kans. State U., 1974; postgrad., Pittsburg State U., 1974-75; MA in Clin. Psychology, U. Kans., 1978, PhD in Clin. Psychology, 1982. Lic. psychologist. Psychology trainee I Wichita VA Med. Ctr., 1977-78, psychology trainee II, 1978-79; psychology intern Wichita Guidance Ctr., 1979-80, staff psychologist, 1980-85; pvt. practice psychology Linden and Mahoney, Wichita, 1985—. Alumni Grad. Merit scholar Pittsburg State U. Alumni Assn., 1974. Mem. Wichita Psychol. Assn. (pres. 1984-85), Am. Psychol. Assn., Kans. Psychol. Assn. (com. mem.), Kans. Assn. Profl. Psychologists (treas. 1987-88), Phi Beta Kappa, Phi Kappa Phi, Psi Chi. Democrat. Office: Linden and Mahoney 1650 Georgetown Suite 160 Wichita KS 67218

GOSSETT, DEBBIE COLLEEN, manufacuturing professional; b. Wichita Falls, Tex., July 29, 1958; d. Kenneth Harold Sluder and Patricia Ann (Sintek) Measley; m. Sherman Allen Gossett, Aug. 12, 1981 (div. Sept. 1985). Dept. head Sprague Electric Co., Wichita Falls, 1976-85; mgr. mfg. Beacon Lighthouse for the Blind, Wichita Falls, 1985—. Mem. Nat. Assn. for Female Execs. Office: Beacon Lighthouse For Blind 300 7th St Wichita Falls TX 76301

GOSSMAN, THERESA DIANE, social services administrator; b. Decorah, Iowa, Sept. 20, 1942; d. Arland E. and Kathleen M. (Knox) G. BA, Briar Cliff Coll., Sioux City, Iowa, 1967; MA, DePaul U., Chgo., 1979. Cert. counselor. Tchr. St. John Brebeuf Sch., Niles, Ill., 1967-74; sch. counselor, social worker St. John Berchman's Sch., Chgo., 1974-80; adminstr. Mercy Boys Home, Chgo., 1980—; cons. various child care homes, 1984—; co-founder Logan Sq. N., Chgo. Mem. Nat. Assn. Homes for Children (bd. dirs. 1987—), Am. Assn. Counseling and Devel., Child Care Assn. Ill. (bd. dirs. 1987—), Ill. Assn. Child Care Workers, Nat. Assn. Female Execs. Roman Catholic. Office: Mercy Boys Home 1140 W Jackson Blvd Chicago IL 60607

GOTCH, LOU ANN MEYER, banker; b. Ft. Wayne, Ind., June 23, 1947; d. Donald LeRoy and Marjorie Ruth (Dyer) Meyer; m. John Raymond Gotch, Oct. 7, 1967; 1 child, Andrew John. Student, So. Ill. U., 1965-66, Am. Inst. Banking, 1979-81; cert. Sch. Bank Mktg., 1982. Teller Carbondale Savs. & Loan, Ill., 1974-76; customer service/advt. mgr. State Savs., Bowling Green, Ohio, 1976-78; mktg. asst. Pk. Nat. Bank, Newark, Ohio, 1978-79; dir. mktg. Central Trust Co., Newark, 1979-85; v.p. mktg. United Nat. Bank, Canton, Ohio, 1985—; cons. pub. speaking Bus. and Profl. women, Newark, 19; cons., mktg. Bldg. Better Bds., Newark, 1984. Newspaper columnist 1984-85. Loaned exec. United Way, Licking County, Ohio, 1978; bd. dirs. Am. Cancer Soc., Licking County, 1978-85, Named Outstanding Women of Am., 1983. Mem. Nat. Assn. Bank Women, Ohio Sch. Bank Mktg. Alumni Assn., C. of C. Licking County. Avocations: teaching aerobics, public speaking, music, Sunday Sch. Lit., sewing. Office: United Nat Bank PO Box 24190 Canton OH 44701

GOTHARD, DONITA, psychologist, educator; b. Minden, La., June 9, 1932; d. Donald Elmer and Nita (Brunt) Gothard. BA, Northwestern State U. La., 1954, MEd, 1961; PhD, U. Ala., 1970. Tchr. Bossier (La.) Parish Schs., 1954-61, counselor, 1961-67; instr. Northwestern State U. La., 1967-68; dir. human relations Caddo (La.) Parish Schs., 1970-71; sch. psychologist

Caddo (la.) Parrish Schs., 1971-73; asst. prof. psychology La. State U., Shreveport, 1973-76; assoc. prof., Shreveport, 1976-81; prof. prof., 1981-85, prof. emeritus, 1981-85, also coordinator specialist degree sch. psychology; founder, pres. West Park Psychol. Services, Inc. Mem. Am. Psychol. Assn., La. Psychol. Assn., NW La. Psychol. Assn., Soc. Personality Assessment, the Am. Regidstry Lic. Psychologists and Mental Health Profls., La. Acad. Scis., Am. Miniature Schnauzer Assn. Home: 10126 Keatchie-Marshall Rd Keatchie LA 71046

GOTLIB, LORRAINE, judge, former lawyer; b. Toronto, Ont., Can., May 13, 1931; m. Christopher B. Paterson. B.A., U. Toronto, 1952; grad., Osgoode Hall. Bar: Ont. 1959; named Queen's Counsel 1973. Former ptnr. Kingsmill, Jennings, Toronto, McMillan Binch, Toronto; apptd. to bench Dist. Ct. Ont., 1985—; past mem. Bd. Trade Met. Toronto, mem. house com., 1977-79, mem. council, 1979-83; group seminar instr. Bar Admission Course 1968-72. Mem. council Ont. Coll. Art, 1976-79. Recipient Jubilee medal, 1977. Mem. Canadian Bar Assn. (nat. exec. com. 1976-78, pres. Ont. br. 1983-84), County of York Law Assn., Women's Law Assn. Ont., Med.-Legal Soc. Toronto, Univ. Coll. Alumnae Assn., Kappa Beta Pi (nat. dir. 1968-72). Clubs: Royal Can. Yacht, Lawyers of Toronto, Empire of Can. (past bd. dirs.). Address: The Court House, 361 University Ave, Toronto, ON Canada M5G 1T3

GOTOWALA, DIANE GERTRUDE TOCE, small business owner; b. Hartford County, Conn., July 26, 1935; d. Dominic Anthony and Ebba (Johnson) Toce; m. George Robert Gotowala, June 4, 1955; children: Kandy Mae, Gary Thomas, Michael Grant. Grad. high sch., Newington, Conn. Instr. Frank Davis Resort, Moodus, Conn., 1979-83, social dir., 1982-84; social dir. Day Care Cen., Newington, 1983-84, Cen. Conn. State U., New Britain, 1984-85; judge Miss Greater New Britain Pageant, Southington, Conn., Miss Southington Pageant. dir., choreographer Nurse Yr., Rocky Hill, Conn., Miss Dance Conn., East Hartford; TV co-host Ranger Andy TV Show, Hartford; guest TV-3 "This Morning Am.", Hartford; demonstrator gymnastics All New Sports World Show, Hartford, numerous other choreographies for local variety shows. Designed float Newington Bicentennial Parade; dir. Newington Children's Hosp. Recipient 1st prize Ted Mack's Original Amateur Hour. Mem. Nat. Dance Exercise Instrs. Tng. Assn., Dance Masters Am., Dance Tchrs. Club Conn., Profl. Dance Tchrs. Orgn., Am. Soc. Composers Authors and Pub., Conn. Assn. Health Phys. Edn. Recreation and Dance, Newington Bus. Women's Assn. (treas.) (honorary award), Sense (sec.). Democrat. Roman Catholic.

GOTSOPOULOS, BARBARA LYNN, brokerage firm executive; b. Paterson, N.J., Mar. 16, 1948; d. Albert Raymond and Vivian Betty (Polkoph) Parker; m. Nicholas Solon Gotsopoulos, Mar. 15, 1970. BS, Rensselaer Poly. Inst., 1969. Prin. in wholesale distbg. co. Hollywood, Fla., 1981-84; pvt. practice commodities trading cons. Hollywood, 1984-87; pres. Blue Springs Capital Corp., Hollywood, 1985-86, 1st Fla. Commodities, Inc., North Lauderdale, 1987; ptnr. Multinat. Services, Inc., Hollywood, 1986-87; br. office mgr. Ind. Brokers Group, Inc., North Lauderdale, 1987; asst. sr. v.p. E.F. Hutton and Co., Inc., North Miami Beach, Fla., 1987-88, Prudential-Bache Securities, North Miami Beach, 1988, Telus Communications, North Miami, 1988—. Mem. Nat. Assn. Female Execs. (charter), Nat. Futures Assn., United Greeks Am. (co-founder), Alpha Psi Omega. Republican. Home: PO Box 183 Hallandale FL 33009

GOTT, SUSAN DARNELL, social services administrator; b. New Britain, Conn., June 14, 1946; d. Victor Clement and Jane Clarissa (Pritchard) Darnell; divorced; children: Heather, Elise. BA in Langs., Middlebury Coll., 1968; MA in Health Care Adminstrn., Framingham State U., 1983. Unit supr. Vocat. Rehab., Brandon, Vt., 1971-73; chief mental retardation services Vocat. Rehab., Montpelier, Vt., 1973; regional supr. Vocat. Rehab., Barre, Vt., 1973-74; coordinator projects Wrentham (Mass.) Research Found., 1979-82; exec. dir. Horace Mann Ednl. Assn. Inc., Wrentham, 1982—; cons. Mass., 1985—. Mem. Am. Mgmt. Assn., Nat. Assn. Female Execs., Mental Retardation Providers Council (bd. dirs. 1986—), Mass. Council Human Service Providers, Mass. Assn. ICF-MR Providers (bd. dirs. 1986—). Home: 7 Mohegan St Norfolk MA 02056 Office: Horace Mann Ednl Assn 29 Franklin St Wrentham MA 02093

GOTTESFELD, ILENE BURSON, nurse, educator; b. Kew Gardens, N.Y., Dec. 25, 1948; 2 children. Student U. Ala., 1966-67; B.S. in Nursing, Boston U., 1971; M. Nursing, U. Fla., 1974. R.N. N.Y. Staff nurse New Eng. Med. Ctr. Floating Hosp., Boston, 1971-72; pediatric community health nurse, emergency room coordinator, inservice instr. Columbia Point Health Ctr., Boston, 1972-73; teaching asst. Sch. Nursing, U. Fla., Gainesville, 1974; clin. nursing specialist in pediatrics L.I. Jewish-Hillside Med. Ctr., New Hyde Park, N.Y., 1974-75; specialist in pediatric cardiology, 1975-77; adj. clin. instr. Sch. Nursing Adelphi U., Garden City, N.Y., 1978-81; nurse clinician in pediatric cardiology North Shore Univ. Hosp., Manhasset, N.Y., 1982—; instr. continuing edn. program SUNY-Farmingdale, 1976; instr. CPR, Nassau Heart Assn., 1976-79. Mem. Am. Nurses Assn., Am. Heart Assn., NE Pediatric Cardiology Nurses Assn. (treas. 1984-86), Sigma Theta Tau. Address: 1405 Plaza Ave New Hyde Park NY 11040-4920 Office: North Shore Univ Hosp Dept of Pediatric Cardiology Manhasset NY 11030

GOTTFRIED, MARTHA ANN, real estate broker; b. Evansville, Ind., Apr. 21, 1937; d. Francis J. and Mildred E. (Schatz) Heines; student U. Evansville, 1958, Palm Beach Jr. Coll., 1971; m. Robert W. Gottfried, Nov. 13, 1970. Sec. production control Mead Johnson & Co., Evansville, 1956-61, sec., v.p. internat. div., 1961-63, sec., pres. internat. div., 1963-67, adminstrv. asst., chmn. bd., 1967-70; corp. sec.-treas., dir. Robert W. Gottfried, Inc., Palm Beach, Fla., 1970—; pres. Martha A. Gottfried, Inc., Real Estate, Palm Beach, 1977—; Mem. Internat. Fedn. Real Estate Fedn., Nat. Womens Council Realtors, Palm Beach Bd. Realtors, Palm Beach Civic Assn. Roman Catholic. Clubs: Poinciana, Govs. (Palm Beach). Home: 748 HiMount Palm Beach FL 33480 Office: 219 Worth Ave Palm Beach FL 33480

GOTTLIEB, BARBARA WEINTRAUB, psychologist, educator; b. N.Y.C.. BA, U. Pitts., 1971; MEd, Lesley Coll., 1974; EdD, Northern Ill. U., 1980. Dir. Community Unit 304/Title I, Geneva, 1977-78; asst. dir. Ctr. for Ednl. Research, Larchmont, N.Y., 1980-81; assoc. prof. Lehman Coll., coordinator graduate program in Emotional Handicaps CUNY, Bronx, 1981—; cons. N.Y.C. Bd. Edn., 1980-87. Author, editor Advances in Spl. Edn., 1987; author various book chpts.; contbr. articles to profl. jours. Mem. Am. Psychol. Assn., Westchester Psychol. Assn., Council on Exceptional Children, Am. Assn. Univ. Profs.

GOTTLIEB, ELIZABETH GEYER, choreographer, educator; b. N.Y.C., Nov. 22, 1951; d. Edward and Gertrude (Cohen) G.; m. Joseph Karpienia, Mar. 2, 1984. Student L.I.U., 1972-73; B.S., NYU, 1976. Dancer N.Y.C. Ballet Co., 1969-72; free-lance dancer, 1972-77; dir. E.G.G. & Dancers Inc., N.Y.C., 1977—; coach for profl. performers, 1977—. Producer, choreographer video films: Journey, 1980 (Bronze Internat. Filmfest award 1981), Videodances, 1982; choreographer (ballet) Choreotunes, 1980, 81, 82 (Criterion Found. grantee 1980, 81, 82). Vol. Crisis Intevention Ctr. C.W. Post Coll., Greenvale, N.Y., 1972-73; dir., founder Harvest, NYU, 1973-74. Mem. Dance Theater Workshop, Sutton Movement Shorthand Soc., NYU Alumni Assn. Democrat. Avocation: music. Office: EGG and Dancers 287 Broadway New York NY 10007

GOTTLIEB, LUCILLE MONTROSE FOX, retired state official; b. Hartford, Conn., May 30, 1929; d. Louis Paul and Rose Tomasina (Vignone) Montrose; student Cambridge Sch. Bus. Sci., 1948, Hillyer Jr. Coll., 1950; m. Francis R. Fox, Jr., June 26, 1954; m. Ralph Gottlieb, Sept. 28, 1979. Adminstrv. fiscal mgmt. officer Conn. Hwy. Dept., Hartford, 1950-61, asst. pub. relations dir., 1961-65, personnel asst., 1965-70; liaison officer Conn. Dept. Transp., from 1970; v.p. TV 58, Shoreline Communications Inc., 1976—. Chmn. Rocky Hill Park Com., 1968, Pool and Teen Center Com., 1976-77, Park and Recreation Adv. Bd., 1969; mem. Govs. Environ. Policy Com., 1972-74; chmn. Park and Recreation Adv. Bd., 1970; v.p. Gov's. Environ. Policy Panel on Travel and Transp.; trustee Council 13 Original States, 1978. Mem. NCCJ, Antiquarian Landmarks Soc. Conn., Fedn. Bus. and Profl. Women (chmn. pub. relations), Pub. Personnel Assn. Greater Hartford (v.p.), Conn. Employees Assn., Nat. Resources Council Conn., Great Meadow Conservation Trust, Conn. Pub. Health Assn., Women in Communications (v.p. Conn. chpt. 1978), Conn. Hist. Com., Conn. Italian-Am. Cultural Assn. (pres. 1978), Smithsonian Inst., Met. Opera Guild, Ft. Lauderdale Symphony Soc., Ft. Lauderdale Opera Guild, Audubon Soc., Am. Mus. Natural History, Internat. Platform Assn. Republican. Roman Catholic. Clubs: Lady Hilton VIP, Cosmopolitan Hartford, Officers of Conn. (sec.). Creator Gertie Glitter anti litter symbol. Home: 3500 Galt Ocean Dr Fort Lauderdale FL 33308 Other: 16 Judd Rd Wetherfield CT 06109

GOTTLIEB, MARILYN ANN, advertising agency, public relations executive, writer; b. N.Y., Dec. 2, 1942; divorced; children—Michael Jedd Molinoff, Joel David Molinoff. Student Skidmore Coll., 1962-64; B.S., NYU, 1964, M.S., 1968. Tchr., Los Angeles, 1964-65, New Rochelle, N.Y., 1965-68, Scarsdale, N.Y., 1973-74; with pub. relations staff Woman's Sch., N.Y., 1974-75; pub. relations coordinator N.Y.C. Bicentennial Corp., N.Y.C., 1975-76; writer N.Y. Med. Coll., N.Y.C., 1976-78; dir. pub. relations Am. Assn. Advt. Agys., N.Y.C., 1979-83; mgr. pub. relations Ogilvy & Mather, N.Y.C., 1983-84; v.p., dir. pub. relations; Lintas: N.Y., N.Y.C., 1984—. Faculty New Sch., N.Y.C. Contbr. articles to profl. publs., columns to mags. and newspapers. Pro bono pub. relations Skidmore Coll., Saratoga Springs, N.Y., Experiment in Internat. Living, Brattleboro, Vt. Recipient Founders Day award NYU, 1964. Mem. Advt. Women of N.Y. (past mem. bd. dirs., chmn. pub. relations com. 1985), Am. Assn. Advt. Agys. (pub. relations com.), Women in Communications, Inc., Pub. Relations Soc. Am. Avocations: swimming, tennis, sailing, jogging, music, dance, travel. Home: Larchmont NY 10538 Office: Lintas NY 1 Dag Hammarskjold Plaza New York NY 10017

GOTTSCHALK, JENNIFER LEIGH, lawyer; b. Bethesda, Md., Feb. 15, 1955; d. George Francis and Betty Jane (Butler) G. BA, U. Del., 1976; JD, Rutgers U., 1979. Bar: N.J. 1980. Jud. law clk. U.S. Bankruptcy Ct., Trenton, N.J., 1979-80; asst. prosecutor Monmouth County (N.J.), Freehold, 1980-82; assoc. Thompson & Stoller, Aberdeen, N.J., 1982-83; asst. counsel N.J. Casino Control Commn., Lawrenceville, 1983-84; dep atty. gen. N.J. Div. Criminal Justice, Trenton, 1984—. Mem. Monmouth Civic Chorus, Little Silver, N.J., 1981—; mem. Aberdeen Twp. Women's Softball League, 1984—. Mem. Bar U.S. Supreme Ct., N.J. Bar, Md. Bar, Monmouth Bar Assn. Democrat. Christian Scientist. Home: 118 Strathmore Gardens Aberdeen NJ 07747 Office: Div Criminal Justice 25 Market St CN 085 Trenton NJ 08625

GOUDY, JOSEPHINE GRAY, social worker; b. Des Moines, Nov. 30, 1925; d. Gerald William and Myrtle Maria (Brooks) Gray; B.A., State U. Iowa, 1953, M.S.W., 1966; m. John Winston Goudy, June 5, 1948; children: Tracy Jean, Paula Rae. Lic. social worker, Iowa. Child welfare supr. Iowa Dept. Social Services, 1960-68; psychiat. social worker Community Mental Health Center Scott County (Iowa), 1966-71; social work instr. Palmer Jr. Coll., Davenport, Iowa, 1967-70; psychiat. social worker, chief social services Jacksonville (Ill.) State Mental Hosp., 1971-74; coordinator community mental health outpatient services McFarland Mental Health Center, Springfield, Ill., 1974; exec. dir. Macoupin County Mental Health Center, Carlinville, Ill., 1974—; chmn. Human Services Edn. Council, Springfield, 1979-81; bd. mem. Alzheimer's Disease and Related Disorders Assn., Springfield Ill. Area Chpt., past exec. Davenport Community Welfare Council. Mem. Nat. Assn. Social Workers (Social Worker of Yr. Central Ill. area 1983), Acad. Cert. Social Workers, Am. Personnel and Guidance Assn., AAUW (br. pres. 1964-66, mem. state bar 1966-68, br. grantee 1975), Internat. Fedn. U. Women, U. Iowa Alumni Assn., Bus. and Profl. Women (Woman of Yr. 1983), Delta Kappa Gamma, Kappa Delta Pi. Republican. Methodist. Club: Carlinville Women's (pres. 1975-77). Home: 364 W Tremont St Waverly IL 62692 Office: 100 N Side Sq Carlinville IL 62626

GOUGÉ, SUSAN CORNELIA JONES, microbiologist; b. Chgo., Apr. 18, 1924; d. Harry LeRoy and Gladys (Moon) Jones; student Am. U., Washington, 1942-43, La. Coll., 1944-45; B.S., George Washington U., 1948; postgrad. Georgetown U., 1956-58, 66-69, Vt. Coll. of Norwich U., M.A. in Pub. Health, 1984; m. John Oscar Gougé , Aug. 7, 1943; children: John Ronald, Richard Michael (dec.), Claudia Renée Gougé Carr. Med. technician Children's Hosp. Research Lab., Washington, 1948-49; bacteriologist George Washington U. Research Lab., D.C. Gen. Hosp., 1950-53; med. microbiologist Walter Reed Army Inst. Research, Washington, 1953-61; research asst. Dental Research, Walter Reed Army Med. Ctr., 1961-62; microbiologist antibiotics div. FDA, 1962-63; supr. quality control John D. Copanos Co., Pharms., Balt., 1963-64; research tng. asst. infectious diseases and tropical medicine Howard U. Med. Sch., 1964-65; research assoc. Georgetown U. Lab. Infectious Diseases, D.C. Gen. Hosp., 1966-69; mycologist Georgetown U. Hosp. Lab., 1969-70; microbiologist Research Found. of Washington Hosp. Ctr., 1971-73; dir. quality control Bio-Medium Corp., Silver Spring, Md., 1973-76; microbiologist Alcolac, Inc., Balt., 1976-77; microbiologist div. labs., dept. human resources Community Health and Hosps. Adminstrn., Washington, 1978-79; microbiologist div. ophthalmic devices, Office Device Evaluation Ctr. for Devices and Radiol. Health, FDA, Silver Spring, Md., 1979—. Sec. to exec. bd. Bethesda Project Awareness, 1970-71; vol. lead poisoning detection testing project, D.C. Office Vols. Internat. Tech. Assistance, 1970-71; vol. Zacchaeus Free Clinic, Washington, 1979-84. Mem. Nat. Capital Harp Ensemble, 1941-65; mem. parish social concerns com. Roman Cath. Ch. Recipient medal community service; registered microbiologist Nat. Registry Microbiologists; specialist microbiologist Am. Acad. Microbiology. Mem. AAAS, Am. Soc. for Microbiology, Am. Inst. Biol. Scis., Am. Chem. Soc., Internat. Union Pure and Applied Chemistry, N.Y. Acad. Scis., Am. Pub. Heath Assn., Albertus Magnus Guild, Capital Bus. and Profl. Women's Club (rec. sec. 1973-74, 1st v.p. 1974-75, pres. 1975-76), Winchester Bus. and Profl. Women, World Affairs Council of Washington D.C., Pi Kappa Delta. Roman Catholic. Club: Toastmasters (sec. 1979-80). Office: FDA Div Ophthalmic Devices Office Device Evaluation 8757 Georgia Ave Silver Spring MD 20910

GOUGH, JESSIE POST (MRS. HERBERT FREDERICK GOUGH), retired educator; b. Nakon Sri Tamaraj, Thailand, Jan. 26, 1907 (parents Am. citizens); d. Richard Walter and Mame (Stebbins) Post; B.A., Maryville Coll., 1927; M.A. in English, U. Chgo., 1928; Ed.D., U. Ga., 1965; m. Herbert Frederick Gough, June 30, 1934; children—Joan Acland (Mrs. Alexander Reed), Herbert Frederick. Tchr. English, Linden Hall, Lititz, Pa., 1930-32; tchr. Fairyland Sch., Lookout Mountain, Tenn., 1955-64; research asst. English curriculum studies center U. Ga., 1964-65; assoc. prof. elem. edn. LaGrange (Ga.) Coll., 1965-73, prof., 1973-75; prof. N.W. Ga. area tchr. edn. services, 1969-71. Mem. Walker County (Ga.) Curriculum Council, 1959-61, Walker County Ednl. Planning Bd., 1958-60. Mem. Am. Ednl. Research Assn., Internat. Reading Assn., East Tenn. Hist. Soc., Nat., Ga. edn. assns., Delta Kappa Gamma. Home: 8111 Savannah Hills Dr Ooltewah TN 37363

GOUGH, PAULINE BJERKE, magazine editor; b. Wadena, Minn., Jan. 7, 1935; d. Luther C. and Zita Pauline (Halbmaier) Bjerke; B.A., U. Minn., Mpls., 1957; B.S., Moorhead (Minn.) State Coll., 1970; M.S., Ind. U., Bloomington, 1972, Ed.D., 1977; children—Mary Pauline, Sarah Elizabeth, Philip Clayton. Reporter women's page San Jose (Calif.) Mercury-News, 1957-58; with research dept. Campbell-Mithun Advt., Mpls., 1958-60; tchr. Univ. Elem. Sch., Bloomington, 1970-79; freelance writer Agy. Instructional TV, Bloomington, 1974-80; mem. adj. faculty Ind. U.-Purdue U., Indpls., summers 1976, 77; asst. editor Phi Delta Kappan, Bloomington, 1980-81, mng. editor, 1981-88; editor, 1988—; mem. profl. staff Phi Delta Kappa, 1981—, also leader insts. on writing for publ. Recipient Disting. Alumna award Moorhead State U., 1982. Mem. Women in Communications, Phi Beta Kappa, Phi Delta Kappa. Author articles in field. Home: 3570 Oakridge Dr Bloomington IN 47401 Office: Phi Delta Kappan 8th & Union Box 789 Bloomington IN 47402

GOUGIS, LORNA GAIL, financial executive; b. New Orleans, Aug. 19, 1948; d. Chester Arthur and Dorothy (Thomas) C. BA in Psychology, Newcomb Coll., 1969. Research assoc. Harvard U. Bus. Sch., Cambridge, Mass., 1970-71; test editor Ginn & Co., Lexington, Mass., 1972-75; v.p. Wallace and Assocs., Chgo., New Orleans, Washington, 1975-81; dir. of research and devel. Omega Group, Washington, 1981-84; dir. sales Polytech. Inc., Atlanta, Wash., 1984-86; v.p. Inter City Fin. Services, Washington, 1987—; freelance cons., Washington, 1985—. Mem. Nat. Forum for Black Pub. Adminstrs., Am. Pub. Transit Assn. Democrat. Roman Catholic. Home: 1019 Connecticut Ave NW Apt 702 Washington DC 20008 Office: Inter City Fin Service 3001 Georgia Ave NW Washington DC 20001

GOULD, ELAINE HOFFPAUIR, educator, librarian; b. Crowley, La., June 22, 1935; d. Marion Mason and Pearl Mildred (Pedigo) Hoffpauir; m. Howard Gould, Dec. 21, 1956; 1 child, Brett Howard. B in Music Edn., U. Southwestern La., 1957, MA, 1975. Cert. tchr. Tex., La. Tchr. vocal music Pasadena (Tex.) Ind. Sch. Dist., 1957-61; tchr. English, Journalism Church Point (La.) High Sch., 1961-64, Crowley (La.) High Sch., 1965-75; librarian, yearbook advisor Church Point Elementary Sch., 1975-85, Crowley Jr. High Sch., 1985—; mem. numerous evaluation coms. So. Assn. Colls. and Schs. Active Acadia Arts Council, Acadia Parish, La., 1977—, Crowley First Baptist Ch.; chmn. Acadia Parish Profl. Improvement Program, Crowley, 1980-86; mem. Crowley Centennial Com. Recipient Community Woman of Yr. award Crowley Bus. and Profl. Women, 1982, SAI Rose of Honor and Sword of Honor Acadia Bus. and Profl. Women; grantee La. Legis., 1953-57. Mem. Acadia Librarians Assn., Kappa Delta Pi, Phi Kappa Phi, Sigma Alpha Iota, Delta Kappa Gamma. Democrat. Baptist. Home: Rte 1 Box 65-B Rayne LA 70578 Office: Crowley Jr High Sch 401 W Northern Ave Crowley LA 70526

GOULD, GEORGIA AGATHA, creative services executive; b. Glencoe, Minn., July 29, 1934; d. George Casper and Ruth Agatha (Lippert) G. Student, U. Minn., 1952-56. Jr. editor TV Guide mag., N.Y.C., 1957-58; research writer The Perry Como Show, Roncom Prodns., N.Y.C., 1958-62; creative asst. Marschalk Advt., N.Y.C., 1965-69; creative services mgr. Sta. WTCN-TV, Mpls.and St. Paul, 1970-80; advt., publicity mgr. Sta. KTCA-TV, Mpls.and St. Paul, 1980—; publicity cons. Met. Boy's Choir, Mpls., 1969-72; PBS adv./promotion com. 1987—. Author teleplay. Mem. So. Theater Bd., 1987—. Recipient PBS Promotion award, 1982, 86. Mem. Am. Women in Radio and TV. Lodge: Order Eastern Star. Office: KTCA-TV 1640 Como Ave Saint Paul MN 55108

GOULD, MARTHA B., librarian; b. Claremont, N.H., Oct. 8, 1931. BA in Edn., U. Mich., 1953; MS in Library Sci., Simmons Coll., 1956; cert., U. Denver Library Sch. Community Analysis Research Inst., 1978. Childrens librarian N.Y. Pub. Library, 1956-58; adminstr. library services act demonstration regional library project Pawhuska, Okla., 1958-59; cons. N.Mex. State Library, 1959-60; childrens librarian then sr. childrens librarian Los Angeles Pub. Library, 1960-72; acctg. dir. pub. srvices, reference librarian Nev. State Library, 1972-74; pub. services librarian Washoe County (Nev.) Library, 1974-79, asst. county librarian, 1979-84, county librarian, 1984—. Contbr. articles to jours. Treas. United Jewish Appeal, 1981; bd. dirs. Temple Sinai, RSVP; trustee N. Nevadans for ERA. Recipient Nev. State Library Letter of Commendation, 1973, Washoe County Bd. Commrs. Resolution of Appreciation, 1978; Named Civil Libertarian of the Yr., Nev. ACLU. Mem. ALA (bd. dirs. intellectual freedom round table 1977-79, intellectual freedom com. 1979-83, council 1983-86), Nev. Library Assn. (chmn. pub. info. com. 1972-73, intellectual freedom com. 1975-78, govt. relations com. 1978-79, v.p., pres.-elect 1980, pres. 1981, Spl. Citation 1978, 87). Office: Washoe Country Library 301 S Center St PO Box 2151 Reno NV 89505

GOULD, MAXINE LUBOW, marketing professional, consultant; b. Bridgeton, N.J., Feb. 28, 1942; d. Louis A. and Bernice L. (Goldberg) Lubow; B.S., Temple U., 1962, J.D., 1968; m. Sam C. Gould, June 17, 1962 (div. Dec. 1984); children—Jack, Herman, David. Head resident dept. student personnel Temple U., 1962-66; dir., treas. Hilltop Interest Program, Inc., Los Angeles, 1973-74; law clk. law firms, Los Angeles, 1975-77; with Buffalo Resources Corp., Los Angeles, 1978-82, corp. sec., 1979-82; corp. sec., securities prin. Buffalo Securities Corp., Los Angeles, 1979-82; corp. sec. LaMaur Devel. Corp., Los Angeles, 1979-82; contracts analyst, land dept. Texaco Inc., Los Angeles, 1982-83; exec. dir. Sinai Temple, West Los Angeles, 1983-85; pres. Cutting Edge, Los Angeles, 1986; adminstr. law firm Robinson, Wolas & Diamant, Century City, 1986, acctg. firm Roth, Bookstein & Zaslow, Los Angeles, 1986-87; project coordinator Cipher, 1987; mktg. dir. Am. Bus. Capital, Beverly Hills, Calif., 1988—. Mem. Roscomare Valley Assn. Edn. Com., Bel Air, Calif., 1975-76; subcom. chmn. Roscomare Rd. Sch. Citizens Adv. Council, Bel Air; active various community drives. Recipient Joseph B. Wagner Oratory award B'nai B'rith, 1959, Voice of Democracy award, 1958-59, award Commentator Club, 1959. Mem. ABA (law office econs. sect.), Los Angeles Bar Assn. (assoc., law office econs. sect.), Nat. Assn. Legal Adminstrs. (Beverly Hills chpt.), Nat. Assn. Female Execs. (network dir.), Nat. Assn. Law Firm Mktg. Adminstrs., Calif. Women Lawyers, Women in Bus. (co-chmn. membership com.), Calif. CPA Soc. (adminstr. com.), Nat. Assn. Synagogue Adminstrs., Am. Assn. Petroleum Landmen, Los Angeles Assn. Petroleum Landmen, Phi Alpha Theta, Alpha Lambda Delta. Jewish. Home: 4101 Knob Hill Dr Sherman Oaks CA 91403

GOULDER, CAROLJEAN HEMPSTEAD, psychologist; b. Houston, Minn., Apr. 9, 1933; d. Orson George and Jean Helen (Lischer) H.; m. L. Lynton Goulder, Jr., May 26, 1956 (div. 1978); children: Jean Virginia, David Thomas, Ann Rachel; m. John T. Blake, Apr. 12, 1986. BS, Hamline U., 1956; CAGS, R.I. Coll., 1975; MA in Sch. Psychology, 1972; postgrad., Nova U., 1977-78. Profl. sch. psychologist, R.I. Dept. head, instr. Highsmith Hosp., Fayetteville, N.C., 1956-57; instr. nursing New Eng. Deaconess Hosp., Boston, 1957-58; dir. psychol. services Burrillville Sch. Dept., Harrisville, R.I., 1972-79, sch. psychologist, 1979—, coordinator presch. handicapped, 1985-86; lectr. pediatric problems Sturdy Meml. Hosp., Attleboro, Mass., 1970-72; cons. Wheeler Sch., Providence, 1970-73. Chmn. 2d Congl. Ch. Sch., Attleboro, Mass., 1962-65, mem. religious edn. com., kindergarten com. and choir, 1965; active 1st Unitarian Ch., Providence, 1982—. Mem. R.I. Sch. Psychologists Assn., Nat. Assn. Sch. Psychology, Am. Psychol. Assn., Mass. Psychol. Assn. (assoc.), Council for Exceptional Children. Avocations: creative cooking, knitting, crewel embroidery, nature study, concerts. Office: A T Levy Sch Spl Services Office Harrisville RI 02830

GOULET, THERESE, professional association administrator; b. Winnipeg, Manitoba, Can., May 20, 1959; d. George Richard Donald and Marie-Therese (de la Giroday) G. BA, U. Calgary, Alta., Can., 1981, MA, 1986. Editorial cons. Atgood Publs. Ltd., Calgary, 1979-85; adminstr. Can. Inst. Resources Law, Calgary, 1985—; media cons., tchr. continuing edn. Calgary Bd. Edn., 1983-84; lectr. U. Calgary, 1988. Author: Sell Yourself, 1982; mng. editor: Calgary: A Year in Focus, 1987; editor; Internat. Jour. Mini- and Microcomputers, 1985; editor: (legal newsletter) Resources, 1985—. Media vol. 1988 Olympic Winter Games, Calgary, 1987-88; active Amnesty Internat.; bd. dirs. Libertarian Party of Can., Toronto, 1987. Recipient Province of Alta. Achievement award, 1988; culture Arts study grantee, Banff, Alberta, 1984. Mem. U. Calgary Student Union (bd. dirs. 1986-87, pres. 1986-87), Kappa Kappa Gamma. Office: U Calgary, Can Inst Resources Law, Calgary, AL Canada T2N 1N4

GOULSON, JO PINNELL, science writer; b. Birmingham, Ala., July 31, 1926; d. John W. and Frances (Moores) Pinnell; m. Hilton T. Goulson, Aug. 21, 1954; children: Daniel Thomas, Amy Frances. BS, U. Ala., 1947; postgrad., Yale U., 1947-48, Woman's Med. Coll., 1948-50, U. Mich., 1950; MS, U. N.C., 1954. Research asst. Sch. Medicine, U. N.C., Chapel Hill, 1954-61, research assoc. Ctr. Research in Toxicology, 1965-67, edit. cons. Schs. Medicine and Dentistry,, 1968, research assoc. Dental Research Ctr.,, 1968-82, lectr. Continuing Edn. Program,, 1982, lectr. dept. parasitology and lab. practice, 1977—. pres. Chapel Hill chpt. Ch. Women United, 1972. Mem. AAAS, Am. Med. Writers Assn., Soc. Tech. Communication, Internat. Assn. Bus. Communications, N.Y. Acad. Scis., U. N.C. Pub. Health Alumni Assn. (sec. 1979-80, chair tech. session 1984-85, mem. planning commn. 1984-85), N.C. Fedn. Women's Club (dist. pres. 1968-72), Sigma Xi, Alpha Epsilon Delta, Delta Omega. Club: Chapel Hill Women's (pres. 1985-86). Home: 52 Oakwood Dr Chapel Hill NC 27514

GOURLEY, MARY MARGARET, clinical laboratory scientist; b. Pitts., Nov. 30, 1942; d. Andrew William and Mary (Boros) Matta; m. John Patrick Gourley, Nov. 16, 1968; 1 child, Christine Denise. Student, Juniata Coll., 1960-63, Montefiore Hosp. Sch. Med. Tech., 1964. Chemistry technologist J.R. Sugarman Lab., Pitts., 1964-65; technologist St. Joseph's Hosp., Pitts., 1965-66, 72-77, chief technologist, 1968-72; supr. blook bank South Hills Health System, Pitts., 1977-79; chief technologist Med. Chek Labs., Pitts.,

1979-82; mgr. lab. South Side Hosp., Pitts., 1982—; presenter in field, 1979—. Deacon Swissvale (Pa.) Presbyn. Ch., 1987—. Mem. Nat. Certifying Agy. for Med. Lab. Personnel (cert. clin. lab. scientist, clin. lab. dir.), Am. Soc. Clin. Pathologists (cert. med. technologist), Am. Soc. Med. Tech. (bd. dirs. 1987—), Pa. Soc. for Med. Tech. (pres. 1983-84, bd. dirs. 1983-88, recipient Dolbey award 1984, pres. SW chpt. 1972-73, 82-83, bd. dirs. 1970-77, 80-83), Clin. Lab. Mgmt. Assn. (bylaws com. 1987-88, bd. dirs. Western Pa. chpt. 1983-84, 87-88, pres. 1985-86), Am. Assn. Blood Banks. Republican. Office: South Side Hosp 2000 Mary St Pittsburgh PA 15203

GOVAK, JUDITH ANN, real estate executive; b. N.Y.C., May 25, 1952; d. Frank and Beatrice (Wilton) G.; m. Edward D. Horowitz, Oct. 11, 1977 (div. 1984). AAS in Bus. Adminstrn., Coll. Staten Island, 1977, BA in Econs./Psychology, 1982. Asst. dir. fin. aid Pratt Inst., Bkln., 1979-81; asst. v.p. Halevi and Assocs., N.Y.C., 1981-84; adminstrv. coordinator Time Equities, Inc., N.Y.C., 1985—; cons. Screen Struct, Inc., Bkln., 1986—. Mem. Nat. Assn. Female Execs. Democrat. Roman Catholic. Office: Time Equities Inc 55 Fifth Ave New York NY 10003

GOVAN, DENISE ALEXANDRA, systems analyst, researcher; b. Balt., June 26, 1953; d. Abraham Govan and Willie Ester (Gaston) Furrs. BS, U. Balt., 1975, MBA, 1978. Placement officer Delta Personnel, Towson, Md., 1972; pub. info. asst. Police Dept. City of Balt., 1972-73, Better Bus. Bur., Balt., 1973-74; claims specialist State of Md., Balt., 1976-79, researcher, 1979, systems analyst, 1979-85, coordinator, supr., 1985—. Mem. steering com. City of Balt. Fair; parade marshal Port City Power Co. Mem. Edgar Allan Poe Soc. (corr. sec. 1973—), Phi Alpha Theta. Democrat. Roman Catholic. Lodge: Order Ea. Star. Home: 3638 Paskin Pl Apt #4A Baltimore MD 21207 Office: State of Md Dept Human Resources 311 W Saratoga St Baltimore MD 21201

GOVE, DOROTHY BERYL, civic worker; b. Haverhill, Mass., Apr. 14, 1905; d. Maurice Leslie and Minnie Evelyn (Tilton) McDaniel; m. William Lionel Gove; children—Inez Beryl Gove Riley, Barbara Evelyn, William Lionel, Donna Ilene Gove Matthews. Student Hall Hosp. Nurses Tng.; grad. Lincoln Inst. Practical Nursing, 1952. Lic. practical nurse, Mass. Treas., sec., founder Pioneer Nursing Assn., Malden, Mass., 1950-60; treas., founder WWI Vets., Woburn, Mass., 1944-60; vol. ARC, Mass., 1952-59; girl scout leader Boston council Girl Scouts U.S.A., 1942-54; leader, founder 4-H, Woburn, 1942-55; mem. Mayor's Dem. race, Woburn, 1943; vol. Health and Rehab. Services Hillsborough County, Tampa, Fla., 1979—(Vol. of Yr. 1986, 87); vol. James A. Haley Vets. Hosp., Tampa, 1979—(1,000 hour pin for vol. services 1988); officer DAV orgns., Brandon, Fla.; nat. aux. commdr. Wm. L. Gove Sr. Veterans Inc., Valrico, Fla., 1979-87. Mem. D.A.V., Aux. (life), Marine Corps League in Fla. (hon.), Angus R. Goss detachment Marine Corps League aux., 1987, Wm. L. Gove Sr. Vets. Aux. (life, founder), Brandon C. of C. Lodges: Women of Moose (founder aux.), Order Eastern Star. Office: Wm L Gove Sr Vets PO Box 369 Valrico FL 33594

GOVINE, BELICIA, therapist, educator; b. Chgo., Mar. 19, 1933; d. James Hart and Margaret (Eisenstaedt) Freudenthal; children: Deborah Sue Lillo, Richard Kenneth Weiner. BS, UCLA, 1955; MA, Pepperdine U., 1972; postgrad., Columbia Pacific U., 1984—. Cert. hypnotherapist, Calif., 1984, lic. family therapist, 1984. Activities therapist psychology unit Los Angeles County-U. So. Calif. Med. Ctr., 1964-65; social case worker Los Angeles Dept. Social Services, 1965-69; social rehab. counselor Los Angeles Dept. Mental Health, 1969-74; mem. clin. staff Holistic Health Ctr., Beverly Hills, Calif., 1976-79; pvt. practice therapy, transpersonal counseling Pacific Palisades, Calif., 1974-79, Arcata, Calif., 1979-83, Berkeley, Calif., 1984—; part-time clin. movemetn therapist Brotman Meml. Hosp., Culver City, Calif., 1973-77; mem. staff 9 Gates Mystery Sch., Sonoma, Calif., 1985—; creator Journey of the Soul, 1982—. Contbr. chpt. to book, numerous articles; presenter workshops, 1965—. Recognized among Women as Heroes Redwood Broadcasting, Eureka, Calif., 1982. Mem. Am. Assn. Family Therapists, Am. Dance Therapy Assn. (bd. dirs. 1972-76), Assn. Past Life Research and Therapy, Assn. Transpersonal Psychology, Acad. Dance Therapists Registered. Democrat. Taoist.

GOVONI, CHERYL ANN, educator; b. Grand Junction, Colo., Dec. 30, 1957; d. Donald P. and Joan Marie (Swiersz) G. BS in Home Econs. Edn., No. Ill. U., 1980, MS in Edn. Adminstrn., 1987. Cert. elem. tchr., Ill.; cert. home econs. tchr., Ill. Tchr. home econs., sponsor Home Econs. Club Arbor Park Mid. Sch., Oak Forest, Ill., 1980—, coach cheerleader team, 1980; Tchr. summer sch.; instr. aerobics Kelly Dance Sch., Joliet, Ill., Arbor Park Mid. Sch., Oak Forest, 1982-83. Choreographer sch. musicals, 1985-86. Mem. faculty council Nat. Jr. Honor Soc., 1987-88. Mem. NEA (bargaining com. 1983). Roman Catholic.

GOWENS, VERNEETA VIOLA, journalist; b. South Holland, Ill., Mar. 19, 1913; d. William and Mary Cawthorne (Fowler) Gibson; ed. public schs., Bryant and Stratton Bus. Coll.; m. Albert Gowens, July 17, 1936; children—Victoria Ann Gowens Utke, Mary Ann Gowens Weiss. Clk., pub. relations worker Chgo. and Riverdale Lumber Co., Chgo., 1934-45; feature writer, women's editor Tribune Publs., Harvey, Ill., 1960-62; feature writer, women's editor Star-Tribune, Williams Press, Chicago Heights, Ill., 1963-78; freelance writer; script writer variety shows Ship Ahoy, 1963, Fair 'n' Square, 1964; contbr. to Internat. Altrusan, 1974, Church Herald, 1977. Sunday sch. tchr., youth leader 1st Ref. Ch., South Holland; mem. editorial council Ch. Herald, Ref. Ch. in Am., 1976-82; pres. Dist. 150 PTA, 1965-66; adv. com. program in ltd. occupation tng. Thornton High Sch., 1963-69; mem. South Holland Indsl. Commn., 1965-68; bd. dirs. Family Service and Mental Health Center of South Cook County, Ill., 1974-77; mem. South Holland unit Salvation Army, 1958—; judge Internat. Teen Pageant, 1969; mem. South Holland Community Chest, 1978—; adv. bd. Thornton Community Coll. nursing program, 1976-83; active South Holland Diamond Jubilee, 1969; mem. South Holland Cable Commn., 1984—. Recipient award South Holland C. of C., 1970, Genoa council K.C., 1974, Village of South Holland, 1969, 1st pl. in contest No. Ill. U., 1974, 75, award Suburban Press Found., 1969, 1st pl. award Ill. Press Assn., 1973, 50 other awards in writing. Mem. Ill. Women's Press Assn. (Woman of Yr. 1974, award 1978), Nat. Fedn. Press Women (1st pl. Sweepstakes award 1976). Home: 16830 S Park Ave South Holland IL 60473

GOWER, ELIZABETH ANN, pharmacist; b. Methuen, Mass., June 24, 1957; d. Charles Ralph and Dorothy Mary (Vandecasteele) Smulkowski; m. David Edward Gower, Sept. 20, 1980. BS in Pharmacy, Mass. Coll. of Pharmacy and Allied Health Scis., 1980. Lic. Pharmacist, N.H. Staff pharmacist Salem (N.H.) Pharmacy, Inc., 1980-87, mgr., 1987—. Justice of the Peace State of N.H., 1986. Mem. Am. Pharm. Assn., Rho Chi. Home: 13 Cross St Salem NH 03079 Office: Salem Pharmacy Inc 300 Main St Salem NH 03079

GRABHORN, JUANITA JONES, dietitian; b. Vinegar Bend, Ala., Mar. 6, 1944; d. Johnnie abd Sarah Jane (Walley) Jones; m. Larry Lee Grabhorn, Jan. 25, 1975; 1 child, Kenneth John. BS, U. So. Miss., 1962-66; MS, U. Ala., 1975. Registered dietitian, Tex. Commd. 2d lt. US. Army, 1965, advanced through grades to lt. col., 1980; staff dietitian Brooke Army Med. Ctr., Ft. Sam Houston, Tex., 1967-69; asst chief food service div. Madigan Army Med. Ctr., Tacoma, 1969-71; C food service div. Lyster Army Hosp., Ft. Rucker, Ala., 1971-74; chief food service div. Darnall Army Hosp., Ft. Hood, Tex., 1975-78; asst. chief food service div. Womack Army Hosp., Ft. Bragg, N.C., 1978-81; chief nutrition care div. Reynolds Army Hosp., Ft. Sill, Okla., 1981-85; chief production and service br. Brooke Army Med. Ctr., 1985-86; studies officer Acad. Health Scis. Army Med. Specialist Corps, Ft. Sam Houston, 1986-87; dir. food & beverage Army Residence Community, 1987—. Mem. Am. Dietetic Assn. Democrat. Methodist. Home: 8607 Autumn Sunset San Antonio TX 78239

GRABOWSKI, JANICE LYNN, school board executive, civic leader; b. Parma, Ohio, Dec. 28, 1948; d. Philip Edward and Marjorie (Woodrig) Konscak; m.Gary Michael Grabowski, June 23,1967; children: Michael John, Jennifer Lynn. Student, Cleve. State U., 1966-67. Pres. Brunwick City Bd. Edn., 1987—, bd. mem., 1982—, legis. liaison, 1983—; pres., bd. mem. Medina County Vocat. Ctr., 1982—, legis. liaison, 1983—; trustee Ohio Schs. Bd. Assn., 1987—, exec. com. NE Region, 1983—, treas., 1984, regions rep. state policy and legis. com., 1984-86, 88—, moderator state conf., 1985-87, del. 1982-87; chmn. 13th Congrl. Dist. Nat. Sch. Bds. Assn., Fed. Relations Network, 1984-86; del. nat. cong. Houston, San Francisco, Anaheim Calif. 1983-85, mem. arrangement and hospitality com. 1986. Mem. Nat. Audubon Soc., LWV. Home: 3968 Keller-Hanna Dr Brunswick OH 44212 Office: Brunswick City Schs Bd Edn 3643 Center Rd Brunswick OH 44212

GRACE, HELEN KENNEDY, foundation administrator; b. Beresford, S.D., Mar. 30, 1935; d. Walter James and Ethel Elvira (Soderstrom) Kennedy; B.S. in Nursing, Loyola U., Chgo., 1963; M.S. in Nursing, U. Ill., Chgo., 1965; Ph.D. in Sociology, Northwestern U., 1969; m. Elliott A. Grace, Nov. 20, 1961; 1 dau., Elizabeth Ann. Nursing adminstr. Ill. Dept. Mental Health, 1963-67; faculty Coll. of Nursing, U. Ill., Chgo., 1967-82, instr., 1967-69, asst. prof., 1969-71, assoc. prof., 1971-73, prof., assoc. dean for grad. study, 1973-77, dean coll. of Nursing 1977-82; program dir. W.K. Kellog Found., Battle Creek, Mich., 1982—. Recipient Disting. Alumnus award Loyola U., Coll. of Nursing U. Ill., Centennial Alumni award Am. State and Land Grant Univs. Mem. Am. Nurses Assn., Nat. League for Nursing (governing bd. 1978-86), Am. Acad. of Nursing (governing council 1976-80), Am. Sociol. Assn. Author: Mental Health Nursing: A Psychosocial Approach, 1977, 2d edit., 1981; Families Across the Life Cycle: Family Studies for Nursing, 1977; The Development of a Child Psychiatric Treatment Program, 1971; Current Issues in Nursing, 1981, 2d edit., 1985, 3d edit., 1988. Office: 400 North Ave Battle Creek MI 49015

GRACE, JULIANNE ALICE, manufacturing company executive; b. Riverdale, N.J., Oct. 29, 1937; d. Arthur Edward and Julia May (McCarthy) Thompson; m. Daniel Vincent Grace, July 2, 1960; children: Daniel Vincent III, Deirdre Elizabeth. BA, Marymount Manhattan Coll., 1959; MA, Fordham U., 1960. Dir. admissions Marymount Manhattan Coll., N.Y.C., 1966-72; mgr. human resources The Perkin-Elmer Corp., Norwalk, Conn., 1972-78, dir. human resources, 1978-81, asst. sr. v.p. semiconductor equipment, 1981-83, asst. pres., 1983-85, v.p., asst. to chief exec. officer, 1985-86; v.p. adminstrn. The Perkin-Elmer Corp., Norwalk, 1986—. Bd. dirs. Norwalk and Wilton Red Cross, 1975-85; bd. trustees Norwalk YMCA, 1986; bd. of friends Norwalk Community Coll., 1986—, Fairfield 2000. Woodrow Wilson Nat. Found. fellow, 1959-60. Mem. Econ. Soc. Conn., Nat. Investor Relations Inst., Am. Soc. Personnel Adminstrn., Regional Plan Assn. Com. Clubs: Millrose Athletic Assn. (N.Y.C.), Roton Point (Rowayton, Conn.), Economic (Conn.). Home: 54 Louises Ln New Canaan CT 06840 Office: The Perkin Elmer Corp 871 Main Ave Norwalk CT 06877

GRADISON, HEATHER JANE, government official; b. Houston, Sept. 6, 1952; d. David Lowe Stirton and Dorothy Johanne (Flatt) Cox; m. Willis D. Gradison, Jr., Nov. 29, 1980; children: Maile Jo, Benjamin David, Logan Jane. B.A., Radford U., 1975; postgrad., George Washington U., 1976, 78. Summer intern So. Ry. System, Washington, 1974, mgmt. trainee, market research asst., asst. rate officer, rate officer, 1975-82; mem. ICC, Washington, 1982—; vice chmn. ICC, 1985, chmn., 1985—. Mem. Rep. Congl. Wives Club, Level IV Presdl. Appointees Orgn., Women's Transp. Seminar. Office: ICC Office of Chmn 12th & Constitution Ave NW Washington DC 20423

GRADY, CAROL ANN, nurse; b. Lowell, Mass., June 6, 1942; d. Harry Ephrem and Rena Marion (Rondeau) Ayotte; m. Robert Joseph Grady, Sept. 5, 1964 (div. 1974); 1 child, Sheryl Lynn. Diploma, Somerville Hosp. Sch. Nursing, 1963; grad. Lee Inst. Lic. real estate broker, Mass., N.H.; notary pub. nurse, Cen. Hosp., Somerville, Mass., head nurse ICU, 1986-88; night supr. Long-term Care Facility, Mediplex Lexington, 1988—. Mem. Am. Assn. Critical Care Nurses, Nat. Wilderness Soc., Nat. Audubon Soc., Am. Nurses Assn., Nat. Assn. Female Execs., Am. Soc. Notaries, Mass. Nurses Assn., Mass. State Rifle and Pistol Assn., Nat. Rifle Assn., Nat. Trust for Historic Preservation. Lodge: Rosicrucians. Home: 126 Clifton St Malden MA 02148

GRADY, DOROTHY HOLLAND, small business owner, interior designer; b. Dunn, N.C., Sept. 27, 1932; d. Marvin B. and Vada Mae (Warren) Holland; m. Forrest C. Shaw II, Aug. 20, 1963 (div. Jan. 1979); children: Forrest C. Shaw III, Gloria R. Shaw Whiteheart; m. Roy C. Grady, Oct. 4, 1987. Owner Dot's Drive-In, Spring Lake, N.C., 1961-85, Star-Light Restuarant, Spring Lake, 1963-64, Continental Beauty Salon, Spring Lake, 1964-65, Heritage Tea Room, Fayetteville, N.C., 1967—; v.p. Shaw Real Estate, Fayetteville, 1975—, So. Furniture, Fayetteville, 1976—. Counselor Girl Scouts U.S., Fayetteville, 1959-61; precinct worker Fayetteville Dems., 1973-76; mem. Cape Fear Valley Hosp. Aux., Fayetteville, 1975-76. Mem. Interior Design Soc., Lafayette Soc. Methodist. Home: 3301 Lennox Dr Fayetteville NC 28303 Office: So Furniture 1983 Skibo Rd Fayetteville NC 28304

GRAEB, THELMA SAVARD, registered representative, insurance agent; b. Rochester, N.Y., July 16, 1934; d. Basil Eugene and Thelma Lucile (Daus) Savard; B.S., Syracuse U., 1956, Ph.D., 1974; M.A., Northwestern U., 1958; ins. cert. Am. Coll., Bryn Mawr, Pa., 1986; m. Harold Sigfreid Graeb, Jr., July 19, 1958; children—Bruce, Jacqueline, Sharon, T. Randall. C.L.U. Supr., Hearing and Speech Center, Yale Sch. Medicine, New Haven, 1956-57; pvt. practice speech pathology, Newport, R.I., 1959-62; supr. hearing and speech Suffolk Rehab. Center for the Physically Handicapped, Inc., Commack, N.Y., 1963-66; asst. prof. spl. edn. N.J. State Coll., Jersey City, 1966-67; cons. speech and hearing dept. Mountainside Hosp., Montclair, N.J., 1967-69; dir., div. audiology Hearing & Speech Center of Rochester (N.Y.), Inc., 1969-71; U.S. Office Edn. fellow Syracuse U., 1971-73, dir. BOCES, 1973-75; ednl. cons. Organizational Change & Staff Devel., Manlius, N.Y., 1976; prin. Rockwell Elem. Sch., Nedrow, N.Y., from 1976; agt. Donohue Mapstone Agy., Equitable Fin. Cos., Syracuse, N.Y., 1985—; dir. Environ. Tech., Inc., Buffalo. Mem. Am. Assn. Sch. Adminstrs., Nat. Council for Exceptional Children, Am. Speech and Hearing Assn., Assn. Profl. Women in Mgmt., Nat. Assn. Women Bus. Owners, Million Dollar Round Table, Nat. Assn. Life Underwriters, Greater Syracuse C. of C. (pres.' cabinet), Phi Delta Kappa, Pi Lambda Theta, Zeta Phi Eta, Kappa Alpha Theta. Contbr. articles to profl. jours. Home: 7619 Glencliffe Rd Manlius NY 13104 Office: Donohue-Mapstone Agy 120 Madison St Suite 1200 Syracuse NY 13202

GRAEBE, ANNETTE MULVANY, university administrator, educator; b. Benton, Ill., Feb. 11, 1943; d. Augusta (Magnabosco) Mulvany; m. William Fredrick Graebe, Jr., Feb. 23, 1974; 1 child, Justin William. B.S., So. Ill. U.-Carbondale, 1962, M.A., 1964. Research asst., speech instr. So. Ill. U.-Carbondale, 1962-64; chmn. speech and theater dept. McKendree Coll., Lebanon, Ill., 1964-68; dir. info. center, So. Ill. U., Edwardsville, 1968—, assoc. prof. speech communication, 1968—, mem. faculty bd. govs.; cons. communications, pub. speaker. Coordinator Edwardsville Autumn Festival Children. Recipient Ill. and U.S. Bicentennial Commn. citation, 1976, Council Advancement and Support of Edn. exceptional achievement community relations award, Washington, 1976, 77, 81, Toronto, Can., 1982, Silver Medal for Pub. Relations Projects, Council Advancement and Support of Edn., 1986, Bronze Quill award Internat. Assn. Bus. Communicators, 1986; named Outstanding Faculty Adviser, Pub. Relations Soc. Am., 1982; named Woman of Year, Bus. and Profl. Women's Club, Edwardsville, 1983, Outstanding Faculty Advisor of Midwest Pub. Relations Student Soc. Am., 1988. Mem. Pub. Relations Soc. Am. (edn. chmn., treas., bd. dirs. St. Louis chpt. 1987-88), Univ. Ambassadors (hon.), Pi Kappa Delta, Kappa Delta Pi, Zeta Phi Eta, Alpha Phi Omega. Contbr. articles to profl. jours.; book reviewer. Office: So Ill U Campus Box 1017 Edwardsville IL 62026

GRAEBNER, LINDA SUSAN, marketing executive; b. Lakewood, Ohio, Mar. 28, 1950; d. Herman F. and Marilynn J. (Baumer) G.; m. Vincent L. Schantz, June 13, 1981; 1 child, Tracy L. BS, Purdue U., 1972; MBA, Stanford (Calif.) U., 1974. Cons. Guffenhagen-Kroeger, San Francisco, 1974-75; cons. Booz Allen & Hamilton, San Francisco, 1975-77, assoc., 1977-79; bus. planning assoc. Crown Zellerbach Corp., San Francisco, 1979-80, mgr. bus. planning, 1980-81, dir. mktg., 1981-85, dir. mktg. and bus. devel., 1985-88; v.p. strategy and bus. integration Dole Food Co., San Francisco, 1988—. Mem. commn. Bay Area Council, San Francisco, 1980-82; mgr. corp. campaign United Way, San Francisco, 1983. Office: Dole Food Co 50 California St San Francisco CA 94111

GRAEFE, SUSAN WEBER, social worker, psychotherapist; b. New Britain, Conn., July 19, 1945; d. Samuel Lewis and Norma Margaret (Hein) Weber; m. Richard F. Graefe, June 17, 1967; children—Karin Elizabeth, Christopher William. B.A., Wilson Coll., Chambersburg, Pa., 1967; M.S.W., U. Pitts., 1969. Psychiat. social worker Western Psychiat. Inst. and Clinic, Pitts., 1969-71; clin. social worker St. Francis Hosp. Community Mental Health Center, Pitts., 1972-76; pediatric social worker R.I. Hosp., Providence, 1976; clin. social worker Providence Mental Health, 1976-78, coordinator elderly services, 1978-83; psychiat. social worker Family Inst. R.I., Warwick, 1983—. Leader R.I. council Girl Scouts U.S.A., North Kingstown, 1980-83; bd. dirs., v.p. Tockwotton Home, 1984-86. Recipient Eleanor Slater award R.I. Coll. Gerontology Ctr., 1983. Mem. Nat. Assn. Social Workers (sec. R.I. chpt. 1982-85), Acad. Cert. Social Workers, Am. Group Psychotherapy Assn., N.E. Gerontol. Soc. Democrat. Unitarian-Universalist. Clubs: Wilson Coll. (sec. 1981—) (Boston); Appalacian Mountain. Home: 70 Meadowland Dr North Kingstown RI 02852 Office: Family Inst RI 335E Centerville Rd Warwick RI 02886

GRAESCH, ALICE IRENE, banker; b. Maynard, Iowa, Mar. 8, 1930; d. George Edward and Irene Esther Trower; student public schs., Maynard; m. Walter R. Graesch, Mar. 11, 1951; children—Allan Lee, Marcia Ann Graesch Hughson. With Oelwein State Bank (Iowa), 1947-50, 53—, asst. cashier, 1971-79, asst. v.p., 1979—; with Security State Bank, San Diego, 1951-52. Republican. Lutheran. Home: Rural Route 1 Box 66 Maynard IA 50655 Office: Oelwein State Bank Oelwein IA 50662

GRAESE, JUDITH ANN, visual and performance artist; b. Loveland, Colo., Nov. 8, 1940; d. Erwin Herman John and Hildegarde Christina (Spieler) G. Student, Augustana Coll., Sioux Falls, S.D., 1958-59, U. Colo., 1964-67. Artist Rocky Mountain Pottery, Loveland, 1956-59; display artist, designer Neusteters, Denver, 1959-62; instr. modern dance N.Mex. State U., Las Cruces, 1963-64; display artist, designer May Co., Denver, 1964-69; artist Denver, 1967—; choreographer, costumer Third Eye Theatre, Denver, 1968-73; dancer, actress, costumer Murray Louis Dance Co., N.Y.C., 1976; instr. modern dance Kent Denver Country Day Sch., 1968—; co-founder Colo. Contemporary Dance, Denver, 1973, sec. 1985—. Illustrator: (books) The Treasure is the Rose, 1973, The Song of Francis, 1973. Democrat. Home and Office: 2055 S Franklin Denver CO 80210

GRAF, DOROTHY ANN, business executive; b. Nashville, Mar. 21, 1935; d. Henry George and Martha Dunlap (Hill) Meek; student Montgomery Coll., 1979—; m. Peter Louis Graf, Oct. 28, 1971; children—Sidney E. Pollard, Deborah Lynn Pollard, Robert George Pollard, Michelle Joy Graf. Office mgr. Pa. Life Ins. Co., Miami and Dallas, 1957-72; exec. sec. to med. dir. Pitts. Children's Hosp., 1974; sec. G.E./TEMPO, Washington, 1974-76; adminstrv. asst. to sr. v.p. Logistics Mgmt. Inst., Washington, 1976-81, dir. adminstrv. services, 1981—; dir. KHI Services, Inc. Mem. Washington Tech. Personnel Forum. Democrat. Baptist. Home: 10000 Stedwick Rd Unit 303 Gaithersburgh MD 20879 Office: 6400 Goldsboro Rd Bethesda MD 75886

GRAFFO, KAREN FRANCES, sales executive; b. Birmingham, Ala., July 6, 1956; d. Joe Lawrence and Helen Marie (George) G. AA, Valencia Community Coll., 1976; student, U. Cen. Fla., 1977-78, U. South Fla., 1979-80. With sales dept. Burdines, Orlando, Fla., 1974, J.C. Penney, Winter Park, Fla., 1977; money-counter Walt Disney World, Lake Buena Vista, Fla., 1975-76; policy analyst So. Security Life, Altamonte Springs, Fla., 1978; claims clk. St. Paul Fire and Marine, Winter Park, Fla., 1979; user support technician U. Commnunity Hosp., Tampa, Fla., 1980-83; customer support rep. Travenol, Annson Systems, Tampa, 1983-85; dist. support mgr. Kansas City, 1985—. Vol., tchr. Head Start Program, Orlando, 1977. Mem. Nat. Assn., Female Exec., Inc. Republican. Roman Catholic. Home: 9816 W 118th St #3 Overland Park KS 66210 Office: Annson Systems 11300 Glenwood Overland Park KS 66211

GRAGG, SARA ELIZABETH, motel executive; b. Malvern, Ark., Mar. 28, 1930; d. Alymer James and Martha Thelma (Cross) Wells; m. Glen E. Keller, Dec. 18, 1949 (div. 1964); children—Michael, Kathryn, Kim; m. Paris R. Green, Sept. 15, 1968 (dec. 1969); m. Billy Max Gragg, May 14, 1970. B.A., U. Ark., 1949, M.A., 1950, Ph.D., 1971. Exec. asst. dept. psychiatry U. Ark. Med. Ctr., Little Rock, 1951-56; asst. prof. English Ark. State U., Jonesboro, 1962-66; instr. English dept. U. Ark.-Fayetteville, 1966-69; asst. prof. U. Mo.-Rolla, 1968; pres. Gragg Motels, Inc., Fayetteville, 1970—. Author: The Artistic Unity of Carlyle's French Revolution, 1971. Pres. Ark. Med. Soc. Aux., Jonesboro, 1963-64; Republican county chmn., Jonesboro, 1962-63. Named Woman of Yr., Bus and Profl. Women, Mountain View, Ark., 1961. Mem. Ark. Motel Assn., Am. Hotel and Motel Assn., Ark. Retail Mchts. Assn., Fayetteville C. of C., Phi Beta Kappa, Lambda Tau, Psi Chi. Methodist. Avocations: writing; travelling. Home: Route 11 Smokehouse Rd Fayetteville AR 72701 Office: Gragg Motels Inc 215-229 N College St Fayetteville AR 72701

GRAH, KAREN ELIZABETH, military officer; b. Phila., Mar. 10, 1953; d. Ernest and Margaret (Alper) G. BA in Psychology, Columbia Coll., 1979; postgrad., Webster U., 1984-85. Enlisted USN, 1972, advanced through grades to lt., 1983; adminstrv. officer, asst. intelligence officer Strike Fighter Squadron, Lemoore, Calif., 1980-84; personnel officer Service Sch. Command, Great Lakes Naval Base, Ill., 1984-87; chief testing mgmt. El Paso (Tex.) Mil. Entrance Processing Sta., 1987—. Republican. Methodist. Home: 5852 Devontry El Paso TX 79934 Office: El Paso MEPS 700 E San Antonio El Paso TX 79901

GRAHAM, ALBERTA NEWSOME, personnel specialist; b. Quitman, Ga., Sept. 1, 1955; d. Ted and Mamie (Newsome) Davis; m. Alfred Graham, Oct. 29, 1983; children: Tangela Adams, Rashaan Nicole. Cert., Valdosta State Coll., 1981, BBA in Mgmt., 1985. Clk. Ga. Power Co., Valdosta, 1981, sec., 1983-84, personnel specialist, 1984—. Chmn. United Way of Ga. Power Co., Valdosta, 1985-86; mem. Laurel St. Ch. of Christ, Quitman, Ga. Mem. Profl. Secretarial Internat., Women of Ga. Power (corr. sec. 1987—, 2d v.p. 1988—, chmn.), Zeta Phi Beta. Democrat. Home: 908 Bethune St Valdosta GA 31601 Office: Ga Power Co 901 N Patterson St Valdosta GA 31601

GRAHAM, CAROL ELIZABETH, psychology educator, administrator; b. Kingston, N.Y., Dec. 25, 1941; d. John Joseph Connors and Ellen Caroline (Ensign) Keresman; m. Alex Lon Graham, Mar. 19, 1964 (div. 1976); children—Alex Lon, Ellen Katherine. B.S., Troy State U., 1975, M.S., 1976, 83. Nat. cert. counselor. Coordinator prep. program Troy State U., Montgomery, Ala., 1975-76, acad. counselor and instr. psychology, 1976-78, dir. admissions and records, registrar European div., Wiesbaden, W.Ger., 1978-80, asst. prof. psychology, registrar, Ft. Benning, Ga., 1980-86 , chmn. Gen. Studies Program, 1986—, assoc. prof. psychol., 1986—. Mem. Troy State U. Personnel Assn. (faculty advisor student chpt. 1982—), Columbus Area Personnel Assn. (faculty advisor to Troy State U. student chpt. 1982—), Am. Assn. Counseling and Devel. (Ga. chpt.), Columbus Area Network Assn. Republican. Methodist. Home: Rt 1 Box 260 Waverly Hall GA 31831 Office: Troy State Univ PO Box 2456 Fort Benning GA 31905

GRAHAM, CAROL ETHLYN, insurance company administrator; b. Guthrie, Okla., Nov. 28, 1941; d. Brance Alma Woodard and Rachel Ione (Brown) Meininger; m. Morton J. Graham Dec. 14, 1965 (div. Apr. 1985); children: Brance D., Kelly L., S. Robert, M. Jeff III. AS in Civil Tech., Okla. State U.-Tech. Inst., 1978; cert. in flood plain analysis, U. Okla., 1979. Cert. premium auditor, Okla. Factory worker Aero Comdr., Bethany, Okla., 1963-66; legal asst. Whit Ingram Atty., Oklahoma City, 1966-75; bookkeeper Joe Roselle Atty., Oklahoma City, 1966-78; hydraulic analyst Cunningham Cons. Inc., Oklahoma City, 1978-80; premium auditor loss control Atwell, Vogel and Sterling, Dallas, 1982-83; premium auditor Mid-Continent Casualty Co., Tulsa, 1983—. Mem. Ins. Auditors Assn. Oklahoma City (sec. 1985-86, pres. 1986-87), Ins. Auditors Assn. of S.W., Nat. Assn. Female Execs., Women Execs. Cen. Okla. Democrat. Home: PO Box 1613 Guthrie OK 73044 Office: Mid-Continent Casualty Co 1646 S Boulder PO Box 1409 Tulsa OK 74101

GRAHAM, CELESTE MARILYN GOTCHER, business executive; b. Santa Monica, Calif., July 12, 1937; d. Leslie Louis and Winnie Viola (Miller) Gotcher; B.A. in Sociology, Calif. State U., Los Angeles, 1974; divorced; children—Leslie Dawn, Cindy Celeste, Wendy Ione, Linda Marie. Propr., C. Graham Graphics, Santa Monica, 1977—; editor Illumination mag., 1979—; adminstrv. dir. Inst. Psycho-Dynamics, Inc., Fla., 1975—; pres. Hawk

Diversified; dir. Celestial Visions Software Pub. Corp.; instr. Fla. Dept. Recreation, 1976-77; dir. info. mgmt. and graphics U. So. Calif. Sch. Music, 1983-86; pres., Coll. Fin. Aid Found. Author: Layman's Guide to Enlightenment, or Cosmic Consciousness on the American Plan, 1980; Residential Treatment System for the Chronically Mentally Ill, 1981; The Utilization of Graying America, 1981; (fiction) Love in High Places, 1986, Dos Does It, 1987; co-author: American Square Dancing, 1961. Originator techniques for meditation. Home and Office: 3175 S Hoover St 513 Los Angeles CA 90007

GRAHAM, CHRISTINE PRISCILLA, foundation administrator; b. Bklyn., July 19, 1947; d. David and Audrey C. (Eurich) G.; m. Louis Calabro, Dec. 19, 1976; children: Finnegan John, Max David. BA, Bennington (Vt.) Coll., 1969; MEd, Antioch Sch., 1982. Dir. devel. Hoosac Sch., Hoosick, N.Y., 1973-76, 1973-76; dir. coll. relations and spl. projects Hoosac Sch., 1976-82; pres. CPG Enterprises, Shaftsbury, Vt., 1982—; coordinator Gov's. Inst. Vt., Shaftsbury, 1983—. Editor: Nonprofit Vermont and Vermont Directory of Founds., 1985—; contbr. articles to mags.; presenter workshops in field. founder and mgr. Sage City Symphony, Vt., 1973—; trustee Vt. Council on the Arts, 1982-85; trustee Preservation Trust of Vt., 1987. Recipient citation Vt. Council on the Arts, 1986. Mem. Women Bus. Owners Vt. Office: CPG Enterprises One Main St Box 199 Shaftsbury VT 05262

GRAHAM, DEBORAH JANE, psychologist, consultant; b. Uvalde, Tex., Oct. 29, 1953; d. Archie Jackson Graham and Della Jane (Reitzer) Holland. BS, Baylor U., 1976; MA, Azusa (Calif.) Pacific U., 1980; PhD, U.S. Internat. U., 1982. Dir. youth program T Bar M Racquet Clubs, Inc., Dallas, 1976-77; instr. Newport-Mesa Sch. Dist., Newport Beach, Calif., 1977-79; marriage and family therapist Lister Psychol. Services, Costa Mesa, Calif., 1979-82, psychologist, sport psychologist, 1982-87; coordinator disabled student programs and services North Orange County Community Coll. Dist., Fullerton, Calif., 1979-86; dir., cons., sports psychologist Internat. Sports Cons., Costa Mesa, 1985—. Author: Analysis of Personalities of Professional Golfers, 1982, Analysis of Personalities of Champion Professional Race Car Drivers. Mem. Am. Psychol. Assn., Am. Coll. Sports Medicine, Am. Assn. Marriage, Family and Child Therapists, Am. Orthopsychiat. Assn., Pres.'s Com. for Employment of the Handicapped, Am. Legion, Delta Psi Kappa. Baptist. Home and Office: Internat Sports Cons 2790 Harbor Blvd Suite 210 Costa Mesa CA 92626

GRAHAM, JENNIFER C., interior designer; b. Bridgetown, Barbados, Apr. 30, 1968; d. Albert C. and and Margaret L. (McCurdy) (stepmother) G. BFA in Interior Architecture, N.Y. Sch. Interior Design, 1985, Design diploma, 1984; student, Hunter Coll., 1984-85. Asst. mgr. designer Alleyne, Aguilar & Altman, Real Estate Developers, Barbados, 1981-82; draftsperson Edmund Mothka Assocs., N.Y.C., 1983-85; project mgr. ITHA Internat., N.Y.C., 1985-85; designer Interior Resources Internat., N.Y.C., 1985-86; assoc. interior designer Total Concept N.Y., Inc., N.Y.C., 1986—; cons. R. Protas Assocs., N.Y.C., 1986—; coordinator program Acad. Environ. Scis., N.Y.C., 1985. Mem. Waterside Volleyball League. Recipient Service award N.Y. State Soc. Interior Designers, 1984. Mem. Nat. Assn. Female Execs., Am. Soc. Interior Designers (asst. coordinator mentor program 1986). Mem. Anglican Ch. Club: Barbados Equestrian Assn. Home: 20 Waterside Plaza New York NY 10010 Office: Total Concept NY Inc 12 East 49th St Tower 49 New York NY 10017

GRAHAM, KATHARINE, newspaper executive; b. N.Y.C., June 16, 1917; d. Eugene and Agnes (Ernst) Meyer; m. Philip L. Graham, June 5, 1940 (dec. 1963); children: Elizabeth Morris Graham Weymouth, Donald Edward, William Welsh, Stephen Meyer. Student, Vassar Coll., 1934-36; AB, U. Chgo., 1938. Reporter San Francisco News, 1938-39; mem. editorial staff Washington Post, 1939-45, mem. Sunday, circulation and editorial depts., pub., 1968-79; pres. Washington Post Co., 1963-73, 77, chmn. bd., 1973—; bd. dirs. Bowater Mersey Paper Co., Ltd., Urban Inst., Fed. City Council, Conf. Bd. Trustee U. Chgo., George Washington U. Mem. Am. Soc. Newspaper Editors, Nat. Press Club, Sigma Delta Chi. Clubs: Cosmopolitan (N.Y.C.); 1925 F Street. Office: Washington Post Co 1150 15th St NW Washington DC 20071

GRAHAM, LAURA MARGARET (LAURA GRAHAM FORBES), artist; b. Washington, Ind.; d. Ray Austin and Eugenia Bruce (Winston) Graham; student Sacred Heart Convents (Grosse Pointe, Mich., Noroton, Conn., N.Y.C.) Westover and Nightingale Schs.; studied art Art Students League, with Bridgman and Frank du Mond; Grand Central Art Sch.; Traphagen Art Sch.; pvt. study with Mead Schaeffer, Henry Rittenberg, N.A. and Edward Dufner, N.A.; grad. Sch. Adult Edn., N.Y. U., 1965; m. Clifford Lee Forbes, May 4, 1940 (div.); 1 son. Exhibited paintings John Herron Art Mus., Indpls., N.Y. Water Color Club, Am. Water Color Soc., N.A.D. (youngest artist exhibiting Nov. 1932), Pa. Acad. Boston Art Club, Montclair Art Mus., World's Fair 1940, Contemporary Art Bldg., Conn. Acad. Fine Arts Exhibit, Allied Arts of Am., Ogunquit (Maine) Art Center, 50th Anniversary Celebration Westover Sch., Newport Art Assn., Nat. Arts Club. A sponsor N.Y. U. Chamber Music Concert, 1954—, concerts in Washington Sq. Park, 1954-55. Recipient Alexander Wall prize, 1943, Allied Artists Am. exhbn., N.Y. Nat. Arts Club, 1st prize for painting, 1939; 2d prize, 1940, 41, hon. mention, 1947, 48, 72; hon. mention Allied Artists, 1948, Art Assn. Ogunquit, Maine, 1947, 49; hon. mention and war bond, Terry Art Exhbn., Miami, Fla., 1952. Mem. Nat. Assn. Women Artists, Allied Artists of Am. (hon. artist mem.), Conn. Acad. Fine Arts (artist mem.), N.Y. U. Alumni Assn., N.Y. Hist. Soc., Museum City N.Y., Nat. Trust Historic Preservation, Victorian Soc. Am., English Speaking Union, Friends of the Philharmonic, Am. Artists Profl. League, Art Students League (life). Clubs: Nat. Arts, Pen and Brush, Women's Nat. Republican (N.Y.C.). Address: 10 Washington Sq N New York NY 10003

GRAHAM, LOLA AMANDA (BEALL) (MRS. JOHN JACKSON GRAHAM), photographer, author; b. nr. Bremen, Ga., Nov. 12, 1896; d. John Gainer and Nancy Caroline Idella (Reid) Beall; student Florence Normal Sch., 1914; m. John Jackson Graham, Aug. 3, 1917 (dec.); children—Billy Duane, John Thomas, Helen (Mrs. D. Hall), Donald, Beverly (Mrs. Bob Forson). Tchr. elem. public sch., Centerdale, Ala., 1914, Eva, Ala., 1915; free lance photographer and writer, 1950—; editor poetry column Mobile Home News, 1968-69; designer jacket cover for Reader's Digest book Our Amazing World of Nature. Recipient numerous nat. prizes, 1950—; Crossroads of Tex. grand nat. in poetry for For Every Monkey Child, 1980; executed prize-winning Sioux Indian and heirloom photog. quilts. Mem. Nat. Poetry Soc. Ina Coolbrith Poetry Soc., Chapparal Poets. Author: (booklet) How to Recycle Ancestors and Grandcestors, (poetry) Recycling Center, 1988. Contbr. photographs to Ency. Brit., also numerous mags. and books. Address: 225-93 Mount Hermon Rd Scotts Valley CA 95066

GRAHAM, LYNDSAY, advertising executive; b. London, June 3, 1948; d. Maitland Fozard and Doreen Iris (Rawlings) Harding; m. Ian Paterson Graham, May 1, 1971; children: Robert Harding, Jaclyn Sarah. BBA, Bromsgrove Coll., Eng., 1966. Exec. asst. to mng. dir. Lenco A.G., Berne, Switzerland, 1970-71; mgr. Olympic Trust of Can., Toronto, Ont., 1971—; v.p., sec.-treas. Specialty Air Svcs., Inc., Toronto, 1980—. Office: Specialty Air Services Inc, Toronto Island Airport, Toronto, ON Canada M5V 1A1

GRAHAM, MARTHA, dancer, choreographer; b. Pitts., May 11, 1894. Studied with Ruth St. Denis and Ted Shawn; LL.D., Mills Coll., Brandeis U., Smith Coll., Harvard, 1966, also numerous others. Faculty Eastman Sch., 1925. Soloist, Denishawn Co., 1920, Greenwich Village Follies, 1923, debut as choreographer-dancer, 48th St. Theatre, N.Y.C., 1926; founder, artistic dir., Martha Graham Dance Co., 1926—, also Martha Graham Sch. Contemporary Dance; choreographer with music composed by Aaron Copland, Paul Hindemith, Carlos Chavez, Samuel Barber, Gian-Carlo Menotti, William Schuman, others of more than 170 works including Appalachian Spring, Cave of the Heart, Errand into the Maze, Clytemnestra, Frontier, Phaedra, Herodiade, Primitive Mysteries, Night Journey, Seraphic Dialogue, Lamentation, Acts of Light, Rite of Spring, Judith, Heretic, Diversion of Angels, Witch of Endor, Cortege of Eagles, A Time of Snow, Plain of Prayer, Lady of the House of Sleep, Archaic Hours, Mendicants of Evening, Myth of a Voyage, Holy Jungle, Dream, Chronique, Lucifer, Scarlet Letter, Adorations, Point of Crossing; guest soloist leading U.S. orchs. in solos Judith, Triumph of St. Joan; fgn. tours with Martha Graham Dance Co., 1950, 54, 55-56, 60, 62-63, 67, 68; some under auspices U.S. Dept State; collaborated in over 25 set designs with Isamu Naguchi, also Alexander Calder; also designed costumes for many of her dances; Author: Notebooks of Martha Graham, 1973. Recipient Aspen award, 1965, Creative Arts award, Brandeis U., 1968, Disting. Service to the Arts award, Nat. Inst. Arts and Letters, 1970, Handel medallion, City of N.Y., 1970, N.Y. State Council on Arts award, 1973, Presdl. Medal of Freedom, 1976, Kennedy Center honor, 1979, Samuel H. Scripps Am. Dance Festival award, 1981, Meadows award, So. Meth. U., 1982, Gold Florin, City of Florence, 1983, Paris Medal of Honor, 1985, Arnold Gingrich Memorial award, N.Y. Arts and Bus. Council, 1985, Nat. Medal for Arts, 1985, Decorated knight Legion of Honor (France), 1983; Guggenheim fellow, 1932. Office: Martha Graham Dance Co 316 E 63d St New York NY 10021

GRAHAM, NANCY KEOGH, psychotraumatologist, consultant; b. Chgo., July 12, 1932; d. Frank Belfort and Dorothy Elizabeth (Cavanaugh) Keogh; m. Edward Ralph Graham, May 12, 1956 (div. 1972); children—Scott, Ted, Sarah. Student Stanford U., 1949-51; B.S., Northwestern U., 1953; M.A., Azusa-Pacific U., 1978. Cert. marriage and family therapist. Copywriter, Young & Rubicam, N.Y.C., 1953-59; clin. assoc. Suicide Prevention Center, Los Angeles, 1971-74; med. social worker St. Francis Med. Ctr., Lynwood, Calif., 1974-76; psychotraumatologist, 1976—; asst. prof. grad. nursing program Calif. State U., Long Beach, 1979-84; guest instr. Los Angeles County Paramedic Tng. Inst., Torrance, 1977—; cons. Hosp. Satellite Network. Contbr. chpt. to book, articles to profl. jours. Mem. Psychosocial Clinicians in Emergency Medicine (dir.), Calif. Rescue and Paramedic Assn., Stanford Profl. Women. Democrat. Office: St Francis Med Ctr 3630 Imperial Hwy Lynwood CA 90262

GRAHAM, PATRICIA ALBJERG, educator; b. Lafayette, Ind., Feb. 9, 1935; d. Victor L. and Marguerite (Hall) Albjerg; m. Loren R. Graham, Sept. 6, 1955; 1 child, Marguerite Elizabeth. B.S., Purdue U., 1955, M.S., 1957, D.Lett. (hon.), 1980; Ph.D., Columbia U., 1964; M.A. (hon.), Harvard U., 1974; D.H.L. (hon.), Manhattanville Coll., 1976; LL.D. (hon.), Beloit Coll., 1977, Clark U., 1978; D.P.A. (hon.), Suffolk U., 1978, Ind. U., 1980; D.Litt. (hon.), St. Norbert Coll., 1980; D.H. (hon.), Emmanuel Coll., 1983; D.H.L. (hon.), No. Mich. U., 1987. Tchr. high sch. Norfolk, Va., 1955-56, 57-58, N.Y.C., 1958-60; lectr., asst. prof. Ind. U., 1964-66; asst. prof. history of edn. Barnard Coll. and Columbia Tchrs. Coll., N.Y.C., 1965-68; assoc. prof. Barnard Coll. and Columbia Tchrs. Coll., 1968-72, prof., 1972-74; dean Radcliffe Inst., 1974-77; also v.p. Radcliffe Coll., Cambridge, Mass., 1976-77; prof. Harvard U., Cambridge, Mass., 1974-79, Warren prof., 1979—; dean Grad. Sch. Edn. 1982—; dir. Nat. Inst. Edn., Washington, 1977-79, trustee Northwestern Mut. Life., 1980—. Author: Progressive Education: From Arcady to Academe, 1967, Community and Class in American Education: 1865-1918, 1974. Bd. dirs. Dalton Sch., 1973-76, Josiah Macy, Jr. Found., 1976-77, 79—; trustee Beloit Coll., 1976-77, 79-82, Found. for Teaching Econs., 1980-87; dir. Spencer Found., 1983—, Johnson Found., 1983—, Carnegie Found. for the Advancement of Teaching, 1984—. Am. Council on Edn. fellow Princeton U., 1969-70. Mem. Sci. Research Assocs. (dir. 1980—), Nat. Acad. Edn. (pres. 1985—), Am. Hist. Assn. (v.p. 1985—), Phi Beta Kappa. Episcopalian. Office: Harvard U Grad Sch Edn Cambridge MA 02138

GRAHAM, POLLY ANN, automobile dealership executive; b. Conway, S.C., Mar. 18, 1938; d. William David and Ina Mae (Hardee) Harrell; m. William Paul Graham, Feb. 29, 1956. Student pub. schs. Bus. mgr. Pinckney Volkswagen, Pensacola, Fla., 1972-75, Carroll Motors, Conway, 1975-79, Hewett Chevrolet Corp., Myrtle Beach, S.C., 1981-86; office mgr. Scott Cars of Myrtle Beach, Inc., 1986—. Recipient cert. of excellence Chevrolet Corp., Charlotte, N.C., 1983-86. Fellow Am. Soc. Notaries. Baptist. Home: Route 1 Box 167 Conway SC 29526 Office: Scott Cars of Myrtle Beach Inc 1251 Hwy 501 Myrtle Beach SC 29577

GRAHAM, SUSAN MARIE, nurse; b. San Antonio, Tex., Sept. 6, 1948; d. Robert Henry and Doris Inez (Thomas) Vermersch; (div.); children: Lauren Marie, Christopher Michael. Diploma nursing, Brackenridge Hosp., Austin, Tex., 1969; BS in Nursing, U. Tex. Health Sci. Ctr., 1972, MS in Nursing, 1986. Staff nurse Med. Ctr. Hosp., San Antonio, 1969-72, clinician II, 1972-79, per diem coordinator, 1979-80, clinician III, 1980-81, dir. area I, 1981-82, dir. emergency ctr., 1982—. Active Conservation Soc., San Antonio, 1983—, March of Dimes, San Antonio, 1985-86, Alamo Area Rape Crisis Ctr. Mem. Nat. League for Nursing, Emergency Nursing Assn. (sec. San Antonio chpt., pres. 1987), Sigma Theta Tau. Democrat. Roman Catholic. Home: 5514 Ben Hur San Antonio TX 78229 Office: Med Ctr Hosp 4502 Medical Dr San Antonio TX 78284

GRAHAM, WINIFRED CLIO, consulting engineer; b. Lufkin, Tex., Jan. 8, 1933; d. Fred and Lillian (Russell) G. BS in Elec. Engring., La. State U., 1955. Jr. engr. Cen. Power & Light Co., Corpus Christi, Tex., 1955-57; field engr. Gulf Interstate Gas Co., Houston, 1957-59; sr. engr. Packard Bell Computer Co., Los Angeles, 1959-62; project engr. Advance Data Systems, Los Angeles, 1962-64; sr. assoc. Planning Research Corp., Los Angeles, 1964-71; pvt. practice engring. cons. Los Angeles, 1971—; cons. NASA, Washington, 1976—, McDonnell-Douglas Helicopters, Mesa, Ariz., 1973-87. Bd. dirs. Topanga Symphony. Mem. Calif. Native Plant Soc., The Nature Conservancy (conservator). Home and Office: 17201 Lanark St Van Nuys CA 91406

GRAHAME, PAULA EASTER PATTON, artist, writer; b. Clearfield, Iowa; d. Harry T. and Betsey J. (Jacobs) Patton; B.A., U. Iowa, 1926; m. Orville F. Grahame, Nov. 3, 1923; 1 dau., Sarah G. Cairns. Artist, sculptor exhibited Ind. Artists, N.Y.C., Worcester Art Mus., Rockport Art Assn. Bd. dirs. Corporator, Worcester Girls Club; bd. dirs. Worcester Children's Friends Soc., 1963-67, Edward St. Day Nursery, 1954-60, Worcester Youth Guidance Ctr., 1963-66; founder Art Scholarship Fund, U. Iowa. Recipient Disting. Service award U. Iowa, 1969; Rotary Found. fellow. Mem. Nat. Soc. Lit. and Arts, Worcester Hist. Soc., Art Mus., Hudson Hoagland Soc. Worcester Found. Exptl. Biology, Music Festival Assn., Worcester Sci. Mus., Am. Mus. Natural History (asso.), Met. Opera Guild, Worcester Heritage Preservation Soc., Nat., Iowa hist. socs., Assocs. Nat. Archives, Smithsonian Assocs., Rockport Art Assn., AAUW (pres. 1959-61), Soc. Profl. Journalists/Sigma Delta Chi, Nat. Trust for Hist. Preservation, Amigo Orgn. Am. States, Unitarian Universalist Alliance (pres. 1966-68), DAR. Republican. Author: Palimpsest Stories; also short stories, poems; editor Meml. Hosp. News, 1951-54. Co-donor Rodin Statue to Orville and Paula Grahame Courtyard, U. Iowa. Home: 6 Bancroft Tower Rd Worcester MA 01609

GRAHN, BARBARA ASCHER, editor; b. Chgo., Mar. 26, 1929; d. Harry L. and Eleanor (Simon) Ascher; m. Robert D. Grahn, Dec. 23, 1952; children: Susan Grahn Gantz, Nancy Grahn, Wendy Grahn O'Brien. BA, Miami U., Oxford, Ohio, 1950. Promotion dir. George Williams Coll., Chgo., 1950-52; sales mgr. Chatham Mfg., Chgo., 1952-54; research asst. Standard Rate and Data Service, Skokie, Ill., 1968-70, adminstr. editorial services, 1970-75, asst. editor, 1975-77; editor Wilmette, Ill., 1977-87, mng. editor, 1987—. Precinct capt. Ill. Reps., 1956-58; pres. Community Club of Jewish Women, Skokie, 1958-60; bd. dirs., treas. North Shore Towers Condo Assn., Skokie, 1986-87. Mem. Nat. Assn. Female Execs., Chgo. Ad Club, Alpha Epsilon Phi. Office: Standard Rate & Data Service 3004 Glenview Rd Wilmette IL 60091

GRALA, JANE MARIE, account executive; b. Phila.; d. Stanley Frank and Anna Stephanie (Yurkiewicz) Grala. BS, Rutgers U., Camden, 1976; MBA, Winthrop Coll., 1979; postgrad., Am. Mgmt. Assn., N.Y.C., 1980-82, Am. Inst. Real Estate Appraisers, Chgo., 1985. Mgr. acctg. dept. NDI Engring. Co., Pennsauken, N.J., 1968-72, project mgr., 1972-76; rep. sales Am. Cyanamid, Wayne, N.J., 1976-80; dist. mgr. Am. Appraisal Assocs., Phila., 1980-86; account exec. Prudential-Bache Securities, Clearwater, Fla., 1986—. Mem. Nat. Assn Accts (dir. advt. So. Jersey chpt. 1983-86), Assn. MBA Execs., Bus and Profl. Women's Assn. (Westshore chpt.), Nat. Assn. for Female Execs., Chi Delta, Phi Chi Theta. Republican. Office: Prudential-Bache Securities 2536 Countryside Blvd Suite 110 Clearwater FL 34623

GRAM, JO ANN, trade association executive; b. Summersville, W.Va., Oct. 24, 1939; d. Mildred Garrett; m. Jerry R. Gram, Dec. 14, 1959 (div. 1983); children: Robin, Dawn, Richard, David, Sherri. Grad. high sch., 1959. With Albert Pick Hotels, Columbus, Ohio, 1960-73; successively gen. office, trade paper editor, asst. exec. v.p. Indep. Sewing Machine Dealers Assn., Columbus, Ohio, 1973-85, exec. v.p., 1985—. Troop leader Camp Fire Girls, Columbus, Ohio, 1965, Girl Scouts U.S., Columbus, Ohio, 1975. Mem. Nat. Assn. Female Execs., Am. Soc. Assn. Execs., Women's Internat. Bowling Congress. Republican. Lodge: Moose. Office: Ind Sewing Machine Dealers Assn PO Box 338 Hilliard OH 43026

GRAMLICH, JEAN MCDOUGALL, clinical psychologist; b. Buffalo, Apr. 5, 1938; d. Arnott Alexander and Jean (McDougall) Moore; m. Michael J. Gramlich, Sept. 28, 1963 (div. Jan. 1975); children: Bryan, Scott. BA with high honors, Swarthmore (Pa.) Coll., 1959; MEd, SUNY, Geneseo, 1961; MA, Oakland U., Rochester, Mich., 1975; PhD, U. Detroit, 1983. Lic. psychologist, Mich. Children's librarian Rochester (N.Y.) Pub. Library, 1959-61; head circulation dept. Swarthmore Coll. Library, 1962-64; dir. community orgns. OEO Franklin County, Greenfield, Mass., 1968-69, dir. social work operation head start, 1967-69; head librarian Roeper Sch., Bloomfield Hills, Mich., 1973-75; vocat. tester State of Mich., Mt. Clemens, 1974-76; psychologist Substance Abuse Ctr., St. Clair Shores, Mich., 1975-77, Oakland County Community Mental Health Clinic, Pontiac, Mich., 1977—; pvt. practice psychology Birmingham, Mich., 1985—; cons. Counseling Resource Ctr., Walled Lake, Mich., 1984—; mem.adv. bd. Havenwyck Hosp., Auburn Hills, Mich., 1986—. Mem. Am. Psychol. Assn., Phi Beta Kappa. Home: 1732 Bradford Dr Birmingham MI 48008 Office: Oakland County Child and Adolescent Clinic 31 Oakland Ave Suite B Pontiac MI 48058

GRAMM, WENDY LEE, government official; d. Joshua and Angeline (AnChin) Lee; m. Phil Gramm, Nov. 2, 1970; children—Marshall Kenneth, Jefferson Philip. B.A. in Econs., Wellesley Coll., 1966; Ph.D. in Econs., Northwestern U., 1970. Staff dept. quantitive methods U. Ill., 1969; asst. prof. Tex. A&M U., 1970-74, assoc. prof. dept. econs., 1975-79; research staff Inst. Def. Analyses, 1979-82; asst. dir. Bur. Econs., FTC, 1982-83, dir., 1983-85; adminstr. Office Info. and Regulatory Affairs, OMB, 1985-87; chmn. Commodity Futures Trading Commision, 1988—. Contbr. articles to profl. jours. Address: Commodity Futures Trading Commn Office of the Chairman 2033 K St NW Washington DC 20581

GRANADOS, CANDACE MICHELE, physical therapist; b. Albuquerque, Nov. 5, 1958; d. Lewis Ray and Pristina (Chavez) G. BS in Phys. Therapy, U. N.Mex., 1981. Chief phys. therapist CHI, Albuquerque, 1981; adminstr. Sports Phys. Therapy & Rehab., Albuquerque, 1982-83; v.p. N.Mex. Phys. Therapist Inc., Albuquerque, 1983—; v.p. Northeastern NMPT Inc.; mem. admissions com. U. N.Mex. Dept. Phys. Therapy, 1982—, mem. clin. edn. staff, 1982—; com. Bernalillo County Sports Medicine Com., 1986—; bd. dirs. N.Mex. Phys. Therapist Inc., Northeastern N.Mex. Phys. Therapist Inc. Mem. C. of C., Am. Phys. Therapy Assn., Nat. Assn. Female Execs., N.Mex. Phys. Therapy Assn., Albuquerque Medicine/Bus. Coalition, Am. Coll. Sports Medicine. Democrat. Roman Catholic. Avocations: water skiing, jogging, weight training, racquetball. Office: S Star Route Box 4088 Corrales NM 87048

GRAND, MARCIA, civic worker; b. N.Y.C., Aug. 9, 1933; d. Irving and Dorothy (Miller) Kosta; m. Richard Grand, Jan. 27, 1952; 1 child, Cindy Deborah. Student U. Ariz., 1950-52, 59-60. Docent, coordinator, docent trainer Tucson Mus. Art, 1965-71, chmn. edn. com., 1975-79, bd. dirs., 1972-79; v.p., sec. Richard Grand Found., 1966-80, pres., 1980—; bd. dirs. Greenfields Schs., 1977-82; bd. dirs., sec. U. Ariz. Found., 1979—, v.p., 1986-87, chmn. exec. com. 1986-87; bd. dirs. Tucson Airport Authority; bd. fellows Ctr. Creative Photography, 1983—; mem.-at-large, bd. dirs. Tucson Mus. Art League, 1977-78. Recipient YWCA Woman on the Move award, 1982; Community Service award Mortar Board, 1978; Disting. Citizen award U. Ariz. Coll. Fine Arts, 1979. Office: 127 W Franklin St Tucson AZ 85701

GRANDE, SARINA D'AMATO, designer, civic worker; b. N.Y.C., June 22; d. Francis and Maria D'Amato; pvt. tutors; numerous coll. courses; m. Frank Grande, Dec. 7, 1962. In various design and mfg. positions, garment industry, 1929-35; prin. design studio, clothing designs, N.Y.C., 1935-65; cons. to garment trade; cons. interior design; participant, coordinator Pageant of Lace for Ziegfield Club, 1941; cons. on synthetic fabrics I.E. DuPont de Nemours & Co., 1942-50; feature writer Italian Am. Rev. Active fund raiser for arts, charitable orgns., 1974—; mem. exec. bd., treas. Stanley Richter Assn. for Arts, Danbury, Conn., Scott Fanton Mus., Danbury, Hist. Soc. Danbury, Met. Opera Guild, N.Y.C., Am. Mus. Natural History, N.Y.C.; bd. dirs. Dante Found. Inc.; chmn. bd. Italian Am. Democratic Orgns. N.Y. N.Y.C., 1960-65; bd. dirs. Don Monte Oncology Found., New England Opera Co., NEMI Cultural Found.; bd. dirs., founder, pres. D'Amato-Grande Scholarship Found. Inc.; mem. Danbury Cultural Commn., 1982-84; active Boys' Towns Italy, Girls' Towns Italy, Children's Day Treatment Ctr. and Sch. Recipient George B. DeLuca award Fedn. Italian Am. Dem. Orgns., 1959, Humanitarian award United Jewish Appeal and Friendship Internat., 1959; named Lady of Month, Italian Am. mag., 1962; cert. of recognition Vol. Bur. Greater Danbury, 1982. Mem. Ams. Italian Descent Inc. (chmn. bd. 1971-79), Am.-Italy Soc., Nat. Italian Am. Found., French Alliance, Les Grands Vivants (founder and pres. 1974), Play Schs. Assn. (exec. bd.), N.Y. Mus. Modern Art, N.Y. Met. Mus., N.Y. Council Navy League of U.S. Roman Catholic. Club: Princeton (N.Y.). Designer for films: Three Men on a Horse, 1938; Black Magic, 1945; Power Unlimited, 1945; designer spl. garments for series This is America, 1945; patentee garment constrn., U.S., Can.; author Social Scene and Opera Scene columns Il Popolo weekly nat. newspaper, 1962-64. Home and Office: 400 E 56th St New York NY 10022

GRANER, JANICE MARIE, personnel administrator; b. Wabasha, Minn., Dec. 1, 1952; d. Donald Eugene and Joyce (Marie) Serum; m. Keith William Graner, Apr. 19, 1975; children: Brian Donald, Anne Marie. BS, U. Wis.-Stout, 1973; postgrad., U. Ind., 1974. Registered dietitian, Minn. Dietitian Mayo Clinic, Rochester, Minn., 1974-78, dietitian dir., 1978-81, employment counselor, 1981-84, employment coordinator, 1985—. Chairperson PSAT com. Elgin (Minn.) High Sch., 1986, Rochester Job Service Employer Com.; mem. PER com., 1987; mem. Am. Luth. Ch. Women. Mem. Am. Dietetic Assn., Rochester Personnel Assn. Lutheran.

GRANGE-HOLMES, JANET LENORE, tax lawyer; b. Chgo., Sept. 5, 1958; d. Albert Edward and Marie Loretta (Hart) G. BS in Acctg., U. Ill., Chgo., 1980; JD, U. Ill., 1983. Bar: Ill. 1983; CPA, Ill. Sr. tax cons. Grant Thornton, Chgo., 1983-85, Deloitte, Haskins & Sells, Chgo., 1985-86, Kraft, Inc., Northbrook, Ill., 1986—. Mem. Chgo. Bar Assn. (fed. taxation com.), ABA (fed. taxation sect.), Am. Inst. CPA's, Ill. CPA Soc., U. Ill. Alumni Assn. (bd. dirs. 1987—), Beta Gamma Sigma. Office: Kraft Inc Kraft Ct Glenview IL 60025

GRANGER, LINDA C., producer, director, writer; b. Duncan, Okla., June 30, 1955; d. Stanley Clark Granger, Jr. and Linda Faye (Wright) Granger-McNutt; m. Rick A. Hall, Sept. 5, 1987. Co-owner Studio 43, Denver, 1981-82; owner, chief exec. officer Mt. Ocean Productions, Bel Air, Calif., 1982—; cons. Dream Quest, Culver City, Calif. Author: (screenplays): Blades, 1983, Street Legal, 1985, Border Zone, 1985-86, Heart Dances, 1985-87. Recipient Love award Colo. Gen. Hosp., Denver, 1982. Mem. Am. Film Inst. Office: Mountain-Ocean Productions 612 N Sepulveda Bel Air CA 90049

GRANICK, LOIS WAYNE, association administrator; b. Weatherford, Okla., Mar. 5, 1932; d. Johnny Wayne and Lois Bernice (Wells) Cox; m. Robert Eugene Granick, June 6, 1951; children—Bruce, Leslie Granick Knipling, Jeffrey, Andrea. Student. U. N.Mex., 1949-51. Programmer, systems analyst Documentation, Inc., Bethesda, Md., 1961-66; cons. Mexican Govt., Mexico City, 1966-69; info. specialist Autocomp, Inc., Bethesda, 1970-72; dir. Autocode div. of Autocomp, Inc., Bethesda, 1972-73; exec. editor Psychol. Abstracts Am. Psychol. Assn., Washington, 1974—; dir., PsycINFO Am. Psychol. Assn., 1977—. Mem. Nat. Fedn. Abstracting and Info. Services (bd. dirs. 1977-82, pres. 1980-81), Info. Sci. Abstracts (bd. dirs. 1978-79), Info. Industry Assn. (bd. dirs. 1982—, chmn. 1988—), Assn. Info. and Dissemination Ctrs., Internat. Council Sci. and Tech. Info. (gen. sec.

1986—), Am. Soc. Info. Sci. Home: 5414 Center St Chevy Chase MD 20815 Office: Am Psychol Assn 1200 17th St NW Washington DC 20036

GRANN, PHYLLIS, publisher, editor; b. London, Sept. 2, 1937; d. Solomon and Louisa (Bois-Smith) Eitingon; m. Victor Grann, Sept. 26, 1962; children: Alison, David, Edward. B.A. cum laude, Barnard Coll., 1958. Sec. Doubleday Pubs., N.Y.C., 1958-60; editor William Morrow Inc., N.Y.C., 1960-62, David McKay Co., N.Y.C., 1962-70, Simon & Schuster Inc., N.Y.C., 1970; v.p. Simon & Schuster Inc., 1976; pres., pub. G. P. Putnam's & Sons., N.Y.C., 1976-86; pres. Putnam Pub. Group, Inc.(now Putnam Berkley Group), N.Y.C., 1986—, chief exec. officer, 1987—. Office: Putnam Berkley Group 200 Madison Ave New York NY 10016

GRANNUM, DIANE FARLEY, special education educator; b. Peekskill, N.Y., Sept. 9, 1951; d. James Howard and Constantia W. A. (Price) Pankey; m. Michael Anthony Grannum; 1 child, Sean Michael. BA in Liberal Arts, Coll. New Rochelle (N.Y.), 1981; postgrad., Herbert Lehman Coll., Bronx, N.Y., 1982; MS in Spl. Edn., L.I. U., 1988. Cert. tchr. spl. edn., N.Y.C. Family assoc. N.Y.C. Bd. Edn. div. of High Schs., 1974-82; tchr. spl. edn. George Washington High Sch., N.Y.C., 1982; tchr. A. Philiph Randolph Sch., N.Y.C., 1982-83; readiness instr. Mary L. Murray Sch., N.Y.C., 1983-85, Ira Strauss Classes for Emotionally Disturbed Students, N.Y.C., 1985-86, Chelsea Sch., N.Y.C., 1986—; cooperating tchr. Sch. Visual Arts, N.Y.C., 1984-85. Grantee Manhattan Regional Office div. Spl. Edn., 1984, Lehman Coll., 1982. Mem. United Fedn. Tchrs., Writing Tchrs. Consortium, Coll. New Rochelle Alumni Assn. (dir. info. 1982-85, author Alumni Expressions, 1983), Nat. Council Geocosmic Research. Democrat. Roman Catholic. Home: 807 E Carl Ave Baldwin NY 11510 Office: Chelsea Sch 281 9th Ave New York NY 11550

GRANT, BETTY LOU, English language teacher; b. Foley, Ala., Dec. 26, 1951; d. Clifford and Margaret (Flowers) G. BS, U. South Ala., 1974, MA, 1975. English tchr. Baldwin County Bd. Edn., Foley, 1975—. Mem. St. Paul's Episcopal Ch., Foley. Home: Wolf Bay Estates HC 70 Box 2800-H Foley AL 36535 Office: Foley High Sch 201 N Pine St Foley AL 36535

GRANT, CHERYL, producer, television syndicator; b. Phoenix, Mar. 1, 1944; d. William Edward and Mary Louise (Weldon) Grant; m. Louis Tancredi, Nov. 27, 1976; children—John Francis, Jennifer Grant. Student U. Fribourg, Switzerland, 1963-64; B.A., Coll. of Notre Dame of Md., 1965; M.S., Syracuse U., 1966. Assoc. producer Girl Talk ABC Films, N.Y.C., 1968-70, New Jersey Speaker for Itself, WNDT-TV, N.Y.C., 1966-68, Communications and Education, WNDT-TV, N.Y.C., 1967, The Virginia Graham Show, RKO, Los Angeles, 1970-71, Manhattan Townhouse, Source Internat., N.Y.C., 1971-72, Collision Course, Wolper Prodns., Los Angeles, 1972, Living Easy with Dr. Joyce Brothers, Capricorn Prodns., N.Y.C., 1972-73, Mike Douglas Show, Westinghouse, Phila., 1974, Beverly & Vidal Sassoon, Sta. KCOP, Los Angeles, 1975, Dinah, 20th Century Fox, Los Angeles, 1975; hostess A.M. Miami, Sta. WPLG-TV, Miami, Fla., 1972; exec. producer/pres. Carter-Grant Prodns., Inc., Los Angeles, 1976—, Sherry Grant Enterprises, Inc., Los Angeles, 1982—. Programs have been honored by the Freedom Found. award, Internat. Film and TV Festival of N.Y. Gold Award and Calif. Motion Picture Assn. Golden Halo award. Mem. Acad. T.V. Arts and Sci., Women in Bus., Women in Film, Am. Women in Radio and TV, AFTRA, Women in Cable. Roman Catholic. Home: 18120 Sweet Elm Dr Encino CA 91316 Office: Sherry Grant Enterprises 17915 Ventura Blvd Suite 208 Encino CA 91316

GRANT, CYNTHIA ELIZABETH, museum director, teacher, consultant; b. Asheville, N.C., Oct. 4, 1948; d. Roger Alpine Grant, Jr. and Mary Elizabeth (Scott) Winterling. B.A., Salem Coll., 1970; M.A. in History, Wake Forest U., 1986. Cert. tchr. social studies. Tchr. Asheville City Schs., 1970-71; buyer Navy Exchange, U.S. Navy, Roosevelt Roads, P.R., 1971-72; staff asst. Tulane U., New Orleans, 1972-74; ombudsman Am. Bankers Assn., Washington, 1977-78; mus. dir. City of Alexandria, Va., 1978-81; dir. Hist. Columbia Found., S.C., 1981-86; cons. Kensington Plantation, Eastover, S.C., 1985-86, Hist. Beaufort Found., S.C., 1985; mem. resource com. Cultural Council, Columbia, 1983-86. Bd. dirs. Young Profls. of Columbia Mus., 1984-85; com. chmn. Leadership Columbia, 1983-86; event chmn. Champions of Children's Hosp., Columbia, 1984-86; mem. stewardship com. Shandon Presbyn. Ch., Columbia, 1983-86. Recipient Pres.'s prize Salem Coll., 1970; John H. Stibbs award Tulane U., 1973; named to Outstanding Young Women Am., 1985. Mem. Am. Assn. Mus., Southeast Mus. Conf., Mid-Atlantic Assn. Mus., S.C. Fedn. Mus. (sec. 1983-84), Am. Assn. for State and Local History (award of merit for mus. 1984), Nat. Trust for Hist. Preservation, Columbia Forum. Democrat. Presbyterian. Avocations: photography, hiking, travel. Home: PO Box 21 Annandale-on-Hudson NY 12504-0021 Office: Hist Hudson Valley River Rd Annandale on Hudson NY 12504

GRANT, ELLESTINE JOHNSON, educator, administrator; b. Balt., Dec. 12, 1938. BS, Coppin State Coll., 1964; MS, Morgan State U., 1972; EdD, Temple U., 1985. Elem. sch. tchr. Balt. Pub. Sch. System, 1964-69, ednl. specialist, 1971-73, project mgr., 1973-75, coordinator specialist program, 1975-87; sr. tchr., dir. Balt. Pub. Schs. and Coppin State Coll., 1069-71; coordinator Mayor's Council City of Balt., 1984-87, ednl. cons., 1986-87; commr. Mayor's Literacy Commn. Author: Students and the Law, 1972. Vol. advisor to Gov. State of Md., 1986; pres. Ret. Sr. Vol. Program, Balt., 1981-87. Mem. Nat. Alliance Black Sch. Educators (chmn. 1979-80, Excellence awrd 1980), Nat. Assn. Female Execs., NAACP, Vol. Adminstrs. Assn. (pres. 1986), Las Compañeras Educational Assn. (pres. 1986), Phi Delta Kappa. Democrat. Roman Catholic. Home: 217 Denison St Baltimore MD 21229

GRANT, HELEN LILLIAN, health spa chain exec.; b. Joliet, Ill., Jan. 2, 1925; d. Carmen and Lucia L. (Pistilli) Palleschi; student Met. Bus. Coll., 1943-44; student Budde Flying Sch., 1947-49, U. Houston, 1967-68; m. Michael D. Grant, June 20, 1958 (dec.); children—Laura Grant Chamblin, Mary Helen, Michael Daniel. Bookkeeper, acct., comptroller, v.p., cost clk. Am. Can. Co., Joliet, Ill., 1943-45; bookkeeper Aylin Advt. Agy. and Naman Hotel Supply, Houston, 1951-55; acct. Houston Bus. Service, 1955-65; comptroller Slenderbolic Health Spa, Houston, 1965-72, Dynamics Health Equipment Co., Houston, 1972-77; comptroller Figure World, Inc., San Antonio, 1972-79, v.p., 1980-86, cons., 1986—. Active Blue Bird Aux., S.W. Tex. Meth. Hosp., San Antonio, 1980—. Served with WAVES, 1945-47. Roman Catholic. Club: Tex. A&M Mother's. Home: 200 Prinz St San Antonio TX 78213 Office: 508 W Rhapsody St San Antonio TX 78216

GRANT, JOANNE CATHERINE, auctioneer; b. Cornwall, N.Y., Nov. 25, 1940; d. Martin Emmett and Josephine Mary (Randazzo) Smith; m. Martin B. Grant, Jan. 11, 1964; children: Martin Andrew, Jennifer Allison. RN, Vassar Bros. Hosp. Sch. Nursing, 1961. RN Vassar Bros. Hosp., Poughkeepsie, N.Y., 1961-64, Dr. Morris Goldberger, N.Y.C., 1964-66, Dr. Martin Grant, New Windsor, N.Y., 1971-75; auctioneer Mid Hudson Galleries, Cornwall on Hudson, N.Y., 1976—, Guernseys, N.Y.C., 1984—. Author: The Painted Lamps of Handel, 1976, Price Guide to American Victorian Figural Napkin Rings, 1978. Bd. dirs. Orange County Assn. for Help of Retarded Children, Middletown, N.Y., 1973-84; mem. com. for spl. edn. Cornwall Sch. Dist., 1986-87. Mem. N.Y. State Auctioneers Assn., Appraisal Assn. Am. Office: Mid Hudson Galleries 1 Idlewild Ave PO Box 305 Cornwall on Hudson NY 12520

GRANT, JUANITA G., librarian; b. Princeton, W.Va., July 25, 1930; d. William Randle and Cora (Fitch) Grant; BS, Concord Coll., 1953; BS in Library Sci., U. N.C., 1955; M in Liberal Arts, Johns Hopkins U., 1970. Librarian, Spl. Services, U.S. Army, Germany, France, 1956-58; asst. librarian Carson Newman Coll., Jefferson City, Tenn., 1959-63; librarian Judson Coll., Marion, Ala., 1964-67; dir. Blount Library, Averett Coll., Danville, Va., 1967—; library adv. com. Va. Council Higher Edn., 1976-78; mem. adv. com. Danville Pub. Library; chmn. library com. Danville Mus. Fine Arts and History, 1976-80; mem. Louisa County Hist. Soc. Mem. ALA, Nat. Geneal. Soc., Va. Geneal. Soc., Va./N.C. Geneal. Soc., Southeastern Library Assn., Va. Library Assn., Am. Hist. Soc., Danville Hist. Soc., Phi Delta Kappa. Baptist. Club: Wednesday (Danville). Home: 126 Primrose Ct Danville VA 24541

GRANT, LILLIAN LYNN GIVENS, utilites executive; b. Louisville, Sept. 19, 1946; d. Latton Willis and Virginia (Wilcox) Givens; (div. Feb. 1978); 1 child, Heather Noel. BA, U. Ky., 1969. Cert. tchr. Ky. Tchr. Jefferson County Sch., Louisville, 1970-75; rep. customer service Louisville Gas & Electric, 1977-79, advisor mkt. services, 1979-80, advisor energy utilization, 1980—. Mem. speakers bur., Louisville, 1983-86; mem. steering com. Family Focus, Louisville, 1985-88, Family Place (child abuse treatment agy.). Mem. Bluegrass Elec. Women Rountable (pres. 1984-85, chpt. service award, mem. yr. 1987), Derbytown Bus. and Profl. Women (pres. 1983-84, Woman Achievement award 1984). Democrat. Baptist. Office: Louisville Gas & Electric Co 311 W Chestnut PO Box 32010 Louisville KY 40232

GRANT, LINDA KAY (SCOTT), small business owner, sales executive; b. Galesburg, Ill., Oct. 15, 1949; d. Claire Arline Tabb and Addie Mae (Smith) Stedman; m. James G. Scott, Feb. 20, 1968 (div. Dec. 1977); children: Angela Cristine, Aaron Cristopher; m. Daryl Quinn Grant, Sept. 20, 1986; 1 child, Rachel Jane. Student, Balckhawk East Coll., 1984-86. Sec. Flynn Beverage, Inc., Rock Island, Ill., 1972-76, Lee's Place, Inc., Rock Island, 1976-81; merchandising rep. Polaroid Corp., Boston, 1981-84; sales rep. Drawing Bd. Greeting Cards, Dallas, 1984-86; owner Card Creations, Galva, Ill., 1986—; sales mgr. Evans Printing, Geneseo, Ill., 1987—. Mem. Dem. Women for Henry County, Cambridge, Ill., 1985—. Mem. Nat. Assn. for Female Execs. Methodist. Home: RR 1 Kewanee IL 61443 Office: Card Creations 352 Front St Galva IL 61434

GRANT, MARGARET ELLEN, psychiatrist; b. Clinton, Okla., July 5, 1948; d. Gilbert Richard and Bernice (Bledsoe) G.; B.A. in Biology, Rice U., 1970; M.D., U. Ark., 1975. Research asst. U. Ark. Sch. Medicine, Little Rock, 1970-72, intern, 1975-76; resident in psychiatry U. Colo., Denver, 1976-80; career resident Colo. State Hosp., Pueblo, 1978-79; practice medicine specializing in psychiatry, Denver, 1980—; psychiat. cons. Jefferson County Mental Health Center, Lakewood, Colo., 1980-86 ; vol. U. Colo. Med. Center, 1980—; mem. staff Bethesda, Mt. Airy, St. Joseph hosps.; dir. Denver Women's Ctr. Diplomate Am. Bd. Psychiatry. Mem. Am. Psychiat. Assn., Colo. Psychiat. Soc., Colo. Women's Med. Assn. Democrat. Office: 3773 Cherry Creek Dr N Suite 225 Denver CO 80209

GRANT, PATRICIA LOUISE, manufacturing executive; b. New Orleans, Jan. 12, 1949; d. Lanis and Albert (Clark) Domio; m. Jemmie Grant; 1 child, Rosalind. BA, Wilberforce U., 1971; MA, Calif. State U., Los Angeles, 1977. Subcontract adminstr. Hughes Aircraft Co., Los Angeles, 1974-79, Northrop Corp., Hawthorne, Calif., 1979-81; sr. subcontract adminstr. Northrop Corp., Hawthorne, 1981-83, subcontract adminstr. specialist, 1983-84, unit mgr. gen. procurement, 1984, branch mgr. gen. procurement, 1984—, auditor, 1984—. Mem. Mgmt. Club, Sigma Omega. Home: 10921 Roberta St Cerritos CA 90701

GRANT, RUBY JAYNE JOHNSON, insurance executive; b. Glen Cove, N.Y., June 28; d. Alfred Lloyd and Ora Mae (Gibson) Pendleton; m. Nolan Eugene Floyd Grant; 1 child, Kristale Michelle. Grad. high sch., Glen Cove. Telephone operator N.Y. Phone Co., Roslyn, 1958-60; bookkeeper Town and Country, Roslyn, 1961-65; real estate sales agt. Parkview Realty, Westbury, N.Y.; salesperson Parkview Realty, Westbury, N.Y., 1965-66; teller Meadowbrook Bank, Jericho, N.Y., 1966-67; cons. Met. Life Ins. Co., Hicksville, N.Y., 1968-73; agt. AllState Ins. Co., Glen Cove, 1973—. Chmn. election dist., bd. inspector New Cassel Rep. Club, Westbury, N.Y., 1985—; pres. Glen Cove Youth Club, 1980-85, advisor, 1986—; chmn. insps. Nassau County Election Bd., 1987—. Mem. Nat. Assn. Negro Bus. and Profl. Women (life; rec. sec. 1985-87, chaplain 1987—), 100 Black Women L.I., Inc. Mem. Ch. of God in Christ. Avocations: interior decorating, bicycling, roller skating. Home: 261 Brook St Westbury NY 11590 Office: Allstate Ins Co 75 Forest Ave Glen Cove NY 11542

GRANT, SARA CATHERINE, training and development specialist; b. Johnstown, Pa., Mar. 28, 1950; d. James Walter and Bernetta (Bewak) G. BS in English, Lock Haven U., 1973; MA in Adult Edn., Ind. U. of Pa., 1978. Tchr. English Williamsport (Pa.) Sch. Dist., 1973; adminstr. adult basic edn. Somerset (Pa.) Sch. Dist., 1973-77; dir. tng. Girl Scouts U.S. Council, Harrisburg, Pa., 1977-79, adult devel. cons., N.Y.C., 1979-82, dir. tng., N.Y.C., 1982-86; tng. and devel. specialist Tchrs. Ins. and Annuity Assn., Coll. Retirement Equities Fund, N.Y.C., 1986—. Contbr. articles to mags. Visitor for the elderly St. Patrick's Cathedral Social Services, N.Y.C., 1985—. Mem. Am. Soc. Tng. and Devel., Phi Delta Kappa. Democrat. Avocation: tennis. Home: 104-20 Queens Blvd Forest Hills NY 11375

GRANTHAM, JOYCE CAROL, small business owner; b. Alameda, Calif., Jan. 4, 1940; d. John Charles and Shirley Anne (Maze) G. AB in Music Composition, Mills Coll., 1961; student, LaSalle Extension U., 1965-69; MBA in Gen. Mgmt., Golden Gate U., 1980. Various secretarial and supervisory positions UNIVAC div. Sperry Rand Corp., San Francisco, 1962-68; various mgmt. positions Decimus Corp., San Francisco, 1969-77, sec. policy rev. com., 1976-81, v.p. personnel, 1977-81; product mgr. Bank of Am., San Francisco, 1981-83, asst. v.p., mgr. ops., mktg. and product mgmt., 1984-85; owner Grantham Assocs./White Rabbit Bus. Graphics, Walnut Creek, Calif., 1985—; tchr. piano Joyce Grantham Piano Studio, Walnut Creek, 1985—. Composer (piano piece) Sarabande, 1959, (song cycle) Sing the Forsaken, 1960, String Trio, 1961 (Elizabeth Mills Crothers, 1961). Bd. dirs. San Leandro Symphony Assn., 1965-66. Francis J. Hellman scholar, 1957, Calif. State scholar, 1957. Mem. Nat. Guild of Piano Tchrs. (scholar 1957), Am. Coll. of Musicians. Republican. Episcopalian. Office: Grantham Assocs/White Rabbit 1365 Milton Ave Walnut Creek CA 94596

GRANTHAM, SHIRLEY LEE, banker; b. Napoleon, Ohio, Mar. 25, 1945; d. Andrew Ellsworth and Jeanette Mildred (Shively) Couch; m. Robert O. (Bud) Grantham, Jr., Mar. 9, 1966; children: Michelle, Robb. Degree in banking, Fla. Sch. Banking, Gainesville, 1988. Sucessively teller, sec., loan interviewer, asst. br. mgr. Park Fed. Savs. & Loan, Mt. Dora, Fla., 1975-78; br. mgr. Heritage Fed. Savs. & Loan, Mt. Dora, 1978-80; asst. v.p., br. mgr. 1st Nat. Bank Mt. Dora, Sorrento, Fla., 1985—; mem. adv. com. Umatilla (Fla.) High Sch., Fla., 1985. Mem. Bus. and Profl. Women's Assn. (pres., 1st v.p. Mt. Dora chpt., dist. dir. Fla. fedn., named most vital club mem., 1986, speech making dist. winner, state runner-up, 1984), Nat. Assn. Bank Women. Republican. Lodge: Order of Rainbow (worthy advisor for girls, 1962-63). Home: Rt 2 Box 152 Umatilla FL 32784 Office: The 1st Nat Bank of Mount Dora 7th & Donnelly Mount Dora FL 32757

GRASSE, WANDA GENE, lawyer, writer; b. Baird, Tex., July 28, 1940; d. William Eugene and Alta Roberta (Dickerson) George; m. Weldon Morris Carriker, Jan 27, 1960; div. 1968; 1 child, Conrad Ray; m. 2d, John Lee Grasse, Mar. 28, 1970; 1 child, Karen Diane. LLB, LaSalle-Whittier Coll. Law, Los Angeles, 1977; postgrad. entertainment law studies, U. So. Calif., 1983. Bar: Calif. 1978, U.S. Tax Ct. 1981, U.S. Supreme Ct., 1987. Continuity dir. Sta. KLBK-TV and WTTN, Lubbock Tex., 1960-66; promotion writer, dir. KTTV and KCOP, Los Angeles, 1966-72; sole practice law, Los Angeles, 1978-81; assoc. Laurence E. Clark, Law Corp. Monterey Park, Calif., 1981—. Mem. Los Angeles County Bar Assn., San Gabriel Valley Bar Assn., ABA. Republican. Mem. Sci. Mind, Mensa. Club: Bus. and profl. Women's (v.p. 1980-81, woman achievement award 1980) (Los Angeles). Home: 1300 Fulton Ave Monterey Park CA 91754 Office: Laurence E Clark Law Corp 631 S Atlantic Blvd Monterey Park CA 91754

GRASSI, ELLEN ELIZABETH, electronics company service administrator; b. N.Y.C., July 27, 1949; d. Dante J. and Mary D. (Olivieri) G. BA in Teaching, High Point Coll., 1971; postgrad., L.I. U., Brookville, N.Y., 1976, 83-84. Cert. tchr., N.Y. Tchr. Yonkers (N.Y.) Schs., 1971-76; electronics tech. Canon U.S.A., Inc., Lake Success, N.Y., 1977-82, supv. eastern regional service, 1982-84, asst. mgr. nat. serv., 1984-85, mgr. nat. service adminstrn., 1985-88, nat. mgr. customer relations, 1988—. Polling booth elector Bd. of Elections, N.Y.C., 1971-77; founding mem. Little Neck Hills (N.Y.) Assn., 1984. Mem. Nat. Assn. Service Mgrs., Nat. Assn. Female Execs., Douglaston Civic Assn., High Point Coll. Alumni Assn., Kappa Delta Pi. Club: Tower. Office: Canon USA Inc 1 Jericho Plaza Jericho NY 11753

GRASSO, DOREEN MARIE, art dealer; b. Pitts., Jan. 12, 1955; d. Frank Jules and Laverne (Damico) G.; 1 child, Sarah Elizabeth Dadisman. BA, U. Pitts., 1976. Dir. appraisal dept. Childs Gallery, Boston, 1977-78; asst. dir. painting dept. William Doyle Galleries Inc., N.Y.C., 1978-79, dir. print dept., 1983-84; art dealer, appraiser Doreen M. Grasso Fine Paintings, Pitts., 1979-83, 85—; dir. Dargate Fine Arts, Pitts., 1984-85; cons. Gallery G, Pitts., 1986-87, lectr. 1987; cons. Concept Art Gallery, Pitts., 1986; lectr. U. Pitts., 1985. Curator numerous exhbns. Mem. Nat. Fedn. Ind. Bus. (Pitts. dist. rep. 1988). Office: 2145 Wightman St 5 Pittsburgh PA 15217

GRATZ, PAULINE, former nursing science educator; b. N.Y.C., Mar. 30, 1924; d. John and Rose (Berman) G.; m. Sidney Aaronson, July 25, 1969. B.A., Hunter Coll., 1945; M.A., Columbia U., 1948, Ed.D., 1961. Jr. bacteriologist Queens Gen. Hosp., 1945-47; research technician Jewish Hosp. Bklyn., 1947-48; instr. biology and phys. sci. Bayonne (N.J.) Hosp. Sch. Nursing, 1948-51; sci. coordinator N.Y. Med. Coll. Sch. Nursing, 1951-56, New Rochelle (N.Y.) Hosp. Sch. Nursing, 1956-61; instr. nursing edn. Columbia U., 1961-62, asst. prof. natural scis. and nursing edn., 1963-65, asst. prof. natural scis., 1965-67, assoc. prof., 1967-69; prof. human ecology Duke U., Durham, N.C., 1969-85; prof. emeritus Duke U., 1985—; vis. prof. physiology N.C. Health Manpower Project, summer 1973; cons. in field. Author: Integrated Science, 1966, (with others) Human Physiology, 1987, Experiments in Physiology, 1987, Teachers Edition in Human Physiology, 1987; contbg. author chpts. to books. NSF fellow, 1965; Shell fellow, 1969. Fellow AAAS; mem. Kappa Delta Pi, Pi Lambda Theta, Iota Sigma Pi, Sigma Theta Tau (hon.). Home: 102 Montrose Dr Durham NC 27707

GRAU, MARCY BEINISH, investment banker; b. Bklyn., Aug. 7, 1950; d. Joseph Beinish and Gloria (Rosenbaum) Bennett; m. Bennett Grau, Nov. 19, 1978; 2 children. A.B. with high honors, U. Mich., 1971; postgrad. Columbia U., 1972, N.Y. Inst. Fin., 1973. Asst. to chmn. Bancroft Convertible Fund, N.Y.C., 1973-75; precious metals trader J. Aron & Co., N.Y.C., 1975-81, mgr. metals mktg., 1981-83; v.p. Goldman, Sachs & Co/J. Aron, N.Y.C., 1983—; bus.-related translator Augustus Clothiers, N.Y.C., 1979—. Editor, contbr. Precious Metals Rev. and Outlook, 1980—. Vol. worker, pediatrics dept. Lenox Hill Hosp., N.Y.C., 1978-79; asst. The Holiday Project, The Hunger Project, N.Y.C., 1978-83; vol. Yorkville Common Pantry, N.Y.C., 1984; tutor Yorkville Neighborhood Assn., N.Y.C., 1984; assoc. Child Devel. Ctr., N.Y.C. Mem. Alliance Francaise, Phi Beta Kappa. Democrat. Jewish. Avocations: interior design, fashion, cooking, swimming. Home: 300 W End Ave New York NY 10023 Office: Goldman Sachs & Co 85 Broad St New York NY 10004

GRAU, SHIRLEY ANN (MRS. JAMES KERN FEIBLEMAN), writer; b. New Orleans, July 8, 1929; d. Adolph and Katherine (Onions) G.; m. James Kern Feibleman, Aug. 4, 1955; children—Ian, James, Nora Miranda, William, Katherine. B.A., Tulane U., 1950. Writer for, Holiday, New Yorker, New World Writing, Mademoiselle, Sat. Eve. Post, Atlantic, The Reporter, 1954—; Author: The Black Prince and Other Stories, 1955, The Hard Blue Sky, 1958, The House on Coliseum Street, 1961, The Keepers of the House, 1964 (Pulitzer prize for fiction 1965), The Condor Passes, 1971, The Wind Shifting West and Other Stories, 1973, Evidence of Love, 1977, Nine Women, 1986. Mem. Phi Beta Kappa. Office: care Brandt and Brandt 1501 Broadway New York NY 10036

GRAUBARD, CARLA LAURA, publishing executive; b. Newark; d. Myron and Ruth (Iskowitz) G. BS in Econs., U. Pa., 1971; PMD, Harvard U., 1985. Economist U.S. Office of Econ. Opportunity, Washington, 1971-72; dir. ops. Saturday Rev. Co., Inc., San Francisco, 1972-74; asst. circulation dir. Redbook Publishing Co., N.Y.C., 1974-75; dir. planning and ops. N.Y. Mag. Co., Inc., N.Y.C., 1975-78; gen. mgr., dir. strategic devel. Newsweek, Inc., N.Y.C., 1978-86; pres., chief operating officer City Home Pub. Co., Inc., N.Y.C., Houston, 1986—; bd. dirs. U. Pa. Pub. Com., Phila., 1985—; cons. in field. Coauthor: Not of One Mind. Bd. dirs. Houston Symphony. Mem. Tex. Mag. Pubs. Assn. (bd. dirs., sec., treas., chmn.-elect 1986—). Office: City Home Pub 420 E 55 #5-0 New York NY 10022

GRAUBART, ALICE VISION, psychiatric social worker, psychotherapist; b. Chgo., Sept. 9, 1945; d. Myron and Shirley (Goldberg) Vision; m. Judah L. Graubart, June 23, 1968. MA in social work, U. Ill., Chgo., 1975. Cert. social worker. Pvt. practice psychotherapy Oak Park, Ill., 1975—; cons. Flexible Careers, Chgo., 1975-81, Search Sch., Chgo., 1975-78; instr. Mundelein Coll., Chgo., 1980-81; bd. dirs. Sarah's Inn, Oak Park. Coauthor: Decade of Destiny, 1978. Exec. dir. Ind. Dem. Coalition, Chgo., 1969-71; staff mem. ind. polit. campaigns, 1969-71; com. mem. Evening of Remembrance village Oak Park, 1987; bd. dirs. Ind. Voters Ill., 1971, village Oak Park Mgrs. Assn., 1985—. Mem. Nat. Assn. Social Workers, Chgo. Assn. for Psychoanalytical Psychology, Soc. for Advancement Self Psychology, Chgo. Assn. Mental Health Pvt. Practitioners (bd. dirs.), Assn. for Mental Health Affiliates with Israel (bd. dirs., v.p. membership 1987—), Assn. Mental Health Pvt. Practitioners (bd. dirs. 1984-85). Home: 321 N Harvey Oak Park IL 60302

GRAUDONS, SALLY ANN, systems specialist; b. Little Falls, N.Y., Sept. 3, 1939; d. Arthur Marmaduke and Elizabeth Graudons; B.A. in Math., Syracuse U., 1960. Programmer trainee Mutual of N.Y., 1961; computer communications software programmer Univac, London, 1965-68; computer specialist Citibank, N.Y.C., 1968-71; edn. mgr. Basic Four Computer Co., N.Y.C., 1971-77; mktg. rep. Edutronics McGraw-Hill, N.Y.C., 1977-79; v.p. systems devel. N.Y. State Urban Devel. Corp., 1981-83; cons. in field. Mem. Data Processing Mgmt. Assn., Am. Soc. Tng. and Devel. Home: 440 E 79th St New York NY 10021

GRAVAT, LOIS J., retail executive; b. St. Louis, July 12, 1938; d. Charles John and Elsie Louise (Dungan) Maehringer; m. John J. Gravat, June 24, 1957 (div. Feb. 1981); children: James, Eric, Darren, John, Jeffrey. Grad., Miss Hickeys Bus. Sch., 1957; student, Max Factor, Hollywood Calif., 1970. Make-up advisor, sales rep. Max Factor & Co. Mil. Div., Charleston, S.C., 1970-75; exec. cons. Exec. Personnel Search, Charleston, 1976; asst. mgr. Brooks Fashion, Charleston, 1976-77; mgr. U.S. Shoe Women's Specialty Retail Div., Arlington, Va., 1977-87; freelance fashion cons., Alexndria, Va., 1981—; freelance nutrition cons., Alexandria, 1986—; freelance executive image and motivation cons. Mem. Nat. Assn. Female Execs. Home: 517 Armistead St #202 Arlington VA 22312

GRAVEL, NANCY, nurse administrator; b. Lewiston, Ma., June 26, 1946; d. Edwin E. and Adele A. (Chlosta) Thompson; children: Charlene, Edward, Elizabeth; m. Robert E. Gravel; 1 child, Erica. BS in Nursing, U. Mass., 1973, postgrad. RN Mass., Conn. Staff nurse Franklin County Pub. Hosp., Greenfield, Mass., 1973; respiratory nurse clinician Hampshire County, Mass., 1973-75; pulmonary clin. specialist Baystate Med. Ctr., Springfield, Mass., 1975-77; instr. nursing Holyoke (Mass.) Community Coll., 1977-80; inservice coordinator Holyoke Geriatric and Convalescent Ctr., 1977-80; asst. dir. nursing services Hebrew Home and Hosp., Hartford, Conn., 1980-84; dir. patient care services Western Mass. Hosp., Westfield, 1984-87; dir. nursing services Mediplex of East Longmeadow, Mass., 1988—; adj. faculty Springfield Tech. Community Coll., 1975-77. Contbr. articles to profl. jours. Bd. dirs. Hampshire County unit Am. Cancer Soc., 1974-75; bd. dirs. Am. Lung Assn. Western Mass., 1975—, mem. bldg. com. 1986-87, exec. com. 1978-82, fin. devel. com. 1979-81, others. Mem. Am. Orgn. Nurse Execs., Mass. Orgn. Nurse Execs., Western Mass. Orgn. Nurse Execs. (sec. treas. 1987—, mem. middle mgrs. task force 1986, nat. nurse recognition day com. 1986, chairperson pub. relations com. 1985-86, mem. nomination com. 1985, by-laws com. 1984-85, mktg. com. 1988), Dept. Pub. Health Hosp. Nurse Exec. Council (sec. 1985-86, pres. 1986-87), Am. Nurses Assn. (cert.), Mass. Nurses Assn. (pub. relations com. 1973-75, ad hoc com. status women 1974-75), Mass. Thoracic Soc., Sigma Theta Tau. Democrat. Roman Catholic. Home: 276 S West St Feeding Hills MA 01030

GRAVES, JUDY TWIEHAUS, museum administrator; b. St. Louis, Apr. 28, 1947; d. John Edward and Alma Louise (Deuser) Twiehaus; m. Robert E. Busby, Oct. 9, 1971 (div. 1978); m. Edward V. Graves, Jan. 19, 1980. BS, St. Louis U., 1978. Office mgr. Sta. WKDL, Clarksdale, Miss., 1968-70; acct. St. Louis County Juvenile Ct., 1972-74; auditor, acct. Mo. Law Enforcement Council, St. Louis, 1973-77; fin. officer Greater St. Louis Police Acad., 1977-79; acct. mgr. St. Louis Police Dept., 1979-84; controller St. Louis Art Mus., 1984—. Mem. Am. Bus. Women Assn. (treas. 1982-84), Am. Assn. Mus., Am. Assn. Mus. Adminstrs. Home: 13317 Westerman Rd

Saint Louis MO 63122 Office: St Louis Art Mus #1 Fine Arts Dr Saint Louis MO 63110

GRAVES, MAXINE ELIZABETH, personnel administration executive; b. Emporia, Va., Dec. 23, 1962; d. Bernard and Doris Marie (Woodley) Graves. BS, Old Dominion U., 1985. Library asst. Old Dominion U., Norfolk, Va., 1984-85; mental health therapist Community Mental Health and P.I., Norfolk, 1985-86; psychiatric technologist No. Va. Med. Health Inst., Falls Church, Va., 1986-87; personnel assoc. Britches of Georgetowne, Herndon, Va., 1986—; profl. model Barone Modeling Agy., Alexandria, Va. Mem. Big Sisters Washington Met. Area, Inc.; participant community service program Venture in Voluntary Action. Mem. Nat. Assn. for Female Execs. Democrat. Baptist. Home: 6299 Maxwell Dr Camp Springs MD 20746 Office: Britches of Georgetown 544 Herndon Pkwy Herndon VA 22070

GRAVES, MELANIE WALLBILLICH, accountant, small business owner; b. New Orleans, Apr. 2, 1963; d. Robert Murphy and Joanna (Charrier) Wallbillich; m. James E. Graves Jr., Oct. 11, 1986. BS in Acctg., U. New Orleans, 1985. Registered rep. Acct. Robert M. Wallbillich, CPA, Metairie, La., 1983-86; pvt. practice acctg. Metairie, 1987—. Contbr. article to profl. jour. Recipient Sales Talk Champion award Dale Carnegie, Greater New Orleans, 1988. Mem. Women Bus. Owners Assn. of La. (state bd. rep. 1987-88, treas. 1988-89), Bus. and Profl. Women (1st v.p. Jefferson Parish chpt. 1988-89, Young Careerist of Yr. 1988), Internat. Assn. Fin. Planners (symposium com. 1987—), U. New Orleans Alumni (awards and scholarship com. 1987). Club: Premier Athletic. Office: Taxes & Fin Planning Services One Galleria Blvd Suite 1702 Metairie LA 70001

GRAVES, NANCY ANN, insurance underwriter; b. Brattleboro, Vt., Dec. 3, 1951; d. Wilfred Paul and Grace Adams (Miller) LaFountain; m. Bruce Floyd Graves, Sept. 21, 1980. BA, U. N.H., 1973. Ins. policy rater Peerless Ins. Co., Keene, N.H., 1973-75, accident and health claims examiner, 1975-77, underwriter trainee, 1977-79, underwriter, 1979—. Mem. Nat. Assn. Ins. Women. Office: Peerless Ins Co 62 Maple Ave Keene NH 03431

GRAVES, NANCY STEVENSON, artist; b. Pittsfield, Mass.. BA, Vassar Coll., 1961; BFA, Yale U., 1961, MFA, 1964. Numerous one-woman shows, including Whitney Mus. Am. Art, N.Y.C., 1969, Nat. Gallery Can., Ottawa, 1971, Neue Galerie der Stadt Aachen, Ger., 1971, Mus. Modern Art, N.Y.C., 1971, Inst. Contemporary Art, U. Pa., Phila., 1972, La Jolla (Calif.) Mus. Art, 1973, Art Mus. South Tex., Corpus Christi, 1973, André Emmerich Gallery, Inc., N.Y.C., 1974, 77, Janie E. Lee Gallery, Houston, 1977, 78, M. Knoedler & Co., 1979, 80, 81, Bklyn. Mus., 1988; retrospective show travelled to Albright Knox Gallery, Buffalo, Akron (Ohio) Art Inst., Contemporary Arts Mus., Houston, 1980, Brooks Art Gallery, Memphis, Neuberger Mus., Purchase, N.Y., Des Moines Art Center, Walker Art Center, Mpls., 1981; numerous group shows including Whitney Mus. Am. Art, N.Y.C., 1970, 76, Corcoran Gallery Art, Washington, 1971, 76, Parc Floral, Paris, 1971, Neue Galerie, Kassel, Germany, 1972, Serpentine Gallery, London, 1973, Project 74, Cologne, Germany, 1974, Berlin Nat. Galerie, 1976, Vancouver (B.C.) Art Gallery; represented in permanent collections, Mus. Modern Art, N.Y.C., Whitney Mus. Am. Art, N.Y.C., Ludwig Mus., Cologne, Nat. Gallery Can., Ottawa, Des Moines (Iowa) Art Center, La Jolla Mus. Contemporary Art, Art Mus. South Tex., Corpus Christi, Berkeley (Calif.) Mus. Art, Albright-Knox Art Gallery, Buffalo, N.Y., Chgo. Art Inst. Vassar Coll. fellow, 1971-72; Fulbright-Hayes grantee, 1965-66; Paris Biennale grantee, 1971; Nat. Endowment for Arts grantee, 1972-73; Creative Artist Pub. Service grantee, 1974-75; recipient Skowhegan medal for Drawing and Graphics, 1980, Disting. Artistic Achievement award Yale U. 1985. Office: care Knoedler & Co Inc 19 E 70th St New York NY 10021 *

GRAVES, PIRKKO MAIJA-LEENA, clinical psychologist, psychoanalyst; b. Tampere, Finland, Jan. 20, 1930; came to U.S., 1957; d. Frans Vilho and Bertta Katariina (Katajisto) Lahtinen; Mag.Phil. (Finnish State scholar 1949-52), 1954; French Govt. scholar, U. Paris, 1954-55; Ph.D. (Fulbright scholar 1957-58, Lucy E. Elliott scholar 1958-59), U. Mich., 1964; postgrad. Washington Psychoanalytic Inst.; m. Irving Lawrence Graves, Dec. 31, 1969. Psychologist, U. Mich. Psychol. Clinic, 1960-63, asst. study dir. Survey Research Center, 1961-63, instr. psychology, 1964-70; asst. prof. Johns Hopkins U., 1970-76, prin. investigator under-nutrition and infant devel. Internat. Ctr. for Research, Calcutta, India and Kathmandu, Nepal, 1970-73, lectr., sr. research psychologist precursors study Med. Sch., 1979—; assoc. clin. prof. U. Md. Med. Sch.; dir. research Mental Health Study Center, NIMH, 1976-79; cons. in field. Fellow Md. Psychol. Assn.; mem. Am. Psychol. Assn., Am. Psychoanalytic Assn. Author articles in field, chpts. in books. Home: 2235 Kentucky Ave Baltimore MD 21213 Office: 550 N Broadway Baltimore MD 21205

GRAVES, SUSAN L. AKERS, marketing specialist; b. Garden City, Kans., Feb. 4, 1948; d. Riley D. and Clara F. (Pallissard) Akers. Student Ariz. State U., 1982-83; BS, U. Calif.-San Diego, 1972; post-grad. in bus. Loyola Marymount U., 1977-80. Pub. info. dir. Coll. Medicine, U. Calif.-Irvine, 1974-77; dir. pub. relations and publs. Loyola Marymount U., Los Angeles, 1977-82; v.p. Ralph Jackson Assocs., Beverly Hills, Calif., 1980-82; dir. pub. affairs Ramada Inns, Inc., Phoenix, 1982-83; pub. relations dir. Am. Med. Internat., Brea, Calif., 1983-84; mktg. dir. Irvine Office & Indsl. Cos. divs. The Irvine Co., Newport Beach, Calif., 1984—; prin. The Creative Consortium, mktg. firm. Active Scottsdale Arts Ctr. Assn., 1982-83, No. Ariz. Hist. Mus., Flagstaff, 1982, Los Angeles County Art Mus.; cons. LWV, Jr. Achievement, Phoenix, 1983; bd. dirs. Irvine Symphony, 1984-87, adv. bd. U. Calif., Irvine; chmn. adv. com. on mktg. Calif. Community Coll., 1985-87; mem. adv. bd. Irvine Sci. Edn. Inst., U. Calif., Co-recipient Silver Anvil award U. Calif.-San Diego, 1973; Council for Advancement and Support of Edn. grantee, 1976. Mem. Women in Communications, Inc. (Best Communications Student of Yr. 1970; editor regional newsletter 1970-72, regional student dir. 1970-72, v.p. 1982), Pub. Relations Soc. Am., Sigma Delta Chi. Democrat. Home: 20612 Reef Ln, Huntington Beach, CA 92646 Office: Irvine Co Newport Beach CA 92660

GRAVLEY, NANCY CARROLL, state agency administrator; b. Dublin, Ga., Sept. 19, 1940; d. Otis Iverson and Rubye Louise (Hudson) Carroll; children: Vicki Chaffin Bennett, Bryan R., Jennifer Carroll Gravley. BS, North Tex. State U., 1975. Cert. tchr., Tex. Qualified mental retardation profl. Denton (Tex.) State Sch., 1975-79; supt. Edmond Oaks Ctr., Lewisville, Tex., 1979-84; program dir. Grand Junction (Colo.) Regional Ctr., 1985-86; supr. Pueblo (Colo.) Regional Ctr., 1986—. Mem. Am. Assn. on Mental Deficiency (State Leadership award 1987), Nat. Assn. Supts., Pueblo C. of C. (com. 1986-87), The Twins Found. Republican. Mem. Christian Ch. Lodge: Order Ea. Star. Office: Pueblo Regional Ctr 1330 W 17th St Pueblo CO 81003

GRAY, ANN MAYNARD, broadcasting company executive; b. Boston, Aug. 22, 1945; d. Paul Maynard and Pauline Elizabeth MacFadyen; m. Richard R. Gray, Jr.; children: Richard R. Gray III, Dana Maynard. B.A., U. Mich., 1967; M.B.A., N.Y. U., 1971. With Chase Manhattan Bank, N.Y.C., 1967-68; with Chem. Bank, N.Y.C., 1968-73; asst. sec. Chem. Bank, 1971-73; asst. to treas., then asst. treas. ABC, Inc., 1974-76, treas., 1976-81, v.p. corp. planning, 1979-86; v.p. Capital Cities/ABC, Inc. (merged 1986), 1986—; sr. v.p. fin. ABC TV Network Group, 1988—; dir. Carteret Savs. Bank, Morristown, N.J., 1984—. Address: Capital Cities/ABC Inc 1330 Ave of Americas New York NY 10019

GRAY, ANNETTE MYERS, planner; b. Dayton, Ohio, Oct. 21, 1956; d. Floyd Eugene and Netha Jean (Roe) Myers; m. Wilburn Wayne Gray, Aug. 11, 1984. BA in History and Sociology, Wright State U., 1980; MA in History, Middle Tenn. State U., 1984. Hist. preservation cons. Thomasson & Assocs., Nashville, 1981-83; hist. preservation project mgr. Robert Seals Architect, Chattanooga, Tenn., 1984; planner Tenn. Dept. Econ. and Community Devel., Chattanooga, 1984-87; dir. Marion County Office Planning and Devel., South Pittsburg, Tenn., 1987—; advisor Marion County Hist. Soc., Jasper, Tenn., 1986—. Author: Neighborhood Conservation: North Maney Avenue, Murfreesboro, Tennessee, 1983. Mem. Nat. Trust for Hist. Preservation; adv. bd. Marion County Mental Health, 1986—, Southeast Tenn. Devel. Corp., Chattanooga, 1987—, Tenn. River Gorge Project, Chattanooga, 1987—; bd. dirs. Tenn. River Gorge Natural Areas Trust. Democrat. Episcopalian. Office: Marion County Office Planning and Devel 202 W 3d St South Pittsburg TN 37380

GRAY, CAROL GREVER, office temporary and personnel executive; b. Tulsa, July 20, 1940; d. Clyde M. and Merietta L. (Stroud) Grever; m. James Rowland Gray, Jan. 31, 1961; children:Stephen Scott, Gary Matthew. BA in Lang. Arts with honors, Phillips U., 1962; MA in English with distinction, Pacific U., Oreg., 1966; doctoral candidate Okla. State U., 1971-72. High sch. tchr., Fort Worth, 1961-62, Beaverton, Oreg., 1963; asst. prof. Phillips U., Enid, Okla., 1966-73; v.p., Express Temp., Boulder, Colo., 1973—; tng. cons. Express Services, Inc., Oklahoma City, 1984—; bd. dirs. Colo. Nat. Bank. Author: Sun of a New Dawn, 1983; contbr. articles to newspapers. Bd. dirs. Boulder YWCA, 1984, Community Food Share, 1985. Mem. Nat. Assn. Temp. Services, Nat. Assn. Personnel Cons., Colo. Assn. Personnel Cons., Bus. and Profl. Women, Boulder C. of C. (exec. council 1984—, dir. 1984—, pres.-elect 1986, chair ambassadors council 1983, chmn. bd. dirs. 1987, grad. Leadership Boulder 1984). Democrat. Clubs: Soroptimists (past pres.) (Boulder). Lodge: Rotary. Avocations: travel, writing, water sports, cats. Office: Express Services 2741 Mapleton Ave Boulder CO 80302

GRAY, CAROL HICKSON, chemical engineer; b. Atlanta, Jan. 3, 1958; d. Ronald Allen and Charlotte Patricia (Blitch) Hickson; m. Randy Lee Gray, June 25, 1983; 1 child, Amanda Christine. BSChemE, Ga. Inst. Tech., 1979. Process engr. Air Products and Chems., Inc., Calvert City, Ky., 1979-83, sr. process engr., 1983-86, sr. prodn. engr., 1986-87, prin. prodn. engr., 1987—. Mem. Nat. Assn. Female Execs. Office: Air Products and Chemicals Inc Box 97 Calvert City KY 42029

GRAY, CAROLYN MARGARET, library administrator; b. Judsonia, Ark., Feb. 26, 1945; d. Robert Vernon and Edna Irene (Poindexter) G.; m. James R. Cox, May 16, 1965 (div. 1979); children: Jason Edward. BA in English, U. Mo., St. Louis, 1968; MLS, U. Okla., 1976; postgrad., Brandeis U., 1983—. English tchr. Cabool (Mo.) Pub. Schs., 1969-71; librarian Judsonia (Ark.) Pub. Schs., 1972-75; reference librarian U. Okla. Library, Norman, 1976-77; asst. to dir. AMIGOS Bibliographic Council, Dallas, 1977-79; head of cataloging Western Ill. U. Library, Macomb, 1979-81; cons. in field 1981-82; assoc. dir. Brandeis U. Library, Waltham, Mass., 1982—; cons. Resource Sharing Alliance for West Cen. Ill, Quincy, 1980-81, Shanghai Jiao Tong U., People's Republic of China, 1985; researcher, cons. Minuteman Library Network, Framington, Mass., 1987. Co-author: (book) Microfilm Catalogs, 1977; contbr. articles to profl. jours.. Asst. leader Girl Scouts of Am., Cabool, 1970; mem. Georgetown Homeowners Assn., Macomb, 1979-81; mem. service com. Arlington St. Ch., Boston, 1982-83. Grantee Edith C. Blum Found., 1985—, Pew Meml. Trust, 1985-87, Roblee Found., 1986. Mem. Library & Info. Tech. Assn. (pres. 1981-82), Am. Library Assn., Am. Soc. for Info. Scis., Library Hi-Tech (asst. editor 1983-85). Democrat. Unitarian. Office: Brandeis U Library 415 South St Waltham MA 02254

GRAY, CATHERINE GARRISON, personnel executive; b. Allen, Tex., Dec. 30, 1926; d. Larkin Guy and Ella Ruth (Keyworth) Garrison; m. Hoyle Mack Gray, June 6, 1945; 1 child, Jim Mack. Office clk. Tex. Bond Reporter, Dallas. 1944-45; acctg. clk. Dallas Title & Guaranty Co., 1946-48, sec., bookkeeper, 1949-70; personnel coordinator USLIFE Title Ins. Co., Dallas, 1971-75, v.p. personnel adminstrn., 1975-85; sr. v.p. human resources Title USA Ins. Corp., 1985—. Mem. Internat. Graphoanalysis Soc., Tex. Graphoanalysts (treas. 1982), Dallas Personnel Assn. Mem. Ch. of Christ. Avocations: camping, handwriting analysis. Home: 208 Whisenant Dr PO Box 157 Allen TX 75002 Office: 580 Decker Dr Irving TX 75062

GRAY, CRYSTAL GRACE, communications executive; b. Anderson, Ind., Oct. 16, 1954; d. Aaron Leon and Mary (Wesley) Bales; m. Philip Alan Gray. BA in Sociology, Hanover Coll., 1977; teaching cert., Temple U., 1981; MSBA, Boston U., 1982. Mgr. Marlo Mortgage Co., Austin, Tex., 1982-84, Tex. Instruments, Johnson City, Tenn., 1985—. Bd. dirs. Am. Cancer Soc. (pub. info. officer), 1987-88. Mem. Nat. Assn. Female Execs. Methodist. Club: Mt. Laurel Coop. (asst. treas. 1987). Office: Tex Instruments Erwin Hwy Johnson City TN 37604

GRAY, DAHLI, accounting educator; b. Grand Junction, Colo., Dec. 28, 1948; d. Forrest Walter and Mary (Crockett) G.; m. Paul Victor Konka, Jan. 23, 1981. BS, Ea. Oreg. State U., 1971; MBA, Portland (Oreg.) State U., 1976; D of Bus. Adminstrn., George Washington U., 1984. Instr. acctg. Portland State U., 1976-79, George Mason U., Fairfax, Va., 1980, George Washington U., Washington, 1981-82; asst. prof. Oreg. State U., Corvallis, 1983-86; research fellow U. Notre Dame, South Bend, Ind., 1986-88; assoc. prof. Am. U., Washington, 1988—. Contbr. articles to profl. jours. Named Tchr. of Yr., Alpha Lambda Delta, 1986; Peat Marwick Mitchell & Co. fellow, 1986. Mem. Internat. Assn. Acctg. Research and Edn., Am. Inst. CPA's, Nat. Assn. Accts. (Andrew Barr award 1982, 84, Cert. Merit 1982), Am. Acctg. Assn., Inst. Cert. Mgmt. Accts. Democrat. Home: 5564 Burnside Dr Rockville MD 20853-2457 Office: Am U Kogod Coll of Bus Washington DC 20016

GRAY, DEBORAH ANN, health agency administrator; b. North Adams, Mass., Oct. 19, 1951; d. Samuel and Grace (O'Neil) Scarfone. BA, U. Mass., 1974; MSW, Adelphi U., 1979. Investigator's aide Commonwealth of Mass., Boston, 1973-74; editorial asst. West Pub. Co., Mineloa, N.Y., 1974-76; project supr. Suffolk Community Council, Smithtown, N.Y., 1977; with Nassau-Suffolk Health Systems Agy., Plainview, N.Y., 1977—, info. coordinator, 1979-81, dep. dir., 1981-88; adminstr. accreditation/regulation North Shore Univ. Hosp., Manhasset, N.Y., 1988—. Active Norfolk Environ. Council, Suffolk County, 1977-82, Nassau County Legis. Network, 1986, Suffolk County Environ. Task Force, 1987; bd. dirs. Nassau Health and Welfare Council, 1987. Mem. Am. Health Planning Assn., Am. Pub. Health Assn., L.I. Communicators Assn., Nat. Assn. Social Workers (bd. dirs. Suffolk chpt. 1979-80). Home: 140 Scudder Ave Northport NY 11768

GRAY, DEBORAH J., public relations executive, consultant; b. Sydney, Australia. M. in Sociology, U. New South Wales, Sydney, 1981. Market researcher George Patterson Advt., Sydney, 1980-81; research asst. dept. sociology U. New South Wales, Sydney, 1981-83; ops. mgr., coordinator Houston Internat. Film Festival, 1983-84; dir. projects Shifrin-Blocher REsearch, N.Y.C., 1983-84; publicity assoc. E.P. Dutton, N.Y.C., 1984—; market researcher The Brit. Market Research Bur., London, 1983, Consumer Connection, London, 1983, Choice Consumer Reports Mag., Sydney, 1983; fund raiser Houston Grand Opera, 1983-84; documentary researcher Gittelman Film Assocs., N.Y.C., 1983; pubs. tchr., cons. Planned Parenthood of Mineola, N.Y., 1983—.

GRAY, DONNA MAE, agricultural products executive; b. Wing, Ill., Dec. 17, 1933; d. Sylvester Roy and Mary Henreitta (Watkins) Fosdick; m. Joyce Glenward Gray, June 1, 1952; children: Allen Keith, Glenda Mae, Cindy Lee, Burton Roberts, Terry Lynn. Nurses aid graduate, Fairbury Hosp.; student, Ill. State U., 1969-70, Winston Churchill Coll., Elec. Computor Programming Inst. Mgr., co-owner Glenn Donna Grocery Store, Fairbury, Ill., 1957; assembler Am. Screen Factory, Chatsworth, Ill., 1957; clk. Tullis News Stand, Chatsworth, Ill., 1958; nurses aide Fairbury Hosp., 1959-65; supr. cost accounting Pontiac (Ill.) Chair Co., 1966-69; balancing clk. Mid Ill. Data Ctr., Pontiac, Ill., 1970-71; office mgr. Grant City Dept. Store, Pontiac, Ill., 1972-75; bookkeeper Pontiac (Ill.) Farm Store, 1976-77, mgr., v.p., 1977—. Mem. Small Bus. Conf., (delegate 1984-85) , Retail Farm Equipment Assn., (pres. zone 4, 1978-80). Republican. Methodist. Office: Pontiac Farm Store Inc 1503 N Division Pontiac IL 61764

GRAY, DORIS MACK, information specialist; b. Balt., Feb. 1, 1950; d. Silas James and Lelia Elizabeth (Coleman) M.; divorced; children: Jonathan Derrell, Donita Montré. AA, Community Coll. Balt., 1974; BS in Econs., Towson (Md.) State U., 1976. Lic. real estate agt., Md. Instr. Bay Coll. Md., Balt., 1977-79; tech. writer Sci. Mgmt. Corp-Data Tech. Industries, Inc., Lanham, Md., 1979-80; sr. tech. writer L.R. Davis & Co., Silver Spring, Md., 1980-81, Maxima Corp., Bethesda, Md., 1981-83, Bus. Methods and Systems Inc., Lanham, 1983-84; specialist documentaton Montgomery County Sch. System, Rockville, Md., 1984-85, Citicorp Fin., Inc., Lutherville, Md., 1985—; real estate aft. Preston T. Johnson & Co., Balt., 1978—; cons. writing numerous contractors, Balt., 1979-82. Contbr. articles to profl. jours., dir. community theater group, 1986 (award 1986). Bd. dirs. Student Day Care Ctr., Towson, 1974-77; organizer various polit. campaigns, Balt., 1978-82; organist, choir dir. Caroline St. Meth. Ch., Balt., 1981-86; lobbyist Lida Lee Tall PTA, Towson, 1982; arbitrator Better Tus. Bur., Balt., 1987. Mem. Nat. Assn. Female Execs., Coll. Reunion Alumni Com. (treas. 1987—), Community Coll. Balt. Student Govt. Assn. (reunion alumni com.). Democrat. Home: PO Box 11866 Baltimore MD 21207

GRAY, DORIS WILLIAMS, marriage and family counselor; b. Dodge County, Ga., Nov. 7, 1936; s. Harry Melton and Evelyn Louise (NeSmith) Williams; m. Robert Floyd Gray, June 14, 1959; children—Pamela, John, Karen. B.S., Ga. Coll., 1958; M.Ed., U. Ga., 1975. Cert. addiction counselor. Tchr. home econs., Quincy, Fla., 1958-61; extension home economist DeKalb County, Mo., 1963-65; tchr. adult edn. Milledgeville, Ga., 1970-73; psychologist Peachbelt Mental Health Center, Warner Robins, Ga., 1975-79; marriage and family counselor, addiction counselor Warner Robins, 1975—. Mem. Ga. Assn. Marriage and Family Therapists (pres. Middle Ga. chpt.), Ga. Addiction Counselors Assn. (bd. dirs., v.p. 1984, pres. 1985—), Nat. Fedn. Parents for Drug-Free Youth, Am. Assn. Marriage and Family Therapy, Nat. Assn. Alcohol and Drug Addiction Counselors (coordinator nat. counselor 1985, bd. dirs. 1985—). Democrat. Baptist. Office: 1764 Watson Blvd Suite 204 Warner Robins GA 31093

GRAY, ENID MAURINE, city official, director of libraries; b. Galveston, Tex., Sept. 2, 1943; d. Willis James and Enid (Childress) G. BA, NE La. State U., 1966; MLS, North Tex. State U., 1969. Sch. librarian Caddo Parish Sch. Bd., Shreveport, La., 1966; dir. libraries City of Beaumont, Tex., 1966-84, 87—, sr. dir. community services, 1984-87; prof. Sch. Library Sci., Sam Houston State U., Huntsville, Tex., 1976; chmn. Library Systems Act adv. bd. Tex. State Library, Austin, 1976-79. Author: History of Medicine in Beaumont, Texas, 1969; Beaumont Libraries, Then and Now, 1976. Pres. Beaumont Civic Opera, 1976-77, Jefferson Theatre Preservation Soc., 1984, Crime Stoppers Beaumont, 1988; bd. dirs. United Way North Jefferson County, 1987—; arbitrator Beaumont Better Bus. Bur., 1981—. Recipient Disting. Alumnus award Sch. Library and Info. Service, North Tex. State U., 1980. Mem. Tex. Library Assn. (life; pres. 1974-75, chmn. polit. action com. 1983—), ALA, Tex. Mcpl. Library Dirs. Assn. (pres. 1971-72), Beaumont Jr. League. Club: Altrusa (pres. Beaumont 1981-83, Community Service award 1981). Methodist. Avocations: civic activities, reading, gardening. Office: City of Beaumont PO Box 3827 Beaumont TX 77704

GRAY, FALINE MATHER, educator; b. Manchester, Conn., Mar. 29, 1943; d. Gilbert LaPlace and Antoinette R. (Rathbone) Mather; m. William Kenworthy Gray, Aug. 28, 1968; children: William Jr., Jeffrey M. BS, Tusculum Coll., 1965; postgrad., Temple U., 1966-75. Cert. elem. tchr., Pa. Counselor, dir. YMCA Day Camps, Deep River, Conn., 1961-65; spl. edn. tchr. N. Pa. Sch. Dist., Lansdale, Pa., 1965-68, substitute tchr., 1972-77; cons., dir. Bright Beginnings Sch., Lansdale, Pa., 1976; dir. Bldg. Blocks Christian Nursery Sch., Lansdale, Pa., 1980—; foster mother Bethany Christian Services, Phila., 1982-85, Bethanna Home for Children, Phila., 1985—. Contbr. articles to profl. jours. Chmn. Centennial Town of Lansdale, 1976. Named one of Outstanding Young Women of Am., 1974. Mem. Questers, Inc. (pres. 1975, nat. 2d prize 1976, chmn. bicentennial display 1976), Nat. Edn. for the Young Child (bd. dirs. 1980), Pa. Home Schoolers (bd. dirs. 1984), Lansdale Hist. Soc. (v.p. publicity 1975). Republican. Presbyterian. Home: 605 Delaware Ave Lansdale PA 19446 Office: Lansdale Presbyn Ch PO Box 664 Lansdale PA 19446

GRAY, GEAN CHATHAM, ceramicist; b. Bay City, Tex., Apr. 15, 1939; d. J.C. and Myra Carola (Hill) Chatham; m. James Wesley Kelly, May 15, 1956 (div.); m. James Carrell Gray, July 27, 1957; children—Joseph Allen, Clara Nell Gray Green, Myra Lee Gray Duke, Jennifer Marie Gray Smith. Student La. State U.-Eunice, 1968-69, Sam Houston State U., 1979-80, Lee Coll., 1980. PBX operator, Madison County Hosp., Madisonville, Tex., 1975-79; ceramicist Gray & Gray Enterprises, Madisonville, 1984-87. Mem. Nocona Adult Right to Read Program Council, Nat. Rifle Assn. Democrat. Baptist. Club: Chico Quilting. Lodge: Order Eastern Star. Avocations: reading; sewing; swimming; cards and letters; writing poems. Home: Rt 1 Box 171 Madisonville TX 77864

GRAY, GEORGIA NEESE, banker; b. Richland, Kans.; d. Albert and Ellen (O'Sullivan) Neese; A.B., Washburn Coll., 1921; D.B.A. (hon.), 1966; student Sargent's, 1921-22; L.H.D. (hon.), Russell Sage Coll., 1950; m. George M. Clark, Jan. 21, 1929; m. 2d, Andrew J. Gray, 1953. Began as actress, 1923; asst. cashier Richland State Bank, 1935-37, pres., 1937—; pres. Capital City State Bank & Trust Co., Topeka, 1964-74; dir. Capital City State Bank and Trust, Topeka; treas. of U.S., 1949-53; mem. Commn. Jud. Qualifications Supreme Ct. Kans. Del.-at-large nat. adv. com. SBA; Democratic nat. committeewoman, 1936-64; hon. chmn. Villages project C. of C. Bd. dirs. Kans. A.A.A., 1950—; bd. dirs., former chmn. Kans. div. Am. Cancer Soc.; mem. bd. exec. campaign and maj. gifts com. Georgetown U.; bd. dirs. Seven Steps Found., Harry S. Truman Library; chmn. Alpha Phi Found., 1962-63; mem. nat. bd. Women's Med. Coll. Pa.; chmn. bd. regents Washburn U., 1975-86; mem. bd., treas. Sex Information and Edn. Council U.S.; mem. White House Com. on Aging. Recipient Disting. Alumni award Washburn U., 1950. Mem. Am. Bus. Women's Assn., Topeka C. of C., Met. Bus. and Profl. Women's Club, Women in Communications, Alpha Phi (nat. trustee), Alpha Phi Upsilon, Alpha Delta Kappa. Clubs: Soroptimist (hon. life), Met. Zonta, Topeka Country. Address: 2709 W 29 St Topeka KS 66614

GRAY, GWEN CASH, agricultural finance manager; b. Cowpens, S.C., Oct. 24, 1943; d. Woodrow C. and Marie (Hamrick) Cash; m. Charles H. Gray, Oct. 24, 1987 ; children: Dianne Marie Young, Teena Michele Bulman. BS, Limestone Coll., Gaffney, S.C., 1984. Sec., treas. Cash Farms, Inc., Cowpens, 1963—; sales agt. Hammett-Miller Real Estate, Spartanburg, S.C., 1985—; bd. dirs. Citizens and So. Nat. Bank, Gaffney; lectr. in field. Contbr. articles to profl. jours. Advisor Clemson U. Extension Service, Clemson, S.C., 1987—, S.C. Peach Festival, Gaffney, 1977—; bd. dirs. Palmetto Health Ctr., Cowpens, 1985—. Named Woman of Yr. Bus. and Profl. Women, 1979, Woman of Yr. S.C. Rural Electric Coop., 1984. Mem. Am. Farm Bur. (chair deciduous fruits adv. com.), Nat. Peach Council, Nat. Bd. Realtors, S.C. Farm Bur. (chmn. fruit com.), S.C. Peach Council, S.C. Bd. Realtors, S.C. Hort. Soc. (bd. dirs.), S.C. Assn. Agriculture Agts. (friend of extension award 1986). Republican. Baptist. Home and Office: Hwy 110 Cowpens SC 29330

GRAY, HANNA HOLBORN, university president; b. Heidelberg, Germany, Oct. 25, 1930; d. Hajo and Annemarie (Bettmann) Holborn; m. Charles Montgomery Gray, June 19, 1954. AB, Bryn Mawr Coll., 1950; PhD, Harvard U., 1957; MA, Yale U., 1971, LLD, 1978; LittD (hon.), St. Lawrence U., 1974; HHD (hon.), St. Mary's Coll., 1974; LHD (hon.), Grinnell (Iowa) Coll., 1974, Lawrence U., 1974, Denison U., 1974; LLD (hon.), Union Coll., 1975, Regis Coll., 1976; LHD (hon.), Wheaton Coll., 1976; LLD (hon.), Dartmouth Coll., 1978, Trinity Coll., 1978, U. Bridgeport, 1978, Dickinson Coll., 1979, Brown U., 1979, Wittenburg U., 1979; LHD (hon.), Marlboro Coll., 1979, Rikkyo (Japan) U., 1979; LittD (hon.), Oxford (Eng.) U., 1979; LHD (hon.), Roosevelt U., 1980, Knox Coll., 1980; LLD (hon.), U. Rochester, 1980, U. Notre Dame, 1980, U. So. Calif., 1980, U. Mich., 1981; LHD (hon.), Coe Coll., 1981, Thomas Jefferson U., 1981, Duke U., 1982, New Sch. for Social Research, 1982, Clark U., 1982; LLD (hon.), Princeton U., 1982, Georgetown U., 1983; LHD (hon.), Brandeis U., 1983, Colgate U., 1983, Wayne State U., 1984, Miami U., Oxford, Ohio, 1984, So. Meth. U., Dallas, 1984; LLD (hon.), Marquette U., 1984, W.Va. Wesleyan U., 1985, Hamilton Coll., 1985; LHD (hon.), CUNY, 1985, U. Denver, 1985; LittD, Washington U., St. Louis, 1985; LHD (hon.), Am. Coll. Greece, 1986; LLD, Smith Coll., 1986, U. Miami, 1986; LLD (hon.), Columbia U., 1987; LHD (hon.), Muskingum Coll., 1987, Rush Presbyn. St. Lukes Med. Ctr., Chgo., 1987. Instr. Bryn Mawr Coll., 1953-54; teaching fellow Harvard, Pa., 1955-57; instr. Harvard, 1957-59, asst. prof., 1959-60, vis. lectr., 1963-64; asst. prof. U. Chgo., 1961-64, asso. prof., 1964-72; dean, prof. Northwestern U., Evanston, Ill., 1972-74; provost, prof. history Yale U., 1974-78, acting pres., 1977-78; pres., prof. history U. Chgo., 1978—; dir. Cummins Engine Co., J.P. Morgan & Co., Morgan Guaranty Trust Co., Atlantic Richfield Co., Ameritech; fellow Center for Advanced Study in Behavioral Scis., 1966-67, vis. scholar, 1970-71. Editor: (with Charles Gray) Jour. Modern History,

1965-70; contbr. articles to profl. jours. Mem. Nat. Council on Humanities, 1972-78; trustee Yale Corp., 1971-74; bd. dirs. Chgo. Council Fgn. Relations, Andrew W. Mellon Found.; trustee Mus. Sci. and Industry, Bryn Mawr Coll., Field Found. Ill., Howard Hughes Med. Inst., Nat. Humanities Ctr. Recipient Medal Liberty award, 1986; Fulbright scholar, 1950-52; U. Chgo. Newberry Library fellow, 1960-61; Phi Beta Kappa vis. scholar, 1971-72; hon. fellow St. Anne's Coll., Oxford U., 1978—. Fellow Am. Acad. Arts and Scis.; mem. Renaissance Soc. Am., Am. Philos. Soc., Nat. Acad. Edn., Phi Beta Kappa. Office: U of Chgo 5801 S Ellis Ave Chicago IL 60637

GRAY, JACQUELINE SUE WESTFAHL, psychologist; b. Enid, Okla., Sept. 2, 1951; d. Harold Wiley and Peggy Onita (Hedges) Westfahl; m. Jan Livingston Gray, May 14, 1971 (div. May 1975); children: Doug, David. BS in Lab. Tech., U. Okla., 1977, MEd in Counseling Psychology, 1984. Histology aide Norman (Okla.) Regional Hosp., 1981-82; math. and sci. aide Norman High Sch., 1982-83; counselor adv. Women's Resource Ctr., Norman, 1983-86; psychol. asst. Creek County Dept. Health, Sapulpa, Okla., 1986—; therapist Sexual Abuse Treatment Team, Sapulpa, 1986—; cons. Shelter for Friends, Norman, 1983-86. Bd. dirs. Domestic Violence Intervention Service, Tulsa, 1986-87; advisor Sapulpa Met. Area Response Team, 1986; adv. bd. Sapulpa Pub. Schs. Drug Prevention Program, 1987. Mem. Am. Assn. Counseling and Devel., Am. Mental Health Counselors Assn., Assn. for Measurement and Evaluation in Counseling and Devel., Nat. Vocat. Guidance Assn., Nat. Assn. for Female Execs. Republican. Baptist. Home: PO Box 2215 Sapulpa OK 74067 Office: Creek County Dept Health PO Box 609 Sapulpa OK 74067

GRAY, JEANNE (MRS. JOHN B. MC DONALD), television producer; b. Seattle, Sept. 10, 1917; d. George Patrick and Mary Edna (Gray) Murphy; m. John B. Mc Donald, June 30, 1951; children: Gregory Roland Stoner, Margaret Jeanne Eve. Student, Columbia U., 1940, Art Students League, 1940-43, Nat. Acad. Dramatic Art, 1945. Radio producer, commentator The Woman's Voice Sta. KMPC, Los Angeles, 1947-50; TV producer, commentator, writer The Woman's Voice Sta. KTTV-CBS, Los Angeles, 1950-51; TV producer, commentator The Jeanne Gray Show Sta. KNXT-TV CBS, Los Angeles, 1951-53; West Coast editor Home Show NBC network, Los Angeles, 1955-56; TV film producer documentaries and travelogues Virgonian Prodns., Los Angeles, 1953—. Author: The Power of Belonging, 1978. Women's chmn. Los Angeles Beautiful, 1971; mem. Women's Aux. St. John's Hosp.; trustee Freedoms Found. at Valley Forge, 1966—, founder, pres. women's chpt., Los Angeles County chpt., 1965-66, Western dir women's chpt., 1967-68, nat. chmn. 1968-71, nat. chmn. women vols., 1973-75, hon life mem. Recipient Francis Holmes Outstanding Achievement award, 1949, Silver Mike award, 1948, Emmy award Acad. TV Arts and Scis., 1951, Lulu award Los Angeles Advt. Women, 1952, Genii award Radio and TV Women, 1956, George Washington Honor award Freedoms Found. Valley Forge, 1967, honor cert., 1972, Morale award Christians and Jews for Law and Morality, 1968, Exceptional Service award Freedoms Found., 1975, Liberty Belle award Rep. Women's Club, 1975, Leadership award Los Angeles City Schs., 1976, Theodore Roosevelt award USN League, 1986. Mem. Am. Women in Radio and TV, Radio and TV Women So. Calif. (hon. life, founder, 1st pres. 1952), Footlighters (v.p. 1958-59), Los Angeles C. of C. (dir. women's div. 1954-54, mem. exec. bd., women's div. 1954-66, pres. women's div. 1963-64, hon. past pres. women's div. 1979), Los Angeles Orphanage Guild, DAR, The Muses, Les Dames de Champagne. Clubs: Bel Air Garden (Calif.), Yacht, Les Dames de Champagne. Home: 910 Stradella Rd Bel Air Los Angeles CA 90077

GRAY, JO ANNA, economist; b. July 8, 1950; m. Wesley Warren Wilson; 1 child, Kelsey Gray. BA, Rockford Coll., 1971; AM in Econs., U. Chgo., 1973, PhD in Econs., 1976. Instr. econs. U. Rochester, N.Y., 1975-76; asst. prof. U. Penn., 1976-78; economist Bd. Govs. Fed. Res. System, 1978-83; assoc. prof. econs. Washington State U., 1983—; visiting asst. prof. econs. U. Washington, spring 1981. Mem. editorial bds. Am. Econ. Review; contbr. articles to profl. jours. Fellow NSF, 1971-74, Earhart 1974-75; grantee NSF, 1986-88. Mem. Phi Beta Kappa. Home: SW 525 Henry St Pullman WA 99163 Office: Washington State U Dept Econs Pullman WA 99164

GRAY, JODE A., theatre facilities manager; b. Manhattan, N.Y., Sept. 23, 1962; d. Robert and Nicki (Stang) G. BS in Speech, Emerson Coll., 1982; MA, NYU, 1988; postgrad., New Sch. Social Research. Prodn. asst. Major League Baseball Prodns., N.Y.C., 1983-85; mgr. audio-visual services Chase Manhattan Bank, N.Y.C., 1985-86; mgr. theatre facilities Auditorium at Equitable, N.Y.C., 1986—. Writer, producer, dir.: (video) Intro. to Values in Hidden Curriculum, 1988. Mem. Ednl. Communication & Tech., Soc. Satellite Profls., Nat. Assn. Female Execs., Am. Library Assn. Office: Tishman Speyer Properties 1285 6th Ave New York NY 10019

GRAY, JUDITH MONROE, librarian; b. Big Spring, Tex., Dec. 26, 1940; d. Wilson Adams and Katharine (Hanson) Monroe; m. James Isiah Gray Jr., Nov. 3, 1967 (div. 1977). AA, Bakersfield Coll., 1960; BA in German, UCLA, 1964; MLS, U. So. Calif., Los Angeles, 1967. Librarian reference Kern County Library, Bakersfield, Calif., 1966-67; children's librarian Santa Monica (Calif.) Pub. Library, 1967-68; librarian Los Angeles County Library, Montebello, Calif., 1968-69; regional children's librarian Los Angeles County Library, Rosemead, Calif., 1969-71; librarian Grummond Coll., U. So. Miss. Library, Hattiesburg, 1971-72; sch. librarian Pascagoula (Miss.) Sch. Dist., 1973-78; dir. Howard County Library, Big Spring, 1980—; resource person Region 18 Edn. Service Ctr., Midland, Tex., 1983—; mem. vocat. edn. adv. council Big Spring Ind. Sch. Dist., 1986—; mem. Future Program Planning Com. West Tex. Library System, Lubbock, 1983-86, mem. Automation Rev. Commn., 1983, mem. collection devel. com., 1982, 86, 87, mem. continuing edn. com., 1980-83. Mem. exec. com. Caprock Chpt. March of Dimes, Big Spring, 1982-84; co-organizer, pres. Crossroads Adult Need to Read Literacy Council and Bd., 1986—; mem. Symphony Guild, 1987—, Spring City Players Community Theater. Mem. ALA, Tex. Library Assn. (chmn. dist. 1983-84, councilor 1985—), Permian Librarians Coop., Big Spring Area C. of C. (Citation 1983, pub. relations com., sec. 1984, chmn. 1985-86, sec. exec. com. 1985-86, women's div.), AAUW (3d v.p. 1982-83, 1st v.p. 1984-85). Presbyterian. Office: Howard County Library 312 Scurry St Big Spring TX 79720

GRAY, KATHLEEN ANN, lawyer; b. Reading, Pa., May 16, 1947; d. Sebastian and Helen Mary (Zajac) Vespico; m. George A. Gray, Oct. 22, 1966 (dec. 1968). BSBA, Drexel U., 1971, MBA, 1978; JD, Wake Forest U., 1977. Bar: Pa. 1977. Computer programmer Ednl. Testing Service, Princeton, N.J., 1971-73, dir. EDP tng., 1973-74; assoc. Barley, Snyder, Cooper & Barber, Lancaster, Pa., 1977-83, ptnr., 1983—. Mem. Wake Forest Law Rev., 1975-77. Bd. dirs. Hist. Preservation Trust of Lancaster County, 1978—, v.p., 1984; sec. bd. dirs. Lancaster Integrated Specialized Transp. System, 1981-85; bd. dirs. Am. Lung Assn. of Lancaster County, 1982—, v.p. 1987—, Leadership Lancaster; sec., treas. Found. Lancaster Chamber, 1985—, Lancaster Pub. Library, 1987—; mem. arbitration panel Better Bus. Bur. Mem. ABA, Pa. Bar Assn., Lancaster County Bar Assn., Pa. Sch. Bd. Solicitors Assn., Nat. Assn. of Bond Lawyers. Republican. Office: Barley Snyder Cooper & Barber 126 E King St Lancaster PA 17602

GRAY, LINDA, actress; b. Santa Monica, Calif., Sept. 12; m. Ed Thrasher (div. 1983); children: Jeff, Kelly. Studied with Charles Conrad. Worked as model; appeared in over 400 television comml.s; appeared in film Dogs; television films include: The Two Worlds of Jenny Logan, Haywire, Chimps, Not in Front of the Children, The Wild and Free; appeared in television series All That Glitters, 1977, Dallas, 1978—; other television appearances include Marcus Welby, M.D; host CBS documentary: The Body Human: The Loving Process, 1981; co-host: Golden Globe awards, 1981. Emmy nominee for Dallas, 1981; recipient Bambi award for best actress Germany, 1982; Il Gato award for best actress Italy, 1983, 84; named Woman of Yr., Hollywood Radio and TV Soc., 1982. Office: PO Box 1370 Canyon Country CA 91351 *

GRAY, LOUISE MAXINE, paramedical examiner; b. Wichita, Kans., Feb. 18, 1938; d. Cliff Calvin and Pearl Rose (Edgar) Robey; m. Raymond E. Sanborn, Mar. 16, 1963 (div. 1968); 1 child, Lloyd Leslie.; m. Morris Wilson Gray, July 31, 1981. Cert. nurse's aide, med. aide, EKG technician, hematologist. Nurses aide Regency Health Care, Wichita, 1981-83; pres., owner L&M EKG, Inc., Wichita, 1987—. Mem. Nat. Assn. Female Execs., Internat. Mounted Police Assn., Am. Fedn. Police, Kans. Advocacy & Protective Services Assn. Home: 3300 N Waco Wichita KS 67204

GRAY, MARCIA TOMPANE, publishing executive, consultant; b. Dover, N.J., Feb. 14, 1941; d. Albert Benton and Dorothea Mae (McGinnis) Tompane; m. John Dana Wise Jr., Dec. 23, 1962 (dec.); children—Anne Stuart, John Dana III; m. 2d, Horace Alfred Gray III (div.). B.A.A., Bennett Coll., 1961; postgrad. U. Va., 1970-76. Ptnr. TBH Ltd., Richmond, Va., 1970-76; pres. The Inside Job Ltd., Aspen, Colo., 1976-82, DIMA Group Ltd., Denver, 1982-85; pres. Gray Design Group, 1985—; pub. Denver Design Directory, 1986; Design Directories Inc., 1986—; v.p. Designers Market Place, 1984—. Guest editor Colo. Homes & Lifestyle, 1981. Bd. dirs. Belle Bryan Day Nursery, Richmond, Va., 1965-76, Valentine Mus., Richmond, 1970-76; alumnae rep. Bennett Coll., Millbrook, N.Y., 1969-71. Fellow Aspen Inst. Humanities; mem. Downtown Denver Inc., Historic Denver Inc. Republican. Episcopalian. Club: Oxford (Denver).

GRAY, MARGARET ANN, management educator, consultant; b. Junction City, Kans., Sept. 19, 1950; d. Carl Ray and Mayme Louise (Kopmeyer) G.; m. Dennis Wayne Stokes, June 9, 1973 (div. July 1981); m. Robert Frederick Carlson Jr., Nov. 21, 1987. BEd, Pittsburg State U., Kans., 1972; MBA, Wichita State U., 1981. Tchr., Sch. Dist. 1, Kansas City, Mo., 1972-73; tchr. Haysville Sch. Dist., Kans., 1974-81, dist. coordinator, 1979-81; instr. mgmt. Wichita State U., 1981-85; mgmt. devel. rep. Beech Aircraft Corp. a Raytheon Co., Wichita, 1985-87, mgr. mgmt. devel. and tng., 1988—; cons. Dartnell Inst., Chgo., 1983—; assoc. dir. Ctr. for Entrepreneurship, Wichita State U., 1984-85. Bd. dirs. Kans. Found. for partnerships in Edn., 1986—; mem. United Way (Speakers' Bur., 1986—, Vol. Training Dir., 1987—, tng. com. 1987—). Mem. ASTD, Beta Gamma Sigma. Democrat. Roman Catholic. Club: Turnip (Wichita). Avocations: ballet, cross country skiing, classical music, hot air ballooning. Office: Beech Aircraft Corp 9709 E Central St Wichita KS 67206

GRAY, MARGARET EDNA, nursing educator; b. Norfolk Va., June 11, 1931; d. William E. and Margaret E. (Smith) G.; diploma Norfolk Gen. Hosp. Sch. Nursing, 1952; B.S. in Nursing, Columbia U., 1956; M.S., U. Md., 1966; Ed.D., Va. Poly. Inst. and State U., 1980. Staff nurse Norfolk Gen. Hosp., 1952-55, asst. night supr., 1953-54, instr. med.-surg. nursing, 1956-58; instr. med.-surg. nursing Riverside Hosp. Sch. Nursing, Newport, Va., 1958-64; ednl. dir. Va. Bd. Nursing, Richmond, 1965-69; coordinator health technology Va. Dept. Community Colls., Richmond, 1969-72; asso. prof. nursing, dir. nursing program, Va. Appalachian Tricoll., Abingdon, 1972-78; grad. research asst. Va. Poly. Inst. and State U., Blacksburg, 1979; asst. prof. nursing grad. program U. Va. Sch. Nursing, Charlottesville, 1980-82, mem. adj. faculty outreach grad. program, 1977-79; chmn. dept. nursing Va. State U., Petersburg, 1982-87; chmn. div. nursing Ga. Southwestern Coll., Americus, 1988—; cons. nursing programs various community colls. in Va., 1969—; mem. adv. com. ARC Health Systems Agy., Va. and Tenn. 1977-78. Mem. human rights com. Southside Tng. Ctr. and mem. adv. com. allied health programs John Tyler Community Coll., Chester, Va. Mem. Nat. League Nursing, Va. League Nursing (fin. com. 1981—, dir. 1982), Am. Nurses Assn., Va. Nurses Assn. (sec. 1976-79, com. mem. 1980—). Presbyterian. Contbr. articles on health care edn. to profl. publs. Office: Ga Southwestern Coll Div Nursing Americus GA 31709

GRAY, MARIANNE WEBSTER, artist; b. Gary, Ind., Dec. 20, 1941; d. Darwin Gray and Marion Blanche (Yarnold) Webster; m. William Morgan Hickman, Jr., Oct. 23, 1961 (div. 1987); children: Elizabeth Gray, Melanie Wray. BA, U. Del., 1974. Exec. dir. Literacy Vols. of N.Y. State, Sherrill, 1974-76; copywriter Oneida (N.Y.) Silversmiths, 1977-79, asst. mgr. pub. relations, 1979-81, mgr. creative planning and publicity, 1981-82, asst. mktg. mgr., 1982-83, mktg. mgr., 1983-86, mgr. design, new product devel., 1986-88, project mgr. new product devel., 1988—. Group shows include 5th Ann. Open of N.Y., DeWitt, 1970 (Purchase Prize), Adironack Exhbn. of Am. Watercolors, Old Forge, N.Y., 1982 (Forest Runes award); two woman shows include Fynmore Galleries, Boonville, N.Y., 1986. Commr. dept. civil service City of Oneida, 1976-79. Mem. Cen. N.Y. Watercolor Soc. Republican. Office: Oneida Silversmiths Kenwood Station Oneida NY 13421

GRAY, MAURISSE TAYLOR, investment banking firm executive; b. Buffalo, July 25, 1954; d. James Graham and Joan Maurise (Fitzpatrick) G.; m. Salim Akbarali Valimahomed, Apr. 24, 1982; 1 dau., Zahra. B.A., Mt. Holyoke Coll., 1976; M.P.A., NYU. Research asst. Rockefeller U., N.Y.C., 1976-77; assoc. Kidder, Peabody & Co. Inc., N.Y.C., 1977-80, asst. v.p., 1980-81, v.p., shareholder, 1981—. Democrat. Roman Catholic.

GRAY, NICOLIN JANE PLANK, botanist, educator; b. Yakima, Wash., Apr. 24, 1921; d. Laurence Lubin and Clara Nicoline (Larsen) Plank; B.S., U. Wash., 1942, M.S. (Alpha Chi Omega scholar), 1945; m. Alfred Orren Gray, Sept. 5, 1947; children—Robin, Richard. Instr. biology Yakima Valley (Wash.) Jr. Coll., 1942-44; instr. Whitworth Coll., Spokane, Wash., 1944-46, asst. prof., 1946-48, 1956-72, asso. prof., 1972-78, prof. biology, 1978-80, prof. emeritus, 1980—, chmn. natural sci. div., 1977-79; bot. cons. Inland Empire Poison Center, Spokane, 1963—; herbarium curator Whitworth Coll., 1963—; cons. Ragged Ridge Outdoor Ednl. Opportunities Center, Spokane, 1973-80; cons. mycologist to various groups, 1975—; bot. illustrator, 1981—. Whitworth faculty research grantee, 1960, 64, 69; NSF grantee, 1962, 65, 71-72; NIH grantee, 1960-61; recipient Woman of Distinction award Women in Communications, 1987. Mem. N.Am. Mycol. Assn., N.W. Sci. Assn., Washington Native Plant Soc., Eastern Wash. State Hist. Soc. (trustee 1979-85), Phi Beta Kappa (sec.-treas. Inland Empire assn. 1951-52, 66-67, 70-71), Sigma Xi, Pi Lambda Theta. Democrat. Presbyterian. Author: A Manual of Common Fungi of the Inland Northwest, 1982; Many Lamps, One Light, A Centennial History of First Presbyterian Church, Spokane, Washington, 1984; An Illustrated Guide to Plants of the Spokane Area, 1985. Contbr. articles to profl. jours.

GRAY, PAMELA, educator; b. Newark, Nov. 11, 1940; d. Irving William and Helen (Gail) G.; m. Robert Emil Kohn, Feb. 19, 1962 (div. 1978); children: Randall Evan Kohn, Andrew Robert Kohn, Cynthia Lee Kohn. BA, Upsala Coll., 1970; MA in Teaching, Seton Hall U., 1972, EdS, 1980, EdD, 1986. Cert. prin., supr., tchr., N.J. Tchr. 2d through 5th grade South Orange-Maplewood Bd. Edn., N.J., 1972-81, adminstv. and supervisory intern, 1980-81, tchr. of gifted, 1981; enrichment coordinator Mountainside (N.J.) Bd. Edn., 1982-85; coordinator, tchr. of gifted Livingston (N.J.) Bd. Edn., 1985—; mem. adminstrv. com. Northeast Olympics of the Mind, N.J., 1984-85. Author: Happy Birthday U.S.A., 1975, America Is Having A Birthday, 1976. Bd. dirs., treas., jour. chmn. Ruth Kohn Community Service, 1972-78. Boston U. scholar, 1979-80; State Dept. Gifted Edn. grantee, 1988-89. Mem. NEA, N.J. Edn. Assn., Livingston Ednl. Assn., Nat. Assn. Gifted Children, Assn. for Supervision and Curriculum Devel., Kappa Delta Pi. Home: 138 Marion Dr West Orange NJ 07052

GRAY, PAULINE BARITEAU, nutritionist; b. Bklyn., Nov. 19, 1934; d. Edward Edmund and Pauline (Robich) Bariteau; m. James Thomas Gray; children: Douglas, Wayne, Russell. BS, St. Joseph's U., Bklyn., 1953; MS, Donsbach U., 1984; PhD, I.U.N.E., 1988. Registered clin. nutrition. Yoga instr. The Meeting Place, Lindenhurst, N.Y., 1972-81; yoga instr. Roslyn, N.Y., 1979-80, Albany, N.Y., 1981—; yoga instr. NE N.Y. State Nursing Home, Latham and Troy, N.Y., 1981—; dance instr. Dept. Edn., Lindenhurst, Levittown and Babylon, N.Y., 1973-74; pvt. practice clin. nutrition Albany and Cohoes, N.Y., 1981—; lectr. in field. Author: Yoga, 1982, (booklet and cassette) Weight Loss, 1986, 87, (cassette tape) Yoga Postures, 1987. Recipient Disting. Achievement in Nat. Nutrition award Nutritional Science Assn., 1985. Mem. Am. Assn. Nutritional Cons., Internat. Acad. Cons., Nat. Assn. Female Execs. Republican. Roman Catholic. Club: Internat. Lodge: Soroptimists (v.p. Albany club 1985—). Home and Office: 101 Edward St Cohoes NY 12047

GRAY, PHYLLIS JEAN, banker; b. Hugoton, Kans., Oct. 6, 1933; d. Herman L. and Ada May (McClure) Hicks; m. Jack Gray, July 29, 1950 (div. Sept. 1978); children: Debra Jean, David Ralph. Grad. in banking, U. Wisconsin, 1972. Agt. Satanta (Kans.) Ins. Agy., 1960—; exec. v.p. State Bank Satanta, 1960—, also bd. dirs. Bd. dirs. Satanta Arts Council, 1987. Mem. Nat. Assn. Bank Women (chmn. state pub. affairs 1982-84, state chmn. membership com. 1988), Satanta C. of C., Kans. Bankers Assn. Bancpac (adv. dir. 1982-83, mem. com.), SW Kans. Bank Adminstrn. Inst. (bd. dirs. 1980-83, pres. 1982-83), Western Kans. Nat. Assn. Bank Women (pres. 1972). Republican. Methodist. Lodge: Order Eastern Star (worthy matron, others). Office: State Bank Satanta 110 Sequoya Satanta KS 67870

GRAY, S(ARA) ELIZABETH, controller; b. Jackson, Tenn., Dec. 19, 1945; d. William Gilbert and Sara Poole (Garner) G.; divorced; children: Margaret, Bonnie, Scott. Student, Emory U., 1963-67; B Vocat. Agr., Ga. State U., 1966-67. Staff exec. Weight Watchers, La., So. Miss., 1976-77; dir. tng. Century 21 Today Realtors, Detroit, 1977-81; mgr. office, exec. asst. Craiger Precision Products, Plymouth, Ill., 1981-83; dir. accounts receivable N. Am. Interstate, Berkley, Mich., 1983-85; mgr. office N. Am. Interstate, Berkley, 1984—, mkgt. analyst, 1986—; controller, gen. mgr. N. Am. Interstate, %, 1985—; fin. cons. Profl. Vending Corp., Berkley, 1984, Omne Fin. Inc., Berkley, 1986—. Home: 29416 Murray Crescent Southfield MI 48076 Office: N Am Interstate 3842 W 11 Mile Rd Berkley MI 48072

GRAY, SHEILA HAFTER, psychiatrist, psychoanalyst; b. N.Y.C., Oct. 19, 1930; m. Oscar Shalom Gray, Apr. 8, 1967. MD, Harvard U., 1958. cert. Washington Psychoanalytic Inst., 1969. Intern St. Elizabeths Hosp., Washington, 1958-59; resident McLean Hosp., Belmont, Mass., 1959-61; clin. and research fellow Mass. Gen. Hosp., Boston, Mass., 1961-62; staff psychiatrist Chestnut Lodge, Inc., Rockville, Md., 1962-64; practice medicine, specializing in psychiatry and psychoanalysis Washington, Rockville, Md., 1964—; clin. asst. prof. psychiatry U. Md. Sch. Medicine, Balt., Md., 1968-75, clin. assoc. prof., 1975-83, clin. prof., 1983—; instr. Washington Psychoanalytic Inst., Balt., Md., 1971-75, teaching analyst, 1975—; mem. staff U. Md. Hosp., Balt.; physician mem. Commn. on Mental Health, Superior Ct. of D.C., 1972—; bd. govs. Nat. Capital Reciprocal Ins. Co., 1981—; cons. Walter Reed Army Med. Ctr., Washington, 1983—. Mem. D.C. Mayor's Adv. Com. on Mental Health Services Reorgn., 1984; exec. com. D.C. Fedn. Civic Assns., 1984—, asst. rec. sec., 1985, rec. sec., 1986—; v.p. programs Women's Equity Action League of Met. D.C., 1986; commr. D.C. Adv. Neighborhood Commn., 1986—. Fellow Am. Psychiat. Assn.; mem. Am. Psychoanalytic Assn. (diplomate Bd. of Profl. Standards), Washington Psychiat. Soc. (councillor 1981-83) Med. Soc. D.C. (exec. bd. 1982), Washington Psychoanalytic Soc. (dir. psychoanalytic clinic and councillor ex officio 1987—), Palisades Citizens Assn. (exec. com. 1980—, treas. 1983-84, pres. 1984-86). Office: PO Box 40612 Palisades Sta Washington DC 20016

GRAYSON, LISA JEANNE, deputy press secretary; b. Flint, Mich., June 20, 1961; d. Robert Lewis and Shirley Jane (Attwood) G.; m. James Allan Mitzelfeld, Sept. 28, 1985. BA, Mich. State U., 1983. Pub. relations asst. U.S. Olympic Com., Colorado Springs, Colo., 1983; media relations asst. Gov.'s Office, Lansing, Mich., 1984, asst. press sec., 1985-86, media coordinator Nat. Govs. Assn., 1987, dep. press sec., 1987—; account asst. PR Assocs., Inc., Detroit, 1984-85; campaign press sec. Blanchard for Gov. Com., Lansing, 1986. Mem. Pub. Relations Soc. Am. Democrat. Roman Catholic. Office: Exec Office The State Capitol Lansing MI 48913

GRAZIANO, LAURA ELLEN, marketing executive; b. Suffern, N.Y., Nov. 22, 1955; d. Frank and Rose Mary (DiBenedetto) Campi; m. Joseph Robert Graziano, June 4, 1983; children: Anthony Joseph, Cristina Marie. B.S. magna cum laude, Fairleigh Dickinson U., 1982, postgrad. 1983—. Adminstrv. asst. in mktg. Thomas J. Lipton, Inc., Englewood Cliffs, N.J., 1978-83; with mktg. dept. Good Humor Corp., Fairfield, N.J., 1983, brand asst., 1983-85, asst. product mgr., 1985-86; mktg. dir. Creative Computer Systems, Inc., Wayne, N.J., 1986—. Roman Catholic.

GREAR, EFFIE CARTER, educational administrator; b. Huntington, W.Va., Aug. 15, 1927; d. Harold Jones and Margaret (Tinsley) Carter; Mus.B., W.Va. State Coll., 1948; M.A., Ohio State U., 1955; Ed.D., Nova U., 1976; m. William Alexander Grear, May 16, 1952; children—Rhonda Kaye, William Alexander. Band dir. Fla. A&M High Sch., Tallahassee, 1948-51, Smith-Brown High Sch., Arcadia, Fla., 1951-56; band dir. Lake Shore High Sch., Belle Glade, Fla., 1956-60, dean of girls, 1960-66, asst. prin., 1966-70; asst. prin. Glades Central High Sch., Belle Glade, Fla., 1970-76, prin., 1976—. Bd. dirs. Palm Beach County Mental Health Assn. Recognized for outstanding achievement by Fla. Sugar Cane League, 1985; recipient Community Service award ElDorado Civic Club, Martin Luther King Jr. Humanitarian award Palm Beach County Urban League, 1988. Mem. Nat. Assn. Secondary Sch. Prins., Nat. Community Sch. Edn. Conf., Nat. Sch. Public Relations Assn., Assn. Supervision and Curriculum Devel., Fla. Assn. Secondary Sch. Prins., Palm Beach County Sch. Adminstrs. Assn., Belle Glade Assn. Women's Clubs (pres.), Belle Glade C. of C. (chmn. beautification Com., citizen yr. 1986), Phi Delta Kappa, Alpha Kappa Alpha. Clubs: Elite Community, Women's Civic. Office: Glades Cen High Sch 425 W Canal St N Belle Glade FL 33430

GREASER, CONSTANCE UDEAN, research organization executive; b. San Diego, Jan. 18, 1938; d. Lloyd Edward and Udean Greaser; B.A., San Diego State Coll., 1959; postgrad. U. Copenhagen Grad. Sch. Fgn. Students, 1963, Georgetown U. Sch. Fgn. Service, 1967; M.A., U. So. Calif., 1968; Exec. M.B.A., UCLA, 1981. Advt., publicity mgr. Crofton Co., San Diego, 1959-62; supr. Mercury Publs., Fullerton, Calif., 1962-64; supr. engring. support services div. Arcata Data Mgmt., Hawthorne, Calif., 1964-67; mgr. computerized typesetting dept. Continental Graphics, Los Angeles, 1967-70; v.p., editorial dir. Sage Publs., Inc., Beverly Hills, Calif., 1970-74; head publs. RAND Corp., Santa Monica, Calif., 1974—. Mem. nat. com. Million Minutes of Peace Appeal, 1986, Dept. Commerce Nat. Info. Standards Orgn., 1987—, nat. com. Global Cooperation for Better World, 1988. Mem. Women in Bus. (pres. 1977-78), Soc. for Scholarly Pubs. (nat. bd. dirs.), Women in Communication, Soc. Tech. Communication, World Future Soc., Brahma Kumaris World Spiritual Orgn. Co-author: Quick Writer-Build Your Own Word Processing Users Guide, 1983; Quick Writer-Word Processing Center Operations Manual, 1984; editor: Urban Research News, 1970-74; mng. editor Comparative Polit. Studies, 1971-74; assoc. editor New Realities mag., 1988—; contbr. articles to various jours. Office: The Rand Corp 1700 Main St Santa Monica CA 90406

GREATHOUSE, PATRICIA DODD, psychometrist, counselor; b. Columbus, Ga., Apr. 26, 1935; d. John Allen and Patricia Ottis (Murphy) Dodd; m. Robert Otis Greathouse; children: Mark Andrew, Perry Allen. BS in Edn., Auburn (Ala.) U., 1959, M in Edn., 1966, AA in Counselor Edn., 1975. Cert. secondary tchr., Ala., Ga. Tchr. Columbus High Sch., 1959-61, Phoenix City Bd. Edn., 1957-58; tchr. pub. schs. Russell County (Ala.) Bd. Edn., Phenix City and Seale, 1961-69, 71-80, 82-83, counselor pub. schs., 1969-82, 83—; psychometrist Russell County (Ala.) Bd. Edn., Seale, 1980-82; county psychometrist Russell County (Ala.) Bd. Edn., Phenix City, 1983—. Editor: (ann.) Tiger Tales, 1973 (award 1980). Treas. Ladonia PTA, Phenix City, 1966-68, parliamentarian, 1987—; leader Ladonia chpt. 4-H Club, Phenix City, 1961-80; active March of Dimes, Am. Heart Assn.; rep. Mardi Gras; tchr. Sunday Sch., Vacation Bible Sch. N. Phenix Bapt. Ch.; vol. Reach to Recovery Am. Cancer Soc., 1980—. Named Mardi Gras Queen Phenix City Moose Club, 1987, hon. life mem. Ladonia PTA, 1967, Outstanding Tchr. of Yr., 1972; recipient Silver Clover award 4-H Club, 1966, Outstanding PTA Performance award 1986-87; nominated to Tchr. Hall of Fame, 1980-81, 81-82, 82-83. Mem. Russell County Edn. Assn. (pres.-elect 1973), Ala. Edn. Assn., NEA, Ala. Personnel and Guidance Assn., Ala. Assn. Counseling and Devel., Council Exceptional Children, Am. Bus. Women's Assn. (pres. Phoenix City charter chpt. 1986-87, woman of yr. 1987, Perfect Attendance award), Delta Kappa Gamma (sec. 1979-80), Kappa Iota. Democrat. Baptist. Lodge: Daus. of Nile (pres. Phenix City club 1984-85), Shrinettes (sec. Phenix City club 1980-81, 83-84, outstanding service award), Jetettes (v.p. Phenix City club 1976, 80), Jaycettes, Order Eastern Star (Worthy Matron 1981-82). Home: 1502 Nottingham Dr Phenix City AL 36867 Office: Ladonia Sch Rt 4 Box 982 Phenix City AL 36867

GREAVER, JOANNE HUTCHINS, mathematics educator, author; b. Louisville, Aug. 9, 1939; d. Alphonso Victor and Mary Louise (Sage) Hutchins; m. James William Greaver, Dec. 17, 1977; 1 child, Mary Elizabeth. BS in Chemistry, U. Louisville, 1961, MEd, 1971; MAT in Math., Purdue U., 1973. Cert. tchr. secondary edn. Specialist math Jefferson County (Ky.) pub. schs., 1962—; part-time faculty Bellarmine Coll., Louisville, 1982—, U. Louisville, 1985—; project reviewer NSF, 1983—; advisor Council on Higher Edn., Frankfort, Ky., 1983-86. Author: (workbook) Down Algebra Alley,

1981; co-author curriculum guides. Charter mem. Commonwealth Tchrs Inst., 1984—; mem. Nat. Forum for Excellence in Edn., Indpls., 1983; metric edn. leader Fed. Metric Project, Louisville, 1979-82. Recipient Presdl. award for excellence in math. teaching, 1983; named Outstanding Citizen, SAR, 1984, mem. Hon. Order Ky. Cols.; grantee NSF, 1983, Louisville Community Found., 1984-86. Mem. Greater Louisville Council Tchrs. of Math. (pres. 1977-78, Outstnading Educator award 1987), Nat. Council Tchrs. of Math. (reviewer 1981—), Ky. Council Tchrs. of Math. (Jeff County Tchr. of Yr. 1985), Math. Assn. Am., Kappa Delta Pi, Zeta Tau Alpha. Republican. Presbyterian. Avocations: tropical fish; gardening; handicrafts; travel; tennis. Home: 11513 Tazwell Dr Louisville KY 40222 Office: J M Atherton High Sch 3000 Dundee Rd Louisville KY 40205

GREAVES, CYNTHIA ANN, trade association administrator; b. Providence, Jan. 20, 1955; d. Hollis Smith and Barbara Ann (Burke) Hawkins; m. John Charles Greaves, Jr., June 21, 1975 (div. Apr. 1987). A, Bryant Coll., 1975. Asst. dir. East Greenwich (R.I.) C. of C., 1981-86; exec. dir. North Kingston (R.I.) C. of C., 1986—. Mem. East Greenwich Bus. and Profl. Women (pres. 1986-87, Young Careerist award 1984). Roman Catholic. Home: 7 Maplewood Dr East Greenwich RI 02818 Office: N Kingstown C of C 55 Brown St North Kingstown RI 02852

GREEN, ADELINE MANDEL, psychiatric social worker; b. St. Paul; d. Meyer and Eva Ulanove; B.S., U. Minn., M.S.W.; m. Nathan G. Mandel (div.); children—Meta Susan (Mrs. Richard Katzoff), Myra (Mrs. Jeffrey Halpern); m. Maurice L. Green. Past investigator, Ramsey County Mothers Aid and Aid to Dependent Children, Ramsey County Welfare Bd., St. Paul; then psychiat. social worker Wilder Child Guidance Clinic, St. Paul; then psychiat. social worker, supr. outpatient psychiatry clinic U. Minn. Hosps., Mpls., subsequently supr., clin. instr. psychiatry-social service, outpatient psychiatry clinic; currently in pvt. practice family and marriage counseling South Bay Clinic. Past pres. St. Paul sect. Council Jewish Women; past chmn. Diagnostic Clinic for Rheumatic Fever-Wilder Clinic, St. Paul; assoc. Family and Child Psychiat. Med. Clinic. Lic. social worker. Mem. Nat. Assn. Social Workers, Acad. Certified, Social Workers, Minn. Welfare Conf., Am. Assn. Marriage and Family Counselors, Brandeis U. Women. Democrat. Home: 2365 Oakcrest Dr Palm Springs CA 92264 Office: 14651 S Bascom Suite 225 Los Gatos CA 95030

GREEN, ALLISON ANNE, educator; b. Flint, Mich., Oct. 5, 1936; d. Edwin Stanley and Ruth Allison (Simmons) James; m. Richard Gerring Green, Dec. 23, 1961 (div. Oct. 1969). B.A., Albion Coll., 1959; M.A., U. Mich., 1978. Cert. tchr., Mich. Tchr. phys. edn. Southwestern High Sch., Flint, 1959-62; tchr. math. Harry Hunt Jr. High Sch., Portsmouth, Va., 1962-63; receptionist Tempcon, Inc., Mpls., 1963-64; tchr. phys. edn. and math. Longfellow Jr. High Sch., Flint, 1964-81, tchr. math., 1981-87, tchr. lang. arts and social studies, 1986-87. Mem. Fair Winds council Girl Scouts U.S.A., 1943—, leader Lone Troop, Albion, Mich., 1957, sr. tchr. aide adviser, 1964-67; mem. Big Sisters Genesee and Lapeer Counties, 1964-68; mem. adminstrv. bd. Court St. United Methodist Ch.; treas. edn. work area, mission commn., sec. council on ministries United Meth. Women Soc. Christian Service, also chmn. meml. com. Mem. NEA, Mich. Edn. Assn., Mich. Assn. Mid. Sch. Educators, United Tchrs. Flint (bldg. rep.), Delta Kappa Gamma (treas. 1982—, profl. affairs chmn. 1978-80, legis. chmn. 1980-82, pres. 1988—), Alpha Xi Delta (pres. Flint, alumnae, v.p., treas., corp. pres. Albion Coll., alumnae dir. province 1972-77, Outstanding Sr. Albion Coll. 1959), Embroiderers Guild Am. (sec. 1977-80, maps rep. 1980-82). Home: 1002 Copeman Blvd Flint MI 48504 Office: 1255 N Chevrolet Ave Flint MI 48504

GREEN, AVRIL MAXINE, health care executive; b. Lloydminster, Sask., Can., Feb. 10, 1943; came to U.S., 1964; d. Stanley Charles and Hulda Louise (Bjork) Cottrell; m. Vernon Green, Aug. 12, 1967; children: Michele Lynne, Teresa Anne. Grad. in nursing, U. Alta., Edmonton, Can., 1963; M in Pub. Adminstrn., Golden Gate U., 1985. Charge nurse U. Alta., 1963-64, El Camino Hosp., Mountain View, Calif., 1964-66; staff nurse Kaiser Permanente, Honolulu, 1966-67; dept. supr. Sunnyvale (Calif.) Med. Clinic, 1967-74; supr. Roseville (Calif.) Community Hosp., 1975-79; coordinator utilization rev. Profl. Standards Rev. Orgn., Sacramento, Calif., 1980-81; mgr. profl. rev. Found. Health Plan, Sacramento, 1981-84; dir. provider services, quality assurance NW Americare Health Plan, Portland, Oreg., 1984-86; mgr. profl. services Affordable Health Care Concepts, Sacramento, 1986—. Mem. Am. Bd. Quality Assurance and Utilization Rev. (diplomate, by-laws com.), Bus. and Profl. Women, Am. Coll. Utilization Rev. Physicians. Democrat. Lodge: Soroptomists (asst. treas. Portland Lodge 1986). Home: 9437 Shumway Dr Orangevale CA 95662

GREEN, BARBARA STRAWN, psychotherapist; b. Cleve., May 31, 1938; d. Charles Everard and Dorothy Haring (Strawn) G. BA, Pa. State U., 1960; MS, Columbia U., 1962; postgrad. in psychotherapy and psychoanalysis, Postgrad. Ctr. for Mental Health, N.Y.C., 1975. Cert. social worker, N.Y.; cert. Rutgers Summer Sch. Alcoholism Studies, 1982. Social worker VA, N.Y.C., 1962-66; sr. psychiat. social worker in child psychiat. Downstate Med. Ctr., Bklyn., 1966-71; staff therapist Inst. for Contemporary Psychotherapy, N.Y.C., 1971-73; social worker Lower East Side Service Ctr., N.Y.C., 1975-77; intake coordinator alcoholism program Postgrad. Ctr. for Mental Health, N.Y.C., 1981-82; program coordinator Bowery Residents Com., N.Y.C., 1984-86; pvt. practice psychotherapy N.Y.C., 1973—. Mem. Nat. Assn. Social Workers (sec. alcoholism com. N.Y.C. chpt. 1987-89), Social Workers Helping Social Workers (chmn. 1982-84). Club: Artists at Waterside (N.Y.C.).

GREEN, BELVA JEAN, free-lance writer; b. Eaton County, Mich., Aug. 16, 1927; d. Phillip Clem and Gladys M. Green; student Mich. State Coll., 1945-47, Ind. U., 1959, Purdue U. Ins. Mktg. Inst., 1967. Sec. to pres. Rea Magnet Wire Co., Ft. Wayne, Ind., 1958-63; sec. to corp. purchasing v.p. Magnovox Co., Ft. Wayne, 1963-67; nat. exec. dir. United Cancer Council, Ft. Wayne and Indpls., 1967-71; exec. dir. Allen County Cancer Soc., Ft. Wayne, 1971-88; guest lectr. Ind. U., St. Francis Coll., IV-Tech. Coll., nursing, med. assts., LPN, 1971—; also lectr. Editor (newsletters): Make Today Count, Soundoff; contbr. articles to various publs. Co-founder local unit Make Today Count, 1976, regional coordinator nat. group, 1980, nat. bd. dirs., 1985; nat. pres. United Cancer Council Staff Assn., 1982-83; vol. United Way of Allen County Bd., 1974-76, Speakers Bur., 1975—, mem. public relations com., 1975-76; v.p. adv. bd. Salvation Army, 1976—; charter mem. Friends and Families of Nursing Home Residents, 1978-81; vol. Mental Health Assn., 1978; mem. med. assts. adv. bd. Ind. Vocat. Tech. Coll., 1980-81; mem. No. Ind. Health Systems Agy. Hospice Panel, 1979; co-founder, bd. dirs. Hospice of Fort Wayne, Inc.; vol. Allen County Cancer Soc. Speakers Bur., Am. Assn. Retired Persons pub. relations com.; coordinator Am. Assn. Retired Persons writer's contest, 1988. Recipient Woman of Influence awards Toastmistress Clubs, Fort Wayne Club and Council #6, 1971, United Way Leadership awards, 1974, 76, Community Service award Seventh-day Adventist Ch., 1979, Community Leaders and Noteworthy Ams. award, Am. Assn. Retired Persons Volunteer award, 1988. Mem. Pub. Relations Soc. Am., Internat. Assn. Bus. Communicators, Women in Communication, Soc. Children's Book Writers (chmn. programs local soc.), Christian Writers (coordinator Ball State U. midwest writers Fort Wayne conf. 1986—), Internat. Platform Assn., Allen County Social Service Agy. Adminstrs. Presbyterian. Clubs: Fort Wayne Press, Foster Park Lioness (charter mem., dir. 1980), World Wide Travel, Fort Wayne Toastmistress Internat., Order Eastern Star, Eaton County Mich. Writers (founder 1987), Everywriter's, Curios Antique, Antique Comb Collectors.

GREEN, CAROL H., lawyer, educator, journalist; b. Seattle, Feb. 18, 1944; B.A. summa cum laude in History and Journalism, La. Tech. U., 1965; M.S.L. (Ford Found. fellow), Yale U., 1977; J.D., U. Denver, 1979. Intern, Shreveport (La.) Times, 1964, reporter, 1965-66; reporter Guam Daily News, 1966-67; city editor Pacific Jour., Agana, Guam, 1967-68; reporter, editorial writer, Denver Post, 1968-76, legal affairs reporter, 1977-79, asst. editor editorial page, 1979-81, house counsel, 1980-83, labor relations mgr., 1981-83; assoc. Holme Roberts & Owen, 1983-85; v.p. human resources and legal affairs Denver Post, 1985-87; mgr. circulation sales & adminstrn. Newsday, 1988—; mem. corrections task force Colo. Criminal Justice Standards and Goals, 1985 speaker for USIA, India, Egypt. Bd. dirs. YWCA, Mile Hi Red Cross, Trans. Council, Denver C. of C. Recipient McWilliams award for juvenile justice, Denver, 1971; award for interpretive reporting Denver Newspaper Guild, 1971-1979. Mem. ABA (forum on communications law), Colo. Women's Bar Assn., Colo. Bar Assn. (bd. govs. 1985-87, chairperson BAR-press com. 1980), Denver Bar Assn. (co-chairperson jud. selection and benefits com. 1982-85, 1st v.p. 1986), Alliance Profl. Women (exec. com.), Women's Forum, Leadership Denver. Clubs: Denver Press. Episcopalian. Office: Newsday 235 Pinelawn Rd Melville NY 11747

GREEN, ELAINE K., educator; b. N.Y.C., Aug. 3, 1932; d. Samuel and Rae (Siegel) Klenosky; m. George Green; children: Lauren Dee, Tammy Jane. BA, Queens Coll., 1954. Tchr. elem. N.Y.C. Bd. Edn., 1954-57. Sponsor bicycle safety legis., N.Y. State legis., 1962, 72; v.p. Oceanside (N.Y.) PTA, 1970, pres., 1972; v.p. Dem. Club Oceanside, 1974-76; pres. Miami Salon Group, Fla., 1987—, Guild Greater Miami Opera, 1987—. Mem. Opera Guild Internat. (sec. SE region 1988—). Home: 19667 Turnberry Way North Miami FL 33180

GREEN, FRANCES HOPE, health care specialist; b. Mt. Vernon, Ill., Jan. 29, 1937; d. Walter Bryon and Myrtle Fern (Sulenski) Green. Student, Mt. Vernon Jr. Coll., 1956; diploma. Triton Coll., 1967; student Calif. U. Advanced Studies, 1985—. Registered respiratory therapist. Office mgr. De Sota Chem. Co., Chgo., 1965-66; therapist Hines VA Hosp., Hines, Ill., 1966-67, West Sub. Hosp., Oak Park, Ill., 1965-67; clin. instr. Rose Meml. Hosp., Denver, 1967-68; dir. respiratory therapy Children's Hosp., Denver, 1968-80, staff assoc. human resources, 1980-85, dir. hosp. security, 1983-85, compensation analyst, 1985—; cons. neonatal/pediatric respiratory care Aspen Valley Hosp., 1977-79, Respiratory Care, Inc., Arlington Hts., Ill., 1978-80; clin. instr. U. Stony Brook, N.Y., 1977-80; bd. advs. and clin. instr. Community Coll. Denver, 1969-77, Aurora Tech. Ctr. & St. Anthony Hosp., 1977-79; speaker in field. Designer, transport isolette for newborns, 1975, asst. designer, aircraft for transport of newborns, 1975; designer/evaluator, pediatric respiratory equipment, 1978-80. Bd. dirs., Fed. Credit Union (Midtown), Denver, 1983, treas., 1983-84; pres., Mid-town Service Orgn., Denver, 1983-84. Served to AK2, USN, 1962-69, Memphis and San Diego, Calif. Recipient Outstanding service award U.S. Navy, San Diego, 1964. Mem. Am. Assn. Respiratory Therapy, Nat. Bd. Respiratory Therapists, Am. Lung Assn. Colo. Democrat. Lutheran. Contbr. article to profl. jour. Home: 2560 Field St Lakewood CO 80215 Office: The Children's Hosp 1056 E 19th Ave Denver CO 80218

GREEN, FRANCINE LOUISE, management information services director; b. Johnstown, Pa., Jan. 14, 1942; d. Frank Yanko and Ann Louise (Salem) Karwowski; m. Timothy John Green, June 4, 1966. BS, Kennedy Western, 1986. Programmer Farrington Mfg. Co., Springfield, Va., 1966-68; systems analysis Farrington Mfg. Co., Springfield, 1968-70; sr. programmer Fairfax County Water Authority, Annandale, Va., 1971-74; project mgr. Fairfax County Pub. Schs., Alexandria, Va., 1974-81; dir., computer systems Fairfax County Pub. Schs., Alexandria, 1981-84, dir., data adminstrn., 1984—. Author, designer: Personnel, Payroll and Position Control Application Systems, 1980. Recipient Outstanding Performance award Fairfax County Pub. Schs., 1981. Mem. Soc. for Information Mgmt. Office: Fairfax County Pub Schs 3701 Franconia Rd Alexandria VA 22310

GREEN, FREIDA STRICKLAND, paralegal, real estate salesman; b. Clayton, Ala., Aug. 27, 1953; d. William Freeman Sr. and Wilma (White) Strickland; m. Roger Dale Green, Aug. 14, 1970; children: Dale, Clint. Student, Sparks State Tech. Coll., 1972; AA, Troy State U., 1982; course in paralegal, So. Career Inst., 1984. Personnel officer State Mental Health, Eufaula, Ala., 1971-72; dist. sec. State Hwy. Dept., Eufaula, 1972-76; div. sec. State Forestry Dept., Ozark, Ala., 1976-77; legal asst. William J. Adams, Clayton, 1977-83; paralegal Lynn Robertson Jackson, Clayton, 1983—. Sec. and mem. exec. com. Barbour County Dem. Party, 1981—; treas. Louisville Athletic Club, Louisville High Sch., 1986—; coach Little League, Louisville, 1980; active mem. PTA Louisville Elementary Sch., 1982—; pastor, parish com. chmn. Street Meml. Meth. Ch., 1980—. Named one of Outstanding Young Women Am., 1984. Mem. Ala. Assn. Legal Assistance. Office: Lynn Robertson Jackson PO Box 10 Clayton AL 36016

GREEN, GERALDINE DOROTHY, lawyer; b. N.Y.C., July 14, 1938; d. Edward and Lula M. (Albro) Chisholm. Student, CCNY, 1961-64; JD, St. John's U., 1968. Bar: N.Y. 1968, Calif. 1972. Tax acct. Coopers & Lybrand, N.Y.C., 1966-68; staff atty. IBM, 1968-69, Gaithersburg, Md., 1969-71, Los Angeles, 1971-72; sr. atty., asst. corp. sec. Atlantic Richfield Co., Los Angeles, 1972-80; commr. corps. State of Calif., Los Angeles, 1980-83; ptnr. Rosenfeld Meyer & Susman, Beverly Hills, Calif., 1983-85; of counsel Burke, Robinson & Pearman, Los Angeles, 1985-87; sole practice, Los Angeles, 1987—. Bd. dirs. Los Angeles area USO, 1978-86. Mem. NAACP, Nat. Bar Assn., ABA, Nat. Legal Aid and Defender Assn., Calif. Assn. Black Lawyers, Calif. Women Lawyers' Assn., Black Women Lawyers' Calif., Los Angeles World Affairs Council, Women Lawyers Assn. Los Angeles, U.S. Olympic Soc. Office: 3325 Wilshire Blvd Suite 1250 Los Angeles CA 90010

GREEN, JOYCE, book publishing company executive; b. Taylorville, Ill., Oct. 22, 1928; d. Lynn and Vivian Coke (Richardson) Reinerd; A.A., Christian Coll., 1946; B.S., MacMurray Coll., 1948; m. Warren H. Green, Oct. 8, 1960. Assoc. editor Warren H. Green, Inc., St. Louis, 1966-78, dir., 1978—; v.p. Visioneering Advt. Agy., 1972—; exec. sec. Affirmative Action Assn. Am., 1977—; pres. InterContinental Industries, Inc., 1980—; asst. to pres. Southeastern U., New Orleans, 1982-86; mem. bd. regents, v.p. adminstrn. No. Utah U., Salt Lake City, 1986—. Mem. Am. Soc. Profl. and Exec. Women, Direct Mktg. Club St. Louis, C. of C. Democrat. Methodist. Clubs: Jr. League, World Trade, Clayton, Media. Home: 12120 Hibler Dr Creve Coeur MO 63141 Office: 8356 Olive Blvd Saint Louis MO 63132

GREEN, JOYCE HENS, federal judge; b. N.Y.C., Nov. 13, 1928; d. James S. and Hedy (Bucher) Hens; m. Samuel Green, Sept. 25, 1965 (dec. Oct. 23, 1983); children: Michael Timothy, June Heather, James Harry. B.A., U. Md., 1949; J.D., George Washington U., 1951. Bar: D.C. 1951, Va. 1956, U.S. Supreme Ct. 1956. Practice law Washington, 1951-68, Arlington, Va., 1956-68; ptnr. Green & Green, 1966-68; judge Superior Ct., D.C., 1968-79, U.S. Dist. Ct. for D.C., 1979—. Trustee D.C. div. Am. Cancer Soc., 1963-76. Named Woman Lawyer of Yr., 1979. Fellow Am. Acad. Matrimonial Lawyers, Am. Bar Found.; mem. Fed. Judges Assn. (bd. dirs.), ABA, Va. Bar Assn., Bar Assn. D.C., D.C. Bar, D.C. Women's Bar Assn. (pres. 1960-62), Exec. Women in Govt. (chmn. 1977), Kappa Beta Pi, Phi Delta Phi (hon.). Club: Nat. Lawyers (Washington). Office: US Dist Ct US Courthouse 3rd & Constitution Ave NW Washington DC 20001

GREEN, JUDY LINDQUIST, communications and development executive; b. Baraboo, Wis., Mar. 10, 1942; d. Durward Walter Louis and Alice Marie (Fabian) Lindquist; m. James M. Green, Aug. 4, 1978 (div. 1985); children: Joseph Durward Lewandowski, Rebecca Nora Lewandowski; m. Daryl Arthur Durant, Apr. 30, 1987. B of Music, Lawrence U., 1963; MA, U. Minn., 1964; PhD, Marquette U., 1980. Cert. elem. tchr., Wis. Instr. Wis. Conservatory of Music, Milw., 1964-70; tchr. Alverno Campus Elem. Sch., Milw., 1972-77; asst. mng. editor Milw. IMPRESSIONS Mag., 1980-81; spl. projects dir. ARTREACH Milw., 1981-82; dir. communications and devel. Sacred Heart Sch. Theology, Hales Corner, Wis., 1982-86; v.p. communications and devel. Unitarian Universalist Assn., Boston, 1986—; arts cons. CESA #10 Arts in Edn. Project, Plymouth, Wis., 1981-82, Milw. Artists Found: Cable TV, Milw., 1983; dir. music St. Paul Episc. Ch., Milw., 1980-85. Author: (monographs) Arts Research: Emotionally Disturbed Children, 1982, The Effect of Arts Programming on Emotionally Disturbed Adults, 1983. Historian Milw. Symphony Chorus, 1980-86. Mem. Am. Guild Organists, Am. Soc. Aesthetics, Nat. Soc. Fund Raising Execs., Pi Kappa Lambda, Phi Delta Kappa. Office: Unitarian Universalist Assn 25 Beacon St Boston MA 02108

GREEN, JULIA M., nursing agency owner; b. Phila., Apr. 2, 1943; d. Julius Green and Annie Mary (Tramel) Green Turner; 1 child, Rachel Lynette Hunter. M in Bus. Arts, Queens (N.Y.) Bus. Coll., 1966; grad., Pinallas (Fla.) County Sch. Practical Nursing, 1973. With Palm Health Care Ctr., 1976, Hill Crest Nursing Home, 1973-77, Highlands Gen. Hosp., 1977-79, Med. Personnel Pool, 1980-86, New Hope of Highlands County, 1981; pres., chief exec. officer Celebrity Med. Personnel Inc., Avon Park, Fla., 1985—. Bd. dirs. Ridge Area ARC, Avon Park, 1986—. Mem. NAACP (chairperson fund raising local chpt. 1987—), Nat. Assn. Female Execs., Ridge Area Assn. Retarded Citizens (exec. bd. dirs. 1986—). Democrat. Seventh Day Adventist. Office: Celebrity Med Personnel 1685 Pardee Rd Avon Park FL 33825

GREEN, JUNE LAZENBY, federal judge; b. Arnold, Md., Jan. 23, 1914; d. Eugene H. and Jessie T. (Briggs) Lazenby; m. John Cawley Green, Sept. 5, 1936. JD, Am. U., 1941. Bar: Md. 1943, D.C. 1945. Sole practice Washington, 1947-68, Annapolis, Md., 1950-68; claims adjuster Lumbermans Mut. Casualty Co., Washington, 1942-43, claims atty., 1943-47; judge U.S. Dist. Ct. D.C., 1968—; examiner bar, Washington, 1963-68. Named Woman Lawyer of Yr., 1965; recipient Lifetime Achievement award Alumni Assn. of Am. U., 1986. Mem. ABA, Md. Bar Assn., Bar Assn. D.C. (bd. dirs. 1966-68, cert. of appreciation 1984), Women's Bar Assn. D.C. (pres. 1955-57), Kappa Beta Pi. Club: Nat. Lawyers. Home: 464 Joyce Ln Arnold MD 21012 also: 550 N St SW Washington DC 20024 Office: US Ct of Appeals US Courthouse 3rd & Constitution Ave NW Washington DC 20001

GREEN, KAREN BLEIER, advertising agency executive; b. N.Y.C., Apr. 18, 1945; d. Benjamin and Sally (Karger) Bleier; m. Joseph H. Green, Sept. 3, 1966; children—Jessica, Adam. B.A., Simmons Coll., 1967; M.B.A, Harvard U., 1969. Media planner Ogilvy & Mather Inc., N.Y.C., 1969-71, asst. media dir., 1971-74, v.p., account supr., 1974-79, v.p., mgmt. supr., 1979-82, sr. v.p., mgmt. supr., 1982—. Office: Ogilvy & Mather Inc 2 E 48th St New York NY 10017

GREEN, LAQUITA STEPHENS, pharmaceutical company executive; b. Birmingham, Ala., Nov. 10, 1957; d. Roy Allen and Ouida (Camp) Stephens; m. John Alton Green, May 7, 1977 (div. Jan. 1981); m. Joseph Charles Zito, July 25, 1987. Student, Jefferson State Jr. Coll., Birmingham, Ala., 1976. Div. mgr. Tech. Products, Inc., Birmingham, Ala., 1979-81; pres., prin. Design Equipment, Inc., Birmingham, 1981-83; sales rep. ConvaTec div. E.R. Squibb & Sons, Princeton, N.J., 1983-87; regional mgr. ConvaTec div. Squibb Pharm., Princeton, 1987—. Pres. Vestavia Highlands Assn., Birmingham, 1984-87; adv. bd., Met. Devel., Birmingham, 1981-82, bd. dirs. City of Birminham. Mem. Nat. Inst. Bus. Mgmt. Republican.

GREEN, LAURA MARIE, marketing, communications executive; b. Balt., Aug. 31, 1961; d. Karl Mathias and Sue Emma (Harman) Green. BA cum laude, U. Richmond, 1982; grad. Am. Campaign Acad., 1986. Fed. lobbyist Nat. Right to Work Com., Washington, 1984-86; developmental sales rep. Procter & Gamble, Charlotte, N.C., 1983; legis. asst. Va. Retail Mchts. Assn., Richmond, 1983; legis. intern Va. Soc. Profl. Engrs., Richmond, 1982; program dir health facilities assn. Md. Service Corp., Annapolis, 1987—. Dir. Communications Neall for Congress, Md., 1986; pres. The Anne Arundel Bipartisan Action Com., 1986—. Served with U.S. Army, 1981. Mem. Mortar Board, Omicron Delta Kappa. Republican. Presbyterian. Avocations: sailing, flying, traveling, horseback riding, dancing.

GREEN, LINDA LOU, logistics engineer; b. Cape Girardeau, Mo., Sept. 12, 1946; d. Barney Oldfield and Opal (Jeffries) G. BA, East Carolina U., 1967, MA, 1969; postgrad., U. Utah, 1969-70; grad. with honors, Naval War Coll., Newport, R.I., 1985. Cert. in collegiate teaching. Asst. prof. history Jackson (Miss.) State U., 1970-72, Va. State U., Petersburg, 1972-74; commd. 1st lt. U.S. Army, 1974, advanced through grades to maj., 1983, resigned, 1983; logistics engr. Land Systems div. Gen. Dynamics Corp., Warren, Mich., 1983-84; systems analyst Raytheon Service Co., Huntsville, Ala., 1984-86; pres. Green & Assocs. Inc., Huntsville, 1985-86; logistics engr., cost analyst Applied Research Inc., Huntsville, 1986—; instr. U. Md., Fed. Republic of Germany, 1975-77. Author: Study Guides for American History, 1969. Mem. Rep. Nat. Com., Washington, 1986—. Mem. Soc. Logistics Engrs., Assn. U.S. Army, Res. Officers Assn., LWV. Baptist. Office: Applied Research Inc 5025 Bradford Dr Huntsville AL 35805

GREEN, LINDA SUE, correctional administrator, consultant; b. Oklahoma City, July 24, 1953; d. Lewis Ernest and Juliene Marie (Greenhaw) G. A in Sociology, So. Oklahoma City Jr. Coll., 1975; BA in Criminal Justice, Cen. State U., Edmond, Okla., 1979. Cert. peace officer. Probation and parole officer Okla. Dept. Corrections, Shawnee, 1981-82, community resource officer, 1982-83; coordinator program Treatment Alternatives to Street Crime Okla. Dept. Corrections, Oklahoma City, 1983-84, dep. dir. div. Probation and Parole, 1984-86; dir. tng. Okla. Dept. Corrections, Taft, 1986—; cons. Nat. Inst. Corrections, Boulder, Colo., 1984—. Active Crown Heights United Meth. Ch. Mem. Am. Corrections Assn., Okla. Corrections Assn., Muskogee (Okla.), C. of C., Nat. Assn. Correctional Trainers (cert.). Home: 323 S 38 Muskogee OK 74401 Office: Okla Dept Corrections George Nigh Staff Devel Ctr Drawer AO Taft OK 74463

GREEN, LYNNE, producer, writer, director; b. Krsko, Yugoslavia, Oct. 16, 1944; came to U.S., 1949, naturalized, 1966; d. Robert and Albina (Schmuck) Prusak; m. Sam Robert Bass, Oct., 1974 (div. 1975). BFA with honors in Directing, Webster Coll. Conservatory of Theatre Arts, 1979. Intern Sta. KSDK-TV, 1987-88; producer-dir. videos Kurt Landberg, Architect and Seja Systems, 1987—. Dir. stage shows including: Second Verse, N.Y.C., 1980, Button Button, N.Y.C., 1982, Atmosphere of Enforced Discipline, N.Y.C., 1981, Friend of a Friend, N.Y.C., 1982, The Other Woman: A Farce Closing Saturday Night, N.Y.C., 1983, Question Marks and Periods, 1981-83, Mrs. Michaelangelo, N.Y.C., 1983, Crimes of the Heart, Las Cruces, N.Mex., 1984, Antigone, St. Louis, 1985, Vol., Harriett Woods Com., St. Louis, 1986. Recipient Best Dir. award Internat. Dirs. Festival, 1980. Mem. NOW, Ms. Found. for Women, Nat. Abortion Rights Action League. Democrat. Avocation: photography.

GREEN, MARIA LAPI, lawyer, consultant; b. Rochester, N.Y., Sept. 17, 1940; d. Louis L. and Edith (Harman) Lapi; m. Harry Green, 1962; children: Edith, Stella, Anna, Harry II, William, Margaret. B.A. in Econs., George Washington U., 1962; J.D., Syracuse U., 1979. Bar: N.Y. 1979, Fla. 1980. Sole practice, Canandaigua, N.Y., 1979—; cons. for small bus.; mem. 1st del. women attys. People's Republic of China, 1984. NEH fellow, 1980. Mem. ABA (family bar sect.), N.Y. State Bar Assn. (family bar sect.), Fla. Bar Assn. (bus. law sect.), Ont. County Women's Bar Assn. (founder, pres.), Lee County Bar Assn., AAUW (chmn. by-laws com.), Pilot Internat. Democrat. Clubs: Ft. Myers (bd. dirs.); Bus. and Profl. Women (chmn. pub. relations com., Bus. Woman of Yr. 1983). Home: 1440 Larkspur Dr Fort Myers FL 33901 Office: 6201 Presidential Ct SW Suite 104 Fort Myers FL 33919

GREEN, MARJORIE, automotive distribution, import and manufacturing company executive; b. N.Y.C., Sept. 27, 1943; d. Benjamin Maxon and Harriet (Weslock) Gruzen; m. Thomas Henry Green, May 31, 1964. Student Antioch Coll., 1961-63, CCNY, 1964-65. Adminstrv. asst. ednl. research U. Calif.-Berkeley, 1965-76; v.p., co-owner Automotion, Santa Clara, Calif., 1973—. Adv. bd. Import Car mag. Mem. Am. Fedn. State, County and Mcpl. Employees (pres. U. Calif. chpt. 1967), Porsche Club Am (v.p. Golden Gate region 1974, treas. region 1975). Home: 688 Cupples Ct Santa Clara CA 95051 Office: Automotion 3535 Kifer Rd Santa Clara CA 95051

GREEN, MARY HESTER, nurse; b. Oxford, N.C., May 6, 1941; d. Melvin and Martha Elizabeth (Bridges) Hester; m. Joe Lewis G., Dec. 24, 1962; children: Reginald, Reneee G. Johnson, Terri Lynatta. AA in Applied Sci., SUNY, 1979; diploma in Christian Edn., Am. Bible Coll., 1984; postgrad. in Christian Edn., Ohio U., 1982-83. Charge nurse Newark City Hosp., 1967-69, Lincoln Hosp., Durham, N.C., 1974-79; team leader Duke Med. Ctr., Durham, 1969—. Deaconess Pine Grove Ch., Creedmoor, N.C., 1971—, Sunday Sch. tchr., 1972-80, mem. choir, 1970—; mem. staff Bapt. Tng. Union, 1974—; leader Girl Scout U.S., 1976-78. Recipient Cert. Recognition YWCA, Durham, 1985, Disting. Service award Lincoln Hosp., 1976. Mem. Nat. Assn. Female Execs., Am. Soc. Notaries. Democrat. Lodges: Masons, Order Ea. Star. Home: 5301 Whippoorwill St Durham NC 27704

GREEN, MEYRA JEANNE, banker; b. Cleve., Oct. 17, 1946; d. Meyrick Evans Green and Jeanne Bynon (Griffiths) Strauss; m. Frank W. Horn, Dec. 10, 1977 (dec. 1983); 1 stepchild, Donna; m. John Joseph Fleming, Aug. 29, 1987; 1 stepchild, Kerry. BA, Lake Erie Coll., 1968; MBA, NYU, 1973. Corp. planner Chem. Bank, N.Y.C., 1968-72, 1st Nat. City Bank, N.Y.C.,

1972; security analyst Bank of N.Y., 1972-74; asst. treas. Credit Lyonnais, 1974-84; v.p. 1st Fidelity Bank, N.A., N.J., Newark, 1985—. Vol. Overlook Hosp. Hospice, Summit, N.J., 1985—. Mem. NYU Grad. Sch. Bus. Alumni. Republican. Home: 2 Pearl St New Providence NJ 07974 Office: 1st Fidelity Bank NA NJ 550 Broad St Newark NJ 07192

GREEN, NANCY LOUGHRIDGE, publisher; b. Lexington, Ky., Jan. 19, 1942; d. William S. and Nancy O. (Green) Loughridge; BA in Journalism, U. Ky., 1964; MA in Journalism, Ball State U., 1971; postgrad. U. Ky., 1968, U. Minn., 1968. Tchr. English and publs. adv. Clark County High Sch., Winchester, Ky., 1965-66, Pleasure Ridge Park High Sch., Louisville, 1966-67, Clarksville (Ind.) High Sch., 1967-68, Charleston (W.Va.) High Sch., 1968-69; asst. publs. and pub. info. specialist W.Va. Dept. Edn., Charleston, 1969-70; tchr. journalism and publs. dir. Elmhurst High Sch., Ft. Wayne, Ind., 1970-71; advisor student publs. U. Ky., Lexington, 1971-82; gen. mgr. student publs. U. Tex., Austin, 1982-85; pres., pub. Palladium-Item, Richmond, Ind., 1985—; dir. Harte-Hanks urban journalism program, 1984; pres. Media Cons., Inc., Lexington, 1980; dir. urban journalism workshop program Louisville and Lexington newspaper pubs., 1976-82; sec. Kernel Press, Inc., 1971-82. Contbr. articles to profl. jours. Bd. dirs. Jr. League, Lexington, 1980-82, Manchester Ctr., 1978-82, pres., 1979-82, chmn. Greater Richmond Progress Com., 1986-87, pres. leadership Wayne county, 1986-87, bd. Richmond Community Devel. Corp., 1987—, bd. advisers Ind. U. East, 1985—. Recipient Coll. Media Advisers First Amendment award, 1987—; named to Ball State Journalism Hall of Fame, 1988. Mem. Student Press Law Ctr. (bd. dirs., pres. 1985-87), Assoc. Collegiate Press, Journalism Edn. Assn., Nat. Council Coll. Publs. Advs. (pres. 1979-83, Disting. Newspaper Adv. 1976, Disting. Bus. Adviser, 1984). AP Mng. Editors, Columbia Scholastic Press Assn. (Gold Key 1980), So. Interscholastic Press Assn. (Disting. Service award 1983), Nat. Scholastic Press Assn. (Pioneer award 1982), Internat. Newspaper Advt. and Mktg. Execs., Sigma Delta Chi. Home: 411 S 22d St Richmond IN 47374 Office: Palladium Item 1175 N A St Richmond IN 47374

GREEN, NANCYE LEWIS, marketing communications and design firm executive; b. Monterey, Calif., Dec. 4, 1947; d. Robert Ben Lewis and Ruth (Grad) Leebron; m. Michael Patrick Donovan, Oct. 3, 1981. B.A., Tulane U., 1968; B.F.A. cum laude Parsons Sch. of Design, 1973. Co-founder, ptnr., pres. Donovan & Green, Inc., N.Y.C., 1974—; instr. Parsons Sch. of Design, 1974-75, 87, Pratt Inst., 1978-79, Bank St. Coll. Grad. Mus. Program, 1980-81; cons., lectr. in field. Producer, editor The Wood Chair in America, 1983. Pres. Am. Inst. Graphic Arts; mem. Young Pres. Orgn., 1985—; advisor Architect-in-Schs.-Program, Nat. Endowment for Arts, 1978-79. Recipient numerous awards in multi-media, graphic design and advt. Office: Donovan & Green Inc 1 Madison Ave New York NY 10010

GREEN, NETTIE FARMER, school system administrator; b. Alexandria, La., Mar. 22, 1926; d. Percy Hennington and Mary Inez (Davison) Farmer; m. McRay Sullivan, May 25, 1949 (dec. Feb. 1951); 1 child, John; m. Henry G. Green Sr., May 29, 1954 (dec. Nov. 1981); children: Henry Gilbert Jr., James Percy, George David. BS, La. Poly. Inst., 1946; MEd, U. So. Miss., 1982. Cert. edn. tchr., La. Tchr. Jos. M. Davidson High Sch., St. Joseph, La., 1946-47; teller Bank of St. Joseph, 1947-49, Concordia Bank & Trust Co., Vidalia, La., 1951-57; sec. Vidalia High Sch., 1965; instr. Concordia Vocat.-Tech. Sch., Ferriday, La., 1965-85, dept. head, 1985—. Named Vocat. Tchr. of Yr., State Dept. Edn., 1985. Mem. Am. Vocat. Assn., La. Vocat. Assn., Office Occupations Assn., Phi Kappa Phi. Democrat. Baptist. Lodge: Order Eastern Star. Home: 208 Cross St Vidalia LA 71373 Office: Concordia Vocat-Tech Sch E E Wallace Blvd Ferriday LA 71334

GREEN, PATRICIA ANN, data processing executive; b. Taylor, Tex., June 18, 1950; d. Raymond William and Lillian Marie (Hajda) Naizer; m. Kenneth Ray Green, May 31, 1969; children: Keith, Kevin. AA, Temple (Tex.) Jr. Coll., 1969; B in Applied Sci., U. Mary Hardin-Baylor, Belton, Tex., 1978; MPA, S.W. Tex. State U., 1981; PhD, North Tex. State U., 1987. Fin. services caseworker Dept. Human Resources, Temple, 1972-77; data processing operator 3M Corp., Brownwood, Tex., 1977; data processing instr. Temple Jr. Coll., 1978—; computer cons. Temple, 1980-88; data processing dept. chmn. 1988—; mem. speakers' bur. Temple Jr. Coll., 1982—, sponsor Newman club, 1979-81; mem. com. for data processing workshop Tex. Edn. Agy. Task Force, Austin, 1982-83, 85; seminar leader Temple Ind. Sch. Dist., Temple, 1983-84, Temple Assn. for Gifted, Temple, 1981-84; cons. Tex. Soil Conservation Bd., Temple, 1985. Mem. Lamar Middle Sch. PTA, Temple, 1983—, treas., 1986-87; vol. Meredith Elem. Sch., Temple, 1984-85, mem. PTA, 1982-85, v.p. PTA, 1982-83; vol. Jefferson Elem. Sch., Temple, 1980-82, mem. PTA, 1978-82; bd. dirs. Temple Family Services, 1974-77; mem. St. Luke's Cath. Ch. Women's Orgn., Temple, 1978-85, Temple Assn. for Gifted, 1981-87, seminar leader, 1981-84. Named Outstanding Young Woman of Am., 1978. Mem. Data Processing Mgmt. Assn, Tex. Assn. Ednl. Data Systems, Soc. Data Educators (cert.), Tex. Jr. Coll. Tchrs. Assn. (sec. data processing sect. 1981, 86, chairperson data processing sect. 1982, 87), Temple Apple Computer Users Group (founder; pres. 1983-85), Bell County Personal Computers Users' Group (v.p. 1984-85, pres. 1986-87), Beta Sigma Phi, Pi Alpha Alpha, Phi Theta Kappa. Democrat. Roman Catholic. Home: 210 Mitchell Temple TX 76501

GREEN, PATRICIA GAIL, nurse; b. Savannah, Ga., Jan. 31, 1959; d. William and Lena (Hall) G. AA, Armstrong State U., 1984. RN, Ga. Charge nurse Meml. Med. Ctr., Inc., Savannah, 1984—. Mem. Am. Assn. Critical Care Nurses, Port City Bus. and Profl. Women, Inc. Club: La Rose Civic (Savannah). Home: 10725 Abercorn Extension Apt 148 Savannah GA 31419 Office: Meml Med Ctr Inc Waters Ave Savannah GA 31401

GREEN, RHONDA BEVERLY, academic administrator; b. Bklyn., June 18, 1958; d. Lawrence and Miriam (Hodosh) Stern; m. Jeremy Eric Green. BA summa cum laude, Bklyn. Coll., 1979, postgrad., 1983—. Instr., dept. chairperson, adminstr. Adelphi Inst., Bklyn., 1980-84; dir. edn. Crown Bus. Inst., N.Y.C., 1984-85; dir. N.Y. schs. Robert Fiance, Am. Hi-Tech Bus Schs., N.Y.C., 1985-87; v.p. Elle! Internat., N.Y.C., 1987—. Mem. Am. Mgmt. Assn., Bus. Edn. Assn., Nat. Assn. Female Execs., Assn. Supervision and Curriculum Devel., Phi Beta Kappa, Pi Delta Phi.

GREEN, ROSE BASILE (MRS. RAYMOND S. GREEN), poet, author, educator; b. New Rochelle, N.Y., Dec. 19, 1914; d. Salvatore and Caroline (Galgano) Basile; BA, Coll. New Rochelle, 1935; MA, Columbia U., 1941; PhD, U. Pa., 1962; LHD (hon.), Gwynedd-Mercy Coll., 1979, Cabrini Coll., 1982; m. Raymond S. Green, June 20, 1942; children—Carol-Rae Hoffmann, Raymond Ferguson St. John. Tchr., Torrington High Sch., Conn., 1936-42; writer, researcher Fed. Writers Project, 1935-36; free-lance script writer Cavalcade of Am., NBC, 1940-42; assoc. prof. English, univ. registrar Tampa U., Tampa, 1942-43; spl. instr. English, Temple U., Phila., 1953-57; prof. dept. English, Cabrini Coll., Radnor, Pa., 1957-70, chmn. dept., 1957-70. Exec. dir. Am. Inst. Italian Studies; dir. lit. com. Phila. Art Alliance; bd. dirs., trustee Free Library of Phila.; v.p., dir. Nat. Italian-Am. Found.; chair Nat. Adv. Council Ethnic Heritage Studies; adv. bd. Women for Greater Phila.; dir. Balch Inst. Phila. Decorated cavalier Republic of Italy; named Woman of Yr. Pa. Sons of Italy, 1975, Disting. Dau. of Pa., 1978; recipient Nat. Amita award for lit., 1976, Nat. Bicentennial award for poetry DAR, 1976, other awards for contbns. to lit. and edn. Mem. Am. Acad. Polit. and Social Sci., Acad. Am. Poets, Acad. Polit. Sci., Am. Studies Assn., Ethnic Studies Assn., AAUW (dir.-at-large), Nat. Council Tchrs. English, Am.-Italy Soc. (dir. 1952—), Eastern Pa. Coll. New Rochelle Alumnae (pres. 1951-54), Kappa Gamma Pi. Club: Cosmopolitan (Phila.). Author: Cabrinian Philosophy of Education, 1967; (poetry) To Reason Why, 1971, Primo Vino, 1974, 76 for Philadelphia, 1975, Century Four, 1981, Songs of Ourselves, 1982; (criticism) The Italian-American Novel, 1974; Woman, The Second Coming, 1977; Lauding the American Dream, 1980; The Life of Mother Frances Cabrini, 1984; Songs of Ourselves, 1982; (poems) The Pennsylvania People, 1984; editor faculty jour. A-Zimuth, 1963-70. Home: 308 Manor Rd Philadelphia PA 19128

GREEN, RUTH NELDA (CUMMINGS), educator; b. Greenway, Ark., Aug. 25, 1928; d. William Harrison and Opal Lee (Davis) G.; B.S. in Edn., U. Omaha (now U. Nebr., Omaha), 1966, postgrad.; m. Robert C. Green, Jr., Apr. 22, 1951 (dec.); children—Dana Lynn Green Schrad, Lisa Jane Green Noon. Tchr., Public Schs. Greenway, 1948-51, Hancock County (Miss.), 1951-53, Bellevue (Nebr.), 1961-86; sec. Nebr. Ornithologists' Union, 1986—. Vol. tchr./naturalist Fontenelle Forest Nature Ctr., 1968—, bd. govs. edn. com. NSF scholar, 1968-73; active Nebr. Coordinating Commn. for post-secondary edn., 1986-88. Mem. NEA, Greater Nebr. Assn. Tchrs. Sci. (state pres. 1984-85), Nebr. Wildlife Assn., Nat. Audubon Soc. (Edn. award 1975), Omaha Audubon Soc., Bellevue Edn. Assn., Nebr. Edn. Assn., Inland Bird Banding Assn., Am. Birding Assn., Nebr. Ornithologists Union (pres. 1982, v.p. 1983-85, bd. dirs., sec. 1986—), Alpha Delta Kappa. Mem. Ch. of Christ. Columnist for Audubon Soc. Omaha Newsletter, Nebr. Ornithologists Union Newsletter. Home: 506 W 31st Ave Bellevue NE 68005 Office: 700 Galvin Rd Bellevue NE 68005

GREEN, RUTH R., health agency administrator; b. N.Y.C.; d. William and Ethel (Trachtenberg) Relkin; m. Darwin Green, Sept. 2, 1950; children: Robert L., Sandor A. BS, CCNY, 1950; MA, Columbia U., 1952. Intake counselor Vocat. Rehab. div N.Y. State, N.Y.C., 1950-51; asst. adminst., dir. counseling N.Y. League for the Hard of Hearing, N.Y.C., 1951-79, adminstr., 1979—; advisor Vocat. Rehab. Commn. Counsel on Deafness, 1986—. Advisor N.Y.C. Bd. Edn. Adv. Com. Occupational Edn., 1976—. Fellow World Rehab. Fund., 1979. Mem. Am. Psychol. Assn., Am. Assn. Counseling and Devel., Nat. Rehab. Counseling Assn. (site vis. for certs.), Am. Speech-Hearing-Lang. Assn. (mem. clin. cert. bd.), Am. Personnel and Guidance Assn., Nat. Vocat. Guidance Assn., Am. Deafness and Rehab. Assn. Home: 1669 Hendrickson Ave Merrick NY 11566 Office: NY League for the Hard of Hearing 71 W 23d St New York NY 10010

GREEN, SELMA BLOCK, lawyer; b. N.Y.C., June 4, 1916; d. Abraham J. and Pauline (Hutner) Block; m. Emanuel Green, June 7, 1942; children—Lori, Frederick S., Nancy Green-Schieken. Student Cornell U., 1933-35; LL.B., NYU, 1938. Bar: N.Y. 1939. Spl. corp. counsel Corp. Counsel N.Y.C., 1939-40; asst. dir. Bur. Prevention Juvenile Delinquency, N.Y.C., 1940-42; atty. U.S. Army Legal Claims Div., Newport News, Va., 1943-44; assoc. Green & Green, N.Y.C., 1944—; owner, mgr. Plaza Pharmacy, Inc., N.Y.C., 1959-87. Pres., Rego Park PTA, 1955; exec. bd. Halsey Jr. High Sch., Rego Park, 1956-57; commr. Girl Scouts U.S.A., 1955-57; dist. capt. Democratic Club, N.Y.C. and Forest Hills, N.Y., 1946-59; del. United Parents Assn., Rego Park, 1956-58; asst. sec., charter mem. Trylon Regular Dem. Club, Rego Park, 1956-69. Mem. N.Y. Women's Bar Assn. (v.p. 1940-41), Nat. Assn. Women Lawyers, ABA, Empire City Pharm. Assn., Nat. Assn. Retail Druggists. Club: Hadassah. Home: 15 Weaver St Scarsdale NY 10583

GREEN, SHIA TOBY RINER, therapist; b. N.Y.C., July 1, 1937; d. Murray A. and Frances Riner; student CCNY, 1954-57; B.A., Antioch Coll., 1974, M.A., 1976; m. Gary S. Green, Sept. 4, 1957; children—Margot Laura, Vanessa Daryl, Garson Todd. Press. and legis. sec. U.S. Ho. of Reps., Washington, 1960-71; cons. Rehab. Services Adminstrn., Social and Rehab. Services, HEW, 1972-73; asst. dir. State of Md. Foster Care Impact Demonstration Project, 1977-78; therapist Alexandria (Va.) Narcotics Treatment Program, 1979-84, Assocs. Psychotherapy Ctrs, Giburg, Md.; mem. treatment com. Alexandria Case Mgmt. and Treatment of Child Sexual Abuse. Mem. exec. bd. Children's Adoption Resource Exchange, Washington; vol. worker Girl Scouts U.S.A., also Boy Scouts Am., 1970-74. Mem. Am. Psychol. Assn., Md. Psychol. Assn., Am. Assn. Marriage and Family Therapy. Co-author: Permanent Planning in Maryland—A Manual for the Foster Care Worker. Home: One Lake Potomac Ct Potomac MD 20854 Office: 8915 Shady Grove Ct Gaithersburg MD 20877

GREEN, SHIRLEY MOORE, federal agency administrator; b. Graham, Tex., Dec. 21, 1933; d. N. Edgar and Cora Day (Morrow) Moore; m. Paul M. Green, Aug. 26, 1967 (div. 1981); children: Ruth Lynn, Tracy Moore. Student, Midwestern U., Wichita Falls, Tex., 1952; BBA, U. Tex., 1956. Staff asst. Rep. Party, Austin, Tex., 1965-67; press asst. Bob Price U.S. Rep., Washington, 1967; coordinator Tex. and Ark. Bush for Pres. Campaign, Houston, 1979-80; dep. press sec. V.p. Bush, Washington, 1980-85, acting press sec., 1983, dir. pub. affairs NASA, Washington, 1985-86, dep. assoc. adminstr. communications, 1987—; adv. bd. Office Personnel Mgmt., Washington. Local chmn. Jim Baker for Atty. Gen., 1978, Pres. Ford Com., San Antonio, 1976; trustee S.W. Found. Forum, San Antonio, 1974-78; bd. dirs. Child Welfare Bd. Bexar County, 1975-79. Mem. Internat. Platform Assn., Am. Newswomen's Club, Tex. Fedn. Rep. Women (editor Partyline mag. 1969-72, one of 10 Outstanding Rep. Women Tex. 1979). Presbyterian. Home: 1642 32nd NW Washington DC 20007 Office: NASA 400 Maryland Ave SW Washington DC 20546

GREEN, VICKI LYNN, lawyer; b. Shreveport, La., Jan. 1, 1956; d. Charles Abner and Cleolis Cloteal (Hudson) G. B.A., La. Tech. U., 1977; J.D., Tulane U., 1980. Bar: La. 1980, U.S. Ct. Appeals (5th cir.) 1982, U.S. Dist. Ct. (we. dist.) La. 1982. Asst. dist. atty. Ouachita Parish (La.), Monroe, 1980-81; assoc. McLeod, Swearingen, Verlander & Dollar, Monroe, 1981-85, Sockrider, Bolin & Anglin, Shreveport, 1986, Shafto & Ashbrook, Monroe, 1986, Barnes, Jefferson, Robertson & Green, 1987-88; sole practice Monroe, 1988—. Mem. ABA, La. Bar Assn. (family law sect. 1983—, ho. of dels. 1984-85), 4th Jud. Dist. Bar Assn. (adv. bd. young lawyers sect. 1983-85, ethics com. 1983-85, ct. laison com. 1986—), Delta Theta Phi.Club: Quota of Moroe (chmn. scholarship com. 1987—, chmn. ways & means com. 1988—, bd. dirs. 1988—). Home: 426 Isabelle St Monroe LA 71201 Office: PO Box 3003 Monroe LA 71210

GREENAWALT, KAREN LOUISE, financial specialist; b. Reading, Pa., Apr. 18, 1951; d. Donald Benjamin and Cynthia (Levan) G. BS in Art Edn., Kutztown U., 1973. Mgr. Foxmoor Casuals, Lancaster, Pa., 1975-76; free-lance artist and pilot Oklahoma City and Tulsa, 1976-82; clk. parts dept. Tulsair Beechcraft, Tulsa, 1982-83; money mgr. 1st State Securities Inc, Tulsa, 1983—; preparer tax, mgr. H&R Block, Oklahoma City and Tulsa, 1977-88. Club: Cacti and Succulent Soc. Tulsa (editor newsletter 1982-86, pres. 1986-87). Office: 1st State Securities 2250 E 73d St #440 Tulsa OK 74136

GREENAWALT, PEGGY TOMARKIN, advertising executive; b. Cleve., Apr. 27, 1942; d. Bernard H. and Gyta Elinor (Arsham) Freed; m. Gary Tomarkin, Aug. 7, 1966 (div. 1981); children: Craig William, Eric Lawrence; m. William Sloan Greenawalt, Oct. 31, 1987. BS, Simmons Coll., 1964. Asst. account exec. Howard Marks/Norman, Craig & Kummel, Inc., N.Y.C., 1964-66; account exec. Shaw Bros. Advt. Co., N.Y.C., 1966-67; copywriter Claire Advt. Co., N.Y.C., 1967; ptnr. Copywriters Coop., Hartsdale, N.Y., 1970-73; copy chief Howard Marks Advt., N.Y.C., 1973-80; sr. copywriter Wunderman, Ricotta & Kline, N.Y.C., 1980-82; v.p., assoc. creative dir. Ayer-Direct (N.W. Ayer), N.Y.C., 1982-84; sr. v.p., creative dir. D'Arcy Direct (D'Arcy, MacManus & Masius), N.Y.C., 1984-86; creative and mktg. cons., 1986-87; pres. Tomarkin/Greenawalt, Inc.; judge various advt. awards. Author: Kiss, The Real Story, 1980. Mem. Direct Mktg. Creative Guild, Direct Mktg. Assn., Direct Mktg. Club N.Y., Westchester Assn. Women Bus. Owners. Office: 24 Lewis Ave Hartsdale NY 10530

GREENBERG, BEVERLY LEE, zoological society administrator; b. Milw., July 6, 1946; d. Jack and Julia (Reitman) Young; m. Martin J. Greenberg, Mar. 29, 1969; children: Kari, Steven. BS in Secondary Edn., U. Wis.-Milw., 1968. Tchr. Brookfield (Wis.) Cen., 1968-72, Shorewood (Wis.) High, 1979-81, MATC, Milw., 1981—; devel. dir. Zool. Soc. Milw. County, Milw., 1984—; cons. Milw. Jewish Fedn., 1981—. Pres. PTO Lake Bluff Sch., Milw., 1978-79, PTA Maple Dale Sch., Milw., 1984-85; bd. dirs. Milw. Jr. Showcase, 1982—, The Theatre Sch. Ltd., Milw., 1983—, Congregation Emanuel B'n Jeshurun, Milw., 1983, Jewish Family-Children's Service, Milw., 1981—. DAR scholar, 1965; recipient Xi Telesis award Alverno Coll. Mem. Nat. Soc. Fund Raising Execs., Am. Assn. Zool. Parks and Aquariums, Wis. Tchr. Cert., Nat. Educators Assn., Wis. Communications Assn., Sigma Tau Delta. Home: 9429 N Broadmoor Rd Milwaukee WI 53217 Office: Zool Soc Milw County 10001 W Bluemound Rd Milwaukee WI 53226

GREENBERG, BLU, author; b. Seattle, Jan. 21, 1936; d. Sam and Sylvia (Genser) Genquer; m. Irving Greenberg; children: Jeremy, David, Deborah, Jonathan, Judith. BA, Bklyn. Coll., 1957; BA in Religious Edn., Yeshiva U., 1958; MA in Clin. Psychol., City U., N.Y.C., 1967; MS in Jewish History, Yeshiva U., 1977. Instr. Dept. Religious Studies Coll. Mt. St. Vincent, N.Y.C., 1970-77; lectr. Pardes Inst., Jerusalem, 1974-75; guest lectr. Harvard U., Princeton U., Dartmouth U., U. Ind., and various other colls. Author: How to Run a Traditional Jewish Household, 1983, On Women and Judaism: A View from Tradition, 1982; mem. editorial bd. Lilith mag., Journal Women and Judaism; contbr. articles to religious jours. Named Woman Yr. United Jewish Appeal-Bronx Div., 1984, Woman Valor Riverdale Jewish Ctr. 1971; recipient Myrtle Wreath Lit. award Hadassah 1976, Lit. award B'nai Brith women 1981. Mem. Sh'ma (mem.editorial bd. 1979—), Jewish Publ. Soc. (mem. editorial bd. 1985—), Hadassah Mag. (mem. editorial bd. 1984—), Jewish Women's Resource Ctr. (mem. adv. bd. 1982—), Jewish Book Council Am. (pres. 1983-86), Fedn. Commn. Synagogue Relations (chmn. exec. bd. 1982-86), U.S.-Israel Women to Women (co-founder, mem. exec. bd. 1978—), Women Faith Eighties (mem. steering com. 1980—), Zionist Acad. Council, B'Nai Brith Commn. Adult Edn. (mem. exec. bd.). Home and Office: 4620 Independence Ave Bronx NY 10471

GREENBERG, CAROLE NAGELSMITH, family therapist, consultant; b. N.Y.C., Nov. 7, 1941; d. Louis and Bernice (Goldberg) Nagelsmith; m. Richard A. Greenberg, Aug. 28, 1964 (div. Oct. 1981); children: Danna, Michael. BS, U. Vt., 1963; MS, U. Bridgeport, 1978. RN, cert. clin. mental health counselor. Psychiat. nurse Mt. Sinai Hosp., N.Y.C., 1963-64; asst. supr. psychiatry Met. Hosp., N.Y.C., 1964-66; sch. nurse, tchr. Clarkstown High Sch., N.Y.C., 1965-67; pub. health nurse Town Greenwich, Conn., 1972-75; co-founder, cons. Kinematics, Greenwich, 1978-80; co-dir. family prog. Moran, Stahl, & Boyer Inc., N.Y.C., 1980-83; pvt. practice family therapy Old Greenwich, Conn., 1983—. Contbr. articles to profl. jours. Mem. Youth Services Council, Greenwich, 1987, Dometic Abuse Service, Greenwich, 1982—. Mem. Am. Assn. Marriage and Family Therapy, Am. Assn. Counseling and Devel., Am. Soc. Training and Devel., NOW. Democrat. Jewish. Home and Office: 4 Lockwood Ave Old Greenwich CT 06870

GREENBERG, ELINOR MILLER, college administrator; b. Bklyn., Nov. 13, 1932; d. Ray and Susan (Weiss) Miller; m. Manuel Greenberg, Dec. 26, 1955; children—Andrea, Julie, Michael. BA, Mt. Holyoke Coll., 1953; MA, U. Wis.-Madison, 1954; EdD, U. No. Colo., 1981; LittD (hon.), St. Mary-of-the-Woods, Ind., 1983; LHD (hon.), Profl. Sch. Psychology, Calif., 1987. Exec. dir. Arapahoe Inst. for Community Devel., Littleton, Colo., 1969-71; founding dir. Univ. without Walls, Loretto Heights Coll., Denver, 1971-79, asst. acad. dean, 1982-84, asst. to pres., 1984-85; regional exec. officer, mgr. Council for Adult and Experiential Learning, Columbia, Md., 1979—; program adminstr. Internat. Bell/CWA, Pathways to the Future, 1986—, Communications workers of Am.; cons. in field. Co-editor, contbr.: Educating Learners of All Ages, 1980; co-author: Designing Undergraduate Education, 1981, Widening Ripples, 1986, Leading Effectively, 1987; editor, contbr.: New Partnerships: Higher Education and the Nonprofit Sector, 1982; contbr. articles to profl. jours. Bd. dirs., exec. com. Anti Defamation League of B'nai B'rith, Denver, 1981—; vice chair Colo. State Bd. for Community Colls. and Occupational Edn., 1981-86; bd. dirs. Nat. Women's Forum, Griffith Ctr., Golden, Colo., 1982-86, Colo. Bd. Continuing Legal and Jud. Edn., 1984—; pres. Women's Forum of Colo., 1986; v.p. Women's Forum Colo. Found., 1987; mem. adv. bd. Anchor Ctr. Blind Child, Colo. Coalition Prevention Nuclear War; mem. Nat. Conf. on Edn. for Women's Devel., Community Adv. Bd. Colo. Woman News, Gov.'s Women's Econ. Devel. Taskforce; co-chair Women's Econ. Devel. Council, 1988—. Named Citizen of Yr. Omega Psi Phi, Denver, 1966; Woman of Decade Littleton Ind. Newspapers, 1970; grantee W. K. Kellogg Found., 1982, Weyerhauser Found., 1986, Fund for Improvement of Post Secondary Edn., 1977, 80; recipient Sesquicentennial award Mt. Holyoke Coll. Alumni Assn., 1987. Mem. Am. Assn. for Higher Edn., Assn. for Experiential Edn. (editorial bd. 1978-80), ACLU, Am. Council in Edn., Kappa Delta Pi. Democrat. Jewish. Home: 6725 S Adams Way Littleton CO 80122

GREENBERG, JEANNE LECRANN, corporate executive; b. N.Y.C., Dec. 23, 1935; d. Vincent and Anne LeCrann; m. Herbert M. Greenberg, July 30, 1969; children: Scott, Phillip, Holly. Student Fairleigh Dickenson U., 1959-60, Rider Coll., 1974-78, Princeton U. Dir. field ops., then v.p., dir. govt. services Mktg. Survey and Research Corp., Princeton, N.J., 1961-70, pres., 1975—; dir. placement and counseling OEO, New Opportunities Program, San Juan, P.R., 1965-66; dir. placement and counseling Social Research Corp., 1968-70; pres., gen. mgr. Progressive Communications, Inc., Sta. WIMG, Trenton, N.J., 1973-85; co-chmn., prin. Caliper Mgmt. Co., 1985—; chmn., chief exec. officer Caliper Co., Human Strategies Cons., 1985—; exec. v.p. Personality Dynamics, Inc., Princeton, 1970-83; founder, 1977, pres. N.J. Radio Network, 1977-81; workshop leader, speaker in field. Contbr. articles to profl. jours. Trustee Del. Valley United Way, 1978-80, chmn. publicity com., 1979—. Mem. Women's Equity Action League, Princeton C. of C. Democrat. Home: 132 Hunt Dr Princeton NJ 08540 Office: PO Box 2050 Princeton NJ 08540

GREENBERG, JUDITH LYNN, social worker; b. N.Y.C., Feb. 9, 1947; d. Sam Paul and Celia (Lidofsky) G. BA with distinction (Adelia Cheever scholar 1966), U. Mich., 1967; MA, U. Chgo., 1970; postgrad. (univ. grantee) Adelphi U., 1979—. Cert. clin. social worker. Elem. sch. tchr. Willow Run Pub. Schs., Mich., 1967-68; urban planner Chgo. Dept. Devel. and Planning, 1970-71; social worker Inst. Juvenile Research, Chgo., 1971; med. social worker St. Luke's Hosp., N.Y.C., 1972-73; social worker immigration and absorption dept. Jewish Agy., Jerusalem, 1973-74; social worker, student supr. Jewish Bd. Family and Children's Services, N.Y.C., 1974-82; dir. Queens Family Ct. Preventive Services, Jewish Bd. Family and Children's Services, Forest Hills, N.Y., 1982—; instr. St. Joseph's Coll., Bklyn., 1979-82, Adelphi U. Sch. Social Work, Garden City, N.Y., 1985—; participant TV programs, family life edn. workshops. HEW fellow, 1968-70; NIMH fellow, 1979-80. Mem. Nat. Assn. Social Workers, Am. Assn. Sex Educators, Counselors and Therapists, Soc. Sex Therapy and Research, Acad. Cert. Social Workers. Jewish. Home: 210 W 89th St Apt 1C New York NY 10024 Office: Queens Family Ct Preventive Services 116-16 Queens Blvd Forest Hills NY 11375

GREENBERG, ROSALIE, child psychiatrist; b. Bklyn., Dec. 21, 1950; d. Sam and Molly G.; BA, NYU, 1972; student Upstate Med. Ctr., Syracuse, 1972-73; MD, Columbia U., 1976. Intern Overlook Hosp., Summit, N.J., 1976-77; resident in gen. psychiatry Columbia Presbyn. Med. Ctr., N.Y. State Psychiatric Inst., N.Y.C., 1977-80, fellow in child and adolescent psychiatry, 1979-81, dep. dir. pediatric psychiatry outpatient clinic, 1981-82; dir. child and adolescent outpatient services Fair Oaks Hosp., Summit, N.J., 1982—; instr. Columbia U., 1981—. Mem. Am. Psychiat. Assn., Am. Acad. Child and Adolescent Psychiatry, AMA. Office: Fair Oaks Hosp 19 Prospect St Summit NJ 07901

GREENBERGER, ELLEN, psychologist, educator; b. N.Y.C., Nov. 19, 1935; d. Edward Michael and Vera (Brisk) Silver; m. Michael Burton, Aug. 26, 1979; children by previous marriage—Kari Edwards, David Greenberger. B.A., Vassar Coll., 1956; M.A., Harvard U., 1959, Ph.D., 1961. Instr. Wellesley (Mass.) Coll., 1961-63, asst. prof., 1963-67; sr. research scientist Johns Hopkins U., Balt., 1967-75; prof. social ecology U. Calif., Irvine, 1975—; dir. program in social ecology U. Calif., 1976-80. Author: (with others) When Teenagers Work, 1986; contbr. articles to profl. jours. USPHS fellow, 1956-59; Margaret Floy Washburn fellow, 1956-58; Ford Found. grantee, 1979-81; Spencer Found. grantee, 1979-81, 87, 88-91. Fellow Am. Psychol. Assn., Soc. Research on Child Devel., Soc. Research on Adolescent Devel. Office: Univ Calif Program in Social Ecology Irvine CA 92717

GREENBERGER, MARCIA D., attorney; b. 1946. AB, U. Pa., JD. Mng. atty. Nat. Women's Law Ctr., Washington. Office: Nat Womens Law Ctr 1626 P St NW Washington DC 20036 *

GREENBERGER, MARSHA MOSES, industrial executive; b. Lakewood, N.J., Mar. 15, 1943; d. Bernard David and Ethel (Gordon) Moses; m. Paul Edward Greenberger (div. 1969); 1 child, Nathan, Scott. Student, Kent (Ohio) State U., 1961-62. Mgr. gen. sales Ellison Products, Fairfield, N.J., 1972-79; gen. mgr. Indsl. Maintenance Corp., Cherry Hill, N.J., 1979-83; co-owner corp. sect. Ven-Mar Sales, Inc., Blairstown, N.J., 1983—. Mem. NE

Pastner Assn. Office: Veri Mar Sales Inc PO Box 648 Lambert Rd Blairstown NJ 07825

GREENBERG-SOLOMON, IRIS LINN, television sales professional; b. Englewood, N.J., July 21, 1960; d. Donald R. and Susan L. (Deitchman) Greenberg; m. Ronald B. Solomon, Sept. 21, 1986. BS in Mass and Bus. Communications, Emerson Coll., 1982. Prodn. asst. Cable News Network, N.Y.C., 1980-82; prodn. coordinator Iris Films, Inc., N.Y.C., 1982-83; dir. scheduling Videoworks, Inc., N.Y.C., 1983-85; account exec. Tapepower, Inc., N.Y.C., 1985-86, VCA/Teletronics, Inc., N.Y.C., 1986—. Mem. Nat. Assn. Female Execs., Am. Film Inst., Internat. Teleprodn. Soc. (co-chairperson judging com. 1986-87), Internat. TV Assn., Videotape Producers Assn. Home: 65-60 Booth St Rego Park NY 11374

GREENBLATT, DEANA CHARLENE, educator; b. Chgo., Mar. 13, 1948; d. Walter and Betty (Lamasky) Beisel; B.S. in Edn., Chgo. State U., 1969; M.A. in Guidance and Counseling, Roosevelt U., 1973; m. Mark Greenblatt, June 22, 1975. Tchr., counselor Chgo. Pub. Schs., 1969-75, City Colls. of Chgo. GED-TV, 1976; tchr. Columbus (Ohio) Pub. Schs., 1976-86; participant learning exchange, Chgo. Active B'nai B'rith; vol. Right-to-Read, Columbus; mem. Community Learning Exchange, Columbus. Certified tchr. K-9, Ill., Ohio; certified personnel guidance, Ill., Ohio; certified Chgo. Bd. Edn. Mem. Am. Personnel and Guidance Assn., Internat. Platform Assn. Democrat. Club: B'nai B'rith Women (chpt. v.p.). Home: 4083 Vineshire Dr Columbus OH 43227

GREENBLATT, MIRIAM, author, editor, educator; b. Berlin; d. Gregory and Shifra (Zemach) Baraks; B.A. magna cum laude, Hunter Coll.; postgrad. U. Chgo., Spertus Coll.; m. Herbert Halbrecht (div. 1960); m. 2d, Howard Greenblatt, 1962 (div. 1978). Tchr., New Trier (Ill.) High Sch., 1978-81; editor Am. People's Ency., Chgo., 1957-58; editor Scott, Foresman & Co., Chgo., 1958-62; pres. Creative Textbooks, Evanston, Ill., 1972—. V.p. Chgo. Chpt. Am. Jewish Com., 1977-79, mem. nat. exec. council, 1980-84; treas. Glencoe Youth Services, 1981-83. Mem. Nat. Council Social Studies, Ill. Council Social Studies, Am. Hist. Assn., Chgo. Women in Publishing, Women in Mgmt. Jewish. Author: James Knox Polk, 1988; (with others) The American People, 1986; (with Cox and Seaberg) Human Heritage, 1985; (with Jordan and Bowes) The Americans, 1985; The History of Itasca, 1976; (with Cuban) Japan, 1971; (with Chu) The Story of China, 1968; edit. cons. Peoples and Cultures Series, 1976-78; contbg. editor A World History, 1979. Address: 550 Sheridan Sq Evanston IL 60202

GREEN-DORSEY, JEAN AUDREY, information systems executive; b. Cleve., Oct. 27, 1940; d. Sydney Howard and Bennie Irene (Blake) Green; B.A., L.I. U., 1962; m. William R. Dorsey, Nov. 1, 1980. With IBM, N.Y.C., 1966-72; mktg. mgr. office automation Olivetti, N.Y.C., 1972-80; dep. dir. N.Y.C. Mgmt. Info. Systems, 1981-85, computer systems mgr. Inter-agy. Task Force, 1985-86; pres. Inst. Mgmt. Devel., N.Y.C., 1986—; dir. PolySoft Systems Inc.; sr. cons. Inst. Mgmt. Devel., 1980—; adv. editor Hearst Pubs., 1981—, Today's Office, 1986—, others; lectr. in field; bd. dirs. Nat. Inst. Mgmt. Bd. dirs. Fair Harbor Community Assn., 1981—; leader Citizen Ambassador Program People to People office automation del. to People's Republic China, 1988. Recipient cert. Fresh Air Fund, 1980. Mem. Assn. Computing Machinery, Assn. Info. Systems Profls. (pres. N.Y.C. chpt., leader sci. and technology delegation to People's Republic China 1988). Clubs: Soroptimists Internat., The Club at N.Y. World Trade Center. Contbr. articles to profl. jours. Office: PolySoft Systems Corp 2901 Druid Park Dr Suite 207 Baltimore MD 21215

GREENE, ADELE S., management consultant; b. Newark, N.J.; d. Adolph and Sara (Schubert) Shuminer; m. Alan Greene (div.); 1 child, Joshua. Student, Juilliard Sch. Music, 1942-44, NYU, 1942-44, New Sch. Social Research, 1944-47; diploma in mgmt., Harvard Bus. Sch., 1978. Account exec. Ruder and Finn Inc., N.Y.C., 1964-66, sr. assoc., 1966-68, v.p., 1968-72, sr. v.p., 1972-76; v.p. pub. affairs Corp. Pub. Broadcasting, Washington, 1976-78; pres., chief operating officer TV Program Group, Washington, 1978-80; pres. Greene and Assocs., N.Y.C., 1981—; instr. pub. relations and community affairs, NYU 1974-76; bd. dirs. Sci. Program Group, Washington 1976-81. Co-author: Teen-Age Leadership, 1971. Advisor The Acting Co., Understudies, N.Y.C. 1987—; pres., chief operating officer Am. Craft Council 1980-81, trustee 1976-81; bd. dirs. Union Settlement, N.Y.C. 1987—; trustee Duke Ellington Sch. Arts, Washington, 1977-81. Mem. Pub. Relations Soc. Am. (silver anvil award 1971), Nat. Assn. Edn. Broadcasters, Am. Women Radio and TV. Home and Office: 30 W 60th St New York NY 10023 also: 31 Pond Dr W Rhinebeck NY 12572

GREENE, AURELIA, state legislator; b. N.Y.C., Oct. 26, 1934; d. Edward Henry and Sybil Elaine (Russell) Holley; children—Rhonda, Russell; m. 2d, Jerome Alexander Greene, Apr. 18, 1975. B.A., Rutgers U., 1974. Dep. exec. dir. Morrisania Community Corp., N.Y.C., 1969-76; exec. dir. Bronx Area Policy Bd. No. 6, N.Y.C., 1980-82; mem. N.Y. State Assembly, 1982—. Dist. leader 76th Assembly Dist., Bronx, 1979-82; sec. Community Sch. Bd. No. 9, Bronx, 1980—; exec. mem. Bronx Unity Democratic Club; del. Dem. Nat. Conv., 1984; mem. credentials com. Dem. Nat. Conv., Atlanta, 1988. Mem. Morrisania Edn. Council, Bronx NAACP (Woman of Yr. award 1974). Democrat. Office: 1188 Grand Concourse Suite D Bronx NY 10456

GREENE, BARBARA ALLEN, physicist; b. Danville, Ill., Jan. 22, 1943; d. MacLean Jack and Irene Eunice (Highberg) Babcock; m. Samuel Laurie Greene, Sept. 1, 1966 (div. 1978). BA in Math., Sonoma State U., Calif., 1975; BS in Physics, Sonoma State U., 1975, MA in Humanistic Psychology, 1976; postgrad., U. Calif., Berkeley, 1976-78. Lic. energy auditor, Calif. Staff scientist, economist Lawrence Berkeley Lab., 1977-78; solar energy specialist, electric generation system specialist Calif. Energy Commn., 1978-80; field rep. Solar Energy Sales, Inc., 1980-81; math tchr. Ursuline High Sch., 1982-83; sr. energy project mgr. North Coast Energy Services, 1983-84; project mgr. Multi-Contact USA, Calif., 1984-85; cons. in field. Author: numerous books including Solar Energy in the 80's and Analysis of the California Energy Industry. Apptd. rep. 2nd dist. Sonoma County Energy Task Force, Calif., 1980. Recipient Hon. cert. Nat. Sci. Talent Search, 1960; Nat. Sci. Found. scholar, 1959. Mem. No. Calif. Solar Energy Assn. (bd. dirs. 1977-80), Soc. Tech. Communication, Nat. Assn. Female Execs., Mensa. Office: Specialized Computer Systems Inc PO Box 758 Cotati CA 94928

GREENE, BARBARA JACKSON, innkeeper; b. Salt Lake City, Oct. 29, 1922; d. Nathaniel and Ella Matilda (Nilsson) Jackson; m. Mark Hindley Greene; children: Mark Hindley III, Richard N., Karen G. Romney, Anne G. Parrish, John. BS, U. Utah, 1943. Bus. mgr. Orthopedic Hand Clinic (name now Hand Care Ctr.), Salt Lake City, 1971—; innkeeper Greene Gate Village Bed and Breakfast, St. George, Utah, 1986—. Pres. PTA, Salt Lake City, 1966, Utah Opera Guild, Salt Lake City, 1975; parliamentarian South Utah Symphony Guild, St. George, 1987—. Recipient Silver Beaver award Boy Scouts Am., 1978. Republican. Mormon. Home: 212 S 200 East Saint George UT 84770

GREENE, BARBARA LOUISE, mortgage company executive; b. Chgo., July 1, 1951; d. John William Miller and Lylas Dian (Stanley) Womack; m. Charles Richard Greene II, July 29, 1978; children: Tara Lynn, Alaina Louise. Underwriter approved Fed. Nat. Mortgage Assn., direct endorsement underwriter approved FHA. Loan processor Ryan Fin. Services, Inc., Columbus, Ohio, 1974-75; closing officer Ryan Fin. Services, Inc., Columbus, 1975-78, asst. mgr., 1978-80, br. mgr., 1980—. Mem. Columbus Mortgage Bankers Assn. Republican. Lutheran. Office: Ryan Fin Services Inc 3630 Corp Dr Suite 101 Columbus OH 43229

GREENE, BARBARA LOUISE, computer consultant, educator; b. Chgo., May 18, 1952; d. Stephen H. and Ruth Elaine (Stanton) G. BS in Edn, Ill. State U., 1974. Tchr. Romeoville (Ill.) Sch. Dist., 1974-76; programmer Spiegel, Inc., Chgo., 1978-80, Ace Hardware, Chgo., 1981-82; dir. data mgmt. U. Albuquerque, 1984-86; coordinator mgmt. info. system Coll. Santa Fe, Albuquerque, 1986-87; assoc. Spectra Research, Albuquerque, 1987—; tchr. Nat. Coll., Albuquerque, 1983—; cons. in field. Mem. Friends of Art, Albuquerque, 1986—; donor Sta. KHFM Classical Radio, Albuquerque, 1986—. Mem. Data Processing Mgmt. Assn., Nat. Assn. Female Execs.

GREENE, BEVERLY ANN, clinical psychologist; b. Orange, N.J., Aug. 14, 1950; d. Samuel and Thelma G. B.A., NYU, 1973; postgrad. Marquette U., 1973-74; M.A., Adelphi U., 1977, Ph.D., 1983. Lic. psychologist, N.Y. Fellow in psychology Mental Retardation Inst., N.Y. Med. Coll., Valhalla, N.Y., 1974-76; psychol. cons. Williamsburg Child Devel. Ctr., Bklyn., 1976-78; psychology intern East Orange VA Med. Ctr., 1978-79; research asst. dept. neurosci. N.J. Coll. Medicine and Dentistry, Vet.'s Hosp., 1979-80; psychology trainee, Children's Partial Hospitalization Unit, Brookdale Hosp. and Med. Ctr., 1980; sch. psychologist N.Y.C. Bd. Edn., 1980-82, staff psychologist, 1982-84; sr. psychologist, dir. inpatient child and adolescent psychol. services King's County Psychiat. Hosp., 1984—; clin. instr. in psychiatry Downstate Med. Sch., 1982-85, clin asst. prof., 1985—, acting dir. Children's Inpatient Unit, 1985-86. Contbr. articles to profl. jours. Martin Luther King scholar, 1968-72, NIMH fellow, 1976-77. Mem. Am. Psychol. Assn. (chmn. subcom. ethnic minor women's div.), Internat. Neuropsychol. Soc., Nat. Assn. Black Psychologists, N.Y. Soc. Black Psychologists, Nat. Assn. Women in Psychology, N.Y. Assn. Women in Psychology, N.Y. Coalition of Hosp. and Instnl. Psychologists. Office: 26 St Johns Pl Brooklyn NY 11217

GREENE, DOLORES EVANGELINE, university official; b. Pilot Grove, Mo., Sept. 21, 1929; d. David Hadley and Mary Esther (Chasteen) Simms; m. James Lincoln Greene, Nov. 18, 1950; children—Gary Alan, Jeffrey Warren, David Morgan. B.S., U. Wis., 1951, M.S., 1965. Cert. tchr., remedial reading tchr., notary pub., Wis. Tchr., Madison Area Tech. Sch. (Wis.), 1954-55, Milw. Pub. Schs., 1955-66; manpower specialist, supr., dir. Wis. Employment Service, Madison, 1967-72; area services specialist Wis. Dept. Health and Social Services, Madison, 1972-75; asst. to chancellor U. Wis. Extension, Madison, 1975-84; chmn. Milw. Reading Tchrs., 1962-63; cons. Milw. Urban League, 1957-60; support specialist Madison Pub. Schs., 1978-80; artist; actress stage and TV. Author: (with others) Ambidextrous (Natural) Tennis, 1979, 2d edit., 1982. Bd. dirs. Dane County Community Action Commn., 1969-72, Madison Urban League, 1974-76; del. Internat. Women's Yr., Houston, 1977; core council, dir. Coalition Minority Women, 1975-82; dir. Madison Civic Repertory Theatre, 1980-84; pres., sec. Brown St. PTA, 1960-64. Recipient Outstanding Pub. Service award Ethnic Heritage Award Com., 1978, award for advancement women's equality Wis. Women's Polit. Caucus, 1980, Meritorious Service award United Way of Dane County and YWCA, 1981, Affirmative Action/EEO Individual award Madison Urban League, 1982, state service award Gov.'s Affirmative Action Council, 1983, Disting. Citizen award U. Wis. Afro-Am. Alumni Assn., 1986. Mem. Internat. Reading Assn., Am. Assn. Affirmative Action, Wis. Assn. Affirmative Action and Equal Opportunity Profls., Madison Black Affirmative Action Officers Assn., Madison Minority Bus. Assn., Epsilon Sigma Phi, Delta Sigma Theta. Democrat. Methodist. Home: 302 S Bassett St Madison WI 53703

GREENE, DOLORES SIMMONS, social services administrator; b. N.Y.C., Mar. 26; d. Andrew and Cornelia (Johnson) Simmons; children: Kevin, Troy, Kimberly. BA, Morgan State U.; MSW, U. S.C., 1976. Counselor Employment Security Commn., Charleston, S.C., 1970-74; title XX planner Trident United Way, Charleston, 1976-78; adminstrv. coordinator Florence Crittenton Home, Charleston, 1978-82; project dir. Peterfield Human Services, Yonges Island, S.C., 1982-83, Beaufort-Jasper Economic Opportunity Commn., Charleston, 1983-85; exec. dir. Reid House of Christian Service, Charleston, 1985—. Pres. Black Women's Coalition, Charleston, 1983—; vice chmn., bd. dirs. Charleston County Dept. of Social Services, Charleston, 1987, State Bd. of Social Services, S.C., 1987; grad. Leadership S.C., 1985; mem. Morris Brown A.M.E. Ch. Recipient Community Service award, Charleston YWCA, 1979, Salem Bapt. Ch., 1972. Mem. S.C. Bd. of Social Work Examiners. Home: 22 Peachtree St Charleston SC 29403 Office: Reid House of Christian Service 165 St Philip St Charleston SC 29403

GREENE, ELAINE D.G., environmental science educator; b. Hartford, Conn., Aug. 3, 1937; d. George A. and Helene (Meyen) Gianopoulos; m. Jeremiah Evarts Greene Jr., June 5, 1971; children: Anne (dec.), Anthony, Meredith, Edward. BS in Biology, U. Hartford, Conn., 1970; MEd, Fitchburg (Mass.) State Coll., 1987. Staff technologist Hartford Hosp., 1957-61; asst. chief technologist Office Dr. Gilbert Heublein, Hartford, 1961-67; faculty, adminstr. Middlesex Community Coll., Middletown, Conn., 1969-71; staff technologist Mass. Gen. Hosp., Boston, 1971-72; supply tchr. William Penn High Sch., New Castle, Del., 1973-76, Catholic Sch., Leominster, Mass., 1980—. Editor Health newsletter. Mass. Opportunity Council, 1985-86. Mem. Am. Registry Radiologic Technologists (cert.), Mass. Audubon Soc. (sanctuary interpretor).

GREENE, GAYLE JACOBA, English language educator; b. San Francisco, June 23, 1943. B.A., U. Calif.-Berkeley, 1964, M.A., 1966; Ph.D. in English Lit., Columbia U., 1974. Edn. asst. Harper & Row Pub., 1967-68; lectr. English lit. Queens Coll., 1968-72, Bklyn. Coll., 1972-74; asst. prof. Scripps Coll., Claremont, Calif., 1974-80, prof. English lit., 1980—. Mem. MLA, Shakespeare Assn. Am., Nat. Women's Studies Assn. Co-editor: The Woman's Part: Feminist Criticism of Shakespeare, 1980; Making a Difference: Feminist Literary Criticism, 1985; contbr. articles to profl. jours. Address: Scripps Coll Claremont CA 91711

GREENE, IDA, educator; b. Minters, Ala., May 28, 1938; d. Willie O'Neal and Rosetta (Ulmer) Greene; 1 child, Christopher. B.A., San Diego State U., 1970, M.S., 1973; Ph.D. in Psychology; D.D. R.N., Calif.; lic. marriage family and child counselor. Charge nurse Univ. Hosp., San Diego, 1967, dir. nursing, 1971; sch. counselor San Diego State U., 1972; psychiatric nurse El Cajon Valley Hosp. (Calif.), 1973; sch. nurse Morse High Sch., San Diego, 1985—; tchr./counselor S.D. City Schs.; lectr. in field. Founder, Henry William Scholarship, 1973. Mem. Women in Mgmt., Women in Sales, Nat. Council Negro Women, Grow, Marriage and Family Child Counselors. Methodist. Club: Toastmasters. Author: Black Triumph, 1975. Address: 2910 Baily Ave San Diego CA 92105

GREENE, KAREN SANDRA, singer, actress, educator; b. N.Y.C., Jan. 7, 1942; d. Nathan and Natalie (Barashick) Stein; m. Richard Greene, July 1, 1962 (div. 1980); children: Barry Randall, Lauren Jennifer. BA, U. Conn.U., 1988. Singer, Broadway actress N.Y.C., 1960-62; pres., educator Karen Greene Studios, Norwalk, Conn., 1962—; pres., dir. voice On Stage Acad., Ltd., Westport, Conn., 1982-84; dir., educator theater arts Westport YMCA, 1981-85; educator Temple Shalom, Norwalk, 1975-87; dir. theater arts Bridgeport (Conn.) Jewish Ctr., 1985, dir. Norwalk Jewish Ctr., 1985. Voiceover artist nat. performing tours. Coordinator Southwestern Conn. Women's Issues Conf., 1988. Mem. Actor's Equity Assn., AFTRA, Screen Actors Guild. Home and Office: 4 Suburban Dr Norwalk CT 06851

GREENE, KATHLEEN JAN, public relations consultant; b. Toledo, Feb. 18, 1949; d. Raymond Philip Greene and Joanne (Jorgensen) Greene Deatrick; m. Thomas Arne Olkkonen, May 24, 1980; 1 child, Dana Joanne. B.A., Kent State U., 1972. Media dir. Gauge Public, Traverse City, Mich., 1973-74; copywriter Sta. WGTU/WGTQ-TV, Traverse City, 1974-78, asst. dir., 1978-79, dir. creative services, 1979-80; mktg. coordinator Sta. WPBN/WTOM-TV, Traverse City, 1980-82; pub. relations cons. KG Unltd., Traverse City, 1982—; media relations and sales Okerstrom Assocs., Traverse City, 1983-87; pub. relations rep. N.Am. Vasa, Traverse City, 1983— bd. dirs. 1987—); communications coordinator Grand Traverse Area United Way, 1983-85. Co-producer/dir.: Central Lake (Am. Legion award), 1978; producer/dir.: Band Classics (music award), 1979, Reach Out (United Way award), 1980. Communications com. Grand Traverse Area United Way, 1977—; publicity com. Community Theatre Mich., 1983-85, Traverse City Civic Players, 1975— (pres. Old Town Playhouse, 1987—), exec. dir. Downtown Traverse City Assn. 1986—, active Grand Traverse County Sesquicentennial Com. 1986-87, Grand Traverse Area Conv. and Visitors Bur. (coordinator Soc. Am. Travel Writers Conv., 1985), coordinator Community Theatre Assn. of Mich., 1986—, bd. dirs. Quota Club, Traverse City, 1987—. Mem. Women in Communications, Inc. (founder, treas. No. Mich. chpt., 1987—), Women's Econ. Devel. Orgn., Traverse City. Traverse Advt. Club (pres. 1978-79), Nat. Assn. Female Execs. Republican. Episcopalian. Home: 1711 Blackbark Ln Traverse City MI 49684

GREENE, LUCIA MURRAY, writer; b. N.Y.C., Aug. 5, 1954; d. Philip M. and Constance (Clarke) G.; m. Thomas Girard Connolly, Sept. 20, 1980; children: Nora Clarke, Sophie Gordon, Luke Philip. Student, U. Dijon, 1975; BA in English and French, Colgate U., 1975. Asst. editor E.P. Dutton Co., N.Y.C., 1976-78; photo researcher, editor, People Mag., N.Y.C., 1979-82, mgr. People Syndication, 1982-83, asst. editor, writer, 1983-85; also freelance writer. Democrat. Roman Catholic. Address: 56 N Pease Rd Woodbridge CT 06525

GREENE, LYNNE JEANNETTE, fashion designer; b. Albany, N.Y., Aug. 27, 1938; d. Zebulon Stevens and Helen Matilde (Maier) Robbins; m. Stanley E. Greene, Jan. 31, 1962 (dec. June 27, 1987); 1 child, Stuart Nathaniel. Student, Goucher Coll., 1956-57; BA, Parsons Sch. Design, 1960. Asst. designer Haymaker Sportswear (David Crystal), N.Y.C., 1959-61; designer Craig Craely Sportswear and Dresses, N.Y.C., 1961-63, Flair Lingerie, N.Y.C., 1964-66; designer, owner Kaleidoscope Lingerie, N.Y.C., 1966-67; head designer Contessa/Monique/Fisher Lingerie, N.Y.C., 1967-71; head designer, owner Lynne Greene Designs Retail, Montclair, N.J., 1972-74; designer, pres. Little Greene Apples Inc., Montville, N.J., 1971—; designer, dir. mktg. Lady Lynne Lingerie, Guy Laroche Lingerie, N.Y.C., 1973—; lingerie critic Pratt Inst., 1984—. Patentee in field. Active participant Montville Soccer Assn, 1972—, fund drives for Am. Heart Assn., Cancer Inc. Mem. The Fashion Group. Republican. Episcopalian.

GREENE, MARGARET LYFORD, banker; b. New Rochelle, N.Y., Sept. 12, 1942; d. Lyford Norman and Margaret Emma-Louise (Kluge) G.; m. Edwin H. Yeo, III, Sept. 30, 1978; stepchildren—Andrew Yeo, Douglas Yeo. B.A. in Econs., Wellesley Coll., 1964; M.A. in Econs., Columbia U., 1966, Ph.D. in Econs., 1972. Research asst. Internat. Econs. Workshop Columbia U., N.Y.C., 1964-66; economist internat. research and fgn. depts. Fed. Res. Bank, N.Y.C., 1967-72, chief fin. stats. div., stats. dept., 1972, mgr. fgn. dept., 1972, asst. v.p. fgn. dept., 1974, v.p. fgn. exchange function, 1977-83, sr. v.p. fgn. exchange function, 1984—; lectr. Sch. Mgmt., Vanderbilt U., Nashville. Contbr. articles to profl. jours. Wellesley Coll. scholar, 1963-64; Columbia U. presdl. fellow, 1966-67; Garth fellow, 1966-67. Mem. Am. Econ. Assn., FOREX U.S.A., Council on Fgn. Relations. Clubs: Orleans Yacht (Mass.); Stone Horse Yacht (Harwich Port, Mass.). Home: 190 Riverside Dr New York NY 10024 Office: Fed Res Bank of New York 33 Liberty St New York NY 10045

GREENE, NANCY ELLEN, infosystems specialist, physicist; b. Worcester, Mass., Nov. 4, 1947; d. William Arthur II and Dorothy Goddard (Fuller) Green; m. Arthur Edward Greene, Sept. 12, 1970; 1 child, Ellen Dorothy. BS in Physics, Ohio State U., 1969, MS in Physics, 1971. Instr. physics U. Colo., Colorado Springs, 1971-73; physics programmer U. N.Mex., Albuquerque, 1973-76; data analyst Controlled Thermonuclear Reaction div. Los Alamos (N.Mex.) Sci. Lab., 1975-77, programmer, 1977-78, mem. staff, 1978-81; mem. staff Accelerator Tech. div. Los Alamos Sci. Lab., 1981-84, Adminstrv. Data Processing div. Los Alamos Sci. Lab., 1984-85, Dynamic Testing div. Los Alamos Sci. Lab., 1985—; mem. exec. com. N.Mex. Digital Equipment Computer Users Soc., Albuquerque, 1984-87; registration chairperson computer conf., Albuquerque, 1984-87; program chairperson Particle Accelerator conf., Sante Fe, 1982-83. Spkr. in field. Vol. Los Alamos Schs., 1980—. Nat. Merit scholar, Mich. State U., 1965, Nat. Defense Edn. Act Title IV fellow, Ohio State U., 1969. Mem. VAX Computer Local Users Group (chmn. 1981-82). Office: Los Alamos Nat Lab PO Box 1663 MS P940 Los Alamos NM 87545

GREENE, REGINA, accountant; b. San Francisco; d. George and Olivia (Crunk) G.; 1 child, Volana. AA, San Francisco State U., 1972. Mgr. Bank of Am., San Francisco, 1969-73; supr. Am. Express, Karlshrue, Fed. Republic Germany, 1973-74, Bank of Orient, San Francisco, 1974-86, Cen. Bank, Concord, Calif., 1985-86; acct., fin. counselor Green's Fin. Services, Oakland, Calif., 1986—. Mem. Nat. Assn. Female Execs., Am. Bus. Women's Assn. Lodge: Order Eastern Star. Home: 71 Anair Way Oakland CA 94605

GREENE, SHARON LOUISE, business manager, editor; b. Washington, Sept. 8, 1960; d. Gary Edward and Lorna Sybil (Herzog) G. Student U. Colo., 1980-82. Office mgr. Irving Kerner Literary Agy., Boulder, 1979-81; bus. mgr. Alpha Micro Users Soc., Boulder, 1979—, editor, 1983—, meeting planner, 1984—, sec.-treas., 1983-86; cons. Club Mac, Boulder, 1984-85. Mem. Nat. Assn. Female Execs., Meeting Planners Internat., Colo. Press Assn. Democrat. Jewish. Avocations: fishing; camping; hiking; reading; sports. Office: Alpha Micro Users Soc 735 Walnut St Boulder CO 80302

GREENE, STEPHANIE HARRISON, marketing executive; b. Lake Forest, Ill., June 20, 1950; d. Howard Harrison and Gloria Juliet (Christensen) Greene. BA in Journalism and Advt., Syracuse U., 1972; MBA in Mktg., Cornell U., 1975. With Weeden & Co., Boston, 1972-73; product rep. Allis Chalmers, Matteson, Ill., 1975-76; asst. product mgr. Midwest Am./Am. Hosp. Supply, Des Plaines, Ill., 1976-77; product mgr. Borden, Inc., Columbus, Ohio, 1977-80; product line mgr. John Sexton & Co./Beatrice, Chgo., 1980-82; product mgr. non-foods PYA/Monarch/Sara Lee, Greenville, S.C., 1982-84; mktg. mgr. Fuller Brush/Sara Lee, Winston-Salem, 1984—; pres. Corbett Harrison Greene, Mundelein, Ill., 1984—; bd. dirs. Career Pub., Mundelein. Editor: The Quotation Dictionary, 1968. Mem. Print Prodn. Club, Cornell U. Alumnae Assn. (pres.), Pi Beta Phi. Republican. Episcopalian. Clubs: Holly Tree Garden (treas. 1983-84), Serendipity Garden (treas. 1978-79). Home: 2533 Buena Vista Rd Winston-Salem NC 27104 Office: Fuller Brush Co 5635 Hanes Mill Rd Winston-Salem NC 27105

GREENE, WENDY SEGAL, educator; b. New Rochelle, N.Y., Jan. 9, 1929; d. Louis Peter and Anne Henrietta (Kahan) Segal; m. Richard M. Greene Jr. (div. Mar. 1976); children: Christopher S., Kerry William, Karen Beth Greene Olson; m. Richard M. Greene Sr., Aug. 29, 1985 (dec. 1986). Student, Olivet Coll., 1946-48, Santa Monica Coll., 1967-70; BA in Child Devel., Calif. State U., Los Angeles, 1973, MA in Elem. Edn., 1975. Counselor Camp Watitoh, Becket, Mass., 1946-49; asst. tchr. Outdoor Play Group, New Rochelle, 1946-58; edn. sec. pediatrics Syracuse (N.Y.) Meml. Hosp., 1952-53; with St. John's Hosp., Sant Monica, Calif., 1962-63; head tchr. Head Start, Los Angeles, 1966-77; tchr. spl. edn. Los Angeles Unified Sch. Dist., 1977—. Bd. dirs. Richland Ave. Youth House, Los Angeles, 1960-63, Emotional Health Assn., Los Angeles, 1961-66, Richland Ave. Sch. PTA, 1959-63; vol. Hospice of St. Joseph Hosp., Orange, Calif., 1985—. Mem. AAUW, So. Calif. Assn. Young Children, Olivet Coll. Alumni Assn. United Tchrs. Los Angeles, Kappa Delta Pi. Jewish. Club: Westside Singers (Los Angeles). Home: 14291 Prospect Ave Tustin CA 92680

GREENE-CURTIS, SALLY JANE, manufacturing company executive; b. Bedford, Ohio, June 25, 1953; d. Herman Joseph and Eileen Maude (Fenton) Greene; m. Howard Detroy Curtis Jr., Sept. 27, 1986; children: Marisa Anne, Emily Kathleen. BE, Ohio State U., 1975. Salesperson Scott and Assocs., Columbus, Ohio, 1975-77, Columbus Coated Fabrics, Columbus and Atlanta, 1977-81; mgr. product Columbus Coated Fabrics, Columbus, 1981-85; ptnr., pres. Chromagraphics Corp., Dallas, 1985—. Mem. Screenprinters Assoc. Internat. Office: Chromagraphics Corp 260 Bank St Southlake TX 76092

GREENFIELD, ANNE LOUISE, librarian; b. Rochester, N.Y., July 2, 1953; d. Leigh Silburn and Edria (Rathbun) G. BA in Liberal Arts, Bradley U., 1975; MLS, Florida State U., 1977. Legal specialist Baxter Travenol, Deerfield, Ill., 1978-79, asst. librarian, 1979-80; supr. records adminstrn. FMC Corp., Chgo., 1980-82; records analyst Nat. Gas Pipeline, Chgo., 1982-85; supr. library and legal records MidCon Corp., Lombard, Ill., 1985-87. Mem. Assn. Records Mgrs. and Adminstrs. (sec. 1986, Chpt. Mem. of Yr. award 1985), Scottish Cultural Soc. Roman Catholic. Home: 12 A High Gate Trail Apt 8 Fairport NY 14450

GREENFIELD, HELEN MEYERS, real estate executive, publishing company executive, inspection and test service executive; b. Albany, N.Y., Aug. 4, 1908; d. Stephen and Catherine (Bronkov) Meyers; grad. Baker's Bus. Sch., 1924; m. Frank L. Greenfield, Apr. 1, 1929; children—Stuart Franklin, Val Shea. Accounts supr. George G. McCaskey Co., N.Y.C., 1924-29; spl.

assignments purchasing dept. McCall's Pub. Co., 1929, Fgn. Affairs Publs., Inc., 1929-31; with purchasing dept. Glidden-Buick Corp., 1931-32; interviewer Civil Works Adminstrn., supr. filing and payroll systems Houston St. Project Center, 1933-36; with dept. accounting Reuben H. Donnelley Co., 1936-37; supr. layouts, makeup prins. of semi-monthly publs. Tide Publs., Inc., 1939-41; asst. to purchasing agt., supr. maintenance perpetual inventory Hopeman Bros., 1941-43; with money order div., corr. dept. U.S. Govt., P.O. Dept., N.Y.C., 1943-44; v.p. Frank L. Greenfield Co., Inc., N.Y.C., 1945-59; v.p. All Purpose Chair Corp., 1950-55; pres. VAL Equipment, Inc., 1950-62; v.p. Am. Testing Labs., Inc., 1950-63; supr. personnel, purchases Irving Lampert Co., 1951-52; account assignment coordinator, advt. contracts dept. Newsweek, N.Y.C., 1970-78; owner, operator Princess Helen Antiques; pres. Helen M. Greenfield Realty Corp., 1968-79; bus. cons., 1979—. Active New York Heart Assn.; founder, coordinator, show producer, dir. and hostess ann. banquet honor of Dr. Manuel Cabral, composer-dir. Mt. Laurel Ctr. Performing Arts, 1960-84. Named Hon. princess Cherokee Tribe by Chief Rising Sun of Richmond, Va. Mem. Internat. Platform Assn. Club: Order Eastern Star (past matron).

GREENFIELD, JUDITH CAROL, librarian; b. Stamford, Conn., Feb. 16, 1935; d. Yale Jerome and Florence Janet (Cramer) Kweskin; m. Jay Greenfield, Sept. 8, 1957; children—Susan, Mark, Benjamin. B.A., Brown U., 1956; M.L.S., Simmons Coll., 1960; M.A., NYU, 1970. Cert. pub. librarian, library media specialist, N.Y. Head cataloging dept. Watertown Pub. Library (Mass.), 1959-60; cataloguer, bibliographer Nat. Library Medicine, 1960-61; reference librarian Queens Coll., Flushing, N.Y., 1966-70; library media specialist Washington Ave Sch., Greenburgh, N.Y., 1973-74; head children's room Rye Free Reading Room (N.Y.), 1974—; mem. children's services adv. bd. Westchester Library System, 1976-78, 80-82, mem. tech. services adv. bd., 1978—. Contbr. articles to profl. jours. Regional dir. alumni schs. program Brown U., 1978-81; chmn. regional screening com. Am. Field Service, Westchester, N.Y., 1981, 83; mem. Family Interest and Resource Service Team, Rye, 1981—. Mem. ALA, N.Y. Library Assn. (speaker children and young adult service sect. conf. 1981), Westchester Library Assn. (speaker panel on computers 1982). Democrat. Jewish. Club: Brown of Westchester (pres. 1984—). Home: 539 Oakhurst Rd Mamaroneck NY 10543 Office: Rye Free Reading Room Boston Post Rd Rye NY 10580

GREENFIELD, LOIS BRODER, educator; b. Chgo., Feb. 5, 1924; d. Samuel and Rose (Michel) Broder; B.S., U. Chgo., 1945, M.S., 1946; Ph.D., U. Calif., Berkeley, 1953; 1 dau., Ellen Beth. Faculty, U. Wis., Madison, 1956—, prof. engring., 1958—. Mem. Am. Soc. Engring. Edn., Am. Psychol. Assn., Am. Ednl. Research Assn., Soc. Women Engrs. Contbr. articles to profl. jours. Office: U Wis Gen Engring Bldg Madison WI 53706

GREENFIELD, THELMA NELSON, English language educator; b. Portland, Sept. 11, 1922; d. Ivar Emanuel and Lulu Ruth (Maxwell) Nelson; B.A., U. Oreg., 1944, M.A., 1947; Ph.D., U. Wis., 1952; m. Stanley B. Greenfield, Jan. 22, 1951; children—Tamma L., Sayre N. Instr., Queens (N.Y.) Coll. Sch. Gen. Studies, 1955-56; mem. faculty U. Oreg., Eugene, 1963— , prof. English, 1972— , dept. head, 1983-86; vis. prof. U. Regensburg, 1974-75; disting. vis. prof. Rennaissance U. Ariz.; guest lectr. Oreg. State Penitentiary. Mem. MLA, Shakespeare Assn. Am., Renaissance Soc. Am., Philol. Assn. Pacific Coast. Club: Shakespeare (Eugene). Author: The Induction in Elizabethan Drama, 1969; The Eye of Judgment, 1982; contbr. articles in field to profl. jours. Office: U of Oregon Dept of English Eugene OR 97403

GREENGOLD, BONNIE B., pension fund consultant; b. N.Y.C., Sept. 14, 1955; d. Henry and Toby (Sklar) Blum; m. David G. Greengold, July 31, 1977. BS in Applied Math., SUNY, Stonybrook, 1976. Pension analyst N.Y. Life Ins. Co., N.Y.C., 1976-77; actuarial assoc. Actuaries Unltd., Inc., N.Y.C., 1977-79; pension cons. Actuaries Unltd., Inc., 1979-83; pres. Advanced Pension Actuaries, Inc., Rockville Centre, N.Y., 1983-86, Actuaries Unltd., Inc., Rockville Centre, N.Y., 1983-86, Pension Actuarial Cons., Inc., Gt. Neck, N.Y., 1986—. Home: 29 Windsor Gate Dr North Hills NY 11040 Office: Pension Actuarial Cons 111 Great Neck NY 11021

GREEN-GONAS, CAMI, academic administrator; b. Helsinki, Finland, June 28, 1946; came to U.S., 1969; m. Roy Bonder Gonas, Dec. 20, 1968; children: Bothwell Carl, Samuel Winston. LLB, U. Helsinki, 1968; MCL, U. Miami, 1971. Freelance writer 1969—; cons. Roy B. Gonas Law Office, Coral Gables, Fla., 1976-84; parliamentarian Consul of Finland, Miami, 1979—; assoc. dir. grad. program Law Sch. U. Miami, 1985—. Contbr. to profl. jours. Founder, pres. Bicentennial Finnish Group, Miami, 1976; trustee United Protestant Appeal. Recipient Bicentennial medal Pres. of Finland, 1976. Mem. Finnish Lawyers Assn., Nat. Assn. Parliamentarians, Fla. State Assn. of Parliamentarians, Am. Scandinavian Found. (trustee), Nat. Assn. Fgn. Student Advisors. Lutheran. Club: Riviera Country (Coral Gables). Lodge: Zonta (founder Miami Lakes club, Nassau (Bahamas) chpt., Downtown Miami chpt., Coral Gables chpt., pres. several local chpts.). Office: U Miami Sch Law Coral Gables FL 33124

GREENLEE, BEVERLY ADELE, army officer, health care administrator; b. Lamesa, Tex., May 29, 1947; d. Cleo Wilson and Tommy Adele (Henley) Greenlee. B.S. in Nursing, Tex. Woman's U., Denton, 1970; M.S. in Health Care Adminstrn., Baylor U., 1976; grad. Comd. and Gen. Staff Coll., Ft. Leavenworth, Kans., 1978. Commd. 2d lt. U.S. Army, 1968, advanced through grades to lt. col., 1984—; staff nurse Ft. Benning Army Hosp., Columbus, Ga., 1970-71, U.S. Army Hosp., Bangkok, Thailand, 1971-72; staff nurse Walter Reed Army Med. Ctr., Washington, 1972, head nurse, 1973, supr., 1974; nursing methods analyst Madigan Army Med. Ctr., Tacoma, Wash., 1975-77, Hdqrs. 7th Med. Comd., Heidelberg, Fed. Republic Germany, 1977-80; asst. chief dept. nursing Winn Army Hosp., Ft. Stewart, Ga., 1980-83; asst. inspector gen. Hdqrs. U.S. Army Health Services Command, San Antonio, 1983-86; chief dept. nursing Fox Army Hosp., Redstone Arsenal, Ala., 1986-87; sr. nurse adminstr. U.S. Army Health Services Command, Ft. Sam Houston, Tex., 1988—. Mem. Am. Nurses Assn., Tex. Nurses Assn., Sigma Theta Tau, Beta Beta Beta. Lodge: Order Eastern Star. Home: 1901 Orba Dr Ne Huntsville AL 35801-1549 Office: US Army Health Services Com Office Insp Gen Hdqrs Fort Sam Houston TX 78234

GREENMAN, JILL DANFORTH, public relations executive; b. Lafayette, Ind., Oct. 9, 1947; d. Frederick Snow and Eugenie (Doran) Greenman. B.A., DePauw U., 1969; M.S.J., Northwestern U., 1976. Pub. relations specialist Harris Trust & Savs. Bank, Chgo., 1976-78; account supr. Burson-Marsteller, Chgo., 1978-81; v.p. Golin/Harris Communications, Inc., Chgo., 1982-84; dir. corporate communications Holiday Corp., Memphis, 1984-86; v.p. John Malmo Advt. Inc., Memphis, 1987—; pub. relations cons.; media relations mgr. for Ill. State Rep., 1978. Recipient award Internat. Assn. Bus. Communicators, 1978. Mem. Pub. Relations Soc. Am., Northwestern U. Alumni Assn., Alpha Phi. Republican. Roman Catholic. Home: 1683 Kimbrough Rd Germantown TN 38138

GREENSPAN-MARGOLIS, JUNE RITA EDELMAN, psychiatrist; b. N.Y.C., June 28, 1934; d. Benjamin Robert and Theresa (Cooperstein) Edelman; divorced; 1 child, Alisa Greenspan; m. Gerald J. Margolis. AB, Bryn Mawr Coll., 1955; MD, Med. Coll. Pa., 1959. Pvt. practice medicine specializing in pediatrics Cinnaminson, N.Y., 1961-67; psychiat. resident Hahnemann Med. Coll., Phila., 1967-71; practice medicine specializing in adult and child psychiatry, psychoanalysis Jenkintown, Pa., 1971—; instr. U. Pa. Sch. Medicine, Phila., 1975-77, clin. assoc. 1977-81, clin. asst. prof. 1981-85, clin. assoc. prof. 1985—; tng. and supervisory analyst Inst. of the Phila. Assn. Psychoanalysis, Bala Cynwyd, Pa., 1985—. Mem. AMA, Am. Psychiat. Assn., Am. Psychoanalytic Assn. (cert. adult and child psychoanalysis), Am. Acad. Child Psychiatry. Office: Benson East Suite 223-C Old York Rd Jenkintown PA 19046

GREENSPOON, JULIE, guide service business owner; b. Washington, Sept. 8, 1961; d. Benjamin and Irma Rose (Naiman) G. BA in Econs., Washington U., St. Louis, 1983; MBA, U. Md., 1985. Sec.-treas., owner Guide Service of Washington, 1984—. Democrat. Office: Guide Service of Washington 733 15th St NW #1040 Washington DC 20005

GREENSTADT, INEZ MCCOY, health science facility administrator; b. Walnut, Miss., June 1, 1930; m. William Greenstadt, Dec. 24, 1964; 1 child, Amy. BA, Millsaps Coll., 1951; MA, Columbia U., 1959; Cert., NYU, 1966. Cert. program dir. Program dir. YMCA, Bklyn., 1955-58; dir. recreation Mt. Sinai Sch. Nursing, N.Y.C., 1958-66; mgr. spl. services Mt. Sinai Med. Ctr., N.Y.C., 1969—. Contbr. articles to profl. jours. Mem. Indsl. Recreation Dirs. Assn., Women's Assn. for Research in Menopause (nat. co-founder 1984-85). Unitarian. Home: 35 E 30th New York NY 10016 Office: Mt Sinai Med Ctr 100th St and Fifth Ave New York NY 10029

GREENSTEIN, RHONDA, lawyer; b. N.Y.C., Dec. 12, 1954; d. Zigmund and Annette (Berman) Greenstein; m. Spencer Adam Kravitz, Aug. 31, 1980. B.A. magna cum laude, CUNY, 1974; J.D. cum laude Temple U., 1977. Bar: N.Y. 1978. Asst. pub. defender Office of Monroe County Pub. Defender, Rochester, N.Y., 1977-80; sole practice law, N.Y.C., 1980-81; asst. atty. gen. N.Y. State Dept. Law, Office of Atty.-Gen., N.Y.C., 1981—; gen. counsel Automated Alternatives, Nassau County N.Y., 1983—. Counsel, Self-Help Community Services, N.Y.C., 1983—; legal cons. Pub. Interest Law Ctr., Phila., 1976; asst. coordinator Creedmore State Sch. and Hosp., N.Y.C., 1972-74. Mem. N.Y. State Bar Assn., ABA, Nat. Lawyers Guild, Phi Beta Kappa. Home: 23 Executive Dr Manhasset Hills NY 11040 Office: NY State Dept Law Office Atty Gen 2 World Trade Center New York NY 11047

GREENSTEIN, RUTH LOUISE, corporation executive, lawyer; b. N.Y.C., Mar. 28, 1946; d. Milton and Beatrice (Zutty) G.; m. David Seidman, May 19, 1972. B.A., Harvard U., 1966; M.A., Yale U., 1968; J.D., George Washington U., 1980. Bar: D.C. 1980. Fgn. service info. officer USIA, Washington and Tehran, Iran, 1968-70; adminstrv. asst. Export-Import Bank U.S., Washington, 1971-72; asst. dean Woodrow Wilson Sch. Pub. and Internat. Affairs, Princeton U., 1972-75; budget examiner U.S. Office Mgmt. and Budget, Washington, 1975-79; budget coordinator U.S. Internat. Devel. Coop. Agy., 1979-81; dep. gen. counsel NSF, 1981-84; treas., then v.p. and gen. counsel Genex Corp., Gaithersburg, Md., 1984—; mem. academic adv. panel to com. on exchanges, CIA, 1983—. Mem. D.C. Bar Assn., Nat. Acad. Scis. (panel on impact of nat. security controls on internat. tech. transfer 1985-87), AAAS (com. on freedom and responsibility 1987—). Home: 2737 Devonshire Pl NW Apt 511 Washington DC 20008 Office: Genex Corp 16020 Industrial Dr Gaithersburg MD 20877

GREENWOOD, AUDREY GATES, librarian; b. Buffalo, Mar. 27, 1917; d. Marc Herbert and Genevieve Cecelia (Naab) Gates; B.A., D'Youville Coll., 1939; B.S. in Library Sci., Cath. U. Am., 1940, M.A., 1944; m. Clayton Edward Greenwood, Sept. 2, 1944; children—Mary Ellen, Nancy Jane, Susan Jean. Head librarian Gonzaga High Sch., Washington, 1940-45, Southeastern U. Evening Sch., 1941-45; reference librarian Cath. U. Am., evenings 1942-43; librarian St. Joseph's Collegiate Inst., Buffalo, 1945-46; head librarian Canisius High Sch., Buffalo, 1949-50; head librarian Eden (N.Y.) Central Schs., 1950-83, coordinator state and fed. funds, 1969-83, dir. adult edn., 1973-83. Mem. Eden Tchrs. Assn. (past pres.), Erie County Ednl. Assn. (past v.p.), NEA, N.Y. State Tchrs. Assn., N.Y. State United Tchrs. (state del., legis. chmn. Western zone, chmn. retirees of western N.Y. 1984—, mem. ROC com. 1985—, mem. editorial bd. The Active N.Y. State United Tchrs. Retiree, mem. Commn. 100), N.Y. State Retired Tchrs. Assn. (pres. Southtowns chpt. 1987—, legis. commn. 1987—), Am. Fedn. Tchrs. (nat. del.), Sch. Librarians Assn. Western N.Y. (past pres.), N.Y. Educators Assn., Delta Kappa Gamma. (state legis. chmn.), Beta Zeta. Democrat. Roman Catholic. Home: 3688 Briarwood Ct Hamburg NY 14075

GREENWOOD, HARRIET LOIS, environmental consultant, researcher; b. Detroit, Oct. 4, 1950; d. Samuel H. and Elizabeth Ann (Bode) G.; m. Michael E. Carlson, Aug. 23, 1981 (div. Sept. 1986); m. Eric J. Halbeisen, Sept. 5, 1987. B.A. in Biology, Antioch Coll., 1972; M.S. in Teaching, Antioch Coll. of New Eng., 1975; postgrad. U. Mich., 1985—. Dir. environ. studies Swanson Environ., Southfield, Mich., 1978-80; project mgr. ESEI, Ecol. Scis., Detroit, 1981-82; pres. Greenwood & Assocs., Detroit, 1982-83; mgr. environ. studies Environ. Research Group, Ann Arbor, Mich., 1983-85; environ. policy specialist Clayton Environ., Southfield, 1985—. Rec. clk. Detroit Friends Meeting, 1985-88; bd. dirs., Friends Sch. Detroit, 1987—. U. Mich. fellow, 1985-86. Mem. Soc. Risk Analysis, Internat. Assn. Bus. Communicators, Cranbrook Inst. Sci., Mich. Assn. Environ. Profls., Nat. Assn. Environ. Profls. Quaker. Avocations: English country dancing; cross country skiing. Office: Clayton Environ Cons 22345 Roethel Dr Novi MI 48050

GREENWOOD, JANET KAE DALY, psychologist, educational administrator; b. Goldsboro, N.C., Dec. 9, 1943; d. Fulton Benton and Kelminy Ethel Esther (Ball) Daly; 1 child, Gerald Thompson. A.A., Peace Coll., 1963; B.S. in English and Psychology, East Carolina U., 1965, Ed.M. in Counseling, 1967; postgrad. N.C. State U., 1967-69, U. London, 1969; Ph.D. in Counseling and Higher Ednl. Adminstrn., Fla. State U., 1972. Tchr. English, Kinston City Schs., N.C., 1965-66, Goldsboro City schs., 1966-67; counselor and psychometrist primary and secondary schs. of Wake County, N.C., 1967-69; coordinator for Am. Inst. for Fgn. Study, 1969, supr. of student tours in Eng., France, Switzerland, Italy and Capri, 1969; counselor Fla. State U., Tallahassee, 1969-72; asst. dir. counseling Rutgers U., New Brunswick, N.J., 1972-73; cons. to v.p. for student services, 1973-74, lectr. in counseling psychology, 1972-74; coordinator and assoc. prof. counselor edn. U. Cin., 1974-77; adviser to grad. students, from 1974, vice provost student affairs, from 1977; cons. guidance South Plainfield Pub. Schs., 1973-76; adviser Parents Without Partners, 1976; pres. Longwood Coll., Farmville, Va., 1981-87, U. Bridgeport, Conn., 1987—; bd. dirs. The Hydraulic Co. Contbr. articles to profl. jours. Mem. Gov.'s Ad Hoc Edn. Com. on Tchr. Edn. and Counselor Edn., State of Ohio, 1975; mem. state planning commn. Nat. Identification of Women Project; chairwoman of Twin Rivers Tenants Rights Assn., 1972-74; bd. dirs. Bridgeport Hosp., Bridgeport, Bus. Council; mem. adv. com. Bridgeport Pub. Edn. Fund; Recipient Tchr. We Honor award Goldsboro City Schs., 1967, Stunt Night Dedication award, 1967, Black Arts Festival spl. award; Meritorious Service award Am. Assn. State Colls. and Univs. Mem. Am. Coll. Personnel Assn. (editor chairperson media bd. 1975—), Am. Personnel and Guidance Assn., Cin. Personnel and Guidance Assn., Ohio Psychol. Assn., Cin. Psychol. Assn., Organizational Behavior Assn., AAUP, Am. Sch. Counselors Assn., Ohio Sch. Counselors Assn., Assn. for Women Faculty, Ohio Counselor Edn. and Supervision Assn., Kappa Delta Pi. Office: U Bridgeport Office of the Pres Bridgeport CT 06601

GREENWOOD, SYLVIA RUTH, educator; b. Detroit, July 10, 1951; d. Lawson Cullen and Annie Alfreda (Smith) G. B.S. Central State U., 1973; MusM Wayne State U., 1988. Tchr., Detroit Bd. Edn., 1974—; producer Vol. Devel. of Youth Talent, Detroit, 1975—; mezzo soprano Brazeal Dennard Chorale, 1985—; producer mus. tour of Japan, Mich. Dept. Commerce. Choir dir. Youth Second Grace Ch., Detroit, 1977-85, Broadstreet Presbyn. Ch., Detroit, 1985—. Named Outstanding Tchr. in Area D, Detroit Pub. Schs., 1985, other honors. Democrat. Methodist. Avocation: sewing.

GREER, ANN LENNARSON, sociology educator; b. Chgo., Dec. 3, 1944; d. Vernon E. C. and Dee Ellen (Wing) Lennarson; m. Scott Greer, Dec. 22, 1969; 1 child, Scott Edward Lennarson. BA, Lake Forest Coll., 1967; MA, Northwestern U., 1968, PhD, 1970. Asst. prof. sociology Lake Forst (Ill.) Coll., 1969-72; from asst. prof. to prof. U. Wis., Milw., 1972—; dir. Urban Research Ctr. U. Wis.-Milw., 1976-82; cons. Health Resources Adminstrn., Rockville, Md., 1976-79, Nat. Ctr. for Health Services Research, Rockville, 1978—, Inst Medicine Nat. Acad. Scis., Washington, 1980, Nat. Cancer Inst. NIH, Bethesda, Md., 1983-86; field assoc. Conservation Human Resources div. Columbia U., N.Y.C., 1977-84; sr. research assoc. Brunel U. Health Services Ctr., Uxbridge, Eng., 1984-85. Author: The Mayor's Mandate, 1974; (with Scott Greer) Understanding Sociology, 1974; editor: (with Scott Greer) Neighborhood and Ghetto, 1974, Cities and Sickness, 1983; contbr. articles to profl. jours. Trustee Citizen's Govtl. Research Bur., Milw., 1976-84. Fellow NDEA, 1966-69, Nat. Assn. Schs. Pub. Affairs and Adminstrn., 1974-75, NIH, 1984-85. Mem. Phi Beta Kappa. Home: 9430 N Upper River Rd River Hills WI 53217 Office: U Wis Dept Sociology PO Box 413 Milwaukee WI 53201

GREER, ANNE LINDSAY, food writer, menu and restaurant designer, consultant; b. Chgo., July 8, 1940; d. John Ralston and Elisabeth (Wood) Lindsay; m. Donald Merrill Greer, Jr., June 11, 1966 (div. 1979); children—Donald Merrill, William Wright. Student Foothill Jr. Coll., 1959-61, Morningside Coll., 1963-66; student bus. adminstrn. U. Calif.-Long Beach, 1966-67. Cons., Cuisinarts, Inc., Greenwich, Conn., 1975-88; menu cons., 1776, Inc., San Antonio, 1983-84; concept and menu developer, Anatole Expansion Restaurants, and Verandah Club, Leows Anatole, Dallas, 1982, cons. restaurant and food concepts, 1982—; industry cons. product devel. Author: (cookbooks) Culinary Renaissance, 1975; Cuisine of the American Southwest, 1983 (Book of the Month selection spring 1984 Tastemaker award); Creative Mexican Cooking, 1975; Food of the Sun, 1987; PBS series Great Chefs of the West. Sustainer Jr. League, San Antonio and Dallas, 1973—; mem. Jr. Symphony. Mem. Internat. Assn. Cooking Schs. (charter), Am. Inst. Wine and Food, Maitre de Table Restaurateur - Confrerie de la Chaine des Rotisseurs (San Antonio and Dallas), Les Dames d'Escoffier. Republican. Episcopalian. Club: Aerobic Center (Dallas). Home: 6805 Midcrest Dallas TX 75240

GREER, BONNIE BETH, educator; b. Toledo, Sept. 13, 1946; d. Therron Otto and Betty Mae Kleckner; A.B., Ind. U., 1968; M.Ed., Okla. U., 1969, Ph.D., 1971; m. John Garland Greer, July 9, 1977; children—Christopher John, Tiffany Maye. Instl. tchr. No. Ind. Children's Hosp., South Bend, 1968; tchr. 6th grade Blanchard (Okla.) public schs., 1968-69; successively grad. asst., spl. instr., lectr. Okla. U., 1969-72; program dir. Stone Belt Center Retarded, Bloomington, Ind., 1972-73; asst. prof. Bridgewater (Mass.) State Coll., 1973-74; mem. faculty Memphis State U., 1974—, asso. prof. spl. edn. and rehab., 1976—; lectr. edn. Ind. U., part-time, 1972-73. Mem. Council Exceptional Children, Am. Assn. Mental Deficiency, Delta Kappa Gamma. Author articles in field, chpts. in books; co-editor: Practical Strategies in Working with the Trainable Mentally Retarded, 1975. Office: Memphis State U Dept Spl Edn Memphis TN 38152

GREER, JEANETTE MULDER, broadcast executive, small business owner; b. Beaumont, Tex., Feb. 18, 1924; d. Herbert Thomas and Annie (Colichia) M.; m. Autry Micajah Greer, Dec. 31, 1971 (dec. 1979). Student, Dequesne U., 1941-42, Lamar U., 1947-50. Clk. Pure Oil Co., Nederland, Tex., 1942-43; billing clk. Norvell-Wilder Supply Co., Beaumont, Tex., 1943-45; traffic mgr. Beaumont Broadcasting Corp., 1945-47, acct., 1947-55; bus. mgr. Beaumont Broadcasting/TV Corp., 1955-63; asst. to mgr. Beaumont TV Corp., 1963-69; asst. sec., bus. mgr. Belo Broadcasting Corp., Beaumont, 1969-78, v.p., bus. mgr., 1978-84; bus. mgr. Sta. KFDM-TV div. Freedom-TV Sub, Inc., Beaumont, 1984—. Bd. dirs. Beaumont YWCA; active Beaumont Art Mus., Gallery Guild, 1985—. Mem. Pilot Club of Beaumont (pres. 1962-63), Am. Women in Radio and TV (sec.-treas. 1978-80, trustee 1987—), Beta Sigma Phi (bd. dirs. Beaumont chpt. 1980—). Roman Catholic. Home: 1440 Edson Dr Beaumont TX 77706 Office: Sta KFDM-TV PO Box 7128 Beaumont TX 77706

GREER, ROBERTA LESLIE, convention bureau executive; b. Seattle, Nov. 14, 1935; d. Vanis Wells and Eleanor Clyde (Rossman) Elson; m. Glendon Alfred Greer, Mar. 22, 1957; children: Scott Allen, Eric Glen. BS in Adminstrn., Fin., City U., Seattle, 1980. Treas., ptnr. Jean's Fabrics, Kirkland, Wash., 1964-68; office mgr. various orgns., Kirkland, 1968-81; gen. ptnr. Land Devel. Co., Seattle, 1968-71; v.p. Seattle/King County Conv. and Vis. Bur., 1982—. Pres. Altrusa Internat., Kirkland, 1964, Kirkland Creative Arts Ctr., 1965; bd. dirs. Woodland Park Zool. Soc., Seattle, 1987, Seattle Aquarium, 1987-88, Hearing, Speech, Deafness Ctr., 1987-88; vice chair region V Wash. State Tourism Devel., 1987-88. Club: Washington Athletic (Seattle). Office: 1815 7th Ave Seattle WA 98101

GREER, SHARI BETH ROTHENSTEIN, software consulting firm executive; b. Reading, Pa., Mar. 1, 1959; d. Martin and Francine Rita (Gross) Rothenstein; m. Martin Brad Greer, Dec. 31, 1979; children: Shannon Leigh, Krista Heather. BA in Biochemistry, Wellesley Coll.-MIT, 1980; postgrad. in bus. adminstrn. Colo. State U., 1982-83. Lead thermal engr. Rockwell Internat. Space div., Downey, Calif., 1980-81; systems engr. Martin Marietta Aerospace, Denver, 1981-82, aerospace new bus. analyst, 1982-84; v.p. Miaco Corp. (Micro Automation Cons.), Englewood, Colo., 1984-87, pres., 1987—. Co-designer life systems monitor for Sudden Infant Death Syndrome, 1980. Recipient Recog. award for satellite work Martin Marietta Aerospace, 1982; VIP at 1st Space Shuttle landing, Rockwell Internat., Vandenberg, Calif., 1981. Mem. Intermountain Humane Soc., MIT Enterprise Forum of Colo. Democrat. Office: Miaco Corp Harlequin Plaza S 7600 E Orchard Suite 230 Englewood CO 80111

GREESON, GAYLA LEE, accountant; b. Austin, Tex., Dec. 22, 1956; d. Howard Gaylon and Nancy Diane (Thomas) Brown; m. David Thomas Greeson, Aug. 25, 1979; children—Timothy David, Samantha Lea. B.B.A., U. Tex., 1979; grad. Sch. Banking of South, La. State U., 1986. C.P.A., Tex. Accounts examiner Office of State Comptroller, Austin, 1979-80; auditor Tyler, Willingham & Tuffly, C.P.A.s, Houston, 1981-82; advt. dir. Security Bank & Trust Co., Wharton, Tex., 1982-86, comptroller, chief fin. officer, 1982—, treas. Security Capital Leasing Corp., Wharton, 1982—; treas. Wharton Capital Corp. Treas., Wharton Christian Sch., 1984-86. Mem. Am. Inst. C.P.A.s, Tex. Soc. C.P.A.s. Home: 600 Country Club Dr Richmond TX 77469 Office: Security Bank & Trust Co 112 N Fulton St Wharton TX 77488

GREESON, JANET ROSEMARY, clinical director, psychotherapist; b. N.Y.C., May 28, 1943; d. Arthur Charles and Rosemary Margaret (Duffy) Durr; m. Eugene W. Boyle, Nov. 28, 1964 (div. 1969); children: Eugene, Jimmy; m. Charles W. Jowers, June 14, 1969 (div. Aug. 1977); 1 child, Rosemary; m. Alden N. Greeson, Apr. 21, 1984. BA in Psychology, U. Cent. Fla., 1978; MA in Clin. Counseling, Rollins Coll., 1979; PhD, Columbia Pacific U., 1987. Cert. addictions, eating disorders, mental health counselor. Counselor alcoholism alcohol rehab. drydock USN, Orlando, Fla., 1978-79, program coordinator alcohol safety action program, 1979-82; assoc. prof. U. West Fla., Pensacola, 1981-82; psychotherapist Met. Alcohol Council Orlando, 1983-85; cons. eating disorders Brookwood Recovery Lodge, Birmingham, Ala., 1985; dir. Alcohol Rehab. Service div. Naval Hosp., Orlando, 1982-86; pvt. practice psychotherapy Orlando, 1981—; founding dir. New Life Ctr. For Depression, Anxiety and Eating Disorders, Orlando, 1986—; trustee exec. bd. Overeaters Anonymous Nat., Torrance, Calif., 1978-85; coordinator conf. on teenage alcohol abuse, Washington, 1983; supr. clin. practice site Rollins Coll., Winter Park, Fla., 1986-87. Mem. adv. bd.Profl. Counselor mag. Pres., treas., trustee Cen. Fla. Intergroup Alcoholics Anonymous, Winter Park, 1977—; bd. dirs. Grove, Altamonte Springs, Fla., 1981-82; mem. Chem. Dependency Network, Orlando, 1983—; founder, corp. dir. Freedom Walk, Inc., 1985; trustee exec. bd. dirs. Overeaters Anonymous, Torrance, Calif., 1978-85; organizer Superwoman Anonymous, cen. Fla., 1986—. Served with USN, 1961-64. Recipient Service to Mankind award Sertoma Club, 1979, appreciation award Lowell State Prison, 1979, cert. achievement U. Tex., 1986, award 30th Fla. Alcoholics Anonymous Conv., 1986. Mem. Internat. Assn. Eating Disorders (bd. dirs.), Am. Eating Disorders Assn. (cert.), Am. Mental Health Counselors (cert.), Am. Counseling and Devel. Assn., Nat. Assn. Alcoholism Counselors, Chem. Dependency Network, Fla. Alcohol and Drug Abuse Assn., Fla. Group Psychotherapy, Fla. Mental Health Counselors, Am. Labor Mgmt. Adminstrs. (sec., presenter conf. 1986-87), Nat. Assn. Female Execs., Am. Orthopsychiat. Assn. Republican. Roman Catholic. Clubs: Rebos (Casselberry, Fla.) (v.p. 1978-85, appreciation award 1983, pres., trustee), Alco-An (Orlando, Fla.). Office: New Life Ctr for Depression Anxiety & Eating Disorders 7727 Lake Underhill Orlando FL 32822

GREGERSON, REBECCA OSTAR, accountant, business services consultant; b. Madison, Wis., Dec. 1, 1955; d. Allan William and Roberta (Hutchison) Ostar; m. James Charles Gregerson, Sept. 25, 1982. BS in Bus. Adminstrn., Appalachian State U., 1977. Acct. Boker-Dick and Co., Silver Spring, Md., 1977-78, Fox and Co., Washington, 1978-80; sr. internal auditor Va. Poly. U., Blacksburg, 1980-82; acct. Teepeedashary, Ltd., Wappingers Falls, N.Y., 1982-83, Leland G. Oathout, CPA, West Hurley, N.Y., 1983-84; owner Gregerson Bus. Services, Hyde Park, N.Y., 1984—. Mem. Hyde Park C. of C. Democrat. Unitarian. Home and Office: 28 Matuk Dr Hyde Park NY 12538

GREGG, DEBORAH MARRS, automobile dealer; b. Orlando, Fla., Oct. 27, 1955; d. David and Arleen (Turner) Marrs; m. Peter Gregg. Dec. 6, 1980 (dec. Dec. 1980). AA, Art Inst. Atlanta, 1975. Creative asst. McDonald & Little, Atlanta, 1975-76; freelance artist Atlanta, 1977-78; art dir. The Boardroom, Tucker, Ga., 1978-79, The Malone Group, Jacksonville, Fla., 1979-80; automobile dealer Brumos Porsche Audi, Jacksonville, 1980—, Gregg MotorCars Inc., Jacksonville, 1980—, Brumos Atlanta, 1980—; profl. road racing driver Jack Roush Racing, 1981—. Named Trans-Am. Rookie of Yr., 1987. Republican. Episcopalian. Office: Brumos Jacksonville 10211 Atlantic Blvd Jacksonville FL 32225

GREGG, DOROTHY ELIZABETH, marketing, opinion research and public relations executive; b. Tempe, Ariz.; d. Alfred Tennyson and Mamie Elizabeth (Walker) G.; B.A., U. Tex., 1944, M.A. (grad. fellow), 1945; Ph.D. (all-univ. grad. fellow), Columbia U., 1951, L.H.D. (hon.), 1967; m. Paul Hughling Scott, 1952; children—Kimerly, Gregg. Lectr., Columbia U., 1946-52, asst. prof. econs., 1952-54; asst. dir. public relations U.S. Steel Corp., N.Y.C., 1956-74; dir. corp. communications Celanese Corp., N.Y.C., 1974-75, corp. v.p. communications, 1975-81, corp. v.p. external affairs, 1981-83; exec. v.p. Research & Forecasts Inc., 1983-84; pres. D.E. Gregg Assocs., 1984—. Mem. civilian pub. relations adv. com. U.S. Mil. Acad.; mem. Gov. Cuomo's Com. on Productivity and Mgmt.; trustee Inst. for Future, WNYC Found. Mem. Found. Pub. Relations Research and Edn., Women in Communications (Nat. Headliner award 1980), Phi Beta Kappa, Pi Sigma Alpha. Clubs: Princeton, Zonta (N.Y.C.). Contbr. articles profl. mags., P.F. Collier & Son Ency. Home: 425 E 58th St New York NY 10022 Office: 301 E 58th St New York NY 10022

GREGG, NANCI CAROL PETERSON, magazine editor; b. Mpls., Oct. 16, 1953; d. Clell Thomson and Cynthia Eileen (Chisholm) Peterson; m. Steven W. Givens (div.); m. John Holman Gregg, May 29, 1982. BS, Murray State U., 1974, MS, 1976; MBA, Cameron U., 1980. Reporter Hobbs (N.Mex.) Daily News-Sun, 1976-78; pub. relations dir. Hobbs Mcpl. Sch. Dist., 1978-79; adminstrv. asst. Delta Child Devel. Ctr., Duncan, Okla., 1980-81; editor Tenn. Monthly mag., Clarksville, 1981-82; dir. communications 1st Presbyn. Ch., Nashville, 1983-86; mng. editor Greysmith Pub. Co., Franklin, Tenn., 1984—. Contbr. articles to periodicals. Mem. Nat. Assn. Bus. Press Editors, Internat. Assn. Bus. Communicators, Nat. Fedn. Press Women, Sigma Delta Chi. Democrat. Presbyterian. Club: Bus. and Profl. Women (Nashville). Office: Greysmith Pub Inc 128 Holiday Ct Suite 116 Franklin TN 37211

GREGG, NANCY LEE, lawyer, army officer; b. Cin., Dec. 26, 1950; d. Robert Victor and Anna Mae (McWhirter) G. B.A. with distinction in Psychology, Southwestern at Memphis (name now Rhodes Coll.), 1972; J.D., U. Ark., 1978; postgrad., Judge Adv. Gen.'s Sch., 1978, 85-86. Bar: Ark. 1978, U.S. Dist. Ct. (western dist.) Ark. 1978, U.S. Ct. Mil. Appeals 1978, U.S. Supreme Ct. 1982, U.S. Army Ct. Military Rev. 1986. Adminstrv. asst. to v.p. support ops. Sunstate Builders, Inc., Tampa, Fla., 1973-74; commd. capt. U.S. Army JAGC, 1978, maj., 1986; trial and def. counsel 2d Armored div., Ft. Hood, Tex., 1979-81, trial counsel, 1st Cav. div., Ft. Hood, 1981-82; chief adminstrv. law div. Hdqrs. V Corps, Office of Staff Judge Adv., Frankfurt, W.Ger., 1982-84, chief claims div. 4th infantry div. mechanized, Ft. Carson, Colo., 1986-87, asst. judge adv. adminstrv. law, 1987—. Legal adviser Frankfurt Mil. Community, Child and Spouse Abuse Case Mgmt. Teams, 1983-85, 4th Aviation Brigade, Ft. Carson, 1987. Decorated Army Commendation medal with oak leaf cluster. Office: Office of Staff Judge Adv 4th Infantry Div Mechanized Fort Carson CA 80913-5003

GREGOIRE, JEANNINE DIANE, radio station executive; b. Pocatello, Idaho, May 8, 1949; d. Edward Paul and Ruth Mardene (Nelson) Gregoire. B.S. in English Lit., Westminster Coll., 1972. Asst. sales promotion, advt. mgr. Sta. KTVX-TV, Salt Lake City, 1975-76, writer, producer, sales promotion/advt. mgr., 1976-78; writer, producer, asst. creative services mgr., audience promotion mgr. Sta. KPIX-TV, Channel 5, San Francisco, 1978-79; sales rep. Xerox Corp., Salt Lake City, 1979-80; dir. advt. and pub. info. Channel 7 Sta. KUED-TV, Salt Lake City, 1980-84; dir. mktg., sales and pub. relations Triad-La Caille Ventures and La Caille at Quail Run, 1984-86; account exec. Sta. KDAB-FM, Salt Lake City, 1985-86; account exec. Sta. KMGR FM/AM, Salt Lake city, 1986-87; account exec. Sta. KSFI/KDYL FM/AM, Salt Lake City, 1987—. Mem. pub. info. bd. dirs. Am. Cancer Soc., Salt Lake City; fundraiser Ballet West, 1985, Glass Slipper Found. and Trust, other Salt Lake City charities. Mem. Women in Communications, Broadcast Promotion Assn. Republican.

GREGOR, DOROTHY DEBORAH, librarian; b. Dobbs Ferry, N.Y., Aug. 15, 1939; d. Richard Garrett Heckman and Marion Allen (Richmond) Stewart; m. A. James Gregor, June 22, 1963 (div. 1974). BA, Occidental Coll., 1961; MA, U. Hawaii, 1963; MLS, U. Tex., 1968; cert. in Library Mgmt., U. Calif., Berkeley, 1976. Reference librarian U. Calif., San Francisco, 1968-69; dept. librarian Pub. Health Library U. Calif., Berkeley, 1969-71, tech. services librarian, 1973-76; reference librarian Hamilton Library U. Hawaii, Honolulu, 1971-72; head serials dept. U. Calif., Berkeley, 1976-80, assoc. univ. librarian tech. services dept., 1980-84; chief Shared Cataloging div. Library of Congress, Washington, 1984-85; univ. librarian U. Calif.-San Diego, La Jolla, 1985—; instr. sch. library and info. studies U. Calif., Berkeley, 1975, 76, 83; cons. Nat. Library of Medicine, Bethesda, Md., 1985, Ohio Bd. Regents, Columbus, 1987. Mem. ALA, Library Info. Tech. Assn., Program Com. Ctr. for Research Libraries, Linked Systems Project Policy Com. Office: U Calif-San Diego Univ Libraries Mail Code C-075-G La Jolla CA 92093

GREGOR, HARRIET ELIZABETH WILSON, physician; b. Rock Island, Ill., Jan. 30, 1950; d. Harry Rex and Eleanor (Fisher) Wilson; m. Peter William Gregor, Aug. 12, 1972; children—Joel Alexander, Ian Russell, Neil Fraser, Elizabeth Marjorie. B.A. in Biology magna cum laude, Mt. Holyoke Coll., 1971; B.A. in Biology, St. Andrews U., Scotland, 1969-70; M.D., McMaster U., Hamilton, Ont., 1974. Diplomate Am. Acad. Family Practice, 1981. Intern, Hotel Dieu Hosp., 1974-75, Kingston Gen. Hosp., 1974-75; resident family medicine Queens U., Kingston, Ont., Can., 1974-76, anesthesia resident, Kingston, 1977, pediatric resident anesthesia, 1977-78, physician student health, instr. family medicine, 1978-79; physician Golden Clinic and Meml. Hosp., Elkins, W.Va., 1979-81; practice family medicine, Gilroy, Calif., 1980—; mem. staff Wheeler Hosp. Sponsor, Gilroy Community Theatre, Gilroy, 1983-84; mem. Planned Parenthood Santa Clara County, 1983-84; mem. Hand Gun Control No. Calif., 1981-86; me. speakers bur. Santa Clara County Cancer Soc., 1986—; mem. Gilroy Blue Ribbon Com., 1987—; vol. Childrens' Home Soc. Calif., 1986—; mem. World Wildlife Fund, 1985. Fellow Am. Acad. Family Physicians; mem. Ont. Med. Assn., Can. Coll. Family Physicians, Can. Med. Assn., AMA, Phi Beta Kappa. Presbyterian. Home: 1570 Welburn Ave Gilroy CA 95020 Office: 7995 Princevalle St Gilroy CA 95020

GREGORCZYK, EVELYN FOJTIK, human resources specialist; b. Beeville, Tex., July 30, 1948; d. Edward Felix and Lela Mae (O'Neal) Fojtik; m. Gilbert Andrew Gregorczyk, June 3, 1967; children: Shane, Sheri. AS, Bee County Coll., Beeville, 1978; BA in Psychology, Corpus Christi State U., 1980, MA in Psychology, 1981. Cert. psychol. assoc., Tex.; lic. profl. counselor, Tex. Switchboard operator Southwestern Bell Telephone Co., Sinton, Tex., 1966-67; head teller Sinton Savs. Assn., 1968-75; intern Ada Wilson Children's Hosp., Corpus Christi, Tex., 1980, Physicians and Surgeons Gen. Hosp., Corpus Christi, 1981; dir. psychol. testing, evaluations and report writing Gridley, Fisher & Assocs., Corpus Christi, 1982-83, Alan T. Fisher, Ph.D., Corpus Christi, 1983; counselor relocation ctr. H.E. Butt Grocery Co., Corpus Christi, 1983, supr., Corpus Christi and San Antonio, 1983-86, coordinator human resources corp. hdqrs., San Antonio, 1986-87, mgr. corp. personnel and relocation corp. hdqrs., 1987—; cons. TRW, Corpus Christi, 1982-83. Coordinator Meml. Med. Ctr., Corpus Christi, 1983. Mem. Am. Psychol. Assn., Tex. Psychol. Assn., Bexar County Psychol. Assn., Am. Personnel and Guidance Assn., Tex. Personnel and Guidance Assn., Assn. Specialists in Group Work, Tex. Mental Health Counselors Assn., AAUW, Nat. Assn. Female Execs., Corpus Christi State U. Alumni Assn., Phi Theta Kappa. Roman Catholic. Club: Parent Teacher (pres.). Avocations: tennis, skeet shooting, gardening, helping with children's activities. Home: 131 Mitch Thomas Rd Pleasanton TX 78064 Office: H E B Corp Hdqrs Human Resources Devel PO Box 9999 San Antonio TX 40999

GREGORIUS, BEVERLY JUNE, obstetrician-gynecologist; b. Ottawa, Ill., June 21, 1915; d. Henry Godfrey and Arline (Barry) Pruette; B.S., Madison (Tenn.) Coll., 1935; M.D., Loma Linda (Calif.) U., 1946, M.S., 1953; m. Hans Harvey Gregorius, Apr. 6, 1939 (dec.); 1 dau., Joan Gregorius Jones. Intern, Los Angeles County Gen. Hosp., 1946-47; resident in ob-gyn, White Meml. Hosp., Los Angeles, 1949-52; practice medicine specializing in ob-gyn, Burbank, Calif., 1953-77; assoc. clin. prof. Loma Linda U. Med. Sch., also U. So. Calif. Med. Sch., 1956—; clin. prof. ob-gyn U. So. Calif. Med. Sch., 1985—; program dir. ob-gyn residency program Glendale (Calif.) Adventist Med. Center, 1977-81, chmn. dept. ob-gyn, 1981-83, cons., 1983—. Bd. dirs. Arroyo Vista Family Health Found. Diplomate Am. Bd. Ob-Gyn. Fellow Am. Coll. Ob-Gyn, ACS, Internat. Coll. Surgeons; mem. Los Angeles Ob-Gyn Soc. (council 1979-86, pres. 1984-85). Adventist (mem. adminstrv. bd. dirs. 1985—). Home: 10635 Landale St North Hollywood CA 91602 Office: 1530 E Chevy Chase Suite 101 Glendale CA 91206

GREGORY, ANGELA, sculptor; b. New Orleans, Oct. 18, 1903; d. William Benjamin and Selina Elizabeth (Brès) G. B of Design, Tulane U., 1925, MA, 1940; studies with Antoine Bourdelle, Academie de la Grand Chaumière, Paris, 1926-28. Instr. Newcomb Art Sch., Newcomb Coll., Tulane U., New Orleans, 1935-37, artist-in-residence, 1940-41; state supr. Works Progress Adminstrn. Art Program, New Orleans, 1941-42; dir. art Gulf Park Coll., Gulfport, Miss., 1950-59; instr. art St. Mary's Dominican Coll., New Orleans, 1962-64, sculptor-in-residence, 1964-74, prof. art, 1975, prof. emeritus, 1976. Prin. works include sculptural decorations New Orleans criminal cts., monuments in New Orleans and Port Allen, La. Co-founder La. Landmarks Soc., New Orleans, 1950; chmn. City Hall Centennial Exhibit, New Orleans, 1950; chmn. New Orleans Sculpture Exhibit, 1967; profl. cons. Gettysburg Meml. Commn., State of La., 1967-71. Recipient Chevalier de L'Ordre Des Arts et Lettres Republique Françcaise, 1985; honored by U. New Orleans for contbg. to city and founding the La. Landmarks Soc., 1985, Disting. Alumnae award Tulane U., 1988. Democrat. Unitarian. Home and Studio: 630 Pine St New Orleans LA 70118

GREGORY, ANGIE ETHELENE, printing executive; b. Strang, Okla., Aug. 12, 1933; d. Lawrence Leroy and Gertie Ovela (Parsons) Duncan; m. Jimmy L. Gregory, Sept. 3, 1953; children: Lea Ann, Timothy, Shelly. G-rad. high sch., Strang, 1951. Purchasing sec. GMAC, Tulsa, 1951-53; cashier Assocs. Finance, Tulsa, 1953-54; bookkeeper Scott Rice Co., Tulsa, 1954-59; exec. sec. Tulsa Manpower Service, 1962-63; girl Friday Tulsa Paper, 1963-70; purchasing sec. Jones-Laughlin Supply, Tulsa, 1970-72; exec. sec. Crosby Group, Tulsa, 1972-73; office mgr. Midwest Paper, Tulsa, 1973-74; printing cons. A&J Printing, Tulsa, 1974—. Mem. Am. Bus. Women's Assn. Democrat. Baptist. Home: 1424 S Erie Tulsa OK 74112 Office: A&J Printing 1919 D S 129th E Ave Tulsa OK 74108

GREGORY, ANN YOUNG, editor, publisher; b. Lexington, Ky., Apr. 28, 1935; d. David Marion and Pauline (Adams) Young; m. Allen Gregory, Jan. 29, 1957; children: David Young, Mary Peyton. BA with high distinction, U. Ky., 1956. Sec. Ky. edit. TV Guide, Louisville, summer 1956; traffic mgr. Sta. WVLK, Lexington, 1956-61; part time tchr. adult basic edn. Wise County (Va.) Sch. Bd., St. Paul, 1966-72; adminstrv. asst. Appalachian Field Services, Children's TV Workshop, St. Paul, 1971-74; editor, co-pub. Clinch Valley Times, 1974—; pres. Clinch Valley Pub. Co., Inc., St. Paul, 1974—. Editor, text writer: The Flood of '77 in the St. Paul Area, 1977; weekly newspaper columnist Of Ships ...and Shoes...and Sealing Wax, 1974—. V.p. St. Paul PTA, 1970-73; trustee Lonesome Pine Regional Library Bd., 1972-80, chmn., 1978-80; chmn. com. to establish br. library in St. Paul, opened 1975; mem. adv. bd. Pro-Art, Wise County chpt. Va. Mus. Fine Arts, 1979-86; co-leader Brownie troop Girl Scouts U.S.A., 1971-76, bd. dirs. Appalachian council, 1st v.p. Appalachian council, 1985—; mem. adv. bd. Wise County YMCA, 1977-80; mem. Wise County Bd. Edn., 1975—, vice chmn., 1981—; pres. So. Region Sch. Bds. Assn., 1987-88; mem. Va. Edn. Block Grants Adv. Com., 1981-86, Va. Council on Vocat. Edn., 1987—, Region I State Literacy Council, 1988—; mem. exec. com. Va. High Sch. League, 1984-88; past pres. Wise County Humane Soc., Inc.; bd. dirs. Va. Sch. Bds. Assn., 1979—, pres., 1985-86; bd. dirs. Va. Literacy Found., 1987—. Named Outstanding Clubwoman of Yr., St. Paul Jr. Women's Club, 1964, 66, Outstanding Citizen, S.W. Va. dist. Va. Fedn. Women's Clubs, 1968, Woman of Yr. Wise County/ Norton Dem. Women's Club, 1986; Ky. Broadcasters Assn. scholar, 1956. Mem. Va. Press Assn. (1st place award for editorial writing 1976), Nat. Press Women, Va. Press Women, Nat. Newspaper Assn., Women in Communications, Nat. Sch. Bds. Assn. (pub. relations com., nominating com. 1987), Mortar Bd., Delta Kappa Gamma (hon. mem. Alpha Psi chpt.), Phi Beta Kappa, Alpha Delta Pi. Democrat. Methodist. Home: PO Box 303 Longview Dr Saint Paul VA 24283 Office: PO Box 817 Russell St Saint Paul VA 24283

GREGORY, BETTINA LOUISE, journalist; b. N.Y.C., June 4, 1946; d. George Alexander and V. Elizabeth Friedman; m. John P. Flannery, II, 1981. Student, Smith Coll., 1964-65; diploma in acting, Webber-Douglas Sch. Dramatic Art, London, 1968; B.A. in Psychology, Pierce Coll., Athens, Greece, 1972. Reporter Sta. WVBR-FM, Ithaca, N.Y., 1972-73, Sta. WCIC-TV, Ithaca, 1972; reporter, anchorwoman Sta. WGBB, Freeport, N.Y., 1973, Sta. WCBS, N.Y.; freelance reporter, writer AP, N.Y.C., 1973-74; freelance reporter N.Y. Times, 1973-74; with ABC News, 1974—; corr. ABC News, Washington, 1977-79; White House corr. ABC News, 1979—, sr. gen. assignment corr., 1980—; elected rep. for corr.'s ABC News Women's Adv. Bd. Recipient 1st Place award Nat. Feature News, Odyssey Inst., N.Y., 1978, Clarion award Women in Communications, Inc., 1979, hon. mention Nat. Commn. on Working Women, 1979; named one of top 10 investigative reporters TV Guide, 1983. Mem. Radio TV Corrs. Assn., White House Corrs. Assn. Clubs: Newswomen's N.Y. (recipient Front Page award 1976); Nat. Press; Washington Press. Office: 1717 De Sales St NW Washington DC 20036

GREGORY, BONITA BELINDA, educator; b. Washington, Jan. 4, 1956; d. James Leon and Catheryn Evelyn (Albright) G.; adopted children: La Keisha Danielle, Latisha Michelle. BS in Spl. Edn., Brescia Coll., 1980. Cert. secondary tchr., Md. Spl. edn. tchr. Richmond County Schs., Warsaw, Va., 1981-85, Dallas Ind. Sch. Dist., 1985-86, Prince George County Schs., Clinton, Md., 1986—; cons. Gregory Day Camp, Silver Spring, Md., summers 1982—. Tchr. to mentally retarded Brescia Coll., Owensboro, Ky., 1978-80; vol. McKinney Hills Downs Syndrome Children, Silver Spring, 1975-76, Prince Georges County Spl. Olympics, 1987-88; severely handicapped tchr. Md. Nat. Capital Park and Planning Commn., Calverton, Md., 1986; sec. Clifton Park Citizens Assn. Recipient B award Brescia Coll., 1980. Mem. Prince Georges County Edn. Assn., Council for Exceptional Children. Democrat. Baptist. Home: 14100 Castle Blvd #304 Silver Spring MD 20904

GREGORY, CANDACE LYNN, firefighter; b. Gridley, Calif., Sept. 10, 1957; d. Wallace Edward and Cynthia Rosemary (Wicker) G. BS, Humboldt State U., 1980. Firefighter U.S. Forest Service, Waldport, Oreg., 1976, Calif. Dept. Forestry, Oroville, Calif., 1977-78; forestry aid Calif. Dept. Forestry, Redding, Calif., 1979, fire apparatus trainer, 1980-81; graduate trainee Calif. Dept. Forestry, Fresno, Calif., 1982, fire capt., 1983; fire capt. Calif. Dept. Forestry, Oroville, 1984-86; battalion chief Dept. Forestry and Fire Protection, Crestline, Calif., 1987—. Mem. Calif. Dept. Forestry Employees Assn., Calif. State Employees Assn., So. Calif. Forestry & Fire Wardens. Democrat. Presbyterian. Office: Calif Dept Forestry and Fire Protection 3800 Sierra Way San Bernardino CA 92405

GREGORY, CLAIRE DISTELHORST, TV producer; b. Chgo., Mar. 6, 1926; d. Robert Henry and Genevieve (McCall) Distelhorst; student Cornell Coll., 1943-46; A.B., Ind. U., 1947, M.S., 1954, ArtsD1969; children—Charles, Martha. Tchr. public schs., Bismarck and Rossville, Ill., 1947-50, Helmsburg, Ind., 1950-51; grad. asst. Audio Visual Center of Ind. U., 1953-55, lectr., dir. women's, children's and social service programs radio and TV, 1956-59; exec. dir. Community Service Council, Inc., Bloomington, Ind., 1971-75; asst. supr. instructional TV program devel. Ind. U. Radio and TV Service, 1975-81, dir. spl. projects, 1982—; chmn. Bloomington Telecommunications Council, 1975-80. Writer, producer: Russian Revolution and Arts, Parts I and II, 1976, Intro. to Immediate Access, 1977-80, Teleconference on Mass Transportation, 1976, Transportation Briefing, 1977, videotapes on profl. devel. Internat. Devel. Inst., 1975-80, 16 videotapes on computer instrn., 1978-80, Getting There, 1980, Living Africa, 1979-82, Programming for Microcomputers, 1982, Negotiation, 1984, Ind. Collection, 1987, Joshua's Battle: The Story of Lyles Station, 1988, Charting New Courses teleconferences, 1988. TV advisor Mostly Moliere Troupe, 1981—. Mem. United Way of Monroe County, 1982; treas. Blue Ridge Assn., 1978-81, Theta Sigma Phi, Psi Iota Xi. Club: Univ. Office: Ind. U. Radio and TV Service 212 Radio and TV Bldg Bloomington IN 47405

GREGORY, CYNTHIA KATHLEEN, ballerina; b. Los Angeles, July 8, 1946; d. Konstantin and Marcelle (Tremblay) G.; m. Terrence S. Orr, May 14, 1966 (div.); m. John Hemminger, 1976 (dec. 1984); m. Hilary B. Miller. Grad. high sch. Ford Found. scholar, San Francisco Ballet, 1961, soloist, 1962-65; principal, San Francisco Opera, 1964-65; with Am. Ballet Theatre, N.Y.C., 1965—, soloist, 1966, prin. dancer, 1967—, choreographer: Solo, 1979; created roles in Eliot Feld's Harbinger, At Midnight, Dennis Nahat's Brahams Quintet, Michael Smuin's The Eternal Idol, Gartenfest, Twyla Tharp's Bach Partita, John McFall's Interlude; dances leading female roles in classic repertory; guest artist with dance cos. including Zurich State Opera Ballet, Nat. Ballet of Cuba, Berlin State Opera Ballet, San Francisco Ballet, Ballet West, N.Y.C. Opera; permanent guest artist, Cleveland San Jose Ballet, 1986—; appeared on TV with San Francisco Opera, 1963-64; made TV appearance on The Edge of Night, 1981; author Ballet is the Best Exercise. Recipient Dance Magazine award 1975, Harkness Ballet Found. First Annual Dance award, 1978, Cyril Magnin award for outstanding achievement in the arts San Francisco C. of C., 1986. Office: Cleveland San Jose Ballet 1 Playhouse Sq Suite 330 Cleveland OH 44115 *

GREGORY, ELEANOR ANNE, artist, educator; b. Seattle, Jan. 20, 1939; d. John Noel and Eleanor Blanche G.; BA, Reed Coll., 1963; MFA, U. Wash., 1966; MEd, Columbia U., 1978, EdD., 1978. Art tchr. Seattle Public Schs., 1970-75; instr. N.Y.C. Community Coll., 1977, Manhattan Community Coll., N.Y.C., 1978; asst. prof. N.Mex. State U., Las Crucas, 1978-79; asst. prof. art Purdue U., West Lafayette, Ind., 1979-82, West Tex. State U., Canyon, 1982-84; lectr. Calif. State U., Long Beach, 1985—; one woman shows: Columbia U. Tchrs. Coll., 1976, Watson's Crick Gallery, West Lafayette, 1980, 81, Gallery I, Purdue U., 1980, W. Tex. State U., 1983, Amarillo Art Ctr., 1984, Sch. Visual Concepts, Seattle, 1985; group shows include: El Paso (Tex.) Art Mus., 1979, Ind. State Mus., Indpls., 1980, Lafayette (Ind.) Art Mus., 1982, T. Billman Gallery, Long Beach, 1987; represented in permanent collection: Portland (Oreg.) Art Mus.; mgr. Watson's Crick Gallery, West Lafayette, 1982-83. Mem. Nat. Art Edn. Assn., N.Y. Soc. Scribes, Chgo. Calligraphy Collective, Internat. Soc. Edn. Through Art. Episcopalian. Office: Calif State U Dept Art 1250 Bellflower Blvd Long Beach CA 90840

GREGORY, JEAN WINFREY, ecologist, educator; b. Richmond, Va., Feb. 13, 1947; d. Thomas Edloe and Kathryn (McFarlane) Winfrey; m. Ronald Alfred Gregory, Dec. 13, 1973. BS in Biology, Mary Washington Coll., 1969; MS in Biology, Va. Commonwealth U., 1975, postgrad. in pub. adminstrn., 1982—; MA in Environ. Sci., U. Va., 1983. Cert. ecologist, fisheries scientist. Lab. specialist A Cardiovascular Div. Med. Coll. Va., Richmond, 1969-70; pollution control specialist A State Water Control Bd., Richmond, 1970-77, pollution control specialist B, 1977-81, ecologist, 1981-85, ecology programs supr., 1985—; adj. faculty Va. Commonwealth U., Richmond, 1978—. Contbr. articles to profl. jours. 1972-73. Named One of Outstanding Young Women of Am., 1974; EPA fellow, Va., 1974-76. Mem. Am. Soc. Pub. Adminstrn., North Am. Benthological Soc., Ecological Soc. Am., Am. Soc. Limology and Oceanography, North Am. Lake Mgmt. Soc. (bd. dirs. 1983-86). Democrat. Methodist. Office: State Water Control Bd Office Environ Research and Standards PO Box 11143 2107 Hamilton St Richmond VA 23230

GREGORY, JUSTINA WINSTON, classics educator; b. Brattleboro, Vt., Sept. 24, 1946; d. Richard and Clara (Brussel) Winston; m. Patrick Bolton Gregory, Aug. 2, 1969; children—Tobias, Nora. A.B., Smith Coll., 1967; M.A., Harvard U., 1972, Ph.D., 1974. Asst. prof. classics Yale U., New Haven, 1974-75; asst. prof. Smith Coll., Northampton, Mass., 1975-80, assoc. prof., 1980—. Fulbright Commn. fellow, 1967-68, Woodrow Wilson Found. fellow, 1968-69; Am. Council Learned Socs. grantee, 1977. Mem. Am. Philol. Assn., Classical Assn. New England, Pioneer Valley Classical Assn. Office: Smith Coll Dept Classics Northampton MA 01063

GREGORY, KAY RISH, home economist; b. Greenwood, S.C., June 15, 1947; d. Ernest L. and Elberta E. Rish; m. Derrell P. Gregory; children: S. Lauren, Nolan R. BS in Home Econs., Lander Coll., 1969; MEd in Guidance and Counseling, Clemson U., 1986. Aging planner Upper Savannah Council of Govts., Greenwood, S.C., 1972-77; county extension agt. Clemson Coop. Extension Service, Greenwood, 1978—. dir. Salvation Army, Greenwood, 1985-88, Shelter for Abused Women, Greenwood, 1986—. Mem. Am. Home Econs. Assn., S.C. Home Econs. Assn., Nat. Assn. Ext. Home Economists, S.C. Assn. Ext. Home Econs. (3d v.p. 1986-88, Rookie of Yr., 1980, Outstanding Home Econs. 1984). Methodist. Home: 139 Roman Circle Greenwood SC 29646

GREGORY, LYN GAIL, accountant; b. Guatemala City, Guatemala, Dec. 29, 1952; d. Thomas R. and Gail M. (Larson) Herrick; m. Mark D. Gregory, June 24, 1972; children: Shane E., Brian T. Student, St. John's Coll., 1970-72, Meridian (Miss.) Jr. Coll., 1977-80, Portland State U., 1981-83, City U., Bellevue, Wash., 1983—. Acct. Computer Devel., Inc., Beaverton, Oreg., 1980-84; staff acct. Johnson, Stone, Deaton, Pagano & Co., Tacoma, 1985—. Vol. tax preparer IRS, Meridian, 1978. Mem. Am. Soc. Women Accts. Episcopalian. Office: Johnson Stone Deaton Pagano & Co 820 A St Suite 300 Tacoma WA 98403

GREGORY, MAUNALLEN, infosystems executive; b. London, Feb. 24, 1935. BS in Acctg., Phila. Coll. Textiles and Scis., 1976; MBA, Temple U., 1979. Cert. internal auditor, cert. info. systems auditor. Sr. v.p., ops. and data processing Western Savs. Bank, Phila., 1965-82; dir. mgmt. info. systems and devel. Paper Corp. Am. subs. Alco Standard Corp., Wayne, Pa., 1982-83; v.p. mgmt. info. Alco Standard Corp., Valley Forge, Pa., 1983—; adj. faculty women's programs Pa. State U., Abington, 1977—; mem. adv. council Pa. State U. Mem. Soc. Info. Mgmt., Nat. Speakers Assn., Beta Gamma Sigma. Clubs: Bryn Mawr, Kennel. Home: 1032 Hartranft Ave Fort Washington PA 19034 Office: Alco Standard Corp 825 Duportail Rd Wayne PA 19087

GREGORY, WANDA JEAN, paralegal, court reporter, singer, musician; b. Little Rock, Sept. 7, 1925; d. John Albert and Angie (Thompson) Deming; student Del Mar Jr. Coll., Corpus Christi, Tex.; m. G. C. Gregory, Jan. 15, 1945 (div.); 1 son, Rex Carleton. Ofcl. ct. reporter, Nueces County, Tex., 1959-76, 36th Jud. Dist. Ct., San Patricio, Live Oak, McMullen, Aransas and Bee Counties, Tex., 1979-82; freelance court reporter, Corpus Christi, 1976-78, 82-85, Honolulu, 1979. Vocalist with dance bands and jazz combos; pvt. tchr. jazz, pop singing and ballroom dancing; a founder Tex. Jazz Festival, 1960, appeared, 1961-82, 84-86, master of ceremonies, 1983; soloist Corpus Christi Interdenominational Choir. Mem. Tex. Jazz Festival Soc. (founder 1969, past pres., now bd. dirs.), Am. Fedn. Musicians. Democrat. Methodist. Home: 6440 Everhart Rd #2D Corpus Christi TX 78413 Office: 3751 S Alameda Corpus Christi TX 78411

GREGORY-GOODRUM, ELLNA KAY, educator, artist; b. Houston, Oct. 3, 1943; d. A. N. and Harriet (Christensen) Gregory; m. Craig R. Goodrum, Aug. 11, 1983; 1 child, Emily K. BFA, U. Okla., 1965; MFA, North Tex. State U., 1979. Tchr., Dallas Ind. Schs., 1965-85; instr. art Richland Coll., Dallas, 1981—; lectr. in field; group exhibits include: Watercolor Soc. of Ala., 1979, Clifford Gallery, Dallas, 1982-83; Nat. Watercolor Soc., 1985, 87, 88, San Diego Watercolor Soc., 1985, Edith Baker Gallery, 1986, 87, Women and Watercolor, Transco. Energy Ctr., Houston, 1988, Watercolor U.S.A., 1988, Rocky Mountain Nat. Watermedia, 1988, Springfield Art Mus.; works represented in permanent collections: Rockwell Internat., Brown Found. and Cons., Atlantic Richfield, Renaissance Ctr., Detroit, Southwestern Watercolor Soc. (mem.). Recipient Cash awards Tex. Watercolor Soc., 1978, Dallas Art Mus., 1978, So. Watercolor Soc., 1979. Mem. Pastel Soc. Am. (best abstract 1979, Mixed Media award 1987), Pastel Soc. S.W. (2d award 1987), Coll. Art Assn., Nat. Watercolor Soc., Tex. Watercolor Soc., Pastel

Soc., Women's Caucus on Art. Methodist. Home: 7214 Lane Park Dr Dallas TX 75225

GREICO, LINDA ANN, mathematics educator; b. Fergus Falls, Minn., Mar. 8, 1947; d. Maynard Sheldon and Dorothy Blanche (Schnetzer) Fletcher; m. William Warren Greico, Dec. 14, 1985; children by previous marriage—Fletcher, Zachary; stepchildren—Paul, Bobby, Maria, Warren. B.S., Moorhead State U., 1968; M.A., U. Ark., 1972; postgrad. U. South Fla., 1981—. Tchr. math. Leto High Sch., Tampa, Fla., 1972-78; prof. math. Hillsborough Community Coll., Tampa, 1974—; adj. prof. U. South Fla., Tampa, 1981—. Mem. Easter Seal Guild, Tampa, 1980—; bd. dirs. Symphony Guild, Tampa, 1978; mem. Red Cross Angels, Tampa, 1980—, Sword of Hope, Tampa, 1980—, Children's Home, Tampa, 1985—. NSF grantee, 1971-72. Mem. Nat. Council Tchrs. of Math., Math. Assn. Am., Fla. Assn. Community Colls., Nat. Assn. Female Execs. Democrat. Roman Catholic. Avocation: tennis. Office: Hillsborough Community Coll PO Box 75313 Tampa FL 33675

GREIG, JOAN MARIE, retail company administrator; b. Sept. 7, 1945; m. Curtis G. Greig; children: Tyron Curtis, Tiffanie Marie. BS in Bus. Mgmt., U. Minn., 1979. Mgr. sales Koscot Kosmetics, St. Paul, 1967-71; owner, operator Dairy Queen, Mpls., 1971-75; with Greig Designs, St. Paul, 1972-1976; asst. mgr. Lynn Rose Clothing, St. Paul, 1975-76; dept. mgr. Target Discount Stores, St. Paul, 1976-79, mgr. customer service, 1979-81; mgr. mdse. Target Discount Stores, Mpls., 1981-84, mgr. ops., 1984—; instr. mgmt. tng., 1980-87, communications and supervision seminar, 1981-87, Target, mem. advt. planning com., 1979-81. Pres. Bel Air PTA, St. Paul, 1974-76; mem. adv. bd. New Brighton City Council, 1971-76. Mem. LWV (bd. dirs. 1969-79). Republican. Presbyterian. Home: 980 Oakwood Dr New Brighton MN 55112

GREIST, MARILYN LEE, advertising agency executive; b. Phila., May 21, 1945; d. David and Florence Gertrude (Wolfe) Vernik; m. Lewis Charles Greist, May 21, 1972. Student, Temple U., 1966; cert., HB Studios, N.Y.C., 1979. Media buyer Brownstein Advt., Phila., 1969-71, media dir., 1971-73, account exec., 1973-75; media cons. Marilyn Greist Media, Phila., 1975-77; dir. advt. Cottman Transmissions, Ft. Washington, Pa., 1977-79; research analyst Katz Communications, Inc., N.Y.C., 1979-83; media dir., account exec. Gregory & Clyburne, Inc., Stamford, Conn., 1983-85; v.p. and sr. account exec. Gregory & Clyburne, Inc., Stamford, 1985—. Mem. Westport Community Theater, 1982-83; mem. North Park Civic Assn., Bridgeport, Conn., 1985-87; mem. ch. choir, Bridgeport. Mem. Ad Club of Fairfield County (v.p. 1985-86, Matty awards 1984, 85, 86), Women in Communications (Fairfield County chpt.). Republican. Home: 578 Cleveland Ave Bridgeport CT 06604 Office: Gregory & Clyburne Inc 45 Church St Stamford CT 06906

GRENN-SCOTT, DEBBI, public relations executive; b. N.Y.C., Oct. 20, 1951; d. Walter Joachim and Rita Rosalind (Kolb) Grenn; m. Charles B. Scott, Aug. 31, 1975. B.A. in Communications, San Francisco State U., 1971; postgrad. N.Y. Inst. Advt., Alliance Francaise, New Sch. Social Research. Jr. media buyer Richard K. Manoff Inc., N.Y.C., 1972-74; freelance writer/publicist, N.Y.C., 1974-78; account exec. Samuel Krasney Assocs., N.Y.C., 1978-81; asst. v.p. R.C. Auletta & Co., N.Y.C., 1981-83; sr. v.p. Howard J. Rubenstein Assocs., N.Y.C., 1983—. Active Stephen Wise Free Synagogue. Mem. Pub. Relations Soc. Am., Nat. Investor Relations Inst. Office: Howard J Rubenstein Assocs Inc 1345 Ave of Americas New York NY 10105

GRENZEBACH, ELIZABETH STEWART, medical technologist; b. Richlands, Va., July 12, 1939; d. Frederick Fitzgerald and Margaret (Bronson) Stewart; student Mary Washington Coll., 1957-60; B.S., Med. Coll. Va., 1961; m. James Austin Grenzebach, May 12, 1973. With dept. pathology, Med. Coll. Va., Richmond, 1961-63, chief technologist Kidney Transplant Lab., 1963-66; research technologist Med. Coll. Wis., Milw., 1966-70, research asso. dept. environ. medicine, 1970-72; lab. dir. Silver Hill Found., New Canaan, Conn., 1973—. Mem. Am. Soc. Clin. Pathologists, The Profl. Collective. Republican. Episcopalian. Club: Country of New Canaan. Home: 106 Elm Pl New Canaan CT 06840 Office: PO Box 1177 Valley Rd New Canaan CT 06840

GRESHAM, JANICE TATE, state agency administrator; b. Athens, Ga., Apr. 11, 1943; d. Gerald Lafayette and Malissa Avis (Sims) Tate; m. John L. Gresham Jr., June 12, 1971; children: John L. III, Frederick, Stanley. BA, J.C. Smith U., 1964; MSW, U. Ga., 1971. With social services dept. N.Y. State Dept. Welfare, Bklyn., 1964-65; tchr. music Wingate High Sch., Bklyn., 1965-68, Smith High Sch., Atlanta, 1968-69; with social services dept. Ga. Dept. Human Resources, Atlanta, 1971-79, with aging services, 1979—; pvt. piano tchr. Atlanta, 1980—; coordinator ch. music, various chs., Atlanta, N.Y.C., 1960—; cons. vocal music, Atlanta, 1986-87. Bd. dirs. Quality Living Services, Inc., Atlanta, 1986—, Recordings for Recovery, Atlanta, 1987—. Recipient Quaker Oats Gospel award Quaker Oats Co., Atlanta, 1981. Mem. Ga. Gerontol. Soc., Metro Atlanta Music Tchrs. Assn., Older Women's League, James Cleveland Gospel Workshop. Baptist. Office: Ga Dept Human Resources Office of Aging 878 Peachtree St NE Atlanta GA 30309

GRESS, ANN MARIA, medical company executive, graphics and technical writing consultant; b. Latrobe, Pa., Dec. 24, 1955; d. Peter and Ella Margaret (Uhall) Uschak; m. David George Gress, July 30, 1983. BA in Secondary Edn. and Communications, U. Pitts., 1977; M in Communications, Pa. State U., 1981, M in Architecture and Art, 1982. Cert. tchr., N.J., Pa. Prin. actress TPC Prodns., Pitts., 1978-79; jr. English and drama tchr. Derry (Pa.) Jr. High Sch., 1977-79; bus. communications teaching asst. Pa. State U., University Park, 1979-81; script writer, narrator Pa. State Info. Telephone System, University Park, 1979-81; sr. English tchr. Kingsway Regional High Sch., Swedesboro, N.J., 1981-84; sr. tech. writer in creative communications DuPont, Wilmington, Del., 1983-84; sr. med. prodn. account rep. DuPont External Affairs, Wilmington, 1984—. Pres. Womens Altar Soc., Carneys Point, N.J., 1987; active Del. Pub. Edn.-Am. Cancer Soc.; soloist, actress Best of Broadway, Wilmington, 1987. Recipient Stanton Chapman Meml. award U. Pitts., 1977, Univ. Residential award, John F. Kennedy Ctr. for Performing Arts, Washington D.C., 1978. Mem. Women in Bus., Am. Theatre Assn., Pitts. Alumni Golden Panthers, Pa. Edn. Assn., N.J. Edn. Assn., Grad. Assn. (treas. 1981-82), U. Pitts. Symphony Band (sec. 1976-77), Nat. Forensic Assn. (pres. local chpt. 1970-73), Alpha Omega (advisor 1981—), Delta Zeta (social chmn. 1977-78). Home: 263 Harding Hwy Carneys Point NJ 08069 Office: DuPont External Affairs Div Taylor Mill BldgRoom 118 Wilmington DE 19898

GREY, CAROLYN ANN, eduator, social worker; b. Bronx, N.Y., Apr. 11, 1943; d. John H. and Hattie (Lewis) G. AB, Hunter Coll., 1966, MA, 1977; MSW, Smith Coll., 1982. Tchr. N.Y.C. Bd. Edn., 1966—; staff therapist Queens Child Guidance Ctr., Jamaica, N.Y., 1986—. Home: 609 Warren St Brooklyn NY 11217

GREY, JEAN S., accountant; b. N.Y.C., June 14, 1925; d. Isdore and Edithe (Sarette) Schwartz; m. Charles Grey, Nov. 22, 1945; children: Scott, Shari. BBA, CCNY, 1950. CPA., N.Y. Acct. Kipnis & Karchmer, CPA's, N.Y.C., 1942-44; acct., then head tax dept. Clarence Rainess Co., CPA's, N.Y.C., 1944-54; ind. tax specialist, estate acct. Syosset, N.Y., 1950—; organizer Cee-Jay Extruders, Inc., 1952, now treas, bd. dirs.; lectr. cons. in field. Mem. Am. Soc. Women Accts. (pres.), Am. Women's Soc. CPA's, N.Y. State Soc. CPA's, Nat. Conf. CPA Practioners, Acctg. Inst. C.W. Post Coll. Art League, Nat. Assn. Pub. Accts., Bus. and Profl. Women's Club, USCG Aux., Société des Vignerons. Clubs: Tappan Beach Yacht. Home: 9 Spruce Ln Syosset NY 11791 Office: 5 Sidney Ct Lindenhurst NY 11757

GRIBBLE, CAROLE L., wholesale distributing executive; b. Toppenish, Wash., May 19, 1940; d. Harold Max and Gertrude Louisa (Spicer) Smith; m. Duane E. Clark, Aug. 1959 (div. 1963); 1 child, David Allen; m. Vance William Gribble, May 19, 1966. Student, Seattle Pacific Coll. With B.F. Shearer, Seattle, 1959-60, Standard Oil, Seattle, 1960-62, Seattle Platen Co., 1962-70; ptnr. West Coast Platen, Los Angeles, 1970-87, Waldorf Towers Apts., Seattle, 1970—, Cascade Golf Course, North Bend, Wash., 1970-88; ptnr. Pacific Wholesale Office Equip., Seattle and Los Angeles, 1972-87, owner, 1988—; owner Bob Bianco Sales, San Francisco, 1988—, Pac Electronic Service Ctr., 1988—. Republican. Methodist. Office: Pacific Wholesale Equipment 1512 7th Ave Seattle WA 98101

GRIBIN, ELIZABETH ANNE, artist; b. London, Mar. 30, 1934; came to U.S., 1939; d. Jack and Margaret (Salomon) Poser; m. Nathaniel D. Griblin, June 17, 1956; children—Eric, Elisa, David. B.F.A., Boston U., 1956; student Art Students League, 1946-51, Mus. Modern Art, N.Y.C., 1944-46; student David Aronson, 1953-56, Margit Beck, 1979-80, Leo Manso, 1970-71, Paul Wood, 1971-84. One-woman show: Great Neck House (N.Y.), 1983; group shows include: City Hall Gallery, Boston, 1983, Knickerbocker Artists, N.Y.C., 1983, NAD, N.Y.C., 1984, Nat. Assn. Women Artists, N.Y.C., 1984, Long Beach Mus. (Calif.), 1984, Salmagundi Club, N.Y.C., 1984, Mussavi Gallery, N.Y.C., 1984., Audubon Artists Nat. Arts Club, N.Y.C., 1985, Isis Gallery, Port Washington, N.Y., 1985, Sarah Lawrence Coll., Bronxville, N.Y., 1985 Frostburg (Md.) State Coll, 1985, Nabisco Brands Hdqrs, East Hanover, N.J., 1986, L'Avenier Gallery, Great Neck, N.Y., 1986, Audubon Award Winners, Lever House, N.Y.C., 1986, Salmagundi Club, N.Y.C., 1986, Sabbeth Art Gallery, Glen Cove, N.Y., 1986, Art Ctr. of Spartanburg, S.C., 1986, Nat. Assn. Women Artists Exhibit Fed. Bldg., N.Y.C., 1986, Jesse Besser Mus., Alpena, Mich., 1986, Southeastern Ark. Arts Ctr., Pine Bluff, 1986, McPherson (Kans.) Coll., 1986, Lighthouse Gallery, Tequesta, Fla., 1986, Knickerbocker Artists at Salmagundi Club, N.Y.C., 1986, Schenectady (N.Y.) Mus., 1987, Adelphi U., Garden City, N.Y., 1987, Audubon Artists Nat. Arts Club, N.Y.C., 1987; represented in permanent collections; pvt. and corp. judge, lectr. L.I. Art Leagues; N.Y.C. coordinator Boston U. Visual Arts Com., 1982-84. Mem. Boston U. Alumni Schs. Com., 1979-84. Recipient award of Excellence, Suburban Art League, 1978; award of Excellence, Ind. Art Assn., 1980, hon. mention, 1982; hon. mention Nassau County Art Mus., 1982, Sole award Nassau County Art Ctr., Nat. League Am. Pen Women, 1982; Grumbach Gold medallion Knickerbocker Artists, 1982, award for oils and acrylics, 1983; 1st prize in acrylics Salmagundi Art Club, 1984, 1st prize in acrylics Manhasset Art Assn., 1985, medal of honor Audubon Artists, 1985, Susan Kahn award Nat. Assn. Women Artists, 1986, Julia Lucile award Knickerbocker Artists, 1986. Mem. Nat. Assn. Women Artists (Doris Klein prize for oils and acrylics 1984), N.Y. Soc. Women Artists, Contemporary Artists Guild, Manhasset Art Assn. (First prize in oils and acrylics 1979, Grumbacher Art award 1982).

GRIEDER, KAREN SUZANNE, producer, radio station executive; b. Paterson, N.J., Apr. 26, 1957; d. John Robert and Suzanne Jeanne (Ferrand) G. AA with honors, Golden West Coll., Huntington Beach, Calif., 1982; student in Spl. Arts Studies, Richmond Coll., London, summer 1983; BA with distinction, Calif. State U., Long Beach, 1984. News and pub. affairs asst. Sta. KBIG, Los Angeles, 1984; mktg. and fundraising asst. Sta. KLON, Long Beach, Calif., 1984-87; program coordinator, producer Sta. KABC and ABC Talkradio Network, Los Angeles, 1987—. Mem. Nat. Assn. Broadcast Employees and Technicians. Office: KABC Radio 3321 S La Cienega Los Angeles CA 90016

GRIER, BARBARA G. (GENE DAMON), editor, lecturer, author; b. Cin., Nov. 4, 1933; d. Phillip Strang and Dorothy Vernon (Black) Grier; grad. high sch. Author: The Lesbian in Literature, 1967, (with others) 2d edit., 1975, 3d edit., 1981; The Least of These (in Sisterhood is Powerful), 1970; The Index, 1974; Lesbiana, 1976; The Lesbian Home Jour., 1976; The Lavender Herring, 1976; Lesbian Lives, 1976; pub. The Ladder mag., 1970-72, fiction and poetry editor, 1966-67, editor, 1968-72; dir. promotion Naiad Press, Reno, Nev., 1973—, treas., 1976—, v.p., gen. mgr., Tallahassee, Fla., 1980—. Democrat. Home: Route 1 Box 3319 Havana FL 32333 Office: Naiad Press Inc PO Box 10543 Tallahassee FL 32302

GRIES, MARION WALTON (MRS. JOSEPH P. GRIES), occupational health and safety consultant; b. Milw., Sept. 14, 1935; d. Ray Guy and Ruth (Schumann) Walton; R.N. cum laude, St Mary's Hosp. Sch. Nursing, Milw., 1957; postgrad. Coll. Nursing, Marquette U., Milw., 1957-59, 75-76; B.S.N. (hon.), Alverno Coll., 1980; M.S.M. (hon.). Cardinal Stritch Coll., 1983; m. Joseph P. Gries, Aug. 22, 1959; children—Rita, Michael, Patrick, Robert, Lori. Staff nurse, supr. hosp., 1957-58; occupational health nurse, 1958-63; pvt. duty nurse, 1963-67; asst. dir. geriatric nursing, 1967-69; owner, mgr. HFM Textile Co., 1969-73; supr. occupational health nursing A.C. Spark Plug div. Gen. Motors Corp., Milw., 1973-78; occupational health and safety cons., v.p. Milw. Indsl. Clinics, 1978—; lectr. alcoholism-drug abuse, 1971—; edn. cons. Wis. Mental Health Assn., 1971-75; lectr. occupational health, 1974—. Chmn., United Cerebra Palsy campaign, 1966; leader, adviser Milw. council Girl Scouts U.S.A., 1968-73; chmn. Council on Drug Abuse, 1972-73; cert instr. ARC, 1973—, chmn. disaster nursing, 1974-78; mem. Intergroup Council Milw., Para-Medic Study Com.; sec. Oak Creek Police and Fire Commn., 1985—. Recipient Civic award Easter Seal Soc., 1965, 66, 67; C.A.R.O.L. award South Milwaukee, 1965, Oak Creek, Wis., 1966, West Allis, Wis., 1967; Leadership award United Cerebral Palsy, 1966; Distinguished Service award St. Mary's Alumni, 1969; Service award Milw. Safety Council, 1976; Citizen of Year, 1979. Mem. Am Assn. Occupational Health Nurses, S.E. Wis. Occupational Health Nurses (pres.-elect 1984, staff editor jour. 1981—, Shering award 1983), Milw. Assn. Occupational Health Nurses (treas.), Am. Assn Safety Engrs., Wis. Assn. Indsl. Hygrene, DAR, St. Mary's Alumni Assn., Wis. Jaycettes (life, v.p. 1967-68), Marquette U. Nursing Club (pres. 1957-58). Contbr. articles to profl. jours. Home: 7934 S Verdev Dr Oak Creek WI 53154 Office: 500 N 19 St Milwaukee WI 53233

GRIEST, DOROTHY, college administrator, marketing consultant; b. Iota, La., Sept. 30, 1924; d. Henry R. and Dicie (Stakes) Hebert; B.S., U. Colo., 1945, M.B.E., 1951; Ph.D., La. State U., 1966; children—Gibson H. Sandham, Jennifer S. Guillory. Prof., Northeast La. U., 1973-76; prof. Coll. Bus. Adminstrn., U. Colo., Boulder, 1956-77, chmn. bus. environment and policy, 1978-81; head dept. mgmt., mktg. and adminstrv. studies U. Southwestern La., 1981—. Dir., Monroe Civic Center, 1973-76. Mem. Acad. Mgmt., Southwest Fedn. Adminstrv. Disciplines, Beta Gamma Sigma, Phi Kappa Phi, Pi Sigma Epsilon, Beta Sigma. Democrat. Presbyterian. Home: 601 Camellia Blvd Lafayette LA 70503 Office: Univ Southwestern LA PO Box 43570 Lafayette LA 70504

GRIEST, GUINEVERE LINDLEY, government official; b. Chgo., Jan. 14, 1924; d. Euclid Eugene and Marianna (Lindley) Griest; A.B., Cornell U., 1944; A.M., U. Chgo., 1947, Ph.D., 1961; postgrad. (Fulbright fellow) Cambridge (Eng.) U., 1953-55. Instr., U. Ill., Chgo., 1947-61, asst. prof., 1961-66, assoc. prof. English, 1966-72; program officer div. of fellowships and seminars Nat. Endowment for Humanities, Washington, 1969-73, dep. dir. div. of fellowships, 1973-85, acting dir., 1985-86, dir., 1986—. Mem. MLA, Phi Beta Kappa, Phi Kappa Phi. Episcopalian. Author: Mudie's Circulating Library and the Victorian Novel (MLA scholars' library award 1971), 1971; contbr. articles to profl. jours. Office: Nat Endowment for Humanities Div Fellowships and Seminars 1100 Pennsylvania Ave NW Washington DC 20506

GRIFF, MERLE DAWN, counselor; b. Phila., Sept. 8, 1948; d. Joseph and Lea (Hoffman) Krouse; m. Franklin Wolfe Griff, Dec. 22, 1968; children: Adam Michael, Richard Asher. BA, Temple U., 1970; MS, U. Pitts., 1973. Cert. counselor Nat. Bd. Cert. Counselors. Play therapy aide St. Christopher's Hosp. for Children, Phila., 1967-69; child care worker Western Pa. Sch. for Blind Children, Pitts., 1969-71; tchr. Exptl. Program for Multipally Handicapped Children, Pitts., 1971; tchr., therapist Parents League for Emotional Adjustment, Pitts., 1972-74; program coordinator Child and Adolescent Service Ctr., Canton, Ohio, 1977-79; trainer Summit County Childrens Services Bd., Akron, Ohio, 1979-81; dir. Interactive Arts, Inc., Canton, 1981—; project mgr. McKinley Centre, Canton, 1986—. Contbr. articles to profl. jours. Founding pres., bd. dirs. Parents Anonymous, Canton, 1980—; dir. Project Kid Gloves, Canton, 1985; chairperson Stark County chpt. Am. Heart Assn., Canton, 1981; mem. Nat. Com. on Child Care Edn. and Tng., Washington, 1977-83. Grantee Dept. Helath and Human Services, 1979, U. Pitts., 1980, Heinz Found., 1985. Mem. Am. Soc. Tng. and Devel., Ohio Assn. Adult Day Care, Nat. Assn. Female Execs., Environ. Design Research Assn., Nat. Orgn. Child Care Workers Assn. (charter del. 1975-77). Office: Interactive ARts Inc 800 Market Ave N Canton OH 44702

GRIFFEE, CAROL MADGE, journalist; b. Washington, Dec. 30, 1937; d. John Franklin and Leda Mae (Woodruff) G.; B.A. with honors, U. Tulsa, 1959, M.A., 1966. Reporter. Ft. Smith (Ark.) Times-Record, 1955, Tulsa Daily World, 1958-60; news editor Annandale (Va.) Free Press, 1961-62; staff writer Washington Star, 1963-66; city editor No. Va. Sun, Arlington, Va., 1967-69, exec. editor, 1969-72; capitol reporter WEHCO Media, Camden, Ark., 1973; reporter Ark. Gazette, Little Rock, 1973-85; pres. Editorial Services, Inc., Little Rock, 1982—. Past pres. George Mason Republican Women's Club; past bd. dirs. Arlington chpt. ARC; past bd. visitors George Mason U., Fairfax, Va.; mem. adv. bd. Greater Little Rock Community Mental Health Ctr., 1986—; mem. com. on environ. and occupational safety Ark. Dept. Health, 1988—. Recipient Very Spl. Lady award Advt. Club Met. Washington, 1967, Spl. award Ark. Sanitarians Assn., 1977, Conservationist of Yr., Ark. Wildlife Fedn., 1985. Mem. Nat. Fedn. Press Women (dir. 1977-78, legislations-resolutions dir. 1978-80, dir. nat. conf., award recipient), Ark. Press Women (pres. 1977-78, Woman of Achievement award 1977, 84), Ark. Hist. Assn., Ark. Polit. Sci. Assn., Ark. Women's History Inst., Phi Delta Epsilon, Phi Gamma Kappa, Phi Delta Theta, Pi Gamma Mu, Phi Mu, Sigma Delta Chi.-Soc. Profl. Journalists (v.p. 1980, 81, Region 12 deputy dir. 1984-87). Co-author, Horizons: 100 Arkansas Women of Achievement, 1980. Home and Office: 2610 N Taylor St Little Rock AR 72207

GRIFFEN, AGNES MARTHE, library administrator; b. Ft. Dauphin, Dem. Madagascar, Aug. 25, 1935; d. Frederick Stang and Alvilde Margrethe (Torvik) Hallanger; m. Thomas Michael Griffen (div. Nov. 1969); children: Shaun Helen Griffen D'Antoni, Christopher Patrick, Adam Andrew; m. John H.P. Hall, Aug. 26, 1980. BA cum laude in English, Pacific Luth. U., 1957; MLS, U. Washington, 1965; Urban Exec. cert., MIT, 1976. Cert. librarian, Wash., Md. Area children's librarian King County Library System, Seattle, 1965-68, coordinator instl. libraries, 1968-71, dep. librarian, staff and program devel., 1971-74; dep. library dir. Tucson Pub. Library, 1974-80; dir. Montgomery County Dept. Pub. Libraries, Rockville, Md., 1980—; lectr. grad. library sch. U. Ariz., Tucson, 1976-77, 79; vis. lectr. Sch. Librarianship U. Wash., Seattle, 1983; treas., bd. dirs. Universal Serials & Book Exchange, Washington, 1984-87, pres.-elect, 1988. Contbr. articles to library periodicals and profl. jours. Active Md. Humanities Council, Balt., 1986—, Ariz. Humanities Council, Phoenix, 1977-80; charter mem. Exec. Women's Council of Southern Ariz., Tucson, 1979-80. Recipient Helping Hand award Md. Assn. of the Deaf, 1985, Cert. Recognition Montgomery County Hispanic Employees Assn., 1985; Henry scholar U. Washington Sch. Librarianship, 1965. Mem. ALA (div. pres. pub. library assn. bd. 1981-82, councilor-at-large 1972-76, 86—, chmn. com. on program evaluation and support 1987-88), Md. Library Assn., Washington Met. Library Council (chmn. 1984). Democrat. Home: 14729 Pebble Hill Ln Gaithersburg MD 20878 Office: Montgomery County Dept of Pub Libraries 99 Maryland Ave Rockville MD 20850-2374

GRIFFIN, BETTY JO ANN, goldsmith, conservator, consultant; b. Dallas, Sept. 22, 1935; d. James Frederick and Mary Audrey (West) G. B.B.A., So. Meth. U., 1957. Prodn. asst. Neiman-Marcus, Dallas, 1957-59; advt. dir. Ramsey Winch Mfg. Co., Tulsa, 1959-60; prodn. mgr. Bloom Advt. Co., Dallas, 1960-61; advt. dir. Swest, Inc., Dallas, 1965; self-employed goldsmith/conservator, Dallas, 1965—; objects conservator Dallas Mus. Art, 1976—; tchr. ptnr. Argent Jewelers Inst., Dallas, 1971—; tech. cons. Museo del Oro, Bogota, Colombia, S.Am., 1977—; presenter 45th Congress Americanists, Bogota, Colombia, 1985. Recipient Gold award Dallas Mus. Art, 1963; 1st award jewelry 18th Nat. Decorative Arts Exhibition, Wichita, Kans., 1964; Diamonds Today awards DeBeers-Diamond Info. Ctr., 1973, 74. Mem. Tex. Designer Craftsman, Am. Inst. Conservators, S.W. Assn. Conservators. Republican. Presbyterian. Home: 6206 Vanderbilt Ave Dallas TX 75214 Office: Dallas Mus Art 1717 N Harwood St Dallas TX 75201

GRIFFIN, JO ANN THOMAS, tax specialist; b. Dallas, July 20, 1933; d. John Baxton and Joan Marion (Ament) Thomas; m. John Barrett Brown, June 29, 1963 (div. 1972); children—John Barrett, Daniel Thomas; m. Thomas Reese Griffin, Jan. 25, 1976; stepchildren—Gregory Crawford, Kevin Bradley. B.A., U. Miss., 1955; B.S. magna cum laude, Lamar U., 1964; M.Edn., U. Del., 1972. Site mgr. Motivational Ctr., Inc., Wilmington, Del., 1976-78; asst. dir. Indochinese Social Services, Associated Cath. Charities, New Orleans, 1978-79; dir. continuing edn. St. Mary's Dominican Coll., New Orleans, 1979-80; with fin. mgmt. U.S. Dept. Agr., New Orleans, 1981; tax auditor IRS, New Orleans and Phila., 1981-86, revenue agt., Wilmington, 1987—; tax specialist Horty & Horty, C.P.A.s, Wilmington, Del., 1986-87; specialist customer relations M Bank USA, Wilmington, 1987. Docent Winterthur, New Orleans Mus. Art, Wilmington and New Orleans, 1966-85; sustaining mem. Jr. League of Wilmington, lay reader Episc. Ch. Diocese of Del., Wilmington, 1971—; regent DAR Vieux Carre chpt., New Orleans, 1984; bd. dirs. Neighborhood Watch, New Orleans, 1983-85. Recipient Grad. Scholarship award AAUW, 1971, Sustained Superior Performance award IRS, New Orleans, 1984. Mem. Nat. Assn. Accts., Am. Soc. Women Accts. (sec. 1986—), Wilmington Tax Group, Nat. Assn. Female Execs., Wilmington Women in Bus. Democrat. Episcopalian. Club: Blue & Gold, Newark.

GRIFFIN, MARY ELIZABETH WILSON (MRS. DONALD F. GRIFFIN), metals manufacturer, educator, county official; b. Yuba City, Calif., May 24, 1932; d. Zacharias Walters and Mary (Nickerson) Wilson; m. Donald F. Griffin, Sept. 6, 1958; children: John Malcolm, Mimi Elizabeth, Zachary Paul. AA, Yuba Coll., 1952, AB cum laude, Chico State Coll., 1954; postgrad. Sacramento State Coll., 1956, San Francisco State Coll., 1957-58. Tchr. pub. elem. schs., Santa Rosa, Calif., 1954-57; assoc. prof. edn. San Francisco State Coll., 1957-59, temporary tchr. Campus Elem. Sch., 1960-67; v.p. Griffin Metal Products, San Francisco, 1960-63, sec.-treas., 1963-80, pres., 1980—; tchr. South San Francisco Sch. Dist., 1973—. Treas. library trust fund French-Am. Bi-Lingual Sch., San Francisco, 1965-67; active PTA, 1967—, dir. county parent edn. program, 1972-73; mem. Millbrae (Calif.) Beautification Com., 1971-78; bd. dirs. San Francisco Boys Chorus, until 1981; mem. Millbrae City Council, 1976-87, mayor, 1980-81, 84-85; chmn. North San Mateo County Council of Cities, 1978-79, San Mateo Bd. Suprs., 1987—; bd. dirs. San Mateo County Easter Seal Soc., 1977-82, 1st v.p., 1981-82; chmn. legis. com. San Mateo City Council of Mayors, 1980-87; 1st v.p. Peninsula div. League Calif. Cities, 1981-82, pres., 1982-83. Recipient appreciation cert. Cub Scouts Am., 1969, 70, 71, Hon. Service award Calif. Congress PTA, 1973; named Woman of Yr., Calif. Fedn. Women's Clubs, 1980, Woman of Distinction Millbrae Soroptimists, 1987; Calif. Congress PTA scholar, 1954. Mem. Millbrae C. of C. Democrat. Presbyterian. Club: Millbrae Woman's. Home: 67 Aura Vista Millbrae CA 94030 Office: 1320 Underwood Ave San Francisco CA 94124

GRIFFIN, MARY FRANCES, retired library media consultant; b. Cross Hill, Laurens County, S.C., Aug. 24, 1925; d. James and Rosa Lee (Carter) G. AB, Benedict Coll., 1947; postgrad., S.C. State Coll., 1948-51, Atlanta U., 1953, Va. State Coll., 1961; MLS, Ind. U., 1957. Tchr.-librarian Johnston (S.C.) Tng. Sch., Edgefield County Sch. Dist., 1947-51; librarian Lee County Sch. Dist., Dennis High, Bishopville, S.C., 1951-52, Greenville County (S.C.) Sch. Dist., 1952-66; library cons. S.C. Dept. Edn., Columbia, 1966-87; vis. tchr. U. S.C., 1977. Recipient Cert. of Living the Legacy award Nat. Council Negro Women, 1980. Mem. ALA, Assn. Ednl. Communications and Tech. S.C., Assn. Curriculum Devel., AAUW (pres. Columbia br. 1978-80), Southeastern Library Assn. (sec. 1978-80), S.C. Library Assn. (sec. 1979), S.C. Assn. Sch. Librarians, Nat. Assn. State Ednl. and Media Personnel. Baptist. Home: PO Box 1652 Columbia SC 29202 Other: 1100 Skyland Dr Columbia SC 29210

GRIFFIN, MELANIE HUNT, accounting firm executive; b. Corpus Christi, Tex., Oct. 25, 1949; d. Roy Albert and Ola Emma (Hunt) G.; m. Robert Thompson; children: Maurice Dale, Donald Dwight, Merideth Thompson, Laura Thompson. BBA summa cum laude, Corpus Christi State U., 1977. CPA, Tex.; cert. fin. planner. Sec.-treas. Roy Hunt, Inc., Corpus Christi, 1970-78, dir., 1970—; v.p. White, Sluyter & Co., Corpus Christi, 1978-80; pres. Whittington & Griffin, Corpus Christi, 1980-82, also dir.; sec.-treas., dir. Sand Express, Inc., Corpus Christi, 1975—; prin. Melanie Hunt Griffin CPA, Corpus Christi, 1982—; ptnr. Fields, Nemec & co., Corpus Christi, 1984—. Devel. chair Am. Heart Assn., 1987, Leadership Corpus Christi Alumni, 1982-83. Mem. Tex. Soc. CPA's (v.p. 1988—, dir. 1987-88, pres.

Corpus Christi chpt. 1987-88), Corpus Christi State Univ. Alumni (dir. 1987—), Exec. Women Internat. (chair philanthropy com. 1986-87), Internat. Assn. Cert. Fin. Planners, Internat. Assn. Fin. Planners, Am. Inst. CPA's (personal fin. planning div.), Bus. and Estate Planning Council. Home: 10817 Stonewall St Corpus Christi TX 78410 Office: Fields Nemec & Co Po Box 23067 501 S Tancahoa Corpus Christi TX 78403

GRIFFIN, PRISCILLA LORING (MRS. JOHN J. GRIFFIN), wax manufacturing company executive; b. Winchester, Mass., Apr. 1, 1930; d. John Alden and Madeleine (Libby) Loring; m. John J. Griffin, Jan. 27, 1951; children: Patricia, Michael, Peter. Student, Pembroke Coll., Brown U., 1947-49, Katherine Gibbs Coll., 1949-50. Adminstrv. asst., asst. treas. Roger A. Reed, Inc., Reading, Mass., 1971-72, pres., treas., 1972-87, chmn. bd., treas., 1987—; trustee Roger A. Reed, Inc. Profit Sharing and Trust, 1968. Chair Camp Fire Girls of Reading, 1964-66, mem. state bd., 1966-68; mem. Reading Town Meeting, 1957-68, Small Bus. Task Force; sec. Friends of Libby Mus. Mem. New Eng. Women Bus. Owners Assn. Industries Mass., Small Bus. Assn. New Eng., LWV (chmn. Ipswich club 1969-70). Unitarian. Club: Ipswich Bay Yacht. Home: Mountain Shadows PO Box 406 Melvin Village NH 03850 Office: 167 Pleasant St Reading MA 01867

GRIFFIN, RITA PAULETTE, rehabilitation psychologist; b. Morganton, N.C., July 30, 1949; d. Paul Alexander and Genettie Olene (Poteet) G. AA, Western Piedmont Community Coll., 1973; BA, Appalachian State U., 1975, MA, 1976. Instr. psychology James Sprunt Inst., Kenansville, N.C., 1976-77; vocat. evaluator Sampson County Mental Health Ctr., Clinton, N.C., 1977; vocat. rehab. counselor Vocat. Rehab. div. State N.C., Charlotte, 1978-79, vocat. rehab. counselor-in-charge, 1979-84, vocat. rehab. unit mgr., 1984-86; asst. v.p. human services Goodwill Industries of So. Piedmont, Charlotte, 1987—. Vice chairperson Mayor's Commn. for People with Disabilities, Charlotte, 1986—. Mem. Nat. Rehab. Assn., Nat. Rehab. Adminstrs. Assn., Nat. Assn. Female Execs. Office: Goodwill Industries So Piedmont 2422 Freedom Dr Charlotte NC 28209

GRIFFIN, RUTH MCCRUM, occupational therapy educator; b. Hartford, Conn., Oct. 4, 1923; d. Robert Carlisle and Amy (Sawyer) McCrum; divorced; 1 child, Robert Douglas. BS in Occupational Therapy, Tufts U., 1946; BS in Edn., U. Hartford, 1966, MEd, 1967; PhD in Ednl. Adminstrn., U. Conn., 1973; JD, So. Eng. Sch. Law, 1988. Dir. occupational therapy Newington (Conn.) Childrens' Hosp., 1946-54, St. Francis Hosp., Hartford, Conn., 1955-57; dir. research and edn. Norwich (Conn.) Hosp., 1957-59; asst. dir. ednl. therapy Inst. Living, Hartford, 1959-68; prof. emeritus occupational therapy Quinnipiac Coll., Hamden, Conn., 1969—; rehab. cons. Arden House, Hamden, Winthrop Health Care Ctr., New Haven; vis. Mellon Found. scholar Yale U., 1985-86. Contbr. articles to profl. jours. Bd. dirs. Am. Assn. Alzheimer's Disease and Related Diseases, Hartford. Fellow Am. Occupational Therapy Assn.; mem. Conn. Occupational Therapy Assn. (past pres., Cert. Appreciation), AAUW. Roman Catholic.

GRIFFIN, SHEILA, marketing executive; b. Chgo., June 17, 1951; d. George Michael and Frances Josephine (Sheehan) Spielman; m. Woodson Jack Griffin, Dec. 30, 1972; children: Woodson Jack, II, Kelly Sheehan. BS, U. Ill., 1975, MBA, 1979. Personal banking rep. Am. Express Banking, Boeblingen, Fed. Republic Germany, 1973-74; market research analyst Market Facts, Chgo., 1975-77; mgr. strategic research Motorola, Inc., Schaumburg, Ill., 1977-83, mgr. mktg. resource, 1985-88, mgr. spl. projects Corp. Strategy Office, 1988—; gen. mgr. mktg. research and info. Ameritech Mobile Communications, Inc., Schaumburg, 1983-85. Trustee, Ill. Math. and Sci. Acad., 1985—. Mem. Am. Mktg. Assn., U. Ill. Chgo. MBA Alumni Assn. (founder, pres. 1984-86), U. Ill. Alumni Assn. (bd. dirs. 1984-86, Disting. Alumni 1985). Home: 53 Highgate Course St Charles IL 60174 Office: Motorola Inc 1301 E Algonquin Rd Schaumburg IL 60196

GRIFFIN, STEPHANIE RUTH, psychotherapist, consultant; b. Nevada, Mo., Apr. 27, 1955; d. John Ezekiel and Zofia (Mudrak) Greer; m. Henry Wesley Griffin, Aug. 4, 1982; 1 child, Melissa Dawn. Student, Baylor U., 1973, Richland Coll., 1975-76; AS, Paris (Tex.) Jr. Coll., 1983; BS, East Tex. State U., Commerce, 1983, MS, 1984. Diplomate Internat. Acad. of Behavorial Medicine, Counseling and Psychotherapy, Inc. Pvt. practice psychotherapy Paris, 1985—. Vol. Family Haven Crisis Ctr., Paris, Paris Outreach Clinic, Paris, Group Therapist for Battered Women, Paris. Served with U.S. Army, 1974. Mem. Am. Assn. for Counseling and Devel., Am. Bd. of Med. Psychotherapists (clin. assoc.), Am. Assn. of Family Counselors and Mediators (cert.), Am. Assn. Profl. Hypnotherapists (cert.). Baptist. Office: 1349 Lamar Ave Paris TX 75460

GRIFFIN, TAMIRA JO, personnel executive; b. Sherman, Tex., July 20, 1959; d. Roy Lee and Joan (Nelson) G. BBA, North Tex. State U., 1981; MBA, Amber U., 1987. Sales agt. Tex. Real Estate Commn., Austin, 1979—; mfg. supr. Tex. Instruments, Sherman, Tex., 1981-82; buyer Tex. Instruments, Dallas, 1982-84, staffing adminstr., office mgr., 1984-86, EEO/Affirmative Action Program mgr., 1986—. Dir. Dallas Mayor's Com. for the Employment of the Disabled, 1985—; bd. dirs. Tex. Alliance for Minorities in Engring., 1988—, v.p. 1987—; mem. adv. bd. Dallas SER, 1987—; mem. Tex. Gov.'s Com. Disabled Persons, 1987—, pres.'s com. employment of people with disabilities. Mem. Dallas Personnel Assn., 1987—. Republican. Baptist.

GRIFFIN-HOLST, (BARBARA) JEAN, marketing administrator; b. Pasadena, Calif., May 20, 1943; d. DeWitt James and Jean Marie (Donald) Griffin; m. Rodney C. Holst, Mar. 22, 1969 (div. May 1975); 1 child, Justin D. Griffin-Holst. BA cum laude, San Jose State U., 1967. Designer integrated cir. mask Fairchild Semicondr., Mountain View, Calif., 1967-69; sr. custom integrated cir. mask designer Nat. Semicondr., Santa Clara, Calif., 1969-71; sr. specialist Advanced Micro Devices, Sunnyvale, Calif., 1971-75; mgr. mask design and computer-aided design groups Precision Monolithics, Santa Clara, 1975-76; mgr. analog mask design and graphic services Signetics Corp., Sunnyvale, 1976-82; dist. mgr. tech. mktg. Computervision Corp., Santa Clara, 1982-84, mgr. dist. sales, 1984-85, mgr. distbr. sales, 1985-87; mktg. mgr. Edn. Products div. program Sun Microsystems Inc., Mountain View, 1987—. Mem. Nat. Assn. Female Execs., AAUW, Navy League U.S., San Francisco Mus. Modern Art, Alpha Chi Omega. Republican. Club: St. Francis Yacht (San Francisco). Office: Sun Microsystems Inc 2550 Garcia Ave Mountain View CA 94043

GRIFFIS, KATHERINE MILLICENT, municipal agency administrator; b. Dallas, Feb. 20, 1954; d. Thomas Farr and Barbara Ann (Cloyd) G. BA, Birmingham-So. Coll., 1975; JD, Birmingham Sch. Law, 1981. Tax mapper Cole-Layer Trumble, Birmingham, Ala., 1975-76; sales assoc. Rich's, Inc., Birmingham, 1976-77; aide legal research, sec. John Lair, Atty. at Law, Birmingham, 1977-79; program coordinator Ctr. for Labor Edn. & Research, U. Ala.-Birmingham, 1979-84; contract adminstr. fed. job tng. Job Tng. Ptnrship. Act Adminstrv. Offices, City of Birmingham, 1984—; instr. labor/personnel law U. Ala.-Birmingham, 1986—; cons. women in employment Mayor's Commn. on Status of Women, Birmingham, 1986—. Editor (film) Work in Alabama: A Photographic Essay, 1983; cons. Ala. Pub. TV documentary on sexual harassment in the workplace. Cons. Ramesses II Exhbn., Memphis, 1987—, Birmingham Mus. Art Egyptian Exhibit, 1988, Egyptian History and Culture Birmingham Festival of Arts, 1988, lectr., So. Coll., U. Ala., Birmingham, 1988; exhibition dir. Birmingham Festival Arts Internat. Fair, 1988. Mem. Am. Soc. Personnel Adminstrs., Southeastern Employment and Tng. Assn., Birmingham Personnel Assn., Nat. Assn. for Female Execs. (Network Birmingham), Earthwatch Expdns.(edn. com. BFA, 1988). Democrat. Lutheran. Office: JTPA Adminstrv Office City of Birmingham 2015 Second Ave N Birmingham AL 35203

GRIFFITH, CAROLE LOTSTEIN, communications consultant; b. Forest Hills, N.Y., Sept. 16, 1953; d. Raymond Sidney and Joan Barbara (Kastil) L. BA cum laude, Fairleigh Dickinson U., 1975. Asst. mgr. The Singer Co., Paramus, N.J., 1976-77; tech. writer instrn. manuals Elizabeth, N.J., 1977-79; supr. instrn. manuals worldwide 1979-82, communications cons., 1982—. Mem. Home Economists in Bus., Phi Omega Epsilon. Club: Navigators. Home and Office: 112-4D Bluebird Dr Somerville NJ 08876

GRIFFITH, DOROTHY AUBINOE, interior designer; b. Washington, Feb. 19, 1927; d. Alvin Love and Dorothy (Barron) Aubinoe; A.B., Rollins Coll., 1948; grad. teaching cert. U. Md., 1949; diploma Internat. Inst. Interior Design, 1958; children—June, Paul, Tod, Holly. Owner, interior designer Griffith Assos., Inc., Bethesda, Md., 1958-78; owner, dir. Griffith Gallery, Miami, Fla., 1978—; owner, pres. Griffith Investments. Mem. alumni council Rollins Coll., 1983—, trustee, 1983-86, nat. dir. Coll. Fund, 1985-87. Recipient Disting. Service award Rollins Coll. Alumni Assn., 1988. Mem. Am. Soc. Interior Designers. Home: 322 Toll Gate Shores Dr Islamorada FL 33036

GRIFFITH, DOTTY (DOROTHY GRIFFITH STEPHENSON), journalist, speaker, author; b. Terrell, Tex., Nov. 4, 1949; d. Edward Morrill and Dorothy (Koch) Griffith; m. Thomas Lee Stephenson, June 4, 1977; children: Kelly Griffith, Caitlin Lee. BJ, U. Tex., 1972; MLA, So. Methodist U., 1980. Gen. assignment reporter Dallas Morning News, 1972-73, edn. writer, 1973-74, gen. assignment reporter, 1974-76, polit. writer, 1976-78, food editor, 1978—; guest host Warner-Amex, Qube Cable TV, Dallas, 1982-83. Mem. nutrition task force Am. Heart Assn., Dallas, 1981-87. Author: Wild about Chili, 1985; editor: The Mansion On Turtle Creek Cookbook (Dean Elaring), 1987. Mem. Newspaper Food Editor's and Writer's Assn. (v.p. 1984-86, pres. 1986-88), Les Dames d'Escoffier (founding mem. Dallas chpt.).

GRIFFITH, KATHERINE SCOTT, communications executive; b. Atlanta, Jan. 16, 1942; d. Robert Sherrill and Emily Howell (Reynolds) G.; m. Henry Armand Terjen, Sept. 4, 1970 (div. Nov. 1979); 1 child, Henry Foster Terjen. AB, Sweet Briar Coll., 1964; Masters, Emory U., 1968. Editor South Today, So. Regional Council, Atlanta, 1969-72; editor Phoenix, Bklyn., 1972-73; dir. communications N.Y. C. of C. and Industry, N.Y.C., 1978-79; dir. pub. liaison N.Y.C. Dept. Ports. and Terminals, 1978-79; sr. pub. affairs officer Citicorp/Citibank, N.Y.C., 1981-84, asst. v.p., 1985-87; v.p. First Atlanta Corp., Atlanta, 1984; sr. mgr. Can. Imperial Bank of Commerce, N.Y.C., 1987—. Pres. 78th Precinct Community Council, Bklyn., 1977-78; com. mem. Community Bd. 6, Bklyn., 1978-80; council mem. So. Regional Council, Atlanta, 1984—; bd. dirs.Atlanta Chamber Players, 1984. Mem. Pub. Relations Soc. Am., Internat. Assn. Bus. Communications, Internat. Pub. Relations Assn., Beta Phi Mu. Democrat. Episcopalian. Club: Jr. League (N.Y.C.). Office: Can Imperial Bank Commerce 237 Park Ave New York NY 10017

GRIFFITH, LINDA MARIE, principal; b. New Bedford, Mass., Jan. 9, 1953; d. George Jesse and Helen Costa (Frias) Morris; m. Thomas Louis Dale Griffith, July 11, 1981. A. in Bus., Golden West Coll., 1974; B.A. in Liberal Studies, Calif. Poly. State U., 1977; M.A. in Ednl. Adminstrn., U. Las Vegas, 1982; EdD in Ednl. Leadership Brigham Young U., 1987. Cert. elem. tchr., adminstr. Tchr. Clark County Sch. Dist., Las Vegas, 1977-79, 80-84, tchr. gifted children, 1979-80, curriculum cons., 1984-85, prin. 1986—; instr. Clark County Community Coll., Las Vegas, 1978-79; mem. Com. for Profl. Standards, Las Vegas, 1984-86. Author handbooks: News to Discuss, 1984; (with others) Crossroads, 1985. Mem. Nev. Women's Polit. Caucus, Las Vegas, 1983-85. Recipient Excellence in Edn. award Clark County Sch. Dist., 1984. Mem. Assn. for Supervision and Curriculum Devel., Internat. Reading Assn., So. Nev. Council of Math., Nat. Council Adminstrn. Women in Edn., Phi Delta Kappa. Republican. Roman Catholic. Avocations: gardening; swimming; cycling; music. Home: 7121 Tempest Pl Las Vegas NV 89128 Office: Clark County Sch Dist 2832 E Flamingo Rd Las Vegas NV 89121

GRIFFITH, LORI ANN, physical therapist; b. Detroit, July 16, 1957; d. Richard Gary and Mary Barbara (Vail) G.; m. Joseph Kurtyka, Nov. 22, 1980 (div. Sept. 1984); B.S., U. Mich., 1979; postgrad., Kennesaw Coll., 1986—. Phys. therapist Lansing Sch. Dist., Mich., 1979-81, Mich. Sch. for Blind, 1980-81, Ingham Med. Ctr., 1980-81; pediatric phys. therapist Toledo Hosp., 1981-84, Childrens Ortho Hosp. and Med. Ctr., Seattle, 1984-85; pediatric clin. specialist Kennestone Hosp., Marietta Ga., 1985—; phys. therapist Am. Home Health Care, 1987—. Mem. Am. Phys. Therapy Assn., Neurodevelopmental Treatment Assn. Avocations: stained glass; furniture refinishing; collection of Oriental art; backpacking; cooking. Home: 113 Misty Hollow Way Woodstock GA 30188 Office: Kennestone Hosp Rehab Dept 677 Church St Marietta GA 30060

GRIFFITH, MARTHA H., controller; b. Brockton, Mass., Sept. 9, 1945; s. Ishmael Hayes and Jettie L. (Dudley) Davis; m. Jack C. Griffith, May 29, 1965 (dec. June 1984); Micheal S., David M. Student, U. Ark., 1960-62; BA, Ball State U., 1967. Prin. Griffith Acctg. Co., Indpls., 1968-70; probate adminstr. Johnson & Weaver, Indpls., 1970-74; personnel adminstr. Hercules Inc., Houston, 1974-76; adminstr. Lapin Totz & Mayer, Houston, 1976-78, Sowell & Ogg, Houston, 1978-80; bus. mgr. Pasadena (Tex.) Citizen, 1980-84; controller Houston Community Newspapers, 1984—. Commr. Houston council Boy Scouts Am., 1983. Recipient Dist. Merit awards Boy Scouts Am., Houston, 1983. Mem. Internat. Newspaper Fin. Execs. (com. mem. 1986-89), Collier Jackson Users Group (moderator 1986-89), Nat. Assn. Female Execs. Democrat. Baptist. Office: Houston Community Newspapers 1136 Sheldon Rd Channelview TX 77530

GRIFFITH, MARY LOUISE KILPATRICK (MRS. EMLYN I. GRIFFITH), civic leader; b. Gadsden, Ala., Mar. 22, 1926; d. Lewis A. and Willie (Reid) Kilpatrick; m. Emlyn I. Griffith, Aug. 13, 1946; children: William L., James R. AB, Huntingdon Coll., 1947. Pres. Evergreen Twig, Rome, N.Y., 1966-67, Rome Home, 1973-75; mem. Rome City Sch. Dist. Bd. Edn., 1967-77; rep. Joint Session on Trade, Investment, and Law, Beijing, 1987, Soviet-Am. Conf. Comparative Edn., Moscow, 1988; trustee Utica (N.Y.) Coll. Found., 1974-80, George Jr. Republic, 1974—, Pub. Broadcasting Council Cen. N.Y., 1977-83, 1st Presbyn. Ch., Rome, 1979-85; bd. dirs. Rome Art and Community Ctr., 1967-72, Rome chpt. Am. Field Service, 1969-77. Recipient Rose for Living award Rotary Club, 1973, Civic award for conspicuous pub. service Colgate U., 1978. Mem. PEO (pres. 1965-66), AAUW, Nat. Soc. Lit. and Arts. Club: Wednesday Morning (Rome) (pres. 1968-70). Home: Golf Course Rd Rome NY 13440

GRIFFITH, REGINA M., financial consultant; b. Camden, N.J., Dec. 8, 1952; d. Lewis Kenneth and Mary Gertrude (Connors) Griffith. A.A., Camden County Coll., 1980; B.A., Glassboro State U., 1982. Paralegal Griffith & Burr, Phila., 1980-82; fin. cons. Cigna, Cherry Hill, N.J., 1983—; investment products coordinator Cigna, 1984—, fin. planner, 1984—. Mem. Nat. Orgn. Securities Dealers, Nat. Assn. Securities Dealeers. Avocations: art; music; poetry. Address: Cigna 1800 Chapel Ave Suite 300 Cherry Hill NJ 08002

GRIFFITHS, MARTHA, lieutenant governor; b. Pierce City, Mo., Jan. 29, 1912; m. Hicks G. Griffiths. B.A., U. Mo.; J.D., U. Mich.; postgrad., Wayne State U. Mem. Mich. Ho. of Reps., 1949-52; judge Recorders Ct., Detroit, 1953; U.S. rep. from Mich. Washington, 1955-75; lt. gov. State of Mich., 1983—; ptnr. Griffiths & Griffiths, Detroit. Democrat. Office: PO Box 407 Romeo MI 48065-0407 *

GRIGGS, DEBRA JANE, realtor; b. Bluefield, W.Va., Nov. 11, 1953; d. Carvel Lee and Ellen Mae (Munsey) G.; m. Gary Stephen Ballard, Dec. 15, 1979. Student, Converse Coll., 1971-72; BA, Radford U., 1974, MA, 1976; student, Vienna Internat. Music Ctr., Austria, 1976-77; postgrad., Memphis State U., 1978-79. Tchr. Sullins Acad., Bristol, Va., 1977-78; various operatic roles Tenn., 1979-81; instr. pvt. voice Delta State U., Cleveland, Miss., 1980-82; dir. music St. George's Episcopal Ch., Clarksdale, Miss., 1981-82; sales assoc. GSH Residential Real Estate, Norfolk, Va., 1983—. Vol. AIDS Housing and Edn., Norfolk; bd. dirs. Tidewater AIDS Crisis Taskforce; provisional mem. Jr. League, Norfolk. Recipient first place Nat. Assn. of Tchrs. of Singing, 1980. Mem. Tidewater Bd. Realtors, Nat. Assn. Realtors, Va. Soc. Profl. Engrs. (pres. Tidewater chpt.). Democrat. Episcopalian. Home: 129 Conway Ave Norfolk VA 23505 Office: GSH Residential Real Estate 4141 Granby St Norfolk VA 23504

GRIGGS, PHYLLIS KAY, fast food chain executive; b. Grand Island, Nebr., Aug. 26, 1937; d. Fritz and Kathryn Rieger; m. Norman E. Griggs, Dec. 31, 1956 (div. 1971); 1 child, Tracy Kay. Grad., Nat. Sch. Bus., 1957. With Corner Constrn. Co., Rapid City, S.D., 1957-71; owner Mister Donut franchises, McAllen, Edinburg, Weslaco, Harlingen and Brownsville, Tex., 1972—; chief exec. officer Ahora Que, Inc., McAllen, 1972—; owner Laundry Basket Laundromat, Weslaco, 1983—, Carousel Laundromat #1, McAllen, 1984—, Carousel Laundromat #2, McAllen, 1986—, Ms. Carol's Dress Store, McAllen, 1984—; mem. adv. council SBA, 1982—. Co-chmn. United Way, 1983; pres. McAllen Boys' Club, 1984—; assoc. mem. Boy's Club of Am.; pres. Am. Heart Assn., 1987-88; mem. Small Bus. Council, Firemen's Pensions Fund Bd., Housing Services Bd., Sr. Citizens Adv. Bd., Humane Soc. Bd., Hidalgo County Elected Officials Assn.; elected commr. City of McAllen, 1986-90. Named Businessperson of Yr. for Tex. SBA, 1983, 5 State Region Businessperson ofYr., 1983. Mem. Orgn. Women Execs., Orgn. Outstanding Businesses (mem. steering com.), McAllen C. of C., Valley C. of C. (merit life mem.). Home: 1700 Fern St McAllen TX 78501 Office: 3616 N 23d #8 McAllen TX 78501

GRIGGS, RUTH MARIE, retired journalism educator, writer, publications consultant; b. Linton, Ind., Aug. 11, 1911; d. Roy Evans Price and Mary Blanche (Hays) P.; m. Paul Philip Griggs, Aug. 4, 1940. BS, Butler U., 1933; postgrad. U. So. Calif., 1938, Northwestern U., 1939; MA, U. Wyo., 1944. Cert. tchr. journalism, English, speech, bus. edn. Travel writer Indpls. Star, 1927-37; summer reporter Worthington Times, Ind., 1928-33; journalism, speech tchr. Warren Central High Sch., Indpls., 1937-37; tchr. bus. edn., journalism Greene Twp. High Sch., South Bend, Ind., 1937-38; tchr. journalism, English, bus. edn. Howe High Sch., Indpls., 1938-46; tchr. journalism Butler U., Indpls., 1946-48, evenings 1972-76; dir. publs. Broad Ripple High Sch., Indpls., 1948-77; summer journalism workshop instr. numerous univs. 1949-80. Author: History of Broad Ripple, 1968; co-author: Handbook for High School Journalism, 1951; Teacher's Guide to High School Journalism, 1965. Dow Jones Newspaper Fund fellow U. Minn., 1967; named Nat. Journalism Tchr. of Yr., Wall Street Jour., 1968, Woman of Achievement, Woman's Press Club of Ind., 1984, Rabb award, 1988. Mem. Journalism Edn. Assn. (v.p., pres. 1963-69, Towley award 1965), Women in Communications (pres. Indpls. 1969-70, Wright award 1969, Kleinhenz award 1978), Nat. Fed. Press Women (youth projects bd. 1979-87), Columbia Scholastic Press Assn. (Gold Key award 1964, Golden Crown 1975, life mem. 1977), Ind. High Sch. Advisers Assn. (pres. 1972, Sengenberger award 1965), AAUW, DAR, Butler Univ. Alumni Bd., Delta Zeta (Ind. Woman of Yr. 1984). Republican. Presbyterian.

GRIGGS, SHIRLEY SAUNDERS, educational administrator; b. Kansas City, Mo., Jan. 11, 1931; d. Robert DeRice Saunders and Anna Van Dalen (Shackelford) Wiseman; m. Carroll C. Griggs, Nov. 16, 1952 (div.). BSc in Edn., Ohio State U., 1967, MA in Edn. Adminstrn., 1969; postgrad., Am. U., 1981-86. Dir. Head Start Program, Mt. Vernon, Ohio, 1968-69; tchr. Mt. Vernon Pub. Schs., 1969-70; prin. Alexandria (Ohio) Elem. and Middle Sch., 1971-74, Perry Middle Sch., Worthington, Ohio, 1975-76; cons. edn. Ohio Dept. Edn., Columbus, 1976-79; specialist edn. U.S. Dept. Edn., Washington, 1979-80, Dept. Def. Dependents Schs., Alexandria, Va., 1980—. Author program guidance manuals. Mem. Assn. Ednl. Communications and Technology, Profl. Women's Orgn., Phi Delta Kappa. Club: Parents without Ptnrs. (McLean, Va.) (bd. dirs. 1985-86). Home: 8350 Greensboro Dr #719 McLean VA 22102 Office: Dept Def Dependents Schs 2461 Eisenhower Alexandria VA 22331-1100

GRILL, PAULA CLARE, fashion designer; b. Chgo., Aug. 22, 1956; d. Frank T. and Rita Ann (Smith) G. Cert. in Fashion Merchandising, Ray Vogue, Chgo., 1975; BA cum laude, Rosary Coll., River Forest, Ill., 1980. Asst. to owner Giggles Boutique, Oak Park, Ill., 1972-73; clerical asst. Robert E. Derby Assocs., Franklin Park, Ill., 1975; mgr. make-up artist Marilyn Mighlin Make-up, Chgo., 1975-76; make-up-artist Cosmetique, Glendale Heights, Ill., 1976-81; pres. designer Paula for St. Andrew, Inc., River Forest, Ill., 1981—. Photgraphs of original designs displayed in Womens Wear Daily. Mem. Rosary Coll. Alumni Network, Chgo. Fashion Guild. Democrat. Roman Catholic. Avocations: painting, reading, skiing. Home and Office: 1500 Lathrop St River Forest IL 60305

GRILLI, JO-ANN, pension administrator; b. Montreal, Que., Can., Mar. 11, 1963; d. Joseph J. and Antoinetta J. (Niosi) G. AS, SUNY, Farmingdale, 1983; BA, Adelphi U., 1987. Pension adminstr. DK Pension Cons., Melville, N.Y., 1985-87, WIA Cons., Inc., Hicksville, N.Y., 1987—. Mem. Nat. Assn. Female Execs. Republican. Home: 489 French Ave North Babylon NY 11703

GRILLS, CAROLINE MARGARET, micropublishing company executive; b. Washington, June 4, 1936; d. Silas Milo and Christine Irene (Donahue) Ransopher; m. Mervyn Joseph Grills, Mar. 27, 1968 (div. Nov. 1974); 1 child, George Glidden. BA cum laude in Radio-TV Prodn. and Directing, Kans. U., 1959; postgrad. UCLA, 1961. Head print prodn. NEA/Assn. Supervision and Curriculum Devel., 1974-76; editor Nat. Micrographics Assn., 1970-71; mgr. microforms and back issues Am. Chem. Soc., Washington, 1976-80; pres. Lasercom Prodns., Balt. and Washington, 1980—; mem. standards bd. color microfilm Nat. Micrographics Assn./Am. Nat. Standards Inst., 1978-81; mem. publs. bd. Internat. Micrographic Congress, 1979-81; del. White House Conf. Library and Info. Services, 1979. Author: Micropublishing in the 80's, 1980; A Buyer's Guide to Videodiscs, 1981; (with others) Micrographics Technology, 1976. Mem. Nat. Micrographics assn. (award), Am. Soc. Info. Sci., Assn. Info. Mgrs., Soc. Photog. Engrs. and Scientists, Am. Chem. Soc., Internat. Info. Mgmt. Congress, Columbia Assn., Wash. Independent Writers. Democrat. Unitarian. Office: Lasercom Prodns 8984 Watchlight Ct Columbia MD 21045

GRIM, PATRICIA ANN, bank executive; b. Everett, Pa., Sept. 7, 1940; d. Harry Grant and Nellie Elizabeth (Koontz) Foor; m. James Woodrow Grim, Feb. 21, 1970. Student, Am. Inst. Banking, Rolling Meadows, Ill., Bank Adminstrn. Inst., The Bus. Women's Tng. Inst. Sec. William H. Snyder, Atty. at Law, Bedford, Pa., 1958-60; sec., loan teller First Nat. Bank of Everett, Pa., 1960-70; teller Orrstown (Pa.) Bank, 1970-81, asst. cashier, asst. sec., 1981-82, v.p., asst. sec., 1982—. Recipient Family Tng. Hour Leader of Yr. award Ch. of God State of Pa., Lyaman of Yr. award, 1979; nat. nominee Layperson of Yr., 1984. Mem. Ch. of God. Office: Orrstown Bank 3580 Orrstown Rd PO Box 60 Orrstown PA 17244-0060

GRIMES, BARBARA LAURITZEN, state legislator; b. Burlington, Vt., Nov. 14, 1945; d. L. Bruce and Elizabeth (Gurney) Lauritzen; m. James G. Grimes III; children: James, Adam. Mem. Vt. Ho. of Reps. Mem. Am. Legis. Exchange Council. Democrat. Episcopalian. Address: 733 North Ave Burlington VT 05401

GRIMES, MARTHA, author; b. Pittsburgh, Pa.; d. D.W. and June (Dunnington) G.; div.; 1 s.: Kent Van Holland. BA, MA, U. Md. Formerly instr. English U. Iowa, Iowa City; asst. prof. Frostburg State Coll., Frostburg, Md.; prof. Montgomery Coll., Takoma Park, Md., from 1970. Author: mystery novels The Man With a Load of Mischief, 1981, The Old Fox Deceiv'd, 1982, The Anodyne Necklace (Nero Wolfe Award for best mystery of yr.), 1983, The Dirty Duck, 1984, The Jerusalem Inn, 1984, Help the Poor Struggler, 1985, The Deer Leap, 1985, I Am the Only Running Footman, 1986, The Five Bells and Bladebone, 1987. Address: care Little Brown & Co 34 Beacon St Boston MA 02106 *

GRIMES, MARY ANNE, nurse; b. Kansas City, Kans., June 19, 1936; d. John Andy and Bertha Helen (Ball) G. R.N., St. Joseph's Hosp. Staff nurse St. Joseph's Hosp., Phoenix, 1957-61; office nurse Family Med. Clinic, Phoenix, 1961-62; pvt. duty nurse Central Registery, Phoenix, 1962-65; office nurse, mgr. Phoenix Urologic Clinic, 1965-79; sch. nurse Wilson Sch. Dist. 7, Phoenix, 1980-84, Balsz Sch. Dist. #31, 1984—. Primary fund raiser Classical Chorus Bach and Madrigal Soc., also sec., bd. dirs.; campaign worker Republican gubernatorial election, Phoenix, 1968, 70. Mem. Am. Bus. Women's Assn. (pres. 1974-75). Republican. Roman Catholic. Home: 1805 N 21st Pl Phoenix AZ 85006 Office: Balsz Sch Dist 31 4309 E Belleview Phoenix AZ 85008

GRIMES, RUTH ELAINE, city planner; b. Palo Alto, Calif., Mar. 4, 1949; d. Herbert George and Irene (Williams) Baker; m. Charles A. Grimes, July 19, 1969 (div. 1981); 1 child, Michael; m. Roger L. Sharpe, Mar. 20, 1984; 1 child, Teresa. AB summa cum laude, U. Calif.-Berkeley, 1970, M in City Planning, 1972. Research and evaluation coordinator Ctr. Ind. Living, Berkeley, 1972-74; planner City of Berkeley, 1974-76, sr. planner, 1983—, analyst, 1976-83; pres. Vets. Assistance Ctr., Berkeley, 1978—, also bd. dirs.; treas. Berkeley Design Advs., 1987—, also bd. dirs.; bd. dirs. Ctr. Ind. Living. Author: Berkeley Downtown Plan, 1988; contbr. numerous articles to profl. jours. and other publs. Edwin Frank Kraft scholar, 1966. Mem. Am. Planning Assn., Am. Soc. Pub. Adminstrn., Mensa, Phi Beta Kappa. Club: Lake Merritt Joggers and Striders (sec. 1986—). Home: 1330 Bonita Ave Berkeley CA 94709 Office: City of Berkeley 2180 Milvia St Berkeley CA 94704

GRIMM, KATHLEEN, lawyer; b. Troy, N.Y., Mar. 21, 1946; d. Frederick Henry and Helen (Johnson) G. B.A., Manhattanville Coll., 1967; J.D. cum laude, N.Y. Law Sch., 1980; LL.M. in Taxation, NYU, 1984. Bar: N.Y. 1981. Tchr., Colegio de Vera Cruz, Cd. Obregon, Son., Mex., 1967-68; social worker, adminstr. Menorah Home & Hosp., Bklyn., 1969-78; atty. U.S. Dept. Treasury, IRS, N.Y.C., 1981-83; assoc. Parker, Duryee, Zunino, Malone & Carter, N.Y.C., 1983-85, 1st dep. commr., N.Y.C. Dept. Fin., 1988—; dep. commr. audit and enforcement N.Y.C. Dept. Fin., 1985-88. Research coordinator casebook: Law, Medicine & Forensic Science, 1980. Mem. ABA, N.Y. State Bar Assn., Assn. Bar City of N.Y., N.Y. Law Sch. Alumni Assn. (bd. dirs.), Manhattanville Alumni Assn. (bd. dirs.). Roman Catholic. Club: Manhattanville of N.Y. (past pres.). Home: 333 E 69th St New York NY 10021 Office: NYC Dept Finance 1 Centre St New York NY 10007

GRIMMER, MARGOT, dancer, choreographer, director; b. Chgo., Apr. 5, 1944; d. Vernon and Ann (Radville) G.; m. Weymouth Kirkland; 1 child, Ashley Samantha Grimmer Kirkland; student Lake Forest; 1963, Northwestern U., 1964-68. Dancer, N.Y.C. Ballet prodn. of Nutcracker Chgo., 1956-57, Kansas City Starlight Theatre, 1958, St. Louis Mcpl. Theatre, 1959, Chgo. TentHouse-Music Theater, 1960-61, Lyric Opera Ballet, Chgo., 1961, 63-66, 68, Ballet Russe de Monte Carlo, N.Y.C., 1962, Ruth Page Internat. Ballet, Chgo., 1965-70; dancer-choreographer Am. Dance Co., Chgo., 1972—, artistic dir., 1972—; dancer, choreographer Bob Hope Show, Milw., 1975, Washington Bicentennial Performance, Kennedy Center, 1976, Woody Guthrie Benefit Concerts, 1976-77, Assyrian Cultural Found., Chgo., 1977-78, Iranian Consulate Performance, Chgo., 1978, Israeli Consulate Concert, Chgo., 1980 Chgo. Council Fine Arts Programs, 1978—, U.S. Boating Indsl. Show, 1981—; dir.-tchr. Am. Dance Sch., 1971—; tchr. master classes U. Ill, 1975, 83, Anderson Hall, Sebastapol Community Ctr., Calif., 1988; appeared in TV commls. and indsl. films for Libbys Foods, Sears, Gen. Motors, others, 1963—, also in feature film Risky Business, 1982; soloist in ballet Repertory Workshop, CBS-TV, 1964, dance film Statics (Internat. Film award), 1967; soloist in concert Ravinia, 1973; important works include ballets In-A-Gadda-Da-Vida, 1972, The Waste Land, 1973, Rachmaninoff: Theme and Variations, 1973, Le Baiser de la Fee and Sonata, 1974, Four Quartets, 1974, Am. Export, 1975, Earth, Wind and Fire, 1976, Blood, Sand and Empire, 1977, Disco Fever, 1978, Pax Romana, Xanadu, 1979, Ishmael, 1980, Vertigo, 1982, Eye in the Sky, 1984, Frankie Goes to Hollywood, 1986, Power House Africano, 1987, others; dance critic Mail-Advertiser Pubis., 1980-82; host cable TV show Spotlight, 1984-85, View-points, 1987. Ill. Arts Council Grantee, 1973-74; Nat. Endowment Arts grantee, 1973-74. Mem. Actors Equity Assn., Screen Actors Guild, Am. Guild Mus. Artists. Home: 970 Vernon Ave Glencoe IL 60022 Office: 442 Central Ave Highland Park IL 60035

GRINBERG, LINDA GWEN, film librarian; b. Los Angeles, May 26, 1951; d. Sherman and Edna (Tract) G. BA in English, Calif. State U., Northridge, 1973. Freelance paralegal 1973-75; chmn., chief exec. officer Sherman Grinberg Film Libraries, Inc., Hollywood, Calif., 1975— Mem. Women in Film, Internat Documentary Assn. (treas., bd. dirs. Los Angeles 1984-87). Democrat. Office: Sherman Grinberg Film Libraries 1040 N McCadden Place Hollywood CA 90038

GRINWIS, MARILYN FLORENCE, educator; b. Paterson, N.J., July 3, 1927; d. John and Florence May (Abert) G. BS in Edn., Trenton (N.J.) State Coll., 1948; MA, NYU, 1968. Cert. elem. tchr., N.J.; cert. music tchr., N.Y. Tchr. kindergarten Ctr. Sch., Bloomfield, N.J., 1948-54; tchr. music Bloomfield Pub. Schs., 1948, Travell Sch., Ridgewood, N.J., 1954-82, Future Musicians, Inc., Cranford, N.J., 1985-88, St. John's Sch., Bergenfield, N.J., 1985-88, St. Catharine Sch., Glen Rock, N.J., 1986—, Ch. of the Nativity Sch., Midland Park, N.J., 1988—; ins. agt. John Hancock Mut. Life Ins. Co., Mut. of Omaha, 1983-84. Contbr. articles to newspapers. Dir. children's music Ridgewood Meth. Ch., 1964-70, 1st Presbyn. Ch., 1970-72; pres. Ch. Women's Guild. Mem. Delta Kappa Gamma, Sigma Alpha Iota. Club: Wyckoff Women's (music and drama chmn., treas.). Home: 383 Sunset Blvd Wyckoff NJ 07481

GRISE, WILMA MARIE, small business owner; b. Kingfisher, Okla., Sept. 4, 1937; d. William and Martha (Brandt) Krittenbrink; m. Paul Grise, Aug. 23, 1956 (div. May 1962); children: Mary Monica MacMartin, Marti Gile. Founder, owner Wichita (Kans.) Auto Auction, 1966—. Democrat. Roman Catholic. Home: 4635 S Broadway Wichita KS 67216 Office: Wichita Auto Auction 3820 S Broadway Wichita KS 67216

GRISEUK, GAIL GENTRY, financial consultant; b. Providence, Jan. 24, 1948; d. Marvin Houghton and Gertrude Emma (Feather) Gentry; m. Steven Paul Griseuk, Oct. 20, 1979; 1 child, Christina Deborah. Student (Fla. Power Corp. scholar), Fla. State U., 1966-70. Registry of Fin. Planning Practitioners. Cert. fin. ops. prin.; cert. gen. securities prin.; registered investment advisor. Asst. div. controller Mobile Home Industries, Tallahassee, 1968-70; owner, mgr. BDI Services, Tallahassee and Lake Charles, La., 1970-78; fin. cons. Aylesworth Fin., Inc., Clearwater, Fla., 1978-82; chmn. bd., chief exec. officer Griseuk Assocs. Inc., 1982—; chief exec. officer GAI Internat. Investment Advisors, Inc., 1985—; instr., dir. vet. outreach Angelina Coll., Lufkin, Tex., 1975-76. Contbr. short stories to Redbook, McCall's, Christian Home. Vol., Sunland Tng. Center, 1970-72, George Criswell House, 1969-73. Mem. Inst. Cert. Fin. Planners, Internat. Platform Assn., Internat. Assn. Fin. Planners. Methodist. Home: 1024 Woodcrest Ave Clearwater FL 33516 Office: 5301 Central Ave Saint Petersburg FL 33710

GRISHAM, EDITH PEARL MOLES, librarian; b. Pinch, W.Va., Mar. 27, 1926; d. Edward Lawrence and Effie (Christy) Moles; m. Charles M. Grisham (div.). A.A., San Antonio Coll., 1958; B.B.A. cum laude, St. Mary's U., 1961; postgrad. Our Lady of the Lake, San Antonio, 1964; M.L.S., Tex. Woman's U., 1973. Billing, sales service asst. Uvalde Rock Asphalt Co., San Antonio, Tex., 1953-62; office mgr. Data Processing Ctr., Inc., San Antonio, 1962-64; serials librarian Houston Pub. Library, 1964-65, head lit. biography dept., 1966-68, head bus. and tech. dept., 1968-73; head Tech. Library Brown & Root, Inc., Houston, 1973-83; reference librarian Incarnate Word Coll., 1984—. Editor, compiler: Union List of Engineering Standards, Specifications, and Codes in Selected Texas Libraries, 1978. Served sgt. USAAF and USAF, 1944-53. Mem. Spl. Libraries Assn., Kappa Pi Sigma, Alpha Beta Alpha. Democrat. Lutheran.

GRISHAM, SANDRA ANN, judge; b. Washington, Sept. 14, 1949; d. Wilber Glenn and Wyndoleen (McCarty) G.; m. Ronald Paul Ratkevich, Sept. 14, 1974 (div. 1982); m. 2d, Wayne Allen Jordon, June 4, 1983; 1 child, Addie Brieanne Jordon. B.A. in Polit. Sci., U. N.Mex., 1970, J.D., 1973. Bar: N.Mex., U.S. Dist. Ct. N.Mex., U.S. Ct. Appeals (10th cir.), U.S. Supreme Ct. Spl. asst. dist. atty. Bernalillo County, Albuquerque, 1973-77; sole practice, Albuquerque, 1973-78; mem. Durrett, Jordon & Grisham, P.C., Alamogordo, N.Mex., 1979-84; dist. judge State of N.Mex. 12th Jud. Dist., 1985—; state chair N.Mex. Council on Crime and Delinquency, 1987-88; bd. dirs. Otero County CHINS (Children in Need of Services), 1987—; steering com. mem. Regional Resource Ctr. for Child Abuse and Neglect, Austin, Tex., 1979-82; chmn. Alamogordo City Charter Commn., 1982-83, Mayor's Com. on Alcoholism and Driving While Intoxicated, Alamogordo, 1983-84; mem. Youth Authority Commn., 1988—. Williston research fellow, 1972-73. Mem. ABA, N.Mex. Bar Assn. (task force on women and the profession 1988—), N.Mex. Trial Lawyers Assn., Otero County Bar Assn, N.Mex. Dist. Judge's Assn. (bd. dirs. 1988—). Republican. Club: Arabian Horse Assn. N.Mex. (dir. 1978). Office: Dist Ct Div 1 PO Box 687 Alamogordo NM 88310

GRISI, JEANMARIE CONTE, finance executive; b. Queens, Sept. 10, 1958; d. Salvatore A. and Rose Marie (Russo) Conte; m. Diodato F. Grisi, Mar. 5, 1983; 1 child, Thomas. BS, St. John's U., 1980. CPA, N.Y. Asst. sr. auditor Peat Marwick Mitchell, N.Y.C., 1980-83; gen. acctg. mgr. N.Y. Pub. Library, 1983-84; controller, asst. and assoc. treas. Carnegie Corp. N.Y., N.Y.C., 1984—. Mem. Am. Inst. CPA's. Roman Catholic. Home: 21 Sarah Dr Hauppauge NY 11788 Office: Carnegie Corp NY 437 Madison Ave New York NY 10022

GRISKEY, PAULINE BECKER, educator, researcher; b. Pitts., Oct. 30, 1933; d. William and Dorothy (Dzienis) Becker; m. Richard G. Griskey, June 11, 1955; children—Paula Louise, David Richard. B.S., Duquesne U., 1955; M.S., Radford U., 1966; ED.D., Nova U., 1985; postgrad. U. Denver, U. Del., Carnegie Mellon U. Tchr. Pitts. Pub. Schs., 1955-58; concertmistress Eastern Shore Symphony, Salisbury, Md., 1958-60; tchr. Blacksburg High Sch., Va., 1962-66; lectr. Arapahoe Jr. Coll., Littleton, Colo., 1966-68; head English dept. Mt. Pleasant High Sch., Livingston, N.J., 1968-71; acting dir., coordinator, lectr., researcher dept. learning skills U. Wis.-Milw., 1971—; reviewer Houghton, Mifflin, Boston, 1983—, Holt, Rhinehart Winston, N.Y.C., 1982—; adj. prof. Milw. Area Tech. Coll., 1981—. Author: Critical Reading, 1978; Speed Reading, 1982; editor Effective Study Strategies, 1978. Solicitor, Pub. TV Fund Raising, Milw., 1981, March of Dime, Milw., 1980, Univ. Sch. Milw., 1978-79. Recipient Outstanding Achievement award U. Wis.-Milw., 1975, Disting. Service award, 1980; U. Wis. System Minority Disadvantaged grantee, 1977; HEW fellow, 1964-66. Mem. Coll. Reading Assn., Western Reading Assn., Internat. Reading Assn., Adult Edn. Assn., MLA. Office: U Wis Dept Learning Skills PO Box 413 Milwaukee WI 53201

GRIVNA, MARY ALLENE, management services officer; b. Dexter, Minn., Sept. 30, 1942; d. Kenneth Ray and Lois Lorene (Schiefelbein) Coleman; student Des Moines Area Community Coll., 1975-78, Am. River Coll., 1984—; m. Donald Lee Grivna, Aug. 5, 1961; children—Mark Allen, Ellen Kay. Sec. dept. vet. physiology and pharmacology Iowa State U., Ames, 1972-77, adminstrv. asst. dept. biochemistry and biophysics, 1977-81; adminstrv. asst. dean's office Sch. Law, U. Calif.-Davis, 1982-85, mgmt. services officer, 1985—. Mem. Nat. Assn. Female Execs., Am. Bus. Women's Assn. Democrat. Lutheran. Home: 2600 Del Mar Ave Penryn CA 95663 Office: U Calif 1011 King Hall Davis CA 95616

GRIZZLE, MARY R., state senator; b. Lawrence County, Ohio, Aug. 19, 1921; ed. Portsmouth Interstate Bus. Coll.; m. Ben F. Grizzle (dec.); children—Henry, Polley, Lorena, Mary Alice, Betty, Jeanne; m. Charles H. Pearson. Mem. Fla. Ho. of Reps., 1963-78; mem. Fla. Senate, 1978—, chmn. Exec. Bus. Com., vice chmn. Natural Resources and Conservation Com., Appropriations Com. Past chmn. Fla. Commn. on Status of Women; govt. rep. Nat. Conf. Women Community Leaders for Hwy. Safety; active P.T.A.; mem. Pinellas County (Fla.) Civil Service Com., Pinellas County Planning Com. Former town commr.; past pres. Women's Rep. Com. Named One of Ten Outstanding Women, St. Petersburg Times, 1966; recipient Achievement award Fla. Rehab. Assn., 1979; hon. life mem. Pinellas County Sch. Food Services, 1979; Largo Jr. Women's Club Woman of Year, 1980. Mem. League Women Voters, Largo Bus. and Profl. Womens Club, Altrusa, Woman's Club, Nat. Soc. Arts and Letters, Delta Kappa Gamma (hon. Alpha Phi chpt.). Episcopalian. Author: (with others) Thimbleful of History. Office: 2601 Jewel Rd Suite C Belleair Bluffs FL 34640

GROAH, LINDA KAY, nursing administrator and educator; b. Cedar Rapids, Iowa, Oct. 5, 1942; d. Joseph David and Irma Josephine (Zitek) Rozek; diploma St. Luke's Sch. Nursing, Cedar Rapids, 1963; student San Francisco City Coll., 1976 77; BA, St. Mary's Coll., Moraga, Calif., 1978; BS in Nursing, Calif. State U.; m. Patrick Andrew Groah, Mar. 20, 1975; 1 dau., Kimberly; stepchildren: Nadine, Maureen, Patrick, Marcus. Staff nurse to head nurse U. Iowa, 1963-67; clin. supr., dir. operating and recovery room Michael Reese Hosp., Chgo., 1967-73; dir. operating rooms Med. Center Central Ga., Macon, 1973-74; dir. operating and recovery rooms U. Calif. Hosps. and Clinics, San Francisco, 1974-82, asst. dir. hosps. and clinics, 1982-86; clin. instr. U. Calif. Sch. Nursing, San Francisco, 1975—; cons. to operating room suprs., to dir. ednl. resources and programs Assn. Am. Med. Colls., 1976—; condr. seminars. Mem. Nat. League for Nurses, Am. Nurses Assn. (vice chmn. operating room conf. group 1974-76), Assn. Operating Room Nurses (com. on nominations 1979-84, treas. 1985-87, Award for Excellence in Preoperative Nursing 1989), Center for Study Dem. Instns. Author: Perioperative Nursing Practice, 1983; contbr. articles on operating room techniques to profl. jours. and textbooks; author, producer audio-visual presentations; author computer software. Home: 5 Mateo Dr Tiburon CA 94920 Office: M423B 3d and Parnassus Sts San Francisco CA 94143

GROBELNY, LORI JO-ANN, manufacturing executive; b. New Brunswick, N.J., June 14, 1954; d. Stanley Joseph and Rose Marie (Toth) G. BA, Douglass Coll., 1976. Mgr. prod. N.Am. Container Corp., North Brunswick, N.J., 1976—, adminstrv. asst. to pres.; bd. dirs. Indsl. Capital Corp., Lawrenceville, Housing Capital Corp., New Hyde Park. Mem. Nat. Rep. Com. Mem. Douglass Coll. Alumnae Assn. Roman Catholic. Club: Douglass Coll. Alumnae Assn. Home: 1 Apple St Edison NJ 08817 Office: N Am Container Corp 501 Finnegans Ln North Brunswick NJ 08902

GRODE, RYKANDA DAWN (KANDY), business analyst; b. Detroit, Mar. 14, 1957; d. Gerald Henry and Nadine Gayle (Clifford) G. Student Schoolcraft Coll., 1977, Internat. Corr. Schs. Ctr. Degree Studies, 1982-84. Bookkeeping mgr. Hall Real Estate Group, Southfield, Mich., 1977-80; head acctg. clk. Edward Rose & Sons, Southfield, 1981; sr. acctg. supr. Mode O'Day, Burbank, Calif., 1981-84; bus. user analyst, acctg. specialist Cardkey Systems, Chatsworth, Calif., 1984-86; bus. analyst installing human resource package Hamilton/Avnet, Culver City, Calif., 1987—; cons.; owner, mgr. Kandy's Kounting Service, Tujunga, Calif., 1985—. Mem. Nat. Assn. Female Execs. Republican. Baptist. Avocations: cross-stitch, embroidery, bowling. Home and Office: 8335 Grenoble #30 Sunland CA 91040

GRODECKI, SISTER MARY REGINELLA, nun, health science facility administrator; b. Chgo., Nov. 7, 1912; d. Valentine and Victoria (Bochenek) G. Diploma in Nursing, St. Mary of Nazareth Hosp., Chgo., 1941; BS, DePaul U., 1946. Entered Sisters of Holy Family of Nazareth order, Roman Cath. Ch., 1932; RN, cert. nurse anesthetist, Ill., Tex. Nurse anesthetist, dir. Sch. Anesthesia St. Mary of Nazareth Hosp., 1941-57, adminstr., 1957-59, superior, 1959-62; vice-provincial supr. Sisters of Holy Family of Nazareth, Grand Prairie, Tex., 1962-74; adminstr. Bethania Regional Health Care Ctr., Wichita Falls, Tex., 1974-87, pres. found bd. and devel., 1987—; chmn. bd. trustees Bethania Regional Health Care Ctr., 1962-74, v.p., 1974—, bd. dirs.; chmn. bd. trustees Mother Frances Hosp., Tyler, Tex., 1962-74, bd. dirs.; mem. bd. trustees Tex. Conf. of Cath. Healthcare Facilities, 1981; ex-officio del. Sisters of Holy Family of Nazareth gen. chpt. 1966, 69, 71, elected del., 1977; mem. nominating com., sec.-treas. Chgo. Archdiocesan Conf. Cath. Hosps.; presenter, speaker in field. Contbr. articles to profl. jours. Recipient Citation award Am. Hosp. Assn., Chgo., 1950, Plaque and Recognition awards Women's Hall of Fame of North Tex., Wichita Falls, 1986. Home and Office: Bethania Regional Health Care Ctr 1600 11th St Wichita Falls TX 76301

GRODER, JUDITH REILLY, health sciences administrator; b. Jersey City, N.J., Aug. 14, 1938; d. Charles William Reilly and Helen (Decker) Tucker; m. Roland Edward Groder, Sept. 2, 1965; children: Charles William, Jill Ellen, Karen Emily. Grad., Sch. Nursing Buffalo Gen. Hosp., 1960; BS in Nursing, U. Buffalo, 1965. RN. Head nurse Buffalo State Hosp., 1960-65; nurse Am. Export Isbrandtsen Shipping Lines, 1965; instr. psychiat. nursing Augusta (Maine) State Hosp.; instr. Lamaze Maine, 1970-75; head nurse labor and delivery Parkview Meml. Hosp., Brunswick, Maine, 1973-75; clin. instr. psychiatry Brookdale Community Coll., Lincroft, N.J., 1980-81; owner, pres. All Health Care Services, Inc., Middletown, N.J., 1983—; apptd. participant Women in Health Care Trade Mission, Japan, 1986; cons. home health care. Mem. Nat. Assn. for Home Care, Assn. Home Care Profls., Home Health Agy. Assembly N.J., Am. Soc. for Psychoprophylaxis in Obstetrics, Home Health Services and Staffing Assn. N.J., N.J. Assn. Women Bus. Owners (pres. 1988), U. Buffalo Gen. Hosp. Alumnae Assn. Republican. Episcopalian. Office: All Health Care Services Inc Penelope Ln Middletown NJ 07748

GROEN, ELAINE SHARON, nutritionist, educator; b. Artesia, Calif., Feb. 28, 1944; d. Gradus Albert and Margaret (Toering) Vander Broek; m. Glenn Verlin Groen, Apr. 9, 1965 (div. 1975); 1 child, Melanie Marie. BA cum laude, Calif. State U., Long Beach, 1970. Pvt. practice cons. dietitian Laguna Beach, Calif., 1971-72; dietitian, asst. food service mgr. South Coast Community Hosp., Laguna Beach, 1972-74; sales rep. Mead Johnson div. Bristol-Myers, Orange County, Calif., 1974-75; specialist nutrition sales Mead Johnson div. Bristol-Myers, So. Calif., 1975-77; sales trainer Mead Johnson div. Bristol-Myers, Evansville, Ind., 1977-79; regional cons. dietitian Mead Johnson div. Bristol-Myers, Western U.S.A., 1979-80; pvt. practice cons. nutritionist Walnut Creek, Calif., 1980—. Author: Healthy Cooking on the Run, 1983; co-author (newspaper column) Successfully Slim, 1981-86. Recipient Betty Crocker award Gen. Mills., 1969. Mem. AAUW (chmn. network women groups 1986—), Am. Dietetic Assn. (registered dietitian), Calif. Dietetic Assn. (chmn. legislation, info. and pub. policy 1980—, third party reimbursement taskforce cons. nutritionists 1984—, nutrition services payment system 1986-87), Bay Area Speakers Service, Nat. Assn. Female Execs., Nat. Council Against Health Fraud, Omicron Nu, Phi Kappa Phi. Democrat. Office: Relationship Counseling Ctr 33 Quail Ct Suite 201 Walnut Creek CA 94596

GROESBECK, ELISE DE BRANGES DE BOURICA, artist; b. Versailles, France, Jan. 31, 1936 (parents Am. citizens); d. Vicount Louis de Branges de Bourcia II and Diane (McDonald) de Branges de Bourcia; student Phila. Coll. Art, 1954-55; m. James Richard Groesbeck, Oct. 3, 1958 (div. June 1969); children: Gretchen Atlee, Genevieve de Branges. One-man shows The Agnes Irwin Sch., Rosemont, Pa., 1973, Phila. Cricket Club, Chestnut Hill, Pa., 1973. Recipient prize Rehoboth Beach Art League, 1944; Agnes Allen Art prize Agnes Irwin Sch., 1954. Repubican. Episcopalian. Home: 3204 Leigh Rd Pompano Beach FL 33062 Office: Box 58 Pompano Beach FL 33061

GROFF, JANET YVONNE, physician, educator; b. Arkadelphia, Ark., July 24, 1954; d. Marion Allen and Betty Joyce (Deaton) G. BA, So. Ill. U., Edwardville, 1976; MD, U. Tex., Galveston, 1980; MSPH, U. Mo., 1986. Diplomate Am. Bd. Family Practice. Intern, resident physician dept. family and community medicine U. Mo. Hosp., Columbia, 1980-83; med. dir. substance abuse unit Mid.-Mo. Mental Health Ctr., Columbia, 1983-84; asst. prof. dept. family medicine U. Tex. Med. Br., Galveston, 1986—, residency program dir., 1987—. Robert Wood Johnson Fellow U. Mo. Sch. Medicine, 1984-86. Mem. Am. Acad. Family Practice, Am. Pub. Health Assn., Tex. Acad. Family Practice, Alpha Omega Alpha. Office: U Tex Med Br Dept Family Medicine 415 Texas Ave Galveston TX 77550

GROFF, JOANN, state legislator, banker; b. Ft. Leonardwood, Mo., Oct. 10, 1956; d. Barry T. Groff and Ann (Ferry) Ragsdale. Student Georgetown U., 1974-76; B.S. in Bus. Adminstrn., Babson Coll., Wellesley, Mass., 1978. Office mgr. Morgan Smith for Congress, Northglenn, Colo., 1978; fair and rodeo asst. Adams County Commrs., Brighton, Colo., 1979; mktg. devel. officer Columbine Title Co., Lakewood, Colo., 1979-80; express agt., loan officer Wells Fargo Credit Corp., Englewood, Colo., 1981-84; pub. banking rep. Cen. Bank of Denver, 1985—; mem. Colo. Ho. of Reps., Denver, 1983—, mem. audit com., fin. com. Mem. Colo. State Democratic Com., 1980—, Colo. State Exec. Com., 1983—, del. Nat. Conv., 1980, 84, alternate del., 1976. Bd. dirs. Westminster (Colo.) Community Artist Series, Marycrest High Sch., Colo. Food Bank Coalition. Mem. Met. North C. of C. Roman Catholic. Office: State of Colo State Capitol Denver CO 80203

GROFT, JAN AGNEW, advertising executive, writer; b. Pitts., Jan. 18, 1951; d. Michael A. and Josephine C. (Trangate) Coco; m. Bryant L. Agnew, May 29, 1971 (div. June, 1979); 1 child, Darcy J.; m. Randy L. Groft, Nov. 14, 1987. B.A. in English, Dickinson Coll., 1971. Health careers coordinator, Pa. Health Council, Camp Hill, 1971-72 copy expeditor, correspondent Lancaster Newspapers, Pa., 1973-74; copywriter Kelly Advt., Lancaster, 1974-78; promotion supr. Armstrong World Industries, Lancaster, 1978-80; founder, pres., creative dir. Agnew & Corrigan Advt., (formerly J.J. Agnew & Co., Inc.), Lancaster, 1980—, chmn. bd. dirs., 1980—. Creative dir. and writer for numerous award-winning print and broadcasting advt. campaigns. Bd. dirs. BizPAC, polit. action com., Lancaster, Pa., 1984-85; vol. instr. Sch. dist. of Lancaster, writing connection program, 1985, cons.; mem. mktg. task force com. Easter Seal, 1986-87; bd. dirs. Sta. WITF-TV/FM Radio, 1986—. Recipient Woman of Yr. award, Am. Bus. Women's Assn., 1979. Mem. Am. Advt. Fedn., (2nd Dist. Addy Awards 1982, 84, 85, 86, 87), Central Pa. Advt. Fedn. (bd. dirs. 1986-87, Addy awards 1982, 83, 84, 85, 86, 87). Lancaster Advt. Club (bd. mem. 1983-84). Democrat. Episcopalian. Avocations: writing, piano, reading, classical music, interior design. Office: Agnew & Corrigan 131 E Grant St Lancaster PA 17602

GROFT, MARY LARUE, corporate information coordinator; b. Russellville, Ky., Sept. 4, 1947; d. Sam and Mary (Mackey) Pillow; m. Steven D. Groft, May 10, 1968 (div. 1971); 1 child, André LaRue. BA, Bellarmine Coll., Louisville, 1971; MLS, Spalding U., 1977. Librarian Community Action Agy., Louisville, 1977-78; supr. info. and research Peat Marwick Main & Co., Chgo., 1978—. Mem. Am. Soc. Info. Scientists, Spl. Library Assn. (div. hospitality chair 1985). Democrat. Roman Catholic. Office: Peat Marwick Main & Co 303 E Wacker Dr Chicago IL 60601

GROGAN, BETTE LOWERY, wholesale steel fastener distribution company executive; b. Seminole, Okla., Nov. 18, 1931; d. C.J. and Martha C. (Eakin) Lowery; m. Morris Rowell, Feb. 8, 1947 (div. Oct. 1960); children—Ronald Michael, Kathy D. Rowell Burkard; m. John Kenneth Grogan, Oct. 28, 1967. Student Del Mar Coll., 1949-51, So. Meth. U., 1963-65. Sec., office mgr. Carrigan Realty, Orlando, Fla., 1958-61; dist. sec. Tektronics, Inc., Orlando, 1961-63; legal sec. Jenkens, Anson, Spradley & Gilchrist, Dallas, 1963-67; real estate broker, Dallas, 1967-77; v.p. Grogan & Co., Dallas, 1972-77; pres. Fla. Threaded Products Inc., Orlando, 1977—; dir. Women's Bus. Ednl. Council (pres. 1986, chmn. bd. 1987), Inc., Orlando, pres., 1986. Mem. Planning and Zoning Commn., Carrollton, Tex., 1972-74; bd. dirs. Jr. Achievement, Orlando, 1981-83. Named Cen. Fla. Small Bus. Person of the Yr., SBA-C. of C., 1981. Mem. Women's Bus. Ednl. Confs. Fla. (bd. dirs. 1984-85, exec. v.p. 1985-86, pres. 1986, chmn. bd. dirs. 1987), Nat. Fedn. Ind. Bus. (guardian adv. council), Fastener Assn. (bd. dirs. 1980-84), Central Fla. Leadership Council (bd. dirs. 1984—), C. of C. Orlando, Nat. Fedn. Ind. Businesses (Guardian Adv. Council Fla. 1987), Fla. Exec. Women, Better Bus. Bur. Central Fla. (bd. dirs., mem. exec. com., chmn.-elect 1988), Beta Sigma Phi (pres. Orlando 1957-59). Republican. Episcopalian. Avocations: tennis; golf; reading. Office: Fla Threaded Products Inc 3060 Clemson Rd Orlando FL 32808

GROGAN, PATRICIA JO, psychiatry resident; b. Buffalo, July 5, 1954; d. Joseph William and Martha Ann (Bliss) G. AS, Empire State Coll.; student, SUNY, Buffalo; MD, SUNY, Bklyn. Intern in internal medicine U. Conn. Health Ctr., Farmington, 1985-86; psychiatry resident Emergency Physicians, Inc., Longmeadow, Mass., 1986-87, U. Calif. at San Diego, La Jolla, 1987—; cons. to Mother Theresa Missionaries of Charity, Calcutta, India, 1982, Rosebud Indian Reservation, S.D. contbr. articles to profl. jours. Vol. firefighter, ambulance aid Harris Hills Fire Co., Williamsville, N.Y., 1980-82. Home: 4885 Kane Rd San Diego CA 92110

GRONEMEYER, SUZANNE ALSOP, medical physicist; b. Tulsa, July 29, 1941; d. Thomas M. and Alberta (Hubbard) Alsop; m. Lee Gronemeyer, Nov. 1966 (div. 1975); m. Larry Kent Revelle, Jan. 14, 1987. BA in Chemistry, Washington U., 1964, MA in Chemistry, 1967, PhD in Physics, 1979. Instr. of physics U. Mo., St. Louis, 1968-74; profl. asst. NSF, Washington, 1975-76; sr. research aide Argonne (Ill.) Nat. Lab., 1977-79; postdoctoral research fellow Mass. Gen. Hosp., Boston, 1979-80; engring. physicist Fermi Nat. Accelerator Lab., Batavia, Ill., 1980-83; applications scientist Siemens Med. Systems, St. Louis. Contbr. articles and papers to profl. jours. Mem. Soc. for Magnetic Resonance in Medicine, Soc. for Magnetic Resonance Imaging, Am. Assn. Physicists in Medicine, Am.

Physical Soc. Home: 7228 Chamberlain Saint Louis MO 63130 Office: Siemens Med Systems 1906 Craigshire Saint Louis MO 63146

GRONER, BEVERLY ANNE, lawyer; b. Des Moines, Jan. 31, 1922; d. Benjamin L. and Annabelle (Miller) Zavat; m. Jack Davis, Dec. 31, 1940; children—Morrilou Davis Morell, Lewis A. Davis, Andrew G. Davis; m. 2d, Samuel Brian Groner, Dec. 17, 1962. Student Drake U., 1939-40, Catholic U., 1954-56; J.D., Washington Coll. Law, Am. U., 1959. Bar: Md. 1959, U.S. Supreme Ct. 1963, D.C. 1965. Sole practice, Bethesda, Md., 1963—; chmn. Md. Gov.'s Commn. on Domestic Relations Laws 1977—; trustee Montgomery-Prince George's Continuing Legal Edn. Inst.; lectr. to lay, profl. groups; participant continuing legal edn. programs, local and nat.; participant trial demonstration films Am. Law Inst., ABA Legal Consortium; participant numerous TV, radio programs; seminar leader Harvard Law Sch., 1987. Named One of Leading Matrimonial Practitioners in U.S., Nat. Law Jour., 1979, 87, Best Divorce Lawyer in Md., Washingtonian Mag., 1981, One of Best Matrimonial Lawyers in U.S., Town and Country mag., 1985, Best Lawyers in Am.; recipient Disting. Service award Va. State Bar Assn., 1982. Fellow Am. Acad. Matrimonial Lawyers; mem. Bar Assn. Montgomery County (exec. com., chmn. family law sect. 1976, chmn. fee arbitration panel 1974-77, legal ethics com.), Md. State Bar Assn. (gov., chmn. family law sect. 1975-77, vice chmn. com. continuing legal edn., ethics com.), ABA (sec. Family Law Sect. 1983-84, vice chmn. 1984-86, chmn. 1986-87, sect. council 1982-83, co-chmn. sect. marital property com., assn.'s adv. to Nat. Conf. of Commrs. on Uniform State Laws Drafting Com. on Uniform Marital Property Act), Phi Alpha Delta. Contbr. numerous articles to legal publs.

GRONOWETTER, FREDA, musician; b. Toronto, Feb. 10, 1918; came to U.S., 1938; d. Max and Sabina (Spindell) G. Student, Royal Conservatory Music, Toronto, 1930; studies with Serge Stupin, studies with Alfred Wallenstein, studies with Joseph Schuster, studies with Emmanuel Feuermann. With Toronto Symphony Orchestra, Am. Symphony Orchestra, N.Y.C. Opera Co. Orchestra, Ballet Theatre Orchestra; soloist Markova-Dolin Ballet Co. Author: (musical composition) In a Sacred Mood, 1941. Recipient 1st prize Can. Nat. Exposition, 1930, award Royal Conservatory Music, 1931, award N.Y.C. Women's Club, 1935. Mem. Am. Fedn. Musician. Home: 557 W Market St Long Beach NY 11561

GRONSKE, SUSAN A., interior designer; b. Paterson, N.J., Aug. 30, 1956; d. Richard J. and Irene (Herold) Dirienzo; m. Edward Gronske, Dec. 1, 1984. Student, Rutgers U., 1979-80; AA, Fashion Inst. Tech., 1981. Paralegal Shanley & Fisher, Esquires, Morristown, N.J., 1974-81; sr. designer, project mgr. Office Planning Inc., N.Y.C., 1981-86; owner, designer Gronske Designs, Rutherford, N.J., 1986—. Office: Gronske Designs 167 Prospect Pl Rutherford NJ 07070

GROOME, SALLY LUCYNTHIA, former army officer; b. Pelham, N.C., Oct. 9, 1936; d. John Whitlock and Addie Estelle (Vass) G. BA, Furman U., 1959; MPA, Shippensburg U., 1983; diploma Naval Coll. of Command and Staff, 1975, U.S. Army War Coll., 1981; postgrad. Old Dominion U. Commd. 2d lt. U.S. Army, 1960, advanced through grades to col., 1982; mil. asst. to sec. of army Dept. of Army, Washington, 1977-78; exec. officer personnel info. systems dir. U.S. Mil. Personnel Ctr., Alexandria, Va., 1978-79; chief personnel actions br., officer personnel mgmt. dir., 1979-80; dep. chief of staff U.S. Army War Coll., Carlisle, Pa., 1981-83; dir. nat. security studies dept. corr. studies, 1983-84; dir. tng. Hdqrs. U.S.A. ROTC Cadet Command. Ft. Monroe, Va., 1984-86. Mem. Assn. U.S. Army, Nat. Assn. Female Execs., Am. Soc. Pub. Adminstrn. Methodist. Avocations: animal welfare, animal conservation, travel, reading, music. Home: 354 Warrington Circle Hampton VA 23669

GROSS, CAROLINE LORD (MRS. MARTIN L. GROSS), state official; b. Laconia, N.H., May 5, 1940; d. William Shepard and Marion (Manns) Lord; AB, Radcliffe Coll., 1963; MAT, Harvard U., 1964; m. Martin L. Gross, Nov. 5, 1960. Research asst. Supr. Schs., Concord, N.H., 1965-66, N.H. Legis. com. ann. sessions, Concord, 1966, N.H. Fiscal com. 1967-68; adminstrv. asst. N.H. gov., Concord, 1969-70; coordinator N.H. fed. funds, Concord, 1971-72, supr. checklist, 1969-84. Mem. N.H. Commn. Status Women, 1972-75; del. N.H. Republican Conv., 1968, 70, 74, 76, 78, 80, 82, 84, 86; legis. policy asst. N.H. Ho. of Reps., 1974-81; trustee Concord Library, 1974-77, Granite State Public Radio, 1979-82; Rep. city chmn., Concord, 1980-84; Rep. candidate N.H. State Senate, 1980; mem. N.H. Ho. of Reps. Com. on Appropriations, 1983—, clk., 1985-86, div. head, 1987—; bd. dirs. Central N.H. Community Mental Health Services, 1984-86. Mem. Concord Bus. and Profl. Women. Club: Harvard-Radcliffe of N.H. (co-pres. 1981-84), Home: 15 Rumford St Concord NH 03301 Office: Room 106 State House Concord NH 03301

GROSS, DONNA LOU, educator; b. Kansas City, Mo., Apr. 9, 1954; d. Donald Lee and Mabel Lucille (Dinwiddie) Dusenberry; m. Allen Wallace Gross, May 24, 1975; children: Craig Allen, Justin Wayne. BS, William Jewell Coll., 1975; MA, U. Mo., Kansas City, 1977. Cert. elem. tchr., Mo. Tchr. North Kansas City Sch. Dist., Mo., 1976-78, 1986—. Nat. Alpha Lambda Delta Dist. Scholar William Jewell Coll., Liberty, Mo., 1975. Mem. Nat. Edn. Assn. Democrat. Baptist. Office: Crestview Elem Sch 4327 N Holmes Kansas City MO 64116

GROSS, HARRIET P. MARCUS, free-lance writer, educator; b. Pitts., July 15, 1934; d. Joseph William and Rose (Roth) Pincus; A.B. magna cum laude, U. Pitts., 1954; cert. Religious Teaching, Spertus Coll. of Judaica, Chgo., 1962; 1972-73; children—Sol Benjamin, Devra Lynn. Asso. editor Jewish Criterion of Pitts., 1955-56; publs. writer B'nai B'rith Vocat. Service, 1956-57; leader recreation program for handicapped adults United Cerebral Palsy of Greater Chgo., 1957-58; group leader Jewish Community Centers of Met. Chgo., 1958-63; columnist Star Publs., Chicago Heights, Ill., 1964-80; public info. specialist Operation ABLE, Chgo., 1980-81; dir. religious sch. Temple Emanu-El, Dallas, 1983-86; tchr. creative writing Homewood-Flossmoor (Il.) Park Dist., Brookhaven Jr. Coll., Dallas; advisor journalism program Prairie State Coll., Chicago Heights, 1978-80; adv. bd. The Creative Woman quar. publ. Governors State U., Governors Park, Ill. Bd. dirs., sec. Family Service and Mental Health Center of South Cook County, Ill., 1965-71; mem. Park Forest (Ill.) Commn. on Human Relations, 1969-80, chmn., 1974-76; bd. dirs. Ill. Theatre Center, 1977-80, Park Forest Bus. and Profl. Assn., 1979-80, Greater Dallas sect. Nat. Council Jewish Women, 1981-87, Jewish Family Service of Dallas, 1982—, exec. com., 1987—; mem. exec. com. Jewish Community Relations Council Dallas, 1983-85. Recipient Fellowship for Action Humanitarian Achievements award, 1974; Anti-Defamation League of B'nai B'rith Honor award, 1978; Dr. Charles E. Gavin Found. Community Service award, 1978. Mem. Nat. Fedn. Press Women, Ill. Woman's Press Assn. (named Woman of Yr. 1978), Intertel (pres. Gateway Forum of Dallas 1984-85), Nat. Assn. Temple Educators, Mensa, Sigma Delta Chi, Phi Sigma Sigma. Jewish. Developed 1st community newspaper action line column, 1966. Address: 8560 Park Ln #23 Dallas TX 75231

GROSS, MARILYN AGNES, artist, business owner, speech audiologist; b. Rolla, Mo., Jan. 23, 1937; d. John Andrew and Florence Margaret (White) Robertson; m. James Dehnert Gross, Jan. 9, 1960; children: Kathleen Ann, Terrence Michael, Brian Andrew, Kevin Matthew. Student, U. Mo., 1955; BS, St. Louis U., 1958; Cert., Washington Sch. Art, 1978. Audiologist Bur. Maternal and Child Health U.S. Dept. Pub. Health, Washington, 1959; pvt. practice speech therapist Millington, Tenn., 1959-60; owner, dir. Marilyns' Studio, Creative Systems for Creative People, Streator, 1983—; bus. mgr. Pathology Services, Streator, 1984—; art represented by Toby Falk Tuscon, Ariz., 1988—; exhbn. coordinator Arts Week Community Project, Streator, 1982; visual arts rep. Ill. Pub. Sch. System on Improvement of Fine Arts Curriculum, 1986; instr. workshop Dillman's Sand Lake Lodge, Lac du Flambeau, Wis., 1988; speaker numerous civi orgns. and clubs; participant numerous art seminars and confs. Exhbns. include: Ill. Valley Art League (award) 1975, 76, Town and Country, Ottawa, Ill. (award), 1975, 76, 77, (award) 78, (2 awards) 79, (award) 81, Streator Centennial, 1976, North Light mag. Competition, Westport, Conn., 1977, Internat. Soc. Artists Competition, N.Y.C., 1978, Ann. Town and Country State Art Show, Peru, Ill., (3 awards) 1979, (4 awards) 80, (award) 81, 82, Urbana, Ill., 1979, 80 (State award), Pekin, 1980, Ill. Valley Art League Silver Ann. Show, 1980, Ducks Unlimited Contest, 1980, Link Gallery, Ogelsby, Ill., 1981, Streator Arts Happening, 1982, Ill. Watercolor Exhbn., Glenview (traveling exhbn. award), 1983, Springfield, 1985, Ill. Art League Lakeview Mus., 1984, Springfield (Ill.) Art Assn., 1985, Gallery 100 Premier Reception, Chgo., 1985, Limelight Club, Chgo., 1986, Galesburg Civic Art Ctr., 1987, N. Coast Coll. Soc., 1988, Hiram (Ohio) Coll., 1988; one-woman shows include: Engle Ln. Gallery, Streator, 1980, 81, 82, 84, 85, Illini Union Gallery, Urbana, 1982, Dai-Ichi Kangyo, Ltd., Chgo., 1983, Atrium Gallery We. Ill. U., Macomb, 1983, John G. Blank Ctr. for Arts, Michigan City, Ind., 1984, 1st Nat. Bank of Morton (Ill.) Gallery, 1985, Birchwood Farms Estate, Harbor Springs, Mich., 1988, Copley Soc., Boston, 1983-86, Lakeview Mus. Gallery, Peoria, Ill., 1983—, Springfield Art Assn. Gallery, 1983—, The Prism Gallery, Evanston, Ill, 1987—, represented in numerous corp. and pvt. collections; author: Gift of Love, 1975 (Peter Herring Poetry award), The President's Book, 1971, Making it Happen-Creative Systems fro Creative People, 1988. Mem. St. Anthony's Parents Club, 1966-82; rep. White House conf. on library and info. services, 1978. Recipient photography award CICCA Interclub Comp., 1981, 82, (3 awards) 83, 2 photography awards Pictorialists Comp., 1982, painting award Binney & Smith Corp., 1982, photography award Fuji Photo Comp., 1983, profl. award Ill. Art League, 1984; named Artist of Month Springfield (Ill.) Art Assn. Gallery, 1983; represented in numerous biographies and revs. in newspapers and books. Mem. Am. Med. Soc. Aux., Assn. Clin. Scientists Aux., Am. Soc. Clin. Pathologists Aux., Coll. Am. Pathologists Aux., LaSalle County Med. Soc. Aux., Am. Speech and Hearing Assn. (cert.), Internat. Soc. Artists (charter), Associated Photographers Internat., Am. Watercolor Assn., Nat. Watercolor Assn., Midwest Watercolor Assn., North Coast Collage Soc., Ill. Watercolor Soc., Ill. Art League, Ky. Watercolor Soc., Chgo. Artists Coalition, Pictoralists Club, Delta Sigma Epsilon, Sigma Alpha Eta, Delta Zeta (State Day award 1958). Republican. Roman Catholic. Lodge: KC (aux. 1962—). Home: 54 Sunset Dr Streator IL 61364

GROSS, MIMI, sculptor, painter; b. N.Y.C. Ed., Bard Coll., 1957-59; Skowhegan Sch. of Painting and Sculpture, Maine, 1959; Kokoschka Sch. of Painting, Salzburg, Austria, 1960. Solo exhbns.: Castagno Gallery, N.Y.C., 1966; Area Gallery, N.Y.C., 1966; Collegiate Sch. for Boys, N.Y.C., 1978, Karen Lennox Gallery, 1984, Galerie Laura Vincy, Paris, 1986, Ruth Siegel Gallery, N.Y.C., 1986; group exhbns. (most recent): Postcards, N.Y.C., 1979, Italy, 1979, numerous others; commd. work: O'Neal's Restaurant, The New Room, N.Y.C., 1978-79, Vera List Graphics, Jewish Mus., N.Y.C., 1983, polychrome outdoor sculpture Wards' Island, N.Y.C., 1983; theater: sets, costumes Seven Days of Mourning, N.Y.C., 1977; designer exterior and interior entrances and decorations Big Apple Circus, N.Y.C., 1977; costumes Douglas Dunn & Dancers, Pulcinello, 1984, Foot Rules, 1979, backdrop Echo, 1980, Matches, 1988; performances: Il Piccolo Circo d'Ombra di Firenze, No. Italy, 1961; Berkeley Eruption, U. Calif.-Berkeley, 1968; Hippodrome Hardware, 1972; numerous films including; Ruckus Manhattan, 1975-76; vis. artist dept. painting Syracuse U., 1978; dept. painting Art Inst., Chgo., 1979; marathon workshop Time & Space Theater Ltd., N.Y.C., 1980. Author: Ruckus Manhattan, 1977. Nat. Endowment Arts grantee, 1977, 85; Am. Acad. and Inst. Arts and Letters grantee, 1981; N.Y. Found. Arts grantee, 1985.

GROSS, NANCY LYNN, accountant; b. St. Joseph, Mo., Nov. 2, 1952; d. Claude C. and Helen Fay (Oliver) Boner; B.S. in Acctg., U. Ky., 1975; M.B.A., U. Cin., 1980; m. Gary Lloyd Gross, May 29, 1976. CPA, Ohio. With Armco Steel Corp., Kansas City, Mo. 1974-80, Middletown, Ohio, 1980, credit rep., Middletown, 1975-80; acct. Armco, Inc., Middletown, 1980-81, sr. acct., 1981-85, supr. acctg., 1985; founder Miami Valley Acctg. Service, 1985—; lectr. Miami U., Middletown, 1980-86, instr. Miami U., Oxford, Ohio, 1987—. Mem. Am. Women's Soc. CPA's, Ohio Soc. CPA's, Am. Inst. CPAs, Beta Alpha Psi, Beta Gamma Sigma. Baptist. Home: 607 S Highview Rd Middletown OH 45044

GROSS, PRIVA BAIDAFF, art historian, retired educator; b. Wieliczka, Poland, June 19, 1911; came to U.S., 1941, naturalized, 1955; d. Israel and Leopolda (Friedman) Baidaff; Ph.M., Jagellonian U., Cracow, Poland, 1937; postgrad. (N.Y. U. scholar 1945-47), N.Y. U. Inst. Fine Arts, 1945-48; m. Feliks Gross, July 25, 1937; 1 dau., Eva Helena Gross Friedman. Mem. faculty Queensborough Community Coll., CUNY, 1961-81, assoc. prof. art history, 1971-81, ret., 1981, co-chmn. art and music dept., 1966-68, chmn. art dept., 1968-74, dir. coll. gallery, 1968-77. SUNY grantee, 1967. Mem. AAUW (dir. 1972-76, 1980-82), Coll. Art Assn. Am., Soc. Archtl. Historians, Gallery Assn. N.Y. State (dir. 1972-73), N.Y. State Assn. Jr. Colls., AAUP, Polish Inst. Arts and Scis. Am., Council Gallery and Exhbn. Dirs. (dir. 1970-72). Contbr. articles, revs. to profl. publs. Home: 310 W 85th St New York NY 10024

GROSS, RUTH TAUBENHAUS, physician; b. Bryan, Tex., June 24, 1920; d. Jacob and Esther (Hirshenson) Taubenhaus; B.A., Barnard Coll., 1941; M.D., Columbia U., 1944; m. Reuben H. Gross, Jr., Aug. 22, 1942; (div. June 1952); 1 son, Gary E. Intern, Charity Hosp., New Orleans, 1944; resident in pediatrics Tulane U., New Orleans, 1945, Columbia U., N.Y.C., 1946, 47; instr. Radcliffe Infirmary, Oxford, Eng., 1949-50; instr. pediatrics Stanford (Calif.) U., 1950-53, asst. prof., 1953-56, asso. prof., 1956-60, prof., 1973—, acting exec. pediatrics, 1957-59, assoc. dean student affairs, 1973-75, dir. div. gen. and ambulatory pediatrics, 1975-85, dir. Stanford-Children's Ambulatory Care Center, 1980-85, nat. study dir. Infant Health and Devel. Program, 1983—; assoc. prof. pediatrics, co-dir. div. human genetics Albert Einstein Coll. Medicine, Yeshiva U., N.Y.C., 1960-64, prof. pediatrics, 1964-66; clin. prof. pediatrics U. Calif. Med. Center, San Francisco, 1966-73; dir. dept. pediatrics Mt. Zion Hosp. and Med. Center, San Francisco, 1966-73. Commonwealth fellow human genetics Instituto de Genetica, Pavia, Italy, 1959-60. Mem. Inst. Medicine, Nat. Acad. Scis., Am. Fedn. Clin. Research, Am. Pediatric Soc., Soc. Pediatric Research, Am. Acad. Pediatrics, Ambulatory Pediatric Assn., Soc. Research in Child Devel., Phi Beta Kappa, Alpha Omega Alpha, Sigma Xi. Contbr. articles to profl. jours. Office: Stanford U Med Sch Dept Pediatrics Stanford CA 94305

GROSS, SHIRLEY MARIE, farm manager, artist; b. Beardstown, Ill., Apr. 4, 1917; d. Robert Lee and Marie Elizabeth (Ellrich) Northcutt; A.A., Stephens Coll., 1936; B.A., Ill. Coll., 1938; m. Carl David Gross, Oct. 4, 1941; children—David Lee, Susan Jean Gross Conner. Med. technologist St. John's Hosp., Springfield, Ill., 1938-41, Schmidt Meml. Hosp., Beardstown, 1957-64; librarian Beardstown Public Library, 1970-76; pvt. practice farm mgmt., Beardstown, 1958—; dir. First State Bank Beardstown; exhibitor various art shows, Ill., 1969—. Bd. dirs. Beardstown Hosp., Head Start; trustee First Congregational Ch. Beardstown. Winner art awards various shows. Mem. Am. Soc. Clin. Pathologists (med. technologist), Beardstown Bus. and Profl. Women's Investment Club, Beardstown Restoration Soc. Jacksonville Area Artist League. Democrat. Clubs: Beardstown Woman's, Cass County Council for the Arts, Beardstown Bus. and Profl. Women's (pres., 1968-70). Home: 1116 Jefferson Beardstown IL 62618

GROSS, WENDY S., public relations consultant; b. Cleve., Oct. 6, 1942; d. Alton E. and Jeanne (Schoen) G. BA in English, U. Mich., 1963. Asst. dir. pub. relations Girl Scouts of Chgo., 1964-66; account exec. Beveridge Orgn., Inc., Chgo., 1966-71; free-lance consultant Chgo., 1971-78; sr. v.p. Golin/Harris Communications, Chgo., 1978—. Mem. Pub. Relations Soc. Am. Club: Publicity of Chgo. (Golden Trumpet award, 1981, 87). Home: 50 E Bellevue Chicago IL 60611 Office: Golin/Harris Communications 500 N Michigan Ave Chicago IL 60611

GROSSER, MARILYN GAIL, marketing, development and management services executive; b. New Braunfels, Tex., Feb. 20, 1951; d. Elmer and Geneva (Mayer) G.; m. Mark Paul Goldman, June 9, 1979 (div.). BS, Tex. Woman's U., 1972, MS, 1976, PhD, 1984. Research fellow Tex. Woman's U., Denton, 1975-76, asst. to grad. dean, summer 1978, teaching fellow, 1976-78; asst. to dir. Denton Sr. Citizens Ctr., 1977-78; instr. dept. anthropology, sociology and social work S.W. Tex. State U., San Marcos, 1978-79; research assoc. group research United Services Automobile Assn., San Antonio, 1980-85, dir. product devel. fin. services div. real estate group, retirement communities, 1985-87; v.p. corp. mktg. and devel. McKerley Mgmt. Services, Inc., Penacook, N.H., 1987—; chmn., mem. council North Chamber Health CAre Task Force, San Antonio, 1987—; cons. in field. NF grantee, 1978. Mem. Gerontol. Soc. Am., SW Social Sci. Assn., Nat. Council on Aging, Am. Mktg. Assn., Am. Mgmt. Assn., Am. Bus. Women's Assn., Nat. Assn. Female Execs., Nat. Assn. Sr. Living Industries, Soc. of Ins. Research. Home: 227 Pleasant St Pleasant View #330 Concord NH 03301 Office: McKerley Mgmt Services One Fisher Ave PO Box 6506 Penacook NH 03303

GROSSET, JESSICA ARIANE, computer analyst; b. Paris, Aug. 31, 1952; came to U.S., 1970; d. Raymond Louis and Barbara Ann (Byrne) G.; m. Bruce Edward Kaskubar, May 23, 1986. AA, Berkshire Community Coll., Pittsfield, Mass., 1972; BS, SUNY, Potsdam, 1979; postgrad., Ariz. State U., 1980, U. Minn., 1980-81. Computer programmer Kay-Bee Toy and Hobby Shops, Lee, Mass., 1974-78; computer analyst Mayo Clinic, Rochester, Minn., 1981—. Mem. Nat. Assn. Female Execs. Office: Mayo Clinic 200 SW 1st St Rochester MN 55905

GROSSETETE, GINGER LEE, gerontology administrator, consultant; b. Riverside, Calif., Feb. 9, 1936; d. Lee Roy Taylor and Bonita (Beryl) Williams; m. Alec Paul Grossetete, June 8, 1954; children: Elizabeth Gay Blech, Teri Lee Zeni. BA in Recreation cum laude, U. N.Mex., 1974, M in Pub. Adminstrn., 1978. Sr. ctr. supr., Office of Sr. Affairs, City of Albuquerque, 1974-77, asst. dir. Office of Sr. Affairs, 1977—; conf. coordinator Nat. Consumers Assn., Albuquerque, 1978-79; region 6 del. Nat. Council on Aging, Washington, 1977-84; conf. chmn. Western Gerontol. Soc., Albuquerque, 1983; mem. Council on Phys. Fitness and Health. Contbr. articles to mags. Pres. Albuquerque Symphony Women's Assn., 1972; exec. com. mem. Jr. League Albuquerque, 1976; campaign dir. March of Dimes N.Mex., 1966-67. Recipient N.Mex. Disting. Pub. Service award N.Mex. Gov.'s Office, 1983, Disting. Woman on the Move award YWCA, 1986. Fellow Nat. Recreation and Park Assn. (bd. dirs. Southwest Regional Council, pres. N.Mex. chpt. 1983-84, Outstanding Profl. 1982); mem. U. N.Mex. Alumni Assn. (bd. dirs. 1978-80, Disting. Alumni award 1985), Southwest Soc. on Aging (pres. 1984-85, bd. dirs.), Am. Soc. Pub. Adminstrn. (pres. N.Mex. Council 1987—, pres. N.Mex. Council 1987-88), Pi Alpha Alpha, Chi Omega (pres. alumni 1959-60). Club: Las Ampolas Garden (Albuquerque) (pres. 1964). Home: 517 La Veta NE Albuquerque NM 87108 Office: Office of Sr Affairs 714 7th St SW Albuquerque NM 87102

GROSSFIELD, RENA ELLEN, free-lance financial writer, editor; b. Bklyn., June 24, 1946; d. Avery Jonah and Harriet Beatrice (Okanst) G.; m. Robin MacDonald Burns, May 14, 1976; 1 stepdaughter Jenny Eastment Burns. BA summa cum laude, Emory U., 1968; MBA, Bernard M. Baruch Coll. div. CUNY, 1974. Research analyst Stevenson, Jordan & Harrison, mgmt. cons., N.Y.C., 1968-70; various editorial, research positions Bus. Internat. Corp., N.Y.C., 1970-78, mng. editor, 1978-79; assoc. editor World Bus. Weekly Mag., N.Y.C., 1979-81; sr. editor Boardroom Reports, Inc., N.Y.C., 1981-82; dir. pub. relations, investment products group J. Aron div. Goldman Sachs & Co., N.Y.C., 1982-83; v.p. ECOM/DDB, N.Y.C., 1984-87; ptnr. Expert Connections the Writing Resource For Bus., N.Y.C., 1984-87; lectr. fin. writing, LARIMI Communications, N.Y.C. Author: (book) Managing Global Marketing, 1976, Operating in a Changing Canada, 1978; editor: Foreign Investment in the U.S., 1977; contbr. articles to profl. mags., jours. V.P. Park Place Assn. of Neighbors, Bklyn., 1987. Mem. Beta Gamma Sigma, Phi Beta Kappa. Jewish.

GROSSHANS, MERILYN LA VONNE, librarian, consultant; b. Plaza, N.D., July 16, 1939; d. John Rudolph and Lillian (Erickson) Willey Peterson; m. Dennis Arthur Grosshans, June 20, 1942 (div. Sept. 1983). B.A., Northwestern Coll., Mpls., 1961; postgrad. Valley City State Coll., 1962; M.L.S., U. N.D., 1969. Tchr. Engish, Stanley (N.D.) High Sch., 1963-65, Williston (N.D.) High, 1965-67; children's librarian Los Angeles Pub. Library, 1969-70; librarian Vermillion (S.D.) High, 1970-72, Las Vegas (Nev.) High Sch., Clark County Sch. Dist., 1973—. Contbr. articles to profl. jours. Vol. worker Nev. State Prison, Jean and Indian Springs. Recipient Exceptional Tchr. award Clark County Bd. Sch. Trustees and PTA, 1983. Mem. ALA (com. best books for young adults, young adult div. 1970-82), Nev. Library Assn. (membership chair 1984-85), Nev. Assn. Sch. Librarians (pres. 1983), Am. Assn. Sch. Librarians (com. 1984-86), Clark County Sch. Library Assn. (pres. 1976-77), ALA (Young Adult Services div.), Mountain Plains Library Assn. (pres. children's and sch. div. 1987-88), Alpha Delta Kappa (sec. 1986, treas. 1986-87). Democrat. Home: 7129 Grasswood Las Vegas NV 89117 Office: Las Vegas High Sch 315 S 7th St Las Vegas NV 89101

GROSSI, GAIL LEE, educational administrator; b. Pitts., Sept. 30, 1946; d. Alexander Neely and Charlene May (Inman) Hamburg; m. Donald Grossi, May 31, 1969; children: Heidi Lynn, Dawn Carole, Troy Alexander. BS, Clarion State U., 1967; MA in Applied Linguistics, Interamericana U., Saltillo, Mex., 1968; postgrad., U. Hawaii, 1968-69. Cert. tchr., Pa., Hawaii. Lectr. U. Hawaii, Honolulu, 1968-69; tchr. Spanish, German, Latin North Alleghany High Sch., Pitts., 1970-80; coordinator ESL instruction program Alleghany Intermediate Unit, Pitts., 1980-82; coordinator corp. program The Learning Ctr., Pitts., 1982—; coordinator Project Literacy U.S., Pitts, 1986. Vol. Youth City, Pitts., 1971-79, March of Dimes, Pitts., 1972-87, Am. Heart Assn., Pitts., 1979-84. Mem. Am. Soc. for Tng. and Devel., Pitts. Advt. Assn. (assoc., fund raising coordinator, 1985), Literacy Coalition, Am. Bus. Women's Assn. (Merit award 1986, Citation of Appreciation 1987), Pitts. C. of C., Alpha Gamma Mu. Democrat. Episcopalian. Clubs: N.H. Historic Auto (treas. 1979-80), Horseless Carriage (tour chair 1975-77), Antique Auto of Am. (tour cahir 1981-84). Home: 8171 Edwood Rd Pittsburgh PA 15237 Office: The Learning Ctr 921 Penn Ave Pittsburgh PA 15222

GROSSINGER, TANIA SELFER, author, public relations consultant; b. Evanston, Ill., Feb. 17, 1937; d. Max and Karla (Selfer) Grossinger. BA, Brandeis U., 1956. Dir. broadcast promotion Playboy Club div. Playboy Mag., N.Y.C., 1963-69, Rogers-Cowan Pub. Relations, N.Y.C., 1969-70; dir. publicity Stein & Day Pubs., N.Y.C., 1970-76; pres. Grossinger Assocs Pub. Relations, N.Y.C., 1972—; ptnr., exec. v.p. Nat. Telecommunications Network, N.Y.C., 1985—; cons. media Hebrew Union Coll., N.Y.C., 1985-86. Author: The Book of Gadgets, 1974, Growing Up At Grossinger's, 1975; (with others) Weekend, 1980. Mem. Village Ind. Dems., N.Y.C., Christopher Bast Block Assn., N.Y.C. Mem. Am. Soc. Journalists-Authors (exec. bd. 1982). Jewish. Home and Office: 1 Christopher St New York NY 10014

GROSSMAN, ELIZABETH KORN, nursing administrator, retired college dean; b. S.I., N.Y., May 15, 1923; d. George and Ethel (Elliot) Korn; B.A., Hunter Coll., 1944; M.N., Western Res. U., 1947; M.S. in Nursing Edn., Ind. U., 1960, Ed.D., 1972; m. Thomas Grossman, Feb. 23, 1952 (dec. 1987); 1 son, Thomas. Researcher, Columbia Carbon Corp., Bklyn., 1944; staff nurse, asst. head nurse, head nurse, supr. Univ. Hosp., Cleve., 1947-52; Instr. Mt. Sinai Hosp. Sch. Nursing, Cleve., 1952-53; supr. maternity nursing Meth. Hosp., Indpls., 1953-57; instr. maternity nursing, 1957-59; instr. DePauw U., Indpls., 1959-62; asst. prof., asso. prof., grad. maternity Ind. U., Indpls., 1959-66, chairperson grad.-undergrad. maternity nursing, 1966-73, dean Sch. Nursing, 1973-88; civilian nat. cons. emeritus USAF Nurse Corps, 1983-86. Fellow Am. Acad. Nursing; mem. Am. Nurses Assn., Nat. League Nursing, Am. Assn. Colls. Nursing (treas. 1981-85), Nurses Assn. of Am. Coll. Ob-Gyn (7th nat. program meeting com. 1987-88), Midwest Alliance Nursing (treas. 1979-81), Sigma Xi, Sigma Theta Tau (Disting. Service award 1977, co-chmn. campaign for Ctr. for Nursing Scholarship), Am. Assn. Maternal Child Health, Delta Kappa Gamma, Alpha Xi Delta (Woman of Distinction 1988). Republican. Roman Catholic. Contbr. articles to profl. jours. Home: 11201 Westfield Blvd Carmel IN 46032 Office: 610 Barnhill Dr Indianapolis IN 46223

GROSSMAN, LISA ROBBIN, clinical psychologist, lawyer; b. Chgo., Jan. 22, 1952; d. Samuel R. and Sarah (Kruger) G. B.A. with highest distinction and departmental honors in Psychology, Northwestern U., 1974, J.D. cum laude, 1979, Ph.D., 1982. Bar: Ill. 1981; registered psychologist, Ill. Jud. intern, U.S. Supreme Ct., Washington, 1975; pre-doctoral psychology intern Michael Reese Hosp. and Med. Center, Chgo., 1979-80; therapist Homes for Children, Chgo., 1980-83; psychologist Psychiat. Inst., Cir. Ct. Cook County, Chgo., 1981-87; pvt. practice, 1984—; invited participant workshop HHS, Rockville, Md., 1981. Contbr. articles to profl. jours. Mem. Am. Psychol. Assn., Ill. Psychol. Assn., Chgo. Assn. for Psychoanalytic Psychologists (parliamentarian 1982), ABA, Ill. State Bar Assn., Chgo. Bar

Assn., Mortar Bd., Phi Beta Kappa, Shi-Ai, Alpha Lambda Delta. Office: 500 N Michigan Suite 1116 Chicago IL 60611

GROSSO, MADELINE MARY, election supervisor; b. Bklyn., Oct. 24, 1938; d. Gregory and Adeline Rose (Sinni) Mariano; m. Maurice C. Grosso Jr., May 21, 1960; children: Maria, Maurice, Melina. Cert., Am. Inst. Banking, 1957. Ins. sales Bushwick Savs. Bank, Bklyn., 1956-60, exec. sec., 1958-59; campaign fin. dir. Suffolk County Bd. Elections, Yaphank, N.Y., 1980-87, supr., 1986—; supr. election coordinator Suffolk County Bd. Elections, Yaphank, 1986—. Mem. Brookhaven Town Rep. Com., Farmingville, 1966—, mem. exec. com., leader seminars; sec. Patchogue-Medford Adv. Bd. for Continuing Edn.; active St. Sylvester Roman Catholic Ch. Home: 216 Mt Vernon Ave Medford NY 11763 Office: Suffolk County Bd Elections Yaphank Ave Yaphank NY 11980

GROSSO, REBECCA LOCKE, health promotion administrator; b. Jackson, Tenn., Feb. 23, 1953; d. John Henry Lock and Annabelle Lee Winfrey; m. Robert John Grosso; stepchildren: Eric Robert, Peter Daniel. BBA, Western Mich. U., 1981, MA in Communications, 1987. Dept. head Grinnell's Music, Jackson, Mich., 1973-75; sec., asst. Nat. Bank of Jackson, 1975-79; sec., intake worker Domestic Assault, Kalamazoo, Mich., 1979-80; dir. health promotion Borgess Med. Ctr., Kalamazoo, 1981—; faculty Nat. Ctr. for Health Promotion, Ann Arbor, 1981-84; cons. IRSA, Boston, 1986—. Contbr. articles to Club Bus. and Optimal Health mags. Pres. Kalamazoo Women's Festival, 1987. Mem. Assn. Quality Clubs (cons., speaker), Assn. for Fitness in Bus. (speaker), Am. Coll. Healthcare Mktg., Women in Communications, Nat. Assn. for Female Execs. Roman Catholic. Office: Borgess Med Ctr 1521 Gull Rd Kalamazoo MI 49001

GROTECLOSS, NONA LOUISE, educational administrator; b. Sayre, Pa., Jan. 23, 1925; d. Stanley Burton and Florence Kimmick (Bach) Severance; B.A., Syracuse U., 1945; M.A. in Guidance, U. South Fla., 1968, M.A. in Adult Edn., 1975; Ed.D., Nova U., 1979; m. Robert Grotecloss, Apr. 15, 1952; children—Robert, Gary, Steven, Bruce. Case Worker Dept. Vet. Assistance, Onondaga County, N.Y., 1945-50; social worker Fla. Welfare Dept., St. Petersburg, 1951-66; guidance coordinator St. Petersburg Vocat. Tech. Inst., 1969-77; counselor Pasco County Adult Edn., Dade City, Fla., 1977-80, supr. adult and community edn., Land-O'Lakes, Fla., 1980—. Mem. Am. Personnel and Guidance Assn., Fla. Personnel and Guidance Assn., Am. Vocat. Assn., Fla. Assn. Sch. Adminstrs., Adult Edn. Assn., Fla. Adult Edn. Assn., Commn. Adult Basic Edn., Pasco County Adminstrs. and Suprs. Assn., Tampa Bay Regional Planning Council, Phi Delta Kappa, Bus. and Profl. Women's Club, Alpha Chi Omega. Methodist. Home: PO Box 1661 Dade City FL 33525 Office: Pasco County Adult and Community Edn 2609 US Hwy 41 N Land O'Lakes FL 33539

GROTH, BETTY, conservationist, author, photographer; b. Oak Park, Ill.; d. Herman A. and Bertha L. (Luepke) G.; grad. Vassar Coll., 1932. Sec., Oak Park YMCA, 1935-42; sec. Ill. Commn. for Handicapped Children, 1943-46; pvt. sec. Chgo. Assn. of Commerce and Industry, 1947-53, Chgo. Heart Assn., 1953-75. Mem. Save-The-Dunes Council, North Central Audubon Council; sec., dir. Natural Resources Council of Ill., 1967-71, v.p., 1969-71; v.p., dir. Du Page County Clean Streams, 1967-69; founder, chmn. Northern Conservation Cabinet, 1971-75; landscape gardener Audubon Sanctuary, Wayne, Ill., 1977-79; color film nature lectr. Mem. Nat. Audubon Soc., Ill. Audubon Soc. (v.p. conservation, dir. 1962-73, sec. bd. dirs. 1973-74), Big Bluestem Audubon Soc. (dir., sec.), Du Page Audubon Soc., Nat. Wildlife Fedn., Conservation Explorers Club (pres. 1975-76), Morton Arboretum, Sarasota Jungle Gardens, Am. Bald Eagle Club. Baptist. Club: Wis. Vassar. Author: Open Spaces in Illinois, 1962; Surprise in the North Woods, 1966; Wildlife by John Burroughs Cabin, 1967; King's Ransom to Save a Prairie, 1968; Ivory Bills Found Alive in Texas Big Thicket, 1969; Great Swamp Wildlife Refuge Versus Jetport, 1970; The Fate of Thorn Creek Woods, 1971; Man's Dominion of the Green Earth, 1972; Country Estate, 1973; King of Sky, Land and Water, 1974; North Woods Shoreline, 1975; Vanished Illinois Prairie Returns, 1976; Florida Conservation and Environmental Survey, 3 vols. for Conservation Ctr., Univ. Wyo., 1983, 4 vols. for Vassar Coll. Library, 1984; Wisconsin Wilderness, 3 vols. for Conservation Ctr., Univ. Wyo., 1985; Yellowstone Park 1914; North with Springtime Florida to Maine, 4 vols. for Vassar Coll. Library, 1986; Toward More Beautiful Gardens, 1988, 3 vols.; The Four Seasons, 1988. Contbr. articles to profl. jours. Home: Gull Shores Gills Rock Ellison Bay WI 54210

GROTTA, SANDRA BROWN, interior designer; b. Detroit, June 7, 1934; m. Louis William Grotta, Sept. 8, 1955. Student U. Mich., 1952-55, N.Y. Sch. Interior Design, 1964. Pres. S.G. Interiors, Maplewood, N.J., 1964—. Mem. Am. Soc. Interior Designers.

GROTZINGER, LAUREL ANN, university dean; b. Truman, Minn., Apr. 15, 1935; d. Edward F. and Marian Gertrude (Greeley) G. B.A., Carleton Coll., 1957; M.S., U. Ill., 1958, Ph.D., 1964. Instr., asst. librarian Ill. State U., 1958-62; asst. prof. Western Mich. U., Kalamazoo, 1964-66; assoc. prof. Western Mich. U., 1966-68, prof., 1968—, asst. dir. Sch. Librarianship, 1965-72, chief research officer, 1979-86, interim dir. Sch. Library and Info. Sci., 1982-86, dean grad. coll., 1979—. Author: The Power and the Dignity, Scarecrow, 1966; editorial bd.: Jour. Edn. for Librarianship, 1973-77, Dictionary Am. Library Biography, 1975-77; contbr. articles to profl. jours. Mem. AAUW, ALA (sec. treas. Library History Round Table 1973-74, vice chmn., chmn.-elect 1983-84, chmn. 1984-85), Assn. Library Info. Sci. Edn., Am. Assn. Higher Edn., Council Grad. Schs., Mich. Council Grad. Deans (chmn. 1983-84, 86), Nat. Council Research Adminstrs., Mich. Acad. Sci., Arts and Letters (mem.-at-large, exec. com. 1980-86, pres. 1983-85), Phi Beta Kappa (pres. SW Mich. chpt. 1977-78), Beta Phi Mu, Pi Delta Epsilon, Alpha Beta Alpha, Delta Kappa Gamma. Home: 2729 Mockingbird Dr Kalamazoo MI 49008

GROVE, HELEN HARRIET, historian, artist; b. South Bend, Ind.; d. Samuel Harold and LaVerne Mae (Drescher) Grove; grad. Bayle Sch. Design, Meinzinger Found., 1937-39, Washington U., 1940-42; spl. studies, Paris, France. Owner studios of historic research and illustration, St. Louis, Chgo., 1943—; dir. archives, bus. history research Sears, Roebuck & Co., 1951-67; commmns. art and research for Northwestern U., Chgo.-Sears Roebuck & Co., art Lawrence U., Appleton, Wis. Home: 6326 N Clark St Chicago IL 60626 Studio: 6328 N Clark St Chicago IL 60626

GROVE, JEAN DONNER (MRS. EDWARD R. GROVE), sculptor; b. Washington, May 15, 1912; d. Frederick Gregory and Georgia V. (Gartrell) Donner; m. Edward R. Grove, June 24, 1936; children: David Donner, Eric Donner. Student, Cornell U., 1932, Hill Sch. of Sculpture, 1934-35, Corcoran Sch. of Art, 1935-37, 42-44, Cath. U. Am., 1936-37, Phila. Mus. Art Sch., 1967; B.S., Wilson Tchrs. Coll., 1939. Exhibited one-man shows, Wilson Tchrs. Coll., Washington, 1939, Grove Family Exhbns., Cayuga Mus. History and Art, Auburn, N.Y., 1964, Episcopal Acad. Gallery, Phila., 1966, group shows, Pa. Acad. Fine Arts, Phila., 1947, 48, 51, 53, N.A.D., N.Y.C., 1949, 78, 81, 83, 85, 87, Nat. Sculpture Soc. at Archtl. League, N.Y.C., Topeka, 1957, Lever House, N.Y.C., 1974, 75, 86, Port of History Mus., Phila., 1987, Equitable Gallery, N.Y.C., 1976, 78, 83, Park Ave. Atrium, N.Y.C., 1985, Art U.S.A., Madison Sq. Garden, N.Y.C., 1958, Corcoran Gallery Art, Washington, 1943-47, Internat. Gallery, Washington, 1946, Phila. Mus. Art, 1955, 59, 62, Phila. Art Alliance, 1957, 60, 66, Phila. Civic Ctr., 1968, Flagler Art Ctr., West Palm Beach, Fla., 1972, Norton Gallery Art, West Palm Beach, 1974, 81, 83; represented in permanent collections, Rosenwald Collection, Phila., Ch. of Holy Comforter, Drexel Hill, Pa., Fine Arts Commn., City Hall, Phila., Palm Beach County Govt. Ctr., West Palm Beach, Fla., Port of History Mus., Philadelphis; sculptor numerous portrait commns., garden figures and fountains, 1940—; (with E.R. Grove) Am. Express Goldpiece, 1982. Recipient 1st prize sculpture Nat. Mus. Washington, 1946; recipient 1st Prize Sculpture Arts Club, 1946, Portrait Prize Sculpture Arts Club, 1947, Morris Goodman award John Herron Art Mus., Indpls., 1957, Competition prize for design and sculpture Artists Equity Phila. award, 1960, Humane award Animal Rescue League of Palm Beach, 1974, 80, 85, Tallix Foundry award NSS Bicentennial Exhbn. Equitable Gallery, N.Y.C., 1976, Acad. of Italy with gold medal, 1979, Golden Centaur award, 1982, Competition prize and commn. Palm Beach County Commn.'s Meml. Chambers portrait plaque, 1986. Mem. Nat. Sculpture Soc., Nat. Acad. Design (assoc.), Artists Equity Assn. (dir. Phila. chpt. 1964-66), Phila. Art Alliance, Soc. of Four Arts, Norton Gallery Art, Soc. Washington Artists, Am. Medallic Sculpture Assn. (edit. bd. jour.), English Speaking Union, Animal Rescue League of Palm Beach (com. chmn. 1972—, dir. 1975—), St. Mary's Guild of Episcopal Ch. Women (v.p. 1974-76), Nat. Women's Bd. Northwood Inst. (exec. com.), Kappa Delta Pi. Home and Studio: Sea-Lake Studio 3215 S Flagler Dr West Palm Beach FL 33405

GROVE, JUDITH COEN, social services finance specialist; b. Washington, Pa., Nov. 23, 1952; d. Charles Richard and Nancy Leslie Coen; m. Steven D. Grove, May 9, 1986. BA, Wilson Coll., 1974. Fiscal technician Pa. Dept. Pub. Welfare, Harrisburg, 1976—. Mem. Nat. Assn. Female Execs., Wilson Coll. Alumnae Assn. (bd. dirs. 1986-88).

GROVE, MYRNA JEAN, educator; b. Bryan, Ohio, Oct. 24, 1949; d. Kedric Durward and N. Florence (Stombaugh) G. Student, Bowling Green State U., 1970-71; BA in Edn., Manchester Coll., 1971; postgrad., U. No. Colo., 1974-76, Purdue U., 1977, St. Francis Coll., Ft. Wayne, Ind., 1986, Coll. Mount St. Joseph, Ohio, 1986. Cert. elem. tchr., Ohio. Tchr. elem. sch. Bryan City Schs., 1972—. Editor newspaper column Education Today, 1975-82, newsletter Northwest Ohio Emphasis, 1981-83, (award 1981). Dir., violinist Bryan String Ensemble, 1981—; organist Trinity Episc. Ch., Bryan, 1979—; trustee Bryan Area Cultural Assn., 1984—. Jennings scholar Martha Holden Jennings Found., Bowling Green State U., 1982-83. Mem. Bryan Edn. Assn. (exec. com., pres. 1985-86), Ohio Edn. Assn. (presenter 1984, del. global issues 1986), Nat. Edn. Assn. (Ohio del., state contact 1986, 87), Nat. Assn. Female Execs., Ohio Assn. Gifted Children, Bus. and Profl. Women Ohio (individual devel. com. 1986—, speaking skills cert. 1987), Northwest Ohio Tchrs. Uniserv (sec. 1975-78), Northwest Ohio Manchester Coll. Alumni Assn. (past pres.).

GROVER, ROSALIND REDFERN, oil and gas company executive; b. Midland, Tex., Sept. 5, 1941; d. John Joseph and Rosalind (Kapps) Redfern; m. Arden Roy Grover, Apr. 10, 1982; 1 child, Rosson. BA in Edn. magna cum laude, U. Ariz., 1966, MA in History, 1982; postgrad. in law, So. Meth. U., Dallas. Librarian Gahr High Sch., Cerritos, Calif., 1969-70; pres. The Redfern Found., Midland, 1982—; ptnr. Redfern & Grover, Midland, 1986—;chmn. bd. dirs. Flag-Redfern Oil Co., Midland. Sec. park and recreation commn. City of Midland, 1969-71, del. Objectives for Convocation, 1980, mem., past pres. women's aux. Midland Community Theatre, 1970, chmn. challenge grant bldg. fund, 1980, chmn. Tex. Yucca Hist. Landmark Renovation Project, 1983, trustee, 1983-88; chmn. publicity com. Midland Jr. League Midland, Inc., 1972, chmn. edn. com., 1976, corr. sec., 1978; 1st v.p. Midland Symphony Assn., 1975; chmn. Midland Charity Horse Show, 1975-76; mem. Midland Am. Revolution Bicentennial Commn., 1976; trustee Mus. S.W., 1977-80, pres. bd. dirs., 1979-80; trustee Midland Meml. Hosp., 1978-80; co-chmn. Gov. Clements Fin. Com., Midland, 1978; bd. dirs. Mountain States Legal Found., 1986—. Recipient HamHock award Midland Community Theatre, 1978. Mem. Ind. Petroleum Assn. Am., Tex. Ind. Producers and Royalty Owners Assn. (bd. dirs.), Phi Kappa Phi, Pi Lambda Theta. Republican. Clubs: Petroleum, Racquet (Midland); Tower (Dallas). Home: 1906 Crescent Pl Midland TX 79705 Office: PO Box 236 Midland TX 79702

GROVES, NANCY ANN, accountant; b. Rochester, N.Y., Feb. 23, 1950; d. Donald Pendell and Vera Umpleby; m. Thomas Castaneda, 1974 (div. 1976); 1 child, Castaneda. Student, Ithaca Coll., 1967-68; student, Santa Barbara City Coll., 1971-74, U. Calif., Santa Barbara, 1986-87. Clk. Raytheon, Santa Barbara, Calif., 1968-69; keypuncher DA-Com, Santa Barbara, 1972-73, Raytheon, Santa Barbara, 1973-77; cost acct. Applied Magnetics Co., Goleta, Calif., 1977-80; data coordinator U. Calif., Santa Barbara, 1980-87; acct. Santa Barbara Mus. of Art, 1987—. Author: Isle of the Blessed, 1982, Catch the Sparrow, 1986, Single Man's Cookbook, 1987. Sec. Parents Without Partners, Santa Barbara, 1986. Mem. Nat. Assn. Female Execs. Republican.

GROVES, ROSALIND GANZEL, corporate communications specialist; b. Phila., Aug. 1, 1934; d. John Edward and Flora Edith (Shultz) Ganzel; m. Harold Eber Woodbridge, Dec. 7, 1951 (div. June 1966); children: John Arthur, Martin Alan, June Marie; m. Gary Wayne Groves, Aug. 7, 1975 (div. 1980). AA, Fla. Keys Community Coll., 1972; BA, U. N. Fla., 1975. Cert. profl. Hypnotist, Fla.; registered ins. agt., Fla. Program analyst USN Officer-in-Charge Constrn. Trident, St. Marys, Ga., 1981-83; with acctg. dept. USN Officer-in-Charge Constrn. Trident, St. Marys, 1983-84; telephone communications USN, NAS Jacksonville, Jacksonville, Fla., 1985—; ins. agt. Hill and Co., Jacksonville, 1986—; also freelance writer/editor; dir. Behavior Modification Ctr., Jacksonville, 1983—; cons. hypnosis, Jacksonville, Fla., 1983—. Counselor Vo. Jacksonville, 1975-76; tchr. Duval County Sch. System, 1984; mem. Key West Art & Hist. Soc., 1984—; speaker Naval Air Station Jacksonville Speakers Bur., 1985—; vol. Jacksonville Upbeat Program, 1986—. Named Honorary Fire Reservist #772 Phila. Fire Dept. Mem. Inst. Advanced Hyponology (newsletter editor 1983-85, sec. 1983-85, v.p. 1986-87), Navy League U.S., Fla. Assn. Profl. Hypnosis (newsletter editor 1985-87), The Exec. Female, Assn. to Advance Ethical Hypnosis, Navy League, Jacksonville C. of C., Offshore Power Boat Racing Assn. Republican. Mem. Ch. of Christ. Club: Internat. Toastmistress (sponsored new club). Home: 7212 Cypress Cove Rd Jacksonville FL 32244

GROWE, JOAN ANDERSON, state official; b. Mpls., Sept. 28, 1935; d. Arthur F. and Lucille M. (Brown) Anderson; children: Michael, Colleen, David, Patrick. B.S., St. Cloud State U., 1956; cert. in spl. edn, U. Minn., 1964; exec. mgmt. program State and local govt., Harvard U., 1979. Tchr. elem. pub. schs. Bloomington, Minn., 1956-58; tchr. for exceptional children elem. pub. schs. St. Paul, 1964-65; spl. edn. tchr. St. Anthony Pub. Schs., Minn., 1965-66; mem. Minn. Ho. of Reps., 1973-74; sec. of state State of Minn., St. Paul, 1975—; mem. exec. council Minn. State Bd. Investment; bd. dirs. Women Execs. in State Govt. Mem. Women's Campaign Fund, Women s Polit. Caucus, Minn. Women's Econ. Roundtable; candidate U.S. Senate, 1984; bd. dirs. Greater Mpls. council Girl Scouts U.S., Wayside House, Epilepsy Support Program. Recipient Minn. Sch. Bell award, 1977, YMCA Outstanding Achievement award, 1978; Disting. Alumni award St. Cloud State U., 1979; Charlotte Striebel Long Distance Runner award Minn. NOW, 1985. Mem. Nat. Assn. Secs. of State (pres. 1979-80), Bus. and Profl. Women, Inc., Minn. Equal Rights Alliance, AAUW, LWV. Roman Catholic. Office: Sec of State's Office 180 State Office Bldg Saint Paul MN 55155

GRUBB, KITTY GOLDSMITH, lawyer; b. Bennettsville, S.C., July 29, 1952; d. Harry Simon and Carolyn (Davis) Goldsmith; m. Lawrence Logan Grubb, Aug. 6, 1972. AB, U. Ala., Tuscaloosa, 1974; JD cum laude, Cumberland Sch. Law, 1977; LLM in Taxation, NYU, 1981. Bar: Ala. 1977, U.S. Ct. Appeals (5th cir.) 1979, Tenn. 1981, U.S. Ct. Claims 1981, U.S. Tax Ct. 1981, U.S. Ct. Appeals (4th cir.) 1980, U.S. Dist. Ct. (ea. dist.) Tenn. 1982, U.S. Ct. Appeals (6th and Fed. cirs.) 1984, U.S. Ct. Mil. Appeals 1984, U.S. Dist. Ct. (mid. dist.) Tenn. 1988. Staff atty. TVA, Knoxville, 1977-79; assoc. Lockridge & Becker, P.C., Knoxville, 1981-82; ptnr. Dunaway, Harrell, Grubb, Van Hook & Cotton, LaFollette, Tenn., 1982-85; assoc. Wagner & Myers, P.C., Knoxville, 1985-86; prin. ptnr., McGehee & Grubb; P.C., Knoxville, 1986—; lectr. St. Mary's Hosp., Knoxville, Knoxville Women's Ctr., various other orgns.; mem. So. Pension Conf., Atlanta, 1981-82, Am. Pension Conf., N.Y.C., 1981-82. Assoc. editor Cumberland Law Rev., 1975-77. Chmn. fund drive, eastern Tenn. region Cumberland Sch. Law, 1979-80; apptd. by Tenn. Supreme Ct. Bd. Profl. Responsibility, 1987—. Recipient Curia Honoris award Cumberland Sch. Law, 1978, cert. merit Cumberland Sch. Law chpt. Phi Delta Phi, 1977, cert. appreciation Knoxville Women's Ctr., 1983-86, Annie P. Selwyn award, 1986. Mem. Knoxville Bar Assn. (continuing legal edn. 1982-84), ABA (Tenn. membership chmn. Young Lawyer's Conf. div. 1984-86), Ala. Bar Assn., Tenn. Bar Assn. (profl. responsibility com.), Assn. Trial Lawyers Am., Cumberland Law Sch. Alumni Assn., NYU Law Sch. Alumni Assn., U. Ala. Alumni (v.p. eastern Tenn. chpt. 1983, pres. chpt. 1984, merit awards eastern Tenn. chpt. 1982, 83, 84, nat. award 1984), AAUW, Knoxville Assn. Women Execs. (v.p. 1986, pres. chpt. 1987), Nat. Assn. Women Execs., Knoxville Zool. Soc., Polit. Button Collectors (Dixie chpt., Am. chpt.), Century Club of U. Ala. Alumni (eastern Tenn. chpt.), Am. Platform Soc., Omicron Delta Epsilon, Pi Sigma Alpha. Democrat. Methodist. Lodge: Kiwanis. Office: McGehee & Grubb PC 1634 Plaza Tower Knoxville TN 37929

GRUBE, REBECCA SUE, elementary educator, consultant; b. Lancaster, Pa., June 27, 1945; d. Warren Landis and Ruth Rebecca (Hackman) Newcomer; m. Terry Wayne Grube, Aug. 27, 1966; children: T. David, Joy Lynn, Matthew Warren. Student Juniata Coll., 1963-65; BA, Franklin and Marshall Coll., 1976; MEd, Millersville U., 1979; postgrad. Temple U., Wright State U. Cert. spl. edn., neurolinguistic programmer. Grad. asst. Millersville U., Pa., 1978-79; tchr. gifted and learning disabled Sch. Dist. of Lancaster, Pa., 1979-80; tchr. pvt. sch., Lancaster, 1980-81; elem. tchr. Lancaster Country Day Sch., 1981-85, tchr. resource room, 1985—, chmn. elem. lang. arts curriculum, 1985—, mem. curriculum com., 1986-87; pvt. practice ednl. cons., tutor, Lancaster, 1981—; dir. program Teaching Talented and Outstanding Pupils for Success, 1987, 88—; instr. Performance Learning Systems, 1987—, Wilkes Coll., 1987—. Contbg. editor United Evang. 1975; contbr. articles to profl. quars.; author research report. Pres. bd. dirs. Contact Lancaster, 1986, chairperson support workers, 1987-88; bd. dirs. Listening Ear, Parents of Adoptive Children Orgn., 1981-85; mem. Cen. Pa. Friends of Jazz. Christa McAuliffe fellow U.S. Dept. Edn., 1988-89; recipient award Lancaster Assn. Retarded Citizens, 1978-79, Cert. of Appreciation, AFL-CIO Community Services, 1983, CONTACT award City of Lancaster, 1988, Literacy award for T.T.O.P.S. Lancaster-Lebanon Reading Council, 1988. Mem. Assn. for Supervision and Curriculum, Nat. Council Tchrs. of English, Orton Dyslexia Soc., Assn. for Children with Learning Disabilities (past bd. dirs. Lancaster Lebanon chpt.), Internat. Platform Assn., Assn. for Psychol. Type, Pa. Assn. for Gifted Children, Council Exceptional Children ,Nat. Assn. for Gifted Children, Pi Lambda Theta (chmn. Lehman Home Project 1984-86). Republican. Lutheran. Avocations: tennis, walking, piano, drums, reading. Home: 18 Gordon Rd Lancaster PA 17603

GRUBER, HOLLY ELIZABETH, design engineer; b. Berwyn, Ill., Jan. 8, 1961; d. Raymond Leon and Myrtle Elizabeth (Fisher) Richey; m. Eddy Jeff Gruber; children: Amber Elizabeth. BChemE, Auburn U., 1983; postgrad. in Bus. Adminstrn., U. Tenn., Chattanooga, 1984—. Power utilization engr. TVA, Chattanooga, 1983-86, McKee Baking Co., Collegedale, Tenn., 1986—. Canvasser United Way, Chattanooga, 1984, U.S. Savings Bonds, Chattanooga, 1985. Mem. Auburn Alumni Assn. Baptist. Home: Rt 6 Box 345 Cleveland TN 37311 Office: McKee Baking Co PO Box 750 Collegedale TN 37315

GRUBER, KIMBERLEY ANN, programmer/analyst; b. Hagerstown, Md., Oct. 26, 1960; d. Lee Baker and Elizabeth Virginia (Shuman) G. BA in Edn., Shepherd Coll., Shepherdstown, W.Va., 1982, BS in Math., 1985. Cer. tchr. Tchr. North Highland Sch., Shreveport, La., 1983-84; system engr.trainee EDS, Southfield, Mich., 1986-87; programmer/analyst CDSI, Germantown, Md., 1987—. Mem. Nat. Assn. Female Execs. Home: 13210 Bristlecore Way #33 Germantown MD 20874

GRUBER, ROSALIND H., counseling psychologist; b. Bronx, N.Y., Feb. 10, 1943; d. Lazarus L. and Beatrice (England) G.; B.A. cum laude, SUNY, New Paltz, 1974; M.A., Suffolk U., 1978. Nat. Cert. Counselor; lic. clin. social worker. Sch. registrar Assn. Help Retarded Children, N.Y.C., 1970; counselor Neighborhood Youth Corps, Poughkeepsie, N.Y., 1971-73; liason Govt. Subsidized Housing, Cambridge, Mass., 1975-77; dir., counselor Aradia Counseling, Boston, 1978—; ptnr.-owner real estate investment co., 1982—. Mem. Nat. Assn. Social Workers, Am. Personnel and Guidance Assn., Assn. Humanistic Edn. and Devel., Mass. Mental Health Counselors Assn., Assn. Women in Psychology, U.S. Power Squaron. Home: 251 Mill St Newtonville MA 02160 also: 2150 Old Kings Hwy PO Box 272 West Barnstable MA 02668 Office: 520 Comm Ave Boston MA 02215

GRUDE, WANDA A., economist, futures trader; b. N.Y.C., May 2, 1948; d. Fabio Renzo and Marie Perfumo Goldschmied; m. John Edward Grude, Sept. 20, 1969. BA in Econ., U. Utah, 1968; MA in Econ., DePaul U., 1972. Econ. research analyst No. Trust Bank, Chgo., 1969-72; instr. Regis Coll., Denver, 1972-73; asst. treas. econ. and pension investment Colo. Pub. Service Co., Denver, 1973-80; corp. economist Petro-Lewis Corp., Denver, 1980-84; pvt. practice consulting economist Denver, 1984—, pvt. practice futures trader, 1986—. Bd. dirs. Pub. Service Employees Credit Union. Woodrow Wilson fellow, 1969. Mem. Am. Econ. Assn., Internat. Assn. Bus. Economists (chpt. pres. 1983-84, newsletter editor 1984-86), Nat. Assn. Energy Economists (chpt. pres. 1974-75), Am. Ski Assn., Pi Kappa Alpha. Republican. Home: 4435 W 94th Ave Westminster CO 80030

GRUEBEL, BARBARA JANE, internist, pulmonologist; b. Honolulu, May 12, 1950; d. Robert William and Elenor Jane (Perry) G.; B.S., Stephen F. Austin State U., 1977; M.D. (Robert Wood Johnson Found. scholar, Coll. Women's Club scholar), Baylor Coll. Medicine, 1974. Intern in internal medicine U. Rochester, 1974-75, resident in internal medicine, 1974-77; pulmonary fellow U. Mich., 1977-79; mem. med. staff Anthony L. Jordan Health Center, Rochester, N.Y., 1976-77, Univ. Health Service, Ann Arbor, Mich., 1978-79; med. dir. progressive respiratory care unit Meth. Hosp. of Dallas, 1979-80; asst. prof. medicine U. Tex. Health Sci. Center, Dallas, 1979-80; cons. in pulmonary disease, Dallas, 1980—; med. dir. pulmonary services Southeastern Meth. Hosp.; clin. asst. prof. medicine U. Tex. Health Sci. Center; nat. affiliate faculty Am. Heart Assn. Active TEXPAC. Recipient award for gen. excellence in pediatrics, 1974, Stanley W. Olson award for acad. excellence, 1974, John Richard Fox award, 1974, Stuart A. Wallace award in pathology, 1974; Welch Found. grantee, 1970; Am. Lung Assn. tng. fellow, 1977-79. Diplomate Nat. Bd. Med. Examiners. Fellow Am. Coll. Chest Physicians (named Young Pulmonary Physicians of Future 1979); mem. Am. Med. Women's Assn. (scholastic excellence award 1974), Am. Thoracic Soc., Am. Lung Assn., AMA, Dallas County Med. Soc., Tex. Med. Soc., Soc. Critical Care Medicine, Nat. Assn. Female Execs., Nat. Assn. Med. Dirs. Respiratory Care, Dallas Acad. Internal Medicine, Am. Cancer Soc. (dir. Oak Cliff area), Women Meeting Women, Dallas Acad. Medicine, Dallas C. of C., Oak Cliff C. of C., Alpha Omega Alpha, Beta Beta Beta. Office: 221 W Colorado St Suite 470 Dallas TX 75208

GRUEN, ERICA MARLENE, television producer, advertising executive; b. Chgo., May 15, 1951; d. Dieter Martin and Dolores (Colen) G.; m. J.M. Levy, June 22, 1986. B.A. with honors, U. Mich., 1972; M.S., U. Wis., 1975. Sch. psychologist, Madison, Wis., 1975-76; concert mgr. U. Tenn., Knoxville, 1976-78; promotion dir. Aspen Music Festival, N.Y.C., 1978-80; mktg. dir. Rainbow Programming, Woodbury, N.Y., 1980-82; v.p., assoc. dir. electronic media Saatchi & Saatchi DFS, N.Y.C., 1982—; speaker New Sch. Social Research; mem. adv. bd. N.Y. Internat. Home Video Show. Contbr. articles to advt. and cable TV publs. Recipient award for Cable Excellence, 1984, 85. Mem. Soc. Advancement Judaism (adv. bd. 1984-86, retreat chmn. 1983-84), Nat. Acad. Cable Programming, Am. Assn. Advt. Agys. (new techs. com. 1982—), Pinewoods Folk Music Club (edn. chmn. 1979-81), Sierra Club, Appalachian Mountain Club.

GRUEN, EVELYN JEANETTE, lawyer, accountant; b. Vancouver, B.C., Can., Oct. 13, 1956; came to U.S., 1960; d. Kurt and Mary Rose (Spörk) G. B.S., Calif. State U.-Northridge, 1977; M.Bus. Taxation, U. So. Calif., 1981, M.B.A., J.D., 1981. Bar: Calif. 1981, Calif. State Supreme Ct. 1981, U.S. Dist. Ct. (cen. dist.) Calif. 1981, U.S. Ct. Appeals (9th cir.) 1981, U.S. Tax Ct. 1984, U.S. Supreme Ct. 1988. Law clk. Dreisen, Kassoy & Freiberg, Los Angeles, 1979-80, Katz, Simon, Weiss & Horwich, Los Angeles, 1980-81; assoc. Pepper, Hamilton & Scheetz, Los Angeles, 1981-83; mng. atty. Los Angeles office Reynolds, Hagendorf, Vance & Deason, 1983-84; sole practice, Simi Valley, Calif., 1984—. Mem. ABA, Calif. State Bar, Los Angeles County Bar Assn., Phi Alpha Delta, Phi Kappa Phi. Office: PO Box 202 Simi Valley CA 93062

GRUENEWALD, PATRICIA MARY, securities trader; b. St. Louis, Mar. 17, 1953; d. Joseph Charles and Ruth Ann (Mueller) Taschler; m. Gary Allen Gruenewald, Nov. 7, 1975 (div. Apr. 1986); 1 child, Kevin Gary. BSBA, U. Mo., St. Louis, 1975; MA in Computer Data Mgmt., Webster U., 1985. Supr. estates and legal securities Edward D. Jones & Co., St. Louis, 1978-80, mgr. money market fund processing, 1980-84, mgr. mut. fund processing, 1983-84, gen. prin. funds processing, 1984—; mem. ICI Mut. Fund. Adv. Com., Washington, 1986—. Campaign worker Kit Bond for Senate, St. Louis, 1986, John Danforth for Senate com., 1987. Mem. Single Profls. Assn., Nat. Assn. for Female Execs., St. Louis Fin. Assn., Parents without Ptnrs. (sec. 1987-88). Office: Edward D Jones 201 Progress Pkwy Maryland Heights MO 63043

GRUHL, ANDREA MORRIS, librarian; b. Ponca City, Okla., Dec. 9, 1939; d. Luther Oscar and Hazel Evangeline (Anderson) Morris; m. Werner Mann Gruhl, July 10, 1965; children—Sonja Krista, Diana Krista. B.A., Wesleyan Coll., 1961; M.L.S., U. Md., 1968; M. Liberal Arts Program, Johns Hopkins U., 1971; postgrad. U. Md., 1968, 71-73. Tchr., Broward County, Fla., Dept. Def. Montgomery County, Md., 1961-66; librarian Prince Georges County (Md.) Pub. Library, 1966-68, 81-83, U. Md., College Park, 1970-72; art history researcher Joseph Alsop, Washington, 1972-74; librarian Howard County Pub. Library, Columbia, Md., 1969-70, 74-79; European exchange staff Library of Congress, Washington, 1982-86; cataloger fed. documents, GPO, Washington, 1986—; processing dept. rep. women's program adv. com. Library of Congress, 1983-86, mem. ofcl. del. Internat. Fedn. Library Assns. ann. conf., Munich, 1983, Chgo., 1985; state del. White House Conf. on Libraries, 1978. Indexer, editor: Learning Vacations, 3d edit., 1980; LCPA Index to Library of Congress Info. Bull., 1984. Trustee, Howard County Pub. Library, Columbia, Md., 1979-87; publ. chmn. LWV of Howard County, Md., 1974; citizen's rep. for Howard County and exec. bd. Balt. Regional Planning Council Library Com., 1976-79; Friends of the Library, Howard County, Md., pres., 1976; vol. Nat. Gallery of Art Library, Washington, 1978-80. Mem. Art Libraries Soc. N.Am. (coordinator, pub. exhbn. 1980-82), ALA (mem. trustee assn. 1982-87, resources and tech. services div., cataloging sect. 1988—, govt. documents roundtable 1988—), Library of Congress Profl. Assn. (coordinator ann. staff art show 1982, 83, chmn. spl. interest group on library sci. 1985-87), Library of Congress Am. Fedn. State County and Mcpl. Employees Union 2477 (program chmn. 1984-86), Md. Library Assn. (pres. trustee div. 1982-83), Kappa Delta Epsilon, Beta Phi Mu. Democrat. Methodist. Lutheran. Home: 5990 Jacob's Ladder Columbia MD 21045 Office: Govt Printing Office Washington DC 20401

GRUMET, PRISCILLA HECHT, fashion specialist, consultant, writer; b. Detroit, May 11, 1943; d. Lewis Maxwell and Helen Ruth (Miller) Hecht; m. Ross Frederick Grumet, Feb. 24, 1968; 1 child, Auden Lewis. AA, Stephens Coll., 1963; student, Ga. State Coll., 1983-85. Buyer Rich's Dept. Store, Atlanta, 1963-68; instr. fashion retail Fashion Inst. Am., Atlanta, 1968-71; pres., lectr., cons. Personally Priscilla Personal Shopping Service, Atlanta, 1971—; instr. Emory U. Cont. Edn. Program, Atlanta, 1976—; fashion merch. coordinator Park Pl. Shopping Ctr., Atlanta, 1979-83; writer Altanta Bus. Mag., 1984—; cons., buyer Greers-Regensteins Store, Atlanta, 1986—; Guest lectr. Fashion Group of Am., Rancho La Puerta Resort, Tecate, Mex., 1985—, adv. bd. Bauder Fashion Coll., 1986—, fashion panel judge Weight Watchers Internat., 1981. Author: How to Dress Well, 1981; reporter, Women's Wear Daily, 1976—; writer, Atlanta Bus. Mag., 1984—; columnist, Altanta Scene Mag.; contbr. numerous articles to mags. including Seventeen, Nat. Jeweler's. Pub. relations dir., Atlanta Jewish Home Aux., 1986—; admissions advisor, Stephens Coll., 1979—. Named Tchr. of Excellence continuing edn. program Emory U., 1983; recipient Outstanding Alumna award Stephens Coll., 1983. Mem. Fashion Group, Inc., Atlanta Press Club, Women in Communications, Nat. Council of Jewish Women. Clubs: Temple Sisterhood (speaker, spl. events com. 1983—). Home: 2863 Careygate NW Atlanta GA 30305

GRUNLOH, ELLEN JO, entrepreneur; b. Effingham, Ill., Mar. 12, 1962; d. Don S. and Dorothy (Jones) G. Diploma in computer operation, Lakeland Coll., 1982. With Mid-Am. Corvette Supplies, Effingham, 1982-88; creative dir. Mid-Am. Corvette Supplies, 1985-88; prin. Media Maker, Effingham, 1988—. Mem. Nat. Assn. Female Execs., Heartland Computer Club. Home and Office: 500 E St Louis Effingham IL 62401

GRUNNER, JOCELYN SARI, accounts professional; b. N.Y.C., Mar. 15, 1958; d. Bernard and Ruth Rosa (Jaslove) G. Student, CUNY, 1975-79. Advt. broadcast negotiator Sawdon & Bess Advt., N.Y.C., 1979-80, Marschall Advt., N.Y.C., 1980-81, Wells, Rich & Green Advt., N.Y.C., 1981-83; assoc. broadcast dir. Media Gen. Broadcast, N.Y.C., 1983-86; nat. broadcast account mgr. Katz Communication, N.Y.C., 1986—. Mem. Advt. Women of N.Y. Office: Katz Communications 1 Dag Hammarskjold Plaza New York NY 10017

GRUNNET, MARGARET LOUISE, pathologist; b. Mpls., Feb. 20, 1936; d. Leslie Nels and Grace Harriet (Thomson) Grunnet; m. Irving Noel Einhorn, Mar. 10, 1972; stepchildren: Jeffrey Allan, Franne Ruth, Eric Carl, Stanley Glenn. BA summa cum laude, U. Minn., Mpls., 1958; MD, U. Minn., 1962; MS, Ohio State U., 1969. Resident in psychiatry U. Pa. Sch. Medicine, Phila., 1963-64; resident anatomic pathology Presbyn.-U. Pa. Med. Ctr., Phila., 1965-66; fellow neuropathology Phila. Gen. Hosp., 1967, Ohio State U. Hosp., Columbus, 1968-69; instr. Ohio State U., 1969; asst. prof. U. Utah Sch. Medicine, Salt Lake City, 1970-76, assoc. prof., 1976-80; assoc. prof. pathology U. Conn. Sch. Medicine, Farmington, 1980—. Contbr. articles to profl. jours. Mem. Am. Med. Women's Assn., Internat. Soc. Neuropathologists Conn. Soc. Pathologists, Am. Assn. Neuropathology, Phi Beta Kappa, Alpha Omega Alpha. Mem. Ch. of Christ. Home: 1550 Asylum Ave West Hartford CT 06117 Office: U Conn Health Ctr Dept Pathology Farmington CT 06032

GRUSH, MARY ELLEN, computer company executive; b. Aurora, Ill., Oct. 28, 1947; d. Byron Edward and Olga Marion (Olson) Grush; m. Kenneth Takagi Takara, Oct. 25, 1981; 1 child, Stephanie Suzanne Grush. B.A., Ft. Wright Coll., 1971; M.A., U. Denver, 1975. Mgr. met. info. retrieval network Bibliog. Ctr. for Research, Denver, 1975-77; customer services rep. tng. Lockheed Dialog Info. Systems, Palo Alto, Calif., 1977-78, computer ops. supr., 1978—. Mem. ALA, Spl. Libraries Assn., Beta Phi Mu, Pi Delta Phi. Home: PO Box 1378 Los Altos CA 94023

GUARALDI, SHARON ANNE, real estate executive; b. Lebanon, N.H., Dec. 14, 1947; d. Clayton Walter and Irene Agness (Withington) Stark; m. Lawrence V. Guaraldi, Feb. 14, 1970; children: Timothy, Luke, Storme, Matthew, Naomi, Kimberly. BS, U. N.H., 1969. Instr. sewing Singer Sewing, Lebanon, 1967-69; salesperson, mgr. Guaraldi Ins., Lebanon, 1970—; owner, mgr. Century 21 Guaraldi, Lebanon, 1978—. Chairperson bloodmobile ARC, Lebanon, 1986—. Mem. Nat. Assn. Realtors, Bus. and Profl. Women. Republican. Roman Catholic. Home: 85 Bank St Lebanon NH 03766 Office: Guaraldi Agencies Hanover St at the Mall Lebanon NH 03766

GUARD, MARY BETH, lawyer, small business owner; b. Carmi, Ill., Aug. 19, 1955; d. William Frank and Jacqueline Lee (Galloway) Sharp; m. Lynndon Michael Guard, May 28, 1978. AA, Kaskaskia Coll., 1975; BS, So. Ill. U., 1977, JD, 1980. Bar: Okla., U.S. Dist. Ct. (we. dist.) Okla., U.S. Ct. Appeals (10th cir.). Atty. oil and gas dept. Commrs. Land Office State of Okla., Oklahoma City, 1980-84; gen. counsel Banking Dept. State of Okla., Oklahoma City, 1984—; gen. ptnr. Sweatshirt Chic, Oklahoma City, 1987—; lectr. continuing legal edn. courses, Okla. 1981—; magician Oklahoma City, 1982—. Vol. various orgns.; mentor Search Sch. for Gifted Children, Moore, Okla., 1986, 87; bd. dirs., 3d v.p. YWCA, Oklahoma city, 1985—. Mem. Okla. Bar Assn. (com. post 1982-85), Oklahoma City Magic Soc. (v.p. 1985-86), Internat. Brotherhood Magicians, Bus. and Profl. Women's Club (pres. 1983-84, Outstanding Woman of Yr. 1982, Outstanding Young Careerist 1985), Order of the Barrister, Phi Alpha Delta (justice 1979-80). Democrat. Methodist. Home: 201 NW 33d St Oklahoma City OK 73118 Office: State Okla Dept Banking 4100 N Lincoln Oklahoma City OK 73105

GUARDO, CAROL J., college president; b. Hartford, Conn., Apr. 12, 1939; d. C. Fred and Marion (Biase) G. B.A., St. Joseph Coll., 1961; M.A., U. Detroit, 1963; Ph.D., U. Denver, 1966. Asst. prof. psychology Eastern Mich. U., Ypsilanti, 1966-68; assoc. prof., staff psychologist U. Denver, 1968-73; assoc. prof., dean Coll. Utica Coll. of Syracuse U., Utica, N.Y., 1973-76; prof., dean Coll. Liberal Arts, Drake U., Des Moines, 1976-80; provost, prof. U. Hartford, 1980-85; pres. R.I. Coll., Providence, 1986—; mem. Iowa Humanities Bd., 1976-80, pres., 1978-80; bd. dirs. Am. Council Edn., People's Bank. Author: The Adolescent As Individual: Issues and Insights, 1975; contbr. articles to profl. jours. Trustee St. Joseph Coll., Monmouth Coll. NSF fellow, 1964; NIMH fellow, 1964-66. Mem. Am. Assn. Higher Edn., Assn. Am. Colls. (vice chair 1987, chair 1988), Am. Psychol. Assn., Assn. Gen. and Liberal Studies (pres. 1979-81), Soc. Research in Child Devel., Phi Beta Kappa. Office: Rhode Island College Providence RI 02908

GUARINO, MARGARET, urban planner, real estate developer; b. Bklyn., Oct. 1, 1949; d. Victor Emanuel and Teresa (Fuoti) Lopez; m. John Edward Guarino, Mar. 24, 1968; children: Jon-Paul, Christopher. BA in Urban Studies, Pratt Inst., MS in City and Regional Planning. VISTA vol. U.S. Peace Corps, 1977-78; VISTA project mgr. Bklyn., 1978-79; founder, exec. dir. East N.Y. Local Devel. Corp., N.Y.C., 1978-79; exec. dirs. Southwest Bklyn. Indsl. Devel. Corp., 1979-81; v.p. N.Y.C. Pub. Devel. Corp., 1981—; vis. prof. Pratt Inst., Bklyn., 1986—; adj. prof. John Jay Coll. for Criminal Justice, N.Y.C., 1984-86. founder Canarsie Vol. Ambulance Corp., Bklyn., 1976; trustee Adelphi Acad., Bklyn., 1984—. Mem. Nat. Orgn. Corp. Real Estate Execs., Am. Planning Assn., Nat. Assn. Rev. Appraisers, Am. Assn. Cert. Appraisers. Home: 492 Henry St Brooklyn NY 11231 Office: NYC Pub Devel Corp 161 William St New York NY 10038

GUENIN, PATRICIA ANNE, industrial engineer; b. Port Lavaca, Tex., Feb. 19, 1958; d. Ernest Arthur and Monique Evelyn (Demaurex) G. BS in Indsl. Engring., Pa. State U., 1980; MBA, U. Dallas, 1987. Mfg. engr. Owens-Illinois, Inc., Toledo, Ohio, 1980-81; prodn. supr. Owens-Illinois, Florence, Ky., 1981-82; indsl. engr. Kodak Corp., Dallas, 1982-85, Boeing Electronics, Dallas, 1985—. Mem. Am. Inst. Indsl. Engrs., Am. Prodn. and Inventory Control Soc., Sigma Iota Epsilon. Club: Toastmasters (Dallas) (adminstrv. v.p. 1984—). Home: 16301 Ledgemont #260 Dallas TX 75248

GUERIN, LINDA G., finance company executive; b. Dothan, Ala., Nov. 4, 1947; d. William Marvin Cain and Ana Nell (Hamn) Dennard; m. Gene Guerin, Nov. 5, 1975 (div. Apr. 1984); children: Randall, Brian; m. Donald Bremer, Sept. 19, 1987. Assoc. Realtek div. Coldwell Banker, West Palm Beach, Fla., 1975-82, Martin Downs, Developer, Stuart, Fla., 1982-84; acct. exec. Lawyers Title Ins. Corp., West Palm Beach, 1984-87; mortgage broker Congress Mortgage, West Palm Beach, 1987; wholesale acct. exec. Profl. Bancorp Mortgage, W. Palm Beach, Fla., 1987—. Mem. Assn. Profl. Mortgage Women (bd. dirs. 1987—), Fla. Assn. Realtors (co-chmn. and chmn. legis. com.), Mortgage Bankers. Republican. Methodist. Home: 1509 15th Ln Palm Beach Gardens FL 33410

GUERNETTE, JOANNE GERDES, psychologist; b. Sacramento, Calif., Mar. 22, 1931; d. Fred Paul and Pauline Clements (Haines) Gerdes; B.A., Sacramento State U., 1954, M.A., 1966; Ph.D., Tex. A&M U., 1974; m. Gene Sutphen; children—Eric, Keslie. Speech pathologist, therapist Sacramento County Supt. of Schs. Office, 1957-60; sch. psychologist Sacramento County Office of Edn., 1960-66; staff psychologist St. Joseph Community Mental Health Center, Houston, 1967; clin. psychologist Hauser Neuropsychiat. Clinic, Houston, 1967-70; cons. Brazos County Mental Health Center also Milam County Mental Health Center, 1972-74; sr. psychologist, clin. dir. Devereux Found., Victoria, Tex., 1974-84; pvt. practice clin. psychology and neuropsychology, Victoria, Tex., 1979—; vol. cons. Brazos County Mental Health Center; Child Study Clinic, Victoria. Mem. Sacramento Area Sch. Psychologists Assn. (pres.-elect 1966), Calif. Assn. Sch. Psychologists and Psychometrists (dir. 1965), Am. Psychol. Assn., Tex. Psychol. Assn., Southwestern Psychol. Assn., Council for Exceptional Children. Home: 403 W Stayton Ave Victoria TX 77901 Office: BehavioraLearn Clinic 104 Kelly Dr Suite A Victoria TX 77904

GUERNSEY, NANCY PATRICIA, mechanical engineer; b. Newark, Oct. 12, 1955; d. Orville Wendell and Dorothy Elizabeth (Maccia) Guernsey. BE in Mech. Engring., Manhattan Coll., Riverdale, N.Y. 1977; MS in Nuclear Engring. Polytech. Inst., 1986. Cert. aircraft single engine pilot. Asst. engr. systems engring. Grumman Aerospace Co., Bethpage, N.Y., 1977-83; engr. product support, Govt. Support Systems div., Harris Corp., Syosset, N.Y., 1983-86, pub. health engr. Nassau County Dept. Health bur. water pollution control, 1987-88. Mem. Nat. Rifle Assn., Soc. Women Engrs., Am. Nuclear Soc. (exec. com. L.I. sect.), ASME, The Ninety-Nines (sect. air age edn. chmn. 1982-84), Aircraft Owners and Pilots Assn., Mensa. Republican. Episcopalian. Clubs: Sperry Flying (sec. 1981-85), Long Island Early Fliers. Home: 14 3d St Ronkonkoma NY 11779

GUEST, BARBARA LEE, clothing store owner; b. Orange, N.J., June 17, 1938; d. Harry Sr. and Lula Iona (Gordon) Schwarz; m. Donald G. Guest, May 3, 1958; children: Susan Carole, Paul Jeffrey, Margaret Doris, David Allen. Grad. high sch., Middletown, N.J. Salesperson Kislin's Dept. Store, Red Bank, N.J., 1955-56, Grand Union, Keansburg, N.J., 1957-58; sec. Les Stewart Lincoln-Mercury, Mt. Holly, N.J., 1959-60; salesperson W.T. Grant, Mt. Holly, 1970-71; traffic sec. radio sta., Mt. Holly, 1971-72; salesperson, independent rep. Avon Products Inc., Newark, Del., 1973-81; mgr. SHE, Burlington, N.J., 1981-84; mgr., salesperson Leroy's, Lawrenceville, N.J., 1984; mgr., buyer Fashion Corner, Mt. Laurel, N.J., 1984-87; owner A Lady's Choice, Inc., Marlton, N.J., 1987—. Sec. N.J. Foster Parents Assn., Mt. Holly, 1962, Easthampton Helping Hand, Mt. Holly, 1975; mem. Easthampton Neighborhood Watch, Mt. Holly, 1982. Mem. Nat. Assn. Female Execs. Democrat. Methodist. Home: 1162 Woodlane Rd Mount Holly NJ 08060 Office: 42 Marlton Greene Plaza Marlton NJ 08053

GUETZKOW, DIANA, corporation executive; b. Munich, Fed. Republic Germany, July 21, 1947; came to U.S., 1954; d. Genrich Gulbinowicz and Gita Gulbin; m. Daniel Guetzkow. BS in Physics, CCNY, 1967; PhD in Internat. Studies, CUNY, 1976. Analyst internat. energy U.S. Dept. Energy, Washington, 1976-79; founder, pres., chmn. bd. Netword Inc., Washington, 1981—. Fellow AAUW, 1970, Carnegie Endowment Internat. Peace, 1971, Law Enforcement Assistance Adminstrn., 1976. Home: PO Box 444 College Park MD 20740 Office: Netword Inc PO Box 888 Riverdale MD 20737

GUIDER, CATHENIA, media specialist; b. Eutaw, Ala., Oct. 8, 1932; d. Curlie James and Alice (Coleman) Spencer; m. Raymond L. Guider, Dec. 10, 1958; children; Cora A., Cathenia D. BS, Benedict Coll., 1954, postgrad., 1962; postgrad., W. Ga. Coll., 1964. Cert. media specialist, elem. tchr. Media specialist Warren County Bd. Edn., Warrenton, Ga., 1962-66; adult edn. tchr. Warren County Bd. Edn., Warrenton, 1964—, media specialist, tchr., 1967-85, media specialist, 1986—. Chairperson Ga. Dept. Edn. PACE and NEA Polit. Action Com., Warrenton chpt., 1962— (Ga. Dept. Edn. voters com. Atlanta 1986); mem. YWCA, Columbia, S.C., 1964—; mem. Warren County Gospel Singers, 1983-85. Named Tchr. of Yr., Norwood Elem. Sch., 1964. Mem. NAACP, NEA (local chairperson polit. action com. 1962—), Ga. Library Assn., Ga. Dept. Edn. (Warren county pres. 1970, 87, excellence award 1972), Warren County Assn. Educators (pres. 1985, excellence award 1986). Democrat. Methodist. Club: Turtle of Warrenton (pres. 1964—).

GUIDI, DORIS FRASER, university provost, educator; b. Pittsfield, Mass., Sept. 14, 1934; d. Walter Frank and Ina Lawson (Fraser) Jordan; m. William Richard Guidi, June 16, 1956; children: Eric Jordan, Cynthia Fraser. BA, U. Rochester, 1956; student, Oxford (Eng.) U., 1958; MS, L.I. U., 1975; EdD, Fairleigh-Dickinson U., 1983. Acad. advisor C.W. Post Campus, L.I. U., 1975-77, instr., 1977-82, asst. prof., 1982-87, assoc. prof., 1987—, chairperson health scis. dept., 1982-85, asst. dean. Sch. Health Professions, 1985-86, provost, 1986—; summer intern The Hastings Ctr., Hasting-on-Hudson, N.Y., 1981; cons., evaluator Empire State Coll. SUNY, Old Westbury, 1977-81. Named Outstanding Alumna Sch. Health Professions L.I. U., 1987. Mem. Am. Soc. Clin. Pathologists (affiliate, cert.). Office: Long Island U CW Post Campus Northern Blvd 25A Brookville NY 11548

GUIDO, JUDITH COOPER, higher education administrator; b. Nyack, N.Y., d. Russell Seabury and Marjorie May (Osborne) Cooper; m. Fred J. Guido, Nov. 30, 1974. BA cum laude, Dominican Coll., N.Y., 1973; MA with honors, Manhattanville Coll., N.Y., 1974. Asst. to supt. for bus. Nyack Pub. Schs., N.Y., 1970-74; asst. to dean bus. program Dominican Coll., Orangeburg, N.Y., 1970-72; treas., bus. mgr. Elizabeth Seton Coll., Yonkers, N.Y., 1974-79; v.p. for fin. and adminstrn., treas. Union Theol. Sem., N.Y.C., 1979-86, v.p. fin. and adminstrn., treas. Manhattanville Coll., Purchase, N.Y., 1986—. Mem. friends com. Mus. Am. Folk Art, 1978—; founding mem. Friends Union Theol. Sem. Burke Library, N.Y.C., 1982—; mem. Pelham (N.Y.) Art Ctr., 1984—; trustee fin. com. The College Bd., N.Y.C., 1985-88; mem. steering com. Friends of the Performing Arts, Wave Hill, Riverdale, N.Y., 1985—; bd. dirs. Morningside Area Alliance, N.Y.C., 1981-85. Mem. Nat. Assn. Coll. and Univ. Bus. Officers (bd. dirs. 1984—), Ea. Assn. Coll. and Univ. Bus. Officers (bd. dirs. 1979-88), Mgmt. Inst. for Religious Orgns. (adv. bd. 1983-88), Am. Mgmt. Assn., Nat. Assn. Coll. Aux. Services, Am. Hist. Assn., N.Y. Geneaol. and Biog. Soc., Nat. Trust for Hist. Preservation, Preservation League N.Y. Avocations: ballet, jazz, reading, genealogical research, historic preservation. Office: Manhattanville Coll Purchase St Purchase NY 10577

GUIDO, SHAREON CHRISTINE, mechanical contractor; b. Washington, Aug. 5, 1946; d. James Harold and Edna Louise (Mills) McCullough; m. Frank Michael Guido, June 7, 1975; 1 child, Craig Scott. Diploma, George C. Marshall Sch., 1964. Asst. corp. sec. First Charter Land, Falls Church, Va., 1969-70; sec. to v.p. Liberty Loan Corp., Falls Church, 1970-71; gen. mgr. Richards A/C Co. Inc., Falls Church, 1971-83; founder, pres. Precision Air, Inc., Falls Church, 1983—; sponser Va. Apprenticeship Program, Fairfax, 1983—. Contbr. articles to profl. jours. Bd. dirs. Boys Clubs of Am., Falls Church, Va., 1975-76; leader Boy Scouts Am. Falls Church, 1975-78; instr. religious edn. Diocese of Arlington, Va., 1976-77; counselor Telecommunications for the Deaf, 1982; guest lectr. Am. Lung Assn., 1983; notary pub. Va., 1971—; ofcl. Nat. Assn. Stock Car Auto Racing, 1972-74. Recipient Outstanding Service award Am. Lung Assn., 1983. Mem. Air Conditioning Contractors of Am. (mgmt. edn. com. 1987—), Falls Ch. Preservation Soc., Western Eastern Roadracers Assn., Plumbing, Heating, Cooling Contractors Assn., Am. Motorcyclist Assn., Am. Soc. Notaries. Roman Catholic. Avocations: poetry writing, skiing, camping, reading. Office: Precision Air Inc 6048 Glen Carlyn Dr Falls Church VA 22041

GUIDRY, KAREN LOUISE, communications systems coordinator; b. Riverside, Calif., Dec. 3, 1956; d. Arthur H. and Helen Louise (Fraser) Tufft; m. Donald R. Guidry, may 27, 1978. BSBA, Colo. State U., 1978; MBA, La. State U., 1985. Communications analyst Ethyl Corp., Baton Rouge, 1980-86, communications system coordinator, 1986-87; communications system coordinator Ethyl Corp., Richmond, Va., 1987—; jr. achievement coordinator Ethyl Corp., Baton Rouge, 1983-87. Fund raiser Jr. Achievement, Baton Rouge, 1983-86. Mem. Ethyl Mgmt. Club (mem. chmn. 1986-87), Internat. Communications Assn. (alt. voting com.). Republican. Presbyterian. Office: Ethyl Corp 330 S 4th St Richmond VA 23219

GUILFORD, MARJORIE BRYAN, marketing executive; b. Wilson, N.C., May 11, 1957; d. James Jones and Laura Frances (Croswell) G. BA, U. N.C., Greensboro, 1979. Mgmt. trainee Donnelley Mktg., Elm City, N.C., 1979-80, systems mgr., 1980-82, mgr. prodn., 1983-84; sales support specialist Donnelley Mktg., Stamford, Conn., 1985-86; acct. rep. Carolina Mfr.'s Service, Winston-Salem, N.C., 1985-86, ops. mgr., 1986—. Democrat. United Methodist. Home: 6013 Allington Ct Winston-Salem NC 27104 Office: Carolina Mfr's Service Inc 2601 Pilgrim Ct Winston-Salem NC 27106

GUILL, DOROTHY BROWN, logistics officer; b. Portsmouth, Va., May 20, 1935; d. Jerry Alton and Geneva Alice (White) Brown; m. Tommie David Phelps, May 12, 1957 (div. May 1978); children: Tommie David Jr., Gary Scott; m. Fred Lynnwood Guill, May 12, 1978. BA in Edn., Mgmt., William and Mary Coll. Extension, 1957. Records clk. U.S. Army C.E., Norfolk, Va., 1961-64; records mgmt. asst. U.S. Army C.E., Norfolk, 1965-70, office of adminstrv. services asst. chief, 1970-75, office of adminstrv. services chief, 1976-85, mgr. EEO officer, 1985-86, logisitics mgmt. office chief, 1986—. Foster parent Chesapeake (Va.) Social Services, 1965-85; counselor Suicide Crisis Prevention Ctr., Ports, Va., 1967-69. Mem. Norfolk Dist. C. of C. Democrat. Methodist. Lodge: Order Eastern Star (line officer 1983-86). Home: PO Box 5122 Suffolk VA 23435-0122 Office: US Army Corps of Engrs Norfolk Dist 803 Front St Norfolk VA 23510-1096

GUILLEBEAU, JULIE GRAVES, public relations executive; b. Springfield, Mo., Apr. 3, 1948; d. Willard Lee and Winifred (Yadon) Graves; m. James Lester Guillebeau, Sept. 11, 1976; children: Christopher Lee, Thomas James, Julie Elizabeth. AB, Drury Coll., 1969. Newscaster Sta. WRDW-TV-12, North Augusta, S.C., 1972-73; editor Med. Coll. Ga., Augusta, 1974-81; contbg. editor Healthcare, Springfield, Mo., 1983-84; dir. pub. relations Drury Coll., Springfield, 1981—; seminar dir. Greene County Med. Soc., Springfield, Mo., 1984-85; state chmn. Ga. Hosp. Assn., Augusta, 1978; seminar dir. Council on Ind. Colls., N.Y.C., 1984, 85; mediator Media-Pub. Relations Socs., Springfield, Mo., 1983-84. Author: Springfield, A Singular City, 1988; editor League Light newsletter Jr. League of Springfield, 1986; writer: Humpty Dumpty Syndrome, 1981; co-producer: Super Soybean, 1981; ILGA, 1983; Holli, 1985; Architecture, 1986; exec. producer: Gradua Medicinae Doctoris, 1979. Dir., sec. Health Ctr. Credit Union, Augusta, Ga., 1980, 81; dir. Summerscape, Springfield, Mo., 1984—; vol. WINGS, Springfield, Mo., 1983, 84; bd. dirs. Jr. League Springfield, 1986, rep. Leadership Springfield, 1987. Mem. Pub. Relations Assn. Springfield (pres. 1986, 87), Springfield Ad Club (bd. dirs., treas. 1982—), Delta Delta Delta (vol alumni advisor). Democrat. Presbyterian. Club: Springfield Ad (bd. dirs. 1982—, treas. 1984-86). Office: Drury Coll 900 N Benton Ave Springfield MO 65802

GUILLEMETTE, GLORIA VIVIAN, dressmaker, designer; b. North Attleboro, Mass., June 27, 1929; d. Wilfred Anthony Roy and Sylviana (Bonnoyer) King; student Nat. Sch. Dress Design, 1976; m. Thomas William Guillemette, Mar. 24, 1963; children—Sylvia Marie, Katherine Anne, John Thomas. Machine operator dress mfg. cos., 1945-60; asst. to dressmaker and designer, Windsor, Conn., 1960-63; owner Mrs. G's Studio, Enfield, Conn., 1963-87; dir. Fashion Show, 1973, 76. Cub Scout commr. Boy Scouts Am., 1979-85; mem. Enfield Fair Rent Commn., 1979—; justice of peace Conn., 1979—; mem. Republican Town Com., 1976—; sec. United Meth. Women, 1977-82; mem. Enfield Fair Rent Commn., 1979-87, Presdl. Task Force, 1982-83. Club: Republican Women.

GUILLERMO, LINDA SUE, social worker; b. Chgo., July 4, 1951; d. Triponio Pascua and Helen Elizabeth (Moskal) G.; B.A., U. Ill., Chgo., 1973, M.S.W., 1975, postgrad., 1980; postgrad. Jane Addams Coll. Social Work, 1980-82; Diplomate in clin. social work, 1987. Mktg. research interviewer Rabin Research Co., Chgo., 1970-73; mktg. research interviewer, coder Marcor Mktg. Research, Inc., Chgo., 1973-75; social work intern Child and Family Services, Chgo., 1973-74, Chgo. Bd. Edn., 1974-75; social worker, therapist child abuse and neglect, case investigator, case planning cons., social service program planner Ill. Dept. Children and Family Services, Chgo., 1975-78, social service program planner, contract negotiator, monitoring agt. Central Resources Contracts and Grants, 1978-79; real estate sales person Sentry Realty, Chgo., 1976—; social worker, therapist, program coordinator, casework supr. of child abuse assessment and intervention program, proposal writer Casa Central, Chgo., 1979-82, casework cons. of child abuse assessment and intervention program, proposal writer, program dir. and casework supr. of early intervention program, 1979-85; social worker Chgo. Bd. Edn., 1985—; tng. specialist City Coll. of Chgo., 1980; adj. asso. researcher Asher Feren Law Office, Chgo., 1980-81. Treas. Greenleaf Condominium Assn., Chgo., 1980-81, sec., 1987-88, interim pres. 1988—, regional rep. North Ill. Assn. of Sch. Social Workers, 1986—, Lic. real estate salesperson, Ill. Mem. Nat. Assn. Social Workers (register clin. social workers), Acad. Cert. Social Workers, Ill. Cert. Social Workers, North Side Real Estate Bd. Home: 3600 N Lake Shore Dr Chicago IL 60613

GUILLET, KAREN ANN, computer programmer; b. Fall River, Mass., Aug. 22, 1963; d. Roland and Adeline Helen (Torres) G. AS in Computer Programming, Bristol Community Coll., Fall River, 1982; BS in Computer Info. Systems, Roger Williams Coll., 1985. Computer operator Gen. Dynamics, Middletown, R.I., 1982-83; research analyst Computer Sci. Corp. div. Naval War Coll., Middletown, 1983-85; assoc. mem. tech. staff Computer Sci. Corp. div. Naval War Coll., Newport, R.I., 1985-86, programmer, analyst, 1986—. Mem. Nat. Assn Female Execs., Assn. Systems Mgmt., Soc. Mgmt. Profl. Computing. Episcopal. Club: Seaview Collectors (Providence). Office: Computer Scis Corp Naval War Coll Sims Hall Newport RI 02893

GUILLORY, MARJORIE FRANK, engineer; b. Hiedelburg, Fed. Republic of Germany, Mar. 9, 1962; came to U.S., 1964; d. John Joseph and Carol (Willman) Frank; m. Blake Clarence Guillory, Apr. 5, 1986. BS, Tex. Agrl. and Mech. U., 1985. Engr. Reed Tool Co., Houston, 1985-86; project engr. Tampa Bay Engring., Inc., Clearwater, Fla., 1986-87, Anderson Parrish Assocs., Inc., St. Petersburg, Fla., 1987-88; planning engr. City of Tampa Water Dept., 1988—; instr. computer-aided design, Pinellas Park, Fla., 1986-87. Fundraiser Leukemia Soc., Dallas, 1983-84; instr. swimming Dallas Red Cross, 1983-84. Mem. NSPE, ASCE, Soc. Petroleum Engrs., Fla. Engring. Soc. (chmn. Jets com.), Women's Service Circle, Computer-aided Design User's Group. Republican. Mem. First Christian Ch. Home: 1409 Swann Ave Tampa FL 33606 Office: Tampa Water Dept 306 E Jackson 5E Tampa FL 33602

GUIN, GRACE HUGHES, physician; b. Birmingham, Ala., July 23, 1912; d. Ernest Smith and Grace Allen (Hawkins) Hughes; B.S., Birmingham-So. Coll., 1938; M.D., Vanderbilt U., 1943; 1 dau., Grace Guin Schiff. Intern, Albany (N.Y.) Hosp., 1945-46; resident pathology Garfield Hosp., Washington, 1950-52, Children's Nat. Med. Center, Washington, 1952-53; fellow pathology Meml. Hosp., N.Y.C., 1953-54; assoc. dir. lab. Children's Nat. Med. Center, Washington, 1954-60, dir. lab., 1960-64; staff pathologist Arlington (Va.) Hosp., 1964-67; staff pathologist VA Med. Center, Washington, 1967-80, asst. to dir. pathology service VA Central Office, Washington, 1967—; clin. prof. pathology George Washington U. Med. Center, Washington, 1960—. Nat. Cancer Inst. postdoctoral fellow, 1952. Diplomate Am. Bd. Pathology (AP and CP). Mem. Internat. Acad. Pathology, Coll. Am. Pathologists, Washington Soc. Pathology, Med. Soc. D.C. Republican. Contbr. articles in field to med. jours. Home: 3600 N Abingdon St Arlington VA 22207 Office: VA Cen Office 810 Vermont Ave NW Washington DC 20420

GUINN, NORMA JOANNE, nurse, writer. d. Robert Dale and Donna Jeanette (Heckert) Clough; m. Patrick Brent Guinn, May 18, 1974; children: Ryan Paul Wesley, Brent Tyler. Diploma in nursing, Merch Sch. Nursing, 1966; BS, Eastern Mich. U., 1974. RN, Mich. Surg. nurse E.W. Sparrow Hosp., Lansing, Mich., 1974-77, McKee Med. Ctr., Loveland, Colo., 1982—. Contbr. numerous articles to profl. jours. Mem. Assn. Operating Room Nurses. Republican. Home: 1516 Rancho Way Loveland CO 80537 Office: 2000 Boise Ave Loveland CO 80538

GUINN, SUZANNE KAY, speech language pathologist; b. Kalamazoo, Mar. 4, 1944; d. Kenneth Jeremiah and Ruth Minnie (Baker) Yeomans; m. Howard Christopher Guinn, Apr. 26, 1968; 1 child, Ian Christopher. BS, Western Mich. U., 1966; MS, U. Wis., 1967. Presch. supr. Kalamazoo Valley Intermediate Sch. Dist., 1967-68; speech-lang. pathologist State operated schs., Eielson AFB, Alaska, 1968-74; coordinator speech-lang. and presch. services Fairbanks (Alaska) North Star Borough Sch. Dist., 1974-88; dir., owner Communicaid, 1988—. Recipient DiCarlo award Am. Speech and Hearing Found., 1983. Mem. NEA, Alaska Speech Lang. Hearing Assn. (pres. 1974-75, 80-81), Am. Speech and Hearing Assn. (Frank Kleffner award 1987), Delta Kappa Gamma (pres. Fairbanks chpt. 1978-80). Home: 1438 Dupont Ln Fairbanks AK 99709 Office: Communicaid 600 University Ave Fairbanks AK 99709

GUISEWITE, CATHY LEE, cartoonist; b. Dayton, Ohio, Sept. 5, 1950; d. William Lee and Anne (Duly) G. B.A. in English, U. Mich., 1972; L.H.D. (hon.), R.I. Coll., 1979, Eastern Mich. U., 1981. Writer Campbell-Ewald Advt., Detroit, 1972-73; writer Norman Prady, Ltd., Detroit, 1973-74, W.B. Doner & Co., Advt., Southfield, Mich., 1974-75; group supr. W.B. Doner & Co., Advt., 1975-76, v.p., 1976-77; creator, writer, artist Cathy comic strip Universal Press Syndicate, Mission, Kans., 1976—. Author, artist: The Cathy Chronicles, 1978; What Do You Mean, I Still Don't Have Equal Rights??!!, 1980; What's a Nice Single Girl Doing with a Double Bed??!, 1981; I Think I'm Having a Relationship with a Blueberry Pie!, 1981; It Must Be Love, My Face Is Breaking Out, 1982; Another Saturday Night of Wild and Reckless Abandon, 1982; Cathy's Valentine's Day Survival Book, How to Live through Another February 14, 1982; How to Get Rich, Fall in Love, Lose Weight, and Solve All Your Problems by Saying "NO", 1983; Eat Your Way to a Better Relationship, 1983; A Mouthful of Breath Mints and No One to Kiss, 1983; Climb Every Mountain, Bounce Every Check, 1983; Men Should Come with Instruction Booklets, 1984; Wake Me Up When I'm a Size 5, 1985; Thin Thighs in Thirty Years, 1986, A hand to hold, an opinion to reject, 1987. Office: Universal Press Syndicate 4900 Main St Kansas City MO 64112

GUITERMAN FREUND, LAURA MAYER, university program administrator; b. N.Y.C., Sept. 15, 1925; d. Francis Randolph and Laura (Walker) Mayer; m. Franklin William Guiterman, May 14, 1949 (wid. Dec. 1974); children: Franklin William Jr., Eric Randolph; m. Paul D. Freund (dec.), Dec. 29, 1977. BA, Adelphi U., 1945; postgrad., N.Y.U., 1945. Pub. relations assoc. Hotel Pierre, N.Y.C., 1947-51; owner, mgr. E.Colony House Inn, E.Hampton, N.Y., 1953-56; pub. relations cons. Union News Co., N.Y.C.ton, 1955; mgr. pub. relations Brass Rail Restaurants, N.Y.C.ton, 1957—; pub. relations cons. Jr. Leagues of Am. and Marymount Coll., 1961-64; alumni, devel. officer, freelance editor sch. of social work, Columbia U., 1964—. Vol. Dem. Orgn., N.Y.C., St. Lukes Hosp., N.Y.C., Community Council, N.Y.C.; mgr. community club St. Bartholomew's Ch., N.Y.C., 1958-61; mem. Council for the Advancement of Edn. Mem. Geneological Soc. Democrat. Episcopalian. Clubs: Regency, Columbia (N.Y.C.), Ocean. Home: 305 E 86th St New York NY 10028 Office: Columbia U McVickar 622 W 113th St New York NY 10025

GULAJSKI, JOAN JANET, principal; b. St. Clairsville, Ohio, Mar. 12, 1933; d. Leo Michael and Rose (Bashour) Gonot; m. David Martin Gulajski, Aug. 4, 1956; children: Lisa Lynn, David Allen. BS in Edn., Kent State U., 1955, M in Edn. Adminstrn., 1974. Cert. elem. tchr., Ohio, elem. prin. Elem. tchr. Cleve. City Schs., 1955-58, Parma (Ohio) City Schs., 1958-61, Toledo City Schs., 1962-64; elem. tchr. Cuyahoga Falls (Ohio) City Schs., 1966-76, cadet prin., 1976-78, elem. prin., 1978—. Adv. bd. YMCA, Cuyahoga Falls, 1985—. Martha Holden Jennings Found. scholar, 1972-73, scholar adminstr., 1979-80. 11m. Nat. Assn. Elem. Adminstrs., Ohio Assn. Adminstrs., Summit County Elem. Adminstrs. (dir. 1985-86), Cuyahoga Falls Congress Adminstrs. (treas.), Silver Lake Fedn. (pres. 1961-62), Pi Lambda Theta. Republican. Roman Catholic. Lodge: Civitan (dir. 1986-87). Home: 2915 Elmbrook Dr Silver Lake OH 44224 Office: Silver Lake Elem Sch 2970 Overlook Silver Lake OH 44224

GULAS, JEAN MARIE, retail executive; b. Woodside, N.Y., July 9, 1957; d. Richard Michael and Joan Diane (Keating) G. BA, Hunter Coll., 1979. Asst. mgr. Master Mt. Corp., Flushing, N.Y., 1979-84; buyer asst. JC Penney, N.Y.C., 1984—. Mem. Nat. Assn. Female Execs. Democrat. Roman Catholic. Home: 147-43 41 Ave Flushing NY 11355 Office: JC Penney Co 1301 Ave of Americas New York NY 10019

GULBRANDSEN, NATALIE WEBBER, religious association administrator; b. Beverly, Mass., July 7, 1919; d. Arthur Hammond and Kathryn Mary (Doherty) Webber; m. Melvin H. Gulbrandsen, June 19, 1943; children: Karen Ann Bean, Linda Jean Goldsmith, Eric Christian, Ellen Dale Williams, Kristin Jane. BA, Bates Coll., 1942. Social worker Bur. Child Welfare, Bangor, Maine; moderator Unitarian Universalist Assn., Boston, 1985—. Exec. dir. Girl Scouts U.S., Belmont, Mass., leader 1941-44, 52-65, leadership trainer 1946-63, bd. dirs., Wellesley, Mass., 1950-63, pres. 1960-63; mem. permanent sch. accomodations com., Wellesley, 1970-76, Wellesley Youth Commn., 1968-70, Wellesley town meetings, 1967—; trustee Wellesley Human Relations Service, 1965-76, pres. 1973-78; bd. dirs. Newton Wellesley Weston Needham Area Mental Health Assn., 1975-78, Am. Field Service, 1964-70; co-chair METCO Program of Wellesley, 1965-69; trustee Unitarian Universalist Women's Fedn., 1971-81, pres. 1977-81. Recipient Wellesley Ctr. Community award, 1981. Mem. Boston Bates Alumnae Assn., Internat. Assn. Religious Freedom (mem. council 1981—). Lodge: Sons of Norway. Home: 35 Riverdale Rd Wellesley MA 02181 Office: Unitarian Universalist Assn 25 Beacon St Boston MA 02108

GULLAND, MELINDA BETH, speech pathologist; b. Clearwater, Fla.; d. Frederick Bethel and Vallie Mae (Reed) McMullen; m. James Edward Gulland, Dec. 23, 1977; children: Amanda Bethel, Megan Eileen. AA, St. Petersburg Jr. Coll., 1971-73; student, U. Fla., 1974-75; MS, U. S. Fla., 1977. Speech pathologist Polk County Schs., Lakeland, Fla., 1978-79, Los Angeles County Schs., 1980-81; v.p. Marina Profl. Services, Long Beach, Calif., 1981-87; pres., chief exec. officer PACE Therapy Inc., Torrance, Calif., 1987—; pres., chief exec. officer Gulland & Assocs., La Palma, Calif., 1986—, also bd. dirs.; bd. dirs. Creative Quality of Life Found., Glendale, Calif. 1984—; vice chmn. bd. dirs. Inst. Profl. Health Service Adminstrs. V.p. Pomona (Calif.) Continuity of Care Council, 1986—; mem. Rep. Nat. Com., Washington, 1983—. Mem. Am. Speech-Lang.-Hearing Assn., Calif. Speech-Lang.-Hearing Assn., Occupational Therapy Assn. Calif., Calif. Assn. Speech Pathologists and Audiologist in Pvt. Practice, So. Calif. Hosp. Dirs. Council, Calif. Assn. Health Facilities. Presbyterian. Home: 5082 Malaga Dr La Palma CA 90623 Office: PACE Therapy Inc Torrance CA 90504

GULLEDGE, KAREN STONE, educator, consultant; b. Fayetteville, N.C., Feb. 3, 1941; d. Malcolm Clarence and Clara (Davis) Stone; m. Parker Lee Gulledge Jr, Oct. 17, 1964. BA, St. Andrews Presbyn. Coll., Laurinburg, N.C., 1963; MA, East Carolina U., 1979; EdD, Nova U., 1986. Social worker Lee County, Sanford, N.C., 1963-64; tchr. Asheboro (N.C.) City Schs., 1964-67, Winston-Salem (N.C.)/Forsyth County Schs., 1967-70; research analyst N.C. Dept. Pub. Instrn., Raleigh, 1971-76, sch. planning cons., 1976—; cons. N.C. elem. com. of So. Assn. Colls. and Schs., 1978—, N.C. secondary com. 1982—; leader profl. seminars; speaker in field. Vol. N.C. Cancer Soc., Raleigh, 1970—, Am. Heart Assn., Raleigh, 1970—, N.C. Cystic Fibrosis Assn, Raleigh, 1970—, Raleigh Rescue Mission, 1975—; charter mem. St. Andrews Presbyn. Ch., Raleigh; mem. N.C. State Capitol Presevation Found., 1988—, N.C. Mus. of Art, 1988—. Mem. Women in State Govt., N.C. Assn. Sch. Adminstrs., Council Ednl. Facility Planners, Delta Kappa Gamma. Democrat. Home: 7405 Fiesta Way Raleigh NC 27615 Office: Div Sch Planning 217 W Jones St Edn Annex I Raleigh NC 27601-1712

GULLETTE, ETHEL MAE BISHOP, pianist; b. St. Paul, Mar. 29, 1908; d. Clarence Eugene and Alma (Beckman) Bishop; m. William Brandon Gullette, Sept. 5, 1936; children: Ethel Mae, Charlene Ann. MusB, MacPhail Sch. Music, Mpls., 1928; BA, U. Minn., 1931; diploma, Juilliard Sch. Music, 1936; pvt. study piano with Donald N. Ferguson, James Friskin. Pianist and accompanist in concerts and radio appearances, Midwest U.S., 1925-33; voice accompanist Juilliard Sch. Music, also pvt. piano tchr., N.Y.C., 1933-47; duo-pianist, accompanist, Fairfield County, Conn., 1951—, also Hartford, Conn., N.J. and N.Y.C., 1967—; concert pianist, Ea. U.S., 1953—; 30 concerts Fairfield Hills Hosp., Newtown, Conn., 1957-71; concerts, Savannah, Ga., Hilton Head Island and Beaufort, S.C., 1972; accompanist Darien Troupers, 1968, 69, New Canaan High Sch. Summer Theater, 1972-73; recent concert appearances include Dallas, 1983, Scottsdale, Ariz., 1985, Lebanon, Bridgeport, Greenwich, New Canaan, Norwalk and Darien, Conn., 1980—; mem. New Canaan Piano Quartet, 1960-68; mem. New Canaan Town Players, 1952—, accompanist, 1958-63, 73; mem., accompanist Nutmeg Music Theatre, 1957-61, Demi-Opera Co., Brookfield Summer Theatre, Conn., 1961, many others. Bd. govs., rehearsal pianist Norwalk Symphony Orch., 1955-62; mem. New Canaan Community Concerts Assn., 1954—, membership chmn., 1967-69, bd. dirs. 1961-69, 84—; active fund drives charitable orgns.; co-pres. New Canaan High Sch. Parent's Council, 1964-65. Recipient Hon. Golden Eaglet award Southwestern Conn. council Girl Scouts U.S.A., 1985; also citations for work in Am. Cancer Soc. and ARC drives. Mem. N.Y. Singing Tchrs. Assn., New Canaan Hist. Soc. (photographer gown exhibits 1968-86), Darien Community Assn. (bd. dirs. 1982-84, chmn. duo piano group 1962-64, 82-84, sec. duo piano group 1984—), New Canaan Library, New Canaan Audubon Soc., Norwalk Symphony Orch. Women's Assn. (mem. bd. 1976-82), Am. Shakespeare Guild, AAUW (charter 1970—, named Outstanding Mem. Conn. chpt. 1980), Friends N.Y. Philharm. Orch. (New Canaan chmn. 1968-71), Fairfield County Panhellenic Council, Juilliard Alumni Assn., U. Minn. Alumni Assn. (past dir. N.Y.), New Canaan Community Concerts Assn. (hon. life, Membership and Service award 1974, hon. life mem. bd., citation for 25 yrs. outstanding achievements 1979), Mu Phi Epsilon (recognition as 50 yr. mem. 1977), Delta Zeta (alumni charter; pres. local alumnae chpt. 1961-63, treas. 1982-84, named Outstanding New Eng. Alumna 1980, Nat. Woman of Yr. 1982; Golden Rose 50 yr. mem. award 1981; ann. alumna service award established in her name by Fairfield County chpt. 1983). Congregationalist. Clubs: Schubert (St. Paul); Atlantic Beach (L.I., N.Y.); Schubert of Fairfield County (duo piano group sec. 1980-82). Home: 85 West Hills Rd New Canaan CT 06840

GULLIVER, ADELAIDE CROMWELL, sociology educator; b. Washington, Nov. 27, 1919; d. John Wesley, Jr. and Yetta Elizabeth (Mavritte) Cromwell; 1 son by previous marriage, Anthony C. Hill. A.B., Smith Coll., 1940; M.A., U. Pa., 1941; certificate social work, Bryn Mawr Coll., 1943; Ph.D., Radcliffe Coll., 1952; L.H.D., U. Southwestern Mass., 1972. Mem. faculty Hunter Coll., 1942-44, Smith Coll., 1945-46; mem. faculty Boston U., 1951—, prof. sociology, now prof. emerita sociology; mem. adv. com. vol. fgn. aid AID, 1964-80; mem. Nat. Council Humanities, 1968-70; adv. com. corrections Commonwealth Mass., 1955-68, mem. commn. instns. higher edn., 1973-74; adv. com. to dir. IRS, 1970-71, to dir. census, 1972-75. Mem. bd. Wheelock Coll., 1971-80, Nat. Center Afro-Am. Artists, 1971-80, African Am. Scholars Council, 1971—, Nat. Fellowship Fund, 1974-75; mem. bd. Sci. and Tech. for Internat. Devel., 1984-86. Mem. African Studies Assn. (dir. 1966-68), Am. Acad. Arts and Scis., Am. Sociol. Assn., Council on Fgn. Affairs (bd. fgn. scholarships 1980-84), Phi Beta Kappa. Home: 51 Addington Rd Brookline MA 02146 Office: Boston Univ 138 Mountfort St Brookline MA 02146

GULLO-JENNE, CAROL ANNE, clinical social worker; b. Camden, N.J., Dec. 25, 1953; d. Peter Anthony and Mary Hunter (Ernst) Gullo; m. Craig C. Jenne, Oct. 18, 1980; 1 child, Peter Christian. BA in Psychology, Montclair State Coll., 1976; MSW, W.Va. U., 1978. Diplomate in clin. social work Nat. Register Clin. Social Workers. Psychiat. social worker Chenango County Mental Health Clinic, Norwich, N.Y., 1978-81; clin. social worker Community Mental Health Ctr. and Psychiat. Inst., Norfolk, Va., 1981-87; clin. social worker, dir. presch. and child partial hosp. programs Portsmouth (Va.) Psychiat. Ctr., 1987—; cons. Day Care and Child Devel. Ctrs. of Tidewater, Norfolk, 1985—. Sen. faculty senate Eastern Va. Med. Sch., 1984-87. Mem. Acad. Cert. Social Workers, Psi Chi. Club: Salem Woods Garden (treas. 1986). Office: Portsmouth Psychiat Ctr Crawford Parkway at Fort Ln Portsmouth VA 23704

GULLOTTE, STEPHANIE DERAN WIGGINS, nursing director; b. Mobile, Ala., Oct. 12, 1956; d. James Andrew and Mary Frances (Wright) Wiggins; m. Henry Samuel Gullotte, Aug. 14, 1981. A in Nursing, Mobile Infirmary, 1976; BS in Nursing, U. South Ala., 1978; MS in Nursing, U. Ala., Birmingham, 1979, postgrad. in nursing, 1986—. Operating room nurse, med. surg. nurse Mobile Infirmary, 1976-78, staff nurse in intensive care, 1978; instr. Mobile Coll. div. Nursing, 1979-81; asst. prof. Oral Roberts U. Anna Vaughn Sch. Nursing, Tulsa, 1981-84; dir. nursing Univ. Village, Tulsa, 1984-85; chief med./surg. nurse City of Faith, Tulsa, 1985-86, dir. skilled nursing, 1987—; dir. home health City of Faith Home Health Care, Tulsa, 1986—. Mem. Am. Coll. Healthcare Execs., Oral Roberts U. Anna Vaughn Sch. Nursing Honor Soc. (pres. 1984-85). Mem. Assembly of God.

GULYAS, TERESA STONE, nurse; b. Boulder City, Nev., Oct. 21, 1954; d. Mark Henry and Patricia Ann (Finder) Stone; m. Leslie Stephen Gulyas, Apr. 25, 1987. BS in Nursing, U. Wis., 1976; MEd, Auburn U., 1980; MS in Nursing, Cath. U. Am., 1986. Staff nurse VA Hosp., Madison, Wis., 1976-77; head nurse Washington Hosp. Ctr., 1980—. Served as capt. USAF, 1977-80. Mem. Oncology Nursing Soc. (cert.). Home: 12508 Kavanaugh Ln Bowie MD 20715

GUMMERSON, ANNE MCCLELLAND HESS, photographer, educator; b. Phila., Sept. 13, 1946; d. Arleigh Porter and Sarah Morrill (Greene) Hess; m. Kenneth Scott Gummerson (div.); 1 child Elizabeth Anne. BA, Goucher Coll., 1968; postgrad., Sorbonne U., Paris, 1968-69; MFA, Md. Inst. Coll. Art, 1972. Asst. photographer Donald Milne Photography, Glasgow, Scotland, 1974-75, Dan Forer Photography, Miami, Fla., 1977-79; owner, photographer architecture Anne Gummerson Photography, Balt., 1979—; instr. photography Md. Inst., Essex Community Coll., No. Va. Community Coll., Balt. Friends' Sch., Balt., 1980—. Contbr.-photographer articles to mags., 1983-84; photographer numerous articles in mags. including So. Accents, Architecture Remodeling, Family Cirle, Washington Post, 1985—. Democrat. Home and Office: 811 S Ann St Baltimore MD 21231

GUNDELFINGER, MARGARET ELLEN, construction company executive, real estate agent; b. Columbus, Ohio, Aug. 3, 1956; d. Boyd Allen and Juanita Melody (Sadler) G.; 1 dau., Justine Marie. B.A., Ohio Wesleyan U., 1977; postgrad. Miami U., Oxford, Ohio, 1979-80, Ohio State U., 1978, 80, 81, Columbus Tech. Coll., 1985. Adj. faculty mem. Ind. U., Richmond, 1980; exec. v.p. Boyd's Constrn. Co., Delaware, Ohio, 1980—; real estate agt. Dublin Realty, Ohio, 1985-87, Williams & Assocs., 1987—; cons. Del. C. of C., 1986. Mem. Delaware Area Women's Network (founder 1984), Nat. Assn. Female Execs. (network dir. 1984—), Delaware Area Bus. and Profl. Women (Young Careerist 1985), Delaware Bd. Realtors, Delaware Area C. of C., Delaware Women's Republican Club, Alpha Gamma Delta. Roman Catholic. Avocations: dancing, cooking. Home: 440 S Section Line Rd Delaware OH 43015 Office: Boyds Constrn Co Inc 34 Reid St Delaware OH 43015

GUNDERSEN, ALICE MARSHALL, business executive; b. Groveton, N.H., Nov. 19, 1934; d. Daniel Weeks and Eleanor Marshall; student Fisher Jr. Coll., Boston, 1952-53, Boston U., 1956, Northeastern U., 1957-59, Madonna Coll., 1966; B.M., U. Mich., 1970; m. Carl A. Gundersen, Apr. 11, 1959; children—Daniel Carl, Scott M. Exec. sec. with New Eng. Colls. Fund, Boston, 1956-58, with John Hancock Mut. Life Ins. Co., Boston, 1958-59; office supr. dept. human genetics U. Mich., Ann Arbor, 1964-67; adminstrv. coordinator and mgr. brokerage adminstrn. Alexander Hamilton Life Ins. Co., Farmington, Mich., 1973-75; supr. data services Delta Dental Plan of Mich., Southfield, 1976-83; cons. Nat. Med. Mgmt. Systems, Flint, Mich.; music dir. St. Timothy Presbyn. Ch., Livonia, Mich., 1964-72, Trinity Episcopal Ch., Farmington, 1975-77; CESA cons. Presbytery of Detroit, 1975-77, mem. task force on women, 1978-80, chair budget div., 1987—; mem. Livonia City Council, 1980-86; cons. women re-entering work force; systems cons. Adv. com. Livonia Sch. Bd., 1967-68; campaign coordinator City Council Candidate, 1970; active Livonia Com. for Better Human Relations, 1965-74; mem. Madonna Coll. Bus. Adv. Council, 1987—; chair outcounty adv. council, bd. dirs. Family Service Detroit and Wayne County, 1987. Cert. systems profl. Mem. Assn. Systems Mgmt. (publicity chmn. 1978, membership chmn. 1979-80, officer 1980-81, v.p., 1981-82, pres. 1983-84), Micro Mgrs. Assn., Women's Econ. Club Detroit (membership com., 1976, program com., 1977), Mich. Women's Polit. Caucus (polit. action chmn. 1979-81, state chmn. 1981-83), Nat. Women's Polit. Caucus (adminstrv. com. 1981-83), Livonia Hist. Soc. (pres., chair fund raising com. 1987—). Home: 15715 Southampton St Livonia MI 48154 Office: 17177 N Laurel Park Dr Livonia MI 48152

GUNDERSON, JOANNA, writer, publisher; b. N.Y.C., May 14, 1932; d. Earle and Margaret (Henderson) Bailie; m. Warren Gunderson, May 2, 1970; children: Lucy, Tom. BS in Gen. Studies, Columbia U., 1954. Pub. Red Dust, N.Y.C., 1963—, writer, 1955—. Contbr. numerous stories to mags. NEA grantee. Mem. Poets and Writers, Dramatists Guild. Home: 1148 5th Ave New York NY 10128

GUNDERSON, JUDITH KEEFER, golf association executive; b. Charleroi, Pa., May 25, 1939; d. John R. and Irene G. (Gaskill) Keefer; student public schs., Uniontown, Pa.; m. Jerry L. Gunderson, Mar. 19, 1971; children—Jamie L., Jeff S.; stepchildren—Todd G. (dec.), Marc W., Bookkeeper, Fayette Nat. Bank, 1957-59, gen. ledger bookkeeper, 1960-63; head bookkeeper First Nat. Bank Broward, 1963-64; bookkeeper Ruthenberg Homes, Inc., 1966-69; bookkeeper, asst. sec./treas. Pennisular Properties, Inc. subs. Investors Diversified Services Properties, Mpls., 1969-72; comptroller, stockholder, pres. dir. Am. Golf Fla., Inc., dba Golf and Tennis World, Deerfield Beach, 1972—; sec.-treas., stockholder, dir. Internat. Golf, Inc. County committeewoman, Broward County, Fla., 1965-66. Mem. Nat. Golf Found., C. of C., Beta Sigma Phi

GUNDRUM, LAETTA JUNE, retired petrochemical company executive; b. East St. Louis, Ill., June 13, 1927; d. Norman Henry and Fern L. (Seibel) Gundrum; student Rockford Coll., 1943-44; B.S. in Chemistry, U. Chgo., 1947. Tech. editor U.S. Dept. Agriculture, Peoria, Ill., 1950-51; tech. writer E. I. DuPont deNemours & Co., Wilmington, Del., 1951-58; advt. mgr. Amoco Chems. Corp., Chgo., 1965-83. Named Person of Yr., Soc. Plastics Industry, 1977. Mem. Am. Chem. Soc.

GUNN, CHRISTY HOWARD, actuary; b. Evanston, Ill., Oct. 6, 1954; d. Coydel Sandford and Ethel Marie (Franklin) Howard; m. Raymond Flynn Gunn, Aug. 26, 1978; children: Raymond Christopher, Justin Howard. BA, Oberlin Coll., 1976; MS in Stats., Carnegie Mellon U., 1979, MS in Pub. Policy and Mgmt., 1979. Analyst CNA, Chgo., 1979-83, mgr., 1983—. Fellow Casualty Actuarial Soc.; mem. Am. Acad. Actuaries. Office: CNA CNA Plaza Chicago IL 60685

GUNSTER-KIRBY, CLAIRE ELIZABETH, county government agency administrator; b. Washington, May 20, 1949; d. John George and Mary Lillian (Kessler) Gately; m. Robert Donald Gunster, Feb. 17, 1970 (div. May 1978); 1 child, Douglas Robert; m. James Alexander Kirby, June 23, 1983; 1 stepchild, Michael Buckley. Student, Wilkes Coll., 1967-70; BA, U. Md., 1973; MS, Johns Hopkins U., 1984. Cert. correctional employee, Md. Tchr. I Md. Dept. Social Services, Frederick, 1973-74; agt. parole/probation Md. Dept. Pub. Safety, Rockville, 1974-78; coordinator community release Montgomery County Dept. Correction, Rockville, 1978-79, dir. area resource ctr., 1979-82, correctional screener, 1982-84, specialist program adminstrn., 1984—; cons. Nat. Inst. Corrections, Boulder, Colo., 1980—. Active campaign United Way, Rockville, 1980; mem. Parent/Tchr./Students' Assn., Poolesville, Md., 1985—, Sugarloaf Citizens' Assn., Dickerson, Md., 1986—; mem. criminal justice adv. bd. Montgomery Coll., Rockville, 1986—. Recipient Silver award United Way, 1980, Gold award United Way, 1982, proclamation of appreciation Caroline County chpt. Md. Commrs., 1980. Mem. Am. Correctional Assn. (state chair policy conf. 1986—, state co-chair women's task force Md. chpt. 1987), Inst. Reality Therapy (cert.), Md. Correctional Adminstrs. Assn., Md. Criminal Justice Assn. (com. chair 1984—), Nat. Assn. for Female Execs., Johns Hopkins U. Alumni Assn. Democrat. Episcopalian. Home: 19700 Westerly Ave Poolesville MD 20837

GUNTER, BONNIE CAROLYN, realtor; b. Piggot, Ark., Apr. 2, 1941; d. William T. and Lema O. (Dixon) Bradshaw; m. Robert Sharp Gunter, Aug. 17, 1960; children—Michelle, Robert Jr., Lori. Student S.E. Mo. State U., 1959-60; Realtors Inst., 1979, 83. Realtor Rainey Realty Co., Little Rock, 1978-84, assoc. v.p., 1984—. Vice pres. Little Rock PTA, 1977, pres., 1979; pres. chpt. Nat. Kidney Found., Little Rock, 1982-83. Recipient numerous sales awards, 1979-84. Mem. Little Rock Bd. Realtors, Women's Council Realtors, Home Builders Assn. Little Rock. Republican. Presbyterian (elder). Club: Bus. Women (Little Rock). Home: #1 Northwest Court Little Rock AR 72212 Office: Rainey Realty Co 10515 W Markham St Little Rock AR 72205

GUNTER, GRETCHEN, beverage company executive; b. Ft. Worth, Tex., Apr. 13, 1942; d. William Clinton and Frances Virginia (Spinks) Weeden; student Gulf Park Coll., 1960; BA, Tex. Christian U., 1963; MA, U. Denver, 1979; children: Garrett Edward, Holli Gretchen. Tchr., Ft. Worth (Tex.) public schs., 1963-64, Denver public schs., 1965-69; pub. relations dir. Classic Chorale, Denver, 1974-75; asso. producer Noonday-KOA-TV, Denver, 1978; with Mountain Bell, Denver, 1979; dir. Vols. Callaway for Senate, 1980; orgnl. dir. Bradford for Congress, 1980; producer Pub. Access, United Cable TV, 1980; local govt. lobbyist Adolph Coors Co., Denver, 1980-84, regional mgr. govt. affairs, 1984-87; prin. The Public Affairs Group, Inc., Denver, 1987—; Mem. Women in Communications (pres-elect 1980-81), Leadership Denver Assn. (dir. 1984-86). Republican. Episcopalian. Clubs: Mile High Republican Women's Forum (charter pres. 1982-84), Colo. Fedn. Rep. Women, Nat. Fedn. Rep. Women, Cherry Creek Rep. Women's. Home: 10020 E Maplewood Ave Englewood CO 80111 Office: 1830 Platte St Denver CO 80202

GUNTHARP, ELIZABETH ANNE, librarian; b. Tulsa, Nov. 26, 1940; d. Edward Wallace and Anna Louise (Sims) Austin; m. John Gill Guntharp,

Aug. 17, 1966. BA, U. Tex., 1962, MA, St. Mary's U., San Antonio, 1967; MLS, Our Lady of Lake Coll., San Antonio, 1972. Tchr. San Antonio Schs., 1962-65, Northside Schs., San Antonio, 1966-68; librarian Austin (Tex.) Pub. Library, 1969, Shenandoah Library, San Antonio, 1970-72, Sul Ross Sch., San Antonio, 1973-88, John Marshall High Sch., San Antonio, Tex., 78240. Contbr. articles to profl. jours. Mem. Bexar Library Assn., Tex. Library Assn., South Tex. Archael. Soc., Tex. Archeol. Soc., SW Archaeol. Soc., Alpha Delta Kappa (pres. 1986-88), Phi Alpha Theta. Republican. Presbyterian. Office: Sul Ross Library 3630 Callaghan San Antonio TX 78228

GUNZER, SHIRLEY ANNE, management consultant; b. Rockville Centre, N.Y., Sept. 4, 1938; d. Charles Richard and Margaret Elizabeth (Sheridan) G. A.A., Centenary Coll., 1958; student NYU, 1960-61. Instr., Pan Am. Airways, N.Y.C., 1965-67, sr. sales instr., 1967-69, needs assessment project mgr., 1969-74, mgr. mgmt. devel., 1974-79, dir. tng. program devel., 1979-81; dir. tng. and communications Hertz Corp., N.Y.C., 1981-88; v.p. Case Abbington Assocs., N.Y.C., 1988—; client instr. Kepner Tregoe, Princeton, N.J., 1972-81, Xerox Corp., Stamford, Conn., 1975-81, Bus. Processes Inc., Denver, 1979-81, Air Transp. Travel Industry Tng. Bd. of Gt. Britain, London, 1979-81. Mem. Am. Soc. Tng. and Devel., Mensa. Democrat. Episcopalian. Home: 426 W 23d St New York NY 10011 Office: Case Abbington Assocs 510 E 20th St New York NY 10007

GURA, JUDITH BETTE, public relations executive; b. N.Y.C., May 15, 1935; d. Abraham and Mildred Pearl (Jacobs) Jankowitz; m. Martin Paul Gura, Mar. 27, 1960; children—Meryl, Jeremy. A.B., Cornell U., 1956, M.B.A., 1956. Promotion asst. Simon & Schuster, N.Y.C., 1956-57; asst. promotion mgr. Modern Bride Mag., N.Y.C., 1958-60; spl. events publicist Abraham & Straus, N.Y.C., 1960-65; account exec. Siesel Co., N.Y.C., 1965; prin. Gura Pub. Relations, Inc., N.Y.C., 1965—. Contbr. articles to profl. jours. Mem. Nat. Home Fashions League, Am. Soc. Interior Designers. Jewish. also: Gura Pub Relations Inc 156 Fifth Ave New York NY 10010

GURAK, KATHLEEN THERESA, multimedia producer; b. Passaic, N.J., Oct. 25, 1943; d. Edward Thomas and Mary Theresa (Glowacki) G. Prodn. coordinator, programmer 1492 Prodns., Inc., N.Y.C., 1968-70; pvt. practice video prodn. N.Y.C., 1971-75; sec., treas., co-owner Media House Inc., N.Y.C., 1976-80; co-owner Gurak/Santry Studios, N.Y.C., 1977-81; producer Jim Sant'Andrea, Inc., N.Y.C., 1982; instr. DMA, Inc., N.Y.C., 1982—; pvt. practice multimedia prodn. N.Y.C., 1983—. Mem. adv. com. to vol. dept. Ea. State Sch. & Hosp. For The Emotionally Disturbed, 1983; vol. Cabrini Hospice, N.Y.C., 1985—; mem. Candlelight Childhood Cancer Found. Recipient Bronze award Internat. Film and TV Festival, 1974, Gold award Internat. Film and TV Festival, 1976, 83, Silver award Internat. Film and TV Festival, 1980, Cabrini Hospice Vol. Service Recognition award, 1986. Mem. Assn. for Multi-Image, Nat. Hospice Orgn., N.J. Hospice Orgn., N.Y. State Hospice Assn., Pa. Hospice Network, Nat. Gardening Assn.

GURFEIN, HADASSAH NEIMAN, clinical psychologist; b. Bklyn.; d. Morris and Dorothy (Wagner) Neiman; B.A., Barnard Coll., 1960; M.A., CCNY, 1962; Ph.D., Fordham U., 1977; postdoctoral in psychoanalysis and psychotherapy NYU, 1977, in hypnosis Inst. of Pa. Hosp., 1982; m. Elisha Gurfein, July 31, 1966; children—Joshua Noah, Jonathan Daniel, David Michael. Diplomate Am. Bd. Marital and Family Therapy. Clin. psychologist Hadassah Hosp., Israel, 1962-63; psychologist, clin. fellow Bklyn. Coll., 1963-64; cons. psychologist L.I. Consultation Center, 1963-64; psychologist Lynbrook and Fairfield Public Schs., 1964-67; adj., dept. psychology Fairleigh Dickinson U., Teaneck, N.J., 1977-78; psychologist, chmn. child study team Dumont (N.J.) Pub. Schs., 1977-83; cons. psychologist Tourette and Tic Lab., Mt. Sinai Hosp., N.Y.C., 1981—, clin. instr. psychiatry; pvt. practice clin. psychologist, N.Y.C., 1977—; mem. Fedn. of Jewish Philanthropies Task Force on Mental Health. Mem. Am. Psychol. Assn., N.Y. State Psychol. Assn., N.J. Psychol. Assn., N.Y. Assn. Clin. Psychologists, N.J. Assn. Psychologists, Soc. Clin. and Exptl. Hypnosis, Psi Chi, Phi Delta Kappa (Ph.D. dissertation award, 1976). Jewish. Home: 156 Sherwood Pl Englewood NJ 07631 Office: 1155 Park Ave New York NY 10128

GURGANIOUS, VALORA SMITH, investment banker; b. Winter Park, Fla., Nov. 29, 1963; d. Warner Washington and Constance (Lark) Reid; m. LeRoy Gurganious, Dec. 28, 1985. BA, Vanderbilt U., 1985; postgrad. in bus. adminstrn., Harvard U., 1987—. Mktg. asst. 1st Am. Nat. Bank, Nashville, 1983-85; investment officer Boston Safe Deposit and Trust Co., 1985—; bd. dirs. INROADS, Boston, Inc. Active Big Sisters Greater Boston. Mem. Boston Urban Bankers Forum (com. chair 1985—), Nat. Assn. Female Execs. Democrat. Baptist. Home: 171 Swanton St Apt 63 Winchester MA 01890

GURIK, DIANE GREEN, personnel company executive; b. Mansfield, Ohio, Apr. 21, 1949; d. Charles Vernon and J. Pauline Green; m. John Carl Gurik, Mar. 13, 1942; children: Jennifer, Brian, Scott, Christine. Student, Olivet Coll., 1968-69; cert. in nursing, Mid-Ohio Nursing Program, 1972; postgrad. in bus. adminstrn., mansfield Bus. Coll., 1975. Adminstr. Wee Care Day Care Ctr., Mansfield, 1974-78; dir. nursing Allied Pvt. Duty Nurses Registry, Mansfield, 1978-83; corp. pres. N. Cen. Personnel Pool, Inc., Mansfield, 1983—, also chmn. bd. dirs.; Mem. adv. bd. Pioneer Sch., Shelby, Ohio, 1988. Mem. Better Bus. Bur., Mansfield, 1985—. Mem. Am. Entrepreneurs' Assn., Luth. Ch. Nurses (bd. dirs. 1982-86), Mansfield C. of C. Republican. Home: 1091 Belmar Dr Mansfield OH 44907 Office: N Cen Personnel Pool Inc 491 Lexington Ave Mansfield OH 44907

GURITZ, KAREN NOREEN, nurse, educator; b. Chgo., Apr. 16, 1950; d. Kenneth Edwin and Lucille Delores (Lee) G. BSN with honors, U. Fla., 1973; M of Nursing, U. Miss., Jackson, 1976. Cert. Lamaze childbirth educator. Charge nurse Johns Hopkins Hosp., Balt., 1973-74, L.W. Blake Hosp., Bradenton, Fla., 1974-75; instr. inservice obstetrics Orlando (Fla.) Regional Med. Ctr., 1976-77, ednl. coordinator, 1977-80, coordinator patient edn. obstetrics, 1980-86, specialist prenatal edn., 1986—. Mem. Fla. Network for Family and Patient Edn., Orlando, 1984—. Mem. Internat. Childbirth Edn. Assn., Am. Soc. Psychoprophylaxis in Obestetrics (coordinator 1982—), Coalition Fla. Childbirth Educators (bd. dirs. 1985—, pres. bd. dirs. 1987-88). Republican. Lutheran. Office: Orlando Regional Med Ctr 1414 S Ruhl Ave Orlando FL 32806

GURKE, SHARON MCCUE, naval officer; b. Bklyn., Apr. 4, 1949; d. James Ambrose and Marion Denise (Coombs) McCue; B.A., Molloy Cath. Coll., 1970; M.S. in Systems Mgmt., U. So. Calif., 1977; m. Lee Samuel Gurke, Apr. 16, 1977; children—Marion Dawn, Leigh Elizabeth. Commd. ensign U.S. Navy, 1970; advanced through grades to comdr., 1979; aircraft maintenance duty officer Orgn.-Intermediate Maintenance Officer, Comdr. Naval Air Force U.S. Pacific Fleet, Naval Air Sta., North Island, San Diego, 1974-77; head quality assurance div. Intermediate Maintenance Dept. Supporting Aircraft, Naval Air Sta., Miramar, San Diego, 1977-78, avionics div. officer, 1978-80; officer in charge Naval Aviation Engring. Service Unit Pacific Naval Air Sta., North Island, 1980-82; aircraft intermediate maintenance officer Naval Air Sta., Alameda, Calif., 1982-84; aircraft intermediate maintenance officer Naval Sta., Rota, Spain, 1984-86, comdr. Naval Air Systems Command Aviation Maintenance Policy Br., 1986-88, asst. prodn. officer Naval Air Rework Facility North Island, 1988—, asst. program mgr., NACOLMIS, 1987—. Decorated Naval Commendation medal, Meritorious Service medal, 1982, 84. Lic. pilot; first female naval officer selected for aero. engring. tng.; recipient Capt. Winifred Q. Collins award USN, 1980. Mem. Ninety Nines, San Diego Naval Women Officers Network (chmn.).

GURLEA, COLLEEN ANN, reporter; b. Salem, Ohio, Feb. 23, 1965; d. James Charles and Charlene Ann (Welker) G. BA in Communications and Journalism, Carlow Coll., 1987. Announcer Sta. WISR, Butler, Pa., 1985-87; reporter Butler Eagle, 1987—. Vol. March of Dimes, Butler, 1986—. Carlow Coll. Presdl. scholar, 1983, GFWC Jr. Women's League scholar, 1985, Robert Fellows scholar, 1987. Mem. Nat. Assn. Female Execs., Speech Communications Assn. Pa., Am. Fedn. TV and Radio Artists, Delta Epsilon Sigma. Democrat. Roman Catholic. Home. RD 1 Cupec Rd Butler PA 16001

GURNE, PATRICIA DOROTHY, lawyer; b. Phila., May 25, 1941; d. George Albert and Dorothy (Hammett) G.; B.A., MacMurray Coll., 1965; J.D., George Washington U., 1969; grad. Nat. Inst. Trial Advocacy, 1974. Bar: , pres. 1984), 1969, D.C. 1971. Law clk. to Judge Joyce H. Green, Superior Ct. D.C., Washington, 1969-71; assoc. Jackson & Campbell, P.C., and predecessors, Washington, 1971-75, partner, 1975—; mem. D.C. Ct. Appeals Jud. Conf., 1977—, D.C. Circuit Jud. Conf., 1979—; mem. U.S. Dist. Ct. Grievance Com., 1983—. Trustee, George Washington U., 1981—; bd. dirs. D.C. Women's Com. for Crime Prevention, 1978-79. Mem. ABA, Bar Assn. D.C. (exec. council young lawyers sect. 1974-77, vice chmn. young lawyers sect. 1976-77, dir. 1986—, Young Lawyer of Yr. award 1979), Women's Bar Assn. (pres. 1978-79, dir. 1980-83), Women's Bar Found. (dir. 1981—, pres. 1984—), D.C. Bar (sec., dir. 1978-79, ethics com. 1979-82, judicial evaluation com. 1986—), George Washington Law Alumnae Assn. (bd. dirs., pres. 87—). Office: 1120 20th St NW Washington DC 20036

GURNEY, CAROL ANN, office expansion service executive; b. East Orange, N.J., June 1, 1949; d. William John and Lily May (Curran) G. Student Franklin Jr. Coll. (Mass.), 1967. Exec. sec. NL Industries, West Caldwell, N.J., 1972-73; v.p. personnel and office mgmt. Dancer Fitzgerald Sample, Inc., Torrance, Calif., 1973-83; prin., owner Carol Gurney Assocs., Office Expansion Services, Los Angeles, 1983-87, Agoura, Calif., 1988—. Vol., Mary Manning Walsh Home, N.Y.C., 1972-74, Jr. Blind Assn., Los Angeles, 1980-81. Mem. Los Angeles Advt. Women (dir. 1981-82, Most Profl. award 1982). Office: 29712 Triunfo Dr Agoura CA 91301

GUSCIORA, AUDREY JOAN, small business owner; b. Mpls., Dec. 4, 1950; d. Franklin Howard and Clara Josephine Irmen; m. Terrance Gusciora, June 14, 1970 (div.); children; Jeffrey, James; married 1983; children: Jennifer, Joseph. Student, U. Minn., Duluth, 1968-69; BA in Nursing, St. Luke's Coll., Duluth, 1971; student, Normandale Community Coll., Bloomington, Minn., 1985-86. Dir. Olathe Nursing Home, Kansas, Minn., 1971-73; head nurse St. Michael's Hosp., Sauke Centre, Minn., 1973-75; nurse specialist Minn. Dept. of Health, St. Cloud, 1975-77; supr. Buffalo (Minn.) Meml. Hosp., 1977-79; dir. Olsten, Mpls., 1979-80; br. mgr. Progressive Health, Hopkins, Minn., 1981-82; pres. P.T.I., Inc., Mpls., 1983-87, Paycheck Plus of Minn., Inc., 1987—; med. cons. Headstart, St. Cloud, 1973-75; small bus. cons. Hennepin-Lake Service, Mpls. Author: (manuals) Telemarketing, 1985, Marketing Techniques, 1985. Foster parent Hennepin County (Minn.) retarded div., Mpls., 1983-85; active Boy Scouts Am., Annandale, Minn., 1975-78, Assn. for Retarded Citizens, 1976-78; vol. Woman's Resource Ctr., Bloomington, 1985-86. Fellow Nat. Assn. Female Execs., Soc. Behavioral Medicine (small bus. mgmt. award 1986); mem. Nat. Assn. Self Employed. Democrat. Roman Catholic. Club: Chart House, Women's Bus. Leads. Home: 11233 Ewing Ave S Bloomington MN 55431 Office: PTI Inc 3112 Hennepin Ave S Minneapolis MN 55408

GUSSIN, ELLEN BETH SHAPERA, marketing executive; b. Chgo., Apr. 30, 1948; d. Louis M. and Julie Miriam (Zuckerman) Shapera; m. Lee E. Gussin, Mar. 26, 1972; children: Grant, Marnie. Student, Miami U., Oxford, Ohio, 1966-68; BBA, U. Mich., 1970; postgrad., U. Minn., 1984. Dir. admissions, auditor Advance Schs. Inc., Chgo., 1971-77; systems analyst Shure Bros. Inc., Evanston, Ill., 1977-79; account executive Allen Levis Orgn., Northfield, Ill., 1986—. Bd. dirs. Adult Edn. Congregation Solel, Highland Park, Ill., 1982-85, fin. v.p., 1987—; exec. v.p., bd. dirs. Nat. Council Jewish Women Info., Thomas Wayne/Northwood Schs. PTAs, Highland Park, 1982—; mem. Com. for Interdistrict Cooperation Roundtable, Com. for Interstate Cooperation, Legislative Action for Edn., Highland Park, 1982—; grant writer for local twps. Nat. Council Jewish Women, TeleHelp and Youth Employment Service, Services of Nat. Council Jewish Women Info., 1984-86; mem. caucus and nominating com. Highland Park High Sch. Dist. 113, 1987—; mem. Joint Action Com. Mem. Nat. Council Jewish Women Info. (bd. dirs., cent. dist. officer 1980—, co-pres. north shore sect. 1977—, field service com., human resource devel., 1987, treasurer met. area, 1986-88), Assn. Reformed Zionists Am., Hadassah, Women's Am. Orgn. Rehab. Through Tng., Brandeis Women. Clubs: Standard; Elms, 41 Sports (Highland Park). Home: 2937 Priscilla Highland Park IL 60035 Office: Allen Levis Orgn 466 Central Northfield IL 60093

GUSTAFSON, BARBARA ANN HELTON, lawyer; b. Washington, Ill., Apr. 26, 1948; d. Joseph and Marilou (Buckles) Balogh; m. Lee Alan Gustafson, Dec. 20, 1969. B.Music, So. Ill. U., 1969; M.Mus. Edn., Vandercook Coll., 1972; J.D., U. Chgo., 1983. Bar: Ill. 1983. Tchr. music Harrison Sch., Wonderlake, Ill., 1969-72, Cook County Dist. 125, Alsip, Ill., 1972-73; dir. orch. Kankakee Dist. III, Ill., 1973-80; atty. MidCon Corp., Lombard, Ill., 1983—. Asst. dir. Kankakee Youth Symphony (Ill.), 1973-76; violinist Kankakee Orch., 1977-80; musician Kankakee Valley Theater, 1976-80. Mem. Ill. State Bar Assn., Chgo. Bar Assn., AAUW, Mu Phi Epsilon (treas. 1968-69). Lutheran. Home: 176 Hickory Creek Dr Frankfort IL 60423 Office: MidCon Corp 701 E 22nd St Lombard IL 60148

GUSTAFSON, CAROLYN GOODRICH, mental health center administrator; b. Chgo., Jan. 13, 1942; d. Paul Wallace and Virginia (Davis) Goodrich; m. Harvey Michael Gustafson, Dec. 23, 1978. BA, Denison U., 1964; MSW, Loyola U., Chgo., 1969. Radio/TV traffic coordinator Compton Advt., Chgo., 1964-66; caseworker Ill. Dept. Pub. Aid, Chgo., 1966-67; social work supr. Ill. Dept. Children and Family Services, Chgo., 1969-74; sch. social worker Sch. Dist. 300, Dundee, Ill., 1974-80; youth and family outreach counselor J. Daviess County, Galena, Ill., 1982-86; dir. Jane Addams Community Mental Health Ctr., Jo Daviess Office, Galena, 1986—. Mem. LWV, Woman in Mgmt. Inc. Republican. Lodge: Rotary. Home: Box 207 Scales Mound IL 61075 Office: Jane Addams Community Mental Health Ctr 300 Summit Galena IL 61306

GUSTASON, GERILEE, educator of hearing impaired, educational consultant, publisher; b. Blair, Nebr., July 5, 1939; d. Arthur D. and Martha (Andersen) G. MA in Edn. of Deaf, Gallaudet Coll., 1963; MA in Adminstrn. and Supervision, Calif. State U., Northridge, 1968; MA in English, U. Md., 1972; PhD in Edn., U. So. Calif., 1972. Cert. tchr. of hearing impaired. Tchr. Va. Sch. for Deaf, Staunton, 1963-64; instr. English Gallaudet U., Washington, 1964-68, from asst. prof. edn. to prof., 1972—; tchr. Brookhurst Jr. High Sch., Anaheim, Calif., 1968-69, Selaco-Downey (Calif.) High Sch., 1970-72; exec. dir. SEE (Signing Exact English) Ctr. for Advancement of Deaf Children, Los Alamitos, Calif., 1985—; chmn. bd. Modern Signs Press, Inc., Los Alamitos, 1980—; internat. and nat. cons. for the deaf, 1972—. Co-author: Signing Exact English, 1972, 3d edit. 1980; editor several books related to sign lang., 1972—; contbr. articles to profl. jours. Named one of Outstanding Young Women Am.; World Rehab. Fund fellow, Israel, 1987; grantee U.S. Dept. Edn. 1986-87. Mem. Conv. Am. Instrs. of Deaf (pres. 1983-85), Am. Soc. for Deaf Children (cons. 1983—), Council on Edn. of Deaf (bd. dirs. 1983—), Assns. on Edn. of Deaf (bd. dirs. 1981-86). Office: SEE Ctr for Advancement of Deaf Children 10443 Los Alamitos Blvd Los Alamitos CA 90720

GUT, MICHELLE CLAIR, operations facilities planner; b. Pitts., May 11, 1954; d. Francis Thomas G.; divorced. BBA, Western State U., 1987. Supr. Doig Optical Co., Pitts., 1972-76; adminstrn. asst. mktg. Zotos Internat., Darien, Conn., 1976-81; info. services tng. specialist Continental Baking Co., Stamford, Conn., 1981-85; ops. facilities planner Wang Fin. Info. Services Corp., N.Y.C., 1986—; asst. to dir. Shearman & Sterling, N.Y.C., 1985-86. Mem. Nat. Assn. Female Execs., Internat. Lotus Users, Internat. Tamdem Users. Republican. Roman Catholic. Office: Wang Fun Info Services Corp 120 Wall St New York NY 10005

GUTGESELL, VICKI JEAN, ophthalmologist; b. Wausau, Wis., Feb. 26, 1947; d. Howard Philip and Myrtle Eileen (Sand) G. BS, U. Wis., 1970, MD, 1978. Diplomate Am. Bd. Ophthalmology. Intern St. Mary's Hosp. and Med. Ctr., San Francisco, 1978-79; resident in ophthalmology U. Fla. Coll. Medicine, Gainesville, 1979-82; fellow in vitreo-retinal U. Wis. Sch. Medicine, Madison, 1982-83; staff ophthalmologist The Permanente Med. Group, Oakland, Calif., 1984—. Contbr. articles to profl. jours. Friend San Francisco Bach Choir, 1987—. Recipient N.A., Nat. and Wis. Speedskating Championships, 1959, 61. Mem. Am. Acad. Ophthalmology, Alameda-Contra Costa Med. Assn., Calif. Med. Assn., West Coast Retina Study Club, The Vitreous Soc., San Francisco Opera Guild, Friends of Filoli, Sigma Epsilon Sigma, Phi Kappa Phi, Alpha Omega Alpha, Phi Beta Kappa. Home: 6525 Glen Oaks Way Oakland CA 94611 Office: Kaiser Permanente Med Group 280 W MacArthur Blvd Oakland CA 94611

GUTH, CAMILLE ANNE, research associate, graphic artist; b. Menomonie, Wis., Mar. 29, 1957; d. Bernard E. and Margaret V. Golden; m. David C. Guth; 1 child, Sylvia K. Student, U. Wis., Menomonie, 1975-77; BS, U. Utah, 1986, MHRM, 1988. Graphic artist Dunn County News, Menomonie, 1975-76, Finns & Feathers Mag., St. Paul, 1976, Quality Press, Salt Lake City, 1981-82, Imperial Printing, Charlotte, N.C., 1982-83, Snow Litho, Salt Lake City, 1983; research Inst. for Human Resources, Salt Lake City, 1986—; job analyst Arben O. Clark, Salt Lake City, 1986—. Sommer/Viehman scholar Master Printers of Am., 1987, Reed C. Richardson scholar, U. Utah, 1987. Mem. Am. Soc. Personnel Adminstrs. (pres. 1987-88, Olsten scholar 1987), Am. Soc. Tng. and Devel. Roman Catholic. Home: 2826 McClelland Salt Lake City UT 84106 Office: Univ Utah 412 Kendall Garff Bldg Salt Lake City UT 84112

GUTH, KATHERINE D., management consultant; b. Moline, Ill., June 17, 1955; d. Robert F. and Shirley Joy (Sammon) Albrecht; m. Marshall C. Guth, Aug. 6, 1977; 1 child, Tyler Marshall. BA, Augustana Coll., Rock Island, Ill., 1977; postgrad., U. Iowa, 1986—. Mgmt. trainee Union Bank, Tuscon, 1977-78; market stimulator Northwestern Bell, Des Moines, 1978-79; account exec. Ill. Bell, Moline, 1979-83; nat. account mgr. AT&T, Peoria, 1983-86; cons. Network Cons., Inc. (formerly Network Systems, Inc.), Peoria, 1986—. Mem. Friends of St. Genevieve Mus. Assn.,Davenport, 1986—, Jr. League Quad Cities, Bettendorf, 1987—; vol. Franciscan Mental Health Ctr., Rock Island, 1980—; bd. dirs. River Valley Mental Health Found., 1988—. Mem. Phi Beta Kappa, Psi Chi. Republican. Lutheran. Home: 2401 27th St Moline IL 61265 Office: Network Cons Inc PO Box 1403 Peoria IL 61655

GUTHMAN, PATRICIA ROSENAU, antiques dealer, writer; b. Glencoe, Ill., Oct. 31, 1926; d. Gustave E. and Irma (Goldstine) Rosenau; m. William Guthman, Sept. 11, 1948 (div. 1980); children: Pamela, William Scott. BA, Northwestern U., 1948. Prin. Pat Guthman Antiques, Southport, Conn.; columnist Antiques & the Arts Weekly, The Newtown (Conn.) Bee, 1976—; cons., advisor for various hist. socs. and museums on creating authentic period kitchens. Office: Pat Guthman Antiques 281 Pequot Ave Southport CT 06490

GUTHRIE, ANN GERTRUDE, administrator, physical therapist, consultant; b. Boulder, Colo., Aug. 4, 1943; d. John T. and Ruth I. Guthrie; B.S. in Phys. Therapy, 1966; M.S., U. Notre Dame, 1977. Phys. therapist Mass. Gen. Hosp., Boston, 1965-67, Univ. Hosp., Denver, 1967-70; dir. phys. therapy Mercy Med. Center, Denver, 1970-72, dir. allied services, 1972-76, patient rep., 1976-83, adminstrv. dir., 1979-83; dir. rehab. services Nat. Jewish Ctr. Immunology and Resp. Medicine, Denver, 1983-87, rehab. adminstr. Univ. Hosp., Denver, 1987—; instr. U. Colo., 1967-70; cons. HEW, 1973-79, grant reviewer, Rockville, Md., 1979; acting dir., adminstr. McNamara Hosp. and Nursing Home, Fairplay, Colo., 1975; mem. State Bd. Phys. Therapy, 1973-76. Lic. phys. therapist, Colo. Democrat. Baptist. Contbr. articles on phys. therapy to profl. jours. Office: 4200 E 9th Ave Box C-243 Denver CO 80206

GUTHRIE, ANN JOYCE, federal agency administrator; b. Columbus, Ohio, Oct. 21, 1946; d. Mahlon Gilbert and Joyce (Baker) G. BS in Pub. Administrn., Georgetown U., 1972. Asst. to dir. W.Va. Arts and Humanities Council, Charleston, 1969-71; writer, editor, info. officer Nat. Endowment Arts, Washington, 1971-76, program officer for challange grants, 1976-78; cons. Fed. Council Arts and Humanities, Washington, 1978-79, Norfolk Historic Preservation Project, Wroxham, Eng., 1980; exec. asst. arts and humanities Pub. Liaison Office White House, Washington, 1981; staff asst. Presdl. Speechwriting Office White House, Washington, 1981-83; exec. dir. Cultural Propert Adv. Com. U.S. Info. Agy., Washington, 1984—. Mem. U.S. Com. Internat. Monuments and Sites (exec. com. 1988—), Nat. Trust Historic Preservation, D.C. Preservation League, World Monuments Fund. Roman Catholic. Office: US Info Agy 301 4th St SW #247 Washington DC 20547

GUTHRIE, ELEANOR YOUNG, lawyer; b. Annawan, Ill., Aug. 12, 1915; m. George B. Guthrie; 1 child, Richard. BA, U. Ill., 1937; LLB, Chgo.-Kent Coll. Law, 1940; JD, IIT-Chgo.-Kent Coll. Law, 1971. Bar: Ill. 1940. Editor Commerce Clearing House Inc., Chgo., 1940-42; assoc. Defrees and Fiske Attys., Chgo., 1942-52; ptnr. Defrees and Fisk Attys., Chgo., 1953—; mem. hearing panel Atty. Registration and Disciplinary Commn. Ill. Supreme Ct., 1973-79, 1985—. Asst. sec. Chgo. chpt. USO, 1972-74; mem. Zoning Bd. Appeals, Oak Park, Ill., 1985—; trustee Celia M. Howard Fellowship Fund, 1983—; pres. Met. Chgo. YWCA, 1979-80, cert. achievement, 1978, bd. dirs., 1971—; bd..dirs. United Way Chgo., 1980-83. Named Woman Yr. Women's Share Pub. Service, 1978. Mem. ABA (labor law sec., vice chmn. OSHA com., fair labor standards com. 1974-76), Nat. Assn. Women Lawyers (del. Ill. chpt. 1950-51), Women's Bar Assn. Ill. (pres. 1950-51), Nat. Fedn. Bus. Profl. Women's Clubs Inc. (parliamentarian 1972-73), Nat., Ill. and Chgo. Assns. Parliamentarians, Alliance Bus. Profl. Women's Club (pres. 1964-65), AAUW, Ill. Fedn. Bus. Profl. Women's Clubs (state parliamentarian 1958—, Woman Yr. 1979), Carl Sandburg Cen. Bus. Profl. Women's Clubs (v.p. 1981-82), Chgo. Bar Assn. (chmn. house com. 1970-72, labor law com. 1966—), Executive's Club Chgo. (capt. youth com. 1979, 1981-83, membership com. 1979-81), Art Inst. Chgo., Field Mus. Chgo., Chgo. Pilot Club (pres. 1955-56), Ill. State C. of C. (com. health care cost containment 1982—), Chgo. Sch. Profl. Psychology (bd. dirs. 1985—), IIT-Chgo.-Kent Coll. Law Alumni Assn. (bd. dirs.). Clubs: 19th Century (Oak Park), Fortnightly (Chgo.). Home: 547 Belleforte Ave Oak Park IL 60302

GUTHRIE, HELEN ANDREWS, educator; b. Sarnia, Can., Sept. 1925; came to U.S., 1946, naturalized, 1957; d. David and Helen Parker (Sweet) Andrews; B.S., U. Western Ont., 1946; M.S., Mich. State U., 1948; Ph.D., U. Hawaii, 1968; D.Sc., U. Western Ont., 1982; m. George M. Guthrie, June 4, 1949; children—Barbara, Jane, James. Asst. prof. nutrition Pa. State U., 1948-69, assoc. prof., 1969-72, prof., 1972—, head dept. nutrition Coll. Human Devel., 1979—; dir. Nabisco Brands Inc. Chmn., State College (Pa.) Bd. Health, 1978-82. Editor: NutrToday, 1987—. Mem. Am. Inst. Nutrition (pres. 1987—), Soc. Nutrition Edn. (pres. 1979-80), Am. Dietetic Assn. Home: 1316 S Garner St State College PA 16801 Office: 106 Human Devel University Park PA 16802

GUTHRIE, JANET, professional racing driver; b. Iowa City, Mar. 7, 1938; d. William Lain and Jean Ruth (Midkiff) G. B.S. in Physics, U. Mich., 1960. Comml. pilot and flight instr. 1958-61; research and devel. engr. Republic Aviation Corp., Farmingdale, N.Y., 1960-67; publs. engr. Sperry Systems, Sperry Corp., Great Neck, N.Y., 1968-73; racing driver Sports Car Club Am. and Internat. Motor Sports Assn., 1963—; profl. racing driver U.S. Auto Club and Nat. Assn. for Stock Car Racing, 1976-80; highway safety cons. Met. Ins. Co., 1980-87. Mem. athlete adv. bd. Women's Sports Found. Recipient Curtis Turner award Nat. Assn. for Stock Car Racing-Charlotte World 600, 1976; First in Class, Sebring 12-hour, 1970; North Atlantic Road Racing champion, 1973; named to Women's Sports Hall of Fame, 1980. Mem. Madison Ave. Sports Car Driving and Chowder Soc., Women's Sports Found. (adv. bd.), Ballet Aspen (bd. trustees).

GUTIERREZ, IRENE, program administrator; b. Littlefield, Tex., Nov. 19, 1949; d. Luis and Jovita (Hernandez) Castilleja; m. Vincente Gutierrez; children: Sonia, Sophia, Celeste. BA in Romance Langs., U. Wash., 1973, JD, 1979. Paralegal Evergreen Legal Services, Seattle, Wash., 1972-75; immigration counselor Hispanic Legal Action, Seattle, 1982-86; dir. Hispanic Immigration Program, Seattle, 1986—. Producer: (video) El Pueblo Hispano, 1986. Roman Catholic. also: 3600 S Graham St Seattle WA 98118

GUTMAN, BONNIE SUE, public relations executive; b. Newark, Nov. 2, 1949; d. Edwin Lesser and Edith Selma (Meit) G. BS, Rutgers U., 1972; MS, Boston U., 1973. Asst. press sec. Gov.'s Office State of N.J., Trenton, 1973-74, asst. to dep. commr. Dept. Transp., 1974-78; account supr. Burson-Marsteller, N.Y.C., Los Angeles, San Juan, 1980-85; v.p. Rogers Assocs., Los Angeles, 1985-86; prin. Bonnie Gutman Pub. Relations, Santa Monica,

Calif., 1986—. Vol., mem. communications com. Am. Cancer Soc., Los Angeles, 1987. Mem. Women in Communications, Inc. (v.p. fin. com. 1987—), Hispanic Pub. Relations Assn., Internat. Assn. Bus. Communicators. Office: 712 Wilshire Blvd Suite 10 Santa Monica CA 90292

GUTSHALL, CAROL LAVON, educator; b. Trenton, Mo., Sept. 23, 1934; d. Roy Alfred and Mildred Erie (Armstrong) Frazier; m. Bill Frank Gutshall, Aug. 17, 1952; children, Douglas, Daniel, Dennis, William. Assoc. in Edn., S.W. Bapt. Coll., Boliver, Md., 1954; BS in Edn., Mo. Western State Coll., 1970; postgrad., U. Mo., 1987—. Cert. elem. tchr., Mo. Tchr. spl. needs Bishop Hogan Cath. Sch., Chillicothe, Mo., 1972-75; tchr. Chillicothe Pub. Schs., 1976-78, tchr.-coordinator gifted classes, 1978—; cons. Future Problem Solving Program, state adv. com., 1986, task force, 1982, coach interstate, internat. acad. competitions, 1982—. Presentor gifted program activities. Chmn. twp. elections, Livingston County, Mo.; supt. Bible sch. 1st Bapt. Ch., Chillocothe, 1981-86. Fellow Gifted Assn. Mo. (liaison Future Problem Solving 1986, Educator of Yr. 1987); mem. Mo. State Tchrs. Assn. (Chilliothe chpt.), Delta Kappa Gamma. Home: Rt 5 Box 168 Chillicothe MO 64601 Office: Cen Sch 321 Elm Chillicothe MO 64601

GUTSHALL, CHARLOTTE FAYE, nurse; b. La Cygne, Kans., Jan. 9, 1940; d. Herman Levi and Marjorie Faye (Bartles) Hewitt; m. Charles Robert Gutshall, Aug. 31, 1961; children: Sherry Lynn, Ellen Elaina, Charles Herman. Cert. records technician, Am. Med. Record, Chgo., 1975; BS in Nursing cum laude, Cen. Mo. State U., 1985, MS in Social Gerontology, 1986. RN, Mo. Dir. med. records Countryside Nursing Home, Butler, Mo., 1975-81; cons. med. records Country View Nursing Home, Prescott, Kans., 1981-84; charge nurse Medicalodge of Butler, 1985-86; primary care nurse Lakeside Hosp., Kansas City, Mo., 1986; dir. nursing service Wornale Health Care, Kansas City, 1986-87; nursing supr. Foxwood Springs Living Ctr., Raymore, Mo., 1987-88; dir. nursing services Experiences Health Care, Kansas City, Mo., 1988—; sec., treas. Tri-Country Med. Records, Butler, 1976-80. Historian Tri Kapps Student Nursing Assn., Warrensburg, Mo., 1983-84. Mem. Nat. Gerontol. Nursing Assn., Phi Eta Sigma, Alpha Phi Delta, Lambda Sigma Psi, Phi Kappa Phi, Sigma Phi Omega. Republican. Office: Experiences Health Care 5331 Highland Ave Kansas City MO 64110

GUTTERMAN-REINFELD, DEBRA ELLEN, physician, consultant; b. N.Y.C., Nov. 13, 1948; d. George and Nettie (Liss) Gutterman; m. Stuart Glenn Reinfeld, June 20, 1982; children: Alan Jeffrey, Naomi Rebecca. B.S., R.N. magna cum laude, SUNY Downstate Med. Ctr., 1972; postgrad. U. Auton, Guadalajara Sch. Medicine (Mex.), 1973-75; M.D., Coll. Medicine and Dentistry N.J., 1977. Intern, Boston City Hosp., 1977-78; resident in medicine Maimonides Med. Ctr., Bklyn., 1978-79, 79-80, Mt. Sinai Med. Ctr., Miami Beach, Fla., 1982-83; fellow Jackson Meml. Hosp., Miami, Fla., 1980-82; internist, cons. infectious diseases, former chief dept. internal medicine, former assoc. med. dir. Maxicare/Health Am., Ft. Lauderdale, Fla.; med. dir. Humana/Health Am., Plantation, Fla., 1988—.

GUTTERSON, JANET MIRIAM, foundation administrator; b. Brockton, Mass., Mar. 9, 1939; d. Axel Harold and Jennie Alberta (Ellmes) Anderson; m. Donald E. Cooper, May 25, 1962 (dec. 1966); m. Lyman P. Gutterson Jr., May 4, 1968; children: Melody Gutterson-Russell, Freya Diane. BS, Bridgewater State Coll., 1961; postgrad., Stetson U. Tchr. Montverde (Fla.) Acad., 1961-62; with personnel office S. Shore Nat. Bank, Quincy, Mass., 1964-72; program coordinator Lake County Bd. Commrs., Tavares, Fla., 1977-81; counselor State of Fla., Eustis, 1982-85; area supr. Green Thumb Program, Jacksonville, Fla., 1985-86; exec. dir. Lake County Family Health Council, Eustis, 1986—; bd. dirs. Haven Inc., Leesburg, Fla., 1983—; founding dir. Lake County Child Advisory Council, Tavares, 1987-88. Mem. Lake County Service League, Leesburg, Fla., 1986—; mem. adv. bd. Lake County Community Coll., 1987—, Lake Sumter Community Coll., 1987-88. Recipient Service award Fla. Choices, 1985. Mem. LWV, Chi Sigma Iota. Democrat. Episcopalian. Club: U.S. Pony (Altoona, Fla.) (sec. 1980-86). Home: 1225 Eastland Rd Mount Dora FL 32757 Office: Lake County Family Health Council Inc 20 S Eustis St Eustis FL 32726

GUY, DIANE FRANCES, restaurant company executive; b. Missoula, Mont., Oct. 19, 1954; d. Arthur Carl and Clara Dorothy (Dahlinger) Weber; m. Gregory William Guy, Mar. 11, 1973. AA in Acctg., Coll. Great Falls, Mont., 1985, BS in Acctg., 1987. Mgr. El Comedor, Great Falls, 1970-80; pres., gen. mgr. El Comedor, Inc., Great Falls, 1980—. Sr. mem. Nat. Ski Patrol, Great Falls, 1976-87. Mem. Nat. Restaurant Assn., Great Falls C. of C. Office: El Comedor Inc 1120 25th St S Great Falls MT 59405

GUY, MILDRED DOROTHY, educator; b. Brunswick, Ga.; d. John and Mamie Paul (Smith) Floyd; BS in Social Sci., Savannah State Coll., 1949; MA in Am. History, Atlanta U., 1952; postgrad. U. So. Calif., U. Colo.; m. Charles H. Guy, Aug. 18, 1956 (div. 1979); 1 child, Rhonda Lynn. Tchr. social studies L.S. Ingraham High Sch., Sparta, Ga.; tchr. English and social studies North Jr. High Sch., Colorado Springs, 1958-84; ret., 1984; cooperating tchr. Tchr. Edn. Program, Col. Coll., 1968-72. Fund raiser for Citizens for Theatre Auditorium, Colorado Springs, 1979; bd. dirs. Urban League, 1971-75; del. to County and State Dem. Conv., 1972, 76, 80, 84; mem. Pike's Peak Community Coll. Council, 1976-83; mem. council of 500, Colorado Springs Opera; mem. nominating com. Wagon Wheel council Girl Scouts U.S.A., 1985-87. Recipient Viking award North Jr. High Sch., 1973; Outstanding Black Woman of Colorado Springs award, 1975; named Pacesetter, Atlanta U., 1980-81, Outstanding Black Educator of Yr., Black Educators of Dist. II, Colorado Springs, 1981; Outstanding Achievement in Edn. award Negro Hist. Assn. of Colorado Springs, 1983, Outstanding Ednl. Service award Colo. Dept. and State Bd. Edn., 1983, Dedicated Service award Pikes Peak Community Coll., 1983; Outstanding Community Leadership award Alpha Phi Alpha, 1985; award Colo. Black Woman for Polit. Action, 1985, Sphinx award, 1986; named in recognition sect. Salute to Women, Colorado Springs Gazette Telegraph, 1986. Mem. NEA, (life mem.), AAUW, Colo. Council of Social Studies, Assn. for Study of Afro-Am. Life and History, Colo. LWV, Friends of Pioneers Mus. (life mem.), NAACP, Alpha Delta Kappa, Alpha Kappa Alpha (chpt. pres. 1984-86, award 1986). Baptist. Home: 3132 Constitution Ave Colorado Springs CO 80909

GUYNES, KAREN LEA, management training administrator; b. Dallas, Feb. 19, 1960; d. Vernon Albert and Adrienne Ann (Leslie) Guynes Jr.; m. Roger Whitfield Christian, Oct. 1, 1980 (div. Feb. 1982). Sales dir. Lincoln Property Co., Dallas, 1980-86; tng. dir. Summit Mgmt. Co., Charlotte, N.C., 1986—. Actor theater and film, Dallas, 1973-81. Mem. Am. Soc. for Tng. and Devel. Office: Summit Mgmt Co 212 S Tryon St Suite 800 Charlotte NC 28281

GUYRE, JUDITH PITZO, industrial drive company executive; b. Phila., Nov. 27, 1945; d. Frank Joseph and Carolyn Marie (Miller) Pitzo; student parochial schs., spl. courses; m. Ronald T. Guyre, Aug. 19, 1978; children: Garrett M., Aubrey Eve. Sec. to pres. Alpha Lithograph, Camden, N.J., 1964-67; adminstrv. asst. Transam. Ins. Co., Phila., 1967-70; office mgr. Power Quip/C.J. Kitching Assocs., Pennsauken, N.J., 1972-78; v.p. Brisbane Indsl. Drive Co., Jim Thorpe, Pa., 1978-87; founder, owner indsl. distbn. co. of adhesives and sealants, Itech, 1987—; seminar leader; mgr. distbn. sales. Asst. to dir. Voorhees Community, Edn. and Recreation Program; sec./treas. Top O'the Mountain Ecumenical Council for 8 area chs.; bd. dirs. community youth group. Recipient Pres.'s award Leeson Electric, Grafton, Wis., 1987. Mem. Nat. Assn. Female Execs., Power Transmission Reps. Assn. Republican. Roman Catholic. Home: PO Box 661 Blakeslee PA 18610 Office: Box 12 2d Star Rt Jim Thorpe PA 18229

GUZY, MARGUERITA LINNES, educator; b. Santa Monica, Calif., Nov. 19, 1938; d. Paul William Robert and Margarete (Rodowski) Linnes; m. Stephen Paul Guzy, Aug. 25, 1962 (div. 1968); 1 child, David Paul. AA, Santa Monica Coll., 1959; student, U. Mex., 1959-60; BA, UCLA, 1966, MA, 1973. Cert. secondary tchr., Calif. Tchr. Inglewood (Calif.) Unified Sch. Dist., 1967—, chmn. dept., 1972-82, mentor, tchr., 1985—; clin. instr. series Clin. Supervision Levels I, II, Ingelwood, 1986-87; tchr. Santa Monica Coll., 1975-76; cons. bilingual edn. Inglewood Unified Sch. Dist., 1975—; mem. edn. teaching com. Monroe Jr. High Sch., 1985-86, staff devel. com., 1985—, chmn. drug and alcohol awareness com., 1986—. Author: Elementary Education: "Pygmalian in the Classroom", 1975, English Mechanics Workbook, 1986. Named Tchr. of Yr., 1973. Mem. NEA, Calif. Tchrs. Assn., Inglewood Tchrs. Assn. (local rep. 1971-72, tchr edn. and profl. services com. 1972-78), UCLA Alumnae Assn. (life), Prytanean Alumnae Assn. Republican. Club: Westside Alano (Los Angeles)(bd. dirs., treas. 1982-83). Lodge: Masons. Office: Monroe Jr High Sch 10711 10th Ave Inglewood CA 90303

GWALTNEY, ANNE BROOKS, federal government administrator; b. New Haven, June 5, 1957; d. John Langdon and Yvette (Gittleson) Brooks; m. Thomas Stewart Gwaltney, June 19, 1982. BA, Vassar Coll., 1979. Mem. policy devel.-research dept. campaign staff George Bush Pres. Com., Alexandria, Va., 1979-80, Reagan-Bush Com., Arlington, Va., 1980; spl. asst. to dir. transition resources-devel. group Reagan-Bush Transition Planning Group, Washington, 1980-81; dep. White House liaison office undersec. mgmt. U.S. Dept. State, Washington, 1981-82; spl. asst. to chmn. NEH, Washington, 1982—, agy. liaison White House initiative historically black colls. univs., 1985-87, mem. adv. com. fed. women's program, chair 1984-87, 1982—; mem. U.S. Dept. Commerce Interagy. Women's Bus. Enterprise, 1984, U.S. Govtl. Steering Com. World Food Day, 1986—; agy. rep. to Fed. Interagy. Com. on Edn. Subcom. on Rural Edn. and on Occupational Literacy, 1987—. Instr. CPR ARC. Named Outstanding Young Woman Am. Outstanding Ams., Montgomery, Ala., 1986. Republican. Episcopalian. Office: NEH 1100 Pennsylvania Ave NW Washington DC 20506

GWIN, DAWN SIMMONS, graphic designer; b. Marshall, Tex., Aug. 23, 1951; d. Aura L. and Janette Fason (Ryan) Simmons; B.A., Trinity U., 1973; postgrad. U. Tex., San Antonio, 1978-80. Communications mgr. Frost Nat. Bank, San Antonio, 1976-80; editor San Antonio Mag., 1980-81; dir. mktg. 1776, Inc., San Antonio, 1981; owner The Drawing Room, San Antonio, 1981—. Mem. Internat. Assn. Bus. Communicators (awards of merit 1980, award of excellence 1978, dir. 1982), Women in Communications (award of excellence 1981), Am. Mktg. Assn. (dir.), San Antonio Press Club (1st v.p.), Chi Beta Epsilon, Kappa Delta Pi. Republican. Roman Catholic. Home: 14806 Gallant Fox San Antonio TX 78248 Office: 1100 NW Loop 410 Suite 402 San Antonio TX 78213

GWINN, NAOMI JEAN, railroad quality control inspector; b. Greeneville, Tenn., May 10, 1952; d. Robert Walter and Ima Jean (Ferguson) G. Grad. high sch., Greeneville, Tenn., 1974. Cert. journeyman electrician. Supr. Midstate Electronics, Beech Grove, Ind., 1975-77; elec. apprentice Amtrak, Beech Grove, Ind., 1977-80, elec. technician, 1980-86, quality control insp., 1986—. Mem. editorial staff Amtrak co. news, 1985—; contbr. articles to mags. Mem. Nat. Assn. R.R. Bus. Women (Circle City chpt. #74, rec. sec. 1985-86, chmn. pub. affairs, press and publicity 1984-85, chair welfare com. 1986, nominating com. 1986), Nat. Assn. Female Execs., Internat. Brotherhood Elec. Workers. Democrat. Office: AMTRAK 202 Garstang Beech Grove IN 46107

GYENESE, PATRICIA ANNE, home loan processor; b. Compton, Calif., Dec. 26, 1952; d. Michael J. and Pauline R. (Karnow) Dingillo; m. Richard E. Gyenese; stepchildren: Rick E., Vincent M. Receptionist United Calif. Mortgage, Tustin, 1978-81; home loan processor Mason McDuffie Co., Santa Ana, Calif., 1981-82, Churchill Fin. Co., Irvine, Calif., 1982-84, Trust Deed Corp., Tustin, 1984-85, Mid-Am. Fin. Services, Inc., Orange, Calif., 1985—; receptionist, home loan processor United Calif. Mortgage.

GYETTERMAN, NANCY JO, insurance agency owner; b. Springfield, Ill., Oct. 2, 1950; d. Elmer Charles and Edna Virginia (Lowe) Forcade; m. Scott Alan Guetterman, Mar. 1, 1969 (div. May 1978); children: Stephanie Ann, Marsha Lynn. Student, Belleville Area Coll., 1980-82. File clk. Forcade Ins. Agy., Granite City, Ill., 1964-69, typist, 1972-80, ins. agt., 1980-82, ins. broker, 1982-86, owner, 1986—. Pres. Collinsville Jaycees 1987-88, chmn. bd. 1988—; mem. disciplinary com. Ill. Jaycees, 1987-88; mem. Community Concerts, Collinsville, Ill., 1988. Recipient Speak-Up award Collinsville Jaycees, 1985, 86; named Outstanding Officer of Yr., Collinsville Jaycees, 1986, one of Outstanding Young Women Am., 1987, Outstanding Officer of Yr. Gateway Region Jaycees, 1986, Outstanding Local Pres., 1987, Blue Chip Chapter Pres Ill. Jaycees, 1987. Mem. Ind. Ins. Agts. Am., Granite City C. of C., Collinsville C. of C. Democrat. Roman Catholic.

HAAG, CAROL ANN, environmental service executive; b. Jamestown, N.D., May 22, 1947; d. Richard C. and Grace A. (Miller) Joyce; m. Roger T. Haag, Sept. 14, 1968; children: Staci, Kelly, Chad. BS in Edn., Valley City (N.D.) State Coll., 1969; MS in Edn., N.D. State U., 1972; cert. in adminstrn., Kans. State U., 1981. Fin. sec. Butler Machinery Co., Fargo, N.C., 1969; instr. Moorhead (Minn.) Vocat. Sch., 1969-72; coordinator, instr. Moorhead State U., 1973-74; corp. sec. Jet-Way, Inc., Moorhead, 1974-77; coordinator Johnson County Community Colls., Overland Park, Kans., 1978; spl. edn. coordinator, high sch. counselor Unified Sch. Dist. #305, Salina, Kans., 1978-81; instr. Lansing (Mich.) Community Coll., 1982-86; pres., chief exec. officer EnviroLand, Inc., Dewitt, Mich., 1985—; speaker on small bus. mgmt. Mem. Nat. Assn. Female Execs. Lutheran. Club: City (Lansing).

HAAG, CAROL ANN GUNDERSON, marketing professional, consultant; b. Mpls.; d. Glenn Alvin and Genevieve Esther (Knudson) Gunderson; m. Lawrence S. Haag, Aug. 30, 1969; 1 child, Maren Anne. BJ, U. Mo., 1969; postgrad., Roosevelt U, Chgo., 1975—. Pub. relations writer, advt. copywriter Am. Hosp. Supply Corp., Evanston, Ill., 1969-70; asst. dir. pub. relations Rush-Presbyn. St. Luke's Med. Ctr., Chgo., 1970-71; asst. mgr. pub. and employee communications Quaker Oats Co., Chgo., 1971-72, mgr. editorial communications, 1972-74, mgr. employee communications programs, 1974-77; dir. pub. relations Shaklee Corp., San Francisco, 1978-82; pres. CH & Assocs., San Francisco, 1982-84; dir corp. communications BRAE Corp., San Francisco, 1984; dir. mktg. St. Francis Meml. Hosp., San Francisco, 1985—; cons. in field. Bd. dirs. Calif. League Handicapped; mem. adv. bd. San Francisco Spl. Olympics; mem. pub. relations com. San Francisco Recreation and Parks Dept., San Francisco Vol. Bur. Recipient 1st Place cert. Printing Industry Am., 1972, 74, 1st Place Spl. Communication award Internat. Assn. Bus. Communicators, 1974; 1st Place citation Chgo. Assn. Bus. Communicators, 1974. Mem. Nat. Acad. TV Arts and Scis., Indsl. Communication Council, Pub. Relations Soc. Am., San Francisco C. of C. Club: San Francisco Press. Home: 133 Fernwood Dr Moraga CA 94556 Office: St Francis Meml Hosp 900 Hyde St San Francisco CA 91409

HAAG, CARRIE A., non-profit association executive; b. Chgo., July 7, 1950; d. Arthur L. and Janice (Tidmarsh) H. BA, Purdue U., 1972; MA, Eastern Ky. U., 1977, EdS, 1978; postgrad., U. N.C., Greensboro, 1978-79. Dir. nat. championships Assn. for Intercollegiate Athletics for Women, Washington, 1979-82; asst. dir. athletics Dartmouth Coll., Hanover, N.H., 1982-84; exec. dir. U.S. Field Hockey Assn., Inc., Colorado Springs, Colo., 1984—. U.S. Olympic Found. grantee, 1986, 87, 88. Mem. Am. Alliance for Health, Phys. Edn., Recreation and Dance, Colo. Amateur Sports Corp., Nat. Assn. for Girls and Women in Sports, Women's Sport Found. Home: 405 Bear Creek Pl Colorado Springs CO 80906 Office: US Field Hockey Assn Inc 1750 E Boulder St Colorado Springs CO 80909-5773

HAAG, VELMA MAY, psychotherapist; b. Gackle, N.D., Aug. 31, 1955; d. Harold R. and Joyce E. (Ziebart) H.; m. Daniel W. Conway, Dec. 15, 1985; 1 child, Rachel. BA, Moorhead State U., 1977; MSW, U. Wis., 1980. Cert. social worker. Youth worker Fargo (N.D.) Youth Commn., 1975-77, acting program dir., 1978-79; unit coordinator S.E. Mental Health Services, Fargo, 1976-78; clin. social worker Columbia County Mental Health, Portage, Wis., 1981-83, program mgr., 1983-86; chem. dependency specialist Dane County Mental Health, Madison, Wis., 1986—; clin. assoc., coordinator Wis. Inst. Psychotherapy, Madison, 1985—. Recipient NIMH Stipend, 1980. Mem. Nat. Assn. Social Workers. Office: 415 N Main St Poynette WI 53955

HAAKE, CATHARINE ANN, lawyer; b. St. Joseph, Mo., Apr. 29, 1954; d. Henry Elmer and Mary Catharine (Growney) H. BS, U. Ill., 1976; JD, Northwestern U., 1979. Bar: Ill. 1979, U.S. Dist. Ct. (no. dist.) Ill. 1979, Colo. 1981, U.S. Dist. Ct. Colo. 1984. Assoc. Mayer, Brown & Platt, Chgo., 1979-81; assoc. Mayer, Brown & Platt, Denver, 1981-85, ptnr., 1986—. Mem. ABA, Ill. Bar Assn., Colo. Bar Assn., Denver Bar Assn. Office: Mayer Brown & Platt 600 17th St Suite 2800 Denver CO 80202

HAALAND, KATHLEEN YORK, neuropsychologist; b. Newport, R.I., July 9, 1946; d. Arthur Alexander and Martha Mary (McGann) York; m. David Michael Haaland, June 6, 1968; 1 child, Ryan. BS, U. N.Mex., 1968; PhD, U. Rochester, 1972. cert. psychologist, N.Mex.; diplomate Am. Bd. Profl. Psychologists. Postdoctoral fellow VA, Albuquerque, 1973-74, Neurology dept. U. Wis., Madison, 1974-75; dir. neuropsychology VA Med. Ctr. Psychology Service, Albuquerque, 1975—; adj. assoc. prof. psychology, neurology, psychiatry U. N.Mex., Albuquerque, 1984—; clin. cons. Lovelace Med. Ctr., Albuquerque, 1980—, cons. scientist Lovelace med. Found., Albuquerque, 1981—; collaborating scientist Los Alamos Nat. Labs., 1985—. Contbr. articles to profl. jours. Mem. Internat. Neuropsychol. Soc. (bd. govs. 1982-86, program chair 1983), Am. Psychol. Assn. (program com. 1983-85, 1987-88), Am. Bd. Profl. Psychologists (bd. dirs. intermountain region 1987—). Office: VA Med Ctr Psychology Service 2100 Ridgecrest SE Albuquerque NM 87108

HAAR, ANA MARIA FERNÁNDEZ, advertising/public relations executive; b. Oriente Province, Cuba, Mar. 25, 1951; came to U.S., 1960, naturalized, 1970; d. Gilberto and Esmeralda Emiliana (Díaz) Fernández. Grad. Miami Dade Community Coll., 1971; student Barry Coll., 1972-78. Adminstrv. asst. thru asst. v.p. nat. accounts Flagship Bank, Miami Beach, Fla., 1971-77; v.p. comml. lending Jefferson Nat. Bank, Miami Beach, 1977-78; pres. IAC Advt. Group, Miami, 1978—; instr. Miami Dade Community Coll. Women in Mgmt. Program, 1980-81; hostess Sta. WPBT Program Viva. Mem. Dade County Commn. on Status of Women, 1979-82; chmn. Econ. Devel. Task Force of Commn. on Status of Women, 1979-82; bd. dirs. Downtown Miami Bus. Assn., 1979-82, Fla. Counseling Services, Miami; Internat. Ctr. of Fla., chmn. healthcare com.; mem. Dist. Export Council; hostess (program) Viva, WPBT-TV; mem. community Services Cedars Med. Ctr. Recipient Gran Orden Martiana of Cuban Lyceum for excellence in community service, 1976, Up and Comers award South Fla. Bus. Jour., 1988. Mem. Advt. Fedn. Greater Miami, Greater Miami Advt. Fedn. (bd. dirs.), Asociación de Publicitarios Latino-Americanos (v.p.), Miami Beach C. of C. (hon. life), Greater Miami C. of C., Hispanic Heritage Festival Com., Home: 2451 Brickell Ave Miami FL 33129 Office: 2725 SW Third Ave Miami FL 33129

HAAS, CAROLYN BUHAI, writer, publisher, consultant; b. Chgo., Jan. 1, 1926; d. Michael and Tillie (Weiss) Buhai; m. Robert Green Haas, June 29, 1947 (dec. June 30, 1984); children—Andrew Robert, Mari Beth, Thomas Michael, Betsy Ann, Karen Sue. B.Ed., Smith Coll., Northampton, Mass., 1947; postgrad. Nat. Coll. Edn., Evanston, Ill., 1956-59; Art Inst. Chgo., 1958-59. Tchr., Francis W. Parker Sch., Chgo., 1947-49; tchr. art Glencoe Pub. Schs., Ill., 1967-68, substitute tchr., 1964-72; co-founder PAR Leadership Tng. Found., Northfield, Ill., 1969-81; pres., editor CBH Pub., Inc., Northfield, 1979—; cons., writer, adv. bd. The Learning Line; cons. presch. sci. program Mus. Sci. and Industry, Chgo.; adv. bd. My Own Mag.; cons. in field. Author: (with Ann Cole and Betty Weinberger) I Saw a Purple Cow, 1972; A Pumpkin In A Pear Tree, 1974; Children Are Children Are Children, 1976; Backyard Vacation, 1978; Purple Cow to the Rescue, 1982; Recipes for Fun and Learning, 1982; author: The Big Book of Recipes for Fun, 1979; Look At Me: Activities for Babies and Toddlers, 1985. Contbr. articles to profl. jours. Pres., West Sch. PTA, Glencoe; pres. Jr. Bd. Scholarship and Guidance, Chgo.; bd. dirs. Family Counseling Service of Glencoe, Glencoe Human Relations Com.; pres., sec., bd. dirs. Glencoe Pub. Library; pres. Friends of Glencoe Pub. Library; co-founder Glencoe Patriotic Days Com.; co-chmn. Frank Lloyd Wright Bridge Com., Glencoe; pres., bd. dirs. Chgo. League Smith Coll.; mem. women's bd. Northwestern U.; bd. dirs. Chgo. chpt. Am. Jewish Com.; mem. regional adv. bd. Am. Found. for Blind; mem. women's com. Chgo. Symphony Orch. Clubs; bd. dirs., Art Resources in Teaching. Mem. Soc. Children's Bookwriters, Children's Reading Roundtable, Nat. Assn. Edn. Young Children, Assn. Childhood Edn. Internat., IRA, NEA, Phi Delta Kappa. Democrat. Jewish. Club: Northmoor Country (Highland Park, Ill.); Monroe, Carlton (Chgo.). Avocations: art; reading; sports; travel. Office: CBH Pub Inc Box 11738 Chicago IL 60611

HAAS, ELEANOR (MRS. PETER RALPH HAAS), business development consultant; b. Jersey City, Mar. 12, 1932; d. Nicholas Mark and Eleanor (Cochran) Alter de Csanytelek; BA, Smith Coll., 1953; cert. N.Y. Sch. Interior Design, 1960; m. Peter Ralph Haas, Oct. 22, 1966. Exec. sec. MCA Artists, Ltd., N.Y.C., 1954-56; exec. sec. Young & Rubicam, Inc., N.Y.C., 1956-58; exec. sec. J. Walter Thompson Co., N.Y.C., 1958-59; exec. sec. Stanford Research Inst., N.Y.C., 1959, Deafness Research Found., N.Y.C., 1960, Earl Newsom & Co., N.Y.C., 1961-65; account exec. Ruder & Finn, Inc., N.Y.C., 1965-68; founder, pres. The Haas Group, Inc., N.Y.C., 1968—; founder, pres. HTL Ventures, Inc., N.Y.C., 1986—; adj. asso. prof. dept. journalism N.Y. U., 1980-83, lectr. Sch. Continuing Edn., 1981-83. Mem. Info. Industry Assn., Am. Mktg. Assn., Electronic Banking Econ. Soc., Pub. Relations Soc. N.Y., N.Y. Women in Communications, Nat. Acad. TV Arts and Scis., Fin. Communications Soc., Electronic Banking Econs. Soc., Advt. Women N.Y., Hajji Baba Club. Office: HTL Ventures Inc 59 E 54th St New York NY 10022

HAAS, ELLEN R., publishing executive; b. N.Y.C., Oct. 28, 1942; d. Nathan and Lillian (Minkoff) Charney; m. Bert Robert Haas, Mar. 11, 1967 (dec. Sept. 1983); children—Caroline Audrey, Paul Edward. B.A., Hunter Coll., 1965. Tchr. speech improvement N.Y. Bd. Edn., Bklyn., 1965-69; mgr. Parker Finch Assocs., N.Y.C., 1978-81; permanent div. mgr. Towne Personnel, N.Y.C., 1981-82; office mgr. Harvey Marcus Personnel, N.Y.C., 1982; employment cons. Payson Ruby Agy., N.Y.C., 1982-85, D.J. Hertz & Assocs., N.Y.C., 1985-87, dir. personnel Am. Jour. Nursing Co., 1987-88; asst. treas., personnel officer Credit Lyonnais, 1988—. Rep., Parents League, N.Y.C., Bentley Sch., N.Y.C., 1974-75, pres. Parents Assn., Rhodes Sch., 1976-78, 85-87; fund raising chmn. Rhodes Sch., N.Y.C., 1982-85, Baldwin Sch. co-chmn., 1987. Home: 315 E 86th St New York NY 10028 Office: Credit Lyonnais 95 Wall St New York NY 10005

HAAS, MIRIAM LEVIEN, sculptor, civic worker; b. N.Y.C., Sept. 21, 1921; d. Maurice Flexner and Louisa (Davis) Levien; m. Raymond S. Robinson, June 2, 1940 (div. Mar. 1962); children: Donald Alan, Barbara Ellen Schwartz, James Alfred; m. Adrian Lawrence Haas, Apr. 29, 1962 (dec. Nov. 1984). Student, Art Students League, N.Y.C., 1938-39, Elaine Journet Studio, New Rochelle, N.Y., 1945-47, Westchester County Ctr. Art Studios, White Plains, N.Y., 1968-70, 78-79, Art Life Craft Studios, North White Plains, N.Y., 1982—. Exec. sec. to sr. v.p. fin. Flinkote Co., White Plains, 1969-77; profl. fund raiser United Jewish Appeal Fedn. Joint Campaign, Hartsdale, N.Y., 1977-81; mounted NASA exhibit at Sinai Temple, Mt. Vernon, N.Y., 1966. Exhibited at Nelson Rockefeller Collection, N.Y.C., 1984; exhibited in group shows at Va. Mus. Fine Arts, Richmond, 1936, Met. Mus. Art, N.Y.C., 1939, Cork Gallery of Avery Fisher Hall-Lincoln Ctr., 1984, 87, Lever House, N.Y.C., 1984, 88; represented in permanent collections Calif., Fla., Ill., N.Y., N.J. and Va.; pres., producer Theatre Workshop, Mt. Vernon, N.Y., 1956-61; stage mgr. Philharm. Symphony Westchester, Inc., 1979—, v.p., bd. dirs., 1985—. Chmn. Interfaith Inst., Sinai Temple, Mt. Vernon, 1968-69; nat. chmn. cancer service fundraising United Order True Sisters, Inc., N.Y.C., 1957-59. Recipient numerous art awards. Mem. Mamaroneck Artists Guild (v.p., chmn. fund raising 1982-84, bd. dirs. 1982—), Women and Arts Westchester (bd. dirs. 1982—, chmn. nat. open juried show awards 1984-87—, chmn. nominating com. 1986-87, membership sculptor juror 1987—), Art Life Guild (pres. 1986—), N.Y. Artists Equity Assn., Internat. Platform Assn. Republican. Club: Woodlands Golf (tournament chmn. 1985). Avocations: golf, bridge, reading, music. Home: 100B High Point Dr Hartsdale NY 10530

HAAS, RUTH SHERWOOD, librarian; b. Peoria, Ill., Nov. 28, 1937; d. Abijah Minor and Elizabeth Ida (Krumpe) Sherwood; m. Howard Wendell Dillon, July 27, 1957 (div.); children—Maureen Rachel, Jason Giles; m. 2d, Howard Clyde Haas, May 28, 1971. B.A., Knox Coll., 1959; M.S. in Library Sci., Ind. U., 1961. Adminstrv. asst. Ind. U. div. library sci., Bloomington, 1960-61; cataloguer Harvard Coll. Library, Cambridge, Mass., 1965-68, asst. head, sr. cataloger CONSER office, 1981—; reference librarian Robbins Library, Arlington, Mass., 1976-81. Recipient Lawrence Latin prize Knox Coll., Galesburg, Ill., 1959; Mem. ALA (resources and tech. services div.), Soc. Scribes and Illuminators, Beta Phi Mu. Methodist. Home: 140 Pleasant

St Arlington MA 02174 Office: Harvard U Widener Library Cambridge MA 02138

HAASE, JACQUELYN, food company executive; b. Wilbur, Wash., Sept. 6, 1947; d. Howard Neal and Helen Lucille (Wachter) Anderson; m. Wayne Ray Flower, Aug. 16, 1973 (div. Nov. 1980); m. Herbert John Haase, May 29, 1982. Student, Wash. State U., 1965-67, Big Bend Community Coll., 1967, Highline Community Coll., 1967-68. Real estate assoc. House & Home Realtors, Spokane, Wash., 1977-78; purchasing specialist MGM Grand Hotel-Casino, Reno, Nev., 1978-80; spl. order coordinator Nobel/Sysco Foodservices Co., Albuquerque, 1980-82, tabletop merchandiser, 1982-83, dir. non food purchasing, 1983-85, asst. to pres., 1985-87, v.p. merchandising and mktg., 1987—. Mem. Nat. Assn. for Female Execs. Republican. Lutheran. Home: 8604 Monitor NE Albuquerque NM 87109 Office: Nobel/Sysco Food Services Co 601 Comanche Rd NE Albuquerque NM 87107

HABBESTAD, KATHRYN LOUISE, financial analyst; b. Spokane, Wash., Sept. 29, 1949; d. Bernard Malvin and Gertrude Lucille (Westberg) H. BA, U. Wash., 1971; postgrad., Seattle U., 1981-82. Mgr. bus. Seattle Sun, 1974-75; analyst, dep. dir. Research and Planning Office, Seattle, 1975-83; account exec. Southmark Fin. Services, Seattle, 1983-84; stockbroker Interstate Securities, New Bern, N.C., 1985-86; co-founder, assoc. pub. Havelock (N.C.) News, 1986-87; pvt. practice stockbroker ISIS Enterprises, Spokane, 1988—; sec.-treas. Seattle Sun Pub. Co., 1974-75, Veritas Services, Seattle, 1978-83; chmn. Energy Com. Nat. Congress for Community Econ. Devel., Washington, 1979-82. Treas. Havelock Chili Festival, 1985-87. Mem. Havelock C. of C., Mensa, Nat. Assn. Female Execs. Home: E 803 26th Ave Spokane WA 99203 Office: West 314 7th Ave Spokane WA 99204

HABELITZ, THORA GRAHAM, small business owner; b. Martinsville, Mo., Feb. 2, 1923; d. George Leslie and Lula Ruth (Kidwell) Graham; m. Gus William Habelitz, DEc. 11, 1943 (dec. 1979); 1 child, Gary William. Student, Cen. Bus. Sch., 1940-41. Accounts receivable clk. Western Ins. Co., Kansas City, Mo., 1943-44; co-owner Habelitz Press, Kansas City, 1946-52; From clk. to gen. mgr. Constrn. Anchors, Inc., Kansas City, 1969-76; owner Clock Bait Shop, Kansas City, 1961—; mem. adv. bd. Fishing Tackle Trade News, 1983. Den mother Boy Scouts Am., Phoenix, 1960-61. Office: Clock Bait Shop 7910 N Oak Kansas City MO 64118

HABER, AUDREY RUTH, psychologist, author; b. N.Y.C., Feb. 4, 1940; d. Eugene Jerome Friedman and Sally (Reit) Brenner; B.A., Adelphi U., 1960, Ph.D. (USPHS fellow), 1963; m. Jerome Jassenoff, Dec. 19, 1969; children—Laurie Beth, David Scott. Diplomate Am. Bd. Med. Psychotherapists. Lic. psychologist, N.Y., N.J. Asso. prof. psychology C.W. Post Coll., Greenvale, N.Y., 1964-70; research psychologist UCLA, 1971-78; now dir. psychology Garden State Rehab. Hosp., Toms River, N.J. Author, 1967—; books include Business Statistics, 1982; Fundamentals of Behavioral Statistics, 6th ed., 1987; Fundamentals of Psychology, 14th edit., 1988; General Statistics, 3d edit., 1977; Psychology of Adjustment, 1984; contbr. articles profl. jours. Recipient Acad. of Distinction award Adelphi U., 1977, Psychologist Recognition award, 1984-86. Mem. Eastern Psychol. Assn. Am. Psychol. Assn., N.J. Acad. Psychology, Nat. Acad. Neuropsychologists, Psi Chi. Home and Office: 14 Hospital Dr Toms River NJ 08753

HABERMANN, PHYLLIS, merger and acquisition professional; b. Bklyn., Feb. 7, 1949; d. Henry and Jane (Lanier) H. BS, Simmons Coll., 1970; MBA, Columbia U., 1972; Inst. European Studies, Vienna, Austria, 1968-69. Fin. analyst Celanese Corp., N.Y.C., 1972-74, mgr. fibers analysis, 1974-76; mgr. mktg. planning Celanese Fibers Group, N.Y.C., 1977-79; mgr., planning and bus. devel. Celanese Internat. Co., N.Y.C., 1980-84; assoc. Charterhouse Group Internat., N.Y.C., 1985—; trustee Film/Video Arts, Inc., N.Y.C., 1983—. Mem. Fin. Women's Assn. N.Y., Planning Forum. Club: Columbia Bus. Sch. (N.Y.C.). Office: Charterhouse Group Internat 535 Madison Ave New York NY 10022

HABERSANG, PIA ERIKA, academic administrator; b. Basel, Switzerland, May 22, 1945; came to U.S., 1970; d. Oskar and Pauline (Willman) Geisinger; m. Rolf W. O. Habersang, June 24, 1967; children: Marion Tirza E., Nicole Rahel. Diploma in nursing, Sch. Nursing div. Univ. Hosp. Basel, Switzerland, 1967; BS in Nursing, Avila Coll., 1978; MS in Nursing, West Tex. State U., 1986. Head nurse neonatal intensive care unit North West Tex. Hosp., Amarillo, 1978-81; exec. dir. Birth Defect Found. subs. March of Dimes, Amarillo, 1981-84, bd. dirs.; clin. nurse specialist Tex. Tech U. Sch. Medicine, Amarillo, 1984-86, dir. quality assurance and risk mgmt., 1986—; pres. Mini Mundo, Kansas City, 1974-75. Bd. dirs. Parenting Service, Inc., Amarillo, 1983-85. Mem. Internat. Council Nurses, Am. Nurses Assn., Tex. Nurses Assn. (bd. dirs. dist. 2 1985—), Tex. Perinatal Assn. (bd. dirs. 1983-86, pres. 1985-86), Sigma Theta Tau. Roman Catholic. Home: 4211 Southpark Amarillo TX 79109 Office: Tex Tech Sch Medicine 1400 Wallace Amarillo TX 79106

HABLUTZEL, NANCY ZIMMERMAN, lawyer, educator; b. Chgo., Mar. 16, 1940; d. Arnold Fred Zimmerman and Maxine (Lewison) Zimmerman Goodman; m. Philip Norman Hablutzel, July 1, 1980; children—Margo Lynn, Robert Paul. B.S., Northwestern U., 1960; M.A., Northeastern Ill. U., 1972; J.D., Ill. Inst. Tech. Chgo.-Kent Coll. Law, 1980; Ph.D., Loyola U., Chgo., 1983. Bar: Ill. 1980, U.S. Dist. Ct. (no. dist.) Ill. 1980. Speech therapist various pub. schs. and hosps., Chgo. and St. Louis, 1960-63, 65-72; audiologist U. Chgo. Hosps., 1963-65; instr. spl. edn. Chgo. State U., 1972-76; asst. prof. Loyola U., Chgo., 1981-87; adj. prof. Ill. Inst. Tech. Chgo.-Kent Coll. Law, 1982—; legal dir. Legal Clinic for Disabled, Chgo., 1984-85, exec. dir., 1985-87; of counsel Whitted & Spain P.C., 1987—. Mem. Ill. Gov.'s Com. on Handicapped, 1972-75; mem. Council for Exceptional Children, faculty moderator student div., 1982-87, Ill. Atty. Gen. adv. com. for disabled, 1985—. Loyola-Mellon Found. grantee, 1983. Fellow Chgo. Bar Found.; mem. ABA, Ill. Bar Assn. (standing com. on juvenile justice, sec. 1986-87, vice chmn. 1987-88, Inst. Pub. Affairs 1985—), Chgo. Bar Assn. (exec. com. of corp. law com. 1984—), Am. Ednl. Research Assn. Republican. Avocations: sailing, travel, swimming, cooking. Office: Whitted & Spain PC One N La Salle St #1750 Chicago IL 60602

HABSHEY, THERESA ANNE, medical center administrator; b. Birmingham, Ala., Oct. 21, 1938; d. Norman Joseph and Matilda (Resha) H. BS in Commerce and Bus. Adminstrn., U. Ala., 1960; MBA, Samford U., 1983. Asst. buyer Loveman's Dept. Store, Birmingham, 1960-61; sec. Am. Bridge, USS, Birmingham, 1961-65, IBM Corp., Huntsville, Ala., 1966-67; programmer trainee IBM Corp., Huntsville, 1967-68; sec. South Cen. Bell, Birmingham, 1968-72, staff asst., 1972-73, supr., 1973-74, staff supr., 1974-75; asst. to chmn. U. Ala. at Birmingham, 1976-81, dir. adminstrv. and fiscal affairs, 1981—. Neighborhood zoning spokesman, Hoover, Ala., 1986-87; sec. Hoover Homeowner's Assn., 1986-87. Mem. Birmingham Bd. Realtors, Women's Jr. C. of C. Roman Catholic. Home: 2220 Myrtlewood Dr Birmingham AL 35216 Office: U Ala Univ Sta Birmingham AL 35294

HACK, LINDA, lawyer; b. Chgo., Nov. 30, 1949; d. Paul K. and Lorraine B. (Johnston) H.; m. Thomas E. Barnes, Nov. 30, 1967 (div. May 1977); m. Gary J. Derer, Aug. 15, 1979. MA, Roosevelt U., 1975; JD, DePaul U., 1979. Bar: Ill. 1979, Tex. 1980, U.S. Dist. Ct. (no. dist.) Ill. 1980, U.S. Dist. Ct. (no. dist.) Tex. 1981, U.S. Ct. Appeals (5th cir.) 1981, U.S. Ct. Internat. Trade 1982, U.S. Supreme Ct. 1983. Judge adminstrv. law Ill. Dept. Labor, 1979-80; assoc. Law Offices F. Ward Steinbach, 1981-83; ptnr. Hack & Derer, Dallas, 1983—; magistrate Dallas County, 1987—; of counsel Hicks, Gillespie, James & Lesser, 1983-84; magistrate, Dallas County, 1987—; arbitrator Chgo. Mercantile Exchange. Mem. subcom. med. and legal ctrs. Goals for Dallas, 1984-85, steering com. CHOICE, 1984-86, polit. action com. Oak Lawn Dems., 1984-85, voter registration com. Dallas Area Women's Polit. Caucus, 1984, vice chmn. 1985-86, bd. dirs. 1984-85; bd. dirs. Tex. Abortion Rights Action League, 1985-86. Mem. ABA (various coms.), Ill. Bar Assn., Tex. Bar Assn. (various coms.), Dallas Bar Assn. (various coms.), Nat. Conf. Women's Bar Assns. (speakers bur. 1984-85, chmn. directory 1984-85, sec. 1985-86, v.p. 1986-87, bd. dirs. 1987-88), Nat. Assn. Women Judges, Am. Judicature Soc., Tex. Young Lawyers Assn. (co-chmn. alt. dispute resolution com. 1984-86, liaison alt. dispute resolution com. 1983-84), Dallas Assn. Young Lawyers (chairperson alt. dispute resolution com. 1984-85), Dallas Women Lawyers Assn. (v.p. 1982-83, pres. 1983-84, pub. relations liaison 1984, liaison nat. conf. women's bar assn. 1984-86), Women's Bar Assn. Ill., Assn. Trial Lawyers Am., Ill. Trial Lawyers Assn., Tex. Trial Lawyers Assn., Acad. Family Mediators (full), Mediation Council Ill., Tex. Assn. Family Mediators, Inc. (founding mem.), Soc. Profls. in Dispute Resolution, Indsl. Relations Research Assn., Chgo. Mercantile Exchange, Nat. Fedn. Bus. and Profl. Women's Club (del. nat. convention 1983), Tex. Fedn. Bus. and Profl. Women's Club (chmn. pub. relations convention 1984-85, treas. 1984-85, chmn. individual devel. 1983-84, chmn. pub. relations 1983-84, dist. treas, recipient Tex. Nat. Program award 1983), White Rock Bus. and Profl. Women's Club (chmn. individual devel. 1983-84, chmn. goals com. 1984-85, pres. 1985-86), Bus. and Profl. Women, Dallas, Inc. (program chmn. 1982-83), Nat. Futures Assn., Nat. Panel Arbitrators, Am. Arbitration Assn. Lodge: Zonta. Home: 3607 Charming Ln Dallas TX 75204 Office: PO Bos 595314 Dallas TX 75359

HACKER, KAREN KAY, educator; b. Pasadena, Tex., Feb. 22, 1958; d. Andrew Jackson and Gloria Jean (Allen) Hickerson; m. James Alexander Hacker, Sept. 17, 1979 (Oct. 1981); 1 child, Dustin Travis. AA, San Jacinto Jr. Coll., 1978; BS, U. Houston, 1983, MEd, 1987. Cert. elem. tchr., Tex., counselor, ESL tchr. Flight attendant Tex. Internat. Airlines, Houston, 1979-80; tchr. Channelview (Tex.) Ind. Sch. Dist., 1984-85, Alief (Tex.) Ind. Schs., 1985-86, Houston Ind. Sch. Dist., 1986—. Mem. Nat. Orgn. Women, Houston, 1984-85, League of Women Voters, Houston, 1984-85. Mem. Am. Fedn. Tchrs., Houston Fedn. Tchrs. Home: 3100 Jeanetta #1403 Houston TX 77063 Office: Browning Elem Sch 607 Northwood Houston TX 77009

HACKER, RANDI, humor writer, magazine editor; b. Bklyn., Dec. 13, 1951; d. Charles Herman and Sylvia (Sukoff) H. B.A. magna cum laude, U. Mich., 1973. Humor writer with Jackie Kaufman contributed articles to Savvy, Punch, Spy, New York Woman; included with Jackie Kaufman in The Pick of Punch, 1987; scriptwriter with Jackie Kaufman for Nickelodeon; co-creator with Jackie Kaufman Captain Strong, No Vacany; co-founder, ptnr. The Fun Group, N.Y.C., 1986—; editor Electric Co. Mag. Children's TV Workshop, N.Y.C., from 1985.

HACKETT, CAROL ANN HEDDEN, physician; b. Valdese, N.C., Dec. 18, 1939; d. Thomas Barnett and Zada Loray (Pope) Hedden; B.A., Duke, 1961; M.D., U. N.C., 1966; m. John Peter Hackett, July 27, 1968; children—John Hedden, Elizabeth Bentley, Susanne Rochet. Intern. Georgetown U. Hosp., Washington, 1966-67, resident, 1967-69; clinic physician DePaul Hosp., Norfolk, Va., 1969-71; chief spl. health services Arlington County Dept. Human Resources, Arlington, Va., 1971-72; gen. med. officer USPHS Hosp., Balt., 1974-75; pvt. practice family medicine, Seattle, 1975—; mem. staff, chmn. dept. family practice Overlake Hosp. Med. Ctr., 1985-86; clin. instr. U. Wash. Bd. dirs. Mercer Island (Wash.) Preschool Assn., 1977-78; coordinator 13th and 20th Ann. Inter-profl. Women's Dinner, 1978, 86; trustee Northwest Chamber Orch., 1984-85 . Mem. Wash. Med. Soc., King County Med. Soc. (chmn. com. TV violence), DAR, Bellevue C. of C., NW Women Physicians (v.p. 1978), Seattle Symphony League, Eastside Women Physicians (founder, pres.), Sigma Kappa. Episcopalian. Clubs: Wash Athletic, Lakes. Home: 4304 E Mercer Way Mercer Island WA 98040 Office: 1128 112th Ave NE Bellevue WA 98004

HACKETT, JEAN BATES, counselor; b. Haverhill, N.H., Oct. 27, 1943; d. Guy Wilbur and Rowena Jeanette (Monette) Bates; m. Thomas Ross Hackett, Apr. 6, 1963 (div. Jan. 1984); children: Thomas Jeffrey, Timothy Ross, Todd Christopher. Assoc. in Bus. Sci. with honors, Champlain Coll., Burlington, Vt., 1964; BA with honors, Trinity Coll., Burlington, 1974; MS in Community Counseling, St. Michael's Coll., Winooski, Vt., 1977. Counselor Interfaith Counseling, Scottsdale, Ariz., 1980; assoc. United Campus Christian Ministry, Tempe, Ariz., 1979-82; pvt. practice counseling Scottsdale, 1982—; lectr. various workshops and retreats. Speaker local and nat. TV and radio talk shows. Vol. Boy Scouts Am., Vt., 1973-79; mem. Phoenix Art Mus. Mem. Am. Assn. for Counseling and Devel., Lupus Found. Am., Inc., Arthritis Found., Spirit of Senses. Republican. Congregationalist. Clubs: P.E.O. (Phoenix) (sec., chaplain), Toastmasters. Office: 7119 E 1st Ave Scottsdale AZ 85251

HACKETT, LOUISE, personnel services company executive, consultant; b. Sheridan, Mont., Nov. 11, 1933; d. Paul Duncan and Freda A. (Dudley) Johnson; m. Lewis Edward Hackett, June 24, 1962; 1 child, Dell Paul. Student U. Oreg., 1959-61; B.A., Calif. State U.-Sacramento, 1971. Legal sec. Samuel R. Friedman, Yreka, Calif., 1952-58, Barber & Cottrell, Eugene, Oreg., 1958-59; paralegal Elmer Sahlstrom, Eugene, 1959-62; legis. aide Calif. Legislature, Sacramento, 1962-72; owner Legal Personnel Services, Sacramento, 1973-78, corp. pres., 1979—; pres. Legalstaff, Inc., 1987—; curriculum adv. dept. bus. Am. River Coll., Sacramento, 1974-79; founder, adminstr. Pacific Coll. Legal Careers, Sacramento, 1973-84; cons. legal edn. Barclay Schs., Sacramento, 1984. Designer, pub. Sacramento/Yolo Attys. Directory, 1974—. Author operations manual and franchise training textbook; contbr. articles to profl. jours. Adv. bd. San Juan Sch. Dist., 1975—. Mem. Sacramento Women's Network, Calif. Assn. Personnel Cons., Sacramento Council Pvt. Edn. (pres. 1976-77), Pi Omega Pi. Clubs: Sierra Sail and Trail, Soroptimist Internat. Lodge: Order of Rainbow. Avocations: skiing; sailing; sports car rallying. Office: Legal Personnel Services 1415 21st St Sacramento CA 95814 also: 353 Sacramento St #1520 San Francisco CA 94111

HACKETT, MOLLY LYNN, small business owner, consultant; b. Lakewood, Ohio, Oct. 10, 1934; d. John Wilson and Marion Harriet (Shepard) Duffell; m. Benjamin Prescott Hackett, June 25, 1961 (div. 1981); children: Scott, Bruce. Student, Coll. of Wooster, 1952-55; BA, U. Mont., 1956, MA, 1957. Editor U. Chgo. Press, 1957-59; tchr. Stevensville (Mont.) Pub. High Sch., 1959-61; co-owner cattle ranch Sweathouse Creek Ranch, Victor, Mont., 1961-81; owner, operator The Frame Shop, Hamilton, Mont., 1981—. Editor: Montana Genesis, 1971. Mem. Rural Conservation & Devel. Com., Hamilton, 1970-72; sec. Hamilton County Planning Bd., 1973-77. Mem. Profl. Picture Framers Assn. Presbyterian. Lodge: Soroptimist (chairperson com. 1982—), Order of Eastern Star (matron 1975-76). Office: The Frame Shop 108 Bedford Hamilton MT 59840

HACKLANDER, EFFIE HEWITT, university administrator; b. Walnut Grove, Minn., Oct. 10, 1940; d. Kenneth and Ruth (Weaver) Hewitt; m. Duane Hacklander, Sept., 1961; children: Jeffrey, Alan, Craig. BS, U. Minn., 1962; MA, Mich. State U., 1968, PhD, 1973. Sec., spl. asst. Marriott Corp., 1962-66; lectr. Wayne State U., 1969; asst. prof. U. Md., College Park, 1973-79, asst. provost, div. human and community resources, 1979-80, assoc. dean, 1982-86; cons. chmn. music com., trustee Congl. Christian Ch. of Fairfax County, 1975—. Mem. Assn. Consumer Research, Am. Home Econs. Assn., Am. Mktg. Assn., Eastern Econ. Assn., World Future Soc., Assn. Adminstrs. in Home Econs. (pres.-elect N.E. region, pres. 1987-89). Office: 1100 Marie Mount Hall U Md College Park MD 20742

HACKMAN, HELEN ANNA HENRIETTE, home economist; b. New Melle, Mo., Oct. 8, 1908; d. John Henry and Lydia Eliza (Meier) Hackman; A.B., Central Wesleyan Coll., Warrenton, Mo., 1929; B.S., U. Mo., 1942, postgrad., 1942; postgrad. U. Wis., 1934, U. Colo., 1953, 75, U. Ariz., 1975, 77. Prin., Wright City High Sch., 1929; home econs. tchr., Cape Girardeau, Mo., 1930-42; sr. extension adviser home econs. U. Ill., Pittsfield, 1942-78; sec. Pike County Health and Social Services Coordinating Com. Dietitian, buyer Oshkosh Wis. Camp Fire Girls Camp, summers 1935, 36, 37; sec.-treas. Western Ill. 4-H Camp Assn., 1952-54; mem. Western Ill. Fair Bd. Com., Griggsville, 1946—; v.p. Tri-county Assn. for Crippled, 1960—; tech. cons. White House Conf., 1960, 70; pres. Pike County Heart Assn., 1969, organizer Family Planning Centers, Diabetic and Blood Pressure Clinics, Pike County Health Dept., 1971; sec. Illini Hosp. Aux., 1978; Bd. dirs. Pike County Mental Health. Recipient Distinguished Service award Nat. Home Demonstration Agts. Assn., 1952; Meritorious Service award Heart Assn., 1960, 61. Mem. Ill. Home Advisers Assn. (sec. 1948), Nat. Assn. Extension Home Economists (3d v.p. 1951-53, pub. relations chmn. 1951-53), Am. Home Econs. Assn. (sec. Ill. nutrition com. 1967-69), Pittsfield Hist. Soc. Epsilon Sigma Phi (chief 1962), Gamma Sigma Delta. Clubs: Pittsfield Woman's (pres. 1979, 80, 81, 82), Pike County Bus. and Profl. (pres. 1970-71). Home: 230 S Illinois St Pittsfield IL 62363 Office: Hwy 36 and 54th St E Po Box 227 Pittsfield IL 62363

HACKMAN, (MARY) JUDITH DOZIER, university administrator, researcher; b. Springfield, Ill., Dec. 30, 1940; d. John Burrel and Elva Hannah (Smith) Dozier; m. (John) Richard Hackman, Sept. 1, 1962; children: Julia Beth, Laura Dianne. Student MacMurray Coll., 1959-62; BA, U. Ill., 1963; MS, So. Conn. State U., 1970; postgrad., Yale U., 1979-80; PhD, U. Mich., 1983. Tchr. Oakwood High Sch., Fithian, Ill., 1963-66; researcher Yale U., New Haven, 1966-71, dir. criteria study, 1971-73, spl. projects, 1974-79, assoc. dir. instl. research, 1979-82, dir. instl. research, 1982-87, assoc. dean Yale Coll., 1987—; cons. Edn. Research Assocs.; guest lectr. numerous univs. Contbr. articles to profl. jours. Bd. dirs. Info. and Counselling Service for Women, New Haven, 1972-77, 79-80, New Careers for Women, New Haven, 1974-80, Bethany Community Schs., Conn., 1978-79; mem. Town Dem. Com., Bethany, 1984—; moderator, ch. council Battell Ch. of Christ in Yale, New Haven, 1985-86. Recipient Outstanding Alumnus award So. Conn. State U., 1983. Mem. Assn. Instl. Research (forum panel com. 1985-86, nominating com. 1986-87, publs. bd. 1987—), North East Assn. Instl. Research (program chmn. 1984-85, pres. 1985-86, chmn. nominating com. 1986-87), Assn. Study Higher Edn. (program vice chmn. 1984-85, program chmn. 1987), New England Assn. Schs. and Colls. (accreditation liaison officer for Yale 1983—, Coll. Bd., adv. bd. Washington office 1987—), Soc. Coll. and Univ. Planning (editorial bd. 1986—). Avocation: playing baritone horn. Home: 109 Sperry Rd Bethany CT 06525 Office: Yale Coll Yale Sta Box 1604-A New Haven CT 06520

HACKMANN, KATHY ALENE, lawyer; b. Alton, Ill., Dec. 15, 1952; d. Alvin Harrison and Mildred Evelyn (Talbert) Petitt; m. William Sterling Hackmann, Dec. 22, 1973. B.A., U. Ill., 1973, M.S., 1974; J.D., Stanford U., 1980. Bar: Calif. 1980, Minn. 1983. Indsl. engr. Sears, Roebuck & Co., Chgo., 1974-77; research asst. Stanford U. (Calif.), 1978-80; law clk. Pacific Telephone Co., San Francisco, 1979, atty., 1980-85; atty. Pacific Telesis Group, 1985—. Mem. ABA, Calif. Bar Assn., Minn. Bar Assn., Bar Assn. San Francisco. Republican. Office: Pacific Telesis Group 130 Kearny #3651 San Francisco CA 94105

HACKWOOD, SUSAN, electrical and computer engineering educator; b. Liverpool, Eng., May 23, 1955; came to U.S., 1980; d. Alan and Margaret Hackwood. BS with honors, Leicester Poly., Eng., 1976, PhD in Solid State Ionics, 1979. Research fellow Leicester Poly., Eng., 1976-79; postdoctoral research fellow AT&T Bell Labs., Homdel, N.J., 1980-81, mem. tech. staff, 1981-83, supr. robotics tech., 1983-84, dept. head robotics tech., 1984-85; prof. elec. and computer engring. U. Calif., Santa Barbara, 1985—, dir. Ctr. Robotic Systems in Microelectronics, 1985—. Editor: Jour. of Robotic Systems, 1983, Recent Advances in Robotics, 1985; contbr. 64 articles to tech. jours.; 7 patents in field. Mem. IEEE, Electrochem. Soc. (treas. 1985-87). Office: U Calif Ctr Robotic Systems 6740 Cortona Santa Barbara CA 93106

HADAWAY, EILEEN, religious organization executive, nurse; b. Buffalo, Mar. 31, 1949; d. Joseph M. and Mary Evelyn (Quinlan) Klein; m. William J. Hadaway, Sept. 8, 1973; children: Shannon, Lindsay; stepchildren: William, Jeffrey, John. AAS, Trocaire Coll., 1969. R.N., N.Y., Fla. Nurse Sisters Hosp., Buffalo, 1969-71, Roswell Park Meml. Hosp., Buffalo, 1971-74, Deaconess Hosp., Buffalo, 1974-78, Lee Meml. Hosp., Ft. Myers, Fla., 1978-80; pres. World Life Scriptures, Cape Coral, Fla., 1980—. Author: Poems for the Weary, 1982. Appearing in the top ten best sellers list Spring Arbor Distbrs., 1984—. Office: Word of Life Scriptures PO Box 150609 Cape Coral FL 33915

HADDA, JANET RUTH, Yiddish language educator, lay psychoanalyst; b. Bradford, Eng., Dec. 23, 1945; came to U.S., 1948; d. George Manfred and Annemarie (Kohn) H.; m. Allan Joshua Tobin, Mar. 22, 1981; stepchildren—David, Adam. B.S. in Edn., U. Vt., 1966; M.A., Cornell U., 1969; Ph.D., Columbia U., 1975. Assoc. prof. Yiddish UCLA; research psychoanalyst So. Calif. Psychoanalytic Inst., Los Angeles, 1988—. Author: Yankev Glatshteyn, 1980, Passionate Women, Passive Men: Suicide in Yiddish Literature, 1988; editorial bd. Prooftexts; contbr. articles to profl. jours. Mem. Assn. Jewish Studies, MLA, Phi Beta Kappa; affiliate mem. Am. Psychoanalytic Assn. Office: UCLA Dept Germanic Langs 310 Royce Hall Los Angeles CA 90024

HADLEY, CAROLYN BETH, physician, educator; b. Dallas, Nov. 22, 1945; d. Charles Franklin and Sadie Beth (Humphreys) Hadley; m. Richard G. Suchan, Dec. 28, 1985; 1 child, Richard C. B.A. with honors in Microbiology, U. Kans., 1968; M.S. in Clin. Microbiology, Columbia U. Coll. Physicians and Surgeons, 1974; M.D., U. Pa., 1981. Diplomate Am. Coll. Med. Examiners. Lab. technologist St. Joseph Mercy Hosp., Ann Arbor, Mich., 1968-70; sr. technologist, diagnostic microbiology service Columbia Presbyn. Med. Ctr., N.Y.C., 1970-73, sr. asst. supr., 1973-75; asst. microbiologist Hosp. of U. Pa., Phila., 1975-77, resident in ob gyn, 1981-85, fellow in maternal fetal medicine, 1985-87; teaching asst. in microbiology U. Kans., 1968; teaching fellow microbiology U. Mich. Med. Sch., 1969; asst. prof. Med. Coll. Pa., 1987—. Recipient Undergrad. Research award U. Kans., 1967; Phillip Williams prize in obstetrics, 1984; S. Leon Israel prize in obstetrics, 1985; Henrietta Ottinger/Huston MacFarlane scholar, 1978—. Fellow Am. Coll. Ob-Gyn (jr. fellow); mem. Am. Soc. Microbiology (specialist in microbiology), Am. Soc. Clin. Pathologists (specialist microbiologist), Soc. for Perinatal Obstetricians (assoc.), DAR, U. Kans. Alumni Assn., Phila. Obstet. Soc., Phi Beta Kappa. Office: Med Coll Pa Dept Ob-Gyn 3300 Henry Ave Philadelphia PA 19129

HADLEY, CORNELIA Q. (CONNIE), insurance agent; b. Dermott, Ark., Mar. 29, 1930; d. Benjamin James and Lillie Rosetta (Herron) Franklin; m. Robert Lawrence Hadley Sr., Sept. 3, 1950; children: Vanessa C. Hadley Cobbins, Robert L. Jr., Walter D. Student, U. Mo., Kansas City, 1967-69. Button maker, stone setter Mendels Garment Mfr., Kansas City, Mo., 1956-61; cashier, asst. mgr. Famco Resturant, Kansas City, 1961-62; bookkeeper Bonner Springs (Kans.) Sanitation Dept., 1962-63; telephone receptionist Leaders Clothing Co., Kansas City, Kans., 1963-66; powder press supr. Army Ammunition Plant, Desoto, Kans., 1966-67; exec. dir. Econ. Opportunity Found., Kansas City, 1967-84; program coordinator, adminstrv. asst. to city mgr. City of Bonner Springs, 1975-77; ins. agt. Farmers Ins. Group of Cos., Los Angeles, 1984—; cons. Nat. Council on Aging, Denver, 1972, Kansas City 1973, Des Moines, Iowa, 1974. Mem. Nat. Assn. for Community Devel. Local, State, Regional Orgns., 1973-82; co-author on Black Alcoholic Proposal for DRAG Ctr., Kansas City, 1974; author first citizen participation plan, first affirmative action plan, updated personnel policy for City of Bonner Springs, 1975-77; resource person, student voter edn. Black Motivation Ctr., Kansas City, 1980; dirs. Wyandotte Mental Health Ctr., Kansas City; vol. Kans. chpt. ARC; legis. com. Bonner Springs; fund raiser LWV, Kansas City, 1985; mem. Women Div. Ea. Diocese, Kansa Ch. of God in Christ. Mem. Nat. Assn. Life Underwriters, Kans. City C. of C., Bonner Springs Bus. and Profl. Women (chair legis. com. 1987), Nat. Assn. Female Execs. Republican. Club: Equal Rights Investors Investment Club. Home: 1530 S 94 St Kansas City KS 66111 Office: Farmers Ins 8245 Neiman Rd Suite 104 Lenexa KS 66214

HADLEY, DEBORAH JOYCE, ballet dancer; b. San Diego, July 4, 1951; d. Raoul Berdet Hadley and Barbara Beverly (Gould) Abbott; m. Bill Edward Kickbush, July 14, 1972 (div. Feb. 1979); children: Brandon Wesley, Brian Anthony; m. Earl Paul Hadler, June 18, 1988. Student, San Diego State U., 1971-72. Soloist, prin. dancer San Diego Ballet Co., 1963-69; corps de ballet Joffrey II, N.Y.C., 1969; co-dir. Springfield (Ill.) Ballet Co., 1976-79; prin. dancer Pacific NW Ballet, Seattle, 1979—; guest artist Godunov and Stars, Detroit, 1985, Kozlovs and Stars, San Francisco, 1986. Mem. Am. Guild Musical Artists. Office: Pacific NW Ballet 4649 Sunnyside Ave N Seattle WA 98103

HADLEY, KAREN MARIE, landscape contractor, musician, songwriter; b. Pasadena, Calif., May 1, 1945; d. Donald Russel and Virginia Frances (Jones) H.; student Los Angeles City Coll., 1967, Orange Coast Coll., 1973-84. Mail carrier U.S. Post Office, 1963-64; musician, singer, songwriter, 1964—; owner, operator Hadley Gallery, Newport Beach, Calif., 1968-72, Hadley Landscape Co., Costa Mesa, Calif., 1972-82. Mem. Am. Fedn. Musicians, Costa Mesa C. of C., Long Beach C. of C. Democrat. Office: PO Box 11082 Costa Mesa CA 92627

HADLEY, LEILA ELIOTT-BURTON, author; b. N.Y.C., Sept. 22, 1925; d. Frank Vincent and Beatrice Boswell (Eliott) Burton; m. Arthur T. Hadley, II, Mar. 2, 1944 (div. Aug. 1946); 1 child, Arthur T., III; m. Yvor H. Smitter, Jan. 24, 1953 (div. Oct. 1969); children—Victoria C. Van D. Smitter Barlow, Matthew Smitter Eliott, Caroline Allison F.S. Nicholson; m. William C. Musham, May 1976 (div. July 1979). Student, U. Witwatersrand, Johannesburg, S. Africa, 1954-55. Author: Give Me the World, 1958; How to Travel with Children in Europe, 1963; Manners for Children, 1967; Fielding's Guide to Traveling with Children in Europe, 1972, rev., 1974, 84; Traveling with Children in the U.S.A., 1974; Tibet-20 Years After the Chinese Takeover, 1979; (with Theodore B. Van Itallie) The Best Spas: Where to Go for Weight Loss, Fitness Programs and Pure Pleasure in the U.S. and Around the World, 1988; Assoc. editor: Diplomat mag., N.Y.C., 1964-65, Saturday Evening Post, N.Y.C., 1965-67; editorial cons. TWYCH, N.Y.C., 1985-87; book reviewer Palm Beach Life, Fla., 1967-72. Contbr. articles to various newspapers, mags. Mem. Soc. Woman Geographers (exec. council 1984—), Authors Guild, Nat. Writers Union, Nat. Press Club. Republican. Presbyterian. Home: 300 E 75th St New York NY 10021 Office: care Peter Matson Literistic 264 Fifth Ave New York NY 10001

HADLOCK, DEBORAH JOYCE, veterinarian; b. Portland, Maine, Sept. 23, 1951; d. Edson Barry and Barbara (Whalen) H.; m. John Nevil Hawkins, June 18, 1977 (div. Jan. 1984). Student Purdue U., West Lafayette, Ind., 1969-71; B.S., U. Ill.-Champaign, 1974; V.M.D., U. Pa.-Phila., 1980. Intern in small animal medicine and surgery The Animal Med. Ctr., N.Y.C., 1980-81; assoc. veterinarian Gramercy Park Animal Clinic, N.Y.C., 1981-85; veterinarian cardiology cons. Cardiopet-Animed Roslyn, 1983—. Mem. The New Alliance Party, N.Y.C., 1983—. Mem. N.Y.C. Veterinary Med. Assn., N.Y. State Veterinary Med. Assn., AVMA, Acad. Veterinary Cardiology, U.S. Cycling Fedn. Club: Century Rd. (N.Y.C.). Home: 330 W 56th St Apt 20H New York NY 10019 Office: Cardiopet 25 Lumber Rd Roslyn NY 62105

HADLOCK, JUDITH PASAHOW, fashion marketing consultant, home furnishings consultant; b. Waterloo, Iowa, Nov. 17, 1944; d. Bernard David and Kathryn Elizabeth (Gaffney) Pasahow; m. John Matthew Hadlock, Aug. 31, 1969; 1 dau., Meghan Elizabeth. BS, U. Wis., 1966; MA, New Sch. Social Research, 1973. Copywriter, Sears Roebuck and Co., Chgo., 1966-68, copy chief, N.Y.C., 1968-72, apparel buyer, fashion dir., 1972-79; cons. Federated Dept. Stores, N.Y.C., 1979-80, Humphrey, Browning, Macdougall, N.Y.C., 1980—, Trustee Rogers Meml. Library, Southampton, N.Y. Mem. Fashion Group Found., New Eng. Appraisers Assn., Fashion Group N.Y. Democrat. Presbyterian. Clubs: Southampton Bath and Tennis (N.Y.); Shinecock Golf. Home: 1136 Fifth Ave New York NY 10128 also: 82 Main St Southampton NY 11968 also: 39 Toylsome Southampton NY 11968

HAEFLINGER, SHARON KAY, writer; b. Dickinson, N.D., June 13, 1949; d. Paul and Perpetua Jean (Wandler) Jahner; m. Charles Stephen Haeflinger, Dec. 14, 1974. BA in Social Work, U. N.D., 1971; MS in Counseling and Guidance, Cen. Mo. State U., 1975. Cert. tchr., Ill., guidance and counseling, Ill. Recreation specialist Am. Nat. Red Cross, Korea, 1971-72; social worker Am. Nat. Red Cross, Ft. Leonard Wood, Mo., 1972-74; tchr. St. Angela Sch., Chgo., 1976-79; project editor The Econ. Co. div. McGraw-Hill, Glendale, Calif., 1981-86; freelance writer Chino Hills, Calif., 1986—; vocat. exploration instr. Nat. Football League, Thousand Oaks, Calif., 1980; cons. Concept Spelling Inc., Newport Beach, Calif., 1981. Author: (book) Medical Care, 1985; contbr. articles to pubs. Urgent action writer Amnesty Internat., 1983—; religion tchr. St. Paul the Apostle Parish, Chino Hills, 1987. Mem. Soc. of Children's Book Writers, Ind. Writers of So. Calif., Nat. Assn. for Female Execs., So. Calif. Booksellers Assn., Am. Overseas Assn. Roman Catholic. Club: Married Couples (co-pres. 1987). Home: 15683 Tern St Chino Hills CA 91709

HAEGER, PHYLLIS MARIANNA, association management company executive; b. Chgo., May 20, 1928; d. Milton O. and Ethel M. H. B.A., Lawrence U., 1950; M.A., Northwestern U., 1952. Midwest editor TIDE mag., 1952-55; exec. v.p. Smith, Bucklin & Assos., Inc., Chgo., 1955-78; pres. P.M. Haeger & Assos., Inc., Chgo., 1978—. Mem. Am. Soc. Assn. Execs., Chgo. Soc. Assn. Execs., Inst. Assn. Mgmt. Cos., Nat. Assn. Women Bus. Owners, Com. of 200, Chgo. Network, Nat. Assn. Bank Women (exec. v.p.).

HAERER, CAROL, artist; b. Salina, Kans., Jan. 23, 1933; d. Alfred Vesper and Helen Margaret (Bozarth) H.; m. Philip W. Wofford, Nov. 1962; 1 child, Sara Gwyn Haerer-Wofford. Student, Doane Coll., 1950-51; B.F.A. cum laude, U. Nebr., 1954; student, Chgo. Art Inst., Summers 1952, 53; M.A., U. Calif., Berkeley, 1958. Dir., instr. Summer Painting Workshop, Bennington Coll., 1976-80; dir. Hand Hollow Artists' Found., 1984; lectr. NYU, 1964-69; instr. art Bennington (Vt.) Coll., 1973-86, U. Vt., Burlington, 1980; prof. art Fordham U., N.Y.C., 1986—. One-person shows include, Galerie Prismes, Paris, 1956, Berkeley Gallery, 1958, Albright Coll., Reading, Pa., 1964, Max Hutchinson Gallery, N.Y.C., 1971, 73, Bennington (Vt.) Coll., 1978, Landmark Gallery, N.Y.C., 1979, Oscarsson-Hood Gallery, N.Y.C., 1981, 83, Sherkat Gallery, N.Y.C., 1988; group shows include, Whitney Mus., N.Y.C., 1970-72, Syracuse (N.Y.) U. Mus., Bklyn. Mus., 1980-81; represented in numerous permanent pvt., mus. collections including, Guggenheim Mus., N.Y.C., Whitney Mus., N.Y.C., Bklyn. Mus., Oakland Art Mus. (Calif.), Sheldon Art Galleries, U. Nebr., Lincoln, Williams Coll. Mus. of Art, Williamstown, Mass. MacDowell Colony fellow, 1969, 79; Woolley fellow Paris, 1955; Fulbright scholar Paris, 1954; Yaddo resident, 1982; NEA grantee, 1985; Guggenheim fellow, 1988. also: 90 Bedford St New York NY 10014 Studio: Rd 2 Box 63B Hoosuck Falls NY 12090

HAESSLY, JACQUELINE, peace education specialist, writer, consultant, family life education specialist; b. Milw., Feb. 18, 1937; d. Jerome Francis and Janice (Ball) Haessly; m. Daniel G. Di Domizio, July 8, 1972; children: Michael, Ernest, Randolph, Francis, Kristyn. LPN, Sacred Heart Sch. Practical Nursing, Milw., 1958; student Alverno Coll., 1958-67; BS in Edn. U. Wis., 1971, MS in Edn., 1976. Staff nurse various local hosps., Milw., 1959-72; founder, dir. Milw. Peace Edn. Resource Ctr., 1974—; founder, pres. Peacemaking Assocs., Milw., 1983—, Creative Playtime, Milw., 1985—; cons., facilitator bus. and profl. orgns., 1974—; organizer prodn. Peace Child, Milw., 1985; cons. U. Wis., Milw., 1983—. Author: Peacemaking: Family Activities for Justice and Peace, 1980. Editor Peacemaking for Children mag., 1983—. Contbr. numerous articles to profl. publs. Bd. dirs. Milw. Mental Health Agy., 1975-78; coordinator food policy conf. The Peace Ctr., Milw., 1975-77; mem. peace studies task force Milw. Pub. Schs., 1983—; chmn. peace studies com. Parent Tchr. Council, Milw., 1983-86, 85-86. Mem. Fellowship of Reconciliation (mem. bd., chmn. com. 1984-85), Nat. Speakers Assn., Wis. Speakers Assn., Parenting for Peace and Justice (mem. bd. 1981-84), Wis. Writer's Council, Nat. Writer's Club, Nat. Profl. Speakers Assn., Wis. Profl. Speakers Assn. Roman Catholic. Avocations: swimming, hiking, biking, knitting, reading. Office: Peacemaking Assocs 2437 N Grant Blvd Milwaukee WI 53210

HAFEN, VICKI A., financial service company executive; b. St. George, Utah, July 22, 1951; d. M. Kent Hafen and Ellie (Cox) Simons; m. Turner, Apr. 7, 1970 (div. 1977). BS in Edn., U. Nev., 1971, MEd, 1975; postgrad., Nat. U., San Diego. Cert. fin. planner, tax preparer, life and disability agt., variable life agt.; registered investment advisor, real estate broker, securities prin. CETA supr., career counselor Roseville (Calif.) Union High Sch., 1974-77; asst. prin. Sweetwater High Sch., Chula Vista, Calif., 1977-80; pres. Hafen and Assocs., San Diego, 1980—; spl. project developer San Diego Regional Youth Employment Council, 1978-80; master trainer in career edn. State of Calif., 1979-80; profl. career cons. Mel Thompson and Assocs., 1981. Contbr. articles to profl. publs. Active Crime Victims Fund, San Diego County Adopt-a-Sch. program, San Diego Conv. and Visitors Bur. Mem. LWV, Calif. Assn. Sch. Adminstrs., Speakers Bur., Women's Council Realtors, San Diego C. of C., AAUW, Nat. Assn. Tax Cons. Office: Hafen and Assocs 1420 Kettner Blvd #511 San Diego CA 92101

HAFER, MARY STEWART, museum curator; b. Newburgh, N.Y., Sept. 7, 1924; d. Thomas A. and Mary L. (Warden) Stewart; m. Frederick L. Hafer, June 8, 1946; children—Thomas F., John S., Abigail Ann. B.A. in Chemistry, Swarthmore Coll., 1945; M.S.L.S., Simmons Coll., 1968. Research Chemist Bartol Found., Franklin Inst., Phila., 1945-46; spl. instr. Patrick A.F.B., Fla., 1960-62; docent Nat. Gallery of Art, Washington, 1963-66; docent orgnr. Bedford (Mass.) pub. library volunteers, 1971—; curator Job Lane house, Bedford, 1980—, Bedford Hist. Soc., 1975—; mem. Historic dist. commn., Bedford, 1979—. Active library and mus. fund raising projects, Bedford, Lincoln, Mass., Boston, 1969-78. Mem. ALA, New Eng. Archivists. Republican. Home: 137 North Rd Bedford MA 01730 Office: Bedford Hist Soc 15 The Great Rd Bedford MA 01730

HAFFNER, MARLENE ELISABETH, physician, health care administrator; b. Cumberland, Md., Mar. 22, 1941. Student Western Res. U., 1958-61; M.D., George Washington U., 1965. Intern, George Washington U. Hosp., Washington, 1965-66; fellow in dermatology Columbia-Presbyn. Med. Ctr., N.Y.C., 1966-67; resident in internal medicine St. Luke's Hosp., N.Y.C., 1967-69; fellow in hematology. Albert Einstein Coll. Medicine, Bronx, 1969-71, asst. clin. prof. medicine, 1971-73; vis. asst. attending Bronx Mcpl. Hosp. Ctr. (N.Y.), 1969-71; clin. assoc. in family, community and emergency medicine U. N.Mex. Sch. Medicine, Albuquerque, 1974-83, clin. assoc. dept. medicine, 1974-83; acting clin. dir. Gallup Indian Med. Ctr. (N.Mex.), 1973-74, chief adult outpatient dept., 1971-74, chief dept. internal medicine, 1971-74; dir. Navajo Area Indian Health Service, Indian Health Service, Window Rock, Ariz., 1974-81; assoc. dir. for health affairs Bur. Med. Devices, FDA, Rockville, 1981-82, dir. Office Health Affairs, Ctr. for Devices and Radiol. Health, 1982-87; dir. office of orphan products devel. FDA, 1987—; asst. clin. prof. dept. medicine Uniformed Services Univ. of Health Scis., Bethesda, Md.; med. dir. USPHS. Home: 11616 Danville Dr Rockville MD 20852 Office: Orphan Products Devel FDA 5600 Fishers Lane (HF-35) Rockville MD 20852

HAFFORD, PATRICIA ANN, electronic company executive; b. Springfield, Mass., Feb. 11, 1947; d. Arthur Charles and Sophie Louise (Piesyk) Rood; m. Jerry William Hafford, May 1, 1971; children: Mark Dutton, Lauren Melynn. BA in Liberal Arts and Scis., U. Conn., 1968. Elem. tchr. East Granby (Conn.) Schs., 1968-69; presch. tchr. RCA-Discovery Ctr., East Hartford, Conn., 1969-70; tng. specialist Travelers Ins. Co., Hartford, 1970-73; scriptwriter ednl. TV Ednl. Satellite Tech. Demonstration Fedn. of Rocky Mt. States, Ft. Collins, Colo., 1973; with computer documentation dept. Hewlett-Packard Corp., Ft. Collins, Colo., 1973-77, tech. writer, documentation mgr., 1977-82, engr. market devel., 1982-83, product mgr., 1983—. Editor: Writing and Designing Operator Manuals. Mem. Soc. for Tech. Communication (v.p. Rocky Mountain chpt. 1979-81, chmn. Art and Writing Competition 1980-81, dir.-sponsor and bd. dirs. Region 8 Washington 1981-84). Republican. Methodist. Office: Hewlett-Packard 3404 E Harmony Rd Fort Collins CO 80525

HAFNER, CATHERINE COURTNEY, physics educator; b. N.Y.C., Nov. 14, 1946; d. Patrick Brendon and Mary Teresa (Feeley) Courtney; m. Carl John Hafner, June 15, 1968; children: Lisa Ann, Steven David. BS, Fordham U., 1968; MA in Sci. Edn., Columbia U., 1969. Cert. secondary tchr., N.Y., N.J. Physics, math. tchr. Mother Cabrini High Sch., N.Y.C., 1969-70; sci. tchr. Cardinal Spellman High Sch., Bronx, N.Y., 1970-71; physics and earth sci. tchr. Monroe-Woodbury Sr. High Sch., Central Valley, N.Y., 1984—. Leader Sarah Wells Council Girl Scouts USA, Middletown, N.Y., 1981-84, service team chmn., 1982-84. Research grantee NSF, SUNY at Stony Brook, 1985-88. Mem. Am. Assn. Physics Tchrs., N.Y. State Sci. Tchrs., N.Y. State United Tchrs.,Earth Sci Tchrs. Assn. Democrat. Home: 27 Half Hollow Turn Monroe NY 10950 Office: Monroe-Woodbury Sr High Sch Old Dunderberg Rd Central Valley NY 10917

HAFT, MARILYN GEISLER, lawyer; b. N.Y.C, Aug. 1, 1943; d. Frank and Sarah (Engelsohn) Geisler; m. Kenneth W. Bowser; 1 child, Samantha Danielle. BA, Bklyn. Coll., 1965; JD, NYU, 1968. Bar: N.Y. 1969, U.S. Supreme Ct. 1973, D.C. 1978. Staff counsel Nat. ACLU, N.Y.C., 1970-76; dep. counsel govt. ops. com. U.S. Congress, Washington, 1976-77; assoc. dir. office of pub. liaison The White House, Washington, 1977-78, dep. counsel V.P. Walter Mondale, 1978-79; N.Y. Primary campaign dir. Re-election for Carter/Mondale, N.Y.C., 1979-80; U.S. rep. Mission to the U.N., N.Y.C., 1980-81; sole practice entertainment law N.Y.C., 1981—; film producer Barking Dogs Prodns., N.Y.C., 1987—. Author: Time Without Work, 1984; author, editor: Prisoner's Rights Sourcebook, 1972, Rights of Gay People, 1973; producer (film) In a Shallow Grave, 1988. Democrat. Jewish. Home: 111 E 10th St New York NY 10003 Office: 865 W End Ave 14D New York NY 10025

HAGAN, ANN ARTHUR, physiologist; b. Oak Park, Ill., Mar. 22, 1948; d. Arthur L. and Ruth Marie (Stillwell) Pelz; 1 child, Philip. BS in Biology, U. Ill., 1970, MS in Biology, 1972, PhD in Physiology, 1976. Cert. biology tchr. Vis. prof. in physiology U. Ill., Urbana, 1975; asst. prof. biology George Williams Coll., Downers Grove, Ill., 1976-78, George Mason U., Fairfax, Va., 1978-79; staff fellow NIMH, Bethesda, Md., 1979-81; asst. prof. biology Am. U., Washington, 1981-87; guest researcher Nat. Inst. Neurol. and Communicative Disorders and Stroke, NIH, Bethesda, Md., 1984-87; exec. sec. div. extramural activities Nat. Cancer Inst., NIH, Bethesda, Md., 1987—; asst. dir. academics Nat. Ctr. Health/Fitness Mgmt., Am. U., Washington, 1986-87; cons. physiology Benjamin Cummings Publs., Menlo Park, Calif., 1985-86, Glenco Publ., Peoria, Ill., 1986. Mem. choir St. James Episc. Ch., Leesburg, Va., 1978—; judge Fairfax County Regional Sci. Fair, 1978-87. Mem. AAAS, Am. Soc. Zoologists, Sigma Xi. Home: 4001 Peppertree Ln Silver Spring MD 20906 Office: Grants Rev Br Div Extramural Activities Nat Cancer Inst Bethesda MD 20892

HAGAN, DARLENE DOLORES, accountant; b. Tucson, Ariz., Dec. 9, 1955; m. Joe L. Senter, Nov. 22, 1986; 1 child, Aaron. AA, Scottsdale Community Coll., 1975; BS in Acctg., Ariz. State U., 1977, MA in Acctg., 1985. CPA, Ariz. Acct. Miller Wagner & Co., Phoenix, 1977-81; controller Park Homes Co., Scottsdale, Ariz., 1982-84; owner Darlene D. Hagan CPA, Scottsdale, 1984-85; acct., shareholder Hunter Hagan & Co. Ltd., Scottsdale, 1985—. Pres., bd. dirs. YWCA of Maricopa County, Phoenix, 1979-85. Mem. Am. Inst. CPAs, Am. Women's Soc. CPAs, Ariz. Soc. CPAs, Estate Tax Study Group, Current Tax Discussion Group. Office: 6991 E Camelback #D-280 Scottsdale AZ 85251

HAGBERG, VIOLA WILGUS, lawyer; b. Salisbury, Md., July 3, 1952; d. William E. and Jean Shelton (Barlow) Wilgus; m. Chris Eric Hagberg, Feb. 19, 1978. BA, Furman U., Greenville, S.C., 1974; JD, U. S.C., 1978, U. Tulsa, 1978; DOD Army Logistics Sch. honor grad. basic mgmt. def. acquisition, def. small purchase, advanced fed. acquisition regulation, Fort Lee, Va., 1981-82. Bar: Okla. 1978, Va. 1979, U.S. Ct. Appeals (4th cir.). With Lawyers Com. for Civil Rights, Washington, 1979; pub. utility specialist Fed. Energy Regulatory Commn., Washington, 1979-80; contract specialist U.S. Army, C.E., Ft. Shafter, Hawaii, 1980-81; contract officer/supervisory contract specialist Tripler Army Med. Ctr., Hawaii 1981-83; supervisory procurement analyst and chief policy sect. Procurement Div. USCG, Washington, 1983; contract officer and chief Avionics Enging Branch sect. engring., 1984; procurement analyst office of sec. Dept. Transp., 1984-85; contracting officer Naval Regional Contracting Ctr., Long Beach, Calif., 1985—. Mem. Nat. Contract Mgmt. Assn., ABA (law student div. liaison 1977-78), Va. State Bar Assn., Okla. Bar Assn., Phi Alpha Delta, Kappa Delta Epsilon. Home: 9810 Meadow Valley Dr Vienna VA 22180 Office: USN NRCC Bldg 53 Long Beach CA 90822-5095

HAGE, ROSEMARY, computer systems analyst, soprano, actress, producer, director; b. Cortland, N.Y., d. Nahra Abdo and Jeannette (Chakra) Cortland. B.A., SUNY-Geneseo, cert. secondary edn. in English and drama. Computer systems adminstr., analyst, operator, corp. legal dept. ABC, Inc., N.Y.C., 1981-85; freelance computer systems adminstr., analyst, operator, N.Y.C., 1985-86; computer systems adminstr., analyst, operator Law Sch., Columbia U., N.Y.C., 1986—; teacher and performer Middle Eastern dance, Washington and San Francisco. Performed with various opera cos. and other orgns., including Bel Canto Opera, N.Y. Opera Theatre, N.Y.C., N.Y. Gilbert and Sullivan Players, N.Y.C., Opera Theatre of Berkeley, Calif., The New Shakespeare Co. of San Francisco; appeared in various operas, operettas, and regional dinner theatre, theatre and summer stock prodns.; concert soloist; producer, dir. Gaslight Opera, Inc., (operas) Don Giovanni, 1981, The Old Maid and the Thief, 1985, (concerts) An Evening of Amadeus, A Day in New York, a Night in Vienna, Offenbach's Birthday, An Evening of Gilbert & Sullivan, (summer stock) A Musical Revue, 1973, (concert series) Montauk Club's Operetta Concert Series, Bklyn., 1982-85, Operetta Concert Series, touring N.Y.C., 1982-86, program coordinator opera dept. Bklyn. Conservatory Music. Mem. Nat. Assn. Female Execs. Democrat. Roman Catholic. Home: 402 Bayridge Pkwy Apt 64 Brooklyn NY 11209 Office: Columbia U Law Sch Law Placement Office New York NY 10027

HAGEN, MARIE LOUISE, lawyer; b. Plainfield, N.J., Oct. 23, 1956; d. Richard A. and Mary Louise (Moore) H. AB, Cornell U., 1978, JD, 1981; student Oxford U. (Eng.), 1979. Bar: N.Y. 1981, Mass. 1982, U.S. Dist. Ct. (so. dist.) N.Y. 1982, U.S. Dist. Ct. (ea. dist.) N.Y. 1982, D.C. 1988. Assoc., Dickerson, Reilly & Mullen, N.Y.C., 1981-82; trial atty. U.S. Dept. of Justice, N.Y.C., 1982-87, asst. atty in charge, 1985-87, assoc. atty. Dyer, Ellis, Joseph & Mills, Washington, D.C., 1987—; judge Philip C. Jessup Internat. Law Moot Ct. Competition. Mem. Maritime Law Assn., ABA, Am. Soc. Internat. Law. Democrat. Roman Catholic. Office: Dyer Ellis Joseph & Mills 600 New Hampshire Ave NW Suite 1000 Washington DC 20037

HAGEN, TRACY LEE, hotel executive; b. Wadsworth, Ohio, Sept. 6, 1962; d. Ralph Arthur and Ruth Marie (Wilson) H.; 1 child, Tyler Allen Powell. Student in sales and mktg., U. Akron, 1982; student in real estate, Pa. State U., 1986. From front desk clk. to mgr. Red Roof Inn, Hillard, Ohio, 1982-85; gen. mgr. Luxury Budget, Clarks Summit, Pa., 1985; dir. sales Ramada Inn, York, Pa., 1985-86; sales mgr. Holiday Inn, York, 1986-88; mems. service Metlife Health Care Network, Beechwood, Ohio, 1988, mktg. liasion, 1988—. Home: 720 Hancock Apt A-1 Akron OH 44314 Office: Metlife Health Care Network 4 Commerce Sq 23200 Chagrin Blvd Beechwood OH 44122

HAGEN, UTA THYRA, actress; b. Göttingen, Fed. Republic of Germany, June 12, 1919; came to U.S., 1926; d. Oskar F. L. and Thyra A. (Leisner) H.; m. Herbert Berghof, Jan. 25, 1957; 1 child, Leticia. DFA (hon.), Smith Coll., 1978; LHD (hon.), De Paul U., 1981, Wooster Coll., 1982. Tchr. acting Herbert Berghof Studio, N.Y.C., 1947—. Played: Ophelia, Dennis, Mass., 1937, Nina in Sea Gull, N.Y.C., 1938, Key Largo, 1939, Vicki, 1942, Othello, 1943-45; appeared in: plays Masterbuilder, 1947, Angel Street, 1948, Street Car Named Desire, 1948, 50, Country Girl, 1950, G.B. Shaw's Saint Joan, 1951-52, Tovarich, City Center, 1952, In Any Language, 1952, The Deep Blue Sea, 1953, The Magic and the Loss, 1954, The Island of Goats, 1955, A Month in the Country, 1956, Good Woman of Setzuan, 1957, Who's Afraid of Virginia Woolf, 1962-64, The Cherry Orchard, 1968, Charlotte, 1980;also univ. tour 1981-82, Mrs. Warren's Profession, Roundabout Theatre, N.Y.C., 1985—, You Never Can Tell, Circle in the Square, 1986—; appeared in films The Other, 1972, The Boys from Brazil, 1978; TV appearances include A Month in the Country, 1956, Out of Dust, 1959; appeared in numerous TV spls.; numerous guest star appearances including Lou Grant, 1982, A Doctor's Story, 1984; author: Respect for Acting, 1973, Love for Cooking, 1976, Sources, a Memoire, 1983. Recipient Antoinette Perry award, 1951, 63; N.Y. Drama Critics award, 1951, 63; Donaldson award best actress, 1951; London Critics award for best actress, 1963-64 season; Outer Circle award; named to Theatre Hall of Fame, 1981; Mayor's Liberty Medal, 1986. Address: Herbert Berghof Studio 120 Bank St New York NY 10014

HAGER, DORIS GEORGETTE, interior designer; b. Sudbury, Ont., Can., May 21, 1957; arrived in West Germany, 1960; came to U.S., 1969; arrived in Can., 1980; d. Georg Hager and Elfriede (Hertle) McLean. BS in Home Econ., U. Ga., 1980. Registered interior designer, Ont. Interior designer Woodhurst and O'Brien Architects, Augusta, Ga., 1980, Murray Architects, Augusta, 1980; sr. interior designer Wood Wilkings Ltd., Toronto, 1980-1984, John Stevenson Interiors, Toronto, 1984; pres. Hager and Assocs. Inc., Toronto, 1984—. Mem. Assn. Registered Interior Designers Ont., Canadian Assn. Photographers and Illustrators in Communication, Am. Soc. Interior Designers. Office: Hager and Assocs Inc, 160 Eglinton Ave E Suite 400, Toronto, ON Canada M4P 1A6

HAGER, ELIZABETH SEARS, state legislator; b. Washington, Oct. 31, 1944; d. Hess Thatcher and Elizabeth Grace (Harper) Sears; m. Dennis Sterling Hager, Sept. 3, 1966; children: Annie Elizabeth, Lucie Caroline. BA, Wellesley Coll., 1966; MPA, U. N.H., 1978. Prin. Philbrook Ctr., Concord, N.H., 1970-71; rep. N.H. Gen. Ct., Concord, 1973-76, 85—; del. N.H. Constitutional Conv., Concord, 1974, 84; campaign coordinator Anderson for Pres. Rep. Primary, N.H., 1980-81; councilor Concord City Council, 1982-88, mayor, 1988—; bd. dirs. Chubb Investment Funds, Concord, 1987—. Commr. N.H. Commn. on the Status of Women; pres. Greater Concord United Way, 1980-81; campaign chair United Way of Merrimack County, Concord, 1986. Republican. Episcopalian. Home: 5 Auburn St Concord NH 03301 Office: Two Eagle Square Concord NH 03301

HAGER, KATHY ELAINE, financial analyst; b. Haskell, Tex., Sept. 17, 1951; d. Walter Richard Jr. and Joyce A. (Grand) H. BBA, Tex. Tech. U., 1972; postgrad., West Tex. State U., 1981-82, Amarillo Coll., 1982. Staff acct. Edwin E. Merriman & Co. CPAs, Lubbock, Tex., 1973-77; asst. controller F-S-W Cattle Co., Wildorado, Tex., 1977-79; with Santa Fe Energy Co., 1980-87; sr. fin. analyst Santa Fe Energy Co., Houston, 1987—. Mem. Nat. Assn. Accts. (pres. Amarillo chpt. 1984-85, pres.-elect Tex. council 1988—, nat. bd. dirs. 1987—). Republican. Methodist. Office: Santa Fe Energy Co 1616 S Voss Suite 1000 Houston TX 77057

HAGERTY, POLLY MARTIEL, banker; b. Joliet, Ill., Aug. 17, 1946; d. George Albert and Gene Alice (Roush) Jerabek; m. Theodore John Hagerty, Feb. 12, 1972. BS in Elem. Edn., Midland Luth. Coll., 1968; MEd in Early Childhood Edn., U. Ill., 1977; MBA in Fin., U. Tex., 1986. Elem. tchr. Madison Heights (Mich.) Sch. Dist., 1968-70, Taft Sch. Dist., Lockport, Ill., 1970-72; systems clerk U.S. Army, The Pentagon, Washington, 1972-74; psychology aide U. Ill. Psychology Clinic, Urbana, 1974-75; elem. tchr. Champaign (Ill.) Sch. Dist., 1975-77; with recruitment Standard Oil of Ohio, Cleve., 1977-78; v.p. First RepublicBank Houston, 1981—. Pres. Christus Victor Luth. Ch., League City, Tex., 1986—. Mem. Nat. Assn. Female Execs., Houston Mortgage Bankers Assn., U. Ill. Alumni Club Houston, Longhorn Assn. Republican. Lutheran. Home: 2310 Hampton Rd League City TX 77573 Office: First RepublicBank Houston 700 Louisiana Houston TX 77002

HAGGARTY, MAUREEN LUCILLE, personnel director; b. Chgo., Oct. 3, 1951; d. Joseph Conrad and Carol Mary (Osborne) H.; m. Michael David Zeiler, May 28, 1978 (div. Nov. 1982). BA in Philosophy, U. Wis., 1973; MBA in Indsl. Relations, U. Minn., 1977. Personnel specialist Cenex, St. Paul, 1978; mgr. plant personnel ITT Continental Baking Co., Mpls., 1978-79; dir., cons. Employee Relations Assn. Inc., Mpls., 1979-81; asst. dir. personnel Yoplait USA, Mpls., 1981-83; dir. personnel GMAC Mortgage Corp., Waterloo, Iowa, 1983-86; v.p. personnel GMAC Mortgage Corp., Phila., 1986—; speaker Mortgage Bankers Assn., Washington, 1987. Tchr., cons. Jr. Achievement, Phila., 1986-87. Mem. Am. Soc. Personnel Adminstrs., Am. Soc. Tng. and Devel. (speaker 1987), Am. Mgmt. Soc., World Future Soc. Roman Catholic. Office: GMAC Mortgage Corp 8360 Old York Rd Elkins Park PA 19117

HAGGERT, SONJA MULLER, filter manufacturing company official; b. Wallenfels, Bavaria, Fed. Republic Germany, May 5, 1953; came to U.S., 1959; d. Christian and Elisabeth (Woletz) Muller; m. Brian Edward Haggert, Oct. 15, 1953. BS in Commerce and Fin., Villanova U., 1975. Asst. buyer Strawbridge and Clothier, Phila., 1975-76, dept. mgr., 1976-78; with Westinghouse Corp., Bala Cynwyd, Pa., 1978; mgr. consumer products Keystone Filter div. Met Pro Corp., Hatfield, Pa., 1978-87, distbr., sales mgr, 1987—. Author: Wholesaling vs. Direct Selling, 1982, Trade Shows, 1985, Industrial Distribution, 1985. Mem. Nat. Assn. Female Execs., Bus. and Profl. Women Ambler (2nd v.p. 1987-88). Roman Catholic. Office: Keystone Filter Div Met Pro Corp 2385 N Penn Rd Box 380 Hatfield PA 19440

HAGGERTY, DONNA MARIE, educational consultant; b. Allentown, Pa., Aug. 30, 1953; d. Stanley Theodore and Emma Anna (Hendricks) Sosnowski; m. Terrence Bernard Haggerty, Mar. 3, 1979. B.S., West Chester U., 1975; M.Ed., Temple U., 1980. Cert. tchr. secondary edn. English, journalism. Teaching asst., curriculum planner West Chester U. (Pa.), 1973-75; sec., computer operator William Taylor Co., Allentown, 1975-76; tchr. English, Salisbury High Sch., Allentown, 1975-78; writer, edr.coordinator Morning Call Newspaper, Allentown, Pa. 1978-80, dir. edn. services, writer, 1980-85, pub. relations dir. Morning Call Newspapers, 1985-87, ednl. cons., 1977-78, 87—; exec. dir. School Works, 1987—; grad. level tchr. intermediate units, Allentown and Nazareth, Pa., 1979-85. Bd. dirs. Lehigh Valley Child Care Assn., Allentown, Pa., 1983—; Bd. dirs Allentown Literacy Council; Author weekly edn. column, 1979—, Make It Relevant, 1986—; author, editor teaching materials; editor: Headlines, Hometowns & History teaching guide, 1980. Mem. Pa. Newspaper Pubs. Assn. (chair 1981-86), Nat. Fedn. Press Women (youth dir. 1983), Nat. Council Tchrs. of English, Phi Delta Kappa. Democrat. Roman Catholic. Office: Allentown C of C 5th and Walnut Sts Allentown PA 18105

HAGLAND, CAROLYN KNIGHT, nurse; b. Camden, S.C., Aug. 10, 1946; d. Walter Lewis Sr. and Hattie Bell (Fletcher) Knight; m. Bryce Harold Smith, Jan. 29, 1970 (div. 1981); children: Ronald Bryce, Anna Cherie; m. Paul Irving Hagland, Dec. 19, 1985. BS in Nursing, U. S.C., 1969, MA in Nursing, 1976, postgrad., 1981. RN. Nurse Columbia (S.C.) Hosp., 1969, S.C. Bapt. Hosp., Columbia, 1970; sch. health nurse Sembach AFB Elem. and Jr. High Schs., Fed. Republic Germany, 1972-73, Kaiserslautern Am. High Sch., Fed. Republic Germany, 1973-74; clin. nurse specialist multiphasic screening Dept. Health and Environ. Control State of S.C., Columbia, 1976-78, clin. nurse specialist crippled children's program, 1978-79; relief nurse Med. Personnel Pool, Columbia, 1979-80; program nurse specialist S.C. Dept. Mental Health, Columbia, 1980-82; psychiat. nurse U.S. Dept. Army, Frankfurt, Fed. Republic Germany, 1982; sch. health nurse Sportfield Elem. Sch. U.S. Dept. Def. Dependent Schs., Hanau, Fed. Republic Germany, 1982—; Sch. rep. Family Advocacy Mgmt. Team, 1982—. Served to capt. U.S. Army, 1970-72. Mem. NEA, Overseas Edn. Assn., Sigma Theta Tau. Office: Sportfield Elem Sch APO New York NY 09165

HAGLER, MARY ANNE TYLER, physician; b. Nashville, Jan. 30, 1927; d. John Luck and Edythe (Belton) Tyler; BS, U. Ga., 1947, postgrad. Sch. Medicine, 1947-48; MD, Med. Coll. Ga., 1975; m. John Carroll Hagler, III, Oct. 16, 1948; children: Mary Anne, John Carroll IV, Richard B., Katharine W., Elizabeth T. Family practice resident Med. Coll. Ga., Augusta, 1975-78; med. dir. St. Joseph Hosp. Home Health Care and Hospice, Augusta, 1978-81; practice medicine specializing in family practice, Augusta; med. staffs St. Joseph Hosp., Univ. Hosp., Doctors Hosp. of Augusta, Humana Hosp.-Augusta. Diplomate Am. Bd. Family Practice. Fellow Am. Acad. Family Physicians; mem. AMA, Med. Assn. Ga., Richmond County Med. Soc., Ga. Acad. Family Physicians, Am. Geriatrics Soc., Historic Augusta, Inc., Ga. Trust for Hist. Preservation, Jr. League of Augusta, Nat. Soc. Colonial Dames Am. in State of Ga. Roman Catholic. Clubs: Augusta Country, Pinnacle. Home: 999 Highland Ave Augusta GA 30904 Office: 1417 Pendelton Rd Augusta GA 30904

HAGNER, JUTTA NAHRGANG, association executive; b. Niederklein, Germany, Sept. 18, 1947; d. Werner Nahrgang and Hildegard (Kaczmarek) Kereluck. B.A., U. Md., 1972, M.A., 1978, postgrad. Fielding Inst. Intern, Zero Population Growth Inc., Washington, 1972-73, VA, Washington, 1973-74; instr. family and community devel. and health edn. U. Md., College Park, 1974-78; health edn. specialist Prince George County Health Dept., Cheverly, Md., 1978-79, Balt. City Health Dept., 1978-79; sr. program specialist Am. Assn. Ret. Persons, Washington, 1979-81; adminstrv. assoc. for profl. affairs Am. Psychol. Assn., Washington, 1981-84; cons. systems analyst Planning Research Corp., U.S. EPA, Gen. Services Adminstrn., bd. dirs. IRM Council Internat. Exchange of Scholars; pvt. practice occupational psychology, College Park; pres. Health Promotion Assocs., College Park, 1974—. Author: (with B. Rogosvsky) Feeling Great: A Book of Healthy Mind and Body, 1979; contbr. articles to profl. jours. Recipient Spl. Achievement award U.S. VA. Mem. Am. Soc. Assn. Execs., Assn. Tng. and Devel. Dirs., Soc. for Psychol. Study of Social Issues, Assn. Polit. Psychology, World Fedn. for Mental Health, Capitol Area Assn. Health Educators. Home: 7512 Sweetbriar Dr College Park MD 20740

HAHN, BESSIE KING, library administrator, lecturer; b. Shanghai, People's Republic of China, May 14, 1939; came to U.S., 1959; d. Jen Fong and Wei (Lok) King; m. Roger Carl Hahn, 1962 (div. 1983); children—Angela Yee-mei, Michael King-yau, Belinda Shee-wei. B.A., Mt. Marty Coll., Yankton, S.D., 1961; M.S.L.S., Syracuse U., 1972. Librarian Carrier Corp., Syracuse, N.Y., 1972; life sci. bibliographer Syracuse U. Libraries, 1973-75, head sci. and tech., 1975-78; asst. dir. reader services Johns Hopkins U. Library, Balt., 1978-81; dir. libraries Brandeis U., Waltham, Mass., 1981—; cons. Shanghai Jiao Tong U. Library, Shanghai, 1983—, hon. prof., 1984. Editor Jour. Ednl. Media and Library Scis., 1983—; contbr. articles to profl. jours. Recipient Golden Cup award Johns Hopkins U. Class of 1980, 1980; hon. benefactor Brandeis U. Nat. Women's Com., 1986. Mem. ALA, Chinese-Am. Librarians Assn. (pres. 1982-83). Home: 148 Sudbury Rd Weston MA 02193 Office: Brandeis U Library Waltham MA 02254

HAHN, CYNTHIA LEIGH, client support specialist; b. Harrisburg, Pa., Mar. 2, 1950; d. Arthur John Jr. and Fern Elizabeth (Exner) Hack; m. Gary S. Hahn, Apr. 24, 1988. Student, U. East Anglia, Norwich, Eng., 1970-71; BA in Liberal Arts, Hollins Coll., 1972. Programmer/analyst Spectra-Physics, San Jose, Calif., 1980-83; customer support mgr. Multidata Corp., San Jose, 1983-85; installation/tng. mgr. Gill Mgmt. Services, San Jose, 1985; dir. client support Edn. Systems Corp., San Diego, 1985—. Mem. Am. Soc. Tng. and Devel. Office: Edn Systems Corp 6170 Cornerstone Ct E San Diego CA 92121

HAHN, HELENE HIRSH, graphics company owner; b. Balt., May 22, 1946; d. Allan T. and Eleanor (Rosenthal) Hirsh, Jr.; m. Joseph Edward Hahn, Aug. 4, 1968; children—Andrew Charles, David Stuart. B.S. in Early Childhood Edn., U. Md., 1968; M.Ed., U. N.C., 1972. Tchr. Gaston County Schs., Gastonia, N.C., 1969-72; instr. Gaston Community Coll., Dallas, N.C., 1972-76; dept. head Ottenheimer Pubs., Inc., Balt., 1979-80; owner Hahn Graphics, Inc., Balt., 1981—; supr. internship Md. Inst. Art, Balt., 1983—, Loyola U., Balt., 1984—; facilitator color reprodn. Port City Press, Balt., 1985, Printing Industries of Md., 1987, 88. Author: Dictionary of Great Events in U.S. History, 1969, Learn About Animals, Birds, Flowers and Insects, 1973, Websters Vest Pocket Dictionary, 1977. Editor: Mischievous Kitten: Porky the Explorer, 1974. Chmn. Religious Sch., Temple Emanuel, Gastonia, 1975-79, pres. Sisterhood Hadassah, 1978-79, bd. dirs., 1975-78, sec., 1978-79; v.p. Gaston County Assn. Childhood Edn., Gastonia, 1969-73; mem. Children's 100 Inst. N.C., Durham, 1973-77, county survey chmn., 1973, mem. steering com., 1974-76; bd. dirs. Gaston County Headstart, Dallas, N.C., 1974-76, Jr. League Gaston County, Gastonia, 1976-79; v.p. Mid-Atlantic region Nat. Fedn. Temple Sisterhoods, 1977-83, pres., 1983-85, bd. dirs., 1983-89, exec. com. mem., 87-89; bd. dirs. Jr. League Balt., 1986-88, v.p., 88-89; bd. dirs. Women's Housing Coalition, 1985-87; mem. Hadassah, Balt., 1979—, Nat. Council Jewish Women, Balt., 1981—, Walters Art Gallery, Balt., 1982—, Jewish Hist. Soc. Md., Balt., 1982—; mem. Sisterhood bd. Balt. Hebrew Congregation, 1982-85; Assn. Jewish Charities-Womens div., Balt., 1985-88, Nat. Fedn. Temple Sisterhood, N.Y.C., 1985-89; mem. steering com. Md. Low Income Housing Coalition, Balt., 1985—. Mem. Printing Industries Md. (bd. dirs. 1988—), Advt. Assn. Balt., Nat. Assn. Female Execs. Democrat. Jewish. Avocations: reading; travel; home decorating; tennis; bridge. Office: Hahn Graphics Inc 8422 Bellona Ln 101 Baltimore MD 21204

HAHN, JOAN CHRISTENSEN, drama educator, travel agent; b. Kemmerer, Wyo., May 9, 1933; d. Roy and Bernice (Pringle) Wainwright; m. Milton Angus Christensen, Dec. 29, 1952 (div. Oct. 1, 1971); children—Randall M., Carla J. Christensen Teasdale; m. Charles Henry Hahn, Nov. 15, 1972. B.S., Brigham Young U., 1965. Profl. ballroom dancer, 1951-59; travel dir. E.T. World Travel, Salt Lake City, 1969—; tchr. drama Payson High Sch., Utah, 1965-71, Cottonwood High Sch., Salt Lake City, 1971—; dir. Performing European Tours, Salt Lake City, 1969-76; dir. Broadway theater tours, 1976—. Dir. Salem City Salem Days, Utah, 1965-75; regional dir. dance Latter-day Saints Ch., 1954-72. Named Best Dir. High Sch. Musicals, Green Sheet Newspapers, 1977, 82, 84; recipient 1st place award Utah State Drama Tournament, 1974, 77, 78; Limelight award, 1982; Exemplary Performance in teaching theater arts Granite Sch. Dist., Salt Lake City, 1982. Mem. Internat. Thespian Soc. (sponsor 1968—, internat. dir. 1982-84, trustee 1978-84), Utah Speech Arts Assn. (pres. 1976-78), NEA, Utah Edn. Assn., Granite Edn. Assn., Profl. Travel Agts. Assn., Utah High Sch. Activities Assn. (drama rep. 1972-76), AAUW (pres. 1972-74). Republican. Mormon. Avocations: reading; travel; dancing. Home: 685 S 1st E Box 36 Salem UT 84653 Office: Cottonwood High Sch 5715 S 1300 E Salt Lake City UT 84121

HAHN, KAREN VIRGINIA, holding company executive; b. Detroit, Jan. 9, 1947; d. A. Kurt and Virginia (Claspill) H. m. R. Eugene Neal, Jr., May 29, 1965 (div. 1973); children—Patricia, David. A.S., Sacred Heart U., 1975; B.A., Sarah Lawrence Coll., 1979. Legal asst. chems. group Comml. Olin Corp., Stamford, Conn., 1980-82; asst. to pres. H.K. James Co., Westport, Conn., 1982; asst. sec. Moore & Munger, Inc. and subs., Shelton, Conn., 1983-85, dir. adminstrv. services, 1984—, sec. corp., 1985—. Mem. Choraliers (sec. 1982-83), Am. Soc. Corp Secs. Republican. Mem. United Ch. of Christ. Office: Moore & Munger Mktg and Refining Inc 230 Long Hill Cross Rd Shelton CT 06484

HAHN, LUCILLE DENISE, paper company executive; b. Stony Point, N.Y., Oct. 8, 1940; d. Raymond and Catherine (Nobert) Hoyt. Lab. asst. Champion Internat. (formerly St. Regis Paper Co.), West Nyack, N.Y., 1972-74, technician, 1974-77, tech. asst., 1977-79, research asst., 1979-82, technologist, 1982-84, sr. technologist, 1984-86, assoc. testing coordinator, 1986—. Mem. Nat. Assn. Female Execs., TAPPI (sec. process and product quality control div. 1987—). Office: Champion Internat West Nyack Rd West Nyack NY 10994

HAHN, SHARON LEE, city official; b. Kenosha, Wis., Sept. 22, 1939; d. Vincent B. and Mary Lee (Vaux) McCloskey; m. Robert W. Hahn, Jan. 1967 (div. June 1977); 1 child, John V. Calhoun. Student Kent State U., 1983. Cert. mcpl. clk., notary pub., Ohio. Sec., Simmons Bedding Co., Columbus, Ohio, 1960-61; exec. sec. Westinghouse, Columbus, 1962-68; legal sec. Bricker Law Firm, Columbus, 1969-70; asst. to prosecutor Whiteleather Law Firm, Columbia City, Ind., 1970-77; legal sec. Metz, Bailey & Spicer, Westerville, Ohio, 1977-80; clk. of council, sec. to city mgr. City of Westerville, 1981-87; clerk of council, records mgr. City of Westerville, 1981—. Mem. Ohio Mcpl. Clks. Assn. (bd. dirs. 1984-86), Internat. Inst. Mcpl. Clks. (CMC award 1984, records mgmt. com. 1986—). Presbyterian. Avocations: golf; organ; rug hooking; interior decorating. Home: 356 MacIntosh Way Westerville OH 43081 Office: City of Westerville 21 S State St Westerville OH 43081

HAI, CAROL SUE, interior designer; b. Ithaca, N.Y., Sept. 16, 1938; d. Norman Charles and Edna (Voronoff) Epstein; m. Richard B. Hai, June 18, 1961 (div. Apr. 1984); children: Jill Ilene, Paul Bradley. BS, Cornell U., 1960. Showroom asst. Jack Lenor Larsen, N.Y.C., 1960; sportswear sales mgr. Davison-Paxon Co., Columbus, Ga., 1962-63; owner, interior designer Carol Sue Hai Interiors, N.Y.C., Rochester, N.Y., 1964—. Trustee Soc. Preservation of Landmarks, Western N.Y., 1971-85, Temple B'rith Kodesh; dir. Opera Theatre Rochester. Recipient Helen Bull Vandervort Alumni Achievement award Cornell U., 1987. Mem. Interior Design Soc., Am. Soc. Interior Designers, Council Meml. Art Gallery U. Rochester. Home and Office: 172 Allens Creek Rd Rochester NY 14618

HAIKO, GERALDINE MAE, auto damage appraiser; b. Hartford, Conn., Nov. 5, 1940; d. Frank Joseph and May Lillian (Brandt) Haiko; m. Douglas Allen Gallant, May 27, 1961 (div. Mar. 1965); 1 child, Douglas Allen. A.A., Vt. Coll., 1960. Rating clk. Travelers Ins. Co., Hartford, 1961-65; teller, adminstrv. asst., Soc. for Savs., Wethersfield, 1965-69; teller, asst. head teller, customer service officer Coral Ridge Nat. Bank, Fort Lauderdale, Fla., 1970-74; with customer service dept. Bank Coral Springs, Fla., 1974-76; pres. Frank J. Haiko, Inc., Wethersfield, 1976—. Mem. Ind. Auto Damage Appraisers (sec. treas. NE region 1981—, nat. sec. 1985—), Wethersfield C. of C., U.S. C. of C., Greater Hartford C. of C. Republican. Avocations: cross country skiing; singing; dancing; spectator sports. Office: Frank J Haiko Inc 36 Silas Deane Hwy Wethersfield CT 06109

HAILEY, WANDA WALKER, interior designer; b. New Orleans, Aug. 5, 1953; d. Edgar Andrew and Lou (Moreau) Walker; m. Timothy Richard Hailey, Aug. 28, 1976. B of Interior Design, La. State U., 1976. Interior designer Valeton J. Dansereau, AIA, New Orleans, 1976-80, The Judy Girod Design Group doing bus. as The Girod-Hailey Design Group, New Orleans, 1980—; profl. liaison Delgado Coll., New Orleans, 1984—. Mem. Am. Soc. Interior Designers (sec. La. chpt. 1987, bd. dirs. 1981-86, chairperson New Orleans assn. 1983-84, sec. 1981-82, Presdl. citations 1982-87), Alpha Omega Pi Alumnae Assn. Democrat. Roman Catholic. Home: 3429 River Oaks Dr New Orleans LA 70131 Office: The Girod-Hailey Design Group 1943 Magazine St New Orleans LA 70130

HAILS, BARBARA GELDERMANN, artist; b. N.Y.C., Mar. 15, 1944; d. Edward Joseph and Helena Monica (McCann) Geldermann; m. Robert Louis Hails Sr., July 2, 1966; children: Robert Louis Jr., Charlotte Lynne. BA, Catholic U. Am., Washington, 1965. Instr. art Montgomery County Pub. Schs., Silver Springs, Md., 1965—; freelance artist Hails Studio, Gathersburg-Olney, Md., 1965—; speaker Montgomery Coll., Rockville 1987; exhibition juror Md. Fedn. Art, Annapolis 1987. Work exhibited in Capricorn Galleries, Bethesda, Md. 1982—, Cudahy's Gallery, Richmond, Va. 1981—, McBride Gallery, Annapolis, Md. 1985—; one-man show exhibited in Capricorn Galleries, 1984, 87; artist in residence City Rockville, Md. 1975; publ. Dimensional Aesthetics, Olney 1985; contbr. articles to profl. jours. Fundraiser Parks and History Assn., Great Falls, Md. 1987, Sandy Spring Mus., Olney 1984. Recipient grant Montgomery County Arts Council, Rockville 1986; named Outstanding Artist Yr. Nat. League Am. Penwomen, Chevy Chase, Md. 1983; invited exhibitor Société Des Patellistes de France, Lille 1987. Mem. Pastel Soc. Am., Md. Pastel Soc., Artists Equity Assn. Office: Dimensional Aesthetics 3902 Ashland Brooke Way Olney MD 20832

HAINSWORTH-STRAUS, CHRISTINE LOUISE, commercial real estate broker; b. Alton, Ill., Oct. 29, 1962; d. Joseph Richard and Nola Jo (Harwood) Hainsworth; m. Michael Wolcott Straus, Aug. 31, 1985. BBA, Principia Coll., 1983, BA in English Lit., 1983. Leasing agt. Murdoch & Coll., Inc., St. Louis, 1983-84, mktg. mgr., 1984-86; comml. real estate broker William D. Feldman Assocs., Culver City, Calif., 1986—. Editor Praxis, 1982, bus. mgr., 1983. Mem. Citizens for Light Rail Transit, St. Louis, 1984, 85; mem. telecommunications task force Los Angeles Cen. City Assn.; pres. Los Angeles Women's Exchange, 1987-88; bd. dirs. 1st Ch. of Christ Scientist South Pasadena. Mem. Nat. Assn. Female Execs., Los Angeles Women's Exchange (pres. 1987-88), Comml. Real Estate Women, Am. Indsl. Real Estate Assn., Friends of Huntington Library, Principia Alumni Assn., Los Angeles Jr. C. of C. Christian Scientist. Avocations: tennis, soccer, Japanese art and French Impressionist art. Home: 1272 E Loma Alta Altadena CA 91001 Office: William D Feldman Assocs 5995 S Sepulveda Blvd Culver City CA 90230

HAIR, MARCIA ELIZABETH, corporate art consultant; b. Miami, Fla., Oct. 16, 1948; d. James Ralph Hair and Marie Louise (Shonter) Yorra; m. Keith Terence Kelley, Jan 10, 1970 (div. Oct. 1975); children: Patrick Shonter, Benjamin James; m. Ronald Elias Hickman, Mar. 15, 1986. Student, U. Ga., 1966-70; BA, Ga. State U., 1981. Asst. dir. Apple Tree Sch., Atlanta, 1971-74; dir. Mini Sch., Atlanta, 1974-76, Kinder Care, Atlanta, 1976-77, A Learning Place, Decatur, Ga., 1977-78; with sales/design div. Frameworks Gallery, Marietta, Ga., 1978—, corp. cons., 1985—; art cons. Marietta City Schs., 1986—. Contbr. articles to profl. jours. Mem. Cobb Insiders, Marietta, 1986—. Recipient Community Achievement award Marietta City Schs., 1987. Mem. Nat. Assn. Female Execs., Profl. Picture Framers Assn. Democrat. Roman Catholic. Club: Atlanta Track. Home: 3350 Bryant Ln Marietta GA 30066 Office: Frameworks Gallery 26 Mill St Marietta GA 30060

HAIRALD, MARY PAYNE, education educator; b. Tupelo, Miss., Feb. 25, 1936; d. Will Burney and Ivey Lee (Berryhill) Payne; m. Leroy Utley Hairald, May 31, 1958; 1 child, Burney LeShawn. BS in Commerce, U. Miss., 1957, M in Bus. Edn., 1963; postgrad., Miss. Coll., 1964, Miss. State U., 1970. Bus. edn. tchr. John Rundle High Sch., Grenada, Miss., 1957-59; youth recreation leader City of Nettleton (Miss.), summers 1960-61; tchr. social studies Nettleton Jr. High Sch., 1959-70; tchr., coordinator coop. vocat. edn. program Nettleton High Sch., 1970—; area mgr. World Book, Inc., Chgo., 1972—; bus. instr. Itawamba Community Coll., Tupelo, 1975-80; sponsor Coop. Vocational Edn. Club, Nettleton, 1970—; advisor Distributive Edn. Clubs Am., Nettleton, 1985—. Contbr. articles on coop. edn. to newspapers. Co-organizer Nettleton Youth Recreation Booster Club; fundraiser Muscular Dystrophy Assn. Named Star Tchr., Miss. Econ. Council, 1978, Am. Vocat. Assn. Region IV Outstanding Coop. and Mktg. Educator of Yr., 1988. Mem. Am. Vocat. Assn. (Region IV coop. vocat. edn. educator of yr. 1985, mktg. and coop. edn. tchr. of the yr. 1988), Coop. Work Experience Edn. Assn., AAUW (charter), Miss. Assn. Vocat. Educators (dist. sec.), Miss. Assn. Coop. Vocat. Edn. Tchrs. (Miss. Tchr. of Yr. 1984, 87), Miss. Assn. Mktg. Educators. Democrat. Methodist. Home: PO Box 166 Nettleton MS 38858

HAIRSTON, BRENDA COLBY, insurance company executive; b. Biloxi, Miss., Aug. 23, 1947; d. Russell Sterling and V. Margaret (Allen) Colby; m. Robert E. Hairston, Jr., Sept. 4, 1971 (div. Apr. 1981). B.A., U. Fla., 1969. Adminstrv. asst. Mutual of Omaha, Miami, Fla., 1973-77; mktg. rep. Tab Products Co., Miami, 1977-80; 2d v.p. Mutual of Omaha, Miami, 1980-81, v.p., 1981—; 2d v.p. United of Omaha, Miami, 1980-81, v.p., 1981—; bd. dirs. Fla. Ins. Council, Tallahassee, 1981—; pres. Fla. Ins. News Service, Tallahassee, 1983-84, 1st v.p., 1984-86; dir. Fla. Life & Health Ins. Guaranty Assn., Jacksonville, 1983—. Bd. dirs. Jr. Achievement of Greater Miami, 1984—. Recipient Disting. Service award Fla. Ins. Council, 1986. Mem. YWCA Women's Network, LWV (bd. dirs. Dade County chpt. 1987—), Brickell Area Assn. (bd. dirs. 1981-83, treas. 1983-84, sec. 1984-85, v.p. 1985-86, pres. 1987). Republican. Office: Mut of Omaha Ins Co PO Box 010711 1201 Brickell Ave Suite 601 Miami FL 33101

HAITHMAN, DIANE ROLLINS, journalist; b. Detroit, Apr. 26, 1957; d. Charles Harrison and Charlotte Lois (Watts) H. BA, U. Mich., 1979. Entertainment writer Detroit Free Press, 1979-84; corr. West Coast Bur. Detroit Free Press, Los Angeles, 1984-87; TV writer Los Angeles Times, 1987—. Critic fellow Eugene O'Neil Theater Ctr., 1983. Office: Los Angeles Times 145 S Spring St Los Angeles CA 90012

HAJASH, VICKIE LYNN, career planning administrator; b. Cin., Sept. 7, 1962; d. Beverly Ann (Seurkamp) Desmarais; m. Paul Gregory Hajash. Grad. high sch., Largo, Fla. Office adminstr., acct. Albertsons Stores, Clearwater, Fla., 1982-83; bookkeeper, data processor Broward Window Shades, Inc., Clearwater, 1984; writer, mgr. Prowriter Services, Dunedin, Fla., 1984-85; office adminstr. Energy Scis., Inc., Miami, 1985-86; owner, cons., writer, advisor Career Mktg. Services, Dunedin, 1986—. Evangelist explosion adminstr. Country Side Chapel, 1987. Mem. Nat. Assn. Female Execs.

HAJNY, DESIREE ANN, artist; b. Hamburg, Iowa, Feb. 8, 1957; d. Eldon L. and Judy Kathleen (Shonka) Kline; m. Bernard E. Hajny; 1 child, Jeffrey Thomas. BA, Peru State Coll., 1979. Instr. high sch. art Rock County Edn., Bassett, Neb., 1979-85; artist free-lance, Columbus, Neb., 1985—. Exhibited in numerous art mags. and shows. Recipient of numerous awards. Mem. Affiliated Woodcarver's Ltd., Nat. Woodcarvers Assn., Guild Mastercraftsman.

HAKIMOGLU, GERALDINE ANN, electronics executive; b. Doylestown, Pa., May 16, 1950; d. Joseph James and Marion Gertrude (Haly) Crilley; m. Ayhan Hakimoglu, Nov. 19, 1982. BA in English, Pa. State U., 1972; postgrad., Temple U., 1978. Asst. to v.p. pub. affairs Children's TV Workshop, N.Y.C., 1972-76; asst. sec., dir. corp. communications Aydin Corp., Horsham, Pa., 1976—. Mem. Women's Bd. for Senator Arlen Specter, Phila., 1985—; bd. trustees Assembly Turkish Am. Orgns., 1987—. Office: Aydin Corp 700 Dresher Rd Box 349 Horsham PA 19044

HALBERSTAM, MALVINA, legal educator, lawyer; b. Kempno, Poland, May 2, 1937; came to U.S., 1947; d. Marcus and Pearl (Halberstam) H.; m. Wolf Z. Guggenheim, 1963; children: Arye, Achiezer. B.A. cum laude, Bklyn. Coll., 1957; J.D., Columbia U., 1961, M.I.A., 1964. Bar: N.Y. 1962, U.S. Dist. Ct. (so. dist.) N.Y. 1963, U.S. Ct. Appeals (2d cir.) 1965, U.S. Supreme Ct. 1966, Calif. 1968. Law clk. Judge Edmund L. Palmieri, Fed. Dist. Ct. (so. dist.) N.Y., 1961-62; research assoc. Columbia Project on Internat. Procedure, 1962-63; asst. dist. atty. N.Y. County, 1963-67; with Rifkind & Sterling, Los Angeles, 1967-68; sr. atty. Nat. Legal Program on Health Problems of the Poor, Los Angeles, 1969-70; prof. Loyola U. Sch. Law, Los Angeles, 1970-76, Benjamin N. Cardozo Sch. Law, Yeshiva U., N.Y.C., 1976—; vis. prof. Gould Law Ctr., U. So. Calif., Los Angeles, 1972-73, U. Va. Sch. Law, 1975-76, U. Tex. Sch. Law, summer 1974; Hebrew U. Jerusalem, 1984-85; counselor on internat. law U.S. Dept. State, 1985-86, cons., 1986-88. Author: (with De Feis) Women's legal Rights: International Agreements An Alternative to ERA?, 1987; articles and rev. editor Columbia Law Rev., 1960-61; contbr. articles, commentary, book revs. to profl. publs. Kent Scholar, Stone Scholar; recipient Jane Marks Murphy prize. Mem. Am. Law Inst. (reporter model penal code project 1977-79), Am. Soc. Internat. Law (exec. council 1987), Internat. Law Assn. Am. Br. (exec. com.), Columbia Law Sch. Alumni Assn., Columbia U. Seminar on Human Rights, Phi Beta Kappa. Home: 160 Riverside Dr New York NY 10024 Office: Yeshiva U Benjamin N Cardozo Sch Law 55 Fifth Ave New York NY 10003

HALE, DAWN LOUISE, librarian; b. Reading, Pa., Nov. 19, 1950; d. Robert Harvey and Hilda Margaret (Ruth) Heinly; m. William C. Hale, Sept. 12, 1969 (div. Jan. 1983). B.S., Indiana U. of Pa., 1973; postgrad. U. Pa., 1974-76; M.Music, Temple U., 1978; M.L.S., Drexel U., 1980; postgrad. Columbia U., 1981-82; NYU, 1984. Pvt. piano tchr., Phila., 1977-79; library asst. Drexel U., Phila., 1978-79; original monographic cataloger Columbia U. Tchrs. Coll., N.Y.C., 1981-83; cataloger NYU, N.Y.C., 1983-86; head cataloging Johns Hopkins U., 1986—; NYU rep. to music program com. Research Libraries Group, Stanford, Calif., 1984-86. Presser scholar Indiana U. of Pa., 1972-73. Mem. ALA (resources and tech. services div.), Library and Info. Tech. Assn. of ALA, Md. Library Assn., Potomac Tech. Processing Librarians, N.Y. Tech. Services Librarians (sec.-treas. 1985-86), Assn. Coll. and Research Libraries (sec. Greater N.Y. met. area chpt. 1983-86), Music Library Assn. Democrat. Lutheran.

HALE, DEBRA ANN, computer software company executive; b. San Francisco, Mar. 12, 1955; d. Jerry Louis and Merdis Marie (Normand) Cole; m. Lee Alan Hale, Aug. 25, 1978; 1 child, Jeffrey Lee. BS cum laude, La. Coll., 1975. Bus. tchr. Alexandria (La.) Sr. High Sch., 1975; legal sec. Stafford, Randow, O'Neal & Scott, Alexandria, 1975-76, Craven, Scott & Murchison, Alexandria, 1976-79; adminstrv. asst. Clark-Dunbar Inc., Alexandria, 1979-84, corp. auditor, 1984-86, exec. sec., 1985-86; sec., acct. Dunbar Enterprises, Alexandria, 1987—; ops. specialist System Specialists Inc., Alexandria, 1984-86, v.p., 1987—; sec. Rapides Media Ctr., Alexandria, 1975. Ch. sec. Alexandria Ch. Nazarene, 1975; music dir. Pineville (La.) Ch. Nazarene, 1977—, soloist, 1976—, asst. children's dir., 1986—; historian Cen. La. Adoptive Parents Orgn., Alexandria, 1984-86. Mem. Nat. Assn. Female Execs., Pi Delta Pi, Alpha Chi, Kappa Delta Pi. Democrat. Home: 112 Deer Creek W Pineville LA 71360 Office: Dunbar Enterprises PO Box 7416 Alexandria LA 71306

HALE, JACQUELINE ANNE, day care and preschool director; b. Des Plaines, Ill., Aug. 29, 1945; d. Daniel Webster and Grace Evadinee (Burns) Brown, m. Ronald Keith Hale, Sept. 17, 1966; children: Michelle (dec.), Randall, Carrie; 1 foster child, Kimberly. Student, Prairie Bible Inst., 1963-66. Tchr.'s aide, band dir. Woodcrest Bapt. Acad., Fridley, Minn., 1975-78; tchrs., band and choir dir. Yellowstone Valley Christian Sch., Laurel, Mont., 1978-83; tchr., band dir. Bible Bapt. Sch., Missoula, Mont., 1983-85; tchr. Brookdale Christian Ctr., Bklyn. Ctr., Minn., 1985-86; dir. daycare and presch. Brookdale Christian Ctr., Bklyn. Ctr., 1986—; tchr. Good News Club, West Dundee, Ill, 1965-66, Pioneer Girls Club, 1968-70, Sunday Sch., various locations, 1973-83. Mem. primary com. Rep. Party, Missoula, 1982; dir. children's choir Chgo. Lakes Bapt. Ch., 1987—. Named an Outstanding Camper Exland Bible Camp, 1961-62. Mem. Greater Mpls. Daycare Assn. Club: Teacher Book (Mpls.). Home: 7401 Jeanne Dr Lino Lakes MN 55014

Office: Brookdale Christian Ctr Daycare and Presch 6030 Xerxes Ave N Brooklyn Center MN 55430

HALE, MARY HELEN PARKER, university administrator; b. Merryville, La., May 25, 1920; d. James Carroll and Mollie (Dear) Parker; BA in English (scholar), La. Coll., 1940, BA in Music, 1940; MA in English (fellow), La. State U., 1942; PhD in Fine Arts (hon.), U. Alaska, 1965; m. George Erwin Hale, June 12, 1942; children: John Parker, James Milton, Nancy Anne. Instr., dir choral music, Boston 1944-45, Albany, N.Y., 1945, Washington, 1946-49, Anchorage, 1949-50; dir. Anchorage Community Chorus, 1951-59; founder, dir. Alaska Festival of Music, 1956-62; vice chmn. N.Am. Assembly Arts Agys., 1968-70; coordinator arts and community affiliates offices Anchorage Community Coll. and U. Alaska, Anchorage, 1970-76; dir. pub. services Anchorage Community Coll., 1977-81, asst. to pres., 1979-81. Founder Alaska Southcentral High Sch. Music Festival, 1950; mem. Alaska Centennial Commn., 1963-65; charter mem. Alaska State Council on Arts, 1966, chmn., 1967-71; founder, mem., sec. Alaska Humanities Forum, 1974-79; mem. adv. bd. No. TV, Inc., 1979—, trust com.Anchorage Sr. Ctr., 1987—; vice-chmn. citizens adv. council Anchorage Community Coll., 1981, mem. adv. council, 1981-86, founder Arts Fair and Women's Ctr. adv. com. Celebrating Alaska's Women, 1945-65, 86, 87; vice chmn. Coalition Community Colls. in Alaska, 1986—. Recipient Mayor's Disting. Service award, Anchorage, 1965; 49'er award, elected to Hall of Fame, Alaska Press Club, 1970, 72; Outstanding Vol. award U. Alaska, Anchorage, 1976; Outstanding Alumni award La. Coll., 1979; President's citation Anchorage C. of C., 1979; Disting. Service award Anchorage Community Coll., 1983. Mem. Anchorage Arts Council (charter mem.), U. Alaska Anchorage Alumni Assocs., Internat. Platform Assn., LWV, AAUW, Nat. Assn. Women Deans, Adminstrs. and Counselors, Mu Phi Epsilon, Beta Sigma Phi (hon.). Presbyterian. Clubs: Anchorage Woman's, Soroptimists (hon. mem., pres. 1956) (Anchorage). Home: 11601 Birch Rd Anchorage AK 99516

HALE, REBECCA HENDRICKS, lawyer; b. Cape Girardeau, Mo., Feb. 17, 1959; d. Oliver Peter and Edna (Baker) Hendricks; m. James Otis Hale, Dec. 26, 1983; children: James Beacher II, Matthew Jacob. BA in Journalism, U. S.C., 1980, JD, 1983. Atty. S.C. Sch. Bds. Assn., Columbia, 1983-85; assoc. Novit, Scarminach and Johnson, P.A., Hilton Head Island, S.C., 1985—. Contbr. articles to S.C. Sch. Bd. Assn. Jour. Mem. ABA, S.C. Bar Assn., Hilton Head Island Bar Assn., Beaufort County Bar Assn. Office: Novit Scarminach & Johnson PA JADE Bldg 52 New Orleans Rd Hilton Head Island SC 29928

HALE, SANDRA JOHNSTON, state official; b. Glen Cove, N.Y., Dec. 9, 1934; d. Alexander Henry and Marian (Baker) Johnston; m. Roger Loucks Hale, June 10, 1961; children—Jocelyn, Leslie, Nina. B.A., Wellesley Coll., 1957. Asst. editor Little Brown & Co., Boston, 1957-61; office mgr., editorial assoc. Johns Hopkins Med. Sch., Balt., 1961-62; owner, mgr. The Book Tree, Mpls., 1968-70; assoc. prof. Met. State U., St. Paul/Mpls., 1973—(on leave); commr. adminstrn., chmn. exec. mgmt. sub-cabinet State of Minn., St. Paul, 1983—; cons. Nat. Endowment for Arts, Washington, 1976-79; host TV spls. KTCA-TV, St. Paul, 1978-79; book reviewer Mpls. Tribune, 1969-77; research project interviewer Johns Hopkins Med. Sch., Balt., 1963-68. Trustee. Macalester Coll., St. Paul, 1979—; past pres., past chmn. bd. dirs., Guthrie Theater, Mpls., 1980—; council mem. Nat. Council on Arts, Washington, 1979-80; commn. mem. 8th Circuit Ct. Appeals Nominating Com., St. Louis, 1978-80; chmn. Minn. Arts Bd., Mpls., 1976-79. Recipient Disting. Service award Minn. chpt. Am. Soc. Pub. Adminstrn., 1986. Office: Adminstrn Bldg Room 200 50 Sherburne Ave Saint Paul MN 55155

HALECKY, BENEDICTA MARTHA, food manufacturing executive; b. Hazleton, Pa., July 17, 1958; d. Joseph John and Lillian Helen (Kontir) H. BS in Biology, Pa. State U., 1980; MBA, Rutgers U., 1986. Asst. mgr. McDonald's Hamburgers Corp., Hazelton, 1975-82; food mfg. engr., team mgr. Procter & Gamble, Staten Island, N.Y., 1981-83, food dept. mgr. mfg. engring., 1983-85; ops. mgr. mfg. engring. food dept. Procter & Gamble, Lexington, Ky., 1986—; guest speaker U. Ky. Mktg. Program, Fugazzi Bus. Sch., 1986. Greek Cath. Union scholar, 1979; recipient Silver Cycling medal Bluegrass State Games. Mem. Am. Assn. of Masters of Bus., Nat. Assn. Female Execs., Soc. Women Engrs., Bluegrass Wheelman's Assn., U.S. Softball Assn. Republican. Roman Catholic. Clubs: Cath. Singles, Am. Soccer League (Lexington). Home: 3751 Appian Way #92 Lexington KY 40502 Office: Procter & Gamble 767 E 3d St Lexington KY 40508

HALES, LISA LINN HERMAN, food merchandiser; b. Omaha, Nov. 25, 1961; d. Larry Lee and Judy Kaye (Ensminger) Herman; m. Ronnie Hales, June 25, 1988. B.S.B.A., U. Fla., 1983. Cashier Publix Supermarkets, Gainesville and Lakeland, Fla., 1978-84; meat merchandiser Fleming Cos., Inc., Geneva, Ala., 1984—. Nat. Food Brokers Assn. scholar, 1983; George Jenkins Found. scholar Publix Supermarkets, Inc., 1980-83; Nat. Honor Soc. scholar, 1980. Mem. Nat. Assn. Female Execs., Phi Chi Theta, Alpha Xi Delta. Office: Fleming Cos Inc 1015 W Magnolia Ave Geneva AL 36340

HALES, ROBERTA LOUISE, respiratory care supervisor; b. Norristown, Pa., Feb. 21, 1962; d. Raymond R. and Mary Louise (Scheetz) Salamone; m. Thomas E. Hales, Jan. 6, 1982. BS, Ind. U. Pa., 1984. Respiratory technician Presbyn. Hosp., Pitts., 1982, Monte Fiore Hosp., Pitts., 1982-84; respiratory therapist Children's Hosp. Phila., 1984-86, supr. respiratory care, 1986—; instr. CPR Am. Heart Assn., Phila., 1984-86; preceptor, Children's Hosp. Phila., 1985-86. Mem. Am. Assn. for Respiratory Care. Home: 314 E Brown St Norristwon PA 19401 Office: Children's Hosp Phila 34th and Civic Ctr Blvd Philadelphia PA 19104

HALEVY, HILDA MARIA, physician, anesthesiologist; b. Havana, Cuba; d. Juan and Raimunda (Valdes) Cheng; B.S., Instituto de Segunda Enseñanza de la Habana, Havana, 1949; M.D., U. Havana, 1957; m. Simon Halevy, 1968; 1 child, Daniel A. Sr. house physician and surgeon Mother Cabrini Meml. Hosp., N.Y.C., 1957-58; resident in anesthesiology Met. Hosp., N.Y.C., 1958-60; fellow in anesthesiology, various hosps., N.Y.C., 1960-67; attending anesthesiologist Astoria (N.Y.) Gen. Hosp., 1967—; vis. scholar to Mexico, Holland, Israel. Recipient Physician's Recognition award. Mem AMA, Am. Soc. Anesthesiologists, Med. Soc. State N.Y., N.Y. State Soc. Anesthesiologists, Med. Soc. County Queens, Am. Soc. Magnesium Research, N.Y. Soc. of Acupuncture for Physicians and Dentists. Democrat. Jewish. Office: Astoria Gen Hosp Dept Anesthesia 25-10 30th Ave Astoria NY 11102

HALEY, DEBRA ANN, educator; b. Wichita, Kans., June 14, 1953; d. Robert Gail and Anna Ellen H.; B.S. in Bus. Adminstrn. (acad. scholar), Kans. Newman Coll., 1975; M.B.A., Emporia State U., 1979; PhD in Bus. Adminstr, Okla. State U., 1986. News reporter KFH-Radio, Wichita, summer 1974; acct. Koch Oil Co., Wichita, 1975-78; instr. mktg., mgmt. Wichita State U., 1979-81, faculty adv. bus. and univ. students, 1980-81; grad. asst. mktg. Okla. State U., Stillwater, 1981-84; asst. prof. U. No. Iowa, 1984-88; asst. prof. U. N.Mex., 1988—. Mem. Am. Mktg. Assn., We. Mktg. Educators Assn., Beta Gamma Sigma. Roman Catholic. Office: U NMex Robert O Anderson Sch Mgmt Albuquerque NM 87131

HALEY, JOHNETTA RANDOLPH, musician, educator, university administrator; b. Alton, Ill., Mar. 19; d. John A. and Willye E. (Smith) Randolph; Mus.B. in Edn., Lincoln U., 1945; Mus.M., So. Ill. U., 1972; children—Karen, Michael. Vocal and gen. music tchr. Lincoln High Sch., E. St. Louis, Ill., 1945-48; vocal music tchr., choral dir. Turner Sch., Kirkwood, Mo., 1950-55; vocal and gen. music tchr. Nipher Jr. High Sch., Kirkwood, 1955-71; prof. music Sch. Fine Arts, So. Ill. U., Edwardsville, 1972—, dir. East St. Louis Campus, 1982—; adjudicator music festivals; area music cons. Ill. Office Edn., 1977-78; program specialist St. Louis Human Devel. Corp., 1968; interim exec. dir. St. Louis Council Black People, summer 1970. Bd. dirs. YWCA, 1975-80, Artist Presentation Soc., St. Louis, 1975, United Negro Coll. Fund, 1976-78; bd. curators Lincoln U., Jefferson City, Mo., 1974—, pres., 1978—; mem. Nat. Ministry on Urban Edn., Luth. Ch.-Mo. Synod, 1975-80; bd. dirs. Council Luth. Chs., Assn. of Governing Bds. of Univs. and Colls.; mem. adv. council Danforth Found. St. Louis Leadership Program, nat. chmn. Cleve. Job Corps, 1974-78; trustee Stillman Coll. Recipient Disting. Citizen award St. Louis Argus Newspaper, 1970; Cotillion de Leon award for Outstanding Community Service, 1977; Disting. Alumnae award Lincoln U., 1977; Disting. Service award United Negro Coll. Fund, 1979, SCLC, 1981; Community Service award St. Louis Drifters, 1979; Disting. Service to Arts award Sigma Gamma Rho, Fred L. McDowell award, 1986, Nat. Negro Musicians award, 1981, Sci. Awareness award, 1984-85, Tri Del Federated award, 1985, Bus. and Profl. Women's Club award, 1985-86, vol. yr. Inroad's Inc., 1986; named Duchess of Paducah, 1973; received Key to City, Gary, Ind., 1973. Mem. Council Luth. Chs., AAUP, Coll. Music Soc., Music Educators Nat. Conf., Ill. Music Educators Assn., Nat. Choral Dirs. Assn., Assn. Tchr. Educators, Midwest Kodaly Music Educators, Nat. Assn. Negro Musicians, Jack and Jill Inc., Women of Achievement in Edn., Friends of St. Louis Art Mus., The Links, Inc., Alpha Kappa Alpha, Mu Phi Epsilon, Pi Kappa Lambda. Lutheran. Club: Las Amigas Social. Lodge: Elks. Home: 30 Plaza Sq Saint Louis MO 63103 Office: So Ill U Box 1200 Edwardsville IL 62026

HALEY, PATRICIA (MAGILL), insurance company official; b. St. Louis, May 17, 1944; d. James Chauncey and Virginia Marie (Foley) Magill; m. Richard Bland Haley, Aug. 25, 1962; children—Michael Shawn, Timothy Shamus. Cert. Gen. Ins., Ins. Inst. Am., 1979; student Marymount Coll., 1985—. Accredited personnel mgr., profl. in human resources. Teller, sec. Citizens Nat. Bank, Maplewood, Mo., 1960-64; sales sec. Statis. Tabulating Co., St. Louis, 1964-70; life sales sec. Home Ins. Co., Kansas City, Mo., 1971-73; sr. mgr. Am. States Ins. Co., Santa Ana, Calif., 1973—. Notary public, Calif., 1978—; team mother Little League Assn., Brea, Calif., 1975-87. Mem. Am. Soc. Personnel Adminstrn., Personnel Employee Relations Mgmt. Assn. (chairperson). Roman Catholic. Club: Dana West Yacht. Home: 26823 Poveda Mission Viejo CA 92692 Office: Am States Ins Co 400 N Tustin Santa Ana CA 92705

HALEY, PEGGY JEAN, emergency medical techniciam; b. Delaware, Ohio, Jan. 6, 1957; d. Roy Claton Mathews and Doris Jean (Hopfer) Mathews Willits; m. Dean Ivan Mack II, June 14, 1974 (div. May 19, 1982); children: Brandon Brady Mack, Dean Ivan Mack III; m. Duke Clayton Haley, May 28, 1983. Grad. in emergency med. tech., Columbus (Ohio) Tech. Inst., 1982. Cert. emergency med. technician, Ind. Park supr. Delaware County Parks, 1977; receptionist, clk. Delaware County Council on Alcoholism, 1977-78; acctg. specialist Mental Health Clinic, Delaware, 1978-82; sales assoc. J.C. Penney Co., Terre Haute, Ind., 1982-84; emergency med. technician AID Ambulance, Terre Haute, 1983—; fin. analyst Vis. Nurse Assn., Terre Haute, 1984-86. Vol. Delaware County Juvenile Ct., 1982. Home: RR 53 Box 181 Terre Haute IN 47805

HALEY-ASPNES, GRACE BERLENE, correctional center business administrator; b. Eastover S.C., Feb. 22, 1943; d. Hugh Wilder and Gladys Berlene (Hendren) Christmas; m. Thomas Ross Haley, Oct. 1, 1961 (div. June 1977); children—Tammy, Thomas Ross, Judy; m. Dale Jennings Aspnes, Mar. 9, 1983; children—Anita, Christopher. B.B.A., Eastern N.Mex. U., 1982. Profl. pub. buyer, 1980; cert. pub. purchasing officer, 1981. Mgr., Commonwealth Theatres, Inc., Gallup, N.Mex., 1970-76; bus. mgr. Roswell Correctional Ctr., Hagerman, N.Mex., 1976-85; bus. mgr. Western N.Mex. Correctional Facility, 1985—. Recipient Exemplary Performance award Dept. Corrections, Santa Fe, N.Mex., 1983. Mem. Am. Correctional Assn., Nat. Inst. Govtl. Purchasing, N.Mex. Correctional Assn. (corr. sec. 1983), Delta Mu Delta, Phi Kappa Phi. Republican. Baptist. Clubs: Moose (Belen, N.Mex.); Lions (Gallup, N.Mex.). Home: 1204 N 4th St Grants NM 87020 Office: PO Drawer 250 Grants NM 87020

HALEY-RUSSO, SALLY FULTON, artist; b. Bridgeport, Conn., June 29, 1908; d. John Poole and Elizabeth (Akers) Haley; m. Michele Russo, June 29, 1935; children: Michael Haley, Gian Donato. BFA, Yale U., 1931. One-woman shows include Portland Art Mus.; exhibited in group shows at San Francisco Mus. of Art, Denver Art Mus., Portland Art Inst., 1959, Seattle Art Mus., The Seattle World's Fair, 1961-62, Expo Vancouver, B.C., Walker Art Ctr., Mpls.; represented in permanent pub. and pvt. collections AT&T, The State of Oreg., The Philip Morris Collection, Willamette U., Salem, Oreg., others. Home: 3227 NW Thurman Portland OR 97210

HALINA, MME. (HALINA JOZEFA LUTOMSKI, MRS. FLOYD MARTIN LUTOMSKI), dance educator, choreographer; b. Lwow, Poland, Feb. 4, 1930; came to U.S., 1947, naturalized, 1950; d. Adam and Katarzyna (Jezierska) Dziekan; student Warsaw Opera Ballet Sch., 1936-38, Wielki Theatre, Lwow, 1939-41; grad. Politechnik, Lwow, 1944; m. Floyd Martin Lutomski, Oct. 31, 1946; children—Norbert Michael, Ilona Maria, Kevin. Dancer, Warsaw Opera Ballet, 1938-39, World's Olympiade, Kiev, Russia, 1939, USO, Germany, 1945-46; producer Dance Capades, 1948—; owner, dir., resident choreographer Sch. of Dance Arts, Elmira and Corning, N.Y.; tchr. Nat. Dance Tchrs. Orgns., U.S., P.R., 1950; choreographer children's and classical ballets Kimbo Dance Records, 1954—; founder, artistic dir., choreographer Elmira-Corning Ballet, Inc., 1955—, artistic dir. Nutcracker Suite, 1980; coordinator, also dir. ednl. programs; lectr. Steuben, Chenung, No. Pa. counties, Elmira-Corning Sch. Dists., 1969-72, Schulyer County Schs., 1968-71; producer, choreographer Four Seasons, 1950, Fairy Doll, 1951, Sleeping Beauty, 1953, 59, 65-67, Nutcracker, 1954, 78-82, Hansel and Gretel, 1955, Cinderella, 1957, 81-82, Les Ballet de Elements, 1958, Schlagobers, 1959, Gaite Parisienne, 1960-61, La Boutique Fantasque, 1961, adaptation of Les Sylphides, 1962, Swan Lake, 1952-64, Masquerade, 1962-63, Snow Maiden, 1964, Copelia, 1965, 68, 70, 77-78, Karnival Kontrasts, 1966, La Bayadere, 1966, Nutcracker, 1969, Aurora's Wedding, 1971, Wooden Prince, 1971, Americana, 1972, La Fille Mal Gardee, 1972, Vignete's Classique-Comedia, 1973, Sylvia, 1974, Cirque, 1975, Am. Alphabet Ballet, 1976, Magic Forest, 1978, Stars and Stripes, 1979, Stardust Trail, 1980, The Americas, 1981; dir., choreographer ballet Nutcracker for Elmira-Corning Ballet, 1965-66, also Red-White and Blue, Comedia del Arte, Masque; dir. Les Petits Riens, 1967; dir. Bicentennial ballet: Witching, Am. Gayeties, Peter and the Wolf, 1976, 80-83, Carnival, Snow White, 1977, Snow Maiden, 1980, Cinderella (Prokofiev), Jewels, 1982, Tale to Tale, 1983, The Magic Key, 1983, prodn. dir. Fete De Jour, Hansel and Gretel, 1984, full length coppelia, Clemen's Performing Arts Ctr., Elmira-Corning, 1985, Centre Themes, Alice, 1985, LaFille Mal Gardee; dir. tour for Bambi, The Magazine Rack Elmira-Corning Ballet; commned. ballet especially arranged music, produced, directed, Rudolph's Great Original Work, Axmas Ballet, 1986, The Magic of Gershwin, Greeting Sentiments, guest artist in Israel, 1987, Rudolph's Great Escape, 1987, New Nutcracker Corning Glass Ctr. and Clemens Ctr., Corning and Elmire; staged Once upon a Piper, Interplay, Openspace, 1979; staged, directed The Woodcutter's Tale, Fete de Jour, The Emperor's New Clothes, 1984; originated Pre Ballet album for presch. age Roper Records, 1977, now chmn. performing arts dept.; tchr. ballet, Tokyo, 1983, Buenos Aires, Argentina and Rio de Janeiro, Brazil, 1984, ballet seminar, Israel, 1987; supr. ballet records Roper label, dir. and supr. 52 new series ballet records; rep. ballet dept. for Dance Educators Am. to Nat. Council Dance Tchrs.' Orgns.; dir. Sch. Dance Arts, Elmira, N.Y., Corning, N.Y. Recipient Steuben Crystal and Gold award Corning community; named Woman of Yr., So. Asian-Am. Assn. Women, 1987. Mem. Dance Educators Am. (chmn. ballet exam., com. 1966-67, exec. bd. 1967-69, exec. dir. 1969-71). Roman Catholic. Recs. 36 ballet albums Roper Label, 41 ednl. records. Home: 933 Fassett Rd Elmira NY 14905 Office: Sch Dance Arts 410-14 W Gray St Elmira NY 14905 also: 258 Dennison Pkwy E Corning NY 14830

HALL, ADRIENNE ANN, advertising agency executive; b. Los Angeles; d. Arthur E. and Adelina P. Kosches; m. Maurice Hall; children: Adam, Todd, Stefanie, Victoria. B.A., UCLA. Founding ptnr. HaLL & Levine Advt., Los Angeles, 1960-80; vice chmn. bd. Eisaman, Johns & Laws Advt. Inc., Los Angeles, Houston, Chgo., N.Y.C., 1980—; chmn. Eric Bovy Inc., 1986—. Trustee UCLA; bd. regents Loyola-Marymount U., Los Angeles; mem. Blue Ribbon of Music Ctr., Pres. Circle, Los Angeles County Mus. Art, Calif. Gov.'s Commn. on Econ. Devel.; bd. dirs. Wonder Women Found., N.Y.C.; mem. adv. council Girl's Clubs Am., Girl Scouts U.S.; mem. adv. bd. Asian Pacific Women's Network, fashion group Downtown Women's Ctr. and Residence, Leadership Am., Washington; mem. exec. bd. Greater Los Angeles Partnership for Homeless, Los Angeles Shelter Partnership Bd.; mem. Nat. Network for Hispanic Women. Recipient Nat. Headliner award Women in Communications, 1982; recipient Profl. Achievement award UCLA Alumni, 1979; named Woman of Yr. Am Advt. Fedn., 1973, Ad Person of the West award Mktg. and Media Decisions, 1982; Bus. Woman of Yr. award Boy Scouts Am., 1983; Women Helping Women award Soroptimist Internat., 1984; Bullock's 1st ann. portfolio award for exec. women, 1985; Communicator of yr. award Ad Women, 1986; Leader award YWCA, 1986; named One of 20 Top Corp. Women, Savvy mag., 1983. Mem. Internat. Women's Forum (bd. dirs., Woman Who Made a Difference award 1987), Am. Assn. Advt. Agys. (bd. dirs., chmn. bd. govs. western region), Western States Advt. Agys. Assn. (pres.), Hollywood Radio and TV Soc. (dir.), Nat. Advt. Rev. Bd., Overseas Edn. Fund, Com. 200 (western chmn.), Women in Communications, Orgn. Women Execs., Calif. Women's Forum (founder, chmn. The Trusteeship), Los Angeles Area C. of C. (bd. dirs. 1987—), Rotary Internat. Los Angeles Chpt. Clubs: Calif. Yacht; Stock Exchange, Los Angeles Advt. (pres.) (Los Angeles). Lodge: Rotary. Office: Eisaman Johns & Laws Advt 6255 Sunset Blvd Los Angeles CA 90028

HALL, AMANDA MCFARLAND, real estate broker; b. Van Nuys, Calif., Oct. 20, 1940; d. Robert Emmett and Virginia Winifred (Phillips) McF.; m. Edwin Lanier King, Jan. 25, 1957 (div. July 1958); 1 child, Keith McFarland; m. Archie A. Hall, Oct. 20, 1966. Student, Cedar Valley Jr. Coll., Lancaster, Tex., 1981-83. Sec. YMCA, Dallas, 1958-62; sec. Vought Corp. div. LTV, Dallas, 1963-65, adminstrv. sec., 1965-75, exec. sec., adminstrv. asst., 1975-84; owner, broker A&A Real Estate Services, Cedar Hill, Tex., 1984—; mem. bus. devel. bd. Duncanville (Tex.) Nat. Bank, 1985—, investigative rev. bd. Dallas Eye Inst., Duncanville, 1985—. Contbg. columnist Cedar Hill Chronicle, 1977-79. Mem. park bd. City of Cedar Hill, 1977-79; fin. chair First United Meth. Ch., Cedar Hill, 1987—, also active vol. work; del. 1984 Rep. Nat. Conv., Dallas; sec. S.W. Dallas County Reps., 1982-84, pres., 1984-85, v.p., 1987-88. Mem. Greater Dallas Bd. Realtors, Am. Bus. Women's Assn. (membership chair 1987, v.p. 1987-88, pres. 1988-89). Lodge: Eastern Star. Home: 823 Cherlyne Dr Cedar Hill TX 75104 Office: A&A Real Estate Services PO Box 430 Cedar Hill TX 75104

HALL, BERNICE LUCIA, minister of music; b. Bronx, N.Y., Mar. 4, 1928; d. Adolphus Christopher and Ada Idalia (Cruse) Edwards; m. Edgar Waker, June 30, 1956 (dec. Sept. 1958); m. Eugene Hall, July 28, 1963. B in Music, New Eng. Conservatory of Music, 1949; cert., Longy Music Inst., Paris, 1954; AA, Annes Coll., N.Y.C., 1955; HHD, Universal Coll., 1982. Soloist New Eng. Conservatory Orch., Boston, 1951; violinist Hinton Orch., Boston, 1951-53; singer City Ctr. Opera Co., N.Y.C., 1953-54, Nat. Negro Opera Co., Washington, 1954-60; minister of music The Bapt. Temple Ch., N.Y.C., 1968-74, Caldwell Meth. Ch., Bronx, 1980-86, Transfiguration Luth. Ch., N.Y.C., 1975-80, Greater Hood Meth. Ch., N.Y.C., 1986—; voice tchr. The Henry Street Music Sch., N.Y.C., 1974-84; founder, dir. youth music Besma Assn., N.Y.C., 1960—, The Luth. Ch., N.Y.C., 1984—; cons. Christian Edn., N.Y.C., 1984—. Author: (poems) Seeds of Hope, 1970; edn. editor The Urban Life Newspaper, Bklyn., 1968. Cons. Republic of Liberia U., Monrovia, 1964; chmn. Ams. for Ethiopia Assn., N.Y.C., 1965. Recipient community service award Sachs Furniture Stores, N.Y.C., 1971; named Woman of Yr. 1978. Mem. Nat. Assn. Colored Women (supr. 1972, Youth Achievement award 1970), Nat. Council Negro Women, Nat. Key Women Assn., New Eng. Conservatory Alumni, Layman League (cons.). Methodist. Lodge: Zion. Office: The Besma Assn PO Box 539 New York NY 10025

HALL, BETTY HYNSON, business educator; b. Foneswood, Va., Aug. 26, 1946; d. Theodore Lawson and Irene Elizabeth (Smith) H.; m. James Ernest Hall. BS in Bus. Edn., Longwood Coll., 1968; MS in Bus. Edn., Va. Commonwealth U., 1975. Bus. educator, vocat. dir., coop. office edn. coordinator, adult edn. supr. Town of Colonial Beach (Va.) Pub. Schs., 1967-77; bus. educator, vocat. dept. chair Washington and Lee High Sch. Westmoreland County Pub. Schs., Montross, Va., 1977—; mem. task force State Dept. Edn. and Bus., Richmond, Va., 1977-79, 84, com. for articulation of secondary/possecondary programs in secretarial sci., 1988; conf. presenter, 1982, 83. Mem., sec. Am. Cancer Soc. Westmoreland Chpt., Montross, 1978-79; mem., sec. Town of Montross Bd. of Zoning Appeals, 1980—. Mem. NEA., Va. Edn. Assn., Westmoreland Edn. Assn. (sec. 1985-86), Nat. Bus. Edn. Assn., Va. Bus. Edn. Assn., Am. Vocat. Assn., Va. Vocat. Assn., Delta Pi Epsilon (Gamma Gamma chpt. corr. sec. 1987—). Mem. Disciples of Christ. Office: Washington and Lee High Schs PO Box 366 State Rt 3 Montross VA 22520-0366

HALL, BEVERLY ELAINE, television director; b. Port Arthur, Tex., Feb. 18, 1957; d. Milton Crawford and Jacqueline Ruth (Pevoto) H. BS in Mass Communications, Lamar U., 1979. Lic. real estate agt., Tex. Tech. dir. Port Arthur Cablevision, 1975-76; prodn. asst. Sta. KJAC-TV affiliate NBC, Port Arthur, 1976-80; word processor The Mansion on Turtle Creek, Dallas, 1980-81; prodn. asst. Sta. KBMT-TV affilate ABC, Beaumont, Tex., 1982; air dir. Sta. KFDM-TV affilate CBS, Beaumont, 1982—; coordinator TV talent Bum Phillips Celebrity Golf Tournament, Bob Hope Birthday Celebration, Port Arthur, 1980; real estate agt. Am. Real Estate, Port Neches, Tex., 1982. Producer, dir.: Life in America, 1982; author: (tng. jour.) Air Director's Manuel, 1987. Republican. Baptist. Home: 2714 S Kitchen Dr Port Neches TX 77651 Office: Sta KFDM-TV 2955 Interstate 10 E Beaumont TX 77706

HALL, BRENDA YVONNE, lawyer; b. Shelbyville, Tenn., Sept. 26, 1957; d. William G. and Alene (Russell) Hall; m. Gary L. McDonald, Sept. 4, 1982. A.S., Columbia (Tenn.) State Community Coll., 1976; B.A., U. Tenn., 1978, J.D., 1980. Bar: Tenn. 1981, U.S. Dist. Ct. (ea. dist.) Tenn. 1981. Student atty. U. Tenn. Legal Clinic, Knoxville, 1980; law clk. Meares and Meares P.C., Maryville, Tenn., 1981; ptnr. Gamble & Hall, Wartburg, Tenn., 1981-82; ptnr. McDonald & Hall, Kingston, Tenn., 1982—; adv. bd. to bd. dirs. Rural Legal Services and Pub. Defenders Office, Oak Ridge, 1981-82. Research editor Tenn. U. Law Rev. 1979-80. Area dir. Knoxville Opera Co., 1982. Mem. ABA, Am. Trial Lawyers Assn., Tenn. Bar Assn. (House of Del. 1987—, bd. dirs. Young Lawyers Conf. 1985—), Roane County Bar Assn. (sec., treas. 1985-87), Roane County Bar Assn., Gamma Beta Phi, Phi Kappa Phi, Pi Delta Phi., Alpha Gamma Rho, Phi Delta Phi. Democrat. Mem. Ch. Christ. Office: McDonald & Hall 145 Court Sq Kingston TN 37763

HALL, CARYL R., marketing executive; b. N.Y.C., May 11, 1949; d. Jacob Sidney and Marian (Werner) Brod; m. Richard Wein, June 20, 1970 (div. 1981); m. Roger Wayne Hall, July 3, 1982; 1 child, Christy. A in Applied Sci., Fashion Inst. Tech., 1969; BA in Mgmt., U. Redlands, 1981. Supr. word processing Coldwell Banker Mgmt. Corp., Los Angeles, 1973-75; sr. text processing operator Jet Propulsion Lab., Pasadena, Calif., 1975-77; office automation analyst Union Oil Co., Los Angeles, 1977-79; supr. word processing Gen. Electric, El Monte, Calif., 1979-81; supr. sales support Wang Labs., Culver City, Calif., 1981-87; sr. systems cons. Wang Labs., Los Angeles, 1987-88, sr. mktg. specialist Western ops., 1988—. Club: Toastmasters (Los Angeles).

HALL, CHERYL ANN, data processing executive; b. San Diego, Sept. 29, 1954; d. Leo Franklin and Anita Lillian (Beuerlein) H. BA, U. Cin., 1979. Intern Lomark, Inc., Middletown, Ohio, 1974-78, mgmt. info. systems operator, 1978-79; dir. accounts Home Care, Inc., West Chester, Ohio, 1979-81; installation dir. SMS, Inc., Malvern, Pa., 1982-85, sr. installation dir., 1985—. Patron Sta. WVXU-FM, Cin., 1984—; sustaining mem. Cin. Zool. Soc., 1984—; advisor youth commn. United Synagogue Youth, Hamilton, Ohio, 1985—; mem. Leadership Council Jewish Fedn., Cin., 1985—, Jewish Community Ctr., Cin.; trustee Congregation Beth Israel, Hamilton, 1985—. Mem. Assn. for Systems Mgmt., Orgn. for Rehab. through Tng. (v.p. 1985-86). Home: 5543 Winton Rd Fairfield OH 45014 Office: SMS Inc 1801 Park 270 Suite 200 Saint Louis MO 63146

HALL, CHRISTINE ANN, marketing executive; b. Los Angeles, June 27, 1958; d. Sidney Munn and Dorothy Mae (Johnston) H. AA, Monterey Peninsula Coll., 1979; BA, U. Wash., 1981. Mgr. Fads and Frames, Monterey, Calif., 1981-83; dir. mktg. Ogden (Utah) City Mall The Hahn Co., 1983-86; dir. mktg. The Fashion Show Mall The Hahn Co., Las Vegas, 1986; dir. mktg. Sunnyvale (Calif.) Town Ctr. The Hahn Co., 1987; dir. mktg. Solano Mall The Hahn Co., Fairfield, Calif., 1987—. Home: 591 Peabody #211 Vacaville CA 95688

HALL, CYNTHIA HOLCOMB, judge; b. Los Angeles, Feb. 19, 1929; d. Harold Romeyn and Mildred Gould (Kuck) Holcomb; m. John Harris Hall, June 6, 1970 (dec. Oct. 1980); 1 child, Harris Holcomb; 1 child by previous marriage, Desma Letitia. A.B., Stanford U., 1951, J.D., 1954; LL.M., NYU,

1960. Bar: Ariz. 1954, Calif. 1956. Law clk. to judge U.S. Ct. Appeals 9th Circuit, 1954-55; trial atty. tax div. Dept. Justice, 1960-64; atty.-adviser Office Tax Legis. Counsel, Treasury Dept., 1964-66; mem. firm Brawerman & Holcomb, Beverly Hills, Calif., 1966-72; judge U.S. Tax Ct., Washington, 1972-81, U.S. Dist. Ct. for central dist. Calif., Los Angeles, 1981-84; U.S. circuit judge 9th Circuit, Pasadena, Calif., 1984—. Served to lt. (j.g.) USNR, 1951-53. Office: US Ct of Appeals 125 S Grand PO Box 91510 Pasadena CA 91109-1510

HALL, ELEANOR WILLIAMS, public relations executive; b. Boston; d. James Murray and Julia Eleanor (Williams) H. A.B. cum laude, Radcliffe Coll., 1945. Exec. sec. Am. Express Co., N.Y.C., 1950-62, adminstrv. asst. corp. mktg., 1963-65, mgr. corp. mktg., 1965-69, mgr. corp. pub. relations, 1969-71; mgr. mktg. services Am. Express Internat. Banking Corp., N.Y.C., 1971-72, asst. treas. advt. and pub. relations, 1972-76, asst. v.p. advt. and pub. relations, 1976-82; pres. Eleanor Hall Assocs., Inc., 1982—. Club: Harvard. Home: 201 E 79th St New York NY 10021

HALL, ELIZABETH LEA, lawyer; b. Paducah, Ky., Dec. 20, 1954; d. Clarence Elton and Anna Kathryn (Humphrey) Hall. BA History, La. State U., 1976, JD, 1981. Bar: La. 1982. Research assoc. La. State U., Baton Rouge, 1980-81; law clk. 14th Jud. Dist. Ct., Lake Charles, La., 1981-82; dir. Criminal Staff State La. 3d cir. Ct. Appeals, Lake Charles, 1982—; adj. prof. dept. criminal justice McNeese State U., 1987—. Mem. ABA, La. State Bar Assn., S.W. La. Bar Assn., Beta Sigma Phi. Republican. Mem. Ch. of Christ.

HALL, ELLA TAYLOR, clinical psychologist; b. Macon, Miss., Nov. 30, 1948; d. Essex and Mamie (Roland) Taylor; B.A., Fisk U., 1971, M.A., 1973; Ph.D., George Peabody Coll., 1978; children—Banyikaai Monique (dec.), Motiqua Shante. Mental health specialist behavioral sci. div. Meharry Med. Coll., Nashville, 1976-77; asso. psychologist Bronx (N.Y.) Psychiat. Center, 1979; clin. psychologist Wiltwyck Residential Treatment Center, Ossining, N.Y., 1979-81; clin. cons. Abbott House, Irvington, N.Y., 1982-85; asst. psychologist Abbott Union Free Sch. Dist., 1985—; active Girl Scouts Am., Yonkers Schs. PTA. Mem. Yonkers PTA; co-leader Yonkers troup Girl Scouts U.S. NIMH trainee; Crusade fellow; Kendall grantee. Mem. Am. Psychol. Assn., Delta Sigma Theta. Episcopalian. Research in field (lit.).

HALL, FRANCES HUNT, librarian; b. Panama City, July 14, 1919; came to U.S., 1919; s. Franklyn Evelyn and Ida Sue (Hunt) Hall. B.A., U. N.C.-Greensboro, 1940; M.A., U. N.C.-Chapel Hill, 1955, M.S.L.S., 1957, J.D., 1959. Bar: N.C. 1959. Asst. law librarian U. N.C.-Chapel Hill, 1959-63, asst. prof. Sch. Library Sci., 1968-72; reference librarian U. Chgo. Law Sch., 1963-66; documents librarian U. N.C.-Greensboro, 1966-68; assoc. prof., asst. law librarian U. Va., Charlottesville, 1972-73; assoc. prof., law librarian So. Meth. U., Dallas, 1975-77; librarian N.C. Supreme Ct., Raleigh, 1977—; bd. dirs. Cinema, Inc., Raleigh. Contbr. articles to profl. jours.; author: Cases and Materials on Librarianship and the Law, 1971. Bd. dirs. Bagger-Iredell Found., Raleigh, 1983—, Triangle Area ARC, Raleigh, 1981—. Served to lt. comdr. USNR, 1942-54. Mem. N.C. Bar, N.C. Bar Assn., N.C. Library Assn., ABA, Am. Assn. Law Libraries, Spl. Library Assn., ALA. Democrat. Episcopalian. Home: 3939 Glenwood Ave Raleigh NC 27612 Office: NC Supreme Ct Library 2 E Morgan St Raleigh NC 27611

HALL, HELEN, interior and environmental designer; b. N.Y.C., Jan. 24; d. Maxwell and Bertha Neuhoff; student N.Y. Sch. Interior Design Architecture, 1982—; m. Sidney Manne, Mar., 1937; children—Belinda Elaine Manne Pokorny, Stephen Anthony Manne. Founder Dumont Hall and Helen Hall Studios, N.Y.C., 1955, pres. Dumont Hall, 1955-60, Helen Hall Studios, 1955—; dir. interior design Sherwood Hotels, 1955-65, other hotel chains, 1956—. Pres., founder League for Cardiac Children, 1948-52; founder Sprout Lake Camp for Cardiac Children; mem. Assoc. Nat. Trust for Historic Preservation, 1987—. Served with ARC, Halloran Hosp. with mil. forces, 1942-50. Recipient cert. of merit, 1947. Mem. Am. Soc. Interior Designers, Assn. Antique Dealers. Active restoration and redesign Hotel Lexington, N.Y.C., 1955-65; design works pub. Interior Design mag., 1955-65, N.Y. Times.

HALL, JACQUELINE YVONNE, lawyer, administrative law judge; b. Detroit, Jan. 8, 1953; d. William Hamilton and Evelyn Virginia (Callaway) H. B in Indsl. Adminstrn., Gen. Motors Inst., 1976; JD, Detroit Coll. Law, 1980. Bar: Mich. 1980. Corp. selection coordinator Ford Motor Co., Dearborn, Mich., 1978-80, position evaluation analyst, 1980-81, staff atty., 1981-84; adminstrv. law judge Mich. Dept. Labor, Detroit, 1984-87; magistrate Worker's Compensation Bd. Magistrates, 1987—. Mem. Nat. Bar Assn., Women Lawyers Assn., Nat. Assn. Women Judges, Mich. Assn. Adminstrv. Law Judges, Assn. Black Judges Mich., NAACP, Wolverine Bar Assn., Founders Soc., U. Detroit Black Alumni Assn. (bd. advisors 1983—), Delta Sigma Theta. Office: Mich Dept Labor 1200 Sixth St Mich Plaza Bldg Detroit MI 48226

HALL, JAMIE LYNN, mortgage company official; b. Indpls., Jan. 17, 1962; d. Gilbert Reagan and Connie Lynn (Farley) Reagan Lamm; m. Jerry Lee Hall, Nov. 1, 1986. Br. mgr. Aresnal Savs. Assn., Indpls., 1982-85; loan processor Mcht's Mortgage Corp., Indpls., 1985-87, processing coordinator, 1987—. Mem. Mortgage Bankers Assn. Republican. Home: 10733 E 96th St Indianapolis IN 46256 Office: Mchts Mortgage Corp 1 N Capitol St Suite 1000 Indianapolis IN 46255

HALL, JANET, corporate international affairs specialist; b. Detroit, Dec. 13, 1942; d. Roy and Alma Isabelle (Thomas) H.; m. Charles Diggs, Nov. 6, 1971 (div. May 1982); 1 child, Cindy Carter. BA in Govt., Barnard Coll., 1964; MA in Internat. Law and Diplomacy, Georgetown U., 1969. Intelligence research analyst U.S. Bur. of Intelligence and Research, Washington, 1967-69; internat. relations officer Am. Embassy, Dakar, Senegal, 1969-71; career mgmt. officer U.S. Bur. Personnel, Washington, 1971-73; country officer U.S. Dept. State, Washington, 1973-75, sr. secretarial officer, 1977-79; dir. internat. affairs geographic area support Westinghouse Electric Corp., Washington, 1979—; cons. Pres.'s Exec. Exchange, Washington, 1975-77; lectr. Georgetown U., Washington, 1985—; mem. Bus. Adv. Council on Internat. Programs, Washington, 1986—. Mem. Mayor's Internat. Adv. Council of D.C., 1982—, Bd. of Equity Policy Ctr., Washington, 1984-85, Bd. of Family Practice Ctr., Washington, 1984-85; alt. del. ward Dem. com., Washington, 1985—. Mem. Barnard Coll. Alumnae Assn. (pres. 1982-84), Am. Soc. Internat. Law (panel chairperson Howard U. 1986—). Democrat. Methodist. Home: 4627 Yuma St NW Washington DC 20016 Office: Westinghouse Electric Corp 1801 K St NW Washington DC 20006

HALL, JOANN, retired publishing company executive; b. Auburn, Ky., Apr. 2, 1927; d. Everett Bluford and Geneva Mae (Maxwell) H.; student public schs., Detroit; m. Dec. 15, 1945 (div. 1964); 1 son, Mark Stephen Rudolph. With Daily News Broadcasting Co., Bowling Green, Ky., 1950-73, women's dir., dir. music and public affairs, 1960-70, ops. mgr., 1970-73; bus. mgr. Cockrel Corp., Bowling Green, 1974-88, editor Back Home in Ky. mag., 1983-84. Hon. Ky. col.; recipient public service award USAF, 1971, Distbv. Edn. Clubs Am., 1970. Mem. Am. Bus. Women's Assn. (pres. 1967, Woman of Year award 1967), Bowling Green C. of C. Cumberland Presbyterian. Home: 661 Hampton Dr Bowling Green KY 42101

HALL, KATHLEEN JULIA, contractor, financial administrator; b. Detroit, Nov. 30, 1932; d. Daniel Joseph and Noreen Mary O'Shea; m. Wendell George Hall, Sept. 20, 1969. Student, Detroit Bus. Inst., 1954-57, Oakland Community Coll., 1980-81. Mem. corp. staff Ex-Cello Corp., Detroit, 1964-69; staff asst. internat. div. Burroughs Corp., Detroit, 1969-77, Detroit Edison Co., 1979—; contractor VA, Detroit, 1983—. V.p. shelter for indigents Wensel Corp., Detroit, 1982. Mem. Property Owners Better Am. Living (sec. 1982—). Address: 2717 Admore St Royal Oak MI 48073

HALL, KATHRYN EVANGELINE, author, lecturer; b. Biltmore, N.C.; d. Hugh Canada and Evangeline Haddon (Jenkins) Hall; B.A., U. N.C., M.A.; diploma Adams Sch. Music, Montreat, N.C.; postgrad. Yale, U. London, Fla. Atlantic U. Author: The Papal Tiara, History of the Episcopal Church of Bethesda-By-The-Sea, 1964, The Architecture and Times of Robert Adam, 1969, The Pictorial History of the Episcopal Church of Bethesda-By-The-Sea, 1970-71, 86, Joseph Wright of Derby, A Painter of Science, Industry, and Romanticism, 1974, A History of English Architecture, 1976-82; Sir John Vanbrugh's Palaces and the Drama of Baroque Architecture, 1982-84; lectr. history, art and architecture, U.S., Eng. and Scotland, 1961—. Vice pres. The Jr. Patronesses, Palm Beach, Fla., 1964. Mem. Nat. League Am. Pen Women (Owl award 1972, 76, 77, pres. Palm Beach chpt. 1975-80), Palm Beach Quills (historian), Palm Beach County Hist. Soc. (gov.), Internat. Platform Assn., Nat. Soc. Arts and Letters, Soc. Four Arts, Cum Laude Soc., Palm Beach Civic Assn. Episcopalian. Clubs: Everglades (Palm Beach); English Speaking Union (Palm Beach and London). Home: Acadie PO Box 648 Palm Beach FL 33480

HALL, KAY CHARLOTTE, medical center official, nurse; b. Dallas, Oreg., Sept. 14, 1942; d. Kenneth Charles and Wilma (Winstead) Blanchard; m. W. Jay Hall, Feb. 14, 1982 (div. 1984). Student, Idaho State U., 1960-62. Nurse Cassia Meml. Hosp., Burley, Idaho, 1961-63, cons., 1982—; nurse Burley Nursing Home, 1963-66, Hillcrest Haven Convalescent Ctr., Pocatello, Idaho, 1966-69; nurse St. Anthony Community Hosp., Pocatello, 1970-72, med. records analyst, 1972-77; instr. med. terminology Idaho State U., Pocatello, 1978-83, lectr., 1983—; mgr. med. info. services Pocatello Regional Med. Ctr., 1977—; cons. med. info. services various regional hosps., nursing homes, 1978—; cons. Lost Rivers Hosp., Arco, Idaho, 1982-84, Star Valley Hosp., Afton, Wyo., 1983—. Author: Policy/Procedure Manual for Hospital Ward Clerks, 1980. Mem. Am. Med. Record Assn. (accredited, del. 1980-82), Idaho Med. Record Assn. (chmn. legal legis. com. 1978-79, pres. 1979-80), Gems Med. Record Assn., Idaho Mus. Natural History. Republican. Presbyterian. Home: 553 Cheyenne Ave Pocatello ID 83204 Office: Pocatello Regional Med Ctr 777 Hospital Way Pocatello ID 83201

HALL, KAY MARGARET, nurse; b. Lima, Ohio, July 24, 1943; d. Harold Ray and Ruth (Gordon) H.; m. Robert G. Jarvis, Oct. 23, 1976 (div. 1983). Diploma Miami Valley Hosp. Sch. Nursing, Dayton, Ohio, 1965; student Wright State U., 1974-77, U. Dayton, 1971, Universidad Technologica De Santiago, Santo Domingo, Dominican Republic, 1984—. R.N., Ohio. Charge nurse recovery room Miami Valley Hosp., Dayton, 1965-66; indsl. nurse Harris Seybold Co., Dayton, 1966-68; office nurse to physician, Dayton, 1968-69, 80-82; coordinator nurse Mobile Unit Clinics, OEO, 1969-72; emergency nurse Kettering Med. Ctr., Ohio, 1972-80, radiology nurse, 1979-80; chair N.A. delegation to world health council World's Children's Health, Geneva; nominated internat. chair over Americas by Mex., 1987—. Author: (manual) Procedures for Nursing Care in Radiology, 1977. Big sister Big Bros.-Big Sisters, Dayton, 1979-83. Recipient Citation Dominican Govt. Mem. Miami Valley Hosp. Sch. Nursing Alumni, Critical Care Nurses Dayton. Home: PO Box 1961 Kettering OH 45429

HALL, LEE, artist, educator, design school president; b. Lexington, N.C., Dec. 15, 1934; d. Robert Lee and Florence (Fitzgerald) H. BFA, U. N.C., 1955; MA, N.Y. U., 1959, PhD, 1965; postgrad., Warburg Inst. U. London, 1965; DFA (hon.), U. N.C.-Greensboro, 1976. Asst. prof. N.Y. State U. Coll., Potsdam, 1958-60; assoc. prof., chmn. art dept. Keuka Coll., 1960-62; assoc. prof. art Winthrop Coll., 1962-65; asst. prof., chmn. art dept. Drew U., Madison, N.J., 1965-67; assoc. prof., chmn. art dept. Drew U., 1967-70, prof., chmn. art dept., 1970-74; dean visual arts State U. N.Y. Coll. at Purchase, 1974-75; pres. R.I. Sch. Design, Providence, 1975-83; sr. v.p. Acad. for Ednl. Devel., N.Y.C., 1984—, dir. div. arts and communications. Exhibited in group shows in, London, N.Y.C., Winston-Salem, Eugene, Oreg., also others; represented by Betty Parsons Gallery, N.Y.C., Armstrong Gallery, N.Y.C.; dir. research on Pres. Kennedy's image in recent art, John F. Kennedy Meml. Library, panelist, Nat. Endowment for Humanities, 1972-80; author: Wallace Herndon Smith: Paintings, 1987; contbr. articles to profl. jours. Recipient research grant Am. Philos. Soc., 1965, 68; Childe Hassam Purchase award Am. Acad. Arts and Letters, 1977; RISD Athena medal, 1983. Mem. Am. Soc. Aesthetics, Coll. Art Assn., Pi Lambda Theta. Office: Acad for Ednl Devel 680 Fifth Ave New York NY 10019

HALL, LESLIE CARLTON, artist, consultant; b. Rockville Centre, N.Y., May 14, 1952; d. Robert Wilson and Barbara Louise (Lyon) H. Student So. Conn. State Coll., 1970-72. BA in Psychology, U. Conn., 1975. Freelance artist PBC Advt. Co., New Canaan, Conn., 1978-80; graphics artist Stamford (Conn.) Weekly Mail, part-time 1978-80; art dir. Tru-Line Publs., Spring Valley, N.Y., 1974-80; owner Creative Intentions, Wilton, Conn., 1980—; cons. for creative design, logos. Editor: Pipeline, 1980-83; artist for cover Doberman World mag., 1985. Active Rescue and Placement of Abused or Stray Doberman Pinschers, Wilton, 1976—; frequent judge Doberman Sweepstakes, Match Shows. Mem. Internat. Platform Soc., Doberman Pinscher Club of Am., Doberman Pinscher Club of Tappan Zee (treas. 1976-82), Doberman Pinscher Club of Danbury (Conn.). Republican. Episcopalian. Home and Office: 341 Olmstead Hill Rd Wilton CT 06897

HALL, LINDA ANNE, entomologist, agency administrator; b. N.Y.C., Aug. 8, 1953; d. Edward J. and Gladys R. (Bedigian) Bormann; m. Perry L. Hall, Aug. 14, 1986; B.S. in Agr. with honors and distinction (Outstanding Sr. Woman Coll. Agr.), U. Del., 1975; M.S., Wash. State U., 1977; Ph.D., Iowa State U., 1983. First woman extension entomologist in U.S., mem. faculty Iowa State U., 1977-84, dept. animal sci., 1983-84; entomologist Ga. Dept. Agr., 1985; dir. Farm and Community Life Ctr., Ft. Valley, Ga., 1985—. Mem. Entomol. Soc. Am., Am. Registry Profl. Entomologists., Entomol. Soc. Can., Sigma Xi, Alpha Zeta, Phi Delta Gamma.

HALL, LISA LYNN, state official, auditor; b. Aurora, Ill., Oct. 13, 1948; d. Kenneth F. and Veva R. Hall; B.A. cum laude (Ill. State scholar, Sigma Lambda Sigma scholar, Helen R. Messenger, univ. grantee, High Ridge Sch. PTA scholar, Ill. PTA scholar), No. Ill. U., 1970; M.B.A. magna cum laude, Sangamon State U., Springfield, Ill., 1980; m. H. Huckaby, Oct. 12, 1980. Pres., owner, broker Hall Real Estate Enterprises, Springfield, 1972—; mgr. internal audit Ill. Dept. Adminstrv. Services, 1977-79; mgr. audit and investigation Ill. Dept. Commerce, 1979-80, chief audits and investigations, 1980—; ptnr./owner H & L Investments Co., 1981—. Del., Ill. Republican Conv., 1980. Cert. info. systems and data processing auditor. Mem. Inst. Internal Auditors (internat. com. 1979—, charter pres. Springfield chpt. 1978; seminar instr. 1979—), No. Ill. U. Alumni Assn. (gov. 1979—), Nat. Assn. Female Execs., Ill. Audit Mgrs. Assn., Assn. M.B.A. Execs., Internat. EDP Auditors Assn., Am. Bus. Women's Assn., Cwens. Contbr. articles to profl. jours.

HALL, MAMIE BARTON, home economics teacher; b. Roanoke, Va., Apr. 22, 1928; d. Clifton Early and Annie Lee (Ayers) Barton; m. William Pembroke Hall, June 23, 1951; 1 child, Carolyn. BEd, James Madison u., 1949; postgrad., U. Va., Charlottesville, 1958, 66-67, U. Va., Roanoke, 1972-73, 77-78, 82-84. Chartered cert. home economist, Va. Asst. postmaster U.S. Post Office Dept., Hardy, Va., 1943-49; clerical sec. U.S. Treas; home econs. tchr. Clifton Forge (Va.) Sch. Bd., 1949-52, Alleghany County Sch. Bd., Covington, Va., 1952-53; home econs., catering, Eng. tchr. City of Covington Sch. Bd., 1954—; Adv. Future Homemakers Am., Clifton Forge and Covington, 1949—; designer Va. Home Econs. Curriculum, 1955. Cons. Fall Foliage Festival/Miss Alleghany Highlands Pageant, Clifton Forge, 1975-85; 1st runner-up Mrs. Virginia Pageant, 1957; organizer, leader Covington-Alleghany County March of Dimes, 1978-85; judge arts and crafts shows, Clifton Forge and Covington; adv. com. Alleghany Highlands Arts and Crafts, 1987—. Mem. AAUW, Am. Vocat. Assn., Am. Home Econs. Assn., NEA, Va. Edn. Assn., Covington Edn. Assn., Rainbow Mountain Garden Club, Kappa Delta Pi, Delta Kappa Gamma (parliamentarian 1979-81, sec. 1981-83), Beta Sigma Phi. Baptist. Club: Clifton Forge Women's (various offices). Home: 1701 Ridgevue Ave Forest Hills Clifton Forge VA 24422 Office: Covington City Sch Bd Walnut St Covington VA 24426

HALL, MARCIA JOY, non-profit organization administrator; b. Long Beach, Calif., June 24, 1947; d. Royal Waltz and Norine (Parker) Stanton; m. Stephen Christopher Hall, March 29, 1969; children: Geoffrey Michael, Christopher Stanton. AA, Foothill Coll., 1967; student, U. Oreg., 1967-68; BA, U. Washington, Seattle, 1969. Instr. aide Glen Yermo Sch., Mission Viejo, Calif., 1979-80; market research interviewer Research Data, Framingham, Mass., 1982-83; adult edn. instr. Community Sch. Use Program, Milford, Mass., 1982-83; career info. ctr. coordinator Milford High Sch., 1983-86; corp. relations dir. Sch. Vols. for Milford, Inc., 1985-86; NE Area Coordinator YWCA of Annapolis and Anne Arundel County, Severna Park, Md, 1987—. Pres. PTO, Mission Viejo, 1979-80, Milford, 1981-84; consumer assistance vol., Calif. Pub. Interest Research Group, 1977-78. Mem. AAUW. Club: Toastmasters (treas. 1988—). Home: 507 Devonshire Ln Severna Park MD 21146 Office: YWCA NE 17 Cypress Creek Rd Severna Park MD 21146

HALL, MARY DIANNE, nurse; b. Mt. Clemens, Mich., May 14, 1951; d. Carlton Doram and Virginia Grace (Garlick) Semos; m. William James Hall Jr., Feb. 5, 1983. Diploma in Practical Nursing, St. Clair Community Coll., 1972, AS, 1979. RN, Mich., Tex. Practical nurse ortho/neurosurgical unit St. Joseph's Hosp., Mt. Clemens, 1972-79; nurse emergency and operating rooms St. John Hosp., Detroit, 1979-83, nurse operating room, 1986—; nurse operating room Brownsville (Tex.) Med. Ctr., 1983-86. Mem. Conservative Caucus, Washington, 1986—. Mem. Nat. Orthopedic Nurses Assn. (v.p., pres. Mich. chpt. 1975-78). Republican. Home: 33450 Bordman Rd Memphis MI 48041 Office: St John Hosp Moross Rd Detroit MI 48236

HALL, PAMELA S., environmental consulting firm executive; b. Hartford, Conn., Sept. 4, 1944; d. LeRoy Warren and Frances May (Murray) Sheely; m. Stuart R. Hall, July 21, 1967. B.A. in Zoology, U. Conn., 1966; M.S. in Zoology, U. N.H., 1969, B.S. in Bus. Adminstrn. summa cum laude, 1981; student spl. grad. studies program, Tufts U., 1986—. Curatorial asst. U. Conn., Storrs, 1966; research asst. Field Mus. Natural History, Chgo., 1966-67; teaching asst. U. N.H., Durham, 1967-70; program mgr. Normandeau Assocs. Inc., Portsmouth, N.H., 1971-79, marine lab. dir., 1979-81, programs and ops. mgr., Bedford, N.H., 1981-83, v.p., 1983-85, sr. v.p., 1986-87, pres., 1987—. Mem. Conservation Commn., Portsmouth, 1977—, Wells, Estuarine Research Res. Review Commn., 1986—, Great Bay (N.H.) Estuarine Research Res. Tech. Working Group, 1987—. Graham Found. fellow, 1966; NDEA fellow, 1970-71. Mem. Am. Mgmt. Assn., Water Pollution Control Fedn., Am. Fisheries Soc., Estuarine Research Fedn., Nat. Assn. Environ. Profls., ASTM, Sigma Xi. Home: 4 Pleasant Point Dr Portsmouth NH 03801 Office: Normandeau Assocs Inc 25 Nashua Rd Bedford NH 03201

HALL, PATRICIA EILEEN, legislative coordinator; b. N.Y.C., Aug. 6, 1962; d. Martin J. and Mildred (Carney) H. BA, SUNY, Stony Brook, 1985. Reporter Pennysaver News of Brookhaven, Medford, N.Y., 1985-86; legis. coordinator, press sec. N.Y. State Assemblyman I. William Bianchi Jr., Hauppauge, N.Y., 1986—. Mem. Stony Brook Alumni Assn.

HALL, SOPHIA HARRIET, judge; b. Chgo., July 10, 1943; d. John B. and Beverly N. (Doyle) H. BS, U. Wis., Madison, 1964; JD, Northwestern U., 1967. Bar: Ill. 1967, U.S. Dist. Ct. (no. dist.) Ill., U.S. Ct. Appeals (7th cir.) 1970, U.S. Supreme Ct. 1971. Assoc. McCoy, Ming & Black, Chgo., 1967-77; ptnr. Mitchell, Hall, Jones & Black, Chgo., 1977-80; judge Cir. Ct. of Cook County, Chgo., 1981—; dep. clk. Cook County Bd. of Commrs., Chgo., 1973-77. Mem. Nat. Assn. of Women Judges (sec. 1987—), Chgo. Bar Assn. (bd. mgrs. 1979-80), Cook County Bar Assn. (Civil Rights award 1973), Ill. Judges Assn. (bd. dirs. 1985-87). Office: 2508 Richard J Daley Ctr Chicago IL 60602

HALL, SYLVIA CHRISTINE, corrosion engineer; b. Orange, Calif., July 4, 1954; d. Clarence Loring and Dorothy Mary (Greenwood) H.; B.S. in Animal Sci., Calif. State Poly. U., 1974, M.S., 1979, M.B.A., 1983; postgrad. San Diego State U., 1979-81, San Jose State U., 1981-82; m. Ronald Raymond Walker, Sept. 9, 1978 (div. Dec. 1987). Registered profl. engr. Calif. Chem. technician Occidental Research Corp., La Verne, Calif., 1974-76; lectr. dept. chemistry. Calif. State Poly. U., Pomona, 1978; chemist Lockheed Aircraft Service Co., Carlsbad, Calif., 1979-81; research engr. Lockheed Missiles and Space Co., Sunnyvale, Calif., 1981-82; corrosion engr. Ameron, 1983—. Mem. Am. Chem. Soc., Nat. Assn. Corrosion Engrs., Am. Water Works Assn., Phi Kappa Phi. Home: 4502 Elizabeth St #5 Cudahy CA 90201

HALL, SYLVIA DUNN, entrepreneur; b. Kewanee, Ill., June 21, 1949; d. Martin Orrill and Elizabeth Jean (Boase) Dunn; m. James Vernon Hall, Jan. 14, 1977. B.A., Rockford Coll., 1971; M.L.S., N. Tex. State U., 1972; M.A., U. Tex., 1975; Ph.D.,U. Pitts, 1985. Library asst. Rockford Pub. Library (Ill.), 1966-71; librarian Holding Inst., Laredo, Tex., 1972-73; system coordinator San Antonio Pub. Library, 1973-76; tech. services librarian Corpus Christi Pub. Library (Tex.), 1976-78; asst. dir. So. Tier Library System, Corning, N.Y., 1978-81; devel. officer Pitts. Regional Library Ctr., 1981-85; pres. The Blue Bear Group, Inc., 1984—; pres. Eldora Data Ctr., Ltd., 1985— ; cons. S.D. State Library, Pierre, 1981-83, State Library of Pa., Harrisburg, 1982-83, Dept. Def., Washington, 1983-84; State Library of Iowa, 1984—. Author: Retro Conversion for Major Libraries in South Central N.Y., 2 vols., 1979; History of Library Development in Pennsylvania, 1982; contbr. articles to profl. jours. U. Pitts. fellow, 1982. Mem. ALA (student staff award 1982), Pa. Library Assn. (dir. 1983-85), Am. Soc. Info. Scientists, Colo. Library Assn. Democrat. Home: 227 Eureka St Central City CO 80427 Office: PO Box 709 Central City CO 80427

HALL, TERRY LEE, accountant; b. Champaign, Ill., Dec. 10, 1949; d. Albert L. and Catherine A. (Comstock) Hall; m. Thomas F. Johnston, Sept. 27, 1973 (div. Jan. 1979); 1 child, Daniel K. BA, Barat Coll., Lake Forest, Ill., 1984. CPA, Ill. Acct. Terry Hall, CPA, Waukegan, 1985—. Bd. dirs. YWCA of Lake County, Waukegan, 1987—. Mem. Am. Inst. CPA's, Ill. Soc. CPA's, Chgo. Soc. Women CPA's, Lake County Estate Planning Council, Nat. Assn. Tax Preparers.

HALL, VICTORIA ELLEN (VICKI), employee and community relations manager; b. Balt., Aug. 30, 1944; d. Robert G. and Della Vern (Chesshir) H.; m. Duane E. Sweatland, Feb. 2, 1963 (div. 1965); 1 child, Michael Gray. Student, Delta Coll., 1968, U. of Ark., Little Rock, 1979, U. Cen. Ark., 1980. Sec. U.S. Dept. Navy, Washington, 1965-68; bookkeeper Aero-Craft Boats, St. Charles, Mich., 1968-71; sec. Franklin Electric Co., Jacksonville, Ark., 1971-74; supr. employee relations Franklin Electric Co., Jacksonville, 1974-85; mgr. employee and community relations Brinkley (Ark.) Motor Products, 1985—; owner retail bus. Cabot Country, 1987. Recipient Recruiter award ARC, 1979. Mem. Ark. Personnel Assn., Nat. Assn. Female Execs., Am. Entrepreneur Assn. Baptist. Office: Brinkley Motor Products 1st and Grand St Brinkley AR 72021

HALLANAN, ELIZABETH V., U.S. district judge; b. Charleston, W.Va., Jan. 10, 1925; s. Walter Simms and Imogene (Burns) H. AB, U. Charleston, 1946; JD, W.Va. U., 1951; postgrad., U. Mich., 1964. Atty. Crichton & Hallanan, Charleston, 1952-59; mem. W.Va. State Bd. Edn., Charleston, 1955-57; mem. Ho. of Dels., W.Va. Legis., Charleston, 1957-58; asst. commr. pub. instns., Charleston, 1958-59; men., chmn. W.Va. Pub. Service Commn., Charleston, 1969-75; atty. Lopinsky, Bland, Hallanan, Dodson, Deutsch & Hallanan, Charleston, 1975-84; judge U.S. Dist Ct. (so. dist.) W.Va., 1983—. Mem. White House Conf. on Children and Youth. Mem. ABA, W.Va. Bar Assn. Office: US Dist Ct PO Drawer 5009 Beckley WV 25801

HALLAS-GOTTLIEB, LISA GAIL, film assistant director; b. Rahway, N.J., Feb. 22, 1950; d. Taras and Mary (Lapchinski) Hallas; m. David N. Gottlieb, May 2, 1980; children: Gabriel, Jamie. B.A. in Broadcasting, Film and English with distinction, Stanford U., 1972. Second asst. dir. films: Opening Night, 1977, World's Greatest Lover, 1977, The Driver, 1977, Old Boyfriends, 1978, Just You and Me, Kid, 1978, A Small Circle of Friends, 1979; 2d asst. dir. TV show M*A*S*H, 1976; 1st asst. dir. TV shows Nobody's Perfect, 1979, Shirley, 1979, Hellinger's Law, 1980, Dynasty; 1980-81, Cagney and Lacey, 1983, Lottery $, 1983-84, Condor, 1984, Buck James, 1987. Home: 1406 N Topanga Canyon Blvd Topanga CA 90290

HALLAUER, JULIE ANN, engineer; b. Dearborn, Mich., May 22, 1961; d. William John and Nancy Ann (Stalker) H. BS in Mech. Engring. Tech., U. Toledo, 1984; postgrad., Calif. Luth. U., 1987. Design engr. Allied Bendix Electrodynamics, Sylmar, Calif., 1983-86; project engr. Aerospace div. Abex Corp., Oxnard, Calif., 1986—. Mem. Soc. Automotive Engrs., Nat. Mgmt. Assn. (chair awards com. 1987), Am. Soc. Metals Internat. Republican. Presbyterian. Office: Abex Corp Aerospace Div 3151 W Fifth St Oxnard CA 93030

HALLBAUER, ROSALIE CARLOTTA, business educator; b. Chgo., Dec. 8, 1939; d. Ernest Ludwig and Kathryn Marquerite (Ramm) Hallbauer; B.S.,

Rollins Coll., 1961; M.B.A., U. Chgo., 1963; Ph.D., U. Fla., 1973. Assoc. prof. bus. Fla. Internat. U., Miami, 1972—. C.P.A., Ill.; certified mgmt. accountant; cert. cost analyst. Mem. Am. Inst. C.P.A.s, Am. Accounting Assn., Nat. Assn. Accountants, Am. Woman's Soc. C.P.A.s, Ill. Soc. C.P.A.s, Inst. Mgmt. Accounting, Beta Alpha Psi, Pi Gamma Mu. Office: Fla Internat Univ Tamiami Trail Miami FL 33199

HALLENBECK, JILL MARIE JUMP, electrical engineer; b. Evanston, Ill., Mar. 10, 1958; d. Cecil James and Gwendolyn Josephine (Wambaugh) Jump; m. Peter Dorr Hallenbeck, May 20, 1978. BSEE, Purdue U., 1980, MSEE, 1982. Coordinator user services engring. computer network Purdue U., West Lafayette, Ind., 1982-83; research engr. Research Triangle Inst. Ctr. for Digital Systems, Research Triangle Park, N.C., 1983—; cons. engr. Petronics, Inc., West Lafayette and Durham, N.C., 1980—. Contbr. articles to profl. jours., 1985—. Mem. IEEE, IEEE Computer Soc., NSPE, Assn. for Computing Machinery. Democrat. Roman Catholic. Office: Research Triangle Inst 3040 Cornwallis Rd PO Box 12194 Research Triangle Park NC 27709

HALLENBECK, SUSAN L., educational administrator; b. New Haven, Conn., July 10, 1958; d. Wayne Jay and Shirley Joyce (Loveday) H.; m. David M. Crookshank, Dec. 20, 1985. BA in Psychology and Pre-Law, Ohio Wesleyan U., 1979; MBA in Exec. Mgmt., Ashland Coll., 1986. Community edn., pub. relations coordinator St. Louis Abused Women's Support Project, Inc., 1979-80; dir. community edn. and counsel Planned Parenthood of Mansfield, Ohio, 1981; adminstrv. asst. Ashland (Ohio) Coll., 1982-83; asst. dir. MBA/BSBA program, 1983-84, dir. transfer admissions, 1984-86; asst. dir. Columbus (Ohio) Council World Affairs, 1987; assoc. dir. admissions Capital U., Columbus, 1987—. Assoc. producer Miss N. Cen. Ohio Scholar, Mansfield, 1984; del. Ohio Fed. Bus. and Profl. Women, Cleve., 1987; team capt. March of Dimes Walkamerica team, Ashland, 1985, 86; mem. dependent care task force Ohio Bus. and Profl. Women, 1988. Named one of Outstanding Women of Am., 1984. Mem. Worthington Bus. and Profl. Women (pres. 1987-88), Ashland Bus. and Profl. Women (2d v.p. 1985-86, Young Career Woman 1986), Ohio Assn. Coll. Admissions Counselors (mem. spring conf. planning com. 1988), Mortar Bd., Omicron Delta Kappa. Republican. Club: Toastmasters. Home: 682 Oxford St Worthington OH 43085 Office: Capital U Admissions Office 2199 E Main St Columbus OH 43215

HALLER, DONNA LOU, insurance company executive; b. Springfield, Ill., Oct. 7, 1956; d. Donald E. and Elsie P. (Simpson) Edwards; m. Arthur W. Haller, Sept. 25, 1976; children: Brian J., Melissa M. Grad. high sch., Argenta, Ill. Ins. agt. Prudential Ins., Dwight, Ill., 1984—. Mem. Dwight Sch. Bd. Edn., 1987—. Mem. Nat. Assn. Female Execs., Ill. Valley Life Underwriters, United Food and Comml. Workers, Dwight Bus. and Profl. Women (sec. 1985-86, chairperson 1986). Lodges: Lioness (chmn. 1986-87), Woman of Moose. Home and Office: 620 N Chicago Dwight IL 60420

HALLERBERG, GRETCHEN ANNE, medical librarian; b. Jacksonville, Ill., Dec. 10, 1949; d. Arthur Edward and Katherine (Rausch) H.; m. J. Walton Tomford, Feb. 5, 1983. BS, Valparaiso U., 1970; MS, Case Western Res. U., 1972, MLS, 1973. Reference librarian Cleve. Health Scis. Library, 1973-76; coordinator collection devel. U. Minn. Libraries, St. Paul, 1976-77; dir. med. library Univ. Hosps. Cleve., 1977-81; mgr. library services dept. Cleve. Clinic Found., 1981—. Cellist, Heights Civic Orch., Cleveland Heights, Ohio, 1983—; council 1st English Luth. Ch., Cleveland Heights, 1986—. Mem. Med. Library Assn. (cert. 1975), Med. Library Assn. Northeastern Ohio (pres. 1987), Med. Library Assn. (pres. Midwest chpt. 1986), Spl. Libraries Assn. Democrat. Office: Cleve Clinic Found 9500 Euclid Ave Cleveland OH 44195

HALLETT, CAROL BOYD, diplomat; b. Oakland, Calif., Oct. 16, 1937; married. Student, U. Oreg.; student, San Francisco State Coll. Field office rep. Calif. State Assemblyman, 1966; staff asst. U.S. Congressman, 1967-76; assemblywoman Calif. State Assembly, Sacramento, 1976-82; cons., dir. Found. for Individual and Econ. Freedom, Sacramento, 1982-83; dir. of parks and recreation Calif. State Assmbly, 1982-83; western regional dir. Citizens For Am., Sacramento, 1984; nat. field dir. Citizens For Am., Washington, 1985-86; U.S. ambassador to the Bahamas 1986—; asst. to U.S. Sec. Interior, 1984-85. Office: Am Embassy Bahamas, Mosmar Bldg Queen St, PO Box N 8197, Nassau The Bahamas *

HALLETT, KAY A., educator; b. Galion, Ohio, May 6, 1946; d. Ralph Howard and Eliza Fern (Hartman) Ernst; m. Thomas James Hallett, Aug. 2, 1969; children: Marnie Kay, Thomas James II. BS in Edn., Bowling Green State U., 1968, MEd, 1986. Cert. elem. and secondary tchr., Ohio. Tchr. Galion Pub. Schs., 1968-69, Wauseon (Ohio) Pub. Schs., 1969-70, P-D-Y Schs., Delta, Ohio, 1971-72, Hicksville (Ohio) Schs., 1972-78, Benton-Carroll-Salem Schs., Oak Harbor, Ohio, 1978-86, 1986—; chmn. Benton-Carroll-Salem Schs. inservice dept. meeting, 1985-86; mem. computer course of study Benton-Carroll-Salem Schs., 1986-87, English curriculum course of study Ottawa County Schs., 1987-88, spl. edn. curriculum, Ottawa County, 1983-86; bd. dirs. adult edn. curriculum Benton-Carroll-Salem Schs. Active bd. elections, Wauseon, 1970; chmn. festival com. St. Boniface, Oak Harbor, 1979-81, 86. Recipient Tchr. of Yr. award Future Tchr's. Am., 1972. Mem. Internat. Reading Assn., Ohio Edn. Assn., Nat. Edn. Assn., Oak Harbor Edn. Assn., Altar Rosary Soc. (lit. chmn. 1976-78). Democrat. Roman Catholic. Home: 118 E Main St Oak Harbor OH 43449 Office: Oak Harbor Jr High Church St Oak Harbor OH 43449

HALLIDAY, HARRIET HUDNUT (HOLLY), free-lance editor; b. Springfield, Ill., Dec. 7, 1941; d. William Herbert and Elizabeth Allen (Kilborne) Hudnut; B.A., Coll. Wooster, 1963; postgrad. McCormick Theol. Sem.; m. Terence C. Halliday, June 14, 1980; children: Tyler Hudnut Colman, Richard Terence, Kimberly Anne, Alastair Charles. Exec. sec. women's bd. Presbyterian Med. Ctr., San Francisco, 1965-68; editor Am. Bar Found., Chgo., 1968-70, asst. dir. publs., 1970-75, mng. editor Am. Bar Found. Research Jour., 1975-80; research asst. dept. philosophy Australian Nat. U., Canberra, 1980-82; mng. editor Chiron Publs., 1983-86; acad. asst. to dean social scis. U. Chgo., 1986-87; dir. BCH Corp., 1985—. Mem. exec. com. jr. governing bd. Chgo. Symphony Orch., 1969-70, 75-76; officer adv. bd. Unitarian Presch. Center, Chgo., 1974-77; mem. Assocs. Rush-Presbyn.-St. Luke's Med. Ctr., 1974-79; mem. alumni bd. Coll. Wooster, 1978-80, also chmn. pub. relations com., mem. nominating com., by-laws revision com.; pres. Women's Exchange, 1988—; bd. dirs. Children's Theatre of Winnetka, Ill., 1984-85; exec. com. Chgo. Bible Soc., 1983-86. Republican. Presbyterian. Home and Office: 955 Vernon Ave Winnetka IL 60093

HALLIDAY-CASMIR, MINA G., communications and arts consultant; b. Hamburg, Iowa, Oct. 16, 1945; d. Ralph Hoover and Florence (Hummel) Halliday; m. Fred L. Casmir. BS, N.W. Mo. State U., 1967; MS, So. Ill. U., 1968. Cert. secondary tchr., Ill. Teaching asst. So. Ill. U., Carbondale, 1967-68; tchr. Belleville (Ill.) West High Sch., 1968-73; edn. cons. Ill. Bd. Edn., Springfield, 1973-86; owner, mgr. Halliday-Casmir Assocs., Los Angeles, 1986—; founder Ill. High Sch. Theatre Festival, 1975-86; adviser, panel mem. Ill. Arts Council, 1981-86. Editor: Teaching Speech Today, 1979, (series) Basic Oral Communication, 1981-82; former mem. editorial bd. Communication Edn. Mem. IAAE.

HALPER, JUNE ANN, human resource development consultant; b. N.Y.C., Dec. 13, 1949; d. Harold Herbert and Sophy (Cohen) H. BS in Edn., Syracuse U., 1970; MA in Guidance and Counseling, Columbia U., 1971, MEd, 1973. Asst., mgmt. devel. and training Philip Morris, USA, N.Y.C., 1971-75; mgr. orgn. devel. and training RCA Missile and Surface Radar, Moorestown, N.J., 1975-80; prin. cons. Ebasco Services, Inc., N.Y.C., 1980-86; ind. cons. N.Y.C., 1986—. Mem. N.Y. Human Resource Planners, N.Y. and Nat. Orgn. Devel. Networks. Office: 445 E 77th St Suite 3H New York NY 10021

HALPERIN, CORRINE SANDRA, association executive; b. Providence, Feb. 8, 1936; d. Barney and Rose Ruth (Bilsky) Gordon; student Behrend Coll., Wayne State U., U. Mich.; B.A., Mercyhurst Coll., 1980; m. Leo William Egan, Nov. 28, 1986; children—Karen Halperin Shor, Micheal Jay, Amy Marlene. Freelance market researcher, 1968-72; exec. dir. Council Vols. Erie County, 1971-78; exec. dir. YWCA, Erie, 1978-81; unit dir. Am. Cancer Soc., Erie, 1982; adj. faculty Mercyhurst Coll., dir. community edn., 1982-84, dir. spl. events, 1984-85; program dir. Northwest Pa. Area Labor Mgmt. Council, Erie, 1985-86, exec. dir., 1986—; adviser Hospitality House for Women, 1975—. Chmn. Erie County Commn. Drug and Alcohol Abuse, 1978-80; bd. dirs. Pa. Women's Campaign Fund. Recipient Community Service award, 1977, 498 Hardworking Women in Pa., 1987. Mem. Am. Soc. Tng. and Devel., AAUW, Nat. Council Jewish Women, The Erie Eighty (pres. 1985—). Contbg. editor: Vol. Adminstrn., 1973-83. Home: 2948 Willow Wood Dr Erie PA 16506 Office: NW Pa Area Labor Mgmt Council 1001 State St Erie PA 16501

HALPERN, JO-ANNE ORENT, lawyer; b. Balt., Apr. 13, 1944; d. Max Howard and Marjorie (Ginsburg) Orent; m. M. David Halpern, Aug. 22, 1965; children—Hugh Nathanial, Lee Randall (dec.), Lauren Gail. B.A. Dickinson Coll., 1966; J.D., Dickinson Sch. Law, 1968. Bar: Pa. 1968. Law clk. Daupin County and Commonwealth Ct. Pa., 1965-68; assoc. Hurwitz Klein, Benjamin & Angino, Harrisburg, Pa., 1968-70; sole practice, Hollidaysburg, Pa., 1970—; legal asst. to Blair County Cts., Hollidaysburg, 1974—; solicitor Blair County Assn. Citizens with Learning Disabilities, 1979—, Family Violence Intervention, Inc., Altoona, Pa., 1980—; lectr., atty. Hospice Program of Home Nursing Agy. Blair County, 1979—. Adviser, bd. dirs. Agudath Achim Sisterhood, 1970—, pres., 1985-88; mem. Fedn. Jewish Philanthropies Bd, 1985—. Mem. ABA, Pa. Bar Assn. (family law sect., rights of handicapped children sect.), Blair County Bar Assn., Am. Arbitration Assn. (arbitrator), Blair County Assn. Lawyers Wives, Phi Alpha Delta, Phi Mu. Republican. Jewish. Lodge: Hadassah. Home: 8 Hickory Hill Hollidaysburg PA 16648

HALPERN, PATRICIA, sales promotion and premiums company executive; b. San Francisco, Jan. 13, 1934; d. William and Alice (Dewey) O'Shaughnessy; student U. Ill., m. Harold Halpern, Apr. 1; children: Rebecca, Jay. Account exec., v.p. sales React Enterprises, N.Y.C., 1974-87; v.p. nat. accounts Logo Promotions, Inc., N.Y.C., 1987—. Mem. Ad Specialty Assn., NOW. Home: 132 E 35th St New York NY 10016 Office: Logo Promotions Inc 230 Fifth Ave Suite 1210 New York NY 10001

HALPIN, LISA SCHMID, banker; b. Evanston, Ill., July 26, 1947; d. David Simpson and Aliceve (Winters) Schmid; m. Thomas Kevin Halpin, June 7, 1975. BSBA cum laude, Boston U., 1971. Staff Continental Ill. Nat. Bank and Trust Co., 1971-72, Ins. Co. N.Am., 1972-74; staff 1st Nat. Bank Chgo., 1974-79, staff officer, mng. purchasing and inventory control, 1979-81, staff officer process cons., 1981-84, asst. v.p., 1985—, product mgr., 1985, bus. systems specialist, 1986-87, mgr. process control, 1987—; pres. 1364 Boa Tr. Corp. (Boa Limousine Service), Carol Stream, Ill., 1985—. Mem. zoning commn. Village Carol Stream, 1987. Republican. Episcopalian. Office: 1st Nat Bank Chgo 525 W Monroe Suite 261 Chicago IL 60670

HALPORN, ROBERTA JOAN, association executive; b. Bklyn., Sept. 9, 1927; d. Benjamin Margolies and Eva (Ganz) Krugman; m. James Halporn, June, 1951 (div. 1958); 1 child, constance. BA in English, N.Y.U., 1949, MA in Edn., 1951. Tchr. N.Y. Bd. Edn., Queens, 1954-61; area mgr. sales Macmillan Pub. Co., N.Y.C., 1961-63; asst. sales mgr. Riverside Press, N.Y.C., 1963-70; promotion mgr. Health Scis. Pub. Corp., N.Y.C., 1970-74; founder., dir. Ctr. for Thanatology Research and Edn., Inc., Bklyn., 1976—; adj. prof. Bklyn Coll., 1981-84; cons. in field. Author: Lessons From the Dead The Graveyard as Classroom, 1981, An Annotated Hospice Bibliography, How to Create and Manage a Small Thanatology Library, 1988; editor: (with Phyllis Silverman) If You Will Lift Your Load, 1977, Helping Each Other in Widowhood, (with Bruce Danto) So You Want to See a Psychiatrist, 1980, (with Jerome Silverman) The Child/Adolescent and Urban Psychiatric Clinics, 1975, How to Run a Hospice Volunteer Training Program, 1980; exec. editor Thanatology Abstracts, 1986—; contbr. articles to profl. jours.; presenter confs., seminars in field. Sec. Atlantic Ave. Assn., Bklyn., 1985-87. Mem. Am. Library Assn., Med. Library Assn., Pubs. Library Promotion Group (past pres.), Ch. and Synagogue Library Assn., Found. Thanatology, Forum for Death Edn. and Counseling, St. Francis Inst. Counseling, Assn. for Gravestone Studies, Soc. Scholarly Pub., Children's Hospice Internat., Nat. Hospice Assn.

HALSBAND, FRANCES, architect; b. N.Y.C., Oct. 30, 1943; d. Samuel and Ruth H.; B.A., Swarthmore Coll., 1965; M.Arch., Columbia U., 1968; m. Robert Michael Kliment, May 1, 1971; 1 son, Alexander H. Architect with Mitchell/Giurgola Architects, N.Y.C., 1968-72; partner R.M. Kliment & Frances Halsband Architects, N.Y.C., 1972—; vis. critic archtl. design Columbia U., 1975-78, N.C. State U., 1978, Rice U., 1979, U. Va., 1980, Harvard U., 1981, U. Pa., 1981, Columbia U., 1987; mem. N.Y.C. Landmarks Preservation Commn., 1984-87. Projects include: Computer Sci. Bldg., Columbia U., Gilmer Hall addition U. Va., Town Hall, Salisbury Conn., Computer Sci. Bldg., Princeton U.; author: Annotated Bibliography of Technical Resources for Small Museums, 1983. Mem. Archtl. League N.Y. (exec. bd. 1975-81, v.p. arch. 1981-85, pres. 1985—), AIA (exec. bd. N.Y.C. 1979), Alliance Women in Architecture, Am. Assn. Museums, Catskill Center for Conservation and Devel., Gallery Assn. N.Y. State. Office: 255 W 26th St New York NY 10001

HALSTEAD, CAROL POPE, public relations executive; b. Norwich, Conn., June 18, 1941; d. Charles Stoddard and Elizabeth (Mersbach) Pope; m. Clark P. Halstead, Nov. 30, 1968, children: Heather Lynn, Hilary Pope. Student, Inst. European Studies, Vienna, Austria, 1962; BA in German, Bucknell U., 1963; MA in Communications Arts, Columbia U., 1972. Info. specialist Fgn. Broadcast Info. Service, Washington and Tokyo, 1964-66; asst. dir. info. services The Coll. Bd., N.Y.C., 1968-71, asst. to pres., 1971-72, dir. pub. info., 1972-79, exec. dir. pub. affairs, 1979-80; pres. Coll. Connections, N.Y.C., 1980—. Author: (with others) Assessing the Performance of the Public Relations Office, 1984. Mem. adv. com., bd. trustees Ind. Coll. Fund of N.Y., 1985—; mem. dean's alumni council Bucknell U., Lewisburg, Pa., 1979—, bd. trustees, 1983-88. Recipient Clio award Am. TV and Radio Commls. Festival, 1972, Internat. Broadcasting award Hollywood (Calif.) Radio and TV Soc., 1977, Bronze award Internat. Film and TV Festival, 1977, Andy award Advt. Club of N.Y., 1978. Mem. Pub. Relations Soc. Am., Council for the Advancement and Support of Edn., Edn. Writers Assn. Club: Publicity of N.Y. Home and Office: Coll Connections 329 E 82d St New York NY 10028

HALTERMAN, CAROLYN, records management consultant; b. Spring Grove, Minn., Sept. 2, 1943; d. Gilman Martin and Helen Charlotta (Solie) Storlie; m. C.D. Halterman III, Dec. 11, 1964 (div. Nov. 1971); children: Helen Marie, Karen Louise, Carole Lynn. BA cum laude, U. Minn., 1974. Cert. records mgr. Program coordinator Heritage Prodns.: Sons of Norway Internat., Mpls., 1975-76; office mgr. regional environ. impact study N.D. Natural Resources Council, Bismarck, 1976-78; adminstrv. officer N.D. Land Dept., Bismarck, 1979-84, profl. devel. supr., 1985-86; records mgmt. cons. Author bio entries in Dictionary of Scandinavian History, 1986; compiler, editor, illustrator Cookbook: A Collection of Recipes, 1978; designer doll costume State Bank of Burleigh County and Dress-A-Doll Program (1st Nationality and Grand Prize 1980), petitpoint reprodn. Our Lady of Vladimir (1st place 1983). Coordinator Marine Corps League, Bismarck, 1978-80; hosp. vol. St. Alexius Med. Ctr., Bismarck, 1981-84; on air host vol. KCND Prairie Pub. Radio, Bismarck, 1982-83; mem., sec. Bismarck-Mandan Civic Chorus, Bismarck, 1981-86. Served with USMC, 1964-65. Mem. Assn. Records Mgrs. and Adminstrs., Inst. Cert. Records Mgrs. Democrat. Lutheran. Home: 1721 Exuma Dr Saint Louis MO 63136-1815

HALVERSON, CATHERINE VIRGINIA, production supervisor; b. LeMars, Iowa, Dec. 26, 1945; d. Leonard Allen and Doris Kathleen (Dickman) Brooks; m. Richard Francis McGee, Sept. 21, 1974 (div. 1978); 1 child, Chad Richard McGee; m. Dale Elliot Halverson, Apr. 5, 1985. B.S., U. No. Iowa, 1969, M.Ed., 1972. Mgmt. trainee Sears, Roebuck & Co., Waterloo, Iowa, 1969-71; dept. mgr. Montgomery Ward Co., Cedar Falls, Iowa, 1972-74; chem. analyst John Deere, Waterloo, 1974-78, prodn. supr., 1978—. Mem. Nat. Assn. Female Execs. Republican. Lutheran. Avocations: golf; aerobics. Home: 1525 W 3d St Waterloo IA 50701 Office: John Deere Component Works 400 Westfield Waterloo IA 50702

HALVORSEN, SUSAN MARIE, accountant; b. Chgo., Mar. 30, 1955; d. George Walter and Evelyn Irene (Wodzin) H. AA, Moraine Valley Community Coll., 1974; BA, Gov.'s State U., 1976; MBA, Lewis U., Romeoville, Ill., 1982. CPA, Fla. Specialist stats. Nat. Tea Co., Rosemont, Ill., 1971-77; supr. warehouse Carson Pirie Scott and Co., Chgo., 1977-78; asst. v.p., controller Fasano Pie Co., Chgo., 1978-83; controller ctr. Distron, div. Burger King, Lakeland, Fla., 1983—. Pres. St. Anthony Parish Council, Lakeland, 1986-89. Mem. Nat. Assn. Female Execs. Office: Distron div Burger King 5300 Great Oak Dr Lakeland FL 33801

HALVORSON, DEBORA ANNE, actuary, consultant; b. Omaha, Jan. 16, 1951; d. Gordon Allen and Carolyn Ann (Visek) Johnston; m. Robert Jon Halvorson, Nov. 29, 1975. Student Stephens Coll., 1969-70; B.A., Gustavus Adolphus Coll., 1973. Actuary, Delta Dental Plan Minn., Mpls., 1974—, asst. v.p., 1984-87, v.p., 1987—; Chmn., Mpls. Aquatennial, 1979; bd. dirs. Shoreline Early Childhood Devel. Ctr., St. John's Early Childhood Edn. Ctr. Mem. Am. Acad. Actuaries (recognition award), Delta Dental Plans Assn. (chmn. nat. actuarial com 1982—). Republican. Lutheran. Home: 26170 Birch Bluff Rd Shorewood MN 55331 Office: Delta Dental Plan Minn 7807 Creekridge Circle Minneapolis MN 55440

HAM, DEBORAH E., nursing supervisor; b. Phila., Mar. 14, 1955; d. William Josesph and Flora (Gruby) H. Degree in nursing, St. Agnes Med. Ctr. Sch. Nursing, 1977. RN, cert. hemodialysis nurse and in critical care nursing. Head nurse ICU Nazareth Hosp., Phila., 1980, acute hemodialysis coordinator, 1980-84; renal nurse mgr. Abington (Pa.) Meml. Hosp., 1984-85, nurse mgr. critical care unit, 1985—.

HAMADA, RENEÉ MERELYN, psychologist; b. N.Y.C., June 2, 1948; d. Carl A. and Hilda (Reichman) H.; m. David A. Adler, Apr. 10, 1947; children: Michael, Edward. BA, Queens Coll., 1970; MS in Edn., CCNY, 1971; MA, Tchrs. Coll., N.Y.C., 1983; PhD, Columbia U., 1986. Lic. psychologist, N.Y. Research asst. Office Edn. Research CCNY, N.Y.C., 1971-72; sch. psychologist Bethpage Pub. Schs., L.I., N.Y., 1972-75, Island Trees Pub. Schs., L.I., 1975-80, Hewlett-Woodmere Pub. Schs., L.I., 1984-86, Long Beach City Sch. Dist., L.I., 1986—; teaching asst. Tchrs. Coll., N.Y.C., 1981-82. NIMH fellow, 1980-82; recipient Ted Bernstein Meml. award N.Y. State Sch. Psychologists, 1986. Mem. Am. Psychol. Assn., N.Y. State Psychol. Assn., Nassau City Psychol. Assn., Phi Beta Kappa, Kappa Delta Pi. Democrat. Jewish. Office: Long Beach City Sch Dist Neptune Blvd Long Beach NY 11561

HAMAN, SHIRLEY ANN, retail executive; b. Detroit, Sept. 11, 1921; d. William Harold and Grace Elizabeth (Hall) Tucker; student Wayne U., 1940-43; m. Edward A. Haman, Sept. 1, 1943 (dec.); children—Edward A., Ann Elizabeth. Account and bus. mgr., Mitchell Buick Sales, Mt. Clemens, Mich., 1945-53, sec.-treas., bus. mgr., 1973—. Mem. City Planning Commn., Mt. Clemens, Base Community Council. Roman Catholic. Home: 1212 Burlington Dr Mount Clemens MI 48043 Office: 165 N Gratiot Ave Mount Clemens MI 48043

HAMANN WOLFE, MARCIA JOANNE, environmental scientist; b. Seattle, July 25, 1945; d. Donald Woodrow and Jane Geraldine (Lind) Hamann; m. Gary John Wolfe, Apr. 8, 1972 (div. 1979); m. Richard L. Winegar, Mar. 15, 1986; stepchildren: Todd, Andrew. BS, U. Puget Sound, 1968; MS, Wash. State U., 1972; postgrad., Colo. State U., 1978-79. Ranger U.S. Nat. Park Service, Longmire, Wash., 1970-72; naturalist Pennzoil-Vermejo Park Ranch, Raton, N.Mex., 1974-78; reclamation engr. Kaiser Steel Corp., Raton, N.Mex., 1978-85; habitat restoration specialist EG&G Energy Measurements, Tupman, Calif., 1985; wildlife mgmt., reclamation specialist Bechtel Petroleum Ops. Inc., Tupman, 1986—; cons., speaker in field. Contbr. articles to profl. jours. and chpt. in book. Mgr. Raton Little League Baseball Team, 1983. NSF Grantee, 1970. Mem. Am. Soc. Surface Mining and Reclamation (pub. com. 1985), Ecol. Soc. Am., Wildlife Soc., Soil Conservation Soc. Am. (Cert. of Merit 1987), NW Sci. Assn., Internat. Erosion Control Assn., Bakersfield Bus. and Profl. Women (2d v.p. 1987, pres.-elect 1988—), Gamma Phi Beta (treas. 1967). Republican. Methodist. Home: 7600 Las Cruces Bakersfield CA 93309-2215 Office: Bechtel Petroleum Ops Inc PO box 127 Hwy 119 Tupman CA 92376

HAMBURG, BEATRIX ANN, medical educator and researcher; b. Jacksonville, Fla., Oct. 19, 1923; d. Francis Minor and Beatrix (Downs) McCleary; married, May 25, 1951; children: Eric N., Margaret A. A.B., Vassar Coll., 1944; M.D., Yale U., 1948. Diplomate: Nat. Bd. Med. Examiners. Intern Grace-New Haven Hosp., 1948-49; resident Yale Psychiat. Inst., New Haven, 1949-50; resident in pediatrics Children's Hosp., Cin., 1950-51; resident in psychiatry Inst. Juvenile Research, 1951-53; research assoc. Stanford U. Med. Sch. (Calif.), 1961-71, assoc. prof. psychiatry, 1976-80; assoc. prof. Harvard Med. Sch., Boston, 1980-83; exec. dir. Div. Health Policy Research, 1981-83; prof. psychiatry and pediatrics Mt. Sinai Med. Sch., N.Y.C., 1983—, dir. div. child and adolescent psychiatry; assoc. dir. Lab. of Stress and Conflict, Stanford U. Med. Sch., 1974-76; sr. research psychiatrist NIMH, Bethesda, Md., 1978-80; dir. studies Pres.'s Commn. Mental Health, 1977-78; mem. vis. com. Sch. Pub. Health, Harvard U., 1977-80, commn. on behavior and soc., Nat. Acad. Scis., 1983—. Author: Behavioral and Psychosocial Issues in Diabetes, 1980, School Age Pregnancy and Parenthood, 1986; contbr. numerous sci. articles to profl. jours. Trustee W.T. Grant Found., 1978—; bd. dirs. New World Found., 1978-83, Bush Found., Greenwall, Fla., 1986—; mem. Pub. Health Council State of N.Y., 1978-80. Vis. scholar Ctr. Advanced Study Behavioral Scis., 1967-68; recipient Outstanding Achievement award Alcohol, Drug Abuse and Mental Health Adminstrn., 1980. Fellow Am. Acad. Child Psychiatry; mem. AAAS (bd. dirs. 1987—), Inst. of Medicine of Nat. Acad. Scis., Soc. Profs. Child Psychiatry (program com. 1972-74), Am. Acad. Child Psychiatry (adolescent com. 1977-81), Soc. Adolesent Medicine, Am. Pub. Health Assn. (adolescent com. 1978-80), Soc. Study of Social Biology, Acad. Research in Behavioral Medicine (exec. council 1980), Phi Beta Kappa. Office: Mount Sinai Med Ctr One Gustave L Levy Pl New York NY 10029

HAMBURGER, MARY ANN, management consultant; b. Newark, Aug. 25, 1939; d. Herman and Sylvia (Strauss) Marcus; div. June 1966; children: Bruce David, Marc Laurence. AA, U. Bridgeport (Conn.), 1960. Office mgr. Millburn, N.J., 1970-84; med. mgmt. cons. Maplewood, N.J., 1984—; tchr. adult edn. South Orange Maplewood Bd. Edn., 1975-83; cons. Wellcare of N.Y.; profl. physician recruiter, N.Y., N.J. Democrat. Jewish. Home: 74 Hudson Ave Maplewood NJ 07040

HAMBY, CATHY YAWN, insurance company executive; b. Greensboro, N.C., Apr. 23, 1953; d. Myron Cornell and Lizzie Viola (Jackson) Yawn; m. John Wesley Hamby Jr., Dec. 13, 1980; children: John III, Megan. BA, Newberry Coll., 1974; postgrad., U. S.C., 1975-77. Examiner Seibels, Bruce Ins. Co., Columbia, S.C., 1974-75; adjuster Underwriters Adjusting Co., Columbia, 1975-78, James C. Greene Co., Columbia, 1978-80; benefits assoc. Nassau AT&T, Gaston, S.C., 1980-81; asst. v.p. Seibels, Bruce Ins. Co., Columbia, 1981—. Mem. Cola Assn. of Ins. Women (editor bulletin, 1979-81), Claims Assn., Claims Mgrs. Assn., Epsilon Sigma Alpha (sec., treas. 1983-84). Republican. Methodist. Club: Toastmasters (pres. 1984-85). Home: 6517 Crossfield Rd Columbia SC 29206 Office: Seibels Bruce Ins Co 1501 Lady St Columbia SC 29210

HAMBY, JEANNETTE, state legislator; b. Virginia, Minn., Mar. 15, 1933; d. John W. and Lydia M. (Soderholm) Johnson; m. Eugene Hamby, 1957; children—Taryn Rene, Tenya Ramine. BS, U. Minn., 1956; MS, U. Oreg., 1968, PhD, 1976. Vice chmn. Hillsboro High Sch. Dist. Bd., 1973-81; mem. Washington County Juvenile Services Com., 1980—; mem. suggested legis. com. Council State Govts., 1981—, Oreg. state rep., 1981-83; mem. Oreg. State Senate from 5th dist., 1983—. Mem. Oreg. Mental Health Assn., Am. Nurses Assn., Oreg. Nurses Assn., Am. Vocat. Assn., Oreg. Vocat. Assn., Oreg. Vocat./Career Adminstrs., Phi Kappa Phi, Phi Delta Kappa. Lutheran. Republican. Office: Oreg State Capitol Bldg Salem OR 97310 Home: 952 Jackson School Rd Hillsboro OR 97123 *

HAMED, MARTHA ELLEN, government administrator; b. Washington, Jan. 14, 1950; d. Rockford Norris and Dorothy Hope (Lough) H. Student George Washington U., 1972-87, AA, 1985, BA in Psychology, 1988.

Command fed. women's program mgr. U.S. Atlantic Fleet, Norfolk, Va., 1978-79; fed. women's program mgr. Naval Ordnance Sta., Indian Head, Md., 1979-80; personnel mgr., EEO course dir. Naval Civilian Personnel Command, Arlington, Va., 1980-83; dep. EEO officer, site mgr. Ship Research and Devel. Ctr., Bethesda, Md., 1983-85, Naval Surface Weapons Ctr., Silver Spring, Md., 1985; command fed. women's program mgr. Naval Sea Systems Command, Washington, 1985-87, mgr. command tng. programs, 1987—. Recipient Sustained Superior Performance award Naval Civilian Personnel Command, 1982, Spl. Achievement award, 1983, Sustained Superior Performance award Naval Surface Weapons Ctr., 1985, Performance Mgmt. award Naval Sea Systems, 1986, 87; named to Outstanding Young Women Am., U.S. Jaycees, 1983. Mem. Federally Employed Women (chpt. pres. 1977-78, 79, registration chairperson nat. tng. program 1980), NOW, Nat. Assn. Female Execs. Democrat. Episcopalian. Avocations: geology, cats, salt-water fishing. Office: Naval Sea Systems Command 90DT Washington DC 20362

HAMEISTER, LAVON LOUETTA, farm manager, social worker; b. Blairstown, Iowa, Nov. 27, 1922; d. George Frederick and Bertha (Anderson) Hameister; B.A., U. Iowa, 1944; postgrad. N.Y. Sch. Social Work, Columbia, 1945-46, U. Minn. Sch. Social Work, summer 1952; M.A., U. Chgo., 1959. Child welfare practitioner Fayette County Dept. Social Welfare, West Union, Iowa, 1946-56; dist. cons. services in child welfare and pub. assistance Iowa Dept. Social Welfare, Des Moines, 1956-58, dist. field rep., 1959-64, regional supr., 1964-65, supr., specialist supervision, adminstrn. Bur. Staff Devel., 1965-66, chief Bur. Staff Devel., 1966-68; chief div. staff devel. and tng. Office Dep. Commr., Iowa Dept. Social Services, 1968-72, asst. dir. Office Staff Devel., 1972-79, coordinator continuing edn., 1979-86; now co-mgr. Hameister Farm, Blairstown, Iowa. Active in drive to remodel, enlarge Oelwein (Iowa) Mercy Hosp., 1952. Mem. Bus. and Profl. Women's Club (chpt. sec. 1950-52), Am. Assn. U. Women, Nat. Assn. Social Workers (chpt. sec.-elect 1958-59), Am. Pub. Welfare Assn., Iowa Welfare Assn., Acad. Cert. Social Workers. Lutheran. Home: 1800 Grand Ave West Des Moines IA 50265

HAMEL, JANE SEEGER, national seminar corporation executive; b. Winona, Minn., June 12, 1939; d. John Dunning and Dorothea Luse (Seeger) Tearse; m. Arthur Bernard Hamel, Jan. 30, 1965; children—John, James. B.S., Northwestern U., 1961. Tchr. kindergarten Jefferson Union Sch. Dist., Sunnyvale, Calif., 1961-62; tchr. kindergarten S. San Francisco Unified Sch. Dist., 1962-66; owner Sahara Motel & Pizza Inn, Modesto, Calif., 1966-72, Rumah Corp., San Jose, Calif., 1972—; owner, corp. officer Business Mktg. Corp., San Jose, Calif., 1975-82, pres., 1982—; Nat. Business Mktg. Corp., San Jose, 1981—. Editor: The Institute Business Newsletter, 1976-79; assoc. editor Arthur Hamel Business Report, 1980-87 ; owner, corp. officer, sec., bd. dirs. Glassware Internat. Inc., San Francisco. Bd. dirs., chmn. health welfare Foothill Family Faculty Club, Saratoga, Calif., 1979-80. Mem. Inst. Cert. Bus. Counselors (past sec.). Republican. Episcopalian. Office: Bus Mktg Corp 1777 Saratoga Ave Suite 107 San Jose CA 95129

HAMEL, JUDITH ANNE, social worker; b. Boston, Sept. 10, 1954; d. Harvey Harding and Myrtle Elaine (Goldberg) H.; B.Social Work, N. Tex. State U., Denton, 1977; m. Jeffrey A. Kaufman, Sept. 5, 1982; 1 child, Jared Hamel. From psychiat. counseling asst. to intensive psychiat. counselor Brookhaven Med. Center, Dallas, 1977-79; social worker, then dir. rehab. services Avodah Work Center, Dallas, 1979-82; child protective services worker Dallas County Child Welfare, Tex. Dept. Human Services, 1983-86. Mem. Nat. Assn. Social Workers, Assn. Jewish Vocat. Service Profls., Sigma Alpha Mu. Jewish. Club: B'nai B'rith (life). Home: 3815 Furneaux Carrollton TX 75007

HAMEL, MARILYN, screen writer, consultant; b. Toronto, Ont., Can., Mar. 28, 1942; d. John and Sally (Nodelman) S.; m. Alan Hamel, Oct. 9, 1960 (div. 1972); children: Leslie, Stephen. BFA, Ont. Coll. Art, 1961. Fashion illustrator J.C. Hudsons, T. Eaton Co., other advt. agys., Detroit, Toronto, 1961-68; ind. toy developer Milton Bradley, Ideal, Mattel, Kenner, various, 1972-84; screen writer Shadowdance, Inc., Los Angeles, 1984—; ind. gen. product developer, 1975-86; cons. toy devel. Gen. Mills mktg. and design Kenner Toys, Los Angeles, N.Y., Cin., 1983—; writer women's self help Delecorte & Dell Pub., N.Y.C., 1984—. Author: Painless Guides to Instant Happiness (4 books) 1982, Sex Etiquette 1984, 2 edit. 1986; exhibitions include McCaffrey Gallery, Los Angeles, 1968-72; TV guest appearances include various periodicals, 1984—. Mem. Am. Fed. Radio and TV Artists.

HAMEL, RHONDA DENNIS, accountant, insurance executive; b. Hobbs, N.Mex., Sept. 17, 1956; d. Jerry L. and Eva Gayle (Griffin) Dennis; m. Jon E. Hamel; children: Jonna Caryn, Jenna Gayle. A in Acctg., Tyler (Tex.) Jr. Coll., 1976; BBA in Acctg., Midwestern State U., 1978; postgrad., U. Dallas-Irving, 1982-83, 87. Asst. mgr. AV&S div. Equifax, Dallas, 1978-83; acct. Accountemps div. Robert Half Co., Dallas, 1983, Hamel Acctg., Dallas, 1983; ptnr., ins. auditor J and R Enterprises, Dallas, 1983—; v.p. sales Hamel, Watkins and Co., Little Rock, 1985—. Mem. East Tex. State Orch., Tyler, 1975-76, com. Preston Green Homeowners Assn., Dallas, 1985-87; pres. Mothers of Preschoolers Group, Dallas, 1986—. Mem. S.W. Ins. Auditors Assn. (sec. 1988), Nat. Assn. Female Execs., Premium Audit Adv. Service. Office: J and R Enterprises PO Box 795006 Dallas TX 75379

HAMEL, VERONICA, actress; b. Phila., Nov. 20, 1943. Student, Temple U. Model 10 yrs. First stage role in The Big Knife, off-Broadway; appeared with road company in Cactus Flower; appeared in TV miniseries 79 Park Avenue, 1977, Jacqueline Susann's Valley of the Dolls, 1981, Kane and Abel, 1985; star TV series Hill Street Blues, 1981-87 (Emmy nomination 1981, 82, 83); TV movies include The Gathering, 1977, Ski Lift to Death, 1978, The Gathering, Part II, 1979, The Hustler of Muscle Beach, 1980, Sessions, 1983; films include Cannonball, 1976, Beyond the Poseidon Adventure, 1979, When Time Ran Out, 1980, A New Life, 1988; appeared on stage in The Miracle Worker, St. Louis, 1982. Office: care MTM Enterprises 4024 Radford Ave Studio City CA 91604 *

HAMEL, VICKI OTTO, retirement services officer; b. Chgo., May 25, 1947; d. Earle W. and Paula Mae (Holman) Otto; m. Francis H. Hamel, July 7, 1969. Student Western Ill. U., 1965-66, Berlitz Sch. Langs., 1967, U. N.C., Wilmington, 1984-85, Brunswick Tech. Coll., N.C., 1986. Office mgr. Admiral Coated Products, Inc., Skokie, Ill., 1966-69; paralegal law firm, Southport, N.C., 1972-74; credit mgr. Augusta Furniture Co., Staunton, Va., 1976-78; trust/tax clk. Franklin-Lamoille Bank, St. Albans, Vt., 1978-80; customs teller U.S. Customs Service, St. Albans, 1980-82; mgmt. analyst Dept. Army, Mil. Ocean Terminal, Southport, 1982-86, retirement services officer, Ft. McCoy, Wis., 1987, fed. women's program mgr., 1983-86. Mem. Boiling Spring Lakes Planning Bd., 1985-86. Named Woman of Yr., Southport Jr. Women's Club, 1975; recipient profl. awards U.S. Govt. Mem. Gen. Fedn. Women's Clubs, N.C. Fedn. Women's Clubs (dist. v.p. 1974-75), Am. Soc. Profl. and Exec. Women, Am. Bus. Women's Assn., Nat. Assn. Female Execs. Republican. Roman Catholic. Clubs: Southport Jr. Women's (pres. 1975), Southport Women's (pub. affairs dept. 1984). Home: 1310 North St Sparta WI 54656 Office: Fort McCoy WI 54656-5000

HAMELINK, CRYSTAL MARY, human resources executive; b. Little Falls, N.Y., Dec. 6, 1947; d. Harold J. and Marian Louise (Hood) Settle; m. Drew R. Hamelink, Aug. 4, 1973; children—Craig A., Michael M. B.A., Wagner Coll., 1969; M.P.A., SUNY-Albany, 1984. Dir. employee advancement program N.Y. State Dept. Civil Service, Albany, 1984-87, dir. external program services div., 1988— . Treas., emergency med. technician Ballston Lake Emergency Squad, Ballston Lake, N.Y., 1979—. Mem. Internat. Personnel Mgmt. Assn., Pi Alpha Alpha. Unitarian. Home: 122 Westside Dr Ballston Lake NY 12019 Office: NY State Dept Civil Service Bldg 1 State Office Bldg C ampus Albany NY 12239

HAMILL, JUDITH ELLEN, municipal administration administrator; b. Chgo., Mar. 8, 1953; d. William Patrick and Dolores Jean (Lhamon) H. MusB, Roosevelt U., 1975; M of Urban Planning and Policy, U. Ill., Chgo., 1979; M of Pub. Adminstrn., Harvard U., 1982. Staff asst. Thomas H. Miner & Assocs., Chgo., 1972-75; project dir. Chgo. Council on Fine Arts, 1977-78; project planning city of Chgo. Dept. Planning, 1978-81; research staff Stevenson/Stern for Ill., Chgo., 1982; ind. cons. Chgo., 1982-86; city planner Dept. Aviation, Chgo., 1986-87; dir. noise abatement office Dept. of Aviation, Chgo., 1987—. Vice chairperson Ill. Women's Polit. Caucus, Chgo., 1975-82; active Women in Govt. Relations, Chgo., 1977-82, Ill. Dem. Women, Springfield, Ill., 1981—, Cook County Dem. Women, Chgo., 1982—; mem. jr. governing bd. Chgo. Symphony Orch., 1981—. Harvard U. Scholar, Cambridge, Mass., 1981-82. Club: Harvard of Chgo. Home: 1847 W Touhy Ave Chicago IL 60626

HAMILTON, ANN STANLEY, marketing executive; b. Phila., Mar. 25, 1960; d. Russell and Helen Marcia (Brown) H. B.A. in Psychology, Temple U., 1982. Customer service rep. Continental Bank, Phila., 1977-82; mgr. pub. div. Hay Assocs., Phila., 1983-84; pres. Hamilton Assocs. mktg. cons., Phila., 1985—. Rep. Senatorial Inner Circle, Washington, 1986. Mem. Alliance Française de Philadelphie, Christian Endeavor, Nat. Assn. Female Execs. Republican. Presbyterian. Avocations: travel; reading; foreign cultures and languages.

HAMILTON, BARBARA, human services director; b. Hartford, Conn., Jan. 3, 1943; d. Harry and Rose Ida (Cohen) Karpman; m. Benjamin Theodore Sporn, Sept. 4, 1960 (div. 1967); children: Mindy Rebecca Sporn, Sarah Ann Sporn. BA, Eckerd Coll., 1983; MA, Norwich U., Vt., 1985. Asst. publicity mgr. Estee Lauder Inc., N.Y.C., 1972-74; owner, ptnr. Strongstarr Inc., N.Y.C., 1975-77; owner Barbara Hamilton Cons. Services, N.Y.C., 1977-81; co-founder The Life Ctr., Tampa, 1981-83; co-founder, co-dir. Project Rainbow, St. Petersburg, Fla., 1983-87; dir. project Rainbow Cons. Services, Inc., 1987—; mem. adv. bd. Suncoast Children's Dream Fund, St. Petersburg, 1986—; cons. Cancer/Clergy Residency, St. Petersburg, 1983-87. Mem. Eckerd Coll. Alumni Bd. Recipient Service to Mankind awards Sertoma Club, 1984-85. Mem. Assn. Care Children's Health, Forum Death Edn. and Counseling, Internat. Imagery Assn., Nat. Soc. Fund Raising Execs., Assn. Humanistic Psychology, Eckerd Coll. Alumni Bd. Avocations: meditation, crystals, holistic health. Home: 7529 1/2 3rd Ave N Saint Petersburg FL 33710

HAMILTON, BARBARA KADISH, auditor, lawyer, educator; b. Kingston, Pa., July 9, 1941; d. Albert Thomas and Sophie Pauline (Putro) Kadish; m. Thomas Harold Hamilton, Arp. 4, 1959; 1 child, Thomas Albert. BS in Mgmt., Widener U., 1973, MBA, 1977; JD, Del. Law Sch., 1980. Bar: Pa. 1980, U.S. Dist. Ct. Pa. 1980, U.S. Supreme Ct. 1984. Contract adminstr. Boeing-Vertol Co., Phila., 1976-78, adminstr. product support dept., 1978-85; sole practice Media, Pa., 1981—; internal auditor Boeing-Vertol Co., Phila., 1986-88; assoc. Law Offices of Jonathan DeYoung, King of Prussia, Pa., 1988—; prof. Del. County Community Coll., Media, 1985—, Pa. State U., Lima, 1985, Widener U., Chester, Pa., 1987—. Contbr. articles to profl. jours. Bd. dirs. Selective Service System, Del. County, Pa., 1981-87; bd. mgrs. Widener U. Alumni Assn., 1982-87. Mem. Pa. State Bar Assn., Del. County Bar Assn. (legal jours. com. 1981-88), Boeing Mgmt. Assn. (v.p. 1984-86). Republican. Roman Catholic. Home: 26 Dundee Mews Media PA 19063 Office: Law Offices of Jonathan DeYoung 144 E DeKalb Pike King of Prussia PA 19406

HAMILTON, BEVERLY LANNQUIST, investment company executive; b. Roxbury, Mass., Oct. 19, 1946; d. Arthur and Nancy L. B.A. cum laude, U. Mich., 1968; postgrad., Grad. Sch. Bus., NYU, 1969-70. Prin. Auerbach, Pollak & Richardson, N.Y.C., 1972-75; v.p. Morgan Stanley & Co., N.Y.C., 1975-80, United Technologies, Hartford, Conn., 1980-87; dep. comptroller City of N.Y., 1987—; bd. dirs. Conn. Natural Gas Co., Northeast Savs., Conn. Mut. Investment Mgmt., TWA Pilots Annuity Fund, Nat. Conf. Christians and Jews. Trustee Hartford Coll. for Women, 1981-87; bd. dirs. Inst. for Living, 1983-87. Mem. Fin. Women's Assn., Hartford C. of C. (bd. dirs.). Clubs: Hartford, Economic of N.Y. Office: City of NY Mcpl Bldg 1 Center St New York NY 10007

HAMILTON, DAGMAR STRANDBERG, lawyer, educator; b. Phila., Jan. 10, 1932; d. Eric Wilhelm and Anna Elizabeth (Sjöström) Strandberg; A.B., Swarthmore Coll., 1953; J.D., U. Chgo. Law Sch., 1956; J.D., Am. U., 1961; m. Robert W. Hamilton, June 26, 1953; children—Eric Clark, Robert Andrew Hale, Meredith Hope. Admitted to Tex. bar, 1972; atty., civil rights div. U.S. Dept. Justice, Washington, 1965-66; asst. instr. govt. U. Tex.-Austin, 1966-71; lectr. Law Sch. U. Ariz., Tucson, 1971-72; editor, researcher Assoc. Justice William O. Douglas, U.S. Supreme Ct., 1962-73, 75-76; editor, research Douglas autobiography Random House Co., 1972-73; staff counsel Judiciary Com., U.S. Ho. of Reps., 1973-74; asst. prof. L.B. Johnson Sch. Pub. Affairs, U. Tex., Austin, 1974-77, assoc. prof., 1977-83, prof., 1983—, assoc. dean, 1983-87; vis. prof. Washington U. Law Sch., St. Louis, 1982; vis. fellow Univ. London, 1987-88. Mem. Tex. Bar Assn., Am. Law Inst., Assn. Pub. Policy Analysis and Mgmt. (mem. policy council), Kappa Beta Phi (hon.), Phi Kappa Phi (hon.). Democrat. Quaker. Contbr. to various publs. Home: 403 Allegro Ln Austin TX 78746 Office: U Tex LBJ Sch Pub Affairs Austin TX 78712

HAMILTON, DEBORAH A., broadcast journalist, public relations consultant; b. Bryn Mawr, Pa., May 7, 1949; d. Perrin C. and Bette Jane H.; m. James K. Brengle, June 6, 1970; children: Stephen Carpenter, Alexander Preston. Student Mary Baldwin Coll., Staunton, Va., 1967-69; B.S. in Polit. Sci., U. Santa Clara (Calif.), 1972. Talk radio producer Sta. KQED-FM, San Francisco, 1975; news reporter Nat. Pub. Radio, San Francisco, 1975-76, reporter, documentary producer, Washington, 1976-78; dir. pub. affairs and relations, producer, host Inside Phila., Stas. WPEN-AM and WMGK-FM, Phila., 1979-85; pres. Performance Plus, Haverford, Pa., 1982—. Bd. mgrs., chmn. pub. relations Jr. League Phila., 1979-81. Mem. Pub. Relations Soc. Am., Am. Women Radio and TV (bd. dirs. Phila. chpt. 1984-87, treas. 1985, pres. elect 1988-89), Women in Communications, Nat. Soc. Colonial Dames, Sigma Delta Chi (bd. dirs. local chpt.). Office: Performance Plus Box 65 Haverford PA 19041

HAMILTON, GIOVANNA MARIA, hospital executive; b. Sequals, Udine, Italy, June 5, 1947; came to U.S., 1949; d. Primo and Giuseppina Pina (Kovacic) Carnera; m. Philip Barry Alderson, Feb. 8, 1966 (dec. 1976); children: Anne Marie, Karl Umberto; m. Virgil Joseph Hamilton, Aug. 19, 1983. BA, UCLA, 1969; Laureata, Educadato Uccellis, Italy, 1965; postgrad., Sangamon State U., Springfield, Ill. Cert. alcoholism counselor. Adminstrv. asst. Glendale Fed. Savs., Los Angeles, 1976-78, Sitmar Cruises, Los Angeles, 1978-80; internat. relations specialist Bernardin SpA, Milan, 1980-82; employee assistance program specialist Sangamon-Menard Alcoholism & Drugs Council, Springfield, Ill., 1982-87, St. John's Hosp., Springfield, 1987—; cons. in field. Contbr. articles to profl. jours. Chmn. Mother's Against Drunk Drivers, Springfield, 1982; bd. dirs. The Parent Place, Springfield, 1988—. Mem. Nat. Assn. Female Execs., Assn. Labor and Mgmt. (cons. on alcoholism), Springfield C. of C. Democrat. Roman Catholic. Home: 1837 Hastings Rd Springfield IL 62702 Office: St John's Hosp 800 E Carpenter St Springfield IL 62729

HAMILTON, JACQUELINE, art consultant; b. Tulsa, Mar. 28, 1942; d. James Merton and Nina Faye (Andrews) H.; m. Richard Sanford Piper, Jan. 2, 1968 (div. June 1976). BA, Tex. Christian U., 1965; postgrad., Stockholm U., 1965-67, Harvard U., 1972-73, Tufts U., 1971, Rice U., 1982-83, Houston Community Coll., 1986-87. Drama tchr. Buckingham Lower Sch., Cambridge, Mass., 1970-71; tchr. creative drama Fayerweather Sch., Cambridge, 1971-72; tchr. art, music Garden Cooperative Nursery, Cambridge, 1971-72; pvt. practice art cons. Houston, 1979—. Active Cultural Arts Council of Houston. Mem. Assn. Corp. Art Curators, Rice Design Alliance, Tex. Arts Alliance, Women's Art Caucus, Art League of Houston, Meml. Bus. Women's Exchange (v.p. 1985), Galleria Bus. and Profl. Women's Club of Houston. Presbyterian. Clubs: Houstonian Breakfast, L'Alliance Française, Swedish. Office: PO Box 1483 Houston TX 77251-1483

HAMILTON, JANE, financial officer; b. Mercer, Mo., Oct. 2, 1952; d. Wayne Earl and Lucy Tressa (Henley) H.; m. Chesda Meak, June 9, 1979 (div. Jan. 1988); 1 child, Tiffany Hamilton. Student, U. Minn., 1972-74, Ames Bus. Sch., 1976. Clk. Bankers Life Ins. Co., Des Moines, Iowa, 1970-71; nursing asst. Iowa Methodist/Younkers Rehab., Des Moines, 1971-72; bookkeeper Tong II Enterprises, N.Y.C., 1976-77, Couristan, Inc., N.Y.C., 1978, Etra, Inc., N.Y.C., 1978-80; treas. Electron Energy Corp., Landisville, Pa., 1980—. Mem. Adminstrv. Mgmt. Soc. Internat. (com. 1985-86, Citation of Contbn. 1986), Adminstrv. Mgmt. Soc. (bd. dirs. 1985-87, 3d v.p. 1987—, editor Lancaster chpt. newsletter 1983-87), Nat. Assn. Female Execs., Am. Mgmt. Assn. Republican. Roman Catholic. Office: Electron Energy Corp 924 Links Ave Landisville PA 17538

HAMILTON, JEAN CONSTANCE, judge; b. St. Louis, Nov. 12, 1945; d. Aubrey Bertrand and Rosemary (Crocker) H. A.B., Wellesley Coll., 1968; J.D., Washington U., St. Louis, 1971; LL.M., Yale U., 1982. Bar: Mo. 1971. Atty. Dept. of Justice, Washington, 1971-73, asst. U.S. atty., St. Louis, 1973-78; atty. Southwestern Bell Telephone Co., St. Louis, 1978-81; judge 22d Jud. Circuit, State of Mo., St. Louis, 1982—. Mem. ABA, Bar Assn. Met. St. Louis, Women Lawyers Assn. Met. St. Louis, Nat. Assn. Women Judges. Episcopalian. Office: 22d Jud Cir Mo 10 N Tucker Blvd Saint Louis MO 63101

HAMILTON, JOYCE KAY, marketing company executive; b. Indpls., Mar. 7, 1950; d. John Samuel and Agnes June (Stribling) McPheeters; m. Gary Roger Hamilton, Aug. 30, 1975 (div. 1981). B.S., U. Tex., 1983; postgrad. SMU, 1987—. Tax payer asst. IRS, Dallas, 1979-80; tech. asst. Dallas Dept. Edn., 1980-81 exec. adminstv. asst. Mass. Mut., Dallas, 1981-82; v.p. Excalibur Mktg., 1983—; mgr. corp. services, Louis G. Reese Inc., Dallas, 1984-85; owner, prin. Creative Visions...Creative Results, Dallas, 1985—; also seminar and workshop leader. Served with USAF, 1974-77. Mem. Nat. Exec. Women's Assn. Republican. Club: Toastmistress.

HAMILTON, JUANITA BOWEN, educator; b. Terre Haute, Ind., Dec. 28, 1947; d. Joseph Arthur and Helen Juanita (Leminger) Bowen; m. Danny D. Hamilton. BS, Ind. State U., 1969; MS, U. Dayton, 1975, postgrad., 1976—; postgrad., Miami (Ohio) U., 1984. cert. elementary tchr., prin., Ohio. Tchr. 3d grade Huber Heights (Ohio) City Schs., 1969-75, tchr. jr. high reading, 1975-76, elem. prin., 1976-79, personnel dir., 1979-82, tchr. first grade, 1982-83, tchr. chpt. 1, 1983—. Active Profl. Coalition Rep. Party, Dayton, 1982-87. Martha Holden Jennings Found. scholar, 1974-75. Mem. Internat. Reading Assn., Ohio Reading Assn., Montgomery County Reading Assn. (treas., v.p. 1975-85). Republican. Prebyterian. Club: Racquet (Dayton). Lodge: Eastern Star.

HAMILTON, JUDITH COURTNEY, nurse, institutional sales person; b. Roanoke, Va., June 14, 1950; d. Carl Cannaday and Mary Lee (Anderson) H.; m. W. Grant Brownrigg, Apr. 28, 1984. BS in Nursing, U. Va., 1972, MBA, 1982. RN, Va. Staff, charge nurse No. Va. Drs. Hosp., Falls Church, 1972; librarian John Hopkins Sch. Internat. Studies, Bologna, Italy, 1974-75; English instr. Politzer Sch. Langs., Bologna, 1975-76; staff, charge nurse Alexandria (Va.) Hosp., 1975, Roanoke (Va.) Meml. Hosp., 1972, 76-77; head nurse intensive care U. Va. Hosp., Charlottesville, 1972, 77-79, staff nurse clinic, 1979-80; mgmt. assoc. Equitable Life Assurance Soc., N.Y.C., 1982-84, product mgr., 1984-86; v.p., instl. account exec. Equitable Real Estate Investment Mgmt., Inc., N.Y.C., 1986—. Baptist. Home: 305 N Mountain Ave Upper Montclair NJ 07043 Office: Equitable Real Estate Investment Mgmt 787 Seventh Ave New York NY 10019

HAMILTON, LAURA ANN, social worker; b. Cordele, Ga., Nov. 16, 1939; d. Herbert Williams and Janie LaVerne (Lumpkin) Hamilton; student Valdosta State Coll., 1957-58; B.S., Fla. State U., 1961, M.S.W., 1965; postgrad. U. Ga., 1961-62, U. Chgo., summer 1967, W. Ga. Coll., 1969, Ga. State U., 1970; postgrad. U. Tex.-Arlington, 1985—; PhD, 1988. Vis. tchr. Crisp County Schs., Cordele, 1961-63; social service worker Social Service Dept., Milledgeville (Ga.) State Hosp., 1963; med. social worker Crippled Children's Service, Birmingham, Ala., 1964; psychiat. social worker Fla. State Hosp., Chattahoochee, 1965, Milledgeville State Hosp., 1965-66; cons. for social work projects ESEA Title I, Ga. Dept. Edn., Atlanta, 1966-68, ESEA Title III, 1968-71; cons. program evaluations and audits Robert Davis Assos., Inc., Atlanta, 1971-72; chief Div. Planning, Evaluation, Monitoring and Analysis, S.C. Dept. Social Services, Columbia, 1973-76; regional dir. social services Regions 01 and 02, Tex. Dept. Public Welfare, Lubbock, 1976-77; partner Kaye Fleming Boutique and Bridal Corner, Ft. Worth, 1978-83; pvt. practice social work, Ft. Worth, Tex., 1978—; dir. Tarrant County Dept. Human Services, Ft. Worth, 1985—; field supr. Kirschner Assos., Inc., Albuquerque, 1972, 73; evaluator for edn. professions devel. act project Waycross (Ga.) City Schs., 1972, W. Ga. Ednl. Service Center, Carrollton, 1972; program auditor Clarke County Schs., Atlanta, 1972; instr. Human Resource Center, U. Tex., Arlington, 1977-79; lectr. in field. Mem. Acad. Cert. Social Workers, Am. Pub. Welfare Assn., Am. Soc. Pub. Adminstrn., Nat. Assn. Social Workers. Address: 1611 Trailridge Dr Arlington TX 76012

HAMILTON, LISA TOMALYNN, lawyer; b. Columbia City, Ind., Apr. 9, 1958; d. Thomas G. and L. Anne (Biddle) Hamilton. B.A., Oberlin Coll., 1979; J.D. cum laude, Ind. U., 1982. Bar: Ind. 1982, U.S. Dist. Ct. (so. dist.) Ind. 1982, U.S. Dist. Ct. (no. dist.) Ind. 1983, U.S. Ct. Appeals (7th cir.) 1985, U.S. Supreme Ct. 1985, Ill. 1988, U.S. Dist. Ct. (no dist.) Ill. 1988. Jud. clk. to justice Ind. Ct. Appeals, Indpls., 1982-83; jud. clk. U.S. Dist. Ct., Ft. Wayne, Ind., 1983-85; assoc. Baker & Daniels & Shoaff, Ft. Wayne, 1985-87, Chapman and Cutler, Chgo., 1987—. Mem. ABA, 7th Cir. Bar Assn., Ind. Bar Assn. Republican.

HAMILTON, MARIAN ELOISE, housing authority official; b. Salt Lake City, Mar. 21, 1931; d. Frederic William and Kathryn Eloise (Core) Wrathall; m. Stanley Keith Hamilton, Feb. 2, 1951 (dec. 1983); children—Edmond Scott, Perri Collette, Deena Kathryn. Student U. Utah, 1949-51, U. Calif.-Santa Barbara, 1951-52, U. Mont., 1952-53. Cert. pub. housing mgr. Field exec. Cross Timbers Girl Scouts, Denton, Tex., 1971-76; camp dir. Camp Kadohadacho, Pottsboro, Tex., 1971-75, acting dir. Wesley Pre-Sch., Denton, 1976-78; field dir. 1st Tex. Council, Campfire, Ft. Worth, 1979-81; housing mgr. Denton Housing Authority, 1981-88, exec. dir., 1988—; cons. on shared housing Tex. Agy. on Aging, Austin, 1984—; area rep. City of Denton Land Use Com., 1986—. Editor Heritage Highlights, 1981—. Mem. Nat. Assn. Housing and Redevel. Ofcls., Am. Assn. Homes for Aging, Nat. Council on Aging, Nat. Trust for Hist. Preservation, Nat. Assn. Female Execs., First Tex. Council of Camp Fire (bd. dirs. SuRaHa), Kimbell Mus. Fine Arts, Ft. Worth Bot. Soc., MedCare Home Services (mem. review com.), Austin Writer's League, Altrusa Internat. Democrat. Avocations: writing; travel; reading. Home: 900 Sierra Dr Denton TX 76201 Office: Denton Housing Authority 308 S Ruddell Denton TX 76205

HAMILTON, MARY RUTH, federal government executive; b. Sharon, Pa., Jan. 29, 1944; d. Edwin Lawrence and Helen Bess (McMillan) H.; m. Irvin L. (Jack) White, May 6, 1978. BA, Bethel Coll., 1966; MA, U. N.C., 1969; PhD, U. Md., 1976. Research asst. Northland Regional Med. Program, St. Paul, 1966-67; research asst. sociology and pub. health depts. U. N.C., Chapel Hill, 1967-69; instr. sociology St. Mary's U., San Antonio, 1969-72, Incarnate Word Coll., San Antonio, 1972-73; research asst. sociology dept. U. Md., College Park, 1973-74; mgr. energy policy dept. BDM Corp., McLean, Va., 1974-79; group dir. and technology U.S. GAO, Washington, 1979-83; asst. regional mgr. U.S. GAO, N.Y.C., 1983-85, regional mgr., 1985—. Contbr. articles to profl. jours. Mem. Nat. Council of Career Women (treas. 1975), Nat. Assn. Exec. Women, Am. Sociologists Assn., Internat. Assn. for Impact Assessment, Intergovtl. Audit Forum, Assn. for Govt. Accts., Am. Soc. Pub. Adminstrs., AAAS (subcom. on univ.-industry relations 1978-79). Home: 25 Tree Top Lane Poughkeepsie NY 12603 Office: US Gen Acctg Office 26 Fed Plaza Rm 4112 New York NY 10278

HAMILTON, NANCY BETH, law company official; b. Lakewood, Ohio, July 22, 1948; d. Edward Douglas and Gloria Jean (Blessing) Familo; m. Thomas Woolman Hamilton, June 10, 1970; children: Susan Elizabeth, Catherine Anne. BA, Denison U., 1970. Cert. secondary edn. tchr., Fla. Tchr. Orange County (Fla.) Bd. Edn., 1970-71; registrar Jones Coll., Orlando, Fla., 1971-72; mgr. service dept. Am. Lawyers Co., Cleve., 1972-79, mgr. data processing dept., 1980—. Trustee, treas. Westshore Montessori Assn., Rocky River, Ohio, 1984—; bd. dirs. Holly Ln. Sch. PTA, Westlake, Ohio, 1988—. Mem. Comml. Law League Am., Alpha Phi (pres. Cleve. Westshore chpt. alumnae 1986-88). Republican. Methodist. Clubs: Westwood Country, Cleve. Yachting (Rocky River). Office: Am Lawyers Co 24441 Detroit Rd Suite 200 Cleveland OH 44145

HAMILTON, NANCY CORINNE MILLER, university publishing executive; b. El Paso, Tex., Aug. 22, 1929; d. Harold Fred and Corinne Miller; m. Ralph Eugene Hamilton, June 15, 1968; stepchildren: James R., Jeannie. BA, U. Tex., El Paso, 1949, MA, 1954. Info. specialist El Paso Pub. Schs., 1959-68; reporter The El Paso Times, 1950-59, El Paso Herald-Post, 1972-76; asst. dir. news service U. Tex., El Paso, 1976-86, assoc. dir. Tex. Western Press, 1986—. Mem. Pub. Relations Soc. Am. (cert.), Western Writers Am. (v.p. 1988—). Democrat. Lutheran. Home: 416 Bedford El Paso TX 79922 Office: U Tex-Tex Western Press El Paso TX 79968-0633

HAMILTON, PAULA HAYDEN, library director; b. Bklyn., Aug. 11, 1946; d. Richard Alfred and Anne Frances (Keating) Hayden; m. Robert Earl Hamilton, Apr. 22, 1972; children—Hayden David, Michael Robert. Student Gonzaga U.-Florence, Italy, 1966-67; B.A., San Francisco Coll. for Women, 1968; M.L.S., U. Wis.-Madison, 1969. Circulation asst. head Northwestern U., Evanston, Ill., 1969-71, reference librarian newspaper and microfilm, 1971-72; reference and cataloging librarian U. Sci. and Tech., Kimasi, Ghana, 1972-73; br. librarian Chgo. Pub. Library, 1973-75; dir. Clackamas County Library, Oregon City, Oreg., 1975-76; dir. Marylhurst Coll. Library, (Oreg.), 1977—, dir. librarian's continuing edn. program Marylhurst Coll., 1980—, instr., 1982—; cons. USIS, Kumasi, 1972-73, Don Barney & Assos., Portland, Oreg., 1983. Author: Computers and Small Libraries: Toward Desktop Libraries, 1987. Campaigner various Democratic campaigns, 1972; eucharistic minister St. Clare Roman Catholic Ch., 1980, co-chmn. parish family life. Mem. ALA, NW Assn. Pvt. Coll. and Univ. Libraries (pres. 1982-83), Oreg. Library Assn. (com. 1980-83), Wash. Library Assn. (joint conf. com. 1985-87), Assn. Coll. and Research Libraries (Oreg. adv. bd. 1983-85), Library and Media Groups of Oreg. Home: 7110 SW Burlingame Ave Portland OR 97219 Office: Marylhurst Coll Shoen Library Marylhurst OR 97036

HAMILTON, PAULETTE LOUISE, computer company executive; b. Kingston, Jamaica, June 19, 1957; came to U.S., 1973; d. Alfred E. Bernard and Joyce Veronica (Small) John; m. Robyn Eugene Hamilton, Apr. 14, 1984. BBA, Baruch Coll., 1980. Account exec. Endorsco, N.Y.C., 1980-82; account adminstr. Select Mailing Lists, N.Y.C., 1982-84; research asst. Prudential Bache Securities, N.Y.C., 1984-85; trainer microcomputer Lehrer McGovern, N.Y.C., 1985-86; pres. Communication Studio, N.Y.C., 1986—. Office: Communication Studio 44 Fifth Ave Suite 203 Brooklyn NY 11217

HAMILTON, RHODA LILLIAN ROSEN, educator; b. Chgo., May 8, 1915; d. Reinhold August and Olga (Peterson) Rosen; grad. Moser Coll., Chgo., 1932-33; B.S. in Edn., U. Wis., 1953, postgrad., 1976; M.A.T., Rollins Coll., 1967; postgrad. Ohio State U., 1959-60; postgrad. in clin. psychology Mich. State U., 1971, 76; postgrad. Yale U., 1972, Loma Linda U., 1972; postgrad. in computer mgmt. systems U. Okla., 1976; postgrad. in edn. U. Calif., Berkeley, 1980; m. Douglas Edward Hamilton, Jan. 23, 1936 (div. Feb. 1952); children: Perry Douglas, John Richard. Exec. sec. to pres. Ansul Chem. Co., Marinette, Wis., 1934-36; personnel counselor Burneice Larson's Med. Bur., Chgo., 1954-56 adminstrv. asst. to Ernst C. Schmidt, Lake Geneva, Wis., 1956-58; asso. prof. fin. aid Ohio State U., 1958-60; tchr. English to speakers of other langs., Istanbul, Turkey, 1960-65; counselor Groveland (Fla.) High Sch., 1965-68; guidance counselor and psychol. cons. early childhood edn. Dept. Def. Overseas Dependents Sch., Okinawa, 1968-85; pres. Hamilton Assocs., Inc., Groveland, Fla., 1985—; co-owner plumbing, heating bus., Marinette, 1943-49; journalist Rockford (Ill.) Morning Star, 1956-58, Istanbul AP, 1960. Vol. instr. U.S. citizenship classes, Okinawa, 1971-72. Mem. Fla. Retired Educators, Nat. Assn. Retired Fed. Employees, Am. Personnel and Guidance Assn., Nat. Vocat. Guidance Assn., Assn. Measurement and Eval. in Guidance, Am. Fedn. Govt. Employees, Nat. Council Measurement in Edn., Am. Sch. Counselor Assn., Phi Delta Gamma. Episcopalian. Clubs: Order Eastern Star (organist Shuri chpt. 1); Ikebana Internat. Author poetry on Middle East, 1959-64; Career Awareness, 1978. Home and Office: 255 E Waldo St Groveland FL 32736

HAMILTON, SHIRLEY SIEKMANN, arts administrator; b. South Bend, Ind., Aug. 31, 1928; d. George F. and Clarice B. (Rapp) Burdick; student St. Mary's Coll., 1946-47; B.A., DePauw U., 1950; postgrad. Ind. U., South Bend, 1951; m. Max R. Siekmann, June 23, 1951; children—Sheryl, Pamela, David; m. Keith L. Hamilton, Sept. 3, 1983. Tchr. public schs., St. Joseph County, Ind., 1950-51, Greencastle, Ind., 1951-52, Ft. Lauderdale, Fla., 1952-53; exec. dir. Michiana Arts and Scis. Council, Inc., South Bend, Ind., 1973-86; tech. asst. cons., adv. panelist Ind. Arts Commn.; treas. Ind. Alliance Arts Councils, 1982. Mem. St. Joseph County Parks and Recreation Bd., 1971-81; pres. Mental Health Assn. of St. Joseph County, 1972; bd. dirs. Century Center Found., South Bend, 1974-88, St. Joseph County Scholarship Found., 1977-82; pres., bd. dirs. United Way St. Joseph County, 1981-82. Recipient Community Service award Michiana Arts and Scis. Council, 1968, Arts award, 1987, Arts Service award, Ind. Assembly of Local Arts Agys., 1987. Mem. Ind. Arts Advs., Ind. Alliance Arts Councils, Nat. Assn. Arts Councils. Club: Jr. League South Bend (pres.). Producer 13 week TV series: Inside Our Schools (Jr. League of South Bend Outstanding Community Service award 1964). Office: 120 S St Joseph St South Bend IN 46601

HAMILTON, SUSAN OWENS, transportation company executive, lawyer; b. Birmingham, Ala., Aug. 7, 1951; d. William Lewis and Vonnette (Wilson) Owens; m. M. Raymond Hamilton, June 8, 1974. BA, Auburn U., 1973; JD, Cumberland/Samford U., 1977. Bar: Ala., Fla. Claim agt. Seaboard System R.R. and predecessor cos., Birmingham, Ala., 1977-78; atty. Seaboard System R.R. and predecessor cos., Louisville, 1978-80, claims atty., 1980-81; asst. gen. atty. Seaboard System R.R. and predecessor cos., Jacksonville, Fla., 1981-83, asst. gen. solicitor, 1983-84, gen. mgr. freight claim services, 1984-85; asst. v.p. casualty prevention Chessie System R.R.'s, Balt. and Jacksonville, 1985-86; asst. v.p. freight damage prevention and claims CSX Transp., Jacksonville, 1986-87, dir. risk mgmt., asst. v.p. adminstrv. services, 1987—. Mem. United Way Allocations Com. Mem. ABA, Jacksonville Bar Assn., Bus. and Profl. Women (pres. Jacksonville chpt. 1984-85), Fla. Bus. and Profl. Women (outstanding young careerwoman 1982). Democrat. United Methodist. Lodge: Uptown Civitan (bd. dirs. Jacksonville club 1982-84). Home: 12154 Hidden Hills Dr Jacksonville FL 32225-1601 Office: 500 Main St Suite 717 Fort Worth TX 76102

HAMILTON, VIRGINIA (MRS. ARNOLD ADOFF), author; b. Yellow Springs, Ohio, Mar. 12, 1936; d. Kenneth James and Etta Belle (Perry) H.; m. Arnold Adoff, Mar. 19, 1960; children: Leigh Hamilton, Jaime Levi. Student, Antioch Coll., 1952-55, Ohio State U., 1957-58, New Sch. for Social Research. Author: children's novels Zeely, 1967 (Nancy Block Meml. award Downtown Community Sch. Awards Com.), The House of Dies Drear, 1968 (Edgar Allan Poe award for best juvenile mystery 1969), The Time-Ago Tales of Jadhu, 1969, Planet of Junior Brown, 1971; W.E.B. Dubois: A Biography, 1972; children's novels Time-Ago Lost: More Tales of Jahdu, 1973, M.C. Higgins the Great (John Newbery medal 1974), 1974 (Nat. Book award 1975), Paul Robeson: The Life and Times of a Free Black Man, 1974, Arilla Sun Down, 1976, Illusion and Reality, 1976, The Justice Cycle: Justice and Her Brothers, 1978, Dustland, 1980, Gathering, 1980, Jahdu, 1980, Sweet Whispers, Brother Rush, 1982 (Boston Globe/Horn Book award 1983), The Magical Adventures of Pretty Pearl, 1984, A Little Love, 1984, Junius Over Far, 1985, The People Could Fly, 1985, The Mystery of Drear House, 1987, A White Romance, 1987; editor: Writings of W.E.B. Dubois, 1975. Recipient Ohioana Lit. award, 1969, 84, Ohioana Lit. award for body of work, 1981, Coretta Scott King award for Fiction, 1980, 85. Address: Box 293 Yellow Springs OH 45387

HAMILTON, VIRGINIA VAN DER VEER, historian, educator; b. Kansas City, Mo., Sept. 7, 1921; d. McClellan and Dorothy (Rainold) Van der Veer; A.B., Birmingham (Ala.)-So. Coll., 1941, M.A. (Ford Found. Fund for Adult Edn. fellow), 1961; Ph.D., U. Ala., Tuscaloosa, 1968; m. Lowell S. Hamilton, Aug. 4, 1946; children—Carol, David. Staff writer AP, Washington, 1942-46, Birmingham News, 1948-50; asst. prof. history U. Montevallo (Ala.), 1951-55; asst. prof., asst. to pres. for pub. relations Birmingham-So. Coll., 1955-65; lectr. in history U. Ala., Birmingham, 1965-68, asst. prof., 1968-71, asso. prof., 1971-75, prof., 1975-87, prof. emerita, 1987—. U. Ala. at Tuscaloosa faculty research grantee, 1969; U. Ala. at Birmingham faculty research grantee, 1973-74, 74-75. Mem. So., Am. hist. assns., Orgn. Am. Historians, Soc. Am. Historians, Am. Assn. State, local History, Ala. Assn. Historians, Ala. Hist. Soc., Oral History Assn. Author: Hugo Black: The Alabama Years, 1972, Alabama: A History, 1977, The Story of Alabama, 1980, Your Alabama, 1980, Seeing Historic Alabama, 1982, Lister Hill: Statesman from the South, 1987; editor: Hugo Black and the Bill of Rights, 1978. Home: 3246 Overbrook Rd Birmingham AL 35213

HAMLIN, SONYA B., communications specialist; b. N.Y.C.; d. Julius and Sarah (Saltzman) Borenstein; m. Bruce Hamlin (dec. 1977); children: Ross, Mark, David. BS, MA, N.Y.U.; LLD (hon.), Notre Dame Coll., 1970. Host arts program Sta. WHDH-TV, Boston, 1963-65; host, producer, writer Meet the Arts program Sta. WGBH-TV, Boston, 1965-68; cultural reporter Sta. WBZ-TV, Boston, 1968-71, TV host, producer The Sonya Hamlin Show, 1970-75; host, producer Sunday Open House program Sta. WCVB-TV, Boston, 1976-80; host, producer, writer Speak Up and Listen program Lifetime Cable Network, N.Y.C., 1982-84; pres. Sonya Hamlin Communications, Boston and N.Y.C., 1977—, Different Drum Prodns., N.Y.C., 1982-86; pvt. practice communications cons., U.S. and Can., 1977—; adj. lectr. Harvard Grad. Sch., Cambridge, Mass., 1974-76, Harvard Law Sch., 1977-81, Kennedy Sch. Govt., Harvard U., 1978-79; adj. asst. prof. Boston U. Med. Sch., 1977-80; mem faculty Nat. Inst. Trial Advocacy, South Bend, Ind., 1977—, U.S. Dept. Justice, Washington, 1979-87, ABA, Chgo., 1979—; chmn. Law/Video Co., N.Y.C. and Waltham, Mass., 1987—. Author: What Makes Juries Listen, 1985, How to Talk So People Listen, 1988; contbr. articles to profl. jours.; dir., writer (films) China: A Different Path, 1979 (Emmy nominee), Paul Revere: What Makes a Hero, 1976, others. Bd. dirs. Gov. Commn. Status of Women, Mass., 1973-83; campaign co-chair Mass. ERA Campaign, 1975-76; cons. Gov. Michael Dukakis, 1978, Dem. Nat. Party, Washington, 1979; mem. nat. vol. action com. United Way, Washington, 1986—. Recipient Best Program award Internat. Ednl. TV Assn., Tokyo, 1969, Ohio State Cultural Reporting award, 1970; named Outstanding Broadcaster New Eng. Broadcasters, Boston, 1973; Sonya Hamlin Day named in her honor Mayor of Boston, 1974.; archive of her works established Boston U. Library, 1983. Mem. Am. Fedn. TV and Radio Artists, Nat. Acad. TV Arts and Scis. (two Emmy nominations).

HAMM, NORMA BETH, accountant; b. Oakland, Calif., Aug. 25, 1945; d. Albert Berger and Ruth Emma (Elmer) Thaxter; m. Jimmie D. Hamm, May 28, 1966. BBA, U. Cen. Fla., 1973. CPA Ken., Colo. Staff acct. Milzer, et al, Denver, 1973-75, Wilkins & Bishop, Denver, 1975-76, Robert McKenna, Durango, Colo., 1976-78, Van R. Prince, Mayfield, Ky., 1978-86; internal auditor Murray (Ky.) State U., 1986-87, asst. dir. acctg. and fin., 1987—. Mem. AAUW (treas. Ky. div. 1983-87), Am. Inst. CPA's, Colo. Soc. CPA's, Ky. Soc. CPA's, Am. Women's Soc. of CPA's, Bus and Profl. Women. Office: Murray State U Acctg and Fin Services Sparks Hall Murray KY 42071

HAMMAN, SHIRLEY CAROLINE, home economist; b. South Haven, Mich., Apr. 12, 1930; d. Dewey McKinley and Lucia Vivian (Krogel) Peterson; m. Harold L. Hamman; children: Kathy, Mark, Eric, Craig. BS, Western Mich. U., 1952, postgrad. Tchr. home econs. Otsego, Mich., 1952-53, Darien, Ga., 1953-54; home economist Westing House, Corpus Christi, Tex., 1954-56; home economist Cooperative Extension Service Mich. State U., Allegan, 1969—. Mem. Mich. Assn. Extension Home Economists (w. ctl. dir. 1985—, Disting. Service award 1981), Epsilon Sigma Phi. Lodge: Lioness (pres. Martin 1987—). Office: Coop Extension Service 108 Chestnut Allegan MI 49010

HAMMES, TERRY MARIE, advertising executive; b. Chgo., Mar. 27, 1955; d. Howard John and Lorna Marie (Jeans) H. BFA, U. Miami, Coral Gables, Fla., 1976. Lic. real estate broker, Fla. Pres. Hammes Advt. Agy., Coral Gables, Fla., 1978—; pres., broker Hammes Realty Mgmt. Corp., Coral Gables, 1986—; bd. dirs. Coral Gables Bus. Leaders, Ponce de Leon Devel. Assn., Coral Gables. One-woman show includes U. Miami, Fla., 1975; juried art show Lowe Art Mus., 1976. Bd. dirs. Young Democrats, Dade County. Named Miss Minn. Council of State Socs., 1975; Valley Forge Freedom Found. scholar, 1971. Mem. Nat. Assn. Women Bus. Owners (pub. relations chmn. 1986—, pac chmn. 1988—), Builders Assn. South Fla. (editor, publisher 1986-87), Advt. Fedn. Greater Miami, Ponce Devel. Assn. (dir. 1985—), Coral Gables C. of C., Orange Key, Alpha Lambda Delta. Democrat. Home: 9234 SW 132d St Miami FL 33176 Office: Hammes Advt Inc 896 S Dixie Hwy Coral Gables FL 33146-2674

HAMMOND, ALICE FAY, military officer; b. Alexandria, La., Apr. 10, 1949; d. James and Annie Mae (Edwards) H.; 1 child, Noland James. Student, Southern U., 1967-68; AA, Spokane Falls Community Coll., 1975; BA in Human Services, Ft. Wright Coll., 1977; MEd, Whitworth Coll., 1977; MS in Procurement and Materials Mgmt., Webster U., 1985. Substitute tchr. Rapides Parish Pub. Sch. System, Alexandria, 1969-70; sec., clk. library, audio visual Rapedes Parish Sch. Bd. Media Ctr., Alexandria, 1970-73; enlisted USAF, 1973, advanced through grades to capt., 1983. Supporter St. Jude Children's Research Hosp. 1986—, sponsor Korean Orphanage, Osan 1983; bd. dirs. Am. Heart Assn., 1981-82, also supporter 1981—, Am. Cancer Soc., 1980-82, also telephon chmn. 1981.;. Named Outstanding Young Woman Am., 1984. Mem. NAACP, Nat. Assn. Female Execs., Nat. Council Negro Women, Delta Sigma Theta. Democrat. Methodist. Club: Panama City Women's (Fla.). Lodges: Daus. Isis, Order Ea. Star. Home: 3107 9th St Alexandria LA 71301 Office: Falcon Air Force Sta Peterson AFB Colorado Springs CO 80914

HAMMOND, DEANNA, educator; b. Terre Haute, Ind., Feb. 13, 1945; d. DeForest and Dorothy Illen (Spaulding) H. BS in Edn., U. Houston, 1970, MEd, 1983. Cert. tchr., reading specialist, Tex. Tchr., Gregg Elem. Sch., Houston, 1970, Fairchild Elem. Sch., Houston, 1970-77, Cen. Elem. Sch., Palacios, Tex., 1977-79, Foster Elem. Sch., Houston, 1979—, also grade chmn. Block capt. crime watch Huntington Village Civic Assn., Houston, 1982; exec. bd. PTA, Foster Sch.; dir. Vols. in Pub. Schs. (V.I.P.'s), Foster Sch. Mem. Tex. State Council of Internat. Reading Assn., Greater Houston Area Reading Council, Congress Houston Tchrs. (bldg. rep. 1983, 85-86), Assn. Children with Learning Disabilities, Am. Assn. Ret. Persons, PTA. Republican. Clubs: Young Homemakers (Palacios); Christian Womens Fellowship (Houston). Home: 12426 South Dr Houston TX 77099 Office: ME Foster Elem Sch 3919 Ward St Houston TX 77021

HAMMOND, DEANNA LINDBERG, linguist; b. Calgary, Alta., Can., May 31, 1942; d. Albin William and Emma Lou (Thompson) Lindberg; m. Jerome J. Hammond, 1968 (div. 1980). B.A., Wash. State U., 1964; M.A., Ohio U., 1968; Ph.D., Georgetown U., 1977; student summer sch., U. Ariz., Guadalajara, Portland State U. With Peace Corps., Colombia, 1964-66; prof. English Universidad Industrial, Bucaramanga, Colombia, 1966-67; tchr. English, Spanish Pullman High Sch., Wash., 1969-74; lectr. Georgetown U., Washington, 1974-77; dir. summer sch. program Georgetown U., Quito, Ecuador, 1977; head lang. services Congl. Research Services, Library of Congress, Washington, 1977—; mem. adv. bd. traduction, terminologie, rédaction U. Quebec; bd. dirs. Interlingua Inst., Westchester, N.Y. Translator: Psychological Operations in Guerrilla Warfare. Recipient Community Service award Sec. Califano, 1978. Mem. Am. Translators Assn. (nat. pres. elect 1987—, rep., mem. policy com. to joint nat. com. on langs., chmn. domestic liaison com., accreditation com.), Copyright Commn., Internat. Fedn. Translators (program chmn. 1986 regional congress 1986, del. to congress 1987, mem. steering com. Regional Ctr. for N.Am.), Nat. Capital Area Translators Assn., Am. Assn. Tchrs. Spanish and Portuguese, N.E. Conf. on the Teaching Fgn. Langs. (adv. council), Nat. Council Returned Peace Corps Vols., Phi Beta Kappa, Phi Kappa Phi. Democrat. Home: 3560 S George Mason Dr Alexandria VA 22302 Office: Congl Research Lang Services Library of Congress Washington DC 20540

HAMMOND, DEBRA LAUREN, educational administrator; b. Plainfield, N.J., Jan. 15, 1957; d. Luther William and Dolores Odessa (Minor) H. BA in Sociology, Criminal Justice, Rutgers U., 1979, postgrad., 1986—. Asst. to dean minority affairs Cook Coll., New Brunswick, N.J., 1980, asst. dean, dir. campus ctr., 1982-88; dir student union Calif. State U., Los Angeles, 1988—; adv. bd. rep. Paul Robeson Cultural Ctr., New Brunswick, 1981—; chairperson adv. bd. Ednl. Opportunity Fund, New Brunswick, 1981—. Pres. Cent. Jersey's Women's Softball, N.J., 1980-82, v.p. 1982-83. Mem. Assn. Coll. Unions (steering com. internat. chairperson 1985—), YWCA (bd. dirs.), Nat. Assn. for Campus Activities, Nat. Assn. Female Execs. Home: 330 E Cordova St #164 Pasadena CA 91101 Office: Calif State U Student Union 5154 State University Dr Los Angeles CA 90032

HAMMOND, DOROTHY LEE, author, publisher, columnist; b. Fairfax, Mo., Sept. 24, 1924; d. Lee O. and Ella E. (Brunk) Martin; B.S., Maryville (Mo.) State Tchrs. Coll., 1949; m. Robert Byron, Sept. 1, 1944; children—Robert K., Kristy R., Byron K. Syndicated columnist Antiques and Collectibles, Columbia Features, Inc., N.Y.C., 1967—; assoc. editor Colonial Homes mag., 1980—; pres. Hammond Publs., Inc., pubs. The Country Calendar, Western Calendar, Wildlife Calendar, 1978—; author 19 books in field including: Confusing Collectibles, I-III; Mustache Cups; Collectible Advertising; Price Guide to Country Collectibles; The Pictorial Price Guide, Vol. I-X; pub. E.P. Dutton; cons. Smithsonian Instn. Methodist. Office: PO Box 8212 Munger Sta Wichita KS 67208

HAMMOND, ELIZABETH EOLYNE, lawyer; b. Detroit, Sept. 6, 1957; d. Harry Richard and Constance (Landen) H. B.A., Kent State U., 1979; J.D., U. Akron, 1983. Bar: Ohio 1983. Adminstr. Alside, Inc. subs. U.S. Steel Co., Akron, Ohio, 1980-82; mgr. Workers' Compensation Service Co., Cleve., 1982-84; assoc. Weltman, Weinberg & Assocs., LPA, Columbus, Ohio, 1985—; cons. in field. dir. Jem Products, Columbus. Adviser 4-H clubs, Ohio, 1977—. Mem. ABA, Ohio State Bar Assn., Assn. Trial Lawyers Am., Phi Alpha Delta (chpt. clk. 1980-81), Eta Sigma Phi (pres. chpt. 1978-79). Republican. Episcopalian. Home: 2563 N 4th St Columbus OH 43202 Office: Weltman Weinberg & Assocs LPA 527 S High St Columbus OH 43215

HAMMOND, IDA B., educational administrator; b. Supply, Va., Feb. 21, 1931; d. Thomas and Lucille (Welch) Coleman; m. William Henry Hammond; children: Harolyn Terese, William Henry Jr. BA, Thomas A. Edison State Coll., 1978; postgrad., U. Pa., 1982—. Coordinator adminstrv. services, Rutgers U., New Brunswick, N.J., 1970-72; program asst. office of program devel. N.J. Dept. Edn., Trenton, 1974-76, adminstrv. asst., 1979-81, edn. planner, 1981-83, edn. program specialist, 1983-87, div. coordinator, 1987—; coordinator library services Edn. Improvement Ctr., Princeton, N.J., 1976-79; ptnr. William Hammond Contracting, Trenton, 1964—. Chair dept. N.J. State Heart Fund Campaign, 1985; mem. presdl. search com. Thomas A. Edison State Coll., Trenton, 1982, student counselor, 1984, chmn. alumni assn. scholarship fund, 1986-88, dir. alumni assn. exec. bd., 1986-88, co-chmn. Ann. Nat. Phonathon, 1986-87; divisional rep. Vol. Literacy Program N.J. Dept. Edn., 1987. Recipient Outstanding Services award Acad. Council Thomas A. Edison State Coll., 1985, cert. of appreciation N.J. Commr. of Edn. for Vol. Literacy Program, 1987, plaque in recognition of spl. services Thomas A. Edison State Coll., 1987. Mem. Nat. Assn. Female Execs., Am. Soc. Profl. and Exec. Women. Club: La Chaperones. Avocations: fashion design, dressmaking, reading, yoga, photography.

HAMMOND, JANE LAURA, librarian, lawyer; b. nr. Nashua, Iowa; d. Frank D. and Pauline (Flint) H. B.A., U. Dubuque, 1950; M.S., Columbia U., 1952; J.D., Villanova U., 1965. Bar: Pa. 1965. Cataloguer Harvard Law Library, 1952-54; asst. librarian Sch. Law, Villanova (Pa.) U., 1954-62, librarian, 1962-76, prof. law, 1965-76; law librarian, prof. law Cornell U., Ithaca, N.Y., 1976—; Adj. prof. Drexel U., 1971-74; mem. depository library council to pub. printer U.S. Govt. Printing Office, 1975-78. Mem. Am. Assn. Law Libraries (sec. 1965-70, pres. 1975-76), Council Nat. Library Assns. (sec.-treas. 1971-72, chmn. 1979-80), ALA, ABA (com. on accreditation 1982-87, chmn. com. on accreditation 1983-84, council sect. on legal edn. 1984—), PEO. Episcopalian. Office: Cornell Law Library Myron Taylor Hall Ithaca NY 14853

HAMMOND, JEANETTE FRANCIS, air traffic controller; b. Tokyo, Oct. 2, 1958; d. William Nelson and Marion Caroline (Francis) H. BA in Journalism, U. S.C., 1981. Cert. tower operator FAA. Studio mgr. Instrnl. Services, olumbia, S.C., 1978-82; air traffic control specialist FAA, Columbia, 1983-88; automation specialist Nashville, 1988—. Vol. ARC, Colulmbia, 1985—. Mem. Alpha Delta Pi. Republican. Lutheran. Home: 156 Seafarer Ln Columbia SC 29212 Office: Nashville Metro Airport Air Traffic Control Tower Nashville TN 37221

HAMMOND, KAREN SMITH, remodeling company executive; b. Baton Rouge, Dec. 20, 1954; d. James Wilbur Smith and Carolyn (May) Carper; m. Ralph Edwin Hammond, Dec. 17, 1985. Student, La. State U., 1973-75, Colo. Women's Coll., 1976; BJ, U. Colo., 1978; cert. paralegal, U. Tex., 1981. Legal asst. Oscar H. Mauzy Atty.-at-Law, Dallas, 1981; editor Ennis (Tex.) Press, 1981-82; sales rep. VEU Subscription TV, Dallas, 1983-84; comml. account rep. U.S. Telecom, Dallas, 1984; mktg. rep. Allnet Communications, Dallas, 1985-87; owner Smith, Hammond & Assocs., Dallas, 1986—; sales rep. Telecable Inc., Richardson, Tex., 1988—; triex agt. Pkwy. Pontiac, Dallas, 1983-86. Bus. writer Mid-Cities Daily News, 1981. Campaign mgr. Mark Bielamowicz for Mayor, Cedar Hill, Tex., 1979; active campaigns Martin Frost for U.S. Congress, Dallas, 1978, Jimmy Carter for Pres., Ft. Worth, 1980. Mem. Press Club Ft. Worth, Women in Communications (fin. com. 1979), Dallas Assn. Legal Assts., Soc. Profl. Journalists, Dallas C. of C., Nat. Assn. Female Execs. Democrat. Home: 18809 Lina St #2102 Dallas TX 75252 Office: Smith Hammond & Assocs 18809 Lina St #2102 Dallas TX 75252

HAMMOND, KARLA MARIE, writer, editor; b. Middletown, Conn., Apr. 26, 1949; d. Lester Arthur and Angelina (Lillian) Lorraine (Fusillo) H.; B.A., Goucher Coll., 1971; M.A., Trinity Coll., 1973. Freelance writer and editor, 1973—; research cons. Futures Group, Glastonbury, Conn., 1981; personnel cons. Barbara Chazan Assocs., Hartford, Conn., 1981; exec. staff adminstr. CT Student Loan Found., Hartford, 1982-83, Aetna Life & Casualty Co., 1983-88, Adro-System Inc., 1988— ; freelance book reviewer Sachem Pub. Assocs., Guilford, Conn., 1981-84. Recipient several prizes local colls. Democrat. Contbr. articles, essays, short stories, interviews, poems, fiction, and revs. to over 185 publs. in U.S.A., Eng., Can., Japan, Australia, Greece, Sweden and Italy. Home and Office: Rural Route 7 12 West Dr East Hampton CT 06424

HAMMOND, KATHLEEN DOORISH, publishing executive; b. N.Y.C., Nov. 29, 1950; d. John Thomas and Anne (O'Connor) Doorish; m. Caleb Dean Hammond III, July 8, 1978; children: Connor Dean, Kathleen Treacy, Joshua. BA, Cornell U., 1972. Mgr. circulation Avant Garde Media, N.Y.C., 1975-76; various sales and mgmt. positions The N.Y. Times, N.Y.C., 1976-80, suburban advt. mgr., 1981-82; dir. copr. devel. Hammond Inc., Maplewood, N.J., 1982-84, v.p. mktg., 1984-87, exec. v.p., 1987—; also bd. dirs.; bd. dirs. Maplewood (N.J.) Bank & Trust Co. Editor jour. What's Doing in—, 1978-79; contbr. articles to profl. jours. Mem. Assn. Am. Publs., Publs. Publicity Assn., Premium Merchandising Assn. Am., Publs. Ad Club. Roman Catholic. Office: Hammond Inc 515 Valley St Maplewood NJ 07040

HAMMOND, MARGARET ANN, social services administrator; b. Burlington, Vt., June 19, 1947; d. Francis Henry and Bertha (Shanks) H.; children: Kristin, Joshua, Jennifer. BA, U. Vt., 1976; MSW, Adelphi U., 1980; cert. in family therapy, Phila Child Guidance Tng. Ctr., 1984. Social worker Vt. Regional Cancer Ctr., Med. Ctr. Hosp. Vt., Burlington, 1980-82; family therapist Del. Valley Psychol. Clinics, Phila., 1982-85, Northside Ctrs., Inc., Tampa, Fla., 1985-87; assoc. dir. Brandon (Fla.) Ctr. for Family Therapy, 1987—. Asst. leader Girl Scouts U.S., Brandon, 1984-88; vol. Hospice of Hillsborough, Tampa, 1986-88. Mem. Nat. Assn. Social Workers (diplomate, award 1982), Am. Orthopsychiat. Assn., Tampa Bay Assn. Marriage and Family Therapists (treas. 1988—), Fla. Soc. Clin. Social Workers. Democrat. Episcopalian. Home: 4502 Country Gate Ct Valrico FL 33594 Office: Brandon Ctr for Family Therapy 602 Vonderberg Dr #203 Brandon FL 33511

HAMMOND-KOMINSKY, CYNTHIA CECELIA, optometrist; b. Dearborn, Mich., Sept. 1, 1957; d. Andrew and Angeline (Laorno) Kominsky; m. Theodore Glen Hammond, Sept. 21, 1985. Student Oakland U., Rochester, Mich., 1976-77; OD magna cum laude, Ferris Coll. Optometry, 1981. Lic. optometrist, Mich. Intern, Optometric Inst. and Clinic of Detroit, 1980, Ferris State Coll., Big Rapids, Mich., 1980, Jackson Prison (Mich.), 1981; assoc. in pvt. practice, Warren, Mich., 1981-82; optometrist Pearle Vision Ctr., Sterling Heights, Mich., 1982-87, K-Mart Optical Ctr., Sterling

Heights, 1982-87, provided eye care to nursing homes, Mt. Clemens, Mich. Inventor binocular low vision aid device. Avocations: music, sports, bicycling. Home: 47626 Cheryl Ct Utica MI 48087 Office: K Mart Optical Ctr 2051 18 Mile Rd Sterling Heights MI 48078

HAMMONS, KAREN GWEN, shopping mall and marketing executive; b. McComb, Miss., Nov. 28, 1959; d. James Aubrey and G. June (Smith) H. AS in Tech. and Merchandising Mktg. with high honors, Southwest Miss. Jr. Coll., Summit, 1985. Owner, mgr. Baker & Baker Employment Service, McComb, 1982-83; adminstrv. asst. Days Inn Hotel, Nashville, 1985; from sales rep. to regional mktg. dir. Holiday Inns, Jackson, Miss., 1985-87; mktg. dir., mall mgr. Edgewood Mall, McComb, 1987—; motivational speaker various orgns. and schs., McComb. Author numerous poems. Zone chmn. United Way, McComb, 1983; membership chmn. Pike County Arts Council, McComb, 1984. Mem. Internat. Council Shopping Ctrs., Southwest Miss. Jr. Coll. Alumni, Delta Epsilon Chi-Deca Alumni (nat. & state judge for career devel. conf. competitions 1987-88), Pike County C. of C. (com. chmn. 1983-85), Bus. and Profl. Women Club (v.p. McComb 1983-84). Baptist. Home: 1127 College St McComb MS 39648 Office: Edgewood Mall PO Box 1205 McComb MS 39648

HAMPL, GLORIA JANE, psychology educator; b. New Britain, Conn., Sept. 5, 1942; d. William Frank and Jane Mildred (Cerkanowicz) H. BS in Edn., Cen. Conn. State Coll., 1964, MS in Edn., 1966; postgrad., U. Hartford, 1970. Asst. instr. Cen. Conn. State U., New Britain, 1967-70, instr., 1970-84, asst. prof., 1984—, mem. com. on concerns of women. Mem. Am. Psychol. Assn., Conn. Psychol. Assn. Office: Cen Conn State U 1615 Stanley St New Britain CT 06053

HAMPTON, CAROL MCDONALD, educator, administrator, historian; b. Oklahoma City, Sept. 18, 1935; d. Denzil Vincent and Mildred Juanita (Cussen) McDonald; m. James Wilburn Hampton, Feb. 22, 1958; children—Jaime, Clayton, Diana, Neal. BA, U. Okla., 1957, MA, 1973, PhD, 1984. Teaching asst. U. Okla., Norman, 1976-81; instr. U. of Sci. and Arts of Okla., Chickasha, 1981-84; coordinator Consortium for Grad. Opportunities for Am. Indians, U. Calif., Berkeley, 1985-86; trustee Ctr. of Am. Indian, Oklahoma City, 1981—; vice chmn. Nat. Com. on Indian Work, Episcopal Ch., 1986, field officer Native Am. Ministry, 1986—. Contbr. articles to profl. jours. Trustee Western History Collections, U. Okla., Okla. Found. for the Humanities, 1983-86; bd. dirs. Okla. State Regents for Higher Edn., mem. adv. com. on social justice; mem. World Council of Chs. Program to Cambat Racism, Geneva, 1985—; bd. dirs. Caddo Tribal Council, Okla., 1976-82. Recipient Okla. State Human Rights award, 1987; Francis C. Allen fellow, Ctr. fot the History of Am. Indian, 1983. Mem. Western History Assn., Western Social Sci. Assn., Orgn. of Am. Historians, Am. Hist. Assn., Okla. Hist. Soc., Assn. Am. Indian Historians (founding mem. 1981—). Democrat. Episcopal. Club: Jr. League (Oklahoma City). Avocation: travel. Home: 1414 N Hudson Oklahoma City OK 73103 Office: Field Office Native Am Ministry 1224 N Shartel Oklahoma City OK 73103

HAMPTON, DOLORES H., army officer; b. Englewood, N.J., Oct. 18, 1946; d. Charles Milford and Kathleen (Steele) H. B.S., Fairleigh Dickenson U., 1971; M.A., Fla. A. &M. U., 1978; M.S., U.S. Army Command and Gen. Staff Coll., 1980. Enlisted in U.S. Army, 1965, advanced through grades to H. col., 1979; med. technologist Columbia-Presbyn. Med. Ctr., N.Y.C., 1971-76; counselor Pensacola Community Mental Health Ctr., Fla., 1978-80; career devel. specialist Urban League, Englewood, N.J., 1980; personnel counselor Army Med. Dept. Recruitment, 1981-84, N.E. regional dir., 1984-85; Author/editor: U.S. Army Stress Management Training Program, 1979. Mem. 369th Vets. Assn., Assn. Mil. Surgeons U.S., Am. Legion, Res. Officers Assn., Psi Chi (chpt. v.p. 1976-77), Alpha Kappa Alpha. Democrat. Methodist. Avocations: poetry; theare; tennis; swimming; running. Home: 292 Liberty Rd Englewood NJ 07631

HAMPTON, LUCILE PAQUIN SMITH, artist, educator; b. Dubuque, Iowa, Jan. 7, 1904; d. Albert Hugo and Lola (Lichtenberger) Smith; m. Lawrence Charles Hampton, Dec. 16, 1930 (dec. 1960); children: Lawrence Charles Jr., Nancy Jeane Hampton Asper, Elizabeth Mary Hampton Erskine. Diploma, Chgo. Acad. Fine Arts, 1923; postgrad., Pasadena (Calif.) City Coll., 1947-48, 64, 67-68, UCLA, 1965-66; BA in Art, Calif. State U., Los Angeles, 1973. Cert. tchr., Calif. Artist advt. dept. Union Lithographing Co., Little Rock, 1923-24; art dir. advt. dept. M. Rich & Bros. Co., Atlanta, 1924-25; head fashion layout artist advt. dept. May Co., Los Angeles, 1925-29; sr. artist advt. dept. David Jones, Ltd., Sydney, Australia, 1929-30; cover designer Women's Budget Mag., Sydney, Australia, 1929-30; fashion illustrator Home Mag., Sydney, 1930; free-lance artist dept. stores J.W. Robinson & Co. Dept. Stores, Los Angeles, 1930-35; fashion illustrator Robinson Accents Mag., Los Angeles, 1935; freelance artist Lucile Hampton Greeting Cards, San Marino, Calif., 1960—; head dept. art, tchr. Anoakia Sch. Girls, Arcadia, Calif., 1963-66; substitute tchr. San Marion Unified Sch. Dist., 1973—. Troop Leader Girl Scouts U.S., San Marino, 1948-56, pres., 1950-51; active San Marino PTA; mem. San Marino Rep. Women's Club Federated, mem. Opera Guild Los Angeles; bd. dirs. Euterpe Opera Reading, Los Angeles, 1956-59; guild leader San Marino Community Ch. Women. Mem. AAUW (bd. dirs. Newport Beach-Costa Mesa br. 1982-83), DAR (regent San Marino chpt. 1960-61), Children Am. Revolution (sr. advisor, sr. pres. El Molino Viejo chpt. 1958-64), Kappa Pi. Republican. Presbyterian. Clubs: Women's Athletic, Pacific Coast, San Marino Women's, PEO Sisterhood. Home: 234 Sherwood Pl Costa Mesa CA 92627

HAMPTON, MARGARET JOSEPHINE, educator, decorating consultant; b. Princeton, Mo., Nov. 25, 1935; d. Leland Isaac and Margaret Ellen (Wendt) Heriford; m. Ronald Keith Hampton, July 20, 1957; children: Kevin Keith, Ronda René. BS, Samford U., 1957; MEd in Home Econs., U. Mo., 1974. Cert. vocat. home econs. tchr., Mo., Ala. Elem. tchr. Birmingham (Ala.) Pub. Schs., 1957; vocat. home econs. tchr. Licking (Mo.) High Sch., 1957-68; tchr. Pattonville High Sch., Maryland Heights, Mo., 1968—; cons. North Cen. Schs. Accreditation Team, Columbia, Mo., 1970—, interior decorating Home Interiors, Dallas, 1981—; cons. lighting, home economist Intercounty Electric, Licking, 1963-67; supervising tchr. U. Mo., Columbia, 1972—; ednl. adv. council J.C. Penny Stores, St. Louis, 1978-80; cons. to food editor St. Louis County Star News, 1982-86. Author (with others) Mo. Family Relations Curriculum Guide, 1961-63. Mem. adv. council Parkway Sch. Dist., St. Louis, 1979-80, Mo. Gov.'s Conf. on Health and Drug Abuse, Jefferson City, 1986—. Mem. Nat. Assn. Vocat. Home Econs. Tchrs. (sec. 1983-85, pres. 1986-88, editor and pub. jour. 1983-85), Am. Home Econs. Assn. (Mo. conf. chmn. 1979-80), Am. Vocat. Assn. (exec. bd. 1986—), Mo. Home Econs. Tchrs. Assn. (pres. 1979-81, Tchr. of Yr. award 1985 -86), St. Louis Suburban Home Econs. Tchrs. Assn. (pres. 1978-79), Future Homemakers Am. (advisor St. Louis chpt. 1957-86). Baptist. Home: 1514 Sugargrove Ct Creve Coeur MO 63146 Office: Pattonville High Sch 2497 Creve Coeur Mill Rd Maryland Heights MO 63043

HAMPTON-KAUFFMAN, MARGARET FRANCES, corporate finance and banking consultant; b. Gainesville, Fla., May 12, 1947; d. William Wade and Carol Dorothy (Maples) Hampton; B.A. summa cum laude with honors in French, Fla. State U., 1969; postgrad. U. Nice (France), summer 1969; M.B.A. in Fin. (Alcoa Found. fellow), Columbia U., 1974; m. Kenneth L. Kauffman, May 12, 1973; 1 child, Robert Lee. Fin. analyst, economist Bd. of Govs. of Fed. Res. System, Washington, 1974-75; v.p. corp. fin. Mfrs. Hanover Trust Co., N.Y.C., 1975-76; v.p., dir. corp. planning and fin., security asset and liability mgmt. and strategic planning coms. Nat. Bank of Ga., Atlanta, 1976-81; sr. v.p. corp. planning and devel. Bank South Corp., Atlanta, 1981-85; mng. ptnr. Hampton Mgmt. Cons., Atlanta, 1985—; dir. Accent Enterprises, Inc., Atlanta, TOMAK, Inc., Atlanta. Trustee Leukemia Soc. Am., 1986—; trustee Ga. chpt. Leukemia Soc., 1980—, treas., 1981-82, 1st v.p., 1982-84. Recipient Outstanding Angel Merit award Angel Flight, 1968; named Trustee of Yr., Leukemia Soc., 1982, 85. Mem. Planning Execs. Inst., Inst. of Mgmt. Scis., Am. Inst. Banking, Inst. of Fin. Edn., Am. Fin. Assn., Downtown Atlanta C. of C., (govt. affairs subcom. 1976-77) Atlanta C. of C. (high tech. task force 1982-83), Ga. Women's Forum (sec./treas., bd. dirs. 1985-86), Ga. Exec. Women's Network (sec. 1982-83, dir. 1982-84), Mortar Bd., Alliance Française, Kappa Sigma Little Sisters (pres., treas., sweetheart), Phi Beta Kappa, Beta Gamma Sigma, Phi Kappa Phi, Alpha Lambda Delta, Pi Delta Phi, Alpha Delta Pi. Episcopalian. Club: Women's Commerce (charter mem., steering com. 1985-86).

HAMRA, ARMEL JEAN CLAXTON, purchasing and general services assistant director; b. Seymour, Mo., May 10, 1932; d. Elvin Ferris and Metta Allene (Duggins) Claxton; divorced; 1 child, Philip Muschell. Student, Murray State U., 1979-86. Mdse. clk. USN Exchange, Naples, Italy, 1960-64; mgr. exchange USAF Hosp., Jacksonville, Ark., 1964-66; with purchase and selling dept. Broadway Store, Las Vegas, Nev., 1966-67; cen. stores clk. Murray (Ky.) State U., 1968-72, adminstrv. sec., 1972-74, buyer and risk claims specialist, 1972-74, sr. buyer, 1978-83, asst. dir., 1983—. Contbr. articles to profl. jours. Mem. Nat. Assn. Female Execs., Ky. Pub. Purchasing Assn., Ky. Women Deans, Adminstrs. and Counselors, Ky. Edn. Purchase Coop. (vice chmn. 1985-86, chmn. 1986—), Ky. Nat. Assn. Ednl. Buyers (vice chmn. 1975-76, chmn. 1976-77). Democrat. Methodist. Office: Murray State U Purchasing & Gen Services Murray KY 42071

HAMROFF, ELLIE, records management company executive; b. N.Y.C., Apr. 17, 1933; d. Benedict Leo and Lillian Edith (Katzen) Lurie; m. Sheldon Hamroff, June 5, 1955; children—Robin Hamroff Boehler, Debra Hamroff Levi, Michael. Student Goucher Coll., 1950-51; B.A., Adelphi U., 1954. Social worker N.Y.C. Dept. Welfare, 1954-55; asst. adminstr. Kew Gardens Hosp., N.Y., 1975-78; pres. Comprehensive Archives, Inc., N.Y.C., 1978—. Pres., Naomi Hadassah, Jamaica Estates, N.Y., 1968-70; v.p. fund raising Hillcrest Hadassah, Jamaica Estates, 1971-73. Democrat. Office: Comprehensive Archives Inc 87-46 123d St Richmond Hill NY 11418

HANAS, SUZANNE ELAINE, manufacturing company sales executive; b. Pitts., July 27, 1950; d. George and Helen (Kalnicky) H. R.N. diploma Shadyside Hosp. Sch. Nursing, Pitts., 1971; B.S., Am. U., 1976. R.N., Ohio, Va., D.C. Head nurse cardio-vascular intensive care Cleve. Clinic Hosp., 1971-73; spl. duty nurse Georgetown U. Hosp., Washington, 1973-75; team coordinator Vis. Nurses' Assn. No. Va., Arlington, 1975-76; ter. mgr. Hollister Inc., Chgo., 1976-79; sr. account rep. 3M Co., West Caldwell, N.J., 1979—, sales trainer, 1984—; pres. Skyline Dance Studio, Inc., Falls Church, Va.; instr. Montgomery Coll., Rockville, Md., 1977-80. Del., Arlington County Civic Fedn. (Va.), 1978-81; v.p. Fairlington Citizens Assn., Arlington, 1978-80, pres., 1980-81; del. Va. Republican Conv., 1981; precinct chmn., mem. Arlington County Rep. Com. (Va.), 1982-83; mem. Presdl. Inaugural Com., 1984. Recipient Order of the Golden Scalpel award 3M Co., 1985. Mem. Am. Cancer Soc., Am. U. Alumni Assn., Nat. Assn. Female Execs. Lutheran. Club: Arlington Rep. Women's Club Federated. Office: 15 Henderson Dr West Caldwell NJ 07006

HANAU, LAIA, educator; b. Boston, June 4, 1916; d. Samuel B. and Lucy A. (Greenwood) Pearlmutter; A.B., Smith Coll., 1937; M.A., U. Rochester, 1960; postgrad. U. Mich., 1942-45, U. Ky., 1951-53, U. Ariz., 1973-74; m. Richard Hanau, Jan. 2, 1941; 1 dau., Loren Michael. Copy editor Am. Horseman, Lexington, Ky., 1947-49; asst. editor pubs. Dept. Pub. Info., U. Ky., Lexington, 1949-50, editorial asst. dept. animal pathology, 1950-52; editorial cons. Optical Soc. Am., Rochester, N.Y., 1959; tchr. English, Lexington pub. schs. and Sayre Sch., 1960-66; instr. study methods U. Ky. Coll. Medicine, Lexington, 1967-69, asst. prof., 1970-73; cons. in field; tchr. Sayre Sch., 1974-76; contbr. Breadloaf Writers Conf., 1953; editorial cons. U. Ky. Coll. Medicine, 1963-66; tchr., cons. Hanau Method of Study and Writing Techniques. Recipient Avery and Jule Hopwood Award in nonfiction, 1942. Mem. Authors Guild. Author: The Study Game, How to Play and Win With "Statement Pie", 1972, 73, 74; The Study Game Workbook: A Guide to Writing and Note Taking, 1976; The Study Game: How to Play and Win, 1979; Play the Study Game for Better Grades, 1985. Address: 517 Spring Lakes Blvd Bradenton FL 34210

HANBACK, HAZEL MARIE SMALLWOOD, management consultant; b. Washington, Sept. 19, 1918; d. Archibald Carlisle and Mary Louise (Mayhugh) Smallwood; m. William B. Hanback, Sept. 26, 1942; 1 child, Christopher Brecht. AB, George Washington U., 1940; MPA, Am. U., 1968. Archivist, U.S. Office Housing Expediter, 1948-50; mgmt. engr. U.S. Archives, 1950-51; spl. asst.-indsl. specialist Sec. Def., 1951-53; dir. documentation div. Naval Facilities Engring., Alexandria, Va., 1953-81; mgmt. cons., 1981—. Author: Military Color Book, 1960, Status of Women in a Cybernetically Oriented Soc., 1968, (newsletter) Worms Eye View, 1982. Pres., West End Citizens Assn., Washington, 1956-58; trustee George Washington U., 1979—. Nominee Rockefeller Pub. Service award, 1969, Fed. Woman's award, 1969; recipient cert. of merit Dep. Def., 1965. Mem. Mortar Bd., Phi Delta Gamma, Sigma Kappa. Democrat. Episcopalian. Clubs: George Washington U. (chmn. bd. 1971-75), Columbian Women (pres. George Washington U. 1967-69), Order Eastern Star. Home: 2152 F St NW Washington DC 20037 Office: 2154 F St NW Washington DC 20037

HANCOCK, MORGAN, construction executive; b. Los Angeles, July 10, 1941; d. John Howard Brooks and Carol G. (Henley) Harper; m. Roger Lester Edwards, July 10, 1959 (div. Dec. 1964); 1 child, Laura Anne; m. Taylor Hancock, Mar. 29, 1969 (div. Apr. 1980); 1 child, Heather. MBA, Calif. State U., 1977. V.p. Bolo Corp., Los Angeles, 1965-72; mng. dir. Feminist Book Club, Los Angeles, 1972-74, Morgan Mktg., Los Angeles, 1977—; pres., chief exec. officer Catalyst Constructors Inc. (formerly Piper Hydro Inc.), Irvine, Calif., 1986-88; v.p., sec., treas. Piper-Hancock, Inc., Irvine, 1988—. Author: Only a Damn Fool: The Pacific Voyage of the Dagny Taggart, 1979. Mem. Internat. Assn. Plumbing and Mechanical Officials, Bldg. Officials and Code Adminstrs. Internat., Internat. Conf. Bldg. Officials. Libertarian. Episcopalian. Club: The Ferrari (Anaheim, Calif) (run chmn. 1986—). Office: Piper-Hancock Inc 10 McLaren Suite C Irvine CA 92718-2820

HANCOCK, TAMMY RAE, accountant; b. Omaha, June 21, 1961; d. Gerald Lee Sr. and Edna Mae (Petersen) Bonney; m. James Steven Hancock, May 30, 1981. Student, Doane Coll., 1979; BS in Bus. Adminstrn., U. Nebr., 1983. CPA, Nebr. Bookkeeper, teller Washington County Bank, Blair, Nebr., 1978-80; cashier, salesperson Sears, Roebuck and Co., Omaha, 1980-82; teller Omaha State Bank, 1982-83; clk. No. Natural Gas Co., Omaha, 1983; mgr. Arthur Andersen & Co., Omaha, 1983—. Treas. Omaha Com. UNICEF, 1984-85; vol. Am. Cancer Soc., 1985, Nebr. Easter Seal Soc., 1986. Mem. Am. Inst. CPA's, Nat. Assn. Accts., Healthcare Fin. Mgmt. Assn. (chmn. reimbursement com. 1985-86, program com. 1988), Nebr. Soc. CPA's, Beta Alpha Psi (v.p., treas. 1983), Beta Gamma Sigma. Republican. Lutheran. Home: 4711 N 131 Omaha NE 68164 Office: Arthur Andersen & Co 1700 Farnam St Omaha NE 68102

HANCSARIK, MARGARET ANN, electronics company administrator; b. Saugus, Mass., Dec. 1, 1962; d. John Michael and Pauline Jean (Thurlow) H. BSBA, Boston U., 1984; postgrad., Babson Coll., 1987—. Network support rep. Fidelity Systems Co., Boston, 1984-86; user system analyst The Boston Co., Malden, Mass., 1986; supr. network control ctr. Baybanks System Inc., Waltham, Mass., 1986—. Democrat. Methodist. Home: 57 Bellrock St Malden MA 02148 Office: 295 Weston St Waltham MA 02154

HAND, DIANE TELESCO, public relations executive; b. San Francisco, Oct. 4, 1946; d. Lee A. and Charlotte Umbreit Telesco; m. William Allen Hand, Jan. 19, 1968 (div. Aug. 1983). B.A., San Jose State U., 1967. Reporter, Santa Clara (Calif.) Jour., 1967-68, Seneca (S.C.) Jour., 1968-70; info. officer Va. Inst. Tech., Blacksburg, 1970-72, U.S. Dept. Agr., Washington, 1972-73; food editor The Times Mag., Army Times Pub. Co., Washington, 1973-76; communications specialist Dorn Communications, Mpls., 1976-82, account exec., 1982-83, account dir., 1983-84, v.p., 1984-85; account mgr. Fleishman-Hillard Inc., Kansas City, Mo., 1985-86, v.p., 1986—; cons. Va. Tech. Inst. Food Technologists Food Editors Conf., 1973-77. Mem. Nat. Fedn. Press Women (first place awards communications contest 1974, 75, 83), Pub. Relations Soc. Am., Press Women Minn. (founder, pres. 1977-79, Woman of Achievement 1982). Office: Fleishman Hillard Inc 2405 Grand Ave Suite 700 Kansas City MO 64108

HAND, SHERRY ELAINE, banker; b. Athens, Ga., May 9, 1949; d. Clarence Hardman Bullock and Lily Helen (Hall) Boleman; m. William J. Hand Jr., Dec. 19, 1987. Student, U. Ga., 1968-69. Lic. real estate agt., Calif. Loan processor Western Mortgage Corp., Atlanta, 1968-76; office mgr. Sentinel Real Estate, Los Angeles, 1977-84; sr. loan processor FPM, Thousand Oaks, Calif., 1986; compliance officer Western Bank, Irvine, Calif., 1986-87; adminstrv. asst. Nat. First Mortgage Corp., Atlanta, 1987—. Methodist.

HANDELMAN, ALICE ROBERTA, public relations official, freelance writer; b. Bklyn., Mar. 17, 1943; d. Ned Harlan and Margaret (Isaacs) Samuels; m. Howard Talbot Handelman, Aug. 29, 1965; children—Karen Leigh, Patricia Gail, Marjorie Lynn. B.J., U. Mo., 1965. Intern reporter Miami (Fla.) News, summer 1964; staff feature writer St. Louis Blues, 1968-77; freelance writer, St. Louis, 1967—; also community relations assoc. Jewish Ctr. for Aged of Greater St. Louis, Chesterfield, Mo., 1981-85, dir. community relations and devel., 1985—; instr. hockey for women Meramec Community Coll., St. Louis, 1976-77; pub. relations cons. Jewish Family and Children's Service, St. Louis, 1983; adv. com. vis. prof. program JCA Assocs., 1981-83, Gerontol. Inst., St. Louis, 1981-83. Author, photographer: LaSalle Street--A History of the St. Louis Wholesale Flower Market, 1987; freelance writer, contbr. to St. Louis Globe-Dem., St. Louis Post-Dispatch, St. Louis Jewish Light, Hockey News, Hockey World, Sporting News, Hockey Pictorial, Suburban Jour. Newspapers; writer copy for Knight's Catalogue, 1983. Pub. relations chmn. Nat. Council Jewish Women, 1981-83, publicity chmn. fashion sale, 1985; pres. Weber Sch. PTA, Creve Coeur, Mo., 1982; mem. Women's Am. ORT, 1965—; life mem. Jewish Hosp. Aux., 1965—, Jewish Ctr. for Aged, 1986—, pres. Young Women's Council on Edn. of Jewish Fedn. St. Louis, 1969; mem. central advancement team Pkwy. Central High Sch., 1985—. Recipient William Randolph Hearst award Hearst Found., Columbia, Mo., 1965, United Way Graphic Design award, 1986, United Way Photography award, 1987, Star Communicator Photography award, 1987, 1st place award communications contest Nat. Fedn. Press Women, 1988; Besse Marks Meml. scholar, 1964-65. Mem. Jewish Ctr. for Aged Auxilliary, Fellows of Jewish Hosp., Mo. Press Women (1st place corp. newsletter category state feature writing communications contest, 1988), Women in Communications (Ruth Philpott Collins award 1984). Republican. Jewish. Club: Meadowbrook Country (Ballwin, Mo.). Home: 12 Terryhill Ln Saint Louis MO 63131 Office: Jewish Ctr for Aged 13190 S Outer 40 Rd Chesterfield MO 63017

HANDLER, CAROLE ENID, lawyer, city planner; b. N.Y.C., Dec. 23, 1939; d. Milton and Marion Winter (Kahn) Handler; m. Peter U. Schoenbach, May 30, 1965 (div. Sept. 1979); children: Alisa, Ilana. AB, Radcliffe Coll., 1957; MS, U. Pa., 1963, JD, 1975. Bar: Pa. 1975. Planner Boston Redevel. Authority, 1959-61; head gen. plans sect. Phila. City Planning Commn., 1963-66; ednl. facilities planning cons. Phila. Sch. Dist., 1966-67, coordinator and dir. policy planning, 1967-69; instr. U. Sao Paulo, Rio de Janeiro, Brazil, 1970-71, Cath. U., Rio de Janeiro, Brazil, 1970-71; law clk. presiding judge Pa. Superior Ct., Phila., 1975-76; assoc. Goodman & Ewing, Phila., 1976-78, Schnader, Harrison, Segal & Lewis, Phila., 1978—; sr. v.p., gen. counsel MGM/UA Distbn. Co., Los Angeles, 1985-87; ptnr. Le Boeuf, Lamb, Leiby & MacRae, Los Angeles, 1987—. Bd. dirs. St. Peter's Sch., Society Hill Synagogue; panel mem. Thomas Jefferson U. (family law and psychiatry). Mem. Phila. Vol. Lawyers for the Arts (v.p.). Jewish. Office: LeBoeuf Lamb Leiby & MacRae 725 S Figueroa St Suite 2205 Los Angeles CA 90017

HANDLER, ELISABETH HELEN, public relations executive; b. Greenwich, Conn., Aug. 10, 1944; d. Meyer Srednick and Helen Eulalah (Sennette) H.; m. Joseph Paul Ozawa, Mar. 18, 1968 (div. Sept. 1978); children: Alison Jane, Susan Hilary. BA, Radcliffe Coll., 1966. Adminstrv. asst. Office for Health Affairs, Office Econ. Opportunity, Washington, 1966-68; acting adminstrv. dir.community mental health service Mass. Mental Health Ctr., Boston, 1969-71; tech. writer Job Corps., Office Econ. Opportunity, Washington, 1972, Merle Norman Cosmetics, Los Angeles, 1973-74; account supr. Wallace Jamie Resource Group, Los Angeles, 1977-79; account supr., v.p. Berkhemer and Kline, Inc., Los Angeles, 1979-82; v.p., creative dir. Fleishman-Hillard, Inc., Los Angeles, 1982—; tchr. pub. relations The Ad Ctr., Los Angeles, 1985—. Contbr. article to profl. jour. Mem. Pub. Relations Soc. Am., Internat. Assn. Bus. Communicators. Democrat. Office: Fleishman Hillard Inc 515 S Flower St Seventh Floor Los Angeles CA 90071

HANDLER, EVELYN ERIKA, university president; b. Budapest, Hungary, May 5, 1933; d. Donald D. and Ilona Sass; m. Eugene S. Handler; children: Jeffrey, Bradley. BA, Hunter Coll., 1954; MSc, NYU, 1962, PhD, 1963; LLD (hon.), Rivier Coll., 1981. Research asst. Sloan Kettering Inst., N.Y.C., 1956-58; research asso. Merck Inst. Therapeutic Research, Rahway, N.J., 1958-60; mem. faculty, dept. biol. scis. Hunter Coll., N.Y.C., 1962-77; dean div. scis. and math Hunter Coll., 1977-80; pres. U. N.H., Durham, 1980-83, Brandeis U., Waltham, Mass., 1983—; Mem. nat. adv. gen. med. sci. council NIH, 1981-84; mem. Am. Council Pharm. Edn., 1978-82; mem. exec. com. Nat. Assn. State Univs. and Land Grant Colls., 1981-83, mem. com. on policies and issues, 1981—. Contbr. articles and abstracts to profl. publs. Mem. New Eng. Bd. Higher Edn., 1980—; mem. New Eng. Council Presidents, 1980-83, N.H. Coll. and Univ. Council, 1980-83, Post-Secondary Edn. Commn., 1980—; corp. mem. Woods Hole Oceanographic Instn., 1983—. Mem. Assn. Ind. Colls. and Univs. Mass. (exec. com. 1986—), Assn. Am. Univs. (sci. and research com. 1985—), New Eng. Council, Inc. (bd. dirs. 1983 chmn. edn., edn and tech. 1985—), The New Eng. (bd. dirs. 1983—).

HANDLEY, JEAN M., telephone company executive; b. Manchester, Conn., Aug. 28, 1926; d. Francis P. and Margaret (Ivers) H. B.A., Conn. Coll., 1948; M.A., Northwestern U., 1949. Pub. relations asst. So. New Eng. Telephone Co., New Haven, 1960, advt. and employee info. staff, 1960-66, dist. mgr., 1966-72; dist. mgr. AT&T, N.Y.C., 1972-73; gen. info. mgr. So. New Eng. Telephone Co., 1973-75; press relations dir. AT&T, N.Y.C., 1976-78; v.p. pub. relations So. New Eng. Telephone Co., 1978-84, v.p. personnel and corp. relations, 1984—; vice chmn. Sci. Park Devel. Corp., New Haven. Trustee Conn. Coll., New London; bd. dirs. New Haven Symphony Orch., women's steering com., Greater New Have C. of C.;assoc. fellow Calhoun Coll., Yale U. Recipient Women in Leadership award YWCA of New Haven, 1979; Greater New Haven C. of C. Community Leadership award, 1984, Women Achievers award, YWCA of N.Y., 1984. Mem. Pub. Relations Soc. Am., Pub. Relations Soc. N.Y., Women in Communications, Inc., Am. Women in Radio and TV. Office: So New Eng Telephone Co 227 Church St New Haven CT 06506

HANDLEY, MARGIE LEE, asphalt and aggregates manufacturing company executive, real estate development company executive, engineering contractor; b. Bakersfield, Calif., Sept. 29, 1939; d. Robert E. and Jayne A. (Knoblock) Harrah; m. Gordon Daniel Lovell, Feb. 17, 1956 (div. Sept. 1973); children—Steven Daniel Lovell, David Robert Lovell, Ronald Eugene Lovell; m. Leon C. Handley, Sr., Oct. 28, 1975. Grad. high sch., Willits, Calif. With Firco, Inc., Willits, 1955-57; receptionist, typist Remco Hydraulics, Inc., Willits, 1958-62; tchrs. aide Montague Sch. Dist., 1964, sec. to dist. supr., 1965-68; owner, operator Shasta Pallet Co., Montague, 1969-70; owner, operator Lovell's Tack 'n Togs, Yreka, Calif., 1970-73; v.p. Microphor, Inc., Willits, 1974-81; pres. Harrah Industries, Inc., Willits, 1981—, Hot Rocks, Inc., Willits, 1983—. Sec. Willits Community Scholarships, Inc., 1962; trustee Montague Methodist Ch., 1966-73; sec. Montague PTA, 1969; clk. bd. trustees Montague Sch. Dist., 1970-73; del. Calif. State Conf. Small Bus., 1984; alt. del. Rep. Nat. Conv., Kansas City, Detroit, 1976, 80; 3d dist. chmn. Mendocino County Rep. Central Com., 1978-84; mem. Calif. State Rep. Central Com., 1985, 86, 87; charter mem. Senatorial Inner Circle, 1980—; mem. Rep. Congl. Leadership Council, 1980-82; Mendocino County chmn. Reagan/Bush, 1980, 84; Mendocino County cochmn. Deukmejian for Gov., 1982; mem. Region IX Small Bus. Adminstrn. Adv. Council, 1982—; mem. Gov.'s Adv. Council, 1983—; del., asst. sgt. of arms Rep. Nat. Conv., Dallas, 1984, del., New Orleans, 1988; vice chmn. Mendocino County Rep. Central Com., 1985; mem. Willits C. of C. (hon.), Calif. Transp. Commn., 1986—; state dir. North Bay Dist. Hwy. Grading and Heavy Engring. div. 1986. Named Mendocino 12th Dist. Fair Woman of the Year, 1987. Mem. Assn. Gen. Contractors Calif. Home: PO Box 1309 Willits CA 95490 Office: Hot Rocks Inc 42 Madrone St Willits CA 95490

HANDLEY, MARY THERESE, sales executive; b. Detroit, Mar. 29, 1927; d. Charles Bernard and Marie (Wheelan) Weiner; m. Michael J. Handley, Aug. 5, 1950 (dec. May 1982); children: Patricia, Alice, Barbara, Daniel, Elizabeth, Kathleen; m. John Desso, Jan. 18, 1986. BS, Mary Grove Coll., 1949. Home economist Detroit Pub. Sch. System, 1949-50; with sales and instrn. Dale Carnegie & Assocs., Saginaw, Mich., 1968-71; sales rep. Dale Carnegie & Assocs., Detroit, 1977-79, instr. Dale Carnegie course, 1979—, sales mgr., 1979-82, sponsor Dale Carnegie Tng., 1982—. Republican. Roman Catholic. Home: 2417 Lakeview Meadow Bay City MI 48706 Office: Handley & Assocs Inc 3131 Davenport Ave Saginaw MI 48602

HANDLIN, AMY HARWOOD, small business owner; b. Neptune, N.J., Jan. 28, 1956; d. Louis Jay and Edna Ceclia (Epstein) Harwood; m. David Stephen Handlin, Aug. 20, 1977. BA, Harvard U., 1977; MBA, Columbia U., 1979. Acct. exec. Wells, Rich, Greene, Inc., N.Y.C., 1978-80, Ted Bates Advt., Inc., N.Y.C., 1980-82, Young and Rubicam Advt., Inc., N.Y.C., 1983-85; owner, dir. Sylvan Learning Ctrs. of Monmouth County, Ocean, 1985—; adj. faculty Sch. Bus., Monmouth Coll. Chair task force Middletown (N.J.) Township Citizen's on Mt. Laurel; elected mem. Middletown Twp. Com., 1987; chair domestic affairs task force Jewish Community Relations Council; mem. Monmouth County Prosecutor's Task Force on Child Abuse; mem. Greater Red Bk. Hadassah; mem. Middletown Township Com. on Productivity and Efficiency; founding mem. Monmouth County Commn. on Women. Mem. AAUW (bd. dirs.), LWV, Jewish Fedn. Greater Monmouth County (exec. bd.), Harvard Club N.J., N.J. LWV (local and state bd. dirs.). Office: Sylvan Learning Ctr 1300 Hwy 35 Bldg II Ocean NJ 07712

HANDY, PAMELA JEAN, infosystems specialist; b. Argentia, Nfld., Can., Mar. 29, 1965; came to U.S., 1965; d. Robert William and Carol Ann (Gaines) H. A in Bus., Hesser Coll., Manchester, N.H., 1986; B in Bus., Daniel Webster Coll., Nashua, N.H., 1988. With Sanders Assocs., Inc., Hudson, N.H., 1986—, release and control dept., 1987—; part-time model FOLIO, Nashua, 1986-87. Mem. Nat. Assn. Female Execs. Roman Catholic. Clubs: Sanders Putter, Power Golf League, Tyngsboro Country. Home: 160 Isaac Frye Hwy Wilton NH 03086 Office: Sanders Assocs Inc 65 River Rd PTP1-2361 Hudson NH 03051

HANEK, PATRICIA ANN, claims representative; b. Cleve., July 25, 1951; d. Leonard William and Marjorie Alwilda (Fulton) Schultz; m. Gary W. Gifford, Sept. 8, 1973 (div. Feb. 1980); m. John Nicholas Hanek, Sept. 26, 1980; children: Nicholas, William, Joel. BA, Cleve. State U., 1973; postgrad., Miami U., Oxford, Ohio, 1976-77. Med. intake worker Butler County Welfare, Middletown, Ohio, 1974-77; head cashier Montgomery Ward, Akron, Ohio, 1977-78; claims approver John Hancock Ins., Shaker Heights, Ohio, 1978-79; claims rep. Social Security Adminstrn., Painesville, Ohio, 1979-81, Parma Heights, Ohio, 1981—. Office: Social Security Adminstrn 6325 York Rd Parma Heights OH 44130

HANES, DARLENE MARIE, finance company executive; b. St. Mary's, Pa., Mar. 24, 1956; d. Donald Frank and Martha Mary (Krug) H. CLU degree, Am. Coll., Bryn Mawr, Pa., 1986, Chartered Fin. Cons. degree, 1988. CLU. Underwriter N.Y. Life Ins. Co., Concord, Calif., 1980-87; v.p. East Bay Fin. Ctr., Concord, 1987—, v.p. agy. devel., 1988—. Pres. Am. Cancer Soc. League, 1985-86, bd. dirs. 1984—; bd. dirs. Airport Commn., St. Mary's, 1975. Named Person of Day, Am. Heart Assn., 1985. Mem. Nat. Assn. Life Underwriters (Nat. Quality award 1985, 86, 87, Pres.'s trophy 1986), Mt. Diablo Assn. Life Underwriters (bd. dirs. 1982—, pres. 1986-87), East Bay CLU Soc. (chmn. membership com. 1987—), Calif. Assn. Life Underwriters (regional coordinator 1987—). Republican. Roman Catholic. Office: East Bay Fin Ctr 3227 Clayton Rd Concord CA 94519

HANES-JENKINS, DEBRA LEE BLAYLOCK, probation officer, family therapist; b. Indpls., Mar. 4, 1947; d. Learmon Cleo Sr. and Doris Lee (Banks) Blaylock; m. Norris Henry Hanes II, June 3, 1967 (div. 1972); 1 child, Norris Henry III; m. Gary F. Jenkins, Feb. 14, 1988. Student, N.C. Agrl. and Tech. State U., 1966-67, Butler U., 1968; BA in Clothing and Textiles, Marian Coll., Indpls., 1972; MS in Family and Child Devel., Ohio State U., 1973. Lic. in real estate. Family therapist Nisonger Ctr., Ohio State U., Columbus, 1973; head div. Clinician Urban Affairs Ctr., Toledo, 1974; investigator Colo. Civil Rights Commn., Denver, 1975; cons. dept. health and hosps. City of Denver, 1976-77; cons., assoc. Planners, Inc., Denver, 1978-79; research assoc. Human Resources Research Orgn., Alexandria, Va., 1979-80; officer dept. corrections State of D.C., Washington, 1981-86; probation officer D.C. Superior Cts., Washington, 1986—; early intervention coordinator, dept. head , child devel. specialist Zucker Ctr., 1973-77; child devel. specialist, div. head Urban Affairs Ctr., 1974; mem. adv. bd. Human Services Inc., Denver, 1977, trustee, 1978; owner Stitchmasters, Silver Spring, Md., 1981—; cons. D.L.H. Enterprises, Silver Spring, 1985—; cons. custom interiors and garments. Copyright Designer Dolls Collection, Heritage Collection. Mem. Toledo Bicentennial Coordinating Com., 1974, headstart compliance steering com., 1973; facilitator Images, Montgomery County, Md., 1986; mem. Friends of the Kennedy Ctr., 1986-87. Named one of Outstanding Young Women in Toledo, Toledo Jaycettes, 1975; Nisonger Ctr. fellow, 1973. Mem. Nat. Assn. for Children with Learning Disabilities, Mid. Atlantic States Correctional Assn., Nat. Assn. Female Execs., Nat. Assn. Black Caths., Smithsonian Inst. (assoc.). Home: 13009 Tamarack Rd Silver Spring MD 20904 Office: DC Superior Cts 409 E St NW 114-B Washington DC 20001

HANEX, TAYLOR ANNE, financial consultant; b. Washington, Mar. 30, 1953; d. John Joseph and Eileen Mildred (Diamondson) H. MusB, Peabody Conservatory of Music, Johns Hopkins U., 1975, MusM, 1978; MBA, Fordham U., 1980; postgrad., U. Nebr., 1975, Conservatorio Municipal de Musica, Barcelona (Spain), 1976. Performer, royalty sales rep. G. Schirmer Music Publs., N.Y.C., 1977-78; research asst. Bill Communications, N.Y.C., 1978-79; account exec. Microband Corp. Am., N.Y.C., 1981-82, nat. accts. mgr., 1983-85; asst. v.p. for bus. ops. Irving Bank Corp., N.Y.C., 1986, asst. v.p., 1986-87; fin. cons. Merrill Lynch, N.Y.C., 1987—; guest lectr. Kean Coll., 1983-87; solo concert pianist East and Midwest U.S.; performed with Orquesta Mcpl. de la Teatro de Barcelona, 1976. U. Nebr. teaching fellow, 1975; recipient Mabel H. Thomas award Peabody Conservatory of Music, Balt., 1970; Fordham U. grad. fellow, 1979; Joseph Mullan scholar Peabody Conservatory of Music, 1975. Mem. Am. Mktg. Assn. Republican. Roman Catholic. Club: Toastmasters Internat. Home: 233 E 69th St New York NY 10021 Office: Merrill Lynch 717 Fifth Ave New York NY 10022

HANEY, MARY BELL, civil engineer; b. Miami, Fla., Nov. 10, 1946; d. James Bell and Suzanna (Allen) Trout; m. Donald Lee Haney, Aug. 15, 1967; children: James Reuben, Donald Louis. BSCE, Clemson U., 1967, MS in Environ. Systems Engring. (USPHS trainee), 1968, postgrad. in mgmt., 1968-76; postgrad. in chemistry, U. Tex., San Antonio, 1980-81; doctoral candidate, Calif. Coast U. Vis. lectr. and adj. prof. U. N.Mex., 1970-72; v.p. engring. Ruben Rodriguez Land Devel. Inc., Albuquerque, 1970-74; asst. project mgr. Pape-Dawson Cons. Engrs., Inc., San Antonio, 1976-78, project engr., 1978-82, project mgr., 1982—. Mem. properties com. Girl Scouts U.S.A., San Antonio; sec. Universal City Planning and Zoning Commn., 1984-86; trustee Judson Ind. Sch. Bd. 1987—; chmn. bldg. com. Windcrest United Meth. Ch. Registered profl. engr., Tex. Mem. Nat. Soc. Profl. Engrs., Tex. Soc. Profl. Engrs. (dir. 1980, 84, treas. 1981, sec. 1982, pres.-elect 1986, pres. 1987, mem. Speakers Bur. 1979—, Outstanding Young Engr. of Yr. award Bexar chpt. 1982, Tex. 1982), Soc. Women Engrs., Assn. Women in Sci., Nat. Assn. Female Execs., Am. Statis. Assn., Am. Assn. Cost Engrs., Water Pollution Control Fedn., Planetary Soc., ASCE, San Antonio Council Engring. Edn., NOW, YWCA, AAUW, Tau Beta Pi (Women's Badge 1965), Phi Kappa Phi, Sigma Tau Epsilon. Clubs: Altrusa; Protestant Women of Chapel (pres. club 1975-76). Contbr. articles to profl. publs. Office: 9310 Broadway San Antonio TX 78217

HANEY-POWELL, BARBARA ALLISON, economist, consultant; b. Kenmore, N.Y., May 21, 1959; d. Van Allison and Mildren Adele (Utter) Haney; m. Mitchell Lum Powell; children: Steven Lum, Vanessa Allison. BA, Ea. Ill. U., 1980, MA, 1983. Cert. system planning FAA. Instr. Lakeland Jr. Coll., Mattoon, Ill., 1983; instr. Ea. Ill. U., Charleston, 1982-83, 87—, dir. Ctr. Econ. Edn., 1988—; instr. in research U. Notre Dame, Ind., 1983-86, dir. forensics, 1985-86; planner land use and aviation East-West Gateway Coordinating Council, St. Louis, 1986-87; instr. McKendree Coll., Lebannon, Ill., 1987. Editor: Aviation Newsletter, 1986. Mem. AFL-CIO (Ill. delegate, Local 1400), Am. Econs. Assn., Com. Status Women Econ. Profession, Midwest Econs. Assn., Ctr. Policy Alternatives, Nat. Assn. Female Exec., Mo. Valley Econ. Assn., Univ. Profls. of Ill. (treas.), Phi Kappa Delta, Omicron Delta Epsilon. Democrat. Luthern. Home: 116 Chateau Dr Belleville IL 62221 Office: Eastern Ill U Dept Econs Charleston IL 61920

HANFT, RUTH S. SAMUELS (MRS. HERBERT HANFT), economist; b. N.Y.C., July 12, 1929; d. Max Joseph and Ethel (Schechter) Samuels; m. Herbert Hanft, June 17, 1951; children: Marjorie Jane, Jonathan Mark. B.S., Cornell U., 1949; M.A., Hunter Coll., 1963. Cons. Urban Med. Econs. Project, Hunter Coll., N.Y.C. and D.C. Dept. Health, 1962-63; health economist Office of Research and Stats., Social Security Adminstrn., Washington, 1964-66; chief grants mgmt., health div. Office Econ. Opportunity, Washington, 1966-68; sr. health analyst Office of Asst. Sec. Planning and Evaluation, HEW, Washington, 1968-71; spl. asst., asst. sec. health Office of Asst. Sec. Planning and Evaluation, HEW, 1971-72, dep. asst. sec. for health policy, research and stats., 1977-79, dep. asst. sec. for health reserach, stats. and tech., 1979-81; health care cons. 1981-88; cons., research prof. dept. health services adminstrn. George Washington U., 1988—; vis. prof. Dartmouth Med. Sch., 1976—; sr. research asso. Inst. Medicine-Nat. Acad. Scis., Washington, 1972-76. Contbr. articles to profl. jours. Mem. Med. Assistance Service bd. Commonwealth Va. Mem. Inst. Medicine of Nat. Acad. Sci. Jewish. Home: 3609 Cameron Mills Rd Alexandria VA 22305 Office: 600 21st St NW Washington DC 20052

HANKIN, CAROLE G., school system administrator; b. N.Y.C., June 7, 1942; m. Joseph N. Hankin; 3 children. BA, Sarah Lawrence Coll., 1973; MA, Columbia U. Tchrs. Coll., 1974, MEd, 1975, EdD, 1978; postgrad., Harvard U. Summer Inst., 1980, Suprs.' Acad., 1986, Cornell U. Sch. Indsl. and Labor Relations, 1987. Cert. sch. dist. adminstr., tchr. Vol. in fundraising, pub. relations Harford Day Sch., Bel Air, Md., 1966-71; tchr., tutor 1973-76; student tchr. remedial reading Purchase Elem. Sch., Harrison, N.Y., 1973-74; adj. lectr. Bronx Community Coll., CUNY, N.Y.C., 1975-77; reading and study skills specialist 1976-83; coordinator of pupil personnel services Edgemont Sch. Dist., Scarsdale, N.Y., 1980-83; dir. of pupil personnel services Port Chester-Rye Union Free Sch. Dist., Port Chester, N.Y., 1983-87; supt. schs. Enlarged City Sch. Dist., Middletown, N.Y., 1987—; cons. Lynbrook (N.Y.) High Sch.; mem. various high sch. steering and accreditation coms.; dir. Summer Title I program in reading and math. for all grades, Middletown. Author: Guide to the College and University Admissions Process, 1983; contbr. coll. conf. manuals, handbooks; panelist, copresenter numerous ednl. programs. V.p. high sch. adv. bd. College Digest; mem. Friends of the Harrison Pub. Library, Friends of the Neuberger Mus., Hartford Community Coll. Adminstrn. Bldg. restoration com.; mem. legis. adv. council Assemblyman Peter Sullivan; mem. N.Y. State Assembly, Manhattanville Coll. Women's Leadership Council and Steering Com., MONY (Port Chester Pub. Schs. Adv. Steering Com. for Adopt-a-Sch. program), Admissions Adv. Council, Westchester Community Coll.; head United Way Edn. Campaign; mem. Orange County Cancer Soc. Recipient hon. life membership N.Y. State Congress of Parents and Tchrs., plaque Am. Assn. Sch. Adminstrs. and Nat. Assn. of Sch. Execs. Nat. Supts.' Acad., 1986; named One of 100 Exec. Educators for 1988 by the Exec. Educator mag., Woman of Yr. A&S Spirited, 1987. Mem. Am. Assn. Sch. Adminstrs., Assn. For Supervision and Curriculum Devel., Council for the Arts in Westchester (ann. benefit com.), LWV, Hartford Opera Theater Assn., Nat. Assn. Secondary Sch. Prins., N.y. State Assn. Jr. Colls., N.Y. State Assn. Spl. Edn. Adminstrs., N.Y. State Reading Council, Orton Soc., Sch. Adminstrs. Assn. N.Y. State, Tchrs. Coll. Adminstrv. Women in Edn., Urban League of Westchester County, Westchester Assn. for Children with Learning Disabilities, Westchester County Hist. Soc., Westchester Putnam Rockland Assn. of Pupil Personnel Adminstrs., Westchester Putnam Rockland Personnel and Guidance Assn., Westchester Putnam Rockland Dirs. Guidance, Westchester Reading Council (exec. com., pub. chmn.), Westchester 2000 Leadership Com., Com. on Edn. and the Arts, Yonkers Reading Council, Phi Delta Kappa, Pi Lambda Theta. Home: Four Merion Dr Purchase NY 10577

HANKIN, ELAINE KRIEGER, psychologist, researcher; b. Scranton, Pa., Oct. 17, 1938; d. Maurice and Beatrice (Blumberg) Krieger; m. Abbe Hankin, Dec. 22, 1957; children: Susan Hankin-Birke, Elyse Rae. BA, Temple U., 1979, MEd, 1980; PhD, Bryn Mawr Coll., 1984. Therapist Comac Youth Service Bur., Willow Grove, Pa., 1975-76; therapist intern Aldersgate Youth Service Bur., Willow Grove, 1975-84; staff psychologist Buck's County Guidance Ctr., Doylestown, Pa., 1981-84; psychologist, ptnr., clin. dir. Abington (Pa.) Psychol. Assocs., 1984—; v.p., adminstr. dir. Corp. Devel. Systems, Abington, 1984—; adj. staff NW Inst. Psychiatry, Ft. Washington, Pa., 1986—, Eugenia Hosp., Ft. Washington, 1986—; bd. dirs. Aldersgate Youth Service Bur. Mem. AAUW, Am. Psychol. Assn., Nat. Council on Family Relations, World Fedn. for Mental Health, Assn. for Mental Health Affiliation, Pa. Psychol. Assn., Pa. Council on Family Relations, Pa. Soc. Behavioral Medicine, Phila. Folk Song Soc., Phi Beta Kappa, Psi Chi. Home: 542 Willow Grove Ave Glenside PA 19038 Office: Abington Psychol Assocs 1408 Old York Rd Abington PA 19001

HANKIN, LOIS DUREITZ, management consultant, construction company executive; b. Cleve., Aug. 6, 1945; d. Arthur Frank and Ruth Gertrude (Renner) DuReitz; student (grantee) Mt. Union Coll., 1963-64, Ohio State U., 1964-65; B.S., Case Western Res. U., 1970; m. Norman Hankin, Oct. 31, 1976. Bookkeeper, Chem. Rubber Co., Cleve., 1965-70; office mgr. Importa Ltd., Washington, 1970-71; controller Nat. Coordinating Council on Drug Edn., Washington, 1971-72; v.p. fin. Am. Footwear Industries Assn., Arlington, Va., 1972-76; legal adminstr., controller Lane and Edson, P.C., Washington, 1977-81; pvt. practice mgmt. cons., 1976-77, 81—; pres. Hankin Constrn., Inc., 1984—. Treas., Sierra Villas Homeowners Assn., 1975; active Young Democrats, 1966-69, Stokes for Mayor campaign, 1968; nat. judge Distbv. Edn. Clubs Am., 1978. Recipient Service award Howard County Handicapped, 1977; resolution of appreciation for service, fin. mgmt. com. of Am. Footwear Industries Assn., 1976. Mem. Nat. Assn. Women in Constrn., ABA, Assn. Legal Adminstrs. (nat. and capital chpt.), Nat. Council Jewish Women. Home: 7165 Deer Valley Rd Highland MD 20777

HANKINS, SHIRLEY, state representative; b. Colby, Kans., Nov. 9, 1931; d. Mack Olif Williams and Florance (Wheaton) Williams Richard; m. Myron M. Hankins, Sr., Aug. 6, 1950 (dec.); children—Myron M., Jr., Shelley D., Sherrey A. Communications program coordinator UNC Nuclear Industry Inc., 1981-86; mem. Wash. Ho. of Reps.; issues analyst Westinghouse Hanford Co.; mem. acad. adv. bd. Pa. Power and Light; bd. advisors Inst. for Regulatory Sci. Mem. Richland Rep. Women; past chmn. Tri-City Tech. Council; mem. adv. bd. Far West Fed. Lab. Consortium, exec. com. Nat. Conf. State Legislatures. Mem. Richland Fedn. Women's Clubs, Richland Bus. and Profl. Women's Clubs, Health Physics Soc. (Columbia chpt.), Am. Nuclear Soc., Inc. (Ea. Washington sect.), Thomas County Hist. Soc., Am. Legion Aux. #71, U.S. Navy League (hon.), Washington Women.

HANKS, BEVERLY JOAN, accountant, town official; b. Middlebury, Vt., Mar. 7, 1934; d. Hugh Lewis and Dorothy Emeline (Crossman) Atwood; A.S., Becker Jr. Coll., 1954; B.S. magna cum laude in Bus. Adminstrn., Nathaniel Hawthorne Coll., 1980; m. John King Hanks, Dec. 26, 1954; children—John Hugh, Donna Lynn, Cynthia Jean, Bruce Barton. Bookkeeper to controller Semikron Internat., Hudson, N.H., 1977-79; controller Commonwealth Chem. Corp., Tewksbury, Mass., 1979-80, cons., 1981; town acct. Town of Hudson (N.H.), 1981-83; co-owner, treas., clk., Harbor's Head, Inc., Boothbay Harbor, Maine, 1983—, Something Spl. Ceramics and Crafts. Town chmn. Reagan for Pres., 1976; treas. Town of Hudson, 1975-77, mem. budget com., 1976-77. Recipient Babe Ruth award, 1952. Mem. Boothbay Harbor C. of C. (fin. advisor), Boothbay Harbor Budget com., 1988—. Home and Office: 7 Union St Boothbay Harbor ME 04538

HANKS, KATHERINE LYNNE DANIEL, chemical engineer; b. June 27, 1961; d. William Eugene Sr. and Patricia Claire (Davis) Daniel; m. Lee William Hanks. BS in Chem. Engring., Clemson U., 1984. Process controller computer applications Dartco Mfg., Inc., Augusta, Ga., 1984-87; process control engr. Nutrasweet Corp., Augusta, 1987—. hosp. vol. ARC, Augusta, 1976—. Mem. Am. Inst. Chem. Engrs., Soc. of Women Engrs., Am. Nuclear Soc., Clemson Alumni Assn. (Silver Tiger club 1985). Home: 821 W Five North Rd North Augusta SC 29841 Office: Nutrasweet Corp 1750 Lovers Ln Augusta GA 30901

HANLEY, ALYCE A., state legislator; b. Pawtucket, R.I., Nov. 5, 1933; d. Lewis Rowland and Sarah (Carnaghan) Baxter; m. Monte E. Hanley, Sept. 28, 1956; children: Mark, Michael, Todd, Tim, James. RN, New Eng. Deaconess Hosp. Sch. Nursing, 1954. Mem. Alaska Ho. of Reps., Anchorage, 1985—. Mem. Youth for Christ, 1980-84, Mayor's Sch. Budget Adv. Com., 1980-81, Anchorage Sch. Bd., 1981-84; del. Rep. Dist. Conv., 1980, 84; Rep. precinct chmn. Dist 9. Mem. Gen. Fedn. Women's Clubs, Rep. Assn. Profl. and Bus. Women, New Eng. Deaconess Hosp. Alumni Assn. Home: 4007 Brentwood Circle Anchorage AK 99502 Office: Alaska State Legislature 3111 C St Suite 410 Anchorage AK 99503

HANLEY, GAIL MAUREEN, principal; b. Glen Ridge, N.J., May 3, 1953; d. Robert Patrick and Maurine Emily (Palmer) H. Student, U. Madrid, 1973; BS in Edn., Cabrini Coll., 1974; MA in Counseling, Villanova U., 1977; Cert. prin., supr., Glassboro (N.J.) State Coll., 1979. Cert. elem. tchr., student personnel services, prin., supr., sch. adminstr. Elem. tchr. Hatboro-Horsham (Pa.) Schs., 1976; migrant tchr. Fairfield Twp. Schs., Fairton, N.J., 1976-77; tchr., adminstr. Swedesboro (N.J.)-Woolwich Schs., 1977-84; prin. Riverside (N.J.) Twp. Schs., 1984-85; prin. Medford (N.J.) Twp. Schs., 1985—, effective parenting facilitator, 1987—; tchr. parenting Riverside High Sch., 1984-85; guest speaker on interviewing Glassboro State Coll., 1984-87; assessor of new prins. for the state Assessment and Devel. Ctr., Manalapin, N.J., 1987. Mem. N.J. Assn. Suprs. and Curriculum Devel. (exec. com. 1986—, Cert. of Appreciation 1987), N.J. Assn. Sch. Adminstrs., N.J. Prins./Suprs. Assn., Burlington County Elem. and Middle Schs. Adminstrs. Assn., Phi Delta Kappa (pres. 1986—). Republican. Roman Catholic. Office: Medford Twp Schs Stokes Rd Medford NJ 08055

HANLON, CAMILLE CAROL, psychology educator; b. New Orleans, Dec. 25, 1937; d. Philip Samuel Hanlon and Mary Sue (Berthelot) Banks. BA with highest honors, U. Tex., 1958, MA, 1959; PhD, Stanford U., 1964. Asst. prof. psychology U. Iowa, Iowa City, 1964-67; asst. prof. psychology Conn. Coll., New London, 1968-73, assoc. prof., 1973-86, chmn. dept., 1979-81, prof., 1986—; vis. scholar Harvard U., Cambridge, Mass., 1974-75; lectr. Harvard U., 1967-68. NIH fellow, 1959-62, 1967-68; NIH grantee, 1975. Mem. Internat. Assn. Study Child Lang., Am. Psychol. Assn., Soc. Research Child Devel., Phi Beta Kappa (pres. New London chpt. 1986-87). Democrat. Roman Catholic. Home: 640 Williams St New London CT 06320 Office: Conn Coll Box 1488 New London CT 06320

HANLON, DEBORAH ANN, environmental scientist; b. Riverside, Calif., Apr. 13, 1950; d. George Allan and Janice (Renfered) H. BS in Microbiology, San Jose State U., 1976; MPA, Calif. State Consortium, Ventura, 1986. Registered sanitarian. Sanitarian Stanislaus County, Modesto, Calif., 1976-80; hazardous materials specialist Ventura County, 1980—. Author reference manuals; contbr. articles to sci. jour. Mem. Nat. Environ. Health Assn., Calif. Environ. Heatlh Assn. (sec. 1984-86), Hazardous Materials Cen. Research Inst. Home: 1746 E Morada Pl Altadena CA 91001 Office: Jacobs Engring Group 251 S Lake Ave Pasadena CA 91101

HANLON, PAMELA, communications executive; b. Sioux Falls, S.D., Sept. 24, 1946; d. Virgil T. and Edna C. (Petersen) H.; m. Charles J. Hanley, May 28, 1976. BJ, U. Mo., 1968. Flight attendant Pan Am. World Airways, N.Y.C., 1968-71; news reporter AP, N.Y.C., 1971-73; rep. pub. relations Nat. Airlines, N.Y.C., 1973-75; mgr. pub. relations Pan Am. World Airways, 1975-79; dir. investor relations Pan Am. World Airways, N.Y.C., 1979-82; system dir. corp. communications Pan Am. Corp./Pan Am. World Airways, N.Y.C., 1982—. Mem. Nat. Investor Relations Inst., Wings Club. Office: Pan Am Corp 200 Park Ave New York NY 10166

HANLON, PAMELA IRENE (KASKIW), health service administrator; b. Park Falls, Wis., Aug. 10, 1948; d. James and Irene Leah (Schwall) Katchis; m. E. Andrew Kaskiw, July 7, 1984; 1 child, Stacey Irene Hanlon. BS in Acctg. Mgmt., U. Evansville, 1983; MBA in Health Care Mgmt., U. Colo., 1986. Cert. Health Care Fin. Mgmt. Cost acct. Isothermics, Inc., Franklin, N.J., 1975-76; dir. fiscal services Benjamin Rush Ctr., Syracuse, N.Y., 1976-78; fin. analyst Mead Johnson, Evansville, Ind., 1978-81; dir. fin. planning St. Mary's Med. Ctr., Evansville, 1981-84; controller Luth. Med. Ctr., Wheat Ridge, Colo., 1984-86; v.p. hosp., physician networks Integrated Med. Systems, Golden, Colo., 1986—; lectr. various seminars. Contbr. articles to profl. jours. Active Title XX Rev. Bd., Sussex, N.J., 1975; bd. dirs. Argyle Sq. Park. Mem. Health Care Fin. Mgmt. Assn. (advanced, matrix com. 1982), Am. Coll. Health Care Execs., Nat. Assn. Female Execs., Soc. Hosp. Planning and Mktg., Colo. Healthcare Adminstrs. Forum. Clubs: Newburg Swim Team (pres., treas. 1980-82), Deer Blvd Corp. (treas. 1984-86). Home: 11861 Bryant Circle Denver CO 80234 Office: Integrated Med Systems 1500 W 6th Ave Golden CO 80401

HANNA, INGA HAUGAARD, financial planner; b. Portland, Maine, Jan. 6, 1930; d. Ejnar Nielsen and Helene Martine (Buje) Haugaard; B.S., Simmons Coll., Boston, 1954; M.B.A., U. Mo., Columbia, 1973; m. John G. Hanna, July 2, 1949; children—Erik H., Charlotte H. Stock broker Putnam, Coffin & Burr, Portland, 1964-67; investment research officer Canal Nat. Bank, Portland, 1967-70; exec. dir. Treemont of Dallas, 1973-75, Portland YWCA, 1976-80; ind. fin. planner, Portland, 1980—; corporator Maine Savs. Bank. Mem. bd. World Affairs Council Maine, 1980-85. Recipient Thomas P. Weill award U. Mo., 1973; Danforth asso., 1981. Mem. Inst. Fin. Planners (cert.), Internat. Assn. Fin. Planners, Am. Soc. Profl. Cons., Maine Econ. Soc. (bd. dirs. 1983-85).

HANNA, VICKI LYNNE, geologist, consultant; b. Noel, Mo., Jan. 26, 1953; d. John Paul and Shirley Jean (Goss) H. BS, Pan-Am. U., 1975; postgrad. Bowling Green State U., 1980-81; AA in Bus., Crowder Coll., 1988. Geologist, Mo. Dept. Natural Resources, Rolla, Mo., 1978-79; geologic asst. Weller & Bates, Edinburg, Tex., 1974-76, Bates & Rodgers, 1974-76; geology cons., Pineville, Mo., 1981—. Mem. Am. Assn. Petroleum Geologists, Soc. Econ. Paleontologists and Mineralogists, Assn. Women Geoscientists. Baha'i. Home: Roland and King Ave Pineville MO 64856 Office: Rt 1 Box N Pineville MO 64856

HANNAH, BARBARA ANN, nurse, educator; b. Pawnee, Okla., Sept. 25, 1943; d. Harold Ray and Betty Jean (Newport) Norris; m. Charles Bush Hannah, Mar. 25, 1971; children: Charles Douglas, Harry William. AS, Rogers State Coll., Claremore, Okla., 1974; BS in nursing, Tulsa U., 1976; MS, Okla U., 1985. Registered nurse. Nurse St. Francis Hosp., Tulsa, 1968-77; dir. clin. prodn. CSI Prodns. for Medcom Inc., Tulsa, 1977-86; edn. specialist St. Francis Hosp., Tulsa, 1986—; cons. St. Anthony Hosp., Okla. City, 1985; affiliate faculty, mem emergency cardiac care com. Am. Heart Assn., 1986—; ACLS faculty, mem. NMA program com. St. Francis Hosp., Tulsa, 1986—. Producer audio-visual programs for nursing edn., 1977-86. Mem. Food & Refreshment Com. Channel 8 fund raising drive, Tulsa, 1985, 86. Mem. Tulsa Greater Area Chpt. Acute Care Nurses Assn. (seminar dir.), Nat. Assn. Female Execs., Sigma Theta Tau. Home: Box 112 Skiatook OK 74070 Office: Saint Francis Hosp 6161 S Yale Tulsa OK 74101

HANNAN, BRADLEY, publishing company executive; b. Rochester, N.Y., Apr. 24, 1935; d. Jack Seymour MacArthur and Alice E. (Knapp) Staley; m. William J. Hannan, Jr., June 15, 1957 (div. 1976); children: Megan Lee, Timothy, Patrick, Moira. BA, Ariz. State U., 1957. Tchr. various sch. dists. Ariz., 1957-62; English language cons. Evanston (Ill.) Twp. High Sch., 1963-65; editor, then sr. editor Harper & Row Pubs., Evanston, 1965-75; sr. reading text editor Scott, Foresman & Co., Glenview, Ill., 1975-78, sr. editor lang. arts, 1982-87; dir. reading McDougal Littell & Co., Evanston, 1978-81; project dir. spelling Ednl. Challenges, Alexandria, Va., 1981-82; dir. curriculum and product mgmt. for reading and lang. arts texts Open Court Pub. Co., Chgo. and Peru, Ill., 1987—; speaker Internat. Reading Assn., New Orleans, 1981, Chgo. Women in Publishing, 1981, Childrens' Reading Roundtable, Chgo., 1985; developer reading textbook series. Mem. Internat. Reading Assn., Nat. Council Tchrs. English, Chgo. Book Clinic. Home: 8500 N Trumbull St Skokie IL 60076 Office: Open Court Pub Co 315 5th St Peru IL 61354

HANNAY, HILDA JULIA, psychologist; b. Lincoln, Eng., May 21, 1944; came to U.S., 1969; d. Christopher Lynton and Hilda Mabel (Beamish) H. BA, U. Western Ont., London, 1965, MA, 1968; PhD, U. Iowa, 1972.

Asst. prof. psychology Auburn (Ala.) U., 1973-77, assoc. prof., 1977-83, prof., 1983-87; prof. U. Houston, 1987—; cons. dept. neurology U. Ala., 1981-87, cons. dept. psychology Tuskegee VA Med. Ctr., Ala., 1978-87. Editor: Experimental Techniques in Human Neuropsychology, 1986. Contbr. articles to profl. jours. V.p. Ala. Head Injury Found., 1986-87. Mem. Am. Psychol. Assn., Ala. Psychol. Assn. (Disting. Sci. award 1982), Southeastern Psychol. Assn., Internat. Neuropsychol. Assn. (bd. govs. 1987-90). Office: U Houston Dept Psychology 4800 Calhoun Rd Houston TX 77004

HANNEGAN, MARTHA MARIE, fraternity executive; b. Kansas City, Mo., Nov. 8, 1932; d. Joseph F. and Mayme A. (Overbay) Carolan; student Baker U., 1950-53; B.A., U. Wichita, 1959; m. Robert Eugene Hannegan, Aug. 30, 1958 (dec.); children—Lawrence David, Thomas Joseph, John Patrick; m. George T. Hanlon, Mar. 12, 1988. Elem. tchr. pub. schs., Wichita, Kans., 1954-58; vol. officer, alumna pres. Alpha Chi Omega, Lincoln, Nebr., 1963-65, province pres., Nebr. and Iowa, 1969-73, asst. collegiate v.p., Phoenix and Houston, 1973-76, nat. collegiate v.p., Houston, 1976-80, nat. pres., 1980-83; dir. devel. Alpha Chi Omega Found., 1983-87. Democrat. Mem. United Ch. of Christ. Home: 5963 Preston Valley Dr Dallas TX 75240 also: Waterwood Box 53 Huntsville TX 77340

HANNEN, ADA LORELEI, marketing professional; b. High Point, N.C., Nov. 8, 1942; d. Pearl Clayton and Germaine Rose (Slover) Jones; m. Charles Floyd Hannen, Apr. 6, 1960; children: Kimberly Rose, Paula Tamala, Scott Kevin. Grad. high sch., Apopka, Fla. Operator directory assistance So. Bell Tel. & Tel. Co., Orlando, Fla., 1969-72; clk. service orders So. Bell Tel. & Tel. Co., Orlando, 1972-74; clk. customer service So. Tel.& Tel.Co., Orlando, 1974-75, clk. dist. office, 1975-79; sales rep. So. Bell Tel. & Tel. Co., Orlando, 1979-85; mgr. directory sales Bell South Advt. and Pub. Co., Orlando, 1988—; staff mgr., tng. So. Bell Tel. & Tel. Co., Orlando, 1988—; staff mgr. trainer Bellsouth Advt. and Pub. Co., 1988—; ptnr. retail clothing store Ladies' Consignment Shop. Mem. Nat. Assn. Female Execs. Office: 3670 Maguire Blvd Orlando FL 32803 also: Ladies Cosignment Shop Orlando FL 32803

HANNIGAN, VERA SIMMONS, federal agency administrator; b. Bklyn., Aug. 20, 1932; d. John Albert and Sadie Marion (Ziegler) Rogel; student U. Md., 1965-71; m. John J. Hannigan, June 15, 1974; children by previous marriage—Stephen F. Simmons, Vera Marifay Simmons King, Susan G. Simmons Bolle. Mem. staff Sen. William B. Saxbe of Ohio, 1972-74; confidential asst. Asst. Atty. Gen. for Legis. Affairs W. Vincent Rakestraw, Dept. Justice, 1974-75; with Office of Legis. Affairs, The White House, Washington, 1975-77; Washington rep. land devel. Union Pacific Corp., Washington, 1977-87; deputy dir. for congressional liason, EPA, 1987—. Active local Va. politics, Republican Party. Home: 11220 Wedge Dr Reston VA 22090 Office: 401 M St SW Suite 835 WT Washington DC 20460

HANNOLD, SHIRLEY BOUILLET, small business owner; b. Phila., Aug. 5, 1925; d. Eugene Silvain and Sara Mae (Oxley) Bouillet; m. Frank Colligan Hannold (div. 1981); children: Frank Eugene, Kathleen Sue, Scott Edward, Bruce Charles. Student, Hillsboro Jr. Coll., Tampa, Fla.; cert., Wellesley Coll., 1986. Sec., receptionist Charleston (S.C.) Rubber Co., 1961-63; adminstrv. asst. Jim Walters Doors, Tampa, 1976-78; travel agt. Travel Advs., San Antonio, 1981-83; owner Buccaneer Travel Cons., Naples, Fla., 1983—. Vol. chmn. ARC, Panama City, Fla., 1966-69; chmn. internat. affairs Naples Women's Club, 1988. Mem. Inst. Cert. Travel Agts., S.W. Travel Industry Assn. Republican. Club: Officer's Wives (Tyndall AFB, Fla., Bentwaters, Eng.), Naples Shores Country, Naples Women's. Home: 3300 Binnacle Dr Apt 213 Naples FL 33940 Office: Buccaneer Travel Cons 3562 N Tamiami Trail Naples FL 33940

HANNON, KITTY SUE, airline pilot; b. San Antonio, Oct. 10, 1954; d. Stanley Edgar and Barbara Lea (Owens) H.; m. Candler Gerald Schaffer, June 10, 1976 (div. 1983). MusB, U. Miami, Coral Gables, Fla., 1976. Flight attendant Eastern Airlines, Miami, Fla., 1977-84; pilot, instr. Tibben Flight Lines, Cedar Rapids, Iowa, 1981, Watham Flying Service, Cedar Rapids, 1981; pilot Mid Continent Airlines, Dubuque, Iowa, 1981-83, Cav Air/Jimmy Jet, Ft. Lauderdale, Fla., 1983, Airlift Internat. Airlines, Miami, 1983-84, Larken, Inc., Cedar Rapids, 1984, Life Investors, Cedar Rapids, 1984; pilot Eastern Airlines, Miami, 1984—, check airman, 1987—, instr. Boeing 727, 1985—, supr. pilots, 1985—, co-pilot, 1986—, flight engr., 1984—; speaker in field. Author, producer: boeing 727 Emergency and Abnorman Training Video, 1988. Vol. pilot Spl. Olympics Fla., Miami, Tallahassee, Fla., 1988; career day guest speaker Miami Schs., 1986, 88. Music and Band Scholar U. Miami, 1972-76; named Honoree, YWCA, 1984. Mem. YWCA Women's Network, Airline Pilots Assn., Aircraft Owners and Pilots Assn., Orange Key, Smithsonian Air and Space, Mortar Bd., Phi Kappa Lambda, Mu Alpha Theta, Phi Kappa Phi, Alpha Lambda Delta. Republican. Lutheran. Home: 3420 Torremolinos Ave Miami FL 33178

HANRETTY, JULIE CLAIRE, criminal investigator, educator; b. Sacramento, Calif., Jan. 30, 1950; d. Peter Thomas Sr. and Ada Margaret (Giannoni) H. BA in Pol. Sci., Gonzaga U., 1972; BA in Criminal Justice, Calif. State U., Sacramento, 1973, MA in Criminal Justice, 1977; M in Pub. Adminstrn., U. So. Calif., 1978, postgrad. Criminal investigator Sacramento County. Pub. Defender, 1974—; instr. Los Rios Community Coll., Sacramento, 1981—; lectr. Calif. State U., Sacramento, 1983—. Bd. dirs. Families First, Davis, Calif., 1985—; vol. Oak Park Food Locker, Sacramento, 1987; active city council meetings Sacramento, 1982—. Mem. Def. Investigators Assn. (sec./treas. 1987—, bd. dirs. 1984—, v.p. 1988), Nat. Def. Investigators Assn., Am. Soc. Pub. Adminstrs., Am. Legion Aux. Democrat. Roman Catholic. Club: Caledonian. Lodge: Daus. Scotia. Office: County Sacramento Pub Defender 700 H St #0270 Sacramento CA 95814

HANSBURG, FREDA KELNER, mental health consultant; b. N.Y.C., Apr. 18, 1950; d. Leon M. and Muriel L. (Goldstein) Forman; m. Frederick Kelner (div. 1984); m. Daniel Hansburg, Jan. 19, 1985. AB magna cum laude, Barnard Coll., 1972; MSS, Bryn Mawr Grad. Sch. of Social Work, 1977; PhD, Temple U., 1988. Cert. trainer in psychiat. rehab. Social worker NE Community Mental Health Ctr., Phila., 1977-78, Community Life Services, Darby, Pa., 1978-79; assoc. Ctr. for Integrated Therapy and Edn., Devon, Pa., 1979-80; dir. aftercare services Intercommunity Action, Inc., Phila., 1980-82; coordinator mental health Bridgeway House Tech. Assistance Ctr., Monmouth Junction, N.J., 1982—; psychiat. rehab. trainer Ctr. for Psychiat. Rehab., Boston U., 1985—; assoc. Mental Health Cons., Furlong, Pa., 1988—. Mem. Acad. Cert. Social Workers, N.J. Psychiat. Rehab. Assn. Home: 304 S Beaver Hill Jenkintown PA 19046 Office: Bridgeway House Tech Assistance Ctr 10 Wynwood Dr US Rt 1 Monmouth Junction NJ 08852

HANSBURY, VIVIEN HOLMES, educator; b. Richmond, Va., Feb. 5, 1927; d. Arthur Jefferson and Mary (Spain) Holmes; m. Horace Trent, Dec. 24, 1942 (div. Feb. 1958); children: Sandra, Horace Jr., Vernard; m. Leonard Andrew Hansbury, Oct. 28, 1962. Cert. elem. and spl. edn. tchr., Pa. Fiscal acct. VA, Phila., 1950-62; intermediate unit tchr. Delaware County (Pa.) Pub. Schs., 1966-68, supr. spl. edn., 1968-69; counselor, instr. Pa. State U., Ogontz, 1969-74; spl. edn. tchr. Phila. Schs., 1974-76, program mgr., 1976-78, instrnl. advisor, 1978-84, resource tchr., cons., 1984—; ednl. cons. NIA Psychol. Assocs., Phila., 1982—; Pa. coordinator Assault on Illiteracy, 1983—, Northeastern sectional dir., 1988—; tutor Mayor's Commn. on Literacy, Phila., 1984—. Den mother Boy Scouts Am., Phila., 1957; dir. adult basic edn. Pinn Meml. Bapt. Ch., Phila., 1985—; pres. Phila. chpt. Pan-Hellenic Council, 1982; exec. bd. Phila. Opportunities for Industrialization Ctr., 1984—. Recipient numerous community service awards; named Tchr. of Yr. Sch. Dist. Phila., 1988. Mem. Northeastern Fedn. Women. (recording sec. Phila. 1987), Phila. Coalition Federated Women (pres. 1988), Pa. Fedn. Women's Clubs (fin. sec. 1986—, Disting. Service award 1987), AAUW, Sigma Pi Epsilon Delta (pres. Phila. 1983, Spl. Educator of Yr. 1986), Kappa Omega Zeta, Zeta Phi Beta (pres. Phila. 1981-86, Woman of Yr. 1986). Democrat. Clubs: Monday Evening (pres. 1984—), Thirty Clusters (pres. 1985-87). Office: Phila Sch Dist Amy Six Sch Washington Ln and Musgrave St Philadelphia PA 19144

HANSEN, CAROL DIANNE, federal agency administrator; b. Memphis, Oct. 15, 1948; d. Stanley Frederick and Rheba (Elizabeth) H. Student, Western Ill. U., 1966-68, BS, U. Ill., 1970, MA in History Edn., 1972; PhD, U. N.C., 1985. Cert. secondary tchr., Ill., N.Y., N.C., Switzerland. Tchr. various schs., Switzerland and U.S., 1970-75; research asst. Internat. Program for Tng. in Health, Chapel Hill, N.C., 1981-83; teaching asst. Sch. Edn. U. N.C., Chapel Hill, 1983; intern Arthur Andersen & Co., St. Charles, Ill., 1983-84; sr. instructional designer Washington, 1984-85; asst. prof. Sch. Edn. Am. U., Washington, 1985; program mgr. ednl. design and evaluation services Bur. Diplomatic Security Tng. Ctr. U.S. Dept. State, Washington, 1986—. Co-author: (with Wallace Hannum) Instructional Systems Development in Large Organizations, 1988, Educational Technology, 1988. Fulbright-Hay scholar, 1973. Mem. Am. Ednl. Research Assn. (Spl. Interest Group evaluation), Am. Soc. for Tng. and Devel., Nat. Soc. for Performance and Instrn., Alliance Francaise, Am. Evaluation Assn. Episcopalian.

HANSEN, CORAL JUNE, nurse, respiratory therapist; b. Seattle, June 5, 1950; d. Raymond Leland and Rosalie (Van Deman) H. Cert. in respiratory therapy, Seattle Cen. Coll., 1975; BS in Nursing summa cum laude, Seattle U., 1987, postgrad. in psychosocial nursing. Reg. respiratory therapist, nurse, Washington. Respiratory therapist Cura-Care Inc., Modesto, Calif., 1975-84, Northwest Hosp., Seattle, 1984-88; critical care and rehab. nurse University Hosp., Seattle, 1986-87. Contbr. letters to profl. jours. Mem. Am. Nurses Assn., DAR, Sigma Theta Tau.

HANSEN, DEBORAH ANN, corrections official; b. East Brunswick, N.J., July 25, 1950; d. Oscar and Julia (Keleman) H. Student, Worcester (England) Coll., 1971-72; BS in Psychology, Trenton (N.J.) State Coll., 1972; MS in Criminal Justice, Rutgers U., 1980. Parole officer N.J. Dept. Corrections, Trenton, 1972-77, sr. parole officer, 1977-79, chief bur. interstate services, 1980-84, dep. compact administr., 1984—; Cons. Washington Dept. Corrections, 1986, Maine Dept. Corrections, 1983, also trainer; trainer affirmative action N.J. Dept. Corrections, Trenton, 1985-86; coordinator and project mgr. Nat. Commn. to Restructure the Interstate Compact for Parolees and Probations, 1985—. Contbr. articles to profl. jours. Twp. coordinator Jim Courtier for Congress, East Brunswick, N.J. 1984; campaign writer, advisor Flemming/Bowen for State Assembly, East Brunswick, 1983; mem. Middlesex County (N.J.) Rep. Orgn. Recipient Proclamation N.J. Legis., 1987, Gov.'s award Outstanding Women in State Govt., 1988, Frederick's award Parole and Probation Compact Adminstrs. Assn., 1987. Fellow Council of State Govts. (com. on suggested state legis.); mem. Am. Parole and Probation Assn. (nat. program com. 1985-87), Parole and Probation Compact Adminstrs. Assn. (pres. 1986-87), Psi Chi. Roman Catholic. Office: NJ Dept Corrections Whittlesey Rd Trenton NJ 08625

HANSEN, DIANA VICTORIA, communications company executive; b. Mobile, Ala., Feb. 25, 1947; d. LeRoy T. and Nella V. (Franz) H. A.A., San Antonio Jr. Coll., 1967; student U. of Ams., 1968, Am. Inst. Banking, 1971; B.A., U. Tex.-Austin, 1969. Curriculum writer SW Ednl. Research Lab, Austin, 1979-70; sec. First City Bank, Houston, 1971-72; secretarial stenographer SW Bell Telephone Co., Houston, 1972-74, dist. sec., 1974, asst. v.p., sec., Dallas, then Austin, 1974-77, exec. sec. Dallas, 1977-78, staff mgr., 1978-83; mgr. AT&T, Austin, 1983-87 , mgr., Chgo., 1987—. Active Tex. Republican Party. Mem. Nat. Assn. Female Execs. (bd. dirs. 1983), Telecommunications Network in Tex. (founder, bd. dirs.), Community Assn. (bd. dirs.). Roman Catholic. Author: Bilingual Education, 1970. Home: 4250 N Marine Dr Apt 2035 Chicago IL 60613-1715 Office: AT&T 1 N Wacker Dr Chicago IL 60606

HANSEN, FLORENCE MARIE CONGIOLOSI (MRS. JAMES S. HANSEN), social worker; b. Middletown, N.Y., Jan. 7, 1934; d. Joseph James and Florence (Harrigan) Congiolosi; B.A., Coll. New Rochelle, 1955; M.S.W., Fla. State U., 1960; m. James S. Hansen, June 16, 1959; 1 dau., Florence M. Caseworker, Orange County Dept. Pub. Welfare, N.Y., 1955-57, Cath. Welfare Bur., Miami, Fla., 1957-58; supr. Cath. Family Service, Spokane, Wash., 1960, Cuban Children's Program, Spokane, 1962-66; dir. Spokane and Inland Empire Artificial Kidney Ctr., 1967—, Social Service Dept. Sacred Heart Kidney Ctr. (formerly Sacred Heart Med. Ctr.), Spokane, 1967-85, bd. dirs. kidney ctr., 1962—. Asst. in program devel. St. Margaret's Hall, Spokane, 1961-62; trustee Family Counseling Service Spokane County, 1981—, also bd. dirs.; mem. budget allocation panel United Way, 1964-76, mem. planning com., 1968-77, mem. admissions com., 1969-70, chmn. projects com. 1972-73, active work with Cuban refugees; mem. kidney disease adv. com. Wash.-Alaska Regional Med. Program, 1970-73. Mem. Spokane Quality of Life Commn., 1974-75. Mem. Nat. Assn. Social Workers (chpt. pres. 1972-74), Acad. Cert. Social Workers (charter). Roman Catholic. Home: 5609 Northwest Blvd Spokane WA 99205 Office: Sacred Heart Med Ctr W 101 8th St Spokane WA 99204

HANSEN, FRANCES FRAKES, art educator; b. Harrisburg, Mo.; d. Eugene Nelson and Cyrene (Graham) Frakes; m. Claude B. Hansen. BFA, U. Denver, 1937; MA, U. No. Colo., 1941. Prof. of art Colo. Women's Coll., Denver, 1942-73; art instr. U. Denver, Denver, 1942-45, 52-57; research and display design, anthropology dept. Denver Mus. of Natural History, 1973-78; artist editorial bd. Denver Botanic Gardens, 1976—. Illustrator: Song of the Ghost Trains, 1981; contbr. numerous articles to profl. jours. Active Cen. City Opera Assn., Denver Lyric Opera Guild, Denver Art Mus., Denver Mus. of Natural History. Faculty research grantee Colo. Women's Coll. Mem. AAUP (emeritus mem.), Alpha Gamma Delta, PEO. Democrat. Disciples of Christ. Home: 700 Pontiac St Denver CO 80220

HANSEN, JOANNA LYNNE, molecular biologist; b. Rochester, Minn., Dec. 30, 1953; d. Gerald E. and Harriet (Wilson) H. BA, UCLA, 1976; PhD, U. Utah, 1982. Lab. tech. Wadsworth VA Hosp., Los Angeles, 1974-77; staff fellow NIH Lab. Infectious Diseases, Bethesda, Md., 1982-83, NIH Lab. Parasitic Diseases, Bethesda, 1983-85; asst. prof. hematology U. Utah Med. Ctr., Salt Lake City, 1985—. Contbr. articles to sci. jours. Grantee U. Utah Research Com., 1985-86; Biomed. Research Support grantee U. Utah, 1986-87. Office: U Utah Med Ctr Div of Hematology Salt Lake City UT 84132

HANSEN, JOYCE KAY, accountant, tax consultant, educator; b. Cedar Springs, Mich., Sept. 26, 1946; d. Raymond A. and Mildred Ruth (Mc Intyre) Wesche; m. John Raymond Hansen, Sept. 3, 1966; children—James K., Jeffrey K. BS in Journalism and Edn., Cen. Mich. U., 1968, MA in Math., 1971. Instr. math Clare Pub. Schs., Mich., 1968-72; adj. prof. Davenport Coll., Grand Rapids, Mich., 1974-79; prof., head dept. Jordan Coll., Cedar Springs, 1978-79; founder, dir. Mich. Tax Cons., Lansing, 1979-83; adj. asst. prof. Aquinas Coll., Grand Rapids, 1979—; pres., acct. J & J Bus. Services, Inc., Cedar Springs, 1980—; pres., prin. Ascii Systems Corp., 1987—, Four J Enterprises Inc., 1987—. Columnist Cedar Springs Clipper, 1979-80. Treas. Cedar Springs Econ. Devel. Corp., 1982-85. Named 1st woman to 200 Club, Mich. Tax Cons., 1980. Mem. Nat. Assn. Enrolled Agts., Ind. Accts. Assn. Mich. (edn. co-chmn. 1985-86, edn. chairperson 1986-87, vice chmn., chmn. Grand Rapids chpt. 1985-88), Nat. Soc. Pub. Accts. (rules com. 1986), Accreditation Council for Accountancy, Cedar Springs Area C. of C. (co-founder 1980, bd. dirs., pres., v.p. 1980-87). Republican. Methodist. Club: West Mich. Bus. (Grand Rapids). Avocations: reading, camping, travel, movies. Home: 4171 Indian Lakes Rd Cedar Springs MI 49319 Office: J & J Bus Services Inc PO Box 560 20 E Beech St Cedar Springs MI 49319

HANSEN, KATHRYN GERTRUDE, former state official, association editor; b. Gardner, Ill., May 24, 1912; d. Harry J. and Marguerite (Gaston) Hansen; BS with honors, U. Ill., 1934, MS, 1936. Personnel asst. U. Ill., Urbana, 1945-46, supr. tng. and activities, 1946-47, personnel officer, instr. psychology, 1947-52, exec. sec. U. Ill. Civil Service System Ill., also sec. for merit bd., 1952-61, adminstrv. officer, sec. merit bd., 1961-68, dir. system, 1968-72; lay asst. firm Webber, Balbach, Theis and Follmer, P.C., Urbana, Ill., 1972-74. Bd. dirs. U. YWCA, 1952-55, chmn., 1954-55; bd. dirs. Champaign-Urbana Symphony, 1978-81; sec. Women's Assn. 1st Presbyn. Ch., Champaign, 1986. Mem. Coll. and Univ. Personnel Assn. (hon., life mem., editor jour. 1955-73, newsletter, internat. pres. 1967-68, nat. publs. award named in her honor 1987), Annuitants Assn. State Univs. Retirement System Ill. (state sec.-treas. 1974-75), Pres.'s Council U. Ill. (life), Library Friends, U. Ill. (bd. dirs.), U. Ill. Alumni Assn. (life), U. Ill. Found., Campus Round Table U. Ill., Nat. League Am. Pen Women, AAUW (state 1st v.p. 1958-60, 50 yr. mem.), Champaign-Urbana Symphony Guild, Secretariat U. Ill. (life), Grundy County Hist. Soc., Delta Kappa Gamma (state pres. 1961-63), Phi Mu (life), Kappa Delta Pi, Kappa Tau Alpha. Presbyterian. Clubs: Monday Writers, Fortnightly (Champaign-Urbana). Lodge: Order Eastern Star. Author: (with others) A Plan of Position Classification for Colleges and Universities; A Classification Plan for Staff Positions at Colleges and Universities, 1968; Grundy-Corners, 1982; Sarah, A Documentary of Her Life and Times, 1984, Ninety Years with Fortnightly, Vols. I and II, an historical compilation, 1986; editor: The Illini Worker, 1946-52; Campus Pathways, 1952-61; This is Your Civil Service Handbook, 1960-67; author, cons., editor publs. on personnel practices. Home: 1004 E Harding Dr Apt 307 Urbana IL 61801

HANSEN, LAURIE JO, executive administrator; b. Arcadia, Calif., Apr. 26, 1960; d. Mark Herman and Sally Jo (High) H. BA in Social Sci., Communications, U. So. Calif., 1982. Staff cons. Calif. State Senate, Sacramento, 1981, 1982; staff cons. Calif. State Assembly, Glendale, 1981; campaign cons. John Garamendi for Gov., Santa Ana, Calif., 1981-82; lobbyist, cons. Murdoch, Mockler & Assoc., Sacramento, 1982-85; exec. adminstr. Calif. State Sen. John Seymour, Sacramento, 1985—. Mem. Nat. Charity League, Newport Beach, Calif. Mem. U. So. Calif. Scapa Praetors (v.p. 1985-86). Republican. Lodge: Internat. Order of Jobs Daus. (honored queen 1977). Office: Office of Sen John Seymour State Capitol Room 3074 Sacramento CA 95814

HANSEN, LISA YOUNG, municipal agency administrator; b. Rexburg, Idaho, Apr. 28, 1957; d. Rulon Squires and Lucille Cole (Young) McCarrey; m. Darrel Chancy Hansen, Mar. 23, 1984. A, Ricks Coll., 1977; student, Harvard U., summers 1977, 78, Brigham Young U., 1980-82. Geneal. clk. Stevensons Geneal. Ctr., Provo, Utah, 1977; typesetter, news clk. Valley News, Rexburg, Idaho, 1977-78; credit clk. Credit Bur. Idaho Falls, 1982-83; adminstrv. asst. Bonneville County Civil Defense, Idaho Falls, 1983—; speaker in field; radiol. defense officer State of Idaho, Bureau of Disaster Services, 1984—; sec. Bonneville Tricentennial Commn., 1983—, Bonneville Flood Control Coordinatig com., 1983—, Bonneville Bicentennial of the Constn. com., 1983—. Contbr. articles to profl. jours. Rep. United Way, Idaho Falls, 1980; vote clerk Bonneville County Elections Dept., Idaho Falls, 1980, 81. Mem. Am. Civil Defense Assn. (co-resolutions chmn. 1985-87), Idaho Civil Defense Assn., Lamba Delta Sigma. Republican. Mormon. Home: 874 W Goldie St Idaho Falls ID 83402 Office: Bonneville County Civil Def 605 N Capital Ave Idaho Falls ID 83402

HANSEN, LORRAINE SUNDAL (SUNNY), counselor, educator; b. Albert Lea, Minn., Oct. 11, 1929; d. Rasmus O. and Cora B. Sundal; m. Tor Kjaerstad Hansen, Dec. 15, 1962; children—Sonja, Tor S. B.S., U. Minn., 1951, M.A., 1957, Ph.D., 1962; postgrad. U. Oslo, 1959-60. English tchr., St. Louis Park, Minn., 1951-53, Lab. Sch., U. Chgo., 1953-54; tchr. English and journalism Univ. High Sch., U. Minn., Mpls., 1954-57, counselor, dir. counseling, 1957-70; asst. prof., assoc. prof., prof. ednl. psychology, 1962—, dir. project BORN FREE; cons. schs. and colls.; worldwide lectr., dir. workshops on career devel. and career edn. Author: Career Guidance Practices in School and Community, 1970; An Examination of Concepts and Definitions of Career Education, 1976; (with others) Educating for Career Development, 1975, 80; Career Development and Planning, 1982; Eliminating Sex Stereotyping in Schools, 1984. Editor: Career Development and Counseling of Women, 1978; numerous BORN FREE publs., videotapes and TV courses. Contbr. articles to profl. publs., chpts. to books. Fulbright scholar, 1959-60; named Outstanding Leader in Edn. Mpls. YWCA, 1984; recipient Career Devel. Profl. Award S.E. Minn. chpt. Am. Soc. for Tng. and Devel., 1986. Fellow Am. Psychol. Assn.; mem. Minn. Psychol. Assn., Adminstrv. Women in Edn., Am. Assn. for Counseling and Devel., Minn. Assn. for Counseling and Devel. (pres.-elect, cert. recognition 1976, research award 1980, Outstanding Achievement award 1986), Nat. Career Devel. Assn. (pres. 1985-86), Minn. Career Devel. Assn. (pres. 1982-83), Internat. Assn. Ednl.-Vocat. Guidance, Internat. Round Table for Advancement of Counseling (exec. council, v.p. 1986—), Am. Sch. Counselors Assn., Am. Coll. Personnel Assn., Assn. for Counselor Edn. and Supervision (Nat. Disting. Mentor award 1985). Democrat. Congregationalist. Club: Minn. Women's Consortium. Office: U Minn Dept Ednl Psychology 139 Burton Hall 178 Pillsbury Dr Minneapolis MN 55455

HANSEN, MARGARET RYAN, financial consultant; b. Jersey City, Aug. 20, 1919; d. Charles A. and Olive E. (Tompkins) Ryan; m. Russell H. Hansen, Oct. 10, 1942; children: Jane Elizabeth, Joyce Elaine. BA in Math. and Econs., NYU. Asst. engr. PSE&G Co., Newark, 1942-50; exec. dir. Community Child Guidance Clinic, Jersey City, 1958-60; treas., mgr. Bus. Roundtable, N.Y.C. and Washington, 1969-84; freelance acct., tax acct., fin. specialist 1984—. Mem. Am. Assn. Ret. Persons. Roman Catholic.

HANSEN, MARIE SABATA, civic worker, former gas company executive; b. nr. Bruno, Nebr.; d. Alois and Marie (Egr) Sabata; m. Gilbert P. Hansen, Nov. 16, 1945 (dec. Mar. 1956). Grad., Am. Bus. Coll., Omaha, 1929; postgrad., U. Nebr., Omaha, 1929. With No. Natural Gas Co. (now Enron Corp.), Omaha, 1931-72, dir. investor research and relations, 1969-72. Charter mem. Omaha Mayor's Commn. on Status of Women, 1969; bd. dirs., treas. Uta Halee Girls Village, Omaha, 1982—, chmn. policy and procedures com., 1984—; bd. dirs., parliamentarian Vols. Intervening for Equity, Omaha, 1981-82. Mem. Nat. Assn. Parliamentarians (registered profl.), Nebr. Assn. Parliamentarians (treas. 1983-84, 1st v.p. 1984-86, pres. 1988—), Cath. Daus. Am. (ct. parliamentarian 1981-82), Omaha C. of C. (past pres. women's div.). Clubs: Omaha Press (charter), Omaha Altrusa (pres. 1968-69, dist. treas. 1972-74, parliamentarian 1980-82).

HANSEN, PAMELA GAY, controller; b. Pascagoula, Miss., Dec. 27, 1963; d. John Carl and Elois (Loper) H. Student, Gulf Coast Jr. Coll., Goutier, Miss., 1980-82; BS in Acctg., U. So. Miss., 1984. Acct. Nat. Am. Cos., Goutier, 1984-85; sales rep. Contel Cellular, Mobile, Ala., 1985; co-owner, v.p. Alpha Cellular Communications, Inc., Semmes, Ala., 1985-86; asst. contoller Fla. Environ. Waste div. Waste Mgmt., Inc., Pensacola, 1986; controller Environ. Waste System div. Waste Mgmt., Inc., Ft. Walton Beach, Fla., 1986—. Mem. Nat. Assn. Female Execs., Delta Sigma Pi. Republican. Baptist. Home: 510 Sheffield Rd Fort Walton Beach FL 32561 Office: Environ Waste System PO Box 4490 Fort Walton Beach FL 32549

HANSEN, SHARON LEE, insurance company executive; b. Mt. Vernon, Wash., Jan. 28, 1950; d. Richard A. and Helen B. (Parker) Burch; m. Clyde J. Markey Jr., July 17, 1970 (div. 1977); 1 child, C.J. III. Student, Skagit Valley Coll., 1982-83. Acctg. asst. Branom Instrument Co., Seattle, 1969-71; retail supr. U.S. Navy Exchange, Taipei, Republic of China, 1972-75; v.p., owner Am. Internat. Rent-A-Car, Everett, Wash., 1976-80; sales agt. Bankers Life and Casualty, Everett, Wash., 1980; owner, pres. Nat. Fin. Services, Mt. Vernon, 1980—. Sec. Mt. Vernon Youth Soccer Assn., 1982-85, now bd. dirs. Mem. Nat. Life Underwirers Assn. (bd. dirs.), Women in Bus. (treas. Skagit chpt.). Lutheran. Club: Soroptimist. Home: 1108 S 16th St Mount Vernon WA 98273 Office: Nat Fin Services 1910 Riverside Dr Suite 9 Mount Vernon WA 98273

HANSEN, SUSANA, real estate corporation officer, consultant; b. Montevideo, Uruguay, June 21, 1943; came to U.S., 1968; d. Jorge Valdemar and Paula (Maruri) H.; m. Federico Padovan (div. 1974); 1 child, Paola Padovan; m. Rodolfo Careri, 1983. BS in French, Alliance Française, Montevideo, Uruguay, 1964; BS, Fla. Internat. U., 1977. Cert. soc. studies tchr., Fla. Internat. U. Special asst. to pres. Hornblower, Werks, Hemphill, Noyes, Beverly Hills, Calif., 1968-71; v.p. special services Alitalia Airlines, N.Y.C., 1971-74, special asst. to pres. Interterra Inc., Miami, Fla., 1976-78; v.p. Grove Isle Realty, Coconut Grove, Fla., 1979-82; pres., broker Turnberry Realty Corp., Miami Beach, Fla., 1982—; cons. Latin Am. Assn. Real Estate Profl., Buenos Aires, 1978—. Fundraiser Restoration Statue Liberty, N.Y.C., 1985. Mem. Internat. Exec. Women Assn., London, Exec. Women's Edn. Travel, N.Y.C. Republican. Roman Catholic. Home: 300 Atlantic Rd Key Biscayne FL 33149 Office: Turnberry Realty 19735 Turnberry Way Miami Beach FL 33180

HANSEY, RENEE JEANNE, corporate executive; b. Tacoma, Wash., Apr. 24, 1927; d. Francis J. and Genevieve (Hewitt) Payette; m. James Burpee, Mar. 13, 1947 (dec. 1950); children: James, Victoria; m. Orville D. Hansey; children; Dan, Terri, John, Bill. Student in Layout and Design, Art Inst.

Chgo., 1943; BS in Psychology, St. John's U., 1988; postgrad. in Graphics, U. Alaska, 1985. Copy writer Sta. KIT, Yakima, Wash., 1942-44; program mgr. Sta. KING FM, Seattle, 1945-47; advt. mgr. Sequim (Wash.) Press, 1967-70, editor, 1970-76; tv producer Municipality of Anchorage, 1976-86; publisher Retired Sr. Vol. Program /Sr. Voice, Port Angeles, Wash., 1986—; also dir. Retired Sr. Vol. Program, Port Angeles, Wash.; founder Widowed Persons Service, Anchorage, 1983-85; owner Frontier Pub., Anchorage, 1983-85; dir. Far North Network, Anchorage, 1982-86. Author: Go to the Source, 1977, One Way to the Funny Farm, 1978; producer (tv show) Opportunities for Seniors, 1981-86 (TV Prodn. award, 1982-85). Sec. dem. council com., 1969-75; founder Olympic Women's Resource Ctr., Port Angeles, 1966-75; councilwoman City Sequim, 1973-76; active Affirmative Action Callam County, Wash., 1974, Sr. Companions, Elder Abuse Task Force; bd. dirs. Port Angeles Sr. Ctr. Roman Catholic. Club: Alaska Press Women (pres. 1981-82, 85-86). Home: 235 N Sunnyside Sequim WA 98382 Office: RSVP 215 1/2 S Lincoln Port Angeles WA 98362

HANSON, ANN H., state legislator; b. May 10, 1935; m. Daniel J. Hanson, 1958; children—Julie, Jennifer, Rebecca, Erica. B.S., U. Vt., 1956. Mem. R.I. Ho. of Reps. from 88th Dist., 1980-83, dep. minority leader, 1983; mem. R.I. State Senate from 44th Dist., 1983—, dep. minority leader, 1983. Active Barrington Town Council, 1975-80, v.p., 1976-78, pres., 1978-80; active R.I. Save the Bay. Mem. LWV, R.I. Women's Polit. Caucus. Roman Catholic. Republican. Office: RI State Capitol Bldg Providence RI 02903 Address: 116 Nayatt Rd Barrington RI 02806 *

HANSON, ANNE COFFIN, art historian; b. Kinston, N.C., Dec. 12, 1921; d. Francis Joseph Howells and Annie Roulhac (Coffin) Coffin; m. Bernard Alan Hanson, June 27, 1961; children by previous marriage: James Warfield Garson, Robert Coffin Garson, Ann Blaine Garson. B.F.A., U. So. Calif., 1943; M.A. in Creative Arts, U. N.C., 1951; Ph.D., Bryn Mawr Coll., 1962. Instr. Albright Art Sch., U. Buffalo, 1955-58; vis. asso. prof. art Cornell U., 1963; asst. prof. Swarthmore Coll., 1963-64, Bryn Mawr Coll., 1964-68; dir. Internat. Study Center, Mus. Modern Art, N.Y.C., 1968-69; adj. asso. prof. NYU, 1969-70; prof. history art Yale U., New Haven, 1970—; chmn. dept. Yale U., 1974-78, acting dir. Art Gallery,, 1985-86; resident Am. Acad. Rome, spring, 1974. Author: Jacopo della Quercia's Fonte Gaia, 1965, Edouard Manet, 1966, Manet and the Modern Tradition, 1977, The Futurist Imagination, 1983; contbr. articles to profl. jours; editorial bd. The Art Bull., 1971—; editor monograph series Coll. Art Assn., 1968-70; mem. governing bd. Yale U. Press, 1977—; mem. editorial com. Art Jour., 1979-83. NEH fellow, 1967-68; Am. Council Learned Socs. grantee, summer 1963, fellow, 1983-84; fellow Inst. Advanced Study, fall, 1983. Mem. Coll. Art Assn. Am. (pres. 1972-74), Comité Internationale de l'histoire de l'Art (nat. mem.). Office: Yale U Dept History Art 56 High St New Haven CT 06520

HANSON, DIANE CHARSKE, management consultant; b. Cleve., May 15, 1946; d. Howard Carl and Emma Katherine (Lange) Charske; m. William James Hanson, June 30, 1973. BS, Cornell U., 1968; postgrad., U. Pa., 1986—. Home service rep. Rochester Gas and Electric, N.Y., 1968-70; home economist U. Conn., Storrs, 1970-72; job analyst personnel dept. State of Conn., Hartford, 1972-73; sales rep. Ayerst Labs., Waterbury, Conn., 1973-80, sales trainer, 1979-80; dist. sales mgr. Phila., 1980-87; pres. Creative Resource Devel., W. Chester, Pa., 1986—; developer, pres. Womens Referral Network, West Chester, 1987—. Bd. dirs. Chester County Soc. for Prevention Cruelty to Animals, 1986—. Mem. Nat. Assn. Female Execs. (network dir. 1987—), Great Valley Sales and Mktg. Group, Sales and Mktg. Execs. Phila., Bus. and Profl. Women West Chester (found. chmn. 1987), West Chester C. of C., Del. State C. of C., Delaware County C. of C. (human services com. 1987), Exton C. of C. Home and Office: Creative Resource Devel 824 W Strasburg Rd West Chester PA 19382

HANSON, JANET CURTIS, lawyer; b. Chgo., Jan. 9, 1948; d. Bruce B. and Marie Katherine (Marsh) Curtis. B.A. magna cum laude, Denison U., 1969; M.A., U. Minn., 1970; A.A., Edmonds Community Coll., 1978; J.D., Stanford U., 1981. Bar: Oreg., 1981, D.C., 1987, Calif., 1987Instr., So. Conn. State Coll., New Haven, 1973-74; parent edn. instr. N. Seattle Community Coll., 1974-76; paralegal George Wm. Cody, Lynwood, Wash., 1978, Davis, Wright, Todd, Riese & Jones, Seattle, 1977-78; assoc. Miller, Nash, Wiener, Hager & Carlsen, Portland, Oreg., 1981-84; assoc. gen. counsel N.W. Power Planning Council, Portland, 1984-86; atty. Fed. Home Loan Bank San Francisco, 1987—. Contbr. articles to profl. jours. Bd. dirs., crime watch chmn., historic preservation chmn. Irvington Community Assn., Portland, 1982-86. Mem. ABA, Oreg. State Bar Assn., D.C. Bar Assn., Calif. State Bar Assn., Lawyers' Club San Francisco, San Francisco Bar Assn., Multnomah County Bar Assn., Nat. Trust Hist. Preservation, Phi Beta Kappa, Sigma Xi, Psi Chi, Kappa Delta Pi. Presbyterian. Clubs: City (Portland), Commonwealth (San Francisco). Home: 701 Waller St San Francisco CA 94117-3224 Office: Fed Home Loan Bank One Montgomery St Suite 400 San Francisco CA 94104

HANSON, JANET LUNDSTROM, marketing professional; b. Kansas City, Mo., July 15, 1961; d. Paul Thomas and Eileen Louise (Jontz) Lundstrom; m. Bryan Eric Hanson, July 7, 1984. BS in Radio/TV/Film with honors, Northwestern U., 1983; postgrad., Rockhurst Coll., Kansas City, 1984—. Assoc. producer, programming NBC-TV, Chgo., 1983-84; div. analyst mut. funds DST Sytems Inc., Kansas City, 1984-85, mgr. mut. funds, 1984-86; mgr. mktg. Investors Fiduciary Trust Co., Kansas City, 1987—; v.p. Moneymarket Fund Inc., Grand Rapids, Mich., 1986-87; TV news anchor, producer Scripps Howard Broadcasting, Kansas City, 1985-86. Mem. Friends of Art-Nelson Art Gallery, Kansas City, 1984-85. Mem. Nat. Assn. Female Execs., Alpha Lambda Delta, Kappa Alpha Pi, Alpha Chi Omega, Zeta Phi Eta. Republican. Methodist. Home: 306 W 7th St #204 Kansas City MO 64105 Office: Investors Fiduciary Trust Co 127 W 10th St Kansas City MO 64105

HANSON, JEAN ELIZABETH, lawyer; b. Alexandria, Minn., June 28, 1949; d. Carroll Melvin and Alice Clarissa (Frykman) H.; m. H. Barndt Hauptfuhrer, May 15, 1982; children: Catherine Jean, Benjamin Colman (twins). BA, Luther Coll., 1971; JD, U. Minn., 1976. Bar: N.Y. 1977, U.S. Dist. Ct. (so. dist.) 1977. Probation officer Hennepin County, Mpls., 1972-73; law clk. Minn. State Pub. Defender, Mpls., 1975-76; assoc. Fried, Frank, Harris, Shriver & Jacobson, N.Y.C., 1976-83, ptnr., 1983—. Named one of People to Watch Fortune Mag., 1985, Big Deals Savvy Mag., 1986. Mem. ABA, N.Y. State Bar Assn., N.Y. Women's Bar Assn., U. Minn. Law Alumni Assn. Democrat. Lutheran. Office: Fried Frank Harris Shriver & Jacobson 1 New York Plaza New York NY 10004

HANSON, JEANNE CAROL, health care administrator; b. New Haven, May 3, 1947; d. John Fletcher and Jeanne (Huttlinger) H. Diploma, Bryn Mawr (Pa.) Sch. Nursing, 1968; BS in Psychology, Eastern Coll., 1978; MBA in Health and Med. Service, Widener U., 1986. RN. Staff nurse pediatric unit Bryn Mawr (Pa.) Hosp., 1968-69; staff nurse psychiat. unit Haverford (Pa.) State Hosp., 1969-71, head nurse psychiat. admissions unit, 1971-73, instr. psychiat. nursing, 1973-80, dir. nursing edn. dept., 1980-87; asst. adminstr. Kendal-Crosslands, Kennett Square, Pa., 1987—. Bd. dirs. Media (Pa.) Child Guidance and Community Mental Health Ctr. Mem. Pa. Nurses Assn., Am. Soc. Health Care Edn. and Tng., Am. Mgmt. Assn., Widener Grad. Alumni Assn. (v.p. 1987—). Republican. Mem. Soc. of Friends. Home: PO Box 283 West Chester PA 19381 Office: Kendal-Crosslands PO Box 100 Kennett Square PA 19348

HANSON, JEWEL LOUISE, marketing executive; b. Washington, July 20, 1962; d. John Dudley and Marjorie Louise (Bowie) H. BA in Polit. Sci. and Criminology, U. Tampa, 1984. Scheduler Mondale-Ferraro Campaign, Washington, 1984; exec. asst., legal adminstr. Barrett, Montgomery & Murphy, Washington, 1984-87; asst. to chief exec. officer Vitrifix of N.Am., Washington, 1987—. Mem. Hazardous Waste Treatment Council, Washington; vol. Am. Red Cross, Washington, 1987, Gallaudet Coll. for Deaf, Washington, 1986—. Mem. Am. Assn. Univ. Women, Assn. Legal Adminstrs., U. Tampa Alumni Assn., Delta Zeta. Office: Vitrifix of N Am 1700 K St NW Suite 302 Washington DC 20006

HANSON, MARY LOUISE, banker, political worker; b. Bremerton, Wash., Apr. 24, 1944; d. Lawrence Grant and Ruth Louise (Johnson) Dix; student U. Wash., 1962-64, U. Colo., 1973-77; m. Michael Zabinski, Aug. 19, 1983. Adminstrv. asst. U. Pa., Phila., 1965-70, Provident Mgmt. Corp., Providence, 1970-72; with First Nat. Bank of Denver, 1972-80; v.p., exec. banking dept. United Bank of Denver, 1980-87; dir. Integrated Media; mem. adv. bd. Network mag., 1984-86; lectr.; chmn. adv. council Aton Found.; various state bd. positions Colo. Libertarian Party, 1976—; nat. vice chmn. Libertarian Party, 1977-83, mem.-at-large nat. com., 1981-83, regional rep. on nat. com., 1977, nat. fin. chmn., 1980; Libertarian candidate for treas. of Colo., 1978. Bd. trustees AMC Cancer Research Inst., 1982—. Mem. Nat. Fedn. Bus. and Profl. Women, Colo. Fedn. Bus. and Profl. Women (state pres. 1984-85), Downtown Denver Bus. and Profl. Women (pres. 1978-80, state legis. chmn. 1980-81), Robert Morris Assos. Office: YWCA Met Denver Suite 700 535-16th St Denver CO 80202

HANSON, ROBIN ELAINE, accountant; b. Jacksonville, Fla., Oct. 19, 1956. BBA, U. North Fla., 1978, M in Acctg., 1986. CPA, Fla. Staff acct. Peter Suess and Co., CPA's, Jacksonville, 1979-80; tax acct. Peat, Marwick, Mitchell, CPA's, Jacksonville, 1980-83, tax mgr., 1983; tax acct. The Charter Co., Jacksonville, 1983-84; tax supr. Touche, Ross & Co., CPA's, Jacksonville, 1984-85; dir. tax Fla. Rock Industries, Inc., Jacksonville, 1985—. Mem. Am. Inst. CPA's (tax div.), Fla. Inst. CPA's. Office: Fla Rock Industries Inc 155 E 21st St Jacksonville FL 32206

HANSON, SANDRA J. MCKENZIE, educational administrator; b. Amery, Wis., Jan. 15, 1949; d. Earl Edward and Ariel Gloria (Benson) McKenzie; m. Craig W. Hanson, June 14, 1969; 1 child, Andrea McKenzie. B.A., U. Wis.-Eau Claire, 1970; M.P.A., U. Puget Sound, 1978. Instr. S.W. Wis. Tech. Inst., Fennimore, Wis., 1970-72; account exec. Ad Factors Advt., Spokane, Wash., 1972-74; dir. spl. projects Wash. Community Colls. of Spokane, 1974-76; instr., pubs. advisor Community Coll. Dist. 12, Olympia, Centralia, Wash., 1978-81; dir. coll. relations South Puget Sound Community Coll., Olympia, Wash., 1981-85; dir. coll. relations and devel. Pierce Coll. Tacoma, Wash., 1985—; dist. rep. 2-yr. coll. com. CASE, 1982-83, 84-86; dir. Graphic Identity Program, 1984. Editor, creative dir. Admissions Brochure Series, 1984. Co-dir. N. Thurston Citizens for Schs., 1978-80. Recipient Award of Merit, Olympia Tech. Community Coll., 1980-81. Mem. Council for Advancement and Support of Edn., Wash. Community Coll. Adminstrs. Assn. (exec. bd. dirs., sec-treas.), Wash. Info. Council (Nat. Admissions/Mktg. Report awards 1986-88), Nat. Council for Community Relations, Wash. State Community Coll. Pub. Info. Com., Nat. Council for Resource Devel. (cons. publs). Avocations: writing, sailing, skiing. Office: Pierce Coll 9401 Farwest Dr SW Tacoma WA 98498

HANSON, SUSAN JANE, real estate credit analyst; b. Columbus, Ohio, Dec. 21, 1958; d. Paul Edward and C. Jane (White) Hanson Van Hoose. BA, Capital U., 1980, MBA, 1986. Staff acct. Vantage Properties Inc., Columbus, 1980-81, asst. controller, 1981-84, controller 1984-87; real estate specialist credit adminstrn. Huntington Nat. Bank, Columbus, 1987—. Mem. Nat. Assn. Female Execs., Am. Mgmt. Assn., Nat. Assn. Office and Indsl. Parks., Columbus Women in Real Estate. Republican. Methodist. Avocations: sewing, swimming, bowling, ceramics, travel. Home: 1738 Brice Rd Apt 10 Reynoldsburg OH 43068 Office: Huntington Nat Bank 41 S High St Box 1558 Columbus OH 43215

HANSON-MARSH, KAREN GRACE, hospital administrator; b. Walla Walla, Wash., Feb. 2, 1948; d. Franklin Bertram and Ruth Elizabeth (Silven) Hanson; m. Carl H. Marsh, Jr., Apr. 7, 1987; children: Rob, Elizabeth, Heather. BA in Social Work, Ea. Wash. State U., 1969; BS in Nursing, Wash. State U., 1971; M.Ed., Walla Walla Coll., 1987. Nurse CCU and med. unit Deaconess Hosp., Spokane, Wash., 1971-72; charge nurse VA Hosp., Walla Walla, Wash., 1972-73, U.S. Army Med. Ctr., Camp Kue, Okinawa, 1973; nurse Walla Walla Gen. Hosp., 1973-76; coordinator health continuing edn., clin. instr. nursing program Walla Walla Community Coll., 1982-85; asst. health care adminstr. Wash. State Penitentiary, 1985-86, health care adminstr., 1986—. Bd. dirs., v.p. Walla Walla Symphony, 1978-80. Mem. Am. Heart Assn. Wash. (Silver award 1978, pres. Ea. Wash. sub. area council 1979, gov. 1978-79), Am. Correctional Assn., Am. Correctional Health Care Assn., AAUW, Am. Assn. Higher Edn., Phi Delta Kappa. Episcopalian. Home: 50 Brookside Dr Walla Walla WA 99362 Office: Box 520 Walla Walla WA 99362

HANSOTIA, HOOTY NOSHIR, manufacturing exective; b. Haregaon, India, June 24, 1949; d. Keki Shapurji and Dina Rustomji (Jamasji) Sagar; m. Noshir Louji Hansotia, May 4, 1969; children: Michelle, Mark. BS in Econs., U. Bombay, India, 1970. Accts. clk. Graham Mortgage Co., Detroit, 1970, Sealright Corp., Kansas City, Mo., 1975-76; co-owner, v.p. Cottman Transmission (now Better Transmission), Independence, Mo., 1976—, Shawnee, Kans., 1977—, Kansas City, 1981—, St. Joseph, Mo., 1984-85, Gladstone, Mo., 1984-85. Mem. Nat. Assn. Female Execs. Republican. Zoroastrian. Office: Better Transmission 8342Bridle Dale Lenexa KS 66220

HANTKE, MARY KLOER, computer company executive; b. Sacramento, Calif., July 19, 1955; d. Jay and Frances (Vaughn) Kloer; m. Paul Werner Hantke, Jan. 20, 1980; 1 child, Emily Frances. AS, Ventura (Calif.) Coll., 1975; BS, Calif. Poly. U., 1977. Regional tng. mgr. May Dept. Stores, Los Angeles, 1977-81; sales instr. Vector Graphic Inc., Thousand Oaks, Calif., 1981-83; tng. dir. Compaq Computer Corp., Houston, 1983-86; sr. dist. mgr. ITT/Alcatel Info. Systems, Los Angeles, 1986—. Recipient various outstanding contribution awards Compaq Computer Corp., ITT. Mem. Ambassador C. of C. (Marina Del Rey, Calif.). Office: ITT/Alcatel Info Systems 6331 Bristol Pkwy Suite 280 Culver City CA 90230

HANWACKER, PATRICIA AILEEN LUDWIG, real estate consultant; b. Bklyn., Mar. 22, 1951; d. Henry Raymond and Margaret Adelaide (Binz) Ludwig; divorced; children—Jessica, Jarrod. B.S. in Math., St. John's U., 1971; M.S. in Computer Sci., Stevens Inst. Tech., 1974. Lic. real estate broker. Planning, equipment engr. N.Y. Telephone Co., N.Y.C., 1971-74; computer systems engr. AT&T, N.Y.C., 1974-76; staff supr. market research and forecasting AT&T Long Lines, Bedminster, N.J., 1976-78, dist. mgr. fin. planning, 1978-80, dist. mgr. tech. sales support, Somerset, N.J., 1980-82; nat. account mgr. for ABC, AT&T Communications, N.Y.C., 1982-84; v.p. mktg. and sales Dama Telecommunications Corp., Parsippany, N.J., 1985-86; nat. acct. mgr. IBM, MCI Telecommunications, Rye Brook, N.Y., 1986-88; real estate cons. Kohere & Cohen, Iselin, N.J., 1988—; pres. PLH Assocs., Millburn, N.J.; cons. Curriculum Concepts, N.Y.C., 1976; v.p. Quantum Investment Corp., Millburn, N.J., 1978—. Mem. Soc. Women Engrs., Internat. Radio and TV Soc., YWCA, Pi Mu Epsilon. Republican. Office: MCI 5 Internat Dr Rye Brook NY 10013

HANZL, KAREN ANN, marketing professional; b. Pompton Plains, N.J., Mar. 14, 1958; d. Walter Frank and Joan (Hoferer) H. BS cum laude, Caldwell Coll., 1980; MBA with distinction, Pace U., 1982. Rep. customer service Stop & Shop Corp., Wayne, N.J., 1974-80; asst. placement Pace U., White Plains, N.J., 1980-82; rep. broker Dun & Bradstreet, Parsippany, N.J., 1983-84; exec. account Dun & Bradstreet, Parsippany, 1984-85, mgr. sales support, 1986—. Mem. Assn. MBA Execs., Nat. Assn. Female Execs., Dir. Mktg. Assn., Am. Mktg. Assn. Roman Catholic. Home: 59 West Pkwy Pompton Plains NJ 07444 Office: Dun & Bradstreet 3 Century Dr Parsippany NJ 07054

HAPPE, SUSAN MARIE, general contractor; b. Mpls., Feb. 18, 1963; d. Gene Francis and Joleen Mae (Kuker) H. BS, Ariz. State U., 1985. Lic. real estate agt. Sales rep. Am. Equity Properties, Phoenix, 1983; comml. mktg. Gosnell Devel. Corp., Phoenix, 1984-85; v.p. EFH Co., Burnsville, Min., 1985—; mem. Econ. Devel. Com., Phoenix, 1985. Vol. Mpls. Aquatennial, 1987. Mem. Nat. Assn. Indsl. and Office Parks. Republican. Office: EFH Co 1601 E Highway 13 #204 Burnsville MN 55337

HAQUE, MALIKA HAKIM, pediatrician; b. Madras, India; came to U.S., 1967; d. Syed Abdul and Rahimunisa (Hussain) Hakim; M.B.B.S., Madras Med. Coll., 1967; m. C. Azeez ul Haque, Feb. 5, 1967; children—Kifizeba, Masarath Nashr, Asim Zayd. Rotating intern Miriam Hosp., Brown U., Providence, 1967-68; resident in pediatrics Children's Hosp., N.J. Coll. Medicine, 1968-70; fellow in devel. disabilities Ohio State U., 1970-71; acting chief pediatrics Nisonger Center, 1973-74; staff pediatrician Children and Youth Project, Children's Hosp., Columbus, Ohio, also clin. asst. prof. pediatrics Ohio State U., 1974-80; clin. asso. prof. pediatrics Ohio State U., 1981—; pediatrician in charge community pediatrics and adolescent services clinics Columbus Children's Hosp., 1982—; cons. Central Ohio Head Start Program, 1974-79. Contbr. articles to profl. jours. and newspapers. Charter mem. Republican Presdl. Task Force, 1982—, Nat. Rep. Senatorial Com., 1985—, U.S. Senatorial Club; charter founder Ronald Reagan Rep. Ctr. Recipient Physician Recognition award AMA, 1971-86, 88—, Gold medals in surgery, radiology, pediatrics and ob/gyn; Presdl. medal of Merit, 1982; diplomate Am. Bd. Pediatrics. Fellow Am. Acad. Pediatrics (Prep Fellowship award 1986, Ohio chpt.); mem. Ambulatory Pediatric Assn., Acad. Medicine, Ohio State Med. Assn., Cen. Ohio Pediatric Soc. (mktg. and community edn. coms.). Islam. Research on enuresis. Home: 5995 Forestview Dr Columbus OH 43213 Office: 700 Children's Dr Columbus OH 43205

HARA, SHERYN LOUISE GREENE, public relations and marketing executive; b. Gt. Falls, Mont., Oct. 14, 1943; d. Charles Andrew and Louise Jane (Oxe) Greene; m. Lloyd F. Hara, Jan. 3, 1970; children: Jennifer, Todd, Stephanie. BA, Mont. State U., 1964. Translator Weyerhaeuser, Tacoma, 1964-66; mktg. analyst Seattle 1st Nat. Bank, 1966-67; statistician Port of Seattle, 1967-68; research analyst Wash. State Dept. Health, Olympia, 1968-70, Spl. Levy Study com., Bellevue, Wash., 1970-72; project dir. Columbia Club, Seattle, 1970-72; event planner Tom Hopkins Tng. Ctr., Bellevue, 1982-84; chief exec. officer Hara and Assocs., Seattle, 1984—. Author, editor Networking mag., 1987. Campaign mgr. Seattle City Treas., 1979, 83, 87; leader Campfire Girls, Seattle, 1979—; chairperson Queen Anne Community Cuncil, Seattle, 1978-80; mem. adv. bd. Seattle Internat. U., 1987—. Mem. Nat. Speakers Assn., Pacific Northwest Speakers Assn. (pres. local chpt. 1984-86, Mem. of Yr. 1986). Home: 466 Smith St Seattle WA 98109 Office: Hara and Assocs 2 Nickerson St #301 Seattle WA 98109

HARA-ISA, NANCY JEANNE, art director; b. San Francisco, May 14, 1961; d. Toshiro and Masaye (Nakahira) Hara; m. Stanley Takeo Isa, June 15, 1985. Student, UCLA, 1979-82; BA in Art and Design, Calif. State U., Los Angeles, 1985. Salesperson May Co., Los Angeles, 1981; service rep. Hallmark Cards Co., Los Angeles, 1981-83; prodn. artist Calif. State U., Los Angeles, 1983, Audio-Stats Internat. Inc., Los Angeles, 1983; prodn. asst. Auto-Graphics Inc., Pomona, Calif., 1984-85, lead supr., 1985-86; art dir., contbg. staff writer CFW Enterprises, Burbank, Calif., 1987—. Writer Action Pursuit Games mag. Parade asst., mem. carnival staff Nisei Week, Los Angeles, 1980-84; asst., mem. Summit Orgn., Los Angeles, 1987—; creator, chair Paintball/Wargame Charity Benefit, Make-a-Wish Found. Mem. Nat. Assn. Female Execs. Republican. Presbyterian. Home: 922 W Mabel Ave #B Monterey Park CA 91754

HARALSON, LINDA JANE, health care company marketing executive, consultant; b. St. Louis, Mar. 24, 1959; d. James Benjamin and Betty Jane (Myers) N.; married. BA summa cum laude William Woods Coll., 1981; MA, Webster U., 1982. Radio intern Stas.-KFAL/KKCA, Fulton, Mo., 1981; paralegal Herzog, Kral, Burroughs & Specter, St. Louis, 1981-82; staffing coordinator, then mktg. coordinator Spectrum Emergency Care, St. Louis, 1982-85, mktg. mgr., 1985-87; dir. mktg. and recruitment Carondelet Rehab. Ctrs. Am., Culver City, Calif., 1987—; mktg. dir. outpatient and corp. services Calif. Med. Ctr., Los Angeles, 1987-88; mktg. dir. Valley Meml. Hosp., Livermore, Calif., 1988—. Party chmn. Heart Assn., St. Louis, 1982—. Recipient Flair award Advt. Fedn. St. Louis, 1984, Hosps. award Hagen Mktg. Research and Hospitals mag., 1984; presdl. acad. scholar William Woods Coll., Fulton, 1977-81. Mem. Am. Mktg. Assn., Internat. Assn. Bus. Communicators, Nat. Assn. Female Execs., Alpha Phi Alumnae Assn. (pres. chpt. 1985-87). Republican. Presbyterian. Club: Bon Amis (program com. 1985—) (St. Louis). Avocations: running, travel, sports, French, needlepoint.

HARBACH, CYNTHIA LEE, social service executive; b. Jersey Shore, Pa., July 14, 1953; d. Robert C. and Anna Mae (Heggenstaller) H. BS, Messiah Coll., 1975; MS, Hood Coll., 1982. Cook supr. New Windsor (Md.) Service Ctr., 1976-81; resident support person Hood Coll., Frederick, Md., 1982-83; exec. dir. Family Life Ctr., Frederick, 1982—; trainer HomeCall, Inc., Frederick, 1981-83; mem. program adv. council Frederick County Extension Service, 1984—; mem. Frederick County Children's Council, 1983—. Named Outstanding Young Marylander, 1986, one of Outstanding Young Women of Am., 1984. Mem. Am. Home Econs. Assn. (Named one of New Faces to Watch 1984), Md. Home Econs. Assn. (chair 1986—), Nat. Assn. Female Execs., Kappa Omicron Phi. Democrat. Office: Frederick County Family Life Ctr 35 E Church St Frederick MD 21701

HARBART, GERTRUDE C., artist, educator; b. Michigan City, Ind., Dec. 25, 1908; d. Charles H. and Maude A. (Hackett) Felton; m. Frank F. (dec. 1977); children: James, Joy. Student, U. Ind., 1930, U. Ohio, 1940, Art Inst. Chgo., 1950; studies with Hans Hoffman, Provence Town, Mass.; studies with Aron Bor, U. Ohio. Tchr. Pub. Schs., Ind., 1957-61, South Bend (Ind.) Art Ctr., 1960-70, Michigan City Art Ctr., 1976—; officer So. Bend NA, 1960—, SAWG, Tucson, Ariz., 1978 Mich. City Art Ctr. Guild, 1979—. One-man shows include Chgo. Pub. Library, St. Mary's Notre Dame, Hoosier Salon Indpls., So. Bend Art Ctr.; group exhibitions include Chgo. and Vicinity Show, Art Inst. Chgo., Old NW Territory, Springfield, Ill, Sarasota Art Assn., Kalamazoo Art Ctr.; nat. competitions include Art U.S.A., Corcoran Gallery, Washington, Acad. of Design N.Y.C., Butler Inst. Am. Art, Youngstown, Ohio, Nat. Painters in Casein, N.Y.; one-man show Tucson Murphy Gallery; permanent collections include Ind. U., Purdue U., Indiana State U., Community Ctr. for the Arts, Michigan City. Presbyterian. Clubs: Skyway Women's, Tucson Women's; Mich. City Women's Study. Home: 5578 N LaCasita Tucson AZ 85718 Studio: 2201 Maryben Long Beach Michigan City IN 46360

HARBAUGH, VIRGINIA WAYNE, govt. adminstr.; b. Savannah, Ga., Dec. 15, 1930; d. Adrian Bancker and Jeannette Butler (Strong) Talbot; B.A., Smith Coll., 1952; M. Planning and Urban Design, U. Va., 1971; m. William Henry Harbaugh, Aug. 15, 1953; children—Lyn Hartridge Harbaugh Brennan, William Talbot, Henry Richmond. Sr. planner Thomas Jefferson Planning Dist. Commn., Charlottesville, Va., 1973-79, exec. dir., 1979-86; lectr. U. Va., 1987—. Pres. League of Women Voters, Mansfield, Conn., 1957-59, Lewisburg, Pa., 1964-66; pres. Va. Citizens Planning Commn., 1976-78. Mem. Am. Inst. Cert. Planners, Am. Planning Assn. Democrat. Unitarian. Home: 1930 Thomson Rd Charlottesville VA 22903 Office: Univ Va 225 Campbell Hall Charlottesville VA 22903

HARBERT, PAMELA ANNETT, personnel administrator; b. Dumas, Tex., Jan. 21, 1963; d. Robert Lewis and Constance Inez (Colston) H. BBA, North Tex. State U., 1986. Clk. North Tex. State U., Denton, 1983, 86; asst. mgr. Memory Lane of Tex., Denton, 1983-84; mgr. Edison Bros. Apparels, Denton, 1984-85; personnel adminstr. TTI, Inc., Ft. Worth, 1986—. Mem. Nat. Assn. Female Execs., Ft. Worth Personnel Assn. (membership com.). Democrat. Methodist. Office: TTI Inc 4033 E Belknap Fort Worth TX 76111

HARBISON, MARGARET WARLICK, physical education educator; b. Cleveland County, N.C., Dec. 19, 1935; d. Walter Theodore and Lessie Lawrence (Downs) Warlick; B.S., Appalachian State U., Boone, N.C., 1957, M.A., 1963; Ed.D., U. Miss., 1974; m. Clyde Hilton Waters, May 31, 1964 (div.); 1 son, Jack Hilton; m. Paul Dean Harbison, May 16, 1981. Instr. phys. edn. jr. high schs., N.C., 1957-61, Fla., 1961-62; asst. prof. health, phys. edn. and recreation U. Miss., 1963-67; asst. prof. phys. edn. Kennesaw Coll., Marietta, Ga., 1967-70; asst. prof. health, phys. edn. and recreation Delta State U., Cleveland, Miss., 1970-74; prof., assoc. athletic dir. East Tex. State U., Commerce, 1974—; mem. Nat. Collegiate Athletic Assn. Postgrad. Scholarship com., 1985—; area coordinator Spl. Olympics, 1975-84; asst. recreation dir.; supr. summer playgrounds. Bd. dirs. United Way, 1977-80, treas., 1978-80; mem. Commerce Parks and Recreation Adv. Bd., 1982—, chmn. 1986—. Recipient Presdl. citation AAHPER, 1974; Disting. Community Service award, 1981. Mem. Am. Alliance for Health, Phys. Edn., Recreation and Dance, Tex. Assn. Health, Phys. Edn. and Recreation, Tex. Assn. Coll. Tchrs., So. Assn. Phys. Edn. for Coll. Women, Nat. Assn. Phys. Edn. in Higher Edn., Nat. Assn. Intercollegiate Athletics (exec. com. 1980-83), C. of C. (dir., 1978-81), Delta Kappa Gamma, Kappa Delta Pi. Democrat. Baptist. Club: Psychology (pres., 1978-80), Sand Hills Golf and

Country (dir. 1984-87). Home: 2824 McCarley Dr Commerce TX 75420 Office: E Tex State U Dept Health and Phys Edn Commerce TX 75428

HARBOE, RUTH STEINFURTH, nursing educator; b. Springfield, Ohio, Aug. 3, 1922; d. Albert William and Hilda (Burghart) Steinfurth; m. Edward Miller Harboe, Sept. 28, 1946; children—Joyce Harboe Baldwin, William, Ronald, Kathryn Harboe Kalal, Sherrill Lojewski. Student Wittenburg Coll., 1940-42; B.S., Carnegie-Mellon U., 1945; M.S., U. Colo., 1967. R.N. Various teaching and nursing service positions, Denver, 1947-62; instr. Presbyterian Hosp. Sch. Nursing, Denver, 1962-66; asst. prof. U. Md.-Balt., 1967-68; coordinator nursing N. Campus, Community Coll. Denver, 1968-74; asst. prof. U. No. Colo., Greeley, 1975-77; asst. prof. nursing Sch. Nursing, U. Colo. Health Scis. Ctr., Denver, 1977-86; adv. bd. Practical Nurse Sch., Beth Israel Hosp.; cons. I.M. Injections, Venereal Disease Clinic, 1980; speaker; mem. nursing com. Colo. Cancer Soc., Denver, 1980-83. Author in field. Asst. Westland Health Fair, 1972-77; med. coordinator 9 Health Fair Denver Fed. Ctr.; visitor probate ct., Denver, 1987—; vol. chaplain Swedish Hosp., 1987—; mem. Chautauqua Planning com., 1982—; active Jefferson County Comprehensive Health Planning, 1970-73; adv. com. Continuing in Nursing, Red Rocks Campus Community Coll., Denver, 1974-76; mem. nursing and health programs com. Mile High chpt. ARC, 1973-76; mem. council, choir, women's orgn., Sunday/Sch. tchr. Lutheran Ch. of the Master, also mem. bldg. com., 1980-82; active Health and Wellness Ctr., Lakewood (Colo.) Dept. Parks and Recreation, 1983. Mem. Am. Nurses Assn., Colo. Nurses Assn. (dir. 1980-83, pres. Dist. 20, 1971-72, affirmative action com. 1977-79). Am. Cancer Soc., Oncology Nurses Soc., Sigma Theta Tau (pres. 1979-80, dir. 1980—), Delta Phi Alpha, Phi Kappa Phi. Home: 867 S Cole Dr Lakewood CO 80228 Office: U Colo Health Scis Ctr 4200 E 9th Ave C-288 Denver CO 80262

HARBOUR, NANCY CAINE, lawyer; b. Cleve., July 30, 1949; d. William Anthony and Bernadette (Frohnapple) Caine; m. Randall Lee Harbour, Sept. 29, 1979. B.A. magna cum laude, U. Detroit, 1970; J.D., Cleve. State U., 1978. Bar: Mich. 1978. Writer, Project Map, Inc., Washington, 1971-72; newspaper reporter Alexandria Gazette, Va., 1972-73, Times Herald Record, Goshen, N.Y., 1973-75; atty. Conklin, Benham, et al., Detroit, 1978-82, Miller, Cohen, Martens, and Ice, P.C., Detroit, 1982—. Mem. Am. Trial Lawyers Assn., Mich. Trial Lawyers Assn., Mich. Bar Assn., State Bar Mich. (mem. compensation council 1983-85), Gamma Pi Epsilon. Democrat. Office: Miller Cohen Martens & Ice PC 1400 N Park Plaza 17117 W Nine Mile Rd Southfield MI 48075

HARCHA, MARY ANN, controller; b. McKees Rocks, Pa.; m. John Michael Harcha; 1 child, Corey Michael. BSBA cum laude, Robert Morris Coll., 1977. Mgmt. trainee U.S. Steel Corp., Joliet, Ill., 1977-78; acctg. mgr. Pitts. Gear Co., 1978-86; controller SMS Sutton Inc., Pitts., 1987-88, SMS Engring. Inc., Pitts., 1988—; cons. in field, 1980—. Mem. Nat. Assn. Accts. (assoc. dir. 1986-88), Nat. Assn. Female Execs., NOW, Wilderness Soc., Nat. Park Assn. Office: SMS Engring Inc 4 Station Sq Pittsburgh PA 15219

HARDAGE, SUSAN JEANNINE PATTERSON, academic program administrator, educator; b. Lubbock, Tex., Sept. 29, 1942; d. Nathan Howard and Affanell (Brock) Patterson; m. Billy Dean Hardage, Sept. 2, 1962; children: Timothy Dean, Cynthia Susan. Student, Hardin-Simmons U., 1961-63; BS, Wayland Bapt. U., 1965, MEd, 1987. Tchr. Lubbock Ind. Sch. Dist., 1965-66, Plainview (Tex.) Ind. Sch. Dist., 1974-83; coordinator, instr. acad. achievement program Wayland Bapt. U., Plainview, 1983—. Mem. Internat. Reading Assn., Western Coll. Reading and Learning Assn., Nat. Assn. Female Execs., PTA. Baptist. Home: Rt #HC01 Box 280 Plainview TX 79072 Office: Wayland Bapt U WBU Box 320 Plainview TX 79072

HARDCASTLE, MILDRED TUCKER, civic worker, genealogist, historian; b. Warren County, Ky.; d. James Harvey and Mildred (Carpenter) Tucker; m. John Vernon Hardcastle. Student, Transylvania U., Lexington, Ky., 1930-32. Regent Samuel Davies chpt. DAR, Bowling Green, Ky., 1965-89; vice-chmn. Seimes Microfilm Ctr. nat. DAR, 1979-85, mem. membership com., 1975-78; librarian Ky. DAR, 1962-65, registrar, 1959-62, organizing sec., 1971-74; officer Ky. Officers Club, 1959-62, sr. state officer Children of Am. Revolution; chaired various state DAR coms., including protocol com., 1981-83, resolutions com., 1980-83; founder, contbr. vols. of records Geneal. Library, DAR, Bowling Green, 1965-89; organizer Western Ky. Waterland chpt. Daus. of Am. Colonists, 1980, regent, 1980-83; pres. Huguenot Soc. Ky., 1971-73, v.p., 1984-88; pres. Warren County Hist. Soc. (Ky.), 1965-68, v.p. 1969-87; charter mem. Mus. Assocs. and Century Club, Western Ky. U., 1983-88; bd. dirs. Hist. Hobson House Assn., 1979-83, hon. mem., 1984-88; organizer 7 DAR chpts., 1 SAR chpt.; DAR chmn. Jubilee 1984 Festival, Warren County, Ky. Compiler: Nat. Society DAR Yearbook (Nat. Soc. DAR Outstanding designation) 1981-88. Recipient Medal of Appreciation Nat. Soc. DAR, 1975; Medals of Appreciation, Nat. Soc. SAR, 1962, 68, 83, Good Citizenship medal, 1983; Ky. Col., 1984-89. Mem. Nat. Soc. Huguenots (charter), DAR (state pres. 1984-86, state pres. 50 Yr. Club 1985-89), Chi Omega. Democrat. Mem. Christian Ch. (Disciples of Christ). Lodges: Magna Charta Dames and Barons, Colonial Dames, Founders and Patriots Am., Washington Family Descs., Washington's Army at Valley Forge.

HARDEBECK, NANCY COLLEEN DEW, personnel director; b. Ponca City, Okla., Nov. 21, 1957; d. John Norman and Marjorie Ann (Schairer) Dew; m. Edward James Hardebeck Jr., Nov. 14, 1987. BS in Bus., Okla. State U., 1980. Personnel analyst Conoco, Inc., Ponca City, 1980-81; adminstrv. asst. Exec. Resources, Tulsa, 1981-82; benefits coordinator AnSon Corp., Oklahoma City, 1982-87, asst. personnel dir., 1987—. Vol. Met. Fair Housing Authority, Oklahoma City, 1987. Mem. Okla. City Personnel Assn., Internat. Found. Employee Benefit Plans, Alpha Lambda Delta, Gamma Phi Beta. Republican. Episcopalian. Office: AnSon Corp 3814 N Santa Fe Oklahoma City OK 73118

HARDEN, ANITA JOYCE, nurse; b. Jackson, Tenn., May 17, 1947; d. Percy Lawrence and Majorie (Robison) H.; B.S. in Nursing, Ind. U., 1968; M.S. in Nursing, Ind. U.-Purdue U., Indpls., 1973; 1 son, Brian Robison Weir. Staff nurse Indpls. hosps., 1968-71; instr. Ind. U. Sch. Nursing, 1973-75; dir. continuing care Gallahue Mental Health Center, Indpls., 1975-80; mgr. psychiatry Community Hosp., Indpls., 1980-87, product line mgr. for psychiat. and mental health services, 1986—; dir. Psychiat. Services Community Hosp. North, 1987—; clin. asst. prof. Ind. U., 1977-82, clin. asso. prof., 1982—; clin. asso., trainer Suicide Prevention Service, Indpls., 1974-77; chmn. adv. bd. de-institutionalization project Central State Hosp., Indpls., 1978-79; mem. Ind. Council Community Mental Health Center, 1979-80. Recipient Outstanding Achievement in Professions award Center Leadership Devel., 1981. Mem. Ind. U. Alumni Assn., Christian Women's Fellowship, 500 Festival Assos., Coalition 100 Black Women (bd dirs.), Neal-Marshall Alumni Club, Alpha Kappa Alpha, Sigma Theta Tau, Chi Eta Phi. Mem. Christian Ch. (Disciples of Christ). Author articles in field. Home: 4057 Clarendon Rd Indianapolis IN 46208 Office: 7150 Clearvista Dr Indianapolis IN 46256

HARDENBURG, LINA, data processing executive; b. Schenectady, N.Y., Oct. 23, 1949; d. Allen Jeffers and Lulo Mae (Nelson) Peek; m. Mark Thomas Hardenburg, Sept. 27, 1969; 1 child, Marta Lynn. Student, Am. U., 1967-69; cert. computer programming, Chubb U., 1985. Cert. quality analyst. Quality control supr. Captive Plastics, Inc., Piscataway, N.J., 1975-85; EDP quality assurance mgr. R.H. Macy & Co., Inc., N.Y.C., 1985—; facilitator Quality Circle Inst., Red Bluff, Calif., 1984. Del. N.J. Dem. Party Convention, Atlantic City, 1980; corr. sec. Mcpl. Dem. Orgn., Piscataway; pres. Lady Vols. of Arbor Hose Co., Piscataway, 1983-85; trusteePiscataway Library, 1986—. Mem. Quality Mgmt. Assn., Quality Assurance Inst., N.J. Quality Assn., Phi Mu. Baptist. Home: 1838 Brunella Ave Piscataway NJ 08854 Office: 131 Market St 5th Floor Newark NJ 07102

HARDENDORF, KRISTEN LOUISE, printing company executive; b. Denver, Nov. 14, 1946; d. Owen F. and Margaret Louise (Ganson) H. BA, Simmons Coll., 1968. Rep. customer service Conn. Printers, Inc., Bloomfield, 1968-83, dir. customer service and prodn. planning, 1983-87; dir. customer service and prodn. planning Treasure Chest Advt. Co. Inc., 1987—. Contbr. articles to profl. jours. Class treas. Simmons Coll., Boston, 1978—. Republican. Home: 82 Victoria St Windsor CT 06095 Office: Treasure Chest Advt Co Inc 3 Choice Rd Windsor Locks CT 06096

HARDER, HEATHER ANNE, child care center administrator; b. Henderson, Tenn., Mar. 2, 1948; d. Wendell Anderson and Anne (Gibbs) Stacks; m. Robert Alan Harder, Apr. 3, 1971; children—Kerry Anne, Stacie Elizabeth. B.S., Ind. U., 1970, M.S., 1974, postgrad. Ind. State U. Tchr., reading specialist Crown Point Community Schs., Ind., 1970-79; mem. adj. faculty Ball State U., Muncie, Ind., 1977-79, Purdue U.-Calumet, Hamond, Ind., 1981-82, Gov.'s State U., University Park, Ill., 1985; owner, exec. dir. Small World Child Care Ctr., Merrillville, Ind., 1980—; founder Human Resources Unltd., Inc. Mem. adv. com. Purdue U.-Calumet, 1982—, Home Econ. Relations Occupations Crown Point High Sch., 1983—. Grantee Lake County Job Tng. Corp., 1984-85. Mem. Ind. Assn. Edn. Young Children (N.W. rep. 1984-86), Midwest Assn. Edn. Young Children, Nat. Assn. Edn. Young Children, So. Assn. Children Under Six, Resource for Infant Edn. Methodist. Avocations: Reading; painting; watching old movies. Home: 501 S Main St Crown Point IN 46307 Office: Small World Child Care Ctr 86 E 70th Ave Merrillville IN 46410

HARDER, SARAH SNELL, university administrator; b. Chgo., Sept. 9, 1937; d. Frank Wen and Margaret Louise (Bryne) Snell; student U. Iowa, 1955-58; B.A., B.S. cum laude, U. Wis., LaCrosse, 1963; M.A., Bowling Green State U., 1966; m. Harry R. Harder, Feb. 7, 1964; children—Richard, Bentley, Jennifer, Aaron. Mem. faculty in English, Bowling Green State U., 1967-68; mem. faculty English, U. Wis., Eau Claire, 1968, adv. to older students, 1975-77, asst. to chancellor for affirmative action, 1975-78, asst. to chancellor for affirmative action and ednl. opportunity, 1978—; mem. U. Wis. regents' task forces on basic skills, status of women, minority/disadvantaged students; cons. women's employment and equity, non-traditional programs in higher edn. Co-chmn. Nat. Women's Conf. Com., 1979-85; trustee Eau Claire Public Library, 1980-85, pres., 1984-85; chmn. bd. dirs. AAUW Ednl. Found., 1985—; founding bd. dirs. Wis. Women's Network; exec. Leadership Eau Claire, C. of C. Named one of 80 Leaders for the Eighties, Milw. Jour., 1979; 1st Excellence in Service award U. Wis.-Eau Claire, 1984. Dept. Edn. grantee, 1978—. Mem. AAUW (nat. pres. 1985—, dir. women's com., dir. legis. program com. mem. 1975—), LWV, Nat. Women's Polit. Caucus (award Wis. br.), Wis. Women's Council (chairperson), Delta Kappa Gamma (chpt. pres.), Alpha Lambda Delta. Democrat. Co-designer Beyond ERA—an Action Plan, 1982; contbr. articles to Redbook, Grad. Woman, Stateswoman. Home: U Wis Eau Claire WI 54701 Office: U Wis Library 2058 Eau Claire WI 54701

HARDESTY, MARY JANE, sports stadium executive; b. Okemah, Okla., Apr. 21, 1937; d. Richard Floyd and Mary May (Hooley) Day; M. Edwin Eugene Hardesty, Oct. 31, 1953; children—Richard Scott, Bryan Eugene. B.A. in Bus. Adminstrn., Okla. Bapt. U., 1969. Secondary edn. tchr. Shawnee High Sch. (Okla.), 1969-70; personnel asst. Plantation Pipe Line Co., Atlanta, 1970-75; office personnel adminstr. Cities Service Corp., Houston, Tex., 1977-78; mgr. personnel Foreman Dyess Law Firm, Houston, 1978-79; sr. employee relations rep., Mitchell Energy & Devel. Corp., Woodlands, Tex., 1979-81, mgr. employee relations, 1981-85; dir. human resources, Houston Sports Assn. Inc., 1987—. Woman of yr. award, 1982. Republican. Office: Mitchell Energy & Devel Corp 2002 Timberloch Pl PO Box 4000 The Woodlands TX 77380

HARDESTY, NANCY ANN, author, historian; b. Lima, Ohio, Aug. 22, 1941; d. Byron Tapscott and Ruth Lucille (Parr) H. A.B., Wheaton (Ill.) Coll., 1963; M.S.J., Northwestern U., 1964; Ph.D., U. Chgo., 1976. Editorial asst. Christian Century, Chgo., 1964-65; asst. editor Eternity mag., Phila., 1966-69; asst. prof. English, Trinity Coll., Deerfield, Ill., 1969-73; asst. prof. Am. ch. history Emory U., Atlanta, 1976-80; tchr. English, Gwinnett County Schs., Lawrenceville, Ga., 1980-82; ind. scholar, freelance writer/editor, 1982—; founder Evangelical Women's Caucus, 1973; founder Daus. of Sarah newsletter, Chgo., 1974. Author: (with Letha Scanzoni) All We're Meant to Be: Biblical Feminism Today (Eternity Book of Yr. 1974), 1974, rev. edit., 1986; Great Women of Faith, 1980; Women Called to Witness, 1984, Inclusive Language in the Church, 1987; contbr. articles to religious jours. Recipient Milo Jewett Prize, U. Chgo., 1976. Mem. Am. Soc. Ch. History, Wesleyan Theol. Soc., Publs. Services Guild, Coordinating Com. for Women in Hist. Professions. Democrat. Episcopalian. Home and Office: 7 Woodridge Dr Greenville SC 29611

HARDESTY, SARAH JANE, violinist; b. Kansas City, Mo., Sept. 14, 1946; d. Egbert M. and Margaret E. H.; B.Mus. Drake U., 1967; postgrad. Ind. U., 1967-68. Mem. 1st violin sect. Dallas Symphony Orch. 1968—; lectr. in field; owner, breeder champion Gt. Danes and English Setters. Mem. Greater North Tex. Orchid Soc. (past sec.).

HARDGROVE, CLAIRE ANN, college dean, communications educator; b. Columbus, Ohio, Nov. 11, 1930; d. James Henry and Florence Isabell (McDonnell) H.; m. J. Blair Thackeray, July 8, 1971 (div.). BA, Ohio Dominican Coll., 1958; MA in Speech and Drama, Cath. U., 1963; PhD in Theatre, U. Wis., 1970. Tchr. St. Lawrence High Sch., Pitts., 1958-60, Bishop Waterson High Sch., Columbus, 1960-61, Newark (Ohio) Cath. High Sch., 1961-63; asst. prof., chair Ohio Dominican Coll., Columbus, 1963-67; assoc. prof. Valparaiso (Ind.) U., 1970-75; instr. Trenton (N.J.) State Coll., 1978-79, dir. continuing studies, 1980-84, dean grad. and continuing studies, 1984—, cons. dir. profl. devel. ctr., 1986—. Dir. theater prodns. The House of Bernarda Alba, Sophocles, Electra, and others, 1958-75; contbr. articles to profl. jours. Univ. fellow, 1968-70. Mem. Speech Communication Assn., Am. Assn. Higher Edn., Assn. Continuing Higher Edn., Nat. Assn. Acad. Advisement. Lodge: Zonta. Home: 777 W State St Trenton NJ 08618 Office: Trenton State Coll Hillwood Lakes CN 4700 Trenton NJ 08650-4700

HARDIMAN, THERESE ANNE, lawyer; b. Chestnut Hill, Pa., Mar. 2, 1956; d. Edward Joseph and Grace Joan (Shaw) Hardiman. BA in History, Mt. St. Mary's Coll., 1978, BA in Psychology, 1978; JD, Thomas M. Cooley Law Sch., 1983. Bar: Pa. 1983. U.S. Dist. Ct. Pa. 1983, U.S. Ct. Appeals (3d cir.) 1984. Staff research asst. Internat. Brotherhood of Teamsters, Washington, 1978-79; law clk. Richard R. Rashid, Atty. at Law, Lansing, Mich., 1981-82; law clk. Pearlstine, Salkin, Hardiman & Robinson, Landsdale, Pa., 1981; staff asst. Employment Relations Bd., Mich. Dept. Civil Service, Lansing, 1982; mem. Pearlstine, Salkin, Hardiman & Robinson, Landsdale, 1983-86; v.p. Edward J. Hardiman & Assocs. P.C., 1986—. Editor-in-chief Pridwin, 1978, layout editor, 1977. Recipient Golden Key award, Delta Theta Phi, 1981; Outstanding Student award Student Bar Assn., Thomas M. Cooley Law Sch., 1982. Mem. ABA, Assn. Trial Lawyers Am., Pa. Assn. Trial Lawyers, Pa. Bar Assn., Monroe County Bar Assn., Montgomery County Bar Assn., Delta Theta Phi. Republican. Roman Catholic. Office: PO Box 850 Rt 940 Pocono Pines PA 18350

HARDIN, TERRI LYNN, investment company executive; b. Lebanon, Ky., Mar. 15, 1950; d. Jack Douglas and Thelma Theresa (Mattingly) VanDyke; m. Robert George Sanders Jr., Sept. 25, 1971 (div. Oct. 1982); children: Tina Lynn, Lori Anne; m. William Murray Hardin Jr., Dec. 15, 1984; children: Mari Beth, Tami Kaye. Cert. in dental assistance, Jefferson County Sch. for Dental Assts., Louisville, 1971. Nurse's aide Mary Immaculate Hosp., Lebanon, 1966-68; asst. Barnes Med. Lab., Louisville, 1969-70; dental asst. Sch. Dentistry U. Louisville, 1971-75; receiving asst. Bacon's Retail Store, Louisville, 1976-85; researcher, real estate cons. Wm. Hardin & Assocs., Louisville, 1984-86; pres., researcher Terri Lynn Corp., Louisville, 1986—, also bd. dirs. Mem. Nat. Assn. Female Execs. Democrat. Roman Catholic. Office: Terri Lynn Corp PO Box 16157 Louisville KY 40216

HARDING, ETHEL M., state legislator; b. Fishtail, Mont., Oct. 19, 1927; m. Warren Harding; 2 children. Student, Heald's Bus. Coll. Clk., recorder Lake County Mont., 1967-84; owner, operator Mission Valley Concrete, 1967-84; rep. State of Mont., 1985-86, senator, 1987—. Republican. Mem. Ch. of Nazarene. Office: PO Box 251 Polson MT 59860 *

HARDING, JACQUELINE JOYCE, producer; b. Memphis, Nov. 21, 1949; d. Shedrick Donnell and Ella Ruth (Ross) Jones; m. Geoffrey Gillespie Harding; children: Ashley Elizabeth, Jessica Marie. BA, UCLA, 1971; MA, Memphis State U., 1973. Producer, dir., writer Sta. WMC-TV, Memphis, 1972-75; cons. Sta. WTTW-TV, Chgo., 1975; producer, dir., writer Sta. CTN, Chgo., 1975-78; producer, writer Sta. WMAQ-TV, Chgo., 1981-87; owner, producer Harding Entertainment Group, Los Angeles, 1981—; story analyst Paramount Pictures, Los Angeles, 1985; co-owner Manchester Mgmt. Inc., Los Angeles, 1982—. Mem. Mus. African Am. Art, 1987, Black Womens Forum, 1987, Greenpeace, 1987. Recipient Emmy award TV Acad., Chgo., 1981, Gabriel award, Cath. Film Bd., DuPont-Columbia award, Columbia U. Mem. Women in Film (co-chmn. writers' com. 1985-86), Am. Film Inst., UCLA Theatre Arts Alumni Assn., Artist and Writers Guild. Office: Harding Entertainment Group 1450 W Manchester Ave Los Angeles CA 90047

HARDING, MARY, social worker; b. Washington, Aug. 9, 1940; d. Joseph Harding and Virginia Murray (Cobb) Stickler; m. Barry McCallion, Dec. 26, 1961 (divorced); Brian, Eamon; m. Jochen Sieckmann, Oct. 31, 1982. BA in English, Columbia U., 1964; cert. in Edn., Claremont (Calif.) Grad. Sch., 1967; postgrad. in social work, Adelphi U. Cert. tchr., N.Y., Calif. Freelance writer, photographer Berlin, Claremont, Exeter, Eng., 1965-80; editor Edition AM Mehringdam, Rensselaer Falls, N.Y., 1978—; tutor North County Tutorial, Potsdam, N.Y., 1981-83, adolescent coordinator in migrant edn., 1983—; v.p., program chair Brainard Art Gallery, 1982-83. Work exhibited in group shows Amerika Haus, West Berlin, 1974, American Artists Living in Berlin Exhibition, West Berlin, 1978, one woman show Ecart Art Gallery, Geneva, 1977; author: (with Dorothy Iannone) Speaking to Each Other, 1978, From The Passion Texts, 1979, A Klondike Journal, 1980, Taco Tia and the Cows of Aberdeen, 1981. Mem. appropriations com. St. Lawrence County Youth Bd., 1985—. Home: PO Box 148 Rensselaer Falls NY 13680

HARDING, VICKI RUTH, lawyer; b. Huntsville, Ala., Oct. 3, 1954; d. John W. and Ora Mae (Welcher) H.; m. Barry I. Hastie, July 1974 (div.); m. Kenneth S. Herring, Sept. 1986. BA, U. Tex., 1974; JD, Harvard U., 1977. Bar: D.C., 1977, Md., 1985, Mich., 1987. Lawyer office of exec. legal dir. U.S. Nuclear Regulatory Commn., Bethesda, Md., 1977-78; lawyer office of Commr. Ahearne U.S. Nuclear Regulatory Commn., Washington, 1978-83; lawyer Shaw, Pittman, Potts & Towbridge, Washington, 1983-85; computer cons. S2D, Rockville, Md., 1985-86; lawyer Pepper, Hamilton & Sheetz, Detroit, 1986—. Home: 3810 Oxley Troy MI 48083 Office: Pepper Hamilton & Scheetz 100 Renaissence Ctr Detroit MI 48243

HARDWICK, ELIZABETH, author; b. Lexington, Ky., July 27, 1916; d. Eugene Allen and Mary (Ramsey) H.; m. Robert Lowell, July 28, 1949 (div. Oct. 1972); 1 child, Harriet. A.B., U. Ky., 1938, M.A., 1939; postgrad., Columbia U., 1939-41. Adj. assoc. prof. Barnard Coll. Author: novels The Ghostly Lover, 1945, The Simple Truth, 1955, Sleepless Nights, 1979; essays A View of My Own, 1962; Seduction and Betrayal, 1974; Bartleby in Manhattan, 1983. Editor: The Selected Letters of William James, 1960; adv. editor: N.Y. Rev. Books; Contbr.: to New Yorker. Guggenheim fellow, 1947; recipient George Jean Nathan award, dramatic criticism, 1966. Mem. Am. Acad. and Inst. Arts and Letters. Home: 15 W 67th St New York NY 10023

HARDWICK, KAREN LEE, elementary school counselor; b. High Point, N.C., Nov. 17, 1952; d. Herman Warren and Josie Mae (Gilliam) Brower; m. Wallace Edward Hardwick Jr., Dec. 16, 1979. BS in Home Econs., U. N.C., Greensboro, 1975; MS in Human Devel. Counseling, George Peabody Coll. for Tchrs., Nashville, 1977. Elem. sch. counselor Cumberland County Pub. Sch. System, Fayetteville, N.C., 1977—. Sec. Fayetteville Civic Woman's Club, 1986—, Ponderosa Elem. Sch. PTA, Fayetteville, 1986—. Recipient Kay Stowe award Fayetteville Civic Woman's Club, 1983-84, 85-86. Mem. Am. Psychol. Assn., Am. Assn. Counseling and Devel., Am. Sch. Counselor Assn., N.C. Assn. for Counseling and Devel., N.C. Sch. Counselor Assn., Phi Delta Kappa. Baptist. Office: Ponderosa Elem Sch 311 Bonanza Dr Fayetteville NC 28303

HARDY, ANNE DUNLAP, artist, educator; b. Birmingham, Ala., Jan. 15, 1910; d. James Thompson and Georgia Bailey (Dixon) D.; m. Charles Lambdin Hardy Sr., Nov. 18, 1936; children: Albert Sidney II, Charles Lambdin Jr., Georgia Hardy Luck. AB, Brenau Coll., Gainesville, Ga., 1931; postgrad., Mus. Modern Art, L.I., N.Y., 1965, North Ga. Coll., 1966, U. Ga., 1970. Supr. art schs., Dawsonville, Ga., 1963-72; pvt. instr. art, Gainesville, 1960—, Dallas, 1961-63. One women shows include Gainesville, 1960, Piedmont Interstate Fair, Spartanburg, S.C., 1977, Lake Lanier Islands (Ga.) Art Show, 1977; group shows include Telfair Mus., Savannah, Ga., 1952, Columbus Art Mus., 1960, Motorola Art Show, Chgo., 1962, U. Ga. Cortona, Italy, 1970; represented in numerous pvt. collections. Mem. Hall County Library Bd., 1951-61, Atlanta Symphony Orch. Bd., 1953-58; pres. Yonah council Girl Scouts U.S., 1955-57, exec. dir., 1958-61; mem. Gainesville Beautification Com., 1979-81. Mem. Assn. Ga. Artists (v.p. 1952-54), Gainesville Art Assn., Ga. Arts Council, Alpha Delta Pi. Democrat. Episcopalian. Clubs: Garden of Ga. (bd. dirs. 1948-60), Gainesville Garden, Gainesville Book (pres. 1970-71); Chattahoochee Country; Cushman. Avocations: gardening, cooking. Home: 3165 Tan Yard Branch Rd Gainesville GA 30501

HARDY, BEVERLEY JANE, controller; b. Windsor, Ont., Can., Aug. 2, 1944; d. Bill and Thelma Viola (Feere) Karpiuk; m. children from previous marriage: Kristin Lee, Timothy John; m. D.E. Hardy, May 23, 1964 (div.). Student, J.L. Forster Collegiate Inst., Can., 1961-63; cert. in bus. mgmt., Western Inst. of Tech., Can., 1964; cert. in bus. tax law, Alvin (Tex.) Jr. Coll., 1978. Acct. Williams and Jamail Elec. Contractors, Houston, 1978-80; comptroller So. Tennis Ctrs., Houston, 1980-86, Brae-Burn Country Club, Houston, 1986—; cons. acctg. and computers 1987—. Leader Girl Scouts of U.S., 1974-78; coach Girls Softball Assn., Tex., 1978-79; band aide Pearland (Tex. Jr. and Sr. High Schs., Tex., 1979-85. Mem. Nat. Assn. Female Execs., Greater Houston Hospitality Accts. Assn. Home: 1118 Robert St Pearland TX 77581

HARDY, CAROL ELIZABETH, marketing services executive; b. Midland, Mich., Jan. 2, 1951; d. John Lawrence and Barbara Jean (Carris) H.; m. William R. Seikaly, July 16, 1977 (div. 1983). AA, Delta Coll., University Center, Mich., 1971; student, Mich. State U., 1971-73. Sec. Indpls. Pub. Schs., 1974-76; admitting coordinator Turtle Creek Convalescent Ctr., Indpls., 1976-77; adminstrv. asst. Hutzel Hosp., Detroit, 1977-80; office mgr. Billingslea, Godley, Surakomol & Assocs., Detroit, 1980-81; adminstr. Datacom Systems Corp., Detroit, 1981-83; dir. Advt. Audit Service, Bloomfield Hills, Mich., 1983-86; v.p. PMH/Caramanning, Inc., Bloomfield Hills, 1986—. Bd. dirs. Peoples Health Ctr., Indpls., 1975-77; vol. Indpls. Spl. Olympics, 1975-77, Children's Hosp., Detroit, 1981-84. Mem. Nat. Assn. Female Execs. Democrat. Episcopalian. Office: PMH/Caramanning Inc 2550 Telegraph Rd Bloomfield Hills MI 48013

HARDY, DEBORAH WELLES, history educator; b. Milw., Nov. 2, 1927; d. Frank M. and Doris (Berger) Hursley; widowed; children: Scott, Jonathan, Bridget. Student, Swarthmore Coll., 1945-47; BA, Stanford U., 1949; MA, U. Calif., 1950; PhD, U. Wash., 1968. TV writer 1964-72; mem. faculty U. Wyo., Laramie, 1967—, prof. history, 1978—, head dept., 1980-85; free-lance TV writer, 1964-74; mem. Wyo. Council Humanities, 1972-76. Author: Petr. Tkachev: The Critic as Jacobin, 1977, Wyoming University: The First Hundred Years, 1986, Land and Freedom: The Origins of Russian Terrorism, 1987; also articles. Grantee Social Sci. Research Council, summer 1971, Am. Philos. Soc., 1976; Internat. Research and Exchanges Bd. scholar, 1987. Mem. Am. Hist. Assn., Am. Assn. Advancement of Slavic Studies, AAUP, NEA, Western Social Sci. Assn., Western Slavic Assn., Phi Beta Kappa. Home: 2450 Park Ave Laramie WY 82070 Office: U Wyo History Dept Laramie WY 82071

HARDY, JANE ELIZABETH, educator; b. Fenelon Falls, Ont., Can., Mar. 27, 1930; came to U.S., 1956, naturalized, 1976; d. Charles Edward and Augusta Miriam (Lang) Little; B.S. with distinction, Cornell U., 1953; m. Ernest E. Hardy, Sept. 3, 1955; children: Edward Harold, Robert Ernest. Garden editor and writer Can. Homes Mag., Maclean-Hunter Pub. Co., Ltd., Toronto, Ont., 1954-55, 56-62; contbg. editor Can. Homes, Southam Pub. Co., Toronto, 1962-66; instr. Cornell U., 1966-73, sr. lectr. in communication, 1979—; mem. Cornell U. Provost's Adv. Com. on Status of Women, 1977-81; lectr., condr. workshops on writing. Bd. dirs. Literacy Vols. of Tompkins County. Mem. Women in Communications, Inc. (faculty adv. Cornell chpt. 1977—, liaison 1986—), Garden Writers Assn. Am., Royal Hort. Soc., Pi Alpha Xi, Phi Kappa Phi, Alpha Omicron Pi. Clubs: Toronto Garden, Ithaca Garden, Ithaca Women's. Contbr. numerous articles to mags.; author numerous other publs., including brochures, slide set scripts; editor pro tem Cornell Plantations Quar., 1981-82. Home: 215 Enfield Falls Rd Ithaca NY 14850 Office: Cornell U Dept Communication 312 Roberts Hall Ithaca NY 14853

HARDY, JUNE DORFLINGER, portrait painter and photographer; b. N.Y.C., Feb. 2, 1929; d. William Francis Dorflinger, Jr. and Katheryn (Hait) Dorflinger Manchee; grad. Briarcliff Jr. Coll., 1949; student Parsons Sch. Design, 1949-50, N.Y. Sch. Interior Design, 1953-54, 87-88, Nat. Acad. Art-Art Students League, 1966-85, Columbia U., 1963; m. John Alexander Hardy, Jr., May 26, 1956. Asst. tchr. Peck Sch., Morristown, N.J., 1950-51; with personnel dept. McGraw Hill, Inc., 1951-52; editorial asst., then asst. editor Better Homes and Gardens mag., 1952-57; editorial asst., then asst. editor Successful Farming mag., 1952-57; freelance portrait painter and photographer, 1969—; tchr. drawing and pastel painting Onteora Club, N.Y., summer 1977; mem. Twilight Park Exhbn. Com., 1983-87. Nat. Home Fashions League scholar, 1953; recipient 1st prize portrait in oil Twilight Park Art Show, 1976, 79, 1st prize portrait photography, 1977, 2d prize pastel landscape, 1979, 2d prize for flower photography, 1982, 3d prize oil, 1987; 1st prize for flower photography Onteora Garden Club Show, 1982, 1st and 2d prizes for photography Twilight Park Art Show, 1985. Life mem. Art Students League. Republican. Episcopalian. Clubs: Colony (chmn. entertainment 1979-84), Wednesday (past pres.), Badminton, Onteora. Address: 14 Sutton Pl S New York NY 10022

HARGER, SUSAN JEAN, air force officer; b. Detroit, Oct. 23, 1947; d. Robert William and Barbara Bray (Bentley) H. B.A., Denison U., 1969; M.S. in Mgmt., Troy State U., 1976. Commd. 2d lt. U.S. Air Force, 1969, advanced through grades to lt. col., 1986; chief adminstrn. Columbus AFB, Miss., 1970-74; chief base adminstrn., San Vito di Normanni, Italy, 1974-77; chief adminstrn. Air Force Contract Mgmt. Div., Kirtland AFB, N.Mex., 1977-79; weapons dir., Wallace Air Sta., Philippines, 1979-80; weapons dir., staff officer Tactical Air Warfare Ctr., Eglin AFB, Fla., 1980-82; comdr. mission crew Airborne Warning and Control System, Tinker AFB, Okla., 1982—, chief ops. plans div., 1984—. Decorated Air medal, Meritorious Service medal. Mem. Air Force Assn. Republican. Presbyterian. Avocations: horseback riding; raising African violets. Office: 552 AWACS/ADO Tinker AFB OK 73145 other: PSC Box 718 San Francisco CA 96366 *

HARGETT, LYNN MARIE SPOTTS, infosystems specialist; b. Jackson, Miss., July 23, 1961; d. William Max and Aline (Liles) Spotts; m. Michael Van Hargett, Jan. 14, 1984. BS in Bus. and Mktg., U. Fla., 1983; postgrad., Clemson U., 1986—. Customer service rep. Blue Cross and Blue Shield, Jackson, 1983-84; data base coordinator Bowater, Inc., Greenville, S.C., 1984-87, mktg. data analyst, 1987—. Active Greenville Jr. League, 1987—. Mem. Nat. Assn. Female Execs., Am. Mktg. Assn., Alpha Mu Alpha. Republican. Presbyterian. Club: Pebble Creek Country (Taylors, S.C.). Home: 305 Oak Brook Way Taylors SC 29687 Office: Bowater Inc PO Box 1028 Greenville SC 29602

HARGETT, SUZANNE JONES, medical technologist; b. Greenwood, Miss., Sept. 9, 1941; d. Theo Vivian and Katherine Roger (Wilson) Jones; m. Joseph Richard Hargett, June 9, 1960; children—Karen Melissa, Susan Elizabeth, William Robert. Student Cin. Conservatory Music, summers 1958-59; B.A. in Biology, Shorter Coll., 1963; diploma med. tech., Med. Ctr. Sch. Med. Tech., 1963. Staff technologist Med. Ctr., 1964-65; part-time technologist doctor's office, 1967-68; staff med. technologist Meth. Hosp., Dallas, 1969-70; supr. hematology and blood bank St. Francis Hosp., Columbus, Ga., 1971-72; supr. hematology and coagulation Med. Ctr., Columbus, 1972—; adj. asst. prof. med. tech. Columbus Coll., 1981—. Mem. Columbus Symphony Orch., 1963-68, 80-81, 1st Bapt. Ch. Orch., 1981—. Mem. Am. Soc. Clin. Pathologists (affiliate). Home: 4804 Allegheny Dr Columbus GA 31907 Office: 710 Center St Columbus GA 31902

HARGIS, CAROL JEAN LESLIE, publisher; b. Dallas, Dec. 25, 1951; d. John Conrad and Ollie May (Clay) Leslie; m. Glen Edward Hargis, Mar. 25, 1979. Student Southwestern U., 1970-72, So. Meth. U., 1972-74. Adminstrv. asst. Record Pub. Co., Dallas, 1973-74, v.p. and asst. pub., 1975—; auto ins. renewal clk. Roach, Howard, Smith & Hunter, Inc., Garland, Tex., 1974-75; adminstrv. asst. and underwriter Cravens, Dargan & Co. Ins. Mgrs., Dallas, 1975; lectr. in field. Former deacon Midway Hills Christian Ch., Dallas, soprano soloist and choir mem., past sec., treas., trustee, bd. dirs. Mem. N. Tex. Reenactment Soc. (sec., treas.), Fedn. Ins. Women of Tex. (past polit. action chmn.), Dallas Assn. Ins. Women (pres. 1984-85, publicity chmn., bd. dirs.), Ins. Women of Dallas, Nat. Assn. Ins. Women (conv. com. 1981), Delta Zeta. Mng. editor The Ins. Record. Home: 9410 Crestedge Dr Dallas TX 75238 Office: PO Box 225770 Dallas TX 75222 also: 2730 Stemmons Tower W Suite 507 Dallas TX 75207

HARGIS-LYTLE, BETTY LOUISE, archivist; b. Roff, Okla., June 11, 1940; d. Lee Fitzhugh and Lucy Ruby (Dunn) Hargis; m. Jack Witt, Apr. 4, 1958 (div. 1976); children—Rhonda Kaie Luker, Michael Jack Witt, Jenifer Denise Witt; m. James Elbert Lytle, June 22, 1977 (div. 1986). B.A. in Acctg., Okla. State U., 1965. Accountant, T.G. & Y Inc., Oklahoma City, 1968-73, Internat. Environ. Corp., Oklahoma City, 1974-78; auditor K & B Inc., New Orleans, 1979-83; audit supr. Oshman's Inc., Houston, 1983-85; archivist Pentecostal Holiness Hdqrs., Oklahoma City, 1985—. Contbg. author: (manual) Fine Arts of Audit, 1985. Contbr. papers to profl. jours. Mem. Nat. Assn. Female Execs. (network dir. 1980-83, 83-85), Nat. Assn. Internal Auditors, Nat. Soc. Am. Archivists, Soc. Okla. Archivists, Soc. Southwest Archivists, Soc. Houston Execs., Okla. Spl. Collections and Archives Network (bd. dirs.), Okla. Conservation Congress, Soc. Pentecostal Studies, Beta Sigma Phi. Republican. Pentecostal. Avocations: poetry writing; cross-country skiing; tennis; swimming; horses. Home: 12301 N MacArthur Apt 403 Oklahoma City OK 73142 Office: Pentecostal Holiness Ch Internat Hdqrs 7300 NW 39th Expressway Bethany OK 73008

HARGRAVE, CECILLE TERRY, interior designer; b. Paris, Tex., July 23, 1917; d. Carl C. and Una Lila (Sealy) Terry. B.A., East Tex. State U., 1938; postgrad. So. Meth. U. Downtown Coll., 1952-53, Little Sch. of Fine Arts, 1953; m. Glenn M. Hargrave, Oct. 9, 1937. Interior designer; specifiers-interior cons. Garland (Tex.) City Hall; guest editor Tex. Contractor, 1954, Furniture Age, 1956. Recipient Instns. Mag.'s award for Sam Rayburn Meml. Student Center, 1964; named Disting. Alumna, East Tex. State U., 1975. Mem. K.T. Ednl. Found. (hon.), East Tex. State U. Alumni Assn. (pres. Dallas county chpt.), Women in Architecture, Dallas Council World Affairs, Southwest Homefurnishing Assn. Alpha Alpha Gamma, Chi Omega. Episcopalian. Clubs: Park Cities Toastmistress (founder, past pres.) (Dallas); Merriman Park Women's (v.p.). Projects include Sam Rayburn Meml. Student Center, East Tex. State U., Commerce, Tex., Midway Park Elementary Sch., Euless, Tex., 1st Nat. Bank, Garland, 1st Security Nat. Bank Dallas, 1st Security Fin. Systems, Inc., Dallas, Parkdale State Bank, Corpus Christi, Tex., Dallas Mus. Fine Arts, Republic Bank Garland, Parkdale Bank, Corpus Christi. Club: Merriman Park Women's (pres. 1985-86). Home: 6938 Winchester St Dallas TX 75231

HARGRAVE, DEANE MCLURE, English language educator; b. El Paso, Tex., Apr. 3, 1931; d. Charles E. and Dessie Dean (Evans) McLure; m. William E. Hargrave, July 27, 1969 (Div. July 1983); children: Deanna Kemling, Robynn Kleck, Nancy Monroy. BS in English, No. Ariz. U., 1963, MA in Guidance and Counseling, 1964, EdS in Reading and Curriculum, 1966; PhD, Ariz. State U., 1975. Cert. tchr. English, acad. guidance counselor. Tchr. Williams (Ariz.) Pub. Schs., 1963-65; instr. English No. Ariz. U., Flagstaff, 1965-67, asst. prof., 1967-76, assoc. prof., 1976-81, prof., 1981—, interim dir. composition, 1986-87; cons. IBM, Kingston, N.Y., 1984-86, lang. and lit. dept. MA program Rensselaer Poly. Inst., Troy, N.Y., 1984-85, Hopi Tribe, Polacca, Ariz., 1977, Puerco Valley Sch. Dist., Sanders, Ariz., 1980; prof. Bur. Indian Affaris Summer Linguistics Conf., 1975-79. Dir. Sunday sch. Unity Ch. of Flagstaff, 1986; mem. Ariz. State Senate Task Force on Composition, Phoenix, 1983—, Ariz. Literacy Project, Tucson, 1986—, visitation com. to high schs. Ariz. Bd. Regents, 1987-88. Mem. Soc. Tech. Communicators, Ariz. English Tchrs. Assn. (pres. 1976-77, v.p. 1974-75, sec. 1972-73, Spl. Excellence in Teaching English award, 1988), Nat. Council Tchrs. English (com. instrnl. tech. 1985—). Democrat. Mem. Unity Ch. Home: 1805 Hereford Dr Flagstaff AZ 86001 Office: No Ariz U PO Box 6032 Flagstaff AZ 86011

HARGRAVE, MARY ANNE, pharmaceutical company administrator; b. Lewiston, N.Y., Feb. 6, 1959; d. Frank J. and Theresa (DiCamillo) H. BS in Bus., BA in Psychology, SUNY, Geneseo, 1981. Ladies dir. Am. Health Fitness Ctr., Amherst, N.Y., 1981-82; med. sales rep. Rorer Pharm. Corp., Ft. Washington, Pa., 1982-85, cardio-respiratory speciality med. rep., 1985-87, mgr. dept. managed health care, 1988—. Mem. Am. Heart Assn., Am. Lung Assn., Smithsonian Inst. (assoc.), Am. Amateur Racquetball Assn. (nat. ranked). Republican. Roman Catholic. Home: 8370 Greensboro Dr #920 McLean VA 22102 Office: 500 Virginia Dr Fort Washington PA 19034

HARGRAVE, SARAH QUESENBERRY, corporate executive; b. Mt. Airy, N.C., Dec. 11, 1944; d. Teddie W. and Lois Knight (Slusher) Quesenberry. Student, Radford Coll., 1963-64, Va. Poly. Inst. and State U., 1964-67. Mgmt. trainee Thalhimer Bros. Dept. Store, Richmond, Va., 1967-68; Cen. Va. fashion and publicity dir. Sears Roebuck & Co., Richmond, 1968-73; nat. decorating sch. coordinator Sears Roebuck & Co., Chgo., 1973-74, nat. dir. bus. and profl. women's programs, 1974-76; v.p., treas., program dir. Sears-Roebuck Found., Chgo., 1976-87, program mgr. corp. contbns. and memberships, 1981-83, dir. corp. mktg. and pub. affairs, 1983-87; v.p. personal fin. services/mktg. Northern Trust Co., Chgo., 1987—. Bd. dirs. Am. Assembly Collegiate Schs. Bus., 1979-82, mem. vis. com., 1979-82, mem. fin. and audit com., 1980-82, mem. task force on doctoral supply and demand, 1980-82; mem. Com. for Equal Opportunity for Women, 1976; chmn., 1978-79, 80-81; mem. bus. adv. council Walter E. Heller Coll. Bus. Adminstrn., Roosevelt U., 1979—; co-dir. Ill. Internat. Women's Yr. Ctr., 1975; mem. Chgo. Artists Coalition. Named Outstanding Young Women of Yr. Ill., 1976; named Women of Achievement State Street Bus. and Profl. Woman's Club, 1978. Mem. Assn. Humanistic Psychology, Am. Home Econs. Assn., Fashion Group, Eddystone Condominium Assn. (v.p. 1978-86). Home: 421 W Melrose St Chicago IL 60657 Office: Northern Trust Co 50 S LaSalle St Chicago IL 60675

HARGROVE, DEBORAH JEAN, real estate executive; b. Birmingham, Ala., June 21, 1953; d. Perry Gaston and Lillie P. (Hargrove) Anderson; 1 child, Bateast Jordan. BS in Acctg., No. Ill. U., 1976; cert. salesman, Atlanta Inst. Real Estate, 1979, cert. real estate broker, 1983. Acct. I, II Shapiro Devel. Ctr., Kankakee, Ill., 1976-78, supr. payroll, acctg., 1978-79; real estate agt. Harold Dawson Realty Co., Atlanta, 1979-82; acct., real estate agt., office mgr. Treasure Properties, Inc., Decatur, Ga., 1982-83; pvt. practice real estate broker Atlanta, 1983—; acct. U.S. Govt. Gen. Services Adminstrn., Atlanta, 1984-85, realty specialist, 1985—. Pres. PTA Hillside Acad., Atlanta, 1985; team mother East Point (Ga.) Amateur Baseball/T-Ball, 1987; bookstore dir. Jesus Christ Ctr. Truth, Atlanta, 1987; v.p., bd. dirs. East Point Youth Sports, 1987—. Recipient Service award Hillside Internat. Truth Ctr., Atlanta, 1982-83. Mem. Nat. Assn. Female Execs., Mortar Bd., Phi Beta Lamda. Democrat. Club: Toastmaster (treas. 1986, adminstrv. v.p. 1987, best speaker 1986, 87, Toastmaster of Yr. 1987). Lodge: Nubian Excursions (treas. 1984-85), Kiwanis (Govt. Walk chpt.). Home: 2726 Bayard St East Point GA 30344 Office: Gen Services Adminstrn 75 Spring St Room 418 Atlanta GA 30303

HARGROVE, KATHERINE EVELYN CHEAVENS, educator; b. Dallas, Sept. 23, 1936; d. David Anderson and Alice Elizabeth (Dawson) Cheavens; m. Mac Hargrove, Sept. 1, 1956; children: David McCauley, John Martin, Matthew Blake, Brian Hull. BA, Baylor U., 1957; MA, East Tex. State U., 1978. Cert. elem./secondary tchr. Tchr. Louisville Pub. Schs., 1958-62, Hamilton (Tex.) Pub. Schs., 1965-66; newspaper editor Hamilton Herald-News, 1966-67; tchr. Bonham (Tex.) Pub. Schs., 1970-72; tchr. Plano (Tex.) Pub. Schs., 1973-80, dir. acad. studies, 1980—; cons. in field. Mem. Assn. Supervision and Curriculum Devel., Delta Kappa Gamma. Office: Plano Ind Sch Dist 1517 Ave H Plano TX 75074

HARITUN, ROSALIE ANN, clarinetist, music educator; b. Johnson City, N.Y., May 30, 1938; d. George and Helen (Ternosky) H.; B.Music Edn., Baldwin-Wallace Conservatory of Music, Ohio, 1960; M.S. in Music Edn., U. Ill., 1961; profl. diploma Tchrs. Coll., Columbia U., 1965, Ed.D., 1968, postdoctoral, 1971-72. Tchr. instrumental music elem. schs., Patchogue, L.I., N.Y., 1961-63, jr. high schs., 1963-65; instr. music edn. Sch. Music, Temple U., Phila., 1968-71; instr. instrumental music N.Y.C. Bd. Edn., 1971-72; assoc. prof. music edn. Sch. Music, East Carolina U., Greenville, N.C., 1972—, del. to faculty assembly, Raleigh, N.C., 1981-88; chmn. profl. devel. com., faculty assembly, 1988—; clarinetist/saxophonist Greenville Summer-in-the Park Orch., 1975-79; clarinetist Albemarle Players prodn. South Pacific, Elizabeth City, N.C.; cons. curriculum devel., 1976-82; adjudicator choral/instrumental festivals, solo/ensemble contests, 1975-87. Bd. dirs. pres. Greenville Boys Choir, 1986-88. Mem. Coll. Music Soc. (council mem. music edn. div. Mid-Atlantic chpt. 1982-84, sec./treas. 1984-86), Delta Kappa Gamma (chmn. exec. bd. 1980-82, pres. elect 1984-86), Sigma Alpha Iota (chpt. pres. 1966-68), Pi Kappa Lambda (chpt. pres. 1977-83). Democrat. Baptist. Contbr. articles on music edn. to prof. publs. Home: 206 N Oak St Greenville NC 27834 Office: East Carolina U Sch Music 10th St Greenville NC 27834

HARKIN, CATHERINE ROSE (KAY), insurance agent; b. Phila., Sept. 21, 1930; d. Albert James and Elizabeth Agnes (Callaghan) Walsh; m. John Harkin, May 24, 1969. Cert. profl. ins. woman. Jr. underwriter Gen. Accident Ins. Co., Phila., 1948-66; rater Conn. Nat. Am. Ins., Phila., 1966-69; adminstrv. asst. Frank B. Hall Ins., Phila., 1969-72; asst. property underwriter Paul Hertel Ins., Phila., 1972-75; adminstrv. asst. Johnson & Higgins, Phila., 1975-77; underwriting asst. Fireman's Fund Commercial Lines, Phila., 1979—; audit dept. Internal Revenue Service. Mem. Nat. Assn. Ins. Women (state legis. chmn.), Irish Soc., Derry Soc. (ball chmn., stewart), Irish Unity Group, Womens Ins. Soc. Phila. (sec., mem. various coms.), activities commn. Parish Ch. Democrat. Roman Catholic. Office: Fireman's Fund Ins 510 Walnut St Philadelphia PA 19106

HARKINS, ROSEMARY KNIGHTON, university dean; b. Amarillo, Tex., Aug. 5, 1938. BS in Biology, English, West Tex. State, 1964; MS in Anatomy, Okla. U., 1970, PhD in Anat. Sci., 1972; BS in Funeral Service Edn., Cen. State U., Okla., 1976. Med. technologist U. Tex. Med. Br., Galveston, 1958-62, St. Anthony's Hosp., Amarillo, Tex., 1962-66, VA Hosp., Oklahoma City, 1966-68, Bapt. Med. Ctr., Oklahoma City, 1969-72; asst. prof. Coll. Allied Health Professions, Okla. U., Oklahoma City, 1972-77; assoc. prof. Coll. Allied Health, Okla. U., Oklahoma City, 1976-81, assoc. dean, prof., chair, 1981-88; dean Coll. Applied Health Scis. Howard U., Washington, 1988—; grant reviewer U.S. Dept. HHS, Washington, 1986, 87; dir. Allied Health Careers Opportunity Program, Oklahoma City, 1985—. Chair Okla. Bus. Devel. Ctr., 1984—, Okla. Inst. Child Advocacy, Oklahoma City, 1986—, Oklahoma City Br. NAACP, 1987—; co-devel. Oklahoma City-County Health Coalition, 1986—. Mem. AAAS, Am. Soc. Med. Tech., Am. Soc. Allied Health Professions, Nat. Soc. Allied Health, Delta Sigma Theta, Phi Delta Gamma. Democrat. Baptist. Home: 12420 Sussex Rd Midwest City OK 73130

HARKNESS, GAIL ANN, nursing researcher, educator; b. Rochester, N.Y., Mar. 14, 1939; d. Elmore Gibson Harkness and Doris (Wood) Harkness Kerbs; children—Michael D., Karen L. Merrill. B.S. in Nursing, U. Rochester, 1961, M.S. in Nursing, 1963; Dr.P.H., U. Ill., 1981. Instr. Norfolk Gen. Hosp. Sch. Nursing, Va., 1963-64; instr. pediatrics Portsmouth Gen. Hosp., Va., 1965; instr. med.-surg. nursing Lankenau Hosp., Phila., 1966-68; adminstrv. asst. Reading Hosp. Sch. Nursing, Pa., 1969-72; assoc. prof. med.-surg. nursing No. Ill. U., DeKalb, 1972-85; research fellow U. Rochester Sch. Nursing, N.Y., 1983-85; assoc. prof., acting chmn. dept. research and doctoral studies Boston U. Sch. Nursing, 1985-87, dir. New Eng. Deaconess Hosp.Ctr. for Nursing Research, 1987—, Boston . Author: Total Patient Care: Foundations and Practice, 4th-6th edits., 1984; Total Patient Care Workbook, 4th-6th edits., 1984. Bd. dirs. Health Systems Agy., 1978-83, pres., 1980-82; bd. dirs. Vis. Nurses Assn. Aurora, Ill., 1979-83. Recipient Nat. Research Service award HHS, 1977-80; nurse traineeship grantee HEW, 1961-62; Robert Wood Johnson Found. clin. nurse scholar U. Rochester Sch. Nursing, 1983-85. Mem. Am. Nurses Assn. (cabinet on nursing edn. 1980-86), Council Nurse Researchers, Mass. Nurses Assn. (bd. dirs. 1979-83), Sigma Theta Tau, Delta Omega. Democrat. Presbyterian. Office: Boston U Sch Nursing 635 Commonwealth Ave Boston MA 02215

HARLAN, NANCY MARGARET, lawyer; b. Santa Monica, Calif., Sept. 10, 1946; d. William Galland and Betty M. (Miles) Plett; B.S. magna cum laude, Calif. State U., Hayward, 1972; J.D., U. Calif., Berkeley, 1975; m. John Hammack, Dec. 1, 1979; children—Laryssa Maria Rebello, Leea Elyce Harlan. Admitted to Calif. bar, 1975, Fed. bar, U.S. Dist. Ct. for Central Dist., 9th Circuit, 1976; assoc. firm Poindexter & Doutré, Los Angeles, 1975-80; residential counsel Coldwell Banker Residential Brokerage Co., Fountain Valley, Calif., 1980-81; sr. counsel for real estate subs. law dept. Pacific Lighting Corp., Santa Ana, Calif., 1981-87; v.p., gen. counsel The Presley Cos., 1987—. Exec. v.p. student body U. Calif., Berkeley, 1974-75; bd. dirs. La Casa. Mem. State Bar Calif., Am. Bar Assn., Los Angeles County Bar Assn., Orange County Bar Assn. (dir. corp. counsel sect. 1982—), Calif. Women Lawyers Assn., Orange County Women Lawyers Assn., Los Angeles Women Lawyers Assn., Nat. Assn. Female Execs., Bus. and Profl. Women. Office: The Presley Cos 17991 Mitchell South Irvine CA 92714

HARLAN, ROMA CHRISTINE, portrait painter; b. Warsaw, Ind.; d. Charles William and Fern (McCormick) H. Student, Purdue U., Art Inst. Chgo. Art chmn. D.C. Fedn. Women's Clubs. One-man shows, Lake Shore Club, Chgo., Little Gallery of Esquire Theatre, Chgo., Purdue U., W. Lafayette, Ind., Hoosier Salon, Indpls., All.-Ill. Soc. Fine Arts, Chgo., Kaufmann's Galery, Chgo., Lafayette (Ind.) Art Assn., Arts Club, Washington, George Washington U., Washington; exhibited numerous group shows; represented in permanent collections at, U.S. Supreme Ct., D.C. Fed. Ct. House, SEC, U.S. Capitol, Nat. Presbyn. Ch., Va. Theol. Sem., Alexandria, Nat. Guard Bldg., St. Stephen's Sch., Alexandria, Washington Nat. Fedn. Bus. and Profl. Women's Clubs, Washington, Children's Hosp. Nat. Med. Ctr., Alexandria, Lakeshore Club, Chgo. Dau. Ind. scholar. Mem. Nat. Soc. DAR, Ind. State Art Assn. Presbyterian. Club: Arts (Washington). Lodge: Zonta Internat. Address: 1600 S Joyce St Arlington VA 22202

HARLAND, MARY KATHRYN HOLTAN, business and economics educator; b. Forest City, Iowa, Mar. 3, 1946; d. Hans Oscar and Ruth (Hermanson) Holtan; m. Thomas Robert Harland, May 4, 1974. A.A., Waldorf Coll., Forest City, 1966; B.A., Wartburg Coll., Waverly, Iowa, 1969; M.A., Mankato State U. (Minn.), 1981. Instr., Chicago Lakes Area Schs., Minn., 1970-72, Hennepin Tech. Inst., 1972-77, Albert Lea Area Vo-Tech Inst. (Minn.), 1977-80; asst. prof. bus. and econs. Waldorf Coll., 1980—, acad. chair faculty; adj. faculty mem. Mankato State U., Minn., 1984; mem. evaluation team North Cen. Assn. Colls. and Schs.; cons., lectr. in field. Author ednl. materials. Mem. Delta Pi Epsilon. Republican. Lutheran. Avocations: needlework, reading, bicycling. Home: RR 1 Box 44 Forest City IA 50436

HARLESS, KATHRYN FRANCES, government adminstrator; b. Washington, Feb. 13, 1946; d. Joseph Sr. and Kathryn Winifred (Ashley) Zagami; children—Angela Lynn, Joseph Anthony. Student Wheeling Coll., Montgomery Coll., Prince Georges Community Coll., ITT Bus. Inst. Sec., U.S. Parole Commn., Washington, 1968-74; with adminstrn. office, Burlingame, Calif., 1974-76; staff asst. to dir., Office of Mgmt. and Fin., U.S. Dept. Justice, Washington, 1976-77, mgmt. analyst, 1977-79, staff asst. to dep. asst. atty. gen. Office Personnel and Adminstrn., 1979-86; co-dir. Consol. Adminstrv. Office, 1986—; notary pub. U.S. Parole Commn., 1974-76. Democrat. Roman Catholic. Avocations: boating; traveling; handicrafts; reading; computers. Home: 3820 Mt Olney Ln Olney MD 20832 Office: US Dept Justice Consol Adminstrv Office Room 1229 10th & Constn Ave NW Washington DC 20530

HARLEY, ANN, nurse, educator; b. San Juan, P.R.; d. Allen Gotwals and May Miller (Naile) H. Diploma in Nursing, Abington Meml. Hosp., Pa., 1954; B.S. in Nursing, U. Pa., 1960, M.S. in Nursing, 1962; Ed.D., Tchrs. Coll. Columbia U., 1978. Curriculum coordinator Presbyn. U. of Pa. Med. Ctr., Phila., 1968-74; asst. prof. CCNY, 1975-76; assoc. prof. Coll. Nursing U. Nebr. Med. Ctr., 1976-80; prof. nursing Western Wash. U., Bellingham, 1980-86; chmn. dept. nursing Western Wash. U., 1980-86; prof. Meth. Coll., Fayetteville, N.C., 1986—, chmn. dept. nursing, 1986—; cons. in field. Performing mem. Voices of Omaha, 1979. Mem. Am. Nurses Assn., Nat. League Nursing, Internat. Soc. Chronobiology, Assn. Supervision and Curriculum Devel., Sigma Theta Tau, Pi Lambda Theta, Phi Delta Kappa, Kappa Delta Pi. Office: Methodist Coll Fayetteville NC 28311

HARLEY, ROSE MADELINE, training school executive; b. Paris, Ark.; d. Charles V.B. and Ella O. (McVay) H.; B.A. cum laude, Columbia U., M.A. in Adult Edn., 1976. Area mgr. N.Y.-L.I., Dale Carnegie orgn., 1960-63, instr. trainer internat. hdqrs., 1963-67, regional mgr. internat. hdqrs., 1967-76, mgr. Dale Carnegie Inst. of N.Y.C., 1976-79; pres. Harley Inst., Inc., presenting Dale Carnegie courses in No. N.J., Hackensack, 1979— , Accrediting Council for Continuing EDn. and Tng. (former pres. and bd. dirs.).Mem. Mensa, Dale Carnegie Sponsors Assn. (bd. dirs.), Internat. Platform Assn., Commerce and Industry Assn. N.J. (bd. dirs.), Columbia U. Alumni Assn., Sales Execs. Club N.Y.C. Club: Princeton. Home: 280 Prospect Ave Hackensack NJ 07601 Office: 25 E Salem St Hackensack NJ 07601

HARLOW, MARY JANE, audit manager; b. Kansas City, Kans., Aug. 13, 1959; d. Thomas Jackson and Ella (Kuntz) F.; m. Brent Allen Harlow, Sept. 19, 1987. BSBA, Kans. State U., 1981. Sec. HBO, Overland Park, Kans., 1981-83, regional auditor, 1983-87; regional audit mgr. HBO, Overland Park, 1987—; cons. Mary Kay Cosmetics, Lenexa, Kans., 1984—. Mem. Nat. Assn. Female Execs. Republican. Presbyterian. Office: HBO 9401 Indian Creek Pkwy #850 Overland Park KS 66210

HARMAN, DIANE WILEY, data processing executive; b. Glendale, Calif., May 1, 1942; d. Kenneth Raymond and Leonore Evelyn (Dorr) Wiley; children: Lisa R., Anthony L., Terence C., Melissa J. BA, Calif. State U., 1974; MBA in Info. Systems and Fin., U. Colo., 1983. Blueprint clk. RCA, Van Nuys, Calif., 1962; teller Citizen's Nat. Bank, Los Angeles, 1962-63; purchasing data entry System Devel. Corp., Santa Monica, 1963-64; jr. high soccer coach Boulder (Colo.) Valley Sch. Dist., 1979-81; cons. Boulder, 1981-84; computing systems mgr. Highline Fin. Services, Boulder, 1984-87; computing systems analyst Boeing Computer Services, Seattle, 1986—; cons. in field, Boulder, 1981-87. Mem. Data Processing Mgmt. Assn., Assn. for Computing Machinery, Front Range Unit Users Group, Am. Assn. Women In Computing, Boeing Computer Soc., U. Colo. Alumni Assn. Home: 21036 100th Ave Kent WA 98031 Office: Boeing Computer Services PO Box 24346 MS 94-04 Seattle WA 98124

HARMAN, MARYANN WHITTEMORE, artist, educator; b. Roanoke, Va., Sept. 13, 1935; d. John Weed and Clifford Kelly Whittemore; B.A., Mary Washington Coll., 1955; M.A., Va. Poly. Inst., 1974; m. Roger Walke, Aug. 25, 1984; children—Mary Kelly, John Whittemore, Phillip Mears. Faculty, Va. Poly. Inst., Blacksburg, 1963—, prof. art 1981—; guest artist Emma Lake Art Workshop, U. Sask., 1985. One-woman shows include: Andre Emmerich Gallery, N.Y.C., 1976, 78, Rubiner Gallery, Detroit, 1977, 78, Meredith Long Gallery, N.Y.C., 1980, Theodore Haber Gallery, N.Y.C., 1981-82, 84, 85, Osuna Gallery, Washington, 1982, 84, 87, Wade Gallery, Los Angeles, 1986, 87; group shows include: Va. Mus. Art, Richmond, 1973, 74, 75, 80, 81, Southeastern Center for Contemporary Art, Winston Salem, N.C., 1963, 65, 67, 71, 76, Boston Mus. Fine Arts, 1981, 84, Roanoke (Va.) Mus., 1963-79, Butler Inst. Contemporary Art, Youngstown, Ohio, 1969, 72, Anita Shapolsky Gallery, N.Y.C., 1988; represented in permanent collections: Boston Mus., General Motors, Detroit, Hunter Mus., Chattanooga, Roanoke Mus., Phillip Morris Corp., Richmond and N.Y.C., Mfrs. Hanover Trust, N.Y.C., Am. Can Corp., N.Y.C., Shawmut Bank of Boston, Mint Mus., CSX Corp., Ethyl Corp, others. Mem. Coll. Art Assn., Nat. Hon. Art and Architecture Soc., Tau Sigma Delta. Episcopalian. Home: 602 Landsdowne Dr Blacksburg VA 24060 Office: Va Poly Inst Blacksburg VA 24061

HARMON, ARTICE WARD, occupational therapist; b. Hughes, Ark., Oct. 2, 1940; d. William Oscar and Alice Williams (Turner) Ward; B.S., Ind. U., 1973; M.P.H., U. Ill., 1975; m. Luther Harmon, Dec. 5, 1959. Occupational therapy intern St. Elizabeth's Hosp., Washington, 1973, Helen Hayes Rehab. Hosp., W. Haverstraw, N.Y., 1973; staff occupational therapist Mercy Hosp. and Med. Center, Chgo., 1973-76; dir. occupational therapy program Westside Parents Center, of Retarded Children United, Chgo., 1976-77; head occupational therapy dept. Americana Health Care Center, Champaign, Ill.,

1977-81; dir. occupational therapy program Chgo. State U., 1981—, acting dean Coll. Allied Health, 1985-86; program devel. specialist, 1986—. ; guest lectr. allied health curriculum U. Ill., Urbana-Champaign, fall 1975, grad. teaching asso. occupational therapy curriculum Coll. Asso. Health Professions, 1978-80, instr., 1980-81; chmn. steering com. Ill. Council Occupational Therapy Edn.; coordinator statewide internship program, Ill. Bd. Govs. State Colls. and Univs., Springfield, Ill., 1986-87; cons. in field. Mem. Am., Ill. occupational therapy assns., Am. Pub. Health Assn., Am., Ill. vocat. assns., Am. Soc. Allied Health Professions, People United to Save Humanity, Phi Delta Kappa, Kappa Delta Pi. Roman Catholic. Home: 5020 S Lake Shore Dr #806-N Chicago IL 60615 Office: Chgo State U Coll Allied Health 95th St at King Dr Chicago IL 60628

HARMON, DEBBYE KAYE, social services administrator; b. San Antonio, June 10, 1952; d. Gregory Thomas Monroe and Clarice Evelyn (Rouse) Kennedy; m. Ronald Paul Harmon, Feb. 26, 1983; children: Kevin Paul, Dane Ronald. Student, Trinity U., 1970-71, Cen. Tex. Coll., 1987, Kennedy-Western U., 1987—. Lic. real estate agt., Tex. Fgn. visitor coordinator Dr. Michael DeBakey, Houston, 1972-74; med. adminstrv. asst. Tex. Women's Hosp., Houston, 1976-81; adminstrv. asst. Smith Protective Services, Houston, 1981-83; real estate assoc. hanszen Real Estate, Burnet, Tex., 1983-84, Johnson City (Tex.) Realty, 1985-86; dir. social services Llano (Tex.) Meml. Hosp., 1986—, also dir. discharge planning, pub. relations, editor, author and photographer newsletter. Coordinator Friends of Family, Llano, 1987—; chmn. pub. edn. Am. Cancer Soc. Llano chpt., 1987—, bd. dirs., 1987—; founder, dir. support group for parents and tchrs. of learning disabled children, Llano County, Tex. Mem. Nat. Assn. Female Execs. Lodge: Eastern Star (Ruth 1987-88). Home: Rt 8 Box 25 Llano TX 78643 Office: Llano Meml Hosp 200 W Ollie Llano TX 78643

HARMON, GAIL MCGREEVY, lawyer; b. Kansas City, Kans., Mar. 15, 1943; d. Milton and Barbara (James) McGreevy; m. John W. Harmon, June 11, 1966; children: James, Eve. BA cum laude, Radcliffe Coll., 1965; JD cum laude, Columbia U., 1969. Bar: Mass. 1970, D.C. 1976, U.S. Dist. Ct. D.C. Assoc. Gaston Snow & Ely Bartlett, Boston, 1970-75, Steptoe & Johnson, Washington, 1975-76, Roisman, Kessler & Cashdan, Washington, 1976-77; ptnr. Harmon & Weiss, Washington, 1977—. Pres. Women's Legal Def. Fund, 1982-84. Democrat. Episcopalian.

HARMON, KATHY JEANETTE, pharmacist; b. Richlands, Va., Aug. 31, 1961; d. Alva Stone and Phyllis Jeanette (Aliff) H. BS in Pharmacy, Ohio No. U., 1984. Lic. pharmacist. Pharmacist Rite Aid Corp., Beckley, W.Va., 1984-87, Cleve., 1987—. Troop leader Girl Scouts U.S.A., Pax, W.Va., 1986-87. Home: 6811 Mayfield Rd Suite 1579 Mayfield Heights OH 44124

HARMON, LILY, artist, author; b. New Haven, Nov. 19, 1912; d. Benjamin and Bessie (Horowitz) Perelmutter; m. Joseph H. Hirshhorn, 1945 (div. 1956); children: Amy, Jo Ann; m. Milton Schachter, Oct. 1972. Student, Yale Sch. Art, 1929-31, Academie Colarossi Paris, 1931-32, Art Students League, 1932-33. Illustrator: Pride and Prejudice (Jane Austen), 1950, Sounds of a Distant Drum (Bill Martin, Jr.), 1967; Japanese books Buddenbrooks (Thomas Mann), 1965, Symphonie Pastorale (André Gide), 1965, The Counterfeiters (André Gide), 1965, Dirty Hands (Jean Paul Sartre), 1965, The Castle (Franz Kafka), 1965, Metamorphosis (Franz Kafka), 1965, Lafcadio's Adventures (André Gide), 1972, Therese (Francois Mauriac), 1972, House of Mirth (Edith Wharton), 1975, Short Stories of Guy de Maupassant, 1976; author: autobiography Freehand, 1981; One-man shows, Asso. Am. Artists Galleries, N.Y.C., 1944, 50, 53, 56, 57, Silvermine Art Assn., 1954, Westchester County Arts & Crafts, 1950, Ann Ross Gallery, N.Y.C., 1959, Selected Artists Gallery, N.Y.C., 1960, HCE Gallery, Provincetown, Mass., 1961, Yamada Gallery, Kyoto, Japan, 1963, Scargo Lake Gallery, Dennis, Mass., 1964, Tirca Karlis Gallery, Provincetown, Krasner Gallery, N.Y.C., 1966, Provincetown Group Gallery, 1966, Internat. Salon Palace of Fine Arts, Mexico City, 1973, U. Richmond, Marsh Gallery, George M. Modlin Fine Arts Center, 1973, Krasner Gallery, N.Y.C., 1977, 81; One-man shows, Summit Gallery, N.Y.C., 1981; others, retrospective show, Wichita Art Mus., Kans., 1982, Butler Inst. Am. Art, Youngstown, Ohio, 1983, Provincetown Art Assn. and Mus., 1983; represented in permanent collections, Butler Art Inst., Youngstown, Ohio, Whitney Mus. Am. Art, N.Y.C., Newark Mus., Ein Harod and Tel Aviv (Israel) museums, U. Mass. at Amherst, Kalamazoo (Mich.) Art Inst., Smithsonian Art Inst., Washington, St. Lawrence U. Mem. Provincetown Art Assn., Artists Equity Assn., Nat. Acad. Design, Provincetown Art Assn., Fine Arts Work Ctr., Author's Guild. Home: 151 Central Park West New York NY 10023 Other: 629 Commercial St Provincetown MA 02657

HARMON, MARCI JANET, controller; b. Newark, Mar. 6, 1960; d. Harold E. and Lorraine G. (Schulte) Jayson; m. Brian Stewart Harmon, May 6, 1984. BS in Acctg., Pa. State U., 1982; MBA in Fin., Fairleigh Dickinson U., Madison, N.J., 1987. CPA, N.J. Auditor Arthur Andersen & Co., Houston, 1982-83; sr. fin. analyst Kidde, Inc., Saddle Brook, N.J., 1983-85; asst. controller Maritz Communications Co., Parsippany, N.J., 1985—; mem. fin. adv. com. City of Mt. Arlington, N.J., 1986—. Fellow N.J. State Soc. CPA's; mem. Am. Inst. CPA's, Nat. Assn. Accts., Nat. Assn. Female Execs., Women Entreprenuers N.J., Pa. State U. Alumni Assn., Alpha Phi Alumni Assn. Jewish. Home: 39 Kadel Dr Mount Arlington NJ 07856 Office: Maritz Communications Co 1515 Rt 10 Parsippany NJ 07054

HARMON, NADINE MAY, probation officer; b. Alhambra, Calif., Aug. 16, 1943; d. Arthur Edward and Phoebe Margaret (Addoms) Kaufman; m. Ronald Lee Fleming (div. 1973); children: Sandra Jean, Eric Lee; m. Harley Ray Harmon (div. 1977); 1 child, Renee. AA, Sierra Coll., 1978; BA, Calif. State U., 1980. Bus driver Placer Joint Union High Sch., Auburn, Calif., 1969-73, Western Placer Unified Schs., Lincoln, Calif., 1973-77; work project supr. Placer County Probation Dept., Auburn, 1977-84, probation officer I, 1984-85, probation officer II, 1985—. Recipient Nat. County Achievement award, 1980, Nat. Good Neighbor award, 1981. Mem. Placer County Dep. Sheriff Assn. Home: 12177 Elm Ct Auburn CA 95603

HARMON-PUGH, DEBORAH, personnel director; b. Phila., Sept. 12, 1956; d. James Author and Ida (Royal) Harmon; m. Walter Lee Pugh, June 5, 1983. BA, Antioch U., 1986; postgrad., U. Pa. Coll. recruitment coordinator Girard Bank, Phila., 1979-80, employment interviewer, 1980-81, sr. employment interviewer, 1981; exec. recruiter Girard Bank (merged with Mellon Bank, Phila.; mgr. coll. relations and recruiting Mellon Bank, Phila., 1983-84, human resource officer, 1984-87; mgr. human resource St. Paul Ins. Co., Plymouth Meeting, Pa., 1987—. Mem. Urban League of Phila., 1985—. Mem. Urban Bankers Assn., Minority Human Resource Assn., Am. Soc. for Personnel Adminstrs., Nat. Ins. Industry Assn. Office: The St Paul Cos Inc 2250 Hickory Rd Plymouth Meeting PA 19462

HARMSEN, MARYANNE J., insurance company executive; b. Bklyn., Dec. 22, 1945; d. Francis P. and Anne M. (Mannelli) Romano; student St. Peter's Coll., 1963, N.J. State Tchrs. Coll., 1964, Coll. Ins., 1977-78, Bergen Community Coll., 1979; children: Andrea Francesca and Jennifer Patricia Lamendola. Agt., Met. Life Ins. Co., Newark, 1974-76, Western World Ins. Co., Ramsey, N.J., 1977-80; account exec. Foxcroft Agy., Inc., Milford, Pa., 1980-83, asst. v.p. corp. risk analysis, 1984-85; sr. account exec. Met. Life Ins. Co., Hackensack, N.J., 1985-87; mktg. mgr. Metlife Healthcare Network, 1987—. Bd. advisors Acad. St. Aloysius, 1973-74; charter mem., officer, dir. nat. chpt. Ladies of Unico, 1969-70. Recipient Leaders award Met. Life Ins. Co. Leaders Conf., 1975. Mem. Profl. Ins. Women, Risk and Ins. Mgmt. Soc. (asso.), Nat. Assn. Female Execs., N.J. Democratic Assn. Roman Catholic. Club: Franklin Lakes Newcomers (past pres.). Home: 22 Myrtle Ave Ramsey NJ 07446 Office: 365 W Passaic St Rochelle Park NJ 07662

HARNESK, PRISCILLA ANN, training specialist; b. Hartford, Conn., May 13, 1955; d. Eric Adolph and Ruth Irene (Jordan) H.; m. David Allen Sauer. BS cum laude, U. Hartford, 1977; MS, Cen. Conn. State U., 1979. Admissions counselor U. Hartford, West Hartford, 1977-79; career counselor YWCA, Hartford, 1979-80; tng. coordinator G. Fox & Co., Hartford, 1980-83; field rep. Pvt. Industry Council, New Britain, Conn., 1983-85; tng. specialist Hosp. of St. Raphael, New Haven, 1985—. Author: Matchbook, 1979. Vol. Am. Cancer Soc., New Britain, 1984; vol. Spl. Olympics, New Haven, 1985. Mem. Nat. Assn. Female Execs., Cen. Conn. Women's Forum, Am. Soc. Tng. and Devel., Phi Delta Kappa. Democrat. Roman Catholic. Home: 98 Acorn Dr Middletown CT 06457 Office: Hosp of Saint Raphael 1450 Chapel St New Haven CT 06511

HARNSBERGER, THERESE COSCARELLI, librarian; b. Muskegon, Mich.; d. Charles and Julia (Borrell) Coscarelli; B.A. cum laude, Marymount Coll., 1952; M.L.S., U. So. Calif., 1953; postgrad. Rosary Coll., River Forest, Ill., 1955-56, U. Calif., Los Angeles Extension, 1960-61; m. Frederick Owen Harnsberger, Dec. 24, 1962; 1 son, Lindsey Carleton. Free-lance writer, 1950—; librarian San Marino (Calif.) High Sch., 1953-56; cataloger, cons. San Marino Hall, South Pasadena, Calif., 1956-61; librarian Los Angeles State Coll., 1956-59; librarian dist. library Covina-Valley Unified Sch. Dist., Covina, Calif., 1959-67; librarian Los Angeles Trade Tech. Coll., 1972—; med. librarian, tumor registrar Alhambra (Calif.) Community Hosp., 1975-79; tumor registrar Huntington Meml. Hosp., 1979—; pres., dir. Research Unltd., 1980—; free lance reporter Los Angeles' Best Bargains, 1981—; med. library cons., 1979—. Chmn. spiritual values com. Covina Coordinating Council, 1964-66. Mem. Calif. Assn. Sch. Librarians (chmn. legis. com.), Covina Tchrs. Assn., AAUW (historian 1972-73), U. So. Calif. Grad. Sch. Library Sci. (life), Am. Nutrition Soc. (chpt. Newsletter chmn.), Nat. Tumor Registrars Assn., So. Calif. Tumor Registrars Assn., Med. Library Assn., So. Calif. Librarians Assn., So. Calif. Assn. Law Libraries, Book Publicists So. Calif., Pi Lambda Theta. Author: (poetry) The Journal, 1982, To Julia: in Memoriam; contbr. articles to profl. jours. Office: 2809 W Hellman Ave Alhambra CA 91803

HAROIAN, ROSE DOROTHY, audiologist, consultant; b. Waukegan, Ill., Nov. 18, 1923; d. Jacob and Gooleg (Toomasian) Haroian; divorced; children—David Danian, Gillis-Ann Haroian. B.A. in Speech and Drama, Marietta Coll., 1949; M.A. in Speech Communication, Boston U., 1951; Ph.D. in Ednl. Adminstrn., Boston Coll., 1981; student Columbia U., U. Mass., So. Conn. Coll., Marlboro Sch. Tufts U., 1950-70. Cert. spl. tchr., speech pathologist and audiologist, Mass. Nursing tng. Worcester City Hosp. (Mass.), 1942-44; med. tech. U.S. Navy, Long Beach, Calif., 1944-46; spl. edn. tchr. Worcester Pub. Schs., 1949-67; mem. faculty Worcester State Coll., 1967-79, adminstrv. dir. Communicative Disorders Clinic, 1970-72, prof. emeritus, 1979—; editor, writer Digital Equipment Corp., Maynard, Mass., 1981—; cons. Psychol. Therapeutic Learning Ctr., Worcester, 1970-73; diagnostic cons. regional nursing homes, Worcester, Holden, Clinton, Mass., 1973-79; mem. Congl. action com. Am. Speech-Lang.-Hearing Assn., Washington, 1973-79. Author various auditory diagnostic tests in Armenian lang. for children, also pamphlet for awareness of hearing problems in children; editor and writer major documents for use in office computer automation products; creator, developer (with Mary O'Grady) American Roulette board game, 1983-88; contbr. articles in field to profl. jours. Diagnostician, therapist Coll. Community Outreach Services, Central Mass. area, 1967-75; dir., supr. Neonatal Hearing Screening Program, Worcester City Hosp. (1st program of its kind); founder Communications Disorders Clinic, Worcester State Coll., 1967 (Gold Plaque award 1979). Mem. Phi Delta Kappa, Alpha Psi Omega. Mem. Armenian Apostolic Ch. Home: 630 Salisbury St Worcester MA 01609

HARP, BEVERLY ANN, real estate broker; b. Little Rock, Dec. 11, 1942; d. Woodrow Wilson and Emma Lou (Weems) Utley; m. Robert Morris Wright, Jr., June 11, 1961 (div. Apr. 1969); children—Gary David, Karen Angela; m. 2d James William Harrison, Aug. 19, 1969; 1 son, James Wilson (div. 1985); m. 3d William T. Harp, Dec. 20, 1985. Student Henderson State U., 1960-61. Lic. real estate broker, Ark., Ins. Agt., Ark.; grad. Ark. Realtors Inst., 1981. Tenant selection officer North Little Rock Housing Authority (Ark.), 1966-69, 75-77; real estate salesperson Fausett & Co., Inc., Little Rock, 1979-82; relocation dir. Rainey Realty Better Homes & Gardens, Little Rock, 1983; assoc. broker ERA Collins Realty, Inc., Little Rock, 1983-84; sales assoc. Lakehill Realty Co., North Little Rock, 1984-85; broker, sales mgr. Gen. Properties, 1985-86; escrow officer Beach Abstract & Guaranty Co., 1986-88; owner BH Enterprises, Inc., The Home Team, Inc., 1988—; instr. Pike's Peak Community Coll. instr. real estate courses. Sec. Ark. Democratic Women, Little Rock, 1982; v.p. cen. Ark. chpt. Am. on the Move; mem. North Little Rock Sch. Bd., 1978-81. Mem. Ark. Realtors Assn. (chmn. pub. relations 1982-84, liaison to Ark. Legislature 1982—), Greater Little Rock Women's Council Realtors (pres. 1981), Greater Little Rock Home Builders Aux. (pres.-elect 1983-84), North Pulaski Bd. Realtors (v.p. 1981), Nat. Bd. Realtors, Ark. Bd. Realtors, Nat. Home Builders Aux., Ladies Aux. United Transp. Union (local pres. 1975). Methodist. Home: 6313 Rolling Hills Dr North Little Rock AR 72118 Office: Home Team Inc 4008 John F Kennedy Blvd North Little Rock AR 72216

HARP, PEGGY, printing company executive, real estate professional; b. Lexington, Ky., July 4, 1931; d. Richard Simmons Shely and Regina (Orma) Stevens; m. Raymond T. Ayers (div.); children: Tom, Richard, Dianna, Steve; m. Roland Joseph Harp; children: Joe, Dan, Meagan, Sim. Cert. in real estate, Pass Sch., 1976. Salesperson Hurst Printing Co., Lexington, Ky., 1969-72; sec., treas. Harp Enterprises, Inc., Lexington, 1972—. Pres. PTA, Okla., 1956-58; Republican committeewomen, Okla., 1958; chmn. Kentucky Chpt. Myasthenia Gravis, Lexington, 1982. Mem. Ky. C. of C., Lexington C. of C., Lexington Printers Assn., Lexington Real Estate Commn. Mem. Disciples of Christ. Club: Lexington Ad. Office: Harp Enterprises 2400 Merchant St Lexington KY 40583

HARPER, ABIGAIL, accounting executive; b. Richmond, Va., July 14, 1953; d. Thomas Gerdine and Marilyn (Montague) H. BA in Fine Arts, Roanoke Coll., 1975; MBA in Acctg., Fordham U., 1984. Mgr. box office Southbury (Conn.) Playhouse, 1975-76; office mgr. Isabel Noyes & Assocs., N.Y.C., 1976-81; mgr. mkt. analysis Coopers & Lybrand, N.Y.C., 1981—. Mem. DAR. Republican. Baptist. Office: Coopers & Lybrand 1251 Ave of Americas New York NY 10020

HARPER, ANNA LOUISE, entrepreneur; b. Little Rock, Nov. 26, 1960; d. Ernest Haven and Mary Louise (Suddreth) H. BA, U. Little Rock, 1984. Staff asst. Office of Gov., Little Rock, 1982; fin. aid officer U. Ark. Med. Scis., Little Rock, 1982; receptionist Riley's Oak Hill Manor, Little Rock, 1982-83; adminstrv. asst. Bethune for Senate, Little Rock, 1983-84; sales rep. Favorite Check Printers, Little Rock, 1984-86; owner, mgr. Harper's, North Little Rock, 1986—. Mem. ladies aux. Ark. Children's Hosp., Little Rock, 1984—, Friends of Repertory Theatre, Little Rock, 1985—; Pulaski County Rep. Women; del Nat. Rep. Conv., Dallas, 1984. Mem. Nat. Assn. Female Execs., Planned Parenthood Ark., Quapaw Quarter Assn., Pi Beta Phi. Episcopalian. Office: 2821 Lakewood Village Dr North Little Rock AR 72116

HARPER, ANN-ELIZABETH, small business owner, nurse; b. Mt. Hope, W.Va., Aug. 30, 1939; d. William Dexter and Margarite Lousia (Craft) Kessler; m. Michael A. Percy (div. 1980); children: James Percy, Brian Percy; m. Ernest Harper Jr.; children: David, Mark, Cynthia, Diania, Kevin, John. Diploma in Vocat. Nursing, Tucson Skill Ctr., 1976; AS in Nursing and Bus., Pima Community Coll., 1978. RN, Ariz., Calif. Nurse Tucson Med. Ctr., 1976-77, Kino Community Hosp., Tucson, 1977-78, Downey (Calif.) Community Hosp., 1980-82; jeweler, owner, appraiser Indian artifacts Harpers Trading Post, Bellflower, Calif., 1980—. Author: Singing Bells, 1987. Republican. Office: Harpers Trading Post PO Box 1092 Bellflower CA 90706

HARPER, BEVERLY JO, real estate broker; b. Seattle, Nov. 29, 1941; d. Rodger R. and Ruth E. (Barnes) Rosacker;. Cert. fin. planning, Coll. Fin. Planning, 1987. Cert. fin. planner, real estate broker, Oreg. Prin. Sunset Tng. Stables, Hillsboro, Oreg., 1965-72, Lone Pine Pintos, Junction City, Oreg., 1973-85; real estate broker Beverly Harper Realty Inc., Junction City, 1974—, cert. fin. planner, 1987—; prin. BHR Mgmt. Inc., Junction City, 1986—; bd. dir., exec. officer Multiple Horse Orgns., Oreg. and nat. affiliations, 1963-79. Instr. Jr. Achievement, Junction City, 1988. Mem. Nat. Bd. Realtors, Oreg. Bd. Realtors. Office: Beverly Harper Realty Inc 1350A Ivy St Junction City OR 97448

HARPER, DEBORAH ANN FLAMMER, infosystems specialist; b. Red Bank, N.J., Dec. 8, 1953; d. David William and Elizabeth (McMurty) Flammer; m. William Arthur Harper, (div. Nov. 1984); 1 child, John William. BA, Purdue U., 1975. Tchr. Tuppecanoe Sch. Dist., Lafayette, Ind., 1975; sales mgr. ITT Terryphone Corp., Harrisburg, Pa., 1976-78; v.p. Interconnect Installation Corp., Greenville, R.I., 1978-82; office mgr. John Marandola Plumbing and Heating Co., Warwick, R.I., 1983-84; inside ops. mgr. James L. Day Co., Inc., Victor, N.Y., 1985-86; project mgr. Eastern area US West Info. Systems, Denver, 1986-88; exec. search cons. Mgmt. Recruiters Internat. Inc., Rochester, N.Y., 1988—. Mem. Nat. Assn. of Female Execs., Rochester Round Table (bd. dirs.). Presbyterian. Club: Purdue (Rochester).

HARPER, DEBORAH MORSE, clothes designer; b. Cheshire, Conn., Jan. 15, 1954; d. Wesley White and Jane (Guilford) H. Assocs., Chamberlyne Jr. Coll., 1974; student, Fashion Inst. Tech., 1984. Designer Deborah Harper Designs Ltd., N.Y.C., 1983—. Designer: Vogue, 1986, Elle mag., 1986-87, Donna, Italy, 1987, Interview Mag., 1987, Taxi Mag., 1987, Harpers Bazaar, 1987, Foreign Intrique, N.Y.C., 1987-88, Bergdorf Goodman catalogues, 1987-88, Fashion Accessories Exhbn., N.Y.C., 1987, Omni Show, N.Y.C., 1987, Pret Show, N.Y.C., 1987, Adrienne Viitinini, Bern Conrad, Mary Ann Restivo. Recipient Exclusivity award Bergdorf Goodman, 1987. Mem. Am. Womens Econ. Assn., Nat. Assn. Female Execs. Episcopalian. Office: PO Box 7077 New York NY 10163-6026

HARPER, DIANE, English educator; b. Media, Pa., May 12, 1950; d. Jesse and Alice Marie (Mars) H.; married 1976 (div. 1987); children: Khadj M., Khamal M. BA, Boston U., 1972, MA, 1973. Cert. secondary edn. tchr., Mass. Tchr. Excellsior High Sch., Kingston, Jamacia, 1973, New Bedford (Mass.) High Sch., 1973-74; instr. English Massachusetts Bay Community Coll., Wellsley, Mass., 1976-79; asst. prof. Massachusetts Bay Community Coll., Wellsley, 1979-83, assoc. prof., 1983-86, prof., 1986—; acad. counselor, instr. English Northeastern U., Boston, 1974-76, 83—; pres., owner To Find an Image Cons. Firm; teaching asst. Sch. Bus. Extension Sch. Harvard U., Cambridge, Mass., 1981-82; v.p. social and ednl. programs Lena Park Community Devel. Corp., Dorchester, Mass., 1985-88; lectr. on black women writers, non-trad. student. Recipient Black Womanhood award Urban League, Boston, 1973; Massachusetts Bay Community Coll. grantee, 1985—. Mem. Community Colls. Humanities Assn., NEA, Mass. Tchrs. Assn., Nat. Assn. Female Execs., Delta Sigma Theta. Methodist. Office: Mass Bay Community Coll 50 Oakland St Wellsley MA 02181

HARPER, DYAN, educational administrator; b. East Chicago, Ind., Jan. 30, 1942; d. John Henry and Dorothy Ilene (Lidgard) Harper; children: R. Scot McNabb, Sean McNabb. BA in Sociology, Ind. U., 1982. Adminstr. Stanley H. Kaplan Ednl. Ctr., Bloomington, Ind., 1983-86, Durham, N.C., 1987—; profl. entertainer various locations, 1970-84. Bd. dirs. Network of Career Women, Bloomington, Ind., 1986; chmn. bd. dirs. Leadership Bloomington Alumni, 1986; mem. Pub. Edn. Task Force, Durham, 1987, Leadership Durham, 1988. Mem. Nat. Assn. Female Execs. Democrat. Unitarian Universalist. Office: Kaplan Ednl Ctr 2634 Chapel Hill Blvd #112 Durham NC 27707

HARPER, GLADYS COFFEY (MRS. THOMAS A. HARPER), health services adviser; b. Pitts.; d. Clarence William and India Anna (James) Jackson; B.A., U. Pitts., 1970, M.P.A., 1972, M.S.H., 1973; m. Thomas A. Harper, Jan. 21, 1968. With Allegheny County (Pa.) Health Dept., 1958—, chief office tng. and edn. adminstr., 1975-76, adv. curriculum devel. and health adminstrn., 1976—; health technician specialist office health affairs OEO, Washington, 1965; vis. lectr. Grad. Sch. Public and Internat. Affairs, U. Pitts., 1970—; bd. dirs. Heritage Nat. Bank, 1988—; panelist Sta. WQED-TV White House Conf. Food, Nutrition and Health; trustee Mayview State Hosp., 1975—, v.p. bd. trustees, 1978, trustee clin. pastoral edn. program, 1979-80; bd. dirs. United Mental Health, Inc. Program chmn. Law Day, Allegheny County Assn. Lawyers' Wives, 1975, v.p., 1978, pres., 1980; program chmn. Pa. Bar Assn. Wives Program, 1978; trustee Louis Little Meml. Fund, Allegheny County Bar Assn., 1979; founder Judge Thomas A. Harper Meml. Scholarship, Howard U. Sch. Law, 1984. Active Allegheny County Bicentennial Com., 1987, Afro-Am. Heritage Day Parade Com., 1987, Allegheny County Bicentennial Scholarship Com., 1988; exec. v.p. Afro-Am. Heritage Parade Assn., chmn. judging com., 1988; v.p. Hist. Soc. of Western Pa., 1988. Named Woman of Yr., Greyhound Corp., 1967, 1 of 25 Outstanding Pittsburghers, Wayfarer Mag., Chrysler Corp., 1967, Health Services award Pitts. Club United, 1970, Harold B. Gardner award-Md. Citizen Health award, Allegheny County Med. Soc., 1973, Drug Edn. recognition Pitts. Press, 1971, citation for environ. health curriculum devel. and supervision Chatham Coll., 1976, award African Meth. Episcopal Zion Ch., 1984; crowned Bahamas Princess Christmas Queen, Freeport, 1976. Mem. Am. Pub. Health Assn., Royal Soc. Health, Am. Soc. Pub. Adminstrn., Conf. Minority Pub. Adminstrs., Legis. Council Western Pa. (dir., v.p. elect 1982), Western Pa. Genealogy Soc. (pres. 1983), Legis. Council Western Pa. (pres. 1983), League Community Health Workers, AAUW, NAACP (Isabel Strickland Youth Advisor award 1967, Daisy E. Lampkin Human Rights award 1969), Hist. Soc. Western Pa. (trustee 1984, v.p. bd. trustees 1988), U. Pitts. Alumnae Assn. (Bicentennial scholarship com.), Program to Aid Citizen Enterprises. Co-producer documentary: What's Buggin' The Blacks?, Sta. KDKA-TV, 1968. Home: 5260 Centre Ave Coronada Apts 502 Pittsburgh PA 15232

HARPER, LILAH M., nursing administrator; b. Tucson, Apr. 9, 1942; d. Riddley D. and Lilah M. (Earley) Jones; m. Kenneth W. Harper, July 7, 1961 (dec. Aug. 1986); children: Dennis W., Alan D., Kevin D., Brian L. BS in Nursing, U. Ariz., 1962, MA, 1974; postgrad., Harvard U. Sch. Pub. Health, 1978. RN. Nurse team leader St. Joseph's Hosp., Tucson, 1962-63; sch. nurse Tucson Pub. Sch., 1966, nursing inst., 1966-71; nursing adminstrn. Tucson Med. Ctr., 1972-79; dir. nursing services El Cajon, Calif., 1979-80; asst. adminstr. nursing services Palomar Med. Ctr., Escondido, Calif., 1980—; lectr. nursing Pt. Loma Coll., San Diego, 1980-81; mem. Ariz. State Bd. Nursing, 1976-78. Bd. dirs. Boys Choir Soc., Tucson, 1976-79. Recipient TWIN award YWCA, 1987. Mem. Am. Soc. Nursing Service Adminstrs., Calif. Soc. Nursing Services Adminstrs., Nursing Adminstrs Council San Diego, Sigma Theta Tau, Pi Lambda Theta. Baptist. Home: PO Box 486 Alpine CA 92001 Office: Palomar Meml Hosp 555 E Valley Pkwy Escondido CA 92025

HARPER, MARY SADLER, banker; b. Farmville, Va., June 15, 1941; d. Edward Henry and Vivien Morris (Garrett) Sadler; m. Joseph Taylor Harper, Dec. 21, 1968; children by previous marriage: James E. Hatch III, Mary Ann Hatch Czajka. Cert. Fla. Trust Sch., U. Fla., 1976. Registered securities rep., Fla. Dep. clk. Polk County Cts., Bartow, Fla., 1964-67; rep. Allen & Co., Lakeland, Fla., 1967-71; with First Nat. Bank, Palm Beach, Fla., 1971—, sr. v.p., 1984-86, sr. v.p. Southeast Bank N.A., Palm Beach, 1986—; pres., chief exec. officer Palm Beach Capital Services, Inc., 1986-88, mng. dir. Investment Services, Palm Beach Capital Services Div., 1988 ; v.p. investments J.M. Rubin Found., Palm Beach, 1983—; mem. adv. council Nuveen, 1987. Mem. adv. panel Palm Beach County YWCA, 1984—. Mem. Nat. Assn. Bank Women, Nat. Assn. Securities Dealers (registered), Miami Bond Club, Fla. Securities Dealers Assn., Exec. Women of Palm Beaches (mem. fin. com. 1985—), Internat. Soc. Palm Beach (treas. 1986—), Palm Beach Martin County Med. Assn. (pres.'s club 1983—), Loxahatchee Hist. Soc., Sebring, Fla. Hist. Soc., Jupiter/Tequesta C. of C. (assoc.), United Daus. of Confederacy, Lighthouse Gallery of Art. Democrat. Baptist. Clubs: Gov.'s, Jonathans. Avocations: reading, history. Home: 630 Ocean Dr Apt 103 Juno Beach FL 33408 Office: Palm Beach Capital Services 1st Nat Palm Beach 225 S County Rd Palm Beach FL 33480

HARPER, PAMELA CELESTE, preschool marketing executive, school district manager; b. Laredo, Tex., May 29, 1952; d. Samuel Ethelbert and Ruth Elizabeth (Delling) Cunningham; m. James David Harper, Sept. 30, 1976 (div. 1980). BE, Southwest Tex. State Coll., 1974. Art tchr. Randolph AFB, San Antonio, 1974-77; registrar, asst. to dir. Longview (Tex.) Mus. Fine Arts, 1977-78; art tchr. Fort Bend Ind. Sch. Dist., Houston, 1978-79; interior designer Changing Look, Inc., Houston, 1979-80; gen. ops. mgr. Crabtree and Evelyn of London, Houston, 1980-84; mktg., dist. mgr. Children's World Learning Ctrs. Inc. (formerly Daybridge Learning Ctrs. Inc.), Houston, 1984—; chmn. Houston ARA Component Exchange, 1986—; mem. Randall's Customer Adv. Bd., 1987—. Editor Discoveries newspaper, 1987—; artist Marketing Line cartoon strip, 1986; designed several audio-visual and promotional projects on childrens' health, 1986-87. Vol. Am.

Lung Assn., Am. Heart Assn. Houston, 1985—, Harris County Heritage Soc. Mem. West Houston C. of C. Episcopalian.

HARPER, PATRICIA ANN, social services administrator; b. Muskegon, Mich., July 9, 1957; d. Alwain Kenneth and Arlene Ann (Knoll) H. AAS, Muskegon Community Coll., 1977; BBA, Grand Valley State U., 1980; MBA, Grand Valley State Coll., 1983. Office asst. Radiology Muskegon (Mich.) P.C., 1975-80; office mgr. Ottawa County, Grand Haven, Mich., 1980-87, asst. friend of the ct., 1987—; mem. adv. com. Mich. Child Support Enforcement System; mem. State Ct. Adminstrv. Office Forms Com. Bd. dirs. Southwestern Mich. Family Support Council, Grand Rapids, 1984—. Mem. Am. Mgmt. Assn., Nat. Assn. Female Execs., Bus. and Profl. Women (pres. 1984-86; named Young Careerist 1982), Friends of Ct. Assn., FOCUS Users Group (pres.), Mich. NCR User's Group. Office: Ottawa County Friend of Ct 414 Washington Ave Grand Haven MI 49417

HARPER, PAULA, art history educator, author; b. Boston, Nov. 17, 1938; d. Clarence Everett and Maura (Lee) Fish. BA in Art History magna cum laude, CUNY, 1966, MA in Art History, 1968; postgrad. U. N.Mex., 1968-69; PhD in Art History, Stanford U., 1976. Dancer, Munt-Brooks Modern Dance Co., N.Y.C., 1963-65; teaching fellow U. N.Mex., 1968-69; asst. prof. Calif. Inst. Arts, Valencia, 1971-72; dir. Hunter Arts Gallery, CUNY, 1977-78; vis. asst. prof. Mills Coll., Oakland, Calif., spring 1979, 1980-81; Stanford U., Calif., 1979-80; assoc. prof. art history U. Miami, Coral Gables, Fla., 1982—; art critic Miami News, 1982—; frequent lectr. mus., art galleries and univs. Author: Pissarro: (with R.E. Shikes) His Life and Work, 1980 (transl. into French, German, Rumanian), Daumier's Clowns, 1981; contbr. to jours., books, exhbn. catalogues. Film Inst. fellow CUNY, 1966, Tuition fellow CUNY, 1966-67; Ford Found. grantee Stanford U., 1969-73, research grantee French Govt., 1973-74. Mem. Coll. Art Assn. (founder Women's Caucus for Art 1972, pres. N.Y. chpt. 1977-78, mem. nat. adv. bd. 1977-80), Internat. Assn. Art Critics, Soc. Mayflower Descs. Office: U Miami Dept Art and Art History PO Box 248106 Coral Gables FL 33124

HARPHAM, VIRGINIA RUTH, violinist; b. Huntington, Ind., Dec. 10, 1917; d. Pyrl John and Nellie Grace (Whitaker) Harpham; A.B., Morehead State U., 1939; m. Dale Lamar Harpham, Dec. 25, 1938; children—Evelyn, George. Violinist, Nat. Symphony Orch., Washington, 1956—, prin. of second violin sect., 1964—; mem. Lywen String Quartet, 1960-69. Nat. Symphony String Quartet, 1973-82. Episcopalian. Home: 3816 Military Rd NW Washington DC 20015

HARRELL, BARBARA FOWLER, sales manager; b. Grosse Pointe, Mich., May 30, 1961; d. Donald Harry and Mary Jane (Ballard) Fowler; m. Jeffrey Randolph Harrell, Sept. 29, 1984. B of Liberal Arts, Hillsdale Coll., 1983. Sales rep. Procter & Gamble, Detroit, 1983-85; spl. accounts rep. Procter & Gamble, Cleve., 1985-86, mgr. unit, 1986—. Publicist Jr. Women's Club, Bay Village, Ohio, 1986-87. Mem. Nat. Assn. Female Execs., Hillsdale Coll. Alumni Bd., Chi Omega. Home: 547 Juneway Dr Bay Village OH 44140

HARRELL, CAROLYN HARDISON, nursing home administrator; b. Washington, N.C., Feb. 25, 1942; d. Dewey Jasper and Emma Blanche (Lilley) Hardison; R.N., Petersburg (Va.) Gen. Hosp., 1963; B. Nursing, Pacific Western U., 1981, D. Sc. in Health Care Adminstrn., 1982; m. Jerry W. Harrell, Apr. 18, 1979; children by previous marriage—Natalie Dawn and John Michael Cameron. Staff nurse Petersburg Gen. Hosp., 1963-66; staff nurse, supr., inservice dir. Central State Hosp., Petersburg, 1963-73; owner, operator Cameron's Day Care Center, Colonial Heights, Va., 1973-74; dir. nurses Guarian Corp., Petersburg, 1974-76; adminstr. Am. Health Care Corp., Richmond, Va., 1976-77, Beverly Enterprises, Greenville, N.C., 1977-83, Pitt County Meml. Hosp., 1983-85, Britthaven, Inc., Kinston, N.C., 1985—. Vocat. adv. com. Martin Community Coll., 1979. Recipient Citizenship award, 1960; named Employee of Month, Guardian Corp., 1974. Mem. Am. Coll. Nursing Home Adminstrs., Va. Health Care Facilities Assn., N.C. Health Care Facilities Assn. Republican. Club: Bus. and Profl. Women. Home: 1403 Red Banks Rd Greenville NC 27834 Office: 317 Rhodes Ave Kinston NC 28501

HARRELL-SESNIAK, MARY RUNNELS, computer company executive; b. Indpls., Sept. 6, 1954; d. Evans Malott Harrell and Mary Edith (Guckes) Stevens; m. Thomas Warren Sesniak, Jan. 3, 1981; children: Brenda and Brian (twins). BA, Eckerd Coll., 1977; MBA, U. South Fla., 1984. V.p. P.L.I. Computers, Cape Coral, Fla., 1984-86; pres. Computer Services & Tng. Inc., Cape Coral, Fla., 1986—; tchr. computers Lee County Adult Edn., Ft. Myers, Fla., 1986-87. Contbr. articles on computers to Seabreeze Publs., 1986—. Mem. Nat. Assn. for Female Execs. Episcopalian. Club: Ft. Myers Women's Community. Office: Computer Services and Tng Inc PO Box 305 Cape Coral FL 33910-0305

HARRELSON, JANICE MARIE, human resources director; b. Panama City, Fla., Sept. 27, 1953; d. Burl Hulen and Catherine (Lawson) H. BA, U. No. Fla., 1974, MA, 1977. Guidance counselor Duval County Sch. System, Jacksonville, Fla., 1977-81; nat. sales rep. Bales Recruiters, Jacksonville, 1981-83; corp. recruitment Blue Cross, Blue Shield, Jacksonville, 1983-84, mgr. mgmt. devel., 1984-85; mgr. tng. devel. Alliance Mortgage Co., Jacksonville, 1985-86, asst. v.p. tng., employment, 1986-87, v.p., dir. human resource devel., 1987-88; v.p. human resources Barnett Bank, Jacksonville, 1988—. Mem. Am. Soc. Tng. Devel., Nat. Assn. Female Execs., Am. Soc. Personnel Adminstrs. Republican. Episcopalian. Home: 1184 Executive Cove Dr Jacksonville FL 32223 Office: Barnett Bank 1801 Art Museum Dr Jacksonville FL 32207

HARRIES, SUSAN ANN, educator; b. Jackson, Minn., May 1, 1946; d. Richard H. and Irene L. (Plum) H. BS magna cum laude, Mankato (Minn.) State Coll., 1968; MS, Mankato State U., 1978. Cert. tchr., Minn. Tchr. third grade Independant Sch. Dist. #177, Windom, Minn., 1968-69, tchr. fourth grade, 1969-88, asst. to prin., 1980-88; prin. intern Clear Springs Elem. Sch., Minnetonka, Minn., 1988—. Tutor Vietnamese Resettlement Commn., Windom, 1976-77; mem. Windom City Charter Commn., 1983—. Named one of Outstanding Young Women in Am., 1979. Mem. NEA, Minn. Edn. Assn. (Tchr. of Excellance 1981), Windom Edn. Assn. (sec., treas. 1975-77, v.p. 1985-87, Tchr. of Yr. 1981), Southeast Reading Assn., Kappa Delta Pi. Club: Interlochen.

HARRIFF, SUZANNA ELIZABETH, advertising consultant; b. Vicksburg, Miss., Dec. 30, 1953; d. David S. and F. Suzanna (McElwee) Bahner; m. James R. Harriff, Sept. 10, 1977; 1 child, Michael James. B.A. summa cum laude, SUNY-Fredonia, 1976; postgrad. Cornell U. Law Sch., 1981. Media asst. Comstock Advt., Syracuse, N.Y., and Buffalo, 1976-77; media buyer/planner G. Andre Delporte, Syracuse, 1979-81; media dir. Roberts Advt., Syracuse, 1982; dir. media services Signet Advt., Syracuse, 1982-84; owner, pres. MediaMarCon, Syracuse, 1984—. Music dir., pianist Manlius United Methodist Ch., N.Y., 1983—, youth dir., 1983-85; vol. Sta. WCNY-TV pub. TV auction drive. Mem. Syracuse Advt. Club (dir. 1985—, program chair 1986-88, pres. 1988), Nat. Assn. Female Execs., Irish-Am. Cultural Inst. Syracuse, Phi Beta Kappa. Democrat. Avocations: music; theatre. Home: 8180 Bluffview Dr Manlius NY 13104

HARRIMAN, PAMELA DIGBY CHURCHILL, political action committee administrator; b. Farnborough, Eng., Mar. 20, 1920; came to U.S., 1959, naturalized, 1971; d. Edward Kenelm and Constance Pamela Alice (Bruce) Digby; B. Domestic Sci.-Economy, Downham (Eng.) Coll., 1937; postgrad. Sorbonne, Paris, 1937-38; m. Randolph Churchill, 1939; 1 son, Winston Spencer; m. 2d, Leland Hayward, May 4, 1960; m. 3d, W. Averell Harriman, Sept. 27, 1971. With Ministry of Supply, London, 1942-43; with Churchill Club for Am. Servicemen, 1943-46; journalist Beaverbrook Press, Europe, 1946-49; mem. Democratic House and Senate Council; co-chmn. Democratic Congressional Dinner 1979; founder Democrats for the 80's, 1980—; bd. dirs. Comn. on Presidential Debates; trustee Presidential and Democratic 1988 Victory Party Fund, Rockefeller U.; hon. trustee Menninger Found.; mem. Council on Fgn. Relations, adv. council W. Averell Harriman Inst. for Advanced Soviet Studies, World Rehabilitation Fund; mem. trustees council Nat. Gallery Art; adv. com. World Rehab. Fund.; mem. adv. bd. Harriman Communications Ctr.; bd. visitors William and Mary Coll.; mem. bd. friends Kennan Inst. for Advanced Russian Studies; bd. dirs. Atlantic Council, Mary W. Harriman Found., also various philanthropic founds. Named Democratic Woman of Yr., Woman's Nat. Democratic Club 1980. Roman Catholic. Office: 3032 N St NW Washington DC 20007

HARRINGTON, BARBARA CARMELLA, human resource development consultant; b. Yonkers, N.Y., May 27, 1939; d. Stanley Constantino and Ethel Vivian (Holder) Castaldo; children: Harold Boyce III, Kimberly Anne, Glen Thomas. Grad. high sch., Yonkers, 1957. Regional mgr. Coppercraft Guild, Taunton, Mass., 1966-80; agt. Prudential Ins. Co., Poughkeepsie, N.Y., 1980-82; gen. agt. U.S. Life, Franklin United and Aetna Ins. Cos., Poughkeepsie, 1982-85; pres. Harrington Investment and Ins. Agy. Inc., Poughkeepsie, 1982-85; v.p. mktg. Confidential Planning Corp., Hartsdale, N.Y., 1985; pension cons. Guardian Life Ins. Co., Nat. Pension Service, Inc., White Plains, N.Y., 1985—; lectr. Marist Coll., 1984—; bd. dirs. Integrated Tng. Systems, Woodstock, N.Y., 1985-86. Author prep. course for licensing career ins. agts., 1983; contbr. articles to profl. jours. Bd. dirs. Dutchess Community Coll., Poughkeepsie, 1982-84, cons. 1984—; den mother Cub Scout pack #69 Boy Scouts Am., 1967-69; founder Dutchess County Stop DWI Student Awareness Program, 1984; mem. liaison com. Rehab. Sheltered Workshop, Poughkeepsie, 1985-86; pres. Yonkers PTA, 1970; sec. Family Service of Dutchess County, 1986-87; founder The Walk-A-Thon Rehab. Programs, Inc., Poughkeepsie, 1984. Fellow Life Underwriter Tng. Council N.Y. State Assn. Life Underwriters (edn. chairperson 1987—); mem. N.Y. State Assn. Life Underwriters (regional v.p. 1985-87), N.Y. State Women Bus. Owners (treas. 1985), Dutchess County Life Assn. (pres. 1984), Westchester County Life Assn., Women Life Underwriters Conf. (charter pres. Dutchess chpt. 1984, state chairperson 1984, nat. chairperson speakers' bur. 1985). Lodge: Zonta (asst. chairperson status on women com. 1984). Home: 14 Sq S Gerald Dr Poughkeepsie NY 12601 Office: Nat Pension Service Inc 1025 Westchester Ave White Plains NY 10604-3595

HARRINGTON, CANDYCE BETH, human resources administrator; b. Adrian, Mich., July 5, 1957; d. Burton Leroy and Dorothy Virginia (Hall) H.; m. Mitchell A. Blank, Nov. 17, 1984 (div. 1987). BA, Adrian Coll., 1979; MA, U. Mich., 1983. Asst. dir. spl. events Adrian (Mich.) Coll., 1979-82; devel. intern McCarter Theatre, Princeton, N.J., 1983-84; adminstrv. asst. Mt. Vernon Coll., Washington, 1984-85; personnel asst. Fairchild Industries, Inc., Chantilly, Va., 1985-87; staff asst. Contel Fed. Systems, Fairfax, Va., 1987—. Bd. dirs. Marjorie Isom Found. for Cancer Detection in Women, Middleburg, Va., 1987; music dir. Nat. Gardens Bapt. Ch., Falls Church, Va., 1986—; mem. Arlington (Va.) Met. Chorus, 1984—. Mem. Nat. Assn. Female Execs. Presbyterian.

HARRINGTON, DIANE GAIL, retail executive; b. Miami, Fla., Aug. 5, 1963; d. James Thomas and Eva Mae (Stephens) H. BBA, U. Miami, 1985, MBA, 1987. Pres. Fla. Gold Seal Inc., Miami, 1985—; agt., rep. John Hancock Mut. Life Ins. Co., Miami, 1985-86; pres. Stephens Service Ctr., Inc., Miami, 1986—. Counselor New Testament Bapt. Ch., Hialeah, Fla., 1983. Mem. Nat. Assn. Female Execs., Nat. Assn. Life Underwriters, Nat. C. of C., Ctr. Fine Arts. Republican. Baptist. Office: Stephens Service Ctr 9500 NW 27th Ave Miami FL 33147

HARRINGTON, JOAN ANN, civic leader; b. N.Y.C., Feb. 19, 1944; d. James and Concetta (DelRoio) Galiardi; m. John P. Harrington, Sept. 4, 1965; children: John, Tara, Pamela. Sr. case adv./handicapped rights specialist, Advs. for Children of N.Y., Inc., reps. parents at com. meetings, at due process impartial hearings, advises parents on preparation of appeals and representation Spl. Edn. students at suspension confs., visits and evaluates Spl. Edn. programs, specialist on vocat. ednl. services, develops spl. edn. treatment plans in consultation with Dr's. in field, instr. classes of tchrs. regarding parents and student's rights, 1979—; cons. Assn. for Help of Retarded Children, N.Y., 1979—, United Cerebal Palsy, N.Y. 1984—; founder, pres. spl. edn. PTA; mem. dist. 24 com. on handicapped, 1977-80; active various testimonial coms. for handicapped children, 1977—. Office: Advs for Children 24 16 Bridge Plaza S Long Island City NY 11101

HARRINGTON, SISTER NORA, college official; b. Holyoke, Mass., July 3, 1921; d. Maurice John and Mary T. (Courtney) Harrington; B.S., Coll. of Our Lady of Elms, 1944; M.S. in Chemistry, Fordham U., 1960. Joined Sisters of St. Joseph, Roman Catholic Ch., 1939; tchr. Sister Joseph's High Sch., Pittsfield, Mass., 1944-50; faculty Our Lady of Elms, 1950—, now assoc. prof. chemistry and physics, acad. dean, 1973-79, v.p., 1979—; mem. Sisters Senate, 1971-78, pres., 1972-74. NSF grantee Oak Ridge Summer Inst., 1968, Renssalaer Poly. Inst., 1970. Recipient Disting. Alumna award Coll. Our Lady of Elms, 1977; Nora Harrington Chemistry lecture established 1983. Mem. AAUP, AAUW, Am. Chem. Soc. Home and Office: 291 Springfield St Chicopee MA 01013

HARRINGTON, SANDRA MAY, educator, administrator; b. Geneva, N.Y., Sept. 21, 1948; d. James Jerome and Julia Mary (Deeb) H.; AA, Niagara County Community Coll., 1968; BS in Secondary Edn., SUNY, Buffalo, 1970; M.S., Nova U., 1979. Tchr. trainable mentally handicapped Okeechobee (Fla.) Public Schs., 1971-79, tchr. educable mentally handicapped, 1979-81, dean of students Okeechobee High Sch., 1981-82, Okeechobee Jr. High Sch., 1982-83; tchr. Mt. Dora High Sch. (Fla.), 1983-85, Dabney Elem. Sch., Leesburg, Fla., 1985—. Recipient Entricy Herald Achievement award Niagara County Community Coll., 1968, Cert. of Appreciation, Okeechobee Cub Scouts, 1977; winner Fla. Learning Resources System/Alpha contest, 1979; Fla. Dept. Edn. grantee, 1976. Mem. Assn. Supervision and Curriculum Devel., Council Exceptional Children, Internat. Platform Assn., Bus. and Profl. Women (past pres. Mt. Dora chpt., chmn. com. Eustis chpt.), Lake County Edn. Assn., Nat. Mus. Women in Arts (charter). Democrat. Home: 1224 Palmetto Rd Eustis FL 32726

HARRINGTON-CONNORS, ERIN MARIE, editor; b. Huntington, N.Y., Sept. 3, 1959; d. Dennis Joseph and Bridget Elizabeth (Toolan) Harrington; m. Brian Christopher Connors, May 2, 1986; 1 child, Kerry Elizabeth Connors. BA, Adelphi U., 1981. Reporter Charlottesville (Va.) Observer, 1982; editor Synergy Gas Corp., Farmingdale, N.Y., 1982-83; assoc. editor Nightlife Mag., Deer Park, N.Y., 1983-85; freelance writer various nat. and regional mags., N.Y.C., 1985-86; editorial mgr. Dunhill Personnel System, Inc., Carle Place, N.Y., 1986—; freelance copywriter Internat. Mktg. Cons., Merrillville, Ind., 1987, Mascia Design, N.Y.C., 1986-87; freelance resumé writing, Babylon, N.Y., 1985-87; mem. scriptwriting workshop Rosemarie Santini, N.Y.C., 1985-86. Contbr. articles to profl. jours. Counselor Huntington (N.Y.) Assn. for Retarded Children, 1972-77. Roman Catholic. Home: 63 Park Ave Babylon NY 11702 Office: Dunhill Personnel System Inc One Old Country Rd Carle Place NY 11514

HARRIS, ALICE KESSLER, history educator; b. Leicester, Eng., June 2, 1941; U.S. citizen; m. Bertram Silverman; 1 child. AB, Goucher Coll., 1961; MA, Rutgers U., 1963, PhD in History, 1968. Tchr. pub. schs., Md., 1961-62; asst. prof. Hofstra U., 1968-74, assoc. prof., 1974-81, prof. history, 1981-88, co-dir. work/leisure ctr., 1976—; prof. history Temple U, Phila., 1988—; dir. women's studies Sarah Lawrence Coll., 1974-76; sr. lectr. Ctr. Study Social History, U. Warwick, 1979-80; vis. prof. SUNY, Binghamton, 1985. Author: Women Have Always Worked: A Historical Overview, 1980, Out to Work: A History of Wage Earning Women in the United States, 1982; editor: (with others) Women in Culture and Politics: A Century of Change, 1986, (with William McBrien) Faith of a (Woman) Writer, 1988. Fellow Nat. Endowment for Humanities, 1976-77, 85-86, Radcliffe Inst., Harvard U., 1977, Rockefellow Found, 1988—, John Simon Guggenheim Meml. Found., 1989—. Mem. Am. Hist. Assn., Orgn. Am. Historians, Am. Studies Assn., ACLU, Berkshire Conf. Women Historians. Mailing Address: Temple U Philadelphia PA 19122

HARRIS, ANDREA LOVELL, librarian; b. Winnfield, La., Dec. 11, 1944; d. Henry Theron and Vermelle (Porter) L.; m. Kerry Wesley Harris, June 15, 1973 (div. Nov. 1980); 1 child, Mary Katharine. BA, Tex. Christian U., 1965; MLS, La. State U., 1967. Young adult librarian Dallas Pub. Library, 1967-68, 1st asst., 1968-72, adminstrv. asst., 1972-74, br. mgr., 1974-78, 80-85, asst. to br. chief, 1978-80, asst. dir. support services, 1985—. Mem. ALA. Office: Dallas Pub Library 1515 Young St Dallas TX 55201

HARRIS, ANN NOBLE, lawyer; b. Rochester, N.Y., June 2, 1947; d. Mason and Mary Prentis (Loder) Noble; m. David Laurence Harris, Apr. 29, 1978; children: Benjamin, Mary-Margaret, Jae, Rebecca. BA, Western Coll., 1969; JD, George Washington U., 1972. Bar: Colo., Ind., D.C. Atty. U.S. Dept. Labor, Washington, 1972-74, Denver, 1974—; lectr. Arapahoe Community Coll., Littleton, Colo., 1978-79. Active loaned exec. program Combined Fed. Campaign, Denver, 1985. Named Outstanding Fed. Atty. Denver Fed. Exec. Bd., 1980. Mem. Colo. Bar. Assn. Office: US Dept Labor 1961 Stout #1585 Denver CO 80209

HARRIS, BARBARA CAMILLE, broadcast sales manager; b. Heidelberg, Fed. Republic Germany, Mar. 6, 1958; came to U.S., 1959; d. Robert William and Edna Janiece (Alborn) H. BA in Journalism and Psychology magna cum laude, Gonzaga U., 1980; postgrad., U. Seattle, 1987. Admissions counselor U. Portland, Oreg., 1980-82; account exec. Sunriver Broadcasting Corp., Great Falls, Mont., 1982-84, Golden West Broadcasting, Seattle, 1984-85; account exec. Bonneville Broadcasting, Inc., Seattle, 1985-88, sales mgr., 1988—. Mem. Women in Communications. Democrat. Office: Sta KIRO-Bonneville Broadcasting 2807 3d Ave Seattle WA 98111-1010

HARRIS, BARBARA IVEY, financial manager, budget analyst, accountant, management consultant, educator; b. Dothan, Ala., Oct. 19, 1951; d. Willie and Hattie Bell (Barnes) Ivey; BS in Acctg. cum laude, Fla. A&M U., 1973. Internal revenue agt. IRS, Fort Lauderdale, Fla., 1974; adminstrv. asst. Internat. Paper Co., Panama City, Fla., 1974-77; sr. adminstr. fin. services, 1977-78, cost analyst, 1978-79; staff acct. S.W. Forest Industries, Panama City, 1979-82; office mgr. Panama City Devel. Ctr., 1982-83; fin. mgr., budget analyst Dept. Def., 1984—; adj. prof. Gulf Coast Community Coll., 1983—; mgmt. cons., acct. Macedonia Housing Authority, Panama City, 1983-84. Treas., Employees Mut. Benefit Assn., 1978-82; Recipient Outstanding Service award United Way, 1975.Ethel Vereen Meml. scholar, 1969, Union Carbide grantee, 1969. Mem. Am. Soc. Mil. Comptrollers. Nat. Assn. Female Execs., Zeta Phi Beta. Democrat. Methodist.

HARRIS, BARBARA NELSON, librarian; b. Bridgeport, Conn., May 12, 1924; d. Carl Alexander and Helen Ella (Bodie) Nelson; m. John Donald Harris, July 12, 1946; children: John, Ralph, Lisa, Todd, Heather. Student, Jr. Coll. Conn., Bridgeport, 1942-43; cert., Audio-Visual Inst. for Effective Communication, Bloomington, Ind., 1976; cert. pub. relations for libraries and info. service, Simmons Coll., 1978. Circulation and reference asst. Groton (Conn.) Pub. Library, 1964-68, head adult services, 1969-72; reference asst. pub. relations Waterford (Conn.) Pub. Library, 1976—; mem. Groton Pub. Library Bd., 1976-77. Co-author: Reflexions in an Herb Garden, 1981. Sec. New London (Conn.) YWCA, 1970-71; pres. LWV Groton, 1976-77, Friends of Groton Pub. Library, 1975-76. Served with WAVES, USN, 1944-46. Mem. ALA, Conn. Library Assn. (chmn. publicity com. 1980-81, head pub. relations sect. 1981-82, treas. 1983-86), New Eng. Library Assn. Democrat. Unitarian. Home: 230 Prospect Hill Rd Groton CT 06340 Office: Waterford Pub Library 49 Rope Ferry Rd Waterford CT 06385

HARRIS, BELINDA KAY, association executive; b. McComb, Miss., July 18, 1952; d. Isaac Sr. and Willye Mae Shaw; m. James Harris Jr., Dec. 26, 1972; children: Dorian Ashon, Leslie Nicole. BS in English and Secondary Edn., U. So. Miss., 1974. With employee devel. dept. FAA, Anchorage, 1974-78; ctr. dir. Agr. and Labor Program, Inc., Ft. Meade, Fla., 1979-81; child dev. coordinator Agr. and Labor Program, Inc., Frostproof and Winter Haven, Fla., 1981-83; exec. dir. Girl's Club of Lakeland (Fla.), Inc., 1983—; pres. Girl's Club of Fla., Lakeland, 1985-86. Mem. Community Alliance Orgn., Lakeland, 1985—; chmn. pub. relations Talbot House Ministries, Lakeland, 1986—; pres. Winston Elem. PTA, Lakeland, 1983—; mem., fundraising chmn. Neighborhood Service Ctr., Lakeland, 1984-85; chmn. United Way (1986—, sec. 1985-86, Outstanding Service award 1987); treas. Girls Club Am., So. Region, 1987—; treas. Winston Elem. Sch. PTA, 1987-88; mem. sch. age children task force Polk County Sch. Bd., 1987-88. Democrat. African Methodist Episcopalian. Office: Girls Club of Lakeland PO Box 1975 Lakeland FL 33802

HARRIS, BETH, journalist; b. Balt., Aug. 27; d. John J. and Pauline (Seligman) Mendes; m. Maurice Harris, Mar. 30, 1959. Writer, producer radio and TV, San Francisco and Los Angeles; advt. account exec., San Francisco; book reviewer Desert Sun, Palm Springs, Calif., 1977—. Program chmn. Friends of Library, Coll. of Desert. Mem. Nat. League Am. Pen Women, Palm Springs Women's Press Club (charter, Woman of Yr. 1982). Jewish. Address: PO Box 2569 Palm Springs CA 92263

HARRIS, CAROL ANN, trucking company executive, antiques educator; b. Venus, Pa., Nov. 17, 1944; d. Lewis S. and Lulu Grace (Whitton) Ehrhart; m. William Chapman, Apr. 3, 1965 (dec. Apr. 1976); children—Jessica Grace, William Colin; m. Ronald W. Harris, Aug. 22, 1976; 1 child, Jason Wayne. Degree in Comml. Art, Art Inst. Pitts., 1963; various courses Clarion U. Design engr. Knox Glass Inc., Pa., 1963-65; prin. Carol Chapman Antiques, Knox, 1975-76; v.p. motor carrier W.H. Christie & Sons Inc., Knox, 1976—; owner Clarion Antique Mall, Pa.; instr. antiques Clarion Vocat. Tech, Pa., 1984; co-founder Midwest Pa. Antique Assn.; sec., bd. dirs. Sandford Gallery Assn., Clarion U., 1984—. Contbr. chpts. in books. Mem. Clarion Civic Club, Pa., 1975-76; chmn. bd. dirs. Am. Cancer Soc., Knox, Pa., 1968-77. Mem. OC/Franklin Traffic Club, North Central Pa. Traffic Assn. (v.p. 1985-86). Republican. Avocations: antiques; painting; drawing. Home: Petrolia St Box 517 Knox PA 16232

HARRIS, CAROLE RIGGS, dance studio executive; b. Covington, Ky., Nov. 20, 1939; d. George William and Gladys Mildred (Griffin) Truitt; m. Melvin LeRoy Harris, Mar. 14, 1971. Grad. high sch. Ludlow, Ky.; pvt. lessons in piano, violin, drums, baton, and dancing. Owner, Carole Riggs Dance Studio, Lynchburg, Va., 1965-82, chmn., pres., 1982—, chmn., pres. Carole Riggs Franchise Devel. Corp., Lynchburg, 1985—; creator Little Miss Lynchburg Pageant, 1967-75, The Dancing Batons Marching Corps., Lynchburg, 1966-81, Harris Modeling Agy., Lynchburg, 1976—; judge numerous pageants Va., 1970—; founder The Carole Riggs System, method for children to learn the arts, 1965. Choreographer (ballet) The Dolle Shoppe Ballet, 1974, voice tng. aids for students in ballet, 1985; composer music for Barre and Center Floor in ballet and tap for dance students, 1985. Author ops. manual for Carole Riggs franchised studios, 1983-85. Fund raiser Crippled Children's Hosp., Greenville, S.C., 1973-83; choreographer Jr. Miss Pageant, Lynchburg, 1975-82; modeling instr. Miss Bronze Pageant, Lynchburg, 1972—; entertainment Lynchburg Tng. Sch. and Hosp., 1969-80. Mem. Dance Educators Am. Inc. (performing arts cert., ballroom dancing cert.). Republican. Christian Ch. Club: Guggenheimer Ladies Aux. (Lynchburg). Lodges: Eagles; Job Daughters (honored queen 1955-56). Avocations: restoring historic bldgs., tracing family tree, choreographing and composing music. Home and Office: 116 Bateman Bridge Rd Forest VA 24551

HARRIS, CAROLYN NIEMANTSVERDRIET, marketing analyst, educator; b. Lafayette, Ind., Mar. 9, 1947; d. Walter Vincent and Amanda Elizabeth (Kelch) Niemantsverdriet; m. Laurence Neal Harris, Mar. 11, 1967 (div. Oct. 1981); 1 child, Michael. BS, Purdue U., 1969; MS, Iowa State U., 1980. CPA, cert. managerial acct. Market analyst Fisher Controls Internat., Inc., Marshalltown, Iowa, 1976—; adj. prof. Buena Vista Coll., Marshalltown, 1983—. Mem. AAUW, Am. Mktg. Assn., Nat. Assn. Bus. Economists, Inst. Mgmt. Acctg., Nat. Assn. Accts., MENSA, Phi Sigma Alpha. Mem. Christian Ch. Home: 1106 Westwood Dr Marshalltown IA 50158

HARRIS, CATHERINE MARY, land surveyor; b. Dearborn, Mich., Sept. 19, 1961; d. Paul Charles and Catherine Helen (Friedman) Janshego; m. Mark Michael Harris, June 8, 1985; 1 child, John Mark. BS in Land Surveying, Mich. Tech. U., 1984; postgrad. Nova U., 1986—. Computer-drafting technician Keith & Schnars, P.A., Ft. Lauderdale, Fla., 1984-85; project mgr., plat coordinator Craig A. Smith & Assocs., Pompano Beach, Fla. 1985-86; computer aided design technician Heller, Weaver & Cato, Inc., Margate, Fla., 1986-87; project mgr. Michael D. Aivon Land Surveyors, Boca Raton, Fla., 1987—. Mem. Fla. Soc. Profl. Land Surveyors (assoc. rep. 1985—), Am. Congress on Surveying and Mapping (pres. Douglass

Houghton chpt. Houghton, Mich. 1983-84). Republican. Roman Catholic. Avocations: diving, computers. Home: 4200 S Pine Island Rd Davie FL 33328 Office: Craig A Smith & Assocs 1000 W McNab Rd Pompano Beach FL 33069

HARRIS, DALE HUTTER, judge, lecturer; b. Lynchburg, Va., July 10, 1932; d. Quintus and Agnes (Adams) Hutter; m. Edward Richmond Harris Jr., July 24, 1954; children—Mary Fontaine, Frances Harris Russell, Jennifer Harris Haynie, Timothy Edward. BA, Sweet Briar Coll., 1953; MEd in Counseling and Guidance, Lynchburg Coll., 1970; JD, U. Va., 1978; LLD (hon.), Wilson Coll., 1988. Bar: Va. 1978, U.S. Dist. Ct. (we. dist.) Va. 1978, U.S. Ct. Appeals (4th cir.) 1978. Admissions asst. Sweet Briar Coll. (Va.), 1953-54; caseworker Winchester/Frederick Dept. Welfare, Va., 1954-55; vis. lectr. Lynchburg Coll. (Va.), 1971; assoc. Davies & Peters, Lynchburg, 1978-82; substitute judge 24th Dist. Gen. Dist. and Juvenile and Domestic Relations Dist. Cts. Va., 1980-82; judge Juvenile and Domestic Relations Dist. Ct., Lynchburg, 1982—; lectr. law U. Va. Law Sch., 1986—. Vice chmn. bd. dirs. Sweet Briar Coll., 1976-86; vol. coordinator vols. in probation with Juvenile and Domestic Ct., 1971-73; chmn. steering com. for establishment Youth Service Bur., Lynchburg, 1972-73; chmn. bd. dirs. Lynchburg Youth Services, 1973-75; mem. adv. bd. Juvenile Ct., 1957-60, 62-68, sec., 1966-68; bd. dirs. Family Service Lynchburg, 1967-69; Lynchburg Fine Arts Ctr., 1965-67, Seven Hills Sch., 1966-73, Greater Lynchburg United Fund, 1963-65, Lynchburg Assn. Mental Health, 1960-61, Miller Home, 1980-82, Lynchburg Gen.-Marshall Lodge Hosps., Inc., 1980-82; v.p. Lynchburg Mental Health Study Commn., 1966; bd. dirs. Lynchburg Sheltered Workshop for Mentally Retarded Young Adults, 1965-69; bd. dirs. Lynchburg Guidance Ctr., 1959-61, v.p., 1970, pres., 1961; bd. dirs. Hist. Rev. Bd. Lynchburg, 1978-82. Mem. Nat. Council Juvenile and Family Ct. Judges, ABA, Va. State Bar, Va. Trial Lawyers Assn., Va. Bar Assn., Lynchburg Bar Assn., Phi Beta Kappa. Home: 1309 Crenshaw Ct Lynchburg VA 24503 Office: Juvenile and Domestic Relations Dist Ct PO Box 757 Lynchburg VA 24505

HARRIS, DEBRA LYNNE, jewelry sales company executive; b. Columbus, Ohio, Oct. 26, 1956; d. Conrad London and Ruth Evelyn (Bergglas) H. B.S. in Bus., Ind. U., 1978. Founder, owner Gold Connection, Inc., Chgo., 1978—. Mem. Jewelers Bd. of Trade, Jewelers of Am.

HARRIS, DIANA KOFFMAN, sociologist, educator; b. Memphis, Aug. 11, 1929; d. David Nathan and Helen Ethel (Rotter) Koffman; student U. Miami, 1947-48; B.S., U. Wis., 1951; postgrad. Tulane U., New Orleans, 1951-52; M.A., U. Tenn., 1967; postgrad. U. Oxford (Eng.), 1968-69; m. Lawrence A. Harris, June 24, 1951; children—Marla, Jennifer. Advt. and sales promotion mgr. Wallace Johnston Distbg. Co., Memphis, 1952-54; welfare worker Tenn. Dept. Public Welfare, Knoxville, 1954-56; instr. sociology Maryville (Tenn.) Coll., 1972-75; instr. sociology Fort Sanders Sch. Nursing, Knoxville, 1971-78; instr. sociology U. Tenn., Knoxville, 1967—. Chmn. U. Tenn. Council on Aging, 1979—; organizer Knoxville chpt. Gray Panthers, 1978; mem. Gov's. Task Force on Preretirement Programs for State Employers, 1973; mem. White House Conf. on Aging, 1981; bd. mem. Knoxville-Knox County Council on Aging, 1976, Sr. Citizens Info. and Referral, 1979, Sr. Citizens Home-Aide Service, 1977; del. E. Tenn. Council on Aging, 1977. Recipient Meritorious award Nat. U. Continuing Edn. Assn., 1982. Mem. Am. Sociol. Assn., AAAS, Gerontol. Soc. Am., Popular Culture Assn., So. Sociol. Soc., So. Gerontol. Soc. (Pres.'s award 1984), N. Central Sociol. Assn. Clubs: London Competitor's; Nat. Contest Assn.; Knoxville Kontestars. Author: Readings in Social Gerontology, 1975, (with Cole) The Elderly in America, 1977, The Sociology of Aging, 1980; co-author: Sociology, 1984, Annotated Bibliography and Sourcebook: Sociology of Aging, 1985, Dictionary of Gerontology, 1988, Dictionary of Gerontology, 1988; contbr. articles to profl. jours. Home: PO Box 50546 Knoxville TN 37950-0546 Office: U Tenn Dept Sociology PO Box 50546 Knoxville TN 37950

HARRIS, DIANE CAROL, optical products manufacturing company executive; b. Rockville Centre, N.Y., Dec. 25, 1942; d. Daniel Christopher and Laura Louise (Schmitt) Quigley; m. Wayne Manley Harris, Sept. 30, 1978. BA, Cath. U. Am., 1964; MS, Rensselaer Poly. Inst., 1967. With Bausch & Lomb, Rochester, N.Y., 1967—, dir. applications lab., 1972-74, dir. tech. mktg. analytical systems div., 1974-76, bus. line mgr., 1976-77, v.p. planning and bus. programs, 1977-78, v.p. planning and bus. devel. Soflens div., 1978-80, corp. dir. planning, 1980-81, v.p. corp. devel., 1981—; v.p. RID-N.Y. State, 1980-83; bd. dirs. Delta Labs., Inc. Contbr. articles to profl. jours. Pres. Rochester Against Intoxicated Driving, 1979-83, chmn. polit. action com., 1983-86; bd. dirs. Rochester area Nat. Council on Alcoholism, 1980-84, Rochester Rehab. Ctr., 1982-84, Friends of Bristol Valley Playhouse Found., 1983-88; mem. Stop DWI Adv. panel to Monroe County Legislature, 1982-87. Recipient Disting. Citizen's award Monroe County, 1979, Tribute to Women in Industry and Service award YWCA, 1983; NSF grantee, 1963. Mem. Newcomen Soc. N. Am., Am. Mgmt. Assn., Fin. Execs. Inst., Assn. Corp. Growth, C. of C., Phi Beta Kappa, Sigma Xi, Delta Epsilon Sigma. Home: 60 Mendon Center Rd W Honeoye Falls NY 14472 Office: Bausch & Lomb Inc 1 Lincoln First Sq Rochester NY 14601

HARRIS, DONNA CATHLEEN, health educator; b. Viroqua, Wis., Apr. 22, 1957; d. Eldon George and Lillian Evelyn (Benrud) Rumppe; m. Scott Kevin Harris, July 7, 1953. BS in Community Health Edn., U. Wis., La Crosse, 1979. Cert. health educator. Health edn. specialist Goodhue-Wabasha Community Health Service, Red Wing, Minn., 1980-81; StayWell program adminstr. Control Data Corp., Mpls., 1981-83; adminstr. StayWell project Control Data Corp., Eden Prairie, Minn., 1983-85; corp., community edn. mgr. Park Nicollet Med. Found., St. Louis Park, Minn., 1985-86; tng. educator Sandoz Nutrition, St. Louis Park, 1986—. Mem. Am. Soc. Tng. and Devel., Minn. Soc. Tng. and Devel., Soc. Pub. Health Educators. Lutheran. Office: Sandoz Nutrition 5320 W 23d Box 370 Minneapolis MN 55440

HARRIS, DOROTHY YVONNE, human services administrator; b. Phila.; d. Frederick morris and Bessie Lee (Fulton) Young; m. David Perry Roberts, July 11, 1954 (div. 1971); children: Marlene Taylor, Teresa Y., Kathryn R. Howard, Kimberly A. Williams; m. Paul Bernard Harris, Sept. 18, 1973. BS in Social Work, Temple U., 1976, MS in Social Work, 1977. Title XX specialist Pa. Dept. Pub. Welfare, Phila., 1976-77; program specialist Pa. Dept. of Aging, Harrisburg, 1977-78, div. chief, 1978-87; exec. dir. Helphouse, Inc., Harrisburg, 1987—; cons. Alternative Sentencing of Pa., Harrisburg, 1987-87; pres. Cen. Pa. Guidance Assocs., Harrisburg, 1985—. V.p. Girls' Club, Harrisburg, 1986—; bd. dirs. Greater Harrisburg YWCA, 1985—. Alumnae fellow Temple U., 1985; recipient Community Service awards Frontiersman, 1983, Pa. Ho. of Reps., 1987. Mem. Cen. Pa. Assn. Black Soc. Workers (pres., founder 1979-83), Nat. Assn. Black Social Workers (exec. dir.), Pa. Nat. Assn. Blacks Criminal Justice, Delta Sigma Theta. Methodist. Mailing Address: PO Box 11755 Harrisburg PA 17108

HARRIS, EMMA EARL, nurse, nursing home executive; b. Viper, Ky., Nov. 6, 1936; d. Andrew Jackson and Zola (Hall) S.; m. Ret Haney Marten Henis Harris, June 5, 1981; children—Debra, Joseph, Wynona, Robert Walsh. Grad. St. Joseph Sch. Practical Nursing. Staff nurse St. Joseph Hosp., Bangor, Maine, 1973-75; office nurse Dr. Eugene Brown, Bangor, 1975-77; dir. nurses Fairborn Nursing Home, Ohio, 1977-78; staff nurse Hillhaven Hospice, Tucson, 1979-80; asst. head nurse, 1980; co-owner Nu-Life Elderly Guest Home, Tucson, 1980—. Vol. Heart Assn., Bangor, 1965-70, Cancer Assn., Bangor, 1965-70. Mem. Nat. Assn. Female Execs., Assn. of Better Living for the Elderly (cons. 1983—). Democrat. Avocations: theatre; opera. Home: 4558 E Sunrise Dr Tucson AZ 85718

HARRIS, EMMYLOU, singer; b. Birmingham, Ala., Apr. 2, 1947; 2 children: Hallie, Meghann; m. Paul Kennerley, 1985; 1 stepchild, Shannon. Student, U.N.C.-Greensboro. Country music performer, singer, 1967—; assisted Gram Parsons on albums GP, Grievous Angels, 1973; toured with Fallen Angel Band, performed across Europe and U.S.; rec. artist on albums Reprise Records, Warner Bros. Records; appeared in rock documentary The Last Waltz, 1978; albums include Gliding Bird, 1969, Pieces of the Sky, Elite Hotel, Luxury Liner, Quarter Moon in a Ten-Cent Town, Roses in the Snow, Blue Kentucky Girl, Cimarron, Last Date, A Light from the Stable, Evangeline, 1981, White Shoes, Ballad of Sally Rose, 1985, Thirteen, Trio (with Dolly Parton, Linda Ronstadt) 1986, Angel Band, 1987; composer songs. Pres. Country Music Found., 1983—. Recipient Grammy awards, 1976, 77, 80, 81, 84, 87; named Female Vocalist of Yr., Country Music Assn., 1980; co-recipient (with Dolly Parton and Linda Ronstadt) Acad. Country Music award for album of the yr., 1987. Office: care Mark Rothbaum & Assocs Box 2689 Danbury CT 06813

HARRIS, GAIL MARIE, computer specialist; b. Detroit, Aug. 9, 1952; d. Ezell Harris and Irene (Cook) Knight. BS, Tuskegee Inst., 1974. Trainee programming Freeman Math. Lab., Eglin AFB, Fla., 1974-75; programmer Air Force Data Systems Design Ctr., Gunter Air Force Sta., Ala., 1975-77, programmer/analyst Software Devel. Base Communications, 1977-80, system analyst ops. plant and support br., 1980-82; specialist computer ops. div. 57 Fighter Weapons Wing, Nellis Air Force Base, Nev., 1982-85; specialist computers Tactical Fighter Weapons Ctr./Comptroller Directorate, Nellis Air Force Base, 1985—; mem. Civilian Awards Panel, Montgomery, Ala.; mem. Air Force Data Systems Design Ctr. Mgmt. Seminar, Montgomery, 1980-82; rep. mgmt. team to local wage survey, Las Vegas, Nev. Mem. Federally Employed Women, Fed. Women's Program Com., Assn. for Computing Machinery. Democrat. Baptist. Office: TFWC/AC Nellis Air Force Base Las Vegas NV 89191

HARRIS, GENEVA DUKE, information scientist; b. Henderson, N.C., Apr. 27, 1946; d. James Lewis and Queen Esther (Wilburn) Duke; m. Fred Walter Harris; children: Donald Walter, Wanda Lynne. Grad. high sch., Henderson. Database analyst Rose's Stores, Inc., Henderson, 1964-86; sr. database analyst Hanes Knit Products, Winston-Salem, N.C., 1986-88; sr. database analyst, cons. Computer Intelligence, Inc., Raleigh, N.C., 1988—. Mem. Nat. Assn. Female Execs. Democrat. Baptist. Home: Rt 1 Box 166-B-1 Henderson NC 27536

HARRIS, GEORGIA, antiques dealer; b. Edna, Tex., Feb. 8, 1920; d. Lee Thomas and Lillie delilah (Walker) Jacobs; m. Volum Lawrence Harris, Mar. 16, 1938 (dec.); children—Patricia, Martha, Janice, Kathryn. Owner, operator antiques bus., Schulenburg, Tex., 1945-50, Weathervane Antiques, Columbus, Tex., 1950—; mgr. dir. Meml. City Antiques Show, Houston, 1972, Sharpstown Antiques, Houston, 1970-78, Magnolia Antiques Show, Columbus, 1964-68, LaGrange (Tex.) Fair Show, 1969-73; mgr. coordinator Columbus Antiques Show, benefit Am. Legion, 1975-80, Brenham (Tex.) Antiques Show, benefit Heritage Soc., 1979-82, Houston Antiques Show, benefit UN, 1981-82. Baptist. Home and Office: Hwy 90 W Box 187 Columbus TX 78934

HARRIS, GWENDOLYN YVONNE, retail executive; b. Chgo., Dec. 30, 1960; d. Edward Eugene and Vicella Gwendolyn (Carlisle) H. BS, Ill. State U., Normal, 1983. Sales clk. Wieboldts, Oak Park, Ill., 1977-78; teller Citizens Nat. Bank, Chgo., 1978-81; clk., receptionist Richard J. Daley, Chgo., 1981; claim service rep. State Farm Ins. Co., Berwyn, Ill., 1982-85; ter. mgr. Philip Morris U.S.A., Schaumburg, Ill., 1985-88, asst. div. mgr., 1988—. Fellow League of Black Women; mem. Delta Sigma Pi (chairperson mem. com. 1982-83), Alpha Phi Omega (service v.p. 1980-82). Home: 514 S Highland Oak Park IL 60304 Office: Philip Morris USA 310 N Martingale Rd Schaumburg IL 60194

HARRIS, JANINE DIANE, lawyer; b. Akron, Jan. 12, 1948; d. Russell Burton and Ethel Harriet (Smith) H.; m. Robert I. Coward, Sept. 14, 1968 (div. 1977); m. John Richard Ferguson, Feb. 1, 1980; children: Brigit Grace, Rachel Anna. AB, Bryn Mawr Coll., 1970; JD, Georgetown U., 1975. Bar: Va. Supreme Ct. 1975, U.S. Dist. Ct. D.C. 1976, U.S. Ct. Appeals (D.C. cir.) 1976, D.C. Ct. Appeals 1976, U.S. Supreme Ct. 1978, U.S. Ct. Appeals (6th cir.) 1981, U.S. Ct. Appeals (8th cir.) 1981. Assoc. Baker & Hostetler, Washington, 1975-78, Pettit & Martin, Washington, 1978-79, Peabody, Lambert & Meyers, Washington, 1979-82, ptnr., 1983-84; sole practice, Washington, 1984—. Contbr. articles to legal jours. Mem. Nat. Conf. Women's Bar Assns. (bd. dirs. 1984-87, pres.-elect 1987-88, v.p. 1986—, pres. 1988-89), Nat. Found. for Womens' Bar Assn. (pres. 1985-88), Women's Bar Assn. D.C. (pres. 1984-85), D.C. Bar (bd. govs. 1984—), ABA (com. on specialization), Va. Women Attys. Assn. Club: Bryn Mawr. Office: 113 W Franklin St Baltimore MD 21201

HARRIS, JANNA FINDLEY, psychotherapist; b. Ballinger, Tex., Oct. 9, 1950; d. Allen Jackson and Lorene (Haner) Dykes; m. William E. Findley, July 17, 1971 (div. 1979); 1 child, Shawn D.; m. Winston E. Harris, June 1, 1984. BS, U. Tex., Austin, 1971; MS, EdS, Ind. U., 1974. Cert. real estate sales, Tex. Sales mgr. ReMax Realtors, Houston, 1981-83; v.p., sales mgr. John Daugherty Realtors, Houston, 1983-84; v.p. mktg. Tangent Securities, Houston, 1984-85; psychotherapist Village Mental Health Assn., Houston, 1985—. Alternate Houston Com. for Gifted Edn., 1986. Mem. Internat. Assn. Fin. Planners. Republican. Lutheran. Office: Village Mental Health Assn 2236 Bissonnet St Suite 1 Houston TX 77071

HARRIS, JEAN LOUISE, physician; b. Richmond, Va., Nov. 24, 1931; d. Vernon Joseph and Jean Louise (Pace) H.; m. Leslie John Ellis Jr., Sept. 24, 1955; children: Karen Denise, Pamela Diane, Cynthia Suzanne. B.S., Va. Union U., 1951; M.D., Med. Coll. Va., 1955; Sc.D. (hon.), U. Richmond, 1981. Intern Med. Coll. Va., Richmond, 1955-56; resident internal medicine 1956-57, fellow, 1957-58; fellow, Strong Meml. Hosp.-U. Rochester (N.Y.) Sch. Medicine, 1958-60; research assoc. Walter Reed Army Inst. Research, Washington, 1960-63; practice medicine specializing in internal medicine allergy Washington, 1964-71; instr. medicine Howard U. Coll. Medicine, Washington, 1960-68; asst. prof. dept. community health practice Howard U. Coll. Medicine, 1969-72; prof. family practice Med. Coll. Va., Va. Commonwealth U.; also dir. Center Community Health, 1972-77; sec. Human Resources Commonwealth of Va., 1978-82; v.p. state mktg. programs Control Data Corp., 1982-84, v.p. state govt. affairs, 1984-86, v.p. bus. devel., 1986-88; pres., chief exec. officer Ramsey Found., 1988—; lectr. dept. med. care and hosps. Johns Hopkins, Balt., 1971-73; asst. clin. prof. dept. community medicine Charles R. Drew Postgrad. Med. Sch., Los Angeles, 1970-73; adj. asst. prof. dept. preventive and social medicine UCLA, 1970-72; chief bur. resources devel. D.C. Dept. Health, 1967-69; exec. dir. Nat. Med. Assn. Found., Washington, after 1970; Cons. div. health manpower intelligence HEW, 1969—; mem. recombinant DNA adv. com. HEW Public Health Service-NIH, 1979-82; vice chmn. Nat. Commn. on Alcoholism and Alcohol Related Diseases, 1980-81; mem. Ores.'s Pvt. Sctor Initiatives Task Force, 1981-82, Def. Adv. Com. on Women in the Service, 1985-88, Eden Prairie City Council, 1987—, Pres.' Task Force on Pvt. Sector Initiatives. Trustee U. Richmond, active city council, Eden Prairie, Minn., 1987—. Recipient East End Civic Assn. award, 1955; named one of Top 100 Black Bus. and Profl. Women, Dollars and Sense mag., 1985. Fellow Royal Soc. (Eng.); mem. Am. Pub. Health Assn., Richmond Med. Soc., Nat. Med. Assn., Am. Soc. Pub. Adminstrs., So. Inst. Human Resources (pres. 1980-81), Inst. Medicine/Nat. Acad. Scis., Beta Kappa Chi, Alpha Kappa Mu, Sigma Xi. Home: 10860 Forestview Cir Eden Prairie MN 55344 Office: Control Data Corp 8100 34th Ave S Minneapolis MN 55440

HARRIS, JEAN NOTON, music educator; b. Monroe, Wis., Feb. 21, 1934; d. Albert Henry and Eunice Elizabeth (Edgerton) Noton; B.A., Monmouth (Ill.) Coll., 1955; M.S., U. Ill., 1975, adminstrv. cert., 1980, Ed.D., 1985; m. Laurence G. Landers, June 7, 1955; children—Theodore Scott, Thomas Warren, Philip John; m. Edward R. Harris, Nov. 27, 1981; stepchildren—Adrianne, Erica. Tchr. music schs. in Ill. and Fla., 1955-76; tchr. ch. music for children, 1957-72; tchr. music Dist. 54, Schaumburg, Ill., from 1976; teaching asst. U. Ill., 1979. Named Outstanding Young Woman of Yr., Jaycee Wives, St. Charles, Mo., 1968; charter mem. Nat. Mus. Women in Arts. Mem. Music Educators Nat. Conf. (life), Ill. Music Educators Assn., Soc. Gen. Music Educators, Alliance for Arts Edn., NEA (life), LWV, Am. Choral Dirs. Assn., U. Ill. Alumni Assn. (life), Mortar Bd., Mensa, Delta Kappa Pi. Mem. United Ch. of Christ. Home: 914 Roxbury Ln Schaumburg IL 60194

HARRIS, JESSIE G. (MRS. HUBERT LAMAR HARRIS), retired educational administrator; b. Athens, Ga., May 12, 1909; d. Wiley Jackson and Dora (Hilley) Ginn; BBA, U. Ga., 1956; AB, Ga. State U., 1960; m. Hubert Lamar Harris, Nov. 25, 1930 (dec.); children: Mary Ann (Mrs. William Holley), Hubert Lamar, Dorothy (Mrs. Ronald Zazworksy), Martha Susan (Mrs. R. R. McCue, Jr.). Various secretarial positions ins. and law offices, 1923-30; sec. div. gen. extension U. Ga., 1930-35, asst. dir. div. gen. extension, 1935-47; assisted with compilation survey Univ. System Ga., Atlanta, 1949-50, adminstrv. asst. to regents, 1951-63, asst. exec. sec., 1963-67, assoc. exec. sec., 1967-72, asst. vice chancellor personnel, 1972-74, emeritus, 1974—; cattle farmer, 1972—. Asst. exec. dir. Ga. Scholarship Commn., 1965-66; assoc. exec. sec. Ga. Med. Edn. Bd., 1952-72. Mem. AAUW (chmn. study group 1964-66, treas. 1972, 73), Farmer Atlanta Hist. Assn., So. Hist. Soc., Hist. Soc. Walton County (trustee, bd. dirs.), Ga. Trust Hist. Preservation, Crimson Key Honor Soc., Mortar Bd., Phi Chi Theta, Delta Mu Delta, Psi Chi. Club: Atlanta Writers. Home: Rosemont Route 4 Box 274 Monroe GA 30655

HARRIS, KAREN KOSTOCK, manufacturing company executive; b. Chgo., Sept. 11, 1942; d. Kenneth P. and Elsie A. (Raffl) Kostock; student Mundelein Coll., 1979—; m. Roy Lawrence Harris, Feb. 14, 1981. Clerk, loan dept. Evanston (Ill.) Fed. Savs. and Loan, 1960-63, mgr. collection dept., 1963-65; credit adminstr. Packaging Corp. Am., Evanston, 1965-72, adminstrv. asst. to v.p., 1972-74; credit mgr. trainee Am. Hosp. Supply Corp., McGaw Park, Ill., 1974-75; cash mgr, asst. to treas. Pullman Standard, Chgo., 1975-76; nat. credit administr. Gen. Binding Corp., Northbrook, Ill., 1976-77; treas. C. H. Hanson Co., Chgo., 1977-79, sec.-treas., 1980—, dir., 1980—, adminstr., trustee C. H. Hanson Co. Pension Plan, 1979—, Employees Savs. and Profit Sharing Trust, 1978—; owner Stock Enterprises, Highland Park, Ill., 1980-81; partner Harris Enterprises, 1981—; pres. Sirrah Enterprises, Inc., 1982—; pres. cottage Keepers Inc., 1986-87; ptnr. Mont. Co., 1984—; cons. in field; lectr. Founder Mundelein Weekend Coll. Scholar Grant. Recipient Cert. of Merit Chgo. Assn. of Commerce and Industry, 1981, 85. Mem. Mundelein Coll. Women's Network, Nat. Fedn. Republican Women. Clubs: Swedish of Chgo. (sec. 1981-82, steering com. 1982), Venice-Nokomis. Office: C H Hanson Co 303 W Erie St Chicago IL 60610

HARRIS, KAYLENE SLAY, finance executive; b. Santa Barbara, Calif., July 31, 1945; d. Kay Parker Slay and Gwendolyn (Milliron) Montgomery; m. William Peyton Harris Jr., June 6, 1964 (div. Aug. 1985); children: William Parker, Russell Slayton, Sara Lorene. Student, Huntingdon Coll., 1963-65, 84. Bookkeeper, designer Dunn's Florist, Prattville, Ala., 1968-76, owner, mgr., 1976-81; office mgr., system control operator Profl. Billings, Inc., Montgomery, Ala., 1982—. Cubmaster Boy Scouts Am., dir. Cub Scout Dist. Day Camp, Montgomery, 1972. Mem. Nat. Assn. Female Execs., Ala. Bus. Profl. Women's Assn. (state-wide display artist 1976-78), Ala. Wholesale Floral Assn. (bd. dirs. 1979-81), SE Ala. Floorist Assn. Republican. Clubs: Jr. Women's (Prattville), Phoenix Christian Singles. Home: 1822 E Autumn Ct Prattville AL 36067

HARRIS, KITTY S., substance abuse therapist, consultant; b. Lubbock, Tex., Mar. 7, 1951; d. Welborn Boyd and Denece (Scaling) H. BS, North Tex. State U., 1973, MS, 1974; PhD, Tex. Tech U., 1983. Cert. tchr. and counselor. Asst. prof. Wayland Bapt. U., Plainview, Tex., 1977-78; research asst. Tex. Tech U., Lubbock, 1981-82, adminstrv. intern, 1982-83; substance abuse cons. Lubbock Ind. Sch. Dist., Lubbock, 1983—; pvt. practice therapist Guidelines, Lubbock, 1983—; program dir. Charter Plains Hosp., Lubbock, 1986—; cons. Sch. Allied Health Tex. Tech U., Lubbock, 1982-83, NIAAA Grant, 1983-84; part time instr. North Tex. State U., Denton, 1973-74, Tex. Tech U., Lubbock, 1979-81, South Plains Community Coll., 1983. Contbr. articles to profl. jours. Bd. dirs. Lubbock Council Alcohol and Drug Abuse, Lubbock, 1986—; mem. Nat. Orgn. Women, 1986—, Regional Networking Council, Lubbock, 1986—. Named one of Outstanding Young Women Am., 1977. Mem. Tex. Assn. Alcoholism and Drug Abuse Counselors, Nat. Assn. Alcoholism and Drug Abuse Counselors, Southwestern Soc. Research Human Devel., Nat. Council Family Relations, Tex. Speech Communication Assn., Chi Omega. Republican. Methodist. Office: Charter Plains Hosp 1801 N Quaker Lubbock TX 79408

HARRIS, LOUISE, author; b. Warwick, R.I.; d. Samuel P. and Faustine M. (Borden) Harris; A.B., Brown U., 1926; pvt. study organ with T. Tertius, Noble, N.Y., 1938-47. Sec., Samuel P. Harris, Inc., 1928-42; tchr. piano and organ, ch. organist, recitalist, Providence, 1928-48; founder, curator C.A. Stephens Collection. Mem. R.I. Hosp. Corp.; 1st founder Brown U. Med. Sch. Mem. Nat. Archives Assocs., Am. Guild Organists, Hymn Soc. Am., Audubon Soc., Brown Alumnae Assn., Nat. Trust Historic Preservation, Am. Bicentennial Research Inst.; Am. Heritage Soc., Am. Mus. Natural History, Smithsonian Instn. Assos., Nat., Western R.I. Author: A Comprehensive Bibliography of C.A. Stephens, 1965; None But the Best, 1966; A Chuckle and A Laugh, 1967; The Star of the Youth's Companion, 1969; The Flag Over the Schoolhouse, 1971; Our Great American Story-Teller, 1978; Old Glory-Long May She Wave, 1981; compiler: Under the Sea in the Salvador (C.A. Stephens), 1969; C.A. Stephens Looks at Norway, 1970; Charles Adams Tales (C.A. Stephens), 1973; Little Big Heart (C.A. Stephens), 1974; Time For The Truth, 1987. Home: 395 Angell St Apt 111 Providence RI 02906 Office: Box 1926 Brown U Providence RI 02912

HARRIS, MARCELLA H. EASON (MRS. HARLEY EUGENE HARRIS), social worker; b. Augusta, Ark., Apr. 19, 1925; d. William Harvey and Hazel Faye (Haraway) Eason; B.A., Wilberforce U., 1947; M.S.W., Loyola U., Chgo., 1961; M.Ed. in Health Occupations, U. Ill., 1979; m. Harley Eugene Harris, June 15, 1952. Child welfare worker Ill. Dept. Pub. Welfare, 1952-54, caseworker Family Consultation Service, 1954-64; clin. social worker Winnebago County Mental Health Clinic, Rockford, Ill., 1964—, now clin. mgr. emergency services Janet Wattles Mental Health Center. Mem. Rockford Bd. Edn., 1965—, sec., 1965-69; trustee Swedish Am. Hosp.; bd. dirs. Rockford Local Devel. Corp.; mem. Allen Chapel African Methodist Episcopal Ch. Recipient Francis Blair award Ill. Edn. Assn., 1970, Service above Self award Rockford Rotary Club, 1971. Mem. Nat. Assn. Social Workers (chpt. vice chmn. 1960-61), Ill. Welfare Assn., Acad. Certified Social Workers, Nat. Council Negro Women, Rockford Jr. League (hon.), AAUW, Nat. Registry Health Care Providers in Clin. Social Work, Delta Kappa Gamma (hon.), Alpha Kappa Alpha. Club: Taus Sevice. Home: Cloisters Apt 1665 2929 Sunnyside Dr Rockford IL 61111 Office: 1325 E State St Rockford IL 61108

HARRIS, MARILYN, academic administrator; b. N.Y.C.; d. Bernard and Rose (Block) Hochberg; m. Seymour J. Harris; children: Randall, April. AB summa cum laude, Hunter Coll., 1945; MS, Iowa State U., 1947. Faculty dept. math and stats. Hunter Coll., N.Y.C., 1946-48; systems analyst, statistician market research services Gen. Electric Co., N.Y.C., 1962-67; biostatistician comprehensive child care project Einstein Med. Sch., N.Y.C., 1967-69; asst. to dean, acting dir. computer ctr. Baruch Coll. CUNY, 1969-72; dir. data collection and evaluation office univ. mgmt. data Bklyn. Coll., CUNY, 1972-74, dir. mgmt. info. systems, 1974-79, dir. personnel services, 1979-85, asst. v.p. human resources and adminstrv. services, 1985—, bd. dirs. Bklyn. Ctr. Performing Arts, 1982—, chair seat campaign, 1984-86. Mem. Coll. and Univ. Personnel Assn., Assn. Univ. Adminstrs., Phi Beta Kappa, Phi Kappa Phi, Pi Mu Epsilon. Home: 9 Knightsbridge Rd Great Neck NY 11021 Office: Bklyn Coll CUNY Bedford Ave and Ave H Brooklyn NY 11210

HARRIS, MARILYN ANN, government affairs executive; b. Kansas City, Mo.; d. Mechell F. and Marguerite (Azar) H.; s. William K. Dabaghi, Apr. 12, 1980. BS, U. Mo., 1965, MA, 1970; PhD, U. Md., 1982. Tchr. Kansas City Pub. Schs., 1965-70; instr. U. Md., College Park, 1970-73; mem. profl. staff U.S. Senate, Washington, 1974-81; adminstrv. asst. U.S. Ho. Reps., Washington, 1981-83; mgr. govtl. affairs USX Corp., Washington, 1983—. Mem. Speech Communications Assn., Women in Govt. Relations. Home: 5111 Yuma St NW Washington DC 20016 Office: USX Corp 818 Connecticut Ave NW Washington DC 20006

HARRIS, MARITZA, nurse, medical administrator; b. Panama City, Panama, Oct. 6, 1947; came to U.S., 1966; d. Arnold and Lucilda (Forbes) Anglin Irons; m. Audley Leonard Harris, Jan. 17, 1970; 1 child, Lizette Ana Maria Harris. A.A. in Nursing, S.I. Community Coll., 1969; B.S., L.I. U., 1978; M.Health Care, C.W. Post Coll., 1986. R.N., N.Y. Psychiat. nurse Dept. Mental Health, Bklyn., 1972—; med. coordinator Addiction Research and Treatmant Corp., Bklyn., 1981—, sr. assoc., 1987—; cons., lectr. in field. Recipient appreciation award Urban Resources, 1983; Outstanding Achievement award UN, 1983. Fellow Am. Acad. Physician's Assts., N.Y.

State Soc. Physicians Assts.; mem. Exec. Females. Democrat. Roman Catholic. Avocations: music; travel; fasion; computers. Home: 420 E 111th St Apt 2904 New York NY 10029 Office: Addiction Research & Traetment Corp 22 Chapel St New York NY 11201

HARRIS, MARJORIE RHODUS, medical records administrator, educator, consultant; b. Anderson, Ind., Sept. 18, 1934; d. Clifford and Lillie Irene (Boyd) Rhodus; m. James William Harris, Feb. 22, 1955 (dec. 1975); children: Dwight Clifford, William Timothy. BS with high honors, East Carolina U., 1975. Registered record adminstr. Mgr. Med. Rcord Dept. Lenoir Meml. Hosp., Kinston, N.C., 1975-79; dir. Med. Info. Services Lee Mrml. Hosp., Ft. Myers, Fla., 1979-86; instr. med. record tech. Cen. Va. Community Coll., 1986-88; dir. Med. Rec. Dept. Fairfax Hosp., Falls Church, Va., 1988—; adj. prof. East Carolina U., Greenville, N.C., 1977-78; clin. instr. U. Cen. Fla., Emory U., Bowling Green State U., 1980-86. Contbr. articles to profl. jours. Vol., mem. prof. adv. bd. Hospice, Ft. Myers, 1984-86. Mem. Am. Med. Record Assn., Va. Med. Record Assn., Electronic Computing Hosp. Oriented, Am. Med. Transcription Assn., Va. Community Coll. Assn., Southeastern Med. Record Assn., Am. Business-women's Assn. Republican. Presbyterian. Home: 10302 Appalachian Circle #211 Oakton VA 22124

HARRIS, MARY DEE, computer scientist; b. Houston, Jan. 15, 1942; d. Newton Temple and Harriet (Rushing) H.; m. Richard Allen Shorter, Mar. 27, 1965 (div. 1972); 1 child, Scott Allen; m. Ben Fosberg, Oct. 14, 1979 (div. 1983). BS in Math., Tex. Tech U., 1964, MA in English Lit., 1965; PhD in English Lit., Computer Sci., U. Tex., 1975. Diagnostic programmer IBM, Los Angeles, 1965-66; systems engr. IBM, Austin, Tex., 1967-68, Entrex Inc., New Orleans, 1972-73; cons. New Orleans, 1973-74; instr. computer sci. Loyola U., New Orleans, 1975-75, asst. prof., 1979-82, assoc. prof., 1982-86; asst. prof. Cen. State U., Edmond, Okla., 1975-79; mgr. natural lang. processing group Systems Research and Applications Corp., Arlington, Va., 1986—; adj. prof. Georgetown U., Washington, 1988—. Author: Introduction to Natural Language Processing, 1985; contbr. numerous articles to profl. jours., 1978—; software editor Computers and Humanities, 1977-1982; keynote speaker U. S.C. Computer Sci. Symposium, 1987. Reviewer grants NEH, 1981—. Mem. Assn. Computers-Humanities (pres. 1982-86, exec. council 1978-82, 1987—, conf. speaker U. Toronto 1986)), Nat. Ednl. Computing Conf. (steering com. 1982-86, program com. 1984), Assn. Computing Machinery, MLA, Assn. Literacy-Linguistic Computing, Assn. Computational Linguistics, Am. Assn. Artificial Intelligence, Cognitive Sci. Soc. Democrat. Office: SRA Corp 2000 15th St N Arlington VA 22201

HARRIS, MICALYN SHAFER, lawyer; b. Chgo., Oct. 31, 1941; d. Erwin and Dorothy (Sampson) Shafer. AB, Wellesley Coll., 1963; JD, U. Chgo., 1966. Bar: Ill. 1966, Mo. 1967, U.S. Dist. Ct. (ea. dist.) 1967, U.S. Supreme Ct. 1972, U.S. Ct. Appeals (8th cir.) 1974, N.Y. 1981. Law clk. U.S. Dist. Ct., St. Louis, 1967-68; atty. The May Dept. Stores, St. Louis, 1968-70, Ralston-Purina Co., St. Louis, 1970-72; atty., asst. sec. Chromalloy Am. Corp., St. Louis, 1972-76; sole practice, St. Louis, 1976-78, Ridgewood, N.J., 1988—; div. counsel, gen. counsel S.B. Thomas, Inc.; div. counsel CPC N.Am., 1978-84; corp. counsel and asst. sec. CPC Internat., Englewood Cliffs, N.J., 1984-88. Mem. ABA (co-chmn. subcom. counseling the mktg. function, securities law com., tender offers and proxy statements subcom.), Ill. Bar Assn., N.Y. State Bar Assn. (securities regulation com.), Bar Assn. Met. St. Louis (chmn. TV com.), Mo. Bar Assn. (chmn. internat. law com.), Am. Corp. Counsel Assn. N.J. (bd. dirs., chmn. bus. law com.). Address: 625 N Monroe Ridgewood NJ 07450

HARRIS, ORENE ELIZABETH, dance school administrator, educator; b. Sinton, Tex., Oct. 27, 1945; d. Orea Alvin and Norma Jean (Clendennen) Ehlers; m. Wayne Lee Harris, Sept. 28, 1979 (div. Sept. 1986); 1 child, Lawrene Elizabeth. Student Del Mar Coll., Corpus Christi, 1964-65, 74-75. Dance instr. Sylvia Grey Sch., Corpus Christi, 1964-68, Hahn AFB and Bitburg AFB, W.Ger., 1968-70, Gwinn Ind. Sch. Dist., Mich., 1970-71; supr., dance instr. Corpus Christi Park and Recreation Dept., 1972-78; owner, instr. Cinderella Sch. Dance, Corpus Christi, 1972—; choreographer Encore Theatre, Corpus Christi, 1983, So. Charm, Panama City, Fla., 1986; Tex. dir. Am.'s Miss Charm, Jacksonville, N.C., 1985, So. Charm, Jackson, Tenn., 1986; dir. Corpus Christi Sparklettes Dance Team, 1976—, Cindy Girls Dance Team, 1985—, Glass Slipper Vocal Group, 1986—, Tex. Pageant Prodns, 1987—. Choreographer dance for TV comml., 1984. Beauty pageant judge; chmn. Dance-A-Thon, Cystic Fibrosis, Tex. Gulf Coast chpt., 1984-86. Recipient Best Prodn. dance award Regency Talent Competition, 1986, Best Prodn. dance award Encore Talent Competition, 1986, Most Outstanding Group Costume award Encore Talent Competition, 1986. Mem. Profl. Dance Tchrs.' Assn. Am., Nat. Assn. Female Execs., PTA, Encore Travel Club. Democrat. Meth. Avocations: doll collecting, sewing and designing clothes, cake decorating, photography, crocheting. Office: Cinderella Sch Dance 4455 S Padre Island Dr Suite 17 Corpus Christi TX 78411

HARRIS, R. ELEANOR M., educator; b. Cleve., July 28, 1936; d. Henry Edward and Annie Elizabeth (Watkins) Murden; m. Lawrence Leonard Harris, Jr., Aug. 5, 1961; 1 child, Loren L. BS in Elem. Edn., Bowie (Md.) State Coll., 1958, MEd in Reading, 1973; EdD in Adminstrn., Nova U., Ft. Lauderdale, Fla., 1985. Tchr. elem. schs. Anne Arundel County Pub. Schs., Annapolis, Md., 1958-73, adminstrv. trainee, 1973-74, asst. prin., 1974-75, coordinator, 1975-79, adminstrv. asst., 1979—; Mem. instructional TV task force Md. State Dept. Edn., Balt., 1976-80, nutrition adv. com., 1979-83. Contbr. articles to profl. pubis. Mem. Foster Care Rev. Bd. Office of Gov. State of Md., 1980-84, City of Annapolis Human Relations Commn., 1987—; bd. dirs. Anne Arundel County YMCA/YWCA, 1984—, Banneker Douglas Mus. Found., Annapolis, 1977-79, Community Action Agy., Annapolis, 1975-85, Opportunities Industrialization Ctr., Annapolis, 1983—. Recipient Community Service award Community Action Agy., 1980, Disting. Alumni award Nat. Assn. for Equal Opportunity in Higher Edn., 1988. Mem. YWCA, Am. Assn. Sch. Adminstrs. (sec. women's caucus 1983), Nat. Acad. Sch. Execs. (excellence in adminstrn. award 1984), Nat. Assn. Female Execs., The Williamsburg Found., Phi Delta Kappa (pres., treas., sec. 1963-70, human relations award 1977). Democrat. Baptist. Clubs: Frontiers Club Internat. (aux. mem. Annapolis chpt., Civic Betterment award 1987), Links, Inc. (parliamentarian, treas. 1983—), Delicados Inc. (nat. pres. 1981-83). Home: 1999 Forest Dr Annapolis MD 21401 Office: Anne Arundel County Bd Edn 2644 Riva Rd Annapolis MD 21401

HARRIS, ROBERTA LUCAS, social worker; b. St. Louis, Nov. 13, 1916; d. Robert Joseph and Clara Louise (Mellor) Lucas; A.B., St. Louis U., 1955, M.S.W. (NIMH grantee), 1964; m. William F. Sprengnether, Jr., Aug. 21, 1937 (dec. Aug. 30, 1951); children—Robert Lucas, Madelon Sprengnether Littlejohn, Ronald John; m. 2d, Victor B. Harris, Sept. 13, 1955 (dec. June 14, 1960). Field instr. Sch. Social Work St. Louis U., 1967-70; chief of domestic relations City of St. Louis, 1966—. Dir., Citizens' Housing Council, 1956-60; del. to Community Family Life Clinic, 1957; dir. Landmarks Assn., 1957-63; pres. Compton Heights Improvement Assn., 1973. Mem. Nat., Mo. assns. social workers, Assn. Family Conciliation Cts. (dir. 1968—), Greater St. Louis Probation and Parole Assn. (sec. 1976), St. Louis U. Sch. Social Service Alumni Assn. (sec. 1973), LWV (dir. 1956-61). Methodist. Club: Wednesday. Home: 3137 Longfellow St Saint Louis MO 63104

HARRIS, RUTH BATES, retired government agency official, writer. d. Harry B. Delaney and Florence Graham; m. Alfred U. McKenzie, Aug. 25, 1987. B.S., Fla. A&M U.; M.B.A., NYU, 1957. Exec. dir. Washington Human Relations Commn. and; equal employment opportunity officer D.C. 1960-69; dir. human relations dept. Montgomery County (Md.) Pub. Schs., 1969-71; dep. asst. adminstr. NASA, 1971-76; human relations officer Dept. Interior, Washington, 1978-88; ind. lectr., author 1988—. Author: Trigger Words, Personal Power Words, Handbooks for Careerists. Recipient over 70 awards, including; Sojourner Truth award Nat. Assn. Negro Bus. and Profl. Womens' Clubs, 1966; Martin Luther King award D.C. chpt. NAACP, 1969; award Nat. Bus. League, 1974; award space div. Rockwell Internat., 1975; Disting. Service award Federally Employed Women, 1976; award Cosmopolitan Bus. and Profl. Women's Club, 1978; keys to cities of Cocoa Beach and Jacksonville Fla., 1980; award Omega Psi Phi; award Sigma Gamma Rho; award Alpha Phi Alpha, Meritorious Service award Dept. Interior, 1987; named Aerospace Woman of Distinction, Thomas W. Anthony chpt. Air Force Assn., 1987, Nat. Black Women of Distinction, Dollars and Cents mag., 1986, Women of Distinction, Washington Mag., 1986, Nat. Disting. Black Women, Black Women in Sisterhood for Action, 1986. Mem. Delta Sigma Theta, Iota Phi Lambda (hon.), Cosmopolitan Bus. and Profl. Women's Club (pres.). Home: 311 Bonhill Dr Fort Washington MD 20744

HARRIS, SHARON JOY, small business owner; b. Phila., Mar. 18, 1953; d. Stanford Herbert and Ruth Diane (Leabman) H. BA in English, Glassboro State Coll., 1975, MA in Pub. Relations, 1979. Tchr. Delsea Regional High Sch., Franklinville, N.J., 1975, Vineland (N.J.) High Sch., 1975-79, Harriton High Sch., Rosemont, Pa., 1980; sales rep. Pitman Learning Ednl. Publs., Belmont, Calif., 1980-82; sales and pub. relations rep. Stan Harris & Co., Inc., Phila., 1982—; owner, pub. relations exec. Creative Connection, 1986—; adviser action network Nat. Tobacco Inst., Albany, N.Y., 1984—; chairperson bus. edn. adv. bd. Bartram High Sch., Phila., 1985-87. Contbr. articles to trade publs. Bd. dirs. Southeastern Pa. Muscular Dystrophy Assn., 1985. Mem. Pa. Amusement and Music Machine Assn. (bd. dirs. 1982—, Coin Machine Operator of Yr. 1986), Nat. Assn. Convenience Stores, Nat. Assn. Female Execs. Republican. Jewish. Lodge: Hadassah. Office: Stan Harris & Co Inc G and Lycoming Sts Philadelphia PA 19124

HARRIS, SHELLEY RAENA, business executive; b. Miami, Fla., Apr. 11, 1951; d. Benjamin Loeb Harris and Lillian (Grossman) Nestler; m. Raymond Justin Shenfield, Dec. 23, 1972 (div. 1985); children—Melisa Adine, Robert Dustin. Student Northwestern U. Project coordinator Zink Pub. Co., Orlando, Fla., 1983-85; pub. Harris Pub. Co., Miami, 1985; adminstrv. dir. Med. Care Devel. Corp., Miami, 1985—, Doctor's Health Care Group, Inc., Miami, 1985—, Bayside Med. Equipment, Inc., Miami, 1985—, Heritage Health Care Group/PIU, Miami, 1985—, Utilization Mgmt. Services, 1985—; promotional asst. to Lillie Rubin, 1986; account mgr. Miami Beach Mag., Playbill, 1987—. Mem. Nat. Assn. Female Execs., Miami Beach C. of C., Coral Gables C. of C. Avocation: art. Home: 353 W 47th St Miami Beach FL 33160 Office: So Playbill Pub Inc 1001 NW 159th Dr Miami FL 33169

HARRIS, SUSAN, television producer; b. Mt. Vernon, N.Y.; m. Paul Junger Witt. Dir. various episodes Soap, All in the Family, Then Came Bronson; creator, writer, co-producer The Golden Girls (NBC-TV), 1985— (Emmy awards for best comedy series, Acad. Television Arts and Scis, 1986, 1987). Office: Witt/Thomas/Harris Prodns 846 N Cahuenga Hollywood CA 90038 *

HARRIS, SUSAN HUNT, development writer, journalist; b. Cleve., Nov. 5, 1959; d. Warren H. and Rose Marie (Fulkerson) H. B.A., Miami U., 1982. Assoc. editor Herald Pub. Co., Barberton, Ohio, 1982-83; reporter News-Herald Newspapers, Wyandotte, Mich., 1983-84, Mellus Newspapers, Lincoln Park, Mich., 1984-86, fund raising exec. Children's Hosp., Detroit, 1986-87; sr. devel. writer, media relations coordinator, Northeastern U., Boston, 1987—; freelance photographer, 1982—; freelance writer, editor, 1984—. Pub. relations advisor Heritage Soc., Canal Fulton, Ohio, 1981-82; vol. Adult Creative Activities Program, Lincoln Park, 1983; bd. dirs. Community Care Services. Recipient Excellence in Media award Assn., first place enterprise feature award Mich. Press. Assn. Retarded Citizens. Mem Miami U. Alumni Assn., Phi Mu. Office: Northeastern U Office Century Fund Communications 266 HN Boston MA 02115

HARRIS, THÉRÈSE EILEEN, psychotherapist; b. Boston, Nov. 25, 1963; d. Frank Henry and Gertrude Thérèse (McCarthy) H. BS, Boston Coll., 1985; MA, Tufts U., 1988. Territory mgr. Am. Hosp. Supply Corp., Valencia, Calif., 1985-86; adolescent counselor Lynn (Mass.) Youth Resource Bur., 1986-87; weekend mgr. Wild Acre Inn, Lexington, Mass., 1987; therapist Tri-City Mental Community Helath and Retardation Ctr., Malden, Mass., 1987-88; co-instr. Tufts U., Medford, Mass., 1988—; cons. edn. dept. Tufts U., 1988. Mem. Assn. Female Execs., Inst. Environ Scis., Assn. Women in Psychology. Roman Catholic. Club: North Shore Karate.

HARRIS, VERA EVELYN, personnel recruiting and search firm executive; b. Watson, Sask., Can., Jan. 11, 1932; came to U.S., 1957; d. Timothy and Margaret (Popoff) H.; student U. B.C. (Can.), Vancouver; children—Colin Clifford Graham, Barbara Cusimano Page. Office mgr. Keglers, Inc., Morgan City, La., 1964-67; office mgr., acct. John L. Hopper & Assos., New Orleans, 1967-71; office mgr. Elite Homes, Inc., Metairie, La., 1971-73; comptroller Le Pavillon Hotel, New Orleans, 1973-74; controller Waguespack-Pratt, Inc., New Orleans, 1974-76; adminstrv. controller Sizzler Family Steak Houses of So. La., Inc., Metairie, 1976-79; dir. adminstrn. Sunbelt, Inc., New Orleans, 1979-82, sec., dir., 1980—; exec. v.p. Corp. Cons., Inc., 1980-83, pres., 1984-86; pres. Harris Personnel Resources, Arlington, Tex., 1986—, Harris Enterprises, Arlington, 1986—; exec. dir. Nat. Sizzler Franchise Assn., 1976-79. Mem. Am. Bus. Women's Assn., Nat. Assn. Female Execs., La. Assn. Personnel Consultants (treas. 1985-86). Home: 8702 Winding Ln Fort Worth TX 76112 Office: Harris Personnel Resources 2000 E Lamar Blvd Suite 600 Arlington TX 76006

HARRIS, VICKY ANN, financial analyst; b. Tonawanda, N.Y.C., June 29, 1952; d. Edwin Elmer and Opal June (Phillips) H. BA, SUNY, Stonybrook, 1973, MBA, NYU, 1982. Acct. Ampal Am. Israel Corp., N.Y.C., 1982-84, acctg. analyst Bankers Trust Co., N.Y.C., 1985-86; adjunct prof. Borough of Manhattan Community Coll., N.Y.C., 1985-86; fin. analyst Bureau of Treasury City of N.Y., 1986—. Home: 146 Montague St Apt 6 Brooklyn NY 11201 Office: NYC Bur of Treasury Mcpl Bldg New York NY 10007

HARRIS, WINIFRED ELIZABETH (BETTY), library administrator; b. 'Nkana, North Rhodesia, Africa, Apr. 14, 1936; arrived in Can., 1945; d. William Arthur and Dorothy Elizabeth (Dixon) Wall; m. Riad Abdelkader Hanafi, 1955 (div. 1967); children: Waleed A., Rhoda E.A.; m. Robert Harris, Dec. 17, 1980. BA, Carleton U., Ottawa, Ont., 1966; BLS, U. Toronto, 1969. Tech. officer II Nat. Library Can., Ottawa, 1965-67; mgr. bus. library Algonquin Coll., Ottawa, 1967-69; dir. libraries St. Lawrence Coll., Kingston, Ont., 1969-70; head of reference, circulation, cataloguing law library, supr. br. libraries Queen's U., Kingston, 1970-72; chief librarian Centennial Coll., Scarborough, Ont., 1972-74; dir. learning resources Fraser Valley Coll., Abbotsford, B.C., 1974—; mgr. Ministry of Edn. Learning Resources Ctrs. Standards Project, B.C., 1978-79; chmn. B.C. Union Catalogue Consortium, B.C., 1981-82; chmn. external evaluation team Red Deer Coll., Alta., 1984; mem. adv. bd. Nat. Library Can.; lectr. in field. Regional editor: Directory of Community & Technical Colleges, 1975; contbg. editor: Where to Eat in Canada, 1976-83, Feliciter, 1986, 87. Am. Assn. Law Libraries scholar and travel grantee, 1971; Quesnel Dist. Tchrs. Fedn. scholar, 1953-54, Can. Fedn. Univ. Women scholar, 1968-69. Mem. Can. Library Assn. (chmn. community coll. sect. 1974, 75, 76, dir. coll. and univ. libraries sect. 1986-87), Council of Post-Secondary Library Dirs. of B.C. (pres. 1979-81), B.C. Library Assn. (bd. dirs. 1976, 77, 78), Fraser Valley Coll. Faculty and Staff Assn. (pres. 1977-78, chmn. profl. devel. com. 1979-80, 87-88, grievance chmn. 1984-85). Office: Fraser Valley Coll, 33844 King Rd, Rural Rt 2, Abbotsford, BC Canada V2S 4N2

HARRIS, YVONNE LEIGH, financial controller; b. Huntington, W.Va., Sept. 9, 1945; d. Wallace Bailey and Effie Afton (Wikel) H.; m. George Howell Starr, Mar. 10, 1966 (dec. Aug. 1972); 1 child, Kirk Howell; m. Robert Warren Harris, July 3, 1973. BBA, Marshall U., 1969. Acctg. supr. Biochem. Procedures, Inc., North Hollywood, Calif., 1969-72; cash mgmt. supr. Washington Iron Works, Inc., Seattle, 1973-77; corp. acct. Formac, Inc., Seattle, 1977-78; asst. controller Advanced Tech. Labs., Bellevue, Wash., 1978-79; cost and pricing mgr. Wash. Iron Works, Inc., Seattle, 1979-81, corp. acctg. mgr., 1981-83, controller, 1983-85; cons. K & H Trust, Seattle, 1985—; controller Woodinville (Wash.) Water Dist., 1986—; notary pub. State of Wash., Seattle, 1977—. Mem. Am. Soc. Profl. and Exec. Women., Wash. State Fin. Officers Assn., Am. Water Works Assn. Republican. Presbyterian. Club: Country Cousins (Woodinville) (treas. 1978-79, pres. 1980-82). Home: 14906 210th Ave NE Woodinville WA 98072 Office: Woodinville Water Dist 17238 Woodinville-Duvall Rd Woodinville WA 98072

HARRIS-CROUTHERS, REBECCA LOUISE, public relations executive; b. Ft. Smith, Ark., Jan. 26, 1959; d. Udell Wayne and Roberta Louise (Rice) H. BA, U. Ark., Fayetteville, 1983. Engring. sec. Southwestern Bell, Little Rock, 1977-78; mgr. interface Rheem/Rudd, Ft. Smith, 1979-80; intern journalism U. Ark., Fayetteville, 1980-83; account exec. Apple Broadcasting, Fayetteville, 1983-84; dir. pub. relations Hudson Foods Inc., Rogers, Ark., 1984—. Editor: The Hudson Spirit, 1984—. County dir. March of Dimes, Fayetteville, 1986—, chmn. WalkAm., 1985—, state exec. bd. dirs.; photography coordinator Phillips Pro-Celebrity Charity Classic Golf and Tennis Tournaments. Mem. Internat. Assn. Bus. Communicators, Nat. Assn. Female Exec., Sigma Delta Chi. Baptist. Home: 905 Joye St Springdale AR 72764 Office: Hudson Foods Inc PO Box 777 Rogers AR 72757

HARRIS-LANGE, JANET ELLEN, real estate development executive; b. N.Y.C., June 7, 1946; d. M. Martin and Alma Regina (Roberts) Maglio; m. John Madison Harris, Dec. 19, 1970 (dec. Nov. 1981); m. 2d, Donald J. Lange, Sept. 8, 1984; children: Matthew, Joshua. A.A., Palm Beach Jr. Coll., 1966; B.S., Fla. Atlantic U., 1967, M.Ed., 1969. Tchr. French and Spanish, Palm Beach (Fla.) County Pub. Schs., 1968-73; pres., owner, chief exec. officer J & J Mfg. Corp., West Palm Beach, 1972-87; pres., co-owner Branet Investments, Inc., West Palm Beach, 1982—; co-owner Branet Devel. Corp., West Palm Beach, Fla. 1985—; instr. entrepreneurship Palm Beach Jr. Coll., City of West Palm Beach; del. White House Conf. Small Bus., 1986. Inventor measuring device, 1975, magnetic soap hook, 1983. Bd. dirs. Am. Diabetes Assn., Palm Beach, Fla., 1982-87; mem. region 1V Miami adv. council, Small Bus. Adminstrn.; mem. edn. and program design group Small Bus. Devel. Program City of West Palm Beach, 1987—; bd. dirs. Consumer Credit Counseling Service. Mem. Nat. Assn. Women Bus. Owners (v.p. 1982-84, 85-86, 88-89, pres. 1984-85), World Trade Council, Nat. Housewares Mfr. Assn., Nat. Fedn. Ind. Businesses. Club: Forum (West Palm Beach). Avocations: aerobic dancing, reading. Office: Branet Investments Inc 1001 W Jasmine Dr Suite G Lake Park FL 33403

HARRISON, ANNA JANE, chemist, educator; b. Benton City, Mo., Dec. 23, 1912; d. Albert S.J. and Mary (Jones) H. Student, Lindenwood Coll., 1929-31, L.H.D. (hon.), 1977; A.B., U. Mo., 1933, B.S., 1935, M.A., 1937, Ph.D., 1940, D.Sc. (hon.), 1983; D.Sc. (hon.), Tulane U., 1975, Smith Coll., 1975, Williams Coll., 1978, Am. Internat. Coll., 1978, Vincennes U., 1978, Lehigh U., 1979, Hood Coll., 1979, Hartford U., 1979, Worcester Poly. Inst., 1979, Suffolk U., 1979, Eastern Mich. U., 1983, Russell Sage Coll., 1984, Mt. Holyoke Coll., 1984, Mills Coll., 1985; L.H.D. (hon.), Emmanuel Coll., 1983; D.H.L., St. Joseph Coll., 1985, Elms Coll., 1985. Instr. chemistry Newcomb Coll., 1940-42, asst. prof., 1942-45; asst. prof. chemistry Mt. Holyoke Coll., 1945-47, asso. prof., 1947-50, prof., 1950-76, prof. emeritus, 1976—, chmn. dept., 1960-66, William R. Kenan, Jr. prof., 1976-79; Mem. Nat. Sci. Bd., 1972-78. Author: (textbook) Chemistry: A search to Understand, 1988; contbr. articles to profl. jours. Recipient Frank Forrest award Am. Ceramic Soc., 1949; James Flack Norris award in chem. edn. Northeastern sect. Am. Chem. Soc., 1977; AAUW Sarah Berliner fellow Cambridge U., Eng., 1952-53; Am. Chem. Soc. Petroleum Research Fund Internat. fellow NRC Can., 1959-60; recipient Coll. Chemistry Tchr. award Mfg. Chemists Assn., 1969. Mem. AAAS (dir. 1979-85, pres. 1983, chmn. bd. 1984-85), Am. Chem. Soc. (chmn. div. chem. edn. 1971, pres. 1978, dir. 1976-79, award in chem. edn. 1982), Internat. Union Pure and Applied Chemistry (U.S. nat. com. 1978-81), Sigma Xi. Address: Mount Holyoke Coll Dept Chemistry South Hadley MA 01075

HARRISON, ANNE ELIZABETH, government official; b. Santa Maria, Calif., May 12, 1941; d. William Lee and Mary Hampton (Beveridge) H. B.S. cum laude, U. Calif.-Davis, 1964; M.S., U. Mich., 1966. Forest naturalist Coronado Nat. Forest, Forest Service, USDA, Tucson, 1966-72, dir. women's activities, regional office, eastern region, Milw., 1972-73, dir. regional visitor info. service, 1973-77, pub. info. officer Cleveland Nat. Forest, San Diego, 1977-81, pub. affairs officer Rocky Mountain Forest and Range Expt. Sta., Fort Collins, Colo., 1981-85, Pacific S.W. Research Sta., Berkeley, Calif., 1985-87, dir. office of info., 1987—; mem. environ. edn. adv. com. Ohio State U., Columbus, 1975-76; regional dir. S.W. region Assn. Interpretive Naturalists, Derwood, Md., 1979-81; project coordinator Seneca Rocks Visitor Ctr., W.Va., 1974-77. Editor, producer 6 tech. transfer modules Silviculture of Rocky Mountain Species, 1981-85 (Nat. Assn. Govt. Communicators nat. 1st place award for one title 1985). Contbr. tech. papers to symposia procs, bot. jours., 1960-80. Conservation chmn. Greenfield Jr. Women's Club, Wis., 1974; chmn. regional conf. S.W. Wis. Interpreter's Assn., 1975; active Christian Women's Clubs, Calif. Recipient 1st place award for exhibit Colo. State Forest Service, 1981, spl. act award USDA Forest Service, 1985. Mem. Nat. Assn. Female Execs., Pub. Relations Soc. Am., Council Biology Editors. Avocations: weaving; hiking; camping; canoeing; cross-country skiing. Office: USDA Forest Service Pacific Research Sta 1960 Addison St Berkeley CA 94704

HARRISON, BEATRICE MARIE (BINION), academic administrator, small business owner; b. Detroit, Sept. 10, 1958; d. Lamar Clinton Sr. and Mildred Arretta (Blount) Binion; m. Albert Willard Harrison III, Feb. 7, 1981; 1 child, Sophia Marie. BA in Psychology, Mich. State U., 1980; postgrad., Wayne State U., 1980-81, U. Mich., Dearborn, 1982-83. Cert. counselor. Bookkeeper City Nat. Bank, Detroit, 1977; asst. sec. Mich. State U., East Lansing, 1979; co-ptnr., asst. Cordove Rental Co., Holly, Mich., 1980-83; counselor CBN, 700 Club Inc., Royal Oak, Mich., 1985; substitute tchr. Pontiac (Mich.) Sch. Dist., 1985-86; admissions counselor, adminstr. Jordan Coll., Detroit, 1986-87; admissions advisor Marygrove Coll., Detroit, 1988—; mem. Echoes of Gt. Lakes Mutual Life Ins. Co., 1986—. Assoc. mem. Detroit Symphony, 1984—, Detroit Inst. Arts, 1985—, State of Liberty/Ellis Island Found., 1984—; block chief Southfield (Mich.) Neighborhood Watch, 1984-86; mem. Senator Jackie Vaughn III Re-election Com., Mich., 1986—; bd. dirs. downtown Detroit br. YWCA, 1988—; vol. fundraiser Sta. WDIV-TV Easter Seal Telethon, 1988. Mem. Am. Psychol. Assn. (student affiliate), Nat. Assn. Female Execs., NAACP. Roman Catholic. Clubs: Top Ladies of Distinction Inc. (mem. Founders' Day com. Detroit chpt. 1987, 88). Home: 5658 Drake Hollow Dr E West Bloomfield MI 48322 Office: Harrison & Harrison Designs Inc PO Box 2896 Farmington Hills MI 48333

HARRISON, BETTY CAROLYN COOK, vocational educator, administrator; b. Cale, Ark., Jan. 11, 1939; d. Denver G. and Minnie (Haddox) Cook; m. David B. Harrison, Dec. 31, 1956; children: Jerry David, Phyllis Lynley. BSE, Henderson State Tchrs. Coll., Arkadelphia, Ark., 1959; MS, U. Ark., 1971; PhD, Tex. Agrl. and Mech. U., 1975. Tchr. secondary schs., McCrory, Ark., 1962-64, Taylor, Ark., 1964-69, Shongaloo, La., 1969-73, Minden, La., 1974-76, 77-80; adminstrv. intern La. Dept. Edn., 1974; cooperating tchr., supr. student tchrs. Grambling (La.) State U., 1974-76, La. Tech. U., Ruston, 1974-76, 78-80; asst. prof. vocat. edn. Va. Poly. Inst. and State U., Blacksburg, 1976-77; assoc. prof. vocat. edn. Coll. Agr., La. State U., Baton Rouge, 1980-85, assoc. prof. Sch. Vocat. Edn., 1985—, head dept. home econs. edn. and bus. edn. Contbr. articles to profl. jours. HEW fellow, 1973; grantee Future Homemakers Am., 1956, Coll. Acads., 1956, Ark. Edn. Assn., 1956-69, Internat. Paper Co., 1966-68, La. Dept. Edn., 1972. Mem. Am. Home Econs. Assn., La. Home Econs. Assn. (bd. dirs., pres.-elect), La. Vocat. Assn. (bd. dirs.), La. Assn. Vocat. Home Econs. Tchrs. (pres.), Nat. Assn. Vocat. Home Econs. Tchrs., Nat. Assn. Vocat. Home Econs. Tchr. Educators, Home Econs. Edn. Assn. (regional dir., nat. v.p., editor and chair publs. 1987—), NEA (nat. assembly del.), Family Relations Council La. (edn. chmn. officer), Phi Delta Kappa, Delta Kappa Gamma, Gamma Sigma Delta. Democrat. Baptist. Home: 2100 College Dr Apt 157 Baton Rouge LA 70808 Office: La State U Sch Vocat Edn Baton Rouge LA 70803

HARRISON, BETTYE INGLE, real estate executive; b. Chattanooga, Mar. 9, 1924; d. Merle Roy and Irene (Ayers) Ingle; m. George K. Harrison Sr.; children: Elwynn Harrison Bishop, George K. Harrison Jr. Grad., Tenn. Realtors Inst. Cert. real estate brokerage mgr. CRB designation; cert. residential specialist CRS designation. Bookkeeper, sec. E. Cecil Phillips Real Estate Agy., Chattanooga, 1956-62, agt., 1962-64, sales mgr., 1964-67, prin. broker, 1967-77; sales mgr. Gloria Sutton Realtors, Chattanooga, 1977-80, v.p., dir. mktg., 1980-86, sr. v.p., gen. mgr., 1986—. Pres. Tenn. Real Estate Edn. Found., 1982-83. Mem. Chattanooga Bd. Realtors (pres. 1983, Realtor of Yr. 1976), Tenn. Assn. Realtors (Realtor of Yr. 1986), Nat. Assn. Realtors (bd. dirs. 1987, nat. pres. Women's Council Realtors 1986, regional v.p., gov. and state chpt. pres. 1987), Tenn.'s Women's Council Realtors (Woman of Yr. 1982), Pilot Internat. Methodist. Office: Gloria Sutton Realtors 2115 Chapman Rd Suite 105 Chattanooga TN 37421

HARRISON, CANDICE FREDRICA, association executive; b. Chgo., Dec. 16, 1948; d. Carl Fredrick Sperry and Betty Marie (Welch) Tapert. Student U. Ill.-Chgo., 1972-75. Asst. purchasing agent Am. Bakeries, Chgo., 1971-76; asst. office mgr. Am. Soc. Dentistry for Children, Chgo., 1976-78; supr. support personnel A.S. Hansen, Chgo., 1978-82; exec. dir. Aux. to the Am. Osteopathic Assn., Chgo., 1982—. Mem. Am. Soc. Personnel Adminstrs.

HARRISON, CAROLYN CASSELL, counselor; b. Waterbury, Conn., June 19, 1925; d. Kenneth Parker and Elizabeth Rachel (Emery) Wight; R.N., Mass. Gen. Hosp. Sch. Nursing, 1946; B.S. in Nursing Edn., Catholic U., 1953; M.Ed. in Counseling, U. Md., 1969; m. Thomas Richard Harrison, June 16, 1973; children—Donna Cassell, Stafford Cassell, Jack Carlton Cassell. Nursing supr. Monadnock Community Hosp., Peterboro, N.H., 1947-49; staff nurse Doctors Hosp., VA Hosp., Washington, 1949-52; asst. dir. health services Am. U., Washington, 1949-50; dir. admissions Sch. Nursing, Washington Hosp. Center, 1957-67; dir. records office Coll. Edn., U. Md., College Park, 1968-70; counselor Prince George's Community Coll., Largo, Md., 1970-81; bd. dirs. The Women's Career Ctr., Portland, Maine; dir. career devel. Isothermal Community Coll., Spindale, N.C., 1981-87; retired. Trustee, sec. to bd. dirs. Gould Acad., Bethel, Maine, 1971—, chair Ann. Giving, 1987-89; bd. dirs. Task Force on Domestic Violence, Rutherford County, N.C., 1982-84; mem. adv. com. Statewide Assessment of Career Aspiration and Job Attainment Among Women Returning to Coll. in Md., 1978-80; mem. First Congregational Ch., South Portland; bd. dirs. Prevention of Abuse in the Home, Rutherford County, N.C. Mem. NOW, Am. Assn. for Counseling and Devel., Nat. Assn. Women Deans, Adminstrs. and Counselors, NEA, Am. Assn. Retired Persons, Counseling and Personnel Assn.-U. Md., Older Womens League. Clubs: Faculty Women's (Am. U.), Pilot Internat. (dir. 1982-83), Sweet Adelines (bd. dirs. Casco Bay chpt.). Home: 23 Bayberry Way South Portland ME 04106 Office: Isothermal Community Coll PO Box 804 Spindale NC 28160

HARRISON, CHRISTINE DELANE, educational administrator; b. Dearborn, Mich., July 22, 1947; d. Walter Frederick and Marguerite Elaine (Champagne) Hancock; m. Charles Richard Bashawaty, Aug. 31, 1968 (div. 1972); 1 child, Brett Charles; m. Andrew David Harrison, June 14, 1980; 1 child, Andrew David, II. BS, Ea. Mich. U., 1969. Cert. early elem. tchr., Mich. Tchr. Westland Schs., Mich., 1969-71, Dept. Army, Ansbach, Germany, 1971-72; prin. sec. chemistry dept. U. Mich., Ann Arbor, 1973-78; word processing mgr. Great Copy Co., Ann Arbor, 1978-79; dir., v.p. Great Lakes Sch., Clawson, Mich., 1979—. Editorial asst. Herbal Extracts, 1984; Bull. of Thermodynamics and Thermochemistry, 1973-78. Bd. dirs. Perry Nursery Sch., Ann Arbor, 1976-77. Recipient Prodn. award and Dedication award Los Feliz Apple Sch. Mem. Mich. Assn. for Supervision and Curriculum Devel., Nat. Trust for Hist. Preservation, Clawson C. of C. Avocations: reading, bicycling, aerobics, sailing. Office: Great Lakes Sch 529 Grove St Clawson MI 48017

HARRISON, DIANE AMES, human resources executive; b. Summit, N.J., Apr. 12, 1962; d. Philip Henry and Carol Nancy (Coe) Ames; m. David William Harrison, Oct. 12, 1985. BA in English and Communications, Fairleigh Dickinson U., 1984. Personnel asst. Monroe Systems for Bus., Morris Plains, N.J., 1984-85; supr. human resources United Research Co., Inc., Morristown, N.J., 1985-87; mgr. employment Commodities Corp., Princeton, N.J., 1987—. Student writer Institute for Children's Literature, 1986—. Mem. Am. Mgmt. Assn., Am. Soc. Personnel Adminstrn. Democrat. Roman Catholic. Home: 22 Orchard Hill Rd Bernardsville NJ 07924 Office: Commodities Corp 701 Mt Lucas Rd Princeton NJ 08542

HARRISON, DOROTHY GORDY, infosystems specialist; b. Pittsfield, Mass., Jan. 1, 1939. B.A. in Chemistry, U. N.C., Greensboro, 1960; Cert. Info. Sci., Ga. Inst. Tech., 1962, M.S. in Info./Computer Sci., Indsl. Mgmt. and Engring., 1965; Cert. Physics, Math., Wake Forest U., 1964; M.Ln. in Adminstrn., Emory U., 1973. With tech. library and info. services Cone Mills Research and Devel., Greensboro, N.C., 1960-63; chmn. dept. physics Pittsfield High Sch., Mass., 1964; with sci. div. Pittsfield, Pub. Schs., 1964; research asst. Price Gilbert Meml. Library Ga. Inst. Tech., Atlanta, 1964-66, Engring. Expt. Sta., 1965-66; research assoc. Sch. Info. and Computer Sci., 1967; info. scientist and projects dir. Office Computing Activities, U. Ga., Athens, 1971-73; cons. info./computer sci. and administrn., 1962—; dir. computer info. services Clarke County, Ga., 1983—; bd. advs. Ga. Inst. Tech., bd. dirs., pres. Ga. Govt. Mgmt. Info. Scis.; bd. dirs. State Archives Athens Vocat.-Tech. Sch., Ga.; exec. com. internat., nat. Govt. Mgmt. Info. Scis. NSF scholar, 1965-66; NSF fellow 1964-65; NSF grantee 1964; recipient citation Recording for the Blind, 1968-70, Young Info./Computer Scientist award, 1969, Outstanding Tchr. award, 1964; named Young Woman Engr. of Yr., 1964. Mem. Beta Phi Mu.

HARRISON, ELLEN KROLL, lawyer; b. East Orange, N.J., Mar. 2, 1946; d. William and Harriet (Herman) Kroll; m. Donald Harrison, 1970; children: Matthew, Margaret. BA, U. Mich., 1968; JD, Harvard U., 1971. Bar: D.C., U.S. Tax Ct., U.S. Supreme Ct. Ptnr. Morgan, Lewis & Bockius, Washington; adj. prof. Georgetown Law Sch., Washington, 1987—. Mem. ABA (subcom. chair), Phi Beta Kappa. Democrat. Home: 5205 Portsmouth Rd Bethesda MD 20816 Office: Morgan Lewis & Bockius 1800 M St NW Washington DC 20036

HARRISON, EVELYN BYRD, archaeologist, educator; b. Charlottesville, Va., June 5, 1920; d. William Byrd and Eva (Detamore) H. A.B., Barnard Coll., 1941; A.M., Columbia U., 1943, Ph.D., 1952; postgrad., Bryn Mawr Coll., 1942-43. Instr. classics U. Cin., 1951-53; asst. prof. fine arts and archaeology Columbia, 1955-59, asso. prof., 1959-67, prof., 1967-70; prof. art and archaeology Princeton, 1970-74; prof. Inst. Fine Arts, N.Y. U., N.Y.C., 1974—; mem. Inst. for Advanced Study, 1961, 64. Author: The Athenian Agora, I, Portrait Sculpture, 1953, XI, Archaic and Archaistic Sculpture, 1965; contbr. articles to profl. jours. Guggenheim fellow, 1954-55; NEH grantee, 1968-69. Mem. Am. Acad. Arts and Scis., Am. Philos. Soc., Archaeol. Inst. Am., Soc. Promotion Hellenic Studies, German Archaeol. Inst. Home: 500 E 85th St New York NY 10028

HARRISON, GLORIA GIMMA, travel company executive; b. Bklyn., Mar. 19, 1928; d. Mario Vito and Rosaria Elena (Geraci) Gimma; m. A.T. Harrison Jr., Dec. 22, 1948 (div. Mar. 1956); children: Arthur Thomas III, John Gimma; m. Henry J. Balnis (dec. Dec. 1978); m. Daniel A. Norton, Dec. 24, 1985. BA in Merchandising and Mktg., Finch Coll., 1945; MA in Psychol. Scis., Mich. State U., 1947. Cert. travel cons. Sec., account exec. NBC, N.Y.C., 1947-48; sec. Coca-Cola USA, Atlanta, 1967-74; adminstrv. asst. Fulton County, Atlanta, 1974-81; owner, founder Harrison Travel Ltd., Atlanta, 1980—; chmn. Media Games Corp. Bd. trustees Ctr. Visually Impaired, Atlanta, 1985, Village St. Joseph, Atlanta, 1987. Mem. Travel Industry Assn. Ga., Inst. Cert. Travel Agts., Pacific Asia Travel Assn., Am. Soc. Travel Agts., Cruise Line Internat. Assn. Home: 54 Ivy Chase Atlanta GA 30342 Office: Harrison Travel Ltd 6 Piedmont Ctr Suite 220 Atlanta GA 30342

HARRISON, GRETCHEN STEINER, training executive; b. Massillon, Ohio, Apr. 21, 1957; d. Paul Lewis and Margarete Elsa (Kunart) Steiner; m. David Charles Harrison. BBA summa cum laude, Tex. Christian U., 1979; postgrad., U. Pa., 1987—. Cert. employee relations law. Dist. ops. mgr. Am. Hosp. Supply Corp., New Orleans, 1979-80; region ops. supr. Am. Hosp. Supply Corp., Arlington, Tex., 1980-81; customer service supr. McNeil Pharm. div. Johnson and Johnson, Arlington, 1982-83; employment adminstr. McNeil Pharm. div. Johnson and Johnson, Springhouse, Pa., 1983-84; sr. employment adminstr. McNeil Pharm. div. Johnson and Johnson, Springhouse, 1984-85, sr. adminstr. employee relations and tng., 1985-87, mgr. tng. and devel., 1987—; mem. steering com. Operation Native Talent, Phila., 1983-85; pvt. sector rep. Pvt. Industry Council, Norristown, Pa., 1985-87. Com. chmn. Jr. League, Phil, 1986-87, mem., 1985—; Bible study host Tenth Presbyn. Ch., Phil, 1983—; mem. program com. Focus '85 Job Conf., Phil. Recipient Plaque of Commendation, Montgomery County Commrs., Norristown, 1986, Optimus award McNeil Pharm., 1987. Mem. Am. Soc. Personnel Adminstrs. Republican. Club: Century. Office: McNeil Pharm Springhouse PA 19477

HARRISON, JACKITA AMMONS, nurse, funeral director; b. Gary, Ind., Nov. 22, 1947; d. Edwin Griffin Moore and Luella (Johnson) Mitchell; m. Alan Dinand Harrison, Aug. 10, 1966 (div. June 1972); children: Gina Fine Harrison, Janien Derniere Harrison. AS, City Coll. San Francisco, 1978, San Francisco Coll. Mortuary Sci., 1980; BS, U. San Francisco, 1985, M in Pub. Adminstn., 1987. RN; lic. funeral director/embalmer. Lic. practical nurse Victory Meml. Hosp., Waukegan, Ill., 1968-73; vocat. nurse St. Luke's Hosp., San Francisco, 1973-76; operating room nurse San Francisco Gen. Hosp., 1976-78; fun. dir., embalmer Assoc. Funeral Services, Oakland, Calif., 1980-84; staff nurse surgery Seton Med. Ctr., Daly City, Calif., 1981-85, St. Francis Meml. Hosp., San Francisco, 1985-86; operating room nurse U. Calif., San Francisco, 1978-81, RN, 1987-88; asst. clin. supr. Perioperative Services, San Francisco, 1988—. Parent adv. Community Alliance for Spl. Edn., San Francisco, 1978—; parent advisor, prin. adv. bd. Mercy High Sch., San Francisco, 1982-86; mem. Parkmerced Resident's Orgn., San Francisco, 1978—, Stanford Parents Assn., 1986—. Mem. Assn. Operating Room Nurses (del. to Congress 1986 chair scholarship 1986—, nominating com.), Nat. Bd. Funeral Dirs. Democrat. Roman Catholic. Home: 6 Grijalva Dr San Francisco CA 94132

HARRISON, JAN, public relations executive; b. Austin, Minn., Jan. 18, 1952; d. Wallace Grant and Margery Joan (Kennard) H. BA, U. Minn., 1974. Assoc. producer Sta. KSDO, San Diego, 1974; producer, reporter Sta. KFMB-TV, San Diego, 1975-76; anchorperson, reporter Sta. KGTV-TV, San Diego, 1976-78, Sta. KIRO-TV, Seattle, 1978-79, Sta. WNEV-TV, Boston, 1979-82; dir. pub. relations Westin Hotel, Boston, 1983-84; prin. Jan Harrison Assocs., Boston, 1984—. Chairperson media adv. bd. Patriots' Trail council Girl Scouts U.S., 1980—, v.p., bd. dirs., 1986—. Recipient Bay State award AP, 1981, 82, Emmy team program award Nat. Assn. TV Arts and Scis., 1981, 82, Pub. Relations Excellence Recognition award Boston Press Photographers Assn., 1983. Mem. Pub. Relations Soc. Am., Smaller Bus. Assn. New Eng. Office: Jan Harrison Assocs 172 Bunker Hill St Boston MA 02129

HARRISON, JEANNE, television producer and director; b. Phila.; d. David and Henriette (Ketchum) H.; m. Kurt Lassen, 1959 (div. 1980); children—Liza, Lydia. Dir., producer ZIV, N.Y.C., 1959-67; sr. producer J. Walter Thompson, N.Y.C., 1967-70; creative dir. Am. Home Products, N.Y.C., 1970-73; producer, dir., owner Harrison Prodns., N.Y.C., 1973—. Mem. Nat. Acad. TV Arts and Scis., Dirs. Guild Am. Home and office: Harrison Prodns 200 E 36th St New York NY 10016

HARRISON, JOAN S(HIRLEY), college dean; b. Orange, N.J., Apr. 29, 1934; d. Harry and Rose (Marshak) Horowitz; m. David Harrison, Mar. 23, 1958; children: Andrew L., Rachel E. AB magna cum laude, Tufts U., 1956; AM, Radcliffe Coll., 1957; MS, Bank St. Coll., N.Y.C., 1982; PhD, Union Grad. Sch., Cin., 1987. Tchr. Weehawken (N.J.) Pub. Schs., 1959-60; faculty Farleigh Dickinson U., Teaneck, N.J., 1960-61, 64-65; program developer, adminstr. Englewood (N.J.) Pub. Schs., 1964-67; asst. dean studies Sarah Lawrence Coll., Bronxville, N.Y., 1973-81, assoc. dean studies, 1981—; dissemination assoc. Englewood Title III project, 1972; adj. faculty Bank St. Coll., 1981-83; acting assoc. dir. Ctr. for Continuing Edn., Sarah Lawrence Coll., 1980-81; cons. N.Y.C. Bd. Edn., 1983-84. Contbr. articles to profl. jours. Mem. planning bd. met. region Nat. Identification project of Am. Council on Edn., 1980-85. Mem. Phi Beta Kappa. Home: 2 Oxford Rd Hastings-on-Hudson NY 10706

HARRISON, JOYCE VIRGINIA, advertising agency executive, songwriter; b. Flin Flon, Man., Can., May 3, 1939; d. Peter Vincent and Amelia (Ohryn) H.; student U. Man., 1957-58, Laurentian U., 1968-69; children—Kim, Marley, Lindsay. Women's editor, program dir. Cambrian Broadcasting, Sudbury, Ont., Can., 1959-70; ops. mgr. Broadcast Services, Evanston, Ill., 1970-72; asso. creative dir. Arthur Meyerhoff & Assos. (now BBDO), Chgo., 1972-79; creative dir., sr. v.p. Draper Daniels, Chgo., 1979-80; creative dir., v.p. Bozell, Jacobs, Kenyon & Eckhardt, 1980-86; group creative dir., v.p. HCF & Lois/GGK (formerly Grey Advt.), Chgo., 1988—; pres. Rambull Inc., 1973-79; bd. dirs. Intervision, Inc.; dir. Wax & Assos., Chgo., 1980-81. Composer songs. Mem. Nat. Acad. Rec. Arts & Scis., ASCAP, Nashville Songwriters Assn. Internat., Country Music Assn., Songwriters Guild Am. Republican. Roman Catholic. Home and Office: LL Music 2762 Eastwood Evanston IL 60201-1545

HARRISON, LINDA SUE, mortgage company executive; b. Ft. Worth, June 27, 1944; d. Paul Martin and Cora Edna (Daniel) Montgomery; m. Millard Dee Harrison, Jan. 2, 1964; children: Jessie Douglas, Paul David, Ronald Dale. Grad., Nat. Inst. Fin. Edn. Teller First Na. Bank, Plano, Tex., 1973-79; computer interface Edn. Service Ctr., Richardson, Tex., 1979-82; mortgage dept. mgr. Majestic Savs. Assn., McKinney, Tex., 1982-86; v.p. mortgage lending Multibanc Savs. Assn., Dallas, 1986—. Mem. Nat. Assn. Female Execs., Mortgage Bankers Assn., Tex. Mortgage Bankers Assn., Dallas Assn. Profl. Mortgage Women. Mem. Ch. of Christ. Office: Multibanc Savs Assn 12770 Coit Rd Suite 800 Dallas TX 75251

HARRISON, LOIS COWLES, civic worker; b. Des Moines, Iowa, June 23, 1934; d. Gardner and Lois (Thornburg) Cowles; B.A., Wellesley Coll., 1956; m. John Raymond Harrison, June 24, 1955; children—Mark, Pat, Lois; m. Homer E. Hooks, Nov. 27, 1982. Dir., Cowles Media Co. (formerly Mpls. Star and Tribune Co.), 1975-85. Commr. Gov.'s Commn. on Status of Women, 1973-77, Fla. Ethics Commn., 1974-78; mem. Commn. on Fla. Constl. Revision, 1977-78; mem. Fla. Women's Polit. Caucus, 1973-75; v.p. LWV Fla., 1973-77, pres., 1977—, bd. dirs., 1982-83, dir. edn. fund, 1973-77, dir. LWV U.S. ERA chair, 1980-82; bd. dirs. ERAmerica, 1980-82; pres. Planned Parenthood Central Fla., 1982-85; pres. Fla. Assn. Planned Parenthood Affiliates, 1987—; dir. Fla. Fine Arts Council, 1972-80; mem. Mayor's Creative and Performing Arts Council, Lakeland, Fla., 1972-75; mem. Am. Bar Commn. on Evaluation of Profl. Standards, 1978-80; pres. Polk Mus. Art, 1985-86, The Hooks Group, 1985—. Episcopalian. Home: 2311 Nevada Rd Lakeland FL 33803

HARRISON, MARCIE ANNE, marketing executive; b. Chgo., July 11, 1946; d. Stanley A. and Ethel (Lurie) H. BA in Journalism, U. Wis., 1968; MBA, DePaul U., 1981. Copy editor The Patriot Ledger Newapaper, Quincy, Mass., 1968-70; asst. dir. pub. relations Michael Reeses Hosp., Chgo., 1970-75; ptnr. Drucker and Harrison, Chgo., 1974-86; pres. Harrison Group, Chgo., 1986—. Del. White House Conf. on Small Bus., 1986; bd. dirs. Jobs for Youth, Chgo., 1980—, Spl. Children's Charities, Chgo., 1986—, Loop Coll. Bus. and Internat., Chgo., 1985—. Recipient Quality Life award Pub. Club Chgo., 1981, Cert. Appreciation award Small Bus. Adminstrn., 1986. Mem. North Bus. and Inc. Council (bd. dirs. 1986), Pub. Relations Soc. Am. (Cert. Recognition 1981), Young Execs. Club (pres. 1985-86). Office: Harrison Group 500 N Michigan Chicago IL 60611

HARRISON, MARION FOX, violin company official, violin maker; b. Chattanooga, Sept. 1, 1911; d. Cicero Gaston and Lucy Mae (Catlett) Fox; m. Edwin Andrew O'Neal, June 4, 1932 (div. Apr. 1945); children—Anne E. O'Neal Langhaug, Sylvia I. O'Neal Nagel; m. 2d, Benjamin Frederick Harrison, Jr., Sept. 24, 1948; 1 dau., Marion Fredericka Harrison LaBounty. Grad. Ga. State Coll., Milledgeville. Tchr., Rossville (Ga.) Schs., 1930-35; chemist Hercules Powder Co., Tyner, Tenn., 1942-46, Chattanooga Medicine Co., 1946-49; mgr. Harrison Violins, Berkley, Mich., 1966—, lutheir, 1971—, mgr., part owner, 1966—; violin maker, 1971—. Sec., Oak Park Symphony Soc., 1968, dir., 1968; dir. Southfield (Mich.) Symphony Soc., 1981—. Mem. Violin Makers Assn. Ariz. (2d place in tone award 1976, 83). Home: 1415 Woodsboro Dr Royal Oak MI 48067 Office: Harrison Violins 2689 Coolidge Hwy Berkley MI 48072

HARRISON, MARTHA ELAINE, computer programmer, military officer; b. Bitburg, Fed. Republic of Germany, June 30, 1962; d. Zadoc Daniel Jr. and Selina Elizabeth (McLaughlin) H. Student, U. Tenn., Chattanooga, 1980. Register operator Wendy's Old Fashioned Hamburgers, Chattanooga, 1978-79; clk. Provident Life and Accident Ins., Chattanooga, 1980, programmer, 1985—; mgr. Massey Enterprises, Inc., Chattanooga, 1981-82; algebra tutor U. Tenn., Chattanooga, 1982-83; register operator Wendy's Old Fashioned Hamburgers, Chattanooga, 1983, 1984; printer operator TVA/Boandi Temp Service, Chattanooga, 1985; disbursement officer 3397th U.S. Army Garrison, Chattanooga, 1981—. Served as disbursement officer USAR, 1981—. Named one of Outstanding Young Women of Am., 1983. Mem. Nat. Assn. of Female Execs., Res. Officers Assn., DAR, Mil. Order of World Wars. Democrat. Episcopalian. Home: 3623 Fountain Ave Apt 97 East Ridge TN 37412-1834

HARRISON, MARY STYRON, accountant; b. Foley, Ala., Dec. 7, 1949; d. Raymond Charles Styron and Vestel Ilene (Wooten) Barnett; m. Dale M. Harrison, May 1, 1974; 1 child, John Dale. AS in Bus. Adminstrn., Faulkner Jr. Coll., 1980; BS in Bus. Adminstrn., Troy State U., 1981. CPA, Ala. Acct. Jerome C. Olsen Co., Mobile, Ala., 1980-83, Johnson, Dees & Montgomery, Foley, Ala., 1983-84; comptroller Vols. Am. S. Ala., Inc., Mobile, 1984-87; controller Lake Forest Yacht and Country Club, Daphne, Ala., 1987—; part-time instr. Faulkner Jr. Coll., Bay Minette, Ala., 1983—. Mem. Am. Inst. CPA's, Ala. Soc. CPA's, Mobile chpt. of Ala. Soc. CPA's. Republican. Mormon. Home: Rt 1 Box 89 Loxley AL 36551 Office: Lake Forest Yacht & Country Club PO Box 1737 Daphne AL 36526

HARRISON, NEDRA JOYCE, surgeon; b. Buffalo, Apr. 16, 1951; d. Herman Lloyde and Gertrude (Newsom) H.; B.S., Rosary Hill Coll., 1973; M.D., SUNY, Buffalo, 1977. Diplomate Am. Bd. Surgery. Resident in surgery Millard Fillmore Hosps., Buffalo, 1977-82, mem. active attending staff in gen. surgery, 1983—; practice medicine specializing in gen. surgery, Buffalo, 1982—; clin. asst. in surgery SUNY at Buffalo Sch. Medicine; cons. staff Bry-Lyn Hosp., 1986—; provisional staff in gen. surgery St. Joseph Intercommunity Hosp., 1986-87. Chmn. United Thank Offering, Episcopal Ch. Buffalo, 1982; bd. dirs. Niagara Luth. Home, 1987; mem. alumni bd. dirs. SUNY at Buffalo Sch. Medicine, 1986—. Recipient Best Research Paper in Gen. Surgery award Millard Fillmore Hosps., 1978, 81. Fellow ACS; mem. Am. Med. Women's Assn., Buffalo Surg. Soc., Christian Med. Soc., N.Y. State Med. Soc., Med. Soc. Erie County, Delta Epsilon Sigma. Episcopalian. Office: 405 Linwood Ave Buffalo NY 14209

HARRISON, ROSALIE THORNTON (MRS. PORTER HARMON HARRISON), retired educator; b. Birmingham, Ala., Jan. 24, 1917; d. John William and Zora (Whetstone) Thornton; AB, Samford U., 1937; MA, U. Ala., 1945; postgrad. Tchrs. Coll., Columbia U., Cath. U. Am., George Washington U., Am. U., U. Md., U. D.C.; m. Porter Harmon Harrison, Apr. 12, 1941; 1 child, Porter Harmon. Tchr., Pinson (Ala.). Sch., 1937-41; tchr. Children's Sch., U. Ala., summers 1939-41; tchr., asst. prin. Avondale Estates (Ga.) Elem. Sch., 1941-45; asst. tchr. Horace Mann-Lincoln Sch. of Tchrs. Coll., Columbia U., 1946; instr. English, Samford U., 1948; tchr. Lakeview Sch., Birmingham, 1948-49, Hazelwood and McFerran Sch., Louisville, 1950-53; with pub. schs. of Dist. of Columbia, Washington, D.C., 1956-82; tchr. Congress Heights Elem. Sch., Washington, 1956-63; guidance counselor Barnard Elem. Sch., Washington, 1963-82; adminstr. D.C. Project Head Start, summers 1966-69, coordinator parent program, summers 1968-69; prin. Congress Heights-Savoy Elem. Summer Sch., Washington, 1971, Blow-Bowen Elem. Summer Sch., Washington, 1972. Del. Congress of Baptist World Alliance, Rio de Janeiro, Brazil, 1960, Miami, Fla., 1965; dir. D.C. Bapt. Conv. Summer Mission Camp Girls Aux., 1955, assembly officer Dept. Bapt. Women, 1967-71, 73-77; dir. Bapt. Tng. Union, Riverside Bapt. Ch., Washington, 1954-65, also mem. choir, council, mem. numerous coms., officer, 1953—; past pres. Ministers Wives, D.C. Bapt. Conv. Ky. Col. Mem. NEA (life), Am. Assn. for Counseling and Devel. and its following divs.: Am. Sch. Counselor Assn., D.C. Sch. Counselor Assn., D.C. Elem. Sch. Counselor Assn. (past v.p.), D.C. Career Devel. Assn. (past pres.), Nat. Career Devel. Assn., Assn. for Multicultural Counseling and Devel., D.C. Assn. for Multicultural Counseling and Devel., Assn. Specialists in Group Work, D.C. Assn. Specialists in Group Work (charter), Am. Mental Health Counselors Assn., D.C. Mental Health Counselors Assn.; also Internat. Platform Assn., Council for Exceptional Children, Nat. Trust Hist. Preservation, D.C. Ret. Tchrs. Assn., The Columbian Women of the George Washington U. (past 1st v.p.), Smithsonian Nat. Assocs., U.S. Capitol Hist. Soc., Concerned Citizens Council Washington (pres.), Washington City Bible Soc. (bd. dirs.), Alpha Delta Kappa (past state pres. Washington, past pres. Gamma chpt.). Home: 3828 17th Pl NE Washington DC 20018

HARRISON-HINDS, SHARLENE MAVIS, writer; b. Montreal, Que., Can., June 8, 1951; d. Sydney Samuel Harrison and Florence (Beit) Brown; m. Terry Lou Hinds, Aug. 1, 1953; 1 child, Sasha Michelle. BA with honors, York U., Toronto, Ont., 1973. Jr. copywriter J. Walter Thompson, Montreal, 1974-76; mktg. asst., copywriter Consiglio and Assocs., Montreal, 1976; copywriter McConnell Advt., Montreal, 1977-78; copywriter, creative dir. Penthouse Studios, Montreal, 1979; free-lance cons. Montreal, 1980-84; copywriter Dally Advt., Ft. Worth, 1984-85, Phillips Agy., Ft. Worth, 1985-87; owner, mktg., creative cons. Armadillo Communications, Ft. Worth, 1987—. Copywriter: (TV comml.) Right Choice/Harris Hospital (Silver Addy award 1986), (ads) Big Boy (Silver Addy award 1985), Muscular Dystrophy (Bronze Addy award 1985). Jewish. Lodges: B'nai Brith, Lilah Tov.

HARRIS-SMITH, JOAN A., educational administrator; b. Wilkes-Barre, Pa., Apr. 14, 1933; d. George Walter and Marjorie (Halstead) Quigley; m. Joseph Michael Melchiona, Nov. 16, 1952 (div. July 4, 1960); children: Joseph, Joan; m. Lynn Rynearson Harris, Apr. 14, 1962 (div. July 18, 1971); children: Kenton, Lynn R. Jr., Sean, Kelly; m. Charles T. Smith, Feb. 14, 1984. Actress, dancer N.Y.C., 1949-72; owner, tchr. KLS Enterprises, Inc., Edwardsville, Pa., 1967-72; program dir. Coll. for Kids, King's and Wilkes Coll., Wilkes-Barre, 1976-79; exec. dir. Kids on Campus, Wilkes-Barre, 1979-80; dir. Marywood Coll., Scranton, Pa., 1981; owner, tchr. Joan Harris Centre for Gifted and Talented, Edwardsville, 1982—, also dir. Author (with others) Creative Dance, 1977; editor (books) The First of the Three R's: Reason, 1978, True Myths, 1978, vol. II, 1980, A Tribute to Water, 1979, The Wheel, 1979, Our Country, 1979, Philosopher's Index, 1981. Mem. Rep. Nat. Com. Recipient Youth Reserve Fund Talent Contest 1st and 2d place awards, 1984, Small Bus. Devel. award Greater Wilkes-Barre C. of C., 1985, Cert. of Appreciation O.K. Heart, 1985. Mem. Nat. Assn. for Gifted, Dance Educators Am., Nat. Assn. Female Execs. Home: 185 Terrace Ave Trucksville PA 18708 Office: Ctr for Gifted and Talented Narrows Shopping Ctr Edwardsville PA 18704

HARRITY, BERNADINE TERESA, lawyer; b. Phila., Nov. 21, 1948; d. Bernard James and Eleanor Mary (McGoldrick) H. BA, U. Pa., 1970; JD, Duquesne U., 1974. Bar: Pa. 1974, U.S. Ct. Mil. Rev., 1974, U.S. Ct. Mil. Appeals 1975, U.S. Supreme Ct. 1978, U.S. Claims Ct. 1980, U.S. Dist. Ct. (we. dist.) Pa. 1988, U.S. Ct. Appeals (3d cir.) 1988. Atty. advisor Darcom, Alexandria, Va., 1979-80; contracts atty. VA, Washington, 1980-87; sole practice Pitts., 1987—. Dir. Darcom Fed. Credit Union, 1980—, Terr. Townhouses of Annandale, 1981-82. Served to capt. JAGC, U.S. Army, 1974-79, to maj. USAR. Decorated Joint Services Commendation medal, Army Commendation medal with 2 oak leaf clusters. Mem. ABA, Pa. Bar Assn., D.C. Women's Bar Assn., Allegheny County Bar Assn., Am. Legion, AMVETS, Delta Theta Phi. Republican. Roman Catholic. Clubs: Falls Church (Va.) Bus. and Profl. Women's U. Pa. Alumni. Home: 6118 Callery St Pittsburgh PA 15206 Office: 933 Liberty Ave Pittsburgh PA 15222

HARROLD, LOU ANN, home economist, farmer, educator; b. Findlay, Ohio, Dec. 9, 1935; d. Donald Layman and Carolyn Genevra (Mathews) Putnam; B.S. summa cum laude, Ohio State U.; MS in Ednl. Adminstrn., U. Dayton; m. Clyde Ellis Harrold; children—Robert E. Spangler, Jr., Stacia Lee Spangler Westerhausen. Tchr., Alger High Sch.; tchr., dept. head Kenton (Ohio) Jr. High Sch.; tchr. home econs., dept. head Kenton St. High Sch.; secondary coordinator Hardin County Dept. Edn., dir. curriculum, 1986—; cons. Ohio Dept. Edn.; dir. sch.-age parent project. State adv. bd. Ohio Coop. Extension Service, Nutrition Edn. Tng. Program; sec. Cessna Twp. Bd. Zoning Appeals; mem. Rep. exec. com. Named Ohio Tchr. of Yr. in Home Econs.; recipient service award Coll. Agr. and Home Econs. Ohio State U.. Mem. Am. Home Econs. Assn., Ohio Home Econs. Assn. (state pres. 1980-81), Ohio Assn. for Supervision and Curriculum Devel., Nat. Assn. Vocat. Home Econs. Tchrs., Ohio St U. Coll. Home Econs. Alumni (pres. 1988), AAUW, Home Econs. Edn. Assn., Am. Vocat. Assn., Home

Economists in Bus., Ohio Sch. Supervisors Assn., Delta Kappa Gamma, Phi Delta Kappa. Methodist. Club: University II (pres.). Home: 8187 TR 90 Ada OH 45810 Office: Courthouse Kenton OH 43326

HARROP, ANNA OUTLER, material analyst; b. Abbeville, Ga., Mar. 10, 1938; d. Thomas Joshua and Irene (Fogerty) Outler; m. Jerry L. Bunch Jr., Mar. 21, 1957 (div. 1974); children: Anna Lisa, Perry Allen; m. Irving Clinton Harrop, Apr. 10, 1976. Grad. high sch., Hawkinsville, Ga., 1956. Office mgr. Electrolux Corp., Orlando, Jacksonville, Pompano Beach, and Savannah, Fla. and Ga., 1961-76; adminstrv. sec., office supply mgr. Orange County Sch. Bd., Orlando, 1976-79; adminstrv. asst. Borg Warner Leasing, Seattle, 1980-82; material analyst Gulfstream Aerospace Corp., Savannah, 1982—. Mem. Nat. Assn. Female Execs., Am. Bus. Women's Assn. (v.p. 1982-83, pres. 1983-84, 87-88, del. 1983-85, chmn. publicity 1984-86, chmn. inner council 1988—), Gulfstream Mgmt. Assn. Republican. Home: 68 Hidden Lake Ct Savannah GA 31419 Office: Gulfstream Aerospace Corp Travis Field PO Box 2206 Savannah GA 31402

HARSNEY, JOHANNA MARIE OFFNER, nurse; b. Youngstown, Ohio, Oct. 15, 1914; d. Michael and Elizabeth (Untch) Offner; m. Theodore Harsney, Aug. 11, 1941; 1 son, Karl Michael. Grad. Youngstown Hosp. Sch. Nursing, 1939; B.A. in Fgn. Langs., Youngstown U., 1972. Staff nurse Youngstown Hosp., 1939-40; pvt. duty nurse Youngstown Profl. Nurse's Registry, Youngstown, 1940-84. Vol. Red Cross nurses. Mem. Am. Nurses Assn., Profl. Nurses Registry (dir.), Ohio Nurses Assn. (pres. pvt. duty sect. 1979-84), Am. Bus. Women Assn. (v.p. Gold Torch chpt. 1978, Nurse of Yr. Dist. 3, 1983), Phi Lambda Pi, Phi Lambda Pi (sec. 1973-74, pres. 1975). Office: Profl Nurses Registry 3119 Market St Suite 224 Youngstown OH 44507

HART, ANGELA KATHERINE, lawyer; b. Radford, Va., May 10, 1949; d. William James, Jr., and Lina Elda (Filios) H. A.B., Trinity Coll., Washington, 1971; J.D., Loyola U., New Orleans, 1975. Bar: Md. 1975, D.C. 1981. Staff atty. Legal Aid Bur., Inc., Annapolis, Md., 1975-77; asst. county atty. Montgomery County, Md., Rockville, 1977—. Bd. dirs. Anne Arundel County chpt. ARC, 1983—. Mem. ABA, Md. Bar Assn., D.C. Bar Assn., Montgomery County Bar Assn., Anne Arundel County Bar Assn., St. Philip Neri Sodality. Democrat. Roman Catholic. Home: 323 Ardmore Rd Linthicum MD 21090 Office: County Atty's Office Exec Office Bldg 101 Monroe St 3d Fl Rockville MD 20850

HART, BARBARA NORRIS, sales professional; b. Lenoir, N.C., Mar. 1, 1941; d. Charlie Archie and Lois (Sharpe) Norris; div. Sept. 1967; 1 child, Angela. Cert., Clevenger Bus. Coll., 1960-61, Caldwell Community Coll., 1973. Clk. Am. Credit Co., Lenoir, N.C., 1960-63; clk., sec. C&M Motors, Inc., Lenoir, N.C., 1963-72; office mgr. Taylor Constrn. Co., Lenoir, N.C., 1972-76; cons. Fashion Two Twenty, Inc., Lenoir, N.C., 1976-78, dir., 1978-82; regional mgr. Fashion Two Twenty, Inc., Aurora, Ohio, 1982-85, mgr. direct sales, 1985—. Mem. Am. Bus. Women's Assn. (pres. 1984, charter, Woman of Yr. award 1984). Democrat. Methodist. Club: Toastmasters (charter, recording sec. 1984, Accomplished Toastmaster award 1984). Home: PO Box 1056 Lenoir NC 28645 Office: Fashion Two Twenty Inc 1263 S Chillicothe Rd Aurora OH 44202

HART, CYNTHIA LOUISE, finance company executive; b. Marshalltown, Iowa, Apr. 4, 1948; d. Robert Lee and Beverly Ione (Greenfield) M.; m. Stephen Lothaire Brandt, July 20, 1967 (div. 1977); m. Leo Oswald Hart, May 27, 1984; children: Sabrina, Kirsten, Jennie. Student, U. Calif., Fullerton, 1966-69; student in bus. and mgmt., U. Calif., Berkeley, 1984-88. Asst. v.p., br. mgr. Hibernia Bank, San Francisco, 1975-82; sr. v.p. comml. loan and credit dept. Eureka Fed. Savs. and Loan, San Carlos, Calif., 1983-86; assoc. dir. Fed. Home Loan Bank, San Francisco, 1986—; guest speaker Office of Edn. Fed. Home Loan Bank, Dallas, 1985—; mem. curriculum com. Am. Inst. Banking Edn., San Francisco, 1983. Contbr. articles to mags. in field. Bd. dirs. Bayshore Childcare Ctr., San Mateo, Calif., 1985. Mem. Nat. Assn. Credit Mgrs., Nat. Assn. Bus. Women, Harvard Bus. and Profl. Women's Group, Credit Women's Internat., Nat. Assn. Female Execs. Lutheran. Office: Fed Home Loan Bank 600 California St San Francisco CA 94120

HART, DOROTHY CRAMER, banker; b. Scoffield Barracks, Hawaii, Mar. 23, 1940; d. Merritt and Margaret Hazel (Baker) Cramer; m. William Donald Hart, Jan. 21, 1967; children: Lea Grace, Rebecca Kay. BBA in Acctg., U. tex., 1962; postgrad., U. Tex., 1965. CPA. Acct. Exxon Corp., Houston, 1962-70; CPA Henry & Horne, CPA's, Scottsdale, Ariz., 1973; pvt. practice acctg. Tyler, Tex., 1974-78; sr. CPA Ross, Eubanks, Betts & Co., Jackson, Miss., 1980-81; CPA supr. Peat, Marwick & Mitchell, El Paso, Tex., 1982; v.p., trust officer, mgr. tax dept. MBank El Paso, 1982—. Mem. Am. Inst. CPA's, Tex. Soc. CPA's, El Paso Chpt. CPA's, El Paso Estate Planning Council (bd. dirs., treas. 1983-84, v.p. 1984-85, pres. 1985-86), Am. Soc. Women Accts. (v.p. El Paso chpt. 1988-89). Republican. Baptist. Office: MBank El Paso MBank Plaza Suite 400 El Paso TX 79901

HART, EILEEN KELLY, contracting officer; b. Cambridge, Mass., Nov. 9, 1947; d. John Charles and Helen Patricia (Bielaski) Kelly; m. Douglas Ryan Bliven, Jan. 6, 1967 (div. Nov. 1978); children: Christopher Bryan, Jennifer; m. Stephen Christopher Hart, Feb. 25, 1983; stepchildren: Jennifer Lynn, Brian Stephen. Student, Montgomery Coll. With USN, 1965—; analyst cost and price USN, Laurel, Md., 1983-86, contracting officer, 1986—. Mem. Nat. Contract Mgmt. Assn. (pres. local chpt. 1986—). Roman Catholic. Home: 204 Garth Terr Gaithersburg MD 20879 Office: USN Naval Plant Rep Office Johns Hopkins Rd Laurel MD 20707

HART, KITTY CARLISLE, arts administrator; b. New Orleans, Sept. 3, 1917; d. Joseph and Hortence (Holtzman) Conn; m. Moss Hart, Aug. 10, 1946 (dec. 1961); children: Christopher, Cathy. Ed., London Sch. Econs., Royal Acad. Dramatic Arts; DFA (hon.), Coll. New Rochelle; DHL (hon.), Hartwick Coll.; LHD (hon.), Manhattan Coll., Amherst Coll. Chmn. N.Y. State Council on the Arts. Former panelist: TV show To Tell the Truth; actress on stage and in films including The Marx Brothers A Night at the Opera, 1936; Broadway theatre appearance in On Your Toes, 1983-84; singer, Met. Opera, TV moderator and interviewer.; contbr. book revs. to jours. Asso. fellow Timothy Dwight Coll. of Yale U.; bd. dirs. Empire State Coll.; formerly spl. cons. to N.Y. Gov. on women's opportunities; mem. vis. com. for the arts Mass. Inst. Tech. Office: 915 Broadway New York NY 10010

HART, LOIS BORLAND, publisher, consultant; b. Syracuse, N.Y., May 15, 1941; d. Leslie R. and Laura S. (Styn) Borland; m. Arnold L. Hart, July 4, 1969; children: Christopher, Richard. BS, U. Rochester, 1966; MS, Syracuse U., 1972; EdD, U. Mass., 1974. Field services coordinator Program Ednl. Opportunity U. Mich., Ann Arbor, 1975-78; pres. Organizational Leadership Inc., East Lansing, Mich., 1978-80; trainer Mgmt. Devel. Ctr. of Mountain State Employers Council, Denver, 1980-81; pres. Leadership Dynamics Inc., Lyons, Colo., 1980—. Author: Are You Stuck, 1986, Survivors of Successful Sales, 1986, Taming Your Junk Jungle, 1986, Conference and Workshop Planners' Manual, 1979, Moving Up! Women and Leadership, 1980, Learning from Conflict, 1981, The Sexes at Work, 1983, Saying Hello: How to get Your Group Started, 1983, Saying Goodbye: Ending Your Group Experience, 1983. Campaign coordinator county commr. campaign. Mem. AAUW, NOW, Am. Soc. Tng. and Devel., Phi Delta Kappa, Pi Lambda Theta. Home: 3775 Iris Ave Suite 3B Boulder CO 80301 Office: Leadership Dynamics Inc 3775 Iris Ave Suite 3B Boulder CO 80301

HART, LYNN PATRICIA, lawyer; b. Schenectady, N.Y., Sept. 12, 1954; d. H. Philip Hart and M. Patricia (Dinsmore) Hart-Franco; m. Frederick T. Muto, Sept. 8, 1979; children: Daniel Frederick, Christopher Hart. BA cum laude, Westmont Coll., 1976; JD, U. Calif., Berkeley, 1979. Bar: U.S. Dist. Ct. (so. dist.) Calif. Law clk. to presiding justice U.S. Dist. Ct., San Diego, 1979-80; assoc. Heller, Ehrman, White & McAuliffe, San Francisco, 1980-83, Howard, Rice, et al, San Francisco, 1983—. Author: Property not Subject to Probate Administration, 1986, Decedent Estate Practice CEB, 1986. Mem. estate planning councils of San Francisco and East Bay; bd. dirs. Dwight House, Berkeley, 1982. Mem. ABA (real property, probate and trust law sect., vice chair disclaimer com.), Calif. State Bar (estate planning, trust, probate law sects., asst. editor respective newsletters), San Francisco Bar Assn. (probate and trust law sect., outstanding pro bono atty. 1982, 83), Calif. Women Lawyers, Women Tax Lawyers, Queen's Bench. Democrat. Presbyterian. Office: Howard Rice et al 3 Embarcadero Ctr San Francisco CA 94611

HART, MARA KIRK, librarian; b. N.Y.C., Dec. 25, 1933; d. George W. and Lucile D. (Dvorak) Kirk; BA, Miami U., Oxford, Ohio, 1955; MA, NYU, 1957; MA, U. Minn., 1973; m. Robert C. Hart, Aug. 1983; children by previous marriage—Steve Bauer, Jenny Bauer. Teenage dir. Central Br. YWCA, N.Y.C., 1957-58; tchr. English, Cleve., Mpls., 1958-61; dir. bibliography rm. U. Minn. Library, Mpls., 1964-65, Portuguese, Latin Am., Spanish bibliographer, 1965-69, acquisitions librarian, Duluth campus, 1973-84, head reference dept., 1985—; humanities bibliographer Claremont Colls., 1969-71; pub., editor Kirk Press Books. Manor Club scholar, 1956-57; Wis. Arts Bd. awardee, 1979. Democrat. Unitarian. Editor: Corn Village, 1971; poetry editor Plainsong, 1967-69, N. Country Anvil, 1971-77; translator various books from Spanish; author: (poetry) Some Yellow Flowers, 1979; pub.: Second Pond, 1980; Till Hope Creates, 1981; contbr. articles to profl. jours. Home: 205 W Kent Rd Duluth MN 55812 Office: Univ Minn Duluth Library Duluth MN 55812

HART, ROSANA LESLEY, author, publisher; b. Washington, Sept. 24, 1942; d. Paul Myron Anthony Linebarger and Margaret (Snow) Roberts; m. Kelly Hart, Aug. 20, 1972; stepdaughter, Ajila Hart. BA, Stanford U., 1964; MLS, U. Calif., Berkeley, 1969. Registered hypnotherapist. Dep. probation officer Alameda County, Oakland, Calif., 1965-66; librarian Sonoma County Library, Santa Rosa, Calif., 1969-81; hypnotherapist Hartworks, Forestville, Calif. and Ashland, Oreg., 1980-84; llama breeder Juniper Ridge Ranch, Ashland, 1982—; author, pub. Juniper Ridge Press, Ashland, 1984—; workshop leader Continuing Edn. of So. Oreg. State Coll., Ashland, 1981—. Author: Living with Llamas, 1985. Named fellow Woodrow Wilson Found., 1964. Mem. Internat. Llama Assn., Llama Assn. N. Am. Democrat. Office: Juniper Ridge Hartworks PO Box 338 Ashland OR 97520

HART, ROSE, sales executive; b. Manchester, Lancashire, Eng., Apr. 13, 1940; came to U.S., 1965; d. Arthur and Ellen Hallewell; m. Jack Ernest Hart; children: William John, Matthew Ryan. Cert. in bus. mgmt., Bellevue (Wash.) Coll., 1980, cert. in mktg. mgmt., 1983; vocat. cert., Seattle Coll., 1981. Instr. cosmetology Vocat. Bellevue (Wash.) Sch., 1970-74; sales dispatcher Honeywell Comml. Co., Mercer Island, Wash., 1979-80; mem. sales staff ITT Cannon Electronics-Bellevue, Fountain Valley, Calif., 1980-81, 82-84; pres., owner, mgr. Hart Internat. Mktg. Exports, Bellevue, 1981—; tech. sales mgr. Fusecom Liberty Engring. Co., Redmond, Wash., 1985—. Mem. Nat. Assn. Female Execs., Lambda Chi. Methodist. Club: Sammamish Beach (Bellevue). Home: 2414 171st Ave SE Bellevue WA 98008 Office: Fusecom Liberty Engring 14864 NE 95th St Redmond WA 98052

HARTER, JEAN ANN, architect, graphic art consultant; b. Kansas City, Kans., Sept. 28, 1959; d. Donald Lee Harter and Beth Arland (Hobbs) Stanley. B.Interior Arch., Kans. State U., 1983. Designer Michael Fox, Inc., St. Louis, 1983-85; interior architect Pabst Design Group, St. Louis, 1985; archtl. designer Interior Space Inc., St. Louis, 1985—; cons. CL Designs, St. Louis, 1985—. Mem. Inst. Bus. Designers (profl. mem.), Nat. Assn. Female Execs. Democrat.

HARTH, ERICA, educator; b. N.Y.C. B.A., Barnard Coll., 1959; M.A., Columbia U., 1962, Ph.D. in French, 1968. Instr. French, NYU, 1964-66; from instr. to asst. prof. Columbia U., 1967-71; lectr. Tel-Aviv U., Israel, 1971-72; asst. prof. Brandeis U., 1972-75, assoc. prof. French, 1975-85, prof. French and comparative lit., 1985—. NEH fellow, 1970; Am. Council Learned Socs. fellow, 1978. Mem. MLA. Author: Cyrano de Bergerac and the Polemics of Modernity, 1970; Ideology and Culture in Seventeenth Century France, 1983; contbr. articles to profl. jours. Address: Brandeis U Dept Romance and Comparative Lit Waltham MA 02154

HARTIGAN, LYNDA ROSCOE, art museum curator; b. Scranton, Pa., Aug. 26, 1950; d. Francis William and Frances (Meek) Roscoe; m. Roger Thompson, June 2, 1984; 1 stepchild, Kirsten. BA cum laude, Bucknell U., 1972; MA in Art History, George Washington U., 1975. Curatorial asst. Nat. Mus. Am. Art, Washington, 1974-78, asst. curator, 1978-87, curator Joseph Cornell study ctr., 1978—, assoc. curator, 1987—; guest curator, lectr., juror, author for various exhibitions, orgns. and pubs. Guest author: Naives and Visionaries, 1974, Joseph Cornell, 1980, Sited Toward the Future: Proposals for Public Sculpture, 1984, Sharing Traditions, 1985. Bd. dirs. Community Arts Council, Arlington, Va., 1984-85, Spaces, Inc., Los Angeles, 1987—. NEH grantee, 1976-78, Smithsonian Inst. scholar, 1987—. Mem. Art Table, Inc., Coll. Art Assn. Democrat. Office: Nat Mus Am Art Washington DC 20560

HARTIGAN, MAUREEN FRANCES, communications director; b. Doylestown, Pa., Mar. 1, 1948; d. Gerald Jeremiah and Mary Doris (Awckland) H. BBA, North Adams State, 1975. With communications/mktg. Gen. Electric, Phila., 1966-80; advt. mgr. TRW, Inc., Cleve., 1980-86; dir. communications Volvo White Truck Corp., Greensboro, N.C., 1986-87, Volvo GM Heavy Truck Corp., Greensboro, 1987—. Contbr. articles to Corp. Advt., 1984-86. Mem. Am. Mktg. Assn., Bus./Profl. Advt. Assn. (internat. v.p. 1986-87, pres. Cleve. chpt. 1984-85). Republican. Roman Catholic. Home: 19 Ramsgate Ct Greensboro NC 27403 Office: Volvo GM Heavy Truck Corp PO Box 26115 Greensboro NC 27402-6115

HARTLEY, CARLA PAULINE, childbirth educator; b. Lonoke, Ark., June 5, 1953; d. Carlos F. and Carolyn (Douglass) Warner; m. Ray Hartley, June 11, 1971; children: Toby, Heather, Sam, Jessica. Grad. high sch., Lonoke. Childbirth educator Assn. Childbirth Home Internat., Spring, Tex., 1978-81; midwife Houston Homebirth, 1980-81; dir., owner Apprentice Acad., Conroe, Tex., 1981—; dir. Midwives Mailpak; developer seminars Creative Childbirth Edn., 1987—; organizer conf. Helping Hands Homebirth, 1988. Contbr. articles to profl. jours. Mem. Nat. Assn. Parents and Profl. Safe Alternatives Childbirth. Republican. Baptist. Home and office: 3805 Mosswood Dr Conroe TX 77302

HARTLEY, GRACE VAN TINE, foundation administrator; b. San Francisco, Aug. 24, 1916; d. Ellis Charles and Nadine (Allen) Van Tine; m. Frank Brooke Hartley (div. 1974); children: Shirley Hartley Hill, Linda Hartley Sims, Brooke Hartley Hudson, Jessie Hartley Brady, Frank. Student, De Anza Coll., 1975-77, Coll. of Marin, 1985-86. V.p. Barron & Hartley Builders, Alameda, Calif., 1946-72; pres. Aurley Apt. Houses, Sunnyvale, Calif., 1974-86; exec. dir. George Demont Otis Found., San Francisco, 1974—; pres. Western Arts Acad. Found., San Rafael, Calif., 1982—, Grace Group of Calif., Inc., Corte Madera, Calif. and San Rafael, 1983—. Author, producer: (audio visual) American Artists National Parks, 1976 (Bicentennial award 1976); exhibited in group shows at Golden Gate Collection, 1974 (S.W.A. award 1974), Otis Centennial, 1980 (C.H.C. award 1980). Pres. Rep. Women's Club, Alameda, 1960-62; active Rep. State Cen. Com., Alameda, 1964, Ronald Reagan Presdl. Task Force, Corte Madera, 1978-80. Recipient cert. Achievement Internat. Platform Assn., Washington, 1982, Presdl. Achievement award Rep. Party, Corte Madera, 1987. Presbyterian.

HARTLEY-LINSE, BONNIE JEAN, health nurse clinician, administrator, consultant; b. Chgo., July 26, 1923; d. Frank and Anna Kathleen (Koutecky) Kadlec; m. Robert William Hartley, June 23, 1949 (div. Feb. 1961); children: Robert Greig, Franklin James; m. Howard Albert Linse, June 10, 1978 (dec. Nov. 1985); stepchildren: Michael Howard, Janet Stokes. BS in Nursing, St. Xavier Coll., Chgo., 1945; cert. edn. Portland State Coll., 1965; MS in Nursing Edn., U. Oreg., 1972; cert. coll. health nurse practitioner program Brigham Young U., 1976. R.N., Oreg. Mem. faculty nursing St. Xavier Coll., 1945-47; head nurse U. Chgo. Clinics, 1947-48; nurse research newborn neurology U. Oreg. Med. Sch., Portland, summer 1961; coordinator dental assistant program, instr. biology Portland Pub. Schs., Oreg., 1965-67; health service clinician, adminstr. Clackamas Community Coll., Oregon City, Oreg., 1970-84; cons. Health Services Community Colls. of Oreg., 1972-84; pres. Coll. Health Nurses, State of Oreg., 1976-78. Mem. N.W. Oreg. Health Systems, Clackamas County Sub-Area Council, Oregon City, 1980-86. Recipient Recognition for Outstanding Service award Clackamas Community Coll., 1984; USPHS grantee, 1968. Mem. Am. Nurses Assn., Oreg. Nurses Assn. (Clackamas County unit 26), Pacific Coast Coll. Health Assn. (ann. conf. program coordinator 1980), Oreg. Coll. Health Dirs. Assn., Oreg. Health Decisions. Avocations: travel, piano, choral singing, swimming. Home: 18633 Roundtree Dr Oregon City OR 97045

HARTLINE, JESSIE COWAN, economist, educator; b. Phila.; d. Henry Shaw Sr. and Anne (McDougall) Cowan. BS in Econs., U. Md.; MBA in Fin., NYU; PhD in Econs., Rutgers U. Asst. prof. econs. Rutgers U., New Brunswick, N.J., 1968-72, assoc. dean acad. affairs, 1970-72, acting dean, 1972-73; program economist Joint Career Corps USAID, Panama, 1984-86; assoc. prof. econs. and fin. Rutgers U., 1972—; thesis examiner ABA Stonier Grad. Sch. of Banking, Washington. Office: Rutgers U Econs Dept N J Hall New Brunswick NJ 08903

HARTMAN, BRENDA ALANE, newspaper executive; b. Spokane, Wash., Oct. 27, 1952; d. Wilbert James and Letitia May (Taft) H.; m. Richard Allen Frishman, Sept. 24, 1983. Cert., U. Wash., 1987. Customer service rep. The Herald, Everett, Wash., 1972-76, dist. mgr., 1976-78, newsdealer supr., 1978-80, personnel mgr., 1981-85, dir. human resources, 1985—; bd. dirs. Ctr. Career Alternatives, Everett. Mem. vocat. adv. bd. Everett Community Coll., 1985-86. Mem. Am. Soc. Personnel Adminstrn., Am. Soc. Tng. and Devel., Newspaper Personnel Relations Assn., Pacific NW Personnel Mgmt. Assn. (sec. 1983, v.p. mem. 1984). Club: Cascade. Office: The Herald Grand & California Everett WA 98201

HARTMAN, CATHERINE RUDISILL, educator; b. Biscoe, N.C., Mar. 24, 1916; d. Jacob Andrew and Annie (Dietz) Rudisill; B.S., Appalachian State Tchrs. Coll., 1944; M.A., Columbia U., 1950, profl. diploma Tchrs. Coll., 1959; student U. London, Heidelberg U., summer 1953, NYU, summer 1954, UCLA, summer 1956; m. Harold R. Hartman, Dec. 26, 1962. Primary tchr. Park Grace Sch., Kings Mountain, N.C., 1936-39; elem., music tchr. Oakhurst Sch., Charlotte, N.C., 1939-44, Gary Sch., Tampa, Fla., 1945-47; elem. supr. schs. Gaston County Schs., Gastonia, N.C., 1947-55, dir. instrn., 1955-61, asst. supt. in charge instrn., 1961-63; assoc. prof. edn. William Paterson Coll. of N.J., Wayne, 1964-85, assoc. prof. emeritus, 1985—, chmn. gen. elem. program com. for curriculum revision, 1967-68, chmn. dept. secondary edn., 1972-78, chmn. dept. adminstrv., adult and secondary programs, 1979-85. Mem. Assn. Supervision and Curriculum Devel. of NEA (nat. dir. 1958-61), NCCJ (Carolinas regional dir. 1952-62), AAUW (dir. Charlotte 1953-55), Assn. Childhood Edn. (life, treas. N.C. 1955-57, adviser Gaston County br. 1955-63), Am. Assn. Sch. Adminstrs. (life), Kappa Delta Pi, Pi Lambda Theta. Presbyterian.

HARTMAN, DEBORAH STANTON, food company executive; b. Maringa, Parana, Brazil, May 10, 1956; came to U.S., 1960; d. Edward Earl and Dorothy Van Meter (Stanton) H. BS, U. Fla., 1978. Calf raiser and milker Twin Acres Farm, Brooksville, Fla., 1978-79; chemist Fla. Dept. Agriculture, White Springs, 1979-80; mgr. quality control Kraft Dairy Group, Tampa, Fla. and Memphis, 1980-82; mgr. loss control, prodn. coordinator Kraft Dairy Group, Jacksonville, Fla., 1982-83; fats and oils formulation technologist, cheese products customer rep. Kraft Indsl. Foods, Memphis, 1983-86; mgr. food tech. Kraft Food Ingerdients Corp., Anaheim, Calif., 1986—. Docent Memphis Zoo, 1982; vol. Memphis Hemophilia Soc., 1983. Recipient Fla. State Team award of Excellence, 1979. Mem. Inst. Food Technologists, Council for Agrl. Sci. and Tech., Am. Inst. Baking. Evang. Christian. Clubs: Jazz Heritage (Los Angeles); Nat. Geog. Soc. Office: Kraft Food Ingredients Corp 125 W Cerritos St Suite 2-125 Anaheim CA 92805

HARTMAN, NANCY LEE, physician; b. Philipsburg, Pa., July 29, 1951; d. Richard Lee and Ann Hartman; grad. Barbizon Sch. Modeling, 1970; A.A., Harcum Jr. Coll., 1969-71; B.A., Lycoming Coll., 1974; M.S., L.I. U., 1977; M.D., Am. U. of Caribbean in Plymouth, Montserrat, W.I., 1981. Med. technologist Lock Haven (Pa.) Hosp., 1971-72, Williamsport (Pa.) Hosp., 1972-73, Renovo (Pa.) Hosp., 1974; microbiologist and med. technologist Jersey Shore (Pa.) Hosp., 1974; microbiologist N.Y. Hosp. and Cornell Med. Center, N.Y.C., 1974-75, Drekter and Heisler Labs., N.Y.C., 1975, North Shore Labs., Inc., Syosset, N.Y., 1976-78. Lab. technician North Shore Hosp., Manhasset, N.Y., 1981-82, Nat. Health Labs. Inc., Bethpage, N.Y., 1982; resident internal medicine program Interfaith Med. Ctr., Bklyn., 1983-84; med. cons. Shapiro, Baines, Saasto & Shainwald, Mineola, N.Y., 1985-88; resident pathology program Lenox Hill Hosp., N.Y.C., 1986-87, clin. pathology Beth Israel Med. Ctr. N.Y.C. Author: The Pocket Handbook of Infectious Agents and their Treatments. Recipient Allied Health Professions Traineeship grant, 1975-77. Mem. AMA, Am. Women's Med. Assn., Am. Soc. Clin. Pathologists (registered med. technologist), Internat. Platform Assn. Home: PO Box 847 Glenwood Landing NY 11547

HARTMAN, PATRICIA KERN, paper scientist; b. Milw., Mar. 5, 1956; d. John Francis and Rosemary Jean (Kavanagh) Kern; m. David Lee Hartman, Aug. 25, 1978; 1 child, Ruth Anne. BS in Paper Sci., Western Mich. U., 1978. Engr. Westvaco Corp., Covington, Va., 1978-85; supr. Westvaco Corp., 1986-87, sr. engr., 1987—. Mem. TAPPI (vice-chmn. quality control com. 1988—), Am. Inst. Chem. Engrs., Paper Industry Mgmt. Assn., Nat. Assn. Female Execs., Am. Soc. Quality Control. Roman Catholic. Office: Westvaco Corp Riverside at Short St Covington VA 24426

HARTMAN, RUTH ANN, educator; b. Galion, Ohio, Aug. 18, 1938; d. Richard Lewis and Florence Evelyn (Ireland) Campbell; m. Richard Louis Hartman, Jan. 14, 1956; children: Jeffery Lee, Marsha Elaine, Jerry Steven. BS, Ohio State U., 1970; MEd, U. LaVerne, 1976, postgrad., 1985—; postgrad., U. Akron, 1977-85. cert. tchr., Ohio. Tchr. Willard (Ohio) City Schs., 1964-65; educator Mansfield (Ohio) City Schs., 1966—, home tutor, 1971-81, educator, 1977—; cons. Ohio State U., Ashland (Ohio) Coll., Mt. Vernon (Ohio) Nazarene Coll., 1976—. Co-author: Handbook for Student Teachers, 1983. Mem NEA, Ohio Edn. Assn., North Cen. Ohio Tchrs. Assn., Mansfield Edn. Assn. Republican. Methodist. Home: Rt 1 Plymouth OH 44865 Office: Mansfield City Schs 150 W 5th St Mansfield OH 44903

HARTMAN, SHARON ANN, medical technologist, marketing consultant; b. Salt Lake City, Apr. 6, 1951; d. Gerald and Patricia (Pearsall) H. B.S., Westminster Coll., Salt Lake City, 1975; M.A., Central Mich. U., 1982. Med. technologist St. Anthony Hosp., Denver, 1975-78, Children's Hosp., Denver, 1978—; instr. Colo. Assn. Continuing Med. Lab. Edn., Inc., Denver, 1980—; cons. and non-profit bd. devel. Tech. Asst. Ctr., Denver, 1981—. Co-contbr.: Marketability, 1982. Bd. dirs. Colo. Assn. Continuing Med. Lab. Edn., Denver, 1980-84, Breckenridge Outdoor Edn. Ctr., 1986—; mem. steering com. Profl. Reps. Denver, 1988—. Recipient Vol. Recognition award Tech. Assistant Ctr., Denver, 1982-85. Mem. Am. Soc. Clin. Pathologists, Denver Jr. League (v.p. edn. 1983-84, v.p. mktg. 1984-85, chmn. 1988 U.S. figure skating championships 1984-87, exec. v.p. internal affairs 1988-89). Episcopalian. Club: Colo. Mountain (Denver). Avocations: skiing, tennis, windsurfing, reading, cooking.

HARTMAN-GOLDSMITH, JOAN, art historian; b. Malden, Mass., June 3, 1933; d. Hyman and Ruth (Hadler) Lederman; m. Alan Hartman, Jan. 10, 1952 (div.); 1 dau., Hedy Hartman; m. 2d Robert Goldsmith, Aug. 12, 1976. Instr., coordinator, initiator art history program China Inst. in Am., N.Y.C., 1967-77; lectr. Sch. Continuing Edn. NYU, 1967-77; exec. officer Jewish Mus., N.Y.C., 1976-77, dir. pub. info., 1977-80; founder, dir. Inst. for Asian Studies, INc., N.Y.C., 1981—; lectr. Cooper-Hewitt Mus. of Design (Smithsonian Inst.), 1976, 83; lectr. museums Los Angeles, St. Louis, Pitts., Indpls., Buffalo, Rochester, N.Y., Toronto, Can., Denver Art Mus., Seattle Art Mus., Asian Art Mus. San Francisco; lectr. museums Oriental Ceramic Soc., Tokyo, Hong Kong; spl. lectr. tour Archaeol. Inst. Am., 1977; condr. seminars on Chinese jade Met. Mus. Art, N.Y.C., 1977, 81, 83; fellow in perpetuity, mem. vis. com. slide and photograph library Met. Mus. Art; trustee Indpls. Mus. Art; mem. art com. China House Gallery, N.Y.C.; program chmn. ann. conf. MAR-Assn. Asian Studies, Buchnel U., 1974. Am. corr.: Oriental Art mag., London, 1963—; contbr. feature articles to profl. publs.; guest curator, author catalogs; author: Chinese Jade of Five

Centuries, 1969, slide survey Introduction to Chinese Art, 1973, Chinese Jade, 1986; contbr. book revs. to learned jours. Nat. Endowment grantee, vis. specialist Buffalo Mus. Sci., 1972, Indpls. Mus. Art, 1971; reviewer NEH div. pub. programs, 1978—. Mem. Am. Oriental Soc., Assn. for Asian Studies (founding mem. Mid-Atlantic Region 1972, sec.-treas. 1973, adv. council 1974-75), Oriental Club of N.Y., Oriental Ceramic Soc. Office: Inst for Asian Studies PO Box 1603 FDR Station New York NY 10022

HARTMANN, DENICE LEE, mental health counselor; b. Manhasset, N.Y., Sept. 4, 1960; d. Hans-Rudolf and Lenora Kathryn (Fiducia) H. BA, St. Mary's Coll., 1982; MA, NYU, 1985. Career specialist Ctr. of Career Life and Planning, N.Y.C., 1984-85; primary counselor Mental Health Resource Ctr., Jacksonville, Fla., 1985-87, mental health supr., 1987-88; assessment specialist River Region Human Services-Jacksonville Recovery Ctr., 1988—. Mem. Nat. Assn. Female Execs., Am. Psychol. Assn. Republican. Roman Catholic. Home: 8433 Southside Blvd Apt 2302 Jacksonville FL 32216 Office: Jacksonville Recovery Ctr Detoxification Unit 920 Bridier St Jacksonville FL 32206

HARTMANN, RUTH ANNEMARIE, health care education specialist; b. Naumburg, Saale, German Dem. Republic, Mar. 16, 1936; came to U.S., 1957; d. Kurt and Anna (Jöesch) H.; m. Karl-Heinz Falatyk (div. 1983); children: Ulrich, Ute; m. Franklin J. Herzberg, 1987. Diploma in nursing, Medizinische Fachschule, Potsdam, Germany, 1956; BA in German summa cum laude, U. Wis., Milw., 1978, MLS, 1979; EdD in Adult Edn., Nova U., 1987. Info. specialist Fluid Power Assn., Milw., 1980-81; asst. librarian Miller Brewing Co., Milw., 1979-82; patient edn. librarian VA Med. Ctr., Milw., 1982-85, health care edn. specialist, 1986—. Contbr. articles to profl. jours. Bd. dirs. Concord Chamber Orch., Milw., 1982—; vol. Cancer Soc., Milwaukee, 1985—; vol. instr. Literacy Services Wis., 1987—. Mem. Am. Assn. Adult Continuing Edn., Spl. Library Assn. (treas. 1981-83), Library Community of Milw., U. Wis. Alumni Assn., Area Council of Health Educators (chairperson 1986—), Nat. Wellness Council, Soc. Pub. Health Edn. Inc., Am. Soc. Healthcare Edn. and Tng., Phi Kappa Phi. Office: Clement J Zablocki Va Med Ctr Milwaukee WI 53295

HARTNESS, SANDRA JEAN, venture capitalist; b. Jacksonville Fla., Aug. 19, 1944; d. Harold H. and Viola M. (House) H. A.B., Ga. So. Coll., 1969; post-grad., San Francisco State Coll., 1970-71. Researcher Savannah (Ga.) Planning Commn., 1969, Environ. Analysis Group, San Francisco, 1970-71; dir. Mission Inn, Riverside, Calif., 1971-75; developer, venture capitalist Hartness Assocs., Laguna Beach, Calif., 1976—; ptnr. Western Neuro-Care Ctr., Tustin Calif.; former edu. dir. Laguna Bd. Realtors, 1982. V.p., mem. bd. dirs. Evergreen Homes, Inc.; recipient numerous awards for community service. Democrat. Club: Soroptimists (Riverside, Calif.). Home: 32612 Adriatic Dr Laguna Niguel CA 92677 Office: Hartness Assocs 301 Forest Ave Laguna Beach CA 92651

HARTSOCK, JANE MARIE, nurse, educator; b. Rock Island, Ill., Nov. 19, 1948; d. George Vincent and Patricia Anna (Holland) Woeber; m. Donald Lee Hartsock, Jan. 16, 1971; children—Cara Elizabeth, David Vincent. B.S. in Nursing, Marycrest Coll., 1977; M.A., U. Iowa, 1982. Head nurse U.S. Naval Hosp., Great Lakes, Ill., 1970-71; staff nurse Moline Pub. Hosp. (Ill.), 1971-72, instr. Sch. Nursing, 1977-87; nurse bone marrow transplant unit, Univ. Minn., 1987—. Song leader Blue Grass Ch., 1977-87. Mem. Am. Nurses Assn., Nurse Educators Assn. (pres. 1984-85), AAUW. Democrat. Roman Catholic. Club: Pioneer (Blue Grass, Iowa, sec. 1983—). Contbr. chpt. in book. Home: 13427 Fernando Ave Apple Valley MN 55124

HARTSOCK, LINDA SUE, educational and management development executive; b. St. Joseph, Mo., Feb. 20, 1940; d. Waldo Emerson and Martha (Skelkop) H. B.S., Central Meth. Coll., Fayette, Mo., 1962; M.Ed., Pa. State U., 1965; Ed.D., 1971. Cert. assn. exec. Am. Soc. Assn. Execs. Tchr. Jr. High Sch. (North Kansas City (Mo.) Public Sch. System), 1962-63; sr. resident Pa. State U., 1963-64, asst. coordinator residence halls, 1964-65, residence hall coordinator, 1965-66, asst. dean women, 1966-68, asst. dean students, 1968-71; researcher Center for Study Higher Edn., 1971, dir. new student programs, 1971-72; nat. dir. program AAUW, 1972-76; exec. dir. Adult Edn. Assn., Washington, from 1976; now pres. Integrated Options, Inc., assn., edn. and mgmt. devel., Alexandria, Va.; designer tng. and ednl. programs for various orgns. and firms; speaker in field; adj. faculty George Washington U.; mem. Conf. Planning Com. on Adult Human Rights Edn., 1979; v.p. fin. Com. for Full Finding Edn., 1979; mem. first adv. panel convened future directions of a learning soc. project Coll. Entrance Exam. Bd., 1978, mem. planning group for course-by-newspaper exam. project, 1979; bd. dirs. Coalition Adult Edn. Orgns., 1976; mem. White House Conf. on Aging Planning, 1979; mem. nat. adv. bd. Nat. Center Higher Edn. Mgmt. System Project to Develop a Taxonomy for the Field of Adult Edn., 1978; bd. dirs. Nat. Joint Steering Com. on Community Edn., 1978; nat. adv. council on adult edn. Futures and Amendments Project, 1977; adv. Collection of Census Data, Nat. Center Ednl. Stats., 1977; mem. public policy com., program com. chmn. Adv. Council Nat. Orgns. to Corp. for Public Broadcasting, 1976; adv. devel. New Mediated Programs, Office Instructional Resources, Miami Dade Community Coll., 1976; mem. innovative awards com. Nat. Univ. Extension Assn., 1977; field reader U.S. Dept. Edn., 1981-83. Editorial bd.: Off to Coll. mag, 1972—; contbr. articles to profl. jours. Asst. sec. HEW Conf. Women's Issues; mem. White House Conf. Human Resources and World of Work. Recipient Disting. Alumni award Central Meth. Coll., 1978. Mem. AAUW, Am. Soc. Assn. Execs. (individual membership council 1979-81, edn. com. 1985-87), Washington Women's Forum (budget, program and exec. com. 1978-82), Am. Assn. Higher Edn., Alumni Soc. Coll. Edn. Pa. State U. (bd. dirs., Outstanding Alumni award), Pi Lambda Theta. Office: Integrated Options Inc PO Box 10140 Alexandria VA 22310

HARTTER, MARJORIE ANN, communications executive; b. Denver, Dec. 26, 1952; d. Leon Miller and Ellen Victoria (Pearson) Corning; m. Michael James Hartter, Nov. 26, 1976; 1 child, Carl John. Student San Mateo Coll., 1971, Palo Alto Bus. Sch., 1973. With sales dept. J & M Hobby Shop, San Carlos, Calif., 1970-71; exec. sec. Randtron Systems, Menlo Park, Calif., 1972-75; mktg. asst. Marriott Corp., Santa Clara, Calif., 1975-76; coordinator edn. WEMA, 1976-77; customer liasion Moran, Lanig & Duncan Advt., Palo Alto, 1977; program and communications dir. Harman Mgmt. Corp., Los Altos, Calif. 1977—, editor monthly mag., also corp. meeting planner for Ky. Fried Chicken stores in Calif., Colo., Utah, Wash. Mem. adv. bd. Meeting Planners Alert. Contbr. articles to profl. jours. Mem. Am. Soc. Assn. Execs., Meeting Planners Internat., Nat. Restaurant Assn., Nat. Assn. Female Execs., Am. Soc. Assn. Execs. Office: Harman Mgmt Corp 199 1st St Los Altos CA 94022

HARTWIG, CLEO, sculptor; b. Webberville, Mich., Oct. 20, 1911; d. Albert and Julia (Klunzinger) H.; m. Vincent Glinsky, 1951 (dec. Mar. 1975); 1 child, Albert. A.B., Western Mich. U., 1932, D.F.A. (hon.), 1973; student, Internat. Sch. Art, Europe, 1935. Tchr. pvt. schs. N.Y.C., 1935-42; instr. Cooper Union, 1945-46; sculpture instr. Montclair (N.J.) Art Mus., 1945-71. First one man show, 1943; one-man show Montclair (N.J.) Art Mus., 1971, Benbow Gallery, Newport, R.I., 1979, Sculpture Ctr., N.Y.C., 1981, Cuny, Plattsburg, 1986, Harmon-Meek Gallery, Naples, Fla., 1987; group exhbns. include Nat. Acad., Pa. Acad., Detroit Inst. Arts, Art Inst. Chgo., Met. Mus., Phila. Mus., Whitney Mus., Newark Mus., Phila. Art Alliance, Denver Art Mus., Boston Mus. Sci., N.Y. Zool. Soc., Nebr. Art Assn., State U. Iowa, U. Ark., Des Moines Art Center, So. Vt. Art Center, U. Conn., Smithsonian Instn. Natural History, USIA in Europe, Nat. Inst. Arts and Letters, U. Minn., Canton Art Inst., N.Y. Bot. Garden, others, traveling one-man show, Can., U.S.; represented in permanent collections, Brookgreen Gardens, S.C., Newark Mus., Detroit Inst. Arts, Pa. Acad., Montclair Art Mus., Mt. Holyoke Coll., Western Mich. U., Oswego (N.Y.) Univ., Nat. Mus. Am. Art, Smithsonian Instn., Chrysler Mus., Norfolk, Va., NAD, So. Vt. Art Center, Gen. Electric Co., Mus. Internat. Art, Sofia, Bulgaria, Nat. Mus. Women in Arts, Washington. Recipient Kamperman Haass prize Mich. Artists Anu., 1943; Anna Hyatt Huntington prize for sculpture, 1945; L. Reusch & Co. prize N.Y. Soc. Ceramic Arts, 1946; Nat. Assn. Women Artists 1st prize for sculpture, 1951; medal of honor, 1967; Audubon Artists prize for sculpture, 1952; Pres.'s award, 1972; Today's Art award and medal of merit, 1975; award mural and sculpture competition Munson-Williams-Proctor Inst., 1958, Feist Meml. prize, 1968, Salomone prize, 1972; Jeffrey Childs Willis Meml. prize, 1975, 82, 86; Amelia Peabody award, 1976; Silver medal Nat. Sculpture Soc., 1969; Ellin P. Speyer prize NAD, 1979; L. J. Liskin Purchase prize Nat. Sculpture Soc., 1980; Edith H. and Richmond Proskauer prize, 1984; Chaim Gross Found., 1986; Audubon Artists medal of Honor, 1987. Fellow Nat. Sculpture Soc. (C. Percival Dietsch prize 1976, Leonard Meiselman prize 1978); mem. Audubon Artists, Sculptors Guild, Nat. Assn. Women Artists, Nat. Acad. Design (academician). Home: 9 Patchin Pl New York NY 10011 Studio: 41 Union Sq W New York NY 10003

HARTZ, DEBORAH SOPHIA, editor, critic; b. Plainfield, N.J., Apr. 11, 1951; d. Sylvester and Margaret (Buschart) H.; m. Thomas McDonald July 24, 1971 (div. Dec. 1976). BA, U. Pa., 1973; MS, U. Wis., 1977. Asst. editor Whitney Communications Corp., N.Y.C., 1978-79; lifestyles editor News Dispatch, Michigan City, Ind., 1979-80; food editor, restaurant critic Daily Herald, Arlington Heights, Ill., 1980—; cons. newsletter Greenwich Conn., 1985-88; cookbook researcher Am. Restaurant Assn. Fine Dining, Chgo., 1987. Recipient Golden Carnation award, 1986. Mem. Les Dames d'Escoffier, Newspaper Food Editors and Writer's Assn. Office: Daily Herald 217 W Campbell Arlington Heights IL 60006

HARTZ, LUETTA BERTHA, insurance agent; b. Stevens Point, Wis., Sept. 29, 1947; d. Alfred Bernard Carl and Bertha Martha (Stauffer) Janz; student Madison (Wis.) Bus. Coll., 1965-66; m. James Patrick Hartz, Dec. 31, 1975. With Employers Ins. of Wausau (Wis.), 1966-68; casualty rater Sentry Ins. Co., Stevens Point, Wis., 1968-70, casualty supr., 1970-71, casualty trainor, 1971-72, customer service corr., 1972-74, bur. technician, 1974-75, customer service and acctg. mgr., Concord, Mass., 1975-79, personal lines property processing mgr., 1979-81, personal lines casualty processing mgr., 1981-83, comml. lines underwriting services mgr., 1983-85, comml. lines ops. mgr., 1985-87; agent Lewis P. Bither Ins. Agy., Inc., Tewksbury and Tyngsboro, Mass., 1988—; Campaign treas. Republican Party county clk. candidate, Portage County, Wis., 1972. Mem. U.S. Golf Assn. (asso.), Nat. Assn. Ins. Women, Mass. Assn. Ins. Women. (Middlesex chpt.). Lutheran. Clubs: Emblem (1st asst. marshall 1980-81, treas. 1981-83). (Concord, Mass.); Maynard Country (bd. govs. 1984-86) (Mass.). Home: 40 Drummer Rd Acton MA 01720

HARTZELL, IRENE JANOFSKY, psychologist; b. Los Angeles; Vor-Diplom, U. Munich, 1961. BA, U. Calif., Berkeley, 1963, MA, 1965; PhD, U. Oreg., 1970. Lic. psychologist, Calif., Oreg., Wash. Psychologist Lake Washington Sch. Dist., Kirkland, Wash., 1971-72; staff psychologist VA Hosp., Seattle, 1970-71, Long Beach, Calif., 1973-74; dir. parent edn. Children's Hosp., Orange, Calif., 1975-78; clin. psychologist Kaiser Permanente, Van Nuys, Calif., 1979—; clin. instr. dept. pediatrics U. Calif. Irvine Coll. Medicine, 1975-78. Author: The Study Skills Advantage, 1986; contbr. articles to profl. jours. Intern Oreg. Legislature, 1974-75. U. Oreg. fellow, 1969. Mem. Am. Psychol. Assn., Pi Lambda Theta. Office: Kaiser Permanente 13746 Victory Blvd Van Nuys CA 91401

HARTZLER, CHERYL ELAINE, financial planner; b. Kokomo, Ind., Feb. 16, 1945; d. Lowell Jay and Juanita Monell (Gasaway) Somsel; m. Edward W. Hartzler, June 11, 1967 (div. June 1981); children: Bryan Joseph, Andrea Lisabeth. BA, Ind. U., 1968; MBA, So. Ill. U., 1985; postgrad., Pacific Luth. U., 1982-83, Seattle Cen. Community Coll., 1979, S.Seattle Community Coll., 1980, Highline Community Coll., 1980-82, U. Washington, 1978, 83, Coll. for Fin. Planning, 1987—. Boutique mgr., jr. asst. buyer trainee Block's, Indpls., 1967-68; tchr. Indpls. Pub. Schs., 1968-71; with sales and inventory dept. Frederick & Nelson's Dept. Store, Seattle, 1971-72; co-owner video store Video World, Inc., Seattle, 1978-81; fin. planner and account exec. Investors Fin. Planning/Southmark Fin. Services, Bellevue, Wash., 1983—; pres. C.E. Hartzler and Assocs., 1986—; instr. continuing edn. N. Seattle Community Coll., 1985—; coordinated reorgn. of pvt. med. practice, Seattle, 1976; registered rep. Southmark Fin. Services. Mem. Seattle Repertory Orgn., 1973—; bd. dirs. Seattle Opera Guild, 1978-80; cultural chmn. Highline Sch. Dist. Parent Teachers Students Assn., Seattle, 1978-83. Mem. Internat. Assn. Fin. Planners, Wash. Women United, Women's Bus. Exchange, Assn. MBA Execs., Nat. Assn. for Female Execs., Am. Soc. Women Accts., Internat. Platform Assn., Alpha Chi Omega Alumni. Clubs: Olympic View Swim (Seattle); Leads (mgmt. team South Seattle chpt.). Home: 718 SW 199th Pl Seattle WA 98166 Office: Investors Fin Planning/ Southmark 1300 114th Ave SE Suite 232 Bellevue WA 98004

HARVARD, BEVERLY JOYCE BAILEY, deputy chief of police; b. Macon, Ga., Dec. 22, 1950; d. Arcelious and Irene (Perkins) Bailey; m. Jimmy C. Harvard, 1972. BA, Morris Brown Coll., 1972; MS, Ga. State U., 1980. Cert. FBI Nat. Acad. Police officer Police Bur. City of Atlanta, crime analysis officer, exec. protection officer, dep. chief police; spl. asst. to commr. Dept. Pub. Safety City of Atlanta, dir. pub. affairs. Mem. Leadership Atlanta, 1983—; adv. bd. dirs. Big Brothers/Big Sisters, 1986—, Atlanta Victim/Witness Assistance Program, 1985—. Named Outstanding Atlantan, 1983, Alumna Yr., Morris Brown Coll., 1985, Bronze Woman Yr., Iota Phi Lambda, 1986, Woman Achiever Atlanta YWCA; recipient Trailblazer award for Law Enforcement City of Atlanta. Mem. Internat. Assn. Chiefs Police (tng. com. Ga. chpt.), Nat. Orgn. Black Law Enforcement (chmn. program), Bus. System Planning Team, Ga. State U. Alumni Assn. (bd. dirs. Atlanta chpt.), Delta Sigma Theta (parliamentarian). Office: Atlanta Bur Police Services 175 Decatur St SE Atlanta GA 30335

HARVARD, MAXINE SARI, public relations executive; b. Rochester, N.Y., Apr. 20, 1935; d. Louis M. and Edith (Ershler) Siller; 1 child, David A. Peckman. BA, Ithaca Coll., 1957; MA in Art History, Kean Coll., 1962. Dir. pub. relations Essex County Coll., Newark, 1976-80; dir. editorial services Blue Cross of N.J., Newark, 1980-82; v.p. Urban Devel. Resources, Newark, 1982-86; owner Maxine S. Harvard Unltd., Cranford, N.J., 1987—. Office: Exec Suite 2000 6 Commerce Dr Cranford NJ 07016

HARVARD, PATRICIA ANN, nurse, educator; b. Macone, Ga., Feb. 16, 1950; d. John L. and Evelyn (Gillard) Manson. BS in Nursing, Carlow Coll., 1972; MA in Edn., San Diego State U., 1977; EdD, U. San Diego, 1988. RN, Calif. Nurse adminstr. Montifore Hosp., Pitts., 1971-73; clin. coordinator Rio Hondo Hosp., Downey, Calif., 1973-74, 129th Evacuation Hosp., Balboa Naval Hosp., San Diego, 1979—; nursing instr. Vets. Adminstrn. Med. Ctr., La Jolla, Calif., 1974—; presenter in field, Los Angeles, 1984; vis. prof. U. Brit. Columbia, 1982; workshop leader San Diego Community Hosps., 1979-83. Author: How to Prepare for the R.N. State Board Licensure, 1985. Served to maj. USAR, 1979—. Mem. San Diego Black Nurses Assn. (pres. 1979-82), San Diego and Imperial Counties Inservice Edn. Council (pres. 1978-80), Sigma Theta Tau. Home: 1445 Hunsaker St Oceanside CA 92054 Office: Am Edwards Labs 17221 Red Hill Ave Irvine CA 92711-1150

HARVEY, BARBARA, lawyer, legal educator; b. N.Y.C., Feb. 19, 1946; d. William and Sylvia (Abramson) Masin. Student Antioch Coll., 1962-65; B.A., Wayne State U., 1968, J.D., 1975. Bar: Mich., 1975. Law clk. to C.W. Joiner, U.S. dist. judge, Detroit, 1975-77; assoc. firm Barris, Sott, Denn & Driker, Detroit, 1977-79; asst. prof. Law Sch., Wayne State U., Detroit, 1979-82, adj. prof., 1982—; legal dir. ACLU of Mich., Detroit, 1983-86; practice labor law, Detroit, 1982—; mem. nat. adv. bd. Assn. for Union Democracy, N.Y.C., 1981—; mem. lawyers adv. com. Teamsters Rank and File Def. and Edn. Fund, Detroit, 1981-83. Article and book rev. editor Wayne Law Rev., 1975; contbr. articles to publs. Dir. Met. Detroit br. ACLU of Mich., 1977—, mem. lawyers com., 1979—, exec. sec., 1981-85, v.p., 1985-88; hearing referee Mich. Civil Rights Commn., Lansing and Detroit, 1983—. Clin. program grantee U.S. Dept. Edn., 1980, 81; editor's scholar Wayne Law Sch., 1974-75; Law Sch. Fund scholar, 1973-75. Mem. ABA, State Bar Mich., Detroit Bar Assn., Assn. Trial Lawyers, Am., Mich. Trial Lawyers Assn. Office: 925 Ford Bldg Detroit MI 48226

HARVEY, BONNIE NEWCOME, chemistry and microbiology educator; b. Grafton, W.Va., Nov. 9, 1913; d. John Allen and Sallie (Marquess) Newcome; m. Wilson Ward Harvey, Oct. 24, 1941; children—John Calvin, Sarah Susan Harvey Haggerty. A.B., Fairmont State U., 1935; postgrad. W.Va. U., 1936-37, 68-69. Life teaching cert. in scis. Tchr. chemistry, physics, biology and history Flemington High Sch. (W.Va.), 1936-41; tchr. Am. history West Fairmont High Sch., Fairmont, W.Va., 1942-43; tchr. gen. sci. Benjamin Franklin High Sch., Parkersburg, W.Va., 1954-56; tchr. gen. sci. and geography Magnolia High Sch., New Martinsville, W.Va., 1958-61; instr. microbiology, clin. tech. biology and psychology, Potomac State Coll. of W.Va. U., Morgantown, 1966-76, counselor Potomac State Coll. Earth Week, 1969-84, mem. vis. com., 1979—. Counselor Tri High Y Girls, YMCA, New Martinsville, 1958-61; mem. W.Va. Nature Conservancy, 1966-84; Bible class tchr. 1st United Methodist Ch., Keyser, W.Va., 1961-84; treas. Ladies Oriental Shrine Club, Children's Hosps., 1980-84; sec. Romney dist. United Meth. Women, 1961-65, 79-83, group membership chmn.; historian Burlington Home for Children and Youth Aux., 1980-84; sci. fair judge Mineral County Bd. Edn., Keyser, 1967-84. Recipient counselor award Tri High Y, YMCA, 1961. Mem. West August Hist. Soc., W.Va. Acad. Sci. (life), W.Va. Edn. Assn., Mineral County Hist. Soc. (Order of Crozet 1978, mus. curator), DAR (regent Potomac Valley 1977-83), Alpha Delta Kappa (sec., historian 1974-84). Republican. Club: Mineral County. Lodge: Order Eastern Star.

HARVEY, DORIS CANNON, trustee, citrus grower; b. Lake Wales, Fla., Mar. 13, 1930; d. Charles Bertal and Sarah (Holbrook) Cannon; m. O.J. Harvey (dec.); children: Barbara Kay, Nancy Jean. Pres. O.J. Harvey Inc., Tampa; v.p. Elfers Citrus Growers Assn., Palm Harbor, Fla.; personal rep. Estate of O.J. Harvey, Tampa; trustee O.J. Harvey Trust, Tampa; trustee Elfers Citrus Liquidating Trust, Palm Harbor. Bd. dirs. Tampa Home Assn., 1982-84; trustee Doris C. Harvey Marital Trust, Tampa, 1988. Democrat. Methodist. Clubs: Centre, Tampa Woman's, Tampa Yacht and Country, Sword of Hope, Rose Circle, Hearts of Gold. Home and Office: 1114 Culbreath Isles Dr Tampa FL 33629

HARVEY, ELAINE LOUISE, artist, educator; b. Riverside, Calif., Mar. 1, 1936; d. Edgar Arthur and Emma Louise (Shull) Siervogel; m. Stuart Herbert Harvey, June 16, 1957; children: Kathleen Robin, Laurel Lynn, Mark Stuart. BA with highest honors, with distinction, San Diego State U., 1957. Cert. gen. elem. tchr., Calif. Tchr. Cajon Valley Schs., El Cajon, Calif., 1957, 58; free-lance artist El Cajon, 1975—; juror various art exhbns., Calif., 1983—; lectr., 1984—; tchr. painting seminars, 1987—. Editor: Palette to Palate, 1986; contbr. The Artists Mag., 1987. Trustee San Diego Mus. Art, 1985, 86; leader El Cajon council Girl Scouts of U.S., 1968; vol. art tchr., San Diego area pub. schs., 1973-76. Recipient Merit award La. Watercolor Soc., 1984, Arches Canson Rives award Midwest Watercolor Soc./Tweed Mus., Greenbay, Wis., 1984, Winsor Newton award Midwest Watercolor Soc./Neville Mus., Duluth, Minn., 1985; McKinnon award Am. Watercolor Soc. 1985, Creative Connection award Rocky Mountain Nat. Exhibition 1986, 1st Juror's award San Diego Internat. Watercolor Exhibition 1986. Mem. Nat. Watercolor Soc. (bd. dirs. 1987, 88), Watercolor West (bd. dirs. 1986, 87, 88), West Coast Watercolor Soc., San Diego Watercolor Soc. (pres., 1979, 80, exhbns. chmn. 1980, 81, Silver Recognition award 1986), San Diego Mus. Art Artist's Guild (pres. 1985, 86, bd. dirs. 1986-87), Western Fedn. Watercolor Socs. (del. 1983—). Club: Grossmont Garden (La Mesa, Calif.) (Elson Trophy 1977, 79). Home and Studio: 1602 Sunburst Dr El Cajon CA 92021

HARVEY, JUDY VONETTE, English language educator; b. Troy, Ohio, Mar. 20, 1954; d. Von E. Jones and Patty L. (Hunt) Thompson; m. Thomas J. Harvey, May 28, 1983. BA, Ga. State U., 1976, M of Arts in Teaching, 1978. Cert. tchr., Ohio. Writer, arts editor Troy Daily News, 1978-80; editor Free Ride Mag., Tipp City, Ohio, 1981-83; instr. Edison State Coll., Piqua, Ohio, 1983-85, Sinclair Community Coll., Dayton, Ohio, 1983-85, Century Coll., Ironton, Ohio, 1985-87; asst. dean Rutledge Coll., Ironton, 1987—. Author poetry. Mem. Nat. Assn. Tchrs. English, Humane Soc. U.S. Republican. Office: Rutledge Coll 3d St Ironton OH 45638

HARVEY, KATHERINE ABLER, civic worker; b. Chgo., May 17, 1946; d. Julius and Elizabeth (Engelman) Abler; student La Sorbonne, Paris, 1965-66; A.A.S., Bennett Coll., 1968; m. Julian Whitcomb Harvey, Sept. 7, 1974. Asst. librarian McDermott, Will & Emery, Chgo., 1969-70; librarian Chapman & Cutler, Chgo., 1970-73, Coudert Freres, Paris, 1973-74; adviser, organizer library Lincoln Park Zool. Soc. and Zoo, Chgo., 1977-79, mem. soc.'s women's bd., 1976—, chmn. library com., 1977-79, sec., 1979-81, mem. exec. com., 1977-81 ; mem. jr. bd. Alliance Francaise de Chgo., 1970-76, treas., mem. exec. com., 1971-73, 75-76, mem. women's bd., 1977-80; mem. Fred Harvey Fine Arts Found., 1976-78; hon. life mem. Chgo. Symphony Soc., 1975—; mem. Phillips Acad. Alumni Council, Andover, Mass., 1977-81, mem. acad.'s bicentennial celebration com. class celebration leader, 1978, co-chmn. for Chgo. acad.'s bicentennial campaign, 1977-79, mem. student affairs and admissions com., 1980-81; mem. aux. bd. Art Inst. Chgo., 1978-88; mem. Know Your Chgo. com. U. Chgo. Extension, 1981-84; mem. guild Chgo. Hist. Soc., 1978—; mem. women's bd. Lyric Opera Chgo., 1979—, chmn. edn. com., 1980, mem. exec. com., 1980-84, 88—, treas. women's bd., 1983-84, 1st v.p. 1988—; mem. women's bd. Northwestern Meml. Hosp., 1979—, treas., chmn. fin. com., 1981-84, mem. exec. com., 1981—; bd. dirs. Found. Art Scholarships, 1982-83; bd. dirs. Glen Ellyn (Ill.) Children's Chorus, 1983—, founding chmn. pres.'s com., 1983; mem. women's bd. Chgo. City Ballet, 1983-84; trustee Chgo. Acad. Scis., 1986-88; bd. dirs. Grant Park Concert Soc., 1986—; adv. council med. program for performing artists Northwestern Meml. Hosp., 1986—; pres., bd. dirs. William Ferris Chorale, 1988—. Mem. Antiquarian Soc. of Art Inst. Chgo. (life); bd. dirs. Grant Park Concerts Soc., 1986—. Clubs: Arts of Chgo., Friday (corr. sec. 1981-83), Casino (gov. 1982-88, sec. 1984-85, 88—, 1st v.p. 1985-86, 2d v.p. 1986-87), Cliff Dwellers. Home: 1209 N Astor St Chicago IL 60610

HARVEY, KIM, small business owner; b. Indpls., Feb. 18, 1955; d. Jack Elsworth and Joyce Ann (Renfro) Taylor. BS in Home Econs., Ind. U., 1978. Designer Jefferson House Interiors, Ft. Wayne, Ind., 1979, Office Interiors, Inc., Ft. Wayne, 1979-81; adminstrn. asst. Internat. Bus. Coll., Ft. Wayne, 1981-83; dir. sales Sheraton Hotel, Ft. Wayne, 1983-85; owner Le Ritz Modeling & Talent Agy., Inc., Ft. Wayne, 1985—; ptnr. Bayberry Basket Co., Zionsville, Ind., 1986—. Big sister Big Bros. Big Sisters of Am., Ft. Wayne, 1980-82; vol. United Way, Ft. Wayne, 1980, 86; vol. ARC, Ft. Wayne, 1986—; mem. Better Bus. Bur. Mem. Advt. Assn. Ft. Wayne, Ft. Wayne C. of C. Republican. Office: Le Ritz Modeling & Talent Agy 5675 Saint Joe Rd Fort Wayne IN 46835

HARVEY, LYNDA MARY, oil company auditor; b. Pitts., May 30, 1954; m. Robert D. Harvey, Jr.; children: Robert III, Kandace. BS in Acctg., Pa. State U., 1976; postgrad. in bus., Clarion U., 1986—. Cert. internal auditor, cert. info. systems auditor. Staff auditor Quaker State Oil, Oil City, Pa., 1976-79, EDP auditor, 1979-84, sr. EDP auditor, 1984-88, mktg. research analyst, 1988—; instr. Clarion Univ. Pa., 1985—. Mem. Inst. Internal Auditors (newsletter com. 1987—), EDP Auditors Assn. (coll. relations com. 1986-87). Office: Quaker State Corp 255 Elm St Oil City PA 16301

HARVEY, LYNNE COOPER, broadcasting executive, civic worker; b. nr. St. Louis; d. William A. and Mattie (Kehr) Cooper; A.B., Washington U., St. Louis, 1939, M.A., 1940; m. Paul Harvey, June 4, 1940; 1 son, Paul Harvey Aurandt. Broadcaster ednl. program KXOK, St. Louis, 1940; broadcaster-writer women's news WAC Variety Show, Fort Custer, Mich., 1941-43; gen. mgr. Paul Harvey News, ABC, 1944—; pres. Paulynne Prodns., Ltd., Chgo., 1968—, exec. producer Paul Harvey Comments, 1968—; editor, compiler The Rest of the Story. Pres. woman's bd. Mental Health Assn. Greater Chgo., 1967-71, v.p. bd. dirs., 1966—; pres. woman's aux. Infant Welfare Soc. Chgo., 1969-71, bd. dirs., 1969—; mem. Salvation Army Woman's Adv. Bd., 1967; reception chmn. Community Lectures; Woman's com. Chgo. Symphony, 1972—; pres. Mothers Council, River Forest, 1961-62; charter bd. mem. Gottlieb Meml. Hosp., Melrose Park, Ill.; mem. adv. bd. Nat. Christian Heritage Found., 1964—; mem. USO woman's bd., 1983, woman's bd. Ravinia Festival, 1972—; trustee John Brown U., 1980—; bd. dirs. Mus. Broadcast Communications, 1987—. Recipient Little Spirit of Love award, 1987, Religious Heritage of Am. award, 1974. Mem. Phi Beta Kappa, Kappa Delta Pi, Phi Sigma Iota, Eta Sigma Phi. Clubs: Chicago Golf, Woman's Athletic, Nineteenth Century Woman's, Press (Chgo.); Oak Park Country. Home: 1035 Park Ave River Forest IL 60305 Office: Box 77 River Forest IL 60305

HARVEY, MADELINE JEAN, public relations director, assistant hospital administrator; b. Phila., Nov. 2,; d. Arthur and Eva (Palermo) Viola; m.

James Earl Harvey, Apr. 1; children: Arthur J., Alexis J. B.A., in Languages, U. Pa., 1955; student journalism Stockton Coll., 1976, pub. speaking, Atlantic Community coll., 1979. Asst. to med. dir. Phila. Gen. Hosp., 1956-60; dir. pub. relations and devel., asst. to adminstr. Children's Seashore House, Atlantic City, 1968-87 . Bd. mem. Atlantic County Homemakers, Atlantic Performing Arts Ctr., Atlantic City, 1980-83; hostess Miss Am. Hostess com., Atlantic City, 1978—; 1st v.p. Atlantic City Womens Chamber. Recipient Certification award Nat. Assn. Hosp. Devel., 1980, First prize, 1982; Named to People to Watch Atlantic City Mag., 1983. Mem. Am. Soc. Mktg. and Pub. Relations, Nat. Soc. Fund Raising Execs., N.J. Soc. Hosp. Pub. Relations, Nat. Soc. Hosp. Devel., Bus. and Profl. Women's Club (pres. 1980-81), Zonta Club Internat. (pres. 1978-80, pres., chmn. conf. 1977-78, nominated districtor dictor 1982), Greater Atlantic City C. of C. (pub. relations dir. 1978-80, dir. 1980-84), Atlantic City Women's C. of C. (1st v.p. 1985—). Republican. Roman Catholic. Home: 2701 Brigantine Ave Brigantine NJ 08203

HARVEY, MARY LOU, educator; b. Tucson; m. David S. Harvey, Oct. 30, 1945; chidren: Lee Allen, Kent Lawrence. BA in Social Work, Mills Coll., 1945; postgrad., U. Ariz., 1960, MEd in Spl. Edn., 1970, MEd in Adminstrn., 1975. Tchr. Corbett Sch. Tucson Unified Sch. Dist., 1960-71, helping tchr., 1971-74, tchr. learning disabilities Ford Sch., 1974-75, prin. Menlo Park Sch., 1975-80, prin. Blenman Elem. Sch., 1980—; mem. cabinet, supt. Tucson Unified Sch. Dist. 1 Regional, 1986—. Mem. Nat. Assn. Elem. Sch. Prins. (officer, del. 1983-84), Ariz. Sch. Adminstrs. (bd. dirs. 1980—, pres. elem. div. 1983-84), Tucson Adminstrs. Inc. (sec. 1982-83, pres. 1983-85), Alpha Delta Kappa, Phi Kappa Phi. Democrat. Office: Blenman Elem Sch 1695 N Country Club Rd Tucson AZ 85716

HARVEY, MICHELLE MAUTHE, college administrator; b. Bethesda, Md., Dec. 29, 1954; d. Benjamin Camille and Lelia Anne (Webre) Mauthe; m. Don Warren Harvey, Mar. 31, 1979; 1 child: Elise Brandner. BS in Forestry, U. South, 1976; postgrad., Duke U., 1987—. Forester Internat. Paper Co. Inc., Natchez and Brandon, Miss., 1976-80; framer, mgr. Frame Workshop, Lexington, Ky., 1981-83; mgr., dir. Country Stitchery Frameshop, Raleigh, N.C., 1984; dir. corp. and found. relations, placement and internship Sch. Forestry & Environ. Studies Duke U., Durham, N.C., 1984—. Bd. dirs. Wake County Literacy Council, Raleigh, 1984—, Soc. Preservation Hist. Oakwood, Raleigh, 1983-85, Newcomers Club, Raleigh, 1983-84; chair Historic Oakwood City Lights Ball, 1988; fundraiser N.C. Symphony, Raleigh, 1985-86; mem. Humane Assn. Greater Louisville (devel. dir. 1980). Mem. Soc. Am. Foresters (mem. nat. com. on women and minorities 1985-88, N.C. communications chair 1988—), N.C. Placement Assn., Assn. Internat Practical Tng., (regional adv. com. 1985—), So. Coll. Placement Assn., Assn. Women Sci., Nat. Soc. Internships and Experiential Edn. Democrat. Roman Catholic. Club: Oakwood Garden (Raleigh). Office: Duke U Sch Forestry & Environ Studies Durham NC 27706

HARVEY, PATRICIA TRACY, health care executive; b. San Diego, Nov. 29, 1961; d. Eugene Robert and Donna (Richardson) Sullivan; m. Scott Rayman Harvey, Aug. 13, 1983; children: Brittany Anne, Lindsay Nicole. Student, Purdue U., 1979-80, Toledo Community Coll., 1980-82. Cen. supply technician Med. Coll. Ohio, Toledo, 1980-82, nursing asst., 1982-83, registered nurse, 1983-85; utilization review specialist United Health Care, Balt., 1985-87, dir. quality assurance, 1987—. Mem. Am. Assn. Critical Care Nurses, Cert. Critical Care Nurses, Nat. Assn. Female Execs. Republican. Roman Catholic. Home: 17 Sylvanoak Way Baltimore MD 21236

HARVEY, RHOBA JANE NEBLETT, clinical social worker, educator; b. Charlotte, Tenn., Nov. 7, 1928; d. John B. and Augusta Elizabeth (Tippit) Neblett; B.S., U. Tenn., 1952, M.S.S.W., 1968; postgrad. U. Chgo., 1957, U. St. Andrews (Scotland), 1978; 1 dau., Elizabeth Lee. Child welfare worker Tenn. Dept. Pub. Welfare, 1954-59, sr. child welfare worker, Gibson County, 1961-66, field supr., Shelby County, 1966-69; asst. prof. child devel. U. Tenn. Center for Health Scis., Memphis, 1969-82, developer, dir. residential tng. program, 1970-76, clin. social worker, 1969—; supr. psychiat. social work Sequoyah Ctr., Memphis, 1981-86; pvt. practice, 1966—. Diplomate clin. social work; lic. nursing home adminstr., Tenn. Mem. Nat. Assn. Social Workers, Acad. Clin. Social Workers, Am. Assn. on Mental Deficiency, Nashville Psychotherapy Inst., DAR, Zeta Tau Alpha. Presbyterian. Home: Box 112 St Paul Rd Charlotte TN 37036

HARVEY, VANDA LEE, title company financial executive; b. Marietta, Okla., May 24, 1942; d. George Van and Anna Lee (Sanders) Burkhart; m. Jerry Don Harvey, Oct. 16, 1964 (div. 1970); children—Jeffrey Lynn, Kimberly Ann. Student Odessa Jr. Coll., 1960-61, So. Meth. U., 1975, Am. Mgmt. Assn. courses, 1980; student, Brookhaven Coll., 1987—. Statistician, interviewer Tex. Employment Commn., Vernon, 1963-69; office and acctg. mgr. Metro Materials Mktg., Plano, Tex., 1969-75; staff acct. Sanger Harris, Dallas, 1976; office and acctg. mgr. Austin Shoes-Greenco Shoes, Dallas, 1976-79; asst. treas., corp. controller Hexter Fair Title Co., Dallas, 1979—, others; dir., fin. adv. Witts & Wilson, Attys., Dallas, 1980-86; controller Lawyers Title Agy. of Denton, Tex., 1980—; mem. state com. trust fund acctg., Tex. State Bd. Ins.; Speaker univ., high sch. Editor, collaborator: Parity (D.A. Witts), 1979, Theft (D.A. Witts), 1982. Club: Plaza Athletic (gov.). Office: Hexter Fair Title Co 1307 Pacific Ave Dallas TX 75202

HARVEY, V(ELMA) FAYE, health care facility administrator; b. Kerens, Tex., Mar. 30; d. Coy Roberson and Emma (Givens) Wilson; m. Robert Whitted, Feb. 20, 1948 (div. 1955); children: Crosby, Dwight, Debra, Randolph. Student, Thornton Bus. Coll., Fort Worth, 1947, St. Joseph Sch. Nursing, Fort Worth, 1948, Coll. San Mateo (Calif.), 1957. Lic. vocat. nurse, Calif.; RN, Tex. Pvt. duty nurse Menlo Park, Calif.; charge nurse Whitcombs Convalescent Hosp., Menlo Park; staff nurse Sequoia Hosp., Redwood City, Calif., VA Hosp., Palo Alto, Calif.; adminstr. Harvey Residential Care Home for Veterans, Menlo Park, 1979—, also dir. Hon. citizen Boys Town, Lincoln, Neb.; bd. dirs. Neighborhood Housing Service, Menlo Park; mem. City of Menlo Park Tenant/Landlord Rental Bd., 1987—. Nominated 3rd annual Women's Hall of Fame of San Mateo County for Disting. Women, 1987. Mem. Nat. Assn. Female Execs., San Mateo County Adv. Council on Women. Democrat. Baptist. Club: Bay Area Women's. Lodge: Order of Eastern Star (sec., worthy matron), Ancient Arabic Order of DTRs of Sphinx (state dep., Most Worthy Grand Matron), Rose-of-Seven-Seals (grand recorder, Perfect Excellent Rose, Most Excellent Rose). Office: Harvey Residential Care Home For Veterans 1330 Chilco St Menlo Park CA 94025

HARVEY, VIRGINIA GRACE, oilwell service company executive; b. Rockwood, Tenn., Sept. 27, 1920; d. Rufus Norman and Georgia Ann (Long) Erwin; m. Thomas Dexter Harvey, July 14, 1943 (dec. Dec. 1979); children—Georgia Ann, Pamela Lee, Michelle Virginia. Student U. Tenn., 1939. Sec.-treas. Pacific Airlines, Burbank, Calif., 1945-47; v.p. Thomas D. Harvey Co., Dallas, 1960-75; sec. Erwin Oil Water Service Co., Ft. Worth, 1980—. Pres., Cen. Tex. Ladies Golf Assn., Dallas, 1960, Dallas Womens Golf Assn., 1962, Northwood Womens Golf Assn., 1966; pres., tournament dir. Civitan Womens Golf Classic, Dallas, 1963, 66; chmn. ladies com. Byron Nelson Classic, Dallas, 1968-72; pres., chmn. Kidney Found. Tex., 1972; bd. dirs. ARC; precinct chmn. Dallas Republican Com., 1968. Recipient Golden award Exchange Club, Dallas, Sport award City of Dallas, 1966; Golf award Salesmanship Club, Dallas, 1976; charity award Civitan Club, Dallas, 1966. Home: 6222 Waggoner Dr Dallas TX 75230

HARVIE, PEGGY ANN, personnel administrator; b. Middletown, Ohio, Oct. 29, 1936. BA in Sociology, U. Ill., 1972; MA in Human Resource Leadership, Azusa Pacific U., 1988. Mgr. personnel Edward C. Minas Co., Hammond, Ind., 1979-81, Wycliffe Bible Translators, Huntington Beach (Calif.) and Papua New Guinea, 1981-84, Glasrock Home Health Care, Tustin, Calif., 1985-86, Bristol Park Med. Group, Costa Mesa, Calif., 1987—. Mem. Am. Soc. Personnel Adminstrs., Personnel and Indsl. Relations Assn. Office: Bristol Park Med Group 3160 Red Hill Costa Mesa CA 92626

HARVITT, ADRIANNE STANLEY, lawyer; b. Chgo., May 15, 1954; d. Stanley and Maryln (Loye) H.; m. Donald Martin Heinrich, Aug. 27, 1977; 1 child, Patrick Loye Heinrich. AB, U. Chgo., 1975, MBA, 1976; JD with honors, Ill. Inst. Tech./Kent Coll. Law, 1980. Bar: Ill. 1980, U.S. Dist. Ct. (no. dist.) Ill. 1983, U.S. Ct. Appeals (7th cir.) 1985, (9th cir.) 1988, U.S. Supreme Ct. 1985. Fin. analyst Bell & Howell Co., Chgo., 1976-77; staff atty. U.S. Commodity Futures Trading Commn., Chgo., 1980-83; assoc. Hannafan & Handler, Chgo., 1983-85; ptnr. Harvitt & Gekas, Ltd., Chgo., 1985—. Mem. ABA, Ill. Bar Assn. (hon. mention received for article 1982), Chgo. Bar Assn., U. Chgo. Women's Bus. Group, Art Inst. Chgo. Office: Harvitt & Gekas Ltd 135 S LaSalle St #1254 Chicago IL 60603

HARWOOD, ELEANOR CASH, librarian; b. Buckfield, Me., May 29, 1921; d. Leon Eugene and Ruth (Chick) Cash; B.A., Am. Internat. Coll., 1943; B.S., New Haven State Tchrs. Coll., 1955; m. Burton H. Harwood, Jr., June 21, 1944 (div. 1953); children—Ruth (Mrs. William R. Cline), Eleanor, James Burton. Librarian, Rathbun Meml. Library, East Haddam, Conn., 1955-56; asst. librarian Kent (Conn.) Sch., 1956-63; cons. to Chester (Conn.) Pub. Library, 1965-71. Served from ensign to lt. (j.g.) USNR, 1944-46. Mem. Am., Conn. library assns., Chester Hist. Soc. (trustee 1970-72), D.A.V., Am. Legion Aux., Soc. Mayflower Descs. Mem. United Ch. Author: (with John G. Park) The Independent School Library and the Gifted Child, 1956; The Age of Samuel Johnson, LL.D., 1959. sec.,(essay) Remember When, 1987. Recipient The Commemorative medal of Honor Am. Biog. Inst., 1987; biog. tribute Dr. Katie Wilcox, 1975. Home: Maple St Chester CT 06412

HASCHKE, BERNADETTE DEVERS, education educator; b. Shelbyville, Ky., July 8, 1945; d. John M. Haschke, Aug. 31, 1968; children: Allison Marie, Lara Anne. BA, Georgetown Coll., 1967; MA, Mich. State U., 1969; PhD, U. Mich., 1978. Tchr. Scottsdale (Ariz.) Pub. Schs., 1969-70; tchr. presch. Huron Hills Nursery Sch., Ann Arbor, Mich., 1971-73; grad. asst. U. Mich., Ann Arbor, 1973-76; asst. prof. Met. State Coll., Denver, 1977-82; cons. in early childhood devel. U.S. Army, Karlsruhe, Fed. Republic Germany, 1983; dir. children's program Applewood Bapt. Ch., Wheat Ridge, Colo., 1983-85; instr. Front Range Community Coll., Westminster, Colo., 1985-86; curriculum cons. Colo. Community Colls., Denver, 1986-87; with Emily Griffith Opportunity Sch., Denver; cons. Denver Pub. Schs., 1986-87; proj. coordinator Emily Griffith Opportunity Sch., Denver, 1987—. Marguerite Wilker Johnson fellow U. Mich., 1973-75. Mem. Am. Home Econs. Assn., Colo. Home Econs. Assn. (v.p. 1987), Nat. Assn. Edn. of Young Children, Colo. Assn. Edn. Young Children (bd. dirs. 1979-81), Am. Vocat. Assn. Baptist. Home: 7932 Pierson Way Arvada CO 80005

HASHIM, ELINOR M., librarian; b. Pittsfield, Mass., Dec. 13, 1933. B.A., U. Vt., 1955; M.S., So. Conn. State U., 1970. Engring. asst. United Techs. Research Ctr., East Hartford, Conn., 1956-58, tech. research asst., 1958-63, supr. engring. aides and assts., 1963-68; head reference dept. Mary Cheney Library, Manchester, Conn., 1968-71; head circulation dept. New Britain (Conn.) Pub. Library, 1971-72, head bus., sci. and tech. depts., 1972-73, head reference dept., 1973-75; dir. Welles-Turner Meml. Library, Glastonbury, Conn., 1975-81; supr. reference and tech. services Perkin-Elmer Corp., Norwalk, Conn., 1981-85; program dir. spl. libraries Online Computer Library Ctr., Dublin, Ohio, 1985—; mem., chmn. Nat. Commn. on Libraries and Info. Sci., Washington, 1982-86; apptd. Conn. State Library Bd., 1974, chmn., 1976-82. Recipient Disting. Alumni award So. Conn. State U., 1982. Mem. ALA (pub. library assn. membership com. 1979-80, councilor Conn. chpt. 1980-82, councilor-at-large 1987—), Am. Soc. for Info. Sci., New Eng. Library Assn. (bylaws com. 1972-73, rep. Conn. 1973-75, chmn. membership com. 1975-76, v.p. 1976-77, pres. 1977-78, chmn. nominations com. 1978-79), Conn. Library Assn. (chmn. legis. com. 1971-73, chmn. nominations com. 1975-76, rep. to ALA 1980-82, Librarian of Yr. award 1982), Spl. Libraries Assn. (fellows award 1987). Home: 8719 Chloe Ct Powell OH 43065 Office: Online Computer Library Ctr 6565 Frantz Rd Dublin OH 43017

HASHIMOTO, FRANCES KAZUKO, food products executive; b. Poston, Ariz., Aug. 26, 1943; d. Koroku and Haru (Kataoka) H.; m. Joel Lawrence Freidman, Jan. 22, 1972; children: Bryan Koji Hashimoto Friedman, Ryan Koroku Hashimoto Friedman. BS, U. So. Calif., 1966. Cert. tchr., Calif. Elem. tchr. Los Angeles Unified Sch. Dist., 1966-70; pres. Mikawaya, Inc., Los Angeles, 1970—; mem. devel. adv. com. Mayor's Little Tokyo Commn., Los Angeles, 1980—. Treas. Pvt. Industry Council, Los Angeles, 1982—; mem. adv. bd. Human Relations Commn., Los Angeles, 1983—; mem. Mayor's Task Force on Cen. City East Los Angeles, 1986—; bd. dirs. Japanese Cultural Community Ctr., Nisei Week Japanese Festival, Inc., 1978—, chmn., 1982; chmn. Little Tokyo Centennial, 1984. Mem. Little Tokyo Bus. Assn. (bd. dirs., v.p. 1978-85), Japanese Village Plaza Mchts. Assn. (pres. 1987), Los Angeles C. of C., Japanese C. of C. Republican. Office: Mikawaya Inc 800 E 4th St Los Angeles CA 90013

HASKEW, JOYCE ANNETTE, engineering firm executive; b. Westerly, R.I., Mar. 7, 1942; d. John Victor and Isabella (MacGonegal) Biswurm, Sr.; m. Kenneth Lacy Haskew, Apr. 20, 1960; children—Kevin Dean, Scot Lacy. A.A., Am. River Coll., 1961. Delineator, State of Calif., Sacramento, 1961-66; engr. Kenneth L. Haskew, Ft. Bragg, Calif., and Ely, Nev., 1971-77; estimator, engr. Park Shah Abbas Co., Esfahan, Iran, 1977-78; civil drafter Pillsbury Engring., Reno, Nev., 1978-79; real estate saleswoman Preferred Equities, Reno, 1979-80; engr. Haskew Engring. Inc., Ely, Nev., 1979—; vice chmn. Regional Planning Commn., Ely, 1983-84; chmn. No. Nev. Pvt. Industry Council, Reno, 1983. sch. bd. trustee Seat A Esmeralda County, Nev., 1987—; health counselor Sch. Natural Health, Spanish Fork, Utah, 1986. Mem. Nat. Assn. Realtors, Ely C of C. (co-chmn. legis. com. 1983). Republican. Baptist. Club: Sweet Adelines (Ely, Nev., and Valdez, Alaska). Office: 411 2d St Goldfield NV 89013

HASLANGER, MARTHA LOUISE, filmmaker; b. Dearborn, Mich., Sept. 16, 1947; d. John Frederick and June (Loftsgordon) Anderson; A.B. with honors in Germanic Lit., Denison U.; M.F.A., Eastern Mich. U. Fellow in film, Bunting Inst., Cambridge, Mass.; film shows include; Whitney Mus. of Am. Art, N.Y.C., 1976, Berlin's (Germany) Arsenal, 5th Internat. Film Competition at Knokke-Heist, Belgium, London (Eng.) Filmmakers' Co-op, the Millenium, N.Y.C., The Collective, N.Y.C., Chgo. Filmgroup, and Munich (Germany) Stadtmuseum, Whitney Biennial, 1979, 81, 83, 3d Internat. Avant-Garde Film Festival, London, Festival Internat. du Jeune Cinema, Hyéres, France, Film as Art, Arts Council Gt. Britain, Internationale Filmfestspiele, Berlin, Edinburgh Film Festival, Stedelijk Mus., Amsterdam, Robert Flaherty Film Sem., N.Y.; video shows include: Sao Paulo (Brazil) Biennial, Whitney Mus. of Art, Inst. of Contemporary Art, Phila.; judge numerous film festivals, panels. Recipient grant for video work, Nat. Endowment for the Arts, film grant Royal Film Archives of Belgium and the AGFA-GEVAERT Corp., grant Radcliffe Inst. and Harvard Corp., artist grant CAPS, N.Y. State; Jerome Found. grantee. Author: Memory Book, 1977; Goldy Dances 1978; photographs appear in Women See Woman; contbr. works to numerous profl. mags. and jours. Films in collection of Am. Fedn. Arts, Royal Film Archives Belgium, Arts Council Gt. Britain, Internat. Forum of Young Cinema of Berlin, New Eng. Found. for Arts.

HASSETT, CAROL ALICE, psychologist; b. Bklyn., Apr. 19, 1947; d. Joseph and Anna (Portanova) Lusardi; B.S., St. John's U., 1968; M.Ed., Hofstra U., 1974, Ph.D. in Psychology (teaching asst.), 1981; m. John J. Hassett, June 29, 1968; 1 son, John J. Tchr. Day Elem. Sch., Bklyn., 1968-69; psychologist Nassau County Dept. Drug and Alcohol also Mental Health Assn. Nassau County, East Meadow, N.Y., 1981-84; chief supervising psychologist Queens Outreach Project, 1985—; pvt. practice clin. psychology, 1984—; adj. asst. prof. Hofstra U., 1980—. Trustee Malverne (N.Y.) Pub. Libray, 1986—; bd. dirs. Malverne Vol. Ambulance Corps, 1976—; bd. govs. Kings County Cadet Corps, 1966-72; bd. trustees Malverne Pub. Lib., 1986—. Cert. advanced emergency med. technician, prehosp. critical care technician; permanently cert. tchr., N.Y. Mem. Am. Psychol. Assn. Republican. Roman Catholic. Contbr. articles profl. jours. Home: 105 Franklin Ave Malverne NY 11565 Office: 230 Hilton Ave Hempstead NY 11550

HASSETT, JACQUELYN ANN, nurse; b. La Crosse, Wis., Sept. 13, 1930; d. Frank Alois and Anne Helena (Milos) Spika; m. James John Hassett, Aug. 22, 1953; children—Barbara, Linda, Jean, Jane, Nancy, James David. Diploma in Nursing, St. Anthony de Padua Sch. Nursing, Chgo., 1951; BS, Barat Coll., 1977; MS, George Williams Coll., 1983. RN, Ill., Wis. Operating room nurse VA Hosp., North Chicago, Ill., 1951-54; part-time nursing positions St. Therese Hosp., Waukegan, Ill., 1954-58, Johnson Motors, Waukegan, 1958-64, VA Hosp., North Chicago, Ill., 1964-71; dir. health services Coll. of Lake County, Grayslake, Ill., 1971—, co-chmn. Inst. Self-Study for Rehab. Act 1973, 1978. Mem. Project SUCCEED, No. Ill., 1980-81; com. mem. Health Systems Agy. Kane-Lake-McHenry Counties, 1978-80; vol. Lake County Cancer Soc., 1975—, Am. Heart Assn., 1975—; bd. dirs. Med. Service Adv. Com. Lake County Health Dept., 1980—. Recipient Appreciation cert. Lake County Bd. Commrs., 1978; Meritorious Service award Am. Heart Assn., 1979-82; Outstanding award No. Ill. Council on Alcoholism, 1982, Commendation for Service Lake County (Ill.) Health Dept., 1986. Mem. Am. Coll. Health Assn. (council of dels. 1978-80, 83—), Mid-Am. Coll. Health Assn. (v.p. 1981-82, pres. 1983-84), No. Ill. Coll. Health Nurses Assn., Am. Legion Aux. Roman Catholic. Club: Altrusa (Waukegan). Home: 42749 Washington St Winthrop Harbor IL 60096 Office: Coll of Lake County 19351 W Washington St Grayslake IL 60030

HASSINGER, SHARON LYNN, sales executive; b. Scranton, Pa., Nov. 28, 1953; d. James Edward and Lois Edna (Weber) Purcell; m. Robert Anthony Hassinger, Mar. 10, 1979; children: Kiley Lynn, Courtney Leigh. BS in Social Sci., Elizabethtown Coll., 1974. Sales coordinator The Hershey (Pa.) Lodge and Conv. Ctr., 1975-77, acct. exec., 1977-80; sales mgr. The Hotel Hershey, 1980-81, dir. sales, 1981-83, asst. gen. mgr. sales/mktg., 1983-87; dir. mktg. Hershey Entertainment and Resort Co., 1987—. Mem. Hotel Sales Mktg. Assn. Office: Corp Mktg Planning and Devel 400 W Hershey Park Dr Hershey PA 17033

HASSLER, SANDRA LEE, controller; b. Allentown, Pa., Jan. 3, 1949; d. Harold Elmer and Ruth Eleanor (Dahlof) H.; A.A. in Bus. Adminstrn., Northampton County Community Coll., 1969; B.S. in Bus. Mgmt., Indiana (Pa.) U., 1971. Engaged in retail fin., 1971-77; corp. controller, asst. to chmn. bd. Apparel Affiliates, Inc., Quakertown, Pa., 1977-81; ind. fin. and retail cons. computer programming and internal auditing, Phila., 1981-82; div. controller Honeybee, women's retail apparel chain, Huntington Valley Pa., 1982-84; asst. controller Wall to Wall Sound & Video, Inc., Cinnaminson, N.J., 1984—. Mem. Am. Mgmt. Assn., Nat. Assn. Female Execs. Mem. Moravian Ch. Author ops. and retail manuals/booklets for design of data collection devices. Home: 800 Trenton Rd #275 Langhorne PA 19047 Office: 200 S Route 130 Cinnaminson NJ 08077

HASSOLD REES, KERRIN, corporate treasurer; b. Midlum, Island Fochr, Fed. Republic of Germany, Apr. 26, 1941; came to U.S., 1961; d. Johann Lorenz and Anna Maria (Woegens) H.; m. Werner Rees, Dec. 1, 1962; children: Dennis, Britta. Student, Wyk/Foehr Retail Bus. Sch., Schleswig Holstein, 1957-60. Sales clk. Paulsens Fine Kost, Wyk/Foehr, Fed. Republic of West Germany, 1957-60, Kanzler Chocolate Store, Flensburg, Fed. Republic of West Germany, 1960-61; mgr. Rees Cake & Pastry Shop, Inc., Ozone Park, N.Y., 1967-80; sec., treas. Rees Import, Inc., Richmond Hill, N.Y., 1980—. Office: Rees Import Inc 120-05 Atlantic Ave Richmond Hill NY 11418-3217

HAST, JOAN EILEEN, human resource development administrator; b. Denver, Jan. 6, 1955; d. Bernard Arthur and Erma Ann (Pospisil) H. Student U. Denver, 1973-74, Goethe Inst., Munich, 1974-75; B.A. in Internat. Affairs, U. Colo., 1983, postgrad., 1983-85, M.S. in Telecommunications, 1985. Owner, mgr. Celebrity Slickers Custom Jackets, Boulder, Colo., 1978-80; monogram specialist Custom Monogramming, Denver, 1981; summer intern in telecommunications Horizon House Pub., Dedham, Mass., 1983; office mgr. Universal Fuels Oil Co., Denver, 1983-84; sr. engr. GTE-Midwestern Telephone Ops., Fort Wayne, Ind., 1985-86; network adminstr. GTE-Info. Bus., Indpls., 1987-88; mgr.engring. assoc. devel. program, GTE Service Corp., Stamford, Conn., 1988—. Advisor Jr. Achievement, Fort Wayne, 1985-86; vol. Fort Wayne Zoo, 1985; active YMCA, Fort Wayne. Research grantee U. Colo. Dept. Telecommunications, Honolulu, 1984, Las Vegas, 1984. Mem. IEEE, Nat. Assn. Female Execs., Ind. Orgn. of Women in Telecommunications, Women in Indpls. Networking. Avocations: horses, foreign languages, travel, art, ballet. Office: GTE Service Corp 1 Stamford Forum Stamford CT 06904

HASTINGS, DEBORAH, bass guitarist; b. Evansville, Ind., May 11, 1959; d. Mortimer Winthrop Hastings and Margaret Hooper (Smith) Zimmerman. Student music, U. Wis. Bass guitarist N.Y.C. and Madison, Wis., 1975—; freelance photographer Madison, 1976-81; performed with Ron Wood, Bo Diddley, Chuck Berry, Jerry Lee Lewis, George Gobel, Little Anthony and the Imperials, Ben E. King, Sarah Dash and others. Author: Photographers Market, 1981; bass player TV shows Joan Rivers, 1987, Classsics of Rock and Roll, 1988, Live from the Ritz, 1988. Fundraiser, bassist polit. campaigns, Madison. Recipient numerous awards for pottery, award Arts Council, Madison, Arts Council, Ann Arbor, Mich. Mem. Musicians Union. Democrat. Office: Talent Cons Internat 200 W 57th St Suite 1201 New York NY 10019

HASTINGS, EVELYN GRACE, teacher; b. Seguin, Tex., May 25, 1938; d. Ed Howard Coleman and Mae Stella (King) Haywood; m. Marvin Hastings, Oct. 9, 1982. BS, Tex. Luth. Coll., 1960; MA, U. Tex., San Antonio, 1985. Cert. tchr., Tex. Tchr. Seguin (Tex.) Ind. Sch. Dist., 1962—; sec. Guadalupe County Tchr.'s Meeting, Seguin, 1962-65, Juan Seguin Sch. PTA, 1969. Historian, corresponding sec. Tex. Women's Conv. Ch. of Our Lord Jesus Christ, Tex., 1961-69; trea. Tex. State Armor Bears Young People's Union of Our Lord Jesus Christ, 1956-59, v.p., 1961-63, pres., 1963-65, 68-70; sec. Tex. State Sunday Sch. Assn. of Our Lord Jesus Christ, 1960-63, asst. supt., 1968-70, state supt., 1970-74; local missionary pres. and fin. sec. of Refuge Ch., missionary dept. state v.p. Ch. of Our Lord Jesus Christ, 1985; state supr. Tex. Jr. Convention of the Ch. of Our Lord Jesus Christ, 1970; Sunday sch. supr. of Lighthouse Ch. of Our Lord Jesus Christ, Gonzales, Tex., 1975—. Recipient Cert. of Outstanding Service Nat. Youth Congress Ch. of Our Lord Jesus Christ, 1968, Outstanding Service Plaque, 1981. Mem. AAUW (sec. 1968-70), NEA, Tex. State Tchrs. Assn. (minority del. 1982), Seguin Educators Assn., Seguin Bus. Women's Assn. Democrat. Home: 950 Elsik Seguin TX 78155

HASTINGS, SUSAN KAY, auditor, accountant; b. Mason City, Iowa, Mar. 25, 1952; d. Arnold E. and Mildred E. (Thiemann) Hoveland; m. Robert E. Hastings, June 12, 1971. AA, North Iowa Area Community Coll., Mason City, 1973; BS, Nat. Coll. Bus., 1975. CPA, S.D. Staff accountant McGladrey Hendrickson & Pullen, Rapid City, S.D., 1975-80, mgr., 1980-84, ptnr., 1984-87; internal auditor First Fed. Savs. Bank, Rapid City, 1987—. Treas. Rapid City Fine Arts Council, 1987-88, also bd. dirs., 1987-88; active YMCA, Rapid City, 1973-88. Mem. am. Inst. CPA's, S.D. Soc. CPA's. Fin. Mgrs. Soc., Inst. Internal Auditors. Club: Arrowhead Country (Rapid City) (treas. and bd. dirs., 1986-88). Office: First Fed Savs Bank 909 St Joe St PO Box 8170 Rapid City SD 57709

HASTREITER, KIM MARIE, benefits administration executive; b. Manitowoc, Wis., July 3, 1956; d. Alois A. and Grace A. (Decker) Hartman; divorced, 1986; children: Katie Jo, Jason John. Grad. high sch., Manitowoc. Sec. Manitowoc Collection Agy., 1975-76; sec., clk. Manitowoc County Sheriff's Dept., 1976-81; personnel clk. Imperial Clevite, Manitowoc, 1981-82, dept. sec., 1982-83, mgr. benefits adminstrn., 1983-87, personnel adminstr., 1987—. Office: Clevite Industries 1440 N 24th Manitowoc WI 54220

HATCH, MARY WENDELL VANDER POEL, nonprofit organization executive, interior decorator; b. N.Y.C., Feb. 6, 1919; d. William Halsted and Blanche Pauline (Billings) Vander Poel; m. George Montagu Miller, Apr. 5, 1940 (div. 1974); children—Wendell Miller Steavenson, Gretchen Miller Elkus; m. Sinclair Hatch, May 14, 1977. Pres. Miller Richard, Inc., interior decorators, Glen Head, N.Y., 1972—, bd. dirs. Eye Bank Sight Restoration, N.Y.C., 1975—, pres., 1980—; bd. dirs. Manhattan Eye Ear and Throat Hosp., N.Y.C., 1966—, v.p., 1978—; sec. 1985—, bd. dirs. Cold Spring Harbor Lab., N.Y., 1985—; v.p. North Country Garden Club, Nassau County, N.Y., 1979-81, 1983-85; dir. Planned Parenthood Nassau County, Mineola, N.Y., 1982-84, Hutton House C.W. Post Coll., Greenvale, N.Y., 1982—. Republican. Episcopalian. Clubs: Colony (N.Y.C.), Church (N.Y.C.), Order St. John Jerusalem (N.Y.C.). Home: Mill River Rd Box 330 Oyster Bay NY 11771

HATCH, REBECCA BLACKMON, stock broker; b. Live Oak, Fla., Nov. 18, 1955; d. Donald James and Marilyn Webb (Blackmon) H. BA, Fla. State U., 1977. Lic. stock broker; registered rep., Nat. Assn. Securities Dealers and SEC. Asst. dir. Fla. House, Washington, D.C., 1977-78; sec. Sci. and Tech. Commn. U.S. Ho. Reps., Washington, 1978-79; loan originator Cameron Brown Co., Annandale, Va., 1979-81; salesperson, mgr. Dictaphone Corp., Alexandria, Va. and Cin., 1981-83; mktg. rep. Computer Consoles, Inc., Reston, Va., 1983-85; account exec. Dean Witter Reynolds, Inc., McLean, Va., 1985-88, Johnston, Lemon and Co., Alexandria, Va., 1988—. Mem. Prince William Bd. Realtors, Fla. State Soc., Washington Tennis Patrons, Fairfax C. of C., Fla. State U. Alumni Club (pres. 1978-79, treas. 1986-87, v.p. 1987—), Delta Zeta Alumni Assn. Democrat. Methodist. Club: Washington Ski. Home: 5838 Rexford Dr Springfield VA 22152

HATCHER, MADELEINE ALEXANDRIA, small business consultant, literary agent; b. Chgo., June 7, 1938; d. Joseph S. and Helen Rosemary (Stevens) Grandis; m. Hudson LeGrand, Aug. 19, 1967; children: Pamela, Walter, William. Student, Lake Forest Coll., 1958-61; diploma, Am. Acad. Dramatic Art, 1974; BA, Sarah Lawrence Coll., 1988. Asst. to pres. Hertz Internat., N.Y.C., 1961-63; mktg. dir. Caribbean Pavilion N.Y. World's Fair, N.Y.C., 1963-65; asst. sales mgr. Simon & Schuster, N.Y.C., 1965-74; lit. agt. Alexandria Hatcher Agy., N.Y.C., 1976—; bus. cons., N.Y.C., 1974—; mem. faculty New Sch. for Social research, N.Y.C., 1978—, Fashion Inst. Tech., N.Y.C., 1979—, NYU, 1987—; speaker in field, 1982—; pres. 150 W. 55th St. Corp., N.Y.C., 1981-85. Author: Before You Start That Business; also articles. N.Y. State del. White House Conf. on Small Bus., Washington, 1980. Named Women-in-Bus. Adv. Yr., SBA, 1981. Mem. Women Bus. Owners of N.Y. (v.p. pub. affairs 1978-79, pres. 1979-81), Independent Lit. Agts. Assn. (council mem. 1980-81). Roman Catholic. Office: Alexandria Hatcher Agy 150 W 55th St New York NY 10019

HATELEY, ENID ELLEN, real estate broker; b. Guayaquil, Ecuador, Mar. 22, 1925; came to U.S., 1944, naturalized, 1948; d. Harry Hawkes and Silia (Blanco) Shephard; B.S., Colegio Guayaquil, 1942; B.A., U. So. Calif., 1946; m. James Charles Hateley, II, Aug. 24, 1946; children—James Charles, Robert, Donald. Asst. credit mgr. Bank of Calif., 1946-49; with IBEC, 1950-51, E.H. Imports, 1952-60; trust adminstr. Bank of Am., 1973-75; broker Coldwell Banker, Los Altos, Calif., 1976-84; pres. City Resources, 1984—. Mem. Orange County Philharmonic Soc. Mem. Women in Commercial Real Estate, Nat. Assn. Realtors, Calif. Assn. Realtors, Beverly Hills (Calif.) Bd. Realtors, Trojan League. Republican. Roman Catholic. Clubs: Los Angeles Athletic, University. Home: 2 La Quinta Turtle Rock Pointe Irvine CA 92715 Office: City Resources PO Box 9935 Newport Beach CA 92658

HATFIELD, ELAINE CATHERINE, psychology educator; b. Detroit, Oct. 22, 1937; d. Charles E. and Eileen (Kalahar) H.; m. Richard L. Rapson, June 15, 1982. B.A., U. Mich., 1959; Ph.D., Stanford U., 1963. Asst. prof. U. Minn., Mpls., 1963-64, assoc. prof., 1964-66; asso. prof. U. Rochester, 1966-68, U. Wis., Madison, 1968-69; prof. U. Wis., 1969-81; now prof. U. Hawaii at Manoa; chmn. dept. U. Hawaii of Manoa, 1981-83. Author: Interpersonal Attraction, 1969, 2d edit., 1978, Equity: Theory and Research, 1978, A New Look at Love, 1978, Human Sexual Behavior, 1985, Mirror, Mirror: The Importance of Looks in Everyday Life, 1986, The Psychology of Emotions, 1988. Contbr. articles to profl. jours. Fellow Am. Psychol. Assn., Am. Sociol. Assn. Home: 3334 Ano'ai Pl Honolulu HI 96822 Office: U Hawaii 2430 Campus Rd Honolulu HI 96822

HATFIELD, SUSAN LINNIE COOK, banker; b. Whidby Island, Wash., Jan. 16, 1957; d. Walter Lewis and Grace Veronica (Sherbuene) Cook; m. Steven William Hatfield, June 5, 1982. Student, Radford Coll., 1975-77, No. Va. Community Coll., 1977-79; BS in Law Enforcement, George Mason U., 1981. Retirement and tng. specialist Continental Fed. Savs. Bank, Fairfax, Va., 1982-85; mgr. retirement and customer services United Savs. Bank, Vienna, Va., 1985-87; mgr. retirement plans dept. Dominion Fed. Savs. and Loan, McLean, Va., 1987—. Mem. Nat. Assn. Female Execs. Republican. Presbyterian. Home: 8434 Georgian Ct Manassas VA 22110

HATHAWAY, CHERYL KAYE, real estate executive; b. Cleve., July 4, 1947; d. Samuel Paul II and Colleen Westcott (Edixon) H. Student, Case-Western Res. U., 1965-67; BA in Math., Defiance Coll., 1970; postgrad., Lake Erie Coll., Cleve. State U. Cert. emergency med. technician. Systems analyst Lake County Data Processing, Painesville, Ohio, 1971-72; tchr. spl. edn. Lake County Mental Retardation Program, Mentor, Ohio, 1972-84; v.p. Hathaway (Rental) Properties, Madison, Ohio, 1984—. Vol. swim instr. YMCA, Madison, 1966—; bd. mgrs. YMCA, 1972—; pres., v.p. Madison Local Bd. Edn., 1976-83. Recipient grant Martha Holden Jennings Found., 1980; named to Lake County Women's Hall of Fame, 1979. Mem. AAUW, NE Ohio Hosp. Assn. (bd. dirs. long-range planning com. 1987), Mensa. Republican. Congregationalist. Lodge: Order Ea. Star. Office: Route 3 Box 433 Clay Baker Rd Cleveland TN 37311

HATHAWAY, JUANITA, nurse; b. Gonzales, Tex., Mar. 9, 1948; d. Ernest Chauncy and Effie Mae (Dyal) Hendershot; m. William John Hathaway, Jan. 14, 1972; children—William J., Jr., Kenneth Earl. Assoc. Degree Applied Sci., San Antonio Coll., 1971. Registered nurse. Charge nurse, Warm Springs, Gonzales, 1972-73, 74-81; charge nurse Davis Hosp., Luling, Tex., 1973-74, asst. dir. nursing, 1984-87; supr. operating room, 1987—. Asst. den leader Capitol Area council Cub Scouts, 1984, den leader, 1986—; vol. Luling Emergency Med. Service. Baptist. Home: 900 S Magnolia Luling TX 78648

HATHAWAY, SANDRA LEE, dietitian; b. Cleve., June 12, 1942; d. Walter Glendening and Mildred Ardel (Sullivan) LeFavour; m. Melvin Barker Hathaway, Sept. 18, 1965; children: Deborah, Gregory, Elizabeth. BS, Purdue U., 1964; postgrad., U. Cin., 1968, Ohio U., 1986. Lic. tchr., Ohio, Ind. Adminstrv. dietician Stouffer Food Corp., Cleve., 1964-65, test kitchen dietician, 1965-66; dietician Proctor and Gamble, Cin., 1966-68; therapeutic dietician St. Lawrence Hosp., Lansing, 1969-72; cons. dietician Jarvis Acres Nursing Home, Lansing, 1972-73, Ohio Commn. on Aging, Zanesville, 1975-85, various nursing homes, Zanesville, 1980—; sub. tchr. W. Muskingum Sch. Dist., Zanesville, 1986—. V.p. Welcome Wagon, Zanesville, 1976-83; coach Olympic of the Mind, Zanesville, 1983, 84; asst. Brownie troop leader Girl Scouts U.S., Zanesville, 1986—; mem. adv. com. Muskingum, Perry, Guernsey, Noble Vocat. Sch., Zanesville, 1987. Mem. Am. Dietetic Assn., Nutrition Specialists, Kappa Alpha Theta. Lutheran. Home: 349 Mel-Kay Way Zanesville OH 43701

HATLEY, DOROTHY LEE RATLIFF, county official; b. Lometa, Tex., July 29, 1934; d. Robert Lee and Ethel Lucille (Dannheim) R.; m. Presley Lewis Hatley, May 15, 1951; children—Sandra Gwen, Gary Presley. Student Durham Bus. Coll., 1950-51. Abstract sec. Rocksprings Abstract Co., Tex., 1966-67; tax assessor dep. Rocksprings Tax Office, 1967-68, clk., dep., 1969-70; county and dist. clk. Edwards County, Rocksprings, 1970—. Sunday sch. primary tchr. First Bapt. Ch., Rocksprings. Home: PO Box 231 Rocksprings TX 78880 Office: County Clk Edwards County Seat County Courthouse Rocksprings TX 78880

HATTON, MARY KATHERINE, finance director, director computer services; b. Mundelein, Ill., Apr. 13, 1957; d. Harry W. and Dorothy (Ullrich) Hatton. BBA, St. Norberts Coll., 1979; MBA, Lake Forest Grad. Sch., 1987. Asst. fin dir. City Hall Village of Mundelein, 1979-81, fin. dir., 1981—, dir. computer services, 1984—; mem. fin. com. Internat. Risk Mgmt. Agy., Downers Grove, Ill., 1985—, adv. council Lake Forest (Ill.) Grad. Sch., 1986—; fin. adv. com. Carmel High Sch., Ill., 1987—. Com. mem. Lake County (Ill.) Stormwater Planning. Mem. Ill. and Chgo. Govt. Fin. Officers Assn. U.S. and Can., Inst. Mcpl. Treas. and Accts., Mcpl. Treas. Assn. of U.S. and Can. Office: Village of Mundelein City Hall 440 E Hawley St Mundelein IL 60060

HATTOX, DOLORES ORTHELLO, educator; b. Oklahoma City, Mar. 25, 1930; d. Emanuel Britton and Irma Naomi (Cooper) Wood; m. Glenn Newman Hattox, Aug. 5, 1950 (dec. Mar. 31, 1983); children: Kirby Wade, Janet Gail Hattox Gotte, Thomas Walter. BS, Lamar U., 1966. Cert. tchr., counselor. Clk. Fair Store, Beaumont, 1946-49, Gulf States Utilities, Beaumont, 1949-53; tchr. Beaumont Ind. Sch. Dist., 1967—; owner, pres. Spindletop Trophy Co. Sec. French Elem. Sch. PTA, Beaumont, 1964-66, Ogden Sch. PTA, Beaumont, 1980-87; active Beaumont Art Mus. Mem. Assn. Tex. Profl. Educators (sec. 1980-81, faculty rep.), NEA (adv. bd. 1983-87), Tex. State Tchrs. Assn., Beaumont Tchrs. Assn. (faculty rep.), Beaumont C. of C. Lodges: Lioness (pres. Beaumont 1982-83), Order Eastern Star. Home and Office: 2230 Toledo Beaumont TX 77703

HATVANY, NINA GABRIELE, real estate developer; b. Eng, Oct. 8, 1953; came to U.S., 1974; d. Baron Paul Bernard and Ingeborg (Kirchtag) H.; B.Sc. with 1st class honors, Bristol (Eng.) U., 1974; M.A. in Psychology (Univ. fellow), Stanford U., 1976, Ph.D. in Psychology, 1978. Asst. prof. bus. Grad. Sch. Bus., Columbia U., 1978-81; pres. Brit. Pacific Devel. Co., real estate devel., San Francisco, 1981—. Editor: (with D. Nadler and M. Tushman) Managerial Behavior, Concepts and Cases, 1982.

HAUCK, CHRISTINE CLAIRE KRAUS, insurance executive; b. McKeesport, Pa., May 22, 1951; d. Lawrence Elmer and Anne Mae (Seinar) Kraus; m. David T. Hauck, Feb. 6, 1971 (div. April 1986); children: Benjamin David, Christopher Thomas, Andrew Lawrence. Student, Duquesne U., 1969-71, U. Pitts., 1972-78, U. Charleston, 1978-81; BA, Ohio State U., 1984. Cert. ins. counselor. Claims asst. John Hancock Ins., Pitts., 1971-73; underwriter Chubb Ins. Group, Pitts., 1973-76; account rep., ins. agt. Frank B. Hall, Columbus, Ohio, 1982-85; customer service rep., agt. Andrew Ins. Assoc., Columbus, 1986—; pres., sec. Positively Successful, Columbus, 1988—. Author poetry. Mem. Welcome Wagon, Upper Arlington, Ohio, 1981-84, Barrington Sch. Assn., Upper Arlington, 1982-87, Tremont Sch. ASsn., Upper Arlington, 1987-88, Upper Arlington Civic Assn., 1986-88; instr. St. Agatha Dept. Religious Edn., Upper Arlington, 1983-87; foster parent, 1975—. Mem. Nat. Assn. Female Execs., Phi Kappa Phi. Democrat. Roman Catholic. Club: Parents Without Ptnrs. Home: 2121 Jervis Rd Columbus OH 43221-2727 Office: Positively Successful 2121 Jervis Rd Columbus OH 43221-2727

HAUCK, MARGUERITE HALL, broadcasting executive, antique dealer; b. Bayside, N.Y., June 30, 1948; d. Carlyle Washington and Anzonette Marguerite (Asmussen) Hall. Student, Syracuse U., 1966-67; B.A. summa cum laude, Queens Coll., CUNY, 1974. Assoc. producer Animatic Prodns., Ltd., N.Y.C., 1974-75; mktg. analyst BBDO, Inc., N.Y.C., 1975-76; mktg. analyst CBS, Inc., N.Y.C., 1976-77, dir. mktg. and research FM nat. sales, Radio div., 1978-86; dir. mktg. and research Christal Radio Sales div. Katz Communications, 1985-87; pres. Lennon Hall Antiques, Inc., 1986—; v.p. research and mktg. Christal Radio Sales div. Katz Communications, 1987—. Author: The 321 Billion Dollar Market, 1981, The Mid-Day Myth Exploded, 1982; columnist, TV-Radio Age mag., 1982. Bd. dirs. Queens Coll. Student Services Corp., 1973-74. Recipient Queens Coll. Disting. Service award, 1974. Mem. Nat. Assn. Female Execs. Home: 20 Continental Ave Forest Hills NY 11375 Office: Christal Radio Sales 919 3d Ave New York NY 10022 also: Lennon Hall Antiques Inc 50 Forest Ave Locust Valley NY 11560

HAUCK, SHIRLEY MADSEN, affirmative action program manager; b. Camden, N.J., Mar. 21, 1942; d. Robert and Dorothy Rose (Carney) Neubaum; m. Harold Randall Madsen, Nov. 18, 1972 (div. 1978); m. Carl W. Hauck, Oct. 1987. Student, Dundalk (Md.) Community Coll., 1980-82. Affirmative action program mgr. McLean Contracting Co., Balt., 1974-88. Editor (newsletter) M-Anation, 1979-83, (newsletter) Voice of Equality, 1979-87. Sec. Joppatowne Civic Assn., Joppa, Md., 1975; mem. Joppatowne Citizens Patrol, Joppa, 1976. Mem. Md. Assn. Affirmative Action Officers (sec. 1981-83, v.p. 1983-85, treas. 1985-87), Mensa (officer 1979-82). Democrat. Home: 8219 Belair Rd Lot #47-B Baltimore MD 21236 Office: McLean Contracting Co 1301 Fidelity Bldg Baltimore MD 21201

HAUER, HELEN PHYLLIS SCHOEN, chemistry educator; b. N.Y.C., Oct. 27, 1942; d. Sohl and Celia (Permut) Schoen; m. Harold Hauer, Aug. 23, 1964; 1 child, Sharon Beth. BS, CCNY, 1963; PhD, Purdue U., 1969. Prof. Del. Tech. & Community Coll., Newark, 1977—, dept. chair, 1979—; ednl. cons. DuPont de Nemours & Co. Inc., Wilmington, Del., 1979-85, Internat. Tng. Ednl. Co., Boston, 1984, TAssn. Tech. Superiors, Lima, Peru, 1984-86. Fellow Am. Chem. Soc., Nat. Assn. Sci. Tchrs., Nat. Assn. Female Execs.; mem. Iota Sigma Pi (pres. Plutonium chpt. 1967-68). Democrat. Jewish. Office: Del Tech & Community Coll 400 Stanton-Christiana Rd Newark DE 19702

HAUETER, CAROL EASON, educational sales professional; b. Rochester, N.Y., Aug. 13, 1945; d. James D. and Lois M. (Stockwell) Eason; m. James A Haueter (div. Dec. 1971); children: Pamela, Alison. BA, Muskingam Coll., 1967. Tchr. Cadiz (Ohio) Exempted Village High Sch., 1967-68; social worker Franklin County Welfare, Columbus, Ohio, 1968-70; social worker fed. programs SW City Schs., Grove City, Ohio, 1970-82; sales Data Transaction, Columbus, 1982-83, Nystrom Co., Chgo., 1983—. Author: Sage Advice, It's Relative, 1980, the Princes and The frog, 1981. Mem. Ohio Hist. Soc. Mem. Audubon Soc., Nat. Council Social Studies, Ohio Council Social Studies, Nat. Assn. Profl. Saleswomen (Saleswoman of Yr.), DAR. Democrat. Presbyterian. Club: Sierra. Home and Office: 2201 Edington Columbus OH 43221

HAUFLER, CONNIE SUSAN, sales executive; b. Cedar Rapids, Iowa, Jan. 13, 1962; d. Herbert Henry and Deanna Kay (Brinkman) H. BS, Tex. A&M U., 1985. With outside sales div. Pitney Bowes, Irving, Tex., 1985—. Me. Nat. Assn. Female Execs, Inc. Republican. Lutheran. Home: 4804 Haverwood #424 Dallas TX 75252

HAUGEN, ALYS JOY, psychologist; b. Shelby County, Iowa, Jan. 8, 1940; d. Harry Albert and Helen Myrtle (Wendt) Wetzel; m. Arthur Dennis Haugen, Aug. 3, 1958; children: Debra Suzan Haugen-Davis, Lisa Michelle, Jill Danene. Student, Minn. Bible Coll., 1957-61, Marshalltown Community Coll., 1974, Eastfield Community Coll., 1975-76; BA summa cum laude, U. Tex., Dallas, 1977, PhD, 1981. Lic. psychologist, Tex.; registered health service provider in psychology. Staff psychologist Salesmanship Club Youth and Family Ctrs., Dallas, 1981-84; pvt. practice clin. psychology, Granbury, Tex., 1985—; clin. supr. U. Tex. Health Sci. Ctr., Dallas, 1983-86. Active Planned Parenthood; elder Christian Ch. Mem. Am. Psychol. Assn. (div. psychology of women), Tex. Psychol. Assn., Hood County Profl. Women, Nat. Mus. Women in Arts (charter), YMCA (ptnr. Rockies chpt.). Democrat. Avocations: singing, sailing, skiing, hiking, horseback riding. Office: 15B South Harbor Dr Granbury TX 76048

HAUGEN, MARILYN ANNE, nurse practitioner, health center director; b. Colorado Springs, Jan. 11, 1932; d. Arnold H. and Juanita P. (Porter) Miller; m. Halver Herbert Haugen, June 13, 1953; children—Steven Lee, Karen Elaine. B.A., Denver U., 1953; B.S. in Nursing, Miami U., Ohio, 1980. Cert. pediatric nurse practitioner; R.N. Tchr., Denver Pub. Schs., 1953-57; pediatric nurse Middletown Regional Hosp., Ohio, 1973-76, educator, 1976-77, pediatric nurse practitioner, 1978-82, project dir. maternal child health ctr., 1982—. Mem. adv. bd. Miami Valley Child Devel. Ctr., 1983—; chmn. Child and Family Health Services Consortium, 1986—; mem. adv. bd. Butler County Mental Health Assn.; treas. adv. bd. Butler County Mental Health Assn. Mem. Nat. Assn. Pediatric Nurse Practitioners and Assocs. (treas., fin. chair 1982-86, treas. Ohio chpt. 1980-84, Henry K. Silver award 1986, Pediatric Nurse Practitioner of Yr. Ohio chpt. 1986), Am. Nurses Assn., Ohio Nurses Assn., Mortar Board, Kappa Delta. Home: 613 Regent Dr Middletown OH 45044 Office: Middletown Regional Hosp 105 McKnight Dr Middletown OH 45044

HAUGEN, MARY MARGARET, state legislator; b. Camano Island, Wash., Jan. 14, 1941; d. Melvin Harry and Alma Cora (Huntington) Olsen; children: Mary Beth Fisher, Katherine, Richard, James. Mem. Wash. Ho. Reps., Olympia, 1982—, chmn. local govt. com., 1984—, mem. natural resources com., transp. com., Salmon Adv. Council, Mcpl. Research Council, local governance com., adv. com. on intergovtl. relations, mem. joint legis. com. on criminal justice system. V.p. Camano Homeowners Assn.; mem. United Meth. Ch. Mem. LWV, Nat. Order Women Legislators, Wash. State Sch. Dirs. (resolution com.), Elected Wash. Women, Greater Marysville Bus. and Profl. Women. Democrat. Lodge: Order Ea. Star. Home: 1268 W Olsen Rd Camano Island WA 98292 Office: Wash State Legislature HOB 331 Olympia WA 98504

HAUGLAND, BRYNHILD, state legislator, farmer; b. Ward County, N.D., July 28, 1905; d. Nels and Sigurda (Ringoen) H.; BA, Minot State Coll., 1956; LLD (hon.), N.D. State U., 1984. Mem. N.D. Ho. of Reps., 1939—, chmn. com. social services and vets. affairs, mem. com. industry, bus. and labor. Mem. Def. Adv. Com. Women in Services, 1955-58. Vice chmn. N.D. Gov.'s State Health Planning Com., 1944-75; mem. Ward County Zoning Commn., Minot City Planning Commn., N.D. Bicentennial Commn. Bd. dirs. Internat. Peace Garden, 1953—, Minot State Coll. Found., Minot Commn. on Aging. Named N.D.'s Outstanding Woman in Law, 1973; Outstanding Legislator, Nat. Assembly Govt. Employees, 1979; recipient Golden award for Outstanding Service, Minot State Coll. Alumni, 1968; Hon. Mem. Uniformed Fire Fighters N.D., 1976; recipient Milky Way award Dairy Industry N.D., 1977, Disting. Service award Western N.D. Health Systems Agy., 1977-78, N.D. Water Wheel N.D. Water Users Assn./N.D. Water Mgmt. Dists. Assn., 1981, Service to Mankind award Sertoma Clubs, 1983, Merit award Pub. Health Assn. N.D., 1983, Liberty Bell award State Bar Assn., 1983, Disting. Service award Mental Health Assn. N.D., 1983, award Minot Assn. Home Builders, 1984, Good Citizen Scouting award, 1984, Disting. Service award Am. Protestant Health Assn., 1985; recognized state conv. Rep. Party for Half Century of Dedicated Pub. Service, longest serving legislator in nation presently serving; numerous others; inducted into Scandinavian Hall of Fame, 1984. Mem. Bus. and Profl. Women's Club (named Woman of Yr. 1956, 71), Am. Assn. Ret. Persons, Nat. Ret. Tchrs. Assn., Farmers Union and Farm Bur., Minot State Coll. Alumni Assn. (dir.), Eureka Homemakers Club, Delta Kappa Gamma. Lutheran. Club: Quota. Address: Box 1684 Minot ND 58701

HAULSEE, ANNE LOUISE, career management consultant; b. Richmond, Va., Dec. 21, 1946; d. Russell Boykin and Mary Louise (Smith) H.; m. Russell Thomas Boyle, July 21, 1979; stepchildren: Samantha, Dana. BA in Sociology, Roanoke Coll., 1968; MA in Sociology, West Va. U., 1971. Program asst. Nat. Sch. Pub. Relations Assn., Washington, 1969-74; mgr. Western Temp. Services, Washington, 1974; cons. women's program Trans-Century Corp., Washington, 1975-76; career mgmt. cons. Alexandria, Va., 1975—; dir. adminstrv., membership Martha Movement, Washington, 1976-77; dir. membership The Exec. Club, Washington, 1983-85. Mem. Nat. Council Career Women, Federally Employed Women, Nat. Assn. Women Bus. Owners (pres. 1979-80), Nat. Assn. Female Execs., YWCA Women's Network (chmn. 1983-84), Delta Gamma (Katie Hale award No. Va. Alumnae chpt. 1976, Shield award 1983). Presbyterian. Club: Exec. (charter mem.). Home and Office: 205 Yoakum Pkwy # 1511 Alexandria VA 22304

HAUPTFUHRER, BARBARA BARNES, corporate director; b. Greensboro, N.C., Oct. 11, 1928; d. J. Foster and Myrtle (Preyer) Barnes; BA cum laude, Wellesley Coll, 1949; m. George J. Hauptfuhrer, Jr., Sept. 9, 1950; children: George J. III, W. Barnes. Dir., Vanguard Group Investment Cos., Valley Forge, Pa., 1972—, Great Atlantic and Pacific Tea Co., Inc., Montvale, N.J., 1975—, Gen. Public Utilities Corp., Parsippany, N.J., 1976-79, Phila. Saving Fund Soc., 1976—, J. Walter Thompson Co., Inc., N.Y.C., 1977-87, Knight-Ridder Newspapers, Inc., Miami, Fla., 1979—, Mass. Mut. Life Ins. Co., Springfield, 1979—, JWT Group, Inc., N.Y.C., 1980-87, Owens-Ill., Inc., Toledo, 1981-87 ; public mem. regional adv. com. on banking policies and practices 3d Nat. Bank Region, 1976-77; adv. bd. Phila. Fin. Assn., 1980—; bd. dirs. Raytheon Co., Lexington, Mass., 1987—, ALCO Standard Corp., Valley Forge, Pa., 1988—; Trustee emeritus Wellesley (Mass.) Coll., 1970-85, Com. for Econ. Devel., 1979-88; bd. dirs. John and Mary R. Markle Found., 1976-86, Greater Phila. Partnership, 1975-85; bd. dirs. World Affairs Council Phila., 1977-87, vice chmn., 1978-80; bd. dirs. Phila. United Fund, 1960-65, United Way Southeastern Pa., 1979-87; trustee Salem Acad. and Coll., 1967-70, Eisenhower Exchange Fellowships, 1986—; mem. Harvard Vis. com. for Harvard and Radcliffe, 1972-78; mem. Presser Found., 1970-85; pres. Jr. League Phila., 1958-60, Meadowbrook Sch., 1962-63; mem. Phila. Orch. Council, 1979-88em. Mayor's Commn. for Women, Phila., 1981-83; mem. U.S. Sr. Women's Golf Assn. Recipient Disting. Alumna award Salem Acad., 1985. Mem. Wellesley Coll. Alumnae Assn. (pres. 1970-73). Lutheran. Home: 1700 Old Welsh Rd Huntingdon Valley PA 19006

HAUPTMAN, MARY MARGARET, court reporting agency executive; b. Queens, N.Y., May 18, 1955; d. Earl Edward and Margaret Frances (Struckman) H.; m. Ted John Doukas, Mar. 20, 1982. Grad. Verbatim/Stenotype Inst., Hicksville, N.Y., 1974. Court reporter, N.Y.C., 1975-79; pres., owner Hauptman Reporting, Syosset, N.Y., 1979—; pres., owner, founder Ct. Reporting Inst., Sch. of Stenotype, Hicksville, N.Y., 1986—. Bd. dirs. Republican Party, Syosset-Woodbury, N.Y., 1983-85, committeewoman, 1984—. Mem. Nat. Shorthand Reporters Assn., N.Y. Shorthand Reporters Assn. Roman Catholic. Club: Syosset-Woodbury Republican. (bd. dirs. 1983-85). Home and Office: 70 Split Rock Rd Muttontown NY 11791 also: 150 Nassau St Suite 2000 New York NY 10038

HAURI, CHRISTINE GAIL, marketing executive; b. Chgo., Nov. 18, 1949; d. George Edward and Dorothy Eleanor (Kunc) H. BS in Communications, U. Ill., 1972. Copywriter Osco Drug, Inc., Oak Brook, Ill., 1972-74; mgr. advt. White Hen Pantry, Elmhurst, Ill., 1974-77; supr. promotion CNA Ins., Chgo., 1978-80; supr. copy, assoc. creative dir. Foote, Cone & Belding Communications, Chgo., 1980-83; v.p., exec. creative dir. William A. Robinson, Inc., Chgo., 1983—. Contbr. articles to profl. jours. Home: 751 Bonnie Brae River Forest IL 60305 Office: William A Robinson Inc 35 E Wacker Dr Chicago IL 60601

HAUSCH, MARY ELLEN, editor; b. Akron, Ohio, Sept. 6, 1949; d. Walter Richard and Anne Marie McKinniss) H.; m. Bob Coffin, 1986. B.S.J. cum laude, Ohio U., 1970. Reporter Gazette Telegraph, Colorado Springs, Colo., 1970-71; reporter Las Vegas (Nev.) Rev.-Jour., Nev., 1971-74; reporter, asst. city editor Las Vegas (Nev.) Rev.-Jour., 1975, city editor, 1976, mng. editor, 1977—. Bd. dirs. HELP Ctr., Las Vegas, 1980—, pres., 1985-87; vice chmn. Nev. Pub. Radio, Las Vegas, 1984-87; bd. dirs. Planned Parenthood of So. Nev., Las Vegas, 1984-87. Mem. Las Vegas C. of C. (mem. bd. Women's Council, 1986—), Sigma Delta Chi (pres. Las Vegas chpt. 1975-76). Club: Variety. Home: 1139 S 5th Pl Las Vegas NV 89104 Office: Las Vegas Rev-Jour PO Box 70 Las Vegas NV 89125

HAUSE, EDITH COLLINS, college administrator; b. Rock Hill, S.C., Dec. 11, 1933; d. Ernest O. and Violet (Smith) Collins; m. James Luke Hause, Sept. 3, 1955; children—Stephen Mark, Felicia Gaye Hause Friesen. B.A., Columbia Coll., S.C., 1956; postgrad. U. N.C.-Greensboro, 1967, U. S.C., 1971-75. Tchr. Richland Dist. II, Columbia, 1971-74; dir. alumnae affairs Columbia Coll., 1974-82, v.p. alumnae affairs, 1982-84, v.p. devel., 1984—. Named Outstanding Tchr. of Yr., Richland Dist. II, 1974. Mem. Columbia Network for Female Execs., Council for Advancement and Support Edn., Alpha Delta Kappa. Republican. Methodist. Home: Route 4 Box 760 Prosperity SC 29127 Office: Columbia Coll Devel Office Columbia SC 29203

HAUSER, CELLANY ELIZABETH, festival administrator; b. Amarillo, Tex., July 4, 1958; d. Sanford and Margaret Jean (Mosley) H. AS in Recreational Leadership, Green River Community Coll., 1982; AA, U. Alaska, Anchorage, 1983. Cert. festival exec., Purdue U. Recreation leader Maverick Boys Club, Amarillo, 1972-75, asst. dir., 1975-78; dir. ops. Gourmet Catering Inc., Anchorage, 1978, gen. mgr., 1979-80; instr. Green River Community Coll., Auburn, Wash., 1981-82; dir. camp Seattle Parks and Recreation Dept., 1981-82; sec., coordinator parade Anchorage Fur Rendezvous, 1982-84, office mgr., 1984—. Mem. Internat. Festivals Assn., Soc. Nonprofit Orgns., N.W. Festivals Assn. Baptist. Office: Greater Anchorage Inc 737 W 5th Ave Anchorage AK 99501

HAUSER, LAURETTE MARIE, public relations company executive; b. N.Y.C., Aug. 3, 1958; d. Kenneth James and Margaret (Bartro) H.; m. Carlos Guerrero Forcade, Aug. 29, 1981. BA magna cum laude, Columbia U., 1980; MS, Rensselaer Poly. Inst., 1983. Editorial asst. N.Y. Acad. Scis., N.Y.C., part-time 1979-80; pub. relations research coordinator Albany Med. Coll., N.Y., 1980-81; communications specialist Matterson Assocs., Albany, 1981-82; account exec. Burson-Marsteller, N.Y.C., 1983-84; account supr.

Daniel J. Edelman, Inc., N.Y.C., 1984-86, v.p. med./pharm. pub. relations, 1986-87; adj. asst. prof. Fairleigh Dickinson U., Teaneck, N.J., 1985, sr. v.p., group head, 1986-87; sr. v.p., group mgr. Creamer Dickson Basford, 1987—. Relief houseparent N.Y. State Div. for Youth, Albany, 1981-83; active Big Bros./Big Sisters, 1983. Mem. Am. Assn. Med. Writers, Internat. Communications Assn., Nat. Assn. Female Execs. Roman Catholic. Club: Sierra. Avocations: biking, cross-country skiing, travel, comparative literature, wildlife preservation. Home: 100 Parkway W Mount Vernon NY 10552 Office: Creamer Dickson Basford 1633 Broadway New York NY 10019

HAUSER, LYNN ELIZABETH, eye surgeon; b. Cleve., Apr. 11, 1951; d. Cavour Herman and Ruth Natalie (Lageman) H.; B.S. in Medicine, Northwestern U., 1974, M.D., 1976; m. Neil L. Ross, June 20, 1975; children—Michael Hauser Ross, Benjamin Hauser Ross. Resident in ophthalmology Northwestern U., 1976-80; practice medicine specializing in cataract surgery, Sycamore, Ill., 1980—; clin. asst. prof. ophthalmology U. Ill., Chgo.; lectr. in ophthalmology Northwestern U.; project ophthalmologist Nat. Eye Inst. Early Treatment Diabetic Retinopathy Study, 1982. Diplomate Am. Bd. Ophthalmology. Fellow ACS, Am. Acad. Ophthalmology, mem. AMA, Dekalb County Med. Soc., Ill. Assn. Ophthalmology, Ill. Med. Soc., LWV. Office: 2240 Gateway Dr Sycamore IL 60178

HAUSER, RITA ELEANORE ABRAMS, lawyer; b. N.Y.C., July 12, 1934; d. Nathan and Frieda (Litt) Abrams; m. Gustave M. Hauser, June 10, 1956; children—Glenvil Aubrey, Patricia. A.B. magna cum laude, Hunter Coll., 1954; Dr. Polit. Economy with highest honors (Fulbright grantee), U. Strasbourg, France, 1955; Licence en Droit, U. Paris, 1958; student law sch., Harvard U., 1955-56; L.L.B. with honors, NYU, 1959; LL.D. (hon.), Seton Hall U., 1969, Finch Coll., 1969, U. Miami, Fla., 1971. Bar: D.C. 1959, N.Y. 1961, U.S. Supreme Ct. 1967. Atty. U.S. Dept. Justice, 1959-61; sole practice N.Y.C., 1961-67; ptnr. Moldover, Hauser, Strauss & Volin, 1968-72; sr. ptnr. Stroock & Stroock & Lavan, 1972—; Handmaker lectr. Louis Brandeis Lectr. Series, U. Ky. Law Sch.; lectr. on internat. law Naval War Coll. and Army War Coll.; Mitchell lectr. in Law SUNY Buffalo; USIA lectr. constl. law Egypt, India, Australia, New Zealand; bd. dirs. Wickes Cos., Inc.; U.S. pub. del. to Vienna Follow-up meeting of Conf. on Security and Cooperation in Europe, 1986—; mem. adv. panel on internat. law U.S. Dept. of State, 1986—. Contbr. articles on internat. law to profl. jours. U.S. rep. to UN Commn. on Human Rights, 1969-72; mem. U.S. del. to Gen. Assembly UN, 1969; vice chmn. U.S. Adv. Com. on Internat. and Cultural Affairs, 1973-77; mem. N.Y.C. Bd. Higher Edn., 1974-76, Stanton Panel on internat. info., edn., cultural relations to reorganize USIA and Voice of Am., 1974-75, Mid. East Study Group Brookings Inst., 1975, 87-88, U.S. del. World Conf. Internat. Women's Yr., Mexico City, 1975; co-chmn. Com. for Re-election Pres., 1972; co-chair Presdl. Debates project LWV, 1976; adv. bd. Nat. News Council, 1977-79; bd. dirs. March of Dimes of N.Y., Bd. for Internat. Broadcasting, 1977-80; trustee N.Y. Philharm. Soc.; adv. bd. Ctr. for Law and Nat. Security, U. Va. Law Sch/. 1978-84; vis. com. Ctr. Internat. Affairs Harvard U., 1975-81; co-chmn. Coalition for Reagan/Bush; bd. govs.; v.p. Am. Jewish Com.; chmn. adv. panel Internat. Parliamentary Group for Human Rights in Soviet Union, 1984-86; U.S. pub. del. Vienna follow-up meeting Conf. on Security and Cooperation in Europe, 1986—; mem. spl. refugee adv. panel Dept. State, 1981, mem. adv. panel on internat. law, 1986—; former trustee Internat. Legal Ctr., Legal Aid Soc. N.Y., Freedom House. Intellectual Exchange fellow, Japan Soc. Fellow ABA (life, standing coms. on law and nat. security, 1979-85, on world order under law 1969-78, on judicial selection, tenure, compensation, 1977-79, council sect. on individual rights and responsibilities, 1970-73, adv., bd. jour., 1973-78); mem. Assn. Bar City N.Y., Am. Soc. Internat. Law (v.p., exec. com. 1971-76), Am. Fgn. Law Assn. (dir.), Am. Arbitration Assn. (past dir.), Am. Soc. Internat. Law (past exec. com., v.p.-elect 1987), Inst. East-West Security Studies (bd. dirs., exec. com.), Council on Fgn. Relations, Harvard Law Sch. Assn. N.Y.C. (trustee), Friends of The Hague Acad. Internat. Law (bd. dirs.), N.Y. Philharm. Symphony Soc. (bd. dirs., mem. exec. com.). Republican. Home: 700 Park Ave New York NY 10021 Office: Stroock & Stroock & Lavan 7 Hanover Sq New York NY 10004

HAUSER-DANN, JOYCE ROBERTA, public relations and marketing specialist; b. N.Y.C.; d. Abraham and Helen (Lesser) Frankel; B.A., SUNY, 1976; Ph.D., Union Grad. Sch., 1987; m. Asher Dann, Sept. 7, 1987. children—Mitchell, Mark, Ellen; stepchildren: Laurence, Michael. Editor, Art in Flowers, 1955-58; pres. Joyce Advt., 1958-65; partner Hauser & Assocs., Pub. Relations, 1966-75; dir. broadcasting Bildersee Pub. Relations, 1973-75; pres. Hauser & Assocs., Inc., Pub. Relations, 1975-78, Hauser-Roberts, Inc., Pub. Relations/Mktg., N.Y.C., 1978-85, Mktg. Concepts & Communications Inc., N.Y.C., 1985—; moderator show Perceptions, Sta. WEVD, 1975-77, Speaking of Health, WNBC, 1977—, 97 Health Line, Sta. WYNY, 1980-83, Conversations with Joyce Hauser, Sta. WNBC, 1975-86, What's on Your Mind, Sta. WYNY, 1983-84, Talk-Net, 1983—; entertainment critic Sta. WNBC, 1986—; instr. Baruch Coll., CCNY, 1980-85; asst. prof. NYU, 1987—; mem. adj. faculty speech communications NYU, 1986-88. Mem. Citywide Health Adv. Council on Sch. Health, 1970—, treas., 1980—; mem. adv. bd. degree programs NYU Sch. Continuing Edn. Named one of 10 Top Successful Women, Cancer Soc., 1976; recipient Professionalism award Sta. WNBC, 1980. Mem. AFTRA, Am. Women in Radio and TV (corr. sec. 1973, chmn. coll. women in broadcasting 1974). Contbg. editor Alive, 1976-77. Home: 115 E 82d St New York NY 10028 Office: 20 E 53d St New York NY 10022

HAUSHALTER, MARY ANN, civic worker; b. McKees Rocks, Pa., May 30, 1906; d. William Aloysius and Mary Aloysius (Griffin) H. Clk.-typist Recorder of Deeds, Pitts., 1927-44; typist DeMoine Steel Co., Neville Island, Pa., 1944-46; asst. sec., cashier State Inheritance, Pitts., 1946-63; dep. sheriff Sheriff's Office Allegheny County, Pitts., 1963-71. Active Focus-On-Renewal, Father Regis Ryan, McKees Rocks, 1971—, Meals-on-Wheels, McKees Rocks, 1979—; treas. Ohio Valley Gen. Hosp., 1983-87, mem. 1979—. Mem. Am. Assn. Ret. Persons (nominating com. 1979), Am. Bus. and Profl. Women's Club (v.p. 1971-75, Woman of Yr. 1978-79), Cath. Daus. Am. (grand regent 1956-67, past grand regent 1966—). Democrat. Roman Catholic. Club: VFW Ladies Aux. (mem. 1945-88, pres. 1979). Avocations: crocheting; embroidering. Home: 100 Pennsylvania Ave McKees Rocks PA 15136

HAUSWIRTH, CONNIE LYNN, accountant; b. Emmetsburg, Iowa, Dec. 9, 1953; d. Ronald George and Mary Sharlene (Johnson) H. BS, Morningside Coll., 1976; MA, U. Iowa, 1981. CPA, Iowa, Ill. Math. tchr., coach Indianola (Iowa) Community Schs., 1976-79; acct. Cargill, Inc., Carpentersville, Ill., 1981—. Home: 207 College Crossing Rolling Meadows IL 60008 Office: Cargill Inc Cottage Ave and Lake Marian Rd Carpentersville IL 60110

HAUTHER, BRENDA FAYE, author; b. Greensboro, N.C., Sept. 10, 1951; d. Cassie Elizabeth (Depew) Stromer. BA, Columbia U., 1975; JD, U. Conn., 1982. Co-author: Surving the Undergraduate Jungle, 3d edit., 1983. Home: 6266 Rose Hill Dr Alexandria VA 22310 Office: Covington & Burling 1201 Pennsylvania Ave NW Washington DC 20004

HAVARD, GAY ROBINSON, edcational administrator; b. Brookhaven, Miss., Jan. 22, 1949; d. Elige and Anna Ree (Simmons) Robinson; (div. 1987); children: DeRon Coryell, Sharron Pleshette (twins); m. Billy R. Havard, Feb. 1988. BS, Jackson State U., Miss., 1971, MS, 1979; postgrad., Wm. Carey Coll., 1982, U. Miss., 1984. Youth counselor State Community Services Agt., Jackson, 1969-70; reading tchr. Brookhaven (Miss.) Pub. Schs., 1971-72, spl. edn. tchr., 1972-85, approved examiner, 1984-86, adminstrv. asst., 1985—. Bd. dirs. Adult Adv. Planning Com., Brookhaven, Miss., 1981-82; mem. Lincoln Residental bd., Brookhaven, 1986—; pres. Brookhaven Humanitarian Aux., 1982-83, Redmond Pre-Sch. Day Care Ctr., 1982-83; bd. dirs. Miter's Day Care Bd., 1982-83; county council co-chmn. Miss. Action for Progress, 1982; mem. Council for Exceptional Children: adv. bd. Adult Work Activity Ctr., 1981-82, Brookhaven Learning Resource Ctr., 1984; choir dir. Bethel A.M.E. Ch., 1983-84, clerk, 1983-85, mem. ednl. bd., 1984-85. Named Educator of the Yr., Miss. Assn. for Children with Learning Disabilities, 1985; U. Miss. scholar, 1984; Urban Tchr's. Appreciation grantee, 1982; Jackson State U. scholar, 1967-71. Mem. Miss. Edn. Computing Assn., Miss. Assn. for Women in Ednl. Leadership, Miss. Assn. Sch. Adminstrs., Nat. Assn. Female Execs., Phi Kappa Phi, Phi Delta Kappa. Democrat. Methodist. Home: 836 Dissa St Brookhaven MS 39601 Office: Brookhaven Pub Schs PO Box 540 Brookhaven MS 39601

HAVELOCK, CHRISTINE MITCHELL, art historian; b. Cochrane, Ont., Can., June 2, 1924; d. William Waterson and Annie Margaret (Graham) Mitchell; m. Eric A. Havelock, Nov. 21, 1962. B.A., U. Toronto, 1946; Ph.D. (Charles Eliot Norton fellow), Harvard U., 1958. Mem. faculty Vassar Coll., 1953—, prof. art history, 1967—, M.C. Mellon Chair, 1985—, chmn. art dept., 1968-71, asst. to pres., 1972-73, acting. chmn. art dept., 1987—; vis. prof. Yale U., 1986-87. Author: Hellenistic Art, 2d edit, 1981. Mem. mng. com. Am. Sch. Classical Studies, Athens, Greece. Recipient Gold medal Radcliffe Grad. Soc., 1987. Mem. Am. Inst. Archeology, Coll. Art Assn., AAUW. Address: Vassar Coll Box 358 Poughkeepsie NY 12601

HAVENS, MARY MARTHA, social services adminstrator; b. Glens Falls, N.Y., July 11, 1939; d. Harry VanGundy and Nellie Goodman (Maxim) Elmore; m. James Carson Varnum (div. July 1977); children: Michael James, Kathleen Ruth Varnum Davis; m. Ronald Joseph Havens, Aug. 26, 1978. AA with honors, Adirondack Community Coll., 1975; BA, Empire State Coll., 1977; postgrad., SUNY, Albany, 1978-81. Adminstrv. asst. Acousticon Hearing Aids, Glens Falls, 1967-69; bookkeeper Bruce Buick, Inc., Glens Falls, 1969-77; sr. child support investigator Wash. County Dept. Social Services, Granville, N.Y., 1977—; county rep. N.Y. State Pub. Welfare Assn. Child Support Enforcement Unit, Albany, N.Y., 1985—. Mem. Nat. Assn. Female Execs. Republican. Methodist. Home: 50 Mountainview Ln Glen Falls NY 12801

HAVERKOS, SHEILAH JANE, nurse, nursing service executive; b. Welland, Ont., Can., Jan. 17, 1950; came to U.S., 1968; d. Keith F. W. and Margaret Elizabeth (Stephens) L.; m. Bruce Edmund Haverkos, Apr. 25, 1970; children: Stacy Lynn, Shawyn. LPN, Manatee Vocat. Sch., 1976. Nurse Manatee County Blood Bank, Bradenton, Fla., 1976-77, Blake Hosp., Bradenton, 1977-78, Dr. Escalante, Bradenton, 1978-81; owner Nursing Profls., Bradenton, 1982—; bd. dirs. Walt Disney World, Orlando, Busch Gardens, Tampa. Named Female Exec. Southwest Fla., 1985, 86. Roman Catholic. Office: Nursing Profls Inc 6302 Manatee Ave W Suite D Bradenton FL 34209

HAVERSTICK, SUSAN REGINA, manufacturing company executive; b. Jersey City, May 24, 1950; d. Kenneth and Margaret Louise (Hoch) H. BA magna cum laude, Jersey City State Coll., 1972. Cert. transp. mgr. Mgr. Edfor Music, Bayonne, N.J., 1972-77; mgr. traffic Belco Lites, Newark, 1977-78; shipping coordinator Sherwin Williams, Newark, 1978-83; transp. analyst Lightolier, Jersey City, 1983-85; supr. corp. traffic Ingersoll Rand, Piscataway, N.J., 1985—; cons. Logistics Mgmt. Assn., South Orange, N.J., 1986—; bd. dirs. Traffic Club Newark, Inc., 2d v.p., 1985-86, pres. 1986-87. Leader Girl Scouts Am., Nutley, N.J., 1976-78. Mem. Delta Nu Alpha. Democrat. Roman Catholic. Office: Ingersoll Rand 91 New England Ave Piscataway NJ 08854

HAVILAND, CAMILLA KLEIN, lawyer; b. Dodge City, Kans., Sept. 13, 1926; d. Robert Godfrey and Lelah (Luther) Klein; m. John Bodman Haviland, Sept. 7, 1957. A.A., Monticello Coll., 1946; B.A., Radcliffe Coll., 1948; J.D., Kans. U., 1955. Bar: Kans. 1955. Assoc. Calver & White, Wichita, Kans., 1955-56; sole practice, Dodge City, 1956—; probate, county and juvenile judge Ford County (Kans.), 1955-77; mem. Jud. Council Com. on Probate and Juvenile Law. Mem. adv. bd. Salvation Army, U. Kans. Sch. Religion. Recipient Nathan Burkan award ASCAP, 1955. Mem. Ford County Bar Assn. (pres. 1980), S.W. Kans. Bar Assn. (pres. 1968), Kans. Bar Assn., ABA, C. of C., Order of Coif, PEO, Phi Delta Delta. Democrat. Episcopalian. Clubs: Prairie Dunes Country (Hutchinson, Kans.); Soroptimists. Contbr. articles to profl. jours. Home: 2006 E Lane Dodge City KS 67801 Office: 203 W Spruce Box 17 Dodge City KS 67801

HAVILAND, LEONA, librarian; b. Stamford, Conn., Nov. 10, 1916; d. Howard Brush and Ada Grace (Jewell) Haviland; B.S., U. Ala., 1940; M.S., U. Ill., 1951; postgrad. Columbia, 1943, 56-60; m. Warren John Burke, Sept. 10, 1973. Jr. asst. Ferguson Library, Stamford, 1936-37, summers 1938-39, sr. asst., 1940-44; student asst. U. Ala., 1937-40; asst. to cataloguer U.S. Nat. Mus. Library, Washington, 1944-48; librarian Arts and Industries Mus., Smithsonian Instn., Washington, 1948-50; reference librarian U.S. Mcht. Marine Acad., Kings Point, N.Y., 1952-77. Mem. council YWCA, Washington, 1945-47. Mem. A.L.A., Spl. Libraries Assn. (past group membership chmn.), L.I. Hist. Soc., N.Y. Geneal. and Biog. Soc., Smithsonian Assos., South Street Seaport Mus., Alpha Beta Alpha, Alpha Lambda Delta. Home: 809 Pennsylvania Ave Saint Cloud FL 32769

HAVIST, MARJORIE VICTORIA, librarian, educator; b. Johnstown, Pa., Nov. 6, 1931; d. Victor Dale and Lillie Mae (Bross) Mulhollen; m. George I. Melhorn, Aug. 8, 1953 (dec. Dec. 1962); children—Susan Lynn, Bradford George; m. Ewald Jack Havist, Aug. 7, 1969. B.S. in Edn., Bucknell U., 1953; M.L.S., U. Wash., 1966. Cert. librarian, Wash. Engr., Boeing Co., Seattle, 1955, 57-58; librarian Bellevue Community Coll., Wash., 1966-78; head librarian Seattle Central Community Coll., Seattle, 1978-80; assoc. dean library Skagit Valley Coll., Mt. Vernon, Wash., 1980—. Bd. dirs. ARC Skagit County, Mt. Vernon, 1982; loaned exec. United Way Skagit County, 1983-84. Mem. ALA, Community Coll. Librarians and Media Specialists (pres. 1977-78), Community Coll. Library Dirs. Council (pres. 1981-82), Phi Theta Kappa. Republican. Lutheran. Office: Skagit Valley Coll 2405 College Way Mount Vernon WA 98273

HAWBAKER, DIANA SUE, software analyst, consultant; b. Des Moines, Jan. 6, 1953; d. Duane William and Pearl Jean (Zimmerman) H.; m. Gary David Perrin, Nov. 18, 1972 (div. 1974). Systems analyst Gen. Growth Devel., Des Moines, 1976-81, cons., 1981-82; project mgr. Mgmt. Controls, Des Moines, 1981-82; pres. Integrated Bus. Systems, Des Moines, 1982-83; project mgr. Gen. Instrument Corp., Des Moines, 1983-85, programming mgr., Balt., 1985-86; product mgr. software services Scan-Optics, Inc., East Hartford, Conn., 1986—; cons. Wallace-Homestead, Des Moines, 1982-84, Mental Health Assn.; Polk County, Des Moines, 1982-84, Miller Pub., Mpls., 1984-85. Author software packages. Mem. NOW, Am. Bus. Women's Assn. (pres. Challenge chpt. 1981-82), Digital Equipment Corp Users Soc., Nat. Assn. Female Execs. Brethren. Avocations: reading; camping; gardening; crafts; tennis. Home: 205 Vernon Ave Apt 152 Vernon CT 06066 Office: Scan-Optics Inc 22 Prestige Park Circle East Hartford CT 06108

HAWES, DEBRA WINIFRED, lawyer; b. Birmingham, Ala., Apr. 16, 1958; d. William and Precious (Williams) H. B.A., Fisk U., Nashville, 1979; J.D., U. Ala.-Tuscaloosa, 1982. Bar: Ala. 1982. Trial atty. EEOC, Birmingham, 1983—. Mem. ABA, Ala. Bar Assn., Magic City Bar Assn., Magic City Jaycees, Ala. Lawyers Assn., Nat. Bar Assn., Alpha Kappa Alpha, Phi Alpha Delta. Democrat. Methodist. Home: 17 9th Ct SW Birmingham AL 35211

HAWK, SUSAN ALICE, medical information specialist; b. Columbia, Pa., Apr. 24, 1953; d. Willard J. and Nanette F. (Knecht) H.; m. Philip I. Wexler, Apr. 4, 1986. BS in Edn., Millersville (Pa.) State Coll., 1974; EdM, Harvard U., 1977; MS in Info. Sci., Simmons Coll., 1981. Library technician Med. Sch. Boston U., 1974-75, searcher Mugar Library, 1975-76; media librarian Sargent Coll. Allied Health Profls., Boston, 1977-79; library technician Mass. Coll. Pharmacy, Boston, 1979; intern Mt. Auburn Hosp. Library, Cambridge, Mass., 1979-80; library assoc. Nat. Library Medicine, Bethesda, Md., 1980-81, specialist tech. info., 1981—. Mem. Parkview Citizens' Assn., Bethesda, 1987—. Mem. Med. Library Assn. (sect. chair 1985-86, sect. council 1986—, vice-chair sect. council 1987—). Jewish. Home: 9208 Chanute Dr Bethesda MD 20814 Office: Nat Library Medicine Specialized Info Services 8600 Rockville Pike/38A Bethesda MD 20894

HAWKES, ELIZABETH LAWRENCE (BONNIE), occupational therapist, consultant; b. Bryn Mawr, Pa., May 28, 1944; d. Edward Bettle and Anna Correy (Keen) Scull; m. Geoffrey Neale Hawkes, Aug. 12, 1972. BA in Chemistry, Hood Coll., 1966; cert. in occupational therapy, U. Pa., 1968; cert. in health care mgmt., B.C. Inst. Tech., Can., 1981; MS, U. B.C., 1988. Therapist Mary Bridge Children's Hosp., Tacoma, 1968-72; staff occupational therapist Pearson Hosp., Vancouver, B.C., 1972-74; staff occupational therapist Lions Gate Hosp., North Vancouver, B.C., 1974-76, sr. occupational therapist, 1976-78, supr. occupational therapy, 1978-82; researcher med. engring. Dept. Surgery U. B.C., Vancouver, 1983-84; lectr. U. B.C., Vancouver, 1981-86; clin. instr. U. B.C., North Vancouver, 1981—; cons. health services North Vancouver, 1983—; bd. dirs. Lions Gate Med. Research Found., 1988—. Contbr. articles to profl. jours. Bd. dirs First Aid Ski Patrol, (coordinator 1977-79) (patrol 1973-80); first aid instr. St. John Ambulance, 1977-80, CPR instr. 1978. Mem. Can. Assn. Occupational Therapists (bd. dirs., com. chair 1982-87), B.C. Soc. Occupational Therapists, World Fedn. Occupational Therapists, Can. Council Health Service Execs., Am. Coll. Health Care Execs. Home and Office: 1397 Harold Rd, North Vancouver Can V7J 1W9

HAWKINS, ALTONNETTE DENISE, telecommunications executive; b. Bklyn., Sept. 25, 1958; d. Ruben Alton and Lula Mae (Taylor) H. BA in Communications, Rutgers U., 1980; MPS in Telecommunications, NYU, 1986. Communications technician network ops. AT&T, Camden, N.J., 1981-83; staff asst. teleprocessing, data ctr. ops. AT&T, Piscataway, N.J., 1983-84, network design assoc. mgr. interactive network design, 1984-85, technical support mgr. data communications mgmt. ctr., 1985-86; project mgr. network ops. project mgmt. AT&T, Piscataway, 1986-87; quality cons. data processing corp. telecommunications AT&T, South Plainfield, NJ, 1987—; network dir. CareerLink, Piscataway, 1987. Named one of Most Outstanding Young Women Am., 1987. Mem. Alliance Black Telecommunications Employees (nat. chpt. liaison 1986—, chairperson), Nat. Assn. Female Execs., Am. Soc. Quality Control. Home: 301 N Randolphville Rd Piscataway NJ 08854 Office: AT&T 5000 Hadley Rd South Plainfield NJ 07080

HAWKINS, CARMEN DOLORAS, lawyer; b. Los Angeles, Sept. 17, 1955; d. Lenell Herman Hawkins and Doloras Mondy. BA, U. Calif., Santa Cruz, 1977; JD, Georgetown U., 1981. Bar: Washington 1981, Calif. 1982, U.S. Dist. Ct. (cen. dist. Calif.) 1982, U.S. Ct. Appeals (9th cir.) 1982. Assoc. Law Offices of Thomas G. Neusom, Los Angeles, 1982-83; sole practice Los Angeles, 1984—; atty. Los Angeles Community Coll., 1984-85; gen. counsel Los Angeles Trade Tech. Coll. Found., 1986—; of counsel Wilson, Becks & Pyfrom, Los Angeles, 1986—. Bd. dirs. Calif. Dems. for New Leadership, Los Angeles, 1985—; mem. New Frontier Dem. Club, Los Angeles, 1984—, New Dem. Channel, Los Angeles, 1984—; commr. City of Los Angeles Commn. on Bicentennial of U.S. Constitution, 1976, 87—. Recipient Community Service award Los Angeles City Council, 1985, Community Service award Calif. State Senator Diane Watson, 1985, Community Service award Black Women Lawyers, 1986, Community Service award Los Angeles Councilman David Cunningham, 1986. Mem. ABA, Los Angeles County Bar Assn., Los Angeles County Barristers Assn. (exec. com. 1986—), NAACP, Black Women Lawyers of Los Angeles (parliamentarian 1985-86), John M. Langston Bar Assn., Black Women's Forum, Phi Alpha Delta. Democrat. African Methodist Episcopalian. Office: 6255 Sunset Blvd Suite 2000 Hollywood CA 90028

HAWKINS, ELINOR DIXON (MRS. CARROLL WOODARD HAWKINS), librarian; b. Masontown, W.Va., Sept. 25, 1927; d. Thomas Fitchie and Susan (Reed) Dixon; A.B., Fairmont State Coll., 1949; B.S. in L.S., U. N.C., 1950; m. Carroll Woodard Hawkins, June 24, 1951; 1 son, John Carroll. Children's librarian Enoch Pratt Free Library, Balt., 1950-51; head circulation dept. Greensboro (N.C.) Pub. Library, 1951-56; librarian Craven-Pamlico Library Service, New Bern, N.C., 1958-62; dir. Craven-Pamlico-Carteret Regional Library, 1962—; storyteller children's TV program Tele-Story Time, 1952-58, 63—; mem. adv. bd. First Am. Savs. Bank. Mem. New Bern Hist. Soc., 1973—, Tryon Palace Commn., 1974—; mem. adv. bd. Salvation Army. Mem. N.C. Assn. Retarded Children, N.C. Library Assn., Salvation Army Advisory Bd. Baptist. Club: Pilot (pres. 1957-58, v.p. 1962-63). Home: PO Box 57 Cove City NC 28523 Office: 400 Johnson St New Bern NC 28560

HAWKINS, GERI SUE, interior designer, realtor; b. Kansas City, Mo., Sept. 4, 1940; d. William S. McCune and Verla J. (Kempter) McCune Stoll; m. LeRay D. Long, Oct. 12, 1958 (div. Dec. 1961); 1 child, Lori Diane Long Seidl; m. Ray Eldon Hawkins, Oct. 9, 1964; children: Lynn M., John Ted; stepchildren: Celeste, Steve. Student Kansas City Bus. Coll., 1961-62, U. Mo., Kansas City, 1974-75; AA, Maple Woods Coll., 1974. Interior designer Carpenter Bros. Inc., Kansas City, 1975-77; pres., designer Gerry Hawkins Interiors, Kansas City, 1977-81; interior designer R. D. Mann Inc., Kansas City, 1981-83; owner-designer Designs By Geri, Kansas City, 1983—; realtor assoc. ERA Martin House, Platte City, Mo., 1984-85; interior designer Martin House Design, Platte City, 1984-85; sales rep. Ron Wood Real Estate, 1987-88; with J.D. Reece Realtors, 1988—. Mem. Lincoln Coll. Prepatory Acad. Adv. Bd., 1986. Local theatrical appearances, 1972-73. Leader Winding River council Girl Scouts U.S., 1966-71; mem. Grace Notes Singing Ensemble, Kansas City, 1980; fundraiser Muscular Dystrophy Assn., Platte City, 1985; trustee Park Hill Bapt. Ch., Parkville, Mo., 1983-85. Mem. Platte County Bus. and Profl. Assn. (bd. dirs. 1980-81), Am. Soc. Interior Designers, Platte County Women's Exchange, Women in Bus. Republican. Baptist. Avocations: tennis, swimming, golf, theatre, gardening. Home and Office: 7709 NW 69th St Kansas City MO 64152

HAWKINS, IDA FAYE, educator; b. Ft. Worth, Dec. 28, 1928; d. Christopher Columbus and Nannie Idella (Hughes) Hall; student Midwestern U., 1946-48; B.S., N. Tex. State U., 1951; student Lamar U., 1968-70; M.S., McNeese State U., 1973; m. Gene Hamilton Hawkins, Dec. 22, 1952; children—Gene Agner, Jane Hall. Tchr., DeQueen Elem. Sch., Port Arthur, Tex., 1950-54; tchr. Tyrrell Elem. Sch., Port Arthur, 1955-56; tchr. Roy Hatton Elem. Sch., Bridge City, Tex., 1967-68; tchr. Oak Forest Elem. Sch., Vidor, Tex., 1968—. Second vice-pres. Travis Elem. PTA, 1965-66, 1st v.p., 1966-67; corr. sec. Port Arthur City council PTA, 1966-67. Named Tchr. of Yr., Oak Forest Elem., 1984-85. Mem. NEA, Tex. State Tchrs. Assn., Classroom Tchrs. Assn., Am. Psychol. Assn., McNeese State U. Alumni Assn. Presbyterian (Sunday sch. tchr. 1951-53, 60-66). Home: 4075 Laurel Apt 73 Beaumont TX 77707 Office: Oak Forest Elem Sch 2400 Hwy 12 Vidor TX 77662

HAWKINS, KAREN FRANCES, banker; b. Portchester, N.Y., Nov. 30, 1947; d. George Lockwood, II and Helen Athena (Raftes) H.; B.A. in Math. and Spanish, Wells Coll., Aurora, N.Y., 1969; grad. Inst. Coop. Leadership, 1978. Asso. in corp. fin. Morgan Stanley & Co., N.Y.C., 1969-71; fin. analyst pvt. placements Travelers Ins. Co., Hartford, Conn., 1971-72; analyst corp. fin. and research Culverwell & Co., Inc., Springfield, Mass., 1972-74; asst. v.p., comml. loan officer Springfield Bank for Coops., 1974-80; group mgr. tng. comml. lenders Citizens & So. Nat. Bank, Atlanta, 1980-81, mgr. comml. br., 1982-84, v.p., comml. relationship mgr., 1984-86, mgr. Comml. Ctr., 1986—; tchr. classes in field. Mem. recreation com. Cross Creek Homeowners, 1984-85; mem. Gwinnett County Council Quality Growth. Mem. Am. Inst. Banking, Atlanta C. of C. (life), Gwinnett County C. of C. (mem. ambassadors council 1987, 88). Republican. Episcopalian. Clubs: Cross Creek Ladies Twilight Golf League (chmn. 1981-82), Cross Creek Golf Assn. (treas. 1982, co-chmn. 1983), Civitan. Office: 6625 The Corners Pkwy Suite 100 Norcross GA 30092

HAWKINS, LINDA PARROTT, business educator; b. Florence, S.C., June 23, 1947; d. Obie Lindberg Parrott and Mary Francis (Lee) Evans; m. Larry Eugene Hawkins, Jan. 5, 1946; 1 child, Heather Nichole. BS, U. S.C., 1969; MS, Francis Marion Coll., 1978; postgrad. in ednl. adminstrn., U. S.C., 1985-88. Tchr. J.C. Lynch High Sch., Coward, S.C., 1973-80, Lake City (S.C.) High Sch., 1980—; mem. Williamsburg Tech. Adv. Council, Kingstree, S.C., 1985-88, Florence-Darlington (S.C.) Tech. Adv. Council, 1981-87; speaker, presenter leadership workshops. Editor: Parliamentary Procedure Made Easy, 1983; contbr. articles to profl. jours. State advisor Future Bus. Leaders of Am., Columbia, S.C., 1978-86; treas. S.C. State Woman's Aux., 1983—. Named Outstanding Advisor S.C. Future Bus. Leaders of Am., 1985. Mem. Profl. Secs. Internat., Nat. Bus. Edn. Assn. (membership dir. 1986—), S.C. Bus. Edn. Assn. (jour. editor 1985-86, treas. 1986-87, v.p. membership 1987-88), Am. Vocat. Assn., S.C. Vocat. Assn. (parliamentarian 1985-86), Internat. Soc. Bus. Educators, Lake City C. of C. Democrat. Baptist. Home: Rt 1 Box 225 Coward SC 29530 Office: Lake City High Sch PO Box 1157 Lake City SC 29560

HAWKINS, LINDA SARAH COFER, entrepreneur; b. Long Branch, N.J., June 13, 1951; d. James H. and Marion D. (Willis) Cofer; children: Eldridge, Hillary. BABA, Upsala Coll., 1973; postgrad. Monmouth Coll., 1974-76. Adminstr. E. Hawkins Atty., East Orange, N.J., 1976—; pres. Cofer Hawkins Funeral Home, Inc., East Orange, 1981-84; treas. Cofer Willis Corp., Red Bank, N.J., 1984—; pres. Lyn-El Corp., East Orange, 1985—; pres. Cofer-Streleck, Inc., East Orange, 1986—. Founder Carl Lewis Fund, East Orange, 1984; dir. Ms. Essex County Sr. Citizen Pageant, East Orange, 1977-78; treas. Essex County Links, Inc., 1986; provisional mem. Jr. League of Oranges and Short Hills; bd. trustees Hudson and West Essex United Way. Named Outstanding Citizen City of Long Branch, 1974-75, one of Outstanding Young Women in Am., 1985. Mem. Llewellyn Park Ladies Assn. (rec. sec. 1984-86, treas. 1986—), Alpha Kappa Alpha. Clubs: Essex New Direction (treas. 1984—), Jack and Jill of Am. (North Jersey); Llewellyn Park Ladies Assn. (rec. sec. 1984—). Avocations: classical piano, gardening. Home: Llewellyn Park West Orange NJ 07052 Office: Eldridge Hawkins Atty at Law 110 S Munn Ave East Orange NJ 07018

HAWKINS, MARY ELLEN, state legislator, public relations consultant; b. Birmingham, Ala.; student U. Ala., Tuscaloosa, 1945-47; m. James H. Hawkins, Feb. 13, 1960 (div., 1971); children—Andrew Higgins, Elizabeth, Peter Hixon. Congl. aide to several mems. U.S. Ho. Reps., 1950-60; art instr. Sumter County Schs., Americus, Ga., 1971-72; staff writer Naples (Fla.) Daily News, 1972-74; prin. Daniels-Hawkins, Naples, 1982—; mem. Fla. Ho. of Reps., Tallahassee, 1974—; vice chmn. NAFCO Fin. Group Inc., Naples, 1979—, also bd. dirs. Columnist, contbr. articles to local newspapers. V.p. Naples/Marco Philharmonic, 1984—; numerous offices Rep. Party of Ga., Americus, 1965-71. Recipient numerous awards for work in Fla. Legislature. Mem. Zonta Internat. Avocation: painting. Office: Fla Ho Reps The Capitol Tallahassee FL 32399

HAWKINS, MYLAN BARIN, computer consulting company executive; b. Chgo., Sept. 25, 1940; d. Harry Lewis Barin and Ruth (Kromelow) Lesser; m. Henry Roloff, July 26, 1959 (div. Sept. 1981); m. Prince Ashton Hawkins, June 27, 1982; children: Ari L., Kevin Barin. BA, U. Chgo., 1960. Div. dir. United Way Dade County, Miami, Fla., 1975-76; campaign mgr. Equality NOW, Reno, Nev., 1977-79; no. dir. March of Dimes, Reno, 1981-82; v.p. Interface Computer Cons., Reno, 1982—; cons. AT&T Liaison Program, Reno, 1983—, PBS, Reno, 1984-86. Editor (newsletter) Diabetes Edn. Ctr., 1980—; contbr. articles to profl. jours. Founder, chmn. Project Survival, Miami, 1969-75; bd. dirs. Nevadians for ERA, Reno, 1977-79; lobbyist ACLU, Now, Reno, 1977-79; adminstr. Diabetes Edn. Ctr., Reno, 1981—. Home: 4465 Boca Way Apt 5 Reno NV 89502

HAWKINS, PAULA (MRS. WALTER E. HAWKINS), senator; b. Salt Lake City; d. Paul B. and Leoan (Staley) Fickes; m. Walter Eugene Hawkins, Sept. 5, 1947; children: Genean, Kevin Brent, Kelley Ann. Student, Utah State U., 1944-47, H.H.D. (hon.), 1982. Dir. Southeast 1st Nat. Bank, Maitland, Fla., 1972-76; del. Republican Nat. Conv., Miami, 1968, 72; mem. rules com. Republican Nat. Conv., 1972, co-chmn. rules com., 1980, co-chmn. platform com., 1984; mem. Nat. Fedn. Rep. Women, 1965—; bd. dirs. Fla. Fedn. Rep. Women, from 1968; mem. Rep. Nat. Com. for Fla., 1968-87, mem. rule 29 com., 1973-75; mem. U. S. Senate from Fla., 1980-87; v.p. Air Fla., 1979-80. Author: Children at Risk, 1986. Mem. Maitland Civic Center, 1965-76; mem. Fgn. Relations Com. U.S. Senate; charter mem. bd. dirs. Fla. Americans Constl. Action Com. of 100, 1966-68, sec.-treas., 1966-68; del. Rep. Nat. Conv., 1968, 72, 76, 80, 84; mem. Central Fla. Museum Speakers Bur., 1967-68, Fla. Gov.'s Commn. Status Women, 1968-71; Mem. Fla. Pub. Service Commn., Tallahassee, 1972-79, chmn. PSC, 1977-79; mem. Pres.'s Commn. White House Fellowships, 1975; bd. dirs. Freedom Found., 1981—; chmn. subcom. Durg Abuse, U.S. Senate; chmn. Family and Children Subcom., 1982-86; mem. U.S. Senate Durg Force Commn., 1986—; Orgn. Am. States Permanent Subcom. Narcotics Control and Terrorism, 1987; del. U.S. to UN Narcotics Conv., Vienna, Austria, 1987. Recipient citation for service Fla. Rep. Party, 1966-67, award for legis. work Child Fund Inc, 1982, Israel Peace medal, 1983, Tree of Life award Jewish Nat. Found, 1985, Mother of Yr., 1984, Grandmother of Yr., 1985, Albert Einstein Good Govt. award, 1986; named Guardian of Small Bus. Nat. Fedn. Ind. Bus., 1982, Rep. Woman of Yr. Women's Nat. Rep. Club, 1981, Outstanding Woman of Yr. in Govt. Orlando C. of C., 1977, Good Govt. award Maitland Jaycees, 1976, Woman of Yr., KC, 1973. Mem. Maitland C. of C. (chmn. congl. action com. 1967). Mem. Ch. Jesus Christ of Latter-day Saints (pres. Relief Soc., Orlando Stake 1960-64, Sunday sch. tchr. 1964-80). Club: Capitol Hill (Washington). Office: PO Box 2000 Winter Park FL 32790

HAWK-LOVEDAY, CHRISTINE JOYCE, college administrator; b. Johnson City, Tenn., June 1, 1954; d. J.C. and Ruth Lillian (DeWitt) Hawk; m. Robert Earl Loveday, Aug. 9, 1980. BS in Bus. Edn. honors, E. Tenn. State u., 1976, postgrad., 1976-77, 87. Cert. tchr. Tenn. Clk. sales Sears, Roebuck & Co., Johnson, 1973-77; asst. mgr. K-Mart Apparel Corp., Kingsport, Tenn., 1977-78; mgr. K-Mart Apparel Corp., Maryville, Tenn., 1978-79; evening faculty Draughons Jr. Coll., Knoxville, 1979-80, day and evening faculty, 1980-84, dir. evening, 1984-86; dean acad. Draughons Jr. Coll., Johnson city, 1987—. Active March of Dimes, Muscular Dystrophy Assn., Dept. Human Services of Tenn., United Way, ARC, Am. Heart Assn., Cystic Fibrosis Found. of E. Tenn., VITA-Vol. Income Tax Assistance programs, IRS in Knoxville, 1984-86 and Johnson City, 1987-88. Mem. NEA, Tenn. Edn. Assn., E. Tenn. Edn. Assn., Nat. Bus. Edn. Assn., Tenn. Bus. Edn. Assn., Nat. Assn. Female Execs. Democrat. Presbyterian. Home: 1908 Newton St Knoxville TN 37920 Office: Draughons Jr Coll 2220 College Dr Johnson City TN 37601

HAWKS, JANE ESTHER HOKANSON, nursing educator, researcher; b. Sac City, Iowa, Apr. 8, 1955; d. Charles Wesley and Esther Pearl (Langbein) Hokanson; m. Edward Harold Hawks, May 24, 1980; 1 child, Jennifer Jane. B.S. in Nursing, St. Olaf Coll., 1977; M.S. in Nursing, U. Nebr.-Omaha, 1981. Staff nurse Rochester (Minn.) Meth. Hosp., 1977-78; instr. nursing Morningside Coll., Sioux City, Iowa, 1978-79, Jennie Edmundson Sch. Nursing, Council Bluffs, Iowa, 1979-81, 86—, U. Nebr. Med. Ctr. Coll. Nursing, Omaha, 1981-86; pvt. duty supr. Family Home Care, Omaha, 1986; researcher Alcoholism Research Team, Omaha, 1982—. Recipient Rena Boyle award U. Nebr., 1980; named Nurse of Yr., Dist. 9 Iowa Nurses Assn., 1983. Mem. Iowa Nurses Assn. (pres. Dist. 9), Am. Nurses Assn., Am. Urol. Assn., Sigma Theta Tau. Lutheran. Contbr. chpts. in books, articles to profl. jours. Home: 414 3d St Box 273A Rural Route 1 Underwood IA 51576 Office: Bishop Clarkson Coll Nursing 333 S 44th St Omaha NE 68132-3799

HAWLEY, ANNE, state arts administrator; b. Iowa City, Iowa, Nov. 3, 1943; d. Marshall Newton and Leone Ardith (Wilson) Hawley; m. Bruce Ivor McPherson, Sept. 4, 1977; 1 child, Katherine Black. BA, U. Iowa, 1966; MA, George Washington U., 1969, LHD (hon.), Lesley Coll, 1987. Adminstrv. asst. Donald Mitchell, Washington, 1967-69; research assoc. Nat. Urban League, Washington, 1969-71, Ford Found. Study Leadership in Pub. Edn., Washington, 1971-73; exec. dir. Cultural Edn. Collaborative, Boston, 1974-77, Mass. Council Arts/Humanities, Boston, 1977—. Bd. dirs. New Eng. Found. for Arts, 1977—, Nat. Assembly/State Arts Agencies, Washington, 1981-83, Greater Boston Arts Fund, 1985—. Fulbright scholar, 1986; recipient Design Travel Grant, Women's Travel Club, Boston, Mass., 1982, Art award Mass. Coll. Art, 1987. Mem. Nat. Endowment for Arts (museum panel, 1978-81, dance panel 1980-81, design panel 1980-83). Office: Mass Council on Arts & Humanities 80 Boylston St Suite 1000 Boston MA 02116

HAWLEY, CAROL ANN, data processing executive; b. Hagerstown, Md., July 23, 1951; d. Arnold Ralph and Grace Mieyo (Nakamura) Mentzer; m. Richard Earle Hawley, May 21, 1977 (div. Sept. 1983); 1 foster child, Maria Antonio Machuca. Grad. high sch., Williamsport, Md. Bookkeeper Dun & Bradstreet, Los Angeles, 1972-74; sec., purchaser Electronic Mfrs. Assoc., Los Angeles, 1974-75, export mgr., 1977-79; purchaser Respiratory Therapy Services, Santa Ana, Calif., 1975-76; sec., acctg. clk. Rossmoor Corp., Laguna Hills, Calif., 1976; asst. office mgr. Scherba's Auto Stores, San Mateo, Calif., 1976-77; adminstrv. asst. Internat. Printers, Santa Fe Springs, Calif., 1979-81, data processing mgr., 1981-86, v.p. adminstrn., 1986—; v.p. steering com. Profit Control Users Assn., N.Y.C., 1985—. Home: 14741 Henning Dr La Mirada CA 90638 Office: Internat Printers 10225 Greenleaf Ave Santa Fe Springs CA 90670

HAWLEY, SANDRA SUE, electrical engineer; b. Spirit Lake, Iowa, May 7, 1948; d. Byrnard Leroy and Dorothy Virginia (Fischbeck) Smith; m. Michael John Hawley, June 7, 1970; 1 child, Alexander Tristin. B.S. in Elec. Engring., U. Dayton, 1981; B.S. in Math. and Statistics, Iowa State U., 1970; M.S. in Statistics, U. Del., 1975. Research analyst State of Wis., Madison, 1970-71; research asst. Del. State Coll., Dover, 1972-73; asst. prof. math. and statistics Wesley Coll., Dover, 1974-81, chmn. dept. math. and computer sci., 1978-80; elec. engr. Control Data Corp., Bloomington, Minn., 1982-85; sr. elec. engr. Custom Integrated Circuits, 1985—. Contbr. articles to profl. jours. Elder, Presbyn. Ch. U.S.A., 1975—, mem. session Oak Grove Presbyn. Ch., Bloomington, 1985-88. NSF scholar U. Dayton, 1981. Mem. IEEE, Assn. Women in Sci., Soc. Women Engrs., Am. Statis. Assn. Home: 7724 W 85th St Circle Bloomington MN 55438 Office: Custom Integrated Circuits 4100 N Hamline Ave Saint Paul MN 55112

HAWLEY, SHERRI KAY, health company administrator; b. Akron, Ohio, Aug. 26, 1953; d. Billie B. and Dorothy Reed (Hayes) Yeager; m. David Louis Hawley, July 22, 1978; children: Joshua David, Mallory Reed. Diploma, Akron Gen. Med. Ctr. Sch. Nursing, 1974; BS in Nursing, U. Akron, 1983. Staff nurse Akron Gen. Med. Ctr., 1974-80; indsl. nurse Gen. Tire & Rubber Co., Akron, 1980-82; hosp. coordinator Nurse's House Call, Akron, 1982-86, asst. dir. staff devel., 1986-87, dir. staff devel., 1987—; community liaison Red Apple Med. Equipment, Akron, 1986. Mem. Ohio Nurse's Assn., Nat. Assn. for Female Execs., Nat. Standards Council, Embroider's Guild Am. (pres. 1985-86, v.p. 1986—), Am. Needlepoint Guild. Home: 4215 Baird Rd Stow OH 44224 Office: Nurse's House Call 3123 Manchester Rd Akron OH 44319

HAWLEY, VICTORIA GAGE, buyer for mail order catalogues; b. Bridgeport, Conn., Mar. 17, 1946; d. Floyd Edward and Sylvia Blanche (Nevard) H.; m. Stephen W. Thompson, Oct. 18, 1968 (div. Oct. 18, 1973). BS in Clothing, Textiles and Related Arts magna cum laude, U. Conn., 1968. Copywriter McCall Pattern Co., N.Y.C., 1968-70, editor ednl. materials, 1970-72; creative dir. Artcraft Concepts, Ballston Lake, N.Y., 1972-77; prodn. mgr. Hanover House Industries, N.Y.C., 1977-80, buyer, 1977-88; ind. cons. specializing in mail order catalog mdse. 1988—; cons., graphic assoc. N.Y., 1970—; merchandiser, buyer catalog Adam York, 1977—. Editor: McCall Sewing Book, 1972; illustrator Simplicity, 1983. Mem. NOW, Women in Arts Mus., Nat. Assn. Female Execs. Democrat. Office: 321 W 78th St 5B New York NY 10024

HAWN, GOLDIE, actress; b. Washington, Nov. 21, 1945; d. Edward Rutledge and Laura (Steinhoff) H.; m. Gus Trinkonis, May 16, 1969 (div.); m. Bill Hudson (div.); children: Oliver, Kate Garry, Wyatt Russell. Student, Am. U. Profl. dancer, 1965; profl. acting debut in Good Morning, World, 1967-68; mem. company TV series Laugh-In, 1968-70; appeared in TV spl. Pure Goldie, 1971; films include: Cactus Flower, 1969 (Acad. award best supporting actress), There's A Girl In My Soup, 1970, Dollars, 1971, Butterflies Are Free, 1971, The Sugarland Express, 1974, The Girl from Petrovka, 1974, Shampoo, 1975, The Duchess and the Dirtwater Fox, 1976, Foul Play, 1978, Seems Like Old Times, 1980, Best Friends, 1982, Swingshift, 1984, Overboard, 1987; exec. producer and star films Private Benjamin, 1980, Protocol, 1984, Wildcats, 1986; host TV spl. Goldie and Kids: Listen to Us!, 1982. Office: care Creative Artists Agy 1888 Century Park E Suite 1400 Los Angeles CA 90067 *

HAWTHORNE, BETTY EILEEN, educator, emeritus university dean; b. Seattle, Nov. 22, 1920; d. Harry Albert and Marcia (Thompson) Hawthorne; B.S., U. Wash., 1941, M.S., 1944, Ph.D., Mich. State U., 1954. Field nutritionist Pacific area ARC, Wash., 1943-44; instr., asst. prof. Oreg. State U., Corvallis, 1946-55, assoc. prof. foods and nutrition, 1955-62, prof., 1962-83, dean Coll. Home Econs., 1965-83; dir. Curtice Burns Foods, Inc., Rochester, N.Y.; chmn. home economics subcom., expt. sta. com. on orgn. and policy Nat. Assn. State Univs. and Land Grant Colls., 1977-80; dir. Pacificorp., Portland. Bd. dirs. Good Samaritan Hosp., Corvallis, 1970-78, Children's Farm Home Found., Corvallis; hon. trustee Good Samaritan Hosp. Found. Served with ensign to lt. (j.g.). Supply Corps. USNR, 1944-46. Mem. Am. Dietetic Assn., Oreg. Dietetic Assn. (past pres.), Am. Home Econs. Assn. (past. sect. chmn., bd. dirs., bd. dirs. found. 1984-87, pres. 1985-86), Assn. Adminstrs. Home Econs. (pres. 1976-77), AAUW, Soc. Nutrition Edn., Nat. Women's Forum., Altrusa Internat. Phi Beta Kappa, Sigma Xi, Phi Kappa Phi, Omicron Nu, Iota Sigma Pi. Home: 144 NW 29th St Corvallis OR 97330

HAWTHORNE, JEWELL ANN, municipal administrator; b. Marshalltown, Iowa, Feb. 16, 1952; d. Arthur and Miriam Mae (Kreuger) Anselme; m. Richard Lowane Hawthorne, Mar. 16, 1973 (div. 1977); 1 child, Matthew Nathaniel. BS, Ariz. State U., 1974, MS, 1984. Specialist dept. econ. security State of Ariz., Phoenix, 1975-76; adminstrv. aide dept. human resources City of Phoenix, 1977-79; adminstrv. asst. Dept. Police City of Phoenix, 1979-80, sytems and procedures analyst II, 1980-81, research analyst, 1981—. Editor Phoenix Police Dept. Ann. Report, 1986, 87. Sports dir. Theodore Roosevelt Council Boy Scouts Am., Phoenix, 1986-87, asst. den leader 1985-86. Mem. Nat. Assn. Police Planners, Am. Fedn. State County Mcpl. Employees (bd. dirs. local 2960 1978-79), Am. Soc. Pub. Adminstrn., Ariz. Mcpl. Mgmt. Assts. Assn. Office: Phoenix Police Dept 620 W Washington Phoenix AZ 85003

HAY, BETTY JO, civic worker; b. McAlester, Okla., June 6, 1931; d. Duncan and Kathryn Myrtle (Albert) Peacock; m. Jess Thomas Hay, Aug. 3, 1951; children—Deborah Hay Spradley, Patricia Lynn. B.A., So. Meth. U., 1952. Bd. dirs. White House Preservation Fund, 1980-87; bd. dirs. Nat. Mental Health Assn., 1978-87, pres., 1986, mem. fin. com. and child adolescent com., 1978-79, mem. resource devel. com., 1980-83; v.p. fundraising Mental Health Assn. Tex., 1980, bd. dirs., 1974—, pres., 1983-84; bd. dirs. Community Council Dallas, 1984—, bd. dirs. Mental Health Assn., Dallas County, 1972-88, pres., 1981-82; bd. dirs. United Way Met. Dallas, 1983—, Assn. Higher Edn. North Tex., 1980-82, vice chmn., 1982-83, chmn., 1984-85; mem. adv. bd. Sch. Social Work, U. Tex., Arlington, 1983—; mem. Dallas Council on World Affairs, Woman's Div., Dallas Symphony Orch. League, Historic Preservation League, March of Dimes Aux., 1982—, many past involvements in charitable orgns. Address: 7236 Lupton Circle Dallas TX 75225

HAY, ELIZABETH DEXTER, embryology researcher, educator; b. St. Augustine, Fla., Apr. 2, 1927; d. Isaac Morris and Lucille (Lynn) H. A.B., Smith Coll., 1948, Sc.D. (hon.), 1973; M.D., Johns Hopkins U., 1952; M.A. (hon.), Harvard U., 1964. Intern in internal medicine Johns Hopkins Hosp., Balt., 1952-53; instr. anatomy Johns Hopkins U. Med. Sch., Balt., 1953-56, asst. prof., 1956-57; asst. prof. Cornell U. Med. Sch., N.Y.C., 1957-60; asst. prof. Harvard Med. Sch., Boston, 1960-64, Louise Foote Pfeiffer assoc. prof., 1964-69, Louise Foote Pfeiffer prof. embryology, 1969—, chmn. dept. anatomy and cellular biology, 1975—; cons. cell biology sect. NIH, 1965-69; mem. adv. council Nat. Inst. Gen. Med. Sci., NIH, 1978-81; mem. sci. adv. bd. Whitney Marine Lab., U. Fla., 1982—; mem. adv. council Johns Hopkins Sch. Medicine, 1982—; chairperson bd. sci. counselors Nat. Inst. Dental Research, NIH, 1984-86. Author: Regeneration, 1966; (with J.P. Revel) Fine Structure of the Developing Avian Cornea, 1969; editor: Cell Biology of Extracellular Matrix, 1981; editor-in-chief Developmental Biology Jour., 1971-75; contbr. articles to profl. jours. Mem. Scientists Task Force of Congressman Barney Frank, Massach, 1982—. Recipient Disting. Achievement award N.Y. Hosp.-Cornell Med. Ctr. Alumni Council, 1985, award for vision research Alcon, 1988. Mem. Soc. Devel. Biology (pres. 1973-74), Am. Soc. Cell Biology (pres. 1976-77, legis. alert com. 1982—), Am. Assn. Anatomists (pres. 1981-82, legis. alert com. 1982—), Am. Acad. Arts and Scis., Johns Hopkins Soc. Scholars, Nat. Acad. Sci., Internat. Soc. Devel. Biologists (exec. bd. 1977), Boston Mycol. Club. Home: 14 Aberdeen Rd Weston MA 02193 Office: Harvard Med Sch Dept Anatomy & Cellular Biology 25 Shattuck St Boston MA 02115

HAY, MAUREENE GRIFFOUL, advertising executive; b. San Jose, Calif., May 17, 1946; d. Henry Maurice and Eileene (Durkin) Griffoul; m. Macgregor Bruce Hay, Feb. 19, 1966 (div. Mar. 1979); children: Alison Nicole, Morgan Andrew; m. Richard Philip Spencer, Apr. 30, 1983. Student, San Jose State U. Acct., Honig Cooper & Harrington, San Francisco, 1966-67, media buyer, 1967-72; pvt. practice media buyer and planner, Oakland, Calif., 1972-79; v.p., media dir. Davis, Johnson, Mogul and Colombatto, San Francisco, 1979-87; dir. corp. media DJMC, Los Angeles, 1987—. Bd. dirs. Bay Area Star. Mem. San Francisco Media Dirs. Council (pres.), San Francisco Ad Club. Democrat. Roman Catholic. Club: Benefit Guild of East Bay (v.p. 1977, pres. 1978). Home: 13938 Cumpston Van Nuys CA 91401 Office: Davis Johnson et al 818 W 7th St Los Angeles CA 90017

HAY, MILLICENT VICTORIA, writer; b. Long Beach, Calif., May 7, 1945; d. Glenn and Julie (DeLong) Gunnells; m. John Leonard Hay, Dec. 16, 1967; 1 child, Ian Daniel. BA, U. Ariz., 1966; MA, Ariz. State U., 1971, PhD, 1979. Instr. Ariz. State U., Tempe, 1969-73, editor Research News, 1979-82; freelance writer, Phoenix, 1982—; staff writer Phoenix Mag., 1983-84; assoc. editor Ariz. Hwys., 1988—, 1984—; instr. Scottsdale (Ariz.) Community Coll., 1986-88. Author: The Life of Robert Sidney, Earl of Leicester, 1984; contbr. articles to various publs. Mem. Am. Soc. Journalists and Authors, Phi Beta Kappa, Sigma Delta Chi. Home and Office: 201 E Hayward Ave Phoenix AZ 85020

HAYCOCK, KATHRYN PROFFITT, communications company executive; b. Hillsboro, Ore., Jan. 10, 1951; d. Willis Raymond and Phyllis Josephine; m. Paul Wadley Haycock, Sept. 10, 1973; children: Korbin Hal, Hollie Elizabeth, Garron Shepherd, Rachelle Dawn. Cert. dental hygiene, U. Ore., 1972. Staff dental hygienist Farm Workers Family Health Ctr., Toppenich, Wash., 1972-73; acting dir. dental hygiene Yakima (Wash.) Valley Coll. Sch. Dental Hygiene, 1973-74; clin. instr. Phoenix Coll. Sch. Dental Hygiene, 1975-80; pres., chief exec. officer, chmn. bd. dirs. Call-Am. Long Distance Phone Co., Phoenix, 1982—; chmn. bd. dirs. KLP Inc., Mesa, 1983—. Mem. Altel of Ariz. (pres. 1984—, lobbyist 1985), U.S. West Carrier Focus Group, Comptel U.S. C. of C. Republican. Adventist. Office: Call-America 20 E Main St Suite 850 Mesa AZ 85201

HAYDEN, GAIL DRESCHER, financial services executive; b. San Diego, June 13, 1964; d. Robert C. and Anne (Holt) Drescher; m. Charles L. Hayden, May 26, 1984. BA in Bus. and Polit. Sci., U. S.C., 1986. Lic. securities rep., real estate agt. Adminstrv. asst. Seaman & Graham Attys., Columbia, S.C., 1982-84; legal asst. Robert E. Seaman III, P.A., Columbia, 1984-86; exec. asst., v.p. Leasing Services Am., Columbia, 1984-86; sales asst. Thomson McKinnon Securities, Columbia, 1986-87; asst. v.p. Capital Resource Mgmt., Inc., Columbia, 1987—; pres. A.D. Ventures, Ltd., Columbia, 1986—. Publicity chmn. First Lady Benefit Am. Cancer Soc., S.C., 1987-88. James F. Byrnes Found. scholar, 1982. Mem. Nat. Assn. Female Execs., Nat. Bus. Women's Assn. Republican. Methodist. Home: 132 Preston Hills Dr Columbia SC 29210 Office: Capital Resource Mgmt Inc 6941 N Trenholm Rd Suite Q-1 Columbia SC 29206

HAYDEN, JOSEPHINE ELEANOR, military policy consultant; b. South Bend, Ind., Dec. 24, 1947; d. Joseph Clark and Eleanor Vernon (Hall) H. AB in Hist. with distinction, Transylvania U., 1969; MA in Am. Hist., Wake Forest U., 1971; MS in Mgmt., U. So. Calif., Los Angeles, 1977. Asst. buyer John Shillito Co., Cin., 1969-70; research assoc. Hazleton Labs., Vienna, Va., 1971-73; logistics mgr. Naval Air Systems Command, Washington, 1973-77; program mgr. Systems Research Corp, Falls Church, Va., 1977-78; asst. program mgr. Naval Electronics Systems Command, Washington, 1977-83; policy maker Naval Material Command, Washington, 1983-85; program mgr. Naval Air Systems Command, Washington, 1985-86; policy maker Naval Supply Systems Command, Washington, 1986—; seminar speaker Soc. Logistics Engrs., Las Vegas, Nev., 1981, Tech. Mktg. Soc. Am., 1985-86; instr. Navy Acquisition/Logistics Mgmt. Tng. Ctr., Washington, 1983-86; lectr. Defense Systems Mgmt. Coll., Ft. Belvoir, Va., 1984—. Vol. Planned Parenthood of Winston-Salem, N.C., 1971, St. Mark's Episcopal Ch., Washington, 1975—, Planned Parenthood of No. Va., Arlington, 1987—. Transylvania U. scholar, 1965-69; fellow Wake Forest U., 1970-71. Mem. Potomac Valley Dressage Assn. (bd. dirs. 1978-82), Acupuncture Soc. of Va. (founder, v.p. 1987), MENSA, Phi Alpha Theta. Republican. Episcopalian. Home: 613 Lexington Pl NE Washington DC 20002

HAYDEN, VIRGINIA EVA, mamagement consultant; b. Midland, Mich., May 20, 1927; d. Robert James and Altheda Mae (Wood) H.; B.A. in Acctg. and Econs., Mich. State U., 1949; m. Donald Conrad, Feb. 15, 1952 (div.). Stock inventory clk. Dow Chem. Co., 1949-50; budget clk., analyst, specialist, coordinator Upjohn Co., Kalamazoo, 1950-72, mgr. corp. budgeting, 1972-78, exec. devel. cons., 1978-85, sr. cons. exec. devel., 1985-87; pvt. exec. devel. mgmt. cons., 1987—; co-founder, advisor Greater Opportunities for Women (GROW); speaker mgmt. classes; speaker on career planning and women in mgmt. to profl. orgns.; tchr. women in mgmt. Kalamazoo Coll. Chmn. adv. bd. Center for Women's Services of Western Mich. U.; bd. dirs. Kalamazoo Alcohol and Drug Abuse Council. Recipient W.E. Upjohn award, 1970. Mem. Kalamazoo Network (dir., co-founder), Nat. Wildlife Assn., Kalamazoo Nature Ctr., Audubon Soc. Club: Kalamazoo Altrusa (past pres.). Home and Office: 8207 Bruning St Kalamazoo MI 49002

HAYDEN, VIRGINIA WEBB, technical writer, editor; b. Maryville, Tenn., Sept. 28, 1955; d. Eugene Leslie and Ruth Lillian (Freeman) Webb; m. Brian R. Hayden, Apr. 30, 1988. B.A. in English magna cum laude, U. Tenn., 1977, M.A. in English, 1979. Asst. dir. engring. central services Washington U., St. Louis, 1979-81; tech. writer/editor action data services Control Data Corp., St. Louis, 1981—; instr. St. Louis Coll. Pharmacy, part-time 1986—. Vol. Crisis Worker and Newsletter Editor at Life Crisis Services, St. Louis, 1980—. Mem. South Atlantic Modern Lang. Assn., S.E. Conf. Linguistics, Soc. Tech. Communication, Phi Beta Kappa, Phi Kappa Phi, Alpha Lambda Delta. Home: 300 Baker Ave Webster Groves MO 63119 Office: 7822 Bonhomme Ave Clayton MO 63105

HAYEK, CAROLYN JEAN, judge; b. Portland, Oreg., Aug. 17, 1948; d. Robert A. and Marion L. (DeKoning) H.; m. Steven M. Rosen, July 21, 1974; children: Jonathan David, Laura Elizabeth. BA in Psychology, Carleton Coll., 1970; JD, U. Chgo., 1973. Bar: Wash. 1973. Assoc. firm Jones, Grey & Bayley, Seattle, 1973-77; sole practice law, Federal Way, Wash., 1977-82; judge Federal Way Dist. Ct., 1982—. Task force mem. Alternatives for Wash., 1973-75; mem. Wash. State Ecol. Commn., 1975-77; bd. dirs. 1st Unitarian Ch. Seattle, 1986—, vice chair 1987-88; den lead Cub Scouts Mt. Ranier council Boy Scouts Am. Mem. ABA, Wash. Women Lawyers, Wash. State Bar Assn., AAUW (br. pres. 1978-80, chmn. state level conf. com. 1986-87), King County Dist. Ct. Judges Assn. (treas., exec. com., com. chmn.), Elected Wash. Women (dir. 1983-87), Nat. Assn. Women Judges (nat. bd. dirs., dist. bd. dirs. 1984-86), Federal Way Women's Network (bd. dirs. 1984-87, pres. 1985), Greater Federal Way C. of C. (dir. 1978-82, sec. 1980-81, v.p. 1981-82). Republican. Office: Federal Way Dist Ct 33506 10th Pl S Federal Way WA 98003

HAYEK, MARY ANNIE, psychologist; b. Paterson, N.J., Feb. 13, 1925; d. Anthony T. and Mary N. (Sara) Haddad; B.A. with distinction in Psychology, Fla. Internat. U., 1975, M.S. in Counselor Edn., 1978; Ph.D. in Clin. Psychology, Heed U., Hollywood, Fla., 1980; m. James Paul Hayek, Aug. 12, 1945; children—George Anthony, James Paul, Joanne Christine. Alcohol counselor, therapist South Miami Hosp., Miami, Fla., 1977-78; cons. psychologist, psychotherapist Victims Advocates for Sexually Abused Children, Miami, 1980-81; psychotherapist Counseling and Stress Control Center, Coral Gables, Fla., 1978-80, pvt. practice with Center, 1980—. Master and Johnson fellow, 1979-82. Mem. Am. Mental Health Counselors Assn., Am. Assn. Counseling and Devel., Am. Psychol. Assn., Fla. Assn. Practicing Psychologists, Fla. Assn. Profl. Hypnosis, Am. Assn. Marriage and Family Therapy, Nat. Acad. Cert. Clin. Mental Health Counselors, Internat. Acad. Behavioral Medicine Counseling and Psychotherapy, Fla. Mental Health Counselors Assn., Nat. Rehab. Assn., Mental Health Assn. Dade County, Phi Theta Kappa, Phi Lambda Pi, Psi Chi. Author: Recovered Alcoholic Women With and Without Incest Experience, 1981. Home: 1801 SW 84th Ct Miami FL 33155 Office: 1901 Ponce De Leon Blvd Suite 200 Coral Gables FL 33134

HAYES, ALBERTA PHYLLIS WILDRICK, retired health service executive; b. Blakeslee, Pa., May 31, 1918; d. William and Maude (Robbins) Wildrick; diploma Wilkes Barre Gen. Hosp. Sch. Nursing, 1938-41; student Wilkes Coll., 1953-54, Pa. State U., 1969—; m. Glenmore Burton Hayes, Oct. 9, 1942; children—Glenmore Rolland, William Bruce. Nurse, Monroe County Gen. Hosp., East Stroudsburg, Pa., 1941-44; pvt. duty nurse, 1944-56; with White Haven (Pa.) Center, 1956-82, dir. residential services, 1966-82, ret., 1982. Pres. Tobyhanna Twp. Sch. PTA, 1948-49, Top-o-Pocono Women of Rotary, 1975-76; nurse ARC, 1955; adv. council Luzerne County Foster Grandparent Program, 1977—, Health Services Keystone Job Corps, Drums, Pa., 1977—. Mem. Am. Assn. Mental Deficiency, Am. Legion Aux. (unit pres. 1946-47). Club: Pocono Mountains Women's (Blakeslee). Home: PO Box 11 Blakeslee PA 18610

HAYES, ALICE BOURKE, biologist, educator, university official; b. Chgo., Dec. 31, 1937; d. William Joseph and Mary Alice (Cawley) Bourke; m. John J. Hayes, Sept. 2, 1961 (dec. July 1981). B.S., Mundelein Coll., Chgo., 1959; M.S., U. Ill., 1960; Ph.D., Northwestern U., 1972. Researcher Mcpl. Tb San., Chgo., 1960-62; faculty Loyola U., Chgo., 1962—, chmn. dept., 1968-77, dean natural scis. div., 1977-80, asso. acad. v.p., 1980-87, v.p. academic affairs, 1987—; mem. NASA Space Biology program; mem. panel NSF, 1977-81; del. Botanical Del. to S. Africa, 1984; del. Botanical Del. to China, 1988. Contbr. articles to profl. publs. Campaign mem. Mental Health Assn. Ill., Chgo., 1973—; trustee Chgo.-No. Ill. div. Nat. Multiple Sclerosis Soc., 1981—; trustee Regina Dominican Acad., 1984—; trustee Civitas Dei Found., 1984—; trustee St. Ignatius Coll. Prep., 1984—. Fellow in botany U. Ill., 1959-60; fellow in botany NSF, 1969-71; grantee Am. Orchid Soc., 1967; grantee HEW, 1969, 76; grantee NSF, 1975; grantee NASA, 1980-85. Mem. Am. Soc. Plant Physiology, Bot. Soc. Am., AAAS, Am. Inst. Biol. Scis. Acad., Chgo. Assn. Tech. Socs., AAUW (corp. rep. 1980—), Am. Council on Edn. (corp. rep. higher edn. panel), Assn. Research Librarians (nominating com. 1986). Democrat. Roman Catholic. Club: Chgo. Network. Office: Loyola U 810 N Michigan Ave Chicago IL 60611

HAYES, BERNARDINE FRANCES, computer systems analyst; b. Boston, June 29, 1939; d. Robert Emmett and Mary Agnes (Tague) H. BA in Edn., St. Joseph Coll., 1967; MA in Urban Affairs and Pub. Policy, U. Del., 1973, PhD in Pub. Policy, 1978. Elem. tchr. St. Dominick Sch., Balt., 1960-63; tchr. sci., math. and art St. Mary's Sch., Troy, N.Y., 1963-65, Our Lady Queen of Peace Sch., Washington, 1965-68, St. Patrick Sch., Richmond, Va., 1968-69, St. Peter Cathedral Sch., Wilmington, Del., 1969-71; planner health and social services Model Cities Program, Wilmington, 1971-72; dir. research Del. State Dept. Mental Health, Wilmington, 1972-75; dir. planning and evaluation Mental Health, Mental Retardation Services, West Chester, Pa., 1976-78; instr. Boston U., 1978; div. dir. Systems Architects, Inc., Randolph, Mass., 1979-81; group mgr. Unisys Corp., Cambridge, Mass., 1981—; cons. in field. Contbr. numerous articles to profl. jours. Bd. sec. Model Cities, 1969-70; chairperson bd. State Service Ctr., Wilmington, 1972-75; mem. Human Relations Commn., Washington, 1965-68; co-chmn. State-wide Coalition for Human Services, Del., 1972-74; activist Vietnam protest, Del., 1970-74, Civil Rights Movement, 1965—, numerous polit. campaigns, 1972—; alt. del. Mass. Dem. Conv., 1985; bd. v.p. Women's Action for Nuclear Disarmament, Arlington, Mass., 1982—; del. Com. for an Enduring Peace, Soviet Peace Commn., Moscow, 1987. Fellow NSF, 1966. Mem. Women's Inst. Housing and Econ. Devel. (bd. dirs. 1985—), NAACP, Boston Computer Soc., Boston Mus. Fine Arts, NOW. Roman Catholic. Home: 49 Crane Rd Adams Shore Quincy MA 02169

HAYES, BETTINE J. (MRS. M. VINSON HAYES), investment exec.; b. Boston, Sept. 6, 1928; d. Reginald W. P. and Ethel (Thomas) Brown; B.A., Wellesley Coll., 1950; m. M. Vinson Hayes, June 10, 1961; children—M. Vinson III, Juliet Dorothy. Security analyst Merrill Lynch, Pierce, Fenner & Smith, Inc., N.Y.C., 1950-60, 76—, portfolio analyst, 1960-73, Canadian research coordinator, 1967-69; mgr. N.Y. Wellesley Club, 1973-74; researcher Nat. Information Bur., Inc., N.Y.C., 1974-76. Mem. D.A.R. (chpt. treas. 1958-59, historian 1961-62, rec. sec. Colonielles 1961-71, 73-77, treas., 1971-73), N.Y. Soc. Security Analysts. Club: New York Wellesley. Home: 39 Gramercy Park New York City NY 10010 also: 11 Spring Close Ln East Hampton NY 11937 Office: Merrill Lynch World Hdqrs North Tower World Fin Ctr New York NY 10281-1215

HAYES, CAROL J., biology educator; b. N.Y.C., Dec. 13, 1940; d. Arnold C. and Regina (Tighe) H. BS in Biology, St. Joseph's Coll., Bklyn., 1961; PhD in Physiology, NYU, 1975. Research asst. Booth Meml. Hosp., Flushing, N.Y., 1961-63; research assoc. Cornell U. Med. Sch., N.Y.C., 1963-65; instr. biology St. Joseph's Coll., 1965-68, asst. prof., 1968-75, assoc. prof., 1975-80, prof., 1980—, chmn. dept. biology, 1976—. NSF research fellow Ill. Inst. Tech., 1968-69. Mem. AAAS, Internat. Assn. Chronobiology, N.Y. Acad. Sic. Office: St Joseph's Coll 245 Clinton Ave Brooklyn NY 11205 also: St Joseph's Coll 155 Roe Blvd Patchogue NY 11772

HAYES, CAROLYN S., corporate professional; b. Toledo, Jan. 2, 1948; d. Alphonse Anthony and Mary (Stopa) Staskiewicz; m. William Fellows Hayes, May 11, 1973; children: William F., James J. BBA, U. Toledo, 1970, MBA, 1977. Sr. auditor Owens-Ill., Inc., Toledo, 1975-77, fin. planning analyst, 1977-79, sr. bus. planning analyst, 1979-82, fin., adminstn. specialist, 1982-83, supr. gen. accounts, 1983-84, mgr. fin. cons. services, 1984-85, sr. benefits cons., 1985-86, mgr. benefits planning, 1986—. Rep. benefits council U.S. C. of C., Washington, 1987—, healthcare subcom. Nat. Assn. Mfgs., Washington, 1987—; treas., bd. dirs. Family Tree, Toledo, 1973-79; team cpt. bus. campaign Toledo Symphony, 1983-86. Served to lt. CAP, 1986—. Mem. Zeta Tau Alpha (pres. local chpt. 1969-70), Beta Gamma Sigma, Beta Alpha Psi. Republican. Roman Catholic. Home: 29455 Belmont Lake Rd Perrysburg OH 43551 Office: Owens-Ill Inc One Seagate Toledo OH 43666

HAYES, DEBORAH W., government official; b. New Haven, Aug. 24, 1958; d. Francis H. and Ollie N. (Thornton) Williamson; m. Ronald L. Hayes; 1 child, Adia S. BS, Bowie State U., 1985; MBA, Morgan State U., 1987. Adminstrv. Dept. Army, Ft. Bragg, N.C., 1979-81; adminstrv. asst. USAF Civilian, Homestead AFB, Fla., 1981-83; employee relations Civilian Personnel Office, Ft. Meade, Md., 1985-87; equal employee specialist EEOC, Balt., 1987—. William Dorsey scholar Bowie State Coll., 1985-86, Morgan State U. scholar, 1986-87. Mem. Nat. Assn. Female Execs., Nat. Black MBA Assn., Morgan State MBA Assn., NAACP, Delta Mu Delta, Delta Sigma Theta.

HAYES, DENISE LYNETTE, telephone company executive; b. Chgo., July 16, 1952; d. Jarrett Bernard and Odelia Fianna (Griffin) Hayes. A.A., El Centro Jr. Coll., Dallas, 1973; B.B.A., So. Meth. U., 1978, M.B.A., 1984. Data examiner Info. Processing Corp., Dallas, 1976-78; supr. data entry Southwestern Bell Telephone Co., Dallas, 1978, supr. computer batch processing, 1980, asst. mgr. real time ops., 1980-81, asst. mgr. user adminstrn., 1981-84, asst. staff mgr. valuations, 1984-87, mgr. valuations, 1987, mgr. comptrollers, 1988—. Adviser Jr. Achievement Dallas, 1979. Democrat. Church of Christ. Office: Southwestern Bell Telephone Co One Bell Plaza Room 2550-08 Dallas TX 75265

HAYES, DOROTHY EARLINE LORRAINE, artist, educator; b. Mobile, Ala., Dec. 1, 1935; d. Earl and Anne Laurie (Hardy) H. BFA, Ala. State U., 1957; student, Pratt Inst., 1962, Sch. Visual Arts, 1965; cert. in graphic art, Cooper Union Sch. Art, 1967; student, N.Y. Inst. Advt., 1969; BFA (hon.), Cooper Union Sch. Art, 1978. With N.Y.C. Tech. Coll. (formerly N.Y. Community Coll.), 1973; assoc. prof. art N.Y.C. Tech. Coll. (formerly N.Y. Community Coll.), N.Y.C., 1977-82; prof. N.Y.C. Tech. Coll. (formerly N.Y. Community Coll.), Bklyn., 1982, N.Y.C., 1986—, Bklyn., 1982-86; invitational lectr. High Sch. of Art and Design, N.Y.C., 1969, various offices, 1969—, R.I. Sch. of Design, Providence, R.I., Kansas City Art Inst., 1971, Sch. of Visual Arts, N.Y.C., 1972; admissions cons. Cooper Union for the Advancement of Sci. and Art, 1977. One-man shows include Viridian Gallery, N.Y.C., 1977, Dorothy's Door, N.Y.C., 1983, CUNY, 1988; exhibited in group shows at The Mead Library of Ideas, N.Y.C., 1970, Gallery 303, N.Y.C., 1970, The Studio Mus. in Harlem, N.Y.C., 1970, The Fine Art Mus. of the South at Mobile (Ala.), 1971, Grace Gallery, Bklyn., 1971, 72, 74, 77, 78, 81, 82, 84, 85, 86, Kenny Gallery Adv. Commn. Exhibit, N.Y.C., 1984; represented in permanent collections at Ashland (Ky.) Oil, Inc., Los Angeles County Mus., Mus. of Modern Art-Bookstore 2, Dr. Martin Luther King's Ctr. for Social Change, N.Y.C. Tech. Coll., 1986-88; works displayed in pvt. collections; contbr. articles to numerous pubs.; patentee in field. Adv. commn. High Sch. of Art and Design, N.Y.C., 1976, pres. 1982-85, pres. emeritus. Recipient Keys to the City Mobile, Ala., 1982; named Bus. Woman of Yr. The Laurelton Club of Nat. Assn. Negro Bus. and Profl. Women's Clubs, Inc., 1984. Mem. Art Dir.'s Club, Inc., N.Y. Artists Equity Assn., Inc. Home: 30 E 4th St 4th Floor E New York NY 10003 Office: NYC Tech Coll Dept Art & Advt Design 300 Jay St Brooklyn NY 11201

HAYES, EILEEN PATRICIA, opera theater executive; b. Tillamook, Oreg.; d. Clemens and Martha Dandridge (Maddox) H.; m. Gale Southard Martin, Dec. 28, 1985. BS, U. Oreg., 1968; BA, U. Nev., Las Vegas, 1985. Cert. tchr., Oreg.; cert. orch. mgr. Asst. to dir. Los Angeles Athletic Club, 1969-73; tchr. drama, music Tillamook Pub. Schs., 1973-74; mus. artist Portland Opera Co., Oreg., 1975-80, Oreg. Light Opera Co., 1977-78; mng. dir. Las Vegas Chamber Players, Las Vegas Symphony Orch., 1982-84; exec. dir. Nev. Opera Theatre, Las Vegas, 1985—; cons. theater arts dept. U. Nev., Las Vegas, 1983; pub. relations dir. So. Nev. Mus. Arts Meml. Concert, Las Vegas, 1984; Columbia Artists Mgmt. Artist community concerts, 1988—. Newspaper writer, 1983; editor concert series program booklet, 1982-84; performance dir., artist Tribute to Vietnam Vets., 1975, Mus. Portrait (Nat. Endowment for Arts), 1986, 87. Patron Charleston Heights Art Ctr., Las Vegas, 1983—; com. mem. St. Rose de Lima Hosp. Aux., Henderson, Nev., 1983—; mem. Nev. Alliance for Arts Edn., 1986—, Rep. Women of Clark County, 1985—, ball com. Nev. Gov.'s Inauguration, 1987; mgmt. artist for community concert series Columbia Artists, 1988-89; mem. St. Jude's Aux. Recipient Internat. Thespian award Drama Dir. Tillamook, 1973. Mem. Am. Guild Mus. Artists, Nat. Assn. Female Execs., Met. Opera Guild, Internat. Assn. Bus. Communicators, Nev. Alliance for the Arts (bd. dirs. 1988—), Am. Symphony Orch. League, Assn. Calif. Symphony Orchs., Las Vegas C. of C. (nominating com. 1984). Club: Los Angeles Athletic. Lodge: Order of Rainbow (worthy advisor 1963). Avocations: collecting antiques, swimming, dancing. Office: Nev Opera Theatre 3430 E Flamingo Rd Las Vegas NV 89119

HAYES, EVELYN RUTH, nurse; b. N.Y.C., June 4, 1942; d. Justin Ferdinand and Margaret (Koons) H. BS, Cornell U., 1965; MPH, U. N.C., 1967; PhD, Boston Coll., 1978. Lic. nurse, N.Y. Staff nurse mobile health unit Alliance for Progress, Honduras, 1965; staff nurse Cornell Med. Ctr., N.Y.C., 1965-66, Vis. Nurse Service of N.Y., N.Y.C., 1967-68; mem. faculty sch. of nursing U. Conn., Storrs, 1968-72, 1974-83; mem. faculty sch. of nursing Newton (Mass.) Jr. Coll., 1972-74; chairperson, assoc. prof. dept. of nursing Coll. of Nursing, Newark, Del., 1983-87; cons. law practices, Conn., 1978—, faculty of nursing U. Panama, 1985—; mem. adv. bd. Springhouse Pub. Co. Author: (with others) editor Orientation to Hospitals and Community Agencies, 1986, Linking Nursing Education and Practice: Collaborative Experiences in Maternal-Child Health, 1987. Mem. Blood Bank of Del., 1983—, Am. Heart Assn., 1983—. Recipient Disting. Alumna award Cornell U., 1982; grantee Gen. U. Research Fund, U. Del., 1986—. Mem. Del. Nurses Assn. (bd. dirs. 1984-87), Mid Atlantic Regional Nursing Assn. , Nat. League for Nursing (accreditation site visitor 1978—, bd. of rev. 1987—), Sigma Xi (sci. research soc.), Sigma Theta Tau (pres. Beta Xi 1985-87), Phi Kappa Phi. Home: 815 Sheldon Dr Newark DE 19711 Office: U Del Coll of Nursing McDowell Hall Newark DE 19716

HAYES, HELEN, actress; b. Washington, Oct. 10, 1900; d. Francis Van Arnum and Catherine Estell (Hayes) Brown; m. Charles MacArthur, Aug. 17, 1928 (dec. Apr. 1956); 1 son, James. Grad., Sacred Heart Acad., Washington, 1917; L.H.D., Hamilton Coll., Clinton, N.Y., 1939, Smith Coll., 1940, Elmira (N.Y.) Coll.; Litt.D., Columbia U., 1949, U. Denver, 1952; D.F.A., Princeton U., St. Mary's Coll. First appeared on stage, age si; mem. Columbia Players, Washington, 4 seasons; toured with Lew Fields and John Drew; mem. A.P.A. Phoenix Repertory Co., from 1966. Stage appearances include Old Dutch, Prodigal Husband, Pollyanna, Penrod, Dear Brutus, Clarence, Bab, To The Ladies, We Moderns, Dancing Mothers, Caesar and Cleopatra, What Every Woman Knows, Coquette, Mr. Gilhooley, Mary of Scotland, 1934, Victoria Regina, 1937-38, Ladies and Gentlemen, 1939-40, Twelfth Night, 1940-41, Candle in the Wind, 1941-42, Harriet, 1943-45, Happy Birthday, 1948, The Glass Menagerie, London, 1948, Farewell to Arms, 1950, Vanessa, 1950, The Wisteria Trees, 1950, Mrs. McThing, 1952, Mainstreet to Broadway, 1953, Skin of Our Teeth, Europe and U.S., 1955, Harvey, Long Days Journey Into Night, 1971; motion pictures include The Sin of Madelon, Claudet (Acad. award 1932), Arrowsmith, My Son John, 1951, Anastasia, 1956, Airport, 1970 (Acad. award Best Supporting Actress 1971), Herbie Rides Again, 1974, Helen Hayes: Portrait of an American Actress, 1974, One of Our Dinosaurs is Missing, 1975, Candleshoe, 1978, Hopper's Silence, 1981; TV shows The Snoop Sisters, 1972-74, played Mrs. Derth in TV revival Barrie's Dear Brutus, 1956, Twelve Pound Look, Mary of Scotland, Skin of Our Teeth, Christmas Tie, Drugstore on a Sunday Afternoon, Omnibus, A Caribbean Mystery, Murder With Mirrors, others; author: (novels) Our Best Years, 1986, Where The Truth Lies, 1988. Pres. Am. Nat. Theatre and Acad.; hon. pres. Am. Theatre Wing; 2d v.p. Actors Fund, from 1975—; chmn. women's activities Nat. Found. for Infantile Paralysis. Recipient best actressaward Motion Pictures Acad. Arts and Scis., 1932; recipient Emmyaward, 1954, Antoinette Perry award for best actress in Time Remembered, 1958, Medal of City of N.Y., Medal of Arts Finland, Am. Exemplar medal Freedoms Found., 1978, Laetare medal U. Notre Dame, 1979. Republican. Roman Catholic. •

HAYES, IRENE PRICKETT, dietitian, lecturer; b. Clay County, Ala., June 2, 1935; d. Willie John and Maudie (Dison) Prickett; m. Donald Ray Hayes, June 27, 1953; children: Wanda H. Posey, Donald Ray Jr., Ronald, William, Gregory. AS, Gadsden (Ala.) State Jr. Coll., 1967; BS, Jacksonville (Ala.) State U., 1969; MA, U. Ala., 1976. Registered dietitian, Ala. Dietary asst. Bapt. Meml. Hosp., Gadsden, 1969-74; instr., asst. dir. community service program Gadsden State Jr. Coll., 1974-81; instr. Bellows-Evans Amana, Birmingham, Ala., 1979-80; food service dir. McGuffey Health Care Ctr., Gadsden, 1981—; cons. Mountain View Hosp., Gadsden, 1978-80; lect. Women's Ednl. Tng. and Orientation Ctr. Workshops, Gadsden, 1978-80. Coordinator Meals on Wheels, Gadsden, 1978-81; vol. United Cerebral Palsy, Gadsden, 1982—, Com. to Elect Dems., Gadsden, 1986; team mem. Etowah County Hospice Orgn., Gadsden, 1986—; bd. dirs. meals for home bound Met. Area Noon Nutrition Assn., Gadsden, 1987. Named Grandmother of Yr., United Cerebral Palsy, 1982; recipient Spl. Recognition award, Etowah County Hospice Orgn., 1987. Mem. Am. Dietitic Assn., N.E. Ala. Dietitic Assn. (sec. 1983-85), AAUW, Am. Bus. Women's Assn., Ala. Bus. Women's Assn. Baptist. Home: 615 Sherry Ln Gadsden AL 35903

HAYES, JACQUELINE CREMENT, real estate broker; b. Chgo., Aug. 12, 1941; d. John and Lottie (Czech) Crement; m. Larry G. hayes, Mar. 4, 1972 (div. Dec. 1978). BA in Mgmt., DePaul U., 1977. Lic. real estate broker, Ill. Bldg. mgr. LaSalle Bank Bldg., Chgo., 1978-80; v.p., gen. mgr. The Hayman Co., Chgo., 1981-83; propr. Jacqueline Hayes & Assoc., Chgo., 1983-86; ptnr. The Retail Group, Chgo., 1986—. Docent Chgo. Archtl. Found.; mem. Burnham Pk. Planning Bd., Chgo.; bd. dirs., chmn. western sect. Greater North Michigan Ave. Assn., Chgo., 1986—; mem. adv. council Friends of Downtown, 1987—. Named Broker of Yr. Chgo. Sun Times, 1986. Mem. Internat. Council Shopping Ctrs., Comml. Real Estate Orgn. (bd. dirs., v.p., chmn. membership 1986—), Chgo. Office Leasing Brokers, River North Assn., Chgo. Assn. Commerce and Industry, Chgo. Real Estate Exec. Women, Lambda Alpha (Ely chpt.). Office: The Retail Group 321 Clark St #3160 Chicago IL 60604

HAYES, JANET GRAY, former mayor; b. Rushville, Ind., July 12, 1926; d. John Paul and Lucile (Gray) Frazee; A.B., Ind. U., 1948; M.A. magna cum laude, U. Chgo., 1950; m. Kenneth Hayes, Mar. 20, 1950; children—Lindy, John, Katherine, Megan. Psychiat. caseworker Jewish Family Service Agy., Chgo., 1950-52; vol. Denver Crippled Children's Service, 1954-55; vol. Adult and Child Guidance Clinic, San Jose, 1958-59; mem. San Jose City Council, 1971-82, vice-mayor, 1973-74, mayor, 1975-82; trustee U.S. Conf. Mayors, 1977-82, mem. sci. and tech. task force, 1976-80; bd. dirs. League Calif. Cities, 1976-82, mem. property tax reform task force, 1976-82; chmn. State of Calif. Urban Devel. Adv. Com., 1976-77; mem. Calif. Commn. Fair Jud. Practices, 1976-72, client-community relations dir. Q. Tech., Santa Clara, Calif., 1983-85, bus. mgr. Kenneth Hayes MD, Inc., 1985—; bd. dirs., pres. San Jose (Calif.) Mus. Art, 1987—; founder, adv. bd. Calif. Bus. Bank, 1982—. Mem. Dem. nat. campaign com., 1976; mem. Calif. Dem. Commn. Nat. Platform and Policy, 1976; del. Dem. Nat. Conv., 1980; bd. dirs. South San Francisco Bay Dischargers Authority; chmn. Santa Clara County Sanitation Dist.; mem. San Jose/Santa Clara Treatment Plant Adv. Bd.; chmn. Santa Clara Valley Employment and Tng. Bd. (CETA); past mem. EPA Aircraft/Airport Noise Task Group; bd. dirs. Calif. Center Research and Edn. in Govt., Alexian Bros. Hosp., 1985—; bd. dirs., chmn. adv. council Public Tech. Inc.; mem. exec. bd. League to Save Lake Tahoe, 1984—. AAUW Edn. Found. grantee. Mem. Assn. Bay Area Govts. (exec. com. 1971-74, regional housing subcom. 1973-74, regional housing subcom. 1973-74), LWV (pres. San Francisco Bay Area chpt. 1968-70, pres. local 1966-67), Mortar Bd., Phi Beta Kappa., Kappa Alpha Theta. Democrat. Club: Century.

HAYES, KATHLEEN ZIMMERMAN, retail store executive; b. Hammond, Ind., May 9, 1944; d. Warren Lee and Irene Rose (Glass) Zimmerman; B.S., Purdue U., 1967; M.B.A., U. Chgo., 1970; postgrad. in taxation DePaul U., 1979—. Pharmacist, various cos., Indpls. and Chgo., 1967-70; revenue agt. IRS, Des Moines, 1971-72; tax specialist McGladrey, Hendrickson & Co., Des Moines, 1972-75; tax mgr. Clow Corp., Oak Brook, Ill., 1975-79; tax compliance mgr. U.S. Gypsum Co., Chgo., 1979-82; tax mgr. Global Marine Inc., Houston, 1982-86; owner retail store, Houston. Pres. bd. Woman's Hosp. of Tex. Research and Edn. Found., 1986. C.P.A., Iowa, Ill. Mem. Tax Execs. Inst. (treas. Houston chpt., dir., chmn. internat. tax com.), Am. Inst. C.P.A.s, Iowa Soc. C.P.A.s, Ill. C.P.A. Found., Am. Women's Soc. C.P.A.s, Beta Alpha Psi. Home: 18203 Heaton Dr Houston TX 77084 Office: 78 Woodlake Sq Houston TX 77042

HAYES, MARGARET DALY, political scientist, writer; b. Washington, July 10, 1943; d. Thomas Reed and Mary Gertrude (Tubbs) Daly; m. Richard Edward Hayes, Sept. 6, 1969; 1 child, Michael Thomas. BS in Journalism, Northwestern U., 1965; MA in Spanish Lit., NYU, Madrid, 1966; MA in Polit. Sci., Ind. U., 1970, PhD in Polit. Sci., 1975. Sr. assoc. policy scis. div. CACI, Inc., Arlington, Va., 1974-77; assoc. dir. Ctr. of Brazilian Studies The Johns Hopkins U. Sch. Advanced Internat. Studies, Washington, 1977-80; sr. profl. staff mem. western hemisphere U.S. Senate Fgn. Relations Com., Washington, 1981-84; dir. Council of the Ams., Washington, 1984-88; external affairs advisor Inter-Am. Devel.Bank, Washington, 1988—; cons. U.S. Info. Agy., Washington, 1977-79, Fgn. Service Inst., Bipartisan Nat. Commn. on Cen. America; mem. nat. adv. com. Hubert H. Humphrey Internat. Fellowship Program, Washington, 1985—; bd. dirs. Internat. Devel. Conf., Washington; lectr. in field. Author: Latin America and the U.S. National Interest, 1984; contbr. articles to profl. jours. and chpts. to books. Asst. advisor Explorer Scout Post 860 Boy Scouts Am. Fellow Nat. Def. Fgn. Language Title VI, 1967-70; Fulbright Hays grantee, 1971-72, Ind. U., 1972. Mem. Council Fgn. Relations, Inc., Latin Am. Studies Assn., Internat. Studies Assn., Inter-Am. Council Washington (pres. 1981-82). Club: Capital Divers Assn. (Washington) (pres. 1981-83, 86-87). Office: Inter-Am Devel Bank 1300 New York Ave NW Washington DC 20577

HAYES, MARY ESHBAUGH, newspaper editor; b. Rochester, N.Y., Sept. 27, 1928; d. William Paul and Eleanor Maude (Seivert) Eshbaugh; B.A. in English and Journalism, Syracuse (N.Y.) U., 1950; m. James Leon Hayes, Apr. 18, 1953; children—Pauli, Eli, Lauri Le June, Clayton, Merri Jess Bates. With Livingston County Republican, Geneseo, N.Y., summers, 1947-50, mng. editor, 1949-50; reporter Aurora (Colo.) Advocate, 1950-52; reporter-photographer Aspen (Colo.) Times, 1952-53, columnist, 1956—, reporter, 1972-77, asso. editor, 1977—; tchr. Colo. Mountain Coll., 1979. Mem. Nat. Fedn. Press Women (1st prizes in writing and editing 1976-80), Colo. Press Women's Assn. (writing award 1974, 75, 78-85, sweepstakes award for writing 1977, 78, 84, 85, also 2d place award 1976, 79, 82, 83, Woman of Achievement 1986). Mem. Aspen Community Ch. Photographer, editor: Aspen Potpourri, 1968. Home: PO Box 497 Aspen CO 81611 Office: Box E Aspen CO 81611

HAYES, MARY PHYLLIS, savings and loan association executive; b. New Castle, Ind., Apr. 30, 1921; d. Clarence Edward and Edna Gertrude (Burgess) Scott; m. John Clifford Hayes, Jan. 1, 1942 (div. Oct. 1952); 1 child, R. Scott. Student, Ball State U., 1957-64, Ind. U. East, Richmond, 1963; diploma, Inst. Fin. Edn., 1956, 72, 76. Teller Henry County Savs. and Loan, New Castle, 1939-41, loan officer, teller, 1950-62, asst. sec., treas., 1962-69, sec., treas., 1969-73, corp. sec., 1973-84; v.p., sec. Ameriana Savs. Bank (formerly Henry County Savs. and Loan), New Castle, 1984—; exec. sec. Am. Nat. Bank, Nashville, 1943-44; corp. sec. HCSS Corp., New Castle, 1984—; bd. dirs. Ameriana Ins. Co. Treas. Henry County Chpt. Am. Heart Assn., New Castle, 1965-67, 76-87, vol. Indpls. chpt. 1980—; membership sec. Henry County Hist. Soc., New Castle, 1975—; sec. Henry County Chpt. ARC, New Castle, 1976—. Recipient Gold medallian Am. Heart Assn., 1973, diploma of merit Inst. Fin. Edn., 1984, 20-Yr. award, 1983, 25-Yr. award Ind. affiliate Am. Heart Assn., 1987. Mem. Inst. Fin. Edn. (sec., treas. E. Cen. Ind. chpt. 1973—), Ind. League Savs. Insts. (25-Yr. award 1975), Psi Iota Xi (past sec., treas.). Mem. Christian Ch. Lodges: Altrusa (past officer, bd. dirs. New Castle chpt.), PEO (past chaplain, sec.). Office: Ameriana Savs Bank 2118 Bundy Ave New Castle IN 47362

HAYES, PATRICIA ANN, academic administrator; b. Binghamton, N.Y., Jan. 14, 1944; d. Robert L. and Gertrude (Congdon) H. BA in English, Coll. of St. Rose, 1968; PhD in Philosophy, Georgetown U., 1974. Tchr. Cardinal McCloskey High Sch., Albany, N.Y., 1966-68; teaching asst. Georgetown U., Washington, 1968-71; instr. philosophy Coll. of St. Rose, Albany, 1973-75, instr. bus., spring 1981, adminstrv. intern to acad. v.p., 1973-74, dir. admissions, 1974-78, dir. adminstrn. and planning, 1978-81, v.p. adminstrn. and fin., treas., 1981-84; pres. St. Edward's U., Austin, Tex., 1984—; bd. dirs. First Fed. Savs. & Loan, Austin. Bd. dirs. St. Michael's Cath. Acad., St. Norbert's Coll., DePere, Wis.; mem. Leadership Austin class 1985-86; chair edn. div. United Way campaign, 1986-87. Mem. Nat. Assn. Ind. Colls. and Univs. (govt. relations adv. council, tax policy com.), Austin C. of C. (bd. dirs., chmn. 1988). Roman Catholic. Address: St Edwards Univ 3001 S Congress Austin TX 78704

HAYES, PAULA FREDA, government official; b. Providence, Apr. 5, 1950; d. Ario Louis and Elena Marguerite (Gentile) Freda; m. Robert J. Hayes, Sept. 6, 1975; children: Brendan Michael, Lauren Ann. B.A. magna cum laude, R.I. Coll., 1972; M.P.A., Maxwell Sch., Syracuse U., 1973. Criminal Justice planner City of Syracuse (N.Y.), 1973-75, asst. crime control coordinator, 1975-77; supervisory grants specialist Nat. Endowment Arts, Washington, 1977-78; criminal justice program analyst Dept. Justice, Washington, 1978-79, program mgr. arson discretionary grant program, 1979-80, sr. mgmt. analyst, 1980-81; dep. insp. gen. Community Services Adminstrn., Washington, 1981-82; dir. legis. and analysis div. Office of Insp. Gen., Dept. Agr., Washington, 1982—. Recipient Outstanding Achievement awards Dept. Justice, 1979, 80, 81, 82; Spl. Achievement award Atty. Gen., 1981; Spl. Achievement Cash awards HHS, 1982, USDA, 1988. Roman Catholic. Office: US Dept Agr Office Insp Gen 12th and Independence Ave SW Room 447-E Washington DC 20250

HAYES, PHYLLIS REGINA, school librarian; b. Phila., June 2, 1955; d. Richard Wheeler and Aislee (Brown) H. BA, Lincoln U., 1976; MA, West Chester (Pa.) State Coll., 1979; MS, Drexel U., 1987. Cert. tchr. music K-12, library sci. K-12, Pa., N.J. Instr. music Sch. Dist. Phila., 1976-77, Pleasantville (N.J.) Sch. Dist., 1977-78, Lincoln U., Pa., 1979; bail acceptance officer Ct. of Commom Pleas, City of Phila., 1982-87; librarian Penrose Elem. Sch., Phila., 1988—. Phila. Bd. Edn. music scholar, 1972; Woodrow Wilson Nat. Fellowship Found. fellow, 1976. Mem. Am. Musicological Soc., Pa. Sch. Librarians Assn., Assn. Phila. Sch. Librarians, Beta Phi Mu, Pi Kappa Lambda, Alpha Kappa Alpha. Democrat. Baptist. Home: 251 N 59th St Philadelphia PA 19139 Office: Penrose Elem Sch 78th St and Este Ave Philadelphia PA 19153

HAYES, REBECCA ANNE, communications manager; b. Princeton, Ky., June 3, 1950; d. James Luther and Margaret Anne (Sparks) H. AA, Midway Coll., 1970; AB, U. Ky., 1972; MEd, U. Louisville, 1974. Educator Jefferson County Bd. Edn., Louisville, 1972-78; mgmt. asst. S. Cen. Bell, Louisville, 1978-80, engr., 1980-82; engr. AT&T, Tucker, Ga., 1983-84, asst.

staff mgr., 1984-87, systems cons. bus. markets group, 1987-88; staff mgr. hdqrs. sales ops. AT&T, Basking Ridge, N.J., 1988—. Advisor Career Explorers S. Cen. Bell, Louisville, 1979-80. Mem. Nat. Assn. Female Execs. Democrat. Roman Catholic. Office: AT&T 295 N Maple Ave Basking Ridge NJ 07920

HAYES, SANDRA LYNN, nurse; b. Trenton, N.J., Oct. 26, 1959; d. Joe Nathan and Agradean (Carter) H. A.S., Northeastern Christian Jr. Coll., 1979; B.S. Nursing, Thomas Jefferson U., 1982; postgrad. U. Pa. Clin. nurse II, Thomas Jefferson U. Hosp., Phila., 1982—. Mem. Nat. Assn. Female Execs., Oncology Nursing Soc. Democrat. Mem. Ch. of Christ. Avocations: aerobics; ice skating; skiing. Home: 950 Walnut St Philadelphia PA 19107

HAYES, SARAH JANE, nurse; b. Washington, Sept. 29, 1948; d. Luther Benjamin and Mary W. (Bush) Cornell; m. Ralph James Hayes, June 25, 1966; children: Heather Jane, Charity Christine, Ralph James II, Holly Marie Nellie. AS, Broward Community Coll., Pompano Beach, Fla., 1974. RN, Fla. Nursing aide Alexander (Va.) Hosp., 1967-69; practical nurse Holy Cross Hosp., Fort Lauderdale, Fla., 1971-74, nurse intensive care unit, 1974-76; nurse Med. Personnel Pool, Fort Lauderdale, 1977-87, Palm Beach Gardens (Fla.) Med. Ctr., 1987—. Mem. Am. Heart Assn., 1974-87; pres. Palmview Elem. Sch. PTA, Pompano Beach, 1980-82, v.p., 1982-83, sec., treas. 1983-84, adv. co-chmn., 1985-86; mem. adv. bd. Crystal Lake Mid. Sch., 1985-87. Recipient Outstanding Service awards Palview Elem. Sch., Pompano Beach, 1982, 83. Mem. Fla. Nursing Assn. Democrat. Methodist. Clubs: Ladies Nite Out (Pompano Beach), Women's Internat. Bowling Congress. Lodges: Moose, Foresters. Home: 13556 151st Ln N Jupiter FL 33478

HAYES, THELMA ANN, state official; b. Cleve., Dec. 4, 1918; d. Eugene and Beatrice (Thomas) Roberts; m. James Andrew Hayes, Mar. 27, 1963; children by previous marriage—K. Machuma Bondele, Yvonne Parker, Eugene Kilgore, Fabienne Goins. Student Franklin U., 1952. Dep. clk. supr. Cleve. Mcpl. Ct., 1966-79; sec. Zion Chapel Bapt. Ch., 1966—; audit cons. State of Ohio, 1979—. Mem. NAACP, Nat. Council Negro Women. Democrat. Baptist. Avocation: bowling. Home: 694 E 120 Cleveland OH 44108 Office: Zion Chapel Bapt Ch 4234 Lee Rd Cleveland OH 44128

HAYLE, CLAUDETTE FREDERICA, information services executive; b. Kingston, Jamaica, Jan. 24, 1955; came to U.S., 1974; d. Errol Pinnock and Ruth Palmer; m. Carlton Hayle, Mar. 29, 1975 (div. May 1986); children: Keisha, Seretze. BSc, York Coll., 1978; cert., Cornell U., 1982. Supr. fin. systems CBS Inc., N.Y.C., 1980-81, compensation analysis, 1981-82; cons. AT&T, Metro North and Citibank, N.Y.C., 1983; pres., chief exec. officer Goodman and Hayle Info. Systems, N.Y.C., 1984—. Trustee Rep. Presdl. Task Force, Washington, 1985; sec. N.Y. del. to Nat. White House Conf., N.Y.C., 1986. Mem. Nat Assn. Women Bus. Owners, Nat. Minority Council, N.Y./N.J. Purchasing Council. Republican. Club: CEO (N.Y.C.). Office: Goodman and Hayle Info Systems Inc 60 E 42d St #1732 New York NY 10165

HAYLETT, MARGARET WENDY, television director, engineer; b. Ravenna, Ohio, Jan. 11, 1953; d. James Edward and Edith Marie (Campbell) H. Tech. cert., WIXY Sch. Broadcasting, Cleve., 1973. FCC 1st class/gen. radio telephone lic. Engr. Sta. WJKW-TV, Cleve., 1973-81; engr. Sta. WOKR-TV, Rochester, N.Y., 1981-87, dir., 1987—. Home: 26 Harvest Rd Fairport NY 14450

HAYNE, HARRIET ANN, state legislator, rancher; b. Puget Island, Washington, Sept. 11, 1922; d. Albert Greger and Angeline Marie (Benjaminsen) Danielsen; m. Jack McVicar Hayne, Apr. 3, 1946; children: Mary Joan, John David, Alice Sue, Nancy Ann. Student, Healds Bus. Coll., Wash. State U. Rep. Mont. Legis. Assembly, 1979-81, 85-87, 87—. Precinct, then state committeewoman, vice-chmn., active various campaigns Mont. Reps., Pondera County, 1964. Served as staff sgt. USMC, 1943-45. Mem. Am. Nat. Cattlewomen, Nat. Order Women Legislators, Am. Farm Bur., Am. Legion (aux.), Women Marines Assn., Nat. Fedn. Rep. Women. Lutheran. Address: PO Box 285 Dupuyer MT 59432

HAYNER, JEANNETTE C., state legislator; b. Jan. 22, 1919; m. Herman H. Hayner, 1942; children—Stephen A., James K., Judith A. B.A., U. Oreg., 1940, J.D., 1942. Atty., Bonneville Power Co., Portland, Oreg., 1943-47; mem. Wash. Ho. of Reps., 1972-76, Wash. Senate from Dist. 16, 1977—. Mem. Walla Walla Dist. 140 Sch. Bd., 1956-63, chmn. bd. 2 yrs.; mem. adv. bd. Walla Walla Youth and Family Services Assn., 1968-72; active YWCA, 1968-72; majority leader Wash. State Senate, 1981-82, 87, minority leader 1979-80, 83-86; dist. chmn. White House Conf. on Children and Youth, 1970; chmn. Walla Walla County Mental Health Bd., 1970-72; former mem. Wash. Council on Crime and Delinquency, Nuclear Energy Council, Bonneville Power Regional Adv. Council, State Wash. Organized Crime Intelligence Adv. Bd.; former asst. whip Republican Caucus. Recipient Merit award Walla Walla C. of C. Mem. Oreg. Bar Assn., Delta Kappa Gamma (hon.), Kappa Kappa Gamma. Lutheran. Office: Office State Senate State Capitol Olympia WA 98504 also: PO Box 454 Walla Walla WA 99362

HAYNES, COLLEEN MARGARET, elementary educator; b. Tampa, Fla., Dec. 30, 1950; d. Thomas LeRoy and Wilhelmina Lee (Cain) H.; m. Paul William Malgioglio, Apr. 28, 1980 (div. July 1981). BA, U. S. Fla., 1971, MA, 1986. Tchr. Dist. Sch. Bd. Pasco County, Land O' Lakes, Fla., 1971—. Precinct capt. Pasco County Dem. Exec. Com., 1984—. Named one of Outstanding Young Women Am., 1985. Office: Richey Fundamental Elem Sch 800 N Madison Ave New Port Richey FL 34652

HAYNES, ELEANOR LOUISE, public relations executive; b. Warrenton, Ga., July 7, 1929; d. Joe Brown and Alma Ruth (Simmons) Crenshaw; m. Kenneth M. Thomas, Jan. 16, 1954 (div. 1963); 1 child, Jeffrey Maynard Thomas. Cert., Fashion Inst. Tech., 1951, Am. Airline Sch., 1976; student, Queensboro Community Coll., 1978, Queens Coll., Flushing, N.Y., 1982-83. Columnist, reporter N.Y. Voice, Flushing, 1968—; columnist St. Thomas (V.I.) Daily News, 1970-74, N.J. Beat, Phila., 1972-74; editor Jamaica (N.Y.) B&P News, 1973-76, Color Report, Roosevelt Island, N.Y., 1979—; columnist, editor Calvary Voice, Jamaica, 1983-85; chief exec. officer Haynes Enterprises, Jamaica, 1960-67; travel cons. Good Service & Group Travel, Jamaica, 1970-73; liaison Color Community Adv. Bd. Designer Sipkin Corp., N.Y..C, 1969-74, Petite Frocks, Inc., N.Y.C., 1953-59. Del. N.Y. State Jud. Conv., Laurelton, N.Y., 1981—; mem. 126 St. Black Assn., Laurelton, 1981-84; mem. Vi Vants Inc., N.Y.C., 1983; pub. relations rep. SE Queens Regular Dem. Club, 1982. Recipient numerous local and nat. awards for community service. Mem. Nat. Assn. Media Women Inc. (1st v.p. 1983-87), Nat. Assn. Female Execs., L.I. Assn. Media Women (pres., Media Women Yr., 1983), Edges Group, Inc. Lodge: Order Eastern Star. Home: 231-16-126 Ave Laurelton NY 11413 Office: Color Meml Hosp Roosevelt Island New York NY 10044

HAYNES, JANET-LINDA, medical biologist, educator; b. Bklyn., Nov. 26, 1947; d. Fred Howard and Juliette Lillian (Dreifuss) H.; diploma in med. tech. (hosp. scholar) Beekman-Downtown Hosp. Sch. Med. Tech., N.Y.C., 1969; B.S. (N.Y. State Regents scholar, Empire State Assn. Med. Technologists scholar, N.Y. State Soc. Pathologists scholar), L.I.U., 1969, M.S., 1972; M.Phil., N.Y.U., 1982, postgrad., 1982—. Teaching fellow in scis. L.I.U., Bklyn., 1969-72, mem. faculty, 1973—, adj. asst. prof. biology, 1975-80, adj. assoc. prof. biology, 1980—, adj. mem. grad. faculty med. biology C.W. Post Coll., L.I.U., 1979-83; research technologist Jewish Hosp. and Med. Center of Bklyn., 1972-77; faculty mem. Physician Asst. Program, Bklyn.-Cumberland Med. Center, 1976—; adj. asst. prof. biology Pace U., N.Y.C., 1977-78; teaching fellow in biology NYU, 1979-84; asst. prof., clin. coordinator dept. med. tech. Health Scis. Center, Sch. Allied Health Professions, SUNY-Stony Brook, 1981-83; adj. instr. CUNY, 1973-85; adj. lectr. Sch. Continuing Edn., NYU, 1984—. Contbr. articles to profl. jours. Active, Operation Baby Track, ARC, N.Y.C., 1981, Am. Cancer Soc., 1982—; mem. ad hoc. com. on status of women SUNY, Stony Brook, 1982. Recipient Charlotte Pann Meml. award N.Y.U., 1981; Phi Sigma grad. research awardee, 1972; Conn. State fellow, 1974-75; NIH trainee, 1974-75; N.Y.U. grantee in biology, 1980—; Sigma Xi grantee, 1981-82. Mem. Am. Soc. Clin. Pathologists (cert. med. technologist), Am. Soc. Microbiology, Assn. for Women in Sci., AAUW, N.Y. Acad. Scis., AAAS, Sigma Xi, Alpha Epsilon Delta, Phi Sigma. Office: LI U Dept Biology University Plaza Brooklyn NY 11201

HAYNES, JEAN REED, lawyer; b. Miami, Fla., Apr. 6, 1949; d. Oswald Birnam and Arleen (Weidman) Dow; m. William Rutherford Reed, Apr. 15, 1974 (div. Sept. 1981); m. Thomas Beranek Haynes, Aug. 7, 1982. AB with honors, Pembroke Coll., 1971; MA, Brown U., 1971; JD, U. Chgo., 1981. Bar: Ill. 1981, U.S. Dist. Ct. (no. dist.) Ill. 1983, U.S. Ct. Appeals (7th cir.) 1982. Tchr. grades 1-4 Abbie Tuller Sch., Providence, 1971-72; tchr./facilitator St. Mary's Acad., Riverside, R.I., 1972-74; tchr./head lower sch. St. Francis Sch., Goshen, Ky., 1974-78; law clk. U.S. Ct. Appeals (7th cir.), Chgo., 1981-83; assoc. Kirkland & Ellis, Chgo., 1983-87, ptnr., 1987—. Sustaining fellow Art Inst. Chgo., 1982—, mem. aux. bd. 1986—, membership com. aux. bd., 1987—. Mem. ABA (litigation sect., com. on affordable justice 1988—), Chgo. Bar Assn., Ill. Bar Assn. (life), Am. Judicature Soc. (life). Club: Internationale, East Bank. Home: 179 East Lake Shore Dr Chicago IL 60611 Office: Kirkland & Ellis 200 E Randolph Dr Chicago IL 60611

HAYNES, MARGARET ELIZABETH, nurse, educator; b. Hopkinsville, Ky., Feb. 25, 1919; d. Philip E. and Marion (Bell) H.; A.A., Bethel Woman's Coll., 1939; B.S. in Nursing, Vanderbilt U., 1942; M.P.H., U. N.C., 1954. Staff pediatric nurse Vanderbilt U. Hosp., Nashville, 1942-43; head pediatric nurse John Sealy Hosp., Galveston, Tex., 1943-45, U. Colo., Colo. Gen. Hosp., 1947-48, U. Colo., Denver Gen. Hosp., 1948-52; asst. instr. obstet. nursing Vanderbilt U. Sch. Nursing, 1946-47, pub. health staff nurse Dist. Health Dept., Chapel Hill, N.C., 1954-58; asst. prof. U. N.C. Sch. Nursing, Chapel Hill, 1958-65; asst. prof. U. Tenn. Coll. Nursing, Memphis, 1967-69, assoc. prof. community health nursing, 1973-84, assoc. prof. emerita, 1984—, nursing cons. Child Devel. Center, U. Tenn. Med. Units, 1967-71; nursing cons. Arlington (Tenn.) Hosp. and Sch. for Retarded, 1970-71; dir. Coop. Community Health Nursing Edn. Project, 1972-73; adminstrv. asst. Phys. Rehab. Clinic, Memphis, 1986—. Recipient Faculty award U. N.C. Sch. Nursing Class of 1965; John Runyan Community Nursing award, 1984. Mem. Am. Nurses Assn., Am. Pub. Health Assn., Vanderbilt U., U. N.C. nursing alumnae assns., Sigma Theta Tau. Baptist. Contbr. articles to profl. jours. Home: 730 Hedgegrove Dr Apt 4 Memphis TN 38117

HAYNES, PATRICIA SOMERVILLE, personnel management specialist; b. Leonardtown, Md.; d. Agnes Elizabeth (Stevens) Somerville. B.S., Howard U., 1980; M.S., Troy State U., 1983. Phys. therapist St. Francis Hosp., Columbus, Ga., 1980-81; personnel mgmt. specialist Communications-Electronics Command, Fort Monmouth, N.J., 1984—; condr. seminars on career devel. Co-author manual in field. Edn. coordinator Kelly Hill Chapel, Fort Benning, Ga., 1981-82. Named to Outstanding Young Women Am., U.S. Jaycees, 1985. Mem. Personnel Adminstrn. Soc., Alpha Kappa Alpha. Roman Catholic. Avocations: swimming; biking; tennis; flute.

HAYNICZ, LACY ANN, medical records administrator; b. Riverside, N.J., Sept. 12, 1950; d. Joseph Charles and Minnie May (Jones) Hale; student La. State U., 1968-70, Rider Coll., 1971-74; B.A. in Health Info. Mgmt., Stephens Coll., 1984; registered records adminstr.; m. Michael S. Haynicz, Dec. 21, 1974. Salesperson accessories dept. Pomeroy's, Willingboro, N.J., 1970; with Strawbridge & Clother, Cherry Hill, N.J., 1971-72; clk. typist R. M. Hollingshead Co., Camden, N.J., 1972-74; exec. sec. to corporate controller The Hibbert Co., Trenton, N.J., 1974-75; dir. med. records Cumberland Regional Health Plan, Vineland, N.J., 1975-78; asst. dir. med. records Phila. Coll. Osteo. Medicine, 1978; dir. med. records in care pavilion and Mt. Laurel Convalescent Centers, Geriatric and Med. Centers, Phila., 1979-80; dir. med. records, Vineland (N.J.) State Sch. Hosp., 1980-85; med. record adminstr. mgmt. Info. Systems unit Div. Devel. Disabilities, 1985-87; dir. med. records, Coop. Health Care of South N.J., 1987-88, Meml. Hosp. of Salem County, 1988—. Coach Little League cheerleading squad, 1972-73. Recipient Records Technician cert. Am. Med. Record Assn., 1977. Mem. N.J. Med. Record Assn., Hort. Soc., Alpha Chi Omega (pres.). Home: 267 Dogwood Ln Clarksboro NJ 08020 Office: Meml Hosp of Salem County Salem-Woodstown Rd Salem NJ 08079

HAYS, ANNE MORRIS, advertising agency administrator; b. Chattanooga, June 5, 1947; d. George Pierce Morris and Doris Pearl (Holt) Eagan; m. Mark Hanna Hays III, Feb. 26, 1966 (div. Aug. 1972); children: Mark, John, David. Student, U. Tenn., 1965-66. Corp. sec. Morris Rent-All Ctr., Nashville, 1980-82; mgr. prodn. Jan. & Assocs., Nashville, 1982-87, account exec., 1987—. Republican. Episcopalian. Office: Jan & Assocs 5560 Franklin Pike Circle Brentwood TN 37027

HAYS, BONNIE LINN, county official; b. Silverton, Oreg., Aug. 21, 1950; d. Lacy Emmett and Ethel Marie (Hunt) Bowlsby; m. Robert Verne Hays, Mar. 21, 1972 (dec. Aug. 1976); m. Arthur J. Lewis, Aug. 22, 1981. BS, Oreg. State U., 1972; postgrad. Portland State U., 1973-74, Rocky Mt. Inst., 1982, Lewis & Clark U., Northwestern U. Sch. Law, 1985-86. Cert. tchr. secondary edn., Oreg. Tchr. high sch. Astoria Sch. Dist., Oreg., 1972-75; ins. agt. Equitable Life Assurance Co., Portland, Oreg., 1975-77; br. mgr. Transamerica Title Ins. Co., Beaverton, Oreg., 1977-82; county commr. Washington County, Hillsboro, Oreg., 1980—; dir. Washington County Community Corrections, Hillsboro, 1983—, elected chmn., bd. commrs., 1987—; dir. State Job Trng. Coordinating Council, Salem, Oreg., 1985-88, Multnomah-Washington Pvt. Industry Council, Portland, 1983-87; project dir. Washington County Driving Under the Influence of Intoxicants Act Com., Hillsboro. Bd. dirs. Un Lugar para Niños, Hillsboro, 1984—; bd. mgmt., chmn. YMCA of Washington County, Beaverton, 1983—; corp. bd. dirs. YMCA of Columbia-Williamette, 1987—; bd. dirs. Tualatin Valley Econ. Devel. Corp., 1987—; bd. dirs. Washington County Hist. Soc., Hillsboro, 1985—, pres., 1986-88; mem. Young Republicans of Oreg., Salem, 1984—; mem. Oreg. Episc. Sch. Wetlands Adv. Com., 1986. Named One of Washington County's "10 Most Influential People", Valley Times Newspaper Poll, 1985. Mem. Am. Corrections Assn., Assn. Oreg. Counties (com. pub. safety and human resources 1982—, vice chmn. 1982, chmn. 1986-88), Nat. Assn. Counties (justice and pub. safety steering com. 1987—). Republican. Roman Catholic. Club: Multnomah Athletic (Portland). Avocation: gourmet cooking. Home: 15540 SW Village Ct Beaverton OR 97007 Office: Washington County Courthouse 150 N First Ave Hillsboro OR 97124

HAYS, HELEN FUGH, corporate executive; b. Beijing, Peoples Republic of China, Sept. 3, 1931; d. Philip J.P. and Sarah (Liu) Fugh; m. John Gordon Hays (dec.); children: Philip, Patricia Gutzat, Priscilla Keith, John Jr., Jennifer. Founder, pres. Da Hua Corp., Washington, 1980—; coordinator Chinese Extension Service Ctr., D.C., 1975-80, D.C. Cooperative Services of U. of D.C. Active PTA, Cub Scouts, Montgomery County, Md., 1958-60; mem. civic affairs com., U.S.-CHina Study Council, Md., 1963-65; vol. dir. D.C. Chinatown and Cultural Ctr., 1969; founder, dir. Asian-Am. Bicentennial Corp., 1973. Mem. Nat. Assn. Chinese-Ams., Inc. (founding), Orgns. Chinese-Am. Heritage (v.p.). Home: 5312 28th St NW Washington DC 20015

HAYS, JOAN EAMES, state legislator; b. Cin., Feb. 29, 1916; d. Alastair Chatham Comyn and Emma (Faber) Eames; m. Nathan Harris David, July 1937 (div. 1956); children: Steven M. David, Anthony P. David, Deborah David Dewar (dec.); m. John Newton Hayes, Sept. 9, 1964 (dec. 1979); m. Robert Burch Hewett, Nov. 7, 1983. BA, Harvard U., 1936. Freelance writer various mags. Washington, 1940-48; mng. editor Am. Fgn. Service Jour., Washington, 1948-53; registered lobbyist Nat. Counsel Assocs., Washington, 1953-60; stockbroker Prudential-Bache, Washington, 1960-67; elected mem. Hawaii Ho. of Reps., 1982-84, 86-88. Author: Inside the State Department, 1952; contbr. articles to profl. jours. Founder, chmn. Citizens Against Noise, Honolulu, 1970—; bd. dirs. Hawaii Planned Parenthood, Honolulu, 1971-74, 84-87, AAUW, Washington, 1971-72, Honolulu Theater for Youth, Honolulu, 1970-72. Recipient Nat. Vol. Activist award Germaine Monteil, 1977, Thomas Jefferson award Honolulu Advertiser, 1978. Mem. League of Women Voters, Common Cause, Japan-Am. Soc. Hawaii, Pacific and Asian Affairs Council, Friends of East-West Ctr. Democrat. Clubs: Hawaii's Thousand Friends, English-Speaking Union, Waikiki Residents Assn. (Honolulu); Harvard. Home: 1860 Ala Moana Blvd #2001 Honolulu HI 96815 Office: State Capitol Room 324 Honolulu HI 96813

HAYS, KATHLEEN ADELLA, nurse, consultant; b. Latrobe, Pa., Jan. 29, 1947; d. Donald Cleary and Catherine (Graham) H. Diploma, Presbyn. U. Hosp. Sch. Nursing, 1967; BSN, U. Pitts., 1969, M in Nursing, 1977. Staff nurse Presbyn. U. Hosp., Pitts., 1967-69, head nurse med. unit, 1967-72, head nurse hematology/oncology unit, 1972—. Cons. Am. Cancer Soc.; trustee local chpt. Leukemia Soc. Am., 1976—, nat. bd., 1986—. Mem. Oncology Nursing Soc. (v.p. gt. Pitts. chpt. 1985-86, pres. 1988—). Presbyterian. Home: 2220 McNary Blvd Pittsburgh PA 15221 Office: Presbyn U Hosp DeSoto at O'Hara Sts Pittsburgh PA 15213

HAYS, MARILYN PATRICIA, lawyer, rancher, real estate executive; b. Yarrow, Mo., Sept. 19, 1935; d. John Dewey and Ruth (McKim) H.; m. Harold Clifton Ledbetter, Dec. 13, 1953 (div. 1972); children—Latricia Lyn, Lisa Ledbetter Cerio, David Clifton, Laura Lizanne; Harold Clifton, Jr.; m. Dean Leon Fortney, July 21, 1978. B.S., Northeast Mo. State U., 1958; broker cert. U. Fla., 1976; M.A., U. Mo., 1983; J.D., Washburn U., 1987. Lic. real estate broker, Mo., Kans., Fla., Grad. Realtors Inst. Fashion coordinator Ashells, Regina's Co., Kirksville, Mo., 1951-54; instr. pub. schs., Crocker, Novinger, Kirksville and University City, Mo., 1954-61; real estate salestaff Goldman's Assocs., Daytona Beach, Fla., 1975-76; real estate broker Kellogg Century 21, Daytona Beach, 1976-78; pres. M.P. Hays Co., Olathe, Kans., 1978-82, Bucyrus, Kans., 1982—; cons. Goldman, Kellogg, Daytona Beach, 1975-78. Contbr. articles on real estate edn. to profl. jours. Pres. Fla. Osteopathic Med. Assn. Aux., Dist. IV, 1964-65, 73-74, pres.-elect, 1967-68; major chmn. Assn. of Jr. League, Daytona Beach, 1968-69, 72-73; Pan Hellenic del., 1972-78; adviser Ormond Beach Hosp. Guild, Fla., 1972-74; tchr. CCD Holy Rosary Cath. Ch., Bucyrus, 1987—. Scholar, Mo. Council PTAs, 1953, K.C., 1954; recipient Outstanding Sales Achievement award Kellogg Century 21, 1977. Mem. Kans. Bar Assn., Holy Rosary Alter Soc., Miami County Bd. Realtors, Johnson County Bd. Realtors, Nat. Assn. Realtors, Kans. Assn. Realtors, ABA, Kans. Farm Bur., Women's Legal Forum, AAUW, Am. Quarterhorse Assn., Alpha Sigma Alpha, Phi Delta Phi. Republican. Roman Catholic. Clubs: Ormond Beach Woman's, Oceanside Country. Avocations: photography; cooking; horseback riding. Home: Route 1 Box 161 Bucyrus KS 66013 Office: M P Hays Co 223d St and State Line Rd Bucyrus KS 66013

HAYS, MARY KATHERINE JACKSON (MRS. DONALD OSBORNE HAYS), civic worker; b. Flora, Miss.; d. Rufus Lafayette and Ada (Collum) Jackson; student U. Miss., 1925-26, Millsaps Coll., 1926-27, 43-44; grad. Clark Bus. Sch., 1934; student Columbia U., 1935, Strayer Bus. Coll., 1951; m. Halbert Puffer Oliver, Aug. 9, 1927 (dec. 1934); m. 2d, Donald Osborne Hays, Aug. 30, 1937. Sec. to pres. McCullough Box and Crate Co., Pharr, Tex., 1934-36; sec. to field supr. Miss. Unemployment Compensatio Commn., 1936-37; rep. Homes of Tomorrow, 1940 N.Y. World's Fair; sec. to head interior design Lord & Taylor, N.Y.C., 1940; sales dept. Knabe Piano Co., N.Y.C., 1941-43. Active, Little Theatre, Wilkes Barre, Pa., 1937-39; charter mem. and incorporator Conf. State Socs., Washington, 1952; vol. worker Am. Cancer Soc., Washington, 1957; mem. Center City Residents Assn., Phila., 1956; mem. women's com. Nat. Symphony Assn., vol. worker USO, 1945-48, symphony sustaining com. drives, 1957-66; mem. women's com. Corcoran Gallery Art, Washington, 1957-62; mem. Pierce-Warwick Adoption Assn. of Washington Home for Foundlings; vol. Washington Heart Assn., 1959-66; mem. Nat. Capital Area chpt. United Ch. Women, 1957—; mem. D.C. Episcopal Home for Children, 1961—, D.C. Salvation Army Aux., 1962—. Mem. Miss. State Soc. D.C. (sec. 1950-53), Nat. Trust for Historic Preservation, Miss. Women's Club D.C., DAR (vice regent chpt. 1970-72, regent chpt. 1972-74, vice chmn. D.C. com. celebration Washington's birthday 1972-76, state librarian 1974-76), chpt. chmn. DAR Service for Vet. Patients Com., 1986-88, UDC (chpt. historian 1982-84, 86—, chaplain 1984-86), Johnstone Clan Am. (exec. council 1976-81), First Families of Miss. Episcopalian. Club: The Washington. Home: 4000 Massachusetts Ave NW Washington DC 20016

HAYS, RHONDA BRASSFIELD, telecommunications executive; b. Broken Arrow, Okla., Sept. 6, 1952; d. Venson O. and Deloris Lee (Hall) Brassfield; m. Vestal L. Patterson, Apr. 28, 1984; children: Lance Venson, Ginger Elise. Grad. high sch., Tulsa. V.p. ops. Cardiff Cablevision, Inc., Denver and Tulsa, 1977—; v.p. Midway Cablevision, Denver and Tulsa, 1980-84, Blue Water Cable, Inc., Tulsa, 1981—, Crawford County Cable, Inc., Tulsa, 1981—, Quad County Commuications, Inc., Denver and Tulsa, 1981-84, Spring Valley Farms, Oskaloosa, Kans., 1982—; pres. United TV Corp., Tulsa, 1985—; v.p. PM United, Tulsa, 1986—; pres. Pirho Foods Corp., Tulsa, 1986—; cons. Chama Video, Inc., Tulsa, 1984—. Mem. Women in Cable (v.p. 1984-85, pres. 1985-86, bd. dirs. 1985— Okla. chpt.), Am. Women in Radio and TV, Cable TV Antenna Assn. Club: Tulsa Exec. Exchange. Home: 6712 S 74th Ave Tulsa OK 74133 Office: United TV Corp 4545 S Mingo Tulsa OK 74146

HAYWARD, OLGA LORETTA HINES (MRS. SAMUEL E. HAYWARD), librarian; b. Alexandria, La.; d. Samuel James and Lillie (George) Hines; A.B., Dillard U., 1941; B.S. in L.S., Atlanta U., 1944; M.A., U. Mich., 1959; M.A. in History, La. State U., 1977; m. Samuel E. Hayward, July 12, 1945; children: Anne Elizabeth, Olga Patricia (Mrs. William Ryer). Tchr., Marksville (La.) High Schs., 1941-42; head librarian Grambling (La.) Coll., 1944-46; br. librarian br. nine New Orleans Pub. Library System, 1947-48; reference librarian So. U., Baton Rouge, 1948-73, prof. library sci., social scis. librarian, 1973-84, dir. collection devel., 1984-87, chmn. ref. dept. Cade library, 1987—. Bd. dirs. La. Diocese Episcopal Community Services, 1972-78; mem. Human Relations Council of La. Mem. ALA, La. Library Assn. (chmn. subject specialists sect. 1986-87), Spl. Libraries Assn. (pres. La. chpt. 1978-79, chmn. positive action com. 1986-87, 87-88), La. Com. for Library Devel. (mem. steering com. 1986-87). Episcopalian. Author: Graduate Theses of Southern University 1959-71; A Bibliography of Literature By and About Whitney Moore Young, Jr., 1929-71, 1972; The Influence of Humanism on Sixteenth Century English Courtesy Texts, 1977; also other bibliographies. Contbr. articles to profl. jours. Home: 1632 Harding Blvd Baton Rouge LA 70807

HAYWARD, TERESA CALCAGNO, educator; b. N.Y.C., Jan. 28, 1907; d. Vito and Rosalie (Amato) Calcagno; m. Peter Hayward, Feb. 6, 1932; children—Nancy, Peter. B.A., Hunter Coll., 1929; M.A., Columbia U., 1931. Tchr. romance langs. Jr. High Sch. 164, N.Y.C., 1936-57, Jr. High Sch. 141, Riverdale, N.Y., 1957-71; tchr. English to Japanese women Nichibei Fujinkai, Riverdale, 1972—. Chmn. Riverdale chpt. Nichibei Fujinkai, Riverdale, 1976-88; bd. dirs. Riverdale chpt. UN Assn., 1976-88. Mem. Hunger and Social Outreach com. Ch. of Christ, Riverdale. Democrat. Episcopalian. Avocations: concerts; piano; art lectures; travel.

HAZALEUS, MARGARET BENNINGTON, university dean; b. Center, Colo., Mar. 8, 1919; d. Frank and Jessie Lynnanne (Scarff) Bennington; B.S. in Food Sci. and Nutrition, Colo. State U., 1941, M.S. in Sociology, 1960; m. Melvin Harp Hazaleus, Jan. 2, 1943; children—John Melvin, Susan Lynn. Dietitian sch. lunch program, LaJunta, Colo., 1941-42; tchr. chemistry and biology Del Norte High Sch., 1942-43; elem. tchr. Center Consol. Schs., 1945-46; asst. to dean Coll. Home Econs., Colo. State U., 1961-67, coordinator student programs, 1967-71, asst. dean Coll. Human Resource Scis., 1971—; conf. presenter. Mem. Poudre R-1 Citizens Com., Gov.'s Commn. Status of Women; vol. Reach to Recovery unit Am. Cancer Soc., 1974—; leader Cub Scouts, Brownie Scouts; mem. 4-H Devel. Com., Larimer County 4-H Scholarship Com. Named Outstanding Faculty Mem., Colo. State U. Coll. Home Econs., 1969; Outstanding Woman Adminstr., Colo. State U., 1973, Very Important Prof., 1980, recipient Disting. Service award in undergrad. advising, 1980. Mem. Am. Home Econs. Assn., Colo. Home Econs. Assn., Assn. Acad. Affairs Adminstrs., Nat. Council Family Relations, Coll. Home Econs. Alumni Assn., Colo. State U. Alumni Assn. (honor alumna 1977), Coll. Human Resource Scis. Alumni Council (pres. 1983-86), Coll. Home Econs. Alumni Council, Mortar Bd. Alumni Group, Gamma Sigma Delta, Delta Kappa Gamma, Phi Kappa Phi, Omicron Nu, Alpha Delta Kappa, Delta Delta Delta. Republican. Presbyterian. Club: PEO. Student patio on Gifford Bldg., Colo. State U. dedicated to biographee, 1982. Home: 1213 Green St Fort Collins CO 80524 Office: Colo State U Coll Human Resource Scis Gifford 100A Fort Collins CO 80523

HAZARDUNNE, EILEEN EDWINA, retail executive; b. Bridgeport, Conn., July 4, 1962; d. David Edwin and Margaret Alicia (Papineau) Dunn;

m. David Wayne Hazardunne, Nov. 11, 1958. Grad. high sch. Mgr. Brooks Drugs, Derby, Conn., 1978-80; computer operator Curved Glass, Derby, Conn., 1980-82; with E. Coast Tile Imports, Inc., New Haven, 1982—; mgr. Intercorp Systems, 1988—; cons. Budson Ent., Hartford, 1982-85. Vol. Sr. Sis. of Marian Hts., 1975-82; vol. Toys for Tots, Hartford. Mem. Nat. Assn. Female Execs. Office: Standard Tile Distbrs Inc 293 East Street New Haven CT 06511

HAZELBAKER, EILEEN GENEVA, medical technologist; b. Decatur County, Kans., Nov. 2, 1928; d. Clint Leonard and Edith Helen (Vermilion) Huff; degree in gen. sci. Ft. Hays (Kans.) State Coll., 1953; m. Fred R. Hazelbaker, Oct. 5, 1974; 1 son by previous marriage, Wayne Leroy Wohler. Intern, Stormont-Vail Hosp., Topeka, 1953; med. technologist hosps. in Kans. and Wash., 1954-67; med. technologist Syringa Gen. Hosp., Grangeville, Idaho, 1967—. Mem. Am. Soc. Clin. Pathologists. Mem. Christian Ch. (Disciples of Christ). Clubs: Extension, Rebekahs. Home: PO Box 225 Grangeville ID 83530 Office: Syringa Gen Hosp Grangeville ID 83530

HAZELTINE, JOYCE, state official; b. Pierre, S.D.; m. Dave Hazeltine; children: Derek, Tara, Kirk. Student, Huron (S.D.) Coll.; grad., No. State Coll., Aberdeen, S.D., Black Hills State Coll., Spearfish, S.D. Former asst. chief clk. S.D. Ho. of Reps.; former sec. S.D. State Senate; sec. of state State of S.D., Pierre, 1987—. Adminstrv. asst. Pres. Ford Campaign, S.D.; Rep. com. chmn. Hughes County, S.D. Office: Sec of State's Office 500 E Capitol Pierre SD 57501

HAZELTON, NANCY TOLER, banker, culinary expert; b. Long Beach, Calif., July 11, 1949; d. Albert Eugene and Mary Olive (Fager) Toler; m. Charles Y. Hazelton, Mar. 1, 1969; children—Patricia, Christopher. Student Memphis State U., 1967-69, Sullivan Jr. Coll., 1983-84; diploma Inst. Fin. Edn., Chgo., 1977, cert., 1985. Mgmt. trainee Aristar, Inc., Memphis, 1968-76; loan officer Home Fed., Memphis, 1976-79; loan originator Future Fed. Savs. Bank, Louisville, 1979-85, v.p., mgr. residential lending/secondary mktg., 1985—. Adult edn. guest speaker Jefferson Community Coll., Louisville, 1984; active Jeffersontown Booster Club, Ky. Mem. Women's Council Realtors, Mortgage Bankers Assn., Louisville Bd. Realtors (assoc.), Homebuilders Assn. Louisville (assoc.), Ky. Assn. Profl. Mortgage Women (program chmn. 1985-86), Mortgage Bankers Assn. Louisville (sec. 1988). Republican. Roman Catholic. Home: 3603 Pirogue Rd Jeffersontown KY 40299

HAZELTON, PENNY ANN, law librarian, educator; b. Yakima, Wash., Sept. 24, 1947; d. Fred Robert and Margaret (McLeod) Pease; m. Norris J. Hazelton, Sept. 12, 1971; 1 dau., Victoria MacLeod. BA cum laude, Linfield Coll., 1969; JD, Lewis and Clark Law Sch., 1975; M in Law Librarianship, U. Wash., 1976. Admissions counselor Linfield Coll., 1969-71; serials librarian Lewis and Clark Law Sch. Law Library, Lewis and Clark Coll., 1972-75; admitted to Wash. bar, 1976; assoc. law librarian, assoc. prof. U. Maine, 1976-78, law librarian, assoc. prof., 1978-81; asst. librarian for research services U.S. Supreme Ct., Washington, 1981-85, law librarian U. Wash., Seattle, 1985—, prof. law, 1985—; tchr. legal research, law librarianship, Indian law, law and medicine; cons. Maine Adv. Com. on County Law Libraries. Mem. Law Librarians New Eng. (sec. 1977-79, pres. 1979-81), Am. Assn. Law Libraries (cert.; program chmn. ann. meeting 1984, exec. bd. 1984-87), Law Librarians' Soc. Washington (exec. bd. 1983-84, v.p., pres.-elect 1984-85), Am. Bar Assn. Westpac. Republican. Contbr. articles to Environ. Law, Legal Reference Services Quar. Office: 1100 NE Campus Pkwy Seattle WA 98105

HAZZARD, SHIRLEY, author; b. Sydney, Australia, Jan. 30, 1931; d. Reginald and Catherine (Stein) H.; m. Francis Steegmuller, Dec. 22, 1963. Ed., Queenwood Sch., Sydney, to 1946. With Combined Services Intelligence, Hong Kong, 1947-48, U.K. High Commr.'s Office, Wellington, N.Z., 1949-51, UN (Gen. Service Category), N.Y.C., 1952-62; Boyer lectr., Australia, 1984. Author: Cliffs of Fall and Other Stories, 1963; novel The Evening of the Holiday, 1966; fiction People in Glass Houses, 1967; novel The Bay of Noon, 1970; social history Defeat of an Ideal: A Study of the Self-Destruction of the United Nations, 1973; novel The Transit of Venus, 1980; contbr.: short stories to New Yorker mag. Trustee N.Y. Soc. Library. Recipient 1st prize O. Henry Short Story Awards, 1976; grantee in lit. Nat. Inst. Arts and Letters, 1966; Guggenheim fellow, 1974; Nat. Book Critics Circle award for Fiction, 1981; Christian Gauss lectureship award Princeton U., 1982. Mem. Nat. Inst. Arts and Letters. Address: 200 E 66th St New York NY 10021

HEAD, MARIE DOSS, computer specialist; b. Atlanta, Aug. 4, 1956; d. Thomas Pollard Doss and Betty Jean (Wallace) Lindsey; m. Joseph David Head III, Dec. 22, 1972; 1 child, Christopher David. Student, Carrol (Ga.) Area Vo-Tech., 1982-84. Personnel clk. Region IV U.S. Dept. Housing and Urban Devel., Atlanta, 1977-79, sec., 1979-80, computer asst., 1980-84, computer programmer analyst, 1984-87, acting chief computer ops., 1987, housing systems mgr., 1987—. Office: US Dept Housing and Urban Devel Mgmt Systems 75 Spring St SW Atlanta GA 30303

HEAD, VIOLET BERYL, psychologist; b. Picton, Ont., Can., Mar. 30, 1922; d. Andrew Burton and Claribel (Miller) H. BA, Queen's U., Kingston, 1958; AM, U. Chicago, 1963, PhD, 1963. Reg. psychologist, Ont. Bd. Examiners Psychology. Elem. tchr. Ont., 1941-46; various positions in bus. Toronto, Ont., 1946-56; coordinator group services Internat. Inst. Met. Toronto, Ont., 1956-60; psychologist Toronto Psychiat. Hosp., 1963-65; coordinator group psychotherpy Addiction Research Found., Toronto, 1965-70; psychologist The Donwood Inst., Toronto, 1970-87, cons., 1987—; pvt. practice psychology Toronto, Ont., Can., 1980—; cons. Project Turnabout: Ont. Nurses Assistance Prog. Inc., Toronto, 1987—. Contbr. articles to profl. jours. Mem. Ont. Psychol. Assn., Can. Group Psychotherapy Assn., (fellow, pres. 1977-79, bd. dirs. 1980-84), Am. Group Psychotherapy Assn. (bd. dirs. 1977-79, int. aspects com, 1980—), Internat. Assn. Group Psychotherapy, Royal Ont. Mus., Art Gallery Ont. Liberal. Clubs: Toronto Lawn Tennis, U. Chgo. Toronto. Home: 34 Standish Ave, Toronto Can M4W3B1 Office: 216 St Clair Ave W, Toronto Can M4V1R2

HEADDING, LILLIAN SUSAN, writer; b. Milw., Jan. 1, 1944; d. David Morton and Mary Davis (Berry) Coleman; m. James K. Hill (div. 1976); children: Amy Denise; m. John Murray Headding (div. 1987). BA, U. Nev., 1975; MA, U. Pacific, 1976. With Gimbels, Milw., 1963-65; retail mgr. Frandisco Corp., N.Y.C., 1965-66; store mgr. Anita Shops, Los Angeles, 1966-68, Clothes Closet, Sunnyvale, Calif., 1969-70; owner Lillian Headding Interiors & Comml. Design, Pittsburg, Calif., 1976-88; instr. 1st degree black belt, 1972—. Author (as Sara Davis): When Gods Fall; short stories. Bd. dirs. Community Action Against Rape, Las Vegas, Nev., 1972-75; self-def. expert Las Vegas Met. Police Dept., 1972-75, North Las Vegas (Nev.) Police Dept.; co. supr. Family & Children's Services, Contra Costa County, Calif., 1985-86. Mem. NOW, Walnut Creek Writers Group (pres.), Philippine Hawaiian Black Belters Assn., Mensa. Republican. Jewish.

HEADLEY, ANNE RENOUF, financier for technology commercialization; b. N.Y.C., Apr. 3, 1937. Student, Emma Willard Sch., 1954, Inst. World Affairs, 1957; AB magna cum laude, Columbia U., 1959; MA, Yale U., 1962, PhD, 1966; JD with honors, Am. U., 1978; postgrad., Duke U. Asst. prof. U. N.C., Chapel Hill, 1966-71; sr. profl. cons. U.S. Govt., Washington, 1972-75; pvt. practice fin. cons. Washington, 1976—; vis. assoc. prof. George Washington U. Sch. Bus. Adminstrn., Washington, 1983-84; gen. ptnr., v.p. Tech. Mgmt. Corp., Montgomeryville, Pa., 1986—; corp. dir., cons. The Brookings Instn., Washington, 1966, U.S. Dept. State, Washington, 1967; vis. scholar Carnegie Endowment for Internat. Peace, N.Y.C., 1968-69; mem. Nat. Chamber Found. Task Force on Space Commercialization, Washington, 1983-86; bd. dirs. Advanced Technology Orgn. Md., 1986—; northeastern dir. Va. Advanced Tech. Assn., Richmond, 1984-86; advisor D.C. chpt. Internat. Red Cross; speaker on fin. and tech. Contbr. articles on tech. commercialization and fin. to profl. jours. Vice-chmn., charter mem. Beijing/Washington Sister City Council, Washington, 1985—; advisor Greater Washington D.C. Bd. Trade, 1985-86; mem. Mayor's Adv. Council on Trade and Investment. Woodrow Wilson fellow, 1958, Bushnell fellow, 1964, Hon. Officer-Faculty fellow U.S. Dept. State, 1967; recipient citation Washington D.C. Mayor's Office, 1986. Fellow Washington Acad. Scis.; mem. Am. Soc. Internat. Law, Internat. Forum U.S. C. of C., Internat. Energy Seminar-Johns Hopkins Sch. for Advanced Internat. Study, Corcoran Gallery of Art (nat. council), Phi Beta Kappa.

HEALD, CAROL MCCARTHY, travel agent, educator; b. Phila., May 20, 1950; d. Raymond John Kluberton and Mary Jane (Grim) Thompson; m. Denis McCarthy, Nov. 18, 1972 (div. Dec. 1985); children: Michael, Kevin, Brian, Anne; m. Jerry Raymond Heald, July 5, 1986. BA, U. Okla., 1968; MSW, Calif. State U., San Francisco, 1972. Lang. instr. Hacienda el Cobano, Colima, Mex., 1968-70; Spanish instr. Peace Corps, Colima, Mex., 1969-70; flight attendant Pan Am. World Airways, N.Y., 1970-72; freelance watercolorist Albuquerque, 1980-83; prof. U. N.Mex., 1983-87; sr. travel counselor Am. Express/Globetrotters, Albuquerque, 1982-87, Ask Mr. Foster Travel U. N.Mex. Br., Albuquerque, 1987—; dir. arts programs Am. Express Travel, Albuquerque, 1983-87. Mem. Friends of Symphony. Mem. AAUW (editor Bethesda chpt. 1974-78), Am. Soc. Travel Agts., Human Relations Commn. (commr. 1976-78), Pan Am. Roundtable (travel dir. 1984-86), Kappa Kappa Gamma. Democrat. Roman Catholic. Home: 2304 Candelaria NW Albuquerque NM 87107

HEALD, EMILY EASTHAM, civic worker; b. Lawrence, Mass., July 14, 1917; d. Ernest Eugene and Elsie (Eastham) H. Grad. Katharine Gibbs Sch., Boston, 1935. With Mass. Electric Co., 1935-81; ret., 1981; trustee First Essex Savs. Bank, Lawrence, 1977-87. Mem. Girl Scout Council Greater Lawrence, Inc., 1935-63, pres. leaders assn., 1938-42, adviser sr. Girl Scouts planning bd., 1949-51, dir., 1951-63, sec. bd. dirs., 1952-53, v.p., 1957-61, pres., 1961-63, nat. council mem. 1949-51, 63-69, dir., pres. Merrimack River Girl Scout Council, Inc., 1963-70; dir. Methuen chpt. ARC, 1952-54, chmn., 1953-54, dir. Greater Lawrence chpt., 1954-81, sec., 1957-60, 1st vice chmn., 1961-63, chmn., 1963-65; sec. dist. 1 Mass. regional blood program, 1960-63, exec. com., 1963-66; chmn. Methuen div. Community Chest Drive, 1951; mem. budget com. United Fund, Lawrence, 1954-56, chmn. spl. gifts, Methuen, 1960; chmn. social action com. Greater Lawrence Council of Chs., 1959-61; sec. bd. dirs. Greater Lawrence Guidance Center; trustee Methuen Meml. Music Hall, Inc., 1949-81, sec., 1949-53, 55-56, 60-63, clk., 1951-55, 60-66, v.p., 1966-69, pres., 1969-73; pres. Gt. Harbors Residents Assn., East Falmouth, Mass., 1985-87 ; vestryman Grace Episc. Ch., Lawrence, Mass., 1972-75, sr. warder, 1976-78, St. Barnabas Meml. Episcopalian Ch., Falmouth, Mass., 1985-88, clk. vestry, 1988—. Clubs: Quota (Lawrence); Appalachian Mountain (Boston). Home: 54 Striper Lane East Falmouth MA 02536

HEALY, ALICE FENVESSY, psychology educator, researcher; b. Chgo., June 26, 1946; d. Stanley John and Doris (Goodman) Fenvessy; m. James Bruce Healy, May 9, 1970. AB summa cum laude, Vassar Coll., 1968; PhD, Rockefeller U., 1973. Asst. prof. psychology Yale U., New Haven, 1973-78, assoc. prof. psychology, 1978-81; assoc. prof. psychology U. Colo., Boulder, 1981-84, prof. psychology, 1984—; research assoc. Haskins Labs., New Haven, 1976-80; mem. com. NIMH, Washington, 1979-81; co-investigator research contract USAF, U. Colo., 1985-86; prin. investigator research contractor U.S. Army Research Inst., U. Colo., 1986—. Co-author: Cognitive Processes, 2d edit., 1986; editor Memory and Cognition, 1986—; assoc. editor Jour. of Exptl. Psychology, 1982-84; contbr. 58 articles to profl. jours. and chpts. to books. Recipient Sabbatical award James McKeen Cattell Fund, 1987—; NSF Research grantee, 1977-86, Spencer Found. Research grantee, 1978-80. Fellow Am. Psychol. Assn.; mem. Psychonomic Soc. (governing bd. 1987—), Soc. Math. Psychology, Cognitive Sci. Soc., Phi Beta Kappa, Sigma Xi, Am. Assn. for the Advancement of Sci. Club: Univ. Home: 840 Cypress Dr Boulder CO 80303 Office: U Colo Dept Psychology Campus Box 345 Boulder CO 80309

HEALY, ANNE, sculptor; b. N.Y.C., Oct. 11, 1939; d. Robert Timothy and Mary Rita (Essig) H.; m. Richard Alois Synek, Feb. 28, 1960 (div. 1962); 1 child, Deirdre Leigh. B.A., Queens Coll., 1961. One-woman exhbns.: U.S. Theatre Technicians Symposium, 1971; Solow Bldg., N.Y.C., 1971; A.I.R. Gallery, N.Y.C., 1972, 74; CUNY Grad. Ctr., 1974; Hammarskjold Plaza Sculpture Garden, N.Y.C., 1974; 88 Pine St., N.Y.C., 1974-75; Zabriskie Gallery, N.Y.C., 1975, 78; Contemporary Art Ctr., Cin., 1976; Am.'s Cup Ave., Newport Art Assn., Susie Schochet Gallery, R.I., 1976; U. Mass., Amherst, 1976; A.I.R., N.Y.C., 1978; U. of South, Tex., 1979; group exhbns. include: Outdoor Installations, Basel, Switzerland, 1976, Paris, 1976; represented in permanent collections Solow Bldg., N.Y.C.; Mus. Contemporary Crafts, N.Y.C.; Dept. Cultural Affairs, N.Y.C.; N.Y. Cultural Ctr.; Mich. State U.; Allen Art Mus., Oberlin, Ohio; CUNY Grad. Ctr.; commns. include Wayne State U. Health Care Inst., Detroit, 1979; Springfield Mus. Fine Art, Mass., 1979; instr. sculpture St. Ann's Sch., Bklyn., 1973-79; adj. asst. prof. Baruch Coll., CUNY, 1976-81; guest lectr. Mich. State U., 1973; vis. artist Mich. State U., 1973; guest lectr. U. Cin., 1974, 76, Smith Coll., Northampton, Mass., 1975, U. R.I., Kingston, 1975; vis. prof. U. Iowa, Iowa City, 1979; asst. prof. U. Calif. Berkeley, 1981-85, assoc. prof., 1985—. Featured in numerous popular mags. and profl. jours.; contbr. articles to profl. jours. Office: U Calif Dept Art Kroeber Hall Berkeley CA 94720

HEALY, BARBARA ANNE, insurance company executive, financial planner; b. Chgo., May 21, 1951; d. William James Healy and Eileen Mary (Dooley) Dashiell; m. Gerald Lally Angst, June 9, 1973 (div. Sept. 1977). BA, No. Ill. U., 1973; MBA, DePaul U., 1976. Cert. fin. planner. Dept. head, instr. St. Benedict High Sch., Chgo., 1973-76; account rep. Xerox Corp., Chgo., 1976-78, mktg. specialist, 1978-79, high volume sr. sales exec., 1979-81; western dist. mgr. McGraw Hill, N.Y.C., 1981-82; fin. planner United Resources Ins. Service, Torrance, Calif., 1982-83, sales mgr., 1983-85, exec. v.p., 1985-86, regional v.p., 1986—; instr. Trenton Coll., Riverside, Ill., City Coll. Chgo., Northeastern Ill. U., Chgo., Prairie State Coll., Chicago Heights, 1976-81. Author: Financial Planning for Educators, 1987; contbr. articles to prof. jours.; speaker in field. Mem. Internat. Assn. Fin. Planners, Inst. Cert. Fin. Planners, Registry Fin. Planning Practitioners, Nat. Council Fin. Edn. Republican. Roman Catholic. Home: 9 Bellflower Ln San Carlos CA 94070 Office: United Resources Ins Services 950 Tower Ln Suite 1120 Foster City CA 94404

HEALY, JEANNE MARIE, personnel director, consultant; b. Rochester, N.Y., July 9, 1940; d. Ray D. Casaretti and Vera (Goeckel) Wilder; m. James T. Healy (div. 1977); children: Matthew, Sandra. BS, Le Moyne Coll., 1962; MBA, Rochester Inst. Tech., 1984. Adminstrv. intern County of Monroe, Rochester, 1963-64, adminstrv. analyst, 1964-66, 68-69; personnel research specialist Xerox Corp., Rochester, 1966-67; coordinator Genesee Region Sudden Infant Death Syndrome Info. and Counseling Ctr., Rochester, 1976-77; personnel specialist Rochester Inst. Tech., 1977-78, personnel mgr., 1978-81, assoc. dir. of personnel, 1982-83, dir. of personnel, 1983—; pvt. cons. Wheaton Coll., Norton, Mass., 1985-86, St. Bernard Inst., Rochester, 1986-87. Contbr. articles to profl. jours. Co-founder Genesee Valley SIDS Found., Rochester, 1969; career advisor Women's Career Ctr., Rochester, 1978—; bd. dirs. Assn. for Blind and Visually Impaired, Rochester, 1986—; bd. govs. Our Lady of Mercy High Sch., Rochester, 1988—. Mem. Coll. and Univ. Personnel Assn. (bd. dirs. Rohester chpt. 1985—), Am. Compensation Assn., Am. Soc. Ifor Personnel Adminstrn. (bd. dirs. Genesee region chpt. 1986—). Roman Catholic. Office: Rochester Inst Tech One Lomb Memorial Dr Rochester NY 14623

HEALY, JOAN MCDONOUGH, lawyer, nurse; b. Pitts., Aug. 7, 1955; d. Aloysius G. and Julia Ann (Connolly) McDonough; m. Patrick Kevin Healy, May 9, 1981. B.S. in Nursing, Georgetown U., 1977; J.D., Cath. U. Am., 1980. Bar: N.C. 1981, D.C. 1981. R.N. Staff nurse Georgetown U. Hosp., Washington, 1977-78; law clk. Aaron M. Levine, P.A., Washington, 1978-80, firm Jackson, Campbell & Parkinson, Washington, 1980-81; gen. counsel Forsyth Meml. Hosp. Found., Winston-Salem, N.C., 1981-84, corp. sec., 1981-84; gen. counsel, asst. sec. Carolina Medicorp Enterprises, Inc., 1984-86; corp. sec. Salem Health Services, Inc., Winston-Salem, 1982—, Found. Health Systems Corp., Winston-Salem, 1982-84; v.p. legal affairs Carolina Medicorp, 1985—. Mem. ABA, D.C. Bar Assn., N.C. Bar Assn. (mem. health law council), N.C. Soc. Hosp. Attys., Nat. Health Lawyers Assn., Sigma Theta Tau. Office: Carolina Medicorp Inc 3333 Silas Creek Pkwy PO Box 15025 Winston-Salem NC 27103

HEALY, JOYCE ANN KURY, banker, marketing director; b. Pitts., Sept. 23, 1947; d. Andrew G. and Mary Jane (Jacobs) Kury; m. Donall Healy, May 17, 1969; children: Brian, Mary Caitlin. Student U. of Toronto, 1965-68; B.A. in Sociology, U. Pitts., 1969; M.A. in Urban Studies, Boston U., 1973; postgrad. NYU and N.Y. Inst. of Fin., 1974-75. Analyst, Boston Model Cities Adminstrn., 1969-71; mktg. research analyst Mfrs. Hanover Trust, 1971-72, sr. mktg. research analyst, 1972-73, asst. sec., 1973-74, asst. v.p., 1974-75, v.p., 1975-81, sr. v.p., 1981—; speaker in field. Contbr. articles to prof. jours. Trustee, YMCA Greater N.Y. Named Woman of the Year Nat. Kidney Found., 1984. Avocations: bicycling, community activities.

HEALY, THERESA ANN, former ambassador; b. Bklyn., July 14, 1932; d. Anthony and Mary Catherine (Kennedy) H. B.A., St. John's U., 1954, LL.D., 1985. Tchr. elem. and secondary schs. N.Y.C., 1951-55; with U.S. Fgn. Service, 1955—, ambassador to Sierra Leone, 1980-83; with Ctr. for Internat. Affairs, U. South Fla., Tampa, 1983-84; mem. faculty Indsl. Coll. Armed Forces, 1984—. Mem. Am. Fgn. Service Assn., Diplomatic and Consular Officers Ret. Roman Catholic. Clubs: Fgn. Service, DACOR. Home: 6800 Fleetwood Rd #1002 McLean VA 22101

HEALY FOX, LINDA DEBORAH, mental health counselor; b. Chgo., July 8, 1952; d. Donn Merrill Healy Jr. and Joanne Louise (Ott) Healy Mathews; m. David Martin Fox, Oct. 11, 1977 (div. 1980); m. Michael Josef Schneider, Dec. 31, 1980. B.A., Valparaiso U., Ind., 1974; M.A., U. South Fla., 1981. Lic. mental health counselor, Fla. Counselor Health and Rehab. Services, State of Fla., Clearwater, 1981; counselor, cons. Sex, Health, Edn. Ctr., Clearwater, 1981-82; rehab. specialist Boley Manor, St. Petersburg, Fla., 1982; supervising counselor Alternative Human Services, pvt. non-profit instn., St. Petersburg, 1982-85; psycotherapist Cigna Healthplan of Fla., Inc., Tampa, 1985-86; out-patient ctr. dir. Charter Med. Group, Brooksville, Fla.; mental health counselor, cons., Tampa, 1987—. Mem. Am. Assn. Counseling and Devel., Phi Kappa Phi. Avocations: violin, swimming, travel. Home: PO Box 5155 Spring Hill FL 34606 Office: 11371 Cortez Blvd Suite 113 Brooksville FL 33573

HEANEY, FRANCES ANN, television art director; b. Cheasea, Mass., Oct. 11, 1947; d. John Francis and Sarah Mary (Walsh) Heaney. BFA, R. I. Sch. Design, 1969; MA, Harvard U., 1971. Artist Sta. WSBK-TV, Boston, 1970; asst. prof. Newton (Mass.) Coll. Sacred Heart, 1971-72; graphic artist Sta. WNBC-TV, N.Y.C., 1973-76; art dir. news Sta. WPIX-TV, N.Y.C., 1977-80; asst. art dir. Cable News Network, Atlanta, 1980-81; art dir. Cable News Network Headline News, Atlanta, 1981—; cons. Time-Life-Home Box Office, Inc., N.Y.C., 1978; lectr. Parigraph Conf., Paris, 1986. Recipient Emmy awards Nat. Assn. TV Arts and Scis., N.Y.C., 1975,77. Mem. Broadcast Designers Assn. (Silver awards 1984). Democrat. Roman Catholic. Home: 176 Elysian Way Atlanta GA 30327 Office: CNN Headline News One CNN Plaza Atlanta GA 30348-5366

HEAP, SYLVIA STUBER, civic worker; b. Clifton Springs, N.Y., Sept. 25, 1929; d. Stanley Irving and Helen (Hill) Stuber; B.A. cum laude, Bates Coll., 1950; postgrad. U. Conn. Sch. Social Work, 1952-54, Boston U. Sch. Social Work, 1953-54, SUNY, Brockport, 1979, SUNY-Potsdam, 1980, Syracuse U., 1980-83, 85—; m. Walker Ratcliffe Heap, June 9, 1951; children—Heidi Anne, Cynthia Joan, Walker Ratcliffe III. Dir. Y-Teens, YWCA, Holyoke, Mass., 1950-51; social group worker West Haven (Conn.) Community House, 1951-54; program dir. YWCA, Ann Arbor, 1954-55, part-time, 1955-59; mem. adv. bd. div. continuing edn. Jefferson Community Coll., 1965—, chmn. adv. bd., 1968—; pres. Jefferson County Med. Soc. Aux., 1971-72; bd. dirs. St. Lawrence Valley Ednl. TV, 1973-83, sec., 1976-80, treas., 1980-82; v.p., 1982-83, dir. Chem. People Project, 1983; bd. dirs. Watertown Lyric Theatre, 1973-83; bd. dirs. N.Y. State Med. Soc. Aux., 1974-85, 2d v.p. bd., 1979-80; fitness instr. Jefferson Community Coll., Watertown, 1977-86; chmn. health projects N.Y. State Med. Soc. Aux., 1981-85. Named Citizen of Yr. Greater Watertown C. of C., 1975. Mem. Friends of Public TV, AAUW, Coll. Women's Club Jefferson County, Phi Beta Kappa. Unitarian Universalist. (UN office envoy 1978—).

HEAPS, DIANNE JOY, engineer; b. N.Y.C., Nov. 7, 1957; m. Brian Leonard Heaps, Dec. 30, 1978; 1 child, Kevin Charles. Student, Cornell U., 1975-78, U. Tenn., 1979; BSME, U. Ill., Chgo., 1982. Detailer, draftsman Gen. Purpose Control div. Gen. Electric, Bloomington, Ill., 1979-80; engr. Aircraft Engine div. Gen. Electric, Evendale, Ohio, 1980, Western Electric, Naperville, Ill., 1982-83, N.Y. Telephone, N.Y.C., 1983—. Home: 36 Tulip Ln New Rochelle NY 10804 Office: NY Telephone 1095 Ave of the Americas Rm 2727 New York NY 10036

HEARD, JOHNY CAROL, accountant, loan specialist; b. Banner, Va., Dec. 17, 1942; d. James Orbin and Juanita (Young) Hamm; m. William B. Heard, Dec. 24, 1960; children: William B., Rodney D. Student, Kansas City (Kans.) Community Coll. Loan specialist-realty U.S. Dept. HUD, Kansas City, Mo., 1979—, regional coordinator computer homes underwriting mgmt. systems, 1984—; acct., co-owner Heard Constrn. Co., Tonganoxie, Kans., 1983—. Recipient Outstanding Performance award U.S. Dept. HUD, 1983, 86, Spl. Achievement award U.S. Dept. HUD, 1984. Mem. Nat. Assn. Female Execs., Nat. Campers and Hikers Assn. (chpt. pres. 1982-83), Tonganoxie Genealogy Soc. (pres. 1986-87). Democrat. Presbyterian. Home: 118 N Village Tonganoxie KS 66086 Office: US Dept HUD 1103 Grand Kansas City MO 64106

HEAREY TAFFET, MICHELE, occupational therapist; b. Philadelphia, Aug. 15, 1959; d. Charles DeLisle and Michelene Mary (Pilch) Hearey; m. Robert Taffet, July 1, 1984. BS in Occupational Therapy, U. Pa., 1981. Registered occupational therapist. Dept. head occupational therapy Cooper River Convalescent Ctr., Pennsauken, N.J., 1982-84; staff therapist New Rochelle (N.Y.) Hosp. Med. Ctr., 1984-88, sr. therapist, chief, 1988—; with contract home care New Rochelle Hosp. Med. Ctr., 1984—; pvt. practice hand therapist. Mem. Am. Occupational Therapy Assn., N.Y. Occupational Therapy Assn. (Westchester chpt.), N.Y. Soc. Hand Therapy. Democrat. Roman Catholic.

HEARN, JOYCE CAMP, retired educator, state legislator; b. Cedartown, Ga., d. J.C. and Carolyn (Carter) Camp; m. Thomas Harry Hearn (dec.); children—Theresa Hearn Potts, Kimberly Ann, Carolyn Lee Becker. Student U. Ga.; B.A., Ohio State U., 1957; postgrad U. S.C. Former high sch. tchr.; dist. mgr. U.S. Census, 2d Congl. Dist., 1970; mem. S.C. Ho. of Reps., 1975—, asst. minority leader, 1976-78, 86—. Mem. Richland County Planning Commn.; bd. dirs. Meml. Youth Ctr. and Stage South; chmn. Nat. Adv. Com. on Occupational Safety and Health, 1982-84; chmn. Sexual Assault Awareness Week; vice chmn. Dist. Republican Com., 1968; chmn. 2d Congl. Dist., 1969, Richland County Rep. Com., 1972; del., platform com. Rep. Nat. Conv., 1980, 84; moderator Kathwood Bapt. Ch., 1979-80, former asst. Sunday Sch. tchr.; bd. dirs. Small Bus. Devel. Ctr. S.C., Columbia Coll. Bd. Vis., Columbia Urban League, Fedn. of Blind; trustee Columbia Mus. Art. Recipient Outstanding Citizen award Columbia Rape Coalition, 1977, Disting. Service award Claims Mgmt. Assn. S.C., 1977, Nat. Fedn. Blind S.C., 1978, Columbia Urban League, 1983, Mothers Against Drunk Drivers, 1985, Outstanding Legislatorof Yr. award Alcohol and Drug Abuse Assn, 1980, Retarded Citizens Assn., 1982, S.C. Rehab. Assn., 1984, S.C. Assn. of Deaf, 1987; numerous other awards. Mem. Nat. Order of Women Legislators (treas.). Club: S.C. Womens; Columbia Women's Club (bd. dirs.), Larkspar Garden.

HEARN, ROSAMOND ERNST, music service executive; b. Boston, Sept. 17, 1924; d. Harry Benjamin and Mary (Downey) E.; divorced; children: Robert D., Diane G., Mary R., Kathleen Anne. Student, Boston U., 1940-42, Longy Sch. Music, 1947-49, Am. Conservatory Music, 1966-71, 74-77; music fellow, U. Colo., 1974-75. Lab. technician Consol. Rendering Co., Boston, 1942-52; organist, choir dir. Mass., Conn. and Ill., 1948-72; asst. condr., accompanist Am. Conservatory of Music, Chgo., 1970-73; organist, choir dir. Sacred Heart Ch., Lombard, Ill., 1973-78; mgr. music store Manhattan Sch. Music, 1978-79; organist Colesville Presbyn. Ch., Silver Springs, Md., 1979—; gen. ptnr., mgr. Allegro Music Service, Silver Springs, 1985—; mgr. choral music dept. Lyon Healy Co., Chgo., 1975-78; mgr. choral, vocal, organ depts. Harris Music Co., Rockville, Md., 1979-85. Columnist Mitzi's Merit Series, 1984—. Mem. Am. Guild Organists (bd. dirs. 1967-70), Am. Choral Dirs. Assn. (workshop coordinator), Music Educators Nat. Conf., Choristers Guild, Music Industry Council, Silver Spring C. of C., Delta Omicron (Outstanding Service to Music Profession 1968). Office: Allegro Music Service 1398 Lamberton Dr Silver Springs MD 20902

HEARN, SHARON SKLAMBA, lawyer; b. New Orleans, Aug. 13, 1956; d. Carl John and Marjorie C. (Wimberly) Sklamba; m. Curtis R. Hearn. B.A. magna cum laude, Loyola U., New Orleans, 1977; J.D. cum laude, Tulane U. Sch. Law, 1980. Bar: La. 1980, Tex. 1982; cert. tax specialist. Law clk. to presiding judge U.S. Ct. Appeals Fed. Cir., Washington, 1980-81; assoc. Johnson & Swanson, Dallas, 1981-84, Kullman Inman Bee & Downing, New Orleans, 1984—. Recipient Am. Legion award, 1970; Tulane Law Sch. Merit award, 1978, 79. Mem. ABA, La. State Bar Assn., Tex. State Bar Assn., Dallas Women Lawyers Assn. Democrat. Roman Catholic. Home: 44 Swallow Ln New Orleans LA 70124 Office: Kullman Inman Bee & Downing 615 Howard Ave New Orleans LA 70130

HEARON, SHELBY, writer, lecturer; b. Marion, Ky., Jan. 18, 1931; d. Charles Boogher and Evelyn Shelby (Roberts) Reed; m. Robert Hearon, Jr., June 15, 1953 (div. Mar. 1977); children—Anne Shelby, Robert Reed; m. Bill Lucas, Apr. 19, 1981. B.A., U. Tex., 1953. Author: (novels) Armadillo in the Grass, 1968; The Second Dune, 1973; Hannah's House, 1975; Now and Another Time, 1976; A Prince of a Fellow, 1978; Painted Dresses, 1981; Afternoon of a Faun, 1983; Group Therapy, 1984; A Small Town, 1985, Five Hundred Scorpions, 1987, Owning Jolene, 1989; also short fiction, articles, book revs. Pres. Tex. Inst. Letters, 1980; chair lit. panel Tex. Commn. on Arts, 1980; mem. lit. panel N.Y. Council on Arts, 1985. Recipient NEA/PEN Syndication prizes, 1984, 85, 86, 88; Guggenheim fellow, 1982; Nat. Endowment Arts fellow, 1983; Ingram Merrill grant, 1987. Mem. PEN, Authors Guild, Poets & Writers Inc., Women in Communications, Tex. Inst. Letters (Fiction award 1973, 78), Associated Writing Programs. Democrat. Presbyterian. Home: 5 Church St North White Plains NY 10603

HEARST, AUSTINE MCDONNELL, newspaper reporter, free-lance feature writer, columnist; b. Warrenton, Va., Nov. 22, 1928; d. Austin and Mary (Belt) McDonnell; m. William Randolph Hearst, Jr., 1948; children—William Randolph III, John Augustine Chilton. Ed. Warrenton County schs., Convent Notre Dame, Md., King-Smith Jr. Coll. Columnist Washington Times-Herald, 1946-56; syndicated columnist King Features Syndicate; radio commentator CBS, 1946-56. Clubs: Nat. Press (Washington), Sulgrave (Washington); Cosmopolitan. Office: Hearst Corp 959 8th Ave New York NY 10019

HEATH, BRENDA JOYCE, management executive; b. Bedford, Ind., Apr. 20, 1941; d. John Paul and Edith Madelyn (Patton) Jones; m. Jesse Franklin Heath, Sept. 19, 1941; 1 child, Kathleen Denise. Certificate, Porter Bus. Coll., 1961; student, Ind. U., 1978-79. Sec. various ins. co., Atlanta, Indpls., 1964, Parke-Davis, Atlanta, 1967-68; various positions Child Guidance Cen. Riley Hosp., Indpls., 1976-79; sec. Physics Services/Radiation Meth. Hosp., Indpls., 1979-80; pres. So. Ind. Med. Equipment Corp., Orleans, 1984—. Mem. Orleans Bus. Assn. (pres. 1987, v.p. 1986), Orleans C. of C., Nat. Assn. bus. and Profl. Women. Republican. Office: So Ind Med Equipment Corp Route 1 box 104 Orleans IN 47452

HEATH, CYNTHIA STARRETTE, marketing manager; b. Statesville, N.C., Oct. 27, 1954; d. George Albert and Macy (Carter) Starrette; m. Randy Lee Feimster, Aug. 17, 1974 (div. Mar. 1981); 1 child, Randall Vincent; m. Floyd Thomas Heath, Mar. 5, 1983. BA in Sociology, N.C. State U., 1976. Billing clk. Graybar Electric Co., Raleigh, N.C., 1976-78; placement counselor Olsten Services, Raleigh, 1978-79, office supr., 1979-80, mktg. rep., 1980-81, office mgr., 1981-84, mktg. mgr., 1986—; sales assoc. Fonville-Morisey Realtors, Raleigh, 1984-85. Mem. Nat. Assn. Female Execs., Am. Soc. Personnel Adminstrs. Baptist. Lodge: Order Eastern Star (assoc. matron 1986-87, worthy matron). Office: Olsten Services 4325 Glenwood Ave Raleigh NC 27612

HEATH, MARY ANNE, marketing administrator; b. Vincennes, Ind., Jan. 20, 1949; d. John Blaine and Betty Louise (Warner) Hoffner; m. Charles Samuel Heath, Sept. 16, 1979 (div. Apr. 1982). BA, Ind. U., 1981. Office mgr. Greater Delray Beach (Fla.) C. of C., 1973-78; with mktg., customer services depts. Fla. Power and Light Co., Ft. Myers, 1978-86, supr. mktg., 1986—; mem. nat. com. older women and energy cons. Am. Assn. Retired Persons, Washington, Ft. Myers, 1985-86; cons. Human Resource Concepts, Ft. Myers, 1986—. Author plays. Mem. adv. com. tech. studies Edison Community Coll., Ft. Myers, 1983—; mem. media com. United Way Lee County, Ft. Myers, 1985, 87; mem. adv. council career edn. Lee County Sch. Bd., Ft. Myers, 1985—; bd. dirs. Concerned Citizens for Sexually Abused Children, Ft. Myers, 1985—, Am. Cancer Soc., Ft. Myers, 1986—. Mem. Met. Ft. Myers C. of C. (ch-chaire Challenge '87), Christian Women in Bus. (steering com. Ft. Myers chpt.). Republican. Baptist. Home: 2244 Winkler Ave #111 Fort Myers FL 33901 Office: Fla Power and Light Co 1926 Victoria Ave PO Box 40 Fort Myers FL 33901

HEATH, PATRICIA LORENE, insurance claims adjuster; b. Rapid City, S.D., Mar. 26, 1944; d. William Edward and Alice Melvina (Hale) Brown; m. Roger Kenneth Heath, Dec. 28, 1962; children: Tricia L., Ryan M. BS in Edn., U. S.D., 1967; AS in Claims, Ins. Inst. Am., 1983. Classroom tchr. Huron (S.D.) Pub. Schs., 1967-70, program dir., tchr., 1970-78; claims rep. Great Am. Ins. Co., Sioux Falls, S.D., 1978-81; ind. multi-line adjuster Frontier Adjusters, Grand Junction, Colo., 1981-87; sr. casualty field adjuster Prudential Property and Casualty Ins. Co., Thornton, Colo., 1987—; tchr. introduction to ins. Ins. Inst. Am., 1986. Bd. dirs. YWCA, Huron, S.D., 1973-78. Mem. Nat. Assn. Ins. Women, Ins. Women of Western Colo. (charter, treas. 1982-84, pres. 1985-86, Claimswoman of Yr. 1984), Western Colo. Claims Assn. (pres./sec. 1983-84, 87), Colo.Claims Assn., Ins. Women Greater Sioux Falls (edn. chmn. 1978-81, Rookie of Yr. 1980). Office: Prudential Property and Casualty PO Box 33543 Thornton CO 80233

HEATHFIELD, SUSAN MARIE, training coordinator, free-lance writer; b. Detroit, May 15, 1949; d. Robert M. and Catherine (Fanning) H. BS, U. Mich., 1971, MS, 1974. Cert. tchr. Small bus. owner Mall Car Wash, Brighton, Mich., 1977-79; tchr., counselor Howell (Mich.) Pub. Sch., 1971-77, dir. adult edn., 1976-85; mgmt. devel. tng. coordinator Buick-Old-Cadillac div., Lansing, Mich., 1985-86; tng. coordinator Lansing Fabrication, Lansing, Mich., 1986—. Contbr. freelance stories to various jours., software documentation. Mem. Mich./Lansing Arts Council, 1984—, Mich. Assn. Retarded Citizens, Lansing, 1971-77, bd. dirs. Livingston County Spl. Olympics; gen. counselor, chmn. Am. Legion Girl's State, Lansing, 1981. Regents scholar U. Mich., 1967-71; tchr. in-service grantee Staff Devel. Collaborative, 1983. Mem. Am. Soc. Tng. Devel. (publicity chmn. Mid. Mich. chpt. 1984), Mich. Assn. Adult and Continuing Edn. (pres., bd. dirs., 1977-85, conf. chair 1982-83), World Future Soc., Nat. Writers Club, Phi Delta Kappa.

HEATON, JANE, religious educator; b. Centralia, Ill., Nov. 23, 1931; d. Wilbur Estle and Nina (Huddleston) Heaton; B.Music Edn., DePauw U., 1953; M.Religious Edn., Christian Theol. Sem., 1968. Sec., Div. Overseas Ministries, Christian Ch., Indpls., 1953-58, departmental assoc., 1958-61, dir. curriculum and edn. dept. ch. women Div. Homeland Ministries, 1961-72, dir. leadership devel., dept. ch. women, 1972-74; course adminstr. Pan-African Leadership Course for Women, Mindolo Ecumenical Centre, Kitwe, Zambia, 1975-78; asst. in curriculum and program sales Christian Bd. Publ., St. Louis, 1978-79, dir. curriculum and program sales, 1979-80, v.p. curriculum and program sales, 1980-85; dir. religious edn., Fort Belvoir, Va., 1985—; missionary in Zaire, 1959-60; ordained to ministry Christian Ch., 1970; tchr. Mindolo Ecumenical Centre, Kitwe, Zambia, 1973. Sec.-tres. Irvington Community Council, Indpls., 1972-75. Mem. Indpls. Radio Club, Theta Phi. Club: Zonta. Author: And What of Ourselves, Bible study guide on Hebrews, 1968; Journey of Struggle, Journey in Hope, 1983. Home: 4410-D Groombridge Way Alexandria VA 22309 Office: Office of Staff Chaplain Fort Belvoir VA 22060

HEATON, MONICA BAYER, communications executive; b. Louisville, Mar. 5, 1951; d. Ralph Joseph and Catherine Anna (Hanley) Bayer; m. Gary Howard Heaton, Oct. 8, 1977; children—Margeaux, Meredith Andrew. B.A., U. Iowa, 1973. Reporter, Times, Hammond, Ind., 1973, Herald-News, Joliet, Ill., 1973-74; city editor Compass, Hammond, 1974-75; asst. city editor Jour.-Register, Springfield, Ill., 1975-77; regional copy chief Globe-Democrat, St. Louis, 1978-80; dir. info. and multimedia Catholic Health Assn. U.S., St. Louis, 1980—. Recipient first place award Internat. Assn. Firefighters media awards, 1977. Mem. Women in Communications, Inc. (outstanding sr. 1973, founding pres. Springfield chpt. 1977), Pub. Relations Soc. Am., Internat. Assn. Bus. Communicators (Gold Quill 1984), Am. Soc. Assn. Execs., Religious Pub. Relations Council (award of excellence 1984, 88, Annual Report Conf. award 1987, 88), Kappa Tau Alpha. Office: Cath Health Assn US 4455 Woodson Rd Saint Louis MO 63134

HEBENSTREIT, JEAN ESTILL STARK, religious educator, practitioner; d. Charles Dickey and Blanche (Hervey) Stark; student Conservatory of Music; U. Mo. at Kansas City, 1933-34; A.B., U. Kans., 1936; m. William J. Hebenstreit, Sept. 4, 1942; children—James B., Mark W. Authorized C.S. practitioner, Kansas City, 1955—; chmn. bd., pres. 3d Ch., Kansas City, 1953-54, reader, 1959-62; authorized C.S. tchr., C.S.B., 1964—; bd. dirs. First Ch. of Christ Scientist, Boston, 1977-83, chmn. bd., 1981-82; mem. Christian Sci. Bd. of Lectureship, Christian Sci. Bd. Edn. Bd. dirs. Principle Found., Religions and Cultures for Peace, Inc., bd. trustees Christian Sci. Pub. Soc. Mem. Art of Assembly Parliamentarians (charter, 1st pres.), Internat. Platform Assn., Pi Epsilon Delta, Alpha Chi Omega (past pres.). Club: Carriage. Contbr. articles to C.S. lit. Home: 310 W 49th St Kansas City MO 64112 Office: 4849 Wornall Rd Suite 104 Kansas City MO 64112

HEBERT, CAROL ANNE, foundation director; b. Greenville, S.C., Sept. 6, 1946; d. Calvin Edward and Margaret Anne (Rowland) Kennedy; m. James R. Harley, Aug. 26, 1973 (div. May 1982); children: Padraic, Zobeida; m. Cyril W. Hebert, Dec. 10, 1983. BBA, Western Internat. U., 1985, MBA, 1986. Dir. program ops. Ariz. Recovery Ctrs. Assn., Phoenix, 1976-78; regional dir. Women in Community Service, Dallas, 1978-81; exec. dir. Ariz. Women's Employment Edn., Phoenix, 1982-86, Crime Victim Found., Phoenix, 1987—; cons. Ctr. for Non-Profit Devel., Dallas, 1978-81, Maricopa Pvt. Industry Council, Phoenix, 1986—; chair steering com. Women of Achievement, Phoenix, 1986. Author: The Bottom Line. Mem. task forces on welfare to work, women and poverty State of Ariz., Phoenix, 1985-86, task force on women, welfare, and work U.S. Dept. Labor, San Francisco, 1985-86; chairperson mayor's task force on self-sufficiency, Phoenix, 1985—; bd. dirs. Ariz. Women's Town Hall, Phoenix, 1987—. Named one of Women Who Care Gov. of Ariz., 1985. Mem. Nat. Orgn. for Victim Assistance, nat. Soc. Fund Raising, Execs., Wider Opportunities for Women (coordinator Ariz. chpt. 1985-86). Democrat. Office: Crime Victim Found 101 W Jefferson 4th Floor Phoenix AZ 85003

HEBERT, CLAIRE LUCILLE, insurance representative; b. Laconia, N.H., Feb. 17, 1949; d. Norman Joseph and Yvonne Theodora (Hamel) H.; divorced; children: Ryan, Sarah Marie. A in Bus. Sci., Pierce Coll. for Women, 1969; BA in Psychology, U. N.H., 1982. Asst. dir. social therapy Golden View, Meredith, N.H., 1983-84; activities dir. Taylor Home, Laconia, 1984-86; sales rep. Mut. of Omaha, Bedford, N.H., 1986—. Mem. Pi Gamma Mu, Phi Kappa Phi, Phi Beta Kappa. Republican. Office: Mut of Omaha Bedford Farms IV Bedford NH 03102

HEBNER, PATRICIA NOWAK, information systems executive; b. Pensacola, Fla., Oct. 23, 1953; d. Harry and Bertha (Moore) Nowak; m. Allyn Paul Hebner, May 22, 1982. BBA, Fla. State U., 1974. CPA, Tex. Auditor State of Fla., Orlando, 1975-77; internal auditor Gulf Oil Corp., Houston, 1977-78, sr. analyst, 1978-82; acctg. supr. Roy M. Huffington Inc., Houston, 1982-85, mgr. computer ops., 1985—. Vol. M.D. Anderson Cancer Inst., Houston, 1982-85. Mem. Am. Inst. CPA's. Lutheran. Office: Roy M Huffington Inc PO Box 4455 Houston TX 77210

HECHT, ANITA GESSLER, communications company executive; b. Prague, Czechoslovakia, Jan. 5, 1938; d. Alfred and Truda (Lengsfeld) Gessler; m. Melvin Salberg, Jan. 24, 1987. Student, Chatham Coll., Pitts., 1956-59; BA in Psychology, Hofstra U., 1960. Vocat. counselor N.Y. State Employment Service, N.Y.C., 1960-64; personnel mgr. Thomas Y. Crowell Co., N.Y.C., 1964-67; employment supr. Olivetti Corp. of Am., N.Y.C., 1967-68, mgr. employee benefits, 1968-74; employee relations advisor Mobil Corp., N.Y.C., 1974-76; dir. personnel Bantam Books Inc., N.Y.C., 1976-78; dir. employee benefits ABC, N.Y.C., 1978-81, dir. personnel-hdqrs., 1981-85; v.p. personnel Capital Cities/ABC Inc., N.Y.C., 1985—; mem. adv. bd. Hofstra U. Sch. Communications, 1985—. Mem. Murray Hill Assn., N.Y., 1970—. Mem. Am. Women in Radio & TV, Am. Soc. Personnel Adminstrn. Office: Capital Cities/ABC Inc 1330 Ave of the Americas New York NY 10019

HECHT, DIANE MELESKI, interior designer; b. Kingston, N.Y., Oct. 17, 1945; d. Vincent J. and Rose S. (Fasce) Meleski; B.F.A., Boston U., 1967; m. Stephen S. Hecht, Aug. 17, 1968. Interior designer M. Brown & Co., Boston, 1966-67, Hans Kreiks Assocs., Boston, 1967-68, F.A. Stahl & Assos., Boston, 1968-69, Interspace, Inc., Phila., 1969-70, William Sklaroff Design Assocs., Ardmore Pa., N.Y.C., 1970-81; pres. D.M. Hecht & Assocs., Inc., N.Y.C., 1981-87; v.p. John Blatteau Assocs., N.Y.C. Recipient Outstanding Achievement in field of design award Women in Design Internat., 1981; honorable mention Hexter Design award, 1983. Mem. Archtl. League, Nat. Home Fashions League, Women in Design Internat., Preservation League N.Y. State, Westchester Preservation League (past trustee, v.p., dir. county wide archtl. survey), Mcpl. Art Soc., Nat. Trust Hist. Preservation, Classical Am. Democrat. Home: 30 Emerson Rd Larchmont NY 10538 Office: Blatteau & Assocs 20 W 20th St New York NY 10011

HECHT, ETHEL MORELL, construction administrator; b. N.Y.C.; d. Louis and Lillie Morell; m. Al Hecht (dec. 1981); children—Randy, Kenneth, Eric. Cert. women bus. enterprise, N.Y. Pres. Sands & Hecht Constrn. Corp., N.Y.C., 1968—. Mem. Nat. Assn. Women Bus. Owners. Avocations: writing poetry; tennis; golf; bridge. Office: Sands & Hecht Constrn Corp 10 E 39th St New York NY 10016

HECHT, JUDITH NELL, information services executive; b. Allentown, Pa., Mar. 16, 1938; d. Jesse and Mary (Mazo) Rosenberg; m. Norman Louis Hecht, Aug. 16, 1959; children: Michael Jesse, David Phillip, Ellen Debra. BS in Nursing, Alfred U., 1958; MA in Am. Studies, U. Dayton, 1977; MLS, U. Ky., 1978. Pub. health nurse Vis. Nurse Service, N.Y.C., 1958-59; staff nurse Alfred (N.Y.) U. Health Ctr., 1959-60; info. specialist materials documentation ctr. Wright-Patterson AFB, U. Dayton Research Inst., Ohio, 1973-75; mgr. tech. info. services U. Dayton Research Inst., 1975—; del. to Ohio Council of Library and Info. Socs., 1984—. Mem. Spl. Libraries Assn. (chpt. pres. 1981-82), Am. Soc. for Info. Sci. (chpt. sec. 1985-86), Miami Valley Assn. Health Sci. Libraries (pres. 1978-80), Beta Phi Mu. Office: Univ Dayton Research Inst 300 College Park Dayton OH 45469

HECHT, MARIE BERGENFELD, educator, author; b. N.Y.C., Oct. 21, 1918; d. Frank Falle and Marie (Trommer) Bergenfeld; B.A., Goucher Coll., 1939; M.A., New Sch. for Social Research, 1971; m. Morton Hecht, Jr., Dec. 17, 1937 (div.); children—Ann (Mrs. David Bloomfield), Margaret, Laurence, Andrew. Tchr. Am. history Mineola High Sch., Garden City Park, N.Y., 1960-80. Mem. Am. Hist. Assn., Orgn. Am. Historians. Author (with Herbert S. Parmet): Aaron Burr: Portrait of an Ambitious Man, 1967; Never Again: A President Runs for a Third Term, 1968; John Quincy Adams: A Personal History of An Independent Man, 1972; The Women, Yes, 1973; Beyond the Presidency: The Residues of Power, 1976; Odd Destiny: The Life of Alexander Hamilton, 1982, The Church on the Hill, 1987. Address: 5 Hewlett Pl Great Neck NY 11024

HECKART, EILEEN, actress; b. Columbus, Ohio, Mar. 29, 1919; d. Leo Herbert and Esther (Stark) Purcell; m. John Harrison Yankee, Jr., June 26, 1943; children: Mark Kelly, Philip Craig, Luke Brian. B.A., Ohio State U., 1942, L.H.D. (hon.), 1981; student, Am. Theatre Wing, 1944-48; LL.D., Sacred Heart U., Bridgeport, Conn., 1973; D.F.A. (hon.), Niagara U., 1981. Actress: Broadway plays Voice of the Turtle, 1944, Brighten the Corner, 1946, They Knew What They Wanted, 1948, Stars Weep, 1949, The Traitor, 1950, Hilda Crane, 1951, In Any Language, 1953, Picnic, 1953, Bad Seed, 1955, A View From the Bridge, 1956, Dark at the Top of the Stairs, 1958, Invitation to a March, 1960, Everybody Loves Opal, 1961, Family Affair, 1962, Too True To Be Good, 1963, And Things That Go Bump in the Night, 1965, Barefoot in the Park, 1965-66, You Know I Can't Hear You When the Water's Running, 1967, The Mother Lover, 1968, Butterflies Are Free, 1969, Veronica's Room, 1973, The Effect of Gamma Rays on Man-in-the-Moon Marigolds, 1971, Remember Me, 1975, Mother Courage and Her Children, 1975, Mrs. Gibbs in Our Town, 1976; one-woman show Eleanor, 1976, Ladies at the Alamo, 1977; movies Miracle in the Rain, Bad Seed, Bus Stop, Hot Spell, My Six Loves, 1962, Up the Down Staircase, 1966, No Way To Treat A Lady, 1968, Butterflies Are Free, 1972, Zandy's Bride, 1974, The Hiding Place, 1975, Burnt Offerings, 1975, Wedding Band, 1975, Heartbreak Ridge, 1986; TV actress movies, 1947—; TV series: Trauma Center; Oscar nomination 1956, Film Daily citation 1956, Variety Poll of N.Y. Drama Critics award 1958, N.Y. Emmy for Save Me A Place at Forest Lawn 1967, Acad. award for Butterflies Are Free 1973, Straw Hat award 1973, 75, 77). Recipient Outer Circle award, 1953, Daniel Blum award, 1953, Sylvania TV award, 1954, Donaldson award, 1955; Hollywood Fgn. Press award, 1956; March Dimes award, 1970; Aegis award, 1970; Ohio State U. Centennial award, 1970; Gov.'s award of Ohio, 1977; Ohiana Library award, 1978. Mem. Pi Beta Phi. Office: Bauman Hiller & Assocs 9220 Sunset Blvd Los Angeles CA 90069

HECKER, DIANE CLEMENTS, facilities engineering administrator; b. Erie, Pa., Sept. 28, 1945; d. Harold Ralph and Ida Marie (Chimenti) C.; div.; 1 child, Rebecca Elizabeth. Student, So. Methodist U., 1969-72, Tulsa Jr. Coll., 1973-74; MBA, Barry U., 1988, BS in Psychology, 1987, postgrad. in bus., 1987—; postgrad. in bus., Nova U., 1987—. Dept. mgr. Neiman Marcus, Dallas, 1965-69; asst. to v.p. mfg. Lowrance Electronics, Tulsa, 1972-74; flight attendant Braniff Internat., Dallas, 1976-82, night mgr., crew scheduler, 1976-82; coordinator for AIDS Research Labs. U. Miami, Fla., 1984-85; adminstr. Cordis Corp., Miami, 1986—; cons. Valeries and Valeries Too, Abilene, Tex., 1969-76, Stout Fashions, Midland, Tex., 1976—. Vol. Project Literacy for Every Adult in Dade County. Mem. Nat. Acad. Mgmt., So. Acad. Mgmt., Mothers Against Drunk Drivers, Mensa. Republican. Roman Catholic. Club: Miami Runners. Home: 9151-6 Fontainebleau Blvd Miami FL 33172

HECKERLING, AMY, film director; b. Bronx, N.Y. Grad., NYU, 1975; fellow, Am. Film Inst. directing program. Dir. films including (short film) High Finance, Getting It Over With, Fast Times at Ridgemont High, 1982, Johnny Dangerously, 1984, National Lampoon's European Vacation, 1985; film appearance in Into the Night, 1985. Address: Gersh Agy 222 N Canon Dr Beverly Hills CA 90210 *

HECKLER, MARGARET MARY, ambassador; b. Flushing, N.Y., June 21, 1931; d. John and Bridget (McKeon) O'Shaughnessy; children—Belinda West, Alison Anne, John M. B.A., Albertus Magnus Coll., 1953; LL.B., Boston Coll., 1956; student, U. Leiden, Holland, 1952; numerous hon. degrees. Bar: Mass. bar 1956, also U.S. Supreme Ct 1956. Mem. 90th to 97th Congresses, 10th Dist. Mass.; founder co-chmn. Congl. Women's Caucus; sec. HHS, 1983-85; ambassador to Ireland 1985—; mem. Mass. Gov.'s Council, 1963-66; Alternate del. Republican Nat. Conv., 1964, del., 1968, 72, 80, 84. Named Outstanding Mother of Year in Politics, 1984; Prince Henry the Navigator award (Portugal). Office: Am Embassy care US Dept State Washington DC 20520 *

HECKMAN, JOANN, small business owner; b. Newton, N.J., Feb. 23, 1950; d. James Richard and Frances Margaret (Bertram) H. A.S. in Communications, Centenary Coll., 1982, B.A. cum laude in Communications and Journalism, 1984. Freelance reporter, editorial asst. Daily Advance, Roxbury Twp., N.J., 1979-81; asst. mgr., pressperson Jag-Ton Print World, Hackettstown, N.J., 1985; owner, operator Words-Worth Word Processing Services, Budd Lake, N.J., 1984—; word processor MetLife Security Ins. Co., East Hanover, N.J., 1985-87; co-owner, pres. The Crystal Works, Hackettstown, N.J., 1987—. Mem. Nat. Assn. Female Execs., AAUW, Phi Theta Kappa (Merit cert. 1982), Alpha Chi. Republican. Baha'i. Avocations: photography, graphic art and design, freelance writing, crafting. Home: 313 Shore Rd PO Box 114 Budd Lake NJ 07828 Office: The Crystal Works PO Box 7101 Hackettstown NJ 07840

HECKMAN, KARYN COOPER, sales executive; b. Cleve., Dec. 30, 1961; d. George Calvin and Sandra Lee (Vargo) Cooper; m. Mark Alan Dodd (div. 1982); m. Mark Allen Heckman, Jan. 27, 1984. BS, Ind. U., 1982. Regional sales rep. Howard W. Sams & Co., Indpls., 1983-87; account exec. CSA Promotions Inc., Indpls., 1987—. Home: 99 Royal Pine Ln Cicero IN 46034-9691 Office: CSA Promotions Inc 7172 Lakeshore Pkwy W Dr Indianapolis IN 46268

HEDBERG, MILDRED ELAINE PONS, retired army officer; b. Hiller, Pa., Jan. 23, 1929; m. Charles Leroy Hedberg, June 25, 1964 (div. 1972). A.A., George Washington U., Washington, 1954; B.A., U. Md., 1962; M.B.A., Webster U., St. Louis, 1976. Commd. 2d lt. U.S. Army, 1956, advanced through grades to brig. gen.; commdr. WAC Detachment, Ft. Gordon, Ga., 1958-60; chief official reception bur. So. Army Command U.S. Army Europe, 1960-63; asst. sec. to gen. staff 5th Infantry Div., Ft. Carson, Colo., 1963; chief WAC recruitin; personnel staff officer U.S. Army Southwest Regional Recruiting Command, Ft. Sam Houston, Tex., 1973-76; chief recruiting and reenlistment div. Office of Dep. Chief of Staff for Personnel, Washington, 1978-79; chief of staff U.S. Army Corps of Cadets, U.S. Mil. Acad., West Point, N.Y., 1979-81; dir. personnel, insp. gen. U.S. European Command, 1981-84; dep. adj. gen. U.S. Army, Washington, 1984-85; adj. gen. U.S. Army, 1985-86. Decorated D.S.M., D.S.S.M., Legion of Merit. Mem. Phi Kappa Phi. Republican. Roman Catholic.

HEDGE, CYNTHIA ANN, lawyer; b. LaPorte, Ind., June 7, 1952; d. John S. and Edith Rae (Badkey) H. AB, Ind. U., 1975; JD, Valparaiso U., 1978. Bar: Ind. 1978, U.S. Dist Ct. (no. dist., so. dist.) Ind. 1978. Staff writer Ind. Dept. Commerce, Indpls., 1975; pub. relations asst. Ravinia Festival, Chgo., 1976; free-lance writer, LaPorte County, Ind., 1978—; dep. pros. atty. LaPorte County, 1978—; sole practice, Michigan City, Ind., 1978—; dir. Michiana Industries, LaPorte County. Chairperson, Child Abuse Adv. Team, LaPorte County, 1982—; bd. dirs., chairperson Parents and Friends of the Handicapped, Inc., 1986—; mem. bd. Bethany Lutheran Ch., LaPorte, 1982—, United Way, Michigan City, 1987—, also 2d v.p. Mem. ABA, Ind. Bar Assn., LaPorte County Bar Assn., Michigan City Bar Assn., Christian Legal Soc., Ind. U. Alumni Assn., AAUW, Michigan City C. of C. Home: 2912 N Regal Dr LaPorte IN 46350 Office: 601 Franklin Sq Michigan City IN 46360

HEDGE, JEANNE COLLEEN, health physicist; b. Scottsburg, Ind., May 30, 1960; d. Paul Russell and Barbara Jean (Belshaw) H. BS in Environ. Health, Purdue U., 1983. Technician chemistry and health physics Marble Hill Nuclear Generating Sta., Pub. Service Ind., Madison, 1983-84; asst. radiation protection Hope Creek Generating Sta., Pub. Service Electric & Gas Co., Hancock's Bridge, N.J., 1984-85, technician radiation protection, 1985—; mem. People to People Internat. Citizen Ambassador Exchange, People's Republic China, 1988. Mem. AAAS, NOW, Am. Nuclear Soc. (assoc.), Health Physics Soc. (plenary mem.), N.Y. Acad. Scis., The Planetary Soc., Tau Beta Sigma (sec. Purdue U. chpt. 1980-81). Democrat. Methodist.

HEDGE, PATRICIA LYTGENS, environmentalist; b. Palo Alto, Calif., Feb. 19, 1940; d. Norman Julius and Ruth Ellen (Hemmer) Hedge; m. Charles Edward Weesner, Oct. 20, 1957 (div. 1973); children—Kathryn Ellen, James Reid; m. Richard Edwin Hammond, Apr. 8, 1978; children—Matthew Mills, Peter Edwin. B.S., U. Calif.-Berkeley, 1972; M.S., U. Calif.-Davis, 1974. Environ. planner Calif. Coastal Commn., San Francisco, 1974-77; real estate agt. Coldwell Banker Comml., Sacramento, 1977-79; pres., owner Hammond Designs, Sacramento and Mill Valley, Calif., 1979-82; regional dir. (Calif. and Nev.) The Wilderness Soc., San Francisco, 1982-86; pres. Hammond Environ. Designs, 1986— ; dir. Tuolumne River Trust, San Francisco, Planning and Conservation League, Sacramento; mem. com. Calif. State Bd. Forestry, Sacramento, 1978-79; mem. task force Bay Area Council, San Francisco, 1976. Contbr. articles to profl. jours. Regional dir. sta. KQED-TV Acution, San Francisco, 1969-70; docent Oakland Mus. (Calif.), 1968-70; leader Girl Scouts U.S.A., Berkeley, Calif., 1970-72; bd. dirs., officer John Muir Sch. Bd., Berkeley, 1967-70; Mem. Sierra Club, Smith River Alliance, Friends of the Earth, Friends of the River, Wilderness Soc., Phi Beta Kappa. San Francisco Boy Chorus Bd. and Youth Hostel Bd. Home: 10 Heuter's Ln Mill Valley CA 94941 Office: Wilderness Soc 1791A Pine San Francisco CA 94109

HEDGES, KATHLEEN ANN, financial systems executive; b. Santa Monica, Calif., Sept. 7, 1956. BA in Sociology, Pepperdine U., 1977; MBA in Fin. and Mktg., George Mason U., 1985. Research asst. Rand Corp., Santa Monica, 1978-80; research assoc. Sci. Applications Internat. Corp., McLean, Va., 1980-84; researcher Sci. Applications Internat. Corp., McLean, 1984-86; mgr. fin. systems Sci. Applications Internat. Corp., San Diego, 1986—. Mem. Pi Gamma Mu. Home: 517 Stratford Ct Del Mar CA 92014 Office: Sci Applications Internat Corp 10404 Roselle St San Diego CA 92121

HEDIEN, COLETTE JOHNSTON, lawyer; b. Chgo.; d. George A. and Catherine (Bugan) Johnston; m. Wayne E. Hedien; children—Mark, Jason, Georgiana. B.S. with honors, U. Wis., 1960; J.D., DePaul U., 1981. Bar: Ill. 1981. Tchr., Sch. Dist. 39, Wilmette, Ill., 1960-63, Tustin Pub. Schs. (Calif.), 1964-66; extern law clk. to judge, Chgo., 1980, U.S. Atty.'s Office, Chgo., 1980; sole practice, Northbrook, Ill., 1981—; atty. Chgo. Vol. Legal Services; mem. Chgo. Appellate Law Com., 1982-83. Chmn. Northbrook Planning Commn; founder Am. Women of Surrey (Eng.), 1975-77; founding dir. U. Irvine Friends of Library, 1965-66; guidance vol. Glenbrook High Sch., 1984—. NSF scholar, 1962. Mem. Chgo. Bar Assn., Ill. Bar Assn., ABA (com. on real property), Phi Kappa Phi, Kappa Alpha Theta.

HEDLUND, NANCY LEE, nurse, psychologist, researcher; b. Chgo., Dec. 3, 1940; d. Sexton Waldemar Hedlund and Lorraine (De Roche) Hamilton; m. Finis Breckenridge Jeffery, Nov. 2, 1979; 1 child, Marva Jean Jeffery. BS in Nursing, U. Okla., 1964, MS in Human Ecology, 1970; MEd in Nursing, Columbia u., 1971, PhD in Social Psychology, 1977. Dir. nursing Cen. Okla. Mental Health Ctr., Norman, 1967-69; instr. Cornell U. Sch. Nursing, N.Y.C., 1969-71; mental health cons. Cornell U. N.Y. Hosp., N.Y.C., 1971-74; assoc. prof. Tchrs. Coll. Columbia U., N.Y.C., 1976-79; assoc. prof., chair program in nursing research Yale U., New Haven, 1976-82; dir. nursing research U. Mich. Hosps., Ann Arbor, 1982-87; coordinator research, quality assurance Queen's Med. Ctr., Honolulu, 1987—. Contbr. articles to profl. jours. Mem. Am. Orthopsychiatry Assn., Am. Nurses Assn., Am. Psychol. Assn. Democrat. Episcopalian. Home: 930 Kaheka St #3601 Honolulu HI 96814 Office: care Kinau 4 1301 Punchbowl St Honolulu HI 96813

HEDRICK, LOIS JEAN, investment company executive, governor's aide; b. Topeka, Kans., Jan. 25, 1927; d. Arthur Lenard and Nellie Cecelia (Johnson) Lungstrum; m. Clayton Newton Hedrick, Apr. 26, 1949; 1 dau., Carol Beth. Cert., Strickler's Bus. Coll., 1947; student Washburn U., Topeka, 1980-83. Staff sec. Kans. State Senate, Topeka, 1946-65; co-owner Hedrick's Market, Topeka, 1953-67; exec. sec. to sr. legal counsel Security Benefit Life Ins. Co., Topeka, 1963-73; asst. corp. sec. Security Mgmt. Co., Topeka, 1973—, Security Distbrs. Inc., SBL Planning Inc., SBL Fund, Security Action Fund, Security Equity Fund, Security Investment Fund, Security Ultra Fund, Security Bond Fund, Security Cash Fund, Security OmniFund, Security Tax-Exempt Fund, Security Benefit Group, Ins., Security Mgmt. Co.; mgmt. cons. United Way of Greater Topeka, 1981—, mem. pub. relations staff, 1982—, rep. precinct woman. Organizer, chmn. Topeka Crime Blockers, 1976—; vol. fundraiser Am. Heart Assn., Stermont-Vail Hosp. Expansion, 1976-77; chmn. Plant a Tree for Century III, 1976; mem. Greater Topeka Career Edn. Com., 1981—; staff sec., fundraiser Christian Rural Overseas Program, 1951, staff sec. USAF Supply Depot, 1951-53. Named Woman of Year, Am. Bus. Women's Assn., 1970; Sec. of Yr., Profl. Secs. Inc., 1975. Mem. Greater Topeka C. of C. (chmn. edn. com. 1981—, ambassador chmn. high sch. honors banquet, 1982—), Adminstrv. Mgmt. Soc. (dir., pres. 1976—). Republican. Home: 1556 SW 24th St Topeka KS 66611

HEDRICK, SUSAN KAYE, government intelligence analyst; b. Lynchburg, Va., Jan. 7, 1954; d. Floyd Dudley and Rachel Conelia (Childress) H. BA in Edn., Coll. William and Mary in Va., 1976. Cert. tchr. Intelligence analyst U.S. Secret Service, Washington, 1976-87; program analyst def. mobilization systems planning activity Dept. of Def., Washington, 1988—. Republican. Home: 3958 Collis Oak Ct Fairfax VA 22033

HEEDING, MICHELLE ANNE, finance executive; b. Coral Gables, Fla., Nov. 24, 1953; d. Donovan and Wynona Mary (Sheleny) Macfarlane; m. William Carl Heeding, II, June 7, 1975. B.A. cum laude, U. Guam, 1974; student Dale Carnegie course, 1976. Mail officer ARC, Agana, Guam, 1975; officer Lee-Wood Motors Co., Whittier, Calif., 1976-78; office mgr. Horizon Mazda Co., Lakewood Calif., 1979-80; bus. mgr. Astro Mgmt. Services Inc., Buena Park, Calif., 1980-81, v.p. fin., 1981—. Recipient numerous awards. Mem. Volkswagon of Am. Bus. Mgrs. Assn. (sec. 1984, excellence awards Mazda chpts. 1981, 82, 83, 84, 85, 86, 87), Nissan Bus. Mgrs. (1981, 82, 83, 84, 85, 86, 87). Republican. Roman Catholic. Office: Astro Mgmt Services Inc 18707 Studebaker Rd Cerritos CA 90701

HEESCH, ELAINE MAXINE, personnel placement company executive; b. Youngstown, Ohio, Sept. 15, 1942; d. Anthony George and Mary Veronica (Belus) Petrin; m. Oscar E. Tipler II, Nov. 19, 1973 (div. 1978)); m. John Richard Heesch, Apr. 1, 1982; 1 child, Jonathon Russell. BA in History, Siena Heights Coll., Adrian, Mich., 1962; MA in European History, U. Detroit, 1967. Joined Dominican Sisters, Roman Cath. Ch., 1961. Tchr. parochial schs. Oxford, Mich., 1961-72; lay tchr. Cathedral Jr. High Sch., Sioux Falls, S.D., 1973-74; sales rep. Waddell & Reed, Sioux Falls, 1984-85; mgr. Manpower Temp. Services, Sioux Falls, 1985—; media employment cons., 1985—. Editor, compiler: You Don't Have to be Jewish to Cook Jewish, 1986. Co-organizer V.O.I.C.E. Grassroots City Econ. Devel. Com., Sioux Falls, 1988—, Civic Fine Arts Mar. Arts Month, Sioux Falls, 1987, 88; participant, sponsor Vietnam Vets. Job Find, 1987, 88. Mem. Data Processing Mgmt. Assn. (pub. dir. 1985-87), Nat. Assn. Female Execs., S.D. Symphony/Symphonics (docent), VFW. Democrat. Jewish. Clubs: Temple Sisterhood (pres. 1987—), Nat. Fedn. Temple Sisterhoods (historian 1986—). Lodge: Hadassah (program chmn. 1973-78). Home: 834 S Phillips Ave Sioux Falls SD 57104 Office: Manpower Temp Services 4001 Valhalla Blvd Suite 106 Sioux Falls SD 57106

HEESTAND, DIANE ELISSA, learning resources educator; b. Boston, Oct. 9, 1945; d. Glenn Wilson and Elizabeth (Martin) H. BA, Allegheny Coll., 1967; MA, U. Wyo., 1968; edn. specialist, Ind. U., 1971, EdD, 1979. Asst. prof. communication Clarion (Pa.) State Coll., 1971; asst. prof. learning resources Indiana U. of Pa., 1971-72; asst. prof. communication U. Nebr. Med. Ctr., Omaha, 1972-74; assoc. prof. learning resources Tidewater Community Coll., Virginia Beach, Va., 1975-78; ednl. cons. U. Ala. Sch. Medicine, Birmingham, 1978-80, sr. ednl. cons., 1980-81; dir. learning resources, assoc. prof. med. edn. Mercer U. Sch. Medicine, Macon, Ga., 1981—; cons. Lincoln (Pa.) U., summer 1975; vis. fellow Project Hope/People's Republic of China, Millwood, Va., summer 1986. Author (teleplay) Yes, 1968 (award World Law Fund 1968); producer, dir. (slide tape) Finding a Way, 1980 (1st Pl. award HESCA 1981, Susan Eastman award 1981). Advisor Explorers post, Macon, 1983-84; mem. recreation com. Wildwood Homeowners Assn., Macon, 1982. Grantee U. Nebr., 1973, Porter Found., 1984. Mem. Health Scis. Communications Assn. (bd. dirs. 1982-86, pres.-elect 1987—), Assn. Ednl. Communications and Tech. (pres. media design and prodn. div. 1985-86), LWV (bull. co-editor 1987), Beyond War. Republican. Unitarian Universalist. Office: Mercer U Sch Medicine Dept Learning Resources Macon GA 31207

HEFFER, JANET CASSANDRA, skating choreographer; b. Ogden, Utah, Jan. 24, 1947; d. Ward Harris Smith and Florence E. (Empy) Powers; m. James Edward Heffer, June 8, 1968 (div. Apr. 1987); children: Clinton Edward, Kelly Cassandra. Student, U. Colo. Skating soloist and choreographer Sun Valley Ice Skating Club, Idaho, 1965; legal sec. Prieve, Gerlach & Meyer, Milw., 1968-69; skating profl. Denver U., 1969-73; skating profl. and choreographer Denver Country Club, 1969-74; prin. Creative Concepts in Advt., Denver, 1984—; cons. to Denver Civic Ballet, Symphony Guild, Cen. City Opera Assn., golf and tennis assns. Choreographer, dir. numerous skating shows, Sun Valley, U. Colo., 1965-71. Rep. committeewoman, Denver, 1971-74,. Recipient gold medal U.S. Figure Skating Assn., 1962. Mem. U.S. Figure Skating Assn., U.S. Golf Assn. (assoc.), Nat. Assn. Female Execs., Kappa Kappa Gamma. Mormon. Clubs: Cherry Hills Country, Glenmoor Country (Denver). Home: 4505 S Yosemite #117 Denver CO 80237 Office: Birko Corp PO Box 530 Westminster CO 80030

HEFFERNAN, PATRICIA CONNER, management consultant; b. N.Y.C., Oct. 11, 1946; d. Arthur S. and Catherine (Center) Conner; B.A., U. Va., 1968; M.B.A., Suffolk U., 1980; m. John Joseph Heffernan, Sept. 13, 1969. Office restaurant mgr. Wobbly Barn, Killington, Vt., 1968-72; bus. mgr. Woodstock Country Sch., Vt., 1972-74; bus. mgr., treas., assoc. dean Vt. Law Sch., Royalton, Vt., 1974-83; mgmt. cons. Heffernan & Assocs., Killington, 1982-87; mgmt. cons., v.p. Sandage Inc., Burlington, Vt., 1987—. Vt. del. White House Conf. on Small Bus.; mem. Gov.'s Commn. on Women; bd. dirs. Rutland div. Chittenden Bank. Trustee, pres. Killington Mountain Sch., 1978-85; mem. Killington Planning Commn., 1975, vice chmn., 1976, chmn., 1977-79, 83—; mem. Killington Zoning Bd., 1979-84, Vt. Epilepsy Assn., 1977—, Vt. Telecommunications Commn., Vt. Econ. Devel. Adv. Council; mem. Vt. steering com. for ACE Nat. Identification Program for Women in Higher Edn., 1978-83; bd. dirs. Rutland Regional Med. Ctr. Mem. Assn. Mgmt. Cons. (v.p. New Eng. region), Inst. Mgmt. Accts., Women Bus. Owners Vt. (dir. 1983—, founder, pres. 1984-86), Inst. Mgmt. Cons., Nat. Assn. Women Bus. Owners. Office: Sandage Inc 215 College St Burlington VT 05401

HEFFRON, NANCY IRENE, physical therapist; b. N.Y.C., June 20, 1959; d. Ralph Joseph and Ruth Patricia (Toomey) H. BS in Phys. Therapy, N.Y.U., 1981. Lic. phys. therapy. Staff phys. therapist Bklyn. Veterans Adminstrn., 1981-82, N.Y.C. Bd. Edn., 1982-85, N.Y. Childhood Ctr., Bklyn., 1985-86; phys. therapist Jewish Spl. Edn. & Devel. Home Care Program, Bklyn., 1986—. Chaperone, coach, Spl. Olympics, N.Y.C., 1984-85. Mem. Am. Phys. Therapy Assn., Nat. Assn. of Female Execs. Democrat. Roman Catholic. Club: N.Y. Road Runners. Home: 321 23d St Brooklyn NY 11215

HEFNER, CHRISTIE A., publisher, entertainment company executive; b. Chgo., Nov. 8, 1952; d. Hugh Marston and Mildred Marie (Williams) H.; B.A. summa cum laude in English and Am. Lit., Brandeis U., 1974. Free lance journalist, Boston, 1974-75; spl. asst. to pres. Playboy Enterprises, Inc., Chgo., 1975-78, v.p., 1978-82, bd. dirs., 1979—, vice chmn., 1986—, pres., 1982—, chief operating officer, 1984—; bd. dirs. Playboy Found.-Playboy Enterprises, Inc., Ill. chpt. ACLU. Recipient Agness Underwood award Los Angeles chapter Women in Communications, 1984, Founders award Midwest Women's Ctr., 1986, Human Rights award Am. Jewish Com., 1987. Mem. Brandeis Nat. Women's Com. (life); mem. Com. of 200, Young. Pres. Orgn., Chgo. Network, Voters for Choice, Am. Politics, Direct Mktg. Assn. (editorial bd.), Nat. Women's Polit. Caucus, Goodman Theatre, Phi Beta Kappa. Democrat. Office: Playboy Enterprises Inc 919 N Michigan Ave Chicago IL 60611

HEFT, CAROLYN MAE, lawyer; b. Bklyn., Apr. 17, 1942; d. William and Pauline (Haselkorn) H. B.A., Skidmore Coll., 1962; postgrad. Hunter Coll., 1962-63; J.D., Columbia U., 1966. Bar: N.Y. 1967, U.S. Dist. Ct. (so. dist.) N.Y. 1971, U.S. Ct. Appeals (2d cir.) 1972, U.S. Supreme Ct. 1974. Staff atty. Inst. Pub. Adminstrn., N.Y.C., 1966-68; assoc. Shearman & Sterling, N.Y.C., 1968-70; adminstrv. dir. Manhattan Bowery Project, Vera Inst. Justice, N.Y.C., 1970-71; dir. litigation and test case unit M.F.Y. Legal Services, Inc., N.Y.C., 1971-75; sr. atty. Nat. Ctr. Social Welfare Policy & Law, N.Y.C., 1975-78; sole practice, N.Y.C., 1978—; cons. Legal Services Corp., Washington, Phila., 1978-81. Co-author: A New Mental Hygiene Law for New York State, 1968, also articles. Mem. Citizens Housing and Planning Council, N.Y.C., 1983, 86. Bd. dirs. MFY Legal Services, Inc., 1980—, chmn. bd., 1986—; bd. dirs. Lorge Sch., N.Y.C., 1983—. Mem. ABA, N.Y. State Bar Assn., N.Y. County Lawyers Assn., Assn. Bar City N.Y. (moderator panel on foster care 1983), Nat. Legal Aid and Defenders Assn. (chmn. workshop and speaker Washington 1978), Gramercy Park Neighborhood Assn., Skidmore Alumni Assn., Columbia Law Sch. Alumni Assn. Democrat. Home: 70 Irving Pl New York NY 10003 Office: 19 W 44th St Suite 400 New York NY 10003

HEGARTY, MARY FRANCES, lawyer; b. Chgo., Dec. 19, 1950; d. James E. and Frances M. (King) H. B.A., DePaul U., 1972, J.D., 1975. Bar: Ill. 1975, U.S. Dist. Ct. (no. dist.) Ill. 1976, U.S. Supreme Ct. 1980. Ptnr. Lannon & Hegarty, Park Ridge, Ill., 1975-80; sole practice, Park Ridge, 1980—; dir. Legal Assistance Found. Chgo., 1983—. Mem. revenue study com. Chgo. City Council Fin. Com., 1983; mem. Sole Source Rev. Panel, City of Chgo., 1984; pres. Hist. Pullman Found., Inc., 1984-85. Mem. Ill. State Bar Assn. (real estate council 1980-84), Chgo. Bar Assn., Women's Bar Assn. Ill. (pres. 1983-84), NW Suburban Bar Assn., Park Ridge Women Entrepreneurs. Democrat. Roman Catholic. Club: Chgo. Athletic Assn. Office: 301 W Touhy Park Ridge IL 60068

HEGE, GAY LYNN, international communications consultant; b. Ft. Riley, Kans., July 24, 1946; d. Franklin Herman and Emma K. (Kling) H. BA in Polit. Sci., Upsala Coll., 1968. Copywriter, graphic designer Prentice Hall, Inc., Englewood Cliffs, N.J., 1968-70; dir. pub. relations Doubleday & Co., Inc., N.Y.C., 1970-76; cons. dba Gay Lynn Hege's, N.Y.C., 1976-78, owner, mktg. cons., 1986—; dir. customized programming Inflight Services, Inc., N.Y.C., 1978-86. Mem. World Airline Entertainment Assn. (charter, contbr. articles to newsletter), Nat. Assn. TV Producers and Execs., Ednl. Film and Library Assn., Nat. Assn. Female Execs. Democrat. Congregationalist. Home and Office: 155 W 75th St New York NY 10023

HEGEL, CAROLYN MARIE, farmer, farm bureau executive; b. Lagro, Ind., Apr. 19, 1940; d. Ralph H. and Mary Lucile (Rudig) Lynn; m. Tom Lee Hegel, June 3, 1962. Student pub. schs., Columbia City, Ind. Bookkeeper Huntington County Farm Bur. Co-op, Inc. (Ind.), 1959-67; office mgr., 1967-70; twp. woman leader Wabash County Farm Bur., Inc. (Ind.), 1970-73, county woman leader, 1973-76; dist. woman leader Ind. Farm Bur., Inc., Indpls., 1976-80, 2d v.p., 1980—, chmn. women's com., 1980—, exec. com. 1988—; farmer, Andrews, Ind., 1962—; dir. Farm Bur. Ins. Co., Indpls., 1980—, exec. com., 1988; mem. rural task force Great Lakes States Econ. Devel. Commn., 1987-88. Ind. Farm Bur. Service Co., 1980—, dirs. Ind. Farm Bur. Found., Indpls., 1980—, Ind. Inst. Agr., Food and Nutrition, Indpls., 1982—, Ind. 4-H Found., Lafayette, 1983-86; com. mem. Hoosier Homestead Award Cert. Com., Indpls., 1980—; speaker in field. Women in the Field columnist Hoosier Farmer mag., 1980—. Named one of Outstanding Farm Woman of Yr. County Woman Mag., 1987. Organizer farm div. Wabash County Am. Cancer Soc. Fund Dr. (Ind.), 1974; Sunday sch. tchr., dir. childrens' activities Bethel United Meth. Ch., 1965—, pres. Bethel United Methodist Women, Lagro, 1975-81; bd. dirs. N.E. Ind. Kidney Found., 1984—, Nat. Kidney Found. of Ind., 1985—, v.p., 1986—. Recipient State 4-H Home Econs. ward Ind. 4-H, 1960; named Farm Woman of 1987 Country Woman mags. Mem. Leadership Am. Program, Women in Communication, Inc., Ind. Agrl. Mktg. Assn. (bd. dirs. 1980—), Producers Mktg. Assn. (bd. dirs. 1980—), Am. Farm Bur. Fedn. (midwest rep. to women's com. 1986—). Republican. Home: Rural Rt 1 Andrews IN 46702 Office: Ind Farm Bur Inc 130 E Washington St PO Box 1290 Indianapolis IN 46206

HEGENDERFER, JONITA SUSAN, public relations executive; b. Chgo., Mar. 18, 1944; d. Clifford Lincoln and Cornelia Anna (Larson) Hazzard; m. Gary William Hegenderfer, Mar. 12, 1971 (dec. 1978). B.A., Purdue U., 1965; postgrad. Calif. State U.-Long Beach, 1966-67, Northwestern U., 1969-70. Tchr. English, Long Beach schs., Calif., 1965-68; editorial asst. Playboy Mag., Chgo., 1968-70; communications specialist Am. Med. Assn., Chgo., 1970-72; v.p. Home Data, Hinsdale, Ill., 1972-75; mktg. mgr. Olympic Savs. & Loan, Berwyn, Ill., 1975-79; sr. v.p. Golin/Harris Communications, Chgo., 1979—. Editor directory, Fin. Info. Nat. Directory, 1972. Author: Slim Guide to Spas, 1984. Contbr. articles to profl. jours. Co-chmn. pub. relations com. Am. Cancer Soc., Chgo., 1984; com. mem. March of Dimes, Chgo., 1986. Recipient 3 Golden Trumpet awards Publicity Club Chgo., 1983, 86, Silver Trumpet awards, 1984, 86, 88; Spectra awards Internat. Assn. Bus. Communicators, 1984, 85, 87, Gold Quill award, 1985; Silver Anvil award Pub. Relations Soc. Am., 1985. Mem. Am. Mktg. Assn., Publicity Club of Chgo., Internat. Platform Assn. Clubs: Council on Fgn. Relations, Art Inst. Chgo. Avocations: travel, photography. Office: Golin/Harris Communications 500 N Michigan Ave Chicago IL 60611

HEGHINIAN, ELIZABETH ALBAN TRUMBOWER, artist, educator; b. N.Y.C., Jan. 11, 1917; d. Eli Cadwallader and Maria Lucas (Coyle) Trumbower; certificate dept. indsl. design Pratt Inst., 1938; B.S. magna cum laude, N.Y. U., 1950, M.A., 1952, Ph.D., 1957; postgrad. Bklyn. Inst. Arts and Scis., 1963-66, Bklyn. Mus. Art Sch., L.I. U., 1963-66, Fairleigh Dickinson U., 1970; studied under Richard Mayhew, Geogiana Brown Harbeson, Edith Fetterolf, Katheryn I. Young, Howard W. Arnold, I.-Ching Ku; m. Aram Lincoln Heghinian, Aug. 24, 1957; children—Elizabeth Alban, Marie Hunazant. Indsl. designer Belle Kogan Assos., 1938-40; art dir. Norscross Pubs., 1940-42; buyer for battle damaged U.S. naval vessels and equipment Arma Corp., 1942-45; dir. arts and crafts YWCA Camp Program, 1946; designer Cosmopolitan Crafts, Camp Fire Outfitting Co., 1946-47; faculty N.Y. U., 1947-61, asst. prof. edn., 1957-61; specialist consultation services nat. arts and crafts com. Boys' Clubs Am., 1949-65; research and practicum in remedial reading techniques N.Y.C. Pub. Sch., Bklyn., 1966-68; exhibited in group shows Pratt Inst., 1936-38, N.Y. U., 1948-52; represented in permanent collection Bklyn. Mus. Art Sch., pvt. collections. Mem. nat. adv. com. on recreation programs and activities arts and crafts sect. Nat. Recreation Assn., 1958-62; pres. Camp Jefferson, Inc., N.Y.C.; dir. Camp Jefferson, Palisades Interstate Park, N.Y., 1945-86 ; active town wide camping and sch. year program Girl Scouts U.S.A., 1969-73; mem. N.Y. Assn. for Brain Injured Children, 1963-86 . Recipient Founders Day certificate, N.Y. U., 1950. Mem. Am. Watercolor Soc. (asso.), AAUW, Nat. Congress Parents and Tchrs., Tenafly Nature Center Assn., Palisades Interstate Park Camp Dirs.' Assn., Pi Lambda Theta, Kappa Delta Pi, Epsilon Pi Tau. Author: The Contribution of Craft Activities to the Philosophy and Objectives of Boys Clubs of America, 1957; (monograph) Crafts in Boys' Clubs, 1958. Address: 52 Howard Park Dr Tenafly NJ 07670

HEGLER, JEAN ANNE, lawyer, educator; b. Maspeth, N.Y., Mar. 24, 1959; d. Richard John and Lillian Carol (Nigrelli) H. BS in Ct. Mgmt., St. John's U., 1981, JD, 1984. Bar: N.Y., 1985; N.Y. Dist. Ct. (ea., 1987). Assoc. atty. Paul, Weiss, Rifkind, Wharton & Garrison, N.Y.C., 1984-85; prof. St. John's U. Law Sch., Jamaica, N.Y., 1985—; assoc. atty. Schulte Roth & Zabel, N.Y.C., 1987—; mem. middlestates evaluation com. St. Vincent's Coll., St. John's U., 1985—. Mem. Middlestates Evaluation. St. Thomas More scholar, 1981-84. Mem. ABA, N.Y. State Bar Assn., Nassau Bar Assn. Democrat. Roman Catholic. Home: 88-46 Ransom St Bellerose NY 11427 Office: Schulte Roth & Zabel 900 Third Ave New York NY 10022

HEIDELBERG, HELEN SUSAN HATVANI, dentist; b. Greenville, Pa., July 30, 1957; d. Balazs Robert and Ilona Borbala (Nemeth) Hatvani; m. David Raymond Heidelberg, June 4, 1983; children: David William, Laura Shari. AA, Cuyahoga Community Coll., 1977; BS in Biology magna cum laude, Cleve. State U., 1979; DDS, Case Western Reserve U., 1983. Resident in dentistry North Chicago (Ill.) VA Med. Hosp., 1983-84; assoc. dentist Steven D. Miller, DDS, Vernon Hills, Ill., 1984-85; gen. practice dentistry Norwalk, Ohio, 1986—. Mem. ADA, Ohio Dental Assn., N. Cen. Ohio Dental Soc., Great Lakes Dental Soc. (v.p. 1984), Norwalk C. of C. Home: 1945 Sleepy Hollow Rd Milan OH 44846 Office: Fisher-Titus Med Pk 266 Benedict Ave Norwalk OH 44857

HEIDEN, ANTONIETTE LOUISE (TONI), real estate broker; b. Santa Monica, Calif., Feb. 3, 1948; d. Donald Maurice and Marguerite Louise (Rosenberger) Mandrillo Torres; student Pierce Jr. Coll., 1967, San Fernando Valley State Coll., 1968, Mesa Coll., 1973-74, Colo. U., 1978-80; children—Chad Wesley, Trent Ashly. Owner, Clubhouse Crafts, Grand Junction, Colo., 1976-78; real estate broker Target Realtors, 1978-80, Home Owners Realty, 1980-81, Bray & Co., div. Better Homes & Gardens, 1981—. Mem. Nat. Assn. Realtors, Women's Council Realtors (ednl. chairperson), Colo. Assn. Realtors (trustee edn. found. 1983-86), Grand Junction Bd. Realtors. Roman Catholic. Home and Office: 1015 N 7th St Grand Junction CO 81501

HEIDMANN, CAROL D., nurse; b. Cin., Apr. 28, 1928; d. Parker David and Dorothy Amanda (Siemsen) Hunter; m. Armin Roland Heidmann, Jan. 17, 1959; children: Debra Jeanne, Peter David, Jennifer Anne. AA, Concordia Coll., Bronxville, N.Y., 1954; BSN, Cornell U., 1958; MEd, U. Wis., La Crosse, 1984. RN; cert. health unit coordinator. Various nursing positions N.Y., Mich., Wis., 1959-77; program head, instr. Western Wis. Tech. Inst., La Crosse, 1977—. Facilitator Reach to Recover, La Crosse, 1981-85; tour guide La Crosse Hist. Soc. Mem. Am. Nurses Assn., La Crosse Dist. Nurses Assn. (sec. 1984-88), Nat. Assn. Health Unit Coordinators (pres. 1987-88). Democrat. Lutheran. Home: 2491 Hagen Rd La Crosse WI 54601 Office: Western Wis Tech Inst PO Box 900 La Crosse WI 54602-0908

HEIDT, MARLYCE JOYCE, marketing consultant; b. Kenmare, N.D., Dec. 14, 1942; d. Oscar Arthur and Agnes JoHanna (Jensen) Anderson; m. Marvin Walter Heidt, Aug. 19, 1962; children: Teresa Lynn, Andrew Michael. Student, U. N.D., 1960-61; student in elem. edn., Minot (N.D.) State Coll., 1961-62; student, Coe Coll., 1969. Instr. Hatha Yoga, Cedar Rapids, Iowa, 1966-79; host TV program Modern Woman and Weekday Live, Cedar Rapids, 1969-78; producer, host exercise TV series, Cedar Rapids, 1969-81; exec. dir. Cedar Rapids Conv. and Visitors Bur., 1979-87; pres. Marlyce Heidt & Assocs., Cedar Rapids, 1987—; pres. Iowa Travel Council, Des Moines, 1982-83; bd. dirs. Iowa Ambassadors, Des Moines, 1987; speaker in field. Author: Yoga Class at Home, 1976; contbg. author: Destination Marketing, 1987; contbr. articles to Cedar Rapids Gazette. Pres. Voluntary Action Ctr., Cedar Rapids, 1974, St. Andrews Luth. Ch. Women's Orgn., Cedar Rapids, 1969; mem. pres.'s United Way, Cedar Rapids, 1974-75; mem. pub. relations bd. St. Luke's Hosp., Cedar Rapids, 1975-77; bd. dirs., pub. relations com. chairperson Jr. League, Cedar Rapids, 1974-75. Recipient Iris award Nat. TV Programmers Assn., 1977, Communications Achievement award Toastmasters Internat., 1986. Mem. Am. Soc. Assn. Execs., Iowa Soc. Assn. Execs. (program chairperson 1986), Internat. Assn. Conv. and Visitors Burs. (pub. relations chairperson 1984, bd. dirs. 1986), Iowa Assn. Conv. and Visitors Burs. (pres. 1981), Profl. Women's Network (pub. relations chairperson). Home: 2217 Ridgeway Dr SE Cedar Rapids IA 52403 Office: Marlyce Heidt & Assocs 2217 Ridgeway Dr SE Cedar Rapids IA 52403

HEIDT, MARY REBECCA, financial executive; b. Albany, Ga., Aug. 22, 1954; d. Emmett Henry and Octavia (Spies) H.; m. Terrell R. Miller, Oct. 23, 1985. BA in Acctg., Birmingham-Southern Coll., 1976. CPA, Fla. Staff accountant Johnson & Jackson, PA, Birmingham, Ala., 1976-80; sr. staff accountant, assoc. Parks and Niles CPA's, Key West, Fla., 1980-83; chief fin. officer Key West Raw Bar, Inc., 1983—; treas. Fla. Marine Conservancy, Key West, 1987—. Mem. Am. Inst. CPA's, Fla. Inst. CPA's (bd. dirs. 1983-85, sec. 1985-86). Home: 38 Bluewater Dr Key West FL 33040 Office: Key West Raw Bar Inc 231 Margaret St Key West FL 33040

HEIFETZ, SONIA, retired pharmacist; b. Rowne, Poland; d. Zise and Toiba (Ehrlich) Heifetz; came to U.S., 1929, naturalized, 1934; Ph.G., Temple U., 1933. Asst. chief pharmacist Grad. Hosp. U. Pa., Phila., 1937-49, dir. pharmacy services, 1949-77; formerly pharmacist-mgr. Rite-Aide Corp., now ret. Cert. tchr. of Russian, Phila. Bd. of Edn. div. sch. extension; asst. dir. pharmacy Eastern State Sch. and Hosp., Trevose, Pa., 1987—. Mem. Am. Soc. Hosp. Pharmacists, Del. Soc. Hosp. Pharmacists (hon.), Pa. Soc. Hosp. Pharmacists (hon.), Phila. Guild Hosp. Pharmacists (v.p. 1966, treas. 1967-77), AAUW. Home: 2665 Willits Rd Apt 324 Philadelphia PA 19114

HEIFETZ, SUSAN, executive recuiting company manager; b. Bklyn., June 27, 1950; d. Samuel and Molly (Marcus) H. BS in Elem. Edn., L.I. U., 1972, MS in Elem. Edn., 1974. Cert. tchr., N.Y. Tchr. N.Y.C. Bd. Edn., Bklyn., 1972-75; coordinator research United Jewish Appeal/Fedn. Jewish Philanthropies, N.Y.C., 1976-79; cons. research Owen, Reddington & Carroll/Interdatum, N.Y.C., 1979-82; free-lance research cons. various firms, N.Y.C., 1982-83; dir. research dept. Richards Cons. Ltd., N.Y.C., 1983—. Mem. 70th Precinct Community Council, Bklyn., 1978-82; pres., bd. dirs. 414 Elmwood Residenc, Inc., 1985-87. Mem. The Research Roundtable, Nat. Assn. Female Execs., L.I. U. Alumni Assn. (bd. dirs. 1977—, co-chmn. homecoming com. 1980—, co-chmn. 10-yr. reunion 1982). Democrat. Jewish. Home: 414 Elmwood Ave Brooklyn NY 11230 Office: Richards Cons Ltd 55 E 59th St New York NY 10022

HEIGHT, DOROTHY EPHRATES, insurance company executive; b. Albion, Mich., Feb. 23, 1950; d. Woodrow and Lillie Bell (Simpson) Wilson; m. Elbert L. Gibson, Aug. 6, 1968 (div. 1984); children: Illya, Erika; m. Jim F. Height. AA, Kellog's Community Coll., 1982; BA, Eastern Mich. U., 1985. With State Farm Ins. Co., Marshall, Mich., 1971-84, supr. II, 1984-88, supr.

III, sr. agy. adminstrn. specialist, 1988—. Speaker Call Someone Concern, Inc., Albion, 1985-86; chmn. State Farm campaign, United Way, 1988; vol. Black History program, Albion Pub. Schs., 1987; chmn. hospitality com. Albion Community Theater, 1981-84; mem. Table for Black Women, Battle Creek, Mich., 1985. Scholar Am. Bus. Women Assn., 1984, Miller Found., 1982, Eastern Star, 1982; recipient Nat. Stephen Buffon award Am. Bus. Women Assn., 1985. Mem. Nat. Assn. Female Execs., Sch. Social Work Assn., Nat. Mgmt. Assn. (bd. dirs. 1988), NAACP (bd. dirs. 1985-86). Democrat. Baptist.

HEIKKINEN, ELLEN JUNE, retail executive; b. Detroit, June 26, 1957; d. Floyd M. and Judith W. (Bartling) H.; m. Paul R. Schrier, Sept. 6, 1980. B.S. in Dietetics, Eastern Mich. U., 1979; postgrad. Amber U., Garland, Tex., 1981—. Registered dietitian. Clin. dietitian, St. Paul Hosp., Dallas, 1979-80, cost control mgr., 1980-81, asst. dir., 1981-83; pres. H & M Concessions, Grapevine, Tex., 1983—. Named Recognized Young Dietitian, Dallas Dietetic Assn., 1982. Mem. Am. Dietetic Assn., Dietitians in Bus. and Industry, Nat. Assn. Female Execs., Martha Assn. Tex. Home: 2203 Proctor Dr Carrollton TX 75007 Office: H & M Concessions Inc PO Box 101 Grapevine TX 76051 *

HEILBRUN, CAROLYN GOLD, English literature educator; b. East Orange, N.J., Jan. 13, 1926; d. Archibald and Estelle (Roemer) Gold; m. James Heilbrun, Feb. 20, 1945; children: Emily, Margaret, Robert. B.A., Wellesley Coll., 1947; M.A., Columbia U., 1951, Ph.D., 1959; D.H.L., U. Pa., 1984, Bucknell U., 1985; D.F.A., Rivier Coll., 1986; D.H.L., Russell Sage Coll., 1987. Instr. Bklyn. Coll., 1959-60; instr. Columbia U., N.Y.C., 1960-62, asst. prof., 1962-67, assoc. prof., 1967-72, prof. English lit., 1972—; Avalon Found. prof. humanities Columbia U., 1986—; vis. prof. U. Calif., Santa Cruz, 1979, Princeton U., N.J., 1981. Author: The Garnett Family, 1961, Christopher Isherwood, 1970, Towards Androgyny, 1973, Reinventing Womanhood, 1979; 8 novels as Amanda Cross, 1964—(recipient Nero Wolfe award 1981). Guggenheim fellow, 1966; Rockefeller fellow, 1976; recipient Alumnae Achievement award Wellesley Coll., 1984, award of excellence Grad. Faculty of Columbia Alumni, 1984. Mem. MLA (pres. 1984), Mystery Writers Am. (exec. bd. 1982-84), Phi Beta Kappa. Club: Cosmopolitan (N.Y.C.). Office: Columbia U Grad Dept English 613 Philosophy Hall New York NY 10027

HEILIG, KATHLEEN SMITH, marketing executive; b. Syracuse, N.Y., Mar. 30, 1949; d. Englert and Kathleen (Mehl) Smith; 1 child, Lauren Fillmore. BA, Syracuse U., 1971; MA, U. Pa., 1972. Reading specialist Springfield (Pa.) Sch. Dist., 1972-75; realtor Andrews, Dickenson and Pinkstone, Wayne, Pa., 1975-79; cons. Xerox Learning Systems, Wayne, 1979-81; br. mktg. mgr. CGA Computer, Inc., Bala Cynwyd, Pa., 1981-86; v.p. mktg. Data Processing Reference Corp., Wayne, 1986—. Bd. dirs. Picket Post Swim and Tennis Club, Wayne, 1985—; tutor Right to Read program, Media, Pa., 1973-75; vol. Brownie troop, Valley Forge, Pa. Mem. Nat. Assn. Female Execs. Club: Phila. Sailing. Office: Data Processing Reference Corp 175 Strafford Ave Suite 1 Wayne PA 19087

HEILIG, MARGARET CRAMER, nurse; b. Lancaster, Pa., Jan. 17, 1914; d. William Stuart and Margaret White (Snader) Cramer; m. David Heilig, June 1, 1942; children—Judith, Bonnie, Barbara. B.A. in Psychology, Wilson Coll., 1935; M.S.W., U. Pa., 1940; AASci. in Nursing Delaware County Community Coll., 1970. Registered nurse. Caseworker Children's Bur., Lancaster, Pa., 1935-37, 39-42; group worker Ho. of Industry Settlement Ho., Phila., 1937-39; curriculum chmn. Upper Darby Adult Sch. (Pa.), 1958-68; health asst., camp mother Paradise Farm Camp, Downington, Pa., 1960-70, camp nurse, 1970-78, infirmary dir., 1978-86; med. surg. nurse Crozer-Chester Med. Ctr., Chester, Pa., 1970; out-patient nurse Maternal Infant Care, Chester, 1971; coll. nurse Delaware County Community Coll., Media, Pa., 1971-76, dir. health services, 1976-84, health cons., 1984—, writer coll. health newsletter, 1973—, health fair dir., 1979—. Author: First Aid Booklet, 1976; also articles and columns in health field. Nurse for health screening children's program Tyler Arboretum, Media, 1982—, Update on Personal Health, Broadmeadows Women's Prison, 1973, 82; former leader Delaware County Council Girl Scouts U.S.; clk. Lansowne Friends Meeting, 1986—; mem. Upper Darby Recreation Bd., 1956-58, Upper Darby Adult Sch. Bd., 1956-68, curriculum chmn., 1958-68; provider host home for fgn. exchange students, 1965-75; participant Audubon Ann. Bird Count, 1970—; coordinator, dir. Ann. Soc. of Friends Ch. Retreat, 1970—; ARC Speakers' Bur.-AIDS; tchr. Beginning Birding course Del. County Community Coll. Recipient Ollie B. Moten award Am. Coll. Health Assn., 1987. Mem. Am. Coll. Personnel Assn., Am. Nurses Assn., Pa. Nurses Assn., Delaware County Nurses Assn. (membership chmn. 1977-78), Southeastern Coll. and Health Assn., Southeastern Pa. Coll. Health Nurses Assn. (co-founder, pres. 1983-85), Middle Atlantic Coll. Health Assn., Delaware Valley Soc. for Adolescent Health, LWV, Women's Internat. League for Peace and Freedom, Brandywine Conservance. Quaker. Avocations: piano and choral music, nature walking, handicrafts. Home: 605 Mason Ave Drexel Hill PA 19026 Office: Del County Community Coll Media PA 19063

HEIM, KATHRYN MARIE, nurse, author; b. Milw., Sept. 29, 1952; d. Lester Sheldon Wilcox and Laura Dora (Corpie) Wilcox Sears; m. Vincent Robert Gouthro, June 30, 1970 (div. 1976); 1 child, Robert Vincent; m. George John Heim, Sept. 17, 1977. AS in Nursing, Milw. Area Tech. Coll., 1983; BS in Nursing, NYU, 1986; MS in Mgmt., Cardinal Stritch Coll., 1988. RN. Staff geriatric nurse Clement Manor, Greenfield, Wis., 1983; nurse, health educator Milw. Boys Club, 1983-84; nurse mgr. Milwaukee County Mental Health Complex, Milw., 1984—, mem. gero-psychiat. inpatient adv. com., 1986-87; mem. nursing research com. Milwaukee County Mental Health Complex, 1986-88. Active Boy Scouts Am., Milw., 1978-80. Mem. Am. Nurses Assn. (cert. gerontol. nurse), Nat. Assn. Female Execs. (network dir. Milw. chpt.), Wis. Nurses Assn., NYU Alumni Assn., Milw. Area Tech. Coll. Alumni Assn. Clubs: South Shore Yacht, Cornucopie Yacht. Home: 4223 W St Paul Ave Milwaukee WI 53208 Office: Milw County Mental Health 9455 Watertown Plank Rd Wauwatosa WI 53226

HEIMANN, JUDITH ANN, health organization executive; b. Upper Montclair, N.J., Mar. 20, 1951; d. William Davis Jr. and June Elizabeth (Smyth) G.; m. Roger Thye Heimann, Oct. 10, 1987. BS in Nursing, Duke U., 1973; M of Pub. Adminstrn., Golden Gate U., 1984. RN. Staff nurse Duke U. Med. Ctr., Durham, N.C., 1972-73, Langley-Porter, San Francisco, 1973-75; sr. staff nurse Langley-Porter Neuropsychiatric Inst., San Francisco, 1975-77; psychiatric nursing supr. San Francisco Gen. Hosp., 1977-80, asst. dir. psychiatirc nursing for adminstrn. and recruitment, 1980-81; evening supr. St. Francis Convalescent Pavilion, Daly City, Calif., 1982-84; health care adminstr. Kaiser Permanente, Farmington, Conn., 1984-87. Mem. Am. Soc. Pub. Adminstrn., Am. Coll. Hosp. Adminstrs., Nat. Assn. Female Execs., Conn. Women in Health Care Mgmt., Duke U. Alumni Assn., Farmington C. of C. Democrat. Presbyterian. Club: Civic Women's (treas. 1967-68) (Westfield, N.J.). Office: Kaiser Permanente 1103 Central Ave Scarsdale NY 10583

HEIMBAUGH, BARBARA ANN, principal, educator; b. Lewistown, Pa., June 21, 1952; d. Jay Marshall and Dolores Ann (Dressler) H. BS in Elem. Edn., Shippensburg (Pa.) U., 1974, ME in Elem. Counseling, 1979, ME in Ednl. Adminstrn., 1986. Cert. elem. tchr., Pa. Tchr. elem. Waynesboro (Pa.) Area Sch. Dist., 1974-76; prin. elem. Cen. York (Pa.) Sch. Dist., 1986—. Bd. dirs. Waynesboro United Way, 1984-86. Named one of OUtstanding Young Educators, Jaycee's, 1982. Mem. Assn. for Supervision and Curriculum Devel., Pa. Assn. Elem. Sch. Prins., Pa. State Edn. Assn. (state chairperson intergroup commn. 1982-86, Appreciation of Service award 1986), Waynesboro Area Edn. Assn. (pres. 1980-81, 83-84), Delta Kappa Gamma. Democrat. Methodist. Home: 13 Morningside Dr York PA 17402 Office: Hayshire Elem Sch 2801 Hayshire Dr York PA 17402

HEIMBOLD, MARGARET BYRNE, publisher, educator, consultant; b. Tullamore, Ireland, June 24; came to U.S., 1966, naturalized, 1973; d. John Christopher and Anne (Troy) Byrne; m. Arthur Heimbold, Feb. 26, 1984; 1 child, Eric Thomas Gordon. B.A., Queens Coll. Group advt. mgr. N.Y. Times, N.Y.C., 1978-85; pub. Am. Film, Washington, 1985-86, v.p., pub. Nat. Trust for Hist. Preservation, Washington, 1986—; advisor Mag. Pubs. Am. Recipient cert. Dale Carnegie, 1977, Psychol. Corp. Am., 1981, Wharton Sch., 1983. Mem. Nat. Assn. Female Execs., Women's Econ. Alliance. Avocation: golf.

HEIMLICH, JANE MURRAY, journalist, author; b. N.Y.C., July 1, 1926; d. Arthur and Kathryn (Kohnfelder) Murray; m. Henry Jay Heimlich, June 3, 1951; children—Philip, Peter, Janet and Elizabeth (twins). B.A., Sarah Lawrence. Coll., 1948. Columnist Hartford Times (Conn.), 1967-70, Cin. Post., 1972-78, Cin. Enquirer, 1980—. Co-author: Homeopathic Medicine at Home, 1980; contbr. articles to publs. including Parents Mag., Americana, Writer's Digest, others. Mem. Authors Guild, Women in Communications.

HEINE, ELIZABETH, editor; b. N.Y.C., Feb. 3, 1939; d. T.C. and Anne Meade H. BA in English and Math., Cornell U., 1960; MA in English, Radcliffe Coll., 1961; PhD in English Lit., Harvard U., 1965. Resident fellow Radcliffe Coll., 1961-62; teaching fellow in English and gen. edn. Harvard U., 1962-65; instr. English, Bklyn. Coll., 1965-66; asst. prof. English, U. Hawaii, Manoa, 1966-71; lectr. humanities U. of Sains, Penang, Malaysia, 1972-73; assoc. prof. English, U. Tex., San Antonio, 1974-78; assoc. editor Abinger Edition, E.M. Forster, King's Coll., Cambridge, Eng., 1978-79, editor, 1980—. Editor: The Hill of Devi and Other Indian Writings, 1983; The Longest Journey, 1984; co-editor: (with Oliver Stallybrass) Arctic Summer and Other Fiction, 1980. Contbr. articles and reviews to profl. jours. Woodrow Wilson fellow, Nat. Merit scholar. Mem. Modern Lang. Assn., Phi Beta Kappa, Phi Kappa Phi.

HEINEY, SUE PORTER, nurse; b. Pickens, S.C., Mar. 23, 1950; d. Garvin Edward and Effie Elizabeth (Anderson) Porter; m. Michael Vincent Heiney, May 21, 1949; children: Elizabeth Porter, Amanda Jean. BSN, U. S.C., 1979, MN, 1981. Charge nurse Roper Hosp., Charleston, S.C., 1971-72, Greenville (S.C.) Gen. Hosp., 1972-73; charge nurse Bapt. Med. Ctr., Columbia, S.C., 1973-75, head nurse, 1979; staff nurse Richland Meml. Hosp., Columbia, 1978-81, clin. nurse specialist, 1981-83; clin. nurse specialist Children's Hosp. Ctr. for Cancer, Columbia, 1983—. Mem. Am. Nursing Assn. (nat. recruitment com. 1985—), Assn. Pediatric Oncology Nurses (sec. 1987-88), Sigma Theta Tau. Baptist. Home: 108 Greengate Dr Columbia SC 29223

HEINKE, MARILYN BRENNE, optometrist; b. Libertyville, Ill., Oct. 11, 1924; d. Richard Julius and Lillian Elvira (Gurske) Brenne; widowed; children: Brenda, Charleen, Jon, James. OD, No. Ill. Coll. Optometry, 1945. Gen. practice optometry. Chmn. profl. adv. bd. Wis. Assn. Children with Learning Disabilities, 1987. Named Optometrist of Yr. Northeast Optometrist Soc., Green Bay, Wis. Fellow Coll. of Optometry in Visual Devel. (state dir. 1982—); mem. Am. Optometric Assn., Wis. Optometric Assn., Nat. Speakers Assn., Wis. Profl. Speakers Assn. Home and Office: 21 S Kings Way Seymour WI 54165

HEINRICH, BONNIE, state legislator. m. Willis Heinrich; 1 child. Student, Valley City (N.D.) State Coll. Writer, polit. cons; mem. N.D. State Senate. Chmn. Dem. Com. dist. 32, N.D. Address: 1606 E Bowen Ave Bismarck ND 58501 *

HEINRICH, DOROTHEA JOSEPHINE, social services administrator; b. Chgo., May 25, 1917; d. Joseph and Josephine (Kallal) Brod; m. George A. Heinrich; children: Jerrold Joseph, Joel George. BA in Mgmt., DePaul U., 1978; grad. social therapist program, Forest Inst., 1979; MA in Psychology, Govs. State U., 1980; postgrad. in psychology, Kensington U., 1988. Exec. sec. to plant comptroller Douglas Aircraft Co., Park Ridge, Ill., 1940-45; exec. dir. The Ctr. of Concern, Park Ridge, 1978—. Mem. Met. Chgo. Coalition on Aging, Park Ridge C. of C. Lodge: Soroptimists. Home: 616 N Dee Rd Park Ridge IL 60068 Office: The Ctr of Concern S 125 1580 N Northwest Hwy Park Ridge IL 60068

HEINS, MARILYN, college dean, pediatrics educator, author; b. Boston, Sept. 7, 1930; d. Harold and Esther (Berow) H.; m. Milton P. Lipson, 1958; children: Rachel, Jonathan. A.B., Radcliffe Coll., 1951; M.D., Columbia U., 1955. Diplomate Am. Bd. Pediatrics. Intern, N.Y. Hosp., N.Y.C., 1955-56; resident in pediatrics Babies Hosp., N.Y.C., 1956-58; asst. pediatrician Children's Hosp. Mich., Detroit, 1959-78; dir. pediatrics Detroit Receiving Hosp., 1965-71; asst., assoc. dean student affairs Wayne State U. Med. Sch., Detroit, 1971-79; assoc. dean acad. affairs U. Ariz. Med. Coll., Tucson, 1979-83, vice dean, 1983—, prof. pediatrics, 1985— . Author: (with Anne M. Seiden) Child Care/Parent Care, 1987; mem. editorial bd. Jour. AMA, 1981—; contbr. articles to profl. jours. Bd. dirs. Planned Parenthood So. Ariz., 1983—, pres., 1988—; mem. adv. com. Tucson Assn. Child Care, Inc., 1984—, Nat. Bd. Med. Examiners, 1983—; mem. adv. bd. Ariz. State Hosp., 1985-88. Recipient Alumni Faculty Service award Wayne State U., 1972, Recognition award, 1977, Women on the Move Achievement award YWCA Tucson, 1983. Fellow Am. Orthopsychiat. Assn., Am. Acad. Pediatrics; mem. Assn. Am. Med. Colls. (chair group on student affairs 1976-79), Am. Hosp. Assn. (chmn. com. med. edn. 1985), Soc. Health and Human Values, Women in Sci. and Engring. U. Ariz. (bd. dirs. 1979—), Exec. Women's Council Tucson, Ariz. Med. Assn. (com. on med. service 1985—), Pima County Med. Soc., Pima County Pediatric Soc., Ambulatory Pediatric Assn., AAAS, Am. Pub. Health Assn., Assn. Am. Med. Colls., Med. Soc. U.S. and Mex., Western Soc. Pediatric Research. Club: Second Tuesday (co-founder). Home: 6530 N Longfellow Dr Tucson AZ 85718 Office: Univ Ariz Med Coll 1501 N Campbell Ave Tucson AZ 85724

HEINZE, LINDA HOLLI, promotion agency executive, lecturer; b. N.Y.C., Dec. 31, 1939; d. Rudolf Ley and Jessica Mary (Babcock) H. A.A., N.Y.C. Community Coll., 1959; student in bus. adminstrn. Pace Coll., 1964-68, New Sch. Social Research, 1969, Baruch Coll. CCNY, 1970. Asst. mgr. advt. makeup Look mag., N.Y.C., 1959-64; prodn. mgr. McCall mag., N.Y.C., 1964-70; asst. promotion mgr. treasury div. J.C. Penney Co., N.Y.C., 1970-72; sr. v.p. Robert Brian Assocs., N.Y.C., 1972—. Mem. bus. games com. L.I. U.; bd. dirs. N.Y. chpt. Medic Alert, 1984-89. Mem. Am. Advt. Fedn. (Silver medal 1971), Advt. Women N.Y. (ELA award 1972). Office: Robert Brian Assocs 149 Fifth Ave New York NY 10010

HEISE, ELAINE HARRIETT, public relations professional; b. Seattle, June 18, 1923; d. Louis Harry and Sharee Freeman; children from previous marriage: Sherrie Esther Phin, Diane Elaine Phin; m. Robert Edward Heise, Oct. 2, 1975; 1 child, James Robert. BA, U. So. Calif., 1945; MA, Stanford U., 1949. Prin. Elaine Davis and Assocs., San Jose, Calif., 1951-61; freelance pub. relations rep. Colorado Springs, Colo., 1965-74; dir. pub. relations Medaille Coll., Buffalo, 1975-77; mgr. news bur. Bell Aerospace Textron, Buffalo, 1978-88. Chmn. Town of Porter Environ. Commn., Youngstown, N.Y., 1983-86; mem. adv. bd. Sister St. Joseph, Buffalo, 1982-88. Mem. Pub. Relations Soc. Am. (bd. dirs. Niagara Frontier chpt. 1986-88, pres. 1985-86). Republican. Presbyterian. Home: 2880 Shady Ln Apt #29 Highlands Ranch CO 80126

HEISLER, BETTY, publisher, talk show host; b. Havana, Cuba, Aug. 27, 1941; came to U.S., 1960; d. Jaime and Pauline (Kantor) Tuchman; m. Charles Heisler, June 1, 1963 (dec. June 1978); children—Iliana, Steven. Student U. Havana, 1958-60, Miami-Dade Coll., 1973-75. Staff writer Spanish Goodhousekeeping, Miami, Fla., 1975-77; asst. editor spl. edits. Spanish Cosmopolitan, Miami, 1977-78; editor Coqueta Miami, 1978-79; pub. Donde Mag., Miami, 1980—. Mem. Jewish Fedn. Profl. Women's Div., Profl. Women Orgn. Grove Isle (life), Hadassah. Republican. Avocations: travel; aerobics; tennis; gourmet cooking. Home: 7955 Biscayne Point Circle Miami Beach FL 33141 Office: Latin Am Publs Inc PO Box 41-4655 Miami Beach FL 33141

HEISLER, JEANNE MICHELLE, insurance agency owner; b. N.Y.C., Mar. 24, 1954; d. Kenneth F. and Therese (DeRosier) Ronan; m. William J. Heisler, Aug. 10, 1974; William Jr., Christopher, Robert. Grad., Stuart Bus. Sch., 1973. CPCU, CLU, cert. ins. counselor, cert. profl. ins. woman. Treas., owner The Ronan Agy., Inc., Brick, N.J., 1972—; adv. council Norfolk and Dedham Isn. Co., Mass., 1983-85, Harleysville (Pa.) Ins. Co., 1984—. Team mother Toms River (N.J.) little league, 1984—; Ocean County Mother of Twins mem., 1985—; com. chmn. Monsignor Donovan Alumni Assn., Toms River, N.J., 1987. Recipient Vol. Achievement award N.J. Assn. of Assn. Execs., 1985, Presdl. Citation Ind. Ins. Agts. of Am., 1985. Mem. Ind. Ins. Agts. of N.J. (chmn. 1981-82, Young Agt. of Yr. 1981, faculty mem., edn. com. 1983, chmn. young agts. com. 1984-85, edn. and agy. service com. 1987, presdl. citation 1982, Ins. Man of Yr. 1986), INd. Ins. Agts. of Ocean County (pres. 1982-83, Agt. of Yr. 1980). Republican. Roman Catholic. Office: 35 Beaverson Blvd Brick NJ 08723

HEISSERMAN, THERESA ANN, transportation executive; b. Washington, Oct. 29, 1951; d. Robert Franklin Matchett and Shirley Fransis (Malone) England; m. Keith Edwin Heisserman, July 17, 1982. Student, Mt. Diablo Valley Coll., 1970-72, Clark County Community Coll., 1983—. Acct. Perfect Parts Inc., Carlstadt, N.J., 1970-73; credit mgr. ES Levy of Galveston (Tex.) Island, 1973-75; acct. XL Controls Inc., Las Vegas, 1977-80, Nev. Airlines, Las Vegas, 1980-82, Air Cortez Internat. Airlines, Ontario, Calif., 1982-86; gen. mgr., sec., treas. Pub. Domain Software Group, Las Vegas, 1986-87; pres. Sierra Nev. Airways Inc., Las Vegas, 1987—. Mem. Am. Bus. Women's Assn. Republican. Methodist. Office: Sierra Nev Airways Inc 1990 Paradise Rd Las Vegas NV 89119

HEISTER, ELLA, executive; b. Brasstown, N.C., Mar. 23, 1938; d. Gust and Opal Allene (Scroggs) Jorella; m. Paul Jay Heister, Aug. 6, 1960 (div. 1982); 1 dau., Michele Lynn. Student Wayne State U., 1958. Engring. sec. Detrex Chem. Co., Detroit, 1964-69; legal adminstrv. asst. Basil M. Briggs, P.C., Southfield, Mich., 1969-82; v.p. adminstrn., corp. sec. A.F. Campbell & Co., Inc., Dallas, 1982—; corp. sec. Murex Corp., Norcross, Ga., 1984—. Office: AF Campbell & Co Inc 2838 Woodside Dr Dallas TX 75204

HEITE, LOUISE BONO, archaeologist; b. Syracuse, N.Y., July 28, 1947; d. Henry Napoleon and Olive Louise (Gilbert) Bono; m. Edward Francis Heite, Dec. 21, 1968; 1 child, Catherine. BFA in Art History, Va. Commonwealth U., 1970; MA in History, U. Del., 1978, PhD in History, 1987. Mus. aide, curator Del. State Mus., Dover, 1974-77; historian Soil Systems, Inc., Wilmington, Del., 1980-82; cons. archaeologist Heite Cons., Camden, Del., 1982—; guide, researcher Winterthur Odessa (Del.) Properties, 1970-72; instr. U. Del., Newark, 1979-84; importer icelandic wool, Camden, Del., 1986—. Columnist Dover Post, 1974-85. Charter mem. Del. Agrl. Mus., Dover, 1974—; mem. Del. State Arts Council, Wilmington, 1980-86; trustee Del. Art Mus., Wilmington; founder, sec., treas. Thistledown Fibers Guild, Dover. Mem. Soc. Profl. Archaeologists (cert.), Handweavers Guild Am. (state rep.), Phi Alpha Theta. Democrat. Home: 21 S Main St Camden DE 19934 Office: PO Box 53 Camden DE 19934

HEIZER, IDA ANN, real estate broker; b. Oxford, Colo., Mar. 14, 1919; d. Albert Henry and Ella (Engbrook) Ordener; m. Donald Heizer, Apr. 7, 1947; children—Robert John. Diploma, Brown's Bus. Coll., 1939; student Otero Jr. Coll., 1946-47, U. So. Colo., 1962; grad. Realtors Inst., Nat. Assn. Real Estate Bds., 1972. Cert. closer real estate, cert. residential specialist. Clk., Montgomery Ward Co., LaJunta, Colo., 1935-37; bookkeeper Colo. Bank & Trust Co., LaJunta, 1937-38; cashier/bookkeeper Fox Theatre, LaJunta, 1939-40; clk. Civil Service, LaJunta, 1940-45; stenoabstractor Deaf Smith Abstract Office, Hereford, Tex., 1948-50; sec. Otero County Agt. Office, Rocky Ford, Colo., 1953-55; real estate broker Pueblo Realty & Service Co., Inc., Colo., 1958-86; ret., 1988. Mem. Pueblo Bd. Realtors, Nat. Assn. Real Estate Appraisers, Nat. Assn. Realtors, Colo. Assn. Realtors, Women's Council Realtors, Beta Sigma Phi. Lodge: Quota Internat. Home and Office: 331 Van Buren St Pueblo CO 81004

HELBERG, SHIRLEY ADELAIDE HOLDEN, artist; b. Solvay, N.Y., Mar. 9; d. Isaac Edgar and Gladys Evelyn (Tucker) Holden; student Syracuse U.; B.E., Johns Hopkins U., 1969; M.F.A., Md. Inst. Art, 1975; m. Burton Edward Helberg; children—Keir Holm, Kristin Vaughan, Kecia Tucker, Kandace Holden, Kraig Brownlee. Tchr. various schs. in N.J. and Pa.; tchr. Manchester (Pa.) Pub. Schs., 1965-84; one-woman art show U. Va., Charlottesville, 1974, Cayuga Mus. Art and History, Auburn, N.Y., 1974, Hist. Soc. York Mus., Pa., 1977, York Coll., 1984, Country Club of York; Bd. dirs. York (Pa.) Arts Council, 1964-66. Mem. Nat. League Am. Pen Women (Pa. State art chmn. 1972-74, pres. Pa. orgn. 1974-76, nat. scholarship chmn. 1976-88, Disting. service award 1978, 80, 82, 84, 86, Disting. Achievement award 1988), NEA, Pa. State Edn. Assn., Nat. League Am. Pen Women (registrar 1986-88), Internat. Platform Assn., Harrisburg, York Art Assns. Republican. Methodist. Club: Johns Hopkins Faculty. Home: RD #4 Spring Grove PA 17362

HELD, BARBARA SUSAN, psychologist; b. N.Y.C., Mar. 5, 1950; d. Milton H. and Harriette (Kornblum) H.; B.A. in Psychology, Douglass Coll., Rutgers U., 1972; Ph.D. in Psychology (NIMH tng. fellow), U. Nebr., Lincoln, 1979; m. David C. Bellows, Aug. 18, 1974. Intern in psychology Tex. Research Inst. Mental Scis., Tex. Med. Center, Houston, 1978-79; psychol. cons. Bath-Brunswick Area Mental Health Center, Brunswick, Maine, 1979-81; asst. prof. psychology Bowdoin Coll., Brunswick, 1979-85, assoc. prof., 1985—; Mellon Fund new course devel. grantee, 1980; pvt. practice clin. psychology, Brunswick, 1981—; supr., cons. specializing in family therapy for Maine mental health profls. Lic. psychologist, Maine. Mem. Am. Psychol. Assn., Phi Beta Kappa. Contbr. articles to profl. publs. Office: Bowdoin Coll Psychology Dept Brunswick ME 04011

HELD, CORINNE, clothing manufacturing company executive; b. N.Y.C., Jan. 22, 1947; d. Frank and Marjorie Edith (Goldberg) Held. Student Ball State Tchrs. Coll. Sales staff Geoffery Beene, N.Y.C., 1970-71; sales mgr. Albert Capraro, N.Y.C., 1971-73, Richard Assatly, Ltd., N.Y.C., 1973-77; co-gen. mgr. Yves St. Laurent, N.Y.C., 1977-78; mng. dir. Christian Dior Sportswear, N.Y.C., 1978-82; pres. Ron Chereskin for Women, N.Y.C., 1982-85, Lisa Maghazeh Inc., 1985—; owner Held/Feld Sales Inc., N.Y.C., 1987—. Mem. N.Y. Fashion Creators. Office: Lisa Maghazeh Inc 530 7th Ave New York NY 10018

HELD, JOY, advertising executive; b. L.I., N.Y., June 17, 1941; d. Matthew Lally and Eleanor (Shaw) Tylek; m. John E. Held III, Nov. 24, 1964 (div. Feb. 1977); children: Kimberly Joy, John. BA, Kings Coll., 1977. Copy clk. Gardner Advt. Agy., N.Y.C., 1962-63; advt. coordinator The Clarion Herald, New Orleans, 1963-64; pvt. practice calligrapher, designer Miami, Fla., 1965-68; creative dir. John Held, Inc., Miami, 1968-75; creative dir., owner Scroll Design Studio, Miami Shores, 1975-79; co-pub., designer Real Estate Digest, Miami Shores, 1979-82; printing broker Unlimited Printing, Inc., Ft. Lauderdale, Fla., 1982-83; owner Joy Held, Inc., Miami Shores, 1983—. Various calligraphy works. Mem. Mayor's Task Force, Miami Shores. Recipient various awards Civitan Internat., Miami Shores. Mem. Miami Shores Bus. Assn. (sec. 1986), Women for responsible Legis. (pres. 1985), Nat. Assn. Female Execs., Miami Shores C. of C. (bd. dirs. 1974—). Republican. Roman Catholic. Lodge: Civitan (pres. 1976-82). Home: 52 NE 98th St Miami Shores FL 33138

HELD, LILA M., art appraiser; b. Cleve., Oct. 5, 1925; d. Mark and Edythe H. (Dobrin) Bloomberg; m. Jacob Herzfeld, Oct. 20, 1946 (div. 1964); children: Garson, Michael; m. Merle Donald Held, Feb. 19, 1966; children: Joanne, Barbara. Student, Coll. William and Mary, 1945-46, Ohio State U., 1943-44, Case Western Reserve U., 1944-45; postgrad., Case Western Reserve U., 1962-66; student, Akron U., 1960-61; BS in Art Edn., Kent State U., 1961-62; postgrad., Lindenwood Coll., 1987—. Instr. art Canton YMCA, Ohio, 1965, Beachwood (Ohio) Bd. Recreation, 1967-68; substitute tchr. art, art history Cleveland Heights, Ohio, 1967-68; freelance artist, writer, researcher 1940—; art cons., appraiser Art Consultants Assocs., Englewood, Colo., 1985—; curatorial aid Denver Art Mus., 1985—. Works exhibited in museums and galleries in Cleve., Akron, Richmond, Va., St. Louis; speaker in field; judge at numerous art shows. Mem. Am. Soc. Appraisers, Am. Art Soc., Contemporary Art Soc., Nat. Council Jewish Women. Home and Office: 5561 S Jamaica Way Englewood CO 80111

HELDERMON, DONNA KAE, computer company executive; b. Oklahoma City, Apr. 1, 1951; d. Don Duane and Shirley Claudine (Hedrick) White; m. Ray Keith Heldermon, Aug. 29, 1969; 1 child, Coy Don. BS, U. Tulsa, 1981. Ops. analyst Telex Computer Products, Tulsa, 1981-83, supr. master scheduling, 1983, supr. ops. auditing, 1983-84, mgr. sales and repair services, 1984-86, dir. logistics support, 1986-87, dir. distbn., 1987-88, dir. materials, 1988—. Mem. Rogers County (Okla.) Freedom Council, 1986-87. Mem.

Am. Prodn. and Inventory Control Soc. Republican. Methodist. Office: Telex Computer Products 6929 N Lakewood Ave Tulsa OK 74117

HELDRICH, ELEANOR MAAR, publisher; b. Hagerstown, Md, Nov. 4, 1929; d. Richard and Sara (Mish) Maar; m. Frederich Joseph Heldrich; children: Sarah, Susan, Frederick, Philip. Grad. high sch., Balt. Editor Federated Garden Clubs of Md., Balt., 1975-87; pub., founder Prospect Hill, Balt., 1981—. Pres. Beautiful Balt., Inc., 1985-87. Recipient of Publication Award Nat. Council of State Garden Clubs, 1984, 86. Mem. Pub. Mktg. Assn., Balt. Pubs. Assn., Internat. Assn. Ind. Pub. (Com. Small Mag. Editors and Pubs.). Office: Prospect Hill 216 Wendover Rd Baltimore MD 21218

HELFAND, SONDRA RUTH, hospital adminstrator; b. N.Y.C., July 14, 1936; d. Harry and Jean (Jossen) Yoskowitz; m. Eugene Helfand, Nov. 17, 1957; children: Robin Glicker, Dawn Huebner, Russ Helfand. RN, Yale U., 1957; BA in Edn., Jersey City State Coll., 1975. Registered health educator sch. nurse, ARC instr. Various positions in nursing and edn. 1957-76; health edn. tchr. Edison (N.J.) Twp. Bd. of Edn. Woodrow Wilson Sch., 1976-80; nurse recruiter Newark Beth Israel Med. Ctr., 1980-84, dir. personnel, 1984-86, adminstrv. coordinator of nurse recruitment, vols. edn. and tng., 1987—; instr. ARC, Edison, 1976-80. Active Mayor's Com. for Environ. Concerns, Berkeley Heights, N.J., 1972-73. Mem. Am. Soc. Tng. and Devel., N.J. Hosp. Recruiters Assn. (v.p. 1982-83). Office: Newark Beth Israel Med Ctr 201 Lyons Ave Newark NJ 07112

HELFER, MELINDA MURRAY, systems programmer; b. Ft. Leavenworth, Kans., Mar. 14, 1943; d. Byron Leslie and Maretta (Talbot) Paige; m. Thomas Michael Helfer, Jan. 11, 1970; children: Lewis Michael, Alistair Michael. AB, Brown U., 1964; postgrad., U. Tex., 1965-67. Systems engr. Service Bur. Corp. div. IBM Corp., Dallas, 1969-70; programmer Frost Nat. Bank, San Antonio, 1970-71; systems programmer Boeing Computer Services, Seattle, 1974-75; programmer Frost Nat. Bank, San Antonio, 1970-71; sr. programmer/analyst Zales, Dallas, 1975-78; sr. programmer analyst Harris Data Communications, Dallas, 1978-80; profl. systems analyst Sun Exploration and Prodn., Dallas, 1980—. Reviewer Romantic Times, 1982—, Rave Reviews, 1986—. Fellow U. Tex., 1966-67. Home: PO Box 1428 Lewisville TX 75067 Office: Sun Exploration and Prodn 5656 Blackwell Room 1516 Dallas TX 75221 also: Romantic Times/Rave Revs 163 Joralemon Brooklyn Heights NY 11201

HELFINSTINE, KELLY ANN, financial planner, securities company executive; b. Salt Lake City, Nov. 4, 1957; d. James William Helfinstine and Jan Elaine (Bragg) Marshall. BS, U. Ariz., 1979. Mgmt. trainee The Ariz. Bank, Phoenix, 1980-81; mktg. rep. The Ariz. Lottery, Phoenix, 1981; pvt. practice fin. planning Phoenix, 1983-86; regional v.p. Jones Internat. Securities, Phoenix, 1986—. Mem. Internat. Assn. Fin. Planners, Inst. Cert. Fin. Planners (cert.). Home: 4322 N 29th Way Phoenix AZ 85016 Office: Jones Internat Securities 9697 E Mineral Ave Englewood CO 80112

HELGASON, CINDY JONES, accountant; b. Oakland, Calif., Aug. 30, 1959; d. Robert Collier and Grace Theresa (McLaughlin) Jones; m. Michael Alan Helgason, Sept. 20, 1986. BBA, St. Mary's Coll., Notre Dame, Ind., 1981. CPA, Oreg. Sr. acct. Coopers & Lybrand, CPA's, Portland, Oreg., 1981-84; corp. controller Lawrence Photo-Graphic, Inc., Kansas City, Mo., 1984-86; mgr. spl. projects The Case Hoyt Corp., Rochester, N.Y., 1986-87; supr. fin. reporting Schlegel Corp., Rochester, 1987—. Bd. dirs. Health Help Ctr., Portland, 1984; treas. Oregonians for Castagna, Portland, 1984. Roman Catholic. Home: 264 Village Ln Rochester NY 14610 Office: 400 East Ave Rochester NY 14607

HELLER, DIANA LYNN, radio station manager; b. Boston, May 18, 1948; d. William Harry and Mary Annette (Brown) Fairfield m. Michael A. Heller, Apr. 20, 1968; 1 child, Scott William. Student, Virginia Farrel Beauty Sch., 1966, Mott Community Coll., 1974-82. Cosmetologist various orgns., Lapeer, Mich., 1967-70; asst. gen. mgr. Sta. WDEY, Lapeer, 1974—; instr. Co-Operative Extension Service, Lapeer, 1987. Lunch mother Immaculate Conception Ch., Lapeer, 1985-87. Mem. Am. Bus. Women Assn. (commentator, 1987), Lapeer C. of C. (chmn. 1st lady award com. 1987). Republican. Lodge: Zonta Internat. (bd. dir. 1987—, chmn. membership 1987). Office: Sta WDEY-AM&FM 286 W Nepessing St Lapeer MI 48446

HELLER, HELEN EVE, educator, consultant; b. Newcastle upon Tyne, Eng., Sept. 19, 1949; came to Can., 1977; d. Hyman and Rachael (Levine) Krolick; m. Charles Heller, Nov. 11, 1972; 1 child, Sarah Louise. BA in Italian, Philosophy with hons., U. London, 1970. Asst. editor Cassell and Co., London, 1970-74; acquistions editor Harlequin Books, Toronto, Ont., Can., 1979-83; editorial dir. Avon Books of Can., Toronto, 1984-85; editor in chief Fitzhenry and Whiteside, Toronto, 1985—. Author numerous articles and revs. of crime fact and fiction. Mem. Book and Periodical Pubs. Assn., Crime Writers Assn., Crime Writers Assn. of Can. Democrat. Jewish. Home: 32 Bayhampton Ct, Downsview, ON Canada M3H 5L6 Office: Fitzhenry & Whiteside Ltd, 195 Allstate Parkway, Markham, ON Canada L3R 4T8

HELLMANN, NORMA JANELLE, cytotechnologist; b. Honolulu, Jan. 21, 1949; d. Norman Louis and Margaret Janelle (Baker) Hellmann; BA, Carthage Coll., 1971; cert. Johns Hopkins Hosp. Sch. Cytotech., 1972. Asso. cytotechnologist Johns Hopkins Hosp., Balt., 1972-74; supr. cytology lab. Clin. Labs. of Nashville, 1974; ednl. coordinator Sch. Cytotech. Vanderbilt U., Nashville, 1974-76; supr. cytology lab. Clin. Labs. of Black Hills, Rapid City, S.D., 1976—; program coordinator CDC Workshops on Cytology, Rapid City, 1978. Mem. CAP, 1976-84, squadron comdr., 1982-83, dir. blood flight program S.D., 1976-83; exec. sec. Wonderland Homes Water and Service Co., 1979-80; founder, chmn. Literacy Council of Black Hills, 1984—; bd. dirs. Piedmont (S.D.) Vol. Fire Dept., 1985-87; mem. adv. council on community edn. Rapid City Schs. Mem. Am. Soc. Cytology, Am. Soc. Clin. Pathologists (assoc., cert. cytotechnologist), Internat. Acad. Cytology (cert.), Am. Soc. Cytotech., AAUW (S.D. v.p. program 1984-86, Woman of Worth award 1982), S.D. Advocacy Network for Women, Aircraft Owners and Pilots Assn., 99s (S.D. chmn. 1984-87), Exptl. Aircraft Assn., Beta Beta Beta, Alpha Mu Gamma. Republican. Lutheran. Home: 12205 Rena'ta Dr Black Hawk SD 57718 Office: PO Box 238 Rapid City SD 57709

HELLMER, MARY ANN, nurse, educator; b. Bklyn., May 4, 1952; d. Raymond Joseph and Mary (Toporowsky) Hanson; m. George A. Hellmer, Jr., Aug. 29, 1979 (div.); 1 son, George A. III. A.A.S. in Nursing, SUNY, Agrl. and Tech. Coll.-Farmingdale, 1974; B.S. in Nursing, SUNY-Stony Brook, 1977; M.S. in Nursing, Adelphi U., 1979, Ph.D. in Nursing, 1986. Registered profl. nurse, N.Y. Asst. head nurse Brunswick Hosp., Amityville, N.Y., 1974-77, ICU staff nurse, 1977-80; instr. nursing Nassau Community Coll., Garden City, N.Y., 1978-83, asst. prof., 1983—, adj. instr. phys. edn., summers 1981, 82, 83; cons. regents external degree program SUNY Army Nurse Corps Res. component, 808th Sta. Hosp. Recipient Dept. Acad. award Dept. Nursing SUNY Agrl. and Tech. Coll.-Farmingdale, 1974; Nursing Achievement scholar Adelphi U., 1981-82. Mem. Am. Nurses Assn., N.Y. Assn. of Two Year Colls., AD Orgn. of Nurse Educators, Sigma Theta Tau (chpt. award; scholarship, eligibility and publicity coms.), Phi Theta Kappa. Contbr. chpts. in books, test materials; item writer Regents External Degree Program, 1981, 82, 85, 86, 87. Office: Nassau Community Coll Dept Nursing Garden City NY 11530

HELLSTROM, PAMELA DONWORTH, human resource management executive; b. Bangor, Maine, Apr. 4, 1948; d. Clarence Arlowe and Margaret Mary (Donworth) Small; m. Michael Willard Hellstrom, Oct. 12, 1978; 1 child, Kirsten Elyse. BA in English Edn., Merrimack Coll., 1970. Lic. vocat. educator, Wash. Asst. dir. pub. relations, employment counselor Meals-On-Wheels, Seattle, 1970-72; social services asst. Madigan Army Med. Ctr., Tacoma, 1972-73, social work asst., 1974-81; chief counselor drug and alcohol treatment ctr. Am. Lake VA Health Ctr., Tacoma, 1973-74; trainer, cons. alt. chief examiner Gen. Equivalency Diploma program L.H. Bates Vocat. Tech. Inst., Tacoma, 1983-84; founder, pres. Growth Techs., Inc., Tacoma, 1984—, project dir. contract staffing services, on-site daycare and day clinicare program. Mem. Nat. Staff Leasing Assn., Tacoma-Pierce County C. of C. Democrat. Roman Catholic. Home: 8918 Delores Ct NE Olympia WA 98506 Office: Growth Techs Inc 10520 Bridgeport Way SW Suite 102 Tacoma WA 98499

HELM, CAROLYN SMITH, sales consultant; b. Long Branch, N.J., Oct. 5, 1958; d. Baynard Rennick and Peggy (Speir) Smith; m. Spencer R. Helm, July 31, 1988. Student, Limestone Coll., 1974-76; BE, U. Ga., 1979. Tchr. indsl. arts Conyers (Ga.) Middle Sch., 1979-80; elec. estimator Brown & Root, Houston, 1981-82; indsl. engr. LDC/Milton Roy, Riviera Beach, Fla., 1982-86; power boat sales rep. Boat Kingdom, Lake Park, Fla., 1986-87, Maxon Marina, Jupiter, Fla., 1987—; engring. cons., West Palm Beach, Fla., 1986-87. Mem. Palm Beach Gardens C. of C. (mem. edn. com. 1985-87). Home: 701 Lakeside Dr North Palm Beach FL 33408 Office: Maxon Mariana & Club 18701 S Federal Hwy Jupiter FL 33469

HELM, SHERYL LYNN, computer specialist; b. Muskogee, Okla., Apr. 2, 1950; d. John Clinton Jr. and JoAnn Peryl (Boydstun) H.; m. Jon Glenn Gilbert, Aug. 1971 (div. Aug. 1973). AA, Laramie County Community Coll., 1972. Data entry operator First Nat. Bank of Denver, 1974-78, quality assurance, program librarian, 1980-82; programmer trainee Intrawest Bank of Denver, 1982, programmer analyst, 1983—. Mem. Am. Inst. Banking, NOW, Nat. Assn. Female Execs. Democrat. Office: First Interstate Services Co 633 17th St 7-N Denver CO 80217

HELMAN, JOYCE KENT, real estate executive; b. N.Y.C., July 23, 1932; d. Emanuel Harold and Belle (Pomerance) Kent; m. Myron Sanger Helman, Mar. 7, 1954; children: Robin Helman Brown, Michael. BS, Bklyn. Coll., 1954. Legal asst. Dreyer & Traub, N.Y.C., 1977-82; asst. v.p. Del-Val Fin. Corp., N.Y.C., 1982—; panelist Marymount Manhattan Coll., N.Y.C., 1982-87; guest lectr. NYU, 1987—. Mem. Nat. Assn. Female Execs. Office: Del-Val Fin Corp care Kenbee Securities Inc 747 3d Ave New York NY 10017

HELMAN, PHOEBE, artist, educator; b. N.Y.C., Oct. 29, 1929; d. Jake Rubin and Bertha Helman; m. Jack Sonenberg, 1949; 1 child, Maya. Student, NYU, 1945-47, Columbia U., 1948-49; B.F.A., Washington U., St. Louis, 1951. One-man shows: Max Hutchinson Gallery, N.Y.C., 1974, 78, Sculpture Now Inc., N.Y.C., 1978, Andre Zarre, N.Y.C., 1981, Douglass Coll. Rutgers U., N.J., 1984, SUNY, Cortland, 1985, Islip (N.Y.) Mus., 1987, Rathbone Gallery Russell Sage Coll., Albany, N.Y., 1988; exhibited in group shows: Lisbon, Portugal, 1981, State Mus., Albany, N.Y., 1981, Artender, Bilbao, Spain, 1982, Kosan Internat. Exhbn., Chonbuk, Korea, 1985, Large Drawings exhbn., 13 galleries in U.S., Islip Mus., East Islip, N.Y., 1987, Rathbone Gallery Russell Sage Coll., Albany, 1988; represented in permanent collection: Guggenheim Mus., N.Y.C., Ciba-Geigy Corp., Ardsley, N.Y., Olympia and York, N.Y.C., Bayonne Art Ctr., N.J.; prof. art Pratt Inst., Bklyn., 1971—; vis. art prof. Syracuse U., 1985-86. Guggenheim fellow, 1979-80; Nat. Endowment Arts visual art fellow, 1983; Creative Artists Pub. Service program awardee N.Y. State Council Art, 1975, 79. Mem. N.Y. State Council Art of N.Y. Found. on the Arts, 1986. Home: 217 E 23d St New York NY 10010 Office: Pratt Inst 200 Willoughby St Brooklyn NY 11205

HELMS, LAURIE LYNN, defense analyst; b. Camden, N.J., Oct. 12, 1961; d. Walter Clyde and Myrtle Sally (Davis) H. BS, George Mason U., 1983. Sec. Dept. of Housing & Urban Devel., Washington, 1983-85; def. analyst Analysis & Tech., Inc., Arlington, Va., 1985-87, Computer Scis. Corp., Arlington, Va., 1987—. Editor, writer newsletter The Elephant's Ear (Best Newsletter in Va. YRFV award 1986, 87). Corr. sec. Arlington Young Reps., 1986-87; recording sec. Young Reps. Fedn. Va., 1987—. Mem. Nat. Assn. Female Execs. Presbyterian. Home: 4522 Pinecrest Heights Dr Annandale VA 22003

HELMS, MARY ANN, nurse; b. Compton, Calif., Jan. 7, 1935; d. Raymond Whitfield and Amanda Zelpha (Hancock) Spencer; AA in Nursing, El Camino Coll., 1971; BS in Nursing, Calif. State U., Los Angeles, 1976; MA in Mgmt., St. Mary's Coll., 1978; MS in Nursing, Ariz. State U., 1985; cert. clin. specialist; m. Willard Ford Helms, Mar. 15, 1958; children: Michael Steven, Steven Allen. Med. sec., bookkeeper Palm Springs (Calif.) Med. Clinic, 1956-61; office mgr. William R. Stevens Ins. Agy., Santa Ana, Calif., 1961-63, I.J. Weinrot & Son Ins. Agy., Los Angeles, 1963-67; staff nurse Kaiser Found. Hosp., Harbor City, Calif., 1971-76; supr., coordinator pediatrics Maricopa County Gen. Hosp., Phoenix, 1976-80; critical care nurse Phoenix Baptist Hosp., 1980-81, critical care mgr., 1981—, critical care cons., 1986—. Mem. Am. Nurses Assn., Am. Soc. Women Accts., Natural History Mus., Met. Mus. Art, Smithsonian Instn., Phoenix Zoo, Phoenix Art Mus., Cousteau Soc., Calif. State U. Alumni Assn., KAET Public Broadcasting System, Am. Assn. Critical Care Nurses, Ariz. Nurses Assn. Nat. League Nursing, Ariz. State U. Alumni Assn., Phi Kappa Phi, Alpha Gamma Sigma, Sigma Theta Tau. Republican. Mormon. Research on noise pollution on phys. and mental health of citizenry, phenylketonuria testing in Los Angeles, measurement of attitudes toward children in pediatric nurses, nursing practice, physiological changes with back massage, incidence of prolonged Q-T internal in critically ill patients. Home: 1007 E Michelle Dr Phoenix AZ 85022 Office: 6025 N 20th Ave Phoenix AZ 85015

HELMSLEY, LEONA MINDY, hotel executive; b. N.Y.C.; m. Harry B. Helmsley, Apr. 8, 1972. Vice pres. Pease & Elliman, N.Y.C., 1962-69; pres. Sutton & Towne Residential, N.Y.C., 1967-70; sr. v.p. Helmsley Spear, N.Y.C., 1970-72, Brown, Harris, Stevens, N.Y.C., 1970-72; pres. Helmsley Hotels, Inc., N.Y.C., 1980—. Named Woman of Yr. N.Y. Council Civic Affairs, 1970; named Woman of Yr. Town & Country Condos & Coops., 1981; recipient Service award Ort Sch. Engring., 1981, Profl. Excellence award Les Dames d'Escoffier, 1981, Spl. Achievement award Sales Execs. Club N.Y., 1981, Woman of Yr. award Internat. Hotel Industry, 1982. Home: 36 Central Park S New York NY 10019 Office: Helmsley Hotels The Helmsley Palace Hotel 455 Madison Ave New York NY 10022 *

HELOISE, columnist, lecturer, broadcaster; b. Waco, Tex., Apr. 15, 1951; d. Marshal H. and Heloise K. (Bowles) Cruse; m. David L. Evans, Feb. 13, 1981. B.S. in Math. and Bus, S.W. Tex. State U., 1974. Owner, pres. Heloise, Inc. Asst. to columnist mother, Heloise, 1974-77, upon her death took over internationally syndicated column, 1977; author: (books) Hints From Heloise, 1980, Help From Heloise, 1981, Heloise's Beauty Book, 1985; contbg. editor Good Housekeeping mag., 1981; co-founder, 1st co-pilot Mile High Pie in the Sky Balloon Club. Mem. Women in Communication, Tex. Press Women, Screen Actors Guild, AFTRA, Women in Radio and TV, Confrerie de la Chaine des Rotisseurs (bailli San Antonio chpt.); mem. Ordre Mondial des Gourmets De'Gustateurd de U.S.A.; Mem. Good Neighbor Council Tex.-Mex. Club: Death Valley Yacht and Racket. Lodge: Zonta. Home: PO Box 795000 San Antonio TX 78279 Office: care King Features Syndicate 235 E 45th St New York NY 10017

HELPERN, JOAN (MARSHALL), designer; b. N.Y.C., Oct. 10, 1926; d. Edward and Ethel (Tilzer) Marshall; m. David M. Helpern, Aug. 14, 1960; children—David M., Elizabeth Joan. B.A., Hunter Coll., N.Y.C., 1947; M.A. (grantee 1947-48), Columbia U., 1948; postgrad., Harvard U., 1960-67. Coordinator guidance services N.Y.C. Bd. Edn., 1950-60; dir. pupil personnel services Lexington Bd. Edn., Mass., 1960-67; cons. child devel. and pupil personnel programs U.S. Dept. Edn. (state univs. and state depts. edn.), 1948-69; pres., chief exec. officer Joan and David (footwear and accessory design and mfg.), N.Y.C., 1968—; fashion designer, pres. Joan Helpern Designs, Inc., N.Y.C. Author: Guidance of Children in the Elementary Schools. Recipient Coty award Am. design 1978. Club: Harvard (Boston). Office: 4 W 58th St New York NY 10019

HELSING, CHERYL WRIGHT, infosystems executive; b. San Jose, Oct. 24, 1954; d. Edward James and Uva Estelle (Fulton) Wright; m. Blair Gray Helsing, Aug. 21, 1976. BS, Calif. Polytech. State U., 1975; MS, San Jose State U., 1978. Editor GTE Lenkurt, San Carlos, Calif., 1976-77; mgr. Boole and Babbage, Sunnyvale, Calif., 1977-79; systems analyst Bank of America, San Francisco, 1979-81, info. security cons., 1981-84, v.p., 1984-87; pres. Cheryl W. Helsing, Inc., San Fransisco, 1987-88; sr. mgr. Deloitte, Haskins & Sells, San Francisco, 1988—; mem. adv. bd. Datapro Reports on Info. Security, Delran., N.J, 1987—; data security project mgr. GUIDE, Chgo., 1982-84. Mem. Info. Systems Security Assn. (v.p. 1984-86), Am. Soc. for Indsl. Security, EDP Auditors Assn., Assn. for Computing Machinery (adv bd. 1985-87), Am. Bankers Assn. (chair data security com. 1986-87). Office: 44 Montgomery St Suite 2000 San Francisco CA 94104

HELSON, RAVENNA MATHEWS, research psychologist; b. Austin, Tex., Feb. 13, 1925; d. Edward Jackson and Ravenna (Wakefield) Mathews; m. Henry Helson, June 12, 1954; children: David, Ravenna, Harold. BA, U. Tex., 1945, MA, 1949; PhD, U. Calif., Berkeley, 1952. Reporter Corpus Christi (Tex.) Times, 1945-47; asst. prof. Smith Coll., Northampton, Mass., 1952-55; asst. pub. health analyst dept. maternal and child health State of Calif., Berkeley, 1955-57; research psychologist Inst. Personality Assessment and Research, U. Calif., Berkeley, 1957—; adj. prof. psychology, U. Calif., Berkeley, 1980—. Contbr. numerous articles to profl. jours., 1949—. Grantee NIMH, Rockefeller Found., NEH, Wickes Found. Fellow Am. Psychol. Assn. (Div. 8 Personality and Social Psychology com. chmn. 1978-80, div. 10 Psychology and the Arts pres. 1979-80, sec.-treas. 1976-79, council del. 1987, div. 35 Psychology Women, Henry A. Murray award 1984). Home: 15 The Crescent Berkeley CA 94708 Office: U Calif Inst Personality Assessment 3657 Tolman Hall Berkeley CA 94708

HELTON, LUCILLE HENRY HANRATTIE, academic administrator; b. Ft. Worth, Mar. 2, 1942; d. P.D. and Virginia (Clark) Henry; m. Wayne Hanrattie, June 26, 1965 (div. Apr. 1986); children: Clark, Chris; m. William M. Helton, Jr., Mar. 19, 1988. BA, So. Meth. U., 1964; MEd, U. Pitts., 1968; cert. in adminstrn., William Paterson Coll., 1984; cert. in mid-mgmt., Tex. Christian U., 1987. Cert. elem. tchr. N.J., Pa., Tex. Nat. field sec. Kappa Kappa Gamma Sorority, Columbus, Ohio, 1964-65; elem. tchr. Pitts. Bd. Edn., 1965-69; co-dir, chmn. dept. maths. Assn. Children with Learning Disabilities Sch., Pitts., 1969-72; tchr. elem., secondary, gifted and remedial and home instrn. programs West Milford (N.J.) Bd. Edn., 1976-84; sch. dir., prin. Hill Sch., Ft. Worth, 1984—. Mem. adminstrv. bd. First Meth. Ch., Ft. Worth, 1987—, Council of Ministries of First Meth. Ch., 1986-87; bd. dirs. Community Psychiat. Ctr. Oak Bend Hosp., Ft. Worth, 1987—. Mem. Networking for Exec. Women, Tex. Ind. Sch. Consortium, Commn. on Status and Role of Women, Assn. for Children with Learning Disabilities, DAR, Delta Kappa Gamma, Phi Delta Gamma. Democrat. Methodist. Office: Hill Sch 3109 Lubbock Fort Worth TX 76109

HELTON, PAMELA KAY WILLIAMS, merchandiser, writer; b. Montgomery, Ala., July 11, 1956; d. Leslie Edward and Dorothy Ann (Bussie) Williams; m. Ralph Eugene Helton, Feb. 11, 1977; children: Joshua Eric, Jason Michael. BS, Auburn U., Montgomery, 1978. Head checkout K-Mart, Montgomery, 1973-77, merchandiser, 1977-87; retail specialist Nabisco Brands, Montgomery, 1987-88, sales rep., 1988—. Contbr. articles to mags. including Highlights for Children, Boys' Life. Sunday sch. tchr. Dalraida Ch. Christ, Montgomery, 1985—. Democrat. Home: 3061 Shenandoah Dr Montgomery AL 36116

HELWIG, SUSAN MITCHELL, university administrator; b. Bklyn., Mar. 6, 1960; d. Peter T. and Kathleen E. (Tansey) M.; m. Willard F. Helwig III. BS, Bloomsburg U., 1982. Pub. relations asst. Berwick (Pa.) Hosp. Ctr., 1982-83, coordinator indsl. services, 1983-86, program dir. health works, 1986; asst. dir. devel. Bloomsburg (Pa. U., 1986—. Mem. Nat. Assn. Female Execs., AAUW. Republican. Roman Catholic. Office: Bloomsburg U Carver Hall Bloomsburg PA 17815

HEMBY, BARBARA JEAN, educator; b. Washington; d. Joseph Henry and Mildred (Barrett) H. BS, D.C. Tchrs. Coll., 1972; postgrad., Howard U., 1972-80. Tchr. D.C. Pub. Schs., Washington, 1972—. Author: The Spirit of Truth, 1984. Minister Christ Only Hope, Washington, 1984—. Mem. Greater Washington Tchrs. Foreign Languages. Office: DC Pub Sch 1301 New Jersey Ave NW Washington DC 20001

HEMBY, DOROTHY JEAN, counselor; b. Greenville, N.C., Aug. 21; d. Samul Emanuel and Queenie Ester Hemby; student Essex County Coll., 1971, Montclair State Coll., 1973-75, Kean Coll. N.J., 1975-77. Clk.-typist Remco Industries, Newark, IRS, Newark, 1963-66, VA Hosp., East Orange, N.J., 1966-71; part-time tchr. Newark Bd. Edn., 1973-76; coll. counselor/academic adviser Kean Coll. N.J., Union, 1976-77; vol. job evaluator N.J. Vol. Employment Service Team, Newark, 1977-78; coll. counselor/adviser Passaic County Community Coll., Paterson, N.J., 1978—, mem. tenure faculty review com, 1986—; chmn. H.O.P.E. com. Clk., East Orange Bd. Elections, 1971-72; v.p. Econ. Consumer's Community Aid., 1971-73; active local polit. orgn., 1973—; adv. Passaic County Gospel Choir and Christian Club; chairperson Passaic County Coll. Student Life Com., 1983-84; publicity coordinator Crispus Attucks Scholarship Found., 1986-87. Mem. N.J. Assn. Black Educators, Assn. Black Women in Higher Edn., Am. Personnel and Guidance Assn., Am. Counseling Personel Assn., N.J. Social Workers Assn., N.J. Behavioral Sci. Soc., Passaic County Acad. Council, Am. Assn. Counseling and Devel., N.J. Black Issues Assn. Clubs: 700, PTL. Office: Passaic County Community Coll College Blvd Paterson NJ 07509

HEMENWAY, JOAN ELIZABETH, minister, religious education director; b. Phila., Mar. 14, 1938; d. Seymour Harrison and Katherine Jayne (McKewn) H. BA, Conn. Coll., 1960; MDiv, Union Sem., 1968. Ordained to ministry United Meth. Ch. Mng. editor Youth Mag., Phila., 1970-72; assoc. minister First Meth. Ch., Germantown, Pa., 1976-78; pastoral counselor Pa. Found. for Pastoral Counseling, Phila., 1974-78; chaplain Presbyn. Hosp., Phila., 1974-78; chaplain supr. Hosp. Chaplainary, Inc., N.Y.C., 1978-84, Hartford (Conn.) Hosp., 1984—; adj. faculty Union Sem., N.Y., 1979-84, Hartford Sem., 1987—; mem. ea. Pa. conf. United Meth. Ch. Contbr. articles to jours. Bd. trustees Hartford Sem., 1987—; bd. dirs. Concern for Dying, Inc., N.Y.C., 1980-85. Fellow Coll. Chaplains; mem. Assn. Clin. Pastoral Edn. (regional dir. ea. region 1983—), Am. Assn. Pastoral Counselors. Democrat. Office: Pastoral Services Hartford Hosp 80 Seymour St Hartford CT 06115

HEMINGWAY, BETH ROWLETT, author, columnist, lecturer; b. Richmond, Va., May 6, 1913; d. Robert Archer and Evelyn Lucille (Doggett) Rowlett; B.Mus., Hollins Coll., 1934; m. Harold Hemingway, Apr. 2, 1938; children—Ruth Hartley, Martha Scott. Writer, Richmond-Lifestyle mag.; columnist Artistry in Bloom, Richmond Times-Dispatch; author: A Second Treasury of Christmas Decorations, 1961; Flower Arrangement with Antiques, 1965; Christmas Decorations Say Welcome, 1972; Antiques Accented by Flowers, 1975; Beth Hemingway's No Kin to Ernest, 1980; Holidays with Hemingway, 1985; lectr. numerous states, also Australia, 1966, Eng., 1977. Vol., Hermitage Meth. Home, 1977-79. Mem. Nat. League Am. Pen Women, Va. Writers Club, Richmond Hort. Assn., Va. Fedn. Garden Clubs (book rev. chmn.), Richmond Council Garden Clubs (flower arrangement chmn.), Clay Spring Garden Club (pres. 1953-55), Barton Garden Club (pres. 1959-61, 74). Republican. Methodist. Home: 1604 Derek Ln Richmond VA 23229

HEMLOW, JOYCE, English language educator, author; b. Liscomb, N.S., Can., July 30, 1906; d. William and Rosalinda (Redmond) H. B.A., Queen's Coll., Kingston, Can., 1941, M.A., 1942; A.M., Radcliffe Coll., 1944, Ph.D., 1948; LL.D., Queen's, 1967, Dalhousie U., 1972. Mem. faculty McGill U., 1945—, Greenshields prof. English lit. and lang., 1965—, prof. emerita, 1975—. Author: The History of Fanny Burney, 1958 (James Tait Black Meml. book prize for best biography in U.K., also Gov. Gen. Can. medal for academic non-fiction 1958, Rose Mary Crawshay prize Brit. Acad. 1960); editor: Journals and Letters Fanny Burney (Madame d'Arblay), 12 vols., Fanny Burney: Selected Letters and Journals, 1986, 87. Guggenheim fellow, 1951-52, 66-67; Disting. Achievement medal Radcliffe Coll., 1969. Fellow Royal Soc. Can.; mem. Johnsonians, Phi Beta Kappa. Home: Liscomb, NS Canada B0J 2A0

HEMPEL, KATHLEEN JANE, paper company executive; b. Monroe, Wis., Nov. 10, 1950; d. Francis H. and Mary Joan (Martin) Mottley; m. Rolf R. Hempel, Aug. 1, 1970; children: Michelle, Patricia. Student, U. Wis., Platteville; grad., U. Wis., Stevens Point, 1972; MBA, Ariz. State U., Tempe, 1984. V.p. Ft. Howard Corp., Green Bay, Wis., 1973-82, 1st v.p., 1986—, also bd. dirs.; cons. Hewitt Assocs., Phoenix, 1985-86. bd. dirs. Ft. Howard Found., Green Bay. Mem. County Exec. Ad Hoc Orgnl. Panel, Green Bay, 1987. Office: Ft Howard Corp 1919 S Broadway Green Bay WI 54304

HEMPFLING, LINDA LEE, nurse; b. Indpls., July 28, 1947; d. Paul Roy and Myrtle Pearl (Ward) Hempfling; diploma Meth. Hosp. Ind. Sch. Nursing, 1968; postgrad. St. Joseph's Coll. Charge nurse Meth. Hosp., Indpl., 1968; staff nurse operating room Silver Cross Hosp., Joliet, Ill., 1969; charge nurse operating room Huntington (N.Y.) Hosp., 1969-73; night supr. operating room Hermann Hosp., Houston, 1973-76; unit. mgr., purchasing coordinator operating rooms, 1976-83; RN med. auditor, quality assurance coordinator Nat. Healthcare Rev., Inc., Houston, 1984—. Future Nurses Am. scholar, 1965; Nat. Merit scholar, 1965. Mem. Nat. League Nursing, Am. Nurses Assn., Assn. Operating Room Nurses, Tex. Med. Auditors Assn. Office: 1130 Earle Houston TX 77030

HEMPHILL, MAUREEN LUCILLE, Canadian government official; b. Grand Forks, B.C., Jan. 26, 1937; d. Jim Leroy and Elaine Agnes Miller; children—Carol, Jim, Ross, Susan. R.N., Vancouver Gen. Hosp. Nurse, Vancouver Gen. Hosp., N. Vancouver Hosp., Good Samaritan Nursing Home, Edmonton; mem. Man. Legis. Assembly for Logan, 1981—. Minister of Edn., Govt. of Man., 1984—, minister Housing, 1986, minister Bus. Devel. and Tourism, 1986, minister Community Services, 1987. Address: Legis Bldg Room 302, Winnipeg, MB Canada R3C 0V8

HEMPSTEAD, MARY CLAIRE, editor, state agency administrator; b. Peoria, Ill., Mar. 3, 1932; d. George Elgin and Mary Theresa (Hannon) Johnson; m. Charles A. Hempstead, Aug. 18, 1956; children: Charles Jr., Theresa Hempstead-Pearce, Catherine, Jeffrey. AB, Bradley U., 1954. Cert. tchr. Tchr. English, history, Spanish Limestone High Sch., Peoria, 1954-56, Mid-County High Sch., Varna, Ill., 1956-57, Avon (Ill.) Sch., 1961-63, Washington (Ill.) Schs., 1964-71; asst. to dir. sch. services Ill. State Hist. Library, Springfield, 1972-80; editor Ill. Hist. Preservation Agy., Springfield, 1980—. Co-author: Revolutionary War Period: A Bibliography, 1973. Mem. Am. Assn. Univ. Women (v.p. 1987—, honoree 1987), Ill. State Hist. Soc., Sangamon County Hist. Soc. Home: 2819 Ticonderoga Springfield IL 62704 Office: Ill Hist Preservation Agy Old State Capitol Springfield IL 62701

HENARD, ELIZABETH ANN, controller; b. Providence, Oct. 9, 1947; d. Anthony Joseph and Grace Johanna (Lokay) Zorbach; m. Patrick Edward Mann, Dec. 18, 1970 (div. July 1972); m. John Bruce Henard Jr., Oct. 19, 1974; children: Scott Michael, Christopher Andrew. Student, Jacksonville (Fla.) U., 1966. Sec. So. Bell Tel.&Tel., Jacksonville, 1964-69; office mgr. Gunther F. Reis Assocs., Tampa, Fla., 1969-71; exec. sec. Ernst & Ernst, Tampa, 1971-72; exec. sec. to pres. Lamalie Assocs., Tampa, 1972-74; exec. sec. Arthur Young & Co., Chgo., 1975; adminstrv. asst. Irving J. Markin, Chgo., 1975; controller, corp. sec. Henard Assocs., Inc., Dallas, 1983—. Mem. Dallas Investors Group (treas. 1986—). Republican. Roman Catholic. Clubs: Bent Tree Country, Willow Bend Polo (Dallas). Home: 5706 Thames Ct Dallas TX 75252 Office: Henard Assocs Inc 15303 Dallas Pkwy Dallas TX 75248

HENDERSON, BOBBIE ALLEN, child development and family relationship educator; b. Houston, May 30, 1940; d. Theodore Brown and Irma Lee (Hart) Allen; m. Robert Arthur Bingham, June 28, 1959 (div. 1967); children—Eric Courtland, Kevin Troy; m. John Ree Henderson, Jan. 4, 1968; 1 child, Shannon Aryana. B.A., Fisk U., 1959; M.A., Tex. So. U., 1973; Ph.D., U. Wis.-Madison, 1977. Cert. elem. tchr., Tex. Civil service position FBI, Washington and N.Y.C., 1961-65; pre-kindergarden tchr. Bunnyland Acad., Houston, 1965-66, 8th Ave Elem. Sch., 1972; social service coordinator Project Head Start, 1966-72; br. dir. YWCA, 1973-74; assoc. prof. Tex. So. U., Houston, 1973—, also dir. cons. in field. Contbr. articles to profl. jours. Chmn., Head Start Policy Council, Houston, 1983—; bd. sec. Planned Parenthood, 1984—; affilaite rep. Tex. Assn. for Edn. Young Children, 1983—; bd. dirs. Family Service Ctr., 1982—; chmn. com. Mayor's Hearing Children & Youth, 1984-85. Recipient Humanitarian award Social Work Program Tex. State U., 1982, Community Service, Sta. KMJQ, 1984, Outstanding Service, Adopt Black Children, 1983, Outstanding Vol., Am. Heart Assn. Mem. Houston Assn. Edn. Young Children (pres., Outstanding Service award 1982), Nat. Assn. Edn. Young Children, So. Assn. Children Under Six (multi-cultural chmn.), Friends of Head Start, Phi Delta Kappa, Omicron Nu. Democrat. Episcopalian. Clubs: Delta Sigma Theta (sec.), Top Ladies Distinction, Coalition 100 Black Women. Home: 4203 Charleston St Houston TX 77021 Office: Texas So U 3100 Cleburne St Houston TX 77004 also: Neighborhood Ctrs Inc 3401 Fannin St Houston TX 77004

HENDERSON, CATHERINE ANNA, psychotherapist; b. Henry, Ill., June 12, 1942; d. Walter Charles and Dorothy Maxine (Colligan) Baldwin; m. Stephen Campbell Henderson, Aug. 8, 1964; children: James, John. BSN, U. Iowa, 1964; MA in Psychology, Antioch U., 1983. Pub. health nurse New Haven Vis. Nurse Assn., 1964-65; psychotherapist Seattle King County Pub. Health Dept., 1965-76; psychotherapist, chmn. community liasion Community Physicians Bellevue (Wash.) Pub. Schs., 1965-79; pvt. practice psychotherapist Bellevue, 1976—; coordinator, dir. parent and child edn. Bellevue Pub. Schs., 1970-72. Mem. Am. Nurses Assn., Seattle Inst. Psychoanalysis (cert. in child psychoanalytic psychotherapy), Child Therapy Assn., Sigma Theta Tau, Zeta Tau Alpha. Republican. Episcopalian.

HENDERSON, GERALDINE THOMAS, retired social security official, educator; b. Luling, Tex., Jan. 7, 1924; d. Cornelius Thomas and Maggie (Keyes) Thomas; m. James E. Henderson, Feb. 9, 1942 (dec. Apr. 1978); children—Geraldine, Jessica, Jennifer. B.S., Fayetteville State U., 1967. Tchr. Cumberland County Schs., Fayetteville, N.C., 1966-67, Fayetteville City Schs., 1967-68; with Social Security Adminstrn., Fayetteville, 1968-87; substitute tchr. Cumberland County Sch. System, 1987—; claims rep. Pres. Fayetteville State U. Found., 1981-82, NAACP, Fayetteville br., 1983—; bd. dirs. Fayetteville Art Council, 1984—, Cumberland County United Way, 1983—, chmn. div. corp. mission Fayetteville Presbytery, 1986, mem. personnel review bd. City of Fayetteville, 1987—. Mem. League of Women Voters, Am. Legion Aux. (treas. 1981-83), Zeta Phi Zeta (Woman of Yr. 1984), Omega Psi Phi (Citizen of Yr. 1985). Democrat. Presbyterian. Avocations: creative dress design; gardening; travel.

HENDERSON, JANA L., federal agency administrator, infosystems specialist; b. Anamosa, Iowa, Feb. 19, 1944; d. H. Dean and Rosetta I. (Lyon) H.; m. Steven J. Reinking, June 18, 1966 (div. June 1971). BA cum laude, U. Iowa, 1966, MBA, 1975. Cert. secondary edn. tchr., math. Systems analyst Iowa Nat. Mut. Ins. Co., Cedar Rapids, 1966-73; sr. systems analyst Westinghouse Learning Corp. div. Westinghouse Corp., Iowa City, Iowa, 1973-77; sr. computer specialist U.S. Dept. Edn., Washington, 1977—, also cons., 1976. Mem. Nat. Assn. Female Execs., Beta Gamma Sigma. Methodist. Lodge: Order Eastern Star. Office: US Dept Edn 400 Maryland Ave SW ROB3 #4642 Washington DC 20202

HENDERSON, JANE WHALEN, travel company executive; b. Fort Dodge, Iowa, June 24, 1913; d. William L. and Blanche (Tremaine) Whalen; m. Lon St. Clair Henderson, Oct. 16, 1946 (div.); children: Thomas, Clare, Anne. Student Fort Dodge Jr. Coll., Iowa, 1931-32, Fort Dodge Bus. Coll., 1932-33, Armstrong Coll., 1937-38. Travel cons. Capwells Travel, 1938-42, Peck Judah Travel Bur., San Francisco, 1942-48; mgr. World Travel Bur., Anaheim, Calif., 1955-56, Fullerton, Calif., 1958-60; mgr. Travel Advisers, Santa Ana, Calif., 1964-65; internat. travel adviser Anaheim Travel, 1960-64; v.p. sales Orange Empire Travel Bur., Anaheim, 1965-70; owner, pres. Jane Henderson Travel, Orange, Calif., 1970—; cons N.Am. Sch. Travel, Newport Beach, Calif., 1968—; mem. adv. bd. Orange Nat. Bank, PanAm. Airways, Traveling Times, Valencia, Calif. Gold sponsor Miss Orange Pageant, 1976-86; mem. street naming com. City of Orange, 1985—, mem. sister city program, 1985—. Named Orange Citizen of Yr., 1983. Mem. Am. Soc. Travel Agts., Assn. Retail Travel Agts., Pacific Area Travel Assn., Orange County Travel Agts. (pres. 1978), Cruise Lines Internat., Orange C. of C. (bd. dirs.). Roman Catholic. Lodge: Soroptimists Internat. Office: Jane Henderson Travel 1876 N Tustin Ave Orange CA 92665

HENDERSON, JANET LEE, diagnostics laboratory sales executive; b. Dallas, Aug. 12, 1946; d. William D. and Jane (Allen) H. B.S. in Med. Tech., North Tex. State U., 1969. Med. technologist Baylor U. Med. Ctr., Dallas, 1969-72. Baptist Hosp., Miami, 1972-74, Sayet Lab., Miami, 1974-76; tech. sales rep. Electronucleonics, Inc., Fairfield, N.J., 1976-79; sales rep. Smith Kline Instruments, Sunnyvale, Calif., 1979-82, Beckman Instruments, Brea, Calif., 1982-83, Boehringer Mannheim Diagnostics, Indpls., 1983—. Named Rookie of Yr., SKI, 1980; recipient Winner's Circle Plaque awardBoehringer Manheim, 1986. Mem. Am. Soc. Med. Technologists, Women in Sales; Nat. Assn. for Female Execs. Republican. Lutheran. Home: 20643 SW 119th Pl Miami FL 33177

HENDERSON, JOAN BLUST, lawyer, educator, writer; b. Paterson, N.J., July 7, 1936; d. Vincent M. and Ellen Kennedy (Adams) Blust; m. J. Eber Henderson, June 26, 1959 (div. 1976); children—Ian Scott, Heather Jo. B.A., Cedar Crest Coll., Allentown, Pa., 1958; M.A., U. Louisville, 1967, J.D., 1978. Bar: Ind. 1979, U.S. Dist. Ct. (so. dist.) Ind. 1979. Tchr. New Providence Sch. (N.J.), 1960-61, Army Sch., Ft. Campbell, Ky., 1961-62; tchr. chronically ill. Louisville Pub. Schs., 1962-65; exec. dir. Rauch Ctr. for Handicapped, New Albany, Ind., 1965-72; instr. Jeffersonville campus Webster U., St. Louis, 1983; sole practice, Jeffersonville, Ind., 1979—; lectr. various orgns. Author: A Good Worker, 1971; A Good Citizen, 1973; A Good Neighbor, 1976. Adv. com. on child abuse Clark County Welfare, Jeffersonville, 1980-84; edn. com. ARC, Louisville, 1982—. Recipient Jeffersonville United to Make Progress Bus. award, 1985. Mem. Ind. Bar Assn., Clark County Bar Assn., Assn. Trial Lawyers Am., Kappa Delta Pi, Phi Alpha Delta, Am. Bus. Women's Assn. (Jeffersonville chpt.). Home: 400 E Terrace Dr Jeffersonville IN 47130 Office: 521 E 7th St Jeffersonville IN 47130

HENDERSON, LOUISE ELAINE, personnel director; b. Coronado, Fla., June 14, 1947; d. Gene Leon and Virginia Louise (Clark) H. Student, Fla. Keys Community Coll., currently. Gen. mgr. Two Friends Raw Bar and Patio Restaurant, Key West, Fla., 1969-78; acct. clk. City of Key West, Fla., 1978-86, dir. human resources, risk mgmt., 1986—. Bd. dirs. Helpline, Key West, 1980-82, Monroe Assn. Retarded Citizens, 1981. Mem. Nat. Assn. Female Execs., Am. Soc. Notaries, Pub. Risk and Ins. Mgmt. Assn., Fla. Fedn. for Safety, Phi Theta Kappa. Home: 2513 Staples Ave Rear Key West FL 33040 Office: City of Key West Key West FL 33040

HENDERSON, MARILYN ANN, research and engineering company executive; b. Scranton, Pa., Aug. 3, 1949; d. William Joseph and Mary Ann (Banick) Delorey; m. William Edgar Henderson, Oct. 23, 1971. Student U. Scranton, 1968; B.S., Pa. State U., 1970; M.B.A., Fairleigh Dickinson U., 1977. With AT&T, 1970-84, dist. mgr., various N.J. locations, 1977-83, div. mgr., Piscataway, N.J., 1983-84; div. mgr. Bell Communications Research, Piscataway, 1984—; editorial bd. Exchange Mag., 1986—. Recipient various corp. awards and recognitions, 1976-85, Clements award Clements Found., 1967, 68, 69, 70. Mem. AAUW, Am. Mgmt. Assn., Assn. Computing Machinery, Telephone Pioneers Am. (v.p. Cen. State council 1987-88, pres. 1988—), Nat. Assn. Female Execs., Morris Mus., Morris County Hist. Soc., Frelinghuysen Arboretum, Hist. Speedwell, Pa. State Alumni Assn., Omicron Nu. Roman Catholic. Avocations: power boating; cats; golfing, historical preservation. Home: Ten Pond Hill Rd Convent Station NJ 07961 Office: Bell Communications Research 33 Knightsbridge Rd Piscataway NJ 08854

HENDERSON, MARSHAE RHONDETTA, tax specialist, realtor; b. Jackson, Miss., Aug. 12, 1959; d. Alonzo Jr. and Virginia (Foster) H. Student, U. So. Miss., 1977-81; BS in Personnel Mgmt., Memphis State U., 1984. Reservation agt. Holiday Corp., Memphis, 1982-83; asst. mgr. charles Shop, Memphis, 1983-84; clk. control IRS, Memphis, 1984-86, tax examiner, 1986-87; personnel action clk. Def. Logistics Agy., Memphis, 1987—; affiliate broker Crye-Leike Realtors. Mem. Assn. for Improvement Minorities, Assn. Female Execs., Nat. Assn. Realtors, Tenn. Assn. Realtors, Memphis Bd. Realtors. Roman Catholic. Home: 3543 Mediterranean 2 Memphis TN 38118 Office: Crye-Leike Realtors 2220 Union Ave Memphis TN 38104

HENDERSON, MARY BIGELOW, health care executive, consultant; b. Barre, Vt., Jan. 29, 1950; d. Arthur Garfield and Dorothy Christine (Bartlett) Bigelow; m. Robert Wayne Henderson, Oct. 7, 1984; children: Douglas Dalby, Jeffrey Bartlett. BS, U. Vt., 1972. Discharge planning coordinator Arlington Hosp., Va., 1975-78; dir. nursing Carriage Hill Nursing Home, Arlington, 1978-79; dir. hosp. rev. No. Va. Found. Med. Care, Falls Church, 1979-80; profl. services dir. M.D.-IPA Health Plan, Rockville, 1980-83; dir. health services, sr. assoc. Jurgovan & Blair, Rockville, 1983-87, mgr., 1987—; cons. Mohawk Valley Health Plan, Schenectady, 1983. Alumni advisor U. Vt., Burlington, 1980—. HMO Mgmt. fellow Group Health Assn. Am., 1983. Mem. Am. Med. Care Rev. Assn., Am. Assn. Quality Assurance Profls. Avocations: racquetball, bike riding, cello, guitar, gardening. Home: 6103 Pembrook St Frederick MD 21701 Office: Jurgovan and Blair Inc 7811 Montrose Rd Potomac MD 20854

HENDERSON, MARY RUTH, agricultural educator, farmer; b. Sweetwater, Tenn., Oct. 25, 1951; d. Bill Hooper and Edna Lee (Largen) H. BS in Home Econs., U. Tenn., 1973, MS in Agr., 1975. Asst. agt. U. Tenn. Agrl. Extension Service, Sequatchie County, Tenn., 1975-77; asst. prof. 4-H, state 4H specialist U. Tenn. Agrl. Extension Service, Knoxville, 1977-86, assoc. prof., 1986—. Editor: The 4-H Leader, 1977—; author 4-H publs., handbooks, visuals and newsletter. Mem. Tenn. 4-H Alumni, Inc., Knoxville Area Home Econs. Assn. (pres.), Nat. Assn. Extension 4-H Agts. (Nat. Disting. Service award 1983), Tenn. Assn. Extension 4-H Agts., Tenn. Assn. Agrl. Agts. and Specialists, Profl. Adminstrs. Vol. Services, Tenn. Livestock Assn., Epsilon Sigma Phi (v.p. 1984-86), Gamma Sigma Delta (pres. Tenn. chpt. 1986-87). Baptist. Club: U. Tenn. Century. Home: Route 1 Box 112 Philadelphia TN 37846 Office: PO Box 1071 209 Morgan Hall Knoxville TN 37901

HENDERSON, MAUREEN MCGRATH, medical educator; b. Tynemouth, Eng., May 11, 1926; came to U.S., 1960; d. Leo E. and Helen (McGrath) H. MB BS, U. Durham, Eng., 1949, DrPH, 1956. Prof. preventive medicine U. Md. Med. Sch., 1968-75, chmn. dept. social and preventive medicine, 1971-75; asso. epidemiology Johns Hopkins U. Sch. Hygiene and Pub. Health, 1970-75; asso. v.p. health scis. 1979-81; prof. epidemiology and medicine U. Wash. Med. Sch., 1975—, head cancer prevention research program Fred Hutchinson Cancer Research Ctr., 1983—; chmn. epidemiology and disease control study sect. NIH, 1969-72; chmn. clin. trials rev. com. Nat. Heart, Lung and Blood Inst., 1975-79; mem. Nat. Cancer Adv. Bd., 1979-84. Assoc. editor jour. Cancer Research, 1987-88; mem. editorial bd. Jour. Nat. Cancer Inst., 1988; contbr. med. publs. Luke-Armstrong scholar epidemiology, 1956-57; John and Mary Markle scholar acad. medicine, 1963-68. Mem. Inst. Medicine (council 1981-85), Assn. Tchrs. Preventive Medicine (pres. 1972-73), Soc. Epidemiol. Research (chmn. 1969-70), Internat. Assn. Epidemiol. (exec. officer 1971-76), Am. Epidemiol. Assn., Royal Soc. Medicine. Home: 5309 NE 85th St Seattle WA 98115 Office: Cancer Prevention Research Program Fred Hutchinson Cancer Research Ctr 1124 Columbia St Seattle WA 98104

HENDERSON, MAXINE OLIVE BOOK (MRS. WILLIAM HENDERSON III), association executive; b. Rush, Colo., Apr. 22, 1924; d. Jesse Frank and Olive (Booth) Book; B.A., U. Colo., 1945; m. William Henderson III, Apr. 10, 1948; children—William IV, Meredith. Personnel adminstr. Gen. Electric Co., Schenectady and N.Y.C., 1945-54; asst. dir. placement Katherine Gibbs Sch., N.Y.C., 1967-70; v.p., dir. William Henderson Cons., Inc., N.Y.C., 1969-83, pres., dir., 1983-86; dir. recruitment Girl Scouts U.S.A., N.Y.C., 1973-78, dir. human resources, 1978-82, dir. career devel., 1982—. Pres., Goddard-Riverside-Trinity Sch. Thrift Shop, N.Y.C., 1964-65, Trinity Sch. Mothers' Orgn., N.Y.C., 1965-66; treas. Brearley Sch. Parents Assn., N.Y.C., 1966-67. Mem. Am. Portuguese Soc., 1983—. Episcopalian. Clubs: North Suffolk Garden, Nissequoque Beach, Nissequogue Platform Tennis Assn. (St. James, L.I., N.Y.). Home: 606 W 116th St New York NY 10027 also: Nissequogue River Rd Saint James NY 11780 Office: 830 3d Ave New York NY 10022

HENDERSON, NANCY GRACE, marketing executive; b. Berkeley, Calif., Oct. 23, 1947; d. John Harry and Lorraine Ruth (Johnson) H. BA, U. Calif., Santa Barbara, 1969; MBA, U. Houston, 1985. Tchr. Keppel Union Sch. Dist., Littlerock, Calif., 1969-72, Internat. Sch. Prague, Czechoslovakia, 1972-74, Sunland Luth. Sch., Freeport, Bahamas, 1974-75; tchr., dept. head Internat. Sch. Assn., Bangkok, Thailand, 1975-79; exec. search Diversified Human Resources Group, Houston, Tex., 1979-82; data processing analyst Am. Gen. Corp., Houston, 1982-83, personnel and benefits dept., 1983-85, investment analyst, 1985-86, equity security analyst/quantitative portfolio analyst, 1986-87; v.p. mktg. and investment systems Vestek Systems Inc., San Francisco, 1987—; tchr. English as Second Language program Houston Metro. Ministries, 1980-81. Named a Notable Woman of Tex., 1984-85. Mem. Fin. Analysts Fedn. Presbyterian. Club: Toastmasters. Office: Vestek Systems 388 Market St Suite 700 San Francisco CA 94111

HENDERSON, NAOMI HAIRSTON, market research company executive; b. Alexandria, La., Jan. 2, 1944; d. Joseph Henry and Anna Lee (Allen) Hairston; B.A. in Elem. Edn., Am. U., 1964, M.Ed. in Spl. Edn., 1968; m. Lucius Samuel Henderson, III, Aug. 8, 1964. Pres. Prism Corp., market research, Washington, 1978-81; dir. market research Goldberg/Marchesano & Assos., Inc., Washington, 1981-82; partner R.J. Sobus & Partners, Washington, 1982-83; pres. Riva Market Research, Washington, 1983—; focus group moderator; cons. in field; lectr. market research. Mem. Market Research Assn., Leadership Forum Washington (vice chmn. 1981-82), Am. Mktg. Assn., Washington Bd. of Trade, Women in Advt. and Mktg. Bus. Owners. Address: 4417 Brandywine St NW Washington DC 20016

HENDERSON, SUZANNE KATHLEEN, small business owner; b. Bridgeport, Conn., June 29, 1943; d. Peter Joseph Jr. and Gertrude Emma (Lockwood) Clowry; m. Paul Melville Henderson, Nov. 23, 1968; 1 child, Jamie Lynn. AA, Cape Cod Community Coll., 1963; BA in Psychology, Russell Sage Coll., 1965; MEd in Elem. Edn., Bridgewater State Coll., 1971; postgrad., Worcester (Mass.) State Coll., 1979-81. Cert. elem. librarian. Tchr. Webutuck Cen. Schs., Amenia, N.Y., 1965-67, Orleans (Mass.) Elem. Sch., 1967-86; pres., owner Bearly in Bus., Brewster, Mass., 1986—; mgr. Cape Cod Melody Tent, Hyannis, 1967-69, Allegro Theatre, Orleans, 1984-85. Mem. Brewster Fin. Com., 1978-9. Mem. DAR, Mass. Tchrs. Assn., NEA, Acad. Performing Arts. Republican. Episcopal. Home and Office: 3811 Main St Brewster MA 02631

HENDERSON-PIERCE, SHIRLEY ANNE, educational consultant; b. Niagara Falls, N.Y., May 23, 1943; d. Hubert J. Jamieson and Luella (Anderson) De Graves; m. Richard A. Pierce; children: Reneé L., John D. Henderson. BA in Acctg., Southeastern U., 1966; AA in Mgmt., Coll. DuPage, 1984; postgrad., Ill. Benedictine Coll., 1986—. Technician FBI, Washington, 1963-64; mgr. data processing AT&T Long Lines, Washington, 1964-66; system analyst IBM, Washington, 1966-68; adult edn. instr. Lewiston-Porter High Sch., Youngstown, N.Y., 1974; owner Antique Restoration, Youngstown, 1975-78; mgr. Midwest region Comptek Research, Chgo., 1978-80; ednl. designer Multigraphics, Mt. Prospect, Ill., 1980-81, mgr. service publs., 1981-86, mgr. graphic services, 1986—. Mem. Internat. Plant Mgmt. Assn., Nat. Soc. Performance and Instrn., Soc. Tech. Communication. Episcopalian. Home: 6329 New Albany Rd Lisle IL 60532

HENDREN, MERLYN CHURCHILL, furniture company executive; b. Gooding, Idaho, Oct. 16, 1926; d. Herbert Winston and Annie Averett Churchill; student U. Idaho, 1944-47; B.A., Coll. of Idaho, 1986. m. Robert Lee Hendren, June 14, 1947; children—Robert Lee, Anne Aleen. With Hendren's Furniture Co., Boise, 1947-69; co-owner, v.p. Hendren's Inc., Boise, 1969-87, pres. 1987—. Bd. dirs. Idaho Law Found., 1978-84; chmn. Coll. of Idaho Symposium, 1977-78, mem. adv. bd., 1981—; bd. dirs. SW Idaho Pvt. Industry Council, 1984-87; pres. Boise Council on Aging, 1959-60, mem. adv. bd., 1986—; mem. Gov.'s Commn. on Aging, 1960, Idaho del. to White House Conf. Aging, 1961; trustee St. Luke's Regional Hosp., 1981—; mem. adv. bd. dirs. Boise Philharm. Assn., Inc., 1981—; bd. dirs. Children's Home Soc. Idaho, 1988. Mem. Boise C. of C. (bd. dirs. 1984-87). Republican. Episcopalian. Home: 3504 Hillcrest Dr Boise ID 83705 Office: 516 S 9th St Boise ID 83706

HENDRICKS, MARTY WHITELAW, food company executive; b. Pine Bluff, Ark., Nov. 29, 1951; d. Ernest Lyndon and Whitney (Halliday) Whitelaw; m. Gary Kim Hendricks, Mar. 8, 1975; children: Kristin Erin, Jonathan Blake. BS in Speech and English, So. Ark. U., 1974. Adminstrv. asst. dept. fin. and adminstrn. State of Ark., Little Rock, 1974-76; mktg. rep. IBM, Little Rock, 1976-80; mktg. mgr. foodservice div. Oscar Meyer Co., Nashville, 1980—; instr. Rhymic Aerobics, Little Rock, 1982. Bd. dirs. Maumelle (Ark.) Child Devel. Ctr., 1982; vol. Girl Scouts U.S., Maumelle, 1988. Mem. Ark. Profl. Foodservice Assn., Ark. Hospitality Assn., Nat. Assn. Female Execs. Republican. Methodist. Home: 20 Hogan Loop Maumelle AR 72118 Office: Oscar Mayer Foodservice 201 Cartwright Goodlettsville TN 37072

HENDRICKSON, LORRAINE UHLANER, business management educator, consultant; b. Washington, July 28, 1953; d. Julius Earl and Vera (Kolar) Uhlaner; m. Jack Reynold Hendrickson, Jr., Dec. 29, 1978; children: Eric Benjamin, Susan Abigail. A.B., Radcliffe Coll., 1973; Doctorandus, U. Leiden (Netherlands), 1976; M.A., U. Mich., 1976, Ph.D., 1980. Research asst. U. Leiden, 1973-74; asst. study dir. Inst. for Social Research, Ann Arbor, Mich., 1974-78; instr., asst. prof. Mich. State U., East Lansing, 1979-81; asst. prof. dept. mgmt. Coll. Bus., Eastern Mich. U., Ypsilanti, 1981-86, assoc. prof., 1986—, founding dir. Ctr. for Entrepreneurship, 1986 (dir. program devel. and research, 1987-88), Coll. Bus. Service Ctr., 1986; cons. StarPak Solar Systems Corp., Novi, Mich., 1981-85, dir., treas., 1976-85; cons. Livingston County Sheriff's Dept., Howell, Mich., 1981; cons. personnel mgmt. and orgnl. devel., Domino's Pizza Distbn., Inc., Ann Arbor, Mich., 1986—; del. White House Conf. on Small Bus., 1986; mem. adv. bd. Ann Arbor Innovation Ctr., 1986-87; mem. bd. dirs. New Enterprise Forum, Ann Arbor, 1986—. Contbr. book revs. to Personnel Psychology, 1983, 84, papers to profl. confs. Sec., co-chmn. Mich. Alliance Small Bus., Lansing, 1981-83; mem. innovation and tech. task force Gov.'s Conf. on Small Bus., 1981; candidate state Democratic primary, 1982. Council for European Studies pre-dissertation fellow, U. Pitts., 1975. Mem. Acad. Mgmt., Am. Mgmt. Assn., Mich. Assn. Indsl. and Organizational Psychologists, Ypsilanti C. of C. (small bus. council 1986—). Home: 5757 Pontiac Trail Ann Arbor MI 48105 Office: Ea Mich U Coll Bus Dept Mgmt Ypsilanti MI 48197

HENDRIE, ELAINE, public relations executive; b. Bklyn., d. David and Pearl (Saltzhauer) Kostell; m. Joseph Mallam Hendrie, July 9, 1949; children: Susan, Barbara. Asst. account exec. Benjamin Sonnenberg Public Relations firm, N.Y.C., 1953-57; pub. relations cons., writer, editor, 1957-72; dir. pub. relations and media Religious Heritage of Am., Washington, 1973-75; producer, interviewer Woman to Woman radio program, sta. WRIV and stas. WALK-AM and -FM, L.I., N.J., Westchester County, N.Y., Conn., 1974-77; exec. dir. Women in New Directions, Inc., Suffolk County, N.Y., 1974-77, cons. 1978—; nat. media coordinator NOW, Washington, 1978; media dir. Am. Speech-Lang.-Hearing Assn., Washington, 1979-80; pub. info. officer, head media and mktg. Dept. Navy, Washington, 1980-81; pres. Triangle Enterprises, 1982, Hendrie & Pendzick, 1982—; resource person for media Nat. Commn. on Observance of Internat. Women's Yr., 1977—; cons. Multi-Media Prodns. Inc., N.Y.C., 1978—, Women in New Directions, Inc., 1981—. Mem. adv. bd. Women's Ctr., SUNY-Farmingdale; mem. exec. bd. Energy Edn. Exponents, 1983—; chmn. Bellport (N.Y.) Bd. Archtl. Review, 1986—; mem. exec. bd. L.I. chpt. Am. Nuclear Soc. Club: Bellport Bay Yacht. Home: 50 Bellport Ln Bellport NY 11713

HENDRIX, KATHRYN ANN, trade association administrator; b. Olean, N.Y., July 6, 1934; d. George Tobias Whipp and Kathryn Elizabeth (Greene) H.; B.S., Carnegie Mellon U., 1955. Cert. assn. exec. Sec., NASA, 1955-57; with Forging Industry Assn., Cleve., 1957—, corp. sec., 1977—, asst. v.p., 1980—. Mem. Greater Cleve. Soc. Assn. Execs. (dir., sec.-treas., v.p., pres.), Cleve. Area Meeting Planners, Club: Women's City of Cleve. (bd. dirs. 1987-90). Lodge: Altrusa (bd. dirs., v.p.). Home: 4400 Clarkwood Pky #615 Warrensville Heights OH 44128 Office: Forging Industry Assn 25 Prospect Ave Suite 300 LTV Bldg Cleveland OH 44115

HENDRIX, SUSAN CLELIA DERRICK, civic worker; b. McClellanville, S.C., Jan. 19, 1920; d. Theodore Elbridge and Susan Regina (Bauknight) Derrick; m. Henry Gardner Hendrix, June 5, 1943; children—Susan Hendrix Redmond, Marilyn Hendrix Shedlock. B.A., Columbia Coll., 1941; M.A., Furman U., 1961; Ed.D. (hon.) Columbia Coll., 1985. Cert. tchr., S.C. Tchr. Whitmire Pub. Schs., 1941-43, Greenville Pub. Schs., S.C., 1944-46, 58-63, dir. Reading clinic, 1965-68; counselor Greenville Pub. Schs., 1963-65; supr. Greenville County Sch. Dist., S.C., 1965-68, dir. pub. relations, 1968-83; grad. instr. Furman U., 1967-69; cons. Nat. Seminar on Desegregation, 1973.

Author: (with James P. Mahaffey) Teaching Secondary Reading, 1966; Communicating With the Community, 1979; editor: Communique, 1968-83. Contbr. articles to profl. jours. and mags. Chmn. bd. trustees Columbia Coll., 1969-70; chmn. Greenville County Rehab. Bd., S.C., 1974-76; vice chmn. bd. Jr. Achievement, Greenville, 1978-79; chmn. S.C. Commn. on Women, Columbia, 1982—; pres. United Methodist Women, Buncombe St. Ch., Greenville, 1956-57; mem. adminstrv. bd. Buncombe St. Ch., 1968—, bd. trustees, 1980—; mem. United Meth. Ch. Southeastern Jurisdictional Council on Ministries, 1984—; chmn. S.C. Conf. Council on Ministries United Meth. Ch., 1980—; mem. Bd. Global Ministries United Meth. Ch., 1972-80, mem. Commn. Study of Ministry, 1984—. Recipient Medallion Columbia Coll., 1980; Alumnae Disting. Service award Columbia Coll., 1983; Disting. Achievement award Women's History Week, Greenville, 1984. Mem. S.C. PTA (life), Alpha Delta Kappa (pres. 1970-72), Columbia Coll. Alumnae Assn., Democratic Women, S.C. Women in Govt. Home: 309 Arundel Rd Greenville SC 29615 Office: SC Commn on Women 2221 Devine St Columbia SC 29205

HENDRY, LEIGH R., public relations executive; b. Stuttgart, Fed. Republic Germany, Mar. 23, 1956; d. Earl Ronald and Marjorie Ann (Nelson) H. BS in Communications magna cum laude, U. Tenn., 1979. Dir. communications 1982 World's Fair, Knoxville, 1979-83; cons. pub. relations/mktg. Events Internat., Knoxville, 1983-86; dir. pub. relations Knoxville Mus. Art, 1986—; cons. pub. relations Greater Knoxville Arts Council, 1983-86. Author, editor: Photo Finish: The 1982 World's Fair, 1983. Mem. mktg./pub. relations com. Main St. Knoxville, 1987-88; mem. Fair Site Devel. Com., Knoxville, 1988; chmn. pub. relations Multiple Sclerosis Gala Weekend, 1987, Mayor's Auction for Arts, 1986-87; chmn. Knoxville-Knox Co. Homecoming '86 Reunion Breakfast, 1986; bd. dirs. Knox Ct. Humane Soc., 1984-86. Recipient Mark of Excellence award Soc Profl. Journalists, Sigma Delta Chi, 1978, others. Mem. Pub. Relations Soc. Am., Phi Kappa Phi, Kappa Tau Alpha, Sigma Delta Chi. Republican. Presbyterian. Office: Knoxville Mus of Art 1010 Laurel Ave Knoxville TN 37916

HENES, DONNA, celebration artist, ritual maker; b. Cleve., Sept. 19, 1945; d. Nathan and Adelaide (Ross) Trugman. BS, CCNY, 1971, MS in Art Edn., 1972; student Ohio State U., 1963-66. Producer series pub. participatory celebratory events in parks, museums and univs., 50 cities in 9 countries, 1970—; designer Olympic Medalist Tickertape Parade, N.Y.C., 1984; creative cons. Harbor Festival, N.Y.C., 1985; ednl. cons. New Wilderness Foundation, N.Y.C., 1985, ritual cons. Cathedral St. John The Divine, N.Y.C., 1988; judge Jane Addams Peace Assn. Children's Book Award, N.Y.C., 1983—. Author, designer: Dressing Our Wounds in Warm Clothes, 1982, Noting the Process of Noting the Process, 1977, Ms. Liberty Fashions, 1985; contbr. numerous articles to profl. jours; editor Celebration News. Cofounder and pres., STAND (Stand Together Affirmative Neighborhood Devel.), N.Y.C.; composer Chants for Peace/Chance for Peace, Sta. WNYC, first peace message in space, 1982. Nat. Endowment for the Arts fellow, 1982, interarts, 1983, N.Y. Found. for Arts, 1986; grantee N.Y. State Council on the Arts, N.Y.C. State Bicentennial Commn., Com. for Visual Arts, Money for Women, Beard's Fund, Jerome Found., Ctr. for the Media Arts. Mem. Ctr. for Celebration (bd. dirs., co-founder). Avocations: dancing, traveling.

HENG, SIANG GEK, communications executive; b. Singapore, Singapore, Dec. 4, 1960; came to U.S., 1984; BSEE with honors, Nat. U. Singapore, 1983; MSEE in Computer Engring., U. So. Calif., 1985. Research engr. Nat. Univ. Singapore, 1983-84; systems mgr. LinCom Corp., Los Angeles, 1985-87; fin. planner N.Y. Life Ins. Co., Los Angeles, 1987-88; systems engr. AT&T Communications, N.J., 1988—; lectr. Singapore Poly., 1983-84; freelance computer/communications cons., N.J./Los Angeles, 1987—. Contbr. articles to profl. jours. Mem. IEEE, Nat. Assn. Female Execs. Office: AT&T Room 1C-310 307 Middletown-Lincroft Rd Lincroft NJ 07738

HENKE, ANA MARI, education educator; b. Albuquerque, Apr. 21, 1954; d. David Ernest and Mary Anne (Gallegos) Sanchez; m. Michael John Henke, Aug. 14, 1976; children: Kristin Mari, Michelle Lee. BA in Spl. Edn., U. N.Mex., 1976, MA in Spl. Edn., 1983. Cert. elem. and secondary spl. edn. tchr., N.Mex.; cert. elem. and secondary phys. edn. tchr., N.Mex.; cert. elem. and secondary behavior disorder tchr., N.Mex. Tchr., supr. Perceptual Motor Learning Sch. U. N.Mex., Albuquerque, 1976, 82, tchr. phys. edn., 1980-82; tchr. phys. edn. Nat. Youth Sports Program, Albuquerque and San Diego, 1976-82; tchr. multihandicapped Chula Vista (Calif.) Pub. Schs., 1976-77; tchr. adaptive phys. edn. San Diego City Schs., 1977-78; lab asst. Presbyn. Hosp., Albuquerque, 1979-80; tchr. Hermosa Jr. High Sch., Farmington, N.Mex., 1983-85, Heights Jr. High Sch., Farmington, 1985—; in-service exercise therapist Four Corners Regional Ednl. Conf., Farmington, 1985-86; supr. parents workshop Intervention/awareness for Subtance Abuse, Heights Jr. High Sch., 1985-86; instr. workshop Farmington Schs., 1986. Mem. Phi Delta Kappa (sec. 1987—, v.p. 1988—). Republican. Roman Catholic. Home: 4406 N Dustin Ave Farmington NM 87401

HENKEL, ELOISE ELIZABETH, writer, information specialist, educator; b. Chgo., Apr. 23, 1923; d. Milford Franklin and Eloise Elizabeth (Lewis) H. B.S. in Journalism, Northwestern U., Evanston, Ill., 1944; M.A. in English, U. Chgo., 1964. Reporter, Battle Creek Enquirer-News (Mich.), 1944-45; pub. relations writer Office of Mil. Govt. U.S., Berlin, 1946-47; reporter, rewriter UP, Chgo. and Omaha, 1948; corr. Women's News Service, Paris, 1949; pub. relations officer Internat. Refugee Orgn., Bremen, W.Ger., 1950-51; fgn. corr. Worldwide Press Service, Europe, North Africa, Near East., 1952-54; test constructor Navy Project U. Chgo., 1955; freelance writer, India, Afghanistan, 1956-58, Tibet, China, 1983—; tchr. English Chgo. Bd. Edn., 1959-66, 72-75, 84-88; freelance corr., Vietnam, 1967-69; reporter Hammond Times (Ind.), 1971-72; media specialist U. Chgo., 1976-79, Ill. Inst. Tech., Chgo., 1980; developer Rainbow Condominium Assn., Chgo., 1981-82. Author: (with Dick Jones) How to Save Money in Paris, 1950. Recipient Best Feature Story award Ind. AP Mng. Editors, 1971, Best News Story award UPI Mng. Editors (Ind.), 1971, Stick-O-Type award for best feature story Chgo. Newspaper Guild, 1972. Mem. YWCA, YMCA; U.S. China Peoples Friendship Assn. Quaker. Club: Overseas Press. Home: 1454 W Hollywood Chicago IL 60660

HENKIND, JANICE VERONICA, medical journal editor; b. N.Y.C., Feb. 3, 1951; d. William I. and Veronica A. Benjamin; BA, Mercy Coll., 1972; MS, U. Bridgeport, 1977; m. Paul Henkind, May 22, 1977 (dec. 1986); 1 child, Aaron Samuel; m. David L. Joslow, May 6, 1988. Electron microscopist Boyce Thompson Inst. for Plant Research, 1972-74, dept. ophthalmology Montefiore Hosp. and Med. Ctr., 1974-76; exec. adminstr. Assn. for Research in Vision and Ophthalmology, New Rochelle, N.Y., 1977-87, mng. editor Ophthalmology, Jour. Am. Acad. Ophthalmology, 1979-87, also XXIV Internat. Congress Opthalmology; pres. Med. Dialogues, Inc.; corporator Inn at Amherst Corp. Trustee Old Sturbridge Village, Mass., 1988—, mem. fin. com., 1987-88, mem. long range planning com. 1988—, bd. overseers, 1984-87; mem. corp. N.Y. Bot. Garden, 1984—. Winner Martha Stone award in floriculture, 1983, 84. Mem. Assn. Women in Sci., Nat. Assn. Female Execs. Am., Assn. for Research in Vision and Ophthalmology (hon.). Author: (with Keith Zinn) chpt. The Retinal Pigment Epithelium, 1979, Biomedical Foundations of Ophthalmology; contbr. articles to profl. jours. Address: 276 Overlook Rd New Rochelle NY 10804

HENKLE, TERESA, writer; b. Baker, Oreg., Mar. 13, 1955; d. Ray and Ida Mae (Hall) Winn; children—Katy Lynn, Maxwell James. Student U. Oreg., 1973-75. Writer, co-founder Writers Assocs., Eugene, Oreg., 1975-77; writer KASH-KSND, Eugene, 1976-78; writer, creative dir. Brockett Real Estate, Eugene, 1978-82; creative dir. Sta. KVMT, Vail, Colo., 1982—; writer Colle McVoy Advt., Denver, 1984-87; sr. writer Ireland Communications, Denver, 1985-87; writer Moses Anshell Advt., Phoenix, 1987—; writer, cons. to local companies. Author: Inside A Storm, 1981. Contbr. articles and poetry to various pubs. Formerly active PTA, also Gifted Children Orgn., Eugene; pub. relations, advt. chmn. Jim Hale for County Commr., Eugene, 1982; hon. mem. Friends of the Library; mem. Pub. Service Com. Mem. Denver Advt. Fedn. Avocations: aerobics instruction, hiking, running, reading. Home: 11026 N 28th Dr #24 Phoenix AZ 85029

HENLEY, ANDREA LEVINSON, publisher, business executive; b. Pitts., Dec. 21, 1953; d. James Charles and Marilyn (Gasche) Levinson; m. Davis Clemens Henley, July 4, 1983. B.S., U.Cin., 1976; postgrad. U. Toledo, 1977-78; M.S., Bowling Green State U., 1979. Geologist, pres. Ranwell, Inc., Houston, 1980-86; v.p. Airways Travel, Houston, 1983-85, Jerusalem Touring Express, Inc., Houston, 1983-85; mgr. Am. Med. Exporters, Inc., Houston, 1983-85; sales mgr. Hamilton-Hall Inc., Houston, 1986-87; owner, pub. The Restaurant Reference Book, 1987—. Mem. Tex. Restaurant Assn., Houston Hotel & Motel Assn. Republican. Jewish.

HENLEY, BETH, playwright, actress; b. Jackson, Miss., May 8, 1952; d. Charles and Lydy H. B.F.A., So. Meth. U., 1974; postgrad. U. Ill., 1975-76. Performed with Dallas Minority Repertory Theater, pageant Gt. American People Show, New Salem State Park, Ill., 1976; author plays: Crimes of the Heart (Broadway), 1981, The Wake of Jamey Foster (Broadway), 1982, Am I Blue, 1982, The Miss Firecracker Contest (off Broadway), 1984, The Debutante Ball (world premiere South Coast Repertory Theatre), 1985; coscreenwriter: True Stories, 1986; screenwriter: Nobody's Fool, 1986, Crimes of the Heart, 1986. Recipient awards for Crimes of the Heart including Pulitzer prize for drama, 1981, N.Y. Drama Critics Circle Best Play award, 1981, George Oppenheimer/Newsday Playwriting award, 1980-81. Address: care Gilbert Parker William Morrris Agy 1350 Ave of the Americas New York NY 10019 *

HENLEY, SALLIE HAMLET, artist, deaf interpreter; b. Norfolk, Va., Sept. 29, 1933; d. Charles McDowell and Sarah Speight (White) Hamlet; student pub. schs., Norfolk; m. William Franklin Henley, Jr., July 21, 1951; children—William Franklin III, Robert Matthew. Pub. speaker, Milw., 1968-71, Houston, 1971—; book dramatist, Milw., 1969-71, Houston, 1971-72; interpreter for deaf, Milw., 1969-71, Houston, 1971—; free-lance artist, Atlanta, 1963-65, Houston, 1975—; exhibited Sportsmans Gallery, Hanson Gallery, Town and Country Ctr., Houston, 1984, The Galleria, Houston. Interpreter to deaf Elmbrook Ch., Brookfield, Wis., 1969-70; vol. tchr. deaf retardate Fairview North Elem. Sch., Brookfield, 1970; narrator, interpreter Deaf Olympics, 1969; sec. Quail Valley Civic Assn., 1974-75; bd. dirs. Ephphatha, Inc., Milw., 1969-70. Mem. Registry Interpreters for Deaf, DAR, Nat. Soc. Magna Charta Dames. Republican. Home and Office: 532 Waterwheel Rd Chesapeake VA 23320

HENLEY, SANDRA S., economist; b. Marion, Ill., Mar. 2, 1945; d. James Robert and Wilma S. (Johnson) Smithson; m. Robert C. Henley, May 5, 1965; children—Marjorie, Joseph. B.S., So. Ill. U., 1966, M.S., 1968; Ph.D. in Econs., U. Ind., 1970. Mem. faculty dept. econs. Governors State U., Park Forest, Ill., 1970-77; mem. exec. staff Indpls. Econ. Council, 1977—; cons. and lectr. in econs. and politics. Author: The Economic Development of Indiana, 1984; contbr. articles to profl. jours. Active, Girl Scouts Council, Indpls. Mem. Nat. Assn. Female Execs., Am. Econs. Assn., Ind. Assn. Social Scientists. Address: 635 E 6th St Seymour IN 47274

HENNEBURY, MARION EDITH, educational administrator; b. Quincy, Mass., Jan. 27, 1937; d. John Henry and Edith Elizabeth (Danahy) Hennebury. B.S., Boston U., 1959; M.Ed., Fla. Atlantic U., 1969; Ed.D., U. So. Calif., 1978. Tchr., Barton Elem. Sch., Lake Worth, Fla., 1963-66, curriculum asst., 1966-69, dir. Head Start, summer 1968; asst. prin. Palm Beach Pub. Sch., Fla., 1969-78, prin., 1978-83; prin. Palm Springs Elem. Sch., Lake Worth, 1983-87, Boynton Beach Elem., 1988—; curriculum writer Palm Beach County Sch. Bd., summers 1965-67, 71-74. Contbr. articles to profl. jours. Boston U. Dean of Women's scholar, 1955-59, Trustee scholar, 1957-59, News Bur. scholar, 1955-59. Mem. Nat. Assn. Elem. Sch. Prins., Palm Beach County Prins. Assn., Assn. for Supervision and Curriculum Devel., Nat. Assn. Sch. Adminstrs., Nat. Assn. Female Execs., Fla. Assn. Sch. Execs., Palm Beach County Jr. High Prins. Assn. (sec. 1978-79), Smithsonian Instn., Nat. Trust for Historic Preservation, Fla. Consumers Fedn., Fla. Sheriffs Assn., Nature Conservancy, Internat. Platform Assn., Media (chpt. pres. 1959), Nat. Mus. Women in the Arts (charter), Internat. Planetary Soc., Boston U. Alumni Assn., U. So. Calif. Alumni Assn., Alpha Delta Kappa (nat. corr. sec. 1971, pres. 1973), Phi Delta Kappa. Avocations: bicycling; hiking; reading; writing; knitting. Home: 3145 Collin Dr West Palm Beach FL 33406 Office: Boynton Beach Elem Ocean Ave Boynton Beach FL 33435

HENNECKE, LYNNE, psychologist; b. Detroit, May 10, 1935; d. James Francis and Marian Angela (Spindler) H.; m. William C. Johnson, Nov. 26, 1957 (div. 1962); 1 child, Jamie Johnson. BA, Columbia U., 1978, MA, 1981, PhD, 1982. Lic. psychologist, N.Y. V.p. Mayday Prodns., N.Y.C., 1964-74; research coordinator Mount Sinai Hosp., N.Y.C., 1974-80; pvt. practice psychology N.Y.C., 1982—; adj. prof. psychology Union of Experimenting Coll.s and Univs., Cin., 1984—; bd. dirs. N.Y. State Bd. for Porfl. Med. Conduct, N.Y.C.; lectr. in field. Contbr. articles to profl. jours. Cochair Women in Crisis, 1979-81. Mem. Am. Psychol. Assn., The N.Y. Fedn. Alcoholism Counselors. Office: 1031 Fifth Ave New York NY 10028

HENNECY, BOBBIE BOBO, English language educator; b. Tignall, Ga., Aug. 11, 1922; d. John Ebb and Lois Helen (Gulledge) Bobo; AB summa cum laude, Mercer U., Macon, Ga., 1950; postgrad. Oxford (Eng.) U., 1961 English-Speaking Union Scholar; MA (NDEA fellow), Emory U., 1962; postgrad. Cambridge U., Eng., 1987; m. James Howell Hennecy, Dec. 28, 1963; 1 dau., Erin. Adminstrv. asst. to pres., instr. Mercer U., 1950-61, instr. English, 1961-76, asst. prof., 1976—; a founder Tattnall Sq. Acad., Macon, 1968, sec. acad. corp., 1968-73, dir., 1968-78; Bobbie Bobo Hennecy scholarship named in her hon. Tattnall Sq. Acad., Mercer U. . Mem. AAUW (chpt. pres. 1961), MLA, S. Atlantic MLA, So. Comparative Lit. Assn., Am. Comparative Lit. Assn., Internat. Comparative Lit. Assn., Nat. Assn. Tchrs. English, Ga. Assn. Tchrs. English, English Speaking Union, LWV, Pres. Club of Mercer U., YWCA (life), Nat. Soc. So. Dames, Nat. Soc. Magna Charta, DAR (registrar 1980-82), Daus. of 1812, Descendants, Colonial Clergy, Daus. of Am. Colonists, Jamestowne Soc., UDC, Colonial Dames XVII Century (chpt. 1st v.p. 1988-90), Colonial Order of the Crown (descendents of Charlemagne), Mid. Ga. Hist. Soc., Cardinal Key, Sigma Tau Delta, Sigma Mu (past pres.), Phi Kappa Phi, Alpha Psi Omega, Chi Omega (alumnae adviser). Baptist. Home: 1347-B Adams St Macon GA 31201 Office: Mercer Univ Macon GA 31207

HENNEKENS, CANDACE ANNE, personnel director; b. Chippewa Falls, Wis., Jan. 19, 1948; d. Theodore John and Elaine Ella (Deuel) H.; divorced; children: Annette Schutz, Jennifer Louviere. BS in Journalism, Northwestern U., 1969; MS in Mgmt. Sci., Cardinal-Stritch Coll., 1988. Pub. relations asst. Computer Technology, Skokie, 1969-70; editor newsletter midwestern territory Sears & Roebuck, Skokie, 1970-72; salesperson Nolan Realty, Las Vegas, 1975-76; editor newsletter Cray Research, Chippewa Falls, Wis., 1979-81, human resources adminstr., 1982-84, mgr. human resources, 1984-86, human resources mgr. II, 1986—. Mem. adv. Displaced Homemakers Project Dist. 1 Tech. Inst., Eau Claire, 1984—, bd. bus. ext. U. Wis., Eau Claire, 1987—; mem. adv. bd. Chippewa Falls Salvation Army, 1987—. Mem. Am. Soc. of Tng. and Devel., Am. Soc. Personnel Adminstrn., Assn. for Psychol. Type, Chippewa Valley Personnel Assn. Office: Cray Research 1168 Industrial Blvd Chippewa Falls WI 54729

HENNESSEE, E. LEE, securities trader, financial consultant; b. Raleigh, N.C., Sept. 1, 1953; d. William Edward Hennessee and Mary F. Dillon. BA, Randolph Macon Coll., 1975. V.p. Thomson McKinnon Securities, N.Y.C., 1976-78, E.F. Hutton & Co., Inc., N.Y.C., 1978—, Shearson-Lehman, N.Y.C., 1978—; personal and corp. investor E.F. Hutton & Co., Inc., 1987—; advisor to bd. trustees Randolph Macon W.C., 1981-85. Contbr. articles to profl. jours. Founder Campership Funds Ann. Charity Girl Scouts of Greater N.Y. Mem. Jr. League of N.Y.C., N.Y.C. Women's Fellowship. Home: 12 E 86th St New York NY 10019 Office: 650 5th Avenue New York NY 10019

HENNESSEY, ALICE ELIZABETH, forest products company executive; b. Havenhill, Mass., May 24, 1936; d. H. Nelson and Elizabeth E. (Johnson) Pingree; A.B. with honors, U. Colo., 1957; cert. with distinction Harvard-Radcliffe Program in Bus. Adminstrn., 1958; m. Thomas M. Hennessey, June 13, 1959; children—Shannon, Sheila, Thomas N. With Boise Cascade Corp. (Idaho), 1958—, sec. to pres., 1958-60, adminstrv. asst. to pres., 1960-61, 65-71, corp. sec., 1971—, v.p., 1974-82, sr. v.p., 1982—. Dir. First Interstate Bank of Idaho. Bd. dirs. Boise Pub. Library Found.; sustaining mem. Boise Jr. League. Mem. Am. Soc. of Corp. Secs., Nat. Investor Relations Inst., Pub. Relations Soc. of Am., Phi Beta Kappa, Alpha Chi Omega. Office: Boise Cascade Corp One Jefferson Sq Boise ID 83728

HENNIGE, MARIANNE AMALIE, accountant; b. Stuttgart, Germany, Apr. 18, 1926; came to U.S., 1952, naturalized, 1956; d. Eugen Albert and Julie Pauline (Groezinger) H.; B.B.A. magna cum laude, Northwood Inst., Midland, Mich., 1981; children—Shirley I., Sharon C. Office mgr. Dept. Army, Europe, 1946-52; supr. acctg. dept. Mich. Farm Bur. Ins., 1953-58; sec. to prin. Peck (Mich.) Community Schs., 1958-61; asst. treas., mgr. acctg. dept. Proctor Homer Warren, Inc., 1961-77; chief acct., mgr. data processing dept. Mich. Products., Inc., distbrs. ednl. materials, Lansing, 1977-84; supr. cashier's office Clark County Community Coll., North Las Vegas, Nev., 1984-85, bursar, 1985—, fin. budget analyst, 1986—; officer, dir. Sanilac County Bd. Edn. Credit Union, Sandusky, Mich. Mem. Peck Library Bd.; chmn. com. for fgn. student exchange Greater Detroit Area YMCA. Mem. Nat. Assn. Female Execs., Am. Mgmt. Assn., Lansing Accts. Assn., AAUW (treas. Las Vegas br.), Phi Theta Kappa, Beta Sigma Phi (life; chpt. pres. 1962, 64, 69-70). Office: 3200 E Cheyenne Ave North Las Vegas NV 89030

HENNING, EMILIE ANNE, college dean, nursing educator; b. Scotrun, Pa., Dec. 4, 1930; d. Lester Dimmick and Ada (Warner) Detrick. Diploma Methodist Hosp., N.Y.C., 1951; B.S. in Nursng, Seton Hall U., 1962; M.Ed. in Nursing Edn., Columbia U., 1965, Ed.D. in Nursing Edn., 1974. Cons. Newark Maternal/Infant Care Project, 1965-66; from instr. to asst. prof. Rutgers U., Newark, 1966-71, chmn., assoc. prof., 1973-76; dean and prof. Fla. State U., Tallahassee, 1976-82, East Carolina U., Greenville, N.C., 1982—; curriculum and accreditation cons. univ. schs. of nursing, 1971—. Contbr. chpt. to book, articles to profl. jours. Chmn. Capitol Adv. Council, Fla. Panhandle Health Systems Agy., 1981-82; active in polit. campaigns. Recipient honor cords Sigma Theta Tau, 1985. Mem. N.C. Nurses Assn. (chmn. forum 1983-87, edn. com. 1983-87), Nat. League for Nursing (bd. rev. 1980-86), N.C. Deans and Dirs. (sec.-treas. 1983-85), N.J. State Nurses Assn. (bd. dirs. 1975-76), Nat. Assn. Women Deans, Adminstrs. and Counselors, N.C. Assn. Women Deans, Adminstrs. and Counselors. Avocation: travel. Home: 76 Quail Ridge Rd Greenville NC 27834 Office: East Carolina U Sch Nursing Greenville NC 27858-4353

HENNING, RONDA REGINA, computer security analyst, writer; b. Pitts., Oct. 9, 1957; d. Ronald Roy and Julia Ann (Butch) H.; m. Steven Eric Rose, Oct. 2, 1982. BA magna cum laude, U. Pitts., 1978, MS, Johns Hopkins U., 1986. Info. ctr. mgr. Dept. Def., Ft. Meade, Md., 1979-82; mgr. user software applications Nat. Computer Security Ctr., Ft. Meade, 1982-86, dep. chief database security research, 1986-87; staff engr. computer security Harris Corp., Melbourne, Fla., 1987—. Sec. Waning Moon Community Assn., Columbia, Md., 1985-87; troop leader Girl Scouts Am. of Southwestern Pa., Pitts., 1975-79; mem. Friends Nat. Zoo, Washington, NAT. Geog. Soc., Washington. Mem. IEEE (tech. com. 1987—), Honeywell Large System User's Assn., Phi Eta Sigma. Democrat. Roman Catholic. Office: Harris Corp/Govt Info Systems Div Computing Tech Ctr PO Box 98000 Melbourne FL 32902

HENNINGS, DOROTHY GRANT (MRS. GEORGE HENNINGS), educator; b. Paterson, N.J., Mar. 15, 1935; d. William Albert and Ethel Barbara (Moll) Grant; A.B., Barnard Coll., 1956; M.Ed. (NSF Acad. Yr. Inst. grantee), U. Va., 1959; Ed.D. (Field Enterprise grantee), Columbia, 1965; m. George Hennings, June 15, 1968. Tchr., Pierrepont Elementary Sch., Rutherford, N.J., 1956-58, Thomas Jefferson Jr. High Sch., Fair Lawn, N.J., 1959-64; prof. edn. Kean Coll. of N.J., Union, 1965—. Recipient Edn. Press. award, 1974; Author citation N.J. Inst. Tech., Div. Continuing Edn., 1982. Mem. Nat. Council Tchrs. English, N.J. Reading Assn., Internat. Reading Assn., Suburban Reading Council, Phi Beta Kappa, Phi Delta Kappa, Phi Kappa Phi, Kappa Delta Pi. Author: (with B. Grant) Teacher Moves, 1971; Content and Craft: Written Expression in the Elementary Sch., 1973; Smiles, Nods and Pauses: Activities to Enrich Children's Communication Skills, 1974; Mastering Classroom Communication: What Interaction Analysis Tells the Teacher, 1975; (with G. Hennings) Keep Earth Clean, Blue and Green: Environmental Activities for Young People, 1976; Words, Sounds, and Thoughts: More Activities to Enrich Children's Communication Skills, 1977; Communication in Action: Teaching the Language Arts, 1978, 3d edit., 1986; (with D. Russell) Listening Aids Through the Grades, 1979; (with G. Hennings) Today's Elementary Social Studies, 1980; Written Expression in the Language Arts, 1981; Teaching Communication and Reading Skills in the Content Areas, 1982; (with L. Fay) Star Show, 1986, Grand Tour, 1986, Previews, 1986; contbr. articles to Edn., The Record, Lang. Arts, Sci. Tchr., The Reading Tchr., Tchr. to Tchrs., Sci. and Children, Early Years, others. Home: 21 Flintlock Dr Warren NJ 07060 Office: Kean Coll of NJ Morris Ave Union NJ 07083

HENNION, CAROLYN LAIRD (LYN), mutual fund executive, financial planner; b. Orange, Calif., July 27, 1943; d. George James and Jane (Porter) Laird; m. Reeve L. Hennion, Sept. 12, 1964; children—Jeffrey Reeve, Douglas Laird. B.A., Stanford U., 1965. Cert. fin. planner, lic. ins. agt. Portfolio analyst Schwabacher & Co., San Francisco, 1964-66; adminstrv. coordinator Bicentennial Commn., San Mateo County Calif., 1972-73; dir. devel. Crystal Springs Uplands Sch., Hillsborough, Calif., 1973-84; tax preparer Household Fin. Corp., Foster City, Calif., 1982, freelance, 1983-87; sales promotion mgr. Franklin Distbrs., Inc., San Mateo, 1984-86, regional sales mgr., 1986—, v.p., 1988—; v.p. Viatech, Inc., 1986—. Editor: Lest We Forget, 1975. Pres. South Hillsborough Sch. Parents' Group, Calif., 1974-75; sec. Vol. Bur. of San Mateo County, Burlingame, Calif., 1975; chmn. Community Info. Com., Town of Hillsborough, 1984-86; mem., subcom. chmn. fin. adv. com., Town of Hillsborough, 1984-86. Recipient awards Council for Advancement and Support of Edn., 1981, Exemplary Direct Mail Appeals Fund Raising Inst., 1982. Mem. Internat. Assn. Fin. Planners (sec. Oreg. chpt. 1988—, bd. dirs.), Inst. Cert. Fin. Planners, Ashland Shakespeare Festival. Republican. Club: Jr. League (San Francisco); Rogue Valley Country (Medford). Home: 148 Greenway Circle Medford OR 97504 Office: Franklin Distbrs 130 E Main St #282 Medford OR 97501

HENRICH, JEAN MARIE, purchasing director; b. Warren, Ohio, Aug. 13, 1961; d. William Myron and Senja Ellen (Mackey) L.; m. Robert L. Henrich, Aug. 29, 1987. BA in English, Mt. Union Coll., 1984. Cert. secondary tchr., Ohio. With personnel coop. dept. Lewis Research Ctr. div. NASA, Cleve., 1981-83; jr. buyer Sperry Corp., McLean, Va., 1984; mgr. purchasing Distribusoft, Inc., Laurel, Md., 1985; sr. procurement specialist Martin Marietta Corp., Greenbelt, Md., 1985-87; dir. purchasing NDC/Fed. Systems, Inc., Rockville, Md., 1987—. Mem. Nat. Contracts Mgmt. Assn., Nat. Assn. Female Execs. Methodist. Office: NDC/Fed Systems Inc 1300 Piccard Dr Rockville MD 20850

HENRIE, BETTY COLLINS, school administrator, health science educator; b. Bloomsburg, Pa., June 17, 1922; d. Clease Ransom and Mary Margaret Alberta (Rhodes) Collins; m. J. Gilbert Henrie, Jr., June 19, 1948; 1 child, Betty June. BS, East Stroudsburg U., 1944; MA, Columbia U., 1947; postgrad., Pa. State U., 1953-72, Bucknell U., 1958-78; EdD, Nova U., 1981. Cert. tchr., prin. and supt., Pa. Tchr. health and phys. edn. Sr. High Sch., Berwick, Pa., 1944-45, tchr., chmn., 1950-65, dean, asst. prin., 1965-78, prin., 1978—; prof. health sci., dir. phys. edn. Shimer Coll., Mt. Carroll, Ill., 1945-48; adj. prof. Luzerne County Community Coll., 1988. Author: Parachute Play, 1959, revised edit., 1964. Instr. first aid and home nursing ARC, 1952-73; council pres. PTA, Columbia County, Pa. Recipient Outstanding Woman award for exemplary service in edn. Columbia-Montour Counties Women's Conf., 1986. Mem. Nat. Health and Phys. Edn. Assn., Pa. Health and Phys. Edn. Assn., NEA, Pa. Edn. Assn., Pa. Assn. Secondary Sch. Prins. (chair research and stats., chair state membership com. 1987—), AAUW, Delta Kappa Gamma, Kappa Delta Pi. Republican. Club: Bus. and Profl. Women (pres. 1984-86, Woman of Yr. 1979). Lodges: Order Eastern Star, Amaranth. Avocations: travel, fishing, golf, reading, writing. Home: 801 E 3d St Berwick PA 18603 Office: Berwick Area Sr High Sch 1100 Fowler Ave Berwick PA 18603

HENRIKSON, LOIS ELIZABETH, journalist, photographer; b. Lytton, Iowa, Nov. 10, 1921; d. Daniel Raymond and Cora Elizabeth (Thomson) Wessling; m. Arthur Allen Henrikson, July 3, 1943; children: Diane Elizabeth Henrikson Slider, Janet Christine, Michele Charlene Henrikson

Smetana. BS, Northwestern U., 1943. Adminstrv. asst. to v.p., dir. ops. bus. communications div. ITT Telecommunications Corp., Des Plaines, Ill., 1980-82; adminstrv. asst. to exec. v.p. Wholesale Stationers' Assn., Des Plaines, 1982-84, membership services coordinator, 1984-88; Chgo. corr. Office World News, Hearst Bus. Communications, Inc., Garden City, N.Y., 1988—. chair safety com. Cumberland Sch. PTA, Des Plaines, 1957-58, chair publicity, 1960-61; bd. dirs. Maine West High Sch. Music Boosters, Des Plaines, 1967-69; capt. fin. drive YMCA, Des Plaines, 1964; deaconess First Congl. Ch., Des Plaines. Mem. Am. Soc. Assn. Execs. (cert. membership mktg. 1986), Chgo. Soc. Assn. Execs. (registrar 1984-85), Nat. Assn. for Female Execs., Am. Soc. of Profl. and Exec. Women, AAUW (chair social com. 1983-84, editor newsletter 1984-85), Am. Assn. Editorial Cartoonists (aux.), Nat. Soc. Magna Carta Dames (life), Am. of Royal Descent (life), DAR, Art Inst. Chgo., Alpha Gamma Delta. Republican. Home: 27 N Meyer Ct Des Plaines IL 60016 Office: Office World News 645 Stewart Ave Garden City NY 11530

HENRIQUEZ-FREEMAN, HILDA JOSEFINA, fashion design executive; b. Palma Soriano, Oriente, Cuba, June 18, 1938; came to U.S., 1960; d. Matias and Isabel Beatrice (Freeman) H. BA, Bethune Cookman, 1963; postgrad., Tchrs. Coll., 1965-66, Roosevelt U., 1966, Northwestern U., 1969-70; cert., No. Ill. U., 1975; postgrad., Loop Coll., 1972-84. Modiste/couturier Fina Modas, Habana, Cuba, 1952-59; ct. reporter Govt. La Cabana, Habana, Cuba, 1959-60; language instr. Ft. Lauderdale Sch. Dist., Fla., 1963-64; custom design Freeman's Fashion Atelier, Chgo., 1965-68; pres. dir. Freeman's Fashion Acad., Chgo., 1968—; head designer Eur-Am. Creations, Chgo., 1978-81; cons. Freeman's Enterprise, Chgo., 1982—. Mentor Spanish coalition, Youth Career Awareness Program, Chgo., 1987. Mem. Cuban C. of C., Cuban Liceo, Ill. Assn. Trade and Tech. Schs., Nat. Assn. for Female Execs. Office: Freeman's Enterprises 410 S Michigan Ave Chicago IL 60605

HENRY, BARBARA A., newspaper editor; b. Oshkosh, Wis., July 23, 1952; d. Robert Edward and Barbara Frances (Aylesworth) H. BJ, U. Nev. Reporter Reno Newspapers, 1974-78, city editor, 1978-80, mng. editor, 1980-82; asst. nat. editor USA Today, Washington, 1982-83; exec. editor Reno Gazette-Jour., 1981-86; editor, dir. Gannett Rochester Newspapers, Rochester, N.Y., 1986—. Mem. Soc. Profl. Journalists, Associated Press Mng. Editors, Am. Soc. Newspaper Editors, Calif.-Nev. Soc. Newspaper Editors (bd. dirs.). Office: Gannett Rochester Newspapers 55 Exchange Blvd Rochester NY 14614 *

HENRY, CRISTINA RAE, insurance administrator; b. Onawa, Iowa, July 28, 1949; d. Corvin Lee Cox and Elena Irene (Godden) Spencer; m. Jack LaVerne, May 3, 1985 (div.); children: Amy Christine, Jill Marie. Student, Emporia (Kans.) State U., 1968. With Westam. Securities, Emporia, 1969-70; with Mut. Omaha, 1970—, premium processor, 1970-74, unit supr., 1974-76, analyst EDR, 1976-78, asst. supr., 1978-83, staff asst., 1983-84, coordinator systems and service, 1984—. Home: 2957 N 59th St Omaha NE 68104

HENRY, DIANA MARA, photographer; b. Cin., June 20, 1948; d. Carl and Edith Entratter) Henry. A.B., Harvard U., 1969; m. Nöel Oard Mapstead, June 12, 1986; 1 child, Barbara Edith Plantagenet. Gen. reporter S.I. Advance, 1970; originator, dir. community workshop program Internat. Ctr. Photography, N.Y.C., 1975-77, mem. faculty, 1976-79; owner Diana Mara Henry Photography, N.Y.C., 1972—; mem. exec. bd. Friends of Alice Austen, N.Y.C., 1977—; artist-in-residence N.Y. Found. Arts, 1985-86; one-woman shows: Ballard Mill Ctr. for Arts, Malone, N.Y., 1983, Overseas Press Club, N.Y.C., 1983, Brattleboro (Vt.) Mus., 1984, ERPF, Catskill Cultural Ctr., Women's Studio Workshop, 1987; group shows include: Tyler Sch. Art Temple U., Phila., Fashion Inst. Tech., N.Y.C., Art Guild, Guilford, Conn.; represented in permanent collections Nat. Archives, Library of Congress, Smithsonian Instn., Washington, Schlesinger Library on History of Women in Am., Radcliffe Coll.; contbr. articles to So. Exposure. Ofcl. photographer First Nat. Women's Conf., Houston, 1977; Nat. Commn. on Observance of Internat. Women's Yr., Washington, 1978. Recipient Ferguson History prize Harvard U., 1967; grantee N.Y. State Found. for Arts, 1985, N.Y. State Council Arts, 1986. Mem. Soc. Photographic Edn. Home: PO Box 1962 Carmel CA 93921 Office: 1160 Fifth Ave New York NY 10029

HENRY, DONNA EDWARDS, educator; b. Washington, Oct. 1, 1949; d. Conard Paul and Jean Marie (Kemp) E. BS, D.C. Tchrs. Coll., 1971; MA, Columbia U., 1974. Cert. tchr., Md. Tchr. Binghamton (N.Y.) Sch. System, 1971-73; group tchr., supr., acting dir. N.Y.C. Coll., 1974-76; tchr., supr. student tchrs. Balt. City Schs., 1976-87, Prince George's County Schs., New Carrollton, Md., 1987—; asst. volley-ball coach Binghamton Sch. System, 1973; project dir. Fund for Ednl. Excellence, Balt., 1986-87 (ednl. grant). Contbr. articles and photographs to mags., 1973-74. Coach Balt. City Volleyball League, 1979-80; vol. Balt. Neighborhoods, Inc., 1980—. Mem. Nat. Assn. Female Execs.

HENRY, HELGA IRMGARD, liberal arts educator; b. Soppo, Buea, Cameroon, May 30, 1915; d. Carl Jacob and Hedwig (Kloeber) Bender; m. Carl F.H. Henry, Aug. 17, 1940; children: Paul Brentwood, Carol Jennifer. BA, Wheaton Coll., Ill., 1936, MA, 1937; M of Religious Edn., No. Bapt. Theol. Sem., 1945. Dean of women State Tchrs.' Coll., Ellendale, N.D., 1937-40; librarian, instr. in lit., religious edn. No. Bapt. Theol. Sem., Ellendale, N.D., 1940-47; instr. German Wheaton Coll., 1945-47; assoc. prof. edn. Pasadena (Calif.) Coll., 1951-60; vis. instr. religious edn. Ea. Bapt. Theol. Sem., Phila., 1963-66; chmn., treas. The Elmer Bisbee Found., 1986—. Author: Mission on Main Street, 1955; translator: Paulus Scharpff, History of Evangelism, 1966. Trustee Ea. Bapt. Theol. Sem., 1971-73. Home: 3824 N 37th St Arlington VA 22207

HENRY, JEAN BLAIR, college aquatics director; b. Pasadena, Tex., Jan. 27, 1953; d. Ulis Lavern and Evelyn Fae (Brennen) H. BS, Tex. A&M U., 1974; MA, Mich. State U., 1979. Owner, instr. Am. Watersports, Inc., Irving, Tex.; natatorium dir., coordinator corp. wellness program North Lake Coll., Irving, 1982—; cons. in field; scuba instr., dive travel coordinator, Irving, 1986—. Editor several staff tng. manuals for aquatic facilities. Chairperson YMCA Regional Scuba Curriculum Devel. Com.; active ARC, Dallas; legis. liaison Tex. Council on Family Violence, Austin, 1983; bd. dirs. New Tomorrows, Inc., Irving, 1984-86, Am. Heart Assn. of Irving, 1986—. Mem. Running and Fitness Assn., Women's Sports Found., Divers Alert Network (regional rep. 1985—), Council for Nat. Cooperation in Aquatics, Nat. Assn. Female Execs., Bus. and Profl. Women, U.S. Triathlon Assn., Women's C. of C. Dallas. Office: North Lake Coll 5001 N MacArthur Irving TX 75038-3899

HENRY, JEANNE DIANE, country club manager; b. Louisville, Nov. 27, 1946; d. Ernest Von Kannel and Dorothy May (Shofner) Norris; m. Kenneth C. Henry, Aug. 8, 1966 (div. Apr. 1981); children: Kevin Scott, Stephanie Brooks. BA, We. Ky. U., 1968. Mgr. Tupperware, Inc., San Diego, 1976-77; asst. mgr. Pic-A-Dilly, Inc., San Diego, 1977-78; cataloger United States Internat. U., San Diego, 1978-79; mgr. Gentlewomen, Inc., Louisville, 1979-81; adminstrv. asst. St. Anthony Radiation Ctr., Louisville, 1981-85; asst. mgr. River Rd. Country Club, Louisville, 1985—, mgr., 1988; mgr. S. Park Country Club, Fairdale, Ky., 1988. Sec. Young Democrats, Louisville, 1965; mem. Early Childhood Edn. Steering Com. of San Diego County Sch. System, 1973. Mem. Club Mgrs. Assn. Am., Club Mgrs. Assn. (Ohio Valley Chpt.), Beta Sigma Pi (v.p. 1977-80). Republican. Roman Catholic.

HENRY, JUDY MARLOWE, television broadcast administrator; b. Newnan, Ga., Mar. 13, 1948; d. Sawyer Davis and Mattie Louise (Holland) Marlowe; divorced; 1 child, Lisa Marlowe. Student, U. Ga., 1966-68, Oglethorpe U., 1987. With editorial dept. TV Guide mag., Atlanta, 1967-68; dir. KinderCare Learning Ctrs., Atlanta, 1972-76; corp. administrator Turner Broadcast System, Atlanta, 1977-83; assoc. dir. sports Sta. WTBS-TV, 1977—, producer Good News, 1986—; asst. dir. ESPN, 1983—; program coordinator Cable News Network, Atlanta, 1983—, producer Nuclear Arms Conf. at Emory U., 1985, producer Showbiz, 1986—; cons. Very Spl. Arts Festival, Greenville, S.C., 1984—, Veratec Industries, Tucker, Ga., 1984—. Recipient Emmy award Nat. Assn. TV Arts and Scis., Atlanta, 1978, Tetrahedron Presdl. citation, 1986; named one of Finalist Women of Achievement Competition Am. Women in Radio and TV, 1987-88. Mem. Am. Women in Radio and TV. Home: 1646 Esquire Pl Norcross GA 30093 Office: Cable News Network One CNN Ctr PO Box 105366 Atlanta GA 30348

HENRY, LOIS HOLLENDER, human resources executive; b. Phila., Jan. 19, 1941; d. Edward Hubert and Frances Lois (Nesler) Hollender; m. Charles L. Henry, Oct. 24, 1964 (div. 1971); children—Deborah Lee, Randell Huitt, Andrew Edward; m. 2d Thomas C. Mosley, Jr., July 11, 1978 (div. 1984). B.A., Thomas A. Edison Coll., 1979; M.S.W., Fordham U., 1981. Cert. social worker, N.Y., N.J.; lic. service profl., Ariz. Personnel asst., sec. IBM, Paterson, N.J. and St. Louis, 1964-66; minister's asst. Grace Luth. Ch., St. Cloud, Fla., 1966-68; adminstr./tchr. Fla. Finishing Acad., St. Cloud, 1968-70; adminstrv. asst. Newark Book Ctr., 1972-77; intern, med. social worker Jersey City Med. Ctr., 1979-80; intern, psychiatric/med. social worker VA Med. Ctr., Lyons, N.J., 1980-81; sch. social worker Lakeview Learning Ctr., Budd Lake, N.J., 1981-82; mgr. human resources Terak Corp., Scottsdale, Ariz., 1982-85 ; v.p. counseling and bus. devel. Murro & Assocs., Phoenix, 1988—; career cons., individual/family counselor/psychotherapist, speaker, Scottsdale, 1982; mem. employers com. Ariz. Dept. Econ. Security; cons. in field. Coordinator-vol. Job-A-Thon, Phoenix, 1983. Mem. Human Resources Council for Am. Electronics Assn., Am. Orthopsychiat. Assn., Nat. Assn. Social Workers, Am. Soc. Personnel Adminstrs., Phoenix Personnel Mgmt. Assn., Am. Compensation Assn., Ariz. Affirmative Action Assn. Home: 8628 E Granada Rd Scottsdale AZ 85257

HENRY, MARY MARGARET, construction company executive; b. Detroit, July 18, 1946; d. Kenneth Lee and Ethel (Hornok) Eshelman; m. Job Roy Henry, June 24, 1967; children: Jennifer Lynn, John Kenneth. BS, No. Mich. U., 1968. Jr. high tchr. Tawas (Mich.) Area Schs., 1968-73; owner, pres. John Henry Exec. Inc., Tawas, 1987. Republican. Lutheran. Home: 1140 Henry Rd East Tawas MI 48730 Office: John Henry Exec Inc 814 Monument Rd Tawas City MI 48730

HENRY, ROSEANN, editor; b. Bronx, N.Y., Nov. 16, 1958; d. John J. and Anne E. (Henchy) H. BA, Hofstra U., 1980. Vol. VISTA Legal Services Corp., Burlington, Iowa, 1980-81; forms analyst Uniform Printing, N.Y.C., 1981-83; prodn. coordinator CBS mags., N.Y.C., 1983-85; prodn. editor Sci. Digest mag., N.Y.C., 1985-86; mng. editor Computers in Banking mag., N.Y.C., 1986-87, Discover mag., N.Y.C., 1987—. Mem. NOW, Am. Soc. Mag. Editors, Nat. Assn. Female Execs. Democrat.

HENRY, SANDRA KEDNOCKER, civic worker, small business investment corporation executive; m. Charles J. Henry; children: Brendan Allan, Garratt Hill. BA, U. N.C., 1959; postgrad., U. Cin., 1966-67; grad. fin. forum, The Harris Bank, Chgo. Pres. Intervest Group, 1984-85. Bd. dirs. North Shore Country Day Sch., Illinois Club, House of the Good Shepherd; mem. Consular Ball benefit com. of Library of Internat. Relations; chmn. Sept. Ball of the Children's Home and Aid Soc. Ill., 1984; bd. mgmt., v.p. sustaining membership, benefit chmn. Jr. League Chgo., 1984-85; mem. woman's bd., mem. ball com. Chgo. Heart Assn., 1985; mem. benefit coms. Brookfield Zoo, 1985-88, Women's Bd. Goodman Theatre, Women's Bd. USO of Ill., 5 hosp. homebound programs for elderly; history of active leadership in geneal. socs., pub. TV, archtl. preservation, community and ednl. orgns., symphony orchs., convalescent hosp. for children; benefit chmn. Am. Cancer Soc., 1987, 88, mem. woman's bd.; bd. dirs. Midwest region Shakespeare Globe Ctr. N.Am., Inc. Mem. Nat. Soc. Fund Raising Execs., Harris Bank Fin. Network, U. N.C. Alumni Assn., Nat. Soc. Daus. Am. Colonists, Nat. Soc. Daus. Founders and Patriots Am., Nat. Soc. Daus. Colonial Wars (state officer), Nat. Soc. Sons and Daus. Pilgrims, U.S. Daus. 1812, Hotchkiss Family Assn., Descs. Colonial Clergy, numerous others. Clubs: Fortnightly of Chgo., Woman's Athletic, The Glenview.

HENRY, SHERRY LYNN, hotel executive; b. St. Louis, Feb. 26, 1936; d. William Harlow and Opal Jane Thomas; m. Herman J. Roodman, Dec. 5, 1965 (dec. 1979); children: Edie Sue Reshef, Janie Weiss, William U.; m. Michael M. Henry, Feb. 26, 1983; 1 child, Diane Elizabeth. BA, St. Louis U., 1957. Mgr. Ask Mr. Foster Travel, St. Louis, 1960-69, Dr. H.J. Roodman's Office, Scottsdale, 1969-73; dir. pub. relations, advt. Prescott Valley, Phoenix, 1973-80; media buyer, acct. exec. McGuiness-Brock, Advt., Denver, 1980-81; dir. mktg. and sales Fiesta Inn, Tempe, Ariz., 1981-83, asst. mgr., 1983-86, gen. mgr., 1986—. Mem. Fiesta Bowl Com., Phoenix, 1982—, chair block party, 1984-86; chair Fiesta Bowl Parade, Phoenix, 1978, scriptwriter, 1982, 83; founder Tempe Envoys, 1983; bd. dirs. Tempe Leadership, 1986—, United Way, 1986—, Tempe Community Council, 1987. Mem. Tempe Tourism Council (pres. 1986-87). Republican. Home: 5425 E Roanoke Phoenix AZ 85008 Office: Fiesta Inn 2100 S Priest Dr Tempe AZ 85282

HENRY-LEWIS, SABRINA NORINE, computer systems analyst; b. Springfield, Ohio, Dec. 14, 1954; d. Karl Leo Francis and Jane Delores (Spivey) Henry; m. Glenn Anthony Lewis, Sept. 25, 1986. BSBA, Cen. State U., Wilberforce, Ohio, 1979. Coop. edn. computer programmer Naval Air Engrng. Ctr., Lakehurst, N.J., 1978-80, computer systems analyst, 1980—; cons. in field. Vice chmn. Fed. Women's Program Com., 1982—; conselor Fed. Equal Employment Opportunity, 1987; sec. Upward Bound adv. com. Georgian Ct. Coll., Lakewood, N.J., mem., 1987; sec. correspondence NAACP, Lakewood, 1982; leader Ocean County Girl Scouts Assn., Lakewood, 1986—. Mem. Civilian Recreation and Welfare Assn., Phi Gamma Nu. Office: Naval Air Engrng Ctr PO Box 1184 Lakehurst NJ 08733

HENSCHEL, LEONORE KATHERINE, elementary educator; b. Milw.; d. Max and Elisabeth (Mattern) Oettmeier; m. James H. Henschel, June 14, 1958; children: Mark, Lynda, Marylynn. BA, U. Wis., 1959, MS, 1963. Cert. elem. and jr. coll. tchr., Wis., Fla. Tchr. St. Francis and New Berlin, Wis., 1958-62, Oakland Park, Fla., 1972-76, Pompano Beach, Fla., 1976—. Bd. dirs. edn. Christ Meth. Ch., Ft. Lauderdale, 1984-87; sec. Coral Ridge Homeowners Assn., Ft. Lauderdale, 1987—. Mem. Broward Tchrs. Union, Jr. C. of C. (aux.), Coral Ridge Jr. Womans Club, Coral Ridge Jr. Womans Assn. (editor newspaper 1967-71). Republican. Home: 5230 NE 14th Terr Fort Lauderdale FL 33334 Office: Cypress Elem Sch 851 SW 3d Ave Pompano FL 33060

HENSE, ANN LOUISE, artist, educator; b. Toledo, Nov. 16, 1950; d. Robert Elmer and Helen Louise (Davis) H. BA, Ohio State U., 1972; MEd, U. Toledo, 1976; MA, Bowling Green State U., 1982, MFA, 1983. Cert. tchr., Ohio. Elementary and secondary art tchr. Sylvania (Ohio) Schs., 1972-79; jr. high art tchr. Otsego Schs., Grand Rapids, Ohio, 1980-81; art instr. Monroe (Mich.) Community Coll., 1984-86; teaching artist Arts Unltd. Bowling Green State U., 1985-86, instr. weaving, 1986; instr. Saturday Children's Program Toledo Mus. Art, 1973-75, 84-86, instr. adult art program, 1983-86, coordinator Sunday programs, 1986-88; chmn. Fibers Alive Competitive Art Exhibit, Toledo, 1984; part-time art tchr. Springfield Local Schs., Holland, Ohio, 1986—. Work exhibited various galleries, 1983—. Recipient 2d Place award State Weaving Competition, Ohio, 1984. Mem. Toledo Area Weavers Guild (pres. 1979-81), Northwest Ohio Watercolor Soc., Mich. Guild of Artists and Artisans, Ohio Art Edn. Assn., NEA. Home: 791 Brookside Sierra Madre CA 91024

HENSELMEIER, SANDRA NADINE, training and development consulting firm executive; b. Indpls., Nov. 20, 1937; d. Frederick Rost Henselmeier and Beatrice Nadine (Barnes) Henselmeier Enright; m. David Albert Funk, Oct. 2, 1976; children: William H. Stolz, Jr., Harry Phillip Stolz II, Sandra Ann Stolz. AB, Purdue U., 1971; MAT, Ind. U., 1975. Exec. sec. to dean Ind. U. Sch. Law, Indpls., 1977-78; adminstrv. asst. Ind. U.-Purdue U., Indpls., 1978-80, assoc. archivist, 1980-81; program and communication coordinator Midwest Alliance in Nursing, Indpls., 1981-82; tng. coordinator Coll./Univ. Cos., Indpls., 1982-83; pres. Better Bus. Communications, Indpls., 1983—; adj. lectr. Ind. U.-Purdue U. at Indpls., 1971—, U. Indpls. Center Continuing Mgmt. Devel. and Edn., Indpls., 1984—. Author: Successful Customer Service Writing, Winning with Effective Business Grammar, Successful Telephone Communication and Etiquette; contbr. articles to profl. jours. Mem. ASTD, Assn. Bus. Communication, Nat. Assn. Profl. Saleswomen, Indpls. C. of C., Ind. C. of C. Republican. Presbyterian. Avocations: traveling, walking, reading, learning new ideas. Office: Better Bus Communications 6208 N Delaware St Indianapolis IN 46220

HENSINGER, MARGARET ELIZABETH, marketing-advertising executive; b. Jackson, Mich., Aug. 31, 1950; d. John Kenneth and Inez Estelle (McVay) H.; m. William C. Pixley, Apr. 26, 1985; 1 child, Christopher. BS, Eastern Mich. U., 1973. Salesperson Hunter Pub. Co., Winston-Salem, N.C., 1974-76, Josten's-Am., Topeka, 1976-77; editorial asst. Mich. Dept. Agriculture, Lansing, 1977-80, U. Fla., Apopka, 1981-82; pres. Country Carousel, Inc., Mt. Dora, Fla., 1983—; editor, pres. Green Pages Ltd., Mt. Dora, 1984—; owner, pres. Sunbelt Mktg. Services, Inc., Mt. Dora, 1982—. Mem. Tex. Assn. Nurserymen, Nat. Assn. Women in Horticulture (v.p., past pres., organizer), Am. Soc. of Advt. Promotion, Fla. Foliage Assn., Fla. Nurserymen and Growers Assn., Mt. Dora C. of C. Republican. Episcopalian. Home: PO Box 908 Zellwood FL 32798 Office: Sunbelt Mktg Services Box 1485 Mount Dora FL 32757

HENSLEY, KATHLEEN NOELLE, association executive; b. Mpls., Mar. 1, 1960; d. James Hampton and Ruth Ila (Kloppenborg) H. BS in Journalism, U. Md., 1982; MA in Human Resource Devel., Marymount U., 1988. Adminstrv. asst. Office Health Maintenance Orgns. HHS, Rockville, Md., 1981-82; strategic systems div. GTE Products Corp., Rosslyn, Va., 1982-83; mgr. tng. program devel. Giant Food Inc., Washington, 1983-87; mgr. curriculum devel. Nat. Assn. Home Builders/Home Builders Inst., Washington, 1987—. Mem. Am. Assn. Tng. Devel., Nat. Soc. Performance and Instrn., Alpha Xi Delta, Kalgethos. Republican. Lutheran. Office: NAHB Home Builders Inst 15th and M Sts 2d Floor NW Washington DC 20005

HENSLEY, MARGARET ANN, swimming pools distributing company official; b. Knoxville, Tenn., May 6, 1941; d. Herman Geissler and Carrie Lucille (Wilmoth) Ballard; children—Dennis Keith Logan, David Wayne Logan, John Ballard Pecora, Felicia Ann Pecora; m. Bill Clyde Hensley, Mar. 27, 1981. Student, Dale Carnegie Sch., 1969, Watterson Coll., Ft. Lauderdale, 1988—. Head subscriptions New Woman mag., Fort Lauderdale, Fla., 1974-75; med. asst. Medi Lab Systems, Fort Lauderdale, 1975-76; mgr. Swimming Pool Owners Assn., Fort Lauderdale, 1976-78; accts. receivable clk. Outdoor World Distbrs., Fort Lauderdale, 1978-81, purchasing agt., 1984, asst. mgr., 1986; credit mgr. Miller Assocs., Miami, Fla., 1981-83, adminstrv. mgr., Miller Miami Br., 1986-87; with Safety Plus, Inc., Louisville, 1987-88. Named to Hon. Order of Ky. Cols., Gov. of Ky., 1986-87. Mem. Nat. Assn. Female Execs., Gold Coast Women in Credit. Avocations: golfing; bowling; art.

HENSON, GENE ETHRIDGE, legal administrator; b. Lawrenceville, Ga., Sept. 26, 1924; d. Fred Golden and Cora Jewell (Smith) Ethridge; student public schs., Lawrenceville; m. James Arthur Henson, May 2, 1948 (dec.); 1 dau., Gena Arlene. With Smith, Currie & Hancock, Atlanta, 1959—, adminstr., 1965—. Ofcl. hostess for State of Ga., So. Gov.'s Conf., Atlanta, 1971; past adult tchr. First Bapt. Ch., Lawrenceville; mem. adv. council Center for Profl. Edn., Ga. State U., 1980-84. Mem. Am. Bar Assn. (assoc.), Assn. Legal Adminstrs. (nat. v.p. 1979—, dir. 1979-83), Atlanta Assn. Legal Execs. (1st pres. 1975), Assn. Legal Adminstrs. (v.p. Atlanta chpt., pres.-elect 1986-87, pres. 1987-88). Home: 74 Scenic Hwy Lawrenceville GA 30245 Office: Smith Currie & Hancock Harris Tower 2600 Peachtree Ctr Atlanta GA 30043

HENTZ, MARIE EVA, real estate investor and developer; b. Detroit, Sept. 27, 1920; d. Charles and Eva (Follman) Hentz. Student Detroit Bus. U., Wayne State U. Draftsman, Cadillac Motor Co., Detroit, 1941-44; stenographer Great Lakes Steel Co., River Rouge, Mich., 1945-46, Can. Nat. R.R., Detroit, 1946-49; sec. UNOCAL, Los Angeles, 1950-72; real estate investor, mgr., developer, Burbank, Calif., 1950—; gen. ptnr. Hentz & Christensen, Ltd., South El Monte, Calif., 1953-86, Hentz Properties, Ltd., Burbank, 1971—. Mem. UNOCAL Women's Club. Republican. Avocations: gardening, reading, travel.

HENZE, NANCY HARMEL, investent banker; b. Balt., July 7, 1946; d. Merel H. and Armide E. (Chilcoat) Harmel; m. Horace J. Caulkins, III, Sept. 21, 1968 (div. Mar. 1978); m. 2d, William F. Henze II, Oct. 3, 1980. A.B., Vassar Coll., 1968; M.B.A., NYU, 1977. Assoc., Bache Halsey Stuart Shields, N.Y.C., 1977-78, Dillon Read & Co., Inc., N.Y.C., 1978-82; sr. v.p. Shearson Lehman Hutton, Inc., N.Y.C., 1982—. Office: Shearson Lehman Bros Inc Am Express Tower World Fin Ctr New York NY 10285-1600

HEPBURN, KATHARINE HOUGHTON, actress; b. Hartford, Conn., Nov. 8, 1909; d. Thomas N. and Katharine (Houghton) H.; m. Ludlow Ogden Smith (div.). Student, Bryn Mawr Coll, 1928. Appeared in films A Bill of Divorcement, 1932, Christopher Strong, 1933, Morning Glory, 1933 (Acad. award for best performance by actress 1934), Little Women, 1933, Spitfire, 1934, The Little Minister, 1934, Alice Adams, 1935, Break of Hearts, 1935, Sylvia Scarlett, 1936, Mary of Scotland, 1936, A Woman Rebels, 1936, Quality Street, 1937, Stage Door, 1937, Bringing up Baby, 1938, Holiday, 1938, The Philadelphia Story, 1940 (N.Y. Critic's award 1940), Woman of the Year, 1941, Keeper of the Flame, 1942, Stage Door Canteen, 1943, Dragon Seed, 1944, Undercurrent, 1946, Sea of Grass, 1946, Song of Love, 1947, State of the Union, 1948, Adam's Rib, 1949, The African Queen, 1951, Pat and Mike, 1952, Summertime, 1955, The Rainmaker, 1956, The Iron Petticoat, 1956, The Desk Set, 1957, Suddenly Last Summer, 1959, Long Day's Journey into Night, 1962, Guess Who's Coming to Dinner, 1967, (Acad. award for best actress 1968),The Lion in Winter, 1968 (Acad. award for best actress 1969), Madwoman of Chaillot, 1969, Trojan Women, 1971, A Delicate Balance, 1973, Rooster Cogburn, 1975, Olly, Olly, Oxen Free, 1978, On Golden Pond, 1981 (Acad. award for best actress 1981), The Ultimate Solution of Grace Quigley, 1985; appeared in plays The Czarina, 1928, The Big Pond, 1928, Night Hostess, 1928, These Days, 1928, Death Takes a Holiday, 1929, A Month in the Country, 1930, Art and Mrs. Bottle, 1930, The Warrior's Husband, 1932, Lysistrata, 1932, The Lake, 1933, Jane Eyre, 1937, The Philadelphia Story, 1939, Without Love, 1942, As You Like It, 1950, The Millionairess, Eng. and U.S.A., 1952, The Taming of the Shrew, The Merchant of Venice, Measure for Measure, Old Vic Co., Eng. and Australia, 1955, Merchant of Venice, Much Ado about Nothing, Am. Shakespeare Festival, 1957, toured later, 1958, Twelfth Night, Antony and Cleopatra, Am. Shakespeare Festival, 1960, Coco, 1969-70, toured, 1971, The Taming of the Shrew, Old Vic, 1970, A Matter of Gravity, 1976-78, West Side Waltz, 1981; appeared in TV movies The Glass Menagerie, 1973, Love among the Ruins, 1975, The Corn Is Green, 1979, Mrs. Delafield Wants to Marry, 1986; Laura Lansing Slept Here, 1988; author: The Making of the African Queen, 1987. Recipient gold medal as world's best motion picture actress Internat. Motion Picture Expn., Venice, Italy, 1934; ann. award Shakespeare Club, N.Y.C., 1950; award Whistler Soc., 1957; Woman of Yr. award Hasty Pudding Club, 1958; outstanding achievement award for fostering finest ideals of acting profession, 1980; lifetime achievement award Council Fashion Designers Am., 1986. Office: William Morris Agy 151 El Camino Beverly Hills CA 90212 *

HERBEIN, BONNIE FLEMMING, purchasing consultant, former casino-hotel company executive; b. Morristown, N.J., Mar. 27, 1955; d. Douglas Haig and Mildred Lillian (Lachenauer) F.; m. Frank J. Herbein, Feb. 7, 1987; BA, Stockton State Coll., Pomona, N.J., 1977; student Susquehanna U., Selinsgrove, Pa., 1973-75. Exec. trainee, Montgomery Ward's, Johnson City, N.Y., 1977-79; systems analyst Reese Pally-Zipp Ltd., Atlantic City, 1979-80; retail shop mgr. Holiday Inn Harrahs Casino, Atlantic City, 1980; asst. dir. purchasing Ramada Tropicana Casino, Atlantic City, 1980-82; dir. purchasing Del Webb Claridge Casino, Atlantic City, 1982-86; pres. B.F. Inc., 1986; v.p. purchasing Bertram Constrn. div. Perlman Properties, 1987—, Viking Constrn., 1988—. Vice chairperson N.J.-Pa.-Del. Regional Minority Council, Phila., 1985—. Mem. Atlantic City Purchasing Assn. (pres. 1986-87), Nat. Assn. Female Execs. Republican. Episcopalian. Home: 112 Roosevelt Ave Northfield NJ 08225 Office: Bertram Constn 505-507 Tilton Rd Mainland Profl Plaza Northfield NJ 08225

HERBENER, PATRICIA WENDY, risk management executive; b. Portland, Oreg., Dec. 23, 1945; d. Nels Bernhardt Jr. and Diana Dorothy (Hoogstraat) Palmquist. BA in History, North Park Coll., 1969. Claims rep. CNA Ins. Co., Los Alamitos, Calif., 1969-72; mgr. claims Ins. Co. N.Am., Los Angeles, 1972-80; regional supr. Crown Zellerbach Corp., Los Angeles, 1980-82; asst. v.p. Alexsis Risk Mgmt. Services Inc. subs. Alexander and Alexander, West Covina, Calif., 1982—. Mem. Calif. Self-Ins. Assn., Calif. Workers Compensation Coalition, Calif. Mfrs. Assn., West

Covina C. of C. Republican. Office: Alexis Risk Mgmt Services Inc 1501 W Cameron Ave #C-300 West Covina CA 91790

HERBERT, BARBARA RAE, librarian, educational media specialist; b. Neptune, N.J., Apr. 1, 1955; d. Raymond Louis and Grace Caroline (Freiermuth) Swan; m. Edward O. Herbert, Jr., June 7, 1986. A.A. cum laude, Ocean County Coll., 1974; B.A., Georgian Ct. Coll., 1976; M.L.S., Rutgers U., 1982. Ednl. media specialist, N.J., 1983. Substitute tchr. Brick Twp. Schs. (N.J.), 1976-77; dir. Instructional Media Ctr. Georgian Ct. Coll., Lakewood, N.J., 1977—; media cons. Lakewood Learning Ctr., 1980-81. Brick Twp. Fine Arts Guild drama scholar, 1972. Mem. ALA, N.J. Library Assn., Ednl. Media Assn. N.J., Nat. Audio Visual Assn., Assn. Audio-Visual Technicians, Ocean County Coll. Alumni Assn., Delta Tau Kappa, Gamma Sigma Sigma. Republican. Presbyterian. Club: Goebel City Collectors, Ocean County Alumnae of Georgian Ct. Coll.

HERBERT, DOROTHY LOUISE, publisher; b. Quincy, Mass., Aug. 31, 1937; d. David Kennedy and Louise Christine (Geigle) Salvini; m. David Eugene Herbert, Feb. 19, 1972. BSME, Northeastern U., 1961. Pub. relations The Foxboro (Mass.) Co., 1961-69; advt. Digital Equipment Corp., Maynard, Mass., 1969-73; owner Davis-Smith Co., Harvard, Mass., 1973-87, Shiloh Press, Harvard, 1987. Contbr. articles to profl. jours. Mem. U.S. Power Squadron (lt., dist. corr. 1985-87), Pi Tau Sigma. Office: Shiloh Press 36 Hawkins St City Island NY 10464

HERBERT, EUGENIA WARREN, history educator; b. Summit, N.J., Sept. 8, 1929; s. Robert Beach and Mildred (Fisk) Warren; m. Robert Louis Herbert, June 6, 1953; children—Timothy D., Rosemary, Catherine. B.A., Wellesley Coll., 1951; M.A., Yale U., 1953, Ph.D., 1957. Asst. prof. history Quinnipiac Coll., Hamden, Conn., 1970; lectr. history Yale U., New Haven, 1972-73, 76, collaborator with R.S. Lopez, 1971, research affiliate, 1976-79; asst. prof. history Mt. Holyoke Coll., South Hadley, Mass., 1978-82, assoc. prof., 1982-85, E. Nevius Rodman prof., 1985—; sr. assoc. mem. St. Anthony's Coll., Oxford U. (Eng.), 1978. Author: The Artist and Social Reform, 1961; (with Claude-Anne Lopez) The Private Franklin (Boston Globe award 1976), 1975; Red Gold of Africa, 1984; Red Gold: Copper Arts of Africa; film (with Candice Goucher and Carlyn Saltman) the Blooms of Banjeli, 1986; contbr. articles to profl. jours. Mem. Bethany Democratic Com., 1970-77; mem. Bethany Sch. Bd., 1964-68; pres. Ctr. for Ind. Study, New Haven, 1977. Fulbright fellow, Vienna, Austria, 1951-52; Mellon faculty fellow Mt. Holyoke Coll., 1982; Donner Found. fellow, 1982-85; NEH mus. grantee, 1984. Fellow Royal Geog. Soc.; mem. African Studies Assn., Am. Hist. Assn., Hist. Metallurgy Soc., Assn. Concerned African Scholars. Office: Mt Holyoke Coll Dept History South Hadley MA 01075

HERBERT, MARY KATHERINE ATWELL, theatre executive; b. Grove City, Pa., Dec. 9, 1945; d. Perry Stewart and Luella Irene (Brown) Atwell; m. Roland Marcus Herbert, July 20, 1963; children: Stephen Todd, Amy Elizabeth, Jill Anne. BA, Ariz. State U., 1968, MA, 1973; film cert., U. So. Calif., 1978. Dir. promotion and advt. Maricopa County Fair, Phoenix, 1976; film writer Scottsdale Daily Progress, 1976-79; dir. pub. relations Phoenix Little Theatre, 1980—; script analyst 1985-86; exec. asst. to v.p. devel. DeLaurentiis Entertainment Group, 1986; producer's assoc. film TRAXX, 1986-87; with devel. Debin/DeVore Prodns., 1988—; freelance writer. Mem. Encanto Homeowners Assn., Phoenix, 1976-80. Mem. Women in Communications, Ariz. Press Women, AAUW, Kappa Delta Pi, Pi Lambda Theta. Office: Debin/DeVore Prodns MGM-Filmland 10000 W Washington Blvd #304 Culver City CA 90232

HERBERT, THERESA MARIE, insurance executive; b. Berwyn, Ill., May 28, 1958; d. Adrian George and Bertha Priscilla (Schmidt) H. Student, No. Ill. U., 1976-77, DePaul U., 1987—. Lic. life and variable annuity rep., Ill., Ind., Ohio, Minn., Mo. Cashier St. Charles (Ill.) Wholesale Corp., 1975-77, asst. office mgr., 1977-78; pension statistician Shadur, LaVine & Assoc., Encino, Calif., 1978-79; pension adminstrn. mgr. Lubin, Shadur, LaVine, Inc., Lincolnwood, Ill., 1979-82; tech. sales support rep. Penn Mut. Life Ins. Co., Chgo., 1982-86, sales exec. pension, 1985—. Mem. Nat. aSsn. Female Exec., Nat. Assn. Security Dealers. Roman Catholic. Home: 922 Lewis Pl Geneva IL 60134 Office: Penn Mut Life Ins Co 150 N Wacker Dr #630 Chicago IL 60606

HERB-SEPICH, DEBORA KAY, communications specialist; b. Portland, Oreg., Mar. 30, 1959; d. Robert Francis and Kathryn Agnes (Roshak) Herb; m. Gordon Lee Sepich, Sept. 21, 1985; 1 child, Cory Nathan. Student, U. Oreg., 1977-80, Maryhurst Coll., 1981-82, U. Portland, 1984-86. Cons. indsl. maintenance Tektronix, Integrated Circuits Orgn., Beaverton, Oreg., 1980-86; specialist customer service tng. Decision Dynamics, Lake Oswego, Oreg., 1986—; pres. Pacific Data Resources, Lake Oswego, 1986-87; product info. mgr. Decision Dynamics, Lake Oswego, 1987—; cons. tng., mgmt. Decision Dynamics, 1986—. Contbr. editor Dyna Star Group newsletter, 1987. Mem. Nat. Assn. Female Executives. Republican. Office: Decision Dynamics 696 McVey Ave Lake Oswego OR 97304

HERBST, MARIE A., state senator. m. Paul Herbst. BA, Albany State Tchr.'s Coll.; Masters, Columbia U.; postgrad. secondary sch. adminstrn., U. Conn. Former pub. sch. tchr. East Windsor, Conn.; now mem. Conn. State Senate from 35th Dist.; in 4th term as mayor Town of Vernon; chmn. pub. safety com.; mem. edn. com. Lector, Sacred Heart Ch.; past chmn. High Sch. CCD Sch.; past mem. Ladies of Sacred Heart; mem. Tri-Town Disabled Com., Vernon Town Council, 1975-79; past mem. Vernon Bd. Edn.; mem. Adult Edn. Adv. Commn., 1985; treas. Capitol Region Council of Govts., 1985. Mem. Internat. Edn. Assn., Nat. Edn. Assn., Conn. Edn. Assn., Phi Delta Kappa, Gamma Kappa Rho. Democrat. Roman Catholic. Home: 245 Brandy Hill Rd Vernon CT 06066

HERD, CHARMIAN JUNE, educator, singer, actress; b. Waterville, Maine, June 1, 1930; d. Samuel Braid and Jennie May (Lang) Herd; B.A., Colby Coll., 1950; postgrad. Boston U., 1951, EdM, U. Maine, 1965; ednl. cert. No. Conservatory, Bangor, Maine, 1954; also study voice with Roger A. Nye. Dir. music State Sch. for Girls, Hallowell, Maine, 1950-51; head English, French, dramatics depts. St. George High Sch., Tenants Harbor, 1951-52; dir. music pub. schs. Albion and Unity, 1952-54, Troy, Freedom, Maine, 1953-54; dir. music pub. sch. system Belgrade, Maine, Waterville Jr. High Sch., 1954-55; dir. vocal music Waterville Jr. and Sr. high schs., 1954-58; head English and dramatics depts. Besse High Sch., Albion, 1959-62; tchr. French, Skowhegan Jr. High Sch., 1962-63; tchr. French, English, Skowhegan Sr. High Sch., 1963-69; tchr. French, Lawrence Sr. High Sch., Fairfield, Maine, 1969-71, chmn. drama and speech dept., 1972-79; instr. dramatics U. Maine, Farmington, 1969-70; tchr. conversational French, Skowhegan Adult Edn. Sch., 1963-69, drama instr., 1965-69; dance asst. Plaza Studio; producer, appeared in role of Vera, Mame, Waterville; soloist various churches, Maine, 1951—; mus. dir. children's sect., performing mem. Theater at Monmouth, Maine, 1970—, mem. exec. bd., 1976—, sec. bd. trustees, 1977—; performing mem. Augusta Players, Camden Civic Theatre, Portland Lyric Theatre, Waterville Players, Titipu Choral Soc., Waterville Community Ballet, Choral Arts Soc., Portland, Maine, 1980—, Riverside Theatre Co., Vero Beach, Indian River Ctr. for Arts; theatre chmn. ann. Maine Festival Arts, Bowdoin Coll., 1978—; soloist Vero Beach Chorale Soc., numerous club, ch., conv., coll. concerts, oratorios; performing mem. Vero Beach Solo Gates, Encore Alley Theatre, Esprit des Amis, Vero Beach, Ft. Pierce City Ballet, Fla.; treas. Coast Opera Co., Ft. Pierce, Fla., 1986—. Bd. dirs. Opera New Eng., 1980—, Portland Lyric Theatre, 1982—Mem. Waterville Friends Music, DAR, Waterville Theatre Guild (charter mem., pres. 1967—), Vero Beach Theatre Guild (Fla.), Encore Alley Theatre, Vero Beach, Waterville Bus. and Profl. Women's Club (program chmn. 1957-58, v.p. 1958-59, pres. 1959-61, chmn. drama dept. 1961, drama and music chmn. 1961—), Fla. Profl. Theatre Assn., Ednl. Speech and Theatre Assn. Maine (mem. exec. bd., pres. 1972-74), Maine Profl.-Community Theatre Assn. (mem. organizing com.), Actors Equity Assn., Albion-Burnham Tchrs. Club (sec. 1960-61), NEA, Maine Tchrs. Assn., New Eng. Theatre Conf. (exec. bd. 1976—, 1st v.p. 1976-77, conf. chmn. 1977), Theatre Assn. Maine (membership chmn. 1972-73, 2d v.p. 1973-74, exec. bd. 1972—, exec. sec. 1975—, state pres. 1976—), Internat. Platform Assn., Nat. Assn. Tchrs. of Singing (sec. Maine chpt. 1980—), Pine Tree Post Card Club (exec. bd., Spring show chmn. 1979-80, pres. 1982-84), Maine Hist. Soc., Bay State Post Card Club, R.I. Post Card Club. Club: Cecilia (Augusta, Maine). Composer sacred music: Babylon, 1959, The Greatest of These is Love, 1961, Pan; Keep Not Thy Silence, O God, Remember Now Thy Creator, Slow, Slow, Fresh Fount, A Witch's Charm, Hymn to God the Father. Avocations: acting, singing, oil painting, collecting opera and operetta scores. Home and Office: PO Box 714 Roseland FL 32957

HERGENHAN, JOYCE, corporate executive; b. Mt. Kisco, N.Y., Dec. 30, 1941; d. John Christopher and Goldie (Wago) H. B.A., Syracuse U., 1963; M.B.A., Columbia U., 1978. Reporter White Plains Reporter Dispatch, 1963-64; asst. to Rep. Ogden R. Reid Washington, 1964-68; reporter Gannett Newspapers, 1968-72; with Consol. Edison Co. of N.Y., Inc., N.Y.C., 1972-82, v.p., 1977-79, exec. asst. to chmn. bd., 1978, sr. v.p. pub. affairs, 1979-82; v.p. corp. pub. relations General Electric Co., Fairfield, Conn., 1982—. Office: Gen Elec Co 3135 Easton Turnpike Fairfield CT 06431

HERMAN, CAROL KORNGUT, advertising agency executive; b. Atlantic City, Oct. 14, 1952; d. Richard F. and Regina (Kornblau) Korngut; m. Henry Lewis Herman, Dec. 30, 1972; children—Matthew, Gregory. B.A., U. Pa., 1972. Asst. account exec. Honig-Cooper and Harrington Advt., N.Y.C., 1973-74; asst. account exec. Grey Advt., N.Y.C., 1974-75, account exec., 1976-78, account supr., 1978-80, v.p., mgmt. supr., 1981-84, v.p., group mgmt. supr., 1985-87, sr. v.p., 1987—. Office: Grey Advt Inc 777 3rd Ave New York NY 10017

HERMAN, EDITH CAROL, public relations manager; b. Edgewood, Md., July 1, 1944; d. Herbert R. and Thirza E. (Simmons) H.; m. Leonard Wiener. B.A., Purdue U., 1966. Reporter Hollister Newspaper Chain, Wilmette, Ill., 1966-68; reporter Chgo. Tribune Newspaper, 1968-79, edn. editor, 1971-74, feature writer, 1976-79; sr. editor TV Digest Inc., 1980-83; pub. relations mgr. Am. Tel. & Tel., 1983—. Recipient Journalism award Ill. Edn. Assn., 1969-70; Editorial award Ill. Automatic Merchandising Council, 1977. Mem. Sigma Delta Chi. Home: 5501 Burling Ct Bethesda MD 20817

HERMAN, JOAN ELIZABETH, insurance company executive; b. N.Y.C., June 2, 1953; d. Roland Barry and Grace Gales (Goldstein) H.; m. Richard M. Rasiej, July 16. 1977. AB, Barnard Coll., 1975; MS, Yale U., 1977. Actuarial student Met. Life Ins. Co., N.Y.C., 1978-82; asst. actuary Phoenix Mut. Life Ins. Co., Hartford, Conn., 1982-83, assoc. actuary, dir. underwriting research, 1983-84, 2d v.p., 1984-85, v.p., 1985— Contbr. articles to profl jours. Fund raising team capt. Greater Hartford Arts Council, 1986; bd. dirs. Hadassah, Glastonbury, Conn., Temple Beth Hillel, South Windsor, Conn., 1983-84. Fellow Soc. Actuaries; mem. Am. Acad. Actuaries, Group Underwriters Assn. of Am., Am. Leadership Forum, Home Office Life Underwriters of Am. Jewish.

HERMANN, MARY KEVIN HOWARD, nurse, educator; b. St. Lawrence, Ky., Oct. 26, 1934; d. Charles Kevin and Mary M. Howard; R.N., St. Mary's Sch. of Nursing, Evansville, Ind., 1955; B.S. cum laude in Nursing, U. Evansville, 1970, M.A., 1972, M.S. in Nursing, 1974; Ed.D., Ind. U., 1984; m. Robert R. Hermann, Feb. 2, 1957; children—Michael R. (dec.), Barbara K., Leah M., Daniel J. Staff nurse St. Mary's Med. Center, Evansville, Ind., 1955-56, head nurse, 1956-58, asst. dir. nursing service, 1965-68; instr. nursing U. Evansville, 1970-73, asst. prof., 1973-76, assoc. prof., 1976-84, prof., 1984—, asst. dean baccalaureate program, 1974-80. Mem. adv. com. Am. Heart Assn. Program, Evansville, 1981. Mem. Am. Nurses Assn., Ind. Nurses Assn. (co-chmn. commn. on edn., chmn. task force on competencies, dir., dir. dist. 4 1982-84), Am. Assn. Critical Care Nurses. Home: 8011 Maple Ln Newburgh IN 47630 Office: 1800 Lincoln Ave Evansville IN 47702

HERMANOFF, SANDRA MARLENE, public relations administrator; b. Canton, Ohio; d. Max and Sylvia (Levin) Weisbrod; m. Michael Joel Hermanoff, Nov. 27, 1976; 1 son, Jeffrey Howard. BA in Journalism, Pub. Relations, Ohio State U., 1965. With Ont. Brewers Inst., Toronto, 1965; copywriter Miller Advt., Columbus, Ohio, 1965; asst. pub. relations dir. Huntington Nat. Bank, Columbus, 1965; pub. relations dir. Sta. CFTO-TV, Toronto, 1968-69; instr. pub. relations, journalism Humber Coll., Toronto, 1969-71; pub. relations adminstr. Liza Minnelli-Desi Arnaz Celebrity Tennis Tournament for Children's Asthma Research Inst. and Hosp., Denver, 1971; with Investor Relations, Toronto, 1972; with Continental Pub. Relations, Toronto, 1975-76; pub. relations dir. W.B. Doner and Co., Southfield, Mich., 1982-85; pres. Hermanoff & Assocs., Inc., 1985—; spl. events chair United Found. Mem. Pub. Relations Soc. Am. (accredited), Pub. Relations Soc. Am. Counselors Acad. (past pres.), Women in Communications, Women in Econs. Club, Detroit Press Club. Club: Detroit Econs., Detroit. Office: Hermanoff & Assocs 31700 W 13 Mile Rd #112 Farmington Hills MI 48018

HERMANSON, GLORIA JEANE, communications executive; b. Williston, N.D., July 19, 1944; d. Arthur Martin and Lillian Coy (Sims) Hermanson; children: Marni Lee, H. Gordon. Sec. FBI, Washington, 1962-63, U.S. Congress, Washington, 1963-66; vocat. edn. instr. Mendocino County, Ukiah, Calif., 1970-71; owner H&M Equipment Co., Helena, Mont., 1971-77; market adminstr. Mountain Bell, Helena, 1977-78, mgr. pub. relations, consumer affairs dept., 1978—. Bd. dirs. Career Devel. Ctr., Helena, 1978-80, Pvt. Industry Council, Helena, 1979-81, Mont. Career Info. System, Helena, 1980-85, Mont. Foodbank Network, 1984-86, Rural Employment Opportunities, Helena, 1985—, Helena Film Soc., 1985-87, Retired Sr. Vol. Program, Helena, 1985—, Northern Rockies Action Group, 1988—. Mem. Nat. Assn. Female Execs., Mont. Assn. Female Execs. (bd. dirs. 1985-87), U.S. West Women, Women's Lobbyist Fund. Democrat. Home: 727 Bridgeview Ct Helena MT 59601 Office: Mountain Bell 560 N Park Helena MT 59601

HERMANUZ, GHISLAINE, architect, educator; b. Lausanne, Switzerland, Apr. 28, 1942; came to U.S., 1968, d. Max and Manotte (Tavernier) H.; 1 child, Dahoud P. Walker. Architecture degree, ETH/L, Lausanne, 1967; student Harvard U., 1969; M.S. in Urban Planning, Columbia U., 1971. Registered architect, Switzerland. Architect, The Architects Renewal Com., Harlem, N.Y., 1971-72; urban designer Dept. City Planning, N.Y.C., 1972-73; lectr. Cornell U., Ithaca, N.Y., 1972-74; asst. dean for Minority Affairs, asst. prof. Columbia Sch. Architecture, N.Y.C., 1975-82, assoc. prof., 1982-84, dir. Community Design Workshop, 1984-87; assoc. prof., CCNY, 1986—; cons. in field; ptnr. PHD Assocs., N.Y.C., 1982—. Contbr. numerous articles to profl. jours. Fulbright scholar, 1968; fellow German Marshall Fund, 1979; grantee Nat. Endowment for Art, 1982, New York State Council on the Arts, 1984. Mem. Societe D'Ingenieurs et Architectes (Switzerland). Office: City Coll Arch Ctr CCNY New York NY 10031

HERMENET, ARGELIA M. BUTTRAGO, government consultant; b. Panama, Mar. 2, 1934; d. Samuel and Maxima (De Leon) Buitrago; m. Raymond A. Hermenet, Apr. 7, 1955; children—Raymond, Maxine Joy, Melinda, Melanie. Student U. Pacific, 1951-52, U. Panama Sch. Social Work, 1951, 52-54; B.S., Springfield Coll., 1958, M.Ed., 1960; Ed.D. (Acad. fellow), U. Mass., 1971. Exec. sec. Pan-Niram Shipping Co. (Marin, Inc.), Panama City, Panama, 1951-53, medico-social caseworker Inst. Interam. Affairs, Santo Tomas and Children's Hosp., 1953-55; med. sec. Geneva Gen. Hosp., N.Y., 1955-56;' night clk. IBM dept. Springfield-Monarch Life Ins. Co., Mass., 1956-57; social worker North End Area Ministry, Springfield Council Chs., 1959-61; developer Maestros & Amigos, home tutorial English as 2d lang. program, 1959-65; social caseworker Child and Family Service, 1962-72; assoc. prof. Springfield Coll., part-time 1969-72; dir. bicultural programs Springfield Tech. Community Coll., 1972-75; cons. psychologist Boston Sch. System, 1977-83; cons. nat. curriculum series Assn. Supervision and Curriculum Devel., HEW; lectr. in field; cons. to Pres. of Panama, 1983—, coordinator plans and programs, 1983—; mem. State Adv. Council on Bilingual Edn., 1971—, mem. steering com., 1972—, chmn. higher edn. com., 1972-76; chmn. linguistic minority access com. Mass. Adv. Council Vocat. and Tech. Edn., 1973—; founder, producer, dir. Latino, 1st bilingual TV program in New Eng., 1969—; incorporator New Eng. Spanish-Am. Regional Inst., 1970-74, mem. exec. com., 1970-74, sec., 1971-74, chmn. pub. relations, 1971-72; producer, hostess bilingual TV show Sta. WGGB, 1968—. Coordinator Mass. Juan Fiesta Com., 1960-61, 63; mem. Mayor's Minority Group Housing Com., 1962-64; mem. Mayor's Human Relations Commn., 1966-72, sec., 1967-70; sec. Springfield Area Mental Health Bd., 1967-76; mem. exec. com. Area Manpower System, 1970-71; mem. Mass. adv. com. U.S. Commn. on Civil Rights, 1971—, also mem. P.R. com.; mem. com. on rent control Springfield City Council, 1971-72; mem. Springfield's Mayor's com. to negotiate Springfield Plan with trade unions and mgmt. for more minority group participation, 1971-72; co-founder Springfield Free U., 1970; mem. Gov.'s Commn. on Status of Women, 1971-72; mem. exec. com. Gov.'s Comprehensive Health Planning Adv. Council, 1971-76, sec., 1973-75; mem. State Adv. Council Mental Health; founding mem. Hispanic-Am. House, 1963-64, sec., dir., 1963-71; bd. dirs. Casa Credit Union, 1967-75; bd. dirs., incorporator Interfaith Housing Corp.; incorporator, 1st v.p. 1st Hispanic Fedn. Springfield, 1970-71; bd. dirs., chmnm. pub. relations com. Vis. Nurses Assn., 1972-74; mem. steering com. Hartford-Springfield Edn.-Work Council. Recipient award community service Springfield Action Com., 1974; Mujer award for TV contbns., Hartford, 1977. Mem. ASCAP, Panamanian Soc. Composers and Songwriters, Am. Guidance and Personnel Assn. (bd. dirs., exec. bd. Mass. chpt. 1972-74), Spanish Am. Union (bd. dirs., 1971-73, sec. 1971-73, co-chmn. 1972-73), World Affairs Council (bd. dirs. Connecticut Valley 1965-73), Sigma Lambda. also: 37 Westernview St Springfield MA 01108 Office: Pres Republic of Panama, Panama City Republic of Panama

HERMES, PATRICIA MARY, writer, educator; b. Bklyn., Feb. 21, 1936; d. Frederick Joseph and Jessie (Gould) Martin; m. Matthew E. Hermes, Aug. 24, 1957 (div. Oct. 1984); children—Paul, Mark, Tim, Matthew, Jennifer. B.A., St. John's U., 1957. Tchr., Rollingcrest Jr. High Sch., Takoma Park, Md., 1957-58, Delcastle Tech. High Sch. (Del.), 1972-73, Norfolk Schs. (Va.), 1981-82; author Harcourt Brace Jovanovich, Inc., San Diego, 1980—, also for Dell and Scholastic. Author: What If They Knew, 1980; Nobody's Fault, 1981; You Shouldn't Have to Say Goodbye, 1982; Who Will Take Care of Me, 1983; Friends Are Like That, 1984; (young adult novel) A Solitary Secret, 1985, Kevin Corbett Eats Flies, 1986, A Place for Jeremy, 1987, A Time to Listen: Preventing Youth Suicide, 1987; contbr. articles to profl. jours. Mem. Soc. Children's Book Writers, Authors Guild. Democrat. Roman Catholic. Home: 1414 Melville Ave Fairfield CT 06430

HERMINGHOUSE, PATRICIA ANNE, educator; b. Melrose Park, Ill., Mar. 13, 1940; m. 1964, 2 children. B.A., Knox Coll., 1962; M.A., Washington U., 1965, Ph.D. in German, 1968. Asst. prof. German, U. Mo.-St. Louis, 1966-67, vis. lectr., 1968-69; asst. prof. Washington U., St. Louis, 1967-78, assoc. prof. German, 1978-83; Fuchs prof. German studies, U. Rochester, N.Y., 1983 , also chmn. dept. fgn. langs., lits. and linguistics; lectr. German, Fontbonne Coll., 1965-66. Internat. Research & Exchanges Bd. ad hoc grantee, 1976. Mem. MLA, Am. Assn. Tchrs. German (exec. council 1979-81), Soc. Study Multi-Ethnic Lit. U.S., Coalition Women German (coordinator 1974-75, nat. steering com. 1976-79). Contbr. articles to profl. jours.; editor or co-editor: Literatur der DDR in den Siebziger Jaren, 1983; Literatur und Literaturtheorie in der DDR, 1976; Frauen in Mittelpunkt, 1987; editor GDR Bull.: Newsletter Lit. and Culture in German Dem. Republic, 1975-83. Address: Univ Rochester Dept Fgn Langs Lits & Linguistics 500 Joseph C Wilson Rochester NY 14627

HERNANDEZ, ANTONIA, lawyer; b. Torreon, Coahuila, Mexico, May 30, 1948; came to U.S., 1956; d. Manuel and Nicolasa (Martinez) H.; m. Michael Stern, Oct. 8, 1977; children: Benjamin, Marisa, Michael. BA, UCLA, 1971, JD, 1974. Bar: Calif. 1974, D.C. 1979. Staff atty. East Los Angeles Ctr. Law and Justice, 1974-77; directing atty. Legal Aid Found., Lincoln Heights, Calif., 1977-78; staff counsel U.S. Senate Com., Washington, 1979-80; assoc. counsel Mexican Am. Legal Def. Ednl. Fund, Washington, 1981-83; v.p. Mexican Am. Legal Def. Ednl. Fund, Los Angeles, 1984-85, pres., gen. counsel, 1985—; bd. dirs. Fed. Immigration Law Reporter, Washington, Oxfam Am., Boston, The Alan Guttmacher Inst., N.Y.C. Contbr. articles to profl. jours. Co-chmn. enriching diversity com. Los Angeles 2000; mem. Nat. Competition on the Constn., Hon. Com. on 75th Anniversary Dept. Labor. AAUW fellow, 1973-74. Fellow AAUW; mem. Calif. Bar Assn., Washington D.C. Bar Assn. Roman Catholic. Home: 1561 E Mountain Pasadena CA 91104 Office: Mexican Am Legal Def Fund 634 S Spring St Suite 1100 Los Angeles CA 90014

HERNÁNDEZ, CAROLYN BROLL, marketing executive; b. Atlantic City, N.J., July 9, 1956; d. Arthur Gorsuch and Nancy (Tompkins) Broll; m. Luis Carlos Hernández, Sept. 17, 1950; children: Johanna, Natalie. BA in Sociology/Anthropology, Gettysburg Coll., 1978. Translator Travel Agy., Columbia, 1978-79; bilingual tchr. Montessori Sch., Columbia, 1979-81; mktg. coordinator Pepsi Cola, Westchester, Pa., 1981-85, mktg. mgr., 1985—. Mem. Carbonated Beverage Inst., Nat. Assn. Female Execs., Women in Family Owned Bus. Democrat. Home: 1002 Pine Valley Circle Westchester PA 19382 Office: Pepsi Cola Distbg Co 920 S Boehmer St Westchester PA 19381

HERNANDEZ, SONIA CARIDAD, public relations executive; b. Havana, Cuba, July 19, 1954; came to U.S., 1966; d. Carlos P. Hernandez Avila and Ofelia Menendez Cespedes de Hernandez. Student, Barbizon Modeling Sch., 1980; AA, Miami-Dade Community Coll., 1986; student, Fla. Internat. U., 1988. Cert. customer service rep. Rep. ins. LaBella Ins. Agy., Port Chester, N.Y., 1972-76; adminstrv. asst. Avon Products Co., Rye, N.Y., 1977-80; adminstrv. asst. Sun Bank/Miami (Fla.) N.A., 1984-86, rep. customer service, 1986, officer customer service, 1987—. Mem. Miami Women's C. of C. Roman Catholic. Office: Sun Bank/Miami NA 777 Brickell Ave Miami FL 33131

HERNANDEZ, WANDA GRACE, rehabilitation counselor, sales manager; b. Detroit, Apr. 23, 1942; d. Harry Lee and Lillian Delores (Williams) Williams; m. Ignacio Heriberto Hernandez, Nov. 25, 1969 (div. April 1979); 1 child, Heriberto Alejandro. BS, Wayne State U., 1973, MA, 1977. Substance abuse counselor Boniface Community Action Corp., Detroit, 1972-73; vocations rehab. counselor Mich. Rehab. Services, Detroit, 1974—. Named Disting. Rehab. Profl., Nat. Disting. Service Registry Library of Congress, 1987. Fellow Nat. Rehab. Assn.; mem. The Smithsonian Assocs. Jehovah Witness. Home: 9056 Patton Detroit MI 48228 Office: Mich Rehab Services 30 E Canfield Detroit MI 48201

HERNDON, LYNDA LEANNE, health facility administrator, investor; b. Winter Haven, Fla., Apr. 13, 1942; d. Rufus Idus and Mildred Louise (Stout) H.; m. George William Yeagle (div.); children: Eric William, Timberly Brook. Diploma, Gordon Keller Sch. Nursing; BA, Met. State U., St. Paul, 1975-78; MBA, Nova U. RN, Fla., Colo., Pa., Wis., N.H. Staff nurse various hosps., 1962-68; asst. dir. operating room Sacred Heart Hosp., Eau Claire, Wis., 1971-77; asst. dir. nursing Luther Hosp., Eau Claire, 1977-79; prt. practice psychotherapy private practice, Eau Claire, 1978-80; ind. investor Sarasota, Fla., 1980-82; asst. dir. operating room Sarasota Meml. Hosp., 1982-84; dir. Sarasota Meml. Hosp. Cape Surgery Ctr., Fla., 1984—; waterskier, model Cypress Gardens, 1952-60; dogbreeder and exhibitor, Fla. and Wis., 1971-87, (AKC champions 1971-86); quarter horse breeder, race farm owner, Wis., 1971-77. Rep. United Fund, Sarasota, 1986. Fellow Am. Hosp. Assn. Ambulatory Care; mem. Assn. Operating Room Nurses (bd. dirs.), Am. Assn. Individual Investors, Am. Transactional Analysis Assn. Republican. Office: Sarasota Mem Hosp Cape Surgery Ctr 1941 Waldemere St Sarasota FL 33579

HERON, CAROL VOYLES, speech pathologist; b. Byron, Wyo., Sept. 2, 1939; d. Alvin Jesse Voyles and Caroline Mary (Johnson) Denny; m. C.E. Pat Heron (div. 1980); children: Lynn Perri, Patricia, Cinda, Cara; m. James G. Forbes. M in Speech Pathology, Calif. State U., Chico, 1974. Coordinator Lassen County Schs., Susanville, Calif., 1972-77; tchr. Shasta County Schs., Redding, Calif., 1977-78; prin. Teach-A-Tot Presch., Susanville, 1978-80, Redding, 1978-81; prin. Evergreen Ctr. Presch. for Communication Disorders, Redding, 1979—; cons. Shasta Community Coll., Redding, 1980—, Coll. of the Siskoyous, Weed, Calif., 1987. Active Redding YMCA, 1986—, Beyond War, Redding, 1986—, Pub. Broadcasting Sta. KIXE-TV, Redding, 1986—. Mem. Council for Exceptional Children, Assn. for Retarded Citizens, Self-Help for Hard of Hearing. Republican. Lodge: Women of Moose. Home and Office: 2933 Shasta View Dr Redding CA 96002

HERPICH, SUSAN, nurse; b. Torrington, Conn., Jan. 16, 1947; d. William Martin and Lillian Edith (Loyeska) Herpich; divorced; children: Tia Patricia, Thomas Paul Jr. AS in Nursing, U. Bridgeport, 1964-66. Operating room nurse Charlotte Hungerford Hosp., Torrington, Conn., 1966-67, 77-87, Lovelace Clinic, Albuquerque, 1967-69; emergency room, delivery room nurse Winsted (Conn.) Meml. Hosp., 1970-71. History nurse ARC, Litchfield, Conn., 1982—. Mem. Assn. for Operating Room Nurses. Republican. Lutheran. Home: Rural Rt #1 Box 65 Litchfield CT 06759

HERPIN, LINNIE CAIN, poet, retired banker; b. Opelousas, La., Nov. 16, 1945; d. Charles Warren and Patricia Lwellyn (Fontenot) Cain; m. Randal Raymond Herpin; children: James Randal, William Cain, Deon Christopher, Damien Andre, Jeanne Dominique, Merideth Ann, Brandon Charles. Student, U. So. La., 1963-64. Credit clk. Exhange Bank and Trust, Dallas, 1965; auditor City Nat. Bank and Trust, Baton Rouge, 1966-68; sec., teller Cen. Bank, Monroe, La., 1969-74; teller First Nat. Bank, Opelousas, 1975-77; account supr., dir. sales tng. Hub City Bank and Trust, Lafayette, La., 1977-87. Co-author: (song) Emerald Eyes, 1984, The Louisiana Waltz, 1987; contbr. numerous poems to jour., 1985-87. Mem. Lafayette Econ. Devel. Task Force, 1987. Recipient Presdl. citation Am. Bankers Assn., Washington, 1984. Mem. Acadiana Music and Entertainment (sec. 1987). Democrat. Roman Catholic. Home: Rt 3 Box 128 Opelousas LA 70570

HERRE, SAUNDRA SUE, small business owner; b. Columbus, Ohio, Aug. 3, 1936; d. James O. and M. Margaret DeVore Ruvoldt; m. Frank J. Herre, Nov. 28, 1958; children: Margaret Herre Fries, James F. Herre. BS, Miami U., 1958. English tchr. Groveport (Ohio) High Sch., 1958-59; sec. to chief div. of reclamation Ohio Dept. Agriculture, Columbus, 1959; broadcaster, sales exec. Sta. WFNY, Racine, Wis., 1970-75; practice pub. relations Racine, 1975-76; ptnr. Portfolio Ltd., Racine, 1975—; v.p. El Sol Broadcasting, Milw., 1980-85; pres. Herrewood Assocs., Racine, 1982—; speaker in field, 1982—. Chair White House Conf. on Small Bus., Washington, 1986, Gov's. Conf., Madison, 1987; bd. dirs. Racine County Econ. Devel. Corp., Racine, 1985—, Big Bros./Big Sisters, Racine, 1986—, Small Bus. United, 1985—. Mem. Wis. Bus. Women Coalition (co-founder, chair 1987), Wis. Women Entrepreneurs (founder, pres.), Ind. Bus. Assn. Wis. (bd. dirs., v.p. 1985-88, apptd. Wis. jobs council 1987—), Nat. Assn. Women Bus. Owners. Office: Herrewood Assocs 4101 Pennington Racine WI 53403

HERRERA, IRMA DOLORES, lawyer; b. Alice, Tex., Mar. 12, 1951; d. Claudio M. and Esperanza (Martinez) H. BA, St. Mary's U., 1971; post-grad., Trinity U., 1971-72; JD, U. Notre Dame, 1978. Bar: Wash. 1979, Calif. 1981, U.S. Dist. Ct. (ea. dist.) Wash., U.S. Dist. Ct. (no., so. and ea. dist.) Calif., U.S. Ct. Appeals (9th cir.). Urban planner Curtis and Davis Architects and Planners, New Orleans, 1973-75; staff atty. Evergreen Legal Services, Wenatchee and Suunyside, Wash., 1978-80; staff atty., dir. ednl. programs Mex. Am. Legal Def. and Ednl. Fund, San Francisco, 1980-83; vis. prof. polit. sci. Colo. Coll., Colorado Springs, 1983-86; assoc. Severson, Werson, Berke & Melchior, San Francisco, 1986—. Contbr. articles to profl. jours. Brachenridge fellow Trinity U., 1971. Mem. ABA, Calif. Bar Assn., San Francisco Bar Assn, San Francisco La Raza Bar Assn. Office: Severson Werson et al 1 Embarcadero Ctr 25th Floor San Francisco CA 94111

HERRERA, SANDRA JOHNSON, school system administrator; b. Riverside, Calif., June 21, 1944; d. William Emory Johnson and Mildred Alice (Alford) Wimer; m. Wynn Neal Huffman, Feb. 19, 1962 (div. May 1967); 1 child, Kristen Lee; m. Steven Jack Herrera, June 21, 1985. AA in Purchasing Mgmt., Fullerton Coll., 1983; BSBA, U. Redlands, 1985, MA in Mgmt., 1988. Sr. purchasing clk Fullerton (Calif.) Union High Sch. Dist., 1969-77, buyer, 1977-79, coordinator budgets and fiscal affairs, 1979-83; asst. dir. fin. services Downey (Calif.) Unified Sch. Dist., 1983-85; dir. acctg. Whittier (Calif.) Union High Sch. Dist., 1985—; cons. Heritage Dental Lab., Mission Viejo, Calif, 1981—. Spl. dep. sheriff Santa Barbara (Calif.) County Sheriff's Mounted Posse, 1986—; spl. dep. marshal U.S. Marshals Posse, Los Angeles, 1987—. Mem. Calif. Assn. Sch. Bus. Ofcls. (treas. S.E. sect. 1985, mem. acct. research and devel. com. 1983—, mem. budgeting and devel. com. 1979-83), so. Calif Paraders Assn. (exec. sec. 1976—), Calif. State Horsemens Assn. (regional v.p. 1986-87, sec. 1988), Alpha Gamma Sigma. Home: 18503 Sordello St Rowland Heights CA 91748 Office: Whittier Union High Sch Dist 9401 S Painter Ave Whittier CA 90605

HERRICK, DONNA SUE, savings and loan executive; b. Oneida, Ky., Dec. 4, 1951; d. Everett William and Zenith (Palmer) Thorpe; m. John Paul Gabbard, Oct. 29, 1971 (div. Mar. 1982); 1 child, Ryan Paul; m. Harlan Douglas Herrick, Nov. 21, 1984. Grad. in Banking with honors, U. Ky., 1980; cert. nat. compliance, U. Notre Dame, 1981. Tax clk. Saunier and Co., CPAs, Lexington, Ky., 1970-72; couselor aide Bur. Rehab., Lexington, 1972-73; audit acctg. aide IRS, Lexington, 1973-77, audit clk., 1982-83; compliance officer, auditor Peoples Exchange Bank, Beattyville, Ky., 1977-82; coordinator student loans 1st Security Bank, Lexington, 1983-84, personal banking processor, 1985; fin. mgr. Solar Age Ky., Lexington, 1984; asst. v.p. audit/compliance Tucson Savs. and Loan, 1985-87; asst. v.p., audit/compliance/security Universal Savings and Loan, 1987—. Bd. dirs. Ariz. Assn. for the Gifted and Talented, Marana, 1986—. Mem. Fin. Mgrs. Assn. (fed. regulations com. 1986—), Inst. Internal Auditors (bd. dirs. 1986—). Congregationalist. Office: Universal Savs and Loan 4141 N Scottsdale Rd Scottsdale AZ 85251

HERRICK, KATHLEEN MAGARA, social worker; b. Mpls., Oct. 18, 1943; d. William Frank and Mary Genevieve (Gill) Magara; B.A. in Social Work and French, Coll. St. Benedict, St. Joseph, Minn., 1965; M.S.W. (Mildred B. Erickson fellow 1975), Mich. State U., E. Lansing, 1976; m. John Middlemist Herrick, Feb. 5, 1966; children—Elizabeth Jane, Kathryn Mary. Social worker II, Carver County Social Services, Chaska, Minn., 1965-70; therapist St. Lawrence Community Mental Health Center, Lansing, Mich., 1974-75; sch. social worker Ingham Intermediate Sch. Dist., Mason, Mich., 1975-76; home/sch. coordinator Eaton Intermediate Sch. Dist., Charlotte, Mich., 1976-81; caseworker St. Vincent Home for Children, Lansing, 1979-80; tchr. cons. for severely emotionally impaired, 1981-83; behavior disorder cons., 1983-85; sch. social work cons., 1985—. Chairperson bd. dirs. Eaton County Child Abuse and Neglect Prevention Council, 1986—; Democratic precinct del.; bd. dirs. Catholic Social Services, Lansing; specialist substance abuse prevention region XIII SAPE, 1987—. Mem. NEA, Mich. Edn. Assn., Okemos High Sch. Parent Orgn., Kinawa Parent Orgn., Nat. Assn. Social Workers, Nat. Assn. Retarded Citizens, Am. Orthopsychiat. Assn., Mich. Assn. Sch. Social Workers, Mich. Assn. Emotionally Disturbed Children, Eaton County Assn. Retarded Citizens, Feingold Assn. SE Mich., NOW, Nat. Women's Health Network, Amnesty Internat., Phi Kappa Phi, Phi Alpha. Democrat. Roman Catholic. Home: 2330 Shawnee Trail Okemos MI 48864 Office: 1790 E Packard Hwy Charlotte MI 48813

HERRICK, PHYLLIS MILLER, librarian; b. Glen Cove, N.Y., Mar. 20, 1930; d. William Selden Native and Mildred (Mandaville) M.; m. David Coulson Herrick, June 28, 1952; children: David Jeffrey, Brian Mandaville, Jonathan Lindsay. Student, Packard Jr. Coll., 1950. With IBM Corp., 1949-53; exec. sec. Sperry Corp., 1953-54; corp. sec. Bellmore (N.Y.) Meml. Pub. Library, 1966-76; librarian Bellmore Union Free Sch. Dist. Elementary Library, 1976—. Republican. Episcopalian. Home: 130 Belmill Rd Bellmore NY 11710

HERRING, EVELYN MAE, leasing company executive; b. Portchester, N.Y., Apr. 13, 1936; d. Carl Gilman and Margaret Anna (Kersten) Wright; m. David Andrew Tilley, Aug. 7, 1965 (div. 1980); 1 child, David Andrew; m. Travis Carlie Herring, Dec. 27, 1981. B.S., Cornell U., 1958. Tchr. dept. home econs. Dept. Kings Park High Sch., Hauppauge, N.Y., 1958-62; real estate broker Jan Realty Co., St. James, N.Y., 1962-72; owner, operator The Village Tub, Plymouth, N.H., 1972-76; engraver, ptnr. The Trophy Shoppe, Sarasota, Fla., 1977-79; owner, mgr. The Plant Shed, Sarasota, 1979—. Mem., sec. Miller Place Fire Dept. Aux., N.Y., 1966-72; organist Trinity Methodist Ch., Plymouth, 1975, 76, Calvary Methodist Ch., Sarasota, 1979-82. Mem. Fla. Foliage Assn., Am. Bus. Women's Assn., Manasota Interiorscapers (founder). Republican. Club: Am. Contract Bridge League (Memphis). Lodge: Enterprise Rebekah. Avocations: band organist, duplicate bridge. Home and Office: 2242 Shadow Lake Dr Sarasota FL 33582

HERRING, FAYE, real estate and mortgage loan broker; b. Mexia, Tex., June 9, 1934; d. Carl Lee and Myrtle Inez (Sykes) Herring; children—Harvey Moody, Jr., Mickey Faye Reagan. Student Henderson County Jr. Coll., student real estate U. Houston; student property mgmt., Ky., La., Can. Cert. Nat. Assn. Ind. Fee Appraisers. Owner-operator Faye Herring Investments, Houston, 1967—. Office: 3408 Crawford St Houston TX 77004

HERRING, RUTH ELLENORE, administrative manager, consultant; b. Anoka County, Minn., May 8, 1934; d. Peter and Tena (Knutson) Frans; m. Joseph C. Herring; 1 child, Karine Renee Beard. Student, Arapahoe Community Coll., 1977. Sec., dist. mgr. Ryder System, Denver, 1954-62; legal sec. Fred W. Vondy, Denver, 1962-66; paralegal Marathon, Littleton, 1966-78; liaison Salt River Project, Phoenix, 1978-81; owner, mgr. Suite Master, Inc., Denver, 1982-83; adminstrv. mgr. Windsor Gardens Assn., Denver, 1983—; cons. J.C. Herring & Assoc., Denver, 1985—. Republican. Home: 3257 S Steele St Denver CO 80210

HERRINGTON, LOIS HAIGHT, government official, lawyer; b. Seattle, Dec. 6, 1939; d. Herbert Schuler and Marie Yvonne (Young) H.; m. John Stewart Herrington, Apr. 10, 1965; children: Lisa Marie, Victoria Jean. B.A., U. Calif.-Davis, 1961; LL.B., Hastings Coll. Law, 1965. Probation officer San Joaquin County, Calif., 1962; counselor Juvenile Hall, Calif., 1963-65; mem. firm Herrington & Herrington, Calif., 1967-76; dep. dist. atty. Alameda County, Oakland, Calif., 1976-81; asst. atty. gen. Dept. Justice, Washington, 1983-86; chmn. White House Conf. For A Drug Free Am., 1987-88; chmn. Pres.' Task Force on Victims of Crime, Washington, 1982; ex-officio mem. adv. bd. Nat. Inst. for Judiciary, Washington, 1983—; mem. Fed. Coordinating Council, Washington, 1983—; U.S. del. to Internat. Conf. on Drug Abuse and Illicit Traffic, Vienna; U.S. del. to UN Commn. on Status of Women, Nairobi, Kenya. Vic-pres. Diablo Scholarships, Calif., 1973-76; sr. advisor USO, 1972-75; vol. high sch. vocat. counselor, 1974-76; coordinator Drug Diversion Program, Calif., 1975-76; mem. Contra Costa Child Devel. Council, 1973-76; hon. mem. Calif. Sexual Assault Investigations; mem. Alemeda County Women's Coalition on Domestic Violence, Calif., 1979-81. Recipient Outstanding Community Service Commendation Concord Police Dept; recipient Crime Victims Rights award Family and Friends of Missing Persons and Violent Crime Victims, 1983, Outstanding Pub. Policy Leadership in Service to Victims award Nat. Orgn. Victims Assistance, 1983, Highest Quality Profl. Service to Criminal Justice and Law Enforcement award Nat. Law Enforcement Council, 1983. Mem. ABA, Calif. Bar Assn., Calif. Dist. Attys. Assn., Queen's Bench Assn., Hastings Law Sch. Alumni Assn. Republican. Episcopalian. Office: White House Conf Drug Free Am 726 Jackson Pl NW Washington DC 20503

HERRINGTON-BORRE, FRANCES JUNE, state government human services executive, school executive; b. Austin, Tex., June 14, 1935; d. George Wilmas Neill and Mildred Lucille (Alexander) Williamson; m. Harold M. Herrington, June 6, 1953 (dec. Dec. 1978); children—Harold M., Cheryl Anne Herrington; m. Thomas Raymond Borre, Apr. 5, 1985. Student, U. Tex., 1967-71. With Tex. Dept. Human Services, Austin, 1961—, adminstrv. technician, 1967-71, field rep., 1971-81, asst. personnel dir., 1981—; freelance profl. interpreter for deaf, 1964—; dir. Austin Sign Lang. Sch., 1964—; cons. in field; project dir. Gov.'s Office, 1980. Gov.'s appointee Joint Adv. Com. on Ednl. Services to Deaf, Austin, 1976-78; chmn. Tex. Commn. for Deaf Bd. Eval. of Interpreters, 1981-84; chmn. Tex. State Agy. Liaisons to Gov.'s Commn. for Women, 1985. Recipient Tex. Rehab. Commn. Merit award, 1977, Gov.'s citation, 1978; named An Outstanding Woman Central Tex., AAUW, 1982, Significant and Meritorious Service to Mankind award Capitol Sertoma Club, 1976, Disting. Service as Adv. and Interpretar award Dal-Tar Lions Club, 1977. Mem. Nat. Assn. of Deaf (Golden Hand award 1987), Tex. Assn. of Deaf (Service citation 1967, Vol. Service award 1971, Interpreter of Decade award 1981), Nat. Registry Interpreters for Deaf, Tex. Soc. Interpreters for Deaf (pres. 1969-70), Austin Interpreters for Deaf. Mem. Ch. of Christ. Home: 2404 Laramie Trail Austin TX 78745 Office: Tex Dept Human Services 701 W 51st St Austin TX 78769

HERRMANN, CHARLENE ALICE, transportation executive; b. Chgo., Nov. 19, 1937; d. Floyd Alvin and Alice Elise (Stach) Schraufnagel; m. George Edward Herrmann, Aug. 5, 1961; children: Kyle Ann, Jeffrey Edward. BS in Edn., No. Ill. U., 1959. Cert. elem. tchr., Ill. Tchr. Sch. Dist. 163, Park Forest, Ill., 1959-61, Sch. Dist. 33, West Chgo., Ill., 1961-65; tax rep. IRS, Chgo., 1979-81; rt. supr. Crosstown Services, Inc., subs. Willett, Inc., Glen Ellyn, Ill., 1981-86, br. mgr., 1986—; mem. transp. task force Special Assn. for Special Edn. in Du Page County (North Region), Roselle, Ill., 1986—. 4-H leader-dir. DuPage County Coop. Extension Service, 1976—. Democrat. Roman Catholic. Club: Winfield Jr. Women's (Ill.) (com. chmn. 1970-75).

HERRMANN, KATHERINE SCOTT, geophysicist; b. Balt., Feb. 7, 1959; d. Louis Grebb and Rose Marie (Hurt) H. BS in Geophysics, Va. Poly. Inst. and State U., 1981. Jr. geophysicist ARCO Exploration Co., Dallas, 1981; geophysicist Arco Exploration Co., Dallas, 1982-85; sr. geophysicist EXXON Corp., Houston, 1985-86, sr. petroleum geophysicist, 1986—. Mem. Nat. Assn. Female Execs., Houston Geol. Soc., Am. Assn. Petroleum Geologists, Houston Jr. C. of C. (sec. 1987, bd. dirs. 1986). Republican. Home: 1519 Plumwood Dr Houston TX 77014 Office: EXXON Co PO Box 4279 Houston TX 77210

HERRON, ELLEN PATRICIA, retired judge; b. Auburn, N.Y., July 30, 1927; d. David Martin and Grace Josephine (Berner) Herron; A.B. Trinity Coll., 1949; M.A., Cath. U. Am., 1954; J.D., U. Calif.-Berkeley, 1964. Asst. dean Cath. U. Am., 1952-54; instr. East High Sch., Auburn, 1955-57; asst. dean Wells Coll., Aurora, N.Y., 1957-58; instr. psychology and history Contra Costa Coll., 1958-60; dir. row Stanford, 1960-61; assoc. Knox & Kretzmer, Richmond, Calif., 1964-65; admitted to Calif. bar, 1965; ptnr. Knox & Herron, 1965-74, Knox, Herron and Masterson, 1974-77 (both Richmond, Calif.); judge Superior Ct. State of Calif., 1977-87; gen. ptnr. Real Estate Syndicates, Calif., 1967-77; owner, mgr. The Barricia Vineyards, 1978—. Active numerous civic orgns.; bd. dirs. Rhonoh Sch., Richmond, YWCA, Econ. Devel. Council Richmond; alumnae bd. dirs. Boalt Hall, U. Calif.-Berkeley, 1980-84. Mem. ABA, Contra Costa Bar Assn. (exec. com. 1969-74), State Bar Calif., Calif. Trial Lawyers, Nat. Assn. Women Lawyers, Nat. Assn. Women Judges, Calif. Women Lawyers, Applicants Attys. Assn., Calif. Judges Assn. (ethics com. 1977-79, criminal law procedure com. 1979-80), Queen's Bench, Juvenile Ct. Judges Assn. Democrat. Home: 51 Western Dr Point Richmond CA 94801

HERRON, LIZA GILPIN, travel compny executive; b. Sewickley, Pa., Aug. 14, 1953; d. Lewis II and Sybil (Adams) H. BA, Schiller Coll., London, 1978. Travel counselor Fairmont Circle Travel, Cleve., 1978-80; travel counselor Ask Mr. Foster Travel Service, N.Y.C., 1980-81, in-plant specialist, 1981—, sr. travel counselor, 1981—, supr., 1982, mgr., 1983, multi-office mgr., 1983—. Mem. Nat. Assn. Female Execs., Women Execs. Internat. Tourism Assn. Avocations: traveling, tennis, bridge, horseback riding, opera. Office: Ask Mr Foster Travel Service 757 3d Ave 11th Floor New York NY 10017

HERRON, LUCINDA DARLENE, account specialist; b. Columbus, Ohio, Feb. 26, 1946; d. Leo James and Ethel (Foth) Pyle; m. Donald J. Herron, Jan. 14, 1972 (div. Nov. 30, 1979); 1 child, Kimberly Dawn. Customer service officer Flagship Nat. Bank, Coral Gables, Fla., 1965-79; mktg. support rep. Lanier Bus. Products, Miami, 1979-82; account exec. Am. Bank Stationery, Ft. Lauderdale, Fla., 1982—. Contbr. articles to profl. jours. Mem. Am. Inst. Banking, Nat. Dog Owner's Assn., Nat. Assn. for Am. Pit Bull Terriers, Everglades Pit Bull Club (founder, 1st pres.), Miami Obedience Club (trial chmn. 1978), South Fla. Schutzhund Club., Greater Miami C. of C., Jaycees. Democrat. Presbyterian. Home: 14240 SW 96th Terr Miami FL 33186

HERRON, MARTHA M., utility company executive; b. Hazleton, Pa., Aug. 28, 1948; d. John Joseph and Regina Mary (Gregoria) Darraugh; m. Terrence Joseph Herron, Aug. 29, 1970; 1 child, Terrence II. Student, Pa. State U., Hazleton, 1967, King's Coll., Wilkes-Barre, Pa., 1984—, Luzerne County Community Coll., Nanticoke, Pa., 1985—. Various positions Pa. Power and Light Co., Hazleton, 1967-1969, customer rep., 1969-73, level 3 stenographer, 1973, supr. div. accounts, 1973-83, area mgr., 1983—; bd. dirs. Econ. Devel. Council of Northeastern Pa., Carbon County Econ. Devel. Chairwoman Leadership Hazleton, 1985-87, steering com. Leadership Pennsylvania; chmn. bd. Hospice St. John; v.p., centennial chairwoman United Way of Greater Hazleton, 1987, campaign chair, 1987, state bd. dirs.; campaign Luzerne County Human Services Task Force; indsl. liaison CAN DO, Inc., Hazleton, 1986-87. Recipient Presdl. Community Service award Hazleton United Way, 1985; PEARL award Hazleton YWCA, 1987; named Woman of Yr. Hazleton Soroptimists, 1987. Mem. Greater Hazleton C. of C. (chairwoman, 1985, 87, cert. of merit award 1986). Republican. Roman Catholic. Clubs: Women's Coalition (v.p. 1984, 88), Legal Aux. (pres. 1984, 87). Office: Pa Power and Light Co 344 S Poplar St Hazleton PA 18252

HERRON, MONICA CHANEY, accountant; b. Burlingame, Calif., June 10, 1956; d. Kenneth Morgan and Olga Teresa (Gaudioso) Chaney; m. Kevin William Herron, June 2, 1985; children: Kevin William II, Andrew Kenneth. Cert. acctg., Am. River Coll., Sacramento, 1985. Office mgr. Thrifty Rent-a-Car, Sacramento, 1975-76; account rep. Morris Plan Co., Sacramento and Santa Barbara, Calif., 1976-78; br. mgr. Avco Fin. Services, Santa Barbara, 1978-80; tng. rep. Avco Fin. Services, Newport Beach, Calif., 1980-81; jr. acct. Sutter Community Hosps., Sacramento, 1982-84; pvt. practice acctg. Carmichael, Calif., 1983—. Democrat. Roman Catholic.

HERRON, WENDY WATTS, wine consultant; b. York, Pa., Oct. 9, 1952; d. Alphonso Irving and Daphne Jean (Gainsford) Watts; m. Frederic Joseph Bonnie, (div. 1986); m. Kenneth Scott Herron, Feb. 14, 1987. BS, U. Cin., 1975. Store mgr. The Grapevine, Inc., Birmingham, Ala., 1978-81; sales rep. Supreme Beverage Co., Birmingham, 1981-84, Internat. Wines Co., Birmingham, 1984—; speaker, instr. various groups, Birmingham, 1978—; v.p. Birmingham Wine Experience, 1987—. Mem. Wine Educator's Soc., Tuesday Group. Democrat. Mem. United Ch. Christ. Office: Internat Wines Inc 288 Snow Dr Birmingham AL 35209

HERSHA, KATHRYN LOUISE JAMIESON, system and data analyst; b. Fort Wayne, Ind., Feb. 12, 1940; d. Norval Eugene and Dorothy Ellen (Turflinger) Jamieson. Student St. Francis Coll., Fort Wayne, 1964-65, Fort Wayne Art Inst., 1967-74; AS, Ind. U.-Fort Wayne, 1973; student U. Evansville, 1977-79, Ringling Art Sch., 1984-88. Programmer Lincoln Nat. Bank, Fort Wayne, 1968-74; programmer, analyst Atlas Van Lines, Evansville, Ind., 1974-77; sr. analyst Nat. Sharedata, Evansville, 1977-79; project leader Fla. Software Services, Orlando, 1979-81; system cons. Anacomp, Sarasota, Fla., 1981-86; bus. analyst Electronic Data Systems, Sarasota, 1986—. Active Sarasota Art Assn., Asolo Festival Theatre Assn., Sarasota Arts Council, Women's Caucus for Art, Sarasota Opera Assn. Mem Nat. Assn. Female Execs., Am. Mgmt. Assn. Methodist. Avocations: art, sculpting. Home: PO Box 1235 Sarasota FL 34230 Office: EDS 1680 Third St Suite 400 Sarasota FL 34230

HERSH-COCHRAN, MONA SHEINFELD, educator; b. Phila., Dec. 3, 1934; m. Kendall P. Cochran; children—Paula, Susan, Kenneth. B.A., Rutgers U., 1956; M.A., Temple U., 1968; M.A., So. Meth. U., 1964, Ph.D., 1966. Teaching asst. So. Meth. U., Dallas, 1961-64; vis. prof. State Coll. Ark., Conway, summers 1967, 68; prof. Tex. Woman's U., Denton, 1969—, prof. econs., 1965—; vis. research scholar London Sch. Econs., London Sch. Hygiene, 1981-82; acad. visitor U. York, Eng., 1981-82; advisor in health econs. World Health Orgn., 1982—; visiting prof. U. Auckland, New Zealand, U. New Castle, New South Wales, Australia, 1985; vis. lectr. U. Barcelona, Spain; cons. U.S. Dept HEW, Bur. Quality Assurance; econ. cons.; computer and systems analysis cons. Contbr. articles to profl. jours. Recipient Outstanding Profs. award Tex. Woman's U., 1969-71; Most Valuable Mem. award Ops. Research Soc. Am.; Tex. Woman's U. Research grantee, 1967, 76, Journalism award, 1973; Danforth Assoc. award, 1977-83; NSF award, 1981-82. Mem. Am. Econ. Assn., Assn. Social Econs. (assoc. editor Forum 1978-81, mem. nat. exec. council 1985-87); Southwestern Social Sci. Assn. (chmn. nominating com. 1978-81), Southwestern Econs. Assn. (sec.-treas. 1970-81), S.W. Soc. Economists, Western Soc. Economists, Western Social Sci. Assn., AAUW, Bus. and Profl. Women, Health Econs. Study Group United Kingdom, Omicron Delta Epsilon (nat. v.p. 1986-87). Home: 3765 Weeburn Dallas TX 75229 Office: Tex Womans U Dept Bus & Econs Denton TX 76204

HERSON, ARLENE RITA, television program host; b. N.Y.C.; d. Sam and Mollie (Friedman) Hornreich; m. Milton Herson, June 16, 1963; children: Michael, Karen. Student, Queens Coll., 1957, New Sch. for Social Research, N.Y.C., 1960. Exec. sec. Tex McCrary, Inc., N.Y.C., 1958-60; asst. to pres. Safire Pub. Relations, N.Y.C., 1960-62; columnist The Advisor, Inc., Middletown, N.J., 1974-78; producer, host The Arlene Herson Show, N.Y.C., 1978—; syndicated nationally on Tempo TV, 1988. Dir. women's activities campaign for Sen. Jacob J. Javits, N.Y.C., 1968; bd. dirs. Monmouth (N.J.) Mus., 1982-86; com. mem. Children's Psychiatric Ctr., 1971—, Monmouth Park Charity Fund, 1980—; corp. exec. bd. Family and Children's Services, 1985—; active Monmouth Ocean Devel. Council, 1981—; life mem. Brandeis U. Library Fund, N.Y. chpt. Recipient Cape award Cable TV Network, 1984-87, Woman of Achievement in Communications award Advisory Commn. on Status of Women, 1986, PAL (Pub. & Leased Access) award for best talk show Paragon Cable TV, Manhattan, 1988, spl. resolution N.J. Assembly, 1988. Mem. Nat. Assn. Female Execs, Nat. Assn. for Profl. Women.

HERSON, DIANE S., microbiologist; b. N.Y.C., Apr. 23, 1944; d. Morris A. and Esther K. (Goldman) H.; B.S., Cornell U., 1964; M.S., Rutgers U., 1966, Ph.D., 1968; m. Stephen H. Franklin, Oct. 21, 1973; children—Pamela Allison Franklin, Daniel Jonathan. Lab instr. Cornell U., Ithaca, N.Y., 1964; research asst. Rutgers U., New Brunswick, N.J., 1964-66, research asso., 1966-68; asst. prof. biol. scis. U. Del., Newark, 1968-74, assoc. prof. 1974—; coordinator microbiology program Sch. Life and Health Scis. U. Del., 1988—; cons. in microbiology N.Y. Acad. Sci. Recipient research grants U. Del. Research Found., 1969-71, 75-76, 86-87, Del. Inst. Med. Edn. Research, 1973-74, Water Resources, 1974-76, 87-88. EPA, 1977-80, 82-85. Mem. Am. Soc. for Microbiology, AAAS, Sigma Xi. Contbr. articles to profl. jours. Office: U Del Sch of Life and Health Sci Newark DE 19716

HERSTAND, JO ELLEN, librarian; b. Iowa City, Sept. 14, 1937; d. Arnold Simpson and Josephine (Jay) Gillette; m. Theodore Herstand, Aug. 23, 1957; children: Sarah Ellen, Michael Simpson. BA, U. Minn., 1970; MLS, Case Western Res. U., 1975. Reference librarian Shaker Heights (Ohio) Pub. Library, 1973-75, head reference librarian, 1975-77; librarian U. Okla., Norman, 1978-80; pub. service librarian Met. Library System, Oklahoma City, 1977-78, chief materials selection, 1980—. Mem. ALA, Okla. Library Assn., Beta Phi Mu. Home: 4418 Manchester Ct Norman OK 73072 Office: Met Library System 131 Dean McGee Oklahoma City OK 73102

HERTE, MARY CHARLOTTE, plastic surgeon; b. Milw., May 31, 1951; d. Clarence H. and Bernadette E. (Storch) H. BS, Mt. Mary Coll., Milw., 1973; MD, U. Wis., 1977. Diplomate Am. Bd. Plastic Surgery. Research fellow in plastic surgery Grad. Sch. Medicine Ea. Va. U., Norfolk, 1978; gen. surgery resident Univ. Hosps., Madison, Wis., 1978-81; plastic surgery resident Univ. Hosps., Madison, 1981-83; practice medicine specializing in plastic surgery Las Vegas, 1983—. Recipient Woman of Promise award Good Housekeeping Mag., 1985. Mem. Am. Soc. Plastic and Reconstructive Surgeons, Nevada State Med. Soc. (del. 1986-88), Clark County Med. Soc. (trustee 1986-88). Lodge: Soroptimist Internat. (treas./fin. sec. Greater Las Vegas chpt. 1985-87). Office: 3006 S Maryland Pkwy Suite 415 Las Vegas NV 89109

HERTZBERG, ROSE, artist; b. Passaic, N.J., Dec. 17, 1912; m. Walter Hertzberg; 1 child, George. Studies with Ben Benn, N.Y.C.; student, Art Students League, N.Y.C. lectr. watercolor demonstrations Ramsey Sch. Systems, Paterson YMCA, adult edn. classes, groups. One-woman shows include Sisti Gallery, Buffalo, N.Y., Woman Art Gallery, N.Y.C., Fullerton Gallery, Montclair, N.J., 1979-81, James Joyce Galler, Nyack, N.Y. and numerous other exhibits; group exhibitions include Thirteen Collection, Sta. WNET, N.Y.C., Nat. Acad., N.Y.C. (Irene Sickle Feist award), Jersey City Mus. (Gruenbacker award), State Mus., Trenton, N.J., 4th Internat. de la Femme, Cannes, France and numerous other galleries. Mem. Artists Equity N.J., Artist Equity N.Y., Art Affiliates Bergen County, Nat. Assn. Women Artists, Painters and Sculptors Soc. N.J., Art Students League, Modern Artists Guild, Altrusa Profl. Women. Bergen County chpt. Address: 27 Buckingham Dr Ramsey NJ 07446

HERTING, CLAIREEN LAVERN, financial planning executive; b. Chgo., Sept. 7, 1929; d. Ernst and Louise Caroline (Wagner) Molzan; m. Robert L. Herting, June 5, 1954; 1 son, Robert L., Jr. B.S., U. Ill.-Champaign, 1951; M.B.A., Northwestern U., Chgo., 1953; J.D., John Marshall Law Sch., 1960. Bar: Ill. 1960. C.P.A., Ill. With Cooper & Lybrands, Chgo., 1951—, dir. personal fin. planning, 1974—; adj. prof. Masters of Taxation program, John Marshall Law Sch., 1987—. Contbr. articles to profl. jours. Bd. dirs., sec. Easter Seal Soc. Met. Chgo., 1974—, Chgo. Soc. Contemporary Composers, 1979-84; bd. trustees John Marshall Law Sch., Chgo.vice chmn. Ill. Dept. Registration and Edn., Springfield, 1984—. Recipient Disting. Service award John Marshall Alumni Assn., Chgo., 1983. Mem. Am. Inst. C.P.A.s, ABA, ISBA, Ill. Bar Assn., Ill. C.P.A. Soc. (bd. dirs. 1987—, treas. 1987—), Chgo. Estate Planning Council (past pres., bd. mem. 1976-84), Chgo. Bar Assn. Home: 1281 N Northwest Hwy Chicago IL 60068

HERTWECK, ALMA LOUISE, educator; b. Moline, Ill., Feb. 6, 1937; d. Jacob Ray and Sylvia Ethel (Whitt) Street; m. E. Romayne Hertweck, Dec. 16, 1955; 1 child, William Scott. A.A., Mira Costa Coll., 1969; B.A. in Sociology summa cum laude, U. Calif.-San Diego, 1975, M.A., 1977, Ph.D., 1982. Cert. sociology instr., multiple subjects teaching credential grades kindergarten-12, Calif. Staff research assoc. U. Calif.-San Diego, 1978-81; instr. sociology Chapman Coll., Orange, Calif., 1982—; instr. child devel. MiraCosta Coll., Oceanside, Calif., 1983-87 ; instr. sociology U.S. Internat. U., San Diego, 1985—; exec. dir., v.p. El Camino Preschools, Inc., Oceanside, 1985—. Author: Constructing the Truth and Consequences: Educators' Attributions of Perceived Failure in School, 1982; co-author: Handicapping the Handicapped, 1985. Mem. Am. Sociol. Assn., Am. Ednl. Research Assn., Nat. Council Family Relations, Nat. Assn. Edn. Young Children, Alpha Gamma Sigma (life). Avocations: foreign travel; sailing; bicycling. Home: 2024 Oceanview Rd Oceanside CA 92056 Office: El Camino Preschs Inc 2002 California St Oceanside CA 92054

HERTZBERG, VICKI STOVER, statistics educator; b. Cin., Aug. 15, 1954; d. William Azel and Betty Marie (Yaden) Stover; m. Richard Carl Hertzberg, Oct. 30, 1946; 1 child, Carl William. BS cum laude, Miami U., Oxford, Ohio, 1976; PhD, U. Wash., 1980. Research asst. U. Wash., Seattle, 1976-79, teaching asst., 1980; asst. prof. U. Cin., 1980-85, assoc. prof., 1985—; cons. Monsanto Corp., 1984-85, Nat. Ctr. for Rehab. Engring., Dayton, Ohio, 1984—. Contbr. articles on biostats. to profl. jours. Mem. Knox Presbyn. Ch., Cin., 1982—. Nat. Inst. Child Health and Human Devel. grantee, 1987. Mem. Am. Statis. Assn. (sec./treas. Greater Cin. chpt. 1982-83, pres. 1984-85, rep. council of chpts. 1986—), Biometric Soc. (regional adv. bd. 1987—), Miami U. Alumni Assn., Weaver's Guild Greater Cin., Kappa Delta. Democrat. Home: 5530 Samstone Ct Cincinnati OH 45242-1323 Office: U Cin Div Biostats Cincinnati OH 45267-0183

HERWIG, JOAN EMILY, educator, researcher; b. Chgo., Apr. 7, 1943; d. Roger Miles and Joyce Ivah (Mahlke) H.; student Merrill-Palmer Inst., 1964; BS, U. Wis., Stout, 1965; MS, Iowa State U., 1971; PhD, Purdue U., 1978. Tchr. jr. high sch., Port Huron, Mich., 1965-69; dir.-tchr. Head Start, Port Huron, summers 1965-69; teaching asst. Iowa State U., 1969-70, assoc. prof. child devel., 1971—, chmn. dept., 1983-86; research asst. Purdue U., 1976-78; cons. child devel., early childhood edn. Bd. dirs. Ames (Iowa) Presch., 1971-73, Pammel Nursery Sch., Ames, 1975-76; mem. governing bd. Episcopal Parish of Ames, 1982-85, sr. Warden, 1984-85. Recipient Amoco Outstanding Tchr. award, 1982-83, Disting. Alumni award U. Wis., 1985, Outstanding Acad. Advisor award, 1982; David Ross fellow Purdue U., 1978. Mem. Soc. Research in Child Devel., Nat. Assn. Edn. Young Children, Midwestern Assn. Edn. Young Children (Iowa rep. council 1985—, v.p. 1986-87, pres. 1987—), Iowa Assn. Edn. Young Children (sec. 1979-82, v.p. 1982-83, pres. 1983-84), Am. Home Econs. Assn., Nat. Assn. Early Childhood Tchrs. Educators, Am. Edn. Research Assn., Internat. Fed. Home Econ., Soc. Internat. Devel., Omicron Nu, Phi Delta Kappa. Contbr. chpts., articles to profl. publs.; research in cognitive devel. of young children's plau, parent involvement and early childhood edn. Office: Iowa State U 212 Child Devel Bldg Ames IA 50011

HERZBERG, SYDELLE SHULMAN, lawyer, accountant; b. N.Y.C., July 24, 1933; d. Hyman and Rose (Green) S.; m. Norman Joseph Herzberg, June 23, 1962; 1 child, Gilbert. BS, NYU, 1955; JD, Bklyn. Law Sch., 1957. Bar: N.Y. 1958; CPA, N.Y. Pub. acct. M. Sharlach & Co., N.Y.C., 1955-62; pvt. practice acctg. and law, New Rochelle, N.Y., 1962—. Mem. bd. edn. Solomon Schechter Sch. of Westchester, White Plains, N.Y., 1975-78, bd. dirs. PTA, 1975-78; pres. PTA bd. Westchester Hebrew High Sch., Mamaroneck, N.Y., 1980-82; mem. budget adv. bd. City of New Rochelle, N.Y., 1975. Mem. Am. Inst. CPA's, N.Y. State Soc. CPA's, ABA, N.Y. State Bar Assn., Westchester Women's Bar Assn., Huquenot-Thomas Paine Hist. Assn. (treas. 1987-88, trustee 1987—), LWV (pres. New Rochelle chpt. 1983-85). Jewish. Home: 46 Longue Vue Ave New Rochelle NY 10804 Office: 519 Main St New Rochelle NY 10801

HERZECA, LOIS FRIEDMAN, lawyer; b. N.Y.C., July 7, 1954; d. Martin and Elaine Shirley (Rapoport) Friedman; m. Christian Stefan Herzeca, Aug. 15, 1980; 1 child, Jane Leslie. B.A. Harpur Coll., SUNY-Binghamton, 1976; J.D., Boston U., 1979. Bar: N.Y. 1980, U.S. Dist. Ct. (so. and ea. dist.) N.Y. 1980. Atty. antitrust div. U.S. Dept. Justice, Washington, 1979-80; assoc. Fried, Frank, Harris, Shriver & Jacobson, N.Y.C., 1980-86, ptnr., 1986—. Editor Am. Jour. Law and Medicine, 1978-79. Mem. ABA, N.Y.C. Bar Assn. Office: Fried Frank Harris Shriver & Jacobson 1 New York Plaza New York NY 10004

HERZINGER, SONJA RAE, communications company manager; b. Twin Falls, Idaho, July 26, 1950; d. William A. and Faye N. (Krupp) Bergadine; m. Ranse L. Herzinger, Aug. 23, 1969 (div. Apr. 1978). B.A. in English, Boise State U., 1972. Office mgr. Mountain Bell, Boise, 1978, applications instr., Salt Lake City, 1978-80, tech. writer, Denver, 1980-83; tech. instr. gen. dept. AT&T, Basking Ridge, N.J., 1983, data administrator, 1984—, strategic planner, 1984—, cons. strategic info. systems planning, 1984—; subject matter expert, data adminstrn. system, 1987—. Author tech. manuals. Scholar Boise State U., 1969. Mem. Nat. Assn. Female Execs. Democrat. Methodist. Avocations: collecting rare and out of print books; antiques; skiing. Home: 8 Ash Ln Morristown NJ 07960 Office: AT&T Communications 295 N Maple Ave Basking Ridge NJ 07920

HERZOG, JOAN DOROTHY, healthcare executive; b. Chgo., July 5, 1938; d. Zigmund and Josephine (Kiras) Zaharski; m. Frederick Jarvis Herzog; children: Gregory Scott, Leslie Ellen, Allison Lynn. BS in Nursing, Loyola U., Chgo., 1961; MS in Health Services Adminstrn., Coll. St. Francis, 1985. RN, Ill. Staff nurse Cook County Dept. Pub. Health, Chgo., 1960-61; clinic nurse Norwood Med. Ctr., Chgo., 1965-70; office nurse Thaddeus Poremski, MD, Chgo., 1974-79; supr., audit/utilization rev. Thorek Hosp. and Med. Ctr., Chgo., 1980-81; dir. quality assurance St. Elizabeth's Hosp., Chgo., 1981-83; cons. Blue Cross & Blue Shield Assn., Chgo., 1983-84; mgr. utilization rev. programs CNA Ins. Cos., Chgo., 1984—; mem. adv. bd. Norell Home Health Care, Northbrook, Ill., 1984, Regional Strategic Planning and Mktg. Com., Northbrook; mem. profl. affairs com. Ancilla Systems, Elk Grove Village, Ill., 1985-87. With pub. relations Cavaliers Drum & Bugle Corps, Park Ridge, Ill., 1977-78; bd. dirs. Council Cath. Women, Park Ridge, Ill., 1974-75, mem. Alexian Bros. Med. Ctr., Elk Grove Village, Ill., 1988—. Mem. Ill. Assn. Quality Assurance Profls. (regional rep. 1984), Chgo. Health Execs. Forum, Am. Coll. Utilization Rev. Physicians (affiliate), Women's Healthcare Exec. Network. Home: 615 S Lincoln Ln Arlington Heights IL 60005 Office: CNA Ins Cos CNA Plaza Chicago IL 60685

HESKEY, KAREN EVELYN, banker; b. Boston, June 2, 1944; d. David Ruble Crawley and Evelyn Pearl (Geer) George; m. George Thomas Heskey, June 2, 1973. BA, William Smith Coll., 1965. Term loan analyst Mfgs. Hanover Trust Co., N.Y.C., 1965-67; credit analyst, real estate lender Bank New England, Boston, 1967-75; real estate lender Comfed Savs. Bank, Lowell, Mass., 1975-82, Arlington Trust Co., Lawrence, Mass., 1982—. Sec. Village Green Condominium Assn., North Andover, Mass., 1975-81; treas. Loon Village Homeowners Assn., Lincoln, N.H., 1981-87, Lawrence Community Housing Resource Bd., 1982-86. Mem. Mass. Mortgage Bankers Assn. (gov. 1974-85), Mass. Housing Fin. Agy. (mem. single family adv. com. 1984—), Mass. Bankers Assn. (mem real estate fin. com. 1988). Home: 110B Hampstead Rd Derry NH 03038 Office: Arlington Trust Co 305 Essex St Lawrence MA 01842

HESS, ALISON LEE, government policy analyst; b. Berkeley, Calif., Oct. 20, 1958; d. Wilmot N. and Winifred E. (Lowdermilk) H. BA in Economics, Environ. Studies, Grinnell Coll., 1980; MA in Pub. Policy, Johns Hopkins U., 1982. Research asst. Ctr. for Met. Planning and Research, Balt., 1980-81; intern Office Technology Assessment U.S. Congress, Washington, 1981, research asst., 1981-82, research analyst, 1982-83, analyst, 1983-84, project dir., 1984—. Editor: (autobiography) All in a Lifetime, 1986; co-editor: (newsletter) Interoceanic Workshop, 1987—. Named one of Outstanding Young Women of Am., 1987. Mem. WorldWide Women in Devel., Phi Beta Kappa, Sigma Xi. Office: US Congress Office of Tech Assessment Washington DC 20510

HESS, BETH BOWMAN, sociology educator; b. Buffalo, Sept. 13, 1928; d. Albert A. and Yetta (Lurie) Bowman; m. Richard C. Hess, Apr. 26, 1953; children—Laurence Albert, Emily Frances. B.A. magna cum laude, Radcliffe Coll., 1950; M.A., Rutgers U., 1966; Ph.D., Rutgers U., 1971. Research asst. Rutgers U., New Brunswick, 1964-69; asst. prof. County Coll., 1969-74, assoc. prof., 1975-79; prof. County Coll., Randolph, N.J., 1979—; Author: (with Elizabeth W. Markson) Aging and Old Age: An Introduction to Social Gerontology, 1980, Sociology, 1988, (with E. W. Markson and P. Stein), 3d edit., 1985; (with Matilda White Riley and Kathleen Bond,) Aging in Society: Selected Reviews of Recent Research, 1983; (with Myra Marx Ferree) Controversy and Coalition: The New Feminist Movement, 1985; (with Myra Marx Ferree) Analyzing Gender: A Handbook of Social Science Research, 1987. Editor: Growing Old in America, 1976, 80, 85; (with Kathleen Bond) Leading Edges: Recent Research on Psychosocial Aging, 1981; assoc. editor Society, 1978-83, Research of Aging, 1980—, Contemporary Sociology, 1981-83, Teaching Sociology, 1987-89; editor SWS Network, 1984—. Bd. dirs. Planned Parenthood N.E. N.J. Fellow Gerontol. Soc. (sec. behavioral and social sci. sect. 1979-81, chair, 1988; mem.-at-large 1984-86); mem. Soc. Study Social Problems (dir. 1981-84), Sociologists for Women in Soc. (treas. 1982-85, pres. 1987-89), Am. Sociol. Assn. (sec. sect. on aging, 1988—), Assn. Humanist Sociology (pres. 1986-87), Eastern Sociol. Soc. (v.p. 1984-85, pres. 1988—). Democrat. Jewish. Home: 2 Hampshire Dr Mendham NJ 07945 Office: County Coll of Morris Randolph NJ 07869

HESS, EILEEN SWEETEN, computer consultant, software developer; b. Malad, Idaho, Jan. 1, 1949; d. Colen Hagel Jr. and Ruth (Gerber) Sweeten; m. Don Lee Hess, Sept. 13, 1968 (div. Nov. 1972); 1 child, Sonya. Student, Brigham Young U., 1967-70. Tchr. Burley Sch. Dist., Oakley, Idaho, 1970-71; keypunch operator DHI Computing Service, Provo, Utah, 1972-76; computer operator Trammel Crow, Inc., Clearfield, Utah, 1976-77; programmer, analyst Davis Computer Services, Provo, 1977-78; owner The Data Doctor, Orem, Utah, 1978-83; programmer, analyst Data Fin. Systems, Scottsdale, Ariz., 1983-84; info. systems dir. Harbor Fin. Group, Phoenix, 1984-85; owner Software Magic, Phoenix, 1985—. Music booster, chaperone Phoenix Country Day Sch., 1985-86. Mem. Data Processing Mgmt. Assn. (cert. com. mem. 1986, newsletter columnist 1986), Ind. Computer Cons. Assn., Micro-Adapt Users Internat. (pres. 1986—), Nat. Assn. Female Execs. Republican. Mormon. Home: 4211 E Camelback Rd Phoenix AZ 85108 Office: Software Magic PO Box 44378 Phoenix AZ 85064

HESS, IRMA, university official, translator; b. Frankfurt, Germany, Feb. 5, 1939; came to U.S., 1957, naturalized, 1960; d. Frederick and Martha (Mahlert) Alban; 1 child, Harold Alban Hess. B.A., New Sch. for Social Research, 1977; B.S., SUNY-Albany, 1976; M.A., NYU, 1979, M.P.A., 1984, advanced profl. cert., grad. of bus., 1986. Asst. to spl. psychol. testing Bd. Edn., Mt. Vernon, N.Y., 1959-65, health chmn., 1959-66; ind. practice bookkeeping, 1959-65; translator N.Y.C. cts. and agys., 1959—, interpreter, 1959-77; counselor Family Ct., Criminal Ct. Youth Div., N.Y.C., 1976-78; tchr. New Rochell Bd. Edn., 1976-78; adminstr. NYU, N.Y.C., 1978—. Vice pres. PTA, Mt. Vernon, 1968-70; chmn. Mt. Vernon Community Chest, 1971-73; sec. N.Y.C. br. ARC, 1975-77. Recipient Mayor of N.Y. accomplishment cert., 1978; scholar State of N.Y., 1976, NYU, 1978. Mem. Am. Soc. Pub. Adminstrs., U.S. Exec. Women, Am. Translators Assn., Am. Pub. Health Adminstrs., Am. Polit. Sci. Assn., N.Y. Acad. Scis., New Sch. for Social Research Alumni Assn., NYU Alumni Assn. Avocations: golf; ballet; tennis; folk music. Office: NYU D'Agostino Hall 110 W 3rd St New York NY 10012

HESS, LORRAINE, health organization administrator; b. Youngstown, Ohio, July 9, 1955; d. John Raymond and Martha Marie (Podolsky) Martinko. BS in Nursing, Coll. Mt. Joseph, 1977; postgrad., Baldwin-Wallace Coll., 1987-89. RN. Nurses aide Parkview Nursing Home, Warren, Ohio, 1973-76; asst. head nurse Doctor's Hosp., Hollywood, Fla., 1978-79, Diamondhead Extensive Care Ctr., North Lima, Ohio, 1979-80, 82-83; asst. dir. rev. Physicians Peer Rev. Assn., Poland, Ohio, 1980-82; dir. utilization mgmt. Western Res. Care System, Youngstown, Ohio, 1983—. Active Animal Charities Inc., Youngstown. Mem. Am. Med. Peer Rev. Assn., Ohio Hosp. Assn. (state utilization com. 1986-88). Roman Catholic. Home: 6764 West Blvd Boarman OH 44512

HESS, MARGARET JOHNSTON, religious writer, educator; b. Ames, Iowa, Feb. 22, 1915; d. Howard Wright and Jane Edith (Stevenson) Johnston; B.A., Coe Coll., 1937; m. Bartlett Leonard Hess, July 31, 1937; children—Daniel, Deborah, John, Janet. Bible tchr. Community Bible Classes Ward Presbyn. Ch., Livonia, Mich., 1959—, Christ Ch. Cranbrook (Episcopalian), Bloomfield Hills, Mich., 1980—. Co-author: (with B.L. Hess) How to Have a Giving Church, 1974, The Power of a Loving Church, 1977, How Does Your Marriage Grow?, 1983, Never Say Old, 1984; author: Love Knows No Barriers, 1979; Esther: Courage in Crisis, 1980; Unconventional Women, 1981, The Triumph of Love, 1987; contbr. articles to religious jours. Home: 16845 Riverside Dr Livonia MI 48154

HESS, PAULA KAY, state legislative assistant; b. Hershey, Pa., Dec. 4, 1947; d. Paul Warren and Judith Alice (Morrett) H.; B.A., Lebanon Valley Coll., 1969; Ed.D., Pa. State U., 1980. Tchr., Cornwall-Lebanon (Pa.) Sch. Dist., 1969-77; fed. curriculum coordinator Joint Task Force New Arrivals, Ft. Indiantown Gap, Pa., 1975; grad. asst. dept. ednl. adminstrn. Pa. State U., 1977-79; dir. profl. devel. Pa. State Edn. Assn., Harrisburg, 1979-80; dir. govt. relations Pa. Assn. Sch. Adminstrs., Harrisburg, 1980-82; adminstrv. asst. to majority leader for legis. ops. Pa. Ho. of Reps., Harrisburg, 1982-83, dir. legis. Office of Rep. whip, 1983—; presenter Edn.-Law Inst., Lehigh U., 1981. Registered Lobbyist, 1980-82. Mem. Nat. Orgn. Legal Problems in Edn., Nat. Assn. Female Execs., Pa. Assn. Sch. Adminstrs., Pi Gamma Mu, Phi Delta Kappa, Pi Lambda Theta. Republican. Home: 5428 Autumn Dr Harrisburg PA 17111 Office: House Post Office Main Capitol PO Box 2 Harrisburg PA 17120

HESSE, MARTHA O., government official; b. Hattiesburg, Miss., Aug. 14, 1942; d. John William and Geraldine Elaine (Ossian) H. B.S., U. Iowa, 1964; postgrad., Northwestern U., 1972-76; M.B.A., U. Chgo., 1979. Research analyst Blue Shield, 1964-66; dir. div. data mgmt. Am. Hosp. Assn., 1966-69; dir., chief operating officer SEI Info. Tech., Chgo., 1969-80; assoc. dep. sec. Dept. of Commerce, Washington, 1981-82; exec. dir. Pres.' Task Force on Mgmt. Reform, 1982; asst. sec. mgmt. and adminstrn. Dept. of Energy, Washington, 1982-86; chmn. Fed. Energy Regulatory Commn., 1986—; vice-chmn. Dean's fund, U. Chgo., 1981-85. Office: Fed Energy Regulatory Commn 825 N Capitol NE Washington DC 20426

HESSEL, ANDREA MICHELE, psychiatrist; b. N.Y.C., Aug. 14, 1952; d. Henry and Bella (Weiss) H. BA magna cum laude, CUNY, Queens, 1973; MD, Rutgers U., 1978. Intern in pediatrics Coll. Medicine and Dentistry Rutgers U. Med. Sch., Piscataway, N.J., 1978-79; resident in psychiatry NYU Med. Sch., N.Y.C., 1979-82; attending psychiatrist NYU Med. Ctr. Bellevue Hosp., N.Y.C., 1982—. Mem. Am. Psychiat. Assn., Internat. Soc. Dissociative Disorder. Office: 330 Third Ave 5B New York NY 10010

HESSELBEIN, FRANCES RICHARDS, organization executive; b. South Fork, Pa.; d. Burgess Harmon and Anne Luke (Wicks) Richards; widowed, 1978; 1 child, John Richards. Student, U. Pitts.; DHL, Buena Vista Coll., 1987. Co-owner Hesselbein Studios, Johnstown, Pa., 1950-70; chief exec. officer Talus Rock Girl Scout Council, Johnstown, 1970-74, Penn Laurel Girl Scout Council, York, Pa., 1974-76, Girl Scouts U.S., N.Y.C., 1976—; bd. dirs. Pa. Power & Light Co., Allentown, 1981-88, Mut. of Am. Ins. Co., N.Y.C., Ind. Sector, Washington; mem. nat. bd. visitors Peter F. Drucker Grad. Mgmt. Ctr., Claremont (Calif.) Grad. Sch., 1987—; mem. adv. com. to bd. dirs. N.Y. Stock Exchange, 1988—. Dir. Youth for Understanding, Washington, 1984—; trustee Am. Humanics, Kansas City, Mo.; mem. Pres.'s Com. on the Employment of People with Disabilities, Washington, 1978—. Recipient Outstanding Achievement award Inter-Service Club Council, Johnstown, 1976, Entrepreneurial Woman award Women Bus. Owners of N.Y., 1984, Nat. Leadership award United Way of Am., Washington, 1985, Disting. Community Service award Mut. of Am. Ins. Co., 1985; named Outstanding Exec., Savvy Mag., 1985. Clubs: Sky, Cosmopolitan, Pa. Soc. (N.Y.C.). Office: Girl Scouts USA 830 Third Ave New York NY 10022

HESSELINK, ANN PATRICE, tax lawyer; b. Tokyo, July 20, 1954; d. Ira John Jr. and Etta Marie (Ter Louw) H. AB, Hope Coll., 1975; JD, St. Johns U., Jamaica, N.Y., 1980; advanced profl. cert. in fin. NYU, 1983. Bar: N.Y. 1981; CPA, N.Y. Tax mgr. Coopers & Lybrand, N.Y.C., 1980-82; asst. v.p. Bankers Trust Co., N.Y.C., 1982-83; dir. internat. taxes PepsiCo, Inc., Purchase, N.Y., 1983-85; v.p., dir. taxes Young & Rubicam, Inc., N.Y.C., 1986—. Mem. ABA, N.Y. State Bar Assn., Am. Inst. CPAs, N.Y. Women's Bar Assn., Am. Sch. in Japan Alumni Assn. (chmn. N.Y. region). Democrat. Home: 16 Oakdale Ave New Rochelle NY 10801-3622 Office: Young & Rubicam Inc 285 Madison Ave New York NY 10017

HESSER, DANIELLE ELAN, aerospace company executive; b. Bklyn., May 19, 1949; d. William and Marie (Nelson) DiBella. Student Prince George's Community Coll., 1981-85. Jr. electronics technician Enviromarine, Inc., Laurel, Md., 1978-80; computer operator Bendix Field Engring. Corp., Columbia, Md., 1980-81; computer operator Ford Aerospace Co., College Park, Md., 1981-83, with command mgmt., 1983-84; satellite controller, obs. engr. OAO Corp., Greenbelt, Md., 1985—. Mem. Assn. for Humanistic Psychology. Republican. Avocations: movies, theater, yachting, flying, metaphysics.

HESTENES, ROBERTA, church foundation administrator, college president, minister; b. Huntington, Calif., Aug. 5, 1939; d. Robert James and Besse Rae (Nipp) Louis; m. John D. Hestenes; children: Joan Hestenes Lehnen, Eric Magnus, Stephen Eastvold. BA, U. Calif., Santa Barbara; M in Divinity, Fuller Theol. Sem., DD. Ordained to ministry Presbyn. Ch., 1979. Dir. adult edn. and small group ministries United Presbyn. Ch., Seattle, 1967-74; assoc. in ministry LaCanada (Calif.) Presbyn. Ch., 1974-84; assoc. prof., dir. Christian Formation and Discipleship program Fuller Theol. Sem., Pasadena, Calif., 1975-87; bd. dirs., chmn. strategic planning com. World Vision U.S., 1980—; bd. dirs. World Vision Internat., 1982—, chmn. bd. dirs., 1985—; pres. Eastern Coll., St. Davids, Pa., 1987—; cons. numerous Presbyn. orgns.; minister Kenya, Australia, South Africa, Singapore, Hong Kong, South Korea, Philippines, Cen. am. Author: (books) Using the Bible in Groups, 1985, Discovering II Corinthians/Galatians, 1986, (taped courses) Building Christian Communicty Through Small Groups, 1985, Helping Christians Grow: Adult Formation and Discipleship in the Local Church, 1987; co-editor: Women and the Ministries of Christ, 1979; contbr. articles to profl. jours.;. Fellow Case Methods Inst.; mem. Am. Acad. Religion, Religious Edn. Assn., Nat. Assn. of Profs. of Christian Edn. Office: Ea Coll Office of Pres Fairview Dr Saint Davids PA 19087

HESTER, CAROLYN LAVAR, hospital administrator; b. Memphis, July 30, 1948; d. James Bateman and Boneta Elmaida (LeBeau) Fite; m. Jimmy Noel Hester, May 22, 1980; 1 child, Matthew James. Student Technol. Inst. Monterrey, Nuevo Leon, Mex., 1968-69; B.S., Okla. State U., 1970. Social worker Okla. Dept. Welfare, Oklahoma City, 1970-72; instr. Pan Am. Airlines, Miami, Fla., 1972-74, Happy Time Sch., Richardson, Tex., 1975-77; sr. account exec. Fite-Davis Inc., Oklahoma City, 1977-80; dir. pub. relations Okla. State U. Tech. Inst., Oklahoma City, 1980-86; dir. pub. relations South Community Hosp., 1986—; dir. Fite-Hester Inc., Oklahoma City; advt. cons. Burl Holmes Ford, Oklahoma City, 1984—, Dodsons Cafeterias, Oklahoma City, 1984—, Sleepe Shoppe, Oklahoma City, 1984—. Author: Mary Lou Likes Blue, 1977, Stop Drop and Roll; also song lyrics, poetry. Active cub scouting, local Boy Scouts Am.; hon. police officer, Chickasaw, Okla. Recipient Appreciation plaque Oklahoma City Hort. Ctr., 1984, Hon. Police Officer Chickasaw, Okla. Mem. PTA (membership chmn. 1983, carnival chmn. 1984, Helping Hands award 1985), Okla. Hosp. Assn., Am. Hosp. Assn., Oklahoma City Power Squadron (pub. relations officer 1985—), Oklahoma City Pub. Relations Assn., Oklahoma City Running Club (bd. dirs. 1985), Oklahoma City C. of C. (vice chmn. econ. devel. council), Kid Safe Assn. Democrat. Methodist. Club: Variety. Lodge: Lions. Avocations: sailing, camping, writing. Office: South Community Hosp 1001 SW 44th St Oklahoma City OK 73109

HESTER, NANCY ELIZABETH, county government administrator; b. Miami, Fla., Jan. 20, 1950; d. George Temple and Lorraine Patricia (Cluney) Hester; B.A., Bucknell U., 1972; M.I.A., Columbia U., 1974; M.B.A., Fla. Internat. U., 1979. Treasury rep. Westinghouse Elec. Co., N.Y.C., 1974-76; adminstrv. officer serving in bldg. and zoning, gen. services, and corrections and rehab. depts. Met. Dade County, Miami, Fla., 1979—; adj. prof. Fla. Internat. U., Miami, 1980-83; realtor-assoc. Keyes Co., 1985—. Mem. Bus. Vols. for Arts, Miami City Ballet Guild, Zool. Soc. Fla., Ctr. Fine Arts; bd. dirs. YWCA greater Miami. Mem. Coral Gables Bd. Realtors, Zool. Soc. Fla., Ctr. for Fine Arts.

HESTERLY, SANDRA CARLENE, nursing educator; b. Abilene, Tex., Nov. 17, 1937; d. William Carl and Ella Virginia (Hutchens) Waters; m. Michael David Hesterly, Dec. 10, 1958 (div. 1967); children: Michael David, Martin Lloyd. AA, San Bernadino (Calif) Valley Coll., 1959; B Social Sci., Calif. State U., San Bernadino, 1972; MS in Ednl. Psychology, Calif. State U., Hayward, 1986. RN. Operating room supr. San Bernadino Community Hosp., 1965-74, dir. nursing, 1974-77; assoc. exec. dir. Calif. Nurses Assn., San Francisco, 1977-80; edn. coordinator Alta Bates Hosp., Berkeley, Calif., 1981-86; dir. nursing edn. and devel. Alta Bates Corp., Acute Care Affiliates, Berkeley, 1986—; mem. clin. faculty in allied health San Bernadino and Chaffey Jr. Colls., San Bernadino and Ontario, Calif., 1970-77; mem. nursing faculty U. Calif., San Francisco, 1981—. Contbr. articles to profl. jours. and chpts. to books. Mem. Am. Nurses' Assn. (del. 1968-76), Calif. Nurses' Assn. (bd. dirs. 1975-77, pres. region 4 1975-76, life mem. region 4 1977—). Democrat. Baptist. Home: 100 Emery Bay Dr Emeryville CA 94608 Office: Alta Bates Acute Care Affiliates 2001 Dwight Way Berkeley CA 94704

HETER, MARTHA LOUISE, engineering manufacturing company administrator; b. Hutchinson, Kans., Nov. 3, 1949; d. Waid and Gladys (Richardson) H.; student Southwestern Coll., 1967-68; B.S., Kans. State U., 1971; postgrad. U. Kans., 1980-81. Adminstrv. asst. Gril-lite, Inc., Shawnee Mission, Kans., 1972-73, sales coordinator, 1973-75, mdse. coordinator, 1975-76; contract adminstr. Chgo. Heater Co., Inc. subs. Marley Co., Mission, Kans., 1976-80, purchasing agt., 1980-87; contracts mgr. Sterling Co., Lenexa, Kans., 1987—; pvt. piano instr., 1977-81. Mem. Lenexa (Kans.) Bicentennial Choir, 1976, Johnson County Republican Run, 1980, Mothers March of Dimes, Spl. Olympics, 1982. Mem. AAUW, Am. Home Econs. Assn., Nat. Assn. Purchasing Mgrs., Kans. State U. Alumni Assn. Republican. Methodist. Clubs: Indian Creek Racquet; Kansas City Ski. Home: 12212 Blackfoor Dr Olathe KS 66062 Office: Sterling Co 8250 Nieman Rd Lenexa KS 66214

HETH, CHARLOTTE ANNE, music educator; b. Muskogee, Okla., Oct. 29, 1937; d. Woodrow Curt and Eula Jewel (Seabolt) Wilson; m. Linton LeRoy Heth, July 5, 1966 (div. Jan. 1970). B.A., U. Tulsa, 1959, M.Mus., 1960; Ph.D., UCLA, 1975. Tchr., Jal (N.Mex.) High Sch., 1960-61, Catoosa (Okla.) High Sch., 1961-62; Peace Corps vol. Maaraga Hiwot Haile Selassie I Sch., Ambo, Ethiopia, 1962-64; tchr. A.B.C. Unified Sch. Dist. Schs., Artesia, Calif., 1965-73; asst. prof., assoc. prof., prof. music UCLA, 1974—, dir. Am. Indian Studies Ctr., 1976-87; dir. Am. Indian program, Cornell U., Ithaca, N.Y., 1987—; vis. prof. music, 1987—; panel mem. for folk arts Nat. Endowment for Arts, 1980-82; bd. mem. Indian Ctrs., Inc., Los Angeles, 1977-78. Editor: Selected Reports in Ethnomusicology, 1980; American Indian Culture and Research Jour., 1982; record producer Songs of Earth, Water, Fire and Sky, etc., 1976; video producer Music of the Sacred Fire, etc., 1978. Ford Found. dissertation fellow, 1973-74; So. Fellowship Fund postdoctoral fellow, 1978-79; sr. postdoctoral award Newberry Library, Chgo., 1978-79, NRC, 1984-85. Mem. Soc. Ethnomusicology (council mem. 1977-84, council chmn. 1980-82), Am. Folklore Soc., Am. Soc. Ethnohistory, Nat. Indian Edn. Assn., Western Social Sci. Assn., Sigma Alpha Iota. Democrat. Baptist. Office: Cornell U Music Dept Lincoln Hall Ithaca NY 14853

HETTLER, MADELINE THERESE, data processing company executive; b. Phila., Feb. 3, 1949; d. Francis Joseph and Cecilia (Freisburg) H. B.S., U. Pa., 1986. With tech. support dept. Martin Marietta, Phila., 1976-84, Sundata, Phila., 1984-85; system support disaster recovery coordinator Nat. Liberties Corp., Frazer, Pa., 1985-87; tech. cons. Micro Tempus Corp., Trerose, Pa., 1987—. Home: 2217 Bond Ave Drexel HI-1 PA 19026 Office: Micro Tempus Corp #3 Neshaminy Interplex Trerose PA 19047

HETU, JOAN LAFFORD, nursing administrator, business executive; b. Southbridge, Mass., Dec. 28, 1926; d. George William and Harriet (Delehanty) Tully; m. Malcolm Howard Lyle, Mar. 17, 1949 (dec. July 1952); m. Joseph Paul Hetu, June 8, 1955 (div. 1978); children—Christine Lyle Hamilton, George David, Jennifer, Wendy Clare, Martin Evan. Nursing diploma, The Meml. Hosp., Worcester, Mass., 1948; B.S. in Health Sci. Adminstrn., Chapman Coll., Orange, Calif., 1983. R.N., Calif., Mass. Asst. head nurse Boston City Hosp., 1949-50; nursing supr. Harrington Hosp., Southbridge, Mass., 1950-66; asst. head nurse Queen of Angels Hosp., Hollywood, Calif., 1970-72; head nurse Am. Med. Internat., Garden Grove, Calif., 1972-77, nursing supr., 1977-80; nursing adminstr. St. Joseph Health Systems, Yorba Linda, Calif., 1980-86; nursing adminstr., clin. supr. Downey (Calif.) Comm. Hosp. 1986—. Mem. Calif. Soc. for Nursing Service Adminstrs., Am. Diabetes Assn., Nat. Assn. Female Execs., Emergency Nurses Assn., AAUW, Am. Soc. Profl. and Exec. Women. Democrat. Roman Catholic. Avocations: ballroom dancing; gourmet cooking. Office: Downey Community Hosp 11500 Brookshire Ave Downey CA 90241

HEUMAN, DONNA RENA, entrepreneur, lawyer; b. Seattle, May 27, 1949; d. Russell George and Edna Inez (Armstrong) H. BA in Psychology, UCLA, 1972; JD, U. Calif., San Francisco, 1985. Owner, Heuman & Assocs., San Francisco, 1978-86. Mem. Hastings Internat. and Comparative Law Rev., 1984-85; bd. dirs. Saddleback, 1987-88. Jessup Internat. Moot Ct. Competition, 1985. Mem. Nat. Shorthand Reporters Assn., Women Entrepreneurs, Calif. Shorthand Reporters Assn., Calif. State Bar Assn., Nat. Mus. of Women in the Arts, Calif. Lawyers for the Arts, ABA, San Francisco Bar Assn., Assn. Trial Lawyers of Am., Nat. Assn. Female Execs. Clubs: Commonwealth (San Francisco), World Affairs Council (San Francisco), Zonta (bd. dirs.) (San Francisco). Home: 611 Cedar Ct Daly City CA 94014 Office: Three Embarcadero Ctr Suite 470 San Francisco CA 94111

HEUMANN, EDITH INGEBORG, educator, inn keeper; b. Traunstein, Fed. Republic of Germany, June 27, 1927; came to U.S., 1953; d. Maximilian and Mathilde (Merkl) Reiss; m. Thomas Heumann, July 13, 1951; children: Michael, Stephan, Carol, Christopher. Student, U. Munich, 1947-51; BA, U. Calif., Berkeley, 1968, MA, 1970. Part-time tchr. Calif. Adult Schs., Albany, Menlo Park, Palo Alto, 1962-79; teaching asst. U. Calif., Berkeley, 1968-71; part-time tchr. German Sch. of Mid-Peninsula, Redwood City, Calif., 1970-73; tchr. Menlo-Atherton (Calif.) High Sch., 1973-78; prof. Cañada Community Coll., Redwood City, 1979-80; owner, innkeeper Bed and Breakfast Neil Creek House, Ashland, Oreg., 1981—; instr. sailing and skiing U. Munich, 1948-50. Contbr. articles on art to various publs. Asst. patrol leader East Bay Ski Patrol, Oakland, Calif., 1962-64 (chair ski safety com. 1962-63); mem. Tudor Guild Shakespearean Festival, Ashland, Oreg., 1981—. Mem. Phi Beta Kappa. Republican. Unitarian. Club: United European American. Lodge: Soroptimists. Home and Office: 341 Mowetza Dr Ashland OR 97520

HEUN, GISELA MARIA, university administrator; b. Stuttgart, Ger., Aug. 4, 1944; came to U.S., 1968, naturalized, 1985; d. Wilhelm Otto and Else Klara Jaeger; B.B.A., U. Frankfurt/Main, 1964; student mgmt. seminars U. Mich., 1974; m. Hartmut Heun, Jan. 9, 1969. Exec. asst. export div. VDO Instruments, Frankfurt/Main, 1962-68, asst. to gen. mgr., Detroit, 1968-69; translator/editor Lang. and Lang. Behavior Abstracts Jour., U. Mich., 1971-72, adminstrv. asst. in Germanic langs. and lit., 1972-73, bus. mgr. Coll. Lit., Sci. and Arts Adminstrn., 1973-79, adminstrv. mgr. physiology Med. Sch., 1979—; cons. in fin. and personnel mgmt., grants mgmt.; translator and interpreter German/English, U. Mich. Mem. Am. Assn. Med. Colls. Club: German/Am. Cultural Exchange. Home: 3120 Pillar Dr Whitmore Lake MI 48189 Office: U Mich 1335 E Catherine St Ann Arbor MI 48109

HEUSCHELE, SHARON JO, college dean; b. Toledo, Ohio, July 12, 1936; 1 child, Brent Philip. B.E., U. Toledo, 1965, M.Ed., 1969, Ph.D., 1973. Cert. elem., secondary tchr., Ohio. Asst. prof. Ohio Dominican Coll., Columbus, 1970-73, St. Cloud U., Minn., 1973-74; assoc. prof. Ohio State U., Columbus, 1974-79; dean instl. planning Lourdes Coll., Sylvania, Ohio, 1980—; cons. U. Hawaii, 1979, others. Bd. dirs. Trinity-St. Paul Inner City Program, Toledo, 1968; cons. Ohio Civil Rights Commn., 1972; active Democratic campaigns. U. Toledo fellow, 1967-69; recipient Citation, U. Toledo, 1979, Journalistic Excellence award Columbia Press Assn., N.Y.C., 1954. Mem. Am. Council Edn., Ohio Conf. Coll. and Univ. Planning, Soc. Coll. and Univ. Planning (com. 1984-85), Phi Theta Kappa, Phi Kappa Phi (Citation 1973), U. Toledo Alumni Assn., U.S. Coast Guard Aux. Lutheran. Avocations: fossil and mineral collecting; poetry; novel writing; horseback riding. Office: Lourdes Coll 6832 Convent Blvd Sylvania OH 43560

HEUSSER, ELEANORE ELIZABETH, painter; b. North Haledon, N.J., June 6, 1922; d. John Jacob and Elsie Elizabeth (Schmedes) H.; m. Edward F. Ferholt, Feb. 25, 1965. Grad., Cooper Union Coll., 1942; student, Columbia U., 1945-46, Innsbruck (Austria) U., 1952-54. Instr. art Sch. Painting and Sculpture, Columbia U., N.Y.C., 1946-52; instr. drawing CCNY, 1960-62; pvt. instr. painting, N.Y.C., 1960-72, North Haledon, N.J., 1972-78, Pound Ridge, N.Y., 1978—; juror Fulbright Painting Fellowships, Inst. Internat. Edn., N.Y.C., 1985-87, Fulbright Collaborative Research Grants, 1987. Contbr. articles to profl. jours; one-woman shows include Cooper Union Gallery, N.Y.C., Kunsthistorisches Inst., Innsbruck, Konzerthaus Gallery, Vienna, 1954, Columbia U. Gallery, N.Y.C.; works exhibited in group shows at Kaufman Gallery, 1965-78, Duveen-Graham Galleries, 1957-58, Newark Mus., 1954 Fulbright Artists traveling exhibit, Pa. Acad. Fine Arts, 1959, 65, Saidenberg Gallery, Mus. Modern Art Lending Library, N.J. Artists show, Trenton State Mus., 1972-79. Fellow Columbia U. Sch. Painting and Sculpture, 1945-46, Fulbright fellow, Inst. Internat. Edn., 1952-55. Home and Studio: 60 Roosevelt Ave North Haledon NJ 07508

HEWETT, BETSY LONG, real estate professional; b. Wilson, N.C., Dec. 4, 1945; d. Cameron D. and Imogene (Pearce) Long; m. Jerry a. Hewett (div. 1980); children: Ginna Strickland, Rod Strickland, Ashley Strickland, Jason Hewett. Grad., Realtors Inst., 1980. With sales and leasing dept. Walden & Kirkland, Albany, Ga., 1975-83; mng. broker 1st Team Realty, Americus, Ga., 1983-85; owner The Jarg Agy., Albany and Atlanta, 1985—; area dir. Remax, Dixie in Birminghan, Ala., 1988—; sales and mktg. mgr. Northside Realty, Atlanta, 1987—; cons. mktg. Crestland Group, Atlanta, 1987—, Northside Realty, Atlanta, 1987—.

HEWING, JEANNE ELLEN, management professional; b. Phillipsburg, N.J., Apr. 11, 1943; d. Leslie and Margaret (Mannon) Smith; m. Alvin N. Hewing III, Aug. 7, 1965 (div. 1972). BS, U. Md., 1965; MEd, U. Ariz., 1971. Tchr. Tucson Pub. Schs., 1967-73; residential rep. Jersey Cen. Power and Light, Morristown, N.J., 1973-77; NE regional dir. Consumers' Inst. Gen. Electric, Phila., 1977-79; realtor Copper Kettle Realty, Clinton, N.J., 1980-81; ind. mfgs. rep. Clinton, 1982-84; bus. mgr. Katharine Gibbs Sch., Montclair, N.J., 1984-87, placement dir., 1987; account exec. Carlyle Cons., N.Y.C., 1987—. Mem. Internat. Assn. Personnel Women. Home: 134 Cooper Ave Upper Montclair NJ 07043

HEWITT, KATHY ANN, realtor; b. San Juan, P.R., Sept. 13, 1958; d. Bill H. and Ann (Adams) H. BS in Fin., U. Tex., 1983. Bus. mgr. Sandra Haynie Enterprises, Dallas, 1979-85; exec. asst. Ross Love and Assocs., Dallas, 1985-87; [illegible] Jim Richardson and Assocs., Dallas, 1987—. Co-chmn. Swing Against Arthritis with Sandra Haynie, Dallas, 1982-87. Home: 5505 Live Oak #14 Dallas TX 75206 Office: Jim Richardson and Assocs 3615 N Hall Dallas TX 75219

HEWITT, MARILYN PATRICIA, graphic artist, exhibits designer; b. Norfolk, Va., June 14, 1947; d. John Arthur Owens and Thelma (Small) Berlin; married, Aug. 14, 1972 (div. Nov. 1975). Student, Old Dominion U., 1970-72. Projection and sound equipment operator Naval Amphibious Sch., Norfolk, 1966-68, office draftsman, 1968-73; topography artist Hammon, Jensen and Wallen, Oakland, Calif., 1973-74; illustrator Comdr. Naval Surface Force, Norfolk, 1974-76, visual info. specialist, 1976-80, dir. graphic arts, 1980—, dep. EEO officer, 1982-85; owner Dynamic Hair & Nail, Norfolk, 1984-86, Abra-Cadabra Nails and Tan Salon, Norfolk, 1982—. Vol. artist Animal Assistance League, Virginia Beach, 1982, Am. Soc. Prevention Cruelty to Animals, Norfolk, 1980—. Recipient Superior Civilian Service medal Comdr.-in-Chief Harry Train, 1982. Mem. Am. Bus. Women Assn. (treas. Tidewater chpt. 1984-85, v.p. 1985-86, mem. Hallmark chpt.). Lutheran. Home: 4908 Preakness Way Virginia Beach VA 23464 Office: Comdr Naval Surface Force CINCLANTFLT Compound Norfolk VA 23511

HEWITT, SANDRA ELAINE STUARD, banker; b. Springfield, Tenn., May 30, 1951; d. Clarence Connell and Madge Delma (White) Stuard; B.S., Austin Peay State U., Clarksville, Tenn., 1973; grad. various banking courses; m. Richard W. Hewitt, Sept. 2, 1972; 1 dau., Lesley Elaine. With Commerce Union Bank, Nashville, 1973-82, asst. v.p., 1981-82, mgr. Madison br., 1980-82; v.p., dir. br. adminstrn. United So. Bank, Nashville, 1982-83; v.p. Union Planters Nat. Bank, 1983—; dir. Transaction Delivery. Chmn., Robertson County chpt. Am. Heart Assn., 1979-80, memls. chmn. Mid Tenn. chpt., 1980; mem. allocations com. Nashville Area United Way, 1978-79. Mem. Nat. Assn. Bank Women (nat. scholar 1983, treas. Met. Nashville, Tenn. awards and scholarship chmn., seminar and nat. workshop presenter), Am. Inst. Banking (counsel Nashville chpt. 1978), Rivergate Mall Mchts. Assn. (treas. 1979), Springfield Bus. and Profl. Women's Club (v.p., treas. 1979; Young Careerist award 1979, Bus. Woman of Yr. award 1979), Chi Omega. Club: Soroptimist (rec. sec. 1982-83). Home: Route 1 Cedar Hill TN 37032 Office: 200 4th Ave N Nashville TN 37219

HEWITT, WENDY ANN, banker; b. Green Bay, Wis., May 17, 1962; d. Ronald Edgar and Nancy Jean (Franken) H. BA, U. Mich., 1984. Lic. real estate broker. Loan officer Washtenaw Mortgage Co., Livonia, Mich., 1984-88, 1st Nat. Bank, Dearborn, Mich., 1988—; real estate agt. ERA, West Bloomfield, Mich., 1986—. Mem. Nat. Assn. Female Execs., U. Mich. Alumni Assn. Roman Catholic. Home: 33823 Eight Mile Rd Livonia MI 48152 Office: 1st Nat Bank One Parklane Blvd Suite 1614 E Dearborn MI 48126

HEWSON, DONNA WALTERS, real estate executive; b. Columbia, S.C., Mar. 28, 1947; d. Jerry William and Rosa (Bryant) Walters; 1 child, Robert Alton Smith Jr.; m. James Robert Hewson Jr., Oct. 1983 (div. 1986). Student, Hollins Coll., 1971-72, Va. Western Coll., 1972, Va. Polytech. and State U., 1972-73, U. S.C., 1978-79, 84, 85. Lic. residential and comml. real estate broker. Sales rep. Russell-Jeffcoat Realtors, Columbia, S.C., 1969-71; broker Russell-Jeffcoat Realtors, Columbia, 1971-72; adminstrv. asst. Roanoke (Va.) Valley Psych. Ctr., 1975-76; sales rep. Moore Bus. Forms, Columbia, 1976-79; project sales mgr. Continental Mortgage Investors, Columbia, 1979-80; broker, project sales mgr. Tom Jenkins Realty, Columbia, 1980-81; sales mgr., broker in charge RELM, Inc., Columbia, 1982-83; sales mgr. So. U.S. Realty/U.S. Shelter, Columbia, 1983-84; pres. WaltersHewson Co., Inc., Columbia, 1984—. Mem. Columbia C. of C. (com. chmn. 1987—), Greater Columbia C. of C., Women's Symphony Assn., Nat. Assn. Real Estate Appraisers (cert., sr. mem.), State Assn. Realtors, Nat. Assn. Realtors, Columbia Bd. Realtors (mem. Million Dollar Club, 1981, 84, 86, Grievance com. mem. 1986-87), S.C. Assn. Realtors (Profl. Standards com. 1986, polit. affairs com. 1987), Realtors Nat. Mktg. Inst. (residential brokerage council), Palmetto Real Estate Educators. Episcopalian. Office: Walters Hewson Co Inc 1600 Park Circle Suite 104 Columbia SC 29201

HEXBERG, KARIN, advertising professional; b. Hayes, Kans., May 17, 1945; d. Caspar Jul and Patricia Marcelle (Phillips) H.; m. Gary Edward Brandt, Sept. 5, 1965 (div. 1977); 1 child, Christopher Gary (dec.); 1 child, Kirsten Annamarie. BA, U. S.D., 1966; postgrad., U. Md., 1972-73, U. Tex., Houston, 1975, U. Houston, 1977-81. Tchr. Wilson Jr. High Sch., Cedar Rapids, Iowa, 1966-68; mng. editor Union Express, Houston, 1975, Am. Jour. Med. Tech., Houston, 1975-77; copywriter Boone Advt., Houston, 1977-79; coordinator advt./tng. FMC Corp., Houston, 1979-80; v.p. LeFevre Assocs., Houston, 1981-83; assoc. creative dir. Pinne Garvin Herbers & Hock, San Francisco, 1983-87; group creative dir. Foote Cone & Belding, Impact, San Francisco, 1987—. Author short stories. v.p. bd. Mem. Kidney Found. No. Calif., 1986-87. Recipient Outstanding Vol. of Yr. award Nat. Kidney Found. No. Calif., 1986, Pres.'s award Nat. Kidney Found. No. Calif., 1987. Mem. Bus./Profl. Advt. Assn. (cert.), Kappa Alpha Theta. Democrat. Presbyterian. Office: Foote Cone & Belding Impact div PO Box 3183 San Francisco CA 94119

HEXT, KATHLEEN FLORENCE, corporate auditor; b. Bellingham, Wash., Oct. 7, 1941; d. Benjamin Byron and Sarah Debell (Youngquist) Gross.; m. George Ronald Hext, June 13, 1964 (div. 1972). BA magna cum laude, Lewis & Clark Coll., Portland, Oreg., 1963; MA, Stanford U., 1964; MBA, UCLA, 1979. CPA; chartered bank auditor; cert. info. systems auditor. Chief exec. officer Internat. Lang. Ctr., Rome, 1970-77; auditor Peat, Marwick, Mitchell & Co., Los Angeles, 1979-81; mgr. fin. audit Lloyds Bank, Los Angeles, 1981-83, mgr. EDP audit, 1983-85; dir. corp. audit First Interstate Bancorp, Los Angeles, 1985—; treas., Arcadia H.O. Assoc., El Monte, Calif., 1982-84, 86—, pres., 1985. Recipient Edward W. Carter award UCLA, 1979. Mem. Am. Inst. CPA's, Inst. Internal Auditors, EDP Auditors Assn., Calif. Soc. CPA's. Republican. Episcopalian. Avocations: photography, microcomputers, reading. Home: 5331A N Peck Rd El Monte CA 91732 Office: First Interstate Bancorp 707 Wilshire Blvd Los Angeles CA 90017

HEYCK, GERTRUDE PAINE DALY, social club administrator; b. Houston, Nov. 30, 1910; d. David and Gertrude (Paine) Daly; m. Theodore R. Heyck, May 1, 1935; children: Jane Peel (Mrs. Donald H. Gaucher), Theodore Daly. Student, Wellesley Coll., 1929; BA, Brown U., 1934. Bd. dirs. Union Stock Yards, San Antonio, 1961-64. Mem. Jr. League. Clubs: Wellesley, Brown-Pembroke (v.p. 1950-60), Brown (Houston); Brown Faculty (Providence). Home: 1907 Bolsover Rd Houston TX 77005

HEYDE, MARTHA BENNETT (MRS. ERNEST R. HEYDE), psychologist; b. New Bern, N.C., Jan. 31, 1920; d. George Spotswood and Katherine (McIntosh) Bennett; AB, Barnard Coll., 1941; MA, Columbia, 1949, PhD, 1959; m. Ernest R. Heyde, Aug. 17, 1946. Instr. psychol. founds. and services Tchrs. Coll., Columbia U., N.Y.C., 1953-60, research asst., career pattern study Horace Mann-Lincoln Inst., Tchrs. Coll. Columbia U., 1957-59, research assoc., 1960-70, cons., 1970-73. Mem. Barnard Coll. Alumnae Council, 1956-61, 69—, pres. class, 1956-61. Trustee, Barnard Coll., 1974-78, vice-chmn. centenary Barnard Coll. Centennial, 1987—. Mem. Am. Psychol. Assn., Am. Personnel and Guidance Assn., Sigma Xi, Kappa Delta Pi, Pi Lambda Theta. Contbr. to research monograph The Vocational Maturity of Ninth Grade Boys, 1960, Floundering and Trial After High Sch, 1967; coauthor: Vocational Maturity During the High School Years, 1979. Home: 140 Cabrini Blvd Apt 109 New York NY 10033

HEYER, ANNA HARRIET, retired music librarian; b. Little Rock, Aug. 30, 1909; d. Arthur Wesley and Harriet Anna (Gage) H. A.B., B.Mus., Tex. Christian U., 1930; B.S. in L.S., U. Ill., 1933; M.S. in L.S., Columbia U., 1939; M.Mus. in Musicology, U. Mich., 1943. Elem. sch. music tchr. Ft. Worth Pub. Schs., 1931-32; high sch. librarian, 1934-38; cataloguer library, U. Tex.-Austin, 1939-40; music librarian, asst. prof. L.S., N. Tex. State U., Denton, 1940-65, librarian emeritus, 1976; cons. music library materials Tex. Christian U., Ft. Worth, 1965-79; ret., 1979. Author: A Check-List of Publications of Music, 1944; A Bibliography of Contemporary Music in the Music Library, North Texas State College, 1955; Historical Sets, Collected Editions and Monuments of Music: A Guide to Their Contents, 1957, 2d edit., 1969, 3d rev. edit., 1980, contbr. articles to profl. publs. Recipient citations for contbn. to music librarianship Music Library Assn., 1980, to music librarianship in Tex., 1983. Mem. ALA, Tex. Library Assn., Music Library Assn., AAUW, DAR. Mem. Disciples of Christ Ch. Clubs: Altrusa, Woman's Club Ft. Worth, Colonial Country. Home: 2538 Greene Ave Fort Worth TX 76109

HEYMANN, MONICA GOLDA, graphic designer; b. Caracas, Venezuela, Jan. 4, 1959; d. George Daniel and Dorothy (Noe) H. BA in Psycho-Biology with distinction, Boston U., 1978; postgrad., Harvard U., 1979-80, Art Inst. Boston, 1980-82; BFA, The Cooper Union Sch. Art, 1984. Cons., exhibition, catalogue designer Rose Art Mus., Waltham, Mass., 1981; creative dir. Triad Press, Boston, 1980-82, Mallory Factor & Assocs., Inc., N.Y.C., 1984-85; art dir. Creative Dirs., Inc., N.Y.C., 1985-86; design dir. Dura Archtl. Signage Corp., L.I., 1986-87; creative dir., pres. Heymann & Ptnrs., N.Y.C., 1987—; design cons. various corps., N.Y.C., 1980—. Art dir., editorial cons.: Ancient American Art: An Aesthetic View, 1981, PreColumbian Art, 1980; cons. holographic design, various corps. Recipient Am. Corp. Identity design award. Mem. Am. Inst. Graphic Arts, Graphic Artists Guild. Office: 227 E 25th St Apt #1A New York NY 10010

HEYN, EILEEN LEONE, aerospace company executive; b. Moose Lake, Minn., Mar. 9, 1945. A.A., Highline Coll., Des Moines, Wash., 1983; student in Bus. Adminstrn., City U., Bellevue, Wash., 1985—. Asst. br. mgr. Cascade Savs. & Loan Assn., Lynnwood, Wash., 1971-72; assoc. br. mgr. Avco Fin. Services, Everett, Wash., 1972-74; quality assurance tech. aide Boeing Co., Seattle, 1975-82; retrofit rev. bd. coordinator Boeing, Seattle, 1982-84, exec. placement specialist, 1984-85, integrated employee records systems analyst, 1985-87, internal auditor, 1987—; cons. and lectr. in field. Author-editor: (Bulletin) Illuminations, 1981-82; contbg. editor: Advisor, 1982. Mem. Seattle Repertory Orgn., 1982, Zonta Internat. Community Club, 1985-88; v.p. Lake Heights Community Club, Bellevue, Wash., 1985-86, pres., 1986-88; Spl. Olympics Vol., 1987-88. Recipient Extra Mile award Boy Scouts Am., Seattle, 1979; Boeing awards, 1980, 82. Mem. Am. Bus. Women's Assn. (pres. 1982-83, Member of Yr., 1982, Nat. Bus. Woman of Yr., 1983), Internat. Tng. in Communications Council (v.p. 1984-85), Seattle Profl. and Managerial Women's Network (bd. dirs. 1986-88), Inst. Internal Auditors, Am. Soc. Quality Control. Avocations: Public speaking; hiking; traveling; theatre-going.

HEYWARD, ILENE PATRICIA, systems chemical engineer; b. Plainfield, N.J., Apr. 9, 1948; d. William Winter and Bonlyn (Pitts) Nesbitt; divorced; 1 child, Eric Eugene. BS in Chemistry, Fairleigh Dickinson U., 1976; MS in Chemistry, NYU, 1987. Lab. assoc. AT&T Labs, Murray Hill, N.J., 1976-77; sr. tech. assoc. AT&T Labs, Murray Hill, 1978-81, assoc. mem. tech. staff, 1981-83, mem. tech. staff, 1983—. Contbr. articles to profl. jours. Active Grant Ave. Community Ctr., Plainfield, 1980—, also sci. adv. council. Named Outstanding Woman Bell Communications Research, 1985. Mem. Am. Chem. Soc., AAAS, Nat. Assn. Black Chemists. Baptist. Home: 1158 Loraine Ave Plainfield NJ 07062 Office: AT&T Bell Labs 600 Mountain Ave Room 7F-227 Murray Hill NJ 07974

HIATT, FLORENCE ELLEN, musician; b. Elwood, Ind.; d. Merrill Paul and Mildred Lenore (Knotts) H.; m. Frank Alvin Robertson, Sept. 1, 1948 (div. 1963); children: Lana Glynn, Bradley Reid; m. Jesse Ben Hines, Feb. 27, 1967; stepdau., Cynthia Fawn. Student, Cin. Conservatory Music, 1945-49; diploma, Ecoles d'Art et Musique, Fontainebleau, France, 1961; B of Music, Auburn U., 1964; M of Music, Ind. U., 1972; postgrad., Fla. State U., 1984-85. Mem. faculty piano and organ Auburn (Ala.) U., 1964-65; asst. mus. dir. then mus. dir. Lakewood Mus. Playhouse, Barnesville, Pa., 1971-72; mus. dir. Clinton (Conn.) Mus. Theatre, 1974-75; concert organist Columbus, Ga., 1960—; mus. dir. Springer Opera House, Springer Theatre, Springer Ballet and Sch. Theatre Arts, Columbus, 1971—; music dir. Temple Israel, Columbus, 1970—; mem. organ and harpsichord faculty Columbus Coll., 1982—; keybd. specialist Columbus Symphony Orchestra, 1967—; organist St. Luke United Meth. Ch., Columbus, 1984—. Author, composer numerous choral, organ and voice pieces. Mem. Am. Guild Organists (cert., past dean), Columbus Arts Council, Mortar Bd. Soc. Home: 2801 Gardenia St Columbus GA 31906

HIATT, JANE CRATER, arts agency administrator; b. Winston-Salem, N.C., May 26, 1944; d. Howard Rondthaler Jr. and Irene (Sides) Crater; m. Wood Coleman Hiatt, May, 1978 (div. June 1973); 1 child, Jonathan David. BA, U. N.C., 1966; MA, Wake Forest U., 1972. Eng. tchr. Winston-Salem (N.C.)/Forsyth County Schs., 1966-70; exec. dir. Tenn. Com. for the Humanities, Nashville, 1973-77; cons. various edn. and cultural agys. Ocean Springs, Miss., 1978-80; asst. dir. Miss. Com. for the Humanities, Jackson, Miss., 1981-85; exec. dir. Arts Alliance of Jackson and Hinds County, Miss., 1985—; participant Arts Leadership Inst. of Humphrey Inst. for Pub. Affairs, Mpls., 1986, Leadership, Jackson, 1987. Co-editor Peoples of the South, 1976; exec. producer (TV series) The South with John Siegenthaler, 1976; host, reporter Miss. Ednl. TV, Jackson, 1981-87. Mem. Miss. Econ. Council, 1986-87, Miss. Research and Devel. Council, 1984—; pres. Mental Health Assn. of Hinds County, Jackson, 1986; treas. Miss. for Ednl. Broadcasting, 1987, 88. Recipient Heritage award City of Biloxi, 1984. Mem. Nat. Assembly of Local Arts Agys., Nat. Council on the Arts, Jackson C. of C., Phi Beta Kappa. Home: 2429 Massena Dr Jackson MS 39211 Office: Arts Alliance PO Box 17 Jackson MS 39211

HIATT, MARY POTT, English studies educator; b. Wusih, China; d. Walter Hawks and Elizabeth Washington (Fisher) Pott (parents Am. citizens); A.B., Elmira Coll.; M.A., Columbia U., Ph.D., 1971; m. Norman W. Storer, Feb. 1975; 1 son, Andrew Hiatt. Instr. English, Rutgers U., Newark, 1969-71; asst. prof. Baruch Coll., CUNY, 1971-75, assoc. prof., 1975-79, prof., 1979—, dept. chmn., 1981-85. Mem. Nat. Council Tchrs. English, MLA, Phi Beta Kappa. Author: Artful Balance: The Parallel Structures of Style, 1975; The Way Women Write, 1977. Office: Baruch Coll English 17 Lexington Ave New York NY 10010

HIBBARD, BEVERLY J., administrative service executive; b. Tyrone, Okla., Feb. 23, 1940; d. Marion E. and Bonnie (Hays) Farmer; m. Sheldon A. Hibbard, Feb. 26, 1966 (div. Nov. 1985); children: Rachael S., Kyle H., Mara K. BA in Psychology, U. Tex., Dallas, 1985; postgrad., Tex. Woman's U., 1986—. Owner, mgr. Peacock Florist & Catering, Dallas, 1966-77; ops. mgr. Kindergard Corp., Dallas, 1977-81; office mgr. Mayrath & Seale, P.C., Dallas, 1982; pres. Hibbard Adminstrv. Services, Dallas, 1983-87; probation officer Dallas County Juvenile Dept., 1988—; sec., treas. Kindergard Corp., 1976—. v.p. fundraising Akiba Acad., Dallas, 1972-74; tutor Dallas Ind. Sch. Dist., 1986. Mem. Psi Chi, Alpha Psi Omega. Home: 7537 Baxtershire Dallas TX 75230 Office: Dallas County Juvenile Dept 4711 Harry Hines Dallas TX 75235

HIBNER, RAE ANNE, nurse; b. Libertyville, Ill., Jan. 31, 1956; d. Richard Douglas and Raelene Ann (Warren) Lyons; m. John Paul Hibner, June 21, 1986; 1 child, Kevin John. Diploma, Luth. Gen. Hosp. Sch. Nursing, Park Ridge, Ill., 1979; BS in Nursing, U. Ill., Chgo., 1984; MS, No. Ill. U., 1987. RN. Staff nurse Cardiac Telemetry Luth. Gen. Hosp., 1979-81, staff nurse CCU, 1981-82; staff nurse CICU U. Ill. Hosp., Chgo., 1982-83, asst. head nurse CICU, 1983-86, head nurse CICU, 1986—. Mem. Am. Nurses Assn., Ill. Nurses Assn., Am. Assn. Critical Care Nurses, Am. Heart Assn. Republican. Roman Catholic. Office: U Ill Hosp 1740 W Taylor Chicago IL 60612

HIBSCHWEILER, BARBARA MARY, wholesale distribution executive; b. Buffalo, Aug. 3, 1945; d. Alvin Jacob and Magdalen Anna (Troidl) H. BA, D'Youville Coll., 1967; MS, Canisius Coll., 1972. Cert. tchr., N.Y. Tchr. St. William's Sch., West Seneca, N.Y., 1968-70, St. Matthew's Sch., Buffalo, 1973-75; mgr. Sterling Bag & Supply Co. Inc., Lackawanna, N.Y., 1976—. Democrat. Roman Catholic. Office: Sterling Bag & Supply Co Inc Foot of Fisher Rd Lackawanna NY 14218

HICKEN, GRACE DOROTHY, social worker; b. Milw., Sept. 15, 1919; d. Rudolph A. and Hildegarde Emma (Brandt) Maurer; m. Edward Oscar Schroeder, Sept. 2, 1942 (dec. 1962); children—David John (dec.), James

Edward, John Frederick; m. William Stevens Hicken, Sept. 12, 1964. B.S.W. cum laude, Mt. Mary Coll., 1976. Sec. Slocum Straw Works, Milw., 1937-42; part time teller West Fed. Savs. & Loan, Milw., 1963-72; social worker Bradley Convalescent Center, Milw., 1977-78, St. Joseph's Hosp., Milw., 1978; dir. social work Community Meml. Hosp., Menomonee Falls, Wis., 1978-80, ret., 1980; vol. coordinator, facilitator Lifeline, support group for suicide prevention, Milw., 1981-86; vol. facilitator Sharing Life, suicide prevention support group, Milw., 1986—; vol. worker refugee families and prison inmates; vol. speaker on suicide prevention; founder living apts. for elderly, 1976. Recipient Madonna medal Alumni Assn. Mt. Mary Coll. Mem. Am. Assn. Suidicology, Nat. Assn. Social Workers, Benedict Ctr. for Criminal Justice, Kappa Gamma Pi. Lutheran. Home: 2869 N 58th St Milwaukee WI 53210

HICKEY, CONSTANCE SUE, oil company executive; b. Auburn, N.Y., July 6, 1958; d. Richard J. and Therese G. (Steigerwald) H. BEE, Rensselaer Poly. Inst., 1980; M in Engring. Adminstrn., George Washington U., 1987. Lic. profl. engr., N.J., Va., Fla. Project engr. Procter & Gamble, S.I., N.Y., 1980-82, prodn. supr., 1982-83; project engr. Mobil Oil Corp., Valley Forge, Pa., 1983-85; supply analyst Mobil Oil Corp., Fairfax, Va., 1985-86, supply coordinator, 1986-87, mktg. planning analyst, 1987-88; field engring. supr. Mobil Oil Corp., Dallas, 1988—. Mem. Soc. Women Engrs., NSPE. Club: Rensselaer (Washington) (pres. 1986-87). Home: 7705 Standish Circle Plano TX 75023 Office: Mobil Oil Corp 4200 Singleton Blvd Dallas TX 75212

HICKEY, DELINA ROSE, educator; b. N.Y.C., Mar. 25, 1941; d. Robert Joseph and Marie (Ripa) H.; B.S. in Edn., SUNY, Oneonta, 1963; M.A., Manhattan Coll., 1967; Ed.D. in Counselor Edn. and Psychology, U. Idaho, 1971; m. David Andrews; 1 son by previous marriage, Jon Robert. Elem. sch. tchr., counselor, Westchester, N.Y., 1963-68; part-time instr. psychology St. Thomas Aquinas Coll., Sparkhill, N.Y., 1971-72; asst. prof. edn. Nathaniel Hawthorne Coll., Antrim, N.H., 1972-75; prof. faculty Keene (N.H.) State Coll., 1975—, assoc. prof. edn., 1978—, prof. edn., coordinator faculty, 1987—; interim dean profl. studies 1987; mem. N.H. Legislature from 13th Dist., 1981-85 ; mem. adv. council Title IV, 1979-82; fellow Nat. Ctr. Research in Vocat. Edn., 1984-85; assoc. in edn. Harvard U., 1984-85. Trustee, Big Bros./Big Sisters, Keene, 1978-80, Family Planning Services S.W. N.H., 1976—; mem. N.H. Juvenile Conf. Com., 1976-81; pres. bd. dirs. CHESCO. Mem. N.H. Order Women Legislators, New Eng. Research Orgn., Am. Vocat. Assn., N.H. Personnel and Guidance Assn. Democrat. Author articles in field. Office: Elliot Hall Keene NH 03431

HICKEY, WINIFRED E(SPY), state senator, social worker; b. Rawlins, Wyo.; d. David P. and Eugenia (Blake) Espy; children—John David, Paul Joseph. B.A., Loretto Heights Coll., 1933; postgrad. U. Utah, 1934, Sch. Social Service, U. Chgo., 1936. Dir. Carbon County Welfare Dept., 1935-36; field rep. Wyo. Dept. Welfare, 1937-38; dir. Red Cross Club, Europe, 1942-45; commr. Laramie County, Wyo., 1973-80; mem. Wyo. Senate, 1980—; dir. United Savs. & Loan, Cheyenne. Pres., bd. dirs. U. Wyo. Found., 1986-87; pres. Meml. Hosp. of Laramie County, 1986—; chmn. adv. council div. community programs Wyo. Dept. Health and Social Services; pres. county and state mental health assn., 1959-63; trustee, U. Wyo., 1967-71; active Nat. Council Cath. Women. Named Outstanding Alumna, Loretto Heights Coll., 1959. Democrat. Club: Altrusa (Cheyenne). Pub. Where the Deer and the Antelope Play, 1967.

HICKINGBOTHAM, BARBARA ANN, association executive; b. Eudora, Ark., Dec. 7, 1937; d. Herren Iveson and Marnette Sophia (Dardelle) Peacock; grad. Center Interior Design, 1964; cert. N.Y. Sch. Interior Design, 1965; cert. achievement Martin McDaniel Sch. Real Estate, 1977; m. Frank D. Hickingbotham, Aug. 21, 1955; children—Herren Curtis, Frank Todd. Interior decorator, Little Rock, 1965-68; with sales dept. Nat. Investor Life Ins. Co., Little Rock, 1968-70; co-organizer A. Q. Restaurants, Little Rock, 1970-72; mgr. restaurants Dogpatch USA, Harrison, Ark., 1972-74; dir. internat. affairs Ark. Sec. State, Little Rock, 1974-77; exec. dir. Nat. Soc. to Prevent Blindness, Little Rock, 1979-82; single parent program devel. Campus Crusade for Christ, 1982—; dir. pub. relations, area field suprs. Green Thumb, Inc., 1983—, also dir. field ops. Fund raiser March of Dimes. Mem. Ark. Health Assn., Ark. Vol. Coordinators Assn. Baptist. Clubs: Pleasant Valley Country, Altrusa (dir.) (Little Rock). Home: 17 Windsor Ct Little Rock AR 72212 Office: 200 S University Suite 100 Little Rock AR 72207

HICKMAN, DIXIE ELISE, writing consultant; b. Harrisburg, Pa., Oct. 26, 1944; d. Thomas William and Eunice McCalip (Hart) H.; m. Thomas Terry Tuggle, Aug. 29, 1970 (div. 1985); m. Glenn Edward Oehms, Feb. 5, 1983; 1 child, Kyla Elise Oehms Hickman. BA, U. Miss., 1966; MA, Duke U., 1967; PhD, U. Iowa, 1977. Instr. English East Carolina U., Greenville, 1967-69; asst. prof. Clemson (S.C.) U., 1975-79, U. So. Miss., Hattiesburg, 1979-86; owner, writing cons., ednl. counselor Communication Resources, Hattiesburg, 1986—; cons. Nat. Space Tech. Lab., Bay St. Louis, Miss., 1980-82, pub. and pvt. schs. and 2-yr. colls., Miss. and La., 1981-84. Author: Friends of Kamper Park and Zoo, 1988; editor: Resources for Writing Consultants, 1987. Publicity chair LaLeche League Hattiesburg, 1985—; publicity dir. Friends of Kamper Park and Zoo. Mem. Nat. Council Tchrs. English, Assn. Profl. Writing Cons. (sec., treas. 1983-86, v.p. 1986-88, pres. 1988—), Miss. Council Tchrs. English, Soc. Tech. Communication, Assn. Tchrs. Tech Writing, Conf. Coll. Composition and Communication, Mortar Bd., Kappa Delta. Office: Communication Resources PO Box 524 Hattiesburg MS 39403

HICKMAN, ELIZABETH PODESTA, counselor, educator; b. Livingston, Ill., Sept. 30, 1922; d. Louis and Della (Martin) Podesta; B.E. summa cum laude, Eastern Ill. State U.; M.A., George Washington U., 1966; postgrad. U. Chgo., 1945, U. Va., 1964-66, (fellow) Northeastern U., 1967-68; Ed.D. (Exxon Found. grantee, Raskob Found. grantee), George Washington U., 1979; m. Franklin Jay Hickman, Mar. 17, 1944 (dec.); children—Virginia Hickman Hellstern, Franklin. Tchr. public schs., Ill., Ohio, Va., Naples, Italy, 1944-64; dir. coll. transfer guidance Marymount Coll. of Va., Arlington, 1964-67, dir. Counseling Center, 1974-81, assoc. dean counseling and residence life, 1981-84; community counselor div. Mass. Employment Security, Newton, 1968-69; tchr. English conversation, Fuchu, Japan, 1969-73; placement dir., career counselor Coll. Great Falls (Mont.), 1973-74; assoc. researcher George Washington U., 1986; lectr. Far East di v. U. Md., Fuchu, 1971-73; spl. adv. Internat. Ranger Camps, Denmark and Switzerland, 1974-81; spl. cons. Internat. Quaker Sch., Wekhoven, Netherlands, 1959-63; mem. steering com. Pres.'s Com. on Employment of Handicapped, 1975—. Vol., ARC, 1967-78, Family Services, 1954-75. Served with WAVES, 1943-44. Recipient Disting. Alumnus award Eastern Ill. U., 1984. Lic. counselor, Va. Mem. Am. Personnel and Guidance Assn., Nat. Assn. Women Deans, Adminstrs. and Counselors (liaison to president's com.), Nat. Vocat. Guidance Assn., Am. Coll. Personnel Assn., No. Va. Counselors Assn., Delta Epsilon Sigma, Pi Lambda Theta. Roman Catholic. Home: 4708 38th Pl N Arlington VA 22207 Office: 2807 N Glebe Rd Arlington VA 22207

HICKMAN, GRACE MARGUERITE, artist; b. Reno, Nev., Nov. 7, 1921; d. Charles Franklin and Jeannie (McPhee) Wolcott; m. Robert Frederick Hickman, Apr. 10, 1943; children—John Charles, Carol Ann Hickman Harp, David Paul. Student Emily Griffiths Opportunity Sch., Denver, 1968-71, Red Rocks Community Coll., Golden, Colo., 1974-75, Loretto Heights Coll., Denver, 1983-85. Tchr. art Aurora Parks & Recreation, Colo., 1979-81; instr. paint workshop Marine Resource Ctr., Atlantic Beach, N.C., 1981, 82; lectr. color theory Aurora Artists Club, 1985; instr. creative color Acapulco Art Workshops, 1987, 88. One woman shows: Internat. House, Denver, 1974, Foothills Art Ctr., Golden, Colo., 1975, Greek Market Place, Denver, 1976, Marine Resource Ctr., Atlantic Beach, N.C., 1983, Depot Art Ctr., Littleton, Colo., 1984, Sheraton DTC, Women's Bank Denver, 1986, NYU Sch. Environmental Medicine, Tuxedo, 1987, Studio Paul Kontny, Denver, 1988. group shows include: Wellshire Presbyn. Ch., Denver, 1975, Brass Cheque Gallery, Denver, 1978, Colo. Women in Arts, Denver, 1979, Garelick's Gallery, Scottsdale, Ariz., 1982; Bold Expressions, Littleton, Colo., 1983. represented in permanent collections: Augustana Luth. Ch., Denver, South Shores Ins. Agy., Huntington Beach, Calif., Texon Gen. Partnership, Englewood, Colo., others. Coordinator figure study Bicentennial Art Ctr., Aurora, 1986; pres. Depot Art Ctr., Littleton, Colo., 1980-82. Mem. Nat. Mus. for Women in the Arts, Artists Equity Assn., Colo. Artists Equity Assn. (chmn. publicity Colo. 1% for Art 1976-77), Pastel Soc. Am., Littleton Fine Arts Guild (pres. 1976-77), Art Students League, Colo. Speakers Bur. (coordinator), Nat. Mus. Women in Arts. Democrat. Lutheran. Club: Aurora Athletic. Avocations: swimming; reading; art history. Home: 12361 E Bates Circle Aurora CO 80014

HICKMAN, JOLENE KAY, banker; b. Omaha, Sept. 5, 1954; d. Thomas Earl and Bernice Leona (McCoy) H. B.A., Otterbein Coll., 1977. Teller, Bancohio Nat. Bank, Columbus, Ohio, 1976-77, auditor, 1977-81; audit supr. Huntington Nat. Bank, Columbus, 1981-85, asst. v.p., mgr., 1985—. Mem. Victorian Village Soc., Columbus, 1983, Up Downtowners, Columbus, 1986. Mem. Nat. Assn. Bank Women (treas. 1985-86, chmn. edn. and tng. 1986-87, Ohio state conf., chmn. Looking at Leadership series 1985-86), Nat. Inst. Auditors, Nat. Assn. Female Execs. Republican. Methodist. Avocations: softball; racquetball. Home: 358 Blenheim Rd Columbus OH 43214 Office: Huntington Trust Co NA 41 S High St 10th Fl Columbus OH 43287

HICKMAN, LINDA MARIE, nurse; b. Ada, Okla., Nov. 10, 1953; d. Charlie Lewis and Bertha Mae (Vinson) Phelps; m. Ronnie Clarence Hickman, May 26, 1972; 1 child, Dustin Jake. RN, Cushing (Okla.) Mcpl. Hosp., 1974-75; AS, Okla. State U. Tech. Inst., 1974; student Cen. State U., Edmond, Okla., 1986—. Staff nurse Cushing Mcpl. Hosp., 1974-75; pub. health nurse Payne County Health, Cushing, 1975-78, 84-88; nurse cons. Care Manor, Stroud, Okla., 1982-83; house supr. Cushing Regional Hosp., 1982-83, asst. dir. home health service, 1983-84; communicable disease nurse Payne County Health Dept., Cushing, 1985-88. Author: Cushing Regional Hospital Home Health Service Policy and Procedure Manual, 1984. Self breast exam. instr. Am. Cancer Soc., 1984—. Cushing Bus. and Profl. Women's Club sr. scholar, 1972, named Career Woman of Yr., 1976. Mem. Okla. Pub. Health Assn. Democrat. Avocations: boating, skiing, camping, ceramics, woodworking. Home: Rt 4 PO Box 300 Cushing OK 74023

HICKMAN, LUCILLE, physical therapist; b. Chgo., July 21, 1949; d. Louis Melvin and Edna (Edwards) H. BA in Sociology, Lake Forest Coll., 1972; BS in Physical Therapy, Chgo. Med. Sch., 1975; M in Health Sci., Gov.'s State U., 1985. Staff phys. therapist Michael Reese Hosp., Chgo., 1975-79; dir. phys. therapy Provident Med. Ctr., Chgo., 1979-83; instr. phys. therapy Chgo. State U., 1983-87; pres. adminstrv. dir. R.O.C. Phys. Therapy Services, Chgo., 1985—; founder, pres. PhysioCare Ltd., Chgo., 1988—; pvt. practice therapy cons., Chgo., 1983—. Mem. Am. Phys. Therapy Assn., Nat. Soc. Allied Health. Democrat. Episcopalian. Office: ROC Phys Therapy Services 5231 S Woodlawn Chicago IL 60615

HICKMAN, MARGARET CAPELLINI, advertising agency executive; b. Hartford, Conn., Sept. 21, 1949; d. Anthony Serafino Capellini and Mary Magdelan (Budash) Zanardi; m. Richard Lonnie Hickman, Nov. 6, 1982. B.A., U. Conn., 1971. Mktg. asst. Advo Systems, Inc., Hartford, 1971-72, mktg. analyst, 1972-75; mktg. asst. Cinamon Assocs. Inc., Brookline, Mass., 1975-77, prodn. supr., 1977-81, v.p. prodn., 1981-84, v.p. client services, 1984-85; dir. client services Bozell, Jacobs, Kenyon & Eckhardt, Boston, 1985-86, v.p. client services Cinamon Assocs., Inc., Boston, 1986—; ptnr. Hickman & Hickman, Merritt Island, Fla., 1987; production mgr. The Direct Mktg. Agy., Stamford, Conn., 1988—. Mem. New Eng. Direct Mktg. Assn. (past sec., treas., v.p.), Cape Ann Child devel. Programs (past dir.), Central Fla. Direct Mktg. Assn. (past mem.), Am. Legion Aux. Democrat. Roman Catholic. Home: 68 Edgewood Pl Fairfield CT 06430

HICKMAN, PATRICIA REED, finance company officer; b. Lakeland, Fla., Mar. 6, 1951; s. John Grant and Juanita (Rushing) Reed; m. Richard Henry Hickman, May 15, 1971 (div. Sept. 1977); 1 child, Richard Reed. Student, Tidewater Community Coll., 1976-77. Loan processor Atlantic Permanent Savs. and Loan, Norfolk, Va., 1980-81; sr. customer service rep. TRW Credit Data Co., Norfolk, 1981-82; internal auditor, comml. loan underwriter, mgr. real estate dept. Va. Beach (Va.) Fed. Savs. and Loan Assn., 1982-87; asst. v.p. Real Estate Fin. div. Ameribanc Savings Bank, Annandale, Va., 1987—; Rep. litigation cases for Va. Beach Fed. Savs. and Loans. Contbr. poetry to Am. Poetry Anthology, 1988. Den mother, sec. Boys Scouts of Am., Va. Beach. Recipient Leadership Sch. award Inst. Fin. Edn., 1986. Democrat. Baptist. Home: 1358 Battleford Dr Virginia Beach VA 23464 Office: Ameribanc Savings Bank 2738 Va Beach Blvd Virginia Beach VA 23452

HICKMAN, PAULA DIANE, lawyer, educator; b. Miami, Fla., July 24, 1947; d. Paul William Hickman and Eva Lena (McCampbell) Melvin; m. Arthur G. Wimer III, Apr. 1, 1973 (div. Apr. 1976); m. Charles J. Rojek, Jan. 2, 1987. Student Longwood Coll., 1965-67; B.A. with honors, U. Tenn., 1969. Bar: Pa. 1980, N.H. 1981, Maine 1981, N.J. 1983, Fla. 1986. Flight attendant Pan Am. World Airways, N.Y.C., 1972-77; law clk. N.J. Superior Ct., Burlington, N.J., 1979-80; atty. Pub. Defender Program, Exeter, N.H., 1981-83; dep. clk. Rockingham County Superior Ct., Exeter, 1983-86; sole practice, Marathon, Fla., 1986; assoc. Spear & Deuschle, P.A., Ft. Lauderdale, Fla., 1988—; instr. McIntosh Coll., Dover, N.H., 1984-85. Past treas. bd. dirs. Rockingham Family Planning. Mem. ABA, N.H. Bar Assn., Rockingham County Bar Assn. (past v.p., past sec./treas.). Office: PO Box 1368 Marathon FL 33050

HICKMAN, SHEILA RENEE, television station executive; b. Monticello, Ill., June 20, 1950; d. Hubert Eugene and Stella Mae (Cody) H. AA in Bus. Adminstrn., Parkland Jr. Coll., Champaign, Ill., 1969. With Sta. WCIA-TV, Champaign, 1969—, sales and traffic clk., 1976-80, program dir., 1980—. Mem. Nat. Assn. TV Program Execs. Club: Exec. (Champaign). Office: Sta WCIA-TV 509 S Neil St Champaign IL 61820

HICKNER, GAIL MARIE, computer analyst; b. South Bend, Ind., Apr. 23, 1953; d. Steve A. and Helen J. (Sieron) Spretnjak; m. Joseph G. Hickner, June 11, 1983. BS in Math., St. Mary's Coll., Notre Dame, Ind., 1975. Jr. programmer St. Mary's Coll., Notre Dame, 1975-76, programmer, 1976-78; assoc. analyst Miles Labs., Elkhart, Ind., 1978-79, analyst, 1979-80, sr. analyst, 1980-84, project leader, 1984—; profl. keyboardist, saxophonist, 1971—; mem. Michiana Jazz Assemblage, 1980—, Elkhart Symphony Pops, 1986—. Mem. Chgo. Info. Mgmt. Services User Group (sec. 1982, 84—). Home: 815 Park Ave South Bend IN 46616

HICKS, BETHANY GRIBBEN, lawyer; b. N.Y., Sept. 8, 1951; d. Robert and DeSales Gribben; m. William A. Hicks III, May 21, 1982; children: Alexandra Elizabeth, Samantha Katherine. AB, Vassar Coll., 1973; MEd, Boston U., 1975; JD, Ariz. State U., 1984. Bar: Ariz. 1984. Sole practice Scottsdale, Ariz., 1984—. Mem. Jr. League of Phoenix, 1984—; parliamentarian Girls Club of Scottsdale, Ariz., 1985-87, bd. dirs. 1988—. Mem. ABA (family law sect.), State Bar Ariz. (family law sect.), Maricopa County Bar Assn. Democrat. Episcopalian. Club: Paradise Valley Country. Office: Cannes Bldg 6623 N Scottsdale Rd Scottsdale AZ 85253

HICKS, FRANCES M., nurse, educator; b. Wasco, Calif., Jan. 1, 1937; d. Clifford L. and Laura Elizabeth (Collins) H. Nursing cert., Okla. Bapt. Hosp., Muskogee, 1957; BS, Northwestern State U. of La., 1960; MS, Case Western Res. U., 1964; PhD, North Tex. State U., 1977. RN, Okla. Staff nurse Valley View Hosp., Ada, Okla., 1957, Okla. Bapt. Hosp., Muskogee, 1957-58; clin. instr. Muskogee Bapt. Hosp., 1959-60; evening med. supr. Muskogee Gen. Hosp., 1960-61, asst. hosp. adminstr., 1964; dir. shc. nursing Confederate Meml. Med. Ctr., Shreveport, La., 1964-71; asst. prof., asst. dean Tex. Woman's U., Denton, 1971-77; prof., asst. dean. U. So. Miss., Hattiesburg, 1977-78; assoc. prof., asst. dean U. Portland, Oreg., 1978—; cons. in field. Contbr. articles to profl. jours.; reviewer nursing texts, 1986—. Active Statewide Master Planning Commn., Portland, 1985—, Oreg. Health 2000 Team, Portland, 1987—. Mem. Am. Nurses Assn. (nat. bd. dirs. 1987—), Oreg. Nurses Assn. (pres. 1984-86), Nat. League for Nursing, Am. Assn. Higher Edn., AAUP, Am. Ednl. Research Assn., Sigma Theta Tau. Democrat. Baptist. Home: 17908 NW 69th Ave Ridgefield WA 98642 Office: U Portland Sch Nursing 5000 N Willamette Blvd Portland OR 97203

HICKS, GRETA PATTERSON, accountant, lecturer; b. Aspermont, Tex., Oct. 14, 1940; d. Herman J. and Zina O'zella (Daniels) Patterson; children—Ted Aaron, Tina Marie. B.S.B.A., U. Tulsa, 1972. C.P.A., Tex., Okla. Revenue agt. IRS, Houston, 1973-79, dist. tng. and recruitment coordinator, 1979-80; tax mgr. Arthur Young & Co., Houston, 1980-81; prin. Greta P. Hicks, C.P.A., Houston, 1981—; lectr.; TV and radio appearances. Author/contbg. editor Money Talk column Houston Woman mag., 1982—; assoc. prof. U. Houston Sch. Optometry; mem. career devel. adv. com. Houston Ind. Sch. Dist., 1980—; active Found. for Edn. and Vision Research, 1987—. Recipient letter of commendation IRS, 1975; cert. of merit U. Tulsa, 1972; named Woman of Yr., Fedn. Bus. and Profl. Women's Clubs, 1984; Am. Soc. Women Accts. scholar, 1972. Mem. Am. Inst. C.P.A.s, Tex. Soc. C.P.A.s, Am. Soc. Women Accts. (pres. Houston 1981-82), Am. Woman's Soc. C.P.A.s (charter), Women's Bus. Support Network (charter), Fedn. Houston Profl. Women (treas. 1986). Office: 2855 Mangum Suite 303 Houston TX 77092

HICKS, HELEN ANNE, data processing executive; b. Chgo., Jan. 18, 1962; d. Harold Francis and Norine Frances (McNamara) H.; m. Terence W. Dempsey, June 6, 1987. BS, U. Ill., Chgo., 1984, MBA with highest honors, 1986. Asst. mgr. Dunkin Donuts, Chgo., 1977-80; research cons. GNP Commodities, Inc., Chgo., 1986; instr. fin. U. Ill., Chgo., 1986; microcomputer mgr., research assoc. Drexel Burnham Lambert, Chgo., 1987—. Mem. Anti-Cruelty Soc. Chgo. Recipient 7 undergrad. scholarships, 3 grad. fellowships. Mem. Nat. Wildlife Fedn., U. Ill. Alumni Assn. (life), Alpha Lambda Delta, Beta Gamma Sigma, Phi Eta Sigma, Phi Kappa Phi. Democrat. Roman Catholic.

HICKS, JOCELYN MURIEL, laboratory medicine specialist; b. Leamington Spa, Warwickshire, Eng., Aug. 17, 1937; came to U.S., 1965; d. Harold Archie and Muriel Ellen (Cumberland) Bingley; m. John Geoffrey Hicks, Aug. 15, 1959 (div. Nov. 1965); m. Melvin Blecher, May 1, 1973. BS, U. London, 1959, MSc, 1962; PhD, Georgetown U., 1971. Fellow Georgetown U. Med. Ctr., Washington, 1969-71; dir. clin. chemistry Children's Hosp. Nat. Med. Ctr., Washington, 1971-75, chmn. dept. lab. medicine, 1975—; instr. George Washington U. Med. Ctr., Washington, 1971-72, asst. prof., 1972-74, assoc. prof., 1975-81, prof., 1981—; mem. profl. staff. The Hosp. for Sick Children, Washington, 1984—; clin. affiliate Cath. U. Am., Washington, 1982—; cons. Eastman Kodak Co., Rochester, N.Y., Technicon Instruments Corp., Tarrytown, N.Y. Author: Selected Analytes of Clinical Chemistry, 1984, Textbook of Pediatric Clinical Chemistry, 1984, Directory of Rare Analyses, 1986, 87, The Neonate, 1974; contbr. articles to profl. jours. Recipient Kone award Assn. Clin. Biochemists, 1987. Mem. Am. Assn. for Clin. Chemistry (bd. dirs. 1978-81, pres. 1981-82, commr. publs. commn. 1982-87, Joseph H. Roe award 1976, Bernard Gerulat Meml. award 1983, Fisher award 1984, cert. of honor, Van Slyke award 1988), Acad. Clin. Lab. Physicians and Scientists. Home: 4329 Van Ness St NW Washington DC 20016 Office: Childrens Hosp Nat Med Ctr 111 Michigan Ave NW Washington DC 20010

HICKS, JOYCE BELLE, personnel administrator; b. Lebanon, Nebr., Nov. 30, 1934; d. Klee and Laura Losetta (Fisher) Bethel; m. Grover Ray Hicks, Dec. 18, 1980; children—Carmen, David. Student U. Nebr.-Lincoln, Opportunity Sch.-Denver, U. Mexico, U. El Paso. Purchasing clk. Chrysler Corp., Cape Canaveral, Fla., 1963-65, contract analyst, 1965-75, budget analyst, 1975-79, personnel adminstr., El Paso, Tex., 1979—. Volunteer, United Way of El Paso, 1979-83. Recipient Citation outstanding achievement, United Way of El Paso, 1979-83. Mem. Am. Soc. Personnel Adminstrn., El Paso Personnel Assn. Clubs: Discover El Paso, others. Home: 11605 Casa View El Paso TX 79936 Office: Chrysler Corp 11210 Armour Dr El Paso TX 79935

HICKS, JUDITH EILEEN, nursing administrator; b. Chgo., Jan. 1, 1947; d. John Patrick and Mary Ann (Clifford) Rohan; m. Laurence Joseph Hicks, Nov. 22, 1969; children—Colleen Driscoll, Patrick Kevin. B.S. in Nursing, St. Xavier Coll., Chgo., 1969; M.S. in Nursing, U. Ill.-Chgo., 1975. Staff nurse Mercy Hosp., Chgo., 1969-70, nursing supr., 1970-73; cons. continuing edn. Ill. Nurses Assn., Chgo., 1974-75; dir. obstetrics and gynecology nursing Northwestern Meml. Hosp., Chgo., 1975-81; v.p. nursing Children's Meml. Hosp., Chgo., 1981-86; pres. Children's Meml. Home Health, Inc., 1986—, Children's Meml. Nursing Services, 1986—; pres. Allied & Children's Home Health and Nursing Services, 1988; dir. Near North Health Corp., Chgo., 1982-85. Mem. Ill. Hosp. Assn. (chmn. Council on Nursing 1982-83), Inst. Medicine, Am. Soc. Nursing Adminstrs., Women's Health Exec. Network (pres. 1984-85). Roman Catholic. Home: 2206 Beechwood St Wilmette IL 60091 Office: Children's Meml Hosp 2300 Children's Plaza Chicago IL 60614

HICKS, KATHRYN KEATON, infosystems executive; b. Cuthbert, Ga., June 28, 1932; d. James Madison and Edna Irene (Dunn) Keaton; m. Lester Melvin Hicks. AB in Math, Biology, Ga. Coll., 1952; MS, U. Tenn., 1985. Statistical clk. TVA, Chattanooga, 1952-56, engring. aide, 1956-59, mathematician, 1959-65, computer specialist, 1965-68, unit supr., 1968-75, staff supr., 1975-77, sect. supr., 1977-80, group mgr., 1980-84, chief of staff, 1984—. Mem. Nat. Mgmt. Assn (bd. dirs. 1984-85, chpt. officer 1986—), Fed. Employed Women, Inst. Cert. Profl. Mgrs. Club: Toastmasters (officer 1987—). Home: 413 S Mission Ridge Dr Rossville GA 30741 Office: Tenn Valley Authority 1010 Georgia Ave Chattanooga TN 37401

HICKS, MARY CARVER, accounting executive; b. Moultrie, Ga., Mar. 8, 1941; d. James Edward and Sudie Mae (Holland) Carver; m. Paul Barnabus Hicks, June 12, 1964 (div. 1976); 1 child, Steven Edward. BS in Acctg., U. Houston, 1964. Bookkeeper A&P Tea Co., Houston, 1955-64; with inventory control Houston Coca Cola Bottling Co., 1964-68, acctg. mgr., 1976—; auditor Moultrie (Ga.) Nat. Bank, 1968-76. Mem. Nat. Assn. Profl. Women. Democrat. Baptist. Home: 8300 Sands Point #907 Houston TX 77036 Office: Houston Coca Cola Bottling Co 2800 Bissonnet Houston TX 77006

HICKS, SUSAN LYNN BOWMAN, social worker; b. Flint, Mich., Mar. 24, 1952; d. Richard and Carol Joanne (Haney) Bowman; m. Duane James Hicks, Aug. 6, 1977. B.A., U. Mich., Flint, 1975; M.A., Central Mich. U., 1981. Med. social worker Flint Osteo. Hosp., 1974-77; dir. med. social work and patient relations Crittenton Hosp., Rochester, Mich., 1978—; mgmt. tng. and devel. cons. Buick, Oldsmobile, Cadillac div. Gen. Motors, Grand Blanc, Mich., 1985. Bd. dirs., chmn. com. Rochester Area Youth Guidance, Mich., 1986, chairperson, 1988. Mem. Soc. for Hosp. Social Work Dirs. (Recognition award 1984, 85, pres.-elect 1985-86, pres. 1986-87, chairperson polit. and social action com. 1988—), Nat. Assn. Social Workers, Nat. Assn. Female Execs., Soc. Patient Representatives. Methodist. Avocations: tap dancing; writing. Home: 20483 Fox Detroit MI 48240-1207 Office: Crittenton Hosp 1101 W University Rochester MI 48063

HICKS, VICKI LYNN, accountant; b. Lubbock, Tex., Aug. 31, 1951; d. Billy Harold and Patsy Sue (Burnett) Jackson; m. Johnny Ray Hicks, Apr. 11, 1970; 1 child, Byron Lee. BBA, Tex. Tech U., 1987. CPA. Staff acct. Davis, Kinard & Co., Abilene, Tex., 1977-79, Wolfe & Roberson, CPA's, Abilene, 1979-85; acct. McDougal Properties, Lubbock, 1988—. Mem. Am. Women's Soc. CPA's, Lubbock Women's Soc. CPA's (bd. dirs. 1988—), Tex. Soc. CPA's, Lubbock Soc. CPA's. Baptist. Office: McDougal Properties 7008 Salem Ave Suite 200 Lubbock TX 79424

HICKS, VIRGINIA GRAY, nurse, educator; b. Lawton, Okla., Oct. 30, 1944; d. John William Gray and Donnie Margaret (Coryell) Nichols; m. Stephen H. Westhafer, Dec. 20, 1966 (div. 1976); children: Stephanie, Lisa, Angela; m. John P. Hicks, May 17, 1986. Diploma in Nursing, Gilfoy Sch. of Nursing, 1967; BS in Nursing, Miss. Coll., 1983; MS, U. So. Miss., 1984. Staff nurse Miss. Bapt. Med. Ctr., Jackson, 1967-68; office nurse Dr. Ralph Sneed, Jackson, 1968-69; nurse St. Dominic Hosp., Jackson, 1969-71; physician asst. Dr. Henry Webb, Jackson Clin., Jackson, 1975-83; asst. prof. NE La. U. Sch. of Nursing, Monroe, 1984—; dir. clin. services MCAN Monroe (La.) Psychiat. Pavilion, 1987—; level coordinator NE La. U. Sch. of Nursing, Monroe, 1985-87; Nat. Council Licensure Exam. RNs coordinator S. Kaplan Co., Dallas, 1987—. Mem. Am. Nurses Assn., State Nurses Assn., Nursing Adminstrs. Council. Baptist. Home: 17 Magnolia Dr Monroe LA 71203 Office: Monroe Psychiat Pavilion Hwy 165 N Monroe LA 71203

HICKSON, CHARLOTTE ANN, librarian; b. Brownfield, Tex., Jan. 8, 1947; d. Rubert Alison and Bernice Viola (Doyle) Martin; B.A., Tex. Woman's U., 1968, M.L.S., 1969; m. Ronnie B. Hickson, Apr. 19, 1965; children—Kurt Leldon, Brandi Katrice. Reference librarian Tex. Tech. U., Lubbock, 1968-70, catalog librarian, 1970-75, acquisitions librarian monograph sect., 1975-79, dept. chmn., acquisitions librarian, 1979-85, catalogue librarian, 1985-86; ins. agt. Horace Mann Ins. Co., Lubbock, 1986—. Mem. Nat. Assn. Life Underwriters, Tex. Assn. Coll. Tchrs. Democrat. Methodist. Club: Lubbock Women's. Author articles in field. Home: 7901 Louisville Ave Lubbock TX 79423 Office: Horace Mann Ins Co PO Box 93242 Lubbock TX 79493

HICKSON, JOAN BOGLE, actress; b. Kingsthorpe, Northamptonshire, Eng., Aug. 5, 1906; d. Harold and Edith (Bogle) Hickson; m. Eric Norman Butler, Oct. 29, 1933; children—Nicholas Andrew Mark, Caroline Margaret Julia. Student Oldfield Sch., Swanage, Dorset, Eng.; diploma Royal Acad. Dramatic Art. Appeared in plays A Day in the Death of Joe Egg, Forget Me Not Lane, The Card, Bedroom Farce, The Freeway, Blithe Spirit, On the Razzle; films include The Guinea Pig, Seven Days to Noon, Yanks, The Wicked Lady, Clockwise; television appearances include Great Expectations, Nanny, Good Girls, Poor Little Rich Girls, Time for Murder, Agatha Christie Novels (Obie award 1987). Recipient "Tony" award League of N.Y. Theatres, 1979, Order of the British Empire, 1987. Mem. Ch. of Eng.

HIDALGO, MARCI L., office products company owner; b. N.Y.C., Apr. 6, 1960; d. Alfred and Nelly (Hernandez) Jimenez; m. Michael John Walczak, Dec. 21, 1985. BA, Drew U.; postgrad. in law, Seton Hall U.; postgrad. in pub. adminstrn., Fairleigh Dickinson U. Profl. asst. Office of gov. of N.J., Trenton, 1981; unit sec. emergency room Overlook Hosp., Summit, N.J., 1980-83; admistrv. asst. Hellring, Lindeman et al, Newark, 1983-84; personnel adminstr. Olsten Corp., Edison, N.J., 1984-86; adminstrv. asst. Chubb Ins. Corp., 1986-87; pres., owner Selective Supply Co., Vauxhall, N.J., 1987—. Vol. worker Irvington Nat. Devel. Corp., N.J., 1977-78. Mem. Nat. Assn. Female Execs., Phi Alpha Delta. Democrat. Roman Catholic. Avocations: reading, writing, public speaking, foreign languages. Home: 176 Milburn Ave Milburn NJ 07041 Office: Selective Supply Co PO Box 115 Vauxhall NJ 07088

HIEATT, CONSTANCE BARTLETT, English language educator; b. Boston, Feb. 11, 1928; d. Arthur Charles and Eleonora (Very) Bartlett; m. Allen Kent Hieatt, Oct. 25, 1958. Student, Smith Coll., 1945-47; A.B., Hunter Coll., 1953, A.M., 1957; Ph.D., Yale U., 1959. Lectr. City Coll., CUNY, 1959-60; from asst. prof. to asso. prof. English Queensborough Community Coll., CUNY, 1960-65; asso. prof. St. John's U., Jamaica, N.Y., 1965-69; prof. English U. Western Ont. (Can.) London, 1969—. Author: The Canterbury Tales of Geoffrey Chaucer, 1964, The Realism of Dream Visions, 1967, Beowulf and Other Old English Poems, 1967, Essentials of Old English, 1968, (with Sharon Butler) Pleyn Delit: Medieval Cookery for Modern Cooks, 1976, rev. edit., 1979, Karlamagnus Saga, Vols. I and II, 1975, 1975, Vol. III, 1980, Sir Gawain and the Green Knight, 1967, The Knight of the Lion, 1968, The Knight of the Cart, 1969, The Joy of the Court, 1971, The Sword and the Grail, 1972, The Castle of Ladies, 1973, The Minstrel Knight, 1974; (with Sharon Butler) Curye on Inglysch, 1985; contbr. articles to scholarly jours. Yale U. fellow, and Lewis-Farmington fellow, 1957-59; Can. Council and Social Sci. and Humanities Research Council grantee. Fellow Royal Soc. Can.; mem. MLA, Medieval Acad. Am., Internat. Arthurian Assn., Early English Text Soc., Internat. Saga Assn., Early English Text Soc., Internat. Assn. Anglo-Saxonists, Children's Lit. Assn., Soc. Advancement of Scandinavian Studies, Assn. Canadian Univ. Tchrs. English, New Chaucer Soc., Anglo-Norman Text Soc. Anglican. Home: 304 River Rd Deep River CT 06417 Office: U Western Ont Dept English, London, ON Canada N6A 3K7

HIEBERT, ELIZABETH BLAKE, civic worker; b. Mpls., July 18, 1910; d. Henry Seavey and Grace (Riebeth) Blake; student Washburn U., 1926-30; B.S., U. Tex. 1933; m. Homer L. Hiebert, Aug. 29, 1935; children—Grace Elizabeth (Mrs. John E. Beam), Mary Sue (Mrs. Donald Wester), John Blake, Henry Leonard, David Mark. Sec. Topeka Regional Sci. Fair, 1958-60, bd. dirs., 1964—; bd. dirs. YMCA 1968-74, Topeka (Kans.) Friends of the 300; water safety instr. and swimming tchr. of handicapped; freelance writer; mem. adv. com. Kans. Ctr.; former mem. Shawnee County Advocacy Council on Aging; Shawnee County chmn. Arthritis Found. Hon. fellow Harry S. Truman Library; recipient Paul Harris award Rotary, 1985. Mem. D.A.R., Daus. Am. Colonists, AAUW (dir. 1944-62, 65—), N.E. Hist. and Geneal. Soc., Tex. U. Alumni, Am. Home Econs. Assn., Shawnee County Med. Aux. (past pres.), Nat. Audubon, Met. Mus. Art, P.E.O. (past local pres. coop. bd.), Topeka Art Guild, Nat. Soc. Ancient and Hon. Arty., Nat. Trust Historic Preservation, Internat. Oceanographic Found., Nat. League Am. Pen Women (pres. Topeka 1970-72), Washburn Alumnae Assn., Am. Assn. State and Local History, Colo. Hist. Assn., Shawnee County Hist. Soc., Mont., Minn., Kans. hist. socs., Smithsonian Assos., Oceanic Soc., Internat. Platform Assn., Topeka Friends of the Library, Cousteau Soc., Am. Assn. Zookeepers, Nat. Assn. for Mature People, Am. Assn. Ret. Persons, K.U. Spencer Mus. Art, Conn. Soc. Genealogists, Nat., New Eng. geneal. socs., Topeka Beautification Assn. (sec.), People to People, Archives Assos., Am. Space Found., Mus. Fine Arts Boston, Kans. Reading Assn., Am. Assn. Museums, San Diego Zool. Soc., Nat. Space Inst., Oriental Inst., Delta Kappa Gamma (hon.), Delta Gamma, others. Club: Topeka Knife and Fork. Editor children's page Household mag., 1934-39. Home: 1517 Randolph Topeka KS 66604

HIEBERT, LESLIE CAROL, nurse; b. Austin, Tex., Oct. 29, 1957; d. Lester Earl and Rachel Josephine (Mancha) H. BS in Nursing, U. Tex. Health Sci. Ctr., 1980; postgrad., Tex. Women's U. RN. Staff nurse Tex. Children's Hosp., Houston, 1980-81, unit tchr., head nurse, 1981-83; nurse clin. research Dept. Urology Baylor Coll. Med., Houston, 1984-85, Dept. Allergy and Immunology Tex. Children's Hosp., Houston, 1985—. Recipient scholarship March Dimes, 1985. Republican. Baptist. Home: 7100 Almeda Rd Houston TX 77054 Office: Tex Childrens Hosp 6621 Fannin St Houston TX 77030

HIENTON, DIANE DEBROSSE, lawyer; b. Fayetteville, Ark., Jan. 30, 1948; d. Joseph Denis and Opal Ruvena (Pitts) DeBrosse; m. James Robert Hienton, July 23, 1977. B.A., U. Hawaii, 1971; J.D., Ariz. State U., 1975. Bar: Ariz. 1975. Asst. atty. gen. State of Ariz., Phoenix, 1976-78, 84—; staff atty. Ariz. Ct. Appeals, 1978-81, 82-84; assoc. firm Jennings, Kepner & Haug, Phoenix, 1981-82. Contbr. articles to profl. jours. Mem. 1984 Phoenix Citizens Bond Com., Ariz. Theatre Guilde, Phoenix, 1982-84; founding life mem. Ariz. Mus. Sci. and Tech., 1984; bd. dirs. Ariz. Women's Town Hall. Mem. ABA, State Bar Ariz., Maricopa County Bar Assn. (pres. pub. lawyers sect. 1988), Jr. League Phoenix. Republican. Club: Soroptimist (pres. 1988—, editor Phoenix SOL Bull 1983-84). Office: Office of Atty Gen Dept Law 1275 W Washington Phoenix AZ 85007

HIERHOLZER, JOAN, artist; BFA, U. Tex., Austin; MFA, Rutgers U.; m. Harlan B. Pratt; children by previous marriage—Charles Cooper Bennett, David Pine Bennett. Fashion illustrator, San Antonio; tchr. art Summit (N.J.) Art Ctr. and Pub. Schs.; one-woman shows of paintings include: Exxon Refinery, Linden, N.J., Marion Koogler McNay Art Mus., San Antonio, Summit Art Ctr., Ednl. Testing Service, Princeton, N.J., Allied Chem. Corp., Morristown, N.J., AT&T Galleries, Basking Ridge, N.J., Phoenix Gallery, N.Y.C., group shows include: Bodley Gallery, N.Y.C., Dallas Mus. Fine Arts, Equitable Life Assurance Co., N.Y.C., Fairleigh Dickinson U., Madison, N.J., Lever House, N.Y.C., Montclair (N.J.) Art Mus., Mus. N.Mex., Santa Fe, Nabisco, N.J., Rutgers U. Art Gallery, New Brunswick, N.J., Witte Mus., San Antonio, N.J. State Mus. Art, Trenton, Fed. Bldg., N.Y.C.; mem. Phoenix Gallery, N.Y.C.; represented in permanent collections: Westinghouse Elevator Co., Exxon Corp., Overlook Hosp., Summit, Schering Plough, Sentry Refining Inc., Chem. Bank., Juniata Coll., Pa., Hiram Coll., Ohio, Deloitte, Haskell & Sells, N.J., Diagnostic/Retrieval Systems, Inc., N.J., also pvt. collections. Trustee Hunterdon Art Ctr. Fellow MacDowell Colony, Peterborough, N.H. Mem. Nat. Arts Club of N.Y.C., Nat. Assn. Women Artists, Artshowcase, Kappa Kappa Gamma. Republican. Christian Scientist. Club: PEO. Address: RD 3 PO Box 380 Pittstown NJ 08867

HIERS, CAROLYN SKINNER, educator; b. Biloxi, Miss., June 1, 1947; d. Shelton Douglas and Ruth (Crimons) Skinner; m. Jerry Lee Hiers; children: Andrew G. Nash, Amanda L. Nash. BS, U. So. Miss., 1965; MS, Loyola U., New Orleans, 1969. Cert. tchr, Miss. Tchr. Biloxi Sch. System, 1965-68, 72-77, St. Francis Cabrini Sch., New Orleans, 1969-70, Fulton County Sch. System, Atlanta, 1970; instr. Upward Bound/Spl. Services Fla. A&M U., Tallahassee, 1978-79, asst. prof., coordinator Ednl. Talent Search, Coll. Reach-Out programs, 1979—. Editor Outreach News, 1979. Bd. dirs. Creative Employment Found., Tallahassee, 1986—. NSF fellow, 1969—. Mem. Fla. Assn. Ednl. Opportunity Program Personnel (sec., newsletter editor 1981-85), Fla. Assn. Student Fin. Aid Adminstrs., Fla. Assn. Counseling and Devel. Democrat. Lodge: Eastern Star. Home: 3238 Yorktown Dr Tallahassee FL 32312-2016

HIGBEE, FLORENCE SALICK, librarian; b. Milw.; d. Otto Thomas and Mary (Reiter) Salick; B.A., U. Wis., 1933; M.S. in Library Sci., Cath. U. Am., 1965; 1 dau., Joan Florence. Reference librarian Shirlington br. of Arlington County Public Libraries, Arlington, Va., 1965-67; br. librarian Glencarlyn br. Arlington County Public Libraries, Arlington, 1967, Columbia Pike br., 1967-73; translator, archivist. Mem. nominating com. Literacy Council No. Va., Inc., 1973-74. State of Va. Grad. fellow, 1964-65. Mem. ALA, Am. Malacological Union. Home: 13 N Bedford Arlington VA 22201

HIGBEE, JOAN FLORENCE, librarian; b. Washington, Dec. 1, 1945; d. Florence Salick H. BA in French, George Washington U., 1967; MA and PhD in Romance Langs., Johns Hopkins U., 1975; MLS, Cath. U. Am., 1976; student, U. Sorbonne, U. Nancy. Librarian Processing Services Dept. Library Congress, Washington, 1976—; collections specialist Internat. Ctr. Scholars, Smithsonian Inst., 1981—; instr. Johns Hopkins U., 1968-72; asst. d'anglais, Lycée Frédéric Chopin, Nancy, France, 1967-68. Contbr. articles to profl. jours. Mem. ALA (councilor at large 1980—, founding coordinator Library Union Task Force, past mem. policy monitoring com., resolutions com., com. profl. standards), Assn. Coll. and Research Libraries (past chair Western European specialists sect.). Office: Library Congress 1st and Independence Ave SE Washington DC 20003

HIGDON, BARBARA, college president; b. Independence, Mo., May 18, 1930; m. 1950; 3 children. B.A., U. Mo., 1951, M.A., 1952, Ph.D. in Speech, 1961. Assoc. prof. English, speech, Tex. So. U., 1958-62; prof. Graceland Coll., Lamoni, Iowa, 1962-75, pres., 1984—; dean, v.p. acad. affairs Park Coll., 1975-84. Address: Graceland Coll Lamoni IA 50140

HIGGINBOTHAM, SARA, hospital education administrator, nurse; b. Hackensack, N.J., June 21, 1926; d. Donald and Theresa (DeLorenzo) Pepe; m. Manning E. Higginbotham, July 1, 1952; children—Nancy June, Miles Dudley. B.S. in Nursing, Alfred U., 1948; postgrad. Columbia U., 1950-52; M.S. in Personnel Counseling, Jacksonville State U., 1972. Staff nurse Hackensack Hosp. (N.J.), 1948-50, Meml. Ctr. Cancer and Allied Diseases, N.Y.C., 1950-51, supr., instr., 1951-55; dir. inservice edn. Bapt. Meml. Hosp., Gadsden, Ala., 1967-80, dir. edn. dept., 1980—; chmn. Inservice Edn. com. Ala. League Nursing, 1967-69. Mem. Am. Soc. Health Edn. and Tng., Am. Nurses Assn., Disabled Am. Vets. Aux. Club: Pilot of Gadsden (pres. 1983-84). Home: Route 2 Box 156 Gadsden AL 35903 Office: Bapt Meml Hosp 1007 Goodyear Ave Gadsden AL 35999

HIGGINS, BARBARA JEANE, financial company administrator; b. Bethany, Mo., Oct. 28, 1949; d. Vurl Oliver and Lorna Mae (Miller) Ellis; m. David Allen Diersen, July 28, 1968 (div. 1974); 1 child, Tamara Jo Diersen; m. Sherman John Higgins, Oct. 16, 1976. Grad. high sch., Sac City, Iowa. Proof operator Citizens Savs. Bank, Sac City, 1967-70; asst. cashier NW Des Moines (Iowa) Nat. Bank, 1974-75; proof, teller Comml. Trust & Savs. Bank, Storm Lake, Iowa, 1975-76; adminstr. hawkeye Bancorp./IHelp, Des Moines, 1980-84; asst. v.p. Home Fed. Savs. & Loan, Phoenix, 1984-86; regional mgr. Marine Midland Bank/Nelc, Tempe, Ariz., 1986—. Sponsor Nat. Rep. Congrl. Commn., 1983—; chair membership com. First Christian Ch., Mesa, Ariz., 1986—, bd. dirs., 1986—. Mem. Nat. Assn. Female Execs., Iowa Assn. Student Fin. Aid. Adminstrs., Ariz. Assn. Student Fin. Aid Adminstrs., We. Assn. Ariz. Pvt. Sch. Assn., Women's C. of C. Republican. Disciples of Christ. Home: 2210 E Fairfield Mesa AZ 85203 Office: Nat Edn Lending Ctr 1600 W Broadway #111 Tempe AZ 85282

HIGGINS, ELIZABETH FLOUNDERS, personnel administrator; b. Phila., Aug. 12, 1944; d. William Joseph and Mary Ann (Gallagher) Flounders; m. Thomas Joseph Higgins, Feb. 5, 1966; children: Timothy Joseph, Maura Douglas. Student, St. Joseph's U., Phila., 1961-67. Position classification specialist USDA Forest Service, Broomall, Pa., 1975—; ptnr. Related Bus. Services, Drexel Hill, Pa., 1986—. Assoc. pub., contbr. Delaware County edit. TV Facts mag., Hicksville, N.Y., 1980-83. Mem. S.E. Lansdowne Civic Assn., 1970-78; sec. Lansdowne Friends Sch. PTA, 1974-78. Mem. Phila. Area Staffing Soc. Democrat. Roman Catholic. Club: Toastmasters (Broomall) (pres. 1982-83, ednl. v.p. 1983-84, treas. 1985—).

HIGGINS, JANINE AUDREY, lawyer; b. Winnipeg, Man., Can., Oct. 21, 1953; d. J.P. Allan and Doris E. (Thompson) Mowat; m. Kevin Barry Higgins, June 25, 1977; children: William James, Erin Kathleen. BA, U. B.C., 1974; LLB, U. Toronto, 1978. Bar: Ont. 1980. Assoc. Siskind, Cromarty, London, Ont., 1980-87, ptnr., 1987—. Pres. London YMCA/YWCA, 1987-88, chair Women of Distinction Awards Program, 1984-86. Mem. Law Soc. Upper Can. (lectr.), Can. Bar Assn. Office: Siskind Cromarty, 471 Waterloo St, London, ON Canada N6B 2J5

HIGGINS, MARGARET M., government agency administrator; b. Meriden, Conn., Dec. 11, 1944; d. Joseph C. and Katherine T. (Roche) H.; BA, Albertus Magnus Coll., 1966; postgrad. Northeastern U., 1973. With U.S. Office of Personnel Mgmt., 1966—, mgr. Augusta (Maine) area office, 1970-72, personnel specialist, Boston regional office, 1972-74, mgr. Providence area office, 1974-79, chief adv. services office, Washington, 1979-82, chief recruiting, testing, and info. br., 1982-84, program analyst, 1984-87, program mgmt. officer, 1987—. Bd. dirs. Opportunities for Women, Providence, 1977-79, Civil Service Employees Credit Union, 1982—. Recipient Office of Personnel Mgmt. Dirs. award for superior accomplishment, 1981, merit pay award, 1984, Dirs. Meritous Service award, 1986, Spl. Service award, 1987. Mem. Internat. Personnel Mgmt. Assn., New Eng. Fed. Personnel Council (chmn. 1978-79), Am. Soc. Pub. Adminstrn. (chpt. pres. 1977-78).

HIGGINS, MARGE, state legislator; b. Lincoln, Nebr., Aug. 3, 1931; m. David Higgins, 1956. Student, St. Joseph's Coll., Owensboro, Ky. Ins. agt; mem. Nebr. State Legislature, 1980—. Office: 125 S 38th St Omaha NE 68131 *

HIGGINS, RUBY JEANETTE DOUGLAS, academic administrator; b. Ruston, La., Mar. 3, 1944; d. Milton James Jr. and Hazel (Greenwood) Douglas; m. Ronald W. Higgins, Apr. 4, 1962 (div. Oct. 1968); children: Renita June, Raynald Wesley. BS in Edn. cum laude, Grambling (La.) Coll., 1964; MS in Edn., La. Tech. U., 1974. Tchr. Vernon Parish Sch. Bd., Leesville, La., 1964-65, St. Louis City Bd. Edn., 1966-73, Berkerly (Mo.) Sch. Dist., 1973-74; coordinator women's activities Grambling State U., 1974-75, coordinator women's area, 1975-77, dean student life, 1977-86, dean student devel., 1986—, also mem. various coms.; chmn. adv. bd. Security Nat. Bank; field reader U.S. Office Edn., 1987—. Mem. Nat. Assn. Personnel Workers (editor newsletter, treas. 1987—), Assn. Fraternity Advisors (Nat. Pan Hellenic Council liaison 1987-88), Nat. Assn. Student Personnel Adminstrs., Am. Coll. Personnel Adminstrs., So. Coll. Personnel Adminstrs., La. Assn. Coll. and Univ. Student Personnel Adminstrs., Nat. Assn. Women Deans and Counselors, La. Assn. Women Deans and Counselors (v.p., then pres.), Nat. Assn. Fgn. Student Affairs, Am. Bus. Women's Assn., Grambling State U. Alumni Assn. (bd. dirs., nat. officer, news editor, chair social com.), NAACP, LWV, Jills Unltd. (treas. Grambling chpt.), Delta Sigma Theta (sec., v.p., then pres. Grambling chpt.). Home: PO Box 185 Grambling LA 71245 Office: Grambling State U PO Drawer 566 Grambling LA 71245

HIGGINS, THERESE, college president; b. Winthrop, Mass., Sept. 29, 1925; d. James C. and Margaret M. (Lennon) H. A.B. cum laude, Regis Coll., 1947; M.A., Boston Coll.; Ph.D., U. Wis.; D.H.L., Emmanuel Coll.; postgrad. in lit. and theology, Harvard U.; LL.D. (hon.), Northeastern U. Joined Congregation of Sisters of St. Joseph, Roman Cath. Ch., 1947; instr. Regis Coll., Weston, Mass., 1963-65; asst. prof. Regis Coll., 1965-67, asso. prof., 1968—, pres., 1974—, also trustee. Book reviewer: Boston Globe, 1965—. Trustee Waltham (Mass.) Hosp., 1978-85, Cardinal Spellman Philatelic Mus., 1976—; mem. Mass. Gov.'s Commn. on Status Women, 1977-79, Nat. Com. Ecclesial Role Women. U. Wis. research grantee Eng. Mem. Nat. Cath. Ednl. Assn., AAUW, MLA, AAUP, Assn. Ind. Colls. and Univs. Mass. (exec. com.), New Eng. Colls. Fund, NEASC (commn.). Office: Regis Coll 235 Wellesley St Weston MA 02193

HIGGS, ELIZABETH JO, savings and loan association executive; b. Chestertown, Md., June 30, 1960; d. Charles Arnold and Mary Elizabeth (Hawkins) Downey; m. Elwood Glenn Higgs, Jr., Aug. 1978; 1 child, Stephanie Lynn. Ed. pub. schs., Centreville, Md. Teller Sudlersville (Md.) Bank, 1978-79; bookkeeper, then proof operator Peoples Bank of Kent County, Chestertown, 1979-80, from new accounts clk. to supr. loan dept., 1980-85; asst. mgr. 2d Nat. Fed. Savs., Salisbury, Md., 1985-87; sr. asst. bank mgr., computer trainer 2d Nat. Fed. Savs., Salisbury, 1987-88; programmer, bookkeeper P. Patrick McClary Real Estate, Golts, Md., 1988—. Treas. Sudlersville Elem. Sch. PTA, 1985-87; leader Chesapeake Bay Council Girl Scouts USA, 1987-88; mem. Sudlersville Vol. Fire Co., 1986-88; rep. Queen Anne's County Council, Centreville, 1987-88. Methodist. Lodge: Moose. Home: Rt 1 Box 182-EF Millington MD 21651 Office: Second Nat Fed Savs 503 Washington Ave Chestertown MD 21620

HIGGS, PATRICIA JANE, software company executive; b. Brewton, Ala., Oct. 30, 1957; d. Jay Darnell and Verla (Jernigan) H. AA, Pensacola Jr. Coll., 1977; BS in Systems Sci. and Bus. summa cum laude, U. W.Fla., 1979, MBA, 1981. Asst. mgmt. S. Cen. Bell. Co., Birmingham, Ala., 1978-79; systems analyst U. W.Fla., Pensacola, 1979-84, Trust Co. Bank, Atlanta, 1984-85; cons. mgmt. Am. Software Inc., Atlanta, 1985—; coordinator mgmt. conf. Profl. Devel. Dept. U. W.Fla., 1982-83; mem. com. curriculum design Dept. Mgmt., 1982; facilitator seminar Personnel Tng. Dept., 1983. Tchr. Sunday Sch. Reorganized Ch. of Jesus Christ of Latter Day Saints, Atlanta, 1984-85; chmn. Dist. Singles Commn., 1986-87; mem. N. Ga. Dist. Council, 1986-87. Mem. Nat. Assn. Female Execs., Am. Inst. Banking, Inst. Cert. Computer Profls. (cert. 1983), Am. Prodn. and Inventory Control Soc. (cert. 1987), Phi Theta Kappa, Phi Kappa Phi. Democrat.

HIGH, DOROTHY HELEN FRANK, city recreation administrator; b. Lincoln, Nebr., Feb 3, 1935; d. Theodore Ludwig and Lillian Winifred (Schellberg) F.; m. Duane High, Nov. 18, 1955; children—Ted Frank, Catherine Nadine. B.S. in Edn., U. Nebr., 1956; M.S. in Edn., Chadron State Coll., 1967. Instr. phys. edn. Lincoln Pub. Schs., Nebr., 1956-58, Alliance City Schs., Nebr., 1964-67, Scottsbluff Pub. Schs., Nebr., 1967-69, Hiram Scott Coll., Scottsbluff, 1969-71; asst. prof. edn., Tarkio Coll., Mo., 1971; recreation supr. City of Scottsbluff, 1973—. Mem. adv. bd. Nebr. Council Ednl. TV, Lincoln, 1968-70, Nebr. Dept. Edn., 1970; bd. dirs. Southeast Recreation Ctr., Scottsbluff, 1975-80, Jaycee Sr. Ctr., Scottsbluff, 1978-82; mem. adv. bd. Foster Grandparent Program, Scottsbluff, 1983—. Mem. Am. Assn. Leisure and Recreation (pres.-elect 1985-86, pres. 1986-87), Am. Alliance Health, Phys. Edn., Recreation and Dance (bd. govs. 1986-87, pres. central dist. 1982-84, Honor award 1975), Nebr. Assn. Health, Phys. Edn., Recreation and Dance (pres. 1972-73, Honor award 1970), Am. Soc. Aging. Republican. Lutheran. Club: Soroptimist Internat. of Scotts Bluff County (pres. 1978-79). Avocations: tennis; swimming. Home: 2210 7th Ave Scottsbluff NE 69361 Office: City of Scottsbluff 1818 Ave A Scottsbluff NE 69361

HIGH, ORPHA HALTERMAN, nurse; b. Moorefield, W.Va., Aug. 18, 1926; d. Lorenzo Dow and Mary Lorena (Henry) Halterman; m. Loy K. High, Dec. 1, 1947; 1 child, James Allen. Diploma in nursing, King's Daughters Hosp. Tng. Sch., 1944. RN. Mem. gen. duty staff King's Daughters Hosp., Martinsburg, W.VA., 1947-48; nurse clinic and office C.E. King, MD, Petersburg, W. VA., 1952-66; nurse Hardy County Bd. Edn., Moorefield, W. VA., 1966—. Deacon, elder local Presbyn. Ch., pres. women's orgn. club. Mem. Nat. Sch. Health Assn. (charter, outstanding contbr. W.Va. chpt.1978, chmn. banquet 1972-76, sec. 1979—, bd. dirs. 1970—), Nat. Sch. Nurses Assn., Am. Nurses Assn., W.Va. Nurses Assn. Democrat. Lodge: Order Eastern Star (worthy matron 1980-81). Home: Rt 4 Box 4 Old Fields WV 26845

HIGHSMITH, CAROL MCKINNEY, photographer; b. Leaksville, N.C., May 18, 1946; d. Luther Carlton and Ruth (Carter) McKinney; m. Mark Steven Highsmith, Dec. 1966 (dec. June 1969); m. Theodore Landphair, June 1988. BA in Photography, Am. U., 1986. Asst. traffic mgr. Peters, Griffin, Woodward, N.Y.C., 1966-67; audience promotion mgr. Sta. WPHL-TV, Phila., 1967-71; regional mgr. Interwest Film Corp., Salt Lake City, 1971-72; account exec. Met. Mag., Phila., 1972-73, Sta. KYW, Phila., 1974-76, Sta. WMAL, Washington, 1976-84; owner, prin. Carol M. Highsmith Photography, Washington, 1984—. Contbr. photography to Time mag., Smithsonian mag., others; one-woman show includes AIA traveling exhibit, 1987—; photog. chronicler hist. renovation projects. Chairperson Occupational Safety and Health Adminstrn., Washington, 1981—; bd. dirs. Columbia Hosp. for Women, Washington, 1981—. Recipient nat. 1st place award Radio Advt. Bur., 1979. Mem. Am. Soc. Mag. Photographers, Washington Bd. Trade (sgt.-at-arms 1980-81, Membership award 1978, 79), U.S. C. of C. (Membership award 1978, 79), Arts Club. Home: 7501 Carroll Ave Takoma Park MD 20912 Office: 1300 G St NW Washington DC 20005

HIGHSMITH, WANDA LAW, association executive; b. Cleveland, Mo., Oct. 25, 1928; d. Lloyd B. and Nan (Sisk) Law; student U. Mo., 1954-56; 1 dau., Holly. Legal sec., firms in Mo. and D.C., until 1960; various staff positions Am. Coll. Osteopathic Surgeons, 1960-72, asst. exec. dir., conv. mgr., Coral Gables, Fla., 1974—. Mem. Profl. Conv. Mgmt. Assn., Washington Soc. Assn. Execs., Am. Soc. Assn. Execs., Assn. Med. Soc. Execs., Nat. Assn. Female Execs. Republican. Methodist. Home: 400 15th St S Apt #1305 Arlington VA 22202 Office: Am Coll Osteopathic Surgeons 123 N Henry St Alexandria VA 22314

HIGHTOWER, ARLENE JANICE, nursing administrator; b. St. Albans, N.Y., Mar. 7, 1949; d. Ernest Charles and Dolores Agnes (Hendel) Krebs; children: Meredith Lynn, Courtney Elizabeth. BS in Nursing, Salve Regina Coll., 1970; MS in Nursing, U. R.I., 1981. Clin. instr. Salve Regina Coll., Newport, R.I., 1977-79, U. R.I., Kingston, 1979-81; supr. maternal child nursing Good Samaritan Hosp., West Islip, N.Y., 1981-85, dir. maternal child nursing services, 1985—. Active Suffolk Perinatal Consortum, Happauge, N.Y., 1986—; sch. bd. Our Lady of Lourdes Sch., West Islip, 1986—. Served to lt. USN, 1970-76, comdr. res., 1986—. Mem. Nurses Assn. Am. Coll. Ob/Gyn (cert.), Naval Reserve Assn., Assn. Mil. Surgeons U.S., Am. Soc. Psychoprophylaxis in Obstetrics. Roman Catholic. Home: 207 Cooper Rd North Babylon NY 11703 Office: Good Samaritan Hosp 1000 Montauk Hwy West Islid NY 11795

HIGHTOWER, CAROL ANN, advertising executive; b. Hanford, Calif., Sept. 22, 1950; d. Russell Malcolm and Carolyn (Brothers) H. AA, West Hills Coll., Coalinga, Calif., 1970; BA, Fresno (Calif.) State Coll., 1972; MA, Calif. State U., Fullerton, 1977. Pub. relations dir. Kings County YMCA, Hanford, 1969-71; reporter Fresno BEE, 1971-72, Sta. KFRE, Fresno, 1971-72; pub. relations dir. Cen. Valley YMCA, Fresno, 1971-73, Anaheim (Calif.) C. of C., 1973-74; with sales dept. Carter Outdoor, Los Angeles, 1974-75; pres. Tower Advt., Santa Ana, Calif., 1975—. Active Santa Ana Comml. Devel. Mem. Sales and Mktg. Council, Sigma Delta Chi. Republican. Baptist. Office: Tower Advt 412 S Lyon Santa Ana CA 92701

HIGHTOWER, CAROLINE WARNER, arts institution executive; b. Cambridge, Mass., Feb. 22, 1935; d. William Lloyd and Mildred (Hall) Warner; children—Amanda Brantley, Matthew Lloyd. Student, Northwestern U., 1953-54, Cambridge U., 1954-55; B.A., Pomona Coll., 1958. Advt. mgr. U. Calif. Press, Berkeley, 1959-61; editor McGraw Hill, N.Y.C., 1961-64, Saturday Rev., N.Y.C., 1967-69; found. officer Carnegie Corp., N.Y.C., 1969-71; cons. Internat. Ctr. Photography, Children's TV Workshop, Rockefeller Found., Ford Found., N.Y.C., 1971-77; dir. Am. Inst. Graphic Arts, N.Y.C., 1977—; vice chmn. creative artists pub. service program N.Y. State Council on Arts, N.Y.C., 1974-84; panelist Nat. Endowment Arts, Washington, 1979, 81, 83; scholarship juror Art Dept. Yale U., 1982, Nat. Inst. for the Deaf, RIT, 1988; commencement speaker, Art Ctr. Coll. of Design, Pasadena, 1987; bd. dirs. Pub. Ctr. for Cultural Resources, N.Y.C., 1984—, Documents of Am. Design, N.Y.C., 1985—; mem. adv. bd. Lubalin Ctr. Cooper Union, Ctr. for Book Library Congress, Innovative Design Fund, Coll. Applied and Fine Arts, Rochester Inst. Tech. Office: Am Inst Graphic Arts 1059 3d Ave New York NY 10021

HIGHTOWER, KATHLEEN MARY, cartoonist, civic leader; b. Washington, Oct. 25, 1956; d. Herbert Earl and Marion Virginia (Spencer) H. Student, Valencia Community Coll., 1986—. Clerical specialist Children's Med. Services, Orlando, Fla., 1980-82, 84—. Illustrator comic strip Belle, 1986—, cartoon series for Praying mag., 1987, others. Vol. Emmaus/ Harlem, N.Y.C., 1982-83. Mem. Bread for the World, Amnesty Internat., Greenpeace, Nat. Assn. Pastoral Musicians, Fellowship of Reconciliation. Roman Catholic. Home: 2135 Minnesota Ave Winter Park FL 32789-5334

HIGHTSHOE, NANCY, expert on rape prevention and investigation; b. St. Louis, May 11, 1947; d. Edwin Jr. and Mary Ann (LaBarge) Kalbfleish. B.A. in Psychology magna cum laude, U. Mo., 1972; M.A. in Human Relations and Adminstrn. of Justice, Webster U., 1977. Commd. police officer sexual assault investigative unit St. Louis County, 1972-81; pres. Rape Prevention Seminars, Inc., St. Louis, 1982—; conv. speaker on rape cause, effect and prevention. Mem. Nat. Speakers Assn., Women's Crusade Against Crime, Women's Info. Network, Psi Chi. Office: PO Box 31339 Saint Louis MO 63131

HIGINBOTHAM, BETTY LOUISE WILSON, botanist, consultant; b. Louisville, July 5, 1910; d. Samuel Gould Wilson and Stella Jane (Robbins) McCracken; m. Noe Higinbotham, Apr. 3, 1937 (dec. Feb. 1980). BA, Butler U., 1932, MA, 1935. Soc. editor New Albany (Ind.) Daily Ledger, 1935-37; editor Williams & Wilkins, Pubs., Balt., 1937-38; botanical writer Columbia Encyclopedia, N.Y.C., 1938-41; head editorial dept. Washington State U. Press, Pullman, 1951-52; assoc. editor Northwest Sci., Pullman, 1952-56; bryological cons. Northrup Space Labs., 1967, Battelle Northwest, Richland, Wash., 1968-71; instr. plants Orcas Island U. Washington, Seattle, 1981; instr. plants San Juan Islands U. Washington, Friday Harbor, 1982-84, Skagit Valley Coll., Friday Harbor, 1985-86; botanical writer Internat. Encyclopedia, N.Y.C., 1938-51, study program Encyclopedia Brittanica, N.Y.C., 1938-41; cons. Nat. Park Service, Friday Harbor, 1986-87. Contbr. articles to profl. jours. Mem. Am. Bryological and Lichenological Soc. (v.p. 1960-61, pres. 1961-62), Am. Radio Relay League, Amateur Radio Emergency Services, Young Ladies Relay League, Delta Zeta, Theta Sigma Phi (hon.), Phi Kappa Phi, Kappa Tau Alpha.

HILBERT, VIRGINIA LOIS, computer training executive; b. Detroit, June 4, 1935; d. Howard G. and Lois (Garner) Swaggerty; m. James R. Hilbert, Nov. 24, 1958; children: James Jr., Jennifer, Douglas, Alexandra. BA with honors, U. Mich., 1957. Govt. analyst personnel dept. City of Detroit, 1957-60; owner, dir. Profl./Tech. Devel., Inc. (doing bus. as Lansing (Mich.) Computer Assn. and Lansing Computer Inst.), 1978—. Sec. Tennis Patrons Bd., Lansing, 1984—, Pro Symphony, 1984—. Mem. Lansing C. of C. (small bus. and ind. council chpt.), Women Bus. Owners Assn., Am. Soc. Tng. and Devel., Alphi Phi (pres. heart equipument fund bd. 1975—), Mich. Tech. Council, Nat. Bus. Edn. Assn. Episcopalian. Home: 938 Wildwood East Lansing MI 48823 Office: Lansing Computer Inst 501 N Marshall St Lansing MI 48912

HILDEBRANDT, CLAUDIA JOAN, banker; b. Inglewood, Calif., Feb. 12, 1942; d. Charles Samual and Clara Claudia (Palumbo) H. B.B.A., U. Colo. Head teller First Colo. Bank & Trust, Denver, 1969-70; asst. cashier First Nat. Bank, Englewood, Colo., 1975-79, asst. v.p., 1979-83, v.p., 1983—; owner CJH Enterprises, Inc., Breckenridge, Colo., 1980—. Mem. Nat. Assn. Bank Women, Am. Soc. for Personnel Adminstrn., Am. Inst. Banking. Roman Catholic. Home: 6602 E Cornell Ave Denver CO 80224 Office: First Nat Bank 333 W Hampden Ave Englewood CO 80110

HILDEBRANDT, DARLENE MYERS, information scientist; b. Somerset, Pa., Dec. 18, 1944; d. Kenneth Geary and Julia (Klim) Myers; m. Byron Howard Johnson, Nov. 4, 1974 (div. 1978 ; m. Peter Anton Hildebrandt, May 26, 1983; 1 child, Robin Adaire. BA, U. Calif., Riverside, 1969; MA, U. Wash., 1970. Info. specialist U. Wash. Acad. Computer Ctr., Seattle, 1970-73, library assoc., 1974-75, mgr. computing info. services adminstr., 1976-85, 86-88, adminstr. computing info. services, 1988—. Editor: (newsletter) Points Northwest, Elaine D. Kaskela award, 1973, 75, Best ASIS, 1974. Recipient Civitan award, 1963. Mem. Am. Soc. for Info. Sci. (founding mem. Pacific Northwest chpt. 1971, chairperson 1975, 76, bd. dirs. 1980, 83, chpt. award 1978). Office: U Wash Acad Computer Ctr HG-45 3737 Brooklyn Ave NE Seattle WA 98105

HILDRETH, SANDRA SUE, stockbroker, publisher; b. Velasco, Tex., Apr. 11, 1944; d. Joseph Weyman and Ethyl Ruth (Henderson) Brown; m. James Edward Hildreth (div. Apr. 1979); children: John Weyman, Jamie Elaine. Student, U. Tex., Arlington, 1962-63, U. Tex., El Paso, 1981. Specification control insp. Tex. Instruments Corp., Richardson, 1965-70; day mgr. Windmill Dinner Theatre, Dallas, 1970-71; sales rep. Cullum Cos., Inc., Dallas, 1972-78, W.G. Haire Textile Co., Dallas, 1978; traffic mgr. Sta. KCOS-TV, El Paso, 1979-81; stock and commodity broker A.G. Edwards & Sons, Inc., Dallas, 1981-87; owner Hildreth Enterprises, Dallas, 1986—, Alexandrite Pub. Co., Dallas, 1987—; adminstr. Uniden Corp. Am., 1988—; v.p. Writer's Edge, Mansfield, Tex., 1986-87; pres. West Tex. chpt. Real Estate Securities and Syndication Inst., El Paso, 1984-85; lectr.; v.p. Breckenridge Fin. Group, 1987—, also bd. dirs. Author: The A to Z of Wall Street, 1987; pub. Contest Master's mag., 1986—; real estate and finance columnist; heard on various radio programs in Tex. Sec., bd. dirs. Cystic Fibrosis Found. Dallas, 1971-72; mem. Women's Div. El Paso C. of C., 1984-85. Named West Side Woman, Upper Valley News, El Paso, 1983, Salesman of Yr. SecurityFirst Group, 1983. Mem. Nat. Assn. Securities Dealers (registered rep.), Dallas Assn. Securities Dealers, Mensa. Republican. Episcopalian. Lodge: Order Eastern Star. Home: 1301 Park Ln Arlington TX 76012

HILFSTEIN, ERNA, science historian, educator; b. Kraków, Poland; came to U.S., 1949, naturalized, 1954; d. Leon and Anna (Schornstein) Kluger; B.A., CCNY, 1967, M.A., 1971, Ph.D., City U. N.Y., 1978; m. Max Hilfstein; children—Leon, Simone Juliana. Tchr. secondary schs., N.Y.C., 1968-84, 86—; vis. prof. Queens Coll., 1973; affiliate Grad. Sch./Univ. Center, City U. N.Y. NEH grantee, 1984-85. Mem. History Sci. Soc., Polish Inst. Arts and Scis. in Am., N.Y. Acad. Scis., United Fedn. of Tchrs. (chpt. chmn. 1978-84, 86—, del. 1980—). Democrat. Jewish. Author: Starowolski's Biographies of Copernicus, 1980; collaborator English version of Nicholas Copernicus Complete Works, vol. 1, 1972, vol. 2, 1978, vol. 3, 1985; contbr. articles and revs. to profl. jours. Editor: Science and History, 1978. Home: 1523 Dwight Pl Bronx NY 10465

HILGEMANN, AMY LUCILLE, social service administrator; b. Ft. Dodge, Iowa, Nov. 9, 1951; d. David Evert McGrath and Laurel Jean (Wilson) Gardner; m. Robert Ernest Hilgemann, Aug. 25, 1973. BA, Wartburg Coll., 1973; MSW, Washington U., St. Louis, 1979; cert. in welding, O'Fallon Tech. Sch., 1975. Clk. Black Hawk Co. Extension Service, Waterloo, Iowa, 1967-69; social service worker State of Mo. Div. of Family Services, St. Louis, 1974-78; ctr. supr. Metroplex, Inc., St. Louis, 1979-80; program dir. Magdala Found., St. Louis, 1980-84, Life Crisis Services, Inc., St. Louis, 1984; regional cons. Mo. Dept. Mental Health, Jefferson City, 1984-87; exec. dir. Crisis Services of Madison Co. Inc., Wood River, Ill., 1987—. Bd. dirs. North I-44 Neighborhood Assn., St. Louis, 1976—; commr. Midtown Enterprise Zone Commn., St. Louis, 1983. Mem. Am. Assn. Suicidology, Mental Health Assn. (bd. dirs. 1985—), Mo. Assn. Social Welfare (bd. dirs. 1986-87), Mo. Assn. of Social Workers, Mo. Federation Social Work (chmn. 1986—), St. Louis City Bus. and Profl. Women (pres. 1987—). Democrat. Methodist. Home: 4131 Blaine Saint Louis MO 63110 Office: Crisis Services Madison County Inc 21 E Acton PO Box 570 Wood River IL 62095

HILKEMEYER, RENILDA ESTELLA, nurse; b. Martinsburg, Mo., July 29, 1915; d. Henry Gerard and Anna Marie (Bertels) Hilkemeyer. Diploma in nursing, St. Mary's Hosp., St. Louis U., 1936; B.S. in Nursing Edn., George Peabody Coll. for Tchrs., Nashville, 1947; postgrad. U. Minn., 1950, U. Tex. Sch. Nursing, 1981; D of Pub. Service (hon.), St. Louis U., 1988. Staff nurse operating room St. Mary's Hosp., Jefferson City, Mo., 1936-37; dist. pub. health nurse Mo. Div. Health, Jefferson City, 1937-40, cons. nursing edn., Mo., 1950-55; asst. dir. nursing Gen. Hosp. No. 1, Kansas City, Mo., 1947-49; asst. exec. sec. Mo. Nurses Assn., Jefferson City, 1949-50; dir. nursing U. Tex. System Cancer Ctr., Houston, 1955-77, asst. to pres. nursing resources, 1977-79, staff asst. to pres., 1979-84; mem. grant rev. com. NIH Nat. Cancer Inst, 1979-83, program rev. com., 1975-77, cons., 1982—; cons. NIH Nat. Heart, Blood and Lung Inst., 1983—, Worker's Inst. Safety, Health, 1983—; chmn., mem. scholarship and professorship com. Cancer Soc., 1980—, mem. nursing adv. com., 1963-80, 85—, profl. edn. com., 1984—; chmn. nursing adv. com., mem. adminstrv. bd. Renilda Hilkemeyer Child Care Ctr., U. Tex. Med. Ctr., 1969—. Book reviewer Am. Jour. Nursing, 1982; contbr. articles to profl. jours. Recipient Outstanding Profl. Women's award Tex. Fedn. Houston Profl. Women, 1983, outstanding contbns. Award, Nat. Cancer Inst., 1983, Disting. Service award Am. Cancer Soc., 1981, Nurse of Yr. Award, Houston Area League Nursing, 1973, Matrix Award, Theta Sigma Phi, Houston, 1963, Disting. Merit award Internat. Soc. Nurses in Cancer Care, 1986; new child care ctr. at U. Tex. Med. Ctr. Houston, named in her honor, 1981 (1st ctr. established 1969); grantee HEW, 1974-77, Am. Cancer Soc., 1974-75, Tex. Fedn. and Profl. Women's Club, 1977-83. Mem. Oncology Nursing Soc., Am. Nurses Assn., Tex. Nurses Assn. (pres. 1962-64, dir. 1964-66, 71-75, Nurse of Yr. award 1979, dist. 9 service award 1970), Am. Med. Writers Assn. (Houston-Galveston sect. 1983-84), Sigma Theta Tau Club: Altrusa (pres. 1983-84) (Houston). Home: 3707 Murworth Houston TX 77025 Office: 6723 Bertner Ave Houston TX 77030

HILL, ANITA CARRAWAY, state legislator; b. Chatfield, Tex., Aug. 13, 1928; d. Archie Clark and Martha (Butler) Carraway; B.A. in Journalism, Tex. Woman's U., 1950; m. Harris Hill, Sept. 20, 1952; children—Stephen Victor, Virginia Evelyn. Reporter Garland (Tex.) Daily News, 1950-51; ednl. dir. First Meth. Ch., Garland, 1951-53; chemist Kraft Foods Co., Garland, 1953-56; legis. aide, Tex. Legislature, 1975-77; mem. Tex. Ho. of Reps., 1977—, mem. mcpl. bond and revenue sharing coms., 1971-74. Awards chmn. City of Garland Environ. Council; mem. City of Garland Park and Recreation Bd., 1971-77, chmn., 1976-77; life mem. PTA. Named Disting. Alumna, Tex. Woman's U., 1981. Mem. Garland C. of C., Rowlett C. of C., Bus. and Profl. Women's Club (Garland Woman of Year, 1980), AAUW, Tex. Assn. Elected Women. Republican. Methodist. Office: 203 Republic Bank Bldg 700 W Ave B Suite 203 Garland TX 75040

HILL, ANNA MARIE, purchasing manager; b. Great Falls, Mont., Nov. 6, 1938; d. Paul Joseph and Alexina Rose (Doyon) Ghekiere. AA, Oakland Jr. Coll., 1959; student, U. Calif., Berkeley, 1960-62. Mgr. ops. OSM, Soquel, Calif., 1963-81; purchasing agt. Arrow Huss, Scotts Valley, Calif., 1981-82; sr. buyer Fairchild Test Systems, San Jose, Calif., 1982-83; materials mgr. Basic Test Systems, San Jose, 1983-86; purchasing mgr. Beta Tech., Santa Cruz, Calif., 1986-87; mgr. purchasing ICON Rev., Carmel, Calif., 1987-88; materials mgr. Integrated Components Test System, Sunnyvale, Calif., 1988—; cons., No. Calif., 1976—. Counselor Teens Against Drugs, San Jose, 1970, 1/2 Orgn., Santa Cruz, 1975-76. Mem. Am. Prodn. Invention Control, Nat. Assn. Female Execs., Nat. Assn. Purchasing Mgmt., Porsche Club Am., Am. Radio Relay League. Democrat. Club: Young Ladies Radio League. Home: 2922 Park Ave Soquel CA 95073 Office: Integrated Components Test System 1350 Bordeaux Dr Sunnyvale CA 94089

HILL, BARBARA ANNE, advertising agency executive; b. Chgo., Aug. 31, 1947; d. Spencer Franklin and Gladys Louise (Jones) H.; m. John Donald Goullet, Jr., Sept. 25, 1982; 1 child, Megan Katherine. AA Stephens Coll., 1967; BS U. Tenn., 1970. Media planner Foote, Cone & Belding, N.Y.C., 1971-73, media supr. 1973-75, account exec. 1977-79; account exec. Ted Bates, N.Y.C., 1975-77; sr. v.p., mgmt. supr. Avrett, Free & Ginsberg, N.Y.C., 1979—. Home: 241 W 108th St New York NY 10025 Office: Avrett Free and Ginsberg 800 Third Ave New York NY 10022

HILL, BETTY JO, medical technologist; b. W. Liberty, Ky., Oct. 9, 1953; d. Arlyn Glen and Thelma Verna (Drake) Allen; m. Terrie Lee Hill, Sept. 22, 1979; children—Terrie Lee, Gaven Ryan. B.S. in Biology, Morehead State U., 1977. Med. technologist staff Licking Meml. Hosp., Newark, Ohio, 1976-81, med. technologist supr., 1981—. Republican. Methodist. Address: 500 Mill Race Rd Granville OH 43023

HILL, BRENDA CAROL, retail executive; b. Portsmouth, Va., Nov. 20, 1954; d. Clarence Cecil and Marie (Cheek) Meece; m. Jeffrey Elwyn Hill, Nov. 9, 1973 (div. 1975); 1 child, Eric Christopher. AA, Hopkinsville (Ky.) Community Coll., 1974. Asst. mgr. Camera World, Inc., Hopkinsville, 1981-83, mgr., 1985—; also bd. dirs. Camera World, Inc.; br. mgr. Michael's Photography, Hopkinsville, 1983-84; exec. sec. Nashville Carpet Ctr., Nashville, 1984. Mem. Christennial Belles, Hopkinsville, 1974; leader Cub Scouts Boy Scouts of Am., Hopkinsville, 1982, 83. Named to Hon. Order Ky. Cols. Commonwealth of Ky., 1987; named one of Outstanding Young Women in Am., 1987. Mem. Nat. Assn. Female Execs. Democrat. Baptist. Home: PO Box 304 Hopkinsville KY 42240 Office: Camera World Inc 117 Susan Ave Hopkinsville KY 42240

HILL, CHARLOTTE RUTH, physics educator; b. Ft. Worth, Nov. 20, 1944; d. Roy Lee and Marjorie Ruth (Parish) Felder; m. Kenneth Dale McAllister, July 10, 1965 (div. Apr. 1981); children: Katharine Marie, Kenneth Lee, Michael Scott II; m. David Bernard Hill, Jan. 8, 1983. Student, Southwestern U., 1962-65; BA, Tex. Tech U., 1966; MA, Tex. A&M U., 1986. Tchr. Fluvanna (Tex.) Pub. Schs., 1966-67; math. tchr. Lamar Jr. High, Snyder, Tex., 1970, Montgomery (Tex.) High Sch., 1977; camp dir. Camp Mission Possible, Houston, 1978-79; research technician Tex. A&M U., College Station, 1982-83, grad. asst., 1980-82, 86, asst. lectr., 1986-87; instr. Blinn Coll., Bryan, Tex., 1987—; co-dir. space sci. seminar A&M Gifted and Talented Inst., College Station, 1982—. Camp staff Camp Mission Possible, Houston, 1972-81; chmn. Interfaith Council Social Concerns, College Station, 1982-84, ch. and soc. Council Ministries A&M United Meth., College Station, 1982-85. Mem. Am. Physical Soc., Tex. Physics Tchrs. Assn. Home: 600 Old Jersey College Station TX 77840 Office: Blinn Coll Bryan TX 77801

HILL, CLAUDIA ADAMS, tax consultant; b. Long Beach, Calif., Oct. 14, 1949; d. Claude T. Adams and Geraldine (Jones) Crosby; m. W. Eugene Hill, Sept. 14, 1968 (div. Oct. 1983); children: Stacia Heather, Jonathan Eugene. BA, Calif. State U., Fullerton, 1972; MBA, San Jose State U., 1978. Systems analyst quality assurance group United Technology Ctr., 1972-73; with commrs. adv. group IRS, 1987; prin., owner Tax Mam, Inc., 1974—; lectr. in field. Chmn. editorial rev. com. The Calif. Enrolled Agt.; contbr. articles to profl. jours. Mem. Nat. Assn. Enrolled Agts., Calif. Soc. Enrolled Agts. (mission chpt., chmn. IRS/Franchise Tax Bd., Tax Bur. liaison com.). Republican. Office: TAX MAM Inc 1080 S Saratoga-Sunnyvale Rd San Jose CA 95129

HILL, DEANN GAIL, construction executive; b. Holyoke, Mass., Apr. 25, 1953; d. Cecil Arthur and Drema Aldene (Mundy) H. BA in Sociology, W.Va. State Coll., 1975; postgrad., W.Va. Coll. of Grad. Studies, 1976-85. Case worker Charleston (W.Va.) Guidance Clinic, 1970-77; social worker W.Va. Dept. Mental Health, Huntington, 1977; office mgr. C/D Hill & Son, St. Albans, W.Va., 1978-83, pres. mktg., 1986—; dep. clk. Kanawha County Circuit Ct., Charleston, 1984-86. Co-exec. dir. Kanawha Dem. Club, Charleston, 1987—; active W.Va. Symphony League, Charleston, 1987—, St. Francis Hosp. Aux., chair fundraising com., 1986-87. Mem. Contractors Assn. W.Va. (program com., legis. com., exposition com. 1988—), Nat. Assn. Female Execs., W.Va. U. Alumni Assn., Charleston Regional C. of C. Roman Catholic. Home and Office: Coal River Rd PO Box 226 Saint Albans WV 25177

HILL, DIANA JOAN, organization representative; b. Pleasant Corner, Pa., June 17, 1936; d. Lawrence Edwin Aaron and Arlene (Wessner) Hausman; m. Bruce Handwerk Hill, June 22, 1957; children: Adrian Bruce, Anita Diann. BS in Edn., Kutztown U., 1958; postgrad., Temple U., 1958-61. Elem. tchr. Cheltenham (Pa.) Twp. Schs., 1958-62, Rockford (Ill.) City Schs., 1965-66; caseworker Lehigh County Children-Youth Services, Allentown, Pa., 1975-85; dist. rep. Luth. Brotherhood, Allentown, 1985—. Publicity chmn. LVW Rockford, 1965-66, human resources chair, Oyster Bay, N.Y. 1968-73; precinct capt. Dem. Party, Massapequa, N.Y., 1973-74. Mem. Lehigh Valley Assn. Life Underwriters. Democrat. Lutheran. Office: Luth Brotherhood 1013 Brookside Rd PO Box 3402 Allentown PA 18106-3402

HILL, ELGIN DILLARD, small business owner, cosmetologist; b. Frierson, La., Aug. 10, 1921; d. Julius and Kittie (Evans) Dillard; 1 child, Elgin Marie Mosley Odom. Cert. in cosmetology, Milam State Trade sch., 1942; BA, Wiley Coll., 1967; cert. in tng. and instrn., Northwestern State U., 1969; MA, Prairie View (Tex.) A&M Coll., 1976. Instr. cosmetology Henrietta Beauty Sch., Shreveport, La., 1946; owner R&E House of Beauty, Shreveport, 1954—, Favrot Student Union Beauty Shop, Grambling, La., 1972—; mem. adv. bd. La. State Bd. Cosmetology, 1968-72, bd. dirs., 1972—; chmn. tchrs. seminar La. Accreditations Cosmetology Assn. Bd. dirs., corr. sec. Friends of Barnwell Garden and Arts Ctr., Shreveport, 1972—; mem. commn. Nat. Accrediting Commn., 1979-83; bd. dirs. Barnwell POlicy Making, Shreveport, 1980—; mem. Futureshape Task Force, Shreveport, 1986—. Recipient Outstanding Achievement award Nat. Info. Research League, 1973, Outstanding Service award Lakeside Bapt. Ch., Shreveport, 1983. Mem. Am. Bus. Women's Assn. (pres. 1983-84, Woman of Yr. 1985), Tchrs. Ednl. Council, Nat. Cosmetologist Assn. (Cosmetologist of Yr. 1983), Delta Sigma Theta. Democrat. Baptist. Office: R&E House of Beauty 1233 Milam St Shreveport LA 71101

HILL, EULA VERTNER, state government official; b. Americus, Ga., Aug. 16, 1928; d. Oscar Thomas and Eula Vertner (Forrest) Harrell; m. Jefferson Perry Hill, Nov. 28, 1946 (dec. Oct. 1985); 1 child, Robert Perry. Ed. Southwestern Coll., Americus, Ga. Cert. tchr., Ga. 6th and 7th grade tchr. Plains (Ga.) Sch., 1946-47; buyer, office mgr. Belk's Dept. Store, Americus, 1949-60; field service mgr. Ga. Dept. Labor, Americus, 1961—. V.p., organizer Inter-Agy. Council, 1970—; active Ga. Council on Aging, 1964-74; organizer Americus unit Ga. Heart Assn., 1975; adv. bd. Ga. Dept. Human Resources, 1976-78; chmn. bd. advisors for bus. edn. South Ga. Tech. Inst., 1973—; mem. career devel. bd. Ga. Southwestern Coll., Americus. Recipient Cert. of Appreciation Kiwanis Club of Americus, 1985. Mem. Nat. Assn. Female Execs., Acad. Women in Mgmt., Internat. Assn. Personnel in Employment Security (chmn. profl. standards com. 1986-87, Ga. chpt. activities chmn. 1987-88, exec. com. 1987—), Americus-Sumter County Bus. and Profl. Women (founder), others. Democrat. Methodist. Home: Rt 4 Vienna Rd Americus GA 31709 Office: Ga Dept Labor 120 W Church St Americus GA 31709

HILL, HYACINTHE (VIRGINIA ANDERSON KAIN), poet; b. N.Y.C., May 24, 1920; d. Joseph Thomas and Angela Virginia (Bradley-Bruen) Cronin; m. Johan Anderson, July 15, 1940 (dec.); children—John Luke Anderson, Matthew Mark Anderson (dec.); m. John Kain, 1978. B.A. cum laude with honors in English, Bklyn Coll., 1961; M.A. in English and Comparative Lit., Hunter Coll., 1965; postgrad., Fordham U., 1965-69; Ph.D. (hon.), No. Pontifical Acad., Sweden, 1969; D.Arts and Letters (hon.), Gt. China Arts Coll., 1969; D.Hum., Coll. Alfred the Great, Hull, Eng., 1970; H.L.D. honoris cause, U. Asia, Pakistan. Tchr. English James Monroe High Sch., Bronx, 1969-82. Author: Shoots of a Vagrant Vine (Avalon Nat. Sonnets prize 1950), 1950; Promethea (Cameo Press book award 1957), 1957; Squaw, No More, 1975, Poetry and the Stars, 1986; also numerous individual poems. Co-editor Diamond Year Anthology, 1970. Editor North Atlantic edit. Great Am. World Poets Anthology, 1973. Named poet laureate internat., 1973, 74, 75; decorated dame Knights of Malta; recipient Poetry Soc. Am. prizes, 1958—, N.Am. Chapbook award, 1966, 1st prize Eleanor Otto award N.Y. Poetry Forum, 1969, 70, 1st prize Internat. Inst., 1970, Commemorative Medal Honor Am. Biog. Inst., 1987, numerous other awards. Mem. Acad. Am. Poets, Poetry Soc. Am., League Am. Pen-Women, Alpha Delta Kappa. Home: c/o Scop and Gleeman 876 Las Ovejas Terra Linda San Rafael CA 94903

HILL, JANICE R., community research facility administrator; b. Alton, Ill., Feb. 15, 1959; d. Paul Robert and Joanne (Wilson) H. B cum laude, cert. in paralegal studies, Webster U., 1984; M, U. Ill., 1986. Legal sec. Quackenbush and Schrimpf, Attys., Alton, 1977-79; adminstrv. asst. Family Service and VNA, Alton, 1980-81; sec. McDonnell Douglas Corp., St. Louis, 1981-83; legal systems analyst Informatics, St. Louis, 1984; instr. U. Ill., Urbana, 1985; legal asst. Angelica Corp., St. Louis, 1986; instr. Webster U., St. Louis, 1986; curriculum writer St. Louis Pub. Schs., 1986-87; tng. and spl. projects coordinator Community Research Assocs., Champaign, Ill., 1987—. Water safety instr. ARC, Midwest chpt., 1976—; pub. edn. specialist Rape and Sexual Abuse Care Ctr., Edwardsville, Ill., 1982. Mem. Amnesty Internat. Democrat. Methodist. Home: 201 W Springfield #806 Champaign IL 61820

HILL, JUDITH DEEGAN, lawyer; b. Chgo., Dec. 13, 1940; d. William James and Ida May (Scott) Deegan; m. Dennis M. Havens, June 28, 1986; children by previous marriage: Colette M., Cristina M. BA, Western Mich. U., 1960; cert. U. Paris, Sorbonne, 1962; JD, Marquette U., 1971. Bar: Wis. 1971, Ill. 1973, Nev. 1976, D.C. 1979. Tchr., Kalamazoo (Mich.) Bd. Edn., 1960-62, Maple Heights (Ohio), 1963-64, Shorewood (Wis.) Bd. Edn., 1964-68; corp. atty. Fort Howard Paper Co., Green Bay, Wis., 1971-72; sr. trust adminstr. Continental Ill. Nat. Bank & Trust, Chgo., 1972-76; atty. Morse, Foley & Wadsworth Law Firm, Las Vegas, 1976-77; dep. dist. atty., criminal prosecutor Clark County Atty., Las Vegas, 1977-83; atty. civil and criminal law Edward S. Coleman Profl. Law Corp., Las Vegas, 1983-84; sole practice, 1984-85; atty. criminal div. Office of City Atty., City of Las Vegas, 1985—. Bd. dirs. Nev. Legal Services, Carson City, 1980-87, state chmn., 1984-87; bd. dirs. Clark County Legal Services, Las Vegas, 1980-87; mem. Star Aux. for Handicapped Children, Las Vegas, 1986—; Greater Las Vegas Women's League; jud. candidate Las Vegas Mcpl. Ct, 1987. Recipient Scholarship, Auto Specialties, St. Joseph, Mich., 1957-60; St. Thomas More Scholarship, Marquette U. Law Sch., Milw., 1968-69; juvenile law internship grantee Marquette U. Law Sch., 1970. Mem. ABA, Nev. Bar Assn., Woman's Bar Assn. of Ill., So. Nev. Assn. Women Attys., Ill. Bar Assn., Washington Bar Assn. Democrat. Club: Children's Village (pres. 1980) (Las Vegas, Nev.). Home: 1110 S 5th Pl Las Vegas NV 89104 Office: City Atty's Office 400 E Stewart 6th Floor Las Vegas NV 89101

HILL, JUDITH LYNN, controller; b. Galesburg, Ill., June 10, 1954; d. Leonard William and Mary Margaret (Still) Anderson; m. Robert Dean Hill, Aug. 21, 1976; children: Douglas Alexander, James Colin. BS Accountancy, U. Ill., 1976. CPA, Ill. Staff acct. Peat, Marwick, Mitchell, CPA's, Chgo., 1976-78, sr. acct., 1978-80; supervising sr. acct. Peat, Marwick, Mitchell, CPA's, Atlanta, 1980-81, audit mgr., 1981-82; asst. corp. controller Health Group, Inc., Nashville, 1982-83; controller CDP Group, Inc., Atlanta, 1983—. Instr. project bus. Jr. Achievement, Atlanta, 1980-81. Mem. Am. Inst. CPA's, Healthcare Fin. Mgrs. Assn. Home: 2810 Fairlane Dr Doraville GA 30340

HILL, JUDITH SWIGOST, business analyst, information systems designer; b. Harvey, Ill., Dec. 31, 1942; d. John Walter and Mary Jean (Kuczaik) Swigost; m. Wallace H. Hill, May 16, 1982; stepchildren: Scott, Amy, Molly, Elizabeth. BA in English/Theater, U. Ill., 1964; postgrad., Am. U., 1967-69, New Sch. for Social Research, N.Y.C., 1977-82, 83-85. Vol. U.S. Peace Corps, Philippines, 1964-66; recruiter U.S. Peace Corps, Washington, 1966-67; program mgr. U.S. Peace Corps, Micronesia, 1968; dir. corr. U.S. Peace Corps, Washington, 1969; editor, prin. Congl. Monitor, Inc., Washington, 1970-76; legis. analyst Philip Morris, Inc., N.Y.C., 1976-77; tech. analyst, writer Jesco, Inc., N.Y.C., 1978-79; assoc. pub. Thomas Pub. Co., N.Y.C., 1980-84; bus. analyst AGS, Inc. Ind. Cons., N.Y.C., 1984—; ind. cons. expert systems research and devel., N.Y.C., 1987—. Contbr. articles to profl. jours. Active Murray Hill Com., N.Y.C., 1986—. Mem. Assn. Systems Mgmt., Am. Assn. Artificial Intelligence, Assn. Computing Machinery, Spl. Interest Group Artificial Intelligence, World Future Soc., Nat. Assn. Returned Peace Corps Vols., Returned Peace Corps Vols. of Greater N.Y. (by-laws com. 1985-86. speakers bur. 1987-88). Republican. Jewish. Home: 155 E 34th St Apt 12-C New York NY 10016

HILL, LARKIN PAYNE, real estate company data processing executive; b. El Paso, Tex., Oct. 30, 1954; d. Max Lloyd and Jane Olivia (Evatt) H.; m. J. Franklin Graves, July 12, 1975 (div. July 1979). Student Coll. Charleston, 1972-73, U. N.C., 1973. Lic. real estate broker, N.C. Sec., property mgr. Max L. Hill Co., Inc., Charleston, S.C., 1973-75, sec., data processor, 1979-82, v.p. adminstrn., 1982—; resident mgr. Carolina Apts., Carrboro, N.C., 1975-77; sales assoc., Realtor, Southland Assocs., Chapel Hill, N.C., 1977-78; cons. specifications com. Charleston Trident Multiple Listing Service, 1985. Mem. Nat. Assn. Female Execs., Scottish Soc. Charleston, Preservation Soc., Charleston Computer Users Group, N.C. Assn. Realtors. Republican. Methodist. Avocations: reading, crossword puzzles, furniture restoration, T'ai Chi. Home: 7 Riverside Dr Charleston SC 29403 Office: Max L Hill Co Inc 632 Saint Andrews Blvd Charleston SC 29407

HILL, LEIGH PATRICIA, trust executive; b. Wilmington, Del., May 15, 1943; d. Malcolm James and Mary Elizabeth (Burns) Bezanson; m. Edward Vernon Hill Jr., Nov. 21, 1964; children: Kirsten Leigh, Christopher Edward. Asst. sec. Del. Trust Co., Wilmington, 1982-84, trust officer, 1984-85, sr. trust officer, 1985—. Contbr. articles to profl. jours. Dir. Del. Singers Inc., 1984-87; trustee Padua Acad., 1988—. Mem. Nat. Assn. Bank Women (Del. group pres. 1987-88, nat. by-laws chair 1988—), Nat. Assn. Female Execs., Del. Alliance of Profl. Women (bd. dirs. 1987—), Wilmington Women in Bus., Mensa. Home: 4402 Miller Rd Wilmington DE 19802 Office: Del Trust Co PO Box 8841 Wilmington DE 19899

HILL, LOLLIE RUTH, social service administrator, check cashing service executive; b. El Dorado, Ark., July 11, 1930; d. Eddie M. and Effie (Byrd) Ento; m. Grandville Eli Hill, Mar. 16, 1957; children: Deidra J., Lorraine, Terence D. Asst. dir. Walter Brown Hosp., El Dorado; adminstr. Hill Farm Care Home, Vallejo, Calif., 1961—; v.p. Express Check Cashing Co., Vallejo, 1985—. Office: Hill Family Home Care 800 Taper Ave Vallejo CA 94590

HILL, MARY LOU, small business consultant; b. Phila., July 8, 1936; d. Norman Findlay and Gladys Louise (Weigand) Tompkins; m. Ernest Clarke Hill Jr., Mar. 15, 1958; children: Sally, Holly, Randy, Chuck, Jim. Student, U. Miami, 1954-55, U. Okla., 1955-57; BBA, Portland State U., 1979, M in Taxation, 1982. CPA, Oreg. Staff acct. Fordham & Fordham, Hillsboro, Oreg., 1982-84; instr. Portland State U., Oreg., 1984-85; owner The Bookshelf, Sunriver, Oreg., 1985-88; instr. Cen. Oreg. Community Coll., Bend, Oreg., 1986. Mem. Oreg. Soc. CPA's, Am. Booksellers Assn., Nat. Fedn. Ind. Businesses, Pacific Northwest Booksellers Assn., Sunriver Mall Assn., Kappa Kappa Gamma. Democrat. Christian Scientist. Home: PO Box 4574 Sunriver OR 97707 Office: PO Box 4574 Sunriver OR 97707

HILL, NOLANDA SUE, broadcast executive; b. Dallas, June 16, 1944; d. Nolan R. and Francile (Morrison) Butler; m. Sheldon K. Turner, Jr., Feb. 14, 1971 (div. 1975); m. 2d, Billy B. Hill, Jr., June 25, 1976; 1 son, Andrew Butler. B.A., B.S., Stephen F. Austin U., Nacogdoches, Tex., 1966. Exec. producer Doubleday Broadcasting, Dallas, 1968-70; pres. U.V. Sports, Los Angeles, 1970-71; chief exec. officer, chief fin. officer Nat. Bus. Network, Dallas, 1972-74; pres. Handel Pub., Dallas, 1974-76; chief exec. officer, chief fin. officer Nat. Bus. Network, Dallas, 1976-84; pres., chief exec. officer Corridor Broadcasting Corp., Dallas, 1984—; mem. bd. Tex. Bd. Archtl. Examiners, Austin, 1983-86; moderator FCC/White House Symosium for Women Ownership in Telecommunications, 1983. Editor: National Directory of Performing Arts and Civic Centers, 1974, 75, 76; National Directory Arts/Canada, 1976. Mem. Speakers' Club Ho. of Reps., 1983; mem. Dallas March of Dimes, Dallas Mus. Art. Mem. Nat. Assn. Broadcasters. Democrat. Home: 3507 Mc Farlin St Dallas TX 75205

HILL, NORMA KATHLEEN, testing coordinator; b. Granite, Okla., Oct. 8, 1932; d. Ranier and Leona Jewel (McCurdy) McMurtry; m. James Arden Hill, July 7, 1956; children: Susan, Dianne, Tim. BS, Abilene Christian U., 1954; MEd, N. Tex. State U., 1972. Cert. tchr., Tex. Tchr. Ft. Worth Pub. Schs., 1954-57, Arlington (Tex.) Pub. Schs., 1957-58, Allen (Tex.) Pub. Schs., 1962-63; tchr. Plano (Tex.) Pub. Schs., 1964-72, counselor, 1972-78, elem. prin., 1978-76, coordinator elem. testing, 1986—. Bd. dirs. Plano Child Guidance Clinic, 1970-72, Plano United to Help People, 1972-78. Mem. Tex. Elem. Prins. and Suprs. Assn., Assn. for Suprs. and Curriculum Devel., Alpha Delta Kappa. Mem. Ch. Christ. Home: Rte 3 Box 380 Plano TX 75074 Office: Plano Ind Sch Dist 1517 Ave H Plano TX 75074

HILL, NORMA LOUISE, librarian; b. Somerville, Mass., Oct. 27; d. Southern G. and Marguerite M. (Smith) Smallwood; m. George Forris Hill, Dec. 30, 1954; children—Gregory Harrison, Jonathan Smallwood. AB, Wheaton Coll., 1952; MSLS, Our Lady of the Lake Coll., 1975. Grad. asst. Our Lady of the Lake Coll., San Antonio, 1974-75; librarian Community Guidance Ctr., San Antonio, 1975, 86th Tactical Fighter Wing, Ramstein, Fed. Republic Germany, 1976-79; info. mgmt. specialist Exec. Office of the Pres., Washington, 1980; dept. head Howard County (Md.) Library, 1980-81, asst. dir., 1981—. Mem. Friends of the Howard County Library, Howard County Literacy Coalition, 1984, Md. Adv. Council on Libraries, 1987-88; adv. bd. State Library Resource Ctr., 1986—, network planning and resource sharing task force, 1988—. Recipient Insp. Gen. Spl. Achievement award USAF, 1977, 78. Mem. Md. Assn. Pub. Library Adminstrs., Md. Library Assn. (chmn. nominations com. 1984-85, co-chmn. fed. relations subcom. 1985-86, 1st v.p., pres.-elect 1986-87, pres. 1987-88), ALA (pub. library div.), Nat. Assn. Female Execs., NAACP, Nat. Council of Negro Women, Alpha Kappa Alpha. Democrat. Office: Howard County Library 10375 Little Patuxent Pkwy Columbia MD 21044

HILL, PAMELA, television executive; b. Winchester, Ind., Aug. 18, 1938; d. Paul and Mary Frances (Hollis) Abel; m. Tom Wicker, Mar. 9, 1974; 1 son, Christopher; stepchildren—Cameron Wicker, Grey Wicker, Lisa Freed, Kayce Freed. B.A., Bennington Coll., 1960; postgrad., Universidad Autonoma de Mexico, 1961, U. Glasgow, 1958-59. Fgn. affairs analyst Nelson A. Rockefeller Presdl. Campaign, 1961-64; researcher, assoc. producer, dir., producer NBC News, 1965-73, dir. White Paper series, 1969-72, producer Edwin Newman's Comment, 1972; producer Edwin Newman's Comment Closeup Documentary series ABC News, N.Y.C., 1973-78; exec. producer Closeup Documentary series ABC News, 1978—; v.p. ABC News, 1979—. Author: United States Foreign Policy, 1945-65, 1968; Contbr. photographs to Catching Up With America, 1969. Trustee Bennington Coll. Recipient Christopher award, 1979, 80, Pinnacle award Am. Women in Radio and TV, 1984, Overseas Press Club Citation for Excellence, Matrix award, 1980; also Ms. Hill and Closeup have received 20 Emmy awards, 10 duPont-Columbia awards, 2 George Foster Peabody awards, 5 Ohio State awards, 7 Christopher awards, 3 Overseas Press Club awards, 9 Clarion awards, 17 CINE awards, others. Mem. Dirs. Guild, Writers Guild, Nat. Acad. Television Arts and Scis. Office: Capital Cities/ABC Inc 1330 Ave of the Americas New York NY 10019

HILL, PATRICIA ARNOLD, management consultant, realtor, former government official; b. Balt., Oct. 29, 1936; d. George Henry and Mildred Mae (Kress) Arnold; student No. Va. Community Coll., part time 1966-76; m. Richard Denzil Hill, Oct. 24, 1970; children—Terry Marlene Fomby, Debra Michelle Hill. Sec. firm McEwan & Walker, Chattanooga, 1955; clk.-typist Bur. Aeros., Washington, 1956-58, security clk., 1958, security asst., 1959-62, security specialist Bur. Aeros. and Naval Weapons Washington, 1962-66; security specialist Bur. Naval Weapons, 1962-66, Naval Ordnance Systems Command, 1966-74; security specialist Naval Sea Systems Command, Washington, 1974-75, head classification mgmt. br., asst. dir. security div., 1975-80, dep. dir., head info. security br. security div., 1980-83, security mgr. and dir. security div., 1983-86; realtor, Town and Country Properties; cons. in mgmt., adminstrn. and security, Alexandria, Va., 1986—. Mem. Nat. Assn. Female Execs., Nat. Classification Mgmt. Soc., Ind. Sec. Assn., Va. State Soc., Profl. Bus. Women. Baptist. Home: 1003 Collingwood Rd Alexandria VA 22308

HILL, PATRICIA FRANCINE, computer engineer; b. Buffalo, Jan. 9, 1955; d. Walter W. and M. Phyllis (Jones) H. BA in Math., Swarthmore Coll., 1977, BS in Engring., 1977; MS in Computer Engring., U. Mich., 1980. Mem. tech. staff AT&T Bells Labs., Middletown, N.J., 1980-86; sr. systems analyst Internat. MarketNet (IMNET), N.Y.C., 1986, Marine Midland Bank, N.Y.C., 1987—; lectr. in field. Active various charitable orgns. Recipient Outstanding Employee award AT&T Worksta. Div., 1986. Mem. Nat. Assn. Negro Bus. and Profl. Women, Nat. Tech. Assn. Democrat. Episcopalian.

HILL, PATRICIA LISPENARD, insurance educator; b. N.Y.C., June 25, 1937; d. George Joseph and Elizabeth (Lispenard) H.; children—George, Christopher, Susan, Daniel, Frederic, Elizabeth. Student Barnard Coll., 1954-55, Pace U., 1972-74, Coll. of Ins., 1980. Lic. ins. broker, 1961—; owner, dir. Hill Sch. of Ins., N.Y.C., 1978—; also ptnr. Hill & Co. Ins. Brokers. Home: Ridgefield Ave South Salem NY 10590 Office: 139 Fulton St New York NY 10038

HILL, PATTY MAYNARD, nursing educator; b. Forsyth County, N.C., June 9, 1944; d. Ray and Etta Mae (Holleman) Maynard; diploma N.C. Bapt. Hosp. Sch. Nursing, 1966; B.S.N., U. N.C., 1969, M.Ed., 1973; Ed.D., N.C. State U., Raleigh, 1986; m. Gary P. Hill, Aug. 20, 1966; children—Gary P., Christopher, Caroline. Office nurse, 1967-69; instr. pediatric nursing Watts Sch. Nursing, Durham, N.C., 1970-74; instr. U. N.C. Sch. Nursing, Chapel Hill, 1974-77, asst. prof., 1977-84; nurse cons., pvt. practice, 1987—; reviewer/cons. Duxbury Press; mem. rev. bd. Appleton Century Croft; condr. workshops. Bd. dirs. Chapel Hill Oasis, 1978-80, Chapel Hill Day Care Ctr., 1977—, Chapel Hill Service League, 1977—; del. St. Thomas More Sch., 1981-82, pres. Home-Sch. Assn. Mem. Am. Nurses Assn., N.C. Nurses Assn., AAUP, Nat. Assn. Adult Edn., Nat. Assn. Care of Hospitalized Child, Durham/Orange Dental Assn. (pres.), Sigma Theta Tau. Methodist. Co-editor, contbg. author: Development throughout Life: A Nursing Perspective, 1982; co-author: Human Development; contbr. articles in field. Home: 414 Sharon Rd Chapel Hill NC 27514

HILL, ROSANNA, laboratory supervisor; b. Macon, Ga., July 1, 1949; d. Henry and Julia (Chambliss) Hill; B.S., Clark Coll., 1971; postgrad. Howard U., 1971-72. Med. technologist Ga. Bapt. Med. Center, Atlanta, 1972-77, lab. mgr., 1977-81; lab. ops. mgr. Acculabs, Inc., Atlanta, 1981—, dir., ptnr., 1981—, v.p., 1988—. Mem. Am. Public Health Assn., Clin. Lab. Mgmt. Assn., Nat. Assn. Female Execs. Mem. A.M.E. Ch. Home: 1305 Camelot Dr College Park GA 30349

HILL, SARA LYNN, architectural company executive, artist, architectural delineator; b. Montclair, N.J., May 25, 1951; d. Lawrence and Mary (Allanson) H.; m. William James Van Cleve., Jr. B.Arch. cum laude, Tulane U., 1974; B.F.A. magna cum laude, Newcomb Coll., 1974. Lic. architect, contractor, La. Archtl. designer J. Buchanan Blitch & Assocs., Architects, New Orleans, La., 1975-76; archtl. cons. F. Monroe Labouisse, Jr., Architect, New Orleans, 1976-79; staff architect, plans examiner Vieux Carre Commn., New Orleans, 1979; ptnr. V.C. Builders, Gen. Contractors, New Orleans, 1980—; sole propr. Hill Co., Architects, New Orleans, 1979—; v.p. Robin Riley & Assocs., Architects, New Orleans, 1981-84; designer, project architect S. Steward Farnet, AIA, Architect & Assoc., Inc., 1984—; founding mem., sec. Art-Op Coop., New Orleans, 1975; agt. Tulane U. Alumni Assn., New Orleans, 1975—. Illustrator: New Orleans Home Care Handbook, 1978; Great Louisiana Recipes, 1977; Razing the Roofs, 1978. Co-editor, founder Marsharch Jour., 1973-74. Mem. Preservation Resource Ctr., New Orleans, Friends of the Cabildo, New Orleans, 1978—, Contemporary Arts Ctr., New Orleans, 1977—. John W. Lawrence fellow Tulane U., 1973, Dorothy Lubbe Dunkerley fellow Tulane U., 1972; recipient 2d place award Reynolds Aluminum Corp., 1973, 1914 prize in Art Newcomb Coll., 1974. Mem. AIA (medal, cert. 1974), Nat. Trust for Historic Preservation, Constrn. Specifications Inst., Urban Land Inst., Internat. Platform Assn., Tulane U. Alumni Assn. (bd. dirs. 1977-82). Methodist. Clubs: So. Yacht, Corinthian Sail (New Orleans). Office: S Stewart Farnet AIA and Assocs Architects 2331 St Claude Ave New Orleans LA 70117

HILL, STEPHANIE HENSLEY, personnel executive; b. Cin., Jan. 6, 1955; d. Raymond Harold and Beverly Jane (Kunz) Hensley; m. Bradley Warren Hill, Aug. 2, 1980; children: Kortney E., Jason T. BA, U. South Fla., 1977. Br. mgr. Kelly Services, Inc., Savannah, Ga., 1977-79, nat. recruiting and retention mgr., Detroit, 1979-80, resident br. mgr., St. Louis, 1980-81, br. mgr., Pensacola, Fla., 1981-85, tng. instr., 1983; nat. mktg. rep., St. Louis, 1985-86. Vol. Muscular Dystrophy Assn., Pensacola, 1982-83; fundraiser Ronald McDonald House, Pensacola, 1983; mem. fin. com. Trinity Presbyn. Ch., Pensacola, 1983. Mem. Am. Soc. Personnel Assocs. (sec. 1983, dir. 1984), Bus. and Profl. Women (sec. 1978), Pensacola C. of C., Phi Kappa Phi. Republican. Home: 4479 Windsor Oaks Dr Marietta GA 30066

HILL, SUSAN SLOAN, safety engineer; b. Quincy, Mass., June 1, 1952; d. Ralph Arnold and Grace Elenore (Sloan) Crosby; m. William Loyd Hill, Dec. 16, 1973 (div. July 1982); m. William Joseph Graham, Sept. 10, 1983 (div. Feb. 1985). Assoc. Sci. in Gen. Engring., Motlow State Community Coll., Tullahoma, Tenn., 1976; BS in Indsl. Engring., Tenn. Technol. U., 1978. Intern, safety engr. Intern Tng. Ctr., U.S. Army, Red River Army Depot, Tex., 1978-79, Field Safety Activity, Charlestown, Ind., 1979, system safety engr. Communications-Electronics Command, Ft. Monmouth, N.J., 1979-84, gen. engr., 1984-85; chief system safety Arnold Air Force Sta., USAF, Tullahoma, 1984; system safety engr. U.S. Army Safety Ctr., Ft. Rucker, Ala., 1985—. Recipient 5 letters of appreciation U.S. Army, 1982. Mem. Assn. Fed. Safety and Health Profls. (regional v.p. 1980-84), Soc. Women Engrs., Nat. Safety Mgmt. Soc., Am. Soc. Safety Engrs., System Safety Soc., Nat. Assn. Female Execs., Order Engr. Republican. Episcopalian. Avocations: bowling, needlework, sewing, cooking, golf. Home: 115 Liveoak Dr Enterprise AL 36330 Office: US Army Safety Ctr Attn CSSC-SE Fort Rucker AL 36362

HILL, SUZANNE, managment corporation executive, entertainment consultant; b. N.Y.C., Dec. 23, 1928; d. Isidore and Surah Tamara (Renert) Kamil; m. Stanley Martin Hiltzik, June 27, 1948 (div.); children—Marcie Bernette Strassner, Robin Leslie Levin, Richard David. Cert. in lang., Am. Sch., Rome, 1973; D.Music (hon.), Sch. for Performing Arts, N.Y.C., 1974. Performing artist Biltmore Hotel, N.Y.C., 1946-47; star program Suzanne Hill Sings, Mut. Network, N.Y.C., 1947-48; actress, singer TV and motion pictures, 1955—; co-owner, mgr. Englewood C.C., Englewood, N.J., 1959-65; exec. dir. Centex Corp., Cliffside Park, N.J., 1977-81; pres. Hill Mgmt. Corp., Fort Lee, N.J., 1981—; entertainment dir. Roosevelt Hotel, N.Y.C., 1980—; entertainment cons. Centre Hotel, Abu Dhabi, United Arab Emirates, 1981-82; cons. Rose Assocs., N.Y.C., 1981, Sulzberger-Rolfe Assocs., N.Y.C., 1982—; dir. Palisadium, Cliffside Park, N.J., 1977-81. Organizer Am. Cancer Soc., N.J., 1979—, Fight for Sight, N.J., 1979—; performing artist USO, 1947-55. Recipient Meritorious Service award Am. Cancer Soc., 1980, Salvation Army, 1982. Mem. USO (Meritorious Service award 1950), Screen Actors Guild, Fedn. TV and Radio Artists, Guild Variety Artists. Home: PO Box 2184 Fort Lee NJ 07024 Office: Hill Management Corp 2 Horizon Rd Fort Lee NJ 07024

HILLEARY, ANNE MEGAN, government official; b. Washington, Nov. 1, 1951; d. Leo Paul and Sally Mary (Meenehan) H. B.S., George Mason U., 1974. Sec., GAO, Washington, 1974-76, budget analyst, 1976, mgmt. analyst, 1976-79, adminstrv. officer, 1979-80, program analyst, 1980-83, sr. evaluator, 1983—, instr. report writing course, 1984—. Recipient Certs. of Appreciation, GAO, 1975, 80, 85, 86. Roman Catholic. Office: US GAO 441 G St NW Room 3820 Washington DC 20548

HILLEGASS, CHRISTINE ANN, psychologist; b. Lancaster, Pa., July 13, 1952; d. Michael and Ann Christine (Wolf) H.; m. E. Cornelius Kocsis, Aug. 6, 1983. BA, Bard Coll., 1975; MA in Forensic Psychol., John Jay Coll. Criminal Justice, 1979; postgrad., Rutgers U. Staff psychologist Dept. Corrections, Adult Diagnostic Treatment Ctr., Avenel, N.J., 1979-84; dir. Monmouth County Sexual Abuse Treatment and Prevention Program, Ocean, N.J., 1984-87; cons. N.J. State Parole Bd., Dept. Corrections, Trenton, 1981-84; cons., trainer various mental health and social services orgns., N.J., 1982—; mem. N.J. State Sexual Abuse Network, Trenton, 1984—; mem. Monmouth Prosecutor's Task Force on Child Abuse, Freehold, N.J., 1985-86; co-chairperson Monmouth County Sexual Abuse Com., WestLong Branch, N.J., 1987-88, chmn. 1986-87. Recipient Woman of Achievement award Monmouth County Adv. Commn. on Status of Women, 1987. Mem. Am. Psychol. Assn., N.J. Psychol. Assn., Am. Assn. Sex Educators, Counselors and Therapists. Office: Monmouth County Sexual Abuse Treatment and Prevention Program 2001 Bellmore St Ocean NJ 07712

HILLER, DONNA LOUISE, dental hygienist; b. Idaho Falls, Idaho, Mar. 6, 1950; d. Reid Hogan Anderson and Uva Louise (Teiser) Baker; m. Thomas G. Williams, Dec. 20, 1969 (div. Dec. 1974); m. Hollen J. Hiller, July 7, 1977; 1 child, Deborah Louise. BS, Idaho State U., 1972. Cert. dental hygienist. Dental hygienist Drs. Loren Hoschouer and Vern Gaffner, Idaho Falls, 1972-73, Dr. Robert Packard, Twin Falls, Idaho, 1973, Oral Health Ctr., Idaho Falls, 1974-76, Dist. 7 Health Dept. State Hosp. South, Idaho Falls, 1976-77, Dr. Hollen Hiller, Idaho Falls, 1977-87; lectr. Gold Leaf Idaho Dental Seminar, Idaho Falls, 1986—. Worship commn., choir, Bible study group, Presbyterian Ch., Idaho Falls, 1986—.ls, 1986—. Mem. Dental Hygiene Soc. (sec. 1984), Dental Aux. (pres. 1985), Ladies Golf Assn. (dir. club championship 1986), Chapter A.A. (sec. 1985-86, v.p. 1987—), Pi Epsilon Omicron (pres. 1986-87). Republican. Home: 11750 Pinehurst Idaho Falls ID 83401 Office: Gold Leaf Idaho Seminar 1820 E 17th St Suite 330 Idaho Falls ID 83401

HILLER, KAREN SUE, medical laboratory administrator; b. Tipton, Ind., Sept. 6, 1952; d. Harold Eugene and Dorothy Mae (Kelley) Goodman; m. Gary Lester Cunningham, Mar. 26, 1972 (div. 1978); m. Gary Dean Hiller, Sept. 6, 1980; children: Bret Christian, Bradley Robert. Student, Ind. U., Kokomo, 1970-72, Purdue U., 1987—. Research asst. Blue Cross/Blue Shield, Indpls., 1975-77; ops. supr. Yellow Freight Systems, Indpls., 1978-80; supr. The Med. Lab., Indpls., 1985—. Mem. Nat. Assn. Female Execs., Clin. Lab. Mgmt. Assn. Republican. Club: Ambassadair. Home: 105 Woodland Dr Mooresville IN 46158 Office: The Med Lab 5940 W Raymond St Indianapolis IN 46241

HILLERY, MARY JANE LARATO, editor, columnist, reserve army officer; b. Boston, Sept. 15, 1931; d. Donato and Porzia (Avellis) Larato; Asso. Sci. (scholar), Northeastern U., 1950; B.S., U. Mass. Harvard Extension, 1962; m. Thomas H. Hillery, Feb. 25, 1961; 1 son, Thomas H. Sales agt., linguist Pan Am. Airways, Boston, 1955-61; interpreter Internat. Conf. Fire Chiefs, Boston, 1966; tchr. Spanish, YWCA, Natick, Mass., 1966-67; community relations cons., adv. bd. dirs., lectr. for migrant edn. project div. Mass. Dept. Community Affairs, Boston, 1967-69; editor-in-chief Sudbury (Mass.) Citizen, 1967-76; asso. editor The Beacon, 1976-79, contbg. editor, 1979-83 ; area editorial adviser Beacon Pub. Co., Acton, Mass., 1970-80, editor, 1976-80; columnist Town Crier, 1987—; contbg. editor Towne Talk, 1975-79, Citizens' Forum, 1975-81; dir. public affairs Mass. Dept. Environ. Quality Engring., 1981-83. Mem. Bus. Adv. Com., 1972-77, Sudbury Sch. Com., 1976-77; mem. Meml. Day Celebration Com., 1972—, master of ceremonies, 1973-87, parade marshal, 1973-75, 82, 84, chmn., 1973-74. Bd. dirs., incorporator Sudbury Nonprofit Housing Corp., 1973-74; mem. Sudbury Town Report, 1967-72, 85-88, chmn., 1969-72; panelist Internat. Women's Year Symposium, 1975, Women in Politics, 1987, Women In Mil., 1987; columnist Town Crier, 1987—. Served with USN, 1950-54; lt. col. USAR; liaison officer U.S. Mil. Acad., 1976—; pub. affairs officer 94th USAR Command, 1982-83; mem. Congl. Nominating bd. USMA, 1985—; editor Hansconian, 1983-85. Named Editor of Year, Beacon Pub. Co., 1970; recipient medal of appreciation Internat. Order DeMolay, 1969, certificates of appreciation U.S. Def. Civil Preparedness Agency, 1975, Mass. Bicentennial Commn., 1976, Res. Officers Assn., 1986; citations Mass. State Senate, 1979, 82; Newswriting award Media Contest, Air Force Systems Command, 1984. Mem. Nat. Editorial Assn., Nat. Newspaper Assn., New Eng. Press Assn., Bus. and Profl. Women's Club (1st v.p. 1973-74, pres. 1974-76, parliamentarian 1978-88, state bylaws com. 1977-78, 79-81, 1986-88, state legis. chmn. 1979-81, 86-88, State Polit. Action Com. Chmn., 1988-89, Woman of Yr. 1979, Woman of Achievement 1982), LWV (dir. 1964-68), Nat. League Am. Pen Women (exec. bd. Boston 1974-76, 78-88, pres. 1976-78, publicity chmn. 1979-80, chmn. bylaws com. 1979-80, parliamentarian 1978-80, 82-84, 84-88, auditor 1980-82, 84-88), Res. Officers Assn. (life; state sec. 1978-79, pres. Boston chpt. 1986-88, army council rep. 1988—; Outstanding Service award 1978-79), Omega Sigma. Home: 66 Willow Rd Sudbury MA 01776

HILLERY, PAMELA LOUISE, banker; b. Danville, Ill., Sept. 16, 1963; d. Pearley H. and Vera L. (Hawkins) Keller; m. Mark Hillery, Sept. 11, 1982; 1 child, Derek Mark. Cert. compliance adminstr. Customer service rep. Palmer Am. Nat. Bank, Danville, 1980-82, data services rep., 1982-86, compliance adminstr., 1986—. Vol. March of Dimes, Danville, 1987, 88; capt. Am. Cancer Soc., Danville, 1988; donor Elks Blood Bank, Danville, 1987, 88; mem. staff United Way, Danville, 1987, 88. Mem. Danville Bus. and Profl. Women (Young Career Woman of the Yr. award 1988, Young Career Woman of the Yr. dist. XII alt., 1988). Office: Palmer Am Nat Bank 2 W Main St Danville IL 61832

HILLIARD, SHAREN ANNE, school program adminstrator; b. Mpls., May 13, 1942; d. Paul Ezetic and Maxene Fern (Carlson) DuFresne; m. Gary Leslie Hilliard, Nov. 16, 1963; children: Wendy, Lynn. BS, U. Minn., 1964; MA, Coll. St. Thomas, St. Paul, Minn., 1986. Tchr. Mpls. Pub. Schs., 1964-68; tchr. Wayzata (Minn.) Pub. Schs., 1978-85, coordinator programs for gifted and talented children, 1985—; lectr. in field. Co-author: (handbook) Nuts and Bolts-A Guide to Beginning an Enrichment Triad, 1987. Recipient Excellence in Edn. award Minn. Assn. Commerce and Industry, 1986; Twincities area Writer's Project fellow, 1981—. Mem. Minn. Educators of Gifted and Talented (pres.-elect 1987), Delta Kappa Gamma, Phi Delta Kappa. Presbyterian. Home: 5920 Maplewood Ln Minnetonka MN 55345 Office: Wayzata Pub Schs 149 Barry Ave Wayzata MN 55391

HILLINGS, JENNIFER ANN, government public affairs official; b. Washington, Oct. 7, 1954; d. Patrick J. and Phyllis Kaye (Reinbrecht) H. B.A., U. So. Calif., 1976. Press sec. Calif. Senate Republican Leader's Office, Sacramento, 1979-81; press sec. Rep. Nat. Com., Washington, 1981-83, White House Conf. on Productivity, Washington, 1983-84; dep. dir. pub. affairs Dept. Commerce, Washington, 1983-84; media coordinator Calif. Dept. Interior, Sacramento, 1984-85; asst. sec. for pub. affairs Dept. Transp., Washington, 1985-87; mgr. media programs N.Y. Stock Exchange, N.Y.C., 1987—. Named one of Outstanding Young Women Am. Mem. U. So. Calif. Alumni Assn., Arcadia High Sch. Alumni Club, Delta Gamma. Home: 155 E 31st St New York NY 10016 Office: NY Stock Exchange New York NY 10005

HILLIS, MARGARET, musician; b. Kokomo, Ind., Oct. 1, 1921; d. Glen R. and Bernice (Haynes) H. B.A., Ind. U., 1947; grad. student choral conducting, Juilliard Sch. Music, 1947-49; D.Mus. (hon.), Temple U., 1967, Ind. U., 1972, Carthage Coll., 1979, Wartburg Coll., 1981; D.F.A. (hon.), St. Mary's Coll., 1977, Lake Forest Coll., 1980. Dir., Met. Youth Chorale, Bklyn., 1948-51; asst. condr., Collegiate Choral, N.Y.C., 1952-53; mus. dir., condr., Am. Concert Choir, N.Y.C. from 1950, Am. Concert Orch. from 1950; condr., instr., Union Theol. Sem., 1950-60, Juilliard Sch. Music, 1951-53; dir. choral dept., Third St. Music Sch. Settlement, 1953-54; founder, music dir., Am. Choral Found., Inc., from 1954; choral dir., N.Y.C. Opera Co., 1955-56, Chgo. Mus. Coll. of Roosevelt U., 1961-62; condr., choral dir., Santa Fe Opera Co., 1958-59, Chgo. Symphony Chorus, 1957—; music dir., N.Y. Chamber Soloists, 1956-60; choral condr., Am. Opera Soc., N.Y.C., 1952-68; mus. asst. to music dir., Chgo. Symphony Orch., 1966-68; music dir., condr., Kenosha Symphony Orch., 1961-68; condr., choral dir., Cleve. Orch. Chorus, 1969-71; prof. conducting, dir. choral orgns., Northwestern U. Sch. Music, 1970-77; vis. prof. conducting, Ind. U. from 1978; resident condr. Chgo. Civic Orch. from 1967; music dir. Choral Inst., 1968-70, 75; mus. dir., condr., Elgin (Ill.) Symphony Orch., 1971-85; condr. Chgo.'s Do-It-Yourself Messiah, 1976—; dir. choral activities San Francisco Symphony Orch., 1982-83; guest condr., Chgo. Symphony, Cleve. Orch., Minn. Orch., Nat. Symphony Orch., others. Artists' adviser Nat. Fedn. Music Clubs Youth Auditions, 1966-70; mem. vis. com. dept. music U. Chgo., from 1971; chmn. choral panel Nat. Endowment for Arts, 1974—; hon. mem. Roosevelt U. Council of 100, from 1976; adv. bd. Cathedral Choral Soc. Washington Cathedral, from 1976. Civilian flight instr. USN CAA, WTS, World War II. Recipient Grammy awards for best choral performances: Verdi's Requiem, 1978, Beethoven's Missa Solemnis, 1979, Brahm's Ein Deutsches Requiem, 1980, Berlioz' La Damnation de Faust, 1983, Haydn's Creation, 1984, Brahm's Ein Deutsches Requiem, 1985, Orff's Carmina Burana, 1987; recipient Grand Prix du Disque for Berlioz' La Damnation de Faust, 1982; recipient Golden Plate award Am. Acad. Achievement, 1967, Alumnus of Year award Ind. U. Sch. Music Alumni, 1969, Steinway award, 1969, Chgo. YWCA Leader Luncheon I award, 1972, Friends of Lit. award, 1973, SAI Found. Circle of 15 award, 1974, Woman of Yr. in Classical Music award

Ladies Home Jour., 1978, Leadership for Freedom award Women's Scholarship Assn. Roosevelt U., 1978. Mem. Nat. Fedn. Music Clubs (hon., citation for contbns. to musical life of nation 1981), Am. Choral Dirs. Assn., Assn. Choral Condrs., Am. Music Center, P.E.O., Sigma Alpha Iota (hon.), Pi Kappa Lambda (hon.), Kappa Kappa Gamma (Alumni Achievement award 1978), Chorus America (formerly Assn. Profl. Vocal Ensembles), Am. Symphony Orch. League, Nat. Soc. Lit. and Arts. Office: care Shaw Concerts 1995 Broadway New York NY 10023 also: Chgo Symphony Orch 220 S Michigan Ave Chicago IL 60604

HILLMAN, CAROL BARBARA, manufacturing company executive; b. N.Y.C., Sept. 6, 1940; d. Joseph Hoppenfeld and Elsa (Spiegel) Hoppenfeld Resika; m. Howard D. Hillman, May 25, 1969. BA with high honors, U. Wis., 1961; Fulbright scholar U. Lyon (France), 1961-62; MA, Cornell Grad. Sch., Ithaca, N.Y., 1966. Staff assoc. pub. relations Eastern Airlines, N.Y.C., 1966-74; pub. affairs mgr. Squibb Corp., N.Y.C., 1974-75; asst. dir. corp. pub. relations Burlington Industries, N.Y.C., 1975-77, dir. corp. pub. relations, 1977-80, v.p. pub. relations, 1980-82; v.p. corp. communications Norton Co., Worcester, Mass., 1982—; mem. Pub. Affairs Council, Machinery & Allied Products Inst., 1982—; mem. dep. policy com., agenda com. Mass. Bus. Roundtable, 1982-87; bd. dirs. Mass. Econ. Stabilization Trust, 1987—. Mem. Cornell Council, Ithaca, 1981-85, pub. relations com. 1981—; mem. adv. council Coll. Human Ecology, Cornell U., Ithaca, 1982-84; mem. adv. bd. Ct. Apptd. Spl. Advocates, Worcester, 1983-87; voting mem. Wis. Union Trustees, U. Wis., Madison, 1982—; mem. Clark U. Assocs., Worcester, 1983—; bd. dirs. Planned Parenthood League Mass., 1986—; trustee Quinsigamond Community Coll., Worcester, 1987—. Cornell Grad. fellow Cornell U., 1962. Mem. Pub. Relations Soc. Am., Women's Econ. Forum, Worcester C. of C. (bd. dirs. 1984-87), Pub. Relations Seminar (com. mem. 1981—), Phi Beta Kappa, Phi Kappa Phi. Clubs: Cornell, Women's City (Boston), Boston. Home: 299 Belknap Rd Framingham MA 01701 Office: Norton Co 120 Front St Worcester MA 01608

HILLMAN, LESLIE WIGINGTON, communications specialist; b. Pawhuska, Okla., Sept. 19, 1954; d. John Henry and Virginia Lee (Conger) Wigington; B.A. (H.H. Herbert hon. pub. relations scholar), U. Okla., 1976; m. Stephen Alan Hillman, May 23, 1976; children—Erica Michelle, Derek Thomas. News reporter Ada Evening News, Okla., 1977-78; editor Southside Times, Tulsa, 1978-79; wire editor Broken Arrow Daily Ledger, Okla., 1979-80; mng. editor Tulsalite mag., Tulsa, 1980-85; communications specialist, 1985—; co-founder Publications Plus, Inc., 1987; editor Spotlite, Tulsa Performing Arts Ctr., 1980, 81. Recipient Irene Bowers Sells award, 1976, Service award Cystic Fibrosis Found., 1981. Mem. Women in Communications (2d v.p. Tulsa 1981-83, 1st v.p. 1983-84, sec. 1984-85). Office: 1308 S Indian Ave Tulsa OK 74127

HILLMAN, RITA, investor; b. N.Y.C., May 16, 1912; d. Rudolf and Bertha (Goodman) Kanarek; m. Alex L. Hillman, Aug. 23, 1932 (dec. 1968); children—Richard Alan (dec.), Alex L. Student NYU, 1929-32. Mem. Met. Mus. Art (mem. vis. com. 20th century art dept.), Am. Friends Israel Mus. (exec. com.), Bklyn. Acad. Music (vice chmn.), Internat. Ctr. Photography (vice chmn.), Alex Hillman Family Found. (pres.). Home: 895 Park Ave New York NY 10021 Office: 630 Fifth Ave New York NY 10111

HILLMAN, SHEILAH ARCHAMBAULT, writer, publisher; b. Quincy, Mass., May 22, 1935; d. Alcide Joseph and Shirley Veronica (Griswold) Archambault; B.A. magna cum laude, Tufts U., 1957; m. Robert S. Hillman, Aug. 31, 1957; children—Kimberly Ann, Robert Joseph. Reporter, The Patriot Ledger, Quincy, 1954-57; mng. editor Gold Medal Books, Fawcett Pubs., N.Y.C., 1957-61; journalism tchr., public relations cons., 1972—. Mem. Women in Communications, Authors Guild. Author: Public Relations for Private Schools, 1976; (with Dr. Robert S. Hillman) Traveling Healthy: A Complete Guide to Medical Services in 23 Countries, 1980, The Baby Checkup Book, 1982, Cradle Kill, 1988.

HILLMAN-JONES, GLADYS CORNELIA, educational administrator; b. Albany, N.Y., Jan. 15, 1938; d. Thomas Benjamin and Minnie Geneva (Colclough) Brooks; m. Harold Jones, Apr. 19, 1980; 1 son by previous marriage, George I. Hillman III. BS, SUNY, Oneonta, 1960; MA, Kean Coll. (formerly Newark State Coll.), Oneonta, 1970. Tchr. public schs. Albany, N.Y., 1960-64, Newark, N.Y., 1964-69; vice prin. Chancellor Ave. Sch., Newark, N.Y., 1969-76; prin. Marcus Garvey Sch., Newark, N.Y., 1976-78, George Washington Carver Elem. Sch., Newark, N.Y., 1978-81, Mt. Vernon Sch., Newark, N.Y., 1984—; dep. exec. supt. Newark Public Schs., 1981-84; mgr. Cernitin Am. Inc.; instructional cons. Barnell Loft Pub. Co. Chmn. bldg. fund com. local Bapt. Ch., South Orange, N.J. Recipient Disting. Alumnus award SUNY-Oneonta, 1983, named One in a Million, 1985, award for outstanding accomplishments in edn. Essex County Civic Club, 1987, award for exemplary adminstrv. leadership Benedetto Croce Ednl. Soc., Woman-on-the-Move award Bethany Bapt. Ch., 1988. Mem. NAACP (life), Am. Assn. Sch. Adminstrs., Internat. Reading Assn., Assn. Supervision and Curriculum Devel., United Council Negro Women, N.J. Reading Assn., Essex County Council Sch. Adminstrs., Delta Sigma Theta (chmn. scholarship com. 1973-77). Baptist (chmn. Black coll. com. 1978-81, chmn. bd. Christian edn. 1982-85). Office: 142 Mt Vernon Pl Newark NJ 07106

HILLS, CARLA ANDERSON, lawyer, former secretary housing and urban development; b. Los Angeles, Jan. 3, 1934; d. Carl H. and Edith (Hume) Anderson; m. Roderick Maltman Hills, Sept. 27, 1958; children: Laura Hume, Roderick Maltman, Megan Elizabeth, Alison Macbeth. A.B. cum laude, Stanford U., 1955; student, St. Hilda's Coll., Oxford (Eng.) U., 1954; LL.B., Yale U., 1958; hon. degrees, Pepperdine U., 1975, Washington U., 1977, Mills Coll., 1977, Lake Forest Coll., 1978, Williams Coll., 1981. Bar: Calif. 1959, U.S. Supreme Ct. 1965. Asst. U.S. atty. civil div. Los Angeles, 1958-61; partner firm Munger, Tolles, Hills & Rickershauser, Los Angeles, 1962-74, Latham, Watkins & Hills, Washington, 1978-86, Weil, Gotshal & Manges, Washington, 1986—; asst. atty. gen. civil div. Justice Dept., Washington, 1974-75; sec. HUD, 1975-77; dir. IBM Corp., Corning Glass Works, Am. Airlines, Fed. Nat. Mortgage Assn., The Henley Group, Chevron Corp.; adj. prof. Sch. Law, UCLA, 1972; mem. Trilateral Commn., 1977-82, Am. Com. on East-West Accord, 1977-79, Internat. Found. for Cultural Cooperation and Devel., 1977—, Fed. Acctg. Standards Adv. Council, 1978-80; bd. dirs. Internat. Exec. Service Corps.; mem. corrections task force Los Angeles County Sub-Regional; adv. bd. Calif. Council on Criminal Justice, 1969-71; mem. standing com. discipline U.S. Dist. Ct. for Central Calif., 1970-73; mem. Adminstrv. Conf. U.S., 1972-74; mem. exec. com. law and free soc. State Bar Calif., 1973; bd. councillors U. So. Calif. Law Center, 1972-74; trustee Pomona Coll., 1974-79, U. So. Calif., Brookings Instn.; mem. at large exec. com. Yale Law Sch., 1973-78; mem. com. on Law Sch. Yale Univ. Council; Gordon Grand fellow Yale U., 1978; mem. Sloan Commn. on Govt. and Higher Edn., 1977-79; mem. advisory com. Princeton U., Woodrow Wilson Sch. of Pub. and Internat. Affairs, 1977-80. Co-author: Federal Civil Practice, 1961; co-author, editor: Antitrust Adviser, 1971, 3d edit., 1985; contbg. editor: Legal Times, 1978—; mem. editorial bd.: Nat. Law Jour, 1978—. Trustee U. So. Calif., 1977-79, Norton Simon Mus. Art, Pasadena, Calif., 1976-80, Lawyers Com. for Civil Rights under Law, 1978-84; trustee Urban Inst., 1978-80, chmn., 1983—; co-chmn. Alliance To Save Energy, 1977—; vice chmn. adv. council on legal policy Am. Enterprise Inst., 1977-84; bd. visitors, exec. com. Stanford U. Law Sch., 1978-81; bd. dirs. Am. Council for Capital Formation, 1978—; mem. adv. com. M.I.T.-Harvard U. Joint Center for Urban Studies, 1978-82. Fellow Am. Bar Found.; mem. Los Angeles Women Lawyers Assn. (pres. 1964), ABA (chmn. publs. com. antitrust sect. 1972-74, council 1974, 77-84, chmn. 1982-83), Fed. Bar Assn. (pres. Los Angeles chpt. 1963), Los Angeles County Bar Assn. (mem. fed. rules and practice com. 1963-72, chmn. issues and survey 1963-72, chmn. sub-com. revision local rules for fed. cts. 1966-72, mem. jud. qualifications com. 1971-72), Am. Bar Inst. Clubs: Yale of So. Calif. (dir. 1972-74); Yale (Washington). Office: Weil Gotshal & Manges 1615 L St NW Suite 700 Washington DC 20036

HILLSMAN, REGINA ONIE, orthopedic surgeon; b. N.Y.C., June 2, 1955; d. David Oka and Laettia Louise (Miller) H.; m. Peter Michael Schmitz, Mar. 18, 1982; children: Michelle Julien Pierre. BA cum laude, Bryn Mawr Coll., 1972; MD cum laude, George Washington U., 1977. Intern Beth Israel Hosp., Boston, 1977-78; resident in surgery Montefiore Hosp., Bronx, N.Y., 1978-79; resident in orthopedics U. Pa., Phila., 1979-81; chief resident Howard U., Washington, 1981-82; practice med. specializing in orthopedics Los Angeles, 1983-87, N.Y.C., 1987—; clin. liaison Martin Luther King, Los Angeles, Calif. Mem. ACS, AMA, Am. Acad. Orthopedic Surgery, Am. Med. Women's Assn., N.Y. Acad. Scis., Am. Orthopedics, N.Y. State Med. Soc., Westchester Polit. Women's Caucus, Westchester Conservatory Music, Phi Delta Epsilon. Democrat. Roman Catholic. Home: 137 Glen Ave Mount Vernon NY 10550 Office: 698 Straib Turnpike Watertown CT 06795

HILPERT, BRUNETTE KATHLEEN POWERS (MRS. ELMER ERNEST HILPERT), civic worker; b. Baton Rouge; d. Edward Oliver and Orvilla (Nettles) Powers; A.B., La. State U., 1930, B.S. in L.S., 1933; post-grad. Columbia U., 1937; m. Elmer Ernest Hilpert, Aug. 1, 1938; children—Margaret Ray, Elmer Ernest II. Catalogue, La. State U. Library, Baton Rouge, 1930-36, La. State U. Law Sch. Library, 1936-38; librarian Washington U. Law Sch. Library, St. Louis, 1940-42; reference librarian Washington U. Library, St. Louis, 1952-54. Drive capt. United Fund, St. Louis, 1956; del. White House Conf. on Edn., St. Louis, 1962; trustee John Burroughs Sch., 1959-63; bd. dirs. Grace Hill Settlement House, 1957-63, v.p., 1960-62; bd. dirs. Internat. Inst., 1964-68; bd. dirs. Neighborhood Health Center, 1964-67, sec., 1964; bd. dirs. Arts and Edn. Council, 1967-87; pres., dir. Women's Assn. St. Louis Symphony Soc., 1969-71; exec. com., dir. St. Louis Symphony Soc., 1969—; bd. dirs. Miss. River Festival, 1969-74; dir. women's adv. bd. Continental Bank & Trust Co., 1970-77, 79-80; bd. dirs. St. Louis Inst. Music, 1971-75; bd. dirs. St. Louis String Quartet, 1971-77, pres., 1975-77; bd. dirs. Community Music Sch., 1973-75, Little Symphony Concerts Assn., 1975-78, St. Louis Conservatory and Schs. for Arts, 1975-84, Dance Concert Soc., 1977-81, Women's Aux. Bd. Bethesda Gen. Hosp., 1981—. Recipient Woman of Achievement award St. Louis Globe Democrat, 1967. Mem. Nat. Soc. Arts and Letters (dir. 1964-65, 80-82), Delta Zeta. Republican. Presbyterian. Clubs: Wednesday (rec. sec. 1963-64), University. Home: 630 Francis Pl Apt 1-N Saint Louis MO 63105

HILTABIDDLE, LINDA LEE, landscape architect; b. Elyria, Ohio, Sept. 18, 1958; d. Robert E. and Marilou (Hoag) H. BS in Landscape Architecture, Ohio State U., 1980. Registered landscape architect, Ohio. Site planner Cardinal Industries, Inc., Columbus, Ohio, 1980-84, dir. site planning, 1984-87, corp. dir. site planning, 1987—. Mem. Am. Soc. Landscape Architects (staff newsletter 1987—, newsletter editor 1988—), Nat. Assn. Female Execs. Republican. Methodist. Office: Cardinal Industries Inc 2040 S Hamilton Rd Columbus OH 43232

HILTON, EVA MAE (EVE), banker; b. Long Beach, Calif., Jan. 19, 1950; d. Albert Martin Wennekamp and Eva Geraldine (Hughes) Wennekamp Johnson; m. Charles H. Hilton, Jr., Nov. 30, 1968 (Div. 1982). Sr. teller Bank of Hawaii, Kailua, 1969-70; asst. mgr. ops. Ariz. Bank, Tucson, 1970-79; teller Valley Nat. Bank, Salome, Ariz., 1979-80; asst. v.p., br. mgr. Citibank (Ariz.), Phoenix, 1980—; instr. Am. Inst. Banking, Tucson, 1981. Mem. Nat. Assn. Female Execs. Avocations: racquetball; water sports; reading. Home: 13233 N 25th Dr Phoenix AZ 85029 Office: Citibank (Ariz) 13651 Phoenix AZ 85029

HILTZ, DAWN PAPP, water purification company executive; b. Norwalk, Conn., Nov. 30, 1959; d. Frank Stephen and Elizabeth Madeline (Mola) Millard; m. Ellis Andrew Hiltz, Jr., Sept. 11, 1982. Student Norwalk State Tech. Coll., Sacred Heart U., Am. Inst. Banking. Clk. Union Trust Co., Norwalk, 1978-82; asst. mgr. Matthew's, Westport, Conn., 1982; asst. to pres. ISP, Inc., Norwalk, 1982-86; asst. to pres. Pure Water Techs., Inc., Westport, 1986—. Vol. Norwalk Seaport Assn., 1985, 86. Mem. Nat. Assn. Female Execs. Republican. Roman Catholic. Club: South Norwalk Boat Club/Aux. Avocations: skiing; scuba diving; photography. Home: 92 Barlow Plain Dr Fairfield CT 06430 Office: ISP Inc 205 Liberty Sq Norwalk CT 06855

HILTZ, STARR ROXANNE, sociologist, educator; b. Little Rock, Sept. 7, 1942; d. John Donald and Mildred V. (Koons) Smyers; A.B., Vassar Coll., 1963; M.A., Columbia U., 1964, Ph.D., 1969; m. Murray Turoff, 1985; children—Jonathan David, Katherine Amanda. Prof. sociology, Upsala Coll., 1969—; assoc. dir. Computerized Conferencing and Communications Center, N.J. Inst. Tech., 1978—; pres. Computerized Conferencing, Inc., 1978—; cons. social impacts of computer systems. Mem. Am. Sociol. Assn., Assn. Computing Machinery, Internat. Communication Assn., Am. Soc. Info. Sci. Unitarian. Author: Creating Community Services for Widows, 1976; (with M. Turoff) The Network Nation, 1978; (with E. Kerr) Computer-Mediated Communication, 1982; Online Communities, 1984. Home: 1531 Golf St Scotch Plains NJ 07076 Office: Upsala College East Orange NJ 07019 also: NJ Inst Tech Newark NJ 07102

HIMLER, MARSHA SUE, state department official; b. Indpls., Mar. 26, 1943; d. John Milton and Ruth Devona (Burks) H. BS, Ind. U., 1964; postgrad. in indsl. and labor relations, Cornell U., 1969-73, in counseling and guidance, Syracuse U., 1968-72. With N.Y. State Dept. Labor, N.Y.C., 1966—, analyst employment systems field support, 1977-80, cons. career info. delivery systems, Albany, 1980-82, supr. adminstrv. analysis Office of Mgmt. Info. Systems, 1982—; pres., chief exec. officer Stonecroft, Inc., 1987—. Charter mem. Rep. Presdl. Task Force, N.Y. State Reps., 1981—; mem. USN Recruiting Dist. Assistance Council, 1982—. Serving as comdr. USNR, 1973 . Recipient cert. of appreciation U.S. Dept. Labor, 1982. Mem. Internat. Assn. Personnel in Employment Security, Welsh Pony Soc. Am. (life), Northeastern Welsh Pony Assn. (bd. dirs. 1975-77, 88—), Am. Driving Soc. (pres. 1975-77, 88, bd. dirs. 1972-86, 88), Mensa. Home: RD2 Rt 423 Stillwater NY 12170 Office: State Campus Bldg 12 Room 314 Albany NY 12240

HIMMS-HAGEN, JEAN MARGARET, biochemist; b. Oxford, Eng., Dec. 18, 1933; d. Frederick Hubert and Margaret Mary (Deadman) H.; m. Paul Hagen, Sept. 29, 1956; children: Anna, Nina. B.Sc., U. London, 1955; Ph.D., Oxford U., 1958. Postdoctoral fellow Harvard U., 1958-59; asst. prof. biochemistry U. Man., 1959-64; asso. prof. biochemistry Queen's U., 1964-67; asso. prof. biochemistry U. Ottawa, 1967-71, prof., 1971—, acting chmn. dept., 1975-77, 87, chmn. dept., 1977-82, acting chmn. dept., 1987. Assoc. editor Can. Jour. Biochemistry, 1967-71, Can. Jour. Physiology & Pharmacology, 1971-75, Am. Jour. Physiology, 1979—; mem. editorial bd. Proceedings Experimental Biology & Medicine, 1984—; council mem. Med. Research Council of Can., 1970-75 (exec. 1970-73); mem. five grants coms. Med. Research Council since 1969; chmn. metabolism grants com., 1972-75; mem. Can. Council Animal Care, 1970-78; author of 85 research publs. and 33 sci. rev. articles (mostly book chpts.). Recipient research grants Med. Research Council, 1960—, career award, 1968-77, Bond award Am. Oil Chemists Soc., 1972. Fellow Royal Soc. Can.; mem. Canadian Biochem. Soc. (Ayerst award 1973), Am. Soc. Pharmacology and Exptl. Therapeutics, Am. Inst. Nutrition, Endocrine Soc., Biochem. Soc. U.K., Canadian Physiol. Soc. Home: 233 Tudor Pl, Ottawa, ON Canada K1L 7Y1 Office: U Ottawa Dept Biochemistry, 451 Smyth Rd, Ottawa, ON Canada K1H 8M5

HIMONAS, JILL SAXON, advertising executive; b. N.Y.C., July 20, 1944, d. Louis Harold and Isobel (Silleg) Saxon; m. James Himonas, May 9, 1969. BA, Hunter Coll., 1966. Sales rep. Lanvin-Charles of Ritz, N.Y.C., 1966-67, dir. dept. store promotions, 1967-69; brand mgr. Prince Matchabelli/Chesebrough-Ponds, N.Y.C., 1969-71; mktg. mgr. Max Factor & Co., Los Angeles, 1972-75, v.p. mktg., 1975-81, sr. v.p. mktg., cosmetics div., 1981-82; sr. v.p., exec. dir. mktg. Ogilvy & Mather Advt., Los Angeles, 1982—; faculty Town Hall Los Angeles, 1981—. Mem. mktg. adv. bd. Calif. State U., Los Angeles, 1986—; bd. councillors U. So. Calif. Coll. Continuing Edn., Los Angeles, 1979-84; mem. fundraising com. Young Musicians Found., Los Angeles, 1982—. Office: Ogilvy & Mather 5757 Wilshire Blvd Los Angeles CA 90036

HIN, JUDITH, travel agency executive; b. Paterson, N.J., Jan. 28, 1954; d. Peter Andrew and Gertrude Patricia (Gavin) Hin. B.A., U. Vt., 1976; diploma, O'Brien's Travel Sch., 1979. Cert. travel cons. Asst. The Wilson Sch., Mt. Lakes, N.J., 1976-77; mgr. Garden State Travel, Teterboro, N.J., 1979-86; mgr. quality control VTS Travel, N.Y.C., 1986—; free lance watercolorist. Mem. Inst. Cert. Travel Agts., Ridgewood Art Inst. Republican. Roman Catholic. Avocations: watercolor painting, piano, skiing, swimming. Home: 284 Godwin Ave Carriage House Ridgewood NJ 07450

HINCHLIFFE, CHERIE ELAINE, internist; b. Woonsocket, R.I., Aug. 10, 1946; d. John and Elaine Alice (Tarr) Aniloski; m. Charles T. Hinchliffe, Nov. 28, 1968 (div. June 1988). AA in Nursing, Riverside City Coll., 1966; BS with highest honors, George Mason U., 1980; MD, Am. U., Plymouth, Montserrat, 1984. RN, Calif. Charge nurse med. clinic Riverside (Calif.) Gen. Hosp., 1967-73; staff nurse Knollwood Community Hosp., Riverside, 1973-74; charge nurse Prince Frederick (Md.) Hosp., 1974-76; pediatric nurse practioner St. Mary's County Health Dept., Leonardtown, Md., 1975-81; resident in internal medicine Waterbury (Conn.) Hosp., 1984-87; practice medicine specializing in internal medicine Colchester, Conn., 1987-88, South Laguna, Calif., 1988—. Cons. Women's Pavilion, South Laguna, 1988—. Fellow Nat. Assn. Pediatric Nurse Assocs. and Practitioners; mem. AMA, ACP (assoc.), Ind. Physicians Assn., Women in Mgmt., Laguna Niguel C. of C., Dana Point C. of C., Sigma Theta Tau, Alpha Chi. Republican. Home: 33571 Binnacle Dr Laguna Niguel CA 92677 Office: 31862 Pacific Coast Hwy Suite 15 South Laguna CA 92677

HINCHLIFFE, GWENDOLYN ANN, adminstrative manager; b. Bristol, Pa., June 26, 1948; d. William and Jane Marie (McElroy) H. AA, Bucks County Community Coll., 1968. Office worker Prudential Ins. Co., Langhorne, Pa., 1968-69; asst. travel mgr. Auto Club Cen. N.J., Trenton, 1969-72; asst. compaid coordinator corp. engring. div. Rohm & Haas Co., Bristol, 1974-82; electronics engring. aide Chessell Corp., Newtown, Pa., 1983-84; communications coordinator G.R. Murray Ins., Princeton, N.J., 1985-87; adminstrv. mgr. S.D. Catalano, Inc., Langhorne, 1988—. Mem. Nat. Assn. Female Execs., Bucks County Community Coll. Alumni Assn., Nat. Geographic Soc. Democrat. Roman Catholic. Home: 2809 Bath Rd Bristol PA 19007 Office: SD Catalano Inc 1252 E Lincoln Hwy Langhorne PA 19047

HINCKLEY, DAWN MARGARET, state government investigator; b. Maywood, Calif., Oct. 31, 1949; d. William Lovejoy and Margaret Hinckley; divorced; children: Robert Sterling, Heather Audrey. AA in Real Estate, Cerritos (Calif.) Coll.; AA in Criminal Justice, Calif. State U., Long Beach, 1984; BA in Sociology; postgrad. in law, Pacific Coast U. Assoc. Bell (Calif.) Realty Co., 1972-83; dep. commr. Calif. Dept. Real Estate, Los Angeles, 1984—; owner apt. bldg. Republican. Roman Catholic. Clubs: Big Bear Ski, Exec. Women, Corvette U.S.A.

HINCKS, MARCIA LOCKWOOD, insurance company executive, lawyer; b. N.Y.C., July 3, 1935; d. John Salem and Dorothy Elinor (Tufts) Lockwood; m. John Winslow Hincks, June 14, 1958; children—Rebecca Towne, Jennifer Winslow, John Morris, Benjamin Lockwood. B.A., Bryn Mawr Coll., 1956; LL.B., Yale U., 1959. Bar: Conn. 1960. Atty. Aetna Life & Casualty, Hartford, Conn., 1961-64, 67-70, counsel, 1970-81, v.p., ins. counsel, 1981—. Chmn. United Way Capital Area, Hartford, 1984-85; bd. dirs. Hartford Hosp., 1983—, Conn. Water Co., Clinton, 1983—; trustee Hotchkiss Sch., Lakeville, Conn., 1973-78, Hartford Coll. Women, 1978—. Recipient Community Service award United Way Capital Area, 1982, Alexis de Tocqueville award United Way of Am., 1987. Mem. ABA, Conn. Bar Assn., Assn. Life Ins. Counsel. Democrat. Congregationalist. Club: Hartford Golf. Office: Aetna Life & Casualty Co 151 Farmington Ave Hartford CT 06156

HINDERLITER, MARIE ANN, advertising and public relations executive; b. Yokusuka, Japan, Mar. 26, 1952; came to U.S., 1954; d. Kenneth Ray and Chizuko (NishYama) H. BA, Old Dominion U., 1974, MBA, 1983. Model Charm Assocs., Norfolk, Va., 1969-85; substitute tchr. Norfolk Pub. Schs., 1974-75; logistics engr. Ceberonics, Inc., Norfolk, 1975-80; systems analyst DALFI, Inc., Chesapeake, Va., 1980-82; mktg. rep. Xerox Corp., Norfolk, 1984-85; exec. dir. corp. affairs Systems Mgmt. Am., Norfolk, 1985—; cons. DALFI, Inc., Chesapeake, Va., 1982-84; mem. adv. bd. CareerCom Sch. of Bus. Bd. dirs. Young Womens Christian Assn, 1988, Big Brothers/Big Sisters Tidewater, 1987-88; mem. fundraising com. Am. Cancer Soc., Norfolk, 1986, Am. Heart Assn., Old Dominion U., Norfolk, 1987; mem. hospitality com. City of Norfolk, 1970-75. Named One of 10 Outstanding Profl. Women of Hampton Rds., 1987, Outstanding Young Women of Am., 1987, Miss Va. World, 1972, finalist Miss World, 1972. Mem. Armed Forces Communications and Electronics Assn., Pub. Relations Soc. Am., Chrysler Mus., CareerCom. Sch. of Bus. (edv. bd.). Republican. Lutheran. Office: Systems Mgmt Am Corp 254 Monticello Ave Norfolk VA 23510

HINDLE, PAULA ALICE, nurse; b. Cambridge, Mass., Feb. 26, 1952; d. Edward Adam and Geraldine Ann (Donahue) H. BS in Nursing, Fitchburg State Coll., 1974; MS in Nursing, Duke U., 1980; postgrad., Simmons Coll., 1985—. Staff nurse Mt. Auburn Hosp., Cambridge, Mass., 1974-75; staff nurse U. Hosp., Boston, 1975-77, head nurse, 1977-79; staff nurse Duke U. Med. Ctr., Durham, N.C., 1979-80, clin. instr., 1980-81, area mgr., 1981; nurse leader, clin. dir. New Eng. Med. Ctr., Boston, 1981-87; cons. Ctr. for Nursing Case Mgmt., Boston, 1984-87; v.p. nursing Faulkner Hosp., Boston, 1987—. Mem. Am. Heart Assn. Mem. Am. Assn. Critical Care Nurses, Mass. Orgn. Nurse Execs. (legis. com.), Am. Orgn. Nurse Execs., Sigma Theta Tau. Democrat. Roman Catholic. Home: 45 Colbrone Rd #6 Brighton MA 02135 Office: Faulkner Hosp Allandale at Centre St Boston MA 02130

HINDMAN, LESLIE S., auctioneer; b. Hinsdale, Ill., Dec. 1, 1954; d. Don J. and Patricia (de Forest) H.; m. Joseph B. Glossberg, Feb. 13, 1988. Student, Pine Manor Coll., 1972-74, U. Paris, 1974-75, Ind. U., 1975-76. Mgr. Sotheby Parke Bernet, Chgo., 1978-82; pres. Leslie Hindman Auctioneers, Chgo., 1982—, Salvage One Archtl. Artifacts, Chgo., 1986—. Named to Nat. Ladies Golf Hall of Fame, 1987. Mem. Com. of 200, Internat. Women's Forum, Arts Club Chgo. Club: Women's Athletic (Chgo.) (bd. dirs. 1988—). Home: 100 E Walton Chicago IL 60611 Office: Leslie Hindman Auctioneers 215 W Ohio Chicago IL 60610

HINDS, PAULA ANDERSON, chemist; b. Lake Charles, La., June 18, 1955; d. Edmund Beard and Nadine (Waldmann) Anderson; m. Brian Livingston Hinds. BS, Armstrong State Coll., 1977. Clin. lab. technician St. Joseph's Hosp., Savannah, 1974-77; process chemistry technician Union Camp Corp., Savannah, 1977-81, quality control supr., 1981—. Mem. Am. Chem. Soc., Am. Soc. Quality Control (cert.), Savannah Women's Network (pres. 1987—), Savannah Area Geneal. Assn. (asst pres.), Nat. Assn. Female Execs. Home: 16 Mulberry Bluff Dr Savannah GA 31406 Office: Union Camp Corp W Lathrop Ave Savannah GA 31406

HINE, DARLENE CLARK, history educator, administrator; b. Morley, Mo., Feb. 7, 1947; d. Levester and Lottie May (Thompson) Clark; m. William C. Hine, Aug. 21, 1970 (div. 1975); m. Johnny Earl Brown, July 25, 1981 (div.); 1 child, Robbie Davine. B.A. in Am. History, Roosevelt U., 1968; M.A., Kent State U., 1970, Ph.D. in Afro-Am. History, 1975. Teaching asst. Kent State U., Ohio, 1968-71; asst. prof. history, coordinator Black studies, S.C. State Coll., Orangeburg, 1972-74; asst. prof. Purdue U., West Lafayette, Ind., 1974-79, assoc. prof., 1980—, interim dir. African Studies and Research Ctr., 1978-79, vice provost, 1981-86; John A. Hannah Prof. History, Mich. State U., East Lansing, 1986—; v.p. 34d World Conf. Found., 1983—; mem. Ind. Com. for Humanities, 1983—; invited lectr. colls. and univs. including Harvard U., 1975, U. Ill., Chgo., 1981, St. Olaf Coll., 1981, Ind. U., 1982, U. Tex., Austin, 1983, So. Meth. U., 1983; grant rev. panelist NEH, 1979-80, Ford Found., NRC, 1980, 81, 82. Author: Black Victory, 1979; When the Truth is Told: A History of Black Women's Culture and Community in Indiana, 1875-1950, 1981; Black Women in the Nursing Profession: A Documentary History, 1984; contbr. chpts. to books, articles to publs., book revs. to jours. Mem. Ind. Com. for Humanities, Indpls., 1982—. Alumni fellow Kent State U., 1971-72, Nat. Humanities Ctr. fellow, 1986, Am. Council Learned Socs. fellow, 1986; research awardee Africana Studies and Research Ctr., 1975, 78; faculty devel. grantee Purdue U., 1978-79; research awardee Rockefeller Archive Ctr., 1978; Rockefeller Found. fellow for minority group scholars, 1980; research grantee Eleanor Roosevelt Inst., 1980-81; project grantee Fund for Improvement of Post-Secondary Edn., 1980-82; NEH grantee, 1982-83; 1st place essay award Degolyer Inst., 1982. Mem. Assn. for Study of Negro Life and History (exec. council 1979, 2d v.p. 1985-88), Orgn. Am. Historians, So. Hist. Assn., So. Assn. Women

Historians (v.p. 1983—), Am. Hist. Assn., Assn. Black Women Historians, Phi Alpha Theta. Democrat. Baptist. Home: 2357 Burcham Dr East Lansing MI 48823 Office: Mich State U Dept History East Lansing MI 48824-1036

HINEMAN, NANCY LEE, protective services official; b. West Chester, Pa., Mar. 23, 1951; d. Leon Joseph and Nancy Josephine (Bruno) Mascaro; 1 child, Marty Hineman. Grad. high sch., Glen Mills, Pa. Lic. cosmetologist, Del. and Pa, private detective, Pa.; cert. in sci. crime detection, Pa. Pvt. practice cosmetologist Wilmington, Del. and Media, Pa., 1969-74; detective criminal investigation div. Delaware County Dist. Atty., Media, Pa., 1975-78; polygraphist Criminal Investigation div. Delaware County, 1975-78; v.p., co-owner Urella's Detective Bur., Media, 1978—. Mem. Pa. Polygraph Assn., Nat. Detective Assn., Nat. Assn. Female Execs. Republican. Roman Catholic. Home and Office: Urella's Detective Bur 160 Paxon Hollow Rd Media PA 19063

HINERFELD, RUTH J., civic organization executive; b. Boston, Sept. 18, 1930; m. Norman Hinerfeld, children: Lee, Thomas, Joshua. A.B., Vassar Coll., 1951; grad., Program in Bus. Adminstrn., Harvard-Radcliffe Coll., 1952. With LWV, 1954—, UN observer, 1969-72, chairperson internat. relations com., 1972-76, 1st v.p. in charge legis. activities, 1976-78, pres., 1978-82; dir. LWV Overseas Edn. Fund., 1975-76, trustee, 1975-86; chairperson LWV Edn. Fund, 1978-82; mem. White House Adv. Com. for Trade Negotiations, 1975-82; sec. UN Assn. of U.S., 1975-78, vice chmn., 1983—, bd. govs., bd. dirs., 1975—; mem. econ. policy council; mem. exec. com., dir. Overseas Devel. Council; mem. U.S. del. auspices of Nat. Com. on U.S.-China Relations and Chinese People's Inst. Fgn. Affairs, 1978. Mem. council Nat. Mcpl. League, 1977-80, 83-86. del.-at-large Internat. Women's Year Conf., Houston, 1977; mem. exec. com. Leadership Conf. on Civil Rights, 1978-82; trustee Citizens Research Found., 1978—; mem. Nat. Petroleum Council, 1979-82; mem. U.S. del. to World Conf. on UN Decade for Women, 1980; mem. adv. com. Nat. Inst. for Citizen Edn. in the Law, 1981—; mem. North South Roundtable, 1978—; mem. nat. gov. bd. Common Cause, 1984—; vice chmn. U.S. com. UNICEF, 1986—; mem. vis. com. Harvard U. Bus. Sch.; mem. Bretton Woods Com. Recipient Disting. Citizen award Nat. Mcpl. League, 1978; Outstanding Mother award Nat. Mother's Day Com., 1981; Aspen Inst. Presdl. fellow, 1981. Mem. Council on Fgn. Relations, Phi Beta Kappa. Office: 11 Oak Ln Larchmont NY 10538

HINES, DAISY MARIE, writer; b. Hanna City, Ill., Dec. 31, 1913; d. Frank W. and Edith Earl (Folger) Humphrey; m. Herbert Waldo Hines, Jr., Dec. 20, 1958; children—Grace Consuelo, Ruby Marie. Student Western Ill. U., 1955-57, So. Ill. U., 1956. Mem. staff advt. dept. Macomb Daily Jour. (Ill.), 1943-47; writer, exec., dir., promoter McDonough County Tb Assn., 1949-58; sec. U.S. Dept. Agr., Macomb, 1955-58; researcher, writer 1st Nat. Bank, Springfield, 1963; adminstrv. asst. to state legislator, 1964-69; newspaper columnist, free-lance writer, mem. survey staff Prairie Farmer Pub. Co., Oak Brook, Ill., 1965-79, Successful Farming, Des Moines, 1982; Springfield corr. Automotive News. Active Altar Soc. Blessed Sacrament Cath. Ch., Springfield; chmn. Illiopolis unit Univ. Ill. Home Extension; pub. relations dir. Springfield chpt. Am. Cancer Soc., 1961-68; 2d v.p. Ill. Conf. Tb Workers, 1952-53; mem. Sangamon County Farm Bur., St. John's Hosp. Auxiliary. Mem. Nat. League Am. Pen Women (pres. Springfield chpt. 1972-73, sec. Ill. br. 1974), Western Ill. U. Alumni Council (sec.; Disting. Alumni award 1982; com. mem. Coll. Applied Scis. Agr. rep. Alumni Council), Ill. Press Assn. USAF Air Def. Team (hon. life), Ill. Women for Agr., Civil War Round Table, Sangamon County Hist. Soc. Club: Republican Women's. Address: 2504 S Holmes Ave Springfield IL 62704

HINES, GLORIA CYNTHELIA, educational administrator; b. Los Angeles, Jan. 29, 1934; d. Earl and Hazel (Magnuss) Jones; m. William E. Hines, Jr., May 20, 1955; children—Tanya Gail, Payton Kevin, William Jones. BA in Edn. and English, Idaho State U., 1957; MA in Supervision and Adminstrn., Montclair State Coll., 1976. Cert. tchr., prin. clk., Dept. Air Force, San Antonio, 1958-61, U.S. Air Force Acad., Colo., 1961-64, English tchr., 1964-66; sec. Dept. Air Force, Bentwaters AFB, Eng., 1967-68; tchr. English, Union Twp. Schs. (N.J.), 1969-75, supr. English dept., 1975-77, vice prin., 1977-83, prin., 1983—; bd. dirs. UTCAO, Inc., Vaux Hall, N.J., 1977-86, Egenolf Early Childhood Ctr. Recipient spl. award 1st Bapt. Ch., 1983. Mem. NEA, N.J. Edn. Assn., Nat. Council Negro Women, Nat. Council Tchrs. English, Assn. Supervision and Curriculum Devel., Nat. Assn. Secondary Sch. Prins., N.J. Assn. Secondary Sch. Prins., Nat. Assn. Negro Bus. and Profl. Women (spl. award 1983), NE Coalition Ednl. Leaders, Internat. Reading Assn., Phi Delta Kappa (rec. sec. 1977-79). Club: Soroptimist Internat. (pres. 1979-81, dir. 1981). Home: Hausman Ct Maplewood NJ 07040 Office: Kawameeh Jr High Sch Golf and David Terrs Union NJ 07062

HINES, MARY KATHERINE, chemist; b. San Diego, Aug. 22, 1950; d. Larry Jack and Virginia Jacqueline (Ourso) H. BS, North Tex. State U., 1972, MS, 1976. Cert. profl. chemist, clandestine lab. drug synthesizer. Receptionist, clk. Med. Surg. Clinic, McKinney, Tex., 1968-70; research asst. biology dept. Tex. Woman's U., Denton, 1970; med. tech. asst. Collin Meml. Hosp., McKinney, 1970; lab equipment monitor chemistry dept. North Tex. State U., Denton, 1971-72, lab. instr. chemistry dept., 1973-75, research assoc. chemistry dept., 1972-76; med. tech. technician Denton Osteopathic Hosp., 1982-86; forensic, toxicological chemist Inst. Forensic Scis., Dallas, 1977—; lectr. in field. Mem. Am. Chem. Soc., Am. Acad. Forensic Scis., Internat. Narcotic Enforcement Officers Assn., N.Y. Acad. Scis., Nat. Assn Female Execs., Am. Quarter Horse Assn., Am. Red Brangus Assn., Am. Dairy Goat Assn., Alpha Chi Sigma. Home: PO Box 933 Argyle TX 76226

HINES, PATRICIA, social worker; b. Watertown, N.Y., Nov. 4, 1947; d. Arthur and Bella (O'Neil) Hines; BS, SUNY, Oswego, 1969; MSW, SUNY, Buffalo, 1975; M in Pub. Adminstrn., Fairleigh Dickinson U., 1982. Supr. social work Ocean County Bd. Social Services, Toms River, N.J., 1973-77, adminstrv. supr. social work, 1977-83, dep. dir., 1983—; social work cons. Medictr. and Rainbow Day Care, Lakewood, N.J., 1975—, Ocean County Vis. Homemaker Service, Inc., Toms River, 1975-80, Community Meml. Hosp., Toms River, 1978-79, Logan Manor Care Ctr., Manchester Manor, Garden State Rehab. Hosp., Country Manor, Bartley Manor Convalescent Ctr., Ocean Convalescent Ctr., Barnegat Nursing Facility, Jackson Health Care Ctr., Harrogate Life Care Community; prin. in Sr. Care Planning Assocs.; instr. social work Georgian Court Coll., Lakewood, 1975—. Chmn., Ocean County Title XX Coalition, 1977-82; bd. dirs. Ocean County Family Planning Program, Toms River, 1969-73, Mental Health Bd., 1983-84; mem. exec. bd. United Way, 1983—. Cert., Dr. Thomas Gordon Parent Effectiveness Trainer. Mem. Acad. Cert. Social Workers, Nat. Assn. Social Workers. Home: 13 Bay Harbor Blvd Brick NJ 08723 Office: 1027 Hooper Ave Toms River NJ 08753

HINES, VONCILE, special education educator; b. Detroit, Dec. 1, 1945; d. Raymond and Cleo (Smith) H. AA, Highland Park Community Coll., 1967; BS in Edn., Wayne State U., 1971, MEd, 1975; MA, U. Detroit, 1978. Tchr. primary unit Detroit Bd. Edn., 1971-79, spl. educator, 1979—; cons. Queen's Community Workers, Detroit, 1977—; ednl. cons. Queen's Community Workers, Detroit, 1977—. Author: I Chose Planet Earth, 1988; inventor in field. Recipient Cert. of Merit State of Mich., 1978, 88, Cert. Appreciation Queen's Community Workers, 1980, Award of Recognition Detroit City Council, 1984. Mem. Assn. for Children and Adults with Learning Disabilities, Assn. Supervision and Curriculum Devel., Nat. Thinking Skills Network, Nat. Assn. Female Execs., Nat. Council Negro Women (presenter 1987). Democrat.

HINKLE, CYNTHIA DAWN, sales and marketing representative; b. Hagerstown, Md., Mar. 23, 1961; d. Darl Wayne and Bonnie JoAnn (Kitchen) Hinkle; m. Frank Steven Selga, June 21, 1980 (div. 1985). BS, Calif. State U., Long Beach, 1984. Retail mgr. Limited Inc., Torrance, Calif., 1983-86; sales and mktg. rep. Gary Steel Co., Long Beach, 1986-87; v.p. so. region Ken Brown and Assoc., Los Angeles, 1987—. Mem. Nat. Assn. Female Execs., Golden Key, Omicron Nu. Home: PO Box 91344 1613 Ximeno #115 Long Beach CA 90809 Office: Ken Brown and Assocs 1722 Westwood Blvd Suite 101 West Los Angeles CA 90024

HINKS, CAROL, tobacco company executive; b. Berlin, May 10, 1944, came to Can., 1953; BA, Sir George Williams U., Montreal, Can., 1968, cert. adv. agy. practitioner, 1969. Media mgr. BCP Advt. (B&B), Montreal, 1969-71; media dir. Can. Advt. Agy., Montreal, 1971-73; v.p., media dir. McKim Advt., Montreal, 1973-77; media planning mgr. Imperial Tobacco Ltd., Montreal, 1977-85; div. mgr. Imperial Tobacco Ltd., Toronto, 1985—; bd. dirs. Can. Outdoor Measurement Bur., Toronto, 1982-86, Print Heasurement Bur., Toronto. Gov. Inter Service Clubs Council, Montreal, 1983-86. Lodge: Zonta. Office: Imperial Tobacco Ltd, 1857 Leslie St, Don Mills CAN M3B 2M2

HINMAN, ELAINE MARIE, aerospace engineer; b. Lincoln Park, Mich., Nov. 18, 1960; d. John Edward and Florence Emelie (Langouse) H. BS in Aero. Engring., U. Mich., 1983. Engr. Marshall (Ala.) Space Flight Ctr. NASA, 1983—. Chmn. robotics informal working group Marshall Space Flight Ctr.; test diver Neutral Bouyancy Simulator, Extravehicular Mobility Unit suit, 1987. Mem. AIAA (Outstanding Young Aero. Engr. of Yr. 1986), NOW, Soc. Photo-Optical Instrumentation Engrs., Robotics Internat. (chmn. robotics informal working group 1986—, sec. Huntsville chpt.), Von Braun Astron. Soc., North Ala. Sci. Fiction Assn. (bd. dirs. 1985-87). Home: 3020C Autumnwood Dr Huntsville AL 35816 Office: NASA Marshall Space Flight Ctr Marshall AL 35812

HINMAN, MYRA MAHLOW, educator; b. Saginaw County, Mich., Jan. 11, 1926; d. Henry and Cynthia (Mims) Mahlow; B.S., Columbia U., 1946; M.A., U. Fla., 1954, Ph.D., 1959; m. George E. Olstead, 1948 (div. 1967); 1 son, Christopher Eric; m. Charlton Hinman, 1968 (dec. 1977); 1 stepdau., Barbara. Asst. prof. Memphis State U., 1959-61; instr. U. Kans., Lawrence, 1961-63, asst. prof., 1963-68, asso. prof. English lit., 1968—. Travel grantee Am. Council Learned Socs., 1966. Mem. MLA, Internat. Arthurian Soc. (conf. speaker), Shakespeare Assn. Am. (conf. presenter), U. Va. Bibliog. Soc., AAUP, Kans. Folklore Soc., Midwest MLA, S. Atlantic MLA, United Burmese Cat Fanciers, Am. Shorthair Cat Assn., Phi Kappa Phi. Asst. editor: Hinman Text, Complete Works of Shakespeare; mem. editorial bd. Computer-Assisted Composition jour.; contbr. articles to profl. jours. Home: 1932 Maine St Lawrence KS 66046 Office: U Kans Wescoe Hall Lawrence KS 66045

HINNRICHS-DAHMS, HOLLY BETH, educator; b. Milw., Oct. 31, 1945; d. Helmut Ferdinand and Rae W. (Beebe) H.; m. Raymond H. Dahms, June 11, 1983 (dec. Oct. 2, 1983). Student U. Wis., Milw., 1963-64, 66, 79—, Chapman Coll., 1965, 67, Internat. Coll. Copenhagen, summer 1968, Temple U., summer 1970, BA, Alverno Coll., 1971; postgrad. Marylhurst Coll., 1972, Chapman Coll. World Campus Afloat, summers 1973, 74, Inst. Shipboard Edn., 1978, 79. V.p. Hinnrichs Inc., Germantown, Wis., 1964-72; tchr. Germantown Recreation Dept., 1965; coach Milw. Recreation Dept., 1966-67; rep. for Wis., Chapman Coll., Orange, Calif., 1967; clk. Stein Drug Co., Menomonee Falls, Wis., 1967-72; tchr. Milw. area Cath. Schs., 1967-72, 83—; asst. mgr. Original Cookie Co. (Mother Hubbard's) Cookie Store, Northridge Mall, Milw., 1977-84, SAU-U Warehouse Deli, 1984-85, mgr. office, 1985—; with Pilgrim Message Ctr., 1987—; substitute tchr. pub. schs. Milw. area, 1975-80, 83—; tchr. Indian Community Sch., Milw., 1971-72, 88—, Martin Luther King Sch., 1973-74, Crossroads Acad., Milw., 1974-75, Harambee Community Sch., 1980-83; tutor Brookfield (Wis.) Learning Ctr., 1986-87; Midwest rep. World Explorer Cruises, 1978-82. Mem. Wis. Math. Council, Nat. Council Tchrs. Math., Internat. Inst. Milw. Friends of Mus., Alpha Theta Epsilon. Christian Scientist. Lodges: Order Eastern Star, Golden Rule. Home: N88W15041 Cleveland Ave #3 Menomonee Falls WI 53051 Office: Indian Community Sch 3134 W State St Milwaukee WI 53208

HINRICHSEN, EVELYN ELIZABETH MERRELL (MRS. WALTER HINRICHSEN), corporate executive; b. Chgo., Nov. 30, 1910; d. Dwight Livingston and Julia (Dodd) Merrell; B.A., Mus.B., Mills Coll., 1938, M.A., 1940; cert. spl. teaching in music, Calif., 1941; m. Walter Hinrichsen, Aug. 2, 1946 (dec. July 1969); children—Martha Eleanor, Henry Hans. Asst. sec. to pres. Mills Coll., Oakland, Calif., 1942-44; sec. to chief asst. and librarian Library of Congress, Washington, 1944-46; v.p., sec. C.F. Peters Corp., N.Y.C., 1948-69, v.p., sec., owner, 1969-70, owner, pres., 1970-78, owner, chmn. bd., 1978—. Mem. AAUW, Met. Mus. Art, Mus. Modern Art, N.Y. Philharmonic, Alumnae Assn. Mills Coll., Sigma Alpha Iota. Home: 431 E 20th St 8C New York NY 10010 Office: 373 Park Ave S New York NY 10016

HINSDALE, MARY JANE, international finance and marketing expert; b. Corry, Pa., June 4, 1950; d. Ernest Raymond and Mary June (Lookenhouse) H. AA, Jamestown (N.Y.) Community Coll., 1970; BS, SUNY, Oswego, 1972; MBA, Nat. U., San Diego, 1984. Export adminstr. O'John Enterprises, Inc., Rochester, N.Y., 1975-78; adminstr. internat. mktg. Datagraphix, Inc., San Diego, 1978-83, internat. sr. fin. analyst, 1984-87; sr. credit analyst Rohr Industries, Inc., Chula Vista, Calif., 1987—. Mem. World Trade Assn.

HINSHAW, PATTY K., interior designer; b. Kannapolis, N.C., June 29, 1939; d. Ralph Clyde Kluttz and Margaret (Pennington) Kirk; m. William Brian Hinshaw, May 29, 1960 (June 29, 1975); 1 child, Damon. Brian. BA in Edn. and Sociology, Lenoir Rhyne Coll., 1961; MA in Social Sci., Hollins (Va.) Coll., 1971; BA in Interior Design, Marymount U., 1988. Bar: Va. 1980; lic. real estate; cert. divorce mediator, tchr., Va. Owner Famous French Gallery, Roanoke, Va., 1972-77; social worker Roanoke Dept. Social Services, 1972-83; dir. sales, mktg. Roanoke Civic Ctr., 1983-85; regional dir. sales Hotel Investors Corp., Chevy Chase, Md., 1985-86; interior designer Capital Interiors, Arlington, Va., 1986—; cons. Amari Internat., Bethesda, Md., 1986. Dir., producer TV Series Mood, 1972; assoc. producer TV Documentary Child Abuse in the 80's. Named Foremost Women of Yr. 20's, Eng., 1985. Mem. Am. Soc. Interior Designers, Nat. Assn. Female Execs., Greater Washington Soc. Assn. Execs., Soc. Govtl. Mktg. Planners, Friends Kennedy Ctr. Democrat. Unitarian. Home: 1200 N Nash St #1111 Arlington VA 22209 Office: Capital Interiors PO Box 12234 Rosslyn VA 22209

HINSON, PEGGY MILDRED, educator; b. Thomaston, Ga., July 19, 1936; d. Robert LeGrand, Sr. and Mildred Sara (Keever) H.; B.S. in Edn., Auburn U., 1958; B.S. in Med. Adminstrn. and Supervision, Ga. State U., 1978. Head English dept. Faith Sch., Ft. Benning, Ga., 1958-61, Daniel Jr. High Sch., Columbus, Ga., 1961-63; tchr. Rothschild Jr. High Sch., Columbus, 1965-75, head English dept., 1976—; secondary English cons., Columbus, 1975-76; curriculum steering com. Columbus Coll. Speaker Ga. Writing Conf., Atlanta, 1986-87. Recipient commendation Pres. of U.S., 1976, commendation U.S. Congress, 1976; named Star Tchr., 1975, Tchr. of Yr., Ga. Council Tchrs. of English, 1988. Mem. Nat. Council Tchrs. of English, NEA, Ga. Assn. Educators, Muscogee Assn. Edn., Columbus Exec. Club, AAUW, Ga. Walking Horse Assn., Phi Delta Kappa, Alpha Delta Kappa, Delta Delta Delta. Home: 3312 Gail Dr Columbus GA 31907 Office: 1136 Hunt Ave Columbus GA 31907

HINTZ ANDERSON, DIANA DAWN, advertising executive; b. Bismarck, N.D., Apr. 22, 1959; d. Wilbur William and Dorothy Ann (Cook) Hintz; m. G. John Anderson, June 16, 1984; 1 child, Garrett William. BA, Augustana Coll., 1981. Office mgr. Harrington Advt., Sioux Falls, 1980-81; with advt. sales The Hendricks (Minn.) Pioneer and Squire, 1981-84; advt. mgr. The S.D. Press Assn., Brookings, 1984—. Newsletter editor The Editorial Page; contbr. newspaper articles. Active Hendricks Community Theater, 1982; county chairperson Am. Heart Assn., Hendricks, 1983. Mem. S.D. Press Woman, S.D. Advt. Fedn. Democrat. Presbyterian. Home: Rural Rt 1 Box 94 Astoria SD 57213 Office: SD Press Assn Communications Ctr Brookings SD 57007

HINZ, DOROTHY ELIZABETH, writer, editor, public relations executive; b. N.Y.C., Nov. 28, 1926. AB, Hunter Coll., 1948; postgrad., Columbia U. Copy editor Colliers mag., 1948-53; asst. to dir. devel. Columbia U., N.Y.C., 1953-55; mng. editor Grace Log, econs. researcher-analyst, writer speeches, white papers, com. reports Latin Am. affairs, public relations dept. W.R. Grace & Co., N.Y.C., 1955-64; staff writer Oil Progress, fgn. news media, speeches, films, internat. petroleum ops., pub. relations dept. Caltex Petroleum Corp., N.Y.C., 1964-68; fin. editor Merrill Lynch, Pierce, Fenner & Smith, 1969-74; asst. sec., mgr. publs., asst. speech writer, editor speeches and reports corp. mktg. and communications dept. Mfrs. Hanover Trust Co., N.Y.C., 1974—. Contbr. articles on multinat. corps., developing nations, trade and fin. to various publs. Mem. Inter-Am. Round Table. Club: Overseas Press. Home: 600 W 115th St New York NY 10025 Office: Mfrs Hanover Corp 270 Park Ave New York NY 10017

HIPSHIRE, LOUISE JOYNER, management consultant; b. Hampton, Va., Nov. 23, 1945; d. Odis B. and Nannie Leigh (Vick) Joyner; student Ga. State U., Mercer U.; m. James R. Hipshire, Sept. 12, 1980. With Peoples Bank and Trust Co., Rocky Mount, N.C., 1966-69, Avco Fin. Services, Rocky Mount, 1969-72, Inventories Co., Garner, N.C., 1972-74; comptroller, officer mgr. Moffett and Henderson, P.C., attys.-at-law, Atlanta, 1974-83; mgmt. cons., Temple Terrace, Fla., 1984—; owner Preferred Bus. Services, Temple Terrace, 1984—, Spl. Arrangements, 1985—; sec.-treas. Charter Oak Mortgage Corp., 1975-83; cons. in acctg. systems. Soc. dir. Fulton County Young Rep., 1975; auditor Ga. Young Rep., 1975. Active local Big Sisters, 1979-83. Recipient Girl of The Year award, Beta Sigma Phi, 1970; mem. Nat. Assn. Legal Adminstrs., DeKalb County Bd. Realtors. Republican. Methodist. Office: PO Box 291365 Tampa FL 33687

HIRAHARA, PATTI, public relations agency executive; b. Lynwood, Calif., May 10, 1955; d. Frank C. and Mary K. Hirahara. A.A., Cypress Coll., 1975; B.A., Calif. State U.-Fullerton, 1977. Pub. affairs dir. United Television, Los Angeles, 1977-80; v.p. Asian Internat. Broadcasting Co., Los Angeles, 1980-81; mktg. cons. Disneyland, Anaheim, Calif., 1982; pub. relations agt. Japan External Trade Orgn., Los Angeles, 1982-86, 87—; owner, pres. Prodns. By Hirahara, Anaheim, 1982—; comml. photographer Hirahara Photography, Anaheim, 1977-83; publicist Tokyo Met. Govt., 1981; advisor State Colo. Trade Mission to Japan, 1986, State Ariz. Trade/Investment Mission to Japan, 1987, County Riverside, Calif. for Japanese trade, investment, tourism, 1986-88; coordinator JETRO's Bus. Study Series, Los Angeles, 1988; advisor Japan External Trade Ordgn., 1987-88. Bd. dirs. Nisei Week Japanese Festival, Los Angeles, 1980-81. Nat. scholar Seventeen Mag. Youth Adv. Council, 1973; named Orange County Nisei Queen, Suburban Optimist Club, Buena Park, Calif., 1975, nat. semi-finalist Outstanding Young Working Women Competititon Glamour mag., 1983-84; recipient service award Suburban Optimist Club of Buena Park, 1975. Mem. Soc. Profl. Journalists (bd. dirs. 1980-81), Nat. Assn. Female Execs., World Trade Ctr. Assn. Orange County, Japanese Am. Citizens League, Am. Women in Radio and TV (bd. dirs. So. Calif. chpt. 1980-82, vice-chair western area conf. 1981), Alpha Gamma Sigma.

HIRANO, JUNE YAMADA, education center administrator; b. Honolulu, Aug. 27, 1943; d. Harry Taketo and Aiko (Endo) Yamada; m. Michael James Hirano, Mar. 31, 1973. BEd, U. Hawaii, 1965, MA, 1967. Instr., assoc. dir. for tng. Speech Communications Ctr., U. Hawaii, Honolulu, 1967-69, asst. to dir., grad./undergrad. coordinator univ. dept. speech communications, 1969-70; asst. coordinator for participant activities East-West Ctr., Honolulu, 1970-73, selections adminstr., 1973-79, award service officer, 1979—. Co-author: (learning manuals) Speech Communication Learning System, vol. I and II, 1st edit., 1968, 3d edit., 1970, Speech Power Learning System, 1969. Mem. Am. Assn. Collegiate Registrars and Admissions Officers (rep. Nat. Council on Evaluation of Fgn. Ednl. Credentials 1985-88), Nat. Assn. for Fgn. Student Affairs, Phi Kappa Phi. Avocations: Oriental art, contemporary prints, ceramics. Office: East-West Ctr 1777 East-West Rd Honolulu HI 96848

HIRASAKI, MARSHA PARRISH, industrial sales company executive; b. Sullivan's Island, S.C., Oct. 27, 1945; d. Louis August Rohde and Ruth Ann (Hynes) Nelson; m. John Kiyoshi Hirasaki, Dec. 29, 1968; children: Kitt Nelson, Parrish Nelson. BSME, Duke U., 1967; MSME, U. Houston, 1971. Aerospace engr. TRW Systems, Houston, 1967-72; design engr. Nat. Maritime Research Ctr., Galveston, Tex., 1972-74; sales mgr. Cooper Valve and Fitting, Inc., LaPorte, Tex., 1974-76; pres., gen. mgr. Eurasia Valve Corp., Houston, 1976-79; gen. mgr. Masoneilan div. McGraw Edison, Houston, 1979-84; gen. mgr. Dresser Valve and Controls, Houston, 1985; pres., gen. mgr. Nelson Controls, Inc., Deer Park, Tex., 1985—. Mem. Instrument Soc. Am. (pres. chpt. 1982-83, internat. bd. dirs. 1986—), NOW (pres. Houston chpt. 1972-73), Portrait Artists Guild (pres. 1984-86). Home: 931 Shady Oak Dr Dickinson TX 77539

HIRN, DORIS DREYER, health service administrator; b. N.Y.C., Dec. 3, 1933; d. James Howard and Dorothy Van Nostrand (Young) Dreyer; student Colby Jr. Coll., 1950-51, Hofstra U., 1953-56; m. John D. Hirn, Oct. 27, 1956; children—Deborah Lynn, Robert William. Owner, Dutchlands Farm, Albany, N.Y., 1957-62, Hickory Hill Farm, Galena, Ill., 1965-75; adminstr. Home Health Service, Chgo., 1972-74, exec. dir. Suburban Home Health Service, 1974-87; exec. dir. Home Health Service Chgo. North, 1987—; pres. Hickory Hill Mgmt. Corp.; dir. Nat. Health Delivery Systems, Serengeti Prodns., Inc.; bd. dirs. Lifeline Pilots, Inc., NAHC, Fin. Mgrs. Forum, Nat. Prospective Pay Task Force, All Long Term Task Force; ptnr. Candor Assocs. Served with WAVES, 1951-52. Mem. Nat. Assn. Home Care (bd. dirs.), Ill. Council Home Health Agys. Clubs: Chgo. Yacht, East Bank. Contbr. articles to various periodicals. Home: 5747 N Sheridan Chicago IL 60660

HIRSCH, IRMA LOU KOLTERMAN, nurse, association administrator; b. Clay Center, Kans., June 11, 1934; d. Arthur Henry and Mildred (Peterson) Kolterman; m. William A. Hirsch, June 8, 1958; children—David William, Brian Duane. B.S. in Nursing, U. Kans., 1957; M.Nursing, U. Washington, Seattle, 1961. R.N. Mo. Instr. Duke U., Durham, N.C., 1961-64; nurse clinician U. Kans. Med. Ctr., Kansas City, 1968-70; project dir., cons. Mo. Regional Med. Program, Kansas City, 1970-74; project dir., program coordinator Am. Nurses' Assn., Kansas City, 1974-79, dept. dir., 1981-83, policy devel., 1983—; supr. VA Med. Ctr., Kansas City, 1979-81; cons. nursing edn. Joint Commn. on Accreditation of Hosps., Chgo., 1973; cons. for project devel. Am. Nurses Found., Kansas City, 1974; cons. nursing standards Health Standards Directorate, Ottawa, Ont., Can., 1978; trustee Presbyterian Manors of Mid-Am., Newton, Kans., 1979-86. Editor: Guidelines for Review of Nursing Care at the Local Level, 1976; Nursing Quality Assurance Management/Learning System, 1982; Peer Review in Nursing, 1982; Issues in Professional Practice, 1985. Mem. Friends of Art, Kansas City, 1975—, Internat. Relations Council, Kansas City, 1980—, Historic Kansas City Found., 1982—; chpt. pres. Am. Field Services, Kansas City, 1978-79. Mem. Am. Nurses Assn., Mo. Nurses' Assn. (pres. Mo. dist. 1980-81), Kans. U. Nurses Alumni Assn. (pres. 1964-66), N.Am. Nursing Diagnosis Assn. (mem. task force 1973-77), Sigma Theta Tau. Club: P.E.O. (Kansas City). Avocations: home and financial management; walking; skiing. Home: 1035 W 57th Terr Kansas City MO 64113 Office: Am Nurses' Assn 2420 Pershing Rd Kansas City MO 64108

HIRSCH, JANET M., communications executive; b. East Chicago, Ind., Mar. 29, 1947; d. Thomas Joseph and Armella (Bronner) Ward; m. Richard H. Hirsch, June 14, 1969. BS in Chemistry, Ill. Inst. Tech., 1969; MBA, Washington U., St. Louis, 1982. Chemist Champion Internat., Chgo., 1969-73; research chemist Sherwood Med., St. Louis, 1974; research chemist Anheuser-Busch, St. Louis, 1975-80, asst. dir. tech. ctr., 1980-82, mgr. industry affairs, 1982-85; pres. Smart Graphics, Inc., Webster Groves, Mo., 1985—; corp. rep. Corn Refiners Assn., 1977-80. Mem. editorial bd. Corn Refiners Assn. Standard Analytical Prodecures Manual, 1978-80; author: (with others) Showoff, 1986; author, presenter visual presentation, Bus. Graphics Using the Z100, 1985-86. Mem. women In Bus. Network (bd. dirs. 1982-84, pres. 1983). Office: Smart Graphics Inc 470 Belleview Webster Groves MO 63119

HIRSCH, JILL SUSAN, physician; b. Bklyn., Nov. 27, 1955; d. Arnold David and Vivian Honey (Agress) Hirsch; m. Randolph Jack Cohen, June 8, 1980. B.S., Columbia U., 1976; M.D., N.Y. Med. Coll., 1980. Diplomate Nat. Bd. Med. Examiners, Am. Bd. Pediatrics. Pediatric resident Brookdale Hosp., Bklyn., 1980-83, attending in charge pediatric emergency services, 1983-84. Fellow Am. Acad. Pediatrics; mem. Royal Soc. Arts (London), Tau Beta Pi, Phi Lambda Upsilon. Democrat. Jewish. Home: Revonah Hill Rd Liberty NY 12754

HIRSCH, JULIA CAROL, management consultant; b. Freeport, Ill., Mar. 18, 1939; d. Muriel Woessner and Lois (Peterman) Woessner Hirsch; m.

Konrad Wedekind, Dec. 4, 1985. BA, Stanford U., 1960. Program dir. Stanford (Calif.) U. Alumni Assn., 1960-68; exec. asst. to pres. Calif. Inst. Arts, Valencia, 1968-72; v.p. Nat. Ctr. for Vol. Action, Washington, 1972-74; Calif. Gubernatorial campaign mgr. for Herb Hafif 1974; pres. J.C. Hirsch and Assocs., San Francisco, 1974-78; v.p. Boyden Assocs., Inc., San Francisco, 1978-83, sr. v.p., 1983—; mem. Stanford U. Alumni exec. bd. 1973-76, trustee York Sch., 1979—. Mem. Women' Forum West, Human Relations Council, Econ. Round Table. Clubs: World Trade, St. Francis Yacht. Home: 2215 Beach St San Francisco CA 94123 Office: Boyden Internat Inc One Maritime Plaza Suite 1700 San Francisco CA 94111

HIRSCH, MICHELLE LINDA, psychiatrist; b. N.Y.C., June 12, 1947; d. Eli and Molly (Kinsler) H.; B.S. cum laude, CCNY, 1968; M.D., Upstate Med. Sch., Syracuse, N.Y., 1973; 2 children. Intern, Westchester div. N.Y. Med. Coll., 1974-75; resident in psychiatry, N.Y. State Psychiat. Inst., N.Y.C., 1975-79; fellow in child psychiatry Columbia-Presbyn. Hosp., 1978-80; asst. clin. prof. psychiatry Columbia U., N.Y.C., 1980—; staff Columbia-Presbyterian Hosp.; researcher, instr. U. Chgo., 1967-68. Diplomate Am. Bd. Psychiatry and Neurology. Mem. AMA, Am. Women's Med. Assn., Am. Psychiat. Assn., Am. Acad. Child Psychiatry, Phi Beta Kappa. Speaker profl. confs. in field. Office: 30 Lincoln Plaza New York NY 10023

HIRSCHBERG, VERA HILDA, writer; b. N.Y.C., Sept. 19, 1929; d. Bernard and Minnie (Margolis) Lieberman; m. Peter Hirschberg, Aug. 21, 1949; children: Karen Hirschberg Tuso, Paul. BJ, Hunter Coll., 1950. Staff writer Pacific Stars and Stripes, Tokyo, 1956-64; corr. Newsweek, Guatemala, 1964-65; transp. staff writer N.Y. Jour. Commerce, Washington, 1969-70; transp. editor Nat. Jour. Mag., Washington, 1970-72; dir. women's programs, presdl. speechwriter The White Ho., Washington, 1972-74; dir. tech. transfer HUD, Washington, 1974-75; dep. spl. asst. to Sec. Pub. Affairs Dept. Treasury, Washington, 1975-77; press. sec. U.S. Sen. William Roth, Jr., Washington, Jan. to Dec. 1977; editorial cons. various govt. and non-govt. clients 1977-78; pub. affairs dir. White Ho. Conf. on Library and Info. Services, 1978-80; sr. writer, adminstr.'s speechwriter NASA, Washington, 1980—. Editor: Israel at the Polls, 1977; author numerous newspaper and mag. articles. Recipient Outstanding Service Citation The White Ho., 1973, Meritorious Service award Dept. Treasury, 1977, Exceptional Performance award NASA, 1982. Mem. Exec. Women in Govt. (founding mem. 1973), Zionist Orgn. Am. Republican. Jewish. Office: NASA Hdqrs Code LM 400 Maryland Ave SW Washington DC 20546

HIRSCHMAN, ELIZABETH CALDWELL, marketing educator; b. Kingsport, Tenn., May 21, 1950; d. John Richard and Virginia (Carter) Caldwell; m. Raymond Hirschman, Mar. 3, 1973; children: Alixandra Chase, Anne Carter. BA, U. Ga. 1971; MBA, Ga. State U., 1974, PhD, 1977. Advt. asst. Eastman-Kodak, N.Y.C., 1971; advt. writer J.C. Penney Co., N.Y.C., 1971-73; market research mgr. Rich's Dept. Stores, Atlanta, 1974-77; asst. prof. bus. adminstrn. U. Pitts., 1977-78; asst. prof. mktg. NYU, N.Y.C., 1978-81, assoc. prof. mktg., 1981-87; prof. mktg. Rutgers U., 1988—; editor Jour. of Retailing, 1980-83, assoc. dir. Inst. of Retail Mgmt., 1978-83; cons. AT&T, N.J., 1980; cons. NCR Corp., Ohio, 1979. Contbr. articles to profl. jours. Recipient George Malanos award Ga. State U., Atlanta, 1974. Fellow Am. Mktg. Assn. (v.p. edn. div. 1985-86); mem. Assn. Consumer Research (program chmn. 1984, treas. 1985), Am. Inst. of Decision Scis., Am. Psychol. Assn. (local div.), Ops. Research Soc. Am., Phi Kappa Phi, Beta Gamma Sigma, Kappa Tau Alpha. Democrat. Presbyterian.

HIRSH, MARY MARGARET, dentist; b. Milw., Oct. 22, 1956; d. Clifford William and Irene Mary (Janes) H.; m. Craig Jeffrey Madsen, July 25, 1981. BS, U. Wisc., 1978; DDS, Marquette U., 1982. Dentist Madsen and Hirsch Family Dentistry, Madison, 1985—, 1985—. Area dir. Quest Seminars Internat., Reno, 1985—. Mem. ADA, Wisc. Dental Assn., Dane County Dental Assn., Am. Assn. Functional Orthodontics, Acad. Gen. Dentistry, Ind. Dentists Am. (bd. dirs. Madison chpt., 1987-89). Roman Catholic. Lodge: Toastmasters. Office: Madsen and Hirsch Family Dentists 6313 Odana Rd Madison WI 53719

HIRSHFIELD, PEARL, artist; b. Chgo., July 5, 1922; d. Louis and Anna (Nissenson) Belly; m. Hyman J. Hirshfield, Dec. 17, 1944; children:Leslie, Laura, Deborah, Jo-Anne. BA, Sch. of Art Inst., Chgo., 1979; AA, Herzl Jr. Coll.; student, Northwestern U. Curator, Midwest Artists for Peace, Chgo., 1967; co-curator art works, Peace March, 1982; organizer, Midwest Arts Festival, Chgo. Author: Conspiracy The Artist as Witness, 1972; film coordinator, Peace Prodns., 1983; creator, organizer Godine Press Art Portfolio, 1972; contb. articles to jours. and newsletters. Organizer, Peace Ctr., Evanston, 1958, bd. mem., 1958-60; co-chmn., organizer, Peace Walk, 1982; coordinator Peace March, N.Y.C., 1982; mem. planning com., Art for a Nuclear Freeze, Chgo., 1983. Recipient scholarship Columbia Coll.; prize Whirlpool Found. Sculpture Competition, 1986; grantee Ill. Arts Council, 1984, grantee tech. assistance Ill. Arts Council, 1983; fellow Ill. Arts Council, 1986. Mem. Nat. Mus. Women in Arts (charter), Chgo. Artists' Coalition, Women's Caucus for Art, Physicians for Social Responsibility, Women's Internat. League for Peace and Freedom. Home and Office: 1333 Ridge Ave Evanston IL 60201

HIRSHMAN, KATHLEEN, former corporate sales executive; b. N.Y.C., June 25, 1953; d. Arthur Anthony and Eleanor Edith (Wray) Walsh; m. Stanley Paul Hirshman. Student, Western Conn. State U., 1986, DePaul U., 1987—. Sec. to gen. mgr. GATX Corp., N.Y.C., 1973-78; sec. Mobil Oil Co., N.Y.C., 1978; sec. Union Tank Car Co., N.Y.C., 1978-79, customer service rep., 1979-82; sales service rep. Union Tank Car Co., Greenwich, Conn., 1982-86; mgr. Util-I-Fax div. Union Tank Car Co., Chgo., 1986-88, ret. Republican. Office: Union Tank Car Co 111 W Jackson Blvd Chicago IL 60604

HIRSON, ESTELLE, retired educator; b. Bayonne, N.J.; d. Morris and Bertha (Rubinstein) Hirson; student UCLA, U. So. Calif., summers 1949-59, San Francisco, summer 1955, U. Hawaii, 1955; B.E., San Francisco State U., 1965. Tchr. High St. Homes Sch., Oakland, Calif., 1949-54, Prescott Sch., 1955-60, Ralph Bunche Sch., 1960-72; owner Puzzle-Gram Co., Los Angeles, 1946-49; pres. Major Automobile Co., 1948-60. Chpt. v.p. City of Hope, San Francisco, 1962-63; bd. dirs. Sinai-Duarte Nat. Med. Center, 1946-50, also parliamentarian, life mem. Mem. NEA, Calif., Oakland, Los Angeles tchrs. assns., Sigma Delta Tau. Democrat. Mem. Order Eastern Star; Scottish Rite Women's Assn. (v.p. Los Angeles 1982). Rights to ednl. arithmetic game Find the Answer 1948, 51. Home: 8670 Burton Way Apt 328 Los Angeles CA 90048

HIRST, WILMA ELIZABETH, consulting educational psychologist; b. Shenandoah, Iowa; d. James H. and Lena (Donahue) Ellis; m. Clyde Henry Hirst (dec. Nov. 1969); 1 dau., Donna Jean (Mrs. Alan Robert Goss). A.B. in Elementary Edn., Colo. State Coll., 1948, Ed.D. in Ednl. Psychology, 1954; M.A. in Psychology, U. Wyo., 1951. Elem. tchr., Cheyenne, Wyo., 1945-49, remedial reading instr., 1949-54; assoc. prof. edn., dir. campus sch. Nebr. State Tchrs. Coll., Kearney, 1954-56; sch. psychologist, head dept. spl. edn. Cheyenne (Wyo.) pub. schs., 1956-57, sch. psychologist, guidance coordinator, 1957-66, dir. research and spl. projects, 1966-76, also pupil personnel, 1973-84; pvt. cons., 1984—; vis. asst. prof. U. So. Calif., summer 1957, Omaha U., summer 1958, U. Okla., summers 1959, 60; vis. assoc. prof. U. Nebr., 1961, U. Wyo., summer 1962, 64, extension div., Kabul, Afghanistan, 1970, Catholic U., Goias, Brazil, 1974; investigator HEW, 1965-69; prin. investigator effectiveness of spl. edn., 1983—; participant seminar Russian Press Women and Am. Fedn. Press Women, Moscow and Leningrad, 1973. Sec.-treas. Laramie County Council Community Services, 1962; mem. speakers bur., mental health orgn.; active Little Theatre, 1936-60, Girl Scout Leaders Assn., 1943-50; mem. Adv. Council on Retardation to Gov.'s Commn.; mem., past sec. Wyo. Bd. Psychologist Examiners, vice chmn., 1965-74; chmn. Mayor's v.p. Model Cities Program, 1969; mem. Gov.'s Com. Jud. Reform, 1972; adv. council Div. Exceptional Children, Wyo. Dept. Edn., 1974; mem. transit adv. group City of Cheyenne, 1974; bd. dirs. Wyo. Children's Home Soc., treas., 1978-84, sec. 1984—; del. Internat. Conv. Ptnrs. of Ams., Jamaica, 1987 ; bd. dirs. Goodwill Industries Wyo., chmn., 1981-83; mem. Wyo. exec. com. Partners of Americas, 1970-86; ambassador to Honduras, summer 1979; del., voice moderator bd. deacons Friendship Force ambassador to Honduras, 1988; chmn. bd. SE Wyo. Mental Health Center; elder 1st Presbyn. Ch., Cheyenne, 1978—; chmn. adv. assessment com. Wyo. State Office Handicapped Children, 1980, 81; mem. allocations com. United Way of Laramie County. Named Woman of Year, Cheyenne Bus. and Profl. Women, 1974. Diplomate Am. Bd. Profl. Psychology. Fellow Internat. Council Psychologists (chmn. Wyo. div. 1980-85); mem. AAUP, Am. Assn. State Psychology Bds. (sec.-treas. 1970-73), Am., Wyo. (pres. 1962-63) psychol. assns., Laramie County (bd. mem., corr. sec. 1963-69, pres.), Wyo. mental health assns. (bd. mem.), Internat. Platform Assn., Am. Ednl. Research Assn., Assn. Supervision and Curriculum Devel., Assn. for Gifted (Wyo. pres. 1964-65), Am. Personnel and Guidance Assn., Am. Assn. Sch. Adminstrs., NEA (life, participant seminar to China 1978), AAUW, Cheyenne Assn. Spl. Personnel and Prins. (pres. 1964-65, mem. exec. bd. 1972-76), Nat. Fedn. Press Women (dir. 1979—), DAR (vice regent Cheyenne chpt. 1975-77), AARP (state coordinator 1988—, preretirement planning specialist 1986—), Psi Chi, Kappa Delta Pi, Pi Lambda Theta, Alpha Delta Kappa (pres. Wyo. Alpha 1965-66). Presbyn. Lodge Soc. Colonial Dames XVII Century, Order Eastern Star, Daus. of Nile. Clubs: Wyo. Press Women, Zonta (pres. Cheyenne 1965-66, treas. dist. 12 1974). Author: Know Your School Psychologist, 1963; Effective School Psychology for School Administrators, 1980. Home and Office: 3458 Green Valley Rd Cheyenne WY 82001

HIRT-KRAVETSKY, PATRICIA CAROL, brokerage house executive; b. Jersey City, Apr. 16, 1948; d. Harold James and Gladys (Nitsch) Hirt; B.A., Upsala Coll., 1969; advanced cert. Am. Inst. Banking, 1973; M.B.A., Fairleigh Dickinson U., 1974. Asst. treas. Bank of N.Y., N.Y.C., 1975-77, asst. v.p., 1977-79, v.p., 1979-80; investment broker Garvin Guybutler, N.Y.C., 1980-83, asst. v.p., 1983-87; v.p. 1987—. Mem. Fin. Women's Assn. Clubs: Binghamton Racquet, Order Eastern Star. Home: 515 Forest Ct Rivervale NJ 07675

HIRYOK, KATHRYN ANN, fundraising organizer; b. Warren, Ohio, June 10, 1942; d. Edward J. and Mary K. (Namton) Lukco; m. Paul Joseph Hiryok, June 16, 1961 (dec. Apr. 1971); children—Janine Marie, Daniel Paul. B.F.A. candidate Kent State U., 1978—. Office mgr. Warren Otologic Group, Ohio, 1963-71, exec. asst., 1971-74, fin. dir., 1975—; property mgr. Northmar Ctr., Warren, 1984—; asst. nat. dir. Israel Tennis Ctrs., N.Y.C., 1975—. Founder/organizer Warren Women's Network, 1981-85; bd. dirs. Warren Family Service Assn., 1984-87, chmn. pub. relations, 1985, v.p., 1986; trustee Trumbull County United Way, 1986-87; mem. Trumbull Art Guild. Mem. Nat. Assn. Female Execs., Am. Assn. Editorial Cartoonists (hon.). Jewish. Lodge: Hadassah (bd. dirs., chmn. major gifts). Home: 160 Winter Ln Cortland OH 44410 Office: Israel Tennis Ctrs 3893 E Market St Warren OH 44484

HIRZEL, NANCY JEANNE, social worker; b. Darby, Pa., Mar. 5, 1948; d. Edwin F. and Irene Doris (Bender) H. BA, Marshall U., 1970; MSW, Fla. State U., 1977. Cert. social worker, La. Social service worker Orange Meml. Hosp., Orlando, Fla., 1971-75; dir. social service New Orleans Home for Incurables, 1977; dir. family counseling Sara Mayo Hosp., New Orleans, 1978-79; coordinator family counseling Metairie (La.) Gen. Hosp., 1979-80; social worker I, II, III Office of Human Devel., New Orleans, 1980-81, social work supr. I, 1981-83; social worker III E. Jefferson Mental Health, Metairie, 1983—. Mem. Nat. Assn. Social Workers (diplomate), NOW. Home: 1010 Lake Ave #B24 Metairie LA 70005 Office: E Jefferson Mental Health 111 N Causeway Blvd Metairie LA 70004

HITCHCOCK, KAREN RUTH, biology educator, university dean; b. Mineola, N.Y., Feb. 10, 1943; d. Roy Clinton and Ruth (Wardell) H. BS in Biology, St. Lawrence U., 1964; PhD in Anatomy, U. Rochester, 1968. Postdoctoral fellow in Pulmonary Cell Biology, Webb-Waring Inst. Med. Research, 1968-70; asst. prof. dept. anatomy Tufts U. Sch. Medicine, Boston, 1970-75, assoc. prof. dept. anatomy, 1975-80, assoc. prof., acting chmn. dept. anatomy, 1976-78, assoc. prof., chmn. dept. anatomy, 1978-80, prof., chmn. dept. anatomy and cellular biology, 1980-82, George A. Bates prof. histology, chmn. dept. anatomy and cellular biology, 1982-85; prof. dept. cell biology and anatomy Tex. Tech U. Health Scis. Ctr., assoc. dean Tex. Tech U. Sch. Medicine, Lubbock, 1985-87, vice chancellor research, dean Grad. Coll., prof. cell biology and anatomy U. Ill., Chgo., 1987—; mem. adv. com. NIH, Nat. Bd. Med. Examiners, 1983-85. Mem. Am. Assn. Anatomy (chmn., exec. council 1979-81), Am. Assn. Anatomists (exec. com. 1981-85, v.p. 1986-88), Nat. Bd. of Med. Examiners, Am. Assn. Anatomy Chmn. (nominating com. 1982-83). Home: 505 N Lake Shore Dr Chicago IL 60611 Office: U Ill Chgo Grad Coll Chicago IL 60680

HITCHCOCK, PATTI ANN, marketing executive; b. Sioux Falls, S.D., Mar. 6, 1945; d. Robert Otto Steineke and Mavis Elaine (Swenson) Cossel; m. William Hitchcock, Jan. 20, 1965 (div. 1979); 1 child, Sean Ralph. AA, Foothills Coll., Palo Altos, Calif., 1965. Dept. supr. San Jose (Calif.) Med. Clinic, 1963-69; gen. mgr. Pacific Health Services Med. Group, 1969-72; dir. ops., mktg. Newport Profl. Clin. Labs., 1972-79; pres., dir. sales Newport Clin. Lab., 1979; mgr., paralegal Brazelton Law Firm, 1980-83; dir. mktg. Allied Physicians, Torrance, Calif., 1984-87; dir. services STAT-PAK Pharms., Santa Fe Springs, Calif., 1986—; exec. v.p. mktg. Hanlester Network, Santa Ana, Calif., 1987—; cons. in field., Los Angeles, Orange County, Calif., 1986—. Host (TV talk show) For Your Information, 1987. Home: 711 Pacific Coast Hwy #322 Huntington Beach CA 92648

HITE, CATHARINE LEAVEY, orchestra manager; b. Boston, Oct. 1, 1924; d. Edmond Harrison and Ruth Farrington Leavey; B.A., Coll. William and Mary, 1945; m. Robert Atkinson Hite, Aug. 28, 1948; children—Charles Harrison, Patricia Hite Barton, Catharine Hite Dunn. Restoration guide Williamsburg Restoration, 1944-45; asst. edn. dept. Honolulu Acad. Arts, 1945-46; sec., tour guide edn. dept. office chief curator Nat. Gallery Art, 1946-48; opera liason/coordinator Honolulu Symphony, 1972-73, asst. to gen. mgr., 1973-75, community devel. dir./opera coordinator, 1975-77, dir. ops./opera prodn. coordinator, 1977-79, orch. mgr., 1979-84, mem. exec. com., 1965-69, pres. women's assn., 1965-66; com. chmn., opera assn. chmn. Hawaii Opera Theatre, 1966-69. Mem. W. R. Farrington Scholarship Com., 1977-82, chmn., 1983-87; mem. community arts panel State Found. Culture and the Arts, 1982, State Found. Music and Opera, 1984. Mem. Jr. League, Phi Beta Kappa. Episcopalian.

HITT, MARY JANE, university administrator; b. Morgantown, W.Va., Sept. 17, 1947; d. James Alfred and Ruth Virginia (Kinney) Ashburn; m. William Herbert Hitt, July 31, 1971; children: Nathaniel Patterson, Amanda Ruth. BA, W.Va. U., 1969; AM, Boston U., 1971; EdD, W.Va. U., 1988. Instr. Waynesburg (Pa.) Coll., 1971, W.Va. U., Morgantown, 1971-72, DeCarteret Coll., Mandeville, Jamaica, 1972-73; compensation analyst W.Va. U., Morgantown, 1978-80, asst. to v.p., 1981-83, asst. to pres., 1984-86, spl. asst. to pres., 1986—. Bd. dirs. Westminster Found., Morgantown, 1983—, southwestern dist. Girl Scouts of U.S., Pitts., 1986—. Mem. Soc. Coll. and Univ. Planning (state coordinator membership com. 1985-87), Am. Assn. Higher Edn., So. Assn. Instnl. Research, Phi Delta Kappa, Phi Beta Kappa. Presbyterian. Home: 353 Rotary St Morgantown WV 26505 Office: WVa U Office of Pres 105 Stewart Hall Morgantown WV 26506-6001

HITTNER, CAROL BRENNER, editorand chief; b. N.Y.C., Aug. 1, 1942; d. Frank and Ida (Josephy) Brenner; m. Steven Bryan Hittner, July 6, 1963; children: Elyse Dawn, Stacy Lynn. AA in Dental Hygiene, N.Y.C. Tech. Coll., 1963; BS in Profl. Studies, Barry U., 1987. Cert. counselor; cert. nutritionist. Prin., owner Covering Dental Hygiene Service, N.Y.C., 1973-80; prin., operator La Cantina Restaurant, Melbourne, Fla., 1980-81; owner, editor in chief Golden Years Mag., Melbourne, 1981—. Contbr. articles to Golden Years Mag. Pres. Temple Beth Shalom, Emerson, N.J., 1976-78; v.p. Emerson Jewish Ctr., 1977-80; youth dir. Temple Beth Shalom, Satellite Beach, Fla., 1981-83; program dir. Women's Networking, Melbourne, 1984-85. Named to Who's How and Why of Successful Fla. Women Currier Davis Pub., 1985. Mem. Fla. Mag. Assn., Brevard Women's Networking, Nat. Assn. Female Execs. Office: Golden Years Magazine 233 E New Haven Ave Melbourne FL 32902-0537

HIVELY, EVELYN THOMAS HELMICK, association executive; b. McKeesport, Pa., July 20, 1928; s. Samuel Blair and Evelyn (Descaunets) Thomas; B.S. (Buhl Found. scholar 1946-50, Andrew Carnegie scholar 1948-50), Carnegie Mellon U., 1950; M.A., U. Miami, 1964, Ph.D., 1969; m. Robert William Hively, June 19, 1972; children—Jon Sommer Helmick, Jennifer Thomas Helmick, Melinda Blair Helmick. Tchr. French and English, Pub. Schs., New Wilmington, Pa., 1950-52; instr. humanities U. Miami, 1964-69, asst. prof., 1969-73, asso. prof. English, 1973-77, dir. Am. studies, 1975-77; acad. dean Salem Coll., Winston-Salem, N.C., 1977-81; v.p. acad. affairs Western Mont. Coll., Dillon, 1982-85; v.p. acad. programs, Am. Assn. State Colls. and Univs., 1985—. Rockefeller Found. fellow, 1963-64. Mem. MLA, Am. Studies Assn., Fla. Coll. English Assn. Contbr. articles to profl. jours. Home: 2836 Kelly Sq Vienna VA 22180 Office: Am Assn of State Coll and U 1 Dupont Circle Washington DC 20036

HIXON, FRANCES MAY, researcher, author; b. Ewington, Ohio, May 15, 1925; d. Seth Almira and Emma Pearl (Libby) Welch; m. John Edwin Hixon, Sept. 4, 1948; children: Barbara Lynne Myers, Mary Jo Hixon. BS, Rio Grande Coll., 1975. Free-lance photographer Jackson, Ohio, 1940—; free-lance writer Jackson, 1978—; tchr. Vinton County Schs., McArthur, Ohio, 1970-83; researcher, editor Poplar Row, Jackson, 1983—; dir. first families Jackson County, 1985—. Author: Cemetry Inscriptions, 1978, Naturalizations and Declarations of Intent, 1980, Marriages of Jackson County, 1982, Wilkesville Township History, 1982, Veterans of Jackson County, 1983, Soldiers of Jackson County, 1983, Annals of Jackson County, 1986, Marriages of Vinton County, 1986, The Last Hanging, 1987, Soldiers of Vinton County, 1987, History of Clinton Township, 1987, Wellston: A History, 1987; compiler various biographical publs. Mem. Ohio Geneal. Soc. (v.p. Jackson chpt. 1982, pres. 1983). Democrat. Methodist. Home: 3289 Petersburg Rd Jackson OH 45640

HIXSON, SHEILA ELLIS, state legislator; b. L'Anse, Mich., Feb. 9, 1933; divorced; children: Denise, Lynn, Andy, Todd. AB, No. Mich. U., 1953. Tchr. Head Start; campaign mgr., aide Congressman William Ford, Mich., 1963-64; adminstrv. aide to state senator 1965-66, legal aide to sec. of Dem. Nat. Conv., 1966-76; mem. Md. Ho. of Dels., Annapolis, 1976—, mem. environ. matters com. Chair task force on child abuse and neglect, joint com. on fed.-state relations, lottery com.; mem. gov.'s task force on time-sharing, Montgomery County Dem. State Cen. Com. Mem. Nat. Assn. Sunday Sch. Instrs., Nat. Profl. and Bus. Women's Orgn., Women's Polit. Caucus, Plowmen and Fishermen, NOW. Home: 1008 Broadmore Circle Silver Spring MD 21401 Office: House Office Bldg Room 221 Rowe Blvd Annapolis MD 21401

HIXSON, SUSAN HARVILL, chemistry educator; b. Orange, N.J., Sept. 26, 1944; 2 children. B.S. in Chemistry, U. Mich., 1965; Ph.D. in Biochemistry, U. Wis.-Madison, 1970. Instr. chemistry Boston U., 1969-70; research assoc. U. Mass., Amherst, 1970-73; asst. prof. chemistry Mt. Holyoke Coll., South Hadley, Mass., 1973-79, assoc. prof. chemistry, 1979-86, prof., 1986—; vis. prof. dept. biochemistry U. N.C., Chapel Hill, 1980, dept. biochemistry, molecular biology U. Tex. Health Sci. Ctr., Houston, 1986-87, vis. scientist, dept. biochemistry, molecular biology. NIH fellow, 1971-72. Mem. Am. Chem. Soc., Am. Soc. Biol. Chemists, AAAS, Am. Soc. Biochemistry, Molecular Biology, Council on Undergrad. Research, Assn. Women in Sci., Sigma Xi. Address: Mount Holyoke Coll Dept Chemistry South Hadley MA 01075

HLAVA, MARJORIE MAXINE KIMMEL, information scientist. Student, U. Minn., 1967; BS in Botany and Secondary Edn., U. Wis., 1970; postgrad., U. N.Mex., 1974-76. Info. scientist Tech. Application Ctr. U. N.Mex., Albuquerque, 1975-77, mgr. info., 1977-79; pres., chief ops. officer Access Innovations, Inc., Albuquerque, 1978—; dir. info. Nat. Energy Info. Ctr. affiliate U.S. Dept. Energy, U. N.Mex., 1976-78, Albuquerque, bd. dirs. Documentation Assocs. Inc. Mem. editorial bd. Info. Services and Use, 1983, Database Update, 1984; tech. columnist ONline Re. 1978-81, Info. Today, 1984; contbr. articles to profl. jours. Mem. Spl. Libraries Assn. (chmn. spl. projects com. 1976, employment com. 1978-79, membership com. 1978-79, nominations com. 1983, v.p. local chpt. 1979-80, pres. 1980-81, chmn. info. techs. div. 1984-85, editor info. techs. div. pub., nat. nominations com. 1988), S.W. Library Assn. (chmn. online bibliographic user group 1976-79), N.Mex. Library Assn. (publicity com. 1981, chmn. nominations com. 1981, chmn. online roundtable 1979, state fair com. 1981-82), Greater Albuquerque Library Assn., Western Info. Network Energy (chmn. edn. com. 1978-81, treas. 1980-84, bd. dirs. 1978-83), N.Mex. Online User Group (chmn. 1976-79), Assn. Info. and Dissemination Ctrs. (pres. 1985-86, 86-87, chmn. 1985, mem. various coms.), N.Mex. Technet Adv. Council, Am. Soc. Info. Sci. (bd. dirs. 1986—). Office: Access Innovations PO Box 40130 Albuquerque NM 87196

HLOZEK, CAROLE DIANE QUAST, business executive; b. Dallas, Apr. 17, 1959; d. Robert E. and Bonnie (Wootton) Quast. BS, Tex. A&M U., 1982, BBA, 1982. Internal auditor Brown & Root Inc., Houston, 1982-84; asst. controller Wilson Supply Co., Houston, 1984-86, sr. acctg. supr., GC Services, Houston, 1987-88; sr. accountant Am. Med. Internat., Houston, 1988—. Mem. Houston Zool. Soc., Nat. Wildlife Assn., Nat. Geog. Soc., Am. Mus. Natural History, Nat. Assn. Female Execs., Assn. Former Students Tex. A&M U., Houston Livestock Show and Rodeo. Lutheran. Home: 8034 Log Hollow Houston TX 77040 Office: Am Med Internat Houston Acctg Office 515 West Greens Rd Suite 1000 Houston TX 77067

HMIELESKI, CAROL LYDIA, local government official; b. Perth Amboy, N.J., June 7, 1950; d. Alexander and Rose (Brozozowski) Shumny; 1 child, K.J. B.A., Rider Coll., 1972; M.A., Rutgers U., 1984. Tchr., South Amboy Bd. Edn., N.J., 1972-73, St. Stephens Sch., Perth Amboy, N.J., 1974-76, St. Theresa's Sch., Linden, N.J., 1976-80; registered pub. purchasing official; ins. analyst The Children's Pl., Pinebrook, N.J., 1980-83; purchasing agt. Borough of Carteret, N.J., 1983—; notary public, State of N.J., 1983—; continuing edn. tchr. Woodbridge Bd. Edn., N.J., 1979—. Mem. Nat. Inst. Govtl. Purchasing (treas. 1984—), Govtl. Purchasing Assn., Carteret Police Athletic League. Roman Catholic. Avocation: antique collecting.

HO, NINA, restaurant executive; b. Hong Kong, Aug. 13, 1953; d. Hsin Y. and Chen Y. (Wu) H. BS, U. San Francisco, 1975. Cert. real estate broker, Calif. Mgr. Goodman Woodworking Corp., Singapore, 1975-81; owner Mr. Chow's Restaurant, San Diego, 1987—; with real estate sales Beach & Bay Realtors, La Jolla, Calif., 1982—. Mem. Nat. Assn. Realtors. Home: 8238 Caminito Modena La Jolla CA 92037 Office: 4619 Convoy St #F San Diego CA 92111

HOADLEY, IRENE BRADEN (MRS. EDWARD HOADLEY), librarian; b. Hondo, Tex., Sept. 26, 1938; d. Andrew Henry and Theresa Lillian (Lebold) Braden; m. Edward Hoadley, Feb. 21, 1970. B.A., U. Tex., 1960; A.M.L.S., U. Mich., 1961, Ph.D., 1967; M.A., Kans. State U., 1965. Cataloger Sam Houston State Tchrs. Coll. Library, Huntsville, Tex., 1961-62; head circulation dept. Kans. State U. Library, Manhattan, 1962-64; grad. asst. U. Mich. Dept. of Library Sci., 1964-66; librarian gen. adminstrn. and research Ohio State U. Libraries, Columbus, 1966-73; asst. dir. libraries adminstrv. services Ohio State U. Libraries, 1973-74; dir. of libraries Tex. A. and M. U. Library, College Station, Tex., 1974—; dir. Higher Edn. Act Inst. Quantitative Methods in Librarianship, Ohio State U., summer 1969; instr. inst. U. Calif. at San Diego, 1970, summer; Mem. steering com. Gov's Conf. on Library and Info. Services, Ohio, 1973-74, joint chairperson, 1974; mem. adv. com. Library Services and Constrn. Act Cuyahoga County Pub. Library, Cleve., 1973. Author: (with others) Physiological Factors Relating to Terrestrial Altitutes: A Bibliography, 1968; Editor: (with Alice S. Clark) Quantitative Methods in Librarianship: Standards, Research, Management, 1972; Contbr. (with Alice S. Clark) articles to profl. jours. Recipient Scarecrow Press award for library lit., 1971; Distinguished Alumnus award Sch. Library Sci., U. Mich., 1976. Mem. ALA, Ohio Library Assn. (chmn. constn. com. 1967-68, chmn. election tellers com. 1969, asst. gen. chmn. local conf. com. 1969-70, sec. 1970-71, v.p., pres.-elect 1971-72, chmn. budget advisory com. 1971-72, pres. 1972-73, bd. dirs. 1970-75), Tex. Library Assn. (com. on White House conf. 1975-77, vice chmn., chmn. coll. and univ. div. 1977-78, exec. bd. 1978-81), Assn. Research Libraries (bd. dirs. 1978-81, search com. for exec. dir. 1980), Midwest Fedn. Library Assns. (exec. bd. 1973-74, chairperson program com. 1974), Online Computer Library Ctr. (pres. User's Council 1983-84, 84-85, bd. trustees 1984—), Phi Kappa Phi, Phi Alpha Theta, Pi Lambda Theta, Beta Phi Mu, Phi Delta Gamma. Home: Route 5 Box 1048 College Station TX 77840

HOAGLAND, PAMELA REDINGTON, educational consultant, administrator; b. Phoenix, June 2, 1937; d. George Appleton and Margaret Tweed (Rae) H. B.A., U. Ariz., 1959; MEd in Reading Edn., 1965, EdD in Reading and Psychology, 1973. Tchr. Tucson Unified Sch. Dist., 1959-73, asst. dir. instruction, reading, lang. arts, library services, 1980—; co-founder, co-dir. Learning Devel. Ctr., Tucson, 1970-74; curriculum specialist and supr. Pima County Spl. Edn. Coop., Tucson, 1973-76; ednl. cons. Redington Cons. Corp., Tucson, 1970—; founder, pres. Redinton Cons. Corp.; lectr. in field; bd. dirs. Behavior Assocs. Chmn. Ariz. Right to Read Council, 1978-80; bd. dirs. Tucson Westside Coalition, 1979-80, bd. dirs. Friends of Tucson Pub. Library, v.p., 1984—, pres. 1986-88; edn. supr. Grace Episcopal Ch., 1965-67; pres. Tucson Area Reading Council, 1968; mem. alumni bd. U. Ariz. Coll. Edn., 1984—, pres. 1986-88. Mem. Nat. Council Tchrs. English, Internat. Reading Assn. (field cons.), Ariz. State Reading Council (pres. 1969), Assn. Supervision and Curriculum Devel., Tucson Adminstrs., Inc. (v.p. 1987-88, pres. 1988-89), Alpha Delta Kappa, Pi Delta Kappa (Disting. lecture series award 1978), Pi Beta Phi. Democrat. Contbr. articles to profl. publs. Office: 2025 E Winsett St Tucson AZ 85719

HOANG, JOY GONZALES, hotel executive; b. Carmel, Calif., Dec. 30, 1949; d. Jose Quijano and Caridad Rodriquez (Martinez) Gonzales; m. Jack Minh Hoang, July 16, 1968 (dec. Aug. 1987); children: Jolene, Mario, Jack, Cherie. Student pvt. schs., Carmel and Monterey, Calif. Front desk mgr. Royal Inn, Monterey, 1972-74; asst. reservations mgr. Hyatt Hotel, Monterey, 1977-78; catering services rep. Casa Munras Hotel, Monterey, 1977-78; reservations mgr. Doubletree Hotel, Monterey, 1980-82, front office mgr., 1982-84, dir. catering, 1984-87, rooms div. mgr., 1987, dir. human resources, 1987—. Chmn. parent adv. council Monterey Sch. Dist., 1984-86; active Leadership Monterey Peninsula. Mem. Nat. Assn. Female Execs., Cen. Coast Personnel Network. Democrat. Roman Catholic. Lodge: Soroptimist. Home: 590 Harcourt Ave Seaside CA 93955 Office: Doubletree Hotel 2 Portola Plaza Monterey CA 93940

HOBAN DOWNEY, KITTY LYN, accountant; b. Dallas, Nov. 20, 1956; d. Eugene David and Peggy Jo (Todd) Fabricius; m. William Patrick Hoban, May 8, 1976 (div. 1982); m. Robert James Downey; stepchildren: Robert J. Jr., Randall Joseph. BS, Calif. Poly St. U., San Luis Obispo, 1978. CPA, Calif. Staff acct. Lawrence E. Baur, Jr., CPA, San Luis Obispo, Calif., 1977-78; staff acct., mgr. Knight, Towle, Sage & Johnson, CPAs, San Luis Obispo, 1978-83; prin. Kitty Hoban, CPA, San Luis Obispo, 1983-86, Commerce Connection, Creston, Calif., 1986; chief fin. officer, head tax services San Luis Obispo County Farm Supply Co., 1987—; counselor Sr. Corps of Retired Execs., San Luis Obispo; treas., pres. dir. Windermere Homeowners Assn. 1983-86; lectr. Calif. Poly State U., San Luis Obispo. Mem. Am. Inst. of CPA's, Nat. Soc. of Accts. for Coops, Calif Soc. of CPAs (active Central Coast Chpt. 1980—), Soc. of Calif. Accts. (pres., mem. steering com. Central Coast Chpt. 1983-86), San Luis Obispo C. of C. (com. mem. 1983-87). Republican. Club: Quota (San Luis Obispo) (pres. 1984-85, active 1980-87). Office: San Luis Obispo County Farm Supply Co 675 Tank Farm Rd PO Box 111 San Luis Obispo CA 93406

HOBART, BILLIE, college educator, consultant; b. Pitts., Apr. 19, 1935; d. Harold James Billingsley and Rose Stephanie (Sladack) Green; m. W.C.H. Hobart, July 20, 1957 (div. 1967); 1 child, Rawson W. BA in English, U. Calif., Berkeley, 1967, EdD, 1988; MA in Psychology, Sonoma State U., 1972. Cert. tchr., Calif. Asst. prof. Coll. Marin, Kentfield, Calif., 1969-78; freelance cons., writer 1969—; asst. prof. Contra Costa Coll., San Pablo, Calif., 1986—; pres. Calif. Visions Inc., Sausalito, Calif., 1986—. Author: (cookbook) Natural Sweet Tooth, 1974, (non-fiction) Expansion, 1972, Purposeful Self: Coherent Self, 1979; contbr. articles to profl. jours. Served with WAC, 1953-55. Mem. Nat. Assn. Female Execs., Phi Delta Kappa. Club: Commonwealth (San Francisco). Home and Office: 6503 Central El Cerrito CA 94530

HOBBS, ANN TODD, sales executive; b. Forrest City, Ark., Nov. 25, 1926; d. William Joe and Maudie (McGee) Todd; m. James Robert Hobbs, Mar. 29, 1948; children: Bardara Ray, Sandra Lynn Davis Hobbs, Brenda Onstott Hobbs. Student, Memphis U., 1948. Bookkeeper Forrest City (Ark.) Wholesale Grocery, 1949-51, Kimdell Wholesale Grocery, Ft. Worth, Tex., 1951-58, A. Brandt & Co., Ft. Worth, 1958-64; saleswoman A.L. Randall Co., Prairie View, Ill., 1964—; Speaker Richland Coll., Dallas, 1986-87. Vol. Al-Anon Drug Program, Ft. Worth, 1986-87; tchr. Beckspur Baptist Ch., Forrest City, 1949-51. Mem. Am. Acad. Florists, Tex. State Florists Assn. (wholesale dir. 1982-84, chair wholesale com., 1983-84, chair membership 1983-84, fin. com. 1986—, chair credit union 1981-87, chair convention 1987, pres. 1987-88), Ft. Worth Florists Assn. (sec. 1982-84). Republican. Baptist. Home: PO Box 211 Hurst TX 76053

HOBBS, JOAN PIZZO, data processing executive; b. Providence, Oct. 11, 1957; d. Ralph Edmund and Albina Margaret (Walsh) Pizzo; m. Walter Romeo Hobbs III, Nov. 22, 1979; children: Kelsey Mackensie, Spencer William. BS, BA, R.I. Coll., 1979; cert., Blake Programming Inst., 1980; MBA, Providence Coll., 1988. Lic. real estate broker, R.I. Substitute tchr., pub. schs. R.I., 1979-80; billing clk. Femic Inc., North Providence, R.I., 1980-81; software cons. I.P.L., Inc., Providence, R.I., 1981-84; programmer, analyst A.S.E. Services Inc., Woonsocket, R.I., 1984-85; mgr. data processing Builders Specialties, Pawtucket, R.I., 1985-88; system installation specialist UPS Software, Cranston, R.I., 1988—. Mem. Am. Congress Real Estate Investors, Nat. Assn. Female Execs., R.I. Real Estate Investors, Boston Computer Soc., Elmwood Found. Archtl. and Hist. Preservation. Home: 1049 Smithfield Ave Lincoln RI 02865 Office: UPS Software 1210 Pontiac Ave Cranston RI 02910

HOBBS, MARILYN MCGUIRE, sales executive, consultant; b. St. Paul, Nov. 1, 1934; d. William Ernest and Virginia (Cheely) Mears; m. Michael John McGuire, Dec. 26, 1955 (div. Sept. 1973); children: Mary Anderson, John McGuire, Margaret Prem; m. George Cannon Hobbs, July 22, 1984. BA, U. Minn., 1956. sec. bd. dirs. Lan-O-Sheen Inc., St. Paul, 1975—. Sec.-treas. Mar-Mac Inc., Bloomington, Minn., 1968-73; dir. sales and catering The Thunderbird Motel, Bloomington, 1973-81; nat. sales and mktg. mgr. Brutger Cos., St. Cloud, Minn., 1981-87; owner, pres. Marilyn McGuire Hobbs Inc Hospitality Cons., Bloomington, 1987—. Mem. Am. Bus. Assn., Nat. Tour Assn., Hotel Sales Mgmt. Assn., Am. Hotel Motel Assn., Travel Industry of Am., Sales and Mktg. Execs. Internat. (nat. officer. past local pres.), Minn. Exec. Women in Tourism, AAUW, Kappa Alpha Theta, Phi Sigma Epsilon. Club: Decathlon. Home and Office: 10543 Dupont Rd Bloomington MN 55431

HOBBS, NILA ALENE, mfg. co. exec.; b. Colorado Springs, Colo., Mar. 11, 1949; d. Harold Carl and Wilma Ella (French) H.; B.S. with high distinction, Colo. State U., 1971, M.B.A., 1973. Systems analyst Colo. div. Eastman Kodak Co., Windsor, 1974-80, sect. supr. systems devel., 1980-84, sr. systems analyst, 1984—. Mem. Am. Prodn. and Inventory Control Soc, Colo. State U. Alumni Assn., Phi Kappa Phi. Republican. Home: 1037 Parkview Dr Fort Collins CO 80525 Office: ISD Bldg C-42 Floor 3 Windsor CO 80551

HOBBS, SANDRA FORRESTER, hospital department manager, educational and wellness director; b. Spartanburg, S.C., Dec. 5, 1947; d. Grover Walter and Catherine Roberta (Barnett) Forrester; m. Stephen Howard Hobbs, Aug. 17, 1978; children: Ansley Catherine, Allen Forrester. BS in Nursing, Med., U. S.C., 1970; MS in Nursing, Med. Coll. Ga., 1976. RN, S.C., Ga. Staff nurse U. S.C., Charleston, S.C., 1970-72; sch. nurse Charleston County Sch. System, 1972-73; instr. Coll. Nursing Med. U. S.C., 1973-74; inservice instr. Talmadge Hosp., Augusta, Ga., 1974-76; asst. prof. Med. Coll. Ga., 1976-82; dir. family life ctr. St. Joseph Hosp., Augusta, 1982—; bd. dirs. N. Augusta Med. Ctr.; ednl. cons. So. Travel Co., Augusta, 1988. Author ednl. workshops: Childbirth Preparation, 1974, Our New Baby, 1983, Be Your Own Best Friend, 1984, You Make the Difference, 1987. 1st v.p. Hammond Hill PTA, N. Augusta, 1988—; chmn. role and status of women com. Grace Meth. Ch., N. Augusta, 1986—; bd. dirs. Girls Scouts of Am., Augusta; mem. Sr. Citizen Adv. com., 1984—, Augusta Coalition for Children and Youth, Leadership Augusta, 1983-84, Leaderhsip Augusta Alumnae Assn., 1984—, family life demostration project Office Adolescent Pregnancy Programs, HHS, 1987—. Recipient Outstanding Faculty award Med. Coll. Ga. Sch. Nursing, 1982; named to Outstanding Young Women in Am., 1983-84. Mem. Nat. Assn. Female Execs., Ga. Fedn. Profl. Health Educators, Nat. Alliance for the Mentally Ill. Republican. Club: N. Augusta Country. Home: 1418 Brookgreen Dr North Augusta SC 29841 Office: St Joseph Hosp 2260 Wrightsboro Rd Augusta GA 30910

HOBEN, SISTER MARIAN WILLIAM, college president; b. Coaldale, Pa. BA in English, Immaculata Coll., 1955; MA in English, Villanova U., 1961; PhD in English, U. Pa., 1968. Joined Servants of Immaculate Heart of Mary, Roman Cath. Ch. Elem. tchr. various schs., 1944-55; secondary tchr. various schs., 1955-60; faculty Immaculata (Pa.) Coll., 1960—, chmn. dept. English, 1971-74, dean coll. devel., 1973-78, acad. dean, 1978-82, pres., 1982—. Chair Gov.'s Citizen's Adv. Com., Pa., 1983-85. Recipient Outstanding Grad. English Dept. medal Villanova U. Grad. Sch., 1982, scroll Newcomen Soc., 1987. Mem. AAUW, Commn. for Ind. Colls. and Univs. (exec. and instl. research coms. 1983—), Pa. Assn. Colls. and Univs. (chair student relations com. 1984—), Nat. Council Tchrs. English, Alpha Sigma Lambda (Iota Kappa chpt.). Office: Immaculata Coll Office of the Pres Immaculata PA 19345

HOBERMAN, MARY ANN, writer, consultant; b. Stamford, Conn., Aug. 12, 1930; d. Milton Gilbert and Dorothy (Miller) Freedman; m. Norman Hoberman, Feb. 4, 1951; children—Diane Hoberman Louie, Perry, Charles, Margaret. B.A. magna cum laude, Smith Coll., 1951; M.A., Yale U., 1985, postgrad. in English lit. Adj. prof. Fairfield U., Conn., 1980-83; program coordinator C. G. Jung Ctr., N.Y.C., 1981; speaker, cons. in field, artist-in-the schs., 1955—. Author children's books: All My Shoes Come in Two's, 1957; How Do I Go?, 1958; Hello and Good-by, 1959; What Jim Knew, 1963; Not Enough Beds for the Babies, 1965; A Little Book of Little Beasts, 1973; The Raucous Auk, 1973; The Looking Book, 1973; Nuts to You and Nuts to Me, 1974; I Like Old Clothes, 1976; Bugs, 1976; A House is a House for Me, 1978; Yellow Butter, Purple Jelly, Red Jam, Black Bread, 1981; The Cozy Book, 1982 (Am. Book award 1983). Contbr. poems to So. Poetry Rev., Small Pond, Harper's Mag.; contbr. children's poems to numerous anthologies, textbooks, mags., U.S. and abroad; contbr. articles to N.Y. Times, Nutmegger Mag., Boston Globe, 1978-86. Active Greenwich Citizens for Nuclear Freeze, 1983—; founder, active mem. The Pocket People, children's theatre group, New Eng., 1968-75; trustee Greenwich Library, 1986—. Recipient children's Book Week Poem award Children's Book Council, 1976, Am. Book award, 1983. Office: c/o Gina Maccoby Lit Agy 19 W 21st St 5th Floor New York NY 10010

HOBLER, SUSAN CAROL, data processing executive; b. Roseberg, Oreg., Mar. 11, 1952; d. Johnny Sitton and Edith Ethel (Rifenberry) Ward; m. John Ellsworth Hobler, Sept. 22, 1950. AS in Data Processing, Fresno (Calif.) City Coll., 1972. Data entry operator Fresno County, 1971-72, control clk., 1972-73, computer operator, 1973-74; computer operator San Luis Obispo (Calif.) County, 1974, computer systems technician II, 1974-77, computer systems technician III, 1977-79, sr. computer systems technician, 1979-82, computer ops. supr., 1982-84, mgr. data processing ops., 1984—. Mem. Am. Bus. Women's Assn. (treas. San Luis Obispo, 1984-85, pres. 1985-86, Woman of Yr. 1985). Methodist. Home: 306 Highland Dr Los Osos CA 93402 Office: Dept Tech Services County Govt Ctr San Luis Obispo CA 93408

HOCHHEIMER, LAURA, musician; b. Worms, Germany, Apr. 18, 1933; came to U.S., 1938, naturalized, 1947; d. Otto and Trude Hochheimer; student Beaver Coll., 1951-52; B.M., Eastman Sch. Music, 1955; M.F.A., Ohio U., 1957; Ph.D., Ind. U., 1966. Tchr. strings and vocal music, conductor Bainbridge (N.Y.) High Sch., Jr. High Sch. Orchs., Bainbridge Elem. and Bainbridge High Sch., 1957-58; tchr. gen. music Chgo. Public Schs., tchr. mentally retarded and physically handicapped children Spalding Sch. for Handicapped Children, 1963-64; mem. Chgo. Chamber Orch., Northwestern U. Chamber Orch., Roosevelt U. Symphony, 1958-64; grad. asst. in violin Ind. U., Bloomington, tchr. strings and orch. Ind. U. Lab. Sch., 1964-66; tchr. music West Liberty (W.Va.) State Coll., 1966-70; vis. asst. prof. music U. B.C., Vancouver, 1970-71; tchr. music edn. Towson State Coll., 1971-73; asst. prof. music edn. U. Cin., 1973-76; asso. prof. music James Madison U., Harrisonburg, Va., 1976-81; asst. prof. music edn. Cin. Coll. Conservatory Music, mem. grad. faculty U. Cin., 1973-76; asso. prof. music Clemson (S.C.) U., 1981—, head prep. dept. music, 1988—; violinist Greenville Symphony Orch., 1984—; violinist solo, chamber music and symphony orchs; cons. music in spl. edn. Orff-Schulwerk and Kodaly approaches in schs. and state convs. throughout U.S. and Can. Recipient George Eastman award Eastman Sch. Music, 1955; Fulbright scholar, Vienna and Salzburg, Austria, 1966-67. Mem. Music Educators Nat. Conf., Am. Orff Schulwerk Assn., Coll. Music Soc., S.C. Music Educators Assn. Author: A Sequential Sourcebook for Elementary School Music, 1980; contbr. articles in field to profl. jours. Office: Clemson U Strode Tower Box 48 Clemson SC 29634

HOCHMAN, ELAINE SCHWARTZ, art historian, author, educator; b. N.Y.C.; d. David and Leah (Altura) Schwartz; m. Raymond B. Hochman, Jan. 27, 1957; children: Elizabeth, Andrew, Russell. Cert., Oxford U., Eng.; BA, Vassar Coll.; MFA, NYU, 1968; PhD, CUNY. Mem. staff Met. Mus. Art, N.Y.C., 1957-58; mem. faculty The New Sch. for Social Research, N.Y.C., 1969—; pres. Art Ventures Internat. Inc., N.Y.C., 1985—; archtl. cons. N.Y.C. Real Estate Developers, 1970—. Contbr. articles to profl. jours. Mem. Coll. Art Assn., Soc. Archtl. Historians.

HOCHRON, BERYL JUDITH, marketing research consultant; b. N.Y.C., Jan. 2, 1947; d. Nathan and Marion (Freedman) Sadowsky; m. Joel Hochron, Jan. 2, 1981; 1 child, Matthew Noah. B.B.A. cum laude, CCNY, 1968; M.B.A., Baruch Coll., 1972. Staff acct. Haskins & Sells, N.Y.C., 1963-65; grad. asst. Baruch Coll., 1968-69; project dir. Batten, Barton, Durstine & Osborn Advt., N.Y.C., 1969-71; sr. project dir. AHF Mktg. Research Co., N.Y.C., 1971-74; mgr. RCA, N.Y.C., 1974-76; sr. research mgr. Clairol Inc., N.Y.C., 1976-83; group mgr. Lever Bros., N.Y.C., 1983-85; cons. mktg. research, 1985—. Mem. Am. Mktg. Assn. (asst. sec. N.Y. chpt. 1980-81, sec. 1981-82), Nat. Assn. Female Execs. Home: 248 Harriman Rd Irvington-on-Hudson NY 10533

HOCHSCHILD, CARROLL SHEPHERD, company administrator, educator; b. Whittier, Calif., Mar. 31, 1935; d. Vernon Vero and Effie Corinne (Hollingsworth) Shepherd; m. Richard Hochschild, July 25, 1959; children—Christopher Paul, Stephen Shepherd. B.A. in Internat. Relations, Pomona Coll., 1956; Teaching credential U. Calif.-Berkeley, 1957; M.B.A., Pepperdine U., 1985. Cert. elem. tchr., Calif. Elem. tchr. Oakland Pub. Schs. (Calif.), 1957-58, San Lorenzo Pub. Schs. (Calif.), 1958-59, Pasadena Pub. Schs. (Calif.), 1959-60, Huntington Beach Pub. Schs. (Calif.), 1961-63, 67-68; adminstrv. asst. Microwave Instruments, Corona del Mar, Calif., 1968-74; co-owner Hoch Co., Corona del Mar, 1978—. Rep. Calif. Tchrs. Assn., Huntington Beach, 1962-63. Mem. AAUW, Bus. Women's Inst., Internat. Dance-Exercise Found., Nat. Assn. Female Execs. Republican. Presbyterian. Clubs: Toastmistress (corr. sec. 1983), Jr. Ebell (fine arts chmn. Newport Beach 1966-67).

HOCHSTADT, JOY, biomedical research scientist, pharmaceutical company executive; b. N.Y.C., May 6, 1939; d. Julius Louis and Edith (Tabatchnick) H.; m. Harvey Leon Ozer, Feb. 3, 1960; 1 child, Juliane Natasha Hochstadt-Ozer. A.B. in Zoology, Barnard Coll., 1960; A.M. in Biologic Scis. (grad. fellow 1961-62), Stanford U., 1963; vis. fellow in tumor biology, Karolinska Inst., Stockholm, 1964-65; research fellow in biol. chemistry, Harvard U., 1965-66; Ph.D. in Microbiology, Georgetown U., 1968; postdoctoral fellow NIH, 1968-70. Diplomate Am. Bd. Clin. Chemistry. Instr. biology Coll. San Mateo, Calif., 1962-63; teaching asst. microbiology Georgetown Med. Sch., 1967-68; established investigator Am. Heart Assn.; lab. biochemistry Nat. Heart and Lung Inst., Bethesda, Md., 1970-72; sr. scientist Worcester Found. Exptl. Biology, Shrewsbury, Mass., 1972-76; adj. prof. biochemistry Central New Eng. Coll., Worcester, Mass., 1974-75; vis. prof. membrane research Weizmann Inst. Sci., Rehovot, Israel, 1976; vis. prof. biochemistry and biophysics U. R.I., Kingston, 1976-77; research prof. microbiology N.Y. Med. Coll., Valhalla, 1977-81; dir. Div. Clin. Biochemistry and Basic Research in Pathology, Cath. Med. Center, Queens, 1981-88; prof. clin. microbiology Cornell U. Med. Sch., 1986—; v.p., scientific dir. Hercon Labs. Corp. subs. Health Chem Corp., N.Y.C., 1988—; mem. NSF postdoctoral fellowship evaluation panel in biology NRC, 1975—, NATO postdoctoral fellowship evaluation panel, 1978—; mem. cell biology study sect. NIH, 1979—, Biomed. scis. fellowship com., 1979—. Editorial bd. Jour. Bacteriology, 1975-80; contbr. research papers, methods articles and monographs to profl. lit. Mem. nat. policy com. Profl. Women's Caucus, 1970-73; mem. alumnae council Barnard Coll., 1975—. Recipient Stanford Grad. award, 1963; Cancer Internat. Research Coop. Snell scholar, 1965; predoctoral trainee USPHS, 1966-67; predoctoral fellow USPHS, 1967-68; postdoctoral fellow USPHS, 1968-70; spl. trainee USPHS, 1973; Am. Heart Assn. investigatorship, 1970-75; NIH grantee, 1973—; NSF grantee, 1978—; Travel award to Stockholm, Am. Soc. Biol. Chemists, 1973, to Hamburg, 1976; Travel award to Jerusalem, Am. Soc. Microbiology, 1973. Fellow Am. Acad. Microbiology, Am. Inst. Chemists (profl. opportunities com., legis. com.), Nat. Acad. Clin. Biochemistry; mem. Am. Heart Assn. (basic sci. council), Am. Soc. Microbiology (status of women com. 1970-73, sec. physiology div. 1972-74, mem. divisional nominating com. 1973), Am. Soc. Biol. Chemists, Am. Assn. Clin. Chemists, AAAS, Am. Soc. Clin. Research, Am. Chem. Soc., Genetics Soc. Am., Harvey Soc., Am. Assn. Cancer Research, N.Y. Acad. Scis., Fedn. Am. Scientists, Assn. Women in Sci. (affirmative goals and actions com. 1973-75), Tissue Culture Assn. (Northeast planning com. 1986—), Am. Soc. for Cell Biology. Home: 300 Central Park W New York NY 10024 also: 1347 Cambridge Ct Saw Creek Bushkill PA 18324 also: Spur Rd Roaring Brook Lake Putnam Valley NY 10579 Office: Health Chem Corp 1107 Broadway New York NY 10010

HODDER, LINDA FAY, product manager; b. Arnprior, Ont., Canada, July 31, 1957; d. Charles Rosier and Doreen Elizabeth (Morphy) H. BBA, Algonquin Coll., Ottawa, Ont., 1980; student, Can. Sch. Mgmt., 1987—. Credit clerk Can. Packers Inc., Toronto, 1980; chem. salesperson, B.C. Can. Packers Inc., Vancouver, 1980-82; chem., key account salesperson Can. Packers Inc., Toronto, 1983, asst. product mgr., 1985-86, product mgr., 1987—. Liberal. Mem. Anglican Ch. Office: Canada Packers Inc, Hospitality Amenities Group, 5100 Timberlea Blvd, Mississauga, ON Canada L4W 2S5

HODES, BARBARA, organizational consultant; b. Chgo., Nov. 30, 1941; d. David and Tybe Zisook; children from previous marriage: Brian, Valery; m. A. Bruce Schimberg, Dec. 29, 1984. BS, Northwestern U., 1962. Ptnr. Just Causes, cons. not-for-profit orgns., Chgo., 1978-86 ; cons. in philanthropy and organizational devel., 1987—; Chgo. cons. Population Resource Ctr., 1978-82. Woman's bd. dirs. Mus. Contemporary Art; bd. dirs., vice chmn. Med. Research Inst. Council, Michael Reese Med. Ctr.; bd. dirs., chmn. Midwest Women's Ctr.; trustee Francis W. Parker Sch. Office: 209 E Lake Shore Dr Chicago IL 60611

HODES, CAROL LYNN, technical writer. BS in Biology, Lock Haven (Pa.) U., 1970; MS in Instl. Systems Design, Pa. State U., 1984. Pesticide research lab. technician Pa. State U., 1973-74; biol. technologist Pa. State U. Dept. of Plant Pathology, 1980-81; high sch. sci. and computer literacy tchr. State College (Pa.) Area Schs., 1981-84; engring. project asst. Pa. State U. Dept. Nuclear Engring., 1984-85; tech. writer Applied Research Lab. Research and Research and Acad. Affairs Dept., 1985—. Author: Understanding the Health Effects of Ionizing Radiation; contbr. articles to profl. jours. Mem. Centre Community Hosp. Aux. Bd., 1976-78, Com. for the Healthy Woman Seminar 1976-78; active Cen. Pa. Festival for the Arts, Cancer Soc., Arthritis Found. Grantee NSF Tchr. Enchancement, Profl. Engring. Review Book, 1984, Nuclear div. Dept. Energy, AAUW L.V. Simmons Project, 1984. Mem. AAUW, Am. Soc. Tng. and Devel. (Nittany Valley chpt.), Pi Lambda Theta, Alpha Kappa, Sigma Delta Epsilon, Penn State Club (bd. dirs. Centre County chpt.), Pa. State Alumni Soc. (life). Home: 1162 Smithfield Circle State College PA 16801 Office: Applied Research Lab PO Box 30 State College PA 16804

HODGE, ALICE MACNAUGHTON, retail advertising executive; b. Honolulu, Feb. 11, 1953; d. Malcolm and Winifred (Sperry) MacNaughton; AB, Stanford U., 1975; postgrad. Foothill Coll., 1975, Golden Gate U., 1981; m. James Blythe Hodge, Jan. 3, 1981; stepchildren—Eric, Terra. With Emporium Capwell Co., San Francisco, 1975—, spl. events, pub. relations dir., 1979-81, dir. broadcast advt., 1981-86, dir. sales promotion mktg. and fin., 1987, v.p. sales promotion, 1987—. Mem. pub. relations com. Vol. Bur., San Francisco, 1980-83; mem. spl. events adv. com. Assn. Merchandising Corp., N.Y.C., 1978-81; mem. mktg. adv. bd. Golden Gate U., 1988—, adv. council; area co-chmn. San Francisco chpt. Stanford Ann. Fund, 1975—; pres. jr. women's com. San Francisco Symphony, 1985-86; trustee Sacred Heart Schs., Menlo Park, Calif., 1986—; bd. dirs. Better Bus. Bur., San Francisco, 1988—. Mem. San Francisco Jr. League, Stanford Assocs. Republican. Episcopalian. Contbr. articles to profl. publs. Home: 2940 Lake St San Francisco CA 94121 Office: 835 Market St San Francisco CA 94103

HODGE, G. JEANNETTE, cultural organization executive; b. Bogalusa, La., Sept. 12, 1935; d. Clarence James and Ruth (Smith) H.; 1 child, Tameka Laverne Jones. Grad., Am. Theatre Wing, 1957; BA, Dillard U., 1959; MA, Columbus U., 1960; MS summa cum laude, CUNY, 1974; EdM, Columbia U., 1977, EdD, 1978. Program dir. Administor-Brownsville Ctr., Bklyn., 1959-60; instr. spl. edn. Shield of David, N.Y.C., 1960-64; instr. early childhood N.Y.C. Bd. Edn., 1964-66; dir. spl. edn. Roslyn (N.Y.) Pub. Schs., 1966-70, spl. edn. tchr., 1970-78; spl. asst. U.S. Office Edn., Washington, 1978-80; dir. pupil personnel service Roosevelt (N.Y.) Pub. Sch., 1980-84; exec. dir., cons., conf. designer Black Arts Nat. Diaspora, N.Y.C., 1982—; researcher U.S. Office Edn. of Roslyn, 1978, 80, 84; lectr. Ind. State U., 1979-80; policy analyst George Washington Inst. for Edn., 1978—. Author: Indomitable Spirit, 1985; editor Black Arts Nat. Diaspora newsletter, Band mag., 1987—. Mem. Cambria Heights (N.Y.) Civic Assn., 1980—, 114th and 222d Block Assn., Cambria Heights, 1985—; active YWCA, Better Boys and Girls, New Orleans. Am. Theatre Wing fellow, 1957, Leadership Policy fellow George Washington Inst. for Edn., 1978, Paul Witty fellow Ind. U., Leadership fellow U. S. Fla., Pearl Cox fellow, Claudia P. Tannage fellow Dillard U. Mem. Sch. Adminstrs. Assn. N.Y. State, African Heritage Studies Assn., St. Albans C. of C., LWV, Phi Delta Kappa. Democrat. Episcopalian. Home: 114-36 222d St Cambria Heights NY 11411 Office: Black Arts Nat Diaspora 143-14 16 Lakewood St Jamaica NY 11435

HODGE, LYNDA SOBCZYK, human resources manager; b. Norfolk, Va., Apr. 28, 1951; d. Walter Frank and Georgia Mae (Fentress) Sobczyk; m. James G. Andrew Hodge, Apr. 25, 1969 (div. Nov. 1979); children: W. Joseph, Andrea Lyn. Student, Mitchell Jr. Coll., New London, Conn., 1976-80, Conn. Coll., 1974, 81, 84. Asst. personnel mgr. Bur. Bus. Practice, Waterford, Conn., 1970-80; corp. mgr. employee relations Analysis & Tech., Inc., North Stonington, Conn., 1980—; bd. dirs., vice-chairperson Thames Services, Inc., Norwich, Conn., 1986—. Organizer Marine Commerce Devel. Council, New London, 1977-78; bd. trustees Thames Valley Community Care Agy., Norwich, 1985—; campaign drive leader St. Joseph's Sch. PTO, New London, 1983—. Mem. N.E. Human Resources Assn., Conn. Personnel Assn. (membership com. 1982—), Ea. Conn. Personnel Assn. (various offices 1976—), S.E. Conn. Task Force on AIDS, 1987. Home: 70 Montauk Ave New London CT 06320 Office: Analysis & Tech Inc Rte. 2 Technology Park Box 220 North Stonington CT 06359

HODGE, MARY GRETCHEN FARNAM, manufacturing company manager; b. DeFuniak Springs, Fla., Sept. 24, 1943; d. Thomas Dewey and Mary Catherine (Mixon) Farnam; m. Spessard L. Hodge, Apr. 28, 1962; children: Jennifer Robin, Monica Leigh, Stephanie, Lea. Student, Orlando Coll. Adminstrv. asst. The Cameron and Barkley Co., Orlando, Fla., 1961-68, office mgr. Machine Tool div., 1975-76; mgr. Frazer Machinery and Supply Co., Orlando, 1976—. Pioneered effort to establish parent support groups for gifted edn., Seminole County, 1979; sec. Parent of Gifted Edn., Seminole County, 1980-87; mem. adv. bd. Exceptional Student Edn., Seminole City, Fla., 1980—; chairperson Maitland (Fla.) Centennial Founders Bd., 1985; tour guide Orlando Opera Guild, Winter Park, Fla., 1985; celebrity waitress Leukemia Soc. Am., Orlando, 1986; co-chairperson Project Graduation Lyman High Sch., Seminole County, 1986—; chairperson Alzheimers Resource Auction Dinner, Winter Park, 1987 88; bd. dirs. Maitland Civic Ctr., 1983-86, v.p. bd. dirs. 1987-88. Recipient appreciation plaque Dividends, Seminole City, 1974-75, cert. appreciation Maitland Civic Ctr., 1986, Alzheimer Resource Ctr., Winter Park, 1987. Mem. Am. Machine Tool Distbrs., Soc. Mfg. Engrs. Democrat. Methodist. Club:

Maitland Woman's (several offices 1976—). Home: 95 Lake Destiny Trail Altamonte Springs FL 32714 Office: 6217 Edgewater Dr Orlando FL 32810

HODGE, MARY JO, health service administrator; b. Talladega, Ala., June 15, 1935; d. John Bowling and Martha Allene (Royal) McKinney; B.S., Auburn U., 1956; M.S. (fellow), U. Miss., 1958; D.Pub. Adminstrn., N.Y. U., 1978; m. Charles Cedric Hodge, Aug. 6, 1955; children—Donna, Holly. Psychometrist, Student Guidance Center, Auburn U., 1956-58; psychologist McGuffey Reading Clinic U. Va., Charlottesville, 1962-64, U. Va. Hosp., 1964-65; psychologist St. Lawrence Psychiat. Center, Ogdensburg, N.Y., 1966-73, mental hygiene treatment team leader, 1973-78; dir. Instn. Edn. and Tng., Gowanda Psychiat. Center, Helmuth, N.Y., 1978, dir. treatment services, 1979— . Bd. dirs. N.Y. Regional Geriatric Ctr., 1983-85. Mem. Am., Eastern psychol. assns., Gerontol. Soc. Am., Northeastern Gerontol. Soc., Acad. Polit. Sci., Assn. Mental Health Adminstrs. (treas. N.Y. chpt. 1985-87), Am. Soc. Pub. Adminstrn., Assn. for Rural Mental Health, Kappa Delta Pi, Chi Delta Phi, Pi Tau Chi. Home: PO Box 112 Helmuth NY 14079 Office: Gowanda Psychiat Ctr Helmuth NY 14079

HODGE, NANCY BATES, director of development, educational consultant; b. Pittsfield, Mass., Sept. 10, 1939; d. H. Ogden III and Mabel (Gilbert) Bates; m. James Edward Hodge, Aug. 24, 1963; children: Stephanie Lynne, Christopher Murray, Timothy James, Michael Bates. BS in Bus. Edn., Fla. State U., 1961; MEd, U. Fla., 1963. Lic. real estate salesman. Devel. asst. The Bolles Sch., Jacksonville, Fla., 1983-85, dir. devel., 1986—; gov.'s appointee com. to select trustee Fla. Jr. Coll., Jacksonville. Mem. Leadership Jacksonville, 1982—; chmn. youth commn. St. Mark's Episcopal Ch.; bd. dirs. Children's Home Soc. Aux., local sch. adv. com. Families in Action, St. Mark's Kindergarten Bd. Mem. Jacksonville Bar Assn. Aux. (bd. dirs.), Nat. Soc. Fund Raising Execs., Mensa, Kappa Delta Alumnae (past pres.). Democrat. Club: The Fla. Yacht. Home: 4984 Ortega Forest Dr Jacksonville FL 32210 Office: The Bolles Sch 7400 San Jose Blvd Jacksonville FL 32217

HODGE, NETA ANN, advertising executive; b. Springfield, Ill., Jan. 4, 1948; d. Earl Leo and Mary Elizabeth (Evans) Lard. BS, St. Louis Coll. Pharmacy, 1971; PharmD, U. Ky., 1978. Pharmacist in charge S&C Drugs, Peoria, Ill., 1971-72; mgr. pharmacy Wal-Mart Drugs, Manhattan, Kans., 1972-75; pharmacist in residence A.B. Chandler Med. Ctr., U. Ky., Lexington, 1975-78; instr. clin. pharmacy Phila. Coll. Pharmacy, 1978-79, asst. prof., 1979-86; adj. asst. prof. in medicine U. Pa., Phila., 1980-86; account exec. Deltakos, USA (J. Walter Thompson), N.Y.C., 1986-87; account supr. Sudler & Hennessey div. Young & Rubicam, N.Y.C., 1987—; clin. pharmacist, cons. U. Pa. Sch. Medicine, Phila. Pa. Diabetic Task Force, Phila., 1985-86. Contbg. editor Pa. State Health Plan, 1986-87; contbr. articles to profl jours. Mem. Pa. Gov's Adv. Bd. on Arthritis, 1985—; vice chair Profl. Edn. Com., 1985—; mem., vice chair Patient/Pub. Edn. Com., 1985-87. Named one of Outstanding Young Women Am., 1980, 84. Mem. Am. Soc. Hosp. Pharmacists, St. Louis Coll. Pharmacy Alumni Assn., Univ. City Hist. Soc., Green Thumb Gardeners Assn. (sec. Phila. chpt. 1986—), Rho Chi, Lambda Kappa Sigma. Democrat. Roman Catholic. Home: 434 S 42d St Philadelphia PA 19104 Office: Sudler & Hennessey 1633 Broadway New York NY 10019

HODGES, JULIA ELMIRA, computer science educator; b. Tupelo, Miss., Nov. 25, 1951; d. Lethal Avon and Methyl Frank (Patterson) H. BS, Miss. State U., 1973, MEd, 1974, MS, 1978; PhD, U. Southwestern La., 1985. Tchr. Starkville (Miss.) Pub. Schs., 1973-76; grad. asst. Miss. State (Miss.) U., 1976-78, instr., 1978-79, prof., 1984—; instr. U. Southwestern La., Lafayette, 1979-83. Named one of Outstanding Young Women Am., 1981, 83, 84, Outstanding Computer Scientist, 1985-86. Mem. IEEE, AAUW (Starkville civic council rep. 1985-86), Assn. for Computing Machinery (Miss. State U. chpt., profl. devel. com. 1985—, tutorial instr. 1986—), Bus. and Profl. Women's Club (sec. 1985-86), Faculty Women's Assn. (treas. 1984-86), Soc. Scholars (pres. 1986-87), United Daus. of Confederacy (pres. 1986-88), Daus. Am. Revolution, Alpha Delta Pi (pres. Starkville alumnae assn. 1985-87), Upsilon Pi Epsilon 1978-79 (sec., treas. 1978-79). Methodist. Home: 118 Briarwood Dr Starkville MS 39759 Office: Miss State U PO Drawer CS Mississippi State MS 39762

HODGES, MARGARET ANN, television editor, newspaper columnist; b. McCamey, Tex., Sept. 7, 1928; d. Ernest Cornelius and Margaret Isabel (Wood) Haynes; m. Cecil Ray Hodges, July 2, 1954 (div. Nov. 1974); children—Craig McNeley, Elizabeth Ann. B.J., U. Tex., 1948. Reporter, Houston Chronicle, 1948-51; society editor The News, Mexico City, 1951-52; reporter Houston Chronicle, 1952-54, TV editor, columnist, 1962—; radio critic Sta. KIKK, Houston, 1981—. Mem. Critics Consensus (dir. 1965-75), TV Critics Assn. (founder, exec. bd., v.p., pres.). Club: Houston Press (pres. 1967-68). Office: Houston Chronicle Texas and Travis Sts Houston TX 77002

HODGES, MELINDA RENEE, academic administrator; b. Detroit, Apr. 2, 1960; d. William Roger Hodges and Joann (Corley) Glenn. Student, Wayne State U., 1978-80; BA in Acctg., Clark Coll., 1980-83. Cash mgmt. clk. Detroit Edison, 1976-78; clerical sec. Rotor Electric, Detroit, 1978-80; word processing typist Southeast Region YMCA's, Atlanta, 1980-83; technician Wayne State U., Detroit, 1983-84, academic services officer, 1984-86, adminstrv. computing systems coordinator, 1986—; mem. com. admissions, records and adminstrn. Wayne State U.; fin. cons. Aisha Shule, Detroit, 1983-84; pub. tax cons., 1983—. Vol. Friends of Sam Turner campaign, Detroit, 1986; bd. dirs., treas., exec. com. mem. Studio African Dance Philosophy, Inc., Detroit, 1985—. Mem. Nat. Assn. Female Execs., NAACP (fin. com. Detroit chpt.). Club: Integral Computing Systems (treas. 1986). Home: 20569 Pierson Detroit MI 48219 Office: Wayne State U 6001 Cass #302 Detroit MI 48202

HODGKIN, GEORGIA ELLEN, nutritionist, educator; b. Minot, N.D., Aug. 9, 1939; d. George Ellis and Thora Eugenia (Nelson) Willey; children: Steven Ellis, Kathryn Elizabeth, Carolyn Yvonne. BS, Walla Walla Coll., 1961; MS, Loma Linda U., 1966. Registered dietitian. Lab instr. Walla Walla Coll., College Place, Wash., 1958-61, instr., 1961; clin. dietitian Glendale (Calif.) Adventist Hosp., 1963-64; research asst. Loma Linda (Calif.) U., 1964-66, asst. prof. nutrition, 1978—; treas. Inland Nutrition Council, Loma Linda, 1984; mem. Pacific Union Exec. Conf., Westlake Village, Calif., 1986—. Editor: cookbook, An Apple-a-Day Vol. 2, 1983. Vol. Shirley Pettis for Congress, 1974-76; leader Children's Sabbath Schs., Univ. Ch., 1964-81; mem. Marital Care and Divorce Recovery Com., Univ. Ch., 1985-87; mem. search com. for pres. and treas. of Southeastern Calif. Conf. of Seventh-day Adventists, Riverside, Calif., 1986, lay adv. council 1979-86. Mem. Am. Dietetic Assn., Calif. Dietetic Assn., Inland Dist. Dietetic Assn. (career guidance chair 1979-81), Dietetic Educators of Practitioners, Seventh-day Adventists Dietetic Assn. (bd. dirs., speaker of house 1985-86). Republican. Seventh-day Adventist. Home: 24360 Lawton Ave Loma Linda CA 92354 Office: Loma Linda U Nutrition and Dietetics Loma Linda CA 92350

HODGKINS, SARA WILSON, former state official; b. Granite Falls, N.C., Nov. 25, 1930; d. Martin Morehead and Doris (Parker) Wilson; m. Norris L. Hodgkins, Jr., June 27, 1953; children—Caroline Eddy, Celeste, Grace. B.S. in Music Edn., Appalachian Coll., 1952. Music specialist Moore County Schs., Southern Pines, N.C., 1953-76; sec. N.C. Dept. Cultural Resources, Raleigh, 1977-84. Vice chmn. N.C. Arts Council, Raleigh, 1971-73; pres. N.C. Symphony Soc., Raleigh, 1972-74; mem. adv. bd. Duke Hosp., Durham, N.C., 1979-83; trustee N.C. Sch. of Arts, Winston-Salem; mem. Southern Pines Town Council, 1975-77. Democrat. Presbyterian. Office: 915 E Indiana Ave Southern Pines NC 28387

HODGMAN, JOAN ELIZABETH, neonatologist; b. Portland, Oreg., Sept. 7, 1923; d. Kenneth E. and Ann (Vannet) H.; m. Amos N. Schwartz, Jan. 30, 1949; children—Ann Vannet, Susan Lynn. B.A., Stanford U., 1943; M.D., U. Calif., San Francisco, 1946. Intern in pediatrics U. Calif. Hosp., San Francisco, 1946-47; resident in pediatrics Harbor Gen. Hosp., Torrance, Calif., 1947-48, Los Angeles County-U. So. Calif. Med. Center, 1948-50; practice medicine specializing in pediatrics South Pasadena, Calif., 1950-52; mem. faculty U. So. Calif. Med. Sch., 1952—, prof. pediatrics, 1969—; dir. newborn div. Los Angeles County-U. So. Calif. Med. Ctr., 1955-86; chmn. med. adv. com. Nat. Found.-March of Dimes, 1972-75; adv. com. Western sect. UNICEF, 1975; med. adv. com. Calif. Legislature, 1970; cons. Calif. Health Dept. Author articles in field, chpts. in books. Recipient cert. appreciation Am. Cancer Soc., 1964, Cameo of Commitment award B'nai B'rith, 1969, Meritorious award Nat. Found.-March of Dimes, 1969; named Woman of Year Calif. Museum Sci. and Industry, 1974, Woman of Year Los Angeles Times, 1976. Mem. Am. Pediatric Soc., Am. Acad. Pediatrics, Am. Thoracic Soc., Western Soc. Pediatric Research, Southwestern Pediatric Soc., Calif. Perinatal Assn., Calif. Med. Assn., Los Angeles County Med. Assn., Los Angeles Pediatric Soc. Home: 494 Stanford Dr Arcadia CA 91006 Office: U So Calif Med Ctr Los Angeles County 1240 Mission Rd Los Angeles CA 90033

HODGSON, AURORA SAULO, food scientist; b. Manila, Philippines, Feb. 24, 1950; came to U.S., 1973, naturalized, 1982; d. Serafin Bumanlag and Natividad David (Alfonso) Saulo; m. Laban Richard Hodgson, 1982. B.S. cum laude in Chemistry, Coll. of the Holy Spirit, Philippines, 1971; M.S. in Chemistry, U. Mass., 1977, Ph.D. in Food Sci., 1978. Flavor chemist, food processing engr. United Brands Corp. Research and Devel.-Quality Control Labs., Newton, Mass., 1978-81; food technologist/sr. food technologist Beatrice Cos., Fullerton, Calif., 1982-84; tech. advisor Orchards Hawaii, Ltd., 1985; food processing cons., 1985—; extension specialist in food tech. U. Hawaii at Manoa, 1985—. Sec., Christian Life Community, Manila, 1968-69, pres., 1969-70. Fulbright Hays scholar, 1973. Mem. Inst. Food Technologists, Am. Chem. Soc. Contbr. in field.

HODGSON, MARY ANN, insurance company executive; b. Manchester, N.H., Jan. 8, 1940; d. A.J. and Paula (Lambert) Veilleux Murphy; m. David Hodgson, Sept. 13, 1958; children: David, Daniel, Donald, Darin. Registered med. asst., Carnagie Inst., 1978. Mgr. Am. Income Life, Waco, Tex., 1975-80; mgr., owner Ins. Services, Port Neches, Tex., 1980—; owner Casual Time Tours, Inc., 1986— . pres. Setex chpt. Muscular Dystrophy; bd. dirs. Sabine Area Cen. Labor Council, 1982-88; co-chmn. Port Neches Pow-Wow Festival, 1985. Mem. S. Jeff County Life Underwriters Assn. (sec./treas. 1986—), Am. Bus. Women's Assn. (corresponding sec. Orange chpt. 1979-80), Sca Rim Estates Assn. (sec./treas. 1978-80), Port Neches C. of C. (bd. dirs. 1982-88). Democrat. Roman Catholic. Office: Ins Services 2044 Nall PO Box 417 Port Neches TX 77651

HODNETT, DIANNE MARIE, risk management executive; b. Neptune, N.J., July 30, 1947; d. Theodore and Betty Jane (Trotta) Griffin; m. Phillip Barry Hodnett, Dec. 31, 1968; children: Phillip Barry, Theodore James. Student, Temple U., 1965-66. Asst. personnel dir. CARE, Inc., N.Y.C., 1969-79; v.p. human resources NICO, Inc., N.Y.C., 1979-87; v.p. risk mgmt. The LVI Group, Inc., 1987—; cons. ICCC, Neptune, 1980—. Active Coalition for Better Govt., Wyandranch, N.Y., 1983-86; v.p. Wyandranch PTA/PTSA Council, 1985-86. Mem. Nat. Assn. Female Execs., Am. Soc. for Personnel Adminstrn. Democrat. Methodist. Home: 11 N 22d St Wheatley Heights NY 11798 Office: The LVI Group Inc 345 Hudson St New York NY 10014

HODNETT, EARNESTINE, labor relations specialist; b. Virginia Beach, Va., Feb. 1, 1949; d. David and Mary Elizabeth (Scott) H. B.S. in Bus. Adminstrn., Norfolk State U., 1978; MBA in Pub. Adminstrn. Valdosta State Coll., 1988. Acctg. technician, Navy Pub. Works Ctr., Norfolk, 1967-78; personnel mgmt. specialist Naval Air Rework Facility, Norfolk, 1978-80, personnel staffing specialist, 1980-83, employee relations specialist, 1982-84; employee relations specialist Naval Submarine Base, Kings Bay, Ga., 1984-85, personnel mgmt. specialist, 1985-86, supervisory labor relations specialist, 1986-88, Eighth Army CPO, Seoul, Republic of Korea, 1988—. Bd. dirs. United Way, Camden County, Ga., 1985. Mem. Black Profl. Women Club Inc. (chairperson scholarship com. 1983-84), Soc. Labor Relations Profls., Federally Employed Women, Personnel Mgmt. Soc., Phi Delta Kappa, NAACP. Democrat. Avocations: reading; golf; aerobics; camping. Office: Seoul CPO Attn: Fast-CP-Mer APO San Francisco CA 96204

HODO, KAREN ANNE, micro computer executive; b. Inglewood, Calif., Feb. 8, 1958; d. Richard D. and Dolores (Jones) Kilpatrick; m. Mark Scott Hodo, May 29, 1980. BS in Animal Sci., Calif. Poly., 1979. Real estate agt. Spring Realty, Torrance, Calif., 1981-82; major account rep. Micro D, Santa Ana, Calif., 1982-84; account mgr. AST Research, Irvine, Calif., 1984-85, dist. mgr., 1985-86; nat. major account mgr. Micro D, Santa Ana, 1986—. Mem. Alpha Zeta, Phi Kappa Phi, Gamma Sigma Delta. Presbyterian. Office: Micro D 2801 S Yale Santa Ana CA 92704

HOEFT, BARBARA ANN, telecommunications professional; b. Milw., Aug. 6, 1950; d. Gordon and Emilie (Kopfmann) Haase; m. Allan Norman Hoeft, Aug. 28, 1971. BA in Bus. Mgmt., Profl. Communications with honors, Alverno Coll., 1982. Mktg. adminstr. Wis. Bell, Milw., 1978-80, account exec., 1980-82; account exec. AT&T, Brookfield, Wis., 1982-83, industry cons., sales mgr., 1983-85, branch ops. mgr., 1985—. Vol. United Way, Milw., 1986. Mem. Telecommunications Profls. Wis. (pres.).

HOEFT, THEA MARIE, college adminstrator, therapist, educator; b. Milw., Feb. 9, 1950; d. Peter Kazin and Renatte Katherine (Kaniewski) Zidonowitz. B.S. in Recreation, U. Wis.-LaCrosse, 1972; M.S. in Leisure Studies, U. Utah, 1973; Ed.D., Va. Poly. Tech. Inst. and State U., 1979. Playground dir. Watertown (Wis.) Dept. Parks and Recreation, 1969; dir. Bluffview playground LaCrosse Dept. Parks and Recreation, 1970; instr. Ind. State U., Terre Haute, 1973-74; day camp dir. Vigo County Extension Service, Terre Haute, Ind., 1974; instr. Radford (Va.) U., 1974-75; phys. edn. tchr. St. Patrick Cathedral Sch., Harrisburg, Pa., 1975; receptionist crisis worker Holy Spirit Hosp. Community Mental Health Center, Camphill, Pa., 1975; adj. faculty U. So. Miss., Hattiesburg, 1976; master recreational therapist Ellisville (Miss.) State Sch. for Mentally Ill and Retarded, 1976; instr. Radford U., 1976-77; mental retardation profl. Hearthside Rehab. Center, Brown Deer, Wis., 1979; asst. prof., coordinator therapeutic recreation curriculum Ariz. State U., Tempe, 1979-83; master therapist Mt. Sinai Med. Ctr. Geriatric Inst. Alzheimer Disease Day Hosp./Phys. Rehab. Hosp., Milw., 1983-84; therapist spinal cord injury unit VA Hosp., Milw., 1984-85; asst. dir. evening coll. and extension programs Milw. Sch. Engring., 1985-88, assoc. dir. admissions and retention, 1988—; cons. 4-H, 1976, Crippled Children's Hosp., Va., 1978, others. Mem. Miss. Com. Spl. Olympics, 1976; rep. United Way Ariz., 1979; mem. Mayor's Adv. Drug Com., 1972; bd. dirs. Youth Treatment and Evaluation Center, Phoenix, 1979-82; mem. Phoenix spl. populations adv. council on recreation, 1980-82; vol. Phoenix Panhellenic Council, 1982; mem. Ariz. State U. Centennial Com., 1981-83, chairperson disabled students services adv. bd., 1981-83. Wis. Leadership grantee, 1968; recipient Disting. Service award Montgomery County Cardiac Therapy Center, 1979, United Way, 1980, Recreation Com. U. Wis., LaCrosse, 1971, 72; H. Roe Bartle Recruiting award, 1981. Mem. Am. Camping Assn., Ariz. Parks and Recreation Assn., Va. Parks and Recreation Assn., Nat. Recreation and Park Assn., Therapeutic Recreation Assn. Greater Milw. (pres. 1983-84), Am. Assn. Adult and Continuing Edn., AAHPER and Dance (editorial bd.), Nat. Leadership Inst., Phi Delta Kappa, Phi Delta Chi (advisor 1986—, mem. grad. program council 1986—), Sigma Kappa Sigma, Sigma Lambda Sigma, Gamma Sigma Sigma. Republican. Catholic. Contbr. numerous articles to profl. jours. Home: 2841 N 54th St Milwaukee WI 53210 Office: Milw Sch Engring Div Continuing Edn 1025 N Milwaukee St Box 644 Milwaukee WI 53201-0644

HOEGER, KAREN LYNN, utilities company professional; b. Pitts., Feb. 26, 1960; d. Charles Philip and Dorothy Jean (Koerts) Zieg; m. Michael Tracy Hoeger, May 17, 1986. AAS in Bus. Adminstrn., Dutchess Community Coll., Poughkeepsie, N.Y., 1980; postgrad., Marist Coll., 1982—. Asst. bookkeeper Rondout/Boyle Electric, Poughkeepsie, 1980-81; co-office mgr. Radiology Assocs., Poughkeepsie, 1981; prodn. staff asst. Cen. Hudson Gas and Electric, Poughkeepsie, 1981-87, prodn. services coordinator, 1987-88, ops. budget coordinator, 1988—. Loaned exec. United Way of Dutchess County, Poughkeepsie, 1984, div. mgr., 1985, group mgr., 1986-88. Mem. Nat. Assn. Female Execs. Republican. Lutheran. Home: 405 Hudson Harbor Dr Poughkeepsie NY 12601 Office: Cen Hudson 284 S Ave Poughkeepsie NY 12601

HOELTERHOFF, MANUELA VALI, editor, critic; b. Hamburg, W.Ger., Apr. 6, 1949; came to U.S., 1957; d. Heinz Alfons and Olga Christine (Goertz) H. B.A., Hofstra U., 1971; M.A., NYU, 1973. Assoc. editor Arete Pub. Co., Princeton, N.J., 1977-80; editor-in-chief Art and Auction Mag., N.Y.C., 1979-81; arts editor Wall Street Jour., N.Y.C., 1981—. Recipient Pulitzer prize Columbia U., 1983; recipient citation for disting. commentary Am. Soc. Newspaper Editors, 1982, 83. Office: Wall Street Jour 22 Cortlandt St New York NY 10007 *

HOEY, JANE KOHRING, health center executive; b. Chgo., Sept. 4, 1940; d. Henry Carl and Jane Hamburg (Decker) Kohring; children: Anne Decker, John Wareham. B.A., Wells Coll., 1962; M.A., Wayne State U., 1979. Asst. art dept. J. Walter Thompson, Detroit, 1962-64, art buyer, N.Y.C., 1964-65; adminstrv. asst. United Found., Detroit, 1965; art asst. Franklin Siden Gallery, Detroit, 1965-66; counselor Macomb County Community Coll., Warren, Mich., 1979-80; mgr. cancer info. service Comprehensive Cancer Ctr. Met. Detroit, 1980—; dir. health edn. dept. Mich. Cancer Found., Detroit, 1986—; cons. service com. Am. Cancer Soc., Lansing, Mich., 1983-84. Bd. dirs., 1st v.p. Jr. League Detroit, 1962—; pres., bd. dirs. Family Life Edn. Council, Grosse Pointe, Mich., 1976-81; bd. dirs. Vis. Nurses Assn., Detroit, 1984—. Recipient Vol. award Jr. League Detroit, 1979. Mem. Mich. Pub. Health Assn., Mich. Health Council, Jr. League Detroit, Tau Beta Assn. Unitarian. Office: Mich Cancer Found 110 E Warren Detroit MI 48201

HOFBAUER, DIANE LYNN, lawyer; b. Milw., July 8, 1957; d. Thomas Anton and Claudia Mary (Billig) Hofbauer. AB, Duke U., 1979; JD, Vanderbilt U., 1982. Bar: Fla. 1983, D.C. 1984, U.S. Dist. Ct. (no. dist.) Fla. 1983. Atty. aide Pub. Defender's Office, Nashville, 1980, Vanderbilt Legal Aid Soc., Nashville, 1981-82; assoc. Maguire, Voorhis & Wells, P.A., Orlando, Fla., 1982-84, Paul, Hastings, Janofsky & Walker, Washington, 1984-87; legal asst. to commr. FCC, Washington, 1987-88; atty., internat. negotiations FCC div. Mass Media Bur., 1988—. Mem. ABA, Fla. Bar (communications com. 1982—), Orange County Bar Assn. (media and communications com. 1983), Fed. Communications Bar Assn. Republican. Roman Catholic. Office: FCC 2025 M St NW Room 8330 Washington DC 20554

HOFBAUER, RITA ANNE, non-profit fundraising organization administrator; b. N.Y.C., Oct. 21, 1936; d. George Clement and Margaret Gertrude (McDonnell) H. BA cum laude, D'Youville Coll., 1966; MA, Villanova U., 1967. Cert. in ednl. adminstrn. Tchr. Parochial Sch. System, Atlanta, 1959-64, ednl. adminstr., 1967-69; tchr. Parochial Sch. System, Phila., 1964-66, ednl. adminstr., 1969-71; dir. tng. Grey Nuns of the Sacred Heart, Yardley, Pa., 1971-75, v.p., 1975-79; asst. dir. Leadership Conf. of Women Religious, Silver Spring, Md., 1979-86; exec. dir. Support Our Aging Religious, Silver Spring, 1987—; mem. adv. bd. Assn. Cath. Colls. and Univs., Washington, 1979-85; cons. Bon Secours Health Corp., Columbia, Md., 1985, Hosp. for Sick Children, Washington, 1986. Co-author: Making Social Analysis Work, 1982; editor: Taking a Corporate Stand, 1980, Women in Ministry, 1981, An Old Voice in a New Age, 1983. Treas. Rachael's Women's Ctr., Washington, 1982; bd. dirs. D'Youville Coll., Buffalo, 1975-83. Mem. Nat. Orgn. Female Execs., Nat. Assn. Fundraising Execs., Beethovan Soc., Smithsonian Assn. Democrat. Roman Catholic. Office: Support Our Aging Religious 8820 Cameron St Silver Spring MD 20910

HOFER, JUDITH K., retail company executive. B.A., Portland State U., 1962. Formerly with Meier & Frank Dept. Store, Portland, Oreg., Emporium-Capwell, San Francisco; v.p. Famous-Barr Stores (subs. The May Co.), 1978-81; pres. Meier & Frank, Los Angeles, 1981-86, pres., chief exec. officer, St. Louis, 1986—. Office: Famous-Barr 601 Olive St Saint Louis MO 63101

HOFER, LUCILLE JOY, marketing and public relations executive; b. Omaha, June 27, 1940; d. Joseph and Frances Edith (Crozier) Kamphuis; m. William Eugene Stewart Oct., 1959 (div. 1966); children: Denise, Stephen, Cherie, David; m. Wesley Richard Hofer, Feb. 16, 1968; children: Wesley Richard Jr., Philip Michael. Student, UCLA, 1957-58, City Colls. of Chgo., 1978-79, Coastline Community Coll. Cons. Joy Hofer Small Bus. Mktg., Calif., 1981-84; mgr. bus. development Fountain Valley and Orange County (Calif.) C. of C., 1984—. Columnist Perspectives, Los Angeles Times, 1986, Huntington Beach Ind., Fountain Valley, 1986-88. Counselor Helpline, Omaha, 1974-76; program chair Protestant Women of Chapel, Ramstein AFB, Fed. Republic of Germany, 1979; treas. Com. to Re-elect George Scott, Fountain Valley, 1984, campaign chair, 1988; chair Protestant Women of the Chapel, Ramstein AFB, Fed. Republic of Germany, 1979; mem. steering com. Citizens for Fountain Valley, 1988; bd. dirs. Huntington Valley Boys and Girls Club, 1986-87. Mem. Omni Bus. Club (bd. dirs. 1984-85, treas. 1986), Nat. Assn. Female Execs., Pub. Relations Soc. Am. Republican. Clubs: Fountain Valley Woman's (dist. chair status of women com. 1986-88); USAF Officer's Wives (bd. dirs. 1969-79). Office: Fountain Valley C of C 10101 Slater Ave Suite 115 Fountain Valley CA 92708

HOFF, JULIENNE NORA, college dean, nurse; b. Detroit, Aug. 10, 1939; d. Basil and Laura Julia (McKenna) Howell; m. William R. Hoff, June 16, 1979. BSN, Mercy Coll., 1963; MEd in Nursing Edn., Columbia U., 1968; PhD, U. Mich., 1984. RN. Staff nurse, asst. head nurse St. Mary's Hosp., Grand Rapids, Mich., 1963-64; nursing supr. Mercy Hosp., Bay City, Mich., 1964-66; asst. prof. nursing Mercy Coll., Detroit, 1968-72, 1976-80, dir., dean of nursing, 1980-86; dean, div. of nursing and health Madonna Coll., Livonia, Mich., 1987—. Co-author: Role of Liberal Arts in Nursing, 1987. Recipient acad. achievement scholarship Mercy Coll., 1957-58, Contbn. to Advancement of Nursing award, Mich. Soc. Hosp. Adminstrs., 1984. Mem. Am. Nurses Assn., Mich. Nurses Assn., Detroit Nurses Assn. (chmn. nominating com. 1987-88), Mich. Assn. of Colls. of Nursing (sec. 1984-86), Am. Assn. of higher Edn., Pi Lambda Theta. Home: 18235 University Park Rd Livonia MI 48152 Office: Madonna Coll Sch Nursing 36600 Schoolcraft Rd Livonia MI 48150

HOFFER, DIANE LYNN, psychologist; b. Coral Gables, Fla., Dec. 29, 1953; d. Harold Herman and Charlotte May (Bernstein) H.; B.A. in Sociology, U. Miami, 1974; M.Ed. in Psychology, Counseling and Psychol. Services, Ga. State U., 1975; Dr. Psychology, Nova U., 1981. Practicum student Community Mental Health S. Dade, Dade County, Fla., 1978-79; clin. psychology intern Univ. Health Services U. Mass., Amherst, 1980-81; psychologist in pvt. practice, Coral Gables, 1981—; co-owner Jazz Workout, dance and exercise studio, 1982-84; dance instr.; instr. Parent Effectiveness Tng. Lic. marriage and family therapist, mental health counselor, clin. psychologist. Mem. Am. Psychol. Assn., AAHPER, Nat. Dance Assn., Internat. Windsurfing Class Assn., Assn. Sex Educators, Counselors and Therapists, Fla. Psychol. Assn. Democrat. Jewish. Contbr. articles to profl. jours. Office: 6851 Yumuri St Suite 17 Coral Gables FL 33146

HOFFMAN, ANN FLEISHER, labor union official, lawyer; b. Phila., June 1, 1942; d. Willis Jr. and Mary (Leffler) Fleisher; m. Charles Stuart Hoffman Jr., June 7, 1964 (div. 1979); m. Arnold Perry Rubin, Jan. 1, 1985. BA, Barnard Coll., 1964; JD, U. Md., 1972. Bar: Md., 1972, N.Y., 1978. Reporter, producer Sta. WBAL-TV, Balt., 1965-68; assignment editor, producer Sta. WJZ-TV, Balt., 1968-69; assoc. Edelman, Levy and Rubenstein, Balt., 1972-77; assoc. gen. counsel Internat. Ladies' Garment Workers Union, N.Y.C., 1977-79, dir. Profl. and Clerical Employees div., 1987—; exec. asst. to Atty Gen. U.S. Dept. Justice, Washington, 1979-81; counsel Dist. 1 Communications Workers Am., N.Y.C., 1981-85; adminstrv. asst. to v.p. Communications Workers Am., N.Y.C. and Cranford, N.J., 1985-87; lectr. U. Md. Sch. of Law, Balt., 1972-77; adj. faculty Cornell U. Trade Union Women's Studies Program, N.Y.C., 1979-85; trustee Botto House Am. Labor Mus., Haledon, N.J., 1986—. Author: (with others) Legal Status of Homemakers in Maryland, 1978, Bargaining for Child Care, 1985. Founding mem. Women's Law Ctr., Balt., 1971-77; mem. Balt. City Charter Review Commn., 1973-76; bd. dirs. ACLU Md. Chpt., Balt., 1975-77, Campfire Girls Chesapeake Council, Balt., 1976-77; co-chair Sachs for Atty. Gen., Md., 1976-77; pub. mem. N.Y. State Banking Bd., N.Y.C., 1984-85. Mem. ABA, Coalition of Labor Union Women (treas. N.Y.C. chpt. 1981-83), Nat. Network of Women Union Lawyers (founder), Lawyers and Legal Workers for Working Women (founder), Cornell U. Adj. Faculty Fedn., Order of Coif. Home: 253 Friar Ln Mountainside NJ 07092 Office: Internat Ladies' Garment Workers' Union 1710 Broadway New York NY 10019

HOFFMAN, BARBARA A., state legislator; b. Balt., Mar. 8, 1940; d. Sidney Wolf and Eve (Simonoff) Marks; m. Donald Edwin Hoffman, 1960; children—Alan Samuel, Michael Stuart, Carolyn Mara. B.S., Towson State U., 1960; M.A., Johns Hopkins U., 1966. Secondary sch. tchr., Balt., 1960-63; supr. student tchrs. Morgan U., Balt., 1968-73; exec. dir. Md. Democratic party, 1979-84; mem. Md. State Senate from 42d Dist., 1983—. Co-author: Journeys in English, 1968. Recipient Appreciation cert. PTC Career Inst., 1984, Outstanding Contbns. to Party award Md. Dem. party, 1984. Mem. Md. Assn. Elected Women (exec. bd. 1985), Nat. Order Women Legislators, Balt. Blews Coalition Blacks and Jews, Md. Com. for Children (pres. 1983), Hadassah (group pres. 1980-82). Jewish. Office: Md State Capitol Bldg Annapolis MD 21401 Other Address: 2905 W Strathmore Ave Baltimore MD 21209 *

HOFFMAN, BETH LYNN, lawyer; b. Buffalo, July 27, 1943; d. Abraham and Bernice (Revo) Rapport; m. Sanford R. Hoffman, June 21, 1964; children: Kevin, Rebecca. BE, SUNY, Buffalo, 1965, JD, 1974. Bar: N.Y. 1975, U.S. Dist. Ct. (we. dist.) N.Y. 1975; cert. elem. tchr., N.Y. Tchr. Kenmore (N.Y.) Schs., 1965-66, Skokie (Ill.) Schs., 1966-67, New Hyde Park (N.Y.) Schs., 1967-70; assoc. Cohen Swados, Buffalo, 1974-76; trial lawyer, ptnr. Bouvier, O'Connor, Cegielski & Levine, Buffalo, 1976—. Active Women for Downtown, Buffalo, 1984—; citizens' ambassador People to People, Eng., Hungary and Fed. Republic Germany, 1985; bd. dirs. Dream Machine Mus., Buffalo, 1984-87, Amherst Y-U, 1988—. Mem. Women Lawyers Western N.Y., Internat. Assn. Defense Counsel (faculty, editor newsletter, vice-chair products liability 1987, automobile ins. com. 1988—), N.Y. State Bar Assn. (tort reparations com. 1986-88), Erie County Bar Assn. (chair negligence com. 1984-85). Home: 696 LeBrun Rd Eggertsville NY 14226

HOFFMAN, BETTY JANE, circuit court clerk; b. Mayville, Wis., Apr. 7, 1933; d. Theodore Henry and Henrietta Elizabeth (Luebke) Machmueller; m. Lyle Eugene Cole, May 12, 1956 (dec. Sept. 1977); children—David Allen, Nanette Rae Cole Mlodzik, Ritchie Brian; m. Clarence Carl Hoffman, May 30, 1981; stepchildren—Judith Ann Aldrich, Clarence Allen Hoffman. Student pub. schs., Ripon, Wis. Cashier Thorp Fin. Corp., Ripon, 1951-56; dep. clk. cir. ct. Green Lake County, Green Lake, Wis., 1968-78, clk. cir. ct., 1979—. Mem. Green Lake County Republican party, 1970—, Wis. Rep. party, 1979—, Green Lake County Rep. Women, 1975—, v.p. elect 1987. Mem. Wis. Clk. of Cts. Assn., Nat. Assn. Ct. Mgmt., Tri-County Officers Assn. Lutheran. Avocations: sewing; cooking; travel. Home: 446 Scott St Green Lake WI 54941 Office: Clk of Cir Ct Courthouse 492 Hill St Green Lake WI 54941

HOFFMAN, CAROL KNIGHT, data processing executive, consultant; b. Lexington, Ky., Feb. 3, 1943; d. Walter E. and Lina K. (Baldauf) Knight; m. John C. Williams; 1 child, Susan. BS in Math. and Secondary Edn., Syracuse (N.Y.) U., 1965; MS in Computer Sci., Rutgers U., 1980. Programmer Litton Industries, Orange, N.J., 1968-70; programmer, analyst Norcross, Inc., N.Y.C., 1971-73; sr. programmer, analyst Ednl. Testing Service, Princeton, N.J., 1974-78; sr. analyst Houston Industries, 1980-83; cons. Computer Horizons, Parsippany, N.J., 1983-85; staff mgr. AT&T, N.J., 1985-87; pres. Hoff-Will Corp., Princeton, 1987—; tchr. Sch. Bus. Partnership, Houston, 1981-83. Photographer Friendswood (Tex.) Soccer Assn., 1983; coach's asst. Princeton Soccer Assn., 1984-85. Mem. Mensa, Ind. Mgmt. Cons. Network of Princeton, Student Parents Orgn., Duchesne Parents Orgn. Presbyterian.

HOFFMAN, DARLEANE CHRISTIAN, chemistry educator; b. Terril, Iowa, Nov. 8, 1926; d. Carl Benjamin and Elverna (Kuhlman) Christian; m. Marvin Morrison Hoffman, Dec. 26, 1951; children: Maureane R., Daryl K. BS in Chemistry, Iowa State U., 1948, PhD in Nuclear Chemistry, 1951. Chemist Oak Ridge (Tenn.) Nat. Lab., 1952-53; mem. staff radiochemistry group Los Alamos (N.Mex.) Sci. Lab., 1953-71, assoc. leader chemistry-nuclear group, 1971-79, div. leader chem.-nuclear chem. div., 1979-82, div. leader isotope and nuclear chem. div., 1982-84; prof. chemistry U. Calif., Berkeley, 1984—; faculty sr. scientist Lawrence Berkeley (Calif.) Lab., 1984—; panel leader, speaker Los Alamos Women in Sci., 1975, 79, 82; mem. subcom. on nuclear and radiochemistry NAS-NRC, 1978-81, chmn. subcom. on nuclear and radiochemistry, 1982-84; mem. commn. on radiochem. and nuclear techniques Internat. Union of Pure and Applied Chem., 1983-87, chmn., 1987—; mem. com. 2d Internat. Symposium on Nuclear and Radiochemistry, 1988; internat. organizing com. for Internat. Conf. on Nuclear and Radiochemistry, Beijing, 1986, planning panel Workshop on Tng. Requirements for Chemists in Nuclear Medicine, Nuclear Industry, and Related Fields, 1988, radionuclide migration peer rev. com., Las Vegas, 1986-87, steering com. Advanced Steady State Neutron Source, 1986—, steering com., panelist Workshop on Opportunities and Challenges in Research with Transplutonium Elements, Washington, 1983. Contbr. numerous articles in field to profl. jours. Recipient Alumni Citation of Merit Coll. Scis. and Humanities, Iowa State U., 1978, Disting. Achievement award Iowa State U., 1986; fellow NSF, 1964 65, Guggenheim Found., 1978-79. Fellow Am. Inst. Chemists (pres. N.Mex. chpt. 1976-78), Am. Phys. Soc.; mem. AAAS, Am. Chem. Soc. (chmn. nuclear chemistry and technology div. 1978-79, John Dustin Clark award Cen. N.Mex. sect., award for Nuclear Chemistry 1983, com. on sci. 1986-88, exec. com. div. of nuclear chem. and tech., 1987—), Am. Nuclear Soc. (co-chmn. internat. conf. Methods and Applications of Radioanalytical Chemistry 1987), Sigma Xi, Phi Kappa Phi, Iota Sigma Pi, Pi Mu Epsilon, Sigma Delta Epsilon. Methodist. Home: 2277 Manzanita Dr Oakland CA 94611 Office: Lawrence Berkeley Lab MS70A-3307 NSD Berkeley CA 94720

HOFFMAN, DEBORAH LYNN, purchasing agent; b. St. Paul, Aug. 10, 1951; d. Warren Hoffman and Francis Rose (Pompilio) Ellis. Student, Lowthian Coll., 1974-75; AA in Materials Mgmt., DeAnza Coll., 1988. Buyer Dialog Info. Services, Inc., Palo Alto, Calif., 1983-88. Home: PO Box 964 Cupertino CA 95015 Office: Dialog Info Services Inc 3460 Hillview Ave Palo Alto CA 94304

HOFFMAN, DONNA MARIE, accountant; b. Chgo., Aug. 7, 1959; d. Joseph and Georgiann (Cox) Hawrysz; m. George A. Hoffman III., Aug. 6, 1983. BA, Lewis Coll., Romeoville, Ill., 1981. CPA, Ill. Acct. Shepard, Schwartz and Harris, Chgo., 1981-82; auditor Nat. Futures Assn., Chgo., 1982-83; acct. Dennis M. Bishop CPA, P.A., Marathon, Fla., 1983—. Mem. Am. Inst. CPA's (liason Fla. chpt.). Democrat. Office: Dennis M Bishop CPA PA 8085 Overseas Hwy Marathon FL 33050

HOFFMAN, DORIS JEAN, accountant; b. Rockford, Ill., June 7, 1929; d. Herschel Herbert and Ollie Mae (Sherlock) Wolfe; student LaSalle Extension U., 1950-51, Broward Community Coll., 1969-71; m. Rodney V. Hoffman, Feb. 14, 1949 (dec. 1968); children: Judith Hoffman Olson, Sandra Hoffman Hardy, Kurt Allyn. Operator, Ill. Bell Telephone Co., Rockford, 1946-49; acct., head tax dept. Fed. & State Tax Record Systems, Rockford, 1949-66, Ft. Lauderdale, Fla., 1966-69; pvt. practice acctg., Ft. Lauderdale, 1969-79; acct., pres. Hoffman & Assos., Inc., Ft. Lauderdale, 1979-87; sec., treas. Auto Busters, Inc., Ft. Pierce, Fla., 1987—; lectr. in field. Mem. bus. edn. adv. com. Fla. Dept. Edn., 1979-87; chmn. Fla. del. to White House Conf. on Small Bus., 1979-80; mem. exec. bd., adminstr. adv. council SBA. Named Bus. Woman of Yr., Broward County Women in Communication, 1979; Woman of Yr., Am. Soc. Woman Accts., 1975; Soroptimist Woman of Yr. in Acctg., 1976, 77; Woman of Yr. in Acctg., Zonta, 1978; Bus. Person of Yr., FBLA, 1980; Broward County Bus. Leader of Yr., 1983; Woman of Yr. Port St. Lucie Charter chpt. ABWA, 1988. Mem. Fla. Accts. Assn. (pres. 1978-79), Nat. Soc. Public Accts., Internat. Platform Assn. Contbr. articles to profl. jours. Office: Auto Busters Inc 4190 Selvitz Rd Fort Pierce FL 34981

HOFFMAN, ELIZABETH GAIL, nurse; b. Stanford, Calif., June 4, 1962; d. Ronald Eugene Switzer and Gail Irene (Siegner) Wiest. BS in Nursing, UCLA, 1984; MPA, U. San Francisco, 1987. Night charge nurse surg. VA med. Ctr., Palo Alto, Calif., 1984-85; emergency room nurse, mobile intensive care nurse Good Samaritan Hosp., San Jose, Calif., 1985—; childbirth educator, San Jose, Calif., 1987. Mem. UCLA Alumni Scholarship Com., No. Calif., 1984—, Flying Drs., 1985—. Chancellors scholar UCLA, 1980. Mem. Calif. Nurses Assn., Nat. Assn. Female Execs. Democrat. Roman Catholic. Club: Bayaria Bruins. Home: 200 Core St #102 San Francisco CA 94117 Office: Good Samaritan Hosp Emergency Dept 2425 Samaritan Dr San Jose CA 95126

HOFFMAN, ELLENDALE MCCOLLAM, psychologist, pastoral counselor; b. Alexandria, La., Apr. 3, 1951; d. William and Hope Flower (Joffrion) McCollam; A.A., Briarcliff Coll., 1971; B.A., Manhattanville Coll., 1973; M.Div., Episcopal Div. Sch., 1976; D.Min., Andover Newton Theol. Sch., 1978; m. Charles L. Hoffman, Nov. 27, 1976. Ordained priest Episcopal Ch., 1977, deacon, 1976; clin. supr. Pastoral Inst. Tng. in Alcohol Problems, Cambridge, Mass., 1976-78; dir. growth and learning center Marion (Mass.) Ctr. for Human Services, 1978-79; clin. dir. Cape Counseling Center, Hyannis, Mass., 1979-82; pvt. practice psychology and pastoral counseling, Falmouth, Mass., 1976-88, Old Saybrook, Conn., 1988—. Chairperson commn. on today's families Diocese of Mass., 1980-82. Roothbert fellow, 1976-78; Epis. Women's scholar, 1976-78. Fellow Am. Assn. Pastoral Counselors (profl concerns com.); mem. Am. Psycol. Assn., Am. Assn. Marriage and Family Therapists (clin.), LWV. Lic. psychologist, Mass. Author course Driver's Alcohol Education Curriculum. Home and Office: 334 Main St Old Saybrook CT 06475

HOFFMAN, JUDY GREENBLATT, preschool director; b. Chgo., June 12, 1932; d. Edward Abraham and Clara (Morrill) Greenblatt; m. Morton Hoffman, Mar. 16, 1950 (div. Jan. 1983); children: Michael, Alan, Clare. BA summa cum laude, Met. State Coll., Denver, 1972; MA, U. No. Colo., 1976. Cert. tchr., Colo. Pre-sch. dir. B.M.H. Synagogue, Denver, 1968-70, Temple Emanuel, Denver, 1970-85, Congregation Rodef Shalom, Denver, 1985-88; instr. Red Rocks Community Coll., Denver, 1988—. Author: I Live in Israel, 1979, Joseph and Me, 1980 (Gamoran award). Coordinator Douglas Mountain Therapeutic Riding Ctr. for Handicapped, Golden, Colo., 1985—. Mem. Nat. Assn. Temple Educators. Democrat.

HOFFMAN, KARLA LEIGH, mathematician; b. Paterson, N.J., Feb. 14, 1948; d. Abe and Bertha (Gutham) Rakoff; BA, Rutgers, U., 1969; MBA, George Washington U., 1971, DSc in Ops. Research, 1975; m. Allan Stuart Hoffman, Dec. 26, 1971; 1 son, Matthew Douglas. Ops. research analyst IRS, Washington, 1970-72; research asst. George Washington U., 1972-75; asso. professorial lectr., 1978-85; NSF postdoctoral research fellow Nat. Acad. Sci., Washington, 1975-76; mathematician Nat. Bur. Standards, Washington, 1976-84; vis. asso. prof. ops. research U. Md., spring 1982; assoc. prof. systems engrng. dept. George Mason U., 1985-86, assoc. prof. ops. research and applied stats., 1986—; cons. to govt. agys. Recipient Applied Research award Nat. Bur. Standards, 1984, Silver medal U.S. Dept. Commerce, 1984. Mem. Ops. Research Soc. Am. (sec.-treas. computer sci. tech. sect. 1979-80, vice chmn. sect. 1981, chmn. sect. 1982, vis. professorial lectr. 1980—, chmn. tech. sect. com. 1983-86, council 1985-88), Math. Programming Soc. (editor newsletter 1979-82, chmn. com. algorithms 1982-85, council 1985-88, exec. com. 1986-88). Club: Clifton Horse Soc. Contbr. articles on ops. research to profl. jours.; assoc. editor Internat. Abstracts of Ops. Research, The Math. Programming Jour., Series B, The Ops. Research Soc. Jour. on Computing. Home: 6921 Clifton Rd Clifton VA 22024 Office: George Mason U Dept Ops Research & Stats 4400 University Dr Fairfax VA 22030

HOFFMAN, LINDA M., chemist, educator; b. N.Y.C., Dec. 18, 1939; d. Theodore and Esther (Schaefer) Weiss; m. Robert G. Hoffman, Feb. 2, 1958; 1 child, Samuel A. B.S., Queens Coll., 1959; M.S., NYU, 1967, Ph.D., 1970. Postdoctoral fellow Sloan Kettering Inst. Cancer Research, N.Y.C., 1972-73; research assoc. Kingsbrook Jewish Med. Ctr., N.Y.C., 1973-77; asst. prof. Baruch Coll. CUNY, N.Y.C., 1977-79, assoc. prof., 1979-82, prof., 1982—. Contbr. articles on Tay-Sachs disease and glycosphingolipids to profl. jours. Mem. edn. com. UN Internat. Sch., N.Y.C., 1981-84. Recipient Moore award Am. Soc. Neuropathologists, 1981, 84. Mem. Am. Chem. Soc., AAAS, Sigma Xi. Office: Baruch Coll Dept Chemistry 17 Lexington Ave New York NY 10010

HOFFMAN, LYNN RENEE, educator; b. Trenton, N.J., Apr. 19, 1957; d. Hugh L. and Thelma B. (Winner) H. BA in Theology, Immaculata Coll., 1983, MusB, 1985. Joined Sisters, Servants of Immaculate Heart of Mary, 1976. Elem. tchr. Diocese of Arlington, Va., 1979-80, Diocese of Allentown, Pa., 1980-82, Archdiocese Phila., 1983-86, Diocese of Trenton, N.J., 1987—. Contbr. articles to children's publs. Moderator Young Astronauts, Trenton, 1987—; mem. Phila. Task Force, 1987—. Recipient Nat. Schs. Excellence award U.S. Dept. Edn., 1988. Mem. Nat. Cath. Ednl. Assn., The Smithsonian Assocs., Nat. Assn. Female Execs. Democrat. Home: 63 Florence Ave Apt 3 Trenton NJ 08618 Office: 333 S Broad St Trenton NJ 08608

HOFFMAN, MARGARET A., banker; b. Phila., Dec. 11, 1945; d. Raymond O. and Helen (Thomas) H. B.F.A., Phila. Coll. Art, 1967; M.Ed., Temple U., 1968; cert. in banking Am. Inst. Banking, 1976. Sr. analyst Glenmede Trust Co., Phila., 1971-75; credit mgr. Lincoln Bank, Phila., 1975-77; dir. credit div. Robert Morris Assocs., Phila., 1977-83; v.p. corp. tng. Barnett Banks, Inc., Jacksonville, 1983-87, v.p. corp. mktg., 1987—; instr. Bank Lending Inst., 1985; adv. bd. Omega, San Francisco, 1984; instr. nat. workshop Robert Morris Assocs., Phila., 1984. Author: Credit Department Management, 1981; contbr. articles to banking jours. Assoc. mem. Robert Morris Assocs. Avocation: watercolors. Office: Barnett Banks Inc 100 Laura St Jacksonville FL 32202

HOFFMAN, MARGARET GROSS, community college administrator; b. Glassport, Pa., Jan. 14, 1940; d. Albert Frederick and Marguerite Bridget (Murphy) Gross; B.S., Slippery Rock State Coll., 1961; M.Ed., U. Pitts., 1972, Ph.D., 1980. children—Daniel Keith, Diane Lynn. Tchr. health and phys. edn. W. Mifflin Sch. Dist., Pa., 1961-63; tchr. Arroyo High Sch., Los Angeles, 1964-65; asst. prof. Community Coll. of Allegheny County, West Mifflin, Pa., 1970-75, athletic dir., 1975-76, asst. to v.p., exec. dean South Campus, 1976-82, asst. dean learning resources, 1982-83; exec. dir. Inst. for Bus., Industry and Govt., Orange County Community Coll., 1984—; bd. dirs. Occupations, Inc. Mem. Am. Assn. Women in Community and Jr. Colls. (participant in Leaders for 80's Program), Am. Council on Edn. (instl. rep. Nat. Identification Program for Women, Pa., 1981-82), Nat. Council on Community Services and Continuing Edn., Women in Mgmt, Orange County C. of C., Eastern Orange County C. of C. Editor and writer: Data from the Dean. Home: 8 Crabapple Ln Middletown NY 10940 Office: Morrison Hall 115 South St Middletown NY 10940

HOFFMAN, MARJORIE NEGELE, nursing adminstrator; b. Cleve., Sept. 1, 1941; d. Charles Frederick and Leah Virgil (Wettich) Negele; m. Walter William Hoffman, Feb. 10, 1968; children—Kevin William, Kimberly Ann, Kathryn Nicole. B.S.N., U. Mich., 1963; M.Nursing Edn., U. Pitts., 1967. Staff nurse U. Mich. Hosp., Ann Arbor, 1963-64; clin. instr. U. Mich., 1964-65; instr. Akron Children's Hosp., Ohio, 1965-66, Ill. Central Community Coll., East Peoria, 1968; clin. nursing specialist Columbus Children's Hosp., Ohio, 1978-80; asst. prof. Otterbein Coll., Westerville, Ohio, 1980-87; asst. dir. nursing staff devel. Children's Hosp. Inc., Columbus, 1987—; participant project facilitating competency devel. Ohio site team of Midwest Alliance in Nursing, 1983-86. Deacon, elder Gahanna Mifflin Presbyn. Ch., Ohio, 1977-82; Sunday sch. tchr. Cen. Coll. Presbyn. Ch., Westerville, 1984-85, deacon, 1985-88; mem. adv. com. Ohio Edn. Program on Smoking and Health, 1982-86; first pres. acad. support group Westerville North High Sch., 1986-87. Mem. Am. Nurses Assn., Ohio Nurses Assn., Sigma Theta Tau. Avocations: crafts; sewing; cooking. Home: 605 Hackberry Dr Westerville OH 43081 Office: Grant-Otterbein Nursing Program Otterbein College Westerville OH 43081

HOFFMAN, MARY CATHERINE, nurse anesthetist; b. Winamac, Ind., July 14, 1923; d. Harmon William Whitney and Dessie Maude (Neely) H.; R.N., Methodist Hosp., Indpls., 1945; cert. obstet. analgesia and anesthesia, Johns Hopkins Hosp., 1949, grad. U. Hosp. of Cleve. Sch. Anesthesia, 1952; Staff nurse Meth. Hosp., 1945-49; research asst., then staff anesthetist Johns Hopkins Hosp., 1949-62; staff anesthetist Meth. Hosp., 1962-64, U. Chgo. Hosps., 1964-66; chief nurse anesthetist Paris (Ill.) Community Hosp., 1966-80; staff anesthetist Hendricks County Hosp., Danville, Ind., Ball Meml. Hosp., Muncie, Ind., 1981-86; instr.-trainer CPR, 1975-81; mem. Terr. 08 CPR Coordinating Com., 1975-80. Mem. Am. Assn. Nurse Anesthetists, Am. Heart Assn., Ind. Fedn. Bus. and Profl. Women's Clubs (Ill. dist. chmn. 1977-78, state found. chmn. 1978-79; found. award 1979). Republican. Presbyterian. Home: 1700 N Maddox Dr Muncie IN 47304

HOFFMAN, MERLE HOLLY, social psychologist, political activist, author; b. Phila., Mar. 6, 1946; d. Jack Rheins and Ruth (Dubow) H.; B.A. magna cum laude in Psychology, Queens Coll., 1972; postgrad. CUNY, 1972-75; m. Martin Gold, June 30, 1979. Founder, pres. Choices Women's Med. Ctr., Forest Hills, N.Y., 1971—, Merle Hoffman Enterprises, N.Y.C., 1986; family planning cons. Health Ins. Plan, N.Y.C., 1973—; founder, pres. Ctr. for Comprehensive Breast Services, N.Y.C., 1979—; founder, pres. Merle Hoffman Enterprises, 1986; speaker, debator on women's rights and political issues. Bd. dirs. Found. for the Creative Community, 1979—; founder, pres. Nat. Liberty Com., 1981. Mem. Am. Health Assn., Nat. Assn. Abortion Facilities (co-founder, pres. 1976-77), Nat. Abortion Fedn. (co-founder, sec. 1977-78), Phi Beta Kappa. Cons. editor Female Health Topics and Diagnostic Reporter, 1979-81; editor, pub. ednl. jour. On The Issues; contbr. articles in field to various publs.; producer documentary film Abortion A Different Light; founder N.Y. Pro-Choice Coalition; host cable TV series MH: On the Issues, 1986. Office: Choices 97-77 Queens Blvd Forest Hills NY 11374

HOFFMAN, NANCY, municipal judge; b. San Francisco, Sept. 13, 1933; d. Franz and Sara (Flaschen) Rosenfeld; m. Daniel N. Hoffman, Dec. 24, 1961; children: Sharon, Jeremy, Carolyn. BA, U. Calif., Berkeley, 1955; JD, U. Santa Clara, 1974. Dep. pub. defender Santa Clara County, San Jose, Calif., 1975-80, judge mcpl. ct., 1980—. Mem. LWV, Calif. Judges Assn. (exec. bd. 1985-88, v.p. 1987-88), Calif. Women Lawyers (governing bd. 1985-87), Nat. Assn. Women Judges, Calif. Preventing Violence (bd. dirs. 1986—). Democrat. Jewish. Office: San Jose Facility Mcpl Ct 200 W Hedding San Jose CA 95110

HOFFMAN, NANCY YANES, health care professional, writer; b. Boston, July 2, 1929; d. William Phillip and Edith Sara (Bernstein) Yanes; m. Marvin J. Hoffman, Feb. 15, 1948; children: William Yanes, Holly Hoffman Brookstein, Jennifer Yanes. Student, Conn. Coll., 1946-48; BA with high distinction, U. Rochester, 1950, MA, 1968. Dir. Am. Guardian Life Ins. Co., Jenkintown, Pa., 1979-85; pub. relations con. Ochsner Med. Insts., New Orleans, 1978-82; asst. prof. English St. John Fisher Coll., Rochester, N.Y., 1969-79; assoc. prof. English St. John Fisher Coll., Rochester, 1979-86; pres. NYH Healthcare Assocs., Rochester, 1986—; freelance writer, lectr. Rochester, 1970—; Spl. clin. investigator Walter Reed Army Med. Ctr., Washington, 1983-85; vis. prof of med. humanities, U. New England, 1985; mem. breast cancer detection awareness task force Am. Cancer Soc., Syracuse, N.Y., 1986—. Author: Change of Heart: The Bypass Experience, 1985; co-author: Breast Cancer: A Practical Guide to Diagnosis, 1988, Doctor! I've Found a Lump!, 1989; columnist, Jour. Am. Med. Assn., 1972-85; contbr. numerous articles to profl. and popular jours., 1970—. Named Instr. of Excellence N.Y. State English Council, 1982; recipient scholarship Nat. Endowment for Humanities, 1978. Mem. Am. Med. Writers Assn., Nat. Assn. of Sci. Writers, Am. Soc. Journalists and Authors, Am. Diabetes Assn. (profl. sect.), Council of Am. Diabetes, Soc. of Diabetes Educators, AAAS, Soc. for Tech. Communication, Women in Communications, Modern Lang. Assn., Am. Heart Assn., Nat. Council Tchrs. English, Am. Culture Assn. Jewish. Home and Office: 77 Southern Pkwy Rochester NY 14618

HOFFMAN, NATHALIE R., lawyer; b. Pitts., Dec. 20, 1946; d. Herb and Rosella (Stein) Cohen; m. Robert L. Ditchey. BS, U. Mich., 1968; JD, UCLA, 1973. Bar: Calif. 1973. Assoc. O'Melveny & Myers, Los Angeles, 1973-76, Mitchell, Silberberg & Knupp, Los Angeles, 1976-78; sole practice, Los Angeles, 1978-80; bus. affairs exec. 20th Century Fox, Los Angeles, 1980-81; ptnr. Graham & James, Los Angeles, 1981-83; of counsel Sidley & Austin, Los Angeles, 1983-85, ptnr., Los Angeles, 1986—. Pres. Brazil-Calif. Trade Assn. Mem. ABA, State Bar Calif., Los Angeles County Bar Assn., Beverly Hills Bar Assn., Copyright Soc. (bd. trustees), Order of Coif, Phi Beta Kappa. Office: Sidley & Austin 2049 Century Park E 35th Floor Los Angeles CA 90067

HOFFMAN, SUSAN RONNIE, psychologist; b. Bklyn., May 5, 1948; d. Harold Abraham and Connie (Ellman) H.; B.S., Boston U., 1970, Ed.D., 1978. Asst. staff psychologist Judge Stone Child Guidance Center, Brockton, Mass., 1972-74; staff psychologist Dorchester Mental Health Center, Boston, 1974-76, Northeastern U. Counseling Center, Boston, 1976-81; psychologist Hurst Assos., P.C., Boston, 1979-82; pvt. practice psychology, Brookline, Mass., 1981—. Lic. psychologist Mass. Mem. Am. Psychol. Assn. Author articles in field. Office: 1180 Beacon St Suite 4C Brookline MA 02146

HOFFMAN, VICTORIA JUNE, lawyer; b. E. Lansing, Mich., Mar. 24, 1953; d. Ralph Alex and Lillian June (McVannel) Klawitter; m. John William Hoffman, Feb. 16, 1974; children—Thomas Clune, William Christopher, Veronica Irene. B.A. summa cum laude, Duquesne U., 1975; J.D. with honors, George Washington U., 1981. Bar: Va. 1981, D.C. 1986, U.S. Dist. Ct. (ea. dist.) Va. 1983, U.S. Ct. Appeals, 4th cir. 1983. Assoc. atty. Charles Kane Schanker, P.C., Fairfax, Va., and Washington, 1979—. Instr. CCD, Burke, Va., 1983-84. Mem. ABA, Assn. Trial Lawyers Am., Va. Trial Lawyers Assn., Trial Lawyers Met. Washington, Fairfax Bar Assn., Alpha Sigma Tau. Lodge: Zonta. Home: 6024 Meyers Landing Ct Burke VA 22015 Office: Charles Kane Schanker PC 1900 L St NW Suite 309 Washington DC 20036

HOFFMANN, CONSTANCE WELLINGS, city manager; b. Pitts., Dec. 11, 1950; d. William John and Marjorie Wellings; m. Stephen Hoffmann, Apr. 10, 1971. BA in Polit. Sci., Fla. Atlantic U., 1971, MA in Polit. Sci., 1972. Research asst. Fla. Atlantic U., Boca Raton, 1970-73; with City of Fort Lauderdale, Fla., 1974—, dep. city mgr., 1979-80, city mgr., 1980—. Bd. dirs. Ft. Lauderdale Neighborhood Housing Services, Inc., 1985—, Ft. Lauderdale Beach Break Blue Ribbon Com., 1987—. Recipient Outstanding Young Leader award Ft. Lauderdale Jaycees, 1981; named Woman of Yr./Broward County Atlantic-Fla. chpt. Women in Communications, 1981, Woman of Yr. South Fla. Bus. & Profl. Women, 1985. Mem. Internat. City Mgrs. Assn., Nat. Trust for Hist. Preservation, Fla. City and County Mgrs. Assn. (bd. dirs. 1983-86). Office: City of Fort Lauderdale PO Box 14250 Fort Lauderdale FL 33302

HOFFMANN, ELLEN BURROWS, data processing executive; b. Medford, Mass., July 24, 1940; d. Robert Bernard and Alice Emma (Fowler) Burrows; m. Francis Roger Hoffmann, Dec. 31, 1964. AB, Brown U., 1962. Programmer Mass. Mutual Life Ins. Co., Springfield, 1968-72; programmer Robertson Factories, Inc., Taunton, Mass., 1972-78, asst. mgr. data processing, 1978-85, data processing mgr., 1985—. Pres. Taunton Civic Chorus, 1986—. Mem. N. Eng. Computer Users Group (pres. 1982-83), Fedn. of NCR User Groups (chair communications 1985—). Office: Robertson Factories 33 Chandler Ave Taunton MA 02780

HOFFMANN, MARY ANN, data processing executive; b. Yonkers, N.Y., Nov. 19, 1946; d. Robert Augustus and Mary Margaret (Mansfield) Neary; B.A., Coll. Mt. St. Vincent, 1968; M.A., Fordham U., 1971; M.S., Fairleigh Dickinson U., 1978; m. Marvin W. Hoffmann, Mar. 9, 1968; children—Karri, Matthew. Project programmer IBM, Kingston, N.Y., 1977-82, devel. programmer, 1983-84, sr. programmer, 1984-86, program mgr., 1986—. NSF fellow, 1968. Roman Catholic. Home: RD 1 Box 386E Woodstock NY 12498 Office: IBM Neighborhood Rd Kingston NY 12401

HOFFMANN, NANCY LARRAINE, state legislator; m. Mark Hoffmann; children—Eva, Anna, Gustav. B.A., Syracuse U.; M.S., U. Md. Former polit. organizer, Tenn., Miss., city councilor Syracuse, N.Y.; mem. N.Y. State Senate from 48th Dist., 1984—, mem. agr., crime and correction, fin., environ. conservation, local govt., tourism, recreation and sports coms. Mem. Gov.'s Council on Fiscal and Econ. Priorities. Democrat. Address: PO Box 268 De Witt NY 13214

HOFFMEISTER, JANA MANCE, cardiologist. MD, SUNY Upstate Med. Ctr., Syracuse, 1976. Diplomate Am. Bd. Internal Medicine. Intern Albany (N.Y.) Med. Ctr., 1976-78, asst. resident, 1978-79, resident, 1979-80, fellow div. cardiology, 1981-83; fellow div. cardiology Emory U., Crawford Long Meml. Hosp., Atlanta, 1984, Emory U., 1984; fellow coronary angioplasty Emory U. Hosp., 1985-86; fellow interventional cardiology Emory U., 1985—; presenter numerous cardiology confs. Contrb. numerous articles to profl. jours. Mem. AMA, Syracuse Med. Alumni Assn., The President's Club, Lamplighters Soc. of Emory U. Home: 7 Reddy Ln Loudonville NY 12211

HOFFNER, MARILYN, university administrator; b. N.Y.C., Nov. 16, 1929; d. Daniel and Elsie (Schulz) H.; B.F.A., Cooper Union; m. Albert Greenberg, May 29, 1949; children—Doren Roe, Peter Cooper. Art dir. Printers' Ink mag., N.Y.C., 1953-63; art dir. Print mag., N.Y.C., 1960-62; corp. art dir. Vision, Inc., Latin Am., 1963-75; dir. alumni relations Cooper Union, 1975-82, dir. devel., 1982—. Bd. dirs. Art Dirs. Club N.Y., 1973-75, 79-82, exec. sec., 1973-75, exec. treas., 1979-82; mem. Citizens Adv. Cultural Arts Com. Dutchess County, 1978-80. Named Alumnus of Yr., Cooper Union, 1968; recipient Gold medal Art Dirs. Club, 1979. Mem. Cooper Union Alumni Assn. (editor-in-chief 1971-74, 1st v.p. 1974-75), Council Advancement and Support of Edn., Type Dirs. Club (numerous awards), Nat. Arts Club (exhbn. com.). Contbg. editor Print mag., 1960-62, Art Direction, 1959-64, Graphics mag., 1959-82; designer mags., advt., books. Home: 51 Fifth Ave New York NY 10003 Office: 41 Cooper Sq New York NY 10003

HOFFNUNG, AUDREY SONIA, speech and language pathologist, educator; b. N.Y.C., Mar. 15, 1928; d. Nathan and Gussie (Karp) Smith; B.A. cum laude, Bklyn. Coll., 1949; M.A., Columbia U., 1950; Ph.D., City U. N.Y., 1974; m. Joseph Hoffnung, Nov. 26, 1950; children—Bonnie Fern, Tami Lynn. Rehab. therapist Ridgewood Cerebral Palsy Center, 1949-50; dir. speech therapy Kingsbrook Med. Center, Bklyn., 1950-55; therapist and cons. Morris J. Solomon Clinic, Bklyn., 1956-58; therapist Speech and Hearing Center Bklyn. Coll., 1958-62, 63-64; pvt. practice speech therapy Hewlett (N.Y.) Med. Center, 1961-63; pvt. practice speech therapy, Oceanside, N.Y., 1964-71; cons. on staff for aphasic patients Phys. Medicine and Rehab. Center, South Nassau Communities Hosp., 1964-65; part-time lectr. Speech and Hearing Center, Queens (N.Y.) Coll., 1970-72; adj. lectr. dept. speech Bklyn. Coll., 1973-74, asst. prof. speech pathology, 1974-77; asst. prof. dept. speech communication and theatre St. John's U., Jamaica, N.Y., 1977-80, asso. prof., 1980—; guest lectr. N.Y. Orton Soc., 1979, Brookdale Med. Center, 1978; mem. profl. adv. bd. Vis. Home Health Services of Nassau County, 1973—. Cert. and lic. speech pathologist, N.Y. Mem. Am. Speech and Hearing Assn., N.Y.C. Speech, Hearing and Lang. Assn., N.Y. State Speech and Hearing Assn. (chairperson student activities 1978-79), L.I. Speech and Hearing Assn., Nat. Student Speech-Lang.-Hearing Assn. (hon. advisor 1988), Aphasia Study Group of N.Y.C., N.Y. Acad. Scis. Contbr. articles on speech pathology to profl. jours. Home: 3282 Woodward St Oceanside NY 11572 Office: St John's U Dept Speech Communication Utopia and Grand Central Pkwys Jamaica NY 11439

HOFMANN, JUDITH L., government official; b. Carlisle, Pa., Feb. 7, 1944. B.A., U. Hawaii, 1966. Tchr. public schs. Hawaii, 1967-68, Fairfax County, Va., 1968-69; personnel mgmt. specialist Dept. Transp., Washington, 1969-71, Dept. Labor, 1971-72; spl. asst. to dep. dir. Cost of Living Council, Washington, 1972-74; spl. asst. to adminstr. Fed. Energy Adminstrn., Washington, 1974-75; dir. for mgmt. Commodity Futures Trading Commn., Washington, 1975-76; dir. exec. secretariat Dept. Labor, 1976-79; dir. adminstrv. services Dept. Labor, Washington, 1979-80; asst. sec. HUD, Washington, 1981—. Office: HUD 451 7th St SW Room 10110 Washington DC 20410

HOFMANN, REVA BUTLER, engineering consulting firm executive; b. Red Bud, Ill.; d. Allen William and Bertha Elizabeth (Conway) Moore; divorced; children: Kathy, Dennis. BS in Bus., U. Mo., 1967. Exec. salesperson Butler Packaging Co., St. Louis, Mo. and Santa Ana, Calif., 1976-82; pres., owner HTS Internat., Laguna Niguel, Calif., 1982—; citizen ambassador to China, Nuclear Tech. delegation, 1985; appeared on TV program Mid Morning Los Angeles, Always on Sunday, Australia. Contbr. articles to Los Angeles Times, Orange Coast Mag., Daily Pilot. Sponsored numerous golf tournaments for Cystic Fibrosis, fund-raising drives for Muscular Dystrophy, March of Dimes. Recipient awards for innovative packaging Midwest Packaging Assn., 1st Lady of the Day award Sta. WORTH-Radio, St. Louis, 1975. Mem. Am. Nuclear Soc. (assoc.), Am. Mgmt. Assn. (bd. dirs.), Sales and Mktg. Execs. (bd. dirs., Woman of Yr. 1975, Entrepreneur of Yr. 1987), CEO, The Exec. Com., Nat. Employment Assn. (ethics com.), Sales and Mktg. Execs. Internat. Office: HTS Internat Inc PO Box 6840 Laguna Niguel CA 92677

HOGAN, GENIE MERRELL, pilot; b. Cleve., Dec. 28, 1946; d. Roswell Pettibone and Madeline (Bliley) Merrell; m. Garland Hogan, Apr. 17, 1986. BS in Pub. and Community Service, Nova U., 1978, postgrad., 1980-85. Customs broker Martin & Merrell, Ft. Lauderdale, Fla., 1977-79, Emery Customs Brokers, Miami (Fla.) and Ft. Lauderdale, 1979-80, Am. Nat. Brokers, 1980-85; pilot Aero Coach Inc., Ft. Lauderdale, Miami, and Palm Beach, Fla., 1985—; pres. Internat. Air Race, Ft. Lauderdale, 1986—; cons. Red Aircraft, Ft. Lauderdale, 1987—. Mem. exec. com. Rep. Party, Ft. Lauderdale, 1978—. Republican. Presbyterian. Club: 99's (chmn. local chpt., Amelia Earhart medal 1980). Lodge: Zonta: (bd. dirs. local chpt.). Home: 4772 NW 2d Ct Fort Lauderdale FL 33317 Office: Merrell Hogan Inc 852 NE 20th Ave Fort Lauderdale FL 33314

HOGAN, LINDA RAE, educator; b. Gary, Ind., Apr. 11, 1948; d. Carl Dorsey and Charlotte L. (Schreiber) Ruley; m. Charles Patrick Hogan, June 10, 1972; children: Colleen Marie, Kelly Kathleen. BS, Ind. U., 1970, postgrad., 1972; postgrad., Gov.'s State U., 1986-87, Lewis U., 1987. Tchr. Crown Point (Ind.) High Sch., 1970-73; tchr. phys. edn. Solon Robinson Elem., Crown Point, 1973-74; coach Lowell (Ind.) Dolphins, 1978-79, 75-87; pvt. practice swimming tchr. Lowell, 1975—; tchr. phys. edn. St. Edward Elem. Sch., Lowell, 1980-86, Hubbard Trail Jr. High, Crete, Ill., 1985—. Mem. NEA, Crete Mone Educators Assn., Pi Epsilon Kappa. Roman Catholic. Home: 503 Driftwood Dr Lowell IN 46356 Office: Hubbard Trail Jr High 1500 Sangamon St Crete IL 46356

HOGAN, MARY THERESA, communications executive; b. Wichita, Kans., Oct. 2, 1956; d. Marion F. and Margaret J. (O'Connor) H. BA, Kans. Newman Coll., 1974-79. Mgr. Lankford Quote Digest, Wichita. Office: Lankford Quote Digest 630 E Douglas Wichita KS 67202

HOGARTY, KATHLEEN CLAIRE, small business owner; b. Albany, N.Y., Dec. 7, 1953; d. Francis Joseph and Claire Mary (Byrnes) H. BS in Bus. Adminstrn., Colo. State U., 1978. Sales rep. Manville Corp., Denver, 1979-81, Griffin Sales, Kansas City, Mo., 1982-83; owner Hogarty & Assocs., Prairie Village, Kans., 1983—. Mem. Nat. Assn. Div. Seven Reps., Constrn. Specifications Inst., Colo. State U. Alumni Assn., Jr. League. Republican. Roman Catholic. Club: Prospectors Investment. Home: 5534 Norwood Rd Fairway KS 66205 Office: Hogarty & Assocs 8611 Delmar Ln Prairie Village KS 66207

HOGE, PATRICIA PATTEN, human service organization administrator; b. Newton, Mass., Mar. 6, 1945; d. Robert Ross and Jean Barnes (Smith) Patten; m. Thomas Philip Seward, Oct. 2, 1965 (div. Mar. 1987); children: Amy, William; m. Philip A. Hoge, Mar. 5, 1988. Diploma in Nursing New Eng. Bapt. Hosp. Sch. Nursing, 1965; B.S. in Psychology, SUNY, 1979; M.S. in Edn., Elmira Coll., 1981; M.S. in Human Services, Cornell U., 1983, Ph.D. in Human Services, 1983. Registered nurse, N.Y., Mass., Del. Staff nurse New Eng. Bapt. Hosp., Boston, 1965-66, 1970-71; nurse. tchr. health Post Sch. Dist., Corning, N.Y., 1973-79; project coordinator Steuben-Alleg BOCES Painted Post, N.Y., 1979-81; teaching asst., lectr. Cornell U., Ithaca, N.Y., 1981-83; exec. dir. ARC, Elmira, N.Y., 1983-87; exec. v.p. Del. div. Am. Cancer Soc., Wilmington, 1987—; cons. N.Y. State Edn. Dept., Albany, 1983, Corning-Painted Post Sch. Dist., Corning, 1981-82. Author: Me, My Baby and Blubber, 1980; A Teacher's Guide to Divorce, 1981, Teacher's Guide to Helping Children of Divorce, 1982. Mem. alumni bd. Coll. Human Ecology. sec., N.Y. State div. Am. Cancer Soc., 1982, bd. dirs. 1979 (recipient Voice of Hope award 1979). Mem. AAUW, N.Y. State Fedn. Profl. Health Educators (pres. 1983), N.Y. State Acad. Scis. Republican. Episcopalian. Avocation: hiking. Home: PO Box 4057 One New London Rd Wilmington DE 18907 Office: Am Cancer Soc Del Div 1708 Lovering Ave Suite 202 Wilmington DE 19806

HOGG, HELEN BATTLES SAWYER, astronomer; b. Lowell, Mass., Aug. 1, 1905; came to Can. 1931; d. Edward Everett and Carrie Myra (Sprague) Sawyer; m. Frank Scott Hogg, Sept. 6, 1930; children—Sarah Longley, David Edward, James Scott; m. Francis Ethelbert Louis Priestley, Nov. 28, 1985. A.B., Mt. Holyoke Coll., 1926, D.Sc. (hon.), 1958; A.M., Radcliffe Coll., 1928, Ph.D., 1931; D.Sc. (hon.), U. Waterloo, 1962, McMaster U., 1976, U. Toronto, 1977, St. Mary's U., Halifax, N.S., 1981; D.Litt. (hon.), St. Mary's U.; D. Sci. (hon.), U. Lethbridge, 1985. Lectr. Smith Coll., Northampton, Mass., 1927; lectr. Mt. Holyoke Coll., South Hadley, Mass., 1930-31, asst. prof., acting chmn. dept. astronomy, 1940-41; research assoc. Dominion Astrophys. Obs., Victoria, B.C., Can., 1931-34; research assoc. David Dunlap Obs. U. Toronto, Ont., Can., 1936—, lectr., 1941-51, asst. prof. astronomy, 1951-55, assoc. prof., 1955-57, prof., 1957-76, prof. emeritus, 1976—; vis. prof. Harvard U., summer 1952; program dir. astronomy NSF, Washington, 1955-56. Contbr. articles to profl. jours.; astronomy columnist Toronto Star, 1951-81. Decorated officer, 1968, companion Order of Can., 1976; recipient medal Rittenhouse Astron. Soc., 1967, Centennial medal, 1967, Queen Elizabeth Silver Jubilee medal, 1967, Klumpke Roberts award Astron. Soc. Pacific, 1983, Sanford Fleming medal Royal Can. Inst., 1985, award of merit City of Toronto, 1985. Mem. Am. Astron. Soc. (councillor 1965-68, Annie J. Cannon prize 1965-68), Royal Astron. Soc. Can. (pres. 1957, hon. pres. 1977-78), Am. Assn. Variable Star Observers (pres. 1940-41), Internat. Astron. Union (past pres. subcom.), Royal Soc. Can. (pres. sect. 3, 1960-61), Can. Astron. Soc. (1st pres. 1971-72). Club: University Women's (Toronto). Home: 98 Richmond St, Richmond Hill, ON Canada L4C 3Y4 Office: David Dunlap Obs, U Toronto, PO Box 360, Richmond Hill, ON Canada L4C 4Y6

HOGGE, SUSAN LOUISE, computer analyst; b. Portsmouth, Va., Mar. 3, 1958; d. Wayne Frances and Jacqueline Palmer (Winston) Hogge; m. Frederic Charles Cale, Dec. 18, 1981 (div.); one child, Rachael Jacqueline. BS, Radford U., 1984. Computer operator Va. Poly. Inst. and State U., Blacksburg, 1980-82, programmer, 1982-85; data base analyst Richmond (Va.) Pub. Schs., 1985—; counselor Career Opportunity Edn., Richmond, 1986—. Mem. Westover Hills Assn., Richmond, 1987—. Mem. Nat. Assn. Female Execs., Research Inst. Am., Richmond Assn. Sch. Adminstrs. Club: Technova (Richmond) (pres. 1987-88). Home: 5108 New Kent Rd Richmond VA 23225 Office: Richmond Pub Schs 301 N 9th St Richmond VA 23219

HOGSETTE, SARAH MARGARET, lawyer; b. Atlanta, May 18, 1948, d. Daniel Lawrence and Dorothy (Hayes) H. B.S., U. Ga., 1970; J.D., Emory U., 1981. Bar: Ga. 1981. Law clk. DeKalb Superior Ct., Decatur, Ga., 1981-83, Supreme Ct. of Ga., Atlanta, 1983-84; atty. Life Ins. Co. of Ga., Atlanta, 1984—. Bd. dirs. The Joel Chandler Harris Assn., 1987—, Greater Atlanta chpt. Lupus Found. Am., 1986—. Recipient award Bur. Nat. Affairs, 1981; Douglas Lee Peabody Meml. award, 1981. Mem. ABA, State Bar Ga., Atlanta Bar Assn. (bd. dirs. 1988—), The Lawyers Club of Atlanta, Corp. Counsel Assn. Greater Atlanta, Atlanta Pub. Affairs Council. Episcopalian. Office: Life Ins Co of Ga 5780 Powers Ferry Rd NW Atlanta GA 30365

HOGSTROM, ROSEANNE, personnel director; b. Colusa, Calif., June 13, 1942; d. Wesley Willow and Marjorie Anne (Miller) Smith; m. George W. Hogstrom, Oct. 17, 1964 (div. 1972); children: Erik Wesley, Inger Marie-Rose. Student, Yuba Coll., 1960-61; AA, Diablo Valley Coll., 1976. Adminstrv. asst. Solano County Dept. Weights and Measures, Vallejo, Calif., 1975-79; exec. sec. The Pasha Group, Corte Madera, Calif., 1979-81, staff asst. pub. relations, 1981-82, corp. communications, 1982-83, personnel mgr., 1983—. Editor: (corp. newsletters) OpenLine, 1981-86, Pasha People, 1986-87; producer: (corp. video show) The Pasha Group, 1987. Mem. Contra Costa Co. Drug Abuse Adv. Bd., Pleasant Hill, Calif., 1977-78, State Calif. Dept. Parks and Recreation Seal Watch, 1986-87. Soroptimist club scholar, 1977. Mem. Federated Employers of Bay Area, Am. Soc. Personnel Adminstrs., No. Calif. Human Resources Council, Marin County Personnel Mgmt. Forum (sec. 1987). Republican. Protestant. Home: 7771 Healdsburg Ave #9 Sebastopol CA 95472 Office: The Pasha Group 5725 Paradise Dr Corte Madera CA 94925

HOGUE, SUSAN CAROL, executive recruitment company executive; b. Atlanta, Ga., Dec. 9, 1949; d. James Carroll and Burdella Gwendolyn (Anderson) Cunningham; m. Robert D. Hogue, Dec. 31, 1984 (div. Mar. 1987); children: James T. Rewis, Melissa K. Rewis. AA, Massey Coll., 1969; student, Ga. State U., 1969-70. Exec. recruiter Parker Page Atlanta, 1980-84; founder, pres. The Hogue Assocs., Lincoln, Nebr., Overland Park, Kans., Plantation, Fla., Atlanta and Chgo., 1984—. Sponsor Nebr. Make-A-Wish, Lincoln, 1986. Recipient Disting. Cons. award Nat. Assn. Personnel Cons., 1984. Mem. Nat. Assn. Female Execs., Nat. Paint Horse Assn., Nat. Pinto Horse Assn. (1987 Champion Barrel Racer award Nebr.), Nat. Quarter Horse Assn., Nebr. Paint Horse Club, Nebr. Pinto Horse Club, PTA. Republican. Episcopalian. Clubs: Lofty Ladies of Lincoln, Salt Creek Wranglers.

HOGYA, MARY GOLDING, government official; b. Essex County, N.J., June 16, 1946; d. Wesley Irwin and Florence Grace (Smith) Golding. Cert., Universite de Grenoble, France, 1967; B.A., Lake Erie Coll., 1968. Editor, writer Bur. Labor Stats., Washington, 1968-72, Employment and Tng. Adminstrn., Dept. Labor, Washington, 1972-78; budget, fiscal officer Interstate Commerce Commn., Washington, 1978-88; dir. adminstrn. U.S. Sentencing Commn., Washington, 1988—. Editor, author lit. jour. Nota Bene, 1967, Monthly Labor Rev., 1968-72. Palisades Citizens Orgn., Washington, 1983—. Recipient Outstanding Performance awards Dept. Labor, 1974, 78; Spl. Achievement Awards, Interstate Commerce Commn., 1983, 85. Avocations: swimming; tennis; music; dancing, reading. Office: US Sentencing Commn 1331 Pennsylvania Ave NW Suite 1400 Washington DC 20004

HOHN, JAYNE MARIE, optometrist; b. Parkston, S.D., May 12, 1957; d. Marlin W. and Wilma A. (Schoenfelder) H. BS, Pacific U., 1979, OD, 1983. Optometrist Dr. J.W. Hanley, Aberdeen, S.D., 1983; pvt. practice optometry Rapid City, S.D., 1984—. Tutor Laubach Literacy Council, Rapid City, 1986—. Named Rossman scholar Pacific U., 1978. Mem. Am. Optometric Assn., S.D. Optometric Soc., Am. Pub. Health Assn., Laubach Literacy Council, Nat. Assn. Female Execs. Republican. Roman Catholic. Office: 501 Kansas City St Rapid City SD 57701

HOINKES, MARY ELIZABETH, federal agency adminstrator, lawyer; b. Washington, Aug. 13, 1940; d. Howard Egger and Elizabeth Mae (Lucas) Wahrenbrock; m. H. Dieter Hoinkes, July 24, 1965. BA, Randolph-Macon Women's Coll., 1962; postgrad. Sch. of Law, U. Va., 1962-63; JD, George Washington U., 1965. Bar: D.C. 1965, U.S. Ct. Appeals (D.C. cir.), U.S. Supreme Ct. Assoc. Clifford & Miller (now Clifford & Warnke), Washington, 1965-68; adminstrv. ofcl. Internat. Labor Office (UN specialized agy.), Geneva, 1969-70, asst. dir. Washington office, 1970-76; atty. adv. U.S. Dept. State, Washington, 1976-77, asst. legal adv. for oceans, environment and sci. affairs, 1977-80, dep. asst. sec. of state for environment, health and natural resources, 1980-81; dep. asst. dir. for multilateral affairs U.S. Arms Control and Disarmament Agy., Washington, 1981-85, dep. gen. counsel, 1985—; mem. bd. appellate rev. U.S. Dept. State, Washington, 1982—; chmn. sr. advisers on environment UN Econ. Commn. for Europe, Geneva, 1980-82; vice-chmn. com. on environment Orgn. for Econ. Coop. and Devel., Paris, 1980-81. Office: US Arms Control and Disarmament Agy 320 21st St Washington DC 20451

HOJNOWSKI, KAY LYNN, real estate investor; b. St. Louis, Sept. 27, 1948; d. Jean Fred and Maxine Florence (Ott) Kallmayer; m. Eugene Leo Hojnowski, Mar. 14, 1981; children: Jessica Ryan, Crystal Danielle; m. Simon Peter Swarbrick, Apr. 17, 1971 (div. Jan. 1976). AA, Am. Coll. in Paris, 1968; BA in Philosophy U. Ill., Chgo., 1970; lic. real estate agt., Ill. Forms analyst Northwestern Meml. Hosp., Chgo., 1970-72; mgr. retail Fabric World, Niles, Ill., 1972; account exec. UARCO Bus. Forms, Chgo., 1973-79, adminstr. health care mktg., 1980-85; real estate investor, Chgo., 1985—. Contbr. articles to trade jours. Named Regional rookie of Yr., UARCO, 1974. Mem. Nat. Assn. Female Execs. Democrat. Presbyterian. Club: Lake Shore Tennis. Co-founder Women in Transition, 1978-79, Chgo. Avocations: reading, writing, painting, crafts.

HOKES, ORA, human services administration fundraiser; b. Memphis, Dec. 30, 1946; d. Albert Lee Hokes and Mary Emma (Owens) Rambert; m. Charles B. Smith, Nov. 12, 1967 (div. 1973); children: Chandre Bion Smith, Terracelyn LaSharones Smith. AA, Mpls. Community Coll., 1985; student, U. Minn., 1972-75, Metro State U., 1987—, Augsburg Coll., 1987—. Social services sec. Pilot City Regional Ctr., Mpls., 1972-74; receptionist, sec. YMCA, Mpls., 1974-75; adminstrv. sec. The Way-Opportunities Unltd., Mpls., 1975-81, asst. adminstr., 1981-82, asst. exec. dir., 1982-85, grant-swriter, 1985; program asst. Mpls. Community Coll., 1986-87; fundraiser Sabathani Community Ctr., Mpls., 1987—. Mem. Mpls. Arts Commn., 1985—; fundraising chmn. Ruth Hawkins YWCA, 1983—; campaign treas. Jackson for Pres., Mpls., 1982-84, del. Dem. Party 57B Dist., Mpls., 1983; bd. dirs. Vacation Bible Sch., Mpls., 1980—. Named one of Outstanding Young Women Am., 1980, recipient U.S. Achievement Acad. Scholastic All-Am. award, 1987. Mem. Nat. Assn. Female Execs., Black Women's Tribute (co-founder), Black Social Workers. Baptist. Club: Serwas, Inc. (officer Mpls. chpt. 1974-80). Home: 1350 Russell Ave N Minneapolis MN 55411

HOKS, BARBARA LOUISE, personnel director; b. Mesa, Ariz., Sept. 9, 1955; d. Adelberto Celaya and Rosalva (Pena) Mendivil; m. Fredrick Thomas Hoks, Nov. 18, 1978. BS in Acctg., Ariz. State U., 1977. Acct. Greyhound Corp., Phoenix, 1978, City of Mesa, 1979; acct. Ariz. State U., Tempe, 1979-81, mgr. ops. and controls, 1981-82, bus. systems analyst, 1982-85, asst. dir. personnel, 1985—. Mem. East Valley Personnel Assn., Univ. Career Women (bd. dirs. 1985-87). Roman Catholic. Office: Ariz State U Personnel Dept Tempe AZ 85287-1403

HOLAHAN, PAULETTE HELDNER, court administrator; b. New Orleans; d. Knute and Colette (Pope) Heldner; m. John M. Holahan, Jan. 15, 1955; children: Shawn Louise, John Michael Jr., Paulette Mary, Gregory Heldner, Odile Riley, Meghan Amy. Student, Loyola U. of the South, New Orleans, 1953-55. Pub. info. officer Orleans Parish Prison, New Orleans, 1974-76; assoc. Ad-Vantage Pub. Relations, New Orleans, 1976-77; pub. info. officer La. Supreme Ct., New Orleans, 1977—. Editor: Classroom Prescriptions for Learning Disabilities, 2 vols., 1974, La. Jud. Newsletter, 1977-84. Chmn. bd. New Orleans Pub. Library, 1979-83, La. State Library Commn., 1978-79, 82-84, 86—; mem. Nat. Commn. on Libraries and Info. Sci., 1979-84; exec. bd. dirs. Urban Libraries Council, 1974—, v.p., 1984-86, pres., 1986—; del. White House Conf. on Libraries and Info. Sci., Washington, 1979. Recipient Modisette award La. Library Assn., 1981. Mem. ABA (assoc.; jud. adminstrn. div.), La. Ct. Adminstrs. Assn. (co-founder, sec.-treas. 1982-86, v.p. 1986—), Nat. Assn. for Ct. Mgmt., Am. Judicature Soc. Democrat. Roman Catholic. Club: New Orleans Press. Avocations: reading, gardening, travel. Office: La Supreme Ct 301 Loyola Ct New Orleans LA 70112

HOLBROOK, NANCY LYN, personnel executive; b. Marietta, Ga., Mar. 9, 1956; d. James Egbert adn Dorothy Julian (Loudermilk) H. Student, Kennesaw Coll., 1978-80, Ga. State U., 1980—. Catalog services asst. J.C. Penney Co., Smyrna, Ga., 1972-74, personnel clk., 1974-75, personnel supr., 1975-76, mdse. mgmt. trainee, 1976-77; mdse. mgr. J.C. Penney Co., Forest Park, Ga., 1977-80, customer service mgr., 1980-83; sr. mdse. mgr. J.C. Penney Co., Atlanta, 1983-85, personnel mgr., 1985—. Mem. Am. Soc. Personnel Adminstrs., Nat. Assn. Female Execs. Baptist.

HOLBROOK, NORMA JEANNETTE, nursing educator; b. Napton, Mo., Oct. 26, 1939; d. R. Milton and Thelma M. (Miller) Cochran; m. Ralph E. Holbrook, June 30, 1961; children—Tamara M., Jennifer L. B.S.N., Central Mo. State U., 1965; M.N., Kans. U., 1982. Staff nurse Menorah Med. Ctr., Kansas City, Mo., 1965-66, head nurse, 1966-67; instr. nursing Met. Community Coll., Kansas City, 1967-68; staff nurse Independence (Mo.) Med. Ctr., 1971-73; staff nurse St. Francis Hosp., Topeka, 1975-80, 84—; instr. nursing Washburn U., Topeka, 1981-85, asst. prof., 1986—; mem. nursing quality assurance com. Stormont Vail Regional Med. Ctr., Topeka, 1982-83, mem. task force for improved implementation nursing care plans, 1983. Chmn. nursing adv. com. ARC, Capital City chpt., Topeka, 1982-83, mem. nursing adv. com., 1980—. Presentor ednl. programs on nursing process and care planning, goal setting, values clarification and ethics in care of the elderly; contbr. articles to profl. jours. Mem. Am. Nurses Assn., Sigma Theta Tau. Republican. Methodist. Office: Washburn U 1700 College St Topeka KS 66621

HOLBROOK, VIVIAN NICHOLAS, artist; b. Mt. Vernon, N.Y., Mar. 31, 1913; d. William and Jessie (Worman) Nicholas; m. Hollis Howard Holbrook, June 26, 1937; children: Ferris H. Caine, Peter Worman, Nicholas. BFA, Yale U., 1936. Art instr. Colby Jr. Coll., New London, N.H., 1936-38; interim art instr. U. Fla., Gainesville, 1943-44; dir. Ctr. of Modern Art, Micanopy, Fla., 1969-72; vol. tchr. A. Quincy Jones Elem. Sch., Gainesville, 1972-74. Exhibited in group shows at: Sarasota Mus. Art., Fla. Nat. Mus. Art, Tampa Fla. Fair, Lowe Gallery, Miami Mus. Art, Patronato de Bellas Artes, Museum Nationales Havana, Columbia Mus. of Art of S.C., Butler Art Inst. Purdue U., Soc. of Four Arts, Palm Beach, Fla., La Universidad Michoacan, Morella, Mexico, Ball State Nat. Drawing Show, Portsmouth (Va.) Arts Ctr., Montgomery Mus. Art, Santa Fe Community Coll., Minn. Mus. Art., 1980; two man shows: U. Fla., Fla. So. Coll., Barry Coll.; one man shows include: J. Hillis Miller Health Ctr., 20 Year Retrospective at Thomas Ctr. Gallery, Gainesville, Fla., 1986. Recipient award Fla. Fedn. Art, 1942, Best Landscape award 1946, Atwater Kent award, 1966. Democrat. Club: Yale (Gainesville) (v.p.). Home: 1710 SW 35th Pl Gainesville FL 32608

HOLCOMB, ALICE WILLARD POWER, diversified investments executive; b. Franklin County, Ga., Sept. 11, 1922; d. William McKinley and Flora Sarah (Cash) Cantrell; m. Fleming Mitchell Power, May 6, 1941 (dec. Sept. 1967); children: Susan Cantrell, Fleming Michael; m. George Waymon Holcomb, June 4, 1982. Student, Toccoa (Ga.) Falls Coll., 1939-40; BS, Perry Bus. Sch., 1941. Owner Power Poultry Co., Toccoa, 1950-61, Fleming Mitchell Power Properties, Toccoa and Athens, Ga., 1962—, Power's (retail shops), Athens, 1968-85; ptnr. Power Constrn. Co., Athens, 1972—, Athens Indsl. Electric, Athens, 1973—. Mem. Athens Hist. Soc. Mem. DAR. Republican. Baptist. Home and Office: 199 Avalon Dr Athens GA 30606

HOLCOMB, DOROTHY TURNER, publicist; b. Roanoke, Va., June 15, 1924; d. Wiley Bryant and Lena Mae (Gray) Turner; m. Joseph E. Baxter, Aug. 1, 1944 (dec. Nov. 1944); m. 2d, G. William Holcomb, May 8, 1948 (div. 1962). Student Coronet Bus. Sch., Roanoke, 1943; interior decorator certificate N.Y. Sch. Interior Design, 1953; student U. Miami, 1962-63. Exec. sec. Am.'s Jr. Miss Pageant, Mobile, Ala., 1962; exec. asst. to pres. Gilbert Mktg. Group, Inc., N.Y.C., 1963-65; br. dirs. Heart Assn., Miami, Fla., 1965-66; publicist in charge on-air promotion Screen Gems, Hollywood, Calif., 1966-68; publicity dir. Mus. of Sci./Planetarium, Miami, 1968-71, Bryna Cosmetics, Inc., Miami, 1973-74; freelance publicist, 1971-73, 76—; pub. relations/communications ECKANKAR, Menlo Park, Calif., 1974-75. Mem. Publicists Guild, Internat. Alliance Theatrical Stage Employees, Moving Picture Machine Operators, Women in Communications. Home: Ridgewood Farm 2400 Gate House Ln Salem VA 24153

HOLCOMB, MARGUERITE KNOWLES, former city ofcl., shorthand reporting co. exec.; b. Dayton Twp., Mich., Apr. 9, 1913; d. Arthur Russell and Catherine (Biermeyer) Knowles; student public schs., Muskegon and Dayton Twp., Mich.; children—Joyce C. Holcomb Filius, John F., June A. Ofcl. circuit ct. reporter 14th Jud. Circuit, Muskegon, 1943-53; pres. Holcomb Reporting Service, Inc., Muskegon, 1953—; commr. City of Muskegon, 1975-84, vice-mayor, 1977-79, mayor, 1980-82; mem. econ. devel. com. U.S. Conf. Mayors. Mem. adv. council Ferris State Coll., Big Rapids, Mich. Recipient Athena award, State of Mich., 1988; named Businesswoman of Yr., Quadrangle Bus. and Profl. Women's Clubs 1970, State Small Businesswoman of Yr., Mich. Fedn. Bus. and Profl. Women's Clubs, 1973, Entrepreneur of Yr., County of Muskegon, 1984, Mich. Woman Entrepreneur of Yr. Mich. Dept. Commerce, 1988. Mem. Nat. Shorthand Reporters Assn., Mich. Shorthand Reporters Assn., Mich. Ct. Reporters Assn. (pres. 1967-68), Muskegon C. of C. (bd. dirs.) Women's Div. Muskegon C. of C. (pres. 1986-87, treas.). Republican. Clubs: Bus. and Profl. Women's (state pres. 1966-67), Zonta (dir. club), Century. Office: 1891 Lakeshore Dr Muskegon MI 49441

HOLDEN, JESSICA ANN, photographer; b. Hartford, Conn., Dec. 18, 1956; d. R. Stuart and Jean Elizabeth (Hanna) H. B.A. in Visual Arts, Mt. Vernon Coll., 1978. Salesman Cape Cod Photo, Orleans, Mass., 1976-77; salesman, Washington Gallery of Photography and Your Lab., Washington, 1977; photographer Friday Publs., Inc., Washington, 1977-78; photographer U.S. Senate, Washington, 1978—. Photographer: Good Housekeeping, 1984. Mem. Mt. Vernon Alumni Assn., U.S Senate Staff Club. Home: 7309 Mallory Ln Alexandria VA 22310 Office: US Senate Photographic Studio Russell Senate Office 31B Washington DC 20510

HOLDER, ANGELA RODDEY, lawyer, educator; b. Rock Hill, S.C., Mar. 13, 1938; d. John T. and Angela M. (Fisher) Roddey; 1 child, John Thomas Roddey Holder. Student, Radcliffe Coll., 1955-56; B.A., Newcomb Coll., 1958; postgrad., Faculty of Law-King's Coll., London, 1957-58; J.D., Tulane U., 1960; LL.M., Yale U., 1975. Bar: La. 1961, S.C. 1960, Conn. 1981. Counsel Roddey, Sumwalt & Carpenter, Rock Hill, S.C., 1960—; atty. criminal div. New Orleans Legal Aid Bur., 1961-62; counsel York County Family Ct., S.C., 1962-64; asst. prof. polit. sci Winthrop Coll., Rock Hill, 1964-74; research assoc. Yale Law Sch., 1975-77, exec. dir. program in law, sci. and medicine, 1976-77; lectr. dept. pediatrics Yale Med. Sch., 1975-77, asst. clin. prof. pediatrics and law, 1977-79, assoc. clin. prof., 1979-83, clin. prof., 1983—; counsel for medicolegal affairs Yale-New Haven Hosp. and Yale Med. Sch., 1977—. Author: The Meaning of the Constitution, 1968, 2d edit., 1987, Medical Malpractice Law, 1975, 2d edit. 1978, Legal Issues in Pediatrics and Adolescent Medicine, 1977, 2d edit., 1985; contbg. editor: Prism mag.; contbg. editor., AMA; mem. editorial bd.: IRB; Law, Medicine and Health Care, Jour. Philosophy and Medicine; contbr. articles to profl. jours. Mem. Rock Hill Sch. Bd., 1967-68; bd. dirs. Family Planning Clinic, chmn., 1970-73. Mem. ABA, S.C. Bar Assn. (medico-legal com. 1973—), La. Bar Assn., Soc. Med. Jurisprudence, Am. Soc. Hosp. Attys., Am. Soc. Law and Medicine (treas. 1981-83, sec. 1983-85, pres. 1986-87). Democrat. Episcopalian. Home: 23 Eld St Apt B New Haven CT 06511 Office: Yale-New Haven Hosp 20 York St New Haven CT 06504

HOLDER, HOLLY IRENE, lawyer; b. Albuquerque, June 16, 1952; d. Howard George and Dorothy Evelyn (Doll) Holzum; m. William B. Holder, June 4, 1974; 1 child, Eric James. BA with honors, U. Colo., 1974; JD with honors, U. Denver, 1980. Bar: Colo., U.S. Ct. Appeals (10th cir.). Chemist Indsl. Labs., Denver, 1974-76; law clk. to presiding justice Colo. Supreme Ct., Denver, 1978; assoc. Calkins, Kramer, Grimshaw and Harring, Denver, 1980—. Active water resources coms. Denver Regional Council of Govt., 1985—, Douglas County (Colo.) Strategic Planning com., 1987; chmn. Chatfield Basin Task Force, Denver, 1986—, Chatfield Basin Assn., 1986. Recipient Govt. Disting. Service award Denver Regional Council, 1987. Mem. ABA, Colo. Bar Assn., Mensa. Office: Calkins Kramer et al 1700 Lincoln St #3800 Denver CO 80203

HOLDER, LILLIAN LYDIA, nursing home administrator; b. Sand Draw, Wyo., July 17, 1936; d. Ezra G. and Lillian Lyon; student U. Wyo., 1955, Central Wyo. Coll., 1972-74; A.S. in Nursing, Casper Coll., 1976, student, 1977-79; m. Willian Holder, Aug. 29, 1964 (div. 1983); children—Kim Marie (Mrs. Clyde Winckler), Mark Darrell. With Farnsworth Ins. Agy., Riverton, Wyo., 1954-55; bookkeeper Hagstrom Constrn., Riverton, 1955-62; supr. Maddox Well Service, Riverton, 1967-68; nursing asst. Bishop Randall Hosp., Lander, Wyo., 1970-72, Meml. Hosp., Riverton, 1973-74, Natrona County Meml. Hosp., Casper, Wyo., 1974-75; charge nurse, 1976-79; dir. nursing Geriatrics Inc. (name changed to ARA Living Ctrs.), Greeley, Colo., 1979-80; adminstr. Poplar Living Ctr., Casper, 1980—; pres.-elect Wyo. Health Care; sec. Wyo. Nat. Fedn. Republican Women. Mem. AARP, Wyo. Am. Nurses Assn., Wyo. Health Care Assn. (bd. dirs.), Bus. and Profl. Women. Republican. United Methodist. Mem. Order Eastern Star. Home: 2351 Sagewood Casper WY 82601 Office: 4305 S Poplar St Casper WY 82601

HOLDSWORTH, JANET NOTT, nurse, educator; b. Evanston, Ill., Dec. 25, 1941; d. William Alfred and Elizabeth Inez (Kelly) Nott; children—James William, Kelly Elizabeth, John David. B.S. in Nursing with high distinction, U. Iowa, 1963; M.Nursing, U. Wash., 1966; postgrad. U. Colo., 1981, U. No. Colo., 1982. Registered nurse, Colo. Staff nurse U. Colo. Hosp., Denver, 1963-64, Presbyn. Hosp., Denver, 1964-65, Grand Canyon Hosp., Ariz., 1965; asst. prof. U. Colo. Sch. Nursing, Denver, 1966-71; counseling nurse Boulder PolyDrug Treatment Ctr., Boulder, 1971-77; pvt. duty nurse Nurses' Official Registry, Denver, 1973-82; cons. nurse, tchr. parenting and child devel. Teenage Parent Program, Boulder Valley Schs., Boulder, 1980—; bd. dirs., treas. Nott's Travel, Aurora, Colo., 1980—; instr., nursing coordinator ARC, Boulder, 1979—, instr., nursing tng. specialist, 1980-82. Mem. adv. bd. Boulder County LaMaz Inc., 1980—; mem. adv. com. Child Find and Parent-Family, Boulder, 1981—; del. Republican County State Congl. Convs., 1972-86, sec. 17th Dist. Senatorial Com., Boulder, 1982—; vol. chmn. Mesa Sch. Parent Tchr. Orgn., Boulder, 1982—, bd. dirs., 1982—, v.p., 1983—. Mem. Am. Nurses Assn., Colo. Nurses Assn. (bd. dirs. 1975-76, human rights com. 1981-83, dist. pres. 1974-76), Soc. Adolescent Medicine, Council High Risk Prenatal Nurses, Council Intracultural Nurses, Sigma Theta Tau. Republican. Presbyterian (elder). Home: 1550 Findlay Way Boulder CO 80303 Office: Teenage Parent Program 3740 Martin Dr Boulder CO 80303

HOLGUIN, ANNABEL MUNIZ, municipal officer; b. Alpine, Tex., June 9, 1959; d. Cruz Huerta and Juanita (Garcia) Muniz; m. Jesus Ramon Holguin, Feb. 2, 1957; 1 child, Jesus M. Grad. high sch., Alpine, Tex. Clk. N.Y.C. Youth Coordinator, Alpine, 1977-78; acct. Pulliam Tax Service, Alpine, 1978-79; admissions clk., payroll clk. Pecos County Hosp., Ft. Stockton, Tex., 1979—; dep. clk. City of Alpine, 1979, cashier, mcpl. court clk., 1980-85, city sec., mcpl. ct. clk., 1985-87. Mem. Internat. Inst. Mcpl. Clks., Tex. Mcpl. Clks. (sec. treas. W. Tex. chpt. 1985), W. Tex. Ct. Clks. Assn. (sec. 1984). Office: City of Alpine 309 W Sul Ross Ave Alpine TX 79830

HOLIAN, GAIL CONCA, educator; b. Jersey City, Sept. 21, 1948; d. Samuel Joseph and Mariejoyee (Contey) Conca; m. John F. Holian, Dec. 26, 1970. BA, Georgian Court Coll., 1970; MA, St. Johns U., 1972; PhD in English Lit., Drew U., 1987. Instr. English, Neptune Twp. (N.J.) Bd. Edn., 1971-80; adj. instr. English, Ocean County Coll., Toms River, N.J., 1974—; teaching fellow English, NYU, N.Y.C., 1978-79; lectr. English, Georgian Court Coll., Lakewood, N.J., 1978-80; assoc. prof. English, Georgian Court Coll., 1988; asst. prof. English, 1980—, dir. writing program, 1982—; judge book rev. div. Ann. Creative Writing Awards, N.J. State Fedn. of Women's Clubs, 1988. Vol., ARC, 1972—; dir. media services and publs. Found. for Research in Optimal Living, Red Bank, N.J., 1984—; chairperson Instl. Integrity Self Study Group for Middle States Accreditation, Georgian Court Coll. Georgian Court Coll. grantee, 1968. Mem. MLA, Nat. Council Tchrs. English (judge Achievement Awards in Writing 1984), AAUP, N.J. Coll. English Assn., Sigma Tau Delta. Lodge: Soroptomists (v.p. 1983-84). Home: 65 Washington St Red Bank NJ 07701

HOLIVER, KIMBERLY LYNN, marketing administrator; b. Los Angeles, Oct. 11, 1956; d. William Leonard and Marilyn Jean (Greenberg) H. BA, UCLA, 1979. Sales rep. E.J. Gallo Winery, Los Angeles, 1983; with key accounts dept. Palm Springs, Calif., 1983-84; dist. mgr. Los Angeles, 1984-85; mgr. field mktg. Sacramento, 1985-86; mgr. regional tng. Los Angeles, 1986—; cons. Supreme Specialties Inc., 1987—. Mem. exec. bd. Concern II Found., Los Angeles, 1981-84; vol. Com. to Cure Cancer through Immunization, Los Angeles, 1981-85. Mem. Nat. Assn. Female Execs., Les Amin du Vin, Delta Gamma (panhellic bd. 1976-78). Office: Gallo Winery 2650 Commerce Way Los Angeles CA 90040

HOLLADAY, JANICE WINCHELL, library administrator; b. W.Va., Jan. 1, 1937; d. John Raymond Winchell and Martha Avinell (Kidwell) Parrott; m. Thomas Melvin Holladay, Dec. 28, 1956; children: Andrea Claire, John Daniel. Student, Berea Coll., 1954-56; BS, U. Tenn., 1959; MLS, SUNY, Geneseo, 1971. Info. specialist Xerox Corp., Rochester, N.Y., 1972-74; dir. library Sybron/Taylor, Rochester, 1974-77; sci. librarian U. Rochester, 1977-79, asst. head sci. libraries, 1979-81, head reference dept., 1981-83, asst. dir. libraries, 1983—; info. specialist Rochester Regional Research Library Council, 1974-76; mem. faculty SUNY, Geneseo, 1980-83. Contbr. articles to profl. jours. Trustee Webster (N.Y.) Library Bd., 1988—. Mem. ALA, Am. Coll. and Research Libraries (mem. legis. com. 1987—), Research Libraries Group (publ. services com., 1985—), Spl. Libraries Assn. (pres. Upstate chpt. 1980-81), Rochester Area Online Users Group (as founder area coordinator 1979), Phi Kappa Phi. Democrat. Presbyterian. Home: 1225 Imperial Dr Webster NY 14580 Office: U Rochester Rush Rhees Library Rochester NY 14627

HOLLADAY, WILHELMINA COLE, real estate and interior design executive; b. Elmira, N.Y., Oct. 10, 1922; d. Chauncy E. and Claire Elizabeth (Strong) Cole; m. Wallace Fitzhugh Holladay, Sept. 27, 1946; children—Wallace Fitzhugh, Scott Cole. BA, Elmira Coll., 1944; postgrad. art history U. Paris, 1953-54, U. Va., 1960-61, HHD (hon.), Moore Coll. Art, 1988. Exec. sec. Howard Ludington, Rochester, N.Y., 1944-45, Chinese Embassy, Washington, 1945-48; staff Nat. Gallery of Art, Washington, 1957-59; dir. interior design div. Holladay Corp., Washington, 1970—; dir. Holladay-Tyler Printing Corp., 1982-86; dir. Adams Nat. Bank, 1978-86, chmn. 1978-86; pres., chmn. bd. Nat. Mus. Women in the Arts; pres. First Corp.-WNB, 1980-86. Founder archival library of periodicals, books, exhbn. catalogs on women's art for research purposes; bd. dirs. Am. Field Service, 1964-80, Internat. Student House, 1973—, Leeds Castle Found.; mem. council Friends of Folger Shakespeare Library, 1978-82; mem. world service council YMCA; trustee Corcoran Gallery of Art, 1980—; pres. Holladay Found., 1980—; mem. profl. adv. com. interior design Mt. Vernon Coll.; mem. Mayor's Blue Ribbon Com., Met. Mus. Art. Recipient Horizon's Theatre award, 1986, Anti-Defamation award, 1987; named Woman of Achievement Washington Ednl. TV Assn., 1984, Woman of Distinction Council Ind. Colls., 1987. Mem. Am. Assn. Mus., Am. Fedn. Art, Women's Caucus for Arts, Met. Mus. Art, Mus. Modern Art, Art Libraries of N.Am., Archives Am. Art, Golden Circle of Kennedy Center, Arttable, Smithson Soc., Internat. Women's Forum, Women's Econ. Alliance (dir. 1984—). Episcopalian. Club: Capital Speakers. Home: 3215 R St NW Washington DC 20007 Office: Nat Mus Women in the Arts 1250 New York Ave Washington DC 20005

HOLLAND, CHERYL ANNE, marketing executive; b. Bryan, Tex., Feb. 20, 1946; d. Curtis Robert and Dorothy (Anderson) H. MusB, Tex. Women's U., 1968. With Sanger Harris, Dallas, 1968-75; buyer Selber Bros., Shreveport, La., 1975-77; div. merchandise mgr. Sanger Harris, Dallas, 1977-82, v.p., 1982-84; sr. v.p. Batus Retail Group, N.Y.C., 1984-86; v.p., gen. merchandisingmgr. Rich's Dept. Store, Atlanta, 1986—. Mem. Atlanta Hist. Soc., New Canaan Hist. Soc., Met. Mus. N.Y., High Mus. of Atlanta. Named Disting. Woman of Atlanta, 1987 Disting. Alumna of Tex. Women's U., 1987. Mem. Nat. Assn. Female Execs., Fashion Group, Atlanta Zoo. Home: 2525 Peachtree Rd Apt 7 Atlanta GA 30305

HOLLAND, DENISE EDGECOMBE, psychiatrist; b. West Palm Beach, Fla., June 13, 1948; d. Erman Wilfred and Mildred Rose (Herndon) Edgecombe; B.S., Howard U., 1970, M.D., 1976; m. Elwood Samuel Holland, June 2, 1973. Adminstrv. asst. NASA, Washington, 1974; extern Alexandria (Va.) Hosp., 1976-78; resident in psychiatry George Washington U. Hosp., Washington, 1976-78, Howard U. Hosp., Washington, 1979-80; physician cons. Dept. Health and Human Services, Balt., 1980-82; physician analyst USPHS, Rockville, Md., 1982-83; fellow Howard U. Hosp., 1983; dir. geriatric program Crownsville (Md.) Hosp. Ctr., 1983-86, clin. dir., 1986—; cons. psychiatrist Bowie (Md.) State Coll., 1979-81, 84—, Palmer Park (Md.) Counseling Center, 1981-83, Prince George's County Dept. Mental Health, 1983—. Recipient awards Dept. Health and Human Services, 1980, Howard U. Hosp., 1979, D.C. Public Schs., 1981. Mem. AMA, Am. Med. Women's Assn., Commd. Officers Assn., D.C. Med. Soc., Howard U. Alumni Assn., Howard U. Med. Alumni Assn., Am. Psychiat. Assn., Nat. Med. Assn., Prince George's County Med. Soc., So. Med. Assn., Nat. Med. Assn. Aux. Democrat. Episcopalian. Club: Links (award 1979). Home: 7812 Lonesome Pine Ln Bethesda MD 20817 Office: Crownsville Hosp Ctr Adminstrn Bldg Crownsville MD 21032

HOLLAND, GENE GRIGSBY (SCOTTY), artist; b. Hazard, Ky., June 30, 1928; d. Edward and Virginia Lee (Watson) Grigsby; B.A., U. S. Fla., 1968; pupil of Ruth Allison, Talequah, Okla., 1947-48, Ralph Smith, Washington, 1977, Clint Carter, Atlanta, 1977, R. Jordan, Winter Park, Fla., 1979, Cedric Baldwin Egeli Workshop, Charleston, S.C., 1984; m. George William Holland, Sept. 22, 1950; 3 children. Various clerical and secretarial positions, 1948-52; news reporter, photographer Bryan (Tex.) Daily News, 1952; clk. Fogarty Bros. Moving and Transfer, Tampa and Miami, Fla., 1954-57; tchr. elem. Schs., Hillsborough County, Fla., 1968-72; salesperson, assoc. real estate, 1984—; owner, operator antique store, 1982-87. One-woman/group shows include: Tampa Woman's Clubhouse, 1973, Cor Jesu, Tampa, 1973, bank, Monks Corner, S.C., 1977, Summerville Artists Guild, 1977-78, Apopka (Fla.) Art and Foliage Festival, 1980, 81, 82, Fla. Fedn. Women's Clubs, 1980, 81, 82; numerous group shows, latest being: Island Gifts, Tampa, 1980-82, Brandon (Fla.) Station, 1980-81, Holland Originals, Orlando, Fla.; represented in permanent collections including Combank, Apopka, also pvt. collections. Vol., ARC, Tampa, 1965-69, United Fund Campaign, 1975-76; pres. Mango (Fla.) Elem. Sch. PTA, 1966-67; pres. Tampa Civic Assn., 1974-75; vol. Easter Seal Fund Campaign, 1962-63. Recipient numerous art awards, 1978-82. Mem. Internat. Soc. of Artists, Council of Arts and Scis. for Central Fla., Fedn. of Women's Clubs (pres. Hillsborough County 1974-75, v.p. Tampa 1974-75), Meth. Women's Soc. (sec. 1976-77), Nat. Trust for Historic Preservation, Nat. Hist. Soc., Central Fla. Geneal. and Hist. Soc., Am. Guild Flower Arrangers, Methodist Soc. Clubs: Internat. Inner Wheel (past chmn. dist. 696, pres. Tampa 1972-73), Musicale (1st v.p. bd. incorporators Tampa 1974-75), Apopka Woman's (pres. 1981-82, dir. 1983-85). Home: 1080 Errol Pkwy Apopka FL 32712 Office: PO Box 700 Plymouth FL 32768

HOLLAND, IRIS KAUFMAN, state legislator; b. Springfield, Mass., Sept. 30, 1920; d. Leo and Sadie Kaufman; grad. Rider Coll., Trenton, N.J.; m. Gilbert S. Holland, Jan. 1, 1941; children—Judy, Richard, Donald. Mem. Mass. Ho. of Reps. from 2d Hampden Dist., 1973—, Republican whip, 1979-82, asst. Republican floor leader, 1983-87, mem. Ho. Com. on Ways and Means, 1987—; columnist Your State Ombudsman; guest lectr. Mt. Holyoke, Smith, Springfield, Am. Internat., Western New Eng. colls.; Robert A. Taft lectr. Tufts U., U. Mass. Bd. corporator Baystate Med. Center, Springfield Day Nursery; chmn. spl. commn. Help for Homeless; adv. bd. Am. Internat. Coll.; trustee Bay Path Jr. Coll.; bd. dirs. Friends of the Homeless, Goodwill Industries, Coalition for the Homeless, Carew Hill Girls Clubs, Western Mass. Radio Reading Service for the Blind; mem. spl. com. Pres. John F. Kennedy Meml. Named Woman of Yr., Women's Div., Greater Springfield C. of C.; recipient Woman of Achievement award Mass. Fedn. Bus. and Profl. Women's Clubs; Outstanding Legislator of Yr. award Mass. League Cities and Towns; Disting. Citizen award Rep. Club of Mass. Mem. LWV, Mass. Caucus Women Legislators (founder). Club: Zonta Internat.

HOLLAND, JARI LYN, small business owner; b. Dawson, Minn., May 25, 1950; d. Alfred Elle and Janice Aileen (Swanson) Ubben. BA, North Cen. Coll., Naperville, Ill., 1972; MA, Northwestern U., 1973; cert. in emergency med. tech., Hennepin County Vocat. Tech. Inst., 1977; cert. in floral design and mgmt., Platt Coll., 1986. Sales and clerical positions Montgomery Ward, Mpls. and Chgo., 1966-73, recruiter, 1973-75; mgr. personnel Dayton Co., Mpls., 1975-78; mgr. personnel and tng. TEAM Electronics, Mpls., 1978-80; dir. tng. Target Stores, Mpls., 1980-85; dir. human resources and adminstrn. Molecular Genetics, Mpls., 1985; dir. human resources and tng. Payless Cashways, Inc., Kansas City, Mo., 1985-86; cons. Human Resource Mgmt. Corp., Kansas City, 1986—; pres. Lynden Greens and Floral, Kansas City, 1986—, The Holland Group, Kansas City, 1987—. Pres., bd. dirs. Euphrates Galery, Kansas City, 1985—. Mem. Am. Soc. Tng. and Devel., Am. Soc. Personnel Adminstrn. Office: Human Resource Mgmt Corp Bd of Trade Ctr 4900 Main Suite 804 Kansas City MO 64112

HOLLAND, JOY, health care facility executive; b. N.Y.C., Oct. 24, 1946; d. Harry Walson and Edna May (Simmons) H.; m. Chesley Roderick Richardson, Sept. 21, 1985; children: Carl Allen Fields, Craig Anthony Fields. AA in Nursing, Olive-Harvey Coll., 1972; BS, St. Joseph Coll., Bklyn., 1976; M in Health Adminstrn., C.W. Post Coll., 1978. Staff nurse U. Chgo. Hosp. and Clinics, Chgo., 1972; head nurse N.Y. Hosp., N.Y.C., 1972; clinic adminstr. Morrisania-Montefiore Hosp., Bronx, N.Y., 1973; head nurse, supr. Pilgrim Psychiat. Hosp., Brentwood, N.Y., 1974, assoc. dir. staff devel., 1974-76, dir. nursing, 1976-78; surveyor, cons Joint Commn. on Accrediation of Hosps., Chgo., 1978—; dir. Ypsilanti (Mich.) Regional Psychiat Hosp., 1986—; dep. commr. State of Ohio dept. of mental health, 1980-82; cons. Joint Commn. on Accrediation of Hosps., bd. dirs. [illegible] specialist Holland-Richardson Assocs., Detroit; bd. dirs. Women in Crisis, Inc., N.Y.C. Contbr. author: (book) Guide to J.C.A.H. Nursing Standards, 1985, 86 editions. Mem. N.Y. Acad. of Sci., (life) Bus. and Profl. Women, Inc. (3rd v.p. local cpt.). Democrat. Lodges: Masons, Order Eastern Star. Home: 315 Willis Rd Saline MI 48176 Office: Ypsilanti Regional Psychiat Hosp 3501 Willis Rd Box A Ypsilanti MI 48197

HOLLAND, LISA ANN, real estate broker; b. Houston, Nov. 11, 1959; d. Robert Gene and Shirley Ann (Collins) H. B.B.A., Southwest Tex. State U., 1982. Sr. property mgr. Century 21, San Marcos, Tex., 1980-83; v.p. Heritage Mgmt., Houston, 1983-84; exec. property mgr., broker U.S.A. Mgmt., Houston, 1984-86; pres. Waterford Mgmt., Houston, 1986—. Mem. Gulf Coast AAU, Profl. Assn. Diving Instrs., Community Assn. Inst., Inst. Real Estate Mgmt. Office: 3400 Timmons St #1 Houston TX 77027

HOLLAND, NANCY MARIE, insurance agency executive; b. Chgo., May 5, 1948; d. Thomas George and Frances Mary (Fister) H. Student, Morraine Valley Community Coll., Ins. Inst. Ill., Chgo. Bd. Underwriters, 1978—. Acctg. clk. Wineman Bros. Ins., Chgo., 1967-72; asst. account exec. Frank B. Hall & Co., Chgo., 1972-78; account exec., v.p. Bayly, Martin & Fay, Inc., Des Plaines, Ill., 1978-83; pres. Holland Ins. Agy., Inc., Willow Springs, Ill., 1983—; cons. Roller Skating Rink Operators Assn., Lincoln, Nebr., 1981—. Mem. Ams. for Legal Reform, Am. Congress Real Estate, Found. Christian Living, Common Cause, Moral Majority, Am. Mus. Natural History. Republican. Home: 39 Ottawa Ct Justice IL 60458 Office: Holland Ins Agy Inc PO Box 128 Willow Springs IL 60480

HOLLAND, ROSE SHEILA, data processing executive; b. Columbus, Ga., Feb. 6, 1952; d. Stanley Rudolph and Carol Justyne (Fellows) P. Student, Meadows Bus. Coll., 1975, IBM GSD Customer Edn., 1978-79. Cert. data processor, cert. systems profl. Data processing mgr. Columbus Packaging, Inc., 1978-81, Rossmark Specialty Products, LaGrange, Ga., 1981-82, Lummus Industries, Columbus, 1983-84; dir. mgmt. info. systems Control Laser Corp., Orlando, Fla., 1984-88; systems cons. Discovery Info. Systems, Maitland, Fla., 1988—. Mem. Data Processing Mgmt. Assn., Nat. Assn. for Female Execs., Assn. for Inst. for Cert. Computer Profls., Mu Alpha Theta. Democrat. Baptist. Home: 4444 S Rio Grande 534C Orlando FL 32809 Office: Discovers Info Systems 1057 Maitland Center Commons Maitland FL 32751

HOLLAND, SANDRA GUNTER, businesswoman, journalist; b. Mount Airy, N.C., Jan. 12, 1952; d. Joseph Bernard and Rondalene Geralda (Stanley) Gunter; m. Gasper O. Holland, Feb. 14, 1981; children: Abraham Justus, Noah Jonah. BS in Journalism, Va. Commonwealth U., Richmond, 1973; postgrad. U. Tex., Austin, 1974, North Tex. State U., Denton, 1975-78. Report writer Va. Dept. Hwys., 1973; newsletter editor Tex. Employment Commn., Austin, 1977-80; former tchr. English, journalism and ESL; part-time reporter Sta. KBOP, 1985-87; columnist, bus. newspaper, 1987-88; owner Holland Secretarial Services (also doing bus. as Holland Editorial Services and Holland Keepsake Clipping Services), 1982—. Pub. (mags.) Austin, Go, Income Opportunities, Lady's Circle, Women's Circle, Woman's World, Income Opportunities; (newspapers) Grit, San Antonio Light, Pleasanton Express, Brush Country Advertiser, Wilson County News, Medina Valley Times, Devine News, Horesville Chronicle-Jour. Mem. Pleasanton Friends of Library, San Antonio Zoological Soc., Friends of the San Antonio Zoo, Friends of Sta. KLRN-TV, Longhorn Mus. Assn., Nat. Arbor Day Found.; mgr. fundraiser bike-a-thon, Cystic Fibrosis; chmn. Atascosa County chpt. ARC, 1987—; media contact congl. candidate, office mgr., election coordinator Rep. Party of Atascosa County, 1986, 88, co-founder and charter pres. Atascosa County Rep. Women's Club, 1986-87, publicity chmn. 1986—, sec. 1988. Served with USAR; mem. Tex. Army N.G. Recipient letter of Appreciation USAR, 1982, cert. of Commendation Tex. Com. for Employer Support of Guard and Res., 1982, U.S. 5th Army Minaret award, 1982, Danforth award, 1973, Freedom Found. awards, 1980, 82. Mem. Mensa, UDC, Pleasanton C. of C., Nat. Soc. Notaries. So. Baptist. Home and Office: 529 Oakhaven Dr Pleasanton TX 78064

HOLLANDER, ELLEN COLLINS, hospital personnel executive; b. Cambridge, Mass., Mar. 6, 1946; d. John Ambrose and Marjorie Emma (Merrifield) Collins; BA, Boston Coll., 1967; MA, Incarnate Word Coll., 1976; 1 child, Christopher Antony Botto. Teaching supr. dept. clin. adminstrn. Mass. Gen. Hosp., Boston, 1963-67; supr. radiology dept. Genesee Hosp., Rochester, N.Y., 1969-70; coordinator edn. S.W. Tex. Meth. Hosp., San Antonio, 1970-77, asst. dir. personnel, 1977—; adj. faculty Sch. Health Professions, S.W. Tex. State U., San Marcos, 1976—; bd. dirs. South Tex. Healthcare Fed. Credit Union, 1986—, vice chair, 1988—. Mem. Am. Hosp. Assn., Am. Soc. Healthcare Edn. and Tng. (dir. 1977-80, Disting. Service award 1982), San Antonio Area Soc. Healthcare Edn. and Tng. (pres. 1972, 74-75), Tex. Soc. Hosp. Educators (Outstanding Service award 1981), Tex. Hosp. Assn. Author: Identifying Healthcare Training Needs, 1984; contbr. articles to profl. jours.; bd. dirs. Inservice Tng. and Edn. Mag., 1972-76. Home: 6123 Walking Galt Dr San Antonio TX 78240 Office: 7700 Floyd Curl Dr San Antonio TX 78229

HOLLANDER, ELLY-LORE, health care industry consultant; b. Stuttgart, Fed. Republic Germany, Feb. 14, 1929; came to U.S., 1949; d. Hermann G. and Erna (Hummel) Brodbeck; m. Fred E. Hollander, Dec. 2, 1950 (dec. Mar. 1986). BA, Pace U., 1976, MBA, 1978. V.p. Robert S. First, Inc., N.Y.C., 1960-77; pres. Hollander Internat. Cons., Inc., Hastings-on-Hudson, N.Y., 1973-80; sr. researcher Channing, Weinberg Inc., N.Y.C., 1980; prin. Hastings Research Assocs., Hastings-on-Hudson, 1981—. Republican. Mem. Unitarian Ch. Club: Ardsley (N.Y.). Home: 21 Floral Dr Hastings-on-Hudson NY 10706 Office: Hastings Research Assocs One N St PO Box 206 Hastings-on-Hudson NY 10706

HOLLANDS, JEAN AUDREY, mental health counselor; b. Minot, N.D., June 18, 1932; d. Carl E. Madsen and Helen (Aver) Madsen Deigan; m. D. Lee Hollands, Apr. 19, 1952 (div. 1977); m. Don E. Wuerflein, May 19, 1979; children: Glenn, Tom, Laura, Todd. BA, San Jose State U., 1974, MS, 1976. Lic. marriage and family counselor. Systems analyst USN and IBM, 1951-56; clin. dir. San Andreas Health Council, Palo Alto, Calif., 1976-80; pres. GLC: Growth and Leadership Cons., Mt. View, Calif., 1980—, also bd. dirs.; cons. French Consulate, Calif., 1986. Author: Silicon Syndrome: How to Survive a High Tech Relationship, 1983 (Clark Vincent award 1986), Human Sexuality Counseling for Helping Professionals, 1976. Mem. Calif. Assn. Marriage Family Therapists (clin. fellow 1986, bd. dirs. 1981-82), MS Soc. (bd. dirs. Santa Clara chpt. 1986—). Home: 257 Bryant Ave Mountain View CA 94040 Office: Growth and Leadership Cons 1451 Grant Rd Suite 102 Mountain View CA 94040

HOLLANDSWORTH, LINDA PADGETT, English language educator; b. Aug. 12, 1947; d. Curtis Jefferson and Aileen (Hodges) Padgett; m. John A. Hollandsworth, June 13, 1970 (div. 1985). BA, Greensboro Coll., 1969; MA, Hollins Coll., 1978; postgrad., Ind. U. Pa., 1988—. Tchr. high sch. 1969-78; adminstr. secondary sch. Henry County, Va., 1978-84; instr. English Coastal Carolina Coll., Conway, S.C., 1984—; asst. in promotion services 1984—. Contbr. articles to profl. jours. Active United Way, Am. Cancer Soc. Mem. Nat. Council Tchrs. English. Democrat. Baptist. Home: 6217 Blynn Dr #7 Myrtle Beach SC 29577 Office: USC Coastal Carolina Coll PO Box 1954 Conway SC 29526

HOLLANDSWORTH, SANDRA S., nurse; b. San Francisco, Jan. 13, 1940; d. Adolph Oscar and Dorothy (Day) Swanson; m. Donald Jay Lawrence, June 25, 1961 (div. 1970); children: James Reynolds, Jennifer Dorothea; m. Terry Lee Hollandsworth, July 24, 1976. BS in Nursing, Calif. State U., San Francisco, 1961; cert. nurse practitioner in ob-gyn, U. Calif., San Francisco, 1973, 77; MS in Nursing, Lewis U., 1986. Cert. family planning nurse practitioner, Calif.; cert. maternity nurse practitioner, Calif. RN Mt. Zion Hosp., San Francisco, 1961; pub. health nurse Montgomery County Health Dept., Clarksville, Tenn., 1962-63, Denver County Health Dept., 1963-66; pub. health nurse Sonoma County Health Dept., Santa Rosa, Calif., 1971-77, nurse practitioner gyn, 1973-77, nurse practitioner ob-gyn, 1977-83; nurse practitioner ob-gyn Drs. Klay and Renfree, Santa Rosa, Calif., 1977-83, Planned Parenthood, Ottawa, Ill., 1984—; preceptor U. Calif.-San Francisco, 1977-83. Vol. Utility Control Program, Santa Rosa, 1976-83, Am. Cancer Soc., Kewanee, Ill., 1984—. Recipient leadership citation Am. Cancer Soc., 1987; USPHS grantee, 1961. Mem. Nurses Assn. Am. Coll. Obstetricians and Gynecologists (cert.), Am. Soc. Psychoprophylaxis in Ob., AAUW, LWV. Democrat. Mem. Ch. of Religious Sci.

HOLLEB, DORIS B., urban planner, economist; b. N.Y.C., Oct. 26, 1922; d. Abraham and Rachel Bernstein; B.A., Hunter Coll., 1942; M.A., Harvard U., 1947; postgrad. U. Chgo., 1959-60, 65-66; m. Marshall M. Holleb, Oct. 15, 1944; children—Alan, Gordon, Paul. Economist Fed. Res. Bd., Washington, 1943-44; freelance journalist, 1945-63; econ. cons. Chgo. Dept. City Planning, 1963-64; research assoc. Center Urban Studies, U. Chgo., 1966-78, sr. research assoc., 1978—, dir. Met. Inst., 1973—, professorial lectr., 1979—; chmn., Francis W. Parker Sch. Ednl. Council, 1965—; mem. adv. council Adlai E. Stevenson Center Inst., 1972-79; bd. dirs. Inter. Am. Found., 1980-84, Pacific Basin Inst., 1981—; mem. nat. adv. com. White House Conf. on Balanced Nat. Growth and Econ. Devel., 1978; mem. Northeastern Ill. Planning Commn., 1973-77; mem. Chgo. Met. Area Transp. Council, 1980-84; mem. adv. council to Nat. Ctr. Research on Vocat. Edn., Dept. Edn., 1979-82, Dept. state adv. com. internat. investment, tech. and devel., 1979-81; commnr. Chgo. Plan Commn., 1987—. Mem. Am. Inst. Cert. Planners, Am. Planning Assn., Am. Econ. Assn., Phi Beta Kappa, Lambda Alpha. Clubs: Arts, Tavern Quadrangle, (Chgo.); Harvard (N.Y.C.). Author: Social and Economic Information for Urban Planning, 1968; Colleges and the Urban Poor; The Role of Public Higher Education in Community Service, 1972; contbr. articles to profl. jours. Home: 2650 Lakeview Ave Chicago IL 60614 Office: U Chgo 5828 S University Ave Chicago IL 60637

HOLLEMAN, SANDY LEE, religious organization administrator; b. Celina, Tex., June 6, 1940; d. Guy Lee and Gustine (Kirby-Sheets) Luna; m. Allen Craig Holleman, June 5, 1959. Cert., Eastfield Coll., 1979. With So. Bapt. Conv., Dallas, 1958—, mgr. personnel annuity bd., 1983-85, dir. human resources annuity bd., 1985—. Mem. Am. Mgmt. Soc. (dir. salary surveys local chpt. 1986—, v.p. chpt. services 1987—), Am. Soc. Personnel Adminstrn., Dallas Personnel Assn. Baptist. Club: Diversity (Dallas) (program chmn. 1976, v.p. 1977). Lodges: Order Eastern Star, Daus. of Nile. Home: 4524 Sarazen Dr Mesquite TX 75150 Office: So Bapt Conv Annuity Bd 511 N Akard Dallas TX 75201

HOLLENBACH, SISTER RUTH, college president. BS in Math. and Sci., Webster Coll., 1952; MA in Philosophy, U. Notre Dame, 1958, PhD, 1960, postgrad.; postgrad., St. Louis U., Cath. U. Tchr. math., sci. St. Joseph High Sch., Conway, Ark., 1952-55; chairperson dept. philosophy Notre Dame Coll., St. Louis, 1958-65; adminstr., tchr. Nanzan U., Nogoya, Japan, 1966-78, dean of studies, 1974-78; fin. dir., dir. devel. Maria Ctr., St. Louis, 1978-84; adminstr. St. Mary's Spl. Sch., St. Louis, 1984-87; pres. Mt. Mary Coll., Milw., 1987—; liaison to Mo. Dept. Mental Health. Exec. dir. dept. spl. edn. Archdiocese St. Louis. Office: Mt Mary Coll Office of the Pres 2900 N Menomonee River Pkwy Milwaukee WI 53222

HOLLENBECK, KAREN FERN, foundation executive; b. Snover, Mich., Mar. 30, 1943; d. Glenn Lee and Ada Gertrude (Robinson) Roberts; m. Marvin Allan Hollenbeck, June 18, 1966. AA, Kellogg Community Coll., 1980; BSBA, Nazareth Coll., 1987. Dir. fellowships W.K. Kellogg Found., Battle Creek, Mich., 1979-85, asst. v.p. adminstrn., 1985—. Bd. dirs. Arc Ministries, Allegan, Mich., 1982—, Vol. Bur., Battle Creek, 1984-86, ARC, Calhoun County, Mich., 1985—. Mem. Am. Mgmt. Assn., Am. Soc. Personnel Adminstrs., Assn. Records Mgrs. and Adminstrs., Nat. Assn. Fgn. Student Affairs, Nat. Assn. Female Execs. Home: 1713 Bridle Creek SE Kentwood MI 49508 Office: WK Kellogg Found 400 North Ave Battle Creek MI 49017-3398

HOLLERAN, PAULA RIZZO, psychology and counseling educator, researcher, consultant; b. N.Y.C.; d. A.M. and Jean T. Rizzo; m. Brian Patrick Holleran, Aug. 22, 1970; children: Tracy Lynn, Brett Daniel. BA, Bklyn. Coll., 1959; MA, U. Conn., 1963; PhD, U. Mass., 1969. Tchr. Shell Bank Jr. High Sch., Bklyn., 1960-62; instr. psychology SUNY, Oneonta, 1963-67, assoc. prof., 1969-70, prof. psychology and counseling, mem. grad. faculty, women's studies faculty, chair dept., 1970—, spl. asst. to assoc. commr. U.S. Office Edn., Washington, 1967-68; cons., specialist Headstart and Followthrough Projects, 1968-71; v.p. Rainbow Assocs./Cons., Oneonta, 1979—; presenter at nat. and regional confs. Contbr. numerous articles to profl. jours.; co-author Nat. Assessment of Women's Studies Programs in Higher Edn.; co-developer Couples Communication Workshop and Gender Summit Game for Marriage Counselors. Officer Oneonta Taxpayers Assn. 1978-79; bd. dirs. Goodyear Lake Assn., Md., N.Y., 1984—. U.S. Office Edn. fellow HEW, 1967-68, research grantee Commonwealth Mass. Bur. Research, 1969-70, Walter B. Ford Faculty grantee, 1988—. Mem. Am. Assn. Counseling and Devel., Am. Ednl. Research Assn., Assn. for Women in Psychology, New Eng. Ednl. Research Orgn. (best paper award 1981, 87), N.E. Ednl. Research Assn. Office: SUNY Dept Psychology and Counseling Oneonta NY 13820

HOLLEY, BARBARA MAY, publisher; b. Rockville Center, N.Y., Apr. 14, 1926; d. Robert Howard and Eva Revenna (Golding) Smith; m. Robert J. Raynor, Apr. 29, 1945 (div. 1955); children: Robert, James, Linda, Michele; m. Joseph Holley, Sept. 11, 1956; children: Deborah, Catherine, Joseph. Student, Barbizon Sch., 1946, Columbia U., 1952-53, Fla. Internat. U. Mgr. med. office Orthopedic Assocs., Hollywood, Fla., 1962-72; transcriptionist radiological North Miami (Fla.) Gen. Hosp., 1976 80; pub. various tabloids and journals, 1982—, producer, host Sta. WLRN, Cable-TV Educational, Miami, 1982—; tchr. Michael Ann Russel Jr. Community Coll., Miami, Aventura, N.E. Regional Library, North Miami. Author: Pieces of a Qoman, 1982 (nominated for Pulitzer Prize); pub. EARTHWISE: A Journal of Poetry, 1984—. Pres. PTA Benjamin Franklin Elem. Sch., 1958-59, also Westview Jr. High Sch., 1959-60. Mem. Fla. State Poets Assn. (pres. 1977—, founder Miami Earth chpt), Laramore Rader Poetry Group (pres. 1979-80). Democrat. Lutheran. Office: Fla State Poetry Assn Earth Chpt PO Box 68036 Miami FL 33168

HOLLEY, LAUREN ALLANA, psychologist, family therapist; b. Balt., Oct. 9, 1948; d. Winston Willouby and Mary Elizabeth (Hart) Holley; B.S., Morgan State U., 1976; M.A., Antioch U., 1978; postgrad. U. Md. Balt. County. Staff Balt. City Schs., 1978—; night communications staff ARC, Balt.; mental health consultant Walter P. Carter Ctr., Interndisciplinary Behavior Mgmt. Program, Balt., behavioral psychologist assoc. for mentally retarded and dually diagnosed clients. Recipient Award of Merit, Voter Registration Com., 1980, award outstanding achievement Jobs Project, Morris Goldseker Found., 1979-80. Mem. NAACP. also: Walter P Carter Ctr 630 W Fayette St Baltimore MD 21201

HOLLEY, SANDRA CAVANAUGH, speech and language pathologist, educator; b. Washington, Mar. 30, 1943; d. Clyde Howard and Rebecca Naomi (Arthur) Cavanaugh; 1 child, David Marshall. AA, George Washington U., 1963, AB with spl. honors, 1965, AM, 1966; PhD, U. Conn., 1979. Supr. speech and hearing East Fairfield Rehab. Ctr., Bridgeport, Conn., 1966-69; faculty teaching So. Conn. State U., New Haven, 1970—. Chairperson Human Commn. City of New Haven, 1978-87; bd. dirs. New Haven Vis. Nurses Assn., 1977-79, ARC, New Haven, 1979-80, Conn. Afro-Am. Hist. Soc., New Haven, 1982-83. Named assoc. Danforth Found., 1974; recipient Excellence in Communications award Howard U., 1987, Disting. Alumnus award George Washington U., 1988. Mem. Nat. Black Assn. Speech, Lang., and Hearing, Am. Speech, Lang. and Hearing Assn. (minority concerns com., v.p. adminstrn. 1982-85, pres.-elect 1987-88, pres., 1988—, fellow 1980, cert., honors 1983). Democrat. Baptist. Home: 215 Stimson Rd New Haven CT 06511 Office: So Conn State U 501 Crescent St New Haven CT 06515

HOLLIDAY, JENNIFER YVETTE, singer, actress; b. Houston, Oct. 19, 1960; d. O.L. Holliday and Jennie V. Eaton. Began singing career in gospel music with Houston Bapt. Ch. choirs; appeared in Don't Bother Me, I Can't Cope, Houston, 1978, Your Arms Too Short to Box with God, Broadway debut, 1979-81, Dream Girls, Broadway, 1981-83, Los Angeles, 1983-84, Sing, Mahalia, Sing, 1985; recs. include Feel My Soul, 1983, Say You Love Me, 1985, Get Close to My Love, 1987. Recipient Grammy award (Rhythm and blues vocal) for And I Am Telling You I'm Not Going, 1982; Tony award for Best Actress in Musical, Dream Girls, 1982; Ace award for Best Performance in a Cable TV Musical Spl., 1988. Address: care Mike Keller Inc 1133 Broadway #911 New York NY 10010

HOLLIEN, PATRICIA ANN, small business owner, scientist; b. N.Y.C., May 11, 1938; d. Leon and Sophia (Biernacki) Milanowski; m. Harry Hollien, Aug. 26, 1969; children: Brian, Stephanie, Christine. AA, Sante Fe Jr. Coll., 1969; ScD (hon), Marian Coll., 1983; student, U. Fla., 1977—. Research asst. Marineland Research Labs., 1965-69; co-owner, exec. v.p. Hollien Assocs., 1969—; owner, dir. Forensic Communication Assocs., Gainesville, Fla., 1981—; vis. assoc. Royal Inst. Spl. Transmission Lab., Stockholm, 1970, Wroclaw Tech. U., Poland, 1974; asst. in research Inst. Advanced Study Communication Scis. U. Fla., 1977-83, assoc. in research, 1983—; adj. asst. prof. Communication Sci. Lab., N.Y., 1982—. Co-author: Current Issues in the Phonetic Scis., 1979; contbr. articles to profl. jours. bd. dirs. Ann. Retirement Village, Waldo, Fla., 1981—. Mem. Internat. Soc. Phonetic Scis. (council reps. 1983—), Am. Assn. Phonetic Scis., Acad. Forensic Application of the Communication Scis., Am. Acad. Forensic Scis. Home: 229 SW 43 Terrace Gainesville FL 32607 Office: Forensic Communication Assocs PO Box 12323 Gainesville FL 32604

HOLLIES, LINDA HALL, pastor, educator, consultant; b. Gary, Ind., Mar. 29, 1943; d. James Donald and Doretha Robinson (Mosley) Adams; m. Charles H. Hollies, Oct. 14, 1962; children—Gregory Raymond, Grelon Renard, Grian Eunyke. B.S. in Adminstrn., Ind. U., 1975; M.A. in Communications, Gov. State U., 1980; M.Div., Garrett-Evang. Theol. Sem., 1986—. Tchr. Hammond Public Schs., Ind., 1975-77; supr. Gen. Motors Corp., Willow Springs, Ill., 1977-79; gen. supr. Ford Motor Co., East Chicago Heights, Ill., 1979-82; coordinator Women in Ministry Evangelical Theol. Sem., Evanston, Ill., 1984-86; pastor New Life Community Fellowship United Methodist Ch., Lansing, Mich., 1983-86; founder, dir., cons. Church Aflame Workshops, Inc., Chgo., 1982—, Woman to Woman Ministries, Inc. Trustee Garrett Evang. Theol. Sem., 1984-86; appointee Mayor's Commn. on Role and Status of Women, Gary, 1982-83. Ford fellow, 1975, Benjamin E. Mays fellow, 1984; Crusade scholar United Meth. Ch., 1984; Lucy Ryder Myer scholar, 1985-86. Mem. Bus. and Profl. Women Assn., Nat. Assn. Pastoral Educators, Urban League, NAACP, Internat. Toastmistress Club (pres. 1976-77). Democrat. Avocations: reading; preaching; creative writing; latch hook. Home: 212 Sherman St Joliet IL 60433 Office: The Richards St United Meth Ch Joliet IL 60433

HOLLIFIELD, NANCY LUCINDA, educator; b. Greenville, S.C., Jan. 29, 1951; d. Jay Terry and Margaret (Chapman) H. BA, Furman U., 1972; MEd, U. Ga., 1973; PhD, La. State U., 1979. Elem. sch. phys. edn. specialist Greenville (S.C.) Sch. Dist., 1973-77; asst. prof. U. N.C.-W, Wilmington, 1979-87, assoc. prof., 1987—. Author: (book) Aerobic Dance: A Focus on Fitness, 1986. Assoc. mem. Girl Scouts Am. Mem. Am. Alliance for Health, Phys. Edn., Recreation and Dance, N.C. Alliance for Health, Phys. Edn., Recreation and Dance (pres. 1972), Aerobics Inst. (cert. group exercise leader), Phi Kappa Phi, Delta Kappa Gamma. Office: U NC Wilmington Health Phys Edn Dept 601 S College Rd Wilmington NC 28403-3297

HOLLINGER, PAULA COLODNY, state senator; b. Washington, Dec. 30, 1940; d. Samuel and Ethel (Levy) Colodny; m. Pal Hollinger, Sept. 16, 1962; children: Ilene, Marcy, David. RN, Mt. Sinai Hosp., N.Y.C., 1961. Mem. Md. Ho. of Dels., 1978-86, Md. State Senate, Annapolis, 1987—; chmn. econ. and environ. affairs com. Gov.'s Task Force on AIDS (adminstrv. exec., legis. rev. com.), Joint Com. on Health Care Cost Containment, Nat. Conf. of State Legislatures (past chair sci. and resource tech. com.), adv. com. Mental Health Laws; Senate chair Joint Commn. on Fed. Relations; chmn. Acid Rain Workgroup, Orgn. Rehab. Tng.; bd. dirs. Nat. Council Jewish Women, Safety First, Women Legislators of Md. (v.p. 1985, past pres.). Recipient Murry Guggenheim award, 1961. Lodge: B'nai Brith Women. Office: Senate Office Bldg State Capitol Room 206 Annapolis MD 21401-1991

HOLLINGSWORTH, MARTHA LYNETTE, educator; b. Waco, Tex., Oct. 9, 1951; d. Willie Frederick and Georgia Cuddell (Bryant) J.; m. Roy David Hollingsworth, Dec. 31, 1971; children—Richard Avery, Justin Brian. A.A., McLennan Community Coll., 1972; B.B.A., Baylor U., 1974. Tchr., Connally Ind. Sch. Dist., Waco, 1974—; with Adult Edn. Night Sch., 1974-78; chairperson for Area III leadership conf. Vocat. Office Careers Clubs Tex., Waco, 1985—; active Lakeview Little League Booster Club, 1985—. Mem. PTA (hon. life), Vocat. Office Edn. Tchr.'s Assn. Tex., Future Homemakers Am. Area VIII (hon.), Tex. Future Farmers Am. (hon.), Delta Kappa Gamma. Baptist. Office: Connally Vocat Dept 715 Rita Waco TX 76705

HOLLINGSWORTH, MEREDITH BEATON, nurse; b. Danvers, Mass., Oct. 5, 1941; d. Allan Cameron and Arlene Margaret (Jerue) Beaton; m. William Paul Hollingsworth, Nov. 19, 1983; stepchild, Brendon R. Diploma, R.I. Hosp. Sch. Nursing, Providence, 1968; BS in Nursing, U. Ariz., 1976; MS in Human Resource Mgmt., Golden Gate U., 1984. Cert. enterostmal therapy nursing. Commd. ensign USN, 1968, advanced through grades to lt. comdr., 1979; charge nurse USN, USA, PTO, 1968—; command ostomy nurse, head ostomy clinic Naval Hosp. Portsmouth, Va., 1985—; pres. PAUMER Assocs., Virginia Beach, Va., 1988. Mem. Thoroughgood Civic League, Virginia Beach, 1979—; mem. adminstrv. bd. Baylake United Meth. Ch., Virginia Beach, 1980-83; mem. Am. Cancer Soc. Mem. Internat. Assn. Enterostomal Therapy, United Ostomy Assn., World Council Enterostomal Therapists, Am. Soc. Healthcare Edn. and Tng. of Am. Hosp. Assn. Republican. Club: Thoroughgood Garden (Virginia Beach). Home: 4528 Biscayne Dr Virginia Beach VA 23455-4242 Office: Naval Hosp Portsmouth Effingham St Portsmouth VA 23708

HOLLINSHEAD, ARIEL CAHILL, research oncologist; b. Allentown, Pa., Aug. 24, 1929; d. Earl Darnell and Gertrude Loretta (Cahill) H.; m. Montgomery K. Hyun, Sept. 27, 1958; children—William C., Christopher C. Student, Swarthmore Coll., 1947-48; A.B., Ohio U., 1951, D.Sc. (hon.), 1977; M.A., George Washington U., 1955, Ph.D., 1957. Asst. prof., fellow in virology Baylor U. Med. Center, 1958-59; asst. prof. pharmacology George Washington Med. Center, 1959-61, asst. prof. medicine, 1961-64, assoc. prof. medicine, head lab. virus and cancer research, 1964-73, prof. medicine, dir. lab. for virus and cancer research, 1974—; cons. in field. Contbr. over 250 articles on active immunotherapy of cancer to profl. jours.; author numerous book chpts. Named Med. Woman of Yr. Joint Bd. Am. Med. Colls., 1975-76, one of Outstanding Woman of Am., 1987; decorated Star of Europe, 1980. Fellow Washington Acad. Sci., Am. Acad. Microbiology, AAAS; mem. N.Y. Acad. Sci., Am. Acad. Microbiology, Grad. Women in Sci. (nat. pres. 1985-86), Internat. Soc. Preventive Oncology, Nat. Soc. Exptl. Biology and Medicine (Disting. Scientist award 1985), Am. Soc. Microbiology, Am. Assn. Cancer Research, Am. Assn. Immunologists, Clin. Immunology Soc., Internat. Soc. Antiviral Research, Am. Soc. Clin. Oncology, Internat. Assn. Study Lung Cancer, Internat. Union Against Cancer (bd. dirs., chair, prof. mgmt.). Clubs: Kenwood Country, Blue Ridge Mountain Country, Washington Forum (pres. 1987). Home: 3637 Van Ness St NW Washington DC 20008 Office: George Washington Univ Dept Medicine 2300 Eye St NW Washington DC 20037

HOLLIS, KATHLEEN SUE, accountant, auditor, state official; b. Champaign, Ill., Sept. 18, 1955; d. James R. and Ellen Louise (Woods) H. Student, DePaul U., 1978-79; BA, U. Ill., Chgo., 1982. Acct. Champaign Nat. Bank, 1978; supr. aircraft services Dept. Def., Chgo., 1978-83; methods and procedures analyst Alexander Proudfoot Co., Chgo., 1983-84; security cons. Excalibur & Assocs., Bridgeview, Ill., 1984-86; examiner Ill. Fin. Instns., Chgo., 1986—. Contbr. articles to profl. publs. Served with USAF, 1974-78, lt. USNR. Ill. Air NG scholar, 1979-82. Mem. Soc. Fin. Examiners, Ill. Soc. Fin. Examiners, Nat. Assn. Female Execs., U.S. Naval Inst., Air Force Assn., Naval Res. Assn., Ill. NG Assn. (legis. comm. 1979-83, membership com. 1981-83). Republican. Episcopalian. Office: Ill Dept Fin Instns 100 W Randolph St Suite 15-700 Chicago IL 60601

HOLLIS-ALLBRITTON, CHERYL DAWN, retail paper supply store executive; b. Elgin, Ill., Feb. 15, 1959; d. L.T. and Florence (Elder) Saylors; m. Thomas Allbritton, Aug. 10, 1985. BS in Phys. Edn., Brigham Young U., 1981; cosmetologist Sch. Beauty Culture, Berwyn, Ill., 1981. Retail sales clk. Bee Discount, North Riverside, Ill., 1981-82, retail store mgr., Downers Grove, Ill., 1982, Oaklawn, Ill., 1982-83, St. Louis, 1983; retail tng. mgr. Arvey Paper & Supplies, Chgo., 1984, retail store mgr., Columbus, Ohio, 1985—. Mem. Nat. Assn. Female Execs. Republican. Mormon. Avocations: cosmetology, reading, travel. Office: Arvey Paper & Supplies 431 E Livingston Columbus OH 43215

HOLLISTER, MONICA A., cosmetics company executive; b. Chgo., Feb. 27, 1946; d. William J. and Joan Poetz; m. Thomas A. Manion, May 22, 1971 (div. 1975); m. 2d, Gary Lewis Hollister, May 6, 1978. Student No. Ill. U.; B.S. in Bus. Adminstrn., Northwestern U.-Chgo. Owner Merle Norman Studios, Hammond, Ind. and Merrillville, Ind., 1969-78; v.p. mktg. Merle Norman, Los Angeles, 1978-83; pvt. cons.

HOLLISTER, PATRICIA CAROL, information systems executive; b. Nashville, July 28, 1950; d. Francis Peter and Frances Rita (Marcisovsky) White; m. John David Hollister, Mar. 13, 1971; children: John Christian, Alyssa Mari. AS, Nashville State Tech. Inst., 1979. Cert. sr. acct. mgr. Programmer/analyst Nat. Life and Accident Ins. Co., Nashville, 1978-81; contract programmer CompuContract, Nashville, 1981-82; sr. acct. mgr. CompuSearch of Nashville, 1982-86; owner Hollister and Assocs., Nashville, 1986—. Den mother Boy Scouts Am., Nashville, 1981-83; cert. tutor Laubach Literacy Action Program; mem. YWCA. Named Account Exec. of Yr., Mgmt. Recruiters, 1984. Mem. Nat. Assn. Female Execs., Assn. Systems Mgmt. (cons., counselor, chmn. membership com. 1984-86), sec. 1985-86, chmn. mktg. com. 1986-87, 2d v.p. 1987—, Cert. Recognition 1984, 85, 86, 87), Data Processing Mgmt. Assn. (speaker ann. conf. 1987, coordinator guest program ann. conf. 1985), Ladies Guild (sec. 1974-75), Nashville C. of C. Roman Catholic. Office: PO Box 248 Hermitage TN 37076

HOLLOWAY, BARBARA JEAN CHAMBERS, educator; b. Pensacola, Fla., June 23, 1938; d. Colon and Annie Bell (Mickles) Chambers; m. John Frederick Holloway Jr., May 11, 1962; children: Frederick Dwayne, Deloris Jeanette. BS, Bishop Coll., 1960; MEd, Cleve. State U., 1979; student, Kent State U., 1980-81. Sec. Horace Mann Jr. High Sch., Omaha, 1960-62; service rep. Northeastern Bell Telephone Co., Omaha, 1963-65; tchr. Pennsauken (N.J.) High Sch., 1969-72, Sawyer Bus. Coll., Cleve., 1972, John Adams High Sch., Cleve., 1972-73; tchr., coordinator Bedford (Ohio) High Sch., 1973—, chmn. bus. edn. dept., 1983—; part-time tchr. Cuyahoga Community Coll., Warrensville, Ohio, 1975-85; speaker Vocat. Edn. Div. Ohio Edn. Dept., 1978-79, Kent (Ohio) State Bus. Edn. Conf., 1979, AM Cleve. Talk Show, 1979, Bedford Rotary, 1979; bd. dirs. Saunder Office and Computer Products, Inc., Solon, Ohio, Datalink Systems, Chagrin Falls, Ohio. Mem. Jay-cettes, Willingboro, N.J., 1971-72, Orange Bd. Edn. Task Force, Orange Village, Ohio, 1982-83; coordinator Vocat. Bus. Edn. Drive-In Conf. Cleve. State U., 1974-75. Recipient Disting. Service award Cory United Methodist Ch., 1980. Mem. N.E. Ohio Bus. Tchrs. Assn. (Tchr. of Yr. 1979, 86), Cleve. Area Bus. Tchrs. (bd. dirs., sec. 1978-80), Ohio Office Edn. Assn. (regional advisor 1975-78), Pi Lambda Theta, Alpha Kappa Alpha, Phi Delta Kappa. Clubs: Couples, Funchasers Camping. Home: 4809 Lander Rd Chagrin Falls OH 44022 Office: Bedford Sch Dist 475 Northfield Rd Bedford OH 44146

HOLLOWAY, CINDY, mortgage company executive; b. Queens, N.Y., Aug. 8, 1960; d. Richard Stephen and Beverly Bunny (Harris) Tannenbaum; m. David Milton Holloway (div. Mar. 1986); 1 child, Benjamin Jerome. BA, Calif. State U., Fullerton, 1981. Lic. real estate broker. Waitress Bob's Big Boy, San Bernardino, Calif., 1984-85; receptionist RNG Mortgage Co., San Bernardino, 1985; loan processor Quality Mortgage Co., Colton, Calif., 1985-88, loan officer, 1988—. Home: PO Box 3187 Crestline CA 92325 Office: Quality Mortgage Co 1060 E Washington Suite 125 Colton CA 92324

HOLLOWAY, DEBORAH KALA, food products executive; b. Honolulu, Aug. 12, 1963; d. Richard Keith and Jan Irene (Dorais) H. BA in Econs. and Internat. Affairs magna cum laude, U. Puget Sound, 1985. New products supr. Cornnuts, Inc., Oakland, Calif., 1985—. Republican. Roman Catholic. Club: Monterey Bay Triathlon (bd. dirs. 1976—).

HOLLOWAY, EDNA LARUE, real estate sales agent; b. Hanover, Pa., July 28, 1942; d. Maurice Edward and Helen Viola (Smith) Wisner; m. Donald LeRoy Holloway, Dec. 29, 1963. BA, Towson State U., 1964, MEd, 1972; cert. in vol. mgmt. U. Colo., 1981. Tchr. Balt. County Pub. Schs., Towson, 1964-74; bookkeeping asst. Gen. Bus. Systems, Parkton, Md., 1974-76; bookkeeper sec. Ret. Sr. Vol. Program, Grand Rapids, Mich., 1976-77, dir., 1977-79; vol. resources coordinator DeKalb County Health Dept., Decatur, Ga., 1981-87; agt. Northside Realty, Snellville, Ga., 1987—; cons., liaison vol. DeKalb, Ga. and Atlanta, 1980-81; cons., trainer First Bapt. Ch. Atlanta, 1983; asst. conv. coordinator Balt. Life Ins. Co., 1974-76; sec., receptionist State Farm Ins. Co., 1980-81. Mem. Nat. Bd. Realtors, Gwinnett Bd. Realtors, Council Vol. Adminstrs. (bd. dirs. 1982-86), Ret. Sr. Vol. Program (v.p. adv. council 1980—), Assn. Vol. Adminstrn. (regional liaison nat. assn.), Charg II. Republican. Club: Rivermist Women's (Lilburn, Ga.). Avocations: piano, tennis, gardening. Home: 3704 Shawnee Run Lilburn GA 30247 Office: Northside Realty 2675 Main St W Snellville GA 30278

HOLLOWAY, JANET STEELE, university department administrator. BA in Spanish and English, Marshall U., 1963; MSW, SUNY, Stony Brook, 1976; ABD, Columbia U. Assoc. dir., asst. prof. Adelphi U. Nat. Tng. Inst., Garden City, N.Y., 1972-77; dir. staff devel. and tng., sch. welfare, title XX project SUNY, Stony Brook, 1977-79, asst. dean, asst. prof. sch. social welfare, 1979-84; dir. programs and publs. grad. sch. mgmt., N.J. Small Bus. Devel. Ctr. Rutgers U., New Brunswick, N.J., 1984-86; state wide dir. N.J. small bus. devel. ctr. grad. sch. mgmt. Rutger U., New Brunswick, N.J., 1986—; owner Mobius Cons. Services, 1982—; adj. instr. sch. social work Columbia U., 1981-83. Editor: The New Jersey Guide to Export Assistance, 1984, The New Jersey Small Business Development Center Newsletter; contbr. articles to profl. jours. Home: 38 Gramercy Park New York NY 10010

HOLLOWAY, JULIA FRANCES, air force officer; b. Indianola, Miss., May 3, 1950; d. Harold Francis and Louise Isabelle (Hall) Holloway; B.A., Miss. State U., 1973; postgrad. U. Denver, 1978-80, St. Mary's U., 1983-84, U. S. Calif., 1986—. Commd. major. USAF, 1974; space surveillance officer Mill Valley AFS, Calif., 1974-77, Clear AFS, Alaska, 1977-78, missile warning officer Cheyenne Mt. Complex, Colo., 1978-79, chief MW Standardization/Evaluation Div., CMC, Colo., 1979-81, dep. dir. MW Ops. Directorate, 1981, MW Software Test/Integration mgr., 1981-82, 1st tech. tng. mgr. Air Force Space Systems Career Fields, 1982-84; space systems acquisition tng. mgr., Randolph AFB, Tex., 1984-85; action officer Joint Chiefs of Staff, Nat. Mil. Command System, Command and Control Div., Washington, 1985-86; chief 1st Space Command liasion office to U.S. European command, tactical warning adviser to comdr.-in-chief European Command, Stuttgart, W. Ger., 1986—; cons. in field. Leader Girl Scouts U.S.A., 1975-76, 87—; disaster preparedness officer Mill Valley AFS, Calif., 1975-77; disaster preparedness evaluation officer Clear AFS, Alaska, 1977-78; acting chief disaster preparedness evaluation team Hdqrs. N. Am. Aerospace Def. Command, 1979-81. Mil. Community Girl Scout Troop Organizer,1987—. Mem. Air Force Assn., AAUW, Nat. Assn. Female Execs., NOW, Amnesty Internat., Smithsonian Inst. Office: HQ USEUCOM/ECJ3 CCD APO NY 09128

HOLLOWELL, MARY LOUISE, editor, publisher; b. Norfolk, Va., Aug. 13, 1941; d. Herbert Pruden and Mary Louise (Bunch) H.; divorced. BA in Edn., Radford (Va.) Coll., 1963; MA, U. Fla., 1970. Tchr. George Washington High Sch., Danville, Va., 1963-65, Kellam High Sch., Virginia Beach, Va., 1965-69, Churchland High Sch., Portsmouth, Va., 1971; librarian The Tobacco Inst., Washington, 1971-72; Washington corr., then editor Broadband Communications Report, contbg. editor Broadcast Mgmt. Engrng., 1972-75; pres., pub. Communications Press Inc., Washington, 1975-86; pub., editor-in-chief ICIT Press, Internat. Ctr. for Info Technologies, 1987—; also editor, writer; singer Dulcimer—Old Time and Traditional Music. Author: (with others) Cable Handbook 1975-76: A Guide to Cable and New Communication Technologies, The Cable Broadband Communication Book, 1978, vol. 3, 1983. Active local polit. campaigns and community services. Mem. Soc. Profl. Journalists, Soc. Scholarly Pub., Washington Book Pubs., Balt. Pubs. Assn., Washington Ind. Writers, Internat. Platform Assn. Home: 2900 Q St NW #102 Washington DC 20007

HOLLOWOOD, JOANN THEOS, marketing professional; b. N.Y.C., Jan. 29, 1951; d. Aristotle G. and Nellie (Ciaston) Theos; m. Edward F. Hollowood, Aug. 8, 1971 (div. 1981). BA, CUNY, 1972; postgrad., NYU, 1972-75. Mgr. installation Med. Info., Dallas, 1976-80; product mgr. Univ. Computing co., Dallas, 1980-82; acct. exec. Software Internat., Dallas, 1982-84; territory mgr. McCormack & Dodge, Dallas, 1984-87; mktg. rep. J.D. Edwards & Co., Dallas, 1987—. Vol. Mental Health and Mental Retardation, 1974—. N.Y. State Regents scholar, 1968. Mem. Nat. Assn. Female Execs., LWV.

HOLLY, PATRICIA ANN, nursing educator; b. Ft. Wayne, Ind., Mar. 30, 1935; d. Jeremiah J. and Loretta M. (Borchers) H.; B.S. in Nursing, U. Dayton (Ohio), 1964; M.N., U. Pitts., 1970. Joined Franciscan Sisters, Roman Catholic Ch., 1951; supr., instr. pediatric nursing St. Elizabeth Hosp., Dayton, 1960-63, 65-68; med.-surg. nursing supr. St. Elizabeth Hosp., Covington, Ky., 1964; tchr. pediatric nursing Wright State U., Dayton, 1972-74; dir. nursing Franciscan Terr., Cin., 1975-79; asst. prof. nursing edn. U. Cin., 1981—; trustee Our Lady of Bellefont Hosp., Ashland, Ky., 1981-85, Schroder Manor Nursing Home, Hamilton, Ohio, 1975-84; speaker, cons. in field. Mem. Am. Nurses Assn., Nat. League Nursing. Home: 60 Compton Rd Cincinnati OH 45215 Office: 9555 Plainfield Rd Cincinnati OH 45236

HOLM, HANYA, choreographer, dancer, dance educator; b. Worms-am-Rhine, Germany; came to U.S., 1931, naturalized, 1939; d. Valentin and Marie (Moerschel) Eckert; divorced; 1 child, Klaus Holm. Ed. pvt. schs., Germany; student of music, Hoch Conservatory and Dalcroze Inst., Frankfurt-am- Main; grad., Dalcroze Inst., Hellerau; dance diploma, Mary Wigman Central Inst., Dresden, Germany; D.F.A. (hon.), Colo. Coll., 1960, Adelphi U., 1969. Chief instr., co-dir. Wigman Inst., Dresden, 10 yrs; dir. dance dept. Mus. Theatre Acad., N.Y.C., 1962—; dir. own sch. N.Y.C., until 1968; dir. summer sessions in dance Colo. Coll., 1941-83; mem. staff Alwin Nikolais/Murray Louis Dance Theatre Lab., N.Y.C., 1972—, Juilliard Sch., N.Y.C., 1975—; tchr., lectr. Bretton Coll., Eng., 1979. Mem. original Wigman Co., performer, dance dir., choreographer, Europe, until 1931, under auspices Sol Hurok, founder, dir., N.Y. Wigman Sch. Dance, 1931, which later became Hanya Holm Sch. Dance; began Am. concert career, 1936; major prodns. Trend, 1937 (N.Y. Times award from John Martin as best dance composition of year), Metropolitan Daily, 1938, Tragic Exodus, 1938 (Dance Mag. award for best group choreography in modern dance); choreographer: Eccentricities of Davey Crockett, 1948, Kiss Me, Kate (Cole Porter), 1948 (best choreographer N.Y. Drama Critics award), Eng. prodn., 1951, Out of this World (C. Porter), 1950, My Darlin Aida, 1952; choreographer, dir.: The Golden Apple, 1954 (Critics Circle citation best musical); Reuben- Reuben, 1955; staged dances for re-make of film Vagabond King, 1956; choreography and mus. numbers My Fair Lady, 1955-56 (Tony nominee), Israeli prodn., 1964, Where's Charley, My Fair Lady; English prodns., 1958; choreography and mus. numbers Camelot, 1960; Christine, 1960-61, Anya, 1965; staged dances television show Pinocchio, 1957, Dinner with the President, 1963, Metropolitan Daily; 1st dance prodn. on TV, 1939; dir., choreographer world premiere opera The Ballad of Baby Doe, Central City, Colo. opera house, 1956; appeared on Am. Cancer Soc. series Tactic, NBC, 1959; dir., choreographer opera Orpheus and Euridice (Gluck), Vancouver Internat. Festival, 1959. Recipient Capezio award, 1978, award Fedn. Jewish Philanthropies, 1959, Colo. Centennial award and Gov.'s award, 1973, 74, Heritage Honor award Nat. Dance Assn., 1976, award and medal of distinction in fine arts City of Colorado Springs, 1978, Samuel H. Scripps Am. Dance Festival award, 1984; subject of film Hanya Holm, Portrait of an Artist/Teacher, 1983; Samuel H. Scripps Am. Dance Festival award, 1984; Astaire award (spl. citation for lifetime achievement) 1987. Mem. Am. Arbitration Assn. (nat. panel arbitrators), Soc. Stage Dirs. and Choreographers (v.p.). Address: care Selma Tamber 45 W 54th St New York NY 10019

HOLMAN, BETTY ANN, manufacturing executive; b. Omaha, Oct. 13, 1937; d. Michael John and Alice Belle (Kelly) Murray; m. Keith David Holman, July 12, 1938; children: Madonna, Lisa, Michael, Julie, Nancy. BSBA, Creighton U., 1959; postgrad., U. Va., Falls Church, 1969, George Mason U., 1969, 78, No. Va. Community Coll., 1980-85. Pres. KABS Bowling Assocs., Vienna, Va., 1976-79; owner, designer House of Quilts, Vienna, Va., 1979-80; mgr. banquets Evans Farm Inn, McLean, Va., 1980; mgr. reservations, asst. front officer Ramada Inn, Bethesda, Md., 1981-82; mgr. reservations, tour/travel Ramada Cen. Hotel, Washington, 1982-83; dir. sales Wellington Hotel, Washington, 1983-84; broker VR Bus. Brokers, Vienna, 1984-86; dir. sales and mktg. hotel div. Stuart A. Bernstein Co., Washington, 1986; pres., chief exec. officer Evergreen Products, Moneta, Va., 1980—; cons. in field; bd. dirs. Holman Enterprises, Moneta. Mem. Isle of Pine Assn., Moneta, 1972—, James Madison's Vols., Vienna, 1978-81, St. Leo's Vols., Fairfax, Va., Smith Mountain Lake Assn., Moneta, 1980—; del. Fairfax Reps., Vienna, 1986, Va. Reps., Vienna, 1986. Mem. Hotel Sales and Mktg. Assn., Govt. Meeting Planners, Delta Zeta. Roman Catholic. Office: Evergreen Products Rt 1 Box 294 Moneta VA 24121

HOLMAN, JEAN MAE, social services administrator; b. Miami, Fla., Aug. 20, 1934; d. Roy Milton Welch and Ruth Jane (Bennett) Simpkins; divorced; children: Rick, Debra, Crystal, Jana, Jill. Grad. high sch., Miami. Sec. USN, Arlington, Va., 1952-53; sec. Welfare Fraud Sect. San Bernardino County, Calif., 1956-58, dep. sheriff, 1958-64; office mgr. Time and Sound Co., Riverside, Calif., 1964-70, Humidial Corp., Colton, Calif., 1970-81; owner Sugar Lake Retirement Homes I, II, III, New Smyrna Beach, Fla., 1981-87, Date Place Care Ctr., San Bernandino, Calif., 1987—. Mem. Fla. Adult Care Assn. (pres. dist. IV 1984-85). Republican. Baptist. Home: 1759 E Date Pl San Bernardino CA 92404

HOLMAN, MARY ALIDA, economist, educator; b. West Point, N.Y., June 26, 1933; d. Jonathan Lane and Anna Alida (Johnson) H.; B.A., George Washington U., 1955, M.A., 1957, Ph.D. (Thomas A. Edison fellow 1962), 1963; m. Theodore Suranyi-Unger, Dec. 15, 1962. Mem. faculty George Washington U., 1963—, prof. econs., 1973—; professorial lectr. Indsl. Coll. Armed Forces, 1965-85, Nat. War Coll., 1966-74, Naval Sch. Health Scis., 1979-86; cons. NASA, 1966-68, Pres.'s Cost of Living Council, 1971-73. Recipient Watson award Am. Patent Law Assn., 1964. Mem. Am. Econ. Assn. Author: The Political Economy of the Space Program, 1974; co-author: Price Theory and Its Uses, 1978. Office: George Washington U Dept Econs Washington DC 20052

HOLMAN, SYLVIA LASH, school system administrator; b. Durham, N.C., Dec. 7, 1938; d. Traugott H. and Nan G. (James) Lash; m. Leon R. Holman, Jan. 28, 1962; 1 child, Theresa L. BA, W.Va. State Coll., 1960; MEd, Ea. Mich. U., 1962. Cert. elem. tchr., spl. edn. tchr., reading cons., Mich. Tchr. spl. edn. Detroit Pub. Schs., 1962-68; crisis tchr., elem. tchr. Ann Arbor (Mich.) Pub. Schs., 1969-74, specialist reading, 1974-86, equity advocate, 1986—. Co-chair Minority Tchrs. Polit. Involvement Conf., 1982; Detroit coordinator Pierce for Gov. Campaign, 1982, Dem. del., 1982-83, 86-88; Dem. co-chair 12th precinct, 1982-83; Dem. sec. 2d Congrl. Dist., Ann Arbor, 1986-88. Mem. Phi Delta Kappa (bd. dirs. 1984-86), Delta Sigma Theta. Methodist. Home: 3455 Yellowstone Dr Ann Arbor MI 48105 Office: Ann Arbor Pub Schs 2555 S State PO Box 1188 Ann Arbor MI 48106

HOLMBERG, JOYCE, state legislator; b. Rockford, Ill., July 19, 1930; m. Eugene Holmberg; 2 daus. B.A., No. Ill. U.; M.A., Alfred Adler Inst., Chgo. Mem. Ill. State Senate from 34th Dist., 1983—. Democrat. Office: Ill State Capitol Bldg Springfield IL 62706 also: 825 N Main Rockford IL 61103

HOLMBERG, SUSAN MARIE, insurance company executive; b. Orange, Calif., Mar. 19, 1958; d. Harry Charles and Anna Jean (Kavulich) H. BA in Environ. Studies, Calif. State U., Sacramento, 1980. Lic. real estate agt., Calif. Air pollution specialist Calif. Air Resources Bd., Sacramento, 1980-81; dir. pub. water supply supr. program U.S. V.I. Dept. Conservation and Cultural Affairs, Christiansted, St. Croix, 1981-82; cons. Santa Ana, Calif., 1982-84; loss control cons. Calif. Casualty Mgmt. Co., Orange, 1984-86; policyholder service rep. Citation Ins. Co., Tustin, Calif., 1986—. CPR instr. ARC, Orange County, 1981. Mem. Air Pollution Control Assn., Am. Indsl. Hygiene Assn., Am. Soc. Safety Engrs., Sigma Delta Pi

HOLME, BARBARA LYNN SHAW, former state senator; b. Long Beach, Calif., May 24, 1946; d. Harry and Lillian (Walton) Shaw; B.A., Stanford U., 1967; Coro Found. intern in pub. affairs, 1967-68; m. Howard Kelley Holme, June 16, 1968; children—Timothy, Lisa. Intern for Rep. Edward Roybal, summer 1966; intern to AID, Washington, D.C., summer 1967; jr. asso. Cogen, Holt and Assocs., New Haven, 1968-69, 71-72; asst. dir. for edn., housing and youth Met. Denver Urban Coalition, 1969-71; housing asst. Denver Housing Adminstrn., 1972-74; mem. Colo. Senate, 1974-84; chmn. senate Dem. caucus, 1977-78; asst. Dem. senate leader, 1979-82; sec. Nat. Assn. Jewish Legislators, 1980-84. Active Mayors Adv. Com. on Youth, Denver, 1969-70; steering com. mem. Colo. Coalition for Social Legislation, 1969-71; co-pres. Colo. Young Dems., 1973-74; bd. dirs. Capitol Hill United Neighborhood, 1974-75; chmn. carbon monoxide subcom. Metro Air Quality, 1985-86; researcher for Romer for Gov. campaign, 1986. Nominated as Outstanding Young Woman Am., Nat. Bus. and Profl. Women's Clubs, 1976. Mem. Met. Air Quality Council. Jewish. Home: 1243 Fillmore St Denver CO 80206

HOLMES, ANNA-MARIE, ballerina, ballet mistress; b. Mission City, B.C., Can., Apr. 17, 1946; came to U.S., 1981; d. George Henery and Maxine Marie (Botterill) Ellerbeck; m. David Holmes, 1962; 1 dau., Lian-Marie. Student U. B.C.; diploma Royal Conservatory of Music. Appeared in Swan Lake, Cinderella, Romeo and Juliet, Sleeping Beauty, Bayadere, Laurencia, Paquita, Graduation Ball, Les Sylphides, Prince Igor, Giselle, Nutcracker, Firebird, Raymonda; guest appearances at numerous theatres including: Berlin Staarts Opera, Royal Albert Hall, London, Roy Alex, Toronto, Ont., Royal Festival Hall, London, Teatro Colon, Buenos Aires, Covent Garden, London; danced with Kirov Ballet, Leningrad, 1963; featured ballerina in dance films including Tour En L'Air, Ballet Adagio, Don Juan, Chinese Nightengale; numerous appearances on European and North Am. TV; artistic dir., prin. choreographer Tenn. Festival Ballet, Oak Ridge, 1981—; staged ballets Am. Ballet Theatre, Dance Theatre of Harlem, Boston Ballet, 1984; ballet mistress Ballet Theatre Francais, 1985, Boston Ballet, co. tchr., 1985, set Giselle for Boston Ballet, 1987; mng. dir. Peforming Arts/Dance Ctr., Oak Ridge, 1982—; co-dir. ballet co. Massimo Opera Theate, Palermo, Italy, 1982-83; guest tchr. Nervi Festival, Genoa, Italy; lectr. in field. Producer film documentation of Kirov Vagonova Teaching system. Office: Boston Ballet 19 Clarendon St Boston MA 02116

HOLMES, BARBARA ANN KRAJKOSKI, educator; b. Evansville, Ind., Mar. 21, 1946; d. Frank Joseph and Estella Marie (DeWeese) Krajkoski; B.S., Ind. State U., 1968, M.S., 1969, specialist cert., 1976; postgrad. U. Nev., 1976-78; m. David Leo Holmes, Aug. 21, 1971; 1 dau., Susan Ann Sky. Acad. counselor Ind. State U., 1968-69, halls dir., 1969-73; dir. residence halls U. Utah, 1973-76; sales assoc. Fidelity Realty, Las Vegas, Nev., 1977-82. cert. analyst Nev. Dept. Edn., 1981-82; tchr. Clark County Sch. Dist., 1982-87, computer cons. Clark County Sch. Dist., 1987—. Named Outstanding Sr. Class Woman, Ind. State U., 1969; recipient Dir's. award U. Utah Residence Halls, 1973, Outstanding Sales Assoc., 1977; Tchr. of Month award, 1983, Dist. Outstanding Tchr. award, 1984, Dist. Excellence in Edn. award, 1984, 86, 87, 88. Mem. Nev. Assn. Realtors, AAUW, Am. Assn. Women Deans, Adminstrs. and Counselors, Am. Personnel and Guidance Assn., Am. Coll. Personnel Assn., Nevadans for Equal Rights Amendment, Alumnae Chi Omega (treas. Terre Haute chpt. 1971-73, pres., bd. officer Las Vegas 1977—), Clark County Panhellenic Alumnae Assn. (pres. 1978-79), Computer Using Educators So. Nev. (sec. 1983-86, pres.-elect 1986-87, pres. 1987-88, state chmn. 1988—). Methodist. Clubs: Job's Daus., Order Eastern Star. Developed personal awareness program U. Utah, 1973-76. Home: 3640 El Toro St Las Vegas NV 89121 Office: Clark County Sch Dist 600 N 9th St Las Vegas NV 89101

HOLMES, BARBARA MARIE, publishing company executive; b. Petaluma, Calif., Sept. 22, 1950; d. Colin and Dorothy (Gamble) H.; spl. student in art Calif. Poly. Inst., San Luis Obispo, 1968-71; B.S. in Graphic Design, San Jose State U., 1974. Art cons., buyer, dir. holiday design Lee Wards, San Jose, Calif., 1974-75; tchr. art Peninsula Sch., Palo Alto, Calif., 1975-76; dist. mgr. sales Nat. Fedn. Ind. Bus., San Mateo, Calif., 1976-79; br. mgr. Datapro Research Corp. subs. McGraw Hill Co., Mountain View, Calif., 1979—, nat. account mgr., 1983-84; mktg. exec. E.W. Communications, Palo Alto, Calif., 1984-88; prin., pres. Holmes & Co., Santa Clara, 1988—. Recipient cert. for dedication to underprivileged children Cuesta Coll., 1969; Sales Achievement award Datapro Research Corp., 1979. Mem. Nat. Saleswomen's Assn., Delta Gamma (Sr. Achievement award 1975, v.p. 1975, rush adv. 1980—). Republican. Episcopalian. Office: EW Communications Palo Alto CA 94301

HOLMES, CYNTHIA MISAO BELL, health services administrator; b. Yokohama, Japan, June 5, 1949; d. Isaac Walter Bell and Chihoko (Adachi) Bell Parker; m. Edward Theodore Holmes, Dec. 21, 1967 (div. Mar. 1973); children—Kenya K., Larik D. B.A., Columbia U., 1975; M.B.A., CUNY, 1977. Teller, N.Y. Bank for Savs., N.Y.C., 1968-69; sec., adminstrv. asst. Columbia U., N.Y.C., 1970-75; asst. day ctr. dir. N.Y. State Dept. Mental Hygiene, N.Y.C., 1976-77; planner, cons. Hosp. Affiliates, Inc., Nashville, 1977-79; program adminstr. Marion County Health Dept., Indpls., 1979—. Bd. dirs. Ind. Black Expo, Inc., 1981, 82; bd. dirs. chmn. Actors Ink Theatre Prodn. Co., Indpls., 1982-86; organizer Health Fair, Ind. Black Expo, 1981, 82. Assoc. U. Programs in Health Adminstrn. scholar, 1975, 76. Mem. Met. Health Council Indpls. (bd. dirs., sec. 1980—), Ind. Primary Health Care Assn. (bd. dirs., treas. 1982-86), Nat. Assn. Community Health Centers (mem. 1982—). Avocations: theatre; sweepstaking; real estate investment. Office: Marion County Health Dept 222 E Ohio St Indianapolis IN 46204

HOLMES, DEBORAH SUE, educational administrator; b. Topeka, Mar. 21, 1953; d. Robert G. and Virginia M. (Slingerland) H.; B.S. in Edn., U. Kans., 1974, M.S. in Curriculum Devel., 1979, cert. adminstrn. instructional tech., 1980, PhD in Ednl. Adminstrn., 1988. Elem. sch. tchr., Lawrence, Kans., 1972-73, 74-79; co-coordinator Green House Child Care Ctr., Lawrence, 1973-74; instr. U. Kans., 1973-75; curriculum developer media, literacy project Lawrence Public Schs., 1979-80; dir. fed. programs/curriculum projects University City, Mo., 1980-82; prin. Jackson Park Elem. Sch., University City, 1982-86, Brittany Woods Middle Sch., University City, 1986—; chmn. personnel com. Hilltop Child Devel. Ctr., Lawrence, 1975-80; cons. in field. Mem. adv. bd. English lang. sch. Recipient Vicki Larason Landman Non-Sexist Teaching award U. Kans., 1975, Jayhawk Tchr. award, 1976, Nat. Recognition for Elem. Sch. Excellence, 1986. Mem. Assn. Supervision and Curriculum Devel., Elem. Sch. Prins. Assn., Assn. Ednl. Communications and Tech., Nat. Assn. Secondary Sch. Prins., Conf., Edn., 99s, NOW, Phi Delta Kappa, Pi Lambda Theta. Author: Thumbs Up, 1978, Nature's Way, 1980, Daily Breaks, 1981; also articles; mem. adv. bd. Oasis mag. Home: 3537 Sidney St Saint Louis MO 63104 Office: 8125 Groby Rd University City MO 63130

HOLMES, DELENA JOANN, sales executive; b. Decatur, Ill, Aug. 5, 1939; d. Chester W. and A. Lurlene (Forehand) Goodman; m. F. Larry Holmes, Aug. 23, 1957; 1 child, David Lynn. Student, Millikin U., 1960, U. Ill., No. Ill. U., 1977, Richland Community Coll., 1981-82, Goshen Coll., 1985, Northwestern U., 1977. Cert. Yamaha presch. music instr. Order writer A.E. Staley, Decatur, 1957-61, asst., 1963-65; piano tchr. Decatur, 1964-86; tchr. music Macon Music, Decatur, 1975-82, mgr. music dept., coordinator music edn., 1982-84, v.p., store mgr., 1984-87; sales exec. Holiday Inn Conf. Resort, Decatur, 1987—. Author: Bible Mountaineers, 1972. Active Gary Anderson for Mayor campaign, Decatur, 1987; solicitor Decatur Area Arts Council, 1986-87. Named Outstanding Christian Educator, Peoples Ch. of God, 1972. Mem. Ill. State Music Tchrs. Assn., Am. Music Tchrs. Nat. Assn., Decatur Area Music Tchrs. Assn., Nat. Assn. Female Execs., Decatur C. of C. (small bus. council 1986, commodore 1985—, Commodore of Month 1986). Republican. Clubs: Christian Women's of Am. (Decatur and Taylorville area rep. 1978-86, Shelbyville area rep. 1983-86, chmn. 1976-77). Office: Holiday Inn Conf Resort Rt 36 West and Wyckles Rd Decatur IL 62522

HOLMES, ELIZABETH, psychologist; b. Boston, Sept. 2, 1951; d. Charles R. and Evelyn M. (Bedia) Holmes; children: Erin Kathleen, Adam Michael. BS in Psychology and Urban/Suburban Studies, U. Bridgeport, Conn., 1974, MS in Sch. Psychology, 1976; PhD in Clin. Psychology, Calif. Sch. Profl. Psychology, 1979. Dir. hall U. Bridgeport, 1974-76; counselor Crisis House, San Diego, 1976-77, Tech. Research, Inc., San Diego, 1977-78; psychology intern County Mental Health, San Diego, 1978-79; commd. lt. (j.g.) Med. Service Corps, USN, 1979; postdoctoral intern Nat. Naval Med. Ctr., Bethesda, Md., 1979-80; chmn. dept. behavioral psychology Nat. Naval Dental Ctr., Bethesda, 1980-84; cons. liaison psychiatry, faculty psychology intern, head HIV/AIDS program U.S. Naval Hosp., Bethesda, 1983-87; psychologist, program developer Trasher Faber Assocs., Norfolk, Va., 1987—; asst. prof. dept. psychiatry and med. psychology Uniformed Services U. Health Scis., 1984—; professorial lectr. Georgetown U. Sch. Dentistry, 1983—; psychol. cons. to dental div. Bur. Medicine and Surgery; trustee Calif. Sch. Profl. Psychology, 1977-79; cons. in field. Mem. Am. Psychol. Assn., Am. Assn. Dental Schs. Home: 2944 Prince of Wales Dr Chesapeake VA 23321 Office: Trasher Faber Assocs 425 W 20th St Suite 4 Norfolk VA 23517

HOLMES, JACQUELIN ANN, personnel administrator, career development consultant; b. Balt., Sept. 5, 1947; d. Paul Chester and Ethel Marie (Parker) Bianchi; m. Larry Lee Lockman, Nov. 29, 1963 (div. Oct. 1972); children: Carole Jean, Gregory Stephen; m. John Stephen Holmes, July 27, 1974. AA in Psychology, Community Coll. of Denver, 1975; BBA, Regis Coll., 1988. Cert. personnel classification, examinations and rules interpretation, Colo.; lic. claims adjuster. With staff support/counseling div. Community Coll. of Denver North Campus, 1973-74, asst. to dir. community services div., 1974-77; claims adjuster State Compensation Ins. Fund, Denver, 1978-80, 82-84; owner day care ctr. Littleton, Colo., 1980-82; personnel analyst Colo. Dept. Labor & Employment, Denver, 1984-88; adminstrv. officer III Colo. Dept. Natural Resources, Denver, 1988—. Student govt. rep. Community Coll. of Denver, 1973-74; organizer Classified Employees Council, Denver, 1975; vol. orgn. support Arapahoe County Family Day Care, Littleton, 1981-82; coach Teen Quiz Team (Champions 79-83), Littleton, 1979-83; marriage enrichment cons. Littleton Ch. of the Nazarene, 1986-87; Sunday sch. tchr., 1980-87. Named an Outstanding Employee Gov.'s Office Colo. State Govt., 1986. Mem. Internat. Personnel Mgrs. Assn., Colo. Council Mediators Assn. Club: Pilot Club Internat. (Denver). Home: 6746 S Dahlia Ct Littleton CO 80122 Office: Colo Dept Natural Resources 1313 Sherman St Room 415 Denver CO 80203

HOLMES, JENANNE NELSON, lawyer; b. Evanston, Ill., Dec. 30, 1941; d. Oscar William and Anne L. (Moll) Nelson. B.S. magna cum laude, U. So. Calif., 1967, J.D., 1976. Admitted to D.C. bar, 1977, Calif. bar, 1983; sec., corp. officer Sta. KUPD-AM-FM, Phoenix, 1959-61; media dir. West, Weir & Bartel, Los Angeles, 1962-65; asso. media dir. Eisaman, Johns & Laws, Los Angeles, 1966-68; media supr. Ogilvy & Mathers, N.Y.C., 1968-69; v.p. media and mktg. services Smith-Gent Advt. Co., N.Y.C., 1969-71; media supr. The Media Dept., N.Y.C., 1971-72; v.p. media Perkal Advt. Co., Los Angeles, 1972-74; research asst. U. So. Calif. Law Center, 1975-76; atty. advisor FCC, Washington, 1977-80; gen. atty. U.S. Dept. Energy, 1980-88; supervisory hearing officer USDA Farmers Home Adminstrn., Memphis, 1988—; pro bono atty. Friends of Animals, N.Y.C. Mem. ABA, Calif. Bar Assn., D.C. Bar Assn., Fed. Bar Assn., Los Angeles Advt. Women, U. So. Calif. Alumni, Presbyterian. Mensa, Cactus and Succulent Soc., Sierra Club, North Shore Animal League, Phi Beta Kappa, Beta Gamma Sigma. Office: Farmers Home Adminstrn Nat Appeals Staff 7777 Walnut Grove Rd Memphis TN 38119

HOLMES, JOAN MARIE WHEELER, health science association administrator; b. Westerly, R.I., Dec. 25, 1938; d. Arthur Gallup and Helen (Perkins) W.; m. Laurence A. Cove (div. 1971); children: David Cove, Ruth Cove; m. Artice William Holmes, Apr. 5, 1980. Diploma, Grace New Haven-Yale Med. Ctr., 1959; cert., Am. U., 1971; student, George Washington U., 1971-73. Project dir. Toby Town (Md.) Hist. Research Project, 1970-72; research supr. Nat. Pub. Radio, Washington, 1972-74; dir. classified advt. Morkap Pub., Gaithersburg, Md., 1974-77; photojournalist Creative Communication, Potomac, Md., 1977-79; nursing supr. Heritage Hall Health Care Ctr., Leesburg, Va., 1979-80; nurse Loudoun Meml. Hosp., Leesburg, 1980-82, Dept. Corrections, Richmond, Va., 1980-83; maternal child health coordinator Dept. Pub. Health, Boydton, Va., 1983-84; chief operating officer Halifax Home Health Ctr., South Boston, Va., 1984—; advisor Southside Community Services Bd., Chase City, Va., 1984—; cons. Rural Home Care Consortium, South Hill, Va., 1985—; faculty Nat. Assn. for Home Care, New Orleans, 1986. Photographer: Chronicle of the Horse Mag., 1969; editor: (newspaper) The Sentinel, 1974-77. Bd. dirs. Am. Heart Assn., South Boston, 1985—, affiliate faculty mem. Glenallen, Va., 1987—; coordinator Lifeline, South Boston, 1986—; mem. South Boston Hosp. Aux. Recipient Community Service award Am. Heart Assn., 1986; Nat. Endowment for the Humanities research grantee, Washington, 1970; Pub. Health Service grantee, Phila., 1984. Mem. Nat. Assn. for Home Care (mem. nominating com. 1985-86, cons. rural health care 1984—), Am. Nurses Assn., N.C. Nurses Assn., Am. Coll. Healthcare Execs. Democrat. Methodist. Clubs: Operation Bass (Ky.); Exec. Women (N.Y.). Office: Halifax Home Health Ctr 2200 Halifax Rd South Boston VA 24592

HOLMES, KAREN FRANCES, television producer, co-host and reporter; b. Cleve., June 30, 1955; d. Clarence Holsey and Etta Marie (Grist) H. BS, Boston U., 1977. Newswriter Sta. WEEI Radio, Boston, 1977-78; news dir., announcer Sta. WILD Radio, Boston, 1978-81; freelance reporter Stas. WGBH-TV, WBZ-TV, Boston, 1977-81; assoc. producer Sta. WCVB-TV, Boston, 1981-83, producer, co-host, 1983—. Mem. bd. dirs., Aswalos House Roxbury YWCA, Boston, 1985, Am. Cancer Soc., 1985. Recipient Emmy award New England Chpt. Nat. Acad. TV Arts and Scis., 1982, 83, 84, 85, Outstanding Radio Journalism award Mass. Legis. Black Caucus, 1979; named Black Achiever Boston YWCA, 1984; named one of Ten Outstanding Young Leaders of Boston Jaycees, 1987. Mem. Boston Black Media Coalition (com. dir. 1985—), Nat. Acad. TV Arts and Scis., Black Achiever Alumni Assn. Office: Sta WCVB-TV 5 TV Pl Needham MA 02192

HOLMES, MARIA LEE, communication consultant, lecturer, writer; b. San Francisco, Mar. 2, 1944; d. Tracy Sherlock Holmes and Alda Maria (Baranzelli) Holmes-Lyddy. B.A., Calif. State U.-Long Beach, 1967; postgrad, Columbia Pacific U. Cert. secondary tchr., Calif. Tchr., Los Angeles City Schs., 1967-80; cons. Maria Holmes Co., Harbor City, Calif., 1971—; owner Maria Holmes Communication Services, Harbor City, 1980—; dir. bus. and program devel. TranSyn, Ltd. Cons., Venice, Calif., 1982; tchr. bus. and psychology Harbor Coll., Wilmington, Calif., 1982, Torrance Adult Sch., Calif., 1980-81; lectr. various community organizations, Greater Los Angeles, 1978—; faculty chair Chapman Sch.; tchr. Long Beach State U. Free Coll., 1967, Orange Coast Coll., 1987—, U. San Diego, 1987—, Pierce Coll., 1987—; cons. Los Angeles County, Carson, Calif., 1980; guest radio and TV talk shows, Los Angeles. Author: Dealing with Difficult People, 1985; Getting Your Message Across: How to Let Others Know You Mean Business, 1985. Mem. AAUW, Nat. Speakers Assn. (corr. sec. greater Los Angeles chpt.), Women in Mgmt., Nat. Speakers Assn., Los Angeles United Tchrs. Office: Maria Holmes & Assocs 760 W Lomita Blvd #144 Harbor City CA 90710

HOLMES, MARIAN MCGRATH, lawyer; b. Chgo., Apr. 1, 1934; d. Harmon Webber and Margaret Helen (Goodman) McGrath; children—Margaret Etta, Karen Chandler. B.A., Wellesley Coll., 1956; M.Ed., Nat. Coll. Edn., 1970; postgrad. Northwestern U., 1975; J.D., Tex. Tech U., 1982. Bar: Tex. 1982. Pres., Hartzell Corp., Evanston, Ill., 1969-70; tchr. North Shore Country Day Sch., Winnetka, Ill., 1970-76; headmistress Trinity Sch., Midland, Tex., 1976-79; assoc. atty. Lemon, Close, Shearer, Ehrlich & Brown, Perryton, Tex., 1982-85; assoc. Bennett, Thomas & Feldman, Dallas, 1986—. Author, editor Tex. Tech Law Rev., 1980-82. Mem. steering com. for Panhandle br. Women's Advocacy Project, Inc., Austin, 1983—; elder Trinity Presbyn. Ch., 1984-86. Centennial Fund grantee, 1972; recipient Oil and Gas law award, 1982. Mem. ABA, Tex. Bar Assn. (mem. state bar forms com. 1985—), Dallas Bar Assn., Northeast Panhandle Bar Assn. (pres. 1984-86), League Women Voters. Republican. Clubs: Bus. and Profl. Women's, Wheatheart Republican Women's (pres. 1983). Home: 3000 Amherst Dallas TX 75225

HOLMES, MARJORIE ROSE, author; b. Storm Lake, Iowa; d. Samuel Arthur and Rosa (Griffith) H.; m. Lynn Mighell, Apr. 9, 1932; children—Marjorie Mighell Croner, Mark, Mallory, Melanie Mighell Dimopoulos; m. George P. Schmieler, July 4, 1981. Student, Buena Vista Coll., 1927-29, D.Litt. (hon.), 1976; B.A., Cornell Coll., 1931. Tchr. writing Cath. U., 1964-65, U. Md., 1967-68; mem. staff Georgetown Writers Conf., 1959-81. Free-lance writer short stories, articles, verse for mags. including McCall's, Redbook, Reader's Digest; weekly columnist: Love and Laughter, Washington Evening Star, 1959-75; monthly columnist: Woman's Day, 1971-77; author: World By the Tail, 1943, Ten O'Clock Scholar, 1946, Saturday Night, 1959, Cherry Blossom Princess, 1960, Follow Your Dream, 1961, Love is a Hopscotch Thing, 1963, Senior Trip, 1962, Love and Laughter, 1967, I've Got to Talk to Somebody, God, 1969, Writing the Creative Article, 1969, Who Am I, God?, 1971, To Treasure Our Days, 1971, Two from Galilee, 1972, Nobody Else Will Listen, 1973, You and I and Yesterday, 1973, As Tall as My Heart, 1974, How Can I Find You God?, 1975, Beauty in Your Own Back Yard, 1976, Hold Me Up a Little Longer, Lord, 1977, Lord, Let Me Love, 1978, God and Vitamins, 1980, To Help You Through the Hurting, 1983, Three from Galilee—The Young Man from Nazareth, 1985, Writing the Creative Article Today, 1986, Marjorie Holmes' Secrets of Health, Energy and Staying Young, 1987, The Messiah, 1987; contbg. editor Guideposts, 1977—; bd. dirs. The Writer, 1975—. Bd. dirs. Found. Christian Living, 1975—. Recipient Honor Iowans award Buena Vista Coll., 1966, Alumni Achievement award Cornell Coll., 1963, Woman of Achievement award Nat. Fedn. Press Women, 1972; Celebrity of Yr. award Women in Communications, 1975; Woman of Yr. award McLean Bus. and Profl. Women, 1976; award Freedom Found. at Valley Forge, 1977; gold medal Marymount Coll. Va., 1978. Mem. Am. Newspaper Women's Club, Va. Press Women, Children's Book Guild, Washington Nat. Press Club, Delta Phi Beta. Home: 637 E McMurray Rd McMurray PA 15317

HOLMES, NANCY RUTH, forester, environmental specialist; b. Grand Junction, Colo., Jan. 19, 1948; d. Richard Walker and Wanda Helen (Dobosz) H. BS, Colo. State U., 1971; MS in Resource Utilization, U. Maine, 1979; MBA in Internat. Bus., Farleigh Dickinson U., 1988. Forestry aid U.S. Forest Service, Rapid City, S.D., 1969, Sheridan, Wyo., 1970; recreation researcher Colo. State U., Ft. Collins, 1971; residential mgr. Dyer Long Pond, South Jefferon, Maine, 1975-76; environ. intern Maine State Planning Office, Augusta, 1977; wood energy specialist Maine Office Energy Resources, Augusta, 1978-85; mgr. fuel & utility contracts Time Energy Systems, Inc., Houston, 1985-86; nat. environ. mgr. Cogeneration Ptnrs. Am., Edison, N.J., 1986—; mem. Maine Forest Service Com., Augusta, 1980-85; mem. coalition NE Govs. Biomass Coordinating Council, Boston, 1983-85; mem. wood energy mkts. Maine Audubon Soc., Freeport, Maine, 1984; mem. Maine Dept. Conservation's Com. on Intensive Forest Harvesting Practices, Augusta, 1985. Speaker various confs., New Eng. and Can., 1979—. Mem. North Star Borough's Citizen Adv. Council, Fairbanks, Alaska, 1975; bd. dirs. Sam Ely Community Services, Augusta, 1978, Crisis and Counseling Ctrs., Augusta, 1981-85; instr. ARC, Augusta, 1983-85. Recipient Walter Priff Meml. award Colo. State U., 1971; named Sr. Patroller, Nat. Ski Patrol, 1982. Mem. Soc. Am. Foresters, Aircraft Owners & Pilots Assn., Nat. Assn. Female Execs., Am. Pulpwood Assn., Northeastern Loggers Assn. Democrat. Home: 827 Valley Brook Ave Lyndhurst NJ 07071

HOLMES, OPAL LAUREL, publisher; b. Laurens, Iowa, Oct. 14, 1913; d. Ila Laurel and Jessie Merle (Hesselgrave) Holmes; ed. pub. and pvt. schs.; m. Vardis Fisher, Apr. 16, 1940. Publisher, Opal Laurel Holmes, Pub. Coauthor: Gold Rushes and Mining Camps of the Early American West. Recipient Golden Spur award, 1969. Mem. Authors Guild, Authors League Am., Nat. Soc. Lit. and Arts, Internat. Platform Assn. Office: PO Box 2535 Boise ID 83701

HOLMES, WILMA K., educational administrator; b. Washington, Apr. 25, 1933; d. Elton F. and Edith King; B.A., D.C. Tchrs. Coll., 1956; M.A., Stanford U., 1970; children—Ricki F. Sharon R. Tchr. various sch. systems, 1960-69; lang. arts tchr.-specialist Montgomery County Public Schs., Rockville, Md., 1969-70, coordinator human relations tng., 1970-71, dir. human relations, 1971-84, EEO officer, 1973-84, elem. supr., 1987—. Second v.p. Nat. Tots and Teens, 1972-73; bd. dirs. YWCA, 1974-75; mem. nat. bd. dirs. Girl Scouts U.S.A., 1974-75. Named Woman of Yr., Montgomery County chpt. NAACP, 1978. Mem. Am. Assn. Sch. Adminstrs., Nat. Assn. Elem. Prins., Nat. Alliance Black Sch. Educators, NAACP (life) NCCJ (bd. dirs. 1982—), Delta Sigma Theta, Phi Delta Kappa. Office: Montgomery County Pub Schs Area 2 Adminstrv Office Tuckerman Ctr 8224 Lochinver Ln Rockville MD 20854

HOLSER, MARY ANN, human services agency executive; b. Detroit, May 21, 1928; d. Ray Ward and Ruth Belle (Ferguson) Harris; m. William Thomas Holser, Dec. 23, 1955; children—Thomas Dana, Alec Stuart, Margaret. B.A., U. Mich., 1950; M.S.W., Ohio State U., 1954; M. Pub. Adminstrn. Harvard U., 1985; postgrad., Community Health, U. Oreg., 1984. Young adult dir. YMCA, Amarillo, Tex., 1950-51; recreation leader Columbus Recreation Dept., Ohio, 1951-53; cottage supr. Juvenile Diagnostic Ctr., Columbus, 1955; group work specialist Spl. Service for Groups, Los Angeles, 1955-56; psychiat. social worker Met. State Hosp., Norwalk, Calif., 1958-60, League of Latin Am. Citizens, Anaheim, Calif., 1965-67, Crisis Intervention Clinic, U. Calif., Irvine Med. Ctr., 1967-70; psychiat. social work cons. Los Angeles County Health Dept., 1970; clin. dir. Alcohol Traffic Safety Program, Eugene, Oreg., 1971-76; co-dir. Drinking Decisions, Eugene, 1977-78; dir. Behanna House, Eugene, 1978-79; exec. dir. Lane County Council on Alcoholism, Eugene, 1979-83; ; mental health examiner mental hearings State of Oreg., 1973—; vis. asst. prof. U. Oreg., Eugene, 1973-76; founder Orange County Free Clinic, 1969. Contbr. articles to profl. jours. Research grantee Max Planck Inst. for Psychiatry, Munich, Fed. Republic of Germany, 1976; winner Eugene Pub. Library Poetry Contest 1st prize, 1983. Mem. rules com. Dem. Nat. Com.; orgn. chmn. Lane County Dem. Cen. Com.; del. Dem. Nat. Conv., 1988. Mem. Nat. Assn. Social Workers, Acad. Clin. Social Workers, Oreg. Substance Abuse Assn., Lane County Affirmative Action Com. (chmn.), Oreg. Alcohol Program Mgrs. Assn. (sec.-treas.), Lane County Alcohol Program Mgrs. Assn. (sec.). Democrat. Home: 2620 Dresta de Ruta Eugene OR 97403 Office: U Oreg Sch Community Health Eugene OR 97403

HOLSEYBROOK, GLORIA ANN, pharmacist; b. Eugene, Oreg., Sept. 21, 1955; d. Ralph Eddy and Emma Stephanie (Juvan) H.; m. Garrett Lyle Tatsumi, July 26, 1980. BS in Pharmacy, Oreg. State U., 1978. Extern drug info. Health Sci. Ctr., U. Oreg., Portland, 1978-79; staff pharmacist Pay-less Drug Store, Eugene, 1978-79; clin. pharmacist Providence Hosp., Anchorage, 1979-81; cons. pharmacist St. Joseph Hosp., Aberdeen, Wash., 1981-83; clin. pharmacist St. Joseph Hosp. and Health Care Ctr., Tacoma, 1983-87; asst. dir. pharmacy St. Francis Community Hosp., Federal Way, Wash., 1987—. Contbr. articles to profl. jours. Mem. Am. Soc. Hosp. Pharmacists, Am. Pharm. Assn., Wash. State Soc. Hosp. Pharmacists (Pharmacist of Yr. 1986), Lambda Kappa Sigma. Republican. Baptist. Club: Tumwater Valley (Wash.) Racquet. Home: 7414 38th Dr SE Lacey WA 98503 Office: St Francis Community Hosp and Health Ctr 34515 9th Ave S Federal Way WA 98003

HOLSMAN, DORENE ENOLA, banker; b. Kanona, Kans., Apr. 19, 1933; d. Darl Abraham and Lavina Gertrude (Anderson) Worley; m. Charley Frank Holsman, Mar. 22, 1950; children—Kelley Dee, Loree Gwendolyn. Student Highland Community Coll., 1982—. Sec. to county atty. Rawlins County, Atwood, Kans., 1950, 51; sec., asst. cashier, asst. v.p., v.p. ops. Bank of Horton (Kans.), 1963—, sec. to bd., 1977—. Ch. sec. United Methodist Ch., Horton, 1960-63, CR. treas., 1966-76. Mem. Horton C. of C. (women's div., officer 1976). Democrat. Methodist. Office: Bank of Horton 108 E 8th St Horton KS 66439

HOLST, MARY-ELLA, religion educator; b. Detroit, Oct. 12, 1934; d. Spencer and Ruth Catherine (McCullough) Holst; B.A., U. Toledo, 1959; M.A., N.Y.U., 1970; m. Bert Zippel, Jan. 18, 1969 (dec. May 1985); children—Patricia Hall, Darcy Hall. Sr. counselor, employment specialist N.Y. Dept. Labor, 1962-75; religious edn. dir. Unitarian Ch. of All Souls, 1976-87; mem. Unitarian Universalist Hist. Scholarship Com. Bd. mgrs. Soc. for Aging, 1974—; bd. dirs. Yorkville Common Pantry, 1982—. Contbg. editor Conversations. . . Journal of Women and Religion; contbr. poetry to lit. jours. Home: 340 E 80 St New York NY 10021 Office: Unitarian Ch of All Souls 1157 Lexington Ave New York NY 10021

HOLSTEIN, MARILYN ANNE, editor; b. Syracuse, N.Y., Feb. 11, 1958; d. Seward North and Helen Margaret (Sedor) H. BS, St. Lawrence U., 1980; MS in Mag. Journalism, Syracuse U., 1981. Editor Syracuse mag., 1981-83; mng. editor Living Publs., Syracuse, 1983-85; assoc. editor Adventure Road-Amoco Traveler, N.Y.C., 1985-86, editor, 1986—; cons. Schueler Communications, Syracuse, 1985. Contbr. articles to profl. jours. Recipient Alexander Black Journalism award St. Lawrence U., 1980. Mem. Syracuse Press Club, Women in Communications, St. Lawrence U. Alumni Club (exec. com. 1987). Club: St. Bartholomew's Community (N.Y.C.). Office: Adventure Road 360 Madison Ave 9th Floor New York NY 10017

HOLSTON, SHARON SMITH, government official; b. Cleve., Dec. 15, 1945; d. Charles Coolidge and Eva Mae (Hall) Smith; m. Joseph Holston, Jr., Dec. 22, 1973; children: Joseph Ikaweba, Eve Denise. AB, Columbia U., 1967; M in Pub. Adminstrn., Harvard U., 1986. Personnel mgmt. specialist U.S. Commn. Civil Rights, 1967-70, HEW, 1970-72; EEO officer FDA, Rockville, Md., 1972-74, personnel mgmt. specialist, 1975-77, acting exec. officer, 1977-79, spl. asst. to assoc. commr. mgmt. and ops., 1979-80, dep. assoc. commr. mgmt. and ops., 1980—, acting assoc. commr. mgmt. and ops., 1986—. Recipient Award of Merit, FDA, 1982, 87, also commr.'s spl. citation, 1985. Fin. sec., mem. Jack & Jill of Am.; active Mt. Calvary Bapt. Ch. Office: 5600 Fishers Ln Rockville MD 20857

HOLT, BARBARA BERTANY, management consultant; b. Bridgeport, Conn., Nov. 4, 1940; d. Stephen Edward and Mary G. Bertany; student Regis Coll., 1958-59; B.A. in English, U. Bridgeport, 1962; m. Robert Holt, Dec. 5, 1971; children—Pamela Maren, Laura Kimbel, Mary Brooke. Instr. speech and theatre, U. Bridgeport (Conn.), 1962-69; gen. mgr. BFL Assos., Exec. Recruitment, N.Y.C., 1969-72; founder, pres. Barbara Holt Assos., mgmt. cons., N.Y.C., 1972—; mem. faculty New Sch. for Social Research. Chmn. bd. advisers Fine Arts Acad. Fairfield. Mem. N.Y. Fashion Group, Women in Mgmt. Club: Atrium (N.Y.C.). Developer, producer video career mgmt. series for public TV, 1976. Office: Barbara Holt Assocs Box 713 Southport CT 06490

HOLT, BERTHA MERRILL, state legislator; b. Eufaula, Ala., Aug. 16, 1916; d. William Hoadley and Bertha Harden (Moore) Merrill; AB, Agnes Scott Coll., 1938; LLB, U. Ala., 1941; m. Winfield Clary Holt, Mar. 14, 1941; children. Harriet Wharton Holt Whitley, William Merrill, Winfield Jefferson. Admitted to Ala. bar, 1941; with Treasury Dept., Washington, 1941-42, Dept. Interior, Washington, 1942-43; mem. N.C. Ho. of Reps. from 22d Dist., 1975-80, 25th Dist., 1980—, chmn. select com. govtl. ethics, 1979-80, chmn. constl. amendments com., 1981, 83, mem. joint commn. govtl. ops., 1982—, chmn. appropriation com. justice and pub. safety, 1985-88 . Pres., Democratic Women of Alamance, 1962, chmn. hdqrs., 1964, 68; mem. N.C. Dem. Exec. Com., 1964-75; pres. Episcopal Ch. Women, 1968; mem. council N.C. Episcopal Diocese, 1972-74, 84-87 , chmn. budget com. 1987—; chmn. fin. dept., 1973-75, parish grant com., 1973-80, mem. standing com., 1975-78; chmn. Alamance County Social Services Bd., 1970; mem. N.C. Bd. Sci. and Tech., 1979-83; bd. dirs. Hospice N.C., State Council Social Legis., U. N.C. Sch. Pub. Health Adv. Bd., Salvation Army Alamance County, N.C., Alternatives for Status Offenders and Burlington (N.C.) Health Adv. Bd. Recipient Outstanding Alumna award Agnes Scott Coll., 1978, Legis. award for service to elderly Non-Profit Rest Home Assn., 1985, health, 1986, ARC, 1987, Faith Active in Pub. Affairs award N.C. Council of Churches, 1987. Mem. Women's Forum N.C., Law Alumni Assn. U. N.C. Chapel Hill (dir. 1978-81), N.C. Bar Assn., NOW, English Speaking Union, N.C. Hist. Soc., Les Amis du Vin, Pi Beta Phi, Phi Kappa Gamma (hon. mem.). Club: Century Book. also: PO Box 1111 Burlington NC 27215

HOLT, BEVERLY ELAINE, educator; b. Little Rock, Aug. 27, 1945; d. Carl Bernard and Artie Mae (Huffman) Cox; m. Dennis Holt, Dec. 21, 1963; 1 child, Dena Elaine. BS in English and Bus. Edn. with honors, Henderson State U., 1966, MS in English, 1969, postgrad., U. Houston, 1981, East Tex. State U., 1981-85. Lang. arts tchr. Helena-West Helena (Ark.) Ind. Sch. Dist., 1966-67; English tchr. Hughes (Ark.) Ind. Sch. Dist., 1967-69; adult bus. edn. tchr. Arkadelphia (Ark.) Ind. Sch. Dist., 1969-70; English tchr. Bismarck (Ark.) Ind. Sch. Dist., 1970-71; tchr. English, bus. Lee Acad., Auburn, Ala., 1976-77; lang. arts tchr. Longview (Tex.) Ind. Sch. Dist., 1977-78; tchr. bus. Kilgore (Tex.) Coll., 1978-79; chmn. English dept., audiovisual dir. Kilgore Ind. Sch. Dist., 1979-85; media specialist Spring Hill Ind. Sch. Dist., Longview, 1985—; teaching specialization panel U. Tex., Tyler, 1983-84; mem. adv. bd. Region VII Edn. Service Ctr., Kilgore, 1984-85; com. mem. Tex. Edn. Study So. Assn., Kilgore, 1984-85. Mem. Tex. Assn. for Gifted/Talented, Tex. Joint Council Tchrs. English, Tex. Library Assn., Tex. Assn. Supervision and Curriculum Devel., Tex. Edn. Assn. (adv. com. 1984-85), Alpha Chi, Phi Beta Lambda, Delta Kappa Gamma. Democrat. Methodist. Home: 2902 Ruidosa Longview TX 75605

HOLT, CHARLENE P., oncologist, pediatrician; b. Memphis, Mar. 2, 1938; d. Clifford Hoyte and Juanita (Smith) Poland; m. Richard C. Holt (div. Sept. 1983); children: Dana, Stephanie. BS, Fla. Southern Coll., 1959; MD, U. Miami, Coral Gables, Fla., 1963. Diplomate Am. Bd. Pediatrics. Intern Bapt. Meml. Hosp., Memphis, 1963-64; resident in pediatrics John Gaston Hosp., Memphis, 1964-66; assoc. in clin. pediatrics St. Jude Childrens' Hosp., Memphis, 1967-69; asst. prof. medicine U. Tenn., Memphis, 1968-69; asst. prof. medicine U. Colo. Sch. Medicine, Denver, 1969-74, assoc. prof., 1974-75, dir. oncology Denver Childrens' Hosp., 1969-75; founding dir. Colo. Regional Cancer Ctr., Denver, 1974-75; dir. pediatrics Mountain States Tumor Inst., Boise, Idaho, 1975-77; pvt. practice family medicine, oncology, pediatrics Weiser, Idaho, 1975-78; dir. Intermountain Youth Cancer Ctr., Boise, 1977-78; assoc. clin. prof. U. Wash., Seattle, 1978-81; pediatrician, oncologist Panama Gorgas Army Hosp., Republic of Panama, 1981-82; sr. oncologist Tawam Hosp., Abu Dhabi, United Arab Emirates, 1982-85; assoc. dir. Adria Labs. div. Erbamont, Inc., Columbus, Ohio, 1985-87; dir. pediatric oncology Harrington Cancer Ctr., Amarillo, Tex., 1987—; prof. pediatrics Tex. Tech U. Health Scis., Amarillo, 1987—; appointed staff numerous hosps. including LeBonheur Childrens' Hosp., Memphis, Presbyn. Med. Ctr., Denver, St. Alphonsus Hosp., Boise, Mercy Med. Ctr., Nampa, Idaho; cons. United Arab Emirates Cancer Com., Abu Dhabi, 1985—, Ministry of Health King Saud Univ., Riyadh, Saudi Arabia, 1986—, Nat. Cancer Inst. Cancer Control Adv. Bd., Blue Mountain Cancer Program of Oregon-Wash., others; adj. prof. pediatrics Tex. Tech U. of the Health Scis., Lubbock, 1987—; author Cancer Control Program for State of Idaho, 1976; mem. edn. com. Madigan Army Med. Ctr. Dept. Pediatrics, Tacoma, 1979-80; lectr., presenter workshops, seminars to numerous internat. and nat. orgns.; tech. advisor for TV series Sunshine, 1975, Shannon, 1981-82 as spl. med. cons. to Universal Studios/NBC-TV. Contbr. numerous articles to profl. jours. Bd. dirs. Tacoma Unit Am. Cancer Soc., 1978-81; chmn. Intra-City Com. on Hodgkins' Disease, Denver, 1971-72; previously active Colo. Commn. on Status of Women. Served as lt. col. USAR, 1978—. Recipient Commendation for Outstanding Service to the U.S. Govt. and the Community, Tacoma Area Exec. Service Assn., 1981; disease research grantee numerous orgns. including Nat. Cancer Inst., Colo.-Wyo. Regional Med. Program. Fellow Am. Acad. Pediatrics; mem. Am. Assn. for Cancer Research, Am. Assn. for Cancer Edn., Am. Soc. for Clin. Oncology, Am. Womens' Med. Soc., Leukemia Soc. Am., Soc. Fed. Med. Agys., Soc. Adolescent Medicine, Rocky Mountain Radiol. Soc., Cen. Ohio Soc. Clin. Oncology, Western Soc. for Pediatric Research, Internat. Soc. Lymphology, Internat. Soc. Pediatric Oncology, Am. Quarter Horse Assn. Club: Woodbrook Hunt (Tacoma). Office: Harrington Cancer Ctr 1500 Wallace Blvd Amarillo TX 79106

HOLT, EVE MAY, advertising agency executive; b. Bklyn., May 22, 1946; d. Harold and June (Mellon) Glicksman; m. Steven C. Holt, June 30, 1966; children—Edward, Jesse. Student Hunter Coll., 1964, U. Hawaii, 1980-83. Lic. real estate salesperson, Hawaii. Asst. converter Donson Fabrics, Inc., N.Y.C., 1965-68; mgr. Sutherland's, Inc., Portsmouth, N.H., 1973-75; gen. mgr. The Small Corp., Berwick, Maine, 1975-77; dept. mgr. Liberty House, Honolulu, 1977-79; account supr. Fawcett, McDermott, Cavanagh, Honolulu, 1979-87; v.p. The Cavanagh Group, Honolulu, 1987—; contbg. arts editor Portsmouth Herald, 1974. Pres. Portsmouth Parade Mall Mchts. Assn., 1975; choreographer Garrison Players, 1972-73; communications cons. to Hawaii state senator Wadsworth Yee, 1982. Recipient Pele award Honolulu Advt. Fedn., 1982, 24 Carat award Affiliated Advt. Agys., Inc., 1983. Mem. Network Mktg. Women (pres. 1984), Am. Mktg. Assn. (dir.), Honolulu Advt. Fedn. Office: Fin Factors Ltd 195 S King St Honolulu HI 96813

HOLT, GWENDOLYN HILL, transportation executive; b. Louisa, Va., Jan. 27, 1952; d. George Edward and Martha Ann (Jackson) H.; m. Robert Dillard Holt, Jr., July 3, 1971 (div. July 1984); 1 child, Courtney Nicole. Cert., Smithdeal/Massey Bus. Coll., 1971, Barbizon Sch. Modeling, 1972; student, Piedmont (Va.) Community Coll., 1973—. Sec. Louisa County Pub. Sch.s, 1968-70; med. transcriptionist Va. Vocat. Rehab., Richmond, 1970-71, U. Va. Hosp., Charlottesville, 1971; sec. Charlottesville Pub. Schs., 1971-79; cons., mgr. Fashion Two Twenty Cosmetics, Charlottesville, 1970-79; sec. Gen. Electric Co., Charlottesville, 1979-81; transp. analyst Gen. Electric Fanuc Automation NA, Charlottesville, 1981—; instr. fashion modeling Charlottesville Pub. Schs., 1973-74, cons. etiquette and poise, 1973, 79; income tax preparer, fashion show cons., antique dealer, Charlottesville. Mem. Parent Adv. Com., Chpt. 1, Charlottesville, 1986-88; judge Miss Pre-Teen Va., Miss Pre-Teen Assn., Charlottesville, 1986; v.p. usher bd. First Bapt. Ch., Louisa. Mem. Nat. Bus. Women's Assn. (newspaper editor 1973), NAACP (top fundraiser 1986). Democrat. Lodge: Order Eastern Star. Home: 2717 Brookmere Rd Charlottesville VA 22901

HOLT, MARILYN JEAN, business development and management company executive; b. Tacoma, Wash., Oct. 22; d. Maynard Ernest and Mable J. (Walker) H.; m. Clifford Rinko Wind, Aug. 25, 1984. Student, Olympic Jr. Coll., 1968-69; BA in History and English, U. Wash., 1972, MA in English Lit., 1979. Freelance writer Seattle, 1970-81; owner, chief exec. officer Holt & Co., Seattle, 1981—; adj. prof. Cen. Wash. U., Edmonds, 1983—; lectr. Western Wash. U., Seattle, 1983-84; instr. Seattle Community Coll., 1983-84; sec., v.p. NW Venture Group, Bellevue, Wash., 1986—, sec., 1986-87. Editor NW Venture Group newsletter, 1986. Recipient Achievement award Soc. Tech. Communications, 1985. Mem. Greater Seattle C. of C. (com. mem. 1984-85, recognition award 1985). Democrat.

HOLT, MARJORIE SEWELL, lawyer, retired congresswoman; b. Birmingham, Ala., Sept. 17, 1920; d. Edward Rol and Juanita (Felts) Sewell; m. Duncan McKay Holt, Dec. 26, 1946; children: Rachel (Mrs. Kenneth Hall Tschantre), Edward, Victoria (Mrs. James Lee Stauffer). Grad., Jacksonville U., 1945; J.D., U. Fla., 1949. Bar: Fla. 1949, Md. 1962. Practiced in Annapolis Md., 1962; clk. Anne Arundel County Circuit Ct., 1966-72; mem. 93d-99th Congresses from 4th Dist. of Md., 1973-86; mem. armed services com.; vice chmn. Office Tech. Assessment, 1977; chmn. Republican Study com., 1975-76; of counsel Smith, Somerville & Case, Balt., 1986—; Supr. elections Anne Arundel County, 1963-65; del. to Rep. Nat. Conv., 1968, 76, 80. Co-author: Case Against The Reckless Congress, 1976, Can You Afford This House, 1978. Recipient; Distinguished Alumna award U. Fla., 1975. Mem. Am., Md., Anne Arundel bar assns., Phi Kappa Phi, Phi Delta Delta. Presbyterian (elder 1959). Office: Smith Somerville & Case 100 Light St Baltimore MD 21202

HOLT, PETRONELLA MARIA, publishing executive, consultant; b. The Hague, The Netherlands, June 12, 1943; came to U.S., 1964; d. Dirk Jan and Johanna Marguerite (van der Roest) Van Boven. BA, Claremont U., Perth, West Australia, 1962; Doctorandus in Ancient History, U. West Australia and U. Cairo, Perth West, 1971. Coll. bookman Harper & Row Pubs., N.Y.C., 1968-69; mgr. European sales Harper & Row Pubs., London, 1969-71; dir. area sales McGraw-Hill Book Pubs., Fed. Republic of Germany, 1975-77; mgr. European sales Hutchinson Pub. Group, London, 1977-81, Feffer & Simons Inc., N.Y.C., 1984; pres. Pubs. Internat. Mgmt., East Windsor, N.J., 1984—; cons. numerous pubs. firms, London, 1985—, Begonia Books Ltd., Melbourne, Australia, 1985—, Asian Books, New Delhi, 1987—; cons./advisor China Nat. Pubs. Import and Export Corp., Beijing, 1987—. Author: Export Strategies for Book Publishers, 1984, Selling Abroad: Rights or Product?, 1986; contbr. articles to profl. jours. Mem. Royal Over-Seas League, Royal Commonwealth Soc. Republican. Club: Netherlands (N.Y.).

HOLT, TODETTE LAPRAIRIE, nurse, educator; b. York, Pa., May 7, 1939; d. Leon Claude and Flo Evelyn (Gentzler) LaPrairie; m. Gerald George Holt, Dec. 24, 1965 (div. 1978); 1 child, Jason Ryan; m. Robert Holt, Sept. 22, 1980 (dec. 1984). BS in Nursing, U. Md., Balt., 1965; MS in Child Devel. and Family Relations, N.D. State U., 1969; EdD in Adminstrn., U. N.D., 1986, postgrad., 1987. Instr. nursing York Hosp., 1960-62, 65; staff nurse No. Itasca Hosp., Bigfork, Minn., 1966; instr. St. Luke's Hosp. Sch. Nursing, Fargo, N.D., 1966-70, maternal-child coordinator, 1970-75, asst. dir. nursing edn., 1975-79, dir. nursing edn., 1979-87; workshop presenter, leader assessor Merit Care St. Luke's Hosp., Fargo, 1986—. Editorial advisor Alumni Newsletter, 1983. Sunday sch. tchr. First Luth. Ch., 1986-87. Mem. Am. Nurses Assn., Nat. League Nursing (bd. rev. diploma programs 1982—, con. student group, 1984-87), Sigma Theta Tau, Phi Delta Kappa. Republican.

HOLTHAUS, KATHERINE DEE, health care marketing professional; b. Denver, Mar. 19, 1961; d. William Philip and Barbara Kristine (Nielsen) H. B in Applied Math. Engring., U. Colo., 1983; postgrad., U. Denver, 1984-85, 87—. Acctg. intern Cooper, Haugen and Co. CPAs, Englewood, Colo., 1982-84; market analyst mktg. dept. Porter Meml. Hosp., Denver, 1985-88; market analyst Tallant/Yates, Denver, 1988—. Judge, vol. 4-H Clubs, Met. Denver, 1979—; supt. Sunday sch. Ascension Luth. Ch., Littleton, Colo., 1985-87. Recipient 2 Advantage awards Adventist Health System, 1987. Mem. Soc. for Hosp. Planning and Mktg. Am. Hosp. Assn., Acad. for Health Services Mktg. Am. Mktg. Assn., Alpha Chi Omega. Republican. Office: Tallant/Yates 5200 DTC Pkwy #400 Englewood CO 80111

HOLTMAN, CAROLYN SUE, arts administrator; b. Kansas City, Jan. 16, 1950; d. Henry Charles and Mary Alice (Sherley) Danielson; m. Stephen Harold Holtman, July 18, 1970; children: Jennifer Elizabeth, Daniel Stephen. Student, Emporia State U., 1968-70; BME, Ill. State U., 1972. Aux. liaison Kansas City Symphony, 1984—, dir. audience devel., 1985—. Mem. Children's Cardiac Ctr. Aux., Kansas City, 1982, Prairie Village (Kans.) Mcpl. Arts Commn., 1984-86; showhouse chmn. Jr. Women's Symphony Alliance, Kansas City, 1983, pres., 1984. Recipient Golden Rule award JC Penney, Kansas City, 1984. Mem. Am. Symphony Orch. League, Sigma Kappa (pres. Greater Kansas City chpt. 1984-85). Presbyterian. Home: 5209 W 83d St Prairie Village KS 66208 Office: Kansas City Symphony 1029 Central Kansas City MO 64105

HOLTMEIER, PAT ANN, nurse, administrator; b. Washington, Mo., Mar. 28, 1949; d. Raymond Frank and Albertine (Glosemeyer) H.; m. Ernest F. Brasier, Dec. 30, 1978; children: Kelly, Jeffrey. BS in Nursing, Incarnate Word Coll., 1979. RN. Staff nurse Santa Rosa Childrens Hosp., San Antonio, 1974-79; dir. Kimberly Nurses, San Antonio, 1979-81, Am. Temporary Resources, San Antonio, 1981; exec. dir. Am. Nursing Resources, Kansas City, Mo., 1981—; realtor Deanne Owens Better Homes and Gardens, San Antonio, 1979; cons. in nursing field. Mem. Nurses in Bus., Nat. Assn. Home Care. Democrat. Roman Catholic. Home: 29 Bopp Ln Saint Louis MO 63131 Office: Am Nursing Resources 141 N Meramec Clayton MO 63105

HOLTON, ANNE LYSBETH, magazine publisher; b. Pitts., June 10, 1950; d. James Leo and Ruth Anna (Homan) H. BS in Psychology, U. Bridgeport, 1972; postgrad. NYU. Legis. aide to Congressman Henry Helstoski of N.J., 1973-74; asst. to advt. dir. New Times Mag., N.Y.C., 1974-75, sales rep., 1975; advt. sales rep. Rolling Stone mag., N.Y.C., 1975-77; advt. sales rep. Ms. mag., N.Y.C., 1977-78, N.Y. adv. mgr., 1978-79, nat. advt. mgr., 1979, advt. dir., 1979-82; mktg. dir. Gentlemen's Quar. Mag., 1982-85; v.p., advt. dir. Parade Mag., 1985-87; pub., US Mag., 1987—. Mem. Mag. Pubs. Assn., Nat. Women's Polit. Party. Republican. Office: US Magazine 1 Dag Hammarskjold Plaza 10th Floor New York NY 10017

HOLTON, VIVIAN, financial administrator; b. Louise, Miss., Sept. 13, 1952; d. Larthyree (Sanders) H.; m. Robert Barnett, June 25, 1983 (div. Mar. 1986). BA, Tougaloo Coll., 1974. Underwriter Towers, Perrin, Forster & Crosby, Hartford, Conn., 1979, Hartford Ins. Co., Shawnee, Kans., 1980-83; collector Montgomery Ward & Co., Inc., Merriam, Kans., 1984-85, Ford Motor Credit Co., Overland Park, Kans., 1985-86; mgr. collections Mitsubishi Acceptance Corp., Leawood, Kans., 1986—. Democrat. Methodist. Home: 12136 W 77th St #306 Lenexa KS 66216 Office: Mitsubishi Acceptance Corp 11100 Ash Leawood KS 66207

HOLTZ, CHARLENE CUNNINGHAM, lawyer; b. Passaic, N.J., Oct. 14, 1948; d. Harrison Groome and Lillian Helen (Feltz) Cunningham; m. William Charles Holtz, Oct. 21, 1972; 1 dau., Kelsey Kristen. A.B. with honors, Rutgers U., 1970; J.D. cum laude, DePaul U., 1976. Bar: Ill. 1976; assoc. firm Coffield, Ungaretti, Harris & Slavin, Chgo., 1976-78, ptnr., 1978—. Ford Found. fellow 1970. Mem. ABA, Ill. Bar Assn., Chgo. Bar Assn., Women's Bar Assn. Ill. Presbyterian.

HOLTZAPFEL, PATRICIA KELLY, health facility executive; b. Madison, Wis., Jan. 29, 1948; d. Raymond Michael and Laura Margaret (Stegner) Kelly; m. Robert Adrian Bunker, Oct. 4, 1975 (div. June 1979); children: Donald, Theresa, Nicole, Douglas; m. Raymond Paul Holtzapfel, Mar. 12, 1983; children: David, Richard. RN; cert. pub. health nurse. Staff nurse Madison Gen. Hosp., 1970-72; bloodmobile staff nurse ARC, Madison, 1972-73; pub. health nurse Dane County Pub. Health Dept., Madison, 1973-75; field health nurse CIGNA Health Plan, Phoenix, 1975-84; dir. nursing Olsten Health Care, Phoenix, 1984-85; mgr. bus. Holtzapfel Phys. Therapy and Pain Control Clinic, Phoenix, 1985—; bd. dirs. Deer Valley Vocat. Arts Adv. Council, Phoenix. Bd. dirs. Deer Valley Vocat. Arts Adv. Council, Phoenix, 1986—. Mem. The Exec. Female Assn., Ariz. Networking Council. Office: Holtzapfel Phys Therapy Pain Control 4025 W Bell Rd Suite #2 Phoenix AZ 85023

HOLTZCLAW, DIANE SMITH, educator; b. Buffalo, May 26, 1936; d. John Nelson and Beatrice M. (Salisbury) Smith; m. John Victor Holtzclaw, June 27, 1959; children—Kathryn Diane, John Bryan. B.S. in Edn. magna cum laude, SUNY-Brockport, 1957, M.S. with honors, 1961; postgrad. SUNY-Buffalo, 1960-65, Canisus Coll., 1979, Nazareth Coll., 1981-82. Tchr. Greece Central Sch., Rochester, N.Y., 1957-60; supr. SUNY-Brockport, 1960-64, assoc. prof. edn., 1960-64; dir. Early Childhood Ctr., Fairport, N.Y., 1968-80; tchr. Fairport Central Schs., 1971—; cons. in field. Ch. music dir. , Rochester, N.Y., 1983—; pres. bd. dirs. Downtown Day Care Ctr., Rochester, 1974-83; mem. exec. bd. Rochester Theatre Organ Soc., 1988—. Mem. Fairport Edn. Assn. (exec. bd. 1982-83, del. 1983), N.Y. State United Tchrs., AAUW (exec. bd. 1973-74, 77-79, 83-84, pres. Fairport br. 1971-73), Kappa Delta Pi. Home: 1455 Ayrault Rd Fairport NY 14450 Office: Fairport Cen Schs 38 W Church St Fairport NY 14450

HOLTZMAN, ELIZABETH, lawyer, district attorney; b. Bklyn., Aug. 11, 1941; d. Sidney and Filia Holtzman. A.B. magna cum laude, Radcliffe Coll., 1962; J.D., Harvard U., 1965; L.D.S., Regis Coll., 1975, Skidmore Coll., 1980, Simmons Coll., 1981, Smith Coll., 1982. Bar: N.Y. Assoc. Wachtell, Lipton, Rosen, Kalz & Kern, N.Y.C., 1965-67; asst. to mayor N.Y.C., 1968-69; assoc. Paul, Weiss, Rifkind, Wharton & Garrison, 1970-72; mem. 93d-96th Congresses from 16th dist., N.Y.; vis. prof. NYU Law Sch. and Grad. Sch. Pub. Adminstrn., 1981; dist. atty. Kings County Bklyn., 1982—. N.Y. State Democratic committeewoman, 1970-72; del. Dem. Nat. Conv., 1972; mem. Select Commn. Immigration Policy, 1979-80; mem. Pres.'s Nat. Commn. on U.S. Observance Internat. Women's Yr.; Dem. nominee U.S. Senate, 1980; mem. Am. Jewish Commn. Holocaust; bd. overseers Harvard U., 1976-82; mem. Helsinki Watch Com., 1981—. Lawyers Com. Internat. Human Rights, 1981—. Recipient Nat. Council Jewish Women's Faith and Humanity award, YWCA Elizabeth Cutter Morrow award, Maccabean award N.Y. Bd. Rabbis, Alumni recognition award Radcliffe Coll. Alumnae Assn., 1973; N.J. and Los Angeles ACLU awards for contbns. to def. of Constn. and preservation of civil liberties, 1981; Am. Traditions award B'nai B'rith, 1984, Athena award N.Y.C. Commn. on Status of Women, 1985; Woman of Yr. award Bus. and Profl. Women, 1985, 5th Kent State Conf. on Holocaust, Humanitarian award, 1986, Queens B'nai B'rith Women's Humanitarian award, 1986, Jewish War Vets. Outstanding and Meritorious Service award, 1986, Child Abuse Prevention award Recognition of Committment to Children, 1986. Fellow N.Y. Inst. Humanities; mem. Nat. Women's Polit. Caucus, Bar Assn. City N.Y., NOW (Equality award for Overall Achievement L.I. chpt. 1987, N.Y.C. task force Cert. of Appreciation 1987), Phi Beta Kappa. Office: 210 Joralemon St Brooklyn NY 11201

HOLVEY, CAROLYN SUE, audit specialist, nurse; b. Weston, W.Va., Jan. 24, 1958; d. Billy Brown and Marjorie Carol (Hardman) Burke; m. William Anthony Holvey, Apr. 10, 1982; children: Burke Ashley, Samantha Carol. BS in Nursing, W. Va. U., 1980. RN. Staff nurse Hermann Hosp., Houston, 1980-81; pvt. duty nurse Staff Builders, Houston, 1981; audit specialist, nurse, Republic Service Bur., Houston, 1981—. Mem. W.Va. Nurses Assn., Tex. Nurses Assn., Am. Soc. Post Anesthesia Nurses, W.Va. U. Alumni Assn., 4-H Allstars. Democrat. Baptist. Home: 9242 Beechnut Houston TX 77036 Office: Republic Service Bur Box 771967 Houston TX 77215

HOM, DORIS SOO, computer and mathematics educator, consultant; b. N.Y.C., May 22, 1953; d. Frank Edward and Ngook Ho (Tow) S.; BA in Math., CCNY, 1977; MS in Stats., Baruch Coll., 1986. Adj. lectr. Hunter Coll., N.Y.C., 1978-79, grant adminstr. to coordinator of field work Research Found., 1980-81, adminstrv. asst. to dean Sch. Social Work, 1981-82; tchr. math. William Alexander Jr. High Sch., Bklyn., 1979; adj. lectr. N.Y. City Tech. Coll., 1979-80; researcher women's bur. U.S. Dept. Labor. NSF grantee, 1979-80. Mem. Nat. Assn. Remedial Devel. Studies in Post Secondary Edn., Assn. Tchrs. Math. N.Y.C., Coalition Asian Am. Profl. Women, Asian Women United, Phi Theta Kappa.

HOMBERGER, KAREN A., loan officer; b. Jeffersonville, Ind., Dec. 31, 1951; d. Bill K. and Patsy R. (Applegate) Schneidtmiller; m. Douglas R. Homberger, May 31, 1975 (div. July 1978). BS in Banking and Fin., Ind. U., 1974; cert. in banking, Am Inst. Banking, 1975; MS in Banking, U. Miss., 1985. Collection mgr. Liberty Nat. Bank, Louisville, 1970-77; with trust dept. Clark County State Bank, Jeffersonville, Ind., 1977-78; loan and collection mgr. Alcorn Bank and Trust, Corinth, Miss., 1978-1982; loan officer Bank of Walnut, Miss., 1983—. Active Am. Cancer Soc., Corinth, 1985-86, Corinth Jr. Auxilary, 1985-86. Mem. Nat. Assn. Bank Women. Republican. Lutheran. Office: The Bank of Walnut 101 S Main St Walnut MS 38683

HOMBS, KAREN KAY, financial planner; b. Denver, Aug. 3, 1942; d. Arthur Clark Eugene and Norma May (Urquhart) Ryman; grad. U. Denver/Colo. Women's Coll., 1984; m. Thomas Gibson Hombs, Apr. 12, 1978; 1 child, Timothy John. With Samsonite Corp., Denver, 1960-75, employee relations rep., supr., 1965-71, labor relations rep., 1971-75; labor relations rep. Climax Molybdenum Co. (Colo.) div. AMAX, 1975-78, prin. labor relations adminstr., 1978-83; registered rep. IDS/Am. Express, 1983—. Mem. council Lord of the Mountains Lutheran Ch., Summit County, Colo., 1979-80, founded women's chpt. Luth. Ch. Women, 1976, chpt. chmn., 1976-77, Sunday Sch. supt., 1976-81. Mem. Indsl. Relations Research Assn., Am. Mgmt. Assn., Internat. Assn. Fin. Planning. Club: Toastmasters (sec.-treas. 1984). Home: 7640 W 24th Ave Lakewood CO 80215 Office: IDS/Am Express Inc 1385 S Colorado Blvd Suite 620 Denver CO 80222

HOMER, JULIA NAOMI, editor, writer; b. Newton, Mass., July 16, 1951; d. Robert Herbert and Jean Marie (Harden) H. BA in Eng. Lit., Mt. Holyoke Coll., 1973. Tchr. Carly Sch., Dover, Mass., 1973-75; editor Resource Planning Inc., Cambridge, Mass. and Washington, 1976-81; writer ADA, Chgo., 1981-82; editor Tech. Illus. Mag., Boston, 1982-83; reporter Inc. Mag., Boston, 1983-84; founding editor and mng. editor CFO Mag., Boston, 1984—; editorial dir. CFO Pub. Group, Boston, 1987—. Co-author: (annotated bibliography) Women and Literature, 1976; editor: The Second Wave: A Magazine of New Feminism, 1975-76; contbr. numerous articles to mags. Vol. various polit. campaigns for state senate and U.S. Congress, Cambridge, 1980—; also NOW and ERA campaigns, Chgo., 1981. Democrat. Home: 100 Lexington St Watertown MA 02172 Office: CFO Pub Group 268 Summer St Boston MA 02210

HOMER, TAMARA KUKRYCKA, advertising executive; b. Warsaw, Poland, Feb. 23, 1932; came to U.S., 1949, naturalized, 1953; d. Basil and Alexandra (Masiuk) Kukrycka; m. Edward John Homer, Sept. 6, 1954. B.A., Hunter Coll., 1954; postgrad. New Sch. for Social Sci., 1956-58. Pres. Sunwear, Inc., N.Y.C., 1964-66; exec. v.p. Allerton, Berman & Dean, N.Y.C., 1966-73; founder, pres. Homer & Durham Advt., Ltd., N.Y.C., 1973—. Author travel guides for European countries. Trustee New Eyes for the Needy, Short Hills, N.J., 1982—; bd. dirs. Nat. Assn. to Prevent Blindness, March of Dimes, N.Y.C., 1983—. Recipient Matrix award Women Execs. in Communication, 1983, Extraordinary Service to Nation's Tourism, Republic of Ireland, 1976; named to Hall of Fame, Hunter Coll., 1983. Mem. Advt. Women of N.Y. (bd. dirs.; pres. 1983-85), Women Execs. in Pub. Relations, Fashion Group, Am. Advt. Fedn. (com. chmn. 1985—). Republican. Ukrainian Orthodox. Avocations: painting; tennis; fresh water fishing. Home: 2 Joanna Way Short Hills NJ 07078 Office: Homer & Durham Advt Ltd 115 Fifth Ave New York NY 10003

HOMER, THERESE, police officer; b. Albany, Ga., Oct. 22, 1954; d. Willie and Ilene (Thomas) H. BS in Sociology, Tuskegee Inst., 1976; MS, Ga. State U., 1982. Research asst. Atlanta Urban League, 1973-78; police officer Ga. State U., Atlanta, 1978-79, Atlanta Bur. of Police, 1979-85; instr. Inst. of Security and Tech., Miami, Fla., 1985—; police officer Palm Beach (Fla.) Police Dept., 1985—. Big sister Big Bros., Big Sisters of Am., Atlanta, 1980; foster parent. Mem. NAACP, Fraternal Order of Police, Nat. Black Police Assn., Atlanta Women Network, Nat. Assn. Female Execs., Suncoast C. of C., Delta Sigma Theta, Alpha Kappa Delta. Democrat. Unity. Home: 612 Executive Center Dr Apt 201 West Palm Beach FL 33401 Office: Palm Beach Police Dept 345 S County Rd Palm Beach FL 33480

HOMESTEAD, SUSAN, psychotherapist, consultant; b. Bklyn., Sept. 20, 1937; d. Cy Simon and Katherine (Haas) Eichelbaum; m. George Gilbert Zanetti, Dec. 13, 1962 (div. 1972); 1 child, Bruce David; m. 2d, Ronald Eric Homestead, Jan. 16, 1973 (div. 1980). B.A., U. Miami-Fla., 1960; M.S.W., Tulane U., 1967. Lic. clin. social worker, Va., Calif. Pvt. practice, cons., Richmond, Va., 1971—; psychotherapist, cons. Family and Children's Services, Richmond, 1981—, Richmond Pain Clinic, 1983-84; cons. Health Internat. Va., P.C., Lynchburg, 1984-86, Santa Clara DSS, Calif., 1986—; co-dir. asthma program Va. Lung Assn., Richmond, 1975-79, Loma Prieta Regional Ctr.; chief clin. social worker Med. Coll. Va., Va. Commonwealth U., 1974-79. Contbr. articles to profl. jours. Active, Peninsula Children's Ctr., Morgan Ctr., Council for Community Action Planning, Community Assn. for Retarded, Comprehensive Health Planning Assn. Santa Clara, Mental Health Commn., Children and Adolescent Target Group Calif., Women's Com. Richmond Symphony, Va. Mus. Theatre, mem. fin. com. Robb for Gov.; mem. adv. com. Lung Assn.; mem. steering com. Am. Cancer Soc. Va. div. Epilepsy Found., Am. Heart Assn., Central Va. Guild for Infant Survival. Mem. Va. Soc. Clin. Social Work, Inc. (charter mem., sec. 1975-78), Nat. Assn. Social Workers, Soc. for Psychoanalytic Psychotherapy, Am. Acad. Psychotherapists. Jewish.

HOMIC, KATHLEEN ANN, business executive; b. Schenectady, N.Y., Aug. 27, 1965; d. Raymond William and Leona Veronica (Paskocim) H. AA, Wade's Fashion Merchandising Coll., Dallas, 1983; student, Fairleigh Dickinson U., 1983. Mdse. asst. Abraham and Straus, Bklyn., 1983; adminstrv. asst. Staff Builders, N.Y.C., 1984-85; showroom mgr. Caltoy, N.Y.C., 1985; asst. to dir. mfg. Crest-Foam Corp., Moonachie, N.J., 1985-87; safety dir. Crest-Foam Corp., 1987; dist. mgr. Kotliar Corp., Paramus, N.J., 1988—. Sponsor Christian Children's Fund, Wagner, S.D., 1986, 87, 88; active fund raising Am. Diabetes Found., United Cerebral Palsy N.Y.C., Am. Lung Assn. Mem. Nat. Assn. Female Execs., N.J. Network Bus. and Profl. Women. Roman Catholic. Home: 319 Stillwell Pl Ridgewood NJ 07450 Office: Kotliar Corp Garden State Plaza Rt 4 & 17 Paramus NJ 07652

HOMICZ, DIANE MARIE, educator; b. Chgo., Mar. 5, 1950; d. Frank Jerome and Mary Louise (Schippits) H. BA with honors, U. Ill., 1972, MEd, 1973. Tchr. Valley View Sch. Dist. 365, Romeoville and Bolingbrook, Ill., 1973—. tchr. rep. exec. bd. PTO, Romeoville and Bolingbrook, 1973-87. Mem. Assn. for Childhood Edn. Internat., Ill. Reading Council, Am. Fedn. of Tchrs. (union rep. 1983-87), Phi Delta Kappa, Alpha Lambda Delta, Kappa Delta Pi, Jaycees (Cert. of Merit 1982-83, Educator of Yr. 1984-85). Democrat. Roman Catholic. Home: 1431 B Haverhill Wheaton IL 60187 Office: Jamie McGee Sch 179 Commonwealth Bolingbrook IL 60439

HOMISAK, THERESA, lawyer; b. Pitts., Jan. 13, 1950; d. John and Mary (Mordovancy) H. BA, U. Pitts., 1971, MA, 1974; JD, Duquesne U., 1980. Bar: Pa. 1980, U.S. Dist. Ct. (we. dist.) Pa. 1980, U.S. Ct. Appeals (3d cir.) 1984, U.S. Supreme Ct. 1985. Assoc. Sharlock, Repcheck and Mahler, Pitts., 1980-87; asst. chief counsel Pitts. regional office Pa. Human Relations Commn., 1987—. Contbg. author: Judicial Review of Children in Placement, 1980, Medical Malpractice, 1987-88. U. Pitts. Provost's Devel. Fund fellow, 1975-76. Mem. ABA, Pa. Bar Assn., Allegheny County Bar Assn. Republican. Byzantine Catholic. Home: 120 S 11th St Pittsburgh PA 15203 Office: Pa Human Relations Commn Suite 1100 300 Liberty Ave Pittsburgh PA 15222

HOMRIGHAUSEN, LINDSLEY HARVEY, foundation executive; b. Wilkes-Barre, Pa., Aug. 30, 1945; d. Robert Burgess and Joan Lindsley (Blackman) Harvey Miner; m. David K. Homrighausen, Apr. 25, 1970; children: Sarah Harvey, Benjamin Burgess. BA, Lake Erie Coll., Painesville, Ohio, 1967. With Mut. of N.Y., N.Y.C., 1967-71, Allied Temp. Service, N.Y.C., 1971-73; adminstr. grants Surdna Found., Inc., N.Y.C., 1973—. Trustee Grace Ch. Sch., N.Y.C.; bd. dirs. Bear Lake Assn. Mem. The Nature Conservancy. Office: 250 Park Ave New York NY 10177

HOMSEY, VICTORINE DUPONT (MRS. SAMUEL E. HOMSEY), architect; b. Grosse Pointe Farms, Mich., Nov. 27, 1900; d. Antoin Bidermann and Ethel (Clark) duPont; m. Samuel E. Homsey, Apr. 27, 1929; children—Coleman duPont, Eldon duPont. A.B., Wellesley Coll., 1923; M.Arch., Cambridge (Mass.) Sch. Architecture, 1925. Practice as architect 1926—; mem. archtl. firm Victorine and Samuel Homsey. Contbr.: Guide to Modern Architecture; major works include Am. Embassy, Tehran, Iran. Mem. exec. com. Greater Wilmington Devel. Council; mem. adv. bd. Historic Am. Bldgs. Survey; mem. Commn. Fine Arts, Washington, 1976—. Recipient 1st prize instl. architecture for Children's Beach House (Lewes, Del.) Pitts. Glass Inst.; regional, state awards for Cambridge Yacht Club Md. Soc. Architects; hon. mention award for design Stubbs Elementary Sch., Wilmington, Del.; hon. mention award for design Sch. Exec. mag. Fellow AIA; mem. NAD (asso.), Colonial Dames. Episcopalian. Club: Wilmington Garden. (Del.). Home: 602 Cokesbury Village Hockessin DE 19707 Office: 2003 N Scott St Wilmington DE 19806 *

HONG, CHUNG-SOOK CHARLOTTE (KIM), librarian; b. Seoul, Apr. 15, 1940; came to U.S., 1963; d. Soon-Kyung and Un-Yun (Kim) Hong; m. Samuel Cynn-Sung Kang, Dec. 19, 1964 (div. Aug. 1978); m. Ben H. (Bong-Hyun) Kim, Nov. 17, 1985; children—Patricia Jean, Claudia Suk-Jin. B.A., Yonsei U., Seoul, 1962; M.Ed., Duquesne U., Pitts., 1967; M.L.S., U. Pitts., 1968; cert. mgmt. devel. program Pa. State U., 1978. Asst. librarian Whitehall Pub. Library, Pitts., 1965-66, children's librarian, 1966-67; asst. children's librarian Carnegie Library of Pitts., 1968-69, children's librarian, 1969-71, br. librarian, 1971-76, div. head., 1976-85; branch head Albany Park Br. Chgo. pub. Library, 1986—; prin. Korean Lang. Sch. Pitts., 1980-85; co-chair Korean-Am. Educators Assn. Spl. Project Com., 1987—, Chgo. Korean Women's Assn., 1988—; trustee Korean-Am. Community Services, Chgo., 1988—. Deaconness Korean Central Ch. of Pitts., 1980-85, editor, 1983-84; historian Pitts. Folk Festival Pitts. Korean Assn., 1983-84; mem. panel Ams., NCCJ, 1984—. Mem. ALA, Pa. Library Assn. (co.-chmn. ann. conf. reception com. 1981, chmn. ann. conf. hospitality com. 1983, chmn. pub. relations com. S.W. chpt. 1984, program com. spring conf. 1984, chmn. pub., p.r. and NLW com. S.W. chpt. 1984), Pub. Library Assn. (mem. standing com. Multilingual Material and Library Service), Yonsei U. Alumni Assn. (trustee Chgo. chpt. 1988—). Democrat. Presbyterian. Club: Altrusa (chmn. internat. relations com. 1982-84) (Pitts.). Home: Hollywood Towers 5701 N Sheridan Rd Unit 25T Chicago IL 60660 Office: Chgo Pub Library Albany Park Br 5150 N Kimball Ave Chicago IL 60625

HONIG, ALICE STERLING, psychologist; b. Bklyn., Apr. 19, 1929; d. William and Ida (Bender) Sterling; divorced, 1979; children: Lawrence Sterling, Madeleine Honig Lenski, Jonathan David. BA magna cum laude, Barnard Coll., 1950; MA, Columbia U., 1952; PhD, Syracuse U., 1975. Lic. psychologist, N.Y. Research assoc. Upstate Med. Ctr., Syracuse, N.Y., 1962-64; family devel. research program dir. Syracuse U., 1964-77, instr. child devel., 1969-71, asst. prof., 1971-75, assoc. prof., 1975-81, prof., 1982—. Author: Discipline, Cooperation and Compliance: an Annotated Bibliography, 1987,author: Parent Involvement in Early Childhood Education, 1979, Playtime Learning Games for Young Children, 1982, (with J.R. Lally) Infant Caregiving: A Design for Training, 1981, (with Wittmer) Infant/Toddler Caregiving: An Annotated Bibliography, 1982; editor: Risk Factors in Infancy, 1986; N.Am. editor: ECDC, 1983—; research rev. editor: Young Children, 1980-87, Early Childhood Ednl. Research Quarterly, 1985—; editor: Early Parenting and Later Child Achievement, 1987. Active Pioneer Women. Recipient Woman Achievement in Child Devel. award State of N.Y., 1983; U.S. Office of Edn. Nat. fellow, 1969-71. Mem. Am. Psychol. Assn., Soc. for Research in Child Devel., Nat. Assn. for Edn. Young Children, Internat. Soc. for Study Behavioral Devel., Am. Ednl. Research Assn., Am. Orthopsychiat. Assn., Jean Piaget Soc., World Assn. for Infant Psychiatry, Internat. Conf. on Infant Studies, Phi Beta Kappa. Jewish. Home: 317 Allen St Syracuse NY 13210 Office: Syracuse U Coll for Human Devel 206 Slocum Hall Syracuse NY 13244

HONIG, JONI ROCHELLE, advertising executive; b. Queens, N.Y., Apr. 20, 1961; d. Herman and Bettyann (Escott) H. Student, Skidmore Coll., Saratoga Springs, N.Y., 1979-81; BA in Biology, NYU, 1983. Adminstrv. asst. Lally McFarland & Pantello, N.Y.C., 1983-84, account coordinator, 1984-86, account exec., 1986-88, acct. supr., 1988—. Home: 365 W 25th St New York City NY 10001 Office: Lally McFarland & Pantello 60 Madison Ave New York City NY 10010

HONNER, (B.) JOAN, advertising executive; b. N.Y.C., Oct. 23, 1952; d. William John and Mary Patricia (Edwards) H.; m. Donald J. Sutherland, Oct. 3, 1987. Student, Endicott Coll., 1970-71. Art dir. Kerrigan Studio, Darien, Conn., 1971-73, Foote Cone and Belding, Phoenix, 1973-77; sr. art dir. Foote Cone and Belding, Chgo., 1977-81; v.p., assoc. creative dir. J. Walter Thompson, Chgo., 1982-86; v.p., exec. art dir. BBDO Chgo., 1986—; cons. J. Walter Thompson, Toronto and San Francisco, 1983-84; owner Fla. Antiques, Geneva, Ill., 1986—. Recipient 1st Place TV local campaign WGN 6th dist. ADDY, 1980, Best Internat. TV campiagn Pepsi Clio, 1985. Roman Catholic. Home: 1969 N Lincoln Ave Chicago IL 60614 Office: BBDO Chicago 410 N Michigan Ave Chicago IL 60611

HONZIK, MARJORIE KNICKERBOCKER PYLES, psychologist emeritus, educator emeritus; b. Johannesburg, Transvaal, Republic South Africa, May 14, 1908; came to U.S., 1927; d. Jay Franklin and Maude Ethel (Knickerbocker) Pyles; m. Charles H. Honzik, Aug. 7, 1935 (dec. 1969); children: Eleanor, Elizabeth. BA, U. Calif., Berkeley, 1930, MA, 1933, PhD, 1936. Research asst. Inst. Child Welfare, Berkeley, 1932-65; lectr. child devel. Mills Coll., Oakland, Calif., 1952-60; lectr. psychology U. Calif., Berkeley, 1954-75, research psychologist Inst. Human Devel., 1965-75, research psychologist IV, lectr. emeritus, 1975—. Gen. Edn. Bd. fellow, Honolulu, 1938-40; NSF, Inst. Aging, Nat. Inst. Neurol. Diseases and Blindness, USPHS grantee, 1958-82. Fellow Am. Psychol. Assn. (G. Stanley Hall award 1983), Am. Assn. Advancement Sci.; mem. LWV. Democrat. Unitarian. Office: U Calif Inst Human Devel Berkeley CA 94720

HOOD, JACKY EMMONS, management consultant, electronics engineer; b. Scottsbluff, Nebr., Jan. 19, 1948; d. Harold LeRoy and Dorthey Pearl (Templar) Emmons; m. David Frederick Hood, Oct. 8, 1945. BSEE, U. Neb., Lincoln, 1970; MS in Engring., Carleton U., Ottawa, Ont., Can., 1975. Project engr. Leigh Instruments, Carleton Place, Ont., 1971-74; mgr. of engrng. Bell-Northern Research, 1975-80; engring. mgmt., program mgr. TRW Vidar, Mountain View, Calif., 1980-82; mgr. product support Rolm (subs. IBM), Santa Clara, Calif., 1982-86; pres. Jacky Hood Inc., Palo Alto, Calif., 1986—; cons. San Jose State U., 1981-82. Author: Vertical Project Mgmt., 1982; inventor; contbr. articles to profl. jours. Trainer Girl Scouts, U.S. Mem. Project Mgmt. Inst., (registrar 1986-87), Assn. Field Service Mgrs. Internat. (edn. chmn. Silicon Valley chpt.; selected for trade mission to Republic of China, 1988). Libertarian. Club: Churchill (Palo Alto). Office: Crescent Project Mgmt 1066 Fife Ave Palo Alto CA 94301

HOOD, KAY MCGHEE, nurse; b. Niagara Falls, N.Y., July 20, 1955; d. K. Burr and Shirley (Aderman) McGhee; m. Charles Lewis. BS in Nursing, Skidmore Coll., 1977; MS in Nursing, U. Pa., 1981. Lic. ob-gyn nurse practitioner. Office nurse Manfred Epstein MD, N.Y.C., 1978-81; clinic coordinator Maternal and Infant Care Project Grady Meml. Hosp., Atlanta, 1982; nurse practitioner Ratchford, McDaniel, Moreland and Sheerer, Atlanta, 1982-83, Hilton Kort, Atlanta, 1983—. Mem. Nurses Assn. Am. Coll. Ob-gyn (conf. chmn. 1987, chmn. program com. 1987), Am. Fertility Soc., Sigma Theta Tau. Lodge: PEO (pres. local chpt. 1982-83). Office: Hilton Kort MD 993 D Johnson Ferry Rd Atlanta GA 30342

HOOD, LOUISE B., state legislator; b. Windsor, Vt., Aug. 27, 1916; d. Albert E., Sr., and Gladys H. (Robinson) Buckman; student schs. Windsor; m. Lee B. Hood, Sept. 4, 1938 (dec.); children—L. Robert, Bonnie Lee, David John. Sec. to attys., payroll clk. Goodyear Tire and Rubber, Windsor, 1947-50; bookkeeper, sec., asst. town clk., justice of peace, notary public, Town of Windsor, 1950-68, treas., 1968-78; mem. Vt. Gen. Assembly, rep. from Dist. 3, 1979—. Trustee, Windsor Library; trustee, sec. Davis Home; sec. Salvation Army, 1975—; vice chmn. Rep. Town Com.; bd. dirs. Windsor Cemetery Assn., 1982—. Methodist. Office: State House Montpelier VT 05602

HOOD, TERESSA MARIE, insurance executive; b. Lynchburg, Va., Dec. 25, 1951; d. Andrew Leroy and Augustine Louise (Hunter) H. AAS, Cen. Va. Community Coll., 1973. Cashier Shoppers Fair, Lynchburg, 1967-69, sec., payroll clk., 1969-74; payroll clk. Nationwide Mut. Ins. Co., Lynchburg, 1973—, underwriter, 1981-83, supr. auto services, 1983-85, supr. fire services, 1985—; defensive driving instr., 1978-80. Active fellow and mem. Cen. Va. Community Choral Ensemble, 1978—, adminstr., 1983—; active fellow and mem. Civic Action Program, Lynchburg, 1979—; fellow, treas. youth dept. New Vine Bapt. Ch., 1980—. Recipient Outstanding Performance and Outstanding Demonstrated Ability awards Dale Carnegie, Lynchburg, 1984, Leadership award, Community Service award. Democrat. Lodge: Toastmistress (local officer 1980-85, treas. 1984-85, sec. 1985-86, 2d v.p. 1986-87, 1st v.p. 1987-88, pres. 1988—). Avocations: singing, piano, trumpet, swimming, tennis. Home: Rt 5 Box 655 Lynchburg VA 24501 Office: Nationwide Mut Ins Co 800 Graves Mill Rd Lynchburg VA 24506

HOOD, VIRGINIA FORD (MRS. FREDERICK REDDING HOOD), civic worker; b. Vinita, Okla., May 1, 1905; d. William Thomas and Demmeria (Byrd) Ford; student Northeastern State Tchrs. Coll., 1920-21, 21-22; A.B., U. Okla., 1924; m. Frederick Redding Hood, Dec. 7, 1924; children—Frederick Redding, William Richard, Virginia Carol (Mrs. Kenneth Lee Pierce). Pres., Ladies Aux. Oklahoma County Med. Soc., 1937, co-chmn. Oklahoma City conv. So. Med. Conv., 1938, chmn. state conv. Okla. Med. Soc., 1950. Dist. chmn. Big One Drive, United Fund, Oklahoma City, 1953; chmn. Okla. Art Center Drive, 1957; capt. spl. gifts div. United Appeal, 1960-69, gen. chmn. Kappa Alpha Theta Found. Drive, 1964-65; chmn. Heritage Hills Hist. Home Tour, 1970-72; pres. Mothers Assn. U. Okla., 1957-58, Okla. Art League, 1960-61, Heritage Hills Aux., 1972-73; mem. Modern Classics, Oklahoma City; dir. YWCA, 1939-41, 66-72, met. bd. dirs., 1969-72, v.p., 1966-69, chmn. personnel com. 1966-68, 70-72, mem. dept. campus Christian life Okla. Assn. Christian Chs., 1964-68; pres. Heritage Hills Women's Com. of Hist. Preservation, 1973—. Mem. Kappa Alpha Theta (Okla. chmn. 1928-31, pres. Oklahoma City alumnae chpt. 1948-51, corp. bd. Alpha Omicron chpt. at U. Okla. 1954-57, 77-83, alumnae dist. pres. 1957-60, grand council 1960-64, v.p. service 1966-70, mem. bd. trustees found. 1966-70 Virginia Ford Hood Scholarship Fund created in her honor by Oklahoma City mems. 1984). Mem. Christian Ch. (deaconess bd. Oklahoma City 1954-57, 65-68, 72-75, 78-81, past chmn.; pres. Christian

Women's fellowship Crown Heights Christian Ch., 1960-61, 61-62, tchr. bus. women's class, sponsor young married class, vice chmn. gen. bd. 1979-80, chmn. gen. bd. 1980-81, elder 1984-87). Club: Coterie Study (Oklahoma City).

HOOK, ALICE PALO, librarian; b. Superior, Wis., Feb. 4, 1909; d. Elmer George and Helen (Payne) Palo; m. Norris M. Hook, June 21, 1945 (dec. 1946). B.S., U. Minn., 1930, Asst. in order dept. U. Minn., 1930; Taft order librarian U. Cin., 1931-37, head acquisition dept., 1943-46; order librarian Temple U., Phila., 1937-43; librarian Hist. and Philos. Soc. of Ohio, Cin., 1947-63; Cin. Art Mus., 1964-74. Mem. vol. canteen corps ARC, 1941-63; bd. dirs. Cin. Met. YWCA, 1957-70, rec. sec. bd. dirs. 1959-61, pub. relations chmn., 1961-64, centennial chmn., 1968; women's bd. dirs. Clovernook Home for Blind, 1974-86, chmn., trustee, 1978-80. Mem. Am. Library Assn., Ohio Library Assn., Spl. Libraries Assn. (past pres. Cin. chpt., past chmn. nat. com. pub. relations, chmn. picture div. 1958-60), chmn. mus. div. 1964-66), Alpha Xi Delta. Clubs: Cin. Woman's (bd. dirs. 1974-77), College (bd. dirs. 1967-74, pres. 1983-84), Altrusa (gov. 5th dist. 1956-58).

HOOK, JULIA JANE, health organization administrator; b. Pasadena, Calif., Feb. 25, 1955; d. Ralph Adam and Kate Ellen (Beisel) King; m. Steven K. Hook, Aug. 31, 1974 (div. 1985); children: Jill Jane, Lisa Marie. BS, Calif. State Poly U., 1979, U. Laverne, 1988. Cert. EEG technician. Nutrition asst. San Dimas (Calif.) Community Hosp., 1972-73; admitting rep. Foothill Presbyn. Hosp., Glendora, Calif., 1973-75; EEG technician Pomona Valley Community Hosp., Pomona, Calif., 1975-79; med. practice mgr. Office of Dr.'s M. Ali and R. Soudmand, San Dimas, 1983, Office Dr.'s David R. Rice and Richard L. Matthews, Pomona, 1983-87; coordinator provider relations CIGNA Pvt. Practice Plan, San Bernardino, Calif., 1987-88; supr. provider relations hdqtrs. CIGNA Health Plan, Glendale, Calif., 1988—; med. practice mgmt. cons., 1983—. Mem. Calif. Med. Assts. Assn. (recording sec. 1987—, chaplain 1985-86, chairperson reservation com. 1986-87), Am. Soc. Electroneurographic Technologists, Nat. Assn. Female Execs., Women in Health Care Adminstrn., San Antonio Liaison Secs. (exec. com. 1984-86). Republican. Episcopalian. Home: 431 Merrimac St Upland CA 91786 Office: CIGNA 505 N Brand Blvd Glendale CA 91203

HOOK, MARY JULIA, lawyer; b. Kansas City, Mo., Oct. 31, 1947; d. Vernon Anthony and Dula Mariah (Wood) H.; m. David Lee Smith, Dec. 30, 1972. BA, So. Meth. U., 1967, MA, 1969, JD, 1972; LLM, Harvard U., 1975. Bar: Tex. 1972, Colo. 1975. Trial atty. U.S. Dept. Justice, Washington, 1972-74, 75-76; assoc. Holland & Hart, Denver, 1976-81, ptnr., 1981—. Contbr. chpts. to legal publs., 2d edit. Mem. ABA, Fed. Bar Assn. (chmn. natural resources com. energy, environ. and natural resources sect.), Tex. Bar Assn., Colo. Bar Assn., Denver Bar Assn., Assn. Trial Lawyers Am., Order of Coif, Phi Beta Kappa. Democrat. Methodist. Clubs: Denver, Denver Athletic. Home: 2036 Dexter St Denver CO 80207 Office: Holland & Hart 555 17th St Suite 2900 Denver CO 80202

HOOK, VIRGINIA MAY, marketing executive; b. Balt., Mar. 11, 1932; d. Arthur M. Monroe McClelland and Margaret (Shipley) McClelland Warfield; m. Donald F. Hook, Aug. 25, 1951 (dec. Dec. 1978); children—Donald F., Jr., Donna J. Hook Kellner. Grad. high sch. Teller, Central Savs. Bank, Balt., 1950-68, tng. dir., 1968-71; ops. mgr. Mature Temps, Inc., Balt., 1971-81; pres. VMH Mktg. Ltd., Glen Burnie, Md., 1982—. Mem. adv. council, sr. aides program D.C. Dept. Labor, 1980-81; active local Democratic party. Mem. Bank Personnel Assn. Md. (sec. 1969-71), Personnel Assn. Md. (sec. 1979-80), Exec. Women's Network, Market Research Assn., Am. Mktg. Assn., Nat. Assn. Women Bus. Owners. Methodist. Lodge: Order Eastern Star. Home: 3 Southerly Ct Towson MD 21204 Office: 8562-A Laureldale Dr Laurel MD 20707

HOOKS, KAREN LEAH, accounting educator; b. Lakeland, Fla., Dec. 27, 1955; d. Wilbur Ocie and Frankie Emily (Grimes) H.; m. Stephen Srygley Walker, July 23, 1983. AA, Polk Community Coll., 1974; BA, U. S. Fla., 1976; PhD, Ga. State U., 1981. CPA, Fla. Staff acct. Touche Ross & Co., Tampa, 1976-77; asst. prof. acctg. U. South Fla., Tampa, 1979-85, assoc. prof. acctg., 1985—; research mgr. Can. Inst. Chartered Accts., Toronto, Ont., 1986-88. Mem. Am. Woman's Soc. CPA (v.p. nat. 1983-85, nat. dir. 1982-83), Nat. Assn. Accts. (dir. 1981-83), Fla. Inst. CPA's, Am. Inst. CPA's, Am. Acctg. Assn., Tampa Jr. League. Contbr. articles to profl. jours. Methodist. Office: U South Fla Sch Accountancy Coll Bus Tampa FL 33620

HOOKS, VANDALYN LAWRENCE, educator; b. Dyersburg, Tenn., Feb. 26, 1935; d. James Bridges and Mary Lucille (Anderson) Lawrence; m. Floyd Lester Hooks, June 15, 1952; children—Lawrence James, Steven Lester. BA, Ky. Wesleyan U., 1967; MA, Western Ky. U., 1970, Edn. Specialist, 1976; postgrad. U. Tenn., 1975. Tchr., Owensboro Bd. Edn., Ky., 1967-71, adminstr., 1976—; dir. career experience Western Ky. U., Bowling Green, 1971-73; dir. career edn. Owensboro Daviess County Sch. Dist., 1973-76; curriculum developer Career Experience Voc. Edn., Frankfort, Ky., 1971-76; cons. Motivation Workshop, Bowling Green, 1971-76, Decision and Goal Setting, 1971-76. Editor; Ky. Assn. Elem. Prin. Jour., 1977-81. Contbr. articles to profl. jours. Organizer, Ky. Council for Better Edn., Owensboro, 1984; legis. advisor Eagle Forum, leadership forum, Washington, 1985, 86-87; Rep. legis. researcher . Recipient Presdl. award, Ky. Wesleyan Coll., 1966. Mem. Concerned Edn. of Am., Nat. Council for Better Edn., Heritage Found., Pro Family Forum, Eagle Forum, Plymouth Rock Found., Nat. Council Christian Educators. Republican. Baptist. Address: 1302 Waverly Pl Owensboro KY 42301

HOOL, IRENE TABAR, real estate broker; b. Owendale, Mich., Mar. 8, 1925; d. Nicholas and Catherine (Welther) Tabar; m. Howard C. Hool, Jan. 26, 1946; children: Lynette R., Loretta R. Grad. high sch., Owendale, Mich. Lic. real estate broker, Fla. Clk.-typist, detail engr. Gen. Motors Corp., Detroit, 1946-51; unemployment claims clk. Mich. Employment Securities Commn., Bay City and Caro, 1952-61; sec.-treas. H.P. Constrn. Co., Inc., Treasure Island, Fla., 1972-80; owner, operator Windjammer Motel, Treasure Island, Fla., 1972-80; pres., bd. dirs. Lai Rene Realty, Inc., St. Petersburg, Fla., 1980—; owner, operator North Grove Inn, Caro, 1955-61, Wagon Wheel Inn, Kinde, Mich., 1961-71. Mem. Nat. Assn. Realtors. Republican. Lutheran. Home: 13000 Gulf Blvd #302 Madeira Beach FL 33708 Office: 5409 Gulfport Blvd Saint Petersburg FL 33708

HOOPER, EDITH FERRY, museum trustee; b. Detroit, Nov. 30, 1909; d. Dexter Mason and Jeannette (Hawkins) Ferry; m. Arthur Upshur Hooper, June 22, 1945; children—Jeannette Williams, Kate Gorman, Queene Ferry. B.A., Vassar U. Indsl. design dept. asst. Mus. Modern Art, N.Y.C., 1939-40; clk. U.S. Procurement Office, Detroit, 1941-43; asst. Roeper City and Country Schs., Detroit, 1944; trustee Balt. Mus. Art., 1957—, pres. bd., 1973-75, accessions com., 1977—. Bd. dirs. Friends Art Gallery, Vassar Coll., Poughkeepsie, N.Y., 1974-76; pres. bd. trustees Bryn Mawr Sch., Balt., 1965-71, chmn. bldg. com., 1971-73; pres. DM Ferry Jr. Trustee Corp. (found.), Balt., 1973. Presbyterian. Clubs: Cosmopolitan (N.Y.C.), Hamilton St. (Balt.). Home: 1100 Copper Hill Rd Baltimore MD 21209

HOOPER, GRACE ISABEL, library educator; b. Cleve., July 1, 1918; d. Cornelius Fitzgerald and Grace Evelyn (True) Maloney; m. John George Hooper, Apr. 18, 1953 (dec. July 1973); children: John David, Dale Thomas. AB, Ursuline Coll. for Women, Cleve., 1941; MLS, Case Western Res. U., 1945. Cert. secondary sch. tchr., Ohio. Media specialist Univ. Sch. for Boys, Hunting Valley, Ohio, 1965-69; library dir. Elyria (Ohio) High Sch., 1969-79; research librarian Magnificat High Sch., Rocky River, Ohio, 1979—. Pres. Great Lakes secondary curriculum Youth for Tomorrow's Lakes, Inc., Elyria, 1983—; trustee Cleve. Waterfront Coalition, 1986—. Recipient Martha Holden Jennings Found. award, 1975, 84. Mem. Am. Assn. Univ. Women, Ohio Ret. Tchrs. Assn., Great Lakes Hist. Soc., Altrusa Internat. (pres. Elyria chpt. 1978-80, Rocky River, 1983—). Republican. Roman Catholic.

HOOPER, KATHERINE ADRIAN, credit union administrator; b. Hilo, Hawaii, July 8, 1922; d. Manuel Freitas and Katherine Isabel (Peter) Adrian; m. Walter F. Mendes (div.); children: Clyde, Wayne, Gary; m. James L. Hooper. Grad. high sch., Hilo; cert., CUNA Mgmt. Sch., UCLA, 1967. Teller Bank of Hawaii, Honokaa, 1955-59; mgr., sec., treas. Honokaa Community Fed. Credity Union, 1979—; bd. dirs. Pacific Corp. Fed. Credit Union, Honolulu, chmn., 1985-87. Sec. County of Hawaii Rep. Party, Kamuela, Hawaii, 1985, treas., 1987; bd. dirs. Salvation Army, Hilo, 1982-87. Mem. Honokaa Hist. Soc., Honokaa Mchts. Republican. Roman Catholic. Home: PO Box 1244 Honokaa HI 96727

HOOPES, JANET LOUISE, educator, psychologist; b. Phila., Mar. 5, 1923; d. Raymond Talmage and Pearl H. (Jacobs) H.; m. John E. Gausmann, June 11, 1977; children: Lenoir Gausmann Heilman, Eric J. A.B., Bryn Mawr Coll., 1944, Ph.D., 1965; M.Clin. Psychology, U. Mich., 1948. Jr. psychologist Rochester (N.Y.) Guidance Center, 1948-51; psychologist Children's Aid Soc. Pa., Phila., 1951-58, chief psychologist, 1958-70; prof. edn. and child devel. Bryn Mawr (Pa.) Coll., 1970-85, prof. emeritus, 1985—; bd. dirs. Hill Top Prep. Sch., Rosemont, Pa., 1971—. Author: An Infant Rating Scale: Its Validation and Usefulness, 1967, A Follow-Up Study of Adoptions: The Functioning of the Children, 1970, Prediction in Child Development: A Longitudinal Study of Adoptive and Non-Adoptive Families-The Delaware Family Study, 1982, Identity Formation in the Adopted Adolescent, 1985. Bd. dirs. Children's Aid Soc. Pa., Phila., 1987. Served as ensign Med. Service Corps, USNR, 1944-46. Mem. Am. Psychol. Assn., Pa. Psychol. Assn., Orton Dyslexia Soc. Presbyterian (elder 1967—). Home: 173 Marlyn Rd Lansdowne PA 19050 Office: Bryn Mawr Coll West House Bryn Mawr PA 19010

HOOSIN, JANICE LAUTT, social worker; b. Chgo., June 22, 1942; d. Herbert and Ruth Jean (Rubenstein) Lapine; B.A., U. Ill., 1964; M.S.W., Jane Addams Grad. Sch. Social Work, 1966; postgrad. U. Utah, summer, 1977. Cert. mental health adminstr., psychiat. social worker, Ill. Psychiat. social worker New Trier Twp. High Sch., East Winnetka, Ill., 1966-70; dir. day hosp. St. Vincent's Hosp., N.Y.C., 1970-73; psychotherapist (part-time) New Trier East High Sch., Winnetka, 1973-74; dir. psychiat. day hosp. dept. psychiatry Evanston (Ill.) Hosp., 1974-78, dir. partial hospitalization, 1978—; clin. assoc., field work supr. U. Chgo. Sch. Social Service Adminstrn., 1974—; cons. in field; pvt. practice marital and individual psychotherapy, specializing in chem. dependency, 1975—. NIMH fellow, 1964-66; cert. psychiat. social worker, Ill. Mem. Nat. Assn. Social Workers, Assn. Mental Health Adminstrs. Jewish. Home: 2638 N Burling St Chicago IL 60614 Office: 2650 Ridge Ave Evanston IL 60201

HOOTKIN, PAMELA NAN, apparel company executive; b. N.Y.C., Nov. 14, 1947; d. Louis Arthur and Sally (Perlman) Mash; BA, SUNY, Binghamton, 1968; MA in Econs., Boston U., 1970; m. Stephen Allen, Aug. 2, 1972; 1 dau., Julie Beth. Diversification analyst Champion Internat., N.Y.C., 1971-75; sr. fin. analyst Squibb Corp., N.Y.C., 1975-77, mgr. fin. analyst, 1977-79, dir. fin. planning, 1979-82; asst. controller Charles of The Ritz Group Ltd., N.Y.C., 1982-83, v.p., treas., 1983-87; sr. v.p. fin. Yves St. Laurent Parfums Corp., N.Y.C., 1987-88; v.p., treas., sec. Phillips Van Heusen Corp., N.Y.C., 1988—; lectr. econs. U. York, Heslington, Eng., 1970-71. Mem. Fin. Women's Assn. of N.Y. Office: Charles of the Ritz Group Ltd 40 W 57th St New York NY 10028

HOOVER, ANNETTE LOUISE, appliance manufacturing company official; b. Dayton, Ohio, Dec. 2, 1944; d. Joseph Vincent and Mary Frances (Dinus) De Saro; m. Clonta Fox, Dec. 5, 1964 (div. Jan. 1976); children: C. Steven, Rodney W.; m. H. Alan Hoover, June 14, 1986. Student, Wright State U., U. S.C., Purdue U. Dental asst. Dayton, 1963-64, realtor, 1966-77; asst. to dir. sales tng. Frigidaire div. Gen. Motors Co., Dayton, 1977; dist. mgr. SE region Charlotte zone Frigidaire div. Gen. Motors Co., Columbia, S.C., 1977-87; dist. mgr. Midwest region Indpls. zone Frigidaire div. Gen. Motors Co., Ft. Wayne, Ind., 1987—. Named Realtor Assoc. of Yr. Dayton Area Bd. Realtors, 1972. Mem. Am. Bus. Women's Assn. Democrat. Roman Catholic. Home: 411 Deep Wood Cove Fort Wayne IN 46845 Office: WCI Appliance Co Frigidaire Div 300 Phillipi Rd Columbus OH 43288 also: 846 E Algonquin Rd Schaumburg IL 60173

HOOVER, BETTY-BRUCE HOWARD, educator; b. Wake County, N.C., Mar. 20, 1939; d. Bruce Ruffin and Mary Elizabeth (Brown) Howard; m. Herbert Charles Marsh Hoover, Sept. 3, 1961; children—David Andrew, Howard Webster, Lorraine VanSiclen. B.A., Wake Forest U., 1961; M.A., U. S. Fla., 1978. Tchr. English, Greensboro Sr. High Sch., N.C., 1961-62, Lindley Jr. High Sch., Greensboro, 1963, Berkeley Prep. Sch., Tampa, Fla., 1976—, chmn. English dept., 1977-85, dir., dean upper div., 1984—, chmn. curriculum com., 1982—. Pres., Suncoast Midshipmen Parents Club, Tampa Bay Area, 1983-84. Mem. Assn. Supervision Curriculum Devel., Nat. Council Tchrs. English, Wake Forest U. Alumni Assn., DAR, Hillsborough County Bar Aux., Cum Laude Soc. (sec. 1981), Nat. Honor Soc., Phi Beta Kappa, Phi Sigma Iota, Sigma Tau Delta. Republican. Episcopalian. Avocations: sewing; gardening. Home: 4504 Beachway Dr Tampa FL 33609 Office: Berkeley Preparatory Sch 4811 Kelly Rd Tampa FL 33615

HOOVER, KIMBERLY HILL, lawyer; b. Ft. Worth, Jan. 22, 1958; d. Richard Harold Hill and Frances Yvonne (Albertson) Cameron; m. Craig Alan Hoover, May 10, 1986. BA, Baylor U., 1980; JD, Duke U., 1983. Bar: Tex. 1984, D.C. 1985. Assoc. Locke, Purnell, Boren, Laney & Neely, Dallas, 1983-84, Akin, Gump, Strauss, Hauer & Feld, Washington, 1984-85, Squire, Sanders & Dempsey, Washington, 1985—. Exec. editor Duke U. Law Jour., 1982-83. Area Coordinator Bread for the World, D.C., 1985-86; rep. Greater Washington Bd. of Trade, D.C., 1987—. Mem. ABA, Tex. Bar Assn., D.C. Bar Assn. Home: 4425 35th St NW Washington DC 20008 Office: Squire Sanders & Dempsey 1201 Pennsylvania Ave NW Washington DC 20004

HOOVER, LOLA MAE, communications company manager; b. Monticello, Ark., Apr. 1, 1947; d. Victor Arthur and Essie (Humphries) Piper; divorced; 1 child, Larry Wayne. With prodn. dept. AT&T, West Chgo., 1965-78, 1st level shop mgr., 1978-83, warehouse mgr., 1983-84, office mgr., 1984-86; with Mfg. Resource Planning project, 1986-87, leader Mfg. Resource Planning project, 1987—; devel. quality excellence program, 1986. Baptist. Home: 207 Briar Ln North Aurora IL 60542 Office: AT&T Info Systems 1700 Hawthorne Ln Chicago IL 60185

HOOVER, MOLLY ANN, automobile sales executive; b. The Dallas, Oreg., May 17, 1948; d. Lile Wendell Hoover and Margaret Ernestine (Howard) Trullinger; m. Denny W. Homer, Mar. 28, 1970 (div. 1977). BS, Oreg. State U., 1970, EdM, 1975. Tchr. bus. Aloha High Sch., Beaverton, Oreg., 1971-75; dental office mgr., Bridgeport, Wash., 1975-77; dist. sales mgr. Chrysler Corp., Portland, 1978-81; leasing mgr. Teague Motor Co., Salem, Oreg., 1981-83; nat. project mgr. A.D.P. Dealer Services, Portland, 1984-85; mng. dir. StyleRight Seminars, Portland, 1985-86; founder, pres. M. Hoover & Assocs. Automotive Mktg., Portland, 1986—; word processing cons. Far West Fed., Portland, 1977; leasing cons. Pacific Coast Leasing, 1984. Comdr., Angel Flight ROTC Women's Aux., Corvallis, Oreg., 1968-70; treas., bd. dirs. Douglas Fed. Credit Union, Bridgeport, Wash., 1976-77; exhibit hall chmn. Small Bus. Adminstrn. Women's Conf., 1984. Named Salem Woman of 80's, Salem Spokesman Rev., 1982. Mem. Inst. Managerial and Profl. Women (v.p. 1985-86 , conf. dir. 1986), Nat. Assn. Female Execs., Zonta Internat., Kappa Alpha Theta, Phi Beta Lambda. Avocations: cross country skiing, painting, needlepoint, travel. Home: 2187 Crown Point Hwy Troutdale OR 97060 Office: PO Box 5515 Portland OR 97228

HOOVER, STEPHANIE PRESSELLER, association executive; b. Hollywood, Calif., Apr. 2, 1936; d. William Andrew and Doris Florence (Hogle) P.; m. David Beall Hoover, Mar. 30, 1985. BS, San Jose State U., 1957; MS, U. Pa., 1971; EdD, Boston U., 1984. Staff occupational therapist John Fremont Sch. for Handicapped Children, Merced, Calif., 1958-61, Bronx Mcpl. Hosp. Cen., Bronx, 1961-65; occupational therapy dept. head Bronx Mcpl. Hosp. Cen., 1965-69; occupational therapy faculty U. Pa., Phila., 1969-71, Columbia U., N.Y.C., 1971-73; faculty, chair. occupational therapy program Hunter Coll. of All. Health, N.Y.C., 1973-76; occupational therapy faculty Boston U., 1976-79; dir. edn. div. Am. Occupational Therapy Assn., Rockville, Md., 1979—; adv. co. mem. Kellogg Allied Health Leadership Project, Washington, 1981-83; cons. U.S. Pub. Health Adminstrn. Allied Health Tng., Rockville, 1983-84. Fellow Am. Occupational Therapy Assn. (assoc. exec. dir. 1987—); mem. Am. Soc. of Allied Health Profls (sec. 1987—, bd. dirs. 1981-85, Pres.'s award 1984), Am. Assn. Higher Edn. Democrat. Home: 7 Tegner Court Rockville MD 20850 Office: Am Occupational Therapy Assn 1383 Piccard Dr Rockville MD 20850

HOOVER, VICKI LYNN, personnel director, b. Union City, Tenn., July 18, 1951; d. Joe Payten and Helen (Crunk) Hodge; m. Lonnie Ray Hoover, Nov. 15, 1975; 1 child, Angela Renee. BBA, Memphis State U., 1977; postgrad in law, Nashville Sch. Law, 1987—. Personnel cons. Hosp. Corp. Am., Nashville, 1978-79; dir. personnel Williamson Med. Ctr., Franklin, Tenn., 1979—; personnel cons. Personnel Devel., Inc., Franklin, 1983-86. Recipient Gov's. award State of Tenn., 1986. Mem. Am. Soc. for Health Care Human Resources Assn., Am. Soc. for Personnel Assn., Tenn. Soc. for Health Care Personnel Assn. Republican. Presbyterian. Lodges: Order Eastern Star, Masons, Civitan. Home: 409 Oakwood Rd Franklin TN 37064 Office: Williamson Med Ctr 2021 Carothers Rd Franklin TN 37064

HOPE, GERRI DANETTE, telecommunications executive; b. North Highlands, Calif., Feb. 28, 1956; d. Albert Gerald and Beulah Rae (Bane) Hope. AS, Sierra Coll., Calif., 1977; postgrad. Okla. State U., 1977-79. Sr. admissions clk. Bass Meml. Hosp., Enid, Okla., 1978-79; instructional asst. San Juan Sch. Dist., Carmichael, Calif., 1979-82; telecommunications supr. Calif. Dental Service, San Francisco, 1982-85; telecommunications coordinator Farmers Savs. Bank, Davis, Calif., 1985-87; telecommunications mgr. Sacramento Savs. and Loan Assn., 1987—; cons. and lectr. in field. Mem. Women in Telecommunications, Nat. Assn. Female Execs. Republican. Avocations: writing, computers, ceramics, animal behavior, participating in Christian ministry. Home: 3025 U St North Highlands CA 95660

HOPE, MARGARET LAUTEN, civic worker, retired; b. N.Y.C., Dec. 17; privately educated; m. Paul C. Debry, Jr., Nov. 9, 1943; m. 2d, Fred H. Hope, Jr., Mar. 30, 1959; 1 son, Frederick H., III. Bd. dirs. Nat. Leukemia Soc., 1974—; co-chmn. giftcom. Heart Ball, Palm Beach, Fla., 1967; mem. ball coms. various charity fund raising events. Mem. Jr. League N.Y.C. Clubs: Everglades, Sailfish (Palm Beach); Women's Nat. Republican (N.Y.C.); St. James (London, Eng.). Address: 236 Dunbar Rd PO Box 601 Palm Beach FL 33480

HOPEWELL, GLORIA GRANDGEORGE, medical association administrator; b. Sandwich, Ill., Oct. 5, 1945; d. Raymond Haas and Patricia Ruth (Curwen) Grandgeorge; m. Sam H. Grayson, May 3, 1969 (div. Dec. 1977); 1 child, Richard; m. Hughes Clayton Hopewell, June 17, 1978; 1 child, Daniel. BS, No. Ill. U., 1968; MBA, Loyola U., Chgo., 1979. Registered med. technologist. Supr. Evanston (Ill.) Hosp., 1968-70; technologist 1101 Clin. Labs., Evanston, 1971-74; supr. Mason Barron Labs., Skokie, Ill., 1974-75, regional supr., 1975-76; div. mgr. Chgo., 1976-78; sales rep. Standard Sci., Rosemont, Ill., 1978; mgmt. analyst Coll. Am. Pathologists, Skokie, 1978-83, dir. edn., 1983-85, mgr. lab accreditation, 1985—; mktg. cons. Savoy-Aires, Wilmette, Ill., 1985—, pres., 1986—, bd. dirs.; cons. and lectr. in field. Mem. women's steering com. 1st Congl. Ch., Wilmette, 1986-88, music com., 1986-88, bd. membership and parish life, 1988. Mem. Clin. Lab. Mgmt. Assn., Am. Soc. Clin. Pathologists. Mem. United Ch. Christ. Club: North Shore Writers (Winnetka, Ill.), Savoy-aires (pres. 1986-87, dir. 1985-88). Home: 116 9th St Wilmette IL 60091

HOPGOOD, DEBRA JO, small business owner; b. Mount Vernon, Ill., June 26, 1958; d. L. John and B. Jean (Stovall) K.; m. Joseph Jefferson Hopgood Jr., Jan. 10, 1981; 1 child, Jillian Denise. Owmer Balloons and Tunes; with Kendrick Paper Stock Co., Mt. Vernon, Ill. Com. mem. Mt. Vernon Civic Ctr., 1983-86, Jefferson County Crime Stoppers, Mt. Vernon, 1984-85; chaperone Loiterers Club, Mt. Vernon, 1987; mem. adv. bd. Good Samaritan Hosp., 1988—; bd. dirs. Mt. Vernon Twp. High Sch. Bd. Edn., 1986—, Mt. Vernon Women's Crisis Ctr., 1988—. Mem. Nat. Fedn. Female Execs., Bus. and Profl. Womens Club, People Against Violent Environments (bd. dirs.). Baptist. Office: Kendrick Paper Stock Co 603 S 12th St Mount Vernon IL 62864

HOPKINS, ANABEL STAFFORD, career consultant company executive; b. Chgo., July 2, 1941; d. Philip Truesdale and Joanna Bartlett (Rogers) Stafford; m. Kris Demetrius, Feb. 2, 1970 (div. 1978); 1 child, Rebecca Bartlett. BA in Edn., U. N.Mex., 1967; MPA, Ind. U., 1983. Personnel officer City of Los Angeles Community Redevel. Agy., 1970-73; cons. supr. Houston-Harris County Community action Assn., 1966-69; vol. U.S. Peace Corps, Philippines, 1962-64; exec. dir. Santa Barbara (Calif.) Community Action Assn., 1974-78; dir. community devel. tng. Santa Barbara County Schs., 1978-81; asst. exec. dir. Ind. Health Care Assn., Indpls., 1983-84; exec. dir. Pi Lambda Theta, Bloomington, Ind., 1984-87; pres. Career Techniques, Bloomington, Ind., 1987—; instr. Santa Barbara City Coll., 1978-81; participation trainer Ind. U., Bloomington, 1982—. Author: Job Hunter's Guide, 1973. Chmn. Adult Day Health Care Planning Com., Santa Barbara, 1976; pres. sub-area council Health Systems Agy., Santa Barbara, 1979; precinct committeeman Monroe County Dem. Party, Ind., 1982; chmn. social concerns com. Unitarian Ch., Santa Barbara, 1978; bd. dirs. Santa Barbara Dem. League, 1977-79. Named to Outstanding Young Women Am., U.S. Jaycees, 1965. Mem. Am. Soc. Assn. Execs., Sch. Pub. and Environ. Affairs (v.p.), Alumni Assn. of Ind. U. (bd. dirs.), Cen. Ind. Assn. Tng. and Devel., Nat. Assn. Female Execs., Spurs (chpt. pres. 1960-61), Pi Lambda Theta, Phi Kappa Phi. Club: Alpine Ski (Bloomington). Avocations: skiing, ski racing, real estate, art, politics. Home: 6636 E State Rd 46 Bloomington IN 47401 Office: Career Techniques 6636 E State Rd 46 Bloomington IN 47401

HOPKINS, BARBARA PETERS, writer, editor; b. Santa Monica, Calif., Sept. 26, 1948; d. Philip Rising and Caroline Jean (Dickason) Peters; m. Philip Joseph Hopkins, May 23, 1981. AA, Santa Monica Coll., 1971; BS, San Diego State U., 1976; postgrad. UCLA, 1981-82, 84. Gen. ptnr. Signet Properties, Los Angeles, 1971-85; tech. editor C. Brewer & Co., Hilo, Hawaii, 1975-76; editor Aztec Engineer, San Diego, 1976-77; regional publicist YWCA, San Diego, 1977-78; campaign cons. Rep. Congl. and Assembly Candidates Los Angeles Times, 1983; pres. Humbird Hopkins Inc., Los Angeles, 1978—; pub. relations cons. ASCE, San Diego, 1975-76, Am. Soc. Mag. Photographers, San Diego, 1980. Author: The Layman's Guide to Raising Cane: A Guide to the Hawaiian Sugar Industry, 1976, The Student's Survival Guide, 1977, 2d edit. 1978. Council mem. Mayor's Council on Libraries, Los Angeles, 1969; mem. Wilshire Blvd. Property Owners Assn., Santa Monica, 1972-78; docent Mus. Sci. and Industry, Los Angeles, 1970; founding mem. Comml. and Indsl. Properties Assn., Santa Monica, 1982—. Recipient Acting award Santa Monica Coll., 1970. Mem. Internat. Assn. Bus. Communicators, Sales and Mktg. Execs. Assn. Avocations: writing, travel, opera. Office: Humbird Hopkins Inc PO Box 39 San Clemente CA 92672

HOPKINS, CECILIA ANN, educator; b. Havre, Mont., Feb. 17, 1922; d. Kost L. and Mary (Manaras) Sofos; B.S., Mont. State Coll., 1944; M.A., San Francisco State Coll., 1958, M.A., 1967; postgrad. Stanford U.; Ph.D., Calif. Western U., 1977; m. Henry E. Hopkins, Sept. 7, 1944. Bus. tchr. Havre (Mont.) High Sch., Mateo, Calif., 1942-44; sec. George P. Gorham, Realtor, San Mateo, 1944-45; escrow sec. Fox & Cars 1945-50; escrow officer Calif. Pacific Title Ins. Co., 1950-57; bus. tchr. Westmoor High Sch., Daly City, Calif., 1958-59; bus. tchr. Coll. of San Mateo, 1959—, chmn. real estate-ins. dept., 1963-76, dir. div. bus., 1976-86, coordinator real estate dept., 1986—; cons. to commr. Calif. Div. Real Estate, 1963—, mem. periodic rev. exam. com.; chmn. Community Coll. Adv. Com., 1971-72, mem. com., 1975—; projector direction Calif. State Chancellor's Career Awareness Consortium, mem. endowment fund adv. com., community coll. real estate edn. com., state community coll. adv. com.; mem. No. Calif. adv. bd. to Glendale Fed. Savs. and Loan Assn.; mem. bd. advisors San Mateo County Bd. Suprs., 1981-82; mem. real estate edn. and research com. to Calif. Commr. Real Estate, 1963—; mem. edn., membership, and profl. exchange coms. Am. chpt. Internat. Real Estate Fedn., 1985—. Recipient Citizen of Day award KABL, Outstanding Contbns. award Redwood City-San Carlos-Belmont Bd. Realtors; named Woman of Achievement, San Mateo-Burlingame br. Soroptimist Internat., 1979. Mem. AAUW, Calif. Assn. Real Estate Tchrs. (state pres. 1964-65, hon. dir. 1962—, outstanding real estate educator of yr. 1978-79), Real Estate Cert. Inst. (Disting. Merit award 1982), Calif. Bus. Edn. Assn. (certificate of commendation 1979), San Francisco State Coll., Guidance and Counseling Alumni, Theta Alpha Delta, Pi Lambda Theta, Delta Pi Epsilon (nat. dir. interchpt. relations 1962-65, nat. historian 1966-

67, nat. sec. 1968-69), Alpha Gamma Delta. Co-author: California Real Estate Principles; contbr. articles to profl. jours. Home: 504 Colgate Way San Mateo CA 94402

HOPKINS, DIANNE MCAFEE, library and information studies educator; b. Houston, Dec. 30, 1944; d. DeWitt Talmadge and Valda Lois (Baker) McAfee; m. Dale William Hopkins, July 7, 1982; children—Brent William, Scott McAfee. B.A., Fisk U., 1966; M.S.L.S., Atlanta U., 1967; Ed.S., Western Mich. U., 1973; Ph.D., U. Wis., 1981. Sch. librarian Houston Ind. Sch. Dist., 1967-71; sch. library specialist Dept. Edn., Lansing, Mich., 1972-73; library media specialist West Bloomfield Sch. Dist., Orchard Lake, Mich., 1973-74; library media cons. U. Mich., Ann Arbor, 1974-77; bur. dir. Dept. Pub. Instrn. Wis., Madison, 1977-87; asst. prof. library and info. studies U. Wis., Madison, 1987—. Contbr. articles to profl. jours., 1973—. Chmn. bd. outreach First Baptist Ch., Madison, 1981, mem. pulpit com., 1982, chmn. bd. edn., 1984; chmn. parents adv. bd. State Day Care Ctr., 1986-87; chmn. Intellectual Freedom award, 1987-88. Recipient Exceptional Performance award Dept. Pub. Instrn. Wis., 1982. Mem. ALA (councilor 1982-86), Assn. Ednl. Communications and Tech. (bd. dirs. 1982-85, exec. com. 1984-85), Am. Assn. Sch. Librarians (rec. sec. 1976-77, parliamentarian 1986, 87, White House Conf. com., 1986—), Wis. Sch. Library Media Assn. (liaison 1977-87 , parliamentarian 1985, 86, 87), Wis. Library Assn. (chmn. intellectual freedom com. 1984), Delta Sigma Theta. Club: Links (Madison). Avocations: piano; reading; cross stitchery; museums; movies. Office: U Wis Sch Library and Info Studies Helen C White Hall 600 N Park St Madison WI 53706

HOPKINS, EDWINA WEISKITTEL, graphic designer; b. Cin., June 7, 1947; d. Edwin and Moody (Bowling) Campbell; m. Michael J. Weiskittel, May 1966 (dec. May 1970); 1 son, Todd Michael; m. Franklin Hopkins, June 1973 (div. June 1977). Student, U. Cin., 1965-66. Asst. to art dir. World Library Publs., Cin., 1965-68; comml. artist Campbell & Assocs. Art Studio, Cin., 1969-73; prodn. mgr. William Wilson Advt. Agy., Palos Verdes, Calif., 1973-74; ptnr. Hopkins & Hopkins Design Studio, Redondo Beach, Calif., 1975-76; owner, graphic designer Winnissa Comml. Art Studio, Rolling Hills, Calif., 1976-81; pres. Winnissa Inc., Redondo Beach, 1981—. U. Cin. hon. scholar, 1965. Home and Office: 718 Ave D Redondo Beach CA 90277

HOPKINS, ELIZABETH BALCH, tobacco company executive; b. Duluth, Minn., June 22, 1932; d. Richard Carlisle and Virginia (Finley) Balch; m. Dwight D. Hopkins, Oct. 23, 1954 (div. 1980); children—D. Douglas, Laura Clark, Timothy Balch. B.A., Wells Coll., 1954; M.A., SUNY-Buffalo, 1968. Tchr. English, Park Sch., Buffalo, 1968-69, Nottingham Acad., 1969; pres. Wonderwoman Employment, Inc., 1973-77; exec. dir. Everywoman Opportunity Ctr., Inc., 1977-80; adminstr. Philip Morris Inc., N.Y.C., 1981-83, mgr., 1983—. Chmn. adv. bd. N.Y. Displaced Homemaker Program, 1981-84; panelist Inter Arts Program, Nat. Endowment Arts, 1984. Mem. Women in Communications, Phi Beta Kappa. Democrat. Office: Philip Morris Inc 120 Park Ave New York NY 10017

HOPKINS, GERRI LYNNE, association executive; b. Elizabeth, N.J., Nov. 5, 1945; d. Dallas Frederick and Irene Dolores (Socha) H.; m. Thomas Edward Still, Apr. 9, 1978 (div. Oct. 1981). Computer operator Para Mfg. Co., Cranford, N.J., 1964-70; exec. sec. Aero-Flow Dynamics, Union, N.J., 1970-73; customer service rep. Basic-Four Computer, Springfield, N.J., 1973-74; v.p. Meredith Assocs., Red Bank, N.J., 1974—; pub. relations asst. Nat. Premium Sales Execs., 1974-81; exec. dir. Soc. Incentive Travel Execs., 1975-79; asst. exec. dir. Trading Stamp Inst., 1979-81; adminstrv. dir. Assn. Retail Mktg., 1981-88; exec. dir. Mktg. Communications Execs., 1982-85; adminstrv. dir. Eastman Research Div. Meredith Assocs., Inc., Sea Bright, N.J., 1979-86. Adminstrv. dir. Mktg. News Bur., 1974-86. Asst. exec. dir. Trading Stamp Inst., Union, 1979-81; mem. Eatontown (N.J.) Rent Monitoring Bd., 1986-87; advisor Eatontown Emergency Maintenance, 1983-86; mem. com. Woman Dems., Eatontown, 1987—; chmn. Eatontown Tenants Rights Commn., 1983-86; Dem. committee person 1st Dist. Eatontown. Mem. Nat. Assn. Female Execs., Meeting Planners Internat., Soc. Incentive Travel Execs. (exec. dir. 1975-79), Mktg. Communications Execs. (exec. dir. 1982-85), Concerned Citizens, Nat. Premium Sales Execs. (pub. relations asst. 1974-81), Assn. Retail Execs. (adminstrv. dir. 1979-82). Home: 97-C White St Eatontown NJ 07724 Office: Meredith Assocs Inc 3 Caro Ct Red Bank NJ 07701

HOPKINS, JEANNE S(ULICK), accountant; b. Fair Lawn, N.J., Oct. 14, 1952; d. Peter and Margaret (McLaughlin) Sulick; m. Ronald T. Hopkins, Aug. 23, 1975. B.S., Syracuse U., 1974, M.B.A., 1975. With Price Waterhouse, Syracuse, 1975-83, staff acct., 1975-78, sr. acct., 1978-80, audit mgr., 1980-83; mgr. cost acctg. United Technologies/Carrier Corp., Syracuse, 1983-85; owner J.S. Hopkins & Co., CPA's, 1985-87, ptnr. Dannible & McKee, CPAs, 1987—; instr. in field. Mem. fund raising com. Syracuse Symphony Orch.; mem. Nat. Assn. Panhellenics. Mem. Am. Inst. C.P.A.s, Planning Execs. Inst., Hosp. Fin. Mgmt. Assn., N.Y. State Soc. C.P.A.s, Syracuse U. Alumni Assn , Delta Delta Delta. Club: Zonta. Office: Dannible & McKee 499 S Warren St Syracuse NY 13202

HOPKINS, LINDA ANN, school psychologist; b. Bristol, Va., Aug. 23, 1937; d. James Robert and Trula Mae (Mink) Broce; A.B., King Coll., 1959; M.A., East Tenn. State U., 1977, postgrad., 1977-79; postgrad. Radford U., 1978-79; m. James Edwin Hopkins, Oct. 8, 1960; children—James Edwin, David Lawrence. Social worker Washington County Welfare Dept., Abingdon, Va., 1959-61; social worker Bristol (Va.) Welfare Dept., 1963-65, Washington County Welfare Dept., 1965-68, Bristol Meml. Hosp., 1968-72; psychologist Washington County Public Schs., Abingdon, 1978-87; pvt. practice psychol. counseling, Abingdon, 1987—; clin. coordinator Critical Incidence Stress Debriefing team. Mem. Nat. Assn. Sch. Psychologists, Va. Psychol. Assn., Va. Assn. Sch. Psychologists, Soc. for Preservation of Bristol's Older Homes, Phi Kappa Phi. Methodist. Home: 423 Pennsylvania Ave Bristol TN 37620 Office: Psychol Services 268 Whites Mill Rd Abington VA 24210

HOPKINS, MARILYN JO, missionary association executive; b. Los Angeles, Nov. 5, 1943; d. Eugene Marvin and Ofa Jane (Bass) H. BS, Dallas Bapt. U., 1971; M, Southwestern Bapt. Theol. Sem., 1973; postgrad., U. Mich., Flint, 1986—. Youth dir. Miss. Bapt. Conv. Bd. div. Woman's Missionary Union, Jackson, 1973-78, cons., 1978-83, cons. adminstrn., 1984-85; exec. dir. Woman's Missionary Union, Southfield, Mich., 1985—. Contbr. articles to youth missionary mags. Office: Bapt State Conv Mich 15635 W Twelve Mile Rd Southfield MI 48076

HOPKINSON, SHIRLEY LOIS, educator; b. Boone, Iowa, Aug 25, 1924; d. Arthur Perry and Zora (Smith) Hopkinson; student Coe Coll., 1942-43; A.B. cum laude (Phi Beta Kappa scholar 1944), U. Colo., 1945; B.L.S., U. Calif., 1949; M.A. (Honnold Honor scholar 1945-46), Claremont Grad. Sch., 1951; Ed.M., U. Okla., 1952, Ed.D., 1957 Tchr. pub. sch. Stigler, Okla., 1946-47, Palo Verde High Sch., Jr. Coll., Blythe, Calif., 1947-48; asst. librarian Modesto (Calif.) Jr. Coll., 1949-51; tchr., librarian Fresno, Calif., 1951-52, La Mesa, Cal., 1953-55; asst. prof. librarianship, instructional materials dir. Chaffey Coll., Ontario, Calif., 1955-59; asst. prof. librarian ship, San Jose (Calif.) State Coll., 1959-64; assoc. prof., 1964-69, prof., 1969—. Dir. NDEA Inst. Sch. Librarians, summer 1966; mem. Santa Clara County Civil Service Bd. Examiners. Mem. ALA, Calif. Library Assn., Audio-Visual Assn. Calif., NEA, AAUW (dir. 1957-58), Bus. Profl. Women's Club, Sch. Librarians Assn. Calif. (com. mem., treas. No. sect. 1951-52), San Diego County Sch. Librarians Assn. (sec. 1945-55), Calif. Tchrs. Assn., League Women Voters (mem. bd. dirs. 1950-51, publs. chmn.), Phi Beta Kappa, Alpha Lambda Delta, Alpha Beta Alpha, Kappa Delta Pi, Phi Kappa Phi (disting. acad. achievement award 1981), Delta Kappa Gamma. Author: Descriptive Cataloging of Library Materials; Instructional Materials for Teaching the Use of the Library. Contbr. to profl. publs. Editor: Calif. Sch. Libraries, 1963-64; asst. editor: Sch. Library Assn. of Calif. Bull., 1961-63. Office: San Jose State U Room LN-608 San Jose CA 95192

HOPPER, CATHERINE VIRGINIA, school system administrator; b. Princeton, Ky., Sept. 6, 1933; d. Fred H. and Elizabeth Belle (Sigler) H.; m. Herbert David Allen, Dec. 20, 1953 (div. 1956). Student, Berea Coll., 1952-53; BA, Western Ky. U., 1955; MA, San Diego State U., 1964. Tchr. Jefferson County Schs., Louisville, 1955-57; tchr. San Diego City Schs., 1957-60, resource tchr., 1960-62, asst. supt., 1983—; tchr. Madison High Sch., San Diego, 1962-64; vice prin. Taft Jr. High, San Diego, 1964-68, Patrick Henn High Sch., San Diego; prin. Wright Bros. Jr. High Sch., Bell Jr. High Sch., San Diego, Univ. City High Sch., San Diego, 1981-83. Author curriculum guides. Chair cancer adv. bd. Scripps ,Meml. Hosp. Cancer Ctr., San Diego, 1985-86; bd. dirs. San Diego Urban League, 1986. Kettering Found. fellow, 1965. Mem. Assn. Calif. Sch. Adminstrs. (v.p., sec., Disting. Educator award 1986), San Diego Adminstrs. Assn. (bd. dirs.). Republican. Episcopalian. Office: San Diego City Schs 4100 Normal San Diego CA 92103

HOPPER, GRACE M., mathematician; b. N.Y.C., Dec. 9, 1906; d. Walter Fletcher and Mary Campbell (Van Horne) Murray; m. Vincent Foster Hopper, June 15, 1930 (div. 1945). BA, Vassar Coll., 1928; MA (Vassar fellow, Sterling scholar), Yale U., 1930, PhD, 1934; postgrad. (Vassar faculty fellow), NYU, 1941-42; DEng (hon.), Newark Coll. Engring., 1972; DSc (hon.), C.W. Post Coll. L.I. U., 1973, Pratt Inst., 1976, Linkoping (Sweden) U., 1980, Bucknell U., 1980, Acadia (Can.) U., 1980, So. Ill. U., 1981, Loyola U., Chgo., 1981; LLD (hon.), U. Pa., 1974; D Pub. Service (hon.), George Washington U., 1981. From instr. to assoc. prof. math. Vassar Coll., Poughkeepsie, N.Y., 1931-44; asst. prof. math Barnard Coll., N.Y.C., summer 1943; research fellow engring. scis., applied physics computation lab Harvard U., Cambridge, Mass., 1946-49; sr. mathematician Eckert-Mauchly Computer Corp., Phila., 1949-50; sr. programmer Eckert-Mauchly div. Remington Rand, 1950-59; systems engr., dir. automatic programming devel. UNIVAC div. Sperry Rand Corp., Phila., 1959-64, staff scientist systems programming, 1964-71; vis. lectr. Moore Sch. Elec. Engring., U. Pa., 1959-63, vis. assoc. prof. elec. engring., 1963-74, adj. prof., 1974; professorial lectr. George Washington U. from 1971. Contbr. articles to profl. jours. Served to comdr WAVES, 1944-46, from 1967, capt. USNR, 1973; later served active duty NAVDAC. Decorated Legion of Merit, Meritorious Service award; recipient Naval Ordnance Devel. award, 1946, Connelly Meml. award, 1968, Wilbur L. Cross medal Yale U., 1972, Sci. Achievement award Am. Mother's Com., 1970, others. Fellow Brit. Computer Soc. (disting.), Assn. Computer Programmers and Analysts, IEEE (McDowell award 1979), AAAS; mem. Nat. Acad. Engring., Assn. Computing Machinery, Data Processing Mgmt. Assn. (Man of Yr. award 1969), Am. Fedn. Info. Processing Socs. (Harry Goode Meml. award 1970), Soc. Women Engrs (Achievement award 1964, Franklin Inst., U.S. Naval Inst., Internat. Oceanographic Found., DAR, Dames Loyal Legion, Hist. Soc. Pa., Geneal. Soc. Pa., N.H. Hist. Soc., New Eng. Hist. Geneal. Soc., Valley Forge Hist. Assn., Ret. Officers Assn., Huguenot Soc. Pa., Nat., N.Y. geneal socs., Pechin Soc, Phi Beta Kappa, Sigma Xi. Home: 1400 S Joyce St Arlington VA 22202 *

HOPPER, SALLY, state legislator. widowed; children: Nancy, Joan, Caroline, Ann. BA, U. Wyo., 1956. Mem. Colo. State Senate, 1987—. Mem. Kappa Kappa Gamma. Republican. Episcopalian. Home: 21649 Cabrini Blvd Golden CO 80401 *

HOPPER, VIVIAN LINDA, training executive; b. Memphis, Tenn., June 8, 1947; d. Leslie Wright Hopper and Vivian Loraine (Beasley) Ray. B.A. in Sociology, Memphis State U., 1973; postgrad., 1975; M. of Gen. Adminstrn., U. Md., 1988. Instr., U. Pitts., 1975-78; media coordinator Amalgamated Clothing and Textile Workers' Union, Pitts., 1976-78; tng. coordinator Wider Opportunities for Women, Washington, 1979-83; tng. specialist Washington Met. Area Transit Authority, 1983-86; dir. tng. Internat. City Mgmt. Assn., Washington, 1986—; dir. D.C. Pvt. Industry Council; cons. Women's Ctr. No. Va., Vienna, McKenna House, Washington, local govts.; mem. speakers bur., program evaluation com. Pvt. Industry Council; workshop leader, panelist; developed and presented tng. for govt. execs. in 12 Arab nations U.N. and Arab Orgn. Adminstrn. Scis., Amman, Jordan, 1988. Co-author: The Ethics Factor, Performance Evaluation: A Manager's Guide to Employee Development, A Manager's Guide to Improving Staf Relations, Motivation; contbr.: Women into Trades and Technology, 1981. Mem. Am. Soc. Tng. and Devel., Nat. Assn. Female Execs. Home: 4770 N 25th St Arlington VA 22207 Office: Internat City Mgmt Assn 1120 G St NW Washington DC 20005

HORACEK, CONSTANCE HELLER, graphic designer, educator; b. Campbell, Nebr., Nov. 7; d. Roy B. and Mildred Bernadine (Holt) Heller; m. Michael Jay Horacek, Aug. 18, 1963 (div. Oct. 1983); children: Kachina Leigh, Marika Sian. BS in Edn., Midland Luth. Coll., 1963; MA in Ceramic Sculpture, Western Ill. U., 1977, postgrad., 1978—; postgrad., U. Kans., 1974-75, Arrowmont Sch. Arts and Crafts, 1978, 79, 81, 82; MFA, Md. Inst. Art, Balt., 1986. Tchr. Ottawa (Kans.) Jr. High Sch., 1964-68, Bardolph (Ill.) Elem. Sch., 1970; mem. faculty Western Ill. U. Lab. Sch., Macomb, 1970-73, instr. clothing textile design dept. home econs., 1975-80; asst. prof. clothing/textiles Albright Coll., Reading, Pa., 1980-86, assoc. prof. fashion merchandising/design, 1986—; acting dir. Freedman Gallery, summer 1981; instr. part-time extension campus Spoon River Jr. Coll., Macomb, 1980; graphic designer for workshops, seminars, and local bus. firms, 1975-80; ptnr. Images Unltd., Macomb, 1980; cons. visual prodn., 1975—; project dir. Outreach program, summer 1981; design cons. Tandy Leather Co., Ft. Worth. Bd. dirs. Kashahasia, Western Ill. U., 1978-80, Downtown Up. Mem. Am. Crafts Council, Am. Home Econs. Assn., Pa. Home Econs. Assn., Surface Design, Kappa Omicron Phi, Kappa Pi, Alpha Psi Omega. Office: Albright Coll Reading PA 19604

HORDEMAN, AGNES MARIE, real estate professional, investment company executive; b. Phila., May 19, 1929; d. Hector and Victoria (Charais) Hill; m. Walter George Hordeman, Sept. 28, 1947; children: Phyllis, Kim, Henry, Rex, Gary. BA in Social Sci., Thomas Edison U., 1978. Relief dir. New Chgo. Trustee's Office, Hobart Twp., Ind., 1962-64; exec. sec. Real Estate Office, Pine Beach, N.J., 1964-65; office mgr. Crestwood Village, Whiting, N.J., 1965-67; reporter Ocean County Daily Times, Lakewood, 1967-69; real estate agt. De-Bow Agy., Lakewood, 1972-73, Century 21 Sullivan Agy. and Centurion and Rimm Howell, 1973-79; dir. Counteract Agy. for Children, Jackson, N.J., 1974-75; pres. Blue Sky Realty, Jackson, 1979—; appraiser Garden State Bank, Jackson, 1986-87; pres. Brassica Inc., Jackson, 1986-87. Contbr. articles to profl. jours. Mem. com. Jackson Twp. Rep. Orgn., 1964-76; rep. to People's Republic China ambassador program SBA. Named Woman of Yr. Girl Scouts U.S., 1975. Mem. Nat. Assn. Real Estate Appraisers, Ocean County Bd. Realtors, Monmouth County Bd. Realtors, N.J. Bd. Realtors, Nat. Bd. Realtors, Nat. Assn. Female Execs., Jackson Twp. C. of C. (v.p., directory chmn.). Republican. Roman Catholic. Clubs: Legion Mary (v.p. 1962-64) (New Chicago); Rosary Sodality (v.p. 1967) (Jackson). Home: RD #4 121 Cooks Bridge Jackson NJ 08527 Office: 277 County Line Rd Jackson NJ 08527

HORELICK, MARY GAIL, physical therapist; b. Westport, Conn., Apr. 27, 1948; d. Michael and Rita (Hermenze) H.; B.S., Ithaca Coll., 1970; M.S., Hartford Grad. Ctr.; student U. Conn. Sch. of Law, 1987—. Staff phys. therapist New Rochelle (N.Y.) Hosp. Med. Center, 1971-73, Misericordia Hosp. Med. Center, Bronx, 1974-77, chief phys. therapist/coordinator rehab. services, 1977-80; dir. rehab. services Newington (Conn.) Children's Hosp., 1980—. Mem. phys. therapy adv. council U. Conn. Mem. Am. Phys. Therapy Assn. (treas. Conn. chpt. 1986-87), Am. Coll. Sports Medicine, Am. Congress Rehab. Medicine, Nat. Spinal Cord Injury Assn. Conn. chpt. (v.p. edn. 1981-83). Home: 24 Conestoga Way Glastonbury CT 06033 Office: Newington Children's Hosp 181 E Cedar St Newington CT 06111

HORN, DEBORAH SUE, organization administrator, writer, editor; b. Cin., July 14, 1954; d. Harry R. and Helen (Ammann) H. B.S., Ball State U., 1977; postgrad., Calif. State U.-Fullerton, 1978-80. Asst. editor Scott Publs., Santa Ana, Calif., 1979-81; publs. mgr. Toastmasters Internat., Santa Ana, 1981-84, edn. mgr., 1984—. Editor Toastmaster mag., 1981-84; contbr. articles to mags. and newspapers. Intern Ind. Republican State Central Com., Indpls., 1976. Mem. Calif. Press Women (pres. Orange County dist. 1984-85, 2d place award 1982, 1st place award 1983), Nat. Fedn. Press Women, Soc. Profl. Journalists. Methodist. Club; Langlaufers Ski (Downey, Calif.) (newsletter editor 1984-85). Home: 2821 S Fairview Santa Ana CA 92704 Office: Toastmasters Internat 2200 N Grand Ave Santa Ana CA 92711

HORN, ESTELLA MCCOY, educational administrator; b. Beauty, Ky., Apr. 16, 1948; d. Robert and Martha (Gandy) McCoy; m. Robert Horn, Aug. 8, 1970; children: Marmanda Gailleen, John Robert. BA, Morehead State U., 1970, MA, 1975. Cert. prin., elem., secondary. Tchr. Warfield (Ky.) High Sch., 1970-73; tchr. Warfield Middle Sch., 1973-83, counselor, 1983-84; tchr. So. Community Coll., Williamson, W.Va., 1980-82; prin. Warfield Elem. Sch., 1984—. Social chmn. PTA, Warfield; mem. pub. relations 4-H Council, Inez, Ky.; coach basketball, Warfield, 1973-77. Mem. Nat. Assn. Female Execs., Ky. Edn. Assn. Club: Homemakers (Warfield) (pres. 1974-83). Home: HC 69 PO Box 905A Inez KY 41224 Office: Warfield Elem Sch Box 407 Warfield KY 41267

HORN, KAREN CAROL, educator; b. Perth Amboy, N.J., Sept. 12, 1957; d. John and Elenore (Wataha) Kowalchek; m. Russell Charles Horn, Oct. 4, 1980. BS, Fairleigh Dickinson U., 1980. Cert. tchr., N.J. Substitute tchr. Bd. Edn., Woodbridge, N.J., 1978-80, Nutley, N.J., 1980; dental asst. Endodontic Assocs. P.A., Engelwood, N.J., 1980; tchr. biology and chemistry Freehold Regional High Sch. Dist. Bd. Edn., Englishtown, N.J., 1980—; v.p. Recovery Data, Inc., Bradley Beach, N.J., 1983—. Recipient cert. Recognition U.S. Army. Mem. The Cousteau Soc., Nat. Geog. Soc., Smithsonian Instn., Am. Mus. Natural History (assoc.). Clubs: Friday Night Mixed Bowling League (Bradley Beach) (sec.-treas. 1985—), Sunday Night Mixed Bowling League (Bradley Beach) (v.p. 1987—). Home: 117 Park Place Ave Bradley Beach NJ 07720

HORN, KAREN NICHOLSON, banker; b. Los Angeles, Sept. 21, 1943; d. Aloys and Novella (Hartley) Nicholson; m. John T. Horn, June 5, 1965; 1 child, Hartley J. B.A., Pomona Coll., 1965; Ph.D., Johns Hopkins U., 1971. Economist bd. govs. FRS, Washington, 1969-71; v.p., economist First Nat. Bank, Boston, 1971-78; treas. Bell of Pa., Phila., 1978-82; pres. Fed. Res. Bank, Cleve., 1982-87; chmn. and chief exec. officer Bank One Cleveland NA, Cleve., 1987—. Trustee Johns Hopkins U., Balt., Case Western Res. U., Cleve., Cleve. Clinic Found., Musical Arts Assn., Cleve., Cleve. Tomorrow, Greater Cleve. Roundtable, United Way, Cleve., Oberlin Coll., Ohio. Mem. Council on Fgn. Relations. Office: Bank One Cleveland NA 1255 Euclid Ave Cleveland OH 44115

HORN, PATRICE DAILY, magazine editor; b. Easton, Pa., June 20, 1927; d. Thomas and Rose (Welch) D.; m. Jack Calvert Horn, Aug. 14, 1948; children: Anthony Calvert, Lisa Ann, Andrew Patrick. Reporter Fortune Mag., N.Y.C., 1947-55; sr. editor Psychology Today, Del Mar, Calif., 1968-76; mng. editor Psychology Today, Washington, 1983, editor, 1984—; sr. editor Self Mag., N.Y.C., 1978-81; mng. editor Technology Mag., N.Y.C., 1982-83. Co-author: Sex in the Office, 1982. Mem. Am. Soc. Mag. Editors. Democrat. Home: 1900 S Eads Arlington VA 22202 Office: Psychology Today 1150 17th St NW Washington DC 20036

HORN, PAULA LOIS, training specialist, consultant, editor, writer; b. N.Y.C., Jan. 20, 1947; d. Herman and Sadie Florence (Spiegelburd) H. BA, Albany State U., 1969; MS, Hofstra U., 1972; MA, NYU, 1974; PhD, U. So. Calif., 1980. Reading cons. and specialist Seaford, N.Y. and Branford, Conn., 1971-74; instructional designer Systems Devel. Corp., Santa Monica, Calif., 1978-79; pvt. cons., 1980—; ednl. tng. cons. U So. Calif., Los Angeles, 1982-85; mktg. tng. cons. Xerox Corp., El Segundo, Calif., 1985-86; software documentation specialist, Ashton-Tate Corp., Torrance, Calif., 1986—; ednl. tng. cons. Nat. Tng. Systems, Santa Monica, 1979-80; ednl. tng. cons. Learning Systems, Encino, Calif., 1980-81; media tng. cons. Media Learning Systems, Pasadena, Calif., 1980; researcher and instructional devel. Northridge U., Calif., 1984-85. Author: Economics Analysis for Business, 1982; (with others) RapidFile, 1987; instr., designer, editor: Consultants' Handbook, 1986. Mem. Nat. Soc. Performance and Instrn., Soc. Applied Learning Tech. (bd. dirs.), Assn. Tng. and Devel., Soc. Tech. Communication, Mensa, Phi Delta Kappa, Phi Delta Epsilon. Avocations: writing, reading, concerts, movies, theater. Home: 11023 Fruitland Dr #4 Studio City CA 91604 Office: Ashton-Tate 20101 S Hamilton Ave Torrance CA 90502-1319

HORNBAKER, ALICE JOY, author; b. Cin., Feb. 3, 1927; B.A. cum laude and honors in Journalism, San Jose State U., 1949; children—Christopher Albert, Holly Jo, Joseph Bernard III. Asst. woman's editor San Jose Mercury-News, 1949-55; owner, mgr. Frisch Big Boy Restaurant, Cin., 1955-68; dir. pub. relations Children's Home Soc. Calif., Santa Clara, 1968-71; asst. dir. pub. relations United Fund Calif., Santa Clara, 1971—; editor Tristate Sunday Enquirer mag., 1986—, columnist Generations; editorial dir. Writers Digest Sch., Cin., 1971-75; columnist, critic, mag. writer, reporter, copy editor Tempo sec. Cin. Enquirer, 1975—, also book editor and critic, columnist for Aging, feature writer Tempo sect.; reporter feature segments on aging WKRC-TV; tchr. adult edn. Forest Hills Sch. Dist., Thomas More Coll., 1973—; author: Preventive Care: Easy Exercise Against Aging, 1974; byline in People, Modern Maturity, Sr. Advocate, NATR Jour., and others; contbr. fiction to Enquirer mag.; freelance mag. writer. Recipient Bronze award in Am. health journalism, Am. Chiropractic Assn., 1977, 78; 1st place for feature writing Cin. Editors Assn., 1983. Mem. Blue Pencil of Ohio State U. (pres. 1981-82), Women in Communications, Ohio Newspaper Women's Assn. (v.p. 1981-83, 1st place human interest story, 1977-85, 2d place columnist award 1979, Tops in Ohio award 1982, M.M. McMullen 2d place award 1982, Recognition award 1985), Soc. Profl. Journalists (treas. 1981-82). Office: The Cin Enquirer 617 Vine St Cincinnati OH 45201

HORNBECKER, JOYCE KILBOURN, town clerk; b. Waterbury, Conn., June 11, 1927; d. Harry Raymond and Erminie (Hassett) K.; m. Howard Arnold Hornbecker, April 28, 1951; children: Shirley Hornbecker Hagyard, Carl H., Laurie Hornbecker Mariano. AS in Bus. Adminstrn., Post Coll., 1982. Cert. emergency med. technician, mcpl. clk., Conn. Cashier Howland Hughes Dept. Store, Waterbury, Conn., 1944-45; stenographer, clk. So. New Eng. Telephone Co., Waterbury, 1945-52; asst. town clk., asst. registrar of vital stats. Town of Southbury, Conn., 1966-81, town clk., registrar of vital stats., 1981—. Sec. Rep. Town Com., 1956-66; various positions and offices Girl Scouts of U.S., Southbury, 1959-81, organizer, chief Lake Zoar Marine Police, Southbury, 1972-80; organizer, pres. Lake Zoar Authority, Southbury, 1972-80; supt. religious edn. So. Britain (Conn.) Congl., 1973-76; vol., emergency med. technician Southbury Ambulance Assn., Inc., 1976-84, 87—, pres. 1982, 84, 85. Mem. Conn. Town Clks. Assn. (v.p. 1981—), Internat. Inst. Mcpl. Clks., New Eng. Assn. City & Town Clks. Lodge: Rotary. Office: Town of Southbury 501 Main St S Southbury CT 06488-2295

HORN-DALTON, KATHY ELLEN, rehabilitation agency administrator; b. Latrobe, Pa., Apr. 12, 1952; d. William Irving and Stella Bertha (Denisiuk) Horn; m. Glenn Holbert Dalton, Aug. 4, 1973. BS in Social Work, W.Va. U., 1975, MSW, 1976; PhD in Adminstrn., Columbia Pacific U., 1983. Registered psychotherapist. Counselor Womens Info. Ctr., Morgantown, W.Va., 1973; psychiatric aid Torrance (Pa.) State Hosp., 1974; group home counselor Sommerset Bedford Mental Health Ctr., Rockwood, Pa., 1974; shop foreman Southwest Wyo. Rehab. Ctr., Rock Springs, 1975-76, exec. dir., 1976-81, pres., administr., 1981—; researcher emotionally disturbed/mentally retarded project Div. Vocat. Rehab., Cheyenne, Wyo., 1985; CD grants adminstr. Sweetwater County, Rock Springs, Wyo., 1982-83. Author: Develop and Design an Energy Efficient Sheltered Workshop, 1983, Job Placement Results of a Job Training Partnership Act Program in a Rural Sheltered Workshop, 1985; contbr. articles to profl. jours. Mem. Wyo. Devel. Disabilities Council, 1978, Wyo. Pvt. Indsl. Council, 1983, adv. bd. U. No. Colo., Greeley, 1978; state advisor U.S. Congl. Adv. Bd., Washington, 1984, YWCA. Mem. Wyo. Assn. Rehab. Facilities (legis. chmn. 1981-83), Nat. Assn. Social Workers (cert.), Exec. Females Assn., Bus. Profl. Women's Assn., Pilot Butte Sand Drag Assn., Intermountain Sand Drag Assn., Nat. Sand Co. Assn., Nat. Hot Rod Assn. Office: SW Wyo Rehab Ctr 2632 Foothill Blvd Suite 107 Rock Springs WY 82901

HORNE, CHARLOTTE ANN HOLCOMBE, real estate executive; b. Anniston, Ala., Feb. 5, 1938; d. Charlie Gardy and Ola Bell (Little) Holcombe; m. Robert (Bobby) Edward Horne, Nov. 6, 1954; children—Robbie Sheila Horne Owen, Gary Wayne Horne, Shannon Michelle Horne Clarke. Cert. real estate appraiser, Ala. With credit dept. Hudson's, Anniston, 1971; sec. Super Valu Warehouse, Anniston, 1972; realtor Service Realty, Anniston, 1978-85, Howell Realty, Anniston, 1985—. Voter, dep. registrar, election poll worker, Anniston, 1970—. Mem. Women's Council of Realtors (charter mem., v.p. 1984, pres. 1985, Woman Yr. 1987), Calhoun County Area Bd.

Realtors (Million Dollar Sales club 1983-87, life mem., named to Sales Honor club 1980, 81, 82, Realtor of Yr. 1986, bd. dirs. state and local 1985-87), DAR. Baptist. Club: Christian Women's (exec. com.). Lodge: Elks (exec. sec. 1983). Home: 1113 Caswell Dr Anniston AL 36201 Office: 1325 Quintard St Anniston AL 36201

HORNE, JO-ALLENE, pediatrician, anesthesiologist; b. Jacksonville, Fla., Dec. 15, 1936; d. Allen Pierce and Bessie Lee (Bruce) H. BS, U. Ga., 1957; MD, Bowman Gray Sch. Medicine, 1962. Diplomate Am. Bd. Pediatrics. Intern Greenville (S.C.) Gen. Hosp., 1962-63; resident in pediatrics U. Okla., Oklahoma City, 1963-65; fellow in neonatology Southwestern Med. Sch. Hosp., Dallas, 1967-69; resident in anesthesiology Parkland Hosp. and Children's Med. Ctr. Hosp., Dallas, 1969-71; practice medicine specializing in anesthesiology Denton, Tex., 1974—. Fellow Am. Coll. Anesthesia; mem. AMA (Recognition award, 1983, 87), Tex. Soc. Anesthesiology, Tex. Med. Assn., Denton County Med. Assn., Am. Soc. Anesthesia, Am. Bd. Pediatrics, Phi Beta Kappa, Phi Kappa Phi, Alpha Epsilon Delta. Home: 4100 Golden Circle Denton TX 76201 Office: 4401 I 35 North Suite 220 Denton TX 76201

HORNER, CONSTANCE, federal office administrator; b. Summit, N.J., Feb. 24, 1942; d. David Earl and Cecelia (Murphy) McN.; m. Charles Edward Horner, May 7, 1965; children: David Bayer, Jonathan Purcell. BA in English Lit., U. Pa., 1964; MA in English Lit., U. Chgo., 1967. Dep. asst. dir. policy planning and evaluation ACTION Agy., Washington, 1981-82, acting assoc. dir. domestic & anti-poverty ops., 1982-83, dep. assoc. dir. for VISTA & service-learning, 1982-83; assoc. dir. for econs. & govt. Office of Mgmt. and Budget, Washington, 1983-85; dir. Office of Personnel Mgmt., Washington, 1985—. Mem. Pres.'s Commn. on White House Fellowships, Pres.'s Commn. on Exec. Exchange. Republican. Office: Office of Personnel Mgmt Office of Dir 1900 E St NW Washington DC 20415

HORNER, LEE, foundation executive, speaker, consultant, computer specialist; b. Sault Ste. Marie, Ont., Can., Mar. 18, 1944; came to U.S., 1976; d. William E. and Gladys (Boomhower) H.; m. Claude Lavallee, Jan. 21, 1960 (div. Sept. 1969); children—Kevin Lauren Lavallee/Petalos, Cynthia Lee Lavallee; m. James G. Petalos, Jan. 9, 1970 (dec. Jan. 1977). Student Concordia U., Montreal, Que., Can., 1975-76, U. Nev.-Las Vegas, 1977. Pres., LHP Investments, Inc., Las Vegas, 1978—; v.p. Casa Mobile Corp., real estate, San Francisco, 1979—; founder, chmn. bd. PMS Research Found., Las Vegas, 1982—; pub. speaker premenstrual syndrome, health, wellness, cycles. Author: How to Chart Your Course to Freedom, 1983; Mini-Nutrition and Exercise Manual, 1983; PMS Minder, 1983; PMS Wellness Workbook, 1985, PMS Support Group Manual, 1985. Mem. Am. Soc. Fund Raising Execs., Am. Bus. Women's Assn., Nat. Speakers Assn. (founding pres. Las Vegas chpt. 1984-85). Club: Toastmasters (ednl. v.p. 1980, adminstrv. v.p. 1983-88). Home: 2754 El Toreador Las Vegas NV 89109 Office: LHP Investments Inc/ PMS Research Found PO Box 14574 Las Vegas NV 89114

HORNER, MATINA SOURETIS, college president; b. Boston, July 28, 1939; d. Demetre John and Christine (Antonopoulos) Souretis; m. Joseph L. Horner, June 25, 1961; children: Tia Andrea, John, Christopher. A.B. cum laude, Bryn Mawr Coll., 1961; M.S., U. Mich., 1963, Ph.D., 1968; LL.D., Dickinson Coll., 1973, Mt. Holyoke Coll., 1973, U. Pa., 1975, Smith Coll., 1979, Wheaton Coll., 1979; L.H.D. (hon.), U. Mass., 1973, Tufts U., 1976, U. Hartford, 1980, U. New Eng., 1987. Teaching fellow U. Mich., Ann Arbor, 1962-66; lectr. motivation personality U. Mich., 1968-69; lectr. social relations Harvard U., 1969-70, asst. prof. clin. psychology dept. social relations, 1970-72; also cons. univ. health services; pres. Radcliffe Coll., 1972—; dir. Time, Inc., Fed. Res. Bank Boston, Liberty Mut. Life Ins. Co., Boston Edison Co. Contbr. psychol. articles on motivation to profl. jours. Mem. adv. council NSF, 1977—, chmn., 1980-86; trustee Twentieth Century Fund, 1973—, Mass. Eye and Ear Infirmary, 1986—; bd. dirs. Revson Found., 1986—, Council for Fin. Aid to Edn., 1985—; bd. dirs. Women's Research and Edn. Inst., 1979—, chmn. research com., 1982—; mem. President's Commn. for Nat. Agenda for 1980s, 1979-80; chmn. Task Force on Quality Am. Life in '80s, 1979-80; mem. adv. com. Women's Leadership Conf. on Nat. Security, 1982—. Recipient Roger Baldwin award Mass. Civil Liberties Union Found., 1982, citation of merit Northeast Region NCCJ, 1982, Career Contbn. award Mass. Psychol. Assn., 1987. Mem. Council Fgn. Relations, Nat. Inst. Social Scis. (award 1973), Phi Beta Kappa, Phi Delta Kappa, Phi Kappa Phi. Office: Radcliffe Coll Office of Pres 10 Garden St Cambridge MA 02138

HORNER, MAXINE, state legislator; b. Tulsa; d. Earl Henry Sr. and Corrine (Burton) Cissel; m. Donald Montell Horner Sr., 1954; children: Shari, Donald Montell Jr. Personnel adminstr. Tulsa Job Corps Ctr., 1971-75; dir. minority women's employment U.S. Dept. Labor, 1975-81; staff asst. U.S Rep. James Jones, Tulsa, 1984-86; mem. Okla. State Senate, 1986—. Mem., v.p. North Tulsa Heritage Found., 1984—; pres. adv. bd. North Tulsa YMCA, 1985-86. Democrat. Baptist. Address: PO Box 351 Tulsa OK 74101 *

HOROWITZ, LOUISE SCHWARTZ, lawyer; b. N.Y.C., Jan. 24, 1932; d. Charles and Bertie (Grad) Schwartz; m. David H. Horowitz, June 20, 1951 (div. 1976); children—Marilyn, Roger, Diana. B.A., Smith Coll., 1953; M.A., Columbia U., 1955, Ph.D., 1969; J.D., N.Y. Law Sch., 1981. Bar: N.Y. 1982. Lectr., Bklyn. Coll., 1966-67; assoc. prof. L.I.U., 1967-75, asst. dir. Learning Ctr., 1975-76; research fellow Wagner Coll., 1976-78; legal intern U.S. Atty.'s Office, Ea. Dist. N.Y., 1980-81; asst. corp. counsel Law Dept. City of N.Y., 1982-86 ; assoc. Budd, Larner, Kent, Gross, Picillo & Rosenbaum, 1986—. Contbr. articles to profl. jours. Mem. N.Y. Woman's Bar Assn., Am. Philos. Assn., N.Y. State Bar Assn., Fed. Bar Council. Democrat. Jewish. Home: 12 W 72d St New York NY 10023 Office: Budd Larner Kent Gross Picillo & Rosenbaum 140 Cedar St New York NY 10006 *

HOROWITZ, MARILYN STEPHENS, biochemist; b. N.Y.C., Sept. 2, 1940; d. William A. and Mary E. (Ambler) Stephens; m. Bernard Horowitz, July 11, 1971; children: Cara Ann, Gregory, Stephen. BS summa cum laude, Marymount Coll., 1962; MS, Georgetown U., 1965; PhD, Cornell U., 1973. Instr. then asst. prof. chemistry Marymount Manhattan Coll., N.Y.C., 1964-69; research fellow N.Y. Blood Ctr., N.Y.C., 1973-77, assoc. dir. quality assurance blood derivatives program, 1977-80, dir. planning, edn. and regulatory affairs, 1980-82, dir. clin. studies and regulatory affairs, 1982-86, dir. office of patents and lics., 1986—; cons. Celltech, Ltd., Berkshire, Eng., 1982-83, Exovir, Inc., Great Neck, 1983-84. Contbr. articles to profl. jours. Pres. HOPE Ctr. for Interfaith Understanding, Washington, Jerusalem, 1985-87; dir., 1984-87. Fellow N.Y. State, 1962, NSF, 1962, NSF, 1963 (intermediate level). Mem. N.Y. Acad. Scis., Am. Chem. Soc., AAAS, Internat. Soc. on Thrombosis and Haemostasis. Democrat. Club: Dessoff Choirs (dir. 1971-73). Office: NY Blood Ctr 310 E 67th St New York NY 10021

HOROWITZ, ROBERTA SHARON, information scientist; b. Bklyn., Aug. 31, 1951; d. Joseph Benjamin and Shirley Beatrice (Streicher) H. BS, Calif. State U., Los Angeles, 1973; MLS, U. So. Calif., 1982; postgrad., Nova U., 1985—. Quality assurance technician Lawry's Foods, Los Angeles, 1975-78; research asst. Am. McGaw Co., Irvine, Calif., 1979-82; sr. info. specialist Allergan Pharms., Irvine, 1982-86; info. scientist Sch. Medicine U. So. Calif., Pasadena, Calif., 1986—; cons. Lit. Analysis Inst., Burbank, Calif., 1983—. Contrb. articles to profl. jours. Mem. Am. Soc. Info. Sci. (dir. membership local chapt. 1986—, outstanding mem. 1986), Am. Assn. Artificial Intelligence, Spl. Library Assn., Drug Info. Assn. Home: PO Box 61211 Pasadena CA 91106

HORRELL, EDNA RICHARDSON, elementary school principal; b. Leitchfield, Ky., Mar. 30, 1929; d. Lannie B. and Vonnie R. (Ramsey) Richardson; m. Billy B. Horrell, June 11, 1949; 1 child: Pamela Joy. B.S., Western Ky. U., 1952; M.A., Ind. U., 1966, postgrad., 1968-69. Cert. tchr., adminstr., Ky. Tchr. elem. sch. Grayson County, Fayette County, Ky., 1947-55; elem. tchr. Jefferson County, Louisville, Ky., 1955-67; curriculum coordinator Daviess County Schs., Owensboro, Ky., 1969-82, remedial reading tchr., 1982-83; prin. Daviess County Elem. Sch., Owensboro, 1983-87; part-time instr. Ky. Wesleyan Coll. Mem. AAUW (sec. 1982-85), Delta Kappa Gamma (2d v.p. 1982-84). Club: Pilot Internat. (coordinator Owensboro, 1983-85). Home: 3000 Frederica St Owensboro KY 42301 Office: Daviess County Bd Edn Southeastern Pkwy Owensboro KY 42301

HORSLEY, PAULA ROSALIE, accountant; b. Smithfield, Nebr., Sept. 7, 1924; d. Karl and Clara Margaret (Busse) Fenske; m. Phillip Carreon (div.); children—Phillip, James, Robert, David, Richard; m. Norby Lumon, Apr. 5, 1980. Student AIB Bus. Coll., Des Moines, 1942-44, YMCA Coll., Chgo., 1944-47, UCLA Extension, 1974. Acctg. mgr. Montgomery Ward & Co., Denver, 1959-62; acct. Harman & Co., C.P.A.s, Arcadia, Calif., 1962-67; controller, officer G & H Transp., Montebello, Calif., 1967-78; comptroller Frederick Weisman Co., Century City, Calif., 1978-80; chief fin. officer Lutheran Shipping, Madang, Papua, New Guinea, 1980-82; prin. Village Bookkeeper, acctg. cons., Monreno Valley, Calif., 1982—; chief fin. officer Insight Computer Products and Tech., Inc., San Diego, 1988—. Vol. crises counselor, supr. and instr. Melodyland Hotline, Anaheim, Calif., 1976-79. Mem. Riverside Tax Cons., Nat. Assn. for Female Execs., Internat. Platform Assn. Republican. Lutheran. Avocations: church activities, reading, cooking, phys. fitness. Home: 4660 N River Rd SP 129 Oceanside CA 92054 Office: Insight Computer Products and Techs Inc 4883 Ronson Ct Suite T San Diego CA 92111

HORSTMANN, DOROTHY MILLICENT, physician, educator; b. Spokane, Wash., July 2, 1911; d. Henry J. and Anna (Hunold) H. A.B., U. Calif., 1936, M.D., 1940; D.Sc. (hon.), Smith Coll., 1961; M.A. (hon.), Yale, 1961; Dr. Med. Scis. (hon.), Women's Med. Coll. of Pa., 1963. Intern San Francisco City and County Hosp., 1939-40, asst. resident medicine, 1940-41; asst. resident medicine Vanderbilt U. Hosp., 1941-42; Commonwealth Fund fellow, sect. preventive medicine Sch. Medicine, Yale U., New Haven, 1942-43; instr. preventive medicine Sch. Medicine, Yale U., 1943-44, 45-47, asst. prof., 1948-52, assoc. prof., 1952-56, assoc. prof. preventive medicine and pediatrics, 1956-61, prof. epidemiology and pediatrics, 1961-69, John Rodman Paul prof. epidemiology, prof. pediatrics, 1969-82, John Rodman Paul prof. emeritus, prof. pediatrics emeritus, sr. research scientist, 1982—; instr. medicine U. Calif., 1944-45. Recipient Albert Coll. award, 1953; Gt. Heart award Variety Club Phila., 1968; Modern Medicine award, 1974; James D. Bruce award ACP, 1975; Thorvald Madsen award State Serum Inst. (Denmark), 1977; Maxwell Finland award Infectious Disease Soc.-Am., 1978; Disting. Alumni award U. Calif. Med. Sch., 1979; NIH fellow Nat. Inst. Med. Research, London, 1947-48. Master A.C.P.; hon. asso. fellow Am. Acad. Pediatrics; mem. Am. Soc. Clin. Investigation, Am. Epidemiol. Soc., Am. Pediatric Soc., Am. Soc. Virology (council 1983-84), Assn. Am. Physicians, Infectious Diseases Soc. Am (pres. 1974-75, council 1971-77), Soc. Epidemiologic Research, Pan Am. Med. Assn., Internat. Epidemiol. Assn., Royal Soc. Medicine (hon. mem. sect. epidemiology and preventive medicine), Nat. Acad. Scis., Conn. Acad. Sci. and Engring., European Assn. Against Virus Diseases, South African Soc. Pathologists (hon.). Home: 11 Autumn St New Haven CT 06511 Office: Yale U Sch Medicine 60 College St New Haven CT 06510

HORTON, ANN MITCHELL, health organization executive; b. Memphis, Apr. 14, 1949; d. Foy B. and Frances Louise (Mashbern) Mitchell; m. Steven Michael Horton, Dec. 20, 1970; children—Matthew William, Emily Frances. B.S., U. Tenn., 1970; M.A. in Speech Pathology, Memphis State U., 1972. postgrad. No. Ill. U., 1973, 74, Chgo. State U., 1974, Nat. Coll. Edn., 1975, U. Tenn., 1976, 84, U. Cin., 1984, 85. Lic. speech pathologist, Tenn., Ga.; cert. speech tchr., Tenn., Ill. Grad. asst. Memphis State U., Osceola, Ark., 1971-72, clin. supr., 1972; coordinator speech and lang. programs Northwest Suburban Spl. Edn. Coop., Palatine, Ill., 1972-75, coordinator reading programs, 1974-75; spl. services coordinator for handicapped children East Tenn. Children's Rehab. Ctr., Knoxville, 1975-76; speech pathologist cons. Nat. Health Corp., Athens, Tenn., 1976-83, eastern regional coordinator for communication disorders services, 1983-87, corp. coordinator communication disorders services, 1986—, founder Athens Out-Patient Rehab. Program. Contbr. articles to profl. publs. Mem. Nat. Assn. Female Execs., Nat. Health Corp. (co-chmn. quality assurance com. 1982—, co-chmn. supportive personnel com. 1985—), Am. Speech, Lang. and Hearing Assn. (supportive personnel com. 1987), Tenn. Speech and Hearing Assn. (peer rev. com. 1979—, adv. bd. to Blue Cross/Blue Shield 1980-84). Home: 404 Cutlas Rd Concord TN 37922 Office: Athens Health Care Ctr 214 Grove Ave Athens TN 37303

HORTON, ENOBIA LIGHTRAIN, recording studio executive; b. N.Y.C., July 4, 1949; d. Robert Strongfeather and Lorraine Anastasia (Ricks-Williams) Ziemoore; children: Quintin Joaquine II, Vanda Ronald III. Student, St. John's Coll., 1970-74, Rutgers U., 1974-75, Jersey City State Coll., 1976-78, Ala. Mil. Police Coll., 1978-80. With IBM, N.Y.C., 1974-75; mgr., field rep. Panasonic, Secaucus, N.J., 1976-78; exec. v.p. Sgt. Whales Recording Studio, Jersey City, 1982—. Mem. council East Orange (N.J.) Sch. Bd., 1980, Spring Dale Block Group, East Orange, 1980; mgr. mayoral campaign, East Orange, 1981. Served with U.S. Army, 1966-70, Vietnam. Mem. DAV (sec. local chpt. 1984). Democrat. Roman Catholic. Office: Sgt Whales Recording Studio 323 N Maple Ave East Orange NJ 07017

HORTON, FAYE T., small business owner; b. Winter Haven, Fla., Jan. 23, 1946; d. Maxwell W. Saxon and Jennie M. (Mathis) Burney; m. Norris H. Horton II, Mar. 13, 1971; children: Rodney D., Norris H. III. Cert., No. Jersey Secretarial Sch., Newark, 1964; student, South Cen. Community Coll., New Haven, Conn., 1973, So. Conn. State Coll., 1984. Adminstrn. cons. Aetna Life & Casualty, Trumbull, Conn., 1971-86; owner Norris-Faye Horton Enterprises, Inc., West Haven, 1986—. Author, editor: Maid Service, 1987. Mem. Elm City Club of Nat. Assn. Negro Bus. and Profl. Women's Assn. (sec. 1987—). Democrat. Baptist. Home: 20 Dix St West Haven CT 06516 Office: Horton Enterprises 422 Front Ave West Haven CT 06516

HORTON, GLADYS MELINDA, nurse; b. Peoria, Ill., Mar. 10, 1956; d. Joseph Herbert and Copprue (Meriam) H. Student, Loyola U., Chgo., 1975-77; BS in Nursing, Howard U., 1980. RN, D.C., Tex. Staff nurse Howard U. Hosp., Washington, 1980-81, Greater S.E. Community Hosp., Washington, 1981-82, 86—; cons. Carlton Med. Specialist, Houston, 1982-86; owner RN's Registry Tex., Houston, 1986—. Mem. Tex. Head Injury Found., Nat. Assn. for Female Execs., Chi Eta Phi (parlimentarian 1977-78). Democrat. Baptist. Home: 7116 Cipraino Springs Dr Lanham MD 20706

HORTON, JEANETTE, municipal government official; b. Paterson, N.J., Dec. 1, 1938; d. David and Mary (Carpenter) Potash; m. Troy Horton, May 14, 1985. Student, Broward Community Coll., 1970-72, Barry U., 1982, Fla. Atlantic U., 1983-84, Fla. State U., 1985. Cert. mcpl. clk., Fla. Bookkeeper Fla. Housewares, Miami, Fla., 1961-65; asst. to comptroller Gulf Stream Press, Miami, 1965-70; comptroller Chrysler Plymouth, Miami, Fla., 1970-75; municipal clk., fin. dir. Village of Biscayne Park, Fla., 1975—. Commr. Cooper City, Fla., 1971-73. Mem. Fla. Assn. City Clks. (scholarship 1985-87), Am. Bus. Women (Woman of Yr. award 1985, pres., v.p. 1985-87), Fla. Assn. City Clks. and Fin. Dirs., Bus. and Profl. Women (pres. 1981), Internat. Mcpl. Clks. Assn., Personnel Mgmt. Assn. Democrat. Roman Catholic. Home: 515 SW 61 Terr Hollywood FL 33023 Office: Village of Biscayne Park 640 NE 114th St Biscayne Park FL 33161

HOSAGE, CATHERINE MARYA, marketing professional, consultant; b. Bristol, Pa., Mar. 27, 1956; d. Paul John and Ann (Hoskey) H. BA in English, Temple U., 1979, MA in Geography, 1981; PhD in Geography, U. Western Ont., London, 1985. Editorial asst. Jour. History of Ideas, Phila., 1977-78; data analyst Energy Mgmt. Cons., Phila., 1980; teaching asst. Temple U., Phila., 1980-81; teaching/research asst. U. Western Ont., 1981-84; engr. ops. research Geog. Systems Inc., Andover, Mass., 1984-85; engr. Digital Equipment Corp., Merrimack, N.H., 1985-87; cons. tech. mktg. Digital Equipment Corp., Marlboro, Mass., 1987—; cons. Computer Mus., Boston, 1987—; researcher engring. Dartmouth Coll., Hanover, N.H., 1986—. Scholar Elizabeth Cadwalader Stoddart, 1974-78; U. Western Ont. scholar Ruse trave, 1984, spl. univ. in grad. studies, 1981-84, univ. admissions, 1981. Mem. Nat. Assn. Female Execs., Assn. Am. Geographers, Urban and Regional Info. Systems Assn., Inst. Mgmt. Scis. Home: 40-1 Nashua St Clinton MA 01510 Office: Digital Equipment Corp MRO3-1/Q17 3 Results Way Marlboro MA 01752-9103

HOSKEN, FRANZISKA PORGES, editor, writer; b. Vienna, July 12, 1919; d. Otto and Mary (Low) Porges; divorced; 3 children: John, Caroline, Andrew. BA, Smith Coll., 1940; MArch, Harvard U., 1944; postgrad. in city planning, MIT, 1963-66. Archtl. designer Skidmore Owings & Merrill, Chgo., 1946-47; owner Archtl. Color Slides, 1947; owner, v.p., treas. Hosken, Inc., 1948-52; designer Contract Interiors, Boston, 1958-59; interior designer M. Brown, Boston, 1958-61; pub., editor Women's Internat. Network News, 1975—; assoc. prof. urban studies Univ. Without Walls, Boston, 1971-74; devel. multi-media urban tchg. programs Harvard, MIT, 1970-71; interior design instr. Tufts U., 1971, Garland Coll., Boston, Cambridge Adult Edn. Ctr., 1958-61; cons. UN habitat confr. human settlements prepatory planning group, 1975, WHO, 1979; lectr. on women's devel. issues; correspondent-at-large Archl. Forum, 1971-74. Author: The Language of Cities, 1968, 2d edit., 1971, The Functions of Cities, 1972, The Kathmandu Valley Towns, 1974, International Directory of Womens Development Organizations, 1977, The Hosken Report: Genital/Sexual Mutilation of Females, 1979, 3d rev. edition, 83 (French transl.), The Facts and Proposals for Action— An Action Guide, 1980, The Childbirth Picture Book, 1981, The Universal Childbirth Picture Book, 1982; creator: (tape program) THe Changing Form and Functions of Cities, 1971, (multi-media programs) The Visual City, The Functions of Cities for Us, City Spaces Around the World, The Living City, The City at Night, Communication; contbr. articles to journals and mags. One women shows: (paintings) Boston City Hall Gallery, 1973, 74; group shows: MIT Hayden Gallery, Boston Visual Artists Union. Served with USCG Women's Res., 1944-45. Named Humanist Heroine Humanist Assn. U.S.A. and Can., 1987. Office: Womens Internat Network 187 Grant St Lexington MA 02173

HOSKINS, CHARLOTTE, psychologist; b. Melrose, Mass., Jan. 24, 1929; d. Roland A. and Effie C. Mangini; m. Robert Graham Hoskins; children: Susan, Pamela, Sarah, Timothy. Student, Pine Manor Coll., 1949-51; BS, Tufts U., 1951; MEd, Boston U., 1953. Lic. psychologist., Wash. Ednl. psychologist child study unit Kans. U., Kansas City, 1953-55; dir. Wellesley (Mass.) Devel. Reading and Counseling Ctr., 1957-60; psychologist Bellevue (Wash.) Sch. Dist., 1969—; cons. St. Christopher Sch. for Learning Disabled, Kent, Wash., 1978—. Mem. Wash. Assn. Sch. Psychologists, Wash. Assn. for Children with Learning Disabilities, King County Med. Aux. Republican. Home: 12425 NE 60th Kirkland WA 98033

HOSKINS, GERALDINE, hospital nursing administrator; b. Maysville, Ky., Aug. 15, 1940; d. Vernon Garrett Hoskins and Ivetti H. Hoskins Candy. Cert., Christ Hosp. Sch. Nursing, Cin., 1961; AA, U. Cin., 1975. Cert. nursing adminstr. Staff nurse, evening supr. Adams County Hosp., West Union, Ohio, 1961-63; staff nurse, then head nurse, then supr. Christ Hosp., Cin., 1963-69; asst. supr., then supr. med. nursing Bethesda Hosp. Oak, Cin., 1969-70; dir. emergency and intensive care Bethesda Hosp. North, Cin., 1970-71, mgr., 1971-72, asst. v.p., 1972-80; ind. contractor, securities salesperson, Fla., 1980-81; asst. v.p. Jewish Hosp., Cin., 1981, v.p., 1981—; ind. neighborhood nurse practitioner, Cin., 1972—; career counselor U. Cin.; mem. adv. bd. co-op. edn. dept. Coll. Mt. St. Joseph on the Ohio, 1982, mem. adv. bd. dept. bus., 1982-88; presenter in field. Mem. Am. Hosp. Assn., Ohio Hosp. Assn., Ohio Soc. Nursing Adminstrs., Cin. Soc. Hosp. Nursing Adminstrs., Nat. League Nursing, Ohio League Nursing, Ohio Coop. Edn. Assn. Republican. Avocations: travel, spectator and participatory sports, swimming, reading, music. Home: 6542 Kentuckyview Dr Cincinnati OH 45230 Office: Jewish Hosp Cin Inc 3200 Burnet Ave Cincinnati OH 45229

HOSMER, HILARY HOLDEN, computer systems educator; b. Worcester, Mass., Sept. 15, 1945; d. Humphrey Buttrick and Janet Wyatt (Pierpont) H.; m. Robert Burrell Holden, June 30, 1973; children: Katherine, Jonathan. BA, Bryn Mawr Coll., 1967; MEd, U. Mass., 1971. Vol. Peace Corps, Guiglo, Ivory Coast, 1967-69; race relations cons. Fed. Desegregation Ctr. Dade County Pub. Schs., Miami, Fla., 1970-71; edn. rep. Honeywell Inc., Wellesley, Mass., 1972-74; programmer Mass. Hosp. Assn., Burlington, 1974-75; cons. Blue Cross/Blue Shield Inc., Boston, 1975-76; edn. specialist Digital Equipment Corp., Maynard, Mass., 1976-77; edn. coordinator, cons. tng. mgr. Interactive Data/Chase Econometrics, Waltham, Mass., 1980-81; instr. Bentley Coll., Waltham, 1981-86; mem. tech. staff MITRE Corp., Bedford, Mass., 1986—; faculty cons., mem. steering com. Bay State Jr. Coll. Bus. Skills Tech. Writing Program, Waltham, 1983-85. Co-founder Students for Internat. Order and World Peace, 1966, Prospect Theater Workshop, 1970. Named citizen ambassador People to People, Europe, 1985, People's Republic China, 1986. Mem. AAAS, Am. Computer Mfrs., Computer Profls. for Social Responsibility, LWV, NOW. Democrat. Unitarian. Clubs: Bryn Mawr (Boston); Bedford Players (Mass.

HOSPITAL, JANETTE TURNER, writer, English language educator; b. Melbourne, Australia, Nov. 12, 1942; came to U.S., 1967, to Can., 1971; d. Adrian Charles and Elsie Evelyn (Morgan) Turner; m. Clifford George Hospital, Feb. 5, 1965; children: Geoffrey, Cressida. BA in English, U. Queensland, Brisbane, Australia, 1964; MA in English, Queen's U., Kingston, Ont., Can., 1973, postgrad., 1974-75. Cert. tchr., Australia, Ont. High sch. tchr., State Dept. Edn., Queensland, 1963-66; librarian Harvard U., Cambridge, Mass., 1967-71; teaching fellow Queen's U., 1971-74; lectr. in English lit. fed. penitentiaries, Kingston, 1975-76; writer, 1976—; lectr. lit. and writers, workshops various univs., 1982—; vis. writer-in-residence MIT, Cambridge, Mass., 1985-87; novels include: The Ivory Swing (Seal First Novel award), 1982, The Tiger in the Tiger Pit, 1983, Borderline, 1985, Charades, 1987; short stories include: Waiting (Atlantic First award Atlantic Monthly), 1978, Our Little Chamber Concerts (1st prize in mag. fiction Found. for Advancement Can. Letters), 1982, Dislocations, 1986, others in U.S., Can., U.K., Australia, 1976—. Named One of Can.'s Top Ten Younger Writers, 1986; recipient Short Story prize Ladies Home Jour., 1986, CBC Literary prize, 1986; Commonwealth scholar, 1961; Ont. grad. fellow, 1972-73; Can. Council doctoral fellow, 1974-75. Mem. Can. Writers Union, Authors League Am., P.E.N. Democrat. Methodist. Office: care Charlotte Sheedy Lit Agt 145 W 86th St New York NY 10024

HOSTETLER, DONNA FORDYCE, corporate administrator; b. Cleve., Oct. 15, 1950; d. Donald Hugh and Ethel Marie (Duncan) Fordyce; m. J. Todd Hostetler. BA, Coll. Wooster, 1972; MBA, Bowling Green (Ohio) State U., 1982. Sec. Mt. Sinai Hosp., Cleve., 1972-73; dir. food services Shamrock Systems, Inc., Atlanta, 1973-79; office mgr. Norrell Services, Inc., Lima, Ohio, 1979-80; systems cons. Ohio Citizens Bank, Toledo, 1983-84, officer productivity, 1984-86; adminstr. The Eye Ctr. Toledo, 1986—; bd. dirs. Crisis Pregnancy Ctr., Toledo. Mem. Internat. Assn Quality Circles (founding v.p. Toledo area chpt. 1985-86, pres. 1986—), Am. Soc. Ophthalmic Adminstrs., Med. Group Mgmt. Assn. Republican. Home: 333 W Fifth St Perrysburg OH 43551 Office: The Eye Ctr Toledo 3915 Sunforest Toledo OH 43623

HOSTETLER, JACQUELINE MICHELE, auditor; b. Oakland, Md., Oct. 8, 1955; d. Donald Jacqueline (Clerget) H.; m. Dennis F. DeBiasio, May 6, 1983 (div. Apr. 1986). Student in adminstrn., Alleghany Coll. Various clerical positions Blue Cross of Western Pa., Pitts., 1974-79, unit leader, 1979-83, internal audit clk., 1983-85, jr. auditor, 1985-87, bus. cons., 1987—, v.p. U.S. Olympic Team sponsorship, 1987—. Vol. Pitts., 1986-87, Spl. Olympics, Pitts., 1987. Mem. Inst. Internal Auditors. Democrat. Home: 3016 Circle Dr Apt #2 Pittsburgh PA 15227 Office: Blue Cross of Western PA 1 Smithfield St Pittsburgh PA 15222

HOSTETTER, MARGARET JONES, retirement community ofcl.; b. Louisville, Feb. 4, 1946; d. Harry W. and Doris (Moreland) Jones; B.A., Ind. U., 1978; postgrad. U. Tenn., 1978-80; m. Andrew Stuart Hostetter, Nov. 9, 1973 (dec.); 1 son, Erik Stuart. Nursing personnel hiring ofcl. Americana Healthcare, Indpls., 1976-78; mgr. Harding House Condominium, Nashville, 1978-79; dir. Deer Lake Retirement Community, Nashville, 1979—. Sec. Foster Grandparent Adv. Council, Social Action Group on Aging of Nat. Council Aging. Active ARC, Mental Health, Nat. Alliance Family Life, PTA, Am. Cancer Soc. Cert. nursing home adminstr. Mem. Bellevue Area C. of C., Am. Assn. Ret. Persons, Tenn. Health Care Assn., Nat. Citizens Coalition for Nursing Home Reform, Nat. Assn. Female Execs. Methodist. Home: 6319 Charlotte Park Ave #B-6 Nashville TN 37209 Office: 6319 Charlotte Ave Nashville TN 37209

HOSTETTER, SHARON SMITH (SHERRY), marketing professional; b. N.Y.C., Nov. 28, 1944; d. Edwin Ely and Priscilla McLintock (Elgas) Smith; m. Henry C. Barnum, Nov. 19, 1966 (div. June 1974); children: Scott C., Todd R.; m. Joseph Arthur Hostetter, Sept. 13, 1980; 1 child, Justin A.; stepchild, William C. BS in Edn., Potsdam (N.Y.) Coll., 1966; cert. in mktg. mgmt., U. Rochester, N.Y., 1976. Cert. elem. and secondary tchr., N.Y. Tchr. elem. and jr. high sch. Corning (N.Y.) Sch. Dist., 1966-68, Rochester Sch. Dist., 1972-74; with customer services dept. Photographic Scis., Inc., Webster, N.Y., 1975-78, mgr. mktg. services, 1978-80; tech. writer, CAI Butler Co. subs. Xerox Corp., Rochester, 1980; copywriter pub. relations dept. Rochester Gas and Electric Co., 1980-84, supr. info. services, 1984-86; gen. mgr. mktg. Rochester Gas and Electric Corp., 1987-88; agt. N.Y. Life, Rochester, 1986-87, registered rep., 1986-88; cons. in field. Producer slide show Energy: Where Do We Go From Here, 1982, Alzheimer's Disease, 1983 (nat. distbn. award 1983). Coach Fairpost Little League, Fairport, N.Y., 1983, 84; dir. pub. relations Rochester chpt. United Negro Coll. Fund, 1982; cons. Women's Career Ctr., Rochester, 1982—; media cons. Alzheimer's Assn., Rochester, 1982—; bd. dir. Legal Aid Soc., Rochester, 1982—, Rochester Women's Network, 1983-85. Named Presdl. Vol. Yr., 1984. Mem. Soc. Tech. Communication (achievement award 1982), U.S. Register Am. Writers, Nat. Assn. Life Underwriters, Rochester Life Underwriters, Downtown Rochester C. of C. (bd. dirs., 1981—, art design/copy brochure Simpson excellence award 1983, downtown council vol. yr. 1986). Home: 4 Gateway Rd Fairport NY 14450 Office: Rochester Gas and Electric Corp 89 East Ave Rochester NY 14649

HOTALING, DENISE LOWERY, chief clinical dietitian; b. Ogdensburg, N.Y., May 11, 1957; d. Vernon H. and Barbara June (Gibson) Lowery; m. Hilton Herschel Hotaling Jr., Oct. 14, 1949; 1 child, Brandon Lee. Student, U. N.C., Greensboro, 1975-76; BS, SUNY, Plattsburg, 1979. Registered dietician. Dietetic intern Office of Mental Health, Albany, N.Y., 1980-81; clin. dietitian St. Lawrence Psychiat. Ctr., Ogdensburg, 1981-82; chief clin. dietitian United Helpers Mgmt. Co., Inc., Ogdensburg, 1981—; cons. speaker Cope, Viewpoint Consortiums, Ogdensburg, 1985—. Bd. dirs., sec. Village of Morristown (N.Y.) Library, 1985—; vol. instr. 4-H Club, Morristown, 1983-84. Mem. Am. Dietetic Assn. (recognized young dietitian N.Y. chpt. 1986), Cen. N.Y. Dietetic Assn. (bd. dirs. 1983—, Seaway Valley subchpt. coordinator 1983-86), N.Y. State Nutrition Council. Office: United Helpers Mgmt Co 732 Ford St Ogdensburg NY 13669

HOTALING, LESLIE ANN, travel company executive; b. Beaumont, Tex., Feb. 7, 1946; d. Edgar Lafayette and Stella Mae (Richardson) Brookins; m. Dale Conrad Clarke, Sept. 10, 1965 (div. 1970); 1 child, Sean Dylan; m. Larry William Hotaling, Mar. 27, 1982. Student, Avarette Coll., 1965-66, Lamar U., 1970-76. With sales dept. Houston Nat. Gas Corp., 1970-76, Entex, Inc., Houston, 1976-77; office mgr. Greyhound Conv. Services, Atlanta, 1976-79; conv. coordinator Hargrove, Inc., Atlanta, 1979-81; asst. dir. Nat. Kidney Found., Albany, N.Y., 1982-85; gen. mgr. Leprechaun Tours, Fishkill, N.Y., 1986—. Author Nat. Kidney Found. newsletter, 1982, Leprechaun Leader newsletter, 1987. Active fund raising United Way, Albany, 1987. Mem. Profl. Staff Assn., Nat. Kidney Found. Home: Rd 2 Box 42 Fox Hill Rd Wallkill NY 12589 Office: Leprechaun Tours Route 9 Dutchess Mall Fishkill NY 12524

HOTALING, TERRI LYNN, comptroller; b. Albany, N.Y., Apr. 8, 1959; d. Stanley Howard and Marjorie Anna (Peter) H. AA, SUNY, Cobelskill, 1979. Bookkeeper Impres T-Shirt Art, Cobelskill, 1979-80; asst. controller Palm Beach (Fla.) Hilton, 1980-83; controller La Famiglia Rest, Palm Beach, 1983-84; comptroller Lifter's Marco Polo Hotel, North Miami, Fla., 1984—. Mem. Internat. Assn. Hospitality Accts. Home: 5144 NW 6th St Delray Beach FL 33445 Office: Marco Polo Hotel 19201 Collins Ave North Miami FL 33160

HOTCHKISS, JUDITH WRIGHT (JUDY), small business owner, writer; b. Dania, Fla., Feb. 16, 1951; d. James Lewis Jr. and Dorothy June (Gillette) Wright; m. Robert Paul Hotchkiss, Aug. 7, 1971. Student, Mercer U., 1969-70, Va. Poly. Inst. and State U., 1970-71, Westfield State U., 1971; BJ, Seattle U., 1973; postgrad., Ga. State U., 1980-81. Lifestyle reporter New London Day newspaper, New London, Conn., 1974-75; writer, editor Equifax Inc., Atlanta, 1976-78; research assoc., writer Atlanta Jour. and Constn., 1978-81; writer, editor News/Sun Pub., Decatur, Ga., 1981-84; mng. editor Eason Publs./Creative Loafing, Atlanta, 1984; prin. Smith & Hotchkiss, Atlanta, 1984-86, Hotchkiss & Randall, Ltd., Atlanta, 1986-87, The Write Co., Atlanta, 1987—; freelance writer So. Homes mag., Norcross, Ga., 1986—. Author Inman Park Cookbook, 1980. Chmn. com. Inman Park Festival, Atlanta, 1979-84, chair printing div., 1984-87; co-chair Citizens Against the Piggyback Noise, Atlanta, 1987—; landscaper Atlanta and Edgewood Street Railway Co., 1986—. Recipient Merit award Internat. Assn. Bus. Communicators, 1979. Mem. Garden Writers Am. Clubs: Hurt Planters, Inman Park Restoration. Office: The Write Co 881 Ponce de Leon Ave NE Atlanta GA 30306

HOTCHNER, BEVERLY JUNE, psychologist; b. East St. Louis, Ill., July 13, 1928; d. Benjamin E. and Jennie Louise (Komar) Novack; m. Selwyn Ross Hotchner, Nov. 22, 1951; children: Kirby Ross, Bradley Ross. BS, U. Ill., 1950; PhD, Washington U., 1972. Lic. psychologist, Mo.; cert. sex therapist, educator, Mo. Asst. prof. dept. behavioral sci. So. Ill. U. Sch. Dental Medicine, Edwardsville, 1973-75, acting chairperson dept. behavioral sci., 1974-75; founder, exec. dir. Ctr. Human Concern, St. Louis, 1975-86; pvt. practice psychology St. Louis, 1979—; adj. instr. Wash. U., 1970-84; cons. St. Luke's Hosp., St. Louis, 1979—. Mem. Am. Psychol. Assn., Mo. Psychol. Assn., St. Louis Psychol. Assn., Am. Assn. Sex. Educators, Cons., Therapists (tng. dir. 1976-77, chairperson Plainstate region 1976-78, mem. nat. sex therapy cert. com. 1977-78), Soc. Sci. Study Sex (nat. bd. dirs. 1987), Am. Assn. Marriage and Family Therapy, Phi Beta Kappa, Alpha Lamba Delta, Kappa Delta Pi. Home and Office: 7206 Cornell Saint Louis MO 63130

HOTES, ELIZABETH ANN, heavy equipment and land development company executive; b. Birmingham, Ala., Oct. 4, 1918; d. Richard and Florence (Ford) Oswald; m. Douglas N. Hotes; children—Richard, Elizabeth, John, Florence, Douglas. Student Hollins Coll., 1937-39, Phila. Sch. Indsl. Art, 1939-40, Art Inst., Chgo., 1941. Engring. draftsman Coast and Geodetic Survey, Washington, 1941-44; cartographer Aero Service, Phila., 1946-48; draftsman, artist C.E., Anchorage, 1968-71; sec., treas. T.E.R.R.A., Inc., Anchorage, 1971—; dir. Amstan, Inc., Anchorage, 1971-87, pres., 1980—; pres. Alaska Contracting Co. Inc., Anchorage. Home: 1900 W Hoteco Ave Anchorage AK 99502 Office: Amstan Inc PO Box 6046 Anchorage AK 99502

HOTING, SHARON KAY, software engineer; b. Glendale, Calif., May 7, 1945; d. Allen Alfred and Katherine Marian (Dressler) H.; 1 child, Shaun Allen. BA, UCLA, 1967, MS, 1972. Mem. tech. staff Logicon, San Pedro, Calif., 1967-73, Sci. Applications Inc., La Jolla, Calif., 1973-75; project leader City of Tucson, 1975-77; program mgr. Bell Tech. Ops., Tucson, 1977-86; mgr. engring. support The Singer Co., Tucson, 1986—. Mem. Tech. Mktg. Soc. Am., Old Crows. Democrat. Methodist. Home: 5520 N Entrada Quince Tucson AZ 85718 Office: The Singer Co 6365 E Tanque Verde Rd Tucson AZ 85715

HOTTENSTEIN, EVELYN JEANETTE KENNY, communications executive; b. Glasgow, Mont., Mar. 4, 1948; d. Daniel Patrick and Miriam (Phelan) Kenny; m. Glenn Hottenstein, 1969 (div.); children: Erin, Kimberly. BA, Carroll Coll., 1970-72. Cert. tchr. English tchr. Mont. State Sch. for Girls, Helena, 1970-72; exec. dir. Camp Fire Council, Helena, 1972-73; mgr. exec. orientation program Camp Fire, Inc., Englewood, Colo., 1974-76; owner, mgr. H&G Devel Co., Cheyenne, Wyo., 1976-78; owner Lifework Assocs., Westminster, Colo., 1978—; prin. Pub. Speaking for the Profl., Denver, 1979—, pres., 1979—; pres. The Ctr. for Intercultural Communication, Denver, 1987—; pub. speaker, instr. U. Colo., Denver, 1982—. cons. Assn. for Vol. Adminstrn.; mem. Gov.'s Commn. on Status of Women, Mont., 1973-79; bd. dirs. Unitarian Universalist service com. Mem. Am. Soc. Tng. and Devel. (career devel. tng. group), Nat. Assn. Women Bus. Owners, Nat. Speakers Assn. Office: Pub Speaking for Profl 1776 Lincoln #614 Denver CO 80203

HOUCK, LINDA ROBINSON, home economist; b. Wadesboro, N.C., Sept. 30, 1949; d. George Jackson and Mattie Lois (Marsh) Robinson; m. Jacob Albert Houck, May 31, 1970. BSHE, U. N.C.-Greensboro, 1971; MEd, Coll. William and Mary, 1978. Extension agt. in home econs. Va. Coop. Extension Service, Hampton, 1971—. Telephone crisis counselor, small group facilitator Contact Peninsula, Newport News, Va., 1978—. Mem. Am. Home Econs. Assn. (cert.), Nat. Assn. Extension Home Economists (Disting. Service award 1986), Peninsula Nutrition Council (chmn. 1984-86), Am. Assn. Counseling and Devel., Peninsula Women's Network. Avocation: reading. Home: 3 Redman Ct Hampton VA 23669 Office: Va Coop Extension Service 1320 LaSalle Ave Room 6 Hampton VA 23669

HOUGAN, ANGELA KAYE, small business owner; b. Olney, Ill., Mar. 8, 1949; d. Bobbie Dale and Elizabeth Ann (Morrison) Hayes; m. Ronald Wayne Green, Aug. 24, 1968 (div. Feb. 1972); m. Robert Martin Hougan, Aprl 2, 1983; step-children: John Edward, Debra Kim, Susan Marie, Kellie Diane. Student, Golden West Coll., 1967—; AA, Orange Coast Coll., 1977; student, Swensen's Tng. Sch., 1986. Acct. Santa Fe Engring. and Cons. Co., Orange, Calif., 1971-82; owner, pres. Osage Engring. and Cons. Co., Placentia, Calif., 1982—; owner Sapphire Imports Co., Santa Ana, Calif., 1980-85; acct. Mission Viejo (Calif.) Co., 1985-86; owner Swensen's Ice Cream Parlour, Anaheim Hills, Calif., 1986-87; fin. advisor Nat. Egyptian Bakeries (joint venture with Osage Engring. and Alfa Internat.), Cairo, 1987—; cons. Team Internat. Ltd. Riyadh, Saudi Arabia 1981-83, Kuwait Sci. Found., Alhamadi 1982; dir. Osage Internat. Inc., Riyadh 1982—. Mem. Orange County Draft Bd. #158 1982-86, Mission Viejo 1987. Mem. Am. Soc. Military Engrs., Assn. Gen. Contractors, ASCE. Republican. Clubs: Desk and Derrick Orange County (chmn. speakers bur. 1978-83), Riyadh's Womens. Home: 121 Casas Bellas Lane PO Box 1408 Santa Teresa NM 88008

HOUGH, JANET GERDA CAMPBELL, research company scientist; b. Glen Ridge, N.J., Dec. 22, 1948; d. Ralph William and Gerda Lydia (Baarck) Campbell; m. John Harrison Hough, Oct. 1, 1966 (div.); 1 child, Laura Leigh. Student Temple U. and Tyler Sch. Art, Phila., 1970-72, Pa. Acad. Fine Arts, 1972, Camden County Coll., Blackwood, N.J., 1973-75; B.S., Thomas Jefferson U., 1977. Lab. animal technician Inst. Med. Research, Camden, N.J., 1972-75; research technician dept. biochemistry Thomas Jefferson U., Phila., 1976, phlebotomist, hematology technician, 1976-78, med. technologist spl. hematology, 1978-79, research technician dept. med. genetics, 1979-80; micromedic Rohm & Haas, Horsham, Pa., 1981-83; micromedic Internat. Clin. Nuclear Inc., Costa Mesa, Calif., and Horsham, 1983—. Collaborator, editor textbook Hematology for Medical Technologists, 1984; poet, illustrator Thought Progressions, 1984. Republican. Roman Catholic. Avocations: drawing, painting, long-distance walking. Office: Micromedic Systems Inc 102 Witmer Rd Horsham PA 19044

HOUGHTALING, PAMELA ANN, business machines company executive; b. Catskill, N.Y., July 8, 1949; d. Stanley Kenneth and Mildred Edythe (Fyfe) H. BA, Princeton U., 1971; cert. Russian Inst., Columbia U., 1976, M in Internat. Affairs, 1974. Internat. relations analyst Library of Congress, Washington, 1974-75, U.S. GAO, Washington, 1976-77; pub. affairs specialist IBM Corp., Washington, 1977-81; sr. external programs analyst IBM World Trade Americas/Far East Corp., North Tarrytown, N.Y., 1981-82; mgr. labor affairs/bus. practices U.S. Council Internat. Bus., N.Y.C., 1982-84; communications specialist-advt. IBM Corp., Boca Raton, Fla., 1984-86; staff communications specialist IBM Corp., White Plains, N.Y., 1986—. Mem. Women in Communications, Nat. Trust Historic Preservation, Nature Conservancy, Am. Mktg. Assn.

HOUGHTON, JUDITH DEAN, choreographer, consultant; b. Rawlins, Wyo., Dec. 4, 1939; d. Irvin C. and Dorothy H. (Ingram) Houghton. Student U. Tex., Austin, 1957-59. Cert. meeting profl. Faculty dance dept., So. Meth., U., Dallas, 1964-65; choreographer numerous themes parks, U.S., 1965-76, Miss Teenage America telecast, Dallas, 1964-80, Miss U.S.A. and Miss Universe Inc., telecasts, 1977—, numerous civic groups, Dallas, 1954—; sr. ptnr. Charles Meeker, Jr. and Assoc., Dallas, 1967-76; cons., dir. corp. meetings, exec. producer Dr Pepper Co., Seven-Up Co., Dallas, 1964—, producer centennial events, 1984-85; ptnr., choreographer Charlie's Place, Fort Worth, 1973-76, Incredible Charlie's Dinner Theatre, Dallas, 1976-78. Active Nat. Cheerleaders Assn., Dallas area orgns., 1965—. Mem. Meeting Planners Internat. (pub. relations com. 1982-84, edn. com. 1985-86, bd. dirs. 1986-87, v.p. pub. relations 1987-88). Republican. Author: Miss Teenage America Tells How to Make Good Things Happen, 1976.

HOUGHTON-ALICO, DOANN, communications and information executive; b. Mt. Kisco, N.Y., Aug. 3, 1940; d. John and Stella (Houghton) Alico; m. C. Samuel Haines III, Feb. 6, 1960 (div. 1974); children: Daraya Haines Haddock, Charles Samuel Haines IV, Peter John Haines. BA, Cedar Crest Coll., 1971; postgrad., Poly. Inst., N.Y., 1986. Legis. analyst Environ. Action, Washington, 1971-73; editor, pub. Deep Creek Rev., Telluride, Colo., 1974-75; cons. Telluride and Denver, Colo., 1975-79; pres. Tech. Info. Assocs. Inc., Denver, 1980—, adj. prof. Poly. Inst. N.Y., Bklyn., 1985-86. Author: Creating Computer Software User Guides: From Manuals to Menus, 1985; Alcohol Fuels: Policies, Production, and Potential, 1982 (Top Hand award Colo. Authors League 1982); also articles; co-originator (film) What Can I Tell You?, 1979 (Red Ribbon award, 1979). Exec. Dialogue Centennial C. of C., Littleton, Colo., 1984-85; commr. Commn. on the Status of Women, Denver, 1976-77. Mem. Human Factors Soc. (assoc.), Assn. Computing Machinery, Soc. Tech. Communication, Colo. Authors League, Computer Soc. IEEE. Club: Sporting. Office: Tech Info Assocs Inc 600 S Cherry St Suite 1100 Denver CO 80222

HOUGLAN, SANDRA L., nurse; b. Denver, Mar. 27, 1950; d. Kenneth E. and Jean E. (Vandenberg) Whitlow; m. Roger D. Houglan, Aug. 18, 1973 (div. 1987). BS in Nursing with honors, U. Colo., Denver, 1974, MS in Nursing with honors, 1977. RN. Charge nurse Gen. Rose Meml. Hosp. & Med. Ctr., Denver, 1974-75; obstet. team nurse U. Colo. Med. Ctr., Denver, 1975-77; asst. prof., clin. specialist Sch. of Nursing Oreg. Health Scis. U., Portland, 1977-81; instr. dept. continuing edn. Oreg. Health Scis. U., Portland, 1982—; sr. research assoc. sch. nursing, 1985-86, asst. dean for student affairs, 1987—; ptnr. JNS Ednl. Perspectives, Beaverton, Oreg., 1982—; chmn. pub. health adv. bd. Oreg. State Health Div., Portland, 1983—; edn. leader obstet. nursing tour, Peoples Republic of China and the Philippines, 1982. Campaign staff Donna Zajone for Sec. of State, Portland, 1984.. Mem. NOW, Oreg. Nurses Assn. (membership services coordinator 1981-83, pres. 1986—), LWV, Sigma Theta Tau. Democrat. Home: 19865 SW Imperial Dr Aloha OR 97006 Office: Oreg Health Scis U Sch Nursing SW Sam Jackson Park Rd Portland OR 97201

HOUSE, CARLEEN FAYE, director management information systems; b. Sparta, Wis., Dec. 14, 1950; d. Clarence Frederick and Ida Mae (Murdock) Anderson; m. Gregory Allen House, Aug. 25, 1984. BS, U. Wis., 1978, MS, 1982. Cert. engr., Wis. Prin. Customized Research and Design, 1979-81; sci. tchr. Wis. Ednl. System, 1981-82; systems engr. Hewlett Packard, 1982-83, systems analyst, 1983-86, MIS dir., 1986-88, project dir., 1988—; chief exec. officer House Research, 1986—; pres. Chisago County Office Supply, Chisago City, Minn., 1988—; dir. devel. House Properties One, 1985—; pres. HPII Ltd. Partnership, 1986—. Mem. Women in Engring., Aircraft Owners and Pilots Assn., Omicron Nu, League of Women Voters. Republican. Lutheran. Home and Office: 10579 Point Pleasant Rd Chisago City MN 55013

HOUSE, CAROL ANN, communications executive; b. Chgo., Jan. 30, 1945; d. Adell and Ruby Lee (Barrett) Childress; m. Henry Arthur House, Jan. 2, 1965 (div. 1976); 1 child, Danielle. BS, DePaul U., 1966; M in Mgmt., Northwestern U., 1982. Prodn. mgr. Selling Areas Mktg. Inc. div. Time Inc., Chgo., 1968-80, staff devel. mgr., 1980-81; v.p. human resources Time Telemarketing Inc. div. Time Inc., Chgo., 1981—; relocation project human resource dir. Time Inc., Chgo., 1986—. Coordinator sponser INROADS, Chgo., 1987—. Mem. Am. Soc. Tng. and Devel. (chairperson nat. com. 1985-86), Am. Mgmt. Assn., Am. Compensation Assn., Women's Direct Response, Direct Mktg. Assn., Affirmative Action Assn., Nat. Urban League. Office: Time Inc 414 N Orleans Suite 301 Chicago IL 60610

HOUSE, KAREN ELLIOTT, editor, reporter; b. Matador, Tex., Dec. 7, 1947; d. Ted and Bailey Elliott; m. Arthur House, Apr. 5, 1975 (div. Sept. 1983); m. Peter Kann, June 4, 1984. B.J., U. Tex., 1970; postgrad. (fellow) Inst. Politics, Harvard U., 1982. Education reporter Dallas Morning News, 1970-71, with Washington bur., 1971-74; regulatory correspondent Wall Street Jour., Washington, 1974-75, energy and agr. correspondent, 1975-78, diplomatic correspondent, 1978-84; fgn. editor Wall Street Jour., N.Y.C., 1984—; bd. dirs. Council Fgn. Relations; mem. dean's adv. council U. Tex. Sch. Journalism, Austin, 1985; mem. adv. bd. Ctr. Strategic Internat. Studies; mem. vis. com. Harvard U. Ctr. Internat. Affairs. Recipient Edward Weintal award for Diplomatic Reporting, Georgetown U., 1980-81, Edwin Hood award for Diplomatic Reporting Nat. Press Club, 1982, Disting. Achievement award U. So. Calif., 1984, Pulitzer prize for Internat. Reporting, 1984, Overseas Press Club Bob Considine award, 1984, 88. Home: 47 Westcott Rd Princeton NJ 08540 Office: Wall Street Jour 200 Liberty St New York NY 10281

HOUSE, LISA ELIZABETH, advertising account executive; b. Hartford, Conn., Sept. 16, 1958; d. Richard Bailey and Ruth (Broman) House; m. Michael Anthony Stanicak, July 18, 1981 (div.). Cert. Katharine Gibbs Sch., 1978, Life Mgmt. Inst. 1977; student Boston U., 1978-80; U. Hartford, 1987—. Policy analyst Security Conn. Life Ins. Co., Avon, 1975-77; sr. adminstrv. asst. Polaroid Corp., Cambridge, Mass., 1978-80; acct. mgr. Keiler Advt., Farmington, Conn., 1980—. Mem. Ad Club of Greater Hartford, Women in Communications. Lutheran. Home: 243 Brickyard Rd Farmington CT 06032

HOUSEMAN, ANN ELIZABETH LORD, educational administrator, state official; b. New Orleans, Mar. 21, 1936; d. Noah Louis and Florence Marguerite (Coyle) Lord; m. Evan Kenny Houseman, June 25, 1960; children—Adrienne Ann, Jeannette Louise, Yvonne Elizabeth. B.A., Barnard Coll., 1957; M.A., Columbia Univ., 1962; Ph.D., Univ. Del., 1969. Cert. elem. prin., secondary sch. prin. State supr. reading Dept. Pub. Instrn., Del., 1977-79; prin. M.L. King, Jr. Elem. Sch., Wilmington, Del., 1979-80; adminstr., exec. dir. Del. State Arts Council, Dover 1980-84; acting dir. Div. Hist. and Cultural Affairs State of Del., Wilmington, 1983-84, prin. P.S. du Pont Intermediate Sch., Wilmington, 1984—; dir. Mid-Atlantic State Arts Consortium, Balt., 1980-84. Mem. adv. bd. Rockwood Mus., Wilmington, 1981—; bd. dirs. Opera Del., Wilmington, 1984—, Del. Theatre Co., Wilmington, 1984—. Contbr. articles to profl. jours. Mem. Diamond State Reading Assn. (pres. 1977-78), Psi Chi, Phi Delta Kappa. Republican. Presbyterian. Office: PS du Pont Intermediate Sch 34th and Van Buren Sts Wilmington DE 19802

HOUSEMAN, CLARE ANITA, nursing educator; b. Cheverly, Md., Feb. 28, 1948; d. Anthony Burnell and Phyllis Lavinia (Butler) Woodell; m. David L. Houseman, June 7, 1969 (div. 1976); m. Igor Magier, Dec. 26, 1980; 1 child, Gregory Ian Magier. Student, Mary Washington Coll., 1966-68; BS, U. Va., 1970; M of Nursing with honors, U. Fla., 1972; PhD, U. Tex., 1985. RN, Va., Fla., Pa. From staff to head nurse U. Va. Hosp., Charlottesville, 1970-71; instr. U. Fla., Gainesville, 1972-73; therapist Mental Health/Mental Retardation Services of Chester County, West Chester, Pa., 1974-75; unit adminstr. Human Services, Inc., West Chester, 1975-77; from instr. to assoc. prof. Sch. Nursing Old Dominion U., Norfolk, Va., 1978—, dir. grad. program, 1987—; cons. Human Resource Inst., Norfolk, 1978-81, Community Mental Health, Norfolk, 1981, 84-87; therapist Psychiat. Assocs. Tidewater, Norfolk, 1983—. Mem. edn. com. Cancer Network, Norfolk, 1974-80. Served to maj. USAR, 1976—. Decorated Gen. Thomas J. Stewart medal Army N.G., 1977. Mem. Am. Nurses Assn. (cert. clin. specialist in psychiat. nursing, CEARP com. 1980-81), Va. Soc. Profl. Nurses (bd. dirs. 1986—), Am. Orthopsychiatirc Assn., Mental Health Assn. (bd. dirs. 1983-84), Sigma Theta Tau, Phi Kappa Phi (officer pub. relations 1985-86). Home: 1223 N Fairwater Dr Norfolk VA 23508 Office: Coll Health Scis Old Dominion U Norfolk VA 23508

HOUSEMAN, MARY S., social services administrator; b. Grand Rapids, Mich., Oct. 23, 1947; d. Walter and Jeanette (Haueman) H. BA in Math., Calvin Coll., 1969; MS in Rehabs. in Adminstrn. with distinction, DePaul U., 1980. Tchr. U.S. Peace Corps, Ethiopia, 1969-71; sales mgr. H. Eikenhout & Sons, Inc., Grand Rapids, 1971-73; dir. Christian Reformed World Relief Com. Jordan Rehab. Program, Amman, 1973-77, Chgo. Assn. for Retarded Citizens Southwest Tng. Ctr., 1978-85; exec. dir. Sunshine House, Inc., Chgo., 1985—. Mem. Social Concerns Assn. Democrat. Home: Werik Ctr 25 E Washington St Chicago IL 60602

HOUSER, LAINE ELIZABETH, project manager, designer; b. Los Angeles, Sept. 28, 1954; d. Wastell Hodgson and Barbara Murrison (Dunn) Dunham; m. Thomas Lloyd Houser, Dec. 15, 1973 (div. 1983); 1 dau., Katrina Leigh. BA, Art Ctr. Coll. Design, Pasadena, 1981. Project designer The Only Co., North Hollywood, Calif., 1981-82, AVG Prodns., Valencia, Calif., 1982, Fredric Hope & Assocs., Venice, Calif., 1982-84, Knott's Berry Farm, Buena Park, Calif., 1985-87, prodn. designer Walt Disney Imagineering, Glendale, Calif., 1987—; cons. Introvision Co., Broggie Elliott Animation, REC, Inc.; ptnr. The Works Partnership, Long Beach, Calif., 1983-85; cons. J.K. Architects, 1988—. Mem. Nat. Assn. Female Execs., KBF Mgmt. Club. Democrat. Presbyterian.

HOUSEWORTH, LAURA JENNINGS, lawyer; b. Kansas City, Kans., Mar. 22, 1927; d. Frank Harvey and Lucile (Pollock) Jennings; m. Richard Court Houseworth, Nov. 1, 1952; children—Louise, Lucile, Court II. B.A. magna cum laude, Lake Forest Coll., 1949; M.Ed., U. Mo., 1951; J.D., Ariz. State U., 1975. Bar: Ariz. 1975. Nat. rep. Chi Omega, Cin., 1949-50; asst. dean women U. Kans., Lawrence, 1951-52; dep. county atty. Maricopa County, Phoenix, 1975—, juvenile div., 1979—, sr. trial atty., asst. supr. juvenile div., 1985—, extradition atty., 1987—, grand jury atty., 1987—; lectr. Nat. Family Support Assn., San Diego, 1977; arbitrator Superior Ct., 1986; judge pro tem Ariz. Ct. Appeals, 1986. Founding bd., pres. Vol. Bur., Tucson, 1969; founding bd. Girl's Club Tucson, 1970; founding bd., 1st v.p. Crisis Nursery, Phoenix, 1978; exec. bd. United Way, Legal Aid, Family Service. Mem. Maricopa County Bar Assn., ABA, Am. Trial Lawyers Assn., Ariz. Women's Lawyers Assn., Ariz. Acad. Republican. Episcopalian. Club: Jr. League Phoenix. Home: Phoenix Towers 2201 N Central Ave 5F Phoenix AZ 85004 Office: Maricopa County Atty 101 W Jefferson St Phoenix AZ 85003

HOUSKA, MARY DITTMER, economics educator; b. Amityville, N.Y., Sept. 20, 1932; s. Bradford and Mary Rose (Umhauer) Dittmer; m. Charles Robert Houska, Aug. 15, 1953; children—Catherine, Robert, Susan. B.S. in Econs., Simmons Coll., 1954; Ph.D. in Econs., MIT, 1963. Asst. to div. controller Dewey & Almy Chem. Co. div. W. R. Grace & Co., Cambridge, Mass., 1954-57; asst. prof., chmn. dept. econs. Radford Coll. (Va.), 1964-66; asst. prof. Hollins Coll. (Va.), 1966-72, assoc. prof., 1972—. Mem. Nat. Council AAUP, Am. Econs. Assn., So. Econs. Assn., Indsl. Relations Research Assn. Democrat. Unitarian. Home: 2301 Spring Hollow Ln Blacksburg VA 24060 Office: Hollins Coll Roanoke VA 24020

HOUSTON, ELIZABETH REECE MANASCO, education educator, consultant; b. Birmingham, Ala., June 19, 1935; d. Reuben Cleveland and Beulah Elizabeth (Reece) Manasco; m. Joseph Brantley Houston; 1 child, Joseph Brantley Houston III. BS, U. Tex., 1956; MEd, Boston Coll., 1969. Cert. elem. tchr., Calif., cert. spl. edn. tchr., Calif., cert. community coll. instr., Calif. Tchr., elem. Ridgefield (Conn.) Schs., 1962-63; staff, spl. edn. Sudbury (Mass.) Schs., 1965-68; staff intern Wayland (Mass.) High Sch., 1972; tchr., home bound Northampton (Mass.) Schs., 1972-73; program dir. Jack Douglas Ctr., San Jose, Calif., 1974-76; tchr., specialist spl. edn., coordinator classroom services, dir. Juvenile Ct. Schs. Santa Clara County Office of Edn., San Jose, Calif., 1976—; instr. San Jose State U., 1980-87, U. Calif., Santa Cruz, 1982-85; cons. Houston Research Assocs., Saratoga, Calif., 1981—. Author: (manual) Behavior Management for School Bus Drivers, 1980, Classroom Management, 1984, Synergistic Learning, 1986. Bd. dirs. Ming Quong Children's Ctr., Los Gatos, Calif. Grantee Santa Clara County Office Edn. Tchr. Advisor Program U.S. Sec. Edn., 1983-84; Recipient President's award Soc. Photo-Optical Instrumentation Engrs., 1979, Classroom Mgmt. Program award School Bds. Assn., 1984. Mem. Assn. for Supervision and Curriculum Devel., Assn. Calif. Sch. Administrs., Council Exceptional Children. Home: 12150 Country Squire Ln Saratoga CA 95070 Office: Santa Clara County Office Edn 100 Skyport Dr San Jose CA 95115

HOUSTON, NANCY MARIE, educator; b. Butler, Pa., Feb. 21, 1948; d. T.H. and Marie G. (McMunigle) Penar; m. Richard L. Houston, Aug. 2, 1969; children: Connie Marie, Stacy Lynn. AB, Grove City Coll., 1970; MS in Edn., Youngstown (Ohio) State U., 1975; EdD in Computer Edn., Nova U., 1987. Tchr. Hickory (Pa.) Sr. High Sch., 1970-73; tchr. adult edn. Mercer (Pa.) County Vocat.-Tech. Sch., 1971-73; instr. mktg. Slippery Rock (Pa.) U., 1975—; prof. Grove City (Pa.) Coll., 1975—, chmn. dept. computer systems, 1986—; owner Peddler's Shop, Ocean City, N.J., 1980—; word-processing cons. Dayton Computer Services, Grove City, Pa., 1982; accreditation cons. Assn. Ind. Colls. and Schs., Washington, 1982—, Mid. States, Phila., 1987. Mem. Assn. for Devel. Computer Based Instructional Systems (mem. program com.), Soc. for Applied Learning Tech., Assn. for Computing Machinery. Republican. Presbyterian. Home: 615 Superior St Grove City PA 16127 Office: Grove City Coll Dept Computer Systems Grove City PA 16127

HOUSTON, SHIRLEY MAE (MRS. THOMAS H. HOUSTON), court reporter; b. Jasper, Tex., Oct. 4, 1938; d. Walter Louis and Effie Marie (Hulett) Gordon; student U. Houston, 1957, South Tex. Jr. Coll., Houston, 1958; grad. Robert Krippner Sch. Reporting, 1965; m. Thomas Harold Houston, Aug. 3, 1957. Various secretarial positions, 1956-65; ct. reporter, owner Houston Reporting Service, 1965—; owner H-R-S, 1975—; v.p. Tradewinds Indsl. Park, Inc., 1974-83, dir., 1984—; partner Houston Video Service, 1977-86; dir. Skate City USA, 1980-86; owner Bear Creek Skating Rink, 1985—, Houston Litigation Support Service, 1986—. Vol. juvenile counselor; advisor Houston Community Coll., 1976-78, Alvin Community Coll., 1980-84. Registered profl. reporter, cert. shorthand reporter, cert. legal video specialist, Tex. Mem. Greater Houston Ct. Reporters Assn. (pres. 1975, chmn. tech. com. 1986-87, disting. service award 1983), Nat. Shorthand Reporters Assn. (state chmn. membership com. 1977-78, dir. 1979-80, placement com. 1980-82, ins. com. 1982-84, co-chmn. word processing com. 1981-83, chmn. videotape com. 1985, mem. 1986, seminar instr. nat. conv. 1978, 79, 81, 82, 83, 84, fund-raising task force 1986-88, chmn. videotape com. 1987-88, nat. membership award 1980), Tex. Shorthand Reporters Assn. (advt. chmn. conv. 1967, dir. 1978-80, spl. advisor to bd. dirs. 1988, state liaison to state bar of Tex. 1986-88, chmn. mktg. & pub. relations 1987-88, disting. service award 1987, seminar instr. 1985, 86, 87, reporters coop. sec. 1986-87, v.p. 1987-88), Nat. Assn. Legal Secs., Tex. Assn. Legal Secs., Greater Houston Legal Secs. Assn. (dir. 1969), Legal Assts. Assn., DAR, UDC, Harris County Heritage Soc., Theatre Under the Stars, Baron Users Group (bd. dirs. 1984-87, treas. 1987-88, seminar instr. 1986, 87, chmn. conv. 1988). Baptist. Club: Cotillion (Houston). Address: 1001 Texas Suite 1100 Houston TX 77002

HOUSTON, WHITNEY, vocalist, recording artist; b. East Orange, N.J., Aug. 9, 1963; d. Cissy Houston. Trained under dir. of mother; mem. New Hope Bapt. Jr. Choir, 1974; background vocalist Chaka Khan, 1978, Lou Rawls, 1978, Cissy Houston, 1978, appeared in Cissy Houston night club act; record debut (duet with Teddy Pendergrass), Hold Me, 1984; albums include: Whitney Houston, 1985, Whitney, 1986; songs include: Greatest Love of All, Saving My Love For You, Didn't We Almost Have It All, You're Still My Man; fashion model Glamour Mag., Seventeen mag., 1981. Recipient Grammy award, 7 Am. Music awards, 4 #1 Single Record awards; named Artist of Yr. Billboard mag., 1986. Grammy award for Best Female Pop Performance, 1985, 87; Winner Am. Music Awd, 1985 (2), 1986 (5). Office: care Solters/Roskin/Friedman Inc 45 W 34th St New York NY 10001

HOUSTON-LUDLAM, GENEVIEVE ANNE, engineer, entrepreneur; b. N.Y.C., July 12, 1959; d. William Myrton and Natalie Merilyn (Elston) Ludlam; m. Mark Douglas Houston, Aug. 18, 1980. BA in Computer Sci. and Psychology, U. Oreg., 1979. Engr. Applied Tech., Sunnyvale, Calif., 1979-80, HRB-Singer, Lanham, Md., 1980-82, Ultrasystems, Hanover, Md., 1982-83; pres. Frontier Techs., Edgewater, Md., 1984—; cons. in field. Mem. Nat. Assn. Female Execs., Assn. Old Crows, Internat. Test and Evaluation Assn., Armed Forces Communications and Electronics Assn., Assn. Advancement Artificial Intelligence. Republican. Presbyterian. Home: PO Box 187 Edgewater MD 21037

HOUX, SHIRLEY ANN, personal and business services company executive, consultant, researcher; b. Claremore, Okla., Nov. 1, 1931; d. George Warren and Alta Zena (Starkweather) Pritchard; m. William Dean Munson, June 1, 1951 (div. June 1962); children—Debra Kay, Diana Sue, Donna Lynn; m. Leonard Houx, June 22, 1963; 1 child, David Leonard. Student in bus. Okla. State U., 1949-50. Sec. Jack Gordon, P.A., Claremore, Okla., 1947-48; sec., personnel mgr. Gulf Oil Corp., Tulsa, 1950-51; exec. sec. to wing comdr. U.S. Air Force, Cocoa Beach, Fla., 1951-53; exec. sec. to gen. counsel Houston So., P.A., Stillwater, Okla., 1957-60; exec. sec. to exec. v.p. and sr. v.p. Williams Cos., Tulsa, 1962-64; owner, chief exec. officer Hallmark Exchange, Inc., Tulsa, 1981—; cons. small bus., Tulsa, 1981—; mem. small bus. adv. bd. Tulsa Jr. Coll., 1983—. Author: (drama) Wedding Rehearsal for the Bride of Christ, 1985. Contbg. editor The Chronicle, 1984. Co-creator, producer foot health program, 1967 (Am. Podiatry Assn. Outstanding award 1968); creator, advt. campaign for Cystic Fibrosis Found.: I'm One...Be One, 1978. Pres. women's aux. Okla. Podiatry Assn., Tulsa, 1966-82; sec.-treas. Okla. bd. examiners Okla. Podiatry Assn., 1969-76; nat. audio-visual chmn. women's aux. Am. Podiatry Assn., 1976; pres. Tulsa Cerebral Palsy Assn., 1977, Cystic Fibrosis Found. Aux., Tulsa, 1979. Named Miss Claremore, Claremore Bus. and Profl. Women, Okla., 1949; recipient Two-Star award Pure D'Lite Co., 1982. Mem. Nat. Assn. Female Execs., Tulsa C. of C. Democrat. Avocations: fashion design; the arts; writing.

HOVEMEYER, GRETCHEN ANNE, editor, bibliographer; b. Erie, Pa., Jan. 2, 1940; d. Ernst Henry and Marjory Etta (Hollister) H. AB, Radcliffe Coll., 1961. Manuscript sec. Internat. Tax Program, Harvard Law Sch., Cambridge, Mass., 1961-63, copy editor, 1963-65, editorial asst., 1965-66, publs. asst., 1966-76, editorial and pub. dir., 1976—. Co-compiler: Bibliography on Taxation of Foreign Operations and Foreigners: 1968-75, 1976, Bibliography on Taxation of Foreign Operations and Foreigners: 1976-82, 1983; author articles on geneal.; designer computer software. Mem. New Eng. Hist. Geneal. Soc., Orange County Geneal. Soc. (pub. cons. 1983—), Sullivan County (N.Y.) Hist. Soc., DAR (chpt. registrar, chpt. historian 1978-83). Home: 10 Agassiz St Apt 21 Cambridge MA 02140 Office: Harvard U Internat Tax Program 1563 Massachusetts Ave Cambridge MA 02138

HOVLIARAS, CHRISTINE ANN, research dental hygienist; b. Dover, N.J., Oct. 3, 1963; d. Crist Dimetrios and Ruth Anne (Rutoski) H. AS in Dental, Fairleigh Dickinson U., 1984, BS in Dental Hygiene, 1985, post-grad., 1985—. Lic. dental hygiene, N.J. Sales assoc. J.C. Penney Co., Inc., Rockaway, N.J., 1979-83; office mgr., dental asst. and hygienist Dr. Jeffrey Gordon, River Edge, N.J., 1983—; dental hygiene faculty Fairleigh Dickinson Sch. Dental Medicine, Hackensack, N.J., 1984-85; research dental hygienist Fairleigh Dickinson Sch. Dental Medicine Oral Health Research Ctr., Hackensack, 1984—; dental hygiene faculty Fairleigh Dickinson Sch. Dental Medicine Oral Health Research Ctr., 1987—. Co-author dental research Jour. Dental Research, 1987; contbr. articles to profl. jours. Recipient Hygiene Advanced Studies award Fairleigh Dickinson U., 1984, Campus Service award, 1985. Mem. N.J. Dental Hygiene Assn., Am. Dental Hygiene Assn., Nat. Assn. Female Execs., Fairleigh Dickinson U. Dental Hygiene Alumni Assn. (v.p. 1986-87, pres., 1987—), N.J. Dental Assn. (liaison 1986—), Fairleigh Dickinson U. Resident Asst. Club (pres. Teaneck chpt. 1984-85), Phi Zeta Kappa, Phi Omega Epsilon. Republican. Greek Orthodox. Home: 11 Mac Spar Dr Randolph NJ 07869 Office: Fairleigh Dickinson U Sch Dental Medicine 140 University Plaza Dr Hackensack NJ 07601

HOWARD, ANASTASIA VICTORIA, editor; b. N.Y.C., Dec. 8, 1958; d. Frederick Sprague and Carol Maria (Hasborne) Weaver; m. Eugene Frederick Howard, Aug. 3, 1980; children: Brandon Christopher, Melanie Amber. BS, Syracuse U., 1980. Intern CBS, N.Y.C., 1979; coordinator Pub. Relations Enterprises, N.Y.C., 1980-82; columnist N.Y. Amsterdam News, N.Y.C., 1982; free lance writer corp. and consumer publs. N.Y.C., 1983-86; dep. features editor Cen. N.J. Home News, New Brunswick, 1986-88; health writer The Greenville (S.C.) News Piedmont Co., 1988—; writer, editor, cons. various Johnson & Johnson corp. publs., 1984-86. Graphic designer in-house publs., corp. newletters, 1984-86. Sec. Civil Ct. Judge Campaign, N.Y.C., 1978. Mem. Newspaper Guild N.Y., Delta Sigma Theta. Democrat. Roman Catholic. Home: 1201 Devenger Rd Greer SC 29551 Office: The Greenville News 305 S Main St Greenville SC 29602

HOWARD, ANN THOMPSON, computer company executive; b. Peoria, Ill., Oct. 2, 1942; d. Chester Wallace and Evelyn (Show) Thompson; m. John Stephen Howard, June 21, 1973. BA, U. Tex., 1964, BS, 1965; PhD, U. Tex, Houston, 1973; postgrad., U. Colo., Denver, 1979-83. Med. technologist Austin, Tex., 1965-68; microbiologist Tex. Childrens Hosp., Houston, 1968-74; supr. microbiology Mt. Sinai Hosp., Cleve., 1974-78; with microbiology research and devel. dept. test instruments div. Honeywell, Denver, 1978-79, sr. software engr. test instruments div., 1979-83; sr. softrware engr. ultrasound div. Johnson & Johnson, Denver, 1983-84; dir. engring. Hathaway Corp., Denver, 1985—. Reader Recording for the Blind, Denver, 1979—. Mem. IEEE. Home: PO Box 685 Franktown CO 80116 Office: Hathaway Corp 5250 E Evans Ave Denver CO 80222

HOWARD, CAROLE MARGARET MUNROE, public relations executive; b. Halifax, N.S., Can., Mar. 5, 1945; came to U.S., 1965; d. Frederick Craig and Dorothy Margaret (Crimes) Munroe; m. Robert William Howard, May 15, 1965. BA, U. Calif., Berkeley, 1967; MS, Pace U., 1978. Reporter Vancouver (Can.) Sun, 1965; editorial assoc. Pacific N.W. Bell, Seattle, 1967-70, employee info. supr., 1970-72, advt. supr., 1972, project mgr. EEO, 1972-73, mktg. mgr., 1973, info. mgr., 1974-75; dist. mgr. media relations AT&T, N.Y.C., 1975-77, dist. mgr. planning, 1977-78, dist. mgr. advt., 1978-80; media relations mgr. Western Electric, N.Y.C., 1980-83; div. mgr. regional pub. relations AT&T Info. Systems, Morristown, N.J., 1983-85; v.p., dir. pub. relations and communications policy The Reader's Digest Assn., Inc., Pleasantville, N.Y., 1985—. Author: (with Wilma Mathews) On Deadline: Managing Media Relations, 1985; contbg. author: Communicators' Guide to Marketing, 1987, Experts in Action: Inside Public Relations, 2d edit., 1988; editor newsletters: Wash. State Rep. Cen. Com., 1973-74; contbg. editor Pub. Relations Quar. Mem. corp. adv. bd. Caramoor Ctr. for Music and the Arts; bd. dirs. The Hundred Club of Westchester, Inc. Mem. Women in Communications (bd. dirs. Wash. state 1973), Internat. Assn. Bus. Communicators, Pub. Relations Soc. Am., Nat. Press Women, Wash. Press Women (bd. dirs. 1972), Am. Cancer Soc., Arthur Page Soc., Pi Beta Phi. Anglican. Clubs: The Aspen; La Paloma Country. Home: 31 Daniel Ct Ridgewood NJ 07450 Office: The Reader's Digest Assn Inc Pleasantville NY 10570

HOWARD, CINDY LEE, programmer, analyst; b. East Patchouge, N.Y., Oct. 14, 1959; d. Marcus A. and Bette Lee (Stinnett) H. Student, Christian Brothers Coll., 1977, State Tech. Inst., 1978-80, Memphis State U., 1985—. Programmer, analyst Hamlin, Williams and Assoc., Memphis, 1979-83; programming cons. Memphis, 1983-84; computer cons. Am. Resources Systems, Memphis, 1984-87; mgmt. info. systems analyst St. Joseph Hosp., Memphis, 1987—. Mem. NOW.

HOWARD, ELIZABETH, public relations company executive; b. Littleton, N.H., Apr. 24, 1950; d. Ellis Woodruff and Elizabeth (Millar) H.; m. Charles A. Schwefel, May 12, 1984. BA, Plymouth (N.H.) State Coll., 1972; MS, Pratt Inst., 1985. Dir. corp. pub. relations Nat. Distillers and Chem. Corp., N.Y.C., 1980-85; dir. pub. relations Transway Internat Corp., White Plains, N.Y., 1985; pres. Corp. Communications Group Millennium Inc., N.Y.C., 1986; pres. Elizabeth Howard and Co., N.Y.C., 1987—. Contbr. articles to profl. mags. Bd. dirs. Katharine Gibbs Sch. Scholarship Found., 1987-88, Hamilton-Madison Settlement House, N.Y.C., 1987— (pres. 1987—). Mem. Global Econ. Action Inst., Women Execs. Pub. Relations (bd. dirs. 1984-87). Home: 4 Coachmen's Sq New Canaan CT 06840 Office: 10 E 39th St New York NY 10016

HOWARD, FLORENCE ROSTRON, home economics educator; b. Chester, Pa., May 11, 1933; d. George Sanderson and Josephine (Dankelman) Rostron. BS, Cedar Crest Coll., Allentown, Pa., 1955; MEd, Western Md. Coll., 1979. Tchr. home econs. Nether Providence High Sch., Wallingford, Pa., 1955-58, Towson (Md.) Town Jr. High., 1958-60; tchr., chmn. dept. home econs. Johnnycake Mid. Sch., Balt., 1960—. Sec. Boy Scouts Am., Balt., 1966—, local unit, 1972—. Mem. United Teaching Profls., Am. Home Econs. Assn., Md. Home Econs. Assn. (com. chmn. 1985-87, mem. nominating com. 1987), Md. Home Econs. Tchrs. Assn. (v.p. 1968-72), Balt. County Home Econs. Tchrs. Assn. (chmn. social com. 1979—), Met. Area Assn. Home Economists (v.p. 1984—). Republican. Presbyterian. Office: Johnnycake Mid Sch 6200 Johnnycake Rd Baltimore MD 21207

HOWARD, FRANCES ESTELLA HUMPHREY, government official; b. Wallace, S.D., Feb. 18, 1914; d. Hubert Horatio and Christine (Sannes) H.; m. Ray Howard, Dec. 7, 1942 (dec. Jan. 1967); children: William, Anne. BA in Sociology, George Washington U., 1937, MA, 1941; HHD (hon.), Lane Coll., 1967. With U.S. Office Civilian Def., Washington, 1941-43; liaison officer various vol. agys. for fgn. relief, Washington, 1942-60; commd. fgn. service officer Dept. State, Washington, 1960; chief liaison officer vol. agys. AID, Washington, 1960-67; chief spl. project div. Office War Hunger, Washington, 1968; liaison officer vol. health orgns., spl. asst. to assoc. dir. Office Asst. Sec. Health and Sci. Affairs HEW, Washington, 1969-70, spl. asst. to assoc. dir. for extramural programs Nat. Library Medicine, NIH, USPHS, Health and Human Services, Bethesda, Md., 1970—; lectr. to various orgns. Contbr. articles to nat. periodicals. V.p. U.S. Com. for Refugees, 1975-82; bd. dirs. Universalist-Unitarian Service Com., 1975-80, Mus. African Art, Smithsonian Instn., 1962—, Washington Opera, 1977—, Nat. Theatre Corp., 1980—, Capitol area Chpt. CARE, 1980—, Washington Ctr., 1982, Am. Council Nationality Services, 1982—, Capitol Children's Mus., 1982-88, Hubert H. Humphrey Inst. Pub. Affairs, U. Minn., 1983—. Recipient Disting. Service award Grand Chpt. Delta Sigma Theta, 1966; Women's Honor award Howard U., 1967; No. Va. service award Altrusa Club, 1967; Emblem of Honor award 6th Ann. Pan Am. Congress Conf. on Social Services, 1968. Fellow Royal Soc. Arts (London); mem. AAUW, Am. Polit. Sci. Assn., Bus. and Progl. Women's Assn., Am. Sociol. Assn., Pan Am. Conf. Social Work, Soc. Internat. Deve., Internat. Council on Social Welfare, UN Assn. (dir. 1980-84), AAAS. Office: NIH Nat Library of Medicine 8600 Rockville Pike Bethesda MD 20209

HOWARD, JOAN ALICE, artist; b. N.Y.C., Apr. 28, 1929; d. John Volkman and Mary Alice Devlin; m. Robert Thornton Howard, June 26, 1949; children: Barbara Jo, Robert Thornton Jr., Gregory Lyon, Brian Devlin. Student, Hunter Coll., 1947-48, UCLA, 1967-68, Los Angeles Valley Coll., 1970-71. Dir., choreographer Acad. Dance, Floral Park and Forest Hills, N.Y., 1947-57; dir. dance. Cath. Parochial schs., N.Y.C., Bklyn., and Floral Park, N.Y., 1948-55; chmn. dept. dance Molloy Coll., 1958-67; artist sta. KNBC-TV, Los Angeles, 1967-74, NBC, N.Y.C., 1974-78, sta. WNBC-TV, N.Y.C., 1978-79; artistic dir. Brookville (N.Y.) Sch., 1980-85; dir. dance N.Y.C. YMCA, 1948; founder, dir. Queens-Nassau Regional Dance Theatre, 1950-55; choreographer Molloy Coll. Dance Theatre, 1959-67; cons. prenatal exercise, L.I., N.Y., 1980—; judge art show Westbury (N.Y.) Mural Project, 1979. One-woman show Dime Savings Bank, Manhasset, 1986-87; exhibited in group shows at Valley Ctr. Arts Gallery, Los Angeles, 1968-72, Home Savs. and Loan Art Exhibits, Los Angeles, 1969-70, Westwood Art Gallery, Los Angeles, 1972, Onion Gallery, Los Angeles, 1972, North Ridge Women's Ctr. Gallery, Los Angeles, 1972, Great Neck (N.Y.) Ctr. Gallery, 1976, A&S Gallery, Manhasset, 1976, Gloria Vanderbilt Designers Showcase, 1978, Manhasset Library Gallery, 1985-86, Great Neck House Gallery, 1986-87, Hutchins Gallery C.W. Post Coll., L.I., 1986-87 (award 1986-87), Dime Savs. Bank, Mass., N.Y., European Am. Bank, 1988; exhibited in juried show Nassau County (N.Y.) Mus. Fine Arts, Roslyn, 1985, Plandome Gallery, N.Y., 1988; choreographer contemporary ballet Crucifixtion, 1960, Persephone, 1961, Cubes of Truth, 1962, Somewhere, 1965; appeared on radio show Coast to Coast on a Bus, 1939-47; Broadway prodn. Lady in the Dark, 1940-42; performed ballet in TV show Stars of Tomorrow, 1942, Sleeping Beauty, 1942. Dem. committeewoman, Glen Cove, N.Y., 1954-58. Recipient Del Rey Perpetual Race championship trophy, 1974, Little Sabot Perpetual Race trophy, 1972-74, So. Calif. Women's Sailing Conf. sabot championship, 1972-74, 1st Woman trophy Olympic Regatta, 1973. Mem. Dance Educators Am., Manhasset Art Assn., Women's Sailing Com. of U.S. Yacht Racing Union (fund raiser 1980-81), Am. Watercolor Soc. (aux.), Women's C. of C. Los Angeles. Clubs: Calif. Yacht (Los Angeles) (Women's Perpetual Race trophy 1972-74), Manhasset (N.Y.) Yacht, Sports Car of Am. Home and Office: RD 1 Autumn Ridge Rd South Salem NY 10590

HOWARD, JOANNE FRANCES, research analyst; b. St. Louis, Feb. 5, 1953; d. Frank Henry and Evelyn Julia (Haeckel) Spellazza; m. Claude Lorrain Howard, May 20, 1978; children: Amy Julia, Laura Ann. B.A., U. Mo.-St. Louis, 1975; M.S., Western Ill. U., 1976. Analyst, Streett Industries, Inc., St. Louis, 1977-78; research analyst Gallup & Robinson Co., Princeton, N.J., 1978-80, Jack Eckerd Corp., Clearwater, Fla., 1980-82, sr. research analyst, 1982-88; mktg. cons. Howard Assocs., 1986—; cons. Anson Lee Rector Inc., Tarpon Springs, Fla., 1982-83, Med-Op Clinics, Tarpon Springs, Fla., 1983-88. Editor monthly newsletter Florida West Coast chpt. Am. Mktg. Assn., 1982-83. Mem. Pinebrook Homeowners Assn., Largo, Fla., 1983-84. Mem. Am. Mktg. Assn. (past sec.-treas.). Democrat. Home and Office: Rural Rt 1 Box 150 Golden City MO 64748

HOWARD, KATHLEEN, computer company executive; b. Norman, Okla., Nov. 3, 1947; d. Robert Adrian and Jane Elizabeth (Morgens) Howard; m. Lawrence W. Osgood, Aug. 10, 1968 (div. Sept. 1970); m. Norman Edlo Gibat, Oct. 15, 1971. Student U. Okla., 1966-68. Typesetter, Selenby Press, Norman, 1968-72; owner, pres. Noguska Industries, Fostoria, Ohio, 1973—; co-founder Home Wine Mchts., Chgo., 1976; cons. Bechtel Corp., Ann Arbor, Mich. and Gaithersburg, Md., 1980—; chairperson Am. Software Project, 1985. Co-author, illustrator: Lore of Still Building, 1972; co-author: Making Wine, Beer and Merry, 1973, Computer Comix Mag., 1986; also jours. and bus. mgmt. software. Treas. United Way of Fostoria, 1986—; bd. dirs. Pvt. Industry Council, 1988-90. Recipient Disting. Service award Bechtel Corp., 1983, Founders award Home Wine and Beer Trade Assn. Chgo., 1976. Mem. Better Bus. Bur., Nat. Fedn. Ind. Bus., C. of C. (bd. dirs. 1986-89), Employer's Assn. Toledo. Club: Altrusa Internat. (sec. Fostoria 1984-85, pres. 1986-88). Avocations: painting, printing, travel, reading. Home: 1030 Columbus Ave Fostoria OH 44830 Office: Noguska Industries 735-741 N Countyline Fostoria OH 44830

HOWARD, MARGARET, lawyer, educator, consultant; b. Rocky Mount, N.C., Oct. 13, 1947; d. William Miller and Edith (Barnes) H. A.B., Duke U., 1969, M.S.W., Washington U., St. Louis, 1975, J.D., 1975; L.L.M., Yale U., 1981. Bar: Mo. 1975. Assoc. Lewis, Rice, Tucker, Allen & Chubb, St. Louis, 1975-77; asst. prof. law St. Louis U., 1977-80, assoc. prof. law, 1980-82; vis. assoc. prof. law Vanderbilt U., 1981-82, assoc. prof., 1982—; cons. Study Group on Internat. Adoption Minors, sec. State's Adv. Com. on Pvt. Internat. Law, Washington, 1983—. Contbr. articles to law publs. Recipient Breckenridge prize Washington U. Law Sch., 1975, Erna Arndt scholar, 1973-75. Mem. ABA, Am. Arbitration Assn. (mem. panel of arbitrators), Mo. Bar Assn., Order Coif. Democrat. Methodist. Home: Kendall Dr Nashville TN 37209 Office: Vanderbilt U Law Sch Nashville TN 37240

HOWARD, MARGUERITE EVANGELINE BARKER (MRS. JOSEPH D. HOWARD), business executive, civic worker; b. Victoria, B.C., Can., July 30, 1921; d. Reuel Harold and Frances Penelope (Garnham) Barker; brought to U.S., 1924, naturalized, 1945; B.A., U. Wash., 1943; m. Joseph D. Howard, June 16, 1952; children—Wendy Doreen Frances, Bradford Reuel. Vice pres., dir. Howard Tours, Inc., Oakland, Calif., 1953—; co-owner, gen. mgr. Howard Travel Service, Oakland, 1956—, mng. dir. Howard Hall, Berkeley, Calif., 1964-75; co-owner, asst. mgr. Howard Investments, Oakland, 1960—; sec., treas. Energy Dynamics Inc. Bd. dirs. Piedmont council Campfire Girls, 1969-79, pres., 1974-79, mem. nat. council, 1972-76, zone chmn., 1974-76, 77-83, zone coordinator, 1976, nat. v.p., 1975, nat. bd. dirs., 1976-83, bd. dirs. Alameda Contra Costa council, 1984—; bd. dirs. Oakland Symphony Guild, 1969—, pres., 1972-74; mem. exec. bd. Oakland Symphony Orch. Assn., 1972-74, bd. dirs., 1972-86; 1st pres. Inner Wheel Club of East Oakland, 1983-84; bd. dirs. Piedmont Jr. High Sch. Mothers Club, 1968-69. Recipient Wohelo Order award Campfire, Inc, 1985. Mem. Oakland Mus. Assn., U. Wash. Alumni Assn., East Bay Bot. and Zool. Soc., Young Audiences, Am. Symphony Orch. League, Assn. Calif. Symphony Orchs., Chi Omega Alumni Seattle, Chi Omega East Bay Alumni Berkeley. Republican. Clubs: Womens Univ. (Seattle); Womens Athletic (Oakland) (bd. dirs. 1986—). Home: 146 Bell Ave Piedmont CA 94611 Office: 526 Grand Ave Oakland CA 94610

HOWARD, MARY JANET ROBISON, library director; b. Mt. Vernon, Ill., June 11, 1937; d. William Leroy and Edith Mary (Hails) Robison; m. David Lorn Howard, June 27, 1959 (div. 1978); children: Steven Lorn, Carol Lynne Howard Dombeck, Mary Leigh. BBA, Coll. of William and Mary, 1959; MA in Library Sci., U. Wisc., Milw., 1976; MA in Exec. Devel., Ball State U., 1986. Library dir. U. Wis. at Washington County, West Bend, 1976-80; dist. librarian Waukesha County Tech. Coll., Pewaukee, Wis., 1980-83; dir. library tech. services Ball State U., Muncie, Ind., 1983-87; dir. Stetson Meml. Library, Mercer U., Macon, Ga., 1987—. Editor: Academic Library Instruction Programs: A Wisconsin Directory, 1980. Mem. ALA (resources and tech. services div., council on regional groups), Library Adminstrn. and Mgmt. Assn. of ALA, Library and Info. Tech. Assn. of ALA, Assn. Coll. and Research Libraries of ALA, Ga. Library Assn., Beta Phi Mu. Office: Mercer U Stetson Meml Library Macon GA 31207

HOWARD, MARY MERLE PRUNTY, environmental engineering executive; b. Columbus, Miss., Nov. 20, 1942; d. Merle Charles Jr. and Eugenia (Wyatt) Prunty; m. William Leroy Phillips Jr., Sept. 7, 1964 (div.); 1 child, William Leroy III; m. Paul King Howard, Nov. 26, 1976. BA, U. Ga., 1964, MA, 1968; diplomate Edn. Ministry, U. the South, 1981. Editor Harland Bartholomew and Assocs. Inc., Memphis, 1973, planner, 1973-79, assoc., 1979-85, head dept. environ. planning, 1978-85; sr. planner Kimley-Horn and Assoc. Inc., West Palm Beach, Fla., 1985-86; pres., chief exec. officer Resource Engring. and Planning Inc., West Palm Beach, 1986—; bd. dir. Resource Engring. and Planning Inc. Active Jr. League, Memphis, The Palm Beaches, 1979-86, sustainer, 1986—; vol. Boy Scouts Am., Memphis, 1978-79; trustee Grace-St. Luke's Sch., Memphis, 1980-83. Mem. Assn. Am. Geographers (panelist 1982-83), Nat. Assn. Female Execs., Am. Planning Assn., Am. Inst. Certified Planners, Memphis Geographic Soc. (founder, pres. 1983-84), Palm Beach County Planning Congress, Chi Omega (pres. 1963-64). Democrat. Episcopalian. Club: Med. Wives (Memphis) (pres. 1972-73). Home: 31 Cambria Rd Palm Beach Gardens FL 33410 Office: Resource Engring Planning 3920 RCA Blvd Suite 2001 Palm Beach Gardens FL 33410

HOWARD, SUSAN, actress; b. Marshall, Tex.; m. Calvin Cecil Chrane; 1 child, Lynn Elizabeth. Student, U. Tex. Various TV appearances including movies The Silent Gun, 1969, Quarantined, 1970, Savage, 1973, Night Games, 1974, Indict and Convict, 1974, Killer on Board, 1977, Superdome, 1978, The Power Within, 1979; actress: (TV series) Petrocelli, 1974-76 (nominated Emmy award 1976), Dallas, 1978-87; featured in Moonshine County Express, 1978, Sidewinder One, 1980; co-host: The 700 Club, 1987—. Office: care Leading Artists Inc 445 N Bedford Dr Penthouse Beverly Hills CA 90210

HOWATT, HELEN CLARE, library director; b. San Francisco, Apr. 5, 1927; d. Edward Bell and Helen Margaret (Kenney) H. B.A., Holy Name Coll., 1949; M.S. in Library Sci., U. So. Calif., 1972. Joined Order Sisters of the Holy Names, Roman Catholic Ch., 1945; cert. advanced studies Inst. Sch. Librarians, Our Lady of Lake U., San Antonio, 1966. Life teaching credential, life spl. services credential, Calif. Prin., St. Monica Sch., Santa Monica, Calif., 1957-60, St. Mary Sch., Los Angeles, 1960-63; tchr. jr. high sch. St. Augustine Sch., Oakland, Calif., 1964-69; tchr. jr. high math St. Monica Sch., San Francisco, 1969-71, St. Cecilia Sch., San Francisco, 1971-77; library dir. Holy Names Coll., Oakland, Calif., 1977—. Contbr. math. curriculum San Francisco Unified Sch. Dist., Cum Notis Variorum, publ. Music Library, U. Calif., Berkeley. Contbr. articles Cath. Library World, 1987, 87. NSF grantee, 1966; NDEA grantee, 1966. Mem. Cath. Library Assn. (chmn. No. Calif. elem. schs. 1971-72), Calif. Library Assn., ALA, Assn. Coll. and research Libraries. Home and Office: 3500 Mountain Blvd Oakland CA 94619

HOWE, PEGGY O'NEILL, public information officer; b. Fairfield, Ala., Nov. 24, 1928; d. Harry Edward and Era Mae (Box) O'Neill; m. Theodore Tyler Howe, Nov. 1, 1952; children: Stephen Tyler Howe, Edward O'Neill Howe. AB, U. Ala., Tuscaloosa, 1949. Info. officer U.S. Steel, Fairfield, Ala., 1950-51; editor Ware Shoals (S.C.) Life, 1951-54; reporter/feature writer The Raleigh (N.C.) Times, 1968-70; editorial asst. Dept. Cultural Resources, Raleigh, 1970-72; pub. info. officer Dept. Cultural Resources, 1972—. Contbr. articles to profl. jours., pub. relations manuals, guidebooks. Recipient 1st place in writing, Internat. Assn. Bus. Communicators, 1986; named Outstanding Pub. Affairs Officer, Civil Air Patrol, N.C. Wing, 1981, 82, 83, 85, 86, 87, Outstanding Chmn., United Way, 1979, Gov.'s Long Leaf Pine award, State of N.C., 1981. Mem. ALA (sec. pub. relations sect., recipient John Cotton Dana award 1979, 83), Raleigh Pub. Relations Soc. (pres. 1986, awards 1977, 79, 80, 83, 84, 85), N.C. Govt. Info. Officers (pres. 1977-79), Pub. Relations Soc. Am. Club: N.C. Mus. of History Assocs. (Mentor of Distinctionaward 1988). Home: 3201 Caldwell Dr Raleigh NC 27607 Office: N C Dept Cultural Resources 109 E Jones St Raleigh NC 27611

HOWE-ELLISON, PATRICIA MARY, investment banker; b. Chgo., Sept. 14, 1928; d. Harry Michael and Helen Mary (Maloney) Howe; student Barat Coll., Lake Forest, Ill., 1944-47, Goodman Theatre, Chgo., 1947; m. Ernest O. Ellison, Sept. 23, 1977. Instl. sales asst. Blyth & Co., 1954-55; with L.F. Rothschild & Co., 1957-82, mgr. San Francisco br., 1965-82, partner, 1968-82; pres. Ellmark Assocs., San Francisco, 1982—; chmn. Corp. Capital Investment Advisors, 1984—; mng. dir. Thrift Investment Services, 1984—. Trustee U. San Diego, Women's Forum West. Mem. Securities Industry Assn., San Francisco Bond Club, Equestrian Order Holy Sepulchre, Opera Guild, San Francisco Symphony Found. Republican. Roman Catholic. Clubs: World Trade, Metropolitan, Bankers, Villa Taverna, Bankers (dir.), Bel Air Bay. Home: 1080 Chestnut St San Francisco CA 94109 Office: 550 Kearny St San Francisco CA 94108

HOWELL, BONNIE HOWARD, hospital administrator; b. Ithaca, N.Y., Dec. 7, 1947; d. Robert Leon and Helen Elizabeth (Ryerson) Howard; m. James Ward Delaney Howell, Jr., Feb. 17, 1950; children: Carolyn Elizabeth, Kathryn Helene. BS, Cornell U., 1970, MPA, 1972. Planning assoc. Areawide & Local Planning Health Action, Syraucse, N.YL, 1972-74; adminstr. Community Med. Ctr., Aurora, N.Y., 1974-76; asst. adminstr. Tompkins Community Hosp., Ithaca, 1974-79, adminstr., 1979—; bd. dirs. Tompkins County Trust Co. Contbr. articles to profl. publs. Bd. dirs. United Way of Tompkins County, Ithaca, 1986—. Mem. Am. Coll. Healthcare Execs., Downtown Bus. Women. Baptist. Home and Office: Tompkins Community Hosp 101 Dates Dr Ithaca NY 14850

HOWELL, DIANE-MARIE, laboratory technician, small business owner; b. San Francisco, Sept. 10, 1944; d. William Norman and Marguriete Antionette (Bujacich) H. BA in Biology, San Francisco State U., 1968; cert. in Lab. Tech., Natividad Med. Ctr., 1978. Diplomate Am. Bd. Pathology. Lab. asst. Community Hosp. Monterey Peninsula, Carmel, Calif., 1973-77; lab. technician Natividad Med. Ctr., Salinas, Calif., 1977-79, Dr. Jerome Rubin, Monterey, 1980—; tchr. in field, Pacific Grove, Calif., 1981-87; owner Artemis Imports, Pacific Grove, 1984-87. Creator Ancient Images Transparencies, 1984, Desert Rider Stationery Line, 1986; contbr. articles to profl. jours. NSF grantee, 1969. Mem. Am. Soc. Lab. Technicians, No. Calif. Oriental Dancers. Club: Arab (Monterey). Office: Artemis Imports PO Box 68 Pacific Grove CA 93950

HOWELL, ELIZABETH FULTON, psychiatrist; b. Pascagoula, Miss., Jan. 24, 1955; d. Earl Octo Jr. and Peggy Jo (Fulton) H. BS in Zoology, U. Ga., 1974, MS in Zoology, 1976; MD, Med. U. of S.C., 1980. Diplomate Am. Bd. Psychiatry and Neurology. Resident in pediatrics Med. U. of S.C., Charleston, 1980-81, resident in psychiatry, 1981-84, chief resident, research fellow in psychiatry, 1984-85, instr. in psychiatry, 1984-87; asst. med. dir. Fenwick Hall Hosp., Johns Island, S.C., 1986-87; asst. prof. dept. psychiatry Sch. of Medicine Emory U., Atlanta, 1987—; cons. psychiatrist Palmetto AIDS Life Support Services, Charleston, 1987—; mem. Trident AIDS Adv. Com., Charleston, 1986—; examiner in psychiatry Am. Bd. Psychiatry and Neurology, Chgo., 1987—. Contbr. articles to profl. jours. King's Fund fellow, 1979. Mem. AMA, Am. Psychiat. Assn., S.C. Med. Assn. (com. on alcohol, drug abuse and impaired physicians 1985-87), Am. Med. Soc. on Alcoholism and Other Drug Dependencies, Am. Acad. Psychiatrists in Alcoholism and Addictions, Am. Med. Women's Assn., Internat. Soc. for Study of Multiple Personality and Dissociation. Office: The Emory Clinic Section of Psychiatry 1365 Clifton Rd NE Atlanta GA 30322

HOWELL, HONOR SHARON, minister; b. Seguin, Tex, Oct. 12, 1947; d. Joe Milam and Mary Elizabeth (McKay) H. BA, Austin Coll., 1970; MDiv, St. Paul Sch. Theology, 1973. Youth minister Key Meml. United Meth. Ch., Sherman, Tex., 1969-71, Second Presbyn. Ch., Kansas City, Mo., 1971-72; pastor Edwardsville United Meth. Ch., Kans., 1972-75; assoc. program dir. Council on Ministries, Topeka, 1975-80; v.p. St. Paul Sch. Theology, Kansas City, 1980-85; sr. pastor St. Mark United Meth. Ch., Overland Park, Kans., 1985-87; exec. program dir., Council on Ministries, Topeka, 1987—; pres. Commn. on Status and Role of Women in United Meth. Ch., Evanston, Ill., 1984-88; chmn. personnel com. Council on Ministries, Topeka, 1984-87. Mem. NOW, ACLU, Christian Educators Fellowship, Nat. Assn. Female Execs., Smithsonian Assocs., Internat. Assn. Women Ministers, Amnesty Internat., Nat. Mus. Women in Arts (charter), Women's Action for Nuclear Disarmament. Democrat. Home: 3012 Tutbury Town Rd Topeka KS 66614 Office: 4201 SW 15th St Topeka KS 66604

HOWELL, JEAN DOROTHY, computer programmer; b. Bath, Maine, May 16, 1946; d. Paul William and Dorothy Mae (Jacobsen) Libbey; m. Philip Alexander Pope, Feb. 4, 1966 (div.); children: Paula Jean, Michel Lee; m. Donald Wilson Howell, Aug. 25, 1979. Student, Pensacola (Fla.) Jr. Coll., 1964-65. Computer aid Navy Regional Data Automation Ctr., Pensacola, 1967-70, computer operator, 1970-74, computer technician, 1974-77, computer programmer, 1977-80, computer specialist, 1980-81, supervisory computer specialist, 1981-85, computer programmer, team leader, 1985-87, supervisory computer programmer, analyst, 1987—. v.p. St. Thomas More Sch. PTA, Pensacola, 1984-85, treas., 1976-77, chmn. adv. employee com., 1980-81. Mem. Federally Employed Women (program chmn. 1975-76). Democrat. Roman Catholic. Club: Toastmasters (pres. 1974-75). Home: 346 Campbellton Lane Pensacola FL 32506 Office: Regional Data Automation Ctr Bldg 603 NAS Pensacola FL 32508

HOWELL, LISA, electrical engineer; b. Phila., Apr. 12, 1962; d. Joseph and Joan Diane (Yancy) H. BSEE, Howard U., 1985. Engring. asst. Phila. Electric Co., 1981, IBM Corp., Manassas, Va., 1982; mktg. rep. IBM Corp., Wilmington, Del., 1987—; assoc. engr. Ideas, Beltsville, Md., 1983-84; engring. asst. Hughes Aircraft, Fullerton Calif., 1984; computer operator Howard U., Washington, 1984-85; devel. engr. Nat. Semiconductor, Santa Clara, Calif., 1985-87. Mem. Nat. Assn. Female Execs. Democrat. Office: IBM Corp 1001 Jefferson Plaza 2d Floor Wilmington DE 19801

HOWELL, M. KAY, financial marketing company executive; b. Mason City, Iowa, Dec. 29, 1938; d. Ray William and Doris Genevieve (Wood) Richmond; m. Gary Lynn Howell, mar. 11, 1968; children: Richard Glenn, Pamela Kay, Lori Diane, Traci Katherine, Bradley Richmond, Christopher Lee, Taimoor Ray. BS, Marylhurst U., Portland, Oreg., 1984. Gen. mgr. G.A.M. & Co., Portland, 1975-84, Cascade Ne, Keasubg, Milw., 1981-84; mktg. mgr. B.O. Drake Willock, Milw., 1981-84; sr. v.p., dir. adminstrn. Mktg. One, Inc., Portland, 1984—. Vol. Muscular Dystrophy Assn., Portland, 1986. Republican. Episcopalian. Home: 6620 Park Way Gladstone OR 97027 Office: Mktg One Inc 400 SW 6th Ave Suite 1000 Portland OR 97204

HOWELL, MARCIA RHODES, state official; b. Dothan, Ala., Dec. 24, 1951. Student, U. Montevalla, Ala., 1970-71, Wallace Coll., Dothan, Ala., 1971-72, Auburn U., 1972-73; BS in BA, Troy State U., 1988. Interviewer, caseworker State of Ala. Houston County Food Stamp Office, Dothan, 1974—. Mem. Ala. Employees Assn. (dir. 1984), Gamma Beta Phi. Club: Shady Brook Study (sec. 1983-84). Home: 2109 Cecily St Dothan AL 36303 Office: Dept Human Resources 1605 Ross Clark Circle Dothan AL 36301

HOWELL, MARY ELIZABETH, small business owner; b. Galesburg, Ill., Feb. 19, 1942; d. John A. Shaner and Elizabeth N. (Bowen) Knowles; m. Murrell D. Howell, Dec. 22, 1969; children: Cherie, Thomas, Dean, Murrell. Cert., Alamo Beauty Coll., 1961; student, Jane Grace Sch. Dress Design, 1973; BS in Bus. Adminstrn., U. Redlands, 1985. Owner, operator Howell's Acctg., Minot, N.D., 1972-78; gen. mgr. Gravel Products, Inc., Minot, 1978-80; controller Bluebird Internat., Inc., Denver, 1981-83; owner, pres. Magnetic Power Systems, Huntington Beach, Calif., 1984—; free-lance cons. Huntington Beach, 1984—; acting controller MRW Inc.; spl. projects cons. Am. Health Ctrs., Newport Beach, Calif.; acctg. advisor Circuit Products West, Anaheim, Calif.; owner Cosmetics For Me, Huntington Beach, 1987—; cons., sr. fin. analyst U. Calif., Irvine, 1987—. Copyright Thin Graille of Insanity etching; patentee rail system, ground effect vehicle; designer award winning needlework; developer cosmetic cream. Leader Girl Scouts USA, Minot, 1973-75, den mother Boy Scouts Am., Minot, 1974, fund raiser Minot AFB Little League and Youth Orgn., 1975; active Hadassah, 1975—, Temple Sharon sisterhood, Costa Mesa, Calif., 1986—. Mem. Nat. Assn. Female Execs., Nat. Assn. Accts. (dir. 1982, 83, v.p. edn. and profl. devel. 1984, 86, sec. 1985, v.p. adminstrn. 1987, pres. 1988), Toastmasters. Republican. Jewish. Office: Magnetic Power Systems PO Box 1115 Huntington Beach CA 92647

HOWELL, MARY L., diversified company executive; b. Springfield, Mass., July 10, 1952; d. Walter Edward and Mary Patricia (Landers) Lynch; m. John N. Howell, Oct. 27, 1980; 1 child, Patrick. B.A., U. Mass.; grad. advanced mgmt. program Harvard U. Dir. legis. affairs Health Industry Mfr.'s Assn., Washington; with Textron Inc., Washington, v.p. govt. affairs. Office: Textron Inc 1090 Vermont Ave NW Suite 1100 Washington DC 20005

HOWELL, REBECCA ELIZABETH, driving educator, pilot, consultant; b. San Antonio, May 23, 1952; d. David Ray and Glenna Ruth (Walters) H.; m. Robert Wayne Sykora, Aug. 22, 1970 (Div. July 1974); m. Donald Homer Kelley, Dec. 23, 1976 (div. Oct. 1977). BS in Pharmacy, U. Houston, 1976; MS, Tex. A&M U., 1983. Clk. Mohrmann Drug Store, Gonzales, Tex., 1968-70, various pharmacies, Houston, 1970-76; staff pharmacist Community Hosp. of Brazosport, Freeport, Tex., 1977-82; owner Safe Cycling Cons., Austin, Tex., 1981—; instr., supr. drivers edn. Austin (Tex.) Driving Sch., 1984—; cons. Tex. Dept. of Pub. Safety, Austin, 1984—; pilot Mandot & Howell Flying Service, Austin, 1986—, Air South Commuter, Inc., Birmingham, Ala., 1987—, Am. Eagle, DFW, Tex., 1988—. Contbr. articles to profl. jours. Cons. contract labor Motorcycle Safety Found., Costa Mesa, Calif., 1983—. Mem. Am. Motorcycle Assn., Tex. Motorcycle Riders Assn., Airplane Owners and Pilots Assn., Tex. Automobile Dealers Assn. (pilot 1983—). Home and Office: Safe Cycling Cons PO Box 858 Manor TX 78653

HOWELL, REBECCA KATHLEEN, nurse; b. Oakland, Calif., Apr. 24, 1959; d. William Charles and Shirley Jean (Choate) Reinhardt; m. Emmitt Shayne Howell, Dec. 6, 1986. B.S. in Nursing, Harding U., 1982. R.N., Ark. Med.-surg. and labor-delivery nurse Mercy San Juan Hosp., Carmicheal, Calif., 1982-86, nursing preceptor, 1985-86, post partum, labor and delivery nurse, newborn nursery Rebsamen Regional Med. Ctr., Jacksonville, Ark., 1986—. Republican. Mem. Ch. of Christ. Avocations: team sports; needlework. Home: 140 Alabama Dr Jacksonville AR 72076 Office: Rebsamen Regional Med Ctr Dept Nursing 1400 Braden Jacksonville AR 72076

HOWELL, SAUNDRA LEAH, nurse; b. Maryville, Tenn., Feb. 20, 1945; d. Frank Huston and Fern (Morrison) Caldwell; m. Roy Lee Goodman, MAy 28, 1967 (dec. 1985); m. Sherill Eugene Howell, June 14, 1986. Diploma in nursing, U. Tenn., 1966. RN, Tenn. Staff nurse Univ. Tenn. Hosp., Knoxville, 1966-67, Good Samaritan Hosp., Cin., 1967-70, Ft. Sanders Hosp., Knoxville, 1970-72; staff nurse VA Med. Ctr., Bay Pines, Fla., 1972-76, Johnson City, Tenn., 1976—. Trainee Johnson City Emergency Rescue Squad, 1988. Mem. Emergency Nurses Assn. (cert.). Republican. Baptist. Club: Thunderbolt Country. Lodge: Order Eastern Star. Home: Rt 3 Box 131 Kentland Dr Johnson City TN 37604 Office: VA Mountain Home Johnson City TN 37684

HOWELL, WILMA JEAN, accountant; b. Sharp County, Ark., May 12, 1943; d. Raymond D. and Grace I. (Hughes) Carver; m. Kenneth Duane Howell, Aug. 26, 1961; children: Kenneth Dale, Kristopher Duane, Korey Dean. BA summa cum laude, Wichita State U., 1980; AA, Butler County Community Coll., 1978. CPA, Kans. Sec., bookkeeper Durling-Richards Ins. Adjusters, Wichita, Kans., 1961-62; staff acct. Alexander Grant and Co., El Dorado, Kans., 1980-85; individual practice acctg., Augusta, Kans., 1986-87; ptnr. Clifton and Howell, Augusta, Kans., 1988—; instr. managerial acctg. Butler County Community Coll., 1981-83. Mem. Kans. Soc. CPAs, Am. Inst. CPAs, Beta Alpha Psi. Mem. Ch. of Christ. Home: Rural Route 1 Leon KS 67074 Office: 407 E Kelly Augusta KS 67010

HOWELLS, KAREN ANNETTE, training and development specialist, consultant; b. Portland, Oreg., Nov. 8, 1955; d. Dale D. and Shirley A. (Mills) Halm; m. Robert M. Howells, Nov. 27, 1976; 1 child, Nathan Robert. BA in Communication, Lewis and Clark Coll., 1977. Account exec. Sta. KWJJ, Portland, 1978, Sta. KXL, Portland, 1978-79; dir. advt. Mercantile, Inc., Portland, 1979-81; pres. Sonrise Prodn. Co., Portland, 1981-85; tng. and devel. specialist, cons. Good Samaritan Hosp., Portland, 1985—; cons. Jim Joeger Cons., Portland, 1987—. Singer, producer record albums, Renewed, 1981, Collection, 1984. Mem. Assn. of Tng. and Devel. Republican. Office: Good Samaritan Hosp 1015 NW 22d Ave Portland OR 97210

HOWERTON, DENISE LYNN, artist; b. Falls City, Nebr., Aug. 21, 1952; d. Darwin Lee and Jacquolyn Sue (Feistner) H. Pvt. studies, Art Students League, Denver; study with Mark Daily and others, Denver, 1971—. Studies with Ramon Kelley 1987. Sculpture displays in art mags.

HOWES, PADDY (LILIAN B.) RUDD, writer/editor; b. Coventry, Eng., May 9, 1909; came to U.S., 1925, naturalized, 1941; d. John Alexander and Mary Elizabeth (Doherty) Rudd; student Liverpool Coll., Huyton, Eng., 1920-25; Oxford U., Sr. Sch. Cert., 1925; student U. Akron, 1934-35, U. Cin., 1941-42, Northwestern U., 1950; m. William R. Howes, Sept. 23, 1946. With Firestone Tire & Rubber Co., Akron, Ohio, 1926-36; sec. Children's Hosp. Research Found., Cin., 1936-42; sr. editor W.B. Saunders Co., Phila., 1942-46; fgn. corre. Country Gentleman Mag., Eng., 1946-48; manuscript editor Jour. Am. Dental Assn., Chgo., 1949-50, news editor, 1950-51; staff writer Survey of Med. Edn., Chgo., 1951-53; free lance writer, editor, publs. cons., Chgo., 1953-56, Phila., 1956-72, Harwich, Mass., 1972—. Bd. dirs. Cape Cod Family and Children's Service, Cape Cod chpt. UN Assn. U.S.A.; corp. mem. bd. dirs. United Way of Cape Cod, 1978-82; mem. Cape Cod Community Council, 1975—. Mem. Women in Communications (Chgo. chpt. pres. 1952-53 pres. Phila. chpt. 1962), Phila. Art Alliance, Asso. Country Women of World (life mem.; exec. com. 1946-48, press officer 1946). Writer-Collaborator Medical Schools in the United States at Mid-Century, 1953. Contbr. articles to mags., newspapers and profl. jours. Address: 17 Haromar Heath RFD 3 Harwich MA 02645

HOWLAND, ANN, clinical psychologist; b. Cleve., Jan. 7, 1944; d. Richard Moulton and Natalie (Fuller) H.; stepfather—William F. Merrill, III; B.A., Goucher Coll., 1965; M.A., U. Fla., 1971, Ph.D., 1973; children—Andrea Merrill and Joshua Howland Sarver. VA trainee, 1971-72; treatment dir., therapy supr. Clin. Services Community Mental Health Clinic, Nelsonville, Ohio, 1973-75; pres. Athens (Ohio) Psychology Clinic, Inc., 1975-81; pres. Ann Howland, Ph.D. and Assos., Athens, 1981—; chief of staff psychology service O'Bleness Hosp., 1977-80; cons. W.Va. Head Start, 1975-78; instr. case mgmt. for mental health technicians Ohio U., 1975; cons. Athens County Probate Ct., 1975—; mem. Masters and Johnson Inst. Vol. Peace Corps, Colombia, S.A., 1966-68; active Athens Humane Soc., Animal Protection Inst., Save the Whales, Conservation of Endangered Species, NOW; bd. dirs. Ohio Hills Health Planning Agy. Mem. Am. Psychol. Assn., Ohio Psychol. Assn., Southeastern Ohio Psychol. Assn., Nat. Register Health Service Providers in Psychology, Nat. Acad. for Advancement Sci., Nat. Arbor Day Found., Common Cause, Ctr. for Environ. Edn., Audubon Soc., Greenpeace, Defenders of Wildlife, Am. Soc. for Prevention Cruelty to Animals. Club: Sawgrass (Fla.). Contbr. chpt. in book. Home and Office: Route 3 Box 163 Athens OH 45701

HOWLAND, BETTE, writer; b. Chgo., Jan. 28, 1937; d. Sam and Jessie (Berger) Sotonoff; m. Howard C. Howland (div.); children—Frank, Jacob. B.A., U. Chgo., 1955. Author: W-3, 1972; Blue in Chicago, 1978 (1st prize Friends of Am. Writers); Things to Come and Go, 1983. Fellow Rockefeller Found., 1969, Guggenheim Found., 1978, Nat. Endowment for the Arts, 1981, MacArthur Found., 1984. Jewish. Office: care Knopf Books 201 E 50th St New York NY 10022

HOWLAND, JOYCE ELIZABETH, college administrator; b. Corvallis, Oreg., Sept. 13, 1946; d. James Chase and Ruth Louise (Meisenhelder) H.; m. Roosevelt Lucio Adolfo Fernandes, Dec. 29, 1972; children: Benjamin James, Von Patricio. AB, Wellesley Coll., 1968; PhD, Vanderbilt U., 1972. Research asst. GASCO, Santiago, Chile, 1967; instr. Vanderbilt U., Nashville, 1972; asst. prof., coordinator SUNY, Oswego, 1972-78; asst. prof. Onondaga Community Coll., Syracuse, N.Y., 1979; mentor Empire State Coll., Syracuse, 1979; dir. Columbia Coll., Hancock Field, N.Y., 1979—; tutor Empire State Coll., Syracuse, 1979—. Contbr. articles to profl. jours. Den leader Cub Scouts Am., 1985—, tiger cub coordinator, 1986-87. Fellow NDEA Title IV, 1968-70. Mem. N.Y. St. Latin Americanists (pres. 1979-80), Am. Econs. Assn., Latin Am. Studies Assn. Home: 104 Ruby Rd Liverpool NY 13088 Office: Columbia Coll 174th Tactical Fighter Wing NY Air NG Hancock Field Syracuse NY 13211

HOWLAND-EARLEY, ARDEN RAE, publisher; b. Chgo., Nov. 8, 1958; d. Ellis King and Elaine (Wood) Howland; m. Thomas John Earley XIII, Aug. 5, 1978; 1 child, Calnen Illeene Earley. BS, Western Ill. U., 1981; MA, Loyola U., Chgo., 1987. Tchr. Knox-Warren Spl. Edn. Dist., Galesburg, Ill., 1981, Lakeshore Hosp., Chgo., 1981-83; cons., owner The Kid's House, Chgo., 1983—; pub., owner Solo Publs., Chgo., 1986—. Editor Today's Provider mag., 1986—. Mem. Nat. M.S. Soc., Nat. Assn. Edn. Young Children, Nat. Assn. Family Day Care, Assn. Childhood Edn. Internat., Ill. Assn. Edn. Young Children, Chgo. Assn. Edn. Young Children.

HOWLETT, CAROLYN CHANCE, association executive, civic worker; b. Millville, N.J., Aug. 28, 1915; d. R. Robinson and Carolyn Davidson (Abbott) Chance; m. Duncan Howlett, Apr. 26, 1943; children—Margaret, Albert Duncan, Richard Chance, Carolyn Abbott (Mrs. Stephen Korth). Cert., Grad. Inst. Internat. Studies, Geneva, 1934; A.B. magna cum laude, Mt. Holyoke Coll., 1935; J.D., Yale U., 1938; D.H.L., Meadville/Lombard Theol. Sch. Chgo., 1983. Bar: N.J. bar 1939, N.Y. bar 1942. Atty. Kellogg & Chance, Jersey City, 1938-40, Hines Rearick Dorr & Hammond, N.Y.C., 1942-43; Bd. dirs. Barney Neighborhood House, Washington, 1965-69; Bd. dirs. Western Maine Counseling Service, 1975-77, treas., 1976-77; mem. Area V Mental Health Bd., Maine, 1976-77; treas. Lovell (Maine) Library, 1981-82, pres., 1982, 85-88; bd. dirs. No. Cumberland Meml. Hosp., 1982—, sec., 1986-87. Mem. steering com. Unitarian Universalist Peace Network, 1986-88. Mem. LWV (dir. Boston chpt. 1953-57), Unitarian Universalist Women's Fedn. (dir. 1965-67, 2d v.p. 1967-69, treas. 1969-71), Unitarian Universalist Assn. (mem. com. study ch. and state relations 1965-68, social responsibility and investment 1969, com. appraisal 1973-77, del. to world congresses 1972, 75, 78, 81, 84, 87 Unitarian Universalist Retired Ministers Assn. (dir. 1985—), Soc. Promoting Theol. Edn., Capital Area UN Assn. (dir. 1962-69, sec. 1964-69), Leadership Conf. Civil Rights (dir. 1967-69), Washington Urban League (5 Year Service award 1967), Internat. Assn. Liberal Religious Women (pres. 1969-78 archivist 1980—), Internat. Assn. Religious Freedom (exec. com. 1972-81, chmn. nominating com. 1974-75, pres. 1978-81, outstanding service award 1980), Mt. Holyoke Coll. Alumnae Clubs (dir. Boston chpt. 1953-57, sec. Washington chpt. 1962-64, chmn. Maine leadership fund dr. 1975-78), Phi Beta Kappa. Home: Eastman Hill Rd RR1 Box 13 Center Lovell ME 04016

HOWLETT, PHYLLIS LOU, athletic conference administrator; b. Indianola, Iowa, Oct. 23, 1932; d. James Clarence and Mabel L. (Fisher) Hickman; m. Jerry H. Howlett, Jan. 2, 1955 (dec.); children—Timothy A., Jane A.; m. Ronlin Royer, Dec. 30, 1977. B.A., Simpson Coll., 1954. Psychometrist Drake U., Des Moines, 1956-57, asst. to men's athletic dir., 1974-79; asst. dir. athletics U. Kans., Lawrence, 1979-82; asst. commr. Big Ten Conf., Schaumburg, Ill., 1982—; mem. NCAA Football TV Com., 1980-87, chmn. NCAA com. on women's athletics, 1987—; exec. com. Nat. Assn. Collegiate Dirs. of Athletics, 1986—; NCAA Women's Golf Com., 1983—. Chmn. Iowa Commn. Status of Women, 1976-79; pres. Vol. Bur. of Greater Des Moines, 1969-70, Arts and Recreation Council of Greater Des Moines, 1975, Iowa Children's and Family Services, 1973; nat. pres. Assn. Vol. Burs., Inc., 1972-73, service award. Recipient certs. of appreciation Des Moines C. of C., State of Iowa, Drake U. Mem. Nat. Assn. Dirs. of Collegiate Athletics, Council Collegiate Women Athletic Adminstrs. (bd. dirs.), Jr. League, Simpson Coll. Alumni Achievement award, 1988. inductee Simpson Coll. Hall of Fame. Republican. Office: 1111 Plaza Dr Suite 600 Schaumburg IL 60195

HOWLETT, SANDRA EILEEN, training and development specialist; b. Lynchburg, Va., Mar. 12, 1953; d. Ernest and Doris (Hicks) H. BSc, Radford U., 1974; MSc, Va. Poly. Inst., 1977, EdD, 1981. Tchr. Roanoke (Va.) City Schs., 1975-77; prog. dir. Dairy & Food Nutrition Council, Roanoke, 1977-78; faculty Va. Poly. Inst., Blacksburg, Va., 1978-82; mgmt. trainer Ramada, Inc., Phoenix, 1984-87; pres. Howlett & Co., Phoenix, 1987—; cons. in field. Tng. dir. Valley of Sun United Way, Phoenix. Mem. Ariz. Speakers Assn. (officer 1985—), Nat. Speakers Assn., Am. Soc. Tng. and Devel., Nat. Assn. Female Execs., Phi Delta Kappa. Presbyterian. Home and Office: 12226 N 39th Pl Phoenix AZ 85032

HOWLETT, STEPHANIE ANN, nurse; b. Kansas City, Kans., Dec. 23, 1957; d. Wayne Stewart and Anna Marie (Barancik) H. AA, Kansas City Community Coll., 1979. RN. Critical care nurse Providence-St. Margarets Health Ctr., Kansas City, Kans., 1979-82; primary pvt. duty nurse Quality Care In, Kansas City, Mo., 1980-81; dir. nursing Profl. Nursing Service, Kansas City, Mo., 1981-86; med. services cons. Crawford Health and Rehab. Services, Kansas City, Mo., 1986; sales rep. Nat. Med. Homecare (now HOMEDCO), Lenexa, Kans., 1986—; mem. adv. bd. Olsten Health Care Services, Kansas City, Mo., 1986—, utilization rev. com., 1986—, budget com., 1987. Mem. Mo. Voters Freeze, Kansas City, 1986, Kansas City (Kans.) Jr. League, 1987. Named one of Outstanding Young Women Am., 1987. Mem. Nat. Rehab. Assn., Assn. Rehab. Nurses, Support Hospice Oncology Profls., Kansas City Met. Discharge Coordinators, Nat. Assn. Female Execs. Republican. Home: 10507 College Kansas City MO 64137 Office: HOMEDCO 14653 W 95th St Lenexa KS 66215

HOWLEY, MARGUERITE A., food service executive; b. Dayton, Ohio, July 18, 1930; d. John Francis and Marguerite Frances (Horan) H. BS, U. Dayton, 1952; MBA, Xavier U., 1963. Intern U. Mich. Hosp., Ann Arbor, 1953; therapeutic dietitian Bent Brigham Hosp., Boston, 1953-54; adminstrv. dietitian New Eng. Med. Ctr., Boston, 1954-55, Good Samaritan Hosp., Dayton, 1955-56; food service specialist civil service USAF, Dayton, Memphis, and Marietta, Pa., 1956-68; v.p., gen. mgr. Greyhound Food Mgmt. Inc., Irvine, Calif. and Detroit, 1969-77; assoc. dir. residence and dining halls food service Ohio State U., Columbus, 1978—; bd. dirs., sec. exec. com., chair nominating com. Life Care Alliance, Columbus, 1986—. Mem. Ohio Ops. Improvement Taskforce, Columbus, 1983; specialist mass care food preparation Columbus chpt. ARC, 1986. Recipient Alumni award U. Dayton, 1964; named one of Outstanding Young Women of Am., 1965. Mem. Am. Dietetic Assn. (registered dietitian), Nat. Restaurant Assn. Democrat. Roman Catholic. Home: 369 Olentangy Forest Dr Columbus OH 43214 Office: Ohio State U Residence and Dining Halls 1800 Cannon Dr #600 Lincoln Tower Columbus OH 43210

HOWORTH, LUCY SOMERVILLE, lawyer; b. Greenville, Miss., July 1, 1895; d. Robert and Nellie (Nugent) Somerville; m. Joseph Marion Howorth, Feb. 16, 1928. A.B., Randolph-Macon Woman's Coll., 1916; postgrad., Columbia U., 1918; J.D. summa cum laude, U. Miss., 1922. Bar: Miss. 1922, U.S. Supreme Ct. 1934. Asst. in psychology Randolph-Macon Woman's Coll., 1916-17; gauge insp. Allied Bur. Air Prodn., N.Y.C., 1918; indsl. research nat. bd. YWCA, 1919-20; gen. practice law Howorth & Howorth, Cleveland, Greenville and Jackson, Miss., 1922-34; U.S. commr.

So. Jud. Dist. Miss., 1927-31; assoc. mem. Bd. Vet. Appeals, Washington, 1934-43; legis. atty. VA, 1943-49; v.p., dir. VA Employees Credit Union, 1937-49; assoc. gen. counsel War Claims Commn., 1949-52, dep. gen. counsel, 1952-53, gen. counsel, 1953-54; ptnr. James Somerville & Assocs. (overseas trade and devel.), 1954—; atty. Commn. on Govt. Security, 1956-57; pvt. law practice Cleveland, Miss., 1958—; mem. nat. bd. cons. Women's Archives, Radcliffe Coll.; mem. lay adv. com. study profl. nursing Carnegie Corp. N.Y., 1947-48; chmn. Miss. State Bd. Law Examiners, 1924-28; mem. Miss. State Legislature, 1932-36, chmn. com. pub. lands, 1932-36; treas. Com. for Econ. Survey Miss., 1928-30; mem. Research Commn. Miss., 1930-34. Editor: Fed. Bar Assn. News, 1944; assoc. editor: Fed. Bar Assn. Jour., 1943-44; editor: (with William M. Cash) My Dear Nellie-Civil War Letters (William L. Nugent), 1977; contbr. articles profl. jours. Keynote speaker White House Conf. on Women in Postwar Policy Making, 1944, at conf. on opening 81st Congress. Recipient Alumnae Achievement award Randolph-Macon Woman's Coll., 1981, Lifetime Achievement award Schlesinger Library of Radcliffe Coll., 1983. Mem. AAUW (nat. dir., 2d v.p. 1951-55, mem. found. 1960-63), Nat. Fedn. Bus. and Profl. Women's Clubs (nat. dir.; rep. to internat. 1939, chmn. internat. conf. 1946), Nat. Assn. Women Lawyers, Miss. Library Assn. (life), Miss. Hist. Soc. (dir. 1982—, Merit award 1983), DAR, Daus. Am. Colonists, Am. Legion Aux. (past sec. Miss. dept.), Assembly Women's Orgns. for Nat. Security (chmn. 1951-52), Phi Beta Kappa, Pi Gamma Mu, Phi Alpha Delta, Alpha Omicron Pi (Wyman award 1985), Delta Kappa Gamma, Omicron Delta Kappa, Phi Kappa Phi (hon.). Democrat (del. nat. conv., 1932). Methodist. Club: Soroptimist (Washington). Address: 515 S Victoria Ave Cleveland MS 38732

HOWSE, ANITA LOUISE, financial analyst; b. Los Angeles, Feb. 12, 1955; d. John Edward Sr. and Elsie (Rogers) H.; divorced 1985; children: Curtis, Jeanine, Michael. Student, Los Angeles Community Coll., 1974, West Los Angeles Community Coll., 1982-83, 87, UCLA, 1986-87. Prin. acctg. clk. Cedars-Sinai Med. Ctr., Los Angeles, 1980-81, scheduling staff asst., 1981-82, asst. dept. mgr., 1982, staff asst., 1982-83, staff acct., 1983, sr. acct., 1983-86, fin. mgmt. analyst, 1986—. Campaign worker Geneva Cox for City Council, Los Angeles, 1987; chair West Blvd. Child Devel. Ctr., Los Angeles, 1986-87; mem. Neighborhood Watch, Concerned Citizens for Better Govt. Mem. Nat. Assn. for Female Execs., Am. Mgmt. Assn. Democrat. Roman Catholic. Home: 4532 W 18th St Los Angeles CA 90019

HOY, MARJORIE ANN, entomology educator, researcher; b. Kansas City, Kans., May 19, 1941; d. Dayton J. and Marjorie Jean (Acker) Wolf; m. James B. Hoy; 1 child, Benjamin Lee. A.B., U. Kans., 1963; M.S., U. Calif.-Berkeley, 1966, Ph.D., 1972. Asst. entomologist Conn. Agrl. Expt. Sta., New Haven, 1973-75; research entomologist U.S. Forest Service, Hamden, Conn., 1975-76; asst. prof. entomology U. Calif.-Berkeley, 1976-80, assoc. prof. entomology, 1980-82, prof. entomology, 1982—; chairperson Calif. Gypsy Moth Sci. Adv. Panel, 1982—. Editor or co-editor: Genetics in Relation to Insect Management, 1979, Recent Advances in Knowledge of the Phytoseiidae, 1982, Biological Control of Pests by Mites, 1983, Biological Control in Agricultural IPM Systems, 1985; contbr. numerous articles to profl. jours. NSF fellow U. Calif.-Berkeley, 1963-64; recipient Bussart award for research in agrl. entomology Entomol. Soc. Am., 1986. Mem. Entomol. Soc. Am. (mem. Pacific br. governing bd. 1985, Bussart award 1986), Am. Genetic Assn., Internat. Orgn. Biol. Control (v.p. 1984-85), AAAS, Acarological Soc. Am. (governing bd. 1980-84), Soc. for Study Evolution, Phi Beta Kappa, Sigma Xi (sec. chpt. 1979-81). Home: 1004 Grizzly Peak Blvd Berkeley CA 94708 Office: U Calif Dept Entomology 201 Wellman Hall Berkeley CA 94720

HOYLE, RUTH PAMELA, art dealer, art historian; b. Biloxi, Miss., July 16, 1945; d. Daniel Scarborough and Hazel Ruth (Starnes) H. AB, U. N.C., 1969, MA, 1971. Curator Boston Athenaeum, 1976-81; gen. mgr. Boston Concert Opera, 1983-84; dir. Alfred J. Walker Fine Art, Boston, 1984-87; pres. The Hoyle Gallery, Boston, 1987—; instr. Dickinson Coll., 1973-74; vis. asst. prof. George Washington U., 1974-75. Contbr. numerous articles to profl. jours. Co-chair ARTCETERA, Boston, 1985, 86; bd. trustees Opera Co. of Boston, 1985—; bd. dirs. Gay and Lesbian Counseling Services, Boston, 1987—. Democrat. Mem. Christian Ch. Home: 30-34 E Concord St Boston MA 02118 Office: The Hoyle Gallery Inc Box 544 Boston MA 02117

HOYT, CHARLEE ILDORA, management executive, former city official; b. Bluefield, W.Va., Mar. 21, 1936; d. Charles Ives Van Cleve and Kathryn Margarete (Harden) Perrow; m. Ronald Reiner Hoyt, 1959 (div. 1983); children: Dean Christopher, Jason Allen. BA in Edn., U. Fla., 1959, MEd, 1962, postgrad., 1963-64. Cert. spl. edn. tchr. Tchr. Amherst County Schs., Elon, Va., 1958; tchr. spl. edn. Marion County Schs., Ocala, Fla., 1959-61; counselor Univ. Counseling Ctr., Gainesville, Fla., 1962-63, Sunland Tng. Ctr., Gainesville, 1963; mem. community faculty Minn. Met. State Coll., Mpls., 1972-83; mem. council City of Mpls., 1975-86; ptnr. Van Cleve Assocs., 1980-87; pres. Van Cleve, Doran & Bruno, Inc. 1987—; corp. officer BAM Leasing Co., Inc., 1987—; mem. faculty Govt. Tng. Service, St. Paul, 1978-86, Ariz. Govt. Tng. Services; pres. Minn. Women in City Govt., St. Paul, 1978-79; mem. Met. Land Use Adv. Bd., St. Paul, 1978-83; bd. dirs. Transp. Adv. Bd., St. Paul, 1979-81; mem. conf. faculty League of Minn. Cities, St. Paul, 1979-82; bd. dirs. Met. Council Criminal Justice Adv. Bd., St. Paul, 1979-82; pres. Women in Mcpl. Govt., Nat. League of Cities, Washington, 1980-81, founder minority caucus coalition, 1982, dir., 1982-84; curriculum cons. Nat. Women's Edn. Fund, Washington, trainer, 1982—. Presenter numerous workshops; contbr. articles to profl. jours. Mem. Women Helping Women YWCA, 1987—; various offices with Republican Party, Minn., 1970-86 ; pres. Burroughs Elem. Sch. PTA, Mpls., 1973-74; panelist White House Conf., 1981; chmn. Senator Durenburger's Task Force on Women's Issues, Mpls., 1981-84; bd. dirs. Nat. Conf. Rep. Mayors and Council Mems., 1984-85; mem. Senator Durenburger's Intergovtl. Relations Adv. Com., Mpls., 1984-86; bd. dirs. Twin Cities Internat. Program, Mpls., 1983-86; participant Women's Dialogue US/USSR, Moscow, 1985; trustee Council Internat. Programs, Cleve., 1985—; bd. dirs. At the Foot of the Mountain Theater, Mpls., 1985-86, Tucson Ctrs. for Women and Children, 1988—; bd. dirs. GOP Feminists, Hamline U. Ctr. for Women in Govt.; mem. Nat. Women's Polit. Caucus, Hennepin County Women's Polit. Caucus; mem. Tucson Support for Success Team, 1986—. Mem. Am. Soc. Training and Devel., Minn. Women Elected Ofcls. (pres. 1983-85), Izaak Walton League, Tucson C. of C. Methodist. Club: Remington Investment (pres. 1968-70) (Mpls.). Avocations: lapidary, music, handwork, camping, science fiction. Home: 6932 E Second St Tucson AZ 85710

HOYT, FRANCES WESTON, artist; b. Elizabeth, N.J., Nov. 15, 1908; d. Edward Faraday and Edith Ross (Parker) Weston; m. Malcolm Burrows Hoyt, June 1, 1944 (dec. Jan. 1984); children—Edith Hoyt Garrett, Edward Weston. Student Art Students League, N.Y.C., 1931-35. One-woman shows: Newark Art Club, 1942, Montclair Woman's Club (4), 1948-73, Pocono Lake Preserve, Pa., 1976; Montshire Mus., Hanover, N.H., 1986, N.H. Audobon Soc., Concord; exhibited in one-woman show: Audubon Soc. N.H., 1988; exhibited in group shows: Nat. Arts Club, N.Y.C., 1943, Los Angeles Mus., 1946, Allied Artists Am., N.Y.C., 1980; represented in permanent collection: Bloomfield Art League N.J., Berkeley Sch., Bloomfield, N.J.; instr. Montclair Adult Sch., N.J., 1962-72; pvt. instr., N.Y.C., 1934-44. Recipient 1st prize Council Am. Artists Soc. N.Y.C., 1980. Fellow Am. Artists Profl. League (Gold medal Grand Nat. 1974); mem. Hudson Valley Art Assn. (bd. dirs. 1978—), Nat. Assn. Women Artists, Salmagundi, Acad. Artists Assn., Copley Soc. Boston.

HRANITZKY, JEANNE BEVERLY, academic administrator; b. New Rochelle, N.Y., Dec. 20, 1935; d. Henry Ervay and Irene Dorothy (McSherry) Crooks; m. Dennis Rogers Hranitsky, Dec. 19, 1959; children: Rachel, Dennis, Patrick. Student, Midwestern U., 1957, So. Meth. U., Dallas, 1958-59; BS in Biology, Chemistry, Yale U., 1959; MEd, Tex. Women's U., 1979, PhD, 1981. Research technician U. Tex. Southwestern Med. Sch., Dallas, 1957-58; biology tchr. Highland Park Ind. Sch. Dist., Dallas, 1958-62; teaching asst. Tex. Women's U., Denton, 1979-82, asst. prof., 1982-87; dir. Dean Learning Ctr., Dallas, 1987; acad. devel. coordinator Carrollton (Tex.)-Farmers Brach Ind. Sch. Dist., 1987—; cons. Tex. schs. and businesses, 1980—; adv. com. Jane Marshall Sch., 1985—; dir. Willow Creek Adolescent Ctr., 1985—. Author: Logically Speaking, 1981; contbr. articles to profl. jours. Chmn. Citizen's Adv. Com., Grapevine, Tex., 1975; v.p. PTA, Grapevine, 1975, 76; v.p. Grapevine/Colleyville Ind. Sch. Dist. Bd., 1976—. Mem. Tex. Assn. Gifted and Talented (v.p.), Nat. Assn. Gifted Children, Council for Exceptional Children, Tex. Sch. Bd. Assn., Tex. Elem. Principals Assn. Republican. Methodist. Home: 3211 Wintergreen Ter Grapevine TX 76051 Office: Carrollton-Farmers Brach Ind Sch Dist 1445 N Perry Rd Carrollton TX 75006

HROMADKA, PAMELA J., corrections administrator; b. Friend, Nebr., Nov. 23, 1948; d. Frank and Elsie Mae (Stetina) Hromadka. B.S., U. Nebr., 1971, M.A., 1977; postgrad. U. S.C., 1981, U. Pa., 1980, Kearney State Coll., 1980. Tchr. home econs. Republican Valley Sch., Indianola, Nebr., 1971-72; social services worker York County div. Pub. Welfare, York, Nebr., 1972-73; social services worker Saunders County div. Pub. Welfare, Wahoo, Nebr, 1974; with Nebr. Ctr. for Women, York, 1974—, counselor, 1975-77, adminstrv. asst., 1977-86, acting asst. supt., 1986, asst. supt., 1987; beauty cons. Mary Kay Cosmetics. Vol. York Community Theatre, 1980—; mem. pub. relations adv. com., treas. All Faiths Chapel, York. Mem. Nebr. Corrections Assn. (sec., conf. chmn.), U. Nebr. Alumni Assn., Am. Corrections Assn., Bus. and Profl. Women of York, LWV, Western Bohemian Fraternal Assn., York Home Econs. Club, Catholic Daughters, York Coll. Bus. Person, Greater York Women's Council (sec. 1984—), Phi Beta Lambda. Republican. Club: Toastmaster (sec. 1983-84). Avocations: reading, travel, horticulture. Home: 1208 Kiplinger Ave York NE 68467 Office: Nebr Ctr for Women Rural Rt 1 Box 33 York NE 68467

HRUBIK, SARAH, financial planner; b. Royal Oak, Mich., Jan. 19, 1931; d. MIllan and Julia (Dejanski) Illich; m. William R. Feldman, June 20, 1954 (dec. Aug. 1966); children: Denise Feldman Reynolds, Valerie Feldman Stern, Laura Feldman; m. Joseph Hrubik, April 15, 1972. BS, Wayne State U., 1953; MS, Akron State U., 1966. Field underwriter Home Life Ins. Co., Richmond, Va., 1975-80; ind. agt. Richmond, 1980-85; dist. mgr. Waddel & Reed, Richmond, 1985-88, Investment Assocs. Ltd., Richmond, 1988—. Mem. Am. Soc. CLU's and Chartered Fin. Cons., Internat. Assn. of Fin. Planning. Office: Investment Assocs Ltd 2010 Bremo Rd Suite 112 Richmond VA 23226

HRYCYK, STEPHANIE ANN, educator, management consultant; b. Cleve., June 7, 1948; d. John and Stephanie Hrycyk. BA, Youngstown (Ohio) State U., 1970; MA, Ohio State U., 1978, PhD, 1981. Tchr. Youngstown Sch. System, 1970-77; adminstrv. assoc. Ohio State U., Columbus, 1977-81; health educator Ft. Sanders Med. Ctr., Knoxville, Tenn., 1982; prin. Aerobex Inc., Amarillo, Tex., 1983-85; dir. Ctr. Community Health, N.W. Tex. Hosp., Amarillo, 1985-87; owner, operator The Wellington Agy., Amarillo, 1987—; grad. instr. West Tex. State U. Canyon, 1985-87; freelance mgmt. advisor, health educator, ins. broker. Mem. AAHPER and Dance, Amarillo C. of C. (chmn. health com. 1986-87), Phi Delta Kappa. Democrat. Roman Catholic. Lodge: Rotary. Home: 1531 S Alabama Amarillo TX 79102 Office: The Wellington Agy PO Box 1859 Amarillo TX 79105

HSU, GRACE HEI-MIN CHEN, biochemist; b. Tainan, Taiwan, Oct. 27, 1940; d. Shou-Tou and Fong-Tuey (Chern) Chen; m. Robert Chung-Ying Hsu, Sept. 3, 1966; children: Bradford, Lawrence, Joshua. BS, Nat. Taiwan Normal U., 1963; MS, Kans. State Tchrs. Coll., 1967; PhD, U. Ill., 1971. Vis. fellow chemistry dept. Northwestern U., Evanston, Ill., 1971-72; resident dept. pathology U. Ill. Hosp., Chgo., 1972-74; cons. Clin. Lab. Holy Cross Hosp., Chgo., 1973-75; sect. dir. Clin. Lab. St. James Hosp., Chicago Heights, Ill., 1974—; adj. prof. Coll. Environ. of Applied Scis., Gov.'s State U., University Park, Ill., 1974—. Mem. Am. Assn. Clin. Chemists, Nat. Acad. Clin. Biochemists, Am. Bd. Clin. Chemistry (diplomate), Sigma Xi.

HSU, JIANN-PING, statistician; b. Soochow, Peoples Republic of China, July 24, 1947; came to U.S., 1968; BS, Nat. Taiwan U., 1968; MA, Columbia U., 1970; PhD, U. Calif., Berkeley, 1977. Research asst. Calif. State Dept. Health, Sacramento, 1977-78; biostatistician Kaiser-Permanente Med. Ctr., Walnut Creek, Calif., 1978-79; math. statistician FDA, Rockville, Md., 1979-86; sr. investigator Smith, Kline and French Lab., King of Prussia, Pa., 1986—. Mem. Am. Statis. Assn., Biometric Soc., Drug Info. Assn. Office: Smith Kline and French Lab Div Research and Devel PO Box 1539 King of Prussia PA 19406-0939

HU, EVELYN LYNN, electrical and computer engineering educator; b. N.Y.C., May 15, 1947; d. David Hosheng and Carolyn Jui-chen (Hsu) H. BA in Physics, Barnard Coll., 1969; MA in Physics, Columbia U., 1971, PhD in Physics, 1975. Mem. tech. staff AT&T Bell Labs., Holmdel, N.J., 1975-81; supr. AT&T Bell Labs., Murray Hill, N.J., 1981-84; prof. elec. and computer engrng. U. Calif., Santa Barbara, 1985—; assoc. dir. Ctr. Robotic Systems in Microelectronics, 1985—; mem. MIT vis. com. EECS, 1983—; mem. program com. Nat. Research and Resource Facility for Submicron Structures; mem. steering com. Internat. Symposium on Electron, Ion and Photon Beams; chmn. Gordon Conf. on Chemistry and Physics of Microstructures, 1986. Contbr. articles to profl. jours.; patentee in field. Mem. IEEE, Am. Phys. Soc., Am. Vacuum Soc., Phi Beta Kappa, Sigma Xi. Office: U Calif Ctr Robotic Systems 6740 Cortona Santa Barbara CA 93106

HU, SCARLETT HSICHIA, information systems administrator; b. Chia-I, Republic of China, Dec. 28, 1957; came to U.S., 1979; d. Frank Y.C. and Ging-Sheng (Cheng) H. BBA with honor, Nat. Taiwan U., 1979; MBA, UCLA, 1981; MS in Computer Sci., U. So. Calif., 1988. Lic. real estate salesman, Calif. Aplications cons. Sci. Time Sharing Corp. Inc., Los Angeles, 1980-83, account mgr., 1983-84; sr. system analyst Home Savs. Am., Los Angeles, 1984-86; supr. info. ctr., asst. v.p. Irwindale, Calif., 1986—; pres., founder Hu & Cheng Career Strategists, Los Angeles, 1987—. Columnist China Ladies mag., Taipei, Republic of China, 1983—. Group leader Voice of Los Angeles Choir, 1980—. Mem. Chinese MBA Assn. (co-chairperson 1985—), Info. Ctr. Mgmt. Assn., So. Calif. Profl. Office Systems Users Group, Assn. Female Execs. Office: Home Savs Am 1001 Commerce Dr Irwindale CA 91706

HUANG, THERESA C., librarian; b. Nanking, China; m. Theodore S. Huang, Dec. 25, 1959. B.A., Nat. Taiwan U., 1955; M.S. in L.S., Syracuse U., 1958. Cataloger, Harvard U., Cambridge, Mass., 1958-60; with Bklyn. Pub. Library, 1960-78, regional librarian, 1978—. Joint compiler bibliography: Asia: A Guide to Books for Children, 1966; Nuclear Awareness, 1983; The U.S.A. through Children's Books, 1986, 88. Mem. ALA, Assn. Library Service to Children, Pub. Library Assn., Chinese Am. Librarians Assn., Asia Pacific Am. Librarians Assn. Office: Bklyn Pub Library 240 Division Ave Brooklyn NY 11211

HUARD, CATHLEEN M., community advocate; b. Frankfort, Fed. Republic Germany, June 5, 1953; came to U.S., 1953; d. David Edward and Evelyn Therese (Perry) Mangsen; children: Paula, Adrian. AA, Quinsigamond Community Coll., Worcester, Mass., 1982. With United Way of Cen. Mass., Worcester, 1983—, Community activist Fair Share program, 1983—, adminstrv. asst. Family Day Care Health Project, 1986—, office mgr. Child Care Connection program, 1986—; news coordinator Sta. WCUW Community Radio, Worcester, 1985-87, mem. programming com., 1987—; co-organizer Women's Campaign for Social Justice, Worcester, 1987; mem. adv. com. Mass Soc. for the Prevention of Cruelty to Children Teen Parent program, Worcester, 1987—; organizer Mother's Day benefit for the homeless, Worcester, 1987, bd. dirs. Worchester Connection. Contbr. articles to the sch. newspaper at Quinsigamond Community Coll. Apptd. to City Mgr.'s adv com. on Status of Women, Worcester, 1985—; del. Dem. Issues Conv., Springfield, Mass., 1987; del. Dem. Nat. Conv., 1988; publicity chairperson Women's Energy Against Violence; mem. Teen Recreation Council (Parks and Recreation dept. at City Hall). Mem. ACLU. Office: United Way of Cen Mass 484 Main St Worcester MA 01608

HUBBARD, ELIZABETH LOUISE, lawyer; b. Springfield, Ill., Mar. 10, 1949; d. Glenn Wellington and Elizabeth (Frederick) H.; m. A. Jeffrey Seidman, Oct. 27, 1974 (div. May 1982). Student Millikin U., 1967-69; B.A., U. Ky., 1971; J.D. with honors, Ill. Inst. Tech.-Chgo. Kent Coll. Law, 1974. Bar: Ill. 1974, U.S. Dist. Ct. (no. dist.) Ill. 1974, U.S. Ct. Appeals (7th cir.) 1976, U.S. Supreme Ct. 1984. Atty. Wyatt Co., Chgo., 1974-75, Gertz & Giampietro, Chgo., 1975-76, Baum, Sigman, Gold, Chgo., 1976-81, Elizabeth Hubbard, Ltd., Chgo., 1981—; legal counsel NOW, Chgo., 1978—, sec., 1977. Editor Chgo. Kent Law Rev., 1970. Bd. dirs., mem. The Remains Theatre, 1985—. Mem. Chgo. Bar Assn. (fed. civil procedure com.), Ill. State Bar Assn. Democrat. Home: 441 E Erie St Chicago IL 60611 Office: 55 E Monroe Chicago IL 60603

HUBBARD, INEZ TERESA, anesthesiologist; b. Memphis; d. Friendloyd and Fannie (Fitzgerald) H. RN, Harlem Hosp., N.Y.C., 1964; cert. nurse anesthetist, Grad. Hosp. U. Pa., Phila., 1971; BS in Biology, Upsala Coll., 1977; MD, U. Medicine and Dentistry N.J., 1981. Diplomate Nat. Bd. Med. Examiners. Flexible internship Overlook Hosp., Summit, N.J., 1981-82; resident in anesthesiology Mass. Gen. Hosp., Boston, 1982-84; locum tenens Underwood Meml. Hosp., Woodbury, N.J., 1985; with med. staff N.J. Sports Expn. Authority, Rutherford, 1985—; locum tenen anesthesiology CompHealth, Salt Lake City, 1985—, World Wide Anesthesia Assocs., Inc., Ukiah, Calif., 1986—; fellow in obstet. anesthesia N.Y. Med. Coll., Valhalla, N.Y., 1987. Mem. Am. Soc. Anesthesia, N.J. Soc. Anesthesia, North Jersey Med. Soc., U. Medicine and Dentistry N.J. Alumni Assn. (bd. dirs. 1985—), Harlem Hosp. Alumni Assn. Democrat. Roman Catholic. Home: PO Box 1161 Orange NJ 07051-1161 Office: 14 N Warwick Rd Somerdale NJ 08083

HUBBARD, JULIA FAYE, accountant; b. Lebanon, Tenn., Apr. 27, 1948; d. Joe Pate Jr. and Rachel (Trice) H.; m. Teddy Clifton Wallin, Sept. 4, 1971 (div. June 1981). BSBA, Tenn. Technol. U., 1970; postgrad. in Acctg., U. Tenn., 1974-77. Sec. Sch. Nursing Vanderbilt U., Nashville, 1970-71; bookkeeper Ingram Corp., Nashville, 1971-72; acct./bookkeeper White & Ensor CPA's, Birmingham, Ala., 1972-74, Internat. Div. Joe M. Rodgers Constrn. Co., Nashville, 1974-79; supr. Ryan, Connelly, Primm & Outhier CPA's, Nashville, 1979-83; prin. Taylor & Assocs. CPA's, Nashville, 1983-86; owner, mgr. Julia F. Hubbard, Acctg. & Cons., Nashville, 1986—; asst. to developer, project coordinator R.B. Investments Co., Nashville, 1985; owner, designer Juliana Fashion Accessories, Nashville, 1986—. Mem.-at.-large Hendersonville (Tenn.) Arts Council, 1985—; bd. dirs., cons. Tenn. Assn. Dance. Fellow Nat. Assn. Accts. (officer, bd. dirs. 1981-85). Republican. Methodist. Office: 25 Music Sq E Nashville TN 37203

HUBBARD, MARION RITA, credit manager; b. Waterbury, Conn., Sept. 11, 1948; d. Orrin J. and Marion E. (Wolfe) H. BS in History, U. Bridgeport, 1982; profl. cert. in credit mgmt., Quinnipiac Coll., 1985. Asst. credit mgr. Barclay Knitwear Co., Newtown, Conn., 1975-76; credit mgr. Tower Olschan Corp., Bridgeport, Conn., 1977-78; credit adminstr. Royal Bus. Machines, Hartford, Conn., 1978-80; credit mgr. Raymark Corp., Trumball, Conn., 1980-84, mgr. credit and receivables, 1985-86, corp. mgr. credit, receivables, cash mgmt., 1986-88; mgr. corp. credit Superior Electric Co., Bristol, 1988—. Contbr. St. Vincent DePaul Shelter for Homeless, Waterbury, 1984-87, Women's Emergency Shelter, Waterbury, 1986-87, Animal Rescue Found., Middlebury, Conn., 1977-87, also vol. Recipient Assoc. award Nat. Inst. Credit, N.Y.C., 1985. Mem. Nat. Assn. Credit Mgmt., Motor Credit Assn., Women's Network Waterbury, Nat. Assn. Female Execs. Democrat. Roman Catholic. Office: Superior Electric Co 383 Middle St Bristol CT 06010

HUBBARD, MARSHA ANN, state government administrator; b. Utica, N.Y., June 28, 1947; d. John Field and Sally (Sinnott) H. Student Webster Coll., St. Louis, 1965-69, George Washington U., 1970-71, St. Louis U., 1972-73. Legis. asst. Congressman James Symington, Washington, 1969-72, Congresswoman Bella Abzug, Washington, 1973-74; adminstrv. asst. Senator Genie Chance, Alaska, 1974-76; budget analyst Health and Social Services, Juneau, Alaska, 1976-78; dir. mgmt. and budget, 1979-83, dir. budget and fin., 1983-84; mgr. lease processing U.S. Leasing Corp., San Francisco, 1979; spl. asst. Office of Gov. Juneau, 1984-85; commr. Medicaid Rate Commn., Juneau 1983-84; mem. Longevity Bonus Task Force, Juneau, 1983; dep. commr. Dept. Adminstrn., 1985—. Chmn. Women's Caucus-Alaska State Dem. Party, 1984-86; mem. Women's Lobby, Alaska; mem. state cen. com. Dem. Party Alaska, 1986-88. Roman Catholic. Club: Juneau Golf and Country (bd. dirs. 1982). Home: 6737 Marquarite Juneau AK 99801 Office: State of Alaska Office of Gov Pouch A Juneau AK 99811

HUBBARD, STEPHANIE ANN, physical education educator; b. Nashville, Jan. 31, 1952; d. Ralph Hunt Drake and Peggy Ann (Jones) Nielsen; m. Douglas Alan Hubbard, June 20, 1981; children: Brandon Keith, Amber Victoria. AA, L.A. Pierce Jr. Coll., Woodland Hills, Calif., 1971; BPE, Calif. State U., Northridge, 1974, MPE, 1979. Instr. phys. edn. Los Angeles City Schs., Van Nuys, Calif., 1975—; volleyball referee Los Angeles, 1974-75; coach Valley Alternative Sch., Van Nuys, 1986—. Parade judge tabulator So. Calif. Band and Orch. Assn., Los Angeles; sales and office counselor United Spirit Assn., Mountain View, Calif., 1975—. Recipient single subject Ryan life credential in Phys. Edn. State of Calif., 1983. Mem. So. Calif. Dance Team (U.S. champion in amateur ballroom dancing), Calif. chpt. of AAHPERD. Home: 22934 Schoolcraft St West Hills CA 91307

HUBBARD, SUSIE DEE, nursing director; b. Hereford, Tex., Dec. 2, 1954; d. John Robert and Joyce Marie (Lewis) Hickman; m. Charles Bruce Hubbard, Aug. 11, 1978; children: Christopher Todd, Toby Brannon, Kaci Michelle. BS in Nursing, West Tex. State U., 1978. CPR instr. Nurse Midland (Tex.) Meml. Hosp., 1978-79; service coordinator Upjohn Healthcare Services, Midland, 1979-80, dir. service, 1980-81; RN surgery St. Anthony's Hosp., Amarillo, Tex., 1981-84; dir. nursing Amarillo Diagnostic Clinic, 1985—. Mem. Patient Edn. Network (pres. 1987—), Nat. Assn. for Female Execs., Sigma Theta Tau, Tri Beta. Republican. Mem. Christian Ch. Home: 5306 Granada Amarillo TX 79109

HUBER, BARBARA MOODY, financial analyst, consultant; b. Buffalo, Sept. 27, 1933; d. Ralph Henry and Edith Florence (Schalk) Moody; m. Donald J. Huber Sr., Sept. 5, 1953 (div. May 1974); children: Donald J. Jr., Gary M. (dec.), Cynthia M. Koelbl, Randy W. Christine M. Student, Rosary Hill Coll., Amhest, N.Y., 1968. Salesperson various real estate cos., Williamsville, N.Y., 1968-80, Empire Nat. Securities, Williamsville, 1981-86, Dean Witter Reynolds, Williamsville, 1986—. Pres. Alden Women's Republican Club, 1970. Recipient Millionaire award Buffalo Bd. of Realtors, 1976-77. Mem. Clarence C. of C. Club: Bond. Home: 6089 Long St PO Box 162 Clarence Center NY 14032 Office: Dean Witter Reynolds 4701 Transit Rd PO Box 1300 Williamsville NY 14221

HUBER, CAROL SMITH, small business owner; b. Detroit, July 8, 1942; d. Ben J. and Flossie Katherine (Callaghan) Smith; m. Barry Wayne Sheldon (div. 1975); 1 child, Chesca Rynn; m. Stephen Thomas Huber, Feb. 6, 1976. BS, Ea. Mich. U., 1965. Tchr. home econs. Peace Corps., Jamaica, 1963-64, Ypsilanti (Mich.) High Sch., 1966-67; tchr. colonial crafts Henry Ford Mus., Dearborn, Mich., 1969-73, Conn. Coll., New London, 1973-80; co-owner S&C Huber Am. Classics, East Lyme, Conn., 1984—; owner spinning and weaving shop Colonial Textiles, Ann Arbor, Mich., 1967-73; owner colonial crafts studio Colonial Textiles, East Lyme, 1973-82; co-owner spl. textiles, antiques Stephen & Carol Huber, Inc., East Lyme, 1973—; tchr. colonial crafts U. Mich., Ann Arbor, 1970-71, U. Conn., Storrs, 1973-78. Author: CountryKnits, 1987, CountryKnits for Kids, 1987, CountryKnits II, 1988. Bd. trustees East Lyme Hist. Soc., 1985-87. Home: 82 Plants Dam Rd East Lyme CT 06333 Office: S&C Huber Am Classics 82 Plants Dam Rd East Lyme CT 06333

HUBER, JOAN ALTHAUS, sociology educator; b. Bluffton, Ohio, Oct. 17, 1925; d. Lawrence Lester and Hallie Moser (Althaus) H.; m. William Form, Feb. 5, 1971; children: Nancy Rytina, Steven Rytina. B.A., Pa. State U., 1945; M.A., Western Mich. U., 1963; Ph.D., Mich. State U., 1967. Asst. prof. sociology U. Notre Dame, Ind., 1967-71; asst. prof. sociology U. Ill., Urbana-Champaign, 1971-73; assoc. prof. U. Ill., 1973-78, prof., 1978-83, head dept., 1979-83; dean Coll. Social and Behavioral Sci., Ohio State U., Columbus, 1984—; coordinating dean Coll. Arts and Sciences, Ohio State University, Columbus, 1987—. Author: (with William Form) Income and Ideology, 1973, (with Glenna Spitze) Sex Stratification, 1983. Editor: Changing Women in a Changing Society, 1973, (with Paul Chalfant) The Sociology of Poverty, 1974. NSF research awardee, 1978-81. Mem. Am. Sociol. Assn. (v.p. 1981-83, pres. 1987—), Sociologists for Women in Soc., Midwest Sociol. Soc. (pres. 1979-80). Home: 2880 North Star Rd Columbus OH 43221 Office: Ohio State U 166 Denney Hall 164 W 17th St Columbus OH 43210

HUBER, MARGARET ANN, college president; b. Rochester, Pa., July 27, 1949; d. Francis Xavier and Mary Ann (Socash) H. B.S. in Chemistry, Duquesne U., 1972; M.S.A., U. Notre Dame, 1975; Ph.D., U. Mich., 1979. Joined Sisters of Divine Providence of Pittsburgh, Pa.; jr. high tchr. St. Martin Sch., Pitts., 1971-72; asst. to acad. dean LaRoche Coll., Pitts., 1972-75; research assoc. U. Mich., Ann Arbor, 1978; dir. planning LaRoche Coll., 1978-80, exec. v.p., 1980-81, pres., 1981—. Mem. Am. Assn. for Higher Edn. Democrat. Roman Catholic. Office: LaRoche Coll 9000 Babcock Blvd Pittsburgh PA 15237 *

HUBER, RITA NORMA, civic worker; b. Cin., July 16, 1931; d. Andrew Elwood and Mary Gertrude (Hille) Stewart; student Cin. Coll. Conservatory Music, 1949-50, Berlitz Sch., Cin., 1951-52; m. Justin G. Huber, July 17, 1954; children—Monica Ann, Sarah Marie, Rachel Miriam Tchr. Russian lang. for officers' wives Ft. Sill, Okla., 1955-56; bd. dirs. United Community Services, Cedar Rapids, Iowa, 1969; founder, chairperson Linn County Consumers League, 1969-70; founder, public relations dir. Cedar Rapids Rape Crisis Services, 1974—; owner/operator Hurber Janitorial Services; chairperson Linn County Democratic Womens Club, 1966-67, Linn County Com., Eugene McCarthy for Pres., 1967-68; campaign mgr. Delores Cortez for Iowa Legislature, 1968, Jan V. Johnson for Iowa Legislature, 1970, Stanley Ginsberg for county supr. Linn County, 1974, E.L. Colton for Cedar Rapids pub. safety commr., 1977; chairperson Linn County Dem. Central Com., 1976-77, 88—; state coordinator Jerry Brown for Pres., 1976; chairperson Pat Kane for Linn County Recorder, 1982; mem. Iowa and Nat. Women's Polit. Caucus; chmn. Linn County Bd. Health; instr. parliamentary procedures Cedar Rapids Women's Community Leadership Inst., 1975-77; lectr. local colls. and service orgns.; tchr. conversational Russian, Pierce Elementary Sch., Cedar Rapids, 1976; instr. Russian, Community Edn. div. Kirkwood Community Coll.; mem. care rev. com. Pineview Care Ctr., Cedar Rapids, 1987—. Named to Iowa Dem. Party DVP Hall of Fame, 1986. Mem. Am. Inst. Parliamentarians. Roman Catholic (extraordinary minister of Eucharist). Composer: She is Risen, 1973. Home: 2050 Glass Rd NE Cedar Rapids IA 52402

HUBLITZ, SUE, sales professional; b. N.Y.C., June 6, 1940; d. Lincoln and Katherine (Daly) H. BA in Speech Therapy, Hofstra Coll., 1962; M, Columbia U., 1968. Head occupational therapy dept. St. Agnes Hosp., White Plains, N.Y., 1971-76; program coordinator devel. disabilities North Shore U. Hosp., Manhasset, N.Y., 1976-78; sales rep. Becton-Dickinson, Rutherford, N.J., 1978-81, Argus Surg. Co., Inc., Mt. Vernon, N.Y., 1981—. Mem. Am. Assn. Occupational Therapist (cert.). Home: 765 N Broadway 18B Hastings-on-Hudson NY 10706 Office: Argus Surg Co Inc 6 North St Mount Vernon NY 10550

HUCKABONE, ELIZABETH FRIED, real estate development and management executive; b. Buffalo, June 13, 1947; d. Martin B. and Isabel (Peek) Fried; A.B., SUNY, Coll. at Buffalo, 1979; postgrad. SUNY-Buffalo 1979-81; m. Darrell A. Huckabone, July 1, 1981; 1 child, Sara Elizabeth. Mgr., Belmont Mgmt. Co., Inc., Buffalo, 1976-84; pres. Belmont Shelter Corp., Buffalo, 1977—, also chmn. bd.; partner Belmont Housing Assos., Buffalo, 1981—. Recipient Property Mgr. merit award Nat. Assn. Home Builders, 1982. Registered apt. mgr.; lic. real estate broker, N.Y. Mem. Nat. Leased Housing Assn. (dir. 1980-83, 85—, sec. 1983-85). Office: 560 Delaware Ave Buffalo NY 14202

HUDAK, CHRISTINE ANGELA, hospital official, nurse; b. Cleve., Dec. 13, 1950; d. Ernest John and Helen Marie (Orovets) H. BS in Nursing, Case Western Res. U., 1974; MEd, Cleve. State U., 1980, doctoral student, 1987—. Staff nurse Vis. Nurse Assn., Cleve., 1974-75; clin. preceptor physicians asst. program Cuyahoga Community Coll., Cleve., 1975-77; staff nurse Sunny Acres Skilled Nursing Facility, Cleve., 1977-78; staff devel. instr. med. service Cleve. Met. Gen. Hosp., 1978-82, staff devel. instr. central programs/computers 1982-85, health care analyst/info. specialist, 1985-87, coordinator clin. info. systems, 1987—; cons. curriculum devel. Ctr. Health Affairs, Cleve., 1981-85, Kidney Found. Ohio, 1979-85; instr. continuing edn. Cleve. State U., 1983—; instr. health care info. systems Capital U., 1986—. Mem. women's com. Cleve. Orch., 1982—. Mem. Assn. Devel. Computer Based Instructional Systems, Ednl. Computer Consortium Ohio, Assn. Ednl. Communication and Tech., Mensa, Am. Assn. Artificial Intelligence, Phi Delta Kappa, Pi Lambda Theta, Sigma Theta Tau. Roman Catholic. Office: Cleve Met Gen Hosp 3395 Scranton Rd Cleveland OH 44109

HUDDLE, WANDA J., educator; b. Batesville, Ark., Mar. 25, 1946; d. E. Wayne and Wanda Lea (Elumbaugh) Jeffrey; m. George D. Love, 1967 (div. 1971); 1 child, Jeffrey Dean; m. Roy V. Huddle, Oct. 27, 1979. BSE, Ark. State U., 1966; MLS, U. Okla., 1972; cert. Ednl. Specialist, U. Ark., 1981. Librarian Searcy (Ark.) Pub. Schs., 1966-67; librarian, media specialist Pulaski County Schs., Little Rock, Ark., 1967-82, personnel adminstr., 1982-84, dir. staff devel., 1984-86; program advisor Ark. Dept. of Edn., Little Rock, 1984—, facilitator Restructuring Schs., 1988—; pres. Vision Resources & Assocs., Little Rock, 1986—; cons. Ark. Pub. Schs., 1984—, Performax Effective Mgmt., WE Care. Bd. dirs. Am. Cancer Soc., Little Rock, 1984—, bd. trustees Nat. Staff Devel. Council, 1986—; mem. Otter Creet Home Owners Club. Grantee Ark. Dept. of Edn., 1985, Winthrop Rockefeller Found., 1985, Met. Life Found., 1986. Mem. Am. Library Assn., Ark. Edn. Assn. (polit. action com. 1966-82), Nat. Assn. Female Execs, Ark. Soc. Tng. and Devel. (Outstanding mem. 1985), Ark. Assn. Curriculum and Supervision (bd. dirs. 1987—), Nat. Assn. Curriculum and Supervision, Phi Delta Kappa, Alpha Gamma Delta, Delta Kappa Gamma. Democrat. Baptist. Clubs: Ark. Ski (Little Rock), Hunting and Retriever (Forest City, Ark.). Office: Ark Dept Edn #4 Capitol Mall Little Rock AR 72201

HUDDLES, LINDA SUE, psychotherapist; b. Balt., July 5, 1939; d. Louis Cyrus and Beatrice (Freedman) Schwartz; B.S. summa cum laude, U. Md., 1962; M.S., Loyola Coll., Balt., 1980; grad. Jay Haley Family Therapy Inst., 1982; m. Gary Huddles, Dec. 16, 1961; children—John David, Kirk. Jr. exec. trainee Williams & Wilkens Med. Pubs., Balt., 1958-59; elem. tchr., Balt., 1962-63; vol. worker Sinai Hosp., Balt., 1970-71, Asso. Jewish Charities, Balt., 1970-75; counselor Planned Parenthood of Md., Balt., 1977-79; psychologist Northwestern Community Mental Health Center, Randallstown, Md., 1981—; pvt. practice psychotherapy, Towson, Md., 1981—. Former mem. Balt. County Arts Council; former chmn. div. Asso. Jewish Charities, award for service. Mem. Am. Psychol. Assn., Md. Psychol. Assn., Am. Personnel and Guidance Assn., Phi Kappa Phi, Kappa Delta Pi. Democrat. Jewish. Oil painter, works exhibited Balt. area, 1976-77. Home: 7 Swanhill Dr Baltimore MD 21208 Office: 28 Allegheny Ave Towson MD 21204

HUDDLESTON, LAUREN BEULAH, oil company executive, human resource developer; b. Nashville, Nov. 19, 1933; d. John and Chattie (Rich) H.; m. Gilbert Taylor, Aug. 25, 1950 (div. July 1972); children: Jeffrey, Charles, Marianne; m. Robert W. Fisher, Apr. 5, 1976. BA, Stephens Coll., 1980; MSW, U. Denver, 1984, PhD, 1988. Clinician, psychotherapy tchr. Halcyon, Inc., Lafayette, Ind., 1972-76; biofeedback specialist New Orleans Ctr. for Psychotherapy, 1976-78; with organizational design and human resource devel., orgnl. design The Anchoring System, Denver, 1972—; adminstrv. dir., v.p. Bradden Exploration, Denver, 1981-86; pres., chief exec. officer Fisher Energy Group, Denver, 1986—; developer wellness and peer counseling program Srs. Resource Ctr. Jefferson County, Denver, 1982-84. Co-organizer Citizens for Responsible Devel. of Bergen Park, Evergreen, Colo., 1983; dean search com. Grad. Sch. Social Work, Denver U., 1982—. Mem. Nat. Assn. Social Workers, World Future Soc., Internat. Transactional Analysis Assn. (clin. cert.), Nat. Assn. Female Execs., Ind. Petroleum Assn. Mountain States, Am. Mgmt. Assn., Internat. Platform Assn. Office: Fisher Energy Group 1020 15th St 4 L Denver CO 80202

HUDDLESTON, MARILYN ANNE, business and financial consultant; b. Fayetteville, N.C., Jan. 28, 1953; d. Allen Paul and Julia Jewel (Hill) Miller; m. Roby Dwayne Huddleston, Sept. 13, 1946; children—Michelle, Christopher, Mathew, Danyel, Michael. B.A. in Real Estate and Fin., Central Tex. U., 1974; diploma Acad. of Coll. of Real Estate, 1977; postgrad. El Paso Community Coll. Owner, fin. cons. Cherokee Fin. Investments, Killeen, Tex., 1983—; owner, broker All Am. Ins. Agy., Killeen, 1984—; realtor, assoc. Exec. Fin., Austin, Tex., 1986—; owner Geodesic Homes of Tex., Killeen, 1984—. Author: Miracle Baby at Bracken Ridge Hospital, 1979; Financial Consulting Made Easy, 1983. Pres. Mil. Council of Catholic Women, Stuttgart, Fed. Republic Germany, 1980, Non-Commnd. Officers Wives, Stuttgart, 1980-82, Ciudad del Niño Orphanage Assn., Killeen, 1979—; instr. Christian Religion, Killeen, 1976—. Mem. Nat. Assn. Female Execs., Internat. Assn. Bus. and Fin. Cons. (hon.), Fort Hood Bd. Realtors, Nat. Assn. Realtors, Tex. Assn. Realtors Soc. Female Execs. (v.p. 1984-86), Internat. Soc. Financiers (cert.). Republican. Roman Catholic. Avocations: singing; writing; tennis; golf; macrame. Home: Rural Rt 5 Box 5760 Belton TX 76513 Office: Cherokee Fin Investments PO Box 1299 Killeen TX 76540

HUDDLESTON, MARY LOUISE, bus company executive; b. Chattanooga, Dec. 28, 1945; d. Howard Pierce and Francis Louise (Talifereo) H.; m. Claude Herman, June 12, 1969 (div. 1976). B.S., U. Tenn., 1967. Tchr., Titusville High Sch., Fla., 1969-70, Bishop Byrne High Sch., Memphis, 1970-72; dir. sales Sea Life Park, Honolulu, 1972-74; v.p. sales Greyhound Royal Hawaiian, Honolulu, 1974-77; v.p. group sales Greyhound Lines, Phoenix, 1977-79; v.p. group sales Trailways, Inc., Dallas, 1979-87; v.p. sales charter and group div., Greyhound/Trailways Corp., Dallas, 1987; exec. v.p., gen. mgr. Hawaiian Adventure Co., Honolulu, 1988—. Named Travel Woman of Yr., Travel Industry Assn. Am., 1983. Mem. Am. Soc. Travel Agts., Am. Bus. Assn. (bd. dirs. 1980-85), Women in Transp. Dallas. Republican. Home: 14333 Preston Rd #1604 Dallas TX 75240 Office: Hawaiian Adventures 444 Hobron Ln Vista Level Honolulu HI 96815

HUDGENS, ELNORA, pianist; b. Baytown, Tex., Jan. 3, 1943; d. John Eugene and Mabel Allene (Elder) H. Student, Southwestern U., 1961, Wharton County Jr. Coll., 1962, 64, 87, Houston Community Coll., 1975-77. Accompanist Meth. Bible Sch., Katy, Tex., 1957-61, various clubs, functions, Katy, 1961—. Vol. Ronald Reagan Campaign, Houston, 1986, others. Mem. Houston Music Tchrs. Assn., Katy Music Tchrs. Assn. (historian), Dist. Leadership Am. Home: PO Box 941 Katy TX 77492

HUDGINS, CATHERINE HARDING, business executive; b. Raleigh, N.C., June 25, 1913; d. William Thomas and Mary Alice (Timberlake) Harding; m. Robert Scott Hudgins IV, Aug. 20, 1938; children: Catherine Harding, Deborah Ghiselin, Robert Scott V. BS, N.C. State U., 1929-33; grad. tchr. N.C. Sch. for Deaf, 1933-34. Tchr. N.C. Sch. for Deaf, Morganton, 1934-36; sec. Dr. A.S. Oliver, Raleigh, 1937; tchr. N.J. Sch. for Deaf, Trenton, 1937-39; sec. Robert S. Hudgins Co., Charlotte, N.C., 1949—, v.p., treas., 1960—, also bd. dirs. Mem. Jr. Service League, Easton, Pa., 1939; project chmn. ladies aux. Profl. Engrs. N.C., 1954-55, pres., 1956-57; pres. Christian High Sch. PTA, 1963; program chmn. Charlotte Opera Assn., 1959-61, sec., 1961-63; sec. bd. Hezekiah Alexander House Restoration, 1949-52, Hezekiah Alexander House Aux., 1975—, treas., 1983-84, v.p., 1984-85, pres., 1985—; sec. Hezediah Alexander Found., 1986—; past chmn. home missions, annuities and relief Women of Presbyn. Ch., past pres. Sunday Sch. class. Mem. N.C. Hist. Assn., English Speaking Union, Internat. Platform Assn., Mint Mus. Drama Guild (pres. 1967-69), Daus. Am. Colonists (state chmn. nat. def. 1973-74, corr. sec. Virginia Dare chpt. 1978-79, 84-85, state insignia chmn. 1979-80), DAR (mem. nat. chmn.'s assn., nat. officers club; chpt. regent 1957-59, chpt. chaplain 1955-57 N.C. program chmn. 1961-63, state chmn. nat. def. 1973-76, state rec. sec. 1977-79, state regent 1979-82, hon. state regent 1982—), Children Am. Revolution (N.C. sr. pres. 1963-66, sr. nat. corr. sec., 1966-68, sr. nat. 1st v.p. 1968-70, sr. nat. pres. 1970-72, hon. sr. nat. pres. life 1972—; 2d v.p. Nat. Officers Club, 1st v.p. 1977-79, pres. 1979-81), Huguenot Soc. N.C. Club: Carmel Country (Charlotte), Viewpoint 24 (v.p. 1986, pres. 1987). Home: 1514 Wendover Rd Charlotte NC 28211 Office: PO Box 17217 Charlotte NC 28211

HUDGINS-BONAFIELD, CHRISTINE ANN, editor; b. Chilocothe, Ohio, Dec. 1, 1954; d. Malcolm M. and Ruby Helen (Star) H.; m. Michael J. Bonafield, Apr. 8, 1981. BS, Auburn U., 1977; postgrad., U. Ala., 1977-79. Reporter Huntsville (Ala.) Times, 1975; asst. press sec. Sen. John Sparkman, Washington, 1976; reporter Wash. Post, 1977, Minn. Star/Tribune, 1979-84, Nuclear Energy McGraw-Hill, Washington, 1984-85; writer internat. corr. McGraw-Hill, Geneva, 1985-86; data editor Communications Week, Washington, 1986—; Author: Auburn Alabama Jokes, 1975. Mem. LWV, AP, Minn. Edn. Assn., Sigma Delta Xi. Club: Nat. Press.

HUDSON, ARLENE, environmental activist; b. Oakland, Calif., Aug. 11, 1959; d. Clyde Edward and Helen Therese (Cerutti) McIrvin; m. James Joseph Coté, Mar. 28, 1958 (div. 1963); 1 child, Steven Michael. BA in Psychology, Calif. State U., Sacramento, 1976, postgrad., 1977-78. Campaign mgr. various state, fed. and local campaigns, Sacramento, 1967-72; exec. field dir. Dem. State Cen. Com., Sacramento, 1967-68; mem. staff Calif. Legis., Sacramento, 1969-72; founder The Group for Alternatives to Spreading Poisons, Nevada City, Calif., 1983—, also bd. dirs., editor newletter, 1986—; co-founder, liaison, del. Calif. Coalition for Alternatives to Pesticides, Arcata, 1983—; mem. Nev. County Toxic and Hazardous Waste Task Force, 1987—, chair tech. subcom., 1988—. Founding mem. Toxics Coordinating Project, 1985; mem. mktg. order subcom. Steering Com. for Sustainable Agr., 1986—; bd. dirs. N.W. Coalition for Alternatives to Pesticides, Eugene, Oreg., 1987—; mem. citizens adv. com. on Nev. County Restrictions on Open Burning and Edn. Program, 1988—. Mem. Sierra Club (chairperson toxic subcom. Sierra Nev. Group of the Mother Lode chpt. 1985-87), Amnesty Internat., Better World Soc., Council for a Livable World, Nat. Peace Inst. Found., People's Med. Soc., Earth First, Nat. Resources Def. Council, Nev. County C. of C., Greenpeace (planning and conservation league). Mem. Universal Life Ch. Home and Office: 10984 Ridge Rd Nevada City CA 95959

HUDSON, COURTNEY MORLEY, interior landscape designer; b. Shreveport, La., Nov. 19, 1955; d. Morley Alvin and Lucy (North) H. Student, So. Meth. U., 1973-74; BS in Horticulture Tech., La. State U., 1978. Owner Interiorscapes, Shreveport, 1978-83, Dallas, 1983-85, C. Hudson, Dallas, 1985—. Vol. Rep. Nat. Conv., 1976; Rep. del., La., 1975; mem. Jr. League Dallas. Mem. Am. Soc. Landscape Architects, North Tex. Interiorscape Assn. (pres. 1984-85), Assn. Landscape Contractors Am. (exec. bd. 1984-86). Office: 746 Lingco Suite 112 Richardson TX 75081

HUDSON, JACQUELINE, artist; b. Cambridge, Mass.; d. Eric and Gertrude (Dunton) H.; student Columbia U., Art Students League, Sch. of the Nat. Acad. One-woman shows: Burr Gallery, N.Y.C., Rockport (Mass.) Art Assn., Present Day Club, Princeton, N.J., Maine Art Gallery, Wiscasset, Moulson Union, Bowdoin Coll., 1979; group shows: NAD, Pa. Acad. Fine Arts, Library of Congress, Cin. Mus., Riverside Mus., Portland (Maine) Mus. Art, Dayton Art Inst., Bixler Mus., Colby Coll., Maine Art Gallery, Wiscasset, Bowdoin Coll., Farnsworth Mus., Rockland, Maine, Vallombreuse Gallery, Palm Beach, Fla., Galerie Salammbo, Paris, many others; represented permanent collection Library of Congress, Galerie Salammbo, Paris; pvt. collections. Recipient Pennell Purchase prize Library of Congress, 1951; Allen Kander Found. award Rockport Art Assn., 1957, Thelma Karr Graphic Prize, 1986; Edith Wengenroth Meml. prize, 1971, 75; Alice Standish Buell Meml. prize Nat. Assn. Women Artists, 1968, Helen Turner Graphic prize, 1974, Donna Miller Meml. prize, 1980; 3d graphic prize Butler Inst. Am. Art, 1983. Mem. Art Students League, Nat. Assn. Women Artists. Rockport Art Assn., Lincoln County Cultural and Hist. Assn., Monhegan (Maine) Assos. (chmn. mus. com. 1963-67). Home: Monhegan Island ME 04852 Other: Federal St Wiscasset ME 04578

HUDSON, JANE SMITHER, furniture manufacturing company executive; b. Altavista, Va., July 5, 1937; d. Victor Nelson and Elois Reynolds Smither; A.A.S. summa cum laude in Mgmt., Central Va. Community Coll., 1978; m. J. Lee Hudson, May 15, 1954; 1 son, Michael Edward. Adminstrv. asst. Altavista (Va.) High Sch., 1954-55; with Lane Co., Inc., Altavista, 1956—, exec. sec. to chmn. bd., 1976-81, exec. sec. to chmn. exec. com., 1981-84, spl. asst. for pub. relations communications, 1984-86, acct. exec. nat. accts, 1986, asst. sales mgr. contract div., 1986-87, mktg. adminstr., 1988—; realtor R. B. Carr & Co., Altavista, 1980—, assoc. broker, 1985—; mem. adv. bd. Am. Fed. Savs. and Loan, 1985—. Mem. town council Town of Altavista, 1980-86; sec. Altavista Community Improvement Council, 1981-82; mem. bd. deacons First Bapt. Ch., Altavista, 1980-83. Mem. Va. Assn. Realtors, Nat. Assn. Realtors. Corr. Lynchburg (Va.) News., 1966-72. Home: 1102 Commonwealth Dr Altavista VA 24517 Office: Lane Co Inc Franklin Ave Altavista VA 24517

HUDSON, MARGARET STOVER, educational administrator; b. Roanoke, Va., Sept. 27, 1947; d. Charles Marvin and Magdalene Virginia (Hobson) Stover; m. John David Hudson, Mar. 1, 1974; 1 stepchild, John David, Jr. B.B.A. cum laude, Roanoke Coll., 1971. Cashier, bookkeeper Roanoke Coll., Salem, Va., 1965-74, controller, 1974-79, dir. fin. and adminstrv. services, 1979-84, bus. mgr., 1984—; customer relations rep. Nat. Cash Register Co., Roanoke, 1974; trustee Diuguid-Spencer Trust, Salem, 1976—, Harold Harris Unitrust, Salem, 1983—, James W. Sieg Unitrust, Salem, 1984—, Lois C. Fisher Unitrust, Salem, 1984—, June Sheelsman Unitrust, 1984—, Rural and Thelma Meadors Annuity Trust, Salem, 1985—. Bd. dirs. Va. Choral Soc., Salem, 1974. Mem. Nat. Assn. Coll. and Univ. Bus. Officers, Nat. Assn. Accts., Coll. and Univ. Personnel Assn., So. Assn. Coll. and Univ. Bus. Officers, Va. Dressage Assn., U.S. Dressage Fedn.. Methodist. Club: Roanoke Valley Figure Skating. Lodge: Rotary. Home: 6539 Laban Rd NW Roanoke VA 24019 Office: Roanoke Coll Salem VA 24153

HUDSON, MARY, oil company executive; b. Athens, Tex., Sept. 30, 1912; d. John Thurmond and Lou Allie (Dewberry) H.; m. Cecil Wayne Driver, Sept. 20, 1939; 1 child, Joyce Driver Cady; m. Frank Bane Vandgrift, June 2, 1945 (dec. 1977). Student U. Okla., U. Kans. Co-founder, 1932, since chmn., chief exec. officer Hudson Oil Co., Kansas City, Kans.; pres., chief exec. officer Hudson Refining Co., 1977—; adv. com. Nat. Petroleum Council, 1976; counsel Republic Colombia in Kansas City, 1959-84. Hon. bd. dirs. Rockhurst Coll., Kansas City. Named Hon. Citizen of Kansas City (Mo.), 1971, Ky. col., 1964. Mem. Soc. Ind. Gasoline Marketers Am. (a founder, pres. 1965-68), Ind. Gasoline Marketeers Council (a founder), Women's Kansas City Assn. Internat. Relations and Trade (pres. 1971-74), Counsular Corps Greater Kansas City (dean), Am. Petroleum Inst., Am. Petroleum Refiners Assn., 25 Year Club Petroleum Industry, DAR. Clubs: Kansas City. Lodge: Order Ea. Star. Office: Box B Kansas City KS 66103

HUDSON, MOLLY ANN, advertising executive; b. Detroit, Apr. 27, 1941; d. Gabriel Nathanial and Beatrice Meriam (Joshel) Alexander; m. Leonard Atkins, June 18, 1961 (div. 1963); 1 child, Sidney Louis; m. Patrick Hudson, May 4, 1968 (widowed 1974); m. Arnold Leonard Rosen, June 20, 1982. Student, U. Colo., 1958-59, Wayne State U., 1959-61. Supr. creative dept. D'Arcy, MacManus, Benton & Bowles, Detroit, 1965-71, Campbell-Ewald Co., Detroit, 1971-83; sr. v.p. Lintas, N.Y.C., 1987—, group sr. v.p., 1986-87, sr. v.p., 1987—. Food editor Met. Detroit, 1983-84; pub. (newsletter) The Food Enthusiast, 1983-85. Recipient Outstanding Achievement award Am. Women in Radio and TV, 1977; named Ad Woman of Yr., Women's Ad Club, 1980; named to Acad. Women Achievers, YWCA, 1986. Mem. Advt. Club N.Y., Advt. Women N.Y. Jewish. Office: Lintas New York One Dag Hammarskjold Plaza New York NY 10017

HUDSON, MONICA SUE, artist, teacher; b. Rockford, Ill., Nov. 2, 1951; d. William Voorhees Doran and Venita Darlene (Zant) Enright; m. Russell Leland Thompson, July 10, 1970 (div. Dec. 1975); m. John Buford Hudson, Oct. 22, 1983; 1 child, Lauren Elizabeth. BFA, Art Inst. of Chgo., 1983. Cert. tchr., Ill. Artists asst. Bradford/Cout Graphic Design, Skokie, Ill., 1980-81; freelance artist Chgo., 1981-82; graphic designer and sculpture Monica's Studio, Springfield, Ill., 1983—; tchr. Springfield Sch. Dist. 186, 1988—; art therapist McFarland Ctr. for Mental Health, Springfield, 1988—. Designer poster Children's Arts Festival, 1986, 87, 88, sculpture Mayor's Art award, 1987, Sr. Olympics poster, 1985; participant light sculpture America Now, Zagreb, Yugoslavia, 1979. Coordinator Artist on the Plaza art series, Springfield, 1986, 87, 88, First Night Springfield laser show, 1988. Mem. Springfield Art Assn. (docent 1985, Springfield Area Arts Council (dir. 1985—), Womens Art Alliance (v.p. 1987—). Democrat. Roman Catholic. Lodge: Elks. Home: 200 N Douglas Springfield IL 62702

HUDSON, MYRA LINDEN FRANK, banker; b. Richmond, Va., Oct. 26, 1950; d. J. C. and Myra Teresa (Lanzarone) Frank; m. Timothy Franklin Long (div. Jan. 1981); m. Robert Andrew Hudson. BA, Erskine Coll., 1972; student, Inst. Fin. Edn., 1982-88. Chief activities therapist S.C. Dept. Corrections, Columbia, 1973-75, acting prin., 1975-77, coll. coordinator, 1977-78; owner, operator Carolina Coast Seafood, Aiken (S.C.) and Beaufort (S.C), 1978-80; from teller to savs. counselor Security Fed. Savs. & Loan, Aiken, 1981-83; rep. customer service Bankers 1st Savs. & Loans, Augusta, Ga., 1983-84, mgr. br. adminstrn., 1984-85; coordinator automated teller machines, banking officer 1st Fed. Savs. Bank, Brunswick, Ga., 1985—; lectr. S.C. Edn. Tchrs. Assn., Columbia, 1974, S.C. Assn. Social Workers, Columbia, 1975, Bus. & Profl. Women's Club, Columbia, 1978; small bus. owner, distbr. Nuskin product line, 1987—. Appeared with Aiken Community Theatre, 1981. Mem. hospice com. Am. Cancer Soc., Augusta, 1981; lectr. St. John's United Meth. Ch., 1981-82. Mem. Nat. Assn. for Female Execs. Democrat. Home: 32 Seminole Rd Brunswick GA 31520

HUDSON-KIMBROUGH, LINDA, health care executive; b. Tuscaloosa, Ala., Feb. 12, 1950; d. Elvin and Clara (Duke) Hudson; m. Charles Garrett Kimbrough, May 26, 1984. BS in Edn., U. Ala., 1971; MS in Psychology, U. So. Miss., 1984. Recreational therapist West Ala. Rehab. Ctr., Tuscaloosa, 1971-72; flight attendant Delta Air Lines, Miami and New Orleans, 1972-80; pvt. practice psychotherapist Hattiesburg (Miss.) and Atlanta, 1984—; program dir. Eating Disorders Adventist Health System/West, Atlanta, 1985-88, regional dir./cons., 1986-87, exec. dir mental health services, 1988—, nat. cons., 1986-88. Contbr. articles to profl. jours. Mem. Covington Jr. Service League, La., 1981-83; co-chmn. St. Tammany Rep. Polit. Action Com., 1980-81; coordinator United Way of St. Tammany Parish, 1979-80. Mem. NOW, Am. Assn. Marriage and Family Therapists, Nat. Assn. Female Execs., Atlanta Women's Network. Democrat. Baptist. Office: Advance Treatment Services Smyrna Hosp 4200 Notrhside Pkwy Atlanta GA 30327

HUEY, SANDRA AGEE, state agency administrator; b. Charleston, W.Va., Sept. 28, 1948; d. Homer Ray and Roberta Star (Hudnall) Agee; m. P.E. Gee Jr., Nov. 27, 1969 (div. Jan. 1986); 1 child, Adam Creighton; m. Cleveland A. Huey, Jan. 16, 1987; children: John B. League III, Micah Merrit. AA, Columbia Comml. coll., 1969; student, Furman U., 1966-67; postgrad., U. S.C., 1972-76. Legal sec. Johnson & Jones, Attys., Gulfport, Miss., 1970; staff asst. State Treas. of S.C., Columbia, 1970-74, adminstrv. asst., 1974-79, sr. asst. state treas., 1979-84, dep. state treas., 1985—; asst. to chmn. State Bd. of Fin. Inst., Columbia, 1972—. Pres. Lexington United Meth. Women, 1986; youth dir. Lexington United Meth. Ch., 1979-83, sec. adminstrv. bd. 1978-86; youth dir. Corpus Christi Cath. ch., 1978-83; bd. dirs. State Employees Assn., Columbia, 1973-75, Lexington Elem. PTA, 1984, 85. Mem. Govt. Fin. Officers Assn. Club: Lexington Jr. Women (sec. 1985-86). Home: 116 Middlebrook Dr Lexington SC 29072 Office: State Treas Office PO Box 11778 Capitol Station Columbia SC 29211

HUF, CAROL ELINOR, tax service company executive; b. Milw., Apr. 21, 1940; d. William Weiss and Florence H. (Melcher) Weiss Lange; m. Walter Franklin Huf, Sept. 9, 1961; children—Mardell Leslie, Walter Albert III. Student Valparaiso U., 1958-60, Waukesha County Tech. Inst., 1968-69. Tax preparer H & R Block, Milw., 1967-84, instr. tax sch., 1969-83; job service interviewer State of Wis., Waukesha, 1984; pres. Personalized Tax Service, Inc., West Allis, Wis., 1984—, div. mgr. A.L. Williams, 1986. Vol. worker Girl Scouts US, Waukesha, 1970-80, Boy Scouts Am., Waukesha, 1975—; swimming referee Wis. Interscholastic Athletic Assn., Milw., 1972-84. Recipient awards Boy Scouts Am. Mem. Wis. Womens Pub. Links Golf Assn. (sr. v.p. 1986—, state tournament chairperson 1987), Wis. Assn. Accts., Met. Swimming Ofcls. Lutheran. Clubs: Edgewood Golf (Big Bend, Wis.) (pres. 1984—). Home: 17825 Westward Dr New Berlin WI 53151 Office: Personalized Tax Service Inc 10533 W National Ave West Allis WI 53227

HUFF, LAURA WEAVER, printmaker; b. Mt. Vernon, N.Y., Dec. 24, 1930; d. Ernest Mason and Marjorie (Calendar) Weaver; m. Alvin Warren Saile, June 10, 1950 (div. Dec. 1972); children: Carol Saile Jeffers, David Warren Saile, Marjorie Saile Fabian, Patty Saile Koehler; m. Eskin Huff, Apr. 7, 1973 (div. Feb. 1988). BA, U. Del., 1964; MFA, George Washington U., 1968. Tchr. Montgomery County Adult Edn., Rockville, Md., 1968-70; instr. Howard Community Coll., Columbia, Md., 1970-71; illustrator project LIFE Nat. Found. for Improvement Edn., Washington, 1971-73; tchr. Graphics Workshop, Glen Echo, Md., 1974-76; lectr. No. Va. Community Coll., Alexandria, 1976; graphics specialist Hazeltine Corp.,

McLean, Va., 1979-80; printmaker Mezzanine Multiples, Alexandria, 1982—; tchr. The Art League, Alexandria, 1985. Illustrator: Copy Cat Sam, 1982; printmaker calendar, 1979—; works included in Fine Print Collection Library Cong., Washington; designed official poster for Spirit of Houston Conf., 1987. Chair esthetics commn. Unitarian Ch. Rockville, 1965-83. Mem. The Art League, Washington Printmakers Gallery, Washington Area Printmakers, So. Graphics Council, The New Art Ctr., Phi Kappa Phi. Democrat. Unitarian-Universalist. Home: 11636 Brandy Hall Ln Gaithersburg MD 20878 Studio: Mezzanine Multiples Studio #225 105 N Union St Alexandria VA 22314

HUFF, NANCY RUTH, citrus groves administrator, investments executive; b. Cin.; d. Norman Vincent and Marie (Voss) H.; m. William H. Brady, Sept. 9, 1961 (div. Apr. 1971); children—William Huff, Sherry Lynn. B.A., Newton Coll. of the Sacred Heart, Mass., 1961. Asst. to pres. Star Fruit Co., Lake Alfred, Fla., 1961-71; mgr., pres. Huff Groves, Winter Haven, Fla., 1971—; pres Star Investments, Winter Haven, 1980—; v.p. Allapattah Operating Co., Fort Pierce, Fla., 1982—, pres. Alpat Grove care Co., Fort Pierce, 1982—. Mem. Fla. Citrus Mutual, Indian River Citrus League (com. mem.), Women in Citrus, Fla. Citrus Women. Republican. Clubs: Lake Region Yacht and Country, Gardania Garden. (v.p. 1974-78) (Winter Haven); Citrus (Orlando, Fla.). Avocations: photography; dance; tennis. Office: PO Box 7167 Winter Haven FL 33883

HUFFMAN, IRENE DOROTHY, wine marketing specialist; b. Joliet, Ill., Oct. 8, 1947; d. Bernard John McShane and Dorothy C. (Cheney) Boster; m. James Earl Huffman, Nov. 29, 1969. Student, No. Ill. U., 1964-66; AAS, Black Hawk Coll., 1979; BA, Western Ill. U., 1983. Computer operator Joliet Army Arsenal, 1966-72; computer programmer Bear Mfg., Rock Island, Ill., 1974-76; computer operator Deere Harvester Works, East Moline, Ill., 1976-80, computer programmer, 1980-83; computer standards coordinator Deere & Co. Harvester Works, East Moline, 1983-85; wine mktg. specialist Dimitri Wine & Spirits, Inc., Rock Island, Ill., 1986—; instr. wine Black Hawk Coll., Moline, Ill., 1984—; guest appearance Sta. WHBF-TV, Moline. Wine judge Miss. Valley Fair, Davenport, Iowa, 1981-82, Midwestern Wine Seminar, Lacrosse, Wis., 1985; mem. tech. team Nat. Restaurant Assn. Wine Competition, Chgo., 1985; contbr. articles on wine to profl. jours.; filmed wine segments for Sta. WQPT-TV, Moline, 1986-87. Vol. Friends of Lane Evans, Rock Island. Recipient 3d place award profl. div. Gejas Wine Competition, Chgo., 1986. Mem. NOW, Career Women's Network (bd. dirs. 1984-86), Soc. Wine Educators (Cert. Proficiency in Wine Knowledge 1987), Les Amis du Vin, Am. Inst. Wine and Food. Methodist. Home: 1225 W 5th St Milan IL 61264

HUFFMAN, NONA GAY, investment retirement specialist; b. Albuquerque, June 22, 1942; d. William Abraham and Opal Irene (Leaton) Crisp; m. Donald Clyde Williams, Oct. 20, 1961; children—Debra Gaylene, James Donald. Student pub. schs. Lawndale, Calif. Lic. ins., securities dealer, N.Mex. Sec. City of Los Angeles, 1960, Los Angeles City Schs. 1960-62, Aerospace Corp., El Segundo, Calif., 1962-64, Albuquerque Pub. Schs., 1972-73, Pub. Service Co. N.Mex., Albuquerque, 1973; rep., fin. planner Waddell & Reed, Inc., Albuquerque, 1979-84; broker Rauscher Pierce Refsnes, Inc., 1984-85; rep., investment and retirement specialist Fin. Network Investment Corp., 1985—; tchr. money mgmt. seminars for sr. citizens ctr.; instr. U. N.Mex. Sr. Citizen Continuing Edn. Mem. Profl. Orgn. Women (co-chmn.), Women in Bus. (Albuquerque chpt.), Internat. Assn. Fin. Planners. Office: Fin Network Investment Corp One Exec Ctr 8500 Menaul Blvd NE Suite A-301 Albuquerque NM 87112

HUFFMAN, ROSEMARY ADAMS, lawyer, corporate executive; b. Orlando, Fla., Oct. 18, 1939; d. Elmer Victor and Esther (Weber) Adams; divorced; 1 child, Justin Adams Fruth. A.B. in Econs., Ind. U., 1959, J.D., 1962; LL.M., U. Chgo., 1967. Bar: Ind. 1962, Fla. 1963. Dep. prosecutor Marion County, Ind., 1963; ct. adminstr. Ind. Supreme Ct., 1967-68; pro-tem judge Marion County Mcpl. Ct., 1969-70; jud. coordinator Ind. Criminal Justice Planning Agy., 1969-70; dir. ctr. for Jud. Edn., Inc., 1970-73; pub. Jud. Xchange, 1972-73; instr. bus. law Purdue U., Indpls., 1962-63, Ind. U., Indpls., 1963-64; asst. Ind. Jud. Council, 1965; legis. intern Ford Found., 1965; sole practice, Indpls., 1962—; pres., owner Abacus, Inc., Indpls., 1980—. Mem. Ind. Bar Assn., Fla. Bar Assn., Indpls. Bar Assn. Home and Office: 6630 E 56th St Indianapolis IN 46226

HUFFMAN, TEELA LOUISE LEWELLEN, medical center administrator; b. Tulsa, May 17, 1948; d. Delmar Huron and Joliet Arlie (Russell) Lewellen; m. Clyde Dean Huffman, Sept. 30, 1980. Student, Okla. State Tech. Inst. Keypunch operator T.G.&Y. Co., Oklahoma City, 1966-68; keypunch supr. Nat. Sharedata Co., Oklahoma City, 1968-71; computer operator Insured Aircraft Title Co., Oklahoma City, 1972-74; prodn. supr. Computer Mgmt. Corp., Oklahoma City, 1974-79; acct. mgr. Automatic Data Processing Co., Tulsa and Chgo., 1979; ops. mgr. Baptist Med. Ctr., Oklahoma City, 1979-86; dir. mgmt systems South Community Hosp., Oklahoma City, Okla., 1986—. Mem. Assn. for Computers Ops. Mgrs., Nat. Assn. Female Execs., Southwest Software Users Group, Am. Health Assn., Electronic Computing Health Oriented, Healthcare Info. and Mgmt. Systems Soc. of Am. Hosp. Assn. Republican. Baptist. Avocations: photography; travel; working with children. Home: 1617 College Ave Oklahoma City OK 73106 Office: South Community Hosp 1001 SW 44th St Oklahoma City OK 73109

HUFFMAN-HINE, RUTH CARSON, adult education administrator, educator; b. Spencer, Ind., Sept. 13, 1925; d. Joseph Charles Carson and Bess Ann Taylor; m. Joe Buren Hine; children: Paulette Walker, Larry K., Annette M. AA in Fine Arts, Ind. Cen. Coll., 1967, BS in Edn., Butler U., 1971; MS in Adult Edn., Ind. U., 1976. Cert. elem. edn. Subs. tchr. Met. Sch. Dist. Wayne Twnshp., Indpls., 1956-60; tchr. of homebound Met. Sch. Dist. Decatur Twnshp., Indpls., 1964-66; adult edn. tchr. Met. Sch. Dist. Wayne Twnshp., Indpls., 1971-75, adminstr. adult edn., 1975—; cons. Ind. Adoption System, Indpls., 1985—; regional rep. Ind. Assn. Adult Adminstrs., 1984—; program rep. Ind. Literacy Coordinators, Indpls., 1985—; speaker, mem. literacy research and evaluation com. Ind. Adult Literacy Coalition, Indpls., 1980-86. Author: Driving Regulations and Courtesies; coauthor Learning for Everyday Living, 1978, Table Approach to Education, 1984, Developing Educational Competencies for Individuals Determined to Excel, 6 vols., 1980 (ERIC System award 1980), (ERIC System award 1985), Collection, Evaluation, Dissemination of Special Research Projects, 1984, Automobile Driving Rules and Regulations, 1988. Vice com. person Rep. Orgn., Indpls., 1968-72; charter mem., sec. Project READ, LITERACY, 1988. Mem. Internat. Reading Assn. (Celebrate Literacy award 1984), Ind. Assn. for Adult Edn. (treas. 1984—, Outstanding Adult Educator 1979), Beta Phi Delta (pres. 1986—), Beta Phi, Delta Kappa Gamma (v.p. 1985-86, fellowship chmn. 1982-84), Phi Delta Kappa. Republican. Mem. Christian Ch. Home: 50 Abner Creek Pkwy Danville IN 46122 Office: Met Sch Dist Wayne Twnshp 1200 N Girls School Rd Indianapolis IN 46214

HUFFNUSS-TOWNLEY, BARBARA, health care executive; b. Chgo., Oct. 6, 1953; d. Klaus and Katharina (Gutti) Huffnuss. B.S. in Pharmacy, U. Ill.-Chgo., 1977. Registered pharmacist, Ill. Pharmacist, store mgr. Medicare Pharmacy, Chgo., 1977-78, Skokie, Ill., 1978-83; dist. dir. Medicare-Glaser Corp., Chgo., 1983—. Mem. Ill. Pharm. Assn., Am. Pharm. Assn. Democrat. Roman Catholic. Office: Medicare Pharmacy 4874 Dempster Skokie IL 60077

HUFNAGLE, BARBARA A., child care center executive; b. Brookville, Ohio, Apr. 18, 1939; d. Kenneth Harry and Gladys Iola (Lesher) Protzman; m. David R. Hufnagle, July 24, 1954 (div. June 1975); children—Eleanor Ruth, Julie Anne, Robert Walter. B.S. in Edn., Miami U., Oxford, Ohio, 1969, M.Ed. in Guidance and Counseling, 1972, M.Ed. in Curriculum and Supervision, 1975. Cert. ednl. adminstr. First grade tchr. West Carrollton Pub. Schs., Ohio, 1968—; pres., owner, mgr. Little Sch. Child Care Ctr., West Carrollton, 1976—. Author: Instructional Centers, 1983. Asst. band dir. West Carrollton High Sch. Band, 1983-85. Mem. NEA, Ohio Edn. Assn., West Carrollton Edn. Assn. (v.p. 1982—), Assn. for Supervision and Curriculum Devel., Nat. Assn. Edn. Young Children, U.S. Power Squadron, Ohio Assn. Child Care Providers, also yacht clubs and square dance clubs. Home: 6410 Blossom Park Dr West Carrollton OH 45449 Office: Little Sch Child Care Ctr 1049 Alex Rd Dayton OH 45449

HUFSCHMID, NANCY KAY, nurse; b. Charleston, Ark., Oct. 11, 1937; d. Daniel G. and Jocie M. (Fitzgerald) Keith; m. Wallace L. Hufschmid, Sept. 29, 1956 (div. Feb. 1971); children: Ramona, Kimley, Donald, Rebecca. Diploma Nursing, Sparks Meml. Hosp., Ft. Smith, Ark., 1958; BS, St. Joseph's Coll., North Windham, Maine, 1984; MBA, Oklahoma City U., 1987. Staff nurse St. John's Hosp., Tulsa, 1958-62; night nursing sup. Capitol Hill Hosp., Oklahoma City, 1963-66; staff nurse Bapt. Med. Ctr. of Okla., Oklahoma City, 1962-63, 1966-68, night nursing supr., 1968-71, clin. supr., 1971-72; night nursing supr. St. Anthony Hosp., Oklahoma City, 1973, Veterans Med. Ctr., Oklahoma City, 1973-80; dir. nursing South Community Hosp., Oklahoma City, 1980—. Republican. Mem. Ch. of Christ. Office: South Community Hosp 1001 S 44th St Oklahoma City OK 73109

HUFSTEDLER, SHIRLEY MOUNT (MRS. SETH M. HUFSTEDLER), lawyer, former federal judge; b. Denver, Aug. 24, 1925; d. Earl Stanley and Eva (Von Behren) Mount; m. Seth Martin Hufstedler, Aug. 16, 1949; 1 son, Steven Mark. B.B.A., U. N.Mex., 1945, LL.D. (hon.), 1972; LL.B., Stanford U., 1949; LL.D. (hon.), U. Wyo., 1970, Gonzaga U., 1970, Occidental Coll., 1971, Tufts U., 1974, U. So. Calif., 1976, Georgetown U., 1976, U. Pa., 1976, Columbia U., 1977, U. Mich., 1979, Yale U., 1981, Rutgers U., 1981, Claremont U. Center, 1981, Smith Coll., 1982, Syracuse U., 1983, Mt. Holyoke Coll., 1985; P.H.H. (hon.), Hood Coll., 1981, Hebrew Union Coll., 1986, Tulane U., 1988. Bar: Calif. 1950. Mem. firm Beardsley, Hufstedler & Kemble, Los Angeles, 1951-61; practiced in Los Angeles, 1961; judge Superior Ct., County Los Angeles, 1961-66; justice Ct. Appeals 2d Dist., 1966-68; circuit judge U.S. Ct. Appeals 9th Circuit, 1968-79; sec. U.S. Dept. Edn., 1979-81; partner firm Hufstedler, Miller, Carlson & Beardsley, Los Angeles, 1981—; dir. Hewlett Packard Co., US West, Inc., Harman Industries Internat. Mem. staff: Stanford Law Rev, 1947-49; articles and book rev. editor, 1948-49. Trustee Calif. Inst. Tech., Occidental Coll., 1972—, Aspen Inst. for Humanistic Studies, Colonial Williamsburg Found., 1976—, Constl. Rights Found., 1978-80, Nat. Resources Def. Council, 1983-85, Carnegie Endowment for Internat. Peace, 1983—; bd. dirs. John T. and Catherine MacArthur Found., 1983—. Named Woman of Year Ladies Home Jour., 1976; recipient UCLA medal, 1981. Mem. ABA, Los Angeles Bar Assns., Town Hall, Am. Law Inst. (council 1974-84), Am. Bar Found., Women Lawyers Assn. (pres. 1957-58), Am. Judicature Soc., Assn. of Bar of City of N.Y., Council on Fgn. Relations, Order of Coif. Office: Hufstedler Miller Carlson & Beardsley 355 S Grand Los Angeles CA 90071

HUG, BARBARA LEE, home economist; b. Newton, Iowa, Jan. 18, 1943. BS, Iowa State U., 1965, MS, 1976. Tchr. Colfax (Iowa) High Sch., 1965-66, Maxwell (Iowa) High Sch., 1966-68; tchr. adult edn. Des Moines Pub. Schs., 1969-74; home economist U. Wis. extension, Mauston, 1976-87, chair univ. com., 1986-87; mem. bd. edn. Mauston Sch. Dist., 1981—, pres., 1986—; mem. Wis. Child Abuse and Neglect Prevention Bd., Madison, 1983—, pres., 1986-88. Recipient Child Advocacy award Wis. Women's Network, 1982. Mem. Nat. Assn. Extension Home Econs. (author, editor child care youth program 1981, Pub. Affairs Edn. award 1982), Am. Home Econs. Assn., Wis. Home Econs. Assn., Wis. Assn. Extension Home Econs. Presbyterian. Home: 316 N Union Mauston WI 53948 Office: U Wis Coop Extension Service 220 E State St Mauston WI 53948

HUG, EILEEN MARIE, accountant; b. Ann Arbor, Mich., Sept. 6, 1952; d. Arnold Carl and Alice Godelieve (DeRycke) Johnson; m. Paul Anthony Hug, May 26, 1973; children: Daniel Vincent, Laura Elizabeth. BS in Math., No. Ariz. U., 1973; MS in Acctg., Ariz. State U., 1978. CPA, Ariz. Account receivable clk. Az-Tech Graphics, Phoenix, 1973-75; acctg. clk. II State of Ariz. Dept. Revenue, Phoenix, 1975; acctg. clk. II, asst. acct. Ramada Inns, Inc., Phoenix, 1975-77; staff accountant Bernard Scarborough, CPA, Scottsdale, Ariz., 1978-80; acctg. analyst Ramada Inn, Phoenix, 1980, fin. analyst, 1980-83, fin. analyst, 1983-84, mgr. fin. planning, 1984-85, dir. fin. planning and analysis, 1985-87, dir. devel. acctg., 1987—; treas., bd. dirs. Ramada Credit Union, Phoenix, 1984-87. Mem. Am. Soc. Women CPA's, Ariz. Soc. CPA's, Am. Inst. CPA's. Republican. Roman Catholic. Club: Phoenix Folk Dancers (co-pres. 1980-87). Home: 6902 E Moreland Scottsdale AZ 85257 Office: Ramada Inc 3838 E Van Buren Phoenix AZ 85008

HUGGARD, EILEEN ELISABETH, lawyer; b. N.Y.C., Apr. 12, 1957; d. Raymond Francis and Carol Jean (Kinsella) H. AAS, Agrl. and Tech. Coll. SUNY, Farmingdale, 1977; BA summa cum laude with highest honors in Communication Arts, Hofstra U., 1980; JD, Georgetown U., 1983. Bar: D.C. 1983. Assoc., Pellegrin & Levine, Chartered, Washington, 1983-86; atty., FCC, Washington, 1987—; atty., telecommunications policy analyst, N.Y.C. Energy and Telecommunications Office, 1988—. Mem. ABA, Women's Bar Assn. of D.C., Women in Communications, Fed. Communications Bar Assn., D.C. Bar, Phi Beta Kappa, Pi Sigma Alpha. Roman Catholic. Office: NYC Energy and Telecommunications Office 49-51 Chambers St New York NY 10007

HUGGENS, JANET LEE, educator; b. Camden, N.J., Aug. 8, 1949; d. Earl A. and Jane F. (Hearn) Clark; m. John E. Huggens, Nov. 13, 1972 (div. 1977). BS in Music Edn., West Chester U., 1971, MusM in Music Edn., 1978. Cert. music educator, Pa.; cert. elem. and secondary prin., Pa., N.J. Educator Upper Darby (Pa.) Sch. Dist., 1970, Exeter Twp. Sch. Dist., Reading, Pa., 1972, Owen J. Roberts Sch. Dist., Pottstown, Pa., 1972—; pvt. practice music teaching, 1972-84; head coach track Owen J. Roberts High Sch., Pottstown, 1977—; pres., bd. dirs. Inter-County Band, 1982—. Dir. ch. choirs 1st Presbyn. Ch., Pottstown, 1979—; mem. Pottstown Hist. Soc., Pottstown Symphony Orch. Mem. NEA, Assn. Supervision and Curriculum Devel., Music Educators Nat. Conf. (chmn. dist. 12), AAUW, U.S. Olympic Soc., Women's Sports Found. Republican. Lutheran. Lodge: Order Eastern Star. Home: 505 E Second St Boyertown PA 19512-1604 Office: Owen J Roberts Sch Dist RD #1 Pottstown PA 19464

HUGGINS, CANNIE MAE COX HUNTER, retired educator; b. Belton, Tex., July 16, 1916; d. Jesse Daniel and Mary Alice (Hamilton) Cox; B.S., Mary Hardin Baylor Coll., 1940; M.S., San Marcos Tchrs. Coll., 1942; postgrad. U. Tex., 1946-47, Tex. Tech U., 1956-70, U. San Diego, 1975, St. Mary's U., 1976; m. William Dudley Hunter, June 5, 1938 (div. 1967); children—Darline, Bob Roy; m. 2d, Bertrand Huggins, Aug. 4, 1979 (dec. July 19, 1980). Tchr. pub. schs., Belton, 1935-38, Galveston, Tex., 1938-42; mem. staff testing dept. U. Ariz., 1942-43; reading cons. Phoenix Pub. Schs., 1943-45; tchr.-counselor pub. schs., Killeen, Tex., 1946-54; classroom tchr., Lubbock, Tex., 1954-74; tchr. first grade bilingual lang. devel. Posey Elementary Sch., Lubbock, Tex., 1974-82; pres. CM Corp. First aid chmn. ARC, Lubbock County, 1960-63, first aid instr., 1956—; area dir. March of Dimes, 1958-63; tchr. high sch. dept. First Bapt. Ch., Lubbock, 1960—; state advisor U.S. Congl. Adv. Bd., 1985—; mem. Lubbock Hospice Vol. Program. Recipient Outstanding Service award ARC, 1966; Bronze award CONTACT Lubbock. Cert. educator, Tex. Mem. Assn. Childhood Edn. Internat., NEA, Tex. Tchrs. Assn., Tex. Classroom Tchrs. Assn., Nat. PTA, Tex. Edn. Assn., Lubbock Educators Assn., Lubbock Classroom Tchrs. Assn., AAUW, Am. Bus. Women's Assn., S. Plains Writers Guild, YWCA, Lubbock, Killeen chambers commerce. Baptist. Club: University City (Lubbock). Home: 4626 30th St Lubbock TX 79410

HUGHES, ANN HIGHTOWER, economist, government official; b. Birmingham, Ala., Nov. 24, 1938; d. Brady Alexander and Juanita (Pope) H. B.A., George Washington U., 1963, M.A., 1969. Asst. U.S. trade rep. Exec. Office of Pres., Washington, 1978-81; dep. asst. sec. trade agreements Dept. Commerce, Washington, 1981-82, dep. asst. sec. Western Hemisphere, 1982—. Recipient Meritorious Exec. award Pres. of U.S., 1982. Office: Dept Commerce 14th & Constitution Ave NW Room 3826 Washington DC 20230

HUGHES, BARBARA ANN, dietitian, public health administrator; b. McMinn County, Tenn., July 22, 1938; d. Cecil Earl and Hannah Ruth (Moss) Farmer; B.S. cum laude in Home Econs. Carson Newman Coll., Jefferson City, Tenn., 1960; M.S. in Instl. Mgmt., Ohio State U., Columbus, 1963; M.A. (Adonarium Judson scholar), So. Bapt. Theol. Sem., 1968; M.P.H. in Public Health Adminstrn., U. N.C., Chapel Hill, 1972; postgrad. in nutrition U. Iowa, 1974, U. N.C., 1975-85, Case Western Res. U., 1979, Walden U.; PhD 1988 ; m. Carl Clifford Hughes, Oct. 13, 1962. Dietitian, instr. Riverside Meth. Hosp., Riverside Whitecross Sch. Nursing, Columbus, 1963-66; consulting dietitian eastern region N.C. Bd. Health, Raleigh, 1968-73; dir. Nutrition and Dietary Services br., div. Health Services, N.C. Dept. Human Resources, Raleigh, 1973—, also dir. Women-Infants-Children Program; cons. dietitian Mt. Holly Nursing Home, Louisville, 1967-68; adj. asst. prof. dept. nutrition Sch. Public Health, U. N.C., Chapel Hill, mem. adv. bd. Hospitality Edn. program N.C. Dept. Community Colls., 1974—, adv. com. Ret. Senior Vol. Program, Raleigh and Wake County, N.C., 1975-79, N.C. Network Coordinating Council for End-Stage Renal Disease, 1975, Nat. Adv. Council on Maternal, Infant, and Fetal Nutrition, Spl. Supplemental Food Program for Women, Infants, and Children, Dept. Agr., 1976-79, adv. com. Nutrition Edn. and Tng. program N.C. Dept. Public Instruction, 1978-80; coordinator undergrad. program in gen. dietetics East Carolina U.; adv. council N.C. Gov.'s Office Citizen Affairs; lectr., cons.; cons. dietitian Augusta Victoria Hosp. and Jerusalem (Israel) Crippled Childrens Center, 1968; witness U.S. congressional and Senate hearings in field. Active edn. programs Pullen Memorial Bapt. Church, Raleigh, deacon, 1976-80, area ministry capt., 1977-78, personnel com., 1978-80; dietitian/dir. food service archeol. expedition to Israel, 1978; bd. dirs. N.C. Literacy Assn. 1978-83, pres., 1981-83; v.p. Wake County Literacy Council, 1986-87; trustee Gardner-Webb Coll., Boiling Springs, N.C., 1979-82, chmn. curriculum com., 1981-82; chmn. Coalition Pub. Health Nutrition, 1983-85; del. various Democratic Convs., 1981-84, precinct sec.-treas., 1981-83, 1st vice chmn., 1983-85, chair, 1985-87; chmn. adv. bd. dept. home econs. Carson-Newman Coll. Named Woman of Yr., Wake County, 1975, N.C. Outstanding Dietitian of Yr., 1976, N.C. Outstanding Dietitian, Southeastern Hosp. Conf. for Dietitians, 1978; Disting. Alumna award Carson-Newman Coll., 1983. Mem. AAUW (life, pres. Raleigh br. 1971-75, pres. N.C. div. 1978-80, nat. bd. dirs. 1980-82, area rep. 1980-82), Am. Dietetic Assn. (del. 1971-74, 87—, pres. N.C. state assn. 1976-77, N.C. network legis. coordinator 1978-81, nat. nominating com. 1979-80, nat. chmn. council on practice 1982-83, chair legislation and pub. policy com. 1985-87), Am. Public Health Assn. (exec. com. So. br. 1977—, sec.-treas. 1979-80, 1st v.p. 1980-81), So. Health Assn. (pres. 1982-83, chair nominating com. 1985-86), Assn. State and Territorial Public Health Nutrition Dirs. (pres. 1977-79, dir. 1981—, liaison to Assn. Faculties Grad. Program in Pub. Health Nutrition, chair legis. and pub. policy com. 1984—), N.C. Council Foods and Nutrition (dir. 1976-78, chmn. membership 1975, nominating com. 1979). N.C. Council Women's Orgns., Am. Acad. Health Adminstrn., Soc. Nutrition Edn., Nutrition Today Soc., N.C. Acad. Public Health, Ohio State U. Alumni Assn. (life), U. N.C. Gen. Alumni Assn. (life), U. N.C. Public Health Alumni Assn. (life), Altrusa Internat. (pres. Raleigh club 1973-74, dir. 1976-78, 1st vice gov. 1978-79, chmn. nomination com. 1980-82, gov. dist. Three, 1979-80, internat. vocat. services chmn. 1977-79, 1st v.p. 1985-87, pres. 1987—), Altrusa Internat. Found. (1st v.p., pres.-elect 1987—), Women's Forum N.C., AAUW Ednl. Found., (bd. dirs. 1987—); Co-author: Diet and Kidney Disease, Assn. for N.C. Regional Med. Program, 1969; contbr. numerous papers, articles to symposia, periodicals in field, vol. areas. Home: 4208 Galax Dr Raleigh NC 27612 Office: PO Box 2091 Raleigh NC 27602

HUGHES, BARBARA BRADFORD, nurse; b. Bragg City, Mo., Jan. 21, 1941; d. Lawrence Hurl Bradford and Opa Jewel (Prater) Puttun; m. Robert Howard Hughes, Dec. 9, 1961; children: Kimberly Ann, Robert Howard II. ASN, St. Louis Community Coll., 1978; student, Webster U., 1980. RN, Mo. Med. surgical nurse Alexian Bros. Hosp., St. Louis, 1979-80; staff nurse Midwest Allergy Cons., St. Louis, 1980; nurse high altitude Aviation Nurse, Ltd., St. Louis, 1980-81; med. surgical staff charge nurse Bethesda Gen. Hosp., St. Louis, 1987—; pvt. practice real estate mgmt., 1962—. Vol. Luth. Hosp., St. Louis, 1967-70; mem. Mo. Botanical Garden, St. Louis, 1976—, St. Louis Aviation Mus., 1984—, St. Louis Zoo Friends Assn., 1986-87, Sta. Channel 9-Ednl. TV, St. Louis, 1986—; vol. blood drive ARC, St. Louis, 1980; vol. health tchr. Spartan Aluminum Products, Sparta, Ill., 1984. U. Mo. scholar, 1959. Mem. U.S. Nurses Assn., Mo. Nurses Assn., Internat. Flying Nurses Assn., Mo. Pilots Assn., U.S. Pilots Assn. Republican. Club: Tyospaye. Home: 4827 Laketon Ct Saint Louis MO 63128 Office: Bethesda Gen Hosp 3655 Vista Ave Saint Louis MO 63110

HUGHES, BARBARA LYNN, broadcasting executive; b. Morton, Wash., Mar. 2, 1961; d. Robert Carroll and Eleanor Margaret (King) H. AA, Western Bapt. Coll., Salem, Oreg., 1981. Tchr. piano East Wenatchee, Wash., 1976-79; announcer Sta. KWWW-Radio, Wenatchee, Wash., 1979; announcer, religious editor Sta. KSLM-Radio, Salem, 1981-83; tchr. music Kinder Coll., Inc., Portland, Oreg., 1983-85; announcer, dir. contemporary music Sta. KPDQ-Radio, Portland, 1985—. Composer: (songs) Psalm 142 Collection, 1986, Turn Me Off, 1986. Western Bapt. Music scholar, 1979, Eagles Past Pres. scholar, 1979. Mem. Women In Communications. Home: 3511 NE Schuyler Portland OR 97212 Office: Salem Media of Oreg Sta KPDQ Radio 5110 SE Stark Portland OR 97215

HUGHES, CAROLYN JEANNE, brokerage house executive; b. Bklyn., Jan. 17, 1957; d. Anthony Arthur and Carmela Marie (Ranieri) Stanganelli. BBA in Fin. magna cum laude, Adelphi U., 1979, MBA in Fin. and Investments, 1982. Asst. domestic cash mgr. Sterling Drug, Inc., N.Y.C., 1979-80; cash mgr. Quality Care, Inc., Rockville Centre, N.Y., 1980-82; asst. v.p. Bank of Am., N.Y.C., 1982-83; mgr. Merrill Lynch & Co., N.Y.C., 1983-84; cash mgr. to v.p. Prudential-Bache Securities, Inc., N.Y.C., 1984-88; mktg. officer Associated Capital Investors, San Francisco, 1988—. exec. asst. to chmn. Prudential-Bache Securities, Inc./Dem. Bus. Council, Washington, 1985. Mem. Delta Mu Delta (series 7 registered rep.). Office: Associated Capital Investors 555 California St San Francisco CA 94104

HUGHES, CAROLYN LAYMON, hotel manager; b. Aug. 30, 1940; d. Carl Warren Laymon; m. John Rogers Egermayer, Aug. 13, 1960 (div. Sept. 1970); children: Michael John, Scott David, Robert Warren. BA, Lic. Practical Nurse, U. Minn., 1961. Office nurse Mpls., 1960-71; mktg. rep. 1st Nat. Bank Commerce, New Orleans, 1971-73; dir. mktg. Bienville St. Corp., New Orleans, 1973-77; gen. mgr. Bienville St. Corp. doing bus. as St. Louis and St. Ann Hotels, New Orleans, 1977-80; v.p. mktg. Arnaud's Restaurant, New Orleans, 1981-82; mgr. Hotel Carlyle, N.Y.C., 1982—; cons. in field, 1984—. City hotel rep. United Way, N.Y.C., N.J. and Conn., 1985; rep. La. Nature Ctr., New Orleans, 1978-81. Mem. N.Y. Hotel Assn., Hotel Execs. Club (sec. 1985-87). Republican. Episcopalian. Home: 205 E 69th St 9-B New York NY 10021 Office: Hotel Carlyle 35 E 76th St New York NY 10021

HUGHES, CHRISTINE GEORGETTE, infosystems specialist; b. San Francisco, Nov. 1, 1946; d. George F. Hughes and Patricia M. (Connolly) Anderson; m. Abraham E. Ostrovsky, July 17, 1980. BA, San Francisco Coll. for Women, 1968. Pub. relations asst. Macy's, San Francisco, 1969-71; sales mgr. Lanier Products, San Francisco, 1976-77; systems analyst Xerox Corp., Stamford, Conn., 1976; product mgr. Savin Corp., Stamford, 1972-75, 77-80; dir. ops. Quantum Sci., N.Y.C., 1981-83; v.p. office techs. Gartner Group, Stamford, 1983—. Precinct chmn. Reps., Coral Gables, Fla., 1980. Mem. Office Systems Research Assn., Inst. Info. Research, Soc. Office Automation Profls. (pres. 1986-87). Republican. Roman Catholic. Office: Gartner Group Inc 56 Top Gallant Rd Stamford CT 06902

HUGHES, DOLORES THERESA, nurse; b. Abington, Pa., Dec. 22, 1948; d. John Francis and Catherine Marie (Fisher) H. Diploma in Nursing, Thomas Jefferson U. Hosp., 1969; BA in Health Care, Antioch U., 1976; MA in Health Edn., St. Joseph's U., 1979. Registered nurse, Fla.; cert. emergency nurse, critical care nurse, cert. in advanced cardiac life support. Staff nurse Thomas Jefferson U. Hosp., Phila., 1969-71, head nurse critical care unit, 1972-78, coordinator health edn. program, 1978-81; asst. head nurse ICU Mount Sinai Med. Ctr., Miami Beach, Fla., 1982-84; asst. head ICU nurse Mt. Sinai Med. Ctr., Miami Beach, Fla., 1982-84; staff nurse, trauma specialist Boca Raton (Fla.) Community Hosp., 1984—; co-owner Status Quo, Inc.; cons. in field. Instr. Am. Heart Assn. Recipient Allumni Achievement award Thomas Jefferson U., 1979. Mem. Am. Trauma Soc., Am. Heart Assn., Am. Assn. Critical Care Nurses, Emergency Nurses Assn. Republican. Roman Catholic. Home and Office: Status Quo Inc 20762 Concord Green W Boca Raton FL 33433

HUGHES, HARRIET S., armed forces executive; b. San Francisco, May 22, 1946; d. Nathan and Nellie (Gourse) Sternsher; m. Thomas S. Hughes, July, 1969 (div. 1975); 1 child, David William. AB in Adminstrn. and Planning, U. Calif., Berkeley, 1967; MS in Orgn. and Staff Devel., Calif. State U., Hayward, 1974; MA in Pub. Fin. Mgmt., Am. U., 1981. Rep., examiner

Social Securities Adminstrn., San Francisco, 1967-70, cons. 1973-75; planning analyst Dept. Navy, Ventura, Calif., 1975-78; budget analyst Naval sea Systems Command, Washington, 1978-79; bus. mgr. Joint Cruise Missiles Project Office, Washington, 1979-80; budget analyst Navy Comptroller, Washington, 1980-82, Office Sec. Def., Washington, 1982-85; spl. asst. for aviation budget and acquisition Office Chief Naval Ops., Washington, 1985—; instr. Ventura (Calif.) Community Coll., 1975-78. Mem. Women in Def., Am. Soc. Mil. Comptrollers (v.p. 1977-78, Contributing award 1977), Assn. for Humanistics Psychology (exec. bd. 1978-80), Exec. Women in Govt., Pi Sigma Alpha. Republican. Roman Catholic. Office: Dept Navy Chief Naval Ops The Pentagon (OP-05C) Washington DC 20350-2000

HUGHES, J. DEBORAH, health care administrator; b. Pitts., Mar. 24, 1948; d. James Francis and Margaret Veronica (Wiullmier) H. Diploma in nursing, Columbia Sch. Nursing, Pitts., 1969; BSN, La Roche Coll., 1987; postgrad. in health care adminstrn., Carnegie-Mellon U., 1987—. Cert. nursing administr. Staff nurse Forbes Health System, Pitts., 1969-78, head nurse recovery, 1978-79, supr. nursing, 1979-84, clin. asst. to med. dir., 1984—. Mem. Am. Assn. Critical Care Nurses, Am. Assn. Operating Room Nurses, Assn. Female Execs. League of IV Therapy Edn., Am. Hosp. Assn., Sigma Theta Tau. Office: Forbes Health System 2570 Haymaker Rd Monroeville PA 15146

HUGHES, JUDITH, diplomat; b. Pocatello, Idaho, Jan. 19, 1942; d. Frank D. and Burva Daun (Astle) H. BS in Merchandising, U. Utah, 1967; postgrad. in Psychology, George Washington U., 1974; postgrad. in Econs., Fgn. Service Inst., Rosslyn, Va., 1977, postgrad. in French and Italian, 1970, 78. Roving adminstrv. officer Bur. African Affairs, 1971-73; pub. affairs officer U.S. Dept. State, Washington, 1974-77; consul, comml. officer Am. Consulate Gen., Milan, 1978-82; first sec., personnel officer Am. Embassy, Ottawa, Can., 1982-86; adminstrv. officer, first sec. Am. Embassy, Vientiane, Lao Peoples Dem. Republic, 1986—. Democrat. Office: US Embassy, 3570 Vientiane, Vientiane Lao Peoples Democratic Republic also: American Embassy Box V APO San Francisco CA 96346

HUGHES, KATHARINE LYNNE, computer company owner; b. Kingston, Pa., Nov. 20, 1939; d. Thomas V. and Mary C. (Corrigan) H. BA in Math., Pa. State U., 1961. Systems engr. IBM Corp., various cities, 1961-72; program mgr. Bunker Ramo Corp., Munich, 1972-75, Westlake Village, Calif., 1975-77; asst. v.p. Citicorp, Marina Del Rey, Calif., 1977-81; owner, pres. Specialized Computer Services, Inc., Portland, Oreg., 1981—. Mem. Oreg. Sanitary Service, Oreg. Petroleum Marketer Assn. (conv. program mgr. 1986). Republican. Roman Catholic. Office: Specialized Computer Services Inc 37 SW Woods St Portland OR 97201

HUGHES, LINDA RENATE, lawyer, educator; b. Hanau, Germany, Oct. 25, 1947; came to U.S. 1950; d. J.A. and Ilga (Vankins) Eglite. B.A. magna cum laude, U. Minn., 1968; J.D. cum laude, Wayne State U., 1980. Bar: Mich. 1980, Ga. 1982, Fla. 1984. Human resource mgr. Browning Marine Co., St. Charles, Mich., 1973-76; law clk. to judge U.S. Dist. Ct. (ea. dist.) Mich., 1980-81; assoc. Miller, Cohen, Martens & Surgerman, Detroit, 1982, Thompson, Sizemore & Gonzalez, Tampa, 1984-85; asst. county atty. Hillsborough County, Fla., 1985—; instr. Valdosta State Coll. (Ga.), 1981; adj. prof. U. Detroit Law Sch., 1982; researcher comparative labor policy, Leigh Creek, Australia, 1983. Editor-in-chief Advocate, Wayne State U. Law Sch., 1979-80, also law rev. Vol. Community Mental Health Crisis Intervention, Saginaw, Mich., 1975-76, Ann Arbor, Mich., 1976-78, Clearwater Fla., 1984; dept. registrar Voter Registration Program, Pinellas County, Fla., 1983-84. Author: Employer's Price for Polygraph, 1986. Mem. State Bar Mich., Ga. State Bar, Fla. State Bar Assn. (chair govt. lawyers sect. 1986-88, mem. midyr. mktg. com. 1988—), Hillsborough County Bar Assn. (jud. evaluation com. 1986-87, 87-88), Fla. Women Lawyers Assn. (officer, bd. dirs.), ABA, AAUW (Saginaw chpt. sec. 1974-75). Club: Tampa.

HUGHES, LYNDA B., legal administrator. BBA in Mgmt., U. Tex. Permian Basin, 1982; postgrad., Tex. Tech U., Inst. Law Office Mgmt., Toronto, Can., 1987. Mgmt. cons. Pruett Redi-Mix Co., Odessa, Tex., 1982-83; coordinator Kent Hance campaign for U.S. Senate, 1983-84, Jay Gibson campaign for State Rep., Aug.-Dec., 1984; legal adminstr. Fowler, Gibson & Morgan, Attys. at Law, Odessa, 1985—; adv. com. legal assts. course Odessa Jr. Coll., 1984—; group facilitator Superconf.: Matching Workforce to Workplace, Odessa, 1986. Treas. U. Tex. Permian Basin Polit. Action Com., 1985—; sec. bd. Odessa Council on Alcoholism and Drug Abuse, 1985-87; co-chairperson Leadership Odessa, 1986-87; participant John Ben Shepperd Leadership Forum, 1986. Mem. Permian Basin Legal Adminstrs. Assn. (sec. 1987—), Legal Adminstrs. Div. State Bar Tex., Greater Odessa C. of C., Women's Info. Network. Home: 2520 Bob White Odessa TX 79761

HUGHES, MARIJA MATICH, law librarian; b. Belgrade, Yugoslavia; came to U.S., 1960, naturalized, 1971; d. Zarija and Antonija (Hudowsky) Matich. BA in Music, Mokranjac, Belgrade; BA in English, U. Belgrade and Calif. State U.; MLS, U. Md.; student, McGeorge Sch. Law; MHA in Health Care Adminstrn., George Washington U., 1985, M in Mgmt. Info. Systems, 1988. Counselor, gen. mgr. Career Counseling Service, Sacramento, Calif., 1962-64; sec. to mgr. Sacramento State Coll., 1965-66; student librarian "High John" program U. Md., Fairmont Heights, 1967; reference librarian State Law Library, 1968; head reference library-faculty liasion librarian Hastings Coll. Law U. Calif., San Francisco, 1969-72; head law librarian Am. Tel. & Tel. Corp., Washington, 1972-73; chief law librarian Nat. Clearinghouse Library, U.S. Commn. on Civil Rights, Washington, 1973—; owner, pub. Hughes Press. Author, compiler: The Sexual Barrier, Legal and Econ. Aspects of Employment, 1970-73; Author, compiler: The Sexual Barrier: Legal, Medical, Economic and Social Aspects of Sex Discrimination, 1977; contbr. articles to profl. jours. Mem. Am. Assn. Law Libraries, Assn. Internat. Law Libraries, Washington Ind. Writers. Home: 500 23d St NW Apt B-203 Washington DC 20037 Office: Nat Clearinghouse Library US Commn on Civil Rights 1121 Vermont Ave NW Washington DC 20425

HUGHES, MARY KATHERINE, lawyer; b. Kodiak, Alaska, July 16, 1949; d. John Chamberlain and Marjorie (Anstey) H.; m. Andrew H. Eker, July 7, 1982. B.B.A. cum laude, U. Alaska, 1971; J.D., Willamette U., 1974; postgrad. Heriot-Watt U., Edinburgh, Scotland, 1971. Bar: Alaska 1975. Ptnr., Hughes, Thorsness et al, Anchorage, 1974—; trustee Alaska Bar Found., pres., 1984—; bd. visitors Willamette U. Coll. Law, Salem, Oreg., 1980—; bd. dirs. Alaska Repertory Theatre, 1986—, pres., 1987—; commr. Alaska Code Revision Commn., 1987—; mem. Coll. of Fellows U. Alaska Found., 1985—. Mem. Alaska Bar Assn. (bd. govs. 1981-84, pres. 1983-84), Anchorage Assn. Women Lawyers (pres. 1976-77), AAUW, Delta Theta Phi. Republican. Roman Catholic. Club: Soroptimists (v.p. 1981-83, pres. 1986-87). Home: 2240 Kissee Ct Anchorage AK 99517 Office: Hughes Thorsness Gantz Powell & Brundin 509 W 3d Ave Anchorage AK 99501

HUGHES, MICHELE JOAN, executive search consultant, publisher; b. Natick, Mass., Nov. 1, 1945; d. Harry G. and Mildred (Goldstein) Feldman; m. Justin P. Hughes, June 16, 1968. BA in English, U. Mass., 1967; MA in English and Edn., Hofstra U., 1972. Tchr. Mass. and N.Y., 1967-72; pres. Scott Parker Anderson, San Francisco, 1972-75, M.J. Hughes and Co., San Francisco, 1975-76; ptnr. William H. Clark Assocs., San Francisco, 1976-78, Ward Howell Internat., San Francisco, 1978-86; pres. M.J. Hughes Internat., San Francisco, 1986—; pres., pub. Grand Voyage Travel Newsletter, 1985—; co-anchor Viacom Cable 6, San Francisco, 1981-82; anchor Sta. KSFO Radio, San Francisco, 1981-82; bd. dirs. Risk Mgmt. Resources, San Francisco. Hon. trustee Nat. Jr. Tennis League, 1975—; mem. Nat. Olympics Com., 1978-81. Named Top Ten Profl. Woman, 1980, All Time Profl. Woman, 1984 Glamour Mag. Mem. Internat. Womens Forum (bd. dirs. 1986—), Womens Forum West (pres. 1986-88, bd. dirs. 1976-78, 86-88). Clubs: Tiburon (Calif.) Peninsula. Home: 6 Rolling Hills Tiburon CA 94920 Office: M J Hughes Internat 100 Shoreline Hwy Suite B-140 Mill Valley CA 94941

HUGHES, N. SUE, school counselor; b. Ballinger, Tex., Jan. 17, 1931; d. Hubert Edgar and Susie M. (Smith) Cothran; B.S., Centenary Coll. of La., 1951; M.Ed., So. Methodist U., 1971; m. Bennie Dee Hughes, Dec. 16, 1950; 1 dau., Vicki Lynn. Tchr. home econs. Caddo Parish Sch. Bd., Shreveport, La., 1951-54; tchr. elementary and jr. high sch. Refugio (Tex.) Ind. Sch. Dist., 1957-61; tchr. home econs. Assumption Parish, Napoleonville, La., 1962, Lafayette (La.) Parish Sch. Bd., 1963-68; tchr., counselor Richardson (Tex.) Ind. Sch. Dist., 1968—. Mem. Am., Tex., N. Central Tex. counseling and devel. assns., Richardson C. of C., Richardson Civic Art Soc., Southwest Watercolor Soc., Phi Delta Kappa, Chi Omega. Baptist. Home: 1217 Ashland Dr Richardson TX 75080 Office: 1600 Spring Valley RD Richardson TX 75080

HUGHES, PAMELA CAMILLE, publisher, writer; b. Santa Monica, Calif., Oct. 19, 1953; d. Vernon Charles and Hariett (Weber) Brown; m. Michael J. Hughes, July 12, 1982. BA, Stanford U., 1982. Editor Crosscurrents mag., Westlake, Calif., 1979-87; pub. Freedom Lights Press, Chimney Rock, Colo., 1988—; freelance writer, Pagosa Springs, 1979—. Author: Step On A Crack, 1987; contbr. articles to profl. jours. Mem. NOW (colo. chpt.), Nat. Assn. Female Execs., Pubs. Mktg. Assn., COSMEP Small Pubs. Assn. Democrat. Buddhist. Office: Freedom Lights Press PO Box 87 Chimney Rock CO 81127

HUGHES, PEGGY LOUISE, gas and oil executive; b. Harleton, Tex., Oct. 2, 1933; d. Travis Houston Sr. and Annie Mozelle (Allen) Fried; m. James Patrick Hughes, July 4, 1953; children: Jeff Anthony, Angela Kay, Debra Jean. Student, Kilgore Jr. Coll., 1976-77, Tyler Jr. coll., 1979-83. Div. order analyst, adminstr. asst. Western Gas Corp., Longview, Tex., 1975-79; mgr. land and right-of-way Excelsior Oil Corp., Western Gas Corp., Longview, 1979-1981; v.p. land Excelsior Oil Corp., Longview, 1981-85; mgr. gas mktg. Tex. Gasmark, Inc., Longview, 1987—; dist. mgr. land Western Oil Corp., Longview, 1985—; v.p. land Bright Prodn. Co., Inc., Longview, Tex., 1987—. Tchr. seminar Tex. Dept. Human Resources, Longview, 1982. Mem. Am. Assn. Petroleum Landmen (cert.), East Texas Assn. Petroleum Landmen. Republican. Baptist. Office: Western Oil Corp 107B Wain Dr Longview TX 75606

HUGHES, ROSEMARY, corporate executive; b. Rockville Centre, N.Y., Sept. 5, 1959; d. Everett George and Elizabeth Marie (Kelly) H. Cert. sec., Berkley Clarmont Secretarial Sch., 1977. Sec. Hallman and Lorber Assocs., Valley Stream, N.Y., 1979-80; dir. of ins. service Hallman and Lorber Associates, Valley Stream, 1980-85, asst. v.p., 1985—. Mem. Nat. Assn. Female Execs. Roman Catholic. Home: 210 Atlantic Ave Apt B4D Lynbrook NY 11563 Office: Hallman and Lorber Assocs Inc 70 E Sunrise Hwy Valley Stream NY 11581

HUGHES, SUE MARGARET, librarian; b. Cleburne, Tex.; d. Chastain Wesley and Sue Willis (Payne) H. BBA, U. Tex., Austin, 1949; MLS, Tex. Woman's U., 1960, PhD, 1987. Sec.-treas. pvt. corps. Waco, Tex., 1949-59; asst. in public services Baylor U. Library, Waco, 1960-64; acquisitions librarian Baylor U. Library, 1964-79, acting univ. librarian, summer 1979; librarian Moody Library, 1980—. Mem. AAUP, ALA, Southwestern Library Assn., Tex. Library Assn., AAUW, Delta Kappa Gamma, Beta Phi Mu, Beta Gamma Sigma. Methodist. Club: Altrusa. Office: Box 6307 Waco TX 76706

HUGHES, SUZANN, nurse, management consultant; b. Hartford, Conn., Aug. 21, 1948; d. James Edward and Mary (Durkin) Scanlon; m. Gerald David Hughes, June 3, 1972; 1 child, Chelsea Ayne. B.S. in Nursing, U. Conn., 1971, M.S. in Nursing, 1981. Instr. Curry Coll., Milton, Mass., 1979; recovery room staff nurse Boston Hosp. for Women, 1979-80; clin. nurse specialist St. Lukes Hosp., Phoenix, 1981-83; dir. nursing Valley Luth. Hosp., Mesa, Ariz., 1983-84; mgmt. cons., Mesa, 1984—; instr. U. Phoenix, 1985—; nursing cons. St. Luke's Hosp. Med. Ctr., Phoenix, 1985. Vol. Morris Udall Campaign for Pres., Boston, 1976. Mem. Ariz. Nurses Assn. (treas. polit. action com. 84-85, trustee 1984—), Am. Soc. Law and Medicine, Ariz. League for Nursing, Sigma Theta Tau. Home and Office: 813 N Robson Mesa AZ 85201

HUGHES, VIRGINIA MARIE, electric utility public relations and communications executive; b. Faribault, Minn., Dec. 7, 1954; d. Alfred Thomas and Lenore Marie (Weum) Hughes; m. Charles Arnold Berg, June 23, 1984. B.S., Mankato State U., 1976. Acctg. asst. Steele Waseca Cooperative, Owatonna, Minn., 1974-77; owner Geraldine's Dress Shoppe, West Concord, Minn., 1977-78; mgr. Maurices, Inc., Faribault, Minn., 1978-79; mem. service asst. FROST-BENCO Electric, Mankato, Minn., 1979—, energy auditor, 1981—; chmn. Farm, Home and Energy Show, Mankato Minn., 1983; mem. mem. service adv. bd. Cooperative Power Assn., Eden Prairie, Minn., 1982-86; mem. steering com. Minn. Youth Energy Camp, 1984—, sec. 1985-86; nat. adv. task force Nat. Rural Electric Cooperative Assn., 1987. Editor News of FROST-BENCO, 1981—. Organizer Minn. Women for Agriculture-Dist. 9, Southern Minn., 1982; sec., newsletter editor Mankato Area Christian Singles, Mankato, 1979-80. Mem. Am. Agri-Women, Rural Electric Mgmt. Assn. (service edn. com. 1982—), Minn. Women for Agriculture (sec., treas. 1982-83, pub. relations com. 1984-86, pres. 1987), Nat. Assn. Female Execs., Elec. Women's Round Table, Phi Kappa Phi, Phi Upsilon Omicron. Club: Goosedowners (Mankato, Minn.). Office: FROST-BENCO Electric Assn PO Box 8 Mankato MN 56002

HUGHES, WAUNELL MCDONALD (MRS. DELBERT E. HUGHES), psychiatrist; b. Tyler, Tex., Feb. 6, 1928; d. Conrad Claiborne and Bernice Oletha (Smith) McDonald; B.A., U. Tex. at Austin, 1946; M.D., Baylor U., 1951; m. Delbert Eugene Hughes, Aug. 14, 1948; children—Lark, Mark, Lynn, Michael. Intern VA Hosp., Houston, 1951-52; resident Parkland Hosp., Dallas, 1964-67; practiced gen. medicine in Tyler, Tex., 1952-64; acting chief psychiatry service VA Hosp., Dallas, 1967-68, asst. chief, 1968-73, chief Mental Hygiene Clinic and Day Treatment Center, 1973-82, unit chief acute inpatient psychiatry Med. Center, 1982—; clin. instr. psychiatry Southwestern Med. Sch., U. Tex. Health Sci. Center, Dallas, 1968—. Chmn. pre-sch. vision and hearing program Pilot Club, Tyler, 1960-64. Mem. Am. Med. Women's Assn. (pres. Dallas 1980-81), Am. Psychiat. Assn., Am. Group Psychotherapy Assn., (pres. Dallas chpt. 1984-86), Dallas Area Women Psychiatrists (archivist 1985—), Alpha Epsilon Iota (pres. 1950-51). Home: 3428 University Blvd Dallas TX 75205 Office: 4500 Lancaster Rd Dallas TX 75216

HUGHEY, LUCINDA KAY, ballet dancer; b. Ridgecrest, Calif., Oct. 25, 1962; d. William Henry and Karen Arline (Covert) H. Student, The Evergreen State Coll. Corps de ballet Pacific Northwest Ballet, Seattle, 1980-83, soloist dancer, 1983-85, prin. dancer, 1985—. Choreographer Improvisations, 1986, Images, 1987, Crystaline Lattice, 1988. Mem. Am. Guild Mus. Artists. Office: Pacific NW Ballet 4649 Sunnyside Ave N Seattle WA 98103

HUGHS, MARY GERALDINE, accountant, social service specialist; b. Marshalltown, Iowa, Nov. 28, 1929; d. Don Harold, Sr., and Alice Dorothy (Keister) Shaw; A.A., Highline Community Coll., 1970; B.A., U. Wash., 1972; m. Charles G. Hughs, Jan. 31, 1949; children—Mark George, Deborah Kay, Juli Ann, Grant Wesley. Asst. controller Moduline Internat., Inc., Chehalis, Wash., 1972-73; controller Data Recall Corp., El Segundo, Calif., 1973-74; fin. adminstr., acct. Saturn Mfg. Corp., Torrance, Calif., 1974-77; sr. acct., adminstrv. asst. Van Camp Ins., San Pedro, Calif., 1977-78; asst. adminstr. Harbor Regional Center, Torrance, Calif., 1979-87; active bookkeeping service, 1978—; instr. math. and acctg. South Bay Bus. Coll., 1976-77. Sec. Pacific N.W. Mycol. Soc., 1966-67; treas., bd. dirs. Harbor Employees Fed. Credit Union. Recipient award Am. Mgmt. Assn., 1979. Mem. Beta Alpha. Republican. Methodist. Club: Holiday Health Spas. Author: Iowa Auto Dealers Assn. Title System, 1955; Harbor Regional Center Affirmative Action Plan, 1980; Harbor Regional Center - Financial Format, 1978—; Provider Audit System, 1979; Handling Client Funds, 1983. Home and Office: 18405 Haas Ave Torrance CA 90504

HUGON, NANCY SUSAN, small business owner; b. Kounz, Tex., Oct. 15, 1957; d. Patrick Morgan and Catherine Anderson (Poole) Brown; m. Joe Frank Hugon Jr., Dec. 3, 1977 (div. June 1985). AA, Blinn Coll., 1980; BS, Tex. A&M U., 1987. Clk., bookkeeper Sheridan Bank and Trust, Lawton, Okla., 1978-80; sec., clk. Mercury Drilling Co., Oklahoma City, 1980-81; office mgr. Adams Affiliates, Bryan, Tex., 1981-83; owner Check Services, College Station, Tex., 1983—. Vol., campaign worker Phil Gramm for Congress, College Station; mem. Brazos Valley Rep. Women, College Station. Mem. Tex. State Tchrs. Assn., Am. Petroleum Inst., Phi Kappa Phi, Kappa Delta Pi. Methodist. Club: Petroleum (historian 1986—). Office: Check Services 602 SW Parkway St 12 College Station TX 77840

HULIN-SALKIN, BELINDA, writer; b. Lafayette, La., July 3, 19[illegible]; d. Adam Joseph and Audrey Mae (Breaux) Hulin; m. Richard Alan Salkin, Nov. 24, 1979. BA in Communications, Loyola U., New Orleans, 1975; MS in Urban Studies, U. New Orleans, 1983. Reporter, producer Sta. WYLD Radio News, New Orleans, 1975; entertainment editor Monroe (La.) Morning World, 1975-77; pub. info. dir. Mental Health Assn., New Orleans, 1978-79; asst. editor Focus mag., Phila., 1980-82; freelance writer Collingswood, N.J., 1982—; contbr. Money mag., N.Y.C., 1982—, Advt. Age, Chgo., 1983—, Jewish Exponent, Phila., 1986—, Incentive Mktg. mag., N.Y.C., 1986—, Meetings and Convs. mag., Secaucus, N.J., 1986—, N.J. Monthly, Morristown, 1987—, Continental mag., Austin, Tex., 1987—, Cosmopolitan mag., N.Y.C., 1988—. Editor: Home Improvement Workbook, 1979, Springhouse Report newsletter, 1985; contbg. editor Phila. mag., 1986—. Counselor Crisis Line, New Orleans, 1979. Mem. Phila. Writers Orgn., Nat. Assn. for Female Execs., Women's Equity Action League, Sigma Delta Chi. Democrat. Home: 100 Woodlawn Ave Collingswood NJ 08108

HULKA, BARBARA SORENSON, epidemiology educator; b. Mpls., Mar. 1, 1931; d. Herbert Fritchof and Mable (Alquist) Sorenson; m. Jaroslav Fabian Hulka, Nov. 13, 1954; children: Carol Ann, Gregory Fabian, Bryan Herbert. B.S., Radcliffe Coll., 1952; J.D., Juilliard Sch. Music, 1954; M.D., Columbia U., 1959, M.P.A., 1961. Diplomate: Am. Bd. Preventive Medicine; Lic. physician, Pa., N.C. Research asst. prof. U. Pitts., 1966-67; asst. prof. U. N.C., Chapel Hill, 1967-71, assoc. prof., 1972-76, prof., 1977—, chmn. dept. epidemiology, 1983—, Kenan prof., 1987—; adj. prof. medicine Duke U. Med. Ctr., Durham, N.C., 1982—; chmn. epidemiology and disease study sect. NIH, 1979-83; bd. sci. counselors Nat. Cancer Inst., 1980—; mem. Inst. of Medicine com. toxic shock syndrome Nat. Acad. Sci., 1981-82; mem. Sci. Rev. and Evaluation Bd. subcom. VA, 1983—; mem. subcom. on long-term effects of short-term exposure to chem. agts. Nat. Acad. Scis., 1985—; mem. preventive medicine and pub. health test com. Nat. Bd. Med. Examiners, 1985—; mem. consensus conf. on smokeless tobacco Nat. Cancer Inst. Panel, 1986. Mem. editorial bd. Postgrad. Medicine, 1985—; contbr. articles to profl. jours., chpts. to books. Health Resources Adminstrn. grantee, 1975-77; tng. grantee in cancer epidemiology Nat. Cancer Inst., 1980—; prostate cancer grantee Nat. Cancer Inst., 1983-85; travel study fellow WHO, 1978. Mem. Soc. Epidemiol. Research (pres. 1975-76, exec. com. 1973-77), Am. Pub. Health Assn. (governing council 1976-78, chmn. epidemiol. sect. 1976-77), Am. Epidemiol. Soc., N.C. Pub. Health Assn. (award for excellence, stats. and epidemiology sect. 1975), Am. Coll. Preventive Medicine (bd. regents 1986), Nat. Acad. Scis. (com. on passive smoking 1985—), Delta Omega. Home: 2317 Honeysuckle Dr Chapel Hill NC 27514 Office: U NC Sch Pub Health Rosenau Hall CB#7400 Chapel Hill NC 27599

HULL, DORIS M., librarian; b. Quantico, Md., May 14, 1926; d. Orrensy and Lottie (Conway) Hull. B.S. in Edn., Va. State U., 1947; M.S. in L.S., Drexel U., 1951; M.A. in History, Howard U., 1957; Ph.D., Am. U., 1966. Tchr. librarian Salisbury (Md.) High Sch., 1947-50, Pomonkey (Md.) High Sch., 1951-52; head reference dept., supr. serials Founders Library, Howard U., Washington, 1952-64, reference librarian Moorland Spingarn Research Ctr., 1980—; UNESCO librarian Advanced Tchr. Tng. Coll., Ondo, Nigeria, 1964-66; exchange prof. Drexel U., Phila., 1967-68; head pub. service library Lagos (Nigeria) U., 1968-71; sr. history master Ministry of Edn., Oyo State, Nigeria, 1971-79; mem. faculty Grad. Sch., U.S. Dept. Agr., 1980—; cons. U.S. Dept. Agr. Grad. Sch., 1980—. Editor-in-chief Current Bibliography African Affairs, 1984-86; contbr. articles to profl. jours. Recipient 10 Yr. Service award Howard U., 1962; Md. State scholar, 1943-51. Mem. African Studies Assn. (archives libraries com.), Council of Library Technicians, Mid-Atlantic Regional Africanist Assn., ALA. Contbr. articles to profl. jours. Office: Howard U Moorland Spingarn Research Ctr Washington DC 20059

HULL, ELLA ELIZABETH, auditor; b. Manhattan, N.Y., Dec. 5, 1959; d. Aloysius and Anna Elizabeth (Edmonds) H. BBA, CUNY, 1981. Tchr. in charge Jacob A. Riis Settlement, L.I., N.Y., 1981-82; acct. dept. environmental protection City of N.Y., Manhattan, 1982-87; tax auditor dept. fin. City of N.Y., Bklyn., 1987—. Mem. YWCA; trustee Antioch Bapt. Ch., Corona, L.I., N.Y. Recipient Outstanding Young Women Am. award Gen. Fedn. Women's Clubs, Montgomery, Ala., 1981. Mem. Nat. Assn. Female Execs. Office: Dept Fin 345 Adams St Brooklyn NY 11201

HULL, JANE LAUREL LEEK, nurse, administrator; b. Ontario, Calif., July 4, 1923; d. William Abram and Susan Bianca (Pethick) Leek; R.N., Columbia Presbyn. Sch. Nursing, 1944; B.A., Redlands U., 1977; ; m. James B. Hull, Oct. 10, 1944 (dec.); children—James W., William P., Kenneth D. Supr. obstetrics Sch. Nursing, Mid-Valley Hosp., Peckville, Pa., 1945-46; surg. nurse acute nursing Scranton (Pa.) State Hosp., 1947-52; nurse San Antonio Community Hosp., Upland, Calif., 1953-55; office nurse H.L. Archibald, Upland, 1965; vis. nurse Pomona West End Inc., continuity of care coordinator, Montclair, Calif., 1968-73, exec. dir., 1973—; tchr. ARC nursing course to high sch. students. Treas. PTA, Pomona, Calif.; vol. exec. dir. Inland Hospice Assn., 1979-80. Mem. Calif. Nurses Assn. (pres. dist. 53 1958), Calif. Assn. for Health Services at Home (dir.), Calif. League Nursing, Nat. Homecaring Council (dir.). Republican. Club: Zonta (Ontario, Upland, pres., 1976). Organizer Homemaker Dept. in Vis. Nurse Assn., 1972; developer (with Don Baxter Corp.) plugs for in-dwelling Foley catheters, 1963. Home: 543 W F St Ontario CA 91762 Office: 4959 Palo Verde Montclair CA 91763

HULL, JANICE LYNN, accountant; b. Birmingham, Ala., July 27, 1953; d. James Barney and Gulma (Traywick) H. Student, U. Montevallo, 1971-72; BS, U. Ala., 1982. CPA, Ala. Acct. Thomas R. Day, CPA, Clanton, Ala., 1970—. Mem. Ala. Soc. CPA's, Am. Inst. CPA's, Am. Women's Soc. CPA's. Baptist. Home: Rt 1 Box 4575 Thorsby AL 36171 Office: Thomas R Day CPA 502 Second Ave S Clanton AL 35045

HULL, LOUISE KNOX, retired elementary educator, administrator; b. Springfield, Mo., May 24, 1912; d. William E. and Ruby Joe (Bradshaw) K.; m. Berrien J. Hull, Jan. 1, 1953. B.S. in Edn., Southwest Mo. State U., 1933; postgrad. Colo. U., 1939, Northwestern U., 1945; M.A., NYU, 1952. Cert. elem. and secondary tchr., Mo. Elem. tchr. R12 Sch. Dist., Springfield, 1936-70, supr. tchr., 1956-70, mem. adv. com. to supt., 1955-57. Chmn. Christian edn. com. Westminster Presbyn. Ch., 1953-66, trustee, 1983-86, chmn. bd. trustees, 1986, circle chair; pres. Women of Ch., 1970-73, pres. bd. trustees, 1983—; life mem. Wilson Creek Found., Springfield, 1954-67; sec. Greene County Hist. Soc., Springfield, 1960—; mem. Springfield Little Theater Guild, 1970—, Hist. Preservation Soc., Springfield, 1980—; docent Mus. Ozarks, Springfield, 1976; chmn. dist. Ill, John Calvin Presbterial, 1974-76, sec., 1977-80. Mem. Springfield Retired Tchrs. Assn. (life), Ozarks Genealogy Soc (sec. 1985-87, pub. info. rep. 1987—), DAR (Rachel Donelson chpt.), Mo. Fedn. Women's Clubs (chmn. home life com. 1986—), Alpha Delta Pi (treas. house corp. 1932-60), Alpha Delta Kappa (sec. 1965-67). Club: Sorosis (Springfield) (pres. 1980-82, chmn. hobby dept. 1986-88, chmn. fine arts dept. 1988-90).

HULL, MARGARET RUTH, artist, educator, consultant; b. Dallas, Mar. 27, 1921; d. William Haynes and Ora Carroll (Adams) Leatherwood; m. LeRos Ennis Hull, Mar. 29, 1941; children: LeRos Ennis, Jr., James Daniel. BA, So. Meth. U., Dallas, 1952, postgrad., 1960-61; MA, North Tex. State U., 1957. Art instr. W.W. Bushman Sch., Dallas Ind. Sch. Dist., 1952-57, Benjamin Franklin Jr. High Sch., Dallas, 1957-58; art instr. Hillcrest High Sch., Dallas, 1958-61, dean, pupil personnel counselor, 1961-70; tchr. children's painting Dallas Mus. Fine Art, 1956-70; designer, coordinator visual art careers cluster Skyline High Sch., Dallas, 1970-71, Skyline Career Devel. Ctr., Dallas, 1971-76, Booker T. Washington Arts Magnet High Sch., Dallas, 1976-82; developer curriculum devel./writing art, 1971-82; artist, ednl. cons., 1982—; mus. reprodns. asst. Dallas Mus. Art, 1984—. Group shows include Dallas Mus. Fine Arts, 1958, Arts Magnet Faculty Shows, 1978-82, Arts Magnet High Sch., Dallas Art Edn. Assn. Show, 1981, D'Art Membership Show, Dallas, 1982-83; represented in pvt. collections. Trustee Dallas Mus. Art, 1978-84. Mem. Tex. Designer/Craftsmen, Craft Guild Dallas, Fiber Artists Dallas, Dallas Art Edn. Assn., Tex. Art Edn.

Assn., Nat. Art Edn. Assn., Dallas Counselors Assn. (pres. 1968), Delta Delta Delta.

HULL, SUZANNE WHITE, former library administrator, writer; b. Orange, N.J., Aug. 24, 1921; d. Gordon Stowe and Lillian (Siegling) White; m. George I. Hull, Feb. 20, 1943; children: George Gordon, James Rutledge, Anne Hull Cabello. B.A. with honors, Swarthmore Coll., 1943; M.S. in L.S., U. So. Calif., 1967. Mem. staff Huntington Library, Art Gallery and Botanical Gardens, San Marino, Calif., 1969-86, dir. adminstrn. and pub. services, 1972-85, dir. pub. adminstrn. and edn., 1985-86. Author: Chaste, Silent and Obedient, Books for Women, 1475-1640, 1982, 88; editor: State of the Art in Women's Studies, 1986. Charter pres. Portola Jr. High Sch. PTA, Los Angeles, 1960-62; pres. Children's Service League, 1963-64, YWCA Los Angeles, 1967-69; mem. community adv. council Los Angeles Job Corps Center for Women, 1972-78; mem. alumni council Swarthmore Coll., 1959-62, 83-86, mem.-at-large, 1986—; mem. adv. bd. Hagley Mus. and Library, Wilmington, Del., 1983-86; hon. life mem. Calif. Congress Parents and Tchrs.; bd. dirs. Pasadena Planned Parenthood Assn., 1978-83, mem. adv. com., 1983—; founder-chmn. Swarthmore-Los Angeles Connection, 1984-85, bd. dirs., 1985—; founder Huntington Women's Studies Seminar, 1984, mem. steering com. 1984—; bd. dirs. Pasadena Girls Club, 1988—. Mem. Monumental Brass Soc. (U.K.), Renaissance Soc., Brit. Studies Conf., Beta Phi Mu (chpt. dir. 1981-84). Home: 1465 El Mirador Dr Pasadena CA 91103 Office: 1151 Oxford Rd San Marino CA 91108

HULME, DARLYS MAE, banker; b. Buckingham, Iowa, Apr. 2, 1937; d. Leland James and Dorothy Mae (Nation) Philp; m. Harlan Dale Hulme, Dec. 4, 1955 (div. Nov. 1971); children: Debra Jean Hulme Hanneman, Richard Dale. Student Iowa Sch. Banking, 1974, Sch. Bank Adminstrn. U. Wis.-Madison, 1982. Bookkeeper, Farmers Savs. Bank, Traer, Iowa, 1954-55, asst. cashier, 1962-72, v.p., 1973-83, sr. v.p., 1983—; acct. North Tama Housing, Inc., Traer, 1974—; sec. to bd. Traer Shares, Inc., Talen Aviation, Ltd., Traer, Farmers Savs. Bank and Trust, Vinton, Iowa, 1988—; dir., sec. to bd. Sunrise Hill Care Ctr., Traer; mem. Iowa State Banking Bd., 1985—. Mem. Nat. Assn. Bank Women (group treas. 1980-81, group v.p. 1981-82, group pres. 1982-83, state membership chair 1983-84, regional membership chair 1984-85), Iowa Bankers Assn. (mem. edn. com. 1985-86). Republican. Methodist. Club: PEO (Traer) (corr. sec. 1988). Avocations: gardening, traveling. Home: 701 S Main St Traer IA 50675 Office: Farmers Savs Bank 611 2d St Traer IA 50675

HULSEBUS, SHARON DAWSON, finance company executive, consultant; b. Niagara Falls, N.Y., Nov. 10, 1947; d. Chester Clarence and Mary Ann (Hehir) Dawson; m. M. Thomas Nichols, Aug. 12, 1978 (div. April 1983); m. M. Lee Hulsebus, June 13, 1986; 1 child, Laura Ann. Student, Trocaire Jr. Coll., 1965-69; BA in English, Niagara U., 1972; MBA, SUNY, Buffalo, 1983. Lic. broker. Tchr. Our Lady of Am.'s Sch., Kansas City, Mo., 1972-73, Martin Luther King Jr. High Sch., Kansas City, 1973-74; life ins. agt. Aetna Life and Casualty, Buffalo, 1974-75; sr. fin. cons., asst. v.p. Merrill Lynch and Co., Inc., Buffalo, 1975-86; asst. v.p. Merrill Lynch and Co., Inc., Atlanta, 1986—. Mem. Sisters of Mercy Catholic Ch., Buffalo, 1965-69. Mem. The Bond Club of Buffalo. Republic. Roman Catholic. Club: Atlanta Athletic. Home: 4496 Ridgegate Dr Duluth GA 30136 Office: Merrill Lynch and Co Inc 3500 Piedmont Rd NE Suite 600 Atlanta GA 30305

HULTMAN, TAMELA JEAN, news agency editor; b. Asheboro, N.C., Apr. 7, 1947; d. Robert Clifford and Ruby Jean (Lucas) Hultman; m. John Reed Kramer; children: Kwindla H., Robert Arnold H. BA, Duke U., 1968. Researcher, writer Meth. Ch. of South Africa, 1969-71, Nat. Council of Chs., N.Y.C., 1971-72; founder, editor Africa News Service, Durham, N.C., 1972-82, exec. editor, 1982—; reporter, producer Africa news for various broadcasters including Nat. Pub. Radio, MonitoRadio and BBC, 1980—. Author, photographer numerous articles for newspapers and mags. including Washington Post, N.Y. Times, Los Angeles Times, Christian Sci. Monitor, Phila. Enquirer, The Nation, others, 1972—. Recipient Media award for radio series on African hunger World Hunger Yr., N.Y.C., 1986. Methodist. Office: Africa News Service Box 3851 Durham NC 27702

HUMMEL, KAREN LUCILLE KOSZUTA, state agency administrator, finance executive; b. Buffalo, May 3, 1956; d. Richard Joseph and Mary Helen (Kaminski) Koszuta; m. Michael Ray Hummel Sr.; May 28, 1983; children: Michael Ray Jr., Jonathan Richard. Student in acctg., Del. Tech. and Community Coll., 1980—. Adminstrv. asst., bookkeeper Sunbeam Appliance Service, Buffalo, 1974-76, Niagara Frontier Tariff Bur., Williamsville, N.Y., 1976-78; acct., supr. parks and recreation div. Dept. Nat. Reservation and Environ. Control State of Del., Dover, 1979-86, fiscal adminstrv. officer, acct. Dept. Transp., 1986—; acct. Roots and Branches, Dover, 1984—, Mist Ltd., Dover, 1986—, Mist Trucking, Dover, 1987—. Mem. Nat. Assn. for Female Execs., Phi Theta Kappa. Home: 327 Mockingbird Ave Dover DE 19901 Office: Dept Transp PO Box 778 Dover DE 19903

HUMPHREY, CARLETTA SUE, fiber optics executive; b. Longmont, Colo., Dec. 4, 1954; d. Robert Edward and Shirley (Ann) H. Materials mgr. Ball Corp., Boulder, Colo., 1978-82; document control mgr. Raycom Systems, Boulder, 1983-85, purchasing agt., 1985—; cons. City of Greeley (Colo.), 1986. Mem. Nat. Assn. Purchasing Mgmt. (Achievement award 1986). Office: Raycom Systems Inc R-6395 Gunpark Dr Boulder CO 80301

HUMPHREY, JAYNE HULBERT, government official; b. Oakland, Calif., Apr. 1, 1947; d. Jack W. and Clare Roberta (Hittle) Hulbert; m. Donald James Humphrey, Nov. 11, 1983. Student Northwestern U., 1964-66, San Francisco State U., 1969-70. With various fed. govt. agencies, Washington, 1964-67; program asst. U.S. Dept. HUD, Washington, 1968, elderly housing program technician, San Francisco, 1969-70, housing rep., coordinator, 1970-75, dir. housing devel. div., 1975-83, dep. regional housing dir., 1983-87 , mgr. Honolulu office, 1986-87, dir. housing devel. div., 1987—; pres. Hulbert Humphrey, Inc., Fairfax, Calif., 1985—; instr. Calif. Mortgage Bankers Assn., Calif. Dept. Real Estate, Sacramento, 1985—; chief negotiator, mem. mgmt. contract with union HUD, San Francisco, 1983-84; mem. rev. bd. performance standards HUD, 1986-87. Named Woman of Yr., U.S. HUD, 1985, recipient 7 outstanding performance awards, 1976-87, superior accomplishment award, 1988, Disting. Service nominee, 1979, spl. achievement award, 1972, 73, 75, Commendation 19th Guam Legislature; named hon. citizen City of Alameda, Calif., 1971. Mem. Fed. Mgrs. Assn., Nat. Soc. Female Execs., Am. Soc. Pub. Adminstrn. Democrat. Presbyterian. Club: Commonwealth. Avocations: music; computers. Office: Dept Housing and Urban Devel 450 Golden Gate Ave Box 36003 San Francisco CA 94102-3448

HUMPHREY, KATHLEEN ELAINE, marketing development manager; b. Moscow, Idaho, Mar. 20, 1958; d. Howard D. and Carol J. (Anderson) H. Student, Vienna (Austria) Internat. Music Ctr., 1978; BS, Duke U., 1980. Mktg. engr. Hewlett-Packard Co., Cupertino, Calif., 1980-82, sales devel. mgr., 1982-84; account exec. Regis McKenna Inc., Portland, Oreg., 1984-86; mktg. mgr. Aldus Corp., Seattle, 1986-87, mgr. mkt. devel., 1987—; cons. Sequent Computer Systems, Portland, 1984. Mem. Nat. Adv. Council on Women's Edn., Washington, 1978-82; ESL tutor Bishop's Fund for Refugee Relief, Seattle, 1987. Mem. Nat. Assn. Female Execs., CitiClub of Portland, CitiClub of Seattle, Earthwatch. Democrat. Office: Aldus Corp 411 First Ave S #200 Seattle WA 98109

HUMPHREY, LOUISE IRELAND (MRS. GILBERT W. HUMPHREY), civic worker, horsewoman; b. Morehead City, N.C., Nov. 1, 1918; d. R. Livingston and Margaret (Allen) Ireland; m. Gilbert W. Humphrey, Dec. 27, 1939; children—Margaret (Mrs. K. Bindhart), George M. II, Gilbert Watts; ed. pvt. schs. Mem. corp., adv. bd. Tall Timbers Research Inc. Nurse's aide ARC, 1944—; past. dir. Nat. City Bank, Cleve., Nat. City Corp., Cleve., 1981-86; trustee Mus. Arts Assn.; hon. trustee, past pres. Vis. Nurse Assn.; hon. trustee Lake Erie Coll., life trustee United Way Cleve., trustee Archbold Hosp., Thomasville, Ga.; hon. trustee Case Western Res. U.; bd. dirs. Monticello (Fla.) Opera House; mem., past trustee, 2d v.p. Jr. League; pres. bd. dirs. Met. Opera Assn.; bd. dirs. Thomas County Entertainment Found.; past pres. No. Ohio Opera Assn.; past mem. Ohio Arts Council; treas., trustee Wildlife Conservation Fund Am.; former master foxhounds Chagrin Valley Hunt, Gates Mills, Ohio; past dir., zone v.p. U.S. Equestrian Team, Inc., now hon. life dir.; mem. Garden Club Cleve.; bd. dirs., past pres. Nat. Homecaring Council; treas., bd. mem. Wildlife Legis. Fund Am.; bd. dir. Thomasville Cultural Ctr.; mem., vice chmn. Fla. Game and Fresh Water Fish Commn. Home: Woodfield Springs Plantation Miccosukee FL 32309

HUMPHREY, PHYLLIS JEAN, writer; b. Oak Park, Ill., July 22, 1929; d. Richard William and Antoinette (Chalupa) Ashworth; m. Herbert A. Pihl, Sept. 13, 1946 (div. 1957); children: Christine Pihl Gibson, Gary Fraizer Pihl; m. Curtis H. Humphrey, June 21, 1965; 1 child, Marc. AA, Coll. San Mateo, Calif., 1972; postgrad., Northwestern U., 1945-47. Ptnr. Criterion House, Foster City, Calif., 1972—. Author: Wall Street on $20 a Month, 1986, Golden Fire, 1986; author radio scripts Am. Radio Theatre, 1983-84; contbr. short storis and articles to popular mags. Recipient 2d prize award Readers Digest Mag., 1980. Mem. Nat. Writers Union, Mensa. Republican. Mem. Christian Sci. Ch. Club: Cupertino Writers, Commonwealth. Office: Criterion House PO Box 4144 Foster City CA 94404

HUMPHREYS, JANET BARNETT, hospital administrator; b. Washington, Dec. 19, 1951; d. Robert James and LaNita Ruth (Ainsworth) Barnett; m. Larry Jones Humphreys, Aug. 15, 1949; children: Brian Anthony, Andre Marie. BA, U. Miss., 1973; MPH, Tulane U., 1974. Geriatric research asst. Jackson-Madison County Mental Health Ctr., Jackson, Tenn., 1974; office mgr. Barnett Orthopedic Clinic, Jackson, 1974-75; dir. plan devel. W. Tenn. Health Improvement Assn., Jackson, 1975-79; dir. planning ARCHA Health Systems Agy., Johnson City, Tenn., 1977-80; adminstrv. asst. Quillen-Dishner Coll. Medicine, Johnson City, 1980-84, instr., 1981-87; asst. adminstr. Woodridge Hosp., Johnson City, 1984-87; adminstr. Elder Inst. of Bapt. Hosp., Knoxville, Tenn., 1987—; asst. prof. Dept. Health Edn. East Tenn. State U., Johnson City, 1983—; bd. dirs. for Sr. Citizens Info. and Referral Service, Knoxville, 1988—. Sec. Johnson City Symphony Guild, 1981-87; den leader Boy Scouts Am., Johnson City, 1986-87; bd. dirs. March of Dimes Team Walk, Johnson City, 1986, 87; bd. dirs. Presch. Age Choir, Cen. Bapt. Ch., Johnson City, 1981-87. NIH grantee, 1982. Mem. Nat. Assn. Female Execs., Nat. Assn. Health Care Execs. (affiliate). Baptist. Office: Elder Inst Bapt Hosp PO Box 1788 Knoxville TN 37901

HUMPHRIES, DEBORAH ANN, computer accessories company executive; b. Hope, Ark., Jan. 27, 1955; d. Wayburn Dean and Joretta Ann (Sims) H. BBA, U. Tex., 1976. Adminstrv. asst. Here's Life New York, N.Y.C., 1976-77; pres. D.A. Humphries and Assocs., N.Y.C., 1977-78, Express Computer Supplies, San Francisco, 1984-87; v.p. Clean Image, Inc., San Francisco, 1985—; pres. Win//Win Co., San Francisco, 1987—; flight attendant Am. Airlines, San Francisco, 1978—; cons., San Francisco, 1983—. Author: Passenger Power, 1987; contbg. editor: Passengers' Best Friend, 1987; patentee in field. Mem. Friends of the Library, San Francisco. Mem. Nat. Office Products Assn., Nat. Orgn. Machine Dealers, Bay Area Career Women. Democrat. Club: Tex. Ex (Austin). Office: Clean Image Inc 1684 Market St San Francisco CA 94102

HUMPHRIES, ELLEN THOM, banker; b. Oskaloosa, Iowa, Aug. 4, 1947; d. Theodore A. Thom and Catherine A. (Wilkes) Betts; m. Quinn F. Humphries, Jr., Dec. 4, 1965 (div. Feb. 1979); 1 child, Laura Amanda Kelly Humphries. Diploma, Killeen Comml. Coll., Tex., 1966. Banking officer, asst. mgr. First Nat. Bank, Metairie, La., 1967-78; banking officer Jefferson Bank & Trust, Metairie, 1978-80; banking officer, mgr. First Nat. Bank, Metairie, 1980-84; v.p. Gulf Fed. Savs. Bank, Metairie, 1984-85; account exec. First Fin. Bank, New Orleans, 1985-87; mgr. Sussex Trust Co., 1987—. Bd. dirs. New Orleans YWCA, 1982-85. Lutheran. Clubs: Metairie Central Bus. Dist. Assn. (sec. 1982-83, pres. 1983-84). Avocations: drama, dance, swimming, reading, youth counseling.

HUNGAR, JULIE YEARSLEY, community college administrator, educator, consultant; b. Bismark, N.D., May 30, 1931; d. Julian Clayton and Gertrude Ethel (Bang) Yearsley; m. Gordon Earle Hungar, Aug. 30, 1953; children—Ann Alison, Susan Lynn, Thomas, George, Paula Jane. B.A. in English Lit., U. Wash., 1954, M.A. in English Lit., 1960; Ed.D., Seattle U., 1982. News editor, traffic mgr. Sta. KBRC Radio, Mt. Vernon, Wash., 1948-51; traffic, promotion dir. KCTS-TV, Seattle, 1955-57; mem. faculty Seattle Community Coll., 1972-77, 80-82, devel. coordinator, 1978-80, div. chmn., 1982-84, vice chancellor, 1984—; cons. Mills Cons. Assocs., Seattle, 1982—. Moderator, producer TV series The Artist Among Us, 1965. Contbr. articles to newspapers. Bd. dirs., concert chmn. Seattle Symphony Family Concerts, 1963-65; bd. dirs. Allied Arts of Seattle, 1965-68; founding chmn. Citizens for Quality Integrated Edn., Seattle, 1968-69; v.p., bd. dirs. New Dimensions in Music, Seattle, 1968-71.; active Seattle Econ. Devel. Comm. Mem. Wash. Assn. Community Coll. Adminstrs., Wash. Community Coll. Humanities Assn. (treas. 1984—), Phi Beta Kappa, Phi Delta Kappa. Office: Seattle Community Coll Dist 1500 Harvard Seattle WA 98122

HUNGATE, SUE CAROL, financal analyst; b. San Antonio, Nov. 4, 1957; d. Joseph Irvin and Betty Lou (Hatzenbuehler) Hungate. BA, U. S.C.-Columbia, 1978. Student asst. U. S.C., Columbia, 1975-78, research asst. Affiliated Computer, Dallas, 1978-79; media planner/buyer Bloom Advt., Dallas, 1979-81; customer service EDS/Cunadata, Dallas, 1981-82, regional rep., Charlotte, N.C., 1982-86; account mgr. Broadway & Seymour, Charlotte, 1986-87. Mem. AAUW, Am. Mgmt. Assn., Am. Bus. Women's Assn., Nat. Assn. Female Execs., Pi Beta Phi. Methodist. Avocations: piano, reading, outdoor sports, sailing, water skiing. Home: 2709 New Hamlin Way Charlotte NC 28210 Office: Broadway & Seymour Inc 302 S Tryon St Charlotte NC 28202

HUNGERFORD, CONSTANCE CAIN, art educator; b. Chgo., Apr. 26, 1948; d. Craig John and Jocelyn Enid (Mason) Cain. B.A., Wellesley Coll., 1970; M.A., U. Calif.-Berkeley, 1972, Ph.D., 1977. Instr. to assoc. prof. history of art Swarthmore (Pa.) Coll., 1975—, chmn. dept. art, 1981-86 . Contbr. articles to profl. jours. Samuel H. Kress nat. fellow, 1973-75; Am. Council Learned Socs. grantee-in-aid, 1978; Am. Philos. Soc. grantee 1980. Mem. Coll. Art Assn. Am., AAUW (award 1983), Phi Beta Kappa. Office: Swarthmore Coll Dept Art Swarthmore PA 19081

HUNLEY, W. HELEN, Canadian provincial government official; b. Acme, Alta., Can., Sept. 6, 1920. Student pub. schs., Rocky Mountain House, Alta.; LL.D., U. Alta., 1985. Telephone operator Carstairs, Acme and Calgary, Alta.; with implement and truck dealership, ins. agy. Rocky Mountain House, 1948-57, owner, 1957-68; owner, mgr. Helen Hunley Agys. Ltd., ins. agy., Rocky Mountain House, 1968-71; town councillor Rocky Mountain House, 1960-66, mayor, 1966-71; elected mem. Legis. Assembly Province of Alta., Edmonton, 1971-79, minister without portfolio, 1971-73, solicitor-gen., 1973-75, minister social services and community Health, 1975-79, lt. gov., 1985—. Formerly active numerous community affairs and vol. agys., including Can. Red Cross, Can. Boy Scouts, Recreation Bd., Alta. Girls Parliament, Provincial Mental Health Adv. Council; hon. patron numerous assns. Served to lt. Can. Women's Army Corps, 1941-45. Office: Province of Alberta, Legis Bldg, Edmonton, AB Canada T5K 2BC

HUNNEWELL, MARGARET BLAKE, film, television production executive; b. Boston, Mar. 18, 1950; d. Carroll G. Hunnewell and Dorothy (Swearingen) Brownlee. Grad., U. De Grenoble, France, 1970; BFA, Bennington Coll., 1972. Co-dir. Castalia Enterprises, Inc., N.Y.C., 1975-77; freelance unit prodn. mgr. United Artists, Columbia Pictures, CBS-TV, Antenne 2, Orion Pictures, Paris and N.Y.C., 1977-80; pres. Hunnewell Prodns., Inc., N.Y.C., 1980—, The Hunnewell Group, Inc., N.Y.C., 1986—, Prodns. Internat., N.Y.C., 1986—; exec., treas. Media & People, Inc., N.Y.C., 1988—. Mem. Dirs. Guild Am., Women in Film, Soc. Motion Picture and TV Engrs. Office: 24 E 23d St New York NY 10010-4401

HUNSINGER, NANCY MARGARET, advertising and public relations executive; b. Hamilton, Can., Jan. 5, 1954; d. William Robert and Sarah Leone (McLachlan) Slack; m. Ray Christian Hunsinger, Apr. 6, 1974 (div. May 1987); children: Ryan Christian, David Ray, Sarah Ruth. Student, George Brown Coll., Toronto, 1985. Tchr. Bruno's Hair Design, Toronto, 1985-86; adv., promotion exec. Cayuga Speedway Ltd., Caledonia, Ont., 1966-86; pub. relations exec. Slack Transport Ltd., Slack Lumber & Supplies, Caledonia, 1954—; mem. Festival Country Tourist Bur., Brantford, Ont. Recipient Recognition for Performance award, Expo '86, Vancouver. Mem. Am. Speed Assn., Nat. Tractor Pullers Assn. Mem. Conservative party. Office: Cayuga Speedway Ltd, 172 Argyle St, Caledonia CAN N0A 1A0

HUNT, ANITA M. HEARD, health care marketing executive, educator, consultant, literary agent; b. Sayre, Okla., Oct. 14, 1943; d. William Lynn and Lydia Ethel (Boyer) Heard; m. Virgil Eugene Medley, Mar. 27, 1959 (div. 1970); children: Donald Eugene, Vicki Lea Medley-Wickham, Robert Lynn, Gary Duane. AS in Med. Tech., Sayre Coll., 1972; BS in Tech. Edn., Okla. State U., 1974; MPH in Health Adminstrn., Okla. U., 1985; post-grad. Calif. State U.-Bakersfield, 1979. Cert. clin. lab. scientist, med. technologist. Profl. relations rep. Blue Cross & Blue Shield, Oklahoma City, 1977-78; med. technologist Kern County Hosp., Bakersfield, Calif., 1979; practice mgmt. cons. Med. Mgmt. Group, Oklahoma City, 1980-81; clin. lab. supr. South Community Hosp., Oklahoma City, 1982-85, hosp. services rep., 1985—; adj. asst. prof. Okla. U. Health Scis. Ctr., Oklahoma City, 1983-85. Editorial reviewer Jour. Med. Tech., 1984-86; author papers in field. Scouting coordinator Last Frontier council Boy Scouts Am., Oklahoma City, 1985; planning com. Okla. county chpt., Am. Heart Assn.; candidate Am. Coll. Health Care Execs. Sci. Products med. tech. grantee, 1973. Mem. Okla. Soc. Am. Med. Technologists (v.p. 1976-77), Okla. City Bus. and Profl. Women, Okla. Women's Forum, Okla. Pub. Health Assn., AAUW, Mensa. Republican. Presbyterian. Club: Toastmasters, Safari Internat. Lodge: Lions. Avocations: piano, vocal music, photography, water and snow skiing, yachting. Home: PO Box 95682 Oklahoma City OK 73143 Office: S Community Hosp Offices 1001 SW 44 Oklahoma City OK 73109

HUNT, ANNICE ELIZABETH, editor; b. Palmetto, Fla., Mar. 30, 1934; d. William Alva and Doris Elizabeth (Mann) H. BS, Abilene Christian U., 1961; postgrad., Fla. State U., 1962-63. Asst. acquisitions librarian Nat. Bur. Standards, Washington, 1963-65; info. specialist Def. Documentation Ctr., Alexandria, Va., 1965-67; cataloguer Dept. Health and Rehab. Services, Jacksonville, Fla., 1967-69; editor Calli's Tales mag., Palmetto, 1981—. Democrat. Mem. Ch. of Christ. Club: Palmetto Garden. (historian 1987). Home: 2103 5th St W Palmetto FL 34221 Office: Calli's Tales Mag PO Box 1224 Palmetto FL 34221

HUNT, CAROLYN ANN, law firm administrator, career counselor; b. Amarillo, Tex., Dec. 12, 1931; d. Grover Cleveland and Leora (Britian) Elder; m. Charles Elmore Hunt, May 30, 1952; 1 son, Timothy Ray. B.S., U. Tex.-Dallas, 1978, M.S., 1984. Bookkeeper, Forrest Builders Supply, Lubbock, Tex., 1958-59, Modern TV Co., Ogden, Utah, 1959-65; office mgr. Austin Shoe Stores, Dallas, 1969-76; adminstrv. mgr. Slaughter Industries, Dallas, 1976-79; adminstrv. mgr. Internat. Paper Co., Dallas, 1979-80, office supr., 1980-86; career ctr. mgr. Drake Beam Morin, Dallas, 1986—; personnel adminstr. Moore & Peterson, 1987—. Chmn., United Way Internat. Paper Co., 1980-82. Mem. Am. Bus. Womens Assn. (v.p. 1984-85, woman of yr. 1982, Exec. dir. Dallas Area Council), Network Career Women (v.p. Dallas 1984-85), Am. Soc. Personnel Adminstrs., Dallas Personnel Assn. Democrat. Baptist. Office: Moore & Peterson 2800 First City Center Dallas TX 75201-4621 also: Drake Beam Morin 14180 Dallas Pkwy Dallas TX 75240

HUNT, KATHY CALLAHAN, educational consultant; b. Lorain, Ohio, Sept. 6, 1951; d. Herbert and Annabel (Helle) Tellman; m. Richard Callahan, July 1, 1980 (div. July 1984); m. Raymond Bradley Hunt, July 9, 1988. BS, Ohio State U., 1973, MA, 1976; postgrad. in adminstrn., U. Colo., 1984-86. Cert. elem. and middle sch. tchr. Tchr. middle sch. math Southwestern City Schs., Grove City, Ohio, 1974-79, instrnl. leader, 1979-81; tchr. jr. high sch. math. Boulder Valley Pub. Schs., Boulder, Colo., 1981-82, Broomfield, Colo., 1982-83; tchr. jr. high sch. math. Louisville, Colo., 1984-87, asst. prin. middle sch., 1984-87; ednl. cons. Nat. Research Ctr. for Middle Grades Edn., U. South Fla., Tampa, 1987—; presenter numerous state, nat. and internat. ednl. confs., 1984—, including 1st European Middle Schs. Conf., Brussels, 1987. Co-author: How to Set Up an Advisory Program, 1988. Named Outstanding Young Educator, Southwestern City Schs., 1979. Mem. Nat. Assn. Secondary Sch. Prins., Assn. for Supervision and Curriculum Devel., Nat. Middle Sch. Assn., Colo. Assn. Middle Level Educators (sec., pres.-elect 1986-87), Phi Delta Kappa. Democrat. Methodist. Home: 1110-A Milo Circle Lafayette CO 80026 Office: U South Fla Nat Resource Ctr for Middle Grades Edn EDU-115 Tampa FL 33620-5650

HUNT, LENORE RUTH SISLER, nurse; b. Friendsville, Md., Jan. 24, 1926; d. Daniel C. and Ida Fay (Chidister) Sisler; m. John W. Hunt, Nov. 6, 1948 (dec.); children—John, George, Bruce. R.N., Lutheran Hosp. Md., 1948; B.S., Mt. St. Mary's Coll., 1977. Relief supr. Lutheran Hosp. Md., 1948-65; relief supr. Greater Balt. Med. Center, 1965-70, med. surg. coordinator, 1970-87; cons. Community Services of Md., Inc. Sec. White Rock Recreation Corp., 1975-78. Mem. Lutheran Hosp. Md. Alumnae Assn., Am. Nurses Assn., Md. Nurses Assn. Republican. Methodist. Club: Homemakers of Bel Air Acres. Home: 23 Idelwild St Bel Air MD 21014

HUNT, LINDA, actress; b. Morristown, N.J., Apr. 2, 1945. Student Interlochen Arts Acad.-Mich., Goodman Theatre and Sch. of Drama-Chgo. Off-Broadway theater debut in Down by the River, 1975; Little Victories, 1983; Top Girls, 1983; films include Dune, 1984, The Year of Living Dangerously, 1983 (Academy award for best supporting actress), The Bostonians, 1984, Eleni, 1985, Silverado, 1985, Popeye, 1980, Waiting for the Moon, 1987; Broadway appearance in Ah, Wilderness!, 1975, End of the World, 1984; in N.Y. Shakespeare Festival prodn. Aunt Dan and Lemon, 1985. Office: care Triad Artists Inc 10100 Santa Monica Blvd 16th Floor Los Angeles CA 90067 *

HUNT, MICHELLE SHARRON, federal investigator; b. Concord, Calif., May 4, 1961; d. Zane Bradford and Sharron Adelle (Richardson) H. AA in French, Brigham Young U., 1983, BA in Internat. Relations, 1983; MBA, John F. Kennedy U., 1987. With FBI, 1984—; fed. investigative specialist FBI, San Francisco, 1985—; assoc. tng. instr. Joint Fed. Agy. seminars, 1987. Mem. Nat. Assn. Female Execs., Assn. MBA Execs. Republican. Mormon. Club: Commonwealth of Calif. Office: FBI 450 Golden Gate PO Box 36015 San Francisco CA 94101

HUNT, PATRICIA STANFORD, judge; b. Dunn, N.C., June 9, 1928; d. Lewis Knox and Florence Hibbette (Cooper) Denning; student Sweet Briar Coll., 1946-48; A.B., U. N.C., 1950, M.A., 1966, J.D., 1978; m. Donald M. Stanford, June 30, 1949 (dec. May 1970); children—Donald M., Randolph Lewis, Charles Ashley, James Cooper; m. Thomas M. Hunt, June 17, 1972. Tchr., Chapel Hill (N.C.) Carrboro Schs., 1963-69, counselor, 1969-73; admitted to N.C. bar, 1978; practiced in Chapel Hill, 1978—; mem. N.C. Gen. Assembly, 1972-81; dist. ct. judge, 15B Judicial Dist., Hillsborough, N.C., 1981—. Pres., Jr. Service League, 1960. Recipient Cert. of Appreciation, N.C. Autistic Soc., 1981, N.C. Assn. Attys., 1981, N.C. Acad. Trial Lawyers, 1981; Rockefeller scholar, 1968-70; R. J. Reynolds fellow, 1970. Mem. Conf. Dist. Judges, N.C. State Bar Assn., N.C. Acad. Trial Lawyers, N.C. Assn. Women Attys. Democrat. Presbyterian. Co-author: (with Hugh Lefler) N.C. History, Geography and Government, 1970. Home: 100 Northwood Dr Chapel Hill NC 27516 Office: Clk Superior Ct Hillsborough NC 27278

HUNT, SUE WHITTINGTON, accountant; b. Greenville, Miss., Nov. 23, 1952; d. Robert Bryan Sr. and Dale (Montgomery) W.; m. Ronnie Charles Hunt, Dec. 28, 1974; children: Andrew W., Emily P. AA in Bus., Holmes Jr. Coll., Goodman, Miss., 1972; BBA, Delta State U., 1974; MBA, Miss. Coll., Clinton, 1985. Acct. J. Milton Newton, Inc., Jackson, Miss., 1975-76; acct., auditor Dept. of Pub. Welfare, Jackson, Miss., 1976-81; chief fiscal officer Miss. Worker's Compensation Commn., Jackson, Miss., 1982-85; budget analyst IV Fiscal Mgmt. Bd., Jackson, Miss., 1985—. Mem. Clinton Park (Miss.) PTA, 1986—. Mem. Assn. Govt. Accts. (sec. 1986, pres.-elect 1986-87, pres. 1987-88), Am. Soc. Women Accts. (pres. 1986—, 1st v.p. 1985-86, treas. 1985-86), Miss. Assn. Govt. Purchasing Agts. Methodist. Home: 1707 Melrose Pl Clinton MS 39056 Office: Fiscal Mgmt Bd 901 Walter Sillers Bldg Jackson MS 39201

HUNT, SUSANNE CAROL KRAFT, nurse; b. Plainfield, N.J., Dec., 25, 1943; d. Rudolph A. and Helen A. (Thomas) Kraft; diploma East Orange

Gen. Hosp. Sch. of Nursing, 1964; cert. intravenous therapy technician, R.N.; m. Kenneth G. Hunt, Oct. 29, 1965 (div.); children—Kenneth G., Kristen S. Nurse, Overlook Hosp., Summit, N.J., 1965-67; head nurse Woodbine Nursing Home, Alexandria, Va., 1967-68; staff nurse Circle Terrace Hosp., Alexandria, 1969-70; head intensive care Manassas (Va.) Manor Nursing Home, 1976-77, dir. nurses, 1977-79; charge nurse Martin Meml. Hosp., Stuart, Fla., 1979-85. Bd. dirs. Am. Cancer Soc., chmn. pub. edn. Cert. intravenous therapy technician; cert. chemotherapy nurse. Mem. Va. Nurses Assn., No. Va. Dirs. of Nursing Assn., Am. Heart Assn., Martin County Hist. Soc., United Meth. Women. Home: 6631 NW 21st St Margate FL 33063 Office: 5300 NE 13th Way Pompano Beach FL 33064

HUNT, WANDA HOLDER, state legislator; b. Bakersville, N.C., Mar. 22, 1944; d. Farrell Robert and Jane (Ledford) Winterhalter Holder; m. Robert Frank Hunt, Mar. 24, 1962; 1 dau., Donna Lynn. Student Appalachian State U. Asst. purchasing Appalachian State U., Boone, N.C., 1965-70; with purchasing/personnel Ceralon Mfg., Aberdeen, N.C., 1972-77; with purchasing office N.C. Dept. Transp., Raleigh, 1977-82; account exec. Pinehurst, Inc. (N.C.), 1984—; mem. N.C. Senate, 1983—, vice-chair edn. com., 1983-84, chmn. sr. citizens com., 1985-86. Mem. bd. edn., Carthage, N.C., 1976-82; precinct chair Democratic party, Pinehurst, N.C., 1974-75; sec. Democratic party, Carthage, N.C., 1975. Recipient award Heart Fund; Disting. Service awards Moore County, 1983, Social Services Bd., Moore County, 1983; Vol. Service award Nat. Cystic Fibrosis, Pinehurst, N.C.; named Disting. Woman, State of N.C., Raleigh, 1984. Mem. Women in State Govt., N.C. State Govt. Employees Assn., N.C. Status of Women, N.C. Heart Fund Assn., Nat. Conf. State Legislatures (pensions com. 1985-86), State Legislators' Network (So. legis. conf. 1985-86), Travel Council N.C. (legis. com.), N.C. Council Hearing Impaired. Democrat. Presbyterian. Home: PO Box 1335 Pinehurst NC 28374 *

HUNT, WANDA SUE, marketing executive; b. Weiser, Idaho, July 28, 1950; d. Donald M. and Ruth Ann (Jones) H. Grad., N.W. Coll. Bus., 1969. With trust dept. First Interstate Bank of Wash., Seattle, 1969-78, with investment dept., 1978-82, investment officer, 1982-84, asst. v.p., 1984-86, mgr. investments, 1986—. Active Big Sisters; vol. fireman King County, Seattle, 1986—; pres. Lewis & Clark Condo's, Seattle, 1985-88; active various charitable orgns.; bd. dirs. U. Child Devel. Sch., 1985-88. Recipient Banker of Yr. award First Interstate, 1987. Mem. Women's Bus. Exchange. Home: 15625 42d Ave S #7 Seattle WA 98188 Office: First Interstate Bank PO Box 160 Seattle WA 98111

HUNTER, BARBARA WAY, public relations executive; b. Westport, N.Y., July 14, 1927; d. Walter Denslow and Hilda (Greenawalt) Way; m. Austin F. Hunter, Jan. 24, 1953; children: Kimberley, Victoria. BA, Cornell U., 1949. Assoc. editor Topics Pub. Co., N.Y.C., 1949-51; publicist Nat. Dairy Product Corp., N.Y.C., 1951-53; account exec. Sally Dickson Assn., 1953-56; assoc. D-A-Y Pub. Relations (div. Ogilvy & Mather Co.), N.Y.C., 1964-70, exec. v.p., 1970-84, pres., 1984—; bd. dirs. Mr. Steak Inc., Denver. Trustee Cornell U., Ithaca, N.Y., 1980-85; bd. dirs. Point O'Woods Assn., Fire Island, N.Y., 1980-87. Recipient Sparkplug award Internat. Foodservice Mfrs. Assn., 1970, Matrix award N.Y. Women in Communications Inc., 1980, Entrepreneurial Woman award Women Bus. Owners, 1981, Nat. Headliner award Women in Communications Inc., 1984. Mem. Pub. Relations Soc. Am. (pres. 1984, pres.-elect 1983, treas. 1982, pres. N.Y. chpt. 1978, John Hill award N.Y. chpt. 1986), Found. Pub. Relations Research and Edn. (trustee 1982, 84). Club: The Club at Point O'Woods. Home: 137 E 38th St New York NY 10016 Office: D-A-Y Pub Relations 40 W 57th St New York NY 10019

HUNTER, CANDACE ELLEN, business executive, computer scientist, research chemist; b. Tampa, Fla., Feb. 9, 1936; d. Melville Gunby and Grace Florence (Robinson) Hunter; B.S. in Chemistry, Stetson U., DeLand, Fla., 1957; M.S. in Organic Chemistry, George Washington U., 1968; m. Robert Gene Plato, Dec. 17, 1955 (div. 1965). Public sch. tchr., Tampa, 1957-58; supr. chemistry labs. Stetson U., 1958-59; biochemist Nat. Inst. Arthritis and Metabolic Diseases, NIH, Bethesda, Md., 1960-66; analytical chemist pesticides standards FDA, Washington, 1966-74, computer systems analyst Bur. Foods, 1974-84, also com. chmn. Fed. Women's Program, fed. govt. project officer Low Acid Canned Food Filing Improvement Project; ptnr. Wiencke & Plato, Chevy Chase, Md., 1972 ; pres Semi-Custom Software Ltd., Chevy Chase, 1984—; tchr. seminars on differential scanning calorimetry U. Md. and George Washington U.; tchr. computer programming. Recipient awards from fed. govt. Mem. Am. Chem. Soc., AAAS, N.Y. Acad. Sci., Delta Delta Delta, Psi Chi, Gamma Sigma Epsilon, Sigma Pi Kappa. Republican. Office: Semi-Custom Software Ltd 6807 Brennon Lane Chevy Chase MD 20815

HUNTER, CHARLOTTE RAE, bank personnel officer, educator; b. Denver, Nov. 7, 1942; d. Ralph Emil and Edmae Marie (Landry) H.; m. Michael Eugene Waters, July 28, 1962 (div. 1977); children—Paige D., Michelle R.; m. Brent M. Knight, June 21, 1986. B.A., DePaul U., 1971; M.Ed., U. Ill., 1974, Ph.D., 1979. Cert. profl. in human resources. Publs. editor Ill. Office Edn., Springfield, 1972-73; dir. research Triton Coll., River Grove, Ill., 1976-78; personnel dir. G.D. Searle & Co., Dallas, 1978-81, Saxon, Chgo., 1981-84; personnel officer World Bank, Washington, 1984-85, internat. recruitment chief, 1985—; adj. faculty Elmhurst Coll. (Ill.), 1983-84; mem. State Adv. Council on Adult, Vocat. Edn., Ill., 1977-79. Editor: Ill. Career Ednl. Jour., 1972; contbr. writings to publs. Commr. Ill. Commn. on Status of Women, 1975-79; bd. dirs. Nat. Assn. Commns. for Women, 1976-77; coordinating com. Internat. Women's Yr., Ill., 1977. EPDA fellow, 1973-75; recipient cert. of leadership YWCA Chgo., 1977. Mem. Am. Soc. Personnel Adminstrs., Employment Mgmt. Assn., Nat. Assn. Corp. and Profl. Recruiters, Phi Delta Kappa. Office: World Bank 1818 H St NW Washington DC 20433

HUNTER, DIANNE MARY, biotechnology company executive; b. Mansfield, Ohio, July 29, 1946; d. William George Brooker and Helen B. (Hickey) Dickson. Student biology Mt. Union Coll., 1969. Product mgr. Technicon Instruments subs. Revlon Corp., Tarrytown, N.Y., 1976-77, product mgr. hematology, 1977-79; mktg. mgr. Ortho Instruments subs. Johnson & Johnson, Westwood, Mass., 1979-80; v.p., gen. mgr. Genetic Diagnostics Corp., Great Neck, N.Y., 1980—; mktg., mgmt. cons., 1980—. Mem. Biomed. Mktg. Assn., Japan Export Trade Orgn. (adv. com. 1982—). Office: Genetic Diagnostics Corp 160 Community Dr Great Neck NY 11021

HUNTER, EDWINA, theology educator; b. Coushatta, La., Apr. 4, 1932; d. Edison Everette and Cora Lee (Jones) H; m. James Robert Snyder, June 2, 1969 (div. 1975); 1 child, Wendy Jo Snyder. BA, La. Coll., 1952; MRE, Southwestern Bapt. Theol. Sem., 1955; MA, Northwestern U., 1958, PhD, 1965. Dir. youth Parkview Bapt. Ch., Shreveport, La., 1952-53, Univ. Bapt. Ch., Ft. Worth, 1954-55; dir. edn. 1st Bapt. Ch., Galax, Va., 1955-57; instr. Bapt. Missionary Tng. Sch., Chgo., 1957-58; prof. speech Georgetown (Ky.) Coll., 1958-75; assoc. prof. oral interpretation U. South Fla., Tampa, 1975-76; lectr. homiletics Pacific Sch. Religion, Berkeley, 1976-83, assoc. prof. preaching, 1983—; pastor Bancroft Ave. Bapt. Ch., San Leandro, Calif., 1979-83. Author: sermon in Modern Liturgy, 1985; contbg. editor Jour. Women and Religion, 1985; contbr. articles to profl. jours. Assn. Theol. Schs. grantee, 1984. Mem. Acad. Homiletics (chmn. pedagogy/evaluation div. 1986), Ministers Council Am. Bapt. Ch. (pres. 1986—), Religious Speech Communication Assn. Democrat. Office: Pacific Sch Religion 1798 Scenic Ave Berkeley CA 94709

HUNTER, ELIZABETH KRISTINE, corporate tax examiner, consultant; b. Troy, N.Y., May 18, 1943; d. Harry Bernhardt and Elizabeth Mae (Stufflebeam) Jensen; m. Robert John Hunter; 1 child, Kristine Elizabeth. AS, Hudson Valley Community Coll., 1963; BS, Empire State Coll., 1981. Account clk. fin. State of N.Y. Dept. Edn., Albany, 1964-65, sr. clk., 1965-68, prin. clk., 1968-69; corp. franchise tax technician N.Y. State Tax & Fin., Albany, 1979-85, bank franchise tax technician, 1985—. Mem. Danish Sisterhood Am. (trustee eastern gen. com. dist. 1984-85, treas. 1985-86, sec. 1986-87, v.p. 1987-88, pres. 1988—). Lutheran. Lodge: Sunshine (pres. 1987—). Home and Office: 6902 Columbus Dr Holiday FL 34691-1027

HUNTER, KIM (JANET COLE), actress; b. Detroit, Nov. 12, 1922; d. Donald and Grace Mabel (Lind) Cole; m. William A. Baldwin, Feb. 11, 1944 (div. 1946); 1 dau., Kathryn Emmett; m. Robert Emmett, Dec. 20, 1951; 1 son, Sean Emmett. Ed. pub. schs.; student acting with Charmine Lantaff Camine, 1938-40, Actors Studio. First stage appearance, 1939, played in stock, 1940-42; Broadway debut in A Streetcar Named Desire, 1947; appeared in: tour Two Blind Mice, 1950, Darkness at Noon, N.Y.C., 1951, The Chase, 1952, N.Y.C., They Knew What They Wanted, 1952, The Children's Hour; revival, N.Y.C., 1952, The Tender Trap, N.Y.C., 1954, Write Me a Murder, N.Y.C., 1961, Weekend, N.Y.C., 1968, The Penny Wars, N.Y.C., 1969; And, Miss Reardon Drinks a Little; tour, 1971-72, The Glass Menagerie, Atlanta, The Women, N.Y.C., 1973, In Praise of Love, 1975, The Lion in Winter, N.J., 1975, The Cherry Orchard, N.Y.C., 1976, The Chalk Garden, Pa., 1976, Elizabeth The Queen, Buffalo, 1977, Semmelweiss, Buffalo, 1977, The Belle of Amherst, N.J., 1978, The Little Foxes, Mass., 1980, To Grandmother's House We Go, N.Y.C., 1981, Another Part of the Forest, Seattle, 1981, Ghosts, 1982, Territorial Rites, 1983, Death of a Salesman, 1983, Cat on a Hot Tin Roof, 1984, Life with Father, 1984, Sabrina Fair, 1984, Faulkner's Bicycle, 1985, Antique Pink, 1985, The Belle of Amherst, 1986, A Delicate Balance, 1986, Painting Churches, 1986, Jokers, 1986, Remembrance, 1987, Man and Superman, 1987-88, The Gin Game, 1988; frequent appearances summer stock and repertory theater, 1940—; appeared, Am. Shakespeare Festival, Stratford, Conn., 1961; film debut in The Seventh Victim, 1943; other motion pictures include Tender Comrade, 1943, When Strangers Marry (re-released as Betrayed), 1944, You Came Along, 1945, A Canterbury Tale, 1949, Stairway to Heaven, 1946, A Streetcar Named Desire, 1951, Anything Can Happen, 1952, Deadline U.S.A., 1952, Storm Center, 1956, Bermuda Affair, 1957, The Young Stranger, 1957, Money, Women, and Guns, 1958, Lilith, 1964, Planet of the Apes, 1968, The Swimmer, 1968, Beneath the Planet of the Apes, 1970, Escape from the Planet of the Apes, 1971, Dark August, 1975, The Kindred, 1987; made TV debut on, Actors' Studio program, 1948; numerous TV appearances include Requeim for a Heavyweight, 1956, The Comedian, 1957, both on Playhouse 90, Give Us Barabbas on, Hallmark Hall of Fame, 1961, 63, 68, 69, Love, American Style, Colombo, Cannon, Night Gallery, Mission Impossible, The Magician, 1972-73, Marcus Welby, Hec Ramsey, Griff, Police Story, Ironside, Med. Center, Bad Ronald, Born Innocent, 1974, Ellery Queen, 1975, Lucas Tanner, This Side of Innocence, Once an Eagle, Baretta, Gibbsville, Hunter, 1976, The Oregon Trail, 1977, Project: U.F.O., Stubby Pringle's Christmas, 1978, Backstairs at the White House, 1979, Specter on the Bridge, 1979, Edge of Night, 1979-80, F.D.R.'s Last Year, 1980, Skokie, 1981, Scene of the Crime, 1984, Three Sovereigns for Sarah, 1985, Hot Pursuit, 1985, Private Sessions, 1985, Martin Luther King, Jr.: The Dream and the Drum 1986, (CBS TV film) Drop Out Mother, 1987; rec. From Morning 'Til Night (and a Bag Full of Poems), RCA Victor, 1961, Come, Woo Me, Unified Audio Classics, 1964. Author: Kim Hunter-Loose in The Kitchen, 1975. Recipient Donaldson award for best supporting actress in A Streetcar Named Desire 1948, also on Variety N.Y. Critics Poll 1948, for film version 1952, winner Acad. award, LOOK award, Hollywood Fgn. Corrs. Golden Globe award, Emmy nominations for Baretta 1977, Edge of Night 1980, Fla. Carbonell (for Big Mama in Cat on a Hot Tin Roof) award 1984. Mem. Acad. Motion Picture Arts and Scis., ANTA, A.E.A. (council 1953-59), Screen Actors Guild, A.F.T.R.A.

HUNTER, LEAH BREAZEALE, nurse; b. Augusta, Ga., June 29, 1951; d. Osman Harrison and Bettye (Huff) Breazeale; m. Keith Ray Hunter, Oct. 10, 1977; 1 child, Brenda Michelle. Assoc., U. S.C., Aiken, 1974. RN, S.C., Ga., Fla. Nursing asst. Andress Nursing Home, Augusta, 1969-71; sr. nursing asst. St. Joseph's Hosp., Augusta, 1971-72; sr. nursing asst. U. Hosp., Augusta, 1972-74, staff nurse, 1974-76, asst. head nurse, 1976-77; staff nurse VA Med. Ctr., Augusta, 1977-80; dir. of nursing Evans Health Care, Augusta, 1980-81; dir. nursing Forrest Lake Manor, Augusta, 1981-84, Ga. War Veterans Nursing Home, Augusta, 1984—; adv. Med. Coll. Ga. Undergraduate bd., Augusta, 1986-88; adv. U. Ga. Master's in Gerontology Planning com., Athens, 1987-88; adv. Augusta Coll. Long Term Care com., 1987-88. Mem. Ga. Assn. Nurses in Long Term Care (v.p. 1986-87, council pres. 1986-87, pres. 1987-88), Omicron Theta Alpha. Home: 958 Fury Ferry Rd Evans GA 30809 Office: Ga War Veterans Nursing Home 1101 15th St Augusta GA 30910

HUNTER, MARLENE SELF, county legislative aide; b. Morganton, N.C., Feb. 9, 1934; d. Richard James and Azalee (Ritchey) Self; comml. cert. U. N.C., 1953; student U. Del.; m. Bill Roper Hunter, Nov. 28, 1953; children—Pamela Dawn, Charles Phifer, Gregory Scott, Susan Azalee. Adminstrv. asst. Charles County C. of C., La Plata, Md., 1974-78, exec. dir., 1978-84; legis. aide Prince Georges County Council, Md., 1985—. Pres. Charles County Democratic Club, 1976-78; bd. dirs. Charles County Handicapped and Retarded Citizens, 1978-80, sec., 1982; bd. dirs. Easter Seal Soc. for Disabled Children and Adults; mem Charles County Career Edn. Adv. Council. Mem. Am. C. of C. Execs. (chmn. chpt. 1982), Md. Council Small Bus. Execs. Methodist. Clubs: Crescent Cities Jaycee-Ettes (pres. 1972); Zonta (pres. 1982-83) (Charles County). Home: Hunter Hill Farm Route 232 Box 148 Bryantown MD 20617 Office: Council Offices County Adminstrn Bldg Upper Marlboro MD 20772

HUNTER, SUE PERSONS, former state official; b. Hico, Tex., Aug. 21, 1921; d. David Henry and Beulah (Boatwright) Persons m. Charles Force Hunter; children—Shelley Hunter Richardson, Kathy Hunter McCullough, Margaret Hunter Brown. BA U. Tex., 1942. Air traffic controller CAA (now FAA), San Antonio and Houston, 1942-52; writer Bissonet Plaza News, 1969-72; coordinator Goals for La., 1971-74; adminstrv. dir. Jeff Publs. Inc., 1974; press sec. Jefferson Parish Dist. Atty., 1972-75, communications cons., 1975-78; adminstr. Child Support Enforcement Div., 1979-85; contbg. editor The Jeffersonian, 1975-76. Pres. United Ch. Women East Jefferson (La.), 1958-59, LWV Jefferson Parish, La., 1961-64; pres. LWV La., 1967-71, also bd. dirs., 1962-67; mem. probation services com. Community Services Council, Jefferson, 1966-73, v.p., 1970-72; mem. Library Devel. Com. La., 1967-71, Nat. Com. for Support of Pub. Schs., 1967-72; mem. Goals Found. Council Met. New Orleans, 1969-75, sec. 1970, 72; mem. Goals La. Task Force State and Local Govt., 1969-70; pres. MMM Investment Club, 1969-72; bd. dirs. New Orleans Area Health Planning Council, 1969-75, Friends of Westminster Tower, 1986; mem. adv. council La. State Health Planning, 1971-76; title I adv. council La. State Dept. Edn., 1970-72; vice chmn. Jefferson Women's Polit. Caucus, 1977-78, chmn., 1979, treas., 1980; bd. dirs. New Orleans Area/Bayou-River Health Systems Agy., 1978-82, pres., 1980, 81; mem. Task force for La. Talent Bank of Women, 1980; exec. bd. La. Child Support Enforcement Assn., 1980-86, pres., 1982-84; bd. dirs., legis. chmn. Nat. Child Support Enforcement Assn., 1983-86; mem. Gov.'s Commn. on Child Support Enforcement, 1984-88; mem. La. Statewide Health Coordinating Council, 1980-83, mgmt. com. edn. fund League of Women Voters La., 1988—. Recipient Outstanding Citizens award Rotary Club, Metairie, La., 1962, River Ridge award, 1976. Mem. Am. Assn. Individual Investors (pres. New Orleans chpt. 1986-88), New Orleans Panhellenic (pres. 1956-57), Les Pelicaneers (pres. 1988—), Alpha Xi Delta. Presbyterian (elder). Home: 210 Stewart Ave River Ridge LA 70123

HUNTER, SUSAN G., publishing executive; b. Akron, Ohio, Aug. 3, 1950; Robert A. and Genevieve G. (Reneker) H. BA, Wittenberg U., 1972. Prodn. editor Charles E. Merrill Pub., Columbus, Ohio, 1972-75; copy editor W.B. Saunders Co., Phila., 1975-77, assoc. med. editor, 1977-79, mktg. dir., 1979-83; dir. mktg. Am. Chem. Soc., Washington, 1983-85; v.p., dir. mktg. Butterworth Pubs., Stoneham, Mass., 1985—. Mem. STM Internat. Pubs., Am. Med. Pubs. Assn., Soc. Scholarly Pub., Boston Bookbuilders, Mensa, Sigma Kappa (sec. 1987—). Home: 15 Terrace Park Reading MA 01867 Office: Butterworth Pubs 80 Montvale Ave Stoneham MA 02180

HUNTER, VALERIE JEAN DEXTER, real estate broker; b. Hackensack, N.J., Sept. 27, 1943; d. Perry and Vera May (Bates) D.; married, Sept. 5, 1965 (div. Mar. 1986); children: Kevin David, Keith Perry; m. William G. Hunter, Aug. 22, 1987. Grad. high sch., Lyndon Center, Ver. Dept. sec. U.S. C. of C., Washington, 1961-63; sec. The Cosmodyne Corp., Hawthorne, Calif., 1963; receptionist, pvt. sec. Sta. WTWN radio, St. Johnsbury, Ver., 1964-65; adminstrv. sec. Sanders Assocs., Inc., Nashua, N.H., 1967-72; co-owner, sec., bookkeeper Gallup Adjustment Service, Skowhegan, Maine, 1975-82; realtor Century 21 Whittemore's Real Estate, Skowhegan, 1981-87; realtor-broker Century 21 Nason Realty, Winslow, Maine, 1987—. Mem. Maine Assn. Realtors, No. Kennebec Valley Bd. Realtors, No. Kennebec Valley Multiple Listing Service, Lakewood Ladies Golf Assn. Home: Fire Rd 7 Neck Rd China ME 04926 Office: Century 21 Nason Realty 11 Bay St Winslow ME 04901 Mailing Address: PO Box 598 Waterville ME 04901

HUNTLEY, ALICE MAE, mfg. exec.; b. Atoka, Okla., May 3, 1917; d. Joseph LaHay and Lula May (Stapp) Howe; B.A. U. Okla., 1939; m. Loren Clifford Huntley, Nov. 7, 1942; children—Loren Lee, Marcia Lynn. Reporter, McAlester (Okla.) News Capital, 1939-41; sec., asst. to pres. and chmn. bd. N.Am. Aviation, Los Angeles, 1941-63; v.p., co-owner Tubular Specialties Mfg., Inc., Los Angeles, 1966—. Former sec. 1st Baptist Ch. of Westchester; sec. Westchester-Del Rey Republican Women, 1959-60; asso. mem. Rep. State Central Com., 1973. Cert. profl. sec.; named Outstanding Sec. in So. Calif., So. Calif. chpt., 1954, Internat. Sec. of Year, 1955 (both Nat. Secs. Assn.). Home: 8238 Calabar Ave Playa del Rey CA 90293 Office: 13011 S Spring St Los Angeles CA 90061

HUNTTING, CYNTHIA COX, artist; b. San Francisco, Sept. 2, 1936; d. E. Morris and Margeret (Storke) Cox; m. Edward Tyler Huntting Jr., Mar. 8, 1969 (div. 1974). BA, Smith Coll., 1958; San Francisco Art Inst., 1959. Artist Emporium White House, San Francisco, 1958-61; artist, staff Pace Program Stanford U., 1962-64; artist World Affairs Council No. Calif., San Francisco, 1964-67; artist pvt. practice San Francisco, 1968—; mem. Modern Art Council Bd. San Francisco Mus. Modern Art, 1970-78. Active Jr. League San Francisco, Inc. Republican. Episcopalian. Clubs: Town and Country, Metropolitan, Calif. Tennis. Home and Office: 2720 Lyon St San Francisco CA 94123

HUPALO, MEREDITH TOPLIFF, artist, illustrator; b. Tarpon Springs, Fla., Apr. 28, 1917; d. Walter and Maurine (Martin) Topliff; cert. in design Pratt Inst., 1938; m. Nicholas Hupalo, July 13, 1940 (dec. Sept. 1977); children—Walter Topliff, John Nicholas. One-woman shows: Tarpon Springs Public Library, 1945, Valley Stream (N.Y.) Mus., 1962, Contemporary Arts, Inc., N.Y.C., 1966, Jet Clubs Internat., N.Y.C., Henry Waldinger Library, Valley Stream, N.Y., 1977, East River Savs. Bank, Valley Stream, 1978; two-person show: Art League of Daytona Beach, 1986; represented in permanent collection Valley Stream Public Library, Tarpon Springs (Fla.) Public Library, Eastern Airlines Exec. Offices, N.Y.C.; tchr. printmaking Nassau County (N.Y.) Home Extension Service; art adviser Valley Stream Mus., 1962-64; illustrator Eastern Airlines, 1964-68; artist Shell Oil Co., 1968-70; designer Continental Can Co., N.Y.C., 1970-73; art tchr. Astor (Fla.) Community Center, 1980-82. Recipient spl. award oil painting 34th Nat. Spring Exhbn. Nat. Art League L.I., 1964, gold medal in oil painting 35th Membership Show, 1965; 1st pl. fine art Fla. Silver Springs Arts & Crafts Festival, 1980; 1st place award Umatilla Fall Festival (Fla.), 1983 merit award, 1985; merit award Tampa Realistic Artists, 1984; Best in Show award Nat. League Am. Pen Women, 1984; 1st pl. Fla. Extension Homemakers Cultural Arts; Award of Distinction, Pioneer Art Settlement, 1987. Mem. Fla. Watercolor Soc. (assoc.), Nat. Art League L.I. (treas. 1959-60), Tampa Realistic Artists, Art League of Daytona Beach (Lillian Gittner Meml. award 1988), Fla. Watercolor Soc. (assoc.), Nat. League Am. Pen Women (2d. pl. Daytona Beach, Fla. br. 1987), Mus. Arts and Scis., DeLand Mus., Astor Area C. of C. (dir. 1981-82). Methodist. Works include Paintings With Markers, 1972. Home: 55821 Dale Circle Astor FL 32002

HURAJT, ANDREA RUTH, controller; b. Cleve., Feb. 29, 1948; d. Andrew Steve and Ruth (Gamary) Hurajt; m. Larry Edward Buehner, May 12, 1988. Student, Dyke Coll., Cleve., 1971-72, Cuyahoga Community Coll., Parma, Ohio, 1984-88. Acct. C.E. Basic, Inc., Cleve., 1973-83; office mgr., acct. Bassichus Co., Cleve., 1983-85; office mgr. Ross Equipment, Cleve., 1985-87; controller Thrifty Car Rental, Cleve., 1987—; sec.-treas. Associated Equipment Corp., Cleve., 1985-87. Mem. Profl. Women's Assn. Democrat. Lutheran. Home: 4790 Andrea Ln Cleveland OH 44109

HURBANIS, BRENDA LOUISE, educator; b. Chgo., Nov. 3, 1949; d. Paul Hurbanis and Mary Jane (Adams) Della Toffalo. BS, Frostburg State Coll., 1972; MEd, Western Md. Coll., 1976; EdD, U. Md., 1986. Elem. tchr. Washington County Pub. Schs., Hagerstown, Md., 1972-74, Anne Arundel County Pub. Schs., Annapolis, Md., 1974-75; tchr. language, arts Anne Arundel County Pub. Schs., Annapolis, 1975-77, guidance couselor, 1977-79, guidance dept. chairperson, 1979-81, guidance resource counselor, 1981-83, coordinator instructional leadership program, 1983—; coop. tchr. Anne Arundel County Pub. Schs., 1976-77, counselor trainer 1981-82; cons. Queen Anne's County Pub. Schs., Centerville, Md., 1983-85. Author (handbooks): Guidance Curriculum Handbook, 1982, Discipline, 1982, School Climate Survey, 1986. Bd. dirs. Ocean Time Homeowners Assn., Queen City, Md., 1986—. Recipient Community Service award United Way Cen. Md., 1978, Counselor of Yr. award Md. Sch. Counselors Assn., 1981, Counseling Contbns. award Md. Personnel and Guidance Assn., 1981, Disting. Service award Anne Arundel County Tchrs. Assn., 1981, Pres.' Service award, 1981. Mem. Assn. for Supervision and Curriculum, Md. Assn. Counseling and Devel. (bd. dirs. 1980), Md. Edn. Assn. (rep. 1975-81), Md. Mid. Sch. Assn., Nat. Orgn. Devel. Network, Anne Arundel County Counselor's Assn. (pres. 1980, Pres.'s Service award 1981). Democrat. Lutheran. Home: 8403 High Ridge Rd Ellicott City MD 21043 Office: Anne Arundel County Pub Schs Annapolis Jr High Instructional Leadership Program Annapolis MD 21401

HURD, EDITH GERMANE, small business owner; b. Columbia, Mo., Aug. 8, 1926; d. Charles E. and Edith (Gayton) Germaine; m. Kenneth Badger Hurd, Jr., Aug. 28, 1948; children: Kenneth B. III, Steven K., Robert G., Jeffrey G. BS in Edn., U. Mo., 1947; postgrad., Columbia U., 1947. Tchr. New Hampton, N.H., 1947-48, Post Rd. Sch., White Plains, N.Y., 1948-50, Mamaroneck Ave Sch., White Plains, 1967-69; co-owner, office and warehouse mgr., buyer, dir. Flowers of the Week, White Plains, 1969—. Vol. Westchester Coalition for Legal Abortion, White Plains, N.Y., 1980-86, Met. Opera Lincoln Ctr., N.Y., 1988. Episcopalian. Clubs: Sierra, Westchester Trails Assn. Office: Flowers of the Week 798 Sleepy Hollow Rd Briarcliff NY 10510

HURLBUT, ROWENA JOSEPHINE, retail card and gift shop owner; b. Webster City, Iowa, May 20, 1917; d. Arthur C. and Eathel R. (Robinson) Bennett; m. Walter C. Hurlbut, June 10, 1942; (dec. 1973); children—Terrill C., Gary D., Cherie K. Student Morningside Coll. Pres., owner Ames News Agy. (Iowa), Inc., 1950—; gen. mgr. Walt's Hallmark Shops, Ames, 1952—, Boone, Iowa, 1969—, Jefferson, Iowa, 1975—, Des Moines, 1977—, Ames, 1978—, West Des Moines, 1983—. Bd. dirs. Story County, Am. Heart Assn., 1985-87. Mem. C. of C., Delta Zeta. Republican. Mem. Church of Christ (deaconess 1980—). Clubs: Ames Women's (chmn. group 1952-53). Lodge: Mem. Order Eastern Star. Home: 1421 Clark St Ames IA 50010 Office: Ames News Agy Inc 2110 E 13th St Ames IA 50010

HURLEY, ALLYSON KINGSLEY, dentist; b. Buffalo, June 15, 1949; d. Norman and Marion (Legler) Kingsley; m. Lawrence Joseph Hurley, May 28, 1977. Student, Barat Coll., 1967-68; degree in dental hygiene, Marquette U., 1970, BS, 1971; DDS, Howard U., 1977. Pvt. practice dental hygiene, Washington, 1971-77; resident VA Hosp., Lyons, N.J., 1977-78; gen. practice dentistry, Chatham, N.J., 1978—; attending dentist Overlook Hosp., Summit, N.J., 1979—, dir. resident adminstrn., 1980—, mem. edn. com., 1981—; clin. instr. dental hygiene Union County Tech. Inst., Scotch Plains, N.J., 1979-81, mem. selection com. for dental dept., 1987; coordinator kindergarten-4th grades dental health program Chatham Boro Sch. System, 1978—; active oral cancer screening program Chatham Boro Jr. Women's Club, 1980-82. Editor, contbg. author: (newsletter) Word of Mouth, 1981—; author: (booklet) Your Child's Teeth, 1984. Alumni recruiter Marquette U., Morris County, N.J., 1977—; bd. dirs. Am. Cancer Soc., Morris County, 1981-83; chair Scholarship Found. of the Chathams, Inc., 1985—. Fellow Acad. Gen. Destistry; mem. ADA, Tri-County Dental Soc. (bd. dirs. 1982-83), Internat. Platform Assn., N.Y. Acad. Scis. Republican. Roman Catholic. Clubs: Columbia U. Dental Study (treas. 1980—), No. N.J. Women's Study (pres. 1980-82, 86—, sec. 1983—), Newcomer's. Office: Allyson Kingsley Hurley DDS 585 Main St Chatham NJ 07928

HURLEY, ANN MARIE, municipal official; b. N.Y.C., July 13, 1925; d. Timothy Charles and Mary Frances (Lacey) O'Neill; ed. N.Y.C. public schs., bus. courses and seminars; m. John D. Hurley, Jr., Aug. 24, 1947; children—John Edward, Patty Ann Hurley McGovern. Clk., bookkeeping supr. Guaranty Trust Co., N.Y.C., 1942-47; bookkeeping supr. Continental Bank & Trust Co., N.Y.C., 1947-48, N.Y. Trust Co., N.Y.C., 1948-49; head bookkeeper, prin. clk., dep. receiver of taxes Town of Huntington, N.Y., 1960-67, receiver of taxes, 1967—; spl. com. revision Suffolk County Tax Act, mem. Blue Ribbon com. to revise Suffolk County Tax Act, 1982; mem. adv. bd. N.Y. State Community Affairs. Pres. Heatherwood Civic Assn., South Huntington Democratic Club; exec. bd. Suffolk County Dem. Party; Dem. zone leader, Huntington Station, N.Y.; committeeperson Dem. Party, 1960—; mem. Spl. Com. on Women's Issues, 1983—; parish council St. Elizabeth Roman Catholic Ch.; grand marshal Huntington ann. St. Patrick's Day Parade, 1976; bd. dirs. ARC; mem. adv. bd. Immaculate Conception Seminary; mem. Cancer Care, Deborah Hosp. Found.; chmn. fundraising Paulist Fathers. Named Woman of Yr., Nassau and Suffolk Bus. and Profl. Women's Clubs, 1983; recipient Clara Barton award Red Cross, 1988. Mem. N.Y. State Receivers and Collectors of Taxes Assn. (v.p. 1979-82, pres. 1982), Suffolk County Receivers of Taxes Assn. (pres. 1969-83). Club: Soroptimist (Grand Pres. Huntington chpt. 1977-80, bd. dirs., Woman of Distinction 1987). Home: 2 Coe Pl Huntington Station NY 11746 Office: Huntington Town Hall 100 Main St Huntington NY 11743

HURLEY, JOAN ELIZABETH, real estate executive; b. St. Paul, Dec. 13, 1953; d. William Joseph and Delores Florence (Stevens) H. BA, Coll. St. Benedict, St. Joseph, Minn., 1975; MBA, U. Iowa, 1977. Membership analyst U.S. C. of C., Washington, 1978; dir. advt. Cliff Co., Houston, 1978-80; dir. mktg. U.S. Home Corp., Houston, 1981-84; v.p. mktg. Randy Morine Homes, Austin, Tex., 1984-85; leasing agt. Johnson/Randolph Devel. Co., Austin, 1985-86; dir. leasing Prime Holding Corp., Austin, 1986—. Mem. Office Leasing Brokers Assn., Austin Retail Marketers Assn. Republican. Roman Catholic. Home: 8017 Pinedale Cove Apt B Austin TX 78758 Office: Prime Holding Corp 600 Congress Ave Suite 1630 Austin TX 78701

HURLEY, LUCILLE SHAPSON, nutritionist, educator; b. Riga, Latvia, May 8, 1922; came to U.S., 1925, naturalized, 1929; married 1945 (div. 1963); children: Barbara Hurley, Michael Hurley; m. Kenneth Thompson, 1967; stepchildren: Tamara, Marcus, Nicholas. BS in Nutrition, U. Wis., 1943; PhD in Nutrition (minors in Physiology, Biochemistry, Histology), U. Calif., Berkeley, 1950. Biochemist Child Research Council U. Colo. Sch. Medicine, Denver, 1951-52, research assoc. div Chem. Embryology, 1952-55; asst. research biochemist to asst. prof. U. Calif. Dept. Home Economics, Davis, 1955-61, assoc. prof. Nutrition, 1961-66, dept. chmn., 1963-65; prof. Nutrition dept. Nutrition U. Calif., Davis, 1966—, acting chmn. of dept., 1966-67, prof. Nutrition Sch. Medicine, 1971-77, prof. internal medicine, 1986—; sabbatical leave Laboratoire d'Embryologie U. Paris Med. Sch., 1962-63, Laboratoire de Biophysique, fall 1969; spl. leave Dept. Biochemistry U. Calif., Berkeley, summer 1961; vis. scientist Laboratoire des Isotopes Pasteur Inst., Paris, summers 1964, 65, Polish Acad. Sci., Nov. 1976; research collaborator Brookhaven Nat. Lab., 1966-68; vis. prof. Oreg. State U., July 1970, Wash. State U., July 1975; chercheur étranger, Inst. Nat. pour la Santé et la Recherche Médicale, Paris, Sept. 1974, 76; disting. lectr. Nutrition Research Inst. Oreg. State U., Feb. 1978, La. State U. Med. Ctr., Shreveport, Jan. 1980, Ga. Med. Coll., Augusta, 1981, 82, 83, 84, 85; Margaret Eppright lectr. Nutrition U. Tex., Austin, Apr. 1979; Marie Curie lectr. Sci., Tex. Women's U., 1983; York lectr. Auburn U., 1984; bd. dirs. sci. counselors Nat. Inst. Dental Research NIH, 1971-75, adv. council 1985-88; mem. Nutrition study sect. NIH, 1975-79; Nat. Acad. Scis. NRC subcom. Environ. Geochemistry in Relation to Health and Disease, 1976-79, chmn. subcom. Nutrient Requirements of Mouse, 1974-78, com. on Nutrition in Med. Edn., 1984-85, com. on Diet and Health, 1986—; sci. adv. council The Nutrition Found., 1980-84. Editor: Jour. Nutrition, 1984—; mem. editorial bd. Teratology, 1967-75, Am. Jour. Clin. Nutrition, 1977-80, Jour. Inorganic Biochemistry, 1978—, Biol. Trace Element Research, 1978—, Magnesium Bull., 1980-84, Nutrition Research, 1981-84, Magnesium, 1983-86, Annales de Recherches Vétérinaires, 1983-87, Issues and Revs. in Teratology, 1985—. Guggenheim fellow, 1962, 69; awardee Fundamental Research in Nutrition and Exptl. Foods, Borden, 1965, Osborne and Mendel award, 1981, Lederle award, 1985; medallist IntraScience Research Found., 1978, médaille de Vermeil, Acad. Nat. de Médecine, France, 1983; 2nd E.V. McCollum Internat. Lectr., 1980; faculty research lectr. U. Calif., Davis, 1987. Fellow AAAS, Am. Inst. Nutrition (nominating com. 1970, membership com. 1970-72, sec. 1972-75, councillor 1979-82, pres.-elect 1982-83, pres. 1983-85); mem. Teratology Soc. (charter mem., recorder 1968-72, pres.-elect 1974-75, pres. 1975-76), Soc. for Experimental Biology and Medicine (Nat. Membership com. 1978-81, councillor 1985—), European Teratology Soc., The Nutrition Soc., Am. Soc. Clin. Nutrition, Soc. Environ. Geochemistry and Health (pres.-elect 1973-74, pres. 1974-75, nominating com. 1979-80), Perinatal Research Soc., Sigma Xi (ann. meeting theme lectr. 1985), Trace Elements in Man and Animals (internat. parent com.), Iota Sigma Pi, Sigma Delta Epsilon. Office: U Calif Davis Dept Nutrition Davis CA 95616

HURLEY, MARY KATHERINE, school food service executive; b. Oakman, Ala., Mar. 27, 1933; d. William Isaiah and Abbie Eugenia (Carter) Allen; B.S., Blue Mountain (Miss.) Coll., 1955; M.S., U. Tenn., Martin, 1980; m. Lee L. Hurley, Jan. 30, 1970; 1 son, James. Food service supr. F. W. Woolworth Co., 1955-75; dir. food service Jackson City Schs. (Tenn.), 1975—. Mem. NEA, Tenn. Edn. Assn., Jackson Edn. Assn., Am. Sch. Foodservice Assn., Tenn. Sch. Foodservice Assn. (pres. 1983-84), Jackson City Sch. Foodservice Assn., Phi Delta Kappa. Republican. Baptist. Home: 106 Southshore Jackson TN 38305 Office: 1341 N Parkway Jackson TN 38301

HURST, CAROLYN JEAN, editor, writer; b. Rapid City, S.D., Jan. 21, 1958; d. Gene R. and Alice Louise (Oshner) H.; m. Steven L. Perry, Aug. 8, 1980; children: Natalie Hurst Perry, Evan Hurst Perry. Student, U. Idaho, 1976-77, 78-79; BS in Broadcast Journalism, S.D. State U., 1980. Asst. producer Sta. KUID-TV, Moscow, Idaho, 1978-79; asst. editor Volga (S.D.) Tribune, 1979-81; editor Crow Publs., Denver, 1981-82; news editor Kitsap County Herald, Poulsbo, Wash., 1983; editor Oudoor Empire Pub., Seattle, 1982-83, asst. to pres., 1983-85, cover editor, 1983—; cons. Windemere Real Estate, Silverdale, Wash., 1987—. Editor Fishing and Hunting News Freshwater Fish Maps, 1985. Mem. Phi Kappa Phi, Pi Gamma Mu, Kappa Tau Alpha. Home: 13718 Hillcrest Ave NW Poulsbo WA 98370 Office: Outdoor Empire Pub 511 Eastlake Ave E Seattle WA 98109

HURST, LAURA JEAN, infosystems specialist; b. St. Johns, Mich., Aug. 14, 1959; d. Paul Edward and Margaret Elizabeth (Moore) H. BS in Bus. Data Processing, Ferris State Coll., 1981. Programmer Data Systems for Industry, Long Beach, Calif., 1981-82; programmer, analyst Data Systems for Industry, Los Alamitos, Calif., 1982-83, project mgr., 1983-87, complex project mgr., 1987—. Mem. Am. Prodn. Inventory Control Soc. (cert., seminar instr., mem. curriculum com.), Nat. Assn. Female Execs. Roman Catholic. Office: Data Systems for Industry 5400 Orange Ave Cypress CA 90630

HURST, MARGARET ANNE, lawyer; b. Raleigh, N.C., Dec. 30, 1957; d. William Wesley and Elizabeth Wray (Lester) H. B in Music, Greensboro Coll., 1979; postgrad., Harvard U., 1981-82; JD, Wake Forest U., 1982. Bar: Fla. 1982, N.Y. 1984, U.S. Ct. Appeals (11th cir.) 1983, U.S. Dist. Ct. (ea. dist.) N.Y. 1987, U.S. Ct. Internat. Trade 1987, U.S. Tax Ct. 1987, U.S. Ct. Mil. Appeals 1987, U.S. Supreme Ct. 1987. Reginald Smith fellow Jacksonville (Fla.) Area legal Aid, Inc., 1982-84; sr. asst. dist. atty. Nassau County Dist Atty.'s Office, Mineola, N.Y., 1984—. Mem. Dem. Nat. Com., Washington, 1984—. Named one of Outstanding Young Women Am., 1978. Mem. ABA, N.Y. State Bar Assn., N.Y. State Dist. Attys. Assn., Nassau County Bar Assn., Phi Delta Phi Internat. Democrat. Methodist. Home: 22-17 Harman St Ridgewood NY 11385

HURT, CHARLENE SCHMIDT, library director; b. St. Louis, Aug. 10, 1940; d. Lester John and Loretta Mary (Doyen) S.; m. James E. Hurt, Aug. 22, 1959 (div. 1978); children—Andrew Pol, Lisa Jan. B.A., Culver-Stockton Coll., 1964; M.L., Emporia State U., 1974; M.P.A., U. Kans., 1979. Cataloger Washburn U., Topeka, 1974-76, asst. librarian pub. service, 1976-77, dir. library and media services, 1977-84; dir. libraries George Mason U., Fairfax, Va., 1984—; vis. lectr. library sci. Emporia State U., Kans., 1981. Author: (film script) Battered Women: A Public or Private Problem, 1977; contbr. book revs. to publs. Mem. steering com. Kans. Com. on Humanities, Topeka, 1979-84; panel mem. grantsmaking panel Unitarian Universalist Assn., Mpls., 1983—; mem. Mayor's Commn. on Status of Women, Topeka, 1981-84; bd. dirs. YWCA, Topeka, 1982-84, Interfaith of Topeka, 1981-83; pres. Unitarian Universalist Fellowship, Topeka, 1981-83. Grad. scholar Emporia State U., 1973-74; grantee Mountain Plains Library Assn., 1978-79; Kansas Com. on Humanities, 1981. Mem. ALA (Olafson Meml. Novia award 1979), Library Dir.'s Council Consortium of Washington Met. Area, D.C. Library Assn., Women Adminstrs. Discussion Group (co-chmn. 1981-82), Women Acad. Library Dirs., Phi Kappa Phi. Democrat. Home: 3714 Persimmon Circle Fairfax VA 22031 Office: George Mason Univ div Libraries 4400 University Dr Fairfax VA 22030

HUSBY, VONNA KAY, brokerage house executive; b. Colfax, Wash., Feb. 8, 1944; d. George W. and Patti (Chase) Von Arb; m. Fredric M. Husby, Sept. 2, 1971; children: Kimberly C., Martin F. AA, Stephens Coll., 1964. Asst. br. mgr. Foster & Marshall, Fairbanks, Alaska, 1982-83, Shearson Lehman Bros., Fairbanks, 1983-85; account exec. Dean Witter Reynolds, Inc., Fairbanks, 1985—. Past pres. Univ. Womens Assn., Fairbanks. Recipient Buz Lukens award for Outstanding D.C. Young Rep. of Yr., Nat. Sales Dirs. Achievement award Dean Witter Reynolds, Inc., IRA Achievement award Dean Witter Reynolds, Inc., Nat. Sales Tng. award Dean Witter Reynolds, Inc., Pacesetters award Dean Witter Reynolds, Inc., 1986. Mem. Univ. Womens Assn., DAR (state chairwoman). Clubs: Kiwanis (bd. dirs.), Soroptimists. Home: 1354 Chena Ridge Fairbanks AK 99701 Office: Dean Witter 305 Lacey St Fairbanks AK 99701

HUSSAINI, EMOLYN MARIN, physician; b. Iloilo, Philippines, Aug. 9, 1946; came to U.S., 1973; d. Jose A. and Concepcion (Marin) Defensor; m. Syed Aijaz Hussaini, June 1976; children: Yasmeen, Amed. MD, U. Philippines, 1971. Diplomate Am. Bd. Pediatrics. Resident Newark Beth Israel Med. Ctr., 1973-75; gen. practice medicine Geneva, Ohio. Mem. Ashtabula Med. Soc. Home: 5542 Forest Glen Rd Madison OH 44057 Office: 810 W Main St Geneva OH 44041

HUSSELMAN, GRACE, innkeeper, educator; b. Paterson, N.J., July 24, 1923; d. Edward and Lydia (Kliphouse) Van Allen; B.A., William Paterson Coll.; m. Samuel Husselman, June 3, 1944; children—Samuel Glenn, Howard Lloyd. With personnel office Wright Aero. Corp., Fairlawn, Pub. 1942-45; library asst. Wyckoff (N.J.) Pub. Library, 1964-66; library dir. Allendale (N.J.) Pub. Library, 1967-81; elem. sch. tchr., assoc. ednl. media specialist, 1981-84; owner Ye Olde Buckmaster Inn, 1984—. Reading Merit Badge counselor Boy Scouts Am.; pioneer guide Pioneer Girls, nat. youth v.p., sec. friendship circle; sec. bookstore com. Christian Growth Ministries; sec. Ladies Aid Soc., Shrewsbury Community Ch.; bd. deacons Shrewsbury Community Ch.; bd. dirs. Shrewsbury Library, Vt. Mem. N.J., Bergen-Passaic library assns., Hist. Soc. of Shrewsbury (sec.), Kappa Delta Pi. Club: Captains and Mates Yacht. Home: Lincoln Hill Rd Shrewsbury VT 05783

HUSTON, ANJELICA, actress; b. Los Angeles; d. John and Enrica Huston. Student, Loft Studio. Actress appearing in Hamlet, Roundhouse Theatre, London, Tamara, Il Vittorale Theatre, Los Angeles; appeared in films including A Walk with Love and Death, 1967, Sinful Darey, 1969, Swashbuckler, 1976, The Postman Always Rings Twice, 1981, This is Spinal Tap, 1984, The Ice Pirates, 1984, Prizzi's Honor, 1985 (Academy award for best supporting actress, N.Y. and Los Angeles Film Critics award), Captain Eo, 1986, Gardens of Stone, 1987, The Dead, 1987; appeared in TV film The Cowboy and the Ballerina, 1984. Address: care William Morris Agency Inc 151 El Camino Beverly Hills CA 90212 *

HUSTON, MARGO, journalist; b. Waukesha, Wis., Feb. 12, 1943; d. James and Cecile (Timlin) Bremner; student U. Wis., 1961-63; A.B. in Journalism, Marquette U., 1965; m. James Huston, Dec. 9, 1967 (div.); 1 son, Sean Patrick. Editorial asst. Marquette U., Milw., 1965-66; feature editor, reporter Waukesha Freeman, 1966-67; feature reporter Milw. Jour., 1967-70; reporter Spectrum, women's and food sections, 1972-79, editorial writer, 1979-84, polit reporter, 1984—, asst. picture editor, 1985—. Recipient Penney-Mo. award for consumer abortion series, 1975, Pulitzer Prize for investigation into plight of elderly, 1977, Clarion award, 1977, Knight of Golden Quill award, Milw. Press Club, 1977, Wis. AP writing award, 1977, special award Milw. Soc. Profl. Journalists, 1977, Penney-Mo. Paul Myhie award for excellence, 1978; By-Line award Marquette U. Coll. of Journalism, 1980; Wis. UPI best editorial award, 1982; Wis. Women's Network award for journalist achievement for women's issues, 1983 Mem. Nat. News Council (dir.), Investigative Reporters and Editors, Nat. Conf. Editorial Writers, Sigma Delta Chi. Club: Milw. Press. Home: 3289 N 50th St Milwaukee WI 53216 Office: Milwaukee Journal 333 W State St Milwaukee WI 53201 *

HUTCHESON, RUTH ANN, accountant; b. Lewiston, Idaho, July 9, 1957; d. Robert James and Vera Rosamond (Ulinder) H. AAS, Lewis-Clark State Coll., 1977. Office mgr. Taxmasters, Billings, Mont., 1977-82; owner Taxmasters, Glasgow, Mont., 1983—; bookkeeper Van Pittack, CPA, Billings. Active Glasgow Swim Team, 1983—. Mem. Nat. Soc. Pub. Accts., Nat. Assn. Female Execs., Nat. Assn. Tax Practitioners. Democrat. Methodist. Lodge: Soroptimists (bd. dirs. 1985-87). Home: 112 Lomond Ave Glasgow MT 59230 Office: Taxmasters Box 248 Hwy 2 East Glasgow MT 59230

HUTCHESON, SHIRLEY JUNE ROBERTS, city official; b. Booneville, Miss., June 25, 1948; d. A.C. and Martha Geraldine (Houston) Roberts; m. Jerry Ronald Hutcheson, June 28, 1969; children—Dena Nicole, Joshua Allen. A.A., N.E. Miss. Jr. Coll., 1968; B.S., Miss. State U., 1972. Cert. city clk. Miss. Sec. to br. mgr. Bank of Miss., Booneville, 1970-72; acctg. technician Corinth Community Devel., Miss., 1973; mayor's sec. City of Booneville, Miss., 1973-75, mcpl. clk., 1975—; co-owner Merry Maids Home Cleaning, Memphis. Mem. Miss. Mcpl. Clks. Assn., Internat. Mcpl. Clks. Assn. (cert.). Baptist. Avocations: reading; ceramics; needlework. Home: PO Box 187 Booneville MS 38829 Office: City of Booneville 203 N Main St Booneville MS 38829

HUTCHESON, TERESA BEE, educator; b. Oakland City, Ind., Sept. 15, 1953; d. Vernon Roy and Peggy Ann (Woolsey) Richardson; m. Michael E. Ebert, Sept. 25, 1971 (div. 1981): children: Teala Ann, Christopher Michael Sean; m. Michael J. Hutcheson, July 23, 1983. AS in Bus., Marion (Ind.) Coll., 1984, BS in Mgmt., 1986. Office mgr. No. Ind. Fin. Services, Marion, 1984-86; tchr. Ind. Bus. Coll., Marion, 1986, dir., 1986—. Poll worker Dem. Party, Marion, 1971. Home: 4620 S Selby St Marion IN 46953 Office: Ind Bus Coll 417 S Branson St Marion IN 46953

HUTCHINGS, LEANNE VON NEUMEYER, communications executive, research consultant, writer and lecturer; b. Los Angeles; d. F. Louis and Greta Catherine (Clifford) von Neumeyer; children: Marc Lane, Kristin Le-Anne, Michael Lane, Jamie Laird, Jeremy Leif, Bret Louis. Student Brigham Young U., 1962. V.p. Steenhoek Neeley von Neumeyer Assocs., Cons.; researcher, writer, owner Heritage Tree, Arcadia, Calif., 1970—; internat. bd. advisors, dir. protocol Neeley Scholarship Found., 1985—; dir. pub. communications Ch. of Jesus Christ of Latter-day Saints, So. Calif., 1975—, dir. community relations, 1984—, asst. dir. area council, 1984—; seminar coordinator R.E.D.I., Inc., Los Angeles, 1982—, corp. relations dir., 1984—; design cons. H.M.J. Jewelers, Los Angeles, 1985—; mem. nat. adv. council motion picture studio Brigham Young U., Provo, Utah, 1986—; adminstrv. dir. Pasadena Geneal. Library, Calif., 1977-82; writer, co-producer KBIG, Sideband Div. Radio, Los Angeles, 1979-80; exec. assoc adminstr. Calif. Bicentennial Found. for the U.S. Constitution, 1987; regional cons. Latter-Day Sentinel Newspaper, Los Angeles, 1985—; mem. internat. bd. advisors, dir. protocol Neeley Internat. Scholarship Found., Los Angeles, 1985—; mem. com. on child pornography legis. Los Angeles County Commn. on Obscenity & Pornography, 1988; artist. Author: Honored Heritage, 1975, Woman's Place of Honor, 1976, Prologue and Tapestry, 1976, Moments with the Prophets, 1977, You're Elected Charlie Brown, 1977, Reaching for the Stars, 1975, Up, Up and Away, 1978, Traditions, 1979, All About You, 1980, Southern California: The Earthquake Threat, 1981, Quake!: Preparing Home, Family and Community, 1982, The Peregrine Papers, 1986; columnist: Heritage Tree Foothill Intercity News, 1977-79, Women's Exponent Southern Calif. edition; Sentinel; journalism series, 1978-80; also articles, collected works, stage trilogy; art exhibits include Wilshire Alma Exhibit, 1985, The Grand Artists Hall, 1986-88. Pres. Dau. Utah Pioneers-Los Angeles County, 1983-85; instr. Arcadia chpt. ARC, Los Angeles, 1983-85; mem. Community Coordinating Council, Arcadia, 1983-86; mem. exec. bd. Calif. Utah Women, Los Angeles, 1977-79, 85-86. Recipient Mother of Yr. award Ch. of Jesus Christ of Latter-day Saints, Arcadia, 1979. Best of Exhibit award Sculptor's West Workshop, 1982. Mem. Assn. Latter-Day Media Artists (assoc. editor Voice of ALMA 1978-83, exec. bd. 1977-81, chmn. spl. events, 1985—, internat. bd. govs. fellow 1981-83), Nat. Assn. Female Execs., Bus. Industry Conf. Earthquake Preparedness Project, Am. Film Inst., Deseret Bus. and Profl. Assn., Nat. Mus. Women in the Arts (charter), Arcadia Tournament of Roses Assn., Arcadia C. of C. (chmn. industry commn. of women's div. 1983-85, mem. exec. bd. 1985-86). Republican. Mormon. Avocations: sculpting, oil painting, violin, pistol marksmanship. Office: REDI Inc 112 W 9th St Suite 922 Los Angeles CA 90015

HUTCHINS, CYNTHIA ANN, optician; b. Beverly, Mass., Aug. 1, 1962; d. Warren Bertram and Carole Marie (Poor) H. AS, Salem State Coll., 1982. Cert. dispensing optician, Mass. Optometric technician Cambridge Eye Assocs., Danvers, Mass., 1984-85; ops. mgr. Precision Optics, Danvers, 1985—; exec. mgr. Parrelli Optical, Danvers, 1985—; asst. dir. edn. Essex Optical Corp., Hamilton, Mass.; cons. Cape Ann Optical, Danvers. Foster parent Christian Children's Fund, Va., sponsor Covenant House, N.Y., mem. Ctr. for Environmental Edn., Washington, mem. Audubon Soc., Mass. Mem. Mass. Assn. Registered Dispensing Opticians, Nat. Assn. Female Execs., The Bus. Women's Tng. Inst. Roman Catholic. Home: 26 Burley St Wenham MA 01984 Office: Parrelli Optical 40 Enon St Beverly MA 01915

HUTCHINS, ELIZABETH ANN, planning consultant; b. Rochester, N.Y., Dec. 18, 1950; d. Frank Asbury and Dorothy (Kaiser) H. BS with honors, MIT, 1972; MBA with honors, Harvard U., 1975. Advt. sales analyst Newsweek div. Washington Post Co., 1975-76, mgr. circulation planning, 1976-77, dir. new venture devel., 1977-80; mgr. corp. planning and devel. Tech. Publishing div. Dun and Bradstreet Corp., 1981-82; dir. acquisitions and strategic planning Tech. Data Resources div. Dun and Bradstreet Corp., 1983-86; planning con. Hutchins and Assocs., 1986—. Rotary scholar, 1972. Clubs: Harvard Bus. Sch. (N.Y.C.), Crafts Student League.

HUTCHINS, JANET M., environmental scientist; b. Washington, Aug. 16, 1947; d. James Otis and Lydia Merrick (Cummins) Taylor; children—Aaron Benjamin, Cristina-Marie, Ernst Frederick. A.A., U. N.D., 1974; B.S., Calif. State U.-San Bernardino, 1977; Cert., U.S. Coast Guard Pacific Strike Team, 1983, Calif. Spl. Tng. Inst., 1984, Monterey County Fire Tng. Officers Assn., 1984. Eviron. technician County of San Bernardino, Calif., 1974-77; environ. specialist U.S. Air Force Systems Command, Edwards AFB, Calif., 1980-81, environ. program mgr., U.S. Air Force, 1981-82; environ. specialist, U.S. Army, Ft. Ord, Calif., 1982-85; bioenviron. scientist HQ Forces Command, Ft. Gillem, Ga., 1985—; pres. H&H Environ. Services, Inc., 1986—; hazardous material specialist, County of Santa Barbara, Calif., 1987—. Author: Hazardous Waste in San Bernardino, 1976. Vol. firefighter Marina Pub. Safety, Calif., 1984-85; hazardous material spill coordinator, instr. Ft. Ord, Calif., 1982-85. Mem. Calif. Firefighters Assn., Nat. Assn. Environ. Profls. Avocations: photography; piano and synthesizer; hiking; canoeing.

HUTCHINS, JEANNE BAHN, town official; b. Rochester, N.Y., Mar. 12, 1922; d. Carl E. and Marie (Hall) Bahn; B.A., Wells Coll., 1943; M.P.A., SUNY, Brockport, 1980; m. Frank McAllister Hutchins, Aug. 24, 1945; children—Katharine H. Welling, Virginia H. Valkenburgh, Patricia H. Murphy, Constance H. Mills. Bacteriologist/chemist Manhattan Project Atomic Energy U. Rochester/Strong Meml. Hosp., 1943-45; library asst. Fort Benning, Ga., 1946-47, Dartmouth Coll., Hanover, N.H., 1947-48; town bd. legislator Town of Brighton, Rochester, N.Y., 1976—; notary pub., County of Monroe, 1976—; trustee Monroe Savs. Bank, 1978—. Trustee, Wells Coll., 1977-86, adv. council bd. trustees, 1986—; trustee Colgate Rochester Div. Sch., 1984—, treas., 1987—; trustee Bexley Hall Episcopal Sem., 1984—, treas., 1986—; vestrywoman St. Paul's Episcopal Ch., 1977-83, treas., 1983-87, warden, 1987—; bd. dirs. United Way of Greater Rochester, 1974-84; trustee Center for Govt. Research, 1979—; pres. Jr. League Rochester, 1957-59; bd. dirs. Vis. Nurse Service, Northaven Adoption Agy., 1965-69, Genesee Region Health Planning Council; bd. dirs. St. Ann's Home, 1982—, v.p., 1986—; pres. bd. dirs. Council Social Agys., 1969-70; bd. dirs. Nat. Com. on Social Work Careers, 1964-65, Monroe County Human Resources Council, 1975-81, Health Care, Rochester Gen. Hosp., 1985—, Family Service Am., 1985-87 ; v.p. bd. dirs. Family Service Rochester, 1962-69, Planned Parenthood, 1960-69; mem. women's council Rochester Inst. Tech., 1970—, N.Y. State Communities Aid Assn., 1970—; pres. Rochester Female Charitable Soc., 1983-85, trustee, 1975—; bd. dirs. Rochester Area Found., 1973-76. Recipient Forman Flair award, 1973, Civic Medal award Rochester Mus. and Sci. Ctr., 1986. Grant Garvey award Am. Soc. Public Adminstrn., 1980; Shumway award Family Service of Rochester, 1983; Wells Coll. Alumnae award, 1988. Mem. Mo. County Bar Assn. (profl. rev. panel 1986—), Brighton C. of C., LWV, Compeer Inc. (bd. dirs. 1982—). Republican. Clubs: Mid Town Tennis, Rochester Dist. Golf, Western N.Y. Golf Assn. Home: 75 Indian Spring Ln Rochester NY 14618 Office: Brighton Town Hall 2300 Elmwood Ave Rochester NY 14618

HUTCHINSON, LESLIE E, fiscal programs manager, consultant; b. Balt., Oct. 14, 1961; d. P. David Hutchinson and J. Leslie (Wilson) Duer; 1 child, Brent David. Student, Essex Community Coll., 1979-82, Villa Julie Coll., 1981-82, Johns Hopkins U., 1984 . V.p. Family Days, Inc., Balt., 1982; asst. clinic coordinator Johns Hopkins U., Balt., 1983-84, adminstrv. asst., 1984-85, budget coordinator, 1985-86; fiscal programs mgr. Balt. County Govt. Criminal Justice Coordinator's Office, Balt., 1986—; cons. Ctr. for Hosp. Fin. and Mgmt. Johns Hopkins U., Balt., 1986-87, Plake Properties, Inc., Balt., 1987—. Mem. Dean's Ad Hoc Com. on Status of Women, Johns Hopkins U., 1985; adv. com. United Way of Johns Hopkins U., 1985-86; exec. dir. Family Day '87, Balt. 1987; campaign coordinator for United Way, Criminal Justice Coordinator's Office, 1987; mem. Am. Council of Young Polit. Leaders, Washington, 1987; treas. Hutchinson Com. for Good Govt., Hutchinson for Senate Com., Balt.,1987—; sec. Balt. County Young Dems., 1987-88; v.p. programs Maryland Young Dems., 1987-88; elected mem. Md. Dem. State Cen. Com., 1986-1990. Named Outstanding Young Dem. of Yr., 1987. Methodist. Home: 331 Lorraine Ave Baltimore MD 21221 Office: Balt County Criminal Justice Coordinator's Office 312 Courthouse 400 Washington Ave Towson MD 21204

HUTCHINSON, MARJORIE, small business owner and operator; b. Nashville, Ga., Mar. 19, 1922; d. Johnie and Fanie (Harrell) Kent; m. Carlos Hutchinson, July 4, 1942; children: Hilda Ann Howington, Linda Kay Slade. Student, Bainbridge Jr. Coll., U. Ga. Dir., owner Children's World at Hutchinson's Day Care Ctr., Bainbridge, Ga., 1966—. Baptist. Office: Children's World Hutchinson Day Care Ctr 914 Palm Bainbridge GA 31717

HUTCHINSON, PATTY S., insurance agency executive; b. Springfield, Mo., Mar. 25, 1933; d. Bernie E. and Macie W. (Israel) Armstrong; m. Robert O. Hutchinson, May 11, 1952 (div. 1975); children: Kevin D., Karen M. Student pub. schs. Pleasant Hope, Mo. Sec. various agts. and adjusters in Las Vegas, Nev., 1950-55; underwriter Peccole Ins. Agy., 1955-60; adjuster Key Adjustment Co., 1960-66; agent, office mgr. Harrington-Horsey Ins. Co., 1966-81; co-owner, agt. McFadden Ins. Agy., 1981—. Pres., Century Meadows Homeowners Assn., 1983-85, Nev. Ins. Edn. Found., 1987-89. Mem. Ins. Women of Las Vegas (pres 1983-84), Nev. Ind. Ins. Agents (bd. dirs. 1988-89), Ind. Ins. Agents of So. Nev. (dir. 1982-83, pres. 1986-87). 1982-83, pres. 1986-87). Office: McFadden Ins Agy Inc 1570 S Rainbow Blvd Las Vegas NV 89102

HUTCHINSON, SANDRA PRICE, advertising executive; b. St. Louis, Feb. 20, 1944; d. Harry Edward and Anna Sue (Woodard) Price; m. James Hutchinson, June 24, 1967 (dec. Dec. 1979). AA in Communications, Forest Park Community Coll., St. Louis, 1981. Supr. ins. St. Louis Globe-Dem. Newspaper, 1965-78; advertisement taker St. Louis Post-Dispatch Newspaper, 1979-80, advt. account exec., 1981—. Active White House Conf. on Domestic and Econ. Affairs, St. Louis, 1975; bd. dirs. Southside Child Devel. and Day Nursery, St. Louis, 1986. Roman Catholic. Home: PO Box 1234 Saint Louis MO 63101 Office: St Louis Post-Dispatch Newspaper 900 N Tucker Blvd Saint Louis MO 63101

HUTCHINSON, THELMA AURELL, real estate executive, travel agency executive; b. Sublette, Ill., Oct. 8, 1930; d. Lawrence Lee and Mary Frances (Dudgeon) Watson; m. John Orvis Hutchinson, June 12, 1949; children: Jill Aurelle Hutchinson Kern, Saralyn Jae Hutchinson Wendelken, Jeffrey John. Student, Beloit Coll., 1948-49; diploma in Italian culture and tourism, Italian U. Fgn. Studies, Perugia, 1984. Sch. tchr. Mendota, Ill., 1950-51; real estate salesperson E.H. Holdren Real Estate, Mendota, 1966-76; real estate broker, owner Rainbow Realtors, Mendota, 1976—; owner Rainbow Travel, Mendota, 1982—; instr. Ill. Valley Community Coll., Oglesby, 1977-79, 82; lectr. in field. Columnist on travel, 1987; radio broadcasts, 1983—. Counselor Am. Field Service, No. Ill., 1970; advisor to Congressman John Grotberg, Springfield, Ill. and Washington, 1977-86. Mem. Illini Valley Bd. Realtors (sec. 1971-73, Outstanding Service award 1973-74), Mendota Area C. of C. (bd. dirs. 1977-80, charter ambassador 1980—), Kappa Delta. Republican. Baptist. Clubs: Mendota Golf, Jr. Women's (sec. v.p., pres. 1949-60), West End (Mendota). Home: 1311 Monroe St Mendota IL 61342 Office: Rainbow Realtors/Travel 910 Washington St Mendota IL 61342

HUTCHISON, DORRIS JEANNETTE, microbiologist, educator; b. Carrsville, Ky., Oct. 31, 1918; d. John W. and Maud (Short) H. B.S., Western Ky. State Coll., 1940; M.S., U. Ky., 1943; Ph.D., Rutgers U., 1949. Instr. Russell Sage Coll., 1942-44, Vassar Coll., 1944-46; research asst. Rutgers U., 1946-48, research assoc., 1948-49; instr. Wellesley Coll., 1949-51; asst. Sloan-Kettering Inst., N.Y.C., 1951-56; assoc. Sloan-Kettering Inst., 1956-60, assoc. mem., 1960-69, mem., 1969—, sect. head, 1956-72, acting chief div. exptl. chemotherapy, 1965-66, div. chief drug resistance, 1967-72, co-head lab. exptl. tumor therapy, 1973-74, lab. head drug resistance and cyto-regulation, 1973-84, coordinator field edn., 1975-81; instr. Sloan-Kettering div. Cornell U. Grad. Sch. Med. Sci., N.Y.C., 1952-53, research assoc., 1953-54, asst. prof., 1954-58, assoc. prof. microbiology, 1958-70, prof. microbiology, 1970—, chmn. biology unit, 1968-74, assoc. dir., 1974-87; assoc. dean Cornell U. Grad. Sch. Med. Sci., 1978-87, asst. dean, 1978-87; mem. Meml. Sloan-Kettering Cancer Ctr., 1984—; del. dir. Am. Cancer Soc., Inc., 1986—. Bd. dirs. Westchester div. Am. Cancer Soc., 1976—, exec. com., 1976—; project chmn. Target 5, 1977-80, v.p., 1979-81, pres., 1981-83, sec., 1983-87, charter mem. So. Westchester Unit, 1984, pres., 1984-86. Faculty fellow Vassar Coll., 1946; USPHS fellow, 1951-53; Philippe Found. fellow Paris, 1959. Fellow N.Y. Acad. Sci., Am. Acad. Microbiology (charter), N.Y. Acad. Medicine (asso.); mem. AAAS, Am. Assn. Cancer Research, Harvey Soc., Genetics Soc. Am., Am. Inst. Nutrition, Am. Soc. for Microbiology (councilor N.Y.C. br. 1954-58, pres. N.Y.C. br. 1958-60, nat. councilor 1961-63, chmn. nat. meeting 1967, mem. pres.'s fellowship com. 1973-76, chmn. 1975-76), Soc. for Cryobiology, Am. Genetic Assn., Internat. Soc. Biochem. Pharmacology. Home: Southgate Bronxville NY 10708 Office: Sloan-Kettering Inst 145 Boston Post Rdst Rye NY 10580

HUTCHISON, PAT, nurse, administrator; b. Omaha, Mar. 4, 1943; d. Earl Edward and Sylvia Lorraine (Kronen) Moore; m. James M. Hutchison, June 23, 1963; children—Michael, Danny. Diploma in nursing, St. Joseph's Sch. Nursing, 1968; student Central Ariz. Coll., 1976-82; BS in Health Service Adminstrn., U. Phoenix, 1983; BS in Nursing, U. Phoenix, 1988. R.N.; cert. in advanced cardiac life support, Ariz. Nurse Armish Maag Hosp., Teheran, Iran, 1969-71; supr. Hoemako Hosp., Casa Grande, Ariz., 1973-84; asst. dir. nursing Casa Grande Regional Med. Ctr., 1984-86, nursing supr., 1986—. Nursing chmn. ARC, Casa Grande, 1986—, also bd. dirs., instr. disaster tng., 1982—; instr. cardiopulmonary resuscitation Am. Heart Assn., Casa Grande, 1978—. Recipient Care award Ariz. Hosp. Assn., 1984, Service and Appreciation award Bus. and Profl. Women's Assn., 1984. Mem. Ariz. Nurses in Mgmt., Emergency Nurses Assn. Democrat. Roman Catholic. Avocations: traveling; camping; boating; reading. Home: 1308 N Center St Casa Grande AZ 85222 Office: Casa Grande Regional Med Ctr 1800 E Florence Blvd Casa Grande AZ 85222

HUTH, ELISABETH HAMILL (BETTY), photographer; b. Charleston, W.Va., Sept. 23, 1940; d. Gordon Mealy and Margaret Elisabeth (Joachim) Hamill; m. Bernard Gene Huth, June 22, 1963; children: Stephen C., Catherine M., Kevin L. BS in Nursing, Case Western Res. U., 1963. RN, cert. profl. photographer. Staff RN Permanente Med. Group, Redwood City, Calif., 1963-64; staff RN Permanente Med. Group, Santa Clara, Calif., 1964, charge nurse, 1964-65, dir. clin. nursing, 1965-67; owner Betty Huth Photography, San Jose, Calif., 1980—; trustee, sec. West Coast Sch. Profl. Photography, Santa Barbara, 1986—, Cert. Commn. Profl. Photographers Calif., San Francisco, 1986—. Bd. dirs. The Women's Fund, Santa Clara County, 1987. Mem. Profl. Photographers Am. (photographs on nat. exhibit, 1986, 87, 88), Profl. Photographers Calif., Profl. Photographers Santa Clara Valley (v.p. 1986-87, pres. 1988, Outstanding mem. 1986), Profl. Photographers No. Counties, Calif. Women in Profl. Photography. Republican. Presbyterian. Home and Office: Betty Huth Photography 6851 Eldridge Dr San Jose CA 95120

HUTSON, GENEVA, refining company executive; b. Tyler, Tex., Nov. 6, 1923; d. Lonnie Frederick and Sylvia Louise (Allen) Wallace; student Sam Houston Tchrs. Coll., 1946, U. Houston, 1973, 74; m. Walter Murphy Hutson, May 23, 1941; children—Wayne Murphy, Mark Farrell. Stenographer Lone Star Def. Corp., Texarkana, Tex., 1942, Montgomery & Ward, Denver, 1943; sec.-bookkeeper William Steinkamp Lumber Co., Groveton, Tex., 1944-45; sec. to plant mgr. Continental Can Co., Houston, 1948-49; sec.-bookkeeper Wherry & Green Ind. Oil Co., Houston, 1951-59; exec. sec., bookkeeper, office mgr. Holmes Drilling Co., Houston, 1961-83; sec., treas. Hartcap Refining Corp., Houston, 1974-83; office mgr. Mildred M. Holmes Interests, Houston, 1983-86, Jameson & Jameson, Houston, 1986-87; retired. Lic. real estate broker, Tex.; cert. profl. sec. Mem. Profl. Secs. Assn. Republican. Episcopalian. Home: 4302 Sarong Dr Houston TX 77096

HUTTENSTINE, MARIAN LOUISE, journalism educator; b. Bloomsburg, Pa., Jan. 26, 1940; d. Ralph Benjamin and Marian Louise (Engler) H.; B.S., Bloomsburg State U., 1961, M.Ed., 1966; postgrad. (NDEA fellow, Newspaper Fund fellow), Rutgers U., 1962-63; Ph.D., U. N.C., 1985. High sch. English, journalism tchr., dept. chmn., 1961-66; asst. prof. Lock Haven (Pa.) U., 1966-73, asso. prof. English, 1973-74; teaching asst., lectr. Sch. Journalism, U. N.C., Chapel Hill, 1974-76; cons., dir. Diener & Assos., Research Triangle Park, N.C., 1975-86; asst. prof. journalism Sch. Communication, U. Ala., Tuscaloosa, 1977—; cons. various publs., Ala., 1977—. Adult leader, vol. worker Luth. Ch., 1962—, Boy Scouts Am. Mem. Assn. Edn. in Journalism and Communication, Internat. Communication Assn., Nat. Fedn. Press Women, Ala. Media Women, Nat. Assn. Female Execs., ACLU, Am. Advt. Fedn., Kappa Tau Alpha. Clubs: Tuscaloosa Advt., Ala. SPJ-SDX. Contbr. papers to profl. lit. Home: K-1 Woodland Trace Tuscaloosa AL 35405 Office: U Ala Dept Journalism Box 1482 Tuscaloosa AL 35487-1482

HUTTNER, MARIAN ALICE, library administrator; b. Mpls., Apr. 10, 1920; d. Frederick August and Hilda Christina (Anderson) Huttner; m. Russell R. Christensen, Apr. 15, 1950 (div. 1961). B.A. summa cum laude, Macalester Coll., 1941; B.S.L.S., U. Minn., 1942. Jr. librarian U. Minn., Mpls., 1941-42, librarian, 1942-43, sr. librarian, 1943-44, prin. librarian serials, 1944-46, prin. librarian archives, 1946-53; serials librarian Hamline U., St. Paul, 1954-56; adult librarian Mpls. Pub. Library, 1956-60, research asst., 1961-64, adult group cons., 1964-67, head sociology dept., 1967-69, head main library subject depts., 1969-75; dep. dir. Cleve. Pub. Library, 1976-85, interim dir., 1986; automated systems cons. 1987—; adj. prof. Case Western Res. U., 1983-84; lectr. Kent State U., 1982-83. Author: Program for Branches, 1976-80 of the Cleveland Public Library, 1976; contbr. articles to profl. jours. Mem. ALA (reference services com. 1973-76), Minn. Library Assn. (sec. 1961-67), Ohio Library Assn. (awards com. 1984-85). Republican. Presbyterian. Home: 12000 Marion Ln Apt 1213 Minnetonka MN 55343

HUTTON, HELENA CLAIRE, industrial relations specialist, government relations specialist; b. Oklahoma City, Dec. 9, 1951; d. Robert Michael and H. Claire (LaFave) H. BS, Oklahoma State U., Stillwater, 1974; postgrad., George Washington U., 1985-87. Staff asst. U.S. Ho. of Eps., Washington, 1975-78; legis. asst. Health Ins. ASsn. of Am., Washington, 1978-79; nat. dir. of pub. affairs NAt. Assn. Mfgs., Washington, 1979-84; gov. relations mgr. 3M, Washington, 1984—; mem. Nat. Adv. com., The Washington Ctr., Washington; chmn. Washington Rep. Com. Employees Council on Flexible Compensation, Washington, 1988; bd. dirs., WGP Leader Fund, Washington, 1982-85. Author: Contbr. articles on pol. activity to "Enterprise" mag., 1980, book chpt., The PAC Handbook, 1980. Mem. Jr. League of Washington. Named Outstanding Young Women in Am., 1981; leadership Am. participant Found. for Women's Resources, 1988. Mem. Women in Gov. Relations, Variety Clubs Internat. Office: 3M 1101 15th St NW Washington DC 20005

HUTTON, MARILYN ADELE, lawyer; b. Cin., July 21, 1950; d. James C. and Ruth (Hutton) Payne. BA, Fisk U., 1972; JD, Harvard U., 1975; Cert., Hague Acad. Internat. Law, 1983. Bar: D.C., U.S. Ct. Internat. Trade, U.S. Ct. Mil. Appeals, U.S. Ct. Appeals (D.C. Cir.). Legis. aide U.S. Sen. Lloyd M. Bentsen, Washington, 1975-76; corp. counsel Procter and Gamble Co., Cin., 1976-81; legis. counsel NAACP, Cin., 1984-87; human and civil rights specialist Nat. Edn. Assn., Cin., 1987—; mem. legal adv. com. Nat. Bowling Assn., N.Y.C., 1978-80; corp. sec. Cin. Queen City Bowling Senate, 1980-82; exec. com. Leadership Conf. on Civil Rights, 1988—. Mem. ABA, Internat. Bar Assn., Am. Soc. Internat. Law, Fed. Bar Assn., D.C. Bar Assn., Am. Assn. Art Mus., Nat. Coalition Against Censorship (bd. dirs. 1988—). Episcopalian. Clubs: Ski of Washington, YWCA. Home: 1500 Massachusetts Ave NW Apt 660 Washington DC 20005 Office: NAACP 1025 Vermont Ave Suite 20005 Washington DC 20005

HUTTON, MARY JOAN, management consultant; b. Windsor, Ont., Can., May 27, 1942; d. John William and Jemetta Eleanor (Touscany) Spray; m. Clifton J. (Bud) Hutton, Oct. 12, 1964 (div. Aug. 1973); children: J. Scott Hutton; m. Danny Goldstein, Apr. 12, 1981. RN, Hotel Dieu of St. Joseph Sch. Nursing, Windsor, Ont., Can., 1963; diploma in nursing edn., U. Windsor, 1964; BA in Psychology, Marygrove Coll., 1973. Cert. personnel cons. Clin. instr. Harper Hosp. Sch. Nursing, Detroit, 1964-68; clin. coordinator Hotel Dieu of St. Joseph Sch. Nursing, Windsor, 1968-70; charge nurse Children's Hosp. Mich., Detroit, 1971-74; dir. nursing Renaissance Continuing Care Ctr., Highland Park, Mich., 1974-75, Park Community Hosp., Detroit, 1975-77; dir. allied health, sr. cons. Harper Assoc., Southfield, Mich., 1977—; pub. relations liaison Mich. Med. Records Assn., 1985—; nat. profl. resource person Nat. Assn. Quality Assurance Profls., 1984—; presenter, workshop leader Nat. Conf. Am. Med. Record Assn., Nat. Assn. Quality Assurance, Regional Confs. Women in Communications; chmn. curriculum adv. com. Ferris State Coll., Big Rapids, Mich., 1985-88. Contbr. articles to profl. jours. Mem. Internat. Tng. in Communications, Mich., Ohio region, 1979—, holder numerous offices. Mem. Nat. Assn. Quality Assurance Profls., Am. Med. Records Assn. (assoc.). Republican. Roman Catholic. Office: Harper Assocs 15659 W 10 Mile Rd Southfield MI 48075

HUXLEY, CAROLE CORCORAN, state education commissioner; b. Evanston, Ill., Jan. 1, 1938; d. Harold Francis and Angela Mary (Dawson) Corcoran; B.A., Mount Holyoke Coll., 1960; M.A. in Teaching, Harvard U., 1961; m. Michael Remsen Huxley, Mar. 27, 1971; children—Samuel Dawson, Ian Matthew Remsen. Tchr., Woodbury (Conn.) High Sch., 1961-62; area supr. to divisional dir. Am. Field Services, N.Y.C., 1962-71; program officer Nat. Endowment for the Humanities, Washington, 1971-79, dep. dir. state programs, 1979-80, dir. spl. programs, 1980-82; dep. commr. cultural edn. N.Y. Dept. Edn., Albany, 1982—. Trustee, Mount Holyoke Coll., 1982-87, Albany Med. Coll., Albany Med. Ctr., 1983—; mem. Commn. on Preservation and Access, Council on Library Resources; mem. adv. com. Albany Cultural Park. Mem. Am. Assn. Mus., Am. Assn. State and Local History, N.Y. Council on Humanities (v.p.), Albany Tricentennial Commn. Roman Catholic. Office: State Education Dept Albany NY 12234

HUXLEY, LAURA ARCHERA, human interest organization executive, author; b. Turin, Italy, Nov. 2, 1914; came to U.S., 1937; d. Felice and Fede (Bellini) A.; m. Aldous Huxely, Mar. 19, 1956 (dec. Nov. 1963). Studies with C. Flesh, Berlin; studies with G. Enesco, Paris; student, Curtis Inst., Phila., 1938-39; D of Human Services, Sierra U., 1961. Concert violinist Europe and U.S., 1927-39; prof. music Conservatory of St. Cecilia, Rome, 1929-40; free-lance assoc. producer documentary films U.S., 1940-45; film editor RKO, Los Angeles, 1950-51; pvt. practice psychotherapy Los Angeles, 1952-60; free-lance writer U.S. and Europe, 1963—; founder, dir. Our Ultimate Investment, Los Angeles, 1978—, an orgn. for the nurturing of the possible human. Author: You Are Not the Target, 1963, This Timeless Moment, 1969, Between Heaven and Earth, 1974, One a Day Reason to be Happy, 1986; (with Dr. Piero Ferrucci) The Child of Your Dreams, 1987. Recipient Maharishi award World Govt. of the Age of Enlightenment, 1981; honoree UN, NYC, 1978. Mem. Authors Guild, Assn. for Humanistic Psychology, Assn. for Transpersonal Psychology, The Huxley Inst. Office: Our Ultimate Investment 6301 Sunset Blvd Suite 133 Los Angeles CA 90028

HYATT-SMITH, ANN ROSE, non-profit organization executive, consultant; b. Portchester, N.Y., Sept. 25, 1953; d. David M. and Lenore (Moerschelle) Hyatt; m. Geoffrey D. Smith, June 24, 1984. BA in Lit., State U. Coll., Oneonta, N.Y., 1975; M in Profl. Studies, New Sch. for Social Research, 1986. Asst. to sec.-gen. Israel Interfaith Com., Jerusalem, 1977-79; field rep. United Jewish Appeal/Fedn. Jewish Philanthropies, N.Y.C., 1979-81; asst. v.p. United Way of N.Y.C., 1981-83; dir. devel. Hebrew Arts Sch., Merkin Concert Hall, N.Y.C., 1983-84; asst. dir. devel. St. Vincent's Hosp. and Med. Ctr. N.Y., N.Y.C., 1984-86; program mgr. Bernd Brecher and Assocs., Inc., N.Y.C., 1986—; adj. faculty New Sch. for Social Research and Learning Alliance. V.p., treas. Village Ind. Dems., N.Y.C., 1985-86. Mem. Nat. Soc. Fund Raising Execs. (cert., fund raising exec.), Nat. Assn. Hosp. Devel., Planned Giving Group N.Y., Am. Mktg. Assn. Jewish. Office: Bernd Brecher and Assocs 25 W 43d St New York NY 10016

HYDE, PAMELA S., mental health administrator, lawyer; b. Thayer, Mo., Nov. 7, 1950; d. Gaston Clark Hyde and L. Vineta (Cross) Hyde Sponsler; Student S.W. Baptist Coll., 1963-65; B.A., S.W. Mo. State U., 1972; J.D., U. Mich., 1976. Bar: Ohio. Staff atty. Ohio State Legal Services Assn., Columbus, 1976-77, staff atty. Ohio Legal Rights Service, Columbus, 1977-79, chief mental health unit, 1979-80, exec. dir., 1980-83; dir. Ohio Dept. Mental Health, Columbus, 1983—. Author: Patient's Rights Rules, 1978, Civil Committment in Ohio, 1980, Homlessness and Mental Health Policy: Developing and Appropriate Role for the 1980's, 1986. Treas., trustee YWCA, Columbus, 1980-83; gov.'s club mem. Ohio Democratic Party, Columbus, 1983-84; trustee, pres. Women's Music Union, Columbus, 1976-83; atty. Choices for Battered Women, Columbus, 1977; organizer Pro Se Divorce Clinic, Columbus, 1977. Recipient Edwin Rakow award Mich. Fed. Practice Bar, 1975, Community award S.W. Community Health Ctrs., Columbus, 1984, Citation of Young Women of Achievement, Nat. Council Women, N.Y., 1984, Award for Distinguished Service to Sate Govt. Nat. Gov.'s Assn., 1987, Gov.'s Spl. Recognition award Gov.'s Task Force on Black and Minority Health, 1987. Mem. Ohio State Bar Assn., Columbus Bar Assn. (family law com. 1976-83, mental disorder law com. 1981-83), Nat. Lawyers Guild. Office: Ohio Dept Mental Health 30 E Broad St Room 1180 Columbus OH 43215

HYDEN, DOROTHY L., marketing consulting executive; b. Fort Collins, Colo., July 19, 1948; d. Douglas Stewart and Elizabeth L. (Stewart) Neilson; m. Michael J. Daley, Dec. 27, 1969; 1 child, Shannon; m. Howard E. Hyden, July 17, 1976; children: Kent, Tiffany. BA, U. Calif., Santa Barbara, 1970; MBA, Pepperdine U., 1980. Head tchr. Sawyer Bus. Coll., Anaheim, Calif., 1974-75, admissions rep., 1975-76; mktg. specialist Anthony Schs., Orinda, Calif., 1976-77; adminstrv. dir. Escrow Tng. Ctr., Orinda, 1977-78; pvt. practice consulting Mpls., 1979-88; exec. v.p. Hyden, Hyden and Assocs., Edina, Minn., 1988—. Author: Training in Excellence, 1986; also marketing curriculum. Mem. Chi Omega (Outstanding Woman of Quarter Fall 1969). Republican. Episcopalian. Home and Office: 7415 Hyde Park Dr Edina MN 55435

HYDER, JOANNE ANNETTE, national bank examiner, consultant; b. Norfolk, Va., Mar. 18, 1957; d. Joseph and Josephine (Simon) H. BBS, W.Va. U., 1977. Asst. nat. bank examiner Office of Comptroller of Currency, Richmond, Va., 1977-79; assoc. nat. bank examiner Office of Comptroller of Currency, Richmond, 1979=82; dist. tng. officer Office of Comptroller of Currency, Chgo., 1983-86; nat. bank examiner Office of Comptroller of Currency, Richmond, 1982—, Washington, 1986—; guest speaker Nat. Assn. Bank Women, Fairmont, W.Va, 1982, Soc. Govt. Meeting Planners, Chgo., 1984; nat. trainer Comptroller of Currency, Washington, 1983—. Bd. dirs. Buena Condominium Assn., Chgo., 1985-86. Mem. W.Va. U. Alumni Assn. Lodge: Soroptimists (sec. of bd. Chgo. chpt. 1984-85). Office: Comptroller of Currency 490 L'Enfant Plaza SW Washington DC 20219

HYMAN, BETTY HARPOLE, technical equipment consultant; b. Jasper, Tex., Nov. 20, 1938; d. Russell Charles and John Francis (Hilton) Harpole; m. Arthur Siegmar Hyman (dec.); children: Norma Sullivan, Eric, Jonathan, Lee Ann. BA in Psychology, U. Tex., San Antonio, 1979. Spl. project coordinator Tex. Stores, San Antonio, 1975-79; communications cons. Southwestern Bell Telephone, Midland, Tex. and San Antonio, 1980-82; tech. cons. AT&T, San Antonio, 1983-85, 88—, Intelliserve Corp., Dallas, 1987-88; cons. IMS Group, San Antonio, 1985-87. Mem. devel. com. San Antonio Spl. Olympics; mem. San Antonio Conservation Soc., 1975—, San Antonio World Affairs Council, 1985—; bd. dirs. South Tex. Childrens' Habilitation Ctr., San Antonio, 1985-87. Mem. Am. Bus. Women's Assn. (program com. 1987-88), Tex. Tennis Assn. (ranked player 1976—). Republican. Presbyterian. Club: Prime Time Tennis (v.p. 1985-86). Home: 14031 Fairway Oaks San Antonio TX 78217 Office: AT&T 4400 Piedras Dr S Suite 200 San Antonio TX 78228

HYMAN, JOHANNA JESSICA, electrical engineer; b. Washington, Oct. 21, 1955; d. John Ernest and Ophelia (Lee) H. BSEE, Brown U., 1978; MS in Engring. Mgmt., Cath. U. Am., 1986. Product testing engr. IBM Corp., Manassas, Va., 1978-83, product test mgr., 1983—. Democrat. Baptist. Office: IBM Corp Manassas VA 22110

HYMAN, MARY BLOOM, education director; m. Sigmund M. Hyman, 1947; children—Carol Ann Hyman Williams, Nancy Louise. B.S., Goucher Coll., 1971; M.S., Johns Hopkins U., 1977. Asst. dir. Edn. Md. Sci. Ctr., Balt., 1976-81, dir. edn., 1981—. Bd. dirs. Md. Health and Welfare Council, Balt.; trustee Goucher Coll. Recipient Disting. Women award Gov.'s Office, Annapolis, Md., 1981; Meritorious Service award Johns Hopkins U., 1983. Mem. Fund for Ednl. Excellence (bd. dirs.), Md. Assn. Sci. Tchrs. (bd. dirs.), Women in Math/Sci. Task Force Md. State Dept Edn., Phi Beta Kappa, Phi Delta Kappa.

HYMAN, PAULA E(LLEN), history educator; b. Boston; d. Sydney Max and Ida Frances (Tatelman) H.; m. Stanley Harvey Rosenbaum, June 7, 1969; children: Judith Hyman Rosenbaum, Adina Hyman Rosenbaum. B.J.Ed., Hebrew Coll., Brookline, Mass., 1966; B.A., Radcliffe Coll., 1968; M.A., Columbia U., 1970, Ph.D., 1975. Asst. prof. Columbia U., N.Y.C., 1974-81; assoc. prof. history Jewish Theol. Sem., N.Y.C., 1981-86, dean Sem., Coll. Jewish Studies, 1981-86; Lady Davis. vis. assoc. prof. Hebrew U. of Jerusalem, 1986; Lucy Moses prof. history Yale U., New Haven, 1986—. Series editor Ind. U. Press. Bloomington, 1982—; contbg. editor Sh'ma Mag., N.Y.C., 1977—; author: From Dreyfus to Vichy, 1979; co-author: The Jewish Woman in America, 1976; co-editor: The Jewish Family; Myths and Reality, 1986. Contbr. articles to publs. Vice chmn. Zionist Acad. Council, N.Y.C., 1982-83. NEH summer grantee, 1977; Am. Council Learned Socs. fellow, 1978; grantee N.Y. Council for Humanities, 1980, NEH fellow, 1986-87. Mem. Am. Hist. Assn. (com. 1983), Assn. for Jewish Studies (bd. dirs. 1978-81, 83-85, 86-88), Leo Baeck Inst. (bd. dirs. 1979—), Yivo Inst. for Jewish Research, Phi Beta Kappa. Jewish. Office: Yale U Dept History New Haven CT 06520

HYMANS, NANCY JEAN, communications executive; b. Glen Rock, N.J., Dec. 6, 1949; d. Edward Loomis and Lucille (Krohn) H. BA in Am. History summa cum laude, Catholic U. Am., 1971. Comml. accounts service rep. N.J Bell Telephone Co., Fairlawn, 1972-74, acct. exec., 1979-83; corp./litigation legal asst. Milgrim, Thomajan & Lee, N.Y.C., 1975-77; v.p. Nitze-Stagen Co, Inc., N.Y.C., 1977-79; bus. controls mgr., sales mgr., HQ staff mgr. AT&T, 1983-86; tech. mgr. integrated applications AT&T, Atlanta, 1987—. Mem. Interested Mems. of Performing Arts Ctr. Team, Ft. Lauderdale, Fla., 1986—. Mem. Nat. Assn. Female Execs., LWV (treas., 1978-80, budget chair 1980-82), Phi Beta Kappa, Phi Alpha Theta, Kappa Gamma Pi, Sigma Epsilon Phi. Office: AT&T 200 West Cypress Creek Rd Fort Lauderdale FL 33309

HYMEL, PATRICIA LOUISE LYON, computer manufacturing company executive; b. Clarksdale, Miss., Sept. 4, 1948; d. Richard Bailey and Mignonne Louise (Stanford) L.; m. Eugene Walet Hymel Jr., Apr. 4, 1987; AB with distinction, Mary Baldwin Coll., 1970; M in Computer Sci., U. Va., 1972. Instr., U. Va., Charlottesville, 1970-72; with Honeywell, 1972-82, regional mktg. mgr., Atlanta, 1979-80, nat. mktg. product mgr., computers, 1980-82; supr. mgmt. info services product evaluation and support Ga. Power Co., Atlanta, 1982-84; account mgr. La. br. Honeywell, Lafayette, 1984-85; with Digital Equipment Corp., Lafayette, La., 1985—; sales rep., 1985-86; account exec., Memphis, 1987—; cons. CII-Honeywell Bull, Honeywell French affiliate. Past pres. Wieuca's Way single's program Wieuca Rd. Bapt. Ch., Atlanta, 1981-82; mem. Germantown United Meth. Ch. Mem. Assn. Computing Machinery, Nat. Assn. Female Execs., Aircraft Owners and Pilots Assn., Republican. Club: Metro Flying. Home: 2587 Cowdrie Cove Memphis TN 38119

HYNES, MARY ANN, publishing executive, lawyer; b. Chgo., Oct. 26, 1947; d. Ernest Mario and Emma Louise (Noto) Iantorno; m. James Thomas Hynes, Dec. 27, 1944; children: Christina, Nicholas. Degree in Math. and Polit. Sci., Loyola U., 1967; JD, John Marshall Law Sch., 1971, LLM, 1975. Bar: Ill. 1971, U.S. Dist. Ct. (no. dist.) Ill. 1971. Exec. editor, law editor Commerce Clearing House, Inc., 1971-79, asst. sec, counsel, 1979-80, v.p., gen. counsel, 1980—. Chief crusader United Way/Crusade of Mercy; v.p., bd. dirs., legis. and policy chmn. Chgo. Crime Commn.; mem. nat. strategy forum Midwest Council Nat. Security; adv. council Chgo. Symphony Orchestra Chorus; advisor New Music Chgo.; deanery del. Chgo. Archdiocesan Pastoral Council; pres. local sch. bd. Mem. ABA (chmn. publs. com., corp. law depts. com., sect. corp., banking and bus. law; membership chair, computer law com., litigation sect.), Ill. State Bar Assn., Chgo. Bar Assn., Internat. Bar Assn., Internat. Fedn. Women Lawyers, Nat. Assn. Women Lawyers (corp. counsel reporter coordinator), Women's Bar Assn. Ill. (former dir., found. adv. bd. mem.), Am. Corp. Counsel Assn., Am. Soc. Corp. Secs., Computer Law Assn., Justinian Soc. Lawyers. Clubs: Legal of Chgo. (exec. com. 1987), Execs. of Chgo, Law of City of Chgo. Office: Commerce Clearing House Inc 2700 Lake Cook Rd Riverwoods IL 60015

HYSNER, KATHY LOWE, nurse, marketing professional; b. Oneida, N.Y., Nov. 22, 1951; d. Billy Felix Lowe and Marion Beryl (Herlan) Baldwin; m. Barry Noel Gardner, Oct. 7, 1975 (div. Oct. 1985); children: Stephanie, Shellie; m. Eugene Robert Hysner, Apr. 1, 1987; children: Jamie, Micheal. ASN, Ga. State U., 1971. Staff nurse Atlanta Hosp., 1971-73; shift supr. Decatur (Ga.) Hosp., 1973-75, coordinator admissions nurses, 1973-75; staff nurse Northside Hosp., Atlanta, 1975-76; asst. head nurse DeKalb Gen. Hosp., Decatur, 1978-83; head nurse DeKalb Cardiac Rehab. Ctr., Decatur, 1983—; sales rep. Specialty Med. Systems, Tucker, Ga., 1985-87; v.p. mktg. H-Comm, Inc., Lawrenceville, Ga., 1987—; instr. basic cardiac life support, Decatur, 1978-86; provider advanced cardiac life support, Decatur, 1986—. Mem. Am. Heart Assn., Am. Assn. Cardiovascular Pulmonary Rehab. Methodist. Club: Walking (pres.). Office: H-Comm Inc PO Box 2083 Norcross GA 30091 Office: DeKalb Cardiac Rehab Ctr 755 Commerce Dr Suite 100-A Decatur GA 30030

HYTIER, ADRIENNE DORIS, French educator. d. Jean and Katharine Hytier Matson. B.A. summa cum laude, Barnard Coll., 1952; M.A., Columbia U., 1953, Ph.D., 1958. Instr. French Vassar Coll., 1959-61, asst. prof., 1961-66, assoc. prof., 1966-70, prof. French Vassar Coll., Poughkeepsie, N.Y., 1970—, Lichtenstein Dale prof. French, 1974—; vis. assoc. prof. Columbia U., 1966, U. Calif., 1968-69. Collaborator: The 18th Century: A Current Bibliography for French Literature since 1970, 13 Vols. to date, Two Years of French Foreign Policy: Vichy 1940-42, 1958, 2d edit., 1974, Les Dépêches diplomatiques du Comte de Gobineau en Perse, 1959, La Guerre, 1975, 2d edit., 1985; editor for French lit.; contbr. revs. and articles in field. Decorated chevalier des Palmes Académiques, 1974; fellow Guggenheim Found., 1967-68. Mem. MLA, Am. Soc. 18th Century Studies, North East Soc. for 18th Century Studies, Middle Atlantic Soc. 18th Century Studies, Internat. Soc. 18th Century Studies, Phi Beta Kappa. Home: 71 Raymond Ave Poughkeepsie NY 12601 Office: Vassar College Box 372 Poughkeepsie NY 12601

IACHETTI, ROSE MARIA ANNE, educator; b. Watervliet, N.Y., Sept. 22, 1931; d. Augustus and Rose Elizabeth Archer (Orciuolo) Iachetti; B.S., Coll. St. Rose, 1961; M.Ed., U. Ariz., 1969. Joined Sisters of Mercy, Albany, N.Y., 1949-66; tchr. various parochial schs. Albany (N.Y.) Diocese, 1952-66; tchr. Headstart Program, Troy, N.Y., 1966; tchr. fine arts Watervliet Jr. and Sr. High Sch., 1966-67; tchr. W.J. Meyer Sch., Tombstone, Ariz., 1968-71, Colonel Johnston Sch., Ft. Huachuca, Ariz., 1971-78; tchr. Myer Sch., Ft. Huachuca, 1978—, coordinator program for gifted and talented, 1981-85. Ann. chmn. Ariz. Children's Home Assn., Tombstone, 1973-74; trustee Tombstone Sch. Dist. #1, 1972-80; active Democratic Club; mem. Bicentennial Commn. for Ariz., 1972-76, Tombstone Centennial Commn., 1979-80, chmn. Centennial Ball, 1980; pres. Tombstone Community Health Services, 1978-80; mem. Tombstone City Council, 1982-84; governing bd. Southeast Ariz. Area Health Edn. Ctr., 1985—; bd. dirs. S.E. Health Edn. Council, 1985—. Mem. Ariz. Edn. Assn. (so. regional dir. 1971-73), Ft. Huachuca Edn. Assn., Tombstone Dist. 1 Edn. Assn. (pres. 1969-71), Ariz. Sch. Bd. Assn., NEA (del. 1971-73), Ariz. Classroom Tchrs. Assn. (del. 1969-71), Internat. Platform Assn., Tombstone Bus. and Profl. Womens Club, Am. Legion Aux., Tombstone Assn. Arts, Pi Lambda Theta, Delta Kappa Gamma, (pres. 1982-84), Phi Delta Kappa (historian 1979-82, 2d v.p. 1982-83). Home: Round Up Trailer Ranch Box 725 Tombstone AZ 85638 Office: Myer School Fort Huachuca AZ 85613

IACONE, MARGE, small business owner; b. Bklyn., Feb. 13, 1943; d. Thomas and Margaret Lucy Fiore; children: Donna Avanti, Debra Iacone. Student, Adelphia Sch. Bus., Bklyn., 1958, Morris Co. Vocat. Sch., 1977. Gen. mgr. Guaranteed Premium Loan Co., Bklyn., 1963-65; claims inspector Universal Car Loading & Distbn., N.Y.C., 1965-68; quality motor control insp. Nash Controls, Fairfield, N.J., 1968-69; gen. mgr. Roman's Mobile Elec. Co., Caldwell, N.J., 1969-72; gen. mgr. Exptl. Plastic Molds Corp., Fairfield, 1972-86, owner, pres., 1986—. Contbr. articles to profl. jours. Indsl. commr. Fairfield Indsl. Commn., 1986-87; vice chmn. Mayor's Adv. Com., Fairfield, 1987-88; mem. The Steeple Fund Com., 1986-88. Fellow Soc. Plastics Industry, West Essex C. of C.; mem. Fairfield Bus. Industrialists (pres. 1986-88). Lodge: Rotary (treas. 1987—). Office: Exptl Plastic Molds Corp 3 Spielman Rd Fairfield NJ 07006

IANDOLI, MARIE ANN, small business owner; b. Bklyn., Mar. 8, 1944; d. Lewis Emil and Beatrice (Salomone) I. BA, Miami U., Oxford, Ohio, 1965; MSW, U. Mich., 1967; cert. in teaching, Fla. Atlantic U., 1976. Clin. social worker United Cerebral Palsy, Roosevelt, N.Y., 1968-70, Youth and Family Counseling Agy., Ft. Lauderdale, Fla., 1970-75; tng. supr. Broward County Social Service, Ft. Lauderdale, 1976-78; substitute tchr. Broward County Schs., Ft. Lauderdale, 1979-81; co-owner Oceanside Shopping Ctr., Pompano Beach, Fla., 1982—. Contbr. articles to profl. jours. Active Caldwell Theatre, Boca Raton, 1983-87, Ft. Lauderdale Mus. Art, 1984-88; bd. dirs. Friends of Pompano Library, Pompano Beach, 1984-85; mem. Jr. Opera Soc., 1984-86; lecture chairperson bus. unit group Boca Mus. Art, Boca Raton, 1986; publicity com. co-chair Boca Raton (Fla.) Heart Assn., 1986-87; membership com. chair Allegro Soc., Boca Raton, 1986-87. Mem. Mental Health Assn. (bd. dirs. 1983-87, fin. devel. com. 1985-87, Golden Bell award 1986), Young Women in the Arts, Light Brigade. Clubs: President's Miami U.; STARS (Ft. Lauderdale) (pres. Miami U. chpt. 1984-88). Lodge: Zonta (bd. dirs. Ft. Lauderdale chpt. 1984-86).

IANNELLI, DONNA MARIE, copywriter; b. N.Y.C., Apr. 12, 1964; d. Carmine T. and Judith Ann (Nazzaro) I. BA, NYU, 1987. Stringer Ramsey-Mahwah Reporter, Ramsey, N.J., 1981, asst. editor, 1984; copy editor Money ene, Haledon, N.J., 1981-84, columnist, 1982-83; paste-up artist Shopper Newspapers, Fair Lawn, N.J., 1983-84, corr., 1984; asst. social editor The Ridgewood (N.J.) News, 1984-85; advt. asst. Schlott Realtors, Fair Lawn, 1985; advt. writer Obrig and Kelley Advt., Wyckoff, N.J., 1986; freelance writer Hawthorne, N.J., 1986—. Contbr. articles to profl. jours. Club: PICA (exec. officer 1987, scholarship 1984).

IASIELLO, DOROTHY BARBARA, brokerage company executive; b. Bklyn., Oct. 6, 1949; d. Albert William and Josephine (Accardo) Rehorn; m. John Joseph Iasiello Jr., May 5, 1974. AAS in Mktg., N.Y.C. Community Coll., 1969; BS in Econs., Coll. Staten Island, 1978. Sec. Lady Manhattan, N.Y.C., 1969-70, Biscayne Fed. Savs. and Loan Assn., Miami, Fla., 1971, Morgan Guaranty Trust Co., N.Y.C., 1971-78; with sales dept. J.P. Morgan Securities, N.Y.C., 1978-81, asst. treas. sales, 1981-84, asst. v.p. sales, 1984-88, v.p. sales adminstrn. mgmt., 1988—. Roman Catholic. Office: JP Morgan Securities 23 Wall St New York City NY 10015

ICENHOWER, JANIS (BOLTON), cosmetology company executive; b. Jacksonville, Tex., Sept. 14, 1928; d. William Curtis and Goldie (Fox) Bolton; m. George Nolan Icenhower, Jan. 22, 1955 (dec.); children: George Nolan, Mark Crew. Cert., Palestine (Tex.) Bus. Sch., 1947. Cert. tchr. cosmetology, Tex. Cosmetologist Oates Plaza Beauty Salon, Dallas, 1956-57, owner, 1957-63; owner Icenhower Beauty Sch., Dallas, 1959-80, 83-86; chief exec. officer, pres. Beauty Schs., Inc., Dallas, Houston, 1961—. Mem. Nat. Assn. Cosmetology Schs., Tex. Cosmetology Tchrs. Assn., Nat. Hairdressers Assn. Republican. Methodist. Home: Rt 3 Box 168A Kemp TX 75143 Office: Beauty Schs Inc 8327 Long Point Rd Houston TX 77055

ICHINO, YOKO, ballet dancer; b. Los Angeles. Student, Mia Slavenska, Los Angeles. Mem. Joffrey II, N.Y.C.; mem. Joffrey Ballet, N.Y.C., Stuttgart Ballet, Fed. Republic Germany; tchr. ballet 1976; soloist Am. Ballet Theatre, 1977-81; guest appearances 1981-82; prin. Nat. Ballet Can., Toronto, Ont., 1982—; various guest appearances including World Ballet Festival, Tokyo, 1979, 82, with Alexander Godunov and Stars, summer 1982, Sydney Ballet, Australia, N.Z. Ballet, summer 1984, Ballet de Marseille, 1985-86, Deutsche Opera Ballet Berlin, Fed. Republic Germany, 1985—, No. Berlin Ballet, 1987, Munich Opera Ballet, 1987-88, Australian Ballet, 1987; tchr. numerous ballet workshops and summer sessions. Recipient medal Third Internat. Ballet Competition, Moscow, 1977. Address: Nat Ballet Can, 157 King St E, Toronto, ON Canada M5C 1G9

IDDINS, MILDRED, retired librarian; b. Fountain City, Tenn.; d. Joseph Franklin and Lucy (Chandler) I.; A.B., Carson-Newman Coll., 1936; B.S., George Peabody Coll., 1941. Tchr., Bell House Sch., Knoxville, Tenn., 1936-37; tchr. Roane County High Sch., Kingston, 1937-41; librarian Dandridge (Tenn.) High Sch., 1941-43; Army librarian, Ft. Oglethorpe, Ga., 1943-44; librarian Carson-Newman Coll., Jefferson City, Tenn., 1944-81. Former mem. ALA, Southeastern, Tenn. library assns.; mem. AAUW (br. treas. 1964-66). Baptist. Clubs: Monday Literary, Modern Literary. Home: 403 Russell St Jefferson City TN 37760

IDLEWINE, SHERRY LYNN, business management educator; b. Indpls., May 24, 1959; d. Lenord George and Mary Walteen (York) I. B.A., U. Indpls., 1981, M.A., M.B.A., 1984. Dept. mgr. Target Corp., Indpls., 1976-81; job placement coordinator Lockyear Coll., Indpls., 1981-86, instr. secretarial work, 1981-83, instr. computer sci., 1983-85, instr. mgmt. and acctg., 1985—; supr. data entry Indpls. Police Dept., 1985—; cons., mem. Partners 2000, Indpls., 1984—; cons. Foremost Ins. Co., Indpls., 1985; supr. data entry Indpls. Police Dept., Indpls., Ind., 1985—. Active Indpls. Alliance for Jobs, 1984—; judge Jr. Miss Pageant for Ind., Brownsburg, 1985. Mem. Nat. Assn. for Female Execs., U. Indpls. MBA Alumni (exec. council), Mu Phi Epsilon (co-organizer internat. conf. 1980, Sterling Staff award 1981, 1st v.p. 1982-83, mag. chmn. 1982-83). Republican. Baptist. Avocations: music, art, writing, travel, tennis. Office: Lockyear Coll Bus Dept 5330 E 38th St Indianapolis IN 46218

IGLE, DIANE CHRISTINE, nurse, nursing services administrator, psychotherapist; b. Wilmington, Del., Apr. 21, 1946; d. Edward A. Igle and Mary Vincent (Caruso) Sassi. Diploma in registered nursing, St. Mary's Sch. of Nursing, 1967; BS, Seton Hall U., 1969; MS, Columbia U., 1971. Staff nurse psychiatry Bergen Pines County Hosp., Paramus, N.J., 1968-69; nurse clinician in psychiatry Hackensack (N.J.) Hosp. and Community Mental Health Ctr., 1971-74; psychiatric nurse therapist Jefferson County Mental Health Ctr., Lakewood, Colo., 1974-77, program mgr. emergency in-patient service, 1977-81; head nurse adolescent unit Denver Health & Hosps., 1981-83; substitute instr. psychiatric nursing Denver Auraria Community Coll., 1983—; asst. nursing service adminstr. Ft. Logan Mental Health Ctr., Denver, 1983-84, nursing service adminstr., 1984—; pvt. practice psychotherapist, Lakewood, 1982—; mem. planning com. 4th ann. Inst. for Psychiatric Nurse Clinicians, 1982. Author and presentor: Cost Effectiveness of the Emergency/In-Patient Program, 1981; presentor nat. day treatment forum on Clin. Supervision: Process and Problems, 1983. Mem. Am. Nurse Assn. (item writer cert. exam in psychiatric nursing), Colo. Nurse Assn., Colo. Soc. for Clin. Specialists in Psychiatric Nursing (legis. com.). Democrat. Roman Catholic. Office: Ft Logan Mental Health Ctr 3520 W Oxford Ave Denver CO 80236

IGLEHART, ALISON ROWE, securities trader; b. Cin., June 22, 1956; d. Joseph H. and Sara Lee (Rodgers) Rowe; m. Stephen Iglehart, Aug. 25, 1984. BA, Catawba Coll., 1978; postgrad., U. Cin., 1979; cert., Katherine Gibbs, Boston, 1982. Cert. tchr. of Spanish; registered commodities and stock broker. Tchr. Wooster Sch., Danbury, Conn., 1980-81; commodity broker EF Hutton, N.Y.C., 1982-84; investment broker Prudential-Bache Securities, Danbury, 1984—. Columnist: Danbury Bus. Digest, 1984—. Translator Town of Danbury; mem. Danbury Alliance Francaise; bd. dirs. Spanish Learning Ctr. Mem. Am. Assn. Tchrs. of Spanish; LWV; Spanish Am. Soc., Women for Personal and Profl. Devel. (co-founder). Office: Prudential Bache Securities 1 Plaza W Danbury CT 06810

IGLESIAS, MARIA ADELA, education specialist; b. Sancti Spiritus, Las Villas, Cuba, Oct. 3, 1950; came to U.S., Nov. 1960; d. Jorge Antonio and Adela (Orizondo) I. BA, Fla. State U., 1972; MEd, Fla. Atlantic U., 1976; postgrad. U. Mass., 1985—. Spl. edn. dept. head, tchr. Palm Beach County Schs., Boynton Beach, Fla., 1976-80, Dade County Pub. Schs., Coral Gables, Fla., 1980-84; bilingual spl. edn. tchr. Boston Pub. Schs., Jamaica Plain, Mass., 1984-85; ednl. specialist III, Mass. State Dept. Edn., Arlington, 1985-87; program advisor/compliance dept. spl. edn. Boston Pub. Schs., 1987—; cons. Fla. Career Coll., Miami, 1982-83; adj. prof. dept. spl. edn. U. Mass., Boston, 1987—; tutor SW Miami Boys Clubs, 1983-84. Mem. Council Exceptional Children, Am. Fedn. Tchrs., Boston Tchrs. Union, Boston Assn. Sch. Adminstrs. and Suprs. Democrat. Roman Catholic. Avocations: tennis, biking, jogging.

IKEDA, DONNA RIKA, state legislator; b. Honolulu, Aug. 31, 1939; d. William G. and Lillian (Kim) Yoshida; div.; children: Rika, Aaron, Julie. BA in Speech, U. Hawaii. Substitute tchr. 1969-71; legis. researcher Hawaii Rep. Research Office, 1971-74; former mem. Hawaii Ho. of Reps.; mem. Hawaii State Senate. Office: State Senate State Capitol Honolulu HI 96813 *

IKLE, DORIS MARGRET, energy conservation corporation executive; b. Frankfort, Germany, May 28, 1928; came to U.S., 1937, naturalized, 1945; d. Richard and Sonia (Pappenheimer) Eisemann; m. Fred Charles Ikle, Dec. 23, 1959; children—Judith, Miriam. B.A., NYU, 1949, M.A., 1953; postgrad. Columbia U., 1957. Economist, Nat. Bur. Econ. Research, N.Y.C., 1949-56, Rand Corp., Santa Monica, Calif., 1957-60, Inst. Energy Analysis, Washington, 1976-77; cons. U.S. Dept. Commerce, Washington, 1975-76; pres. Conservation Mgmt. Corp., Bethesda, Md., 1977—; adv. council Am. for Energy Independence, 1985—; cons. in field. Author: The Complete Energy Audit Book, 1980, (software) RCS and CACS Audit Systems, 1984. Contbr. articles to profl. jours. Home: 7010 Glenbrook Rd Bethesda MD 20814 Office: Conservation Mgmt Corp 1155 W Chestnut St Union NJ 07083

ILAO, TINA MARIANNE, medical services administrator; b. Jersey City, July 6, 1948; d. Louis John and Josephine Jean (Pecoraro) Rizzo; m. Democrito C. Ilao, Jr., Sept. 28, 1975; children: Kimberly Jo, Christopher Jon. BS in Biology, Notre Dame U., 1970; Microbiology, Hosp. Adminstrn. cert., Wagner Coll., 1985; postgrad., Northland U., Temple U. Med. tech. St. Francis Hosp., Jersey City, 1970-72, asst. supr., sr. med. technologist, 1973-79; lab. mgr. South Amboy (N.J.ú Meml. Hosp., 1979-81; lab. adminstr. Muhlenburg Hosp., Plainfield, N.J., 1981-84; adminstr. lab. services St. Francis Med. Ctr., Trenton, N.J., 1984—; assoc. prof. med. technology, Hudson Community Coll.; bd. dirs. med. adv., ednl. coms. Lupus Found., N.J. Mem. Lab. Mgmt. Assn., N.Y. Acad. Scis., Am. Soc. Clin. Chemists, Am. Soc. Med. Technologists, Assn. Clin. Scientists, N.J. Soc. Med. Technology (past pres., chmn. govt. liaison com.). Democrat. Roman Catholic. Home: 8 Sycamore Way Hamilton Square NJ 08650

ILCHMAN, ALICE STONE, college president, former government official; b. Cin., Apr. 18, 1935; d. Donald Crawford and Alice Kathryn (Biermann) Stone; m. Warren Frederick Ilchman, June 11, 1960; children: Frederick Andrew Crawford, Alice Sarah Crawford. B.A., Mt. Holyoke Coll., 1957; M.P.A., Maxwell Sch. Citizenship, Syracuse U., 1958; Ph.D., London Sch. Econs., 1965; L.H.D., Mt. Holyoke Coll. Asst. to pres., mem. faculty Berkshire Community Coll., 1961-64; lectr., asst. prof. Ctr. for South and Southeast Asia Studies U. Calif.-Berkeley, 1965-73; prof. econs. and edn., dean Wellesley (Mass.) Coll., 1973-78; asst. sec. ednl. and cultural affairs Dept. State, 1978; asso. dir. ednl. and cultural affairs Internat. Communication Agy., 1978-81; advisor to sec. Smithsonian Instn., 1981; pres. Sarah Lawrence Coll., Bronxville, N.Y., 1981—; intern, asst. to Sen. John F. Kennedy, 1957; seminar leader, dir. Peace Corps Tng. Program for India, 1965-66; chmn. com. on women's employment Nat. Acad. Scis.; bd. dirs. N.Y. Telephone. Author: The New Men of Knowledge and the New States, 1968, (with W.F. Ilchman) Education and Employment in India, The Policy Nexus, 1976. Trustee Mt. Holyoke Coll., 1970-80, Mass. Found. for Humanities and Pub. Policy, 1974-77, East-West Center, Honolulu., 1978-81 Expt. in Internat. Living, The Markle Found., The Rockefeller Found., The U. of Cape Town, South Africa, Corp. Adv. Bd.; mem. Smithsonian Council, Yonkers Emergency Fin. Control Bd., Am. Ditchley Found. Program Com., Internat. Research and Exchange Bd.; bd. dirs. N.Y. Telephone Co. Mem. Nat. Acad. Public Adminstrn., NOW Legal Defense Edn. Fund, Council Fgn. Relations. Clubs: Cosmopolitan (N.Y.C.); Bronxville Field (N.Y.). Home: 935 Kimball Ave Bronxville NY 10708 Office: Sarah Lawrence Coll Bronxville NY 10708

IMES, SHARON KAY, labor arbitrator; b. Grand Island, Nebr., Mar. 31, 1943; d. George Stark and Julieanne Marie (Ayoub) McC.; m. Roger Loren Imes, Sept. 4, 1963; children: Loren, Matthew. BA, U. Wis., 1969, MA, 1980. Instr. Western Wis. Tech. Inst., La Crosse, 1974-75; dir. Omni, Inc., La Crosse, 1975-76; dir. disaster housing assistance program State of Wis., La Crosse and Madison, 1978-79; labor arbitrator La Crosse, 1979—; instr. U. Wis., La Crosse, 1979-86; bd. dirs. La Crosse Luth. Hosp. Found. Mem. Citizens Environ. Council State of Wis., Madison, 1975-78; mem. La Crosse City Council, 1973-79; moderator-elect, bd. dirs. First Congl. Ch., La Crosse, 1985—; bd. dirs. La Crosse Festivals, Inc., 1975-77, La Crosse Community Theatre, Inc., 1986—. Recipient CAROL award Wis. Jaycettes, 1975; Bush fellow, Bush Found., 1976. Mem. LWV, AAUW, Nat. Acad. Arbitrators, Soc. Profls. in Dispute Resolution, Am. Arbitrations Assn., Industrial Relations Research Assn., La Crosse County League of Women Voters (pres., bd. dirs. 1984—). Democrat. Home: 3465 Ebner Coulee Rd La Crosse WI 54601

IMHOFF, CAROL ANN, nursing administrator; b. Los Angeles, June 15, 1934; d. Neal and Frances M. (Roberts) Vogelsang; m. James C. Imhoff, Aug. 10, 1957; children: Jean, Robert, Christopher, Mary Angela. BSN, U. Utah, 1973; diploma Holy Cross Hosp. Sch. Nursing, 1955. Cert. rehab. registered nurse (CRRN). Staff nurse Holy Cross Hosp., UCLA Med. Ctr., 1955-58, staff nurse, part time supr., 1960-66, unit supr. rehab., 1978-82, rehab. clinician, 1982-83; dir. nursing Bountiful Care Convalescent Ctr., 1983-87; dir. nurses Washington Terr. Nursing Ctr., Ogden, Utah, 1987—; vis. staff nurse Community Nursing Service, Salt Lake City, 1966-69; head nurse supportive care med. rehab. McKay Dee Hosp., Ogden, 1969-78. Mem. edn. com. Am. Heart Assn., 1969-81, chmn., 1972-73; bd. dirs. Utah Heart Assn., 1976-83; sec. Home Sch. Assn.; gov.'s appointee Utah State Bd. Nursing, 1987—. Mem. Am. Nurses Assn., Assn. Rehab. Nurses (certs. for service, nat. pres. 1982-83, sec.-treas. 1979-80), Rehab. Services Adv. Council, Utah Nurses Assn. (past dist. treas., bd. dirs., 2d place Nurse of Yr.), Utah Dirs. Nurses of Long-Term Care (pres. 1984-87), Beta Sigma Phi, Sigma Theta Tau. Roman Catholic. Club: Does. Home: 4581 Taylor S Ogden UT 84403 Office: Washington Terr Nursing Ctr 400 E 5350 So Ogden UT 84405

IMMEL, NANCY KAY, business administrator; b. St. Paul, Aug. 25, 1946; d. Robert Ellsworth and Norma Mae (Judkins) Wheaton; m. Donald R. Waller, Mar. 5, 1966 (div. July 1981); children: Deborah, Gregory; m. Howard Ernest Immel, Feb. 25, 1984; stepchildren: Diane, Nancy Howard, Steven, Charles, Michael. Student, Macalester Coll., 1965; AA, Lakewood Community Coll., 1985; student, Met. State U., 1986—. With gen. office Gould Batteries, St. Paul, 1965-66; with payroll Collins Electric, St. Paul, 1967-69; with acctg., office mgr. White Bear Travel, Inc., White Bear Lake, Minn., 1975-80; treas., chief fin. officer Smarte Carte, Inc., White Bear Lake, Minn., 1980-86; adminstr. bus. Rerat Law Firm P.A., Mpls., 1986—; pres., owner Rose Lake, Inc., White Bear Lake, 1985—, E-Z Roller, Inc., White Bear Lake, 1986—, NKI Fin., Inc., Mpls., 1986—. Mem. Am. Legion Aux., Nat. Assn. for Female Execs. Democrat. Lutheran. Office: Rerat Law Firm PA 1735 Piper Tower 222 S 9th St Minneapolis MN 55402

IMPELLIZZERI, ANNE ELMENDORF, insurance company executive, social services executive; b. Chgo., Jan. 26, 1933; d. Armin and Laura (Gundlach) Elmendorf; m. Julius Simon Impellizzeri, Oct. 12, 1961; children—Laura, Theodore (dec.). BA Smith Coll., 1955; M.A., Yale U., 1957. CLU; chartered fin. cons. Tchr., Amity Regional High Sch., Woodbridge, Conn., 1957-58; adminstrv. and editorial asst. East Europe Inst., N.Y.C., 1958-59; health educator Met. Life Ins. Co., N.Y.C., 1959-62, 71-76, adminstrv. asst. pub. affairs, 1976-78, asst. v.p., 1978-80, v.p., 1980-85, v.p. group ins., 1985-88; chmn. summer jobs adv. com. N.Y.C. Partnership, 1980-82, v.p. 1988—. Pres. Am. Assn. Gifted Children, 1975-85, chair, 1985—; bd. dirs. Nat. Safety Council, 1974-80; trustee Lakeland Bd. Edn., Westchester County, N.Y., 1967-71, pres., 1970-71. Named to Acad. of Women Achievers, YWCA N.Y., 1978; Fulbright grantee, 1955-56. Mem. Assn. Yale Alumni (bd. govs. 1985—), Phi Beta Kappa. Office: NYC Ptnrship 200 Madison Ave New York NY 10016

IMPERIAL, MELANIE KAY, health care products company executive; b. Denver, Dec. 28, 1962; d. Marvin Otto and Nancy Lee (Martin) Maul; m. Brooks Charles Imperial, May 23, 1986. Student, U. So. Calif., 1980-82; BA with honors, U. Calif., Berkeley, 1984. Office mgr. Container Freight Corp., Oakland, Calif., 1983-84; container yard supt. Am. President Lines, Ltd., Oakland, 1984-85, freight sta. supt., 1985; mgr. adminstrn.-distbn. Medisystems Corp., San Francisco, 1986—, mgr. nat. accounts, 1988—. Mem. Women in Transp., Calif. Geneal. Soc., Phi Beta Kappa. Republican. Presbyterian. Home: 8067 Lt William Clark Rd Parker CO 80134 Office: Medisystems Corp 345 California St 21st Floor San Francisco CA 94104

INCAGNOLI, THERESA MARIE, clinical neuropsychologist; b. N.Y.C., June 22, 1949; d. Thomas Marcel and Marie Incagnoli. B.A. cum laude, Bklyn. Coll., 1970; Ph.D., St. John's U., 1978. Diplomate in clin. neuropsychology Am. Bd. Profl. Psychology. Psychologist, St. Vincent's Med. Ctr., N.Y.C., 1973-79; postdoctoral fellow in clin. neuropsychology U. Okla. Health Scis. Ctr., 1979-80; clin. neuropsychologist VA Med. Ctr., Northport, N.Y., 1981—; asst. prof. dept. psychiatry (psychology) Sch. Medicine SUNY-Stony Brook, 1982—. Editor textbook: Clinical Application of Neuropsychological Test Batteries, 1986. NIMH fellow, 1979-80. Mem. Am. Psychol. Assn., Internat. Neuropsychol. Soc., Nat. Acad. Neuropsychologists, N.Y. State Head Injury Assn. Home: 240 Central Park S New York NY 10019 Office: VA Med Ctr Psychology Dept Northport NY 11768

INCIVILITO, DIANA, import and customs manager; b. Bklyn., June 1, 1953; d. Joseph Paul and Mary Jean (Maltese) I. BBA, Pace U., 1987. Import, customs mgr. Warnaco, Inc., N.Y.C., 1979—; cons. K & K Sports, N.Y.C., 1986—. Mem. Nat. Assn. Female Execs., Am. Assn. Exporters and Importers. Roman Catholic. Home: 275 Bay 37th St Brooklyn NY 11214

INDICK, JANET, sculptor, educational administrator; b. Bklyn., Mar. 3, 1932; d. Charles and Sarah (Goldsmith) Suslak; m. Benjamin Philip Indick, Aug. 23, 1953; children: Michael Cory, Karen Leigh Indick Maizel. B.S. in Art, Hunter Coll., 1953, postgrad., 1953; postgrad. New Sch., 1961-62. Tchr. kindergarten pub. schs., Elizabeth, N.J., 1953-54; dir. nursery sch. Teaneck Jewish Ctr., N.J., 1964—. Executed commd. sculpture Netzach Yisroel, Teaneck Jewish Ctr., 1974, Etz Chaim 1981, Sanctuary Wall Menorah 1983, Temple Beth Rishon, Wyckoff, N.J., 1981, 83, Menorah, Franklin Lakes Pub. Sch., 1983; exhbns. include Morris (N.J.) Mus., 1979, 84, Bergen (N.J.) Mus., 1981, Newark Mus., 1982, Jersey City Mus., 1983, Hebrew Tabernacle, N.Y.C., 1984, Parsons Gallery, N.Y.C., 1984, Lillian Heidenberg Gallery, N.Y.C., 1984—, Chubb Corp., N.J. solo, 1985, N.J. Art Ctr., Summit, 1985, Galleria Maray, N.J., 1986, Vineyard Gallery, N.Y.C., 1986, Edward Williams Gallery Fairleigh Dickinson U., solo 1986, Artforms Gallery, Red Bank, N.J., 1987. Advisor Teaneck Arts Adv. Bd., 1982—. Recipient sculpture prize Nat. Assn. Painters and Sculptors, 1970-80, Merit award IFFRA/AIA Forum on Religion, Art and Architecture, 1984; N.J. State Council Arts fellow, 1981. Mem. Sculptors Assn. N.J. (v.p. 1988—), Sculptors League Internat., Nat. Assn. Women Artists (juror; sculpture prize 1974), N.Y. Soc. Women Artists (juror), Women's Caucus Art (juror). Democrat. Jewish. Home: 428 Sagamore Ave Teaneck NJ 07666 Other: care Lillian Heidenberg Gallery 50 W 57th St New York NY

INFANTE, DAISY INOCENTES, sales and real estate executive; b. Marbel, Philippines, Aug. 3, 1946; came to U.S., 1968; d. Jesus Infante and Josefina (Inocentes) I.; m. Enerico Malong Sampang, Sept. 20, 1968 (div. 1981); children: Desiree Josephine, Dante Fernancio, Darrell Enerico; m. Rosben Reyes Ogbac, Jan. 30, 1987; children: Peter Ross, Analisa Frances. AA with highest honors, Notre Dame of Marbel, Philippines, 1963; AB in English magna cum laude, U. Santo Tomas, Manila, 1965, BS in Psychology, 1966; MA in Communications, Fairfield U., 1971. Columnist, writer Pinoy News mag., Chgo., 1975-76, Philippine News, Chgo., 1977-80; cons. EDP Cemco Systems, Inc., Oak Brook, Ill., 1980-81; pres. Daisener, Inc., Downers Grove, Ill., 1980-82; cons. EDP Robert J. Irmen Assocs., Hinsdale, Ill., 1981-82; pres. Data Info. Systems Corp., Downers Grove, Ill., 1982-84; broker, co. mgr. Gen. Devel. Corp., Chgo., 1984-86; columnist, writer Via Times, Chgo., 1986-86; owner, pres. Marbel Realty, Chgo., 1984—; exec. v.p. Dior Enterprises, Inc., Chgo., 1986—. Author: Poems of My Youth, 1982, (lyrics and music) My First Twenty Songs, 1981; inventor fryer-steamer. Mem. Nat. Assn. Female Execs., Am. Soc. Profl. Exec. Women, Philippine C. of C. (sec. Chgo. chpt. 1985). Roman Catholic. Lodge: Lions (twister Chgo. Fil-Am club 1978-79). Home: 2019 W School St Chicago IL 60618 Office: Dior Enterprises Inc 5906 1/2 N Clark St Chicago IL 60660

INFANTE, ISA MARIA, political scientist, educator; b. Santo Domingo, Dominican Republic, Sept. 8, 1942; came to U.S., 1945; d. Rafael Infante and Dolores Nieves; student Woodbury Coll., 1960-61; B.A., U. Calif.-Santa Cruz, 1973; M.A. in Comparative Polit. Systems, Yale U., 1975; postgrad. U. Santa Clara Law Sch. and People's Coll. of Law, 1975-77; Ph.D. in Polit. Sci. (Ford Found. fellow), U. Calif.-Riverside, 1977; 1 child, Ninette Maria. Mgmt. trainee Calif. Savs. and Loan Assn., Los Angeles, 1960-61; asst. fgn. corr. Los Angeles Times, Mexico City, 1961-62; bus. enterprise officer, Los Angeles, 1962-64; regional mgr. advt. Strout Realty, Pasadena, Calif., 1964-66; dir. ops. Branford, Inc., N.Y.C., 1966-68; entrepreneur retail stores, Los Angeles, Lake Elsinore, Calif., Anaheim, Calif.; exec. dir. coll. adult rehab. program U. Calif., Riverside, 1970-71; research asso. U. Calif., Santa Cruz, 1972-73; dir. human resources project SUNY, Binghamton, 1973-75; instr. social scis. div. Riverside (Calif.) Community Coll., 1976; dir. nat. immigration bd. Nat. Lawyers Guild, Los Angeles, 1977; acad. adv. and exec. asst. to provost Antioch Coll. West, Antioch U., San Francisco, 1977-78; sr. devel. officer U.S. Human Resources Corp., San Francisco, 1978; mem. profl. staff Interdepartmental Task Force on Women, White House, Washington, 1978-79; policy fellow and program officer Inst. for Ednl. Leadership/Fund for Improvement of Postsecondary Edn., HEW, Washington, 1978-79; assoc. dean Labor Coll., Empire State Coll., SUNY, N.Y.C., 1979-81; pres. I. Infante Assocs., internat. cons., 1980—; prof. polit. sci., dir. Latin Am. studies dept. Jersey City State Coll., 1983—; cons. to various ednl. orgns. and govt. agys. Pres., Nat. Hispanic Coalition, Washington, 1978-80; notary public, 1980—; mem. Am. Council on Edn., 1980—, Community Bd. 12, Borough of Manhattan, N.Y., 1980—; bd. dirs. Nagle House Co-op, N.Y.C., 1980—, Solidaridad Humana, Inc., N.Y.C., 1980—; trustee Center for Integrative Devel., N.Y.C., 1979. P.R. Legal Defense and Edn. Fund scholar, 1975-77, Pease Barker scholar, 1972-73, Council on Legal Edn. Opportunity scholar, 1975-76. Fellow Am. Polit. Sci. Assn.; mem. Soc. for Internat. Devel., Internat. Polit. Sci. Assn., Am. Ednl. Research Assn., Latin Am. Studies Assn., Univ. and Coll. Labor Edn. Assn., Nat. Women's Polit. Caucus, Nat. Women's Health Network, Nat. Assn. Female Execs. Club: Yale of N.Y.C. Author: (with others) Field Preparation Manual, 1973; contbg. author: Voices From the Ghetto, 1968; The Politics of Teaching Political Science, 1978; Labor Studies Jour., 1981; Black Studies Jour., 1983; Political Affairs, 1984. Address: Route 1 Box 119-I Holladay TN 38341

INGEBRIGTSTEN, CATHERINE WILLIAMS, rehabilitation consultant, health education specialist; b. Lake Charles, La., May 28, 1955; d. Thomas Humphrey and Jane Catherine (Caldwell) Williams; 1 child, Jennifer Catherine Bittle. BS, Old Dominion U., 1978, MS summa cum laude, 1983; diploma profl. nursing, Norfolk Gen. Hosp., 1978. Intensive care unit nurse DePaul Hosp., Norfolk, Va., 1979-80; cons. Internat. Rehab. Assn., Virginia Beach, Va., 1980-82; ptnr., pres., cons. OccuSystems, Norfolk, 1982-85, prin., pres. Cathy Bittle & Assocs., Norfolk, 1985—; health edn. cons. Peninsula Health Dept., Newport News, Va., 1985—, dir. grant writing program, 1985-86; educator Diabetes Inst., Virginia Beach, 1984—; speaker in field. Com. mem. Tidewater Health Fair Task Force, Norfolk, 1983. Mem. Am. Assn. Counseling and Devel., Am. Assn. Phys. Health, Edn., Recreation and Dance, Old Dominion U. Grad. Student Assn. (pres. 1982-83), Phi Kappa Phi. Republican. Roman Catholic. Avocations: sailing, biking, skiing, running, rollerskating. Home: 122 Cathedral Dr North Wales PA 19454 Office: Cathy Bittle & Assocs PO Box 8551 Norfolk VA 23503

INGENITO, JANE ELIZABETH, health science facility association; b. Newark, Jan. 18, 1947; d. Alban Eugene and Rita Esther (Keyes) Esche; m. Gregory Francis Ingenito, July 17, 1971; 1 child, Cristina Caryn. BS in Nursing, Wagner Coll., N.Y.C., 1969; MA in Edn., NYU, 1971. Clin. nurse specialist Yale New Haven Hosp., Yale U. Sch. Medicine, 1971-73; asst. prof. clin. psychiatry, clin. nurse specialist U. Pitts., 1973-85; nurse psychiat. and mental health St. John's Hosp. Home Health Care, Pitts., 1986-87; clin. nurse specialist Woodville State Hosp., Carnegie, Pa., 1987—. Contbr. articles to profl. jours. Active Girl Scouts U.S., Pitts., 1984—. NIMH grantee, 1968-71. Mem. Am. Nurses Assn. (cert. clin. specialist; div. psychiat. and mental health nursing), Pa. Nurses Assn., Nat. Assn. for Female Execs. (charter), Sigma Theta Tau. Home: PO Box 11329 Pittsburgh PA 15238 Office: Woodville State Hosp Adminstrn Bldg Carnegie PA 15106

INGERSOLL, DIANE SUE, librarian sales professional; b. Mason City, Iowa, July 24, 1952; d. Robert Earl and Mary Dean (Braatz) Waite; m. Douglas Alan Ingersoll, Nov. 10, 1972; 1 child, Katherine. AA, North Iowa Area Community Coll., 1972; BS in Elem. Edn., U. Iowa, 1976, MLS, 1980. Tech. services coordinator Iowa City Pub. Library, 1976-82; installation cons. CLSI, Newtonville, Mass., 1982-85, sales rep., 1985—. Mem. ALA. Office: CLSI 320 Nevada St Newtonville MA 02160

INGERSOLL, FAY E., nursing administrator; b. Manokin, Md., Dec. 7, 1933; m. Norris E. Ingersoll, Jan. 21, 1956; 1 child, Debora A. BS, U. Maine, 1969, MEd, 1974. Staff nurse Penisula Gen. Hosp., Salisbury, Md., 1954-55, U.S. Pub. Health Service Hosp., Balt., 1955-56; head nurse Deer's Head State Hosp., Salisbury, 1956-57; staff nurse Cen. Maine Gen. Hosp., Lewiston, 1957; instr. Cen. Maine Gen. Hosp. Sch. Nursing, Lewiston, 1957-72, asst. dir., 1973-76; dir. Cen. Maine Med. Ctr. (formerly Cen. Maine Gen. Hosp. Sch. Nursing), Lewiston, 1976—; corporator Cen. Maine Med. Ctr., 1977—. Bd. dirs. Maine High Blood Pressure Council, 1986—; trustee Dr. Gard Twaddle Nurses Endowment Fund, 1978—; ombudsman Maine Com. Aging, Augusta, 1984—; mem. Women's Lit. Union, Auburn, Maine, 1984—. Helene Fuld Health Trust grantee, N.Y.C., 1987. Mem. Nat. League Nursing, Am. Nurses Assn., Maine State Nurses Assn., Maine Assn. Continuing Edn., Lisbon (Maine) Area C. of C., Phi Kappa Phi. Roman Catholic. Clubs: Slovakian (Lisbon), Emblem (Lewiston). Office: Cen Maine Med Ctr Sch Nursing 300 Main St Lewiston ME 04240

INGLE, JOAN MARIE, nurse practitioner; b. Balt., Nov. 2, 1943; d. Edgar Allen and Mary Virginia (Reese) Peppler; m. Elbert L. Fisher, Nov. 12, 1966 (div. Mar. 1976); children—Heather Marie, Todd Perry; m. 2d, William Kenneth Ingle, Dec. 25, 1979. R.N., Bon Secours Sch. Nursing, Balt., 1964; student U. N.C., 1979-82. Staff nurse Doctors Hosp., Coral Gables, Fla., 1965-68, charge nurse CCU, 1976-78; staff nurse CCU, South Miami Hosp., Miami, Fla., 1978-79; home care supr. Med. Personnel Pool, Asheville, N.C., 1980-81, dir. nurses, 1981-82, dir. home health, 1982-84, 86; nurse practitioner, York Hosp. Trauma/Emergency Ctr., 1987—. Mem. N.C. Nurses Assn. (chmn. legis. com. 1983-84). Democrat. Baptist. Club: Altrusa (Asheville). Home: Sheffield Dr York PA 17313 Office: York Hosp 1001 S George St York PA 17405

INGLEHART, LORRETTA JEANNETTE, physicist; b. Cleve., July 14, 1947; d. Trevor Gordon and Lois Jeannetta (Kolterman) Kopp. BS, Wayne State U., 1979, MS, 1982, PhD, 1984. Asst. prof. physics Lab. d'Optique Physique Ecole Supervieure de Physique et de Chimie, Paris, 1984-85; assoc. research scientist Johns Hopkins U., Balt., 1985—, asst. prof., 1987—; professorial lectr. physics Am. Univ., Washington, 1986-87; guest scientist Nat. Bur. Standards, Gaithersburg, Md., 1985—. Contbr. articles on thermal wave NDE to profl. jours., 1980—. Fulbright scholar, 1986; research grantee Bendix Corp., 1979-81. Mem. AAAS, Am. Phys. Soc., Optical Soc., Sigma Xi. Office: Johns Hopkins U 34 and Charles St Baltimore MD 21218

INGLETT, BETTY LEE, media services administrator; b. Augusta, Ga., Oct. 6, 1930; d. Wilfred Lee and Elizabeth Arelia (Crouch) I. BS in Edn., Ga. State Coll. for Women, 1953; MA in Library, Media and Edn. Adminstrn., Ga. So. U., 1980; EdD in Edn. Adminstrn., Nova U., 1988. Tchr. James L. Fleming Elem. Sch., Augusta, Ga., 1953-63, Murphey Jr. High Sch., Augusta, 1963-64, Sego Jr. High Sch., Augusta, 1964-68, Glenn Hills High Sch., Augusta, 1968-75; media specialist Nat. Hills Elem. Sch., Augusta, 1975-80; prin. Lake Forest Elem. Sch., Augusta, 1980-84, Joseph R. Lamar Elem. Sch., Augusta, 1984-86; dir. ednl. media services Richmond County Bd. Edn., Augusta, 1986—; owner, operator Betty Inglett Enterprises, Augusta. Contbr. articles to profl. jours. Bd. dirs. Am. Heart Fund, 1975-80, Am. Cancer Fund, 1986—; del. Dem. State Conv., 1982; council mem. PTA. (life), 1985. Mem. Richmond County Edn. Assn. (sec. v.p. 1961-63), AAUW (v.p. 1957-59), NEA, Ga. Assn. Edn., Ga. Assn. Ednl. Leaders, Ga. Library Media Dept., Ga. Library Assn., Ga. Assn. Instructional Tech., Ga. Assn. Curriculum Instructional Supr., Profl. Leadership Assn., Cen. Savannah River Area Library Assn., Alpha Delta Kappa, Phi Delta Pi, Phi Delta Kappa. Baptist. Office: Ednl Media Services 3148 Lake Forest Dr Augusta GA 30909

INGRAHAM-PARSON, VIVIAN JUNE LOWELL, fed. program adminstr.; b. Omaha, June 1, 1922; d. John Calvert and Pearl Mabel (Whitscell) Lowell; student schs. Omaha; m. Clarence Parson, Sept. 7, 1969 (div. Nov. 1982); m. Edwin L. Ingraham; children—Richard D. Ingraham, Leroy Lowell Ingraham, John Edwin Ingraham, Jeffrey Scott Ingraham. Supr. customer service Met. Utilities Dist., 1940-46; news reporter Sta. KBON, Omaha, 1962-67; med. transcriber VA Hosp., Omaha, 1971-73; exec. dir. Gt. Plains council Girl Scouts U.S.A., Omaha, 1973-75; job developer City of Omaha, 1976-81; employment coordinator Iowa CETA, 1981-83; owner, mgr. VIP Enterprises Real Estate, 1984—. Exec. com. Mid-Am. council Boy Scouts Am., 1960—, Fontenelle Dist. Boy Scouts Am., 1958-76; youth coordinator Douglas County ARC, 1965-70; dist. II dir. Nebr. State PTA, 1964-68; v.p. Omaha PTA Council, 1966-68; pres. Walnut Hill Sch. PTA, 1958-60, Monroe Sch., 1965-67, Fontenelle Schs., 1962-64; dist. del. Republican Party. Recipient hon. life membership award, nat. and state PTA, 1972; Good Neighbor award Ak-Sar-Ben, 1970; Brotherhood Week-Good Neighbor award NCCJ, 1967; Service award ARC, 1968; nat. officer (Stewards) Nat. Presbyn. Mariners, 1960-66; hon. adm. Nebr. Navy. Mem. Profl. Assn. Girl Scout Execs. Presbyterian. Panelist: Discrimination and Its Effect on Children, 1970; author booklet: A Look at PTA, 1966; contbr. articles to religious mags. Office: VIP Enterprises Real Estate PO Box 44604 Omaha NE 68104

INGRAM, BETTY EILEEN, airline company executive; b. Ravenna, Ohio, Nov. 18, 1942; d. John Daryl and Sibyl Marie (Marshall) I. Grad. high sch., Rootstown, Ohio. With communications dept. Trans World Airlines, N.Y.C., 1961-62; sales exec. Nat. Airlines, San Francisco, 1962-67, Aer Lingus Irish Airlines, San Francisco, 1967-73; owner, pres. Tara Travel, San Francisco, 1973-84, Travel Resources, Inc., San Francisco, 1984-86; pres. SystemOne Travel Resources, Larkspur, Calif., 1986—. Office: System One Corp 2929 Allen Pkwy Houston TX 77019

INGRAM, HELEN MOYER, political science educator; b. Denver, July 12, 1937; d. Oliver Weldon and Hazel Margaret (Wickard) Hill; m. W. David Laird; children by previous marriage: Mrill, Maia, Seth. BA, Oberlin (Ohio) Coll., 1959; PhD, Columbia U., N.Y.C., 1967. Lectr., asst. prof. polit. sci. U. N. Mex., 1962-69; cons. Nat. Water Commn., Washington, 1969-72; assoc. prof. polit. sci. U. Ariz., Tucson, 1972-77, prof. polit. sci., 1979—; sr. fellow Resources for the Future, Washington, 1977-79; mem. panel on climate variability and U.S. water resources AAAS, 1986—. Mem. Policy Studies Orgn., (pres. 1985), Am. Polit. Sci. Assn. (council, treas. 1985-87), Western Polit. Sci. Assn. (past pres., v.p.). Author: (with Dean Mann) Why Policies Succeed or Fail, 1980; (with Nancy Laney and John McCain) A Policy Approach to Representation: Lessons from the Four Corners States, 1980; (with Martin, Laney and Griffin) Saving Water in a Desert City, 1984, (with Brown) Water and Poverty in the Southwest, 1987; book rev. editor Am. Polit. Sci. Rev., 1987—. Home: 2811 E 3d St Tucson AZ 85719 Office: U Ariz Dept Polit Sci Tucson AZ 85721

INGRAM, SYBIL LOUISE, pharmaceutical representative; b. Chgo., Mar. 23, 1959; d. Emmett Julian and Louise (Henderson) I. BS, Tenn. State U.; MEd, Vanderbilt U. Chief technologist Riverside Hosp., Nashville, 1982-83; mgr. lab. Meharry Med. Coll., Nashville, 1983-85, instr. clin., 1983; rep. CooperVision Ophthalmic Products, San Jose, Calif., 1985-87, Abbott Labs., North Chicago, Ill., 1987—. Mem. Am. Soc. Med. Technologists, Am. Soc. Clin. Pathologists, Nat. Assn. Female Execs., Delta Sigma Theta. Home: 10529 Roseton Ct Saint Louis MO 63114 Office: Abbott Labs Abbott Park North Chicago IL 60064

INNES, P. KIM STURGESS, transportation company executive; b. Ottawa, Ont., Can., Mar. 29, 1955; d. Roy and Sydney Claire (Chamberlain) S.; m. W. Campbell Innes, May 12, 1984. BSc in Engring. Physics, Queen's U., Kingston, 1977; MBA with distinction, U. W. Ont., 1984. Registered profl. engr., Alta. Gas pipelines engr. Nat. Energy Bd., Ottawa, 1977-78; reservoir engr. Esso Resources Can. Ltd., Calgary, Alta., Can., 1978-80, corp. planning analyst, 1980-82; cons. McKinsey and Co., Toronto, Ont., 1984-88; v.p., asst. to pres. Greyhound Lines of Canada, Calgary, 1988—; trustee Queen's U. 1987—, bd. dirs. bookstore 1975-77, mem. univ. council, 1979—. Mem. Assn. Profl. Engrs., Geologists and Geophysicists Alta, Queen's U. Alumni Assn. (pres. 1980-82). Club: Esso Calgary (treas. 1980-82). Home: Box 1 Site 32, Rural Rt 12, Calgary Can T3E6W3 Office: Greyhound Lines of Canada, 877 Greyhound Way SW, Calgary Can T3C 3V8

INNIS, GAIL MARIE, counselor; b. Highland Park, Mich., June 3, 1957; d. William Archie and Leila Marie (Schoen) I. AA in Liberal Arts, Concordia Coll., Ann Arbor, Mich., 1977; BA in Edn., Art, Concordia Tchrs. Coll., River Forest, Ill., 1979; MA in Counseling, Oakland U., 1985. Tchr., ch. worker Immanuel Luth. Sch., Houston, 1979-80, St. John Luth. High Sch., Ocala, Fla., 1980-84; counselor, coordinator, acad. advisor Oakland U., Rochester, Mich., 1984-86; counselor, adj. faculty Oakland Community Coll., Auburn Hills, Mich., 1985—; counselor, instr., dir. testing Concordia Coll., Ann Arbor, Mich., 1986—. Author: (with others) Cultural Values and Individual Work Values, 1985. Cons. numerous agys. Mem. Am. Assn. for Counseling and Devel., Mich. Assn. Counseling and Devel., Luth. Edn. Assn., Chi Sigma Iota. Lutheran. Office: Concordia Coll Counseling Services 4090 Geddes Rd Ann Arbor MI 48105

INNIS, PAULINE, author, newspaper company executive; b. Devon, Eng.; came to U.S., 1954; m. Walter Deane Innis, Aug. 1, 1959. Attended U. Manchester, U. London. Author: Hurricane Fighters, 1962; Ernestine or the Pig in the Potting Shed, 1963; The Wild Swans Fly, 1964; The Ice Bird, 1965; Wind of the Pampas, 1967; Fire from the Fountains, 1968; Astronumerology, 1971; Gold in the Blue Ridge, 1973, 2d edit., 1980; My Trails (transl. from French), 1975; (with Mary Jane McCaffery) Protocol, 1977; Prayer and Power in the Capital, 1982, The Secret Gardens of Watergate, 1987, Attention: A Quick Guide to the Armed Services, 1988. Bd. dirs. Washington Goodwill Industries Guild, 1962-66; membership chmn. Welcome to Washington Club, 1961-64; co-chmn. Internat. Workshop Capital Speakers' Club, 1961-64; pres. Children's Book Guild, 1967-68; dir. Ednl. Communications; bd. dirs. Internat. Conf. Women Writers and Journalists; mem. criminal justice com. D.C. Commn. on Status of Women; founder vol. program D.C. Women's Detention Center; chmn. women's com. Washington Opera, 1977-79; mem. Liaison Com. for Med. Edn., 1979—; nat. trustee Med. Coll., Pa., 1980—; bd. dirs. Kahill Gibran Found., 1983—; mem. Edn. Council for Fgn. Med. Grads., 1986—. Named Hoosier Woman of Yr., 1966. Mem. Soc. Woman Geographers, Authors League, Smithsonian Assocs. (women's bd.), English-Speaking Union (dir.), Spanish-Portuguese Group D.C. (pres. 1965-66), Brit. Inst. U.S. Clubs: Am. Newspaper Women's (pres. 1971-73), Nat. Press. Home: 2700 Virginia Ave NW Washington DC 20037 also: Skipper's Row Gibson Island MD 21056

INSCOE, JENNIFER LYNN, loan company executive; b. Washington Island, Wis., Sept. 13, 1947; d. Clifford Charles and Betty Delores (Greenfeldt) Young; m. Robert Daniel Inscoe, Dec. 31, 1966 (div. 1981); children: Stephanie Lynn, Robyn Elizabeth. Student, Trinity Coll., Deerfield, Ill., 1965-67, Community Coll., 1979, 80, 87. Real estate agt. Merrill Lynch, Manassas, Va., 1980-82, ReMax Olympic, Manassas, 1982—; loan officer Mfrs. Hanover Mortgage, N.Y.C., 1981-83, Epic Mortgage Co., Woodbridge, Va., 1983-84, Sovran Mortgage, Manassas, 1984-86, Am. Home Funding, Manassas, 1987—. Mem. Fauquier Bd. Realtors (Warrenton, Va.), Prince William Bd. Realtors (Manassas, Va.), Mortgage Bankers Assn., No. Va. Builders Assn. Republican. Baptist. Club: HOA Outlook (sec. 1985). Home: 10384 Rapidan Ln Manassas VA 22110 Office: Am Home Funding 7691 Donegan Dr Manassas VA 22110

INSELMAN, LAURA SUE, pediatrician; b. Bklyn., Nov. 2, 1944; d. Alexander M. and Rae (Bloom) Inselman. BA, Barnard Coll., 1966; MD, Med. Coll. Pa., 1970. Intern and resident St. Lukes Hosp. Ctr., N.Y.C., 1970-73; fellow in pediatric pulmonary disease Babies Hosp., N.Y.C., 1973-76; chief pediatric pulmonary div. Interfaith Med. Ctr., Bklyn., 1976-81; chief pediatric pulmonary div. North Shore Univ. Hosp., Manhasset, N.Y., 1981-86; clin. dir. pediatric pulmonary div. Newington Con. Children's Hosp., 1987—; asst. prof. pediatrics Cornell U. Med. Coll., N.Y.C., 1981-86; asst. clin. prof. pediatrics, Yale U. Sch. Medicine, New Haven, 1987—; asst. prof. pediatrics, U. Conn. Health Ctr., Farmington, 1987—; mem. staff Good Samaritan Hosp., West Islip, N.Y., 1982-87. Bd. dirs. Am. Lung Assn. Nassau-Suffolk, East Meadow, N.Y., 1983-86. Fellow Am. Acad. Pediatrics, Am. Coll. Chest Physicians; mem. Am. Thoracic Soc., Am. Fedn. Clin. Research, N.Y. Acad. Medicine, Harvey Soc., Soc. Pediatric Research. Office: Newington Children's Hosp 181 E Cedar St Newington CT 06111

INTILLI, SHARON MARIE, television associate director; b. Amsterdam, N.Y., Aug. 11, 1950; d. Francisco Joseph Intilli and Virginia Eleanor (Tallman) Monaco. Cert., Paralegal Inst., 1973; student, Fordham U., 1975-79. Group assoc. editor Matthew Bender & Co., N.Y.C., 1974-77; prodn. sec. 20/20 program, ABC, N.Y.C., 1977-78, prodn. assoc., 1979-80, program prodn. asst., 1980-82; legal contract adminstr. ABC Sports, N.Y.C., 1978-79; assoc. dir. Capitol Cities/ABC, N.Y.C., 1982—; dir., assoc. dir. freelance projects. Contbg. editor Bender's Forms of Discovery, Vols. 15 & 16, 1975. Recipient Outstsanding Individual Achievement cert. Nat. Acad. TV Arts & Scis., 1980-81. Mem. Dirs. Guild of Am.

IOANNIDIS, LESLIE PAMELA COOK, mathematics educator, researcher; b. Kingston, Ont., Can., Aug. 23, 1946; came to U.S., 1956; d. Leslie G. and Alfreda M. Cook; m. George A. Ioannidis, Nov. 26, 1972; children—Alexander, James. B.A., U. Rochester, 1967; M.S., Cornell U., 1969, Ph.D., 1971. NATO postdoctoral fellow U. Utrecht (Netherlands), 1971-72; research assoc., instr. Cornell U., Ithaca, N.Y., 1972-73; asst. prof. UCLA, 1973-80; assoc. prof. math., 1980-83; assoc. prof. math. U. Del., Newark, 1983—; NSF vis. prof. U. Md., College Park, 1987-88. Author: Transonic Aerodynamics. NDEA Title IV fellow Cornell U., 1967-70; NSF grad. fellow, 1970-71; NSF grantee UCLA, U. Del., 1977—. Mem. Soc. Indsl. and Applied Math. (council 1984-87), Am. Phys. Soc. Office: Math Dept Ewing Hall U Del Newark DE 19716

IORFIDA, DIANE MARY, health care executive; b. Chgo., Sept. 21, 1954; d. Boleslaus and Genevieve Marie (Sumara) Laskowski; m. Samuel Joseph Iorfida, Sept. 13, 1975. B.A. in English, DePaul U., 1975, postgrad. 1975-76; M.S., Notre Dame U. (Ind.), 1984; M.M.O.B., Ill. Benedictine Coll., 1987. Lic. tchr., Ill., Ind. Tng. coordinator Saxon Home Care Ctrs., Chgo., 1971-75; reading specialist Dept. Spl. Edn., LaGrange, Ill., 1975-76; tng. coordinator LaGrange State Bank, 1976-78; dir. tng. and personnel Garatoni & Assocs., South Bend, Ind., 1978; asst. dir. personnel Elkhart Gen. Hosp. (Ind.), 1978-80, dir. personnel, 1980-84; corp. asst. v.p., dir. human resources Ravenswood Health Care Corp., Chgo., 1984-88; sr. v.p. human resources Univ. Hosps. of Cleve., 1988—. Editorial bd. Jour. Am. Soc. Personnel Adminstrn. Mem. Ind. Soc. Hosp. Personnel Adminstrn. (bd. dirs. 1980-84, pres. 1983-84), Am. Compensation Assn., Ind. Personnel Assn., Am. Soc. Personnel Adminstrn., Chgo. Healthcare Human Resources Mgmt. Assn., Human Resources Mgmt. Assn. Chgo., Am. Soc. Healthcare Human Resources Adminstrn. (bd. dirs. 1987—). Office: Univ Hosps of Cleve 2074 Abington Rd Cleveland OH 44106

IPP, LINDA SUE, zoo executive; b. Dayton, Ohio, May 23, 1957; d. Leonard J. and B. June (Wolf) I. BA in English Lit., U. Cin., 1984. Pub. relations intern Nat. History Mus., Cin., 1983-84, Cin. Fire Mus., 1984; dir. communications, devel. Dr. Michael Tillery, Inc., Indpls., 1985; asst. campaign mgr. Cin. Zoo, 1986, pub. relations asst., 1986-87, spl. events asst., 1987—; freelance writer, Cin., 1984; freelance model, Cin., 1985—. writer ZooNews., 1986-87. Democrat. Jewish. Office: Cin Zoo 3400 Vine St Cincinnati OH 45220

IPPOLITO, ELAINE ROSE, artist, educator; b. Dover, Del., July 20, 1953; d. Peter Paul and Sara (Lepore) DeMarie; m. James Clement Ippolito, June 1, 1974; 1 child, Jacy Clement. BA, U. Del., 1975; MA, W.Va. U., 1980. Program coordinator Kent County Recreation Programs, Dover, Del., 1977-78; art instr., program dir. Del. State Arts Council, Georgetown, Del., 1980-84; artist in residence Del. State Arts Council, Wilmington, 1981—; tchr., program dir. Rehoboth (Del.) Art League, 1983—, gallery mgr., 1983-86; tchr. Del. Tchr.'s Ctr., Dover, 1984—; lectr. various Del. arts orgns., 1983—, workshop cons. Headstart Program Tchrs., 1980; coordinator, dir. outreach program Sussex County Schs., 1986; asst. to state registrar hist. and cultural affairs Sate Del., Lewes, 1985—. Recipient 2d, 3d Place awards Wicomico Art League Exhibit, Salisbury, Md., 1982, Art award Merit of Work Sussex County Arts Council, Georgetown, Del., 1985: Very Spl. Arts Program Del. Grantee, 1986. Mem. Nat. League Am. Pen Women (sec. Holly Br. 1983-86, 1st Place annual exhibit 1986), Internat. Graphics Arts Found., Del. State Arts. Co. (artist in residence 1981—), Pyramid Atlantic Prints and Paperworks Assn., Sussex County Arts Council. Democrat. Roman Catholic. Club: Phila. Print. Home: 609 Savannah Rd Lewes DE 19958

IRBY, LEILANI JUNE, nursing educator; b. Idaho Springs, Colo., Feb. 26, 1939; d. Robert C. and Bernice M. (Reimer) McClain; R.N., Grace-New Haven Sch. Nursing, New Haven, 1958; B.S.N., U. Okla., 1967, M.S., 1974, Ph.D., 1983; m. Michael Eugene Irby, Aug. 27, 1966; children—Michelle, Michael. Staff nurse/supr. Presbyn. and Mt. Sinai hosps., N.Y.C., Good Samaritan Hosp., Phoenix and Cedars-Sinai Hosp., Los Angeles, 1958-66; chief nurse Central Okla. Mental Health Center, Norman, 1967-72; nurse epidemiologist, asst. dir. nursing St. Anthony Hosp., Oklahoma City, 1974-77; instr. Central State U., Edmond, Okla., 1977-81, asst. prof., 1981-85, assoc. prof., 1985—. Active public edn. and screening for diabetes and hypertension; resource person Redlands council Girls Scouts U.S.A., local PTA; Sunday sch. tchr. New Convenant United Methodist Ch., 1968—. Mem. Am. Nurses Assn., Okla. Nurses Assn., Phi Delta Kappa, Sigma Theta Tau. Democrat. Club: Edmond Garden. Edmond Soccer. Home: 616 S Firelane Rd Edmond OK 73034 Office: 100 N University Dr Edmond OK 73034

IRELAND, PAIGE VALENTINE, institutional director; b. Englewood, N.J., Apr. 28, 1954; d. Lloyd Owen and Frances (Valentine) I. B.S., Cornell U., 1976, M.B.A., 1983. Research specialist, v.p. research Cornell U., Ithaca, N.Y., 1974-79; research planning assoc. Instl. Planning and Analysis, Cornell U., Ithaca, 1979-83; dir., 1983-87; cons. Mgmt. Dynamics, 1987—. Product sales chmn. Camp Fire, Ithaca, 1983-87, bd. dirs., 1983-87. Mem. Assn. Inst. Research, N.E. Assn. Instl. Research (pres.-elect 1986-87, pres. 1987—), Kappa Kappa Gamma. Home: 1155 Warburton Ave #1W Yonkers NY 10701 Office: Mgmt Dynamics Treetops Estate 612 E Grassy Sprain Rd Yonkers NY 10710

IRELAND, PAMELA WOODHULL, department store buyer; b. Englewood, N.J., May 14, 1957; d. Lloyd Owen and Frances Woodhull (Valentine) I. BA magna cum laude, Hobart and William Smith Coll., 1979. Asst. buyer B. Altman & Co., N.Y.C., 1979-80, sr. asst. buyer, 1980-82, buyer children's accessories and sleepwear, 1982-83, buyer infants and toddler apparel, 1983—, buyer children's sleepwear, 1987—. Mem. St. Bartholomews Community Club, N.Y.C., 1985—. Mem. Phi Beta Kappa. Avocations: tennis, travel. Office: B Altman & Co 361 5th Ave New York NY 10016

IREY, CHARLOTTE YORK, educator; b. Oklahoma City, Arp. 29, 1918; d. Charles William and Annie Charlotte (Upsher) York; B.S. with honors, U. Wis., 1940; M.A., U. Colo., 1965; m. Eugene Floyd Irey, June 10, 1942; 1 dau., Susan Gail. Instr. dance Stephens Coll., Columbia, Mo., 1940-43; prof. dance U. Colo., Boulder, 1945-88, chmn. dance div., dept. theatre and dance, 1973-88. Recipient Robert L. Steans award U. Colo., Boulder, 1973, Thomas Jefferson award, 1980; Mem. Nat. Dance Assn. (pres. 1975-76, Scholar of Yr. 1982-83), AAHPERD, Am. Coll. Dance Festival, Council Dance Adminstrs., Congress Dance Research, Am. Dance Guild. Episcopalian. Author: (with Frances Bascom) Costume Cues, 1952. Charlotte York Irey Studio/Theatre at U. Colo., Boulder named in her honor, 1984. Office: U Colo Box 261 Boulder CO 80309

IRLAND, LORRAINE, telecommunications analyst; b. Newark, Dec. 21, 1946; d. Allen Robert and Evelyn (Lusardi) Zensen; m. Michael Joseph Berger, Feb. 13, 1966 (div. 1971); 1 child, Michael Louis Berger; m. James Frederick Irland, Dec. 28, 1983; 1 child, Kevin Frederick. AA in Bus. Mgmt., Diablo Valley Coll., 1979; BA in Bus. Adminstrn., Upper Iowa U., 1983; MS in Corp. Planning, U. Pa., 1986. Communications cons. Pacific Telephone & Telegraph Co., San Francisco, 1969-80; industry cons. AT&T, Basking Ridge, N.J., 1981-84; systems cons. Pitney Bowes, Inc., San Antonio, 1985-86, NURSEFINDERS, San Antonio, 1986-87; telecommunications analyst United Services Automobile Assn., San Antonio, 1987—. Mem. pub. info. com. Am. Cancer Soc. Mem. Am. Mktg. Assn., Nat. Assn. Female Execs., Inc., AAUW. Republican. Roman Catholic. Clubs: Goebel Collector's (N.Y.); Model A Ford (Calif.). Avocations: antiques, needlepoint, fashion design, antique Model A cars, floral arranging. Home: 5801 Spring Village San Antonio TX 78247 Office: United Services Automobile Assn 9800 Fredericksburg Rd San Antonio TX 78288

IRONS, PATRICIA DOUBLEDAY, magazine editor; b. N.Y.C., Mar. 25, 1934; d. George Chester and Mary (Kelley) Doubleday; m. Henry Clay Irons, July 10, 1954; children—Henry Clay Jr., G. Chester, Carol Irons Ross. B.A., Vassar Coll., 1956. Asst. editor Ladies Home Jour., N.Y.C., 1952-54; assoc. editor Baby Talk Mag., N.Y.C., 1957-76, editor-in-chief, 1976—. Mem. Am. Soc. Mag. Editors. Republican. Roman Catholic. Office: Baby Talk Mag 185 Madison Ave New York NY 10016

IRVIN, KATHRYN JEANETTE, educator; b. Tallahassee. B.A., Fla. A&M U.; M.Ed., Fla. Atlantic U. Tchr., Palm Beach County Schs., West Palm Beach, Fla., 1969—, head tchr. adult spl. edn., 1985—, media rep. adult edn., 1985-86, chair self-study, exceptional student edn., philosophy and objectives coms., 1986-87. Author: Black, Brown and Amber, 1979, Comes a Riderless Horse, 1983, reading home tutoring system Tutor Your Child, 1983; compiler, editor Where to Find Thrift Treasures, 1988. Dir. Kambi

Youth Theatre, West Palm Beach, 1979-82; tech. dir. Performing Arts Summer Sch., Palm Beach Gardens, Fla., 1983-84, 85; mem. Palm Beach Council Arts. Recipient 1st place award Cleveland Creative Arts, Tenn., 1981, Walter Bogle award Creative Arts Guild, 1983; grantee Palm Beach County Edn. Found., 1987. Mem. Nat. Writers Club (hon. mention 1983), NEA, Fla. Freelance Writers (1st pl. awards 1984, 85), Classroom Tchrs. Assn., North Palm Beaches Arts Soc. Avocations: drawing, painting, collecting art objects. Home: 312 Baker Dr West Palm Beach FL 33409

IRVINE, PHYLLIS ELEANOR KUHNLE, university administrator; b. Germantown, Ohio, July 14, 1940; d. Carl Franklin and Mildred Viola (Erisman) Kuhnle; m. Richard James Irvine, Feb. 15, 1964; children: Mark, Rick. BSN, Ohio State U., 1962, MSN, 1979, PhD, 1981; MS, Miami U., Oxford, Ohio, 1966. Staff nurse VA Ctr., Dayton, Ohio, 1962-66; mem. nursing faculty Miami Valley Hosp. Sch. Nursing, Dayton, 1968-78; teaching asst., lectr. Ohio State U., Columbus, 1979-82; assoc. prof. Ohio U., Athens, 1982-83; prof., dir. NE La. U., Monroe, 1984—; cons. Drexel U., Phila., 1986; reviewer Addison-Wesley Pub. Co., Phila., 1984—, Health Edn. jour., Phila., 1987, Jour. Profl. Nursing, Phila., 1986. Contbr. articles to profl. jours. Mem. Mayor's Commn. on Needs of Women, La., 1984—; 1st v.p., bd. dirs. United Way of Ouachita, La., 1986—. Tandy Corp. grantee, 1986. Mem. Am. Nurses Assn., La. Nurses Assn., Monroe Dist. Nurses Assn. (bd. dirs. 1985—), Internat. Council Women's Health Issues (bd. dirs. 1986—), Assn. for the Advancement Health Edn., Sigma Theta Tau. Office: NE La Univ 700 University Ave Monroe LA 71209-0460

IRVING, AMY, actress; b. Palo Alto, Calif., Sept. 10, 1953; m. Steven Spielberg, Nov. 27, 1985; 1 child, Max Samuel. Student Am. Conservatory Theatre, London Acad. Dramatic Art. Films include Carrie, The Fury, Voices, Honeysuckle Rose, The Competition, Yentl, Mickey and Maude, Rumplestiltskin; TV appearances include: The Rookies, Policewoman, Happy Days, Panache, I'm A Fool, Dynasty, Voices, Once An Eagle, Showtime, 1985, (miniseries) Anastasia: The Mystery of Anna Anderson, 1986; appeared as Juliet in Romeo and Juliet, Seattle Repertory Theatre, 1982-83; appeared on Broadway in Amadeus, 1981-82, Heartbreak House, 1983-84, off Broadway The Road to Mecca, 1988; Office: D Hunter Kimball Parseghian & Rifkin 10100 Santa Monica Blvd Los Angeles CA 90067-4002 *

IRVING, GITTE NIELSEN, educator; b. Copenhagen, Nov. 5, 1954; came to U.S., 1976; d. Sven Aage and Aase (Espersen) Nielsen; m. Richard Frederick Irving, June 5, 1976; children: Erik Christian, Emilie Jessica. BA, U. Iceland, Reykjavik, 1976; MEd, Lesley Coll., 1977. Cert. elem. tchr., spl. edn. tchr., Mass. Spl. edn. aide Brookline (Mass.) Pub. Schs., 1977-78; spl. edn. tchr. Ashland (Mass.) Pub. Schs., 1978-81, Greater Lawrence Ednl. Collaborative, Andover, Mass., 1981-82; owner, dir. Comprehensive Academics, Inc., Winchester, Mass., 1983—; tutor Learning Disabilities and Reading Clinic, Arlington, Mass., 1981-83; guest columnist Winchester Star, 1986; mem. com. early edn. planning Winchester Pub. Schs., 1986, com. missions and social concerns United Meth. Ch., Winchester, 1987, co-chair 1988, adv. council Spl. Edn. Parents, Winchester, 1985—. Editor spl. edn. presch. newsletter, 1985-86. Second v.p. Neighborhood Cooperative Nursery Sch., Winchester, 1986, 88. Home: 12 Stone Ave Winchester MA 01890 Office: Comprehensive Academics 573 Main St Winchester MA 01890

IRWIN, DIANNE E., psychology educator; b. Madison, Wis., July 22, 1946; d. Donald J. and Dorothy R. (Shaw) I. A.A., Valley Coll., 1970; B.A., Calif. State U., San Bernardino, 1972; M.A., Calif. State U., Fullerton, 1974; Ph.D., U.S. Internat. U., 1979. Lectr., instr. Calif. State U.-San Bernardino, 1973, psychometrist, 1974-78, dir. learning ctr., 1974-84; assoc. prof. psychology Glendale (Calif.) Community Coll., 1985—; lectr. Valley Coll., San Bernardino, 1973, Calif. State U., Fullerton, 1974; cons. nat. tests, psychol. corp., Harcourt Brace Jovanovich, Inc., 1985-86; mem. Calif. Statewide Legal Compliance com. instructionally related material review, 1979-84; speaker in field. Editor, author (with Sherman) Writing Tutor's Training Manual, 1985. Mem. Am. Psychol. Assn., Student Personnel Assn., Western Coll. Reading Assn., Western Psychol. Assn., Am. Personnel and Guidance Assn. Co-author: (with L. Sherman) Writers Tutor Training, 1986; contbr. numerous articles to profl. jours. Home: 918 W Edgemont Dr San Bernardino CA 92405 Office: Glendale Coll 1500 N Verdugo Rd Glendale CA 91208

IRWIN, HEATHER MAY, interior designer; b. Troy, N.Y., Feb. 19, 1949; d. Richard Jay and Helen Irma I. Student, SUNY, 1969, New Sch. Contemporary Radio, 1979, Interior Design Soc., 1984. Reporter Capital Newspaper Group, Albany, N.Y., 1969-73; freelance writer Insight Mag., Latham, N.Y., 1973-76; owner, pub. The Daily Woman, Watervliet, N.Y., 1976-79; interior designer Mayfair Home Furnishings, Albany, 1980-85; owner, pres. Wingate House of Design, Albany, 1985—. Pres. Woman's Counseling Collective, Albany, 1977. Mem. Interior Design Soc. (pres. ea. N.Y. chpt. 1986-88). Methodist. Club: Ecology (Mechecsville, N.Y.) (v.p. 1971). Home: 49 Hillcrest Rd Latham NY 12110

IRWIN, MIRIAM DIANNE OWEN, miniature book publisher, writer; b. Columbus, Ohio, June 14, 1930; d. John Milton and Miriam Faith (Studebaker) Owen; m. Kenneth John Irwin, June 5, 1960; 1 child, Christopher Owen Irwin. BS in Home Econs., Ohio State U., 1952, postgrad. in bus. adminstrn., 1961-62. Editorial asst. Am. Home Mag., N.Y.C., 1953-56; salesman Owen Realty, Dayton, Ohio, 1957-58, Clevenger Realty, Phoenix, 1958-59; home economist Columbus and So. Ohio Electric Co., 1959-60; pub. Mosaic Press, Cin., 1977—; owner, Bibelot Book Bindery, 1987—. Author: Lute and Lyre, 1977, Forty is Fine, 1977, Miriam Mouse's Survival Manual, 1977, Miriam Mouse's Costume Collection, 1977, Miriam Mouse's Marriage Contract, 1977, Miriam Mouse, Rock Hound, 1977, Silver Bindings, 1983; editor: Tribute to the Arts, 1984; illustrator: Corals of Pennekamp, 1979. Daytime crew chief Wyoming Life Squad, Ohio, 1966-71. Mem. Internat. Guild Miniature Artisans, Miniature Book Soc. (bd. dirs. 1983—, chairperson 1987-89), Am. Philol. Assn., DAR, Soc. for Promotion of Byzantine Studies, Wyo. Women's Club. Republican. Presbyterian. Avocation: book collecting. Home and Office: 358 Oliver Rd Cincinnati OH 45215

IRWIN, NAN KELLY, real estate executive; b. Lubbock, Tex., May 15; d. Samuel Edgar and Molly (Stratton) Kelly; m. Raulie Lee Irwin, Oct. 6, 1945 (dec.); children—Raulie Lee Jr., Lenora Mae. Grad. Real Estate Inst. Cashier, Humble Oil & Refinery Co. (now Exxon), Ingleside, Tex., 1941-49; Irwin Real Estate, ptnr. Irwin & Irwin Devel. Co., Rockport, Tex., 1955—; sec.-treas. Brashear-Irwin Industries, Inc., 1959-66, Irwin Industries, Inc., 1972-80; v.p. Aransas-San Patricio County Bd Realtors, 1960-61, sec.-treas., 1967-68. Republican. Methodist. Club: Ingleside Woman's (pres. 1954-55). Office: Irwin Properties & Investments Hwy 35 S Rockport TX 78382

IRWIN, NANCY BARBARA, chemical company executive; b. Cleve., Apr. 16, 1944; d. L.M. and Barbara L. (Boer) I.; m. Joseph Wilson Prejean, Jr., June 2, 1979; 1 child, Lawrence Kapaekukui Irwin Prejean. BA, Miami U., Oxford, Ohio, 1965; MBA, Cleve. State U., 1977. Internat. mktg. mgr. The Harshaw Chem. Co., Cleve., 1975-79; regional mgr. AKZO Chemie Americas, Houston, 1980-83; treas. The KIP Co., Cleve., 1983—; cons. in field; speaker, condr. various workshops. Served to capt. WAC, U.S. Army, 1965-72. Mem. 1st Spl. Forces Group (hon.), Am. Soc. Internat. Execs. (SCORE chpt. #33), Ohio Fgn. Commerce Assn., Cleve. Alumnae Panhellenic Endowment Fund Inc. (fund adminstr.), Sigma Kappa (pres. Cleve. chpt.). Episcopalian.

IRWIN, SHAROLYN ANN, state agency administrator; b. Chrisman, Ill., Jan. 26, 1938; d. Daniel Francis Perisho and Jessie Irene (Fulton) Rudisill; m. Thomas Lee Irwin, Apr. 20, 1958; children: Timothy Lee, Sallee Ann, Daniel Jeffrey. Student, Richland Community Coll., 1972—. Head cashier Liberty Loan Corp., Decatur, Ill., 1956-61; credit clk. Ford Motor Credit Corp., Decatur, 1961-72; with Bur. Unemployment Ins. State of Ill., Decatur, 1975-85, claims adjudicator unemployment ins., 1978-80, asst. mgr., 1980-85; consol. mgr. Dept. Employment Security State of Ill., Decatur, 1985—; chmn. Internat. Assn. Personnel in Employment Security, Decatur/Springfield, Ill., 1985-86. Mem. Indsl. and Personnel Relations Assn., Ill. Unemployment Ins. Adjudicators Assn. (past chairperson cen. region 1981-83, chairperson state conv. 1984), Adult Edn. Adv. Bd., Dislocated Workers Adv. Com., Pvt. Industry Council and Planning Sub Com., Decatur Met. C. of C. Republican. Methodist. Home: 2151 Hoyt Dr Decatur IL 62526 Office: Ill Dept Employment Security 347-357 N Main St Decatur IL 62523

ISAAC, TERESA ANN, lawyer, law educator; b. Lynch, Ky., July 3, 1955; d. Samuel Thomas Sr. and Barbara Ann (Thomas) I.; m. James Isaac Lowry IV, Dec. 30, 1978; children: Jacob, Alicyn. BA, Transylvania U., 1976; JD, U. Ky., 1979. Bar: Ky. 1979, U.S. Dist. Ct. (ea. dist.) Ky. 1979, U.S. Ct. Appeals (6th cir.) 1980, U.S. Supreme Ct. 1981, U.S. Ct. Appeals (D.C. cir.) 1984. Sole practice Lexington, Ky., 1979—; asst. atty. Fayette County Prosecutors Office, Lexington, 1986—, prosecutor, 1986-87; judge U. Ky. Trial Adv. Competition, Lexington, 1981; acting dir. Eastern Ky. U. Paralegal Program, Richmond, 1985; legal counsel Ky. Women's Heritage Mus., Inc., 1986—, v.p. 1987. Editor newsletter At Issue, Lexington Forum, 1983-85; pub. The Full Ct. Press, 1986—; author: Sex Equity in Sports Leadership: Implementing the Game Plan in Your Community, 1987. Mem. Human Resources Adv. Bd., Lexington, 1982-85, Ky. Displaced Homemaker Adv. Bd., Lexington, 1982-84, NCAA Final Four Host Com., Lexington, 1985; chmn. Ky. Women's Suffrage Day Celebration, 1986—; project dir. Sports Equity Program A Model for the South, Ky., 1986—; mem. Philharm. Guild, 1986—; chair Ky. Nat. Women in Sports Day Celebration, 1988. Recipient Outstanding Service award Lexington Forum, 1985. Mem. ABA (exec. com. delivery of legal services to women, chair 1987-88, spl. com. on housing and urban devel. law, recipient Silver Key award 1979), AAUW (sec. 1986, state bd. dris. 1987-88) Fed. Bar Assn., Ky. Bar Assn. (bd. of editors 1983-85, mem. Task Force on Gender Bias in Cts. 1987—), Ky. Acad. Trial Lawyers Assn., Am. Soc. for Pub. Adminstrn., Am. Assn. for Paralegal Edn., Nat. Assn. Women Lawyers (brief bank coordinator 1985—), ACLU (chairperson legal panel 1983—), League of Women Voters (voter service com. 1985—), Ky. Women Advocates (treas. 1987—), Leadership Am., Lexington C. of C., Phi Mi (legal advisor 1985—). Democrat. Roman Catholic. Home: 335 Garden Rd Lexington KY 40502 Office: Fayette County Atty PO Box 22163 Lexington KY 40522

ISAAC NASH, EVA MAE, educator; b. Natchitoches Parish, La., July 24, 1936; d. Earfus Will Nash and Dollie Mae (Edward) Johnson; m. Will Isaac Jr., July 1, 1961 (dec. May 1970). BA, San Francisco State U., 1974, MS in Edn., 1979, MS in Counseling, 1979; PhD, Walden U., 1985. Nurse's aide Protestant Episcopal Home, San Francisco, 1957-61; desk clk. Fort Ord (Calif.) Post Exchange, 1961-63; practical nurse Monterey (Calif.) Hosp., 1963-64; tchr. San Francisco Unified Schs., 1974; counselor, instr. City Coll. San Francisco, 1978-79; tchr. Oakland (Calif.) Unified Schs., 1974—; pres. Sch. Adv. Council, Oakland, 1977-78; advt. writer City Coll., San Francisco, 1978; instr. vocat. skill tng., Garfield Sch., Oakland, 1980-81; pub. speaker various ednl. insts. and chs., Oakland, San Francisco, 1982—. Mem. Internat. Reading Assn., Nat. Assn. Female Execs., Am. Personnel and Guidance Assn., Assn. Supervision and Curriculum Devel., Calif. Personnel and Guidance Assn., Phi Delta Kappa. Democrat. Office: Oakland Unified Sch Dist 1025 Second Ave Oakland CA 94606

ISAACS, FLORENCE, writer; b. Bklyn., July 2, 1937; d. Joseph and Sylvia (Tanklow) Satow; m. Harvey A. Isaacs, Sept. 1, 1962; children—Jonathan, Andrew. B.B.A., Baruch Sch., CCNY, 1957. Copywriter Fisher Radio Corp., Long Island City, N.Y., 1957-58, Cosmair Inc., N.Y.C., 1958-59; advt.-promotion mgr. mag. div. Dell Pub. Co., Inc., N.Y.C., 1960-71; free-lance writer specializing in health and medicine, marriage and family, N.Y.C., 1971—, contbr. articles to Reader's Digest, Family Circle, N.Y. Times, N.Y. News Sunday Mag., Family Weekly, Parade, Newsday, Cosmopolitan, Good Housekeeping, Mademoiselle, Rx: Being Well; free-lance pub. relations writer. Mem. membership com. The New Mus., N.Y.C., 1983-84 (activites com. 1987—); mem. fund raising com. Nat. Found. for Ileitis and Colitis, N.Y.C. 1983-84, 1987—. Mem. Am. Soc. Journalists and Authors (mem. exec. bd.).

ISAACS, HELEN COOLIDGE ADAMS (MRS. KENNETH L. ISAACS), artist; b. N.Y.C., Jan. 17, 1917; d. Thomas Safford and Martha (Montgomery) Adams; student Miss Hewett's classes, N.Y.C., Miss Porter's Sch., Farmington, Conn., Fontainbleau (France) Sch. Art and Music, 1935, Art Students League, 1936; m. Kenneth L. Isaacs, Mar. 10, 1949; children—Kenneth Coolidge, Anne Isaacs Merwin. Agt., Child's Gallery, Boston; one-woman shows at Child's Gallery, 3 times exhibited in group shows Allied Artists, N.Y., Boston Arts Festival; portraits of various prominent persons; murals in various public bldgs., Boston, Rochester, N.Y., Pittsfield, Mass., Daytona, Fla.; represented in painting and drawing collections Fogg Mus., Cambridge, Mass. Mem. Colonial Dames Am. Clubs: Colony (N.Y.C.); Chilton (Boston). Home: 68 Beacon St Boston MA 02108

ISAACSON, ARLINE LEVINE, food and beverage/hotel executive; b. Bklyn., Jan. 28, 1946; d. Harry and Sally (Fogelman) Levine; m. Leslie Robert Isaacson, Oct. 31, 1964 (div. July 1970); 1 child, Eric Michael. A.A.S. in Hotel and Restaurant Mgmt., N.Y.C. Tech. Coll., 1983. Restaurant and lounge mgr. Holiday Inn, N.Y.C., 1982-83; mgr. Astors, St. Regis Hotel, N.Y.C., 1983-84; banquet and conf. mgr. Mariner 15 Conf. Ctr., N.Y.C., 1984-85; dir. banquets, confs. and sales Sardi's Restaurant Corp., N.Y.C., 1985-87; dir. catering sales Days Inn Hotel, N.Y.C., 1987—. Dem. vol. Koch Relection Campaign, N.Y.C., 1985. Mem. Food and Beverage Mgrs. Assn. (sec. 1984-88), Roundtable for Women in Food Service (treas. 1986-87), Meeting Planners Internat., Soc. Incentive Travel, Hotel Sales and Mktg. Assn., Internat. Food Service Execs., N.Y.C. Tech. Coll. Alumni Assn. (bd. dirs. 1986—, v.p. 1986-87). Jewish. Avocations: dancing; travel; theatre; gourmet cooking. Home: 1836 E 18th St Brooklyn NY 11229 Office: Days Inn Hotel 440 W 57th St New York NY 10019

ISAACSON, EDITH LIPSIG, civic leader; b. N.Y.C., Jan. 8, 1920; d. I.A. and Bertha (Evans) Lipsig; m. Selian Hebald, June 28, 1940 (dec. Feb. 1959); children: Anne Mandelbaum, Selian Jr.; m. William J. Isaacson, 1975. Student, Radcliffe Coll., 1941; LLB, St. Lawrence U., 1943. Pres. Forest Knolls Corp., N.Y.C., 1960—, Norman Homes Corp., N.Y.C., 1968—; cataloguer Nat. Collection Fine Arts, Smithsonian Instn., 1969-72. Author biographies Am. artists; writer club handbooks. Fellow Pierpont Morgan Library, N.Y.C.; mem. Carnegie Council Ethics Internat. Affairs, founders com. Am. Symphony Orch., N.Y., 1962; nat. sec. Women's Am. Orgn. Rehab. through Tng., 1950; trustee Allergy Found. Am. Mem. Radcliffe Coll. Alumni Assn. (chmn. clubs 1966). Clubs: Harvard (N.Y.C.), Cosmopolitan (N.Y.C.) (bd. govs. 1987—); Radcliffe (pres. Washington chpt. 1969) (pres. N.Y. chpt. 1959, 63, bd. sponsors 1974).

ISADORE, MARJORIE ANNE, contracting company executive; b. New Britain, Conn., June 29, 1945; d. Manuel Martin and Rose Mary (Sorbello) Franco; married; children: Elyse A., Michael A. AA in Acctg., Morse Bus. Coll., 1965. Office mgr. Kay's Trucking, Hartford, Conn., 1964-67; office mgr. Kahn Constrn., Hartford, Conn., 1967-75, realtor, broker, 1975-79; plumbing contractor Aetna Mech. Services, Inc., West Palm Beach, Fla., 1979—. active Palm Beach Round Table, 1983—, Rep. Club Palm Beach, 1983—. Mem. Exec. Women Palm Beach, League Women Voters, Palm West C. of C., Nat. Assn. Women Bus. Owners, Home Builders and Contractors Assn., Nat. Fedn. Independent Businesspeople. Roman Catholic. Club: Glastonbury (Conn.) Jr. Women's. Home: 11630 Anhinga Dr West Palm Beach FL 33414

ISALY, SHARON MARTIN, interior designer, contractor; b. Columbus, Ohio, July 31, 1946; d. John W. and Patricia M. Martin; student in edn. No. Ariz. U., 1964-66; m. Charles W. Isaly, Nov. 5, 1966; children—Jeffrey Scott, Bradley William. Interior designer John Martin Constrn., Phoenix, 1967-72; interior designer Martin Devel. Co., Missoula, Mont., 1972-79; v.p., ptnr. Security-West Devel. Co., Missoula, 1979-82; dir.; pres., owner SMI Interiors, Missoula; Prospect Assos./Devel. Co., Missoula, 1979-82; v.p. Martin Constrn. Co., Phoenix and San Antonio, 1983-86. Vice-pres. C.W. Isaly Corp., Mesa, Ariz., 1983—, Missoula Civic Symphony, 1977-78; bd. dirs. Missoula Children's Theatre, 1977-78. Mem. Am. Soc. Interior Designers, LWV, Delta Delta Delta. Republican. Methodist. Home: 615 W Lawrence Rd Phoenix AZ 85013 Office: 535 S Dobson Rd Mesa AZ 85202

ISEL, DEBRA ANNE, nurse; b. Ft. Worth, Nov. 5, 1956; d. John William and Grace Ann (Murphy) I. BS in Nursing, Tex. Christian U., 1979. RN, Tex. Staff nurse St. Joseph's Hosp., Ft. Worth, 1979-80, Tarrant County Nephrology Ctr., Ft. Worth, 1980-81; staff nurse Providence Hosp., Anchorage, 1981—, asst. mgr. thermal unit, 1984-86, edn. coordinator thermal unit, 1986—, thermal outreach coordinator, 1986—. Mem. Am. Assn. Critical Care Nurses (treas. 1986—), Am. Burn Assn., Alaska Sled Dog and Racing Assn., Sigma Theta Tau. Home: 3041 Brookridge Circle Anchorage AK 99504 Office: Providence Hosp Thermal Unit 3200 Providence Dr Anchorage AK 99508

ISELIN, SALLY CARY, writer; b. Nahant, Mass., June 16, 1915; d. Charles Pelham and Edith Goddard (Roelker) Curtis; m. Lewis Iselin, June 14, 1935; children: Edith Byron, Sarah Morrison. Student, Harvard U., 1933. Editorial asst. sports and fgn. news depts. Newsweek mag., N.Y.C., 1942-45; soc. and non-fiction editor Town & Country Mag., N.Y.C., 1945-48; reporter, researcher Life Mag., N.Y.C., 1948-50; writer-contact CBS, N.Y.C., 1951; fashon editor Women's Home Companion, N.Y.C., 1956; freelance writer. Fund raiser Planned Parenthood, 1935—, Robert Kennedy for Senate, 1964. Democrat. Episcopalian. Club: Colony. Home: Belfast Rd Camden ME 04843

ISELY, MARGARET, nutritional consultant, food stores executive; b. Orion, Ill., Aug. 13, 1921; d. John Henry and Sadie Mae (Durman) Sheesley; m. Henry Philip Isely, June 12, 1948; children—Zephyr, LaRock, Lark, Robin, Kemper, Heather. Student Antioch Coll., 1941-46. Acting dietitian Antioch Coll., Yellow Springs, Ohio, 1942; nutritional cons. Vitamin Cottage, Lakewood, Colo., 1955—; gen. ptnr., mgr. 5 health food stores in Denver area; pres. Nat. Found. for Nutritional Research, Lakewood, 1982—. Mem. Rocky Mountain Nutritional Foods Assn. (pres. Denver 1978-82), Nat. Nutritional Foods Assn. (dir., mem. exec. council 1978-83), Orthomolecular Med. Soc., World Constn. and Parliament Assn. (treas. 1982—, U.S. del. to World Constn. Assembly, Interlaken, Switzerland, 1968, Wolfach, Fed. Republic Germany, 1968, Innsbruck, Austria, 1977, Colombo, Sri Lanka, 1979; U.S. del. to Provisional World Parliament, Brighton, Eng., 1982, New Delhi, India, 1985, Miami Beach, Fla., 1987; mem. Presidium Provisional World Govt., 1987—). Home: 241 Zephyr Ave Golden CO 80401 Office: Vitamin Cottage 8800 W 14th St Lakewood CO 80215

ISENOR, LINDA DARLENE, grocery retailer, marketing professional; b. Calgary, Alta., Can., Oct. 3, 1955; d. Frank Carl and Mavis Ella (Jarnett) Kachmarski; m. Larry Douglas Isenor, Oct. 13, 1973. Grad. high sch., Calgary. Cashier to asst. mgr. G&S Restaurants Balmoral Ltd., Calgary, 1972-74; cashier, supr. Calgary Coop. Assn. Ltd., 1974-75, supr., 1975-78, head cashier, 1978-80, asst. grocery merchandiser, 1980-81, grocery merchandising specialist, 1981-82, grocery procurement specialist, 1982-83, supr. pricing and costing, 1983—. Office: Calgary Coop Assn Ltd, 8818 Macleod Trail, Calgary, AB Canada T2H 0M5

ISHAM, BERNICE JEAN, musician, educator; b. Salem, Oreg., Mar. 30, 1929; d. Earl and Tillie Charlotte (Kildahl) I.; B.Mus., Willamette U., 1950; M.Mus., U. Oreg., 1957, D.M.A., 1976. Tchr. music Taft (Oreg.) High Sch. and Elem. Sch., 1950-56, Beaverton (Oreg.) High Sch., 1956-59, Elmhurst Jr. High Sch., Oakland, Calif., 1959-60; instr. music West Hills Community Coll., Coalinga, Calif., 1960-84; condr.; ch. choir dir.; dir. opera workshop; dir. ann. Christmas madrigal feast. dir. St. Peter the Fisherman Luth. Ch. Choir; part-time music instr. Oreg. Coast Community Coll.; musician, various community orgns. Recipient disting. services citation Sec. Treasury, 1944, community services award Masons, 1974. Mem. Music Assn. Calif. Community Colls. (state sec. 1970-72, sr. v.p. 1972-74), Am. Choral Dirs., Music Educators Nat. Conf., Nat. Assn. Tchrs. of Singing, Delta Kappa Gamma. Lutheran. Home: 3540 NE Surf Dr PO Box 137 Lincoln City OR 97367

ISHII, HELEN MAREKO, nuclear engineering company executive; b. Lexington, Ky., Oct. 1, 1959; d. Washio and Jean Pogue (Gartrell) I. BS in Mktg., U. Ala., 1981. Salesperson The Bed, Inc., Huntsville, Ala., 1981-83; ptnr. Digital Systems, Huntsville, 1984; sales/mktg. Digital Engring., Inc., Huntsville, 1985, tech. librarian, purchasing, adminstrv. support services mgr., 1986—. Presbyterian. Home: 205-1 Utica Pl Huntsville AL 35806 Office: Digital Engring Inc 658 Discovery Dr Huntsville AL 35806

ISKANDER, SUZANNE SHAKIR, financial services executive; b. Khartoum, Sudan, May 7, 1959; came to Can., 1979; d. Shakir and Mary Shabib (Bushara) I. BSc in Math., U. London, 1979. Lic. stock broker Can. Securities Inst. Customer service rep. Royal Bank Can., Toronto, Ont., Can., 1980-84; branch mgr. Deak-Perera, Toronto, 1984-86; regional mgr. Deak Internat., Niagara Peninsula, Ont., Can., 1986-88; v.p. resource ctr. (trading) Deak Internat. Can. Ltd., Toronto, 1988—. Contbr. articles to profl. jours. Mem. Ont. Underwater Council; bd. dirs. Niagara Falls Visitor and Conv. Bur., 1987-88. Mem. Niagara Falls C. of C. (bd. dirs. 1987), Nat. Assn. Underwater Instrs. (asst. instr.). Coptic Orthodox. Club: Diver Down (Toronto) (asst. instr. 1987—). Office: Deak Internat, 1 University Ave, Toronto, ON Canada M5J 2P1

ISLAS-WALTERS, EUGENIA MICHELLE, personnel services executive; b. Farmington, N.Mex., Nov. 2, 1953; d. Eugene Fredrick and Corrine (Wiggins) Islas; m. Robert Whit Waller, June 12, 1982 (div. 1984); children: Joshua Adrian Islas, Michael Justin Waller; m. George Thomas Walters, Dec. 31, 1986. Student, N.Mex. State U., 1973, 85. Restaurant mgr. Far West Services, Newport Beach, Calif., 1974-75; adminstrv. mgr. Pre-Hire Services, Farmington, 1975-79; dist. mgr. Thrifty Rent a Car, Farmington, 1979-80; ops. mgr. Temporarily Yours, Inc., Farmington, 1980-81; pres. E.M.W., Inc./E. Mint, Inc., Farmington, 1981—. Mem. N.Mex. Assn. Personnel Cons. (bd. dirs. 1986-87), Nat. Assn. Personnel Cons., Nat. Assn. Temporary Services, Farmington Women's Network, Farmington C. of Co, Better Bus. Bur. Republican. Roman Catholic. Home: 621 Meseta St Farmington NM 87401 Office: EMW Inc E Mint Inc 653 W Broadway Farmington NM 87401

ISLES, ELEANORA M., educator; b. Trinidad and Tobago, Sept. 11, 1939; came to U.S., 1962; m. Ericson J. Isles, June 12, 1966; children: Erica, Adrian. MS in Nutritional Sci., Tuskegee U., 1974; BS in Food and Nutrition, Howard U., 1966, PhD in Community Nutrition, 1985. Registered dietitian. Instr. Tuskegee (Ala.) U., 1974-76, Morgan State U., Balt., 1976-80, Howard U., Washington, 1981—. Mem. Inter-Am. Caribbean Cultural Orgn., Washington, 1981-85. Mem. Am. Dietitian Assn., D.C. Dietitian Assn., Am. Home Economics Assn. Adventist. Home: 2025 Powder Mill Rd Silver Spring MD 20923

ISRAEL, DONNA ALEXANDER, dietitian, consultant, health promotion company executive; b. Dallas, Feb. 22, 1942; d. James Weldon and Aileen (Morrison) Alexander; m. John Winslow Israel, Dec. 6, 1934; Kelly Susan, Karen Elaine, Dabney Anne, Clifford Winslow, Alexander Kent. BA cum laude, Baylor U., 1964; MEd, North Tex. State U., 1970; PhD, Tex. Women's U., 1982. Lic. profl. counselor, dietitian. Social worker Tex Hosps. and Schs., Austin, Big Springs, 1964-67; coordinated acad.-vocational edn. instr. Big Spring, Richardson (Tex.) Instructional Systems Devel., 1968-74; vocational counselor Richardson Instructional Systems Devel., 1974-76; adminstr. Dallas Community Coll. Dist., 1976-78; research asst., cooperative edn. adminstr. Tex. Women's U., Denton, 1979-82; pres. The Fitness Formula, Inc., Dallas, 1983—; cons. Home Bodies, Dallas, 1985—; task force mem. Am. Heart Assn. Heart at Work, Dallas, 1986—; cons. Tex. State Bd. of Examination for Dietitians, Austin, 1987; instr. Am. Lung Assn., ARC. Author: Diet Modification, 1987; contbr. articles in nutrition and counseling. Mem. Heart at Work Task Force Am. Heart Assn., Dallas, 1986—. Recipient Presdl. scholarship Baylor U., 1964; Cert. of Excellence, Am. Counseling Assn., 1978; Outstanding Service award Dallas Ednl. Counselors Assn., 1975; named one of Outstanding Young Women in Am., 1980. Mem. Am. Dietetic Assn., Dallas Dietetic Assn., Tex. Dietetic Assn., Assn. for Fitness in Bus., Sigma Xi. Home: 3611 Dartmouth Dallas TX 75205 Office: The Fitness Formula 1131 Rockingham Suite 121 Richardson TX 75080

ISRAEL, MARGIE OLANOFF, psychotherapist; b. Atlantic City, Apr. 30, 1927; d. Herman and Mary (Salter) Olanoff; student U. Miami, 1945-46, 50, Am. Acad. Dramatic Arts, 1946-47; B.A. in Psychology cum laude, Hunter Coll., 1970; M.S.W. with honors in fieldwork, Hunter Sch. Social Work, 1972; psychoanalytic tng. N.Y. Soc. Freudian Psychologists, 1965-70,

Manhattan Center for Advanced Psychoanalytic Studies, 1972-74, 76; m. Allan Edward Israel, Sept. 20, 1953; 1 child, Janet. Bd. cert. clin. soc. work, N.Y. Celebrity interviewer Lunchin' with Marge radio show Sta. WFPG, Atlantic City, 1947-48; co-host Steel Pier Midnight radio show, 1949; publicity writer Hy Gardner Astor Hotel, N.Y.C., 1948; writer theatrical interviews Miami (Fla.) Daily News, 1950-51; sec. to exec. dir. Hebrew Old Age Center, Atlantic City, 1951-55; sec. to dir. TV-films and radio Nat. Office, Am. Cancer Soc., N.Y.C., 1959-66, asst. to dir. TV-films and radio, 1966-70; social worker Bellevue Hosp., N.Y.C., 1972-76; field instr. social work N.Y. U., 1975-76; practice psychotherapy, N.Y.C., 1973—. Fellow N.Y. State Soc. Clin. Social Work Psychotherapists, Am. Orthopsychiat. Assn.; diplomate Nat. Assn. Social Workers; mem. Acad. Cert. Social Workers, N.Y. Acad. Scis., Psi Chi. Office: 201 E 28th St Suite 1F New York NY 10016

ISRAEL, NANCY DIANE, lawyer; b. Fall River, Mass., Apr. 20, 1955; d. David Joseph and Charlotte Millicent (Epstein) I. AB magna cum laude, Harvard U., 1976, JD, 1979. Bar: Mass. 1979, N.Y. 1986. Mem. Hale & Dorr, Boston, 1980-83; atty. Harvard U., Cambridge, Mass., 1983-85, asst. gen. counsel internat. div. Arthur Young and Co., N.Y.C. and Boston, 1985—; chmn. 21st, 22d ann. practical skills seminar, curriculum com., Mass. Continuing Legal Edn., Boston, 1985-86, Ctr. House, Inc., Boston, 1980-86, also bd. dirs. Mem. editorial bd. Mass. Lawyers Weekly, 1988. Mem. energy and environ. issues task force Dukakis gubernatorial campaign, Boston, 1982, southeastern Mass. coordinator, 1974, mem. nat. fin. com. Dukakis Presdl. Campaign, 1987—; bd. dirs. nominating com. Mass. Council for Pub. Justice, Boston, 1971-76; mem. ad hoc com. Coalition for Better Judges, Boston, 1971-72; judge N.E. and Mid.-Atlantic Regionals of Jessup Moot Court Competition, 1988. Named an Outstanding Young Woman of Am., 1986. Fellow Mass. Bar Found. (mem. nominating com. 1988), Am. Bar Found.; mem. Mass. Bar Assn. (computer coll. steering com. 1984-86, del. bd. dels. 1984-87, chmn. young lawyers div. 1986-87, chmn. bus. law sect. 1987-88, commn. on delivery of legal services 1988, exec. com. 1985-86, commn. on professionalism 1985—, chmn. elect young lawyers com. 1987, chmn. young lawyers com. 1988, Silver Gavel award for outstanding leadership 1986), Am. Corp. Counsel Assn. (chmn. nonprofit counsel com. 1983-85, exec. bd. dirs. young lawyers com. 1985—, chmn. young lawyers com. 1988), ABA (exec. council young lawyers div., dist. rep. 1984-86, Mass. del. to ABA Ho. of Dels. 1987—, bd. dirs. continuing legal edn. young lawyers div. 1985-87, Barrister bd. dirs. 1987—, sect. council internat. law sect. 1987—, affiliate outreach team young lawyers div. 1986—), Radcliffe Alumnae Assn., Boston Bar Assn. (bd. dirs. vol. lawyers project 1985—), Women's Bar Assn., Mass. Assn. Women Lawyers, Am. Judicature Soc., Internat. Bar Assn., Internat. Law Soc. (Am. branch), Interests on Lawyers Trust Accounts (mem. implementation com. 1987—). Clubs: Harvard (Boston Schs. and Scholarships com.), Radcliffe, New Bedford Yacht. Office: Office of Gen Counsel Arthur Young & Co 277 Park Ave New York NY 10172

ISRAEL, VIVIANNE WINTERS, nurse; b. Inglewood, Calif., Mar. 29, 1954; d. Robert Reynolds and Annie Laura (Ripley) Winters; m. Richard Clyde Israel, May 30, 1976 (div. 1985); 1 child, Tiffany Carissa. RN, El Camino Coll., Torrance, Calif. Fashion model Los Angeles, 1957-70; critical care nurse Northridge Med. Ctr., Reseda, Calif., 1977-80, St. Joseph Med. Ctr., Burbank, Calif., 1980-81; exotic animal handler, trainer Gentle Jungle, Corona, Calif., 1980-81; coronary care nurse Mercy Med. Ctr., Reading, Calif., 1981-85; critical care nurse Norrell/CCSI, Los Angeles, 1985-87, St., 1986—. Vol., co-dir. edn. Wildlife Way Sta., Little Tajunga, Calif., 1987—. Mem. Pubs. Mktg. Assn., Book Publicists of So. Calif., Book Publicists of San Diego, Execs. of S. Bay, Nat. Assn. Female Execs., Womens Internat. Network, Walters Internat. Speakers Bur., Internat. Assn. of Ind. Pubs. Baptist. Home: 304 S Miraleste Dr Unit 29 San Pedro CA 90732 Office: Pacific Coast Publishers 710 Silver Spur Rd Suite 126 Rolling Hills Estates CA 90274

ISRAELOV, RHODA, financial planner, writer; b. Pitts., May 20, 1940; d. Joseph and Fannie (Friedman) Kreinen; divorced; children—Jerome, Arthur, Russ. BS in Hebrew Edn. Herzlia Hebrew Tchr.'s Coll., N.Y.C., 1961; BA in English Language and Lit. U. Mo.-Kansas City, 1965. Cert. Fin. Planner, Chartered Life Underwriter. Tchr. Hebrew, various schs., 1961-79; ins. agt. Conn. Mut. Life, Indpls., 1979-81; fin. planner Shearson, Lehman Hutton, Inc., Indpls., 1981—, v.p., 1986—; instr. for mut. fund licensing exams. Pathfinder Securities Sch., Indpls., 1983—; cons. channel 6 News, 1984-85. Weekly fin. columnist Indpls. Bus. Jour., 1982—; bi-weekly fin. columnist Jewish Post & Opinion, 1982—. Recipient Gold Medal award Personal Selling Power, 1987; named Bus. Woman of Yr. Network of Women in Bus., 1986. Mem. Inst. Cert. Fin. Planners, Nat. Assn. Life Underwriters, Women's Life Underwriters' Conf. (treas. Ind. chpt. 1982, v.p. chpt. 1983), Internat. Assn. Fin. Planners (v.p. Ind. chpt. 1983—, bd. dirs.), Am. Soc. Chartered Life Underwriters, Women's Life Underwriters Conf., Nat. Council Jewish Women, Nat. Assn. Profl. Saleswomen (nat. bd. dirs.), Nat. Speakers Assn. (pres. Ind. chpt.), Registry Fin. Planning Practitioners. Lodge: Toastmasters (chpt. ednl. v.p. 1985—), Soroptimists (bd. dirs.). Avocations: piano; folk and square dancing; needlepoint; theatre. Office: E F Hutton 1 American Sq Suite 180 Indianapolis IN 46282

ISREAL, LESLEY LOWE, political consultant; b. Phila., July 21, 1938; d. Herman Albert and Frances (Segal) Lowe; m. Fred Isreal, Dec. 18, 1960; children: Herman Allen, Sanford Lawrence. BA, Smith Coll., 1959. Dir. media advance Humphrey for Pres., Washington, 1967-68, dir. politic. intelligence, 1972; dir. scheduling Bayh for Pres., Washington, 1971; spl. asst. Jackson for Pres., Washington, 1975-76; coordinator nat. labor Kennedy for Pres., Washington, 1979-80; sr. v.p. The Kamber Group, Washington, 1981-87; pres., chief exec. officer Politics, Inc., Washington, 1987—; bd. dirs. The Kamber Group, Washington. Pres. Jewish Community Ctr. of Greater Washington, Rockville, Md., 1981-83; bd. mgrs. Adas Israel Synagogue, 1981-88; mem. Dem. Charter Commn., 1972-73, Dem. Del. Selection Commn., 1983-84, Nat. Dem. Club, 1986—. Recipient Spl. Service award Jewish Community Ctr., 1984. Mem. Am. Assn. Politic. Cons. Jewish. Home: PO Box 69 Royal Oak MD 21662 Office: Politics Inc 1920 L St NW Washington DC 20036

ISSEKS, EVELYN, retired educational administrator; b. N.Y.C., Feb. 9, 1925; d. David S. and Sadye (Jaffa) Sher; m. Jack Isseks, Dec. 22, 1946; children: Frederick Edward, Robert Nathan. BEd, SUNY, Oneonta, 1947; MS, SUNY, New Paltz, 1967, CAS, 1975. Tchr. Middletown (N.Y.) Sch. Dist., 1947-67; asst. prin. Monroe-Woodbury Sch. Dist., Central Valley, N.Y., 1967-69, prin., 1969-85; mem. Middletown Bd. of Edn., 1986—. Membership chair Horton Hosp. Aux., Middletown, 1947-49; pres. Middletown Players Club, 1950s; chair ward drive Middletown Cancer Soc., 1950's; mem. exec. com. local PTA, 1967-85; life mem. Nat. PTA; mem. Childhood Services Cons. Com., 1983—, Middletown Bd. Edn., 1986—; bd. dirs. Orange County Mental Health Bd, 1985-86. Recipient Nat. Disting. Service award PTA, 1983. Mem. Middletown Tchrs. Assn. (treas. 1965-67), Phi Delta Kappa (charter; membership com.). Democrat. Jewish. Club: Women's Univ. Home: 37 Watkins Ave Middletown NY 10940

ISTOMIN, MARTA, performing arts administrator; b. P.R., Nov. 2, 1936; d. Aguiles and Angelica M. (Martinez) Montanez; m. Pablo Casals, Aug. 3, 1957 (dec. 1973); m. Eugene Istomin, Feb. 15, 1975. Student, Mannes Coll. Music, N.Y.C., 1950-54; Mus.D. (hon.), World U., P.R., 1972; L.H.D. (hon.), Marymount Coll., 1975; D (hon.), U. P.R., 1984, Dickinson Coll., Carlisle, Pa., 1986. Prof. cello Conservatory Music, San Juan, P.R., 1961-64; vis. prof. cello Curtis Inst., Phila., 1974-75; co-chmn. bd., music dir. Casals Festival, 1974-77; artistic dir. John F. Kennedy Center for Performing Arts, Washington, 1980—; dir. Harcourt Brace Jovanovich, Inc., N.Y.C., cons. Latin Am. ednl. projects. Trustee Marlboro Sch. Music and Festival; trustee Marymount Sch., N.Y.C., World U. Recipient Puerto Rican Fedn. Women's Clubs award, 1967; award for cultural achievements City of San Juan, 1975; Nat. Conf. Puerto Rican Women award, 1975; Casita Maria medal for outstanding contbns. to culture N.Y.C., 1978; Outstanding Contbns. Performing Arts in Nation's Capitol award, 1983; Family Place Outstanding Community Service award, 1986; Mayor's Excellence in Service Arts award, Washington, 1986; Nat. Fedn. Music Clubs citation, 1987; named Outstanding Woman of Yr. P.R., 1975; Woman of Achievement Sta. WETA-TV, Washington, 1981; Order of Isabella the Cath. govt. Spain, 1986; Officer, Order Arts and Letters govt. France, 1986; Officer's Cross Order Merit govt. Fed. Republic Germany, 1987. Roman Catholic. Office: John F Kennedy Ctr for Performing Arts Washington DC 20566

ITTELSON, MARY ELIZABETH, management consultant; b. Dayton, Ohio; d. Richard W. and Lois (Koblitz) I.; m. Richard Carl Tuttle. BA, NYU, 1979; MBA, Stanford U., 1985. Dir., choreographer Premiers Dance Theatre, N.Y.C., 1976-78; exec. dir. Crossroads Inc., N.Y.C., 1978-79; asst. prof. dance Northwestern U., Evanston, 1979-83; assoc. McKinsey & Co., Inc., Chgo., 1985—. Choreographer: (dance) In Three Places, 1977, Garland Epitaphium, 1981, Sir Gawain and the Green Knight, 1982, Little Children Lost, 1983. Am. Dance Festival fellow, 1980. Office: McKinsey & Co Inc 2 First Nat Plaza Chicago IL 60611

ITURRALDE, IRAIDA, writer, poet; b. Havana, Cuba, Jan. 28, 1953; came to U.S., 1962; d. Fernando Alfonso and Iraida (Bustillo) I.; m. Robert Joseph Loizzo, Dec. 7, 1985. BA, St. Peter's Coll., Jersey City, 1972; cert. in soc. sem., U. Madrid, 1973; MA in Politics, NYU, 1975; postgrad., Columbia U., 1976-81. Asst. program coordinator Met. Mus. Art, N.Y.C., 1973-76; instr. polit. sci. N.Y. Inst. Tech., Old Westbury, 1976-78, Touro Coll., N.Y.C., 1978-84; sr. cons. Internat. Rescue Com., West New York, N.J., 1984—; v.p. Giralt Editorial, N.Y.C., 1985—; panelist Mid-Am. Conf. Hispanic Lit., Boulder, Colo., 1986; founding mem., organizer N.Y.C. I & II Latin Am. Book Fair, N.Y.C., 1985-87; del. Internat. Poetry Biennial, Belgium, 1984, 86, Pablo Neruda Internat. Writers' Congress, Dominican Republic, 1983, Internat. Conf. Hispanic-Am. Writers, Venezuela, 1981. Author: (poetry) The Book of Josaphat, 1982, Hubo La Viola, 1979; co-editor lit.jour. Lyra, 1986—; editor-in-chief NYU lit. rev. Romanica, 1975-80; contbr. numerous writings to journs., anthologies, bibliographies in Europe, Latin Am., U.S., 1971—. Cintas Poetry fellow, 1982-83; grantee Mid-Atlantic States Arts Consortium, 1984, Ford Found., 1980. Mem. Emporium Assn. Writers Artists (pres. 1976-78), Assn. Hispanic Arts, J.M. Heredia Artistic Lit. Guild (v.p. 1978-82). Clubs: Latin Am. (pres. 1970-72), St. Thomas More Polit. Sci. (Jersey City) (sec. 1968-70). Home: 6040 Blvd East (26-H) West New York NJ 07093 Office: Giralt Editorial Inc PO Box 450 Times Sq Sta New York NY 10108

IVANAJ, DRITA A., computer systems and information professional, consultant; b. Novara, Italy, June 15, 1933; came to U.S., 1952; d. Martin and Giuseppina (Pogliotti) I. Sci. degree, Sci. Lyceum, Mortara, Italy, 1951; B.A., Hunter Coll., 1960; certs. in Mgmt. Devel. Program, Assn. Systems Mgmt., 1974-85; spl. cert. IBM Systems Sci. Inst., 1982. Cert. systems profl. 1986. With Fiat U.S., N.Y.C., 1954-69; program analyst Columbia U., N.Y.C., 1969-71, project leader, 1971-74, DP ops. mgr., 1974-79, mgr. adminstrv. systems control ops., 1979-83, adminstrv. and planning mgr., 1983-85, mgr. computer ctr., 1985—. Author procedural and operational manuals for computer installations, 1982-83, research projects reports depts., 1984-85. Mem. Assn. Systems Mgmt. (research chairperson 1982-83, pres.-elect 1983-84, pres. 1984-85, long-term planning chair 1985-86), World Future Soc. (sec. 1982-83, bd. dirs. 1984), Am. Mgmt. Assn., Assn. Computer Operator Mgrs., Nat. Assn. Female Execs. Republican. Roman Catholic. Office: Columbia U Ctr Computing Activities 119 th St and Broadway New York NY 10027

IVANJACK, JOAN EDGEKOSKI, health care official, soup company executive; b. Mt. Vernon, Wash., Apr. 1, 1941; d. Albert Theodore and Lillian (Ostrom) Edgekoski; m. Allen John Ivanjack, Oct. 5, 1963; children: Susan Elaine, Robert Allen. Student, Everett Community Coll., 1975. Sec., bookkeeper, office mgr. Gen. Hosp. Everett (Wash.), 1960-62; acctg. clk. Marine Corps Exchange, Twenty Nine Palms, Calif., 1962-63; personnel sec. Hughes Aircraft Co., Culver City, Calif., 1963-64; playground supr. Everett Sch. Dist., 1972-74; payroll asst. Gen. Hosp. Med. Ctr., Everett, 1974-77; bus. mgr. Channing Phys. Therapy, Everett, 1977—; owner, mgr. Joan E. Ivanjack Unltd. (Hill O'Beans Soup Co.), Everett, 1987—. Author, editor: Credit the Cook, 1985. First v.p. Madison Sch. PTA, Everett, 1970-71; fundraising chmn. Navy League U.S., Everett, 1985-87; v.p. West Point Parents Club Wash., 1985-86; vol. Everett Community Schs., 1986—. Recipient Golden Acorn award Madison Sch., 1971. Mem. Credit Woman Internat.: Credit Profls. (pres. 1983-84, 87—, Woman of Yr. award 1985), Beta Sigma Phi (pres. Everett chpt. 1973-74, 77-78, Girl of Yr. awrad 1974, 77, Sweetheart 1974, 78). Republican. Roman Catholic. Lodge: Zonta (Everett) (1st v.p. 1988—). Office: Channing Phys Therapy 4220 Hoyt Ave Everett WA 98203

IVENS, J(ESSIE) LOREENA, science editor, writer; b. nr. Mt. Carmel, Ill., Apr. 5, 1922; d. Elisher and Gertrude Arletta (McKibben) Moudy; m. Creighton Carl Webb, Dec. 24, 1946 (dec. 1950); m. 2d, Ralph Wilson Ivens, Sept. 30, 1950. B.S., U. Ill.-Urbana-Champaign, 1945, M.S., 1947. Instr. rhetoric U. Ill.-Urbana-Champaign, 1947-48, asst. editor Inst. Aviation, 1950-51; instr. English-journalism Ill. State U., 1948-50; newspaper editor Chanute AFB, Rantoul, Ill., 1951-60; tech. editor Ill. State Water Survey, Champaign, 1960-80, head communications unit, 1980-87, scientist emerita; interim exec. dir. Soc. Ill. Sci. Surveys, 1984. Assoc. editor Man-Made Lakes: Their Problems and Environmental Effects, 1973; author, co-author, editor NSF reports, Water Survey Report, 1977, 81, 83. Served with USNR, 1943-44. Recipient YWCA Achievement award, 1984; Rotary Paul Harris fellow, 1983. Mem. Soc. Tech. Communications, Nat. League Am. Pen Women, AAAS, Women in Communications. Republican. Club: Altrusa Internat. (past pres., past dist. sec.). Home: 802 S Busey St Urbana IL 61801

IVENS, KATHY, marketing consultant, writer; b. Phila., July 23, 1941; d. Irving and Marie (Fred) L.; m. Bernard Ivens, Jan. 31, 1960 (div. Nov. 1975); children: Deborah, Beverly, Judith; m. Harvey H. Klein, May 22, 1976. Student, Temple U., 1959-60. Exec. producer CBS Sta. WCAU-TV, Phila., 1981-83, mktg. mgr., 1983-84; pvt. practice polit. cons. Phila., 1980—, pvt. practice mktg. cons., free-lance writer, 1984—. Contbr. articles to profl. jours. Sec. Phila. Com. on City Policy, 1980—. Democrat.

IVENS, MARY SUE, microbiologist, mycologist; b. Maryville, Tenn., Aug. 23, 1929; d. McPherson Joseph and Sarah Lillie (Hensley) I.; B.S., E. Tenn. State U., 1949; M.S. (NIH research trainee), Tulane U. Sch. Medicine, 1963; Ph.D., La. State U. Sch. Medicine, 1966; postgrad. Oak Ridge Inst. Nuclear Studies, Emory U. Sch. Medicine. Dir. microbiol. and mycol. labs. Lewis-Gale Hosp., Roanoke, Va., 1953-56; research mycologist Ctrs. Disease Control, Atlanta, 1957-60; research assoc. La. State U. Sch. Med., 1963-66, instr. medicine, 1966-72, clin. prof., 1972—; dir. mycology lab, La. State U. Sch. Med., 1963-72; lectr. Sch. Dentistry, La. State U. Med. Ctr., 1968-70; assoc. prof. natural scis. Dillard U., New Orleans, 1972—; assoc. Marine Biol. Lab., Woods Hole, Mass., 1978—; cons. in field. Commr. WHO conf. on center for Mycotic sera 1969; chmn. Gold Medal Award Com. Sigma Xi, 1978; mem. La. assn. defense counsel expert witness bank, 1985—; Bd. dirs. Girl Scouts Council La., Community Relationships Greater New Orleans, Zoning Bd. River Ridge (La.); mem. exec. bd. River Ridge Civic Assn., 1982—, sec., 1982-84; chmn. personnel bd. Riverside Bapt. Ch., River Ridge. Recipient Rosicrucian Humanitarian award, 1981; Macy fellow, MBL, Woods Hole, 1978-79; grantee NSF, NIH; diplomate Am. Bd. Microbiology. Mem. Internat. Soc. Human and Animal Mycology, Med. Mycological Soc. Am., Am. Soc. Microbiology (nat. com. on membership 1983—), AAAS, Nat. Inst. Sci., Sigma Xi. Author articles in field. Home: 408 Berclair Ave New Orleans LA 70123 Office: Dillard U Div Natural Sci New Orleans LA 70122

IVERSON, KAREN MARIE, lawyer; b. Urbana, Ill., June 16, 1946; d. Leroy Cook and Evelyn Mae (Wright) I.; m. Daniel Brook Bartlett, Feb. 16, 1980. B.A., Stephens Coll., 1968; J.D., U. Mo., 1972. Adminstrv. asst. U. Mo., Columbia, 1968-69; asst. atty. gen. State of Mo., Jefferson City, 1972-77; assoc. Lathrop, Koontz & Norquist and predecessor firms, Kansas City, Mo., 1977-83, ptnr., 1983—; curator Stephens Coll., Columbia, 1973-76, 77—. Bd. dirs. Univ. Assocs., Kansas City, Mo., 1983-86. Named Outstanding Woman of Yr., Mo. Bus. and Profl. Women, 1974. Mem. ABA, Mo. Bar, Kansas City Bar Assn. Republican. Office: Lathrop Koontz & Norquist 2345 Grand Ave Suite 2600 Kansas City MO 64108

IVERSON, SUZANNE, publishing executive; b. Chgo., Dec. 13, 1937; d. Joseph Francis Winkes and Edna Mary (Paulauskis) Burke; m. Michael Gavin Nolan, June 1, 1960 (div. Nov. 1970); m. Robert Nels Iverson, Nov. 14, 1970; 1 stepchild: Deborah Leah Koves. Grad. high sch., Phoenix. Payroll clk. Acme Steel, Chgo., 1964-66; purchasing agent Whiting Corp., Harvey, Ill., 1966-67, shipping clk. Rollenex Corp., Chgo., 1967-69; sec. Encyclopedia Britannica, Chgo., 1969-78, exhibits mgr., 1978—, prin. The Mud Hut Ceramic Studio, Chgo., 1980—. Mem. Nat. Assn. for Female Execs., Health Care Exhibitors Assn., Trade Show Bur., Internat. Ceramic Assn., Town and Country Ceramic Assn. (sec. 1982-83). Republican. Roman Catholic. Office: Encyclopedia Britannica USA 310 S Michigan Ave Chicago IL 60604

IVES, ADRIENE DIANE, real estate executive; b. Washington, Oct. 6, 1951; d. Edwin Forrest and Carolyn Elizabeth (Wray) Warner; m. Perry Nelson Ives, May 12, 1972; children: Jesse Warner, James Robert. BS, U. Md., 1973. Tchr. Charles County (Md.) Bd. Edn., 1973-83, Broad Creek Day Sch., Ft. Washington, Md., 1983-85; sales counselor L.K. Farrall, Ltd., Camp Springs, Md., 1985—; tchr. Christian Children's Ministry, Washington, 1982-83; bd. dirs. Nat. Plumbing Supply, Inc., Washington; v.p., bd. dirs. Warner Corp., Washington, 1982-83. Bd. dirs. Broad Creek County Day Sch., Ft. Washington, 1982-83. Recipient Citizenship award Prince Georges County Police, Forestville, Md., 1986. Mem. Nat. Assn. Realtors, Md. Assn. Realtors (CRS award 1986). Republican. Mem. Christian Ch. (Disciples of Christ). Office: LK Farrall Ltd Realtors 6339 Allentown Rd Camp Springs MD 20746

IVEY, JUDITH, actress; b. El Paso, Tex., Sept. 4, 1951; d. Nathan Aldean and Dorothy Lee (Lewis) I. B.S., Ill. State U., 1973. Actress plays in Chgo., N.Y.C.: The Sea, 1974, The Goodbye People, The Moundbuilders, Oh, Coward, 1977-78, Bedroom Farce, 1979, Dusa, Fish, Stas and Vi, 1980, Piaf, 1980-81, The Dumping Ground, 1981, The Rimers of Eldritch, 1981, Pastorale, 1982, Two Small Bodies, 1982, Second Lady, 1983, Hurlyburly, 1984; Broadway plays: Steaming, 1982-83, Blithe Spirit, 1987; films include: Harry and Son, 1984, The Lonely Guy, 1984, The Woman in Red, 1984, Brighton Beach Memoirs, 1986, Hello Again, Sister Sister; TV films include: The Shady Hill Kidnapping, Dixie Changing Habits, We Are The Children. Winner Tony award 1983 (for Steaming), 85 (for Hurlyburly). Office: care Triad Artists Inc 10100 Santa Monica Blvd 16th Floor Los Angeles CA 90067 *

IVEY, KAY ELLEN, state educational agency administrator; b. Repton, Ala., Oct. 15, 1944; d. Boardman Nettles and Barbara Elizabeth Ivey. BS, Auburn U., 1967; cert. in mktg., U. Colo.; cert. in banking, U. South Ala. Tchr., coach forensics Rio Linda (Calif.) High Sch., 1968-69; asst. v.p. Mchts. Nat. Bank, Mobile, Ala., 1970-79; cabinet officer Office of the Gov., State of Ala., Montgomery, 1979-81; reading clk. Ala. Ho. Reps., Montgomery, 1981-82; exec. v.p. St. Margaret's Hosp. Found., Montgomery, 1982-85; asst. to exec. dir., nat. chmn. for govt. relations and communications Ala. Commn. Higher Edn., Montgomery, 1985—; owner, cons. Ivey Enterprises, Montgomery, 1982—; speaker in field. Editor (audio-visual presentation) What Price Freedom (award of Excellence), 1976, St. Margaret's Hosp. Heart tabloid, 1983. Mem. adv. bd. Sch. Bus. Auburn U., 1980-83; candidate Ala. State Auditor, 1982; sec. Ala. div. Am. Cancer Soc., 1985—; bd. dirs. Ala. Girl's State Sch., 1983-85, Stetson Hoedown Rodeo Queen's Pageant, Montgomery, 1986—; bd. trustees Sheriff's Boys and Girls Ranches. Mem. Indsl. Developers Ala., Young Men's Bus. Orgn., Pub. Relations Council Ala. (bd. dirs. 1976-82), DAR (state chmn. 1985-86), Alpha Gamma Delta (disting. citizen award 1986). Republican. Baptist. Home: 609 Thorm Pl Montgomery AL 36106

IVIE, DOROTHY ANNE, city clerk, realtor; b. Richmond, Ky., Oct. 26, 1941; d. David Pryse and Eleanor Henry (Best) Azbill; m. Thomas Garner Ivie, Sept. 10, 1960; children—Karen Elaine, Kathleen Margaret, David Reid. A.A., Eastern Ky. U., 1960; B.A., No. Ky. U., 1984. Lic. real estate broker, Ky. Reporter, Campbell Co. News, Newport, Ky., 1975-76; fin. clk. City of Ft. Thomas, Ky., 1976-79, city clk., 1979—; realtor assoc. Jim Huff Realty, Highland Heights, Ky., 1982-88; realtor assoc. Matt Franck Realtors, Ft. Thomas, 1988—. Poet, writer anthology pamphlet Collage (Poet of Yr. award 1975). Editor, writer: Mcpl. News, Cannon Cues, From the Fountain. Treas., Ft. Thomas Jr. Woman's Club, 1972-73; chmn. com. Youth Haven Guild, Ft. Thomas, 1973-74; sec. Ky. Prof. Firefighters, 1983-87. Mem. Ky. Mcpl. Clks. Assn., Ft. Thomas Heritage League (sec. 1983-85), Internat. Inst. Mcpl. Clks. (pub. relations com. 1985—), Kenton Boone Bd. Realtors, Cambell County Bd. Realtors, Democrat. Methodist. Club: Circle #11 (Ft. Thomas). Lodge: Order of Eastern Star. Avocations: swimming; golfing; writing. Home: 67 Stacy Ln Fort Thomas KY 41075 Office: City of Fort Thomas 130 N Ft Thomas Ave Fort Thomas KY 41075

IVRY, PATRICIA W., social worker, educator; b. N.Y.C., Sept. 9, 1950; d. Irving and Rose (Lubin) Weisman; m. Robert Jonathan Ivry, Jan. 7, 1973; children: Elizabeth Jae, Gregory Matthew. BA in English, Goucher Coll., Towson, Md., 1972; MSW, U. Md., 1974; postgrad., CUNY. Cert. social worker. Community relations specialist United Way of Cen. Md., Balt., 1974-75; community organizer N.W. Balt. Corp., 1975-77; community relations assoc. Balt. Jewish Community Relations Council, 1977-80; prof. social work Western Conn. State U., Danbury, 1980—; community resource cons. Rotondo Real Estate, Katonah, N.Y., 1986—. Bd. dirs. Katonah Village Improvement Soc., 1981—, Ahome, Bedford, N.Y., 1985—; chair Katonah Hist. Preservation Com., 1981-85, Katonah Neighborhood Preservation Area Adv. Com., 1987; mem. allocations com. United Way of North Fairfield County, Danbury, 1987—, Katonah-Lewisboro Bd. Edn. Mem. Nat. Assn. Social Workers, Council on Social Work Edn., Am. Assn. Univ. Profs., Assn. Baccalaureate Social Work Educators (house of dels 1987). Democrat. Jewish. Office: Western Conn State U 181 White St Danbury CT 06810

IWAMOTO, COREEN AKIKO, advertising executive; b. Honolulu, Oct. 11, 1959; d. Douglas Masao and Betty Masako (Munesue) I. BBA, U. Hawaii, 1981. Mktg. coordinator Am. Savs. & Loan Assn., Honolulu, 1981-83; acct. coordinator Bernard Hodes Advertising, Palo Alto, Calif., 1983-86, account coordination supr., 1986—. Sunday Sch. tchr. Kaimuki Evang. Ch., Honolulu, 1977-81, bd. deacons, 1981-83. Mem. Phi Eta Sigma (activities officer 1979-80, pres. 1980-81), Alpha Lambda Delta. Democrat. Congregationalist. Home: 1760 California St Apt #11 Mountain View CA 94041 Office: Bernard Hodes Advt 1101 Embarcadero Rd Palo Alto CA 94303

IWANCHUK, ROXANA, programmer, analyst; b. Cleve., Nov. 28, 1958; d. William and Nadia (Romaniuk) I. BS, Bowling Green State U., 1981; MBA, DePaul U., 1983. Jr. programmer Cardinal Fed. Savs. & Loan Assn., Cleve., 1981-82; assoc. programmer DeCarlo, Paternite & Assocs., Inc., Independence, Ohio, 1983-84, programmer, analyst, 1984-87, sr. programmer, analyst, 1987—. Mem. Nat. Assn. Female Execs., Beta Gamma Sigma. Orthodox. Office: DeCarlo Paternite & Assocs Inc Independence OH 44131

IZENOUR, CHRISTINE, lighting designer; b. San Antonio, Jan. 22, 1949; d. Charles Stevens and Elizabeth Christine (Lien) I. AA in Fine Arts, Pensacola (Fla.) Jr. Coll., 1970; BA in Metaphysics, Am. Nat. Inst., Calabasas, Calif., 1986; Bachelor Interdisciplinary Studies, U. South Fla., 1983. Sr. stage operator Walt Disney World, Orlando, Fla., 1971-74; lighting designer Ch. St. Sta., Orlando, 1974-76; prodn. asst. Quinn Martin Prodns., Hollywood, Calif., 1977-79; lighting designer Walt Disney Prodns., Epcot, Fla., 1979-83; design engr. Hubert Wilke, Inc., North Hollywood, Calif., 1984-86; researcher, writer Am. Nat. Inst., 1986-87; freelance designer, writer, Glendale, Calif., 1986-88, Santa Monica Mountain Conservancy, Malibu, Calif., 1988—. Columnist Westar Courier newspaper, 1986. Water safety instr. ARC, Ft. Walton Beach, Fla., 1966-76; vol. Cerebral Palsy Telethons, Orlando, 1974-75; co-founder Cathedral Players, Orlando, 1975; marshal Olympic Torch Run, Los Angeles, 1984. Fellow Nat. Thespian Soc., 1967. Mem. Nat. Assn. Female Execs., Phi Kappa Phi. Republican. Home: 427-B Raymond Ave Glendale CA 91201 Office: 3700 Solstice Canyon Rd Malibu CA 90265

IZZO, FRANCES SUSAN, nursing educator; b. Glen Cove, N.Y., Aug. 11, 1947; d. Joseph Lawrence and Angeline Marie (DeMaio) Belfiore; m. Joseph May, 13, 1979 (div. May 1983). A.A.S., Nassau Community Coll., 1968; B.S.N., Adelphi U., 1973, M.S.N., 1978. Staff nurse, asst. head nurse Community Hosp., Glen Cove, N.Y., 1965-77; nurse practitioner St. Francis Hosp., Roslyn, N.Y., 1978-81; instr. nursing Molloy Coll., Rockville Centre, N.Y., 1982-85; adj. faculty Adelphi U., Garden City, 1975-82; adj. faculty

Nassau Community Coll., 1981-85, asst. prof. nursing, 1985—; cons., instr. continuing edn. SUNY-Farmingdale/N.Y. State Nurses Assn. Dist. 14, Bklyn., 1981—. Corr. sec. Glen Cove Republican Club, 1979-81. N.Y. State Regents scholar, 1965. (USPHS trainee, 1972-73, 77-78); chairperson nursing edn. com. Nassau County chpt. Am. heart Assn., also bd. dirs. Mem. N.Y. State Nurses Assn., Alpha Omega Sigma, Theta Tau. Roman Catholic. Contbr.: Assess Test, 1982-88. Office: Nassau Community Coll Dept Nursing Garden City NY 11530

JACK, NANCY RAYFORD, electronics company executive; b. Hughes Springs, Tex., June 23, 1939; d. Vernon Lacy and Virginia Ernestine (Turner) Rayford; m. Kermit E. Hundley, Dec. 19, 1979; 1 child by previous marriage: James Bradford Jack, III. C.B.A., Keller Grad. Sch. Mgmt., 1980; cert. in acctg, Harper Coll., 1972, cert. in corp. law and tax law, paralegal, 1973. Sr. sec. Gould, Inc., Rolling Meadows, Ill., 1971-73; staff asst. Gould, Inc., 1973-74, asst. sec., 1974-77, corp. sec., 1977—, v.p., 1985—; sec. numerous subs. Recipient cert. of leadership YWCA Met. Chgo., 1975. Mem. Am. Soc. Corp. Secs., Midwest Corp. Transfer Agts. Assn., Beta Sigma Phi. Republican. Clubs: Meadow, St. Charles Country. Home: 1040 Creekside Dr Wheaton IL 60187 Office: Gould Inc 10 Gould Center Rolling Meadows IL 60008

JACK, VALERIE MARIE, recording industry executive; b. Bklyn., Nov. 6, 1956; d. Paul Peter and Rose Violet (Todaro) Tsakos; m. Thomas Allen Jack, June 1, 1986. Adminstr., registrar Bankers Trust, N.Y.C., 1978-81; adminstr. Arista Records, N.Y.C., 1981-82; adminstr. artists contracts RCA Records, N.Y.C., 1982-83; coordinator artists and repertoir RCA/Ariola Records, N.Y.C., 1983-86; coordinator internat. mktg. artists and repertoir RCA/BMG Music, N.Y.C., 1986—; cons. Thomatron Prodns., N.Y.C., 1984-87. Project coordinator record albums: (by Grim Reaper) Fear No Evil, 1985, (by White Lion) Fight to Survive, 1986, (by PseudoEcko) Living in a Dream, 1987. Mem. Nat. Acad. Recording Arts and Schis., Nat. Assn. Female Execs. Democrat. Roman Cathlic.

JACKER, CORINNE LITVIN, writer; b. Chgo., June 29, 1933; d. Thomas Henry and Theresa (Bellak) Litvin. Student, Stanford U., 1950-52; BS, Northwestern U., 1954, MA, 1955, postgrad., 1955-56. Editor Liberal Arts Press, 1959-60, MacMillan Co., 1960-63; story editor Sta. WNET-TV, N.Y.C., 1969-71, CBS-TV, N.Y.C., 1972-74; instr. playwrighting NYU, 1976-78; vis. prof. playwriting Yale U., 1979-81; adj. prof. Princeton U., 1986—, Columbia U., 1988—, Breadloaf Sch. of English, 1988; sci. cons. Benton Project for Broadcasting, U. Chgo., 1988. Exec. story editor, head writer (TV series) Best of Families, PBS, N.Y.C., 1975-77; head writer (TV series) Another World, 1981-82; author: Man, Memory, and Machines, 1964 (N.Y. Pub. Library 50 Best Books of Yr. 1964), Window on the Unknown, 1966 (AAAS 50 Best Books of Yr. 1966), A Little History of Cocoa, 1966, The Black Flag of Anarchy, 1968 (Pubs. Weekly 25 Best Books of Yr. 1968), The Biological Revolution, 1971; playwright: The Scientific Method, 1970, Seditious Acts, 1970, Travellers, 1973, Breakfast, Lunch, & Dinner, 1975, Bits and Pieces, 1975 (Obie award 1975), Harry Outside, 1975 (Obie award 1975), Night Thoughts & Terminal, 1976, Other People's Tables, 1976, My Life, 1977, After the Season, 1978, Later, 1979, Domestic Issues, 1981, In Place, 1982, Songs from Distant Lands, 1985; TV writer, including: 3 episodes Actors' Choice, NET, 1970 (Emmy citation 1970); Virginia Woolf: The Moment Whole, NET, 1972 (CINE Golden Eagle award 1972); story editor: 4 episode series Benjamin Franklin, CBS, 1974 (Emmy citation 1974); The Adams Chronicles, 1975 (Peabody award 1975), Loose Change, 1978; 3 episode series, NBC, 1978; 3 episodes of Best of Families, NET, 1978, The Jilting of Granny Weatherall, NET, 1980, Night Thoughts and Terminal BBC, 1978; Overdrawn at the Memory Bank, NET, 1983 (Rotterdam Film Festival award, Am. Film Inst. Feature Film Festival award). Rockefeller Found. grantee, 1979-80; residency Villa Serbelloni, Bellagio, Italy, 1987. Mem. Dramatists Guild, Writers Guild Am. East, PEN. Home and Office: 110 W 86th St New York NY 10024

JACKSON, ANDREA CARROLL, public relations executive, writer, photographer; b. Lockesburg, Ark., Jan. 8, 1945; d. Jake Charles and Lola Evelyn (Hale) Carroll; m. Ronald William Jackson, Dec. 23, 1967 (div. Jan. 1978). B.S. in Edn., Henderson State U., 1967, postgrad. in journalism La. State U., 1981-82. Phys. edn. tchr. Lamar Consol. Schs., Ark., 1967-68; field advisor Ark. Post council Girl Scouts U.S.A., Pine Bluff, 1969-74, pub. relations dir. Ouachita council, Little Rock, 1974-79; program and pub. relations dir. Baton Rouge Area YWCA, 1979-81; editor Bayou Country Pubis., Plaquemine, La., 1981-83; communications dir. Am. Lung Assn. of Ark., Little Rock, 1984—; owner, operator TLC Pet Care Service. freelance writer, photographer. Editor: (tng. manual) Safe Homes Project for Battered Women, 1981; Ark. Women's Rights OURS newspaper, 1985-86. Recipient Excellence in color slide photography awards Ouachita Girl Scout Council and Girl Scouts U.S.A., 1978; Outstanding Service award Baton Rouge Area YWCA, 1980. Mem. Ark. Press Women (feature writing awards, 2 in 1982, 3 in 1983, 2 interview awards 1984, 2 broadcast awards 1984, 87, writing editing and interviewing, 1985, 86), Congress of Lung Assn. Staff, Sierra Club (chmn. state chpt., council del. so. plains regional conservation com.), . Avocations: movies, hiking, whitewater rafting. Home: 323 S Valmar Little Rock AR 72205 Office: 211 Natural Resources Dr Little Rock AR 72205

JACKSON, ANNE (ANNE JACKSON WALLACH), actress; b. Pitts.; d. John Ivan and Stella Germaine (Murray) J.; m. Eli Wallach, Mar. 5, 1948; children: Peter, Roberta, Katherine. Studied with Sanford Meisner and Herbert Berghof at Neighborhood Playhouse, with Lee Strassberg at Actor's Studio. Profl. debut: Cherry Orchard; mem. Am. Repertory Co.; Broadway plays include: Summer and Smoke, Oh, Men! Oh, Women!, Middle of the Night, Major Barbara, Rhinoceros, Luv, Waltz of the Toreadors, Diary of Anne Frank, 1978, Twice Around the Park, 1982-83, Nest of the Woodgrouse, 1984, off-Broadway plays: The Typists, The Tigers; film appearances include: So Young, So Bad, 1950, Secret Life of an American Wife, 1968, Dirty Dingus McGee, 1970, Lovers and Other Strangers, 1970, The Shining, 1980, Sam's Son, 1985; TV appearances include: 84 Charing Cross Road, Private Battle, Everything's Relative, 1987—; TV films: Family Man, Golda I and II, Out on a Limb; author: (autobiography) Early Stages, 1979. Recipient Obie award. Office: care Internat Creative Mgmt 8899 Beverly Blvd Los Angeles CA 90048

JACKSON, ARLENE L., family therapist; b. Rockford, Ill., July 16, 1943; d. John E. and LaVern R. (Hazzard) J.; divorced; children—Jan Arlene, James Paul. A.A., Rock Valley Coll., 1978; B.A. summa cum laude in Clin. Psychology and Eng. Lit., Beloit Coll., 1979; postgrad. Ill. State U., 1981-82; M.S. in Community Mental Health, No. Ill. U., 1985, postgrad., 1986—. Advocate, coordinator Ill. Status Offender Service, Rockford, 1979-80; dir. Pathways, Inc., Rockford, 1980-81; therapist Family Life Ctr., Rockford, 1982-86; rational interventions therapist, 1986— exec. dir. Youth Services Network, Inc., Rockford, 1982—; prin. J & J Cons., 1986—; cons. in field. Chmn. task forces Youth Services Network, Inc., 1982—; mem. Peace and Justice Commn., Rockford, 1982—; bd. dirs. Knights Community Complex, Rockford, 1984-87. Named One of Outstanding Working Women of Yr. Ill. Bus. and Profl. Women; Bingham fellow Beloit Coll., 1979. Mem. NOW, Nat. Assn. Social Workers, Rockford Network, Nat. Assn. Women Bus. Owners, Rockford C. of C., Phi Beta Kappa, Psi Chi. Unitarian. Avocations: writing poetry; dancing; interior decorating; travel; theater. Office: Youth Services 4402 N Main St Rockford IL 61105

JACKSON, BECKY ROBERTA, publishing executive; b. Denver, June 20, 1945; d. Robert and Iletha (Overturf) Payte; m. Dennis Lloyd Jackson, Jan 21, 1967; children: Justin A., Garrette A. Grad. high sch., Arvada, Colo. Legal sec. Davis & Michael, Denver, 1963-64, Sidney Ohr, Denver, 1964-67; ins. sec. Northwestern Mut. Life, Denver, 1967-71; sales person Med. Adminstrn. Co., Denver, 1976-78, adminstrv. asst., 1978-80, gen. mgr., 1980-84, dir., 1984—. Office: MAC Pub Co 5005 E 39th Ave Denver CO 80207

JACKSON, BETTY EILEEN, music educator; b. Denver, Oct. 9, 1925; d. James Bowen and Fannie (Shelton) J. B.Mus., U. Colo., 1948, M.Mus., 1949, B.Mus. Edn., 1963; postgrad. Ind. U., 1952-55, Hochschule fur Musik, Munich, 1955-56. Cert. educator Colo., Calif. Tchr., accompanist H.L. Davis Vocal Studios, Denver, 1949-52; teaching assoc. U. Colo., Boulder, 1961-63, vis. lectr., 1963-69; tchr. Fontana Unified Sch. Dist., Calif., 1963—, pvt. studio, 1966—; lectr. in music Calif. State U., San Bernardino, 1967-76; performer, accompanist, music dir. numerous musical cos. including performer, music dir. Fontana Mummers, 1980—, Riverside Community Players, Calif., 1984—; performer Rialto Community Theatre, Calif., 1983—. Performances include numerous operas, musical comedies and oratorios. Judge, Inland Theatre League, Riverside, 1983—; mem. San Bernardino Cultural Task Force, 1981-83. Fulbright grantee, Munich, 1955-56; named Outstanding Performer Inland Theatre League, 1982-84. Mem. AAUW (bd. dirs., cultural chair 1983-86), Nat. Assn. Tchrs. Singing (exec. bd. 1985—), NEA, Music Educators Nat. Conf., Calif. Tchrs. Assn., Fontana Tchrs. Assn., Music Tchrs. Assn., San Bernardino Valley Concert Assn. (bd. dirs. 1977-83), Kappa Kappa Iota (v.p. 1982-83). Lodge: Eastern Star. Avocations: Community theater and opera; travel; collecting Hummels and plates. Home: PO Box 885 Rialto CA 92377

JACKSON, CAROL FRANCES, moving company executive; b. Falmouth, Ky., Sept. 15, 1938; d. Roy Wilson and Alma C. (Field) Johnting; m. Forrest Edward Jackson, Aug. 23, 1957; children: Mary Ann Jackson Pennington, David A., Marsha, Douglas, Roy Andrew. Student, Transylvania Coll., 1956-57; grad., Miller Bus. Coll., Cin., 1957. Sec. Cin. Gas and Electric Co., 1958-59; bookkeeper moving co. Cin., 1968-71; now owner, sec.-treas. Apollo Moving Specialist, Inc., Daytona, Fla., 1985—. Vol., Cannon Falls (Minn.) Elem. Sch., 1980-83, Boy Scouts Am., Brownies. Democrat. Office: Apollo Moving Specialists Inc 771 Fentress Blvd Daytona FL 32015

JACKSON, CAROLE EDYTHE, computer laboratory executive; b. Bloomfield Hills, Mich., Apr. 20, 1956; d. William Carlton Warrick and Joan Ruth (Hessler) Jackson. B.A. in Art History, U. Mich., 1976, M.B.A., 1978; postgrad. Harrington Inst. Interior Design, 1985-86, U. Ill., 1986—. Lic. real estate broker, securities sales. Corp. research analyst Ill. Bell Telephone Co., Chgo., 1978-81; mktg. account mgr. Dun & Bradstreet Corp., Chgo., 1981-83; dir. mktg. Monchik Weber Corp., Chgo., 1983-85; v.p. mktg. Walsh Greenwood & Co., Chgo., 1985—; mktg. cons. Triton Coll., River Grove, Ill., 1982-83, Roeper City and Country Sch., Bloomfield Hills, 1974. Artist/designer water color, pencil drawings. Com. mem. Ann Arbor City Planning Commn., 1976-77. Mem. Am. Mktg. Assn., Am. Mgmt. Assn., Am. Assn. Individual Investors, Chgo. Women in Architecture, Am. Inst. Architects, Nat. Assn. Women Bus. Owners. Lutheran. Home: 1818 N Howe St Chicago IL 60614 Office: U Ill Sch Architecture 935 W Harrison St Chicago IL 60680

JACKSON, CONSTANCE CORDICE, reading consultant; b. Winchester, Mass.; d. Conrad and Florence (Smith) Cordice; B.S. in Elem. Edn., Boston U., 1963, M.Ed. in Reading, Lang., Elem. Edn., 1966, Ed.D. in Reading, Elem. Edn., 1974; m. Eugene B. Jackson. Tchr. Scituate (Mass.) Public Schs., 1963-64; tchr. Marshfield (Mass.) Public Schs., 1964-68, reading cons., 1968—; teaching fellow Boston U., 1972. Dir. Marshfield Right to Read Effort, 1973-76. Mem. NEA, Internat. Reading Assn., Mass., Marshfield tchrs. assns., Mass. Reading Assn., Delta Kappa Gamma, Pi Lambda Theta. Home: PO Box 126 North Marshfield MA 02059 Office: Box 126-195 Oak St North Marshfield MA 02059

JACKSON, CORDELL, music production company executive, real estate broker; b. Pontotoc, Miss., July 15, 1923; d. William Langdon and Mary Stella (Plunk) Miller; divorced; children: Bexley Ryan, Dana Miller. Student, U. Tenn., 1962. Pres., broker Greater Memphis Realty, 1952—; pres. Moon Records, Memphis, 1956—, Bexley Publishing Co., Memphis, 1957—, Creative Talent Network, Inc., Memphis, 1985—, Let's Keep Family Together America, Memphis, 1986—. Affiliate writer, publisher, Broadcast Music, Inc., N.Y.C., Nashville, 1954—; syndicated radio program; published songwriter. Campaign worker Senatorial campaign, 1984-85, and others 1984—. Named Outstanding Citizen Memphis C. of C., 1986, Memphis Songwriter of Yr.; recipient World War prodn. award, Dr. Hubert Brewster award, cert. merit Memphis and Shelby County Film, Tape and Music commn., 1986 hon. cert. Shelby County Bs. Commrs., 1986 Tenn. Outstanding Achievement award Gov. Lamar Alexander, 1986, proclamation of accomplishments and contbrs. Tenn. Ho. of Reps. Ned Mcwherter, 1986, letter of merit Sen. Albert Gore Jr., Sen. Jim Sasser, 1986, Outstanding Service award Nat. Conf. Christians and Jews, 1986, cert. appreciation Shelby County Govt., 1986, merit award City of Memphis, 1986, proclamation cert. U.S. Ho. Reps. and State Tenn. Mem. NARAS (alt. trustee, com. chmn. 1974—, named honoree of Yr., Nat. Govs. awaed, Creative and Pioneering Achievement award), Blues Found. (charter, bd. govs. 1980—), Song Writers Assn. Baptist. Home: 3333 Scenic Hwy Memphis TN 38128 Office: Greater Memphis Realty 656 Madison Ave Memphis TN 38103

JACKSON, DENISE VARNELL, educator; b. Cleve., Sept. 5, 1952; d. Walter Alvin and Margaret (Scott) Wolff; m. Eugene Jack Jackson, Jr., June 6, 1976; children: Denise Daniele, Eric Eugene. B.A., Tex. So. U., 1974, M.A. 1978. Asst. principal, Houston Ind. Sch. Dist., 1974-81, 82—; instr. English Houston Community Coll., 1974-75, 78-79; personnel asst. Union Carbide, Houston, 1981-82; mem. French Fgn. Lang. Curriculum Com., Houston, 1975; guest speaker Houston Ind. Sch. Dist. In-Service, Houston, 1980. L'Alliance Francaise scholar, Houston, 1972; Ford Ednl. Found. grantee, Houston, 1983, Impact II grantee, 1984, 87; recipient Tex. Excellence award, 1988. Mem. Assn. Supervision and Curriculum Devel. , Tex. Assn. Supervision and Curriculum Devel. Democrat. Roman Catholic. Home: 3723 Grapevine Dr Houston TX 77045 Office: Houston Ind Sch Dist 1700 Dumble St Houston TX 77025

JACKSON, DONNA JEAN, accountant; b. Chandler, Okla., Feb. 7, 1957; d. Donald L. and Betty J. (Cline) J. BS in Acctg., Okla. State U., 1977, MS in Acctg., 1983. CPA, Okla. Auditor Okla. State U. Internal Audit, Stillwater, 1975-78; acct. Thomas & Co. CPA, Oklahoma City, 1979; auditor, tax acct. ANTA, Oklahoma City, 1979-82; acct. Luton & Co., CPA, Oklahoma City, 1982-83, James Wright & Co., Oklahoma City, 1983—. Mem. Am. Inst. CPA's, Okla. Soc. CPA's. Republican. Home: 6600 Edenborough 204 Oklahoma City OK 73132

JACKSON, ELEANOR ROSS, hospital administrator; b. Pitts., Feb. 23, 1942; d. Jean Theodore and Eleanor (Snowden) Ross; children from previous marriage: Traci Jean, Kelli Lynn; m. Clifford Andrew Jackson, June 21, 1986. BS, Fla. So. U., 1963; MS in Health Care Adminstrn., Trinity U., San Antonio, Tex., 1975. Stenographer FBI, Tampa, Fla., 1964-65; adminstrv. asst. Nat. Ctr. for Primate Biology, Davis, Calif., 1965-66; high sch. tchr. Auburn (Ala.) Pub. Sch. Dist., 1967-69; sr. evaluator Auburn U., 1969-71; adminstrv. asst. Jeff Davis Hosp., Houston, 1972-73; adminstrv. resident Met. Gen. Hosp., San Antonio, Tex., 1974-75; adminstr. Shriners Hosp., Houston, 1975—; acting adminstr. Shriners Hosp., Shreveport, La., 1986-87. Active Missouri City (Tex.) PTA, 1979-87; bd. dirs. Presbyn. Ch. of Houston, 1977-78. Mem. Am. Coll. Health Care Execs. (assoc. sec. Houston chpt. 1986), Tex. Hosp. Assn. (del. 1980-82), Young Hosp. Adminstrs. (pres. 1982). Republican. Presbyterian. Office: Shriners Hosp 1402 Outer Belt Houston TX 77030

JACKSON, EVELYN ARDETH, nurse; b. Great Falls, Mont., Feb. 11, 1929; d. Henry and Esther Lillian (Morris) Bergdorf; m. Elmer Donald Jackson, May 16, 1952; children—Donita Jo, Jenice Evelyn. Student Gonzaga U., 1947-48; R.N., St. Luke's Sch. Nursing, Spokane, Wash., 1950; postgrad. St. Joseph's Coll., Roanoke, Va., 1983-85. Staff nurse in doctors' offices, Spokane, 1950-55, Houston, 1956-68; 76-78; supr. M.D. Anderson Hosp. and Cancer Inst., Houston, 1968-76; nursing supr. Austin Steel Co., Houston, 1978-80; charge nurse Reed Rock Bit Co., Houston, 1980—. Mem. Houston Occupational Health Nurses Assn. (documentation com. 1980-81, telephone com. 1981-82, nomination com. 1982-83, dir. 1982—), Am. Occupational Health Assn., Tex. Occupational Health Assn. (dir. 1986—), Nat. Mgmt. Assn., Profl. and Bus. Women, ARC (instr. 1980—), Am. Security Council. Republican. Methodist. Club: U.S. Senatorial (presdl. task force 1985) (Washington). Home: PO Box 325 Bellaire TX 77401 Office: Reed Rock Bit PO Box 2119 Houston TX 77252

JACKSON, FREDA LUCILLE, clergywoman, church administrator, editor; b. Sikeston, Mo., Sept. 15, 1928; d. Jesse Freda and Ruby Lucille (Carter) Andres; student Three Rivers Jr. Coll., 1969, Central Bible Coll., Springfield, Mo., 1973; B.S., Drury Coll., 1980; M.A. in Bibl. Lit., Assemblies of God Theol. Sem., 1986; m. Thomas Lowell Jackson, Oct. 2, 1947; children—Stephen Andres, Elizabeth Ann, Thomas Dean. Bookkeeper, Aduddel Wholesale Auto Parks, Sikeston, 1947-48; pvt. sec. to v.p. So. Ice & Coal Co., Memphis, 1948-49; sec. firm Bailey & Craig, Sikeston, 1950-56, firm Blanton & Blanton, 1956-57; ordained to ministry Assemblies of God Ch., 1983; promotions coordinator, editor deferred giving and trusts dept., gen. council Assemblies of God, Springfield, Mo., 1974—; tchr. English, Central Bibl. Coll., 1986—. Mem. Alpha Sigma Lambda, Womens Ministries, Maranatha Aux. Editor: New Dimensions, 1979—, Maranatha newsletter, 1977; contbr. articles to denominational publs. Home: 2407 W Atlantic St Springfield MO 65803 Office: 1445 Boonville Ave Springfield MO 65802

JACKSON, GERALDINE MCMILLAN, mathematics educator; b. Lubbock, Tex., Feb. 15, 1949; d. Thawather and Lenora (Morrison) McM.; m. Fabian Wallace Jackson, Dec. 19, 1973; children—Africia, Kafricia. B.S., M.S., Prairie View A&M U. Mgr., Nat. Convenience Stores, Houston, 1972-77; tchr. North Forest Ind. Sch. Dist., Houston, 1977—, curriculum writer, 1979—, mem. textbook com., 1983. NSF scholar, 1980. Mem. Delta Sigma Theta, Kappa Delta Pi. Office: North Forest Ind Sch Dist 7525 Tidwell St Houston TX 77018

JACKSON, JANE W., interior designer; b. Asheville, N.C., Aug. 5, 1944; d. James and Willie Mae (Stoner) Harris; m. Bruce G. Jackson; children: Yvette, Scott. Student, Boston U., 1964; BA, Leslie Coll., 1967; postgrad., Artisan Sch. Interior Design, 1980-82. Tchr. Montessori, Brookline, Mass., 1969-72; interior designer Nettle Creek Shops, Honolulu, 1980-82, owner, 1982—. Active Mayor's Com. for Small Bus., Honolulu, 1984. Mem. Am. Soc. Interior Design Industry Found. Democrat. Club: Honolulu. Office: Nettle Creek Shops 1221 Kapiolani Blvd Honolulu HI 96814

JACKSON, JEANNE ANNE, educational consultant; b. Lakewood, Ohio, Aug. 21, 1922; d. Edward Adam and Elsa Wilhelmina (Stengel) Roege; A.B., Hiram Coll., 1944; M.A., Kent State U., 1962; Ph.D., Case-Western Res. U., 1970; m. Stuart Ray Jackson, July 12, 1946; children—Stuart Clinton, Philip Clay. With Nat. City Bank Cleve., 1944-47, Geneva Savs. & Trust Co. (Ohio), 1947-52; tchr. Geneva Area City Schs., 1954-68; tchr., guidance counselor Kirtland (Ohio) Middle Sch., 1969-70; adminstrv. asst. Ashtabula (Ohio) County Joint Vocat. Sch., 1970-75; prin., adminstrv. asst. Geneva Area City Schs., 1975-82; pres. Curriculum and Supervision Services, Inc., 1982—; asst. prof. Kent (Ohio) State U., 1980—. Past pres. United Way Ashtabula County; trustee Ohio Citizens Council, Ashtabula Arts Ctr., Overlook House, Cleve.; trustee 1st Ch. of Christ Scientist, Ashtabula. Recipient Status of Women award Zonta 1981; Outstanding Citizen award Ashtabula C. of C., 1982. Mem. AAUW, Women's Service League Ashtabula, LWV, Assn. Supervision and Curriculum Devel., Am. Assn. Sch. Adminstrs., Internat. Reading Assn., Mensa, Nat. Council Tchrs. English, Delta Kappa Gamma. Republican. Clubs: Eastern Star (past matron), Zonta. Home: 1634 Highland Ln Ashtabula OH 44004

JACKSON, JEWEL, state youth authority official; b. Shreveport, La., June 3, 1942; d. Willie Burghardt and Bernice Jewel (Mayberry) Norton; m. Edward James Norman, May 17, 1961 (div. Nov. 1968); children—Steven, June Kelly; m. Wilbert Jackson, Apr. 6, 1969; children—Michael, Anthony. With Calif. Youth Authority, 1965—, group supr., San Andreas and Santa Rosa, 1965-67, youth counselor, Ventura, 1967-78, sr. youth counselor, Stockton, 1978-81, treatment team supr., program mgr., Whittier and Ione, 1981—, affirmative action adv. mem., Sacramento, 1976-78, equal employment adv. mem., 1978-79; speaker U. Pacific Youth Motivational Project, Stockton, Calif., 1985-86. Mem. Women in Criminal Justice-North (co-chair 1974-76), Nat. Assn. for Female Execs., Assn. Black Correctional Workers (chpt. v.p. 1979, editor newsletter 1978-80). Avocations: reading, horseback riding, writing poetry and short stories, designing clothing. Home: PO Box 898 Ione CA 95640

JACKSON, JOANNE REGINA, minority business coordinator; b. Albany, N.Y., Jan. 28, 1949; d. Howard Reginald and Barbara Ann (Noisette) J. BBA, Howard U., 1971; M in Urban and Regional Planning, U. Pitts., 1977. Fin. analyst COMSAT Gen. Corp., Washington, 1974-75; sr. planner Albnay Urban Renewal Agy., 1977-79; devel. specialist dept. housing, community renewal State of N.Y., Albany, 1979-81; bus. devel. specialist Va. Community Affairs, Arlington County, Arlington, 1981-83; exec. dir. H St Community Devel. Corp., Washington, 1983; econ. devel. specialist MATCH Inst., Washington, 1984-85; cons. Brown & Co., CPA, Washington, 1985-86; minority bus. enterprise coordinator Anne Arundel County, Annapolis, Md., 1987—; tech. advisor Shirlington Rd. Community Devel. Corp., 1983—. Mem. Nat. Black Women's Caucus, Washington, 1986-87. Scholar Patricia Bruce Cole Sch., 1967, Howard U., 1968-71, U. Pitts., 1975-76. Democrat. Roman Catholic. Home: 1244 K St SE Washington DC 20003 Office: Anne Arundel County Purchasing Office Arundel Ctr MS 1303 Annapolis MD 21404

JACKSON, JOE ANN, medical association administrator; b. Brewton, Ala., Feb. 13, 1949; d. William Joseph and Missouri (Stokes) J. BS Northwestern U., 1988. Program adminstr. AMA, Chgo., 1974—; editor directories: Opportunity Placement Register, Physician Placement Register. Mem. Am. Mktg. Assn. Mem. Sanctified Ch. Home: 5050 S Lake Shore Dr 2708 Chicago IL 60615 Office: AMA 535 N Dearborn Chicago IL 60610

JACKSON, JOY JUANITA, educator; b. New Orleans, Oct. 8, 1928; d. Oliver Daniel and Oneida Christina (Drouant) Jackson; student La. State U., 1946-49; B.A., Tulane U., 1951, M.A., 1958, Ph.D., 1961. Feature writer New Orleans Times-Picayune, 1951-56; instr. Nicholls State Coll., Thibodaux, La., 1961-62, asst. prof., 1962-66; asst. prof. Southeastern La. U., Hammond, 1966-68, asso. prof., 1968-73, prof. history, 1973—, dir. Center for Regional Studies and univ. archives, 1982—. AAUW Irma E. Voight fellow, 1960-61. Mem. Am., La. (dir. 1966-68, pres. 1977-78), So. Hist. Assn., S.E. La. Hist. Assn. (pres. Hammond 1978), Oral History Assn. Author: New Orleans in the Gilded Age, 1969. Home: 1411 University Dr Hammond LA 70401

JACKSON, JOYCE ELIZABETH MITCHELL, government official; b. Washington, Aug. 21, 1935; d. Clarence Hural and Flora Elizabeth (Washington) Mitchell; m. William I. McAdoo, Feb. 4, 1955; 1 child, Gregory Michael; m. Leo Jackson, June 23, 1962; 1 chld, Gary Leo. AA, Univ. of D.C., 1983, BA cum laude, 1985. Exec. sec. Voice of Am., Washington, 1975-81, staff asst., 1981-82; paralegal USIA, Washington, 1982, personnel specialist, 1982-85, research specialist, 1985—, realtor-assoc., 1984—. Block leader Ft. Lincoln Civic Assn., Washington, 1980-81. Mem. Nat. Assn. Female Execs., Am. Polit. Sci. Assn. (assoc.), Nat. Assn. Realtors (assoc.), Am. Bus. Women's Assn., Washington Bd. Realtors, Nat. Capitol Area Paralegal Assn., Delta Sigma Theta. Democrat. Episcopalian. Avocations: piano, organ, travel. Home: 240 M St SW Apt E-507 Washington DC 20024 Office: USIA 301 4th St SW R562 Washington DC 20547

JACKSON, KATE, actress; b. Birmingham, Ala., Oct. 29, 1949; d. Hogan and Ruth Jackson; m. Andrew Stevens, Aug. 23, 1978 (div. 1981); m. David Greenwald, 1982 (div. 1984). Student, U. Miss.; student, Birmingham U.; grad., Am. Acad. Dramatic Arts, 1971. Worked as model. Appeared in TV series Dark Shadows, 1966-71, The Rookies, 1972-76, Charlie's Angels, 1976-79, The Scarecrow and Mrs. King, 1983-87; TV appearances include Movin' On, The Jimmy Stewart Show; TV movies include: Satan's School for Girls, 1973, Death Cruise, 1974, Killer Bees, 1974, Death Scream, 1975, Charlie's Angels, 1976, Death at Love House, 1976, James at 15, 1977, Topper, 1979, Inmates: A Love Story, 1981, Thin Ice, 1981, Listen to Your Heart, 1983, Baby Boom, 1988; motion picture appearances include: Dirty Tricks, 1981, Making Love, 1982; dir. numerous episodes The Scarecrow and Mrs. King. Recipient 3 Emmy award nominations Nat. Acad. TV Arts and Scis. Mem. AFTRA, Screen Actors Guild, Actors Equity Assn., Dirs. Guild Am. Office: Creative Artists Agency Inc 1888 Century Park E Suite 1400 Los Angeles CA 90067

JACKSON, LADY LOYD APPLEBY, personnel executive; b. Toccoa, Ga., July 8, 1946; d. Samuel Cecil and Lillian Loyd (Collins) Appleby; m. Joseph Howard Torrence, July 27, 1968 (div. 1973); 1 dau., Katherine Loyd; m. Thomas Houston Jackson, May 3, 1974; children—Thomas Houston, Jr., John Andrew. B.A., Mary Baldwin Coll., 1968. Cert. profl. in human resources. Exec. trainee Sears, Roebuck & Co., Phila., 1968-69; tng. adminstr. Genesco, Inc., Nashville, 1969-72; adminstrv. asst. State Tenn. Dept. Human Services, Nashville, 1972-73, dir. office services, 1973-77, dir. personnel, 1977-80; dir. personnel ARC, Nashville, 1980-81; asst. dir. personnel Nashville Electric Service, 1981—; sec.-treas. The Guide Co., Inc., 1984—. Vice chmn. bd. Mcpl. Auditorium Bd., Nashville, 1976-77; sec., treas. Tenn. Personnel Adv. Council, Nashville, 1978-79; mem. Outlook Nashville Personnel Com., Leadership Nashville, 1986-87; bd. dirs. United Methodist Neighborhood Centers, Nashville, 1984—, chmn. personnel com., 1985; cons. Jr. Achievement, 1986. Recipient Laurel Soc. award Mary Baldwin Coll., 1968, Bess Maddox award, 1987; named Woman of Yr. Bus. and Profl. Women's Club, 1987. Indsl. Personnel Assn. (chmn. operating com. 1982-83), Indsl. Personnel Assn. (sec. treas. v.p. 1984, pres. 1985), Am. Soc. Personnel Adminstrs. (program com. chmn. 1984, sec. 1986, v.p. 1987, pres. Nashville chpt. 1988), Internat. Assn. Quality Circles (co-founder, dir. Central Tenn. chpt. 1982-83). Democrat. Mem. Woodmont Christian Ch. Office: Nashville Electric Service 1214 Church St Nashville TN 37203

JACKSON, LELA EVELYNE, company executive; b. Mesilla Park, N.Mex. Feb. 11, 1941; d. Willie L. and Ruth (Boggess) Ashworth; m. Robert C. Jackson, Apr. 21, 1969; children—Cinthia Sams, Edward Taber, Elizabeth Taber; adopted children—Shiela Prokuski, Robert Jackson, Regina Jackson. B.A. in Acctg., Bakersfield Coll., 1970; cert. fed. taxation Tex. A&M U., 1983. Ptnr. Personalized Bookkeeping, Bakersfield, 1969-71, Jackson & Jackson, Vivian, La., 1977-79; pres. Le Jac Inc., Vivian, 1979—. Subsect. mem. Nat. Republican Com., Washington, 1982—. Mem. North Caddo C. of C. (co-founder, sec. 1980-81), Profl. Cons. Baptist. Avocations: fishing; gardening; reading. Home: PO Box 747 Vivian LA 71082 Office: Le Jac Inc 219 W Kentucky Vivian LA 71082

JACKSON, LINDA BLAIR, merchandising executive; b. Troy, N.Y., Oct. 21, 1947; d. William Erle and Dorothy Louise (Baker) Blair; m. James Richard Jackson, April 25, 1970; children: Julie Marie, Emily Anne. BA in History, San Diego State Coll., 1969. Buyer Buffum's, Long Beach, Calif., 1970-77; merchandiser Miller's Outpost, Ontario, Calif., 1977-83; v.p. merchandising Ocean Pacific, Tustin, Calif., 1983—. Various commissions St. Mark Presbyterian Ch., Newport Beach, 1971—.

JACKSON, LINDA SUEING, financial consulting executive; b. Madisonville, Tex., Nov. 24, 1952; d. Bert and Edgar (Nealey) Sueing; m. Governor Jackson, Apr. 28, 1976; 1 child, Governor III. BBA, East Tex. State U., 1974; MBA, North Tex. State U., 1977; postgrad., Tex. Woman's U., 1983. Staff acct. Sears Roebuck & Co., Irving, Tex., 1974-75; acctg. analyst Cooper Industries, Dallas, 1975-77; fin. analyst Hunt Oil Co., Dallas, 1977-80, sr. internat. acct., 1980-81, mgr. internat. acctg., 1981-84; owner, pres. Global Fin. Resource, Dallas, 1984—; cons. tax-deferred annuity Variable Annuity Mktg. Co., Dallas, 1984, tax. cons., Dallas, 1984—. Chairperson fin. com. St. Luke United Meth., Dallas, 1983—, bond program, 1986; bd. dirs., treas. Africare, Dallas, 1986. Recipient proclamation of merit award Dallas Dance Theater, 1986. Mem. Nat. Assn. Securities Dealers, Women Bus. Assn. (v.p. Dallas chpt. 1985), Dallas C. of C. Home: 3735 White Bud Ct Lewisville TX 75028

JACKSON, LOIS ANN, mental disabilities educator; b. Clinton, Iowa, Aug. 23, 1948; d. Alvin E. and Vera Miranda (Barnes) Roberts; m. Darrell John Jackson, Jan. 1, 1972; children—Vanessa Ann, Brian Nicholas, Valerie Rose. B.A., U. No. Iowa, 1970. Cert. tchr. mental retardation, elem., Iowa. Tchr. trainable mentally retarded Pottawattamie County Schs., Council Bluffs, Iowa, 1970-72; head tchr. Skyline Ctr., Inc., Clinton, Iowa, 1972-76, program mgr., 1976-87. mental disabilities, self-contained with integration tchr, Bellevue Community Schs., Bellevue, Iowa, 1987—. Mem. Nat. Assn. Female Execs., Smithsonian Assocs. Lutheran. Avocations: reading; antique and auto shows. Home: 832 3d Ave S Clinton IA 52732 Office: Bellevue High Sch PO Box 46 Bellevue IA 52031

JACKSON, LOIS THIGPEN, former county official; b. Bailey, N.C., May 28, 1935; d. George Washington and Lillie B. (Temple) Thigpen; m. Osco Kermit Jackson, Sept. 21, 1957; 1 child, Elsie Yvonne. Grad. Hradbarger Bus. Sch., Raleigh, N.C., 1956; student Carson-Newman Coll., Walters State Community Coll. Cert. tax preparer, IRS. With Wachovia Bank & Trust Co., Raleigh, 1953-56; exec. sec. N.C. Dairy Products Assn., Inc., Raleigh, 1956-57; legal sec. Daniel & Daniel, Rutledge, Tenn., 1957-69; clk. and master Grainger County Chancery Ct., Rutledge, 1969-87. Vice-chair Grainger County Vocat. Adv. Com., 1983-85, chmn., 1986-87; chair Grainger County Council on Aging, 1980—, Grainger County Republican Women, 1970—; sec. Grainger County Rep. party, 1970—; vol. Ridgeview Terr. Nursing Home, 1980-87; mem. adv. council Walters State Community Coll. Found., 1970-83; chair Grainger County Heart Assn., 1982-83, Grainger County Cancer Drive, various times. Mem. Tenn. County Ofcls. Assn., State Ct. Clks. Assn. Baptist. Avocations: sewing; decorating; gardening; catering. Home: Route 4 Box 77 Rutledge TN 37861 Office: Courthouse Rutledge TN 37861

JACKSON, LORA RUTHE THOMPSON, parliamentarian, corporate executive; b. Ft. Worth, Oct. 29, 1920; d. John Lyle and Florence (Ector) Thompson; m. Vernon Jackson, Sept. 10, 1944; children: Xanna Yvonne Jackson Young, Jorja Annette Jackson Clemson. Student, Ft. Worth Christian Coll., 1960, Christian Coll. of S.W., 1969. Registered profl. parliamentarian. Clk. mail and advt. Mut. Benefit Ins. Co., 1940-42; clk. to exec. sec. N.Am. Aviation, 1942-45; exec. sec. TEMCO Mfg., 1945-47, Luscombe Aircraft, 1947-50; sec., gen. office supr. SA-SO Sign Mfg. Co., 1950-53; co-owner All-Quality Sign Co., 1953-59; co-owner, v.p., office supr., dir. pub. relations Jackson Vending Supply, Inc., Grand Prairie, Tex., 1959—; tchr., judge parliamentary law; bd. dirs. 1st Nat. Bank Red Oak. Host, dir.: (cable TV show) It's Happening in Grand Prairie, 1981—, History of Grand Prairie, 1981—; producer, dir. city council's agenda preview weekly on govt. cable TV channel; contbr. articles on parliamentary law, beautification and community improvement, and cultural arts to mags. Mem. Dallas County Sch. Bd., 1974—, Dallas County Hist. Commn., 1974-82, Grand Prairie Civil Def. Commn., 1959—; chmn. Grand Prairie Arts and Hist. Preservation Commn., 1976-85, Grand Prairie Bi-Centennial, 1974-76; mem., past chmn. Grand Prairie Community and Home Improvements Commn., 1964-85; mem. spl. funds com. Grand Prairie Ind. Sch. Dist.; state treas. Keep Tex. Beautiful, Inc., 1987; active local, council and dist. PTA's; regional v.p. Tex. PTA; hon. life mem. Nat. Congress Parents and Tchrs., Tex. Congress Parents and Tchrs.; Grand Prairie Hosp. Aux.; mem. council City of Grand Prairie, 1985—, mayor pro-tem, 1986-88. Recipient Mrs. Lyndon B. Johnson Environ. Keep Am. Beautiful award, 1977, award in conservation Tex. Forest Service, 1976; named Woman of Yr., Grand Prairie Daily News, 1979. Mem. Grand Prairie Friends of the Library (pres. 1978-80), Grand Prairie C. of C. (pres. 1982, Women of Yr. 1967, Citizen of Yr., 1969), Nat. Assn. Parliamentarians (nat. pub. relations chair 1987-89), Tex. Assn. Parliamentarians (state pres. 1974-75), North Tex. Assn. Parliamentarians (pres. 1988—), Beautify Tex. Council (state pres. 1976-78, Tex. Bluebonnet State award 1978), Grand Prairie Hist. Orgn., (life, sec., founding pres.). Democrat. Mem. Ch. of Christ. Clubs: Grand Prairie Bus. and Profl. Women's (treas., pres. 1983-84, Woman of Yr. 1976, 82), Grand Prairie Garden (pres., Woman of Yr. 1975). Lodge: Soroptimists (corr. sec. Grand Prairie chpt., regional parliamentarian nat. chpt.). Home and Office: 200 Meyers Rd Grand Prairie TX 75050

JACKSON, LYNDA KAY, leasing company executive; b. Ottumwa, Iowa, Sept. 26, 1949; d. James Leon and Evelyn Melosina (Hartwig) J. Student, Iowa State U., 1967-70. From sec. to state comptroller Iowa State Dept. Transp., Ames, 1967-70; cash analyst McCall Pattern Co., Manhattan, Kans., 1970-71; credit analyst Beneficial Fin., Manhattan, 1971-72; mgmt. trainee CIT Fin. Services, Des Moines, 1973-75; loan mgr. CIT Fin. Services, Ft. Dodge, Iowa, 1975-76; dist. sales mgr. CIT Fin. Services, St. Louis, 1976-80; v.p. sales TriContinental Leasing Corp., Paramus, N.J., 1980-86; v.p. Copelco Credit Corp., Maywood, N.J., 1986—. Republican. Baptist. Home: 24 Peach Hill N Ramsey NJ 07446 Office: Copelco Credit Corp 25 E Spring Valley Ave Maywood NJ 07446

JACKSON, MARY CLARE LOKKEN, jeweler, educational and advertising consultant; b. LaCrosse, Wis., July 28, 1949; d. Clayton Marvin and Marian Lucille (Knutson) Lokken; m. William Thomas Jackson, Oct. 2, 1970; 1 dau., MaryJune Lokken. Student St. Olaf Coll., 1967-68; B.S. in Journalism, Iowa State U., 1971. Tchr., Portage (Wis.) Pub. Schs., 1972-76; pres., owner Magi Jewelry Ltd., Ames, Iowa, 1976—; v.p. for salon ops. Finesse Imagemakers, Ames, 1976—; ednl. cons. Profl. Cosmetology Inst., Ames, 1978—. Mem. Iowa Jewelers and Watchmakers Assn., Jewelers Am., Nat. Cosmetologists Assn., Iowa Cosmetology Schs. Assn. Republican. Lutheran. Clubs: Altrusa, Order Eastern Star. Home: 4712 West Bend Dr Ames IA 50010 Office: Magi Jewelry Ltd 707 24th St Ames IA 50010

JACKSON, MARY LEE, legislative advocate executive; b. Norfolk, Va., Oct. 31, 1947; d. Charles Lee Rineheardt and Shirley (Sale) Whitman. AA in Bus., Va. Intermont Coll., 1968. Adminstrv. sec. Rubber Mfrs. Assn., Washington, 1970-75; legis. asst. Rocky Mountain Oil and Gas Assn., Washington, 1975-79; adminstrv. asst. U.S. Nuclear Regulatory Commn., Washington, 1979-80; staff asst. com. energy and natural resources U.S. Senate, Washington, 1980-82; communications and fundraising cons. Sequoia Inst., Sacramento, Calif., 1982-84; legis. coordinatorState and Consumer Services Agy. State of Calif., Sacramento, 1984; sales assoc. MacBride Realty, Sacramento, 1984-85; legis. dir. Advocaton, Inc., Sacramento, 1985—. Del. state conv. Rep. Party, Alexandria, Va., 1975-82, Rep. Assembly, Sacramento, 1983—; vol. congl. and presdl. campaigns, 1975—. Mem. Sacramento Bd. Realtors, Calif. Assn. Realtors, Calif. Assn. Realtors. Episcopalians. Club: Calif. River City Reps. (Sacramento). Home: 200 Cadillac Dr #26 Sacramento CA 95825

JACKSON, MARY LOUISE, health services executive; b. Phila., June 25, 1938; d. John Francis and Helen Catherine (Peranteau) Martin; m. Howard Clark Jackson III, Dec. 17, 1954; children—Michael, Mark, Brian. Student Bucks County Community Coll., 1977-83. Asst. mgr. retail div. Sears Roebuck & Co., Bensalem, Pa., 1972-77; educator, adminstr., dir. Trevose Behavior Modification Program, Pa., 1975—, leadership tng. workshops, 1979—; salesman Makefield Real Estate, Morrisville, Pa., 1977-78; mortgage fin. cons. Tom Dunphy Real Estate, Feasterville, Pa., 1978-81; weight loss cons., Hulmeville, Pa., 1984—. Writer monthly column The Modifier, 1977—. Mem. Bucks County Bd. Realtors, Hulmeville Hist. Soc. (a founder, charter mem.). Democrat. Presbyterian. Avocations: reading; classical music; speed walking; knitting; fishing. Home: 218 Main St Hulmeville PA 19047

JACKSON, MONA BETHEL, educational administrator, assistant prinicipal; b. Miami, Fla., Mar. 7, 1947; d. Charles E. Bethel and Olga Isabel (Goodman) Bethel Williams; m. Herman Jackson, Dec. 31, 1968; children: Keane Sean, Herman. BS, Fla. A&M U., 1969; MEd, Fla. Atlantic U., 1973. Cert. tchr., Fla. Sci. tchr. Dade County pub. schs., Miami, 1970-74, sci. tchr./counselor, 1974-75, counselor, 1975-82, ednl. specialist, 1982-84, project mgr., 1984-86, asst. prin., 1986—; cons.; curriculum coordinator Perrine Crime Prevention Program, Miami, 1979-82. Author: (manual) Dollars and Cents: A Guide for Scholarship Applicants, 1980, Focus on Careers, 1984. Pres., Dade County Sickle Cell Found., 1983-86; sec. bd. dirs. Haitian Refugee Ctr., Miami, 1983-85; vestry Christ Episcopal Ch., 1984-86. Named Tchr. of Yr., Drew Jr. High Sch., 1972; recipient plaque Dade County Sickle Cell Found., 1981. Mem. Dade County Personnel and Guidance Assn. (pres. 1983-84, plaque 1984), Fla. Assn. Counseling and Devel. (pres.-elect 1985-86, pres. 1986-87, conv. exec. 1986-87, plaque 1985, 87), Fla. Assn. Sci. Tchrs., Women Involved Now, Phi Delta Kappa, Delta Sigma Theta (pres. Beta Alpha chpt. 1967-68, pres. Miami chpt. 1976-80). Democrat. Sec. vestry Christ Episcopal Ch., 1984-86.—. Home: 8970 SW 126th Terr Miami FL 33176

JACKSON, MONA MARIA, accountant, educator; b. Stockholm, Apr. 30, 1944; came to U.S., 1964; d. John Sigvard and Elsa Maria (Evert) Alshammar; m. Julius Leon Jackson, Dec. 31, 1976; children: Timothy John, Mercedes Maria, Julios Deon. BA in Bus. cum laude, U. Guam, 1985; postgrad. in edn., Calif. State U., 1986. Mgr. Security Pacific Nat. Bank, Davis, Calif., 1967-73; acct. R.J. Reynolds Co., Davis, 1973-78; supr. Bank Am., North Highlands, Calif., 1978-80; office mgr. U. Guam, Mangilao, 1983-85; instr. acct. banking and fin. Barclay Coll., San Bernardino, Calif., 1985-87; sr. acct. City of Moreno Valley, Calif., 1987-88; instr. acctg. Nat. Bus. Inst., Riverside, Calif., 1988—; tchr. adult edn. Colton (Calif.) Joint Unified Sch. Dist., 1986—; computer cons., Moreno Valley, 1988—. Com. mem. Shared Housing, Riverside, 1988—. Mem. Am. Soc. Pub. Adminstrs., Am. Soc. Women Accts. Democrat. Lutheran. Club: Exchange (Moreno Valley). Home: 24673 Ormista Dr MOreno Valley CA 92388 Office: Nat Bus Inst 4300 Central Ave Riverside CA 92506

JACKSON, MURIEL GRACE, university official; b. Wood-Ridge, N.J., Apr. 21, 1929; d. John David and Lillian Grace (Rogers) Kappeler; B.A., Keuka Coll., 1950; M.S., Columbia U. Sch. Journalism, 1952; grad. U. Mich. Inst. Acad. Adminstrv. Advancement, 1973, Oreg. Mgmt. Devel. Program, 1974; m. Rudolph Lorenz, Mar. 27, 1955 (dec. Nov. 1965); children—John Martin, Tracy Ann, Andrea Grace; m. 2d, Ross E. Jackson, June 10, 1967. Pub. relations asst. St. Lawrence U., 1950-51; editorial asst. Ridgewood (N.J.) News, 1952-53; reporter Binghamton (N.Y.) Press, 1953-56; adminstrv. asst. to pres. San Jose State Coll., 1966-69; asst. to pres. U. Oreg., 1969-75, dir. univ. relations, 1974-79, asst. for adminstrn., 1979-85, asst. v.p. for adminstrn., 1985—, dir. univ. bookstore, 1977-84. Troop leader Western Rivers Council Girl Scouts U.S.A., 1973-74; troop treas. Oreg. Trails Council Boy Scouts Am., 1973-74; sr. warden Episcopal Ch. of the Resurrection, Eugene, Oreg., 1973-74; chmn. Central Convocation Episcopal Diocese of Oreg., 1974-76; spl. events chmn. Lane County (Oreg.) United Way, 1976, 77; bd. dirs. Lane County Cancer Soc., 1978-80; bd. dirs. Lane Meml. Blood Bank, 1979-86, pres., 1984-85. Recipient Disting. Alumna award Keuka Coll., 1975. Mem. Council Advancement and Support of Edn., Eugene C. of C. (chmn. univ. affairs com. 1978, 81, 82), State Bar Assn. Oreg. (mem. bd. state profl. responsibility 1987, 88), Lane County Rubicon Soc. Republican. Home: 2149 Lake Isle Ct Eugene OR 97401 Office: U Oreg 202 Johnson Hall Eugene OR 97403

JACKSON, (AASE) OSA LITTRUP, physical therapy educator; b. Copenhagen, Jan. 3, 1950; d. Gunnar and Gerda (Petersen) Littrup; m. Nils Klykken, Feb. 26, 1982 (divorced); 1 child, Marius. BS, U. Mich., 1972, MA in Ednl. Adminstrn., 1973, PhD, 1979; student, Hartford Family Inst., 1980, Feldenkrais Practioner Tng. Program, 1981-84. Dir. rehab. Roseville (Mich.) Nursing Home, 1973-74, St. Joseph Nursing Home, Hamtramck, Mich., 1972-75; asst. clin. prof. NYU, N.Y.C., 1975-77; dir. rehab. Hartford Hosp., 1977-79; ptnr. Glastonbury (Conn.) Health Assocs., 1980; founder, pres. Geriatric Inst, Inc., Glastonbury, 1980-81; vis. prof. dept physiotherapy U. Queensland, Brisbane, Australia, 1983-85; assoc. prof., chmn. div. kinesiological scis. Oakland U., Rochester, Mich., 1986—; adj. faculty dept. phys. therapy U. Conn., Stoors, 1978-79; asst. prof. dept. phys. therapy U. Md., 1980; lectr. dept. family medicine U. Conn., Farmington, 1981, Diakonissehusets Nursing Sch., Oslo, 1982-85, Oslo Sch. Physiotherapy, 1983-85, Andrew U., Berrien Springs, Mich., 1987—; adj. asst. prof. dept. phys. therapy U. Pitts., 1984—; cons. in field. Author: Physical Therapy of the Geriatric Patient, 1983, Therapeutic Considerations for the Elderly, 1987; coeditor Jour. of Geriatric Phys. and Occupational Therapy, 1980-81; mem. editorial bd. Jour. Gerontology and Geriatric Edn., 1980-83, Internat. Phys. Therapy, 1984—; contbr. articles to profl. jours. Mem. Am. Gerontol. Soc., Am. Geriatric Soc., Norwegian Phys. Therapy Assn. (faculty 1983-85, program devel. 1985—), AAUP, Am. Phys. Therapy Assn. (del. 1978-80, pres. Conn. chpt. 1981, chmn. sect. on geriatrics 1982, Joan Mills award 1987), Am. Heart Assn. (chmn. cardiac rehab.). Home: 450 Maple Hill Rochester Hills MI 48063 Office: Oakland U Sch Health Scis Rochester MI 48063

JACKSON, PATRICIA LEE (MRS. CLIFFORD L. JACKSON), psychologist; b. N.Y.C.; d. Albert George and Lisbeth P. (Lee) Scharf; B.A., Barnard Coll.; M.A., Ph.D., Tchrs. Coll. Columbia U.; m. Clifford L. Jackson. Dir. psychol. testing R. H. Macy & Co., Inc., 1941-49; employment dir. Alexander's Dept. Stores, Inc., Bronx, N.Y., 1949-52; asst. prof. psychology Hunter Coll., N.Y.C., 1951-66, asso. prof., 1966-77, coordinator of counseling services, 1959-71; research dir. Klein Inst. for Aptitude Testing, Inc., N.Y.C., 1953-59, asst. v.p., 1957-59; pvt. practice in psychotherapy, 1964—. Trustee Alfred Adler Inst.; v.p. bd. trustees Ch. of Healing Christ (Emmet Fox Ch.), N.Y.C. Mem. AAAS, Am. Personnel and Guidance Assn., Am. Psychol. Assn., Am. Statis. Assn., Am. Group Psychotherapy Assn., N.Y. Soc. Clin. Psychologists. Author articles in field. Home: 129 E 35th St New York NY 10016

JACKSON, PAULETTE WHITE, nursing administrator, agency executive; b. New Orleans, Jan. 19, 1949; d. Lawrence III and Velma (Jones) White; m. Robert Wardell Tate, June 30, 1964 (div. 1969); children—Robert Jr., Detra Jeanene; m. Tommy Lee Jackson, July 20, 1974; 1 child, Byron. B.S. in Nursing, Southeastern La. U., 1980. Staff nurse Capitol Home Health, Baton Rouge, 1980-81; dir. nursing service Hill Haven Nursing Home, Baton Rouge, 1981; nephrology nurse BMA Baton Rouge, 1981-82; staff nurse Ammon's Home Health, Baton Rouge, 1981-83; supr. Greenwell Springs Hosp., La., 1983; owner, adminstr. Faith Home Health Services, Baton Rouge, 1983—. Recipient Outstanding Bus. Achievement award Wybirk & Assocs. Inc., 1984. Mem. Beta Beta Beta. Democrat. Avocations: reading; skating; swimming. Home: 5589 Monarch Ave Baton Rouge LA 70811 Office: Faith Home Health Services 2034 Wooddale Blvd Suite A Baton Rouge LA 70806

JACKSON, PHILLIS KITCHEN, stock broker; b. Canadian, Tex., June 14, 1948; d. William David Kitchen and Wanda Jane (Shaw) Groff; m. Wesley Richard York (div.); children: Richard Todd, Carmel Lei; m. Kenneth Wayne; children: Ashley Brette; 1 stepchild, Kristi Lynn. Student, Tex. State Tech. Inst., 1979, Amarillo (Tex.) Coll., 1975-82. Owner Touch of Brass, Pampa, Tex., 1979-81; broker Tex. Securities, Amarillo, 1983; br. mgr. Heinold Securities, Amarillo, 1983-86; pres. Panhandle Investments, Groom, Tex., 1985—; instr. Amarillo Coll., 1984—; cons. investment clubs. Mem. econ. devel. com. City of Grom. Mem. Internat. Assn. Fin. Planning, Nat. Assn. Female Execs., LWV, Nat. Fedn. Ind. Bus., Amarillo Womens Network. Baptist. Home and Office: Rt 1 Groom TX 79039

JACKSON, (MARY) RUTH, orthopedic surgeon; b. Jefferson, Iowa, Dec. 13, 1902; d. William Riley and Carolyn Arabelle (Babb) J.; B.A., U. Tex., 1924; M.D., Baylor U., 1928. Gen. intern Meml. Hosp., Worcester, Mass., 1928-29, resident in orthopaedic surgery, 1930-31; intern in orthopaedic surgery Univ. Hosps., U. Iowa, 1929-30; resident in orthopaedic surgery Tex. Scottish Rite Hosp. for Crippled Children, Dallas and asst. at Carrell-Driver-Girard Clinic, Dallas, 1931-32; pvt. practice medicine specializing in orthopaedic surgery, Dallas, 1932—; clin. instr. in orthopaedic surgery Baylor U., Dallas, 1936-43; hon. cons. orthopaedic surgeon Baylor U. Med. Center, Dallas, Parkland Meml. Hosp., Dallas; hon. asst. clin. prof. orthopaedic surgery Southwestern Med. Sch. of U. Tex., Dallas; lectr. in field. Diplomate Am. Bd. Orthopaedic Surgery. Fellow ACS, Internat. Coll. Surgeons; mem. Dallas County Med. Assn., Tex. Med. Assn., So. Med. Assn., AMA, Tex. Orthopaedic Assn., Tex. Rheumatism Assn., Southwestern Surg. Congress, Am. Acad. Orthopaedic Surgeons, Am. Orthopaedic Foot Soc., Am. Assn. for Study Headache, Am. Trauma Soc., Am. Assn. Automotive Medicine, Am. Soc. Contemporary Medicine and Surgery, Western Orthopaedic Assn., Law-Sci. Acad. Am., Pan-Am. Med. Assn. (diplomate sect. orthopaedic surgery), Royal Soc. Medicine (assoc.), Nat. Assn. Disability Examiners, Dallas C. of C., North Dallas C. of C., Kaufman C. of C., Ruth Jackson Soc. Republican. Methodist. Club: Zonta Internat. Author monograph: The Cervical Syndrome, 1956, 4th edit., 1977, Japanese transl, 1967; contbr. articles to profl. jours. Office: 3629 Fairmount Dallas TX 75219

JACKSON, RUTH ROBERTSON, insurance company executive; b. Grady County, Okla., Apr. 17, 1939; d. Gordon James and Rose Viola (Ritter) Robertson; m. Mahlon Bruce Slocum, Dec. 30, 1957 (div. 1972); children: Laura Wynn Robertson, Jill Michele Slocum; m. Gilbert Shepard Jackson, May 31, 1987. Student, Okla. Coll. for Women, 1957-58, Midwestern U., 1961, El Centro Community Coll., 1980. Legal sec. Wichita County Judge, Wichita Falls, Tex., 1960-62, Douglas E. Bergman Law Firm, Dallas, 1962-64; sec. claims Excalibur Ins. Co., Dallas, 1971-75; sr. sec. claims Excalibur Ins. Co., Carrollton, Tex., 1975-79, asst. sec., treas., 1979-84, pres., 1984—; supr. compliance Excalibur Holdings, Inc., Carrollton, 1979-82, dir. compliance and analysis, 1982-84, dir. underwriting, 1984. Mem. Nat. Assn. Female Execs. Republican. Home: 2663 Via Los Altos Carrollton TX 75006 Office: Def Mapping Agy PO Box 1744 APO San Francisco CA 96555

JACKSON, RUTHIE FAY, government official; b. Wynne, Ark., June 2, 1948; d. Tyree and Ruth (Perry) Weaver; m. Charles M. Jackson, July 6, 1974; children: Vanessa Marie, Casey Nathaniel. AAS in Secretarial Sci., Seattle Community Coll., 1968; student U. Wash., 1971. Receptionist Mobil Oil Corp., Seattle, 1969; clk., stenographer HEW (now Dept. Health and Human Services), Seattle, 1970-74, equal opportunity specialist, 1974-78, child support specialist, 1978-80, dep. regional rep. child support office, 1980-81, dir. Office Child Support Enforcement, Region X, Seattle, 1981—. Mem. Wash. Statewide Steering Com. on Adolescent Pregnancy Prevention, Pregnancy and Parenting. Recipient Commendations, Dept. HHS, 1978, Cert. of Merit, Dept. HHS, 1980, Spl. Achievement Cash awards Dept. HHS, 1980, 1984, Merit award Dept. HHS, 1985, 86, Performance cash awards Dept. HHS, 1981-87. Mem. Nat. Assn. Female Execs., Am. Soc. Pub. Adminstrs., Internat. Platform Assn., Am. Soc. Profl. and Exec. Women. Mem. Church of God in Christ. Home: 12734 SE 73d St Renton WA 98056 Office: Office Child Support Enforcement 2901 3d Ave M/S 305 Seattle WA 98121

JACKSON, SALLY A(NN) WARD, state official; b. Springfield, Ill., July 9, 1931, d. Verdun and Marion L (Hult) Randolph. B.S. in Adminstrn. of Justice, So. Ill. U., 1972, M.S. in Adminstrn. of Justice, 1973; fellow state and local program Harvard U. JFK Sch. Govt., 1987. Mem. law enforcement faculty Western Ill. U., Macomb, 1973-76; budget and program analyst Ill. Bur. of Budget, Springfield, 1976-77; asst. to dir. Ill. Dept. Law Enforcement, Springfield, 1977-80; asst. to gov. State of Ill., Chgo., 1980-83; dir. Ill. Dept. of Employment Security, Chgo., 1983—; dirs. Ill. Job Tng. Coordination Council, Chgo., 1983—, Chgo. Pvt. Industry Council, 1983—; mem. cabinet Econ. Devel. Subcabinet, Springfield, 1983—; Mem. Interstate Conf. Employment Security Adminstrs. (chmn. pub. relations 1983, bd. dirs. 1985-86, mem. com. 1985-86), Internat. Assn. Personnel in Employment Security, Women Execs. in State Govt. (vice chair 1987, charter mem. 1983, bd. dirs. 1985—). Republican. Methodist. Office: Ill Dept Employment Security 401 S State 6S Chicago IL 60605

JACKSON, SANDRA KAY, manufacturing company executive; b. Crossett, Ark., May 20, 1950; d. Willie James Hall and Irene (Coleman) Fields; m. Harry James Jackson, Sept. 18, 1986. BS, Ark. AM&N Coll., 1972; postgrad., U. Toledo. Clk. Blue Cross N.W. Ohio, Toledo, 1972-73; clk. Sheller Globe Corp., Toledo, 1973-75, ins. adminstr., 1975-79; ins. adminstr. Owens-Ill., Inc., Toledo, 1979-82, sr. ins. adminstr., 1982-85, mgr. liability ins., 1985—. Vol. probation officer Lucas County Probation Dept., Toledo, 1978-80. Democrat. Office: Owens-Ill Inc One SeaGate Toledo OH 43666

JACKSON, SHARON PATRICE, research analyst; b. Washington, Feb. 4, 1958; d. Archibald and Frances (Armwood) J. B.A., Catholic U., 1980; M.A., Johns Hopkins U., 1982. Pub. info. specialist White House Council on Environ. Quality, Washington, 1980-81; research analyst NAACP, Washington, 1981-82; intelligence analyst U.S. Dept. Def., Washington, 1982—. Mem. Network of Women in Slavic Studies, Nat. Assn. Female Execs., Johns Hopkins U. Alumni Assn. Avocation: cooking, reading.

JACKSON, SHIRLEY CRITE, government agency executive; b. Memphis, June 4, 1940; d. Golden and Lucinda (Berry) Crite; B.A. in Elem. Edn., Northeastern U., 1961, M.A. in Applied Linguistics and English Lang., 1966; postgrad. U. Chgo., George Washington U., 1967-77; Ed.D. in Curriculum and Instrn., Cath. U. Am., 1982; m. Allen D. Jackson, July 5, 1969; 1 son, Dewyane Anthony. Tchr., Chgo. Public Schs., 1961-66, high sch. English cons., 1966-68, coordinator reading, lang. arts, high sch. English programs, 1968-72; communication skills and math. cons., program coordinator D.C. Health Pub. Co., Lexington, Mass., 1972-75; prof. U. Maine, Portland/Gorham, 1975-77; tech. asst. to state depts. edn. Right to Read Program, U.S. Office Edn., Washington, 1975, program devel. br. chief Right to Read Program, 1975-77, dep. dir. program, 1977, dir. program, 1977-78, dir. Nat. Basic Skills Improvement Program, 1978-81, dir. basic edn. programs, 1979-81, acting dep. asst. sec. ednl. support programs, 1981-82, dir. state and local ednl. programs, 1982; asso. dir. Teaching and Learning Research Programs Nat. Inst. Edn., 1982—; dir. edn. Young Astronaut Council; conf. speaker; dir. analysis and data collection service Office Civil Rights, Washington; mem. Nat. Brain Trust on Edn. of Congressional Black Caucus; mem. adv. council Nat. Center for the Book, Library of Congress;

mem. nat. adv. council ERIC Reading/Communication Skills; mem. exec. devel. council Horace Mann Learning Center, also mem. exec. resources bd.; mem. task panel Pres.'s Commn. on Mental Health; mem. literacy task panel White House Conf. on Libraries; speaker. Sr. Usher, missionary Allen Chapel A.M.E. Ch., Washington, 1975—; developer, chairperson Operation Coll. Bound: Hosts, 1980-82; active Boy Scouts Am.; v.p. Shugart Jr. High Sch. PTA, 1976; mem. Prince George's County Parents Integration Task Force, 1975-76. Recipient Outstanding Alumni award Northeastern U., 1987. Cert. tchr., Ill.; recipient profl. certs. U.S. Dept. Edn., 1976, 78, 80, 81; Recognition cert. U.S. Office of Edn., 1981; others. Mem. Internat. Reading Assn., Assn. Supervision and Curriculum Devel., Am. Ednl. Research Assn., Nat. Council Negro Women, NAACP, Nat. Urban League, Alpha Kappa Alpha, Phi Delta Kappa. Author Manuals and articles in field. Home: 2120 Keating St Temple Hills MD 20748 Office: 1211 Connecticut Ave Washington DC 20036

JACKSON, SHIRLEY STROTHER, federal agency programs administrator; b. Washington, Mar. 21, 1940; d. Thomas and Lillian (Washington) Strother. AS in Bus. Adminstrn., Southeastern U., 1987, BS summa cum laude in Mktg., 1988. Payroll clk., then supr. Naval Fin. Office U.S. Naval Sta., Washington, 1958-63; sec. Office of Gen Counsel Fed. Power Commn., Washington, 1963-64; dep. undersec. and asst. sec. community devel. HEW, Washington, 1964-71; adminstrv. asst. ACTION Agy. div. Office of Dep. Assoc. Dir. of VISTA, Washington, 1971-73; staff asst. to commr. Consumer Product Safety Commn., Washington, 1973-76; office mgr., sec. Newman & Hermanson Co., Washington, 1977; staff asst. Consumer and Regulatory Functions div. HUD, Washington, 1976-77; bus. devel. specialist Minority Bus. Devel. Agy. div. Dept. of Commerce, Washington, 1978—; assoc. real estate agt. Colonial Homes, Inc., Ft. Washington, Md., 1978-81, J. Rob Robinson, Inc., Silver Hills., Md., 1981-85. Tutor Operation Rescue, Washington, 1983; vol. Providence Hosp. Ctr. for Life, Washington, 1983. Recipient Group Incentive award Minority Bus. Devel. Agy., 1984, Sustained Superior Performance award Minority Bus. Devel. Agy., 1980, 83, Cert. Recognition, Minority Devel. Agy., 1987, Outstanding Performance award Minority Bus. Devel. Agy., 1987. Mem. Nat. Assn. Female Execs., NAACP, Am. Mgmt. Assn., Am. Mktg. Assn., Les Amis Du Vin, The Pinochle Club (sec. 1982-83). Democrat. Baptist.

JACKSON, SUSAN ADAMS, programmer; b. Missoula, Mont., Mar. 22, 1953; d. Ronald Burton and Elisabeth Helen (Blumenthal) J.; m. Richard C. Wolverton, 1987. BA, U. Mass., 1980. Jr. programmer Filene's, Boston, 1976; programmer Comml. Union Ins., Boston, 1977-78, jr. data base analyst, 1978-79; data base analyst Boston U., 1980-81, systems programmer, 1981-83; systems programmer Lechmere, Inc., Woburn, Mass., 1984-86; sr. data communications programmer, analyst Fed. Res. Bank, Boston, 1987—. Home: 14-1A Leverett Ave East Boston MA 02128 Office: Fed Res Bank of Boston 600 Atlantic Ave Boston MA 02106

JACKSON, THERESA PATRICIA, physician; b. Bronx, N.Y., Oct. 15, 1952; d. Pat Howard and Genevieve (Glover) Jackson. B.A., Hunter Coll, City U. N.Y., 1974; M.D., Cornell U. Med. Coll., 1978. Diploma Am. Bd. Pediatrics. Intern Montefiore Hosp., Bronx, 1978-79, resident, 1979-81, clin. instr., attending pediatrician, 1981-85; assoc. dir. clin. devel. Lederle Labs./Am. Cyanamid, Pearl River, N.Y., 1985—. Louis-Simon scholar, 1970-74; Nat. Med. fellow, 1974-76. Mem. Nat. Med. Assn., Susan Smith McKinney Stewart Found. Democrat. Roman Catholic. Home: 59 Alan Rd Spring Valley NY 10977 Office: Lederle Labs/Am Cyanamid Middletown Rd Pearl River NY 10965

JACKSON, WILMA (DARCY DEMILLE), columnist, public relations consultant; b. Chgo., Dec. 17; d. R.L. and Sophia O. Littlejohn; B.S. in Urban Studies/Sociology, U. Mich., 1977; cert. in urban studies Mich. State U., 1977; m. Gordon Chester Jackson, July 1, 1959; children—Carole Harris, Linda Luten, Jill, Shelley Bethay. Feature writer and columnist Sepia Mag., Fort Worth, 1961-81; columnist Hip Mag., 1963-81, Soul-Teen Mag., 1973-81, Bronze Thrills Mag., 1957—, also feature writer, 1956—, Chgo. Daily Defender, 1959-61; columnist, feature writer Flint Jour. (Mich.), 1981—; pub. relations cons. A. Gail Mazaraki, cons., 1982—; syndicated columnist Associated Negro Press, 1959-64, women's editor, 1959-61; reporter and feature writer Negro Press Internat., 1964-65; market research interviewer Barlow Survey Service, Chgo., 1958-59; owner, mgr. Medi-Rary Lit. Agy., 1963—; assoc. editor Vines mag., 1980—; instr. Jordan Coll., 1982—, Mott Community Coll., 1984—; guest lectr. creative writing U. Mich., Flint, 1977-78; adv. Black Fashion Mus., N.Y.C., 1979-80; public relations dir. The Links, Inc., 1979—, also chmn. internat. trends and services; eval. specialist and instr. The Kennedy Center, Flint, 1979-83; bus. liaison rep., tchr. Flint Community Schs.; cons. Manulife Ins., Timeshares, Inc. Mem. public affairs com. YWCA; bd. dirs., mem. adv. council Mich. League for Human Services. Recipient Woman of Year awards (3), 1983, Media Women Humanitarian award, 1983. numerous writing awards. Mem. Nat. Assn. Media Women (Woman of Yr. award 1978, pres. 1978-80), Flint Writers Club (v.p. 1973-74), Greater Flint Art Guild, U. Mich. Alumni Assn., Paint and Palette Art Group, Grand Blanc Arts Guild, Flint Inst. Arts, Phi Delta Kappa. Democrat. Office: 615 Lippincott Blvd Flint MI 48503

JACKSON-BROWN, IRENE VIOLA, administrator, educator; b. Washington, Aug. 13, 1947; d. Robert and Dorothy (Williams)Jackson; m. Enrique Ricardo Brown, June 15, 1974; 1 child, Guillermo. BA in Music, Howard U., 1969; MA, Smith, 1970; PhD, Wesleyan, 1974. Asst. prof. Yale U., New Haven, Conn., 1973-77; lectr., project dir. U. Conn., Stamford, 1977-79; asst. prof., program dir. Howard U., Washington, 1979-82; vis. specialist Montclair (N.J.) State Coll., 1979; program officer Episcopal Ch. Ctr., N.Y.C., 1982—. Editor: Afro-Am. Religious Music, 1979, More Than Drumming, 1986, More Than Dancing, 1986. Mem. coalition 100 black Women, Fairfield, Conn. Ford Found. grantee, 1971-74. Mem. Soc. For Ethnomusicalogy, Assn. For Study Afro-Am. Life and History. Home: 80 Betsy Brown Circle Port Chester NY 10573

JACKSON-FRANKL, KAY ANN, nurse; b. Cin., Mar. 11, 1958; d. William E. and Mary Helen (Filippine) Jackson; m. Russell Joseph Frankl, Oct. 13, 1957. A in Nursing, Miami U., Hamilton, Ohio, 1978; B in Nursing, U. Cin., 1981, M in Nursing, 1983; postgrad., Ind. U., 1983—. Charge nurse St. Francis Hosp., Cin., 1978-79; staff, team leader Providence Hosp., 1979-82; research asst. U. Cin., 1982-83; instr. Deaconess Sch. Nursing, Cin., 1983-86; cons. to nursing adminstrn. Dearborn County Hosp., Lawrenceburg, Ind., 1986—. Mem. Ams. Nurses Assn., Nat. Assn. Female Execs. Home and Office: RR #1 PO Box 216 Aurora IN 47001

JACKSON-GILLISON, HELEN LUCILLE, lawyer; b. Colliers, W.Va., July 9, 1944; d. George William and Helen Loretta (Wells) Jackson; m. Edward Lee Gillison Sr.; 1 child, Edward Lee II. BS cum laude, West Liberty State Coll., 1977; JD, W.Va. U., 1981. Bar: W.Va. 1981, U.S. Dist. Ct. (so. and no. dists.) W.Va. 1981. Sole practice Weirton, W.Va., 1981—. Mem. adv. bd. Blot Out Litter Today, Inc. Clean Community System, Weirton; with office of sec. W.Va. Northern Community Coll., 1983—, adv. council friends of coll., 1983—, bd. dirs. 1983—; civil service commr. City of Weirton Police Dept., 1987; mem. People to People Internat. Citizen Ambassador Program; bd. dirs. W.Va. Civil Liberties Union, ARC, Weirton, Sheltered Workshop of W.Va., Hancock County, Housing Authority, Weirton, Ft. Steuben council Boy Scouts Am. Recipient Black Atty. Yr. award BALSA W.Va. Coll. Law, 1986. Mem. ABA, Assn. Trial Lawyers Am., Mountain State Bar Assn., Nat. Bar Assn., Hancock Bar Assn., W.Va. Trial Lawyers Assn. (bd. govs. 1986—, pub. relations com.), W.Va. Bar Assn. (bd. govs. 1986—, various coms.), Weirton Bus. and Profl. Women's Club (chmn. polit. action com. 1982-83), Assn. Community Coll. Trustees (assoc.), NAACP (bd. dirs. Steubenville chpt. 1982-84), Million Dollar Club, Internat. Platform Assn., Phi Alpha Delta. Democrat. Baptist. Home: 264 Lakeview Dr Weirton WV 26062 Office: 3139 West St Weirton WV 26062

JACKSON-THOMPSON, MARIE-THERESE OLIVER, judge; b. Pitts., Aug. 14, 1947; d. Warren Joseph and Nettie Marie (Wall) Oliver; m. Peter Jackson, July 8, 1972 (div.); children: Vincent, Alphonso; m. Henry Quentin Thompson, Feb. 14, 1987; 1 stepchild, Joshua Thompson. B.A., Mt. Holyoke Coll., 1969; JD Harvard U., 1972. Bar: Mass. 1973, U.S. Dist. Ct. Mass., 1973. Assoc. Cambridge & Somerville Legal Services, Mass., 1972-74; atty. Mass. Commn. Against Discrimination, Boston, 1974, dir. investigation, 1974-76; adminstrv. judge Div. Hearing Officers, State of Mass., Boston, 1976-77; gen. counsel Exec. Office Adminstrn. and Fin., Boston, 1977-80; judge Cambridge Dist. Ct. (Mass.), 1980—; mem. Juvenile Justice Adv. Com., Gov.'s Anti-Crime Commn., 1983—; teaching faculty Mass. Continuing Legal Edn., Mass. Judicial Inst. Bd. dirs. Adolescent Consultation Service, Cambridge, 1981—, Cambridge and Somerville Mental Health Bd., 1981-84, West Medford Community Ctr. (Mass.), 1979-84; mem. Mass. Commn. on Correction Alternatives, 1985-86; mem. Gov.'s Com. on Foster Care, 1986; mem. sexual abuse task force Middlesex Dist. Atty.'s Office, 1985-86; bd. dirs. Nat. Conf. Christians and Jews, 1985-88 , Boston Youth Symphony Orch., 1984-87, Judge Baker Guidance Ctr., 1988—. Named one of Ten Outstanding Young Leaders, Boston Jr. C. of C., 1981, Outstanding Profl. Leaders, Cambridge YMCA, 1985; recipient citation for advocacy for foster parenting Boston City Council, 1985, Mass. Senate, 1985; Juvenile Justice award, Mass. Justice Resource Inst, 1985. Mem. Nat. Assn. Women Judges (dir. 1982-84) ABA (del. commn. courts, community, Nat. Conf. Spl. Ct. Judges 1983), Nat. Assn. Bus. and Profl. Women (Boston & vicinity group 1st v.p. 1979-80, leadership award 1981, Sojourner Truth Leadership award 1984), Mass. Black Lawyers Assn. (dir. 1978-79, leadership award 1980), Links, Inc. (Middlesex chpt.), Mass. Black Judges Assn., Mass. Judges Conf., Middlesex Chpt. Links, Alpha Kappa Alpha. Baptist. Office: Cambridge Dist Ct 40 Thorndike St Cambridge MA 02141

JACKSON-WILLIAMS, MARY IRENE, educator; b. Hugo, Okla., June 30, 1944; d. Primer and Hylar B. (Tarkington) Jackson; B.Bus. Edn., Langston U., 1967; M.S. in Bus. Edn., Emporia State U., 1973; postgrad. U. Nev., 1975-77, U.S. Internat. U., San Diego, 1987-88; m. Lee A. William, Feb. 10, 1973; 1 dau., Monica Ariane. Bus. instr. Spokane (Wash.) Community Coll., 1967-69; Topeka West High Sch., 1970-71, tchr. bus. Highland Park High Sch., Topeka, Kans., 1972-73; instr. Clark County Community Coll., North Las Vegas, Nev., 1973-78, dir. bus. div., 1978—; cons. Scott Foresman Pub. Co., 1977-80; condr. seminars for Las Vegas C. of C., 1980. Recipient Educator of Yr. award, Bus. and Service award for edn. Clark County Community Coll., 1986, 87. Mem. Am. Bus. Communication Assn., Nat. Bus. Edn. Assn., Am. Assn. Women in Community and Jr. Colls., Internat. Assn. Bus. Communicators, Am. Assn. Female Execs., Am. Assn. Univ. Women, Nat. Council Instructional Adminstrs. Office: Clark County Community Coll 3200 E Cheyenne Ave North Las Vegas NV 89030

JACOB, DELIA LEGGETT, human relations executive; b. Los Angeles, Sept. 16, 1950; d. Charles William and Delia (Marin); B.A. with honors, Stanford U., 1972; M.A., U. Mich., 1975; student U. So. Calif., 1968-70; m. John Edward Jacob, Feb. 14, 1979; 1 son, Jonathon Michael. Study coordinator Soc. Psychol. Study of Social Issues-Am. Psychol. Assn., Ann Arbor, Mich., 1973; teaching fellow U. Mich., Ann Arbor, 1974, 75-76; research asso. Survey Research Center, Ann Arbor, 1977-78; acad. counselor Coll. Lit., Sci. and Arts, U. Mich., 1978-79; adminstrv. mgr. Rackham Grad. Sch., U. Mich., 1979-80; personnel asst. Martec Services, Los Angeles, 1981; asst. dir. personnel Cox, Castle & Nicholson, Century City, Calif., 1981-82; staffing mgr. applied tech. div. TRW, Redondo Beach, Calif., 1982-85, personnel policies mgr. ops. and support group, 1985-86; sector mgr. human relations spl. projects Electronics & Def. sector, 1986-87; corp. human relations mgr. ESL Inc., Sunnyvale, Calif., 1987—. Mem. career mktg. bd. Mademoiselle mag.; mem. program council Women for Richstone. Ford Found. fellow, 1972-77; Calif. State scholar, 1970-72; recipient Book award Calif. State Employees Assn., 1968-69; Gov.'s scholar, Calif., 1968. Mem. Am. Psychol. Assn., Women in Communication, Nat. Network Hispanic Women, Women for Richstone; Chicano Student Psychol. Assn. (chmn.), Theta Sigma Phi. Democrat. Contbr. articles to profl. jours. Home: 2112 Menalto Ave Menlo Park CA 94025 Office: ESL 501 495 Java Dr PO Box 3510 Sunnyvale CA 94088

JACOB, MARY JANE, curator; b. N.Y.C., Jan. 5, 1952; d. Elmer J. and Catherine (Marino) J.; m. Russell L. Lewis. B.F.A., U. Fla., 1973; M.A. in Art History, U. Mich., 1976. Assoc. curator modern art Detroit Inst. of Arts, Mich., 1976-80; curator Mus. of Contemporary Art, Chgo., 1980-83, chief curator, 1983-87; chief curator Mus. Contemporary Art, Los Angeles, 1987—. Author numerous exhbn. catalogues; contbg. author: A Quite Revolution: British Sculpture Since 1965, 86, Jannis Kounellis, 1986, Gordon Matta-Clark, A Retrospective, 1985, The Woven and Graphic Art of Anni Albers, 1985, In the Mind's Eye: Dad and Surrealism, 1984, The Amazing Decade: Women and Performance Art 1970-1980, 1983; Magdalena Abakanowicz, 1982, The Rouge: The Image of Industry in Art of Charles Sheeler and Diego Rivera, 1978; contbr. articles and essays to profl. jours. Office: Mus of Contemporary Art 250 S Grand Ave Los Angeles CA 90012

JACOB, NANCY LOUISE, college dean; b. Berkeley, Calif., Jan. 15, 1943; d. Irvin Carl and Ruby (Roberts) Feustel; m. George B. Fotheringham, Dec. 22, 1972; 1 child, Randy. BA magna cum laude, U. Wash., 1967; PhD in Econs. magna cum laude, U. Calif., Irvine, 1970. Econ. analyst, summer research staff Ctr. for Naval Analysis, Arlington, Va., 1969, chmn. dept. fin., bus. econs. and quantitative methods, 1978-81; with Weyerhaeuser Co. Tacoma, 1963-65; mem. faculty U. Wash., Seattle, 1970—, dean Schs. Bus. Adminstrn., 1981—, prof. fin., 1981—; trustee Coll. Retirement Equities Fund., N.Y., 1980—; bd. dirs. Puget Sound Power and Light Co., Bellevue, Wash., Rainier Bancorp., Seattle. Co-author: Basic: An Intro to Computer Programming Using Basic Language, 1979, Investments, 1984, 88; contbr. articles to profl. jours. Bd. dirs. Pacific Coast Banking Sch., Seattle, 1981—, Jr. Achievement, Seattle, 1982-84, Wash. Council on Internat. Trade, Seattle, 1981—. Recipient Wall St Jour. Achievement award U. Wash., 1967; NDEA Title IV fellow, 1968-70. Mem. Am. Econ. Assn., Am. Fin. Assn. (bd. dirs. 1975-77), Western Fin. Assn. (bd. dirs. 1976-78), Seattle Soc. Fin. Analysts, Fin. Mgmt. Assn. (program com. 1977), Phi Beta Kappa, Alpha Kappa Psi. Club: Rainier, Washington Athletic, Columbia Tower (Seattle). Office: U of Wash Sch Grad Bus Adminstrn Seattle WA 98195

JACOB, RUTH ANN, beauty business owner; b. Flint, Mich., Nov. 14, 1945; d. Theodore Sargis and Charlotte (Isaac) J. A.A., Flint Jr. Coll., 1968; B.F.A., San Francisco Art Inst., 1971; M.F.A., U. Mich., 1974. Asst. buyer, clk. Saks Fifth Ave, Evanston, Ill., 1974-75; receptionist Gazebo Salon, Park Ridge, Ill., 1975-76; receptionist, asst. mgr. Mark Benaim Salon, Chgo., 1976-77; mgr. salon Drake Hotel Salon, Chgo., 1977-78; br. coordinator Glemby Internat., Chgo., 1979-81; owner, bookeeper Mark/James Inc., Chgo., 1981—; instr. fine arts North Shore Arts, Winnetka, Ill., 1975-76, Goddard Coll., Plainfield, Vt., 1974-75; co-owner Creations & Things, Flint, Mich., 1975-76; teaching asst. U. Mich., Ann Arbor, 1973-74. Mem. Old Town Art League, Chgo., 1983. Recipient award Craft Commitment Exhbn., Rochester, Minn., 1974, Scholarship, Assyrian Am. Nat. Exhbn., Chgo., 1974, Plaque, Metro-Help, Chgo., 1981; grantee San Francisco Art Inst., 1971, Kiwanis Club, Flint, 1971. Mem. U. Mich. Alumni Assn. Republican. Presbyterian. Club: Women's Workout (Chgo.). Avocations: painting; sewing. Office: The Hair Salon of Mark/James Inc 1652 N Wells St Chicago IL 60614

JACOBI, MARY JO, financial services executive; b. Bay St. Louis, Miss., Dec. 7, 1951; d. Lawrence John and Delta Mae (Lizana) Jacobi. B.B.A., Loyola U., 1973; M.B.A., George Washington U., 1976; student Cath. U. Am., 1969-70. Chief adminstr. U.S. Senate Commerce Com., 1973-76; dir. mktg. regulations and govt. ops. NAM, 1977-79; mgr. regulatory affairs 3M Co., 1979-81; bus. liaison U.S. Dept. Commerce, Washington, 1981-83; spl. asst. to the Pres. of U.S., The White House, Washington, 1983-85; corp. v.p. Drexel Burnham Lambert, Inc., 1985-87, 1st v.p., 1987—; v.p. Nat. Energy Resources Orgn., Washington, 1983-85. Contbg. author: Mandate for Leadership, 1980; featured author: America's New Women Entrepreneurs, 1986. Mem. Republican Women's Fed. Forum, others. Mem. Women in Govt. Relations, Nat. Women's Econ. Alliance, Acad. Polit. Sci. Roman Catholic. Home: 44 Gramercy Park New York NY 10010 Office: Drexel Burnham Lambert Inc 60 Broad St New York NY 10004

JACOBOWITZ, ELAINE LYNN, sign language professional; b. Bklyn., Mar. 10, 1953; d. Abraham Harry and Miriam (Weintraub) J. BA in Psychology, Gallaudet Coll., 1976; MEd Ednl. Communications, U. Md., 1981; postgrad., Va. Poly. Inst. and State U., 1985—. Instr. Hilda Knoff Sch. for The Deaf, New Orleans, 1977-78, Dept. Sign Communications Gallaudet Coll., Washington, 1978-87; asst. prof. Dept. Sign Communications Gallaudet U., Washington, 1987—; presenter, workshop cons. in field, 1982—. Producer videotapes; author, dir. play, Gallaudet Coll. Alumni Assn. Mem. Am. Edn. and Communication Tech., Nat. Assn. of the Deaf, Registry Interpreters for the Deaf, Sign Instruction Guidance Network. Democrat. Jewish. Home: 8 Musicmaster Ct Silver Spring MD 20904 Office: Gallaudet Coll 800 Florida Ave NE Washington DC 20002

JACOBOZZI, VIVIAN MARIE, retail store executive; b. Montenero, Italy, Apr. 24, 1933 (parents Am. citizens); d. Andrea and Adelia Z. (Tornincasa) Iacobozzi; student public schs., Lorain, Ohio. Acct., Caravan Inn, Phoenix, 1963-67; office mgr. AME Food Service, Scottsdale, Ariz., 1967-70, v.p., 1970-78, pres., 1978-81, also dir.; pres., owner Remembrance Inc., 1983—; treas. Arcos Dress Shop, Sun City, Ariz., 1973—. Recipient plaque March of Dimes, 1978. Mem. Nat. Assn. Meat Purveyors (hon.), Livestock Mktg. Assn. (trustee). Republican. Roman Catholic. Home: 2836 N 76th Pl Scottsdale AZ 85251 Office: 7129 6th Ave Scottsdale AZ 85251

JACOBS, AGNES JACQUELINE EVERINGTON, retired wildlife federation executive; b. Wilkinsburg, Pa., June 17, 1923; d. James Pate and Agnes Kathleen (Scurry) Everington; A.B., Coker Coll., Hartsville, S.C., 1944, D.Letters (hon.), 1986; M.S. U. S.C., 1961, Ph.D. in Biology, 1968; m. Harold Weinberg Jacobs, May 11, 1947; children—Patricia Francyl, Janet Carolyn, James Cecil. Tchr. pub. schs., Columbia, S.C., 1957-64, 71-73; instructional TV specialist S.C. Dept. Edn., 1968-71; coordinator Inst. Environ. Studies, U. S.C., The Citadel, Clemson U., summers 1972-77; exec. dir. S.C. Wildlife Fedn., Columbia, 1974-83; mem. exec. com. S.C. Gov.'s Overall Recreation Plan Exchange Council, 1975—; charter mem. S.C. Environmental Edn. Assn., 1976—. Lectr. to various civic orgns., garden clubs, Rotary clubs, Scouts; mem. choir St. Michael and All Angels' Ch., Columbia, lay reader, 1980, mem. vestry, 1980-83, sr. warden, 1983; trustee Coker Coll., 1971-77, pres. Alumni Assn., 1975-77; bd. visitors Coker Coll., 1977-80; vice chmn. citizens' environ. planning com. Central Midlands Regional Planning Council, 1976-83; mem. S.C. Coastal Council, 1976-77; mem. citizens' adv. com. Riverbanks Zoo, Columbia, 1979—; mem. Russell Dam Task Force, 1979-83; bd. dirs. Yr. of Coast, 1980; mem. S.C. Forestry Study Group, U.S. Dept. Agr., 1979; Wildlife adv. com. Coll. Agrl. Scis., Clemson U., 1976-82; bd. dirs. Harry R.E. Hampton Wildlife Meml. Fund; co-chmn. Gov.'s Council Natural Resources and the Environment, 1983-85; exec. com. S.C. Marine Sci. Mus., 1986—. Served with USMC Women's Res., 1944-46. Decorated Letter of Commendation; recipient Conservation Educator of Year award S.C. Wildlife Fedn., 1970, F. Bartow Culp award, 1975, Conservationist of Yr. award, 1983; S.C. Conservation of Year award Woodmen of World, 1975; Outstanding Service award Nat. Wildlife Fedn., 1977, Disting. Service award, 1983; Outstanding Alumni award Coker Coll., 1980; S.C. Wildlife and Marine Resource Dept. and Commn.'s Meritorious Service award, 1983; Gov.'s Order of Palmetto, 1983; S.C. Trappers Assn. cert. appreciation, 1983; Environ. Edn. Assn. S.C. citation meritorious service, 1983. NSF fellow, summers 1959-60, 63-65, W. Gordon Belser fellow U. S.C., 1964-65; Belle W. Baruch Found. grantee U. S.C., 1967-68; EPA film grantee, 1980. Mem. AAAS, Am. Inst. Biol. Scis., Assn. Southeastern Biologists, Nat. Assn. Biology Tchrs. (Outstanding Biology Tchr. award for S.C. 1963), S.C. Assn. Biology Tchrs. (pres. 1965), S.C. Acad. Sci. (pres. 1973), S.C. Edn. Assn. (life), Richland County Legal Aux. (charter), Wildlife Soc. (charter mem. S.C. chpt.), S.C. Wildlife Fedn. (life bd. dirs. 1986, trustee Ednl. Found. 1986), Embroiderers' Guild Am. (pres. Millwood chpt. 1986-88, sec. Carolinas Region, 1988—), S.C. State Mus. (chmn., mem. exec. bd. S.C. through the Needle's Eye, 1987), Sigma Xi. Episcopalian. (layreader). Author: Life Science-Teacher's Guide to ITV Courses, 1970; also sci. papers. Producer-tchr ITV Life Science series, 1969-70. Producer films The Loggerhead Turtle Story, 1971, South Carolina Coastal Nesting Birds, 1971, Life in the Coral Reef, 1971, The Russell Dam—A Question of Values, 1977; One Percent, 1980. Home: 5 Northlake Rd Columbia SC 29223

JACOBS, ANN ELIZABETH, lawyer; b. Lima, Ohio, July 28, 1950; d. Warren Charles and Virginia Elizabeth (Lewis) J. BA, George Washington U., 1972; JD, Cath. U., 1976. Bar: Ohio 1977, Calif. 1977, U.S. Ct. Appeals (D.C. cir.) 1980, U.S. Dist. Ct. (no. dist.) Ohio 1982. Asst. atty. gen. State of Ohio, Columbus, 1977-78; trial atty. EEOC of Ohio, Miami, Fla., 1978-80; sole practice Lima, 1980—. Chairperson, fundraiser for Lima Symphony Orch., 1985; v.p., bd. dirs. Ottawa Valley Ctr., Lima, 1988; bd. dirs. Allen County Mental Health Assn., Lima, 1987—. Recipient Recognition award US Naval Air Sta., Jacksonville, Fla., 1979. Mem. Ohio Bar Assn., Calif. Bar Assn., D.C. Bar Assn., Allen County Bar Assn., LWV, YWCA. Home: Greentree Circle Apt 13 Cridersville OH 45806 Office: 558 W Spring St Lima OH 45801

JACOBS, ARLEEN GALE, speech pathologist; b. N.Y.C., Oct. 7, 1950; d. Stanley and Marilyn (Fried) Schreck; m. Robert Jeffrey Jacobs, June, 1973; children: Evan, Eric. BA in Speech Pathology, Cleve. State U., 1972; MA in Speech Pathology, SUNY, Buffalo, 1972; cert. in adminstrn., supervision, So. Conn. State U., 1981. Speech pathologist Children Forever, Parma, Ohio, 1973-74, Shield Inst., Flushing, N.Y., 1984-77, Rescue, Regional Ednl. Services, Litchfield, Conn., 1977-78; speech pathologist specializing in adult and pediatric speech and lang. therapy New Fairfield, Conn., 1978—; speech pathologist Stamford (Conn.) Health Dept., 1979-80, Project Interact, Rescue, Birth to 3, Litchfield, 1980—. Bd. dirs. S.O.S. Childcare Placement Service, New Fairfield. Mem. Am. Speech-Lang.-Hearing Assn. (cert. clin. competence), Conn. Speech-Lang.-Hearing Assn., Danbury Area Speech-Lang.-Hearing Assn. (chmn. 1981-82), Danbury Council for Hearing Impaired (cons.).

JACOBS, AUGUSTA ADELLE, educator, recycling company executive; b. Portsmouth, Ohio, Nov. 25, 1925; d. Jacob Harry and Rose (Levine) J. BS, U. Cin., 1947; postgrad. Ohio U., Ohio State U.; grad. Kathleen Bushe and Dody Howard Sch. Modeling, 1954. Tchr. bus. East High Sch., Portsmouth, 1947-51, Green High Sch., Franklin Furnace, Ohio, 1951-87 ; office sec. Eagle Iron Co., Portsmouth, 1957-75, v.p., purchasing agt., 1975-77, v.p., asst. mgr., ptnr., 1977—. Mem. NEA, Southeastern Ohio Tchrs. Assn., Ohio Bus. Tchrs. Assn., Green Local Tchrs. Assn., Am. Assn. U. Women (bd. dirs. 1986-88), Portsmouth C. of C., AAUW (past pres. Portsmouth, rec. sec. Ohio div. 1956-58, bd. dirs. Ohio div. 1956-60, bulletin editor, program com. 1987-88, co-chair Women's Work-Women's Worth seminar), Bus. and Profl. Women's Club Portsmouth (pres.), Portsmouth Women's Networking Orgn. (charter mem.), Delta Kappa Gamma (asst. auditor 1987-88, Alpha Beta chpt.) Sec., Am. Cancer Soc. Scioto County, also bd. dirs.; tchr. Sunday Sch., Temple Beneh Abraham, also bull. editor, pres. Jewish Temple Sisterhood; capt. fund drives United Way, vol. Heart Drive. Republican. Home: 2840 N Hill Rd Portsmouth OH 45662 Office: Green High Sch Bobcat Circle Franklin Furnace OH 45629

JACOBS, BELLA HERTZBERG, gerontologist; b. Bklyn., Mar. 22, 1919; d. Rubin and Pauline (Klaif) Hertaberg; m. Lewis Jacobs; children: Ronald, Paula, Barbara. BA, U. Richmond (Va.), 1940; MA, George Washington U., 1970; EdD, U. So. Calif., 1981. Program asst. Health and Welfare Council, Washington, 1967-68; profl. asst. B'nai B'rith Career and Counseling Service, Washington, 1970-72; sr. program mgr Nat. Council on the Aging, Washington, 1972-88; cons. in field Washington, 1988—; mem. nat. adv. com. later years Am. Found. for Blind, N.Y.C., 1981-83; mem. info consortium Adminstrv. on Aging, Washington, 1983-85. Author: Senior Centers and the At-Risk Older Person, 1980 (with other) A Guidebook for the Educational Goals Inventory, 1984, Organizing a Literacy Program for Older Adults, 1986. Mem. Gerontol. Soc., Assn. Adult and Continuing Edn., Assn. Counseling and Devel. Democrat. Jewish. Clubs: Woodmont, Press. Home and Office: 2925 Greenvale Rd Chevy Chase MD 20815

JACOBS, ELEANOR ALICE, retired clinical psychologist, educator; b. Royal Oak, Mich., Dec. 25, 1923; d. Roy Dana and Alice Ann (Keaton) J. B.A., U. Buffalo, 1949, M.A., 1952, Ph.D., 1955. Clin. psychologist VA Hosp., Buffalo, 1954-83; EEO counelor VA Hosp., 1962-79, chief psychology service, 1979-83; clin. prof. SUNY, Buffalo, 1950-83; speaker on psychology to community orgns. and clubs, 1952—; Mem. adult devel. and aging com. NICHD, HEW, 1971-75. Recipient Outstanding Superior Performance award Buffalo VA Hosp., 1958, Spl. Recognition award SUNY, Buffalo, Spl. Recognition award SUNY, 1971; W.L. McKnight award Miami Heart Inst., 1972; Adminstrs. commendation VA, 1974; Dirs. commendation VA Med. Center, Buffalo, 1978; Disting. Alumni award SUNY, Buffalo, 1983; named Woman of Yr. Bus. and Profl. Women's Clubs, Buffalo, 1973. Mem. Am.

Psychol. Assn., Eastern Psychol. Assn., N.Y. State Psychol Assn., Am. Group Psychotherapy Assn., Am. Soc. Group Psychotherapy and Psychodrama, Psychol. Assn. Western N.Y. (Disting. Achievement award 1976), Group Psychotherapy Assn. Western N.Y., Undersea Med. Soc., Sigma Xi. Home: 221 Pleasant Ave N, Ridgeway, ON Canada LOS 1 NO

JACOBS, JACQUELINE ROSE, economic consultant; b. Bklyn., Jan. 25, 1957; d. Walter Harvey and Dorothy Joan (Kaplan) J. BA, Pomona Coll., 1979; JD, Boston U., 1983; M of City and Regional Planning, Harvard U., 1983. Bar: Calif. Assoc. Loeb & Loeb, Los Angeles, 1983-85, Greenberg, Hennigan & Mercer, Beverly Hills, Calif., 1985-86; econ. cons. Beverly Hills, 1986—. Editor: The Future of the Coastal Zone Management Act, 1982. Mem. New Dem. Channel, Los Angeles, 1984—. Mem. ABA. Jewish. Home: 432 N Palm Dr Beverly Hills CA 90210 Office: Disney Devel Co 500 S Buena Vista St Burbank CA 91521

JACOBS, JANE, author; b. Scranton, Pa., May 4, 1916; d. John Decker and Bess Mary (Robison) Butzner; m. Robert Hyde Jacobs, Jr., May 27, 1944; children—James Kedzie, Edward Decker, Mary Hyde. Author: Downtown Is For People in The Exploding Metropolis, 1959, The Death and Life of Great American Cities, 1961, The Economy of Cities, 1969, The Question of Separatism, 1980, Cities and the Wealth of Nations, 1984. Address: care Random House 201 E 50th St New York NY 10022

JACOBS, JOAN RACHELLE, statistician; b. N.Y.C., June 24, 1947; d. Lester A. and Emma N. (Pinkofsky) Kraus; children—Michael Zev, Lisa Arielle. AB, U. Mich., 1968; MA, U. Calif., Berkeley, 1969. Public health statistician Calif. Dept. Public Health, Berkeley, 1969-72; systems analyst Tex. Inst. Rehab. and Research, Houston, 1972-74; statistician Am. Optometric Assn., Washington, 1974-76; assoc. statistician George Washington U., Washington, 1977-78; cons. statistician Nat. Ctr. for Health Stats., Hyattsville, Md., 1976-79, mem. faculty Applied Stats. Tng. Inst., 1977-81; research analyst Health Care Agy., Orange County, Santa Ana, Calif., 1979-85; adminstrv. and staff analyst Orange County, 1985—. Pres., Sierra Broadmoor Community Assn., 1982. Mem. Am. Statis. Assn., So. Calif. Statis. Soc.

JACOBS, JUDITH CHERYL, casting director, drama educator; b. Chgo., Aug. 27, 1951; d. Lawrence and Lillian (Rabin) J. Student, Drake U., 1969-70; voice study, Northwestern U., 1970-72. Asst. mgr. Lyon-Healy Music Store, Highland Park, Ill., 1969-70; singer, actress various cos., N.Y.C., 1972-73; personal shopper Tiffany's, N.Y.C., 1973; box office mgr. Roundabout Theatre, N.Y.C., 1973-74, North Shore Music Theatre, Beverly, Mass., 1974; asst. agt. Sallee Held Ltd., N.Y.C., 1974-75; asst. casting dir. Young & Rubicam Advt., N.Y.C., 1975-78; casting dir. Bill Williams Casting, N.Y.C., 1978-80, Judith Jacobs Casting, N.Y.C., 1980—; freelance acting tchr., N.Y.C., 1982—; pvt. acting coach, N.Y.C., 1982—; personal mgr., 1987—; guest speaker various schs., 1978—. Democrat. Jewish. Office: Judith Jacobs Casting 336 E 81st #5D New York NY 10028

JACOBS, KAREN LOUISE, medical technologist; b. Kingston, N.Y., May 7, 1943; d. William Charles and Vera Elizabeth (Kelly) Jacobs; BS in Applied Tech., Empire State Coll., 1976; MS in Pub. Service Adminstrn., Russell Sage Coll., 1982. Sr. lab. technician, hosp. lab. supr. City of Kingston (N.Y.) Labs., 1962-68; sr. research asst. Dudley Obs., Albany, N.Y., 1972-75; lab. adminstr. Albany Med. Coll., 1976—, mem. faculty, 1982—; mem. inspection control com. and subcoms. on AIDS mgmt. and human immunodeficiency virus precautions Albany Med. Ctr. Inspection Control, 1987—. Bd. dirs. chpt. Leukemia Soc. Am., 1983. Mem. Clin. Lab. Mgmt. Assn., Blood Banks Assn. of N.Y. State, Am. Soc. Clin. Pathologists, Sierra Club, Earthwatch, Nat. Speleological Soc., Helderburg-Hudson Grotto. Home: 37B Picotte Dr Albany NY 12208 Office: Albany Med Coll Div Oncology 47 New Scotland Ave Albany NY 12208

JACOBS, LIBBY (MARY ELIZABETH MILLER), theater director; b. Omaha, Mar. 31, 1947; d. George Erwin and Hilda Frances (Nevin) Miller; m. John Francis Jacobs Jr., Aug. 16, 1969; children: Michele Nevin, John Francis III. BA, Hood Coll., 1969; MEd, Va. Commonwealth U., 1973; MA, U. Mich., 1976. Tchr. Henrico County Sch. System, Richmond, Va., 1969-70, Richmond City Sch. System, 1970-71; cons. loan dept. Security Fed. Savs. & Loan, Richmond, 1971-73; instr. Concordia Luth. Coll., Ann Arbor, Mich., 1977-78; dir. Coach House Theatre, Akron, Ohio, 1980-85, 87—; founder, dir. Actors' & Playwrights' Theatre, Akron, Ohio, 1985—. Author: (plays) Sparks, 1984, The Gospel According To Omaha, 1985, Harsh Criticism, 1986. Named Woman of Yr. in Creative Arts, Women's History Project, 1987. Mem. NOW, Ohio Theatre Alliance. Episcopalian. Home and Office: 618 N Portage Path Akron OH 44303

JACOBS, LINDA JOAN, special education educator; b. Balt., Mar. 25, 1941; d. Bernard and Freda (Statter) White; m. Martin H. Jacobs. BA, U. Md., 1962, MA, 1965, EdD, 1971. Tchr. Baltimore County Pub. Schs., Towson, Md., 1962-64, resource supr., 1967-68; research teaching asst. U. Md., College Park, 1964-67, asst. prof. spl. edn., 1968-71, undergrad. program coordinator, 1971-73; dir. spl. edn. Anne Arundel County Bd. Edn., Annapolis, Md., 1974-77; asst. supt. Md. State Dept. Edn., Balt., 1977-79; dir. Innovative Learning Ctr., Annapolis, 1979—; sec. bd. dirs. Bernard White & Co., Pikesville, Md., 1970 —; cons. to more than 125 sch. dists. throughout U.S., 1971—. Author: Every Child an Individual, 1987. Mem. Gov.'s Commn. on Funding for Spl. Edn., Annapolis, 1975, Gov.'s Adv. Com. on Handicapped, Annapolis, 1977, Com. to Re-elect Lamb, Anne Arundel, Md., 1986. Recipient Gov.'s Citation for 25 Yrs. Service to the Handicapped, 1987. Mem. Assn. Retarded Citizens, Council for Exceptional Children (Md. state pres. 1970-72), Assn. for Children with Learning Disabilities (advisor 1979—), Kappa Delta Pi. Democrat. Jewish. Home: 8808 Sonya Rd Randallstown MD 21133 Office: Innovative Learning Ctr 1933 Severn Grove Rd Annapolis MD 21401

JACOBS, LINDA LEE, hospital administrator; b. Lincoln, Nebr., Apr. 18, 1949; d. Jacob and Darleen Rose (Worster) J.; B.S. U. Nebr., 1971. Gastrointestinal asst. Bryan Meml. Hosp., Lincoln, Nebr., 1972-78, chief gastrointestinal asst., 1978-81, supr. gastrointestinal lab., 1981-85, clin. instr. Cooper LaserSonics, 1985-86, cons. trainer CORE Assocs., 1987—, mem. employee adv. com., 1973-74; dir. Jacobs Constrn. Co., Inc., Lincoln. Active Vols. in Probation. Mem. Nat. Soc. Gastrointestinal Assts. (pres. 1980-81, chmn. nominating com. 1981-82, ex officio dir. at large 1981-85, editor jour. 1981-85), Nat. Assn. Female Execs., Am. Soc. Tng. and Devel., Am. Legion Aux., Jr. League, Gamma Phi Beta (corp. bd., pres. 1983-85). Home: 2624 Austin Dr Lincoln NE 68506 Office: CORE Assocs 9202 W 90th Overland Park KS 66212

JACOBS, MARIAN BECKMANN, chemical market research analysis; b. Teaneck, N.J., Dec. 20, 1935; d. Frederick J. and Marguerite J. (Thoma) Beckmann; B.A. cum laude (Grace Potter Rice fellow), Barnard Coll., 1957; M.A. (Columbia scholar, Quincy Ward Boese fellow, James Furman Kemp fellow), Columbia, 1959, Ph.D., 1963; m. Warren R. Jacobs Jr., Sept. 5, 1959 (dec.); children—Laura Diane, Anita Michelle; m. 2d, Donald H. Norman, Jan. 9, 1975 (dec.). Research asst. mineralogy dept. Columbia, N.Y.C., 1960-63; research asso. Lamont-Doherty Geol. Obs. of Columbia, Palisades, N.Y., 1963—; asst. prof. oceanography Ramapo Coll. of N.J., Mahwah, 1974-76; sr. analyst market and industry research for polymers and spl. chems. ARCO Chem. Co., Inc. subs. Atlantic Richfield Co., 1976—. NSF grantee, 1965-66, 66-67, 69-71, 71-72, 72-73. Mem. Soc. Plastic Engrs., AAAS, Mineral Soc. Am., Geol. Soc. Am., Phi Beta Kappa, Sigma Xi. Contbr. articles to profl. jours. Research X-ray diffractions and fluorescence studies deep-sea sediments and particulate matter in sea water. Home: 7 Robin Rd PO Box 572 Mahwah NJ 07430 Office: Arco Chem Co 1500 Market St Philadelphia PA 19101

JACOBS, MARY ANN, nurse; b. Eau Claire, Wis., June 16, 1945; d. Thomas DeLos and Jane Victoria (Freid) Pendergast; m. William RObert Jacobs, Nov. 25, 1964; children: Stephanie Ann, Stacy Liz. Lic. practical nurse, Dist. 1 Technical, 1974. Chairside asst. Thomas Staatz, DDS, Eau Claire, 1976-77; practical nurse Sacred Heart Hosp., Eau Claire, 1974-87; health and safety asst. Pope & Talbot, Inc., Wis., 1987—; bd. dirs. Credit Union, Eau Claire, 1984—. Home: 4352 Meadow Lane Eau Claire WI 54701

JACOBS, MARY SHARRON, librarian; b. Endicott, N.Y., June 19, 1947; d. John Arnold and Evelyn Grace Jacobs; student U. Buffalo, 1965-68, M.L.S., SUNY, Geneseo, 1971. Dir., David A. Howe Public Library, Wellsville, N.Y., 1972—. Librarian, Sovereign Grace Ch., 1978—, coordinator women's activities, 1980—, trustee, 1983. Mem. Allegany County Library Assn. (v.p. 1981-83), N.Y. State Library Assn., ALA. Republican. Office: 155 N Main St Wellsville NY 14895

JACOBS, MEREDITH CELESTE, retail company administrator; b. Pasadena, Calif., Dec. 26, 1951; d. Lyle Stanley and Dorothy Ellen (Lindstrom) J. AA, Citrus Coll., 1972. Photographer May Company, Arcadia, Calif., 1973-79; dept. mgr. studio May Company, San Bernardino, Calif., 1979-80; exec. sec. May Company, Cerritos, Calif., 1980-85; regional coordinator May Company, North Hollywood, Calif., 1985-86; staff adminstr. May Company, Sherman Oaks, Calif., 1986-87; regional staffing coordinator May Company, North Hollywood, 1987—. Democrat. Office: May Co Laurel Plaza North Hollywood CA 91606

JACOBS, PHYLLIS, finance professional; b. Newark, Feb. 24, 1932; d. Samuel and Fae Ruth (Farerh) Tapper; m. Martin Leonard Jacobs, Dec. 27, 1953; children: Robert Stewart, Beth Vivian Rose, Leslie Ellen, Michelle Jean. BSc, Rutgers U., 1953. Cert. fin. planner. Asst. buyer L. Bambergers and Co., Newark, 1953-55; tchr., dept. mgr. Holy Child Acad., Portland, Oreg., 1966-72; asst. v.p. Benjamin Franklin Fed. Savs. and Loan, Portland, 1972-82; registered fin. planner Resource Fin. Planning Inc., Portland, 1982—. Mem. Inst. Cert. Fin. Planners, Internat. Assn. for Fin. Planners. Democrat. Jewish. Office: Resource Fin Planning Inc 10300 SW Greenburg Rd #270 Portland OR 97223

JACOBS, RONNE TOKER, management consultant; b. Newark, July 25, 1938; d. William and Helen (Levitin) Toker; m. A. Cecil Jacobs, Nov. 24, 1963; children: Stephen, Andrew. BA, Am. U., 1960; MFA, Va Commonwealth U., 1975. Tchr. Westfield (N.J.) High Sch., 1960-62, Union County Regional High Sch., Clark, N.J., 1962-63, Tucker High Sch., Henrico, Va., 1963-64; finder adoptive homes Richmond (Va.) Social Welfare Agy., 1964-65; cons. Va. Commonwealth U., Richmond, 1974-77; adj. prof. U. Richmond, 1975-77; asst. v.p. United Va. Bank, Richmond, 1977-80; pres. Ronne Jacobs Assocs., Richmond, 1980—. Author: The Speaker's Primer, 1984; co-author: (videotape) The Portfolio of Selling Skills. Bd. dirs. Jewish Community Ctr., Richmond, YWCA, Richmond, 1984, Jewish Family Services, Richmond, 1986—. Mem. Am. Soc. for Tng. and Devel. (pres. Richmond chpt. 1980-81), Richmond Assn. Women Bus. Owners (pres. 1983-84), Orgn. Devel. Network, Jewish Family Services, Richmond Metro C. of C. Avocations: swimming, reading, travel, gardening. Office: 401 September Dr Richmond VA 23229

JACOBS, SHEILA GAIL MCNEIL, health agency administrator; b. Akron, Ohio, May 24, 1953; d. Kenneth Lee McNeil and Lois Lenora (Turpin) Jones; m. Paul Alan Jacobs, Aug. 23, 1987. BS, Bowling Green (Ohio) State U., 1975, MEd, 1976. Instr. health edn. Northeastern U., Boston, 1976-80; coordinator health promotion program U. Mass., Boston, 1980-82, asst. to exec. dir. Health Service, 1982-88; dir. health promotion Beder Health Assocs., Braintree, Mass., 1988—. Rep. speaker's bur. Mass. Passenger Safety program, Boston, 1985—; reviewer citizen's rev. com. on community and youth devel. United Way of Massachusetts Bay, Boston, 1981-84; leader, vol. Patriot's Trail council Girl Scouts of U.S., Dorchester, Mass., 1984-86. Mem. Am. Coll. Health Assn., Soc. Pub. Health Educators, Am. Lung Assn. (chairperson smoking or health guidance com. 1984—, bd. dirs. 1985—, exec. com. 1987—), Mass. Choice and Religious Coalition for Abortion Rights, NOW. Democrat. Unitarian Universalist. Home: 8 Tinson Rd Quincy MA 02169-4843 Office: Beder Health Assocs 759 Granite St Braintree MA 02134-3393

JACOBS, SHERRY RAPHAEL, textile executive, lawyer; b. N.J., June 29, 1943; d. Leon L. and Fay (Silverstein) Raphael; m. Stephen Edward Jacobs, Jan. 4, 1976; children from previous marriage: Jeremiah Raphael and Deborah Feinsmith. BA, Fairleigh Dickinson U., 1967; JD, Loyola U., Chgo., 1970. Bar: Ill. 1970, N.Y. 1975. Assoc. Weil, Gotshal & Manges, N.Y.C., 1972-75, Wachtell, Lipton, & Rosen & Katz, N.Y.C., 1975-76; assoc. counsel Estee Lauder Inc., N.Y.C., 1976-77; v.p. legal R.H. Macy & Co., Inc., N.Y.C., 1977-79; v.p., gen. counsel Saks Fifth Ave., N.Y.C., 1979-83, v.p., gen. counsel, dir. loss prevention, 1983-84, v.p., gen. mgr., 1984-86; v.p. adminstrn., gen. counsel, sec. Guilford Mills, Inc., 1986—, also bd. dirs. Mem. ABA, N.Y. State Bar Assn., N.Y. County Bar Assn., Assn. of Bar City N.Y. Office: Guilford Mills Inc 180 Madison Ave New York NY 10016

JACOBS, SUE CAROL, lawyer; b. N.Y.C., June 21, 1940; d. Harry and Harriet (Rosenblatt) Braunstein; m. Robert A. Jacobs, Aug. 21, 1961; children—Jacqueline Anne, Michelle Keri. B.A. with honors, Hunter Coll., 1960; M.A., Am. U., 1966; J.D., Pace U., 1979; postgrad. New Sch. Social Research, N.Y.C., 1960-62. Bar: N.Y. 1980, U.S. Dist. Ct. (so. dist.) N.Y. 1980. Tchr., N.Y.C. Bd. Edn., 1960-61, 62-64, Arlington County Bd. Edn., 1963-67; atty. Siff, Rosen & Parker, PC, N.Y.C., 1980—; law guardian Family Ct., Westchester, N.Y., 1980-85; arbitrator Civil Ct., 1985—. Bd. dirs. LWV, East Manhattan, Scarsdale, N.Y., 1967-76; founder Hunter Coll. Call for Action, N.Y.C., 1975-77. Alvin Johnson fellow New Sch. for Social Research, N.Y.C., 1960. Mem. ABA, N.Y. State Bar Assn., Westchester Women's Bar Assn. Democrat. Jewish. Home: 40 Fifth Ave New York NY 10011 Office: Siff Rosen & Parker PC 233 Broadway New York NY 10279

JACOBS, SUE-ELLEN, anthropologist, educator, b. Chgo., Oct. 27, 1936; d. William Douglas and Ruth May (Cain) J. BA in Sociology and Anthropology, Adams State Coll., 1963; MA in Anthropology, U. Colo., 1966, PhD in Anthropology, 1970. Asst. prof. Calif. State U., Sacramento, 1968-71; vis. assoc. prof. U. Ill., Champaign-Urbana, 1971-74; asst. prof. women's studies and anthropology U. Wash., Seattle, 1974-81, dir. women studies, 1974-82, assoc. prof. women studies, 1982—; guest prof. U. Bergen, Norway, fall 1982; prin. investigator U.S. Corps Engrs., 1973-74, Bur. Reclamation, 1975, others. Author: Women in Perspective, 1974, Anthropological Studies of Women, 1988, (with others) Women in Commercial Fishing, 1988; co-author, co-editor: AAA Handbook on Ethical Issues, 1987; contbr. articles to profl. jours. Women's Roles in Comml. Fishing Sea grantee, 1980-81, Nat. Endowment for Humanities grantee, 1980-83, others. Fellow Soc. for Applied Anthropology (mem. exec. com. 1979-82, pres. 1983-85), Am. Anthropol. Assn. (mem. ethics com. 1979-82). Democrat. Office: U Wash Women Studies Dept GN-45 Seattle WA 98185

JACOBSEN, JOSEPHINE WINDER BOYLAN, author; b. Coburg, Ont., Can., Aug. 19, 1908; d. Joseph Edward and Octavis (Winder) Boylan; m. Eric Jacobsen, Mar. 17, 1932; 1 son, Erlend Ericsen. Grad., Roland Park Country Sch., 1926; LHD (hon.), Coll. Notre Dame Md., 1974, Goucher Coll., 1974; MDiv. (hon.), St. Mary's Seminary & Coll., 1988. Critic; short story writer; lectr.; poetry cons. Library of Congress, 1971-73, hon. cons. in Am. letters, 1973—; v.p. PSA, 1979—. Author: The Human Climate, 1953, For the Unlost, 1948, The Animal Inside, 1966, (with William Mueller) The Testament of Samuel Beckett, 1968, Genet and Ionesco Playwrights of Silence, 1968, The Shade-Seller: New and Collected Poems, 1974, A Walk With Raschid and Other Stories, 1978 (Notable Books of 1978), The Chinese Insomniacs, New Poems, 1981, Adios Mr. Moyley, 1986, The Sisters: New and Selected Poems, 1987; writing also included in Best American Short Stories, 1966, O. Henry Awards Prize Stories, 1967, 71, 73, 76, 85, Fifty Years of the American Short Story, 1970, Best Poems of, 1961, 64, 68, 72, 73, 74, 75. Mem. panel D.C. Commn. of the Arts and Humanities, 1973; mem. lit. panel Nat. Endowment for Arts, 1980-84; mem. com. Millay Colony for Arts. Recipient best poem of 1981 award Cath. Journalist Assn., award for service to lit. Am. Acad. and Inst. Arts and Letters, 1982, 84; MacDowell Colony fellow; Yaddo fellow; Am. Acad. Poets fellow, 1987. Mem. PEN. Democrat. Roman Catholic. Home: Mountain View Rd Whitefield NH 03598

JACOBSEN, PAMELA, special education coordinator, consultant, counselor; b. Cleve., June 25, 1947; d. Michael Antony and Mary (Pappas) Hoty; m. William Henry Jacobsen, Aug. 21, 1971 (div. 1982). B.S. in Elem. Edn., Baldwin-Wallace Coll., 1969; postgrad. in learning disabilities, Akron U., 1971-72; M.Ed. in Educating Handicapped, Adams State Coll., 1976. Tchr. Strongsville Schs., Ohio, 1969-71, lang. disabilities tchr., 1971-73; educationally handicapped itinerant tchr. Dist. 60, Pueblo, Colo., 1973-74, educationally handicapped lab. educator, 1974-77, educationally handicapped resource tchr., 1977-79, emotional/behavior disorder educator, 1979-86; child study team specialist, 1986—; educator Summer Champ Camp for Asthmatics, Woodland Park, Colo., 1983-86. Author: Correct and Effective Use of Placement and Procedures for Emotionally Disordered Students, 1985. Active Pueblo Nature Ctr., 1981—; area chmn. Channel 8 Pub. TV Auction, 1982-87; bd. dirs. Altrusa Club of Pueblo, 1986; nominating com. Columbine Girl Scout Council, 1984-86. Recipient Hon. Mention award Gov. Colo., 1985; Service award Champ Camp Program, 1984, 85. Mem. Nat. Assn. Female Execs., Bus. and Profl. Women, Phi Delta Kappa (v.p. 1985-87, pres. 1987-89), Delta Kappa Gamma. Greek Orthodox. Club: Pueblo Athletic. Avocations: golf; hiking; reading. Home: 1100 W 26th St Pueblo CO 81003 Office: Keating Staff Devel Ctr Cen Child Study Office 215 E Orman Ave Pueblo CO 81004

JACOBSEN-MCKEAGUE, MARY MAE, state association executive; b. Waterville, Wash., Sept. 4, 1952; d. Adelbert Arnold and Alice Mae (Grandy) Jacobsen; m. William Richard McKeague, July 19, 1986. Student, Wenatchee (Wash.) Community Coll., 1970-72; BA, Central Wash. U., 1975, MA, 1980; student, U. San Jose (Calif), 1980-84. Tchr. Bridgeport (Wash.) Pub. Schs., 1976-78; crisis intervention case worker Wash. Dept. of Social & Health Services, Wenatchee, 1980; adminstr. Wenatchee (Wash.) Area Visitor & Convention Bur., 1980-84; regional sales mgr. Seattle/King County Convention & Visitors Bur., Seattle, 1984; exec. dir. Roofing Contractors Assn. of Western Wash., Seattle, 1984—. Photographer: Self Portrait, 1979, several other photographs on exhibit at various shows, 1979-80. Mem. Wash. Soc. of Assn. Execs. (bd. dirs. 1984-86; cert. of appreciation 1986); Wash. Assn. of Convention & Visitor Bur. Mgrs. (bd. dirs. 1980-85, pres. 1984—; past pres. award, 1986), Central Wash. Tourism Assn. (chmn. of bd. 1983-84), Profl. Ski Instrs. Assn. of Am. Home: 4452-50th Ave SW Seattle WA 98116 Office: Roofing Contractors Assn Western Wash 314 Fairview Ave N #121 Seattle WA 98116

JACOBSOHN, MYRA KRAMER, biology educator, biochemist; b. N.Y.C., Feb. 13, 1939; d. Paul and Sara (Ryshpan) Kramer; m. Gert Max Jacobsohn, June 21, 1959; children: Hannah, Jamie, Diane, Alice. BA, Barnard Coll., 1959; MS, U. Pa., 1962; PhD, Bryn Mawr Coll., 1975. Asst. prof. Beaver Coll., Glenside, Pa., 1976-84, assoc. prof. biology, 1984—; research assoc. prof. Hahnemann U., Phila., 1984—. Contbr. research articles to profl. jours. Recipient Lindback Found. award, 1983. Mem. AAAS, Am. Inst. Biol. Scis. Office: Beaver Coll Glenside PA 19038

JACOBSON, ALICE MARIE, psychiatric social worker; b. Almaville, Tenn., Feb. 13, 1925; d. Shelton Hall and Annie (Barnes) Edwards; m. Arthur Jacobson, July 28, 1974. BA, U. Tenn., 1946; MA, Columbia U., 1952; MSW, NYU, 1956. Postgrad. fellow U. Vt., Burlington, 1946-47; exec. dir. YWCA of U. S.C., Columbia, 1947-52; social worker Bklyn. Juvenile Guidance Ctr., 1956-61, social worker supr. Jewish Bd. Family and Children's Services, Bklyn., 1963—; lectr. on video tapes for Columbia Univ. Sch. of Social Work, N.Y.C., 1985. Mem. East 22d St. Assn., N.Y.C., 1982—. Fellow Am. Group Psychotherapy Assn.; mem. Nat. Assn. Social Workers, Ortho Psychiat. Assn. Home: 102 E 22d St New York NY 10010 Office: Jewish Bd Family and Children's Services 26 Court St Brooklyn NY 11201

JACOBSON, ANN REISNER, organization executive; b. Berlin, Apr. 25, 1926; d. Fred and Eugenia (Goldman) Reisner; m. Elliot Jacobson, Sept. 1, 1946; children: Mark, Steven, Susan. BA, U. Mo., Kansas City, 1946; MSW with high distinction, U. Kans., 1967. Caseworker Kans. Child Welfare Service, Kansas City, 1965-66; group worker Mattie Rhodes Community Ctr., Kansas City, Mo., 1966-67; project dir. Carver Neighborhood Ctr., Kansas City, 1967-71; exec. dir. Vol. Action and Info. Ctr., Kansas City, 1971-85; v.p. vol. and community resources Heart of Am. United Way, Kansas City, 1986—; instr. vol. mgmt. Pioneer Community Coll., Kansas City, 1978—. Author: Volunteer Management Handbook: For Effective Development of Volunteer Programs, 1985, Self Study Manuel for Information & Referral Services, 1987; editor Standards and Guidelines for Field Volunteerism, 1979. Chair, founder Vol. Bur. of Kansas City, Mo., 1966-71; chair Vols. in Edn., 1969; mem. nat. com. Goodwill Industries of Am., 1969-73; bd. dirs. Nat. Ctr. for Vol. Action, 1969-76; v.p. Regional Health and Welfare Council, 1971-72; mem. Mayor's Human Rights Commn., 1972, Mayor's Fair Housing Commn., 1972; del. World Assembly of Jewish Agys. in Israel, 1971—; mem. adv. com. U. Mo. Sch. Social Work, 1975; charter mem., mem. steering com. U. Mos. Kansas City Disting. Fellows Program, 1986—; v.p. Congregation B'nai Jehudah, Jewish Fedn. Recipient Community Service award Regional Health and Welfare Council, 1969, Matrix Table award Theta Sigma Phi, 1972, Germaine Monteil award, 1975; cited for Outstanding Corp. Achievement Kansas City Times, 1986. Mem. Acad. Cert. Social Workers, Am. Soc. Pub. Adminstrs., AAUP, Mo. Assn. Social Welfare, Nat. Assn. Social Workers (chair Mo. state council 1974-75, pres. 1975-77), Mid-Am. Family Mediation Assn. (v.p. 1986—), Alliance Info. and Referral Services (nat. bd. dirs. 1982—), Nat. Assn. Vol. Burs., (chair 1978-80, editor newsletter 1971-77, pres. 1970-72), NCCJ (bd. dirs. 1983—), Nat. Jewish Fedn. and Council (pres. women's div. 1968-71), Nat. Fedn. Temple Sisterhoods (com. 1967-69), Union Am. Hebrew Congregations (commn. 1966-72). Home: 615 W Meyer Blvd Kansas City MO 64113 Office: Heart of Am United Way 605 W 47th St Suite 300 Kansas City MO 64112

JACOBSON, ANNA SUE, financial executive; b. Ft. Smith, Ark., Aug. 13, 1940; d. Ray Bradley and Joy Anna (Person) McAlister, (stepfather) Cleve J. McDonald, Sr.; m. Lyle Norman Jacobson, Nov. 23, 1958; children: Lyle Michael, Daniel Ray, Julie Anne, Eric Joseph. Degree, Coll. for Fin. Planning, 1984. Cert. fin. paraplanner. Office mgr. Twin Cities Lithographic Inst., St. Paul, 1963-66; sec., St. Paul, Mpls., 1971-78; asst. to pres., office mgr. Planners Fin. Services, Mpls., 1978-85, asst. corp. treas., 1987—; fin. paraplanner McAlmont Investment Co., Mpls., 1985—; dir. Planners Fin. Services; mem. bd. advisors Coll. for Fin. Planning, Denver, 1982—; speaker various orgns. Co-creator Paraplanning Profession Advisor. Del., Dem. Farmer Labor Party, St. Paul, 1980; campaign chmn. mayoral election, Roseville, Minn., 1983, county commr., city council election, Roseville, 1980, 84; local chmn. for passage of E.R.A., Minn.; chmn. Am. Lung Assn., St. Paul; past. pres. PTA, Minn. Recipient Volunteerism award Gov. State of Minn., 1981; Cert. of Appreciation, Minn. Bicentennial Com., 1976; mem. exec. council Boy Scouts Am., 1977-81; mem. adv. bd. Sch. Dist. 623, Roseville, Minn., 1978-81; fund raising com. mem. Twin Cities Pub. TV Sta., 1985—. Mem. Internat. Assn. Fin. Planning, Twin Cities Assn. Fin. Planners, Internat. Assn. Bus. and Profl. Women (bd. dirs. 1977-86, pres. 1980-82, named Woman of Yr. 1982), Concordia Acad. Booster Club, Beta Sigma Phi Nu Phi Mu Chpt. Democrat. Lutheran. Avocations: tennis, riding, reading, piano, fencing. Office: McAlmont Investment Co Shelard Plaza N Minneapolis MN 55426

JACOBSON, BONNIE BROWN, utility company executive, statistician; b. Annapolis, Md., Feb. 15, 1952; d. Albert Robert and Ruth Marie (Puhak) Brown; m. Peter Roy Jacobson, Apr. 28, 1979. BS cum laude, LaRoche Coll., Pitts., 1974; MS, U. Pitts., 1976. Research scholar U. Pitts., 1974-76; research assoc. Squibb Inst. Med. Research, Princeton, N.J., 1976-78; assoc. statistician N.E. Utilities Service Co., Hartford, Conn., 1978-80, statistician, 1980-82, sr. statistician, 1982-83, mgr. consumer research, 1983-87, corp. statistician, 1987—; cons. stats., Hartford, 1976—; adviser Electric Power Research Inst., Palo Alto, Calif., 1978—. Research plan developer Conn. Energy Assistance Study Project, Hartford, 1983-84. Mem. Am. Statis. Assn., Am. Mktg. Assn., Nat. Assn. Female Execs., Electric Utility Market Research Council. Club: Sport and Leisure (Wallingford, Conn.). Avocations: golf, skiing, racquetball, gardening, reading. Home: 45 Stephen Dr Meriden CT 06450 Office: NE Utilities Service Co PO Box 270 Hartford CT 06141

JACOBSON, CAROLE RENEE, lawyer, educator; b. N.Y.C., Feb. 10, 1935; d. Daniel and Sally (Leader) Gold; m. David S. Jacobson, Jan. 28, 1962; children: Robin, Mark, Brad. BS with honors, U. Pa., 1956; MA English with honors, Columbia U., 1957; JD, Rutgers U., 1979. Bar: Pa.

1980, Fla. 1982, N.J. 1983; cert. English tchr., N.J. Tchr. Manhasset (L.I., N.Y.) High Sch., 1958-62, Westfield (N.J.) High Sch., 1962; dir. social services South Brunswick (N.J.) High Sch., 1976; asst. counsel N.J. Casino Control Commn., Lawrenceville, 1981—. Editor N.J. Voter, 1974-75. Mem. Hunterdon (N.J.) Cen. Regional Bd. Edn., 1983—, v.p., 1986-87, pres. 1987-88; mem. Raritan Twp. (N.J.) Bd. Adjustment, 1979-82, vice chmn., 1981; chmn. legis. subcom. State Consumer Affairs Adv. Com., 1976—; mem. N.J. State bd. LWV, 1974-75, pres. Hunterdon County, 1972-74, Plainfield, 1968-70; pres. Vol. Bur. Hunterdon County, 1974-76; trustee Hunterdon County Housing Council, 1972-76; mem. Citizens Housing Corp. Raritan Twp. 1971-72; chmn. Hunterdon County Coalition Better Pub. Schs., 1971-72. Recipient resolution of appreciation Bd. Adjustment, Raritan Twp., 1982. Democrat. Home: 1 Pinewood Ct Flemington NJ 08822 Office: Princeton Pike Office Park Lawrenceville NJ 18625

JACOBSON, DEBRA ANN, lawyer; b. Kingston, N.Y., Mar. 20, 1952; d. Charles and Esther (Tasker) Denkensohn; B.A. summa cum laude in Environ. Studies, U. Rochester (N.Y.), 1974; J.D. with honors, George Washington U., 1977; m. David Edward Jacobson, Aug. 10, 1975; 1 son, Andrew Scott. Admitted to N.Y. bar, 1979, D.C. bar, 1985; congressional legis. asst., 1977-79; counsel subcom. on oversight and investigations, com. energy and commerce U.S. Ho. Reps., 1979—; dir.-at-large Women's Council Energy and Environ., 1981-83. Recipient award Delta Labs., 1972. Mem. Nature Conservancy, N.Y. State Bar Assn., Nat. Spinal Cord Injury Assn. Author govt. report. Office: 2323 Rayburn House Office Bldg Washington DC 20515

JACOBSON, DOROTHY REID, foundation executive; b. Manchester, Conn., June 11, 1950; d. Charles Edward Jacobson and Dorothy Agnes (Case) Beach. BA, Williams Coll., 1972; MA, George Washington U., 1980. Staff asst. U.S. Ho. of Reps., Washington, 1973-75; cons. Nat. Park Service, Washington, 1975-76, Nat. Endowment for the Arts, Washington, 1976-78; sr. v.p. Ptnrs. for Livable Places, Washington, 1978-85; dir. spl. projects Nat. Geog. Soc., Washington, 1986-88, exec. dir. edn. found., 1988—. Author: (with others) The Economics of Amenity, 1985, Return of the Livable City, 1986; contbr. articles to profl. jours. Vol. child life program Children's Hosp. Nat. Med. Ctr., Washington, 1985-86. Fellow Nat. Endowment for the Arts, 1982. Office: Nat Geog Soc 17th and M Sts NW Washington DC 20036

JACOBSON, ETHEL THOMAS, librarian, educator; b. Green Mountain, N.C., Apr. 20, 1940; d. Isaac Carper and Hattie (Callahan) Thomas; m. Steven Eugene Jacobson Sr, Oct. 1, 1960; children: Steven Jr., Edward Thomas. BS, Appalachian State U., 1960, MA, 1970. Cert. library sci. tchr., N.C. Librarian Walkertown Elem. Sch., Winston-Slem, N.C., 1960-61, Camden County (N.C.) High Sch., 1961-63 , A.C. Reynolds High Sch., Ashville, N.C., 1963—; instr. library sci. Mars Hill (N.C.) Coll., 1971—. Cheerleading sponsor A.C. Reynolds High Sch., 1968-86. Mem. N.C. Library Assn., N.C. Edn. Assn. Democrat. Baptist. Home: 4 Blueberry Hill Dr Asheville NC 28804 Office: AC Reynolds High Sch Rt 5 Box 592 Asheville NC 28803

JACOBSON, GLORIA NADINE, college administrator; b. Jewell, Iowa, July 12, 1930; d. Christian Frederick and Amanda M. (Englebart) Larson; B.B.A., U. Iowa, 1974; m. Richard T. Jacobson, July 22, 1951 (dec. Feb. 1988); children—Richard Thomas, Douglas L., William Andrew. Mem. adminstrn. staff U. Iowa, Iowa City, 1950—, asst. to the dean Coll. of Pharmacy, 1981—. Mem. Phi Gamma Nu, Kappa Epsilon. Republican. Lutheran. Home: 415 Ridgeview Iowa City IA 52240 Office: U of Iowa Coll of Pharmacy Iowa City IA 52242

JACOBSON, HELEN G. (MRS. DAVID JACOBSON), civic worker; b. San Antonio, Tex.; d. Jac Elton and Rosetta (Dreyfus) Gugenheim; B.A., Hollins Coll.; m. David Jacobson, Nov. 6, 1938; children—Elizabeth, Dorothy (Mrs. Sam Miller). News, spl. events staff NBC, N.Y.C., 1933-38. First v.p. San Antonio, Bexar County council Girl Scouts U.S.A., 1957-63; Tex. State rep. UNICEF, 1964-69; bd. dirs. U.S. com. UNICEF, 1970-80, hon. bd. dirs., 1980—; bd. dirs. Nat. Fedn. Temple Sisterhoods, 1973-77, Temple Beth-El Sisterhood, Youth Alternatives, Inc.; bd. dirs. Community Guidance Center, chmn. bd., 1960-63; bd. dirs. Sunshine Cottage Sch. for Deaf Children, chmn. bd., 1952-54; pres. Community Welfare Council, 1968-70; pres. bd. trustees San Antonio Pub. Library, 1957-61; trustee Nat. Council Crime and Delinquency, 1964-70, San Antonio Mus. Assn., 1964-73; bd. dirs. Cancer Therapy and Research Found. South Tex., 1977—, sec., 1977-83; pres. S.W. region Tex. Coalition for Juvenile Justice, 1977-79; chmn. Mayor's Commn. on Status of Women, 1972-74; del. White House Conf. on Children, 1970; mem. Commn. on Social Action of Reform Judaism, 1973-77; chmn. Foster Grandparent project Bexar County Hosp. Dist., 1968-69; sec. Nat. Assembly for Social Policy and Devel., 1969-74; pres. women's com. Ecumenical Center for Religion and Health, 1975-77; mem. criminal justice planning com. Alamo Area Council of Govts., chmn., 1975-77, 1987-88; mem. Tex. Internat. Women's Yr. Coordinating Com., 1977; co-chmn. San Antonio chpt. NCCJ, 1980-84; chmn. United Negro Coll. Fund Campaign, 1983, 84; v.p. Avance; trustee Target 90/Goals for San Antonio. Recipient Headliner award for civic work San Antonio chpt. Women in Communications, 1958; named Vol. Woman of Yr., Express-News, 1959; honoree San Antonio chpt. NCCJ, 1970, Nat. Jewish Hosp., 1978; Nat. Humanitarian award B'nai B'rith, 1975; Hannah G. Solomon award Nat. Council Jewish Women, 1979, San Antonio Women's Hall of Fame, 1986, others. Mem. San Antonio Women's Fedn., Nat. Council Jewish Women, Symphony Soc. (women's com.). Club: Argyle. Home: 207 Beechwood Ln San Antonio TX 78216

JACOBSON, JUDITH HELEN, state senator; b. South Bend, Ind., Feb. 26, 1939; d. Robert Marcene and Leah (Alexander) Haxton; m. John Raymond Jacobson, 1963; children—JoDee, Eric, Wendy. Student U. Wis.-Milw. and Madison, 1957-60. Mem. Mont. Senate, 1980—. Mem. Nat. Conf. State Legislators (human resources com. 1981—, del. Mont. Med. Aux. (legis. chmn. 1981—). Democrat. Lutheran. Office: Mont Senate State Capitol Helena MT 59620 *

JACOBSON, MARGARET, banker; b. Chgo., Aug. 11, 1944; d. Leon Christian and Kathleen Eileen (Brennan) Eschbach; m. Herbert Jacobson, Dec. 8, 1972. B.S., U. Ill., 1967. Mgmt. trainee Harris Trust, Chgo., 1967-69; asst. to dir. advt. Velsicol Chem. Co., Chgo., 1969-70; account exec. Gardner, Stein & Frank, Chgo., 1970-74; v.p. consumer mktg. Budget Rent-a-Car, Chgo., 1974-82; sr. v.p. Bozell & Jacobs, N.Y.C., 1982-85; v.p. Citibank U.S.A., N.Y.C., 1985—; guest lectr. AMR, Inc., N.Y.C., 1975-76. Treas., bd. dirs. Profl. Women for Brain Rearch, Chgo., 1973-75. Named Mktg. Warrior of Yr., AMR, Inc., 1980; selected finalist as Advt. Woman of Yr., Women's Advt. Club, Chgo., 1978, 79. Avocations: Chinese cooking; travel; racquetball.

JACOBSON, MARIAN SLUTZ, lawyer; b. Chgo., Nov. 10, 1945; d. Leonard Doering and Emily Dana (Wells) Slutz; m. Fruman Jacobson, Sept. 21, 1975; 1 child, Lisa Wells. BA, Ohio Wesleyan U., 1967; JD, U. Chgo., 1972. Bar: Ill. 1972, U.S. Dist. Ct. (no. dist.) Ill. 1972, U.S. Ct. Appeals (7th cir.) 1973. Assoc. Sonnenschein, Carlin, Nath & Rosenthal, Chgo., 1972-79, ptnr., 1979—. Mem. ABA, Chgo. Council Lawyers. Office: Sonnenschein Carlin Nath & Rosenthal 8000 Sears Tower Chicago IL 60606

JACOBSON, NANCY HELEN, nurse, consultant, educator; b. Lansdowne, Pa., Nov. 16, 1947; d. Homer Pierce and Helen Irwin (Duffy) Tillotson; m. Philip William Jacobson, Dec. 11, 1976; children—Jeneane Renee, Abbe Nicole. Diploma Chester County Hosp., 1968; B.S.N., U. Pa., 1973, M.S.N., 1978. Lic. R.N.; cert. med. surg. nurse, Pa.; cert. nutrition support nurse, Pa. Staff nurse Hosp. of U. Pa., Phila., 1968-79, head nurse, 1970-73, staff devel. instr., 1973-79; instr. Holy Family Coll., Phila., 1979-83; cons. nursing, Phila., 1983—; curriculum specialist Med. Coll. Pa., Phila., 1985-87; assoc. dir. continuing nursing edn., The Med. Coll. Pa., 1987—; cons. 1982-85; cons. United Home Health Services, Phila., 1984—, Springhouse Corp., Phila., 1984—, W.B. Saunders Co., Phila., 1986— , Va. Nursing Assn. Eastern Montgomery County; guest lectr. continuing edn. various agys., 1977—. Co-editor RN Bds. Rev. for NCLEX-RN 1987, 88; contbr. articles to profl. jours. Instr. ARC, Phila., 1985, cons. needs assessment, 1985, coordinator student project, 1985. Recipient Profl. Nurse Traineeship award Dept. HEW, 1977. Mem. Am. Nurses Assn. (cert. med., surgical nurse 1987), Pa. Nurses Assn. (continuing edn. approval rev. panel 1987-88), League of I.V. Therapy Edn. (guest lectr. at 1985, 87 convs.), Pa. Assn. for Gifted Edn., Sigma Theta Tau. Home: 617 Elkins Ave Elkins Park PA 19117 Office: Med Coll Pa 3200 Henry Ave PO Box 12608 Philadelphia PA 19129

JACOBSON, RUTH ANNETTE KRAUSÉ, public relations counselor; b. Watertown, N.Y., June 30, 1925; d. Thomas M.R. and Ruth E. (Parmelee) Krausé; married; 1 child, Anne Heyliger Jacobson Nunno. Grad., Medill Sch. Journalism, Northwestern U., 1947; postgrad., U. Chgo., Northwestern U., Washington U. Guest editor Mademoiselle mag., N.Y.C., 1945; with Howard G. Mayer & Assocs., Chgo., 1947-48; Midwest area rep. CARE, Inc., Chgo., 1948-50; account exec. Harshe-Rotman and Druck, Chgo., 1950-51; free-lance pub. relations counselor 1955-57; pub. relations counselor Fleishman-Hillard, Inc., St. Louis, 1957-68; dir. spl. events Fleishman-Hillard, Inc., 1968—, sr. ptnr., 1971—. Bd. dirs. First Street Forum, Chatillon-DeMenil House Found., chmn. pub. relations com.; bd. dirs. Vanderschmidt's Secretarial Sch., chmn. mktg. com.; bd. dirs. St. Louis Conservatory and Schs. for the Arts, chmn. communications com.; chmn. Commerce mag. com. St. Louis Regional Commerce Growth Assn.; bd. dirs. VP Fair Found., Women's Soc. of Washington U.; mem. pres.'s adv. cabinet Greater St. Louis council Girl Scouts U.S.A.; bd. dirs. Downtown St. Louis, Edgewood Children's Ctr., Girls Club St. Louis; bd. govs., chmn. pub. relations com. Assn. Churchill Fellows Winston Churchill Meml. and Library in U.S., Westminster Coll., Fulton, Mo.; trustee Mo. Bapt. Hosp., pres., v.p.; mem. adv. council YWCA; mem. adv. com. Experience St. Louis. Recipient Ann. Signal award St. Louis Sentinel, 1983, Leader Lunch Spl. award YWCA, 1983; named one of Ten Women of Achievement in St. Louis Sta. KMOX and The Suburban Journal's newspaper. Mem. Pub. Relations Soc. Am. (past sec. St. Louis chpt.), St. Louis Soc. Blind (past bd. dirs), Landmarks Assn. St. Louis (counselor-at-large to bd. dirs. on pub. relations 1976-77), Women in Communications (Mentor award 1986), St. Louis Forum, Intertnat. Women's Forum, Mo. Women's Forum, Mo. Hist. Soc. (past bd. trustees), St. Louis Symphony Soc., Friends of St. Louis Art Mus., St. Croix Landmarks Soc., Nat. Trust for Historic Preservation, Mo. Bapt. Hosp. Assn., Vis. Nurse Assn. (past bd. dirs.). Epscopalian. Clubs: Noonday, Media, Whittemore House. Office: Fleishman-Hillard Inc 200 N Broadway Saint Louis MO 63102

JACOBSON, SANDRA W., lawyer; b. Bklyn., Feb. 1, 1930; d. Elias and Anna (Goldstein) Weinstein; m. Irving Jacobson, July 31, 1955; 1 child, Bonnie Nancy. BA, Vassar Coll., 1951; LLB, Yale U., 1954. Bar: N.Y. 1955, U.S. Supreme Ct. 1960, U.S. Dist. Ct. (so., ea. dists.) N.Y. 1972, U.S. Ct. Appeals (2nd cir.) 1975. Ptnr. Mulligan, Jacobson & Langenus, N.Y.C., 1964-88, Hall, McNicol, Hamilton & Clark, N.Y.C., 1988—; lectr. in field. Contbr. articles to profl. jours. and chpts. to books. Mem. ABA (mem. family law sect.), N.Y. State Bar Assn. (mem. family law sect., legis. and custody coms., internat. law and practice sect.), N.Y. Women's Bar Assn. (treas. 1987-88, v.p. 1988, co-chair Matrimonial and Family Law com. 1984—, chmn. 1986—, mem. jud. screening com. 1987—), Women's Bar Assn. of State N.Y. (mem. matrimonial com. 1986—, co-chair 1987—, courts com. 1987—), Assn. Bar N.Y.C. (mem. com. matrimonial law, 1984-87, mem. com. women in the courts 1986—, sec. 1987—, state cts. of superior jurisdiction, 1987—), Westchester County Bar Assn., Am. Acad. Matrimonial Lawyers (mem. bd. mgrs. N.Y. chpt. 1987—, mem. interdisciplinary com.), Com. to Improve Availability of Legal Services, Ind. Jud. Screening Panel. Clubs: Westchester, Vassar. Office: Hall McNicol Hamilton & Clark 220 E 42d St New York NY 10017

JACOBY, KATHARINE WATTS, architecture company executive; b. Providence, May 10, 1953; d. Charles Henry II and Patricia Dorothy (McQuillen) W.; m. Jay David Jacoby, Sept. 26, 1987. BA in Philosophy with highest honors, MusB, Oberlin Coll., 1976. Coordinator Masterworks, CBS Records, N.Y.C., 1976-78; account exec. Dailey & Assocs., San Francisco, 1978-80; account supr. Daniel J. Edelman, Inc., San Francisco, 1980-86; dir. corp. communications Hillier Group, Princeton, N.J., 1986—. Bd. dirs. San Francisco Chamber Orch., 1985-86. Mem. Pub. Relations Soc. Am., Nat. Assn. Real Estate Editors Inc., Phi Beta Kappa. Democrat. Episcopalian. Office: The Hillier Group 500 Alexander Park CN23 Princeton NJ 08543-0023

JACOBY, MARY JEAN, sales executive; b. Westfield, Mass., Apr. 10, 1955; d. Benjamin M. Jacoby and Barbara Ann (Quigley) Smith. BS, Miami U., Oxford, Ohio, 1977; MA, U. Va., 1983; Cert. Communications, Communications Sch., Rep. Nat. Com. Polit. Edn., 1984; Cert. Inst. for Bus. and Community Devel., U. Richmond, 1985. Hospitality hostess Walt Disney World Co., Inc., Lake Buena Vista, Fla., 1977-78; community affairs sec. Sta. KBTV TV, div. Gannett Corp., Denver, 1979-81; instr. U. Va., Charlottesville, 1981-83; mid-atlantic admissions rep. Edn. Mgmt. Corp., Pitts., 1983-84; dir. communications, research Va. Reps., Richmond, 1984-86; ind. pub. relations mktg. cons. Richmond, 1986-87; regional sales mgr. McKendree and Co., Inc., Richmond, Va., 1987—; chairperson pub. relations and recruitment, com. chairperson Met. Richmond, Inc. Chmn. pub. relations, recruitment com., bd. dirs. Big Bros-Big Sisters, Richmond, 1984—; co chmn. pub. relations Va. Spl. Olympics, Richmond, 1986—. Recipient Pub. Service award for Outstanding Service United Way, Denver, 1980, Commendation for Professionalism FBI, 1981, Commendation for Humanitarian Service Disabled Am. Vets., 1981; named Big Sister of Yr. Big Bros. and Big Sisters of Met. Richmond, Inc., 1988. Episcopalian. Home: 9154 Cloisters W Richmond VA 23229 Office: McKendree & Co Inc 4200 Colley Ave Norfolk VA 23508 also: McKendree & Co Inc 1504 Santa Rosa Rd #106 Richmond VA 23288

JACOX, ADA KATHRYN, nurse, educator; b. Centreville, Mich.; d. Leo H. and Lilian (Gilbert) J. B.S., Columbia U., 1959; M.S., Wayne State U., 1965; Ph.D., Case Western Res. U., 1969. R.N. Dir. nursing Children's Hosp.-Northville State Hosp., Mich., 1961-63; assoc. prof., then prof. Coll. Nursing Univ. Iowa, Iowa City, 1969-76; prof., assoc. dean Sch. Nursing U. Colo., Denver, 1976-80; prof., dir. research ctr. Sch. Nursing U. Md., Balt., 1980—. Co-author: Organizing for Independent Nursing Practice, 1977 (named Book of Yr., Am. Jour. Nursing); A Process Measure for Primary Care: The Nurse Practitioner Rating Form, 1981 (named Book of Yr., Am. Jour. Nursing). Editor: Pain: A Sourcebook for Nurses, 1977 (named Book of Yr., Am. Jour. Nursing). Carver fellow, U. Iowa, 1972; cert. Disting. Achievement in Nursing Research and Scholarship, Alumni Assn. Columbia U. Tchrs. Coll., 1975. Fellow Am. Acad. Nursing, Am. Nursing Assn.; mem. Am. Nurses Assn. (dir. 1978-82, 1st v.p. 1982-84), Am. Nurses Found. (pres. 1982-85), Am. Acad. Nursing, Nat. Acad. Scis. (com. on nat. needs for biomed. and research personnel 1984-87), Inst. of Medicine, AMA (mem. health policy agenda work group 1983-86). Office: U Md Sch Nursing 655 W Lombard St Baltimore MD 21201

JACQUES, AIDA CASTRO, small business owner, infosystems specialist; b. Manila, Philippines, July 15, 1947; came to U.S., 1968; d. Severo R. and Honoria (Boquiren) Castro; m. Richard Louis Jacques, July 28, 1968; children: Elizabeth, Louis. BS in Math. and Physics, U. Santo Tomas, Manila, 1968; MBA, N.H. Coll., 1984. Clerical supr. Aetna Life & Casualty Ins., Lowell, Mass., 1970-72; asst. edn. cons. N.H. Dept. Edn., Concord, 1974-77; agt. IDS Life Ins., Manchester, N.H., 1979-81; bus. analyst N.H. Ins. Group, Manchester, 1982-86, bus. systems analyst, 1986—; owner A & RJ Machine Shop, Hooksett, N.H., 1985—. Mem. Nat. Assn. Female Execs., Nat. Assn. Women Bus. Owners, Nat. Fedn. Ind. Bus. Owners (adv. council). Roman Catholic. Home and Office: 103 Goffstown Rd Hooksett NH 03106

JACSO, ILONA M., real estate manager; b. Budapest, Hungary, July 23, 1936; came to U.S., 1957; d. Michael and Irene (Breisach) J.; m. Geza Buidoso, June 10, 1958 (div. 1966); children: Rita, Lillian (dec.). BS in Chemistry, U. Budapest, 1956. Mgr. Ireland's Restaurant, Chgo., 1968-72; sr. adjuster, supr. Carson Pirie Scott, Chgo., 1972-78; personal banker Austin Bank of Chgo., 1978-84, real estate dept. mgr., 1984-85; real estate biller Equitable Relocation Mgmt., Chgo., 1985—. Mem. Nat. Assn. Female Execs. Democrat. Roman Catholic. Home: 869 W Buena Apt 221 Chicago IL 60613

JAEGER, KAREN E., contracting company executive; b. Pampa, Tex., Feb. 25, 1948; d. Perry Enlo and Gwendolyn A. (Maxwell) Davis; m. James B. Haiduk, June 24, 1966 (div. June 1981); children: Wendy L., James B.; m. Danny E. Jeager, Mar. 11, 1983. Degree in computer sci., Odessa (Tex.) Coll., 1966. Pres. Crown Equipment, Ind., Odessa, 1975—. Mem. Assocs. Builders and Contractors, Am. Legion, Odessa C. of C., Midland C. of C. Home: 220 W Hillmont Odessa TX 79764 Office: Crown Equipment Inc PO Box 1321 Odessa TX 79760

JAFFARIAN, SARA, retired library and media services director, consultant; b. Haverhill, Mass. Sept. 7, 1915; d. Mugerdich and Quhar (Nalbandian) J. B.A., Bates Coll., 1937; B.S., Simmons Coll., 1947; M.Ed., Boston U., 1957; postgrad. U. N.C.-Greensboro, 1955-56; postgrad. in Edn., Harvard U., 1963-70. Cert. tchr., librarian, media specialist. Library asst. Haverhill Pub. Library (Mass.), 1937-42; tchr. Ossipee High Sch. (N.H.), 1942-43; librarian, Quincy Jr. High Sch. (Mass.), 1943-53; dir. libraries Greensboro Pub. Schs., (N.C.), 1953-60, Seattle Pub. Schs., 1960-61; dir. library, media, Lexington Pub. Schs. (Mass.), 1961-78; cons. media programs sch. dists. and sch. library design; cons. and adviser to book pubs. and book wholesalers and architects planning sch. libraries; lectr., cons. various regional and state profl. assns., New Eng., Southeast, West Coast; grad. library sch. instr. Queens Coll., L.I., N.Y., summer 1959; dir. sch. library workshop, U. Oreg. Grad. Sch., Eugene, summer 1956; dir. sch. library workshop U.S. Office Edn., U. Hawaii, summer 1968; instr. Grad. Sch. Edn., U. N.H., Durham, summers 1964-71. Editor: Every School Needs a Library, 1952; contbr. chpt. to text series (transl. Japanese); guest editor Jr. Libraries, 1957; contbr. articles to library and ednl. jours. Recipient Britannica Sch. Library award, ALA and Ency. Britannica, 1964; U.S. Govt. grantee Grad. Sch. U. So. Calif., 1969. Mem. ALA (council 1962-66, dir. Nat. Library Week, State N.C. 1958-59), Am. Assn. Sch. Librarians (dir. 1954-56, sec. 1956, Newberry-Caldecott award com.), New Eng. Sch. Library Assn. (v.p. 1950-53, dir.), New Eng. Library Assn. (dir. 1962-66), Am. Sch. Library Suprs. Assn. (sec. treas. and pres. 1954-62), Mass. Sch. Library Assn. (pres. 1964-66), NEA (joint com. on libraries 1959-60), Mass. Tchrs. Assn. (publicity dir. 1950-52), Assn. for Supervision and Curriculum Devel., Assn. for Ednl. Communications and Tech., Simmons Alumni Assn. (dir. 1963-64), Bates Key, Pi Lambda Theta (Boston U. Alumni chpt.), Phi Delta Kappa (Harvard Alumni chpt.), Delta Kappa Gamma. Republican. Lodge: Order Eastern Star. Home: 58 Bateman St Haverhill MA 01830

JAFFE, IRMA BLUMENTHAL, art educator; b. New Orleans; d. Harry and Estelle (Blumenthal) Levy; m. Donald Korshak, July 15, 1935 (div. 1941); 1 child, Yvonne; m. Samuel B. Jaffe, June 12, 1941. BS, Columbia U., 1958, MA, 1960, PhD, 1966. Researcher, curator Whitney Mus. Am. Art, N.Y.C., 1963-66; asst. prof. art Fordham U., Bronx, N.Y., 1966-68, assoc. prof., 1968-70, prof., 1970—; cons. Md. Ctr. Public Broadcasting, 1984-85. Author: Joseph Stella, 1970, John Trumbull: Patriot of the American Revolution, 1975, John Trumbull's Declaration of Independence, 1976, The Sculpture of Leonard Baskin, 1980; co-author: Selections from the Permanent Collection of the Arkansas Art Center, 1983; contbg. author: Genius of American Painting, 1973, The American Revolution and Eighteenth Century Culture, 1986; editor: (with R. Wittkower) Baroque Art The Jesuit Contribution, 1972; mem. editorial bd. Am. Art Jour., 1981—; contbg. editor Art News jour., 1983—; contbr. articles to profl. jours. Chmn. grants application bd. Musician's Emergency Fund, N.Y.C., 1985—. Recipient Owl award Columbia U.; NEH fellow, 1973-74; grantee in field. Mem. Am. Soc. for 18th Century Studies, Am. Studies Assn., Coll. Art Assn., Phi Beta Kappa. Avocation: tennis. Home: 880 Fifth Ave New York NY 10021 Office: Fordham U Bronx NY 10458

JAFFE, LOUISE, English language educator, creative writer; b. Bronx, N.Y., May 17, 1936; d. Joseph and Anna (Movitz) Neuwirth; m. Steven Jaffe, Aug. 26, 1962 (div. 1975); 1 child, Aaron Lawrence. BA, Queens Coll., 1956; MA, Hunter Coll., 1959; PhD, U. Nebr., 1965. Instr. Kingsborough Community Coll., Bklyn, 1965-67, asst. prof., 1967-70, assoc. prof. English, 1970—. Author: Hyacinths and Biscuits, 1985, Wisdom Revisited, 1987, also numerous poetry and fiction stories. Mem. editorial bd. Community Review CUNY, 1984—; faculty adv. student lit. mag., 1983—. Recipient First prize N.Y. Poetry Forum, 1980, First prize, First honorable mention Shelley Soc. N.Y., 1983, 84, and others. Mem. Mensa, Poets and Writers Inc., Shelley Soc. of N.Y., Writers Union, Feminist Writers Guild, Democrat. Jewish. Avocations: creative writing, scrabble, crossword puzzles, people-watching, attending and giving poetry readings. Home: 2411 E 3rd St Brooklyn NY 11223 Office: Kingsborough Community Coll Oriental Blvd Manhattan Beach Brooklyn NY 11223

JAFFE, NORA CROW, educator; b. Los Angeles, Feb. 12, 1944; d. Thomas J. and Helen E. (Beshears) Crow; 1 child, Margaret Collins. A.B. magna cum laude in English and Classics (Univ. scholar, Ford Found. fellow), Stanford U., 1965; A.M., Harvard U., 1968, Ph.D. (Grad. Prize fellow), 1972; m. Arthur M. Jaffe, July 24, 1971. Tutor, teaching fellow Harvard U., 1968-70; asst. prof. English, Smith Coll., Northampton, Mass., 1971-79, assoc. prof., 1979—. Ford Found. fellow, 1965; Harvard U. travel grantee, 1969; Hyder Rollins Found. grantee, 1975. Mem. Am. Soc. 18th-Century Studies, MLA (exec. com. div. Restoration and early Eighteenth-Century English lit.), Phi Beta Kappa. Author: The Poet Swift, 1977; co-editor: The Evil Image. Two Centuries of Gothic Short Fiction and Poetry. The Literary Art of Terror from Daniel Defoe to Stephen King, 1981; contbr. articles to profl. jours., chpts. in books. Home: 27 Lancaster St Cambridge MA 02140 Office: English Dept Smith College Northampton MA 01063

JAFFE, PHYLLIS SHELLEY, lawyer; b. N.Y.C., Feb. 13, 1925; d. Robert and Jessie (Sinick) Shelley; m. Frederick Stanley Jaffe, Aug. 7, 1947 (dec. Aug. 1978); children: Paul, David, Richard. BA, Queens Coll., 1944; JD, Columbia U., 1949. Bar: N.Y. 1949, U.S. Dist. Ct. (so. dist.) N.Y. 1981, U.S. Ct. Appeals (2d cir.) 1984, U.S. Dist. Ct. Mo. 1986. Sole practice, Ossining, N.Y., 1953-69; editor Prentice-Hall, Englewood Cliffs, N.J., 1969-71; specialist labor relations N.Y.C. Bd. Edn., 1971-72; staff atty. Bd. Coop. Ednl. Services, Yorktown Heights, N.Y., 1972-75; ptnr. Plunkett & Jaffe, P.C., White Plains, N.Y., 1975—. Mem., pres. Ossining Bd. Edn., 1964-69. Served as sgt. WAC, U.S. Army, 1944-46. Mem. Westchester County Bar Assn., Women's Bar Assn. N.Y. State. Jewish. Avocations: tennis, gardening. Office: Plunkett & Jaffe PC 1 N Broadway White Plains NY 10601

JAFFE, RONA, author; b. N.Y.C., June 12, 1932; d. Samuel and Diana (Ginsberg) J. BA, Radcliffe Coll., 1951. Sec. N.Y.C., 1952; assoc. editor Fawcett Publs., N.Y.C., 1952-56. Author: The Best of Everything, 1958, Away From Home, 1960, The Last of the Wizards, 1961, Mr. Right is Dead, 1965, The Cherry in the Martini, 1966, The Fame Game, 1969, The Other Woman, 1972, Family Secrets, 1974, The Last Chance, 1976, Class Reunion, 1979, Mazes and Monsters, 1981, After the Reunion, 1985. Office: care Ephraim London Buttenwieser 875 3rd Ave New York NY 10022 *

JAFFE, SUSAN, ballerina; b. Washington; m. Paul Connelly. Student, Md. Sch. Ballet; student, Sch. Am. Ballet, Am. Ballet Theatre Sch. With Am. Ballet Theatre II, 1978-80; with Am. Ballet Theatre, 1980—, soloist, 1981-83, prin., 1983—. Repertoire includes: Le Corsaire, Apollo, La Bayadere, Bouree Fantastique, Carmen, Cinderella, Concerto, Duets, Giselle, The Guards of Amager, Push Comes to Shove, Symphonie Concertante, others; created role Lynne Taylor-Corbett's Great Galloping Gottschalk; appeared Spoleto in An Evening of Jerome Robbins Ballets, 1982. Office: care Ludwig Mgmt Ltd 148 E 74th St New York NY 10021 *

JAFFE, SYLVIA SARAH, art collector, former medical technologist; b. Detroit, May 16, 1917; d. Sam and Rose (Rosmarin) Turner; B.S. in Med. Tech., U. Wis., 1940; m. David Jaffe, Nov. 8, 1942. Med. technologist Watts Hosp. Lab., Durham, N.C., 1940-45; research hematology technologist in leukemia Sloan Kettering Meml. Hosp. Lab., N.Y.C., 1946-47; chief med. technologist in hematology Arlington (Va.) Hosp. Lab., 1948-55; chief technologist in diagnostic hematology Georgetown U. Hosp., Washington, 1959-70; collector 19th century and 20th century art, 1970—. Mem. Col. Williamsburg (Va.) Found., hon. citizen. Mem. Am. Soc. Med. Technologists, Am. Soc. Clin. Pathologists (assoc.), Am. Women in Sci., Corcoran Gallery Art, Pa. Acad. Fine Arts, Sierra Club, Nat. Wildlife Fed., World Wildlife Fund., Nat. Audubon Soc., Nat. Trust Hist. Preservation, The Washington Print Club, U. Wis. Alumni Assn., Boston Mus. Arts, Nat. Mus. Women in Arts (charter), Nat. Wildlife Fedn., Sierra Club, Greenpeace, Audubon Soc., Wilderness Soc. Democrat. Jewish. Club: Pioneer Women.

Contbr. articles to profl. socs. Address: 1913 S Quincy St Arlington VA 22204

JAFFE-BARZACH, AMY EILEEN, marketing executive, consultant; b. Schenectady, N.Y., May 3, 1961; d. Samuel Ellis and Laurie Ellen (Rothstein) J. BS in Econs., SUNY, Albany, 1982; postgrad. in bus. Rennsalear Poly. Inst. Account exec. Retail Mktg. Cons., Albany, 1981-83; regional mktg. mgr. The Pyramid Cos., Glens Falls, N.Y., 1983-84; mktg. mgr., then dir., The Rouse Co., Springfield, Mass., 1984-88; dir. mktg. Bronson & Hutensky, Hartford, Conn., 1988—; cons. Childsplay Mag., Springfield, 1984—; bd. dirs. Creative Edge, N.Y.C. Mem. steering com. Young patrons of the Quadrangle Mus., Springfield, Mass., 1984—; bd. dirs. Leukemia Soc. Am., Springfield, 1984—. Mem. Bus. and Profl. Women's Club (Young Careerist award 1984), New Eng. Mktg. Dirs. Council, Advt. Club Western Mass., Pub. Relations Soc., Women in Communications. Democrat. Jewish. Club: Appalachian Mt. (Hartford, Conn.). Home: 26 Forest Hills Ln West Hartford CT 06117 Office: Bronson & Hurtensky City Place 34th Floor Hartford CT 06103

JAGGERS, ELIZABETH DANIEL, financial executive; b. Nashville, Apr. 23, 1946; d. Eddie Francis and Mary Frances (Ballou) Daniel. BA, U. Ky., 1968, MPA, 1979. Budget examiner Budget Div. State of N.Y., Albany, 1979-81, budget analyst Youth Div., 1981-83, dir. planning Dept. Banking, 1983-85, dir. budget and fin. Dept. Banking, 1985-87, dir. fin. and adminstrn., 1987—. Mem. Am. Soc. Pub. Adminstrs. Office: NY State Dept Banking 194 Washington Ave Albany NY 12210

JAGUSZTYN, BARBARA JEAN, accountant; b. Grove City, Pa., Apr. 26, 1948; d. Roger Ellis Bettie Virginia (Hook) Wood; m. Richard J. Jagusztyn, Jan. 3, 1981; children: Nicole Ellis, Alexis Avril. BBA, Fla. Atlantic U., 1977. Sr. acct. Fox and Co., CPA's, Ft. Lauderdale, Fla., 1977-82; owner, prin. Ft. Lauderdale, 1982-87; ptnr. Jagusztyn & Jagusztyn, PA, CPA, Ft. Lauderdale, 1987—. Mem. Am. Inst. CPA's, Fla. Inst. CPA's, Am. Women's Soc. CPA's (Broward County newsletter chairperson 1985-86, pub. speaking chairperson, dir. 1986, workshop chairperson 1986-87, v.p. 1987-88, pres. 1988—). Republican. Methodist. Home: 5461 NW 56 Ct Fort Lauderdale FL 33319 Office: 5100 NW 33 Ave Suite 240 Lakeshore Fort Lauderdale FL 33319

JAHDE, JUDY ANN, health care educator; b. Beatrice, Nebr., July 23, 1949; d. Harry Lee and JoAnne Roberta (Heble) Scott; m. Marv John Jahde, Apr. 15, 1972; children—Jennifer D., Sarah A., Matthew J. Diploma in nursing Bryan Meml. Sch. Nursing, 1970; student in nursing U. Nebr., 1970-72, Marquette U., 1981, Coll. St. Francis, Joliet, Ill., 1981—. R.N., Nebr., Iowa, Wis., Kans., Ohio. Staff nurse, clinic nurse U. Nebr. Student Health Ctr., Lincoln, 1970-71; clin. instr. med.-surg. nursing Lincoln Gen. Sch. Nursing, 1971-72; patient teaching coordinator Deaconess Hosp., Milw., 1972-73; edn. coordinator, patient tchr., nurse recruiter Family Hosp., Milw., 1973-80; nursing edn. coordinator Norrell Home Health Services, West Des Moines, IA, 1986; RN case mgr., mktg. Home Health Care Related Health Care Services West Des Moines, 1987; cons. RN, 1987—; RN, home health care nurse mgr. St. Francis Hosp. and Med. Ctr., 1987—; speaker in field. Author teaching guides, articles on women's health issues. Mem. Metro Maternal Child Steering Com., Des Moines, 1985—; speaker Iowa Luth. Hosp., 1985—. Mem. Nat. Assn. Female Execs., Met. Women's Network Des Moines (speakers bur.), Resolve Orgn., Exec. Circle Des Moines, Continuing Inservice Educators of Iowa, Iowa Nursing Assn. (commn. on nursing practice), Greater Des Moines Chamber Fedn. (health and human services com.). Republican. Lutheran. Home: 758 Glacier Pass Westerville OH 43081

JAHN, BILLIE JANE, nurse; b. Byers, Tex., Dec. 12, 1921; d. Thomas Oscar and Molly Verona (Kennemer) Downing; student Scott and White Sch. Nursing, 1941-42, U. Mich., 1973-75; B.S. in Nursing, Wayne State U., 1971; M.S., East Tex. State U., 1976, Ph.D., 1982; m. Edward L. Jahn, Dec. 6, 1942; children—Antoinette R., James T., Thomas L., Edward L., Janette E. Staff nurse Warren Meml. Hosp., Centerline, Mich., 1957-61; supr. nursing service Mich. Dept. Mental Health, Northville, 1962-71, Franklin County (Tex.) Hosp., 1972-74; instr. nursing Paris (Tex.) Jr. Coll., 1975-80; nurse educator VA, Waco, Tex., 1981-82; exec. v.p., dir., sr. nursing cons. Dos Cabezas, Inc., Mt. Vernon, Waco and Temple, Tex., 1981—; adj. faculty U. Tex.-Arlington, 1985—; mem. dept. phys. medicine and rehab. Scott and White Hosp., Temple, Tex., 1985—; head nurse dept. physc. med. and rehab.; cons. East Tex. State U., Texarkana, 1978—. adj. faculty U. Tex.-Arlington. Vol., ARC, 1971—; den mother Boy Scouts Am., 1960-62; sec. PTA, Warren, Mich., 1960-62; v.p., Temple, Tex., 1957-58. Mem. AAAS, Nat. League Nursing, Nat. Assn. Rehab. Nurses (rev. bd. Rehab. Nursing Inst. 1986—), Tex. League Nursing, AAUP, Nat. Assn. Female Execs., Am. Assn. Curriculum and Supervision, Phi Delta Kappa, Kappa Delta Pi. Home: 4122 Antelope Trail Temple TX 76504

JAHN, NORMA JEAN, accountant, actress, singer musician; b. Galveston, Tex., Sept. 17, 1926; d. Oran Henry and Helen Angela (Seale) Jahn; m. Lester A. Balaski, Oct. 22, 1944 (div. 1957); children: Beverly Sue, Belinda Lou; m. Charles F. Brass, Dec. 12, 1957 (div. 1959). Grad. high sch. Dancer, singer Florence Coleman Dance Sch., Port Arthur, Tex., 1929-33; dance instr. Ella Lu Pau Dance Sch., Houston, 1934-40; singer Bg Band Era, various locations, 1941-44; with Model-Billboards Orange Crush Chgo., 1942; model-print John Robert Powers, N.Y.C., 1943-44; star Norma King Show WWL Radio, Roosevelt Hotel, New Orleans, 1968-69; musicians payroll acct. Warner Bros. Records Inc., Burbank, Calif., 1973—. Bd. dirs. Toluca Lake Commerce Assn., Calif., 1988—. Named Hon. Citizen, Mayor Victor H. Shiro, City of New Orleans, 1967, Key to the City, 1967; recipient award for outstanding svc., USNR, 1968, Donna King Conkling award Associated Latter-day Media Artists, 1986, Bravo award Associated Latter-day Media Artists, 1986; named outstanding vol., New Orleans Recreation Dept., 1968. Mem. Screen Actors Guild, Am. Fedn. Musicians, Am. Fedn. TV and Radio Artists, Assc. Latter-Day Media Artists (membership dir. 1979-84), Am. Film Inst. Democrat. Mem. Ch. of Jesus Christ of Latter Day Saints. Clubs: The Actor's Ctr., Lincoln Continental Owner's. Office: Warner Bros Records Inc 3300 Warner Blvd Burbank CA 91510

JAIDINGER, JUDITH CLARANN, wood engraver, painter; b. Chgo., Apr. 10, 1941; d. John Henry and Charlotte Violet (Anton) J.; m. Gerald Szesko, June 27, 1970; 1 dau., Loralee C. Kolton. B.F.A. in Drawing, Painting and Printmaking, Sch. Art Inst. Chgo., 1970. Represented in permanent collections including: Ill. State Mus., Kemper Group, Eastern Ill. U., Charleston, Brand Library Art Ctr., Glendale, Calif., Washington and Jefferson Coll., Washington, Pa., Minot State Coll. (N.D.), Prairie State Coll., Chicago Heights; group shows include: NAD, N.Y.C., Boston Printmakers, Needham, Mass., J.B. Speed Art Mus., Louisville, Soc. Wood Engravers and Relief Printers, Eng. Included in portfolio: Face to Face, 1985. Recipient awards including 1st graphics Okla. Art Guild, Oklahoma City, 1974, N.Mex. Art League, Albuquerque, 1974, Okla. Mus. Art, Oklahoma City, 1975, Smithsonian Traveling Exhbn., 1971-74, Norfolk Biennial, 1971. Home: 6110 N Newburg Ave Chicago IL 60631

JAIN, SAVITRI, physician; b. Delhi, India, Dec. 4, 1930; d. Padam Chand and Raj Rani Gupta; m. S. Kumar Jain, Dec. 14, 1960; children: Sanjay, Monica, Neena. BS, Delhi (India) U., 1954, MD, 1958. Diplomate Am. Bd. Internal Medicine, Am. Bd. Cardiology. Intern Lady Hardinge Med. Coll. Hosp., New Dehli, 1954-55, resident in cardiology, 1955-58; asst. prof. Lady Hardinge Med. Coll., New Dehli, 1958-60; tutor, research assoc. Topiwala Med. Coll., Bombay, 1960-62; research assoc. and assoc. attending physician Michael Reese Hosp., Chgo., 1962-65; gen. practice medicine, cons. New Delhi, 1965-67; asst. prof. St. Louis U., 1967-75; practice medicine specializing in cardiovascular diseases, pres. Cardiovascular Assocs. Inc., St. Louis, 1975—; chief of medicine St. Joseph Hosp., Kirkwood, Mo., 1985-87, pres. elect med. staff, 1987—. Contbr. articles to profl. jours. Fellow ACP, Am. Coll. Cardiology, Am. Heart Assn. Office: Cardiovascular Assocs Inc 533 Couch Ave Kirkwood MO 63122

JAKAB, IRENE, psychiatrist; b. Oradea, Rumania; came to U.S., 1961, naturalized, 1966; d. Odon and Rosa A. (Riedl) J. MD, Ferencz József U., Kolozsvar, Hungary, 1944; lic. in psychology, pedagogy, philosophy cum laude, Hungarian U., Cluj, Rumania, 1947; PhD summa cum laude, Pazmany Peter U., Budapest, 1948; Drhc, U. Besançon (France), 1982. Diplomate. Am. Bd. Psychiatry. Rotating intern in neurology and psychiatry Ferencz József U., 1943-44; resident in psychiatry Univ. Hosp., Kolozsvar, 1944-47; resident in neurology Univ. Hosp., 1947-50; resident internal medicine Univ. Hosp. for Internal Medicine, Pecs, Hungary, 1950-51; chief physician Univ. Hosp. for Neurology and Psychiatry, Pécs, 1951-59; staff neuropathol. research lab. Neurol. Univ. Clinic, Zurich, 1959-61; sect. chief Kans. Neurol. Inst., Topeka, 1961-63; dir. research and edn. 1966; resident psychiatry Topeka State Hosp., 1963-66; asst. psychiatrist McLean Hosp., Belmont, Mass., 1966-67; assoc. psychiatrist McLean Hosp., 1967-74; prof. psychiatry U. Pitts. Med. Sch., 1974—, co-dir. med. student edn. in psychiatry, 1981—; dir. John Merck Program, 1974-81; mem. faculty dept. psychiatry Med. Sch., Pecs, 1951-59; asst. Univ. Hosp. Neurology, Zurich, 1959-61; asso. psychiatry Harvard U., Boston, 1966-69, asst. prof. psychiatry, 1969-74, lectr. psychiatry, program dir. grad course mental retardation, 1970-87. Author: Dessins et Peintures des Aliénés, 1956, Zeichnungen und Gemälde der Geisteskranken, 1956; editor: Psychiatry and Art, Proc. 4th Internat. Colloquium of Psychopathology of Expression, 1968, Art Interpretation and Art Therapy, 1969, Conscious and Unconscious Expressive Art, 1971, Transcultural Aspects of Psychiatric Art, 1975; co-editor: Dynamische Psychiatrie, 1974; editorial bd.: Confinia Psychiatrica, 1975-81; contbr. articles to profl. jours. Prinzhorn prize, 1967; recipient 1st prize Benjamin Rush and Gold medal award for sci. exhibit, 1980; Bronze Chris plaque Columbus Film Festival, 1980; Leadership award Am. Assn. on Mental Deficiency, 1980; Ernst Kris Silver award, 1981; Fellow Menninger Sch. Psychiatry, Topeka, 1963-66. Mem. AMA, Am. Psychol. Assn., Am. Psychiat. Assn., Société Medico Psychologique de Paris, Internat. Rorschach Soc., N.Y. Acad. Scis., Internat. Soc. Psychopathology of Expression (v.p. 1959—), Am. Soc. Psychopathology of Expression (chmn. 1965—), Internat. Soc. Child Psychiatry and Allied Professions, Deutschsprachige Gesellschaft für Psychopathologie des Ausdruckes (hon.), Deutschsprachige Gesellschaft fur Psychopathologie des Ausdrucks (Prinzhorn prize 1967). Home: 228 Parkman Ave Pittsburgh PA 15213 Office: U Pitts Med Sch 3811 O'Hara St Pittsburgh PA 15213

JAKUBIC, PATRICIA MARY, manufacturing company administrator; b. Detroit, Mar. 20, 1939; d. John Donald and Marion Hogg (Walker) Niergarth; m. Rodney Thurston, Dec. 27, 1956 (div. Dec. 1981); children: Susan, Michael; m. Thomas James Jakubic, June 28, 1985; children: Kathleen, Mary, Timothy, Michael, Ann Marie, Daniel, Thomas Jr. BFA, Wayne State U., 1972; postgrad., Cen. Mich. U., 1982—. Free-lance graphic designer Kokomo, Ind., 1972-78, Pitts. Plate Glass, Kokomo, Ind., 1978-79; illustrator Def. div. Chrysler Corp., Center Line, Mich., 1979-81, trainer Def. div., 1981-82; mgr. M60 program Info., Land Systems div. Gen. Dynamics Corp., Center Line, Mich., 1982-83; chief tng. Gen. Dynamics Services Co. subs. Gen. Dynamics Corp., Sterling Heights, Mich., 1985-87, mgr. Data Mgmt. dept., 1987—; supr. tng. XMCO, Inc., Troy, Mich., 1983-85. Pres. Birmingham (Mich.) Power Squadron Aux., 1970. Mem. Soc. Logistic Engrs., Gen. Dynamics Mgmt. Club, Mich. Soc. Instructional Tech. Office: Gen Dynamics Services Co PO Box 1420 Sterling Heights MI 48311-1420

JAMES, ALICE HOWRY, educator; b. Evanston, Ill., Apr. 9, 1918; d. Henry Burney and Edyth (Wornall) H.; AB, U. Louisville, 1939, MEd, 1974, EdD, U. Louisville, 1987; m. Thomas James II, July 15, 1941 (dec.); children—Thomas III, Edyth MacMillan, David Buchanan. Tchr., St. Mark's Presch., Louisville, 1959-61; asst. dir., tchr. Crescent Hill Meth. Presch., Louisville, 1961-66; kindergarten tchr. Louisville Bd. Edn., 1966-75; kindergarten tchr. Jefferson County Bd. Edn., Louisville, 1975-79; assoc. prof. early childhood edn. Jefferson Community Coll., Louisville, 1979—. Chmn., Peterson-Dumesnil Restoration Com., 1978; mem. Crescent Hill Community Council Edn. Com., 1979; bd. dirs. Home of the Innocents, 1980-86; mem. career devel. com. Head Start, 1980, chmn. policy council, 1983-84; bd. dirs. Peterson-Dumesnil Found., 1983—, Community Coordinated Child Care, pres. 1987—. Mem. Am. Assn. Community Coll. Early Childhood Educators, Nat. Assn. Edn. Young Children, Ky. Assn. Edn. Young Children, Louisville Assn. for Children Under Six, LWV, Phi Delta Kappa. Episcopalian. Clubs: Pendennis Club, Louisville Country. Home: 240 S Peterson Ave Louisville KY 40206 Office: Jefferson Community Coll 109 E Broadway Louisville KY 40202

JAMES, BARBARA ANN WOODWARD, hospitality industry executive, interior design, business consultant; b. Owensboro, Ky., Feb. 14, 1936; d. J.T. and Thelma (Newman) Woodward; m. William E. James, Feb. 19, 1951 (div. June 1953); 1 child, Keith Douglas. Vice pres., Fla. Containers Inc., Sebring, 1978-81; v.p. Barda Services Inc., Tampa, Fla., 1981-87; v.p., gen. mgr. BJ's of Tampa, Inc., 1982—; founder, owner Flamingo Bar and Grill, Clearwater, Fla., 1987—. Democrat. Roman Catholic. Office: 610 Court St Clearwater FL 34616

JAMES, CATHERINE BENNETT, investment banker; b. Boston, Sept. 5, 1952; d. Robert Gregory and Ardis (Butler) J. B.A. with distinction, Carleton Coll., 1974; M.B.A., Harvard U., 1976. Vice pres. Dean Witter Reynolds Inc., N.Y.C., 1976-82; v.p. Morgan Stanley & Co., Inc., N.Y.C., 1982-84, prin., 1985-86; mng. dir., 1987—. Trustee Carleton Coll., Northfield, Minn., 1984—. Club: Harvard (N.Y.C.). Office: Morgan Stanley & Co Inc 1251 Ave of Americas New York NY 10020

JAMES, DOT (DOROTHY ANN), non-profit organization administrator; b. San Antonio, Sept. 14, 1938; d. Royal Percy and Eloise (Ohlen) J. BA in History, So. Meth. U., 1960; MA in Edn., Stanford U., 1962; postgrad., U. San Francisco, 1984-85. Cert. in secondary edn., Calif. Mgmt. analyst Dept. of Navy, Treasure Island, Calif., 1963-65; tchr. pub. high sch. Gilroy, Calif., 1965-69, Caldwell, Idaho, 1969-71; editor-in-chief Venus mag., Palo Alto, Calif., 1973-75; ptnr., chief exec. officer F.S. Button Mfg. Co., San Jose, Calif., 1975-83; exec. dir. AIDS Found. of Santa Clara County, San Jose, Calif., 1983-84; freelance mgmt. cons. and writer San Jose, 1984—; office mgr. Adult Independence Devel. Ctr., Santa Clara, Calif., 1987; dir. vols. Emergency Housing Consortium, San Jose, 1987-88; coordinator community devel. Shelter Against Violent Environments (S.A.V.E.), Fremont, Calif., 1988—; devel. cons. ARIS Project, Campbell, Calif., 1985—. Designer/mfr. feminist slogan buttons housed in Women's Collection, Smithsonian Inst., Washington; contbr. monographs and articles to profl. pubs. Active various women's rights, environ., animal welfare, orgns. for developmentally and physically disabled, gay rights, pub. health groups, 1962—; bd. dirs. Aris Project, Campbell, Calif.; crisis intervention counselor Suicide Crisis Service of Santa Clara County, San Jose. Grantee Nat. Def. Edn. Act, 1967, Coe Found., 1969; Nonprofit Orgn. Mgmt. Inst. scholar, 1984. Mem. Stanford Bay Area Profl. Women. Democrat. Home: 4260 Camden Ave San Jose CA 95124 Office: SAVE PO Box 8283 Fremont CA 94537

JAMES, EDITH JOYCE, steel company executive; b. Chgo., May 22, 1926; d. John and Rebecca Miriam (Fischer) Shaiova; m. W. Ivan James, Dec. 29, 1958 (div. 1970). Student, Hunter Coll., 1944-45, Northwestern U., 1945-47, Ill. State U., 1963-66, Washington U., 1966-70. Acctg. supr. Panelit, Inc., Skokie, Ill., 1958-62; comptroller Johnstone Constrn., Bloomington, Ill., 1962-66; asst. dir. housing Washington U., St. Louis, 1966-70; v.p., gen. mgr. William A. Miller Machine and Elevator, St. Louis, 1970-76; pres. J & J Installers, Inc., St. Louis, 1976—; pres. Erector and Riggers St. Louis, 1986—; bd. dirs. Nat. Assn. Miscellaneous Ornamental Archtl. Products Contractors. Democrat. Jewish. Office: J & J Installers Inc 4301 Arco Ave Saint Louis MO 63110

JAMES, GENEVA BEHRENS, educator; b. Marietta, Minn., Mar. 23, 1942; d. Siegfried and Dora (Schoenrock) Behrens; BS, Mankato State U., 1963; m. Howard James, Aug. 2, 1963; children: Scott, Dawn. Tchr. English high schs., Minn., 1964-65; instr. acctg., Adult Continuing Edn., Bellevue, Nebr., 1971-75, dir. Adult Basic Edn. Ctr., 1974—, vol. coordinator, 1983—, instr. secondary schs., 1980—, instr. computer literacy, 1984—; Pilot Computer Program, 1987-88, seminar presenter Nebr. State Advt. Edn. Assn., 1986, Commn. on Adult Basic Edn., 1987. Mem. exec. com. Boy Scouts Am., 1974-80; mem. metro community task force, 1986-88. Mem. AAUW, Nat. Assn. Public and Continuing Adult Edn., Adult and Continuing Edn. Assn. Nebr., NEA, Nat. Council Tchrs. English (dist. curriculum com. 1985—), Alpha Delta Kappa. Republican. Lutheran. Home: 1314 Hansen Ave Bellevue NE 68005 Office: 2221 Main St Bellevue NE 68005

JAMES, GLEDA JO, mineral water company executive; b. Atlanta; d. Oscar Lee and Jewell Odessa (Hancock) Brown; m. William Edward James, Jan. 6, 1951 (div. Oct. 1982); children—Jennifer James Camp, Gregory, Susan. Art student, Naples, Italy, 1962-65; student, Wilmington Coll., 1966-67. Owner, James House Restaurant, Lithia Springs, Ga., 1971-84; real estate sales agt. Finch Realty, Lithia Springs, 1984-85; owner, pres., chmn. bd. Lithia Springs Mineral Water Co., Inc., 1983—, also Cave Spring Pure Water Co. Inc., also Deer Lick Springs Inc. Pres., Lithia Springs Civic Club, 1978; curator Family Dr. Mus., 1984—; mem. Ga. Trust for Hist. Preservation, 1985—; chmn. Tourist Hist. Commn. Recipient Best Painting in Show award Jacksonville Artists Club, N.C., 1966, Homemaker of Yr. award Congl. Dist. Ga. Homemakers, 1970. Mem. Internat. Bottled Water Assn. (pub. relations com. 1984, Pub. Relations award 1984, 85), Sweetwater Hist. Soc. (pres. 1979-85), Atlanta Hist. Soc. Methodist. Avocations: collecting medical memorabilia; historical preservation. Home and Office: PO Box 713 Lithia Springs GA 30057

JAMES, JEANNIE HENRIETTA, educator; b. Greenville, S.C., Dec. 5, 1921; d. Portice J. and Essie Virginia (Ross) J.; B.S., Berea (Ky.) Coll., 1945; M.S., U. N.C., 1949; postgrad. Iowa State U., 1955-56; Ed.D., Pa. State U., 1965. Tchr. home econs. Stowe (Vt.) High Sch., 1945-48; asst. prof., asso. prof. home econs. Lincoln Meml. U., Harrogate, Tenn., 1949-59; asst. prof., asso. prof. Ill. State U., Normal, 1959-75; asso. prof. early childhood edn. U. S.C., Columbia, 1975-79, Spartanburg Meth. Coll., 1980; mem. Ill. White House Conf. on Children and Youth, 1969-70. Mem. Nat., S.C. assns. for edn. young children, Soc. for Research and Child Devel., AAUP, World Orgn. for Edn. Children, S.C. Home Econs. Assn., So. Highlands Handicraft Guild, Am. Home Econs. Assn. (program chmn. sect. 1977-79), AAUW, Phi Kappa Delta, Zeta Tau Alpha. Contbr. articles to profl. jours. Home: Belmont Estates #205 Fountain Inn SC 29644

JAMES, JENNIFER, writer; b. Sacramento, Dec. 19, 1947; d. Ralph Edward and Myrlene Augusta (White) J. Student, San Bernardino (Calif.) Valley Coll., 1966-68, Pasadena (Calif.) Playhouse, 1968-69. Actress various commls./films, Los Angeles, 1973-84; billing clk. Capitol Records, Hollywood, Calif., 1984-87; income tax preparer H & R Block, Hollywood, 1987; freelance writer Hollywood, 1987—. Author screenplay The Killing of Felicity, short story Marjorie; contbr. articles to profl. jours.; violinist rock band Rubber Bible, 1987. Contbr. Ayn Rand Inst., Marina del Rey, Calif., 1987. Named Best Actress Pasadena Playhouse, 1969. Mem. Screen Actors Guild, Actors Equity Assn.

JAMES, KATHRYN KANAREK, electrical engineer; b. N.Y.C., July 16, 1949; d. Jesse Jay and Dora Dorothy (Sader) Kanarek; m. Hugh R. James, Aug. 1982 (div.). BS, MIT, 1969, MSEE, EE, 1971. Computer analyst Computer Systems Engrng., North Billerica, Mass., 1971-72; staff mem. MIT Lincoln Lab., Lexington, Mass., 1972-73, MITRE Corp., Bedford, Mass., 1973-76, Analytical Systems Engrng. Corp., Burlington, Mass., 1976-77; elec. engr. Combined Arms Combat Devel. Activity U.S. Army, Ft. Leavenworth, Kans., 1978-86; research staff Inst. Def. Analyses, Alexandria, Va., 1986—. Mem. Jr. Women's Symphony Alliance, Kansas City, 1980-86. Grad. fellow Nat. Sci. Found., 1969-71. Mem. IEEE, Armed Forces Communications and Electronics Assn., Nat. Assn. Female Execs., Tau Beta Pi, Eta Kappa Nu, Sigma Xi. Jewish. Club: Toastmasters (pres. local chpt. 1976). Home: 3726 King Arthur Rd Annandale VA 22003 Office: Inst for Def Analyses 1801 N Beauregard Alexandria VA 22311

JAMES, MARIE MOODY, musician, vocal music educator, clergywoman; b. Chgo., Jan. 23, 1928; d. Frank and Mary (Portis) Moody; m. Johnnie James, May 25, 1968. B Music Edn., Chgo. Music Coll., 1949; MusM, Roosevelt U., 1969, MA, 1976; DD, Internat. Bible Inst. and Sem., Plymouth, Fla., 1985. Ordained to ministry Pentecostal Ch., 1976; cert. vocal music tchr., Ill. Key punch operator Dept. Treasury, Chgo., 1950-52; tchr. Posen-Robbins Bd. Edn., Robbins, Ill., 1952-59; tchr. vocal music Englewood High Sch., Chgo., 1964-84; music counselor Head Start, Chgo., 1965-66. Composer, arranger choral music: Hide Me, 1963, Christmas Time, 1980, Come With Us, Our God Will Do Thee Good, 1986, The Indiana House, 1987. Organist Allen Temple A.M.E. Ch., 1941-45; asst. organist Choppin A.M.E. Ch., 1945-49; organist-dir. Progressive Ch. of God in Christ, Maywood, Ill., 1950-60; missionary Child Evangelism Fellowship, Chgo., 1955-63; unit leader YWCA, New Buffalo, Mich., 1956-58; minister of music God's House of All Nations, Chgo., 1960-80; pastor God's House of Love, Prayer and Deliverance, Robbins, 1982—; chmn. Frank and Mary Moody Scholarship Com., 1984—; dir. music Christian Women's Outreach Ministry, 1984—; mem. Robbins Community Council, 1983-85. Coppin A.M.E. Ch. scholar, 1946. Mem. Music Educators Nat. Conf., AFT. Democrat. Clubs: Good News (tchr. 1955-63 Chgo.). Home: 8154 S Indiana Chicago IL 60619

JAMES, MARY ROSENBLUM, design engineer; b. Cornwall, N.Y., Oct. 13, 1950; d. Hyman and Evelyn (Levy) Rosenblum. BA, NYU, 1972; MA, New Sch. for Social Research, 1975. Pvt. practice psychotherapy Newburgh, N.Y., 1978-85; design engr. CDI Corp., Hopewell Junction, N.Y., 1986-87, L.J. Gonzer Assocs., Beacon, N.J., 1987—; dir. archtl. design team L.J. Gonzer Assocs., Beacon, 1987; tchr. adult edn. Mt. St. Mary Coll., Newburgh, 1980-82; lectr. profl. groups, Newburgh, 1978-84; pres. NJCC Drama Workshop, Newburgh, 1982. v.p. Temple Beth Jacob Sisterhood, Newburgh, 1983. Mem. Nat. Assn. for Female Execs., Am. Fedn. TV and Radio Artists. Office: LJ Gonzer Assocs Box A Sterling St Beacon NY 12508

JAMES, MARYELLEN, executive search company administrator; b. Rockville Centre, N.Y., Nov. 27, 1960; d. Gerard Joseph and Mary Agnes (Mullany) Smith; m. Thomas J. James, June 21, 1985; 1 child, Robert Thomas. BS in Psychology, So. Conn. State U., 1982. Sr. assoc. Richards Cons. Ltd., Westport, Conn., 1982-85; personnel specialist Gen. Datacom Industries, Inc., Middlebury, Conn., 1985-86; research mgr. J. Redmond & Assocs., Inc., Danbury, Conn., 1986-87; research dir. Employment Opportunities, Danbury, Conn., 1987; ind. cons. New Fairfield, Conn., 1987—. Mem. Nat. Assn. Female Execs.

JAMES, REBECCA LOU, educator, consultant; b. Houston, Mar. 4, 1938; d. Ben Allen and Julia Corinth (Wainscott) J.; m. William Fabian Kitchell, June 10, 1961 (dec. Nov. 1982); 1 dau., Julie Ann. B.S., U. Houston, 1959, M.Ed., 1976, Ed.D., 1982. Tchr., Houston Ind. Schs., 1959-73; asst. supr. Timbergrove Christian Acad., Houston, 1974-75; grad. fellow U. Houston, 1975-78; cons. region 4 Edn. Service Ctr., Houston, 1978-79; student tchr. supr. U. Houston, 1979-80; gifted/talented instr. Galena Park Schs., Houston, 1980-84; pres. The Whole Brain Experience, Inc., 1984-85; Bibl. counselor 700 Club, Houston, 1982-84, dir. tng. programs, 1982-83; dir. Accelerated Learning, Fremont, Calif., 1985—; curriculum specialist independent study ctr. Fremont Unified Schs., 1985—; mem. task force, Tex. Council for Personnel Preparation for Handicapped, Austin, Houston, 1976-77; mem. evaluation com. So. Assn. Colls. and Schs., Houston, 1982; cons. region 4 Edn. Service Ctr., Houston, 1979—. Cons., Hope Ctr. for Youth, Houston, 1980-82; counselor rape victims, parents of gifted or handicapped children Evangelistic Temple, 1980—; co-dir. Evangelistic Temple Sch. of Bible, Houston, 1979-82. Internat. Order Alhambra scholar, 1976; Grad. Scholarship Endowment grantee U. Houston, 1980. Mem. Council Exceptional Children, Tex. Council Exceptional Children, Tex. Assn. Gifted and Talented Soc. Accelerated Learning and Teaching, Phi Delta Kappa, Kappa Delta Pi, Delta Delta Delta. Home and Office: 4310 Eggers Dr Fremont CA 94536

JAMES, RHODA ANN MICHAUX, business college administrator; b. Cleve., Sept. 10, 1953; d. Charles Talmadge and Wilma Revella (Jones) Michaux; m. Thomas Harold James, June 24, 1977; children: Tamara Nikole, Kerel Michaux. BEd, Chgo. State U., 1973-75; postgrad., U. Nev., 1976-77, Calif. State U., Carson, 1980-81. Teaching cert., Ill., Nev., Calif. Instr. Clark County Sch. Dist., Las Vegas, Nev., 1975-78; adminstrv. asst. Dorothy Brown Sch., Los Angeles, 1978-83; dir. Watterson Coll., Los Angeles, 1983—; now asst. to pres., dean of academics Sawyer Coll. at Pomona, Calif. Active Los Angeles Urban League. Mem. Calif. Bus. Edn. Assn., Nat. Assn. Female Execs., Exec. Women Internat., NAACP. Baptist. Clubs: Cocker Spaniel of Orange County (membership chairperson 1981-84, Rookie of Yr. 1985), San Gabriel Cocker Fanciers (treas. 1984-85). Home: 4810

Mane St Ontario CA 91762 Office: Sawyer Coll at Pomona 1021 E Holt Pomona CA 91767

JAMES, SHERIDAN FRANCES, licensing corporation executive; b. Bakersfield, Calif., July 3, 1937; d. Chester A. and Bettye Lou (Short) J. B.S., UCLA, 1959; postgrad. Harvard Bus. Sch., 1960. Dept. mgr. Filene's, Boston, 1960-64, I. Magnin & Co., San Francisco, 1964-68; v.p. licensing Determined Prodns., Inc., San Francisco, 1968-82; pres. Claremont Internat., Inc., N.Y.C., 1983—. Republican. Episcopalian. Clubs: Harvard, Radcliffe. Home: 903 Park Ave New York NY 10021 Office: Claremont Internat Inc 157 W 57th St New York NY 10019

JAMES, SUSAN OLIVIA, engineer; b. Balt., Apr. 14, 1951; d. Joseph Edward and Frances Marlene (Kolodziejski) Schmidt; student Community Coll. R.I., 1977-83, Western New Eng. Coll., 1984-86; m. Alan R. James; children—Eileen, Karen. With Victor Corp., West Warwick, R.I., 1971-83, cost estimator, 1973-76, process engr., 1976-79, applications engr., 1979-81, process engring. supr., 1981-82, process engring. mgr., 1982-83; product engr. Mold Con div. K&M Electronics, West Springfield, Mass., 1983-84; harness engr. Am. Electric Cable Co., Holyoke, Mass., 1984-87; applications engr. Century Wire & Cable div. Gehr Industries, Commerce Calif., 1987-88, mgr. engring., 1988—. Mem. Wire Assn. Mem. Soc. Friends. Home: 2851 S LaCadena Dr #253 Colton CA 92324 Office: 7400 E Slauson Ave Commerce CA 90040

JAMES, VICKI DIANE, conversion analyst; b. Hawthorne, Calif., Aug. 26, 1954; d. Jack Monroe and Shirley Ann (Black) Goff; m. Jeffrey George Obitz, Mar. 17, 1979 (div. Oct. 1982); 1 child, Stefanie Diane; m. Stephen John James, Apr. 24, 1987. Customer service officer Liberty Nat. Bank, Oklahoma City, 1978-86; data processing mgr. Eastland Mortgage Co., Oklahoma City, 1986-87; conversion analyst FDIC, Oklahoma City, 1987—. Mem. Nat. Assn. Female Execs. Office: FDIC PO Box 26208 Oklahoma City OK 73010

JAMES-DAUGHERTY, ANN ELOISE, health facility director; b. Russell Springs, Ky., June 15, 1936; d. Clifford D. and Rectie (Whittle) Leach; m. Charles A. Daugherty, Sept. 1959 (div. Mar. 1981); children: Theresa, David, Diana; m. Jimmy James, Nov. 22, 1982. AA, Ind. U., Indpls., 1967, BS in Nursing, 1972, MS in Nursing, 1981; M in Psychiat. Nursing, Ind. U.-Purdue U., 1981. Lic. nursing home adminstr., Ind. Nurse ob-gyn Johnson County Meml. Hosp., Franklin, Ind., 1969-71, acting head nurse, 1972-75; adminstr., dir. nursing Franklin Nursing Home, 1971-72; nurse psychiatry drug detoxification unit VA Med. Ctr., Indpls., 1979-81; asst. supr. Ind. Masonic Home Hosp., Franklin, 1981; with in-patient unit Quinco, Columbus, Ind., 1982, with outpatient unit, 1982-85; exec. dir. Tara Treatment Ctr., Inc., Franklin, 1985—. Named to Hon. Order Ky. Cols. Mem. Nat. and State Assn. Alcoholism and Drug Abuse Counselors (bd. dirs.), Johnson County Mental Health Assn. (pres.), Johnson Mental Health Clinic (pres., bd. dirs.), Franklin C. of C. Baptist. Home and Office: Rural Rt 5 Box 225 Franklin IN 46131

JAMES-O'LOUGHLIN, DEBORAH ANN, entertainment industry consultant; b. Elizabeth, N.J., Dec. 17, 1958; d. Ronald M. and Veronica (Tomko) James; m. Michael D. O'Loughlin, June 15, 1985. Student, Katharine Gibbs Sch., 1977; BA, Rutgers, 1983. Admin. asst., jr. exec. CBS, Inc., N.Y.C., 1978-83; office mgr. BNV, Inc., N.Y.C., 1983—; cons. Elkins Entertainment, West Hollywood, Calif., 1985—, SATIE Prodns., Malibu, Calif., 1987—; prodn. asst. United Service Orgn., Washington, 1986, Sportsco, Calif., 1987; v.p. sales div. Globe Computer Co., N.Y.C., 1987—; cons. Make-A-Wish Found., Newport, Calif., 1986—. Contbr. Am. Poetry Anthology, 1983. Mem. Am. Cancer Soc., 1985—. Roman Catholic. Club: Camp Pendleton Officers' Wives'. Home: 410 B Ferrari Ct Camp Pendleton CA 92055

JAMESON, DOROTHEA, sensory psychologist; b. Newton, Mass., Nov. 16, 1920; d. Robert and Josephine (Murray) Jameson; B.A., Wellesley Coll., 1942; M.A. (hon.), U. Pa., 1973; m. Leo M. Hurvich, Oct. 23, 1948. Research asst. Harvard, 1941-47; research psychologist Eastman Kodak Co., Rochester, N.Y., 1947-57; research scientist N.Y.U., 1957-62; vis. scientist Venezuelan Inst. Sci. Research, 1965; research asso. to prof. Psychol. and Inst. Neurol. Scis., U. Pa., 1962-74, Univ. prof. U. Pa., 1975—; vis. prof. Center Visual Sci., U. Rochester, 1974, Columbia U., 1974-76, fall 1986; cons. in field. Mem. Nat. Adv. Eye Council, NIH, 1985—; corp. bd. Woods Hole Oceanographic Inst., 1978-84, 85—; U.S. Nat. Com. Internat. U. Psychol. Scis., 1985—; Nat. Acad. Sci.-NCR Commn. on Human Resources, 1977-80, chmn. com. on vision, 1980-81. Recipient I.H. Godlove award Inter-Soc. Color Council, 1973; Alumnae Achievement award Wellesley Coll., 1974; Deane B. Judd award Assn. Internationale 'de Couleur, 1985; Hermann von Helmholtz award Cognitive Neurosci. Inst., 1987; fellow Center for Advanced Study in the Behavioral Scis., 1981-82. Mem. Soc. Exptl. Psychologists (Howard Crosby Warren medal 1971), Am. Psychol. Assn. (Distinguished Sci. Contbn. award 1972), Nat. Acad. Scis., Am. Acad. Arts and Scis., AAAS, Assn. Research in Vision and Ophthalmology, Biophys. Soc., Internat. Brain Research Orgn., Internat. Research Group Color Vision Deficiencies, Optical Soc. Am. (Tillyer medal 1982), Psychonomic Soc., Soc. Neurosci., Sigma Xi. Co-author: The Perception of Brightness and Darkness, 1966; co-author introduction and English translation: (E. Hering) Outlines of a Theory of the Light Sense, 1964. Co-editor, author chpt.: Visual Psychophysics: Handbook of Sensory Physiology, Vol. VII/4, 1972. Contbr. articles to profl. jours. Office: Univ of Pa 3815 Walnut St Philadelphia PA 19104

JAMESON, PATRICIA MARIAN, government agency administrator; b. Pitts., Mar. 17, 1945; d. Vernon L. and Dorothy Leam (Wilson) J.; B.A., Northwestern U., 1967; M.A., Ohio State U., 1969, with HUD, 1970—, project mgr., Detroit, 1976-77, acting dir. housing mgmt., 1978, dep. area mgr. Milw. Area Office, 1978-85, acting area mgr., 1979-80, 82, regional dir. adminstrn. Chgo. Regional Office, 1985—. Mem. Chgo. Council on Fgn. Relations. Recipient Quality Performance award HUD, 1973, 75, 80, Outstanding Performance award, 1980, 85, 87; NDEA fellow, 1967-69. Mem. Am. Mgmt. Assn., Nat. Assn. Female Execs., NOW, ACLU, Fed. Execs. Inst. Alumni Assn., Phi Beta Kappa, Pi Sigma Alpha. Office: 300 S Wacker Dr Room 2237 Chicago IL 60606

JAMESON, PAULA ANN, lawyer; b. New Orleans, Feb. 19, 1945; d. Paul Henry and Virginia Lee (Powell) Bailey; 1 child, Paul Andrew. B.A., La. State U., 1966; J.D., U. Tex., 1969. Bar: Tex. 1969, D.C. 1970, Va., 1973, N.Y. 1978, U.S. Dist. Ct. D.C. 1970, U.S. Dist. Ct. (ea. dist.) Va. 1976, U.S. Ct. Appeals (D.C. cir.) 1972, U.S. Ct. Appeals (4th cir.) 1976, U.S. Ct. Appeals (5th cir.) 1978, U.S. Supreme Ct. 1973, U.S. Ct. Appeals (2d cir.) 1985. Asst. corp. counsel D.C. Corp. Counsel's Office, 1970-73; sr. asst. county atty. Fairfax County Atty.'s Office, Fairfax, Va., 1973-77; atty. Dow Jones & Co., Inc., Princeton, N.J., 1977-79, house counsel, 1979-81, asst. to chmn. bd., 1981-83, house counsel, dir. legal dept., 1983-86; sr. v.p., gen. counsel, corp. sec., PBS, Alexandria, Va., 1986—. Mem. ABA, Fed. Communications Bar Assn., D.C. Bar Assn., Assn. Bar City N.Y. Democrat. Roman Catholic. Office: PBS 1320 Braddock Pl Alexandria VA 22314

JAMESON, PRESCILLA KAREN HOLMES, educator; b. Chgo., Sept. 4, 1925; d. Presley Dixon and Mildred Priscilla (Rufsvold) Holmes; A.B. in Speech, U. Mich., 1947, M.A. in Speech, 1953; postgrad. U. Va., James Madison U., George Washington U., George Mason U.; m. Dorence C. Jameson, Aug. 16, 1948; children—Scott Kelly, Terence Alan, Patrick Brian. Dir. drama, Mt. Morris, Mich., 1947; tchr. lang. arts, Albuquerque, 1950; pvt. practice speech pathology, 1959-63; tchr. pub. schs., Marietta, Ohio, 1966-67; speech pathologist, dept. human resources Child Growth and Devel. Center, Arlington, Va., 1967-68; dir. speech activities Washington Irving Intermediate Sch., Springfield, Va., 1969—, dir. gifted talented program, 1976-79; instr. Fairfax County Staff Devel. Mem. Polit. Action Com. for Edn., 1976-79; tchr. Sunday sch. class for exceptional children Grace Presbyterian Ch., 1970. Mem. United Teaching Professions, NEA (rep. caucus for edn. exceptional children), Va. Edn. Assn., Fairfax Edn. Assn. (sec., dir. 1977-78), Am. Speech and Hearing Assn., Council for Exceptional Children, AAUW (v.p. Springfield-Annandale br. 1961-63), Zeta Phi Eta, Alpha Delta Kappa, BPW. Republican. Home: 6024 Selwood Pl Springfield VA 22152 Office: 8100 Keene Mill Rd Springfield VA 22152

JAMISON, DARLENE MARY, university administrator; b. Kansas City, Mo., Nov. 24, 1928; d. Joseph and Caroline E. Broyles; B.A. in Sociology, U. Mo., Kansas City, 1963, M.A., 1969; m. Homer C. Jamison, Feb. 12, 1971; 1 dau., Carolyn Suzanne Love. Mem. adminstrv. staff U. Mo., Kansas City, 1967-74, dir. affirmative action-academic, 1973-74; adminstrv. assoc., affirmative action officer Sch. Optometry, U. Ala., Birmingham, 1974-81, asst. to dean, 1981—. Mem. Ala. Assn. Women Deans, Adminstrs. and Counselors, Personnel Assn. Birmingham, Nat. Conf. Women in Chambers of Conf. (del. 1979-81), Women's Jr. C. of C. Birmingham (pres. 1981-82), Birmingham Met. Bus. and Profl. Women's Club (v.p. 1979-80), Am. Bus. Women's Assn. (chpt. pres. 1984-85, chpt. Woman of Yr. 1986, One of Top Ten Bus. Women of Yr., 1986). Editor various univ. publs. Home: 3586 Rockhill Rd Birmingham AL 35223 Office: U Ala Sch Optometry Birmingham AL 35294

JAMISON, ELEANOR A(GNES), social services administrator; b. Larimer, Pa., July 12, 1927; d. John A. and Virginia (Kowalczk) Rice; m. Boris Vugrincic, Aug. 29, 1948 (dec. 1973); children: Kathleen A. Vugrincic, Michael J. Vugrincic. BS, Youngstown (Ohio) State U., 1968; RN, Braddock Gen. Hosp. Sch. Nursing. Head nurse Shadyside Hosp., Pitts., 1952-56; obstetrics supr. St. Joseph Hosp., Warren, Ohio, 1956-62; dir. nursing Warren Gen. Hosp., 1962-68; mgr., office nurse E.B. McGovern M.D., Warren, 1969-76; asst. dir. Parkview Hosp., Toledo, 1976-77, St. Luke's Hosp., Maumee, Ohio, 1977-80; 5 St. Vincent Med. Ctr., Toledo, 1980—; cons. PE Industries, Dundee, Ohio, 1980-83. Mem. editorial bd. Hosp. Purchasing News. Mem. speakers bur. Am. Cancer Soc., 1968—, Am. Heart Assn., Toledo, 1968—. Mem. Ohio Soc. Cen. Service (past pres.), N.W. Ohio Cen. Service (past pres.), Am. Soc. Hosp. Cen. Service (past bd. dirs.), Am. Bus. Women's Assn. (past pres.), Assn. Operating Room Nurses, Am. Practitioners in Infection Control, Ohio Fedn. Bus. and Profl. Women, Toledo Bus. and Profl. Women's Club (past pres.), Health Clin. Internat. (pres.), Grey Nuns Assn., Nat. Assn. Female Execs., Mich. Basketweavers. Office: St Vincent Med Ctr 2213 Cherry St Toledo OH 43608

JAMISON, SHELIA ANN, finance company executive; b. Hattiesburg, Miss., July 19, 1950; d. Stanley Gear and Vivian (Gillis) English; m. Troy James Creel, Dec. 21, 1968 (div. 1980); m. Richard Allen Jamison, Oct. 24, 1981. BS in Mgmt. magna cum laude, Fairleigh Dickinson U., 1986. Purchasing asst. Dept. Hosps. State La., Independence, 1973-77; sales rep. Fisher Sci., Houston, 1977-79; account v.p. Paine Webber, Clifton, N.J., 1981-87; asst. br. mgr., assoc. v.p. Dean Witter Reynolds, Inc., N.Y.C., 1987—; speaker The Cons. Firm, Saddle Brook, N.J., 1987. Dir. Gene Michael Scholarship Fund, Bergenfield, N.J., 1986; mem. fund raising com. Tomorrow's Children Fund, Hackensack, N.J., 1987; mem. Group Against Smoking Pollution, 1987. Mem. Direct Investment Adv. Bd., Phi Zeta Kappa, Delta Mu Delta, Phi Omega Epsilon. Baptist. Office: Dean Witter Two World Trade Center 73d Floor New York NY 10048

JAMISON, SUSAN CLAPP, librarian; b. Pitts., Mar. 21, 1929; d. Harlan Luther and Irene Julia (Krause) Clapp; m. Robert Beatty Jamison, Dec. 19, 1947; children—Linda Jamison Larkin, Stephen Robert. BA in History and English, Coll. Staten Island, CUNY, 1971; M.A. in Am. Studies, U. Del., 1972, Am. History, 1974; MLS U. Md., 1979. Bus. asst. Dr. Robert L. Jacobson, 1960-71; real estate sales Walter Reno Watson Agy., Staten Island, N.Y., 1960-63; tchr. Dover High Sch. (Del.), 1973-75; adj. prof. Wilmington Coll., New Castle, Del., 1975—; asst. dir. Dover Pub. Library, 1980-85; dir. Corbit-Calloway Meml. Library, Odessa, Del., 1975—; grant writer Del. Humanities Forum, Wilmington, 1979-81; mem. speakers bur., 1982-83, evaluator, 1978—; pres. Central Del. Library Consortium, 1982-85. Author: The Face of a Town: the Corbit-Calloway Meml. Library, 1979; author 8 books and programs Yesterday & Today, series 1979-81; contbr. articles to profl. jours; editor and project dir., Six Tricentennial Views of Kent County, 1983-85; author, advisor A Legacy from Del. Women, 1987. Active in Odessa Women's Club, Del., 1975—; host of open house Christmas In Odessa, 1976—; founder Septemberfest, 1982; art chmn. Del. Fed. Women's Clubs, 1980-82; publicity chmn. Kent County Tricentennial Commn., Dover, 1983. Recipient Facts on File award for reference pub. ideas, 1985. Mem. Kent Library Network (v.p. 1982-84, pres. 1984-85), Del. Library Assn. (pres. pub. library div. 1979-81, pres. 1985-86), ALA, Del. Folklife Assn. (treas. 1987—). Home: Starr-Lore House Main St Odessa DE 19730 Office: Corbit-Calloway Meml Library 2d and High Sts Odessa DE 19730

JANAZZO, DONNA LYNN, sales executive; b. New Britain, Conn., Dec. 8, 1948; d. Maurice Janazzo and Dorothy Joan (Ingerson) Reid; divorced. Student, Quinnipiac Coll., Hamden, Conn., 1966-67. Sales and service rep. L'Eggs Hosiery, West Hartford, Conn., 1974-76; fleet sales mgr. Stephen World Wheels, Bristol, Conn., 1977—. Mem. Nat. Assn. Fleet Adminstrs. (assoc.), Nissan Century Club, Automotive Fleet and Leasing Assn., Pontiac Sales Masters Club, Cadillac Crest Club, Toyota Sales Soc. Club: Sunshine (Bristol) (sec. 1985—). Office: Stephen World Wheels 1097 Farmington Ave Bristol CT 06010

JANDEL, JULIETTE, technical publications writer, consultant; b. Dayton, Ohio, May 18, 1957; d. Walfred Theodore and Patricia Ruth (Reedy) J. BA in English, Miami U., Oxford, Ohio, 1977; MA in English, Wright State U., 1983. Cert. tech. writer, tchr. ESL. Asst. in mcht. banking Wells Fargo Bank, San Francisco, 1978; EEO specialist Levi Strauss & Co., San Francisco, 1978-80; fin. planning adminstr. Mead Corp., Dayton, 1980-81; instr. English grad. sch. Wright State U., Dayton, 1981-83; tech. writer Shaw, Weiss & Denaples, Dayton, 1983; dir. tech. communications Digitec Corp., Dayton, 1983-85; dir. tech. pubs. Hayes Microcomputer Products, Norcross, Ga., 1985—; cons. in communications Hi-Tech Ad Council, Atlanta, 1986—. Author tech. manuals; contbr. tech. articles to profl. jours. Mem. Soc. Tech. Communication (membership mgr. 1987—, 2 publs. awards 1986), IEEE, Nat. Assn. Female Execs. (network mgr. Atlanta chpt. 1987), Am. Mgmt. Assn. Home: 6664 September Eve Dr Norcross GA 30092

JANECKI, JANICE MARIE, marketing professional; b. Chgo., Jan. 6, 1953; d. Richard A. and Billie L. (Duckworth) J. BS in Mass Communications, Ariz. State U., 1978. Advt. mgr. Home Appliance-TV Ctr., Phoenix, 1978-79; account exec. WFC Advt., Inc., Phoenix, 1979-83; asst. v.p., product mgr. The Ariz. Bank, Phoenix, 1983-85; asst. v.p., mgr. mktg. Wells Fargo Credit Corp., Scottsdale, Ariz., 1985—; assoc. prof. Phoenix Coll., 1982-86. Bd. dirs. Ad2 Phoenix, 1982, North Star Behavioral Ctr., Phoenix, 1983; mem. publicity com. Fiesta Bowl, Phoenix, 1982-86. Mem. Am. Mktg. Assn., Bank Adminstrn. Inst., Am. Mgmt. Assn. Republican. Roman Catholic. Home: 7791 E Osborn Rd Scottsdale AZ 85251 Office: Wells Fargo Credit Corp 4141 N Scottsdale Rd Scottsdale AZ 85251

JANESKI, VICTORIA HIGH, insurance company executive; b. Lancaster, Pa., Feb. 25, 1952; d. James Leon and Carolyn Joanne (Kling) H.; m. Jerome Richard Janeski, Nov. 27, 1976. Grad. high sch., Kinzers, Pa. Acct. Sperry New Holland (Pa.), 1970-76; office retail mgr. Kitchen Kettle Foods, Inc., Intercourse, Pa., 1978-81; adminstrv. mgr. Sateco Title Ins., Panorama City, Ca., 1981-87. Mem. Nat. Assn. Female Execs. Republican. Methodist. Home: 848 Olde Hickory Rd Lancaster PA 17601

JANEWAY, ELIZABETH HALL, author; b. Bklyn., Oct. 7, 1913; d. Charles H. and Jeannette F. (Searle) Hall; m. Eliot Janeway; children: Michael, William. Student, Swarthmore Coll.; A.B., Barnard Coll., 1935; Ph.D. in Lit. (hon.), Simpson Coll., Cedarcrest Coll., Villa Maria Coll.; D.H.L., Russell Sage Coll., 1981, Florida Internat. U., 1988. Asso. fellow Yale. Author: The Walsh Girls, 1943, Daisy Kenyon, 1945, The Question of Gregory, 1949, The Vikings, 1951, Leaving Home, 1953, Early Days of the Automobile, 1956, The Third Choice, 1959, Angry Kate, 1963, Accident, 1964, Ivanov Seven, 1967, Man's World, Woman's Place, 1971, Between Myth and Morning: Women Awakening, 1974, Powers of the Weak, 1980, Cross Sections: From a Decade of Change, 1982, Improper Behavior, 1987; contbr. to: Comprehensive Textbook of Psychiatry, 2d edit, 1980, Harvard Guide to Contemporary American Writing, 1979, also short stories and critical writing in periodicals and newspapers. Chmn. N.Y. State Council Humanities, NOW Legal Def. and Edn. Fund; mem. Bd. Fedn. State Humanities Council. Recipient educator's award Delta Kappa Gamma, 1972; named Disting. Alumna Barnard Coll., 1979; recipient Medal of Distinction, 1981. Mem. Authors Guild (council), Authors League Am. (council), PEN, Phi Beta Kappa (hon.). Home: 15 E 80th St New York NY 10021

JANICKE, PATRICIA ANN, technical writer, editor; b. Milw., Aug. 28, 1932; d. John Harold and Dorothy Ellen (Lappen) Carney; student U. Wis., 1950-51; B.A. in Speech, Radio and Dramatics, Mt. Mary Coll., 1954; postgrad. Moorpark Coll., 1974-76; m. Joseph E. Janicke, Jan. 13, 1962 (dec. 1976); 1 dau., Julia Ellen. Exec. sec. Acad. Motion Picture Arts and Scis., Beverly Hills, Calif., 1959-63; computer operator Litton Industries, Van Nuys, Calif., 1969-72; acct. Vetek Computer Systems, Inc., Westlake Village, Calif., 1974-75, Datex, Oxnard, Calif., 1975-76; tech. writer, editor Vitro Labs., Oxnard, 1976-80; tech. writer, logistics analyst Raytheon Service Co., Ventura, Calif., 1980-82; tech. writer L.I. Dimmick Corp., Oxnard, 1982-84; sr. systems analyst System Devel. Corp., Camarillo, Calif., 1984-85, sr. logistician Support Mgmt. Services, Oxnard, 1985-86; sr. tech. writer/editor McLaughlin Research Corp., Camarillo, Calif., 1986—, treas. recreation com. Editor bulletin Camarillo Springs Mobile Home Owners Assn., 1987—, pres. Westlake Village (Calif.) chpt. One Again, Inc., 1977-79, bd. dirs., 1977-79; bd. dirs. Am. Contract Bridge League, Oxnard, 1978-80; v.p. Raytheon Activities Club, 1980-82. Recipient Masque and Gavel award Mt. Mary Coll., 1954. Mem. Am. Soc. Women Accts., N.W. Indsl. Editors Assn., Ventura County Heart Fund Guild. Republican. Roman Catholic. Club: Sweet Adelines. Home: 42 Margarita Camarillo CA 93010 Office: 275 E Pleasant Valley Rd Camarillo CA 93010

JANITELL, KAREN SUE, sales director; b. Heidelburg, People's Rep. Germany, May 13, 1956; d. Frank and Roberta Fay (Hicks) Bartlett; divorced; 1 child, Jennessa Fay Janitell. Student, Colo. State U., 1975, U. Colo., 1976-77. With sales dept. U.S. Swim and Fitness, Colorado Springs, 1982, mgr., 1982-84, with pub. relations, advt. depts., sales trainer, 1984-85, nat. dir. sales, 1985-87. Vol. Chins-up, Zebulon Pike Detention Ctr. Mem. Nat. Assn. Female Execs. Republican. Methodist.

JANKO, MAY, graphic artist; b. N.Y.C., Feb. 27, 1926; d. Jacob and Clara (Schupler) J. B.A., Hunter Coll., 1946, M.A., 1952; student Art Students League, 1949-53. Tchr. art N.Y.C. Pub. Schs., 1953-60; textile designer M. Lowenstein Corp., N.Y.C., 1967-84. Exhibited in group shows: Library of Congress, Washington, 1956, 63; Albany, 1959; Whitney Mus. Am. Art, N.Y.C., 1959; Pa. Acad., Phila., 1959; Bklyn. Mus., 1960; Taipei Nat. Mus. (Taiwan), 1984; represented in permanent collections: Met. Mus. Art, N.Y.C., Rockefeller Collection, N.Y.C., Cin. Mus. Art, Nat. Gallery, Washington. Recipient Achievement award Hunter Coll., 1956; I.B. Markell award in graphics Audubon Artists, N.Y.C., 1961; Leo Meissner award NAD, N.Y.C., 1984; Louis Comfort Tiffany Found. fellow, 1959. Mem. Soc. Am. Graphic Artists (life; mem. council 1977, Henry B. Shope award 1954, Graphic Chem. award 1985), Boston Printmakers, Am. Color Print Soc., Art Students League (life).

JANNONI-MORRISSEY, CHERYL ANNE, architectural engineer; b. Cambridge, Mass., Mar. 29, 1963; d. William Nicholas and Lucy Ann (Porcaro) J.; m. Richard Arthur Morrissey, Apr. 25, 1987. A in Archtl. Engring., Wentworth Inst., 1981, B in Archtl. Engring., 1985. Designer The Nordquist Co. Archtl. Firm, Waltham, 1985-86; designer coop. edn. div. capitol planning and operations Commonwealth of Mass., Boston, 1984-85, architectural engr. State House Constrn. Project, 1986—. Mem. Coalition for Reliable Energy, Andover, Mass., 1987. Mem. Soc. Women Engrs., Nat. Assn. Female Execs. Office: State House Project Office Room 46 State House Boston MA 02133

JANNUCCI, GLORIA ISABELLA, psychologist; b. Elizabeth, N.J., Jan. 16, 1929; d. Louis and Anna Carmella (Vitale) J. AB cum laude, U. So. Calif., 1953; MA, Columbia U., 1954; EdD, Rutgers U., 1964. Lic. psychologist, N.J.; cert. sch. psychologist. Clin. intern N.J. State Dept. Insts. and Agys., 1954-55; clin. psychologist Marlboro (N.J.) State Hosp., 1955-58, from sr. clin. psychologist to prin. psychologist, 1960-65; clin. psychologist Middlesex Mental Health Clinic, New Brunswick, N.J., 1958-60; cons. psychologist N.J. pub. schs., 1965-70; clin. psychologist Monmouth Sch. for Exceptional Children, Eatontown, N.J., 1970-77; sch. psychologist Colts Neck (N.J.) Pub. Schs., 1970—; instr. psychology Kean, Monmouth and Brookdale Colls., N.J., 1968-70; pvt. practice psychology, West Long Branch, N.J., 1960—. Mem. Am. Psychol. Assn., N.J. Psychol. Assn., Monmouth-Ocean City Psychol. Assn. (chairperson membership com. 1958-60), N.J. Assn. Sch. Psychologists, N.J. Edn. Assn., Colts Neck Twp. Edn. Assn., Lambda Sigma Tau. Roman Catholic. Home: 80 Chelsea Ave Long Branch NJ 07740 Office: 265 Monmouth Park Hwy West Long Branch NJ 07740

JANOSKI, LISA-MARIE ANN, executive recruitment executive; b. Somerville, N.J., Sept. 15, 1963; d. Frank Henry and Dorothy (Malinowski) J. BS in Bus. Adminstrn., Marquette U., 1985. Dir. research Burke, O'Brien and Bishop Assocs., Inc., Princeton, N.J., 1985—. Mem. Nat. Assn. Female Execs., Marquette U. Alumni Orgn. Republican. Roman Catholic. Home: 300 Gemini Dr #3C Hillsborough NJ 08876 Office: Burke O'Brien & Bishop Assocs 1000 Herrontown Rd Princeton NJ 08540

JANOUSEK, JUDITH ANN, finacial industry consultant; b. Chgo., July 25, 1940; d. Anton C. and Emily R. (Bajza) J. A.A. in Bus. Morton Coll., 1960; B.S. in Bus. Mgmt., Elmhurst Coll., 1981; postgrad. U. Ill., 1981-82, U. Ga., 1984-85; A.A. in Paralegal Studies, MacCormac Coll., 1984. Lic. real estate broker, Ill. Supr. Olympic Fed. Savs. and Loan Assn., Berwyn, Ill., 1960-65; corp. asst. sec. Clyde Fed. Savs. and Loan Assn., North Riverside, Ill., 1965-75, Proviso Fed. Savs. and Loan Assn., 1975-79; mgr. acctg. dept. Fidelity Fedn. Savs. and Loan Assn., Berwyn, 1979-80; asst. v.p. lending collections Security Fed. Savs. and Loan Assn., Chgo., 1980-86; cons. CEO Assistance, Inc., Oakbrook Terr., Ill., 1986—. Mem. AAUW, Nat. Assn. Bank Women, Soc. Loan Underwriters, Women in Networking, Nat. Assn. Female Execs., Cath. Alumni Club, Dialogue for Blind, Bus. and Profl. Women's Club (local and dist. sec. 1968-70). Roman Catholic. Office: CEO Assistance Inc 18 W 100 22d St Suite 125 Oak Brook Terrace IL 60181

JANOWIAK, SANDRA LOGAN, funeral service company executive; b. Lansing, Mich., Apr. 25, 1955; d. Carol Edward and Ardis M. (West) Rogers; m. James A. Logan, Jr., Oct. 24, 1981 (dec. Sept. 1983); m. Christopher S. Janowiak, Mar. 7, 1987. Student in social work, Eastern Mich. U., 1978—. Office supr. Bur. Vocational Rehab., Ann Arbor, Mich., 1978-79; adminstrv. asst. reception ctr. Jackson State Prison, Mich., 1979-81; co-owner Geer-Logan Funeral Home, Ypsilanti, Mich., 1981-83, pres., owner, 1983—. Exec. bd. Women Bus. Owners Com., Ypsilanti, 1983—; adv. bd. Salvation Army, 1983—; mem. exec. com. Pvt. Industry Council, Washtenaw County, Mich. Mem. Ypsilanti C. of C., Nat. Funeral Dirs., Mich. Funeral Dirs. Assn., Women in Funeral Service Assn. Democrat. Baptist. Club: Zonta Internat. Home and Office: 320 N Washington St Ypsilanti MI 48197

JANSAK, KRISTINA LEA, federal government official; b. Augusta, Ga., Nov. 12, 1951; d. Andrew and Lee (Threlkeld) J. BA in Journalism magna cum laude, U. Ga., 1973; postgrad., U. Wis., 1976, Armed Forces Staff Coll., 1988. Chmn. youth adv. bd. EPA, Atlanta, 1973-74; pub. affairs officer Army Forces Command, Fort McPherson, Ga., 1974-80, chief of joint doctrine, 1980-84, war plans officer, 1984-85; manpower mgr. U.S. Forces Command, Atlanta, 1985-88, chief orgn. and studies, 1988—; orgnl. effectiveness cons. U.S. Army, Ft. McPherson, 1975-80; mem. Manpower Career Program Bd., Washington, 1987—; speaker in field. Editor Ft. Drum newspaper, 1976-77; contbr. articles to mags. and newspapers. Named an Outstanding Young Woman Am., 1976, Woman of Yr. Am. Bus. Women's Assn., 1977. Mem. Am. Soc. Mil. Comptrollers, Delta Gamma (pres. 1974-75). Republican. Baptist. Club: 1st Quarter (Athens, Ga.). Home: 1146 Timberland Dr Marietta GA 30067 Office: US Forces Command Directorate Resource Mgmt Fort McPherson GA 30330

JANSEN, ANGELA BING, artist, educator; b. N.Y.C., Aug. 17, 1929; d. Lester and Jean Bing; m. Gunther Jansen, Mar. 8, 1956; children—Edmund, Douglas. B.A., Bklyn. Coll., 1951; M.A., NYU, 1953; student, Bklyn. Mus. Art Sch., 1947-50, Atelier 17, N.Y.C., 1950-52. Tchr. art, public schs. N.Y.C., 1954—. One-man shows: Madison (Wis.) Art Center, 1977, Gimpel & Weitzenhoffer, N.Y.C., 1974, 78, group shows: Bklyn. Mus., 1950, 70, 76,

Library of Congress, Washington, 1969, 71, Ljubijana Internat. Print Biennale, Yugoslavia, 1971, 73, 75, 77, Venice Biennale, 1972, Internat. Exhbn. Drawing, Rejeka, Yugoslavia, 1972 (award), Internat. Print Biennale, Cracow, Poland, 1978; represented in permanent collections: Mus. Modern Art, N.Y.C., Met. Mus. Art, N.Y.C., N.Y. Pub. Library, Art Inst. Chgo., Tate Gallery, London, Victoria and Abert Mus., London, Bibliotheque Nationale, Paris, Bklyn. Mus., Phila. Mus. Art, Fonds d'Art Contemporain, Centre de Recherche et d'Etude de la Sculpture Contemporaine, Mauberge, France, Museé du Petit Format, Couvin, Belgium, Bklyn. Mus., Francine Tyler Art Forum, summer, 1979. Nat. Endowment for Arts grantee, 1974-75.

JANSEN, BONNIE MAY, transportation company office manager; b. Mankato, Minn., May 12, 1954; d. Werner Joseph and Charlotte Ann (Tacheny) J.; 1 child, Leah Rose. BS, Mankato State U., 1976. Billing clk. Theater Equipment Co., San Francisco, 1976-77; sec. Chem. Dependency Halfway House, Mpls., 1977-78; asst. export mgr. Internat. Freight Forwarder, Mpls., 1978—. Mem. adv. com. Children's Welfare Agy., 1980—; mem. bldg. adv. com. for local elem. sch. Mem. Minn. World Trade Assn. Mem. Dem. Farm Labor Party. Roman Catholic. Home: 3128 3rd Ave S Minneapolis MN 55408

JANSEN, CATHERINE SANDRA, art educator; b. N.Y.C., Dec. 14, 1950; d. George Jansen and Catherine (Janoulis) Matthews; m. William G. Larson, Feb. 14, 1972 (div. 1985); children: Erika Larson, Michaal Larson. BFA, Cranbrook Acad. Art, 1974; MFA, Temple U., 1977. Prof. Bucks County Community Coll., Newtown, Pa. One-woman shows include Rutgers Coll., N.J., 1978, St. Josephs U., Phila., 1981, Ctr. Creative Photography, Tucson, Ariz., 1983, U. Va., Charlottesville, 1985; group exhibits include Mus. Art, N.Y.C., 1973, Mus. Contemporary Crafts, N.Y.C., 1973, Phila. Mes., 1976, Smithsonian Inst., Washington, 1977, Honolulu Acad. Art, 1979, Hong Kong Arts Ctr., 1984, Pa. State U., Middletown, 1985, others; shown in various art mags. Nat. Endowment Arts grantee Pa. State Council of Arts, 1981. Home and Office: #152 Heacock Ln Wyncote PA 19095

JANSEN, ISABEL, civic worker; b. Phlox, Wis., May 26, 1906; d. Mose A. and Clara K. J.; RN, Marquette U., Milw., 1927. Surg. asst. to prof. oral and maxillofacial surgery Marquette U., 1927-52; ret., 1954; chmn. Antigo Freedom Com., 1960—. Recipient Liberty award Congress of Freedom, Inc., annually 1972-78, Keeper of the Flame award Woman Constitutionalist, 1974, cert. of appreciation Nat. Police Officers Assn. Am., 1973, Spl. award for Service to Nursing Marquette U. Nurses Alumni Assn., 1987. Roman Catholic. Research on heart deaths in Antigo, Wis., 1974; research on cancer deaths in Antigo, 1930-80; inventor Jansen Ray Pen, 1947. Home: 608 Gowan Rd Antigo WI 54409

JANSEN, MARTHA, realtor; b. Columbus, Ind., Dec. 22, 1938; d. William Thomas and Lillian Emaline (Stilwell) Brockman; m. James Russell Jansen, June 18, 1960; children: Jennifer, James D., Wendy, Russell, William, Mary. AA, Fullerton Coll., 1958; student, Calif. State U., Fullerton, 1959-60. 67-77, 86. Elem. sch. tchr. St. Juliana Sch., Fullerton, 1959-60; tech. typist tech. manuel writing firm, Los Angeles, 1960-61; sub. tchr. Cath. elem. schs., Fullerton, 1963-66; legal sec. various attys., Santa Ana and Placentia, Calif., 1972-78; real estate agt. Century 21 North Hills, Fullerton, 1978-82; pres., real estate broker Century 21 Achievers, Yorba Linda, Calif., 1982—. Mem. Calif. Assn. Realtors (state dir. 1986—), North Orange County Bd. Realtors (bd. dirs. 1985—, broker of the yr. 1984, 86). Office: Century 21 Achievers Inc 19768 Yorba Linda Yorba Linda CA 92686

JANSEN, PATRICIA GAIL, television producer; b. Bronxville, N.Y., July 3, 1946; d. Patrick Frank and Rita (Twohig) Curry; B.A. in Journalism/Broadcasting, Fordham U., 1968. Exec. producer Skyline series WNET, N.Y.C., 1978-79; coordinating producer Alexander the Great, Time-Life Films, N.Y.C., 1979-80, FYI with Hal Linden, ABC/Network, N.Y.C., 1980-81; assoc. dir. documentary programming HBO Cable, N.Y.C., 1981-83; sr. producer Why in the World series WNET/PBS, 1984-85; coordinating producer Art of the Western World, WNET/PBS, 1986—. Recipient Emmy award FYI series ABC-TV, 1980. Mem. Women in Film, Am. Acad. TV Arts and Scis. Home: 430 W 24th St New York NY 10011

JANSKY, JEANNETTE JEFFERSON, learning disabilities specialist; b. Urbana, Ill., Nov. 27, 1927; d. Bernard Levi and Irma Nicholson (Williams) Jefferson; m. Curtis Moreau Jansky, Aug. 14, 1949 (div. 1976); 1 child, Matthew Jefferson. BS, U. Ill., Urbana, 1949; MS in Edn., CCNY, 1960; PhD, Columbia U., 1970. Speech therapist Blythedale Convalescent Home, Valhalla, N.Y., 1950-51; clinician Lang. Disorder Clinic Columbia-Presbyn. Med. Ctr., N.Y.C., 1951-57, 65-72, dir. Lang. Disorder Clinic, 1972-74, dir. de Hirsch Robinson Reading Clinic, 1974—; pvt. practice learning disabilities specialist, N.Y.C., 1951—; mem. adv. bd. Fisher-Landau Found., N.Y.C., 1986—. Author (with K. de Hirsch): Predicting Reading Failure, 1966, Preventing Reading Failure, 1972; contbr. chpt. to books; assoc. editor Annals Dyslexia, Towson, Md., 1981—. Recipient N.Y. State award Orton Soc., 1977; grantee Health Research Council N.Y., 1966, Babies Hosp. Fund, 1966, Bienecke Found., 1974, 82. Fellow Am. Orthopsychiat. Assn.; mem. Am. Psychol. Assn., Internat. Reading Assn., Orton-Dyslexia Soc., Sigma Xi. Democrat. Presbyterian. Clubs: Cosmopolitan (N.Y.C.); Columbia U. Faculty (N.Y.C.). Home: 120 E 89th St New York NY 10128 Office: 46 E 82d St New York NY 10028

JANUARY, MARY A., sports marketing and public relations consultant; b. Dallas, Feb. 25, 1949; d. Alvin Eugene and Mae Elizabeth (Robinson) Patterson; 1 child, Mariah January. Student, North Tex. State U., 1967-68, Coll. of Marin, 1973-75. Pvt. practice fine arts cons., San Francisco, 1974-78, Dallas, 1978-79; assoc. dir. Allrich Gallery, San Francisco, 1980-81; account exec. Platt Communications, San Rafael, Calif., 1981-82; account exec. and promotions Sta. KFTY-TV, Santa Rosa, Calif., 1982-83; v.p. Sears Point Internat. Raceway, Sonoma, Calif., 1983-86; owner Auto/Sports Internat., 1986—; dir. mktg. Firebird Internat. Raceway, Chandler, Ariz., 1986-88, Corvette Challenge Series/Powell Devel. Am., Wixon, Mich., 1988—. Vol. Students Against Driving Drunk. Fellow Phoenix Press Box Assn., North Bay Advt. and Communications (bd. dirs.), Nat. Assn. for Female Execs., Am. Advt. Fedn. Mailing Address: PO Box 51090 Phoenix AZ 85076

JANZEN, NORINE MADELYN QUINLAN, medical technologist; b. Fond du Lac, Wis., Feb. 9, 1943; d. Joseph Wesley and Norma Edith (Gustin) Quinlan; B.S., Marian Coll., 1965; med. technologist St. Agnes Sch. Med. Tech., Fond du Lac, 1966; M.A., Central Mich. U., 1980; m. Douglas Mac Arthur Janzen, July 18, 1970; 1 son, Justin James. Med. technologist Mayfair Med. Lab., Wauwatosa, Wis., 1966-69; supr. med. technologist Dr.'s Mason, Chamberlain, Franke, Klink & Kamper, Milw., 1969-76, Hartford-Parkview Clinic, Ltd., 1976—. Substitute poll worker Fond du Lac Dem. Com., 1964-65; mem. Dem. Nat. Com., 1973—. Mem. Nat. Soc. Med. Technologists (awards com. 1984-87, chmn. 1986-88), Wis. Assn. Med. Technologists (chmn. awards com. 1976-77, 84-85, 86-87, treas. 1977-81, pres.-elect 1981-82, pres. 1982-83, dir. 1977-84, 85-87, Mem. of Yr. 1982, numerous service awards, chair ann. meeting 1987-88), Milw. Soc. Med. Technologists (pres. 1971-72; dir. 1972-73), Communications of Wis. (originator, chmn. 1977-79), Southeastern Suprs. Group (co-chmn. 1976-77), LWV, Alpha Delta Theta (nat. dist. chmn. 1967-69; nat. alumnae dir. 1969-71), Alpha Mu Tau. Methodist. Home: N 98 W 17298 Dotty Way Germantown WI 53022 Office: Hartford-Parkview Clinic 1004 E Sumner St Hartford WI 53027

JAPAR, SUSAN ELIZABETH, nurse, obstetrical nurse practitioner; b. Bronx, N.Y., Jan. 8, 1949; d. Romeo and Susan (Kuklish) J. BS in Nursing, Hunter Coll., 1970; ob/gyn nurse practitioner cert. U. Kans. Med. Ctr., 1975; MS, U. Calif., San Francisco, 1977. Med.-surg. staff nurse Albert Einstein Hosp., Bronx, 1970-72; staff nurse USAF Hosp., 1972-74; nurse practitioner, Grand Forks AFB, N.D., 1974-75; USAF Hosp., Clark AFB, Philippines, 1977-78; course supr. USAF, 1978-83; gynecol. nurse practitioner USAF Hosp., Myrtle Beach AFB, S.C., 1983—; ob-gyn nurse practitioner cons. to surg. gen. USAF, 1982; ob-gyn nurse practitioner cons. tactical air command USAF, 1986—; vis. lectr. U. Okla. Health Scis. Ctr. Mem. Uniformed Nurse Practitioner Assn., Nurses Assn. of Am. Coll. Ob-Gyn (chmn. Armed Forces Dist. 1983-85). Lutheran. Author: Diagnosis and Treatment of Vulvovaginitis, 1982, 4-part series on contraception, 1983

JAQUET, ADA CHARLOTTE, piano teacher, writer; b. Chgo., Aug. 17, 1912; d. Harry Irving and Bertha Mae (Broom) Thomas; m. Eugene S. Tanner, June 20, 1935 (dec. 1970); children—Joanne Elizabeth, Jane E., Malin, John E., Julie E. Smith; m. Roy R. Hewitt, Mar. 8, 1973 (dec. 1976); m. Felix W. Jaquet, Nov. 14, 1980. B.E., Nat. Coll. Edn., 1933; postgrad. U. N.D., 1935-37, Juillard Sch. Music, 1939, U. Tulsa, 1942-44, Syracuse U., 1969; M.A.T., Coll. of Wooster, 1971. Cert. tchr., Ill. Tchr. Pub. Schs., Libertyville, Ill., 1933-35, Country Day Sch., Tulsa, 1937-42; founder, dir. Women's League Play Sch., Grand Fork, N.D., 1935-37; owner, dir., tchr. Musical K, Tulsa, 1942-54; tchr., dir., mgr. Piano Studio Musical K., Wooster, Ohio, 1954-62; private instr. piano, Jaquet Piano Studio, Wooster, 1953—; freelance reporter Chautauqua Daily, N.Y., 1965-73, Wooster Daily Record, 1970-73. Dir. childrens choir Westminster Presbyterian Ch., Wooster, 1959-60, 1st Presbyn. Ch., Wooster, 1960-62; leader vol. poetry wookshop Community Ctr., Wooster, 1979-84. Author: (poetry) Gleanings, 1972. Mem. Wooster Poetry Soc. (sec. 1964-65), Nat. League Am. Pen Women (pres. Cen. Ohio branch 1982-84), Monday Club (pres. 1967-68), MacDowell Club (pres. 1987-89), AAUW, Nat. Kindergarten Assn. (field sec. 1935-37), Nat. Writers Club, Verse Writers Guild. Democrat. Avocations: Ecology; water coloring; RV travel. Home: 3220 Batdorf Rd Wooster OH 44691

JARAMILLO, MARI-LUCI, educational services corporation executive; b. Las Vegas, N.Mex., June 19, 1928. B.A., N.Mex. Highland U., 1955, M.A., 1959; Ph.D., U. N.Mex., 1970. Lang. arts cons. Las Vegas Sch. System, 1965-69; asst. dir. instructional services Minority Group Ctr., 1969-72; assoc. prof., chmn. dept. elem. edn. U. N.Mex., 1972-75, coordinator Title VII tchr. tng., 1975-76, assoc. prof. edn., 1976-77, prof., 1977, spl. asst. to pres., 1981-82, assoc. dean Coll. Edn., 1982-85, v.p. for student affairs, 1985-87; asst. v.p., dir. Ednl. Testing Service, Emeryville, Calif., 1987—; ambassador to Honduras, Tegucigalpa, 1977-80; dep. asst. sec. for inter-Am. affairs Dept. State, Washington, 1980-81. Contbr. articles to jours., chpts. to books. Trustee Tomas Rivera Ctr. Mem. Nat. Assn. Bilingual Edn., Latin Am. Assn., Am. Assn. Colls. for Tchr. Edn., Nat. Council La Raza. Office: Ednl Testing Service Bay Area Office 6425 Christie Ave Emeryville CA 94608

JAROS, LINDA, sports muscular therapist, nutritional consultant; b. Natick, Mass., Nov. 4, 1959; d. Robert Leo and Irene Victoria (Maslowska) J. AS with honors, Mass. Bay Community Coll., Wellesley, 1979; cert. in muscular therapy, New Eng. Inst., Allston, Mass., 1983. Cert. sports muscular therapist, Mass. Adminstrv. asst. Waters Assoc., Milford, Mass., 1979-81; mgr., instr. fitness and dance Workout Plus, Dedham, Mass., 1981-82; sports muscular therapist, fitness educator, nutritional cons. Myotech, Dedham, 1983—, also bd dirs. Participant various TV shows, 1985—; speaker radio interviews Stas. WBCN and WVBF, 1985—. Mem. Nat. Health Fedn., Am. Massage Therapy Assn. (coordinator sports massage team Boston marathon, 1985, speaker nat. conf. 1985, 1st ann. massage conf. 1987, 88, Appreciation Plaque 1983). Office: Myotech 450 Washington St Dedham MA 02026

JARRAD-MCCRAY, LUCY KAY, marketing professional; b. Cottonwood, Ariz., Mar. 20, 1955; d. Donald Stanley and Jane Marie (Post) J. BS in Sociology, Ariz. State U., 1985. Inbound mgr. Nat. Switchboard, Phoenix, 1978-86, ADDS Telemarketing, South Pasadena, Calif., 1986—. Mem. Customer Service Assn. Republican. Roman Catholic.

JARRELL, IRIS BONDS, educator, business executive; b. Winston-Salem, N.C., May 25, 1942; d. Ira and Annie Gertrude (Vandiver) Bonds; m. Tommy Dorsey Martin, Feb. 13, 1965; 1 child, Carlos Miguel; m. 2d, Clyde Rickey Jarrell, June 25, 1983; stepchildren—Tamara, Cris, Kimberly. Student U. N.C.-Greensboro, 1960-61, 68-69, 74-75, Salem Coll., 1976; B.S. in Edn., Winston-Salem State U., 1981; postgrad. Appalachian State U., 1983. Cert. tchr., N.C. Resource person Winston-Salem Dental Health Plan; substitute tchr. Winston-Salem/Forsyth County Schs., 1967—; tchr. Rutledge Coll., Winston-Salem, 1982-84; owner, mgr. Rainbow's End Consignment Shop, Winston-Salem, 1983-85; tchr. elem. edn. Winston-Salem/Forsyth County Sch. System, 1985—. Contbr. poetry to mags. Mem. Assn. of Couples for Marriage Enrichment, Winston-Salem, 1984-86, Forsyth-Stokes Mental Health Assn., 1985-86. Mem. Internat. Reading Assn., N.C. Assn. Adult Edn., Forsyth Assn. Classroom Tchrs., Nat. Assn. Female Execs. Democrat. Baptist. Avocations: singing; writing; sewing; crewel embroidery; gardening; reading. Home: 1008 Gales Ave SW Winston-Salem NC 27103

JARRETT, JOYCE CRISCOE, media relations executive; b. Greensboro, N.C., Oct. 13, 1938; d. Langester Clayton and Lillian Louise (Joyce) Criscoe; m. Ralph R. Jarrett; 1 child, Patti Lee Jessup Finney. AA, Guilford Coll. Tech. publs. writer Celanese Corp., Asheville, N.C., 1962-65; exec. sec. Lorillard, Inc., Greensboro, 1965-75, mgr., editor employee publs., mgr. community media relations, 1975—. Del. N.C. Gov.'s Conf. for Women, 1982, 83; publicity dir. Jr. Achievement Greensboro, 1983-85; chmn. United Way, 1983, coordinator person to person program, 1983-85. Named Outstanding Greensboro Businesswoman, 1982; recipient of Women's History Community Service award, 1987. Mem. Internat. Assn. Bus. Communicators (Piedmont chpt., compleat communicator awards 1981, 1982, 86). Carolinas Assn. Bus. Communicators, Greensboro C. of C. (council on bus. communications 1985-88), Leadership Greensboro program (grad. 1988), The Bd., A Profl. Women's Consortium (treas. 1987), Quill and Scroll (bd. dirs.), N.C. Human Genetics Assn. (bd. dirs. 1983-84), Adopt-a-Sch. program (steering com.). Republican. Baptist. Home: 122 Pineburr Rd Greensboro NC 27408 Office: 2525 E Market St Greensboro NC 27401

JARRETT, (LYNN) LENTA JOYCE, computer professional, consultant; b. Owings, W.Va., Jan. 25, 1941; d. Jack Calvin and Helen Addie (Sherbs) Girod; m. Robert Henry Jarrett, 1961 (div.); children: Todd and Stephanie. BBA, Nat. U., 1982, MBA, 1983. Sec. Dept. of State, Washington, 1958-59, Watertown (N.Y.) Daily News, 1959-60; printer Times-West Virginian, Fairmont, W.Va., 1960-61; printer Union-Tribune, San Diego, 1961-79, computer specialist, 1979-84, computer mgr., 1984—. Nat. columnist: Digital Rev. mag., Boston. Leader Girl Scouts U.S., San Diego, 1975-79; v.p., fin. chair of bd. dirs. San Diego YWCA, 1987-88. Recipient Twin award YWCA, San Diego, 1985. Mem. Nat. U. Alumni Assn., DECUS Computer Soc. (chair PC SIG 1987-88), Rainbow Users Group (chair 1986-88), Newspaper Computer Users Group (bd. dirs.), Data Processing Mgrs. Assn., San Diego Women in Computers. Democrat. Methodist. Club: Skyliters (San Diego). Office: PO Box 191 350 Camino De La Reina San Diego CA 92112

JARRETT, MARY OLIVE, hotel executive; b. Del Norte, Colo., Oct. 5, 1947; d. Donald Monroe and Mary Edith (Mock) J. Student, U. Colo., Denver, 1972-76. Concierge Cambridge Club Hotel, Denver, 1985, sales mgr., 1985-86, sales dir., 1986-87, sales, mktg. dir., 1987—. Precinct committeewoman Nat. Dem. Party, Englewood, Colo., 1972; mem. Denver Conv. Bur., 1985—. Mem. Brit. Profl. Assn., Nat. Thespian League (nat. honors 1965), Nat. Forensic League (nat. honors 1965), Am. Soc. Profl. Exec. Women, Colo. Bus. Com. for the Arts (mem. program com. 1987-88). Club: Elbert Grange (lectr. 1979-82). Office: Cambridge Club Hotel 1560 Sherman St Denver CO 80203

JARRETT, ROSALIND, television executive; b. Bklyn., June 15, 1948; d. Milton Philip and Harriet Blanche (Josephs) J. BA magna cum laude, SUNY, Buffalo, 1969. Asst. to exec. dir. Assn. Am. Dance Cos., N.Y.C., 1969-70; grants officer spl. programs div. N.Y. State Council on the Arts, N.Y.C., 1970-74, dir. application service sect., 1974-75; publicist Bella Lewitzky Dance Co., Los Angeles, 1976-78; from publicist to sr. publicist Sta. KCET-TV, Los Angeles, 1978-79; assoc. dir. program underwriting TV sta. KCET, Los Angeles, 1979-80; program publicist Capital Cities/ABC, Inc., Los Angeles, 1980-86, mgr. movie/miniseries publicity, 1986-87, dir. program publicity West Coast, 1987—. Mem. Publicists Guild of Am. (exec. bd. 1982-84, Maxwell Weinberg Publicist Showmanship award 1986), Acad. TV Arts and Scis., Women's Sailing Assn. of Santa Monica Bay (bd. dirs. 1986-87), Phi Beta Kappa. Office: Capital Cities/ABC Inc 2040 Ave of the Stars Los Angeles CA 90067

JARRETT, SANDRA LYNN, editor, advertising executive; b. Denver, Apr. 29, 1933, d. Harlan Vernon and Janet Mae (Wells) J. Student, Arapahoe Community Coll., Littleton, Colo., 1972-75, Met. State Coll., Denver, 1977-79. Editor Singles Country U.S.A., Denver, 1979—; dir. publicity and advt. Peaches Sportsbar and Good Time Emporium, Wheat Ridge, Colo., 1986—. Contbr. articles to profl. jours. Dir. advt. and publicity Ginny's Kids, 1986. Recipient award for Ginny's Kids program Arvada (Colo.) Kiwanis, 1986. Office: Singles Country USA 844 S Vine St Denver CO 80219 also: Singles Country USA PO Box 440066 Aurora CA 80014

JARVIS, BARBARA ANNE, lawyer; b. Kansas City, Mo., Apr. 14, 1934; d. Herman Edward and Marjorie Maude (Graber) Spitzenfeil; A.A., Kansas City Jr. Coll., 1953; B.S. in Polit. Sci. magna cum laude, Ariz. State U., 1976, J.D., 1979; m. Thomas B. Jarvis, Sept. 9, 1965; 1 son, Kenneth Mark. Technologist Menorah Med. Center, Kansas City, Mo., 1955-56, Ariz. State U. Student Health Service, 1960-62, Scottsdale (Ariz.) Bapt. Hosp., 1962-65; chief technologist Skyline Lab., Globe, Ariz., 1967-72; practice law, Phoenix, 1979—. Sec. Globe Planning and Zoning Comm., 1970-75; assoc. coordinator Women's Polit. Caucus Ariz.; 1st vice chmn. Ariz. Democratic Com.; mem. Dem. Nat. Com. from Ariz.; chmn. neighborhood rehab. com. Phoenix Urban Form, 1976-77, mem. steering com., 1976-79; mem. Phoenix Bd. Adjustment, 1977-82, chmn., 1980-81; chmn. Village 4 Planning Com., City of Phoenix; chmn. citizens adv. com. Ariz. Dept. Corrections, 1983-85, Paradise Corridor, 1986—; bd. dirs. Salvation Army, Globe, Gila Pueblo campus Eastern Ariz. Coll., Gila County Guidance Clinic. Mem. Am. Bar Assn., State Bar Ariz., State Bar Orge., Maricopa County Bar Assn. (co-chmn. alternatives to sentencing com. 1980-81), Ariz. Assn. Criminal Justice, Nat. Orgn. Criminal Def. Lawyers, Oreg. Criminal Def. Lawyers Assn., Ariz. Women Lawyers, Women in Law (chmn.), Ariz. State U. Law Sch. Alumni Assn., Charter 100, Pi Sigma Alpha, Phi Kappa Phi. Office: 1159 Emma Ashland OR 97520

JARVIS, GALE RALL, retail executive; b. St. Louis, Aug. 3, 1945; d. C.J. and Audrey (Reeves) Rall; m. Peter Leslie Jarvis, Apr. 22, 1972; children: Lauren, Jennifer. BSBA, Okla. State U., 1968; postgrad., NYU. Asst. buyer Lord & Taylor, N.Y.C., 1970-71; from asst. buyer to v.p. R.H. Macy, N.Y.C., 1971-85; exec. v.p. FAO Schwarc, N.Y.C., 1985—. Home: 20 Cottontail Rd New York NY 11747 Office: FAO Schwarz 767 Fifth Ave New York NY 10153

JARVIS, SHIRLEY KAYE, real estate executive; b. Huntington, W.Va., Feb. 11, 1942; d. Thurman Albert and Naomi Elizabeth (Simpson) Chapman; m. James Edward Jarvis, Jan. 3, 1964; children: Donald Christopher, James Courtney. Student, Alderson-Broaddus Coll., 1960-61; Grad. Realtors Inst., Parkersburg Community Coll., 1980. Cert. lab. technician Cabell Huntington (W.Va.) Hosp., 1962-72; realtor Toney Gallery of Homes, Huntington, 1972-79, Era Galaxie, Huntington, 1979-83, H.E. Pilcher and Co., Huntington, 1983; pres., owner The Property Shoppe, Inc. Realty, Barboursville, W.Va., 1983—. Dir. Huntington Womens Bowling Assn., 1981—; photographer Calvin Evans Evangelistic Crusade, Montego Bay, Jamaica, 1986-87. Recipient Winners Circle award ERA, 1982. Mem. Nat. Assn. Realtors (multiple listing service policy com. 1987—), W.Va. Assn. Realtors, Womens Council of Realtors (state sec. 1987—), Huntington Bd. Realtors (bd. dirs. 1982—, multiple listing service and computer affiliates com. 1987—, Realtor of Yr. 1987-88, Life Time Million Dollar award 1978-88). Republican. Baptist. Clubs: W.Va. Womens 600 (Parkersburg) (bd. dirs. 1981-86); Huntington Womens 600 (pres. 1982-87). Home: PO Box 231 Ona WV 25545 Office: The Property Shoppe Inc Realty 6468 Farmdale Rd Barboursville WV 25504

JARZOMBEK, SUSAN MARLENA, investment banker; b. Holyoke, Mass., Mar. 14, 1956; d. Richard Orville Berkwitt and Jacqueline Joyce Largent; m. Bruce Edward Jarzombek, Jan. 2, 1982. BA, George Mason U., 1977; MA, George Washington U., 1980; MBA, NYU, 1988. Research analyst Nat. Econ. Research Assocs., Washington, 1978-79; asst. mgr. First Nat. Bank of Chgo., N.Y.C. and Chgo., 1980-83; asst. v.p. Lloyds Internat. Corp., 1983-84; v.p. Swaps Fin. Group, 1984-86; v.p. corp. fgn. exchange group Bank of America, N.Y.C., 1986-87; futures/options product mgr. Bankers Trust Co., N.Y.C., 1987—. Mem. AAUW, Nat. Options and Futures Soc., Fin. Women's Assn. of N.Y. (mem. internat. com. 1984), NYU Money Marketeers, Council on Fgn. Relations (contbr. articles to newsletter 1982-83). Republican. Roman Catholic. Home: 511 Scofieldtown Rd Stamford CT 06903 Office: Bankers Trust Co 130 Liberty St New York NY 10006

JASPER, CYNTHIA ROSE, educator; b. Escanaba, Mich., May 19, 1953; d. Anthony Joseph and Sally Clare (Luft) J. BS magna cum laude, No. Mich. U., 1974; MS, U. Wis., 1982, PhD, 1984. Tchr. Lac du Flambeau (Wis.) Pub. Sch., 1975-78; adult edn. tchr. Rhinelander, Wis., 1976-78; mem. sales staff Singer Co., Madison, Wis., 1978-81; research asst. U. Wis., Madison, 1980-81, teaching asst., 1982-84, lectr., 1984-86, adminstrv. specialist, 1984-86, asst. prof. retailing textiles and clothing, 1986—. Contbr. numerous articles to profl. jours. Assoc. Am. Hist. Assn., 1987—; mem. State Hist. Soc. Wis., 1984—. Helen Cooper Mercer fellow, 1979. Mem. Internat. Fedn. Home Economists, Assn. Coll. Profs Clothing and Textiles (chmn. fellowship com. 1986-87, mem. council 1987-88), Am. Collegiate Retailing Assn., Am. Home Econs. Assn. (history and archives com. 1985-87), Costume Soc. Am. (publs. com. 1986-87), Am. Sociol. Assn. (assoc.), Omicron Nu (publs. com. 1985-87). Club: Retail (U. Wis.) (advisor 1984-86). Office: U Wis 1300 Linden Dr Madison WI 53706

JASTREBSKI, LINDA MARIE, assistant director academic computing; b. Brick Town, N.J., Jan. 27, 1958; d. Henry John and Gertrude Francis (Yarzab) J. BS, St. John's U., 1981, MBA, 1986. Computer operator St. John's U., Jamaica, N.Y., 1978; programmer St. John's U., Jamaica, 1978-83, supr. acad. computer lab, 1983-86, asst. dir. acad. computing, 1986—; Instr. adult edn., St. John's U., 1985—. Mem. Nat. Assn. Female Execs. Office: St. John's U Grand Central and Utopia Pkwys Jamaica NY 11439

JAVIER, DIANA, physical education educator; b. San Germán, P.R., Feb. 6, 1951; d. Pedro Javier Boscio and Dafne (Montalvo) Javier. BA, InterAm. U. of P.R., 1973, MA, 1977; postgrad. in edn. adminstrn., founds., Ill. State U., 1985; postgrad. in bus., mgmt., Glocester County Coll., Sewell, N.J., 1986. Adminstr. Recreation Ctr. Housing Dept. of P.R., San Juan, 1973-77; adv. Sports and Recreation Com. Senate of P.R., San Juan, 1977-81; supt. planning and tech. services Dept. Recreation Services, City of San Juan, 1977-81; spl. services mgr. U.S. Dept. Transp., USCG Air Sta., Borinquen, P.R., 1981-83; track and field head coach Ill. Wesleyan U., Bloomington, 1983-85; physical edn. instr., volleyball coach Glocester County Coll., Sewell, 1985—; dir. Sports Facilities, PanAmerican Games, San Juan, 1978, Accreditation div. First Pan Am. Master Games, P.R., 1980; coach female cross-country team, Catholic U. of P.R., 1983. Coordinator Latin Am. Little League Football, P.R., 1976; cert. life guard, instr. first aid, CPR, ARC, N.J., 1985—; mem. Puerto Rico Nat. Volleyball team, 1969-73. Recipient numerous gold medals, awards for swimming, volleyball, tennis, softball competitions, P.R., 1969-73, acknowledgement cert. United Service Orgn., 1983. Mem. AAHPERD, N.J. Alliance for Health, Phys. Edn., Recreation and Dance, Nat. Assn. Underwater Instrs., Profl. Assn. Diving Instrs., N.J. Collegiate Athletic Assn., Nat. Assn. Female Execs. Home: 7 Desmond Run Sicklerville NJ 08081

JAWORSKY, JANICE LOVELAND, musical director and conductor, vocal coach, soprano; b. Wichita, Kans., Apr. 9, 1947; d. James Edward and Virginia (Randle) Loveland; m. John Michael Jaworsky. B.M.E. summa cum laude, U. Kans., 1969, M.M.E. with honors, 1980. Mem. voice and music theory faculty U. Kans., Lawrence, 1974-76; lectr. voice Wichita State U., Kans., 1976—, vocal coach, 1976—, also asst. condr. opera, 1978-80, also music dir. and condr. for theatre, 1979-83; music dir. Crown-Uptown Dinner Theatre, Wichita, 1984—; concert singer for various civic, social orgns., Wichita, 1978—; radio and TV commls. backup singer, 1982—; producer dir. various sacred concerts, Wichita, 1980—; dir. music Hillside Christian Ch., Wichita, 1985—; clinician/adjudicator Kans. High Schs. Activity Assn., Topeka, 1976—. Author: A Teaching Guide for Class Voice, 1980; also univ. course and degree design. Mem. Nat. Assn. Tchrs. Singing, Am. Choral Dirs. Assn., P.E.O., Mu Phi Epsilon, Pi Kappa Lambda, Pi Lambda Theta. Republican. Mem. Chirstian Ch. (Disciples of Christ). Home: 252 N

Glendale Wichita KS 67208 Office: Crown-Uptown Dinner Theatre 3207 E Douglas Wichita KS 67218

JAY, NORMA JOYCE, artist; b. Wichita, Kans., Nov. 11, 1925; d. Albert Hugh and Thelma Ree (Boyd) Braly; m. Laurence Eugene Jay, Sept. 2, 1949; children—Dana Denise, Allison Eden. Student Wichita State U., 1946-49, Art Inst. Chgo., 1955-56, Calif. State Coll., 1963. Illustrator Boeing Aircraft, Wichita, Kans., 1949-51; co-owner Back Door Gallery, Laguna Beach, Calif., 1973—. One-woman shows Milcir Gallery, Tiburon, Calif., 1978, Newport Beach City Gallery, 1981; group shows include Am. Soc. Marine Artists ann. exhbns., N.Y.C., 1978-86, Peabody Mus., Salem, Mass., 1981, Mystic Seaport Mus. Gallery, Conn., 1982-85, Grand Cen. Galleries, N.Y., 1979-84, The Back Door Gallery, Laguna Beach, Calif., 1973—, Mariners' Mus., Newport News, Va., 1985-86; represented in permanent collections including James Irvine Found., Newport Beach, Niguel Art Assn., Laguna Niguel, Calif., Deloitte, Haskins & Sells, Costa Mesa, Calif., M.J. Brock & Sons Inc., North Hollywood, Calif., others. Recipient Best of Show award Ford Nat. Competition, 1961, First Place award Traditional Artists Exhbn., San Bernadino County Mus., 1976, Artist award Chriswood Gallery Invitational Exhbn., Rancho California, Calif., 1973. Fellow Am. Soc. Marine Artists (charter); mem. Niguel Art Assn. (first pres. 1968, hon. life mem. 1978), Artists Equity, Am. Artists Profl. League, Laguna Beach C. of C. Republican. Office: Back Door Gallery 352 N Coast Hwy Laguna Beach CA 92651

JAYARAM, SUSAN ANN, professional secretary; b. Stockton, Calif., Nov. 23, 1930; d. George Leroy and Violet Yvonne (Rushing) Potter; m. M. R. Jayaram, July 2, 1960. Student Pasadena Coll., 1951-52; Woodbury Coll., 1961; A.A., Long Beach City Coll., 1979. Cert. profl. Sec. Sec. to mgr. First Western Bank, Los Angeles, 1953-56; sec. to pres. Studio City Bank (Calif.), 1957-60; sec. to exec. vice-pres. Union Bank, Los Angeles, 1962-81; sec. to vice chmn. Imperial Bank, Los Angeles, 1981-82; personal sec. to Howard B. Keck, chmn. W.M. Keck. Found., 1982—. Sec., bd. advisors Citizens for Law Enforcement Needs, 1972-74; dir. Los Angeles/Bombay Sister City Com.; mem. Jeffery Found. Mem. DAR (Susan B. Anthony chpt.), Jeffery Found., Assistance League So. Calif., Freedoms Found. at Valley Forge (Los Angeles chpt.), U.S. Navy League (Beverly Hills, Orange County Councils) League of the Americas (pres. 1988—). Republican. Club: Los Angeles (dir., sec. 1967-81). Editor: Angeles Club Panorama, 1979-80; California Clarion, 1978-80. Office: HB Keck 555 S Flower St Los Angeles CA 90071

JAYNE, CYNTHIA ELIZABETH, psychologist; b. Pensacola, Fla., June 5, 1953; d. Gordon Howland and Joan (Rockwood) J. AB, Vassar Coll., 1974; MA, SUNY, Buffalo, 1978, PhD, 1983. Lic. psychologist, Pa. Instr. dept. psychiatry Temple U. Sch. Medicine, Phila., 1982-84, asst. prof., 1984-85, asst. dir. outpatient services, asst. dir. residency tng., 1982-85, clin. asst. prof., 1985—; pvt. practice psychology Phila., 1985—. Contbr. articles to profl. jours. Soc. for Sci. Study Sex scholar, 1981; Sigma Xi grantee, 1981, Kinsey Inst. Dissertation award, 1983. Mem. Am. Psychol. Assn., Ea. Psychol. Assn., Soc. for Sci. Study Sex (bd. dirs. 1984-86). Office: 1213 Locust St Philadelphia PA 19107

JEANE, JACQUELINE LEE, manufacturing executive; b. Anchorage, Dec. 15, 1952; d. Jerry Lee and Anita Joy (Bowen) Hawes; m. Harold Travis Jeanne II, Jun 4, 1977 (div. Mar. 1987). Student, Weatherford Jr. Coll., 1971-73; BA, Sam Houston State U., 1975. Speech and hearing disorders technician Mineral Wells (Tex.) Ind. Sch Dist., 1975-77; supr. cost control Kobe Systems, Odessa, Tex., 1977-78; supr. customer service and order entry Baker Prodn. Services, Houston, 1978-80; mgr. customer service BWT Corp., Houston, 1980-81; customer service, order control specialist Baker Packers (now Baker Oil Tools), Houston, 1981-85, supr. distribution services, 1985—. Mem. Nat. Assn. Female Execs., Phi Theta Kappa. Mem. Unity Ch. Office: Baker Oil Tools 6023 Navigation Blvd Houston TX 77011

JEANES, SHERRY LYNN, educator, extension agent; b. Cin., June 9, 1959; d. Wesley Albert and Shirley Ann (Clinger) Goenawein; m. Thomas Wesley Jeanes, Aug. 18, 1984. AA, Tyler Jr. Coll., 1978; BS, Stephen F. Austin State U., 1980, MS, 1985. Cert. home econs. tchr., Tex. Extension agt. home econs. Cherokee County Tex. Agrl. Extension Service, Rusk, Tex., 1980-82, San Augustine-Sabine (Tex.) County Tex. Agrl. Extension Service, 1982—; home econs. program leader San Augustine-Sabine County Extension Service, 1982—. County coordinator 4-H Council, San Augustine, 1982—; advisor Sabine County Youth Found., Hemphill. Tex., 1982—, San Augustine County Fair Bd., 1986—; com. chmn. San Augustine County Sesquicentennial Activities, 1986; adult leader Girl Scouts USA, San Augustine, 1987—. Mem. Tex. Assn. Extension Home Economist, Dist. Assn. Extension Home Economist (Rookie of Yr. 1982), Stephen F. Austin State U. Alumni Assn., San Augustin C. of C., Epsilon Sigma Phi (State Early Career award 1987). Club: San Augustine Garden. Lodge: Rotary (Goodwill Ambassador to Australia 1987). Home: Rt 1 Box 389 San Augustine TX 75972 Office: Tex Agrl Extension Service County Courthouse Room 201 San Augustine TX 75972

JEBENS, PATRICIA S., medical occupations educator; b. Berkeley, Calif., July 5, 1936; d. Wesley James and Constance Lord (Brady) Smith; m. Donald R. Jebens, Sept. 15, 1957; children—David Scott, Mark Alan. B.S. in Nursing, Calif. State U.-Fullerton, 1980; M.A., Calif. State U.-Long Beach, 1982. R.N., Calif.; lic. pub. health nurse, Calif. Staff nurse Providence Hosp., Oakland, Calif., 1957; nurse, team leader Garden Park Hosp., Anaheim, Calif., 1961-70; instr. Nurses Tng. Inst., Fullerton, Calif., 1970-73; med. occupations educator North Orange County Community Coll. Dist., Fullerton, 1974—, program coordinator health occupations, 1983—, guest lectr., 1980-83. Active Orange County council Boy Scouts Am., 1964-75; mem. vestry St. Joseph's Episcopal Ch., Buena Park, Calif., 1982; counselor, vol. Orange County Dept. Mental Health, 1978-81. Mem. Am. Soc. Aging, Orange County/Long Beach Nursing Consortium, Phi Kappa Phi. Office: North Orange County Community Coll Dist 1800 W Ball Rd Anaheim CA 92804

JECKLIN, LOIS U., art corporation executive, consultant; b. Manning, Iowa, Oct. 5, 1934; d. J.R. and Ruth O. (Austin) Underwood; m. Dirk C. Jecklin, June 24, 1955; children—Jennifer Anne, Ivan Peter. Student State U. Iowa, 1953-55, 60-61, 74-75. Residency coordinator Quad City Arts Council, Rock Island, Ill., 1973-78; field rep. Affiliate Artists, Inc., N.Y.C., 1975-77; mgr., artist in residence Deere & Co., Moline, Ill., 1977-80; dir. Vis. Artist Series, Davenport, Iowa, 1978-81; pres. Vis. Artists, Inc., Davenport, 1981-88; cons. writer's program St. Ambrose Coll., Davenport, 1981, 83, 85; mem. com. Iowa Arts Council, Des Moines, 1983-84; panelist Chamber Music Am., N.Y.C., 1984, Pub. Art Conf., Cedar Rapids, Iowa, 1984; panelist, mem. com. Lt. Gov.'s Conf. on Iowa's Future, Des Moines, 1984. Trustee Davenport Mus. Art, Nature Conservancy Iowa; mem. steering com. Iowa Citizens for Arts, Des Moines, 1970-71; bd. dirs. Tri-City Symphony Orchestra Assn., Davenport, 1968-83; founding mem. Urban Design Council, HOME, City of Davenport Beautification Com., all Davenport, 1970-72. Recipient numerous awards Izaak Walton League, Davenport Art Gallery, Assn. for Retarded Citizens, Am. Heart Assn., Ill. Bur. Corrections, many others; LaVernes Noyes scholar, 1953-55. Mem. Am. Council for Arts, Ptnrs. for Livable Places, Ann. Coll. Univ. Community Arts Adminstrs., Nat. Assembly Local Arts Agys., Crow Valley Golf Club. Republican. Episcopalian. Club: Outing. Lodge Rotary. Home: 2717 Nichols Ln Davenport IA 52803

JEFFERDS, MARY LEE, environmental edn. assn. exec.; b. Seattle, July 16, 1921; d. Amos Osgood and Vera Margaret (Percival) Jefferds; A.B., U. Calif. at Berkeley, 1943, gen. secondary teaching certificate, 1951; M.A., Columbia, 1947; certificate Washington and Lee U., 1945. Sec., Fair Play Com. Am. Citizens Japanese Ancestry, 1943-44; adminstrv. asst. U.C. Alumni Assn. book Students at Berkeley, 1949; dir. Student Union Monterey Jr. Coll., 1949-50; mgr. Nat. Audubon Soc. Conservation Resource Center, Berkeley, 1951-66; dir. Nat. Audubon Soc. Bay Area Ednl. Services, 1966-71; curriculum cons. Project WEY, U. Calif. Demonstration Lab. Sch., Berkeley, 1972-83. Cons. Berkeley Sch. Dist., Alameda County Schs. Mem. land use com., environ. edn. com. East Bay Municipal Utility Dist., 1968—; mem. steering com. Nat. Sci. Guild, Oakland Mus., 1970-76; community adviser Jr. League of Oakland, 1972-76. Mem. Berkeley Women's Town Council, 1970—. Bd. dirs. East Bay Regional Park Dist., 1972—, pres., 1978-80, 88—; bd. dirs. Save San Francisco Bay Assn., 1969—, People for Open Space, 1977-86, Calif. Natural Areas Coordinating Council, 1968—, Living History Ctr., 1982-85; mem. steering com. Bay Area Environ. Edn. Alliance, 1982-85, regional planning com. Assn. of Bay Area Govts., 1988—, exec. com. Citizens for Eastshore State Park, 1985—; v.p. Friends of Bot. Garden, U. Calif., Berkeley, 1976-80, trustee, 1986—. Served with USAAF, 1944-46. Recipient Merit award Calif. Conservation Council, 1953; Woman of Achievement award Camp Fire Girls, 1976; Merit award Am. Soc. Landscape Architects, 1979, Conservation award Golden Gate Audobon Soc., 1985. Mem. Prytanean Alumnae, Inc. (pres. 1969-71, chmn. adv. council 1971-73), AAUW (Calif. com. 1970-73), Nature Conservancy (chmn. no. Calif. chpt. 1970-71), LWV, Regional Parks Assn., Nat. Women's Polit. Caucus, Golden Gate Audubon Soc., Sierra Club (environ. edn. com. No. Calif. chpt. 1973-77), Urban Care, U. Calif. Art Council, U. Calif. Alumni Assn., Inst. Calif. Man in Nature, NAACP, Calif. Assn. Recreation and Park Dists. (v.p. 1978—), Calif. Elected Women for Edn. and Research, Nat. Assn. Environ. Edn., Preserve Area Ridgelands Calif. Native Plant Soc., Planning and Conservation League, Cousteau Soc., Soroptomists, Pi Lambda Theta, Mortar Board, Gavel (pres.). Democrat. Adv. com. natural history guide series U. Calif. Press, 1972—. Home: 2932 Pine Ave Berkeley CA 94705

JEFFERIS, LU ELLEN, personnel executive; b. Little Rock, Oct. 2, 1952; d. Charles Wesley and Eva Louise (Elmore) Walton; m. Michael Jefferis, Oct. 1, 1982; 1 son, Russell Walton. BA, Miss. State U.-Starkville, 1973; MEd U. So. Miss., 1987. Personnel mgr. Ferro Corp., Jackson, Miss., 1973-83, cons., 1983-88; specialist profl. staffing and compensation Gen. Electric, Burlington, 1988—. Chmn., Rankin County Job Service Improvement Program, Pearl, Miss., 1980-84; panelist Miss. Job Service Job-A-Thon on Ednl. TV, 1983. Recipient Miss. Gov.'s Meritorious Service award, 1980. Mem. Am. Soc. Personnel Adminstrn., Capitol Area Personnel Assn. (com. chmn. 1979-82), Activity Vector Analysis Assn. Republican. Methodist. Home: 83 Old Stage Rd #2 Williston VT 05495

JEFFERS, IDA PEARLE, management consultant, volunteer; b. Houston, Tex., Sept. 5, 1935; d. Stanford Wilbur and Ida Pearle (Kinkead) Oberg; m. Samuel Lee Jeffers, Aug. 29, 1956; children: John Laurence (dec.), Julie Elizabeth, Melinda Leigh. Student, U. Colo., 1953-56; BA in History, U. N.Mex., 1957. Asst. to mayor City of Albuquerque, 1978, dir. capital improvements, 1979-81; pres. Orgn. Plus, 1988—. Chmn. Comprehensive Plan Review, Bond Issue, various coms., Albuquerque, 1968—; mem. Middle Rio Grand Council Govts., Albuquerque, 1972-74; mem. Environ. Planning Commn., Albuquerque, 1972-77, chmn. 1975-76; chmn. Citizen Adv. Group, Community Devel., Albuquerque, 1974-75; mem. Jr. League, Albuquerque, 1966—; mem. N. Mex. Architect, Engrs. Joint Practice Bd. 1978-85, chmn. 1983-85; treas. St. Mark's Episcopal Ch., 1983-86; pres. Eldorado High Sch. Parents, Albuquerque, 1985-86; chmn. Regional Conservation Land Trust, Albuquerque, 1987—; trustee Found., Study and Care of Organic Brain Damage, Houston, 1972-82, pres. 1982—; mem. Urban Transp. Planning Policy Bd., 1972-74; chmn. community advisors Albuquerque Youth Symphony, 1985—; founder, chair Friends of Sandia (N.Mex.) Sch., 1965-68, chmn. devel. pre-sch. bd., 1974; mentor Leadership Albuquerque, 1987—; bd. dirs. Good Govt. Group, Albuquerque, 1988—. Recipient Disting. Pub. Service award, State of N. Mex., 1975, Disting. Woman of N. Mex. award, N. Mex. Women's Polit. Caucus, 1976, Golden Talon award Eldorado High Sch., Albuquerque, 1985, Panhellenic Council Disting. Alumnae award 1979. Mem. Delta Gamma (pres. 1963-67, Cable and Shield awards 1970, 77). Republican. Episcopalian.

JEFFERS, KAY AUDRA, sales executive; b. Ft. Wayne, Ind., Nov. 10, 1953; d. Howard Ben and Audra Mildred (Dalton) Tenny; m. Ronald Thomas Jeffers, May 12, 1979. B.S. in Indsl. Mgmt., Purdue U., 1976. Asst. buyer Block's Dept. Sotre, Indpls., 1976-77, buyer, 1977-79; sales analyst Ford Motor Co., Indpls., 1979-80, zone mgr., Houston, 1980—, light truck merchandising mgr., 1986—; dist. sales mgr. Jaguar Cars, 1986—. Home: 4018 Colquitt Houston TX 77027

JEFFERSON, KRISTIN MARIE, art dealer; b. Tacoma, Jan. 15, 1947; d. Edward Harold and Helen Marie (Chandler) J. BA, Bard Coll., 1968; MFA, Hunter Coll., 1974. Facilities adminstr. Sterling Inst., Washington, 1969-71; prof. art CUNY, 1971-79; art dealer N.Y.C., 1979—; guest lectr. CUNY, 1979, 80, 81, 82, 83. Author: She-Images of Woman in Art, 1983, Magic in the Mind's Eye-Alchemy of Collecting, 1987; curator mus. quality art exhibits, 1982—; film maker documentaries and art pieces, 1971—. Mem. pub. relations staff Sotheby's benefit for Cath. Relief Services to Benefit the Famine Victims of Ethiopia, 1985. Episcopalian. Home and Office: 330 W 56th St New York NY 10019

JEFFERSON, LINDA REBECCA, physical therapist; b. Dover, Del., June 28, 1948; d. Joseph Russell and Helen Russell (Jefferson) J. BS in Phys. Therapy, Med. Coll. Va., 1971. Cert. Tex. State Bd. Phys. Therapy Examiners. Staff phys. therapist Spartanburg (S.C.) Gen. Hosp., 1971-72; staff phys. therapist Riverside Hosp., Newport News, Va., 1972-75, sr. phys. therapist, 1975-77, dir. phys. therapy, 1977-80, dir. phys. contract services, 1980-82; contract phys. therapist San Antonio, 1982—; mem. profl. adv. com. Diversified Nursing Services, Bandera, Tex., 1984-85, Kimberly Services, San Antonio, 1986—. Mem. Am. Phys. Therapy Assn., Tex. Phys. Therapy Assn. Address: 7813 Leafy Hollow San Antonio TX 78233

JEFFERSON, NANCY ZANDERS, engineer; b. Winter Garden, Fla., Sept. 10, 1936; d. William Napoleon Jr. and Grace (Williams) Zanders; m. Sam James Jefferson, June 11, 1953, children: Wendy Alicia, Samuel James, Patricia Ann, Charlotte Gail. Cert. in engring., Iowa State U., 1977; AS in Bus. Adminstrn., Bryant Coll., Smithfield, R.I., 1978. Key punch operator So. Bell Telephone Co., Orlando, Fla., 1965-70; key punch operator New Eng. Telephone, Providence, 1970-72, reports clk., 1972-76; asst. engr. New Eng. Telephone, Boston, 1976-77; engr. New Eng. Telephone, Pawtucket, R.I., 1977—. Pres. missionary circle Olney St. Bapt. Ch., Providence, 1978-84; company rep. Jr. Achievement of R.I., Providence, 1986—. Mem. Telephone Pioneers of Am. (Cert. of Participation 1984), Minority Mgrs. Assn. (sec. 1983), Greater Providence Bowling Assn. (bd. dirs. 1988—). Democrat. Lodges: Order of Eastern Star (Providence chpt. worthy matron 1972-83), Cyrene Crusaders (Providence chpt. Royal Magdalene 1986-87), Queen of Sheba (treas. 1985—, worthy matron 1983, Royal Martha 1987, Royal Commandress 1988—). Home: 101 Apulia St East Providence RI 02914 Office: New Eng Telephone 85 High St Pawtucket RI 02860

JEFFERSON, NAOMI, health science facility administrator; b. New Orleans, Oct. 20, 1936; d. Leonard Alvin and Lurline (Nelms) J.; m. Frederick Joseph Depland, Mar. 23, 1961 (div. Apr. 1976); children: Cyril, Donna, Darlene, Gregory, Dianne. Student, Delgado Coll., New Orleans, 1977-79. Communications rep. South Cen. Bell, New Orleans, 1966-79; residential sales rep. Cen. Telephone Co., Las Vegas, 1979-84; blood donor adminstr. Brookdale Hosp. Med. Ctr., Bklyn., 1985—. Mem. Hosp. Blood Donor Recruiters Assn. (sec. 1985—), Nat. Assn. Female Execs., Brookdale Hosp. Med. Ctr. Blood Transfusion Com., Am. Assn. Donor Recruitment Profls. Democrat. Roman Catholic.

JEFFETT, NANCY PEARCE, tennis administrator, foundation executive; b. St. Louis, July 16, 1928; d. Charles Frederick and Lillian (Schaefer) Pearce; m. Frank A. Jeffett, Dec. 29, 1956; children—Wiliam F., Elizabeth. B.S. in Edn., Washington U., St. Louis, 1951. Co-founder Tyler (Tex.) Tennis Assn., 1954; chmn. jr. devel. com. Tex. Tennis Assn., Dallas, 1963—, chmn. Virginia Slims Dallas Tennis tournament, 1970—, MCB Internat. Teams, U.S. and Gt. Britain, 1973—; chmn., pres. Maureen Connolly Brinker Tennis Found., Dallas, 1968—; mem. Women's Internat. Profl. Tennis Council, 1974-87; chmn. Davis Cup Tie, U.S. vs. Mex., 1965; capt. U.S. Fedn. Cup Tennis Team, 1983; chmn. Wightman Cup and Fedn. Cup Com., 1976-87. Mem. bd. YMCA, Tyler, 1956, Dallas, 1962, Crystal Charity Ball. Recipient Caswell award Tex. Tennis Assn., 1970; Service Bowl award U.S. Tennis Assn., 1970; World Championship Tennis Service to Tennis award, 1983; named Tex. Mus. Tennis Hall of Fame, 1983. Mem. Jr. League Dallas, The All-England Club of Wimbledon, Dallas Tennis Assn. (dir.), Tex. Tennis Assn. (dir.), U.S. Tennis Assn. (exec. com.), Lawn Tennis Assn. U.S., All Eng. Lawn and Crocquet Club. Republican. Episcopalian. Home: 5419 Wateka Dr Dallas TX 75209 Office: Maureen Connolly Brinker Tennis Found 5419 Wateka Dr Dallas TX 75209

JEFFREY, MARGIE SUE, transportation company executive; b. Evansville, Ind., June 19, 1935; d. James Andrew and Eula Madeth (Tucker) Baughn; student McHenry County Coll., 1977-79, Coll. Advanced Traffic, Chgo., 1977; m. Joseph W. Jeffrey, Nov. 28, 1981; children from previous marriage Dan Market, Tony Market, Lee Ann Market. With Market Produce Trucking, Evansville, 1959-70; gen. ops. mgr. Farm Service & Supplies Inc., Marengo, Ill., 1970—, v.p., 1980—; pres. MLB Mktg. Services, Marengo 1981—; admitted to practice transport law ICC, 1977. , Am. Soc. Traffic and Transp., Assn. ICC Practitioners (nat. com. motor fleet supr. tng.), Am. Trucking Assn. (com. regulatory policy), Am. Assn. Handwriting Analysts, Women's Traffic Club Evansville, Soc. Integrative Graphology (founding mem.), Internat. Platform Assn., Notaries Assn. Ill., Cen. States Women's Traffic Conf. (1st v.p.), No. Ill. Transp. Club (founding mem., legis. com.), Mid-West Trucking Assn., Delta Nu Alpha, Traffic Clubs Internat. Home: 9505 Elm Ln Crystal Lake IL 60014 Office: 21606 W Railroad St Marengo IL 60152

JEFFREY-SMITH, LILLI ANN, biofeedback specialist, educator, administrator; b. Bedford, Ind.; d. Charles Constantine and Adelai (Malon) Jeffrey-Smith. Grad. Ind. Bus. Coll., 1963; B.S., Ind. U., 1973; grad. Psychosomatic Medicine Clinic, Berkeley, Calif. (accredited by Albert Einstein Coll. Medicine); PhD, Kennedy-Western U., 1988. Cert. biofeedback specialist. Project assoc., stress mgmt. clinician City of Indpls., 1973-79; cons. Airport Med. Clinic, Indpls., 1981; outreach coordinator Abbot-Northwestern Hosp., Mpls., 1981; dir. biofeedback dept. Sister Kenney Inst., Mpls., 1979-81, Noran Neurol. Clinic, Mpls., 1981-83; instr., dir. Biofeedback Tng. and Treatment Ctr., Edina, Minn., 1979—; pres. Biofeedback Research and Devel. Co. Ltd., Edina, 1983—; cons. to biofeedback depts. St. Joseph Hosp., Mankato, Minn., 1984—, Lakeview Clinic, Waconia, Minn., 1983, Psychiat. Clinic of Mankato, 1983—, Fairview Ridges Hosp., Burnsville, Minn., 1987—. Author, narrator health and wellness tape series. Mem. Republican Presdl. Task Force, 1984—, NSC, 1985; co-chmn. Mayor's Handicapped Task Force, Indpls., 1975; founder, pres. Miss Wheel Chair of Ind., Inc. Named Hon. Lt. Gov., State of Ind., 1978; given Key to the City of Indpls., 1973, Flag of the City of Indpls., 1975. Mem. Am. Inst. Stress, N.Y. Acad. Sci., AAAS, Edina C. of C., Minn. Women's Network, Biofeedback Soc. Am., Biofeedback Soc. Minn., Am. Assn. Control Tension, Am. Assn. Behaviorial Therapists, Am. Assn. Biofeedback Clinicians, Nat. Assn. Women Bus. Owners, Soc. Open Focus and Tng. Research, Assn. Trainers in Clin. Hypnosis, Internat. Stress and Tension Control Assn., Minn. Assn. Rehab. Providers, Nat. Assn. Exec. Women, Internat. Platform Assn. Avocations: music; stamp collecting; shooting; poetry. Office: Biofeedback Tng & Treatment Ctr 6545 France Ave S Southdale Med Bldg Suite 158 Edina MN 55435

JENKINS, ANNE ELIZABETH GREEN, pediatric therapist; b. Richmond, Va., May 18, 1944; d. John P. and Dorothy Mae (Williams) Green; B.S., (Rehab. Service Adminstrn. scholar), N.Y.U., 1972; M.A. (Minority Student grad. fellow), Columbia Tchrs. Coll., 1975, Ed.M., 1976; Ph.D. candidate, U. N.C.-Greensboro; m. Earnest Jenkins, June 1, 1964; children—Frederick Anthony, April Kaché, August Kali. Occupational therapist Harlem Hosp., N.Y.C., 1972-74, Blythedale Children's Hosp., Valhalla, N.Y., 1974-77; developmental disabilities specialist Amos Cottage Bowman Gray Sch. Medicine, Winston-Salem, N.C., 1977; dir. Early Intervention Program, Forsyth/Stokes counties, Winston-Salem, 1977-80, learning disabilities specialist, 1980-84; pvt. practice, 1984—; mem. faculty N.Y.U. Sch. Edn., N.Y.U. Med. Sch., U. N.C.-Chapel Hill, Winston-Salem State U., 1984—; founder, dir. Visions of the Children, Lexington, N.C., 1986; cons. pre-schools and developmental day-care ctrs., U.S. Dept. Edn., 1987—. Mem. Am. Occupational Therapy Assn., Smithsonian Instrn., Assn. Retarded Citizens (dir.), Center Study Sensory Integrations, Am. Burn Assn. Liberal. Roman Catholic. Designer hand orthotics, adaptive equipment for the handicapped. Home: 2931 Springhaven Dr Winston-Salem NC 27103

JENKINS, AUDREY LOVELESS, health care corporation executive; b. McCormick, S.C., Sept. 19, 1924; d. James Wilson and Eula Mae (McMahan) Loveless; m. Joseph Bradford Roberts, May 26, 1945 (dec. 1966); children—Kathy Jo, James Bradford, Susan Roberts Millsap, Thea Frances; m. Winford Lee Jenkins, Dec. 10, 1977. Grad. Anderson Hosp. Sch. Nursing, 1945; postgrad. Mo. U., 1973-74, Lincoln U., 1973-75. Asst. supr. med. floor Vets. Hosp., Fayetteville, Ark., 1947-49; adminstr. Phelps County Health Dept. and Home Health Agy., Rolla, Mo., 1964-73; dir. Waynesville Pub. Sch. Practical Nursing, Mo., 1973-75; pub. health nurse cons. Bur. Pub. Health Nursing Mo. Div. Health, Jefferson City, Mo., 1975-78; cons. community health nurse Bur. Maternal and Child Health, 1978-79, Bur. Hosp. Licensing and Cert., 1979-84; pres. Mo. Health Care Mgmt. Services, Inc., Jefferson City, 1984—; mem. Mo. State Bd. Nursing, 1975-79. Mem. Mo. Pub. Health Assn., Mo. Heart Assn. (bd. dirs. 1972—, chmn. 1968-72), Mo. Assn. Home Health Agys., Beta Sigma Phi. Baptist. Avocations: antiquing; walnut Victorian furniture; crocheting; gardening. Home: Route 3 Box 32 California MO 65018 Office: Mo Health Care Mgmt Services Inc 1022-B Northeast Dr Jefferson City MO 65101

JENKINS, BARBARA JEAN MOSELEY, health management executive; b. Winsted, Conn., May 18, 1944; d. Harry Hayden and Eunice (Cook) Moseley; m. Wayne W. Jenkins, May 1, 1965 (div. May 1985); children: Holly Lynne, Brian Kendall. AS, U. Hartford, 1964. Med. sec. Irving Krall M.D., Hartford, Conn., 1964-65, Francis Gallo M.D., Winsted, Conn., 1965-66; mgr. Elderly Nutrition-Sr. Ctr., Norfolk, Conn., 1978—; coordinator housing Sumner Sch. Music and Art Yale U., Norfolk, 1987—. Leader Girl Scouts Am., Norfolk 1977, tchr. Ch. Christ, Norfolk 1980, deaconess 1983-86. Republican. Lodge: Order Ea. Star (various positions). Home: 32 Grant St Norfolk CT 06058 Office: Norfolk Nutrition Ctr Shepard Rd Norfolk CT 06058

JENKINS, BILLIE BEASLEY, film company executive; b. Topeka, Kans., June 27, 1943; d. Arthur and Etta Mae (Price) Capelton; m. Rudolph Alan Jenkins, Nov. 1, 1935; 1 child, Tina Caprice. Student, Santa Monica City Coll., 1965-69. Exec. sec. to v.p. prodn. Screen Gems, Los Angeles, 1969-72; exec. asst. Spelling/Goldberg Prodns., 1972-82; dir. adminstrn. The Leonard Co./Mandy Films, 1982-85, v.p., 1985-86; exec. asst. to pres. and chief operating officer 20th Century Fox Film Corp., Los Angeles, 1986—; dir. adminstrn. 20th Century Fox Film Corp. Asst. to exec. producer: (films) War Games, 1984, Spacecamp, 1986; (movies for TV) Something about Amelia, 1984, Alex, The Life of a Child, 1985; (series) Paper Dolls, 1985, Cavanaughs, 1987, Charlie's Angels, Rookies, others. Mem. Women in Film Assn., Nat. Assn. Female Execs., Black Women's Network. Office: 20th Century Fox Inc 10202 W Pico Blvd Los Angeles CA 90034

JENKINS, BRENDA GWENETTA, early childhood education specialist; b. Durham, N.C., Aug. 11, 1949; d. Brinton Alfred and Ophelia Arden (Eaton) Jenkins. B.S., Howard U., 1971, M.Ed., 1972, Cert. Spl. Edn., 1973-75; postgrad. Trinity Coll., Am. U., U. D.C., 1976—. Cert. aerobics instr. Nat. Dance-Exercise Instr.'s Tng. Assn. Cheerleader coach Howard U., Washington, 1971—; aerobics instr. D.C. Pub. Schs., 1982—, tchr., 1972—; v.p. Nerdlihc Corp., Washington, 1985—; ptnr. Jenkins, Trapp-Dukes and Yates Partnership; aerobic instr. for handicapped Council for Exceptional Children, Washington, 1982, recreation services City of Rockville, Md., 1986—; instr. aerobics Langdon Park Recreation Ctr. Washington Dept. Recreation, 1988—. Recipient Conscientious Service award D.C. Pub. Schs., 1985; Outstanding Recognition award Howard U. Alumni Cheerleaders Assn., 1984 (award renamed The Brenda G. Jenkins Outstanding Cheerleader Award, 1987); Outstanding Service awards Kappa Delta Pi, 1978, 79, 81, 82, 84; citation Washington Tchrs. Union, 1985; Appreciation cert. D.C. Dept. Recreation, 1985, others; nominee Agnes Meyer Outstanding Tchr. award, 1988, Theodore R. Hogans Jr. Pub. Service award, 1988. Mem. Am. Fedn. Tchrs., Theta Alpha chpt. Kappa Delta Pi (exec. com.), Howard U. Alumni Cheerleaders Assn. (co-founder 1977) Democrat. Avocations: fashion design, cooking, dancing, poetry writing.

JENKINS, CAROLYN VIRGINIA, food service administrator; b. Boque Chitto, Miss., Feb. 15, 1940; d. Robert Clyde and Earline (Walker) Boone; m. John O. Jenkins Jr., Nov. 28, 1963; children: John Michael, Jeffery Clyde. BS in Home Econs., Miss. State Coll. for Women, 1961; MS of Home Econs., U. So. Miss., 1977, MS in Occupation Foods, 1980, AAA in home econs., 1985; MS of Secondary Adminstrn., Jackson (Miss.) State U.,

1982. Cert. vocat. dir., adminstr., occupational food service dir. Home demonstration agt. U. Miss. Extension Service, Hattiesburg, 1961-64; instr. home econs., advisor jr. class Harrisville (Miss.) Attendance Ctr., 1968-73; instr. home econs. and sci., sponsor and advisor jr. class Council Hanging Moss, Jackson, 1974-76; instr. sci. Manhattan Acad., Jackson, 1976-77; instr. vocat. food service Lanier High Sch., Jacskon, 1977-86, advisor youth adv. council, 1981; supr. sch. food service Jackson Pub. Schs., 1986—; advisor home econs., Jackson, 1977-85;. Mem. Am. Sch. Food Service Assn., Miss. Sch. Food Service Assn. (dist. nutrition chairperson 1987), Miss. Sch. Adminstrn. Assn., Am. Vocat. Assn., Miss. Home Econs. Assn. (dist. advisor 1980-85). Baptist. Office: Jackson Pub. Schs 101 Near St Jackson MS 39203

JENKINS, CLARA BARNES, educator; b. Franklinton, N.C.; d. Walter and Stella (Griffin) Barnes; BS, Winston-Salem State U., 1939; MA, N.C. Ctl. U., 1947; EdD, U. Pitts., 1965; postgrad., N.Y.U., 1947-48, U. N.C.-Chapel Hill, 1963, N.C. Agrl. and Tech. State U., 1971; m. Hugh Jenkins, Dec. 24, 1949 (div. Feb. 1955). Tchr. pub. schs., Wendell, N.C., 1939-43, Wise, N.C., 1943-45; mem. faculty Fayetteville State U., 1945-53, Rust Coll., Holly Spring, Miss., 1953-58; asst. prof. Shaw U., 1958-64; prof. edn. and psychology St. Paul's Coll., Lawrenceville, Va., 1964—; vis. prof. edn. Friendship Jr. Coll., Rock Hill, S.C., summer 1947, N.C. Agrl. and Tech. State U., 1966-83. Former mem. bd. dirs. Winston-Salem State U. Notary pub., N.C.; United Negro Coll. Fund Faculty fellow, 1963-64; Am. Bapt. Conv. grantee, 1963-64. Mem. AAUP, Nat. Soc. for Study Edn., NEA, AAUW, Am. Hist. Assn., Va. Edn. Assn., Am. Acad. Polit. and Social Sci., AAAS, Internat. Platform Assn., Assn. Tchr. Educators, History Edn. Soc., Doctoral Assn. Educators, Am. Assn. Higher Edn., Am. Soc. Notaries, Acad. Polit. Sci., Am. Psychol. Assn., Soc. Research in Child Devel., Am. Soc. Notaries, Marquis Biog. Library Soc., Jean Piaget Soc., Philosophy of Edn. Soc., Soc. Profs. Edn., Am. Soc. Notaries, Phi Eta Kappa, Zeta Phi Beta, Phi Delta Kappa, Kappa Delta Pi. Episcopalian. Home: 920 Bridges St Henderson NC 27536 Office: St Paul's Coll Lawrenceville VA 23868

JENKINS, COLLEEN THERESA, marketing professional, consultant; b. Troy, N.Y., Aug. 10, 1961; d. Donald J. and Helen E. (Daley) Gagen; m. Jeffrey Carl Jenkins, Aug. 24, 1985. BA in Pub. Relations, SUNY, Binghamton, 1983. Admissions rep. The Stratford Sch., Syracuse, N.Y., 1983-85; adminstrv. asst. Profl. Mail Services, Inc., Raleigh, N.C., 1985-86, mktg. dir., 1986-87, asst. v.p., 1987-88; mktg. rep. SAS Inst. Inc., Cary, N.C., 1988—. Mem. Nat. Assn. Female Execs., Raleigh Bus. and Profl. Women's Group, Raleigh C. of C. Office: SAS Inst Inc SAS Circle Box 8000 Cary NC 27512

JENKINS, CYNTHIA JANE, infosystems specialist; b. Topeka, Aug. 25, 1955; d. Frank Munn and Patricia Faye (Pratt) J. BS in Applied Maths., U. Ark., 1977, MS in Ops. Research, 1979. Analyst, programmer Ark. Best Corp., Ft. Smith, 1979-80; tech. analyst Cities Service Co., Tulsa, 1981-82; systems analyst Telex Computer Products, Tulsa, 1982-84, sr. analyst, natural adminstr., 1984-85, info. ctr. supr., natural adminstr., 1985—. Mem. Software AG User's Group, Assn. for Mgmt. Systems. Baptist. Office: Telex Computer Products 6422 E 41st Tulsa OK 74135

JENKINS, E(THEL) VALERIE, retired media specialist; b. Amherst, Ohio, Sept. 7, 1913; d. Frank A. and Ethel E. (Dute) Eppley; student Hiram Coll., 1932; B.A., Baldwin-Wallace Coll., 1936; postgrad. Western Res. U., 1936, 41, 66, State U. Iowa, 1938-39, Ohio State U., 1960; M.A., Kent State U., 1962; m. William J. Jenkins, Aug. 13, 1944 (div. May 1964). Dir. dramatics Baldwin-Wallace Coll., Berea, Ohio, 1936-38; tchr. English and speech St. Elmo (Ill.) High Sch., 1939-42; tchr. English, speech, dir. dramatics Clearview-Lorain (Ohio) High Sch., 1942-57, librarian, 1949-57; library coordinator Amherst (Ohio) Pub. Schs., 1957-80, drama dir., 1957-60, 75-77; instr. Kent State U., 1963-66; instr. speech Cleve. State U., 1966-70; lectr. costumes for theatre; owner, operator children's theatre, also costume rental; cons. Amherst Pub. Library Bldg. Program, 1972-73. Founder Workshop Players, Inc., 1948, trustee, 1948—, pres., 1948-49, 56-58, 60, 75-80, now vol. worker; mng. dir. Workshop Theatre, 1980—; mem. bd. Amherst Pub. Library, 1962—, pres., 1963-65, 83-85. Recipient Amherst Gallery Success for Alumni, 1987, Alumni Merit award Baldwin-Wallace Coll., 1986, Community Improvement award Amherst C. of C., 1987; Paul Harris fellow Rotary Internat., 1985. Mem. Nat., Ohio (life) edn. assns., Am. Theatre Assn., ALA, Ohio Ednl. Library Media Assn. (dir. NE chpt. 1974-76), Amherst Tchrs. Assn. (pres. 1962-64), Delta Kappa Gamma, Phi Mu. Republican. Congregationalist. Home: 439 Shupe Ave Amherst OH 44001

JENKINS, FRANCES OWENS, retail executive; b. Leonard, Tex., Nov. 12, 1924; d. R. Melrose and Maureen (Durrett) Owens; m. William O. Jenkins (div. 1961); children: Steven O., Tamara. Student theatre arts East Tex. State U., 1939-42, Ind. U., 1945-48, U. Tenn., 1954-56. Fashion model Rogers Modeling Agy., Boston, 1950-52, Rich's, Knoxville, Tenn., 1955-60; owner, instr. Arts Sch. of Self-Improvement and Modeling, Knoxville, 1959-69; owner, pres. Fran Jenkins Boutique, Knoxville, 1964—; cons. Miss Am. Pageant, Knoxville, 1958-66. Actress Carousel Theatre, Knoxville, 1955 58. Home: 8833 Cove Point Ln Concord TN 37922

JENKINS, GLORIA DELORES, former airline official; d. David and Johnnie Sue (Smith) Barnes; extension student City U. N.Y.; cert. fund raising N.Y. U., 1982; m. John Elmo Jenkins, 1960 (dec.); children—Gloria Susan, Melanie Yvette Treadwell, Carol Lynn, Jonathan Edward. With Pan Am. World Airways, 1955-82, mgmt. prodn. planning aircraft service control maintenance and engring. JFK Airport, N.Y.C., 1979-82, mgmt. powerplant planning A/C engine maintenance and engring., 1982; mem. FAA Speakers Cadre. Exec. bd. Hansel & Gretel Inc., 1977-79; pres. Addisleigh Park Civic Orgn., 1960; mem. John E. Jenkins Meml. Scholarship Fund, 1980; mem. exec. bd. Queens council Boy Scouts Am., chair ethnic outreach com.; chairperson United Negro Coll. Fund Pre-Telethon, 1987-88. Recipient various service awards. Mem. Nat. Assn. Female Execs. (network dir.), NAACP (br. exec. bd.). Mem. A.M.E. Ch. Clubs: Hansel and Gretel (past nat. pres.), Toastmistresses.

JENKINS, LUCINDA SUE, healthcare financial consultant; b. Springfield, Mo., Jan. 28, 1953; d. Roger Wesley and Dorothy June (Williams) J. BBA, U. Mo., 1986, MBA, 1987. Mgr., contract officer We. Mo. Area Health Edn. Ctr., Kansas City, 1972-82; adminstrv. asst. St. Joseph Hosp., Kansas City, 1982-83; mgr. client services United Healthcare Systems, Overland Park, Kans., 1983-85; graduate coordinator Small Bus. Inst., Kansas City, 1986—; fin. cons. Econ. Devel. Agy., Kansas City, 1986—; bd. dirs. NW Mo. Area Health Edn. Ctr., St. Joseph, 1980-82; adv. council Metro Area Health Edn. Found., Kansas City, 1980-82. Adminstrv. staff, U. Mo. Sch. Med. Study Tour, Republic of China, 1981. Recipient Dean Banking Fin. Scholarship Boatman's Bank, 1986; named one of Outstanding Young Women of Am., 1981, Young Entrepreneur of the Yr., U. Mo. Entrepreneurial Com., 1986. Mem. MBA Execs., Am. Mgmt. Assn., Am. Mktg. Assn., Bus. and Profl. Women's Found. (recipient scholarship 1986). Home: 12825 W 117th St Kansas City MO 66210 Office: Univ Mo Sch Bus and Pub Adminstrn 5200 Cherry Kansas City MO 66210

JENKINS, MADGE MARIE, management educator, consultant; b. Dearborn, Mich., Oct. 19, 1938; d. Lem and Margaret Mary (Tulloch) VicKroy; m. Robert Eugene Brennan, Dec. 28, 1958 (div. 1965); 1 child, Richard; m. George Henry Jenkins, Aug. 15, 1967. Student Systems Inst., Detroit, 1965, Henry Ford Community Coll., 1965-67; B.A. cum laude, U. Mich., 1976; M.P.A., Wayne State U., 1978. Ops. mgr. Custom Lab., Dearborn, Mich., 1967-68; mgr. Jenkins Wedding Studies, Dearborn, 1968-74; unit dir. dept. recreation City of Dearborn, 1976-78; enumerator Dept. Agr., Seattle, 1978-79; coordinator Stillaguamish Ctr., Arlington, Wash., 1979-80; asst. prof. mgmt. Lima Tech. Coll., Ohio, 1980—; mem. Adv. Bd. Continuing Edn., Bellingham, Wash., 1978-80, Marysville, Wash., 1979-80; mgmt. cons. Jenkins & Jenkins, Cario, Ohio, 1984—; cons. Ctr. for Bus. and Econ. Research, Western Wash. U. 1979-80. Elder, Columbus Grove Presbyterian Ch., Ohio, 1982-83. Mem. Acad. Mgmt., Am. Mgmt. Assn., Am. Assn. Pub. Adminstrn., Am. Soc. Tng. and Devel., Am. Assn. Personnel Adminstrn. Republican. Club: 8-16 Cine (Detroit). Lodge: Toastmasters (v.p. local chpt. 1981-82). Office: Ohio State U Lima Tech Coll Campus Lima OH 45804

JENKINS, MARGARET AIKENS, educational administrator; b. Lexington, Miss., May 14, 1925; d. Joel Bryant and Marie C. (Threadgill) Melton; m. Daniel Armstrong, May 21, 1944 (div. 1950); children Marie Cynthia, Marsha Rochelle; m. Gabe Aikens, June 29, 1954 (div. 1962); m. Herbert Jenkins, May 21, 1966. Student, Chgo. Conservatory of Music, 1959, Moody Bible Inst., Chgo., 1959, Calif. State U.-Northridge, 1984; HHD (hon.), Payne Acad., 1984; HHD (hon.) Pentacostal Bible Coll., 1988. Clk., U.S. Signal Corp., Chgo., 1943-44, Cuneo Press., Chgo., 1948-52, Ford Aircraft, Chgo., 1952-58, Corp of Engrs., Chgo., 1958-64; progress control clk. Def. Contract Adminstrn. Service Region, Los Angeles, 1966-73; founder, adminstr. Celeste Scott Christian Sch., Inglewood, Calif., 1976—; founder, pres. Mary Celeste Scott Meml. Found., Inc., Inglewood, 1973—; pub., writer, founder Magoll Records, Chgo., 1958-64. Recipient Cert. Appreciation, Mayor of Inglewood, 1984, Mayor of Los Angeles, 1980, State Senator, 1975, State Rep., 1976; named Women of Yr., Los Angeles Sentinel, 1982, Inglewood C. of C., 1982. Mem. Broadcast Music Inc., Am. Fedn. TV and Radio Artists, Nat. Assn. Pentecostal Women and Men Inc. Avocations: religion, writing music, recording music. Home: 11602 Cimarron Ave Los Angeles CA 90047 Office: Celeste Scott Christian Sch 930 S Osage Ave Inglewood Ca 90301

JENKINS, MARY BARNES, lawyer; b. Danbury, Conn., July 5, 1946; d. Charles Thomas and Helen Eva (Bakanau) Barnes; m. Richard Thomas Jenkins, Aug. 7, 1974; 1 child, Elizabeth Alexandra Barnes Jenkins. AB, Barnard Coll., 1968; BS in Nursing, Columbia U., 1974; JD, Fordham U., 1979. Bar: N.Y. 1980. Litigation asst. Sullivan & Cromwell, N.Y.C., 1968-72; pediatric nurse, ICU, Babies Hosp., Columbia-Presbyn. Med. Ctr., N.Y.C., 1974-76; assoc. Paul, Weiss, Rifkind, Wharton & Garrison, N.Y.C., 1979-83; counsel Revlon, Inc., N.Y.C., 1984-85, sr. counsel, asst. sec., 1985-88, asst. gen. counsel Primerica Corp., Greenwich, Conn., 1988—. Mem. ABA, Am. Soc. Corp. Secs., Inc. Democrat. Episcopalian. Home: 24 Prospect Dr Greenwich CT 06830 Office: Primerica Corp Am American Ln Box 3610 Greenwich CT 06836-3610

JENKINS, MYRA ELLEN, historian, archivist; b. Elizabeth, Colo., Sept. 26, 1916; d. Lewis Harlan and Minnie (Ackroyd) Jenkins; B.A. cum laude, U. Colo., 1937, M.A., 1938; Ph.D., U. N.Mex., 1953. Instr. pub. schs., Climax, Colo., 1939-41, Granada, Colo., 1941-43, Pueblo, Colo., 1943-50; fellow U. N.Mex., 1950-52, asst., 1952-53; free-lance historian and hist. cons., Albuquerque, 1953-59; archivist Hist. Soc. N.Mex., Santa Fe, 1959-60; sr. archivist N.Mex. Records Center and Archives, 1960-69, dep. for archives, 1968-70; N.Mex. state historian, 1967-80; ret., 1980; instr. St. Michael's Coll., 1962-63, Coll. of Santa Fe, 1966-74, 81-82; assoc. prof. N.Mex. State U., 1983; assoc. adj. prof. U.N. Mex., summer 1982, 84, 86. Mem. Western History Assn., Hist. Soc. N.Mex., Phi Beta Kappa, Phi Kappa Phi, Phi Alpha Theta, Kappa Delta Pi. Democrat. Episcopalian. Author: (with Albert H. Schroeder) A Brief History of New Mexico, 1974; Guides and Calendars to the Spanish, Mexican and Territorial Archives of New Mexico; contbr. articles to profl. jours. and book revs. Home: 1022 Don Cubero St Santa Fe NM 87501

JENKINSON, JUDITH ELLEN, librarian; b. Monroe, Mich., Apr. 9, 1943; d. Robert Henry Williams and Caroline (Pardee) Stephenson; m. Arnold Apsey, July 1, 1962 (div. 1977); 1 child, Amy Lou; m. Leif Jenkinson, May 21, 1977, 1 stepchild, Karl J. A.A., Alpena Community Coll., 1964; B.A., Mich. State U., 1966; Arts M.L.S., U. Mich., 1969. Elem. tchr., Lincoln, Mich., 1966-68, high sch. librarian, 1969-72; elem. librarian, Ketchikan, Alaska, 1972-75, high sch. librarian, 1975—. Mem. Ketchikan Community Coll. Council, 1980-84, pres., 1984-85; del. Alaska Democratic Conv., 1982, 88; dir., producer, actress, mem. stage crew First City Players, 1972—. Mem. ALA, NEA, AAUW, NOW, LWV, Ketchikan Edn. Assn., NEA-Alaska, Women's Internat. League for Peace and Freedom, Alaska Library Assn. VFW Aux., Swinging Kings Square Dancers (pres. 1985-86). Lodges: Eagles, Women of the Moose. Home: Box 5342 Ketchikan AK 99901 Office: 2610 4th Ave Ketchikan AK 99901

JENKS, BARBARA TZUR, technology company executive; b. Chgo., Dec. 11, 1935; d. Julius and Frieda (Zucker) Samuels; m. Jacob Tzur, Oct. 10, 1959 (div. May 1972); children: Ronny, Naomi, Elana, Yoav; m. Robert R. Jenks, Aug. 18, 1976. BA in Liberal Arts, U. Ill., 1957; MA in Edn., U. Calif., Santa Barbara, 1979. Provost Lawrence U., Santa Barbara, 1974-76; admissions counselor U. Calif., Santa Barbara, 1976-80; dir. extension programs Roosevelt U., Chgo., 1981-83; mgr. tng. and devel. Allnet Telcenter, Chgo., 1983-84; dir. sales The Z Corp., Santa Barbara, 1984-85; owner Brylen Techs., Santa Barbara, 1985—. V.p. Bret Harte Sch. PTA, Chgo., 1965; chairperson Hyde Park Community Orgn., Chgo., 1967-68; bd. dirs., treas. Sci. and Engring. Council of Santa Barbara, 1987—. Mem. ASTM, Am. Soc. Personnel Adminstrn., Am. Soc. Quality Control, Nat. Conf. Standards Labs., Nat. Assn. Female Execs. Democrat. Jewish. Office: Brylen Techs 828 Bond Ave Santa Barbara CA 93103

JENKS, MARY ELLEN, food industry consultant; b. Milw., 1933. Student U. Wis., 1956, 57. Vice pres. consumer affairs Pillsbury Co., Mpls., until 1986, pres. Mary Ellen Jenks and Assocs., Edina, Minn., 1986—. Dir. Better Bus. Bur. of Minn. Mem. Am. Women in Radio and TV, Am. Home Econs. Assn., Grocery Mfrs. of Am. (consumer affairs com.). Address: Mary Ellen Jenks and Assocs 5109 Green Farms Rd Edina MN 55436

JENKS, MONICA LEE, research professional; b. Guatemala City, Guatemala, Oct. 10, 1956; d. William Lee and Joanne Lorraine (Rodgers) J. BFA in Speech, Emporia (Kans.) State U., 1978, postgrad. Asst. mgr. Folger Shakespeare Library, Washington, 1980-81; exec. asst. Soc. Consumer Affairs Profls., Alexandria, Va., 1981-86; sr. research assoc. Tech. Assistance Research Programs, Washington, 1986-87, dir. tng. and devel., 1987—. Editor Update, 1984-86; asst. editor Mobius, 1985-86. Mem. 1st Bapt. Ch. Alexandria, 1983—, exec. com., 1984-86. Mem. Nat. Assn. Service Mgrs., Am. Soc. Tng. Devel., Soc. Consumer Affairs Profls. (editorial rev. bd.), Am. Soc. Profl. and Exec. Women, Nat. Assn. for Female Execs. Republican. Office: Tech Assistance Research Programs 705 G St SE Washington DC 20003

JENKS, SARAH ISABEL, retired nursing administrator; b. Springfield, Mo., May 5, 1913; d. George S. and Mary (Laing) Cuckie; diploma St. Joseph Mercy Hosp., 1934; student U. Calif. Extension, 1959-70, West Coast U., 1974, 78; m. Dean F. Thompson, June 16, 1936 (dec. 1949); 1 son, Dean F.; m. 2d, Kermit Jenks, June 17, 1951. Staff nurse Calif. Hosp., Los Angeles, 1936-37, head nurse, 1937-38, supr., 1938-40; indsl. nurse May Co., Los Angeles, 1940-43; office nurse, Burbank, Calif., 1944-45, Fort Dodge, Iowa, 1946-57; office mgr. Inglewood Med. Clinic ret., 1985; 1957-58; occupational health nurse, Hawthorne, Calif., 1958-72; supervising nurse Occupational Health Service, Los Angeles County, 1972-75; chief occupational health nurse Naval Regional Med. Center, Long Beach, Calif., 1975-81; adminstrv. nurse Occupational Health Center, U. Calif.-Irvine, 1981-85, ret., 1985; nursing chmn. ARC, 1964-70. Recipient Schering Occupational Health Nurse award, 1979; named Nurse of Yr., Harbor Area Assn. Occupational Health Nurses, 1985; Sarah I. Jenks scholarship established in her honor U. Calif.-Irvine, 1985. Mem. Am. Nurses Assn. (chmn. occupational health nurse forum 1968-72), Calif. State Nurses Assn. (pres. Centinela Valley 1963-65), Calif. State Occupational Health Nurses Assn., Am. Assn. Occupational Health Nurses, United Scottish Soc. Democrat. Presbyterian. Home: 1000-6 Williams Dr Fort Dodge IA 50501

JENNE, RUTH MARIE, aerospace company financial executive; b. Providence, Apr. 7, 1947; d. Robert Charles and Concetta Therese (Iacovelli) J. BA, Calif. State Coll., 1970; MBA, U. Phoenix, 1983. Paymaster Charlton Co., Compton, Calif., 1974-79; payroll adminstr. Northrop Corp., Hawthorne, Calif., 1979-82, fin. mgr., payroll, 1982-87, mgr. fin., 1987—; membership chmn. Northrop Mgmt. Club, 1983-86, treas., 1986-87; leader Northrop Integrated Fin. Systems Project, 1984-87. Mem. Nat. Assn. Female Execs., Am. Payroll Assn. Democrat. Roman Catholic.

JENNESS, DEBRA DIANE, medical office administrator; b. Portland, Oreg., Sept. 12, 1954; d. Byron Edward and Emma Bessie (Ghilliasa) McDonnell; diploma Western Bus. U., 1973, Univ. Acad. Music, 1973; cert. Med. Sch. U. Oreg., 1975; m. Gordon D. Jenness, Dec. 31, 1975; 1 child, Tyler Gordon. Adminstrv. sec., Hydronics, Inc., Portland, 1973; exec. sec., claims processor CNA/Ins., Portland, 1973-74; claims analyst Aetna Medicare, Portland, 1973-76; tchr. math. S. Albany High Sch., Albany, Oreg., 1976; exec. sec. Plywood Components, Albany, 1977; exec. sec., office mgr. Wise Personnel, Corvallis, Oreg., 1977 78; sr. loan processor, 1st Nat. Bank Oreg., Salem, Oreg., 1978-83; loan shipping dir., secondary mktg. asst. State Fed. Savs. and Loan Assn., Corvallis, Oreg., 1983-85; med. sec. James R. Price, D.P.M., Albany, Oreg., 1985-86; exec. sec. for div. mgr. Automation Tech. div. Intelledex, Inc., Corvallis, Oreg., 1986-87; owner, operator Elf Express. Mem. Am. Inst. Banking, Nat. Secs. Assn., Am. Bus. Women's Assn., Christian Business Women's Assn., Benton Hospice Service, Beta Sigma Phi. Home: 4176 Durillo Pl SE Albany OR 97321 Office: PO Box 375 Albany OR 97321

JENNINGS, B. JOELLE, educator; b. Phila., Nov. 8, 1944; d. John Joseph and Foresta (Cianfrogna) Rodgers.; m. James T. Jennings, Sept. 25, 1971 (div. 1981). B.A., Holy Family Coll., Phila., 1966; postgrad. in edn. Immaculate Heart Coll., Los Angeles, 1977. Cert. tchr., Calif. Intake worker Mental Health Devel. Ctr., Los Angeles, 1966-69; adminstrv. asst. Los Angeles Mut. Ins. Co., 1969-70; sec. med. staff Queen of Angels Hosp., Los Angeles, 1970-76; tchr. sci. Los Angeles Unified Sch. Dist, 1977-79; sci. chmn. New Jewish High Sch., Los Angeles, 1980-83; research mgr. Heidrick & Struggles, Los Angeles, 1983—; cons. ednl. pvt. psychotherapist, Woodland Hills, Calif., 1979—. Hospice vol. St. Joseph Med. Ctr., Burbank, Calif. Mem. NEA, Calif. Tchrs. Assn. Office: 445 S Figueroa St Suite 2330 Los Angeles CA 90071

JENNINGS, BARBARA JEAN, interior designer, art consultant; b. Redondo Beach, Calif., Nov. 30, 1944; d. Harold Willard and Leone Jeanette (Kuhn) Cole; m. George Alvin Jennings, Oct. 28, 1979; children: Ian David, Euriel Leonae. Student, Pacific ChristianColl., 1962-64. Bookkeeper Household Fin., Long Beach, Calif., 1965-66; exec. sec. Our Saviours's Luth. Ch., Long Beach, 1966-72; prin., owner Nat. Design Assocs., Huntington Beach, Calif., 1972—; lectr. Design Assocs. Internat., Huntington Beach, 1973—. Author: The Job Connection, 1983, Where There's a Wall-There's a Way, 1986; editor: Sentenced to Life, 1987. Named one of Top Ten Recruiting Dirs. Transdesigns, 1984, 85, Girl Athlete of Yr. Can. Acad., Kobe, Japan, 1961, 62; record holder in 2 events Track and Field, 1961, 62. Mem. Nat. Assn. Female Execs. Republican. Office: Nat Design Assocs 19581 Topeka Huntington Beach CA 92646

JENNINGS, DIANE BONNIE, accountant; b. Cedar Rapids, Iowa, July 14, 1953; d. William C. and Patricia Rose (Proskovec) Jennings. BS, Mt. Mercy Coll., 1975; student Coe Coll., 1971-73; postgrad. U. Iowa, 1981—. CPA, Iowa. Bookkeeper (part-time) Eagles Grocery Store, Cedar Rapids, 1969-75; sr. acct. Bell & Van Zee, P.C., Cedar Rapids, 1975-81; treas. (part-time) Kenwood Park Ch., Cedar Rapids, 1977-78; controller LeaseAm. Corp., Cedar Rapids, 1981-82, asst. treas., 1982-84, v.p., chief fin. officer, 1984-87, v.p. info. mgmt., 1988—. Mem. selection com. for Ramsey Scholarship Coe Coll., 1973, vol. Growth Fund Drive, 1981; vol. sr. citizen Thanksgiving dinner, 1983-87, Life Investors Inc., 1983-87, Cedar Rapids, 1983-87; fin. review com. United Way, 1986—; mem. exec. com. Alumni Phonathon, Mt. Mercy Coll., Cedar Rapids, 1985, fin. com. Indian Creek Nature Ctr., 1988—, fin. com. YWCA, Cedar Rapids, 1988—; alumni career cons., 1984—. Mem. Nat. Assn. Accts. (Storm award 1985, 87), Iowa Soc. CPAs, Am. Women's Soc. CPAs, Am. Inst. CPAs, Nat. Assn. Female Execs. Roman Catholic. Avocations: running, golf, racquetball, bicycling, reading. Office: LeaseAm Corp 4333 Edgewood Rd NE Cedar Rapids IA 52499

JENNINGS, LINDA GAIL, information services executive; b. Torrance, Calif., June 15, 1945; d. Herbert Chandler and Olive (Doench) Jennings; m. Kirby Jones, May 21, 1980; 1 child, Samantha Lee Jennings-Jones. BA in English, Coll. of Wooster, 1967; MA in Ednl. Devel., Ohio State U., 1975. With dept. preventive medicine Ohio State U., Columbus, 1967-71, research found., 1971-73; with MCI Communications Corp., 1976-81, mgr. mktg. services, 1981-82, mgr. cop. devel., 1982-84, sr. mgr. corp. info. services, Washington, 1985—. Mem. Internat. Assn. Bus. Communicators, Internat. Customer Service Assn., Assoc. Info. Mgrs., Soc. Consumer Affairs Profls., Nat. Alliance for Women in Communications Industries. Avocations: travel, scuba diving, photography. Office: MCI Communications Corp 1133 19th St NW Washington DC 20036

JENNINGS, MADELYN PULVER, communications company executive; b. Saratoga Springs, N.Y., Nov. 23, 1934; d. George Joseph and Martha (Walsh) Pulver. BA in Bus. and Econs., Tex. Woman's U., 1956. Asst. dir. pub. relations Slick Airways, Dallas, 1956-58; asst. dir. radio-TV promotion VIP Service, Inc., N.Y.C., 1958; asst. to pres. Smith, Dorian & Burman, Hartford, Conn., 1959; bus. mktg. planning Gen. Electric Co., Bridgeport, Conn., 1960-68, mgr. manpower planning, 1968-71, mgr. environ. support operation, 1971-73, mgr. employee relations, 1973-76; v.p. human resources Standard Brands, Inc., N.Y.C., 1976-80; sr. v.p. personnel Gannett Co., Arlington, Va., 1980—; NOW legal def. and edn. fund/corp. adv. bd.; bd. dirs. Detroit News. Bd. sponsor trustees U. Va. Colgate Darden Sch. of Bus. Adminstrn.; trustee Russell Sage Coll., Gannett Found.; bd. dirs. Am. Press Inst., Tex. Woman's Univ. Found. Mem. Am. Soc. Personnel Adminstrn., Human Resources Roundtable, Sr. Personnel Execs. Forum, Human Resources Planning Soc., Newspaper Personnel Relations Assn., Sr. Personnel Execs. Roundtable, Conf. Bd. (adv. council mgmt. and personnel), Am. Newspaper Pubs. Assn. (labor and personnel relations com.), Labor Policy Assn., Bus. Roundtable (employee relations com.), Ctr. Pub. Resources (human resources exec. program). Home: 3520 Duff Dr Falls Church VA 22041 Office: Gannett Co Inc Box 7858 Washington DC 20044

JENNINGS, MARCELLA GRADY, rancher, investor; b. Springfield, Ill., Mar. 4, 1920; d. William Francis and Magdalene Mary (Spies) Grady; student pub. schs.; m. Leo J. Jennings, Dec. 16, 1950 (dec.). Pub. relations Econolite Corp., Los Angeles, 1958-61; v.p., asst. mgr. LJ Quarter Circle Ranch, Inc., Polson, Mont., 1961-73, pres., gen. mgr., owner, 1973—; dir. Giselle's Travel Inc., Sacramento; fin. advisor to Allentown, Inc., Charlo, Mont.; sales cons. to Amie's Jumpin' Jacks and Jills, Garland, Tex. investor. Mem. Internat. Charolais Assn., Los Angeles County Apt. Assn. Republican. Roman Catholic. Home and Office: 509 Mt Holyoke Ave Pacific Palisades CA 90272

JENNINGS, SANDRA CHARLENE, retail store executive, designer; b. Dallas, Apr. 4, 1939; d. Charles Otis and Eula Mae (Williams) J.; children—Charles Haws, Amy Haws Jeffrey, Jay Haws, Larry Haws. Coordinating dir. Zales Corp., Dallas, 1976-77; pres. Fleming & Fleming, Inc., Dallas, 1977-78; sales mgr. Cockrell Wholesale, Dallas, 1979-80; pres. Jael Industries, Inc., Dallas, 1980—; organizer workshops. Trustee Suicide Prevention, Dallas, 1979-81; bd. dirs. Laos House, Austin, Tex., 1983—. Home and Office: 4303 Buena Vista #303 Dallas TX 75205

JENNINGS, TONI, state senator, construction company executive; b. Orlando, Fla., May 17, 1949; d. Jack C. and Margaret (Murphy) J. B.A., Wesleyan Coll., Macon, Ga., 1971; postgrad., Rollins Coll., 1972-73. Tchr. Killarney Elementary Sch., Winter Park, Fla., 1971-73; pres. Jack Jennings and Sons, Inc., Gen. Contractors, Orlando, 1973—; mem. Fla. Ho. of Reps., 1976-80; mem. Fla. Senate, 1980—, Republican leader pro tempore, 1982-86, Rep. leader, 1984, 86-88, chmn. commerce, transp., rules and calender, appropriations, mem. coms. personnel, retirement and collective bargaining, fin., taxation and claims, transp., exec. bus., rules and calendar. Active Sr. Citizens Adv. Council, Sea World, Winter Park Rep. Women's club, Leadership council, Rep. Women's Federated Club of Winter Park. Recipient Appreciation award Fla. Med. Assn. and Physicans of Fla., 1983, Legis. award Fla. Chiropractic Assn., 1983, Outstanding Service award Retail Grocers Assn. of Fla., 1983, Outstanding Efforts award Tampa Missing Children Help Ctr., 1983, Support of Law Enforcement award Fla. Sheriffs' Assn., 1983, Freedom award Women for Responsible Legis., 1982, Disting. Alumni award Wesleyan Coll., 1981, Outstanding Service award Homebuilders Assn. Mid-Fla., 1980, Spl. Commendation award Fla. Restaurant Assn., 1979, Meritorious Service award Fla. Fedn. Humane Socs., 1979; named Legislator of Yr. Fla. Assn. Realtors, 1984, Outstanding Rep. Woman of Yr. Orange County Rep. Exec. Com., 1983, Legislator of Yr. Orange County Young Rep. Club, 1980-81, Legislator of Yr. Assn. Builders and Contractors of Fla., 1978, Outstanding Woman in Govt. Orlando C. of C. Central City Com., 1977. Mem. Orlando Area Bd. Realtors,

Assn. Builders and Contractors, Central Fla. Builders Exchange, Delta Kappa Gamma, Phi Kappa Phi, Kappa Delta Epsilon. Office: Fla Senate Dist #15 1032 Wilfred Dr Orlando FL 32803

JENNINGS, VIVIEN LEE, bookstore management and licensing organization chief executive officer; b. Little Rock, Ark., Mar. 7, 1945; d. Loron and Mildred Louise (Wright) Bolen. B.A., Rhodes Coll., Memphis, 1967. Women's fiction cons. Ballantine Books, Inc., N.Y., 1981-82, Berkeley Pub. Group, N.Y., 1982-83; pres. Rainy Day Books, Inc., Fairway, Kans., 1975—. Editor nat. weekly bus. letter Boy Meets Girl, 1981-86; exec. editor serialized women's fiction project Day Dreams, 1984. Author: The Romance Wars; contbr. articles to profl. publs. Featured on nat. pub. radio and nat. tv programs. Mem. Romance Writers Am. Inc. (bd. dirs.), Soc. of Fellows Nelson-Atkins Mus. of Art, Hist. Kansas City Found. Episcopalian. Clubs: Carriage, Cen. Exchange (Kansas City). Home: 5413 Norwood Rd Fairway KS 66205 Office: Rainy Day Books Inc 2812 W 53d St Fairway KS 66205

JENNY, YOLANDE JEANNE, language professional; b. Zurich, Switzerland, Aug. 9, 1937; came to U.S., 1958; d. Jean and Emma Emilie (Zimmermann) J.; m. Jean-Raymond Audet, 1968 (div. 1977); 1 child, Pierre-Dominique. BA, Meredith Coll., 1960; MA, Duke U., 1962, PhD, 1967. Tchr. Cathedral High Sch., Superior, Wis., 1963-64; prof. French U. Minn., Duluth, Minn., 1965-67, 1969—; prof. English and German Collège de Bex, Switzerland, 1968. Contbr. articles to profl. jours. Co-founder Women's Defense Fund, Duluth, 1983. Mem. Am. Assn. Tchrs. of French, Minn. Council on Teaching of Fgn. Langs. (treas. 1976), Alpha Mu Gamma. Unitarian. Office: U Minn Dept Fgn Langs Duluth MN 55812

JENRETTE, RITA CARPENTER, actress, writer, commodities associate; b. San Antonio, Nov. 25, 1949; d. Carney Hunt and Reba (Garlington) Carpenter; m. John Wilson Jenrette, Sept. 10, 1976 (div. July 1981). BA in History cum laude, U. Tex., 1971. Dir. research Rep. Party Tex., Austin, 1972-74; lectr. Taft Polit. Inst. Trinity U., San Antonio, 1974; dir. research, writer Rep. Nat. Com., Washington, 1974-75; research assoc. Office Tech. Assessment, Washington, 1975-77; dir. mktg. Bridgewater U.S.A., N.Y.C., 1986—. Author: My Capitol Secrets, 1981, Conglomerate, 1986; appeared in Fantasy Island, Edge of Night, Kate & Allie, The Equalizer; stage debuts include The Philadelphia Story, A Girl's Guide to Chaos; feature film End of the Line. Vol. Partnership for Homeless, N.Y.C., 1985-87, Spl. Olympics, N.Y.C., 1980-87; fund-raiser AMFAIR, N.Y.C. and Washington, 1986-87. Recipient Critics award Drama-Logue, 1982. Mem. Dutch Reform Ch. Office: Bridgewater USA One World Trade Center Suite 1547 New York NY 10048

JENSEN, ANNE TURNER, automobile service company executive; b. Upper Providence Twp., Pa., Sept. 15, 1926; d. Ellwood Jackson and Elizabeth Addis (Downing) Turner; student Hood Coll., 1944-45, Phila. Coll. Pharmacy and Sci., 1945-46, 47-48; m. Harry Frederick Jensen, Jr., Apr. 13, 1946; children—Frederick Howard, Richard Jordan, Peter Hielm. Legal sec. Robertson & Turner, Media, Pa., 1950-51; sec. Luncheon-is-Served, Media, 1951-53; asst. sec., treas. Delvale Realty Corp., Media, 1955-59; bookkeeper Turner Realty Co., 1960-64, William H. Turner, Atty., 1960-64, Media Auto Service, 1957-74; sec. Media Auto Service, Inc., 1957-88. Capt. Heard Fund Dr., 1958-60. Republican. Presbyterian. Clubs: DAR (chpt. regent 1971-74, state corr. sec. 1977-80, nat. chmn. 1974-77), Daughters of Am. Colonists, Daughters of Colonial Wars (state treas. 1974-77, 80-83), Magna Carta Soc., Daus. of 1812, Navy League U.S. (N.Y. Council).

JENSEN, BARBARA JOAN, economics educator; b. Mpls., Oct. 20, 1948; d. Kenneth Paul and Lorraine Joan (Peterson) J.; m. David Lloyd Bergerson, June 9, 1972 (div. 1984); children: Jared David, Sarah Kristine. Student, Gustavus Adolphus Coll., 1966-68; BA, U. Minn., 1970, BS, 1972. Cert. tchr., Minn. Tchr. pub. schs. Mpls., 1975-77; pub. info. asst. Fed. Res. Bank, Mpls., 1977-78, cons., 1978-79, ednl. materials coordinator, 1979-84, econ. programs coordinator, 1984—; mem. adv. com. Mpls. Pub. Schs. Acad. Fin., 1986—; bd. dirs. Mpls. Pub. Schs. Learning Ctr. Econs., 1987—. Co-author instructional materials. Loaned exec. United Way Mpls., 1983. Mem. Assn. Supervision and Curriculum Devel., Nat. Council for Social Studies. Democrat. Lutheran. Office: Fed Res Bank Mpls 250 Marquette Ave Minneapolis MN 55480

JENSEN, BARBARA WOOD, interior design business owner; b. Salt Lake City, Apr. 30, 1927; d. John Howard and Loretta (Sparks) Wood; m. Lowell N. Jensen, June 6, 1947; children: Brent Lowell, Robyn Lynn, Todd Wood. Interior decorator paint and wall paper co., 1947-49; cons., interior designer 1950-60; pres., treas. Barbara Jensen Interiors, Inc., Salt Lake City, 1960-79; interior designer 1979—; owner Red Hills Wholesale Distributors, Salt Lake City, Barbara Jensen Designs, Salt Lake City; dir. 1st Women's Bancorp, Utah. Chmn. Utah Legis. Rep. Ball, 1970, Utah Symphony Ball, 1979. Fellow Inst. Profl. Designers (London); mem. Assistance League, Com. Fgn. Affairs, Interior Design Soc. (assoc.). Mormon. Clubs: Ft. Douglas Country, Knife and Fork, Hi-Steppers Dance, Ladies Lit., Pres.'s Utah. Lodge: Elks.

JENSEN, BETTY, physicist; b. Lodz, Poland, June 20, 1949; d. Sam and Gussie (Alter) Klainminc; came to U.S., 1962; m. Richard Alan Jensen, Dec. 19, 1971; children: David Jonathan, Andrew Michael, Penelope Judith, Sandra Rachel. BS in Math. summa cum laude Bklyn. Coll., 1970; MA in Physics Columbia U., 1972, MPhil, 1973, PhD, 1976; MBA St. John's U., 1981. Grad. research asst. recitation instr. Columbia U., 1970-76; sr. physicist research Public Service Electric and Gas Co., 1976-79, prin. staff physicist, 1979-81, prin. physicist, 1981-84, mgr. research and devel. for nuclear and environ. program, 1984-88, mgr. research and devel. for fuels and environ. scis. program, 1988—; adj. lectr. Richmond Coll., S.I., N.Y., 1973-76, N.Y.C. Community Coll., Bklyn., 1973-76; tutor for profl. sch. entrance exams Kaplan Tutoring Sch., Bklyn., 1970; chmn. fusion program adv. com. to Electric Power Research Inst., 1984-85; advisor Electric Power Research Inst., 1987—, Gas-Cooled Reactor Assocs., 1978—, Edison Electric Inst., 1987—; mem. review panel on Magnetic Fusion Office of Tech. Assessment, 1986-87. Mem. Am. Jewish Com. Recipient Math. prize Bklyn. Coll., 1968. N.Y. State Regents scholar, 1967-70; NSF grad. asst., 1970-72. Mem. Am. Phys. Soc., Air Pollution Control Assn., Ams. for Energy Independence, Assn. Women in Sci., Am. Nuclear Soc., IEEE, Phi Beta Kappa, Sigma Xi, Omicron Delta Epsilon, Beta Gamma Sigma. Jewish. Office: Pub Service Electric and Gas Co 80 Park Pl Newark NJ 07101

JENSEN, CAROL ANN, finance and administrative executive; b. Livermore, Calif., Apr. 22, 1951. BA in History cum laude, U. Calif., Santa Barbara, 1973, BA in Art History, 1974; MBA with honors, UCLA, 1976. Budget analyst Lawrence Berkeley Lab., Berkeley, Calif., 1976-79; fin. analyst Trans. Services div. Tymshare, Inc., Fremont, Calif., 1979-80; sr. cons. mgmt. adv. services Price Waterhouse, San Francisco, 1980-82; mgr. fin. systems Cambridge Plan Internat., Monterey, Calif., 1982-83; mgr. info. systems Transam. Corp., San Francisco, 1983-86; controller Am. Internat. Rent a Car/A-I CAL Leasing Corp., Burlingame, Calif., 1986; v.p. Micon Wind Turbines, Inc., Livermore, Calif., 1986—. Mem. APICS, Inst Mgmt. Acctg., Nat. Assn. Accts., U. Calif. at Stanta Barbara Alumni Assn. (past dir., treas.), Bay Area Lawyers for Arts. Office: Micon Wind Turbines Inc 2352 Research Dr Livermore CA 94550

JENSEN, CAROLYN REMINGTON, social worker; b. Central Falls, R.I., May 23, 1912; d. John Alfred and Caroline Nowlan (Allen) R.; m. William Craddock, May 4, 1943 (div. June 1946); m. Wesley Frederic Jensen; 1 child, Charles Wesley. BA, Wellesley Coll., 1933; BS, Simmons Coll., 1934; grad., N.Y. Sch. Social Work, 1940; MA, Framingham State Coll., 1986. Lic. social worker, Mass. Case worker Family Welfare Soc., Providence, 1934-37, Family Soc., Hartford, Conn., 1937-39; psychiatric social worker, pub. relations worker Family Soc., Providence, 1940-42; social work writer ARC, Washington, 1942-44; psychiatric social worker mental health clinic U.S. Pub. Health Service, Washington, 1944; chief social worker VA, Bridgeport, Conn., 1950-54; SW case supr. VA Hosp., West Haven, Conn., 1954-57; edbl. dir. Greater Bridgeport Child Guidance Clinic, 1957-60; psychiatric social worker Trinity Mental Health Clinic, Framingham, Mass., 1981-83; publicity, pub. relations worker South Middlesex Area Mental Health Dept., Framingham, 1987—. Contbr. articles to profl. jours. Mem. Greater New Haven Mental Health Com., 1964-66; attendant Gov.'s Conf. on Aging, Springfield, Mass., 1987; campaign worker Holliston Dems., Mass., 1984-86; del. Mass. Dem. Conv., Springfield, 1985; social action chmn. Sherborn Ch., 1982religious edn. dir., Canton, 1983. Mem. Nat. Assn. Social Workers. Unitarian. Home: 928 Washington St Holliston MA 01746 Office: Council on Aging St Paul's Episc Ch Millis MA 02054

JENSEN, DORIS J., educational administrator; b. Sterling, Colo., Aug. 10, 1939; d. Clarence J. and Lillian Lucille (Lawrie) Buckley; m. R. Blair Jensen, Aug. 28, 1960; children—Steven J., Cheryl B. A.A., Graceland Coll., 1959; B.S., Central Mo. State U., 1961, M.A. in English, 1964; PhD in Higher Edn. Adminstrn., U. Mo.-Kansas City, 1988. English instr. Central Mo. State U., Independence, 1969-74, U. Mo., Kansas City, 1974-80; registrar Cleveland Chiropractic Coll., Kansas City, 1980-81, dean student affairs and admissions, 1981—. Mem. Am. Assn. Coll. Registrars and Admissions Officers, Mo. Assn. Coll. Registrars and Admissions Officers, Nat. Assn. Student Personnel Adminstrs, Phi Lambda Theta. Office: Cleveland Chiropractic Coll 6401 Rockhill Rd Kansas City MO 64131

JENSEN, ELOUISE HENRIE, civic worker; b. Manti, Utah, Jan. 20, 1932; d. Irven Lund and Orlene (Larsen) Henrie; m. Clayne R. Jensen, Mar. 14, 1952; children: Craig R., Michael H., Blake Jensen, Christian Jensen. Student Brigham Young U., 1950-53, Utah State U., 1958-62. Pres., Brigham Young Univ. Women, 1982, Utah Valley Symphony Guild, Utah, 1983-84; mem. housing bd. Brigham Young U., 1972-82. Mem. U.S. Tennis Assn., Utah Valley Symphony Bd. Republican. Mem. Ch. of Jesus Christ of Latter Day Saints. Clubs: Cleafon (pres. 1981), Etienne (pres. 1979), Riverside Country (pres. 1987-88), Ridge Tennis (tournament chmn. 1984). Address: 1900 N Oak Ln Provo UT 84604

JENSEN, HELEN, musical artists mgmt. co. exec.; b. Seattle, June 30, 1919; d. Frank and Sophia (Kantosky) Leponis; student pub. schs., Seattle; m. Ernest Jensen, Dec. 2, 1939; children—Ernest, Ronald Lee. Co-chmn., Seattle Community Concert Assn., 1957-62; sec. family concerts Seattle Symphony Orch., 1959-61; hostess radio program Timely Topics, 1959-60; gen. mgr. Western Opera Co., Seattle, 1962-64, pres. 1963-64; v.p., dir., mgr. public relations Seattle Opera Assn., 1964—, preview artists Coordinator, 1981-84; bus. mgr. Portland (Oreg.) Opera Co., 1968, cons., 1967-69; owner, mgr. Helen Jensen Artists Mgmt., Seattle, 1970—. First v.p. Music and Art Found., 1981-84, pres. 1984-85. Recipient Cert., Women in Bus in the Field of Art, 1973; award Seattle Opera Assn., 1974; Outstanding Service award Music and Art Found., 1984; award of distinction Seattle Opera Guild, 1983. Mem. Am. Guild Mus. Artists, Music and Art Found., Seattle Opera Guild (pres., award of distinction 1983), Ballard Symphony League (sec.), Seattle Civic Opera Assn. (pres. 1981-84), Portland Opera Assn., Portland Opera Guild, Seattle Civic Opera Assn. (pres. 1981-88), 200 Plus One, Aria Preview, Lyric Preview Group, Past Pres. Assembly (pres. 1977-79, parliamentarian 1987-88), Pres.'s Forum (program vice chmn. 1987-88), North Shore Performing Arts Assn. (pres. 1981). Clubs: Helen Jensen Hiking, Kenmore Community. Home: 19029 56th Ln NE Seattle WA 98155 Office: 716 Joseph Vance Bldg Seattle WA 98101

JENSEN, JANE THIELKE, counseling center administrator; b. Lakewood, Wis., May 13, 1933; d. Gilbert William and Laura (Huss) Thielke; children: Colene Jensen Acker, Greg, Grant, Garrett. BS in Psychology, U. Wis., 1978; MS in Profl. Devel., U. Wis., Stout, 1981. Cert. mental health counselor, Wis. Community services specialist Dane County Mental Health Ctr., Madison, Wis., 1973-76; pvt. practice divorce counseling Madison, 1976-78; instr. Madison Area Tech. Coll., Madison, 1973-78; dir., owner, counselor Divorce Counseling and Resource Ctr., Madison, 1978—; divorce cons. clergy cts., attys., sch., colls., employee assts. program to bus., Madison, 1973—; creator, presentor Crisis of the Holidays, Single Parent Burnout workshops, divorce groups and women groups, single parents without custody, 1973—. Mem. Gov.'s Women's Adv. Bd., Madison, 1978-82, Single Women/Single Parent Taskforce, Madison, 1978-82. Recipient Nat. Recognition award Cable TV, Madison, 1974. Mem. Wis. Outpatient Clinics, Investment Club (pres.). Home and Office: 7402 Friendship Ln Middleton WI 53562

JENSEN, JOY DOLORES, real estate broker; b. Cushing, Okla., Jan. 30, 1938; d. J. D. and Nancy Grace (Franklin) Raper; m. Darrel F. Kuhlmann, June 1, 1958 (div. 1967); children—Kirsta Kae, Kari Gae; m. 2d, Victor Robert Jensen, Dec. 6, 1969. Student pub. schs. Legal pvt. sec. Pure Oil Co., Wichita, Kans., 1957-59; builder sec. Hudson Co., Boulder, 1960—, real estate property mgr., 1971; closings broker Time Unlimited, Boulder, 1971-76; real estate broker Remax of Boulder, Colo., 1976-80, Joy Jensen Realty, Boulder, 1980—. Mem. Colo. Real Estate Assn., Nat. Real Estate Assn., Boulder Bd. Realtors, North Suburban Bd. Realtors, Farm and Ranch Inst. Republican. Lutheran. Office: Joy Jensen Realty 3120 Folsom St Boulder CO 80302

JENSEN, MALCYE WISDOMA, psychologist; b. New Haven, June 4, 1930; d. James Wisdom Jones and Malcye Heros (Collins) Toney; m. James Alfred Bush, Apr. 25, 1954 (div. 1981); children: Michael, Kevin, Michele; m. Kurt Alan Jensen, June 21, 1981. BA, Calif. State U., 1957; BS, Loma Linda U., 1952, MS, 1964; PhD, Calif. Grad. Inst., 1983. RN. Nursing instr. Orange Coast Coll., Costa Mesa, Calif., 1963-67; asst. prof. Loma Linda (Calif.) U., 1967-71; rehab. nurse Fireman's Fund Ins. Co., Los Angeles, 1973-76; nursing instr. Calif. Med. Ctr., Los Angeles, 1976-77; occupational health cons. Dept. Indsl. Relations, Los Angeles, 1977-87; pvt. practice psychology, Sierra Madre, Calif., 1987—; co-trainer State of Calif., 1983-85; lectr. Med. Media Assocs., East Hanover, N.J., 1984—; faculty sponsor Calif. Med. Ctr., 1976-77; mental health practitioner Pasadena Family Service, Los Angeles, 1984—. Contbr. articles to profl. jours. Mem. sch. bd. San Gabriel Acad., Calif., 1984—; workshop facilator community chs., Altadena, Los Angeles, 1983—, lectr., 1983—. Mem. So. Calif. Assn. Black Psychologists, Nat. Assn. Black Psychologists, Research Council of Scripps Clinic, The Menniger Found., Nat. Assn. Female Execs., Oakwood Coll. Alumni, Loma Linda Alumni. Avocations: reading, travel. Home: 427-42E Mission Rd Alhambra CA 91801 Office: Life Change 37 Auburn Ave Suite 5 Sierra Madre CA 91024

JENSEN, MARILYN ANNE, educator, consultant; b. Minot, N.D., May 12, 1932; d. Raymond A. and Florence H. (Timmerman) Parcher. BA, San Jose (Calif.) State U., 1954; MA, U. So. Calif., 1965, PhD, 1971. Supr. City of Torrence (Calif.) Recreation Dept., 1955-65; prof. Calif. State U., Long Beach, 1965—, chairperson., 1975—; research assoc. U. So. Calif., Los Angeles, 1965-69; pvt. practice cons. Los Angeles, 1969—; researcher, investigator aerial photography projects, numerous cities, 1975—. Commr. Community Services Commn., City of Huntington Beach, Calif., 1981-86. Mem. Calif. Parks and Recreations Assn. (officer, pres. 1964-67, Citation award 1965, fellow 1977), Nat. Recreation and Parks Assn. (bd. of regents western region Somers Revenue Sch. 1986—, Profl. award 1987), Soc. Parks and Recreation Edn. (bd. dirs. 1982-85). Home: 21436 Via Straits Huntington Beach CA 92646

JENSEN, MARILYN MOORE CONNELL, publishing executive; b. Waukesha, Wis., Jan. 31, 1935; d. John R. and Florence (Evans) Moore; m. William Connell (div.); children: William, Ann, Shawn. Student, Oberlin Coll., 1952-54; BS, Carroll Coll., 1956. Dir. book clubs Christian Herald, Chappaqua, N.Y., 1972-78; editorial dir. books Guideposts, N.Y.C., 1978-84; v.p. publs. C.R. Gibson Co., Norwalk, Conn., 1984-87, v.p., pub., 1987—. Author: Formerly Married, 1983; contbr. articles to profl. jours. Mem. Evang. Christian Pubs. Assn. (bd. dirs. 1987—), Religion Pubs. Group N.Y. (bd. dirs. 1980-81, pres. 1982-84). Episcopalian. Office: The CR Gibson Co 32 Knight St Norwalk CT 06856

JENSEN, MARLENE F., magazine publisher; b. Aurora, Ill., Apr. 16, 1947; d. Benjamin Waldo Fann and Sylvia Ida (Brott) Burch; m. Raymond Neils Jensen, Jan. 11, 1970 (div. Sept. 1975). BA in Psychology, Calif. State U., Los Angeles, 1972; MBA, Fordham U., 1981. Editor, pub., owner Sportswoman Mag., Los Angeles, 1972-76; bus. mgr. ABC Leisure Mags., N.Y.C., 1977-79; dir. acquisitions CBS Mags., N.Y.C., 1979-81, pub. audio mag., 1982-83; v.p., pub. Home Mechanix Mag., N.Y.C., 1983-86; v.p. mags. Springhouse Corp., Pa., 1986—; cons. Bus. Supporting the Arts, Phila., 1987. Author: Women's Sports, 1975, Women Who Want to Be Boss, 1987. Named to Woman Achievers Hall of Fame YWCA, N.Y.C., 1984. Mem. Assn. Bus. Pubs. (chmn, pubs. com., 1987—), Mensa.

JENSEN, MARY BETH, small business owner, legal systems corporate executive; b. Madison, Wis., Jan. 5, 1947; d. William LeRoy and Virginia Mae (Brown) Clapp; m. Richard Albert Boots, Mar. 22, 1968 (div. 1983); 1 child, Beth Carisch; m. Dagfin Jensen, Sept. 25, 1983; stepchildren: Kristina, Karin. BS in Elem. Edn. with high honors, U. Louisville, 1970. Tchr. Madison Pub. Schs., 1971-72, West Lafayette (Ind.) Sch. Corp., 1972-75; transportation authority Solie & Spiegel Law Firm, Madison, 1980-81; asst. to v.p. personnel Cuna Mutual Ins., Madison, 1983; pres., owner Sunlife, Inc., Madison, 1984—; dir., chief exec. officer Versus Services, Chgo., 1986-87; bd. dirs. Sunlife Madison, 1984—, Brookfield (Wis.), 1985, Stevens Point (Wis.), 1984-86, Appleton (Wis.), 1984-85, Mequon (Wis.) Sun Ctr., 1984-86. Design chmn. Purdue Women on Campus, West Lafayette, 1977-78; auction co-chmn. Madison Arts Ball, 1983, Cancer Ball, 1985; bd. dirs. Big Bros., Madison, 1985—, art auction chairperson, 1985—, Scholar Home, Lafayette, Ind., 1977-78, Cancer So., 1984-86. Interviewed by In Business mag., 1984, 1985, Milwaukee mag., 1985. Mem. Nat. Assn. Female Execs., Gamma Phi Beta (dir., v.p. 1986-87, pres. 1987—), Tri Kappa. Roman Catholic. Clubs: Maple Bluff Country (Madison), Wayzata Country Minn.). Office: Versys Inc 320 N Michigan Ave Suite 1805 Chicago IL 60601

JENSEN, REGINA BRUNHILD, psychotherapist; b. Bredstedt, Germany, Oct. 26, 1951; came to U.S., 1973; d. Karl Adolf and Hildegard (Weiss) Schlosser; m. Benny Hvitfelt Jensen, July 31, 1976; stepchildren: Anita, Lisa. BS in Physiotherapy, Krankengymnastik Schule, Tuebingen, 1971; MA in Counseling Psychology, Vt. Coll., 1983; PhD Human Behavior, Ryokan Coll., 1984; PhD Clin. Psychology, Sierra U., 1987. Physiotherapist Urban Krankenhaus, Berlin, 1971-73; staff physiotherapist Werner & Beck Physical Therapy, Santa Maria, Calif., 1976-83; pvt. practice health cons. Santa Ynez, 1982—; cons. Jensen Enterprises, Solvang, 1975—, Alexander & Jensen Assocs., Los Angeles, 1983-85; health cons., Santa Ynez, 1982—; adolescent crisis counselor Santa Ynez Valley High Sch., 1984-86; tutor, program coordinator Sierra U., Santa Monica, 1985—; dir. Inst. for Human Systems Integration, Santa Ynez, 1985—. Author: Education for the Medical Consumer, 1983, To Liberate or to Enslave, 1985, How To Buy Back Your Soul, 1987; contbr. articles to profl. papers and jours. Mem. Am. Psychol. Assn. (divs. for media and health psychology), Calif. Assn. For Marriage and Family Therapists, Am. Assn. for Counseling and Devel., Orgnl. Devel. Network. Home and Office: 2880 Baseline Ave #B Santa Ynez CA 93460

JENSEN, RITA ANN, educator; b. Charles City, Iowa, Sept. 22, 1955; d. John William and Myrtle Laurene (Shipp) J. BA, Grand Rapids (Mich.) Bapt. Coll., 1978; BS, Calvin Coll., 1978; MA in Edn., U. No. Iowa, 1982; PhD, Iowa State U., Ames, 1988. Cert. elem., spl. edn. and lang. arts tchr., Iowa. Tchr. lang. arts Clarksville (Iowa) Community Sch., 1978-81; tchr. gifted edn. Charles City Community Schs., 1982-85; instr. elem. edn. Iowa State U., Ames, 1985—. Del. state conv. Floyd County Reps., Charles City, 1984. Named one of Outstanding Young Women of Am., 1986. Mem. AAUW (legis. chmn. 1984-85), Soc. for Internat. Tng. and Devel., Am. Soc. Tng. and Devel., Phi Kappa Phi, Phi Delta Kappa, Charles City Singers. Baptist. Home: 244 Village Dr Ames IA 50010 Office: Iowa State U N131 Lagomarcino Hall Ames IA 50011

JENSEN, VIVIAN NELSON, educator, state legislator; b. Redmond, Utah, Apr. 16; d. Franklin Theodore and Annette Christine (Willardson) Nelson; m. Moroni Lundby Jensen, Mar. 8, 1934; children—Moroni Leon, Jerold Lynn. B.S., Columbia U., 1950; postgrad. U. Utah, 1952-55. Tchr. Sevier Sch. Dist., Salina, Utah, 1940-50; librarian Granite Sch. Dist., Salt Lake City, 1950-56, tchr., 1956-59, counselor, 1959-76; mem. Utah Senate, 1980-81; mem. Utah Ho. of Reps., 1982-84. Named Woman of Achievement, Bus. and Profl. Womens Club Utah, Salt Lake City, 1983. Mem. Order Women Legislators, Fedn. Dem. Women (pres. Utah chpt. 1988). Democrat. Mormon. Avocation: writing. Home: 2940 Filmore St Salt Lake City UT 84106

JENSEN, YVONNE MARIE, graphic designer; b. Houston, May 30, 1946; d. Owen Franklin Jr. and Mary Jane (Autrey) J. BFA, U. Tex., 1968. Graphic designer Hayes Advt., Houston, 1968-70, Pieper Delineators, Houston, 1970-73; designer, owner Jensen Graphic Design, Houston, 1968—. Patron Acad. Medicine, Tex. Med. Ctr. Library Autrey Collection, Citizens for Animal Protection. Mem. Printing Industries of Gulf Coast, DAR, Nat. Assn. Watchs Clock Collectors, United Daus. of Confederacy, Alpha Gamma Delta (past pres., 2d v.p. Epsilon Delta Chpt.). Methodist.

JEPPESEN, SUSAN QUANDT, marketing executive; b. Milw., Sept. 8, 1954; d. Raymond W. and Ruth M. (Sievers) Quandt; m. Edward Kersten (div.); 1 child, Jennifer Elizabeth; m. Eric Jeppesen; 1 child, Katherine Joan. BS in Acctg., Valparaiso U., 1976; MBA, U. Wis., 1978. Acct. E.C. Hicks & Assocs., Merrillville, Ind., 1976-77; market research analyst Wis. Telephone Co., Milw., 1979, S.C. Johnson & Son Inc., Racine, Wis., 1980; sales fin. cons. Wis. Telephone Co., Milw., 1981-82; mgr. sales support AT&T Info. Systems, Chgo., 1983; comptroller Ameritech Communications Inc., Chgo., 1984, dir. product mgmt., 1984-86, sr. dir. network mgmt., 1988—; dir. New Bus. Devel. and Systems Integration, 1987—; prof. mktg. Alverno Coll., Milw., 1982; instr. mktg. Milw. Area Tech Coll., 1982; chmn. publicity Infant Welfare Ctr. Clarendon, 1987. Tchr. Grace Ch. Sunday Sch.; nominating com. St. Helen's Guild. Mem. Am. Mktg. Assn. (pres. Milw. chpt. 1982-83, pres. elect 1981-82, v.p. communications 1980-81), Chgo. Zool. Soc. Home: 44 Golf Ave Clarendon Hills IL 60514 Office: Ameritech Communications Inc 300 S Wacker Dr Chicago IL 60606

JERABEK, LENORE A., systems specialist; b. Milw., Mar. 23, 1944; d. Joseph and Stephanie (Swedish) J. BA, Alverno Coll., 1966. Systems coordinator Northwestern Mut. Life Ins. Co., Milw., 1966—. Office: Northwestern Mut Life Ins Co 720 E Wisconsin Ave Milwaukee WI 53202

JERNER, BETSY BOWEN, training supervisor; b. Milwaukee, Aug. 13, 1949; d. Fred Everett and Eva Mae (Goff) B.; m. William Vernon Jerner, Sept. 2, 1978; 1 child, Alexandra Drew. BA, U. Ky., 1971, MA, 1977. CLU; chartered fin. cons. Tchr. Fayette County Sch. System, Lexington, Ky., 1972-80; field underwriter N.Y. Life, Lexington, Ky., 1980-82, tng. supr., 1982—. Pres. Soroptimist Internat. Lexington, 1981-82; mem. profl. women's forum, Lexington. Mem. Certl Life Underwriter Soc. (dir. 1987—), Lexington Assn. of Life Underwriters. Office: N Y Life Lexington Fin Ctr Suite 240 250 W Main St Lexington KY 40507

JERNIGAN, JEAN ALLEN, group executive assistant; b. Brookline, Mass., May 26, 1923; d. Langdon and Dorothy (Talbot) Allen; A.A., Garland Jr. Coll., 1942; m. Roger R. Jernigan, May 31, 1943; children—Roger, Jeffrey, Bruce, Linda. Fashion and beauty editorial asst. Boston Herald Traveler, 1942-44; news editor Sun Newspapers, Contra Costa County, Calif., 1958-64; aide to county supr. Contra Costa County, 1964-66; dir. public relations Children's Hosp. Med. Center, Oakland, Calif., 1966-68; women's editor, feature writer Berkeley (Calif.) Gazette, 1968-78; dir. public relations, asst. exec. dir. Berkeley-East Bay Humane Soc., 1978-81; reporter Contra Costa Sun, Lafayette, Calif., 1979-80; adminstrv. asst. to v.p. fin. Cetus Corp., 1981-83; group exec. asst. Triad Systems Corp., 1984—. Recipient McQuade award, 1970. Mem. Women in Communication. Clubs: East Bay Press, Contra Costa Press. Republican. Office: 3055 Triad Dr Livermore CA 94550

JEROME, BETTE, actress, speaker; b. Newport News, Va.; d. Elias and Sophie (Harris) J.; m. Samuel M. Bialek, June 26, 1960; children by previous marriage—Alan Craig Rafel, Lisa Rafel. Stage and radio actress, concert artist, choral condr., TV producer/moderator, writer, 1953—; narrator govt. and industry tng. films; actress, spokesvoice comms.; pres., exec. dir. BJB Prodns., Ltd.; producer radio programs including Mind's Eye Theatre, Foggy Bottom, Interact; tchr. dynamic speech for TV and radio newscasters, announcers; condr. speech and spokespersons workshops. Recipient Emmy award, AAUW award, Dept. Indian Affairs award, Gold Mike award McCalls. Mem. Am. Women in Radio and TV (pres. Washington chpt. 1971-72), AFTRA (pres. Washington/Balt. local 1973-75), Nat. Acad. TV

Arts and Scis., Screen Actors Guild, Actors Equity Assn. Home: 10250 Silver Lake Dr Boca Raton FL 33428

JERRIS, MILDRED CAROL, mathematics educator; b. Buffalo, Feb. 17, 1928; d. Philip J. and Ida P. (Incavo) Scaffidi; BA, U. Buffalo, 1948; MA, N.Y. State Coll. Tchrs., 1955, postgrad., 1970-72; postgrad. Nova U., 1984-86; m. Richard Jerris, Apr. 10, 1950; children—Robert, Janice, Keith, Karen. Tchr., Buffalo Pub. Schs., 1948-53, Amherst (N.Y.) Jr. High Sch., 1957-58, DeLand (Fla.) Jr. High Sch., 1967-72; tchr., dept. head math. Nova Mid. Sch., Ft. Lauderdale, Fla., 1972-88; mem. curriculum devel. com. Broward County Schs., 1980-88; textbook cons. Math. 6, 1983; coach math. competition teams. Treas. DeLand Children's Mus., 1969-71. Stetson U. scholar, 1967; NSF grantee SUNY, 1970. Mem. Fla. Council Tchrs. Math. (dir. dist. VII 1983-85), Broward County Councils Tchrs. Math. (nat. rep. 1987-89, dir. south cen. dist. 1985-87), Broward Tchrs. Union, Delta Kappa Gamma (v.p. 1980-82, 84-86), Gamma Beta (pres. 1986-87). Home: 8550 SW 26th Pl Ft Lauderdale FL 33328 Office: 3602 SW College Ave Ft Lauderdale FL 33314

JERRY, JACQUELINE, interior designer; b. Pitts., July 1, 1939; d. Horace Oscar and Edwinor Jane (Carter) J.; m. Robert Lee Hammond (dec. Jan. 1983); children: Robert Jr., Steven, Mark Aaron; m. Alvin Edward Jerry; children: Gary Alvin, Keith Edwin. AA, Art Inst., Pitts., 1978, Triangle Tech., 1980. Owner, mgr. Le'Shop, Pitts., 1980—; supr. tng. students Goodwill, Pitts. 1986-87; set designer Kuntu Theater, 1977—. Mem. task force Mayor's Office Renaissance II, Pitts. 1984. Mem. Nat. Assn. Female Exec., Urban League Pitts. Democrat. Lodge: Shriners. Office: Le'Shop 2200 Centre Ave Pittsburgh PA 15219

JERVIS, JANIS WILLIAMS, public service organization executive; b. Wilmington, N.C., Apr. 5, 1924; d. R. Saunders and Thelma J. (Pickard) Williams; m. Frederick Martin Jervis, Sept. 23, 1947; children—Bruce Martin, Ellen Day, Jane Winfield. B.A., U. N.C., 1947; postgrad. U. N.H., 1947-49. Freelance writer, Durham, N.H., 1960-71; co-founder, seminar leader, dir. publs., exec. dir. Ctr. for Constructive Change, Durham, 1971—; mgmt. cons., 1974—; treas., dir. Delphi Mgmt. Systems, Durham, 1981-85. Trustee, Gruber Found., 1981—; active City/Town Planning Forums, 1975-84. Saul O. Sidore Found. grantee, 1979-80. Author: Change: Piecemeal or Comprehensive, 1975; contbr. numerous articles to profl. jours. Office: Ctr Constructive Change 16 Strafford Ave Durham NH 03824

JESESEKE, ELLEN FRANCES, computer programmer, graphic artist; b. Saddle Brook, N.J., Sept. 3, 1954; d. Frank Alexander and Helen (Kandravy) J. BFA magna cum laude, cert. in art edn. and computer sci., William Paterson Coll., 1976. Tchr. art N.J. Sch. Systems, 1976-79; visual merchandising artist Hahne's & Co., Montclair, N.J., 1979-80; health aide, art therapy asst. John F. Kennedy Rehab. Ctr., Edison, N.J., 1980-81; interior designer Carriage House, River Edge, N.J., 1981-82; programmer, data processing tech. writer Mchts. Refrigerating Co., Secaucus, N.J., 1982—, corp. computer graphics artist, research coordinator, 1987 ; presenter at confs. and seminars. Mem. Nat. Computer Graphics Assn., Digital Equipment Computers Users Soc., Nat. Assn. Desktop Pubs., Am. Mgmt. Assn., Nat. Assn. Female Execs., Assn. for Women in Computing, Pi Lambda Theta. Russian Orthodox. Home: 260 Fourth St Saddle Brook NJ 07662 Office: Merchants Refrigerating Co 1 Enterprise Ave Secaucus NJ 07094

JESSEN, SHIRLEY AGNES, artist; b. Bklyn., Jan. 23, 1921; d. Arnold Peter and Agnes Veronica (Maguire) Hemmersbach; m. Albert Vern Jessen, Nov. 23, 1944; 1 child, Gregory Vern (dec.). Student, N.Y. Sch. Applied Design, 1939-42, N.Y.C. Fashion Inst., 1942-43, Garden City (N.Y.) Community Art Studio, 1961-83. 37 one-woman shows include N.Y. State Council Arts, 1972, 7-12 Assn., 1972, Wantagh (N.Y.) Library, 1972, Security Nat. Bank, 1972, 73, Bank N.Am., 1972, 73, Expo Fine Arts Instructional Movie, 1973-74, Community Arts Program, Cinema Theatre, 1973, Nat. Bank North Am., 1973, S.E. Nassau (N.Y.) Guidance Clinic, 1973, Nassau County Office Performing and Fine Arts, 1973, N.Y State Council Arts, 1974, Garden City Library, 1975, Merrick (N.Y.) Mall Theatre, 1976, Reynold Securities, Inc. Art Gallery, 1977, Nassau County Mus. Fine Arts, 1979, Adelphi U. Alumni House, 1980, Town of Oyster Bay (N.Y.) Hall and Dept. Community Services, 1981, Cent. Savs. Bank Syosset (N.Y.), 1981, GEICO Art Gallery, Woodbury, N.Y., 1981, Oyster Bay Library, 1981, Cathedral of the Incarnation Mercer Library, 1981, Molloy Coll. Kellenberg Art Gallery, 1984, Expo Art Gallery, 1987; 172 juried shows including St. Frances de Chantal Art Show, 1974, North Shore U. Show, 1974, Union Carbide Art Gallery, 1977, Nat. Soc. Painters in Casein and Acrylic, 1978, Long Beach Mus. Juried Competition, 1979, Rosyln Mus. Fine Arts, 1979, Les Etoiles Galerie D'Art, France, 1980 (Internat. award), Nat. Art Ctr., N.Y., 1980, South Shore Art League, 1981 (first prize), Citibank Gallery, Merrick, 1981, Wilbur Arts Ctr. Molloy Coll., 1981, Xavier Art Gallery, N.Y., 1982. Illustrator Wantagh PTA, 1950-65, pres. 1961-62, Mercy Hosp., Hempstead, N.Y., 1980-82; bd dirs. United Cerebral Palsy, Wantagh, 1955-78, pres. 1959-61, del. to AMA conventions, illustrator 1959-75; bd. dirs. Nassau County Med. Soc. Aux., 1955 87, pres. 1961-62; mem. Pro Arté Symphony Orch., Hofstra U., N.Y., 1969-80; organizer benefits various local hosps., charitable orgns., 1976—. Mem. Internat. Soc. Artists, South Shore Art League (bd. dirs. 1975-85, publicity chmn. 1982), Artists Equity N.Y., Audubon Artists Assn., Ind.'s Art League, L.I. Artists Alliance, Freeport Arts Council. Roman Catholic. Club: Garden City Community.

JESSUP, KAREN LOUISE, historic preservation educator, consultant; b. Detroit, Mar. 20, 1945; d. Robert LeRoy and Vera Louise (Kriegoff) Crispin; m. Richard Jessup Jr., June 24, 1967; children: Dana Leigh, Amy Krieghoff, Kara Buntin. BA, Allegheny Coll., 1967; MA in Preservation Studies, Boston U., 1983. Caseworker Child Welfare Services of Allegheny County, Pitts., 1968-70; pvt. practice cons. Providence, 1983—; mem. faculty Roger Williams Coll., Bristol, R.I., 1985—; adj. assoc. prof. grad. program in historic preservation Boston U., 1987—. Contbr. articles to profl. jours. Mem. distbn. com. Citizens Bank Community Found., Providence, 1986—; sec. R.I. Legis. Commn. on Preservation Law, 1986—; trustee Heritage Found. Rhode Island; panelist Mass. Council on the Arts. Alden scholar Allegheny Coll., 1967; named Providence Disting. Citizen, 350 Yr. Celebration. Mem. Providence Preservation Soc. (exec. com. 1982—, bd. dirs. 1982—, pres. revolving fund 1985—), Preservation Action (nat. bd. dirs. 1984—), Nat. Trust for Historic Preservation (bd. dirs. Antoinette Downing Fund 1986—).

JESSUP, MARY FROST, retired statistician, social and economic researcher; b. N.Y.C., June 18, 1902; d. David Stuart Dodge and Maud Ogden (Heath) J. A.B., Vassar Coll., 1925; M.A., Columbia U., 1930. Cert., U.S. Civil Service Commn. Surveyor, City of N.Y., 1925-26, economist; research asst. Inst. Social and Religious Research-Rockefeller Found., N.Y.C., 1929-32; asst. dir., field dir. consumer purchase study U.S. Depts. Labor, Agri. 1936-37, 42; researcher div. hist. studies, U.S. Dept. Labor, 1943-44, Field Progress Br. U.S. Dept. Army, 1944-46; spl. asst. gen. dir. AAUW, Washington, 1954-56; research analyst Office of Equal Opportunity, U.S. Dept. Labor, 1971-73; research assoc. social research br., U.S. Dept. of Human Resources, Washington, 1973-76; mem. staff Women's Ednl. Research AAUW, Washington br., 1983-86; cons. and lectr. in field. Contbr. articles to profl. jours. Area chmn. United Way, N.W. sect., Washington, 1960's; bd. dirs., pres. All Souls Housing Corp., 1983-86; bd. dirs. Change All Souls Housing Corp., 1975—. Recipient Disting. Service citation All Souls Unitarian Ch., 1983, citation Human Rights Day, AAUW, Washington, 1976, 1985. Mem. AAUW (past v.p. program and mem. com. Washington br.) (pres.'s award, 1985), Nat. Women's Democratic Club, Vassar Coll. Assn. of Washington, Columbia Univ. of Washington (past pres.). Club: Garden of Montrose (Pa.), Montrose. Avocations: bridge; landscape painting; swimming; golf; tennis. Home: 2853 Ontario Rd NW Washington DC 20009

JESTER, JANICE MAY, nurse; b. Muncie, Kans., Jan. 4, 1941; d. Jessie Theodore and Gusta Fern (Bilyeu) J. Diploma Nursing, Bethany Hosp. Sch. Nursing, Kansas City, Kans., 1962. R.N. Staff nurse Bethany Med. Ctr., Kansas City, Kans., 1962-65, head nurse, 1965-70, rehab. coordinator, 1970-74, rehab. and enterostomal therapy nurse specialist, 1974—. Bd. dirs. Cancer Action, Inc., Kansas City, Kans., 1974-86, pres. bd., 1981-83; bd. dirs. Hospice Care Mid-Am., Kansas City, Mo., 1980-86, mem. med. adv. bd., 1986—; bd. dirs. United Cancer Council, Inc., 1984; mem. nat. bd. Make Today Count, since 1986—; dir. children's dept. Faith Temple Family Worship Ctr., singer gospel music group. Recipient J.C. Penney Golden Rule award, 1987; named Woman of Yr., Bus. and Profl. Women, Kansas City, Kans., 1984. Mem. United Ostomy Assn. (nat. bd. dirs. 1984-87, advisor Greater Kansas City chpt. 1974-88, co-founder Nat. Youth Rally, Sam Dubin award 1985), World Council for Enterostomal Therapy, Internat. Assn. for Enterostomal Therapy (bd. dirs. 1977-84, treas. 1980-84. Home: 3144 S 53d St Kansas City KS 66106 Office: Bethany Med Ctr 51 N 12th St Kansas City KS 66102

JETER, CHRYSTAL CARR, librarian, storyteller; b. Los Angeles, June 30, 1948; d. King and Naomi Ruth (Shackles) Carr; m. Abraham Jeter, Jr., Dec. 29, 1979. BA, Calif. State U. Los Angeles, 1970; MLS, U. So. Calif., 1972; postgrad. UCLA, 1976-77, U. Alaska, Anchorage, 1977-78, U. Wash., 1983. Library staff asst. Occidental Coll., Eagle Rock, Calif., 1971-72; librarian trainee Los Angeles Pub. Library, 1972; children's and adult librarian Inglewood (Calif.) Pub. Library, 1972-77; instr. speech dept. Los Angeles S.W. Coll., 1976-77; br. librarian Anchorage Mcpl. Libraries, 1977-84, asst. mcpl. librarian for spl. services, 1984-85, asst. mcpl. librarian for community services, 1985—; community adv. bd. Alaska Pub. TV, Sta. KAKM, 1986—; bd. dirs. Alaska chpt. March of Dimes, 1982-83, Alaska Double Dutch League, 1982-83; storyteller Anchorage Sch. Dist., 1978—; active Alaska Black Caucus, 1982—; music dir. Anchor Ch. of God. Mem. ALA, Alaska Library Assn. (chmn. publicity 1979-80; local v.p. 1983), NAACP, Delta Sigma Theta. Democrat. Home: 740 Bounty Dr Anchorage AK 99515 Office: Anchorage Mcpl Libraries 3600 Denali Anchorage AK 99503

JETER, KATHERINE LESLIE BRASH, lawyer; b. Gulfport, Miss., July 24, 1921; d. Ralph Edward and Rosa Meta (Jacobs) Brash; m. Robert McLean Jeter, Jr., May 11, 1946. B.A., Newcomb Coll. of Tulane U., 1943; J.D., Tulane U., 1945. Bar: La. 1945 U.S. Dist. Ct. (we. dist.) La. 1948, U.S. Tax Ct. 1965, U.S. Supreme Ct. 1971, U.S. Dist. Ct. (ea. dist.) La. 1975, U.S. Ct. Appeals (5th cir.) 1981, U.S. Dist. Ct. (mid. dist.) La. 1982. Assoc. Montgomery, Fenner & Brown, New Orleans, 1945-46, Tucker, Martin, Holder, Jeter & Jackson, Shreveport, 1947-49; ptnr. Jeter, Jackson and Hickman and predecessors, Shreveport, 1980—; judge pro tem 1st Jud. Dist. Ct., Caddo Parish, La., 1982-83; mem. adv. com. to joint legis. subcom. on mgmt. of the community. Pres. YWCA of Shreveport, 1963; hon. consul of France; Shreveport; pres. Little Theatre of Shreveport, 1966-67; pres. Shreveport Art Guild, 1974-75; mem. task force crim justice La. Priorities for the Future, 1978; pres. LWV of Shreveport, 1950-51. Recipient Disting. Grad. award Tulane Law Sch., 1983. Mem. La. State Law Inst. (mem. council 1980—, adv. com. La. Civil Code 1973-77, temp. ad hoc. com. 1976-77), Public Affairs Research Council (bd. trustees 1976-81, exec. com. 1981—, area exec. committeeman Shreveport area 1982), ABA, La. Bar Assn., Shreveport Bar Assn. (pres. 1986), Nat. Assn. Women Lawyers, Shreveport Assn. for Women Attys., C. of C. Shreveport (bd. dirs. 1975-77), Order of Coif, Phi Beta Kappa. Baptist. Contbr. articles on law to profl. jours.; editor Tulane Law Rev., 1945. Home: 3959 Maryland Ave Shreveport LA 71106 Office: 401 Edwards St Suite 905 Shreveport LA 71101-3146

JETT, JANE ELLEN, home economist; b. Terre Haute, Ind., Feb. 26, 1951; d. William H. and Bernadean (Harlan) Heramb; m. James W. Jett, Jan. 18, 1986. BS in Vocat. Home Econs., Ind. State U., 1973, MS in Gen. Home Econs., 1978. Cert. home economist. Sales clk. G.C. Murphy Co., Terre Haute, 1970-74; 4-H leader Vigo County Extension Office, Terre Haute, 1970-74; grad. asst. Ind. State U., Terre Haute, 1973-74; ext. agt. Vanderburgh County Extension Office, Evansville, Ind., 1974-88; substitute tchr. Vigo County Sch. Corp., Terre Haute, Ind., 1974. Bd. dirs., vol. Patchwork Cen., Inc., Evansville, 1983—; bds. dirs., chmn. child devel. com. Community-Action Program Evansville, 1977-87; friend Shakertown at Pleasant Hill, Harrodsburg, Ky., 1984-89. Mem. Am. Home Econs. Assn., Ind. Home Econs. Assn. (sec. 1985-87), Ind. Extension Agts. Assn. (bd. dirs. 1982-86), Nat. Extension Home Economists Assn. (Disting. Service award 1987), Epsilon Sigma Phi. Baptist. Club: Evansville Home Econs. (v.p. 1974-75). Lodge: Order of Eastern Star (Ruth 1970-74), Job's Daus. (honored queen 1960-70).

JEVELI, ELAINE CAROL, clinical researcher; b. Medford, Mass., July 25, 1937; d. Edmund S. and Gia E. (Saggese) J.; m. Russell C. Kraus. BS, Tufts U., 1958; MAT, Harvard U., 1959; MS, Smith Coll., 1965; PhD, U. Mass., 1975. Educator in various biol. scis. U. Wis., Smith Coll., suburban Boston secondary schs., 1960-75; mgr. Fundamental Info. and Testing, sr. research scientist Kimberly-Clark Corp., Neenah, Wis., 1976-80; mgr. disposables prodn., adminstr. clin. and research studies Sybron Corp., Rochester, N.Y., 1980-84; mgr. clin. research services Bausch and Lomb, Rochester, 1985-88, dir. clin. research services, 1988—; indsl. rep FDA, Washington, 1980-82; steering com. for standards HIMA, Washington, 1983-84; cons. in field. Contbr. articles to profl. jours. Recipient Bausch and Lomb Sci. award, 1954; Alfred P. Sloan scholar, 1958-59; NFS teaching grantee, 1972; Smith Coll. teaching fellow, 1973-75. Mem. Soc. Clin. Trials, Regulatory Affairs Profls. Soc. Office: Bausch & Lomb 1400 N Goodman St Rochester NY 14692

JEW, JEAN, hotel communications executive; b. Oakland, Calif., May 6, 1959; d. Ju Wah and Frances (Wong) J. AA, Meritt Coll., 1982; BS in Internat. Bus., San Francisco State U., 1985, BS in Transp. Mgmt., 1985. Banking service miscellaneous clk. Alameda (Calif.) First Nat. Bank, 1977-81, sr. customer service rep., 1981-85, sr. banking service rep. mcht., 1985-86; office mgr. Domino's Pizza, Inc., Alameda, 1986-87; mgr. communictions The Portman Hotel, San Francisco, 1987—. Vol. coordinator Alameda County Spl. Olympics, Fremont, Calif., 1976—, v.p., bd. dirs., 1986—; coordinator handicapped transport, assist to asst. dir. transp. Dem. Nat. Conv., San Francisco, 1984. Recipient Spl. Olympic Vol. award Alameda County Spl. Olympics, 1983. Mem. Nat. Assn. Female Execs. Club: The Commonwealth of Calif.

JEWELL, MARTHA PEARL, marketing professional; b. Brimfield, Ohio, Oct. 10, 1940; d. Roy Delbert and Johnnie Belle (Smith) McPherson; m. Richard Lee Jewell, Oct. 13, 1956; children: Melany Elaine, Brian Lee, Kenneth Richard. Student, U. Kansas, 1974, Dale Carnegie, Kansas City, Mo., 1974, U. Mo., Kansas City, 1975-76. Successively treas., gen. sales mgr., exec. v.p. Arrow Forklift Parts Co., Inc., Kansas City, 1971-81; pres. Jewell Mktg. Service, Inc., Kansas City, 1981—, Matrix Dimensions, Inc., Kansas City, 1986—. Film producer The Master Key, 1986. Treas. Wesleyan Service Guild, Kansas City, 1975. Fellow Nat. Assn. Women Bus. Owners (spl. projects chmn., 1982), Smithsonian Inst., Creative Film Soc., Visual Music Alliance, Nat. Arbor Day Found.; mem. Christian Bus. and Profl. Women (chmn. 1973-74), Sales and Mktg. Execs., Material Handling Equipment Dealers Assn., Kansas City Dir. Mktg. Assn. Presbyterian. Home and Office: 10400 Walrond Kansas City MO 64137

JEWETT, PAULINE, Canadian legislator; b. St. Catharines, Ont., Can., Dec. 11, 1922; d. Frederick Coburn and Ethel Mae (Simpson) J. Student, Queen's U., Can., Harvard U., U. London, London Sch. of Econs. Prof. polit. sci. Carleton U., 1955-74; pres. Simon Fraser U., 1974-78; mem. Can. Ho. of Commons, 1963-65, 79—. Mem. New Democratic Party. Address: 303-9303 Salish Ct, Burnaby, BC Canada V3J 7B7 *

JEWETT, SHIRLEY JOANNE, insurance executive; b. Springfield, Mo., Mar. 8, 1937; d. Keith C. and Erma T. (Metcalf) Wilcox; m. David I. Buffington, May 14, 1956 (div. Jan. 1980); children: Cheryle D., David B., Jeffrey B., Mary B.; m. Maurice J. Jewett, Oct. 3, 1980. Student, S.W. Bapt. U., Bolivar, Mo., 1955-56, LaSalle Extension U., Chgo., 1967-70. Lic. ins. broker, Mo. Real estate sales assoc. Re/Max Realtors, Independence, Mo., 1980-81; custom decorator J.C. Penney Co., Inc., Kansas City, Mo., 1981-83; life ins. agt. Modern Am. Ins. Co., Kansas City, 1983-85; career agt. Farm Bur. Ins. Co. of Mo., Kansas City, 1985—. Life Underwriters Tng. Course fellow. Mem. Nat. Assn. Life Underwriters, Nat. Assn. Female Execs. Baptist. Home: 9025 Lewis Kansas City MO 64138 Office: Farm Bur Ins Co of Mo 2528 S M-291 Independence MO 64057

JEX, MARY KATHRYN, designer, clothing company executive; b. Balt., Mar. 28, 1959; d. Edward Robert and Kathryn Maxine (Pyle) J. BFA, Pa. State U., 1981; BS, Phila. Coll. Textiles and Sci., 1982. Asst. designer The Arrow Co. div. Cluett Peabody, N.Y.C., 1982-83; designer Gant Corp. div. Palm Beach, N.Y.C., 1983-84, mgr. mdse., 1984—. Republican. Methodist. Club: Atrium. Home: 200 E 82d #20A New York NY 10028 Office: Gant Corp 689 5th Ave New York NY 10022

JIMENEZ, ARLENE MARIE, brokerage executive; b. Salinas, Calif., June 20, 1959; d. Melvyn Howard and Gertrude Lorraine (McKernan) Krause; m. Waldo Rafael Jimenez, June 1, 1985. AA in Merchandising, Fashion Inst. Design, Los Angeles, 1981; BS in Bus. Adminstrn., U. La Verne, Calif., 1981; MBA in Mgmt., U. Bridgeport, 1986. Salesperson Bullocks, West Covina, Calif., 1976-81; asst. buyer Bullocks Wilshire, Los Angeles, 1981-82; mgr. ops. Pacific Sunwear of Calif., Newport Beach, 1982-85; research asst. U. Bridgeport, Conn., 1985-86; commodity broker Chilmark Commodities Corp., Stamford, Conn., 1986—. Mem. Nat. Rep. Com., Washington, 1987. Mem. Nat. Assn. Female Execs. Roman Catholic. Home: 1169 Hope St C-5 Stamford CT 06907 Office: Chilmark Commodities Corp 2001 W Main St Suite 110 Stamford CT 06902

JIMENEZ, BETTIE EILEEN, small business owner; b. LaCygne, Kans., June 8, 1932; d. William Albert and Ruby Faye (Cline) Montee; m. William R. Bradley, Aug. 21, 1947 (div. Sept. 1950); 1 child, Shirley; m. J.P. Jimenez, Feb. 20, 1951 (div. Nov. 1978); children: Pamela, Joe Jr., Robin Michelle. Student, Ft. Scott Jr. Coll., Paola, Kans., 1979-81. Reporter LaCygne Jour., 1943-45; union recorder I.L.G.W.U., Paola, 1956-57; mgr. Estes Metalcraft, Osawatomie, Kans., 1977-82; owner El Rey Tavern, Osawatomie, 1980-87. Home: 516 Walnut Osawatomie KS 66064

JIMENEZ-WAGENHEIM, OLGA, history educator; b. Camuy, P.R., Sept. 24, 1941; d. Santos and Victoria (Mendez-Ramos) Jimenez; m. Kalman Wagenheim, June 10, 1961; children: David, Maria. BA, Inter-Am. U., San Juan, P.R., 1970; MA, SUNY, Buffalo, 1971; PhD, Rutgers U., 1981. Coordinator bi-lingual sect. The Learning Ctr. SUNY, Buffalo, 1971; coordinator community adult edn. program Puerto Rican Community, Buffalo, 1971; asst. to the dir. E.O.F. Rutgers U., Newark, 1973; instr., dir. Puerto Rican studies Rutgers U., Newark, 1977-81, asst. prof. history, 1981-86, assoc. prof. history, 1986—; V.p. editing projects Waterfront Press, Maplewood, N.J., 1983—. Author El Grito de Lares: sus causas y sus hombres, 1984, Puerto Rico's Revolt for Independence, 1985; co-editor The Puerto Ricans: A Documentary History, 1973; contbg. editor Caribbean Review, Miami, 1983—; contbr. articles to profl. jours. Researcher Hispanic Women Task Force, Trenton, 1986—; trustee Newark Mus., 1979-85; bd. dirs. Acad. Founds. Rutgers U., Newark, 1986—. Fellow Ford Found., 1973-76, NEH, 1986. Mem. Latin American Studies Assn., Assn. of Caribbean Historians, Asociación de Historiadores Puertorriquenos, Caribbean Studies Assn., N.J. Congress of Latina Women, Oral History Assn., Hispanics in Higher Edn. Democrat. Roman Catholic. Home: 52 Maple Ave Maplewood NJ 07040 Office: Rutgers U 175 University Ave Newark NJ 07102

JOANNIDES, STEPHANIE EVANGELINE, lawyer; b. Tripoli, Libya, July 6, 1954; d. George Efthyfron and Violet (Microutsicos) J. BS in Psychology, U. Santa Clara, 1975; JD, Gonzaga U., 1981. Bar: Alaska 1984, U.S. Dist. Ct. Alaska, 1987. Counselor Boys & Girls Homes of Montgomery County, Bethesda, Md., 1976-77; legal intern, researcher Spokane (Wash.) Pub. Defender's Office, 1979-81; legal researcher Wash. Appellate Pub. Defenders, Seattle, 1982, Juneau, Alaska, 1983; asst. dist. atty. Dist. Atty.'s Office Dept. of Law, Juneau, 1984-87; asst. atty. gen. Criminal Div. Dept. of Law, Juneau, 1987—; vis. instr. Sitka Alaska State Trooper Acad., 1985-87; apptd. Alaska Supreme Ct. adv. com. Pattern Jury Instructions; mem. Council on Domestic Violence and Sexual Assault, Comml. Vehicle Task Force. Mem. Cousteau Soc., Norfolk, Va., 1987, Mem. Alaska Task Force on Comml. Driver & Vehicle Safety, 1988, Domestic Violence & Sexual Assault Council, 1987—. Mem. Alaska Bar Assn., Juneau Bar Assn., Am. Judicature Soc. Democrat. Greek Orthodox. Office: Criminal Div Cen Office PO Box KC Juneau AK 99811

JOBE, ALICE, transportation executive; b. Little Rock, Nov. 24, 1935; student Long Beach City Coll., 1960-61; m. K.L. Jobe, Mar. 12, 1957; 1 dau., Cathy. With Nat. Equity Life Ins. Co., Little Rock, 1954-55, Cash Wholesale Co., Little Rock, 1956-57; with Bekins Internat., subs. Bekins Co., Wilmington, Calif., 1959-77, v.p., 1971-77; v.p. Imperial Internat., Inc., Torrance, Calif., 1977-78, exec. v.p., 1978-80, dir., 1977-81; pres. Imperial Van Lines Internat., Inc., 1980-81; industry cons., 1981-82; founder, pres. Caddo Internat., freight forwarding, Los Alamitos, Calif., 1982—. Mem. Household Goods Forwarders Assn. (exec. com. 1977-78), Nat. Def. Transp. Assn. (life), Am. Soc. Profl. Women. Republican. Office: Caddo Internat 3662 Katella Ave Suite 209 PO Box 739 Los Alamitos CA 90720

JOBS, LORETTA, real estate broker; b. Murray, Ky., Nov. 27, 1938; d. Ivy and Ola (Jones) Culver; m. Sindin Jobs, Mar. 25, 1961; children: Sindin Andrew, Richard Ivan. BS, Murray State U., 1960. Sec. Tappan Co., Murray, 1960-63; social worker Commonwealth of Ky., Murray, 1963-66; ins. rep. Woodmen of the World, Murray, 1966-86; real estate agt. Wilson Real Estate, Murray, 1972-77; real estate broker Century 21 Loretta Jobs Realtors, Murray, 1977—. Bd. dirs. Leadership Murray, 1983-87, vice-chmn. 1984, chmn. 1987-88; bd. dirs., v.p. devel. Econ. Devel. Corp., 1986-87; trustee Murray Ind. Sch. Found. for Excellence in Pub. Edn., Inc., 1986-87; chmn. stewardship commn. First United Meth. Ch., 1984-85, mem. fin. com., 1983-85, mem. adminstrv. bd., 1984-87 chmn. Council on Ministries, 1988; state chmn. Opening Ceremonies, Ky. State Spl. Olympics, 1981-82. Mem. League Women Voters (v.p.), Ky. Assn. Realtors (membership com. 1980,-82, assoc. realtor of yr. 1974), Murray Calloway County Bd. Realtors (pres. 1984), Murray Calloway County C. of C. (dir. 1982-87, pres. 1986-87). Office: Century 21 Loretta Jobs Realtors 303 N 12th St Murray KY 42071

JOBSON, MAREDA BELL, semiconductor company executive; b. Wilkes Barre, Pa., May 17, 1946; d. William Andrew and Kathleen Mary (Kinsey) Bell; m. Charles Thompson Jobson, Aug. 14, 1970; children: Paul Thompson, Adam Robert. BA, Fontbonne Coll., 1968. Actuarial asst. Travelers Ins. Co., Hartford, Conn., 1968-69, Gen. Am. Life Ins. Co., St. Louis, 1969-73; programmer/analyst Allied Supermarkets, Oklahoma City, 1973-78; programmer McGraw-Hill, Hightstown, N.J., 1979-80; data analyst McGraw-Hill, Hightstown, 1980-81; data specialist NSA/ARMS, Cherry Hill, N.J., 1981-82; adminstr. data base RCA Solid State, Somerville, N.J., 1982-84; mgr. data base adminstrn. Gen. Electric Solid State, Somerville, N.J., 1984—. Bd. dirs. Pickwick Pebble Hill Sch., Doylestown, Pa., 1983-84, sec.-treas., 1984-85. Mem. Delaware Valley Cullinet Software Users Group (pres. 1984—), Integrated Database Mgmt. System Users Assn. (bd. dirs. 1985-88, sec.-treas. 1986-88). Home: 46 Pebble Woods Dr Doylestown PA 18901

JOBSON, MARIAN, corporate executive; b. Chgo.; d. George Baigrie and Almira (Giddings) J. AB, Chatham Coll. Founder, ptnr. Hartwell, Jobson & Kibbee, N.Y.C.; chair bd. Jobson Assocs., N.Y.C. Mem. Pub. Relations Soc. of Am. (accredited, Counselors Acad.). Republican. Presbyterian. Home: 235 E 49th St New York NY 10017 Office: Jobson Assocs 1841 Broadway Suite 1203 New York NY 10023

JOE, MELISSA CARVER, legal administrator; b. San Antonio, Aug. 2, 1953; d. Robert W. and Kathryn J. (Raby) Carver; m. Dennis Thomas Joe, Mar. 26, 1983. Student, S.W. TEx. State U., 1971-73, U. Tex., 1973-76. Copywriter advt. Clyde Butter Advt. agy., Austin, Tex., 1974-75; theatre mgr. Am. Multi Cinema, Inc., Austin and Houston, 1975-83; real estate mgmt., sales Austin, 1984-85; legal adminstr. Jenkins & Gilchrist, Austin, 1985—. Mem. Assn. Legal Adminstrs., Nat. Assn. Female Execs. Republican. Office: Jenkens & Gilchrist PC PO Box 2987 Austin TX 78769-2987

JOFFE, BERTHA, textile designer; b. Leningrad, USSR; came to U.S., 1924; d. David and Lydia (Kretzer) Pashkovsky; m. Joseph Joffe; children: Robert, Paul, Richard. Student, N.Y. Phoenix Sch. Design, 1930-31; studies painting with Winold Reiss, N.Y.C., 1934; BS, CCNY, 1940; MA, Tchr.'s Coll., 1941; studies with Oronzio Maldarelli, N.Y.C., 1941, studies with William Zorach, 1942; postgrad., NYU, 1942. Freelance textile designer Waverly Fabrics, 1942-62; fabric designer French Fabrics Corp., N.Y.C.,

1962-66; designer home furnishing fabrics M. Lowenstein & Sons, N.Y.C., 1967-77; freelance textile designer N.Y.C., 1977—. Exhibited in group shows at Provincetown (Mass.) Art Assn., 1940, Met. Mus. Art, N.Y.C., 1942, Weatherspoon Art Gallery, N.C., 1944, Watercolor in Renaissance Fair, Summit, N.J., on air exhbn. Sta. WNET, 1980, 82, 83. Mem. Soc. for the Arts, Religion, and Contemporary Culture Inc., Common Cause, Nat. Peace Found., LWV.

JOFFE, ZERLINE CHARLOTTE HESS, designer; b. N.J., July 25, 1936; d. Richard Hess and Dorothy Kaye (Newman) Hess; student Hunter Coll., 1954-57; cert. Parsons Sch. Design, N.Y. Sch. Interior Design, 1972; m. Martin Lee Joffe, Oct. 8, 1958; children—Paul, Simeon. With Robert Caigan Assos., 1974-77; prin. firm Zerline Joffe Interiors, 1977-87; cons. archtl. firms. Mem. Allied Bd., Am. Soc. Interior Designers (assoc. mem.). Home and office: 145 W Broadway New York NY 10013

JOHANNSEN, LINDA BETH, electronics company executive; b. Columbus, Ohio; d. Lloyd Griffith and Blanche Wanda (Medve) Robey; m. James Reed Schreckengast, Oct. 16, 1965 (div.); 1 child, Heather Lynn; m. Bruce A. Johannsen, Nov. 29, 1981. BA in Art, Fla. Atlantic U., 1978; student, Ohio State U. Mgr. mktg. communications Sensormatic Electronics Corp., Deerfield Beach, Fla., 1979—. Mem. Boca Raton Mus. Art. Recipient Knowledge, Wisdom and Courage to Serve award U. Mich., 1969. Mem. Bus. Profl. Advertisers Assn. (bd. dirs. at large 1986—). Clubs: Gold Coast, T-Bird (Ft. Lauderdale, Fla.). Office: Sensormatic Electronics Corp 500 NW 12th Ave Deerfield Beach FL 33342

JOHANSEN, CYNTHIA DEE ANN, pharmacist; b. Aberdeen, S.D., Oct. 21, 1933; d. Roy Samuel and Sena (Williams) Glover; m. Richard Dean Johansen, Dec. 23, 1953; children—Jay William, James Richard, Jess Douglas. BS, S.D. State U., 1954; MS, U. San Francisco, 1984. Lic. pharmacist, S.D., Kans., Calif. Pharmacist/asst. Palace Drug Store, Manhattan, Kans., 1954-58; mgr., relief pharmacist Med. Ctr. and State Hosp., Yankton, S.D., 1958-61; owner, mgr. Dakota Drug Store, Newell, S.D., 1961-69; asst. dir. pharmacy St. John's Hosp., Rapid City, S.D., 1970-74; clin. pharmacist dir. pharmacy Kings View Corp., Reedley, Calif., 1974—; clin. pharmacist cons., 1974—; mem. adv. bd. Data Med. Inc., Mpls., 1983—. Author: Guidelines for Safe and Effective Use of Medication, 1977; contbr. chpts. in books, brochures on drugs. Mem. Tulare County Profl. Standards com., Calif., 1979-81; bd. dirs. Family Planning for Tulare County, 1976-80; pres. St. John's Hosp. Employee Council, 1971-72. Mem. C. of C. (pres. 1965-66), Am. Soc. Hosp. Pharmacists (mem. council clin. affairs 1982), Am. Soc. Cons. Pharmacists, Calif. Pharmacists Assn., Am. Pharm. Assn., Tulare Kings Pharm. Assn. (pres. 1976-77, bd. dirs. 1978—), Calif. Soc. Hosp. Pharmacists (sec. 1979-82, sec. council clin. pharmacy and therapeutics 1977-78, sec. council organizing affairs 1985, membership com. 1986, chmn. 1987—), Sierra Soc. Hosp. Pharmacists (pres. 1986), Fresno Madera Pharm. Assn. Home: 6050 W Caldwell St Visalia CA 93277 Office: Kings View Corp 42675 Road 44 Reedley CA 93654

JOHN, CAROLINE CARLTON, newspaper executive; b. Winston-Salem, N.C., Dec. 22, 1944; d. Romulus Lancaster and Caroline (Cheney) Carlton; B.A., Duke U., 1967; postgrad. Radcliffe Coll., 1967; m. David Vaughn John, Aug. 31, 1968 (div. 1984); children—Matthew Ian, Caroline Elizabeth. Dir. info. services and publs. Guilford Coll., Greensboro, N.C., 1967-68; asst. editor alumni publs. Duke U., 1968-70; account exec., creative dir. Farnan Advt., Atlanta, 1970-74; with Atlanta Jour.-Constn., 1974-86, mktg. dir., 1981-83, circulation sales and mktg. dir., 1983-86, circulation dir., 1984, v.p., 1986; v.p., gen. mgr. Cox Ariz. Publs. Inc. (pub. Mesa Tribune, Chandler Tribune, Tempe Tribune), 1986-88; v.p. consumer mktg. and research Cox Newspapers, 1988—. Mem. Am. Mktg. Assn. (dir. 1980-82), Ariz. Newspapers Assn. (bd. dirs.), Internat. Newspaper Mktg. Assn. (dir. 1980, treas. 1983-84, v.p. 1984-85, pres. 1986-87), Newspaper Research Council, Internat. Circulation Mgrs. Assn. Democrat. Home: 3003 Vinings Forest Way Atlanta GA 30339 Office: Cox Newspapers PO Box 105720 Atlanta GA 30348

JOHN, YVONNE MAREE, interior designer; b. Leeton, New South Wales, Australia, Sept. 8, 1944; came to U.S., 1966; d. Percy Edward and Gladys May (Markham) Thomas; m. Michael Peter John, Aug. 20, 1966; children: Michael Christian, Stephen Edwin Dennis. Student, Buenaventura Coll., 1969, U. Calif., Santa Barbara, 1975; cert., United Design Guild, 1975; AA, Interior Design Guild, 1976; Diploma, Internat. Correspondence Sch., 1976. Designer Percy Thomas Real Estate, Leeton, 1960-66; cosmetologist, artist Bernard's Hair Stylists, Ventura, Calif., 1966-67, 74-73; cosmetologist Banks Beauty Salon, Chgo., 1968-69; owner, mgr. Yvonne Maree Designs, Ventura and Olympia, Wash., 1978—; owner, cosmetologist Mayfair Salon, Leeton, 1962-66; owner, mgr. Y.M. Boutique, Griffith, Australia, 1965-66. Contbr. numerous short stories and poems to newspapers; artist numerous pen and ink drawings; one man show Royal Mus. Sydney, Australia, 1954. Artist Ventura County Gen. Hosp., 1970's. Recipient Cash and Cert. awards Sydney Newspapers, 1950's, Ribbon awards Sydney County Fairs, 1950's. Office: Yvonne Maree Designs PO Box 2143 Olympia WA 98507

JOHNS, ANN FLORENCE, small business owner; b. Woonsocket, R.I., May 4, 1944; d. Florence Marie Trepanier; m. Charles Paul Johsn, Apr. 20, 1941; children: Christopher, Reneé. Degree in med. tech., St. Joseph's Hosp., Providence, 1964. Co-owner Varna Inn, Ithaca, N.Y., 1969-86, Chuck Johns Auto Rental, Ithaca, 1983-87; owner Lady J Products, Ithaca, 1985—. Mem. Inn Keepers Assn. (co-pres. 1985). Roman Catholic. Office: Lady J/CJ Auto Rental 930 Dryden Rd Ithaca NY 14850

JOHNS, BEVERLEY ANNE HOLDEN, special education administrator; b. New Albany, Ind., Nov. 6, 1946; d. James Edward and Martha Edna (Scharf) Holden; m. Lonnie J. Johns, July 28, 1973. BS, Catherine Spalding Coll., Ky., 1968; MS, So. Ill. U., 1970; postgrad., Western Ill. U., 1973-74, 79-80, 82, U. Ill., 1984-85. Cert. adminstr., tchr. Ill. Demonstration tchr. So. Ill. U., Carbondale, 1970-73; instr. MacMurray Coll., Jacksonville, Ill., 1977-79; intern Ill. State Bd. Edn., Springfield, 1981; program supr. Four Rivers Spl. Edn. Dist., Jacksonville, Ill., 1972—; chmn. Ill. Edn. of the Handicapped Coalition, 1982-87; chmn. Ill. Edn. of Handicapped Coalition, 1982-87; conf. coordinator Ill. Alliance, Champaign, 1982—; v.p. Internat. Council for Exceptional Children, Reston, Va., 1987-88; bd. dirs. Jacksonville Area Assn. Retarded Citizens; lectr. to profl. confs.; cons. in field. Author: Report on Behavior Analysis in Edn., 1972; editor: Position Papers of Ill. Council for Exceptional Children, 1981; contbr. articles to profl. jours. Govt. relations chmn. Internat. Council Exceptional Children, 1984-87; fed. liason Ill. Adminstrs. Spl. Edn., 1985-86. So. Ill. U. fellow, 1968; resolution honoring Beverly H. Johns 60th Ann. Internat. Council for Exceptional Children Conv., 1982; cert. of recognition Ill. Atty. Gen., 1985. Mem. Assn. Retarded Citizens (com. 1982—), Assn. Supervision and Curriculum Devel., Ill. Council for Children With Behavioral Disorders (founder, past pres., presdl. award 1985), Ill. Alliance for Exceptional Children (v.p 1982—), Ill. Council Exceptional Children (past pres., chmn. govt. relations com. 1982—, governing bd. 1984—, Presdl. award 1983), West Cen. Assn. for Citizens with Learning Disabilities (founder, com. chair 197—), Delta Kappa Gamma. Roman Catholic. Avocation: world travel. Home: PO Box 340 Jacksonville IL 62651 Office: Four Rivers Spl Edn Dist 936 W Michigan Jacksonville IL 62651

JOHNS, CAROL JOHNSON, physician, educator; b. Balt., June 18, 1923; d. Ashmore Clark and Elsie Greacen (Carstens) Johnson; B.A., Wellesley Coll., 1944; M.D., Johns Hopkins U., 1950; D.H.L. (hon.), Coll. Notre Dame of Md., 1981; m. Richard James Johns, June 27, 1953; children—James Ashmore, Richard Clark, Robert Shanard. Intern, Johns Hopkins Hosp., 1950-51, asst. resident in medicine, 1951-53, fellow, 1953-54, physician outpatient dept., 1953-64, dir. Sarcoid Clinic, 1962—, active staff, 1964—, dir. med. clinic, 1967-76, dir. hosp. quality assurance, 1974-79, mem. hosp. med. bd., 1971-79; asst. in medicine Johns Hopkins U., 1951-58, instr., 1958-67, asst. prof., 1967-71, assoc. prof., 1971—, adv. bd. Applied Physics Lab., 1974-78; acting pres. Wellesley Coll., 1979-81, asst. dean, dir. continuing edn., 1981—; chmn. bd. Balt. City PSRO, 1975-79; pres. Internat. Sarcoid Conf., 1984; mem. pulmonary allergy adv. com. FDA, 1973-75; faculty adv. editorial bd. Johns Hopkins U. Press, 1981-84. Mem. vestry Ch. of Redeemer, 1967-70, sr. warden, 1976-79, layreader; bd. trustees Calvert Sch., 1968-72; bd. trustees Wellesley Coll., 1971—, exec. com., 1971-80, 84—chmn. nat. devel. fund, 1975-80, trustee fin. com., 1979—, chmn. trustee faculty relations com., 1984—; trustee St. Paul's Sch. for Girls, 1973-75; bd. dirs. Stetler Research Fund for Women, 1971-79, 84—; mem. Armed Forces Epidemiol. Bd., 1985—; bd. regents Univ. Health Scis., 1985—. Named Med. Woman of Yr. Med. Coll. Pa., 1984. Mem. Am. Clin. Climatol. Assn. (v.p. 1987), Am. Thoracic Soc., Balt. City Med. Soc., Johns Hopkins Med. Surg. Assn. (sec.-treas. 1981-87, pres. 1987—), Johns Hopkins Women's Med. Alumni Assn. (pres. 1957-59, dir.), Md. Med. Chirurg. Faculty (council 1978-79), Soc. Med. Coll. Dirs. Continuing Edn., Alliance for Continuing Med. Edn. (council 1987—), Phi Beta Kappa, Sigma Xi, Alpha Omega Alpha (bd. dirs. 1978-87, v.p. 1985-86, pres. 1986-87). Episcopalian. Clubs: Johns Hopkins, Wellesley Coll., Mt. Vernon. Contbr. articles med. jours., chpts. in textbooks. Home: 203 E Highfield Rd Baltimore MD 21218 Office: 17 Turner 720 Rutland Ave Baltimore MD 21205

JOHNS, ELIZABETH JANE HOBBS, educational administrator; b. Roanoke Rapids, N.C., July 18, 1941; d. Florence Eugene and Elizabeth Holt (Massey) Hobbs; m. Lewis Clarence Johns, Apr. 7, 1961; children: Karen Anne Johns Cuccaro. AA with honors, Valencia Community Coll., 1984; BSBA with honors, Fla. So. Coll., 1988. Med. receptionist Dr. Harold Knowles, Orlando, Fla., 1959-61; sec. Martin Marietta Aerospace%, Orlando, 1961-77; edn. adminstr. Martin Marietta Aerospace, Orlando, 1977—; chair bd. credit union Martin Marietta Orlando (Fla.) Aerospace, 1987—; bd. dirs. Martin Marietta Fed. Credit Union, 1978—. Mem. community adv. bd. sch. continuing edn. Hamilton Holt Sch., continuing edn. council for women Valencia Community Coll., 1984—. Named one of Outstanding Women in Bus., 1985, one of Top Ten Employees, Martin Marietta Aerospace, Orlando, 1983, one of Top 100, 1978. Mem. Am. Bus. Women's Assn., Valencia Community Coll. Alumni Assn. (bd. dirs. 1984—), Orlando C. of C. (post secondary edn. task force), Phi Theta Kappa. Democrat. Methodist. Home: 3201 Holliday Ave Apopka FL 32703 Office: Martin Marietta Electronics & Missiles Group Orlando Ops PO Box 5837 MP Orlando FL 32855

JOHNSON, ANN TERRILL, educator; b. Mattoon, Ill., Apr. 2, 1941; div. 1972; children: Terrill Leigh, Scott Eliot. AB in Polit. Sci., Coll. William and Mary, 1963; MEd in Adult Edn. Adminstrn., N.C. State U., 1984. Hostess/guide Colonial Williamsburg (Va.), 1962-64; tchr. Yorktown (Va.) City Schs., 1963-64; registrar's clk. Guilford Coll., Greensboro, N.C., 1964-65; adminstrv. asst. State Senator McNeill Smith, Greensboro, N.C., 1972-76; admissions counselor, law enforcement edn. program counselor Guilford Coll., Greensboro, N.C., 1976-80, assoc. dir. continuing edn. and adminstrn., 1980-81, dir. continuing edn., 1981-86; dir. lifelong learning Greensboro Coll., 1986—; bd. dirs., sec. Touring Theatre Ensemble, Greensboro; chmn. Alliance Bus. and Lifelong Edn., Greensboro, 1985-87. Sec., bd. dirs. ARC, Greensboro, 1976-81. Mem. Assn. Continuing High Edn. (bd. dirs. region V 1983-87), N.C. Adult Edn. Assn. (bd. dirs.), Greensboro Area C. of C. Democrat. Mem. Soc. of Friends. Office: Greensboro Coll 815 W Market St Greensboro NC 27401-1875

JOHNSON, ANNETTE MADELEINE, health administrator, b. Windsor, Ont., Can., Nov. 17, 1950; d. Walter E.A. and Madeleine St. George (Wilson) J. B.S., Mich. State U., 1972; cert. Tuskegee Inst., 1973; M.S. in Health Edn., Columbia U. Tchrs. Coll., 1977; postgrad. Hunter Coll., 1980-81. Registered dietitian. Cclin. nutritionist, health educator Whitney M. Young Health Ctr., Albany, N.Y., 1977-80; nutritional cons. N.Y. State Office of Aging, 1980-81; nutritional edn. cons. N.Y. State Health Dept., 1981-84, dir. edn., 1984-87 adminstr. minority mgmt. devel. fellowship program, 1987—; nat. cons. Assn. Retarded Citizens, Albany, N.Y., 1979-80, N.Y.C. Council Chs. Ctr. for the City, 1985—, others. Mem. steering com. Black Women's Health Project, N.Y.C., 1985-86; co-chmn. Coalition of Blacks in the Nutrition Profession, N.Y.C., 1983-84. Mem. Am. Dietetic Assn. (chpt. sec. 1979), Am. Home Econs. Assn., Am. Pub; Health Assn., Phi Delta Kappa, Pi Lambda Theta (chpt. sec. 1977), Nat. Assn. Female Execs., Bus. and Profl. Women USA (dist. chmn. 1986). Democrat. Avocations: travel; reading; collecting ceramics and glass; dance; theatre. Home: 55 Park Ave Brooklyn NY 12202 Office: NY State Dept Health Empire State Plaza Corning Tower Room 742 Albany NY 12237

JOHNSON, ARLENE MAE, educator; b. Yuba, Wis., Aug. 10, 1930; d. Frederick Ray and Mary (Subera) Stowell; m. C. Gaylord Johnson, June 21, 1952; children: Kent Alan, Todd Earle. BS, U. Wis., Whitewater, 1952; MST, U. Wis., Eau Claire, 1971, EdS in Bus., 1979. Cert. vocat. tech. tchr.; cert. adult edn. tchr., Wis., N.C. Instr. bus. Bangor (Wis.) Pub. Schs., 1952-55, 64-65, Sparta (Wis.) Pub. Schs., 1955-57, 65-69; adminstrv. sec. No. Engraving Co., Sparta, 1961-63; sec. personnel Wis. Child Ctr., Sparta, 1963-64; instr. bus. Dist. One Tech. Inst., Eau Claire, 1969-85; sec. sales Diamond Brand Canvas Co., Naples, N.C., 1985-86; instr. bus. Hendersonville (N.C.) High Sch., 1986—. Tchr. sch. 1st Congl. Ch., Sparta, Eau Claire, 1953-80; chair various coms. Profl. Secs. Internat., Eau Claire, 1971-84. Mem. NEA, N.C. Edn. Assn. Republican. Office: Hendersonville High Sch 311 Eighth Ave W Hendersonville NC 28739

JOHNSON, BARBARA DOMURAT, data processing executive; b. Trenton, N.J., Aug. 12, 1959; d. Eric and Paula (Szygiel) Domurat; m. Edgar Wyles Johnson Jr., Apr. 19, 1986. BSBA, Old Dominion U., 1981, MS in Computer Sci., 1983. Cert. in data processing. System analyst Aux. Enterprises Old Dominion U., Norfolk, Va., 1981-82; instr. data processing Old Dominion U. Sch. Bus., 1982, research asst., 1982-83; instr. Tidewater Community Coll., Virginia Beach, Va., 1982; mgr. systems and tng. Exec. Productivity Systems, Inc., Norfolk, 1983-87, dir. tng., 1987—; guest speaker CUBE Nat. Conv., Washington, Berkeley, Calif., New Orleans, 1986-88. Mem. Ghent Sq. Homeowners Assn., Norfolk, 1985—. Mem. Data Processing Mgmt. Assn., Assn. Computing Machines. Office: Exec Productivity Systems Inc 150 W Brambleton Ave Norfolk VA 23501

JOHNSON, BARBARA JANE, sales representative; b. Chgo., Aug. 19, 1946; d. Sidney and Norma Mona Shaffer; B.A. in Sociology and Psychology, U. Ill., 1968; postgrad. M.B.A. program, Roosevelt U., 1971-72; m. Gary Johnson, Aug. 25, 1968; 1 child, Eric Michael. Asst. personnel dir. Associated Mills, Chgo., 1967-69, Scholl Mfg. Co. Inc., Chgo., 1969-71; nurse recruiter Cook County Hosp. Governing Com., Chgo., 1971-73; recruiter Mt. Sinai Hosp., Chgo., 1973-76; sales rep. Stryker Corp., Kalamazoo, 1976-81, area trainer; sales rep. Physio Control, Schaumberg, Ill., 1981—; with Sensormedics Corp., Anaheim, Calif.; founder Chgo. Area Nurse Recruiters; cons. positions as nurse recruiter. Vice pres. Budlong Community Action Group, 1979—; advisor Jr. Achievement, 1969-72; auction com. Ednl. TV; trustee Mt. Sinai/Schwab Rehab. Ctr., 1983—. Recipient Lee Stryker sales award, 1979. Mem. Assn. of Operating Room Nurses (sponsor). Recipient first place Recruitment Brochure for Chgo. Area Bus. Communicators, 1975; salesman of year, 1979; first woman to achieve nat. award, 1979.

JOHNSON, BARBARA JEAN, lawyer, judge; b. Detroit, Apr. 9, 1932; d. Clifford Clarence and Orma Cecile (Boring) Barnhouse; m. Ronald Mayo Johnson, June 24, 1965; 1 dau., Belinda Etezad. B.S., U. So. Calif., 1953, J.D., 1970. Bar: Calif. 1971. Ptnr. Anglea, Burford, Johnson & Tookay, Pasadena, Calif., 1970-77; judge Los Angeles Mcpl. Ct., 1977-81; judge Los Angeles Superior Ct., 1981—; lectr. U. So. Calif. Law Sch. profl. program; adj. prof. Southwestern U. Law Sch. Recipient Ernestine Stahlhut award, 1981. Mem. Calif. Judges Assn., Nat. Assn. Women Judges, Calif. Women Lawyers Assn., Women Lawyers Assn. of Los Angeles. Office: Superior Ct 111 N Hill St Los Angeles CA 90012

JOHNSON, BARBARA JILL, packaging engineer; b. Binghamton, N.Y., Jan. 21, 1957; d. Thomas Blauvelt and Barbara Ann (Larrabee) Johnson. AS in Bus. Adminstrn., Broome Community Coll., 1977; BS in Packaging Sci., Rochester Inst. Tech., 1982. Recreation leader Dept. Parks and Recreation City of Binghamton, 1976-80; packaging engr. Boehringer Ingelheim, Danbury, Conn., 1982-85, purchasing buyer, 1985-86; packaging engr. Westreco/Nestle, New Milford, Conn., 1986—. Mem. Parks and Recreation Commn., Brookfield, Conn., 1984-87; sec. Rollingwood III Condominium Bd., Brookfield, 1986. Named Champion Women's B Div. Speed Skating, Amateur Speed Skaters. Mem. Soc. Packaging and Handling Engrs. (cert.), ASTM (subcom. 1982-87), Nat. Assn. Female Execs. Republican. Episcopalian. Office: Westreco Inc-Nestle 140 Baordman Rd New Milford CT 06776

JOHNSON, BARBARA JO, nurse; b. Parma, Ohio, Aug. 14, 1952; d. Ralph James and Johanna Bell (Folk) Dee; m. Maurice Bernard Johnson, July 17, 1975; children: Colin Benard Dee, Brian James Dee. BS in Nursing, S.D. State U., 1974; MS in Nursing with distinction, DePaul U., 1978. Mem. nursing staff Northwestern Meml. Hosp., Chgo., 1974-78; clin. cardiovascular specialist Grant Hosp., Chgo., 1978, dir. med. nursing, 1979-87; asst. v.p. patient care services Highland Pk. (Ill.) Hosp., 1988—. Mem. Am. Nurses Assn. (cert. nursing adminstr., del. 1979, 81, 83, 85), Ill. Nurses Assn. (bd. dirs. 1983-85), Chgo. Nursing Assn. (bd. dirs. 1983-85, budget com. 1982—), Women Health Exec. Network, Am. Soc. Hosp. Nursing Service, State Nurses Active in Politics in Ill., Sigma Theta Tau Zeta. Office: Highland Pk Hosp Highland Park IL 60035

JOHNSON, BARBARA VESEY, cosmetic specialist, motivational speaker; b. San Diego, Oct. 1, 1952; d. James Lee and Jean Louise (Hastings) Vesey; m. Kenneth Campbell Johnson, Dec. 28, 1974; 1 child, Lucretia. BS, San Diego State U., 1974. Lic. cosmetologist. Owner, pres. Indian Art Wholesaler, Atlanta, 1973-78; spl. rep. Lydia O'Leary Cosmetics, East Rutherford, N.J., 1980-84; independent cosmetic therapist, make-up artist Atlanta, 1980—; cons. Jacqueline McClure Lupus Ctr., 1982—, Emory U. Egleston Children's Hosp., Atlanta, 1986—. Author: Beauty: Inside/Out, 1983. Coordinator vols. Found. Hosp. Art, Atlanta, 1985—; pres. Pub. Broadcasting Vols., 1978-81. Home and Office: Cosmetic Specialists 1293 Sylvan Cir NE Atlanta GA 30319

JOHNSON, BETH WEST, educator; b. Jacksonville, Ala., Jan. 19, 1950; d. Seymour Jr. and Sara (Fryar) West; 1 child, Stephen Lamar Jr. BS, U. N.C., Willington, 1975; MA, Jacksonville State U., 1978. Tchr. Wellborn Elem Sch., Anniston, Ala., 1975—. Treas. Parents Aux., Jacksonville, 1981-83; leader Girl Scouts U.S., Anniston, 1986-87. Mem. NEA, Ala. Edn. Assn., Calhoun County Edn. Assn. (rep. 1985-86). Methodist.

JOHNSON, BETTY LOU GUGE, dietitian; b. St. Louis, May 19, 1924; d. Lee Brown and Louise Susanna (Reitz) Guge; B.S. in Home Econs., U. Mo., 1945; m. Harold Arthur Johnson, Oct. 1, 1954 (dec. 1986); children—Christopher Arthur, Stephen Paul. Dietetic intern Michael Reese Hosp., Chgo., 1945; dietitian VA Hosp., Van Nuys, Calif., 1945-49, Portland, Oreg., 1949-51; relief cons. dietitian Md. Dept. Health and Mental Hygiene, 1972, 76; dept. head, dir. dietary services Pineview Gardens Nursing Home, Clinton, Md., 1967-70; instr. U. Md. Adult Edn. Center, College Park, 1977; cons. dietitian to 5 health care facilities Washington area, 1970—; mem. dietetic curriculum adv. com. No. Va. Community Coll.; mem. food mgmt. programs adv. com. Montgomery County Community Coll. (Md.); mem. adv. com. dietetic technician program Community Coll. Balt.; preceptor Hood Coll., Frederick, Md., U.S. Air Force dietetic interns Malcolm Grow Med. Ctr., Washington, Health Facilities Assn. Md. Edn. Com. Active PTA; den mother Cub Scouts, 1963-70; mem. Republican Nat. Com. Served with USAF, 1951-55; Korea. Mem. Am. Dietetic Assn. (registered; chmn. Cons. Dietitians-Health Care Facilities 1980-81, treas. 1978-79), Md. Found. Health Care, Md. Dietetic Assn. (chmn. div. consultation and pvt. practice 1985-86, pres. 1988—), Health Facilities Assn. Md. (mem. edn. com.), Nutrition Today Soc. Lutheran. Club: Officers' Wives Andrews AFB. Editor cookbooks for service orgns.; cons. editor Today's Nursing Home, 1980-83 (editorial adv. bd. 1983—); editorial adv. bd. Aging Network News, 1985—. Home and Office: 4080 Norbeck Square Dr Rockville MD 20853

JOHNSON, BEVERLY KAY, marketing executive; b. Ponca City, Okla., May 15, 1939; d. Maynard F. and Flossy N (Lowe) Sallee; children: Debi, Paul; m. Leif Johnson, June 1, 1987. BA, Pt. Loma Coll., 1961; MA, Calif. State U., 1967. Choral conductor Cen. Oregon Community Coll., Bend, 1970-80, Azusa (Calif.) Pacific U., 1980-81; owner Davis & Assoc., Brea, Calif., 1981—. Producer 2 videos, 12 audio tapes, 1986—. Fund raiser Easter Seals. Mem. Nat. Assn. Female Execs., So. Calif. Vocat. Edn. Orgn. (bd. dirs. 1964-69), Nat. Assn. Single Adult Leaders. Republican.

JOHNSON, BIRGITTA W., banker; b. Göteborg, Sweden, June 22, 1937; came to U.S., 1958; d. Sture V. and Rut I. (Andersson) Johansson; m. Roy A. Johnson, Apr. 29, 1967 (dec. 1982); 1 child, Soli R. BS, Quinnipiac Coll., 1976. With Bank of Boston Conn., 1958—, v.p., 1984—. Bd. dirs. St. Raphael Found., New Haven, 1981—, Jr. Achievement So. Cent. Conn., Wallingford, Conn., 1986—; bd. dirs., past pres. Internat. Ctr., New Haven, 1972—; founder Network Inc. of Conn., bd. dirs. 1980-82. Mem. Nat. Assn. Bank Women, New Haven C. of C. (vice chmn., bd. dirs. 1981-87). Lutheran. Club: Quinnipiack. Office: Bank of Boston Conn 135 Church St New Haven CT 06510

JOHNSON, BONNIE LAVERN, advertising executive; b. Atlantic City, N.J., Aug. 19, 1954; d. Lawrence Edward and Verna Mary (McPherson) McCall; m. Leonard Johnson, Nov. 9, 1980; children: Briana, Jason, Wyatt. BA, Hampton Inst., 1976; postgrad., Rutgers U., 1980. Graphic artist Civic Projects Co., Brigantine, N.J., 1976-78, Belford Printing Co., Ocean City, N.J., 1978-80; adminstrn. asst. Harrah's Marina Hotel-Casino, Atlantic City, 1980-81; mktg. dir. Am. Property Group, Inc., Atlantic City, 1984-86; prin. McCall Johnson Assocs., Linwood, N.J., 1986—; cons. econ. devel. adv. com. Galloway Township, N.J., 1986-87. Mem. Nat. Assn. Female Execs. Home: RD 4 Box 405C-1 Pleasantville NJ 08232

JOHNSON, CAROL ANN, book editor; b. Seattle, Aug. 19, 1941; d. Jack Rutherford and Marian Frances (Cole) Schisler; m. Gary L. Johnson, Sept. 8, 1962; children: Deborah Carol Erickson, Barbara Ann. Student, Bethany Sch. of Missions, Mpls., 1962. Typesetter Bethany Printing Div., Mpls., 1960-69; librarian Bethany Sch. of Missions, Mpls., 1969-79; mng. editor Bethany House Pubs., Mpls., 1980-84, editorial dir., 1984—. Office: Bethany House Pubs 6820 Auto Club Rd Minneapolis MN 55438

JOHNSON, CAROLINE, personnel executive; b. Hamburg, Fed. Republic of Germany, July 16, 1960; came to US., 1966; d. Hans Joachim and Ilse (Jansen) B. BA, U. Miss., 1981, BBA, 1985, postgrad., 1985—. Office mgr., trainer Munford, Inc, Majik Market div., Jackson, Miss., 1981-83; personnel, ins. asst. Super Sagless Corp., Tupelo, Miss., 1983—, quality circles coordinator, 1983-85; personnel, safety mgr. H&W Industries, Inc., Booneville, Miss., 1985-86; employee relations mgr. Malone & Hyde, Inc. Mega Market div., Memphis, 1986—; cons. safety seminar NE Miss. Jr. Coll., Booneville, 1986. Mem. lang. bank, World's Fair, Knoxville, Tenn., 1982; youth choir dir., counselor, Holy Trinity Luth. Ch., Tupelo, 1985-86. Recipient German Excellence cert. Groethe Inst., Atlanta, 1980, German Govt. award, U. Miss., 1979. Mem. Nat. Assn. Female Execs., Am. Soc. for Personnel Adminstrs., Miss. Mfrs. Assn. (employee relations com. 1985—), Zeta Tau Alpha. Republican. Lutheran. Club: German (Tupelo). Home: 3200 Pecan Lake Cir #207 Memphis TN 38115

JOHNSON, CATHERINE COMMON, newspaper executive; b. Watertown, N.Y., Feb. 12, 1914; d. James Allison and Minna (Anthony) Common; B.A., St. Lawrence U., 1935; M.S. in Journalism, Columbia U., 1937; m. John Brayton Johnson, June 21, 1941; children—John Brayton, Ann Catherine, Deborah Jane, Harold Bowtell. Reporter, editor Watertown (N.Y.) Daily Times, 1937-41, editorial and spl. features writer, 1950—; v.p., sec. Johnson Newspaper Corp., owners Watertown Daily Times, Batavia Daily News; dir. Creg Systems Corp., Watertown. Vice chmn. Thousand Islands State Park Commn. Recipient Alumni citation St. Lawrence U., 1972, Athletic Hall of Fame inductee, 1987. Mem. Nat. League Am. Pen Women, North Country Artists Guild, AAUW (pres. Jefferson br. 1981-82). Republican. Presbyterian. Club: Coll. Women of Jefferson County (pres. 1954-56). Home: 221 Flower Ave W Watertown NY 13601 Office: 260 Washington St Watertown NY 13601

JOHNSON, CATHERINE GRYMES, sales professional; b. Oklahoma City, Feb. 19, 1952; d. Herman Jr. and Mary (Visant) Grymes; m. Robert Dale Johnson; children: Justin Robert, Mary Elizabeth. Student, U. Tenn., 1970-71, Memphis State U., 1971-74. Rental agent Avis Rent-A-Car, Memphis, 1974; clk. The Galbreath Co., Memphis, 1974-75; sales rep. Cook-Treadwell & Harry, Inc., Memphis, 1975-76; dept. mgr. Internat. Harvester

Credit Corp., Memphis, 1976-81; customer service mgr. Am. Wallcoverings (div. The Arton Group), Memphis, 1981-82, retail store mgr., 1985-86; sales rep. The Arton Group, Memphis, 1985—. Mem. Olive Branch (Miss.) New Beginnings Civic Orgn., 1985—. Mem. Am. Soc. Internal Designers, Constrn. Specifications Inst., Pi Beta Phi. Club: King's Daughters (Memphis) (pres. 1970). Home: 7188 Larkfield Cove Olive Branch MS 38654

JOHNSON, CECILIA ANN, educator, researcher; b. Panama City, Fla., Nov. 22, 1940; d. Lott Warren and Cecilia Ann (Kuhlman) Middlemas; m. Joseph Asberry Johnson, Mar. 21, 1970. B.A., Agnes Scott Coll., 1962; M.A., Emory U., 1964, Ph.D., 1976. Golf profl. 1963; instr. Ga. State Coll., Atlanta, 1964-66; instr. world history Northwestern State U., Natchitoches, La., 1970-74, 85—. Pres. Natchitoches Humane Soc., 1972—; bd. dirs. La. Humane Soc., 1983—. Mem. Inst. Hist. Research (London), South Central Renaissance Conf., Met. Opera Guild, Audubon Soc. Democrat. Roman Catholic. Fla. State Women's Golf Assn. champion, 1956, 59. Avocations: reading; humane work; music. Home: 305 Poete St Natchitoches LA 71457

JOHNSON, CHARLENE ELIZABETH, language arts consultant, educator; b. Aurora, Ill., June 7, 1933; d. Floyd Clark and Marion Priscilla Smith; m. Bennett F. Johnson, July 25, 1955 (div. 1961): children—Roderick Julian, Marshall Floyd. BSE, Butler U., 1960, MSE, 1968, EdS, 1982. Classroom tchr. Indpls. Pub. Schs., 1960-68, reading tchr., 1968-71, lang. arts cons., 1972-82, reading tchr., 1982—; condr. parent workshops in reading Flanner House, 1980, 4 parent workshops, N.E. orgns., 1988. Author: Parent Primer, 1979. Instrumentalist, Butler U. Orch., C 2d Christian Ch. String Ensemble, Indpls. Philharm. Orch.; trainer reading tutors Pub. Housing Authority; vol. Ptnrs. Edn., Harshman Jr. High Sch.; Pres. Christian Women's Fellowship. Mem. Internat. Reading Assn., Indpls. Reading Assn., Ind. Reading Assn., Nat. Council Negro Women, NEA, Indpls. Edn. Assn., Ind. State Tchrs. Assn., NAACP, Delta Sigma Theta, Sigma Alpha Iota.

JOHNSON, CHARLOTTE VERNE, sales account executive; b. Tampa, Fla., Mar. 26, 1944; d. Calvin Phylemon and Theda Karleen J. B, Kans. State U., 1966. Acct. mgr., office mgr. Rainbow Photo, Kansas City, Kans., 1966-70, plant mgr., sales rep., 1970-74; regional mgr. GAF Corp., Wayne, N.J., 1974-78; sales rep. Olympus Corp., Woodbury, N.Y., 1978-80, regional mgr., 1980-81, dir. nat. accts., 1981-83, v.p. sales, 1983-85, v.p. nat. accts., 1985—; supplier rep. Catalog Showroom Merchandiser, 1982-83, Discount Store News, 1984. Photographer Kansas City Zool. Gardens, 1976-78, Breed mag., 1977-78, Am. Kennel Club, 1976-78. Mem. Nat. Premium Sales Execs., Nat. Assn. Female Execs., Photo Mktg. Assn., Nat. Arbor Soc., Nat. Wildlife Soc., Leavenworth (Kans.) Kennel Club. Office: Olympus Corp Crossways Park Woodbury NY 11791

JOHNSON, CHRISTINE MELSTER, business executive; b. Superior, Wis., Mar. 27, 1939; d. Lars Otto and Evelyn Margaret (Melster) Larson; m. Elert Marlin Johnson, June 20, 1959; children—Beverly Melster, Janet Halls, Eric Marlin. Ed. pub. schs. Pres., Identification Services, Inc., Mpls., 1976—. Mem. Twin West C. of C. (exec. com. and sec. 1984-85, bd. dirs. 1980—), Nat. Assn. Women Bus. Owners, Mpls. C. of C., Minn. Direct Mktg. Assn. (treas. 1978-80). Republican. Presbyterian. Avocation: bridge. Home: 3218 Flag N Minneapolis MN 55427 Office: Identification Services Inc 3410 Winnetka N Minneapolis MN 55427

JOHNSON, CONSTANCE HOWIE, academic program director, educator; b. Winston-Salem, N.C., Oct. 29, 1939; d. Ulysses and Susie (Morrison) Howie; m. Victor Johnson, Jr., June 9, 1962; 1 child, La Tanja Kim. BA, N.C. Cen. U., 1961; MS, N.C. A&T State U., 1966; PhD, So. Ill. U., 1973. Tchr. Winston-Salem County Schs., 1962-65, social worker, 1966-67; couselor Winston-Salem State U., 1967-70, prof. psychology, 1967—, dir. counseling, 1971-78, dir. gen. studies, 1978-86, dir. devel. edn. and testing, 1986—; sch. psychologist North Wilksboro (N.C.) City Schs., 1973. Chair Winston-Salem Community Assessment, 1976-77, Human Relations Commn., Winston-Salem, 1983-84; bd. dirs. ARC, Urban League, 1980—. Mem. N.C. Assn. Devel. Studies, Nat. Assn. Devel. Edn., Alpha Kappa Alpha. Republican. Methodist. Home: 2315 Manchester St Winston-Salem NC 27105

JOHNSON, DEBBIE LOUISE, librarian; b. Kinder, La., Dec. 14, 1957; d. Calvin and Mary Jane (Johnson) Delafoisse; widowed; 1 child, Tariq Daniel-le. BA, McNeese State U., 1979. Customer service rep. The Houston Post Co., 1982, sec., 1982-83, account exec., 1983-84; headstart tchr. Allen Action Agy., Kinder, 1984-85; br. librarian Allen Parish Police Jury, Kinder, 1985—; book rev. columnist So. Consumers Times, Lafayette, La., 1987—; storyteller, program dir. Allen Parish Library, Kinder, 1985—, founder credit union, 1987; owner Lucky Heart Cosmetics, 1987. Youth dir. Greater First Bapt. Ch., Kinder, 1987. Mem. ALA, Pub. Library Assn., La. Library Assn., Nat. Assn. Female Execs. Democrat. Home: PO Box 625 Kinder LA 70648 Office: Allen Parish Library PO Box 637 Kinder LA 70648

JOHNSON, DEBORAH JEAN, real estate company executive; b. Phoenix, Apr. 24, 1953; d. Forrest Willard and Pauline Laverne (Childress) Long; m. Barry Williams Eisenach, Feb. 16, 1974 (div. 1980); m. Albert Austin Johnson, Jan. 24, 1981 (div. 1984); children: Justin Edward, Lisa Marie. Student, Mesa Jr. Coll., 1971-72, Westminster Community Coll, 1977; cert., Jones Real Estate Sch., 1983, Legal Awareness Tng. Program, 1987. Receptionist, sec. Telecommunications Inc., Denver, 1972-73; office mgr. United Drywall & Painting Inc., Denver, 1973-80; bookkeeper, asst. acct. Gam & Co., Portland, Oreg., 1981; controller Realities Inc., Denver, 1983-84; real estate assoc. ERA Award RRealty, Arvada, Colo., 1985-86, Re/Max West Inc., Arvada, 1986—; acct. Smith, Brooks, Bolshoun & Co., Denver, 1980. Coach, Arvada Soccer Assn., 1985-86. Mem. Colo. Assn. Realtors, Realtor Corpac 99 Club. Home: 6773 Welch Ct Arvada CO 80004 Office: Re/Max West Inc 8600 Ralston Rd Arvada CO 80002

JOHNSON, DEBORAH SUE, consultant archaeology and forensic civil research; b. Rochester, N.Y., May 18, 1948; d. Hobart Warren and Jean Phyllis (Bassage) Hondorf; m. Michael Chee Johnson, Aug. 14, 1976; children: Kristi Anne, Ryan Michael. BA in Anthropology, SUNY, Binghamton, 1970; MA in Anthropology, U. Ariz., Tucson, 1972; postgrad., Ariz. State U., Phoenix, 1974—. Cert. community coll. tchr., Ariz. Instr. anthropology Mesa Community Coll., Phoenix, 1976-79; civil designer WBC (Griner Engineering), Phoenix, 1979, Collar, Williams and White Engring., Phoenix, 1979-81, Henningson, Durham and Richardson Engring., Phoenix, 1984-88; photogrammetrist, civil designer, archaeologist, dir. mktg. Andrews Atherton, Inc., Phoenix, 1984-87; prin. Research Assocs., Phoenix, 1987—. Contbr. numerous articles to profl. jours. NSF grantee, 1970. Subcom. chmn. Internat. Soc. for Photogrammetry and Remote Sensing Com. II, 1984-88, dir. ISPRS Analytical Instrument Workshop, 1986-87, Phoenix, Mem. Am. Soc. for Photogrammetry and Remote Sensing (editor Guide to Manufacture of Analytical Instruments, 1984-88), Soc. for Am. Archaeology, Soc. for Indsl. Archaeology, Profl. Assn. Diving Instrs. (cert. advanced diver with night specialty). Methodist. Club: Al Houris Middle Eastern and North African Dance Co. (dir. 1976—). Home and Office: 10211 S 43rd Pl Phoenix AZ 85044

JOHNSON, D'ELAINE ANN HERARD, artist; b. Puyallup, Wash., Mar. 19, 1932; d. Thomas Napoleon and Rosella Edna (Berry) Herard; m. John Laffette Johnson, Dec. 22, 1956. B.F.A., Central Wash. U., 1954; M.F.A., U. Wash., 1958, postgrad. U. London, 1975—. Instr. art Seattle Pub. Schs., 1954-78, Mus. History and Industry, Seattle, 1954-56; dir. Mt. Olympus Estate, Edmonds, Wash., 1971; cons. art groups, Wash. State, 1954—. lectr. Cen. Wash. State U., Seattle PTA, Creative Arts Assn., Everett, Everett Community Coll., Women's Caucus for Art, Seattle, numerous others; served as art juror for numerous shows. Founder Mt. Olympus Preserve for Arts, Edmonds, Wash., 1971, sponsor art events, 1971—; active Wash. Coalition Citizens with Disabilities. Exhibited in group shows: Fry Art Mus., Seattle, 1964, Seattle Art Mus., 1959, Henry Art Gallery, Seattle, Vancouver Maritime Mus., B.C., Can., 1981, N.S. Art Mus., Can., 1971, Whatcom Mus., Bellingham, Wash., 1975, State Capitol Mus., Olympia, Wash., 1975, Corvallis State U., Oreg., 1982, Newport Mus., Oreg., Nat. Artist Equity, 1972; over 300 exhibits 1950—, over 1200 paintings through 1970. Elected to Wash. State Art Commn. Registry, Olympia, 1982; recipient numerous awards. Mem. Nat. Artist Equity, Internat. Soc. Artists, The Cousteau Soc., Am. Council for Arts, Nat. Women's Studies Assn., Assn. Am. Culture, Internat. Platform Assn., Kappa Delta Pi, Kappa Pi. Avocations: scuba diving, camping, travel, violin, writing. Home and Office: 16122 73d St Ave W Edmonds WA 98020

JOHNSON, DENA NANCEAN, real estate executive; b. Des Moines, May 31, 1944; d. William W. and Genevieve Garland (Myrick) den Hartog; student Central Coll., Pella, Iowa, 1962-65, Coe Coll., summer 1965; B.A., Central Mo. State U., 1968; student Dijon (France) U., summer 1967; postgrad. Fla. State U., 1969; interior design cert. Griffith Opportunity Sch., 1975; m. Richard K. Johnson, Jan. 9, 1965; children—Scot Richard, Kurt William. Tchr. Gadsen County Sch. System, Quincy, Fla., 1969; with Junction Realty, Evergreen, Colo., 1977-79; salesman Pine Ridge Realty, Evergreen, 1979-80; v.p. Tamarac Ltd., Evergreen, 1978-82, Tamarac II, Ltd., 1982—; salesman, treas. Tamarac Homes, Ltd., Evergreen, 1974-82. Pres. Bear Mountain Homeowners' Assn., 1980-82. Lic. real estate salesman, Colo. Mem. Nat. Assn. Realtors, Colo. Assn. Realtors, AAUW (charter mem. Lakewood), PEO, Beta Constrn. Mgmt., Inc. (v.p. 1985—). Mem. Unity Ch. Office: 2785 W Hampden Ave Englewood CO 80110

JOHNSON, DIANA LYNN, law clerk; b. Pearisburg, Va., Dec. 23, 1954; d. Ted James Sr. and Thelma Ilene (Kirk) J. BS, Radford U., 1977. Law clk. Warren, Gibb and Scheid, P.C., Narrows, Va., 1977—; cons. Anderson and Assocs., Inc., Blacksburg, Va., 1983-84; abstractor Record Data Va., Richmond, 1985—. Author poetry book. Campaign mgr. Dem. Ted Johnson Jr. for Congress, 9th Dist. Va., 1974. Mem. Relief Soc., DAR (invitee). Mormon. Home: 1501 Wenonah Ave Pearisburg VA 24134 Office: Warren Gibb and Scheid PC 225 Main St Narrows VA 24124

JOHNSON, DIANE SEELYE, wholesale distributor executive, accountant; b. Pueblo, Colo., Aug. 25, 1933; d. John Clarence and Vula Vona (Ward) Seelye; m. Leonard L. Johnson, Dec. 26, 1952; children—Michael Owen, Lori Lynn, Charles Leonard. B.S. with distinction in Bus. Adminstrn., U. So. Colo., 1974. X-ray technician, Pueblo, Colo., 1952, 56; treas., dir. Central Pipe and Supply Co., Houston, 1976-79, exec. v.p., dir., 1979—; sec., dir. Central Threading, Inc., Channelview, Tex., 1981—. Recipient Merit award Am. Soc. Women Accts., Denver, 1974. Mem. Now, Women's Equity Action League, Nat. Women's Polit. Caucus, Com. of 200. Office: Cen Pipe and Supply Co 13231 Champion Forest Dr Suite 101 Houston TX 77069

JOHNSON, DIXIE RACHEL, finance executive; b. Wendell, Minn., Jan. 4, 1934; d. Clarence William and Ruth Evelyn (Kube) Lacey; m. Donald Walter Johnson, Aug. 16, 1952; children: Deborah, Garret, Holly. Grad. high sch., Elbow Lake, Minn. Bookkeeper Fergus Falls (Minn.) Hatchery, 1951-52; sec. State Farm Ins. Co., Bemidji, Minn., 1966-67; bookkeeper Rock River Cablevision, Inc., Sterling, Ill., 1968-70; v.p. Lakeland Cablevision, Inc., Detroit Lakes, Minn., 1971-78, pres., 1978-86; v.p. Cablevision, Inc., Detroit Lakes, 1985-86; mgr. personal finances Detroit Lakes, 1986—; mem. Indsl. Devel. Corp., Detroit Lakes, 1979—; bd. dirs. 1st Nat. Bank, Detroit Lakes. Alderman-at-large Detroit Lakes City Council, 1979—, mem. fire dept. com., 1979, mem. ordinance charter com., 1979, chair community devel. com., 1983—; chair Downtown Redevel. Adv. Com., Detroit Lakes, 1979-86, Com. to Re-Elect Congreeman, Detroit Lakes, 1982; chair bd. dirs. Detroit Lakes United Way, 1983—; mem. State Rep. Election Com., Detroit Lakes, 1984, 86; chmn. gov. bd. St. Marys Hosp., 1988—. Named Woman of Yr., Detroit Lakes Bus. and Profl. Women, 1986. Mem. LWV (charter), Detroit Lakes C. of C. (chmn. membership drive 1988), Beta Sigma Phi (pres. Detroit Lakes chpt. 1985-86). Republican. Methodist. Home and Office: 1095 Villa Ln Detroit Lakes MN 56501

JOHNSON, DOROTHY BERTRAM, lawyer; b. Chgo., Mar. 15, 1947; d. Frederick Jacob and Pauline (Otte) Bertram. B.A., Miami U., 1968; J.D., Ill. Inst. Tech., Chgo. Kent Coll. Law, 1973; student S. P. Chase Law Sch., Cin., 1968-70. Bar: Ill. 1973. Ptnr. Bertram & Johnson, Chgo., 1973; asst. Cook County states atty., Chgo., 1973-75; sole practice law, Chgo., 1975-76; ptnr. Johnson & Arnel, Chgo., 1976-85; chmn. bd. dirs., sec., Chgo. Dance Medium, 1983-85; benefit subcom. chmn., com. mem. Chgo. Repertory Dance Ensemble; instr. Walton div. Indsl. Coll. Engring., Chgo., 1981-85; mem. adv. com. Bus. Inst. of Chgo. City-Wide Colls., 1986—. Mem. Christian Indsl. League-Grainger Hall Steering com., 1983—. Mem. ABA, Chgo. Bar Assn. (mem. matrimonial law com. 1981—, co-chairperson tax subcom. 1984, 86, chairperson 1987), Ill. State Bar Assn., Chgo. Kent Alumni Assn. Presbyterian. Club: University (Chgo.). Home: 100 E Walton Chicago IL 60611 Office: Johnson & Assocs 10 N Dearborn St Chicago IL 60602

JOHNSON, DOROTHY PHYLLIS, counselor, art therapist; b. Kansas City, Mo., Sept. 13, 1925; d. Chris C. and Mabel T. (Gillum) Green; B.A. in Art, Ft. Hays. State U., 1975, M.S. in Guidance and Counseling, 1976, M.A. in Art, 1979; m. Herbert E. Johnson, May 11, 1945; children—Michael E., Gregory K. Art therapist High Plains Comprehensive Mental Health Assn., Hays, Kans., 1975-76; art therapist, mental health counselor Sunflower Mental Health Assn., Concordia, Kans., 1976—, co-dir. Project Togetherness, 1976-77, coordinator partial hospitalization, 1978—, out-patient therapist, 1982—; dir. Swedish Am. State Bank, Courtland, Kans., 1960—, sec., 1973-77. Mem. Kans., Am. art therapy assns., Am. Mental Health Counselors Assn., Am. Assn. for Counseling and Devel., Kans. Assn. for Counseling and Devel., Assn. for Humanistic Psychologists, Assn. Transpersonal Psychologists, Assn. Specialists in Group Work, Phi Delta Kappa, Phi Kappa Phi. Contbr. articles to profl. jours. Home: Box 200 Courtland KS 66939 Office: 520 B Washington St Concordia KS 66901

JOHNSON, EDDIE BERNICE, senator; b. Waco, Tex., Dec. 3, 1935; d. Lee Edward and Lillie Mae (White) J.; m. Lacy Kirk Johnson, July 5, 1956 (div. Oct. 1970); 1 child, Dawrence Kirk. Diploma in Nursing, St. Mary's Coll. of South Bend, 1955; BS in Nursing, Tex. Christian U., 1967; MPH in Pub. Adminstrn., So. Meth. U., 1976; LLD (hon.), Bishop Coll. and Jarvis Christian Coll., 1979. Chief psychiat. nurse psychotherapist Vets. Hosp., Dallas, 1956-72; state rep. Tex. Ho. Reps. Dist. 33, Dallas, 1972-77; regional dir. HEW, Dallas, 1977-79; exec. asst. to adminstr. for primary health care policy HEW, Washington, 1979-81; v.p. Vis. Nurse Assn. of Tex., Dallas, 1981-87; cons. div. urban affairs Zales Corp., Dallas, 1976-77; exec. asst. personnel div. Neiman-Marcus, Dallas, 1972-75. Elected mem. Ho. of Reps. Dist. 33, 1972; Tex. senator, Dist. 23, 1986—; bd. dirs. ARC. Recipient Citizenship award Nat. Conf. Christians and Jews, 1985; named an Outstanding Alumnus St. Mary's Coll. of Nursing, 1986. Mem. Alpha Kappa Alpha. Office: Tex State Senate PO Box 12068 Austin TX 78711

JOHNSON, EILEEN MORGAN, lawyer; b. Pitts., Jan. 28, 1957; d. Michael Joseph and Regina Cecelia (Mahoney) Morgan; m. William F. Johnson; 1 child, Jennifer Ann. Student, Rutgers U., 1975-77; BA in Govt., Coll. William and Mary, 1979; postgrad., Oxford U., Eng., 1980; JD, Brigham Young U., 1981. Bar: Va. 1982, Calif. 1984. Assoc. Bagwell & Compton, Grundy, Va., 1982-83, Hyatt Legal Services, Springfield, Va., 1983, Blake & Smith, Del Mar, Calif., 1984-85; assoc. gen. counsel Nat. Wildlife Fedn., Vienna, Va. and Washington, 1986—. Advisor 77th/71st Highlanders, Inc., New Carrollton, Md., 1985—; bd. dirs. Fair Oaks Farms Homeowners Assn., Inc. Chantilly, Va., 1986—. Mem. ABA, Va. Bar Assn., Calif. Bar Assn., Kappa Delta (editor 1987—). Democrat. Office: Nat Wildlife Fedn 1412 16th St NW Washington DC 20036

JOHNSON, ELAINE LOUISE, meetings specialist, consultant; b. Worcester, Mass., July 31, 1942; d. Gladys Louise Davis; m. William Johnson, Feb. 1, 1961 (div. 1966). AS, Becker Jr. Coll., 1962; cert., Pan Am. Sch. Travel, N.Y.C., 1985. Exec. sec. L.W. Frolich & Co., N.Y.C., 1969-75; media planner Medicus Communications, N.Y.C., 1975-76; traffic mgr. Medicus Intercon Internat., N.Y.C., 1976-77, asst. account exec., 1977-79, account exec., 1978-81; account exec. Medicus Intercon Ltd., London, 1982; sr. project dir. Profl. Postgrad. Services, Secaucus, N.J., 1983-85; meetings specialist Conf. Planning, N.Y.C., 1985—. Mem. Meetings Cons. Network, Pharm. Advt. Council, Mass. Soc. Mayflower Descs. Home and Office: 222 E 80th St New York NY 10021

JOHNSON, ELISABETH SUSAN LYNN, data processing executive; b. Bucyrus, Ohio, July 12, 1959; d. James Theodore and Betty Jean (Walker) J. Student, Bliss Coll., 1986—. Dir. data processing Bible Lit. Internat., Columbus, Ohio, 1980—; software cons. Ohio State U., Columbus, 1985, small bus. office automation and database design, 1988—. Author: (poems) American Poetry Anthology, 1987, Cambridge Collection, 1987, Natchez Series, 1987. Vol. Rosemont Bible Sch., Columbus, 1983-85, Teen Challenge, Columbus, 1980, The Better Way; mem. Life Commn., Columbus, Friend of the Library, Upper Sandusky, Ohio. Mem. Nat. Assn. Female Execs., Am. Mgmt. Assn. Office: Bible Lit Internat 625 E North Broadway Columbus OH 43214

JOHNSON, ELIZABETH ANN, research analyst, businesswoman; b. Sanford, N.C., July 21, 1949; d. James Arlon and Freda Elizabeth (Frazier) J. BA summa cum laude, U. N.C., Wilmington, 1976; MBA magna cum laude, Campbell U., Buies Creek, N.C., 1980. Personnel mgr. Miller & Rhoads, Fayetteville, N.C., 1976-77; dir. research and program evaluation Cumberland County Mental Health and Mental Retardation Ctr., Fayetteville, 1977-81; supervisory intelligence research specialist Joint Spl. Ops. Command, Ft. Bragg, N.C., 1982—; EEO officer Joint Spl. Ops. Command, 1987—; v.p. Personal Accents, retail sales, Fayetteville, 1986—. Mem. AAUW, Am. Soc. Profl. and Exec. Women, Nat. Assn. Female Execs., Beta Sigma Phi. Republican. Home: 1219 Stansfield Dr Fayetteville NC 28303 Office: Joint Spl Ops Command PO Box 70239 Fort Bragg NC 28307

JOHNSON, ELIZABETH ANNA EDWARDS, geophysicist; b. Hartford, Calif., Feb. 21, 1956; d. Raymond Wright and Judith Grace (Cooper) Edwards; m. Mark Harold Johnson, June 10, 1978. BS, Harvey Mudd Coll., 1978; postgrad., Calif. State U., Long Beach, 1984. Research helper Union Oil Co., Brea, Calif., 1977; geophys. technician Union Oil Co., Los Angeles, 1978-79; geophysicist trainee Union Oil Co., 1979-80, geophysicist, 1980-84; area geophysicist Unocal, Los Angeles, 1984—. Editor Cucumonga Fault Zone, 1986. Vice chmn. region 67 Libertarian party Calif., San Dimas, 1984; judge Calif. State Sci. Fair, Los Angeles, 1986. Mem. Assn. Women Geoscientists (pres. 1984-85, dir. 1983-86), Soc. Exploration Geophysicists (sec. Pacific Coast sect. 1984), Am. Geophys. Union, Los Angeles Basin Geol. Soc. Club: Union Royal Toastmasters (Los Angeles) (pres. 1985). Home: 1550 Somerset Way Upland CA 91786 Office: Unocal 1201 W 5th St Los Angeles CA 90017

JOHNSON, ELIZABETH DIANE LONG, lawyer; b. Pasadena, Calif., Nov. 16, 1945; d. Volney Earl and Sylvia Irene (Drury) Long; m. Lynn Douglas Johnson, Oct. 22, 1966; 1 child, Barbara Annette. BA, U. of Houston, 1967; JD, Rutgers U., 1980. Bar: N.J. 1980, U.S. Dist. Ct. N.J. 1980, Pa. 1984, U.S. Supreme Ct. 1986. Sole practice Riverside, N.J., 1980—; Pub. defender, Riverside Twp., 1988.; speaker's bur. Comprehensive Justice Ctr. Burlington County, 1987—. Mem. Tenby Chase Civic Assn., Delran, N.J., 1972-87, treas. 1976, v.p. 1974; trustee Drenk Mental Health Ctr., 1988—. Mem. ABA, N.J. Bar Assn., Burlington County Bar Assn., Assn. Trial Lawyers Am. N.J., Internat. Platform Assn., Mensa, Phi Alpha Delta, Delta Gamma. Methodist. Office: 23 Scott St Suite C PO Box 274 Riverside NJ 08075

JOHNSON, ELIZABETH HELEN, real estate broker; b. Atlantic, N.J., Dec. 21, 1936; d. James Daniel and Helen (Figenshu) Byrne; m. Wesley Johnson Jr. (dec. 1974); children: Wesley III, Carolyn, Stephen, James. RN, Misercordia, Phila., 1957. Lic. real estate broker, 1980. Nurse Atlantic City Hosp., 1957-58, head nurse, 1958-62; sales assoc. Fox & Lazo, Inc., Ocean City, N.J., 1976-85; ind. real estate broker Ocean City, 1985—. Organizer Rosco D. Brown Youth Ctr., 1964-74. Mem. Nat. Assn. Realtors, N.J. Bd. Realtors, Ocean City Bd. Realtors (grievance bd. 1986—), Bus. and Profl. Womens, N.J., Pa. RNs, N.J. Assn. Women Bus. Owners, Concerned Parents of N.J. (charter mem.). Lodge: Soroptomist Internat. Office: 1145 Asbury Ave Ocean City NJ 08226

JOHNSON, ELLEN BULLOCK, realtor; b. Luzerne, Pa., Sept. 21, 1949; d. Leonard Samuel and Dolores (Zurinski) B.; m. Wilbur James Johnson Jr., Feb. 14, 1970; children: Adam Michael, Brandon Hamilton. BA, Glassboro State Coll., 1971; MSEd, Monmouth Coll., 1983. Cert. tchr. English, Md. Statistician FBI, Washington, 1972-76; tchr. English City of Balt., 1978-79; supr. transp. Millstone Twsp. Schs., Clarksburg, N.J., 1983-86; cons. E.W. Murray Assocs., Inc., Howell, N.J., 1986-87; realtor Wegner Realty, Howell, 1987—. Bd. dirs. Howell Twsp. Bd. Edn., 1983—, v.p. 1984, pres. 1985, 87; bd. dirs. Help Our Kids of Howell, 1986-87; sec. Howell Twp. Dem. Club, 1987. Mem. Nat. Sch. Bds. Assn., Monmouth County Sch. Bds. Assn., N.J. Sch. Bds. Assn., South Monmouth Bd. Realtors, Ocean County Bd. Realtors. Democrat. Roman Catholic. Home: 31 Monticello Dr Howell NJ 07731 Office: Wegner Realty 2178 Rt 9 Howell NJ 07731

JOHNSON, ELLEN CHRISTINE, health care public relations and advertising; b. St. Paul, Mar. 10, 1948; d. Arnold Elwood and Betty Jane (Bruening) Damsgaard; m. Neal Frank Johnson, June 21, 1969; 1 child, April Holly. BA in Advt., U. Minn., 1971; MBA in Mktg., Coll. St. Thomas, 1985. Dir. pub. relations Children's Home Soc. Minn., St. Paul, 1971-73, asst. dir. devel., 1973-78; coordinator pub. relations Minn. Hosp. Assn., Mpls., 1978-80; dir. mktg., pub. relations Unity Med. Ctr., Mpls., 1980-83; exec. dir. Unity Health Found., Mpls., 1983-85; mgr. mktg. product Health One Corp., Mpls., 1985-87; pres. Stiles/Bradley/Johnson, Inc., Mpls., 1987—. Contbg. author: Fifty Effective Print Ads for Hospitals, 1986, Profiles in Hospital Marketing, 1984; editor (newsletter) Women in Sr Mgmt., 1987. Recipient Mpls. YWCA Leadership award, 1985, MacEachern citation Acad. Hosp. Pub. Relations, 1979. Fellow Am. Soc. for Hosp. Mktg. and Pub. Relations (pres. 1985); mem. Pub. Relations Soc. Am. (accredited, pres. Minn. chpt. 1982, Silver Anvil award 1983), Minn. chpt. Am. Mktg. Assn. Presbyterian. Office: Stiles/Bradley/Johnson Inc Ct Internat 238N 2550 Universtiy Ave W Saint Paul MN 55115

JOHNSON, ELLEN RANDEL, real estate broker; b. Canton, Miss., May 9, 1916; d. Robert Colquhoun and Laura Arabella (Taylor) R.; m. Floyd Everett Johnson Sr.; children: Dolly Mae Johnson Day, Floyd Everett Johnson Jr. Student, Blue Mountain Coll., 1934-35; course in real estate, Miss. Realtors Inst., 1976-77. Bookkeeper E. Constantin, Jr., Yazoo City, Miss., 1951-54, 56-59; draftsman Miss. State Hwy. Dept., Yazoo City, 1955; office mgr. Miss. Chem. Corp. Fed. Credit Union, Yazoo City, 1963-66; freelance journalist Yazoo Herald, 1970-74; broker, owner Ellen Johnson Realty, Yazoo, 1977; broker, assoc. Phyllis Waltman Realtors and Century 21 Beard & McMahan Realtors, Hattiesburg, Miss., 1978-79; broker, owner Ellen Johnson, Realtor, Hattiesburg, 1980—. Author: The Dining Table for Candida Patients, 1988; contbr. articles to profl. jours. Charter dir. Yazoo Arts Council, 1973-75; chmn. civic quiz Am. Bus. Women's Assn., Hattiesburg, 1987. Mem. Nat. Assn. Realtors (Omega Tau Rho medal 1984), Nat. Women's Council Realtors, Miss. Women's Council Realtors (gov. 1984, v.p. 1983-84, by-laws chmn. 1984, Realtor of Yr. 1984), Hattiesburg Women's Council Realtors (v.p. 1982-83, Realtor of Yr. 1984), Miss. Assn. Realtors (by-laws com.), Hattiesburg Bd. Realtors (bd. dirs., com. chmn. 1979, 81, 84, v.p. multiple listing service 1982-83, pres. 1983-84, treas. 1987, Realtor of Yr. 1984). Republican. Baptist. Clubs: Mozart (Yazoo City) (pres. 1969); Miss. Music (Jackson) (jr. festival chmn. 1973-75). Home: 1302 Estelle Hattiesburg MS 39402 Office: 2604 O'Ferrall Hattiesburg MS 39402

JOHNSON, EVELYN BRYAN, flying service executive; b. Corbin, Ky., Nov. 4, 1909; d. Edward William and Mayme Estelle (Fox) Stone; grad. Tenn. Wesleyan Jr. Coll., 1929; student U. Tenn., 1930-32; m. Wyatt J. Bryan, Mar. 21, 1931 (dec. 1963); m. 2d, Morgan N. Johnson, Feb. 25, 1965 (dec. 1977). With Morristown (Tenn.) Flying Service, Inc., 1947—, chief flight instr., 1949—, sec.-treas., 1949-62, pres., 1962-82; mgr. Moore Murrell Airport, 1962—. Gov.'s appointee Tenn. Aero. Commn., 1983-86, v. chmn., 1987—. Recipient Carnegie Hero medal, 1958, Service to Mankind award Morristown Sertoma Club, 1981; named Flight Instr. of Yr., Nashville dist., 1973, 79, So. region, 1979, Nat., 1979 (all FAA); Outstanding Alumnus, Tenn. Wesleyan Coll., 1981. Mem. Morristown Area C. of C., Nat. Assn. Flight Instrs. (dir., treas. 1987—), Ninety-Nines, Whirly Girls, Aircraft Owners and Pilots Assn., CAP, Silver Wings (Woman of Yr. 1981). Republican. Baptist. Home: Rural Rt 1 Osage Hills Jefferson City TN 37760 Office: PO Box 1013 Morristown TN 37816

JOHNSON, FELICIA LYNNE, government official; b. Meridian, Miss., Aug. 10, 1961; d. Earlie Jr. and Barbara Ann (Crosby) Gettis; m. Oscar Johnson Jr., Dec. 28, 1985; 1 child, Cortnea Shondrei. BS in Computer Sci., Miss. Valley State U., 1985. Computer programmer Miss. Valley State U.,

Itta Bena, Miss., 1981-84; gen. supply intern U.S. Dept. Def., Texarkana, Tex., 1985; gen. supply specialist U.S. Dept. Def., Warren, Mich., 1985-87, inventory mgmt. specialist, 1987—. Mem. Nat. Assn. Female Execs. Democrat. Baptist. Home: 21682 Stratford Ct Oak Park MI 48237

JOHNSON, FRANCES FLAHERTY, retired educator, career development specialist; b. Hamlet, N.C., Feb. 23, 1916; d. John Lawrence and Mary Elizabeth (Shortridge) Flaherty; m. Clifton Jerome Johnson, Nov. 27, 1940 (dec. 1953); 1 child, Carolyn Johnson Koch. BS, State Tchrs. Coll., Fredricksburg, Va., 1936; MEd, U. N.C., 1958; postgrad. U. Oslo, 1963, U. Vienna, Austria, 1967; student Shetland Islands tradition and crafts, Leriwck, Eng., 1979. Tchr. Cumberland County Schs., Godwin, N.C., 1936-37; tchr. Aberdeen Schs., N.C., 1937-39, prin., 1939-41; counselor Fayetteville Schs., N.C., 1958-64, Winston-Salem Forsyth Schs., N.C., 1964-65; cons. Dept. Pub. Instrn., Raleigh, N.C., 1965-71; project dir. Dare-Hyde-Tyrrell Schs., Manteo, N.C., 1971-73; vocat. counselor Wake Schs., Raleigh, 1973-74; now ret. contbg. mem. Smithsonian Inst., Washington, 1988— ; active SITES and outreach programs. Mem. Am. Assn. for Adult and Continuing Edn. (del. for people-to-people visit to Soviet Union and to People's Republic China 1983), Am. Assn. for Counseling Devel., Asia Soc. Avocation: traveling.

JOHNSON, GAIL DELORIES, forensic chemist, toxicologist; b. Chgo., Sept. 30, 1957; d. Roger George and Delories B. (Reppert) J. BS in Chemistry, No. Ill. U., 1980. Quality control chemist Standard Pharmacal Corp., Elgin, Ill., 1980; forensic chemist Ill. Racing Bd. Lab., Elgin, 1980-82, Analytical Techs., Inc., Tempe, Ariz., 1982-84; analytical chemist Nichols Inst., San Juan Capistrano, Calif., 1985-87; forensic chemist, toxicologist Reference Lab., Colton, Calif., 1987—. Mem. Am. Chem. Soc., Am. Inst. Chemists. Office: Reference Labs 952 S Mt Vernon PO Box 670 Colton CA 92324

JOHNSON, GERALDINE ESCH, language specialist; b. Steger, Ill., Jan. 5, 1921; d. William John Rutkowski and Estella Anna (Mannel) Pietz; m. Richard William Esch, Oct. 12, 1940 (dec. 1971); children: Janet L. Sohngen, Daryl R., Gary Michael; m. Henry Bernard Johnson, Aug. 23, 1978 (dec. 1988). BSBA, U. Denver, 1955, MA in Edn., 1958, MA in Speech Pathology, 1963; vocat. credential, U. No. Colo., 1978; postgrad., Metropolitan State Coll. Cert. speech therapist, Colo.; cert. tchr., Colo. Tchr. music Judith St. John Sch. Music, Denver, 1946-52; tchr. West High Sch., Denver, 1955-61, chmn. bus. edn. dept., 1958-61, reading specialist, 1977-78; speech therapist, founder South Denver Speech Clinic, 1965-71; tchr. Educationally Handicapped Resource Rm., Denver, 1971-74, Diagnostic Ctr., The Belmont Sch., Denver, 1974-77; speech-lang. specialist elem. and jr. high schs., Denver, 1978 86; itinerant speech-lang. specialist various elem. and jr. high schs., Denver, 1978—; ret. Denver Pub. Sch. System, 1986; home lang tchr. Early Childhood Edn., Denver, 1975; mem. Ednl. TV Adv. com., Colo.; sec. Cen. Bus. Edn. Com., Colo; tchr. letter writing clinics, local bus., Denver, 1960—. Former judge Colo. State Speech Festival; demonstrator, lectr. Speech-Lang. and Learning Disabilities area Colo. Edn. Assn., 1971-73. Recipient Spl. Edn. award Denver Pub. Schs., 1986. Mem. Speech-Lang.-Hearing Assn. (cert.), U. Denver Sch. Bus. Alumni Bd., Beta Gamma Sigma, Kappa Delta Pi, Delta Pi Epsilon. Home: 2780 S Vance Way Denver CO 80227

JOHNSON, GWENAVERE A., artist; b. Newark, S.D., Oct. 16, 1909; d. Arthur E. and Susie Ellen (King) Nelson; m. John Wendell Johnson, Dec. 17, 1937; 1 son, John Forrest. Student Mpsl. Sch. Art, 1930; B.A., U. Minn., 1937; M.A., San Jose State U., 1957. Cert. gen. elem., secondary, art tchr., Calif. Art tchr., supr. Austin (Minn.) Schs., 1937-38; art tchr. Hillbrook Sch., Los Gatos, Calif., 1947-52; art tchr., supr. Santa Clara (Calif.) Pub. Schs., 1952-55; art tchr., dept. chmn. San Jose (Calif.) Unified Schs., 1955-75; owner Tree Tops studio, San Jose, 1975—. Juried shows: Los Gatos Art Assn., 1976, 77, 78, 79, 85, 86 (1st and 2d awards), 83, 84 (Best of Show awards), Treeside gallery, Los Gatos, 1980, 81 (1st awards); Livermore Art Assn., 1977 (2d award), Los Gatos Art Mus., 1981 (1st award), 82 (2d award), Rosicrucean Mus., 1983, Centre d'Art Contemporian, Paris, 1983; creator Overfelt portrait Alexian Bros. Hosp., San Jose, Calif., 1977; exhibited in group shows Triton Art Mus., 1983, 85, 86. Recipient Golden Centaur award Acad. Italia, 1982, Golden Album of prize winning Artists, 1984, Golden Flame award Academia Italia, 1986, others. Mem. San Jose Art League, Los Gatos Art Assn., Santa Clara Art Assn. (Artist of Yr. 1983), Soc. Western Artists, Artists Equity, Nat. League Am. Penwomen (corr. sec., Merit Achiever award), Academia Italia. Home and Office: 2054 Booksin Ave San Jose CA 95125

JOHNSON, HELEN LAURANE, health science facility executive; b. Willmar, Minn., Aug. 27, 1920; d. Werner E. and Elphy C. (Nelson) Berglund; m. Raymond A.E. Johnson, Aug. 7, 1948 (dec. 1970); children: Ruth E., Daniel R. Diploma, Willmar Bus. Coll.; AS, St. Cloud (Minn.) St. U.; cert., Cath. Hosp. Assn., St. Louis, 1973; AA in Edn., St. Cloud State U., 1948; student, U. Minn., 1987—. Lic. nursing home administr., Minn. Tchr. Mound View Sch. Dist., St. Paul, 1948-52; reserve tchr. Mpls. and Brooklyn Center (Minn.) Sch. Systems, 1964-72; dir. personnel Trevilla Homes Inc., Golden Valley, Minn., 1972-73; asst. adminstr. Trevilla of Robbinsdale, Minn., 1973-76; adminstr. Summit Manor Health Care Ctr., St. Paul, 1976-77; exec. v.p. Thro Homes, Mankato, Minn., 1977—; preceptor long-term care program U. Minn., 1976-77. Mem. Colonial Ch. Edina, adv. council Lamb (Bangladesh) Hosp.; exec. bd. dirs. Nat. Luth. Youth Encounter, Mpls. Fellow Am. Coll. Health Care Adminstrs. (Minn. chpt.); mem. Am. Swedish Inst., Care Providers Minn., Golden Valley Health Care Aux., Am. Legion Aux. Republican. Office: The Thro Co Box 1236 Mankato MN 56001

JOHNSON, HOLLY ANNA, computer programmer; b. Lakewood, Calif., May 7, 1962; d. Charles Eugene and Margaret Ann (Crim) Sullenger; m. Brian Arnold Johnson, Dec. 18, 1981. AAS in Computer Sci., Columbia Basin Coll., 1983, AA in Liberal Arts, 1984; BBAsumma cum laude, Cen. Washington U., 1987. Retail sales clk. various retailers, Washington, 1978-82; computer operator Columbia Basin Coll., Pasco, Wash., 1982-83; computer technician Battelle Pacific N.W. Labs., Richland, Wash., 1983-84; computer programmer I City of Kennewick, Wash., 1984-86, computer programmer II, 1987—; instr. Columbia Basin Coll., 1988—. Speech writer campaign Robert L. Johnson Legis. Campaign, Kennewick, 1984. George Washington Found. scholar, 1980, 81. Mem. Colum Basin Regional Users Group, Data Processing Group, Nat. Assn. Female Execs., Toastmasters Internat. Home: 2318 W 16th Ave Kennewick WA 99337-2803 Office: City of Kennewick 210 W 6th Ave Kennewick WA 99336-6108

JOHNSON, JANE G., cosmetics company executive; b. Birmingham, Ala., July 8, 1936; d. Herbert W. and Florence I. (Brown) Gilley; m. James R. Johnson, Apr. 11, 1953; 1 child, Garry M. Grad. high sch., Prichard, Ala. Nurse asst. Riley County Hosp., Manhatten, Kans., 1954-55; credit reporter Credit Bur., Mobile, Ala., 1958-71; clk., asst. mgr. Merle Norman Cosmetics, Mobile, 1971-79; owner Merle Norman Cosmetics, Lucedale, Miss., 1979-84, Gautier, Miss., 1980—, Pensacola, Fla., 1981—; pres., owner Merle Norman Cosmetics, Mobile, 1987—. Pres. Norwood Community Club, Chickasaw, Ala., 1962; active P.T.A., Chickasaw, 1961-73. Republican. Methodist. Clubs: Norwood Garden :(Chickasaw) (treas. 1963); Pierettes (emblem 1980), Ramada Estates Garden (Mobile, Ala.). Home: 5718 Ramada Dr S Mobile AL 36609 Office: Merle Norman Cosmetics Singing River Mall Gautier MS 39553

JOHNSON, JANET A., lawyer, academic dean; b. Bridgewater, Iowa, Mar. 10, 1940; d. Leland Russell and Viola Lydia (Pfundheller) Taylor; m. Kenneth L. Johnson, Jan. 8, 1960 (div. 1981); children—Rodger (dec.), Sheri; m. Burton M. Leiser, Aug. 12, 1984; stepchildren—Shoshana, Illana, Phillip. AB U. Ill.-Chgo., 1968; JD Drake U., 1972; LLM U. Va., 1984. Bar: Iowa 1972. Cts. specialist Iowa Crime Commn., 1972-73; asst. prof. Law Sch., Drake U., Des Moines, 1973-75, assoc. prof., 1975-77, prof., 1977-78; assoc. judge Iowa Ct. Appeals, Des Moines, 1978-83; dean Sch. Law, Pace U., White Plains, N.Y., 1983—; mem. Iowa Bd. of Parole, 1975-78; bd. dirs. Fund for Modern Cts., N.Y.C., 1983—, Fortune Soc., 1983—, Burke Rehab. Ctr., 1985—; mem. Supreme Ct. Adv. Commn. Des Moines, 1980-81, 75. Contbr. articles to legal publs. Pres., bd. mem. Our Primary Purpose, Des Moines, 1981-83; vice chmn. adv. com. State Corrections Master Plan, 1977-78; bd. mem. Iowa Civil Liberties Union, 1974-76. Mem. ABA, Iowa Bar Assn., N.Y. State Bar Assn., Westchester Women's Bar Assn., Westchester County Bar Assn. Office: Pace U Sch Law 78 N Broadway White Plains NY 10603

JOHNSON, JANET HELEN, Egyptology educator; b. Everett, Wash., Dec. 24, 1944; d. Robert A. and Jane N. (Osborn) J.; m. Donald S. Whitcomb, Sept. 2, 1978. B.A., U. Chgo., 1967, Ph.D., 1972. Instr. Egyptology U. Chgo., 1971-72, asst. prof., 1972-79, assoc. prof., 1979-81, prof., 1981—; dir. Oriental Inst. 1983—; research assoc. dept. anthropology Field Mus. of Natural History, 1980-84. Author: Demotic Verbal System, 1977, Thus Wrote 'Onchsheshonqy, 1986, (with Donald Whitcomb) Quseir al-Qadim, 1978, 80; editor: (with E.F. Wente) Studies in Honor of G.R. Hughes, 1977. Smithsonian Instn. grantee, 1977-83; NEH grantee, 1978-81, 81-85; Nat. Geog. Soc. grantee, 1978, 80, 82. Mem. Am. Research Ctr. in Egypt (bd. govs. 1979—, exec. com. 1984-87). Office: Oriental Inst Mus U Chgo 1155 E 58th St Chicago IL 60637

JOHNSON, JANET LOU, real estate executive; b. Boston, Aug. 22, 1939; d. Donald Murdoch and Helen Margaret (Slauenwhite) Campbell; m. Walter R. Johnson, Mar. 31, 1962; children—Meryl Ann, Leah Kathryn, Christa Helen. Student Boston U., 1959, Gordon Coll., Hamilton, Mass., 1962-64. Adminstr., account exec. Fuller/Smith & Ross, Boston, 1958-63; adminstr. Walter R. Johnson, P.E., Gloucester, 1970-76; broker Realty World, Gloucester, 1976-77, Hunneman & Co., Gloucester, 1977-79; pres., owner Janet L. Johnson Real Estate, Gloucester, 1979—. Mem. Mass. Assn. Realtors (bd. dirs. 1985-87), Nat. Assn. Realtors, Cape Ann C. of C., Cape Ann Bd. Realtors (pres. 1984-85, state dir. 1985-86), Greater Salem Bd. Realtors (state dir. 1986-87). Home: 35 Norseman Ave Gloucester MA 01930 Office: Janet L Johnson Real Estate 79 Rocky Neck Ave Gloucester MA 01930

JOHNSON, JANET THERRIEN, banker; b. Montreal, Que., Can., Oct. 20, 1939; d. Achille and Lucille (Remillard) Therrien; came to U.S., 1960, B.B.A. summa cum laude, Western New Eng. Coll., 1969; M.B.A. in Fin., Northeastern U., 1978; 1 dau., Alexandra Tiffany. Chartered fin. analyst. Asst. trust investment officer Third Nat. Bank Hampden County, Springfield, Mass., 1963-73; sr. trust officer Bank of New Eng., 1973-84; v.p. investments Citizens Bank, Providence, 1984—; dir. Bullard Assocs., Inc.; Amos House lectr. Grad. Sch. Bus. Adminstrn., Northeastern U., 1978—, Brown U. Author: Principles of Investment Management, 1980; Personal Financial Planning, 1984. Mem. Nat. Assn. Bank Women, Mass. Bankers Assn. (mem. edn. com. 1973-74), Boston Soc. Security Analysts (dir., edn. com.), Providence Soc. Fin. Analysts, Fin. Analysts Fedn. (edn. com.). Roman Catholic. Lodge: Rotary. Home: 131 Coolidge Ave Apt #215 Watertown MA 02172 also: 107 Windward Ln Bristol RI 02809 Office: Citizens Bank Providence RI 02903

JOHNSON, JANICE LEE, management consulting firm executive; b. Coffeyville, Kans., Aug. 5, 1942; d. Wayne Harold and Opal Jane (Thompson) Ehart. BA in Bus. Edn., Wichita State U., 1965; MA in Orgn. Change and Consultation, Columbia U., N.Y.C., 1985. Instr. Wichita Bus. Coll., 1965-66; edn. support rep. IBM, Oklahoma City, 1966-71; product planner IBM, Lexington, Ky., 1971-75; internat. market requirements manager IBM, Franklin Lakes, N.J., 1975-77, mgr. market research, 1977-79; mgr. internat. product support IBM, White Plains, N.Y., 1979-81; mgr. retail strategy IBM, Rye Brook, N.Y., 1982-83, mgr. mktg. analysis, 1983-85; v.p. Schubert Assocs., Inc., Boston, 1985-87; pres., founder Diversified Solutions, Inc., N.Y and N.J., 1987—; mem. adv. bd. Schubert Assocs., Inc., Boston, 1987—. Bd. dirs. Saddle River Valley Cultural Ctr., Upper Saddle River, N.J., 1985—; treas., fund raising chmn. Hist. Soc., Upper Saddle River, 1986—; mem. LWV Bergen Highlands Chpt.. Mem. Met. N.Y. Assn. for Applied Psychology, N.J. Network of Bus. and Profl. Women., Woman's Club of Upper Saddle River (co-chmn. community devel. project 1987-88). Home: 29 Old Stone Church Rd Upper Saddle River NJ 07458

JOHNSON, JANICE YVONNE, elementary educator; b. Vidalia, Ga., Aug. 25, 1949; d. Eddie Alfonzo Edwards and Lula Mae (Williams) Page; m. Walter Lewis Johnson, Aug. 10, 1975; children: Kale, Justin. BA, Ft. Valley (Ga.) State Coll., 1971, MA, 1972. Tchr. Houston County Bd. Edn., Bonaie, Ga., 1972-74, Bibb County-Alexander Elem. Sch., Macon, Ga., 1974-78, Bibb County-Rosa Taylor Elem. Sch., Macon, 1978—. Bd. Christian Edn. New Pleasant Grove Bapt. Ch., Macon, 1982—, deaconess, 1984—; bible sch. tchr., 1980—. Mem. Middle Ga. Council Internat. Reading Assn., Profl. Assn. Ga. Educators. Democrat. Baptist. Club: Agape (Macon) (pres. 1979-81). Home: 2977 Armstrong Dr Macon GA 31211

JOHNSON, JANIE FIELDER, day care center director, educator; b. Atlanta, June 16, 1957; d. Mary (Wilson) Adams; m. Miller E. Johnson, Aug. 29, 1980; 1 child, Joi Letonya Holmes. BA, Knoxville Coll., 1979; MA, Sangamon State U., 1981. Cert. nat. aerobic instr. Instr. Eastfield Coll., Dallas, 1982—; dir. Mt. Pisgah Early Learn, Dallas, 1982—. Bd. dirs. YMCA, Dallas, 1987, Mt. Pisgah Early Learning Ctr., Dallas, 1984—, Project Care, Dallas, 1987. Grantee Sangamon State U., 1981; recipient Internat. Youth In Achievement award Am. Bio Inst., Raliegh, N.C., 1980. Mem. Dallas Black C. of C., NAACP, Alpha Kappa Alpha. Democrat. Baptist. Home: 6524 Gretchen Ln Dallas TX 75252 Office: Mt Pisgah Early Learning Ctr 11611 Webbs Chapel Dallas TX 75229

JOHNSON, JEAN ELAINE, nurse, psychologist; b. Wilsey, Kans., Mar. 11, 1925; d. William H. and Rosa L. (Welty) Irwin. B.S., Kans. State U., 1948; M.S. in Nursing, Yale U., 1965; M.S., U. Wis., 1969, Ph.D., 1971. Instr. nursing Iowa, Kans. and Colo., 1948-58; staff nurse Swedish Hosp., Englewood, Colo., 1958-60; in-service edn. coordinator Gen. Rose Hosp., Denver, 1960-63; research asst. Yale U., New Haven, 1965-67; asso. prof. nursing Wayne State U., Detroit, 1971-74; prof. Wayne State U., 1974-79; dir. Center for Health Research, 1974-79; prof. nursing, asso. dir. oncology nursing Cancer Center, U. Rochester, 1979—; Rosenstadt prof. health research Faculty Nursing, U. Toronto, fall 1985. Contbg. author: Handbook of Psychology and Health, vol. 4, 1975; contbr. articles to profl. jours. Recipient Bd. Govs. Faculty Recognition award Wayne State U., 1975; award for disting. contbn. to nursing sci. Am. Nurses Found. and Am. Nurses Assn. Council for Nurse Researchers, 1983; grantee NIH, 1972—. Fellow AAAS; mem. Inst. Medicine, Nat. Acad. Sci. (com. on patient injury compensation 1976-77, membership com. 1981-86, governing council 1987-89), Am. Nurses Assn. (chmn. council for nurse researchers 1976-78, mem. commn. for research 1978-82), Acad. for Behavioral Medicine Research, Sigma Xi, Am. Psychol. Assn., Omicron Nu, Phi Kappa Phi. Home: 1412 East Ave Rochester NY 14610 Office: U Rochester Cancer Ctr Rochester NY 14642

JOHNSON, JERMICKO SHOSHANAH, fashion designer; b. Chgo., July 22; d. Albert Johnson and Teary Watson-Johnson. Student, Art Inst. Chgo., 1972, U. Chgo., 1972; cert., Cosmopolitan Sch. Bus., 1973. Designer apprentice Stanley Korshak, Chgo., 1971; with Eucos, Inc., Evanston, Ill., 1972-73, Fureal, Ltd., Skokie, Ill., 1973-74; tchr. Chgo State U., 1974-75; fashion designer, coordinator Pier 1 Imports, Ft. Worth, 1975-77; designer Revere Sportswear, Chgo., 1977-79; pres. Jermicko Shoshanah Johnson Originals, Chgo., 1979—; founder adult edn. fashion design program Olive-Harvey Coll., Chgo. State U.; faculty adviser Acad. Fashion and Merchandising, 1981, Ray-Vogue Sch. Fashion Design, 1982. Active Girl Scouts U.S. Chgo. Pub. Sch. Art Soc.-Sch. Art Inst. grantee, 1971; Stanley Korshak grantee, 1971, Oscar Arronson grantee, 1970. Mem. Chgo. Fashion Group Guild, Chgo. Fashion Exchange, League of Black Women, Fashion Group. Jewish. Home: 21 W Goethe Chicago IL 60610 Office: 1127 W Division Chicago IL 60622

JOHNSON, JOAN BRAY, insurance company adminstrator; b. Kennett, Mo., Nov. 19, 1926; d. Ples Green and Mary Scott (Williams) Bray; m. Frank Johnson Jr., Nov. 6, 1955; 1 child, Victor Kent. Student, Drury Coll., 1949-51, Cen. Bible Inst. and Coll., 1946-49. Staff writer Gospel Pub. Co., Springfield, Mo., 1949-51; sec. Kennett Sch. Dist. Bd. Edn., 1951-58; spl. features corr. Memphis Press-Scimitar, 1959-60; sec. to v.p. Cotton Exchange Bank, Kennett, 1959-60; proposal analyst Aetna Life Ins. Co., El Paso, Tex., 1960-64, pension adminstr., 1964-71; office mgr. Brokerage div. Aetna Life Ins. Co., Denver, 1971-78; office adminstr. Life Consol. div. Aetna Life Ins. Co., Oakland, Calif., 1979-82; office adminstr. PFSD div. Aetna Life Ins. Co., Walnut Creek, Calif., 1983-86; office adminstr. PFSD-Heatth Mktg. div. Aetna Life Ins. Co., Sacramento, 1986—. Officer local PTA, 1964-71; pres. Wesley Service Guild, 1968-71; den mother Boy Scouts Am. Recipient Life Service award PTA, 1970. Fellow Life Office Mgmt. Assn. (instr. classes); mem. Assn. Bus. and Profl. Women, Life Underwriters Assn., DAR. Democrat. Methodist. Clubs: Last Monday, Opti-Mrs., Allied Arts. Home: 4776 Oak Twig Way Carmichael CA 95608

JOHNSON, JOANNE MARY, markting and adminstrative executive, real estate broker; b. Bklyn., Mar. 28, 1947; d. John Peter and Anne Marie (Alesi) Da Prato; m. John Daryl Johnson, Feb. 15, 1969; children: Jodi Lynn, Shaun Bryan. Student, Bkly. Coll., 1969; AA, Coll. of Staten Island, 1986; student, N. Tex. State U., 1987—. Profl. asst. Price Waterhouse, N.Y.C., 1982-86; mktg. supr. real estate services group Price Waterhouse, Dallas, 1986—. Editor (newsletter): Real Estate Update, Real Estate Syndicator. Mem. Nat. Assn. Female Execs., Nat. Assn. Real Estate Editors, Greater Dallas Bd. Realtors. Republican. Roman Catholic. Club: Brookhaven Country (Dallas). Home: 1312 Royal Palm Ln Carrollton TX 75248 Office: Price Waterhouse 16479 Dallas Pkwy Suite 810 Dallas TX 75248

JOHNSON, JORENE KATHRYN, community organization director; b. Rockville Centre, N.Y., Jan. 6, 1931; d. Adam and Kathryn Lillian (Schoen) Freitag; m. Roland E. Johnson, Oct. 10, 1954; children: Lorin, Melissa. BFA, Pratt Inst., 1952; MPA, U. Cin., 1975; postgrad. Mt. St. Joseph Coll., 1977-78. Furniture designer Jacques Bodart, Inc., N.Y.C., 1952-54; interior decorator Albert Parvin Co., Los Angeles, 1955-57, Maria Bergson Assocs., N.Y.C., 1957-61; office mgr., research asst. The Cin. Inst., 1973-74, research mgr., 1974-75; exec. dir. Friends of Cin. Parks Inc., 1975-76; community coordinator College Hill Forum, Cin., 1977-84; sec., insp. Green Twp. Zoning Bd., 1982-84; dir. The Program for Cin., 1984—. Mem. Cin. Mayor's Energy Policy Com., 1982-83; chmn. budget process com. Mayor's Budget Task Force, 1984; vice-chmn. Monfort Heights Civic Assn., 1977, chmn., 1978; mem. Leadership Cin. Class III, 1979-80; mem. planning com. Community Chest, 1982-88; mem. planning com. Program for Cin., 1982-83; mem. steering com. Congress of Neighborhood Groups, 1983-85; bd. dirs. Hamilton County Assn. Retarded Citizens, 1983-87. Mem. Internat. Platform Assn., Cincinnatus Assn., Woman's City Club. Home: 5200 Race Rd Cincinnati OH 45247 Office: 230 E 9th St Cincinnati OH 45202

JOHNSON, JOSEPHINE POWELL, power and light company manager; b. Goldsboro, N.C., Apr. 23, 1941; d. William Howard and Vennie Ann (Johnson) Powell; m. William Gene Stephenson, Dec. 24, 1959 (dec. Feb. 1979); 1 child, Teresa Lynn; m. 2d, Amos James Johnson Jr., Aug. 15, 1981; stepchildren—Amos James III, Edward Spencer, Brian Keith. Student Fayetteville Tech. Inst., 1975-79, Mt. Olive Coll., N.C., 1980-83. With Carolina Power & Light Co., 1961—, adminstrv. asst. to dist. mgr., Goldsboro, N.C., 1979-80, area mgr., Mt. Olive, 1980-86, area bus. mgr., Goldsboro, 1986-87; pres. Mt. Olive Bus. Devel. Corp., 1987—; pres. Bus. Industry Assn. for Duplin, Samson and Wayne County, 1987—. Bd. dirs. United Way, Wayne County, N.C., 1983—, Am. Heart Assn. Wayne County, 1987, Goldsboro Edn. Found., 1987 ; bd. dirs., pres. Mt. Olive Indsl. Com. of 100, 1984; bd. dirs. Com. of 100 Wayne County, 1987; precinct vice chmn. Cumberland County, Manchester Twp., N.C., Mem. Am. Bus. Womens Assn. (v.p. 1983), N.C. Bus. and Profl. Women U.S.A. (v.p. 1982), C. of C. (v.p., bd. dirs. 1980—). Democrat. Home: 117 Club Knolls Mount Olive NC 28365 Office: S Center St Goldsboro NC 27530

JOHNSON, JOYCE, writer, editor; b. N.Y.C., Sept. 27, 1935; d. Daniel and Rosalind (Ross) Glassman; m. James Johnson, Dec. 12, 1962 (dec. 1963); m. Peter Pinchbeck, Nov. 21, 1965 (div. 1971); 1 child, Daniel. Student, Barnard Coll., 1951-55. Assoc. editor William Morrow & Co, N.Y.C., 1965-67; sr. editor Dial Press, N.Y.C., 1967-70, exec. editor, 1977-84; sr. editor McGraw Hill Book Co., N.Y.C., 1970-77, Atlantic Monthly Press, N.Y.C., 1984-87; contbg. editor Vanity Fair, 1987—. Author: Come and Join the Dance, 1962, Bad Connections, 1978, Minor Characters, 1983 (Nat. Book Critics 1983). John Gardner fellow Breadloaf Writers Conf., 1983; co-winner O'Henry awards, 1987. Mem. PEN. Jewish. Office: Vanity Fair 350 Madison Ave 4th Floor New York NY 10170

JOHNSON, JUANITA, social welfare administrator; b. Chgo., June 3, 1950; d. Thomasine Neal. BA, Roosevelt U.; MST, U. Chgo., 1975; MSW, Loyola U., Chgo., 1986; postgrad., Sch. Art Inst., Chgo., 1987—. Tchr. Chgo. Bd. Edn., 1975-83, social worker, 1986—. Illustrator: History Disciplinary Church, 1987. Deacon 1st Christian Ch., Maywood, Ill., 1984—; sec. exec. com. Chgo. Disciplinary Union, 1985-87, del. regional bd. Fellow Loyola U., 1985-86. Mem. Nat. Assn. Social Workers, Ill. Assn. Social Workers. Office: Chgo Bd Edn Dist 7 Office 211 S Kildare Chicago IL 60624

JOHNSON, JUANITA AVIS, civic worker, former life sciences educator, microbiologist; b. Spokane, Wash., July 7, 1909; d. Avery Clarence and Addie Mae (Steele) Rickel; m. James Johnson, Dec. 29, 1938 (div. Dec. 1946); children—Linda Lee, Judith Ann. B.S., U. Wash., 1934; M.S., Ft. Wright Coll., 1971. Microbiologist, Kitsap County Dairy, Bremerton, Wash., 1933-38; lab. technician for Dr. E.B. White, Spokane, 1945-47; microbiologist Early Dawn Dairy, Spokane, 1947-56; tchr. life sci. East Valley High Sch., Spokane, 1956-74, Fort Wright Coll., Spokane, 1974. Mem. Spokane County Democratic Precinct Com., 1952—; trustee Spokane County Library Dist., 1978-85; pres. Am. Bapt. Women for East Wash., North Idaho and West Mont., 1983-86, officer Am. Bapt. Women Pacific N.W., Seattle, 1974-86; 1st v.p. Am. Bapt. Chs. Pacific N.W., 1984-87. Named Woman of Yr., Bus. and Profl. Women, 1961; Outstanding Biology Tchr., Nat. Assn. Biology Tchrs., 1972; recipient award of merit Wash. Sci. Tchrs., 1972; NSF grantee, 1969-71. Mem. NEA. Democrat. Baptist. Home: E 10901 9th Ave Spokane WA 99206

JOHNSON, JUDITH LAWSON, commodity broker; b. Memphis, Jan. 12, 1943; d. David Voss and Julia (Larkey) J.; B.A., Smith Coll., 1965; M.A.T., Duke U., 1966. Sales asst. Howard, Weil, Labouisse, Friedrichs, Inc., New Orleans, 1969-72, analyst, Chgo., 1975-77, 1st v.p., commodity sales mgr., New Orleans, 1977—. Mem. Chgo. Mercantile Exchange, N.Y. Futures Exchange, Futures Industry Assn., Nat. Futures Assn. (western bus. conduct com.). Presbyterian. Home: 3009 Constance St New Orleans LA 70115 Office: Howard Weil Labouisse Friedrichs Inc Inc Energy Ctr 1100 Poydras St Suite 900 New Orleans LA 70163

JOHNSON, JUDITH SUGG, lawyer; b. Washington, Aug. 30, 1945; d. Irvin Douglas and Bernice (Humphrey) Sugg; m. Robert C. Scott, Jan. 2, 1988; children: Carmen Ramona, Nichole Lynette. BBA with honors, Va. State Coll., 1966; post baccalaureate degree in econs., Swarthmore Coll., 1967; JD, Cath. U. Law, Washington, 1975. Bar: Va. 1975. Dep. dir. Halifax County Community Action, South Boston, Va., 1967-68; dir. Alexandria (Va.) Econ. Opportunity Co., 1968-71; asst. atty. gen. Atty. Gen.'s Office, Richmond, Va., 1975—; sr. counsel Va. Housing Devel. Authority, Richmond, 1975-82, Office Gov. of Va., Richmond, 1982-85; corp. v.p., gen. counsel Systems Mgmt. Am. Corp., Norfolk, Va., 1985—; gov.'s appointee State Equal Employment Opportunity Com., 1979. Mem. editorial adv. bd. mag. Met. Woman. Bd. dirs. TheatreVa., Downtown Norfolk Devel. Corp., Va. Cares, The Va. Water Project, Greater Richmond Transit Co., Travelers Health Network, HMO; mem. adv. bd. Colnial Girl Scout Council; past chmn. Gov.'s War on Drugs Task Force; gov.'s appointee Juvenile Justice and Delinquency Prevention Adv. Council. Recipient Outstanding Woman award Iota Phi Lambda, 1976; named one of Outstanding Young Women in Am., Va. Woman of Achievement in Govt., 1984, Va. Outstanding Woman Atty., 1986; Rockefeller Found. fellow. Mem. ABA, Norfolk and Portsmouth Bar Assn., Old Dominion Bar Assn., Va. Perinatal Assn. (mem. legislative com.), The Travelers Health Network (bd. dirs.), The Cultural Alliance Greater Hampton Rds. (bd. dirs.), Alpha Kappa Alpha. Democrat. Episcopalian. Office: Systems Mgmt Am Corp 254 Monticello Ave Norfolk VA 23510

JOHNSON, JUDY SHERRILL, business educator, educational consultant; b. McComb, Miss., Aug. 27, 1944; d. Samuel Benton and Eunice (Ikard) Sherrill; m. Bill Johnson, Dec. 27, 1985; stepchildren: Christie, Karen, Laurie, Leslie. BSC, U. Miss., 1966; postgrad. U. Fla., 1967, Fla. Atlantic U., 1971, 73, 76, U. Central Fla., 1984, Ark. State U., 1981. Lic. tchr. N.C.,

Tenn., Ala., Fla., Miss. Mem. faculty Santa Fe Jr. Coll., Gainesville, Fla., 1966-68, Broward County Bd. Pub. Instrn., Ft. Lauderdale, Fla., 1968-76; tchr. Huntsville City Sch., Ala., 1976-81; ednl. cons., sales rep. McGraw-Hill Book Co., N.Y.C., 1981-85; cons. Hillsborough County Bus. Edn. Tchrs., Tampa, Fla., 1982; mem. adv. bd. Pinellas County Indsl. Arts Dept., Clearwater, Fla., 1982-84; mem. adv. bd. bus. edn. Pinellas County, Clearwater, 1984-85, Hillsborough High Sch., Tampa, 1982-85, Gaither High Sch., Tampa, 1984-85, chmn. adv. bd. adult night sch., 1985; judge state contests Miss., 1977, Fla., 1982-85. Active Republican Party of Fla., 1982-85; mem. Symphony Guild, Ft. Lauderdale; project advisor Huntsville Christian Women's Club, 1987-88; sec. United Meth. Women's Club First United Meth. Ch., 1988; v.p., pres. elect Heritage Quilters Huntsville, 1987-88; chair mini-retreat First United Meth. Ch., Huntsville, 1988; retreat com. worker, mem. planning com. Tenn. Valley Women's Retreat, 1988; tchr., leader Precept Bible Study, Precept Ministeries, 1988. Runner-up Advisor of Yr., Fla. Future Bus. Leaders Am., 1974. Mem. Delta Pi Epsilon, Alpha Delta Kappa (treas. 1980-81, various coms.), Phi Mu Alumnae (pres. 1969-71, collegiate dir. State of Fla. 1968-69, state day coordinator 1970), Beta Sigma Phi, Phi Beta Lambda Alumnae. Avocations: cross stitch, sewing, fishing, gardening. Home: 1409 Governors Dr Huntsville AL 35801

JOHNSON, JULIE ANN, diversified company executive; b. Lemmon, S.D., Jan. 22, 1961; d. Arthur H. and Marilyn Irene (Starr) Christman; m. Randall Lynn Johnson. BS in Computer Sci., S.D. Sch. Mines and Tech., 1983. Assoc. programmer Sperry Univac, Salt Lake City, 1983-84; software engr. Sperry Flight Systems, Phoenix, 1984-85; requirements planner Sperry Flight Systems/Honeywell, Phoenix, 1985—. Democrat. Presbyterian. Home: 6034 W Kings Phoenix AZ 85306 Office: Honeywell-Sperry Comml Flight div 21111 N 19th Ave Phoenix AZ 85036

JOHNSON, JULIE ELIZABETH, accountant; b. Salisbury, Md., Nov. 30, 1962; d. Clyde George and Edith Margaret (Crowther) J.; m. Francis Lafferty, Nov. 24, 1984. BS, Towson St. U., 1984. Internal auditor Cheasapeake Rim & Wheel, Balt., 1984-85; mgr. Princess Anne (Md.) Pharmacy, 1985; tax acct. Ellin & Tucker Chartered, Balt., 1985—. Republican. Methodist.

JOHNSON, JULIE PAYNE, personnel assessment manager; b. Attleboro, Mass., June 13, 1948; d. John Gordon and Claire (Paquin) P.; m. W. Richard Johnson, Oct. 10, 1970 (div. Oct. 1980). BBA, U. R.I., 1970. Service rep. New England Telephone, East Greenwich, R.I., 1970-71, Southern Bell, Jacksonville, Fla., 1971-73; bus. office supr. Southern Bell, Jacksonville, 1973-77, bus. office mgr., 1978-84, staff assessment mgr., 1984-87; dir. human resources assessment State of Fla., Jacksonville, 1987—; dir. human resources assessment State of Fla., 1987—. Bd. dirs. Duval Assn. of Retarded Citizens, Jacksonville, 1981-86, treas. 1983-86. Mem. Nat. Assn. Female Execs., Pioneers of Am. Roman Catholic. Office: So Bell Tower 301 W Bay St 4DD1 Jacksonville FL 32202

JOHNSON, KAREN BREMER, dentist; b. Clark AFB, Philippines, Oct. 24, 1950; d. Charles and Eva-Ann (Dougherty) Bremer; 1 child, Kenneth Brandon. B.S. in Dental Hygiene, U. N.C., 1972, D.D.S., 1978. Practice dentistry, Creedmoor, N.C., 1978-80, Durham, N.C., 1980—; mem. dental faculty, U. N.C., Chapel Hill, 1978-80; mem. dental staff Durham County Gen. Hosp., 1983—. Mem. Acad. Gen. Dentistry, Acad. Implant Dentistry, ADA, N.C. Dental Assn., Durham C. of C., D.A.R. Avocations: raising and training horses, racquetball, swimming, bicycling, skiing. Office: 2702 S Miami Blvd Durham NC 27703

JOHNSON, KAREN CHRISTINE, newspaper editor; b. Manchester, Conn., Aug. 10, 1953; d. Sewall Harvey Emler and Ruth LeJune (pallesen) J.; m. Jeremy L. Driver, May. 23, 1976 (div. Oct. 1980). BA in Am. Studies, U. Sussex, Brighton, Eng., 1975; MA in Communications, Stanford U., 1981. Claims adjuster USF&G Ins. Cos., Phila., 1976-80; new writer, weekend assignment editor KSDO Radio, San Diego, 1981-82; news editor Copley Video, San Diego, 1982-84; copy editor San Diego Union, 1984, asst. news editor, 1984-85, fgn. editor, 1985—; producer community video channel Cox Cable, San Diego, 1981-82. Author: (videotape) Back to Back, 1981. Vol. Art Walk, San Diego, 1986. Stanford U. grantee, 1981. Democrat. Mem. Ch. of Eng. Office: The San Diego Union 350 Camino de la Reina San Diego CA 92108

JOHNSON, KAREN LANMAN, data communications company executive; b. Columbus, Ohio, Jan. 30, 1948; d. Garold T. and Katherine (Swinning) Lanman; m. Thomas G. Johnson, Apr. 19, 1970 (div. 1980); 1 child, Tyler Grant. BS, Ohio State U., 1969, MA, 1972. Dir. corp. communications Carvel Corp., Yonkers, N.Y., 1977-80; mgr. mktg. communications Racal-Milgo, Miami, Fla., 1980-82; mgr. nat. sales support Racal-Milgo, Plantation, Fla., 1982-84; mgr. nat. sales system Racal-Milgo, Sunrise, Fla., 1984-85, mgr. network optimization, 1985—. Mem. Indsl. Devel. Council, Lewisboro, N.Y., 1978-79; media cons. Lewisboro Town Council, 1978-79, Lt. Gov.'s campaign, N.Y.C., 1978. Named Outstanding Undergrad. Instr., Ohio State U., 1970. Mem. Women in Communications. Republican. Home: 5021 SW 87 Terr Cooper City FL 33328 Office: Racal-Milgo 1601 N Harrison Pkwy Sunrise FL 33323

JOHNSON, KATHARYN PRICE (MRS. EDWARD F. JOHNSON), civic worker; b. Smyrna, Del., Mar. 24, 1897; d. Lewis M. and Jennie Cairl (Smithers) Price; grad. Centenary Coll., 1915; student Goucher Coll., 1915-18; m. Edward F. Johnson, Nov. 16, 1920; children—Edward A., Jane Cairl Johnson Kent. With Liberty Loan Com. for Md. and Liberty Loan Assn. of Balt., 1918-20; pres. Women's Guild Hitchcock Meml. Ch., 1930-32; dir. Scarsdale Woman's Club, 1933-36; dir. White Plains Thrift Shop, 1930-43, pres, 1936-43; mem. exec. com. Scarsdale Community Fund, 1934-38; active Scarsdale council Girl Scouts, 1937-53, commr., 1939-41, now hon. mem. Scarsdale-Hartsdale council, 1953-69; mem. region 2 com. Girl Scouts U.S.A., 1942-56, mem. nat. bd., exec. com., 1947-55, chmn. orgn. and mgmt. dept., 1952-55, mem. nat. field com., 1943-55, mem. equipment service com. 1956-69, mem. internat. com., 1956-60, mem. meml. gifts com., 1974-81; mem. Bd. Edn., Scarsdale, N.Y., 1943-46; disaster chmn. Scarsdale chpt. ARC, 1942-45; mem. Commn. Human Rights, 1958-69, Commn. Status of Women, 1957-69; rep. World Assn. Girl Guides and Girl Scouts to UN, 1957-71, mem. NGO com. on UNICEF, 1965-72, sec., 1968-70; participant World Confs., World Assn. Girl Guides and Girl Scouts, Greece, 1960, Denmark, 1963, Japan, 1966, Finland, 1969, Can., 1972, Eng., 1975, Iran, 1978, World Conf., U.S., 1984. Recipient Juliette Low World Friendship medal Girl Scouts USA, 1984. Mem. Nat. Council Women U.S., Scarsdale Hist. Soc., Olave-Baden-Powell Soc. (founder), Pi Beta Phi. Republican. Presbyterian. Clubs: Scarsdale Woman's (life), Scarsdale Golf, Nat. Women's Republican; Shenorock Shore. Home: 165 Brewster Rd Scarsdale NY 10583

JOHNSON, KATHLEEN SUZANNE, funeral director, embalmer, nurse; b. Tilden, Nebr., Oct. 14, 1958; d. Roger Everitt and Marian Agnes (Kent) Johnson. Student, U. Nebr., Lincoln, 1976-77, 79-80; diploma in nursing Bryan Meml. Hosp. Sch. Nursing, 1979; A of Funeral Service Edn., Mt. Hood Community Coll., 1981. RN; lic. funeral dir.; lic. embalmer. Staff nurse Our Lady of Lourdes, Norfolk, Nebr., 1981-82; apprentice Johnson-Stonacek Funeral Home, Norfolk, 1981-83; embalmer Butherus, Maser & Love, Lincoln, 1983; staff nurse Scribner Med. Clinic, Nebr., 1983-85; pres. Spear-Johnson Funeral Home, Scribner, 1983—; mgr. Warne-Johnson Funeral Homes, Hooper and Uehling, Nebr., 1986—. Tchr. 11th grade religion class St. Lawrence Ch., Scribner, 1984-85; alt. bd. dirs. Fremont and Elkhorn Valley R.R. Mem. Nebr. Funeral Dirs. Assn. (edn. com.), Nat. Funeral Dirs. Assn., Nat. Assn. Female Execs., Nat. Ry. Hist. Soc., Nat. Hospice Orgn. (profl.), Hooper Comml. Club, Scribner C. of C. (pres. 1986), Scribner Jaycees. Roman Catholic. Avocations: golf, swimming, travel. Home: PO Box 530 Scribner NE 68057 Office: Spear-Johnson Funeral Home 509 Main St Scribner NE 68057 also: Warne-Johnson Funeral Home 109 W Elk St Hooper NE 68031

JOHNSON, KATHY ANN, insurance agent; b. Portland, Oreg., Sept. 30, 1956; d. Edgar Scott and Bettymae (King) H.; m. Douglas Michael Johnson, Nov. 7, 1981. BS, Oreg. Coll. Edn., 1978; MS, We. Oreg. State Coll., 1981. Cert. elem. tchr., Oreg. Tchr. Glendale (Oreg.) Pub. Schs., 1978-79, Salem (Oreg.) Pub. Schs., 1979-82; owner, agent State Farm Ins., Issaquah, Washington, 1983—. Mem. Toy and Gift Bank of Issaquah, 1984; active Salmon Days, Rotary Run, 1987. Named to Half Millionaire Club State Farm Ins., 1984, named one of Outstanding Young Women of Am., 1984; recipient Legion of Honor award State Farm Ins., 1987. Mem. Issaquah Women Profls. (chmn. 1985), Bus. Womens Inst., Nat. Assn. Female Execs., Issaquah C. of C. Republican. Presbyterian. Lodge: Rotary. Office: State Farm Ins 240 NW Gilman Blvd Suite C Issaquah WA 98027

JOHNSON, KELLEY SMITH, accounting administrator; b. Boulder, Colo., Sept. 2, 1959; d. Gerald Lynn (stepfather) and Joanna Jean (Greenwood) Hotzler; m. James Michael Rio, Aug. 16, 1980 (div. Aug. 1985); m. David F. Johnson. BS in Acctg., Ill. State U., 1981; postgrad., Calif. State U., Fullerton. CPA, Calif., Ill. Auditor Peat Marwick & Mitchell, Chgo., 1981-83; regional mgr. Santa Fe Pacific Realty, Brea, Calif., 1983—. Mem. Am. Inst. CPA's, Am. Mgmt. Assn. (assoc.), Calif. Soc. CPA's, Nat. Assn. for Female Execs. Republican. Office: Santa Fe Pacific Realty Corp 3230 E Imperial Hwy Suite 100 Brea CA 92621

JOHNSON, KIM HADARIA, loan analyst; b. Logan, W.Va., Jan. 17, 1957; d. Osble Alfred and Mary Sydney (Gray) Vance; m. Cecil H. Johnson, Sept. 17, 1975 (div. Feb. 1982). BA in Fin., Marshall U., 1986. Sr. accounts clk. Gen. Electric Credit Corp., South Point, Ohio, 1978-82; sec. Sch. Medicine, Marshall U., Huntington, W.Va., 1982-84; exec. sec. Cilco Inc, Huntington, 1984-85; loan analyst W.Va. Econ. Devel. Authority, Charleston, 1985-87; exec. dir. Upper Kanawha Valley Econ. Devel. Corp., Montgomery, W.Va., 1988—. Speaker W.Va. Soc. Prevention Child Abuse, 1986; vol. W.Va. Soc. Prevention Child Abuse for Kinds on the Block, 1986, Working To Eliminate Child Abuse and Neglect, 1987; mem. W.Va. Econ. Devel. Council, 1988. Mem. Nat. Assn. Female Execs., Alpha Kappa Psi (life, pres. 1985-86, Service award 1984). Republican. Jewish. Home: PO Box 836 Montgomery WV 25136

JOHNSON, LADY BIRD (CLAUDIA ALTA) (MRS. LYNDON BAINES JOHNSON), wife former pres. U.S.; b. Karnack, Tex., Dec. 22, 1912; d. Thomas Jefferson Taylor; B.A., U. Tex., 1933, B.Journalism, 1934, D.Letters, 1964; LL.D., Tex. Woman's U., 1964; D.Letters, Middlebury Coll., 1967; L.H.D., Williams Coll., 1967, U. Ala., 1975; H.H.D., Southwestern U., 1967; m. Lyndon Baines Johnson (36th Pres. U.S.), Nov. 17, 1934 (died Jan. 22, 1973); children—Lynda Bird Johnson Robb, Luci Baines. Mgr. husband's congl. office, Washington, 1941-42; owner, operator radio-TV sta. KTBC, Austin, Tex., 1942-63, cattle ranches, Tex., 1943—. Hon. chmn. Nat. Headstart Program, 1963-68, Town Lake Beautification Project. also cotton and timberlands, Ala. Mem. Advisory council Nat. Parks, Historic Sites, Bldgs. and Monuments; bd. regents U. Tex., 1971-77, mem. internat. conf. steering com., 1969; trustee Jackson Hole Preserve, Am. Conservation Assn., Nat. Geog. Soc.; founder Nat. Wild flower Research Ctr., Austin, 1982. Recipient Togetherness award Marge Champion, 1958; Humanitarian award B'nai B'rith, 1961; Businesswoman's award Bus. and Profl. Women's Club, 1961; Theta Sigma Phi citation, 1962; Disting. Achievement award Washington Heart Assn., 1962; Industry citation Am. Women in Radio and Television, 1963; Humanitarian citation Vols. of Am., 1963; Peabody award for White House TV visit, 1966; Eleanor Roosevelt Golden Candlestick award Women's Nat. Press Club; Damon Woods Meml. award Indsl. Designers Soc. Am., 1972; Conservation Service award Dept. Interior, 1974; Disting. award Am. Legion, 1975; Woman of Year award Ladies Home Jour., 1975; Medal of Freedom, 1977; Nat. Achievement award Am. Hort. Soc., 1984 . Life mem. U. Tex. Ex-Students Assn. Episcopalian. Author: A White House Diary, 1970. Address: LBJ Library 2313 Red River Austin TX 78705

JOHNSON, LEONE NANCY, marketing professional; b. Washington, Nov. 9, 1955; d. William Monroe and Dorothy Esther (Blotner) Pease; m. Robert Malcolm Johnson, May 31, 1986. BA cum laude, Mt. Holyoke Coll., 1978; MBA with high distinction, Babson Coll., 1980. Sales Horizon House Internat., Dedham, Mass., 1980-81; market analyst Venture Devel. Corp., Natick, Mass., 1981-83, sr. market analyst, 1984-85, venture search mgr., 1985-87, mgr. office and computer div., 1987—. Contbr. articles to profl. jours. Mem. Beta Gamma. Club: Mt. Holyoke (dir. alumni admissions 1983-87).

JOHNSON, LILLIAN BEATRICE, sociologist, educator; b. Wilmington, N.C., Nov. 8, 1922; d. James Archie and Mary Gaston (Atkins) J. A.A., Peace Coll., 1940; B.R.E., Presbyterian Sch. Christian Edn., 1942; M.S., N.C. State U., 1965, Ph.D., 1972. Dir. Christian edn. First Presbyn. Ch., Pensacola, Fla., 1945-47, Greenwood, S.C., 1947-48, Durham, N.C., 1948-51; club dir. Army Spl. Services, No. Command, Japan, 1951-53; teenage dir. YWCA, Washington, 1953-56, assoc. exec. Honolulu, 1956-59, exec. dir. Tulsa, 1959-62; instr. N.C. State U., 1962-72; asst. prof. Greensboro Coll., 1972-75; mem. faculty sociology dept. Livingston U., 1975—, now prof. Election law commr. State of Ala. Mem. Am. Sociol. Assn., So. Sociol. Soc., Ala.-Miss. Sociol. Assn. (treas.), Nat. Council Family Relations, Ala. Council on Family Relations (v.p. 1981-83), Alpha Kappa Delta (treas. 1984-86). Home: Meadowbrook Dr Livingston AL 35470 Office: Livingston U Livingston AL 35470

JOHNSON, LINDA ARLENE, oil distributor; b. Sparta, Wis., Mar. 6, 1946; d. Clarence Julius and Arlene Mae (Yahnke) Jessie; children: Darrick, Larissa. With Union Nat. Bank & Trust Co., Sparta, 1964-69, Hill, Christensen & Co., CPA's, Tomah, Wis., 1969-75; owner Johnson of Wis. Oil Co., Inc., Tomah, 1969—; with Larry's Express, Inc., Tomah, 1975-78; owner Johnson Rentals, 1979—, Johnson of Wis. Transport Co., Inc., 1982—. Mem. St. Paul's Luth. Ch., Tomah. Mem. Petroleum Marketers Assn. Am., Nat. Assn. Convenience Stores, Nat. Fedn. Ind. Bus., Am. Trucking Assn., Wis. Assn. Convenience Stores, Oil Jobbers Wis., Wis. Ind. Businessmen, Inc., Tomah Area C. of C. Home and Office: 612 Kilbourn Ave Tomah WI 54660

JOHNSON, LINDA JOYCE, sales executive; b. Lowell, Mass., Nov. 6, 1956; d. Emil and Esther Muriel (Ayer) Zabierek; m. James M. Johnson, Sept. 5, 1975 (div. Nov. 1979). Mfg. adminstr., M/A-Com., Inc., 1979, sales adminstr., 1979-81, sales specialist, 1981-84; regional sales mgr. Hyletronics, Inc., Littleton, Mass., 1984; regional sales mgr. Frequency Sources, Chelmsford, Mass., 1984-86; regional sales mgr. Sanders Assocs., Manchester, N.H., 1986—. Mem. Nat. Contract Mgmt. Assn., Nat. Assn. Female Execs., Women in Electronics, Computer Decisions, Inc. (bd. dirs.). Lodge: Assn. Old Crows. Avocations: golf, piano, reading. Home: 5 Walnut Hill Rd Derry NH 03038 Office: Sanders Assocs Inc 955 Perimeter Rd Manchester NH 03108

JOHNSON, LIZABETH LETTIE, insurance agent; b. Dallas, Aug. 24, 1957; d. Winfred Herschel Johnson and Mary Francis (Flowers) Goff; children: Brandi, Elissa. Student, Georgetown (Ky.) Coll., 1975-76, U. Ky., 1976-78. Staff analyst Met. Ins. Co., Lexington, 1979-81, ins. agt., 1981-82; agt. Allstate Ins. Co., Lexington, 1982—. Vol. Big Bros./Big Sisters, 1979-84; hotline counselor Lexington Rape Crisis Ctr., 1984—, bd. dirs., 1988; vol. Christians in Community Service, 1986—; mem. Ky. Spl. Needs Adoption Support Group, 1985—. Fellow Life Underwriting Tng. Council; mem. NAACP, Nat. Assn. Life Underwriters. Democrat. Baptist. Office: Allstate Ins Co 694 New Circle Rd NE Room 3 Lexington KY 40505

JOHNSON, LOIS JEAN, music educator; b. Los Angeles, Jan. 13, 1950; d. Kenneth Franklin and Iona Jean (Miller) J. BA, Brigham Young U., 1971, MusM, 1975. Grad. teaching asst. Brigham Young U., Provo, Utah, 1972-75, instr. voice, 1975—; instr. music study Vienna, Austria, 1978; chief registrar vital stas. City-County Health Dept., Provo, 1979-85; mus. dir. Utah Valley Choral Soc., Provo, 1980—, trustee, 1983—; mus. dir. Promised Valley Playhouse, Salt Lake City, 1984; dir. choral activities American Fork (Utah) High Sch., 1985—; vocal tchr., Provo, 1972—; mem., soloist Mormon Tabernacle Choir, Salt Lake City, 1972—. em. Am. Choral Dirs. Assn., Nat. Assn. Tchrs. Singing (v.p. local chpt. 1983-84), Assn. Profl. Vocal Ensembles, NEA, Utah Edn. Assn., Music Educator Nat. Conf., Utah Music Educators Assn. Republican. Mormon. Home: 835 North 750 West Provo UT 84604 Office: Am Fork High Sch 510 North 600 East American Fork UT 84003

JOHNSON, LUAN, educational program developer, researcher; b. Provo, Utah, Apr. 27, 1956; d. Jack R. and Colleen (Kesler) J. BA, Brigham Young U., 1981, MA, 1984. Dir. Teaching Resource Ctr., Provo, 1980-84; teaching asst. communications dept. Brigham Young U., Provo, 1982-83, counselor Master Acad., Salt Lake City, 1985; staff asst. Teaching Resource Ctr., DeAnza Coll., Cupertino, Calif., 1986; ednl. designer, community services officer City of Sunnyvale, 1986—; free-lance editor, 1984-85; tutor, 1984-85. Pres. Youth Assn. Retarded Children, Brigham City, 1976-77. Mem. Phi Kappa Phi. Republican. Mormon. Avocation: collecting and flying kites. Home: 205 B Red Oak Dr W Sunnyvale CA 94086 Office: Dept Pub Safety 700 All American Way Sunnyvale CA 94086

JOHNSON, LUCILLE MERLE BROWN, elementary educator, principal; b. Brown's Town, St. Ann, Jamaica, Nov. 5, 1936; came to U.S., 1970; d. Ezekiel and Christina (Hawthorne) Brown; m. Carl Wesley Johnson, Oct. 26, 1958 (div. 1974); children: Carl Anthony, Michael Ian. BE, Bethlehem Coll., 1957; MEd, Nat. Coll. Edn., 1976, cert. advanced study, 1980. Cert. elem. tchr., Ill. Div. head St. Ann Schs., Jamaica, 1968-69; reading facilitator Sch. Dist. #64, North Chicago, Ill., 1973-76, coordinator tchr. inservice, 1976-80, prin., 1980—; supr. Dist. 64 Yeager Elem. Sch., North Chicago, 1980—. Mem. North Chicago I-SEARCH; sec. Lake County Community Service League, Waukegan/North Chicago, Ill., 1985-86; trustee North Chicago Pub. Library. Mem. Nat. Assn. Elem. Sch. Princs., Nat. Alliance Black Sch. Educators, Lake County Alliance Black Sch. Educators (sec.). Office: Yeager Elem Sch Morrow and Lewis Ave North Chicago IL 60064

JOHNSON, LYNN KIMMEL, accountant; b. Rochester, N.Y., July 3, 1958; d. Ronald Kenneth and Gudrun Anna Berta (Degel) Kimmel; m. Harold Franklin Johnson Jr., Sept. 13, 1987. BA in Acctg., Lyola Marymount U., 1980. CPA, Calif. Acct. Ernst and Whinney, Los Angeles, 1980-84, mgr., 1985; chief fin. officer Fremont Ins. Services, Los Angeles, 1985-86; v.p. fin. Cal-Surance Assocs. Inc., Torrance, Calif., 1986—. Treas. Com. to Elect George Nakano, Torrance, 1984. Mem. Ins. Acctg. and Systems Assn., Am. Inst. CPA's, Nat. Assn. Female Execs., Loyola Marymount U. Alumni Assn., Alpha Sigma Nu. Republican. Lutheran. Office: Cal-Surance Assocs Inc 2790 Skypark Dr Torrance CA 90505

JOHNSON, MADGE RICHARDS, business owner, fundraiser, consultant; b. Washington, Oct. 4, 1952; d. Benjamin Ellsworth and Virginia (Oliver) Richards; m. Jeffrey Leonard Johnson, June 25, 1977; children: Jared Benjamin, Jessica Lauren. B.S. in Bus. Mgmt., Strayer Coll., 1973; postgrad. in Bus. Adminstrn., Am. U., 1975-77. Nat. govt. sales rep. G.F.C. Mfg. Co., Bklyn., 1972-75; ter. sales rep. John H. Breck, Am. Cyanamid, Wayne, N.J., 1975-77; ter. sales mgr. Drackett Products Co., Cin., 1977-81, E.J. Brach & Sons., Chgo., Annapolis, Md., 1981-87, owner, pres. Madge Johnson Ltd., 1987—. Mem. Nat. Assn. Female Execs., Grocery Mfrs. Reps., Women in Consumer Product Sales. Home and Office: 625 Rolling Dale Rd Annapolis MD 21401

JOHNSON, MARCELITE ELAINE, computer management executive, consultant; b. Savannah, Ga., Mar. 19, 1949; d. Leon and Jane (Mohr) Dingle; m. Melvin Norman Johnson, Dec. 22, 1968, children -DeAndra Chanet, Monet Nichelle, Melvin Roschaun. B.A. in Math., U. Colo.-Boulder, 1972; M.S. in Edn., Ind. U.-Bloomington, 1979; postgrad. U. So. Calif., Stuttgart, W.Ger., 1984-85. Programmer analyst Hewlitt-Packard, Colorado Springs, 1979-81; sr. systems analyst Penrose Hosp., Colorado Springs, 1982-83; systems mgr. Penrose Cancer Hosp., Colorado Springs, 1981-82; systems mgr. Civilian Personnel Office U.S. Army, Stuttgart, Fed. Republic Germany, 1983-85; br. support mgr. Wang Deutschland GmbH Fed. Systems Dist., Stuttgart, 1985—; lectr. U. Colo., 1980, City Colls. Chgo., Stuttgart, 1983-85. Mem. Nat. Assn. Female Execs., Alpha Kappa Alpha. Episcopalian. Avocations: tennis; bridge. Office: Wang Deutschland GmbH, Vor dem Lauch 25, 7000 Stuttgart 80, Federal Republic of Germany

JOHNSON, MARGARET ANN KIEFT, marquetry company executive; b. Chgo., Nov. 25, 1939; d. Charles Samuel and Betty Marie (Fridrich) Kieft; B.S. in Edn., No. Ill. U., 1961, postgrad., 1963-67, 86—; postgrad. Western Ill. U., 1962-63, (NDEA grantee) Northeastern U., 1967; m. Dale L. Johnson, Aug. 19, 1961; 1 child, Jeffrey Kieft. Tchr., Frew Elem. Sch., Aledo, Ill., 1961-62; tchr. English, Aledo High Sch., 1962-63; tchr. English, head dept. Hiawatha High Sch., Kirkland, Ill., 1963-72; sec.-treas., office mgr., dir. Inlaid Woodcraft Co., Kirkland, 1973—. Mem. adv. bd. Kirkland Parent-Tchr. Orgn., 1977-78; mem. steering com. Sycamore Parent-Tchr. Orgn., Sycamore, Ill., 1980-81; mem. membership com. Ben Gordon Mental Health Center, 1980-81, supporting mem., 1982-85, benefactor, 1986-88; den leader Sycamore Pack #118, Three Rivers council Cub Scouts, Boy Scouts Am., 1981-82; mem. Sycamore Hosp. Aux., 1983-87, dir. Opportunity House, 1987-88. Mem. Marquetry Soc. Am., Nat. Fedn. Ind. Bus., Nat. Small Bus. Assn., Beta Sigma Phi (Order of Rose 1980, pres. exec. council 1982-83). Club: Order Eastern Star. Home: Ellen Dr PO Box 497 Genoa IL 60135 Office: 525 Brickville Rd Sycamore IL 60178

JOHNSON, MARGARET HELEN, welding executive; b. Chgo., June 3, 1933; d. Harold W. and Clara J. (Pape) Glavin; m. Odean Jack Johnson, Nov. 18, 1950; children: Karen Ann, Dean Harold. Student Moody Bible Inst., 1976-78. V.p., sec. Seamline Welding, Inc., Chgo., 1956—, also dir.; trustee SWCEPS, Chgo., 1963—. Author: Living Faith, 1973, 80, Lord's Ladder of Love, 1976, God's Rainbow, 1982; contbr. articles to religion mags. Mem. Rep. Presdl. Task Force, 1982-88, trustee, 1986-88, renew facilitator 1986-88, co-chairperson 1986-88; charter founder Ronald Reagan Rep. Ctr., 1987, mem. Lake View Neighborhood Group, Chgo.; active Mary, Seat of Wisdom Cath. Women's Club, 1970—, Renew facilitator, 1986-87, co-chairperson, 1986-88; Sunday sch. tchr., 1985. Mem. ASCAP, Fedn. Ind. Small Bus., Internat. Platform Assn., Small Group Community (Renew co-chairperson 1986-87). Roman Catholic. Home: 6 S Seminary Ave Park Ridge IL 60068

JOHNSON, MARGARET HILL, educational administrator; b. Dundee, Scotland, June 26, 1923; d. John Barnet and Isabella Rae (Watson) Hill; came to U.S., 1946, naturalized, 1957; student Inverness (Scotland) Royal Acad., 1940, Edinburgh (Scotland) Royal Coll. Art, 1940-43; doctoral candidate U. Mass., Amherst, 1980—; children—Ann Hill Doughty, James Appleton Doughty (dec.), Joanna Elizabeth Johnson. Latin and remedial English tutor Harvey Sch., N.Y.C., 1947-52; tchr. athletics Pingree Sch. for Girls, Hamilton, Mass., 1959-61; tchr. Shore Country Day Sch., Beverly, Mass., 1952-59; asso. dir. Theodore S. Jones & Co., design mgmt. cons., Milton, Mass., 1961-72; dir. career planning and placement Mass. Coll. Art, 1972—, coordinator human services; design cons. Theodore S. Jones & Co.; speaker Lesley Coll., 1977, Cambridge (Mass.) Community Schs., 1977—, MIT, Harvard U., R.I. Sch. Design, Hofstra U. Served with Brit. Women's Royal Naval Service, 1943-46. Mem. Coll. Placement Council, Mass. Assn. Women Deans and Counselors, Nat. Assn. Women Deans, Adminstrs. and Counselors, Am. Assn. Higher Edn., Coll. Art Assn. Am., Eastern Coll. Placement Officers, Arts Dirs. Club Boston, Graphic Artists Guild. Author: (with others) Your Future in Art and Design, 1977. Home: Box 75 Off Summer St Marshfield MA 02051 Office: 621 Huntington Ave Boston MA 02115

JOHNSON, MARGARET KATHLEEN, educator; b. Baylor County, Tex., Oct. 30, 1920; d. George W. and Julia Rivers (Turner) Higgins; m. Herman Clyde Johnson, Jr., July 27, 1949 (dec.); 1 child, Carolyn Kay. B.S., Hardin-Simmons U., 1940; M.Bus. Edn., North Tex. State U., 1957, Ed.D., 1962. Clk. Farmers Nat. Bank, Seymour, Tex., 1940-41; adminstrv. sec. U.S. Navy, Corpus Christi, Tex., 1941-46; adminstrv. asst. Hdqrs. 8th Army, Yokohama, Japan, 1946-49; instr. Coll. Bus. Adminstrn., U. Ark., 1957-60; teaching fellow Sch. Bus. Adminstrn., North Tex. State U., 1960-62, instr., 1962-63; asst. prof. bus., tchr. edn. and secondary edn. Tchrs. Coll., U. Nebr., Lincoln, 1963-65; asso. prof. Tchrs. Coll., U. Nebr., 1966-70, prof., 1970—; guest lectr. U. N.Mex., 1967, Curriculum Devel. in Bus. Edn., N.S. Dept. Edn., 1969, North Tex. State U., 1970, East Tex. State U., 1972; in Policies Commn. for Bus. and Econ. Edn., 1979-83. Author: Standardized Production Typewriting Tests series, 1964-65, National Structure for Research in Vocational Education, 1966; co-author: Introduction to Word Processing, 1980, 2d edit., 1985, Introduction to Business Communication, 1981, 2d edit., 1988; editor: Nat. Bus. Edn. Assn. Yearbook, 1980. Recipient

United Bus. Edn. Assn. award as outstanding grad. student in bus. edn. North Tex. State U., 1957; award for outstanding service Nebr. Future Bus. Leaders Am., 1968; Mountain-Plains Bus. Edn. Leadership award, 1977; merit award Nebr. Bus. Assn., 1979. Mem. Nat. Bus. Edn. Assn. (exec. bd. 1975, 76-78), Mountain-Plains Bus. Edn. Assn. (exec. sec. 1970-73, pres. 1975), Nebr. Bus. Edn. Assn. (pres. 1966-67), Nebr. Council on Occupational Tchr. Edn., Delta Pi Epsilon. Office: U Nebr 529 Nebraska Hall Lincoln NE 68588

JOHNSON, MARGARET KENNARD, artist; b. Madison, Wis., Feb. 3, 1918; d. Dwight Clinton and Florence June (Lott) Kennard; m. Edward Oscar Johnson, Sept. 1, 1947; children: Lonni Sue, Aline Marie. BFA, Pratt Inst., 1941; M in Design, U. Mich., 1943; studied with Josef Albers, 1944. Cert. tchr., Mich. Art. supr. Ypsilanti (Mich.) Schs., 1941-42; acting asst. prof. Drake U., Des Moines, Iowa, 1943-45; asst. prof. Tex. State Coll. for Women, Denton, 1945-46; instr. adult classes Mus. Modern Art, N.Y.C., 1946-71; art. instr. Tokyo American Club, 1981-83; instr. Princeton Art Assn., 1960-75, 85—; instr. found. classes The Art Sch. Pratt Inst., Bklyn., 1946-49; instr. Princeton Adult Sch., 1965-74. Work exhibited in one woman shows Internat. Print Soc., New Hope, Pa., 1983, Gallery Tapies, Kobe, Japan, 1985, Norske Grafikere, Oslo, 1985, Am. Ctr., Tokyo, 1986, N.J. State Mus., Trenton, 1988; group exhibits include Sao Paulo Mus., Brazil, 1973, Tochigi Prefectural Art Mus., Utsunomiya, Japan, 1980, Coll. Womens' Assn. Japan show, Tokyo, 1976-79, 81, 83-87, Met. Mus., Tokyo, 1976-79, 83-88, Pratt Graphs Ctr., N.Y.C., 1986; work exhibited in permanent collections British Mus., London, 1986, Tochigi Prefectural Mus., Japan, 1980; co-author Japanese Prints Today, 1980; contbr. articles to Am. and Japanese art jours. Mem. Print Assn., Japan Hands, Princeton Art Assn., Printmaking Council of N.J. Home: 231 Snowden Lane Princeton NJ 08540

JOHNSON, MARIE LOUISE, college dean; b. Chgo., June 28, 1933; d. Frederick Douglas and Pearl Louise (Bailey) J. BA, U. Ill., 1954, MS, 1958; PhD, Ill. Inst. Tech., 1971. Chief psychometrist student counseling service U. Ill. Navy Pier, Chgo., 1956-61, U. Ill. Chgo. Circle Campus, 1965-71; assoc. dean of students U. Ill., Chgo., 1971—; with Chgo. Bd. Edn., 1961-65; mem. adv. com. long-term care study sect. Nat. Ctr. Health Services Research HEW, Washington, 1976-77, cons., 1977-81; cons. women's identities study Chgo. State U., 1980-81; mem. health services devel. grants Dept. Health and Human Resources, Washington, 1977-81; charter mem. adv. bd. Bur. Child Study Chgo. Bd. Edn., 1981—. Mem. adv. bd. model cities Altgeld Quality of Life Project, Chgo., 1976-77. Mem. Am. Assn. Counseling and Devel., Am. Coll. Personnel Assn., Nat. Assn. Black Psychologists, Nat. Assn. Women Deans, Adminstrs. and Counselors, U. Ill. Black Alumni Assn. (pres. 1985—), Alpha Lambda Delta, Psi Chi, Alpha Kappa Alpha, Alpha Gamma Pi. Mem. United Ch. of Christ. Home: 10722 S Prospect Ave Chicago IL 60643 Office: U Ill at Chgo Box 4348 Chicago IL 60680

JOHNSON, MARIE-LOUISE TULLY, dermatologist, educator; b. N.Y.C., July 26, 1927; d. James Henry and Mary Frances (Dobbins) Tully; m. Kenneth Gerald Johnson, June 10, 1950. AB, Manhattanville Coll., 1948; PhD, Yale U., 1954, MD, 1956. Intern, then resident Yale-New Haven (Conn.) Med. Ctr., 1956-60; asst. prof. medicine, dermatology Yale U., 1961-64, clin. prof. dermatology, 1980—; chief dermatologist med. service Atomic Bomb Casualty Commn., Hiroshima, Japan, 1964-67; asst. prof. dermatology NYU, 1967-69, assoc. prof. dermatology, 1969-70, 74-76, prof. dermatology, 1976-80; assoc. prof. dermatology, coordinator continuing med. edn. Dartmouth Coll., Hanover, N.H., 1971-74; chief dermatology Bellevue Hosp., N.Y.C., 1974-80; dir. med. edn. Benedictine Hosp., Kingston, N.Y., 1980—; cons. Health and Nutrition Exam. Survey I, II, Health Statistics, Washington, 1967-84; bd. dirs. Benedictine Health Found., 1986—. Contbg. author: Cecil's Textbook of Medicine, 15th edit., 1979, 16th edit., 1982, 17th edit., 1985, Dermatology in General Medicine, 2d edit., 1979. Mem. Cardinal Cooke Pro-Life Commn., Albany, N.Y., 1986-87; bd. dirs. Maternity and Early Childhood Found., Albany, 1985—. Named Disting. Alumnae Manhattanville Coll., 1977. Fellow Am. Acad. Dermatology (bd. dirs. 1976-80); mem. Am. Dermatol. Assn. (bd. dirs. 1986—), Nat. Acad. Scis. Inst. Medicine, Internat. Physicians for Prevention of Nuclear War (del. 1982, 83, 87, 88). Democrat. Roman Catholic. Home: Strawberry Bank High Falls NY 12440 Office: Benedictine Hosp 105 Mary's Ave Kingston NY 12401

JOHNSON, MARILYN THERESE CURRAN, sales techniques company executive; b. N.Y.C., Oct. 22, 1936; d. Carl Frederick and Bridget (O'Brien) Bachmann; m. Harold Joseph Curran, Nov. 28, 1959 (div. 1972); 1 child, Jeffrey Francis; m. Ronald Hans Johnson Aug. 8, 1981; stepchildren—Ronald, Kristina. Student, Katherine Gibbs Sch., 1954-55, U. Conn., 1955-57; B.A. in Psychology, Rutgers U., 1969. Asst. to Asst. Sec. State Dept., Washington, 1957-59; broker Merrill Lynch, N.Y.C., 1971-73; asst. mgr. sales Xerox, Princeton, N.J., 1973-80; nat. account rep. Gen. Dynamics Co., Montvale, N.J., 1980-82; sales exec. No. Telecom, N.Y.C., 1982-85; pres., owner Selling Scis., Somerset, N.J., 1985—; cons. Barbizon Modelling Schs., Highland Park, N.J., 1964-69. Mem. Bus. and Profl. Women (chmn. young careerist 1984, chmn. foundation com. 1985). Avocations: French studies; skiing; tennis; travel; reading. Home: 144 Drake Rd Somerset NJ 08873

JOHNSON, MARLENE, lieutenant governor; b. Braham, Minn., Jan. 11, 1946; d. Beauford and Helen (Nelson) J. BA, Macalester U., 1968. Founder, pres. Split Infinitive, Inc., St. Paul, 1970-82; pres., bd. dirs. Face to Face Health and Counseling Clinic, 1977 78; with Working Opportunities for Women, 1977-82; lt. gov. State of Minn., St. Paul, 1983—; founder, past chmn. Nat. Leadership Conf. Women Execs. in State Govt.; mem. exec. com., midwestern chair Nat. Conf. Lt. Govs. Chmn. Minn. Women's Polit. Caucus, 1973-76, Dem.-Farmer-Labor Small Bus. Task Force, 1978, Child Care Task Force, 1987, Nat. Conf. of Lt. Govs., 1987; dir. membership sect. Nat. Women's Polit. Caucus, 1975-77; vice chmn. Minn. Del. to White House Conf. on Small Bus., 1980; co-founder Minn. Women's Campaign Fund, 1982; founder, past chmn., Nat. Leadership Conf. Women Execs. in State Govt.; bd. dirs. Nat. Child Care Action Campaign, Minn. Outward Bound Sch., Mpls., Spring Hill Conf. Ctr., Mpls. Recipient Outstanding Achievement award, St. Paul YWCA, 1980, Disting. Citizen citation, Macalester Coll., 1982, Disting. Contributions to Families award Minn. Council on Family Relations, 1986, Minn. Sportfishing Congress award, 1986; named dir. World Press Inst.; Swedish Bicentennial Commn. grantee, 1987. Mem. Nat. Assn. Women Bus. Owners (past pres.). Office: Office of Lt Gov Room 121 State Capitol Aurora Ave Saint Paul MN 55155

JOHNSON, MARLENE CAROLE, banker; b. Somerville N.J., Apr. 10, 1950; d. Herbert E. and Thelma E. (Westerfield) J. B.A., Glassboro State Coll., 1972; M. Banking, Rutgers U., 1982. Cert. tchr., N.J. Asst. bookkeeper Franklin State Bank, Somerset, N.J., 1972-73; adminstr. North Plainfield (N.J.) State Bank, 1973-76, asst. sec., 1976-78, asst. v.p., 1978-86; v.p. 1986—. Mem. Voluntary Action Com., New Brunswick, N.J.; v.p. Quailbrook Homeowners Assn. Recipient Tribute to Women and Industry, YWCA, Westfield, N.J. Mem. Am. Inst. Banking (v.p. edn. Middlesex, Somerset, Union chpt. 1974-84, pres. chpt. 1984-85), Nat. Assn. Bank Women, Nat. Assn. Female Execs. Contbr. articles to profl. jours. Home: 137 Bayberry Dr Somerset NJ 08873 Office: North Plainfield State Bank Route 22 and Rock Ave Box 1027 North Plainfield NJ 07060

JOHNSON, MARY LEONA, city official; b. Greenville, N.C., Sept. 21; d. Lewis and Leona (Anderson) Blow; B.A. in Sociology, Wayne State U., 1974; M.A., Antioch Sch. Law, 1982; 1 son, Reginald B. Johnson. With U.S. Treasury Dept., Washington, 1944-46; receptionist U.S. Army Tank Automotive Center, 1952-56; supr. Tb Registry, Detroit Dept. Health, 1956-71; Affirmative Action adminstr. Detroit Human Rights Dept., 1977—, cons. women's issues, 1975-77. Mem. Mich. State adv. council vocat. edn., 1980-83; mem. appeal bd. Selective Service System, Eastern Jud. Dist. Mich.; vice chmn. 1st Congl. Dist. Dem. Party Orgn. Recipient Christian Service award, numerous awards for community service. Mem. Nat. Assn. Human Rights Workers of Mich. (pres. Mich. chpt.), Mich. Coalition for Human Rights, Nat. Assn. Exec. Women, Detroit Round Table of Christian and Jews Detroit Women's Forum, Women's Econ. Club. Democrat. Mem. United Ch. of Christ (chair dept. missions, Detroit Metro. Assn., mem. nominating com. Mich. Conf., trustee Plymouth chpt.). Office: Detroit Human Rights Dept 150 Michigan Ave 4th Fl Detroit MI 48226

JOHNSON, MARY MURPHY, social services director; b. N.Y.C., Mar. 5, 1940; d. Richard and Nora (Greene) Murphy; m. Noel James Johnson, Oct. 8, 1961; children: Valerie Johnson Brogan, Donna Homan, Noreen Marie, Richard. BA in English, History and Sociology magna cum laude, Jacksonville State U., 1983, MA in History, 1984, B in Social Work magna cum laude, 1987. Cert. gerontology specialist. Asst. acticities dir. Jacksonville (Ala.) Nursing Home, 1985-86; social services dir. Beckwood Manor, Anniston, Ala., 1987—; Cons. in field. Editor: Vladivostak Diary, 1987. Mem. Ala. Archaeol. Soc., Coosa Valley Archaeol. Soc. (sec. 1982-87), Soc. Ala. Archivists, Human Services Council, Phi Eta Sigma, Phi Alpha Theta, Sigma Tau Delta, Omicron Delta Kappa. Russian Orthodox. Clubs: Non Commd. Officers Ladies Aux. (pres. 1970-71), Non Commd. Officers Wives (Germany) (pres. 1965-66).

JOHNSON, MARY NINA, university program administrator; b. Jamaica, N.Y., June 18, 1943; d. William Joseph and Viola (Osani) Graham; m. William Johnson, May 2, 1965; children: Kim Marie, Scott Edward. Diploma, Wood Secretarial Sch., N.Y.C., 1963. Sec. to regional mgr. Coca Cola Bottling Co., Inc., N.Y.C., 1963-66; exec. sec. Dover Corp., N.Y.C., 1966-68; benefits adminstr. Singer Corp., Woodbury, N.Y., 1968-70; regional mgr. Dart Industries, Tauton, Mass., 1971-80; sr. sec. Rensselaer Poly. Inst., Troy, N.Y., 1980-81, adminstrv. asst., 1981-82, mgr. corp. relations, 1982-86, asst. dir., 1986—; exec. com. IBM Grantee Schs. Consortium, 1983—. Mem. Computer Graphics Soc. (internat. coordinator 1986—, treas. 1987—). Republican. Roman Catholic. Office: Rensselaer Polytechnic Inst 110 Eighth St Troy NY 12181

JOHNSON, MARY THIGPEN (TISH), real estate executive; b. Jacksonville, Fla., Sept. 15, 1951; d. John Jackson and Marie (Currie) Thigpen; m. Terry George Johnson, Mar. 17, 1973; children: Steven, Kimberly, Rebekah. BA, Valdosta State Coll., 1973. Lic. real estate broker, Ga. V.p. Dewar Properties, Inc., 1976—; ptnr. various real estate partnerships. Mem. Council for Rural Housing and Devel. (past bd. dirs., chmn. Ga. State), Nat. Leased Housing Assn., Am. Mgmt. Assn. Methodist. Home: 1205 Ravenwood Circle Valdosta GA 31602 Office: Dewar Properties Inc 2409 Bemiss Rd Valdosta GA 31602

JOHNSON, MARY VERONICA, nurse, private investigator; b. Syracuse, N.Y., Dec. 27, 1945; d. Zachariah Irving and Beulah Therese (Hill) Hotaling; m. Anthony Alan Fugo, July 4, 1964 (div. 1971); m. Wayne Raymond Johnson, July 11, 1974 (div. 1987); children: William John, David Jeffrey. Lic. Practical Nurse, Sheridan Vocat. Coll., Hollywood, Fla., 1972. Staff nurse Hollywood Meml. Hosp., 1972-74; office nursing supr. Drs. Johnson and Cofran, Hollywood, 1974-86; nursing supr. Hollywood Diagnostics Ctr., 1986-87; prin. Guardian Detective Agy., Hollywood, 1987-88; staff nurse Hospice House, Hollywood, 1988—. Pub. Luther Meml. Luth. Ch. newsletter, Hollywood, 1983—. Chmn. adv. bd. McArthur High Sch., Hollywood, 1981, 82, 85, supr. vols., 1984-86, v.p. band boosters, 1982; local capt. Pembroke Pines (Fla.) Citizens' Crime Watch, 1984—; mem. crew "Day Tripper" Cruises Inc., Pompano Beach, Fla., 1987-88; dir. youth group Luther Meml. Luth. Ch., 1976-79, dir. activities, 1980-82. Recipient Outstanding Service award McArthur High Sch., 1985, 86. Mem. Nat. Assn. Female Execs., Older Women's League, United Singles of Am. Home: 7190 SW 14th St Pembroke Pines FL 33023 Office: Hollywood Diagnostics Ctr 4224 Hollywood Blvd Hollywood FL 33021

JOHNSON, MARYANN ELAINE, educational administrator; b. Franklin Twp., Pa., Nov. 1, 1943; d. Mary I. Sollick; B.S. in Elementary Edn., Mansfield State Coll., Pa., 1964; M.S. in Elementary Edn., U. Alaska, College 1973; Ed.D., Wash. State U., Pullman, 1981; married. Tchr. Nayatt Sch., Barrington, R.I., 1964-66, North Sch., North Chicago, Ill., 1966-67, Kodiak (Alaska) On-Base Sch., 1967-71; reading coordinator Eastmont Sch. Dist., East Wenatchee, Wash., 1974-77, now asst. supt. Sec. Parent Advisory Com., 1974-76. Mem. Assn. Supervision and Curriculum Devel., Wash. State Assn. Supervision and Curriculum Devel. (bd. dirs. 1986—, Educator of Yr. 1981), NEA, Wash. Assn. Sch. Adminstrs. (bd. dirs., chmn. curriculum and instrn. Job-Alike, profl. devel. com., Project Leadership, pres. 1986-87, 87-88, leadership award, 1986, Exec. Educator 100 1988), Am. Assn. Sch. Adminstrs., Delta Kappa Gamma (pres. 1982-84), Phi Delta Kappa, Phi Kappa Phi. Named Eastmont Tchr. of the Yr., 1973-74. Office: 460 N E 9th St East Wenatchee WA 98802

JOHNSON, NANCY LEE, congresswoman; b. Chgo., Jan. 5, 1935; d. Noble Wishard and Gertrude Reid (Smith) Lee; m. Theodore H. Johnson, July 16, 1958; children—Lindsey Lee, Althea Anne, Caroline Reid. B.A., Radcliffe Coll., 1957; postgrad., U. London, 1957-58. Vice chmn. Charter Commn. New Britain, Conn., 1976-77; mem. Conn. Senate from 6th dist., 1977-82, 98th-100th Congresses, Washington, 1983—. Lectr. Am. art New Britain Mus. Am. Art, 1968-71; pres. Friends of Library, New Britain Pub. Library, 1973-76; pres. Radcliffe Club No. Conn., 1973-75; bd. dirs., pres. Sheldon Community Guidance Clinic, 1974-75; dir. religious edn. Unitarian Universalist Soc. New Britain, 1967-72, pres., 1973-75; bd. dirs. New Britain Symphony Soc., 1975-77, Plainville Group Home, 1975-76, United Way New Britain, 1976-79. Recipient Outstanding Vol. award United Way, 1976; English Speaking Union grantee, 1958-59. Republican. Home: 141 S Mountain Dr New Britain CT 06052

JOHNSON, NORINE GOODE, psychologist; b. Indpls., Dec. 3, 1935; d. Frank and Marie (Collins) Goode; B.A., DePauw U., 1957; Ph.D., Wayne State U., 1972; postgrad. Harvard Med. Sch., 1975-77; m. Charles W. Johnson, Aug. 23, 1958; children—Cammarie, Kathryn Carroll, Margaret Ellen. Psychology cons. to pediatrics Univ. Hosps. Cleve., 1968-69; asst. clin. prof. dept. neurology Boston U. Med. Sch., 1976—; adj. prof. psychology Boston Coll., 1978-84; dir. psychology Kennedy Meml. Hosp., Brighton, Mass., 1970-88; pres. ABCS Psychology Resources, 1988—. Pres. area bd. Mental Health and Retardation, 1973, regional bd., 1974; mem. Gov.'s Adv. Council Mental Health and Mental Retardation, 1974-76, chairperson children's subcom., 1976. NIMH scholar, trainee. Fellow Mass. Psychol. Assn. (pres. elect 1980, pres. 1981-83, dir., bd. profl. affairs 1977—, chairperson 1977-78, liaison to Mass. Psychiat. Soc. 1978); mem. Am. Psychol. Assn. (co-chair fin. com. 1987—, exec. com. assn. psychology internship ctrs. 1985—, council of reps. 1985-88), Psi Chi. Club: Boston Athletic. Home: 13 Ashfield St Roslindale MA 02169 Office: 111 Willard St Suite 2B Quincy MA 02169

JOHNSON, NORMA HOLLOWAY, federal judge; b. Lake Charles, La.. BS., D.C. Tchrs. Coll., 1955; J.D., Georgetown U., 1962. Bar: D.C. bar 1962, U.S. Supreme Ct. bar 1967. Practiced in Washington, 1963; atty. Dept. Justice, Washington, 1963-67; asst. corp. counsel D.C. 1967-70; judge D.C. Superior Ct., 1970-80, U.S. Dist. Ct. for D.C., 1980—; Bd. dirs. Nat. Children's Center, Washington, National Street Law Inst. Mem. Am. Bar Assn., Nat. Bar Assn., D.C. Bar, Nat. Council Juvenile Ct. Judges, Am. Judicature Soc. (dir.), Nat. Assn. Women Judges (dir.). Office: US Dist Ct US Courthouse 3d & Constitution Ave NW Washington DC 20001

JOHNSON, NORMA J., specialty wool grower; b. Dover, Ohio, Aug. 30, 1925; d. Jasper Crile and Mildred Catherine (Russell) J.; student Heidelberg Coll., 1943; cert. drafting techniques Case Sch. Applied Sci., 1944; student Western Res. U., 1945-47, Ohio State U., 1951, Muskingum Coll., 1965; A.A., Kent State U., 1979, Buckeye Joint Vocat. Sch., 1979-84; m. Robert Blake Covey, Oct. 7, 1951 (div. 1960); 1 dau., Susan Kay. Instr. arts and crafts Univ. Settlement House, Cleve., 1944; mech. drafstwoman Nat. Assn. Civil Aeros., Cleve., 1944-46; mfrs. rep. Nat. Spice House, 1947-49; tchr. econs., home econs., English, math, history, high sch., Tuscarawas County Sch. System, New Philadelphia, Ohio, 1962-69; owner, mgr., operator Sunny Slopes Farm, producer of specialty wools and grains, Dover, Ohio, 1969—. Tchr., Meth. Sunday Sch., 1956-61; chaplain Winfield PTA, 1960; program dir. Brandywine Grange, 1960-62; troop leader Girl Scouts, U.S.A., 1961-70; mem. Tuscarawas County Jail Com., 1981-87. Recipient cert. of merit Tuscarawas County Schs., 1965, Ohio Wildlife Conservation award Tuscarawas County, 1972, 1st and 3d premiums for handspinning fleece, Ohio State Fair, 1984., 8th and 10th premiums, Mich. Stat Fair, 1985. Mem. Mid States Wool Growers, Am. Angus Assn., Club: Nat. Grange. Bldg. designed and constructed interior facilities for the Scheuerhaus. Home and Office: Route 1 Box 398 Dover OH 44622

JOHNSON, NORMA LOU, educator; b. Lubbock, Tex., May 19, 1941; d. Hubert Huston and Wallace Leana (Currey) Foster; m. Charles Kenneth Johnson, Dec. 20, 1958; children: Norma Elizabeth, Victoria Lee. Student, Tenn. Temple U., 1963-65, Liberty U., 1985-86. Dental asst. Caperton Med., Lubbock, 1957-58; lab. technician Porter Med. Clinic, Lubbock, 1958-59; head bookkeeper Graham TV Clinic, Chattanooga, 1960-61; educator Littlefield (Tex.) Pub. Sch. System, 1967-70; missionary Can. Bapt. Missions, Can., 1970-84; educator Can. Bapt. Schs., various locations, Can., 1970-84, Colo. Bapt. Missions, Ft. Collins, 1984—; cons. Partnership mag., 1985—. Pianist Can. Bapt. Missions, Can., 1970-82; organist Victory Bapt. Missions, Ft. Collins, 1983—. Mem. Profl. Homemakers Assn., Vocat. Indsl. Corp. Home: 1038 Boltz Dr Fort Collins CO 80525

JOHNSON, PATRICIA ANN, academic administrator, consultant; b. Mobile, Ala., Dec. 25, 1943; d. Kenneth Nathaniel Johnson and Lula Mae (Bolding) Reed. BA, Knoxville Coll., 1965; MEd, Georgia State U., 1974; EdD, Atlanta U., 1976. Tchr. Nat. Capitol child Care, Washington, 1965-69; mgmt. specialist A.L. Nellum Assocs., Washington, 1969-71; project dir. Roy Littlejohn Assocs., Washington, 1971-73; adminstr. U. South Ala., Mobile, 1979-86; pres. co-owner Future Firm Internat., Inc., Mobile, 1986—; cons. Devel. Assocs., Washington, 1970-71, Va. Commonwealth U., Richmond, 1971-73, Southeastern Tchr. Corp., Atlanta, 1973-74, Dept. Health/Human Services, nationwide, 1973-86. Pres. Ala. Head Start Assn., 1979-83, S.D. Bishop State Health Careers Opportunity Program, Mobile, 1985—, Ala. State Fedn. Planning Bd., Montgomery, 1979-86; v.p. Mobile County Urban League, 1984-86; bd. dirs. Maternal and Child Health Adv. Bd., Ala., 1980-87. Recipient Leadership award Miss. Head Start Dirs. Assn., 1985-86, leadership award Ala. Fedn. Human Resources, 1983, 84, 86; Ford Found. fellow, 1974; named Outstanding Citizen State Ala. Gov. Office, Montgomery, 1985. Mem. Am. Edn. Research Assn., Assn. Supervision/Curriculum Devel., Alpha Kappa Alpha. Democrat. Mem. Unity Ch. Office: Future Firm Internat Inc 1806 Brownlee St Mobile AL 36617

JOHNSON, PATRICIA ELAINE, sales professional; b. Quakertown, Pa., Jan. 9, 1947; d. Robert Hoffert and Elaine Laura (Stowell) Neubert; divorced; children: Marnie L., Alisha S. License in Cosmetology, Empire Beauty Sch., Allentown, Pa., 1965, License Cosmetology Mgmt., 1969. Gen. mgr. Meehan's Beauty Salons, Allentown, Pa., 1970-74; color technician Helene Curtis Industries, Chgo., 1974-75; dist. mgr. Helene Curtis Ind., Chgo., 1975-80; regional mgr. Ardell Inc., Solon, Ohio, 1979-80; gen. mgr. Beethoven's Salons, Buffalo, 1980; ednl. dir. G.A. Kayser and Sons, Buffalo, 1980-81; mfr.'s rep. Art Marshall Inc., Leonia, N.J., 1981-82; territorial mgr. Matrix Essentials Inc., Solon, 1982-87; gen. mgr. DiDonato Corp., Trenton, N.J., 1988—. Republican. Lutheran. Club: Quakertown Soccer. Home: 242 Levian St Apt A Allentown PA 18951 Office: DiDonato Corp 682 Whitehead Rd Trenton NJ 08648

JOHNSON, PATRICIA GAYLE, corporate communication executive, writer; b. Conway, Ark., Oct. 23, 1947; d. Rudolph and Frances Modene (Hayes) J. Student U. Calif., Irvine, 1965-68. Advance rep. Disney on Parade, Los Angeles, 1971-75; mktg. dir./dir. field ops. Am. Freedom Train, 1975-77; publ. relations mgr. Six Flags, Inc., Los Angeles, 1977-81; mgr. corp. communications Playboy Enterprises, Inc., Los Angeles, 1981-82; external relations mgr. Kal Kan Foods, Inc., Los Angeles, 1982-86; v.p. Daniel J. Edelman, Inc., 1986—; lectr. U. So. Calif., UCLA, Calif. State U., Northridge, Calif. State U., Dominguez Hills. Mem. Pub. Relations Soc. Am. (past officer), Pub. Affairs Council, Delta Soc. (advisor). Mem. Foursquare Gospel Ch. Collaborator TV scripts; contbr. articles to various consumer and profl. mags. Office: Daniel J Edelman Inc 10866 Wilshire Blve Suite 550 Los Angeles CA 90024

JOHNSON, PATRICIA MARY, publisher; b. Evanston, Ill., Mar. 14, 1937; d. Harold W. and Florence M. (Miller) J.; children: William, Nancy, Richard. Degree in Interior Design LaSalle U., Chgo., 1972; student Art Inst., Chgo., 1970-73. Owner Decor Interior Design, Chgo., 1972-76; interior design communicator, producer/host weekly syndicated cable TV program on interior design, 1980-86; owner Design Communications, Rosenhayn, N.J., 1976-85; exec. dir. Corp. for Disabled/Handicapped; pub. A Positive Approach mag. Mem. adv. bd. So. N.J. Easter Seal. Recipient award N.J. Gov., 1985, Practitioner of Yr. award N.J. Rehab. Assn., 1987, Humanitarian Service award United Cerebral Palsy, 1987, Jefferson award NBC, 1988. Author: Eliminating Barriers from Your Lifestyle, 1985; contbr. articles to profl. jours. and consumer mags.; also radio broadcaster.

JOHNSON, PRETANGIA, accountant; b. Guin, Ala., Feb. 11, 1960; d. Frank D. and Threcia Jquan (Webster) Bull; m. Michael Vaughn Johnson, Oct. 15, 1983 (div. Apr. 1987); 1 child, Garrett Vaughn. Degree in applied sci. law enforcement, San Antonio Coll., 1981; BBA, U. Tex., 1987. CPA, Tex. Acct. Plano (Tex.) Orthopedic and Sports Medicine Ctr., 1983-85; adminstrv. asst. to treas. Tex. Back Inst., Plano, 1985-87; asst. controller Charter Hosp. Dallas, Plano, 1987—. Baptist. Home: 6538 Bronze Ln Plano TX 75023 Office: Charter Hosp Dallas 6800 Preston Rd Plano TX 75024

JOHNSON, SALLY ANN, hotel manager; b. Phila., July 22, 1960; d. Victor L. and Joan (Markovitz) J. BA, Clark U., 1982; BS in Culinary Arts, Johson and Wales Coll., Providence, 1984. Food service mgr. DAKA, Worcester, Mass., 1978-85; garde manger chef Pleasant Valley Country Club, Worcester, 1984; hotel mgr. Marriott Corp., Atlanta, 1985—. Recipient Woman of Achievement award Ga. YMCA, 1987. Mem. Nat. Assn. Female Execs., Nat. Restaurant Assn. Home: 31 Arpege Way Atlanta GA 30327 Office: Marriott Corp 265 W Peachtree Ave Atlanta GA 30303

JOHNSON, SAMMYE LARUE, communications educator; b. Dallas, Oct. 8, 1946; d. Sam S. and Poppy (Hammond) Malosky; BS in Journalism with distinction, Northwestern U. Medill Sch. Journalism, 1968, MS in Journalism, with highest distinction, 1969. Asst. editor Where Mag., Chgo., 1969; feature writer Chicago Today newspaper, Chgo., 1969-71, Sunday mag. editor, 1971-73; asst. dir., public relations mgr. W. O. Darby Library, Nurnberg, W.Ger., 1974-75; editor San Antonio Mag., 1976-79; communications dir. VIA Met. Transit System, San Antonio, 1979; asst. prof. journalism William Allen White Sch. Journalism, U. Kans., Lawrence, 1979-80; assoc. prof. communication Trinity U., San Antonio, 1980—; cons. public relations Community Guidance Ctr., San Antonio, 1985—, Funding Info. Ctr., San Antonio, 1983—, Bexar County Women's Ctr., San Antonio, 1984—. Named Today's Woman of Achievement, San Antonio Light Newspaper, 1981, Pub. Relations Educator of Yr., Tex. Pub. Relations Assn., 1984-85. Mem. Women in Communications (dir. 1978-80, pres. chpt. 1983-84, Proliner award 1981, 82, 83, 86, 87, 88, Communications Headliner of Yr. 1984), Internat. Assn. Bus. Communicators (bd. dirs. 1979, Gold Quill award 1979, named Communicator of Yr. 1981, numerous other awards 1976-79), Assn. for Edn. in Journalism and Mass Communications (sec., vice chair , chair mag. div. 1985—), Kappa Tau Alpha. Home: 2906 Spring Bend San Antonio TX 78209 Office: Trinity U Dept Communication 715 Stadium Dr San Antonio TX 78284

JOHNSON, SARAH CAROLYN, nutrition educator; b. Paducah, Ky., Oct. 11, 1947; d. Earl Hubbard Hillyard and Pauline (Byrd) Cooke; children: Jennifer Lynn Cruse, Josie Elizabeth Johnson. BS, Ea. Ky. U., 1968; M Bus. Edn., Middle Tenn. State U., 1974. Cert. tchr., Tenn. Tchr. Metro Bd. Edn., Nashville, 1971-78; edn. specialist Vocational Edn., Tenn. Dept. Edn., Nashville, 1978-82; lead cons. Child Nutrition Programs Tenn. Dept. Edn., Nashville, 1982—. Chmn. Role and Status of Women com., First United Meth. Ch., Lebanon, Tenn., 1984-88. Named Ky. Col. by Ky. Cols. Assn., 1981, Tenn. Col. by Gov. Tenn. Mem. Am. Sch. Food Service Assn., Tenn. Sch. Food Service Assn., Dist. Edn. Clubs of Am. (Friend of DECA 1984), Tenn. Vocational Assn. (lifetime, treas. 1981-84), Am. Vocational Assn. (lifetime). Home: Rt 12 PO Box 276 Lebanon TN 37087 Office: Tenn Dept Edn 208 Cordell Hull Bldg Nashville TN 37219-5338

JOHNSON, SARAH LURLINE (CHERYL), sales recruiting agency executive; b. Little Rock, Jan. 21, 1940; d. Foster David and Lurline Fay

(Rice) J.; m. James B. Williams (div. 1961); 1 son, Bradley Foster. Student U. Ark., 1957-59. Med. sales recruiter Dunhill of Houston, 1967-76; owner Johnson Cons., Houston, 1976—. Baptist. Office: Johnson Cons Inc 9801 Westheimer #302 Houston TX 77042

JOHNSON, SARILYN JOAN, real estate broker; b. Kokomo, Ind., June 25, 1932; d. Cleon Frederick Meister and Iris Marie (Detamore) Clark; m. Richard D. Johnson, Dec. 24, 1948 (div. 1963); children: Douglas Kent, Kimberly Mae; m. Glenn E. Johnson, May 3, 1965. Cert. real estate, Edison Coll., Ft. Myers, Fla., 1978. Cert. real estate broker. Office clk. Kimm Paint Co., Muncie, Ind., 1952-56; office mgr. Muncie Reclamation and Supply, 1956-61; office mgr., bookkeeper C.E. Geckler, MD, Muncie, 1961-65; office mgr. C. Bibler Supply Co., Inc., Muncie, 1966-72; real estate broker Raso & Mascarello Realty, Inc., Cape Coral, Fla., 1978-88, owner, pres. Fla. Fleet Supply, Inc., Cape Coral, 1988—. Contbr. articles to profl. jours. Mem. Rep. Nat. Com., Washington, 1987. Mem. Nat. Assn. Female Execs., Am. Bus. Women Assn., Bus. and Profl. Women, Women's Council Realtors (pres. 1981-82, Woman of Yr. 1983), Cape Coral Bd. Realtors (bd. dirs. 1986—, Realtor Assoc. of Yr. 1981), Cape Coral C. of C. Lodge: Order Eastern Star. Home: 1429 SW 57th St Cape Coral FL 33914 Office: Fla Fleet Supply Inc 4812 Cape Coral St Cape Coral FL 33904

JOHNSON, SHARON POWELL, educator; b. Hendersonville, N.C., June 14, 1941; d. James Reid and Edna Una (Love) Powell; m. Larry Rex Bell, July 25, 1964 (div. 1974); 1 child, Beverly Edna; m. John Samuel Johnson, July 22, 1978; 1 child, Shannon Love. BS in Edn., Western Carolina U., 1963. Tchr. Edneyville (N.C.) High Sch., 1963-67, Hendersonville Jr. High Sch., 1968-74, Jefferson Davis Middle Sch., W. Palm Beach, Fla., 1974-77, 1983—; tchr. Congress Middle Sch., Boynton Beach, Fla., 1977-83; coach girl's basketball, N.C., Fla., 1968-85. Mem., sec. Palm Springs Recreation Bd., W. Palm Beach, 1974-77. Named an Outstanding Young Educator Hendersonville Jaycess, 1972. Mem. Nat. Edn. Assn., Classroom Tchr's. Assn., Sci. Tchr's. Assn., Delta Zeta Alumni. (membership com. 1985-86). Democrat. Baptist. Home: 7830 Edgewater Dr West Palm Beach FL 33406

JOHNSON, SHARON SLITER, writer, producer; b. Midland, Tex., July 22, 1950; d. Warren Greenlee and Barbara Jean (Hayslip) Sliter; B.A., DePaul U., 1976; m. Stephan Glenn Johnson, Nov. 7, 1981; 1 son, Luke Daniel. Sec., adminstrv. asst. to chmn. bd. Ency. Brit. Ednl. Corp., Chgo., 1972-77, writer, producer, 1977—; freelance script cons., researcher, writer, 1978—; juror U.S. Indsl. Film Festival, 1981, 82, 83, jury chmn., 1982-83. Democrat. Methodist. Author: I Want to be a Clown, 1985. Home and Office: 4115 N LeClaire St Chicago IL 60641

JOHNSON, SHIRLEY ELAINE, management consultant; b. Terre Haute, Ind., Sept. 15, 1946; d. Mervil Ray and Sarah Kathryn (Tucker) W.; m. Richard E. Johnson Jr., Sept. 23, 1964 (div. 1974); children: Richard Alan, Gary Michael Sr. AA, Coll. Dupage, 1980; student, DePaul U., 1988—. Sec. to v.p. fin. Cenco Inc., Oak Brook, Ill., 1972-74, exec. asst. to group pres., 1974-75, asst. to chmn., 1975-77, corp. personnel/office mgr., 1977-80; corp. sec. Acadia Petroleum Corp., Denver, 1980-82; mgr. office Chapman, Klein & Weinberg, PC, Denver, 1982-84; asst. to chmn. The Heidrick Ptnrs., Inc., Chgo., 1984—. Mem. Am. Mgmt. Assn., Am. Soc. Personnel Adminstrs., DuPage Personnel Assn. (sec. 1979), Exec. Women Internat., Nat. Assn. Female Execs. Home: 7309 Hartford Downers Grove IL 60516 Office: The Heidrick Ptnrs Inc 20 N Wacker Dr Suite 4000 Chicago IL 60606

JOHNSON, SHIRLEY FAY, insurance agent; b. Covington, Ky., Apr. 3, 1936; d. Silas Leonard and Beulah Rich (Smith) Riggs; m. Thomas Ray Johnson. Grad. high sch., Burlington, Ky., 1954. Computer and statistical machine operator Re Polk Co., Cin., 1954-57, Ky. State Police Dept., Frankfort, 1957-58; computer programmer Ky. Dept. Hwys., Frankfort, 1958-59; computer and statistical machine operator Gen. Motors Corp., Cin., 1959-60; office mgr. No. Ky. Sanitation, Walton, 1969-72; exec. asst. J.B. Johnson Ins. Co., Walton, 1972-74, lic. agent, 1974-77, owner, agent, 1977-82, agent, mgr., 1982—. Active Walton Christian Ch., 1959—; treas. Walton Fire Dist., 1983—, Boone County Fire Dist. Assn., 1987—. Mem. Assn. Profl. Ins. Agents (bd. dirs. 1977-86, pres. 1981-82, regional bd. dirs. 1980-82), No. Ky. Profl. Ins. Agents (chmn. bd. dirs. 1985), Profl. Ins. Agts. Ky. (Agt. of Yr. 1985). Democrat. Home: 93 N Main St Walton KY 41094-1130 Office: 24 N Main St Walton KY 41094

JOHNSON, SONDRA LEA, accountant; b. Kansas City, Mo., May 11, 1952; d. Albert John Oscar and Dorothy Mae (Hudgens) J. AA, Longview Coll., 1972; BSBA cum laude in Acctg., Cen. Mo. State U., 1974, MBA, 1980. CPA, Mo. Acct. Farmland Industries, Kansas City, 1974-76; acct., auditor Ernst & Whinney, Kansas City, 1976-79, Laventhol & Horwath, Kansas City, 1980-81; corp. acct., mgr. Butler Mfg. Co., Kansas City, 1981-84; audit supr. Grant Thornton Internat., Kansas City, 1984—; specialized instr. nat. continuing edn. tng. program, Grant Thornton Internat., various locations U.S.A.; acctg. instr. Cen. Mo. State U., Warrensburg, 1979-80, Rockhurst Coll., Kansas City, 1981-82. Mem. Nat. Assn. Accts., Am. Inst. CPA's, Mo. Soc. CPA's, Women's C. of C. of Kansas City, Phi Kappa Phi. Democrat. Lutheran. Office: Grant Thornton Internat 1101 Walnut Kansas City MO 64106

JOHNSON, SUSAN BROOKS, gemology educator, gemology consultant; b. Oregon City, Oreg., July 29, 1952; d. Theodore Reed and Doreen Edith (Gillett) Merrell; m. James-Burr July 21, 1979; 1 child, Summer Brooks. Grad. gemologist Gemol. Inst. Am., 1975; diploma, St. Olaf Coll., 1972. Asst. mgr. Bubar's Jewelers, Santa Monica, Calif., 1977-79; asst. dir. edn. Gemological Inst. Am., Santa Monica, Calif., 1974-77, 1979—. Author: Lab Manual, Properties of "B" Gemstones, 1977. Mem. Am. Gem Soc. (cert.), Accredited Gemologists' Assn. (v.p. 1980-82), Meeting Planners Internat. Club: Golden State Rottweiler (sec., mem. bd. 1982—) (Los Angeles). Office: Gemological Inst Am 1660 Stewart St Santa Monica CA 90404

JOHNSON, SUSAN GILMORE, manufacturing company executive, leasing company executive; b. Ft. Wayne, Ind., Mar. 9, 1941; d. Samuel Edward and Virginia Alma (Northup) G.; m. Donald Johnson, Feb. 1, 1959 (div. 1963). Student, U. Houston, 1957, Rice U. Ptnr. S & S Leasing Co., Houston, 1975—; pres., dir. Fluid Units Corp., Houston, 1976-84; exec. v.p. Collins Machine, Longview, Tex., 1980-84; exec. v.p. Gilmore Valve Co., Houston, 1963-86, pres., chief exec. officer, 1987—; bd. dirs. Tex. Commerce Bank, Houston. Chartered bd. dirs. Joint Interest Mental Health Services, Houston, 1977-78; mem. State Tex. Job Tng. Coordinating Council, 1987—. Mem. Soc. Profl. Women in Petroleum, Nat. Orgn. Women Bus. Owners, Small Bus. Assn., Bellaire C. of C. (trustee, bd. dirs. scholarship found. 1986—, treas., bd. dirs. 1986—), River Oaks Exec. Women's Breadfast Club, Nat. Assn. Mfrs., Tex. Exec. Women. Republican. Home: 10710 Bayou Glen Houston TX 77042 Office: Gilmore Valve Co PO Drawer 39 Bellaire TX 77041

JOHNSON, SUSAN HALL WINSTEAD HAGY, cable television company executive; b. Alexandria, Va., May 17, 1960; d. Harold Henry and Anne (McLawhorn) H.; m. William Eric Johnson, May 7, 1988. BS, Va. Commonwealth U., 1982. Coordinator pub. relations Cen. Va. Safety Council, Richmond, 1981; adminstrv. asst. Office Overload, Richmond, 1982, profl. voice, camera talent, 1983—; customer service rep. Continental Cablevision, Richmond, 1983-84, lead customer service rep., 1984, regional mktg. adminstr., 1984-85, regional trainer, 1985, mgr. regional tng., 1985—, dir. spkr.'s bur., 1987—; profl. voice, camera talent Park Ave. Teleprodns., Richmond, 1986—. Mem. pub. relations com. Va. Spl. Olympics, Richmond, 1984—; tour guide Fan Dist. Assn., Richmond, 1985. Mem. Am. Soc. for Tng. and Devel., Nat. Assn. Female Execs., Internat. TV Assn., Internat. Thespian Soc., Lakewood Research Group. Presbyterian. Office: Continental Cable Vision Va 1520 W Main St Richmond VA 23220

JOHNSON, SUZANNE BENNETT, psychologist; b. Johnson City, N.Y., Feb. 8, 1948; d. Carl Emil and Marion Sisson (Bennett) J.; m. Bruce Henry Taffel, June 14, 1970 (div. June 1977); m. Nathan Warren Perry, July 22, 1978; children: Erika Marion Perry, Marissa Clara Perry. BA, Cornell U., 1970; PhD, SUNY, Stony Brook, 1974. Lic. psychologist, Fla. Postdoctoral fellow in clin. child psychology U. Fla. Health Sci. Ctr., Gainesville, 1974-75, asst. prof. clin. psychology, 1975-81, assoc. prof., 1981-87, prof., 1987—. Research grantee in behavioral childhood diabetes NIH, 1980—; recipient Research Career Devel. award NIH, 1985—. Mem. Am. Psychol. Assn., Fla. Psychol. Assn., Soc. Pediatric Psychology, Am. Diabetes Assn., Assn. for Advancement Behavior Therapy. Democrat. Office: Univ Fla Dept Psychiatry Box J-234 JHMHC Gainesville FL 32610

JOHNSON, TERRI LYNN, journalism educator, public relations consultant; b. Anderson, Ind., July 15, 1947; d. Joseph J. and B. Maxine (Kidwell) Applegate; m. John W. Johnson, June 29, 1968. BS, Ind. U., 1970; MA, Ball State U., Muncie, Ind., 1981, postgrad., 1986. Editor Morgan County Gazette, Martinsville, Ind., 1971-72; pub. info. dir. State Hwy. Commn., Indpls., 1974-79; adminstrv. asst., speechwriter Gov. Bowen, Indpls., 1980-81; instr. Butler U., Indpls., 1981-87; asst. prof. journalism U. Indpls., 1987—; account exec. Borshoff Ketchum Pub. Relations, Indpls., 1985; v.p. FutureSet, Indpls., 1986—. Chmn. pub. relations com. Ind. chpt. Am. Heart Assn., Indpls., 1987—; bd. dirs. Am. Cancer Soc., Marion County chpt., 1986-87; bd. dirs., sec., pub. relations chmn. Morgan County Humane Soc., 1974—. Mem. Internat. Assn. of Bus. Communicators (cert., dir. dist. leadership devel. 1984-85, pres. 1985-86, vice-chmn. educators acad. 1987—, Educator of Yr. 1985, Communicator of Yr. 1986), Pub. Relations Soc. of Am. (accrediation chair Hoosier chpt. 1983-87), Women in Communication Inc. (chmn. freedom of info. com.). Home: 257 E South St Franklin IN 46131 Office: U Indpls 1400 E Hanna Ave Indianapolis IN 46227-3697

JOHNSON, VICKI R., insurance company executive; b. Glens Falls, N.Y., June 19, 1952; d. Leonard H. and Rose (Petrosky) J. A.B., Franklin and Marshall Coll., 1974; postgrad. U. Portland, 1979-80; M.B.A., UCLA, 1986. Product mgr. Prudential Ins. Co. Am., Woodland Hills, Calif., 1974—; mem. Oreg. Accident and Health Claim Assn., 1976-81. Pres., Ridgeview Condominium Assn., 1978-81; mem. Los Angeles Olympic Organizing Com., 1984. Mem. Los Angeles Accident and Health Claim Assn., The Woods Homeowners Assn., UCLA Alumni Bd. (dir. at large, exec. MBA). Home: 21931-16 Burbank Blvd Woodland Hills CA 91367 Office: 5800 Canoga Ave Woodland Hills CA 91367

JOHNSON, VICKI SUE, aerospace engineer; b. Spokane, Wash., May 12, 1959; d. Charles Thomas and Mary Kathryn (Bowman) Johnson. BS in Aerospace Engring. with honors, U. Mo., Rolla, 1982; MS in Flight Scis., George Washington U., 1985; postgrad., U. Kans., 1985—. Engring. co-op Langley Research Ctr. NASA, Hampton, Va., 1978-82, aerospace engr., 1982—. Zonta Internat. Amelia Earhart fellow, 1985, 86; Curator's Scholarships U. Mo., Rolla, 1977-82. Mem. AIAA (sr.), Air Force Assn., Va. Acad. Sci., Va. Peninsula Bus. and Profl. Women's Club (pres. 1987-88), Engrs. Club of Va. Peninsula (pres. 1987-88), Phi Kappa Phi, Sigma Gamma Tau. Methodist. Office: NASA Langley Research Ctr M/S 412 Hampton VA 23665

JOHNSON, VILIA JOCELYN, perfume company executive; b. Bamberg, S.C., Dec. 21, 1953; d. John Franklin and Mary Elizabeth (Covington) J. BA in Lang. and Lit., BA in Social and Behavioral Scis., U. S. Fla., 1974. Sales clk. Sandcastle Swimwear, N.Y.C., 1975-76; market rep. Allied Stores Mktg., N.Y.C., 1976; retail buyer Mabley and Carew, Cin., 1977-78, Richman Gordman, Omaha, 1978-84; account exec. Cosmair Inc., Kansas City, Kans., 1984-85, Dallas, 1985; regional sales mgr. Cosmair Inc., St. Louis, 1986-87; asst. v.p., mgr. field sales Cosmair Inc., Dallas, 1987—. Vol. Literacy Vols. Am. Mem. Nat. Assn. Female Execs. Democrat. Office: Cosmair Designer Fragrances 575 Fifth Ave New York NY 10017

JOHNSON-ALEXANDER, STEPHANIE DIANA, health care administrator; b. Redlands, Calif., Aug. 1, 1961; d. Edna Mae (Goff) Williams; m. Brian Donavan Alexander, Aug. 23, 1986. BS in Health Sci., Calif. State U., Long Beach, 1984, MPA, 1986. Adminstr. Lakewood chpt. Planned Parenthood, Los Angeles, 1985-87; dir. patient services Planned Parenthood World Population, Los Angeles, 1987—; cons. community health, health edn., greater Long Beach, 1986—. Active Planned Parenthood World Population, Los Angeles, 1982—; vol. educator, mem. pub. edn. com. Am. Cancer Soc., Long Beach, 1985—; vol. educator ARC, Long Beach, 1986—; lobbyist Coalition for Freedom, Los Angeles, 1987; mem., cons. Coalition Concerned with Adolescent Sexuality, Long Beach, 1987. Mem. Women in Mgmt., Nat. Assn. Female Execs., Lakewood C. of C. Democrat. Office: Planned Parenthood World Population 1920 Marengo St Los Angeles CA 90033-1317

JOHNSON-BROWN, HAZEL WINIFRED, nurse, retired army officer; b. West Chester, Pa., Oct. 10, 1927; d. Clarence Lemont and Garnett (Henley) J.; R.N. diploma Harlem Hosp., N.Y.C., 1950; B.S.N., Villanova U., 1959; M.S.N., Tchr.'s Coll., Columbia U., 1963; Ph.D. in Nursing Edn., Catholic U. Am., 1978. Commd. 1st lt. U.S. Army Nurse Corps, 1955, advanced through grades to brig. gen., 1979; mem. staff U.S. Army Med. Research and Devel. Command, Washington, 1967-73; dir. Walter Reed Army Inst. Nursing, Washington, 1976-78; asst. for nursing Office of Surgeon, Med. Command, Korea, 1978-79; chief Army Nurse Corps, Office Surgeon Gen., Dept of the Army, Washington, 1979-83; cons. edn. com. Operating Room Nurses Assn. Decorated Distinguished Service Medal, Legion of Merit, Meritorious Service medal, Army Commendation medal, Disting. Service Medal. recipient Evangeline G. Bovard Army Nurse of Yr. award Letterman Army Med. Center, San Francisco, 1964, Dr. Anita Newcomb McGee award DAR, Washington, 1971. Mem. Assn. U.S. Army, Nat. Assn. Military Family, Am. Nurses Assn., Chester County (Pa.) Nurses Assn., Nat. League Nursing.

JOHNSON-CHAMP, DEBRA SUE, lawyer, educator; b. Emporia, Kans., Nov. 8, 1955; d. Bert John and S. Christine (Brigman) Johnson; m. Michael W. Champ, Nov. 23, 1979; children: Natalie, John. BA, U. Denver, 1977; JD, Pepperdine U., 1980; postgrad. in library sci. U. So. Calif., 1983—. Bar: Calif. 1981. Sole practice, Long Beach, Calif., 1981-82, Los Angeles, 1981—; legal reference librarian, instr. Southwestern U. Sch. Law, Los Angeles, 1982-88; adj. prof. law, 1987—. Editor-in-chief: Southern Calif. Assn. Law Libraries Newsletter, 1984-85. Contbr. articles to profl. journs. Mem. law rev. Pepperdine U., 1978-80. West Pub. Co. scholar, 1983; trustee United Meth. Ch., Tujunga, Calif., 1986—. Recipient H. Wayne Gillis Moot Ct. award, 1980, Vincent S. Dalsimer Best Brief award, 1979. Mem. ABA, So. Calif. Assn. Law Libraries, Am. Assn. Law Libraries, Calif. Bar Assn., Southwestern Affiliates, Friends of the Library Los Angeles. Democrat. Home: 5740 Valerie Ave Woodland Hills CA 91367 Office: Contos & Bunch 5855 Topanga Canyon Blvd Suite 400 Woodland Hills CA 91367

JOHNSON-MASTERS, VIRGINIA E. (MRS. WILLIAM H. MASTERS), psychologist; b. Springfield, Mo., Feb. 11, 1925; d. Harry Hershel and Edna (Evans) Eshelman; m. George Johnson, June 13, 1950 (div. 1956); children: Scott Forstall, Lisa Evans; m. William H. Masters, Jan. 7, 1971. Student music, Drury Coll., Springfield, 1940-42, U. Mo., 1944-47; D.Sc. (hon.), U. Louisville, 1978. With St. Louis Daily Record, 1947-50, Sta. KMOX, St. Louis, 1950-51; with div. reproductive biology, dept. obstetrics and gynecology Washington U. Sch. Medicine, 1957-64, research instr., 1962-64; research assoc. Reproductive Biology Research Found., St. Louis, 1964-69, asst. dir., 1969-73; co-dir. Masters & Johnson Inst. (formerly Reproductive Biology Research Found.), 1973-80, pres., dir., 1981-86, now co-chmn. bd. dirs.; pres. MVM Enterprises, Inc., 1981—; Am. Geriatrics Soc. Edward Henderson lectr. Author: (with Dr. William H. Masters) Human Sexual Response, 1966, Human Sexual Inadequacy, 1970, The Pleasure Bond, 1975, Homosexuality in Perspective, 1979, (with Kolodny and others) Textbook of Human Sexuality for Nurses, 1979, Textbook of Sexual Medicine, 1979, Human Sexuality, 1982, 2d edit., 1985, Sex and Human Loving, 1982, (with Masters) Heterosexual Behavior in the Age of AIDS, 1988; editor: (with Masters and Kolodny) Ethical Issues in Sex Therapy and Research, Vol. 1, 1977, Vol. 2, 1980; mem. editorial bd.: Sci. Digest, 1982. Recipient Paul H. Hoch award Am. Psychopathol. Soc., 1971; SIECUS citation award, 1971; Distinguished Service award Am. Assn. Marriage and Family Counselors, 1976; Modern Medicine award for Disting. Achievement, 1977; Biomed. Research award World Assn. Sexology, 1979; named One of 25 Most Influential Women in Am. World Almanac, 1975, 78, 79, 80; Paul Harris fellow Rotary Internat., 1976. Fellow Soc. Sci. Study of Sex; mem. AAAS, Soc. Study of Reprodn., Internat. Soc. Research in Biology Reprodn., Internat. Acad. Sex Research (treas. 1975-76), Am. Assn. Sex Educators, Counselors and Therapists (Modern Medicine award 1977), Internat. Platform Assn., Authors Guild. Episcopalian. Office: 24 S Kingshighway Saint Louis MO 63108 *

JOHNSON-MYERS, GWEN, animal trainer; b. Whittier, Calif., Nov. 2, 1955; d. Carl Emil Jr. and Sieglinde (Henrich) J.; m. Jerry Owens Myers Jr., Oct. 19, 1986. BA in Biology, U. Calif., Santa Cruz, 1978; postgrad., U. Bridgeport, 1983—. Cert. in animal tng. and mgmt. Research asst. Marineland of the Pacific, Palos Verdes, Calif., 1974; animal trainer Animal Actors of Hollywood, Thousand Oaks, Calif., 1975-80, Birds and Animals Unltd., El Toro, Calif., 1980—. Recipient Patsy award Am. Humane Assn., 1985. Democrat. Home: 478 Saint Ann's Dr Laguna Beach CA 92651

JOHNSON-SNYDER, BRENDA FAYE, army officer; b. Fort Leavenworth, Kans., Jan. 13, 1953; d. Hugh Dorsey and Marguerite Elizabeth (Achilles) Johnson; divorced; children: Beth Louise, Barbra Marie; m. Lloyd Howard Snyder. Cert. in lang. and humanities Scripps Coll., Claremont, Calif., 1970; cert. in fine arts U.S. Internat. U., San Diego, 1972; AA in Liberal Arts, Fresno City Coll., Calif., 1973; BA in Psychology/Sociology, Calif. State U.-Fresno, 1975; MA in German, Antioch Internat. U., Yellow Springs, Ohio, 1986; postgrad. in linguistics Union Coll., Cin., 1986-87. Cert. educator, counselor, instr. U.S. Army. Commd. lt. U.S. Army, 1976; adjutant/test officer U.S. Army Armed Forces Entrance and Examining Sta., Mpls., 1978-80, promoted to capt., 1980, asst. area club mgr., U.S. Army Command, Grafenwoehr, Fed. Republic Germany, 1982-83, contbg. editor U.S. Army-Trojan, Fort Leavenworth, 1983, spl. edn. instr. U.S. Army-Acad. div., 1983-84, ops., quality control supr. U.S. Army-Vocat. Tng., 1984-85, behavioral sci. research analyst U.S. Army-Dept. Mental Health, 1985-86; fire inspector Fresno (Calif.) Fire Dept., 1986—; co-owner Spacemakers, Inc., 1988—. Lang. instr., cons. German-Am. relations, 1983-86. Author: Men in Power, 1986; co-author: The Trial, 1986; co-editor: (mag.) Stray Shots-Book of Poems, 1983. Cultural arts dir., phys. edn. dir. Mormon Ch., Mpls., 1978-79; mgr. tonemaster Calif., 1988—; campaign coordinator elections Fresno City Council, 1985; bd. dirs., sec. Burn Aware Bd. Decorated Army Commendation medal; Calif. Gov.'s scholar, 1969-75. Mem. Assn. U.S. Army, Nat. Assn. Female Execs., NOW, Jr. C. of C. (speech cons. 1983), Calif. Scholarship Fedn., Cen. Calif. Psychol. Assn., Summit Orgn., Fire Prevention Officers Assn., Mensa, Phi Beta Kappa, Phi Kappa Phi, Alpha Gamma Sigma, Phi Theta Kappa. Avocations: swimming, sailing, skating, dance, tennis.

JOHNSON-WHEELWRIGHT, JEANNE L(OUISE), management consultant; b. Kenosha, Wis., Nov. 14, 1928; d. Byron Simpson and Amanda (Zeitler) Knight; m. Robert Burk Wheelwright, 1985; B.S. cum laude, U. Dubuque, 1949. Head editing dept. Film Prodn. unit Ia. State U., 1954-56; head Continuity dept. WICS-NBC TV, Springfield, Ill., 1958-59; home service adv. Central Ill. Light Co., Springfield, 1959-61; instr. home economics Centralia (Ill.) City Schs., 1962-66; v.p. Tallman Robbins & Co., Springfield, 1967-77; v.p. Delta Business Forms, Cairo, Ill., 1971-77; mgmt. cons., 1977—; v.p. Adminstrv. Techs. Inc., Springfield, Ill., 1980-82; exec. v.p. Skill-Builders, Inc., San Antonio, 1982—; v.p. Computer Security Engring., Ltd., San Antonio, 1982—; cons., mktg. rep. ComputerLand of San Antonio, 1982-85. Treas. Marion County Humane Soc. (Ill.), 1961-66. Mem. Data Entry Mgmt. Assn., Am. Soc. Tng. Dirs., Women in Bus., Profl. Secs. Assn., Nat. Assn. Female Execs., Greater San Antonio C. of C., Data Processing Mgmt. Assn., Internat. Orgn. Women Execs., Assn. Info. Systems Profls., Zeta Phi. Address: 7667 Callaghan Rd #701 San Antonio TX 78229

JOHNSTON, AUDREY JUANITA, travel business executive; b. Belfast, No. Ireland, Jan. 26, 1934; came to Can., 1963; d. John and Annie (Rice) McMillan; m. Richard Johnston, May 29, 1965; 1 child, Mark Richard. Grad., Belfast Tech. Sch., 1954. Advt. exec. Crawford Advt. Co., London, 1955-61; travel exec. Thomas Cook Travel Co., London, 1961-63; pres. Royal Travel and Tours Can. Ltd., Toronto, Ont., 1963—. Mem. exec. com., pres. Oakville (Ont.) Humane Soc., 1967—. Mem. Can. Inst. Travel Counsellors, Internat. Assn. Tour Mgrs., Ont. Exec. Women in Travel (charter). Office: Royal Tours, Dixie Mall, 1250 S Service Rd, Mississauga Can L5E 1V4

JOHNSTON, CHRISTINA JANE, real estate executive, mortgage broker, educator; b. Toronto, Ont., Can., June 3, 1952; d. George Elmer and Mary Selina (Northey) J. B.A. with honors, U. Western Ont., London, 1975. Researcher, writer House of Commons, Ottawa, Ont., 1975-77; adminstrv. mgr. sales Marco Beach Realty, Marco Island, Fla., 1977-79; pres., owner Marco Summit Realty, Marco Island, 1979-82; v.p., mortgage broker Windjammer of Marco, Marco Island, 1979—; instr. Realty World Acad., St. Petersburg, Fla., 1979—; pres., mgr. Fla. Sun Realty Co., Sarasota, 1982-86; v.p., mgr. Fla. Home Properties & Comml. Realty, Inc., 1986-87; mgr. 1st So. Trust Realty Corp., 1987—; bd. dirs., chmn. edn. com. Sarasota Bd. Realtors, 1985-86, also mem. realtors polit. action com. 1985—; pres. So. Gulf Council Realty World, 1980-82; bd. dirs. First Fla. region Broker's Council, Realty World, 1982-84; pres. Women's Council of Realtors, Marco Island, 1988—; dir. Marco Island Bd. Realtors, 1987—. Contbr. articles to profl. jours. Pres. Young Progressive Conservatives, Cambridge, Ont., 1968-70; Recipient Office of Yr. award Realty World, 1980, Top Listing Office award, 1981, Spl. award for Prodn., 1981, Million Dollar Sales Awards Marco Beach and Realty World, 1979-81. Mem. Sarasota C. of C., Marco Island C. of C. (chmn. Expo '82). Home: 591 Yellowbird Dr Marco Island FL 33937

JOHNSTON, CYNTHIA COCHRAN, physician, educator; b. Kansas City, Mo., Oct. 2, 1952; d. John A. and Mary L. (Leffler) Cochran; B.S. in Zoology with high honors, Ariz. State U., 1974; M.D., U. Ariz., 1976; m. Bruce G. Johnston, Dec. 29, 1973; children—Lauren Elizabeth, Stephen Shepherd. Diplomate Am. Bd. Family Practice. Resident in family practice U. Ariz., Tucson, 1976-79, chief resident in family practice, 1978-79; med. officer San Xavier Indian Health Center, Tucson, 1979, dir., 1979-82; assoc. faculty dept. family and community medicine U. Ariz., Tucson, 1979-81, adj. asst. prof., 1981—; staff physician Tucson Clinic, 1982—; physician ambulatory care dept. Tucson VA Med. Ctr., 1983—; Ariz.'s rep. to Nat. Conf. Family Practice Residents, 1978, 79. Served with USPHS, 1979—. Recipient John Grobe award for outstanding family practice resident in Ariz., 1979. Mem. Am. Acad. Family Physicians (resident rep. com. Indian health, rep. com. minority health affairs 1980-82, Warner-Chilcot award for outstanding tchr. 1979), Ariz. Acad. Family Physicians, (dir. 1981—), Soc. Tchrs. in Family Medicine, Phi Beta Kappa. Contbr. articles to profl. jours. Home: 6307 E Paseo Otono Tucson AZ 85715

JOHNSTON, DOLORES MAE MASCIK (MRS. ROBERT EDGAR JOHNSTON), cultural organization administrator; b. Conneaut, Ohio, May 26, 1927; d. Michael Morris and Roberta Mary (Jacobs) Mascik; m. Robert Edgar Johnston, Mar. 19, 1950; children: Kirk, Christine, Mark. BS, Ohio State U., 1949. Lic. med. technologist; registered profl. parliamentarian. Researcher hematology dept. Ohio State U., Columbus, 1949-54; med. technologist Youngstown (Ohio) Hosp. Assn., 1954-55; med. technologist Eli Lilly Clin. Research Labs., Indpls., 1955-57, Green Bay, Wis., 1958-60. Mem. Green Bay Community Chorus, 1966-70, Bach Choir of Green Bay, 1970-80, St. Norbert Coll. Collegiate Chorale, 1980—; pack officer Boy Scouts of Am., 1970-71; co-chmn. ARC Blood Bank, 1970-72, mem. Lakeland chpt. steering com., 1974-76, 78-79, vol. chmn. blood bank vols., 1976-80; bd. dirs. Lakeland chpt. ARC, 1980-87, chmn. 1983-85, rep. to Badger Region blood services com., 1979-81, 82-83, rep. to Pere/Marquette div. council, 1980-82; vol. worker Mobile Meals, 1971—; pres. Brown County Med. Soc. Aux., 1969-70, dir., 1973-78; mem. Brown County Rep. Women's Club, 1969—; bd. dirs. Wis. Polit. Action Com., 1972-73; bd. dirs. Curative Workshop Rehab. Ctr., 1975-85, sec., 1976-78, pres., 1980-82; chmn. Ind. Living Program Council, 1982-85; sec. bd. dirs. Brown County United Way Council of Agys., 1975-76. Recipient Outstanding Mem. award Brown County Med. Aux., 1973-74, Vol. of Yr. award Lakeland chpt. ARC, 1981, Med. Services award Brown County Med. Soc., 1982, 31st Ann. Brotherhood award B'nai B'rith, 1984; named YWCA Women of Yr., 1977. Mem. Women's Aux. State Med. Soc. Wis. (pres. 1973-74, parliamentarian 1981-87), AMA Aux. (N.C. regional family health chmn. 1974-75, N.C. regional area counselor Project Bank, 1975-76, 76-77, nat. project bank coordinator 1977-78, nat. rec. sec. 1979-80, chmn. nat. health projects 1978-79, nat. historian, 1980-81), Wis. Assn. Parliamentarians (pres. 1987-89), Aesculapian Soc. (charter), Brown County Med. Soc. Aux. (pres. 1969-70), P.E.O. (chpt.

treas. 1970-72, state conv. treas. 1976, chpt. pres. 1985-87), Alpha Lambda Delta, Alpha Chi Omega. Lutheran. Clubs: Federated Women's, Jr. Women's. Lodge: Order Eastern Star, Shriners. Home: 3285 Waubenoor Dr Green Bay WI 54301

JOHNSTON, DONNA FAYE, color consultant, production art director; b. Stromburg, Nebr., Oct. 16, 1941; d. Verlin James and Roberta Carola (Larsen) Fellows; m. Robert Carl Johnston, May 2, 1964 (div. 1965); 1 child, Karla Kathliene. BFA, Kansas City Art Inst., 1963; journeyman cert., Graphic Communications Union, 1980; cert. color correction, Vocat. Tech. Edn., 1980. Prodn. mgr. H.H. Harney Advt., Lincoln, Nebr., 1966-68; lead mech. art and trainer Bozell & Jacobs Advt., Omaha, 1968-70; mech. art spl. account Dudycha Studio, Omaha, 1970-72; prodn. mgr. Oliver Advt., Kansas City, 1972-73; prodn. and color correction artist Vile/Goller Fine Arts, Kansas City, 1973-79; color correction artist K&A Lithographing, Kansas City, 1979-80, Chroma-Graphics, Kansas City, 1980-81; color correction artist and quality control Orent Graphic Arts, Omaha, 1981-86; color correction supr. Epsen-Hillmer Graphics Co., Omaha, 1986—; printing cons. Margo Kries-Entrepreneur, Stromsburg, 1987—, Willie Plith-Photographer, Omaha, 1987—. Author monthly newsletter Am. Singles, 1986. Mem. Landmarks, Omaha, 1986-87, Westport Art Assn., Kansas City, 1979-80, Earthwatch, Watertown. Mass., 1985-87, Nat. Geographic Soc., 1984-85. Mem. Omaha Club Printing House Craftsmen (bd. dirs.), Nat. Assn. Female Execs., Am. Singles of Omaha (pub. relations dir. 1986-87, author monthly newsletter 1986), Parents Without Ptnrs. (Outstanding Service award 1986). Methodist. Office: Epsen-Hillmer Graphics Co 2000 California Omaha NE 68102

JOHNSTON, GWINAVERE ADAMS, public relations consultant; b. Casper, Wyo., Jan. 6, 1943; d. Donald Milton Adams and Gwinavere Marie (Newell) Quillen; m. H.R. Johnston, Sept. 26, 1963 (div. 1973); children: Gwinavere G., Gabrielle Suzanne; m. Donald Charles Cannalte, Apr. 4, 1981. BS in Journalism, U. Wyo., 1966; postgrad., Denver U., 1968-69. Editor, reporter Laramie (Wyo.) Daily Boomerang, 1965-66; account exec. William Kostka Assocs., Denver, 1966-71, v.p., 1971-73; exec. v.p. Slottow, McKinlay & Johnston, Denver, 1973-74; pres. The Johnston Group, Denver, 1974—; bd. dirs. The Lovelace Corp., Denver, Designers Marketplace, Denver; mem. adj. faculty U. Colo. Sch. Journalism, 1988—. Bd. dirs. Leadership Denver Assn., 1975-77, 83-86. Mem. Pub. Relations Soc. Am. (pres. Colo. chpt. 1978-79, bd. dirs. 1975-80, 83-86, nat. exec. com., counselor's acad. 1988-89, profl. award), Colo. Women's Forum. Republican. Clubs: Denver Athletic, Denver Press, Com. of 200. Home: 717 Monaco Pkwy Denver CO 80220 Office: The Johnston Group 1340 Glenarm Pl #200 Denver CO 80204

JOHNSTON, JEANNE MATHIS, educator; b. Ft. Worth, July 26, 1944; d. Edwin D. and Grace F. (Wilson) Mathis; m. David Walker, Nov. 26, 1964 (div. Apr. 1974); 1 child, Lynn Walker; m. John Johnston Apr. 26, 1975; 1 child, Candace. BS in Elem. Edn., Tex. Christian U., 1967; MEd in Reading, Cen. State U., 1981. Cert. elem. tchr., Tex., Okla., La. Tchr. White Settlement Schs., Ft. Worth, 1967, Flower Mound Sch., Lawton, Okla., 1967-68, Westminster Day Sch., Oklahoma City, 1979-85, Trinity Episcopal Sch., New Orleans, 1985—; mem. Okla. Reading Council, Oklahoma City, 1980-81. Chmn. social studies com. Trinity Episc. Sch., 1987-88. Mem. Delta Gamma Alumna, Kappa Delta Gamma. Presbyterian. Home: 2934 Johnston Metairie LA 70001 Office: Trinity Episcopal Sch 2111 Chestnut St New Orleans LA 70130

JOHNSTON, JOANNE SPITZNAGEL, lawyer, writing consultant; b. Peoria, Ill., Mar. 11, 1930; d. Elmer Florian and Anna E. (Kolb) Spitznagel; m. Charles Helm Bennett, June 12, 1951 (div. 1978); children—Mary Jaquelin Bennett Graub, Ariana Holliday, Caroline Helm Bennett Ammerman, Joanne Mary; m. Donald Robert Johnston, Nov. 25, 1981. A.B., Vassar Coll., 1951; M.A., Ind. U., 1970, Ph.D., 1974; J.D., Ind. U.-Indpls., 1980. Bar: Ind. 1980, Minn. 1985. Lectr., Ind. U., Indpls., 1968-81, U.-Indpls., 1970-76; writing cons. U. Minn., Mpls., 1982—; sole practice, Indpls., 1980-86, Mpls., 1986—. Vice-pres. Jr. League Indpls.; pres. Sch. 70 Parent Tchr. Orgn., Indpls. Mem. Assn. Bus. Communications, Ind. State Bar Assn., Minn. State Bar Assn. Methodist. Clubs: Indpls. Womans, Garden Club Am. (Indpls. and Lake Minnetonka); Woman's (Mpls.). Home: 4915 Sussex Pl Shorewood MN 55331

JOHNSTON, JOSEPHINE R., chemist; b. Cranston, R.I., Aug. 9, 1926; d. Robert and Rose (Varca) Forte; student Carnegie Inst., 1945-47; B.S., Mich. State U., 1972, M.A., 1973; postgrad. Mass. Inst. Tech., 1973—m. Howard Robert Johnston, Mar. 7, 1949; 1 son, Kevin Howard. Med. technologist South Nassau Community Hosp., Rockville Centre, N.Y., 1947-50, Mich. State U., East Lansing, 1950-53, dept. pathology Albany (N.Y.) Med. Center, 1953-54; med. lab. supr. Bulova Watch Co., Jackson Heights, N.Y., 1954-57; sr. chemistry technologist Mid Island Hosp., Bethpage, N.Y., 1958-66; faculty specialist Mich. State U., East Lansing, 1966-76; sr. research asso. Uniformed Services Univ., Bethesda, Md., 1976-78, asst. to chmn. dept. physiology, 1978-82, asso. to chmn., 1982—. Mem. Analytical Chem. Soc., Data and Electronic Soc., Internat. Platform Assn. Lutheran. Contbr. articles in field to profl. jours. Office: 4301 Jones Bridge Rd Bethesda MD 20014

JOHNSTON, KAREN LANG, government relations executive; b. St. Petersburg, Fla., Nov. 10, 1949; d. James Talley and Dorothy Louise (Gustafson) Lang; m. Walter Eugene Johnston III, Apr. 13, 1983. B.A., U. Md., 1971. Aide to Congressman C.W. Young, 1972-73; aide Consultation and Guidance Center, 1973-76; legis. rep. Nat. Assn. Small Bus. Investment Cos., 1976-78; asso. dir. regulatory affairs Nat. Assn. Mfrs., 1978-79; congressional liaison U.S. Regulatory Council, 1979-81; spl. asst. to adminstr. for info. and regulatory affairs Office of Mgmt. and Budget, Washington, 1981; dep. dir. Office Congressional Relations, FTC, Washington, 1981-83, dir., 1985—; press sec. N.C. Reagan-Bush '84, 1984. Active Washington Internat. Ctr., 1972, Washington Ear, 1973, Rockville Free Clinic, Planned Parenthood, 1974-76; mem. 1st families com. Am. Children's Home, Lexington, N.C., fine arts com. N.C. Exec. Mansion, Greensboro Civic Ballet Guild; bd. dirs. Greensboro Beatuiful, Inc. Mem. Women in Govt. Relations, Nat. Fedn. Republican Women, Greater Greensboro Rep. Women, Greensboro Symphony Guild, Alpha Delta Pi. Methodist. Club: Jr. League (Washington).

JOHNSTON, LORENE GAYLE, lawyer; b. Wellston, Ohio, Jan. 15, 1952; d. Joseph Lewis and Gladys Leona (Bocook) J.; m. D. Keith Woolum, Apr. 9, 1988. BS in Edn., Miami U., Oxford, Ohio, 1974; MA in Polit. Sci., Ohio U., 1978; JD, U. Dayton, 1982. Bar: Ohio 1982. Tchr. Gallia County Local Shs., Vinton, Ohio, 1974-79; sole practice Wellston, 1982—. Councilman City of Wellston, 1977; committeewomen 10th Dist. Rep. State Com., Columbus, Ohio, 1978-82. Mem. ABA, Ohio Bar Assn., Jackson County Bar Assn. (pres. 1986, v.p. 1985, sec. 1984, treas. 1982), Phi Alpha Delta. Roman Catholic. Lodge: Order Eastern Star. Home: 424 W Broadway Wellston OH 45692 Office: 116 E 2d St Wellston OH 45692

JOHNSTON, MALINDA JO, public relations executive; b. Ft. Hood, Tex., Apr. 4, 1955; d. James Henry Jr. and Jessie Malinda (Durham) Johnston. BJ, U. Mo., 1976. City editor The Daily Forum, Maryville, Mo., 1976-78, mng. editor, 1978-80; asst. mng. editor The Examiner, Independence, Mo., 1980-83; pub. relations supr. AT&T, Kansas City, Mo., 1983-85; pub. relations mgr. AT&T, Basking Ridge, N.J., 1985—. Bd. dirs. United Way of Nadaway County, Maryville, Mo., 1978-80; bd. dirs., chartered mem. Hope House Shelter for Battered Women and Their Children, Independence, 1983-85. Mem. Kansas City Press Club (pres. 1983-84, treas. 1981-83), Soc. of Profl. Journalists (v.p. 1982-83, bd. dirs. N.J. chpt. 1986-87), Internat. Assn. of Bus. Communicators (Bronze Quills 1984), Pub. Relations Soc. of Am., Waller Williams Club (alumni group of Mo. Sch. of Journalism), Nat. Fedn. of Press Women (newspaper editing award 1981), Mo. Press Assn. (editing, editorial writing 1982, 83), Sigma Delta Chi. Baptist. Home: 37 Indian Spring Ln High Bridge NJ 08829 Office: AT&T 4 Campus Dr Room SIJ11 Parsippany NJ 07054

JOHNSTON, MARYANN, religious organization administrator; b. Phila., Sept. 24, 1939; d. Rudolph John and Frances (McGinley) Seppy; m. William James Johnston Jr., Feb. 20, 1965; 1 child, Christopher. BEd, Seattle U., 1978, M of Religious Edn., 1979, postgrad., 1987—. Adminstrv. asst. Cath. Archdiocese of Seattle, 1979-83, asst. to dept. dir., 1983-84, adminstrv. mgr., 1984-85, dir. Faith and Community Devel. Dept. cen. and adminstrv. services, 1985—. Mem. Child and Family Resource Ctr., Seattle, 1986—. Served to sgt. USAF, 1962-65. Mem. Am. Soc. for Tng. and Devel., Nat. Assn. for Female Execs., Lay Ministers Assn. of Western Wash. (past pres.), Alpha Sigma Nu, Kappa Delta Pi. Office: Cath Archdiocese of Seattle Faith and Community Devel Dept 910 Marion St Seattle WA 98177

JOHNSTON, ROBIN LYNNE, travel company owner; b. St. Louis, Mar. 5, 1954; d. William Allen and Jeannette Elizabeth (Schulte) Stark; m. James Robert Murphy(div. Apr. 1982); m. John David Johnston; children: John Clayton, Lindsey Nicole. Grad. high sch., St. Louis, 1972. Reservation agt. Trans World Airlines, St. Louis, 1973-74; sr. trans. agt. Maritz Travel Co., Fenton, Mo., 1974-79; customer service agt. Republic Airlines, St. Louis, 1979-82; deluxe tour operator Intrav, Clayton, Mo., 1982-83; supr. customer service Air One, Inc., St. Louis, 1983-85; pres., founder Midwest Travel Inst., Inc., St. Charles, Mo., 1985—, chief exec. officer. mem. Wolf Sanctuary, St. Louis, 1985; cert. mem. Mo. Coordinating Bd. for Higher Edn. Mem. Airline Ground Services Assn., Human Soc. of Am. Republican. Presbyterian. Home: #8 Donald Dr Saint Charles MO 63303 Office: Midwest Travel Inst Inc 1600 Heritage Landing Suite 102 Saint Charles MO 63303

JOHNSTON, RUBY CHARLOTTE, nurse; b. Freedom, Nebr., Oct. 6, 1918; d. William Murray and Delia Isabel (Morgan) Phillips; student Nebr. Sch. Agr., Curtis, 1932-36, U. Colo., Boulder, summer 1938; R.N., Denver Gen. Hosp., 1945; m. Gerald William Johnston, Sept. 19, 1943; 1 son, Leo F. Rural sch. tchr., 1936-41; sec. supt.'s office Nebr. Sch. Agr., 1941-42; staff nurse Denver Gen. Hosp., 1945-46; office nurse, Cambridge, Nebr., 1946-47; staff nurse St. Catherine's Hosp., McCook, Nebr., 1947-56, LaGrange County Hosp., LaGrange, Ind., 1956-58; obstet. supr. LaGrange County Hosp., 1958-68, dir. nurses, 1968-70; dir. nurses Miller's Merry Manor, LaGrange, 1970-76; county health nurse LaGrange County Health Dept., LaGrange, 1976-80, part-time staff nurse, 1980—; chmn. exec. com. Ind. Nurses Assn. Geriatric Conf., 1975-77; deacon Presbyt. Ch. Bd. dirs. N.E. Ind. chpt. Am. Lung Assn., 1981—; Co-coordinator Focus on Health, LaGrange, 1982-85. Registered Mem. Ind. Nurses Assn., Nurses Assn. Am. Coll. Obstetricians and Gynecologists, Am. Legion Aux. Republican. Clubs: Bus. and Profl. Women's, Eastern Star, River Oaks Extension. Home: Rural Route 2 Box 298 Howe IN 46746 Office: Cour House Annex LaGrange IN 46761

JOHNSTON, RUBY KAY, accountant; b. Grove Hill, Ala., Oct. 29, 1943; d. Christopher Colombus and Tena Lavania (Cobb) Caddy; m. Rolan Lamar Johnston, Mar. 12, 1966; children: Rolan Lamar Jr., Christopher Alan. Cert. in acctg., N.Am. Coll., 1984. Tax asst. Joe Davis, CPA, Thomasville, Ala., 1961-66; bookkeeper Overstreet & McCorguodale, Jackson, Ala., 1974-76, McGowin Oil Co., Jackson, 1976-77; owner Kay's Bookkeeping, Jackson, 1978—, Rainbow Realty, Jackson, 1986—. Mem. Nat. Assn. Female Execs., Nat. Assn. Tax Practioners. Republican. Baptist. Home: Route #3 Coffeeville Rd Jackson AL 36545 Office: Rainbow Realty Hwy 43 S Jackson AL 36545

JOHNSTON, SARAH, communications company manager; b. Bainbridge, Ga., Nov. 11, 1936; d. Wyatt Steadham and Mary Marie (Ward) J. Grad. high sch., Bainbridge. Operator So. Bell, Bainbridge, 1954-60; acctg. asst. So. Bell, Atlanta, 1960-65, staff asst. forecast, 1965-69, supr., 1969-78, staff supr., 1978-80, staff mgr. forecast, 1980—. Trustee Rosebud McCormick Found., 1986—; v.p. Chattahoochee Council Telphone Pioneers Am., 1987-88, pres. 1988—; pres. Roswell Bldg. and Pub. Works, 1981-83, 2nd v.p., 1st. v.p., pres. Bldg. Pub. Works/Ga.; 2nd v.p., treas. Dogwood City Bldg. Pub. Works. Mem. Bus. and Profl. Women's Club (numerous offices). Baptist. Home: 4945 Surrey Dr NE Roswell GA 30075 Office: So Bell 311-125 Perimeter Center W Atlanta GA 30346

JOHNSTON, VIRGINIA EVELYN, editor; b. Spokane, Wash., Apr. 26, 1933; d. Edwin and Emma Lucile (Munroe) Rowe; student Portland Community Coll., 1964, Portland State U., 1966, 78-79; m. Alan Paul Beckley, Dec. 26, 1974; children—Chris, Denise, Rex. Proofreader, The Oregonian, Portland, 1960-62, teletypesetter operator, 1962-66, operator Photon 200, 1966-68, copy editor, asst. women's editor, 1968-80, spl. sects. editor (UPDATE), 1981-83; editor FOODday, 1982—; pres. Matrix Assos., Inc., Portland, 1975—, chmn. bd., 1979—; cons. Democratic party Oreg., 1969, Portland Sch. Dist. No. 1, 1978. Mem. Women in Communications, Inc., Inst. Profl. and Managerial Women, Nat. Assn. Female Execs., Eating and Drinking Soc. Oreg. (pres.), We. Culinary Inst. (mem. adv. bd.), Portland Culinary Alliance (mem. adv. bd.). Democrat. Editor Principles of Computer Systems for Newspaper Mgmt., 1975-76. Home: 4140 NE 137th Ave Portland OR 97230 Office: 1320 SW Broadway Portland OR 97201

JOHNSTONE, PAULA SUE, medical technologist; b. Springfield, Mo., July 5, 1947; d. Nathan Paul and Ima Louise (Glenn) Johnstone. B.S., S.W. Mo. State U., 1969. Cert. med. technologist Am. Soc. Clin. Pathologists. Vol., Cox Med. Ctr., Springfield, 1964-68; lab., office aide Springfield Med. Lab., 1964-68; chief technologist Springfield Gen. Osteo. Hosp., 1969-73; staff technologist St. John's Regional Health Ctr., Springfield, 1973-75, evening supr., 1975-76, asst. adminstrv. dir., 1976-86; clin. lab. coordinator, 1986—. Dir., Glidewell Baptist Ch. Tng., Springfield, 1984-85, chmn. budget and fin. com. 1986-87. Mem. Am. Soc. Med. Technologists, Nat. Cert. Agy. Med. Lab. Personnel, Mo. Soc. Med. Technologists (pres. 1976-77, columnist newsletter 1976-77), Nat. Assn. Female Execs., S.W. Mo. State U. Alumni Assn. Baptist. Clubs: Nat. Travel, $25-A-Day-Travel. Avocations: European travel; reading; knitting; house plants. Home: Route 5 Box 495C Springfield MO 65803 Office: St John's Regional Health Ctr 1235 E Cherokee Springfield MO 65804

JOHNSTON-THOMAS, PAMELLA DELORES, physician; b. Westmoreland, Jamaica, W.I., May 11, 1947; came to U.S., 1976; d. Wellesley and Hyacinth Ida (Muir) Johnston; m. Earl Alfonso Thomas, Apr. 9, 1977; children—Ramogi Odhiamo, Monifa Jamila. M.D., U. W.I., 1974. Intern, Brookdale Hosp., Bklyn., 1976-77; resident in Surgery Cath. Med. Centre, Queens, N.Y., 1978-79; attending physician N.Y.C. Transit, N.Y.C., 1983-86; asst. med. dir. 1986—. attending physician Brookdale Hosp., Bklyn., 1979-83. Mem. Am. Occupational Med. Assn., N.Y. Occupational Med. Assn., Am. Pub. Health Assn., N.Y. Pub. Health Assn.

JOINER, MARILYN SEGURA, marketing consultant; b. Shreveport, La., Oct. 22, 1947; d. Jerry William Taylor and Mary Claire (Murrell) Segura; m. George Edward Seymour, Nov. 30, 1968 (div. 1977); 1 child, Laura Claire; m. Gary Dillard Joiner, Aug. 7, 1982. BA, La. Tech. U., 1968; postgrad., Centenary Coll., 1987—. Tchr. English St. John the Bapt. Parish Sch. Bd., Reserve, La., 1968-69; tchr. social studies Our Lady of Fatima High Sch., Lafayette, La., 1969-71; women's reporter Daily Advertiser, Lafayette, 1971-73; lifestyle reporter Shreveport Times, 1973-78; donor recruiter, pub. relations asst. La. Blood Ctr., Shreveport, 1978-81; dir. community relations Riverside Community Hosp., Bossier City, La., 1981-84; dir. health care mktg. div. Dolph Miller & Assocs., Shreveport, 1984-88; dir. mktg. ANDICARE/The Co. Doctor, Shreveport, 1988—. Editor La. State Report mag., 1977-78. Co-founder Stroke Hope, Shreveport, 1976; mem. steering com. Community Health Fair, ARC, Shreveport, 1984—. Recipient Service Appreciation award Am. Heart Assn., La., 1982. Mem. AAUW (pres. Shreveport chpt. 1975-76), DAR, Pub. Relations Soc. Am. (cert., v.p. North La. chpt. 1987—), Nat. Fedn. Press Women (treas. 5th dist. 1975), La. Fedn. Press Women (awards 1973-78), Am. Soc. Hosp. Pub. Relations, Magna Carta Dames. Republican. Methodist. Lodge: Magna Charta Dames. Office: ANDICARE/The Co Doctor 1666 E Bertkouns Loop Suite 100 Shreveport LA 71105

JOLICOEUR, BERNADETTE, systems analyst; b. Redwood City, Calif., May 2, 1961; d. Joel David Sorem and Joyce Sue (Ross) Pease; m. Maurice Richard Jolicoeur, Feb. 1, 1986. BS in Bus. Adminstrn. and Econs., St. Mary's Coll., 1985. Software librarian Xerox Corp., Palo Alto, Calif., 1985; quality assurance coordinator Sierra Info. Systems, Cupertino, Calif., 1985-86; computer edn. tchr. Fremont Christian High Sch., Calif., 1986-87; systems analyst Blyth Software,Inc., Foster City, Calif., 1987—; cons. Computecture, Sunnyvale, Calif., 1988—. Author: Omnis Express, 1987. Mem. Nat. Women's Ministries, Springfield, Calif., 1985; leader Jr. High Ministries Fremont 1st Assembly, 1985. Republican. Mem. Assemblies of God Ch. Home: 43081 Mayfair Prak Terr Fremont CA 94538 Office: Blyth Software Inc 1065 E Hillside Blvd Foster City CA 94404

JOLICOEUR-SMITH, CHRISTINE ANNE, service executive; b. Cohoes, N.Y., Aug. 15, 1954; d. Leo Albert and Lena Mary (DeKeado) Jolicoeur; m. Kevin Charles Mancino, Apr. 30, 1976 (div. May 1981); m. Warren J. Smith III, June 26, 1982; 1 child, Meredith Anne. AAS, Fulton-Montgomery Community Coll., 1974; student, Siena Coll., 1975, 82-85. Exec. sec. J.L. English Co., Inc., Cohoes, 1976-77; dept. sec. Abbott Labs., Los Angeles, 1977; owner/mgr. Mancino Secretarial Service, Los Angeles, 1978-81; coordinator word processing Cohoes Savs. Bank, 1982-85; owner/mgr. Smith Office Services, Cohoes, 1985—; exec. adminstr. Automated Dynamics Corp., Troy, N.Y., 1985; sec. St. Gregory's Sch., Loudonville, N.Y., 1986-87. Liturgical chmn. St. Rita's Ch., Cohoes, 1983-84. Mem. Alliance for Lobbying, Evaluation, Research & Tng., N.E. Network Exec. Women, Capital Area Office Automation Profls. (sec./treas. 1986—), Nat. Assn. for Female Execs. Democrat. Roman Catholic. Office: Smith Office Services 143 Remsen St Cohoes NY 12047

JOLLEY, JANINA MAE, psychology educator; b. San Pedro, Calif., Aug. 26, 1956; d. Neal Alfred Jolley and Zoë Mae (Davis) Kibbe; m. Mark L. Mitchell, Aug. 2, 1980. BA, Calif. State U., Dominguez Hills, 1978; MA, Ohio State U., 1979, PhD, 1982. Dir. Ohio State U. Poll, Columbus, 1978-80; adj. prof. Franklin U., Columbus, 1980-81; asst. prof. psychology Mansfield (Pa.) U., 1982-83; assoc. prof. Clarion (Pa.) U., 1984—; reviewer MacMillan Pub. Co., N.Y.C., 1983—, Merrill Pub. Co., Columbus, 1985—. Author: How to Write Psychology Papers, 1984, Research Design Explained, 1988; cons. editor Jour. Genetic Psychology, 1984—; contbr. articles to profl. jours. Mem. Am. Psychol. Assn. Gerontol. Soc. Am., Ea. Psychol. Assn., Soc. for the Study of Social Issues, LWV, NOW (v.p. Clarion chpt. 1986-87), Psi Chi. Democrat. Mem. Soc. of Friends. Home: 156 S 6th Ave Clarion PA 16214 Office: Clarion U Pa Dept Psychology Clarion PA 16214

JONAS, HILDA, harpsichordist, pianist; b. Duesseldorf, Ger., Jan. 21, 1913; came to U.S., 1938, naturalized, 1943; d. Moritz and Ann (Lilienfeld) Klestadt; student Hochschule Musik, Cologne, 1932-33; diploma Gumpert Conservatory, Duesseldorf, 1934; pupil of Rudolf Serkin, Wanda Landowska; m. Gerald Jonas, Jan. 30, 1938; children—Susanne Leilani, Linda Irene. Owner pvt. piano studio, Honolulu, 1938-42, Cin., 1942-75; soloist maj. orchs. throughout world, 1932—; solo recitalist throughout world, 1932—; founder Put-in-Bay Harpsichord Festival, 1965, dir., 1965-75; rec. artist Educo, Sanjo Music, 1982—; harpsichordist for rec. Johann Kuhnau: Six Biblical Sonatas, 1982. Life mem. Brandeis, Hadassah. Jewish. Author articles in field. Address: 50 Chumasero Dr San Francisco CA 94132

JONAS, KATHY WOOLF, college dean; b. Worcester, Mass., Aug. 18, 1957; d. Richard Charles and Carol Toby (Hurwitz) Woolf; m. Frederick Jonathan Jonas, Apr. 6, 1986. AB in Am. Studies, Hamilton Coll., 1979; MEd in Student Personnel, Northeastern U., 1983. Vol. VISTA ACTION, Cin., 1979-80; coordinator admissions N.H. Coll. and Univ. Council, Manchester, 1982-84; dean of students Wheelock Coll., Boston, 1984—. Bd. dirs. YMCA, Framingham, Mass., 1987. Mem. Nat. Assn. Student Personnel Administrs., Mass. Assn. Women Deans and Counselors. Democrat. Jewish. Home: 146 Bishop Dr Framingham MA 01701 Office: Wheelock Coll 37 Pilgrim Rd Boston MA 02215

JONES, ALEXANDRA DONALDSON, management consultant; b. Croydon, England, Jan. 2, 1960; d. Frederick Charles and Judy Carlton (Carmalt) J.; m. Andrew Kenan Rose, May 30, 1986. BA with honors, Oxford (England) U., 1983; M of Pub. Adminstrn., Harvard U., 1985. Economist Internat. Monetary Fund, Washington, 1984; intern UN Devel. Programme, Nepal, 1985; mgmt. cons. McKinsey & Co., Inc., London, 1985-86, San Francisco, 1986—. Mem. pub. affairs council Planned Parenthood, San Francisco, 1987—; mem. San Francisco Symphony Chorus. Mem. Nat. Assn. Female Execs. Club: Harvard of San Francisco. Home: 903 Pine St Apt 34 San Francisco CA 94108

JONES, ANITA KATHERINE, data processing executive; b. Ft. Worth, Mar. 19, 1942; d. Park Joel and Helene Louise (Voigt) J.; m. William A. Wulf, July 1, 1977; children: Karin, Ellen. AB in Math., Rice U., 1964; MA in English, U. Tex., 1966; PhD in Computer Sci., Carnegie Mellon U., 1973. Programmer IBM, Boston, Washington, 1966-69; assoc. prof. computer sci. Carnegie-Mellon U., Phila., 1973-81; founder, v.p. Tartan Labs. Inc., Pitts., 1981-87; cons. free lance, Pitts., 1987-88; prof., head computer sci. dept. U. Va., Charlottesville, 1988—; mem. Defense Sci. Bd., Dept. Defense 1985—, U.S. Air Force Sci. Advisory Bd. 1980-85; bd. dirs. Sci Applications Internat. Corp. Editor: Perspectives on Computer Science, 1977, Foundations of Secure Computation, 1971. Mem. Assn. Computing Machinery (editor-in-chief Transactions on Computer Systems, 1983—), IEEE.

JONES, ANNE ELIZABETH, motor license agent, insurance executive; b. Chgo., Nov. 26, 1945; d. George Edward and Betty Jane (Wise) Sybrant; m. Brenton Elvis Jones, Aug. 15, 1965 (div. June 1980); children—James Devon, Douglas Edward, Robert Derrick. Student Ark. City Jr. Coll., Kans., 1962-64, Okla. State U., 1964-65. Credit mgr. Koppel's, Bartlesville, Okla., 1966-67; collector Am. Collection Agy., Bartlesville, 1967-72; office mgr. Paul Stumpff & Assocs., Bartlesville, 1972-82; owner A.J. Leasing, Inc., Tulsa, 1982—, Sooner Assocs., Inc., Tulsa, 1982—; motor lic. agt. Cen. Tag Agy., Tulsa, 1982—. Mem. Motor Lic. Agts. Assn. (exec. v.p. 1984-85, polit. liaison 1984, tchr. ins. and lic. law 1984, legis. chmn. 1986-87, exec. v.p., 1987—), Ins. Women Tulsa (legis. chmn. 1984, pub. relations chmn. 1985, tchr. ins. classes 1979-85, cert. profl. ins. woman, bylaws chmn., 1987), Nat. Assn. Ins. Women (state orgn. chmn. 1985, Rookie of Yr. 1981, regional winner Lace Speak-Off 1985, 1st Runner-up Nat. Speak-Off 1985, Region vi chmn. pub. relations, 1986-87), Tulsa C. of C., Okla. Soc. Chartered Ins. Counselors (charter), Profl. Ins. Agts. Okla. (seminar instr. 1979-88), Ind. Ins. Agts. Okla. (seminar instr. 1979-83). Club: Toastmasters (Tulsa) (various offices, Area 1 Gov., 1987-88). Avocations: pub. speaking, motivational seminars, antique dealing, oil painting, photography. Office: Cen Tag Agy 2702 E 15th St Tulsa OK 74104

JONES, AUDREY HOWARD, utility executive; b. Bklyn., May 13, 1928; d. Edward Richard and Venie Ednora (Jacobs) Howard; BA, Hunter Coll., 1949; MS in Marine Sci., L.I.U., 1969; m. Farrell Jones, June 16, 1951; children: Joanne Kathryn and Jacqueline Elinor (twins). Research biochemist Manhattan Eye, Ear and Throat Hosp., 1949-51, Downstate Med. Coll., SUNY, Bklyn., 1952-58; instr. biology Nassau Community Coll., Garden City, N.Y., also cons. Environ. Assocs. and Urban Edn., Inc., 1970-73; environ. scientist, then EEO mgr. L.I. Lighting Co., Hicksville, N.Y., 1972-79, personnel policies and services mgr., 1979-86, mgr. tng. and devel., 1986—; adj. asst. prof. N.Y. Inst. Tech., 1979-80; field faculty adv. Goddard grad. program Norwich U., 1981-83; lectr. SUNY, Farmingdale; mem. career services adv. bd. Adelphi U., 1981—. Mem. citizens adv. com. N.Y. State Coastal Zone Mgmt. Program; mem. L.I. regional adv. com. N.Y. State External High Sch. Diploma Program; assoc. trustee L.I. Jewish Med. Ctr. Recipient various service awards, certs. appreciation. Mem. Am. Gas Assn. (various coms. 1975-84), Edison Electric Inst. (bvarious coms. 1975-84), L.I. Assn. (chmn. personnel dirs. council 1980-81), LWV, NAACP, L.I. Center for Bus. and Profl. Women (pres. 1982-84), Delta Sigma Theta. Democrat. Unitarian-Universalist. Clubs: Zonta, 100 Black Women of L.I. Home: 22 Driftwood Dr Port Washington NY 11050 Office: L I Lighting Co 175 E Old Country Rd Hicksville NY 11801

JONES, BARBARA CHRISTINE, educator, linguist, creative arts designer; b. Augsburg, Swabia, Bavaria, Fed. Republic Germany, Nov. 14, 1942; came to U.S., 1964, naturalized, 1971; d. Martin Walter and Margarete Katharina (Roth-Rommel) Schulz von Hammer-Parstein; m. Robert Edward Dickey, 1967 (div. 1980); m. Raymond Lee Jones, 1981. Student U. Munich, 1961, Philomatique de Bordeaux, France, 1962; BA in German, French, Speech, Calif. State U., Chico, 1969, MA in Comparative Internat. Edn., 1974. Cert. secondary tchr., community coll. instr., Calif. Fgn. lang. tchr. Gridley Union High Sch., Calif., 1970-80, home econs., decorative arts instr., cons., 1970-80, English study skills instr., 1974-80, ESL coordinator, instr. Punjabi, Mex. Ams., 1970-72, curriculum com. chmn., 1970-80; program devel. adviser

Program Devel. Ctr. Supt. Schs. Butte County, Oroville, Calif., 1975-77; opportunity tchr. Esperanza High Sch., Gridley, 1980-81, Liberty High Sch., Lodi, Calif., 1981-82, resource specialist coordinator, 1981-82; Title I coordinator Bear Creek Ranch Sch., Lodi, 1981-82, instr., counselor, 1981-82; substitute tchr. Elk Grove (Calif.) Unified, 1982-84; freelance decorative arts and textiles designer, 1982—; internat. heritage and foods advisor AAUW, Chico, Calif., 1973-75; workshop dir. Creative Arts Ctr., Chico, 1972-73; workshop dir., advisor Bus. Profl. Women's Club of Gridley, 1972-74; v.p. Golden State Mobile Home League, Sacramento, 1980-82. Designer weavings-wallhangings (1st place 10 categories, Silver Dollar Fair, Chico, 1970). Mem. United European Am. Club, Am. Assn. German Tchrs., U.S. Army Res. Non-Commd. Officer's Assn. (ednl. adv. 1984-86), Kappa Delta Pi. Avocations: weaving, fiber designs, swimming, skiing, internat. travel and culture. Home: 3531 Thunderbird Ln Lake Havasu City AZ 86403

JONES, BEATRICE, television executive; b. Nashville, Jan. 24, 1953; d. Thomas Jefferson and Pearlie Bee (Saunders) J. Student, Bentley Coll., 1974; BS in Commerce, N.C. Cen. U., 1975; postgrad., Rider Coll., 1985—; cert. mgmt. and administrv. analysis program, Trenton State Coll.; postgrad., MIS Tng. Inst., Boston, USDA Grad. Sch. Auditor N.J. Dept. Trans., Trenton, 1976-78; mgmt. compliance officer N.J. Dept. Higher Edn., Trenton, 1978-86; mgr. finance and acctg. N.J. Pub. Broadcasting Authority, Trenton, 1986—. Co-chair recruitment Big Bros./Big Sisters Assn., Trenton; mem. minority arts com. Friends of N.J., Trenton; treas. N.J. Black Adminstrs. Network.; treas. N.J. Black Am. Heritage Festival, 1988; mem. Trenton Dropout Prevetion Planning Collaborative; youth advisor N.J. Black Issues Conv. Youth Leadership Devel. Inst.; mem. adv. council Rider Coll. Ednl. Opportunity Program. Named Mercer County Big Sister of Yr., 1980, 84, one of Outstanding Young Women of Am., 1984; recipient N.J. Black Admisntrs. Network Pres.' award, 1986. Mem. Nat. Assn. Govt. Accts. (social dir. Trenton br.), Nat. Assn. Female Execs., Pub. Telecommunications Fin. Mgmt. Assn., Trenton chpt. NAACP. Home: 1018-B Prospect St Trenton NJ 08638 Office: NJ Pub Broadcasting Authority 1573 Parkside Ave CN777 Trenton NJ 08625

JONES, BETTY HARRIS, educator; b. St. Louis, May 25, 1937; d. Homer and Pearl (Fulgham) Harris; A.B., Rutgers U., 1967; M.A., Bryn Mawr Coll., 1968, Ph.D., 1972; m. Calvin Walter Jones, Dec. 2, 1954; children—Christopher Walter, Nicholas Alexander. Instr. in English, Rutgers U., Camden, N.J., 1969-72, asst. prof., 1972—; mem. Nat. Faculty for Humanities, Arts, and Scis., 1983—; bd. dirs. Burlington County Opportunities Industrialization Ctrs.; cons. Phila. Sch. Dist. Grad. collector in English, Bryn Mawr Coll., mem. bd. cons., 1974-76. Contbr. articles to profl. jours. Danforth Found. fellow, 1967-68; Danforth Found. assoc., 1972; Rutgers U. summer fellow, 1975, faculty fellow, 1977; nominee Lindback award for excellence in coll. teaching, 1970, 77; named one of Ten Top Profs. in the Delaware Valley, Phila. Inquirer, 1986; cited for Outstanding Coll. Teaching Gov. N.J., 1986; recipient Outstanding Faculty award for excellence in classroom and disting. service to campus Rutgers U. Alumni Assn. Camden, 1987. Mem. MLA, AAUP, N.J. Coll. English Assn., Nat. Council Tchrs. English, Alumnae Assn. Bryn Mawr Coll. (3d v.p., exec. bd.). Contbr. articles to profl. jours., essay to book. Home: 42 Norman Ln Willingboro NJ 08046 Office: Rutgers U Camden NJ 08102

JONES, BEVERLY ANN MILLER, nursing executive; b. Bklyn., July 14, 1927; d. Hayman Edward and Eleanor Virginia (Doyle) Miller. B.S.N., Adelphi U., 1949; m. Kenneth Lonzo Jones, Sept. 5, 1953; children—Steven Kenneth, Lonnie Cord. Chief nurse regional blood program ARC, N.Y.C., 1951-54; asst. dir., acting dir. nursing M.D. Anderson Hosp. and Tumor Inst., Houston, 1954-55; asst. dir. nursing Sibley Meml. Hosp., Washington, 1959-61; assoc. dir. nursing service Anne Arundel Gen. Hosp., Annapolis, Md., 1966-70; asst. adminstr. nursing Alexandria (Va.) Hosp., 1972-73; asst. adminstr. patient services Longmont (Colo.) United Hosp., 1977—; instr. ARC, 1953-57; mem. adv. bd. Boulder Valley Vo.-Tech Health Occupations Program, 1977-80; chmn. nurse enrollment com. D.C. chpt. ARC, 1959-61; del. nursing adminstrs. good will trip to Poland, Hungary, Sweden and Eng., 1980. Contbr. articles to profl. jours. Bd. dirs. Meals on Wheels, Longmont, Colo., 1978-80; bd. dirs. Longmont Coalition for Women in Crisis; mem. Colo. Hosp. Assn. Task Force on Nat. Commn. on Nursing, 1982; mem. utilization com. Boulder (Colo.) Hospice, 1979-83; mem. council labor relations Colo. Hosp. Assn., 1982-87; mem.-at-large exec. com. nursing service adminstrs. Sect. Md. Nurses' Assn., 1966-69. Recipient Excellence in Human Caring Nightingale award U. Colo. Sch. of Nursing. Mem. Am. Orgn. Nurse Execs. (chmn. com. membership services and promotions, recipient recognition of excellence in nursing adminstrn.), Colo. Soc. Nurse Execs. (dir. 1978-80, 84-86, pres. 1980-81, mem. com. on nominations 1985-86). Home: 8902 Quail Rd Longmont CO 80501 Office: PO Box 1659 Longmont CO 80501

JONES, BEVERLY JEANNE, postal service executive; b. Carroll County, Ohio, Apr. 1, 1935; d. Raymond L. Clark and Martha Jane (Christian) Carter; m. Charles E. Jones, July 11, 1970; children: Michael, Kevin, Virena, Donna Lee. AS in Bus. Adminstrn., Franklin U., 1976, BSBA, 1978; AS in Bus. Mgmt., Hocking Tech. Coll., Nelsonville, Ohio, 1986. Supr. of mails U.S. Postal Service, Columbus, Ohio, 1973-77, labor relations rep., 1977-78, mgr. employee relations, 1978-80; regional labor relations specialist U.S. Postal Service, Columbus, 1980-82; dir. employee and labor relations U.S. Postal Service, Kalamazoo, 1982-84; dir. employee and labor relations U.S. Postal Service, Columbus, 1984-86, field dir. human resources, 1986—. Mem. adv. bd. Columbus Met. Area Community Action Orgn., Columbus Urban League, NAACP; mem. adv. bd. Ptnrship. in Edn. Adopt-A-Sch. program, Columbus. Mem. Cen. Ohio Fed. Exec. Assn. (Fed. Employee of Yr. award 1986), Women's Network of U.S. Postal Service, Soc. for Advancement Mgmt., Am. Arbitration Assn. (cert. advocate), Columbus, Ohio Personnel Assn., Am. Soc. Personnel Adminstrn., Columbus, Ohio Postal Customer Council. Baptist. Club: Top Ladies of Distinction (Columbus). Lodge: Order Eastern Star, Daughters of Isis. Home: 853 Sheridan Bexley OH 43209-2376 Office: U S Postal Service 850 Twin Rivers Dr Columbus OH 43216

JONES, CAROLYN ELIZABETH, small business owner; b. Middleboro, Mass., Sept. 5, 1931; d. King Israel and Kleo Estelle (Hodges) Evans; m. John Homer Jones, Sept. 9, 1966 (dec. July 1986); 1 child, David Everett. BA in English, Tift Coll., 1952; M of Religious Edn., Carver Sch. Missions and Social Work (now So. Bapt. Theol. Sem.), 1958; BA in Art, Mercer U., 1982. Cert. secondary tchr., Ga. Tchr. McDuffie County Bd. Edn., Thomson, Ga., 1952-53, Colquitt County Bd. Edn., Norman Park, Ga., 1953-55; missionary Home Mission Bd. SBC, New Orleans and Macon, 1958-66; spl. edn. tchr. Bibb County Bd. Edn., Macon, 1968-70, 75-79; owner, operator Laney Splty. Advertising Co., Macon, 1986—. Contbr. numerous articles and poems to profl. jours.; copyright Converts game, 1979. Bible tchr. YWCA, Macon, 1980-85, clk.-trustee, deacon 1st Bapt. Ch., Macon. Mem. Macon-Bibb County C. of C., Alumnae Assn. Tift College (pres., chaplain Macon chpt.). Democrat. Club: Ad of Cen. Ga. Office: Laney Splty Advt Co 2451 Kingsley Dr Macon GA 31204

JONES, CAROLYN ELLIS, publisher, retired employment agency and business service company executive; b. Marigold, Miss., Feb. 21, 1928; d. Joseph Lawrence and Willie Decelle (Forrest) Peeples; m. David Wright Ellis, May 30, 1945 (div. 1966); children—David, Lyn, Debbie, Dawn; m. Frank Willis Jones, Jan. 1, 1980. Student La. State U., 1949. Owner, mgr. Personnel and Bus. Service, Inc., Greenwood, Miss., 1962-88, now v.p.; owner Honor Pub. Co., Greenwood, 1988—. Author: The Lottie Moon Storybook, 1985; Editor: An Old Soldier's Career, 1974. Contbr. articles to religious and gen. interest publs. Mem. adv. bd. career edn. Greenwood Pub. Schs., 1975-76, mem. adv. bd. vocat.-tech. dept., 1975—; conf. leader Miss. Bapt. Convention Singles Retreat, 1980; Mission Service Corps del. Home Mission Bd., So. Bapt. Conv., Hawaii, 1979. Mem. Greenwood C. of C. (edn. com. 1980—), Mothers Against Drunk Drivers, Altrusa Internat., Nat. Fedn. Ind. Bus., Miss Delta Rose Soc., Miss. Native Plant Soc., Gideon Aux. (pres. 1988—). Avocations: writing, rose exhibitions. Office: Honor Pub 802 W President Greenwood MS 38930

JONES, CAROLYN JANE, clergywoman; b. Grove City, Pa., Jan. 28, 1937; d. Hester Clark and Winifred Eleanor (Hoag) J.; m. Thomas Woodward Golightly. B.A., Westminster Coll., 1958; M.A. in Edn., Syracuse U., 1963; M. Div., Pitts. Theol. Sem., 1977. Tchr. Am. Coll. for Girls, Cairo, 1958-61, Bethel Park High Sch., Pa., 1963-66; asst. dean women Syracuse U., N.Y., 1968-71, dir., asst. dir. activities and orgns. Office Student Affairs, 1971-74; assoc. in Christian edn. Pebble Hill Presbyterian Ch., DeWitt, N.Y., 1971-74; dir. Christian edn. Newlonsburg United Presbyn. Ch., Murrysville, Pa., 1975-77; assoc. pastor Glenshaw Presbyn. Ch., Pa., 1977-84; interim minister-at-large Pitts. Presbytery, 1984—; bd. dirs. Pitts. Theol. Sem.; bd. mgrs. New Wilmington Missionary Conf. Recipient Thomas Jamison scholar, 1977; Sylvester S. Marvin Meml. fellow, 1977. Mem. Cleric of Pitts., Internat. Assn. Women Ministers, Interim Network, Assn. Presbyn. Interim Ministry Specialists, Presbyn. Clergywomen's Assn. Home: 1524 King Charles Dr Pittsburgh PA 15237 Office: 801 Union Ave Pittsburgh PA 15212

JONES, CATHY WEAVER, advertising executive, property management company executive; b. Martinsville, Va., July 21, 1955; d. Milford Anderson and Dorothy (Smith) Weaver; m. Robert Alan Jones, Oct. 11, 1980; 1 child, Lindsay Tyler. BBA, Samford U., 1977. Lic. real estate salesperson. Comptroller Hall Devel. Corp., Norfolk, Va., 1977-81; bus. mgr. Va. Stage Co., Norfolk, 1982-83; v.p. fin. TSG Corp., Norfolk, 1983—. Active Horizons Circle Children's Hosp. Kings Daus., Norfolk, 1985-87. Lutheran.

JONES, CHERYL ANN, municipal investments specialist; b. Phila., Apr. 10, 1951; d. Donald D.M. and Ann (Brow) J. BA, Randolph-Macon Woman's Coll., 1973. Estate and trust adminstr. Fidelity Nat. Bank, Lynchburg, Va., 1973-76, Am. Security Bank, Washington, 1976-80; mcpl. bond underwriter Merrill Lynch Capital Markets, Atlanta, 1980-88, asst. v.p. mcpl. bond dept., 1988—. Mem. Jr. League. Office: Merrill Lynch Capital Markets 3414 Peachtree Rd NE Atlanta GA 30326

JONES, CHERYL BEATRICE, medical technologist; b. N.Y.C., July 31, 1948; d. Frederick Douglas and Mary Magdalene (Reid) Campbell; m. Leroy Jones, Aug. 4, 1973; 1 child, Kaleah Marie, Britney Ruth. A.A.S., N.Y.C. Community Coll., 1969; B.S., Richmond Coll., 1973. Lab. technician, Met. Diagnostic Labs., Bklyn., 1969-72; lab. technician in chemistry Bklyn. Hosp., 1972-73; technologist in hematology, coagulation and clin. microscopy Lenox Hill Hosp., N.Y.C., 1973-77; tchr. biology Tehran Am. Sch., Iran, 1978; technologist in serology and immunohematology Path Lab, Inc., Nashville 1979-80; tech. services instr. ARC, Nashville, 1981—; technical adv. com., 1987— Tenn. Assn. Blood Banks, 1987; mem. adv. com. Nashville State Tech. Inst., 1985-86. Author abstract. Mem. Am. Assn. Blood Banks, Tenn. Assn. Blood Banks, Am. Soc. Clin. Pathologists, Nat. Assn. Female Execs. Democrat. Roman Catholic. Avocations: photography; coin collecting; traveling. Home: 278 St Andrews Dr Franklin TN 37064 Office: ARC 2201 Charlotte Ave Nashville TN 37203

JONES, CHRISTINA KAREN, banker; b. Detroit, May 2, 1947; d. William George Rumpa Jr. and Alice Geraldine (Groom) Kraft; m. Michael Dennis Jones (div. Dec. 1986); 1 child, Layna Geraldine. Grad. high sch., Detroit. Legal collector Mich. Nat. Bank, Southfield, 1976-78; exec. loan officer Coop. Services Credit Union, Dearborn, Mich., 1978-81, br. mgr., 1981-83; credit mgr., asst. div. mgr. Guaranty Fed. Savings Bank, Taylor, Mich., 1984-87; mgr. consumer loan, asst. treas. Guaranty Fed. Savings Bank, Taylor, 1987—; chmn. ops. review com. Guaranty Fed. Savings Bank, Taylor, 1986—. Mem. Nat. Assn. Female Execs. Avocation: writing articles. Home: 22420 Madison Dearborn MI 48124 Office: Guaranty Fed Savings Bank 23333 Eureka Taylor MI 48180

JONES, CONNIE R., accountant; b. Joliet, Ill., Mar. 11, 1959; d. Harry T. and Charlotte R. J. BA, Augustana Coll., 1981. Fin. analysis Deer and Co., Moline, Ill., 1980, auditor factory and branch, 1981-84, auditor in charge, 1984; budget acct. John Deere Harvester Works, East Moline, Ill., 1984, forecast acct., 1985-86, acct. inventory, budget, 1986-87, forecast acct., 1987, supr. gen. acctg., 1987—. Mem. Nat. Assn. Accts. (team capt. 1986-87).

JONES, CORA LEE, medical technologist, insurance company administrator; b. Atlanta, Tex., Apr. 8, 1952; d. Charlie and Eloise (Stiger) Peters; m. Nuddie P. Jones, Apr. 1, 1952 (div. Aug. 1986); children: Cedric Ray Peters, Racine H. Jones. Cert. med. technology, St. Michael Sch. Med. Tech., Texarkana, Ark., 1975; BS, U. Tex., Arlington, 1975; MBA, East Tex. State U., 1985. Cert. ins. agt., Tex. Staff med. technologist Titus County Meml. Hosp., Mt. Pleasant, Tex., 1975, Linden (Tex.) Mun. Hosp., 1975-76; supr. blood bank St. Michael Hosp., Texarkana, Ark., 1977-81; supr. phlebotomy Wadley Regional Hosp., Texarkana, Tex., 1981-85; exec. trainee Met. Life Ins., Texarkana, Tex., 1985-87; med. technologist U. Tex. Cancer Hosp., Houston, 1987—; sales mgr. Ky. Cen. Life, Houston, 1987—; resident mgr. Am. Capital Fin. Service, Houston, 1987—. Mem. Am. Soc. Clin. Pathologists (registered), Nat. Assn. Securities Dealers (registered), Nat. Assn. for Female Execs. Democrat. Methodist. Home: 3435 Walnut Bend Apt 3012 Houston TX 77042

JONES, DELORES ELDER, administrative social worker, model, planner; b. Memphis, Jan. 21, 1940; d. Otis Augustus II, and Mary Odessa (Jones) Elder; m. Walter Lewis Spinks, Oct. 26, 1957 (dec. 1966); children—Sedrick Duane Jones, Tedra Shaun Spinks-Hicks; m. Richard Henry Jones, Mar. 10, 1968 (div. Jan. 27, 1988). B.Social Welfare, Memphis State U., 1982, M pf City and Regional Planning, 1986. Master barber. Men's hairstylist Jim's Barber Shop, Memphis, 1962-77; personal aide Isaac Hayes Movement, Memphis, 1970-77; pre-occupancy counselor Memphis Housing, 1977-83; adminstr., community and devel. social worker Diocese of Memphis Housing Corp., 1983—. Mem. housing com. Shelby County Kitchen Kabinet, Memphis; co-chmn. Tenn. Statewide Fair Housing Conf., 1986; bd. dirs. Memphis Area Neighborhood Watch, Inc.; vol. United Way. Named Ms. Inspiration, Big Beautiful Women Mag., 1984, Role Model of Yr. 1985, Fed. Express and Booker T. Washington High Sch., Memphis, 1985; recipient cert. of recognition HUD, 1986. Mem. Nat. Assn. Social Workers, Memphis Community Housing Resource Bd., Memphis Assn. Dirs. of Vols., Nat. Assn. Housing and Redevel. Ofcls. Democrat. Baptist. Clubs: In Good Company, Young Sophisticates (advisor Memphis 1966-84). Avocations: reading; bowling; inspiring big women and women over 40. Home: 4605 White Pine Memphis TN 38109

JONES, DENISE DEE, advertising agency executive; b. Lancaster, Pa., Sept. 16, 1958; d. Neil Helm and Dolores (Wesley) J. B.A., Franklin and Marshall Coll., 1979. Account exec. Kelly/Michener Advt., Lancaster, 1981-83; ptnr. Snyder & Snyder, Lancaster, 1983-85; account exec. Caravetta Allen Kimbrough/BBDO Inc., Miami, Fla., 1985—. Mem. Big Bros./Big Sisters, 1983-85. Mem. Phila. Club Advt. Women, Nat. Assn. Female Execs., Nat. Trust for Historic Preservation. Republican. Methodist. Avocations: piano; writing; theater. Home: 2930 Day Ave Apt N103 Coconut Grove FL 33133 Office: Caravetta Allen Kimbrough/BBDO 7200 Corp Center Dr Miami FL 33126

JONES, DENISE RENEE, accountant; b. Tripoli, Libya, Jan. 23, 1958; d. William Donald and Erma Susan (Howlett) Ferguson; m. Byron Lee Jones, May 2, 1981; 1 child, Dustin Lee. Pub. acct. Pierce Bus. Service, Valley Center, Kans., 1976-83; prin. Exec. Acctg. Service, Wichita, Kans., 1983—. Pres. Valley Center Hist. and Cultural Soc., 1986-87; mem. Valley Center Downtown Improvement Dist., 1986. Mem. Nat. Assn. Female Execs., Nat. Fedn. Ind. Bus., Nat. Taxpayers Union, Valley Center C. of C. (v.p. 1984-85). Home: 1411 E Boston Wichita KS 67211 Office: Exec. Acctg Service 140 N Hydraulic Suite 100 Wichita KS 67214

JONES, DOLORES PHILLIPS, welfare adminstrator; b. Birmingham, Ala., Apr. 3, 1935; d. Edward Love and Lucile (Clark) Phillips; m. J. Douglas Jones, June 2, 1957; children: Karen René, J. Chrystopher, Jamel Terrence. BS, Miles Coll., 1956. Cert. social worker, Ala. Tchr. secondary schs. Birmingham and Jefferson County, 1957-61; researcher Social Security Adminstrn., Birmingham, 1964-66; social worker Ala. Dept. Pensions and Security, Birmingham, 1966-71, cons., 1971-72, case work reviewer, 1972-79, welfare supr., 1979—; mem. Mayor's Commn. on Status of Women, Birmingham, 1984—, Atty. Gen's. Anti-drug Commn., Ala., 1987—. Bd. dirs. Found. for Women's Health in ALa., 1984—. Mem. AAUW, Nat. Assn. Social Workers, Ala. Conf. Social Workers, Assn. for Children and Adults with Learning Disabilities. Roman Catholic. Clubs: Les Precieuses, Rosary Sodality (pres. 1970-76). Home: 930 Hitching Post Ln Birmingham AL 35210 Office: Ala Dept Human Resources 85 Bagby Dr Birmingham AL 35210

JONES, DOLORIS DOROTHEA, marine equipment company executive; b. Salem, Mass., Mar. 26, 1937; d. Rene George and Cecilia C. (Pasquinelli) Duchesne; m. Harry Elmer Jones, Feb. 16, 1957; children—Leslie Carlin, Ross Owen. Student U. Maine, 1966-67, St. Petersburg Jr. Coll., 1968-71, Houston Community Coll., 1978-83, Rice U., 1984-85. Diagnostician, Aldine Sch. Dist., Houston, 1972-75; owner, pres. Dee Paula Fashions, Houston, 1973-76; dept. asst. mgr. Nissho-Iwai Trading Co., Houston, 1976-79; gen. mgr. Hamanaka Internat., Inc., Houston, 1979—; project mgr. floating product platform Placid Oil Co., Dallas, 1984-87; owner Alexandria of Houston. Patentee in field. Mem. LWV, Nat. Assn. Female Execs. Republican. Lutheran. Avocations: music; art; woodworking. Office: Hamanaka Internat Inc 1980 Post Oak Blvd Suite 1000 Houston TX 77056

JONES, DORIS MAE, court reporting company executive; b. Allentown, Pa., Nov. 24, 1938; d. Michael C. and Ann (Fedor) Hardony; m. Lewis M. Horwitz, Mar. 14, 1964 (div. 1984); children: Monica B., Pamela L. BS, Mich. State U., 1960; postgrad. Cleve. Marshall Law Sch., 1962; cert. Emery Sch., 1975. Ct. reporter Doris O. Wong Assocs., Boston, 1975-79; ofcl. reporter U.S. Dist. Cts., Boston, 1979-81; pres. Doris M. Jones & Assocs., Boston, 1980—. Bd. dirs., sec. Lawrence Extended Day Program, Brookline, Mass., 1977-81; steering com. hospitality program, Episcopal Diocese, Boston, 1984—, co-chair, 1987. Men.. Nat. Shorthand Reporters Assn., Mass. Shorthand Reporters Assn. (sec. 1977-79, bd. dirs. 1977-80), Greater Boston C. fo C. (mem. Execs. Club), Phi Gamma Nu, Delta Zeta. Avocations: reading, traveling, cooking, public speaking. Address: Doris M Jones & Assocs Inc 59 Temple Pl Boston MA 02111

JONES, DOROTHY CAMERON, language professional, educator; b. Detroit, Feb. 5, 1922; d. Vinton Ernest and Beatrice Olive (Cameron) J. B.A., Wayne State U., 1943, M.A., 1944; Ph.D., U. Colo., 1965. Attendance officer Detroit Bd. Edn., 1943-44; tchr. English Denby High Sch., Detroit, 1946-56, 57-58; exchange tchr. Honolulu, 1956-57; instr., asst. prof. English Colo. Women's Coll., Denver, 1962-66; mem. faculty U. No. Colo., Greeley, 1966—; prof. English U. No. Colo., 1974—. Contbr. articles to profl. lit. Served with WAVES USNR, 1944-46. Faculty research grantee, 1970, 76. Mem. Internat. Shakespeare Assn., Central States Renaissance Soc., Patristic, Medieval and Renaissance Conf., Rocky Mountain Medieval and Renaissance Soc., Rocky Mountain MLA, Delta Kappa Gamma, Pi Lambda Theta. Home: 1009 13th Ave Apt 312 Greeley CO 80631 Office: U No Colo Dept English 40 Michener Library Greeley CO 80639

JONES, EDITH IRBY, physician; b. Conway, Ark., Dec. 23, 1927; d. Robert and Mattie (Buice) Irby; m. James Beauregard Jones, Apr. 16, 1950; children: Gary, Myra, Keith. BS, Knoxville Coll., 1948; MD, U. Ark., 1952. Intern Univ. Hosp., Little Rock, Ark., 1952-53; gen. practice medicine Hot Springs, Ark., 1953-59; resident in internal medicine Baylor Coll. Medicine, Houston, 1959-62; practice medicine specializing in internal medicine Houston, 1962—; mem. staff Meth. Hosp., Houston, Hermann Hosp., Houston, Riverside Gen. Hosp., Houston, St. Elizabeth Hosp., Houston, St. Anthony Ctr., Houston, St. Joseph Hosp., Houston, Thomas Care Ctr., Houston; mem. staff Town Park, Houston, chief of staff; clin. asst. prof. medicine Baylor Coll. Medicine, U. Tex. Sch. Medicine, Houston; dir. Prospect Med. Lab.; bd. dirs., sec. Mercy Hosp. Comprehensive Health Care Group; ptnr. Jones, Coleman and Whitfield; grand med. exeminer Ct. Calanthe Jurisdiction, Tex.; cons. Social Security Agy., Tex. Pub. Welfare Dept., Vocat. Rehab. Assn., Tex. Rehab. Commn.; bd. dirs. Standard Savs. Assn., Houston; numerous others. Contbr. articles to profl. jours. Bd. dirs. Houston Internat. U., Drug Addiction Rehab. Enterprise, March of Dimes, Houston, Odessey House, Houston; mem. adv. bd. Houston Council on Alcoholism; mem. com. for revising justice code, Harris County, Tex.; chmn. bd. trustees Knoxville Coll.; impartial hearing officer Houston Ind. Sch. Dist.; trustee Mut. Assn. for Profl. Service; mem. Community Welfare Planning Assn., Friends of Youth, Human Services Adv. Council, Houston; mem. bd. visitors U. Houston; numerous others. Dr. Edith Irby Jones Day proclaimed by State of Ark., 1985, City of Little Rock, 1985, City of N.Y.C., 1986; named One of 30 Most Influential Black Women Houston, 1984; inducted into Tex. Black Women's Hall of Fame, 1986; commended by Calif. Senate, 1969; proclamation by city council, Houston, 1985, Mayor of Houston, 1986; recipient cert. of citation Ho. of Reps. State of Tex., 1986; portrait placed in entrance hall U. Ark. for Med. Scis., 1985; numerous others. Mem. AMA, Am. Med. Women's Assn. (v.p. Houston chpt.), Nat. Med. Assn. (past pres.), Lone Star Med. Assn., Harris County Med. Assn., Houston Med. Forum, Tex. Assn. Disability Examiners, Bus. and Profl. Women, Nat. Council of Negro Women, Inc. (v.p. Dorothy Height chpt.), NAACP, PTA, YMCA, Alpha Kappa Mu, Delta Sigma Theta, Eta Phi Beta. Democrat. Clubs: Links, Inc., Top Ladies of Distinction, Girl Friends, Inc., Women of Achievement, Inc. (Hall of Fame 1985). Lodge: Order Eastern Star. Home: 3402 S Parkwood Dr Houston TX 77021 Office: 2601 Prospect St Houston TX 77004

JONES, ELEANOR ILLSTON, foundation executive; b. Ithaca, N.Y., Nov. 6, 1924; d. Cady Pangburn and Laura H. (Buck) Illston; m. Don L. Jones, Dec. 24, 1942 (div. 1980); children: David M., Amy L., Evan W., Anne L., Matthew D., Peter W. Diploma, Practical Bus. Coll. Freelance writer for newspapers, religious periodicals, trade papers 1949-68; dir. pub. relations Harding Hosp., Worthington, Ohio, 1968-85; dir. Harding Evans Found., Worthington, 1985—; cons. Bd. Devel. Network:; founder, 1st pres. Tele-Mom Inc. Trustee Directions for Youth, Zonta Service Found.; trustee, v.p. adminstr. Columbus Area Internat. Program, 1980-86; chmn. adv. com. on mental health and retardation tech. Columbus Tech. Inst., 1970-78. Recipient first award Excellence in Column Writing, Kans. Press Assn., 1956, 58; Outstanding Service award Columbus Tech. Inst., N. Area Mental Health Services, Harding Hosp. Mem. Nat. Assn. Hosp. Devel. (fellow, dir. Region VI), Ohio Assn. Hosp. Devel. Democrat. Methodist. Club: Columbus Metro. Lodges: Zonta, Order Eastern Star. Home: 823 Franklin Ct Worthington OH 43085 Office: 445 E Granville Rd Worthington OH 43085

JONES, ELIZABETH BROWN, writer; b. Kansas City, Mo., Sept. 27, 1907; d. James Riley and Agnes Julia (Gammage) Brown; student U. Mo., Kansas City, 1946, Mid-Am. Nazarene Coll., 1981; m. Clare Hartley Jones, June 4, 1929; children—Elizabeth Ann, Sara Denise, David Hartley, Phyllis Elaine. Free-lance writer, 1940-62, 78—; author numerous books, including: Teaching Primaries Today, 1974; Because God Made Me, 1975; Stories of Jesus, 1977; When We Share the Bible with Children, 1977; Let the Children Come, 1978; contbr. numerous stories, poems to children's publs.; author song lyrics; editor, curriculum planner, writer Nazarene Pub. House, Kansas City, Mo., 1962-78; workshop leader; speaker at writers' confs.; mem. nat. com. for planning Sunday sch. curriculum; book reviewer; speaker at parent's groups. Mem. Ch. of the Nazarene.

JONES, ELODIA LOUISE, computer executive; b. Olsburg, Kans., July 11, 1928; d. George Harold and Anita (McFarland) Taylor; m. Jesse Clarence Jones, Apr. 23, 1953; 1 child, Jesse Lewis. BBA, Ea. Mich. U., 1971, M, 1978. Edn. cons. Mich. Dept. Edn., Lansing, 1971-79, supr. of propriatory vocat. sch., 1979-86; sr. v.p. Hallmark Computer Tng. Inst., Oak Park, Mich., 1986-87; pvt. practice edn. cons. Lansing, 1987—; V.p. MKJ Paralegal Sch., San Francisco, 1986—; cons. Total Life Enrichment, Detroit, 1987—; leader seminars in field. Vice chair Mayor's Human Resource Com., Lansing, 1975-80. Mem. Nat. Assn. Female Execs., Nat. Assn. State Adminstrs. and Suprs. of Proprietary Schs. (v.p., historian). Democrat. Seventh-day Adventist. Home and Office: 421 McPherson Ave Lansing MI 48915

JONES, ETTA MAYS, educator; b. Lawrenceville, Va., May 31, 1955; d. Freddie and Julia Ann Mays; m. Willie H. Jones; children: Christopher Alexander, Collin Alastaire. Cert., Southside Va. Community coll., 1977; BEd, St. Paul's Coll., 1986. Dist. aide Boy Scouts Am., River Edge, N.J., 1978-79; tchr. aide Brunswick County Sch., Lawrenceville, Va., 1980-81; office asst. St. Paul's Coll., Lawrenceville, 1983-86; tchr. Red Oak Elementary Sch., Alberta, Va., 1986-87, Pub. Sch. Number 6, Paterson, N.J., 1987—. Mem. Red Oak Elem. PTA, Alberta, 1986-87, Sturgeon Elem. PTA, Lawrenceville, 1986-87. Mem. Va. Edn. Assn., N.J. Edn. Assn.,

Paterson Edn. Assn., NEA, NAACP. Mem. Reformed Zion Union Apostolic Ch. Home: 1261 Tuxedo Sq Teaneck NJ 07666

JONES, FRANCES SYLVIA, medical technology educator; b. Mangham, La., July 30, 1934; d. Harvel Traylor and Eva Dee (Weems) Jones; B.S., N.E. La. U., 1956; M.S., La. Tech. U., 1970. Chief technologist E.A. Conway Hosp., Monroe, La., 1956-62; staff technologist to supr. VA Med. Center, Shreveport, La., 1962-72; edn. coordinator Sch. Med. Tech., VA Med. Center, Shreveport, 1972-82; program dir. Sch. Med. Tech., clin. prof. Cantenary Coll., Shreveport, 1983—; clin. assoc. prof. La. Tech. U., Ruston; clin. asst. prof. Northwestern State U., Natchitoches, La.; clin. asst. prof. Allied Health Scis., Notheast La. U., Monroe; clin. instr. dept. pathology La. State U. Sch. Medicine, Shreveport; faculty mem. So. Regional Med. Edn. Ctr., 1977, 83; site surveyor Nat. Accreditation Agy. for Clin. Lab. Scis. Chmn., VA Fed. Employees Credit Union credit com., 1972-79, dir., 1978—, pres./bd. dirs., 1983—. Recipient Superior Performance award, VA Med. Center, 1971, 79, 83, 85-87; La. Heart Assn. grantee, 1953-54. Mem. Am. Soc. Clin. Pathologists, Am. Bus. Women's Assn., La. Soc. Med. Tech., Am. Soc. Med. Tech., Clin. Lab. Mgmt. Assn., Phi Mu (charter mem. 1956). Democrat. Baptist. Home: 1823 Pluto Dr Bossier City LA 71112 Office: 510 E Stoner Ave Shreveport LA 71130

JONES, GERALDINE ANN JOHNSON, educator; b. Seaford, Del., July 30, 1939; d. Thomas E. and Marion Frances (Walker) Johnson; 1 child, Monica. BA, Del. State Coll., 1961; MBA, Cen. Mich. U., 1978; postgrad., Temple U., 1986—. Caseworker Div. Social Services, Dover, Del., 1962-64; tchr. English William C. Jason Sch., Georgetown, Del., 1966-67; vis. tchr. Capital Sch. Dist., Dover, 1967—; home and sch. coordinator, migrant edn. program, Dover, 1967; paraprofl. Title I, Dover, 1964, 65; supr. Head Start Program, Camden, Del. 1970. Active local polit. coms.; lay leader; pres. United Meth. Women, Whatcoat, v.p. Peninsula conf.; mem. nominating com. Upper Atlantic regional sch., dir. summer day camp; mem. Yesterdays Youth Choir, Seaford. Named Woman of Yr., Whatcoat Ch., 1986. Mem. Internat. Assn. Pupil Personnel Workers, Del. Assn. Cert. Vis. Tchrs. (sec.treas. 1984), Capital Educators Assn., Nat. Educator Assn., Del. State Coll. Alumni Assn. (pres. Kent County chpt., Alumni of Yr. 1985, Ms. Alumni 1986-87), William C. Jason Alumni Club (treas.), Delta Sigma Theta, Sigma Iota Epsilon. Democrat. Office: Capital Sch Dist 945 Forest St Dover DE 19907

JONES, GLORIA KAY, librarian; b. Perryton, Tex., Oct. 9, 1953; d. Kenneth and Christine (Jarrett) Gibson; m. Steven Karl Branham, May 17, 1975 (div. June 1984); m. Stephen Lewis Jones, Feb. 28, 1987; stepchildren: Marci Kay, Corey Todd. BA, West Tex. State U., 1975; MLS, Tex. Woman's U., 1977. Library tech. asst. Amarillo (Tex.) Coll., 1975-76; jr. librarian West Tex. State U., Canyon, 1976-77, asst. reference librarian, 1977-80, head govt. documents dept. Cornette Library, 1987—; librarian Southwestern Pub. Service Co., Amarillo, 1980-87. Vol. Big Bros./Big Sisters Inc., Amarillo, 1985— (Rookie of Yr. 1986); bd. dirs., treas. Friends of Amarillo Pub. Library. Mem. ALA, Spl. Library Assn., Tex. Library Assn. (councilor 1984-87, polit. action com.). Presbyterian. Office: West Tex State U Cornette Library PO Box 748 WT Sta Canyon TX 79016

JONES, J. DULIN, writer, film producer; b. Hollywood, Calif., Sept. 6, 1957; d. John Dulin and Helen Mae (Weaver) J. BA, Calif. State U., Long Beach, 1980. Developer mini-series and TV series Embassy Communications, Los Angeles, 1981-84; assoc. to producer Hotel Aaron Spelling Prodns., Los Angeles, 1984-85; writing intern Sundance Film Inst., Los Angeles, 1985; feature film story analyst Carson Prodns., Los Angeles, 1985-86; freelance screenplay and play writer Los Angeles and N.Y.C., 1986—. Author: (screenplays) Fade Away, 1986, No Other Love, 1987, Story of the Century, 1988. Mem. Writers Guild Am., Ind. Feature Project, Am. Film Inst., Sundance Film Inst. (pre-selection com. 1985-87), People for Am. Way, Delta Gamma.

JONES, JACQUELINE LEE, occupational therapy educator; b. Ironton, Ohio, Aug. 30, 1934; d. Leslie Marion and Victoria Louise (Greenlee) J.; m. Alfred Q. Cooke, 1960 (div. 1969); 1 child, Victoria Lee Cooke Sims. BS, Milw.-Downer Coll., 1956; MS, Fla. Internat. U., 1975; PhD, U. Ill., 1986. Cert. occupational therapist. Officer in charge dept. occupational therapy Wright-Patterson AFB Hosp., Dayton, Ohio, 1957-60; head, dept. occupational therapy South Fla. State Hosp. Children's Unit, Hollywood, 1969-76; sr. instr. Palm Beach Jr. Coll., Fla., 1976-79; asst. prof. U. Ill. at Chgo., 1979-84, asst. head dept. occupational therapy, 1984-87; complemental faculty Rush U., Chgo., 1984-87; chmn. dept. occupational therapy Elizabethtown (Pa.) Coll., 1987—. Milw.-Downer Coll. scholar, 1952-56. Mem. Am. Occupational Therapy Assn., Pa. Occupational Therapy Assn., Ill. Occupational Therapy Assn. (exec. bd. dirs. 1979-87), Phi Delta Kappa, Pi Kappa Alpha. Republican. Presbyterian. Office: Elizabethtown Coll Dept Occupational Therapy Elizabethtown PA 17022

JONES, JACQUELINE RAE MCBRIDE, city official; b. Cumberland County, N.J., Oct. 3, 1950; d. James Elwood and Lucy Mae (Coursey) McBride; m. Norman Preston Jones, Oct. 19, 1974; children: D'Andre, Pheon, Coyuca, Matoya. BS, Howard U., 1972; MA, Fairleigh Dickinson U., 1976; postgrad., Am. U., 1978, U. Mich., 1979. Asst. dir. social services, psychol., sociol. and social services cons. NARCO, Atlantic County, N.J., 1972-75; therapist Seabrook House, Cumberland County, N.J., 1976-77, Alternatives, Ataintic County, 1978; project dir. Mental Health Assn., Atlantic County, 1978; cons. program dir. Jacobs Youth Shelter, Atlantic County, 1979; pres. Sanctuary Assn., Atlantic County, 1979-80; pension fund supr. Atlantic City, 1980-83. V.p., bd. dirs. Garden State Coalition for Youth and Family Services, 1979—; active Nat. Conf. Christians and Jews, 1980—, InerAgy. Council Atlantic County/CES Network, 1972—; bd. dirs. Empire State Coalition for Youth & Family Services, 1979-82, Nat. Network Runaway and Family Services, 1979—, Boys and Girls Club Atlantic County, 1981—. Mem. Am. Soc. Pub. Adminstrn., Nat. Assn. Female Execs., Atlantic County Juvenile Officers Assn., N.J. Assn. Alcoholism Counselors, Mainland C. of C., Greater Atlantic C. of C. Democrat. Methodist. Home: 9A Power Mill Springs Mays Landing NJ 08330 Office: PO Box 44 Atlantic City NJ 08404

JONES, JEANNIE CROMEANS, publishing executive; b. Helena, Ark., Jan. 19, 1949; d. Ardie Leaton and Ruth Beatrice (Rowan) Cromeans; m. Hugh Allen Noland, Feb. 14, 1968 (div. 1970); children: Jennifer Dana (dec.), Steven Douglas. Student, San Diego State Coll., 1968, Phillips County (Ark.) Community Coll., 1969-70, Memphis State U., 1980. Comml. artist Bradford Printing Co., Helena, 1969-70, Branch-Smith Pub. Co., Inc., Ft. Worth, 1970-71; owner, publisher DeSoto County Tribune and Pub. Co., Inc. & Home Market Mags., Olive Branch, Miss., 1972—. Supporter Disabled Am. Vets Assn., Humane Soc. Am., Miss. Humane Soc., Memphis Humane Soc. Mem. Greenpeace, Miss. Press. Assn. Republican. Home: 8141 Hunters Hill Cove Olive Branch MS 38654 Office: DeSoto County Tribune Pub Co Inc Home Market Mags Olive Branch MS 38654

JONES, JOAN MEGAN, anthropologist; b. Laramie, Wyo., Sept. 7, 1933; d. Thomas Owen and Lucille Lenoir (Magill) J; m. James Caldwell Merritt, June 20, 1980. BA, U. Wash., 1956, MA, 1968, PhD, 1976. Mus. educator Burke Mus. U. Wash., Seattle, 1969-72; anthropologist Quinault Indian Nation, Taholah, Wash., 1976-77; researcher, corp. officer Profl. Anthropology Consulting Team/Social Analysts, Seattle, 1977-79; research assoc. dept. anthropology U. Wash., Seattle, 1982—; research investigator Dept. Social and Health Services State of Wash., Seattle, 1977; vis. lectr. Dept. Anthropology U. B.C., Vancouver, 1978; research specialist Artsplan Arts Alliance Wash. State, Seattle, 1978; vis. instr. Dept. Anthropology Western Wash. U., Bellingham, 1981; cons. in field. Author: Northwest Coast Basketry and Culture Change, 1968, Basketry of Quinault, 1977, Native Basketry of Western North America, 1978, Art and Style of Western Indian Basketry, 1982, Northwest Coast Indian Basketry Styles. Bd. dirs. Anacortes (Wash.) Arts and Crafts Festival, 1981-83. Wenner-Gren Found. Anthrop. Research fellow, 1967-68; Ford Found. fellow, 1972-73; Nat. Mus.'s. Can. grantee, 1973-74. Fellow Am. Anthrop. Assn., Soc. Applied Anthropology; mem. AAUW (bd. dirs. Anacortes chpt. 1982-83), Am. Assn. Mus., Nat. Assn. Practicing Anthropologists, Assn. Women in Sci., Skagit Valley Weavers Guild (v.p. Skagit County chpt. 1985-86), Whidbey Weavers. Office: U Washington Dept Anthropology Seattle WA 98195

JONES, KATHY LUNDY, insurance company executive, nurse; b. Jan. 30, 1951; d. John H. and Thelma (Greenup) Lundy; m. William Lynn Jones; 1 child, Candace L. Assoc. in Nursing, Midway (Ky.) Coll., 1977; BS, U. Ky., 1980. Program coordinator Bluegrass Comprehensive Care, Lexington, Ky., 1972-73; staff nurse Good Samaritan Hosp., Lexington, 1977-78; team leader, nurse U. Ky. Med. Ctr., Lexington, 1978-83; research nurse U. Ky. Coll. Pharmacy, Lexington, 1982-83; pres. Equus Unltd., Inc., Lexington, 1985—. Mem. Profl. Ins. Agts., Am. Nurses Assn., Ky. Nurses Assn. Republican. Roman Catholic. Office: Equus Unltd Inc PO Box 4217 Lexington KY 40544

JONES, KATHY LYN, health care organization director; b. Lubbock, Tex., July 2, 1949; d. D. C. Roberts Jr. and Wylene (Moss) Ball; m. Kenneth Ray Beebe, June 20, 1970 (div. Aug. 1977); 1 child, Kyle Mac Beebe; m. James Robert Jones, July 5, 1980. Student, Tex. Tech U., 1967-70, 74-77. Mgr. bus. J. Taylor Evans, DDS, Lubbock, 1977-80; adminstr. dept. psychiatry Tex. Tech U Health Sci. Ctr., Lubbock, 1980—. Mem. Adminstrs. in Acad. Psychiatry (pres. 1988—). Republican. Methodist. Club: Jr. League Lubbock (chmn. emergency med. services com. 1987—). Lodge: Soroptimists (treas. Lubbock chpt. 1984-85). Office: Tex Tech U Health Sci Ctr Dept Psychiatry 4th and Indiana Lubbock TX 79430

JONES, LAURETTA MARIE, artist, computer art consultant, educator; b. Cleve., Mar. 13, 1953; d. Richard Llewellyn and Loretta (Jares) J. BFA, Cleve. Inst. Art, 1975; postgrad., N.Y. Inst. Tech., 1981, 87. Free-lance artist, designer N.Y.C., 1981—; instr. Sch. Visual Arts, N.Y.C., 1984—; adj. prof. art Manhattanville Coll., Purchase, N.Y., 1985-86; cons. Trintex, White Plains, N.Y., 1986-87, IBM Gallery Sci. and Art, N.Y.C., 1987-88. Exhibited collages, drawings in shows worldwide, 1983—. Mem. Nature Conservancy, 1978—, People Am. Way, 1985—. Mem. Nat. Computer Graphics Assn. (speaker 1987), Small Computers Arts Network (speaker 1984-87), Computer Arts Discipline Graphic Artists Guild (founding, steering com. 1984—), N.Y.C. chpt. Assn. Computing Machinery's Spl. Interest Group Graphics (editor newsletter, bd. dirs. 1986—), Amnesty Internat., Greenpeace, NOW. Home: 437 W 53d St Suite 5A New York NY 10019 Office: Sch Visual Arts 214 E 21st St Computer Ctr New York NY 10010

JONES, LAURIE LYNN, editor; b. Kerrville, Tex., Sept. 2, 1947; d. Charles Clinton and Jean Laurie (Davidson) J.; m. C. Frederick Childs, June 26, 1976; children: Charles Newell (Clancy), Cyrus Trevor; 1 stepchild, Ariel Childs. B.A., U. Tex., 1969. Asst. to dir. coll. admissions Columbia U., N.Y.C., 1969-70; asst. to dir. Office Alumni-Columbia U., N.Y.C., 1970-71; asst. advt. mgr. Book World, 1971-72, Washington Post-Chgo. Tribune, 1971-72; editorial asst. N.Y. Mag., N.Y.C., 1972-74, asst. editor, 1974, sr. editor, 1974-76, mng. editor, 1976—. Mem. Am. Soc. Mag. Editors, Women in Coummunication, Advt. Women N.Y. Republican. Methodist. Home: 40 Great Jones St New York NY 10012 also: 62 Giles Hill Rd Redding Ridge CT 06876 Office: New York Magazine 755 2nd Ave New York NY 10017

JONES, LISA ROLFING, copywriter, editor; b. Cin., May 14, 1955; d. Dudley S. Jones and Joanne (Rolfing) Gehlert; divorced. BFA, U. Ariz., 1977. Bus. mgr. various community music programs, Greensboro, N.C., 1982-84; mktg. dir. High Point (N.C.) Theatre and Exhibition Ctr., 1984-85; assoc. editor PACE Communications, Greensboro, 1985-86, promotions mgr., 1985-86; freelance copywriter Tucson, 1987—; stage mgr. Citystage Celebration, Greensboro, 1984, 85, 86. chair entertainment Festival of Lights, Greensboro, 1983. Home: 5408 N Paseo de la Terraza Tucson AZ 85715

JONES, LOIS MAILOU (MRS. VERGNIAUD PIERRE-NOEL), artist, educator; b. Boston; d. Thomas Vreeland and Carolyn (Adams) J.; m. Vergniaud Pierre-Noel, Aug. 18, 1953. Diploma Boston Mus. Sch., 1927; cert. Boston Normal Art Sch., 1928, Designers Art Sch., 1928, Academie Julian, Paris, 1938, Academie de la Grande Chaumière, 1962; AB magna cum laude, Howard U., 1945, HHD (hon.), 1987; student Harvard U., 1927, Columbia U., 1934-36; PhD, Suffolk U., 1981, HLD, 1981; PhD (hon.), Colo. State Christian Coll.; PhD in Fine Arts (hon.), Mass. Coll. Art, 1986; PhD in the Humanities (hon.), Howard U., 1987. Exhibited in one man shows Vose Galleries, Boston, Barnett Aden Gallery, Washington, Howard U. Gallery Art, Washington, Los Angeles County Mus. Art, High Mus. Art, Atlanta, Pan Am. Union, Ctr. d'Art, Port au-Prince, Haiti, Galerie Internat., N.Y.C., Mus. Fine Arts, Dallas, Lincoln U., Pa., Hampton Inst., Va., Cornell U., Ithaca, N.Y., W.Va. State Coll., Galerie Soulanges, Paris, Mus. Nat. Ctr. Afro-Am. Artists, Boston, Reynolda House Mus. Am. Art, Winston Salem, N.C., Harbor Art Gallery, U. Mass., Boston, Bethune Mus. Archives, Inc., Washington, Le Musee d'Art Haitien, Port au Prince; retrospective exhbn. Howard U. Gallery Art, 1972, Boston Mus. Fine Arts, 1973, Acts of Art Gallery, N.Y.C., 1973, Phillips Collection, Washington, 1979, Cooper Union, N.Y.C., 1986; exhibited group shows Salon des Artistes Français, 1938, 39, 66, Biennial exhbn. Corcoran Gallery Art, NAD, N.Y.C., Nat. Mus., Pa. Acad., Balt. Mus., Oakland Art Mus. (Calif.), Seattle Mus., Wash. State, A.C.A. Galleries, N.Y.C., Grand Cen. Art Galleries, San Francisco Mus. Art, Princeton U., Mus. Modern Art, N.Y.C., Fisk U., San Jose Mus. Art, Smith Coll., Carnegie Inst., Ill. State U., FESTAC, Nigeria, Galerie Jean Charpentier, Paris, Galerie de Paris, Salon des Inds., Paris, Rhodes Nat. Gallery, So. Rhodesia, King George VI Gallery, Port Elizabeth, Republic South Africa, Smith Coll., Harmon Found., Pa. U. Mus., Am. Embassy, Tanzania, Mus. of Nat. Ctr. of Afro-Am. Artists, Boston, 1983, Hofstra U., 1983 84, African-Am. Mus. Art, Los Angeles, 1984, Nat. Collection Fine Art and Nat. Potrait Gallery, Ctr. Gallery, Bucknell U., Pa., Studio Mus. in Harlem, N.Y.C., Nat. Urban League, N.Y.C., Cooper Union, N.Y.C., Bellevue Art Mus., Wash.; represented permanent collections Phillips Collection, IBM Corp. Palais Nationale, Haiti, Howard U. Gallery Art, Atlanta U., Barnett Aden Gallery, Bklyn. Mus., 135th St. Public Library, Rosenwald Found., Retreat for Fgn. Missionaries, Washington, U. Panjab, Pakistan, Internat. Fair Gallery, Izmir, Turkey, Walker Art Mus., Am. Embassy, Luxembourg, Ebony hdqrs., Chgo., Boston Mus. Fine Arts, Met. Mus. Art, N.Y.C., Hirshhorn Mus. and Sculpture Garden, Nat. Portrait Gallery; designed stained glass window Andrew Rankin Meml. Chapel, Howard U. Prof. design and watercolor painting Coll. Fine Arts Howard U., Washington, now prof. emerita; lectr. Afro-Am. Artists, Contemporary Haitian Artists. Conducted 5 week Around the World Tour, summers 1966, 67; Howard U. Research grantee study tour 17 African countries, 1970, 71. Recipient many awards and prizes, including Robert Woods Bliss award, 1st Luban Watercolor award, 1958; Franz Bader award, 1962; 1st hon. mention for oil painting Soc. des Artistes Francais, Paris, 1966; Howard U. Alumni award, 1978; diplome and decoration de l'Ordre Nat. D'Honneur et Merite Haitian Govt., 1954; Candace award Met. Mus., 1982; citation Mass. Ho. of Reps., 1982; D.C. Mayor's 3d Ann. Art award; honor award Women's Caucus for Art, 1986. Fellow Royal Soc. Arts; mem. Nat. Art Dirs. Club, Washington Soc. Artists, Am. Watercolor Assn. (asso.), Washington Watercolor Assn., Alumni Assn. Boston Mus. Sch., Artists Equity, Nat. Conf. of Artists (1st v.p.), Bienfaiteur, Foyer Montparnasse, Paris, Alpha Kappa Alpha. Author: Peintures, Lois Mailou Jones, 1937-51, 1952; Caribbean and Afro-American Women Artists. Home: 4706 17th St NW Washington DC 20011

JONES, LYNN LOUISE, law enforcement professional; b. Chgo., June 13, 1949; d. Ralph Thomas and Virjean Louise (Field) J.; m. Charles Edward Pierce III, Apr. 4, 1975; children: Charles Edward IV, Jeanne Louise. BA, U. Tulsa, 1971, MS, 1975. Patrol officer Tulsa Police Dept., 1972-76, sgt., 1976-84, lt., 1984—; cons. Foley's Career Lifestyle, 1984—, vol. coordinator Tulsa police 1985-87, mediation liason Tulsa Police Dept. Corrections 1985-86, instr. Council on Law Enforcement Edn., and Tng. officer survival 1981-87. Bd. dirs. At Risk Parent-Child Program, 1979, chmn. 1986-87; mem. Tulsa Assn. Vol. Adminstn., 1985—, "Gillies" Thomas Gilcrease Inst. Am. History and Art, 1985—, Statewide Child Abuse Prevention Task Force, 1986—; chmn. Fellowship Congl. Ch. long range planning com. Named Outstanding Vol. of Yr. Tulsa Assn. Vol. Adminstrs., 1984; recipient Paragin award Leadership Tulsa, 1988. Mem. Police Mgmt. Assn., Internat. Assn. Women Police, Jr. League (cen. site com.), Tulsa Urban League, (bd. dirs. 1987), Leadership Tulsa. Republican. Club: Questors, (v.p. 1984-87). Lodge: Frat. Order Police, (bd. dirs. 1975), Optimists (Officer of Yr. 1983). Home: 1320 E 19th Tulsa OK 74120 Office: Tulsa Police Dept 600 Civic Ctr Tulsa OK 74103

JONES, LYSA LYNETTE, interior designer, lecturer; b. Dallas, Sept. 15, 1959; d. William Mesheck and Shirley (Brinkley) J. BA in Art History, So. Meth. U., 1981, MA, 1986. Apprentice Hudson & Hudson Interiors, Dallas, 1976-80; prin., art cons., interior designer Lysa L. Jones Fine Arts, Decorative Arts, Interiors, Dallas, 1982—; cons. Gerald Tomlin & Assocs., ASID, Dallas, 1987-88, Better Homes and Gardens Idea House, 1988; guest lectr. Continuing Edn. Dept. So. Meth. U., Dallas, 1987—, various non profit orgns., Dallas, 1986—. Co-chair season tickets Dallas Ballet, 1986, Multiple Scelorsis Fundraiser, Dallas, 1987-88; ballet liaison Arts Bond Election, Dallas, 1986. Recipient Pollock Art History scholar So. Meth. U., 1980-81, Meadows Found. assistantship, 1984-86. Republican. Office: 5939 DeLoache Ave Dallas TX 75225

JONES, MALINDA THIESSEN, telecommunications company executive; b. Perryton, Tex., Jan. 23, 1947; d. Chester Francis Thiessen and Bobbye Pearson (Wallis) Schwalm; m. Hollis Bass Jones, Mar. 21, 1969 (div. 1972); 1 child, Reshad. B.A. in Psychology, U. Mo.-Kansas City, 1975. Research asst. U. Kans. Med. Ctr., Kansas City, 1975-77; owner, mgr. Metro Shampoo Co., Kansas City, Mo., 1977-79; regional mgr. U.S. Telecom, Dallas, 1981-82, staff asst. to pres., Dallas, 1983-84, sr. planner, 1984-85; dir. mktg. Telinq Systems Inc., Richardson, Tex., 1985-86, dir. bus. devel. and corp. communications, 1986—; cons. in field. Editor conf. presentations, bus. plans. Vol. tchr. Sch. for Learning Disability, Operation Discovery, Kansas City, 1973-75; corp. liaison exec. assistance program Dallas C. of C./Dallas Ind. Sch. Dist., 1984; chmn. com. Therapeutic Riding Tex., Dallas, 1985. Recipient Outstanding Contbr. award Dallas Ind. Sch. Dist., 1984. Mem. Nat. Assn. Female Execs., Nat. Mus. Assn. for Women in Arts, Assn. Women Entrepreneurs Dallas. Home: 1122 Overlake Dr Richardson TX 75080 Office: Telinq Systems Inc 1651 N Glenville Dr Richardson TX 75081

JONES, MARGARET BENDER, fitness salon administrator; b. Dover, Del., July 20, 1956; d. Gomer Edward and Dorothy (Pugh) J. Student, No. Va. Community Coll., 1980-83. Receptionist, sec. Am. Press Inst., Reston, Va., 1977; sec., acctg. technician Sullivan and Co., Ltd., Reston, Va., 1977-80; adminstrv. asst., sec. to treas. Evaluation Research Corp., Vienna, Va., 1980, accts. payable clk., computer operator, 1980-81, mgr. accts. payable dept., 1981-83; cost analyst, program mgmt. specialist Evaluation Research Corp., Arlington, Va., 1983; systems cost analyst The Maxima Corp., Rockville, Md., 1983-85; sr. cost analyst Exec. Resource Assocs., Inc., Arlington, Va., 1985-87; mgr. The Feminine Weigh, Deltona, Fla., 1987—. V.p., treas. Kimberly Place Condominium, Silver Spring, Md., 1984-87. Mem. Inst. Cost Analysis, Nat. Assn. Female Execs. Republican. Presbyterian. Home: 150 Balsam St Deltona FL 32725 Office: The Feminine Weigh 1200 Deltona Blvd Suite 48 Deltona FL 32725

JONES, MARGARET ELAINE, military officer; b. Little Rock, Ark., Nov. 13, 1957; d. Howard Carlton Carlson and Peggy Ruth (Shadle) Hopwood; m. Robert John Jones, Oct. 25, 1985. BA, U. Cen. Ark., 1980. Enlisted USCG, 1980, commd., 1980, advanced through grades to lt.; deck, commns. officer Cutter RUSH USCG, San Francisco, 1980-82; staff officer hdqrs. USCG, Washington, 1982-86; asst. port ops. officer marine safety office USCG, Corpus Christi, Tex., 1986—; adv. Commn. Awarenes in Emergency Response, Port Lavaca, Tex., 1986—, Victoria, Tex., 1986—; USCG coordinator Combined Fed. Campaign, Corpus Christi, 1986—. troop leader U.S. Girl Scouts, Alexandria, Va., 1983-84. Mem. Delta Zeta. Republican. Lutheran. Home: 406 Monette Corpus Christi TX 78412

JONES, MARGO ROSCH, public relations, advertising agency executive; b. Balt., Oct. 9, 1944; d. Randolph Wilson, Sr. and Margaret (Rosch) Jones; m. Jack Saul Katzman, Mar. 14, 1982; 1 child, Linda Joy. B.A. in English, Mt. St. Agnes Coll., Balt., 1966. Prodn. asst. Am. Chem. Soc., Washington, 1972-73; with FPC Advt., Rock Hill, N.Y., 1974-79, v.p., 1978-79; mktg. dir. Cablevision Industries, Liberty, N.Y., 1979-80; pub. relations, tourism dir. Sullivan County Catskills, Monticello, N.Y., 1980—; pres., owner Advt. by Margo Jones, Monticello, 1984—; pres. Catskill Assn. Tourism Services, N.Y., 1983—; dir. adv. council Sullivan County Community Coll. Radio announcer Sta. WSUL Good News show, Monticello, 1982—. Pub. relations dir., treas. Goshen Jaycees, N.Y., 1978-79; pub. relations vol. bd. Am. Heart Assn., Syracuse, N.Y., 1981-83; vol. Peace Corps, Bolu, Turkey, 1966-67. Mem. N.Y. State Travel and Vacation Assn. (2d v.p. 1984-86), Travel Industry Assn. Am., Assn. Travel Mktg. Execs., Am. Bus. Assn., Nat. Townbrokers' Assn. Democrat. Roman Catholic. Avocations: yoga, swimming. Home: PO Box 804 Monticello NY 12701 Office: Sullivan County Catskills County Govt Ctr Monticello NY 12701

JONES, MARGUERITE JACKSON, educator; b. Greenwood, Miss., Aug. 12, 1949; d. James and Mary G. (Reedy) Jackson; m. Algee Jones, Apr. 4, 1971; 1 child, Stephanie Nerissa. BS, Miss. Valley State U., 1969; MEd, Miss. State U., 1974; Specialist in Community Coll. Teaching, Ark. State U., 1983; postgrad. U. Ark. Tchr. English, Henderson High Sch., Starkville, Miss., 1969-70; tchr. creative writing Miami (Fla.) Coral Park, 1970-71; tchr. English, head dept. Marion (Ark.) Sr. High Sch., 1971-78; tchr. East Ark. Community Coll., Forrest City, 1978-79; migrant edn. supr. Marion (Ark.) Sch. Dist., 1979-83; mem. faculty Draughons Coll., Memphis, 1978-83; asst. prof. State Tech. Inst., 1984—; cons. writing projects; condr. workshops for ednl. bus., civic groups; dir. Tng. Inst., The Cathedral of Bountiful Blessings Ch. Mem. Nat. Council Tchrs. English, Ark. Assn. Profl. Educators, Assn. Supervision and Curriculum Devel. Home: 3707 Stallion St Memphis TN 38116 Office: State Tech Inst 5983 Macon Grove Memphis TN 38134

JONES, MARIE REINHART, editor; b. Phila., June 5, 1925; d. Henry Joseph and Kathryn Frances (Finn) Reinhart; m. Charles Nicholas Jones Jr., June 27, 1953; children: Charles J., Maryalice Jones May, Christopher Henry, Kathleen M. BA magna cum laude, Chestnut Hill Coll., 1947. Reporter Chestnut Hill Local newspaper, Phila., 1963-68, assoc. editor, 1968-72, co-editor, 1972-79, editor, 1979—; lectr. in field. Founding dir. Cascade Aphasia Ctr., Phila., 1976—; mem. adv. council La Salle U., Phila., 1979-81, Spring Garden Coll. Archtl. Sch.; bd. dirs. N.W. Unit Am. Cancer Soc., Phila., 1980-87; cons. Chestnut Hill Community Assn., Phila, 1987. Recipient first place feature award Keystone Press, 1982. Mem. Nat. Assn. Newspaper Editors, Pa. Newspaper Editors Assn., Pa. Newspaper Pubs. Assn., Great Books Found. (discussion leader), Sigma Delta Chi, Kappa Gamma Pi, Delta Epsilon Sigma. Office: Chestnut Hill Local 8434 Germantown Ave Philadelphia PA 19118

JONES, MARILYN DAVIS, personnel counselor; b. East Chgo., Ind., Nov. 9, 1952. BS in Mgmt., Ind. State U., 1974; MS in Mgmt. and Devel. Human Resources, Nat. Coll. Edn., Chgo., 1988. Income tax preparer Midwest Tax, East Chgo., 1975-76; substitute tchr. City of East Chgo. Pub. Schs., 1978-80; lab. technician St. Margaret Hosp., Hammond, Ind., 1975-77, unit mgr., 1977-78; info. technician Wm. Wrigley Jr. Co., Chgo., 1980-84, product transmittal coordinator, 1984-86, personnel counselor, 1986—. Chairperson gen. women's day St. Mark A.ME Zion Ch., East Chgo., 1987. Named an Outstanding Resident, U. Wis., Oshkosh, 1971. Mem. Human Resources Mgmt. Assn., Alpha Kappa Alpha (treas. 1980-84, fin. sec. 1986—). Home: 2516 140th Pl East Chicago IN 46312 Office: Wm Wrigley Jr Co 3535 S Ashland Ave Chicago IL 60609

JONES, MARJORIE GILLETTE, writer; b. Bklyn., Oct. 1, 1924; d. Frank LeRoy and Florence Marion (Vincent) Gillette; m. William Henry Jones, Nov. 27, 1947; children: Virginia Ann, Carol Marie, David Scott. RN, Auburn Meml. Hosp., 1946. Pres. Baldwin (N.Y.) Literary Services, 1979—, also bd. dirs.; tchr. creative writing Baldwin Community Coll., Nassau Community Coll., 1981-86, creative writing in continuing education, 1982-86. Author over 150 short stories, 1963-71, (book) The Lighthouse, 1986; contbr. articles to N.Y. Times, 1984—. Instr. 4-H Clubs, Mineola, Cornell, 1959-77. Mem. Internat. Women's Writing Guild (talent bank 1982—), Arista Soc. Home: 935 Hayes St Baldwin NY 11510 Office: Baldwin Literary Service 935 Hayes St Baldwin NY 11510

JONES, MARTHA ELLEN, public relations firm executive; b. Detroit, Nov. 3, 1948; d. Robert Everett and Bess Alice (Johnson) J.; m. John N. Touchstone, Jan. 24, 1987. Student, Williams Coll., 1969; BA, Vassar Coll., 1970. With radio and TV news dept. Burson Marsteller, N.Y.C., 1974; account exec. Hill & Knowlton, N.Y.C., 1975-78; dir. public relations and environ. affairs Fla. Phosphate Council, Lakeland, 1978-81; pres. Jones &

Assocs., Lakeland, 1981-87, Houston, 1987—. Apptd. commr. edn. Fla. Adv. Council on Sci. Edn., 1979, vice chmn., 1980-81, chmn., 1981-82; mem. Gov.'s Task Force on Phosphate-Related Radiation, 1979-80; trustee Learning Resource Ctr., Lakeland, 1979-82; bd. dirs. Campfire Inc., Lakeland, 1982-85; mem. Lakeland Young Life Council, 1985; del. Diocesan Conv., St. Stephen's Episcopal Ch., 1982-85, lay reader, 1983-86, mem. vestry, 1984-86; mem. adv. council Fla. Defenders of Environ., 1980, United Way, 1980, Hist. Lakeland, 1979-80, Fla. Assn. Sci. Tchrs., 1981; active Leadership Lakeland, 1985-86. Recipient nat. 1st place Addy award Am. Advt. Fedn., 1978. Mem. Pub. Relations Soc. Am., Fla. Pub. Relations Assn. (bd. dirs. Polk chpt. 1983-84, Golden Image awards 1979-80, 82, Grand All Fla. award 1982), Leadership Lakeland, Lakeland C. of C. Episcopalian. Club: Jr. League Houston. Home and Office: 2205 Fulham Ct Houston TX 77063

JONES, MARY DAILEY (MRS. HARVEY BRADLEY JONES), civic worker; b. Billings, Mont.; d. Leroy Nathaniel and Janet (Currie) Dailey; m. Harvey Bradley Jones, Nov. 15, 1952; children: Dailey, Janet Currie, Ellis Bradley. Student, Carleton Coll., 1943-44, U. Mont., 1944-46, UCLA, 1959. Owner Mary Jones Interiors. Founder, treas. Jr. Art Council, Los Angeles County Mus., 1953-55, v.p., 1955-56; mem. costume council Pasadena (Calif.) Philharm.; co-founder Art Rental Gallery, 1953, chmn. art and architecture tour, 1955; founding mem., sec. Art Alliance, Pasadena Art Mus., 1955-56; benefit chmn. Pasadena Girls Club, 1959, bd. dirs., 1958-60; chmn. Los Angeles Tennis Patron's Assn. Benefit, 1965; sustaining Jr. League Pasadena; mem. docent council Los Angeles County Mus.; mem. costume council Los Angeles County Mus. Art., program chmn. 20th Century Greatest Designers; mem. blue ribbon com. Los Angeles Music Center; benefit chmn. Venice com. Internat. Fund for Monuments, 1971; bd. dirs. Art Ctr. 100, Pasadena, 1988—; co-chmn. benefit Harvard Coll. Scholarship Fund, 1974, steering com. benefit, 1987, Otis Art Inst., 1975; mem. Harvard-Radcliffe scholarship dinner com., 1985; mem. adv. bd. Estelle Doheny Eye Found., 1976, chmn. benefit, 1980; adv. bd. Loyola U. Sch. Fine Arts, Los Angeles; patron chmn. Benefit Achievement Rewards for Coll. Scientists, 1988; chmn. com. Sch. Am. Ballet Benefit, 1988, N.Y.C.; bd. dirs. Founders Music Center, Los Angeles, 1977-81; mem. nat. adv. council Sch. Am. Ballet, N.Y.C., nat. co-chmn. gala, 1980; adv. council on fine arts Loyola-Marymount U.; mem. Los Angeles Olympic Com., 1984, The Colleagues; founding mem. Mus. Contemporary Art, 1986. Mem. Kappa Alpha Theta. Clubs: Valley Hunt (Pasadena); Calif. (Los Angeles). Home: 10375 Wilshire Blvd Apt 8B Los Angeles CA 90024

JONES, MARY DELLA, accountant; b. Clarksville, Pa., June 2, 1949; d. Will and Maggie E. (Claytor) J.; m. James David West, Dec. 31, 1981; 1 child, Eugenia Michelle (dec.). Student, Community Coll. Allegheny County, Pitts., U. Pitts., 1971—. Sales clk. Sears Roebuck and Co., Pitts., 1967; file clk. Blue Cross/Blue Shield, Pitts., 1967-68; recruiter, bookkeeper Bidwell Tng. Ctr., Pitts., 1968-69; receptionist Homewood Brushton Health Ctr., Pitts., 1969-70; exec. sec. Recreation Ctr. Bidwell Street United Presbyn. Ch., Pitts., 1970-71; cashier, sr. acctg. clk. U. Pitts., 1971-78; data analyst, acct. Volkswagen Am., New Stanton, Pa., 1978—; bookkeeper Black Medium Coffee Shop, Inc., Pitts., 1969-70; fin. chair Sch. Gen. Studies U. Pitts., 1978; chair staff adv. bd. fin. Volkswagon Am., 1985; mem. staff adv. bd. U. Pitts, 1978; mem. James Cleveland Gospel Music Workshop, Pitts. Pres., bd. trustees Mt. Ararat Bapt. Ch., Pitts., 1984—, personnel chmn., 1987. Recipent Community Service award Homewood Brushton YWCA, 1980. Mem. Nat. Assn. Female Execs., Nat. Negro Bus. and Profl. Women's Clubs, Inc. (publicity chmn. Pitts. area 1978-79, pres. 1980, Club award 1979), Phi Chi Theta (pres. U. Pitts. chpt. 1977). Democrat. Baptist. Home: 104 Old Farm Dr Pittsburgh PA 15239 Office: Volkswagen of Am Hwy 119 New Stanton PA 15672

JONES, MARY ELLEN, biochemist; b. La Grange, Ill., Dec. 25, 1922; d. Elmer E. and Laura A. (Klein) J.; B.S., U. Chgo., 1944; Ph.D., Yale U., 1951; children—Ethan Vincent Munson, Catherine Laura Munson. AEC fellow, Am. Cancer Soc. fellow, assoc. biochemist Mass. Gen. Hosp., Boston, 1951-57; asst. prof. grad. dept. biochemistry Brandeis U., Waltham, Mass., 1957-60, assoc. prof., 1960-66; assoc. prof. dept. biochemistry Sch. Medicine, U. N.C., Chapel Hill, 1966-68, prof. depts. biochemistry and zoology, 1968-71; prof. dept. biochemistry Sch. Medicine, U. So. Calif., 1971-78; prof., chmn. dept. biochemistry Sch. Medicine, U. N.C., Chapel Hill, 1978—, Kenan prof. biochemistry, 1980—; mem. study sect. Am. Cancer Soc., 1971-73, NIH, 1971-75; mem. sci. adv. bd. Nat. Heart, Lung and Blood Inst., 1980-84; mem. metabolic biology study sect. NSF, 1978-81; mem. Merit rev. bd. VA, 1975-78; mem. life sci. com. NASA, 1976-78; pres. Chairs of Assn. Med. Sch. Depts. Biochemistry, 1985. Am. Cancer Soc. scholar, 1957-62; NIH grantee, 1957—; NSF grantee, 1957—. Mem. Am. Chem. Soc. (councilor 1975-79, nominating com. 1971-72, chair 1973-74), Am. Soc. Biol. Chemists (councilor 1975-78, 81-84, pres. 1986), Nat. Acad. Scis., Inst. Medicine of Nat. Acad. Scis. (councilor 1984-87), Assn. Women in Sci., AAAS, N.Y. Acad. Sci., Sierra Club, Sigma Xi. Democrat. Unitarian. Club: Appalachian Mountain. Contbr. numerous articles on biochem. research to sci. publs.; editorial bd. Jour. Biol. Chemistry, 1975-80, 82-87, Cancer Research, 1982-86; assoc. editor Can. Jour. Biochemistry, 1969-74. Office: Univ of NC Dept Biochem & Nutrition Chapel Hill NC 27514

JONES, MARY VIRGINIA, mechanical engineer; b. Roanoke, Va., Sept. 19, 1940; d. James Bernard and Evangeline (Jamison) Jones; BS in Mech. Engring. with honors, Va. Poly. Inst. and State U., 1962; MS in Mech. Engring., George Washington U., 1972, postgrad. 1972. Design engr. Atlantic Research Corp., Alexandria, Va., 1962—, head design engring. sect., Gainesville, Va., 1981, chief mech. design group, 1982-86, mgr. design dept., 1986-88, mgr. engring., 1988—; research scholar asst. George Washington U., Washington, 1972. Mem. Va. State Bd. Architects, Land Surveyors, Profl. Engrs. and Landscape Architects, 1983—, chmn. engrs. sect., 1984, 88, pres., 1986. Mem. bd. visitors Va. Poly. Inst. and State U., 1984—, exec. com., 1988, chair acad. affairs com., 1988—; mem. Nat. Council Engring. Examiners, 1983—. Recipient Tau Beta Pi Woman's Badge, 1961; registered profl. engr., Commonwealth of Va. Mem. ASME, AIAA (tech. com.), Soc. Women Engrs. (Balt./Washington v.p. 1981, pres. 83-84), Fedn. Orgns. Profl. Women, Tau Beta Pi, Pi Tau Sigma, Phi Kappa Phi, Omicron Delta Kappa. Methodist. Home: 3137 Stratford Ct Oakton VA 22124 Office: Atlantic Research Corp 5945 Wellington Rd Gainesville VA 22065

JONES, MERRY-GORDON PANNILL, manufacturing executive; b. Columbia, S.C., July 7, 1940; d. Gordon and Ellis (Laidley) Pannill; m. Charles Darnall Jones, Apr. 9, 1960 (div. June 1973); children: Laidley Loretta, Merry Margaret Jones Coggins. Student, Randolph-Macon Woman's Coll., 1958-59, Wake Forest U., 1959-61; BA, U. Ala., Birmingham, 1982. Sec. Shoal Creek Lighting, Anniston, Ala., 1981-88, treas., 1982-88, v.p., 1985—, also bd. dirs.; v.p. Shoal Creek Mfg., Anniston, Ala., 1986—, also bd. dirs.; career planning counselor, 1986-87; bd. dirs. Badge Creations, Birmingham. Mem. Ala. Wake Forest Alumni Assn. (pres. 1984—). Republican. Episcopalian. Home: 536 Turtle Creek Dr Birmingham AL 35226 Office: Shoal Creek Lighting 1401 Commerce Blvd Anniston AL 36201

JONES, MONA P., finance company executive; b. Milan, Tenn., Oct. 2, 1955; d. Don David and Jean Y. J. BBA in Acctg., Memphis State U., 1976. CPA, Tenn. Field examiner FHLBB/FSLIC, Memphis, 1978-84; v.p. ops. Home Fed. Savs. & Loan, Memphis, 1984—. Office: Home Fed Savs & Loan Assn 4700 Poplar St Memphis TN 38117

JONES, MONIKA, data processing executive; b. Burlington, Vt., May 7, 1949; d. Paul and Frieda (Windisch) Desforges; m. Dennis E. Jones (div. 1974); children: Dennis E. Jr., Anthony B. Data processing mgr. Exchange Bank & Trust, Tampa, Fla., 1974-82; asst. v.p., v.p. data processing First Fla. Bank. N.A., Tampa, 1982—. Mem. Am. Inst. Banking (edn. adminstr. Tampa chpt. 1979-83, Banker of Yr. Tampa chpt. 1981-82), Nat. Assn. Female Execs. Home: 14538 Fall Circle Tampa FL 33613 Office: First Fla Bank NA 4109 Gandy Blvd Tampa FL 33611

JONES, NANCY L., brokerage house executive; b. Chgo., June 17, 1931; d. Carlos E. and M. Luverne (Hessler) Anderson; m. Lloyd R. Jones, Aug. 1, 1953 (dec. Apr. 1983); children: Larry, Linda, Laurie, Lee. BA, Western Mich. U., 1953. Registered securities rep., fin. prin., annuity and variable life ins. Soc. Dept. Corrections, Marquette, Mich., 1954-57, Dept. Health, Lansing, Mich., 1957-58, U. Calif., Riverside, 1958-60; sec. Dean Witter Reynolds, San Bernardino, Calif., 1975-78, mgr. office, adminstrv. asst., 1978-79; controller Gt. Am. Securities Inc., San Bernardino, 1979-81, stockbroker, 1981-84, adminstrv. v.p., 1984—; lectr. Riverside City Coll., 1984-85. Seminar leader YWCA, Riverside, 1985; sr. advisor Nat. Charity League, 1986-87; bd. dirs. Calvary Presbyn. Ch., Riverside, 1984-87. Named Outstanding Woman in Bus., San Bernardino Sun Telegram, 1984. Mem. Nat. Assn. Female Execs. (dir. network 1982-86), Nat. Assn. Investment Clubs (dir. club 1982-87), Riverside C. of C., San Bernardino C. of C. (cert. of achievement 1986), Sigma Kappa (advisor to treas. 1986-87). Republican. Clubs: Nat. Panhellenic (Riverside) (pres. 1963), Plus, Para Ninos Aux. to Children's Home Soc. Office: Gt Am Securities Inc 334 W 3d St Suite 201 San Bernardino CA 92401

JONES, NORMA LOUISE, educator; b. Poplar, Wis.; d. George Elmer and Hilma June (Wiberg) J. BE, U. Wis.; MA, U. Minn., 1952; postgrad, U. Ill., 1957; PhD, U. Mich., 1965; postgrad., NARS, 1978, 79, 80; postgrad. info. sci., Nova U., 1983—. Librarian Grand Rapids (Mich.) Public Schs., 1947-62; with Grand Rapids Public Library, 1948-49; instr. Central Mich. U., Mt. Pleasant, 1954, 55; librarian Benton Harbor (Mich.) Public Schs., 1962-63; asst. prof. library sci. U. Wis., Oshkosh, 1968-70; assoc. prof. U. Wis., 1970-75, prof., 1975—, chmn. dept. library sci., 1980-84, exec. dir. libraries and learning resources, 1987—; lectr. U. Mich., Ann Arbor, 1954, 55, 61, 63-65, asst. prof., 1966-68. Recipient Disting. Teaching award U. Wis.-Oshkosh, 1977. Mem. ALA (chmn. reference conf. 1975—), Assn. Library and Info. Sci. Educators, Spl. Library Assn., Soc. Am. Archivists, Phi Beta Kappa, Phi Kappa Phi, Pi Lambda Theta, Beta Phi Mu, Sigma Pi Epsilon. Home: 1220 Maricopa Dr Oshkosh WI 54901

JONES, PAMELA ANN MCALPIN, banker; b. Clarksdale, Miss., May 7, 1958; d. Erskine Carroll and Mildred Catherine (Jackson) McAlpin; m. Jerry Keith Jones, Aug. 9, 1980; 1 child, Danielle Marie. B of Range Sci., Tex. A & M U., 1980, M of Agri., 1981. Grad. asst. to dean Tex. A & M U., College Station, 1981; with computer ops. dept. Altamesa Ch. of Christ, Ft. Worth, 1982-84; mgr. sales office Profl. Mgmt. Assn., Ft. Worth, 1984; mgr. Dillards, Inc., Ft. Worth, 1984-85; asst. bond adminstr. InterFirst Bank Ft. Worth, N.A., 1985—. Republican. Mem. Ch. of Christ. Office: First Republic Bank Fort Worth NA 801 Cherry St 18th Fl Fort Worth TX 76102

JONES, PATRICIA MURPHY, nurse, realtor; b. Cambridge, Md., Oct. 6, 1941; d. Bernard Patrick and Madeline (Hurley) Murphy; m. Robert Bryan Jones, Feb. 13, 1965. Diploma in Nursing, Sinai Hosp., Balt., 1962; BS in Nursing, Washington Coll., 1983. RN, Md. Nurse coordinator Eastern Shore Hosp. Ctr., Cambridge, Md., 1962-78, nursing supr., 1978-87; chief nursing div. Eastern Shore Hosp. Ctr., Cambridge, 1987; realtor Cambridge, 1988—. Recipient Gold award State of Md., 1974, Rosalie S. Abrams Legis. award State of Md., 1987. Mem. Am. Nurses Assn., Assn. Practitioners in Infection Control, Sinai Hosp. Alumnae Assn., LWV (sec. Cambridge chpt. 1981-86), Md. Nurses Assn. (congl. dist. coordinator 1986, legis. chair, mem. state legis. com. 1984—, Nurse of Yr. 1986). Republican. Methodist. Club: Yacht (Cambridge). Lodge: Elks. Home: Box 77 White Hall Rd Cambridge MD 21613 Office: 208 Cedar St Cambridge MD 21613

JONES, PHYLLIS GENE, judge; b. Fargo, N.D., May 29, 1923; d. Joseph C. and Rosina Belle (Pinkham) Bambusch; m. Dwight Bangs Jones, May 29, 1945 (dec.); children—Stephanie, Jacqueline, Kent Carroll; m. David D. Norman, Oct. 9, 1970 (dec.). B.A., Macalester Coll., 1944; J.D., William Mitchell Coll. Law, 1960. Bar: Minn. 60. Wirephoto operator AP, St. Paul, 1943-45; reporter St. Paul Pioneer Press, 1945-46; asst. county atty. Ramsey County (Minn.), St. Paul, 1960-71; gen. counsel Minn. Urban County Attys. Bd.-Minn. County Attys. Council, St. Paul, 1971-75; pvt. practice, St. Paul and Cottage Grove, Minn., 1975-84; judge Minn. Dist. Ct. 10th Jud. Dist., Anoka, 1984—; mem. Minn. Adv. Council to State Investment Bd., 1983-84; mem. Washington County Personnel Com., Stillwater, Minn., 1982—. Supr., Grey Cloud Town Bd. (Minn.), 1971-75. Mem. ABA, Minn. Bar Assn., State Bar Minn. (chmn. victimless crimes com. 1974-75), Ramsey County Bar Assn. (exec. com. 1982-83). Office: 10th Jud Dist 325 E Main St Anoka MN 55303

JONES, RACHEL M., educator; b. Ahoskie, N.C., July 1, 1929; d. George Washington and Lollie Eldo (Gatling) Manly; m. Edward Thomas Jones, Aug. 22, 1970; children: Antonio, Julie, Mark, Kimberely. BS, A & T Coll., 1953; MA, Bklyn. Coll., 1976, MA in Adminstrn. and Supervision, 1980. Tchr. home econs. Jr. High Sch. 265, Bklyn., 1962-64; dean girls med. program Jr. High Sch. 117, Bklyn., 1968-79, tchr. reading, sci., 1980-81, acct. asst. prin., 1985—; realtor Bklyn., 1987—; owner variety store, 1985-87. Pres. East 56th St Block Assn., 1975—. Recipient Cert. Community Planning Bd., 1985. Mem. Bklyn. Coll. Alumni, Am. HEC, Bklyn. Assn. Supervision and Curriculum Devel., N.Y. Nat. Assn. Black Educators. Lodge: Order Eastern Star. Home: 47 E 56th St Brooklyn NY 11203

JONES, REGINA NICKERSON, public relations executive; b. Los Angeles, Sept. 23, 1942; d. Leslie Augustus and Luedelia (Triggs) Nickerson; children: Kenneth Leon, Kevin Christopher, Keith Fitzgerald, Kory Reginald, Karen Regina. Bookkeeper, sec. Carson Realty, Los Angeles, 1958; radio telephone operator Los Angeles Police Dept., 1962-66; owner, publisher Soul Publs., Los Angeles, 1966-83; v.p. pub. relations Solar Records-Dick Griffey Prodns., Los Angeles, 1983-86; pres., owner Regina Jones & Assocs, Los Angeles, 1985—. Mem. Nat. Assn. Media Women, Black Music Assn. (exec. council), NAACP, Urban League.

JONES, RENAE SPENCER, marketing professional; b. Dickson, Tenn., Dec. 15, 1960; d. William Roger and Genny L. Spencer. BA, David Lipscomb Coll., 1983. Mgr. Gen. Distbg. Co., Burns, Tenn., 1975-83; bill clk. Tenn. Ho. of Reps., Nashville, 1982; mktg. coordinator Universal Plastics, Inc., Cookeville, Tenn., 1983—. Mem. exec. bd., water safety chmn. Putnam County Red Cross, Cookeville, 1986—; bd. dirs. Putnam County United Way, 1988; prizes and donations chair Putnam County Cystic Fibrosis Bike-a-Thon; active Upper Cumberland Alliance Against Domestic Violence, Cookeville-Putnam County Clean Commn., Tenn. Council for Future of Women in the Workplace. Mem. Nat. Assn. Profl. Saleswomen, Cookeville Bus. and Profl. Women (1st v.p. 1987-88, pres. 1988—), AAUW (bd. dirs. 1987-88). Club: Toastmasters (Cookeville) (pres. 1988). Home: 191 E 15th Apt 4 Cookeville TN 38501

JONES, RENEE KAUERAUF, healthcare administrator; b. Duncan, Okla., Nov. 3, 1949; d. Delbert Owen and Betty Jean (Marsh) Kauerauf; m. Dan Elkins Jones, Aug. 3, 1972. BS, Okla. State U., 1972, MS, 1975; postgrad., Okla. U. Health Sci. Ctr., 1988—. Statis. analyst Okla. State Dept. Mental Health, Okla. City, 1978-80, divisional chief, 1980-83, adminstr., 1983-84; assoc. dir. HCA Presbyn. Hosp., Okla. City, 1984—; adj. instr. Okla. U. Health Sci. Ctr., 1979—; assoc. staff scientist Okla. Ctr. for Alcohol and Drug-Related Studies, Okla. City, 1979—; cons. in field. Assoc. editor Alcohol Tech. Reports jour., 1979-84; contbr. articles to profl. jours. Mem. Am. Pub. Health Assn., Assn. Health Services Research, Alcohol and Drug Problems Assn. N.Am., N.Y. Acad. Scis., So. Sleep Soc. Democrat. Methodist. Home: 215 NW 20th Oklahoma City OK 73103 Office: HCA Presbyn Hosp NE 13th at Lincoln Blvd Oklahoma City OK 73104

JONES, ROSA LEE WRIGHT, school guidance counselor; b. Waynesboro, Ga., Sept. 16, 1938; d. George and Edith Arilee (Williams) Wright; m. Samuel Wyatt Jones III, Mar. 26, 1963; children: Alan Lenell, Arnold Myles. Student, Bank St. Coll. Edn., N.Y.C., 1961-62; BS, N.C. Agrl. and Tech. State U., 1960, MS, 1972; postgrad., U. N.C., 1969-70, 1987—, The Atlanta U. Tchr. Atlanta City Schs., 1964-65, 67-68, N.Y. div. Day Care, Bklyn., 1961-65, Greensboro Headstart Program, 1968-70; ednl. dir. Greensboro City Schs., 1970-72, guidance counselor, 1973—; parent adv., trainer Advocacy Ctr. for Children's Edn. and Parent Tng., Piedmont Area, 1981—; guest presenter Bklyn. Coll. Guidance and Counseling Assn., 1985. Co-organizer McIver Serteen Club for Exceptional Students, 1978; co-developer Hayes-Taylor-McIver PEP Club, 1978; chmn. SE area Cancer Assn. drive, Greensboro, 1978; mem. Friends of Theatre, Kernersville, N.C., 1984; donation collector Easter Seals Assn., Cystic Fibrosis Assn., Greensboro; mem. Guilford County Humane Soc., 1987. Recipient Lady of Yr. award Hayes-Taylor YMCA, Greensboro, 1977, Outstanding Cultural Arts Program award PTA Council N.C., 1977, Terry Sanford Creative Tchr. of Yr. award McIver Sch., Greensboro, 1975, award for membership recruitment Greensboro Assn. Retarded Citizens, 1979, Ben L. Smith Outstanding Educator of Yr. award Jonesboro Sch., Greensboro, 1981, citation Vol. for State Spl. Olympics, 1978, CUNY-Bklyn. Coll. Guidance and Counseling Dept., 1985, others; Greensboro Woman's Club scholar, 1972; Greensboro Jr. League grantee, 1983. Mem. Am. Assn. for Counseling and Devel. (citation for outstanding work with exceptional children 1984), Nat. Assn. for Counseling and Devel., Am. Black Counselors (steering com.), N.C. Sch. Counseling Assn., Nat. Assn. for Children and Adults with Learning Disabilities, Jack and Jill Am. (membership com.), Phi Delta Kappa, Delta Sigma Theta. Democrat. Episcopalian. Avocations: bowling, golf, gardening, reading, crafts. Home: 1173 Pine Knolls Rd Kernersville NC 27284

JONES, ROXANNE HARPER, state legislator; b. N.C., May 3, 1928; d. Gilford and Mary (Bruton) Harper; m. James H. Jones, 1957 (dec.); children—Patricia Hill, Wanda Crews. Student pub. schs. Bd. mem. Pa. State Transp. Adv. Com., Pa. Legis. Black Caucus, 1985—; minority chmn. urban affairs and housing com., mem. pub. health and welfare com., community and econ. devel. com., Democratic policy coms. Pa. State Senate, 1985—. Recipient Nat. Welfare Rights Orgn. Leadership award Nat. Welfare Rights Orgn., 1972, Woman of Yr. award Zeta Phi Beta, 1985, Achievement cert. Nat. Council Negro Women, 1985. Bd. dirs. Ams. for Democratic Action; co-chmn. Coalition Concerned Citizens; exec. dir. Phila. Citizens in Action; trustee Lincoln U., 1985—; mem. adv. council African-Am. studies Temple U. Mem. Apolstolic Ch. Office: Pa State Capitol Bldg Harrisburg PA 17120 Address: 3133 N Broad St Philadelphia PA 19132

JONES, SALLY DAVIESS PICKRELL, author; b. St. Louis, June 4, 1923; d. Claude Dildine and Marie Daviess (Pittman) Pickrell; student Mills Coll., Oakland, Calif., 1941-43, U. Calif.-Berkeley, 1944, Columbia, 1955-58; m. Charles William Jones, Sept. 2, 1943; 1 son, Matthew Charles. Author: (novel) The Lights Burn Blue, 1947. Mem. UN Women's Guild, Fgn. Policy Assn., Nat. Council Women, Asia Soc., English-Speaking Union, Met. Mus. Art, Internat. Platform Assn. Episcopalian. Address: 311 E 58th St New York NY 10022

JONES, SALLY SUE, educator; b. Advance, Mo., July 4, 1931; d. Benjamin Harrison and Clara Gertrude (Davault) Sample; m. Wilbur R. Jones, Aug. 22, 1953 (div. Aug. 1981); children: Susan Kaye Jones Cartwright, Denise Rae Jones Curry. BS in Edn., No. Ill. U., 1967; MS in Edn., Sam Houston U., 1981. Tchr. Seneca (Ill.) Twp. High Sch., 1967-80, Conroe (Tex.) Ind. Sch. Dist., 1980-85, Klein Ind. Sch. Dist., Spring, Tex., 1985—. Rep. Mental Health Bd., LaSalle County, Ill., 1978-80. Mem. NEA, Nat. Council Tchrs. of Social Studies, Klein Ind. Sch. Dist. Edn. Assn., Tex. Sch. Tchrs. Assn., Seneca Twp. Edn. Assn. (pres. 1970-72, faculty rep. 1972-75), Conroe Ind. Sch. Dist. Edn. Assn. (faculty rep. 1983-85). Republican. Methodist.

JONES, SANDRA MARIE, editor, marketing director; b. Madison, Wis., Aug. 14, 1956; d. Robert Fredrick and May Marie (Guse) J. BA, U. Wis., 1978. Editor, advt. mgr. Wis. Motor Carriers Assn., Madison, 1978-79; advt. dir. Credit Union Execs. Soc., Madison, 1979-83; account specialist CUNA Mut. Ins. Group, Madison, 1983-84; pub. relations dir. Computer Land of Madison, 1984-85; video tng. specialist Wis. Found. Vocat. Tech. and Adult Edn., Inc., Middleton, 1985-86; editor, mktg. dir. Magna Publs., Inc., Madison, 1987—; ind. contractor Directions Mag., Edgerton, 1985. Editor: Patient Referral Ideas for Doctors, 1987. Chmn. pub. relations com. Dane County chpt. ARC, Madison, 1979-84, disaster services, 1980—. Mem. Madison Advt. Fedn. Lutheran. Office: Magna Publs Inc 2718 Dryden Dr Madison WI 53704

JONES, SHALLEY ANN MATTHEWS, savings and loan association executive; b. Moorehead, Miss., Sept. 17, 1954; d. Robert Lee and Rosie Lee (Taylor) Matthews; m. Ernest Jones; children: Shantea K., Ernest J. BA, U. Miami, 1975; MS in Mgmt., Fla. Internat. U., 1983. Lic. mortgage broker, Fla. Asst. v.p., mgr. loan processing Flagler Fed. Savs. and Loan Assn., Miami, Fla., 1976-84; asst. v.p., regional mgr. 1st Union Nat. Bank, Pompano Beach, Fla., 1984-85; v.p. loan adminstrn. Chase Fed. Bank, Miami, 1985—; instr. Inst. Fin. Edn., Miami, 1983—, Miami-Dade Community Coll., 1987—; mortgage counselor Neighborhood Housing Services, Inc., Miami, 1984—; mem. loan com. Miami Capital Devel., Inc., 1984—. Instr. Presdl. Classroom/Young Ams., Washington, 1983—; mem. vol. recognition program com. Dade County (Fla.) United Way, 1988; mem. Planned Process to Stimulate Black Econ. Devel. in Dade County, 1988—; pres. BYW Glendale Bapt. Ch., Miami, 1980-84. Mem. Miami-Dade Urban Bankers Assn. (nat. rep. 1983-87, pres. 1987-88, Banker of Yr. 1986), Inst. Fin. Edn. (bd. dirs. 1988—), Alpha Kappa Alpha. Democrat. Home: 11255 SW 127th St Miami FL 33176

JONES, SHARON LESTER, psychotherapist; b. Stuart, Fla., Mar. 26, 1944; d. Andrew Morrison and Dorothy Virginia (Atkinson) Lester; b. James Baker Jones, June 12, 1965; children—James Timothy, Jennifer Lynn. A.B. cum laude, U. Miami, 1966, M.A., U. Tulsa, 1980; postgrad. in family therapy, Houston Family Inst., 1980-82. Psychotherapist Interface Counseling Ctr., Houston, 1980—; Mem. Am. Assn. Marriage and Family Therapists, Houston Marriage and Family Therapist Assn. (bd. dirs. 1983—, pres.), Nat. Council Family Relations, Am. Assn. Profl. Hypnotherapists, Assn. Neuro Linguistic Programming (master programmer 1983-85), Pi Beta Phi (bd. dirs. Houston 1988—). Republican. Methodist. Avocations: jogging; raquetball; reading; camping. Office: Interface Counseling Ctr 5015 Westheimer Suite 3260 Houston TX 77056

JONES, SONIA JOSEPHINE, advertising agency executive; b. Belize, Brit. Honduras, Nov. 9, 1945; came to U.S., 1962, naturalized, 1986; d. Frederick Francis and Elsie Adelia (Gomez) Alcoser; m. John Marvin Jones, Mar. 21, 1970; children—Christopher William Edward, Joshua Joseph Paul. Student Lamar U., 1964-66. With Foley's Federated Dept. Store, Houston, 1965-67; media buyer Vance Advt., Houston, 1967-68; media buyer, planner O'Neill & Assocs., Houston, 1968-75; media supr. Ketchum Houston, 1975-76; v.p., media dir. Rives Smith Bladwin Carlberg/Y & R, Houston, 1976-86; sr. v.p. media dir. Black Gillock & Langberg, Houston, 1986—; lectr. U. Houston, 1983—, mem. journalism adv. bd., 1983—. Vol., Women in Yellow, Houston, 1966; mem. sch. bd. St. Cecilia Cath. Sch.. Mem. Houston Advt. Fedn., Houston Area Media Council. Republican. Office: Black Gillock & Langberg 5851 San Felipe Suite 100 Houston TX 77057

JONES, SUSAN DORFMAN, writer; b. N.Y.C., Oct. 4, 1939; d. Joseph and Sarah (Sorrin) Dorfman; m. William Harry Jones, Sept. 18, 1960; children: Jeffrey Scott, Eric David, Timothy Mark. BA, Syracuse U., 1961. Pres., owner Antiques Corp. Am., 1972-77; communications officer Riggs Bank, Washington, 1978-81; mgr. publs. Potomac Electric Power Co., Washington, 1981-82; sr. mgr. corp. communications MCI Corp., Washington, 1982-83, dir. corp. communications Sears World Trade, Washington, 1983-85; dir. corp. communications and govt. relations Oxford Devel. Corp., Bethesda, Md., 1985-87; free-lance writer, cons., Washington, 1975—; radio personality Sta. 4KQ, Brisbane, Australia, 1962; adj. prof. communications Am. U., Washington, 1978-82. Author, editor, project mgr. corp. ann. reports; writer sch. bd. candidates and home rule campaign speeches, Washington, 1970-76. Treas. playground D.C. Recreation Dept., 1973-79; bd. dirs. March Elem. Sch., Washington, 1969. Recipient 1st place award for columns N.Y. Press Assn., 1961, Gold Quill award Internat. Assn. Bus. Communicators, 1980. Mem. Internat. Assn. Bus. Communicators (treas. 1981), Nat. Assn. Bank Women, Women in Telecommunications, Nat. Press Club, Pub. Relations Soc. Am. Democrat. Jewish. Home and Office: 7300 Burdette Ct Bethesda MD 20817

JONES, SUSAN SUTTON, educational administrator; b. Nanticoke, Md.; d. Douglas Judson and Emma Jerona (Evans) Sutton; B.S., Fisk U., 1946; M.Edn., Johns Hopkins U., 1965; Ed.D., Temple U., 1983; m. Clifton Ralph Jones, Apr. 2, 1978; 1 son, George Henry Miles, Jr. Caseworker Dept. Pub. Assistance, Phila., 1946-49; tchr. Balt. City Pub. Schs., 1949-63, counselor, 1963-67, adminstr., 1967-84; prin. Edmondson Sr. High Sch., Balt., 1975-84; lectr. Morgan State U., 1986-87. NSF grantee, 1967-68. Mem. NAACP, Nat. Assn. Secondary Sch. Prins., Pub. Sch. Adminstrs. and Suprs. Assn. Balt., Continental Soc. Disadvantaged Youth, Delta Sigma Theta Pub. Service

Sorority (pub. service award 1987, bd. dirs. found.). Democrat. Episcopalian. Home: 1190 W Northern Pkwy Apt 524 Baltimore MD 21210

JONES, THELMA, physician; b. N.Y.C., Nov. 8, 1937; d. Jack and Etta Jones; m. Josua Sack, Nov 19, 1967; children—Amy, Michelle. B.A. cum laude, Barnard Coll., 1959; M.D. cum laude, SUNY-Downstate Med. Ctr., 1963. Intern, Jewish Hosp., Bklyn., 1963-64; resident in internal medicine, hematology Montefiore Med. Ctr., Bronx, N.Y., 1964-67; chief sect. hematology White Plains (N.Y.) Hosp., 1982—, attending physician medicine and hematology; assoc. attending physician Montefiore Hosp., N.Y.C.; asst. attending internal medicine St. Agnes Hosp., White Plains, N.Y.; pres. Central Westchester div. Am. Cancer Soc., 1981-83. Fellow ACP; mem. AMA, Am. Med. Women's Assn., Am. Soc. Internal Medicine, N.Y. State Soc. Internal Medicine, N.Y. State Med. Soc., N.Y. Acad. Medicine, Westchester County Med. Soc. Office: 105 Garth Rd Scarsdale NY 10583

JONES, VALERIE KAYE, insurance company executive; b. Cleve., Oct. 26, 1956; d. Daniel Edward and Katherine (Donaldson) J. BS with high honors, Ohio U., 1978; postgrad., Cleve. State U. Lic. ins. agt. Asst. personnel dir. The Higbee Co., Cleve., 1977-78; tchr. learning disabilities and behavior disorders Cleve. Heights-Univ. Heights (Ohio) Sch., 1978-83; mem. ins. specialist CUNA Mut. Ins. Group, Madison, Wis., 1983-84, rep. group coverages, 1984-87, field communications adminstr. cen. dist., 1987-88, sr. field communications adminstr., 1988—; bd. sec. Liberty Hill Credit Union, Cleve., 1978-83. Asst. to dir. directory project Cuyahoga Spl. Edn. Service Ctr., 1974; mem. 21st Dist. Congl. Caucus, Cleve., 1984. Mem. Nat. Assn. Female Execs., Delta Sigma Theta. Democrat. Home: 37456 Spring Ln Farmington Hills MI 48018 Office: CUNA Mut Ins Group 15600 Providence Dr Southfield MI 48075

JONES, VIRGINIA A., information management consulting company executive; b. Trumbull, Conn., Jan. 3, 1947; d. Raymond C. and Mary (Walters) J.; student Marywood Coll., 1977—. With Sikorsky Aircraft, Stratford, Conn., 1966-70; with Micro-Tech, Inc., New Orleans, 1970-71, Dikewood Corp., Albuquerque, 1971-76; micrographic specialist State Records Center, Santa Fe, 1976-80, chief records mgmt. div., 1980-81, chief micrographics services div., 1981-83; pres. info. mgmt. cons. co., 1983—. Author: Handbook of Microfilm Technology and Procedures. Mem. Nat. Assn., Assn. Record Mgrs. and Adminstrs., Internat. Micrographics Congress, Assn. for Info. and Image Mgmt. Democrat. Episcopalian. Home: 707 Agua Fria Santa Fe NM 87501 Office: 707 Agua Fria Santa Fe NM 87501

JONES, WINONA NIGELS, library media specialist; b. St. Petersburg, Fla., Feb. 24, 1928; d. Eugene Arthur and Bertha Lillian (Dixon) Nigels; m. Charles Albert Jones, Nov. 26, 1944; children—Charles Eugene, Sharon Ann Jones Allworth, Caroline Winona Jones Pandorf. AA, St. Petersburg Jr. Coll., 1965; BS, U. South Fla., 1967, MS, 1968; Advanced MS, Fla. State U., 1980. Library media specialist Dunedin (Fla.) Comprehensive High Sch., 1967-76; library media specialist, chmn. dept. Fitzgerald Middle Sch., Largo, Fla., 1976-87; dir. Media Services East Lake High Sch., 1987—. Active Palm Harbor and Pinellas County Hist. Soc. Named Educator of Year, Pinellas County Sch. Bd. and Suncoast C. of C., 1983. Mem. ALA, NEA, AAUW, Fla. Assn. Media in Edn. (pres.), U. So. Fla. Alumni Assn., Assn. Ednl. Communication and Tech. (div. sch. media specialist, coms.), Am. Assn. Sch. Libraries (com.), Southeastern Library Assn., Fla. Library Assn., Assn. Supervision and Curriculum Devel., Fla. State Library Sci. Alumni, U. South Fla. Library Sci. Alumni Assn. (dir.), Phi Theta Kappa, Phi Rho Pi, Beta Phi Mu, Kappa Delta Pi, Delta Kappa Gamma. Democrat. Club: Inner Wheel (Palm Harbor, Fla.) Pilot (Palm Harbor), Civic (Palm Harbor). Lodge: Order of Eastern Star (Palm Harbor) (past worthy matron). Home: 911 Manning Rd Palm Harbor FL 33563 Office: 1300 Silver Eagle Dr Tarpon Springs FL 34689

JONES-LUKÁCS, ELIZABETH LUCILLE, physician, air force officer; b. Norfolk, Va.; d. Oliver C. and Gertrude (Layden) Jones; B.S., Oglethorpe U., 1955; m. Michel J. Lukacs (dec.); children—Amanda, Laurel, Angelique, Klara. Intern Beth Israel Hosp., N.Y.C., 1964-65; family practice medicine, Goshen, N.Y., 1965-73, Buckingham, Va., 1973-78; commd. maj. U.S. Air Force, 1978; flight surgeon, Andrews AFB, Md., 1978-85; unit charge physician Student Health Ctr., U. Md., College Park, 1985—. Col. USAFR, commd. 459th USAF Clinic. Diplomate, fellow Am. Bd. Family Practice. Mem. Am. Med. Womens Assn. (pres. Br. I), Assn. Aerospace Physicians, Aerospace Med. Assn., Md. Thoroughbred Breeders. Episcopalian. Author: The Curies Radium & Radioactivity, 1962; The Golden Stamp Book of Flying Animals, 1963. Home: Star Route Box 56 Rattle N Snap Farm Buckingham VA 23921 Office: U Md Student Health Office College Park MD 20742

JONES-WILSON, FAUSTINE CLARISSE, education educator; b. Little Rock, Ark., Dec. 3, 1927; d. James Edward and Perrine Marie (Childress) Thomas; m. James T. Jones, June 20, 1948 (div. 1977); children: Yvonne Dianne, Brian Vincent; m. Edwin L. Wilson, July 10, 1981. A.B., Ark. A.M.&N. Coll., 1948; A.M., U. Ill., 1951, Ed.D., 1967. Tchr., sch. librarian Gary pub. schs. (Ind.), 1955-62, 1964-67; asst. prof. Coll. Edn., U. Ill., Chgo., 1967-69; assoc. prof. adult edn. Fed. City Coll., Washington, 1970-71; prof. edn., grad. prof. Howard U., Washington, 1969-70, 71—. Editor: Jour. Negro Edn., 1978—; author: The Changing Mood in America; Eroding Commitment, 1977, A Traditional Model of Educational Excellence: Dunbar High School of Little Rock, Arkansas, 1981. Recipient Frederick Douglass award Nat. Assn. Black Journalists, 1979, Disting. Scholar-Tchr. award Howard U., 1985. Mem. Am. Ednl. Studies Assn. (pres. 1984-85), John Dewey Soc., Soc. Profs. of Edn., Phi Delta Kappa (pres. Howard U. chpt. 1986-87). Democrat. Methodist. Home: 908 Dryden Ct Silver Spring MD 20901 Office: Howard U Sch Edn 2400 6th St NW Washington DC 20059

JONG, ERICA MANN, author, poet; b. N.Y.C., Mar. 26, 1942; d. Seymour and Eda (Mirsky) Mann; m. Allan Jong (div. Sept. 1975); m. Jonathan Fast, Dec. 1977 (div. Jan. 1983); 1 dau., Molly. B.A., Barnard Coll., 1963; M.A., Columbia U., 1965. Faculty, English dept. CUNY, 1964-65, 69-70, overseas div. U. Md., 1967-69; mem. lit. panel N.Y. State Council on Arts, 1972-74. Author: poems Fruits & Vegetables, 1971, (poems) Half Lives, 1973; (novel) Fear of Flying, 1973, (poems) Loveroot, 1975, (novel) How to Save Your Own Life, 1977; (poems) At the Edge of the Body, 1979; (novel) Fanny, 1980, (novel) Parachutes & Kisses, 1984; (poetry and non-fiction) Witches, 1981; (poems) Ordinary Miracles, 1983; (juvenile) Megan's Book of Divorce, 1984; (novel) Serenissima, 1987. Recipient Bess Hokin prize Poetry mag., 1971, Alice Faye di Castagnola award Poetry Soc. Am., 1972; Nat. Endowment Arts grantee, 1973. Mem. Authors Guild (dir. 1975), Poets and Writers Bd., Writers Guild Am.-West, P.E.N., Phi Beta Kappa. Office: care Morton L Janklow Assocs 598 Madison Ave New York NY 10022

JONSSON, ELLEN FLORENCE, cultural organization administrator; b. Bridgeport, Conn., Dec. 1, 1941; d. Gustav Harold and Lela Mildred (Wheaton) Johnson; m. Donald James Binkley, Feb. 2, 1963 (div. Nov. 1981); children: David James, Andrew Evan. BFA, R.I. Sch. of Design, 1963; MBA, U. Okla., 1986. Dir. Norman (Okla.) Arts Council, 1978-81; asst. dir. Assembly of Community Arts Councils, Oklahoma City, 1981-84, State Arts Council, Oklahoma City, 1984—; chmn. Norman Arts Council, 1977-78. Dir. Norman Choral Soc., 1978-80, Sooner Theatre, Norman, 1976-78, Individual Artists of Okla., Oklahoma City, 1977-79; mem. Norman Civic Improvement Council, 1978. Mem. Am. Council on the Arts. Republican. Home: 1632 Franklin Dr Norman OK 73072

JONTZ, DEBORAH LEE, college administrator; b. Newton, Iowa, Sept. 14, 1952; d. Jack Duane and Ruby Lee (Shrum) Jontz. BS, Western Ill. U., 1974; MS in Edn., No. Ill. U., 1978. Tchr. Polo (Ill.) Community Sch. Dist., 19074-78; substitute tchr. Woodstock (Ill.) Community Sch. Dist., 1978-79; coordinator student activities McHenry County Coll., Crystal Lake, Ill., 1979-83, dir. student activities, 1981-83, divisional chairperson, 1983-85, assoc. dean of instrn., 1985—; cons. drug curriculum McHenry County Supt. Schs., Woodstock, 1983-84. Active McHenry County Drug and Alcohol Com., Woodstock, 1981-83; referendum chairperson Friends of McHenry County Coll., Crystal Lake, 1986—. Mem. AAUW, Am. Vocation Assn., Ill. Vocat. Assn., Ill. Council Local Adminstrs. (bd. dirs. 1988-91), Ill. Council Community Coll. Adminstrs., Career Deans Council, Chgo. Area Transfer Adminstrs. (sec. 1988-89), Sigma Sigma Sigma, Beta Sigma Phi. Club: Woodstock Backers. Home: 890 West Ave Woodstock IL 60098 Office: McHenry County Coll Rt 14 and Lucas Rd Crystal Lake IL 60012

JORAM, JOAN MARIE, human resources representative; b. Washington, July 19, 1960; d. Phillip Robert and Helen (Philips) J. BA in Human Services, Elon Coll., 1982. From personnel recruiter to employment mgr. Washington Fed., 1982-84; employment rep., sr. human resources rep. Unisys Corp., McLean, Va., 1984—. Mem. Nat. Assn. Female Execs., Washington Tech. Personnel Forum, Washington personnel Assn. Home: 1954 Kennedy Dr #101 McLean VA 22102 Office: Unisys Corp 8008 Westpark Dr McLean VA 22102

JORDAN, ALICE MACDONALD, lawyer, educator; b. N.Y.C., Oct. 17, 1943; d. Martin E. and Ruth (Rhoads) Macdonald; m. Carl Richard Jordan, Aug. 3, 1962; children: Richard Kent, Jason Kyle. B.S., Murray State U., 1964; student U. Mo.-St. Louis, 1966; J.D., So. Ill. U., 1980. Bar: Ill. 1980. Tchr., St. Louis City Schs., 1964-65, Ritenour Sch. System, St. Louis County, Mo., 1965-67, Harrisburg Schs. (Ill.), 1967-68, Eldorado Schs. (Ill.), 1968-69; mgr., purchasing agt. Jordan Pharm., Eldorado, Ill., 1969-77; law clk. Robert Wilson Law Office, Harrisburg, 1978-80; ptnr. Cochran & Jordan, Fairfield, Ill., 1980—; bus. law instr. Frontier Community Coll., Fairfield, Ill. Bd. dirs. Central Bapt. Family Services, Olney, Ill., 1983-84, Wayne County Vols. for Youth, 1984—, Career Devel. Ctr.; pres., organizer Fairfield Soccer Assn. Mem. ABA, Ill. Bar Assn., Am. Trial Lawyers Assn., Ill. Trial Lawyers Assn., Fairfield C. of C., Phi Alpha Delta, Kappa Delta Phi. Clubs: Fairfield Woman's, Bus. and Profl. Women's Assn. Home: 301 W Center St Fairfield IL 62837 Office: 302 E Main St Fairfield IL 62837

JORDAN, BARBARA C., lawyer, educator, former congresswoman; b. Houston, Feb. 21, 1936; d. and Arlyne J. B.A. in Polit. Sci. and History magna cum laude, Tex. So. U.; J.D., Boston U., 1959. Bar: Mass. 1959, Tex. 1959. Adminstrv. asst. to county judge Harris County, Tex.; mem. Tex. Senate, 1966-72; pres. pro tem, chmn. Labor and Mgmt. Relations Com. and Urban Affairs Study Com.; mem. 93d-95th congresses from 18th Dist. Tex.; mem. com. judiciary, com. govt. ops.; mem. spl. task force 94th Congress; mem. steering and policy com. House Democratic Caucus; Lyndon B. Johnson public service prof. U. Tex., Austin, 1979—; mem. UN panel on multinat. corps. in South Africa and Namibia; dir. numerous cos. Author: Barbara Jordan—Self Portrait, 1979. Named One of 10 Most Influential Women in Tex., One of 100 Women in Touch With Our Time, Harpers Bazaar mag.; Dem. Woman of Year Women's Nat. Dem. Club; Woman of Year in Politics, Ladies Home Jour.; recipient Eleanor Roosevelt humanities award, 1984, Charles Evans Hughes Gold medal Nat. Conf. Christians and Jews; Barbara Jordan Fund established in her honor Lyndon B. Johnson Sch. Pub. Affairs. Mem. ABA, Tex. Bar Assn., Mass. Bar Assn., Houston Bar Assn., NAACP, Delta Sigma Theta. Baptist. Office: U Tex Lyndon B Johnson Sch Public Affairs Austin TX 78712 *

JORDAN, BARBARA MOORE, psychiatrist; b. Petersburg, Va., June 5, 1928; d. Carlisle Seward and Bertha Edna (Beasley) Moore; m. Harmon Geiger Jordan, Oct. 28, 1960; children: Jon David, Lisa Anne, Monica Leigh, Robert Bruce. AB, U. N.C., Greensboro, 1949; MD, U. N.C., 1954. Diplomate Am. Bd. Psychiatry and Neurology. Intern Queens Hosp., Honolulu, 1954-55; resident in psychiatry U. N.C. Med. Sch., Chapel Hill, 1955-57; resident in psychiatry Dorothea Dix Hosp., Raleigh, N.C., 1957-58, chief of female service, 1958-60; clin. dir. Dorothea Dix, Raleigh, 1966-71, asst. supt., 1971-73; gen. practice psychiatry 1960-66; mem. attending staff Rex Hosp., Raleigh, 1960-66; med. cons. disability determination div. N.C. Dept. Pub. Welfare, Raleigh, 1961-66; project physician NIMH, Raleigh, 1965-66; psychiatrist Southeastern Regional Area Program, Lumberton, N.C., 1973—; mem. staff Southeastern Gen. Hosp., Lumberton, 1973—; clin. instr. U. N.C. Med. Sch., 1958-61. Organizer Drug Action Com. Wake County, Raleigh, 1968. Fellow Am. Psychiat. Assn.; mem. Robeson County Med. Soc. (pres. 1986), N.C. Med. Soc. (del. 1984, 85), N.C. Neuropsychiat. Assn., AMA. Episcopalian. Home: 302 Highland Ave Lumberton NC 28358 Office: Southeastern Regional Area Program 207 W 29th St Lumberton NC 28358

JORDAN, BARBARA SCHWINN, painter; b. Glen Ridge, N.J.; d. Carl Wilhelm Ludwig and Helen Louise (Jordan) Schwinn; grad. N.Y. Sch. Fine and Applied Art (Parsons), N.Y. and Paris; student Grand Central Art Sch., Art Students League, Grand Chaumiere, Academie Julien-Paris, Columbia U., NAD; m. Frank Bertram Jordan, Jr.; children—Janine Jordan Newlin, Frank Bertram III. Illustrator mags. including Vogue, 1930's, Ladies Home Jour., Saturday Evening Post, Colliers, Good Housekeeping, Cosmopolitan, McCall's, American, Town and Country, 1940's-50's. Women's Jour., Eng., Hors Zu, Germany, Marie Claire, France, other fgn. publs., 1950's-60's; portrait painter, including Queen Sirikit, Princess Margaret, Princess Grace; free lance painter, 1970—; one-man shows include Soc. of Illustrators, 1940, 50, Barry Stephens Gallery, 1950, Bodley Gallery, N.Y.C., 1971, 80, Community Coll., West Mifflin, Pa., 1973, Duquesne U., 1973; exhibited in group shows including NAD, 1955, Royal Acad., London, Guild Hall, N.Y., 1981, Summit N.J. Art Ctr., 1981, Meredith Long Gallery, Houston, 1983, Mus. Soc. Illustrators, N.Y., 1985, The Marcus Gallery, Sante Fe, 1985, 86, The Gerald Peters Gallery, Santa Fe, 1985, 86, Brandywine Mus., Pa., 1985, 86, New Britain (Conn.) Mus. Am. Art, 1986, works represented Holbrook Collection, Ga. Mus. Art, Eureka Coll., Ill., New Britain Mus. Am. Art, Mus. of the Soc. of Illustrators, N.Y.C., Brandywine Mus., Pa., Sanford Low Meml. Collection, Del. Art Mus., Wilmington, various pvt. and gallery collections; lectr., instr. illustration Parsons Sch., 1952-54; founder adv. council Art Instrn. Sch., 1956-70. Chmn. art com. UNICEF greeting cards, 1950-61 mem. com. Spence Chapin Sch., Philharm. Soc., 1950's-60's. Winner prizes Art Dirs. Club, 1950, Guild Hall, 1969. Assoc. mem. Guggenheim Mus. Club: Cosmopolitan N.Y. Author: Technique of Barbara Schwinn, 1956; World of Fashion Art, 1968. Home and Studio: Mecox Rd Rural Route 1 Box 882 Water Mill NY 11976

JORDAN, BETTY SUE, retired educator; b. Lafayette, Tenn., Sept. 4, 1920; d. Aubrey Lee and Geneva (Freeman) West; m. Bill Jordan, Oct. 22, 1950; 1 child, L. Nicha. Student David Lipscomb Coll., 1939-41; B.S., U. Tenn., 1943; registered dietitian Duke U. Hosp., 1945; M.Ed., Clemson U., 1973. Dietitian, U. Ala., Tuscaloosa, 1945-46, Duke U., Durham, N.C., 1946-48, Stetson U., DeLand, Fla., 1948-50, Furman U., Greenville, S.C., 1950-52; elem. tchr. Greenville County Schs., S.C., 1952-66, tchr. orthopedically handicapped, 1966-85. Mem. NEA, Assn. Childhood Edn. (treas. 1980-85), United Daus. Confederacy (pres. Greenville chpt. 1978-88), Greenville Woman's Club, Lake Forest Garden Club (pres. 1970-71, 77-79, 80-81, historian 1981-87), Greater Greenville Rose Soc. (pres. 1983-84), Am. Rose Soc. (accredited rose judge 1986, cons.), Clarice Wilson Garden Club (pres. 1987-89). Delta Kappa Gamma (pres. Tau chpt. 1976-78, state chmn. communications 1979-81, state chmn. research 1983-85), Clarice Wilson Garden Club (pres. 1987-88), Kappa Kappa Iota (state pres. 1972-73, conclave pres. 1983-85), Democrat. Methodist. Avocations: collecting antiques, growing roses, flower arranging. Home: 21 Lisa Dr Greenville SC 29615

JORDAN, CECILE BLANK, educational administrator; b. Newark, N.J., Aug. 27, 1937; d. Robert and Adele (Schechner) Blank; m. Earl A. Jordan, May 26, 1956 (div. 1977); children: Philip, Ruth Ellen. BA, Case Western Res. U., 1968; MS, U. Bridgeport, 1972; EdD, U. Houston, 1983; MA, NYU, 1986. Tchr. Fox Run Sch., Nowalk, Conn., 1969-72; tchr. math. Plumfield Sch., Noroton, Conn., 1972-73; tchr. Beth Yeshurun Day Sch., Houston, 1975-78, prin., 1978-86; exec. dir. Agy. for Jewish Edn., San Diego, 1986—; mem. Com. on Jewish Edn., Houston, 1979-80. Contbg. editor Private Sch. Monitor, 1981-83; contbr. articles to profl. publs. Mem. Nat. Assn. Elem. Sch. Prins., Nat. Assn. Temple Educators, Am. Ednl. Research Assn., Jewish Edn. Assn., Ind. Schs. Assn. SW (chair minority affairs com.), Tex. Assn. Non-Pub. Schs. (bd. dirs. 1981—). Office: Agy for Jewish Edn 7510 Clairemont Mesa Blvd Suite 108 San Diego CA 92111

JORDAN, ELIZABETH MARTIN, insurance risk management administrator; b. Ahoskie, N.C., Feb. 10, 1952; d. Marvin Earl and Margaret (Griffin) Martin; m. Larry Clifford Jordan, Mar. 19, 1977; children: Caitlin Brianne, Maura Justine. BA in Behavioral Sci., Tift Coll., Forsyth, Ga., 1974; postgrad., Fla. State U., 1983. Social worker State of Fla., Gainesville, 1974-78; supr. social services Bd. County Commrs. of Alachua County, Gainesville, 1978-79, dir. social services div., 1979-83, risk and claims coordinator, 1983-87, risk mgmt. officer, 1987—. Active Allocations com. United Way of Alachua County, 1986-87, bd. dirs.; bd. dirs. Gainesville Community Action Agy., 1978-81, North Cen. Fla. Bus. and Health Care Coalition, Gainesville, 1986—. Mem. Pub. Risk and Ins. Mgmt. Assn., Am. Soc. Tng. and Devel. (treas. 1986), Safety Council of North Cen. Fla. Democrat. Roman Catholic. Office: Alachua County Bd Commrs 21 E University Ave Gainesville FL 32601

JORDAN, JANITH MARY, college administrator; b. Detroit, Oct. 11, 1942; d. Joseph Walter and Wanda (Bonk) J. BA, Wayne State U., 1965; postgrad. Summer Inst., U. London, 1967, Harvard U., 1977; MS, U. Mich., 1968. Curriculum specialist The Coll. Human Services, N.Y.C., 1968-70, acad. dir., 1971, ednl. planner, 1972-76, faculty, 1977, dir. inter-instl. devel., 1978-81, v.p., 1981—. Co-author: Taking Constructive Action, 1980. Roman Catholic. Home: 200 E 84th St New York NY 10028 Office: The Coll for Human Services 345 Hudson St New York NY 10014

JORDAN, JOAN SHEPHERD, real estate executive; b. Maryville, Tenn., July 4, 1950; d. Albert Charles and Mary Elisabeth (Hackler) Shepherd; m. Thomas Garland Cook, Aug. 16, 1969 (div. Feb. 1971); m. Michael Francis Jordan Sr., Mar. 31, 1984; 1 child, Michael Francis Jr. Student, U. Tenn., 1968-70. Lic. real estate broker, Tenn. Gen. mgr. Testerman Mgmt. Co., Knoxville, Tenn., 1973-84; property mgr. Watt Mgmt. Co., Santa Monica, Calif., 1984-85; dir. property mgmt. Jordan & Assocs., Knoxville, 1985-87, R.S. Tatum Co., Knoxville, 1987—. Bd. dirs. Knoxville Beautification Bd., 1981. Mem. Inst. Real Estate Mgmt. (cert. property mgr.), Knoxville Bd. Realtors., Apt. Council of Tenn. (bd. dirs. 1983-84) Knoxville Apartment Council (sec., v.p., pres. 1981-84), Home Builders Assn. (bd. dirs. 1984). Republican. Baptist. Home: 1804 Strathmore Rd Knoxville TN 37922 Office: RS Tatum Co 5731 Lyons View Suite #28 Knoxville TN 37919

JORDAN, JUDITH VICTORIA, clinical psychologist, educator; b. Milw., July 28, 1943; d. Claus and Charlotte (Backus) J.; m. William M. Redpath, Aug. 11, 1973. AB, Brown U., 1965; MA, Harvard U., 1968, PhD, 1973. Diplomate Am. Bd. Profl. Psychology. Psychologist Human Relations Service, Wellesley, Mass., 1971-73; assoc. psychologist McLean Hosp., Belmont, Mass., 1978—; dir. women's studies program McLean Hosp., Belmont; instr. Harvard Med. Sch., 1973—; asst. dir. tng. Psychology Dept. McLean Hosp., 1982—; visiting scholar Stone Ctr. Wellesley Coll., 1985—; instr. psychology Harvard U., 1986; cons. in field. Author: Empathy and Self Boundaries, 1984, (with others) The Self in Relation, 1986; editor, author: Relational Self in Women. Mem. Am. Psychol. Assn., Mass. Psychol. Assn. (bd. dirs. 1983-85), Phi Beta Kappa. Office: McLean Hosp 115 Mill St Belmont MA 02178

JORDAN, JULIA GAY, accountant; b. Modesto, Calif., Feb. 25, 1957; d. Harry J. and Sonja Yvonne (McGee) Holton; m. Jan. 20, 1979 (div. Feb. 1982); m. Mark W. Jordan, Mar. 12, 1982; children: Jared, Jenna. Student, Modesto (Calif.) Jr. Coll., 1975-77; BA in Bus. Adminstrn., Calif. State U., 1977-79. CPA, Calif. CPA Kemper CPA Group, Modesto, 1978—. Mem. Calif. Soc. CPA's, Am. Inst. CPA's. Lodge: Lions. Home: 2012 Goldfield Dr Modesto CA 95351 Office: Kemper CPA Group 1101 Standiford Ave Ste C1 Modesto CA 95350

JORDAN, KATHLEEN CASEY, diplomatic liaison; b. Roseville, Calif., Apr. 7, 1963; d. Stephen Edgington J. BA in Polit Sci., Law and Soc., U. Tulsa, 1985; MA in Criminal Justice, John Jay Coll. Criminal Justice, 1987; postgrad., CUNY, (**. Sales asst. Sears and Roebuck, Tulsa, 1979-85; research analyst U. Tulsa, 1983-85; paralegal The Dreyfus Corp., N.Y.C., 1985; asst. personal aide to ambassador Socialist People's Libyan Arab Jamahiriya Mission to UN, N.Y.C., 1985—. Recipient numerous oratory awards. Mem. Nat. Assn. Female Execs., Women in Communications, Internat. Nat. Forensic League, Oxford Union Debate Soc., Pi Sigma Alpha. Office: Libyan Mission to UN 309 E 48th St New York NY 10017

JORDAN, KATHLEEN MARIE, labor relations executive, lawyer; b. Cambridge, N.Y., July 26, 1949; d. Lewis Francis and Harriet Clair (Fremont) Boex; m. Robert Lawrence Jordan (div. 1971); 1 child, William Lewis Jordan. AA, Va. Intermont, Bristol, 1969, BA, 1972; JD cum laude, Gonzaga Law Sch., Spokane, Wash., 1980. Bar: Idaho, 1981, U.S. Dist. Ct. Idaho, 1981, U.S. Mil. Ct. Appeals, 1982. Psychiat. Social Worker Eastern State Hosp., Williamsburg, Va., 1973-77; student research asst. Gonzaga Law Sch., Spokane, Wash., 1978-79; student legal clk. Spokane Legal Services Ctr., 1980; prosecutor, legal advisor Office of the SJA, Ft. Knox, Ky., 1981-82; legal instr. U.S. Army Armor Sch., Ft. Knox, Ky., 1982; defense counsel Trial Defense Services, Fall Church, Va., 1982-84; asst. prof. Eastern Ky. U., Ft. Knox, 1983-84, Embry-Riddle Aero. U., Ft. Knox, 1983; asst. to supt. for personell, labor relations Coatesville (Pa.) Area Sch Dist., 1984—. Employee chair United Way, Chestor County, Pa., 1986-87. Served to cpt. U.S. Army, 1981-84. Recipient academic scholarship Gonzaga Law Sch., 1980, Am. Juris Prudence award Lawyers Coop. Pub. Co., 1980. Mem. Idaho State Bar Assn., Chester County (Pa.) Bar Assn., Am. Arbitration Assn., Pa. Sch. Bds. Assn. Republican. Roman Catholic. Home: 1330 Manor Rd Coatesville PA 19320 Office: Coatesville Area Sch Dist 1515 E Lincoln Hwy Coatesville PA 19320

JORDAN, MARY ANN, medical sales representative; b. Natrona Heights, Pa., Nov. 25, 1949; d. Raymond George and Bernadean Margaret (Maizland) Faulx; m. Joseph Roger Jordan Jr., Nov. 28, 1970 (div. June 1976); 1 child, Michelle Linette. AS, Community Coll. of Allegheny County, 1969; student, U. Pitts., 1980—. Med. lab. technician Citizens Gen. Hosp., New Kensington, Pa., 1969-70, Community Gen. Osteopathic Hosp., Harrisburg, Pa., 1970-72, Cobb Meml. Hosp., Phenix City, Ala., 1972, Lexington County Hosp., West Columbia, S.C., 1972-75; inside sales rep. Fisher Scientific Co., Pitts., 1975-79, outside sales rep., 1980—. Mem. Assn. of Clin. Pathologists, Clin. Lab. Mgmt. Assn. (spl. recognition award 1984). Office: Fisher Scientific Co 585 Alpha Dr Pittsburgh PA 15238

JORDAN, RUTH ANN, physician; b. Richmond, Ind., Oct. 12, 1928; d. Willard and Esther (Fouts) J.; children: Diane M., Linda J. AB, Ind. U., 1950; MD, Columbia U., 1957. Intern, St. Luke's Hosp., N.Y.C., 1957-58, asst. resident in medicine, 1958-59; physician clinic Met. Life Ins. Co., N.Y.C., 1960-62, Standard Oil Col. of N.J., N.Y.C., 1962; physician in med. dept. MIT, Cambridge, 1963-72; physician clinic New Eng. Mut. Life Ins. Co., Boston, 1963-66, asst. med. dir., 1972-74; fellow internal medicine Mass. Gen. Hosp., Boston, 1974-75; physician Simmons Coll., Boston, 1975-78, Northeastern U., Boston, 1976-78; therapeutic dietitian Meth. Hosp., Indpls., 1951-53, Presbyn. Hosp., N.Y.C., part-time 1954-57; assoc. med. dir. New Eng. Telephone Co., 1978, med. dir. clin. services, 1978-86, gen. med. assoc. dir. occupational medicine, 1986—; nat. coordinator com. on cholesterol Mass. Adv. Council for Workers Compensation, 1986—. Active Brownies Orgn. Fellow Am. Occupational Med. Assn. (membership com. 1985—, health edn. com. 1984—, bd. dirs. 1986—); mem. Ind. Dietitic Assn. (past pub. relations chmn.), AMA, DAR, Norfolk County Med. Soc., New Eng. Occupational Med. Assn. (bd. dirs. 1980—, pres. 1981-84), Mass. Med. Soc. (mem. council 1984—, chmn. environ. and occupational health com. 1985—), Alpha Chi Omega. Clubs: Columbia U. of New Eng. (v.p. 1981-84), Roxbury Clin. Records, Wianno Yacht. Home: 105 Rockwood St Brookline MA 02146

JORDAN, SHARON ANN, clinical social worker, child and family psychotherapist; b. Detroit, July 22, 1953; d. Benneal and Myrtice Marie J. A.B. in Journalism, U. Mich., 1975, M.Urban Planning, 1977, M.S.W., 1979. Social worker, counselor, staff devel. coordinator U. Mich. opportunity program, 1979-84; clin. social worker U. Mich. Children's Psychiat. Hosp., 1984—; mental health profl. Psychiatric Emergency Services U. Mich. Hosp., 1986—; pvt. practice in psychotherapy, 1987—; sr. assoc. Employee Assistance Assn., 1984-87. U. Mich. fellow, 1976-77. Mem. Nat. Assn. Social Workers, Acad. Cert. Social Workers, Am. Ortho-Psychiat. Assn., Nat. Black Child Devel. Inst., Phi Beta Kappa. Office: U Mich Day Hosp Program NI3 A12 Box 0401 Ann Arbor MI 48109

JORDAN-SWEET, JEAN L., research chemist; b. Los Angeles, Aug. 19, 1954; d. Henry James and Edith (Hill) Jordan; m. Robert Mahlon Sweet, Aug. 23, 1986. BS in Chemistry, Physics, Loyola-Marymount U., Los

Angeles, 1976; PhD, UCLA, 1983. Postdoctoral research assoc. Brookhaven Nat. Lab., Upton, N.Y., 1983; postdoctoral research assoc. IBM T.J. Watson Research, Yorktown Heights, N.Y., 1984-86, staff engr., 1986—, equal opportunity coordinator phys. scis. dept., 1987—. Contbr. numerous articles to profl. sci. jours. Mem. Am. Physical Soc., Am. Vacuum Soc., Sigma Pi Sigma. Democrat. Roman Catholic. Office: IBM Beamline X20 NSLS 725A Brookhaven Lab Upton NY 11973

JORDON, DEBORAH ELIZABETH, lawyer; b. Pitts., June 24, 1951; d. Joseph Mitchell and Marjorie Odessa (Glaude) J. BA, Brown U., 1972; JD, Yale U., 1975. Bar: Pa. 1975, N.Y. 1978, U.S. Dist. Ct. (ea. and we. dists.) N.Y., 1978. Law clk. to presiding justice U.S. Dist. Ct. (ea. dist.) Pa., Phila., 1975-77, assoc. Paul, Weiss, Rifkind, Wharton & Garrison, N.Y.C., 1977-79; asst. to mayor City of N.Y., 1979-82; counsel to pres. CCNY, 1982-84; sr. atty. NBC, N.Y.C., 1984-87, asst. gen. atty., 1987—; chmn. bd. dirs. Harlem Legal Services Inc., N.Y.C.; bd. dirs. Met. Assistance Corp., N.Y.C. Bd. dirs. Bennett Coll., Greensboro, N.C., 1985—, Lifelong Learning Program, N.Y. 1981-82, Marymount Manhattan Coll., N.Y.C., 1984-87. Named Achiever in Industry Harlem YMCA, N.Y.C., 1988. Mem. Phi Beta Kappa. Roman Catholic. Home: 200 W 79th St New York NY 10024 Office: NBC Inc 30 Rockefeller Plaza New York NY 10112

JORDON, PEARL, psychotherapist, educator; b. N.Y.C., July 24, 1926; d. Max and Clara (Pineus) J.; B.A., Bklyn. Coll., 1959; M.S., Yeshiva U., 1960; M.S.W., Hunter Coll., 1963. Sr. social worker Manhattan State Hosp., Wards Island, N.Y., 1959-66, psychiat. cons. social service dept., 1967-68; psychiat. cons. Kings County Psychiat. Social Service Dept., Bklyn., 1969-71; asso. dir. dept. social services Montefiore Hosp. & Med. Center, Bronx, N.Y., 1971-77; asst. prof. N.Y.U., N.Y.C., 1966-71; lectr. Hunter Coll., N.Y.C., 1975-77, adj. clin. asso. prof., 1976—; clin. asso. prof. SUNY, Stony Brook, 1979-84, chmn. integrated practice concentration, 1980-83; adj. assoc. prof., coordinator individual treatment program Postmasters Clin. Program, Hunter Sch. Social Work, CCNY, 1984—; pvt. practice psychotherapy, N.Y.C., 1968—. Mem. social service adv. com. March of Dimes, Jericho, N.Y., 1980-81; guest speaker Nassau and Suffolk Health Systems Assn., Melville, N.Y., 1980; mem. com. Suffolk/Nassau Health Systems Agy., 1980-81. Fellow Soc. Clin. Social Work Psychotherapists, Am. Orthopsychiat. Assn.; mem. Nat. Assn. Social Workers. Contbr. articles in field to profl. publs. Office: 160 E 88th St New York NY 10128

JORGENSEN, ESTELLE RUTH, music educator; b. Melbourne, Victoria, Australia, May 28, 1945; came to U.S., 1986; d. Alfred Stanley and Jean Winifred (Cook) J. BA in Econs. with honors, U. Newcastle, New South Wales, Australia, 1967, Diploma in Edn., 1968; MusM, Andrews U., 1970; PhD, U. Calgary, Alta., Can., 1976. Tchr. social studies Epping Boys Sch., Sydney, Australia, 1968; tchr. social studies and music County of Newell, Brooks, Alta., Can., 1968-69; instr. music Andrews U., Berrien Springs, Mich., 1970-71; tchr. music Milton Williams Jr. High Sch., Calgary, 1971-74; tchr. choral music Henry Wise Wood High Sch., Calgary, 1974-76; asst. prof. Sch. Edn. Notre Dame U., Nelson, B.C., Can., 1976-77; assoc. prof. music faculty McGill U., Montreal, Que., Can., 1977-87; prof. music edn. Sch. Music Ind. U., Bloomington, 1987—. Editor: (proceedings) McGill Symposium in School Music Administration and Supervision, 1980; contbr. articles to profl. jours. Mem. Coll. Music Soc., Inc. Soc. Musicians, Royal Coll. Organists, Music Educators Nat. Conf. Office: Ind U Sch Music Bloomington IN 47405

JORGENSEN, JUDITH ANN, psychiatrist; b. Parris Island, S.C.; d. George Emil and Margaret Georgia Jorgensen; B.A., Stanford U., 1963; M.D., U. Calif., 1968; m. Ronald Francis Crown, July 11, 1970. Intern, Meml. Hosp., Long Beach, 1969-70; resident County Mental Health Services, San Diego, 1970-73; staff psychiatrist Children and Adolescent Services, San Diego, 1973-78; practice medicine specializing in psychiatry, La Jolla, Calif., 1973—; staff psychiatrist County Mental Health Services of San Diego, 1973-78, San Diego State U. Health Services, 1985-87; psychiat. cons. San Diego City Coll., 1973-78, 85-86; asst. prof. dept. psychiatry U. Calif., 1978—; chmn. med. quality rev. com. Dist. XIV, State of Calif., 1982-83. Mem. Am. Psychiat. Assn., San Diego Soc. Psychiat. Physicians (chmn. membership com. 1976-78, v.p. 1978-80, fed. legis. rep. 1985-87), Am. Soc. Adolescent Psychiatry, San Diego Soc. Adolescent Psychiatry (pres. 1981-82), Calif. Med. Assn. (alternate del.), Soc. Sci. Study of Sex, San Diego Soc. Sex Therapy and Edn., San Diego County Med. Soc. (credentials com. 1982-84). Club: Rowing. Office: 470 Nautilus St Suite 211 La Jolla CA 92037

JORGENSEN, LOU ANN BIRKBECK, social worker; b. Park City, Utah, May 14, 1931; d. Robert John and Lillian Pearl (Langford) Birkbeck; student Westminster Coll., 1949-51; B.S., U. Utah, 1953, M.S.W., 1972, D.S.W., 1979; grad. Harvard Inst. Ednl. Mgmt., 1983; m. Howard Arnold Jorgensen, June 9, 1954; children—Gregory Arnold, Blake John, Paul Clayton. Social work adminstr. nursing home demonstration project, dept. family and community medicine U. Utah Med. Center, Salt Lake City, 1972-74; mental health ednl. specialist Grad. Sch. Social Work, U. Utah, 1974-77, 77-80, asst. prof., 1974-80, assoc. prof., 1980—, dir. doctoral program, 1984 , assoc. dean, 1986—; regional mental health cons. Bd. dirs. Info. and Referral Center, 1975-82, United Way of Utah, 1976-82, Pioneer Trail Parks, 1977-83, Rowland Hall-St. Marks Sch., 1980-86; Salt Lake County housing commr., 1980-86; pres. Human Services Conf. for Utah, 1979-80. Mem. Council on Social Work Edn., Nat. Assn. Social Workers (pres. Utah chpt. 1978-79), Adminstrs. of Public Agys. Assn., Human Services Assn. Utah, Jr. League of Salt Lake City, Phi Kappa Phi. Republican. Episcopalian. Clubs: Town, Eastern Star. Author: Explorations in Living, 1978; Social Work in Business and Industry, 1979; Handbook of the Social Services, 1981; contbr. articles to profl. jours. Home: 3442 East Oaks Dr Salt Lake City UT 84124 Office: U Utah Grad Sch Social Work Salt Lake City UT 84112

JORGENSEN, VIRGINIA TRIEST, psychiatrist; b. New Orleans, Mar. 22, 1923; d. Kenneth G. and Luise (Schiele) Triest; B.A. cum laude, Hofstra U., 1951; M.D., U. Copenhagen, 1957; postgrad. N.Y. Sch. Psychiatry, 1963; m. Eric Jorgensen, Aug. 5, 1951; children—Ellen Verena, Nina. Intern, Flushing (N.Y.) Hosp., 1957-58; resident in psychiatry Creedmore State Hosp., Queens, N.Y., 1959-62, sr. psychiatrist, 1962-64; practice medicine specializing in psychiatry, Garden City, N.Y., 1963—; psychiat. cons. Sch. for Emotionally Disturbed Children, Nassau County, N.Y., 1962-71, Children's Village, Dobbs Ferry, N.Y., 1964-65; asst. attending physican North Shore Univ. Hosp., Manhasset, N.Y., 1980-86, sr. asst. attending, 1986—; clin. instr. psychiatry Cornell U. Coll. Medicine, 1981. Mem. med. adv. bd. Planned Parenthood of Nassau County, 1966—; bd. dirs. Family Life Center, Garden City, 1981. Diplomate Am. Bd. Psychiatry. Mem. Am. Psychiat. Assn., Am. Med. Women's Assn., Nassau Psychiat. Soc. (dir. 1983-86). Club: Garden City Ski. Office: 520 Franklin Ave Garden City NY 11530

JORGENSON, BARBARA WEISBROD, construction executive; b. Los Angeles, Oct. 23, 1956; d. Harold and Evelyn (Mertzel) W.; m. Michael Allen Jorgenson, June 5, 1983; m. Richard Desmond Wood, Jun 7, 1981 (div. Aug. 1982). Grad. exec. program, UCLA, 1982. Product mgr. Harlyn Products, Inc., Los Angeles, 1981-83, with advt. and promotions dept., 1982-83, bd. dirs., 1983—; owner Mibar Design and Constrn., Inc., Sebastopol, Calif., 1983-86, pres., 1986—; owner Exotic Wood Products, Sebastopol, 1986—. Republican. Jewish.

JORS-CAVANAUGH, THERESA MARIE, sales specialist; b. Jackson, Mich., June 3, 1956; d. Robert Nathan and Barbara Jean (Betts) J. BBA, U. Mich., 1978. Mgmt. trainee Kelsey Hayes Co., Romulus, Mich., 1978; rep. customer relations Kelsey Products div. Kelsey Hayes Co., Romulus, Mich., 1978-79; dist. sales mgr., after market sales Chgo., 1979-81; mktg. rep. Bendix Heavy Vehicle Systems, Elyria, Ohio, 1981-82, sr. mktg. rep., 1982-86, sr. sales engr. Original Equipment Sales, 1986—. Republican. Roman Catholic. Home and Office: 2723 San Onofre Ct Antioch CA 94509

JOSE, PHYLLIS ANN, librarian; b. Detroit, Mar. 15, 1949; d. William Henry and Isobel Eleanor (Mundle) J.; B.A., Mich. State U., 1971, M.A., 1972; M.A. in Library Sci., U. Mich., 1975. Library aide audio-visual div. Dearborn (Mich.) Dept. Libraries, 1973-76, librarian gen. info. div., 1976-77; reference library dir. Oakland County (Mich.) Library, 1977—. Officer Southfield Economic Devel. Corp., 1980—; mem. Southfield Tax Increment Fin. Authority, 1981—; coordinator Southfield Arts Festival, 1984, 85. [illegible] (ALA chpt. councilor). Presbyterian. Office: 1200 N Telegraph Rd Pontiac MI 48053

JOSEFF, JOAN CASTLE, manufacturing executive; b. Alta., Can., Aug. 12, 1922; naturalized U.S. citizen, 1945; d. Edgar W. and Lottie (Coates) Castle; BA in Psychology, UCLA; widow; 1 son, Jeffrey Rene. With Joseff-Hollywood, jewelry rental, Burbank, Calif., 1939—, chmn. bd., pres., sec.-treas., 1948—; exec., aircraft components mfg. co. Mem. Burbank Salary Task Force, 1979—, Los Angeles County Earthquake Fact-Finding Commn., 1981—; bd. dirs. San Fernando Valley area chpt. Am. Cancer Soc.; mem. Rep. Cen. Com.; del. Rep. Nat. Conv., 1980, 84, 88. Mem. Women of Motion Picture Industry (hon. life), Nat. Fedn. Rep. Women (dir. recipient Caring for Am. award 1981), Calif. Rep. Women (dir., treas. 1986—), North Hollywood Rep. Women (pres. 1981-82). Home: 10060 Toluca Lake Ave Toluca Lake CA 91602 Office: 129 E Providencia Ave Burbank CA 91502

JOSELYN, JO ANN, space scientist; b. St. Francis, Kans., Oct. 5, 1943; d. James Jacob and Josephine Felzien (Firkins) Cram. BS in Applied Math., U. Colo., 1965, MS in Astro Geophysics, 1967, Ph.D. in Astro Geophysics, 1978. Research asst. NASA-Manned Space Ctr., Houston, 1966; physicist NOAA-Space Environ. Lab., Boulder, Colo., 1967-78; space scientist NOAA-Space Environ. Lab., Boulder, 1978—; U.S. del. study group 6 Consultive Com. for Ionospheric Radio, 1981, 83; mem. com. on data mgmt. and computation NASA Space Sci. Bd., 1988-90. Mem. U. Colo. Grad. Sch. Alumni Council, 1986—. Recipient unit citation NOAA, 1971, 80, 85, 86, Sustained Superior Performance award NOAA, 1985, 87, 88, group achievement award NASA, 1983, Disting. Engring. Alumnus award U. Colo., 1987. Mem. AIAA, Am. Women in Sci., Am. Geophys. Union, Union Radio Sci. Internat., Internat. Union Geodesy and Geophysics, Assn. Geomagnetism and Aeronomy, Am. Astronautical Assn., AAAS, AAUW, PEO, Sigma Xi, Tau Beta Pi, Sigma Tau. Republican. Methodist. Office: NOAA-Space Environ Lab 325 Broadway St R/E/SE2 Boulder CO 80303

JOSEPH, ELEANOR ANN, director medical records, consultant; b. Cleve., Mar. 6, 1944; d. Emil and Eleanor (Leelais) Dienes; m. Abraham Albert Joseph, Oct. 28, 1984. BS in Math. cum laude, Cleve. State U., 1978. Accredited record technician. Asst. dir. med. records Warrensville Heights, Ohio, 1963-77; coder Shaker Med. Ctr., Shaker Heights, Ohio, 1965, Huron Rd. Hosp., Cleve., 1965; instr. Cuyahoga Community Coll., Cleve., 1970-72; dir. med. records Hillcrest Hosp., Mayfield Heights, Ohio, 1977-84; med. records technician Vis. Nurse Assn., Cleve., 1985; coordinator med. records Services Greater Cleve. Hosp. Assn., 1985-88; dir. coding services Service Ctr. Health Affairs Greater Cleve. Hosp. Assn., 1988—; cons. in field, Cleve., 1976—; mem. speakers' bur. Hillcrest Hosp., Mayfield Heights, Ohio, 1978-84; adv. com. Cuyahoga Community Coll., Cleve., 1973-80, instr. 1970-72; cons. Suburban Pavilion, Manor Care Nursing Homes, Luth. Home, Cleve., 1976—. Co-author: (manual) Qulity Assurance Program for Medical Records Department, 1981; co-editor: Care and Management of Health Care Records, 1988. Active Holden Arboretum, Kirtland, Ohio, 1975—, Ohio Hist. Soc., Columbus, 1975—. Mem. Am. Med. Record Assn., Ohio Med. Record Assn. (coding council 1985-88), NE Ohio Med. Record Assn. (pres. 1982-83, counselor 1983, ednl. com. 1984, 87, chmn. nominating com. 1986, treas. 1978, v.p. 1980; recipient Pres.'s award 1983), Jr. League (Parliamentarian Cleve. chpt. 1987—). Democrat. Lutheran. Club: Luth. Bus. Women. Office: Ctr for Health Affairs Greater Cleve Hosp Assn 1226 Huron Rd Cleveland OH 44115

JOSEPH, GERI MACK (GERALDINE), former ambassador; b. St. Paul, June 19, 1923. B.S., U. Minn., 1946; LL.D. (hon.), Bates Coll., 1982. Staff writer Mpls. Tribune, 1946-53, contbg. editor, 1972-78; ambassador to The Netherlands The Hague, 1978-81; sr. fellow internat. programs Hubert H. Humphrey Inst. Pub. Affairs, U. Minn.; dir. George A. Hormel Co., Honeywell, the German-Marshall Fund; Mem. U.S. Pres.'s Commn. on Mental Health; mem. Minn. Supreme Ct. Commn. on Mentally Disabled and the Cts.; mem., bd. dirs. The German Marshall Fund, 1987; mem. com. on Mid. East, The Brooking's Inst., 1987. Vice chmn. Gov.'s Commn. on Taxation, 1983-84; trustee Carleton Coll., 1975—; mem. Democratic Nat. Com., 1960-72, vice chmn., 1968-72; co-chairperson Minn. Women's Campaign Fund, 1982-84; co-chmn. Atty. Gen.'s Com. on Child Abuse within the Family, 1986.

JOSEPH, JILL ANN, purchasing executive; b. Mpls., Mar. 6, 1955; d. Edward Kenneth and Lorraine Helen (Schullo) Larson; m. Edward Thomas Joseph, Feb. 24, 1979. Student, Inver Hills Community Coll., Inver Grove Heights, Minn., 1987—. Sec. Data 100 Corp., Minnetonka, Minn., 1975-78; buyer Data 100/No. Telecom, Minnetonka, 1978-79, Lee Data Corp., Eden Prairie, Minn., 1979-85; sr. buyer Lee Data Corp., Eden Prairie, 1985-87; pvt. practice property mgmgt. Inner Grove Heights, Minn., 1987—. Home: 1655 68th St W Inver Grove Heights MN 55075

JOSEPH, JUDITH ROSE, editor; b. Newark, Sept. 18, 1948; d. Siegmund and Yolanda (Klein) J., B.A. with honors, N.Y.U., 1970; M.A., U. Va., 1973; m. Alan M. de Vries, June 1982; 1 child, Elizabeth Martha. Sales rep. Prentice-Hall Pub., Inc., 1973-75; pub. social sci. and humanities texts D. Van Nostrand Co., Inc., N.Y.C., 1975-79, v.p., publs. dir., 1979-81; sr. editor vocat. and tech. texts John Wiley & Sons, Inc., N.Y.C., 1981-87, exec. editor Architecture, Design and Hospitality Mgmt., Van Nostrand Reinhold Co., N.Y.C., 1987—. Mem. Am. Assn. Pub., Nat. Assn. Female Execs., NOW.

JOSEPH, SALLY SHAHEEN, lawyer; b. Michigan City, Ind.; d. James Said and Adele Martha (Sawaya) Shaheen; m. Edward P. Joseph, Mar. 8, 1959 (dec. Dec. 1987); children: Barbara, Jacqueline, John, Stephanie, Allison. BA, U. Mich., Flint, 1975; JD, T. M. Cooley Sch., 1983. Bar: Mich. 1983. Budget and credit counselor Genesee County Prosecuting Attorney, Flint, investigator, 1976-79; staff atty. NuVision Inc., Flint, 1984-85; risk mgr., purchasing agt. Genesee County Rd. Commn., Flint, 1985—. Trustee Charter Twp. Flint, 1984—, mem. bd. appeals, 1984—, mem. planning commn., 1982-84; mem. com. promote charter revision, City Flint; bd. dirs. St. George Orthodox Ch., Flint, 1987—. Mem. ABA, Mich. Bar Assn., Genesee County Bar Assn., Pub. Risk and Ins. Mgmt. Assn., Pub. Purshasing Officers Assn., Soc. Syrian Orthodox Youth Orgn. Democrat. Orthodox Catholic. Club: El Bakura (Flint) (past sec.). Lodge: Order St. Ignasius (DAME). Home: 6263 Stonegate Pwy Flint MI 48532 Office: Genesee County Rd Commn 211 W Oakley St Flint MI 48503

JOSEPH-FELDMAN, DIANE, appraiser; b. Chgo., May 21, 1933; d. Wilfried Elmer and Rose (Kopca) Davis; ed. Am. Acad. Art, Art Inst. Chgo., Stone-Camryn Sch. Ballet; m. Z. Albert Joseph, 1957 (div. 1969); m. Hy Feldman, Feb. 14, 1979; children—Diana Jill Joseph, John Alan Joseph. Soloist, tchr. ballet Interlochen (Mich.) Nat. Music Camp, 1954-55; soloist in Brigadoon, N.Y.C. Center, 1956, My Fair Lady, other musicals; dancer WGN-TV and Lyric Opera Ballet, Chgo., 1955-58; founder, pres. Heritage Appraisal Service, Inc., Wilmette, Ill., 1971-82; lectr, instr. continuing edn. series antiques Oakton Community Coll. Vol., Hospice of North Shore, Cancer Care Ctr. of Evanston Hosp., Planned Parenthood; bd. mem., Y-Me Breast Cancer Support Group; moderator, Evanston Hosps. Cancer Self-Help Group. Mem. Simon Wiesenthal Center, Democratic Nat. Orgn. Mem. Internat. Soc. Appraisers (rec. and corr. sec. Chgo. chpt.), New Eng. Appraisers Assn., ACLU, NOW, Audubon Soc. Address: 2201 Crestview Ln Wilmette IL 60091

JOSEPHS, BONNIE PRISCILLA, lawyer; b. Verona, N.J., Oct. 11, 1938; d. Paul and Helen (Joelson) J.; children: Melodie Winawer, Paul. BA, Smith Coll., 1960; JD, NYU, 1966. Bar: N.Y., 1966. Editor MacFadden Publs., N.Y.C., 1960, Hearst Mags., N.Y.C., 1961-62, Del Publs., N.Y.C., 1962, Grosset & Dunlap, N.Y.C., 1962-63; assoc. Cravath, Swaine & Moore, N.Y.C., 1966-69, London, Buttenwieser & Chalif, N.Y.C., 1969-74; ptnr. London, Buttenwieser, Bonem & Valente, N.Y.C., 1975, Buttenwieser & Josephs, N.Y.C., 1976-77; prin. Bonnie P. Josephs, N.Y.C., 1978—. Author: (with others) Political and Civil Rights, 1966, Child's Play, 1965; contbr. articles to profl. jours. Mem. ABA, Assn. Trial Lawyers, Assn. of Bar of City of N.Y. (arbitration and alternate dispute resolution com. 1986—). Democrat. Jewish. Home: 173 Riverside Dr New York NY 10024 Office: 1414 Sixth Ave New York NY 10024

JOSEPHSON, DIANA HAYWARD, aerospace executive; b. London, Oct. [illegible] 1959; d. Robert Hayward and Barbara (Clark) Bailey. BA with honors, Oxford U., Eng., 1958, MA, [illegible] in Comparative Law, George Washington U., 1962. Bar: England 1959, Wales 1959, D.C. 1963. Assoc. Covington & Burling, Washington, 1959-68; asst. dir. Office of the Mayor, Washington, 1968-74; exec. dir. Nat. Capital Area ACLU, Washington, 1975-78; dep. asst. adminstr. policy and planning, satellites NOAA, U.S. Dept. Commerce, Washington, 1978-82; pres. Am. Sci. and Tech. Corp., Bethesda, Md., 1982-83, Space Am., Bethesda, 1983-85; v.p. mktg. Arianespace, Inc., Washington, 1985-87; dir. Martin Marietta Comml. Titan Inc., Washington, 1987—; mem. comml. space adv. commn., U.S. Dept. Transp., Washington, 1984-85. Mem. D.C. Law Revision Commn., Washington, 1975-78, D.C. Internat. Women's Yr. State Coordinating Com., 1977. Recipient Gold medal for Disting. Service, U.S. Dept. Commerce, 1981. Mem. Am. Astronautical Soc. (bd. dirs. 1985—), Nat. Space Club (bd. govs.), Women in Aerospace, Washington Space Bus. Roundtable (adv. bd. 1985-87), Am. Inst. Aeronautics and Astronautics. Office: Martin Marietta Comml Titan Systems 1800 K St NW Suite 724 Washington DC 20006

JOSEPHSON, JANNA WALDINGER, artist, photographer; b. Los Angeles, Mar. 16, 1958; d. Arthur and Gloria (Lieberman) Waldinger; m. Paul Jay Josephson, Apr. 12, 1981. BA, U. Calif., Santa Barbara, 1979. Prin. Janna W.J. Art and Photography, N.Y.C., 1979—; owner, pres., designer Janna: Original Art Plates, N.Y.C., San Francisco, 1985—; guest lectr. Santa Barbara Coll. Creative Studies U. Calif., 1984. Prin. works include Janna orginal art plates. Bd. dirs. Tribeca Owners Corp., N.Y.C., 1984-85. Mem. Nat. Assn. Female Execs., Women's Caucas for the Arts, Foundation of Community Artists, Greenpeace. Democrat. Jewish. Home: 4674 19th St San Francisco CA 94114

JOSLYN, SANDY LYNNE, police officer; b. Owensboro, Ky., Dec. 28, 1958; d. Carl and Emily (Richardson) Phillips; m. Gary Douglas Joslyn, Dec. 29, 1984. BA in Criminology, Corrections and Rehab., Murray State U., 1980; police basic tng., Eastern Ky. U., 1981. Sgt. security Burns Internat. Security, Owensboro, 1980; police officer Madisonville (Ky.) Police Dept., 1980; police officer, detective Paducah (Ky.) Police Dept., 1980—; community edn. speaker civic and religious groups, Paducah, 1985-87. Mem. protocol task force Childwatch, Paducah, 1986—, Citizens and Victims Justice Reform, Paducah, 1987—; in-service speaker Rape Crisis Ctr., Paducah, 1986—, continuing edn. speaker Western Bapt. Hosp., Paducah, 1985—. Mem. Fraternal Order of Police. Democrat. Home: 3620 Minnich Ave Paducah KY 42001

JOYCE, BERNITA ANNE, federal government agency administrator; d. Albert A. and Margaret C. Joyce; B.A., Duchesne Coll.; M.B.A., U. Santa Clara, 1968, Ph.D., 1974; m. Kenneth B. Lucas, Aug. 2, 1975. Adminstr., Soc. of Sacred Heart, Menlo Park, Calif. and Seattle, 1957-71, regional adminstr., San Francisco, 1969-71; with Wolfe & Co., C.P.A.s, Washington, 1971-72; fin. dir. Nat. Forest Products Assn., Washington, 1972-74; budget fiscal officer ICC, Washington, 1974-77, Office Mgmt. and Budget, 1977-80; asst. dir. mgmt. services Bur. Mines, Dept. Interior, 1980-85, asst. dir. Office Policy Analysis, 1985—. Trustee St. Francis Preparatory Sch., Spring Grove, Pa. Author: Financial Viability of Private Elementary Schools. Mem. Am. Inst. C.P.A.s, Sr. Execs. Assn., AAUW, Exec. Women in Bus. (v.p.), Beta Gamma Sigma. Home: 6001 Bradley Blvd Bethesda MD 20817

JOYCE, KATHY ELLEN, corporate communication specialist; b. Butte, Mont., May 10, 1949; d. Joseph William and Mary Jean (Isberg) J. BJ, U. Colo., 1973. Editor Metro Denver mag., 1973-74; reporter, writer, photographer N.J., Maine and N.Y., 1974-78; mng. editor Town and Country, Boulder, Colo., 1978-79; communication mgr. Regional Transp. Dist., Denver, 1979-83; communication and tng. mgr. The Denver Post, 1983—. Bd. dirs. Sudden Infant Death Syndrome, Denver, 1979-85; council mem. Historic Denver, 1985—; active Mile High United Way. Mem. Am. Soc. Tng. Dirs. Office: The Denver Post 650 15th St Denver CO 80202

JOYCE, MARILYN SCHMIDT, training company executive; b. Covington, Ky., Sept. 3, 1942; d. Robert Andrew and Rita Marie (Stadtmiller) S.; m. Clayton Robert Joyce, Nov. 29, 1975; stepchildren—David Joyce, Kathryn Joyce Keehn, Robert Joyce. B.A., Thomas More Coll., 1964; M.Ed., Xavier U., 1968. Tchr., Colerain High Sch., Cin., 1964-68; tchr. N.E. High Sch., Ft. Lauderdale, Fla., 1968-69; chmn. dept. curriculum devel. Henderson High Sch., Atlanta, 1969-75; trainer, mgr. URS Corp., Seattle, 1977-80; founder, pres. Joyce Inst., Seattle, 1981—; ergonomics tng. cons. GTE, 1983—, Boeing Co., Seattle, 1981—; speaker Internat. Sci. Conf.1986, Nat. Safety Council Conf., 1986. Editor tng. courses: Dataspan, 1981, Datahealth, 1985. Co-author tng. manual: Managing Office Ergonomics, 1986, Pro-Read, 1972. Mem. Human Factors Soc., Am. Soc. Tng. and Devel., Am. Mgmt. Assn. Seattle C. of C. Republican. Roman Catholic. Clubs: Columbia Tower, Ranier, Pres. Club. Lodge: Rotary. Home: 2220 40th Ave E Seattle WA 98112

JOYCE, SHEILA MARY, executive search consultant; b. Chgo., May 31, 1953; d. John Leo and Mabel Marie (McGarry) J.; m. James Franklin VerKamp, Apr. 29, 1979. BS, Northwestern U., 1976. Supr. employee services Avon Products, Inc., Morton Grove, Ill., 1972-76; sr. personnel adminstr. Johnson & Johnson, Chgo., 1976-80; ptnr., founder VerKamp-Joyce Assocs., Inc., Oak Brook, Ill., 1980—; mem. exec. com., bd. dirs. pres.' adv. council of Ill. Benedictine Coll., Lisle, 1985—; mem. pres.' council Bus. Assocs. of Elmhurst Coll., Ill., 1986—, adv. com. Congl. Sci. and Tech., Hinsdale, Ill., 1986—; del. White House Conf. On Small Bus., 1986. Mem. Nat. Assn. Women Bus. Owners (v.p. Chgo. chpt. 1986, pres. 1986—), Oak Brook Assn. Commerce and Industry (bd. dirs. 1984—), Ill. Mgmt. and Exec. Search Cons., Nat. Assn. Corp. and Profl. Recruiters. Club: DuPage (Oakbrook Terrace, Ill.). Office: VerKamp-Joyce Assocs Two Mid-America Plaza PO Box 1500 Oak Brook IL 60522-1500

JOYCE, SUSAN VALLONE, state representative; b. Exeter, N.H., Mar. 9, 1951; d. Andrew M. and Marguerite (Fecteau) Vallone; m. Mark V. Joyce (div. 1986); children: Ryan J., Patrick A. BS, Niagara Falls U., 1973. State rep. N.H., 1983, 84; mem. bd. selectman State of N.H., Epping, 1985-86, 1987—. Mem. Gov.'s Council on Arts, N.H., 1983-84, State N.H. Dem. Com., 1984-86, Upstairs/Downstairs Community Theatre, Epping.; N.H. State rep. 1986—. Mem. Orgn. Women Legislators. Democrat. Roman Catholic. Club: Epping Garden. Home: PO Box 735 Epping NH 03042

JOYNER, MICHELLE DENISE, state program analyst; b. Bklyn., July 26, 1961; d. John Brown and Francine (Whittaker) Ifill; m. Barry Edward Joyner, July 26, 1986. AA, Sullivan County Community Coll., 1981; BS in Math., SUNY, Fredonia, 1983; student, Union Coll., 1987—. Planning analyst Bur. Research Planning/Evaluation State of N.Y., Albany, 1985—. Office: Bur Research Planning & Evaluation 194 Washington Ave Albany NY 12210

JOYNER, SUZANNE DIMASCIO, marketing executive; b. Phila., Dec. 2, 1942; d. Placido L. and Lillian G. (Smith) Mosca; m. Richard DiMascio, Dec. 26, 1963 (div. Nov. 1976); children: Christopher, Jeffrey; m. James H. Joyner III, Jan. 1, 1980; children: James IV, Gordon, Christopher, Richard, Jeffrey. RN; cert. nurse specialist in gerontology. Dir. nursing North Pa. Convalescent Home, Lansdale, 1976-78; clin. research assoc. Pharmacia, Piscataway, N.J., 1978-80, product mgr., 1980-85, sr. product mgr., 1985-86, group product dir., 1986-88; mktg. exec. Wyeth Internat. Co., Phila., 1988—, product mgr., 1988—. cons. nursing, 1977-79; cons. Thane Assocs., 1983-86. Author: (manual) Debrisan for Wound Care, 1977. Republican. Roman Catholic. Avocations: walking, swimming, aerobics. Home: 26 Solebury Mountain Rd New Hope PA 18938 Office: Wyeth Internat Co 150 Rodor Chester Rd Radnor PA 19101

JOYNER, SYLVIA PETTIS, fundraiser; b. Galveston, Tex., Sept. 12, 1946; d. Louis James Pettis and Florence Gloria Lawton Cody; B.A., Tuskegee Inst., 1968; 1 son, Michael Pettis. Social service advisor Prichard (Ala.) Housing Authority, 1973-74; community rep. McDonald's of Mobile (Ala.), 1974-76; nat. VISTA worker, VISTA Spl. Project, Fedn. So. Coops., Epes, Ala., 1978; area devel. dir. United Negro Coll. Fund, Inc., Birmingham,

Ala., 1978—. Bd. dirs. Vol. and Info. Center, 1980—, Birmingham Creative Dance Co., YWCA, Birmingham Festival of Arts; mem. Leadership Birmingham. Named one of Powers to Be under 40 award Birmingham Bus. Jour., 1985; recipient Community Leadership award Ala. Conf. Black Mayors, 1986. Mem. Ala. Soc. Fund Raising Execs. (pres. 1986-88, exec. com. 1980—, Outstanding Fundraiser award 1981), Nat. Soc. Fund Raising Execs. (bd. dirs.), Urban League, NAACP, Nat. Assn. Young Children, Nat. Soc. Fundraisers, Continental Socs. Am., Alpha Kappa Alpha (Omicron Omega chpt.).Club: The Links. Office: 310 18th St N Birmingham AL 35203

JOYNER-KERSEE, JACQUELINE, track and field athlete; b. East St. Louis, Ill., Mar. 3, 1962; d. Alfred Sr. and Mary Joyner; m. Bob Kersee, Jan. 11, 1986. Student, UCLA. Winner 4 consecutive Nat. Jr. Pentathlon Championships; winner heptathlon Goodwill Games, Moscow, 1986; winner heptathlon, world record of 7161 points U.S. Olympic Festival, 1986; winner USA/Mobil Outdoor Track and Field Championship, 1987; winner, long jump and heptathlon World Track and Field Championships, 1987. Recipient Sullivan award, 1987, Jesse Owens award, Am. Black Achievement award Ebony Mag., 1987; named Athlete of Yr. Track & Field News, 1986, Female Athlete of Yr. AP, 1987. Address: care Athletics Congress/USA PO Box 120 Indianapolis IN 46206 *

JUANPERE, NIEVES PAZO, business executive; b. Havana, Cuba, Aug. 5, 1955; came to U.S., 1963, naturalized, 1973; d. Raul Heriberto and Evangelina (Rodriguez) Pazo; m. Pedro A. Juanpere, June 27, 1981; children: Peter Andrew, Janelle Marie. Grad. Washington Sch. Secs., 1975. Sec., Am. Pharm. Soc., Washington, 1975; sec. to Congressman Rosenthal from N.Y., 1976; legis. asst. to Congressman Tom Foley, Washington, 1976-86; ptnr. Design Assocs., 1982-85; treas. Intec Group, Inc., Burke, Va., 1984—; with Goodfriend Temporaries Co., 1987—. Mem. campaign for Congressman Thomas S. Foley, 1988—. Roman Catholic. Club: Concord (N. Va.) (pres. 1974). Avocations: photography, gardening. Home: 10137 Walnut Wood Ct Burke VA 22015

JUARBE, NORA, communications professional; b. Canovanas, P.R., Nov. 4, 1960; d. Martin and Moncita (Ortiz) J. AS, City Coll. San Francisco, 1980; BA, San Francisco State U., 1983. Voucher examiner U.S. Army C.E., San Francisco, 1978-81; adminstrv. asst. Westana Publs., San Francisco, 1981; asst. dir. communications Bay Area Council, San Francisco, 1982-86; dir. communications Samuel Merritt Hosp., Oakland, Calif., 1987—; bd. dirs. Artists in Print, San Francisco. Mem. Soc. Profl. Journalists, Nat. Assn. Female Execs., Internat. Assn. Bus. Communicators (bd. dirs., treas. 1986—), San Francisco Soc. Prevention of Cruelty to Animals, Nat. Assn. of Deaf. Home: 554 Moultrie St San Francisco CA 94110 Office: Samuel Merritt Hosp Hawthorne Ave and Webster St Oakland CA 94609

JUDD, DOROTHY HEIPLE, educator; b. Oakwood, Ill., May 27, 1922; d. Eldridge Winfield and Mary Luciel (Oliphant) Heiple; B.A., Ind. U., 1944; M.Ed., U. Toledo, 1971; Ed.S., Troy State U., 1976; Ed.D., No. Ill. U., 1981; m. Robert Carpenter Judd, Sept. 19, 1964; children by previous marriage—Patricia Ann Konkoly, Catherine Rafferty, Deborah Brown, Nancy Lee Arrington; stepchildren—Dianna Kay Judd Carlisi, Nancy Carol Judd Wilber, Linda Judd Marinaccio Pucci. Head lang. arts dept. Eisenhower Jr. High Sch., Darien, Ill., 1961-70; instr. devel. edn. Owens Tech. Coll., Perrysburg, Ohio, 1971-73; instr. edn. Troy State U., Montgomery, Ala., also right-to-read coordinator State of Ala., 1975-76; core dept. chair Community Consol. Sch., Dist. 15, Palatine, Ill., 1977-79; asst. prof. curriculum and instrn. No. Ill. U., 1979-83; asst. prof. edn. Southeastern La. U., Hammond, 1984—; pres. R.C. Judd & Assos., Bloomingdale, Ill., 1980-86; pres. Edn. Tng. Service, Inc., Glandale Heights, Ill., 1986—. Mem. Assn. Supervision and Curriculum Devel., Assn. Tchr. Edn., Internat. Council Computers in Edn., Internat. Reading Assn., Nat. Council Social Studies, Nat. Council Tchrs. of English, Pi Lambda Theta, Phi Delta Kappa. Author: Mastering the Micro, 1984. Contbg. editor Ednl. Computer mag., 1981-84, Electronic Edn., 1984-87, Acad. Technology, 1987—; contbr. articles to profl. jours. Home: 1990 Flagstaff Ct Glendale Heights IL 60139

JUDD, PATRICIA HOFFMAN, social worker; b. Pitts., June 22, 1946; d. Joseph Andrew and Irene Patricia (Bednar) Hoffman; m. Lewis Lund Judd, Jan. 26, 1974. B.A., Marquette U., 1968; M.S.W., San Diego State U., 1970; doctoral candidate Calif. Sch. Profl. Psychology, 1983—. Dir. treatment services DEFY, Health Care Agy. of San Diego County, San Diego, 1973-75; coordinator emergency psychiat. services U. Calif. Med. Ctr., San Diego, 1975-77, mem. attending staff, 1975-85; clin. coordinator crisis and brief treatment service Gifford Mental Health Clinic, U. Calif.-San Diego, 1975-79, coordinator clin. services, 1979-82, asst. dir., 1983—; clin. instr. dept. psychiatry U. Calif.-San Diego Sch. Medicine, 1976—; field instr. Sch. Social Work, San Diego State U., 1970—, lectr., 1978-80; pvt. practice psychotherapy, San Diego, 1979—; mem. staff Chestnut Lodge Research Unit, Rockville, Md., 1988-90, asst. prof. Sch. of Social Work, U. Md., 1988-90. Mem. Nat. Assn. Social Workers, Acad. Cert. Social Workers, Soc. Clin. Social Workers. Office: 500 W Montgomery Ave Rockville MD 20850

JUDELL, CYNTHIA N., craft company executive; b. N.Y.C., Mar. 23, 1924; d. Luma L. and Stella E. (Robins) Kolburne; m. Samuel Judell, Oct. 30, 1949; children—Joy C., Neil H.K. B.S.E.E., Antioch Coll., Yellow Springs, Ohio, 1945; M.A., Columbia U., 1948. Cert. secondary tchr. Engr., Jet Propulsion Lab., Pasadena, Calif., 1946-47; tchr. math., sci. Leonard Sch. for Girls, N.Y.C., 1948-49; substitute tchr. Bd. Edn., Ridgefield, Conn., 1964-67; part-time tchr. Bd. Edn., Brookfield, Conn., 1967-73; ptnr. T W M Enterprises, Wilton, Conn., 1976—. Dep. registrar of voters Town of Wilton, 1977—; elected mem. Bd. of Tax Rev., Wilton, 1980-87; treas. Town Assn., Inc., Wilton, 1980-84. Recipient Intergroup scholar Columbia U., 1948. Mem. LWV (budget chair, treas. Conn. chpt. 1978-86, treas. Wilton chpt. 1986—), Conn. Soc. Women Engrs. (treas. 1971-72). Office: T W M Enterprises PO Box 266 Wilton CT 06897

JUDGE, LAURIE, psychiatric social worker; b. N.Y.C., Feb. 28, 1946; d. Jerome Edward and Ruth (Gerstenfeld) J.; children: Gabriel, Joshua, Benjamin. AA, Nassau Community Coll., 1965; BA, Am. Internat. Coll., 1967; MSW, Mich. State U., 1970; PhD, Case Western Reserve U., 1974. Psychiatric social worker Detroit Mental Health and Drug Treatment Ctr., 1970-72; intern, counselor, psychotherapist student devel. ctr. Case Western Reserve U., Cleve., 1972-75, instr. in sch. medicine clin. services dept., 1979-82, trainee in psychotherapy, 1983-84; dir. social services Parmadale Children's Village, Parma, Ohio, 1984-85; psychiatric social worker Kaiser Permanente Hosp., Cleve., 1985—; adv. faculty sch. applied social sci. Case Western Reserve U., Cleve., 1975; cons. community service dept., University Heights City Sch. Dist., Cleve., 1981-83; clin. counselor Cuyahoga Community Coll., Warrensville Twp., 1982—. Mem. Shaker Heights (Ohio) PTA, 1981—, Nat. Orgn. Women, Cleve., 1972—. Mellan Found. grantee, 1967-68; NIMH fellow, 1968-70. Mem. Am. Psychol. Assn., Nat. Assn. Social Workers, Am. Assn. Counseling and Devel., Ohio Soc. Clin. Social Work, Nat. Assn. Clin. Mental Health Counselors, Phi Alpha, Phi Lambda Theta. Club: Sierra.

JUDKINS, DOLORES ZEGAR, librarian; b. Portland, Oreg., Mar. 1, 1948; d. Frank John and Adeline Angela (Konieczny) Zegar; m. David Carl Judkins, Nov. 19, 1977; 1 child, Stephen Daniel. B.A., Portland State U., 1970; M.L.S., U. Oreg., 1973. Librarian Library Assn., Portland, Oreg., 1974-77; librarian Suffolk Coop. Library System, Bellport, N.Y., 1978-79, Good Samaritan Hosp., Portland, 1980-81; dental librarian Oreg. Health Scis. U., Portland, 1981—. Community organizer VISTA, Scottsbluff, Nebr., 1970-72. Served with Peace Corps, 1973-74. Community Coll. Libraries fellow, 1972. Mem. Med. Library Assn. (cert.), Oreg. Library Assn., Oreg. Health Scis. Libraries Assn. (pres. 1983). Office: Oreg Health Scis U Dental Library 611 SW Campus Dr Portland OR 97201

JUDSON, JEANNETTE ALEXANDER, artist; b. N.Y.C., Feb. 23, 1912; d. Philip George and Gertrude (Leichter) Alexander; m. Henry Judson, Sept. 23, 1945; children: S. Robert Weltz Jr., Pauline Raiff; 1 stepson, E. William Judson. Student, Columbia U., 1930-31, N.A.D., 1956-59, Art Student League, N.Y.C., 1959-61. One-man shows Fairleigh Dickinson U., 1965, Bodley Gallery, N.Y.C., 1967, 69, 71, 73, NYU, 1969, Pa. State U., 1969, Laura Musser Mus. Art, Muscatine, Iowa, 1969, Syracuse U. House, N.Y.C., 1975, Ludlow-Hyland Gallery, 1980, Key Gallery, N.Y.C., 1982; 2 person show, Am. Standard Gallery, 1980; exhibited in group shows, including: anns., Nat. Assn. Women Artists, N.Y.C., France, Italy, 1965—, Audubon Artists, N.Y.C., 1962, 64, 65-67, Allied Artists, N.Y.C., 1966-67, group show Key Gallery, N.Y.C., 1981, Key Gallery small works exhibit, 1983, NYU small works, N.Y.C., 1982; represented in permanent collections, Joseph H. Hirshhorn, N.Y. U., Norfolk (Va.) Mus. Arts and Scis., Brandeis U., Peabody Art Mus., Mus. N.Mex., Sheldon Swope Art Mus., Syracuse U., Evansville Mus. Arts and Scis., Rutgers U., Colby Coll., Butler Inst. Am. Art, Laura Musser Mus., Fordham U., Lehigh U., Ga. Mus. Art, U. Ga., Fairleigh Dickinson U., Lowe Mus., U. Miami, Washington County (Md.) Mus. Fine Arts, Miami Mus. Modern Art, Bruce Mus., Greenwich, Conn., Bklyn. Mus., Hudson River Mus., Dartmouth Coll. Mus., Columbia U., Art In Embassies program Dept. State, Am. embassy., Stockholm, Sweden and Sofia, Bulgaria, NYU Small Works Exhibit, 1984, also numerous pvt. collections. Mem. Nat. Assn. Women Artists (Grumbacher award 1967, Lillian Cottan award 1979, oil nominating com. 1977-79), Artists Equity N.Y., Art Students League (life), Am. Soc. Contemporary Artists (Dorothy Feigin award 1976, House of Heydenrick award 1977, Ralph Mayer Meml. award 1985). Home and Studio: 1130 Park Ave New York NY 10128

JUFFER, KRISTIN ANN, research analyst; b. Omaha, Mar. 2, 1947; d. Theodore Arnold and Adeline (Brinks) J.; m. Gregory Paul Awbrey, Jan. 26, 1985; 1 child, Michael John. BA, U. Nebr., 1969; MA, U. Iowa, 1979, PhD, 1983. Cert. tchr., supt., Iowa. Tchr., acting curriculum coordinator Cedar Rapids (Iowa) Pub. Schs., 1970-80; asst. prof. then assoc. prof. edn. Western Ill. U., Macomb, 1979-86, asst. dir. bilingual edn., 1979-84, adminstrv. asst. to v.p., 1983-84, researcher, 1984-86; program officer, acad. specialist USIA, Washington, 1985-86, research analyst Voice of Am., 1986-88, dir. audience research, 1988—; coordinator European Bus. Seminars, Tempe, Ariz., 1980-84; researcher, test devel. Iowa Testing Program, Iowa City, 1982-83; researcher, cons. U. Nebr., Lincoln, 1984-86; v.p. Am. Fedn. Tchrs., Cedar Rapids, 1973. Co-convenor Cedar Rapids Women's Caucus, 1970, Iowa Women's Polit. Caucus, 1972; pres. Iowa Dem. Women's Caucus, 1971. Mem. Soc. Intercultural Tng. Edn. and Research, Soc. Internat. Devel., Nat. Assn. Fgn. Student Affairs, Am. Assn. Pub. Opinion Research, Phi Delta Kappa. Office: USIA Voice of Am ML 400 6th St SW Washington DC 20547

JUILLERAT, FLORENCE LUCILLE, biology educator; b. Indpls., Oct. 1, 1940; d. James Abner and Florence Lucille (Serak) Burroughs; m. Paul Eugene Goodwin, June 9, 1962 (div. 1973); m. Monte Everett Juillerat, Feb. 10, 1973; children: Phil, Sheila. BS in Biology, Purdue U., 1962, MS in Biology, 1968, PhD in Biology, 1974. Cert. sci. tchr., Ind., N.Y.; cert. real estate broker, Ind.; cert. tng. cons. Sci. tchr. Huntington (N.Y.) Sch. Dist. #3, 1962-63, Great Neck (N.Y.) Pub. Schs., 1963-64, Washington Twp. Pub. Schs., Indpls., 1964-66; biology instr. Indiana U. Purdue U. at Indpls., 1966-74, asst. prof. biology, women's studies, 1974-85, adj. assoc. prof. women's studies, 1985—, assoc. prof. biology, 1985—; biology tchr. Jakarta (Indonesia) Internat. Sch., 1978-79, mem. sch. bd., 1978-79; guest investigator USN Med. Research Unit, Jakarta, 1979-80; speaker on internat. topics to civic groups, Inpls., 1980—; cons. Ind. Dept. Edn. Gifted and Talented Program, 1984—; mem. long range planning com. Women's Studies Program, Ind. U. Purdue U. at Indpls., 1984—; organizer, moderator Women's Studies Forum, 1985—. Author: (books) Study Guide for Contemporary Biology, 1978 (Nat. Univ. Extension Assn. award 1979), Study Guide for the Biology of Women, 1987, (lab manual) Zoology: A Laboratory Manual, 1984; editor: Contemporary Biology: Readings and Conversations, 1984. Bd. dirs. Boone County YMCA, Lebanon, Ind., 1975-76. Fulbright-Hays grantee, 1985. Mem. Nat. Women's Studies Assn., Nat. Sci. Tchrs. Assn. (internat. and pubs. coms.), Nat. Biology Tchrs. Assn. (sec. com. Role and Status of Women, 1984—), Hoosier Assn. Sci. Tchrs. (newsletter editor, 1985-87, v.p., pres. elect 1987—), Purdue Alumni Club (sec. 1985—), Mortar Bd. Republican. Methodist. Club: Boone County Home Econs. (sec. 1984-86). Office: Ind U Purdue U at Indpls 425 N Agnes St Indianapolis IN 46202

JULIAN, ELEANOR SUSAN, mortgage company executive; b. N.Y.C., Feb. 19, 1958; d. Joseph Jack and Paula Dorothy (Mirsky) Cynamon; m. John F. Hennessey, Apr. 21, 1985 (div.); m. Nicholas J. Julian, Feb 14, 1988. BA in Psychology, Framingham State Coll., 1981. Customer service rep. The Gamewell Corp., Medway, Mass., 1982-84, sales application engr., 1984-85; customer service rep. Home Nat. Mortgage Corp., Milford, Mass., 1986-87; homemaker Framingham, 1988—; customer service rep. Franklin Chiropractic, Mass., 1987—. Republican. Jewish. Office: Home Nat Mortgage Corp 258 Main St PO Box 40 Milford MA 01757

JULIANO, PATRICIA, city official; b. E. Orange, N.J., Dec. 8, 1930; d. John and Mildred (Petoia) Tricoli; A.S., Essex County Coll., 1975; B.A., Rutgers U., 1980; m. Carmen Juliano, May 10, 1952; children—John, Frank, Carmen, Angelo, Kathy, Michael, Joseph. Tchrs. aide Oakwood Ave. Sch., Orange, N.J., 1973-75; mem. Orange City Council, 1976—. Pres., PTA, Orange, 1960-61; v.p. Essex County Council PTA, 1963-65; vol. N.J. Assn. Retarded Children, 1965—; sec. to Parents of Orange PAL, 1962; co-founder Parents' Groups for Exceptional Children, 1975—, Orange Parents of Exceptional Children, 1978; mem. Community Service Council, United Way, 1976-84; lobbyist for better edn. for exceptional children; bd. dirs. Orange Child Devel. Corp., 1976-84; mem. Essex County Community Action Bd., 1980-85, Orange Planning Bd., 1984—; mem. governing bd. Community Mental Health Center, Region II, 1982—; mem. adv. bd. Women in Support of Essex County Coll., mem. Nat. Park Found.; co-ordinator Central Jersey Telephone Bank, Floria for Gov., N.J. Dem. Com., 1981; Orange chmn. Mother's March, March of Dimes Found., 1982. Recipient Outstanding Vol. award Community Services Council of United Way, 1977; Achievement award Essex council N.J. State Civil Service Assn., 1982, Outstanding Alumni award Essex County Coll., 1983. Mem. N.J. League of Municipalities (legis. com. 1980—), N.J. Assn. Elected Women Ofcls. (co-founder 1981, treas. 1982-84), Orange Planning Bd. Essex County Community Devel. Block Grant Program, Econ. Devel. Corp. (bd. dirs.), Orange LWV, Am. Mus. Natural History, Smithsonian Inst. (assoc.), N.J. Fedn. Dem. Women, Rutgers U. Alumni Assn. Roman Catholic. Lodge: Soroptomist Internat. (Essex County). Home: 390 Tremont Pl Orange NJ 07050 Office: 29 N Day St Orange NJ 07050

JULIFS, SANDRA JEAN, community action agency executive; b. Jersey City, July 12, 1939; d. Roy Howard and Irma Margrete (Barkhausen) Walters; m. Harold William Julifs, July 22, 1961; children: David Howard, Steven William. BA, U. Va., 1961; postgrad., U. Minn., 1962-63, Mankato State Coll., 1963. Tchr. St. James (Minn.) Pub. Schs., 1961-62; substitute tchr. Sleepy Eye (Minn.) Pub. Schs., 1963-67, home bound tutor, 1967; lay reader, rater U. Wis., Stevens Point, 1968; co-founder Family Planning Service Portage County, Stevens Point, 1970-72; family planning dir. Tri-County Opportunities Council, Rock Falls, Ill., 1971-77, energy programs coordinator, 1977-78, planner, EEO officer, 1978-83, exec. dir., chief exec. officer, 1983—; bd. dirs., sec. Ill. Ventures for Community Action, Springfield, 1983—. Mem. Nat. Community Action Found., Washington, 1987—. Recipient Appreciation award Western Ill. Agy. on Aging, 1980, 81, Spl. Recognition award Ill. Head Start and Day Care Assn., Recognition award Ill. Community Action Fund, 1984. Mem. AAUW, Am. Soc. Pub. Adminstrn., Nat. Assn. Female Execs., Whiteside County Welfare Assn. (chair 1986-87), Lee County Welfare Assn. (sec.-treas. 1983-84), Nat. Community Action Assn., Ill. Assn. Community Action Agys. (com. chair 1985-88, dir. exec. com. 1986—, treas. 1988, Recognition award 1985, 86, 87, 88). Lutheran. Office: Tri-County Opportunities Council 405 Emmons Ave PO Box 610 Rock Falls IL 61071

JUNG, DORIS, dramatic soprano; b. Centralia, Ill., Jan. 5, 1924; d. John Jay and May (Middleton) Crittenden; m. Felix Popper, Nov. 3, 1951; 1 son, Richard Dorian. Ed., U. Ill., Mannes Coll. Music, Vienna Acad. Performing Arts; student of, Julius Cohen, Emma Zador, Luise Helletsgruber, Winifred Cecil. Debut as Vitellia in: Clemenza di Tito, Zurich (Switzerland) Opera, 1955, other appearances with, Hamburg State Opera, Munich State Opera, Vienna State Opera, Royal Opera Copenhagen, Royal Opera Stockholm, Marseille and Strasbourg, France, Naples (Italy) Opera Co., Catania (Italy) Opera Co., N.Y.C. Opera, Met. Opera, also in Mpls., Portland, Oreg., Washington and Aspen, Colo.; soloist: Wagner concert conducted by Leopold Stokowski, 1971; with, Syracuse (N.Y.) Symphony, 1981, voice tchr., N.Y.C., 1970—. Home: 40 W 84 St New York NY 10024

JUNG, LADONNA, physician; b. N.Y.C., Oct. 30, 1960; d. George S. and Kay (Han) Chung. BA magna cum laude, Columbia U., N.Y.C., 1982; MD, NYU, 1987. Research asst. dept. neurology UCLA, 1980-81, Harvard U., Boston, 1982; tchr. chemistry St. Ann's Sch., Brooklyn Heights, N.Y., 1982-83; resident in internal medicine Lenox Hill Hosp., N.Y.C., 1987-88; resident in radiation oncology Hosp. of U. Pa., Phila., 1988—. Marine Biol. Lab. scholar, 1981. Mem. AMA, Med. Soc. State N.Y. Presbyterian. Home: 2400 Chestnut St Apt 2104 Philadelphia PA 19103 Office: Hosp U Pa Dept Radiation Oncology 3400 Spruce St Philadelphia PA 19104-4283

JUNG, LYNNETTE CLAIR, social worker, military officer; b. Billings, Mont., Aug. 7, 1940; d. Joseph Leopold Jung and Margaret Lucille (Keefe) Friedl. BA, Coll. of St. Catherine, St. Paul, 1961; MSW, U. Utah, 1965. Psychiat. social worker Calif. Dept. Mental Hygiene, Pomona, 1965-68; staff devel. and foster care cons. Colo. State Social Services, Denver, 1968-73; team chief family planning program Monterey County Dept. Social Services, Salinas, 1973-74; commd. capt. USAF, 1974, advanced through grades to lt. col., 1987; psychiat. social worker Malcolm Grow USAF Med. Ctr., Washington, 1974-79; team chief human devel. program Lowry AFB, Denver, 1979-81, dir. human devel. program, 1981-82; chief mental health clinic USAF Hosp., Osan Air Base, Korea, 1982-83, Clark Air Base, The Philippines, 1983-85; chief social services USAF Clinic Randolph AFB, San Antonio, 1985; chmn. dept. social work Wilford Hall USAF Med. Ctr., Lackland AFB, San Antonio, 1985—. Mem. Juvenile Parole Bd., Denver, 1968-72. Fellow Am. Orthopsychiat. Assn.; mem. Nat. Assn. Social Workers (steering com. 1986—, chmn. San Antonio unit 1987—), Am. Group Psychotherapy Assn., Am. Assn. Sex Educators, Counselors and Therapists, Tex. Hosp. Assn., Tex. Soc. Clin. Social Workers, San Antonio Hosp. Social Worker Dir.'s Assn., Soc. Sci. Study of Sex, Bus. and Profl. Women's Assn., Family Service Assn. (adv. bd. 1986—), Pi Gamma Mu. Avocations: raising orchids and African violets, travel, golf, reading. Home: 9003 Peuplier San Antonio TX 78250 Office: Wilford Hall USAF Med Ctr SGHMW Lackland AFB TX 78236

JUNGBLUTH, CONNIE CARLSON, investment banker; b. Cheyenne, Wyo., June 20, 1955; d. Charles Marion and Janice Yvonne (Keldsen) Carlson; m. Kirk E. Jungbluth, Feb. 5, 1977; 1 child, Tyler. BS, Colo. State U., 1976. CPA, Colo. Sr. acct. Rhode Scripter & Assoc., Boulder, Colo., 1977-81; mng. acct. Arthur Young, Denver, 1981-85; asst. v.p. Dain Bosworth, Denver, 1985-87, George K. Baum & Assocs., Denver, 1987—; bd. dirs. Security Diamond Exchange, Denver. mem. Denver Estate Planning Council, 1981-85, organizer Little People Am., Rocky Mountain Med. Clinic and Symposium, Denver, 1986; adv. bd. Children's Home Health, Denver, 1986—; fin. adv. bd. Gail Shoettler for State Treas., Denver, 1986; bd. advisors U. Denver Sch. Accountancy, 1986—; campaign chmn. Kathi Williams for Colo. State Legis., 1986. Named one of 50 to watch Denver Mag., 1988. Mem. Colo. Soc. CPA's (instr. bank 1983, trustee 1984-87, pres. bd. trustees, 1986-87, bd. dirs. 1987—, chmn. strategic planning com. 1987—, Pub. Service award 1985-87, chmn. career edn. com. 1982-83), Am. Inst. CPA's, Colo. Mcpl. Bond Dealers, MetroNorth C. of C. (bd. dirs. 1987—), Pi Beta Phi. Club: Denver City (bd. dirs. 1987-88). Office: George K Baum & Co 17th St Suite 2800 Denver CO 80293

JUNKER, CHRISTINE ROSETTA, food products executive; b. Burlington, Iowa, June 10, 1953; d. Roland Lee and Janet Elaine (Kapotas) Wiemann; m. Theodore Henry Junker, Mar. 10, 1977; 1 child, Nolan Robert. Assocs. of Animal Sci., Hawkeye Inst. Tech., 1977; student, U. No. Iowa, 1984-85. Drafstman Confinement Specialists, Mediapolis, Iowa, 1973-75; herdsman X-L Pork, Cedar Falls, Iowa, 1976-77; livestock specialist Tasco, Inc., Shell Rock, Iowa, 1977-81; problem accounts specialist I.F.G. Leasing, Parkersburg, Iowa, 1981-86; pres. Pork Purveyors, Ltd., Parkersburg, 1986—; adv. com. mem. Animal Sci. Dept. Hawkeye Inst. Tech., Waterloo, Iowa, 1988. Contbr. articles to profl. jours. Mediator Iowa Farmer/Creditor Mediation Service, 1987-88. Named Outstanding Alumni All Agrl. Club, Hawkeye Inst. Tech, 1979. Mem. Iowa Pork Producers. Home and Office: Pork Purveyors Ltd Rural Rt 2 Box 100 Parkersburg IA 50665

JUNKMAN, JACALYN MARIE, physical education educator; b. Ft. Dodge, Iowa, Nov. 23, 1953; d. Earl Willis and Rose Marie (Krebs) J. BA, Tarkio (Mo.) Coll., 1977; MS in Edn., Baylor U., 1979. Recreation counselor Devereux Found., Victoria, Tex., 1975-78; asst. volleyball and basketball coach Baylor U., Waco, Tex., 1978-79; head women's basketball coach, instr. San Jacinto Coll. N., Houston, 1979—; sponsor Gator Assn., Houston, 1983—. Mem. Tex. Assn. Health, Phys. Edn., Recreation and Dance, Tex. Jr. Coll. Tchrs. Assn., Tex. Assn. Basketball Coaches, Phi Beta Kappa. Democrat. Lutheran. Office: San Jacinto Coll 5800 Uvalde Houston TX 77049

JURACEK, ARLENE ADAMS, utilities executive; b. Chgo., Aug. 13, 1950; d. Stephen H. and Apolonia Mary (Juszkiewicz) Adams; m. Edward John Juracek, June 16, 1974; children: Grant Edward, Andrea Lynn, Robert Adam. BS in Mech. and Aerospace Engring., Ill. Inst. Tech., 1972; M in Mgmt., Northwestern U., 1976. Registered profl. engr., Ill. Engr. Commonwealth Edison, Chgo., 1972-75, mktg. rep., 1975-76, mktg. engr., 1976-77, dist. staff asst., 1977-78, rate research analyst, 1978-81, supr. mkt. research, 1981-82, supr. load forecasting and analysis, 1982-86, dir. strategic analysis, 1986—. Mem. Am. Soc. Mech. Engrs., Nat. Assn. Bus. Economists, Chgo. Assn. Bus. Economists (Gross Nat. Product Forecasting award 1986), Internat. Assn. Energy Economists, Chgo. Energy Economists (v.p. 1985-86, pres. 1986-87). Roman Catholic. Office: Commonwealth Edison Co PO Box 767 Chicago IL 60690

JURGENSEN, LAURA J., programmer analyst; b. Madison, Wis., Mar. 2, 1962; d. Wayne Henry and Marjorie Ann (Swiggum) J. A in Data Processing, We. Wis. Tech. Inst., 1983; BS in Mgmt., Upper Iowa U., 1987. Analyst adminstrv. support CUNA Mut. Ins. Group, Madison, 1983-87, computer support analyst, 1987—. Mem. Wis. Nuclear Weapons Freeze Campaign, Madison, 1986—. Mem. Nat. Assn. Female Execs. Democrat. Lutheran.

JURZYKOWSKI, MILENA CHRISTINE, film producer; b. N.Y.C., Sept. 25, 1949; d. Alfred and Milena J.; B.A., Boston U., 1968. Prodn. mgr., editor Nat. Assn. Broadcast Employees and Technicians, N.Y.C., 1973-76, editor, 1976-80; pres., exec. producer Cinetudes Film Prodns., Ltd., N.Y.C., 1976—; founder Atelier Cinema Video Stages and Cinetudes Cable Programming Assocs. Producer feature film No Big Deal, 1983. Mem. N.Y. Women in Communications, Nat. Assn. Broadcast Employees and Technicians, Internat. Indsl. TV Assn., Assn. Ind. Film and Video Makers, Info. Film Producers Am., Soc. Motion Picture and TV Engrs., N.Y. Women in Film. Office: 295 W 4th St New York NY 10014

JUST, FAYE JORDAN, antique restoration co. exec.; b. Carthage, Miss., June 6, 1925; d. Neadham Guice and Ethel (Doude) Jordan; student UCLA, 1943-62, U. So. Calif., 1950-52; A.A. in M.E., Pierce Coll., 1965; B.S. in B.A. and Math., U. Calif., Northridge, 1969; m. Virgil Louis Just, May 2, 1970; children—Babetta, Sandra, Audrey. Loftswoman/flying wing Northrope Aircraft, Hawthorne, Calif., 1943-45; with Rockwell Internat., Los Angeles and Canoga Park, Calif., 1947-70, sr. research engr. rocket engines, to 1970; Co-owner Just Marine Engring., 1972-77, Just Enterprises, Ventura, Calif., 1977—. Office: Just Enterprises 2790 Sherwin Ave #10 Ventura CA 93003

JUST, GEMMA R., advertising executive; b. N.Y.C., Nov. 29, 1921; d. Philip and Brigida (Consolo) Rivoli; B.A., Hunter Coll., N.Y.C., 1943; m. Victor Just, Jan. 29, 1955. Copy group head McCann Erickson, N.Y.C., 1958-62; copy. supr. Morse Internat., N.Y.C., 1962-67; v.p., dir. creative services Deltakos div. J. Walter Thompson, N.Y.C., 1967-75; v.p., copy dir. Sudler & Hennessey, div. Young & Rubicam, N.Y.C., 1980-87; sr. v.p., assoc. creative dir. copy, 1987—. Mem. Women of St. Bartholomew's Episcopal Ch., also ch. altar guild. Named Best Writer, Art Dirs. Club N.Y., 1979, Best Writer Young & Rubicam, 1981; recipient Aesulapius awards

Modern Medicine mag., 1980, 86. Mem. Council Communications Svcs., Pharm. Advt. Council, Am. Med. Writers Assn. (exec. com. 1973). Home: 155 E 38th St Apt 5D New York NY 10016 Office: 1633 Broadway New York NY 10019

JUSTESEN, EVELYN O(LGA), principal, deputy mayor; b. Phila., Aug. 17, 1925; d. Henry and Hjördis Marie (Rüüd) Sörensen; m. Roy Clifford Justesen, Dec. 18, 1920; children: Roy Jr., Linda, Jeffrey, Nancy, Susan. BA, William Paterson Coll., 1963; MEd, Harvard U., 1968. Tchr. gifted and talented Pequannock (N.J.) Sch. Dist., 1963-67, 80-83, 85-86, sci. tchr., 1967-80, prin., 1983-85, 86—; chair fairplay Morris County Council of Edn., Denville, N.J., 1972-75. Mem. council Pequannock Township, 1980—, mayor, 1984-85, dep. mayor, 86-87. Mem. NEA (del. 1973-74), Prin. and Supr. Assn., N.J. Edn. Assn., N.J. Fedn. Elected Women Officials, Pequannock Twp. Edn. Assn. (pres. 1970-71), Phi Delta Kappa. Republican. Home: 52 Madison Ave Pequannock NJ 07440 Office: Pequannock Sch Dist Oak Ave Pequannock NJ 07440

JUSTICE, DOROTHY DOBBS, food equipment manufacturing company executive; b. Woodstock, Ga., Apr. 13, 1932; d. Eugene Tiller and Bertha (Roe) Dobbs; m. Lester Joseph Justice, June 10, 1950. Student Marsh Bus. Coll., Atlanta, 1948-49. Office mgr. Norris Candy Co., Atlanta, 1964-68; exec. asst. Cornelius Co., Atlanta, 1968-70; v.p. adminstrn. Remarco, Atlanta, 1970-73; v.p. Refresco Internat., Atlanta, 1973-82, pres., chief exec. officer, 1982—; dir. Modular Engring. Corp., Atlanta. Pres. Mountain Park Homeowners Assn., Stone Mountain, Ga., 1984—. Mem. Nat. Assn. Food Equipment Mfrs. Democrat. Baptist. Clubs: Big Canoe Golf and Tennis (Ga.); Stone Mountain Garden, Stone Mountain Women's. Avocations: interior decorating; flower arranging. Home: 1524 Carlton Ave Stone Mountain GA 30087 Office: Refresco Internat Corp PO Box 1748 Stone Mountain GA 30086

JUSTICE, SUSANNE DOROTHY, medical administrator; b. Flushing, N.Y., Aug. 28, 1942; d. Edward H. and Dorothy E. (Scholl) Lane; m. M.M.T. Justice (dec. Apr. 1980); children: Edward P., Jennifer L.; m. Frank J. Moran, May 18, 1984. Diploma Jackson Meml. Hosp. Sch. Nursing, 1963. R.N., Fla. Group nurse Mt. Saini Hosp., Miami Beach, Fla., 1963-66; part-time group nurse, 1967-72; head nurse Jackson Meml. Hosp., Miami, 1966-67; hosp. coordinator, head coordinator Fla. Home Health Services, Miami, 1972-73; hosp. coordinator, assoc. dir. nursing Unicare, Inc., Miami, 1973-75; pres., adminstr. Medi-Health of Fla., Inc., Ft. Lauderdale, 1975—; cons. in field. Author: Problem Oriented Records for Home Health Agencies; mem. editorial adv. bd. Caring mag., 1983-84; contbg. author: Quality Assurance Workbook, 1978, 83. Mem. Nat. Assn. Women Bus. Owners, Fla. Assn. Home Health Agys. (v.p. 1981-83, pres. 1983-85, chmn. liasion com. 1985—, bd. dirs. 1978-86, 87-88, M.T. Terry Justice Meml. award 1980), So. Fla. In Home Services Consortium (pres. 1981-83), Am. Acad. Med. Adminstrs. (sec.-treas. Fla. chpt. 1983-84, pres. 1985-86, Hardie Lord award 1986, Nat. Disting. Service 1986), Nat. Assn. Home Care (dir. 1982). Lutheran. Home: 2027 NE 121 Rd North Miami FL 33181 Office: Medi-Health of Fla Inc 2331 N State Rd 7 Suite 107 Fort Lauderdale FL 33313

JUVELIS, PRISCILLA CATHERINE, antiquarian bookseller; b. Newark, Sept. 2, 1945; d. Steven and Odelite (Canning) Juvelis. B.A., Boston U., 1967. Dir. internat. dept. Harcourt Brace Jovanovich Internat. Corp., N.Y.C., 1971-76; rights dir. The Franklin Library, N.Y.C., 1976-78; owner, pres. Priscilla Juvelis, Inc., Boston, 1980—. Mem. exec. com. Save Venice, Inc., Boston. Editor, pub.: The Book Beautiful and The Binding as Art, 1983, vols. 1 and 2. Mem. Antiquarian Bookseller's Assn. Am., Mass. and R.I. Bookseller's Assn. (sec. 1983-84, v.p. 1984-86, pres. 1986-88), The Manuscript Soc. (trustee 1987-88). Office: 150 Huntington Ave Boston MA 02115

JUZAK, TATANIA, psychologist; b. Willamantic, Conn.; d. Pafnuty and Constance (Krenichyn) Juszczak. BS in Edn., Willimantic State Tchrs. Coll., 1942; MA in Child Psychology, U. Minn., 1944; PhD in Psychology, NYU, 1953. Diplomate in Clin. Psychology, Lic. psychologist, N.Y., Conn. Psychologist Kings County Hosp., Bklyn., 1946-49; sr. psychologist Bellevue Hosp., N.Y.C., 1953-59; chief psychologist New Rochelle (N.Y.) Guidance Ctr., 1959-60, Westchester County Med. Ctr., Valhalla, N.Y., 1960-86; asst. prof. psychiatry N.Y. Med. Coll., Valhalla, 1972—; cons. psychologist N.Y. State Office Vocat. Rehab., 1972—, Cen. Harlem Med. Ctr., 1986—. Contbr. articles to profl. jours.

JWAIDEH, DARA NARMEEN, banker; b. Washington, Dec. 27, 1955; d. Wadie and Alice Mary (Reid) J. BA in Human Biology, Stanford U., 1977; MBA in Gen. Mgmt., Harvard U., 1980. Asst. buyer, dept. asst. mgr. Emporium-Capwell, Oakland, Calif., 1977-78; project mgr. Crocker Nat. Bank, San Francisco, 1980-82, ops. officer, asst. v.p., 1982-84; asst. v.p. Wells Fargo Bank, San Francisco, 1984-86, v.p., group planning officer, 1986-87, v.p., mgr. br. automation, 1987-88, v.p., mgr. account mgmt. credit card div., 1988—. Cons. Bus. Vols. for Arts, San Francisco, 1984-85. Home: 128 Spring Rd Orinda CA 94563 Office: Wells Fargo Bank 1220 Concord Ave (0314-052) Concord CA 94163

KAANAANA, BONNIE JEAN, personnel executive; b. Cheyenne, Wyo., Feb. 2, 1941; d. Wilfred James Tucker and Beatrice Louise (Wake) Turner; m. Ronald Gary Kaanaana (div.); 1 child, Shawna Lee. Grad. high sch., Aurora, Ill. Sec., personnel asst. Island Holidays, Ltd. subs. Amfac Co., Honolulu, 1969-72, mgr. personnel and benefit plans, 1972-73, employee relations dir., 1973-81, v.p. employee relations, 1981-84; mgr. adminstrv. and personnel services The Estate of James Campbell, Honolulu, 1984—. Vol. Hospice-Hawaii, 1986—. Mem. Am. Soc. Personnel Adminstrs. (bd. dirs. Hawaii br.). Home: 1621 Dole St Apt #607 Honolulu HI 96822 Office: Estate of James Campbell 828 Fort Street Mall Honolulu HI 96813

KAAP, LINDA JEAN, sales executive; b. Green Bay, Wis., Mar. 24, 1962; d. John Paul and Jean Audrey (Koeppe) K.; m. Gregory Eugene Cook, Nov. 7, 1980 (div. 1981). Med. asst. cert., Mt. Scenario, 1980; student, U. Wis., Milw., 1980-82; sales, mktg. cert., Cardinal Stritch Coll., 1982, student, 1986-87. Sales coordinator Packaging Sales, Inc., Butler, Wis., 1982-84; resident trainer Revlon, Inc., Milw., 1984, account mgr., 1984-87; account mgr. Revlon, Inc., Gwynedd Valley, Pa., 1987—; trainer devel. trainer Mount Mary Coll., Wauwatosa, Wis., 1984-85. Mem. Nat. Assn. Female Execs. Republican. Assembly of God. Home and Office: 1357 Gypsy Hill Box 596 Gwynedd Valley PA 19437

KABACK, ELAINE, career counselor-consultant; b. Phila., Feb. 22, 1939; d. Sol and Evelyn Zitman; student Pa. State U., 1956-58; B.A., Temple U., 1960; M.S., Calif. State U., 1977; children—Douglas, Stephen, Michelle. Tchr. English, Sayre Jr. High Sch., Phila. Public Schs., 1960-62; tchr. English and history Beth Tfiloh Pvt. Day Sch., Balt., 1968-72; mgmt. cons., trainer Sandra Winston Assos., Palos Verdes, Calif., 1975—; counselor Career Planning Ctr. and Mid-Life Ctr., Long Beach City Coll., 1977-78, instr. in assertion tng. coll. extension; dir. program devel. Univance Career Ctrs., Inc., Los Angeles, 1978-80; pvt. practice career counseling, 1980—; coordinator career transition program, trainer/presenter UCLA Extension; cons. in career systems and outplacement. Pres. Palos Verdes chpt. NOW, 1974-76, chairperson, lectr. Speaker's Bur., 1977—; treas. S.W. chpt. Nat. Women's Polit. Caucus, 1973, 78; bd. dirs. STEP Adult Edn. Programs, Palos Verdes, 1974—, cert. community coll. life counselor, Calif.; cert. tchr., Pa. Mem. Calif. Counseling and Devel., Am. Soc. Tng. and Devel., Am. Assn. Counseling and Devel., Phi Kappa Phi. Office: 24222 Hawthorne Blvd Suite B Torrance CA 90505 also: 924 Westwood Blvd Suite 850 Westwood CA 90024

KABAT, SYRTILLER DÉLORES MCCOLLUM, psychologist; b. Tampa, June 18, 1937; d. Theodore and Katie (McCoy) McCollum; m. Lucien Kabat, July 16, 1965; children: Luke, Michael (adopted), Soon Yun Kwon (adopted). BA, Montclair State Coll., 1960; MA in Psychol., Wright Inst., 1972, PhD, 1975. Cert. tchr. N.J., Calif.; licensed counselor Calif., Mo. Asst. prof. counseling San Jose (Calif.) St. U., 1972-79; prof. John. F. Kennedy U., Orinda, Calif., 1974-83; instr. U. Mo., Kansas City, 1984-86; private practice psychol. Kansas City, 1984—; bd. dirs. Miramonte Mental Health Services; pres. Shekinah Found. Contbr. articles to profl. jours. Bd. dirs. Ravenswood Sch. Dist., Palo Alto, Calif., 1967-75, Lee's Summit Housing Bd., Adolescent Resource Com., Kansas City; Mem. Calif. Assn. Marriage and Family Therapists (v.p.), Am. Assn. Counseling and Devel. Home: 410 SE Independence Ave Lee's Summit MO 63064 Office: 120 SE Second St Suite 106 Lee's Summit MO 64063

KABATT, DIANE LOUISE, marketing and sales manager; b. Harrisburg, Pa., Sept. 3, 1952; d. Frank John Jr. and Nancy Jane (Kapp) Tezak; m. Daniel John Kabatt, Aug. 6, 1982. BS, Messiah Coll., 1973. Food service dir. M.W. Wood Co., Allentown, Pa., 1976-79; regional sales mgr. Rustco Products, Denver, Pa., 1980-84; mktg. mgr., nat. accounts sales mgr., new products mgr. Knouse Foods, Inc., Peach Glen, Pa., 1984—. Republican. Home: 555 S 3d St Lemoyne PA 17043 Office: Knouse Foods Inc Peach Glen PA 17306

KABRIEL, MARCIA GAIL, psychotherapist; b. El Reno, Okla., Jan. 8, 1938; d. Gail Frederick and Katherine (Marsh) Slaughter; m. J. Ronald Kabriel, May 25, 1957 (div. Sept. 1985); children—Joseph Charles, Jeffrey Gail, Jae B. BA, U. Okla., 1965, MSW, 1968; postgrad. Am. U. Psychiat. social worker Dept. Mental Hygiene, N.Y.C., 1968-69; psychiat. social worker Washington Hosp. Ctr., 1970-72, assoc. mem. dept. psychiatry, 1972-75, sr. psychotherapist Counseling Ctr., 1972-75; psychotherapist Md. Inst. Pastoral Counseling, Annapolis, Md., 1972—; chief dept. social services Washington Hosp. Ctr., 1979-82, cons. spl. projects, 1974-82; supr. continuing protective services State Md., 1983—; exec. v.p. Kent Island Transport, Inc., 1985—; field instr. Cath. U., Washington, 1973-75, U. Md., 1976-87. Mem. Nat. Assn. Social Workers, Acad. Cert. Social Workers. Democrat. Presbyterian. Home: 1416 Regent St Annapolis MD 21403 Office: 104 Forbes St Suite F Annapolis MD 21404

KACIR, BARBARA BRATTIN, lawyer; b. Buffalo, Ohio, July 19, 1941; d. William James and Jean (Harrington) Brattin; m. Charles Stephen Kacir, June 3, 1973 (div. Aug. 1977). BA, Wellesley Coll., 1963; JD, U. Mich., 1967. Bar: Ohio 1967, D.C. 1980. Assoc. Arter & Hadden, Cleve., 1967-74, ptnr., 1974-79; ptnr. Jones, Day, Reavis & Pogue, Washington, 1980-83, Cleve., 1983—; instr. trial tactics Case-Western Res. U., Cleve., 1976-79; legal representative for Warner Bros., Twentieth-Century Fox, MGM/UA, Universal, Orion, De Laurentis, Columbia, Buena Vista, Paramount, Tri-Star in Ohio litigation. Mem. nat. com. visitors, nat. fund raising com. U. Mich. Mem. ABA, Ohio Bar Assn., D.C. Bar Assn., Cleve. Bar Assn. (trustee 1973-76, treas. 1978-79), Assn. Trial Lawyers Am., Am. Law Inst., Def. Research Inst. Republican. Office: Jones Day Reavis & Pogue 901 Lakeside Ave North Point Cleveland OH 44114

KACLIK, DEBI LOUISE, construction executive; b. Pitts., May 15, 1953; d. John G. and Dolores J. (Grekalskis) K. BA, West Liberty State Coll., 1975; cert. in computer aided drafting and design, Pitts. Tech. Inst., 1982. Program dir. YMCA, Pitts., 1975-78; regional supr. United Republic Life Ins. Co., Harrisburg, Pa., 1977-80; phys. therapy asst. The Verland Found., Pitts., 1980-81; estimator, mgr. PPS Enterprises, Inc., Pitts., 1981-83; mgr. Wild Sisters Restaurant, Inc., Pitts., 1983-84; v.p., project mgr. Kreisle Bros. Masonry, Ltd., Georgetown, S.C., 1984-85; owner, ptnr., constrn. mgr. Mastco Masonry/Steel, Georgetown, 1986-87; owner, pres. The Brick People, Inc., Surfside Beach, S.C., 1988—; presenter news spl. Sta. KDKA-TV, Pitts., 1977; guest speaker Sta. WTAE-TV, Pitts., 1978, Sta. WBTW-TV, Myrtle Beach, S.C., 1987. Instr. water safety, first aid and disaster shelters ARC, Myrtle Beach and Pitts., 1969-85; coordinator regional and internat. Cerebral Palsy Games, Pitts., 1981; bd. dirs. North Am. Riding for the Handicapped, Pitts., 1982; team coordinating asst. nat. telethon teamwalk Am. March of Dimes, Myrtle Beach, 1986-88. Mem. Am. Assn. Subcontractors, U.S. Sidewinder Assn. Democrat. Roman Catholic. Home: 28 Bay Dr Salters Cove Murrells Inlet SC 29576 Office: The Brick People Inc South Point Exec Offices Suite 114 1012 16th Ave NW Surfside Beach SC 29575

KADAH, DIANNE, computer graphics administrator; b. Syracuse, N.Y., Feb. 8, 1957; d. Hassan Bedri and Ann Marie (Tylka) K. BFA, Syracuse U., 1979. Computer graphics designer Genigraphics Corp., Chgo., 1979-80; regional trainer Genigraphics Corp., Chgo. and N.Y.C., 1980-83; adminstr. computer graphics dept. Philip Morris, Inc., N.Y.C., 1983-88; active N.Y.C. Commn. on Status of Women, 1984-87; mem. steering com. Philip Morris Women's Adv. Com., 1984-86. Mem. Nat. Computer Graphics Assn. (pres. N.Y.C. chpt. 1986—, judge animation competition 1987), Assn. Computing Machinery Siggraph Assn. (bd. dirs. 1986—), Am. Women's Econ. Devel. Home: 235 Adams St Apt 3 Brooklyn NY 11201

KADEC, SARAH THOMAS, information management consultant, retired government official; b. Winchester, Va., Dec. 15, 1932; d. Lemuel and Mary (Switzer) Thomas; m. Mark Mania Kadec, July 27, 1975. B.A., Madison Coll., 1952; M.L.S., Carnegie Library Sch., 1961. Acquisitions librarian Engr. Research and Devel. Labs., Fort Belvoir, Va., 1952-53; librarian Jeter Jr. High Sch., Covington, Va., 1953-55, J.H. Russell Elem. Sch., Quantico, Va., 1955-57; ref. librarian Def. Atomic Support Agy., Washington, 1975-60; ref. asst. Carnegie Library, Pitts., 1960-61; chief librarian Fairchild Library, Fairchild Stratos Corp., Hagerstown, Md., 1961-63; librarian Booz Allen Applied Research, Bethesda, Md., 1963-66; head reader's services Applied Physics Lab., Johns Hopkins U., Silver Spring Md., 1966-67; lectr., dir. continuing edn. U. Md., College Park, 1967-69; cons. in library and info. sci. Ctr. Sci. and Tech. Info., Tel Aviv, 1969-70; vis. lectr. Hebrew U. Sch. Library Sci., Jerusalem, 1970; librarian Commn. on Govt. Procurement, Washington, 1970-71; lectr. Cath. U. Am., Washington, 1971-75; chief library systems br. EPA, Washington, 1971-78; adj. lectr. U. Md. Sch. Library and Info. Services, College Park, 1972-74; dir. info. mgmt. and services div. Office Adminstrn., Exec. Office of Pres., Washington, 1978-79; dep. dir. Office of Adminstrn., 1979-81; mem. sci. and edn. mgmt. staff U.S. Dept. Agr., Washington, from 1982; dir. library program service Supt. U.S. Govt. Printing Office, 1982; dir. info. mgmt. and services div. EPA, Washington, 1983-84, dep. dir. Office Info. Resources Mgmt., 1984-85; info. mgmt. cons., 1985—; lectr. in field. Contbr. articles to profl. jours. Mem. numerous adv. bds., com. memberships including Environ. Scis. Adv. Com., Washington Tech. Inst., Library of Congress. Div. Blind and Physically Handicapped, Fed. Library Com., Fed. Energy Adminstrn. Library Bd., Fed. Library Networking; bd. dirs. Soc. Library and Info. Technicians, 1973-74. Mem. Spl. Libraries Assn. (assoc. editor documentation div. 1967-68), Am. Soc. Info. Sci., Assoc. Info. Mgrs. Presbyterian. Home: 2833 Gunarette Way Silver Spring MD 20906 Office: PO Box Silver Spring MD 20906

KADILAK, DEBORAH W., sales executive; b. San Francisco, June 18, 1959; d. Neil S. III and Marilyn A. (Augustine) Williamson; m. Stephen A. Kadilak Jr., Oct. 24, 1982; children: Megan Elizabeth, Stephan A. III. AAS, No. Va. Community Coll., 1979. Merchandiser Almay Cosmetics (subs. Esmark Corp.), N.Y.C., 1981-82, ter. mgr., 1982-84, key account mgr., 1984; nat. account mgr. Almay Cosmetics (subs. Playtex Corp.), N.Y.C., 1984-85; key account mgr. Charles of the Ritz Ltd. (div. Squibb Corp.), N.Y.C., 1985-87, Revlon Fragrance Group, N.Y.C., 1988—. Roman Catholic. Office: Revlon 767 Madison Ave New York NY 10019

KADISH, ROSALYN SUNA, lawyer; b. N.Y.C., July 3, 1942; d. Harry and Helen Mae (Buchsbaum) Suna; divorced; children: Ellen Grace Schlossberg, Richard Mark Schlossberg. AB, Clark U., 1963; JD magna cum laude, Woodrow Wilson Coll. Law, 1980. Bar: Ga. 1980, U.S. Ct. Appeals (11th cir.) 1984. Assoc., Kadish, Davis & Brofman, Atlanta, 1980-83; ptnr. Kadish & Kadish, P.C., Atlanta, 1983-85; legal asst. Ct. Appeals for State of Ga., 1986—; asst. to editor Kluwer Law Book Pubs., Inc., 1985—. Contbr. articles, chpts. to profl. pubs.; co-author: The Successful Defense of Narcotics Cases, 2 vols., 1985. Recipient Am. Jurisprudence awards, 1980. Mem. ABA, Ga. Bar Assn., Assn. Trial Lawyers Am., Nat. Assn. Criminal Def. Lawyers, Ga. Trial Lawyers Assn., Ga. Assn. Criminal Def. Lawyers, Atlanta Bar Assn. Democrat. Jewish. Club: Confrerie de la Chaine des Rotisseurs (charge de press 1983—).

KAEL, PAULINE, author, film critic; b. Petaluma, Calif., June 19, 1919; d. Isaac Paul and Judith (Friedman) K.; 1 child, Gina James. Student, U. Calif., Berkeley, 1936-40; LLD (hon.), Georgetown U., 1972; D. Arts and Letters (hon.), Columbia Coll., Chgo., 1972; LittD (hon.), Smith Coll., 1973, Allegheny Coll., 1979; LHD (hon.), Kalamazoo Coll., 1973, Reed Coll., 1975, Haverford Coll., 1975; DFA (hon.), Sch. Visual Arts, N.Y.C., 1980. Movie critic New Yorker mag., 1968—. Author: I Lost it at the Movies, 1965, Kiss Kiss Bang Bang, 1968, Going Steady, 1970, Deeper into Movies, 1973 (Nat. Book award 1974), Reeling, 1976, When the Lights Go Down, 1980, 5001 Nights at the Movies, 1982, Taking It All In, 1984, State of the Art, 1985; contbg. author: The Citizen Kane Book, 1971; contbr. to numerous other mags. Recipient George Polk Meml. award, 1970, Front Page award Newswomen's Club N.Y., 1974, 83; Guggenheim fellow, 1964. Mem. Phi Beta Kappa (hon.). Office: care The New Yorker 25 W 43d St New York NY 10036

KAELIN, JEANNETTE JILL, account executive; b. Springfield, Ohio, Aug. 1, 1956; d. William Jacob and Rosemary Jeanne (Slagle) Stoll; m. William Adelrich Kaelin, Oct. 6, 1979. BA in Communications, U. Colo., 1978. Collegiate cons. Gamma Phi Beta Internat. Sorority, Denver, 1978-79; account exec. Sta. KGWA/KUAL-FM, Enid, Okla., 1979-82; sales mgr. Sta. KPSA-AM-FM, Alamogordo, N.Mex., 1983-87; account exec. Sta. KVOR, Colorado Springs, Colo., 1987-88; sr. account exec. Sta. KRDO-AM-FM, Colorado Springs, 1988—; cons. Gamma Phi Beta, Denver, 1980—. Recipient Top Gun award Alamogordo C. of C., 1986; named one of Outstanding Young Women Am., 1979, 85, 86. Mem. Am. Bus. Women's Assn. (pres. 1981-82), Am. Women in Radio/TV. Club: Jr. Women's (Alamogordo) (Outstanding Mem. award 1986). Lodge: Soroptimist (bd. dirs.). Office: Sta KRDO-AM-FM PO 1457 Colorado Springs CO 80901

KAGAN, JULIA LEE, magazine editor; b. Nurnberg, Fed. Republic Germany, Nov. 25, 1948; d. Saul and Elizabeth J. (Koblenzer) K. A.B., Bryn Mawr Coll., 1970. Researcher Look Mag., N.Y.C., 1970-71; editorial asst., asst. editor McCall's Mag., N.Y.C., 1971-74, assoc. editor, 1974-78, sr. editor, 1978-79; articles editor Working Woman mag., N.Y.C., 1979-85, exec. editor, 1985—. Co-author: Manworks: A Guide to Style, 1980; contbg. author: The Working Woman Success Book, 1981, The Working Woman Report, 1984. Pres. Appleby Found., N.Y.C., 1982-84; bd. dirs. Women's Counseling Project, N.Y.C., 1983-87; chmn. selection com. Alumnae Assn. Bryn Mawr Coll. Recipient 2d Ann. Advt. Journalism award Compton Advt., 1983. Mem. Am. Soc. Mag. Editors, Am. Soc. Pub. Opinion Researchers. Club: Princeton (N.Y.C.). Home: 523 W 121st St Apt 42 New York NY 10027 Office: Working Woman 342 Madison Ave New York NY 10173

KAGAN, MARCIA PESSIN, social worker; b. Hartford, Conn., Jan. 4, 1922; d. Israel George and Gussie Elizabeth (Marcus) Pessin; A.A., Hillyer Coll., 1943; B.A., U. Miami, 1947; M.S.W., U. Conn., 1969; m. Nathaniel D. Kagan, May 9, 1948; children—Larry H., Jeffrey M. With Dept. Children and Youth, Conn. State Dept. Welfare, Hartford and Torrington, 1947-74, program supr., 1969-74; sr. staff social worker Hartford Rehab. Center, 1974-80; pvt. practice social work, West Hartford, Conn., 1980-85, 1987—; Licensed social worker, Conn., 1986. social work cons. Vis. Nurse and Home Care, East Hartford, Conn., 1985-86; freelance social worker Nurses Registry, 1986—. Bd. dirs. CAC 18, North Central Regional Mental Health Bd., 1979-82, Capital Region chpt. Mental Health Assn., 1980-82, Sunshine Group, Inc., 1980-82; trustee sisterhood Temple Beth Israel, 1982-83, mem. social action com., 1985—; mem. consumer adv. bd. Div. Vocat. Rehab., 1982-83; mediation counselor Better Bus. Bur., 1985—. Mem. Nat. Assn. Social Workers, Acad. Cert. Social Workers, Conn. Assn. Human Services, Social Action com. Beth Israel. Democrat. Jewish. Club: B'nai B'rith (v.p. 1964-65). Home and Office: 43 Whitehill Dr West Hartford CT 06117

KAGAWA, KATHLEEN HATSUYO, entrepreneur; b. Honolulu, June 9, 1952; d. Shinso and Jane Fumiko (Murata) K.; m. Masamichi Irimajiri (div. 1977). Student, U. Hawaii, Honolulu, 1970-73, Sophia U., Tokyo, 1973; BSBA, U. Beverly Hills, 1977, MBA, 1979, PhD in Internat. Bus., 1982. Mgr. Flipside Record Shop, Honolulu, 1969-70; producer, singer Victor Records, Tokyo, 1973-76; actress Hawaii Five-O, Honolulu, 1976; co-owner Images Internat. of Hawaii, Honolulu, 1976-79; v.p., sec., hostess East-West Connection TV Show, Los Angeles, 1980-81; dir. pub. relations Fendi, Beverly Hills, 1981-82; pres. Sky Prodns., Inc., Honolulu, 1982-86; adminstrv. exec. New Tokyo-Hi Restaurants, Honolulu, 1983—; v.p., treas. Born Internat., Inc., Honolulu, 1986—; cons. Schlossberg-Cassidy and Assoc., Washington, 1983-86, Yamada Group, Japan and U.S.A., 1987—; sponsor State of Hawaii Nat. Aquaculture Assn., Washington, 1983-86; admissions counselor U. Beverly Hills, Honolulu, 1984-86; adminstrv. exec., corp. sec. New Tokyo-Hawaii Restaurant Co. Ltd., 1981—; pres. K & H Devel. Co., Ltd. Sponsors State of Hawaii Nat. Aquaculture Assoc., Washington, 1983-86. Named Best in Backstroke, State of Hawaii Swim Competition, 1968. Mem. Gemological Inst. Am. Alumni Assn., Japan-Am. Soc. of Honolulu, Honolulu Bd. Realtors, Mortgage Broker Assn., Pacific and Asian Affairs Council, Internat. Ladies Benevolent Assn., Punahou Alumni Assn. Baptist. Club: Oahu Country (Hawaii). Home: 3215 Kaohinani Dr Honolulu HI 96817

KAGEY, F(LORENCE) EILEEN, educator; b. Lima, Ohio, July 29, 1925; d. Joseph Leonard and Florence Elizabeth (Niles) K.; B.S. in Edn., Ball State U., 1952; M.S. in Edn., Ind. U., 1955. Sec., Gen. Electric Co., Ft. Wayne, Ind., 1943-45, 48-49, Farnsworth Telephone and Radio Corp., Ft. Wayne, 1945-48; H.A. Jeep prof. Ball State U., 1949-52; elem. tchr. Harmar Sch., Ft. Wayne, 1952-54, Emerson Sch., Gary, Ind., 1954-58, Sch. 52, Indpls., 1959-61, George Kuny Sch., Gary, 1961—; sec. to v.p. Research and Rev. Service of Am., Indpls., 1958-59. Chmn. public relations Calumet Corner chpt. Sweet Adelines, Inc., Munster, Ind., 1980-82, mem., 1977—, bd. dirs., 1981-82. Mem. NEA (life), Am. Fedn. Tchrs. (bldg. rep. Local 4 1979—), Ind. State Tchrs. Assn., Assn. Supervision and Curriculum Devel., Ind. Assn. Supervision and Curriculum Devel., AAUW (v.p. in-charge program), Kappa Delta Pi. Democrat. Roman Catholic. Author: (juvenile) Jeremy: the People-Dog, 1974. Home: 3040 W 39th Pl Gary IN 46408 Office: 5050 Vermont St Gary IN 46409

KAHIN, AUDREY RICHEY, editor; b. Newcastle Upon Tyne, Eng., May 18, 1934; came to U.S., 1963; d. Charles Joseph and Florence (Anderson) Richey; m. George McTurnan Kahin, Mar. 8, 1967. BA, Nottingham (Eng.) U., 1955; MA, Cornell U., 1975, PhD, 1979. Editorial asst. Longmans, Green & Co., London, 1956-58; tchr. Scuola Interpreti, Bergamo, Italy, 1958-60; interviewer Cen. Office Info., London, 1961-63; adminstr., research aide Cornell Modern Indonesia Project, Ithaca, N.Y., 1963-66, co-editor, mng. editor, editor S.E. Asia program, 1979—. Co-editor: (book) Interpreting Indonesian Politics, 1982; editor: Regional Dynamics, 1985; translator: (monograph) Prisoners at Kota Cane, 1986; contbr. articles to profl. jours. Recipient Assn. South East Asian Nations award Fulbright, 1985; fellow Nat. Def. Fgn. Language, Cornell U., 1973-75, Fulbright fellow, 1975-76; postdoctoral fellow Social Sci. Research Council, 1981. Mem. LWV, Assn. Asian Studies, Soc. Scholary Pub. Democrat. Roman Catholic. Office: Cornell Modern Indonesia Project 102 West Ave Ithaca NY 14850

KAHKEJIAN, DEBORAH CAROL, management information specialist; b. Schenectady, N.Y., June 14, 1957; d. Arthur Joseph and Evelyn Angeline (DeMarco) K.; m. Cary A. Fassler, June 20, 1987. AS in Mgmt., Onandaga Community Coll., Syracuse, N.Y., 1982; BS in Mgmt., Syracuse U., 1985; MS in Mgmt. Info. Systems, Clarkson U., Potsdam, N.Y., 1986. Project analyst Young & Franklin, Liverpool, N.Y., 1985; field support specialist Merchant's Ins. Co., Syracuse, 1986-87; program evaluation specialist Hutchings Psychiat. Ctr., Syracuse, 1987—. Vol. Rosemary Pooler for Congress, Syracuse, 1986. Democrat. Club: Syracuse Microcomputer.

KAHM, VALERIE SARAH, college administrator; b. Phila., Oct. 2, 1952; d. Sarah Champlin; m. Daniel R. Kahm, Sept. 20, 1975. BA magna cum laude, Brockport State U., N.Y., 1974; MEd, Elmira Coll., 1981. Cert. tchr., N.Y., N.J., Calif. Tchr. Sch. Dists., Elmira, Corning and Allamuchy, N.Y., 1974-80; with Elmira Coll., 1980, successively staff asst., asst. to dir. evening programs, asst. dean continuing edn., acting dean continuing edn., acting dir. career planning and placement, dir. career planning and placement, lectr. in writing, communications and lit., 1980—; dir. adult programs, services Ithaca (N.Y.) Coll., 1987—; pvt. human resource cons., 1987—. Contbr. articles to profl. jours.; editor continuing edn. and career planning and placement newsletters. Com. mem. Council for aging, Elmira, 1983-85, Friends Soc. Prevention Cruelty to Animals, Chemung County, N.Y., 1980—; mem. pub. relations com. Am. Cancer Soc., Elmira, 1984-85; core com. Image Group County/VCommunity Pub. Relations, Chemung County, 1987—; mem. task force Women in Transition Cope House, Elmira, 1985—; bd. dirs. Career devel. Council, Chemung, Stueben and Schuyler Counties, 1985—. Mem. Mid Atlantic Placement Assn. (task force pub. and community services subcom.), Career Placement Council, Nat. Assn. Female Execs., Cen. N.Y. Career Consortium (bd. dirs.), Am. Council on Edn. (nat. identification program subcom.), Assn. for Continuing Higher Edn., Ithaca Personnel Assn. Office: Ithaca Coll Danby Rd Ithaca NY 14901

KAHN, ARLENE JUDY MILLER, nurse, educator; b. Chgo., Dec. 16, 1940; d. Fred and Sophie (Schelbe) Miller; R.N., A.B., U. Ill., Chgo., 1963, M.S. in Nursing, 1970; Ed.D., U. San Francisco, 1986; m. Roy M. Kahn, Oct. 25, 1968; 1 child, Jennifer M. Head nurse psychiat. unit Grant Hosp., Chgo., 1966; supervising nurse Ill. Psychiat. Inst., Chgo., 1967; instr. psychiat. nursing Calif. State U., San Francisco, 1968-70; mem. faculty Calif. State U., Hayward, 1974—, assoc. prof. nursing, 1980-86, prof., 1986—; cons. in field. Research grantee Calif. State U., Hayward, 1980-81. Fellow Am. Assn. Psychiat. Nursing; mem. United Profs. Calif., Calif. Nursing Assn., Bay Area Nursing Diagnosis Assn. (officer 1986—), Sigma Theta Tau. Author articles in field. Home: 95 Sonia St Oakland CA 94618 Office: Hayward State U Sch Sci Hayward CA 94542

KAHN, BLOSSOM, motion picture executive; b. N.Y.C., Aug. 16, 1936; d. Jules Franklin and Anita Beatrice (Arkin) K.; B.A. in English, Hofstra Coll., Hempstead, N.Y., 1958; postgrad. Columbia U. Sch. Journalism, N.Y.C. Exec., story dept. Universal Pictures Corp., N.Y.C., 1963-64; head motion picture, TV and play depts. Curtis Brown Lit. Agy., N.Y.C., 1964-68; pres. Kahn-Penney Lit. Agy., Los Angeles, 1968-77; dir. creative affairs First Artists Prodns., Los Angeles, 1977-78; exec. in charge creative projects Avco-Embassy Pictures, Los Angeles, 1978-82; v.p. prodn. Zupnick Curtis Enterprises, Inc., Los Angeles, 1982-83; v.p. West Coast Packaging & Devel., Polymuse, Inc., 1983—; lectr. Sherwood Oaks Coll., Marymount Coll., Los Angeles. Mem. Women in Film, Women in Communication, Inc. Office: 208 S Beverly Dr Beverly Hills CA 90212

KAHN, DEBORAH JEAN, advertising executive; b. Pitts., Oct. 21, 1957; d. Robert Warren and Dorothy Jean (Kohn) Kahn. B.A., Grove City Coll., 1979. With Thompson, Matelan & Hawbaker, Inc., Pitts., 1979-82, asst. account exec., 1979-81, account exec., 1981-82; mgr. media and prodn. account exec. Tandem Inc., Pitts., 1982-83; mgr. advt., promotion, mktg. and merchandising Total Communication Systems, Pitts., 1984-86; mktg. communications mgr. Marc Advt., Pitts., 1986—. Mem. Mademoiselle Mag.'s Career Bd., 1979—. Mem. Pitts. Ad. club (v.p. programming 1986-87, v.p. activities 1987-88, bd. dirs. 1988—), Grove City Coll. Alumni Council. Republican. Presbyterian. Club: University.

KAHN, FAITH-HOPE, nurse, adminstrator, writer; b. N.Y.C., Apr. 25, 1921; d. Leon and Hazel (Cook) Green; RN, Beth Israel Med. Center, N.Y.C., 1942; student N.Y. U., 1943; m. Edward Kahn, May 29, 1942; children: Ellen Leora, Faith Hope II, Paula Amy. First scrub operating room Beth Israel Hosp., N.Y.C., 1942; supr., operating room Hunts Point Gen. Hosp., 1942; gynecol. reconstrn. procedures researcher Phoenixville (Pa.) Gen. Hosp., 1943, Sydenham Hosp., N.Y.C., 1945; supr. ARC Disaster Field Hosp., Queens, N.Y., 1950-51; adminstr., mgr. team coordinator Dr. Edward Kahn, FACOG, Queens Village, N.Y., 1945—. Inventor, publicity chmn. Girl Scouts U.S.A., 1953; exec. dir. publicity Woodhull Schs., 1956-60, pres., 1961-62; exec. dir. publicity N.Y. Dept. Parks Figure Skating, 1956-70; exec. dir. publicity and applied arts St. John's Hosp., Smithtown, N.Y., 1965-66; state advisor N.Y., U.S. Congressional Adv. Bd., Washington, 1981—; nat. adv. bd. Am. Security Council, 1978—; founder Am. Security Found.; bd. trustees, Am. Police Hall of Fame and Mus., 1983—; mem. Republican Presdl. Task Force, 1986, Statue of Liberty and Ellis Island Centennial Commn., N.Y., 1986—. Recipient citation ARC, 1951, Am. Law Enforcement Officers Assn., Bronze medal Am. Security Council Ednl. Found., 1978, spl. recognition award Center Internat. Security Studies, 1979, Meml. Plate, Patriots of Am. Bicentennial, 1976, Great Seal of U.S.A. Plate, cert. Am. Sons Liberty, 1987, Good Smaritan award, 1987, Justice award Cross of Knights, 1987 Knights of Justice award, 1987; named Knight Chevalier Venerable Order of Michael the Archangel, 1987. Fellow, World Lit. Acad. (life), Acad. Nat. Law Enforcement (hon.); mem. Am. Acad. Ambulatory Nursing Adminstrn., Nurses Assn., Nat. League Nursing, Am. Coll. Obstetricians and Gynecologists, Nat. Assn. Physicians' Nurses, Nat. Critical Care Inst., Assn. Operating Room Nurses, AAAS, Nat. Assn. Female Execs., N.Y. Acad. Scis., Am. Police Acad. (cert. appreciation 1979, 83), Am. Fedn. Police, The Retired Officers Assn., Internat. Platform Assn., Security and Intelligence Found. (cert. appreciation 1986), Internat. Intelligence and Orgnd. Crime Investigators Assn., Smithtown Hist. Soc., Nat. Audubon Soc., NRA. Clubs: Tiyospaye, Paul Revere, Sterlingshire Woman's. Author, editor: The Easy Driving Way for Automatic and the Standard Shift, 1954; (with Edward Kahn) The Pelvic Examination, Outline and Guide for Residents, Internes and Students, 1954; (with Edward Kahn) Traction Hysterosalpingography for Uterine Lesions, 1949; contbr. articles profl. and lay jours. Home: 213 16 85th Ave Hollis Hills NY 11427-1324 Office: 213 16 85th Ave QueensVillage NY 11427

KAHN, FLORENCE LEVITT, writer; b. Balt.; d. Joseph and Annie (Arnstein) Levitt; widowed, 1966. BS, Johns Hopkins U., 1940; postgrad., NYU, 1942, U. Mex., Mexico City, 1944. Cert. secondary tchr., Md. Tchr. social studies various secondary schs., Balt., 1930-50; pvt. tchr. painting Miami Beach, Fla., 1968-78; with Earthwise Publs., Miami, Fla., 1978—, staff writer, 1984—. Contbr. column in newspaper and review; poetry published in mags. and anthologies. Mem. Friends of Bass Mus., Miami Beach, Friends of Miami Dade Library. Mem. Nat. League Am. Pen Women (Biennial award 1984, 88), Fla. State Poetry Soc. (treas. local chpt. 1982-84, sec. 1984—). Home: 2301 Collins Ave #323A Miami Beach FL 33139 Office: Earthwise Publs PO Box 680-536 Miami FL 33168

KAHN, JULIANNA B., financial analyst; b. Chgo., Aug. 17, 1953; d. Leroy Hirschfield and Esther (Levine) Blumenthal; B.S. in Acctg., U. Ill., Urbana, 1975; m. Frederick J. Kahn, Sept. 6, 1981; children: Matthew Alexander, Jeremy Chagall. Auditor, B. L. Rosenberg & Co., Chgo., 1975-76; acct. Bankers Life & Casualty Co., Chgo., 1977-78, fin. analyst, 1978-81; prin. fin. analyst Chgo. Bd. Edn., 1981—. C.P.A., Ill. Home: 5354 Suffield Ct Skokie IL 60077

KAHN, KATHY, writer, photographer; b. Seattle, Apr. 2, 1945; d. Robert Arthur Moody and Donna (Green) Kelly; children: Simon Peter, Jesse MacDougall. Author: Hillbilly Women, 1973 (Mademoiselle Woman of the Yr. 1974); Fruits of Our Labor (NEH grant 1981), 1982. Playwright: The Contest, 1983. Contbr. articles and photographs to internat. mags.; photographic exhbns. Seattle, N.Y.C., Moscow, Leningrad. Mem. PEN. Home: 151 1st Ave #4R New York NY 10003 Office: 1609 1st Ave Studio 305 Seattle WA 98101

KAHN, LESLIE RUTH, service executive; b. N.Y.C., Jan. 15, 1947; d. Murrey and Florence (Marine) Kahn; divorced; 1 child, Steven Craig; m. John Schwartz. AAS, N.Y. Tech. Coll., N.Y.C., 1972; BA, CUNY, 1981. Adminstr. coll. dentistry NYU, N.Y.C., 1967-71; dental hygienist Dr. Steven S. Baron, DDS, Rego Park, N.Y., 1974-79; office mgr. Dr. Jerome Levine, DDS, N.Y.C., 1973-74; dental hygienist Dr. Steven S. Baron, DDS, Rego Park, N.Y., 1974-78; pres. Craig Med. and Dental Personnel Agy., Inc., N.Y.C., 1980—; adj. lectr. CUNY Med. Assts. Sch., 1981, Greater N.Y. Dental Meeting, 1980-86; cons. in field. Mem. N.Y. State Dental Hygiene Soc. (hons.), Fla. State Dental Hygienist Soc., Fla. Dental Soc. Office: Craig Personnel Agy Inc 25 W 43d St Suite 1510 New York NY 10036

KAHN, LINDA MCCLURE, maritime industry executive; b. Jacksonville, Fla.; d. George Calvin and Myrtice Louise (Boggs) McClure; m. Paul Markham Kahn, May 20, 1968. B.S. with high honors, U. Fla.; M.S., U. Mich., 1964. Actuarial trainee N.Y. Life Ins. Co., N.Y.C., 1964-66, actuarial asst., 1966-69, asst. actuary, 1969-71; v.p., actuary US Life Ins., Pasadena, Calif., 1972-74; mgr. Coopers & Lybrand, Los Angeles, 1974-76, sr. cons., San Francisco, 1976-82; dir. program mgmt. Pacific Maritime Assn., San Francisco, 1982—. Sec.-Bd. dirs. Pacific Heights Residents Assn., sec.-treas., 1981; trustee ILWU-PMA Welfare Plan, SIU-PD-PMA Pension and Supplemental Benefits Plans, Seafarers Med. Ctr., others. Fellow Soc. Actuaries, Conf. Actuaries in Pub. Practice; mem. Internat. Actuarial Assn., Internat. Assn. Cons. Actuaries, Actuarial Studies Non-Life Ins., Am. Acad. Actuaries, Western Pension Conf. (newsletter editor 1983-85, sec. 1985—), Actuarial Club Pacific States, San Francisco Actuarial Club (pres. 1981). Clubs: Metropolitan Soroptimist (v.p. 1973-74), Commonwealth. Home: 2430 Pacific Ave San Francisco CA 94115 Office: Pacific Maritime Assn 635 Sacramento St San Francisco CA 94111

KAHN, SUSAN BETH, artist; b. N.Y.C., Aug. 26, 1924; d. Jesse B. and Jenny Carol (Peshkin) Cohen; m. Joseph Kahn, Sept. 15, 1946 (dec.); m. Richard Rosenkranz, Feb. 1, 1981. Grad., Parsons Sch. Design, 1945; pupil, Moses Soyer, 1950-57. Subject of: book Susan Kahn, with an essay by Lincoln Rothschild, 1980; One-man shows, Sagittarius Gallery, 1960, A.C.A., Galleries, 1964, 68, 71, 76, 80, Charles B. Goddard Art Center, Ardmore, Okla., 1973, Albrecht Gallery Mus. Art, St. Joseph, Mo., 1974, N.Y. Cultural Center, N.Y.C., 1974, St. Peter's Coll., Jersey City, 1978; exhibited in group shows, Audubon Artists, N.Y.C., Nat. Acad., N.Y.C., Springfield (Mass.) Mus., City Center, N.Y.C., A.C.A., Galleries, N.Y.C., Nat. Arts Club, N.Y.C., Butler Inst., Youngstown, Ohio; represented in permanent collections, Tyler (Tex.) Mus., St. Lawrence U. Mus., Canton, N.Y., Fairleigh Dickinson U. Mus., Rutherford, N.J., Syracuse U. Mus., Sheldon Swope Gallery, Terre Haute, Ind., Montclair (N.J.) Mus. Fine Arts, Butler Inst. Am. Art, Youngstown, Ohio, Reading (Pa.) Mus., Albrecht Gallery Mus. Art, St. Joseph(Mo.), Cedar Rapids (Iowa) Art Center, N.Y. Cultural Center, N.Y.C., Edwin A. Ulrich Mus., Wichita, Kans., Wichita State U., Johns Hopkins Sch. Advanced Internat. Studies, Washington, Joslyn Mus., Omaha, U. Wyo., Laramie. Recipient Knickerbocker prize for best religious painting, 1956; Edith Lehman award Nat. Assn. Women Artists, 1958; Simmons award, 1961; Knickerbocker Artists award, 1961; Nat. Arts Club award, 1967; Knickerbocker Medal of Honor, 1964; Famous Artists Sch. award, 1967. Mem. Nat. Assn. Women Artists (Anne Barnett Meml. prize 1981), Artists Equity, Met. Mus., Mus. Modern Art, Nat. Assn. Women Artists (meml. award 1987).

KAICHEN, LISA M., association executive; b. South Bend, Ind., Feb. 19, 1951; d. John A. and Elizabeth (McGuire) K. BA, U. Detroit, 1972; MSW, U. Mich., 1975. Project coordinator Applied Social Research Project, Birmingham, Mich., 1974-75; exec. dir. The Sanctuary Runaway Program, Pleasant Ridge, Mich., 1975-80; instr. Wayne State U., Detroit, 1977-83; interim dir. Mich. Children's Trust Fund, Lansing, Mich., 1984; exec. dir. Children's Charter of the Courts of Mich., Lansing, 1980—; mem. Juvenile Justice Commn., State of Mich., 1985—; cons. in field. Contbr. articles to profl. jours.; author manuals: Citizen Advisory Councils, 1981, Applied Social Research, 1975, Guidelines for Assessing Parenting Capacities in Child Abuse Cases with Special Reference to Mentally Ill or Retarded Parents, 1986. Office: Children's Charter of Cts 115 W Allegan #500 Lansing MI 48933

KAIL, JO ANN FRESHOUR, media executive; b. Memphis, Sept. 29, 1948; d. Pershing Hall and Mattie Pearl (Bolding) Freshour; m. Raymond Riley Kail, Apr. 13, 1962 (div. Jan. 1979); children: Anthony Keith, Michael Sean, Laura Kathleen. BS in Edn., Memphis State U., 1972, postgrad., 1976. Tchr. Memphis City Schs., 1972-81; dir. mktg. Care Inns, Inc., Memphis, 1981-83; mgr. mktg. Beverly Enterprises, Pasadena, Calif., 1983-84; v.p. Milton Q. Ford & Assocs., Inc., Memphis, 1984—. Mem. Am. Women in Radio and TV, Nat. Assn. Broadcasters, Nat. Assn. Media Brokers (sec. 1987—). Democrat. Roman Catholic. Office: Milton Q Ford & Assocs Inc 5050 Poplar Ave Suite 1135 Memphis TN 38157

KAILO, ANDREA ILENE, managing editor; b. N.Y.C., Sept. 2, 1948; d. Norman Nathan and Marilyn Ruth (Waldman) K.; m. Gary J. Gerber, Aug. 23, 1970 (div. May 1977). BA, Douglass Coll., 1970. Adminstrv. asst. to senate pres. Ill. State Senate, Chgo., 1970, U. Saskatchewan, Saskatoon, 1970-73; research asst., editor Sci. Council Can., Ottawa, Ont., 1974-76; sr. editor Systems Cons., Inc., Washington, 1976-78; editor, dir. pub. affairs Nat. Conf. State Legislatures, Washington, 1978-83; dir. communications Nat. Council for Urban Econ. Devel., 1983-87; mng. editor Optical Soc. Am., 1987—. Author: (with others) Implications of the Changing Age Structure of the Canadian Population, 1976; contbd. articles to profl. jours. Pres. Arena Stage Angels, Washington, 1982-84. Mem. Women in Communications, Inc. (pres. D.C. chpt. 1988—). Democrat. Jewish. Home: 2316 N Nottingham St Arlington VA 22205 Office: Optical Soc Am 1816 Jefferson NW Washington DC 20036

KAINER, DEBORAH MARIE, accountant; b. Welmar, Tex., Sept. 18, 1955; d. George R. and Ethel M. (Drozd) K.; m. Kenneth A. Ripper, July 6, 1974; 1 child, Stephen A. BBA-Acctg., U. Houston, 1983. CPA, Tex. Legal asst. Childs, Fortenbach, Beck & Guyton, Houston, 1974-78, Sullivan, Bailey, King, Randall & Sabom, Houston, 1978-79; staff acct. Peat, Marwick, Mitchell & Co., Houston, 1983-84; sr. tax acct. Kares & Cihlar, Houston, 1984-86; supr. tax acct. Laventhol & Horwath, Houston, 1986-87; fin. v.p. Entry Control Systems Co., Houston, 1987-88; pvt. practice acctg. Houston, 1988—; bd. dirs. Access Security, Inc., Houston; mem. partnership com. Entry Control Systems Co., Houston. Sec., mem. exec. com., bd. dirs. Spring Shadows Civic Assn., Houston. Mem. Am. Inst. of CPAs, Tex. Soc. CPAs, Spring Br. Meml. City Tax Forum. Republican. Roman Catholic. Home: 2735 Kenross Houston TX 77043

KAISER, JOYCE ANN, government official; b. Jersey City, Aug. 30, 1939; d. Frederick and Louise (Feary) Neebling; m. Gordon Allen Biddle, Sept. 21, 1963 (div. 1974); 1 dau., Adrienne Louise; m. Dennis Lee Kaiser, June 5, 1975 (div. Dec. 1983); m. Burt S. Barnow, July 18, 1987. A.A., Coll. San Mateo, 1959; B.A., Calif. State U.-San Francisco, 1961. With Employment Devel. Dept., Sacramento, Calif., 1965-80; owner Adrienne's Furniture, Davis, Calif., 1975-80; personnel dir. Reagan Transition Team, Washington, 1980-81; exec. asst. to asst. sec. Employment and Tng., Washington, 1981-82, adminstr. policy and research, 1981-82; assoc. asst. sec. of labor Employment and Tng. Adminstrn., Washington, 1982-85; asst. dir. Office Internat. Tng., AID, Washington, 1985—; rep. Nat. Commn. on Employment Policy, Washington, 1981-83. Republican. Presbyterian. Office: AID SA-16 Suite 201 Washington DC 20523

KAISH, LUISE CLAYBORN, sculptor; b. Atlanta, Sept. 8, 1925; d. Harry and Elsa (Brown) Meyers; m. Morton Kaish, Aug. 15, 1948; 1 child, Melissa. BFA, Syracuse U., 1946, MFA, 1951; student, Escuela de Pintura y Escultura, Escuela de las Artes del Libro, Taller Grafico, Mexico, 1946-47. artist-in-residence Dartmouth Coll., 1974; prof. sculpture and painting, 1980—, chmn. div. painting and sculpture, Columbia U., 1980—; vis. artist U. Wash., Seattle, Battelle seminars and study program, Seattle, 1979; artist-in-residence U. Haifa, Israel, 1985. One-man shows Rochester (N.Y.) Meml. Art Gallery, 1954, Sculpture Ctr., N.Y.C., 1955, 58, Staempfli Gallery, N.Y.C., 1968, 81, 84, 87, Minn. Mus. Art, St. Paul, 1969, Jewish Mus., N.Y.C., 1973; exhibited (with Morton Kaish), Manhattanville Coll., Purchase, N.Y., 1955, Rochester Meml. Art Gallery, 1958, USIS, Rome, 1973, Dartmouth Coll., 1974, Oxford Gallery, Rochester; represented in permanent collections Whitney Mus. Am. Art, N.Y.C., Met. Mus. Art, N.Y.C., Jewish Mus., N.Y.C., Export Khleb, Moscow, Minn. Mus. Art, Gen. Mills Corp., Minn., High Mus. Art, Atlanta, Rochester Meml. Art Gallery, Lowe Mus., Coral Gables, Fla., Smithsonian Instn., Nat. Mus. Am. Art, Washington, also numerous pvt. collections, commns., Syracuse U., Temple B'rith Kodesh, Rochester, Temple Israel, Westport, Conn., Holy Trinity Mission Sem., Silver Springs, Md., Temple Beth Shalom, Wilmington, Del., Beth-El Synagogue Ctr., New Rochelle, N.Y., Temple B'nai Abraham, Essex City, N.J., Continental Grain Co., N.Y. Trustee Am. Acad. in Rome, 1973-81, mem. exec. com., 1975-81; trustee St. Gaudens Found., 1978—, mem. exec. com., 1980—. Recipient awards Everson Mus., Syracuse, 1947, awards Rochester Meml. Art Gallery, 1951, awards Ball State U., 1963, awards Ch. World Service, 1960, awards Council for Arts in Westchester, 1974; Emily Lowe award, 1956; Audubon Artists medal, 1963; Honor award AIA, 1975; Louis Comfort Tiffany grantee, 1951; Guggenheim fellow, 1959; Rome prize fellow Am. Acad. in Rome, 1970-72. Mem. Eta Pi Upsilon, Pi Lambda Theta. Home: 610 West End Ave #9-A New York NY 10024 Office: Columbia U Sch Arts Div Painting and Sculpture Dodge New York NY 10027

KALAHAR, PAT ANN, marketing and communications executive; b. Fort Collins, Colo., Aug. 1, 1951; d. James N. and Florence B. Kalahar; m. James A. Jamison, Apr. 28, 1977 (div.). B.A. in Tech. Journalism, Colo. State U., Fort Collins, 1974. Info. specialist, tech. writer Tri-State Generation and Transmission Assn., Denver, 1977-79; tech. editor, dir. communications Willard Owens Assocs., Inc., Denver, 1979; self-employed, Golden, Colo., 1980; project mgr. U. Colo. Health Scis. Ctr., Denver, 1981; dir. mktg., tech. editor Muller Engrng. Co., Inc., Lakewood, Colo., 1981-82; v.p. bus. devel. BHCD Engrs., Inc., Denver, 1982-84; founder, owner Mktg. Adv. Assocs., Denver, 1984—; cons. in field. Recipient Best Staffer award Rocky Mountain News, 1969. Mem. Soc. Mktg. Profl. Services (cert. excellence 1983). Contbr. articles to mags. Home: 442 S Eliot Denver CO 80219

KALAW, VIOLETA RECIO, psychiatrist; b. Lipa City, Philippines; came to U.S., 1973.; d. Jaime Javier and Lucia (Recio) K. BS, U. St. Thomas, Manila, 1964, MD, 1969. Resident gen. psychiatry Lafayette Clinic, Detroit, 1977, resident child and adolescent psychiatry, 1978, staff psychiatrist, 1979-81; cons. psychiatrist Caro (Mich.) Regional Ctr., 1976-78; asst. prof. Wayne State U., Detroit, 1980-81; chief service children unit Hatchings Psychiat. Ctr., Syracuse, N.Y., 1981-82; asst. prof. Upstate Mut. Ctr., Syracuse, 1981-82; supr. psychiatrist Fairmount Childrens Ctr., Solvay, N.Y., 1983—; cons. psychiatrist Cath. Charities of Syracuse, 1983—. Mem. Am. Acad. Child Psychiatrists, Am. Assn. Women Physicians. Office: Fairmount Childrens Ctr PO Box 64 Solvay NY 13209

KALAYJIAN, ANIE SANENTZ, educator, consultant, psychotherapist; b. Aleppo, Syria; came to U.S., 1971; d. Kevork and Zabelle (Mardikian) K.; m. Shahé Navasart Sanentz, Dec. 16, 1984. BS L.I. U., 1979; MEd, Columbia U., 1981, EdD, 1985, profl. nurses tng. course, 1984; cert. photography, Pratt Inst., 1979. R.N., N.Y. Psychiat. nurse Met. Hosp., N.Y.C., 1979-84; staff psychiat. mental health nurse Manhattan Bowery Project, N.Y.C., 1978-86; instr. Hunter Coll., N.Y.C., 1980-82; prof. Bloomfield Coll., N.J., 1984-85; lectr. Jersey City Coll., 1985; prof. Seton Hall U., South Orange, N.J., 1985-87, grad. program St. Joseph Coll., 1987—. Recipient Clark Found. scholarship award, 1985; Endowed Nursing Edn., Columbia U., scholar, 1984; Armenian Relief Soc. scholar, 1976-77, Armenian Students Assn. Am. scholar, 1976-78. Fellow Council on Continuing Edn., Am. Orthopsychiat. Assn., N.Y. State Nursing Assn. (planning com. nursing edn.); mem. Psychiat. and Mental Health Nursing (council), Inst. for Psychodynamics and Origins of Mind, Armenian Students Assn. (treas. 1980-81, pres. 1981-83, scholarship chairperson 1983-85, v.p. Cen. Exec. Com. 1987-88, elected nat. pres. 1988—), Kappa Delta Pi, Sigma Theta Tau. Avocations: aerobics; photography; acting. Office: 130 W 79th St New York NY 10024

KALCHBRENNER, THELSEN MARJORIE, small business owner; b. Chgo., Dec. 4, 1936; d. James Russell and Thelsen Clara (Hauk) Hoffheimer; divorced; children: Lori Thelsen, Russell John. Grad. high sch., Chgo. Sec. Continental Bank of Ill., Chgo., 1953-55, Raynor Lithographing, Chgo., 1956-58; adminstrv. and exec. sec. Delta Advt., Chgo., 1974-82; owner, pres., mgr. T.J. Investments and Thelsen Enterprises doing bus. as Fair Muffler Shops, Loves Park, Ill., 1984—. Mem. Loves Park/Machesney Park C. of C. (bd. dirs.). Roman Catholic. Club: YWCA. Lodge: KC. Home: 4555 Trevor Circle Rockford IL 61109 Office: Fair Muffler Shops 130 E Riverside Blvd Loves Park IL 61111

KALEDO, GRACE LUCILLE, public relations executive; b. Adrian, Mich., Dec. 17, 1928; d. Everett Ray and Ethel (Moore) Deken; student Adrian schs.; m. Charles Gordon Kaledo, June 22, 1946; children—Mary Lou Kaledo Mitchell, Kathryn Sue Kaledo DeMeritt, Larry Michael. Editor, publisher Lenawee Tribune, Adrian, 1968-74; pub. relations with community services dept. City of Adrian, 1975-79; adminstrv. dir. Croswell Opera House, Adrian, 1975-79, bd. dirs., 1978—, devel. cons. ; ptnr. Catalyst Promotions. Past mem. continuing edn. com. Adrian Coll.; bd. dirs. Southeast Travel & Tourism Commn.; co-chmn. Lenawee Heritage Festival; Croswell Players; past pres. Greater Adrian Inter Club Council; mem. operational support and outreach com. Mich. Council Arts; active Trenton Hills United Brethren Ch. Recipient Outstanding Community Service award Adrian Kiwanis, 1971, Service to Youth award, 1973. Mem. Nat. Fedn. Press Women, Nat. Assn. Female Execs., League Historic Am. Theatres, Nat. Writers Club, Lenawee C. of C. (travel and tourism com., Maple Leaf award 1986), Mich. Press Women. Clubs: Lenawee Civitan, Zonta. Home: 4555 S Mission Rd #525 Tucson AZ 85714 Office: PO Box 306 Adrian MI 49221

KALFUS, ELYSE RUTH, management consultant; b. Norfolk, Va., Sept. 14, 1947; d. Seymour H. and Irene C. (Chernitzer) Chapel; m. Ira F. Kalfus, Dec. 22, 1972 (div. 1977); 1 son, Brian Eric; m. Marshall Gordon, Dec. 12, 1981 (div. 1987); stepchildren—Howard David, Michael Kenneth, Jack Jay, Sheryl Patricia. Student, Norfolk pub. schs. Acctg. clk. Life Ins. Co. Ga., Atlanta, 1970-72; ind. contractor Atlanta Advertiser, Decatur, Ga., 1973-74; bookkeeper William Harvey Rowland & Co., Mableton, Ga., 1974-77; comptroller Sofas & Chairs, Inc., Atlanta, 1977-79; dir. security and distbn. Simon Mktg. Inc., Atlanta, 1979-80, dir. logistics, 1980-85; mgmt., transp. and Logistics, freight rate audit cons., 1979-85; pres. Traffic Mgmt. Cons., Inc., Marietta, Ga., 1985—, TMCI Internat. Ltd., Marietta, 1987—; computer newsletter editor. Mem. Women's Traffic Club Atlanta, Atlanta Computer Users Group (founder; sec.-treas. 1982-85), Council for Logistics Mgmt., Cobb C. of C., Delta Nu Alpha.. Home: 2665 Moss Ln Marietta GA 30067 Office: Traffic Mgmt Cons Inc/TMCI Internat 2130 Kingston Ct Suite B Marietta GA 30067

KALFUSS, HELENE AARONSON, speech pathologist; b. Phila., Feb. 28, 1941; d. Norman Ralph and Lillian Rose (White) Aaronson; m. Leonard M. Kalfuss, Aug. 29, 1965; children: Lenore, Ronald, Barry. BS, MEd, Wayne State U., 1963, PhD, 1968. Speech pathologist VA Hosp., Allen Park, Mich., 1963-70, chief speech pathology and audiol. depts., 1968-70; assoc. prof. Wayne State U. Med. Sch., Detroit, 1968-70; dir. speech and hearing div. Camarillo (Calif.) State Hosp., 1970-71; pvt. practice speech pathology Palm Springs, Calif., 1971—; cons. Angel View Crippled Childrens Fund, Palm Springs, Calif., 1973—; adminstr., chief fin. officer Bone & Joint Med. Clinic, Inc., 1972—; bd. dirs. Palm Valley Sch., Palm Springs; past pres., bd. dirs., treas. Angel View Crippled Children's Found., Desert Hot Springs, 1974-87; adv. bd. mem. Stroke Activity Ctr., Palm Springs, 1986—. Contbr. articles to profl. jours. Commr. Human Relations Commn. City of Palm Springs, 1976-78; past. v.p. Palm Valley Sch., Palm Springs, 1974—, sec., bd. dirs.; past pres. Sisterhood of Temple Isaiah, Palm Springs, 1973-74, pres. 1986—. Recipient Founders award Angel View Crippled Children's Found, 1980. Mem. Internat. Assn. Logopedics and Phoniatrics, Alexander Graham Bell Assn. for the Deaf, Calif. Speech and Hearing Assn., Am. Acad. Pvt. Practice in Speech Pathology and Audiology (sec. 1982-84, mem. nat. bd. dirs. 1982—, editor nat. jour. 1984—), Am. Speech-Lang. Hearing Assn. (cert.). Republican. Jewish. Office: 225 S Civic Dr Suite 1-1 Palm Springs CA 92262

KALIAN, SUSAN FRANCES, retail executive; b. Whittier, Calif., Oct. 16, 1940; d. John Russell and Dorothy May (Jonkey) Nies; m. Charles Gary Kalian, June 30, 1962 (div. Nov. 1975); children: Barrett Todd, Michelle Suzanne. BA, U. Calif., Berkeley, 1962. Tng. rep. Emporium-Capwell, Oakland, Calif., 1976-81; personal mgr. Emporium-Capwell, Stoneridge, Calif., 1979-81; mgr. design and visual presentation The Sharper Image, San Francisco, 1981-87, sr. mgr. design and visual presentation, 1987—; con. The Shop-Next to New Shop, Oakland, 1986—; cons., adviser Fashion Inst. Design and Merchandising, San Francisco, 1987. Chmn. ways and means com. Jr. Ctr. Art and Sci., Oakland, 1967-68; pres. Jr. League Oakland-East Bay, 1979-80, community adviser, 1986—, community research chmn., rec. sec.; mem. Alameda County (Calif.) Human Relations Commn., 1981-82; pres., bd. dirs. No. Calif. chpt. Cystic Fibrosis Found., 1980-82; bd. dirs. Social Service Bur. East Bay, Alameda County, 1974-79. Democrat. Office: The Sharper Image 650 Davis St San Francisco CA 94111

KALIK, BARBARA FAITH, state legislator; b. Bronx, N.Y., Nov. 8, 1936; d. Albert and Lydia (Cohen) Benowitz; children: Darcie Lynn, Andrew Jay, Lance Jon. Student, CCNY, 1953-56. Owner, operator Jolie Travel Ctr., Inc., Willingboro, N.J., 1968—; mem. N.J. Gen. Assembly, 1978—, dep. minority leader, 1986, chmn. revenue, fin. and appropriations com. 1984-85, vice chmn. joint appropriations com., 1986-87, mem. judiciary com., mem.

higher edn. and regulated professions com., mem. council, 1971 75; Mayor City of Willingboro, 1974, 77; pres. Willingboro Dem. Club, 1967; Dem. committeewoman Willingboro 16th Dist., 1965-85; vice chmn. Burlington County Dem. Com., 1970-77; mem. Nat. Dem. Policy Commn.; bd. dirs. Spl. Services Sch.; mem. N.J. Job Tng. Coordinating Council, 1984, Mt. Laurel Ballet Co., Burlington County Girl Scout Council. Recipient Area Health Edn. Ctr. award, N.J. State Fedn. Women's Clubs award, Motor Vehicle Employees Appreciation award; named Bus. Person of Yr., Rotary Internat., Outstanding Citizen, VFW. Mem. Burlington County C. of C. (pres. 1984). Jewish. Office: Country Club Plaza Beverly-Rancocas Rd Willingboro NJ 08046 also: Park Plaza Mall Rt 130 S Edgewater Park NJ 08010

KALIN, MARCIA FAY, physician; b. N.Y.C., Sept. 12, 1954; d. Milton and Marilyn (Kravetz) Kalin; B.A. cum laude, Brandeis U., 1976; M.D., Mt. Sinai Sch. Medicine, 1980; m. Edward C. Houser, Oct. 12, 1980. Resident in internal medicine Overlook Hosp., Summit, N.J., 1980-81; editor Sci. Am., N.Y.C., 1981-83; resident in internal medicine Beth Israel Med. Ctr., N.Y.C., 1983-85, fellow in endocrinology, 1985-88, attending physician in internal medicine, 1988—. Home: 16 E 98th St 2C New York NY 10029 Office: Beth Israel Med Ctr 1st Ave at 16th St New York NY 10003

KALINS, DOROTHY, magazine editor; b. Westport, Conn., Oct. 9, 1942; d. Joseph M. and Gil G. Kalins. Student, Skidmore Coll., 1960-62, Sorbonne, Paris, 1962-63; B.A., Columbia U., 1965. Design writer Home Furnishings Daily, N.Y.C., 1965-68; freelance writer, various publs. including N.Y. Mag., 1969-74; exec. editor Apartment Life Mag., N.Y.C., 1974-78; editor-in-chief Apartment Life Mag., 1978-81, Metropolitan Home mag., 1981—. Author: Researching Design in New York, 1968, Cutting Loose, 1972, The Apartment Book, 1979, The New American Cuisine, 1981; editor: Renovation Style, 1986. Mem. Am. Soc. Mag. Editors (past exec. bd.). Office: Met Home 750 3rd Ave New York NY 10017

KALLGREN, JOYCE KISLITZIN, political science educator; b. San Francisco, Apr. 17, 1930; d. Alexander and Dorothea (Willett) K.; m. Edward E. Kallgren, Feb. 8, 1953; children: Virginia, Charles. BA, U. Calif., Berkeley, 1953, MA, 1955; PhD, Harvard U., 1968. Jr. researcher to asst. researcher Ctr. Chinese Studies U. Calif., Berkeley, 1961-65, research assoc., 1965—, chair, 1983-88; assoc. dir. Inst. of East Asian Studies, Berkeley, 1987—; from lectr. to prof. polit. sci. U. Calif., Davis, 1965—; cons. in field. Contbg. editor: China After Thirty Years, 1979, Academic Exchanges: Essays on the Sino-American Experience; editor, Jour. Asian Studies, 1980-83; mem. editorial bd. Asian Survey, World Affairs; contbr. articles to profl. jours., chpts. to books. Ford Found. awardee, 1978-79. Mem. Am. Polit. Sci. Assn., Assn. Asian Studies, China Council, Nat. Com. U.S./China Relations. Home: 28 Hillcrest Rd Berkeley CA 94705 Office: U Calif Inst East Asian Studies Berkeley CA 94720

KALLMAN, KATHLEEN BARBARA, marketing professional; b. Aurora, Ill., Mar. 23, 1952; d. Kenneth Wesley and Germaine Barbara (May) Eby; m. John Kenneth Kallman, Sept. 27, 1975; 1 child, Erin Marie. Legal sec. Sidley & Austin, Chgo., 1973-76, Winston & Strawn, Chgo., 1976-78; exec. sec. Beatrice Cos., Inc., Chgo., 1978-81, adminstrv. asst., 1981-83, asst. to chmn. bd. dirs., 1983-84, asst. v.p., 1984-85; pres., mng. dir. Stratxx Ltd., Chgo., 1985—. Mem. Chgo. Council on Fgn. Relations, 1986—. Roman Catholic. Club: Internat. (Chgo.). Office: Stratxx Ltd 840 N Michigan Ave #415 Chicago IL 60611

KALSTAD, KRISTEN ANDREA, transportation executive; b. Annapolis, Md., Mar. 6, 1948; d. Henry Morris and Elizabeth (McKnight) K.; divorced; 1 child, Heidi Kalstad Rork. Student, Bergen Community Coll., 1969-70, Paterson State Tchrs. Coll., 1970; A summa cum laude, Anne Arundel Community Coll., 1979; B, U. N.Mex., 1982, postgrad., 1983; student, Embry Riddle Aero. U., 1981. Flight instr. Sunport Aviation, Albuquerque, 1980-81; co-pilot SW Med. Air Transport, Albuquerque, 1981; flight instr. Crestview Aviation, Albuquerque, 1981-83; flight attendant Trans World Airlines, N.Y., 1970-83; regional airline pilot Big Sky Airlines, Billings, Mont., 1983-85; airline pilot Eastern Airlines, Washington, 1985—. Mem. Internat. Social Affiliation of Women Airline Pilots, Airline Pilots Assn. Republican. Home: 111 Round Bay Rd Severna Park MD 21146

KALUZNIACKI, SOPHIA BARBARA, veterinarian; b. Warsaw, Poland, May 11, 1942; came to U.S., 1952; d. Roman Julius and Stena (Zubrzycki) Kaluzniacki; m. George G. Kulesza, Dec. 27, 1971; 1 child, Christina. Student, U. Ariz., 1960-63, Ariz. State U., 1963-64; D.V.M., Wash. State U., 1968. Asst. prof. U. Ariz., Tucson, 1968-70; staff veterinarian Humane Soc. Ariz., Phoenix, 1970-71; pvt. practice vet. medicine, Green Valley, Ariz., 1971—. Contbr. articles to profl. jours. Adv. bd., sec. Pima County Animal Control, Tucson, 1978—; mem., sec. Ariz. State Bd. Vet. Examiners, Phoenix, 1980—; bd. dirs. Soc. Prevention Cruelty to Animals of Ariz., Inc., Tucson, 1972—; sec. religious edn. bd. St. Luke's Cath. Ch., 1987-88, mem. parish council, co-dir. pre-Sunday sch. religious edn., tchr. kindergarten Sunday sch., lector, eucharistic minister. Mem. AVMA, Ariz. Vet. Med. Assn., So. Ariz. Vet. Med. Assn. Address: Green Valley Animal Hosp 220 E Duval Rd PO Box D Green Valley AZ 85622

KAMALI, NORMA, designer; b. N.Y.C., June 27, 1945; d. Sam and Estelle (Grub) Mariategui; grad. Fashion Inst., 1965. With Kamali Ltd., 1967-78; owner, designer O.M.O. Norma Kamali. N.Y.C., 1978—. Recipient Coty Winnie award, 1981, Return award, 1982, Hall of Fame award, 1983; Women's Fashion Designer of Yr. award Council Fashion Designers Am., 1983; Award for Innovative Use of Video Council of Fashion Designers Am., 1986; Fashion Group honoree, 1986, CEDA award, 1986, Community Service award, 1985. Office: 11 W 56th St New York NY 10019 *

KAMARAS, ELLEN HARRIET, accountant; b. N.Y.C., Oct. 16, 1955; d. Israel David and Marsha (Tau) Geller; m. Philip Louis Kamaras, Aug. 21, 1983; 1 child, Jacob. BS summa cum laude, Bklyn. Coll., 1977; MBA, Baruch Coll., 1984. CPA, N.Y. Auditor, acct. Ernst and Whinney, N.Y.C., 1977-81; fin. mgr., asst. controller Mfrs. Hanover Trust, N.Y.C., 1981—. Mem. Am. Inst. CPA's, N.Y. State Soc. CPA's. Democrat. Home: 1876 E 23d St Brooklyn NY 11229 Office: Mfrs Hanover Trust 130 John St New York NY 10038

KAMBOJ, LYNN MARIE, small business owner; b. Chgo., Aug. 17, 1947; d. Michael Patrick and Dorothy Kathlyn (Geng) Necas; m. Vinod Kumar Kamboj; 1 child, Kiran Jeannine. BA in Math. magna cum laude with honors, San Jose State U., 1969. Cert. secondary tchr. Jr. staff analyst San Jose (Calif.) State U. Found., 1970-75; owner Lynn Taylor Bridal Service, Campbell, Calif., 1975—. Helen Pardee scholar, 1968. Mem. Phi Beta Kappa, Phi Kappa Phi. Office: 880 E Campbell Ave Campbell CA 95008

KAMDAR, JANET IDEN, account marketing representative; b. Ft. Wayne, Ind., June 10, 1954; d. Deloss Leroy and Mary Lou (Weigel) Iden; m. Sadruddin Kamdar, Sept. 25, 1985; 1 stepchild, Megan Alima. BA in French, Ind. U., Ft. Wayne, 1976, BSBA, 1978, MSBA, 1983. Mktg. support rep. IBM, Ft. Wayne, 1976-82, systems engr., 1982-87, account mktg. rep., 1987—; guest instr. IBM edn. class, Dallas, 1980. Mem. Embassey Theatre Found., Ft. Wayne, 1986-87, Civic Theatre, Ft. Wayne, 1986-87, Purdue's Pres.'s Council, Ind. Purdue at Ft. Wayne Strategic Planning and Mgmt. Task Force Subcom. on Alumni Affairs and Devel., 1987-88, Ind. Purdue at Ft. Wayne Strategic Planning and Mgmt. Task Force Subcom. on Athletics, 1987-88, Ft. Wayne Panhellenic Bd., 1986-87. Named One of Outstanding Young Women of Am., 1985. Mem. AAUW, Nat. Assn. Female Execs., Ind. U. Athletic Assn., Ind. U. Exec. Council (bd. dirs. 1985-88), Am. Diabetes Assn., Woodburn Guild, Small Systems User's Group, Ind. U. Alumni Assn., Ind. U. Varsity Club, Delta Gamma Alumni Assn.(scholar 1974, alumnae pres. Ft. Wayne chpt. 1988—). Republican. Lutheran. Club: Ind. U. Allen County. Home: 5723 Sandra Lee Ave Fort Wayne IN 46819 Office: IBM Corp 2827 Rupp Dr Fort Wayne IN 46815

KAMINE, DARLENE MARIS, lawyer; b. Cin., July 20, 1952; d. Jonas and Rose (Jupiter) Greenbaum; m. Charles Stephen Kamine, Aug. 12, 1973; 1 child, Elida Beth. B.A., Brandeis U., 1973; J.D., U. Denver, 1975. Bar: Ohio 1976. Staff atty. Pub. Defender Div., Cin., 1976-79; adj. asst. prof. Law Chase Coll. Law, Highland Heights, Ky., 1979, 87; sole practice, Cin., 1979-82; asst. atty. gen. State of Ohio, 1979-82; referee Hamilton County Juvenile Ct., Cin., 1982—; chmn. Nat. Legal Resource Ctr. for Child Advocacy and Protection, Washington, 1984-85; dir. Guardian Ad Litem Program, Cin., 1978-79; exec. com. mem. Hamilton County Regional Planning Unit for Juvenile Justice, Cin., 1980-83; bd. dirs. Inst. for Child Advocacy, Cleve., 1981-83; trustee Cin. Bar Found., 1980—. Bd. dirs. Parent's Anonymous, Cin., 1981—; bd. dirs., vice chmn. ProKids, Inc., Cin., 1981-84; mem. Jr. League, Cin., 1982—; mem. Community Chest Evaluation Task Force and Children's Services Planning Com., Cin., 1981-83. Mem. Cin. Bar Assn. (pres. Young Lawyers sect. 1979-80, mem. exec. com. 1979-82, chmn. Day Care Com. 1981-87), Ohio State Bar Assn. (pres. Young Lawyer's Sect. 1980-81, del. Council of Dels. 1983-86), Member, American Bar Association House of Delegates 1980-84 Nat. Conf. of Bar Pres. (liaison 1980-82). Author: Child Abuse, Neglect and Dependency in Ohio, 1982. Office: 1309 Gwynne Bldg 602 Main St Cincinnati OH 45202

KAMINSKI-DA ROZA, VICTORIA CECILIA, human resource administrator; b. East Orange, N.J., Aug. 30, 1945; d. Victor and Cynthia Helen (Krupa) Hawkins; m. Thomas Howard Kaminski, Aug. 28, 1971 (div. 1977); 1 child, Sarah Hawkins; m. Robert Anthony da Roza, Nov. 25, 1983. BA, U. Mich., 1967; MA, U. Mo., 1968. Contract compliance mgr. City of San Diego, 1972-75; v.p. personnel Bank of Calif., San Francisco, 1975-77; with human resources Lawrence Livermore (Calif.) Nat. Lab., 1978-86; pvt. cons. Victoria Kaminski-da Roza & Assocs., 1986—; lectr. in field; videotape workshop program on mid-career planning used by IEEE. Contbr. numerous articles to profl. jours. Mem. social policy com. City of Livermore, 1982. Mem. Am. Soc. Tng. and Devel., Western Gerontol. Soc. (planning com. Older Worker Track 1983), Gerontol. Soc. Am. Home and Office: 385 Borica Dr Danville CA 94526

KAMINSKY, ALICE RICHKIN, English language educator; b. N.Y.C.; d. Morris and Ida (Spivak) Richkin; m. Jack Kaminsky; 1 son, Eric (dec.). B.A., NYU, 1946, M.A., 1947, Ph.D., 1952. Mem. faculty dept. English NYU, 1947-49, Hunter Coll., 1952-53, Cornell U., 1954-57, Broome Community Coll., 1958-59, Cornell U., 1959-63; mem. faculty dept. English SUNY, Cortland, 1963—, prof., 1968—, faculty exchange scholar. Author: George Henry Lewes as Critic, 1968, Logic: A Philosophical Introduction, 1974; editor: Literary Criticism of George Henry Lewes, 1964, Chaucer's Troilus and Criseyde and the Critics, 1980, The Victim's Song, 1985; contbr. articles and revs. to numerous jours. Mem. MLA, Chaucer Soc., Author's Guild. Office: SUNY Cortland Dept English Cortland NY 13045

KAMINSKY, PHYLLIS, international organization official; b. Montreal, Que., Can., Dec. 1, 1936; came to U.S., 1945, naturalized, 1958; d. Julius and Betty (Shapiro) Levitt; B.A. in Polit. Sci., U. Mich., 1957; postgrad. Columbia U., 1957-58; m. I. Samuel Kaminsky, June 24, 1971; children—David, Glenn. Sec. speakers bur. Fgn. Policy Assn., N.Y.C., 1957-58; editor disarmament procs. UN, Geneva, 1958; secretarial supr. McKinsey and Co., Geneva, 1963-64; adminstrv. asst. Chrysler Internat. S.A., also Internat. Research Cons. S.A., Geneva, 1959-63, Grey Advt. Internat., N.Y.C., 1965-67; exec. asst. Lee Burdick Advt., Inc., N.Y.C., 1967-68; bilingual press attache S.B.M. Resort Complex, Monte Carlo, 1968-69; public relations asst. Mayor's Com. for 25th Anniversary of UN, N.Y.C., 1970-71; consular corps liaison officer N.Y.C. Dept. Public Events, 1967-68; media cons., public relations adv. United Jewish Appeal, N.Y.C., 1971-80; media cons. Bush for Pres. Campaign, Pa. and Ill., 1980; dep. dir. communications Coalition for Reagan-Bush, 1980; press sec. to sr. fgn. policy adv. Office of President-Elect, 1980-81; press liaison White House, Nat. Security Council, 1981; dir. Office of Public Liaison, USIA, 1981-83; dir. UN Info. Center, Washington, 1983—; mem. U.S. ofcl. del. 29th session UN Commn. on Status of Women, 1982. Co-founder Jerusalem Women's Seminar, 1979—. Recipient Gold Key award PR News, 1984. Mem. Public Relations Soc. Am., Internat. Pub. Relations Soc., AAUW, Women in Communications; (chmn. pub. affairs adv. bd. 1984-85), Exec. Women in Govt., Nat. Women's Forum. Club: Nat. Press (co-chmn. internat. women's media conf. 1986). Office: 1889 F St NW Washington DC 20006

KAMISAR, SANDRA LEE, federal agency administrator, publishing consultant; b. Washington, Apr. 15, 1937; d. Harry and Betty (Bass) K. AA, George Washington U., 1956; cert. med. sec., Strayer Bus. Coll., Washington, 1957. With Office of Prevention, Edn. and Control Nat. Heart, Lung and Blood Inst., Bethesda, Md., 1957—, chief pubs. mgmt. sect., supr. writing and editing, 1977—; cons. printing and pub. NIH, Bethesda, 1979—. Editor: Dietary Management of Hyperlipoproteinemia. V.P. Temple Shalom, Chevy Chase, Md., 1982—; bd. dirs. Mid-Atlantic Council Union of Am. Hebrew Congregations, Washington, 1987—. Mem. Nat. Assn. Govt. Communications. Democrat. Home: 6140 Utah Ave Washington DC 20015

KAMIYA, LURA ANN, insurance company executive; b. Gonzales, La., Sept. 26, 1952; d. Pershing James and Lee Ella (Lanoux) Mire; m. Shingo Kamiya, Dec. 28, 1973; children—Cheryl, Charlotte. B.A. magna cum laude, N. Tex. State U., 1975. Formerly mgr. human resources Presbyn. Ministers Fund, Phila., now asst. v.p. human resources, 1976—. Fellow Life Mgmt. Inst. (sec. Soc. Del. Valley); mem. Am. Soc. Personnel Adminstrs., Nat. Assn. for Female Execs., Am. Mgmt. Soc., Delaware Valley Ins. Personnel Group, Internat. Assn. Personnel Women. Republican. Roman Catholic. Office: Presbyn Ministers Fund 1809 Walnut St Philadelphia PA 19103

KAMLET, BARBARA LYNN, volunteer sevices director; b. Denver, May 3, 1949; d. Sam Henry and Bette Ann (Krim) Kamlet; children: Jennifer, Lisa. BA, Colo. State U., 1971. Adminstrv. asst. Beth Israel Hosp., Denver, 1972-79; pub. relations coordinator St. Luke's Hosp., Denver, 1979-84; program devel. mgr. Norrell Services, Englewood, Colo., 1984-86; dir. vol. services Mercy Med. Ctr., Denver, 1987—; mem. exec. com., co-chairperson Women and Bus. Conf., Denver, 1984—; mem. adv. bd. T.H. Pickens Tech. Coll., Aurora, Colo., 1985—; mem. speaker's bur. Colo. Alliance Bus., Denver, 1985—; mem. Arapahoe/Douglas Pvt. Industry Council, Englewood, 1987—. Vol. Denver Children's Hosp., 1983—, Colo. Sudden Infant Death Syndrome Program, Denver, 1984—; bd. dirs. Meadow Print Elem. Sch., Aurora, 1984-86. Mem. Am. Soc. for Tng. and Devel., Colo. Health and Life Claims Assn. (sec. 1986-87). Home: 18172 E Bellewood Dr Aurora CO 80015 Office: Mercy Med Ctr 1650 Fillmore Denver CO 80206

KAMM, LINDA HELLER, lawyer; b. N.Y.C., Aug. 25, 1939; d. Seymour A. and Mary (Kravitz) Heller; children: Lisa, Oliver. BA in History, Brandeis U., 1961; LLB, Boston Coll., 1967. Bar: Mass., D.C., U.S. Supreme Ct. Counsel Dem. Study Group, Washington, 1968-71; counsel select com. on coms. U.S. Ho. of Reps., Washington, 1973-75; gen. counsel budget com. U.S. Ho. of Reps., Washinton, 1975-77; gen. counsel U.S. Dept. Transp., Washington, 1977-80; ptnr. Foley and Lardner, Washington, 1980-84; of counsel Foley and Lardner, 1984—. Mem. ABA, Fed. Bar Assn. (treas. Environ. Policy Inst.). Office: Foley and Lardner 1775 Pennsylvania Ave NW Washington DC 20006

KAN, BARBARA HUTCHINSON, photographer, travel consultant; b. Grand Rapids, Mich., June 21, 1952; d. Jack and Laura Mae (Coles) Hutchinson; m. Stephen Andrew Kan, Aug. 25, 1979. AA, Grand Rapids Jr. Coll., 1972; BA, Mich. State U., 1974, MA, 1981. Cert. secondary English tchr. English instr., drama coach, reading cons. Hale (Mich.) Area Jr. and Sr. High Sch., 1974-76; English instr., drama coach Traverse City (Mich.) Area High Sch., 1976-85; owner, photographer Photo Graphics Studio and Location Film Art, Traverse City, 1985—; comml. services cons. and rep. Andrew Kan Travel Service, Inc., Traverse City, 1985—; media rep., writer, photographer Traverse City Edn. Assn., 1976-85. Mem. Human Rights Commn., Traverse City, 1987-88. Meisel-Winona Photography scholar, 1986. Mem. Profl. Photographers Am., Associated Photographers Internat., Internat. Freelance Photographers, Am. Freelance Photographers, Kappa Delta Pi, Phi Kappa Phi, Delta Pi Alpha. Clubs: Traverse City Country (evening rep. 1980-82), Cherry Capital Cycling (asst. editor monthly newsletter). Home and Office: Photographics Studio and Location Film Art 1404 Peninsula Dr Traverse City MI 49684 also: Andrew Kan Travel Service Inc 135 E Front St Traverse City MI 49684

KANAGY, JANICE ALISA, pharmaceutical plant manager; b. Glendale, Calif., Aug. 13, 1952; d. Vernon William Jones and Betty Lou (Davis) Alsberg; m. Douglas A. Kanagy, Dec. 24, 1976 (div. 1983). BS in Biochemistry, Calif. Polytech. State U., 1976. Asst. chemist McGaw Lab., Irvine, Calif., 1976-78, asst. research scientist, 1978-80, quality control supr., 1980-82; quality assurance mgr. Allergan Pharms., Irvine, Calif., 1982-83, production mgr., 1983-86, plant mgr., 1986—. Mem. C. of C. Women Bus. Republican. Office: Allergan Pharm 2525 Pullman Ave Santa Ana CA 92705

KANE, ALICE THERESA, lawyer; b. N.Y.C., Jan. 16, 1948. AB, Manhattanville Coll., 1969; JD, NYU, 1972; grad., Harvard U. Sch. Bus. Program Mgmt. Devel., 1985. Bar: N.Y. 1973, U.S. Dist. Ct. (so. dist.) N.Y. 1974. Atty. N.Y. Life Ins. Co., N.Y.C., 1972-83, v.p., assoc. gen. counsel, 1983-85, v.p. dept. personnel, 1985, sr. v.p., gen. counsel, 1986—. Mem. ABA (chmn. employee benefits com., tort and ins. practice sect. 1984-85, mem. corp., banking and bus. law sects., tort and ins. practice sects.), Assn. of Life Ins. Counsel. Office: NY Life Ins Co 51 Madison Ave New York NY 10010

KANE, CANDICE COTTER, real estate and title company executive; b. Darby, Pa., Oct. 13, 1948; d. J. William and Mary Mildred (Hurley) Cotter; m. Daniel Merrick Kane, May 3, 1974; children: Victoria Elise, Alexis Siobhan, Daniel Merrick, Octavia Bevan, Cordelia Grace, Edward William. Student, Miseracordia Sch. of Nursing, 1966-68, Villanova U., 1972, Rosemont Coll., 1974. Pulmonary pump technologist Bryn Mawr (Pa.) Hosp., 1969-74; mgmt. trainee Title Abstract, Newtown Square, Pa., 1974-75, dir., 1981-86; pres. Candice Kane Assocs., Devon, Pa., 1984—. Sec. Women's Com. for Wills Eye Hosp., Phila., 1985-86, v.p. 1986, pres. 1988—; mem. Jr. League of Phila., 1986—. Roman Catholic. Home: 354 Sugartown Rd Devon PA 19333 Office: 227 E Lancaster Pike Devon PA 19333

KANE, CAROL, actress; b. Cleve., June 18, 1952. Appeared with touring co. of plays The Prime of Miss Jean Brodie, 1966, Joseph Papp's Pub. Theatre, Charles St. Playhouse, Boston, Woman of Mystery, Lucky Spot; film appearances include Carnal Knowledge, 1971, The Last Detail, 1974, Dog Day Afternoon, 1975, Hester Street, 1975 (Acad. award nomination for Best Actress), Harry and Walter Go to New York, 1976, Annie Hall, 1977, Valentino, 1977, The World's Greatest Lover, 1977, The Mafu Cage, 1977, When a Stranger Calls, 1979, The Muppet Movie, 1979, La Sabina, 1979, Les Jeux, 1980, Racing With the Moon, 1984, All is Forgiven, 1985-86, Jumpin' Jack Flash, 1986, Ishtar, 1987, License to Drive, 1988; stage appearances include The Effect of Gamma Rays on Man in the Moon Marigolds, 1978, Tales from the Vienna Woods, 1979, Benefit of a Doubt, 1979, The Tempest and Macbeth at Lincoln Center, Sunday Runners in the Rain, 1980, A Midsummer Night's Dream; appeared in TV film Many Mansions, in TV series Taxi, All is Forgiven, 1986. Office: care MSI 370 Lexington Ave Suite 701 New York NY 10017

KANE, CAROLYN RAE, banker; b. Whittier, Calif., Mar. 31, 1960; d. Raymond Earl and Mary Ann (Brooks) Crawford; m. Andrew Joseph Kalkowski, Jan. 21, 1980 (div. Apr. 1982); m. John Vincent Kane, Jr., Apr. 4, 1987. Student, Fullerton Coll., 1982-83, Orange Coast Coll., 1983-86, Coastline Community Coll., 1984-86, Cal. State U., Long Beach, 1987—. Supr. loan services Am. Savs., Fullerton, Calif., 1980-83; office mgr. Imperial Bancorp Mortgage, Huntington BEach, Calif., 1983-85; acct. exec. The Gilsand Co., Newport Beach, Calif., 1985-86; asst. mgr. Security Pacific Nat. Bank, Cypress, Calif., 1986—. Republican. Roman Catholic.

KANE, DEBORAH LANGE, pharmaceutical company executive; b. Orange, N.J., July 28, 1956; d. Howard Francis and Doris Mae (Sandnes) Lange; m. Michael G. Giuliano, Jun. 13, 1981 (div. Apr. 1985); 1 child Danielle Marie; m. John J. Kane, Feb. 22, 1987. BS in Biology, Seton Hall U., 1978. Clin. data coordinator Schering Pharm. Corp., Kenilworth, N.J., 1976-87; mgr. clin. data mgmt. Fidia Pharm. Corp., Washington, 1987—. Vol. Montville Twp. First Aid Squad, 1976-87. Mem. Drug Info. Assn. Home: 6001 Pratt St Alexandria VA 22310

KANE, DOROTHEA SANDERSON, records administrator; b. Chorley, Eng.; d. Joseph Frederick and Anne (Green) Sanderson; m. Thom Gerald Kane, Apr. 1, 1972. Student, Drexel U., 1962-64, U. Pa., 1964-65; BS in Sociology, SUNY, 1975. Librarian Burroughs Corp., Paoli, Pa., 1962-64, tech. writer, 1965-70; systems analyst, records adminstr. Sperry Rand, Blue Bell, Pa., 1970-72; info. services sect. head W,. H. Rorer, Ft. Washington, Pa., 1972-74; sr. analyst Met. Water Dist., Los Angeles, 1974-85; info systems cons. Los Angeles, 1985-87; records adminstr. Henrico County Pub. Schs., Richmond, Va., 1987—. Mem. Assn. Records Mgrs. and Adminstrs., Soc. Tech. Communications, Spl. LIbraries Assn., Am. Assn. Artificial Intelligence. Office: Henrico County Pub Schs PO Box 40 Highland Springs VA 23075

KANE, GLADYS ANN, government official; b. Detroit, Jan. 28, 1934; d. Axel Raymond Kaleva and Elma Engeborg (Oja) Johnson; m. Albert Nicholas Garbukas, Dec. 23, 1954 (div. Nov. 1973); children: Cheryl, Michael, Steven; m. John Edward Kane, July 3, 1974 (dec.). Student, Wayne State U., 1952-54, 69. Women's editor, reporter Community News, Warren, Mich., 1966-68; chief housing counselor City of Warren, 1968-71; relocation rep. HUD, Detroit, 1971-74; assoc. dir. City of Milw., 1974-79; dir. community affairs and human services City of Miami Beach (Fla.), 1979-85; dir. housing mgmt. HUD, Milw., 1985—. Bd. dirs. Pvt. Industry Council South Fla., 1984-85; vol. North Suburban Spl. Olympics, Milw., 1987-88. Recipient Cert. of Appreciatin, ARC, Miami, 1985. Lutheran. Office: HUD 210 W Wisconsin Ave Suite 1380 Milwaukee WI 53202

KANE, JANET EMPIE, interior design firm executive, educator; b. Scotia, N.Y., Oct. 16, 1936; d. Kenneth Alfred and Helen Elizabeth Empie; m. Roger Carl Kane, Dec. 28, 1957 (div. May 1979); children—Peter Carl, Kenneth Chapple. B.F.A., Pratt Inst., 1958. Staff designer Bloomingdales, N.Y.C., 1958-60; project mgr. Van Dyck Corp., Westport, Conn., 1960-62, Thalhimers Bus. Interiors, Richmond, Va., 1968-71; mgr., design dir. Litton Office Products, Richmond, 1971-72; v.p., design dir. Interior Design Assocs., Richmond, 1972-74; pres. Janet Kane Interiors, Inc., Richmond, 1974—; bd. dirs. Futures Council, Va. Tech. State U., Blacksburg, 1984—; asst. prof. dept. interior design Va. Commonwealth U., Richmond, 1979-80. Treas., Republican Senatorial Campaign, Richmond, 1969. Named Interior of Yr., 3-M Co., Inc., Richmond, 1980; recipient Air Tycom-Quality of Life award Dept. Navy, Virginia Beach, Va., 1983. Mem. Am. Soc. Interior Designers (nat. regional v.p. 1981-82, mem. nat. industry found. 1981-85, pres. Va. chpt. 1986; outstanding contract interior 1978, presdl. citation 1982, nat. presdl. citation 1982-83), Retail Mchts. Assn. (membership com. 1979), Richmond C. of C. (membership com. 1986), Richmond Met. C. of C. (newcomers com. 1985). Republican. Presbyterian. Club: Insider's (Richmond) (pres. 1985-86). Avocations: bicycling; bowling; golf. Home: 14309 Winter Ridge Ln Richmond VA 23230 Office: Janet Kane Interiors Inc 1301 N Hamilton St Suite 105 Richmond VA 23230

KANE, JEAN CAROLINE, interior design fabricator; b. N.Y.C., May 2, 1941; d. James Alfred and Theresa Miriam (Schulz) Amoroso; A.S., Endicott Coll., 1961; m. John Francis Kane, May 2, 1964; 1 dau., Cathleen Theresa. Free-lance model with Candy Jones Modeling Agy., N.Y.C., 1950-8; asst. dept. mgr. Lord & Taylor, Scarsdale, N.Y., 1959, multi-br. mdse. mgr., N.Y.C., 1961-62; asst. advt. mgr. Van Raalte, Inc., N.Y.C., 1962-64; free-lance promotion coordinator for Van Raalte, Inc., 1965-68; free-lance interior design fabricator Mamaroneck, N.Y., 1969—; ind. travel cons., 1985-87; co-owner Travel Agy., 1987—; cons. Eye of the Needle, Larchmont, N.Y., 1965-85; Prentice-Hall tng. video on reupholstery, 1982-83; tchr. upholstery Bd. Coop. Ednl. Services, Yorktown, N.Y., 1979. Sec., Rye Neck Sch. Bd.; trustee Selection Com., Mamaroneck, 1976-77, pres., 1977-78; chairwoman club activities F.E. Bellos Sch. Parent Tchr. Student Assn., Mamaroneck, 1977-79, co-chairwoman book and art show, 1980; active Girl Scouts U.S.A., Mamaroneck community dir., 1978-83, del. ann. meeting Sackerah Path council, 1978-79, Westchester/Putnam council, 1979-82; active campaign for mayor of Mamaroneck, 1979. Roman Catholic. Designs include: 2 rooms of Larchmont Shore Club; fabric design for Bloomingdale Mansion, YWCA house tour; 3 rooms of 16th century replica French castle; members' needlpoint for doors of Temple Israel, Scarsdale. Home: 116 Lawn Terr Mamaroneck NY 10543 Office: Honey Travel Inc 11 Elm Pl Rye NY 10580

KANE, MARGARET BRASSLER, sculptor; b. East Orange, N.J., May 25, 1909; d. Hans and Mathilde (Trumpler) Brassler; m. Arthur Ferris Kane, June 11, 1930; children—Jay Brassler, Gregory Ferris. Student, Packer Collegiate Inst., 1920-26, Syracuse U., 1927, Art Students League, 1927-29, N.Y. Coll. Music, 1928-29, John Hovannes Studio, 1932-34; PhD (hon.), Colo. State Christian Coll., 1973. Head craftsman for sculpture, arts and skills unit ARC, Halloran Gen. Hosp., N.Y., 1942-43; 2d v.p. Nat. Assn. Woman Artists, Inc., 1943-45; sec. to exec. bd. Sculptors Guild, Inc., 1942-45, chmn. exhbn. com., 1942, 44; Jury mem. Bklyn. Mus., 1948, Am. Machine & Foundry Co., 1957; com. mem. An American Group, Inc. Work exhibited at Jacques Seligmann Gallery, N.Y., Whitney Ann. Exhbns., all Sculptors Guild Mus. and Outdoor Shows, Nat. Sculpture Soc. Ann. Bas-Relief Exhbn., 1938, Whitney Mus. Sculpture Festival, 1940, Bklyn. Mus. Sculptors Guild, 1938, Bklyn. Soc. Artists, 1942, Lawrence (Mass.) Art Mus., 1938, N.Y. World's Fair, 1939, Sculptors Guild World's Fair Exhbn., 1940, Robinson Gallery, N.Y., 1939, Traveling Mus. and Instns., 1938, Lyman Allyn Mus., 1939, Met. Mus., Internat. Exhbns., 1940, 1949, Roosevelt Field Art Ctr., N.Y.C., 1957, Phila. Mus., N.Y. Archtl. League, Nat. Acad., Penn. Acad., Chgo. Art Inst., Am. Fedn. Arts, Riverside Mus., Montclair Mus., Grand Cen. Art Galleries, Lever House, N.Y.C., 1959-81, Rye (N.Y.) Library, 1962, Lever House Sculptors Guild Ann. Exhbn., 1973-81, N.Y. Bot. Garden, 1981, Sculptors Guild 50th Anniversary Exhbn., Lever House, 1987, Phila. Art Alliance, 1987, also exhbns. of nat. scope, 1938—, solo sculpture exhbn., Friends Greenwich (Conn.) Library, 1962; executed plaque for Burro Monument, Fairplay, Colo.; exhibited N.Y. Bank for Savs., 1968, Mattatuck Mus., Con., 1967, Lamont Gallery, N.H., 1967, Sculptor's Guild 50th Anniversary Lever House, N.Y.C., 1987, Phila. Art Alliance Exhibition Sculpture of the American Scene, 1987; executed: 18 foot carving in limewood depicting History of Man; contbr. articles to mags.; reprodns. in Contemporary Stone Sculpture, 1970, Contemporary American Sculptures. Recipient Anna Hyatt Huntington award, 1942; Am. Artists Profl. League and Montclair Art Assn. Awards, 1943; 1st Henry O. Avery Prize, 1944; Sculpture Prize Bklyn. Soc. Artists, Bklyn. Mus., 1946; John Rogers Award, 1951; Lawrence Hyder Prize, 1952, 54; David H. Zell Meml. Award, 1954, 63; hon. mention U.S. Maritime Commn., 1941 and; A.C.A. Gallery Competition, 1944; Med. of honor for sculpture Nat. Assn. Women Artists, 1951; Med. of honor for sculpture Nat. Acad. Galleries, N.Y.; prize for carved sculpture, 1955; animal sculpture, 1956; 1st award for sculpture Greenwich Art Soc., 1958, 60; 1st award for sculpture Annual New Eng. Exhbns., Silvermine, Conn. Fellow Internat. Inst. Arts and Letters (life); mem. Sculptors Guild (charter), Nat. Assn. Women Artists (2d v.p. 1943-44), Artists Council, U.S.A., Bklyn. Soc. Artists, Greenwich Soc. Artists (council), Pen and Brush, Internat. Sculpture Center, Silvermine Guild Artists, Nat. Trust for Historic Preservation.; Mem. Internat. Soc. Artists (charter). Home and Studio: 30 Strickland Rd Cos Cob CT 06807

KANE, NINA GAROFALO, computer company manager, consultant; b. Greenwich, Conn.; m. Robert Edward Kane. BS, U. Bridgeport, 1972, MS, 1973; MLS, U. Md., 1976. Pvt. practice cons., researcher Columbia, Md., 1976-77; info. services mgr. Morrison-Knudsen Saudi Arabia Consortium, Columbia, 1977-79; project coordinator Texaco, Inc., White Plains, N.Y., 1979-84; sr. analyst IBM, Gaithersburg, Md., 1984-85, staff analyst, 1985-86, mgr., 1986—. Author book rev. Productivity/Records Management, 1983, proceedings Conducting System Analysis, 1981. Mem. Assn. Info. and Image Mgmt., Am. Mgmt. Assn., Assn. Info. Mgrs. Home: Siscowit Rd Box 190A Pound Ridge NY 19576 Office: IBM 44 S Broadway White Plains NY 10600

KANEB, ELIZABETH M., nursing home administrator; b. Massena, N.Y., Jan. 16, 1958; d. Edward John and Catherine Margaret (Meinhold) K. BA, St. Lawrence U., 1979; MBA, Clarkson U., Potsdam, N.Y., 1988. Lic. nursing home adminstr. Asst. adminstr. Highland Nursing Home, Inc., Massena, 1983—; sec. Kaneb Realty Corp.

KANE-VANNI, PATRICIA RUTH, lawyer, consultant; b. Phila., Jan. 12, 1954; d. Joseph James and Ruth Marina (Rameriz) Kane; m. Francis William Vanni; Feb. 14, 1980; 1 child, Christian Michael. AB, Chestnut Hill Coll., 1975; JD, Temple U., 1985. Bar: Pa. 1985. Art illustrator Free-lance, Phila., 1972-80; secondary edn. instr. Archdiocese of Phila., 1980-83; contract analyst CIGNA Corp., Phila., 1983-84; judicial aide Phila. Ct. of Common Pleas, 1984; assoc. atty. Anderson and Dougherty, Wayne, Pa., 1985-86; atty. cons. Bell Telephone Co. of Pa., 1986-87; assoc. corp. counsel Blue Cross Greater Phila., 1987—; cons. Coll. Consortium on Drug and Alcohol Abuse, Chester, Pa., 1986—. Contbr. articles and illustrations to profl. mags. Com. woman Dem. Party, Lower Merion, Pa., 1983—; judge Delaware Valley Sci. Fairs, Phila., 1986, 87. Recipient Legion of Honor award Chapel of the Four Chaplins, 1983. Mem. ABA, Phila. Bar Assn., Pa. Bar Assn., Brehon Law Soc., Phila. Assn. Def. Counsel, Nat. Health Lawyers Assn., Phi Alpha Delta. Democrat. Roman Catholic. Home: 32 E Levering Mill Rd Bala Cynwyd PA 19004 Office: Blue Cross Greater Phila 1500 Market St Legal Dept 20th Floor Philadelphia PA 19102

KANG, BANN C., physician; b. Kyungnam, Korea, Mar. 4, 1939; d. Daeryong and Buni (Chung) K.; came to U.S., 1964, naturalized, 1976; A.B., Kyungpook Nat. U., 1959, M.D., 1963; m. U. Yun Ryo, Mar. 30, 1963. Intern, L.I. Jewish Hosp.-Queens Hosp. Center, Jamaica, N.Y., 1964-65, resident in medicine, 1965-67; teaching asso. Kyungpook U. Hosp., Taegu, Korea, 1967-70; fellow in allergy and chest Creighton U., Omaha, 1970-71; fellow in allergy Henry Ford Hosp., Detroit, 1971-72; clin. instr. medicine U. Mich. Hosp., Ann Arbor, 1972-73; asst. prof. Chgo. Med. Sch., 1973-74; chief allergy-immunology Mt. Sinai Hosp., Chgo., 1975—; asst. prof Rush Med. Sch., Chgo. 1975-84, assoc. prof., 1984-86; assoc. prof. U. Ky. Coll. Medicine, 1987—; cons. allergy-immunology Edgewater Hosp., Chgo., 1976—, St. Anthony's Hosp., Chgo., 1976—. Recipient NIH award U. Mich., 1972-73. Diplomate Am. Bd. Internal Medicine, Am. Bd. Allergy-Immunology. Fellow ACP, Am. Acad. Allergy; mem. Am. Fedn. Clin. Research, AMA, Inter-Asthma Assn. Contbr. over 40 articles to profl. jours. Home: 2716 Martinique Ln Lexington KY 40509 Office: U Ky Coll Medicine 629 Albert B Chandler Med Ctr 800 Rose St Lexington KY 40536

KANG, SURINDER (CINDY) A., educator; b. India, June 10, 1940; came to U.S., 1970; d. K.S. and Swaran Sahi; m. Amarjit S. Kang, Feb. 27, 1970; children: Supriya A., Kavita A. BA, Punjab U., 1966, EdB, 1967; MA, So. Meth. U., Dallas, 1976. Cert. elem. tchr., Tex. Tchr. St. Mary's, New Delhi, 1968-70, Big Springs Elem., RISD, Richardson, Tex., 1978—. Mem. Richardson Educators Assn., Richardson Assn. Tex. Profl. Educators. Office: Big Springs Elem 3301 Big Springs St Garland TX 75042

K'ANG, VERSA CLARICE, museum director; b. Victoria, Va., May 28, 1939; d. Ralph Jennings Holder and Clara Hayworth (Weir) Holder Fischer; m. Jay Stephen Anderson, Aug. 11, 1961 (div. 1973); children: Max Kuika'hi, Mark Kuikawa'; m. Lyle Kekahi K'ang, Dec. 19, 1974; 1 child, Micah Ka'aona. BA in Edn., U. Wash., 1961; MA in Am. Studies, U. Hawaii, 1973; postgrad., Cen. Wash. U., 1980. Cert. tchr., Hawaii. Tchr. South Cen. Sch. Dist., Seattle, 1961-63, Kamehameha Schs., Honolulu, 1963-68; tchr., ctr. supr. lang. arts multi-cultural ctr. Hawaii County Econ. Opportunity Council, Honokaa, 1976-78; counselor, supr. People for People, Yakima, Wash., 1978-83; exec. dir. Yakima Valley Mus. and Hist. Assn., 1983—; cons. dept. interdisciplinary studies Heritage Coll., Toppenish, Wash., 1982-83. Contbr. articles on Yakima Valley heritage to various publs. Co-chmn. Gov.'s Commn. on Youth and Leisure Time Activities, Honolulu, 1972-73, sub-com. Wash. State Centennial Commn., Olympia, 1985—. Mem. Nat. Assn. Female Execs., Am. Assn. State and Local History, Am. Assn. Mus., Wash. Mus. Assn., Wash. State Folklife Council (founding bd. dirs. 1983), Yakima C. of C., U. Wash. Alumni Assn., Phi Kappa Phi. Mormon. Lodge: Kiwanis. Home: 910 S 25th Ave Yakima WA 98902 Office: Yakima Valley Mus and Hist Assn 2105 Tieton Dr Yakima WA 98902

KANNRY, SYBIL, psychotherapist, consultant, b. Tulsa, Okla., Oct. 1, 1931; d. Julius and Celia Bertha (Triger) Zeligson; m. Daniel Kannry, June 12, 1977; children by previous marriage—Jeffrey Alan Shames, Erica Leslie Shames, Jonathan Adam Shames. Student U. Colo., 1949-51; B.A., U. Okla., 1953; M.S.W., NYU, 1974. Diplomate in Clin. Social Work; cert. clin. social worker, N.Y.; credentialled alcoholism counselor; cert. employee assistance profl. Tchr. piano, Tulsa, 1956-61; psychiatric social worker Essex County Hosp., Cedar Grove, N.J., 1974-75, Rockland Psychiat. Ctr., Spring Valley, N.Y., 1975, adult team supr., 1975-78, adult team supr., Haverstraw, N.Y., 1978, clinic supr., Orangeburg, N.Y., 1978-83, clinic dir., Yonkers, N.Y., 1983-84; founder, dir. Indsl. Counseling Assocs., South Nyack, N.Y., 1982-84, ctr. for Corp. and Community Counseling, South Nyack, 1984—; founder, pres. Tulsa Assn. for Childbirth Edn., 1957-59. Fellow Soc. Clin. Social Work Psychotherapists; mem. Am. Assn. Marriage and Family Therapy (clin. mem.), N.Y. Milton H. Erickson Soc. for Psychotherapy and Hypnosis, Nat. Assn. Social Workers, Am. Orthopsychiat. Assn., Acad. Cert. Social Workers, Assn. Labor-Mgmt. Adminstrs. and Cons. on Alcholism, Soc. Clin. and Exptl. Hypnosis. Home and Office: 2 Clinton Ave South Nyack NY 10960

KANRICH, SUSAN AZARIA, management consultant; b. Bklyn., Oct. 8, 1938; d. Steve Johnson and Estelle (Miller) Silverman; m. Murray Azaria, June 19, 1960 (div. Nov. 1977); children: Dale Ellen Azaria, Laurie Azaria; m. Kenneth Kanrich, May 29, 1980. BS in Psychology, Brandeis U., Waltham, Mass., 1960; cert. in spl. edn., William Paterson Coll., North Haledon, N.J., 1970; cert. in dispute resolution, John Jay Coll., 1988. Tchr. Teaneck (N.J.) Pub. Schs., 1960-63, 66-75; with sales dept. Unitemp, Paramus, N.J., 1975-77; cons. Sales Cons., Glen Rock, N.J., 1977-87, Sak Inc., Teaneck, 1987—; mediator Am. Arbitration Assn., N.Y.C., 1987—. Interviewer Teaneck Youth Guidance Council, 1970-77; mem. Nat. Council Jewish Women. Mem. Soc. Profls. in Dispute Resolution (vice-chair N.Y.C. chpt. 1988—). Home and Office: 644 Sagamore Ave Teaneck NJ 07666

KANTER, LORETTA ELAINE, retail executive; b. New Haven, Conn., Nov. 17, 1932; d. Abraham and Rose (Nassiter) K. Grad. pub. high sch., Lebanon, Conn. Sec. A. Werman & Sons, Norwich, Conn., 1951-54, Montgomery Ward & Co., Inc., Oakland, Calif., 1954-80; corp. sec., treas. Am. Delivery Service Co., Walnut Creek, Calif., 1980-83, corp. sec., 1983-87, corp. equipment mgr., 1988—. Home: 2562 Walnut Blvd #69 Walnut Creek CA 94596-4247 Office: Am Delivery Service Co 1990 N California Blvd #700 Walnut Creek CA 94596-3711

KANTER, ROSABETH MOSS, management professor, consultant, writer; b. Cleve., Mar. 15, 1943; d. Nelson Nathan and Helen (Smolen) Moss; m. Stuart Alan Kanter, June 20, 1963 (dec. Mar. 1969); m. Barry Alan Stein, July 2, 1972; 1 child, Matthew Moss Kanter Stein. BA, Bryn Mawr Coll., 1964; MA, U. Mich., 1965, PhD, 1967; postgrad., Harvard U. Law Sh., 1975-76; MA (hon.), Yale U., 1978; LHD (hon.), Bucknell U., 1980, Antioch U., Westminster Coll., 1984, Suffolk U., Regis Coll., Union Coll., N. Adams State Coll., 1987; DSc (hon.), Babson Coll., 1984, Bryant Coll., 1986; MA (hon.), Harvard U., 1986. Vis. prof. mgmt. MIT, 1973-74, Harvard U., 1979-80; from assoc. to asst. prof. Brandeis U., 1967-77; prof. Yale U., 1977-86; chmn. bd. Goodmeasure, Inc., Cambridge, Mass., 1980—; Class of 1960 prof. mgmt. Harvard U. Bus. Sch., 1986—; cons. BellSouth, Apple Computer, Procter & Gamble, IBM, Internat. Harvester Co., Honeywell Corp. and numerous others; trustee Coll. Retirement Equities Fund, N.Y., 1985—. Author: Work and Family in the U.S., 1977, Men and Women of the Corporation, 1977 (C. Wright Mills award 1977), The Change Masters, 1983, plus 5 other books; contbr. over 100 articles to profl. jours., books, mags. (2 articles Harvard Bus. Review McKinsey award). Incorporator Babson Coll., 1984—, Boston Children's Mus., 1984—; bd. dirs. Nat. Orgn. Women Legal Def. and Edn. Fund, N.Y., 1979-86, Ctr. New Democracy, Washington, 1985—. Named Woman of the Yr. New Eng. Women's Bus. Owners, 1981, Internat. Assn. Personnel Women, 1981, MS mag., 1985, Working Woman AT&T Hall of Fame, 1986; recipient Athena award Intercollegiate Assn. Women Students, 1980; Guggenheim fellow; numerous research grants. Mem. Am. Sociol. Assn. (exec. council 1982-5), Eastern Sociol. Soc. (exec. com. 1975-78, Gellman award, 1978), Acad. Mgmt., Com. of 200 (founder). Clubs: Yale (N.Y.).; Harvard (Boston). Office: Goodmeasure Inc 330 Broadway PO Box 3004 Cambridge MA 02139 also: Harvard Sch Bus Boston MA 02163 *

KANY, JUDY C(ASPERSON), state senator; b. June 29, 1937; d. Helmer C. and Florence P. Casperson; m. Robert Kany, Aug. 16, 1958; children—Kristin, Geoffrey, Daniel. B.B.A., U. Mich., 1959; M.P.A., U. Maine-Orono, 1976. Mem. Maine Ho. Reps., 1975-82, Maine Senate, 1982—, chmn. Maine's Adv. Commn. on Radioactive Waste, 1981-87, Joint Standing Com. Legal Affairs; former chmn. Joint Standing Com. on State Govt. and Energy and Natural Resources, 1982-86, mem. Commn. on Maine's Future, 1976, 87—; mayor of Waterville, Maine, 1988—. Democrat. Home: 18 West St Waterville ME 04901 Office: State Senate Office State Capitol Augusta ME 04333 also: City Hall Waterville ME 04901

KAPLAN, AMY LOUISE, teacher; b. N.Y.C., June 14, 1950; d. Max and Anne Esther (Langsam) K. BA, U. Conn., 1972, MA, 1978; postgrad., Fairfield U., 1979-82, N.Y. Med. Coll., 1982-83. Cert. tchr., Conn. Tchr. Columbia (Conn.) Bd. Edn., 1972-73, Manchester (Conn.) Bd. Edn., 1973-74, Trumbull (Conn.) Bd. Edn., 1974-79; project dir. Weston Group, Westport, Conn., 1981; tchr. Easton (Conn.) Bd. Edn., 1983-84; dir. Learning Ctr., Westport, 1983—; tchr. Westport Bd. Edn., 1984—. Mem. Dem. Town Com., Fairfield, 1987; fundraiser Hole-in-the-Wall Gang Day Camp, Westport, 1987-88. Mem. NEA, Conn. Edn. Assn. (assembly rep. 1975). Club: Flying Eagles (Stratford, Conn.) (bd. dirs. 1987—). Office: The Learning Center 10 Bay St Suite 140 Westport CT 06880

KAPLAN, ARLENE LAVENDER, banker; b. N.Y.C., Mar. 4, 1928; d. Michael and Leah Lavender; B.A. in Math. cum laude, SUNY, Albany, 1948; M.A. in Math., Columbia U., 1966; m. Bernard Kaplan, Aug. 23, 1952; children—Lee Michael, Jonathan Harris. Actuarial asst. G.B. Buck, Cons. Actuary, 1948-54; programmer Bankers Trust Co., N.Y.C., 1966-68, mgmt. scientist, 1968-72, asst. treas., asst. v.p. retail planning, 1972-79, v.p., head mgmt. info. systems in strategic planning dept., 1979—. Home: 27 Pryer Manor Rd Larchmont NY 10538 Office: 280 Park Ave New York NY 10015

KAPLAN, DOROTHY ANNE, clinical psychologist; b. N.Y.C., May 7, 1954; d. Milton and Madeleine (Hundert) Kaplan; B.A. with highest honors in Psychology, SUNY-Stony Brook, 1975; Ph.D. in Clin. Psychology (NIMH fellow), U. Vt., 1979. Asst. prof. psychology SUNY Coll. at Brockport, 1979-83; dir. psychol. services Children's Hosp. and Rehab. Ctr., Utica, N.Y., 1983-85; sr. clin. psychologist Nat. Rehab. Hosp., Washington, 1986—; cons. clin. psychologist Orleans County Mental Health, Job Corps., Office Vocat. Rehab., Bur. Disability Determination; lectr. U. Vt., 1978-79. Lic. psychologist, N.Y. Mem. Assn. for Advancement of Behavior Therapy, Am. Psychol. Assn., N.Y. State Psychol. Assn., Gennesee Valley Psychol. Assn. (v.p.), Soc. for Study of Social Issues, Phi Beta Kappa. Contbr. articles to profl. jours. Home: 5 Saddle River Ct Gaithersburg MD 20878 Office: Psychol Services Nat Rehab Hosp 102 Irving St Washington DC 20010

KAPLAN, ERICA LYNN, typing/word processing service company executive, pianist, vocal coach; b. Jamaica, N.Y., Aug. 6, 1955; d. George William and Raylia (Eagle) Kaplan; m. James Laurence Kellermann, Feb. 26, 1982. B.Mus., Manhattan Sch. Music, N.Y.C., 1976, M.Mus., 1979. Clk. dept. edn. 92d Street Y, N.Y.C., 1972-76, assoc. dept. pub. relations, 1977-78, catalogue coordinator, sec. to exec. dir., 1978, assoc. dept. performing arts, 1978-79, assoc. dir. dept. publications, 1979-80; pres. Erica Kaplan Typing/Word Processing/Music Services, N.Y.C., 1980—; piano soloist Huntington (N.Y.) Philharmonia, 1975; rehearsal pianist, performance accompanist The Mikado, Playwrights Horizons, N.Y.C., 1975, Fiona in Swan Song, N.Y.C., 1986; mus. dir., accompanist A Salute to Vaudeville/A Tribute to Fred Astaire, N.Y.C., 1980—; mus. dir., pianist Portrait of a Man, Hyde Pk. (N.Y.) Festival Theatre, 1981, Am. Renaissance Theater, N.Y.C., 1982, 86, The Fantasticks, Dalton Sch., N.Y.C., 1983; performance accompanist Oklahoma, Theatreworks, Bklyn., 1984; resident pianist Am. Renaissance Theater, N.Y.C., 1981—; audition accompanist Interboro Repertory Theatre, N.Y.C., 1986—. Translator and annotator with additional mus. examples: L'Anacrouse dans la Musique Moderne, 1978; composer (songs) Four by Feiffer, 1978, Hey Boys, 1984. Mem. New Eng. Anti-Vivisection Soc., Boston, 1982—, Common Cause, Washington, 1983—. Mem. Am. Fedn. Musicians, Nat. Assn. Female Execs., Union Concerned Scientists. Democrat. Jewish. Avocations: theater, travel.

KAPLAN, HELENE LOIS, lawyer; b. N.Y.C., June 19, 1933; d. Jack and Shirley (Jacobs) Finkelstein; m. Mark N. Kaplan, Sept. 7, 1952; children: Marjorie Ellen, Sue Anne. AB cum laude, Barnard Coll., 1953; JD, NYU, 1967. Bar: N.Y. 1967. Sole practice N.Y.C., 1967-78; assoc. Webster & Sheffield, N.Y.C., 1978-86; counsel Webster & Sheffield, 1986—; bd. dirs. The May Dept. Stores, Met. Life Ins. Co., Chem. Bankip Corp., Chem. Bank, N.Y. Partnership Inc., Verde Exploration Ltd. Trustee N.Y. Council for the Humanities, 1976-82, chmn., 1978-82; trustee Barnard Coll., 1973-83, chmn., 1983—, trustee Columbia U. Press, 1977-80, MITRE Corp., 1978—, N.Y. Found., 1976-86, Mt. Sinai Hosp. Med. Ctr. and Med. Sch., 1977—, John Simon Guggenheim Meml. Found., 1981—, NYU Law Ctr. Found., 1985-87, Carnegie Corp. N.Y., 1979—, vice chmn., 1981-84, chmn., 1984-87; trustee Inst. for Advanced Study, 1986—, Neuroscis. Research Found., 1986—; mem. adv. com. of U.S. Sec. of State on South Africa, 1986-88; mem. N.Y. State Gov.'s Task Force on Life and the Law, 1985—; trustee N.Y.C. Pub. Devel. Corp., 1978-83, vice chmn., 1979-82; trustee Olive Free Library; bd. dirs. Am. Arbitration Assn., 1978-82, Catskill Ctr. for Conservation and Devel., 1981—; mem. Women's Forum, Inc., 1982—; mem. council Rockefeller U., 1984—; mem. Bretton Woods Com., 1985—; mem. Carnegie Council on Adolescent Devel., 1986—, Carnegie Commn. on Sci., Tech., and Govt., 1988—. Mem. N.Y.C. Bar Assn. (com. on philanthropic orgn. 1975-81, recruitment of lawyers 1978-82, com. on profl. responsibility 1980-83), AB A, N.Y. State Bar Assn., Council Fgn. Relations. Club: Cosmopolitan, Coffee House (N.Y.C.). Home: 146 Central Park W New York NY 10023 Office: 237 Park Ave 20th Floor New York NY 10017

KAPLAN, JANET GORDON, music educator; b. Boston, Nov. 30, 1938; d. Morris and A. Ruby (Perlman) G.; children: Beth, Deborah, Paul. AA, Los Angeles Valley Coll., 1968; BA, Calif. State U., 1984, MA in Ednl. Psychology, 1987. Intern social work Los Angeles Children's Bur., 1982, Valley Hosp. Med. Ctr., Van Nuys, Calif., 1983; tchr., coach, judge string music Los Angeles County Schs., 1983—; cons. San Fernando Valley Community Concerts, Van Nuys. Pres. Los Angeles Philharmonic Docents, 1977-80. Mem. Music Tchrs. Assn., Am. String Tchrs. Assn., Mu Phi Epsilon (pres. 1980-82, Outstanding Musician 1958, Music Therapy award 1981-84, Edn. award 1986).

KAPLAN, JOCELYN RAE, financial planning firm executive; b. Lynbrook, N.Y., Apr. 23, 1952; d. Eugene S. and Adeline (Dembo) K. B.S., Northwestern U., 1975. Cert. fin. planner. Ins. agt. Fidelity Union Life Ins. Co., College Park, Md., 1976-77, Bankers Life Ins. Co., Rockville, Md., 1977-80; fin. planner Reutemann & Wagner, McLean, Va., 1980-82; fin. planning casewriter McLean Fin. Group, 1982-83; dir. fin. planning DeSanto Naftal Co., Vienna, Va., 1983-85; pres. Advisors Fin., Inc., Vienna, 1985—. Founding mem., treas. Congregation Bet Mishpachah, Washington, 1981, v.p., 1982, pres., 1983. Recipient Nat. Quality award Nat. Assn. Life Underwriters, 1978; Agt. of Yr. award Gen. Agt. and Mgrs. Assn., 1978. Mem. Internat. Assn. Fin. Planners, Inst. Cert. Fin. Planners, Registry of Fin. Planning Practitioners. Home: 2224 N Pollard St Arlington VA 22207 Office: Advisors Fin Inc 8321 Old Courthouse Rd Suite 250 Vienna VA 22180

KAPLAN, JUDITH HELENE, business executive; b. N.Y.C., July 20, 1938; d. Abraham and Ruth (Kiffel) Letich; m. Warren Kaplan, Dec. 31, 1958; children: Ronald Scott, Elissa Aynn. BA, Hunter Coll., 1955; postgrad., New Sch. for Social Research, 1955-56. Registered rep. Herzfeld & Stern, N.Y.C., 1963; agt. New York Life Ins. Co., N.Y.C., 1964-69; registered rep. Scheinman, Hochstin & Trotta, 1969-70; v.p. Alpha Capital Corp., N.Y.C., 1970-74; pres. Tipex, Inc., N.Y.C., 1966-84; v.p. Alpha Pub. Relations, N.Y.C., 1970-73; pres. Utopia Recreations Corp., 1971-73, Howard Beach Recreation Corp., 1972-73; chmn. bd. Alpha Exec. Planning Corp., 1970-72; field underwriter N.Y. Life Ins. Co., 1974-75; pres. Action Packets Inc., 1978-87, chairperson, 1980—, Ronel Industries, Inc., 1982-84; participant White House Conf. on Small Bus., 1979. Author: Woman Suffrage, 1977; co-author: Space Patches-from Mercury to the Space Shuttle, 1986; contbg. editor: Stamp Show News, M & H Philatelic Report; creator, producer Women's History series of First Day Covers, 1976-81; contbr. articles to profl. jours. Wyo. adv. on woman suffrage; trustee Found. for Innovative Lifelong Edn. Inc., 1986—; named Outstanding Young Citizen, Manhattan Jaycees, Small Bus. Person of Yr. State of Fla, 1986. Mem. NOW (ins. coordinator nat. task force on taxes, v.p. N.Y. chpt., co-founder Ocala/Marion County chpt. 1982, bd. women's adv. council Ocala and Marian Counties 1986—), Nat. Women's Polit. Caucus, Women Leaders Round Table, Nat. Assn. Life Underwriters, Assn. Stamp Dealers Am., Am. First Day Cover Soc. (life), Am. Philatelic Soc. (life), Bus. and Profl. Women, AAUW. Home: 577 Silver Course Circle Ocala FL 32672 Office: 344 Cypress Rd Ocala FL 32672

KAPLAN, MADELINE, law firm administrator; b. N.Y.C., June 20, 1944; d. Leo and Ethel (Finkelstein) Kahn; m. Theodore Norman Kaplan, Nov. 14, 1982. AS, Fashion Inst. Tech., N.Y.C., 1964; BA in English Lit. summa cum laude, CUNY, 1982. Free-lance fashion illustrator N.Y.C., 1965-73; legal asst. Krause Hirsch & Gross, Esquires, N.Y.C., 1973-80; mgr. communications Stroock & Stroock & Lavan Esquires, N.Y.C., 1980-86; dir. adminstrn. Cooper Cohen Singer & Ecker Esquires, N.Y.C., 1986-87, Donovan Leisure Newton & Irvine Esquires, N.Y.C., 1987—. Contbr. articles to profl. jours. Founder, pres. Knolls chpt. of Women's Am. Orgn. Rehab. Through Tng., Riverdale, N.Y., 1979-82, v.p. edn., Manhattan region, 1982-83. Mem. Women Info. Processing, Assn. Legal Adminstrs., Am. Soc. Tng. and Devel., Adminstrv. Mgmt. Soc.

KAPLAN, SHEILA, university official; b. Bklyn.. BA in European History, CUNY, PhD in Modern European History; MA, Johns Hopkins U. Instr. history CUNY System; dir. Spl. Baccalaureate Program CUNY; v.p. acad. affairs Winona (Minn.) State U.; vice chancellor for acad. affairs Minn. State U. System; chancellor U. Wis.-Parkside, Kenosha, 1986—. Bd. dirs. Kenosha Area Devel. Corp., Racine County Econ. Devel. Corp.; chmn. bd. Council for Adult and Experiential Learning. Office: U of Wis-Parkside Box 2000 Kenosha WI 53141-2000

KAPLAN, SYLVIA YALOWITZ KAPLAN (MRS. MILTON I. KAPLAN), librarian, educator; b. Chgo., May 23, 1921; d. Max and Gertrude (Yalowitz) K.; Ph.B., Northwestern U., 1956; M.A. in L.S., Rosary Coll., 1961, postgrad., 1962; postgrad. U. Ill., 1965-69, HEA Inst. on Reclassification, Rosary Coll., 1969, DePaul U., 1970; doctoral candidate (scholar, grad. asst.) U. Pitts., 1980-86; m. Milton I. Kaplan, Apr. 5, 1959. Asst. librarian Argonne Nat. Lab., U. Chgo., 1943-50; chief med. librarian Mcpl. Tb Sanitarium, Chgo., 1953-57; sch. librarian, Gary, Ind., 1957-59; librarian Inst. Applied Research, U. Chgo., 1961-62; chief librarian, instr. med. bibliography Chgo. Med. Sch., 1960-64; librarian Michael Reese Hosp. Sch. Nursing, Chgo., 1964-66; chief librarian Ill. Dept. Mental Health, 1967-70; instr. library sci. Northeastern Ill. State Coll., 1970—; asst. prof. library sci. Eastern Ill. U., Charleston, 1970—. Mem. AAUW, AAUP (officer), Med. Library Assn. (cert.), Am. Assn. Library Schs., Spl. Libraries Assn., Assn. Acad. Librarians, Internat. Assn. Semantics, Hadassah, Internat. Platform Assn. (hon.), Delta Kappa Gamma (hon.; scholar 1979). Democrat. Jewish. Contbr. revs. to profl. jours. Office: Eastern Ill U Dept Library Sci Charleston IL 61920

KAPNICK, LAURA BETH, library administrator; b. N.Y.C., June 8, 1951; d. Emanuel and Shirley (Glassner) K. BA, George Washington U., 1973; MLS, CUNY, 1974. Research librarian Consumers Union of U.S., Inc., Mt. Vernon, N.Y., 1975-77; serials librarian CBS News, N.Y.C., 1977, mgr. library services, 1977-81, dir. reference library, 1981—; mng. librarian CBS Tech. Ctr., Stamford, Conn., 1981. Mem. Spl. Libraries Assn. Office: CBS News 524 W 57th St New York NY 10019

KAPP, NANCY GLADYS, savings and loan executive; b. Oak Park, Ill., Jan. 23, 1945; d. Andrew John and Gladys Abigail (Johnson) McClintock; m. Ted Martin Kapp, Sept. 28, 1973; children—Adam, Natalie, Pamela. B.S.Ed., No. Ill. U., DeKalb, 1968; postgrad. Nat. Coll. Edn., Evanston, Ill., 1969-70. Tchr. elementary/jr. high sch. Dist. 96, Riverside, Ill., 1968-71, high sch. substitute tchr., 1971-72; personnel dept. sec. St. Paul Fed. Bank for Savs., Chgo., 1971-73, sr. exec. sec. to pres., 1973-80, adminstv. asst. legal dept., 1980—. Dir., chmn. Community Sch. of Galewood, Chgo., 1983-84; mem. Republican Nat. Com., 1979—; sponsor GOP Victory Fund, Rep. Party, Washington, 1982—; mem. Rep. Presdl. Task force, 1984—. Mem.

Nat. Assn. Female Execs., AAUW, Nat. Assn. Exec. Secs., Nat. Paralegal Assn. Republican. Episcopalian. Office: St Paul Fed Bank for Savs 6700 W North Ave Chicago IL 60635

KAPPA, MARGARET MCCAFFREY, resort hotel consultant; b. Wabasha, Minn., May 14, 1921; d. Joseph Hugh and Verna Mae (Anderson) McCaffrey; B.S. in Hotel Mgmt., Cornell U., 1944; grad. Dale Carnegie course, 1978; cert. hospitality housekeeping exec.; m. Nicholas Francis Kappa, Sept. 15, 1956; children—Nicholas Joseph, Christopher Francis. Asst. exec. housekeeper Kahler Hotel, Rochester, Minn., 1944; exec. housekeeper St. Paul Hotel, 1944-47, Plaza Hotel, N.Y.C., 1947-51; exec. housekeeper, personnel dir. Athearn Hotel, Oshkosh, Wis., 1952-58; dir. housekeeping The Greenbrier, White Sulphur Springs, W.Va., 1958-84; cons., 1984—; tchr. housekeeping U.S. and fgn. countries; cons.; vis. lectr. Cornell U. Pres. St. Charles Borromeo Parish Assn., White Sulphur Springs, 1962, v.p., 1980, 82; tech. adv., host 2 ednl. videos Am. Hotel and Motel Assn., 1986. Recipient diploma of honor Société Culinaire Philanthropique, 1961. Mem. Cornell Soc. Hotelmen (pres. 1980-81, exec. com. 1981-82), Nat. Exec. Housekeepers Assn. (pres. N.Y. chpt. 1950), N.Y.U. Hotel and Restaurant Soc. (hon. life). Republican. Roman Catholic. Clubs: Nat. Woman's; Quota (charter mem. Greenbrier County). Home and Office: 323 W Main St Wabasha MN 55981

KAPPLER-MEYERS, LYDIA PATRICIA, electronics executive; b. Trenton, N.J., Apr. 15, 1958; d. Harry Patrick and Lydia Jane (Arnold) Kappler; m. Harry A. Meyers. Student, Nova U. Various mgmt. positions Lionel Leisure Inc., Phila., 1976-83; product merchandiser IMAGIC Co., Los Gatos, Calif., 1983; sales rep. CAL-ABCO Inc., Woodland Hills, Calif., 1983-84, area mgr., 1984, dist. mgr., 1984-85, mgr. regional sales east coast, 1985—. Mem. Nat. Assn. Female Execs. Democrat. Roman Catholic. Home: 4491 Crystal Lake Dr #106B Pompano Beach FL 33064 Office: CAL-ABCO Inc 6041 Variel Ave Woodland Hills CA 91367

KAPPMEYER, BETTE JEANE (BETTE KAYE), entertainment agency executive, producer; b. Chgo., Dec. 9, 1922; d. Emanuel Donald and Sophia Lee (Rowitz) Weiser; m. Charles Frank Kappmeyer, Feb. 23, 1946; children—Robert Joseph, Marcia Diane, Phyllis Darlene, Michelle Charlene. B.A., Md. U., 1960. Pres. Bette Kaye Prodns., 1946-69, treas., Sacramento, 1962—; founder, pres. Rete Inc., 1979-82, chmn. bd. dirs., 1982—; producer Mid State Fair, Paso Robles, Calif., 1968-85, Stanislaus County Fair, Calif., 1968—. Organizer Wiesbaden PTA, Germany, 1948, YES Youth Employment Services, Travis AFB, 1954, choral clubs at various bases, 1950-61. Served with U.S. Army, 1944-45. Commended by resolution Calif. State Assembly, 1974, Calif. Senate Rules Com., 1973. Mem. Country Music Assn. (dir. 1981-84), Acad. Country Music (dir. 1984-85). Republican. Lutheran. Avocations: clown collector, travel, thoroughbred horses, sports, sponsoring youth baseball teams. Office: PO Box 61048 Sacramento CA 95860

KAPPY, KATHLEEN ANNE, psychologist; b. Bronxville, N.Y., July 2, 1953; d. Thaddeus Roman and Eileen Marie (McEntee) K. BA, Coll. Mt. St. Vincent, 1974; MA, Fordham U., 1976, PhD, 1979. Research asst. Psychological Corp., N.Y.C., 1974-75; research assoc. Nat. Acad. Scis., Washington, 1978; sr. research asst. Ednl. Testing Service, Evanston, Ill., 1978-79; indsl. psychologist So. Calif. Edison, Rosemead, 1979-82, research adminstr., 1982-85, mgr. HR measurement, 1985-87, mgr., measurement and devel., 1987—; pvt. practice cons., Los Angeles. 1977—; adj. prof. U. San Francisco, 1981—; nat. coordinator Edison Electric Inst., Washington, 1986—. Psychometrics fellow Psychological Corp., N.Y.C., 1974, Ednl. Testing Service Fellow, Princeton, N.J., 1976. Mem. Am. Psychological Assn. Home: 599 S Oakland Ave Pasadena CA 91106 Office: So Calif Edison 2244 Walnut Grove Rosemead CA 91770

KAPSNER, ROSE MARY, information systems specialist; b. St. Cloud, Minn., Dec. 20, 1955; d. Leander Frank and Marcella (Peuringer) K. BA, St. John's U., St. Joseph, Minn., 1977; postgrad., Webster U., 1987—. Trainer Equitable Life Assurance Co., St. Paul, 1977-82; mgr. sect. Equitable Life Assurance Co., Colo. Springs, Colo., 1982-83; assoc. mgr. project Equitable Life Assurance Co., Colo. Springs, 1983-86; rep. bus. support Advanced Systems Applications, Bloomingdale, Ill., 1986—. Mem. Nat. Orgn. Exec. Women. Democrat. Roman Catholic. Home: 384 Hilton Dr Glendale Heights IL 60139 Office: Advanced Systems Applications 1 ASA Plaza Bloomingdale IL 60139

KAPTUR, MARCIA CAROLYN, congresswoman; b. Toledo, June 17, 1946. B.A., U. Wis., 1968; M. Urban Planning, U. Mich., 1974; postgrad., U. Manchester, (Eng.), 1974. Urban planne; asst. dir. urban affairs domestic policy staff White House, 1977-79; mem. 98th-100th Congresses from 9th Dist. Ohio, 1983—. Bd. dirs. Nat. Ctr. Urban Ethnic Affairs; adv. com. Gund Found.; exec. com. Lucas County Democratic Com.; mem. Dem. Women's Campaign Assn. Mem. Am. Planning Assn., Am. Inst. Cert. Planners, NAACP, Urban League, Polish Mus., U. Mich. Urban Planning Alumni Assn. (bd. dirs.), Polish Am. Hist. Assn. Roman Catholic. Clubs: Lucas County Dem. Bus. and Profl. Women's, Fulton County Dem. Women's. Office: US House of Reps 1228 Longworth House Bldg Washington DC 20515 *

KAPUS, KERI LYNN, management training executive; b. Burbank, Calif., Aug. 23, 1963; d. Theodore Edmond and Theresa Marie (Budd) Kapus. B.S. in Bus. Administrn., U. Pacific, 1985. Sr. employee Dialyn Corp., Simi Valley, Calif., 1979-85; intern Senator John Garamendi, Stockton, Calif., 1985; mgr. Gallo Winery, South San Francisco, 1985-87; staff coordinator, account exec. White Collar Personnel Services Inc., San Francisco, 1987—. Contbr. articles to profl. arbitration publs. Mem. AAUW, Nat. Assn. Female Execs., U. Pacific Alumni Assn., Delta Sigma Pi, Lambda Kappa Sigma. Avocations: sports; music; travel. Office: White Collar Temp Services 44 Montgomery St Suite 1200 San Francisco CA 94104

KAPUSTIN, ELEANOR LOUISE, paralegal; b. La Mesa, Calif., Dec. 28, 1960; d. Rudolf and Vera June (Sedorovich) K. AA in Liberal Arts, Catonsville Community Coll., 1981; BA in Polit. Sci., U. Tex., Arlington, 1984; postgrad., U. Tex., Dallas, 1985—. Comml. teller Equitable Bank & Trust Co., Columbia, Md., 1977-78; loan counselor Fraternity Fed. Savs. and Loan, Ellicott City, Md., 1978-79; asst. office mgr. New TV Dating Game, Silver Spring, Md., 1979-81; data base engr. Redifussion Simulation Inc., Arlington, 1981-83; data base adminstr. Univ. Computing Co., Dallas, 1983; paralegal Jackson, Walker, et. al., Dallas, 1983-87, Gibson, Dunn & Crutcher, Dallas, 1987—; legal asst. South Dallas Legal Clinic, 1985-87. Bd. dirs., v.p. Dallas Tenants' Assn., Dallas, 1984-85; counselor Chance Ctr. Child Abuse Prevention, Dallas, 1987. Mem. Nat. Assn. Female Execs., Legal Assts. Div. State Bar of Tex. (Legal Asst. award 1986), Pi Sigma Alpha. Democrat. Lutheran. Office: Gibson Dunn & Crutcher 1700 Pacific Ave Suite 4400 Dallas TX 75201

KARABATSOS, ELIZABETH ANN, federal official; b. Geneva, Nebr., Oct. 25, 1932; d. Karl Christian and Margaret Maurine (Emrich) Brinkman; m. Kimon Tom Karabatsos, Apr. 21, 1957 (div. Feb. 1981); children: Tom Kimon, Maurine Elizabeth, Karl Kimon. BS, U. Nebr., 1954; postgrad., Ariz. State U., 1980; Cert. contemporary exec. devel., George Washington U., 1985. Instr. bus. Fairbury (Nebr.) High Sch., 1954-55; staff asst. U.S. Congress, Washington, 1955-60; with Karabatsos & Co. Pub. Relations, Washington, 1960-73; conf. asst. to asst. adminstr. and dep. adminstr. Gen. Services Adminstrn., Washington, 1973-76; dir. corr. Office Pres.-Elect, Washington, 1980; assoc. dir. adminstrv. services Pres. Personnel-White House, Washington, 1981; dept. asst.to Sec. and Dep. Sec. Def., Washington, 1981-86, asst. to, 1987—. Mem. Nat. Mus. Women in Art, Washington, Rep. Women's Fed. Forum, Washington. Mem. AAUW, Office of Sec. Def. Sr. Profl. Women, Women in Def. (sec. 1987), Pi Omega Pi, Pi Beta Phi. Episcopalian. Lodge: Order Eastern Star. Home: PO Box 726 McLean VA 22101

KARAN, DONNA (FASKE), fashion designer; b. Forest Hills, N.Y., Oct. 2, 1948; m. Mark Karan; 1 child, Gabrielle. Ed., Parsons Sch. of Design. With Addenda Co., to 1968; with Anne Klein & Co., N.Y.C., 1968-84; co-designer Anne Klein & Co., 1971-74, designer, 1974-84; owner, designer Donna Karan Co., N.Y.C., 1984—. Recipient Coty award, 1977, 81; recipient Coty Hall of Fame [illegible] Klein & Co 215 W 39th St New York NY 10018 *

KARASICK, CAROL, advertising agency executive; b. N.Y.C., 1941. Grad., Boston U., 1962; former sr. v.p., Saatchi & Saatchi Compton (now Saatchi & Saatchi DFS Compton), N.Y.C., now exec. v.p., dir. media ops. Office: Saatchi & Saatchi DFS Compton Inc 375 Hudson St New York NY 10014 *

KARASIK, GITA, concert pianist; b. San Francisco, Dec. 14, 1949; d. Monia and Bereni Karasik; pupil of Lev Shorr, Rosina Lhevinne, Karl Ulrich Schnabel. Debut as soloist, San Francisco Symphony, 1958; debut on nat. TV, Bell Telephone Hour, 1964; N.Y.C. debut Carnegie Hall, 1972; film score debut Andy Warhol: Made in China, 1986; solo recitalist, guest soloist with major orchs. throughout world, 1955—; tchr. master classes, 1970—; 1st Am. pianist to make ofcl. concert tour of China, 1980; mem. music adv. panel solo artists Nat. Endowment Arts, 1980; interdisciplinary panel 1st D.C. Arts Commn., 1981; mem. Artists for Nuclear Disarmament, Artists to End Hunger. Recipient Solo Artists award Nat. Endowment Arts, 1981-82, Artists award and commd. concerto Ford Found., 1976, Musicians award Rockefeller Found., 1982, 1st prize Xerox/Affiliate Artists Internat. Piano Competition, 1982; winner Young Concert Artists Internat. Auditions, 1969; Solo artist sponsorship Pro Musicis Found., 1978—, Bösendorfer Piano Co., 1976—. Address: care Lee Caplin Prodns 8274 Grand View Los Angeles CA 90046

KARASOV, PHYLLIS, lawyer; b. St. Paul, Oct. 3, 1951; d. Elliott Karasov and Doris Unger; m. Alan David Olstein, Sept. 2, 1979; 2 children. B.A. with honors, U. Rochester, 1973; J.D., Emory U., 1976. Bar: Minn. 1976, Ga. 1976. Atty., NLRB, Mpls., 1976-81, Moore, Costello & Hart, St. Paul, 1981—; bd. dirs. U. Minn. Student Legal Services, Mpls., 1982-85 . Pres. bd. dirs. Talmud Torah of St. Paul, 1983-85; trustee Minn. Women Lawyers Polit. Action Com., 1982-84; bd. dirs. Resources for Child Caring, 1985—, St. Paul United Jewish Fund Council, 1986— . Recipient Young Leadership award St. Paul United Jewish Fund Council, 1987; acad. scholarships Emory U. Sch. Law, Atlanta, 1973-76, U. Rochester, 1969-73. Mem. ABA, Minn. Bar Assn. (editor labor law sect. newsletter 1982-83), Minn. Women Lawyers (pres. 1979-80). Jewish. Home: 1841 Walsh Ln Saint Paul MN 55118 Office: Moore Costello & Hart 1400 Norwest Ctr Saint Paul MN 55101

KARDON, JANET, museum director, curator; b. Phila.; d. Robert and Shirley (Drasin) Stolker; m. Robert Kardon, Nov. 19, 1955; children: Ross, Nina, Roy. B.S. in Edn., Temple U.; M.A. in Art History, U. Pa. Lectr. Phila. Coll. Art, 1968-75, dir. exhbns., 1975-78; dir. Inst. Contemporary Art, Phila., 1978—; cons., panel mem. Nat. Endowment for Arts, 1975—; vice chmn. visual arts panel Pa. Council on Arts, Phila., 1978—; U.S. commr. Venice Biennale, Venice, 1980. Curated and created essays for 30 exhbns., including Laurie Anderson, Siah Armajani, David Salle. Grantee Nat. Endowment for Arts, 1978. Mem. Assn. Art Mus. Dirs. Club: Cosmopolitan. Home: Rittenhouse Plaza 1901 Walnut St Apt 21-A Philadelphia PA 19103 Office: U Pa Inst Contemporary Art 34th & Walnut Sts Philadelphia PA 19104

KARELITZ-LESHAY, MAXINE HOFFMAN, social service agency executive, educator; b. Bklyn., May 29, 1942; d. Jacob and Jean Lorraine (Fierstein) Hoffman; m. Julian Robert Karelitz, Oct. 2, 1960 (div. Dec. 1963); 1 child, Gavin Alexander Karelitz; m. Steven Vedder LeShay, Apr. 17, 1982. B.A., Bklyn. Coll., 1976; M.S.W., Barry Coll. Sch. Social Work, Miami Shores, Fla., 1978. Cert. social worker, N.Y. Social worker Seminole Indian Reservation, Hollywood, Fla., 1976-78, Children's Home Soc., Fort Lauderdale, Fla., 1977-78, United Cerebral Palsy, N.Y.C., 1978-80; instr. sociology and social work Glassboro State Coll., N.J., 1980—; dir. and cons. social services N.J. Meml. Home, Vineland, N.J., 1980-86; exec. dir., founder Women On Their Own, Inc., Malaga, N.J., 1982—. Mem. Guideposts Women's Consortium, Glassboro State Coll., 1984—, mem. adv. bd. career direction for single parents and homemakers, 1985-87; adv. citizen advocacy Assn. Retarded Citizens, Gloucester County, N.J., 1986-87; mem. Reach planning sub-com., Gloucester County, N.J., 1987—; active People Against Spouse Abuse, Woodbury, N.J., 1986-87. Named hon. capt. U.S. Naval Res., 1980; child welfare trainee Barry Coll. Sch. Social Work, 1977-78. Mem. Nat. Assn. Social Workers, N.J. Assn. Displaced Homemakers. Mem. Christian Science Ch. Office: Women On Their Own Inc PO Box O Malaga NJ 08328

KARKLINS, VIJA L., librarian; b. Riga, Latvia, USSR, Apr. 16, 1929. BA in Comparative Lit., CCNY, 1955; MLS, Columbia U., 1957. Pre-profl. librarian Bklyn. Pub. Library, 1955-57; with pub. relations dept. Socony Mobil Oil Co., 1957-59; librarian Bio-Med. Library U. Minn., 1958-61, 62-63; with NIH, 1963-75, cataloger, 1963-65, 1965-69, head catalog dept., 1969-72, chief tech. services, 1972-75; assoc. dir. libraries for bibliog. systems Smithsonian Inst., 1975—; mem. Fedlinn Exec. Adv. Council, Washington, 1979-82, 86—. Mem. ALA, Southern Library Assn., Fed. Library Network (exec. advt. council 1979—), D.C. Library Assn. Office: Smithsonian Instn Libraries Constitution Ave/10th St NW Washington DC 20560

KARKLIS-CALDWELL, BARBARA LEE PARIS, nurse, director of nursing; b. Oak Park, Ill., June 21, 1942; d. James Archie and Doloris Muriel (Chaput) Paris; m. Zigurds Karklis, Jan. 28, 1966 (div. Aug. 1981); children: Elizabeth Ann, Edward Andrew; m. Leonard A. Caldwell Jr., Apr. 13, 1988. A.A.S., Bklyn. Coll., 1965; student Troy State U. Registered nurse, N.Y., Ga., Ala. R.N., staff nurse, unit coordinator Cobb Hosp., Phenix City, Ala., 1981-84; dir. nursing Chattahoochee Valley Nursing Services, Inc., Columbus, Ga., 1984—. Contbr. poetry and articles to various publs. Instr., Army Community Services, Va., Wash.; vol., instr. A.R.C., Nurnberg; trainer Pacific Peaks council Girl Scout U.S. Mem. Am. Nurses Assn., Ga. Nurses Assn., Nat. Assn. Female Execs., Columbus Area Network Profl. and Exec. Women. Roman Catholic. Clubs: Officers Wives, Non-Commissioned Officers Wives. Avocations: skin diving, macrame, water skiing, snow skiing, hiking, backpacking, sketching, sewing, interior decorating. Home: 979 Trophy Club Dr Roanoke TX 76262 Office: FAA 4400 Blue Mound Rd Fort Worth TX 76193-0150

KARLBERG, KRISTINA ANN, sales professional; b. Chgo., Feb. 18, 1954; d. Wayne Lee Ambroze and June Dolores (Karlberg) Gilmore; children: Michele Danine, Melissa Ann, Alexandra Ann. BS in Liberal Arts, U. Ill., 1975; MA in Edn., Northwestern U., 1977; MBA, Rosary Coll., 1982. Tchr. elem. sch. Rufus Hitch Grammar Sch., Chgo., 1975-76; mktg. support rep. Lanier Bus. Products, Chgo., 1977; br. mgr. Newark Electronics div. Premier Indsl. Corp., Chgo., 1977-78; market coordinator Ultravue Key Market, field sales trainer Am. Optical Corp. div. Warner Lambert, Southbridge, Mass., 1979-80; regional sales mgr. East Cen. region Syntex Ophthalmics Inc div. Syntex Corp., Chgo., 1980-86; regional sales mgr. SE region Sola-Syntex Ophthalmics Inc. div. Sola Internat., 1986—. Republican. Office: Sola/ Barnes-Hind 895 Kifer Rd Sunnyvale CA 94086

KARLE, ISABELLA, chemist; b. Detroit, Dec. 2, 1921; d. Zygmunt Apolonaris and Elizabeth (Graczyk) Lugoski; m. Jerome Karle, June 4, 1942; children: Louise Hanson, Jean Marianne, Madeleine Tawney. BS in Chemistry, U. Mich., 1941, MS in Chemistry, 1942, PhD, 1944; DSc (hon.), U. Mich., 1976, Wayne State U., 1979, U. Md., 1986; LHD (hon.), Georgetown U., 1984. Assoc. chemist U. Chgo., 1944; instr. chemistry U. Mich., Ann Arbor, 1944-46; physicist Naval Research Lab., Washington, 1946—; mem. exec. com. Am. Peptide Symposium, 1975-81, adv. bd. Chem. and Engring. News, 1986—. Mem. editorial bd.: Polymers Jour., 1975—, Internat. Jour. Peptide Protein Research, 1981—; contbr. articles to profl. jours. Recipient Superior Civilian Service award USN, 1965, Fed. Women's award U.S. Govt., 1973, Annual Achievement award Soc. Women Engrs., 1968, Annual Achievement award U. Mich., 1987, Dexter Conrad award Office Naval Research, 1980, WISE Lifetime Achievement award Women in Sci. and Engring., 1986, Gregori Aminoff prize Royal Swedish Acad. Scis., 1988, Rear Adm. Parsons award Sci. and Chem. Progress Navy League, 1988, award for disting. achievement in sci. Sec. of Navy, 1987. Fellow Am. Inst. Chemists. (Chem. Pioneer award 1984); mem. Nat. Acad. Scis., Am. Crystallographic Assn. (pres. 1976), Am. Chem. Soc. (Garvan award 1976, Hillebrand award 1970), Am. Phys. Soc., Biophys. Soc. Home: 6304 Lakeview Dr Falls Church VA 22041 Office: Naval Research Lab Code 6030 Washington [illegible]

KARLEN, JANICE M., academic administrator, consultant; b. Elizabeth, N.J., Oct. 29, 1953; d. Victor Joseph and Leona Mary (Metz) K. BS, Kean Coll., 1974; MBA, Rutgers U., 1975; EdS, Seton Hall U., 1980, EdD, 1984. Auditor Exxon Corp., Florham Park, N.J., 1975-76; asst. registrar Essex County Coll., Newark, 1977-79, instl. researcher, 1979-80; asst. to v.p. N.J. Inst. Tech., 1980-83; dean bus. div. Antelope Valley Coll., Lancaster, Calif., 1984-86; v.p. Erie Community Cpll., Williamsville, N.Y., 1986-88; pvt. practice cons. Elizabeth, N.J., 1988—. Contbr. articles to profl. jours. Mem. AAUW (edn. chair 1986), Phi Delta Kappa, Kappa Delta Pi, Lancaster C. of C. (bd. dirs. 1985), Amherst C. of C. Democrat. Lodge: Soroptimist (internat. leadership chmn. 1985). Home: 635 Magie Ave Elizabeth NJ 07208

KARLIN, DENISE JOY, lawyer; b. Portland, Maine, Feb. 10, 1958; d. Reuben Joshua and Golda (Rudner) K.; m. William R. Jarosz. AB, Harvard U., 1980, JD, 1983. Bar: Mass. 1983, U.S. Dist. Ct. Mass. 1984, U.S. Ct. Appeals (1st cir.) 1984, Pa. 1985, U.S. Dist. Ct. (ea. dist.) Pa. 1985, U.S. Ct. Appeals (3d cir.) 1986. Law clk. Superior Ct. Mass., Boston, 1983-84, dep. chief law clk., 1984-85; assoc. Pepper, Hamilton and Scheetz, Phila., 1985-86; assoc. prosecutor Mass. Bd. Med., Boston, 1986-87, dep. chief prosecutor, 1987—. Mem. ABA, Mass. Bar Assn., Boston Bar Assn., Assn. Women Lawyers, Women's Bar Assn., Mass. Assn. Women Lawyers. Democrat. Jewish. Club: Harvard (Boston). Home: 149 Chiswick Rd #2 Brighton MA 02135 Office: Mass Bd Registration in Med 10 West St Boston MA 02111

KARLIN, MURIEL SCHLOSBERG, information systems analyst, consultant; b. Mt. Vernon, N.Y., Dec. 19, 1940; d. Nat and Lee (Karlin) Schlosberg; children: Leeza Beth Watstein, David Michael Watstein. BA in Psychology, Clark U., 1962; MS in Computer Sci., NYU, 1986. Programming cons. N.Y.C. Bd. Edn., Bklyn., 1983; systems engr. Electronic Data Systems, Woodbury, N.Y., 1983-84; documentation mgr. Instinct Corp., N.Y.C., 1987-88; instr. Info. Techs. Inst., NYU, N.Y.C., 1987. Enrichment coordinator, v.p. Ridge Rd. Elem. Sch. PTA, North Haven, Conn.; mem. North Haven Ednl. Council, 1974-75. Mem. Nat. Assn. Female Execs., Assn. Computing Machinery. Home: 77 Bleecker St New York NY 10012

KARLSON, KAREN LOUISE, radiologist; b. N.Y.C., May 6, 1950; d. Lloyd Alfred and Antoinette Sofia (Petersen) Bolling; B.A., CCNY, 1971; M.D., Columbia U., 1975; m. Thomas J. Karlson, May 19, 1971; children—Aurora, Alexandra. Intern, St. Vincent's Hosp., N.Y.C., 1975-76; resident Columbia Presbyn. Med. Center, 1976-79; fellow, 1979-80, asst. prof., 1980-81; attending radiologist, St. Barnabas Med. Ctr., Livingston, N.J.; chairperson dept. radiology, 1987—; asst. clin. prof. radiology UMDNJ, 1987;, asst. prof. Cornell U. Med. Center-N.Y. Hosp. Mem. Columbia U. Coll. Physicians and Surgeons, Black and Latin Students Orgn., Am. Coll. Radiology, Radiol. Soc. N.Am. Lutheran. Contbr. articles to profl. jours. Home: 6 Orchard Ln Livingston NJ 07039 Office: St Barnabas Med Ctr Dept Radiology Livingston NJ 07039

KARMALI, RASHIDA ALIMAHOMED, biochemist, research scientist; b. Mitalamaria, Uganda, May 12, 1948; d. Alimahomed and Sakina (Walji) Karmali. B.S., Makerere U. (Uganda), 1971; M.S. in Nutrition Aberdeen U. (Scotland), 1973; M.S. in Anatomy, McGill U., 1977; Ph.D. in Biochemistry, Newcastle U., 1976. Postdoctoral fellow Clin. Research Inst., Montreal, Que., Can., 1976-78; research assoc. East Carolina U., Greenville, N.C., 1978-80; research staff Sloan-Kettering Inst. for Cancer Research, N.Y.C., 1980—; assoc. prof. Rutgers U., New Brunswick, N.J., 1984—; cons. Cappel Labs., Malvern, Pa., 1982, United Scis. of Am., 1985, Hoffman-La Roche and Lederle Labs, 1987, Nippon Suisan, 1987. Contbr. numerous articles to sci. jours. Mem. Cell Biology Soc., Leukemia Soc. Am., Am. Assn. Cancer Research, Am. Soc. Clin. Nutrition, Sigma Xi. Club: Health and Raquet (N.Y.C.). Office: Sloan-Kettering Inst Cancer Research 1275 York Ave New York NY 10021

KARNES, ELIZABETH HELEN, academic professional, television producer; b. Los Angeles, July 22, 1951; d. Samuel and Shirley Ruth (Richmond) K. Student, U. Nice, France, 1970, Drew U., 1971; BA, Adelphi U., 1972. Exec. asst. to Bill Moyers PBS, N.Y.C., 1975-78, dir. research dir. Bill Moyers Jour., 1978-82; assoc. producer CBS Evening News, N.Y.C., 1982-83, CBS Crossroads, N.Y.C., 1984-86; exec. asst. to pres. Middlebury (Vt.) Coll., 1986—. dir. research A Coversation with George Steiner, 1981 (Emmy award 1981); assoc. producer CBS Evening Analysis segment, Bill Moyers Commentary, 1982 (Emmy nominee 1983), 1982. Past pres. W. 69th St. Block Assn., N.Y.; bd. dir., treas. Interfaith Housing Corp. Addison County, Vt.; mem. Otter Creek Child Ctr., Addison County Benefit Bd., 1988. Mem. Women in Communication. Office: Middlebury Coll Old Chapel Middlebury VT 05753

KARNIOL, HILDA HUTTERER, artist, educator; b. Vienna, Austria, Apr. 28, 1910; d. Simon and Josephine (Weisman) Hutterer; student Acad. for Women, Vienna, 1926-30, Mrs. Olga Konetzny-Maly and A. F. Seligman, Vienna, 1925-28; m. Frank Karniol, June 25, 1933; 1 son, William George. Over 100 one-man shows, including Susquehanna U., 1952-73, Pa. State Mus., Harrisburg, 1954, Neville Mus., Green Bay, Wis., 1958, Addha Artzt Gallery, N.Y.C., 1960, Cornell Library Gallery, Ithaca, N.Y., 1960, Drexel Inst. Tech., Phila., 1960, Farnsworth Mus., Rockland, Maine, 1960, Mary Buie Mus., Oxford, Miss., 1960, Columbus (Ga.) Mus., 1962, Rutgers U., 1965-66, Laurel (Miss.) Rogers Mus., 1962; La Salle Coll., Phila., 1964; Hallmark Art Gallery, Kansas City, Mo., 1967, U. Ill., Urbana, 1968, U. Minn., St. Paul, 1969, U. Mich., 1969, U. Ky., Elizabethtown, 1970, La. State U., New Orleans, 1971, Kans. State Coll., Pittsburg, 1972, Purdue U., 1973, Invitational Art Exhbn., Painters of Central Pa., State Coll., 1982, 83; represented in permanent collections at St. Vincent Arch Abbey, Latrobe, Pa., Susquehanna U., Selinsgrove, Pa., Lincoln Sch., Honesdale, Pa., Del. Art Center, Wilmington, HEW, Lycoming Coll., Williamsport, Pa., Bloomsburg (Pa.) State Coll., Lewisburg (Pa.) Art Council; instr. fine arts Susquehanna U., 1959-75; lectr., artist-in-residence Fed. Govt. Cultural Enrichment Program for Clearfield, Clinton, Centre and Lycoming counties, Pa., 1967; art adviser Sunbury Bicentennial Com., 1972; demonstrator, exhibitor Laurel State Festival, Wellsboro, Pa., 1975. Recipient 1st prize in portraiture Berwick (Pa.) Arts Center, 1965; purchase prize Lewisburg Arts Festival, 1975, 1st prize, 1978, Distinguished Citizen award, Susquehanna U., Selinsgrove, Pa, 1988. Mem. Susquehanna Art Soc., Société d'Honneur Française, Pi Delta Phi, Sigma Alpha Iota. Home: 960 Race St Sunbury PA 17801

KAROGHLIAN, DIANA A., marketing and sales professional; b. Detroit, Sept. 30, 1950; d. Edward and Margaret Ann (Gurganian) K. BA, Oakland U., 1972; student, Marcel Marceau Internat. Sch. Mime, 1970, U. Sorbonne, Paris, 1971, U. Perugia, Italy, 1971, Detroit Sch. Arts and Crafts, 1974, Parsons Sch. Design, N.Y.C., 1981. Mfg. rep. Stendig Internat., N.Y.C., 1974-82; account exec. Furniture Cons., N.Y.C., 1982-83; dir. mktg./regional sales mgr. Domus Italia, N.Y.C., 1983-85; pres. Dee Karoghlian, Inc., N.Y.C., 1985-87; v.p. Travis Assocs., N.Y.C., 1988—. Democrat. Roman Catholic. Home: 333 E 33 St #3A New York NY 10016 Office: Travis Assocs 45 W 21st New York NY 10016

KARP, JUDITH ESTHER, oncologist; b. San Diego, July 15, 1946; d. Louis Moses and Bella Sarah (Perlman) K.; B.A. in Chemistry, Mills Coll., Oakland, Calif., 1966; M.D., Stanford U., 1971; m. Stanley Howard Freedman, Sept. 21, 1975. Intern medicine, jr. resident in medicine Stanford Hosps., 1971-72; asst. resident in medicine Johns Hopkins Hosp., 1972-73; clin. and research fellow oncology Johns Hopkins Med. Sch., 1973-75, instr. oncology and medicine, 1975-78, asst. prof., 1978-85, assoc. prof., 1985—; speaker Internat. Congress Chemotherapy, Vienna, Austria, 1983; mem. consensus com. Immuno-compromised Host Soc., 1987-88. Recipient Aurelia Henry Reinhardt prize Mills Coll., 1966, Cancer Research award Washington chpt. Awards for Research Coll. Scientists, 1975; San Diego Heart Assn. grantee, 1965-67; Am. Cancer Soc. Jr. clin. faculty fellow, 1976-79. Diplomate Am. Bd. Internal Medicine; recipient Resolution of Commendation, State of Md., 1982; Recognition award City of Balt., 1984. Mem. Am. Soc. Hematology, Am. Soc. Clin. Oncology, Cell Kinetics Soc. (clin. counsellor governing council 1985-87), Am. Soc. Microbiology, Internat. Soc.

Exptl. Hematology, Nat. Bd. Med. Examiners, Phi Beta Kappa. Democrat. Jewish. Home: 15 Farmhouse Ct Baltimore MD 21208 Office: Johns Hopkins Hosp Oncology Ctr 601 N Broadway Baltimore MD 21205

KARP, PHYLLIS KOSACOFF, construction company executive; b. N.Y.C., Apr. 1, 1944; d. Louis and Claire (Rubin) Kosacoff; m. Sheldon I. Karp, May 30, 1964 (div. 1974); children: Andrew, Allyson, Michele, Jamie Greg. Student, SUNY, N.Y.C., 1961-63, 72-77. Constrn. mgr., owner Phyllis Joyce Interiors Inc., Plainview, N.Y., 1969-81; constrn. project mgr. HRH Constrn. Corp., N.Y.C., 1981—. Prin. projects include Manufacturer Hanover Trust World Hdqrs., AT&T World Hdqrs., AT&T Infoquest, Thomson McKinnon Securities Fin. Sq., Hartz Assoc., Loews, Corp, The Mediators. Office: HRH Constrn Corp 667 Madison Ave New York NY 10021

KARPAN, KATHLEEN MARIE, lawyer, journalist, state official; b. Rock Springs, Wyo., Sept. 1, 1942; d. Thomas Michael and Pauline Ann (Taucher) K. B.S. in Journalism, U. Wyo., 1964, M.A. in Am. Studies, 1975; J.D., U. Oreg., 1978. Bar: D.C. 1979, Wyo. 1983, U.S. Dist. Ct. Wyo., U.S. Ct. Appeals (D.C. and 10th cirs.). Editor Cody Enterprise, Wyo., 1964; press asst. to U.S. Congressman Teno Roncalio U.S. Ho. of Reps., Washington, 1965-67, 71-72, adminstrv. asst., 1973-74; asst. news editor Wyo. Eagle, Cheyenne, 1967; free-lance writer 1968; teaching asst. dept. history U. Wyo., 1969-70; desk editor Canberra Times, Australia, 1970; dep. dir. Office Congl. Relations, Econ. Devel. Adminstrn. U.S. Dept. Commerce, Washington, 1979-80, atty. advisor Office of Chief Counsel, Econ. Devel. Adminstrn., 1980-81; campaign mgr. Rodger McDaniel for U.S. Senator, Wyo., 1981-82; asst. atty. gen. State of Wyo., Cheyenne, 1983-84, dir. Dept. Health and Social Services, 1984-86, sec.of state, 1987—. Del. Democratic Nat. Conv., San Francisco, 1984, Atlanta, 1988; del., chmn. platform com. Dem. State Conv., Douglas, Wyo., 1984. W.R. Coe fellow, 1969. Mem. D.C. Bar Assn., Wyo. Bar Assn., Nat. Assn. Secs. State, Bus. and Profl. Women, Women Execs. in State Govt., Am. Pub. Welfare Assn., Nat. Assn. Lt. Govs., Nat. Assn. Secs. of State. Roman Catholic. Lodge: Zonta. Home: 2919 Carey Ave Cheyenne WY 82001 Office: Sec of State State Capitol Bldg Cheyenne WY 82002

KARPEN, MARIAN JOAN, financial executive; b. Detroit, June 16, 1944; d. Cass John and Mary (Jagiello) K.; A.B., Vassar Coll., 1966; postgrad. Sorbonne, Paris, N.Y. U. Grad. Sch. Bus., 1974-77. New Eng. corr. Women's Wear Daily, Fairchild Publs.-Capital Cities Communications, 1966-68, Paris fashion editor, TV and radio commentator Capital Cities Network, 1968-69; fashion editor Boston Herald Traveler, 1969-71; nat. syndicated newspaper columnist and photojournalist Queen Features Syndicate, N.Y.C., 1971-73; account exec. Blyth Eastman Dillon, N.Y.C., 1973-75, Oppenheimer, N.Y.C., 1975-76; v.p., mcpl. bond coordinator Faulkner Dawkins & Sullivan (merged Shearson Hayden Stone), N.Y.C., 1976-77; mgr. retail mcpl. bond dept. Warburg Paribas Becker-A.G. Becker (merger Becker Paribas and Merrill Lynch), N.Y.C., 1977-79, sr. v.p. and prin., 1977-84; sr. v.p., ltd. ptnr. Bear Stearns & Co., 1984-87, assoc. dir., 1987—, also assoc. bd. dirs.; lectr. fin. seminars, 1978—; mem. bus. adv. council U.S. Rep. Senate. Mem. benefit com. March of Dimes, 1983; mem. Torchlight Ball com. Internat. Games for Disabled, 1984, other benefit coms.; friend vol. Whitney Mus. Am. Art. Recipient Superior Prodn. award Becker Paribas, 1983. Mem. Nat. Assn. Securities Dealers (registered rep.), N.Y. Stock Exchange (registered rep.), N.Y.C. Women's Econ. Roundtable, Am. Soc. Profl. and Exec. Women, AAUW, U.S. Figure Skating Assn., Fishing Club of Am. (angler's honor roll), English Speaking Union. Clubs: Vassar, Skating (N.Y.C. and Boston). Editorial bd. Retirement Planning Strategist; contbr. articles and photographs to newspapers and mags. Home: 233 E 69th St New York NY 10021 Office: Bear Stearns & Co 245 Park Ave New York NY 10167

KARPIEJ, ANITA, gymnastic coach, dancer; b. Hampton, Va., Jan. 10, 1961; d. Henry Theodore and Joyce Sarah (Marsh) K. Student, Royal Ballet Sch., London, 1977; grad., Sch. Am. Ballet, 1982. Dancer Hartford (Conn.) Ballet Co., 1977-79; profl. dancer Chgo. Ballet Co., 1982-83, Milw. Ballet Co., 1980-83, Conn. Concert Ballet, Manchester, 1983—; asst. mgr. Valley Pet Care, South Windsor, Conn., 1985—; tchr., coach Gymnastic Tng. Ctr., Simsbury, Conn., 1986—; model Beckett & Beckett, Milw., 1980-83; choreographer and guest tchr. Conn. Concert Ballet, Manchester, 1979-86; dancer Chgo. Lyric Opera, 1982-83; tchr. Parks and Recreation, Manchester, 1984-86. Choreographer (ballets) Pastorale, 1985, Nutcracker, 1985, Chakra, 1988. Mem. YMCA, Greenpeace, Am. Soc. for the Prevention of Cruelty to Animals, People for the Ethical Treatment of Animals, Humane Soc. of U.S., Nat. Wildlife Fedn., Found. for Christian Living. Mem. Am. Guild Musical Artists, World Wildlife Fund, Defenders of Animals Rights, Inc. Baptist. Home: 15 Colby Dr East Hartford CT 06108 Office: Conn Concert Ballet Garden Grove Manchester CT 06104

KARPIEL, DORIS CATHERINE, state legislator; b. Chgo., Sept. 21, 1935; d. Nicholas and Mary (McStravick) Feinen; m. Harvey Karpiel, 1955 (div.); children—Sharon, Lynn, Laura, Barry. A.A., Morton Jr. Coll., 1955; B.A., No. Ill. U., 1976. Real estate sales assoc. Bundy-Morgan BHG; coordinator Bloomingdale Twp. Republican Presdl. Hdqrs., Ill., 1960, 64, 68; former pres. Bloomingdale Twp. Rep. Orgn.; mem. Twp. Ofcls. of Ill.; trustee Bloomingdale Twp., 1974-75, supr., 1975-80; precinct committeewoman Bloomingdale Twp. Rep. Central Com., 1972, chmn., 1978-80; mem. Ill. Ho. of Reps., 1979-82, Ill. State Senate from 25th Dist., 1984—. Mem. Am. Legislators Exchange Council, Rep. Orgn. Schaumberg Twp.; former sec. Dupage County Suprs. Assn.; former sec. Dupage County Twp. Ofcls.; mem. Dupage County Women's Rep. Orgn., Meml. Hosp. Guild, Am. Cancer Soc. Mem. LWV, DuPage Bd. Realtors, Pi Sigma Alpha. Clubs: Bloomingdale Roselle and Streamwood Country, University Women's, St. Walters Women's. Office: Ill State Capitol Bldg Springfield IL 62706 also: 127 W Lake St Bloomingdale IL 60108 *

KARPINSKI, JANIS LEIGH, security manager; b. Rahway, N.J., May 25, 1953; d. Nelson Arthur and Ruth (Sorensen) Beam; m. George Frank Karpinski, Nov. 17, 1974. Ba in English and Secondary Edn., Kean Coll. of N.J., 1975; M in Mgmt., Embry-Riddle Aero. U., 1985. Commd. 2d lt. U.S. Army, 1977, advanced through ranks to capt., 1981, resigned, 1987; intelligence officer 7th Spcl. Forces Group, Ft. Bragg, N.C., 1980-82; ops. and intelligence officer Anti-Terrorism Ctr., Mannheim, Fed. Republic Germany, 1982-83; ops. officer U.S. European Command, Mannheim, 1983-85; commander U.S. Army Military Police Co., Ft. McPherson, Ga., 1985-86; investigations mgr. Argenbright, Inc., Atlanta, 1987—; dep. to dir. plans tng., mobilization and security, chief of security and intelligence Dept. Def., Ft. McPherson, Ga., 1987—; assoc. prof. City Coll. of Chgo., Fed. Republic Germany, 1982-85. Author: various poems. Active Atlanta Zoological Soc., 1986. Served to maj. U.S. Army Reserves. Mem. Nat. Assn. Female Execs., Am. Soc. Indsl. Security, Embry-Riddle Alumni Assn. Republican. Office: DPTMSEC-Security Bldg 65 Fort McPherson GA 30330-5000

KARR, ELIZABETH MCRAE, hospital executive; b. Birmingham, Ala., July 9, 1953; d. James Neal and Donna Mae (Paige) McRae; divorced; children: Kristopher Ryan, Brian Heath. A in Nursing, Jefferson State Jr. Coll., 1974; cert. in Health Services Adminstrv. Devel., U. Ala., Birmingham, 1985, BS in Hosp. Adminstrn., 1987. RN, Ala. Staff nurse Cooper Green Hosp., Birmingham, 1974-83, operating room supr., 1981-83; clin. dir. Druid City Hosp., Tuscaloosa, Ala., 1983-88; dir. surg. services Brookwood Hosp., Birmingham, 1983-88, Huntsville (Ala.) Hosp., 1988—; cons. Tuscaloosa Surg. Ctr. Vol. local March of Dimes, 1980, ARC, 1981. Grantee March of Dimes, 1971, Davis & Geck, 1982. Mem. Assn. Operating Room Nurses (bd. dirs. 1982-84), Surg. Soc. Huntsville Ala. Republican. Methodist. Avocations: camping, canoeing, reading. Home: 8319 Whitesburg Way Apt 901 Huntsville AL 35802 Office: Huntsville Hosp 101 Sivley Rd Huntsville AL 35801

KARR, HELEN EILEEN, beauty company executive; b. Alamosa, Colo., June 4, 1934; d. Carl Herman and Elsie Cecelia (Anderson) Higel; m. Charles Edward Sullivan, Oct. 27, 1955 (div. Aug. 1977); m. Harold Solomon Karr, May 27, 1979. BA cum laude, Calif. State U., Fresno, 1980. Lic. cosmetologist, Calif. Stewardess Frontier Airlines, Denver, 1955-56; salon mgr. Seligman & Latz, Inc., Visalia, Calif., 1966-69, San Leandro, Calif., 1969-72; group supr. Seligman & Latz, Inc., Fresno, 1972-76; account exec. Seligman & Latz, Inc., San Francisco, 1984—. Democrat. Roman Catholic. Club: Commonwealth (San Francisco). Home: 5009 Pacifica #34 Pacifico CA 94044

KARRAS, DONNA CIRIPOMPA, dental hygienist, educator; b. Wheeling, W.Va., Aug. 1, 1951; d. George Henry and Eleanor Jane (Nyles) Ciripompa; m. Donald George Karras, Mar. 6, 1982; children: Dane Anthony, Dillon James. AS/BS, West Liberty State Coll., 1973; MA in Community Health, W.Va. U., 1978. Cert. CPR instr., dental hygienist. Dental hygienist, Morgantown, W.Va., 1973-78; asst. prof. dental hygiene U. S.D., Vermillion, 1979-80, asst. prof., 1980-82, assoc. chmn. dept. dental hygiene, 1980-82; pvt. practice as dental hygienist, Aurora, Colo., 1982-84; clin. asst. prof dept. dental hygiene and periodontics U. Colo., research asst. dept. applied dentistry; instr. CPR various schools, univs. and orgns., geriatric coordinator for Dist. X Outreach Program. Vol. Clay County (S.D.) Ambulance Dept., 1979-82. Named Outstanding Clin. Instr., U. Colo., 1986; revipient Volunteerism award Nat. Council on Aging, 1986. Mem. Internat. Assn. Dental Research, Am. Dental Hygiene Assn., Colo. Dental Hygienist Assn. (v.p.), Colo. Assn. Dental Research (charter mem.), Metro Denver Dental Hygienists Assn. (regional conv. del.), Colo. Hygienists Polit. Action Com., Delta Zeta. Home: 28505 Little Big Horn Dr Evergreen CO 80439

KARRENBAUER, BEVERLY WOLFORD, elementary school administrator, consultant; b. Marion Center, Pa., Aug. 5, 1938; d. Clarence Frederick and Thelma Pearl (MacArthur) Wolford; B.S. in Edn., Indiana U. of Pa., 1959; M.Ed., U. Pitts., 1963; m. Raymond Joseph Karrenbauer, Jr., Aug. 20, 1960; 1 son, Raymond Joseph, III. Supr. perceptual devel. Keystone Oaks Sch. Dist., Pitts., 1967-69; supr. early childhood edn. Dade County (Fla.) public schs., 1969-80; adminstr. Miami Gardens Elem. Sch., Opa-Locka, Fla., 1980-82; adminstr. Treasure Island Elem. Sch., Miami Beach, Fla., 1982—; ednl. cons. children's programming WTVJ-TV, 1981-82; sr. cons. early childhood program Scholastic Mag. Inc. Recipient Internat. Year of Child award, 1979, Kiwanis Appreciation award, 1963; Frick Found. scholar 1962. Mem. Children Learning Disabilities, Elementary Prins. Assn., Assn. Supervision and Curriculum Devel., Dade County Adminstrs. Assn., PTA, Delta Kappa Gamma. Democrat. Author: Perpetual Development, 1968. Home: 9381 E Bay Harbor Dr 203-S Bay Harbor Islands FL 33154 Office: 7540 E Treasure Dr Miami Beach FL 33141

KARSEN, SONJA PETRA, Spanish educator; b. Berlin, Apr. 11, 1919; came to U.S., 1938, naturalized, 1945; d. Fritz and Erna (Heidermann) K. Titulo de Bachiller, 1937; B.A., Carleton Coll., 1939; M.A. (scholar in French), Bryn Mawr Coll., 1941; Ph.D., Columbia U., 1950. Instr. Spanish Lake Erie Coll., Painesville, Ohio, 1943-45; instr. modern langs. U. P.R., 1945-46; instr. Spanish Syracuse U., 1947-50, Bklyn. Coll., 1950-51; asst. to dep. dir. gen. UNESCO, 1951-52, Latin Am. Desk, tech. assistance dept., 1952-53, mem. tech. assistance mission Costa Rica, 1954; asst. prof. Spanish Sweet Briar Coll., Va., 1955-57; assoc. prof., chmn. dept. Romance langs. Skidmore Coll., Saratoga Springs, N.Y., 1957-61, chmn. dept. modern langs. and lits., 1961-79, prof. Spanish, 1961-87, prof. emerita, 1987; Fulbright lectr. Free U., Berlin, 1968; mem. adv. and nominating com. Books Abroad, 1965-67. Author: Guillermo Valencia, Colombian Poet, 1951, Educational Development in Costa Rica with UNESCO's Technical Assistance, 1951-54, 1954, Jaime Torres Bodet: A Poet in a Changing World, 1963, Selected Poems of Jaime Torres Bodet, 1964, Versos y prosas de Jaime Torres Bodet, 1966, Jaime Torres Bodet, 1971, Essays on Eberoamerican Literature and History, 1988; editor: Lang. Assn. Bull., 1980-83; mem. editorial adv. bd.: Modern Lang. Studies; contbr. articles to profl. jours. Decorated chevalier dans l'Ordre des Palmes Academiques, 1964; recipient Leadership award N.Y. State Assn. Fgn. Lang. Tchrs., 1973, 78, Nat. Disting. Leadership award, 1979, Disting. Service award, 1983, 86, Capital Dist. Fgn. Language Disting. Service award, 1987; recipient Spanish Heritage award, 1981, Alumni Achievement award Carleton Coll., 1982; exchange student auspices Inst. Internat. Ednl. at Carleton Coll., 1938-39; Buenos Aires Conv. grantee for research in Colombia, 1946-47; faculty research grantee Skidmore Coll., summer 1959, 61, 63-64, 67, 69-70, 73, ad hoc faculty grantee, 71, 78, 85. Mem. AAUP, MLA (del. assembly 1976-78, Mildenberger medal selection com. 1984-86), Am. Assn. Tchrs. Spanish and Portuguese, Nat. Assn. Self-Instructional Lang. Programs (v.p. 1981-82, pres. 1982-83), AAUW, El Ateneo Doctor Jaime Torres Bodet (founding mem.), Nat. Geog. Soc., Instituto Internacional de Literatura Iberoamericana, Asociacion Internacional de Hispanistas, UN Assn. U.S.A., Am. Soc. French Acad. Palms, Fulbright Alumni, Phi Sigma Iota, Sigma Delta Pi. Home: PO Box 441 Saratoga Springs NY 12866

KARTON, CAROL KAUFMAN, editor, writer; b. Buffalo, Nov. 10, 1941; d. William and Rhea (Olodort) Kaufman; m. Robert M. Karton, Aug. 1, 1964 (div. Feb. 1984); children—Deborah Lynn, Gary Stuart, Jeffrey Alan. B.A., U. Mich., 1963; M.A., Northwestern U., 1964. Cert. tchr., Ill. Tchr., writer Sch. Dist. 72, Skokie, Ill., 1964-67; project assoc. Northwestern U., Evanston, Ill., 1976-79; freelance writer, editor, Glencoe, Ill., 1975—; co-owner Ragtime, Ltd., Glencoe, 1979-81; asst. editor Scott, Foresman & Co., Glenview, Ill., 1981-83, assoc. editor, 1983-85, editor, 1985-88, supr. outside services, 1988—. Mem. Glencoe Sch. Bd. Nominating Caucus, 1983-85; vol. Chgo. Youth Motivation Program, Chgo. Symphony Orch. Radiothon; participant Chgo. Women in Pub. Career Carousel. Jewish. Home: 1182 Carol Ln Glencoe IL 60022 Office: Scott Foresman & Co 1900 E Lake St Glenview IL 60025

KARU, GILDA MALL, lawyer, government official; b. Oceanport, N.J., Dec. 1, 1951; d. Harold and Ilvy (Meriloo) K.; m. Frederick F. Foy, May 23, 1981. AB, Vassar Coll., 1974; JD, Ill. Inst. Tech., 1987. Bar: Ill. 1987, U.S. Dist. Ct. (no. dist.) Ill. 1987. Quality control reviewer food and nutrition service USDA, Robbinsville, N.J., 1974-77, team leader, 1977-78, supr., 1978-81; sect. chief USDA, Robbinsville, 1981—; employer advisor Ctr. for Rehab. and Tng. Disabled Persons, Chgo., 1986—. North-central dir. Estonian Am. Nat. Council, N.Y.C.; elder 1st Estonian Evangelical Luth. Ch., Chgo. Recipient letters of commendation USDA, 1975, 77, 79, 80, cert. of merit, 1985, cert. of appreciation Ctr. for Tng. and Rehab. Disabled, 1986, cert. of recognition William A. Jump Meml. Found., 1987. Mem. Washington Downtown Jaycees (Arthur S. Flemming award, 1987), ABA, Ill. Bar Assn., Chgo. Bar Assn., Am. Pub. Welfare Assn., Nat. Assn. Female Execs., Mensa. Republican. Club: Chgo. Vassar (treas. 1988—). Home: 402 S Evergreen Ave Arlington Heights IL 60005 Office: USDA Food and Nutrition Service 50 E Washington St Chicago IL 60602

KARWOWSKI, JUDITH RAE, health and benefits executive; b. Pontiac, Mich., Jan. 26, 1950; d. John and Josephine D. (Sak) Mathews; m. Robert J. Karwowski, June 30, 1973; children: Jeffery A., Audrey L. and April L. (twins). BA, Oakland U., Rochester, Mich., 1971. RN. Surg. nurse trauma Henry Ford Hosp., Detroit, 1973-74; trauma nurse operating room Med. Coll. Ohio, Toledo, 1974-75; nurse occupational health Ford Motor Co., Ypsilanti, Mich., 1975-80; trauma nurse intensive care unit Wayne County Hosp., Westland, Mich., 1980-81; nurse emergency room Saline (Mich.) Hosp., 1981—, cons. occupational health, 1984—; adminstr. health and benefits Edwards Bros., Inc., Ann Arbor, Mich., 1984-87; mgr. corp. benefits Dominos Pizza Inc, Ann Arbor, Mich., 1987—. Chair Ann Arbor United Way, 1982; coordinator Ann Arbor chpt. ARC, 1984—. Recipient Service award Ann Arbor United Way, 1984-85. Mem. Occupational Health Nurses's Assn., Cert. Benefits Adminstrs. Assn. Roman Catholic.

KARY, SUSAN E., architect; b. Washington, Nov. 16, 1950; d. Reino August and Miriam (Hendrickson) K.; m. Martin Edward Svrcek, Dec. 28, 1973 (div. Sept. 1986). BA in Sociology cum laude, BArch cum laude, Syracuse U., 1973; MS in Fin., Am. U., 1985. Registered architect, D.C., Md., Va. Intern Cohen, Haft, Holtz, Kerxton & Karabekir, Silver Spring, Md., 1973-74; architect John J. Orofino of OKE, Inc., Silver Spring, Md., 1974-77, Benjamin P. Elliott Assocs., Silver Spring, 1977, Wilmot, Bower, Quinlan & Assocs., Silver Spring, 1977-79; product exec.,exec. dir. tech. services, dir. design mgmt., project di Architecture and Constrn. Div. Marriott Corp., Washington, 1980—; mem. adv. council Am. Cons. Engrs. Council Research Found., 1987-88. Mem. AIA (corp. architects com. steering mem.), Comml. Real Estate Women. Office: Marriott Corp Marriott Dr Washington DC 20058

KASABACH, JACQUELYN ARSHALOUS, conference sales and service executive, caterer; b. Detroit, May 20, 1943; d. Vahram Y. and Sarah (Antonian) K. BA, U. Mich, 1964, MLS, 1967. Librarian Chgo. Pub. Library, 1967-71; library cons. Ency. Brittanica, Chgo., 1971; real estate broker Aspen, Colo., 1976—; caterer Mom's Catering, Aspen, 1973—; asst. mgr. Aspen Chateaux Co., 1972-81; dir. conf. The Gant, Aspen, 1981—. Mem. Meeting Planner Internat. Democrat. Office: The Gant Box K-3 Aspen CO 81612

KASABIAN, ANNA, advertising executive; b. Springfield, Mass., Oct. 29, 1949; d. Dominick J. and Agatha K. (Maggio) Lepore; m. David R. Kasabian, Oct. 26, 1950. AA, Endicott Coll., 1970; BA, Emerson Coll., 1972. Reporter Hartford (Conn.) Times, 1973-74; reporter, editor Essex County Newspapers, Beverly, Mass., 1974-78; publicity writer Newsome and Co., Boston, 1978-79; mng. editor Playbill and Panorama, Boston, 1979-80; exec. editor Crosby/Vandenburgh Pub. Co., Boston, 1980-83; account exec. Arnold and Co., Boston, 1983; sr. acct. exec. DRK, Inc., Boston, 1983—. Vol. ad and mktg. rep. Shriners Hosp. for Crippled Children, Boston, 1986—. Home: 4 Longfellow Pl Boston MA 02114 Office: DRK Inc 101 Summer St Boston MA 02114

KASAKOVE, SUSAN, interior designer; b. Newark, N.J., Nov. 11, 1938. BFA, U. Buffalo, 1958, Hunter Coll., 1960; postgrad., N.Y. Sch. of Interior Design, 1960-64, New Sch. for Social Research, 1967-68, Pratt Inst., 1968-69. Asst. interior designer Rodgers Assocs., N.Y.C., 1964-66; interior designer Walter Dorwin Teague Assocs., N.Y.C., 1966-70; sr. interior designer N.Y. State Facilities Devel. Corp., N.Y.C., 1970—. Interior designs include projects for Eli Lilly & Co., Bank of Bermuda, Quaker Oats Corp., N.Y. State Office of Mental Health, N.Y. State Office of Mental Retardation, Cattaraugus County, Warren County. Reading tutor Vols. for Children's Services, N.Y.C., 1976-82; chair Friends of White Plains (N.Y.) Symphony, 1981-83; vol. guide dept. edn. Met. Mus. Art, N.Y.C., 1978—; Rep. treas. 11th Ward, Yonkers, N.Y., 1979-81. Recipient Outstanding Service to Sch. award Rockland County (N.Y.) Lions Club, 1955. Avocations: photography, history of art and architecture, golf, swimming. Home: 793 Palmer Rd Apt 3-F Bronxville NY 10708 Office: NY State Facilities Devel Corp 909 3d Ave New York NY 10022

KASE-POLISINI, JUDITH BAKER, educator; b. Wilmington, Del., Dec. 13, 1932; d. Charles Robert and Elizabeth Edna (Baker) Kase; B.A., U. Del., 1955; M.A., Case Western Res. U., 1956; m. James F. Polisini; stepchildren—James, Elizabeth, John, Katherine, Ann. Tchr., dir. children's theatre Agnes Scott Coll., 1956, U. Tenn., 1957, U. Md., Germany, 1958-60, Denver Civic Theatre, Denver U., Kent Sch. for Girls, 1960-61; dir. children's theatre U. N.H., Durham, 1962-69; dir. theatre resources for youth, Somersworth, N.H., 1966-69; assoc. prof. theatre U. South Fla., Tampa, 1969-74, assoc. prof. edn., 1969-84, prof., 1984—, artistic dir. ednl. theatre, 1976—; project dir. Hillsborough County Artists-in-Schs. Evaluation and Inservice Project, 1980-82. Bd. dirs. Fla. Alliance for Arts Edn., sec., 1976-77, vice-chmn., 1979-82, chmn. 1982-84; chmn. Wingspread Conf. on Theatre Edn., 1977; drama adjudicator Nat. Arts Festival, Ministry of Edn., Bahamas, 1975, 76, 79, 80; regional chmn. Alliance for Arts Edn., chmn. nat. adv. council, mem. edn. adv. com., 1986-88; J.F. Kennedy Center for Performing Arts, 1983—; cons. theatre edn. and prodn. Mem. Children's Theatre Assn. Am. (pres.-elect 1975-77, pres. 1977-79, chmn. symposia 1981—), Am. Theatre Assn. (chief div. pres.'s coordinating council 1977-78 commn. on theatre edn. 1982—), Speech Communication Assn., Southeastern, Fla. theatre confs., Internat. Assn. Theatres for Children and Youth, Fla. Assn. for Theater Edn., Fla. Conf. Tchrs. English, United Faculty Fla., Tampa Mus. Democrat. Episcopalian. Club: Carrollwood Village. Author: The Creative Drama Book: Three Approaches, other books; editor: Creative Drama in a Developmental Context; Children's Theatre, Creative Drama and Learning, Drama as a Meaning Maker; contbr. articles to profl. jours.; pub. playwright; dir. plays. Home: 5311 Taylor Rd Lutz FL 33549 Office: U South Fla Dept Curriculum and Instrn Tampa FL 33620

KASH, FRANCYS KAYGEY, civic worker, service organization executive; b. Sioux City, Iowa, Feb. 25, 1921; d. Jacob David and Ida (Schwab) Maron; student pub. schs., Sioux City; m. Louis Kash, Dec. 17, 1939; 1 dau., Leslie Jo Kash Brodie. Dir., Columbia Savs. and Loan Assn., Beverly Hills, Calif., 1976-81; v.p. 1st Pacific Bank, 1981-83; public affairs/cultural cons. Los Angeles County, 1983—. Vice pres. B'nai B'rith Women, Washington, 1965-76, mem. exec. bd., 1958, treas., 1963-65, internat. pres., 1976-78, chmn. constitution-policy com., 1982-86, former chmn. Anti-Defamation League planning com., life mem. exec. com., hon. life mem. Commn.; former commr. Hillel, B'nai B'rith Youth Orgn.; guest lectr. U. Calif. Extension, Los Angeles, 1977; mem. exec. com. western region, U.S. Com. for UNICEF, 1966; mem. Los Angeles City Human Relations Commn. Adv. Com., 1963—; chair JFC Greater Los Angeles Bd. Govs., 1987—; del. to U.N. End Decade Cof., Nairobi, 1985; mem. Calif. Atty. Gen. Constl. Rights Adv. Com., 1962-64; bd. govs. Jewish Fedn. Council Greater Los Angeles, 1984—. Named Woman of Achievement, N.Y. Women's Div. of Anti-defamation League, 1976; recipient B'nai B'rith Women Dove of Peace award, 1987, Outstanding Service award State of Israel, 1973, Los Angeles Mayor award, 1976-77. Mem. Jewish Fedn. Council (bd. dirs. 1958-76, pres. women's conf. 1960-61, bd.dirs. exec. com. 1987—), Sisterhood Congregation Mogen David (life), JFC, GLA (bd. dirs, exec. com. Lodge: B'nai B'rith Internat. (bd. govs., adm. com.). Home: 9311 Alcott St Los Angeles CA 90035

KASH, KATHLEEN, physicist; b. Corona, Calif., Nov. 28, 1953; m. David A. Smith, Dec. 23, 1978; children: Nathan Smith, Caroline Smith. BA, Middlebury (Vt.) Coll., 1975; PhD, MIT, 1982. Postdoctoral fellow AT&T Bell Labs., Holmdel, N.J., 1982-84; mem. tech. staff Bell Communications Research, Red Bank, N.J., 1984—. Contbr. articles to profl. jours. Mem. Am. Phys. Soc. Office: Bell Communications Research 331 Newman Springs Rd Red Bank NJ 07728

KASHDIN, GLADYS SHAFRAN, painter, educator; b. Pitts., Dec. 15, 1921; d. Edward M. and Miriam P. Shafran; B.A. magna cum laude, U. Miami, 1960, M.A., 1962; Ph.D., Fla. State U., 1965; m. Manville E. Kashdin, Oct. 11, 1942 (dec.). Photographer, N.Y.C. and Fla., 1938-60; tchr. art, Fla. and Ga., 1956-63; asst. prof. humanities U. South Fla., Tampa, 1965-70, assoc. prof., 1970-74, prof., 1974-87, prof. emerita, 1987—; works exhibited in 58 one-woman shows, 38 group exhbns.; maj. touring exhibits include: The Everglades, 1972-75; Aspects of the River, 1975-80; Processes of Time, 1981—; represented in permanent collections: Taiwan, Peoples Republic of China, Columbus Mus. Arts and Sci., LeMoyne Art Found., Tampa Internat. Airport, Tampa Mus. Art, Kresge Art Mus.; lectr.; adv. bd. Hillsborough County Mus., 1975-83. Mem. U. S. Fla. Status of Women Com., 1971-76, chmn., 1975-76. Recipient Women Helping Women in Art award Soroptimist Internat., 1979; Mortar Bd. award for teaching excellence, 1986. Mem. NOW, AAUW (1st v.p. Tampa br. 1971-72), Phi Kappa Phi (chpt.-pres. 1981-83, artist/scholar award 1987). Home: 441 Biltmore Ave Temple Terrace FL 33617 Office: U South Fla Tampa FL 33620

KASICA, CYNTHIA ANNA, lawyer; b. Passaic, N.J., Dec. 12, 1956; d. Matthew and Anna (Wlazlo) K.; m. Jeffrey P. Barasch, May 27, 1984. BS in Nursing, Fairleigh Dickinson U., 1978; MS in Nursing, Columbia U., 1982; JD, NYU, 1985. Staff nurse NYU Hosp., 1978-79; pub. health nurse Bergen County Health Dept., Paramus, N.J., 1979-80; assoc. Sage Gray Todd & Sims, N.Y.C., 1985-87, Weber Muth & Weber, Ramsey, N.J., 1987—. Mem. ABA, N.J. State Bar Assoc. Roman Catholic. Home: 195 Overlook Pl Mahwah NJ 07430

KASINDORF, BLANCHE ROBINS, educational administrator; b. N.Y.C., May 18, 1925; d. Samuel David and Anna (Block) Robins; B.A., Hunter Coll., 1944; M.A., N.Y.U., 1948; postgrad. Cornell U., 1946-50; m. David Kasindorf, July 1, 1960. Tchr. pub. schs., Bklyn., 1945-56; instr. Bklyn. Coll., 1956-57; asst. in research for Puerto Rican study Ford Found. and N.Y.C. Bd. Edn., 1956-57; asst. prin. N.Y.C. Pub. Schs., 1957-59; research asso. ednl. programming and stats. N.Y.C. Bd. Edn., 1959-63, coordinator spl. edn. liaison div. child welfare for Bur. Curriculum Research, 1963-64; jr. prin., integration coordinator Bklyn. Sch. Dist. 44, 1964-65; prin. Pub. Sch. 8, Bklyn., 1965-87; cons. to numerous social agys. Mem. NEA, Council Exceptional Children, N.Y.C. Elementary Sch. Prins., Council Supervisory Assns. Contbr. to profl. publs.; also editor instructional materials. Home: 1655 Flatbush Ave Brooklyn NY 11210 Office: PS 8 37 Hicks St Brooklyn NY 11201

KASMIR, GAIL ALICE, insurance company official, accountant; b. N.Y.C., Aug. 19, 1958; d. Fred and Evelyn Silvie (Mailman) K. BSBA summa cum laude, U. Cen. Fla., 1979. CPA, Fla. Acct. Ernst and Whinney, Orlando, Fla., 1979-83; fin. mgr. Harcourt Brace Jovanovich (Harvest Life Ins. Co.), Orlando, Fla., 1983-85; sr. v.p., treas., asst. sec. LifeCo Investment Group, Inc and subs. Nat. Heritage Life Ins. Co., Farmers and Ranchers Life Ins. Co., Maitland, Fla., 1985—, cons. to bd. dirs., mem. investment com., 1985—. Vol. Am. Cancer Soc., 1987—, Am. Soc. for Cancer Research, 1987—. Fellow Life Office Mgmt. Assn.; mem. Am. Inst. CPAs, Fla. Inst. CPAs, Ins. Acctg. and Systems Assn., Beta Alpha Psi, Beta Gamma Sigma. Republican. Jewish. Home: 1160 Woodland Terr Trail Altamonte Springs FL 32714 Office: LifeCo Investment Group Inc 1101 N Lake Destiny Dr Suite 200 Maitland FL 32751

KASSEBAUM, NANCY LANDON, U.S. senator; b. Topeka, July 29, 1932; d. Alfred M. and Theo Landon; children: John Philip, Linda Josephine, Richard Landon, William Alfred. BA in Polit. Sci, U. Kans., 1952; MA in Diplomatic History, U. Mich., 1956. Mem. Maize (Kans.) Sch. Bd.; mem. Washington staff Sen. James B. Pearson of Kans., 1975-76; mem. U.S. Senate from Kans., 1979—, mem. fgn. relations com., commerce, sci. and transp. com., budget com., select com. on ethics. Republican. Episcopalian. Office: US Senate 302 Russell Senate Bldg Washington DC 20510

KASSEL, MARLENE EDITH, sales representative; b. Washington, Mar. 21, 1961; d. William and Rachel (Berman) K. BS in Mktg. summa cum laude, U. Md., 1983. Sales cons. Auditel, Cockeysville, Md., 1983-85; pharm sales rep. Ortho Advanced Care Products, Washington, 1985, ter. mgr., 1988—. Mktg. cons. Am. Cancer Soc., Silver Spring, Md., 1981-82; co chairperson Great Am. Smokeout, Silver Spring, Md., 1984. Recipient Achievement award Am. Cancer Soc., Silver Spring, 1983. Mem. Nat. Assn. Female Execs., Am. Mktg. Assn. (v.p. fin. 1982-83), Beta Gamma Sigma, Phi Kappa Phi. Democrat. Home: 3929 Wendy Ln Silver Spring MD 20906

KASSEWITZ, RUTH EILEEN BLOWER, hospital executive; b. Columbus, Ohio, May 15, 1928; d. E. Wallett and Helen (Daub) Blower; B.S. in Journalism-Mgmt., Ohio State U., Columbus, 1951; m. Jack Kassewitz, July 28, 1962 (dec.); 1 step son, Jack. Copywriter, Ohio Fuel Gas Co., Columbus, 1951-55, Merritt Owens Advt. Agy., Kansas City, Kans., 1955-56; account exec. Grant Advt., Inc., Miami, Fla., 1956-59; account supr. Venn/Cole & Assocs., Miami, 1959-67; dir. communications Ferendino/Grafton/Candela/Spillis Architects & Engrs., Miami, 1967-69; dir. communications Dade County Dept. Housing and Urban Devel., Miami, 1969-72; dir. communications Met. Dade County Govt., 1972-78; adminstr. community relations and mktg. U. Miami/Jackson Meml. Med. Center, 1978—. Pres., U. Miami Women's Guild, 1973-74; bd. dirs. Girls Scouts Tropical Fla., 1974-76, 81-83, Lung Assn. Dade-Monroe Counties, 1976-87; mem. exec. com. Miami-Dade Community Coll. Found.; pres. Mental Health Assn. Dade County, 1982; mem. Miami Ecol. and Beautification Com., 1978—; bd. govs. Barry U., Miami, 1981-83; trustee Nat. Humanities Faculty, 1981-83; trustee United Protestant Appeal, 1984—; mem. Greater Miami Urban Coalition; treas., past chmn. Health, Edn., Promotion Council, Inc.; adv. bd. Miami's for Me, 1987—; mem. Coral Gables Cable TV Bd., 1983-86; ch. moderator Plymouth Congl. Ch., 1986-88. Recipient Disting. Service award Plymouth Congl. Ch., Miami, 1979; Ann Stover award, 1983, Golden Image award, Fla. Pub. Relations Assn, 1987. Mem. Public Relations Soc. Am. (pres. South Fla. chpt. 1969-70, nat. chmn. govt. sect. 1973-74, nat. dir. 1974-78; continuing edn. council 1981-83; Silver Anvil award 1973, Assembly del. 1986-89), Internat. Platform Assn., Women in Communications (pres. Greater Miami chpt. 1962-63; Clarion award 1973, Community Headliner 1985), Fla. Hosp. Assn., South Fla. Hosp. Public Relations Assn., Miami Internat. Press Club (bd. dirs. 1986-87), Miami Forum, Greater Miami C. of C. (gov. 1983-86), Fla. Women's Network. Conglist. Home: 1136 Aduana Ave Coral Gables FL 33146 Office: Jackson Meml Hosp 1611 NW 12th Ave The Alamo Miami FL 33136

KASSINGER, MARGUERITE MARY, human resources analyst; b. Pensacola, Fla., Mar. 27, 1956; d. John Keating and Marguerite Mary (Sullivan) Owens; m. Kenneth Lee Kassinger Jr., Aug. 24, 1986. BS in Computer Sci., Bus., English, N.Y. Inst. Tech., 1982, MBA in Mgmt. Info., 1988. Engring. aide Fairchild Republic Co., Farmingdale, N.Y., 1977-78, engr. in tng., 1978-81, adminstr., 1981-83, supr. engring. personnel, 1983—. Mem. Nat. Assn. Female Execs., Nat. Mgmt. Assn., Assn. MBA Execs., Assn. Computing Machinery. Democrat. Roman Catholic.

KASWORM, CAROL EDITH, educational administrator; b. Salt Lake City, Nov. 8, 1944; d. William Matthew and Gladys (Backlund) k.; m. John B. Neill, June 6, 1987; stepchildren: Michele, Renee. BA, Valparaiso U., 1967; MA, Mich. State U., 1970; EdD, U. Ga., 1977. Head advisor Mich. State U., East Lansing, 1969-70; resident inst. U. South Fla., Tampa, 1970-72; asst. dir. housing U. Ga., Athens, 1972-75, staff research asst., 1975-77; lectr. U. Tex.-Austin, 1977-80, asst. prof., 1980-84; assoc. v.p., assoc. prof. U. Houston- Clear Lake, 1984-88, interim sr. v.p., provost acad. affairs, 1988—; mem. adv. bd. Eric Adult Career and Vocat. Edn., Columbus, Ohio, 1981-84. Author, editor: Education Outreach to Adult Population, 1983; cons. editor adult Edn. Quar., Washington, 1982—; contbr. to profl. publs. Active Austin Intergovernmental Tng. Council, 1982-84. Mem. Am. Assn. Adult and Continuing Edn. (program chair 1983-85), Adult Edn. Assn. (publicity chair 1980-82, Merit award 1981-82), Am. Ednl. Research Assn. Democrat. Lutheran. Office: U Houston Clear Lake 2700 Bay Area Blvd Houston TX 77058

KATES, CAROL A(NN), philosophy educator; b. Coral Gables, Fla., Nov. 5, 1943; d. Bruce Lawrence and Betty Jane (Caldwell) K. Student, Newcomb Coll., 1961-62; BA, U. Calif., Berkeley, 1965; MA, PhD, Tulane U., 1968; M in Indsl. and Labor Relations, Cornell U., 1986. Asst. prof. philosophy Ithaca (N.Y.) Coll., 1968-71, assoc. prof., 1971-83, prof., 1983—; researcher AFL-CIO, Albany, N.Y., 1986, numerous labor orgns., Tompkins County Dep. Sheriffs Assn., Ithaca, 1987—. Author: Pragmatics & Semantics, 1980; contbr. articles to acad. jours. and labor relations publs., 1969-82; co-editor The Working Press, 1986—. Fellow Am. Council Learned Societies, 1976-77; grantee NEH, 1973. Mem. Husserl Circle. Office: Ithaca Coll Dept Philosophy Ithaca NY 14850

KATHIE, CAROLE AYN, business executive, writer, public relations consultant; b. Jersey City, N.J., July 1, 1949; d. John and Emily (Bures) Kasenchak. B.A. in History, Pace U., N.Y.C., 1971; postgrad. U. Houston, 1972-73; M.A. in Sociology, Hunter Coll., N.Y.C., 1976. With custody dept. Morgan Guaranty, N.Y.C., 1968-72; adminstrv. asst. U. Houston, 1971-72, Citizens Com. for Children, 1973-74, N.Y. State Conf. for Childrens Rights, N.Y.C., 1973-74, N.Y. State Assn. for Human Services, Albany, 1974-75, Girl Scouts U.S.A., N.Y.C., 1976-77; employment counselor Dept. Labor State N.J., Trenton, 1977-81; personnel mgr. Union Photo Co., Clifton, N.J., 1981-84; exec. recruiter Mgmt. Recruiters, Internat., N.Y.C., 1985—. Contbr. newspaper The Palisadian, 1980-85. Bd. dirs. N.Y. Coalition for Juvenile Justice, N.Y.C., 1973-74; pres. Bergen County Women's Polit. Caucus (N.J.), 1978-80; commr. Bergen County Commn. on Status of Women, 1979-82; mem. state adv. com. N.J. Commn. on Women, 1980-81; mem. help line Contact Teleministries, N.Y.C., 1981-82; state chmn. pub. relations N.J. Women's Bus. Owners Conf., 1984. Mem. Am. Soc. Personnel Adminstrs. (sec. 1983-84, v.p. 1984-86), Fifth Ave Forum, Marble collegiate Chs., Internat. Assn. Personnel in Employment Security (sec. 1980-81), N.J. Network of Bus. & Profl. Women, Nat. Assn. Female Execs., AAUW. Democrat. Dutch Reformed. Club: Fleet (v.p. pub. relations 1983) (Ft. Lee, N.J.). Home: 334 Coolidge Ave Fort Lee NJ 07024 Office: Mgmt Recruiters Internat 230 Park Ave New York NY 10169

KATO-WHITE, JANET MIYO, hotel sales executive; b. Los Angeles, Nov. 29, 1953; d. Kazuo and Cherry (Tsuruta) Kato; m. Richard White. BA, U. Calif., Berkeley, 1973. Sales mgr. Miyako Hotel-Western Internat. Hotels, San Francisco, 1975-79; meetings mgr. Am. Mgmt. Assn., N.Y.C., 1979-80; sales mgr. Houstonian Hotel and Club, Houston, 1981-83; nat. sales mgr. Biltmore Hotel, Los Angeles, 1983; dir. sales Harbortown Marina Resort, Los Angeles, 1983-84; regional sales dir. Halekulani Hotel of Hawaii, Los Angeles, 1984—. Mem. Hotel Sales Mgrs. Assn., Meeting Planners Internat., Am. Soc. Assn. Execs., Am. Soc. Travel Agts., Pacific Assn. Travel Agts. Office: Halekulani Hotel Regional Sales Office 9434 Wilshire Blvd Suite 607 Beverly Hills CA 90212

KATSON, ROBERTA MARINA, economist; b. Albuquerque, Oct. 5, 1947; d. Robert V. and Penelope (Papafrangos) Katson; student Emory U., 1966-67, Ga. State U., 1967-69; B.A., U. N.Mex., 1974, M.A., 1977; m. Cyrus Butner, 1980; children—Justin Cyrus, Renee Alexis. Gen. mgr. Window Rock (Ariz.) Motor Inn, Navajo Reservation, 1972-73; research asst. dept. econs. U. N.Mex., Albuquerque, 1974-75, research asso. Resource Econ. Group, 1975-77; economist program analysis Econ. Devel. Adminstrn., Dept. Commerce, Washington, 1977-79; economist Dept. Energy, Washington, 1979-84; cons., Reston, Va.,1987—. Mem. Phi Kappa Phi, Omicron Delta Epsilon. Democrat. Contbr. articles to profl. jours. Home: 11901 St Johnsbury Ct Reston VA 22091

KATTER, MARGARET ANN CASTRO, health organization executive; b. San Francisco, Mar. 30, 1940; d. Clarence Charles and Elaine Ruth (Bullock) Castro; B.A. magna cum laude, U. Colo., 1960; M.B.A., Harvard U., 1983; divorced; children by previous marriage—Richard Todd Radakovich, Michael Keith Radakovich, Gary Douglas Radakovich. Mgr. med. office, Ketchikan, Alaska, 1965-69; public relations asst. to U.S. Senator from Alaska, 1969-71; cons., instr. office staff Seattle Gen. Hosp., 1971-72; editor reports, asst. to dir. Rocket Research Corp., Redmond, Wash., 1972-74; exec. asst. to bd. of trustees Group Health Coop. of Puget Sound, Seattle, from 1974, now dir. bd. trustees, asst. sec., corp. officer; corporate officer subs. bds. Group Health of Wash., Group Health Enterprises; past pres. Hospice and Home Care of Snohomish County subs. Everett (Wash.) Gen. Hosp. Co-chmn. gubernatorial campaign of Wally J. Hickel, 1968-69; Alaska del. to Republican Women's Conf., 1970; vol. bd. trainer United Way of King County. Mem. Am. Mgmt. Assn., Group Health Assn. (editorial bd., membership com.), Am. Aircraft Owners and Pilots Assn. Republican. Lutheran. Club: Redmond Flying. Office: Group Health Coop Puget Sound 1000 E Garfield St Seattle WA 98102

KATZ, ALICE JOAN, psychotherapist; b. N.Y.C., July 1, 1935; d. Murray and Elizabeth (Gold) Jacobs; m. Philip Katz, July 28, 1957; children: Melissa Robin, Adam Eric. BS in Art Edn., NYU, 1956; postgrad., Columbia U., 1957-76; MS in Counseling, U. of Bridgeport, 1979. Tchr. art N.Y.C. Pub. Schs., Queens, 1957-65; tchr. adult edn. program Norwalk and Stamford, Conn., 1967-77, Westport, Conn., 1984-85; tchr. continuing edn. Sacred Heart U., Bridgeport, 1986-87; pvt. practice psychotherapy Westport, 1979—; founder, group leader The ALICE Program for A Life Minus Compulsive Eating, Westport, 1980-87; guest speaker local radio and cable TV shows, 1980-87, Fairfield (Conn.) Pub. Library, 1987. Author: Conquering Compulsive Eating, 1986. Mem. Inst. for Visual Artists, Conn. Commn. on the Arts, Westport-Weston Arts Council, Entreprenurial Women's Network. Home and Office: 13 High Point Rd Westport CT 06880

KATZ, CAROLE S., psychotherapist; b. N.Y.C., Nov. 27, 1936; d. Henry Jonas and Mildred (Fassler) Rosenfeld; divorced; children: David Jonathan, Stephen Charles. BA, NYU, 1968, MA, 1972; MSW, SUNY, Stony Brook, 1979. Cert. psychoanalyst, psychotherapist. V.p. Henry Rosenfeld Inc., N.Y.C., 1954—; asst. therapist Jewish Bd. of Guardians, N.Y.C., 1963-68; dirs. research and evaluation Vera Inst. of Justice, N.Y.C., 1971-72; sr. health program analyst N.Y.C. Health and Hosp. Corp., N.Y.C., 1972-73; founder Found. for Community Innovation, N.Y.C., 1972-78; dir. community edn. and supervision Inst. for Mental Health Edn., Englewood, N.J., 1977—; assoc. dir. N.J. Ctr. for Psychotherapy, Englewood, 1978—; pvt. practice psychoanalyst N.Y.C., 1977—. Contbr. articles to scholarly jours. Vol. Nat. Abortion Rights Action League, N.Y.C.; east side organizer SANE, N.Y.C. Fellow Clin. Social Work Psychotherapists N.Y.C.; mem. Orthopsychiat. Assn. Am. Group Psychotherapy Assn., Nat. Assn. of Social Workers, Assn. Humanistic Psychology (pres. women's caucus 1971-78), Consciousness Raising and Research. Home: 1125 Park Ave New York NY 10128 Office: Inst Mental Health Edn 20 Grand Ave Englewood NJ 02631

KATZ, COLLEEN, editor-in-chief; b. Newark, May 5, 1936; d. John J. and Marion (Dull) Burke; m. Robert A. Katz, Jan. 29, 1956; children: Warren, Howard, Judy. BA in Math., Montclair (N.J.) Coll., 1957. Assoc. editor Fawcett Publs., N.Y.C., 1972-73, editor, 1973-76; editorial dir. Butterick Fashion Mktg. Co., N.Y.C., 1976-77; editor Encyclopedia of Textiles, N.Y.C., 1979; editor in chief N.J. Monthly, Morristown, 1982-85; dir. publs. Ins. Info. Inst., N.Y.C., 1985-88; editor Journal of Accountancy, N.Y.C., 1988—; dir. pub. relations Barbra Holt Assocs., N.Y.C., 1974-78. Editor: N.J. Monthly mag., 1985 (Gold award 1985, Bronze award 1985). Vol. tchr. Elizabeth (N.J.) Sch. System, 1965; vol. editor Nat. Council Jewish Women, N.J., 1967-71; vol. pub. relations worker Essex County Mental Health Assn., N.J., 1980-81. Named Woman of Yr., Cen. N.J. March of Dimes, 1984, Outstanding Alumnus, Montclair Coll., 1984. Mem. Soc. Profl. Journalists, N.J. Press Women, Internat. Assn. Bus. Communicators, Am. Soc. Mag. Editors. Office: Am Inst CPAs 1211 Ave of the Americas New York NY 10036

KATZ, ELAINE MARCIA, nuclear engineering educator; b. Chgo., Oct. 31, 1942; d. Hymen and Esther (Schnidman) K. BSME, Purdue U., 1963; MS, U. Tenn., 1971, PhD, 1975. Mech. engr. Met. Sanitary Dist, Chgo., 1963-64, J.F. Pritchard & Co., Kansas City, Mo., 1964-66, Rust Engring. Co., Birmingham, Ala., 1966-68; research asst. AEC, Knoxville, Tenn., 1969-71; sr. nuclear engr. Combustion Engring. Inc., Windsor, Conn., 1973-76; fgn. research assoc. French AEC, 1976-77; from asst. to assoc. prof. nuclear engring. U. Tenn., Knoxville, 1977—; summer faculty participant Oak Ridge Associated Univs., 1981. Summer faculty fellow NASA-ASEE Johnson Space Ctr., Houston, 1980, ASME congl. fellow as sci. advisor for Sen. Jim Sasser, Tenn., 1985, Lilly Found. fellow, 1978-79. Mem. ASME, Am. Soc. Engring. Edn., Am. Nuclear Soc., Soc. Women Engrs. (student sect.). Home: 1431 Cherokee Trail Apt 106 Knoxville TN 37920 Office: U Tenn Dept Nuclear Engring Knoxville TN 37996-2300

KATZ, ESTHER, historian, editor, administrator; b. Brussels, Aug. 14, 1948; came to U.S., 1951; d. Harry and Rose (Katz) K. A.B., Hunter Coll., 1969; M.A., NYU, 1973, Ph.D., 1980. Instr. SUNY Coll.-Brockport, 1976, NYU, 1976, Coll. New Rochelle, N.Y.C., 1981; asst. prof. NYU, 1983-84, adj. prof. history, 1983-86, 88—; dep. dir. Inst. for Research in History, N.Y.C., 1983-87; dir., editor Margaret Sanger Papers Project, 1984—; bd. dirs. Inst. for Research in History, 1987—; mem. planning com. N.Y.C. Commn. on Status of Women, 1982-84; mem. task force Women's Thesaurus Project of Nat. Council for Research on Women, N.Y.C., 1982-84; mem. nat. council advisors for exhibit censorship: 500 Yrs. of Conflict, N.Y. Pub. Library, 1983-84. Author: A History of Birth Control in the U.S., 1986; assoc. editor: Jour. Trends in History, 1983-86 ; editor: Women's History: East and West, 1986; co-editor: Woman's Experience in America, 1980; Procs. of Conf. on Women Surviving Holocaust, 1983. Contbg. author, editor: Everywoman's Guide to Colleges and Universities, 1982. Moses Coit Taylor fellow, NYU, 1976. Mem. Am. Hist. Assn., Orgn. Am. Historians, Berkshire Conf. Women Historians, Assn. for Documentary Editing. Office: NYU Dept History 19 University Pl New York NY 10003

KATZ, HILDA, artist; b. June 2, 1909; d. Max and Lina (Schwartz) K. Student, Nat. Acad. Design; student (3 awards; New Sch. Social Research scholarship), 1940-41. Author (under pen name Hulda Weber) poems including numerous anthologies, spl. ltd. edit., 1987-88; contbr.: numerous poems, short stories to books and mags. including Humpty Dumpty's Mag. (publ. for children); one-woman exhbns. include: Bowdoin Coll. Art Mus., 1951, Calif. State Library, 1953, Print Club Albany, N.Y., 1955, U. Maine, 1955, 58, Jewish Mus., 1956, Pa. State Tchrs. Coll., 1956, Massillon Mus., 1957, Ball State Tchrs. Coll., 1957, Springfield (Mass.) Art Mus., 1957, Miami Beach (Fla.) Art Ctr., Richmond (Ind.) Art Assn., 1959, Old State Capitol Mus. La., other exhbns. include: Corcoran Bienniale Library of Congress, Am. in the War Exhbn, 26 mus., Am. Drawing anns. at: Albany Inst., Nat. Acad. Design, Conn. Acad. Fine Arts, Bklyn. Mus., Delgado Mus., Art-U.S.A., 1959, Congress for Jewish Culture, Met. Mus. Art., Springfield (Mo.) Art Mus., Children's Mus. Hartford, Conn., Miniature Printers, Peoria (Ill.) Art Ctr., Pa. Acad. Fine Arts, Originale Contemporate Graphic Internat., France, Bezalel Nat. Mus., Israel, Venice (Italy) Bienniale, Royal Etchers and Painters Exchange Exhibit, Eng., Bat Yam Mus., Israel, Paris, France, 1958, 59, Am.-Italian Print Exchange, numerous libraries, artists socs., invitational exhbns. include, Rome, Turin, Venice, Florence, Naples (all Italy), Nat. Academic Mus., France, Israel, USIA exhbns. in, Europe, S. Am., Asia, Africa; represented spl. collections, U.S. Nat. Mus., 1965, U. Maine, 1965, Library of Congress, 1965-71, Met. Mus. Art, 1965-66, 80, Nat. Gallery Art, 1966, Nat. Collection Fine Arts, 1966-71, 78, Nat. Air and Space Mus., 1970, N.Y. Pub. Library, 1971, 78, U.S. Mus. History and Tech., 1972, Naval Mus., 1972, Ft. Lewis Coll., Durango, Colo., 1980-81, Boston Pub. Library, 1980-81, Israel Nat. Mus., Jerusalem, 1980-81, State Mus. Albany, N.Y., 1980; also represented in permanent collections Balt. Mus. Art, Franklin D. Roosevelt, Fogg Mus., Harvard, Santa Barbara (Calif.) Art Mus., Syracuse U., Colorado Springs Fine Arts Ctr., Pennell Collection, Am. Artists Group Prize at Samuel Golden Coll., U. Minn., Calif. State Library, Pa. State Library, Bezalel Nat. Mus., Archives Am. Art Smithsonian Instn. (art and poetry), Washington, Archives and State Mus. Albany, N.Y. (120 works), Newark Pub. Library, Addison Gallery Am. Art, Bat Yam Municipal Mus., Safed Mus., Israel, Pa. State Tchrs. Coll., Richmond Art Assn., Peoria (Ill.) Art Ctr., Boston Pub. Library, St. Margaret Mary Sch. Art, Musee Nat. d'Art Modern, Yad Vashem Meml. Archives, Jerusalem (poetry). Represented as artist and poet: Miss. Art Assn. Internat. Water Color Club award 1947, 51, New Haven Paint and Clay Club, purchase award Peoria Art Ctr. 1950, Print Club Albany 1962, also Library of Congress, U. Minn., Calif. State Library, Met. Mus. Art, Pa. State Tchrs. Coll., Art Assn. Richmond, Ind., N.Y. Pub. Library, Newark Pub. Library, St. Margaret Mary Sch. Art Coll., landscape award Soc. Miniature Painters, Gravers and Sculpture, James Joyce award Poetry Soc. Am. 1975; presented spl. commemoration to Yad Vashem Meml. Hist. Site, Jerusalem, 1987; named Dau. of Mark Twain 1970; life fellow Met. Mus. Art; named to Exec. and Profl. Hall of Fame (plaque of honor 1966). Named Membro Honoris Causa dell'Accademia di Scienze, Letteri, Arti Classe Accademica "Nobel", Milan, 1974, 75, Classe Storia Letter-Atura Americana, Milan, 1978. Fellow Internat. Acad. Poets (founder 1977); mem. Soc. Am. Graphic Artists (group prize 1950), Print Club Albany (N.Y.), Boston Printmakers (award 1955), Washington Printmakers (exhbns.), Conn. Acad. Fine Arts, Am. Color Print Soc., Audubon Artists (group exhbns., award 1944), Phila. Water Color Club (group exhbns.), Nat. Assn. Women Artists (award 1945, 47), Print Council Am., Hunterdon Art Center, Internat. Platform Assn., Poetry Soc. Am., Artists Equity N.Y., Authors Guild, Inc., Accademia Di Scienze, Lettere, Arti-Milano, Italy (Consigliere, named hon. mem. as artist 1974, author/poet 1975); Academia Di Scienze. Lettere, Arti, Classe. Address: 915 West End Ave Apt 5D New York NY 10025

KATZ, JANE, educator; b. Sharon, Pa., Apr. 16, 1943; d. Leon and Dorothea (Oberkewitz) Katz; B.S. in Edn., CCNY, 1963; M.A., NYU, 1966; M.Ed., Columbia Tchrs. Coll., 1972, Ed.D., 1978. Mem. faculty Bronx Community Coll., CUNY, 1964—, prof. phys. edn., 1972—; mem. U.S. Round-the-World Synchronized Swim Team, 1964; synchronized swimming solo tour of Eng., 1969; founding co-organizer, coach 1st Internat. Israeli Youth Festival Games, 1970; mem. winning U.S. Maccabiah Swim Team, 1957; vice chmn. Metro Master AAU Swim Team, 1974—; mem. AAU Nat. Masters All-Am. Swimming Team, 1974—, synchronized swimming solo champion, 1975; speaker, judge in field. Trainee Fed. Adminstrn. Aging, 1971-72; mem. Internat. Hall. of Fame, Ft. Lauderdale, Fla. Named Healthy Am. Fitness Leader U.S. Jaycees and the President's Council on Physical Fitness, 1987. Mem. U.S. Com. Sports for Israel (dir., co-chmn. women's swimming com. 1970—), AAHPER, Nat. Jewish Welfare Bd., Internat. Aquatics. Author: Swimming for Total Fitness, A Progressive Aerobic Program, 1981; Swimming Through Your Pregnancy, 1983; W.E.T. Workouts: Water Exercises and Techniques to Help You and Tone Up Aerobically, 1985; Fitness Works: Blueprint for Lifelong Fitness, 1988; papers in field. Address: 400 2d Ave Apt 23B New York NY 10010

KATZ, JUDITH TERRY, food marketing specialist; b. N.Y.C., Apr. 17, 1946; d. Morris and Beatrice (Miller) K.; m. Arthur J. Schwartz, Nov. 14, 1984. B.A., Bklyn. Coll., 1966, M.A., 1968; grad. chef's cert. Le Cordon Bleu, 1977. Public relations dir., catering mgr. TWTF Restaurant Group, N.Y.C., 1972-76; exec. chef Ashleys, N.Y.C., 1977, LaGriglia, N.Y.C., 1977-78; dir. food service prodn. Macy's, N.Y.C., 1977-78; mgr. Marine Midland Food Service, Service Systems Corp., N.Y.C., 1978-79, Veggies Park Restaurants, N.Y.C., 1979; dir. mktg. and food standards Corp. Food Services Inc., N.Y.C., 1980-82; asst. to corp. dir. food services Allied Stores Corp., 1982-86, corp. mgr. food services, 1986-87; ops. v.p. Maruki U.S.A. Co., N.Y.C., 1987—; free-lance restaurant cons., guest lectr. Restaurant Sch., Nassau Community Coll.; guest lectr. New Sch. Culinary Arts. Fund raiser Kennedy Found. Spl. Olympics, 1981—, Reader In-Touch Networks, 1983—. Mem. Am. Soc. Profl. and Exec. Women, Nat. Assn. Female Execs., Food and Beverage Mgrs. Assn., Mensa. Clubs: Scuba Sport Rites, Bottom Dwellers. Home and Office: 222 E 93d St New York NY 10128

KATZ, LILLIAN VERNON, mail order company executive; b. Leipzig, Germany; d. Herman Feiner and Erna Menasche; m. Sam Hochberg (div.); children—Fred, David; m. Robert Katz, Oct. 24, 1970. Ph.D. (hon.), Mercy Coll., Dobbs Ferry, N.Y., 1984, Bryant Coll., Coll. New Rochelle, Baruch Coll. Pres. Lillian Vernon, Mt. Vernon, N.Y., 1951—. Contbr. articles to profl. jours. Bd. dirs. Westchester County Assn., N.Y.; mem. Com. of 200, Americas Bus. Conf. Recipient Entrepreneural award Women's Bus. Owners of N.Y., 1983. Mem. Women's Forum. Office: Lillian Vernon Corp 510 S Fulton Ave Mount Vernon NY 10550

KATZ, MARTHA LESSMAN, lawyer; b. Chgo., Oct. 28, 1952; d. Julius Abraham and Ida (Oiring) Lessman; m. Richard M. Katz, June 27, 1976; 1 child, Julia Erin. AB, Washington U., St. Louis, 1974; JD, Loyola U., Chgo., 1977. Bar: Ill. 1977, U.S. Dist. Ct. (no. dist.) Ill. 1977, Calif. 1981, U.S. Dist. Ct. (so. dist.) Calif. 1981, U.S. Dist. Ct. (no. dist.) Calif. 1982. Assoc. Fein & Hanfling, Chgo., 1977-80, Rudick, Platt & Victor, San Diego, 1981-82, 84—; asst. sec., counsel Itel Corp., San Francisco, 1982-84. Mem. ABA (corp. banking and bus. law, taxation sects.), Ill. Bar Assn., San Diego County Bar Assn., Lawyers Club San Diego, Phi Beta Kappa. Jewish. Office: Rudick Platt & Victor 1770 4th Ave San Diego CA 92101

KATZ, PHYLLIS POLLAK, magazine publisher; b. N.Y.C., Dec. 29, 1939; d. Henry Abraham and Rose (Chaiken) P.; m. Edward Katz, Sept. 12, 1971; children: Charles Daniel, Jacob Evan. B.A., Cornell U., 1961; postgrad., U. Pa., 1961-68, Am. Sch. Classical Studies, Athens, 1964-66. Dept. asst. Univ. Mus., U. Pa.; lectr. NYU, 1970-71; asst. editor Archaeology mag., N.Y.C., 1968-72; editor Archaeology mag., 1972—, pub., 1978—. Mem. archaeol. excavations, Gordion, Turkey, 1965, Porto Cheli, Greece, 1965, Samothrace, Greece, 1966, Torre del Mordillo, Italy, 1967. Heinemann fellow, 1964-66. Mem. Archaeol. Inst. Am., Soc. Am. Archaeology, Soc. Hist. Archaeology, Am. Anthrop. Assn., Asia Soc. Jewish. Office: Archaeology Archeol Inst of America 15 Park Row New York NY 10038 *

KATZ, SARAH CAROLYN, marketing executive; b. Norwalk, Conn., Dec. 21, 1955; d. J. Leonard and Mildred Doris (Naum) K. BA, George Washington U., 1980. Mktg. coordinator Perkins & Will, Washington, 1982-86, bus. devel. exec., 1986—. Assoc. Smithsonian Inst., Washington, 1985; mem. Nat. Trust for Hist. Preservation, Washington, 1986, Greater Washington Bd. Trade, 1987. Mem. Soc. Mktg. Profl. Services, Women in Sales Assn. (bd. dirs. D.C. chpt. 1987-88), Nat. Assn. Female Execs. Office: Perkins & Will Architects 3299 K St NW Washington DC 20007

KATZEL, JEANINE ALMA, journalist; b. Chgo., Feb. 20, 1948, d. LeRoy Paul and Lia Mary (Arcuri) Katzel; B.A. in Journalism, U. Wis., 1970; M.S. in Journalism, Northwestern U., 1974. Publs. editor U. Wis. Sea Grant Program, Madison, 1969-72; editor research div. agrl. sch. U. Wis., Madison, 1972; research editor Prism mag. AMA, Chgo., 1972-73; free lance writer, 1974-75; lit. editor Plant Engring. mag. Tech. Pub. Co., Barrington, Ill., 1975-76, news editor, 1976-77, asso. editor, 1977-79, sr. editor, 1979—; sr. editor Plant Engring mag Cahners Pub., Des Plaines, Ill., 1987—. Judge assoc. ann. competition Engring. Coll. Mag., 1978-83, 85—. Recipient Elsie Bullard Morrison prize in Journalism, U. Wis., 1969; Peter Lisagor award in bus. journalism, 1983. Mem. Women in Communications, Am. Soc. Bus. Press Editors (pres. Chgo. chpt. 1977-78), Soc. Profl. Journalists, Soc. Fire Protection Engrs., Am. Inst. Chem. Engrs., Am. Chem. Soc., Nat. Audubon Soc., Nat. Fire Protection Assn. (tech. com. on fire pumps), Am. Soc. Safety Engrs., Internat. Soc. Fire Service Instrs., No. Ill. Computer Soc., Phi Kappa

Phi. Home: 16 Boxwood Ln Cary IL 60013 Office: 1350 E Touhy Ave PO Box 5080 Des Plaines IL 60018

KATZEN, ELLEN JOYCE, actress, writer, producer; b. Phila., July 26, 1950; d. Raymond and Sadona Joan (Friedman) K. BA, Temple U., 1976. News editor Sta. KYW-TV, Phila., 1976-78; dir. pub. relations and mktg. Phila. Fin. Group, Phila., 1979-80; dir. announcer relations, talk show host Nat. Broadcasting Service Radio Network, N.Y.C. and Phila., 1980-82; reporter, writer satellite div. Sta. WPIX-TV, N.Y.C., 1982; writer, reporter Satellite News Channel, Stamford, Conn., 1983; columnist, advt. account exec. East Side Express, N.Y. Guides Wisdom's Child, N.Y.C., 1983-85; dir. advt. West Side Spirit, N.Y.C., 1985-88; producer Request TV and Channel 44, N.Y.C., 1984-85, 88—; producer Request TV, N.Y.C., 1984-85; talk show host, producer Mark Carvel TV Show, N.Y.C., 1984-85. Editor Women's Resource Guide, 1978; writer: article Phila. Daily News, 1978; photojournalist West Side Spirit and East Side Express, 1986; contbring. writer to Bulletin, Phila. Jour. (recipient prize Phila. Writers' Conf., 1975); appeared in movies: Hand Me Down Kids (ABC-TV), Sharing Thoughts, Falling in Love, Desperately Seeking Susan, Playing for Time; acted in Off-Broadway, Quaigh Theater, N.Y., various TV commercials. Fund raiser Harlem Children Theater Co., N.Y.C., 1985; fund raiser, actress Tweedle-Dum Theater Co., N.Y.C., 1985. Dion Found. scholar, 1972, 74; recipient Cert. Performing Arts Am., 1978, Cert., Life Office Mgmt. Assn., 1980. Mem. Am. Film Inst., Am. Film Soc., Women in Communications, N.Y. Advt. Club, Advt. Women of N.Y. (letter of Commendation, Screen Actors Guild, Am. Fedn. of TV and Radio Artists. Office: West Side Spirit 1220 Broadway New York NY 10001

KATZEN, SALLY, lawyer, former government official; b. Pitts., Nov. 22, 1942; d. Nathan and Hilda (Schwartz) K.; m. Timothy B. Dyk, Oct. 31, 1981; 1 child, Abraham Benjamin. B.A. magna cum laude, Smith Coll., 1964; J.D. magna cum laude, U. Mich., 1967. Bar: D.C. 1968, U.S. Supreme Ct. 1971. Congl. intern Sente Subcom. on Constl. Rights, Washington, summer 1963; legal research asst. civil rights div. Dept. Justice, Washington, summer 1965; law clk. to judge U.S. Ct. Appeals (D.C. cir.), 1967-68; assoc. Wilmer, Cutler & Pickering, Washington, 1968-74, ptnr., 1975-79, 81—; gen. counsel Council on Wage and Price Stability, 1979-80, dep. dir., 1980-81; mem. Jud. Conf. for D.C. Circuit, 1972-81, 83-88. Editor-in-chief U. Mich. Law Rev., 1966-67. Mem. com. visitors U. Mich. Law Sch., 1972-87. Fellow ABA (ho. of dels. 1978-80, council adminstrv. law sect. 1979-82; chmn.-elect adminstrv. sect. law 1988; governing com. forum com. communications law 1979-82); mem. D.C. Bar Assn., Women's Bar Assn., FCC Bar Assn. (exec. com. 1984-87), Women's Legal Def. Fund (pres. 1977, v.p. 1978), Order of Coif. Home: 4638 30th St NW Washington DC 20008 Office: 2445 M St NW Washington DC 20037-1420

KATZENBACH, SUSAN D., infosystems specialist; b. Chgo., Aug. 27, 1954; d. Robert E. and Merlyn T. (Coyle) Deiss; m. Edward G. Katzenbach, June 30, 1978. Student, Hope Coll., 1972-74; BS in Acctg., Elmhurst (Ill.) Coll., 1981. Jr. acct. Griffin Pipe div. Amsted Industries Inc., Oak Brook, Ill., 1975-76; acct. Clow Corp., Oak Brook, 1976-79, programmer, mgr., 1979-82; programmer/analyst electro-motive div. Gen. Motors Corp., La Grange, Ill., 1982-84; mem. info. systems staff AT&T Technologies, Inc., Warrenville, Ill., 1984—. Mem. Am. Prodn. and Inventory Control Soc. (cert.).

KATZOWITZ, LAUREN, public affairs consultant. B.S. in Comparative Lit. with honors, Brandeis U., 1970; M.S. with honors, Columbia U., 1971. With, Newsweek mag., then Phila. Bull.; free-lance writer, editor, cons., until 1975; cons. Ford Found., 1972-75; mgr. PBS programs Exxon Corp., 1978-81, Great Performances, Live From Lincoln Center, Dance in America, NOVA, The MacNeil/Lehrer Report; communications mgr. Exxon Research and Engring. Co., 1981-84; regional liaison Europe and Africa, Exxon Corp., 1984-86; Exec. director Foundation Service, Federation of Jewish Philanthropies, 1986—; pres. LK Cons., 1986—. Trustee Women's Action Alliance, Bronx Ednl. Services, Community Family Planning Council of N.Y.C., Am. Friends of Institut Internat. d'Etudes Musicales, St. Maximin, France, B'nai B'rith Hillel/Jewish Association for College Youth. Friend N.Y.C. Commn. on Status of Women. Named one of 12 Women to Watch in the Eighties, Ladies' Home Jour., 1979. Regional Finalist President's Commission on White House Fellowships 1984. Office: LK Cons 505 E 79th St New York NY 10021

KAUBLE, AYLENE TILLEY, educator; b. Sparkman, Ark., Dec. 14, 1936; d. Audie and Lena Mae (Fortner) Tilley; m. Michael Anthony Kauble, Feb. 6, 1959; children: Terri Lynn, Reese Everett. BS in Edn., Southern State Coll., 1957; MS in Edn., Henderson State U., 1973. Various clerical positions La., Ark., 1957-63; tchr. bus. edn. Sparkman (Ark.) High Sch., 1964-66, Harmony Grove High Sch., Camden, Ark., 1966-67; bus. instr. Red River Vo-Tech. Sch., Hope, Ark., 1967-69; tchr., chair bus. edn. dept. Hope High Sch., 1969—. Mem. Am. Vocat. Assn., Ark. Vocat. Assn., Ark. Bus. Educators Assn., N. Central Evaluation Com. Baptist. Office: Hope High Sch 1700 Main St Hope AR 71801

KAUDER, KAREN LEE, infosystems specialist; b. San Luis Obispo, Calif., Mar. 2, 1957; d. Wesley Eugene and Loretta Lee (Roberson) K. BS in Speech and Theatre, Houston Bapt. U., 1979, MBA, 1984. Coordinator. mktg. Big Music Am. Corp., Houston, 1980; exec. asst. to pres. A. R. Busse and Assoc., Houston, 1981; specialist end-user computing Superior Oil Co., Houston, 1981-85; sr. analyst Exxon Co., USA, Houston, 1985-86; cons. software Enron Corp., Houston, 1986-87; mgr. bus. systems support Transwestern Pipeline (subs. Enron Corp.), Houston, 1987-88; dir. Houston Pl. Learning Ctr. (subs. Burnett Cos.), Houston, 1988—. Vol. big sister Depelchin Children's Ctr., Houston, 1985-86. Mem. Info. Ctr. Mgmt. Assn.

KAUFFMAN, CHARLINE PUTNEY, accounts management company executive; b. Elmira, N.Y., Sept. 5, 1948; d. J. Forrest and Eleanor Jane (Doty) Putney; m. Eddie L. Kauffman, Aug. 16, 1968 (div. Aug. 1977); children: Kristine, Traci, Teri, Sara. BBA, Elmira Coll. Design dept. adminstr. Eastern Metal, Elmira, 1976-78; receptionist Horwitz Paper and Packaging, Elmira, 1978; aide Assemblyman George Winner, Elmira, 1979-80, 82-87; office mgr. Planned Parenthood, Elmira, 1980-81; abstractor Winner & Denton Law Office, Elmira, 1984; v.p. Bus. Recovery Systems, Horseheads, N.Y., 1980—; prin. Pragmatic Cons., Pine City, N.Y., 1984—. Fundraiser Community Found. of Chemung Co., Elmira, 1978. Mem. Purchasing Mgmt. Assn., Inc. of Elmira (v.p. 1987—). Republican. Home: 974 Dalrymple Ave Pine City NY 14871 Office: Bus Recovery Systems 124 W Franklin St Horseheads NY 14845

KAUFFMAN, JUDITH ANNE, psychologist; b. Peoria, Ill., Sept. 3, 1941; d. Albert Eugene and Hazel Bernice (Hutchinson) K.; m. Melvin L. Inglet, Oct. 4, 1980. AB, Bradley U., 1963, MA, 1967; MA, U. Nebr., 1971; PhD, U.S. Internat. U., San Diego, 1977. Tchr. gifted children Peoria Pub. Schs., 1963-69; psychol. counselor U. Nebr. Counseling Ctr., Lincoln, 1970-72; flight service supr. Am. Airlines, Los Angeles, 1972-74; psychol. asst. Gerson Psychol. Corp., Hawthorne, Calif., 1974-80; pvt. practice psychology Manhattan Beach, Calif., 1977—; speaker aerosapce cos. Author profl. newsletter; speaker to airline industry meetings. Mem. Western Psychol. Assn., Calif. State Psychol. Assn., Los Angeles County Psychol. Assn., Assn. Labor-Mgmt. Adminstrs. and Cons. on Alcoholism, Nat. Assn. Adult Children of Alcoholics. Home: 1406 11th St Manhattan Beach CA 90266 Office: 1726 Manhattan Beach Blvd #G Manhattan Beach CA 90266

KAUFFMAN, M. JANE, guidance counselor; b. Batavia, N.Y., Sept. 2, 1935; d. Edward Joseph and Loretta Viola (Garraghan) K. BS, SUNY, Buffalo, 1957; MS, Canisius Coll., 1964. English tchr. Kenmore (N.Y.) Sch. System, 1957-62; guidance counselor Williamsville (N.Y.) Sch. Dist., 1962—; polit. action com. N.Y. State United Tchrs., 1983—, state chmn., 1985, western N.Y. polit. action coordinator. Labor studies adv. bd. Erie Community Coll., Buffalo, 1986—; govt. relations com. Erie County United Way, 1987—; mem. Erie County Dem. Com., Buffalo, 1986—, nominating com. Amherst (N.Y.) Dem. Com., 1987—. Mem. Am. Fedn. Tchrs., Williamsville Tchrs. Assn. (exec. bd.), Buffalo AFL-CIO Council (polit. del. 1983—), N.Y. State United Tchrs., Western N.Y. Consortium Guidance Counselors, Phi Delta Kappa. Roman Catholic. Office: NY State United Tchrs 5350 Main St Williamsville NY 14221

KAUFFMAN, MARGARET A., advertising executive, marketing consultant; b. Erie, Pa., Apr. 19, 1944; d. Eric Alfred and Agnes Mary (Logue) Jonsson; m. Walter L. Kauffman, July 15, 1966; children—Walter L., Eric Barton, Leslie Ann, Andrew John. Student parochial schs., Erie. Advt. account rep. The Greensheet, Erie, 1983-85, Lake Shore Visitor, Erie, 1985-86; cons. Geary & Hill Mktg., Erie, 1986-88; pres. Kauffman Assocs. Mktg. and Advt., Erie, 1988—. Editor Erie Philharm. Newsletter, 1977-78. Bd. dirs. YWCA, Erie, 1979-80; corr. sec. Hamot Aid Soc., Erie, 1980-81; v.p. Erie Philharm. Women's Assn., 1980-81; active Erie Civic Ballet, Erie Art Mus. Mem. Am. Bus. Women's Assn. (v.p.), Nat. Assn. Female Execs. Democrat. Roman Catholic. Clubs: Woman's of Erie, Erie Advt. Avocations: needle-point, hot air ballooning, walking. Home: 1135 W 10th St Erie PA 16502

KAUFFMAN, MARGARET ANNE, public relations executive, photojournalist; b. St. Louis, Sept. 9, 1945; d. Tom Harry and Margaret Ruth (Siebert) Goddard; m. William Francis Kauffman, June 29, 1968; children—Kathryn Ruth, Juliet Lynn. B.Journalism, U. Mo., 1968, postgrad., 1983, 84; postgrad. Jefferson Coll., 1984, 85, 88. Writer, Am. Nat. Stores, St. Louis, 1968-69, J.C. Penny Co., St. Louis, 1969; dir. pub. info. St. Louis Dept. Health and Hosps., 1969-71, Jefferson Coll., Hillsboro, Mo., 1979—. Editor, Jefferson Coll. News, 1979—. Founding mem., sec.-treas. Friends Jefferson Coll., 1980-87; mem. adminstrv. bd., United Seekers, Union United Methodist Ch., St. Louis, 1976—; chmn. blood dr. ARC, St. Louis, 1976-77. Recipient MacEachern award Am. Hosp. Assn., 1970. Mem. Mo. Assn. Community Jr. Colls., Council Advancement and Support of Edn., Nat. Council for Community Relations, Am. Assn. Community and Jr. Colls., United Methodist Women, Phi Delta Kappa. Home: 6601 Bancroft Saint Louis MO 63109 Office: Jefferson Coll PO Box 1000 Hillsboro MO 63050

KAUFFMAN, MARILYN JOY, small business owner; b. Red Oak, Iowa, Nov. 9, 1930; d. Kenneth Martin and Lotus (Goodner) Sells; divorced; children: Marno Linn Miller, Pamela Marie Dake, Kenneth Harold Kauffman. BA, San Diego State U., 1972. Cert. tchr., Iowa. Tchr. elem. sch., Sidney, Iowa, 1950-51; pres., owner Repair Bus., San Diego, 1972-81; co-owner Gen. Contractor Bus., San Diego, 1981-86; owner Herrepair, Inc., La Mesa, Calif., 1987—; treas., dir. The Network of San Diego County, 1983—. Democrat. Unitarian. Home and Office: Herrepair Inc 7304 Cornell Ave La Mesa CA 92041

KAUFMAN, BEL, author, educator; b. Berlin, Germany; d. Michael J. and Lala (Rabinowitz) K.; divorced; children: Jonathan Goldstine, Thea Goldstine. B.A. magna cum laude, Hunter Coll., M.A. with highest honors, Columbia U.; LL.D., Nasson Coll., Maine. Adj. prof. English CUNY; lectr. throughout country, also appearances on TV and radio.; Mem. Commn. Performing Arts. Editorial bd., Phi Delta Kappan.; Author: Up the Down Staircase, 1965, Love, etc, 1979; also short stories, articles, TV play, translations of Russian, lyrics for musicals. Bd. dirs. Shalom Aleichem Found.; adv. council Town Hall Found. Recipient plaque Anti-Defamation League; award and plaque United Jewish Appeal; Paperback of Year award; Bell Movie award; also ednl. journalism awards; named to Hall of Fame Hunter Coll., winner short story contest sponsored by NEA and PEN, 1983. Mem. Author's Guild (council), Dramatists Guild, P.E.N. (membership com.), English Grad. Union, Phi Beta Kappa. Address: 1020 Park Ave New York NY 10028

KAUFMAN, CHARLOTTE KING, artist, retired educational administrator; b. Balt., Dec. 5, 1920; d. Ben and Belle (Turow) King; A.B., Goucher Coll., 1969; M.P.H., Johns Hopkins U., 1972, M.Ed., 1976; m. Albert Kaufman, July 22, 1945; children—Matthew King, Ezra King. Dir. public relations Balt. Jewish Community Center, 1962-67; research and editor Johns Hopkins U. Sch. Hygiene and Public Health, Balt., 1969-72, admissions officer, 1972-74, dir. admissions and registrar, 1974-86, dir. study cons. program undergraduates, 1986—. Mem. Am. Pub. Health Assn., Am. Assn. for Higher Edn., Am. Assn. Collegiate Registrars and Admissions Officers. Democrat. Jewish. Home: 1 E University Pkwy #1501 Baltimore MD 21218 Studio: 3000 Chestnut Ave Mill Centre 223 Baltimore MD 21211

KAUFMAN, ELIZABETH ANN, postal service supervisor; b. Milw., June 2, 1958; d. Lawrence Edward and Virgina (Libecki) K. Grad. high sch., Waukesha, Wis. City letter carrier U.S. Postal Service, Yakima, Wash., 1981-84, supr., 1984—; mem. women's adv. bd. U.S. Postal Service, Yakima, 1984—. Loaned exec. combined fed. campaign United Way, Yakima, 1984-86, Yakima, 1984-86; chairperson, 1986-87. Served with U.S. Army, 1976-80. Mem. Nat. Assn. Female Execs. Roman Catholic. Lodge: Zonta. Home: 450 Buchanon Rd Selah WA 98942-9521 Office: US Postal Service 205 W Washington Yakima WA 98903-9998

KAUFMAN, JOYCE JACOBSON, chemist, educator; b. N.Y.C., June 21, 1929; d. Abraham and Sarah (Seldin) Deutch; m. Stanley Kaufman, Dec. 26, 1948; 1 child, Jan Caryl. B.S. with honors, Johns Hopkins U., 1949, M.A., 1959, Ph.D. in Chemistry, 1960; D.E.S. with honors in Theoretical Physics, Sorbonne, Paris, 1963. Analytical research chemist Army Chem. Ctr., Md., 1949-52; mem. chemistry research staff Johns Hopkins U., Balt., 1952-60; mem. quantum chemistry group Research Inst. Advanced Studies, Balt., 1960-69, staff scientist, 1965-69, head, 1963-69; prin. research scientist dept. chemistry Johns Hopkins U., Balt., assoc. prof. dept. anesthesiology Sch. Medicine, 1969—, assoc. prof. dept. surgery div. plastic surgery, 1977—; mem. sci. adv. com. Dept. Def., 1977; mem. rev. panel for undergrad. chemistry edn. NSF, 1977; Fogarty Internat. Exchange specialist NIH-USSR Ministry of Health, 1978. Mem. editorial adv. bd.: John Wiley and Intersci. Pubs., 1965—; Molecular Pharmacology, 1970—; Internat. Jour. Quantum Chemistry, 1967—; Jour. Computational Chemistry, 1980—; editor Benchmark Book Series in phys. chemistry-chem. physics, 1975—, overall chemistry editor, 1977—. Contbr. articles to profl. jours. Recipient Garvan medal as outstanding woman chemist Am. Chem. Soc., 1974; Md. Chemist award Am. Chem. Soc. Md. sect. 1974. Fellow Am. Phys. Soc., Am. Inst. Chemists; mem. Am. Chem. Soc. (chmn. Md. sect. 1972, councilor phys. chemistry div. 1971—, budget and fin. com. 1981—), Am. Soc. Pharmacology and Exptl. Therapeutics, European Acad. Scis., Arts and Letters (corr. mem.), Internat. Soc. Quantum Biology, Am. Soc. Anesthesiology, AAUP, Phi Beta Kappa, Sigma Xi. Office: Johns Hopkins U Dept Chemistry Baltimore MD 21218

KAUFMAN, JUDITH LASKER, health association administrator; b. N.Y.C., May 27, 1942; d. Lewis and Miriam (Greenspan) Lasker; m. Jerome B. Kaufman, June 29, 1967; children: Jonathan Lasker, Jeffrey Paul. BA, Alfred U., 1963, MS, 1965. Dir. N.Y.C. campaign Planned Parenthood, 1965-66; mktg. rep. IBM Corp., N.Y.C., 1966-70; chief exec. officer Champaign-Urbana (Ill.) Conv. and Vis. Bur., 1984-86; dir. pub. relations Penta, Champaign, 1986; dir. Leukemia Soc. Am. Inc., Urbana, 1986—. Pres. Champaign Children's Home and Aid Soc. Ill., 1972—; past v.p. Jr. League Champaign-Urbana; founder, mem. regional adv. com. Dept. Family and Children's Services, Champaign, 1978—; chair Urbana Juvenile Justice Rev. Com., 1983—. Mem. Exec. Club Champaign-Urbana, Twin Cities Bus. and Profl. Women's Club, Women's Bus. Council, Champaign-Urbana C. of C. Jewish. Homw: 2104 Zuppke Dr Urbana IL 61801 Office: Leukemia Soc Am Inc 109A N Broadway Urbana IL 61801

KAUFMAN, KATIE EDWINA TRIMBLE, graphic designer; b. Hamilton, Tex., Dec. 26, 1947; d. Joseph Hobart and Carrie Novella (Wilson) Trimble; m. George Lee Daves, Aug. 22, 1970 (div.); m. Gary Paul Kaufman, June 25, 1977. Student, Tex. Tech. U., 1969-70; BS, No. Mich. U., 1974; postgrad., U. Calif., 1979-80. Advt. asst. Sears-Roebuck Co., Odessa, Tex., 1967-69; advt. and pub. relations dir. Cliffs Ridge Ski Area, Marquette, Mich., 1974-78; graphic designer U. Calif., Davis, 1979-80, River City Advt., Sacramento, 1982-83; sr. designer Trendsetters Advt., Riverside, Calif., 1983-84; asst. art dir. Crown Printers, San Bernardino, Calif., 1984—; designer, prin. Katie Kaufman Designs, Vacaville, Calif., 1981-83. Designer symphony posters, 1986. Mem. Nat. Assn. Female Execs., Portfolio, Officers' Wives Club (illustrator mag. 1979). Democrat. Baptist.

KAUFMAN, LOUISE SUSAN, pharmaceutical company executive; b. S.I., N.Y., Dec. 4, 1952; d. Santo Michael and Selma Mary (Sidoti) Repage; m. Peter Joseph Kaufman, Sept. 18, 1976. BS, Wagner Coll., 1975, MS, 1978; MBA, St. John's U., 1983. Vet. technician Hylan Animal Hosp., S.I., 1972-75; vet. abstractor Merck & Co., Inc., Rahway, N.J., 1975-78, regulatory affairs asst., 1978-79, sr. regulatory coordinator, 1979-82, mgr. registration, 1982-85; dir. regulatory affairs internat. Warner-Lambert Co., 1985—. Mem. Pharm. Mfg. Assn. (mem. internat. regulatory affairs com. 1987—, mem. clinical safe surveil com. 1988—), Drug Info. Assn. (publicity dir. 1980-82, treas. 1982-86, gen. chmn. 1st internat. meeting in Rome, Outstanding Acheivement award 1987), N.Y. Acad. Scis., Nat. Soc. Microbiology, Am. Vet. Med. Assn. Aux., N.Y.C. Soc. Microbiology. Office: Warner-Lambert Co 201 Tabor Rd Morris Plains NJ 07905

KAUFMAN, PAULA T., librarian; b. Perth Amboy, N.J., July 26, 1946; d. Harry and Clara (Katz) K. AB, Smith Coll., 1968; MS, Columbia U., 1969; MBA, U. New Haven, 1979. Reference librarian Columbia U., N.Y.C., 1969-70, bus. librarian, 1979-82, dir. library services, 1982-86, dir. acad. info. services, 1986-87, acting v.p., univ. librarian, 1987-88; dean of library U. Tenn., Knoxville, 1988—; reference coordinator McKinsey & Co., N.Y.C., 1970-73; founder, ptnr. Info. for Bus., N.Y.C., 1973-76; prin. reference librarian Yale U., New Haven, 1976-79. Contbr. articles to mags., 1983-87; editor: (book) Social Science (vol. 3 Reader's Adviser), 1986. Mem. Soc. For Scholarly Pub., Am. Library Assn. Office: U Tennessee John C Hodges Library Knoxville TN 37996

KAUFMAN, PHYLLIS CYNTHIA, lawyer, author, theatrical producer; b. Phila., Nov. 4, 1945; d. Harry and Gertrude (Friend) K. BA cum laude, Brandeis U., 1967; JD, Temple U., 1974. Bar: Pa. 1974, U.S. Dist. Ct. (ea. dist.) Pa. 1974. Sole practice entertainment law, Phila., 1977—; exec. producer Playhouse in the Park, Phila., 1979; dir. entertainment Caesar's Hotel-Casino, Atlantic City, N.J., 1980-81; v.p. entertainment Sands Hotel-Casino, Atlantic City, 1981-83; v.p. Kanadus Entertainment Inc., Toronto, 1982—. Co-author: No-Nonsense Financial, Real Estate, Career and Legal Guides, 1985—; assoc. editor Temple Law Quarterly. Bd. dirs. Phila. Coll. Performing Arts, 1977-85, Creative Artists Network, 1986—. Ford Found. grantee, 1965-67. Mem. Phila. Bar Assn. Democrat. Office: 1500 Locust St Suite 3805 Philadelphia PA 19102

KAUFMAN, SHIRLEY A. BEHNKE, educational consultant; b. Clawson, Mich., Aug. 18, 1931; d. Oren Leroy and Delta Mae (Rohrer) Adams; m. William Frederick Behnke, Apr. 18, 1954 (dec. 1982); children—Douglas, Curtis, Pamela; m. John M. Kaufman, Dec. 1, 1985. B.A., Ohio State U., 1953, M.A., 1971, E.A.S. (specialist), 1981, Ph.D., 1983. Cert. in secondary edn. and ednl. adminstrn. Reporter Wellington (Ohio) Enterprise, 1948-49; editor Ohio Council Chs., Columbus, 1953-55; tchr. Upper Arlington Schs., Columbus, 1971-83, adminstrv. asst. to supt., 1983-85; lectr. Ohio State U. Sch. Journalism, 1986; mem. state Adv. Com. for Community Edn., 1979-82; dir. Journalism Assn. of Ohio Schs., 1980-82. Contbr. articles to profl. jours. Mem. Promote Upper Arlington Com., 1983-84. Recipient Journalism Achievement award Newspaper Fund, 1977; Jennings scholar, 1981-82; Presdl. scholar, 1983. Mem. Women in Communications (pres. 1963-64), Mensa, Phi Delta Kappa. Democrat. Home: 2566 Chester Rd Columbus OH 43221

KAUFMAN, SUSAN GAIL, executive search company executive; b. Bklyn., Feb. 28, 1943; d. William and Emma (Pollack) Zipkis; m. Michael David Kaufman, June 30, 1962; children—Robert, Craig. B.A. cum laude, Western Conn. State Coll., 1977; M.S.W., NYU, 1979. Cert. social worker, N.Y., Mass. Sr. clin. social worker No. Westchester Guidance Clinic, Mt. Kisco, N.Y., 1975-80; pres. Kaufman Assocs., Stamford, Conn., 1981-85; v.p. Staub, Warmbold & Assoc., Stamford, 1985-86; pres. Kaufman Assocs., Palo Alto, Calif.; prin. M.K. Global Ventures, Palo Alto, 1986—. Mem. Nat. Assn. Social Workers. Avocation: private pilot.

KAUFMAN, SUSAN JANE, banker; b. Denver, Nov. 13, 1942; d. William Douglas and Catherine Sue (Orrison) Morrison; m. Jerry Allen Kaufman, Mar. 10, 1962; children: Eric Douglas, Carrie Annette. BA, U. Colo., 1968; MA, U. Denver, 1972; MBA, John F. Kennedy U., Orinda, Calif., 1981. Cert. fin. planner. Librarian Littleton (Colo.) Pub. Library, 1972-74, Kent Denver Country Day Sch., 1974-76; exec. dir. Colo. Library Assn., Denver, 1974-76; customer service rep. bus. office Pacific Telephone Co., Berkeley, Calif., 1977-80; br. mgr., asst. v.p. Citicorp Savs., Orinda, 1981-87, area staff officer, Los Angeles, 1987—. Mem. Contra Costa County M-11 Commn. (Calif.), 1983—, Children's Hosp. of Oakland, Alexander Lindsay Jr. Mus. Mem. Jr. League Pasadena, Orinda C. of C. (pres.), Orinda Hist. Soc., Bus. Vol. for the Arts, 1987—. Mem. Internat. Council Fin. Planners, Inst. Cert. Fin. Planners, Delta Gamma. Republican. Lodge: Soroptimists (treas.). Home: 2033-3 Rosemont Ave Pasadena CA 94563 Office: 6750 Van Nuys Blvd Van Nuys CA 91405

KAUFMAN, VICTORIA BOYT, sales consultant; b. New Brunswick, N.J., July 20, 1944; d. Arnold Arpad and Mildred Louise (Mortenson) Boyt; m. Jeffrey Ian Kaufman, Jan. 29, 1966; children—Michael Boyt, Meredith Lara. B.A., Temple U., 1966; postgrad. Columbia U., 1974-77. Biology tchr. Germantown Acad., Ft. Washington, Pa., 1966-68; research assoc. Med. Coll. Ga., Augusta, 1968-69; sales rep. Boehringer Ingelheim, Ridgefield, Conn., 1978-81; nat. sales mgr. PlayCable Co., N.Y.C., 1981—; pres. V. Kaufman Enterprises, River Vale, N.J., 1980-81. Mktg. vol. Bill Bradley for U.S. Senate campaign, Union, N.J., since 1984—. Mem. Nat. Assn. Homebased Bus., Women in Cable (mem. bd. 1983-84), N.Y. Women's Network, Am. Women Entrepreneurs. Democrat. Jewish. Club: Women's City of N.Y. (mem. program com. 1985-88). Avocation: collecting works of American women artists. Office: 373 Walnut St Englewood NJ 07631

KAUFMAN-DRESSLER, BRENDA JOYCE, sex educator, consultant; b. N.Y.C., Jan. 30, 1943; d. Herbert and Betty (Kirshner) Dressler; m. Irving Kaufman, Dec. 30, 1961 (div. Dec. 1979); 1 child, Joshua Ari. BA, CCNY, 1964; MA, CUNY, 1969; PhD, NYU, 1986. Lic. high sch. health tchr., N.Y.C. Educator sex and health N.Y.C. Bd. Edn., 1964-75, 1979—, Sex Info. and Edn. Council U.S., N.Y.C., 1985-86, Bd. Edn., N.Y.C., 1979—; cons. PTA and Curriculum Adv. Com. Steinway Jr. High Sch., N.Y.C., 1985-87, Bayside High Sch., 1987-88, Benjamin Cardozo High Sch., N.Y.C., 1988—. Contbr. numerous articles to profl. jours. Mem. Am. Assn. Sex Educators (cert.), Counselors and Therapists (cert.), Sex Info. and Edn. Council Am., Soc. for Sci. Study of Sex, Am. Pub. Health Assn., Kappa Delta Pi. Home: 162-41 Powells Cove Blvd Beechhurst NY 11357

KAUFMANN, MARY S., insurance executive; b. Buckley, Ill., Nov. 11, 1941; d. William J. and Marcella E. (Williams) Schaumburg; divorced; children: Kathryn, Kristin. Various secretarial positions N.C., Calif., Colo., 1962-82; owner, broker MSK Ins. Cons., Ft. Collins, Colo., 1982—; owner Express Temporary Services, Ft. Collins, 1982-85; lectr. in field, Ft. Collins, 1982—. Contbr. articles to profl. jours. Mem. Nat. Assn. Life Underwriters, Nat. Assn. Health Underwriters, Larimer County Assn. Life Underwriters (pres. 1986-87, sec., treas., v.p. 1983-85), Internat. Assn. of Fin. Planners (v.p. 1982-83, treas. 1985—), Western Assn. Fin. Planners (del. 1985-87), Ft. Collins C. of C. (relations com. 1980-87, univ. affairs com. 1988—). Home: 3005 Anchor Way No 4 Fort Collins CO 80525

KAUFMANN, SYLVIA NADEAU, office equipment sales company executive; b. Eagle Lake, Maine, Dec. 1, 1940; d. Edwin Joseph Nadeau and Emily (Beaulieu) Gabois; m. Max Daniel Kaufmann, Sept. 21, 1958 (div. 1985); children: Mark A., Laura A., Max D. Jr. Grad. high sch., East Hartford, Conn., 1958. Bookkeeper United Bank and Trust, Hartford, Conn., 1959-66; real estate agt. Barcombe Agy., South Windsor, Conn., 1967-74; sales rep. Duplicating Methods Co., East Windsor, Conn., 1974-80; gen. mgr., officer Duplicating Methods Co., East Windsor, 1980—. Mem. Nat. Office Machine Dealers Assn., North Cen. Conn. C. of C., Bus. Profl. Women Greater Hartford, Exec. Females Inc. Democrat. Roman Catholic. Home: 6 Hoover Lane PO Box 2044 Enfield CT 06082 Office: Duplicating Methods Co 170 North Rd East Windsor CT 06088

KAUGER, YVONNE, state justice; b. Colony, Okla., Aug. 3, 1937; d. John and Alice (Bottom) K.; m. Ned Bastow, May 8, 1982; 1 child, Jonna Sinclair. BS magna cum laude, Southwestern State U., Weatherford, Okla., 1958; cert. med. technologist, St. Anthony's Hosp., 1959; J.D., Oklahoma City U., 1969. Med. technologist Med. Arts Lab., 1959-68; assoc. Rogers, Travis & Jordan, 1970-72; jud. asst. Okla. Supreme Ct., Oklahoma City, 1972-84, justice, 1984—; mem. appellate div. Ct. on Judiciary; mem. State

Capitol Preservation Commn., 1983-84; mem. dean's adv. com. Oklahoma City U. Sch. Law. Founder Gallery of Plains Indian, Colony, Okla., Red Earth, 1987; active Jud. Day, Girl's State, 1976-80; keynote speaker Girl's State Hall of Fame Banquet, 1984; bd. dirs. Lyric Theatre, Inc., 1966—, pres. bd. dirs., 1981; past mem. bd. dirs. Civic Music Soc., Okla. Theatre Ctr., Canterbury Choral Soc. Named to Outstanding Young Women Am., U.S. Jaycees, 1967, Byliner Honoree, Women in Communications, 1984, Woman of Yr., Oklahoma City chpt. Bus. and Profl. Women's Club, 1984, Woman of Yr., High Noon, 1985, Judge of Yr., Okla. Trial Lawyer's Appellate, 1987; adopted by Cheyenne-Arapaho tribes, 1984; honored by Okla. Hospitality Club, Ladies in the News, 1985; recipient Dist. Alumni award Southwestern Okla. State U., 1986, Oklahoma City U., 1986; named Outstanding Appellate Judge Okla. Trial Lawyers Assn., 1987. Mem. ABA (law sch. accreditation com.), Okla. Bar Assn. (law schs. com. 1977—), Washita County Bar Assn., Washita County Hist. Soc. (life), St. Paul's Music Soc., Iota Tau Tau, Delta Zeta. Episcopalian.

KAUNITZ, RITA DAVIDSON, religious organization official; b. N.Y.C., Apr. 18, 1922; d. David and Bessie (Golden) Davidson; B.A. magna cum laude, N.Y. U., 1942; M.A., Columbia U., 1946; Ph.D., Radcliffe Coll., 1951; m. Paul E. Kaunitz, Aug. 10, 1947; children—Victoria Moss, Jonathan Davidson, Andrew Moss. Adminstrv. asst. OPA, Washington, 1943-44; columnist planning and housing Progressive Architecture mag., N.Y.C., 1944-46; editor Plan for Rezoning, 1st year's studies, N.Y.C., 1948-49; asso. editor bull. housing and town and country planning UN Secretariat, 1950-52; cons. Center Housing, Bldg. and Planning, UN Secretariat, 1960-66; research asso. grad. program in city planning Yale U., 1955-57; policy and program specialist Model Cities Program, Bridgeport, Conn., 1969; project dir. Conn. Issues and Answers, Regional Plan Assn., N.Y.C., 1976-78; sci. adv. L.I. Sound Regional Study, New Eng. River Basin Commn., New Haven, 1972-75; asst. to dir. N.Y. chpt. Am. Jewish Com., N.Y.C., 1980-85; adv. bd. adminstrv. council Jacob Blaustein Inst. for Advancement Human Rights, Am. Jewish Com., 1980-85; vis. lectr. U. R.I., 1967-69; cons. in field, condr. seminars, planning cons., 1965—. Mem. Conn. Clean Air Commn., 1969-71; chmn. reorgn. task force Conn. Public Utilities Control Authority, 1976-77; chmn. com. housing and urban affairs Nat. Council of Women, N.Y.C., 1968-70; active Commn. Soc. Action (cons. South Africa, 1985—), bd. dirs. Woman's Place, Darien, 1976-80. Recipient service citation Fulbright-Hayes Fellowships, 1975. Mem. Am. Soc. Planning Ofcls. (dir. 1973-76), Union Am. Hebrew Congregations. Democrat. Club: Lower Fairfield County Radcliffe. Author articles. Address: 9 Marine Ave Westport CT 06880

KAVALER, SUSAN ADLER, clinical psychologist; b. N.Y.C., Jan. 31, 1950; d. Solomon and Alice (Zelikow) Weiss; m. Thomas Kavaler, July 12, 1970 (div. 1975); m. Saul Michael Adler, Aug. 14, 1983. PhD in Clin. Psychology, Adelphi U. Inst. Avanced Psychol. Studies, 1974. Cert. psychoanalyst and psychotherapist Nat. Inst. Psychotherapies. Psychologist, Beth Israel Hosp., N.Y.C., 1974-76, Manhattan Psychiat. Children's Ctr., N.Y.C., 1977-80; pvt. practice psychotherapy-psychoanalysis, N.Y.C., 1976—; sr. supr., tng. analyst Internat. Sch. Mental Health Practitioners; mem. faculty Postgrad. Ctr. Mental Health, N.Y.C., 1984-86; mem. faculty, supr. Nat. Inst. Pychotherapies, N.Y.C., 1985—; sr. supr., tng. analyst Internat. Sch. Mental Health Practitioners, 1985—; bd. dirs., supr. Bklyn. Inst. Psychotherapy, 1985—, mem. psychoanalytic inst. faculty; adj. prof. Union of Experimenting; tng. analyst Internat. Sch. Mental Health Practitioners. Contbr. chpts. to books, articles to profl. jours. Recipient Post-grad. Ctr. Hon. award, 1984-85. Mem. Am. Psychol. Assn. (bd. dirs., chairperson pub. info. com. for psychoanalysis div.), Nat. Inst. for Psychotherapies Profl. Assn. (chair writing group 1984-88), Postgraduate Psychoanalytic Soc. (speaker), Nat. Assn. Female Execs., Women's Psychotherapy Referral Service. Jewish. Office: 115 E 9th St New York NY 10003

KAVANAGH, CHERYL ELIZABETH, investor, consultant; b. Marlborough, Mass., May 30, 1949; d. Joaquim Michael Costa and Alice Delores (Morris) Kasaras; m. Richard Patrick Kavanagh, Nov. 10, 1967; children: Richard Christopher, Christopher Noel. Student, Mt. Wachusett Coll., 1972-74, Northeastern U., 1988—. Investor real estate, property mgr. Hudson, Mass., 1973—; part-time fin. cons. Hudson, 1985—. Chairperson parent adv. council Marlborough Sch. Dept., 1982-87; vol. polit. candidates, 1972-74, Right to Life, Marlborough, 1972-75; sponsor Save the Children; tchr. religious instrn., Marlborough, 1981-83, contbg. editor newsletter, 1982-87. Democrat. Roman Catholic. Clubs: Paradise Island, Gulf and Tennis (St. Petersburg). Home and Office: 95 White Pond Rd Hudson MA 01749

KAVANAGH, JANE LAVONNE, academic foundation director; b. Conrad, Mont., Jan. 29, 1961; d. Jerry Stark Kavanagh and Margaret Lavonne (Harris) Eschenbacker. BS in Bus. Edn., Eastern Mont. Coll., 1983. Grant ctr. coordinator Eastern Mont. Coll., Billings, 1980-83, adj. faculty, 1981-83, asst. dir., 1983-86; dir. annual giving Ea. Washington U., Cheney, 1987, acting exec. dir., 1987—; cons. Big Sky State Games, Billings, 1986; bd. dirs., speaker Dist. Council for Advancement and Support of Edn. Conf., Tacoma, Wash., 1986. Vol. Big Sky State Games, Mont., 1986; bd. dirs. Arthritis Found. Mem. Nat. Soc. Fundraising Execs., Bus. and Profl. Women's Club, Spokane and Cheney C. of C. Lodge: Rotary (program chair). Office: Ea Wash Univ MS 122 216 Showalter Cheney WA 99004

KAVANAUGH, BRENDA SWICEGOOD, sales executive; b. Lexington, N.C., Dec. 16, 1948; d. C. Luther and Meredith (Hedrick) Swicegood; m. Barry L. Kavanaugh, May 5, 1973 (div. Nov. 1983); 1 child, Lucas. Student, Davidson County Community Coll., 1968-69, 78-79. With mktg. dept. Integon Ins. Co., Winston-Salem, N.C., 1968-72; sales rep. Lentz Transfer & Storage, Winston-Salem, 1972-75; mgr. Davidson County Country Store, Lexington, 1976-79; sales cons. Booke & Co., Winston-Salem, 1979-82; sales rep. Hart & Cooley, Holland, Mich., 1982-84; sr. sales rep. SunGard Trust Systems, Charlotte, N.C., 1984—. Mem. Presdl. 100% Club (bd. dirs. 1987—).

KAVANAUGH, MARILYN LESLIE, lawyer; b. Morristown, Tenn., Apr. 1, 1945; d. Lynn Jr. and Mary Leslie (Gentry) Sheeley; m. Ben Hudson Kavanaugh Jr., Mar. 1, 1969; children: Ben Hudson III, Margaret Ann. BA, U. Tenn., 1966, JD, 1968. Bar: Tenn. 1968, Ala. 1973. Atty., adviser Space Flight Ctr. NASA, Huntsville, Ala., 1968-73; sole practice Huntsville, 1985—. Mem. Hist. Huntsville Found., 1980-88, Day Care Assn., Huntsville, 1987-88; sec. Juvenile Ct. Adv. Bd., Huntsville, 1987-88; co-leader Brownie Troop 267, Huntsville, 1987-88. Mem. ABA, Ala. Bar Assn., Tenn. Bar Assn., Huntsville-Madison County Bar Assn. Democrat. Methodist.

KAVIN, REBECCA JEAN, health science facility executive, medical consultant; b. Dodge, Nebr., June 29, 1946; d. William Wilber Walsh and Dorothy Eleanor (Watson) Williams; m. Paul Babcock, May 15, 1965 (div. Sept. 1976); m. E. Iraj Kavin, Apr. 23, 1977; children: Mark Bijan, Seana Shereen. Cert., Ohio U., 1963. Claims adjuster San Found. for Med. Care, San Diego, 1968-70; adminstrv. asst. Friendly Hills Med. Group, La Habra, Calif., 1971-77; office mgr. Robert M. Peck and Sergio Blesa, M.D., Pasadena, Calif., 1978-81; pres. Provider Mgmt. Assocs., La Canada, Calif., 1981—; speaker Continuing Edn. Dept. UCLA, 1985, Hosp. Council of So. Calif., Los Angeles, 1986, Am. Acad. Med. Preventics, Los Angeles, 1986. Contbr. articles to profl. jours. Mem. Am. Guild Patient Account Mgrs. (speaker Los Angeles chpt. 1986). Republican. Presbyterian. Office: Provider Mgmt Assocs 2418 Honolulu Ave Montrose CA 91020

KAVY, SUSAN, clothing executive, consultant; b. Ossining, N.Y., Mar. 7, 1955; d. Bert and Rosalie (Voll) K. BA in Am. Studies, Ithaca Coll., 1977; AA in Fashion Buying and Merchandising, Fashion Inst. Tech., 1978. Buyer Allied Stores, N.Y.C., 1979-83; prof. Fashion Inst. Tech., N.Y.C., 1983—; pvt. practice wardrobe cons. N.Y.C., 1978—; coordinator intern program Fashion Inst. Tech., N.Y.C., 1987—. Contbr. articles to local newspaper; guest on WCTC radio show, 1986, 87. Mem. The Fashion Group. Home and Office: 400 E 85th St New York NY 10028

KAWAGUCHI, MEREDITH FERGUSON, lawyer; b. Dallas, Feb. 5, 1940; d. Hugh William Ferguson and Ruth Virginia (Perdue) Drewery; m. Harry H. Kawaguchi, Apr. 22, 1977. B.A., U. Tex., 1962, M.A., 1968; J.D., So. Meth. U., 1977. Bar: Tex. 1977. Legal examiner gas utilities div. Tex. Railroad Commn., Austin, 1977-84, legal examiner oil and gas div., 1984—; cons. in law, lectr. to profl. confs. Author position paper Tex. Energy Natural Resources Adv. Council. Mem., Sorority Adv. Council, Austin, 1980—, Japanese-Am. Citizens League, Houston, 1981—, Exec. Women in Tex. Govt., Austin, 1984. Recipient Cert. of Recognition, Tex. Railroad Commn., 1982, Outstanding Service award, 1987. Mem. ABA, Tex. Bar Assn., Travis County Bar Assn. (oil gas and mineral law sect.), Travis County Women Lawyers Assn., Internat. Platform Assn. Home: 5009 Westview Dr Austin TX 78731 Office: Tex Railroad Commn 1701 N Congress Austin TX 78711-2967

KAWALERSKI, SUSAN MARY, television news director; b. Buffalo, Nov. 9, 1952; d. Thaddeus Daniel and Adele Stella (Widomski) K. B.S. in Broadcast Journalism, Syracuse U. Promotion mgr. Sta. WUTV-TV, Buffalo, 1974-75; owner Image, Buffalo, 1975-76; news producer Sta. WGR-TV, NBC, Buffalo, 1976-78, asst. news dir., 1980-81; sr. producer Sta. WCKT-TV, NBC, Miami, 1978-80; news exec. producer Sta. KDFW-TV, CBS, Dallas, 1981-86, asst. news dir., 1986; news dir. Sta KTVI-TV, ABC, St. Louis, 1986—. Recipient Best Newscast award N.Y. State AP, 1977. Mem. Soc. Profl. Journalists (dir. 1981-85), News Dirs. Assn., Women in Communications. Roman Catholic. Club: Dallas Press. Office: Sta KTVI-TV 5915 Berthold Ave Saint Louis MO 63110

KAWANO, DANA LYNN, infosystems administrator; b. Sacramento, Oct. 1, 1959; d. James and Jean Sachiko (Fujimoto) K.; m. Dave Jack Mahaffey, May 10, 1986. AA, Sacramento City Coll., 1978; BS, San Francisco State U., 1982. Tng. analyst EBI Orion Group Inc., San Jose, Calif., 1982-84, supr. systems user support, 1984—. Office: EBI/Orion Group Inc 1290 N 1st St San Jose CA 95112

KAWAS, ANNE L., accountant; b. New Rochelle, N.Y., Mar. 14, 1957; d. Eugene J.T. and Lucette Ann (Stumberg) Flanagan; m. Paul T. Kawas, Sept. 24, 1949. BS in Econs., SUNY Coll., New Paltz, 1979; MBA in Acctg., Pace U., 1981. CPA, N.Y. Staff acct. Peat Marwick Mitchell and Co., N.Y.C., 1981-83; sr. fin. analyst Time Inc. Corp. Fin., N.Y.C., 1983-85; mgr. corp. devel. Time Inc., N.Y.C., 1985-86; dir. bus. planning SAMI/Burke Inc. subs. Time Inc., N.Y.C., 1986-87; mgr. external devel. Gen. Foods Corp. subs. Philip Morris Cos., White Plains, N.Y., 1987—. Mem. Am. Inst. CPA's, N.Y. State Soc. of CPA's, Advt. Research Found. Club: Westchester Country. Office: Gen Foods Corp 250 North St White Plains NY 10625

KAY, ELIZABETH ALISON, zoology educator; b. Kauai, Hawaii, Sept. 27, 1928; d. Robert Buttercase and Jessie Dowie (McConnachie) K. BA, Mills Coll., 1950, Cambridge U., Eng., 1952; MA, Cambridge U., Eng., 1956; PhD, U. Hawaii, 1957. From asst. prof. to prof. zoology U. Hawaii, Honolulu, 1957-62, assoc. prof., 1962-67, prof., 1967—; research assoc. Bishop Mus., Honolulu, 1968—. Author: Hawaiian Marine Mollusks, 1979; editor: A Natural History of The Hawaiian Islands, 1972. Chmn. Animal Species Adv. Commn., Honolulu, 1983-87; v.p. Save Diamond Head Assn., Honolulu, 1968-87, pres., 1987—; trustee B.P. Bishop Mus., Honolulu, 1983—. Fellow Linnean Soc., AAAS; mem. Marine Biol. Assn. (Eng.), Australian Malacol. Soc. Episcopalian. Office: U Hawaii Manoa Dept Zoology 2538 The Mall Honolulu HI 96822

KAY, HERMA HILL, legal educator; b. Orangeburg, S.C., Aug. 18, 1934; d. Charles Esdorn and Herma Lee (Crawford) Hill. B.A., So. Meth. U., 1956; J.D., U. Chgo., 1959. Bar: Calif. 1960. Law clk. to Justice Roger Traynor, Calif. Supreme Ct., 1959-60; asst. prof. law U. Calif., Berkeley, 1960-62; assoc. prof. U. Calif., 1962, prof., 1963—, dir. family law project, 1964-67; co-reporter uniform marriage and div. law Nat. Conf. Commrs. on Uniform State Laws, 1968-70; vis. prof. U. Manchester, Eng., 1972, Harvard U., 1976; mem. Gov.'s Commn. on Family, 1966. Contbr. articles to profl. jours; contbg. author: Law in Culture and Society, 1969; author: Text, Cases and Materials on Sex-Based Discrimination, 1981, Conflict of Laws; Cases, Comments, Questions, 4th edit. (with R. Cramston and D. Currie), 1987. trustee, Russell Sage Found., N.Y., chmn. bd., 1980-84; trustee, bd. dirs. Equal Rights Advs. Calif., 1976-88, chmn., 1976-83; pres. bd. dirs. Rosenberg Found., Calif., 1987—. Fellow Center Advanced Study in Behavioral Scis., Palo Alto, Calif., 1963-64. Mem. Calif. Bar Assn., Bar U.S. Supreme Ct., Calif. Women Lawyers (bd. govs. 1975-77), Am. Law Inst. (mem. council 1985-87, pres.-elect 1988), Assn. Am. Law Schs. (exec. com. 1986-88), Order Coif (nat. pres. 1983-85). Democrat. Office: Univ of California School of Law Berkeley CA 94720

KAY, M. JANE, utility executive; b. Detroit, Aug. 31, 1925; d. Albert A. and Celia (Betzing) Kay; BS, U. Detroit, 1948; MA, Wayne State U., 1952; MBA, U. Mich., 1963. Sr. personnel interviewer employment Detroit Edison Co., 1948-60, personnel coordinator for women, 1960-65, office employment adminstr., 1965-70, gen. employment adminstr., 1970-71, dir. personnel services, 1971-72, mgr. employee relations, 1972-77, asst. v.p. employee relations, 1977-78, v.p. employee relations, 1978-82, v.p. adminstrn., 1982—; dir. First Am. Bank-SE Mich., Bon Secours of Mich. Healthcare System, Inc.; tchr. U. Detroit Evening Coll. Bus. and Adminstrn., 1963-75; seminar leader div. mgmt. edn. U. Mich., 1968-74, Waterloo Mgmt. Edn. Centre, 1972-77. Mem. Mich. Employment Security Adv. Council, 1967-81; chmn. bd. dirs. Detroit Inst. Commerce, 1976-79; exec. bd. NCCJ, 1980—, nat. trustee, 1984-88. Recipient Alumni Tower award U. Detroit, 1967; Headliner award Women Wayne State U., 1970, Wayne State U. Alumni Achievement award, 1974, Career Achievement award Profl. Panhellenic Assn., 1973; named one of Top Ten Working Women of Detroit, 1970; Alumnus of Yr., U. Detroit, 1981; cert. Adminstrv. Mgmt. Soc., Am. Soc. Personnel Adminstrn. Mem. Internat. Assn. Personnel Women (pres. 1969-70), Women's Econ. Club (v.p. 1971-72, pres. 1972-73), Personnel Women Detroit (pres. 1960-61), U. Detroit Alumni Assn. (pres. 1964-66), Phi Gamma Nu (nat. v.p. 1955-57). Office: 2000 2d Ave Detroit MI 48226

KAY, PATRICIA M., educator; b. Bklyn., June 22, 1934; d. Lawrence Peter and Helena Frieda (Seifert) McGoldrick; B.S., Cornell U., 1956; Ed.D., Rutgers U., 1969; m. Morris I. Kay; children—Mary Katherine, Andrew Stephen. Asst. prof., coordinator research and evaluation, div. tchr. edn. CUNY, 1970-73; asst. prof., assoc. prof., prof. edn. and ednl. psychology Baruch Coll. and Grad. Center, 1973—; cons. in field; mem. N.Y. State Tchr. Edn., Cert. and Practices Bd., 1980-87. Mem. Metuchen (N.J.) Bd. Edn., 1971-77; trustee Chamber Symphony N.J., 1976-78, N.J. Youth Symphony, 1980-83. Mem. Am. Ednl. Research Assn., Nat. Council on Measurement in Edn., Am. Psychol. Assn., Kappa Delta Pi. Cons. editor Jour. Exptl. Edn., Jour. Ednl. Research; guest editor Jour. Tchr. Edn.; contbr. articles to profl. jours. Home: 51 Linden Ave Metuchen NJ 08840 Office: 17 Lexington Ave New York NY 10010

KAY, SUSAN BARCUS, plastic surgeon; b. Stockton, Calif., Sept. 28, 1948; d. Robert Kirkpatrick and Betty Jane (Sullivan) B.; m. Gregory Louis Kay, Sept. 26, 1981; children—Brittany Paige, Morgan Allison. AB with distinction, Cornell U., 1970; MD, U. Rochester, 1975. Diplomate Am. Bd. Plastic Surgery. Intern Johns Hopkins Hosp., Balt., 1975-76, resident, 1976-77; resident U. Louisville, 1977-78, Barnes Hosp.-Washington U., St. Louis, 1978-81; instr. plastic surgery Washington U. Sch. Medicine, St. Louis, 1981-83; asst. prof. plastic surgery Baylor Coll. Medicine, Houston, 1983-85; asst. prof. plastic surgery UCLA, 1985—. Chmn. ad hoc com. on black studies Cornell U., Ithaca, N.Y., 1969; coordinator voter registration drive, Rochester, N.Y., 1972. NSF research grantee Cornell U., 1969; Teaching asst. grantee Cornell U., 1969-70; recipient Faculty Letters of Commendation, U. Rochester Sch. Medicine and Dentistry, 1972, 73. Mem. Am. Soc. Plastic and Reconstructive Surgeons, Am. Med. Women's Assn., Phi Beta Kappa. Office: UCLA Med Ctr Dept Plastic Surgery Los Angeles CA 90024

KAYA, ESTELLE ETSUKO, director of catering; b. Honolulu, Oct. 7, 1956; d. George Kaya and Totsue (Kawachi) K. BBA, U. Hawaii, 1978, MBA, 1987. Mgmt. devel. InterContinental Hotel, Kihei, Hawaii, 1979-82; dir. catering Oahu Country Club, Honolulu, 1982—. Mem. Travel Industry Mgmt. Alumni Assn., Nat. Assn. Catering Execs. Home: 55 South Judd St #2203 Honolulu HI 96817 Office: Oahu Country Club 150 Country Club Rd Honolulu HI 96817

KAYE, JUDITH SMITH, judge; b. Monticello, N.Y., Aug. 4, 1938; d. Benjamin and Lena (Cohen) Smith; m. Stephen Rackow Kaye, Feb. 11, 1964; children: Luisa Marian, Jonathan Mackey, Gordon Bernard. B.A., Barnard Coll., 1958; LL.B. cum laude, NYU, 1962; LL.D. (hon.), St. Lawrence U., 1985, Albany Law Sch., 1985, Pace U., 1985. Assoc. Sullivan & Cromwell, N.Y.C., 1962-64; staff atty. IBM, Armonk, N.Y., 1964-65; asst. to dean NYU Sch. of Law, 1965-68; ptnr. Olwine Connelly Chase O'Donnell & Weyher, N.Y.C., 1969-83; judge N.Y. State Ct. Appeals, N.Y.C., 1983—; dir. Sterling Nat. Bank. Contbr. articles to profl. jours. Former bd. dirs. Legal Aid Soc. Recipient Vanderbilt medal NYU Sch. of Law, 1983. Fellow Am. Bar Found.; mem. Am. Law Inst., Am. Judicature Soc. (bd. dirs. 1980-83). Democrat. Home: 101 Central Park W New York NY 10023 Office: NY Ct of Appeals 20 Eagle St Albany NY 12207 *

KAYS, NANCY ELIZABETH, public relations executive; b. Longview, Tex., Apr. 21, 1948; d. Hugh Stuart and Lillian Elizabeth (Carnegie) K.; m. Curtis John Beckmann, May 5, 1984; 1 child, Alexandra Elizabeth Kays Beckmann. BA, Drake U., 1970. Dir. pub. relations Jostens Inc, Mpls., 1972-77; account rep. Carl Byoir Assoc., N.Y.C., 1977-78; mgr. pub. relations comml. div. Honeywell Inc., Mpls., 1978-79, mgr. pub. relations bldg. services div., 1979-87, mgr. pub. relations comml. bldgs. group, 1987—. Mem. Pub. Relations Soc. Am. (1st pl. Minn. Classics award 1979, 83). Clubs: Mpls. Athletic, Mercedes N.Am. Home: 6201 Saint Albans Circle Edina MN 55435 Address: Honeywell Inc Honeywell Plaza MN27-5231 Minneapolis MN 55408

KAYTES, ROXANNE, architectural company executive; b. Havana, Cuba, Jan. 4, 1954; came to U.S., 1961; d. Carlos and Rose (Wilder) Lew; m. Fred H. Kaytes; children: Jesse, Bennett. AA, U. Fla., 1976; BA, U. Miami, 1979. Pres. archtl. design Arell Design, Inc., North Miami Beach, Fla., 1979—; archtl. cons. Date County (Fla.) Bd. Edn., 1986—. Democrat. Jewish.

KAZAZES, BARBARA ANNE, academic administrator; b. Danville, Va., Dec. 2, 1944; d. James Gregory and Anne (Sakellaris) K. BS, Guilford Coll., 1967; MA, Appalachian State U., 1970; cert. in advanced grad. studies, Va. Poly. Inst. and State U., 1979. Tchr. Greensboro (N.C.) Pub. Schs., 1967-68; counselor Lenoir Community Coll., Kinston, N.C., 1970-72; counselor Guilford Tech. Inst., Jamestown, N.C., 1972-75, coordinator counseling, 1975-78, mem. staff admissions, counseling, 1979-80, mem. staff admissions, 1980-81, coordinator admissions, counselor, 1981-84; dir. student devel., instrl. support Guilford Tech. Community Coll., Greensboro/High Pt. Campuses, 1984-86, dir. literacy, 1986—. Vol. March of Dimes, Greensboro, 1985-86. Named Outstanding Young Women, 1971, Outstanding Young Woman of YWCA, Greensboro, 1986. Mem. Nat. Bd. Cert. Counselors, N.C. Bd. Practicing Counselors. Democrat. Greek Orthodox. Lodges: Order Easter Star, Daus. Penelope (dist. marshall 1966-67, dist. treas. 1967-69, lt. gov. 1969-70). Home: 2901 Northampton DR Greensboro NC 27408 Office: Guilford Tech Community Coll PO Box 309 Jamestown NC 27282

KAZIMIR, GINA ANN, public relations company executive; b. Perth Amboy, N.J., Oct. 9, 1964; d. Andrew Steven and Nancy Carol (Neapolitan) K.; m. Philip Matthew Caruso Jr., July 25, 1986. Student, Georgetown U., 1982-84; BA, Rutgers U., 1986. Art cons. Circle Fine Art, Woodbridge, N.J., 1984-85; asst. creative dir. J.B. Ross-Linea Inc., New Brunswick, N.J., 1985-86; owner, chief exec. officer G.A. Kazimir & Co., Balt., 1986—; dir. arts mgmt. U. Md., 1988; cons. D.B. Prodns., Washington, 1982-85, Jeuesses Musicales-USA, N.Y.C., 1986—. Cons. Nomadic Theatre, Washington, 1986; vol. Balt. Choral Arts Soc., 1987—. Nat. Merit, Rutgers and Leopold Schepp scholar, 1982. Mem. Pub. Relations Soc. Am., Nat. Assn. Female Execs., N.J. Women's Network, Mensa. Office: 8855 Green Needle Dr Baltimore MD 21236

KEACH, E. LOUISE, small business owner; b. Kansas City, Kans., Oct. 26, 1939; d. Fred and Katie Lillian (Stuart) Meier; m. Bob D. Wertz, Aug. 4, 1957 (div. 1972); children: Todd Dee Wertz, Peri Lou Wertz; m. Thomas E. Keach, Dec. 28, 1984. BA, U. So. Colo., 1979. Office mgr. Elliot-Barry Advt. Specialists, Denver, 1960-63; sales rep. Jones Healy Real Estate, Pueblo, Colo., 1972-74; service rep. Kelly Services, Pueblo, 1983; owner, mgr. At Your Service, Inc., Pueblo, 1983—. Mem. investment com. Pueblo Day Nursery Trustees, 1978-87; pres. Colo. Internat. Airshow, Pueblo, 1983-84; mem. Friends of Library, Colo. Recipient Ingrid Ahlberg award Pueblo Beautiful Assn., 1984. Mem. Pueblo Bus. Womens Network, Pueblo Econ. Devel., Pueblo C. of C. (bd. dirs. 1983-86, Citizen of Yr. 1984), Air Force Assn. (Aviation Leadership award 1984), Jr. League Pueblo, Pueblo Met. Mus. Presbyterian. Home: 7 Terr Dr Pueblo CO 81001 Office: At Your Service Inc 201 W 8th Suite 474 Pueblo CO 81003

KEALIHER, CAROLYN LOUISE, human resources executive; b. Helena, Okla., Jan. 19, 1926; d. Amos R. and Martha L. (Werner) K. BA, Colo. State U., 1974. Employment interviewer Martin Marietta, Denver, 1957-65; asst. v.p. 1st of Denver, 1965-78; sr. v.p. human resources 1st Nat. Services, Denver, 1978—; bd. dirs. Francis Heights. Mem. Colo. Soc. for Personnel Adminstrn. (Personnel Adminstr. of Yr. 1972), Women's Forum. Democrat. Roman Catholic. Office: 1st Nat Services Corp 3910 Buchtel Blvd Denver CO 80210

KEALIINOHOMOKU, JOANN WHEELER, anthropologist, dance ethnologist, educator; b. Kansas City, Mo.; B.S.S., Northwestern U., 1955; M.A., 1965; Ph.D., Ind. U., 1976; 1 child, Halla K. Mem. faculty No. Ariz. U., Flagstaff, 1970-72, 75-87 , assoc. prof. anthropology, 1980-87 ; sr. research assoc. Ctr. for Colo. Plateau Studies No. Ariz. U., 1987—; mem. faculty World Campus Afloat, fall 1972, 73; resident scholar Sch. Am. Research, Santa Fe, 1974-75; vis. faculty U. Hawaii, Hilo, spring 1973, summer 1973, 74, U. Hawaii-Manoa, fall 1981, NYU, summer 1980, 84. Bd. dirs. Native Americans for Community Action, Flagstaff Indian Center, 1977-82, sec., 1980-82. Grantee, Am. Philos. Soc. Wenner Gren Found.; Weatherhead fellow Sch. Am. Research, 1974-75; research fellow East-West Center, 1981; NEH grantee, 1986. Fellow Current Anthropology; mem. Soc. Ethnomusicology (councilor; co founder Southwestern chpt.), Dance Research Center (charter), Congress on Research in Dance (bd. dirs. 1974-79), Cross-Cultural Dance Resources (founder 1981). Contbr. articles to profl. jours. Home: 518 S Agassiz St Flagstaff AZ 86001 Office: CU Box 15200 No Ariz U Flagstaff AZ 86011

KEAN, KATHERINE ANN, visual effects designer, artist; b. Huntington, W. Va., Aug. 9, 1956; d. Victor Alden and Betty L. (Berisford) Kean; m. John T. Van Vliet, May 5, 1984. B.F.A., R.I. Sch. Design, 1978. Prodn. art ednl. filmstrips Carr and Assocs./Meta-4, Los Angeles, 1979; animator: Dragonslayer, Conan, Star Trek II, etc., Visual Concept Engring., Hollywood, Calif., 1980-82, The Day After, etc., Praxis Filmworks, North Hollywood, Calif., 1982-83; animation designer, prodn. mgr., v.p. Available Light Ltd., North Hollywood, 1983—; supr. 1st ann. student/alumni art show R.I. Sch. Design, Providence, 1976; animation cons. Allamaze, Providence, 1978; asst. to animation tchr. R.I. Sch. Design, 1977. Vol. art tchr. Ctr. for Arts., Boston, 1975. Recipient Globe Scholastic Portfolio award, Boston, 1974; Cert. of Acknowledgement, Acad. TV Arts and Scis. Home: 8724 1/4 Wyngate St Sunland CA 91040 Office: Available Light Ltd 3110 W Burbank Blvd Burbank CA 91505

KEANE, PATRICIA, telecommunications executive; b. Sugarland, Tex.; d. Roland and Susie (Medina) Rodriguez. BA, No. Tex. State U., Denton, 1976. Assoc. mgr., engr. Southwestern Bell Telephone Co., Houston, 1976-78; sr. engr. Southwestern Bell Telephone Co., San Antonio, 1978-79; tng. mgr. AT&T Gen. Dept., Denver, 1979-82; network designer AT&T Info. Systems, Denver, 1982-85; mgr. telecommunications First Interstate Services Co., Los Angeles, 1985—. Mem. Nat. Assn. Female Execs. Democrat. Roman Catholic.

KEARNEY, CAROL ANN, school library administrator; b. Buffalo, May 6, 1939; d. Robert and Inez (Lenore) Lacey Schubring; m. John Edward Kearney, Jr., July 4, 1959; children—Yvonne Carol, John Edward III, B.S., Geneseo State Tchrs. Coll., 1960; M.S., SUNY-Buffalo, 1970, Specialist Edn. Adminstrn., 1977. Library media specialist West Seneca (N.Y.) Central

Schs., 1964-69, elem. library media specialist, 1967-71, jr. high library media specialist, 1971-73, sr. library media specialist, 1971-73, coordinator library services, 1969-73; dir. sch. library Buffalo Pub. Schs., 1973—; vis. lectr. Sch. Info. and Library Sci., Buffalo, 1978-86; chmn. Regents Adv. Council, N.Y. State Edn. Dept., Bd. Regents, 1981-85. Named Librarian of Yr., Sch. Info. and Library Sci., SUNY-Buffalo, 1975; Boss of Yr., Am. Bus. Women's Assn., 1975. Mem. ALA, N.Y. Library Assn. (pres. 1983-84), Sch. Library Media Sect. (pres. 1980-81), Sch. Media Suprs. N.Y. State (pres. 1976-78), Sch. Libraries Assn. Western N.Y. (pres. 1973-74). Christian Scientist. Home: 54 Suburban Ct West Seneca NY 14224 Office: Buffalo Pub Schs City Hall Rm 418 Buffalo NY 14202

KEARNEY, CHRISTINE ANN, chemist; b. Phila., July 1, 1954; d. Francis Joseph and Edith Doreen (Govier) K. BA in Chemistry, Holy Family Coll., Phila., 1976. Chemist indsl. hygiene Mobil Oil Corp., Princeton, N.J., 1977—. Mem. Am. Indsl. Hygiene Assn. (mem. lab. accreditation com.). Office: Mobil Oil Corp TSL Titusmille Rd Pennington NJ 08534

KEARNEY, ELIZABETH IRENE, consulting firm executive, writer; b. New Burnside, Ill., Dec. 7, 1934; d. E. William Edmondson and Verna P. (Greer) Eppley; m. M.L. Kearney, Feb. 7, 1953 (div.); children—Michael, Kim. B.A., UCLA, 1954; M.A., U. Pa., 1959; doctoral candidate. Tchr., program dir. Pasadena Unified Sch. Dist., Calif., 1959-84; v.p. Managex, Inc., Houston, 1984, Cole/Kearney Co., South Pasadena, 1984; pres. Kearney Enterprises, Los Angeles, 1979—. Author: How to Increase Your Vocabulary, 1964; How To Write A Term Paper, 1965; The American Novel: A Study Guide to 36 Great Books, 1966; The Continental Novel: A Bibliography of Criticism, Vol. I, 1967, Vol. II, 1982; Everyone's A Customer, 1986. Contbr. articles to profl. jours. Past editor CAG Communicator, Pipelines Newsletter, Previews newspaper. Pres. Terr. Park Assn., 1984—; bd. dirs. Pasadena Edn. Found.; vol. Nat. Trust Hist. Preservation, 1980—; adv. gifted children Calif. Advs. Gifted Edn., 1967—. Recipient Best Reference Book award ALA, 1967; fellow NDEA, 1968, Johns Hopkins U., 1971. Mem. Golden Voice, Nat. Speakers Assn., Leads Club, Women's Referral Services, Pasadena C. of C. (chmn. com. 1983-85). Republican. Episcopalian. Avocations: travel; writing; reading; historical preservation.

KEARNEY, PATRICIA ANN, university administrator; b. Wilkes-Barre, Pa., May 15, 1943; d. William F. and Helen L. (Hartz) K. BA, Mich. State U., 1965; MSEd, Ind. U., 1966. Head resident advisor Western Ill. U., Macomb, 1966-68; asst. v.p. SUNY, Buffalo, 1968-70; asst. dean student life Lock Haven (Pa.) State Coll., 1970-72; dir. residential life U. Calif., Davis, 1974-83, bus. mgr., 1983-85, dir. housing and food services, 1985—; speaker nat. and state convs. Contbr. articles to profl. jours. Mem. Am. Coll. Personnel Assn. (pres.), Am. Mgmt. Assn., Am. Soc. Tng. and Devel., Assn. Coll. and U. Housing Officers Internat., Sierra Club. Home: 714 Borchard Ct Woodland CA 95695 Office: U Calif 127 Student Housing Davis CA 95616

KEARNS, MARTHA MARY, humanities educator, author; b. Flint, Mich., Mar. 23, 1945; d. Lewis Gamble and Mary Lucille (Williamson) K. BA, Beaver Coll., 1967; MS in Edn., Antioch U., 1977. Cert. tchr., Pa. Prof. humanities Antioch U., Phila., 1979-88, prof., chair dept. humanities, 1988—; artist-in-residence City of Phila., 1986—; lectr. Coll. Art Assn., New Orleans, 1980, 1986—, New Studies Ctr., U. Arts, 1986— Phila Coll. Art, 1986—, Goethe House, N.Y.C., 1987; book reviewer Phila. Inquirer, 1981-85; drama critic Phila. City Paper, 1981-86; tech. writer City of Phila., 1985. Author: Käthe Kollwitz: Woman and Artist, 1976, 77; critic Voices of Women, 1980; playwright King Christina, 1985; co-arranger My Lifetime Listens to Yours, 1982. Appointed mem. literature com., Mayor's Coutural Adv. Council, Phila., f1984-85; bd. dirs. Wilma Theatre, Phila., 1981-84. Recipient Fulbright scholarship U.S. Gov., 1982, humanities fellow Aston Magna Acad., 1977. Mem. Dramatists Guild (assoc.), Author's Guild, Playwrights Co., Dramatic Risks Theatre Co. Democrat. Methodist. Club: Cosmopolitan, Phila. Home: 339 W Cliveden St Philadelphia PA 19119 Office: Antioch U 1811 Spring Garden St Philadelphia PA 19130

KEARSE, AMALYA LYLE, judge; b. Vauxhall, N.J., June 11, 1937; d. Robert Freeman and Myra Lyle (Smith) K. B.A., Wellesley Coll., 1959; J.D. cum laude, U. Mich., 1962. Bar: N.Y. State 1963, U.S. Supreme Ct. 1967. Assc. firm Hughes Hubbard & Reed, N.Y.C., 1962-69; partner Hughes Hubbard & Reed, 1969-79; judge U.S. Ct. of Appeals, 2d Circuit, 1979—; lectr. evidence N.Y. U. Law Sch., 1968-69. Author: Bridge Conventions Complete, 1975, 2nd edit., 1984, Bridge at Your Fingertips, 1980; translator, editor: Bridge Analysis, 1979; editor: Ofcl. Ency. of Bridge, 3d edit, 1976; Mem., Charles Goren Editorial Bd., 1974—. Bd. dirs. NAACP Legal Def. and Endl. Fund, 1977-79; bd. dirs. Nat. Urban League, 1978-79; trustee N.Y.C. YWCA, 1976-79, Am. Contract Bridge League Nat. Laws Commn., 1975—; mem. Pres.'s Com. on Selection of Fed. Jud. Officers, 1977-78. Nat. Womens Pairs World Champion, 1986. Mem. Am. Law Inst., Assn. Bar City N.Y., ABA, Lawyers Com. for Civil Rights Under Law (mem. exec. com. 1970-79). Office: US Ct Appeals US Courthouse Foley Sq New York NY 10007

KEATING, GLADYS BROWN, state legislator; b. N.Y.C., Aug. 1, 1923; d. Irving Lenton and Emma Frances (Baumbach) Brown; m. John Anthony Keating, Nov. 18, 1950; children: John A. Jr., Lawrence P., Michael L., Margaret K. Jones, Eileen P. Student, Queen's Coll., 1940-41, Weatherford (Tex.) Coll., 1960-61, U. Va., 1962-63, George Mason U., 1976. With acturial div. Metropolitan Life Ins. Co., N.Y.C., 1941-50; elected mem. Va. Ho. of Reps., Fairfax, 1977—; mem. Va. Ho. Dels. com. on corps., ins. and banking, com. on counties, cities and towns, com. on militia and police, com agrl. and consumer affairs; mem. numerous legis. study coms. including chair study car telephones and paging deregulation, study unisured motorist and taxicab liability rates, study removal item prices on food, and others; bd. dirs. Sci., Tech. and Resource Planning Com., Washington, NCSL. Active Lee Dist. Land Use Com., Fairfax, 1970—, Fairfax County Library Bd., 1974-77; mem. exec. bd. Va. Citizen Consumer Council, Arlington, 1975—; softball commr. Franconia Youth Assn., 1969-75; past pres. Edison High Sch. PTA; lay reader, vestry Olivet Epis. Ch., Franconia. Recipient Human Rights award Fairfax County Human Rights Commn., 1979; named Woman of Yr. Bus. and Profl. Women's Club, 1977. Mem. Nat. Orgn. Women Legislators. Democrat. Episcopalian. Office: 5909 Parkridge Ln Franconia VA 22310 Session Office: Va House Dels Capitol St Richmond VA 23219

KEATING, LAUREL, humanities educator, theatrical director; b. Los Angeles, Dec. 29, 1924; d. Charles and June Elaine (Smith) K. BS, UCLA, 1945; MA, Syracuse U., 1952, PhD, 1973; EdD, Arts Complex, Rochester, N.Y., 1988. Instr. Moravian Coll., Bethlehem, Pa., 1952-54; dir. women's program Sta. WSBA-TV, York, Pa., 1954-56; lectr. Hunter Coll., N.Y.C., 1958-60; asst. prof. SUNY, Cortland, 1960-62; assoc. prof. humanities Yeshiva U., N.Y.C., 1962—. Ednl. cons. Rochester Prodns., 1987—; moderator numerous TV series; theatre dir. numerous prodns.; author: Notes on Speech, 1973; contbr. articles to profl. jours. Served with USN Waves, 1945-46. Mem. Popular Culture Assn., Ednl. Film Library Assn., Assn. Ednl. Communication and Tech. Club: New Community Cinema (N.Y.). Home: 1112 Washington Dr Centerport NY 11721 Office: Yeshiva U 500 W 185th St New York NY 10029

KEATING, MARY PIERSON, lawyer; b. White Plains, N.Y., Jan. 1, 1958; d. Pierson and Elizabeth (Nelson) K. BA cum laude, 1979; JD, Yale U., 1985. Bar: N.Y. Internal auditor Bank of N.Y., Harrison, 1979-80; benefits supr. Cummings & Lockwood, Stamford, Conn., 1980-82; law clk. U.S. Dept. Justice, Washington, 1983; atty. IBM, Rye Brook, N.Y., 1985—. Assoc. trustee St. Agnes Hosp., White Plains, 1987—. Mem. N.Y. Bar Assn., Yale Alumni Fund (bd. dirs. 1984-85). Home: 10 Stewart Pl 4EW White Plains NY 10601 Office: IBM 900 King St Rye Brook NY 12977

KEATON, FRANCES MARLENE, sales representative; b. Redfield, Ark., July 1, 1944; d. John Thomas and Pauline (Hilliard) Wells; m. Larry Ronald Keaton, Sept. 17, 1946. Cert. in acctg., Draughon's Sch. Bus., 1972. Lic. ins. agt. Acctg. supr. Home Ins. Co., Little Rock, 1962-70; auditor St. Paul Ins. Co., Little Rock, 1970-74; spl. agt. Continental Ins. Co., Little Rock, 1974—. Vol. Ark. Sch. for the Blind, Little Rock, 1968. Mem. Little Rock Field Club, Casualty Roundtable, Auditor's Assn., Ins. Women, Underwriters Roundtable, The Executive Female, Ind. Ins. Agts. Assn., Profl. Ins. Assn. Democrat. Baptist. Home and Office: PO Box 4131 Little Rock AR 72214-4131

KECK, BARBARA ANNE, management consulting company executive; b. Goshen, Ind., Aug. 10, 1946; d. Howard and Mary Elizabeth (Taylor) Brumbaugh; m. Gerald Nadel, June, 1966 (div. 1972); Chad Whitney Keck, May 16, 1976; children: Martin Whitney, Matthew James Howard. BA cum laude, Rutgers U., 1968; MBA, Harvard U., 1976. Communications specialist U.S. Dept. Agrl., New Brunswick, N.Y., 1968-71; asst. dir. pub. relations dept. Hill & Holliday, Boston, 1971-73; dir. advt. and pub. relations Paperback Booksmith, Boston, 1973-74; mktg. mgr. food packaging Continental Can Co. Hdqrs., Stamford, Conn., 1976-79; chmn., chief exec. officer Keck & Co. Bus. Cons. Inc., N.Y.C., 1979-85; pres. Keck & Co. Bus. Cons., Atherton, Calif., 1985—. Sec. N.J. Tenants Assn., 1969-70; bd. dirs. Puppetry Guild Greater N.Y., N.Y.C., 1981-84. Mem. Assn. Mgmt. Cons., Women in Mgmt. (founder 1978, pres. 1979-80). Episcopalian. Club: Harvard Bus. Sch. (San Francisco). Home and Office: 410 Walsh Rd Atherton CA 94025

KECK, JUDITH MARIE, government agency administrator; b. Springfield, Ohio, Feb. 24, 1938; d. John T. and Mary Elizabeth (Kaliher) Burke; m. Henry J. Reinhardt, Feb. 22, 1958 (div.); 1 child, Lucy L.; m. James E. Keck, Feb. 18, 1978. BS in Mgmt., Park Coll., 1983; MA in Mgmt., Cen. Mich. U., 1985; postgrad., Def. Systems Mgmt. Coll., 1986. Cert. govt. contracting officer, govt. program mgr. Billeting officer USAF, Zweibrucken AFB, Fed. Republic Germany, 1969-72; commissary officer Edwards AFB, Calif., 1972-74; procurement agt. George AFB, Calif., 1974-76; chief contract adminstrn. Nellis AFB, Nev., 1976-78; chief services contracting Grand Forks AFB, N.D., 1978-81; contracting officer aero. systems div./air launched cruise missile div. Wright Patterson AFB, Ohio, 1981-85, program mgr. aero. systems div./B-1 Bomber, 1985-87, program mgr. aero. systems div. project 2000, 1987—; instr. systems mgmt. Air Force Inst. Tech., Wright Patterson AFB, 1985, quality assurance, 1981; dir. fed. women's program George AFB, 1976. Mem. Nat. Contract Mgmt. Assn., Air Force Assn., Nat. Assn. Mil. Comptrollers, Nat. Assn. Female Execs., Sigma Iota Epsilon. Democrat. Roman Catholic. Home: 8022 Philadelphia Dr Fairborn OH 45324

KECK, SUSAN JENNIFER, advertising executive, consultant; b. Oklahoma City, Dec. 21, 1958; d. William Albert and Honey (Heerwagen) K. BA in Journalism, U. Kans., 1981. Account exec. Sta. KLWN/KLZR Radio, Lawrence, Kans., 1979-81; sr. media planner Saatchi & Saatchi Compton, N.Y.C., 1981-84; acct. exec. Ogilvy & Mather Advt., N.Y.C., 1984—; mktg. cons. Zadoc Media, N.Y. Advocate N.Y. Jr. League, 1985-87, chmn. pub. affairs 1986-87; congl. intern Sen. Bob Dole, Washington, 1981. Mem. N.Y. Advt. Club. Republican. Presbyterian. Club: St. Bartholemew's Community. Office: Ogilvy & Mather Advt 2 E 48th New York NY 10017

KECLIK, JANICE LYNN, engineering and construction company executive; b. Chgo., Apr. 23, 1952; d. John and Lillian Lorraine (McCarty) Keclik; BS, U. San Francisco, 1983, MBA,Calif. State U., Long Beach. With Continental Ill. Bank & Trust Co., Chgo., 1970-72, Bruhnke & Silver, Cary, Ill., 1972-73, Libby, McNeill & Libby, Chgo., 1973. Sargent & Lundy, Chgo., 1973-81; dir. personnel Ultrasystems, Inc., now Ultrasystems Power and Environ. Systems, Irvine, Calif., 1981—; cons. to several small firms, Calif., 1983-84. Mem. Personnel and Indsl. Relations Assn., Nat. Assn. Female Execs., Am. Soc. Personnel Adminstrs., Am. Soc. Tng. and Devel. Office: 16845 Von Karman Ave Irvine CA 92714

KEDDERIS, PAMELA JEAN, insurance company executive; b. Waterbury, Conn., May 15, 1956; d. Leo George and Evelyn Helen (Fenske) K. Student, U. Nice, 1976-77; B.A., Assumption Coll., 1978; M.B.A., U. New Haven, 1981. Credit analyst, Citytrust Bank, Bridgeport, Conn., 1980-81, sr. credit analyst, 1981-82, fin. analyst, 1982-83, seminar leader, 1981-83; planning analyst Continental Ins. Co., N.Y.C., 1983-84, sr. planning analyst, 1984-85, dir. planning, 1985-87, asst. v.p 1987—. Active YMCA, Union, N.J., 1985—. Mem. Nat. Assn. Female Execs., North Shore Animal League. Democrat. Lutheran. Avocations: music, traveling. Home: 1166 Schmidt Ln North Brunswick NJ 08902

KEDING, ANN CLYRENE, free-lance copywriter; b. Ft. Benning, Ga., Aug. 31, 1944; d. Porter Bill and Clyreme (Stull) Maxwell; children from previous marriage: Robert, Jeff. BA in Psychology, Calif. State U., Fullerton, 1973, MA in Psychology, 1975; postgrad., U. So. Calif., 1980-83. Instr. psychology Calif. State U., Fullerton, 1974-76, Golden West Coll., Huntington Beach, Calif., 1976-78; mktg. research project dir. Foote, Cone & Belding, Los Angeles, 1980; free-lance advt. copywriter Los Angeles, 1980—. Writer TV commls, advt. campaigns, brochures. Mem. adv. council Los Angeles Commn. on Assaults Against Women, 1985—. Recipient Pub. Citation Govt. Calif., 1985, Humanitarian award Los Angeles Commn. Assaults Against Women, 1986; Gannett fellow, Ind. U., 1987, 88. Mem. Am. Acad. Advt., Calif. State U. Fullerton Alumni Assn., Phi Kappa Phi (bd. dirs. 1974-75).

KEECH, ELOWYN ANN, interior designer; b. Berrien County, Mich., Oct. 5, 1937; d. Earl Docker and Elizabeth Hall (Paullin) Stephenson; 1 child, Robert Earl. Print designer, copywriter newspaper accounts, dept. stores, resorts, service orgns., industry, 1957-75; freelance interior designer, photoset and video set designer, St. Joseph, Mich., 1975—; owner Fog Horn Records & Tapes. Bd. dirs. Blossomland United Way, 1981-86; bd. dirs., mem. steering and long-range planning coms. United Way Mich., 1980-87. Designer interiors 1st Fed. Savs. & Loan Assn., Three Oaks, Mich., 1975, Holland (Mich.) Cen. Trade Credit Union, 1978, 1st. Fed. Savs. & Loan Assn., Holland, 1978, Yonker Realty, Co., Holland, 1979, People's Bank of Holland, 1979, exec. offices Whirlpool Corp., 1980—, human resources St. Joe div., 1985, Claeys Residence, 1984, Calley Dental Office, 1985, Sarett Nature Ctr., 1985, Imperial Printing, 1986, Miller Residence, 1986, Schraders Super Market, 1986, Dave's Garage, 1987, Merritt Residence, 1987-88, Smith Residence, 1988. Mem. AIA (profl. affiliate Western Mich. chpt.), Sarrett Nature Ctr., Nat. Trust Historic Preservation, Chgo. Art. Inst., Assn. Great Lakes Maritime History, Econ. Club of SW Mich., Sierra Club, Nat. Maritime Hist. Soc., S.W. Mich. Nordic Ski Club. Lodge: Rotary. Home and Office: 375 Ridgeway Saint Joseph MI 49085

KEEFE, KATHLEEN LAURA (MACDONALD), educator; b. Coleman, Prince Edward Island, Can., Jan. 9, 1942; d. Adrian E. and Anna Isabel (Lynch) MacD.; children: Janice, Deanna, Sean. Student, York U., 1986—. Cert. tchr., Province Ont. Tchr. Derby (Prince Edward Island) Sch. Dist., 1962-63, Met. Separate Sch. Bd., Toronto, 1963-68, 71-74, Wellington County Separate Sch. Bd., Guelph, Ont., 1968-71, Durham Region Cath. Separate Sch. Bd., Oshawa, Ont., 1975-88; affirmative action rep. Durham Region Cath. Separate Sch. Bd., 1984-87. Religious edn. coordinator, lectr. St. Bernadette's Ajax, Ont., 1986-87;mem. Theatre Durham, T.V. Ont., Friends of Pub. Broadcasting, Foster Parents Plan of Can., Nat. Action Com. on the Status of Women, Can. Ctr. for Arms Control. Mem. Ont. English Cath. Tchrs. Assn., Ont. Tchrs. Fedn., Can. Nature Fedn., Nat. Acid Precipitation Found. Roman Catholic.

KEEFE, MARY MARGUERITE (MARGO), biotechnology company executive; b. Old Town, Maine, Oct. 29, 1946; d. George Ernest and Winifred Mary (Olson) Fortier; children: Brendan Matthew, Daniel Jeffery. BS cum laude, U. N.H., 1968. Lic. med. technologist. Research asst. virology VA Hosp. Yale Lab, West Haven, Conn., 1968-70; med. technologist Middlesex Meml. Hosp., Middletown, Conn., 1970-73; tech. specialist quality control Internat. Biotech. Inc. div. Kodak Co., New Haven, 1982-84, asst. mgr., 1984-85, asst. dir. lab. ops., 1985-86, dir. quality control and custom services, 1986-87, dir. quality assurance, 1987—; organizer Keefe Co. Realtors, Madison, Conn., 1977. Bd. dirs. No. Madison Congregational Ch., Conn., 1973-76. Mem. Nat. Assn. Female Execs., AAUW, Phi Mu Alumni Assn. Republican. Club: Newcomers (Madison) (ways and means com. 1977-78). Avocations: crafts, sewing, tennis, classical music. Home: 13 A Stonegate Briarwood Ln Branford CT 06405 Office: Internat Biotechs Inc 25 Science Park New Haven CT 06511

KEEFE, NANCY QUIRK, editor; b. Pittsfield, Mass., Nov. 20, 1934; d. John Gorman and Ann (O'Laughlin) Quirk; m. Kevin Brian Keefe, Oct. 3, 1959; children—Brendan, Clare, Maura. BA, Coll. New Rochelle, 1956; MS, Columbia U., 1958. Asst. telegraph editor Berkshire Eagle, Pittsfield, Mass., 1958-59; copy editor World Telegram & Sun, N.Y.C., 1959-60; mng. editor, columnist Gannett Westchester Newspapers, White Plains, N.Y., 1981-84, editorial page editor, columnist, 1984—; columnist Berkshire Eagle, 1969—. Recipient Angela Merici medal Coll. New Rochelle, 1981, John Peter Zenger award Westchester chpt. N.Y. Civil Liberties Union, 1988. Roman Catholic. Home: 79 Harmon Dr Larchmont NY 10538 Office: Gannett Westchester Newspapers 1 Gannett Dr White Plains NY 10604

KEEFER, DANA, health care executive; b. Pitts., Feb. 26, 1946; d. Paul Blount and Dorothea Belle (Franklin) K.; m. Reynold Levy, June 18, 1967 (div. 1979); 1 child, Justin Shayne Levy. BA, William Smith Coll., 1968; MA in English, U. Va., 1970; MA in Theatre, CUNY, 1978, postgrad, 1979. Exec. asst. N.Y.C. Health and Hosps. Corp., 1970-73; asst. producer Syzygy Prodns., Ltd., N.Y.C., 1979-80; ptnr. & exec. Health Mgmt. Systems, Inc., N.Y.C., 1980—; free-lance writer N.Y.C., 1978-86. Columnist Bull. N.Y. Personnel Mgmt. Adminstrs., 1983-84; co-author screenplay Dossier on the Sahara, 1981; asst. producer (TV movies) Playing for Time, 1980 (5 emmies), Hardhat and Legs, 1979, Voyage of the Mayflower, 1979. Home: Brooklyn NY 11226 Office: Health Mgmt Systems Inc 401 Park Ave S New York NY 10016

KEEFER, RHONDA JEAN, data processing executive; b. Elmira, N.Y., May 20, 1959; d. Ronald Burger; m. Steven L. Keefer. BS, Pa. State U., 1981. Sr. sales rep. Datapoint Corp., Bala Cynwyd, Pa., 1981-82; dist. sales mgr. Commodore Bus. Machines, West Chester, Pa., 1982-83; sr. account mgr. Digital Equipment Corp., Blue Bell, Pa., 1983—. Mem. Jaycees (bd. dirs. Lansdale br. 1986-87, v.p. 1987—). Home: 100 Hunter Ln North Wales PA 19454 Office: Digital Equipment Corp 1740 Walton Rd Blue Bell PA 19422

KEEFER, YVONNE JUNE KELSOE, religious organization administrator; b. Gotebo, Okla., Oct. 2, 1935; d. Carl Clifford and Zelma Phoebe (Bond) Kelsoe; m. James Albert Keefer, June 8, 1956; children: Steven Dale, Brian Lee. BS in Home Econs., Okla. State U., 1966. Ednl. dir. 1st So. Bapt. Ch., Lawrence, Kans., 1969-70; dir. Bapt. Student Union U. Kans., Lawrence, 1969-82; exec. dir. Woman's Missionary Union, Family Ministry, Partnership Missions Kans. Nebr. Conv. So. Bapts., Topeka, Kans., 1983—; chmn. 1990-91 dated plan Woman's Missionary Union So. Bapt. Conv., Birmingham, Ala., 1987-88. Assoc. editor The Campus Minister, 1980-82. Chaplain Lawrence Police Dept., 1976-83; mem. Friends of Art, Lawrence; exec. bd. Kaw Valley Assn., Topeka, 1970-82; bd. dirs. Wellspring Found., Prairie Village, Kans., 1984—, Douglas County Mental Health Assn., Lawrence, 1979-82. Mem. Assn. So. Bapt. Campus Ministers (nat. v.p. 1982-83), Exec. Dirs. Woman's Missionary Union, Phi Kappa Phi, Omnicron Nu, Phi Upsilon Omnicorn, Pi Zeta Kappa (Outstanding Mem. award, nat. v.p.). Republican. Club: PEO (Lawrence) (pres. 1981-82). Home: 4011 W 13th Lawrence KS 66044 Office: Kans Nebr Conv So Bapts 5410 W 7th Topeka KS 66606

KEEGAN, JANE ANN, insurance executive, consultant; b. Watertown, N.Y., Sept. 1, 1950; d. Richard Isidor and Kathleen (McKinley) K. BA cum laude, SUNY-Potsdam, 1972; MBA in Risk Mgmt., Golden Gate U., 1986. CPCU. Comml. lines mgr. Lithgow & Rayhill, San Francisco, 1977-80; risk mgmt. account coordinator Dinner Levison Co., San Francisco, 1980-83; ins. cons., San Francisco, 1983-84; account mgr. Rollins Burdick Hunter, San Francisco, 1984-85; account exec. Jardine Ins. Brokers, San Francisco, 1985-86; ins. cons., San Francisco, 1986-87, ins. adminstr. Port of Oakland, 1987—. Vol. San Francisco Ballet vol. orgn., 1981—, Bay Area Bus., Govt. ARC disaster conf. steering com., 1987-88; mem. Nob Hill Neighbors Assn., 1982—. Mem. Soc. Chartered Property Casualty Underwriters (spl. events chairperson 1982-84; continuing profl. devel. program award 1985, 88), Risk and Ins. Mgr. Soc. (dep.). Democrat. Roman Catholic. Home: 1635 Clay St Apt 1 San Francisco CA 94109

KEEL, JOLENE MAR-JEN, real estate and insurance administrator; b. Granite City, Ill., Sept. 13, 1951; d. Ellis Newton and Lois Laverne (Thomas) Hackney; m. Harlon Davis Keel, Dec. 20, 1980; children: Eric Lee, Shanna Mar-Jen. Student, Belleville (Ill.) Area Coll., 1979-84. Payroll and accounts payable clk. 3M Bus. Products Ctrs., St. Louis, 1973-75; payroll clk. Peabody Coal Corp., St. Louis, 1975-76; office mgr. Leader's Dept. Store, Granite City, 1976-80; personnel and ins. adminstr. Love Real Estate Co., St. Louis, 1980—. Democrat. Mem. Assembly of God Ch. Lodge: Order Eastern Star. Office: Love Real Estate Co 515 Olive St Suite 1400 Saint Louis MO 63101

KEELAND, DELPHA FLORINE, librarian; b. Glendive, Mont., June 3, 1925; d. Fred Peter and Anna (Buller) Deckert; m. Charles William Keeland, July 25, 1943; children—Charles, Richard James, Norma Lynn, Princess Ann, Ramona Joy, Dixie Lee, Dana Scott. Student pub. schs., Richey, Mont. Nurses aide McCone County Hosp., Circle, Mont., 1962-66, 74-76; owner Trail's End Cafe, Olympia, Wash., 1967-71; librarian Richey Pub. Library, Mont., 1980—. Mem. V.F.W. Aux., Am. Legion Aux. Methodist. Office: Richey Pub Library Richey MT 59259

KEELER, VIRGINIA MARY, university official; b. San Antonio, Aug. 24, 1932; d. Thomas Love and Margaret Therese (Conway) K.; A.B., Chestnut Hill Coll., Phila., 1953. Sec. to Office of Pres., Georgetown U., 1953-54, sec. to pres., 1954-74, asst. sec. of univ., 1968-74, sec. of univ., 1974—. Recipient Vicennial medal Georgetown U., 1973, Patrick J. Healy medal Georgetown U. Alumni Assn., 1984. Mem. Am. Assn. Higher Edn., Assn. Governing Bds. Roman Catholic. Home: 2712 Wisconsin Ave NW 811 Washington DC 20007 Office: Georgetown U Washington DC 20057

KEEN, CHARLOTTE ELIZABETH, marine geophysicist, researcher; b. Halifax, N.S., Can., June 22, 1943; d. Murray Alexander and Elizabeth Randell (Cobb) Davidson; m. Michael J. Keen, May 11, 1963 (div.). B.Sc. with 1st class honors, Dalhousie U., Halifax, 1964, M.Sc. with 1st class honors, 1966; Ph.D., Cambridge U., (Eng.), 1970. Research scientist Atlantic Oceanographic Lab., Energy, Mines, Resources, Dartmouth, N.S., 1970-74, Geol. Survey of Can., Atlantic Geosci. Centre, Dartmouth, 1972—; chmn. Can. Nat. Com. Lithosphere; mem. Can. Nat. Com. Internat. Union Geol. Scis., Geodesy and Geophysics, Iternat. Commn. Marine Geology. Contbr. articles to sci. jours. Recipient Young Scientist medal Atlantic Provinces Inter-Univ. Commn. Sci., 1977. Fellow Royal Soc. Can., Geol. Assn. Can. (past pres.'s medal 1979), Am. Geophys. Union; mem. Can. Geophys. Union. Anglican. Home: 9 Wenlock Grove, Halifax, NS Canada B3P 1P6 Office: Atlantic Geosci Ctr, Bedord Inst Oceanography, Dartmouth, NS Canada

KEEN, MARIA ELIZABETH, academic administrator; b. Chgo., Aug. 19, 1918; d. Harold Fremont and Mary Eileen Honore (Dillon) K. AB, U. Chgo., 1941; postgrad., U. Wyo., summer 1943; MA, U. Ill., 1949; postgrad., U. Mich., 1957. Tchr. high sch. Wyo., 1942-43, Mich., 1943-44; tchr. Am. Coll. for Women, Istanbul, Turkey, 1944-47; mem. faculty U. Ill., Urbana, 1967-88, asst. prof. English as 2d lang., asst. prof. ednl. adminstrn., 1967—, prof. emeritus, 1988—. Mem. Champaign Community Devel. Com.; com. mem. YWCA, YMCA. Mem. AAUP (treas.), Animal Protection Inst., Defenders of Wildlife, LWV, Nat. Assn. Fgn. Student Advisors, Am. Inst. Biol. Scis., Nat. Council Tchr. Educators, U. Ill. Athletic Assn. (sec., dir.), Ont. Geneal. Soc., AAAS, Orton Dyslexia Soc., Phi Kappa Epsilon. Baptist. Home: 608 S Edwin St Champaign IL 61821

KEENAN, BEVERLY OWEN, newspaper manager; b. Medicine Lodge, Kans., July 29, 1948; d. Neil Harrington and Bertie Geneva (Nurse) Owen; m. Donald Joseph Livingston, Jan. 29, 1963 (div. Mar. 1975); children: Virginia, Rebecca, Wesley, Carrie, Lee; m. Theodore Wayne Keenan, Apr. 23, 1975; 1 child, James. Student, Okla. State U., 1978-79. Field research person Nat. Analysts, Phila., 1977-79; agt. Daily Oklahoman, Stillwater, Okla., 1979-80; distbr. Rocky Mountain News, Denver, 1980-82, dist. mgr., 1982—; seminar leader, 1986—. Supporting mem. Women's Crisis Ctr., Castle Rock, Colo., 1986-87; speaker for Women in Transition Groups,

Littleton, Colo., 1987. Mem. Nat. Assn. Female Execs., Mensa. Club: Appaloosa Horse (Moscow, Idaho). Office: Rocky Mountain News 400 W Colfax Ave Denver CO 80201

KEENAN, CATHERINE CHARLOTTE, nursing educator; b. Wilmington, Del., Aug. 3, 1947; d. Charles Edward and Catherine Ann (Murphy) Jackson; m. Joseph J. Keenan, Jr., June 20, 1970; 1 son, John Patrick. B.S. in Nursing, U. Del., 1969. Lic. nurse, Del. Head nurse Del. State Hosp., New Castle, 1969-70; asst. head nurse Norwich State Hosp (Conn.), 1970-71; asst. charge nurse Montgomery Gen. Hosp., Olney, Md., 1971-74; nurse therapist St. Francis Hosp., Wilmington, 1978-81; instr. nursing Del. Tech. and Community Coll., Newark, 1979—. Mus. guide Fort Del. Soc., Wilmington, 1982—; v.p. St. Peter's Parish Council, New Castle, 1982-84; pres. PTA St. Peter's Sch., 1986-87. Mem. Nat. League for Nursing, Beta Beta Beta, Sigma Theta Tau. Democrat. Roman Catholic. Home: 111 Baldt Ave New Castle DE 19720 Office: Del Tech and Community Coll 400 Christiana Stanton Rd Newark DE 19702

KEENAN, CONNIE ANN, fashion educator; b. Hawthorne, Nev., Aug. 10, 1948; d. Robert Eugene and Dorothy Anita (Castle) Carroll; m. Terrence Henry Keenan, May 20, 1972; 1 child, Gina Colleen. Student, Pasadena City Coll., 1966-67, Citrus Coll., 1968-69, U. Calif., 1970-72. Dir. fashion Montgomery Ward, Rosemead, Calif., 1967-72; editor fashion Teen Mag., Los Angeles, 1972-73; v.p. J. Patrick Stebbins Med. Corp., Duarte, Calif., 1976-82; dir. advt. copy Santa Anita Prodns., Arcadia, Calif., 1984-86; instr. El Monte (Calif.) Sch. Dist., 1986—; performer Mark Goodson Prodns., Los Angeles, 1976-85; producer El Monte Cable TV; dir., cons. Miss Ariz. Universe Pageant, Los Angeles, 1979-83; dir., producer "One More Time" Assn., Rosemead, 1986—; host TV show The "Other" Valley, 1987—. Author: How To Be A 'Teen Model, 1973, Teen Money Making Ideas, 1973; contbr. articles to profl. jours. Named one of Outstanding Tchrs. of Yr. Basset Sch. Dist., 1973. Mem. Screen Actors Guild, AFTRA, El Monte Producers Access Channel TV. Republican. Home: 12050 Hallwood Dr El Monte CA 91732

KEENAN, GEORGIA ANN, service representative; b. Denver, Oct. 3, 1936; d. Lawrence Edward and Helen Kathleen (Gray) K.; m. Charles Henry Dupree, May 31, 1958 (div. Nov. 1977); children: Phoenix, Therese, Mark, John. BA, Regis Coll., 1968; MA, St. Thomas U., 1978. With reservations United Airlines, Denver, 1956-57; stewardess Trans World Airlines, Chgo., 1957-58; in elem. edn. Notre Dame Sch., Denver, 1969-72; dir. religious edn. Notre Dame Parish, Denver, 1972-77, Archdiocese Denver, 1977-80; v.p., treas. Kilfinane and Cook, Denver, 1980-82; dir. human resources Cosmopolitan Hotel, Denver, 1982-83, Kaanapali Beach Hotel, Lahaina, Hawaii, 1983-85, Royal Lahaina Resort, Hawaii, 1985—; corp. dir. human resources Hawaiian Hotels and Resorts, Lahaina, 1988—; trainer Amfac Hotels and Resorts, Hawaii, 1984-86; vice chmn. Maui Hotel Assn., 1987—; bd. dirs. Project 714, Lahaina, 1987—. Bd. dirs. Archdiocesan Women's Bd., Denver, 1981-83, Passages, Denver, 1980-83, Maui Econ. Devel. Bd., Kahalui, 1984; chairperson Charity Walk, 1984-86. Named Handicapped Employer of Yr., State of Hawaii, 1987. Mem. Council Hawaii Hotels, Am. Soc. Personnel Assn. Club: Distributive Edn. of Am. (Hawaii) (bd. dirs. 1984—). Home: 4002 Mahinahina Lahaina HI 96761 Office: Royal Lahaina Resort 2780 Kekaa Dr Lahaina HI 96761

KEENAN, RETHA VORNHOLT, nurse; b. Solon, Iowa, Aug. 15, 1934; d. Charles Elias and Helen Maurine (Konicek) V.; B.S.N., State U. Iowa, 1955; M.S.N., Calif. State U., Long Beach, 1978; m. Roy Vincent Keenan, Jan. 5, 1980; children from previous marriage—Scott Iverson, Craig Iverson. Public health nurse City of Long Beach, 1970-73, Hosp. Home Care, Torrance, Calif., 1973-75; patient care coordinator Hillhaven, Los Angeles, 1975-76; mental health cons. InterCityHome Health, Los Angeles, 1978-79; instr. Community Coll. Dist., Los Angeles, 1979-87; instr. nursing El Camino Coll., Torrance, 1981-86, NIMH grantee, 1977-78; instr. nursing Chapman Coll., Orange, Calif., 1982, Mt. Saint Mary's Coll., 1986-87. Contbg. author: American Journal of Nursing Question and Answer Book for Nursing Boards Review, 1984, Nursing Care Planning Guides for Psychiatric and Mental Health Care, 1987-88, Nursing Care Planning Guides for Children, 1987, Nursing Care Planning Guides for Adults, 1988. Cert. nurse practitioner adult and mental health, 1979; mem. Assistance League of San Pedro, Palos Verdes, Calif. Bd. dirs. Luth. Ch. Mem. Am. Nurses Assn., Calif. Nurses Assn., AAUW, Am. Nurses Assn. Council on Psychiatric and Mental Health Nursing, Phi Delta Gamma, Sigma Theta Tau, Phi Kappa Phi, Delta Zeta (bd. dirs.). Home: 27849 Longhill Dr Rancho Palos Verdes CA 90274 Office: West Los Angeles Coll Dept Nursing Culver City CA 90230

KEENAN, ROBERTA MONROE, insurance company executive; b. Webberville, Mich., May 6, 1934; d. Cecil Francis and Edna Almeda (Gowing) Monroe; m. Earl J. Gibson Jr., May 1, 1954 (div. 1972); children—Paula Steele, Christopher; m. 2d, James W. Keenan, Dec. 17, 1983. Student Lansing Community Coll., 1975-77. Cert. Ins. Inst. Am. Mgr. Citizens Credit Union, Howell, Mich., 1961-73; personnel adminstr. Citizens Ins. Co., 1973-77, personnel mgr., 1977-81, asst. v.p., 1981—. Mem. Am. Soc. for Personnel Adminstrn., Nat. Writers Club. Home: 239 Cornell Dr Howell MI 48843 Office: Citizens Ins Co Am 645 W Grand River Howell MI 48843

KEENAN, SHIRLEY ELAINE, engineer; b. Chgo., Dec. 8, 1928; d. Louis and Olga Hilda (Gran) Schultz; m. Vernon Keenan, Dec. 31, 1950 (div. July 1975); 1 child, Vernon III. BSCE, Ill. Inst. Tech., 1950. Registered profl. engr., Ohio, Fla., Maine, Calif. Civil engr. Santa Fe R.R., Chgo., 1950-51; civil/structural engr. Sargent & Lundy, Chgo., 1951-54; structural engr. Yoder & Assocs., Milwaukee, 1954-55; sch. tchr. Benton High Sch., St. Joseph, Mo., 1956-57; project engr. Mead Corp., Dayton, Ohio, 1974-77, sr. project engr. Champion Internat. Corp. (formerly St. Regis), Hamilton, Ohio, 1977—. Pub. relations vol. non-profit health orgn., Dayton, 1971-74. Mem. NSPE, Fla. Soc. of Profl. Engrs., Tech. Assn. of Pulp and Paper Industry. Republican. Methodist. Home: 14 Friars Green Fairfield OH 45014

KEENE, ABIGAIL ASHTON, academic director; b. Boston, Jan. 7, 1958; d. John Willis and Abilgail Richie (McKee) K. BA, Smith Coll., 1981. Bus. mgr. HouseCalls Inc., Hartford, Conn., 1982-85; account exec. So. New Eng. Telephone, New Haven, 1985; devel. officer U. Hartford, 1986—; cons. fund raising, Hartford, 1985—. Chmn. pub. relations Artist Showcase Office Cultural Affairs, Hartford, 1986. Mem. Nat. Assn. Female Executives, Nat. Mus. Women in Arts (charter), Smithsonian Inst., Bus. Profl. Womens Club (legis. chair 1985), Wadsworth Atheneum. Club: Smith Coll. (Hartford) (chmn. 1985). Home: care Ingram 34 Fainiew St UA West Hartford CT 06119 Office: U Hartford 300 Bloomfield Ave Hartford CT 06050

KEENE, ELOISE DOLORES, dietition, nutritionist; b. Huntington, N.Y., July 16, 1952; d. Earl Orville and Louise (Pappalardo) K. BA, U. Miami, 1976; MS, U. Fla., 1980. Cert. tchr., Fla., registered dietitian. Pub. health nutritionist Dade County Dept. Pub. Health, Miami, Fla., 1980-81; coordinator spl. projects Dade County Pub. Schs. Food and Nutrition, Miami, Fla., 1981—; instr. Miami-Dade Community Coll. Restaurant and Insts., 1972-81; coordinator, cons. know your body program Am. Health Found., Miami, N.Y.C., 1982-83; coordinator spl. projects, Dade County Pub. Schs.' Food and Nutrition Miami, Fla., 1981—, restaurant and insts., 1982-87. Bd. dirs. Coconut Grove Assn., Miami, Fla., 1982-83, Coconut Grove Civic Club, Miami, 1983, cons. 1987. Mem. Am. Dietetic Assn., Fla. Dietetic Assn., Miami Dietetic Assn. (Career Guidance chairperson 1987, 88). Office: Dept Food and Nutrition 7042 W Flagler St Miami FL 33144

KEENE-BURGESS, RUTH FRANCES, army official; b. South Bend, Ind., Oct. 7, 1948; d. Seymour and Sally (Morris) K.; m. Leslie U. Burgess, Jr., Oct. 1, 1983; children: Michael Leslie, David William, Elizabeth Sue. BS, Ariz. State U., 1970; MS, Fairleigh Dickinson U., 1978; grad., U.S. Army Command and Gen. Staff Coll., 1986. Inventory mgmt. specialist U.S. Army Electronics Command, Phila., 1970-74, U.S. Army Communications-Electronics Materiel Readiness Command, Fort Monmouth, N.J., 1974-79; chief inventory mgmt. div. Crane (Ind.) Army Ammunition Activity, 1979-80; supply systems analyst Hdqrs. 60th Ordnance Group, Zweibrucken, Fed. Republic Germany, 1980-83; chief inventory mgmt. div. Crane (Ind.) Army Ammunition Activity, 1983-85, chief control div., 1985; inventory mgmt. specialist 200th Theater Army Material Mgmt. Ctr., Zweibruecken, 1985—. Mem. Federally Employed Women (chpt. pres. 1979-80), Nat. Assn. Female Execs., Soc. Logistics Engrs., Assn. Computing Machinery, Am. Soc. Public Adminstrn., Soc. Profl. and Exec. Women, Assn. Info. Systems Profls., AAAS, NOW. Democrat. Jewish. Home: 4916 W Pinchot Ave Phoenix AZ 85031 Office: 200th TAMMC Attention AEAGD-MMC-VS APO NY 09052

KEENHOLTZ, JUDITH K., real estate executive; b. N.Y.C., Dec. 13, 1944; d. Robert J. Kass and Bernice Ruderman; m. Michael Keenholtz, Aug. 14, 1976; 1 child, Robin. BS, NYU, 1965; MS, Queens Coll., N.Y., 1969; cert. in real estate brokerage, U. So. Calif., 1985. Cert. community coll. instr., adminstr. Tchr. Highland Springs Elem. Sch., Richmond, Va., 1964-67, Woodmere (N.Y.) Pub. Schs., 1967-68, 71-72; learning specialist middle sch. level Prince Georges, Va., 1969-70; learning specialist Lexington Sch. for Deaf, Jackson Heights, N.Y., 1970-71, Fieldstone Middle Sch., Montvale, N.J., 1975-77; project specialist Solano County Sch. Dist., Fairfield, Calif., 1977-79; assoc. realtor Valley of Calif. Coldwell Banker, Walnut Creek, 1979-83; resident sales mgr. Coldwell Banker, Walnut Creek, 1983-86; sr. v.p., regional mgr. Coldwell Banker, Contra Costa, Calif., 1986—, Diablo Valley, Calif., 1988—. Mem. Nat. Assn. Realtors, Calif. Assn. Realtors, So. Alameda Bd. Realtors. Home: 704 Miner Rd Orinda CA 94563 Office: Coldwell Banker 3180 Crow Canyon Suite 115 San Ramon CA 94583

KEEP, JUDITH N., federal judge; b. 1944. B.A., Scripps Coll., 1966; J.D., U. San Diego, 1970. With Defenders Inc., 1971-73; sole practice 1973-76; asst. U.S. atty. Calif., 1976; judge Mcpl. Ct., San Diego, 1976-80, U.S. Dist. Ct. (so. dist.) Calif., San Diego, 1980—. Office: US Dist Ct 940 Front St San Diego CA 92189

KEER, JANET S., financial executive; b. N.Y.C., June 8, 1936; d. Martin and Ada (Karnig) Katz; B.B.A., Baruch Sch. Bus. and Public Adminstrn., CUNY, 1956; children—Jennifer, Elizabeth. Asst. to advt. dir. WNEW-TV, N.Y.C., 1959-62; comptroller/ins. sales Joel Katz & Assos., Inc., Roslyn, N.Y., 1969-75; comptroller Am. Bus. & Profl. Program, Inc., Manhasset, N.Y., 1975—; exec. v.p. Arrandale Mgmt. Co., N. Shore Mgmt. Co.; pres. El-Jen Assocs., Inc., 1975—; mng. gen. partner Pueblo Sq. Assos., Manhasset, 1978—. Office: 1205 Northern Blvd Manhasset NY 11030

KEESEE, HELEN LEE, retail drug store chain executive; b. Beaumont, Tex., June 26, 1963; d. Raymond E. and Billie Ruth (Williams) K. Student pub. schs. Courtesy clk. Frey's Thriftway, Salem, Oreg., 1978-80; cashier, clk. Skillerns-Revco, Round Rock, Tex., 1980-81; mgr. Revco D.S., Inc., Round Rock, 1981-83, regional trainer, Austin, Tex., 1983—. Mem. Nat. Assn. Female Execs. Democrat. Methodist. Home: Apt 506 512 Eberhart Ln Austin TX 78745 Office: Revco D S Inc 6800 Westgate Suite 115 Austin TX 78745

KEETER, LISA ANN, marketing assistant; b. Winston-Salem, N.C., July 25, 1959; d. Jerry Manson and Ann Marie (Ellis) K. BA, U. S.C., 1980. Promotion mgr. Sun Pub. Co., Inc., Myrtle Beach, S.C., 1980-81; mgr. promotion Up With People, Inc., Tucson, Ariz., 1981-84; asst. dir. alumni U. S.C., Columbia, 1984-85; materials coordinator Amsterdam (Netherlands) 86 Billy Graham Evang. Assn., 1986; mktg. asst. S.C. Credit Union League, Columbia, 1985—. Author, editor: Amsterdam 86 Conference Book, 1986, Biblical Standards for Evangelists Bible Study, 1986; editor, producer: songbook Songs of Praise, 1986. Ch. newsletter editor, Bible study leader St. Andrews Presbyn. Ch., Irmo, S.C., 1985-87. Democrat. Club: LeagueEmps. Home: 1513 N Woodstream Rd Columbia SC 29212 Office: SC Credit Union League PO Box 1787 Columbia SC 29202

KEETON, KATHY, publisher; b. Republic of South Africa, Feb. 17, 1939; d. Keith and Queenie K.; m. Jan. 17, 1988. Student, Royal Ballet Sch., London. Pres. Omni mag., N.Y.C.; vice chmn. Penthouse Internat. Author: (with Yvonne Baskin) Woman of Tomorrow, 1985; exec. producer TV program Omni: Visions of Tomorrow, The New Frontier. Active Fund for the Aging (City Meals on Wheels), Corp. Blood Drive, Nat. Coalition Against Censorship. Mem. AIAA, Amateur Astronomers Assn., Am. Space Found., Robotics Internat. SME, Space Generation Found., L-5 Soc. Office: Omni Mag 1965 Broadway New York NY 10023

KEGLER, CAROLYN ROSE, marketing professional; b. Wisconsin Rapids, Wis., Jan. 16, 1959; d. Donald William and Lucille Dorothy (Putzier) K. BS in Computer Sci. and Math., U. Wis., 1982. Software engr. McDonnell Douglas Aircraft Co., St. Louis, 1982-84; software design engr. Tex. Instruments, Inc., Dallas, 1984-86; account mgr. MAI Basic Four, Dallas, 1986-87; mktg. rep. IBM Corp., Madison, 1987—. March of Dimes scholar, 1977; recipient award Trust Fund of La Crosse, 1977. Mem. Nat. Assn. Female Execs. Home: 4517 Hammersley Rd #210 Madison WI 53711 Office: IBM Corp 3113 W Beltline Hwy Madison WI 53717

KEGLEY, JACQUELYN ANN, philosophy educator; b. Conneaut, Ohio, July 18, 1938; d. Steven Paul and Gertrude Evelyn (Frank) Kovacevic; m. Charles William Kegley, June 12, 1964; children: Jacquelyn Ann, Stephen Lincoln Luther. BA cum laude, Allegheny Coll., 1960; MA summa cum laude, Rice U., 1964; PhD, Columbia U., 1971. Asst. prof. philosophy Calif. State U., Bakersfield, 1973-77, assoc. prof., 1977-81, prof., 1981—; vis. prof. U. Philippines, Quezon City, 1966-68; grant project dir. Calif. Council Humanities, 1977, project dir. 1980, 82; mem. work group on ethics Am. Colls. of Nursing, Washington, 1984-86. Author: Introduction to Logic, 1978; editor: Humanistic Delivery of Services to Families, 1982, Education for the Handicapped, 1982; mem. editorial bd. Jour. Philosophy in Lit., 1979-84; contbr. articles to profl. jours. Bd. dirs. Bakersfield Mental Health Assn., 1982-84. Mem. N.Y. Acad. Scis., Philosophy of Sci. Assn., Soc. Advancement Am. Phil. soc. (chmn. Pacific div. 1979-83, nat. exec. com. 1974-79), Philosophy Soc., Soc. Interdisciplinary Study of Mind, Soc. Philosophy and Psychology, Dorian Soc., Phi Beta Kappa. Democrat. Lutheran. Home: 7312 Kroll Way Bakersfield CA 93309 Office: Calif State U Dept Philosophy and Religious Studies Bakersfield CA 93309

KEHOE, ALICE BECK, anthropologist, educator; b. N.Y.C., Sept. 18, 1934; d. Roman and Lena (Rosenstock) Beck; m. Thomas Francis Kehoe, Sept. 18, 1956; children—Daniel Miles, Thomas David, Cormac Joel. B.A., Barnard Coll., 1956; Ph.D., Harvard U., 1964. Asst. curator Mus. Plains Indian, Browning, Mont., 1956-58; lectr. U. Sask., Regina, 1964-65; asst. prof. U. Nebr., Lincoln, 1965-68; prof. anthropology Marquette U., Milw., 1968—. Author: North American Indians, 1981. Contbr. articles to profl. jours. Wenner-Gren Found. fellow, 1984. Fellow Am. Anthropol. Assn. (exec. bd. 1979-82); mem. Soc. Am. Archaeology (pub. relations com. 1985—), Archaeol. Inst. Am. (chpt. pres. 1985-87), Am. Ethnological Soc., Nat. Ctr. Sci. Edn. (co-chair Wis. com. corr. 1984—). Jewish. Avocations: bicycling; hiking. Home: 3014 N Shepard Ave Milwaukee WI 53211 Office: Marquette U Milwaukee WI 53233

KEHOE, HELEN GERALYN, human resources executive; b. Evergreen Park, Ill., Sept. 1, 1955; d. Joseph Francis and Margaret Mary (Roach) K. BS in Psychology, Loyola U., Chgo., 1977; MS in Indsl. Relations, U. Wis., 1979. Indsl. relations specialist B.F. Goodrich Co., Akron, Ohio, 1980, employee relations rep., 1980-81; sr. personnel asst. B.F. Goodrich Co., Oaks, Pa., 1981-83, supr. employee relations, 1983-85, mgr. employee relations, 1985-86; regional mgr. human resources Cigna Cos., Bala Cynwyd, Pa., 1986—. Mem. Big Bros./Big Sisters of Chester County, West Chester, Pa., 1982-85—, Beyond War, Phila. chpt., 1986. Named Big Sister of Yr., Big Bros./Big Sisters of Chester County, 1985. Mem. Indsl. Relations Research Assn., Am. Soc. for Personnel Adminstrn., Internat. Assn. for Personnel Women, Indsl. Relations Alumni Assn. (bd. dirs. 1985-88). Roman Catholic. Office: Cigna Cos 3 Bala Plaza W Bala Cynwyd PA 19004

KEHOE, SUSAN, communications and training company executive, consultant; b. Cleve., Dec. 5, 1947; d. John William and Mary Margaret (Swicia) Kehoe; m. Gerald Nicholas, May 15, 1970 (div.); children—Patricia, Mark. B.A., U. Detroit, 1970; M.A., Oakland U., 1980, Ph.D., 1983. Cert. secondary tchr., Mich. Trainer ESL Utica Community Schs., Mich., 1974-78; coordinator program Oakland Univ., Rochester, Mich., 1980-83; adj. prof. mktg. Wayne State Univ., Detroit, 1983-85, U. Mich., Ann Arbor, 1984-85; pres., owner The Kehoe Group, Birmingham, Mich., 1983—; trainer, program designer Gen. Motors, Detroit, 1984—; trainer, cons. Nat. Steel, Ecorse, Mich., 1984—; trainer, speech coach AM Gen., Livonia, Mich., 1984—; presenter Nat. Reading Conf., 1981, 83, Internat. Reading Assn., 1982, Am. Edn. Research Assn., 1982, Conf. on Coll. Composition, 1984; mktg. com. Detroit Symphony Orch. Mem. Pub. Relations Soc. Am. (membership chair). Club: Econ. of Detroit. Avocations: art, travel, music. Home: 3858 Lincoln West Birmingham MI 48010 Office: PO Box 242 Franklin MI 48025

KEIFER, MARY CARTER, law educator; b. Charlottsville, Va., Sept. 21, 1946; d. Carter Lewis and Anne Harrison (Crathorne) Loth; m. John Louis Keifer, Aug. 29, 1970; children—Marcy, Lisa, Kate, Kristin. AB in Math., Converse Coll., 1968; JD, U. Va., 1971. Bar: Ohio 1971, U.S. Dist. Ct. 1974. Staff atty. Toledo Legal Aid Soc., 1971-74; assoc. prof. bus. law, mem. faculty senate Ohio U., Athens, 1974—. Contbr. papers to legal procs. Mem. Athens City Recreation Bd., 1978-83, pres., 1980; mem. Athens City Bd. Edn., 1978—, pres., 1984; sec. bd. govs. J. Warren McClure Athens Edn. Found.; officer Athens Coop. Nursery Bd., 1975-77; bd. dirs. Athens Swim Club. Recipient Faculty-Staff Contbn. award Coll. Bus. Adminstrn. Ohio U, 1988. Mem. Ohio State Legal Services Assn. (trustee), Tri-State Bus. Law Assn. (v.p.), Ohio State Bar Assn., Athens City Bar Assn. Presbyterian. Club: Athens Jr. Women's. Avocations: reading, lap swimming. Home: 201 Longview Heights Athens OH 45701 Office: Ohio U 216 Copeland Hall Athens OH 45701

KEIGHLEY-GRAY, ELIZABETH ANN, management concultant; b. Ithaca, N.Y., Oct. 23, 1958; d. John Frances and Anita Mary (Bunster) Keighley. BS, Syracu U., 1980; M of Health Scis., Johns Hopkins U., 1982. Research assoc. Upstate Med. Ctr., Syracuse, 1978-80; cons. Blue Cross/Blue Shield, Balt., 1980-81; biostatistician Kappa Systems Inc., Washington, 1981-85; mgr. data systems University Research Corp., Rockville, Md., 1985-87; mgr. project Booz, Allen and Hamilton Inc., Bethesda, Md., 1987—. Dir. mktg. Nat. High Blood Pressure Edn. Program, Washington, 1983-84. Mem. Am. Pub. Health Assn. Office: Booz Allen and Hamilton Inc 4330 EW Hwy Bethesda MD 20814

KEIL, LUCY GUTHRIE, accountant; b. Buffalo, July 17, 1937; d. Edward Hosmer and Molly Clapp (Danforth) Guthrie; m. A. Eugene Keil, Sept. 11, 1965; children: Lisa Loring, Katrina Marie. BA, Stanford U., 1959; M.Div., Union Theol. Sem., 1963; M in Acctg., Bowling Green State U., 1977. CPA, Ohio. Assoc. dir. Westminster Found., State Coll., Pa., 1961-65; tchr. math. Highland Jr. High Sch., Medina, Ohio, 1966-67; instr. acctg. dept. Bowling Green (Ohio) State U., 1974-78; sr. internat. acct. Owens-Corning Fiberglas Corp., Toledo, 1978-79, supr. internat. acctg., 1979-82, supr. consol. acctg., 1983-84, mgr. internat. acctg., 1984-86, sr. specialist internat. tax, 1986—. Pres. bd. trustees, chair fin. com. First Presbyn. Ch., 1987—. Mem. LWV (pres. 1971-75). Democrat. Home: 426 Wallace Bowling Green OH 43402 Office: Owens-Corning Fiberglas Fiberglas Tower-2 Toledo OH 43659

KEIL, SUE-ANN, geologist; b. LaGrange, Ill., Oct. 25, 1959; d. Herbert Bruce and Marilyn (Martin) K.; m. David Noyes Powers, Feb. 28, 1987. BA in Geology, Boston U., 1981; MBA in Mgmt. Sci. and Tech. and Innovation, George Washington U., 1986. Geologist NOAA, Rockville, Md., 1981-83; agt. patent Keil and Weinkauf, Washington, 1983-86; asst. to pres. Controlled Environ. Systems Inc., Rockville, 1986—; cons. Express It with Roses, Kensington, Md. 1985-86. Mem. Women Advtg. and Mktg., Balt.-Washington Venture Capital Group. Club: Chevy Chase (Md.). Home: 9319 Kendale Rd Potomac MD 20854

KEIRNS, NANCY ANN, data processing executive, consultant; b. Cleve., Aug. 19, 1942; d. Arthur Frederick and Frances Anna (Graff) Nabinger; m. Phillip Joseph Mesi, June 27, 1962 (div. Aug. 1970); children: Phaedra Ann, Alicia Marie; m. Harry Dayton Keirns, May 6, 1978. Student, Catawba Coll., 1960-61, U. Akron, 1974-76. Systems programmer B.F. Goodrich Co., Akron, Ohio, 1973-78; mktg. mgr. Carroll Touch Tech., Champaign, Ill., 1979; systems programmer Community Tech., Champaign, 1980; mgr. internal systems The Continuum Co., Austin, 1980-84; pres. Keirns Software Factory, Austin, Tex., 1985—; bd. dirs. Ultra Systems Design, Austin. Office: Keirns Software Factory 609 Rocky River Rd Austin TX 78746

KEISER, KAREN LYNNE, health facility executive; b. Dayton, June 29, 1960; d. Charles William and Doris Eloise (Preston) Keiser. B.A., Oglethorpe U., Atlanta, 1983. Program coordinator Muscular Dystrophy Assn., Atlanta, 1983-85, dist. dir., Palm Beach, Fla., 1985-86; dir. women's health ctr. Ga. Bapt. Med. Ctr., Atlanta, 1986—. Author, editor: MDA Monthly News, 1985-86. Recipient Oglethorpe award Student Govt. Assn., 1982. Mem. planning com. Atlanta Dogwood Festival. Mem. Am. Mktg. Assn., Nat. Bus. Assn. Female Execs., Am. Soc. for Hosp. Mktg. and Pub. Relations, Jr. C. of C., Women's C. of C. (chmn. community devel. com.). Roman Catholic. Clubs: Toastmasters; Atlanta Track. Avocations: running; outdoor sports; horseback riding. Home: 8362-R Roswell Rd Atlanta GA 30350

KEISER, LINDA HALLSTEN, music educator, consultant, author; b. New Haven, Jan. 9, 1937; d. Donald Eskil and Elizabeth Marie (Horwath) Hallsten; m. Gordon Delbert Craig, June 29, 1957 (dec. Jan. 1963); m. Harry Robert Keiser, June 11, 1964; children: Harry Rudolph, Robert Hungerford. BA, Mount Holyoke Coll., 1957; MA, Yale U., 1958. Chmn. Dept. Foreign Langs. Walter Johnson High Sch., Bethesda, Md., 1960-65; music dir. Geneva United Presbyn. Ch., Rockville, Md., 1966-79; assoc. dir. ICM Tng. Seminars, Balt., 1979-85; Reiki master Archedigm, Inc., Kensington, Md., 1982—, pres., 1985—; workshop, retreat leader, 1959—; bd. dirs. Well-Springs Found., Madison, Wis., 1980—. Author: Conscious Listening, 1986, Light Search, 1987, (taped music series) Creativity I, II and III: Grieving, Expanded Awareness, Changing Patterns, 1984-88; contbr. articles to profl. publs. Deacon Christ Congregational Ch, Silver Spring, Md., 1981-84. Fellow Inst. Music and Imagery (bd. dirs. 1981—, assoc. exec. dir. 1986—); mem. Am. Assn. for Counseling in Devel., Assn Music and Imagery, The Reiki Alliance, Assn. Transpersonal Psychology, Washington Ind. Service for Edn. Resources, Mt. Holyoke Coll. Alumnae Assn. (bd. dirs. 1978-83). Republican. Home: 11515 Rokeby Ave Kensington MD 20895 Office: Archedigm Inc PO Box 557 Kensington MD 20896

KEISTLER, BETTY LOU, accountant, tax consultant; b. St. Louis, Jan. 2, 1935; d. John William and Gertrude Marie (Lewis) Chancellor; m. George E. Keistler, Aug. 4, 1957 (div. Mar. 1981); children: Kathryn M. Morrissey, Deborah J. Birsinger. AS, St. Louis U., 1956; BBA, U. Mo., 1986. Asst. treas. A. G. Edwards & Sons, St. Louis, 1956-57; owner, mgr. B. L. Keistler & Assoc., St. Louis, 1969-82; controller Family Resource Ctr., Inc., St. Louis, 1982-87; registered rep. Equitable Fin. Services, Mo., 1987; bus. mgr. Mo. Bapt. Coll., St. Louis, 1987—; cons. in field, St. Louis, 1982—; registered rep. Equitable Fin. Services, 1987—. Treas. Pkwy. Townhouses At Village Green, Chesterfield, Mo., 1985—; exec. core United Way Greater St. Louis, 1984—; mem. U. Mo. Alumni Assn., 1987—, 1904 World's Fair Soc., 1987—. Scholar Phillip Morris Corp., St. Louis, 1982-84. Mem. Am. Bus. Women Assn. (v.p. 1978-79, pres. 1979-80, treas. nat. conv. 1981, Woman of Yr. 1979-80), Am. Soc. Women Accts., Ind. Accts. of Mo. (sec. 1978-79, v.p. 1980-81, state sec. 1978-79), St. Louis Women's Commerce Assn., 1904 World's Fair Soc., Beta Sigma Lambda (life, treas. 1985-87). Republican. Baptist. Home: 14524 Bantry Ln Chesterfield MO 63017

KEITH, CAMILLE TIGERT, airline company executive; b. Ft. Worth, Feb. 27, 1945; d. Marvin and Catherine Frances (Tuscany) K. Student, Tex. Tech U.; BA in Broadcasting and Journalism, Tex. Christian U., 1967. Pub. relations, publicity mgr. Sta. WFAA-TV, Dallas; media relations dir. Read-Poland Pub. Relations Co., Dallas; pub. relations dir. Southwest Airlines Co., Dallas, 1972-76, asst. v.p. pub. relations, 1976-78, v.p. pub. relations, 1978-84, v.p. spl. mktg., 1984—. Pub. relations, info. coms. Am. Heart Assn.; bd. dirs. Shakespeare Festival of Dallas, Dallas Repertory Theatre, Jr. Achievement of Dallas, Communities in Schs., Press Club of Dallas, Vis. Nurses of Dallas; mem. adv. bd. Tex. Christian U. Journalism Com., Tex. Tech U. Advertising Com., Women's Ctr. of Dallas; deacon, dept. chmn. Cen. Christian Ch., Dallas. Named Rising Star, Tex. Bus. Mag, 1984. Mem. Discover Tex. Assn. (bd. dirs.), Tex. Pub. Relations Assn., Women in Communications, 500, Inc., Women Entrepreneurs of Tex. (adv. bd.), Tex. Children of the Am. Revolution (nat. chmn.), Dallas C. of C. (pub. service com.), Women's Ctr. (adv. bd.). Clubs: Dallas Press (bd. dirs.), Dallas Advertising League (past pres.). Home: 3257 Lancelot Dr Dallas TX 75229 Office: SW Airlines Co PO Box 37611 Love Field Dallas TX 75235

KEITH, ELIZABETH MILLER, civic worker; b. Wayne, Pa., July 23, 1911; d. Edgar T. and Norah (Schweyer) Miller; grad. Baldwin Sch., 1930; B.A., Vassar Coll., 1934; postgrad. Maria Ouspenskaya Sch. Acting, 1934-36; cert. N.Y. Sch. Design, 1972; m. George R. Vila, Oct. 4, 1941 (div. Feb. 1970); children—John Desmond, Richard Lawrence; m. 2d, Percival Cleveland Keith, Jan. 17, 1976 (dec. July 1976). Actress, Essex (N.Y.) Summer Theatre, 1937, Barter Theatre, Abindgon, N.Y., 1938-39, Drove Players, Greenwich Village, N.Y.C., 1939-41, Canton Workshop (Conn.), 1941, Woonsocket (R.I.) Theatre, 1940. Nurse's aide ARC, Waterbury Hosp., 1942-48; chmn. Planned Parenthood; pres. Woodbury (Conn.) PTA, 1951-53; mem. Citizens Com. to Evaluate Pub. Sch. and Tchr. Tng., 1954; mem. restoration com. Wallace House, Somerville, N.J., 1966-68; chmn. decorating, seminar coms. Wykeham Rise Sch. Festival, 1972-73, mem. public relations com.; edn. chmn. N.Y. Bryant Park Flower Show, 1976-77, 77-78. Bd. dirs. Vis. Nurse Assn., Somerset Hills, N.J., 1962-68, Washington, Conn., 1972-74; trustee Gunnery Sch., Washington, Conn., 1973-76, Wykeham Rise Sch., Washington, Conn., 1982-88. Episcopalian (vestry 1973-76). Clubs: Garden of Am. (hort. zone rep. 1974-76, flower show zone rep. 1978-80, nat. flower chmn. 1980-82, dir. 1982-84), Somerset Hills Garden (historian 1967-69); Vassar, Cosmopolitan (N.Y.C.); Washington (Conn.) Garden (hort. chmn. 1971-73, program chmn. 1973-75, vis. garden chmn. 1978-79, v.p. 1980, 82-83); Washington. Home: Meadow Wind 119 Calhoun St Washington Depot CT 06794

KEITH, GINNI, orchestra manager; b. Seattle, Oct. 1, 1949; d. George Dunlap and Elizabeth Emma (Patz) Paynton; B.A., U. Wash., 1973, B.Mus. cum laude, 1973; m. David Keith, July 5, 1972. Mgr., dir. devel. Los Angeles Mozart Orch., Los Angeles, 1975—; mem. London Symphony Orch. Chorus, 1973-74, Roger Wagner Chorale, 1975-77, Los Angeles Master Chorale, 1975-77. Mem. Phi Beta Kappa. Clubs: Am. Fedn. Aviculture, Nat. Wildlife Fedn.

KEITH, PENNY SUE, educator; b. Louisville, Sept. 15, 1949; d. John G. Jr. and Edna Lee (Butler) K. AS, U. Ky., 1974; BS, U. Louisville, 1978, MEd in Spl. Edn., 1982, MEd in Curriculum Studies, 1984. Cert. tchr., Ky. Adv. tchr. St. Stephan Martyr Sch., Louisville, 1978-80; tchr. learning disabled students S. Oldham Middle Sch., Crestwood, Ky., 1980—; pub. relations liason South Oldham Middle Sch., 1987—. Editor: Through the Eyes of 6th Graders, 1978, Interview with Famous People in the Louisville Times, 1987. Commr. City of Parkway Village, Louisville, 1982-85, treas. 1986. Mem NEA, Ky. Mcpl. League, Ky. Cols., Oldham County Edn. Assn., Atwood Sr. Citizens (pres. 1985—). Democrat. Methodist. Home: 850 Melford Ave Louisville KY 40217 Office: S Oldham Middle Sch 6403 W Hwy 146 Crestwood KY 40014

KEITH, SUSAN ELIZABETH, market analyst; b. Keokuk, Iowa, Apr. 15, 1959; d. Teddy Jr. and Delores Ann (Curless) K. B in Bus. Mktg., Western Ill. U., 1980, MBA, 1982. Dental asst., bookkeeper Bruce Morrow, DDS, Macomb, Ill., 1976-77; mktg. intern Colchester State Bank, Ill., 1979-80; instr. mktg. Western Ill. U., Macomb, 1982-84; fiscal analyst McDonnell Douglas Astronautics, St. Louis, 1984-86, fin. planner, 1986-88, sr. market analyst, 1988—; advisor Western Ill. U. chpt. Am. Mktg. Assn., 1982-84, Sigma Kappa, 1982-84, Alpha Mu Alpha, 1982-84; mem. Western Ill. U. grade appeals com., 1982-84. Author: Consumer Market Behavior: An Instructional Study Guide for Marketing, 333, 1983, Retailing Concepts and Their Management: An Instructional Study Guide for MArketing, 343, 1983. lifeguard, Red Cross instr. Macomb Park Dist., 1979; vol. USO, St. Louis, 1984-88, Better Bus. Bur. St. Louis, 1985-88, McDonnell Douglas Vol. Services Orgn., St. Louis, 1985-86, Leukemia Soc., 1986. Recipient Two-On-Two award, 1986, Two-On-The-Town award, 1986, 87, 88; J. Binnie Wolfe scholar. Mem. Am. Mktg. Soc., Nat. Agra-Mktg. Assn. (advisor 1982-84), Am. Mktg. Assn., Western Ill. U. Alumni Assn., Mortar Bd., U.S. Amateur Confedn. Roller Skating, MDC Roller Skaters (sec., treas.), ., Phi Kappa Phi (fellow 1981), Alpha Mu Alpha, Alpha Lambda Delta, Beta Gamma Sigma, Sigma Iota Epsilon. Republican. Home: 950 Rue de LaBanque E Creve Coeur MO 63141 Office: McDonnell Douglas Astronautics Saint Louis MO 63141

KEITH-MUSELIN, BRENDA KAY, health care facility administrator; b. Middletown, Ohio, Nov. 13, 1947; d. James Edward and Eva May (Alexander) Keith; m. Walter Ellery Muselin, Aug. 30, 1968 (div. Sept. 1978); children: Ellery Linn Muselin, Thomas James Muselin. Nursing diploma, St. Elizabeth Med. Ctr., 1968; cert. in cardiology, Ohio State U., 1968; student, Miami U., Ohio, 1969-70, 80; BS in Health Edn., Cen. State U., Wilberforce, Ohio, 1976; M in Hosp. and Health Adminstrn., Xavier U., 1976. Dist. health nurse Clearcreek Local Schs., Springboro, Ohio, 1969-81; asst. charge nurse emergency dept. Southview Hosp., Dayton, Ohio, 1980-84; relief charge nurse emergency dept. Stubbs Meml. Health Ctr., Waynesville, Ohio, 1983-85; charge nurse emergency dept. Bethesda Care Warren County, Lebanon, Ohio, 1984-86; instr. staff devel. Clinton Meml. Hosp., Wilmington, Ohio, 1985-86; dir. Quaker Heights Health Care Ctr, Waynesville, Ohio, 1986-87; pres. Keilin, Inc., Dayton, 1987—; instr. State of Ohio, Wayne Twp., 1979, asst. instr. Ohio Regents Clinton Meml. Hosp., 1984—. Active Southwestern Ohio Am. Heart Assn., Warren County br. ARC, Wayne Local PTO, Waynesville Soccer Assn., Waynesville Little League, Athletic Assn., Tri-State Health Adminstrs. Forum, Warren County Health Planning Bd., Miami U. Health Edn., Outdoor Edn. Workshop. Mem. Am. Hosp. Assn., Nat. Assn. Female Execs. Methodist. Home: PO Box 482 Waynesville OH 45068 Office: Keilin Inc 2912 Springboro W Dayton OH 45439

KEKICH, BARBARA, lawyer; b. Pitts., Jan. 2, 1948; d. Marcus Stephen and Marie Eunice (Blank) Kekich; m. Joseph Forman, Nov. 12, 1978. B.A., Carlow Coll., 1969; J.D., Southwestern U., 1978. Bar: Calif. 1978, U.S. Dist. Ct. (cen. dist.) Calif. 1979, U.S. Dist. Ct. (so. dist.) Calif. 1986, U.S. Supreme Ct., 1986. Atty., ptnr. King & Williams, Los Angeles, 1978—; judge pro tem small claims div. Los Angeles Mcpl. Ct. Bd. dirs. San Fernando Valley Ednl. Center, Canoga Park, Calif., 1979-83. Mem. ABA, Calif. Women Lawyers, Assn. So. Calif. Def. Counsel, Los Angles County Bar Assn. Home: 2780 McConnell Dr Los Angeles CA 90064 Office: King and Williams 1875 Century Park East 8th Floor Los Angeles CA 90067

KELEHEAR, CAROLE MARCHBANKS SPANN, legal assistant; b. Morehead City, N.C., Oct. 2, 1945; d. William Blythe and Gladys Ophelia (Wilson) Marchbanks; m. Henry M. Spann, June 5, 1966 (div. 1978); children—Lisa Carole, Elaine Mabry; m. Zachariah Lockwood Kelehear, Sept. 15, 1985. Student Winthrop Coll., 1963-64; grad. Draughon's Bus. Coll., 1965; cert. in med. terminology Greenville Tech. Edn. Coll., 1972; grad. Millie Lewis Modeling Sch. Cert. med. asst. Office mgr. S.C. Appalachian Adv. Commn., Greenville, 1964-68, Wood-Bergheer & Co., Newport Beach and Palm Springs, Calif., 1970-72; asst. to Dr. J. Ernest Lathem, Lathem & McCoy, P.A., Greenville, 1972-75, Robert E. McNair, McNair, Konduros, Corley, Singletary and Dibble Law Firm, Columbia, S.C., 1975-77; office mgr. Dr. James B. Knowles, Greenville, 1977-78, Constangy, Brooks & Smith, Columbia, 1978-83; legal asst. to sr. ptnr. William L. Bethea Jr., Jordan & Griffin, P.A., Hilton Head Island, S.C., 1983—; notary pub.; vol. Ladies aux. Greenville Gen. Hosp., 1966-72, South Coast Hosp., Laguna Beach, Calif., 1973, St. Francis Hosp, Greenville, 1974-76, Hilton Head Hosp., 1983—. Mem. Hilton Head Hosp. Aux., Profl. Women's Assn. Hilton Head Island, Am. Bus. Women's Assn., Nat. Assn. Female Execs., Am. Soc. Notaries, Beta Sigma Phi. Home: PO Box 1174 Hilton Head Island SC 29925

KELL, CARLA SUE, federal agency administrator; b. Highland Park, Mich., Sept. 15, 1952; d. Carl William and Margie May (Cannon) Bodner; m. Joseph Mark Kell, Oct. 10, 1971 (div. Dec. 1980). Student, Anderson Coll., 1970-71, Glendale Coll., 1976-77, Ariz. State U., 1978-79, Mesa Coll., 1979-80. Private tutor English, Federal Republic of Germany, 1971-74; office mgr. Bell & Schore, Rochester, Mich., 1974-75, COL Press, Phoenix, 1978-80; publicity mgr. O'Sullivan Woodside & Col, Phoenix, 1980-81, gen. mgr., 1982-84; pub. relations/promotion cons. GPI Publs., Cupertino, Calif., 1985; pub. cons., 1985-88; project adminstr. FAA, 1988—; account coordinator Bernard Hodes Advt., Tempe, Ariz., 1981; cons. freelance mktg., Phoenix, 1983. Vol., Fiesta Bowl Parade Com., Phoenix, 1983, FAA Airport Improvement Program Project. Home: 789 Pepper Dr San Bruno CA 94066

KELLAM, SANDRA, occupational therapist; b. Saginaw, Mich., May 14, 1940; d. I. Lee and Charlotte (O'Neall) Kellam; children: Scott, Richard, Piet. AA, Stephens Coll., 1960; BS, Coll. of William and Mary, 1962. Occupational therapist Met. Hosp., N.Y.C., 1963-65, Gen. Hosp. of Monterey County, Salinas, Calif., 1965-66; supr. occupational therapy Grant-Cuesta Hosp., Mountain View, Calif., 1968-71; dir. occupational therapy services Kennebec County Regional Health Agy., Waterville, Maine, 1976-82; occupational therapist Eastern Shore Regional Ednl. Continuum, Accomac, Va., 1982-86; regiester occupational therapist cons. to spl. learning ctr., Ohancock, Va., 23417, 1986— ; cons. in field. Chmn. For a Safe Park, Rangeley, Maine, 1973, Citizens for Longley for Gov., Rangeley, 1974; field worker Cohen for Senate, Maine, 1978; organizer Citizens for Responsible Govt., Dresden, 1980; chmn. Citizens for Barrier-free Access, 1986—. Recipient cert. Merit Occupational Therapy Club. Mem. Am. Occupational Therapy Assn., World Fedn. Occupational Therapists, Orthotics Unltd. (v.p. 1979-80). Republican. Presbyterian. Clubs: Subron Officers Wives (pres. 1967-68) (Rota, Spain); Skiers Anonymous (v.p. 1973-74) (Rangeley).

KELLEHER, DEBRA LEE, health organization administrator; b. Indpls., May 10, 1958; d. Donnis Leon and Marilyn Lee (Smith) Winegar; m. T. William Kelleher, Sept. 13, 1986. BA, Miami U., 1980. From field rep. to branch dir. Arthritis Found., Ohio, 1981-83, exec. dir., 1984—; mem. Human Health Services for Health Dept., Cin., 1986-88. Dir. Policy Co. for United Way, Cin., 1988—; mem. Edn. Com. Nat. Arthritis Found., Atlanta, 1987—. Mem. Cin. Small Bus. Assn., Nat. Fundraising Execs., Madeira Bus. Assn., Tri-Delta Alumni, Miami U. Alumni. Republican. Presbyterian. Home: 5848 Charter Oak Dr Cincinnati OH 45236 Office: Arthritis Found 7811 Laurel Ave Cincinnati OH 45243

KELLEHER, LISA ANN, insurance company executive; b. Plainfield, N.J., Oct. 15, 1960; d. Henry George Clauer and Georgiana Rose (Wannag) Sweetman; m. Thomas Michael Kelleher, June 12, 1982 (div. Oct. 1985). BA in Journalism, Pace U., 1978—. Documentation closing specialist Mcpl. Issues Servic Corp., White Plains, N.Y., 1982-84, mgr. documentation and closing dept., 1984—; asst. v.p. Mcpl. Bond Investors Assurance Corp., White Plains, 1987—. Mem. Nat. Assn. Female Execs. Republican. Presbyterian. Office: Mcpl Bond Investors Assurance Corp 445 Hamilton Ave White Plains NY 10601

KELLER, FRANCES RICHARDSON, history educator; b. Lowville, N.Y., Aug. 14, 1914; d. Stephen Brown and Sarah Eliza (Bell) Richardson; m. Chauncey A.R. Keller, June 20, 1936 (div. 1964); children—Reynolds, Stephen, Julia, William; m. William P. Rhetta, May 10, 1969. B.A., Sarah Lawrence Coll.; M.A., U. Toledo; Ph.D., U. Chgo., 1973. Lectr., U. Ind.-Gary, 1966-67, U. Ill.-Chgo., 1967-68, Chgo. City Coll., 1968-70, Centre Inter. Universitaire, Paris, 1970-71, U. Calif.-Berkeley Extension, 1972-74, San Jose (Calif.) State U., 1974-78; adj. prof. history San Francisco State U., 1978—; panelist, reader NEH, 1978, 79, 81. Author: An American Crusade: The Life of Charles Waddell Chesnutt, 1978; editor, contbr.: Women in Western Tradition; translator, editor, author interpretive essay: Slavery and the French Revolutionists (Anna Julia Cooper), 1988. Mem. Nat. Women's Studies Assn. (chair publicity and pub. relations, founding conv. 1976, ofcl. historian 1978), Western Assn. Women Historians (program chair 1979, pres. 1981-83), Am. Hist. Assn. (nominating com. 1983—), Orgn. Am. Historians, Women in Hist. Profession (pres. coordinating com. 1985-88), Western Soc. French History. Home: 835 Junipero Serra Blvd San Francisco CA 94127 Office: San Francisco State U Dept History San Francisco CA 94132

KELLER, GLENDA KAY, corporation executive; b. Harrisonville, Mo., Feb. 27, 1951; d. Glyndon Ritner and Shirley Ann (Wills) Divelbiss; div. 1982; children: Anne Elizabeth, Bryan Robert. BA in Polit. Sci., U. Mo., 1973, MA in Edn., 1976. Instr. U.S. Army/Tex. Coll., Kaiserslautern, Germany, 1977-79; mktg. com. specialist Honeywell Inc., Los Angeles, 1980-81, mgr. mktg. services, 1981-83, mgr. venture programs, 1983; dir. market analysis and research, strategic planning computervision, Bedford, Mass., 1984-85, cons. Bain and Co., Boston, 1985—; prin. Synectics, Cambridge. Dir. County Up with People (Music), Harrisonville, Mo., 1970-71 ; recruiter of instrs. Glenkirk Reaching Out to Women, Glendora, Calif., 1979-80; researcher Durenberger for U.S. Senate Campaign, Bloomington, Minn., 1982; bd. dirs. Sylmar Chamber Orch., Mpls., 1983—, Bay State Red Cross, 1987—. Recipient Leadership award Mpls. YWCA, 1981; Individual Recognition award Honeywell, 1980, 81; U. Mo. Regents scholar, 1968; U. Mo. oboe performance scholar, 1968; named Outstanding Young Woman of Am., 1981. Mem. N.Am. Corporate Planning Soc., Assn. Devel. Computer Based Instructional Systems, Nat. Honor Soc.

KELLER, JANET ANN, filtration company executive; b. Rochester, N.Y., Dec. 26, 1949; d. Ronald Leon and Marilyn Ida (Wetzel) K. BA in Chemistry, Coll. Notre Dame, 1971. Sr. lab. technician Eastman Kodak Co., Rochester, N.Y., 1971-85; v.p. Soran, Inc., Sodus, N.Y., 1985—, also sec. bd. dirs. Home: 80 Clematis St Rochester NY 14612

KELLER, JOYCE GARVER, association executive, writer; b. Cleve. Sept. 28, 1947; d. John H. and Zelda (Gershowitz) Garver; m. Steven Ray Keller, 1967; 1 child, Stuart Alan. Assoc. dir. ACLU of Ohio, 1972-78; polit. campaign cons., Columbus, Ohio, 1978-80; ops. supr. U.S. Census Bur., Columbus, 1980; exec. dir. Ohio Women, Inc., Columbus, 1980-82, People for the Am. Way, Columbus, 1982-85; gen. mgr. Health Power of Columbus, Inc., 1986-87 ; QA/UR and compliance mgr. Health Power Mgmt. Co., Columbus, 1987-88, v.p. HMO ops., 1988—; cons. various univs. Contbr. articles to profl. jours. and mags.; creative cons. TV documentary "Focus:-Censorship", 1983 (Ohio State Bar Assn. Media award 1985). Bd. dirs. Alliance for Coop. Justice, Columbus, 1977-80, Ohio Hunger Task Force, Columbus, 1981-84, Columbus Area Women's Polit. Caucus, 1978-82 (Dem. Task Force chmn., 1987); selection com. Ohio Women's Hall of Fame, Columbus, 1983; adv. Ohio Tchr. Edn. and Cert., Ohio Dept. Edn., 1984. Recipient Community Service award Ohio Ho. of Reps., 1982, City of Columbus and Franklin County, 1978, Civil Liberties award ACLU of Ohio Found., 1983, Friend of Edn. award Ohio Edn. Assn., 1986. Mem. Nat. Assn. Female Execs., Nat. Women's Polit. Caucus (nat. site selection com.), Columbus Bus. and Profl. Women's Club, Nat. Council Jewish Women, Columbus Area C. of C. (mem. pres.'s Roundtable, 1986). Democrat. Office: Health Power Mgmt Corp 560 E Town St Columbus OH 43215

KELLER, KAREN MARIE, nurse, educator; b. Bloomington, Ind., Oct. 15, 1952; d. Robert Ross and Theresa (Hessig) McEllininey; m. Lucien Fairfax Jr., Oct. 23, 1982; 1 child, Stephanie. BS in Nursing, U. Evansville, 1975; M in Nursing Adminstrn., U. Tex.-Austin, 1987. Registered nurse, Ind., Wash.; cert. med.-surg. nurse. Commd. 1st lt. U.S. Army, 1973, advanced through grades to Maj. 1984; nurse instr. Acad. Health Scis., Ft. Sam Houston, Tex., 1978-79, phase 2 coordinator, 1979-80, tng. officer, 1980-81, dep. program dir. satellite TV, 1981-82; asst. head nurse Madigan Army Med. Ctr., Tacoma, Wash., 1983, nurse instr., 1983-85; head nurse surg. unit, 1986; exec. officer Spl. Assistance Team, Liberia, 1985. Producer 18 videotapes/live TV programs for health providers, 1981-82. Treas. Fox Glen Homeowners Assn., Tacoma, 1984. Decorated Army Commendation medal with 2 bronze oak leaf clusters, Humanitarian Service medal. Mem. AMSUS, Am. Nurses Assn., Nat. League Nurses, Assn. Fed. Nurses (pres. 1984-85), Emergency Dept. Nurses Assn., Sigma Theta Tau. Republican. Lodge: Order Eastern Star. Home: 8502 Acropolis Dr Universal City TX 78148 Office: Acad Health Scis Student Detachment Fort Sam Houston TX 78234

KELLER, MARGARET GILMER (MRS. GEORGE HENRY KELLER, III), educator; b. Harrisburg, Pa., July 11, 1922; d. Charles Greenawalt and Mary Ellen (Sullivan) Gilmer; m. George Henry Keller III, July 13, 1940; children: Mary Ellen, Margaret Marie, George Henry. AB, Trinity Coll., 1933, AM, Columbia U., 1934; cert. 1942, cert. State Tchrs. Coll. Bloomsburg, Pa., 1934; Acting chmn. history dept., Trinity Coll., Washington, 1935-36, chmn. classical dept., Convent Sacred Heart, 1936-37, Steelton (Pa.) High Sch., 1937-41, adj. prof. English dept., Rutgers U., 1946—, mem. dean's adv. com. U. Coll.,1968, also advisor to women's clubs U. Coll., chmn. classical dept., Glen Rock (N.J.) High Sch., 1956-59, chmn. fgn. lang. dept, 1959—. Active Am. Cancer Soc., Community Chest ARC, Girl Scouts U.S.A.; mem. nominating bd. Ridgewood (N.J.) Nursing Service, 1959-60; Republican county committeeman; trustee Trinity Coll. (life), 1963-67, 1974—, chmn. 75th Anniversary Fund, 1974-75. Honored by Rutgers U., 1953, 61, 65, 71, 82, 87, Newman Province of N.J., 1963, Nat. Jaycees, 1973, Middle States Assn. Comm. on Secondary Schs., 1970, 74; recipient Robert Ax citation Glen Rock High Sch., 1971, Case Inst., 1976, Alumnae Service award Trinity Coll., 1977, 87, Pres.'s medal, 1982; Outstanding Tchr. of Yr., Rutgers U., Newark, 1982. Mem. NEA, N.J. Edn. Assn., Am. Classical Soc., AAUW (former dir.), Archeol. Inst. Am., MLA, Suprs. Assn. N.J. (sec. 1973-76), Am., N.J., Mid-Atlantic States classical socs., AAUP, Chaplain's Aid Assn., Trinity Coll. Alumnae Assn. (nat. pres., recipient Nat. Achievement award, 1987), rutgers Alumnae Assn. (hon., advisor), Phi Chi Theta (hon.), Alpha Sigma Lambda (hon., advisor). Clubs: Newman (adviser Rutgers U.), Univ. Coll. Women (hon. Rutgers U.), Coll. Home: 200 Phelps Rd Ridgewood NJ 07450 Office: Rutgers U New Brunswick NJ 08901

KELLER, MARY ANN, accountant; b. Pawhuska, Okla., May 31, 1953; d. Walter Marion and Mary Margaret (Reale) Harriman; m. Jackson David Keller, Jr., Sept. 6, 1986; 1 child, Robert Jefferson. BS, Okla. State U., 1976. CPA, Okla. Comptroller, mgr. Inngroup, Inc., Oklahoma City, 1976-80; staff acct. Lester Witte & Co. and Foster-Dickinson & Co., CPA's, Tulsa, 1980-85; mgr. Foster-Dickinson & Co., CPA's, Tulsa, 1985, Baird, Kurtz and Dobson, CPA's, Tulsa, 1986; pvt. practice acctg. Tulsa, 1986—. Coordinator Tulsa area Ali Lassen's LEADS Club, 1986-87; treas., deacon 1st bd. Forest Park Christian Ch., Tulsa, 1986—. Mem. Am. Inst. CPA's, Okla. Soc. CPA's, Nat. Assn. Female Execs., Tulsa Profl Network (pres.), Assn. Ind. Bus. Cons. Republican. Home: 6314 S 70th E Ave Tulsa OK 74133 Office: 9726 E 42d St Suite 207 Tulsa OK 74146

KELLER, SHARON PILLSBURY, speech pathologist; b. Los Angeles, Sept. 28, 1935; d. Edward Gardner and Iris Noriene (Hager) Pillsbury; m. Clarence Stanley Keller (dec. 1982); children: Jann Kathleen, Jennifer Beth, Lauren Elaine. AA, Chaffey Community Coll., Alta Loma, Calif., 1971; BA, U. La Verne, 1978, MS, 1983. Lic. speech pathologist, Calif.; lic. sch. audiologist, Calif.; life service credential - clin. and rehabilitative, Calif. Lang. speech and hearing specialist Chino (Calif.) Unified Schs., 1978-86, Rim of the World Sch. Dist., Lake Arrowhead, Calif., 1986—. Mem. AAUW, Am. Speech-Lang. Hearing Assn. (cert. clin. competence speech-lang. pathologist), Calif Speech and Hearing Assn., Calif. Tchrs. Assn. Republican. Presbyterian. Home: PO Box 1745 Crestline CA 92325 Office: Lake Arrowhead Elem Sch PO Box 430 Lake Arrowhead CA 92352

KELLER, SHELLY B., writer, editor, marketing consultant; b. Ranson, W.Va., Dec. 7, 1948; d. Denzil Eugene Greynolds and Rebecca Jane (Propps) Hayes; m. Howard Lee Keller Jr., Aug. 23, 1969 (div. Sept. 1975); children: Laura Christine; m. Robert James Anselmo, July 15, 1986. BS, U. Md., 1971; postgrad., Boston Coll., 1972-73. Mktg. dir. Tennessee Williams Repertory Ctr., Key West, Fla., 1977-79; community relations mgr. The Wis. State Jour. and The Capital Times, Madison, Wis., 1979-81; advt. mgr. The Sacramento Bee's Neighbors, 1981-84; mng. editor Today's Supervisor, Sacramento, 1985-87; mktg. cons. Calif. Dept. Trans., Sacramento, 1984-85. Editor Homegrown Recipes, 1975; co-author: 96 Marketing Ideas for Physicians, 1987. Chair Sacramento Rideshare Campaign, 1984-85; mem. adv. com. Sta. KVIE, Sacramento, 1985—. Mem. Internat. Assn. Bus. Communicators, Women in Communications, Am. Soc. Assn. Execs., Nat. Assn. Female Execs. Office: 1114 21st St Sacramento CA 95814

KELLER, SUSAN AGNES, insurance officer; b. Moline, Ill., July 12, 1952; d. Kenneth Francis and Ethel Louise (Odendahl) Hulsbrink; m. Kevin Eugene Keller, June 20, 1981; 1 child, Dawn Marie. Grad. in Pub. Relations, Patricia Stevens Career Coll., 1971; grad. in Gen. Ins., Ins. Inst. Am., 1986. CPCU. Comml. lines rater Bitiminous Casualty Corp., Rock Island, Ill., 1973-78; with Roadway Express, Inc., Rock Island, 1978-81; front line supr. Yellow Freight System, Inc., Denver, 1982-83; supr. plumbing and sheet metal prodn. Bell Plumbing and Heating, Denver, 1983-84; underwriter Golden Eagle Ins. Co., San Diego, 1985—; cons. real estate foreclosure County Records Service, San Diego, 1986—. Vol. DAV, San Diego, 1985—. Mem. Soc. Chartered Property and Casualty Underwriters, Profl. Women in Ins., Nat. Assn. Female Execs. Roman Catholic. Home: 449 Jamul Ct Chula Vista CA 92001 Office: Golden Eagle Ins Co 7175 Navajo Rd San Diego CA 92119

KELLER, TERESA ANN, food and beverage director, consultant; b. Statesville, N.C., Apr. 13, 1956; d. Spencer Lee and Ann (Brumley) K. Student, Fla. So. Coll., 1974-76; BA, BS, So. Meth. U., 1978. Tng. coordinator TGI Friday's, Dallas, 1978-83; dir. tng. Kelly-Johnston Enterprises, Oklahoma City, 1983-84; mgr. Marriott Corp., Oklahoma City, 1985-86; dir. catering Skirvin Plaza Hotel, Oklahoma City, 1987—; cons. Joe Kelly's Restaurants, Oklahoma City, 1983-84 ; researcher engring. Noise Pollution Project, 1978; tng. cons. Antigua, W.I. Author: (with others) TGI Fridays Employee Manual, 1982, Joe Kelly's Manuals, 1983-84; editor corp. newsletter Kelly Johnston Communications., 1983-84. Vol. Dallas County Chidren's Shelter, 1978, Animal Shelter, Oklahoma City, 1984; campaigner for sch. bd., Dallas, 1977, Chief of Police, Dallas, 1980; coordinator Chidren's Miracle Network Telethon Fundraiser, Oklahoma City, 1987. Mem. Am. Soc. for Tng. Devel., Nat. Assn. Female Execs., DAR, Magna Carta Dames Assn., Psi Chi. Republican. Home: PO Box 20402 Oklahoma City OK 73156-0402 Office: Skirvin Plaza Hotel One Park Ave Oklahoma City OK 73102

KELLER, THERESA FAYE, business development coordinator; b. New Orleans, Mar. 19, 1950; d. Charles and Septemia (Gibson) Keller. BS, Southern U., 1972. Research statistician Southern U., Baton Rouge, 1973, adminstrv. asst., 1973-77, bus. devel. analyst, 1977-79, bus. devel. specialist, 1979-81, bus. devel. coordinator, 1986—; records supr. Sentry Ins. Co., Baton Rouge, 1981-83, supr. underwriting, 1983-84; spl. asst. La. Dept. of Commerce, Baton Rouge, 1984-86; mem. profls. selection bd. Baton Rouge Recreation and Parks Commn., 1986—. Bd. dirs. Audubon Girl Scout council, 1980-86; chairperson Women of Achievement YWCA, Baton Rouge, 1983 (pres., bd. dirs. 1984-86, 1988 nat. conv. rules com., N.Y.C., 1986—); mem. pacesetter campaign Capital Area United Way, 1985-86; mem. exec. council Red River Valley Area Council; pres. Capital Area Network, Baton Rouge, 1987; bd. dirs. Leadership Greater Baton Rouge, 1987—. Mem. Nat. Assn. Female Execs. Democrat. Roman Catholic. Home: PO Box 65294 Baton Rouge LA 70896 Office: So U and A & M Coll Coll of Bus PO Box 9723 Baton Rouge LA 70813

KELLERMAN, SALLY CLAIRE, actress; b. Long Beach, Calif., June 2, 1937; d. John Helm and Edith Baine (Vaughn) K.; m. Richard Edelstein, Dec. 19, 1970; 4 step-daus.; m. Jonathan Krane, 1980. Student, Los Angeles City Coll., Actor's Studio, N.Y.C. Stage appearances include Singular Man, N.Y.C., Breakfast at Tiffany's; films include A Little Romance, Mash, Brewster McCloud, Last of the Red-Hot Lovers, Foxes, Reflection of Fear, Slither, Lost Horizon, The Big Bus, Head On, Rafferty and the Gold Dust Twins, The Boston Strangler, Loving Couples, The April Fools, Welcome to L.A., Serial, For Lovers Only, 1982, Dempsey, 1983, September, Gun, 1983, Back to School, 1986, That's Life, 1986, Meatballs III, 1987; also TV roles Chrysler Theatre, Mannix, It Takes a Thief; TV film Verna: USO Girl, 1978 (Nominee Acad. and Golden Globe awards for M). Mem. Actor's Equity, AFTRA. *

KELLERS, KATHLEEN MARIE, federal government postal administrator; b. Jersey City, Jan. 19, 1956; d. Edward Vincent and Maria Joyce (Mehok) Keegan; m. Timothy Robert Kellers, Sr., Oct. 3, 1981; children: Timothy Robert Jr., Jaye Joyce. B.A., Rutgers Coll., 1978. Letter carrier U.S. Postal Service, Toms River, N.J., 1978-83; supt. postal ops., Brielle, N.J., 1983-87; postmaster, Sea Girt, N.J., 1987—, dist. safety instr., Cherry Hill, N.J., 1985. Recipient cert. appreciation Del. Valley Dist. U.S. Postal Service, 1985, cert. appreciation New Brunswick Div. Career Awareness Conf., 1987. Mem. Nat. Assn. Letter Carriers, Nat. Assn. Postal Suprs., Nat. Assn. Postmasters of U.S. Roman Catholic. Avocations: reading; needlework; gardening. Home: PO Box 391 Brielle NJ 08730 Office: US Postal Service 800 The Plaza Sea Girt NJ 08750-9998

KELLEY, BETTY J.W., securities sales professional, social service organization executive; b. Sacramento, Apr. 27, 1954; d. John Sanford and Madeline A. (Reylea) McA.; m. James W. Kelley, Mar. 26, 1988. Student, Hudson Valley Community Coll., 1979; cert. securities sales asst., Securities Sch. of Miami, 1980. Sec. Shearson Hayden Stone, Huntington, N.Y., 1977-78; ops. mgr. Shearson Am. Express, Palm Beach, Fla., 1979-80; registered sales asst. Shearson Lehman Securities, Palm Beach, 1980-82; registered sales asst. Prudential Bache Securities, Schenectady, N.Y., 1983-85, Palm Beach, 1985-86; registered sales asst. Dean Witter Reynolds Securities, Boca Raton, Fla., 1986—. Recipient Most $ Contbrns. award March of Dimes, 1987. Mem. Guillain-Barré Syndrome Support Group (coordinator, dir. Boca Raton chpt. 1987—). Republican. Episcopalian. Club: Gator Sno Ski (North Palm Beach) (treas. 1985-86). Home: 419 NW 36th Ave Deerfield Beach FL 33442 Office: Dean Witter Reynolds Securities 150 E Palmetto Park Rd Boca Raton FL 33432

KELLEY, DELORES GOODWIN, college dean; b. Norfolk, Va., May 1, 1936; d. Stephen Cornelius and Helen (Jefferson) Goodwin; m. Russell Victor Kelley, Dec. 26, 1956; children: Norma Delores, Russell Victor III, Brian Todd. BA, Va. State U., 1956; MA, NYU, 1958, Purdue U., 1972; PhD, U. Md., 1977. Instr. English, Morgan State Coll., Balt., 1966-70; grad. teaching fellow Purdue U., 1970-72; chmn. dept. lang., lit. and philosophy Coppin State Coll., Balt., 1976-79, dean lower div., 1979—; panelist, reviewer NEH; mem. Md. Dept. Edn. evaluation com. for Hood Coll., 1978—, Md. Commn. Values Edn., 1980—; bd. dirs. Harbor Bank Md., Balt., 1980—, Inst. for Christian Jewish Studies, 1987—; chmn. adv. council Gifted and Talented Edn. Balt. City Schs., 1980—. Mem. Mayor Balt. Adv. Council Mental Health, 1981-84; elected to Dem. Cen. Com. from 42d legis. dist. Md., 1982-86; sec. Md. Dems., 1986—; Dem. del. Nat. Conv., 1988; v.p. Cross Country Improvement Assn., 1980-82; active Fact-Finding Mission to Israel, 1987—. Grantee Md. Com. Humanities and Pub. Policy, 1977, NEH, 1987—; fellow Am. Coll. on Edn., 1982-83. Mem. Nat. Assn. Women Deans, Adminstrs. and Counselors, Nat. Council Tchrs. English, Md. Collegiate Honors Council (sec.-treas. 1981-82), Balt. Urban League (bd. dirs. 1986—), Md. Assn. Higher Edn., Alpha Kappa Mu, Alpha Kappa Alpha. Baptist. Home: 3400 Olympia Ave Baltimore MD 21215 Office: 2500 W North Ave Baltimore MD 21216

KELLEY, GERALDINE MARIE, home economist; b. Wichita, Kans., June 16, 1942; d. James Leon and Ula Mae (Riley) Lane; m. John Austin Kelley, Nov. 9, 1970; children: Craig, Lisa, Kenneth. AA, El Centro Coll., 1969; BS in Home Econ., North Tex. State U., 1971; MS in Consumer Sci., Tex. Woman's U., 1984. Home demonstrator Tex. Agrl. Extension Service, Sherman, 1971-72; agt. Tex. Agrl. Extension Service, Ft. Worth, 1972-73; 4-H agt. Tex. Agrl. Extension Service, Sherman, 1973-83, home economist, 1983—. Adv. bd. Sherman Community Edn., 1984—. Mem. Grayson County Home Econs. Assn. (pres. 1983-84), Tex. Assn. 4-H Agts., Tex. Assn. Extension Home Economists Dist.4, Tex. Home Econs. Assn., Am. Hom Econ. Assns.. Democrat. Methodist. Clubs: Quilt Makers, Sherman, (pres. 1987—), Tex. A&M U. Mother's, Sherman, (pres. 1986). Office: Grayson County Extension Service County Courthouse Sherman TX 75090

KELLEY, JOYCE KAREN, English language educator; b. Greenfield, Mass., Dec. 5, 1942; d. Michael Charles and Felicia Elizabeth (Lapinski) Kostek; m. Earl Francis LaPierre, June 29, 1969 (div. 1980); children: Neal Edward, Danielle Renee; m. Andrew McClure Kelley, Aug. 25, 1982. BA, U. Mass., 1965; MEd summa cum laude, North Adams (Mass.) State U., 1975. Cert. elem., secondary and coll. level instr. of French, Social Studies, Reading and English, Vt., Mass., Fla. Asst. merchandiser Sears, Roebuck and Co., N.Y.C., 1965-66; assoc. designer B. Altman, N.Y.C., 1966-67; elem. tchr. Cen. Berkshire Regional Sch. Dist., Dalton, Mass., 1967-70; asst. editor Mass. State Dept. Edn., Pittsfield, 1970-71; Title IV C reader Pub. Revenue Edn. Council of Mass. Dept. Edn., Pittsfield, 1971; tchr. English Martin County Sch. Dist., Stuart, Fla., 1981-82, tchr. English honors program, 1982—; creator coursework Reading in the Content, Mass., Vt., 1978-81. Contbr. poetry various jours. Mem. scholarship com. Martin County, 1987; active Girl Scouts, chmn. cookie drive Palm Glades council, 1986; sponsor Martin County chpt. Nat. Beta Club, 1982—. Mem. NEA, Fla. Council Tchrs. of English, Delta Kappa Gamma (parliamentarian 1986-87). Democrat. Roman Catholic. Office: Martin County Instrnl Offices E Ocean Blvd Stuart FL 33494

KELLEY, KATHRYN, psychologist, educator; b. Tulsa; d. Lawrence J. and Johnnie A. Kelley; married; 1 child, Lindsey. BA in Psychology, U. Okla.; MS in Social-Personality Psychology, Purdue U., PhD in Psychology. Asst. prof. psychology Marquette U., Milw., 1977-78, U. Wis.-Milw., 1978-79; asst. prof. psychology SUNY-Albany, 1979-85, assoc. prof., 1985—, coordinator indsl. and organizational psychology, 1987—. Author: Females, Males, and Sexuality, 1986; Alternative Approaches to the Study of Sexual Behavior, 1986, The Human Sexual Experience, 1987. Bur. Indian Affairs higher edn. fellow, 1974-77. Mem. Am. Psychol. Assn., Eastern Psychol. Assn., Soc. Sci. Study of Sex, Soc. Exptl. Social Psychology. Office: SUNY Social Sci Dept Psychology Albany NY 12222

KELLEY, KATHY ANN MARCUM, distribution company executive; b. Ft. Worth, Mar. 22, 1952; d. Billy Walter Sr. and Marydee Elizabeth (Peterson) Marcum; m. Thomas Ellis Blessing, Jan. 14, 1972 (div. Jan. 1976); m. Jimmy Ross Kelley, Jan. 23, 1976; children: Jimmy Brett, Mickey Tye; 1 stepchild, Cyndi. BS in Secondary Edn., North Tex. State U., 1974. Sales clk. Boteler's Dry Goods Store, Boyd, Tex., 1967; receptionist Boyd Electric, 1967-68, Big State Constrn., Arlington, Tex., 1969-70; sec. East Tex. State U., Commerce, 1972; speech tchr. Ft. Worth Ind. Sch. System, 1974-75, Decatur (Tex.) Ind. Sch. System, 1975-76; showroom model Apparell Mart, Dallas, 1978-87; with Am. Airlines, Dallas, 1983-84; outside sales rep., corp. sec./treas. F/S Industries Inc., Arlington, 1982—; pres., owner Fourteen Golden Karats; flight attendant Am. Airlines, Dallas, 1988—. Mem. First United Meth. Ch. Mem. Nat. Assn. Female Execs., PTA, U.S. Tennis Assn., Assn. Profl. Flight Attendants. Home: 2709 Shadow Wood Dr Arlington TX 76006

KELLEY, LINDA EILEEN, marketing specialist, sales consultant; b. Osceola, Iowa, June 10, 1950; d. Marion Gale and Frances (Steele) McKinnie; m. Dennis Dean Kelley, Aug. 3, 1969 (div. 1980); 1 child, Jennifer Lynne. Student, U. No. Iowa, 1969. Classified advt. mgr. Creston (Iowa) News-Advertiser, 1971-79, advt./promotion mgr., 1981-82; classified advt. promotion specialist Des Moines Register & Tribune, 1979-81; assoc. cons. K. Bordner Cons., Inc., Bloomington, Minn., 1982-84; commn. sales rep. Mpls. Star & Tribune, 1983—; instr. advt. Hennepin Jr. Coll., Mpls.; cons. small bus. Author: Retail Advertising for the Small Business, 1986—. Methodist. Home: 8440 Quinn Ave S Bloomington MN 55437

KELLEY, MARIE ELAINE, educational administrator; b. St. Johns, Mich., Feb. 6, 1941; d. Berl Louis and Doris Louise (Tait) Foerch; m. Edgar Alan Kelley, Aug. 10, 1963; 1 child, Wesley Lynn. BA, Cen. Mich. U., 1963; MA, Mich. State U., 1965, PhD, 1973; EdS, U. Nebr., Lincoln, 1976. Tchr. Ovid Elsie (Mich.) Area Schs., 1963-67, Colon (Mich.) Community Schs., 1967-68, Lincoln (Nebr.) Pub. Schs., 1970-78; asst. prin. instrn. Lincoln East-Jr. Sr. High Sch., 1978-85; prin. Caledonia (Mich.) Jr. High Sch., 1985—; vis. prof. U. Nebr., Lincoln, 1976-77, 80-81; vis. prof. Western Mich. U., Kalamazoo, 1988—; originator, 1st dir. Lincoln Writing Lab., 1975-78. Contbr. articles to profl. jours. Mem. Nat. Assn. Secondary Sch. Prins., Mortar Board, Phi Delta Kappa, Alpha Lambda Delta. Home: 6875 Glen Creek SE Caledonia MI 49316 Office: 330 Johnson St Caledonia MI 49316

KELLEY, VICKY LYNN MONTGOMERY, nursing supervisor; b. Radford, Va., Apr. 14, 1955; d. Robert William and Albertine Faye (Akers) Montgomery; m. Stephen Ray Kelley, Mar. 10, 1978; children: Stephanie Autumn, Joseph Robert. Profl. Nursing Diploma, Roanoke Meml. Hosp., 1975; student Roanoke Coll., 1981—. Nurse neurol. intensive care unit Roanoke (Va.) Meml. Hosp., 1975-77; nurse oral surgery Dr. John E. Gardner, Jr., Roanoke, 1977-78; staff nurse Roanoke Valley Artificial Kidney Ctr., 1978—, supr. nursing, 1980-83, area dir. nursing, 1983—; acute hemodialysis nurse Valley Nephrology Assocs., Roanoke, 1981—. Lodge: Order Ea. Star. Home: 5540 Deer Park Dr NW Roanoke VA 24019 Office: Roanoke Valley Artificial Kidney Ctr 4330 Brambleton Ave Roanoke VA 24018

KELLISON, DONNA LOUISE GEORGE, accountant, educator; b. Hugoton, Kans., Oct. 16, 1950; d. Donald Richard and Zenha Louise (Lowry) George. BA in Elem. Edn. with honors, Anderson (Ind.) U., 1972; MS in Elem. Edn., Ind. U., 1981. CPA; Ind.; lic. tchr., Ind. Tchr. elem. Maconaquah Sch. Corp., Bunker Hill, Ind., 1972-73; office mgr. Eskew & Gresham, CPA's, Louisville, Ky., 1973-78; para-profl. Blue & Co., Indpls., 1979-83, tax compliance specialist, 1983-84, tax sr., 1984-86, tax supr., 1986-87, tax mgr., 1987—. Vol. Children's Clinic, Indpls., 1985—. Mem. Network Women in Bus., Am. Inst. CPA's, Ind. CPA Soc. Presbyterian. Club: Toastmasters (Indpls.) (sec. 1986). Home: 9318 Embers Way Indianapolis IN 46250 Office: Blue & Co PO Box 80069 Indianapolis IN 46280-0069

KELLOGG, DOROTHY M., state legislator; b. Mpls., July 26, 1920; d. Carl Howard and Marie (Mundhenke) Sorteberg; m. Lawrence Strong Kellogg, 1940; children: Lawrence Edmund, Ralph Curtis, Jean Marie Jostad. Grad. high sch., Watertown, S.D. Former mem. S.D. Ho. of Reps.; mem. S.D. State Senate. Mem. LWV, Bus. and Profl. Women, C. of C. Address: Rt 2 Box 123 Watertown SD 57201 *

KELLOGG, MARY ALICE, writer, editor; b. Tucson, June 6, 1948; d. Bertram Cecil and Alice Katherine (Sawyer) K.;. BA cum laude in Journalism, U. Ariz., 1970. Editorial asst., reporter Newsweek, N.Y.C., 1970-71; Chgo. corr. Newsweek, 1971-73, San Francisco corr., 1973-76; assoc. editor Newsweek, N.Y.C., 1976-77; reporter, writer Newsweek Broadcasting Service, N.Y.C., 1972-77; corr. Sta. WCBS-TV, N.Y.C., 1977, freelance writer, editor and lectr., 1978—; sr. editor Parade Publs., Inc., N.Y.C., 1978-81; adj. prof. journalism NYU; lectr. in field. Author: Fast Track: The Superachievers and How They Make It to Early Success, Status and Power, 1978; contbr. articles to N.Y. Times, GQ, Travel & Leisure, Harper's Bazaar, Vis a Vis TWA Ambassador, New York mag., Glamour, TV Guide, others; columnist. Recipient Easter Seal Soc. Communications award, 1977, Lowell Thomas Travel Journalism award, 1987. Mem. Overseas Press Club, Women in Communications, Authors Guild, Soc. Am. Travel Writers, AFTRA, Am. Soc. Journalists and Authors, N.Y. Travel Writers, Sigma Delta Chi. Club: Dialogue (founder). Home and Office: 287 W 4th St Apt 6 New York NY 10014

KELLUM, CARMEN KAYE, apparel company executive; b. Greensburg, Pa., Oct. 15, 1952; d. Bruce Lowell and Mildred Louise (Montgomery) Taylor; m. John Douglas Kellum, Aug. 2, 1975 (div. May 1987). Student, MacMurray Coll., 1971-72, Elgin Community Coll.; AA, Coll. DuPage, 1975; BA with honors, Nat. Coll. Edn., 1978. Cert. tchr. Aide occupational therapy Mercy Ctr., Aurora, Ill., 1972-76; tchr. behavior disorders Lake Park High Sch., Roselle, Ill., 1978-80, Salk Pioneer Sch., Roselle, 1980-81; mgr. So-Fro Fabrics Stores, Chgo., Lombard and Joliet, Ill., 1981-84; offshore coordinator Florsheim Shoe Co., Chgo., 1984—. Mem. Orton Dyslexia Soc., Nat. Assn. Female Exec., Kappa Delta Pi. Lutheran. Home: 30 W 156 Wood Ct and Hwy 59 Bartlett IL 60103 Office: Florsheim Shoe Co 130 S Canal St Chicago IL 60606

KELLY, ANGELA MASTRACCHIO, nurse, medical facility administrator; b. Waterbury, Conn., Aug. 12, 1944; d. Louis Charles and Angeline Olga (Codianni) Mastracchio; m. Kenneth Francis Kelly, June 18, 1966; children: Brendan David, Glenn Evan. BS in Nursing, U. Conn., 1966; MEd, U. So. Calif., 1977; MS in Nursing Service Adminstrn., U. Hawaii, 1984. RN, Conn., Hawaii; cert. advanced adminstr. for nursing. Asst. head nurse Hillandale Hosp., Killeen, Tex., 1966-67; pub. health nurse Waterbury Vls. Nurse Assn., 1967-68; clin. researcher West Haven (Conn.) VA group dynamics, 1968-69; instr. psychiatric nursing Sch. of Nursing John's Hopkins U., Balt., 1969-70; nurse epidemiologist, supr. emergency room, primary care USPHS Indian Hosp., Lawton, Okla., 1971-72; sr. instr., supr. med., surgical, psychiatric services Cameron U., Lawton, 1972-73; dir. nursing edn., nurse epidemiologists Southwestern Clinic Hosp., Lawton, 1973-74; chief nursing edn. and tng. 121st Evac. Hosp., Seoul, Korea, 1974-75; sch. nurse and med. coordinator for handicapped children Frankfurt Elem. Sch. # 2, Fed. Republic Germany, 1975-78; dir. staff devel. Fauquier Hosp., Warrenton, Va., 1979-80; instr. nursing VA Med. Ctr., Leavenworth, Kans., 1980-81; clin. specialist Castle Med. Ctr., Kailua, Hawaii, 1981-83, clin. specialist, mgr. ICU/CCU, emergency room and acute care units, 1983-84; dir. patient care services and med. surgical nursing Sierra Med. Ctr. div. Nat. Med. Enterprises, El Paso, Tex., 1984-86; instr. nursing edn. Queen's Med. Ctr., Honolulu, 1986, dir. surgical div. nursing adminstrn., 1986—; ARC coordinator Darnell Army Hosp., Ft. Hood, Tex., 1966-67; clin. research specialist, instr. shock and trauma, U. Md., Balt., 1967; edni. advisor Parents of the Hearing Impaired, 1975-78, Med. Explorers' Group 97th Gen. Hosp., Frankfurt, 1975-78, Med. Explorers' Group, Va., 1979-80, regional emergency technicians, Warrenton (Va.) Vocat. Tech. Sch. of Nursing, 1979-80; bd. advisors Germanna Community Coll. Sch. Nursing, Shenandoah Coll. Sch. of Nursing, 1979-80; chmn. nursing mgmt. seminar Nursing Service Adminstrn., U. Hawaii, 1983; faculty mem., advisor, program planner and speaker Cansurmount and I Can Cope seminars Am. Cancer Soc., El Paso, 1984-86; publ. teaching tapes Am. Orgn. RNs Nat. Cong., 1986; chmn. Community AIDS Task Force; chair AIDS Community Care Team; mem. Dept. Health AIDS Adv. Team, Gov.'s Com. on AIDS. Speaker in field. Co-chmn. Frankfurt Spl. Olympics, 1978. Recipient community commendation award, Frankfurt; named Nurse of Day Okla. State Legislature, 1974. Mem. Am. Nurses Assn., Nat. League for Nursing, Hawaii League for Nursing (seminar co-chmn., adv. 1984), Am. Heart Assn., Hawaii Heart Assn. (mem. nurse edn. subcom., products chmn. 1983, speaker 1983), Am. Assn. Critical Care Nurses, Clin. Nurse Specialists' Interest Group, Emergency Room Mgrs. of Oahu (sec.), Nursing Leaders of the Pacific, Inservice Interest Group of Hawaii, Internat. Sch. Nurses Assn. (co-founder), Oncology Conf. for Nurses (adv., co-chmn. 1986)., Am. Hosp. Assn., Sigma Theta Tau. Roman Catholic. Lodge: Elua Allis. Home: 47-265D Hai Iwa St Kaneohe HI 96744 Office: The Queens Med Ctr Nursing Adminstrn 1301 Punchbowl Honolulu HI 96813

KELLY, ANNE C., retired city official; b. Buffalo, Mar. 6, 1916; d. John Patrick and Elizabeth Marie (Edwards) Donohue; m. Thomas Edward Kelly, Apr. 19, 1941; children—Maureen Anne, Michael Thomas, Edward John, Kevin Joseph, Theresa Elizabeth Callahan. Student SUNY-Buffalo. Tchr., St. Teresa Sch., Buffalo, 1956-64; clk. City of Buffalo, 1964, sec. to comptroller, 1967-70, council clk., 1970-76, sr. council clk., 1976-81. Mem. exec. bd. N.Y. Democratic Com., 1970—; vice chmn. Erie County Dem. Com., 1985—; past pres. Mercy League of Buffalo Mercy Hosp., Nash Ladies Guild, South Side Dem. Club; mem. Women for Downtown Buffalo. Roman Catholic. Clubs: Daus. of Erin, Nash Ladies. Lodge: KC (past pres. Nash guild). Home: 9 Haig Place #603 Dunedin FL 33528 also: 9 Haig Pl #603 Dunedin FL 34698

KELLY, BARBARA JEAN, political worker; b. Huntingdon, Tenn., Oct. 16, 1952; d. William Lloyd Sr. and Betty Jean (Umstead) K. Student, U. Tenn., Martin, 1970-71, Jackson State U., 1983-84. Dental office mgr. Huntingdon, 1971-84; field coordinator Albert Gore for U.S. Senate, Nashville, 1984; field rep. Sen. Gore, Jackson, Tenn., 1985—. Mem. adv. bd. Carroll County Vocat. Ctr., Huntingdon, 1982-83; vice-chmn. Huntingdon Beautification Com., 1981-82; pres. Carroll County Dem. Women, 1982-84; div. sec. Carroll County Dem. Exec. Com., 1984—. Named one of Outstanding Young Women of Am., 1981, 82, 84. Mem. Nat. Assn. Female Execs., Bus. and Profl. Women (pres. 1980-81, state program chair 1981, state legis. chair 1981-82, named Woman of Yr. 1984), Carroll County C. of C. Baptist. Club: U.S. Senate Staff (Washington). Home: PO Box 156 Jackson TN 38302 Office: US Senator Albert Gore Jr B-9 Federal Bldg 109 S Highland Jackson TN 38301

KELLY, BEVERLY JOY, managing editor; b. Madison, Tenn., Oct. 4, 1961; d. Larry Franklin and Helen Louise (Bartlell) K. BS, Southern Coll., 1984. Coordinator project Review and Herald Pub. Assn., Hagerstown, Md., 1984-85; editorial asst. Review and Herald Pub. Assn., Hagerstown, 1985-86, managing editor, 1986—. Writer, composer Give Yourself a Hand (United Way theme song), 1986. Seventh-day Adventist. Office: Review and Herald Pub Assn 55 W Oak Ridge Dr Hagerstown MD 21740

KELLY, BIRGITTE THERESA, interior designer; b. Montreal, Que., Can., Aug. 26, 1962; d. Kenneth Bliven and Margit Vibeke (Rasmussen) Gorton. BA, Mt. Vernon Coll., 1985. Owner Design Enterprises, Fairfield, Iowa, Bus. Mgmt. Ctr., Fairfield, Iowa. Mem. Am. Soc. Interior Designers, Inst. Bus. Designers. Office: Design Enterprises 200 W Lowe Fairfield IA 52556

KELLY, CECILIA MARY, artistic director, choreographer; b. Beckenham, England, Mar. 22, 1922; d. James Robert and Emily Monica (Hewitt) Ellis; came to U.S., 1946, naturalized, 1949; student Ballet Sch., LaScala Theatre, Milan, Italy, 1931-36; m. Eugene Joseph Kelly, May 22, 1945; children—Eugene James, Chinta Monica (Mrs. Alvin Tucker). Mem. LaScala Co., Milan, 1936-38; concerts in Far East, Bombay, Cape Town, Penang, Singapore, 1938-41; mem. Sadler's Wells Ballet, England, 1941-46; guest chr., lectr. N.H., 1946-54; master classes, Taiwan, 1955-59; founder, dir. ballet, Ark. Arts Center, Little Rock, 1960-63; founder, dir. Shreveport (La.) Symphony Ballet, 1966-72, El Dorado Civic Ballet (Ark.), 1967-70, Twin City Civic Ballet, Monroe, La., 1970-83, artistic dir. emeritus, 1983—; guest artist So. Methodist U., Dallas, 1968; artist in residence Shreveport Symphony Ballet, 1974-75. Chmn., Save the Whale Com. La.; benefit performances March of Dimes, 1954, 70. Recipient award Gov. Faubus. Mem. Nat. Soc. Arts and Letters (nat. dance chmn. 1970-72, 74-76, 84—, nat. career award chmn. 1976-83). Roman Catholic. Home: PO Box 171 Greenwood LA 71033

KELLY, CHRISTINE ANN, sales executive, educator; b. Bklyn., May 11, 1952; d. William John and Joan Ellen (Sullivan) K. AAS in Acctg., Kingsborough Community Coll., 1973; BS in Physical Edn., Bklyn. Coll., 1976. Cert. physical edn. tchr., N.Y. Head softball coach C.W. Post Coll., Greenvale, N.Y., 1979-84; sales mgr. Karnival Sports Ctr., Bklyn., 1984—; tchr. St. Edmund High Sch., Bklyn., 1979-81; adj. lectr. Kingsborough Community Coll., Bklyn., 1984—; head coach softball Empire State Games, N.Y., 1987—. Dir. holiday basketball tournament Tournament of Champions, N.Y., 1986—. Mem. Sporting Goods Mfg. Assn., N.Y. Bd. Officials for Women Sports. Democrat. Roman Catholic. Office: Karnival Sports Ctr 2505 65th St Brooklyn NY 11204

KELLY, DARLENE OKAMOTO, administrative manager; b. Denver, Dec. 6, 1944; d. Ricky Rikio and Minnie Misao (Okada) Yamamura; m. Steven T. Okamoto, Jan. 11, 1964 (div. May 1974); 1 son, Jeffrey; m. 2d, Ronald William Kelly, Oct. 29, 1983; 1 stepson, Sean. Cert. Ins. Inst. Am., 1977; B.A. in Mgmt., St. Mary's Coll., 1983. Tax cons. H. & R. Block, Oakland, Calif., 1971-72; office mgr. Multi-Fin., Oakland, 1972-75; v.p. Dealey, Renton & Assocs., Oakland, 1975-84; assoc. Levine Fin. Group, San Francisco, 1984-85; adminstrv. mgr. Storek & Storek/Old Oakland, Oakland, 1985—. Trustee Ind. Ins. Agts. & Brokers Found. for Edn. and Research, 1982-84; dir. Asian Community Mental Health Services, 1986—. Mem. Ind. Ins. Agts. and Brokers Calif. (chmn. edn. com. 1982-84), Oakland Assn. Ins. Agts. (dir. 1983-86), East Bay Assn. Ins. Women, A Central Place (dir. 1985—), Bus. Women's Expo. (dir. 1986—). Democrat. Buddhist. Club: Last Monday (council 1986—). Home: 4001 Midvale Ave Oakland CA 94602 Office: Storek & Storek/Old Oakland 484 9th St Oakland CA 94607

KELLY, DOROTHY ANN, college president; b. Bronx, N.Y., July 26, 1929; d. Walter David and Sarah (McCauley) K. B.A., Coll. New Rochelle, 1951; M.A., Catholic U., Washington, 1958; Ph.D., U. Notre Dame, 1970; Litt.D. (hon.), Mercy Coll., Dobbs Ferry, N.Y., 1976; LL.D. (hon.), Nazareth Coll. of Rochester, N.Y., 1979; D.H.L. (hon.), Coll. St. Rose, 1981, Manhattan Coll., 1979. Mem. faculty Coll. New Rochelle, N.Y., 1957—, chmn. dept. history, 1965-67, acad. dean, 1967-72, acting pres., 1970-71, pres., 1972—; trustee, vice chmn. Commn. Ind. Colls. and Univs. State of N.Y., 1977-78, chmn. bd. trustees, 1978-80, mem. govt. relations com., 1980—; chmn. Com. Higher Edn. Opportunity, 1977; mem. commr. edn. Adv. Council on Higher Edn. for N.Y. State, 1975-77, subcom. on postsecondary occupational edn., 1975-77; exec. com. Empire State Found. Ind. Liberal Arts Colls., 1975—, vice chmn., 1977-81, chmn., 1981—; trustee, mem. exec. com. Assn. Colls. and Univs. State of N.Y., 1976—; mem. exec. com. Assn. Colls. Mid-Hudson Area, 1976—, pres., 1979-81; mem. com. on purpose and identity Assn. Cath. Colls. and Univs., 1975-80; mem. Neylan Conf. steering com., 1978—, mem. bishops and pres. com., 1979—; mem. adv. council on fin. aid to students Office Edn., HEW, 1978—; chmn. Women's Coll. Coalition, 1981-83; trustee United Student Aid Funds, 1980—; chmn. govt. relations adv. com. Nat. Assn. Ind. Colls. and Univs., 1981-82, chair, 1987-88; mem. Westchester County Assn., 1980—, bd. dirs. 1985-87, vice chair elect. Mem. AAUP, Am. Hist. Assn., AAUW, Nat. Fedn. Bus. and Profl Women, Am. Assn. Higher Edn., Nat. Assembly Women Religious. Address: Coll New Rochelle New Rochelle NY 10801

KELLY, EILEEN PATRICIA, management educator; b. Steubenville, Ohio, Oct. 24, 1955; d. Edward Joseph and Mary Bernice (Cassidy) K. BS, Coll. Steubenville, 1978; MA, U. Cin., 1979, PhD, 1982. CPA, Pa., Ohio. Lectr. U. Cin., 1981-82; asst. prof. bus. Creighton U., Omaha, 1982-87, chmn. mgmt., mktg. and systems dept., 1986-88, assoc. prof., 1987-88, coordinator project Minerva, 1987-88; assoc. prof. La. State U., Shreveport, 1988—, chmn. dept. mgmt. and mktg., 1988—. Mem. Indsl. Relations Research Assn., Am. Arbitration Assn., Acad. Mgmt., Am. Soc. Personnel Adminstrs., Beta Gamma Sigma (faculty advisor 1985—). Roman Catholic. Office: La State U Coll Bus 8515 Youree Dr Shreveport LA 71115

KELLY, JOAN PATRONITE, urban planner, consultant; b. Lynwood, Calif., Dec. 10, 1954; d. James M. Sr. and Jane (Hallinan) Patronite; m. Eamon N. Kelly Jr., Sept. 24, 1949; children: Laurel Christine, Evan William. BA, U. Calif., Irvine, 1977; M of Urban Planning, Calif. Poly. U., 1983. Housing coordinator, planner City of Pamona, Calif., 1977-80; asst. project mgr. VTN Co., Irvine, 1980-84; sr. project mgr. Michael Brandman Assocs., Costa Mesa, Calif., 1984-86; regional planner Michael Brandman Assocs., Los Angeles, 1986—. Mem. Am. Inst. Cert. Planners, Am. Planning Assn., Assn. Environ. Planners, Nat. Assn. Female Execs. Democrat. Roman Catholic. Lodge: Soroptomists. Office: Michael Brandman Assocs 411 W 5th St #1010 Los Angeles CA 90013

KELLY, JOSEPHINE KAYE, social worker; b. Grand Rapids, Mich., May 30, 1944; d. Clark Everet Peterson and Dorothy Jane (Mudd) Schaefer; m. Raymond Luke Kelly, July 19, 1969; children: William Lawrence, Kenneth James. BA with honors, Grand Valley State Coll., 1967; postgrad., Western Mich. U., 1984—. Exec. dir. Voluntary Action Ctr., Grand Rapids, 1970-77; project coordinator Area Agy. on Aging, Grand Rapids, 1977-79; program coordinator Aquinas Coll., Grand Rapids, 1979-80; psychiat. social worker Kent Oaks Psychiat. Unit, Grand Rapids, 1980-87; continued care social worker St. Mary's Hosp., Grand Rapids, 1987—; co-owner Hidden Lake Farm, Conklin, 1969—; Registered social worker. Trustee Chester Twp., 1984—, mem. canteen services unit, 1984—; mem. planning bd. St. Mary's Hosp., Grand Rapids, 1981-82; mem. lay adv. bd. Cath. Info. Ctr., Grand Rapids, 1983-85, pres., 1984-85; pres. Council on Aging of Kent County, Grand Rapids, 1979-80, mem. 1977—; mem. transp. adv. commn. Coopersville (Mich.) Area Pub. Schs., 1977-81; sec. Conklin Food Coop., 1977-80; bd. dirs. Women's Resource Ctr., Grand Rapids, 1977-79, steering com., 1972-73. Mem. Am. Soc. Pub. Adminstrn., Am. Legion (aux.), Mich. Beefalo Breeders Assn. (sec./treas. 1982-84), Am. Beefalo World Registry, Vol. Mgmt. Assn. Western Mich. (founder, 1st pres. 1975-76), Conklin Brotherhood Assn. Republican. Roman Catholic. Home: 3616 Coolidge St Conklin MI 49403 Office: Continued Care St Mary's Health Services 200 Jefferson SE Grand Rapids MI 49503

KELLY, KAREN MARIE, computer company executive; b. Phila., Oct. 2, 1950; d. Timothy Joseph and Eileen Mae (Nolan) K. BA, Villanova U., 1972, MA, 1974. Systems engr. IBM, Phila., 1976-83, nat. acct. mgr., 1980-83; nat. product mgr. Unisys, Blue Bell, Pa., 1983—. Fellow Pub. Broadcasting System; mem. Sierra Club, Inst. Profl. Exec. Women, Wilderness Soc. Office: 890 Tasman Dr Milpitas CA 95035

KELLY, KATE, writer; b. Pueblo, Colo., Nov. 3, 1950; d. William Bret and Patricia Ruth (Ducy) K; m. George F. Schweitzer, Sept. 8, 1974; 2 children. BA, Smith Coll., 1973. Assoc. dir. CBS Radio Network, N.Y.C., 1973-76; pub. relations cons. Realty Hotels, N.Y.C., 1976-77; freelance writer N.Y.C., 1977—. Author: The Publicity Manual, 1980, How to Set Your Fees and Get Them, 1984, Organize Yourself, 1986; contbr. articles to profl. jours. and mags. Mem. Am. Soc. Journalists and Authors. Home and Office: 11 Rockwood Dr Larchmont NY 10538

KELLY, KATHLEEN MARY, sales professional; b. Bklyn., Feb. 21, 1959; d. Eugene and Mary Kathleen (Carron) K.; m. David Stanton Dolezal, June 22, 1985; 1 child, Lauren Sinead Dolezal. BS in Bus., BS in Liberal Arts, U. Oreg., 1982. Sales rep. Eastman Kodak Co., Portland, Oreg., 1982-86, dist. specialist, 1986, acct. rep., 1987—. Active Big Bros./Big Sister Program, Portland, Oreg., 1984. Mem. Assn. Info. and Image Mgmt. (treas. 1984-85), Assn. Record Mgrs. and Adminstrs., Nat. Assn. Female Execs. Democrat. Roman Catholic. Office: Eastman Kodak Co 5410 SW Macadam Ave Portland OR 97201

KELLY, KATHRYN ELIZABETH, toxicologist; b. Montreal, Mar. 10, 1958; d. Paul Brendan Jr. and Barbara Alden (Carter) K. AB, Stanford U., 1979; MPH, Columbia U., 1982, Dr.P.H., 1985. Environ. scientist Dames & Moore, White Plains, N.Y., 1979-80; environ. toxicologist Dames & Moore, Cranford, N.J., 1980-82; pres. Environ. Toxicology Internat., Inc., Seattle, 1985—. Speaker on toxicology and risk assessment Am. Coll. Toxicology; contbr. articles to profl. jours. Mem. Soc. Environ. Toxicology and Chemistry, Soc. Risk Analysis. Office: Environ Toxicology Internat Inc 600 Stewart St Suite 700 Seattle WA 98101

KELLY, LEONTINE T. C., clergywoman; b. Washington; d. David D. and Ila M. Turpeau; m. Gloster Current (div.); children—Angela, Gloster Jr.; m. James David Kelly (dec.); children—John David, Pamela. Student W.Va. State Coll.; grad. Va. Union U., 1960; M.Div., Union Theol. Sem., Richmond, Va., 1969. Formerly sch. tchr.; former pastor Galilee United Methodist Ch., Edwardsville, Va.; later mem. staff Va. Conf. Council on Ministries; pastor Asbury United Meth. Ch., Richmond, 1976-83; mem. nat. staff United Meth. Ch., Nashville, 1983-84; bishop Calif.-Nev. Conf., San Francisco, 1984-88. Office: United Meth Ch PO Box 467 San Francisco CA 94101 *

KELLY, LESLIE ANN, training and development consultant; b. Hammond, Ind., June 13, 1945; d. Philip C. and Esther A. (Lardie) K.; B.S., Northwestern U., 1967; M.S. summa cum laude, Ind. U., 1973; children: Christine Anna, Raymond Sutton Battey. Assoc. faculty dept. speech, theatre and communications Ind. U., Indpls., 1973-87 ; pres. Kelly & Assocs., tng. and devel. cons., Indpls., 1979—; adj. faculty MBA Sch. Ind. U., Indpls., 1987— ; mem. Ind. Bus. Adv. Council to SBA; chair Indpls. Chamber Tng. Adv. Bd. Indiana Del., mem. nat. rules com. White House Conf. on Small Bus., 1986. Named Ind. Women's Bus. Advocate of Yr., SBA, 1983. Mem. Am. Soc. for Tng. and Devel. (Nat. award for disting. contbn. to community and nation 1985), Am. Soc. for Personnel Adminstrs., Central States Speech Assn. (Outstanding Young Tchr. award 1971), Network of Women in Bus. (Bus. Woman of Yr. 1980), Nat. Assn. Women Bus. Owners (bd. dirs. 1985). Lodge: Rotary. Author: Negotiating Notebook, 1983; Successful Supervision, 1984; Productive Management, 1984; Sales Negotiating, 1985; editor: The Best of Sales and Marketing, 1986; contbg. author various manuals and handbooks on tech. report writing. Home: 6125 Graham Rd Indianapolis IN 46220 Office: 2625 N Meridian Suite 208 Indianapolis IN 46208

KELLY, MARILYN VERONICA, management consultant; b. Jersey City, Jan. 29, 1947; d. William Henry and Agnes (Greener) K. BA, Rutgers U., 1968; MA, Goddard Coll., 1980. Acting project leader RCA Corp. Staff, N.Y.C., 1968-70; systems analyst programmer Litton Ednl. Pub., N.Y.C., 1970-72; dept. mgr. mktg. stats. Melnor Industries, Moonachie, N.J., 1972-75; prin. Movement Therapy, Plainfield, N.J., 1980—; pvt. practice Plainfield, 1981—. Contbr. articles to profl. jours. Mem. N.Y. Acad. Scis., Internat. Transactional Assn., Orgn. Devel. Network.

KELLY, MATTIE CAROLINE MAY, business woman; b. Vernon, Fla., Mar. 12, 1912; d. William W. and Mary Alice (Russ) May; student Rollins Coll., 1944-46, 48-49; A.B., Fla. State U., 1952, postgrad., 1970-71; m. Coleman Lee Kelly, Mar. 26, 1932 (div. June 1971); children—Carnera Lee, Lila Bernarr, Imogene (Mrs. H.J. Toole), Carol Kelly Adams, Cecelia Kelly Sims; m. 2d, Paul Sims, July 13, 1973 (div. May 1979). Tchr. public schs., Fla., 1928-33, 37; pres. Kelly Boat Service, Inc., 1980—, Kelly Homes, Inc., Destin, Fla., to 1978; co-owner, trustee Coleman L. Kelly Trust; co-organizer, owner, pres. Radio Sta. WMMK-FM, Destin. Mem. Okaloosa County Democratic Com., 1958—, exec. adv. bd., 1956-72; mem. State Dem. Exec. Com., mem. adv. bd., 1966-70, del. nat. conv., 1968, 72. Bd. dirs. Destin Library, 1956—, Fla. League Arts, 1980-81; bd. dirs. Okaloosa County chpt. ARC, 1954-60, chmn., 1957-58; adv. bd. diversified coop. tng. Choctawhatchee High Sch., 1960—; camp counsellor Senior Hi, Camp Weed, 1964; patron Stagecrafters, Okaloosa Community Concert Assn.; Benefactor Ft. Walton Beach Ballet Assn., Symphony Assn.; sponsor Playground Mut. Concert Assn.; founder, promoter, supporter Mattie M. Kelly Fine Arts Center, Destin. Mem. coordinating council for arts Okaloosa-Walton Jr. Coll., 1965—, rep. to Fla. Arts Council, 1966—; patron Okaloosa County Symphony, Ft. Walton Beach Ballet Assn.; adv. bd. Okaloosa County Mental Health Assn., 1978—, Women's Theatre Workshop Okaloosa-Walton Jr. Coll., 1978—; chmn. Historic Sites Commn., Okaloosa-Walton. Recipient award ARC, 1960; award for arts for Northwest Fla., Gov. Fla., 1982; Gov.'s citation, 1983; Harmony award SPEBSQSA, 1983. Mem. Am. Camellia Soc., Nat. Writers Club, Geneal. Soc. Okaloosa County, N.Y. Bot. Gardens Club, Okaloosa County Concert Assn., Nat. Hist. Soc., Playground Poets Assn. (coordinator 1977—), Ft. Walton Beach C. of C. (edn. com., mem. host com.; Ross and Nell Marler Citizenship award 1982). Fla. Boatsmen's Assn. (sec. 1972—), Hist. Soc. Okaloosa and Walton Counties, Ft. Walton Beach Woman's Club (chmn. fine arts com. 1957-58), Woman's Club (v.p. 1958-59), Gulf Coast Dem. Women's Club, AAUW (charter, legis. com. 1971—), Assoc. Council Arts, Choctaw Bay Music Club. Mem. Protestant Episcopal Ch. (adminstr., supt. ch. sch. 1953-60, br. chmn. Christian edn. 1955-60, dist. chmn. Christian edn. 1958-61, asst. organist, tchr., del. adult conf. 1957, 59, del. religious TV programming workshop 1955-56; dist. v.p. 1961-64; pres. church-women Diocese Fla. 1965-68). Author: Songs and Sonnets From the Sea (poetry), 1964; donor land and funds for Mattie M. Kelly Fine Arts Center. Address: PO Box 425 Indian Bayou Destin FL 32541

KELLY, MAXINE ANN, property developer; b. Ft. Wayne, Ind., Aug. 14, 1931; d. Victor J. and Marguerite E. (Biebesheimer) Cramer; m. James Herbert Kelly, Oct. 4, 1968 (dec. Apr. 74). B.A., Northwestern U., 1956. Sec., Parry & Barns Law Offices, Ft. Wayne, 1951-52; trust sec. Lincoln Nat. Bank & Trust Co., 1956-58; sr. clerk stenographer div. Mental Health, Alaska Dept. Health, Anchorage, 1958-60; office mgr. Langdon Psychiat. Clinic, 1960-70; propr. A-1 Bookkeeping Service, 1974-75; ptnr. Gonder-Kelly Enterprises & A-is-A Constrn., Anchorage, 1975—; dir. Alaska Mental Health Assn., Anchorage, 1960-61. Pres., treas. Libertarian Party Anchorage, 1968-69, Alaska Libertarian Party, 1969-70. Mem. AAUW (life), Anchorage C. of C., Whittier Boat Owners Assn. (treas. 1980-84). Home and Office: 4000 Steven Dr Wasilla AK 99687

KELLY, PATRICIA SUE HAGGERTY, chemical company executive; b. Pitts., June 12, 1950; d. Bernard Anthony and Helen Rita (Pellegrini) Haggerty; student Duquesne U., 1968-69; BS with highest honors, W. Liberty State Coll., 1972; MBA magna cum laude, U. Pitts., 1974; m. Robert E. Kelly, Apr. 21, 1979 (div.). Sales clk. Gimbels Dept. Store, Pitts., 1969-70; supr. Mktg. Services Center, Pitts., 1973; market research analyst Koppers Co., Pitts., 1974-78; planning asso. Mobil Chem. Co., Pitts., 1978-82, sr. mktg. analyst, 1982-84; sr. mktg. analyst Valspar Corp., Pitts., 1984-85, bus. mgr., 1985—; tchr. indsl. mktg. research Carnegie-Mellon Grad. Bus. U., 1977-78; cons. A. O. Smith Co., Pitts. Nat. Bank, Darlington Clay Products div. Gen. Dynamics Bd. dirs., public notary animal care and welfare Soc. Prevention Cruelty to Animals, 1974—; adv. Explorers Program, 1974-78. Recipient Phi Chi Theta award U. Pitts. Grad. Sch. Bus., 1974. Mem. Assn. Time Share Users (sec.-treas.), Nat. Assn. Female Execs., Am. Mktg. Assn. (v.p. intercollegiate chpt.), Beta Gamma Sigma, Delta Mu Delta (sec.-treas.). Republican. Roman Catholic. Home: 1321 Great Oak Dr Pittsburgh PA 15220 Office: 2000 Westhall St Pittsburgh PA 15233

KELLY, ROCHELLE-LOUISE, marketing professional, clothing designer; b. Pueblo, Colo., July 29, 1961; d. John Russell and Georgina Frances (Woodward) K. BS, U. So. Colo., 1984. Assoc. brand mgr. Better Brands Atlanta, 1984-86; mktg. cons. Peachtree Mktg., Atlanta, 1986; young adult mktg. specialist Coffee Devel. Group, Denver, 1986—; designer, ptnr. KELYCO Western Wear, 1987—; cons. pub. relations, mktg. Nat. High Sch. Rodeo Assn., Denver, 1987—. Mem. Jr. League Denver. Home and Office: 10890 W Evans #2E Lakewood CO 80226

KELLY, SHANNON LYNN, stockbroker; b. Monterey, Calif., Sept. 10, 1956; d. Leonard Howard and Joni Dorothy (Twitchell) Higginbotham; m. Brian Andrew Kelly, Sept. 12, 1982. A.A., U. South Fla., 1974-76; B.A., U. Hawaii, 1979. Outer islands mgr. Gatliff Corp., Honolulu, 1979-81; stockbroker Paine Webber Jackson & Curtis, Honolulu, 1981—, also dir.; freelance poetry writer. Recipient Golden Poet award Am. Poetry Assn., 1987. Mem. Investment Soc. Hawaii (bd. dirs.). Republican, Honolulu Bd. Raltors.

KELLY, SHEILA SEYMOUR, public relations executive, political consultant; b. Bronxville, N.Y.; d. William Joseph and Jane (Seymour) K.; m. Robert Max Kaufman, 1959. BA magna cum laude, Syracuse U., 1949. Reporter Yonkers Herald Statesman, N.Y.C., 1950; editor Close Up column, Herald Tribune, N.Y.C., 1950-52; writer, producer Sta. WNBC-TV, N.Y.C., 1953-54; media cons. to Senator Jacobs K. Javits, Washington, 1956-74; press sec. Senator Jacobs K. Javits, N.Y.C., 1958-60; v.p. Harshe Rotman Druck, N.Y.C., 1961-72; founder, pres. VOTES, Inc., N.Y.C., 1973-75; v.p. Doremus Pub. Relations, N.Y.C., 1976-86, sr. v.p., 1987—. Mem. Pub. Relations Soc. Am., Women Execs. Pub. Relations, WEPR Found. (v.p. 1984-85), Women Execs. Pub. Relations (pres. 1987-88). Republican. Office: Doremus Pub Relations 120 Broadway New York NY 10271

KELLY, SHIRLEY LOUISE, therapeutic recreation executive; b. Harrisburg, Pa., Jan. 23, 1929; d. Alfred Peters and Anna Elizabeth (Shutt) Lego; m. Robert Leonard Kelly, Mar. 28, 1948; children—Donna, Robert E., Rick, Mark, Debra. Student pub. schs., Harrisburg. Nurses aide Bethany Village Retirement Ctr., 1967-72; dir. activities Bethany Village, 1972—. Mem. Pa. Therapeutic Recreation Soc., Nat. Remotivation Technique Orgn. (cert. instr., cons. Keystone chpt. 1978—). Methodist. Office: Bethany Village Retirement Ctr 325 Wesley Dr Mechanicsburg PA 17019

KELLY, SUZANNE WOODWARD, management consultant, trainer; b. Wichita, Kans., Sept. 10, 1946; d. Wallace Wayne and Julianne (Seitz) Woodward; m. Glenn Lochten Kelly, Jan. 27, 1967; children: Scott Lochten, Brian Woodward, Matthew MacFerren. BS in Nursing, U. Colo., Denver, 1969, MS in Bus. Administn., 1985. Reg. nurse. Vis. nurse Denver Vis. Nurses Assn., 1969; founder, childbirth educator Childbirth and Parenting Assn. and Co., Denver, 1969-80; mgmt. cons. Susan Kelly and Assocs., Englewood, Colo., 1980—; adj. prof. Met. State Coll., Denver, 1980, 85; cons., trainer, bd. dirs., Tech. Assistance Ctr., 1980—. Pres. Cherry Hills Rancho Water and Sewer Dist., Englewood 1986—; bd. dirs., pres. Arapahoe County Med. Aux., Englewood pres. 1970-84, bd. dirs. Porter Meml. Hosp. Found., 1979-85; v.p. Jr. League Denver, 1975-87; mem. Leadership Denver, 1982—. Mem. Am. Soc. Training & Devel., Inst. Mgmt. Cons. Presbyterian. Office: 17 Martin Ln Englewood CO 80110

KELMAN, JUDITH ANN, freelance writer; b. N.Y.C., Oct. 21, 1945; d. George Joseph and Flora (Underberg) Edelstein; m. Edward Michael Kelman, June 28, 1970; children—Matthew Steven, Joshua Kenneth. B.S., Cornell U., 1967; M.A. (Fed. fellow), NYU, 1968; M.S., So. Conn. State Coll., 1977. Tchr. educable mentally handicapped Valley Stream (N.Y.) Pub. Schs., 1968-71; recreation supr. Camp A.N.C.H.O.R., extracurricular activities for handicapped children, Town of Hempstead, (N.Y.), 1968-71; speech pathologist Greenwich (Conn.) public schs.; freelance writer, 1981—. Author: (novel) Prime Evil, 1986, Where Shadows Fall, 1987, While Angels Sleep, 1988; contbg. author N.Y. Times, Redbook, Bride's, Glamour, Seventeen, others. Bd. dirs. Stamford (Conn.) Aid for Retarded, 1973-74; founder Touch, Inc., orgn. for parents of handicapped, Stamford, 1975, pres., 1975-76. Mem. Am. Soc. Journalists and Authors, Mystery Writers Am., Author's Guild, Mystery Writers Am. Democrat. Jewish. Club: Cornell of Fairfield County (Conn.) (sec. 1979—). Home: 60 Thornwood Rd Stamford CT 06903

KELSCH, BETTY BEALL, nurse, consultant; b. Elgin, Ill., Mar. 2, 1935; d. John G. and Opal V. (Strube) Beall; m. Buddy D. Kelsch, Dec. 27, 1956 (div. 1974); children: John William, Cynthia Lynn, Michael Scott, Robert Duane. BS in Nursing, U. Mich., 1957, MS, 1981. RN. Charge nurse Killeen (Tex.) Gen. Hosp., 1957-58; instr. obstet. nursing St. Laurence Sch. Nursing, Lansing, 1960-63; staff nurse med., surg. U. Mich. Med. Ctr., Ann Arbor, 1958-60, 1963-65, staff nurse psychiatry, 1965-73, asst. head nurse psychiatry, 1973-74, head nurse psychiatry, 1974-85, staff assoc., 1985—; cons. in field. Mem. Am. Nurses Assn., Mich. Nurses Assn., Sigma Theta Tau. Home: 1715 Saunders Crescent Ann Arbor MI 48103

KELSEY, KATHRYN KENNY, sales representative; b. Coaldale, Pa., Apr. 10, 1955; d. John Francis and Hilda Marie (Schweitzer) Kenny; m. Robert Allen Kelsey, Aug. 5, 1981. BS, Pa. State U., 1977. Sales rep. Allied-Signal Corp., Morristown, N.J., 1977—. NSF grantee, 1975-77. Republican. Lutheran. Home: 601 Clebud Dr Euless TX 76040

KELSH, KAREN TERESA, sales executive; b. White Plains, N.Y., Oct. 10, 1963; d. John Joseph Kelsh and Leila Jane (Nichols) Christman. AA, Gulf Coast Community Coll., 1984; BS in Fashion Mdse., Fla. State U., 1985. Store mgr. Dairy Queen, Panama City Beach, Fla., 1979-83; asst. mgr. Ice Cream Circus, Panama City Beach, 1983; night mgr. Surf Line Shirts, Panama City Beach, 1984; intern Jordan Marsh, Boca Raton, Fla., 1985; exec. trainee Jordan Marsh, Orlando, Fla., 1986; area sales mgr. Jordan Marsh, Altamonte Springs, Fla., 1986—. Mem. Nat. Assn. Female Execs. Republican. Roman Catholic. Home: 275 Cranes Roost Blvd #814 Altamonte Springs FL 32701 Office: Jordon Marsh 451 E Altamonte Dr Altamonte FL 32701

KELSO, LINDA EVELYN, communications executive; b. St. Marys, Pa., Apr. 12, 1936; d. James Allen and Helen Elizabeth (Roher) Hanes; m. Neil Michael Kelso, Apr. 25, 1964 (div. July 1984); children: Douglas James, Aleta Ruth. Grad. high sch. Rating clk. Nationwide Ins., Harrisburg and Butler, Pa.; claims clk. Continental Ins. Cos., Pitts. and San Francisco, 1957-63; office mgr. Beaudry Adjusting, San Francisco, 1963-64; asst. acctg. editor Ga.-Pacific Corp., Portland, Oreg., 1976-82; project developer Dunn-Rowan, Inc., Vancouver, Wash., 1983-85; mgr. human resources devel. Dunn-Rowan, Inc., Birmingham, Ala., 1985-86; sr. project mgr. Dunn-Rowan, Inc., Birmingham, 1986—, sec., bd. dirs., 1985—; freelance writer, Portland, 1977-84, 88—, cons. 1988—; corp. sec., bd. dirs. Dunn-Rowan, Inc., Birmingham, 1985—. Author: Mt. St. Helens-The First 60 Days, 1980, Mt. St. Helens and Other Volcanoes of the West, 1980. Officer, editor Parents Coop. Preschs.Oreg., 1969-72; various positions Wilcox and Glenhaven PTA's, Portland, 1971-76; leader Cub Scouts and Girl Scouts U.S., Portland, 1972-77; vol. Oreg. Mus. Sci. and Industry, Portland, 1972-84. Mem. Oreg. Writers Colony, Mensa.

KEMENYFFY, SUSAN HALE, ceramicist, printmaker; b. Springfield, Mass., Oct. 4, 1941; d. Stuart Dwight and Marjorie (Stebbins) Hale; m. Steven Kemenyffy, Oct. 5, 1968; 1 child, Maya Hale. BFA, Syracuse U., 1963; MA, U. Iowa, 1966, MFA, 1967. Instr. art Midwestern U., Wichita Falls, Tex., 1967-68, U. Wis., Whitewater, 1968-69; asst. prof. art Mercyhurst Coll., Erie, Pa., 1974-78; studio artist McKean, Pa., 1978—; vis. lectr. Escuela Madrilena de Ceramica de la Moncloa, Madrid, 1985, Edinburgh (Scotland) Coll. Art, 1985, South Glamorgan Inst. Higher Edn., Cardiff, Wales, 1985, New Zealand Soc. Potters, Wellington, 1988, "A Festival of Ceramics" Craftsman Potter Assn., Newark, Nottinghamshire, Eng., 1988, and through the U.S. and Can. Works exhibited in Galveston (Tex.) Art Ctr., 1984, Am. Craft Mus. II, N.Y.C., 1984, Carnegie-Mellon U., Pitts., 1985, Nat. Council Edn. Ceramic Arts, San Antonio, 1986, Palo Alto (Calif.), Cultural Ctr., 1986, new Zealand Acad. Fine Arts., Wellington, Rufford Craft Ctr., Newark, Nottinghamshire, Eng., 1988, "Pattern & Decoration Contemporary Approaches", "Recent Acquisitions of Sculpture", Cin. Art. Mus., 1986, "Clay", Contemporary Crafts, Portland, Ofeg., Worcester Craft ctr., Ma., 1988. NEA fellow, 1973; recipient prizes in invitational and juried clay exhibs. Mem. Nat. Council Edn. Ceramic Arts, Associated Artists Pitts., Erie Art Mus. (pres. 1985-88), Craftsman Guild Pitts. Home and Studio: 4570 Old State Rd McKean PA 16426

KEMMERER, MARIANN HOHE, marketing analyst; b. Allentown, Pa., May 24, 1963; d. Donald George and Ann May (Pfeiffer) H. BBA, Bucknell U., 1985. Asst. buyer Abraham & Strauss, Inc., Bklyn., 1985-86; mktg. asst. Meeco Inc., Warrington, Pa., 1986-88; mktg. analyst The Franklin Mint, Franklin Ctr., Pa., 1988—; mgmt. teaching asst. Bucknell U., 1983-85. Mem. Nat. Assn. Female Execs., Nat. Council Tchrs. Eng. (award), Delta Mu Delta. Republican. Moravian. Home: 400 E DeKalb Pike King of Prussia PA 19406

KEMMERER, SHARON JEAN, computer specialist; b. Sellersville, Pa., Apr. 11, 1956; d. John Mussleman and Esther Jone (Landis) K. BS, Shippensburg U., 1978; MBA, Marymount Coll., 1982. Mgmt. analyst Navy Internat. Logistics, Phila., 1978-81; computer systems analyst Navy Supply Systems Commn., Crystal City, Va., 1981-86; computer specialist Nat. Bur. Standards, Gaithersburg, Md., 1986—; mem. com. Fed. Women's Program. Contbr. articles, poetry to newspapers. Deacon Alexandria (Va.) Ch., 1985-86, v.p. council, 1985; moderator Lung Assn., Fairfax, Va., 1986; vol. Project Heart, Washington, 1986-87. Mem. Nat. Assn. Female Execs. Lutheran. Office: Nat Bur Standards NBS/ICST Gaithersburg MD 20899

KEMP, BETTY RUTH, librarian; b. Tishomingo, Okla., May 5, 1930; d. Raymond Herrell and Mamie Melvina (Hughes) K.; B.A.L.S., U. Okla., 1952; M.S., Fla. State U., 1965. Extramural loan librarian U. Tex., Austin, 1952-55; librarian lit. and history dept. Dallas Public Library, 1955-56, head Oaklawn Br., 1956-60, head Walnut Hill Br., 1960-64; dir. Cherokee Regional Library, LaFayette, Ga., 1965-74; dir. Lee County Library, hdqrs. Lee-Itawamba Library System, Tupelo, Miss., 1975—; bd. library commrs. State of Miss., 1979-83, chmn., 1979-80. Active LWV, United Meth. Women. Mem. ALA, Southeastern Library Assn. (sec. pub. library sect. 1987-88), Miss. Library Assn., Beta Phi Mu. Democrat. Club: AAUW. Home: 2112 President Tupelo MS 38801 Office: 219 Madison Tupelo MS 38801

KEMP, JUNE, employment specialist, educator; b. Homestead, Pa., Dec. 16, 1933; d. Patrick H. and Gladys Naomi (Pifer) Cloherty; adopted d. William P. and Grace Kemp; m. Raymond Vargay, Apr. 21, 1953 (div. 1965); 1 child, Rose Marie. B.A. in Sociology, Fla. Internat. U., 1976, B.A. in Religion, 1978, M.P.A., 1980. Sec. U.S. Air Force, various bases, 1959-84; adj. prof. Miami-Dade Community Coll., Fla., 1980-82; equal employment opportunity staffing specialist U.S. Air Force, Homestead AFB, Fla., 1984—. Leader, cons. Girl Scouts U.S.A., 1952-83; lay asst. St. Peter's Luth. Ch., Miami, Sunday sch. tchr., 1974-85, mem. ch. council, women's group, 1988—; bd. dirs. Dade Hire the Handicapped Com., 1985-86. Recipient Outstanding Employee of Yr. award Homestead AFB, 1980, 84 (lectr. 1986—); Fed. Employee of Yr. award Fed. Exec. Bd., 1984. Mem. Am. Soc. Pub. Adminstrn., Am. Bus. Women's Assn. (community Service award 1982), AAUW, Nat. Assn. Retired Fed. Employees, Federally Employed Women, Air Force Assn., Nat. Assn. Female Execs., Irish Soc. of South Fla., Fla. Internat. U. Alumni Assn. (chmn. profl. devel., 1987—, mem. long range planning com.). Phi Lambda Pi. Republican. Lutheran. Club: Toastmasters. Lodge: Lions. Avocation: Irish history. Home: 11350 SW 45th St Miami FL 33165

KEMP, PEGGY SLOAN, educator, lawyer; b. Shepherdsville, Ky., June 5, 1948; d. Samuel Robert Sloan and Ernestine Masden; m. Kenneth Alfred Kemp, July 29, 1976; children—Kenneth N., Alfred C., Paul L. B.A., Berea Coll., 1969; postgrad. U. Mass. 1971-72; J.D., Harvard U., 1980. Bar: Mass. 1982. Tchr., Lewenberg Middle Sch., Boston, 1971-80; pvt. practice law, Cambridge, Mass., 1982—; head dept. history Boston Latin Sch., 1983—. Boston Edison scholar, 1986. Mem. ABA, Mass. Bar Assn., Mass. Black Women's Attys. Address: 59 Rindge Ave Cambridge MA 02140

KEMP, SUZANNE LEPPART, educator, clubwoman; b. N.Y.C., Dec. 28, 1929; d. John Culver and Eleanor (Buxton) Leppart; m. Ralph Clinton Kemp, Apr. 4, 1953; children—Valerie Gale, Sandra Lynn, John Maynard, Renee Alison. Grad. Ogontz Jr. Coll., 1949; B.S., U. Md., 1952. Elem. sch. tchr. Mem. Nat. Soc. Women Descs. of Ancient and Hon. Arty. Co., Nat. Soc. Daus. of Founders and Patriots of Am. (corr. sec.), Nat. Soc. Sons and Daus. of Pilgrims, Nat. Soc. U.S. Daus. of 1812 (chpt. organizing pres. 1977-79, state 2d v.p., chpt. v.p. 1979—), Nat. Soc. New Eng. Women (colony pres. 1978-80, Nat. Soc. Colonial Dames XVII Century (state chmn. heraldry and coats of arms 1977-79), Nat. Soc. D.A.R. (chpt. regent 1970-73, chpt. v.p., Md. soc. chmn. transp. 1976-79), Md. State Officers Club, Md. Hist. Soc., Friends of Animals, Defenders of Animal Rights Inc., U. Md. Alumni, English Speaking Union, Star Spangled Banner Flag House Assn., Potter-Balt. Clayworks, Balt. Mus. Art, Walters Art Gallery, Dames of the Court of Honor, Kappa Delta Alumni. Clubs: Baltimore Country; Towson; Lago Mar (Ft. Lauderdale, Fla.); Roland Park Women's. Editor; The Spinning Wheel, 1973-76. Home: 1206 Doves Cove Rd Towson MD 21204

KEMPCZINSKA, BARBARA ANN, health care planner; b. Bklyn., Apr. 16, 1944; d. Anthony and Irene (Kaczorek) K. BA, St. Joseph's Coll., 1964; MPH, U. Mich., 1971. Peace corps vol. Bolivia, 1964-66; social worker N.Y.C. Dept. Social Services, 1967-68; asst. dir. N.Y.C. Urban Corps., 1969-70; sr. health program planner N.Y.C. Health and Hosp. Corp., 1972-77; assoc. dir. N.J. Found. Health Care Eval., Lawrenceville, N.J., 1977-80; health care adminstrn. faculty St. Mary's Coll., Moraga, Calif., 1980—; sr. planning analyst Alameda/Contra Costa Health Services Assn., Oakland, Calif., 1982-85; cons. Alameda County Health Dept., Oakland, 1985-86; contract mgr. Blue Cross Calif., Oakland, 1986—. Mem. Am. Pub. Health Assn., Home Health Care Agy. (bd. dirs. 1986-87). Home: 4441 Montgomery St Oakland CA 94610

KEMPER, DORLA DEAN (EATON), real estate broker; b. Calhoun, Mo., Sept. 10, 1929; d. Paul McVey and Jesse Lee (McCombs) Eaton; student William Woods Coll., 1947-48; B.S. in Edn., Central Mo. State U., 1952; m. Charles K. Kemper, Mar. 1, 1951; children—Kevin Keil, Kara Lee. Tchr. pub. schs., Twin Falls, Idaho, 1950-51, Mission, Kans., 1952-53, Burbank, Calif., 1953-57; real estate saleswoman Minn., 1967-68, Calif., 1971-73; Deanie Kemper, Realtor (name changed to Deanie Kemper, Inc. Real Estate Brokerage 1976), Loomis, Calif., 1974-76, pres., 1976—, also dir. Pres., Battle Creek Park Elem. Sch. PTA, St. Paul, 1966-67; mem. Placer County (Calif.) Bicentennial Commn., 1976; mem. Sierra Coll. Adv. Com., 1981—. Named to Million Dollar Club (lifetime) Sacramento and Placer County bds. realtors, 1978; designated Grad. Realtors Inst., Cert. Residential Specialist. Mem. Nat., Calif. assns. realtors, Placer County (mem. profl. standards com.) bds. realtors, DAR (chpt. regent 1971-73, organizing chpt. regent 1977—, dist. dir. 1978-80, state registrar Calif. 1980-82, state vice regent 1982-84, state regent 1984-86, nat. resolutions com.); nat. recording sec. gen. NSDAR, DAR (nat. chmn. units overseas 1983-86). Republican. Mem. Christian Ch. Clubs: Hidden Valley Women's (pres. Loomis club 1970-71, recording sec. gen. 1986—), Auburn Travel Study (pres. 1979). Home: 8165 Morningside Dr Loomis CA 95650

KEMPER, MARLYN J., information scientist; b. Balt., Mar. 26, 1943; d. Louis and Augusta Louise (Jacobs) Janofsky; m. Bennett I. Kemper, Aug. 1, 1965; children—Alex Randall, Gari Hament, Jason Myles. B.A., Finch Coll., 1964; M.A. in Anthropology, Temple U., Phila., 1970; M.A. in Library Sci., U. S. Fla., 1983; D. in Info. Sci., Nova U., 1986. Dir., Hist. Broward County Preservation Bd., Hollywood, Fla., 1979-87; automated systems librarian Broward County Main Library, Ft. Lauderdale, Fla., 1983-86; asst. prof., dir. info. sci. doctoral program Nova U., Ft. Lauderdale, 1987—. Pub. info. officer Broward County Hist. Commn., 1975-79. Vice chmn. Broward County Library Adv. Bd., 1987—. Recipient Judge L. Clayton Nance award, 1977; Broward County Hist. Commn. award, 1979. Mem. ALA, IEEE, Am. Soc. for Info. Sci., Spl. Libraries Assn., Assn. Computing Machinery, Info. Industry Assn., Beta Phi Mu, Phi Kappa Phi . Author: A Comprehensive Documented History of the City of Pompano Beach, 1982 A Comprehensive History of Dania 1983, Hallandale, 1984, Deerfield Beach, 1985, Plantation, 1986, Davie, 1987, Networking: Choosing A Lan Path to Interconnection, 1987, A Comprehensive History of Davie, 1987; author weekly columns Ft. Lauderdale News, 1975-76, 77-79; contbr. articles to Managing Micro-computer Collections and Microcomputer Environment: Management Issues and articles to profl. jours. Vice chmn. Broward County Library Home: 2845 NE

35th St Fort Lauderdale FL 33306 Office: Nova U Info Sci Dept Parker Bldg 3301 College Ave Fort Lauderdale FL 33314

KEMPER, PATRICIA LOUISE, financial specialist; b. Dayton, Ohio, Sept. 2, 1948; d. Earl Richard and Elizabeth Ruth (Jacobs) Clark; m. Wendell R. Kemper, May 7, 1977 (div. July 1981); 1 child, Laura Elizabeth. Student, Wright State U., 1966-68. With Air Force Avionics Lab., Wright-Patterson AFB, Ohio, 1970-77, program analyst reconnaissance and weapon delivery div., 1977-82; budget analyst Air Force Wright Aero. Labs., Wright-Patterson AFB, 1982; budget analyst Ramjet engine div. Aero. Propulsion Lab., Wright-Patterson AFB, 1982-84; fin. specialist MANTECH div. Air Force Materials Lab., Wright-Patterson AFB, Ohio, 1984-87; budget analyst F-15 System Program Office, Wright-Patterson AFB, Ohio, 1987—; facilities chair Am. Soc. Mil. Comptrollers Profl. Devel. Inst. V, Dayton, 1984-85; developer Air Force Mfg. Tech. Info. System, Wright-Patterson AFB, 1985—. Pres. Kids, Inc. Coop. Pre-Sch. and Day Care, Dayton, 1982-84. Mem. Nat. Assn. Female Execs., Nat. Fedn. Federal Employees, Am. Soc. Mil. Comptrollers (lab. publicity chair aviation chpt. 1985-87). Democrat. Roman Catholic.

KEMPF, MARTINE, voice control device manufacturing company executive; b. Strasbourg, France, Dec. 12, 1958; came to U.S., 1985; d. Jean-Pierre and Brigitte Marguerite (Klockenbring) K. Student in Astronomy, Friedrich Wilhelm U., Bonn, Fed. Republic of Germany, 1981-83. Owner, mgr. Kempf, Sunnyvale, Calif., 1985—. Inventor Comeldir Multiplex Handicapped Driving Systems (Goldenes Lenkrad Axel Springer Verlag 1981), Katalavox speech recognition control system (Oscar, World Almanac Inventions 1984, Prix Grand Siecle, Comite Couronne Francaise 1985). Recipient Medal for Service to Humanity Spinal Cord Soc., 1986; street named in honor in Dossenheim-Kochersberg, Alsace, France, 1987; named Citizen of Honor City of Dossenheim-Kochersberg, 1985. Home: 655 S Fair Oaks Ave Apt B-3-3 Sunnyvale CA 94086 Office: Kempf 1080 E Duane Ave Suite E Sunnyvale CA 94086

KEMPF, PATTI HEBERT, cultural organization administrator, real estate agent; b. Houma, La., Oct. 3, 1950; d. Patrick Raymond and Gloria (Martin) Hebert; m. John Fredrick Jordan Kempf, Feb. 6, 1943; children: Doty, Ariel, Marisa. Student, Gulf Area Tech. Sch., Abbeville, La., 1970, Charity Hosp. Nursing Sch., New Orleans, 1973; AB, U. La., Lafayette, 1983. Lic. practical nurse, 1970; RN, 1983. Office mgr. Dr. Falgoust, Abbeville, La., 1970-71; oncology nurse South Balt. Gen. Hosp., 1971-72; obstet. nurse Charity Hosp., New Orleans, 1973-75; owner, mgr. Exquisite Delights, Inc., Opelousas, La., 1976-80; exec. dir. St. Landry Arts Assn., Opelousas, 1981—; real estate agt. Andrus, Leger & Wilson, Opelousas, 1984-87; cons. regional arts AAC, Lafayette, La., 1984-85; treas. La. Assn. Arts Educators, Baton Rouge, 1984-85; mem. La. State Arts Council, Baton Rouge, 1985-87. Chmn. Acad. Excellence Honor Card, Opelousas, 1985-87; bd. dirs. Jenn Lafite Acadian Cultural Ctr.; adv. bd. Opelousas Community Cancer Ctr.; active fin. com. to elect Morgan Goudeau to 8th dist. Congress, 1986; v.p. La. Fedn. Dem. Women, Baton Rouge, 1986, St. Landry Fedn. Dem. Women, 1987; Clk. of Ct. St. Landry Parish, 1987—. Named Friend of Edn. St. Landry Assn. Tchrs., 1984, one of Outstanding La. Women La. Women's Health Found., 1987. Mem. Nat. Assn. Master Appraisers, Opelousas Indsl. Devel. Corp., Opelousas-St. Landry C. of C. (woman of yr. award 1985), Opelousas Med. Aux. Democrat. Episcopalian. Club: Opelousas Women's.

KEMPIS, JANET T., hospital executive; b. Kawit, Cavite, The Philippines, Sept. 21, 1944; came to U.S., 1979; d. Isidro A. Toledo and Ursula Fajardo; m. Richard A. Kempis, Jan. 6, 1965 (div. 1970); children: Joyce, Jenny, Denise. BSc, Far Eastern U., Manila, 1964; MPA, U. San Francisco, 1987, postgrad., 1987—. Internal auditor Philippine Airlines, Manila, 1968-70; internal auditor Sarmiento Internat., Manila, 1970-73, pres., 1973-77; adminstrn., fin. mgr. Pacific Woodworks Internat. Inc., Manila, 1977-79; health care billing clk. Laguna Honda Hosp., San Francisco, 1980-84, patient accounts supr., 1984-87; dir. patient acctg. French Hosp. Med. Ctr., San Francisco, 1987—. Vol. Freewheelers, San Francisco; pastoral aide Laguna Honda Hosp. Fellow Healthcare Fin. Mgmt. Assn., Nat. Assn. Female Execs.; mem. U. San Francisco Alumni Assn., Notarial Assn. Calif.

KEMPSTER, LINDA SUE, engineer; b. Washington, Jan. 3, 1950; d. Joseph Murray and Alberta C. (Cross) Decker; m. Mark Andrew Kempster, July 3, 1976. BSBA, Ariz. State U., 1972; MSSM, U. So. Calif., 1984. Casualty claims adjustor Allstate Ins., Tucson, 1972-76; contract programmer EF McDonald/Gen. Motors, Dayton, Ohio, 1977-78; sr. tech. writer Nat. Cash Register, Dayton, 1978-80; systems analyst Internat. Computing Co., Dayton, 1980-81; fin. systems analyst Northrop Aircraft Div., Hawthorne, Calif., 1981-85; optical disk cons. S Systems Corp., Inglewood, Calif., 1985; engr. Computer Tech. Assocs., Lanham, Md., 1986—. Mem. Internat. Info. Mgmt. Congress, Assn. for Info. and Image Mgmt., Internat. Soc. Optical Engring. Republican. Methodist. Office: Computer Tech Assocs 7501 Forbes Blvd Suite 201 Lanham MD 20706

KEMSLEY, SANDRA LEE, director of engineering, software consultant; b. Toronto, Ont., Can., Sept. 2, 1960; d. Donald Herbert and Helen Jean (McCaw) K. B of Applied Sci. in Engring., U. Waterloo, 1984. Registered profl. engr., Ont. Project mgr. PCI Inc., Toronto, Ont., 1984-87; dir. engring., chief exec. officer Software Metaconcepts Inc., Toronto, Ont., 1987—. Mem. Assn. Profl. Engrs. of Ont., Inst. Elec. and Electronic Engrs., Urban and Regional Info. Systems Assn. Office: Software Metaconcepts Inc, 1055 Bay St Suite 1204, Toronto Can. M5S 3A3

KENDA, JUANITA ECHEVERRIA KENDA, artist, educator; b. Tarentum, Pa., Nov. 12, 1922; d. Carlos Porfirio and Jane Amelia (Gummert) Echeverria; m. William Kenda, Aug. 18, 1940; children: Linda Jane, Carlos Paul, William Porfirio. Student, Stephens Coll., 1940-41, Art Students' League, N.Y.C., 1941-42; BFA, Temple U. and Tyler Art Sch., 1945; student, U. Hawaii, 1969-72. Instr. Phila. Mus. Art, 1940-43, Sr. Acad., Punahoo Sch., Honolulu, 1948-49; dir. art edn. Hawaii Dept. Edn., Honolulu, 1952-60; head, creative art sect. Honolulu Acad. Arts, Honolulu, 1958-63; community relations officer, Eastwest Ctr. U. Hawaii, Honolulu, 1967-70; pres. Nat. Soc. Arts and Letters, Downtown Gallery, Honolulu, 1969-76, Am. Women's Club, Asuncion, Paraguay, 1977-79; trustee Tennant Found., Honolulu, 1984—. One woman exhibitions include: Duncan Gallery, N.Y., Da Vinci Gallery, Phila., Downtown Gallery, Honolulu; represented in collections of pres. of Mex., many others. bd. dirs. Hawaii Art Council, Honolulu, 1984—. Mem. Hawaii Artist's League (pres. 1984—), Am. Assn. of Museums, Internat. Council of Museums, PEO, Allentown Art Mus., Peabody Mus.; bd. dirs. Hawaii Art Council, Honolulu Acad. Arts. Republican. Episcopalian. Clubs: Oahu Country (Honolulu), Plaza (Honolulu). Home: 3708 Lurline Dr Honolulu HI 96816

KENDALL, DOLORES DIANE PISAPIA, artist, author, marketing executive; b. Newark, N.J., June 1, 1946; d. Dominick Pisapia and Ann Fanfone Pisapia Kendall. Grad. Berkeley Bus. Coll., East Orange, N.J., 1965; postgrad. Middlesex County Coll., Edison, N.J., 1966-67, Rutgers U., 1967-69, Todd Butler Art Workshop, Edison, 1964-74, Art Inst. Boston, 1976, Graham Art Studio, Boston, 1975-77, Sch. Visual Arts, N.Y.C., 1978, NYU, 1977, Advt. Club N.Y., 1978. Proofreader, supr. N.J. State Diagnostic Ctr., Menlo Park, N.J., 1965-75; apprentice, instr. Graham Art Studio, Boston, 1975-77; dir. direct mktg. Boardroom Reports Inc., N.Y.C., 1977-82; pres., chief operating officer Roman Managed Lists, N.Y.C., 1982; dir. direct mktg. Mal Dunn Assocs., N.Y.C., 1983; dir. lists and card deck mgmt. Warren, Gorham & Lamont Inc., N.Y.C., 1984-86, direct mktg. cons., 1986-87; v.p., Marketry, Inc., N.Y.C. and Bellevue, Wash., 1987—. Exhibited in group art shows: N.Y.C., Boston, Middlesex County, N.J., Somerset County, N.J., Morris, N.J., 1965-74, Greenwich Village Art Show, N.Y.C., 1972, Graham Art Studio, Boston, 1975-77; represented in numerous pvt. art collections throughout the U.S. Author: My Eyes Are Windows, 1972; Feelings and Thoughts (poetry), 1979. Recipient Desi award Direct Mail Mktg. Promotion Package, 1980, Poetry award One Mag., 1972, Internat. Cert. of Recognition for List Day, 1982. Mem. Direct Mktg. Assn. (Echo awards bd. judges 1982-85, List Day lectr., N.Y.C.), Internat. Poetry Assn. (Clover Collection of Verse VI 1973, Danae in Clover 1973—), Direct Mktg. Creative Guild, Nat. Mail Order Assn. (adv. bd. 1979-80), Nat. Assn. Female Execs., NOW, Direct Mktg. Club N.Y.C., Internat. Platform Assn., Nat. Bus. Circulation Assn. Home: 530 Second Ave New York NY 10016 Office: Marketry Inc 312 E 30th St Suite 14B New York NY 10016

KENDALL, DONNA JOYCE, public relations executive; b. Milan, Ill., Jan. 15, 1929; d. Orville Daniel and Marie Grace (Hansen) K. AA, Stephens Coll., 1948; BA, U. Iowa, 1950. Asst. pub. relations manager Modern Woodmen of Am., Rock Island, Ill., 1956-63; pub. relations supr. TICOR, Los Angeles, 1963-69; mktg. officer Comml. & Farmers Bank, Oxnard, Calif., 1969-71; pub. info. dir. Weslein Ins. Info. Service, Los Angeles, 1971-73; asst. v.p., corp. relations mgr. Lloyds Bank, Los Angeles, 1973-74; pub. relations dir. Palmer Coll. Chiropractic, Davenport, Iowa, 1974—. Campaign aid Mayor Fred Leopold, Beverly Hills, Mayor of Oxnard, Calif., 1970. Recipient Achievement award for Best Pub. Relations Campaign Los Angeles Advt. Women. Mem. Pub. Relations Soc. (v.p. 1975-77), Davenport C. of C. (bd. dirs. 1986—). Club: Pinnacle Country. Lodge: DAR. Home: 1804-16th St #108 Rock Island IL 61201 Office: Palmer Coll Chiropractic 1000 Brady St Davenport IA 52803

KENDALL, LAUREL ANN, geotechnical engineer; b. Detroit, Dec. 4, 1956; d. James McNair and Dorothy Mildred (Frost) K. BSE in Environ. Sci., U. Mich., 1979, MS in Civil Engring., 1983. Registered profl. engr., Mich. Student engr. Bechtel Assocs. P.C., Ann Arbor, Mich., 1979, geotech. engr., 1980-81; geotech. engr. Bechtel Civic & Mineral Corp., Gaithersburg, Md., 1981-82, Bechtel Power Corp., Midland, Mich., 1983-84; sr. staff project engr. Neyer, Tiseo & Hindo, Ltd., Farmington Hills, Mich., 1984—; instr. Lawrence Inst. Tech., Southfield, Mich., 1985—. Mem. ASCE (chmn. geotech. com. 1985-87, bd. dirs. 1987—), Mich. Soc. Profl. Engrs., Engring. Soc. Detroit. Congregationalist. Office: Neyer Tiseo and Hindo 38955 Hills Tech Dr Farmington Hills MI 48055

KENDALL, SHARON JEAN, quality control documentation coordinator; b. Chgo., July 8, 1956; d. Harper Newsum and Bernadine Williamson; m. Wellington Earl Kendall; children: Danita, Wellington III. BS in Biology, DePaul U., 1978; student, Abraham Lincoln Sch. Medicine, 1978-79. Sr. technician quality control Glidden Coatings & Chems., Chgo., 1979-81, supr. quality control chemistry, 1982-84; resin chemist Standard T Chem., Chicago Heights, Ill., 1981-82; lab. technician The NutraSweet Co., University Park, Ill., 1984-86, documentation coordinator, 1986—. Mem. South Suburban Action Com., Country Club Hills, Ill., 1986—. Mem. Am. Soc. Quality Control, Total Quality Process (team leader 1986—), Nat. Assn. Female Execs., Am. Records Mgrs. Adminstrs., Delta Sigma Theta. Democrat. Baptist.

KENDEL, DORLA DEAN (MRS. ROBERT LEWIS KENDEL), former industrial relations executive, artist; b. Los Angeles, Apr. 16, 1930; d. Thomas Weston and Lois May (Oliver) Hall; m. Robert Lewis Kendel, Aug. 13, 1949; children—Robert L., Michael L., Richard L. Cert. hypnotherapist. Tchr. oil painting, LaCrescenta, Calif., 1960-62; with Air Conditioning Spltys. Co., Inc., mfrs. rep., LaCrescenta, 1962-79, corp. sec.-treas., 1970-79; artist, 1979—. Active Scouting, sch. and sport activities, 1956-70. Mem. ASHRAE. Address: Drawer 4627 Palm Desert CA 92261

KENDER, LAURA LOGAN, education administrator, special education educator; b. Ponca City, Okla., Aug. 29, 1959; d. John A. and Mary Louise (Brown) L.; m. Theodore David Kender, July 28, 1953. BS in Edn., Southwestern U., 1981; MEd, Tex. Woman's U., 1986. Spl. edn. tchr. Ft. Worth State Sch., 1981-84, ednl. specialist, 1984-86, dir. non-residential community services, 1986—. Office: Fort Worth State Sch 5000 Campus Dr Fort Worth TX 76119

KENDERDINE, GWEN CAMILLE, telecommunications engineer; b. Sask., Can., Oct. 15, 1962; d. Richard Gordon and Mary Olive (Howson) K. Diploma in Computer Programming, Herzing Inst., Winnipeg, Can., 1981; B.S. of Elec. Engring., U. Saskatchewan, 1986; postgrad., U. Regina. Systems analyst HSSG, Saskatoon, 1981-82; tech. asst. Sasktel, Saskatoon, 1984-86; engr. Sasktel, Regina, Saskatchewan, 1986-88; mgr. engring. and support SaskTel Internat., Regina, Saskatchewan, 1988—. Mem. IEEE, Assn. Profl. Engrs. Sask., Working for Women Inc., Coll. Engring. (advancement trust fundraising com.). Office: SaskTel Internat, 2121 Saskatchewan Dr, 11th Floor, Regina Can S4P 3Y2

KENDRICK, PAMELA ANN, mathematics educator; b. Joplin, Mo., July 6, 1943; d. Laymon Harl and Margaret Alice (Stiers) Morrison; m. Anthony Eugene Kendrick , June 9, 1963. EdB, Pittsburg (Kans.) State U., 1965, MS, 1969. Cert. tchr., Mo., Kans. Computer programmer RCA Missile Test Project, Cape Canaveral Air Force Sta., Fla., 1969-72; statistician NASA Pub. Health Service, Cape Canaveral Air Force Sta., Fla., 1972-73; engr., computer analyst Jet Propulsion Lab., Cape Canaveral Air Force Sta., Fla., 1973-74; instr. math Fla. Inst. Tech., Melbourne, 1974-81; asst. prof. Brevard Community Coll., Cocoa, Fla., 1982—; cons. to various textbook pubs.; dir. computer calculus project in conjunction with Fla. Programs in Excellence, 1988. Recipient Outstanding Alumni award Pittsburg State U., 1975-76; named Fla. Outstanding Young Woman, 1976-77, One of Top 20 Outstanding Young Women Am., 1976-77. Mem. AAUW (sec. Brevard County 1983-85, v.p. programming Brevard County 1986-88), Math. Assn. Am. Democrat. Office: Brevard Community Coll 1519 Clearlake Rd Cocoa FL 32922

KENDRICK, PAMELA DALEY, lawyer, educator; b. Springfield, Mass., Oct. 1, 1952; d. Edward Murray and Elizabeth (Bloom) Daley; m. Calvert Tomlin Kendrick, Sept. 20, 1975. AB, Princeton U., 1974; JD, U. Pa., 1979. Bar: Pa. 1979. Ptnr. Morgan, Lewis & Bockius, Phila., 1979—, also prof. tax law U. Pa., 1982—. Recipient Carrye G. Barenkopf award U. Pa., 1978, McCall prize, 1979, Reeves award, 1979; fellow Salzburg seminar in Am. Law and Legal Insts., 1986. Mem. ABA, Pa. Bar Assn., Phila. Bar Assn. Office: Morgan Lewis & Bockius 2000 One Logan Sq Philadelphia PA 19103

KENIMER, KATHLEEN CULLEY, financial analyst, consultant, planner; b. Lexington, Ky., Sept. 19, 1953; d. Robert Lewis and Betty Jean (Dunn) Culley; m. William Curtis Kenimer, Dec. 6, 1975; children—Richard Cameron, Keenan Joel, William Ryan. B.A. in Edn., U. Ky., 1974; M.A. in Edn., Georgetown U., 1984. Tchr. Fayette County Schs., Ky., 1975-80; dist. mktg. dir. Lady Love Cosmetics, Dallas and Lexington, 1980-85; fin. analyst Waddell and Reed, Lexington, 1985—, also seminar instr., 1985—; tchr. fin. planning Bourbon County Schs., Ky., 1986. Adviser Christian Women's Club, Paris, Ky., 1984—. Named Boss of Yr., Am. Bus. Women's Assn., 1984; Scholar Ky. Baptists, 1971, Eta Sigma Phi, 1971. Mem. Phi Mu. Avocations: smocking; horticulture. Home: 311 Redmon Rd Paris KY 40361 Office: Waddell and Reed Inc 870 Corporate Dr Lexington KY 40503

KENNAN, ELIZABETH TOPHAM, college president; b. Phila., Feb. 25, 1938; d. Frank and Henrietta (Jackson) Topham; m. Michael Burns, 1986; 1 child, Frank Alexander Kennan. BA summa cum laude, Mt. Holyoke Coll., 1960; MA, St. Hilda's Coll. Oxford U., Eng., 1962; PhD, U. Wash., 1966; LHD (hon.), Trinity Coll., Washington, 1978, Amherst Coll., 1980, St. Mary's Coll., 1982, Oberlin Coll., 1983, Smith Coll., 1984, Cath. U. Am., 1985. Asst. prof. history Cath. U. Am., Washington, 1966-70, assoc. prof., 1970-78, dir. medieval and Byzantine studies program, 1970-78, dir. program in early Christian humanism, 1974-78; pres. Mt. Holyoke Coll., South Hadley, Mass., 1978—; lectr. in field; dir. NYNEX Corp., White Plains, N.Y., N.E. Utilities, Hartford, Conn., Berkshire Life Ins. Co., Pittsfield, Mass., Shawmut Corp., Boston; cons. to various colls.; pres. Five Colls., Inc., 1985—; dir. Council on Library Resources, 1982—; mem. Indo-U.S. Subcommn. of Am. Secretariat. Translator, author: (with John D. Anderson) On Consideration (St. Bernard of Clairvaux), 1976; contbr. articles to profl. publs. Mem. Dana Found., Higher Edn. Program Commn., 1986—, Am. Council on Edn. Commn. on Internat. Edn., 1985—; trustee U. Notre Dame, South Bend, Ind. Woodrow Wilson fellow, 1962; Marshall scholar, 1962; named Tchr. of Yr. Cath. U. Am., 1977. Mem. Mediaeval Acad. Am. (council 1984-86), Phi Beta Kappa., Council on Fgn. Relations. Home: Pres' House Mt Holyoke Coll South Hadley MA 01075 Office: Office of the Pres Mt Holyoke Coll South Hadley MA 01075

KENNEDY, BETH BLUMENREICH, film studio executive; b. Detroit, Mar. 11, 1950; d. Leonard and Bernice Blumenreich; m. Michael F. Kennedy; 1 child, Joshua Hayes. BA, U. Mich., 1971; MA, UCLA, 1974; JD, Southwestern U., 1984. Mgr. sensurround dept. Universal Studios, Universal City, Calif., 1975; asst. to studio mgr. Universal Studios, Universal City, 1977; adminstr. transp. dept., 1978; dir. info. systems TV & UP, 1980; dir. corp. int. mgmt., 1982-87, v.p. planning and adminstrn., 1987; v.p., dir. corp. internal mgmt. MCA, Inc., Universal City, 1988—. Contbr. articles to profl. jour. Mem. legal com. The Nurtury, Sherman Oaks, Calif., 1988—. Named one of Outstanding Young Women of Am., Outstanding Young Women of Am. awards program, 1980. Mem. ABA, Women in Bus. (mem. com. 1985—), Orgn. of Women Execs. (bd. dirs. 1986—, membership com.), Women in Film, Beverly Hills Bar Assn., Los Angeles County Bar Assn. Office: Universal City Studios 100 Universal City Plaza Universal City CA 91608

KENNEDY, BRENDA, psychotherapist; b. Amityville, N.Y., Mar. 10, 1945; d. Stanley and Ruth Rose (Ludgewait) Rockman; m. Jeffrey Kupke, Sept. 4, 1965 (div. 1976); children: Todd, Jennifer; m. William T. Kennedy, Sept. 15, 1979. BA, SUNY, Old Westbury, 1974; MS, N.Y. Inst. Tech., Old Westbury, 1976. Asst. coordinator family services Nassau County Dept. Drug and Alcohol Abuse, East Meadow, N.Y., 1972-75; dir. Lifeskool, Mineola, N.Y., 1982-84; tchr. Course in Miracles, Mineola, 1984—. Author: Under the Covers, 1985. Mem. Nat. Assn. Female Execs. Home and Office: 341 Latham Rd Mineola NY 11501

KENNEDY, CHERYL LYNN, museum director; b. Pekin, Ill., Nov. 25, 1946; d. Paul Louis and Ann Marie (Bingham) Wieburg; m. Roger Nicholas Kennedy, Feb. 7, 1966; children: Kurt Alan, Kimberly Ann. Grad. high sch., Pekin, Ill. Prin., and profl. quilter Mahomet, Ill., 1976-81; program coordinator Early Am. Mus., Mahomet, 1981-85, dir. mus., 1985-86; dir. mus. and edn., 3 parks Champaign County Forest Preserve, Mahomet, 1986—; chmn. Ill. quilt documentation project Early Am. Mus. and Land of Lincoln Quilt Assn., 1986—. Creator and presenter (slide programs) Our Founding Mothers, 19th Century Life. Historian Meth. Local History Com., Mahomet, 1984-86. Mem. Midwest Mus. Council, Am. Assn. Museums, Am. Assn. State and Local History Museums, Cong. Ill. Hist. Socs. and Museums (dir. regionII), Ill. Heritage Assn., Ill. State Hist. Soc., Champaign County Hist. Soc., Nat. Quilt Assn. and Am. Quilt Soc., Antique Quilt Study Group and the Quilt Conservancy. Home: Rural Rt 3 Box 52 Mahomet IL 61853 Office: Early Am Mus PO Drawer 669 Mahomet IL 61853

KENNEDY, CORNELIA GROEFSEMA, judge; b. Detroit, Aug. 4, 1923; d. Elmer H. and Mary Blanche (Gibbons) Groefsema; m. Charles S. Kennedy, Jr.; 1 son, Charles S. III. B.A., U. Mich., 1945, J.D. with distinction, 1947; LL.D. (hon.), No. Mich. U., 1971, Eastern Mich. U., 1971, Western Mich. U., 1973, Detroit Coll. Law, 1980, U. Detroit, 1987. Bar: Mich. bar 1947. Law clk. to Chief Judge Harold M. Stephens, U.S. Ct. of Appeals, Washington, 1947-48; asso. Elmer H. Groefsema, Detroit, 1948-52; partner Markle & Markle, Detroit, 1952-66; judge 3d Judicial Circuit Mich., 1967-70; dist. judge U.S. Dist. Ct., Eastern Dist. Mich., Detroit, 1970-79; chief judge U.S. Dist. Ct., Eastern Dist. Mich., 1977-79; circuit judge U.S. Ct. Appeals, 6th Circuit, 1979—. Mem. Commn. on the Bicentennial of the U.S. Constitution (presdl. appoinment). Recipient Sesquicentennial award U. Mich. Fellow Am. Bar Found.; mem. ABA, Mich. Bar Assn. (past chmn. negligence law sect.), Detroit Bar Assn. (past dir.), Fed. Bar Assn., Am. Judicature Soc., Nat. Assn. Women Lawyers, Am. Trial Lawyers Assn., Nat. Conf. Fed. Trial Judges (past chmn.), Fed. Jud. Fellows Commn. (bd. dirs.), Fed. Jud. Ctr. (bd. dirs.), Phi Beta Kappa. Office: US Ct of Appeals 744 Fed Bldg 231 W Lafayette St Detroit MI 48226

KENNEDY, DANIELLE RAE, sales company executive, author/lecturer; b. Chgo., Jan. 6, 1945; d. Joseph Daniel and Rose Mary (Dolce) Barrett; m. William P. Kennedy, June 27, 1964 (div. 1980); children: Beth, Joe, Kevin, Daniel, Mary; m. R. Michael Craig; children: Kelly, Bob, Kathleen. BA in Communications, Clarke Coll., 1980. Lic. real estate broker, Calif. Salesperson Mission Viejo (Calif.) Realty, 1972-77; pres. Mission Viejo Assocs., 1977-80, Danielle Kennedy Internat., San Clemente, Calif., 1980—; instr. Grad. Realtors Inst.; mem. adv. bd. Real Estate Profl. Mag., Wellesley, Mass. Author: How to List and Sell Real Estate, 1983, Super Natural Selling, 1984. Mem. Nat. Assn. Bus. Profl. Women, Nat. Assn. Profl. Saleswomen, Nat. Speakers Assn., Nat. Assn. Female Execs., Aerobics Fitness Assn. (cert. instr.), Women's Council Realtors, Calif. Assn. Realtors, South Orange County Bd. Realtors, Internat. Dance Exercise Assn., San Clemente C. of C. Roman Catholic. Home: 39 Monarch Bay South Laguna CA 92677 Office: 219 S El Camino Real San Clemente CA 92672

KENNEDY, DEBRA JOYCE, marketing professional; b. Covina, Calif., July 9, 1955; d. John Nathan and Drea Hannah (Lancaster) Ward; m. John William Kennedy, Sept. 3, 1977 (div.); children: Drea, Noelle. B.S. in Communications, Calif. State Poly. U., 1977. Pub. relations coordinator Whittier (Calif.) Hosp., 1978-79, pub. relations mgr., 1980; pub. relations dir. San Clemente (Calif.) Hosp., 1979-80; dir. pub. relations Garfield Med. Ctr., Monterey Park, Calif., 1980-82; dir. mktg. and community relations Charter Oak Hosp., Covina, 1983-85; mktg. dir. CPC Horizon Hosp., Pomona, 1985—. Mem. Am. Soc. Hosp. Pub. Relations, Healthcare Mktg. Assn., Healthcare Pub. Relations and Mktg. Assn., Covina and Covina West C. of C., West Covina Jaycees. Republican. Methodist. Club: Soroptimists (coord. council Pomona chpt.). Contbr. articles to profl. jours.

KENNEDY, EVELYN SIEFERT, foundation executive; b. Pitts., Nov. 11, 1927; d. Carmine and Assunta (Iacobucci) Rocci; BS magna cum laude, U. R.I., 1969, MS in Textiles and Clothing, 1970; m. George J. Siefert, May 30, 1953 (div. 1974); children: Paul Kenneth, Carl Joseph, Ann Marie; m. Lyle H. Kennedy, II, Oct. 12, 1974 (div. Feb. 1986). With Pitts. Public Schs., 1945-50; with Goodyear Aircraft Corp., Akron, Ohio, 1950-54; clothing instr. Groton (Conn.) Dept. Adult Edn., 1958-68; pres. Sewtique, Groton, 1970, Sewtique II, New London, Conn., 1986; v.p. Kennedy Capital Advisors, Groton, 1973-85, Kennedy Mgmt. Corp., Groton, 1974-85, Kennedy InterVest, Inc., Groton, 1975-85; pres., exec. dir. P.R.I.D.E. Found., Inc., Groton, 1978—; clothing cons. Coop. Extension Service, Dept. Agr.; internat. lectr. on clothing for disabled and elderly; adj. faculty U. Conn., Eastern Conn. State Coll., St. Joseph Coll.; hon. prof. Univ. R.I., assoc. prof., 1987—; fed. expert witness Care Label Law, FTC, 1976; mem. Major Appliance Consumer Action Panel, 1983—. Regional adv. council SBA active corps Execs., Hartford, 1985—; bd. dirs. Easter Seal Rehab. Center Southeastern Conn.; bus. adv. council U. R.I., 1979—, trustee, 1985—; active LWV; mem. Groton Vocat. Edn. Adv. Council. Recipient award of distinction U. R.I., 1969, Small Bus. Adminstrn. Adv. of Year, 1984; named Woman of Yr. Bus. and Profl. Women's Club, 1977, Conn. Home Economist of Yr., 1987. Mem. Internat. Sleep Council (consumer affairs rep.), Nat. Assn. Bedding Mfrs., Conn. Home Economists in Bus. (founder 1977, Women of Yr. 1987), Nat. Home Economists in Bus. (chmn. internat. relations, nat. fin. chmn. 1986), Am. Home Econs. Assn., Coll. and Univ. Bus. Instrs. of Conn., Fashion Group, Omicron Nu, Phi Kappa Phi. Democrat. Roman Catholic. Clubs: New London Zonta, Bus. and Profl. Women's (Outstanding Women of Year 1977). Author: Dressing With Pride, 1980, Clothing Accessibility: A Lesson Plan to Aid the Disabled and Elderly, 1983. Office: 71 Plaza Ct Groton CT 06340

KENNEDY, JANICE MARIE, accountant; b. Wichita, Kans., Jan. 4, 1943; d. Oren L. and Jean H. (Harrison) Shelley; m. David W. Kennedy, Aug. 29, 1964; children: Christopher L., Drue D. BS in Bus. Adminstrn., U. Kans., 1964; MS in Acctg., Wichita State U., 1981. CPA, Kans. Staff acct. Kennedy and Coe, CPAs, Wichita, 1981-84; pvt. practice acctg. Wichita, 1984—. Adv. bd. Kans. Children's Service League, Wichita, 1984—; treas., bd. dirs. Literacy Vols. of Am., Wichita, 1986—. Mem. Nat. Assn. Accts. (treas., pres. 1981—), Am. Inst. CPA's, Kans. Soc. CPA's (com. mem.), Am. Soc. Women Accts. (bd. dirs., v.p. 1982-83). Republican. Episcopalian. Home: 6211 Beachy Wichita KS 67208 Office: 4930 E Lincoln Wichita KS 67218

KENNEDY, JEAN M., magazine editor, journalist; b. St. Louis, Oct. 14, 1957; d. Lawrence L. and Emma W. (Irons) K.; m. Darrel L. Miller, May 1, 1981. BJ, U. Mo., 1980. Manuscript editor C.V. Mosby Co., St. Louis, 1980-81; editor Edwardsville (Ill.) Jour., 1981-83; assoc. editor The Midwest Motorist mag., St. Louis, 1983-85, mng. editor, 1985—. Mem. Internat.

Assn. Bus. Communicators, U. Mo. Columbia Jour. Sch. Alumni Assn. Roman Catholic. Club: Press (St. Louis). Office: Midwest Motorist 12901 N Forty Dr Saint Louis MO 63141

KENNEDY, JEAN THRASHER, writer, poet, educator; b. Atlanta, Aug. 5, 1932; d. Barton Edmonds and Winnie H. (Ham) Thrasher; A.B., Wesleyan Coll., Macon, Ga., 1954; M.A., Northwestern U., 1956; m. Victor N., June 30, 1956 (div. 1985); children—Philip, Elaine, Laura. Staff writer Atlanta Constn., 1952-54; tech. manuscript editor Jour. AMA, Chgo., 1956-57, Jour. ADA, Chgo., 1957-58; asst. to editorial page editor Waterloo (Iowa) Courier, 1972-76; writing tchr. Waterloo Recreation Commn., Iowa Arts Council and Waterloo YWCA, 1980—; instr. in English lang. and lit. U. No. Iowa, 1981—; contbr. fiction, non-fiction, poetry to various publs. Bd. dirs. Waterloo-Cedar Falls Jr. League, 1967-68; pres. Waterloo Reciprocity, PEO Sisterhood, 1981-82; mem. adult program com. YWCA, Waterloo, sec. bd. dirs., 1985-86, chmn. nominating com., 1986. Recipient prizes for poetry and fiction. Mem. Nat. League Am. Pen Women (v.p. Waterloo-Cedar Rapids br. 1980-82; bd. dirs. 1984—), AAUW, Iowa Council Tchrs. English, Nat. Council Tchrs. English. Presbyterian. Contbr. fiction to mags. Home: 857 Sunrise Blvd Waterloo IA 50701 Office: Univ No Iowa Dept English Lang & Lit Cedar Falls IA 50614

KENNEDY, JENNIFER LYNN, nursing administrator, educator; b. Miami, Fla., Mar. 16, 1962; d. Dennis James and Anne Craig (Lewis) K. BS in Nursing, Auburn U., 1984. Mktg. asst. Coral Ridge Ministries, Ft. Lauderdale, Fla., 1984-85; registered nurse Dr. G. David Onstad, Ft. Lauderdale, 1984-85, Life Care Med. Ctr., Pompano Beach, Fla., 1985; staff devel. educator Delray Community Hosp., Delray Beach, Fla., 1986—. Mem. Am. Heart Assn., Fla. Nurses Assn., South Fla. Nurse Educators, Health Educators of Palm Beach County. Republican. Presbyterian. Home: 2750 NE 58th St Fort Lauderdale FL 33308 Office: Delray Community Hosp 5352 Linton Blvd Delray Beach FL 33445

KENNEDY, KATHIE SPRAGUE, day care center administrator; b. Lynwood, Calif., Sept. 12, 1952; d. Elmer Edwin and Catherine Rose (Bush) Sprague; m. John Robert Capozzi, Nov. 1970 (div. Aug. 1973); m. Dennis Lee Kennedy, Mar. 29, 1986; children: Matthew and Nathan (twins). AA, Orange Coast Coll., 1978; BA, Long Beach State U., 1984. Basic Four key punch operator McDonnell Douglas, Tustin, Calif., 1979-80; word processor operator McDonnell Douglas, Long Beach, Huntington Beach, Calif., 1980-82; substitute tchr. Orange County Pub. Sch. System, Calif., 1984-86; owner, dir. New Beginnings, Norco, Calif., 1986—. Sunday sch. tchr. Ch. Jesus Christ Latter Day Saints, Huntington Beach, 1978-86. Mem. Nat. Assn. for the Edn. Young Children. Republican. Club. Orange County Mother of Twins. Home: 6022 Ivory Circle Huntington Beach CA 92647

KENNEDY, KAY J., researcher-writer; b. S.D.; d. Edward James and Marie Amelia (Bowman) K.; B.A. in Geology, U. Wyo., 1931. Reporter, Gt. Falls (Mont.) Leader, 1944-45, Denver Post, 1945, Alaska Daily Empire, Juneau, 1950-51, Fairbanks (Alaska) Daily News-Miner, 1952-56; chief news bur. Alaska Visitors Assn., Seattle, 1957-60; news bur. chief Alaska Travel Promotion Assn., 1961-62; pub. relations Wien Alaska Airlines, Fairbanks and Anchorage, 1966-70; freelance research-writer, 1936—; producer 1st 2 Alaska Travel manuals, 1957-58; 68; author original copy Alaska Sunset Discovery Book, 1963, Wien Brothers Story, 1967. Recipient Lulu award Los Angeles Advt. Women, 1958; named Wash. Woman of Achievement, Wash. Press Women, 1978. Mem. Nat. Fedn. Press Women (Woman of Achievement 1987), Outdoor Writers Assn. Am., Alaska Press Women (founder, pres. 1961; awards 1969, 71, Nat. Woman of Achievment 1987), Wash. Press Women (award 1959), Soc. Am. Travel Writers. Clubs: Alaska Press (award 1959). Address: 330 3d Ave #407 Fairbanks AK 99701

KENNEDY, MARGARET SWIERZ, magazine editor; b. Milford, Mass., Oct. 19, 1941; d. Mitchell Martin and Jennie (Novack) Swierz; m. Eugene Martin Kenndedy Jr., Nov. 7, 1964; 1 son, Eugene Martin. A.B., Clark U., 1963. Sec. Conde Nast. Publs., N.Y.C., 1963—; also asst. editor House and Garden Mag., N.Y.C., editor furniture and design projects; exec. editor House Beautiful Mag., N.Y.C., 1981—; guest editor Mademoiselle Mag., 1962. Mem. Internat. Furnishings and Design Assn., Decorators Club, Decorative Arts Trust, Phi Beta Kappa. Roman Catholic. Home: 46 E 91st St New York NY 10128 Office: House Beautiful 1700 Broadway New York NY 10019

KENNEDY, MARGE M., editor; b. N.Y.C., Oct. 16, 1950; d. William Joseph and Ruth Rita (Keeler) K. B.A., CUNY, 1979; postgrad., Columbia U., 1979—. Editor Random House, Inc., N.Y.C., 1974-83; free lance writer N.Y.C., 1977—; editor-in-chief Sesame Street mag., N.Y.C., 1984—. Author children's books including: Mystery of Hypnosis, 1979. Office: Sesame Street 1 Lincoln Plaza New York NY 10023

KENNEDY, MARY PATRICIA, publisher; b. Norwood, Mass., Mar. 16, 1956; d. Stephen Joseph Jr. and Mary Virginia (Rajab) K. Student, U. Mass., 1977. Mem. Wet Paint Collective, Boston, 1977-78; account exec. Atlantic Publs., Dedham, Mass., 1978; co-owner Community Publs., Boston, 1978-81, Best Pub., Boston, 1981-83; owner M. Kennedy Pub., Boston, 1983—; pub. Boston Best Guide, 1978—, Community Guide, Boston, 1980—; producer Mktg. Mag. (Cable TV), Boston, 1986; co-producer Am. Stonehenge (Cable), Boston, 1987. Co-producer video: Pets in Motron, 1986, 87. Community producer Boston Community Access and Programming Found., Boston, 1986—; mem. Beacon Hill Civic Assn., Boston, 1987. Mem. Mass. Gay and Lesbian Polit. Alliance. Club: YWCA. Home and Office: 105 Charles St #285 Boston MA 02114

KENNEDY, NANCY MCGRAW, accountant; b. Centreville, Miss., June 8, 1950; d. Harry Burnell and Minnie Louisa (Harkey) McG.; m. Charles Woodrow Kennedy, Dec. 8, 1969; children: Karen Leigh, Kathryn Lynn. Student, Millsaps Coll., Jackson, Miss., 1967-69; BS, U. So. Miss., 1981. CPA, Miss., La. Staff acct. Handjis & McGraw CPA's, Natchez, Miss., 1973-83; ptnr. Handjis & Kennedy CPA's, Natchez, 1983—; adj. prof. acctg. U. So. Miss., Natchez, 1982-83, Copiah Lincoln Jr. Coll., Natchez, 1982-83. Classification chmn. United Way of Natchez-Adams County, 1984. Mem. Am. Inst. CPA's, Miss. Soc. CPA's (pres. S.W. chpt. 1985—, bd. govs. 1985—, chmn. pub. relations and publicity com. 1986-87), Phi Kappa Phi. Democrat. Methodist. Club: Pilot (Natchez) (treas. 1984-86).

KENNEDY, ROSE FITZGERALD (MRS. JOSEPH P. KENNEDY), b. Boston, July 22, 1890; d. John Francis and Josephine Mary (Hannon) Fitzgerald; m. Joseph P. Kennedy, Oct. 7, 1914 (dec. 1969); children: Joseph (dec.), John Fitzgerald, (Pres. U.S. 1961-63; dec.) Rosemary, Kathleen (dec.), Eunice (Mrs. Robert Sargent Shriver), Patricia Kennedy Lawford, Robert Francis (dec.), Jean (Mrs. Stephen Smith), Edward M. Ed., New Eng. Conservatory, Convent of Sacred Heart, Boston, Manhattanville Coll. Sacred Heart, Blumenthal Acad., Valls, The Netherlands; LL.D., Manhattanville Coll.; LL.D. hon. degree, Georgetown U., 1977. Author: Times to Remember, 1974. Named Papal Countess Pope Pius XII. Roman Catholic. Address: Hyannis MA 02647 •

KENNEDY, SHEILA SUESS, lawyer; b. Indpls., Oct. 20, 1941; d. Joseph S. and Annette (Marcus) Simkin; m. Roberet E. Suess, June 27, 1964 (div. 1977); children: Michael, Stephen, David; m. Robert N. Kennedy, Mar. 2, 1980. AA, Stephens Coll., 1960; BS, Ind. U., 1964; JD, Ind. U., Indpls., 1975. Bar: Ind. 1975, U.S. Dist. Ct. (so. dist.) 1975, U.S. Ct. Appeals (7th cir.) 1977. Assoc. Baker & Daniels, Indpls., 1975-77; corp. counsel City of Indpls., 1977-80; of counsel Treacy, Cohen, Mears & Crawford, Indpls., 1981-83; ptnr. Mears, Crawford, Kennedy & Eichholtz, Indpls., 1983-87; pres. Kennedy Devel. Services, 1987—; instr. bus. law Ind. Cen. U., 1978; tchr. Eng. composition and lit. Ind. pub. schs. Mng. editor Ind. Law Rev.; contbr. articles to legal jours. Mem. sch. liberal arts adv. com. Ind. U.-Purdue U., Indpls.; vice-chmn. Taxpayers for Better Indpls.; Rep. candidate U.S. Ho. of Reps., 11th Dist. Ind., 1980; vice-chmn. Ind. Women for Reagan-Bush; Rep. precinct committeeman, 1982-84; active Ind. Women's Rep. Club, also Indpls. chpt., numerous local, state and nat. polit. campaigns; bd. dirs. Jewish Community Relations Council, Jewish Welfare Fedn. Mem. ABA, Ind. Bar Assn., Indpls. Bar Assn., Fed. Jud. Merit Selections Commn., Nat. Assn. Women in Constrn., Associated Gen. Contractors Ind., Nat. Inst. Mcpl. Law Officers, NCCJ, Am. Jewish Com. (past nat. bd. dirs., chmn. Indpls. chpt.), Nat. Council Jewish Women, Am. Israel Pub. Affairs Com., Hadassah, Women's Polit. Caucus., Network of Women in Bus., Indpls. Symphony Soc. (jr. group), Channel 20, Hooverwood Guild, Ind. U. Law Sch. Alumni Assn. Club: Columbia (Indpls.). Home: 628 Lockerbie St Indianapolis IN 46202 Office: Kennedy Devel Services 36 S Pennsylvania St Suite 290 Indianapolis IN 46204

KENNEDY, SHIRLEY LOU, accountant; b. New Smyrna Beach, Fla., Dec. 8, 1958; d. Doyle Kennedy and Annie Ruth (Whittle) Lybrand; m. William T. Sanders, Dec. 9, 1983; children: Lindsey Kennedy, Allison Kennedy. BS, U. S.C., 1980. CPA, S.C. Mgr. Smith, Sapp, Bookhoot, Crumpler & Calliham, P.A., Myrtle Beach, S.C., 1980-87; corp. controller Wallaman Clay Products Co., Inc., Myrtle Beach, 1987—; cons. North Strand Equipment Co., North Myrtle Beach, 1984—. Treas. Trinity United Meth. Ch., North Myrtle Beach, 1987. Mem. S.C. Assn. CPA's, Am. Inst. CPA's, Bus. and Profl. Women's Club (treas. 1985). Republican. Office: Wallaman Clay Products Co Inc 3200 Pottery Dr Myrtle Beach SC 29577

KENNEDY, SUSAN JOANNE, management executive; b. Coatesville, Pa., Mar. 5, 1943; d. Lloyd F. and Alice Mae (Jackson) K.; A.A., Brevard Community Coll., 1977, A.S. in Human Service Tech., 1977; B.S. in Social Sci., Rollins Coll., 1979; postgrad. Stetson U., 1980-81; M.S. in Counseling Psychology, Nova U., 1983. Cert. DWI evaluator, Fla. Various positions with hotels and restaurants, Ill., Miss., Fla., 1965-74; social worker Brevard Achievement Center, Rockledge, Fla., 1977, vocat. placement specialist, 1978-84, vol./pub. edn. coordinator, 1984-86; ct. support services dir. Brevard County Bd. Commrs., Rockledge, Fla., 1986—; mem. Brevard Equal Opportunity Com., 1980-84; mem. Brevard Community Coll. Equal Access/Equal Opportunity Adv. Com., 1979-84; mem. Brevard County Job Developers Com., 1981, mem. human service tech. adv. bd. Brevard Community Coll., 1980-83. Sec. exec. com. Family Service Bur., 1976-77; scouting coordinator Boy Scouts Am., 1981-86; loaned exec. United Way, 1980, 81; mem. Brevard County Pvt. Industry Council, 1982-85, Brevard Assn. Counseling Planning com., 1988—. Recipient Community Service award Brevard Community Coll., 1977. Mem. Nat. Rehab. Assn., Brevard Assn. Human Service Agys., Brevard Assn. Counseling Devel., Brevard Personnel Assn. (treas. 1984), Nat. Assn. Human Service Technologists, Fla. Assn. Crime Deliquency, Am. Correctional Assn., Fla. Assn. Alcohol Drug Abuse, Nat. Assn. Female Execs., VFW Aux. Democrat. Episcopalian. Home: 1525 S Fiske Blvd Apt 244 Rockledge FL 32955 Office: 1017 S Florida Ave PO Box 224 Rockledge FL 32955

KENNEDY, SUSAN LOUISE, data processing marketing executive; b. Pasadena, Calif., Oct. 3, 1956; d. Andrew Robert and Lois Adrienne (Olsen) Allegretti; m. Kirk Wayne Kennedy, July 11, 1981; children: Sean Christopher, Nicholas Paul. BA, U. Calif., Davis, 1979. Adminstrv. asst. Orionics, Inc., Bozeman, Mont., 1980-81; customer service rep. Hi-Tek Corp., Garden Grove, Calif., 1981-83; mktg. asst. Hi-Tek Corp., Garden Grove, 1983-84, mktg. adminstr., 1984-85; mktg. communications mgr. Computer Automation Co., Irvine, Calif., 1985-86; mktg. mgr. Applied Data Communications, Tustin, Calif., 1986—. Mem. Bus. Profl. Advt. Assn., Alpha Omicron Epsilon, Alpha Phi. Democrat.

KENNEDY, VARINA (KAY), design and color consultant, writer; b. Newark, Ark., Dec. 4, 1940; d. Estel Charles and Valerie (Murphy) Kuehnert; m. Joseph Kennedy, Nov. 7, 1959. Cert. in interior design Clover Park Tech. Sch., Tacoma, 1972; student Solano Coll., Calif., 1972-73, San Bernardino Valley Coll., Calif., 1980. Designer trainee Breuner's Home Furnishings, Pleasant Hill, Calif., 1972-73; decorator cons. J.C. Penney Co., Concord, Calif. and North Little Rock, Ark., 1973-76; interior designer Walls Galore & More, Inc., North Little Rock, 1976-78, Nickell Flooring, San Bernardino, Calif., 1978-79; freelance designer, San Bernardino, 1980-83; owner Comprehensive Design Services, Tacoma, 1984-87; owner Creative Concepts, Tacoma, 1987—; instr., seminar speaker on color and design. Columnist Decorating Styles, North Beach Beacon, 1984, Business People/Profiles, Pierce County Bus. Examiner, 1987—; v.p. Home Based Bus. Assn., 1987-88, Washington Home Bus. Network, 1987. Contbr. numerous articles on design, color and small bus. to profl. mags. Mem. Am. Soc. Interior Designers (assoc.), Color Mktg. Group, Nat. Trust for Historic Preservation, Pacific N.W. Writers Conf., Nat. Assn. Female Execs. Office: Creative Concepts PO Box 98119 Tacoma WA 98498

KENNELLY, BARBARA BAILEY, congresswoman; b. Hartford, Conn., July 10, 1936; d. John Moran and Barbara (Leary) Bailey; m. James J. Kennelly, Sept. 26, 1959; children: Eleanor Bride, Barbara Leary, Louise Moran, John Bailey. BA in Econs, Trinity Coll., Washington, 1958; grad., Harvard-Radcliffe Sch. Bus. Adminstrn., 1959; M.A. in Govt, Trinity Coll., Hartford, 1971. Mem. Hartford Ct. of Common Council, 1975-79; sec. of state State of Conn., Hartford, 1979-83; mem. 98th-100th Congresses from 1st Dist. Conn.; Hartford rep., sec. exec. com. Capitol Region Council of Govts., 1975-79; mem. exec. com. Eastern Regional Conf., Council of State Govts.; dir. Conn. Bank & Trust Co. Bd. dirs. Hartford Architecture Conservancy; mem. Conn. bd. dirs. Catholic Family Services, Inc. Mem. Internat. Inst. Mcpl. Clks., Nat. Assn. of Secs. of State. Democrat. Roman Catholic. Office: 1230 Longworth House Office Bldg Washington DC 20515

KENNETT, COLETTE ANN, religious organization administrator; b. Breese, Ill., May 2, 1951; d. John Franklin and Virginia Mary (Micheel) K. BA, Park Coll., 1971; MS, So. Ill. U., Edwardsville, 1980; postgrad., Loyola U., Chgo., 1986—. Clk, stenographer U.S. Treasury Dept., St. Louis, 1969-72, U.S. Dept. of Def., Scott AFB, Ill., 1972-79; assoc. dir. Cath. Youth Orgn. Belleville (Ill.) Diocesan, 1979-83, dir., 1983—; legal sec. Listeman, Bandy & Hamilton, New Baden, Ill., 1969-72; coll. instr. Kaskaskia Jr. Coll., Centralia, Ill., 1983-86; bd. dirs. Diocesan Cath. Newspaper, Belleville, Ill., 1980-82; chairperson Diocesan Youth Ministry Coalition, Belleville, 1985-86. Vol. Clinton Manor Shelter Care, New Baden, Ill., 1969-76, Menard Correctional Ctr., Chester, Ill., 1984—, Centralia (Ill.) Correctional Ctr., 1983—, Vienna Correctional Ctr., 1975—, Ill. Youth Ctr., Dixon Springs, Ill., 1980-82, Harrisburg, 1983; campaign chairperson, Cystic Fibrosis Found., St. Louis, 1985-87, Teens Encounter Christ, Belleville, 1978-82; vice chairperson Diocesan mem. Cath. div. Girl Scouts U.S., 1983— (medal 1987, 88); sec. Residents Encounter Christ, Belleville, 1984-85, Clinton County Assn. for Spl. Persons, Breese, 1982-84, Nat. Teens Encounter Christ, Belleville, 1977-81; exec. com. Region VII Youth Coalition, Chgo., 1979-86; bd. dirs. Clinton County Mental Health Bd., Breese, 1970-72; mem. Boy Scouts Am., 1986—, Area 12 Spl. Olympics, 1979—. Recipient voice scholarship So. Ill. U., Edwardsville, 1969, Ill. Tchrs. scholarship, 1969, Spirit of St. Francis award St. Francis Coll., 1987; named Outstanding Am. Woman for State of Ill. Lady Stetson Cologne, 1987. Home: 305 E Cedar St New Baden IL 62265 Office: Cath Youth Orgn 2620 Lebanon Ave Belleville IL 62221

KENNEY, ALISON JOAN, sales professional; b. Boston, July 17, 1958; d. George James and Ann Joan (Maciver) K. BA in Pub. Relations, Advt., U. Mass., 1980. Sales rep. Procter & Gamble, Manchester, N.H., 1980-81; dist. field rep. Procter & Gamble, Boston, 1981-82, unit mgr., 1982-85, sales tech. mgr., 1986-87, dir. sales and info. resources, 1987—; speaker in field. Vol. Christian Children's Fund, Honduras, 1983—; sponsor Boston Mus. Fine Arts, 1986—. Mem. Am. Mgmt. Assn., Nat. Orgn. for Women, U. Mass. Alumni Club. Roman Catholic. Home: 796 Willard St #D5 Quincy MA 02169

KENNEY, DOLORES TORRES, patent lawyer; b. Chgo., Apr. 6, 1934; d. Anastacio and Bibiana Torres; m. Jerome George Kenney, July 11, 1959. BS cum laude, Coll. of St. Francis, Joliet, Ill., 1956; cert. in bus. adminstrn., Keller Grad. Sch. Mgmt., 1977; JD, Ill. Inst. Tech., 1984. Bar: Ill. 1984, U.S. Dist. Ct. (no. dist.) Ill. 1984. Chemist Stepan Chem. Co., Chgo., 1956; research scientist personal care div. Gillette Co. formerly Toni Co., Chgo., 1956-74; pres., dir. Ken-Quest Ltd., Park Ridge, Ill., 1974—; patent atty. Dressler, Goldsmith et al, Chgo., 1984-87, Olson & Hierl, Chgo., 1987—. Author, contbg. columnist Cosmetics and Toiletries mag., 1974—; contbr. articles to profl. jours; co-inventor, 1973, 76. Mem. Niles (Ill.) Concert Choir, Park Ridge Art League. Named Contemporary Woman of Yr., Mex.-Am. Bus. and Profl. Women of Chgo., 1985. Mem. Am. Chem. Soc. (treas. 1985-88, alt. councilor Chgo. sec. 1980—, past treas. div. small chem. bus., past bus. mgr. publs. Chgo. sect., Internat. Exhibitors of Art by Chemists 1973, 75, 77), Chgo. Chemists' Club (trustee 1982—, Past Pres. award 1981), ABA, Chgo. Bar Assn., Womens Bar Assn. of Ill., Am. Intellectual Property Assn., Fed. Cir. Bar Assn., Nat. Assn. of Sci. Writers, Soc. of Cosmetic Chemists, Am. Oil Chemists Soc., Ill. State Bar Assn., Phi Alpha Delta, Delta Epsilon Sigma. Office: Olson & Hierl 20 N Wacker Dr Suite 3000 Chicago IL 60606

KENNEY, DOROTHY HASTINGS, small business owner; b. Rome, N.Y., Oct. 21, 1942; d. Mary Pauline (Daily) Hastings; m. Jack M. Kenney, Aug. 22, 1964; children: Catherine, Cynthia, Peggy. Student, Rome Free Acad., 1960, Mohawk Valley Community Coll., 1972, Erie Community Coll., 1983. Sec. Griffiss AFB, Rome, 1960-64, 67, VA Hosp., Syracuse, N.Y., 1964-66, Upstate Med. Ctr., Syracuse, 1966, Rutgers U., New Brunswick, N.J., 1967-72; exec. sec. Audn Corp., Hamburg, N.Y., 1975, Javco Industries, Blasdell, N.Y.; prin. Dorothy Kenney Secretarial Service, Hamburg, 1976-87; v.p. Kenney Exec. Ctr., Inc., Longwood, Fla., 1987—. Democrat. Roman Catholic. Lodge: Zonta. Office: Kenney Exec Ctr Inc 407 Wekiva Springs Rd #213 Longwood FL 32779-9998

KENNY, SHIRLEY ELISE STRUM, academic administrator; b. Tyler, Tex., Aug. 28, 1934; d. Marcus Leon and Florence (Golenternek) Strum; m. Robert Wayne Kenny, July 22, 1956; children: David Jack, Joel Strum, Daniel Clark, Jonathan Matthew, Sarah Elizabeth. BA, BJ, U. Tex., 1955; MA, U. Minn., 1957; PhD, U. Chgo., 1964; LHD (hon.), U. Rochester, 1988. Asst., assoc. prof. Gallaudet Coll., Washington, 1962-66; assoc. prof. Cath. U. Am., Washington, 1966-71; assoc. prof. U. Md., College Park, 1971-73, prof., 1973-85, chmn. dept. English, 1973-79, provost-div. of arts and humanities, 1979-85; pres. Queens Coll., Flushing, N.Y., 1985—. Author: Richard Steele: The Conscious Lovers, 1968, The Plays of Richard Steele, 1971, The Performers and Their Plays, 1982, British Theatre and the Other Arts, 1984, The Works of George Farquhar, 1988. Mem. Am. Soc. for Eighteenth-Century Studies (exec. bd. 1981-83, steering com. 1982-83), Com. on Careers of MLA (nominating com. 1981-83), Internat. Council Fine Arts Deans, Council of Colls. of Arts & Scis., South Atlantic Grad. Coop. (chair 1977-79). NEH fellow, 1967, 80-82, Folger Shakespeare Library sr. fellow, 1970-71, Guggenheim fellow, 1976-77; Disting. Alumnus award for Profl. Excellence, U. Chgo. Club. of Washington, 1980; Outstanding Women award U. Md., 1983. Office: CUNY Queens Coll Kissena Blvd Flushing NY 11367

KENNY-GRANT, JANE SUSAN THERESA, graphic designer, b. N.Y.C., Aug. 27, 1956; d. James Joseph and Josephene Elizabeth (Tagliaferro) K.; m. Irving L. Grant Jr., Sept. 5, 1987. BFA, Coll. New Rochelle, N.Y., 1982. Artist Ganette Newspaper—Fairpress, Norwalk, Conn., 1983-84; graphic designer, illustrator Med. Edn. Program, Wilton, Conn., 1984-88; free-lance illustrator Joint Med. Products, Stamford, Conn., 1987-88; prin. Seafriend Ltd., Stamford, Conn., 1988—. Home: 55 Kenilworth Dr W Stamford CT 06902

KENOE, LISA BROIDO, lawyer; b. Norwalk, Conn., June 22, 1957; d. Henry Williard and Lois (Richards) Broido; m. Andrew Scott Kenoe, Dec. 27, 1980. B.S., Northwestern U., 1979; J.D., Columbia U., 1982. Bar: Ill. 1982. Assoc. editor ABA, Chgo., 1978-79; assoc. Friedman & Koven, Chgo., 1982-86, Neal, Gerber, Eisenberg & Lurie, Chgo., 1986—. Assoc. editor Update on Law-Related Education, 1982. Contbr. numerous articles to legal jours. Harlan Fiske Stone scholar Columbia U., 1982. Mem. ABA, Chgo. Bar Assn., Ill. Bar Assn. Office: Neal Gerber Eisenberg & Lurie 208 S LaSalle Suite 900 Chicago IL 60604

KENT, DEBORAH LYNN, banker; b. Tampa, Fla., Mar. 3, 1955; d. Shirley Jewell and Vera Juanita (Anderson) Kent. BA in Psychology magna cum laude, St. Leo's Coll., 1977; postgrad. in law, Mercer U., 1978-79, 80-81; MBA, Barry U., 1987; security diploma, Am. Inst. Banking, 1983; cert., Fla. Suprs. Acad., 1982. Clk. 1st Nat. Bank, Homestead, Fla., 1972-73, teller, then head teller, 1973-78; head teller Dadeland Bank, Miami, Fla., 1979-80, Great Am. Bank, Homestead, 1981-82; asst. cashier, teller adminstr. Sunset Comml. Bank, Miami, 1982-83, asst. cashier, ops. officer, asst. v.p., 1984—, also trainer, instr., 1982-83, data processing coordinator, 1983, compliance officer, 1983, owner Acad. Guidance Service, 1988—. Author teller manual and editor policy manual for Sunset Comml. Bank, 1983. Campaign vol. Dan Lewis for Senator, Homestead, 1982. Mem. Nat. Assn. Bank Women (group membership chmn. 1986—, co-chmn. state conf. publicity com. 1986—, publicity chmn. State Testimonial Dinner 1987, treas. 1987, sec. 1988, v.p. 1989), Nat. Assn. Female Execs., Bank Adminstrn. Inst., South Dade Bankers Assn., Am. Inst. Banking. Democrat. Baptist. Clubs: French (pres. 1971-73), Modern Music Masters (treas. 1972-73). Lodges: Homestead Assembly (worthy advisor 1972), Ad Astra. Home: 444 NW 21st St Homestead FL 33030 Office: Sunset Comml Bank 10899 Sunset Dr Miami FL 33173

KENT, ELIZABETH JANE LIPFORD, nursing administrator; b. Cleve., Feb. 23, 1919; d. Charles Meshach and Cora (Wiggins) Lipford; m. Cecil Alexander Kent, June 25, 1955; children: Cecil Alexander Jr., Jane Elizabeth. BA, Spelman Coll., 1942; BS, Med. Coll. Va., 1945; MPH, U. Mich., 1946, PhD, 1955. Instr. nursing Meharry Med. Coll., Nashville, 1946-47; instr., adminstr. health service Spelman Coll., Atlanta U., 1947-50, VA Hosp., Tuskegee, Ala., 1950-51; staff nurse, clin. instr. Providence Hosp., Detroit, 1951-56; pub. health educator Detroit Dept. Health, 1953-57; nurse educator and researcher, dir. psychiat. nursing research Lafayette Clinic, Detroit, 1958-86; nurse cons. Mich. Dept. Mental Health, Lansing, 1986—; home nursing instr. ARC, various cities, 1945-57; adj. prof. nursing Wayne State U., Detroit, 1965-87. Rosenwald Fund fellow, 1945-46. Mem. Am. Nurses Assn., Mich. Nurses Assn., Detroit Nurses Assn., Mich. Mental Health Assn., Mich. Assn. for Emotionally Disturbed Children. Home: 19344 Stratford Rd Detroit MI 48221 Office: Mich Dept Mental Health Lewis Cass Bldg Walnut St Lansing MI 48913

KENT, ELIZABETH NOEL, editor; b. Greensboro, N.C., Dec. 6, 1940; d. William Alfred and Rosa Elouise (Baughn) K. B.S., Ga. So. Coll., 1962; M.A., Ball State U., 1983. Tchr. English, Bd. Edn. Savannah, Ga., 1962-67; tchr. English, Stenography Div., Fort Harrison, Ind., 1974-77; edn. specialist Directorate of Tng. and Doctrine, Dept. Army, Fort Harrison, Ind., 1977-79, editor, 1979-83, chief editor, 1983-86; instr. English Vincennes U., 1979-86; realtor Realty World Sargent and Assocs., 1986-87, Ind. Referral Corp., 1987—; communication cons., lectr. on communication and English to profl. groups; tchr. English Programming and Systems, Inc. Inst., Indpls., 1987—. Served to capt. U.S. Army, 1967-74. Recipient Sustained Superior Performance award U.S. Army, 1976, Spl. Act award for superior editing, 1985. Mem. Federally Employed Women, Am. Legion, DAV, Women's Army Corps Assn., Bus. and Profl. Women. Anglican Catholic. Avocation: reading. Home: 11430 Wolf Ln Indianapolis IN 46229 Office: PSI Inst Indpls 20 N Meridian Indianapolis IN 46204

KENT, JILL ELSPETH, government official; b. Detroit, June 1, 1948; d. Seymour and Grace (Edelman) K.; m. Mark Elliott Solomons, Aug. 20, 1978. BA, U. Mich., 1970; JD, George Washington U., 1975, LLM, 1979. Bar: D.C. 1975. Mgmt. intern U.S. Dept. Transp., Washington, 1971-73; staff analyst Office Mgmt. and Budget, Exec. Office of Pres., Washington, 1974-76; legis. counsel U.S. Treasury Dept., Washington, 1976-78; dir. legis. reference div. Health Care Financing Adminstrn., Washington, 1978-80; sr. Budget Examiner Office Mgmt. and Budget, Exec. Office Pres., Washington, 1980-84; chief Treasury, Gen. Services, OMB, 1984-85; dep. asst. sec. for departmental fin. and planning U.S. Dept. Treasury, 1985-86; dep. asst. sec. for dept. fin. and mgmt., 1986-88; acting asst. sec. of the Treasury, 1988—; pres. S&K Properties Investment Partnership, Washington, 1979—; lectr. D.C. Pub. Schs.; participant charter exec. devel. program Office Mgmt. and Budget, 1984. Recipient Adminstrs. award Health Care Financing Adminstrn., 1980; named one of Top 40 Performers, Management mag., 1987. Mem. ABA, D.C. Bar Assn., Pres's. Council on Mgmt. Improvement. Republican. Jewish. Home: 5300 27th St NW Washington DC 20015 Office: US Dept Treasury Washington DC 20220

KENT, JOAN SWAFFORD, real estate broker; b. Los Angeles, Aug. 14, 1927; d. Henry Watson and Lillian (Stanton) Swafford; m. William Kent III, Sept. 3, 1955; children—Lucinda, Nicholas, Augustus. Student Bennington Coll., 1947-48, U. Calif.-Berkeley, 1945-1947; BA, UCLA, 1950. Cert. real estate broker. Sales assoc. Frank Howard Allen, Stinson Beach, Calif., 1970-75, Seadrift Co. Realtors, Stinson Beach, 1975-76, Cushman and Wakefield,

San Francisco, 1976-80; broker assoc. Hill and Co., San Francisco, 1981—. Bd. dirs. San Francisco Symphony, 1981-87; active in Modern Art Council, San Francisco, 1957—; Edgewood Aux., San Francisco, 1956—; assoc. dir. San Francisco Opera Guild, 1958—; mem. Childrens Theatre Assn., San Francisco, 1958—; charter mem. art mus. council Los Angeles County Mus. Art Volunteer Council, San Francisco Symphony. Mem. Marin County Bd. Realtors, San Francisco Bd. Realtors. Republican. Episcopalian. Clubs: Town & Country, San Francisco Golf, Seadrift Beach and Tennis. Avocations: golf, reading, music, swimming, hiking, gardening. Home: 3196 Pacific Ave San Francisco CA 94115 Office: Hill & Co 2107 Union St San Francisco CA 94123

KENT, KAREN IRENE, transportation executive; b. Ashtabula, Ohio, July 24, 1944; d. Herman Henry and Winifred Melissa (Havens) Smith; m. Larry Leroy Kent, June 26, 1965; children: Ronald Bruce, Donald Bryan. Student, Kent State U., Ashtabula, 1962-63, Durham Bus. Coll., Phoenix, 1964-65. Bookkeeper Osselaer Constrn. Co., Phoenix, 1978; from moulding clk. to jr. auditor S.W. Forest Industries, Phoenix, 1964-68, 74-75, 79-81; asst. bookkeeper Bookbinder Fin. Corp., Phoenix, 1982; gen. auditing clk. Cen. Ariz. Distbg. Co., Glendale, 1983; acct. Inspiration Consol. Copper Co., Phoenix, 1983, SMP Mech. Contractors Inc., Phoenix, 1984; co-owner, v.p. Canyon States Transp. Inc., Phoenix, 1984—. Cons. Birthright of Phoenix, 1969-75; program chmn. Phoenix Bapt. Hosp. Auxiliary, 1969-74; child find advocate Ariz. Dept. Edn., Phoenix, 1978—; team mother Pop Warner Football, 1980-83, Little League Baseball, Phoenix, 1978-83; treas. PTO, Phoenix, 1978-83, Skyhawk Parent Alliance, Glendale, 1986-88; active After 5 Christian and Profl. Women, 1985—. Mem. Phoenix C. of C. (pres.'s exchange 1986—). Republican. Baptist. Home: 2913 W Muriel Dr Phoenix AZ 85023 Office: Canyon States Transp Inc 21630 N 19th Ave Suite B-3 Phoenix AZ 85027-2717

KENT, PATRICIA JEAN TOPEL, graphic designer; b. Great Falls, Mont., May 5, 1959; d. Henry Thomas and Adeline Marie (Sieben) Topel; m. Lee Elworth Kent, Apr. 23, 1983. Student, Ea. Montana Coll., 1977-78; BA, Mont. State U., 1982. Freelance graphic designer Creative Imagery, Bozeman, Mont., 1982, The Marketplace, Bozeman, 1982-83; graphic designer Greenleaf Graphics, Evanston, Ill., 1984; owner The Graphics Shoppe, Arlington Heights, Ill., 1984—; graphic design cons. Montana Chorale, Great Falls, 1984—; advt. cons. Cellular Communications Corp., Las Vegas, Nev., 1987—; freelance graphic designer The Chestnut House Group, Inc., 1987—. Mem. Nat. Assn. Female Execs. Republican. Roman Catholic.

KENT, ROBERTA B., literary agent; b. N.Y.C., Sept. 7, 1945; d. Robert B. and Rose (Linker) K. BA magna cum laude, NYU, 1967, MA, 1969; postgrad., Princeton U., 1967-68. Asst. to head literary dept. Creative Mgmt. Assocs., N.Y.C., 1969-70; asst. to pres. Curtis Brown Ltd., N.Y.C., 1970-72, literary agt., v.p. dept. motion pictures, 1978-79; ptnr., literary agt. W.B. Agy., N.Y.C., 1972-78; literary agt., v.p. dept. motion pictures Kohner-Levy Agy., Los Angeles, 1979-81; literary agt. The Ufland Agy., Beverly Hills, Calif., 1981-83; literary agt., v.p. literary dept. S.T.E. Representation, Ltd., Beverly Hills, 1983—. Mem. Phi Beta Kappa. Democrat. Office: STE Representation Ltd 9301 Wilshire Blvd Beverly Hills CA 90210

KENT, RUTH KIMBALL, lexicographer; b. Auburn, N.Y., Aug. 30, 1920; d. Charles Arthur and Nellie Corrinne (Gove) Kimball; m. Harold Thomas Kent, 1936 (div. 1960); children—Harold Thomas, David Arthur, Grace Ann Kent Richardson. B.A., Syracuse U., 1962, M.A., 1968. Copy editor Kent State U. Press (Ohio), 1964-68; assoc. editor Webster's New World Dictionary (Prentice Hall Press), Cleve., 1964-87; columnist The Plain Dealer, Cleve., 1979-84. Author: Language of Journalism, 1970; editor: Collins Gem Dictionary of Synonyms, 1979. Mem. Women in Communications, Soc. Profl. Journalists, Dictionary Soc. North Am. Republican. Methodist. Club: Press Club. Home: 60 Broadmeadows Blvd 129 Columbus OH 43214

KENTON, AUDREE COKE, editor, public relations official; b. Griffin, Sask., Can., July 24, 1922; d. Raymond Leslie and Clara Edna (Learn) Willsey; m. Stanley Newcomb Kenton, Aug. 30, 1975 (dec. 1979); children: Leslie, Dana, Lance, Cynthia. AA, Santa Ana Coll., 1941; student, UCLA, 1946. Editor-in-chief Western Family Mag., Los Angeles, 1944-49, Your Guide to Hawaii, Honolulu, 1953-56; writer Dudley, Anderson & Yutsy Pub. Relations, N.Y.C., 1949-51; dir. pub. relations TB and Health Assn. Hawaii, Honolulu, 1956-66, Creative World Records, Los Angeles, 1971-83, Estate of Stan Kenton, Los Angeles, 1979—; editor Creative Press Pub., Los Angeles, 1980—. Editor: Stan Kenton: Artistry in Rhythm, 1981 (ASCAP Deems Taylor award 1982). Mem. pub. relations adv. com. Oahu Health Council, 1963; mem. pub. relations com. East-West Ctr., U. Hawaii, 1965. Mem. Women in Communications (pres. Hawaii 1966, Orange County 1969), Pub. Relations Soc. Am. (sec. 1962-63), Pub. Relations Women Hawaii (pres. 1969). Republican. Clubs: Press (Honolulu); Hollywood Women's, Press (Hollywood). Home and Office: 6193 Rockcliff Dr Hollywood CA 90068

KENWORTHY, SHARON LYNNE, manufacturing company manager; b. Long Beach, Calif., Dec. 14, 1944; d. Harvey Wyrill and Doris June (Henneberry) Kenworthy; m. Jeffrey Richard Viscuso, Feb. 28, 1970 (div.). B.A. in Psychology cum laude, Upsala Coll., 1966. Vol. U.S. Peace Corps, Philippines, 1966-68; mgmt. devel. and tng. assoc./specialist Western Electric Co., N.Y.C., 1968-71, sect. chief manpower devel., 1971-72, buyer, East Orange, N.J., 1972-76; mgr. contract adminstrn. Wallace Computer Services, Hillside, Ill., 1976-85, mgr. price and contract adminstrn., 1985—. Mem. Nat. Assn. Female Execs., Upsala Coll. Alumni Assn. (alumni council 1974-76). Republican. Episcopalian. Avocations: singing; reading; photography. Home: 313A Dee Ct Bloomingdale IL 60108 Office: Wallace Computer Services Inc 4600 W Roosevelt Rd Hillside IL 60162

KENYON, JULIA CAROLINE, retired educator; b. Harvard, Nebr., Jan. 3, 1919; d. Peter J. and Anna Marie (Bartholoma) Pauley; m. Meril T. Kenyon, May 10, 1949. BS, U. Nebr., 1941; MEd, Colo. State U., 1968, postgrad., 1980; postgrad., Oreg. State U., 1965, U. No. Colo., 1970, Utah State U., 1979, others. Tchr. home econs., Philips, Nebr., 1941-43, Grand Island, Nebr., 1943-44; FHA supr. home econs. Loup City (Nebr.) Schs., 1945-46; mgr. home extension program Perkins County, Nebr., 1947-59; tchr. home econs. Holyoke (Colo.) High Sch., 1959-84. Hon. vol. local Heart Assn.; chair Holyoke Heart Assn.; vol. Meals on Wheels. Served with WAVES, USN, 1944-46. Recipient Outstanding Home Econs. Humanitarian award State of Colo., 1977. Mem. NEA, Colo. Edn. Assn. (profl. affairs com.), Holyoke Edn. Assn. (pres. 1975), Am. Vocat. Assn., Colo. Vocat. Assn., Colo. Assn. Vocat. Tchrs., Am. Home Econs. Assn., Colo. Home Econs. Assn., Gen. Fedn. Women's Clubs (dist. treas. Nebr. 1954-55, pres. 1954-55), Sigma Kappa, Delta Kappa Gamma (pres. local chpt.). Methodist. Clubs: Venango Fairy Dell (pres.), Mary Jane Extension. Lodge: Order Eastern Star (past matron). Home: 205 S Belford St Holyoke CO 80734 Office: PO Box 193 Holyoke CO 80734

KENYON, LISA ANNE, ship building consultant, yacht captain; b. Providence, May 30, 1958; d. Charles Lincoln and Marilyn (Broden) K. Student, U. R.I., 1977. Lic. USCG 100-ton vessel captain, 1983. First mate Yachts "Topaz" I & II, Greenwich, Conn., 1971-76, 12-Meter Sloop "Gleam", Newport, R.I., 1977-81; proprietor, designer "Dagoils" Restoration and Refinishing, Newport, 1981-83; pres., founder Airwaves Inc., Hovercraft Service, Newport, 1983—; exec. Endeavour, Inc., Newport, 1986—; cons. to yacht refinishing firms, Newport, 1981—, to contracting, design firms, Newport, 1983—. Mem. Mus. Yachting, Newport, 1981—. Mem. Order of the Good Cheer. Club: St. George's Dingy (Bermuda). Office: Endeavour 32 Church St Newport RI 02840

KENYON, PATRICIA BOTHWELL, occupational therapist, consultant; b. Phila., Jan. 22, 1949; d. Thomas Henry and Dorothy Lyle (Galloway) Bothwell; divorced; children: Cynthia, Margaret. BS in Biology, Alma (Mich.) Coll., 1970; cert. program occupational therapist, U. Pa., 1972; MA in Pshycology, U. Colo., 1982; postgrad., Lesley Coll., 1986—. Cert. occupational therapist, Pa. Sr. occupational therapist Hosp. of U. Pa., Phila., 1972-76, Bethesda Hosp., Denver, 1977-80, Littleton (Colo.) Pub. Schs., 1981-88; cons. therapy Denver, 1981—; occupational therapist Children's Hosp., Denver, 1988—; research asst. Children's Hosp., Denver, 1981; intensive care occupational therapist Rose Med. Ctr., Denver, 1982; charter mem. Nat. Spl. Edn. Alliance (Apple Computer), Denver, 1987; mem. steering com. early childhood intervention project Rocky Mountain Child Devel. Ctr., Denver, 1986—. Contbr. articles to profl. jours. Mem. Am. Occupational Therapy Assn. (mental health liaison 1978-81), Occupational Therapy Assn. of Colo. (research com. 1977—, sec. 1986—), Colo. Assn. Severly Handicapped, Soc. Alternative and Augmentative Communication, Colo. Edn. Assn. Presbyterian. Home: 825 Lafayette St Denver CO 80218 Office: Children's Hosp Denver CO

KENYON, PATRICIA JEANNE, real estate broker; b. Chgo., July 15, 1945; d. William August and Marie Louise (DeSchryver) Patera; m. J. Andrew Kenyon, Jr., Aug. 12, 1942; 1 child, Patrick James Orrell. BBA, Wichita (Kans.) State U., 1984. Cert. Comml. Investment Mem., Realtors Nat. Mktg. Inst. of Nat. Assn. Realtors. Regional underwriter Fed. Home Loan Mktg. Corp., Topeka, 1971; asst. v.p. Mid Kans. Fed. Savs. and Loan, Wichita, 1981; broker J.P. Weigand & Sons, Wichita, 1983—. Mem. Hist. Landmark Preservation Com., Wichita, 1983—. Mem. Nat. Assn. Women Bus. Owners (bd. dirs. 1986—), Rho Epsilon (local pres. 1982-83), Nat. Assn. Realtors, Internat. Council of Shopping Ctrs. Office: JP Weigand & Sons 150 N Market Wichita KS 67202

KEOGH, JEANNE MARIE, librarian; b. Toledo, Sept. 20, 1924; d. Thomas Leroy and Agnes Mary (Wenzler) K. BA, Mary Manse Coll., 1946; BLS, Western Res. U., 1947. Asst. librarian tech. dept. Toledo Pub. Library, 1946-54; tech. librarian Libbey Owens Ford Co., Toledo, 1954-83; librarian Libbey Owens Ford Co. (now subs. Pilkington Group), Toledo, 1983—. Established library Riverside Hosp. Nursing Sch., Toledo, 1950-51; gray lady ARC, Toledo, 1966-70; mem. Transp. Safety Info. com., 1972—; mem. fin. com. Mary Manse Coll., Toledo, 1972-75; chmn. bd. Ecumenical Library Toledo, 1976—. Mem. Ohio Library Assn., Cath. Library Assn., Spl. Libraries Assn. (chmn. 1960-70, 72-74, scholarship com. 1968-74, chmn. Detroit conf. hospitality com. 1970, chmn. metals/materials div. 1977-78, metals/materials div. Honors award 1987), Mary Manse Coll. Alumni Assn. (bd. dirs. 1971-76, pres. 1972-73). Club: Quota (Toledo). Office: Libbey Owens Ford Co 1701 E Broadway Toledo OH 43605

KEOGH, NANCY JONES, psychologist; b. Youngstown, Ohio, Oct. 18, 1950; d. Edward Henry Jr. and Ruth Virginia (Jensen) Jones; m. Frederick John Keogh, July 20, 1974. BA in Psychology, Miami U., Oxford, Ohio, 1972; MA in Psychology, U. Akron, 1975, PhD in Counseling Psychology, 1983. Psychology asst. Portage Path Community Mental Health Ctr., Akron, Ohio, 1976-79, U. Akron Testing and Counseling Ctr., 1979-81; research assoc. Northeastern Ohio U. Coll. Medicine, Rootstown, 1981-82; psychology intern Fallsview Psychiat. Hosp., Cuyahoga Falls, Ohio, 1982-83; psychologist Behavioral Cons., Norton, Ohio, 1983-85, Freedman & Assocs., Akron, 1983—; instr. psychology U. Akron, 1984—; cons. psychologist Psychodiagnostic Clinic Summit County Ct. Common Pleas, Akron, 1985—. Active Jr. League, Youngstown, Ohio, 1972-75, Akron, 1975-79. Recipient Mental Health Service award Mental Health Assn. Summit County, 1986. Mem. Am. Psychol. Assn., Ohio Psychol. Assn., Akron Area Profl. Psychologists. Club: Silver Lake (Ohio) Garden. Office: Keogh Bendo Freedman & Assocs 33 North Ave Suite 210 Tallmadge OH 44278

KEOHANE, NANNERL OVERHOLSER, college president, political science educator; b. Blytheville, Ark., Sept. 18, 1940; d. James Arthur and Grace (McSpadden) Overholser; m. Patrick Henry III, Sept. 16, 1962 (div. May 1969); 1 son, Stephan; m. Robert Owen Keohane, Dec. 18, 1970; children: Sarah, Jonathan, Nathaniel. B.A., Wellesley Coll., 1961, Oxford U., Eng., 1963; Ph.D., Yale U., 1967. Faculty Swarthmore Coll., Pa., 1967-73, Stanford U., Calif., 1973-81; fellow Ctr. for Advanced Study in the Behavioral Scis.-Stanford U., 1978-79, 87-88; pres., prof. polit. sci. Wellesley Coll., Mass., 1981—; bd. dirs. State St. Boston Corp., IBM, Consortium on Fin. Higher Edn. Author: Philosophy and the State in France: The Renaissance to the Enlightenment, 1980; co-editor: Feminist Theory: A Critique of Ideology, 1982. Trustee WGBH Ednl. TV Found., from 1981; mem. vis. com. John F. Kennedy Sch. Govt. Harvard U., 1983—; bd. dirs. Am. Ditchley Found., 1986—, Carnegie Found. for Advancement of Teaching, 1986—. Marshall scholar, 1961-63; AAUW dissertation fellow. Mem. Council on Fgn. Relations, Phi Beta Kappa. Democrat. Presbyterian. Clubs: Cosmopolitan (N.Y.C.); Saturday (Boston), Commercial (Boston), Algonquin (Boston). Office: Wellesley Coll Office of the Pres Wellesley MA 02181

KEON, PEGGY LUMPKIN, career management consultant; b. Chgo., Sept. 10, 1931; d. Richard Adamson and Mary Hart (Green) Lumpkin; B.A., Wellesley Coll., 1952; children—Pamela Keon Vitale, Lisa Keon Thompson, Susan Tamara, Margaret Lynley, Joseph John, Katherine Stoddert. Career counselor, San Francisco, 1978-80; owner Careers for Women, San Francisco, 1980-83; owner Keon Assocs., Career Mgmt. Cons., Mill Valley, Calif., 1983—; dir. Utility Bond & Share Co. Mem. Nat. Assn. Female Execs., Chi Psi. Republican. Episcopalian. Clubs: Wellesley Coll. of No. Calif.; San Francisco Yacht. Home and Office: 16 Miller Ave Mill Valley CA 94941

KEOUGH, ANN B., personnel administrator; b. N.Y.C., Sept. 27, 1934; d. George Loyal Ball, Jr. and Helen (Ellsworth) Paget; m. Milton E. McKay, 1958 (div. 1970); children: Tracy O'Brien, Shari, Scott; m. Raymond B. Keough, 1983. BS, Allegheny Coll., 1956; MS, U. Fla., 1958; EdD, Fla. Atlantic U., 1977. Cert. tchr., Fla. Lab. technician U. Pitts., 1956; chemist research lab. U. Fla. Med. Sch., Gainesville, 1958-62; supr. labs. dept. chemistry Fla. Atlantic U., Boca Raton, 1971-77; project mgr. affirmative action Palm Beach County Sch. Bd., West Palm Beach, Fla., 1977-79, supr. employee benefits services, 1979-83, dir. employee services, 1984-86, dir. info. ops., 1986—; cons. environ. waste Belle Glade and Palm Beach, 1966-78. Mem. area planning bd. West Palm Beach, 1974-76, Palm Beach County Sch. Bd., 1969-76, chmn. 1972. Republican. Office: Palm Beach County Schs 3323 Belvedere Rd West Palm Beach FL 33402

KEPNER, RITA MARIE, sculptor, writer, editor, international military public affairs officer; b. Binghamton, N.Y., Nov. 15, 1944; d. Peter Walter and Helena Theresa (Piotrowski) Kramnicz; student Elmira Coll., 1962-63; BA, Harpur Coll., SUNY, 1966; postgrad., Okla. U., 1988. m. John C. Matthiesen; 1 son, Stewart John, Matthiesen. One-woman shows include: Willoughby Wallace Meml. Gallery, Branford, Conn., 1967, Penryn Gallery, Seattle, 1970, 73, 76, Haines Gallery, Seattle, 1975, Zoliborz Gallery, Warsaw, Poland, 1981; group shows include: SUNY, Binghamton, 1966, Manawata Art Gallery, Palmerston North, N.Z., Modern Art Mus., Seattle, 1976, Portland (Oreg.) Art Mus., 1976, Die Roemer Gallery, Wiesbaden, Fed. Republic Germany, 1988; major works include: Peace Pipe, Zalaegerszeg, Hungary, Human Forms in Balance, City of Seattle, 1975, Unity, City of Znin, Poland, 1976, Rough to Smooth, Seattle Pub. Library, 1978; informal visual arts ambassador between U.S. and Poland, 1976-81; pres. fed. women's program council Seattle dist., 1985-86; fed. women's project mgr., Sweinfurt, Fed. Republic Germany, 1986-87, Wiesbaden, 1988; artist-in-residence City of Seattle, 1975, 77-78; del. Internat. Sculptors Conf., Toronto, Ont., Can., 1978; VISTA vol., 1982-84 Paramedic, bd. dirs. Aradia Med. Clinic, Seattle, 1972-74; writer, editor, pub. affairs specialist Seattle dist. U.S. Army CE; pub. affairs officer Wiesbaden (Fed. Republic Germany) Milcom Hdqrs., 1987—; editor Schweinfurt, Fed. Republic Germany, 1986-87. Cofounder Bainbridge Island Arts Council. Recipient merit award for superior journalistic achievement U.S. Army CE, 1984, 85, 2d place news category competition award, 1985, 86; suggestion award Dept. Army, 1984, ofcl. commendation, 1985, 86, 87; Kosciuszko Found. grantee, 1975, 76, 79, 81. Mem. Internat. Artists Assn. of UNESCO, Paris Artists Equity Assn., Internat. Artists Cooperation (Edewecht, W. Ger.), NW Multihull Assn. (commodore 1974). holder USCG capt. lic. for passenger carrying aux. sailing vessels up to 50 tons, 1980—. Contbr. articles to Northwest Arts, Seattle Post Intelligencer, Leonardo mag., Polska Panorama, Poland mag. Home: 6681 Flager Rd Nordland WA 98358 Office: Wiesbaden Milcom HQ Public Affairs Office APO NY 09457

KEPPLER, PATRICIA ANN, personnel director; b. Elmira, N.Y., Aug. 29, 1956; d. Robert Harry and Ellen Patricia (Bird) Huddle; m. Stephen Thomas Keppler, Apr. 21, 1979. BA cum laude, St. Bonaventure U., 1978. Dir. personnel services and communications Louis N. Picciano & Son, Endwell, N.Y., 1979—; owner Woman's World Fitness Ctr. Vol. Am. Cancer Soc., 1984—, March of Dimes, 1984—; com. mem. Broome County Arts Council, Binghamton, N.Y., 1987; bd. dirs. Community Meml. Ctr., Endicott, N.Y., 1987—; participant first Broome County Leadership; pres. Girls Club Western Broome, Endicott, 1987—. Mem. Am. Soc. Personnel Adminstrs. So Tier Personnel Assn. Home: 611 ValleyView Dr Endwell NY 13760 Office: Louis N Picciano & Son 405 Davis Ave Endwell NY 13760

KEPPNER, FLORENCE FERNANDEZ, dietitian, consultant; b. Cabanatuan, Philippines, Nov. 7, 1936; d. Severino Obando and Macaria (Hernando) Fernandez; m. Norbert Johann Keppner, Feb. 8, 1969; children: Michele, Michael. BS, Philippine Women's U., Manila, 1956; MS, Purdue U., 1965. Registered and lic. dietitian. Tchr., therapeutic dietitian St. Mary's Hosp., Rochester, Minn., 1961-63; adminstrv. dietitian Johns Hopkins Hosp., Balt., 1965-66; dir. dietetics Balt. County Gen. Hosp., Randallstown, Md., 1966-68; travelling, supervising dietitian Hosp. Food Mgmt. div. Automatic Retailers of Am., Des Plaines, Ill., 1968-69; therapeutic dietitian Gulf Coast Community Hosp., Biloxi, Miss., 1976-77; dir. food and nutrition South Miss. Retardation Ctr., Long Beach, 1978—; TV and radio cooking demonstrator Inter-Island Gas Service, Inc., Manila, 1956-60; cons. dietitian Med. Facilities Gt. Muskegon, Mich., 1969-73, Gulf Coast Nursing Home, Pascagoula, Miss., 1977—, USN Naval Home, Gulfport, 1988; assoc. prof. Philippine Women's U., Manila, 1973-75; dietary cons. Miss. State Bd. Health, Jackson, 1977-78; adj. instr. Miss. Gulf Coast Jr. Coll., Gulfport, 1982. Event coordinator Miss. Gulf Coast Oktoberfest, 1976—; adv. bd. de l'Epee Deaf Ctr., Gulfport, 1980-84, chairperson fund-raising com. 1982; fin. com. mem. St. Joseph's Ch. parish council, Gulfport, 1980; food com. mem. Miss USA Pageant, Miss., 1980-82; coordinator Gulf Coast Gingerbread contest, 1982—; organizer Miss. Gulf Coast Volksmarch, 1984, pres. 1984-85, spl. event coordinator 1986—; organized Fun Walk for Fitness, 1988; mem. Miss. Coast Jazz Soc., Biloxi, 1977—; com. mem. Developing A Curriculum program at Miss. Gulf Jr. Coll., Gulfport, 1987. Recipient Highest Achievement award Manila Speech Clinic, 1957, Outstanding Profl. Achievement award Mich. Hosp. Assn., 1971. Mem. Miss. Dietetic Assn. (career guidance com. 1977-78, food adminstrn. com. 1979-80, nutritional adminstr. 1977-79), Dietary Mgr.'s Assn. (Gulf Coast chpt. advisor 1981—, meritorious services award 1986). Roman Catholic. Lodge: Kiwanis (mgmt. citation, 1968), Optimist (profl. citation 1972). Home: 18588 Robinson Rd Gulfport MS 39503 Office: S Miss Retardation Ctr 1170 W Railroad St Long Beach MS 39560

KERBER, LINDA KAUFMAN, historian, educator; b. N.Y.C., Jan. 23, 1940; d. Harry Hagman and Dorothy (Haber) Kaufman; m. Richard Kerber, June 5, 1960; children: Ross Jeremy, Justin Seth. A.B. cum laude, Barnard Coll., 1960; M.A., NYU, 1961; Ph.D., Columbia U., 1968. Instr., asst. prof. history Stern Coll., Yeshiva U., N.Y.C., 1963-68; asst. prof. history San Jose State Coll., (Calif.), 1969-70; vis. asst. prof. history Stanford U., (Calif.), 1970-71; asst. prof. history U. Iowa, Iowa City, 1971-75, prof., 1975-85; May Brodbeck prof. U. Iowa, 1985—. Author: Federalists in Dissent: Imagery and Ideology in Jeffersonian America, 1970, paperback edit., 1980, Women of the Republic: Intellect and Ideology in Revolutionary America, 1980, 2d edit., paperback, 1986; co-editor: Women's America: Refocusing the Past, 1982, 2d edit., 1987; mem. editorial bd.: Am. Hist. Rev., Signs: Jour. Women in Culture and Society; contbr. articles and book revs. to profl. jours. Danforth Found. fellow; Barnard Coll. fellow; NEH fellow, 1976, 83-84; grantee Am. Philos. Soc., 1971, Am. Bar Found., 1975, Am. Council Learned Socs., 1975. Mem. Orgn. Am. Historians, Am. Hist. Assn., Am. Studies Assn. (pres. 1988), Am. Soc. for Legal History, Berkshire Conf. Women Historians. Jewish. Office: U Iowa Dept History Iowa City IA 52242

KERBIS, GERTRUDE LEMPP, architect. m. Walter Peterhans (dec.); m. Donald Kerbis (div. 1972); children: Julian, Lisa, Kim. B.S., U. Ill.; M.A., Ill. Inst. Tech.; postgrad., Grad. Sch. Design, Harvard U., 1949-50. Archtl. designer Skidmore, Owings & Merrill, Chgo., 1954-59, C.F. Murphy Assocs., Chgo., 1959-62, 65-67; pvt. practice architecture Chgo., 1967—; lectr. U. Ill., 1969; prof. William Rainey Harper Coll., 1970—, Washington U., St. Louis, 1977, 82; archtl. cons. Dept. Urban Renewal, City of Chgo.; mem. Northeastern Ill. Planning Commn., Open Land Project, Mid-North Community Orgn., Chgo. Met. Housing and Planning Council, Chgo. Mayor's Commn. for Preservation Chgo.'s Hist. Architecture; bd. dirs. Chgo. Sch. Architecture Found., 1972-76; trustee Glessner House Found., Inland Architect Mag.; lectr. Art Inst. Chgo., U. N.Mex., Ill. Inst. Tech., Washington U., St. Louis, Ball State U., Muncie, Ind., U. Utah, Salt Lake City. Prin. archtl. works include U.S. Air Force Acad. dining hall, Colo., 1957, Skokie (Ill.) Pub. Library, 1959, Meadows Club, Lake Meadows, Chgo., 1959, O'Hare Internat. Airport 7 Continents Bldg, 1963; prin. developer and architect: Tennis Club, Highland Park, Ill., 1968, Watervliet, Mich. Tennis Ranch, 1970, Greenhouse Condominium, Chgo., 1976, Webster-Clark Townhouses, Chgo., 1986; exhibited at Chgo. Hist. Soc., 1984, Chgo. Mus. Sci. and Industry, 1985, Paris Exhbn. Chgo. Architects, 1985; represented in permanent archtl. drawings collection Art Inst. Chgo. Recipient award for outstanding achievement in professions YWCA Met. Chgo., 1984. Fellow AIA (dir. Chgo. chpt. 1971-75, chpt. pres. 1980, mem. nat. com. architecture arts and recreation 1972-75, com. on design 1975-80, head subcom. inst. honors nomination); mem. AAUP, ACLU, U. Ill., Ill. Inst. Tech. alumni assns., Art Inst. Chgo., Chgo. Council Fgn. Relations, Chgo. Women in Architecture (founder), Planned Parenthood Assn., Chgo. Network, Lincoln Park Zool. Soc., Lambda Alpha. Clubs: Chgo. Arts (pres. 1988), Cliff Dwellers (bd. dirs. 1987-88, pres. 1988). Office: Lempp Kerbis Assocs 172 W Burton Pl Chicago IL 60610

KERES, KAREN LYNNE, English educator; b. Evanston, Ill., Oct. 22, 1945; d. Frank and Bette (Pascoe) K.; B.A., St. Mary's Coll., 1967; student U. Notre Dame, 1967-68; M.A., U. Iowa, 1969. Asst. to editor U. Chgo. Press, 1968; assoc. prof. English, humanities, fine art William Rainey Harper Coll., Palatine, Ill., 1969—; cons. bus. communications. Mem. MLA, Ill. Assn. Tchrs. English, Am. Fedn. Tchrs., Nature Conservancy, Mensa. Home: 222 Fairfield Dr Island Lake IL 60042 Office: William Rainey Harper Coll Dept Liberal Arts Palatine IL 60067

KERLEY, JANICE JOHNSON, personnel executive; b. Coral Gables, Fla., Nov. 28, 1939; d. Howard Love and Lois Dean (Austin) Johnson; m. Bobby Joe Kerley, May 16, 1959; children: Janice Elizabeth Kerley Vela, Meredith Ann Kerley Tucker. AA, Stephens Coll., 1958; B in Music Edn., U. Miami, Fla., 1960. Tchr. Dade County Pub. Schs., Miami, 1960-69; asst. to v.p. engr. Racal-Milgo, Inc., Miami, 1972-80; dir. sales and mktg. B. Joe Kerley, Realtor, Miami, 1980-83; dir. customer service, ops. mgr. Modern-Age Furniture Co., Miami, 1983-85; chief exec. officer Adia Personnel Services, Greensboro, Winston-Salem, N.C., 1985—. Mem. Am. Bus. Women's Assn. (nat. bd. dirs. 1978-79, trustee nat. scholarship fund 1978-79). Office: Adia Personnel Services 315-B Pomona Dr Greensboro NC 27407 other: 4300 Indiana Ave Suite #35 Winston-Salem NC 27106

KERMEEN, SHARON KAY, social services worker; b. Caledonia, Mich., Dec. 2, 1938; d. Wayne Earl and Crystal Doreen (Johnson) K. Grad. high sch., Middleville, Mich. Clk. State of Mich., Hastings, 1957-69; clerical supr. State of Mich.-Barry County Dept. Social Services, Hastings, 1970-72, eligibility examiner, 1970-72; assistance payments worker Dept Social Services Barry County, Hastings, 1972—. Mem. cast Hastings Civic Players, 1963. Mem. Mich. State Employees Assn. (sec. treas., v.p.), United Auto Workers, Hastings Bus. and Profl. Women's Club)corr. sec., 2d v.p.). Home: 321 S Broadway Middleville MI 49333

KERMIS, MARGUERITE DEYAEGER, psychology educator; b. Rochester, N.Y., Apr. 21, 1948; d. Alphonse Louis and Mary Alice (Tobin) DeYaeger; m. George F. Kermis III, July 28, 1973. BA, Canisius Coll., 1972; MA, Syracuse U., 1975, PhD in Psychology, 1976; MS in Preventive Medicine, U. Buffalo, 1983. Lic. psychologist, N.Y. Asst. prof. Syracuse (N.Y.) U., 1976-77; prof. psychology Canisius Coll., Buffalo, 1977—; vis. prof. U. Rochester (N.Y.) Sch. Medicine, 1984; cons. N.Y. State Edn. Dept., Albany, 1980—, N.Y. State Health Dept., Albany, 1984-85, Sisters of St. Joseph, Buffalo, 1986—; adj. prof. Roswell Park Meml. Cancer Inst., Buffalo, 1982—; mem. Masters Program in Gerontology D'Youville Coll., Buffalo, 1986—. Author: Psychology of Human Aging, 1984, Mental Health in Late Life, 1986. Mem. Gov.'s Council on Aging, Albany, 1985-87, Erie County Mgmt. and Budget Adv. Council, Buffalo, 1987. Named Disting.

Prof. of Psychology, 1984; recipient Book award Am. Jour. Nursing, 1986-87. Mem. Am. Psychol. Assn., Assn. for Geronotology in Higher Edn. (program chmn. 1986—), N.Y. State Assn. Gerontological Educators (pres. 1984-85), Gerontological Soc. Am., Di Gamma, Alpha Sigma Lambda. Home: 6111 Clarence Ln N East Amherst NY 14051 Office: Canisius Coll 2001 Main St Buffalo NY 14208

KERMON, MARGARET ANNE, engineer; b. Chgo., Feb. 27, 1956; d. James Paul and Joan Margaret (Fitzgerald) Morgan; m. Lawrence J. Kermon, Mar. 24, 1979; children: Kathryn, John. BS in Mechanical Engring., U. Notre Dame, 1978; MBA, Washington U., St. Louis, 1985. Process engr. E.I. DuPont de Nemours, Seaford, Del., 1978-79; engr. Vitro Labs., Silver Springs, Md., 1979-80, McDonnell Aircraft Co., St. Louis, 1980-85; project engr. Honeywell, Herndon, Va., 1985—. Mem. Soc. Women Engrs. Roman Catholic. Club: Mulberry (Reston). Office: Honeywell 13775 McLearen Rd Herndon VA 22071

KERN, BARBARA PATRICIA, public health administrator; b. Elizabeth, N.J., Sept. 22, 1935; d. Eugene Louis and Wilma Catherine (Pitula) K. BS, Ithaca Coll., 1957; MA, NYU, 1965. Lic. in phys. therapy, N.J., N.Y. Supr. N.Y. State Dept. Rehab., West Haverstraw, 1958-67; asst. prof. phys. therapy Temple U., Phila., 1967-71; cons. phys. therapy N.J. State Dept. Health, Trenton, 1971-75, coordinator crippled children program, 1975-80, chief spl. child health services, 1980-86, dir. spl. chiefl health services, 1987—; adminstrv. cons. Va. Crippled Children Program, 1985, Ala. Crippled Children Program, 1982; mem. planning com. Nat. Conf. Fin. Servicesfor Handicapped Children, 1983; cons. in field. Contbg. author: Competencies in Physical Therapy, 1977; contbr. articles to profl. jours. Chmn. prevention com. N.J. Assn. Retarded Citizens, 1981. Mem. Am. Pub. Health Assn., Assn. Maternal and Child Health Programs. Office: NJ State Dept Health CN 364 Trenton NJ 08626

KERN, CONSTANCE ELIZABETH, real estate broker; b. Cleve., Dec. 18, 1937; d. Walter Anthony and Irene (Davies) Matthews; divorced; children: James, David, Douglas, Kathleen. Student, John Carroll U., 1957, Case Western Res. U., 1958; BA in Speech and English, Marietta (Ohio) Coll., 1959; postgrad., Sul Ross State U., Midland, Tex., 1967-68, Comml. Coll. Real Estate, Ft. Worth, 1984, 86. Cert. tchr., Ohio, Tex.; lic. real estate broker, Tex. Tchr. South Euclid and Lyndhurst (Ohio) Schs., 1959-60; sec. Pan Am. Petroleum, Midland, 1960-61; tchr. St. Ann's Sch., Midland, 1967-69; real estate agt. McAfee & Assocs., Arlington, Tex., 1985-86; real estate broker Constance Kern Real Estate, Arlington, 1986—; adminstrv. asst. JWJ Enterprises, Arlington, 1986-87; pvt. practice oil operator, investor, Midland and Arlington, 1975—. Vol. Pink Ladies Midland Meml. Hosp., 1970-73; troop leader Brownies Girl Scouts Am., Midland, 1971; vol. speech therapist Children's Service League Cerebral Palsy Ctr., Midland, 1975-76. Mem. AAUW, Nat. Bd. Realtors, Tex. Bd. Realtors, Arlington Bd. Realtors, Women's Golf Assn. (pres.), Pi Kappa Delta. Republican. Roman Catholic. Clubs: Shady Valley Golf (Arlington) (pres. 1982), Woodhaven Country (Ft. Worth).

KERN, KATHRYN CECELIA, hospital administrator; b. Easton, Pa., Mar. 1, 1947; d. Frank Reagle and Kathryn Cecelia (Bonstein) K. BS, Conn. Coll., 1969; MS, Northeastern U., 1977; MBA, Boston U., 1983. Sr. research technologist, infectious disease unit Mass. Gen. Hosp., Boston, 1969-76, first lab. asst., thyroid unit, 1976-83, bus. mgr. for practices, dept. of medicine, 1983-84; assoc. dir., MGH-Community Health Assocs Mass. Gen. Hosp., Chelsea, Mass., 1984—. Author: (with Kathryn Cecelia Kern) Lysozyme, 1974. Mem. Camp Bunker Hill Adv. Bd.,Charlestown, Mass., 1984—. Mem. Am. Mgmt. Assn., Boston U. Health Care Alumni Assn., Mass. Health Council, Women Health Care Mgmt. Assn. Home: 1C Fletcher Way Salem MA 01970 Office: MGH Community Health Assocs 111 Bellingham St Chelsea MA 02150

KERN, LISA MARIE, computer scientist; b. N.Y.C., Dec. 29, 1957; d. John Walter Kern and Joan Ann (Mihalics) Ecker; m. Scott Jay Horowitz, Oct. 23, 1983. BS in Computer Sci., St. John's U., Jamaica, N.Y., 1978; MS in Computer Sci., Ga. Inst. Tech., 1979. Asst. programmer IBM, Cape Canaveral, Fla., 1978; applied computer analyst Univ. Tenn., Knoxville, 1979-81; tech. cons. Computer Scis. Corp., N.Y.C., 1981-83; mgr., end user Motorola, Inc., Scottsdale, Ariz., 1983—; instr. North Am. Coll., Phoenix, 1985-86, Mesa (Ariz.) Community Coll., 1986—. Active Phoenix Rep. Party, 1987—. NSF fellow, 1978. Mem. Am. Mgmt. Assn., Assn. for Computing Machinery, Planetary Soc., Exptl. Aircraft Assn., IBM PC Users Group, Macintosh Users Group. Club: Toastmasters. Home: PSC Box 4212 APO NY 09132

KERN, MARIAN REGINA, computer programmer; b. Winchester, Va., Mar. 17, 1963; d. Wilbur L. and Gloria K. (Graff) K. BS in Computer Sci., Maths. Summa Cum Laude, Bridgewater (Va.) Coll., 1985. Programmer, analyst Rubbermaid Comml. Products, Winchester, 1985—. Big Sister Big Brothers/Big Sisters, Winchester, 1985—; mem. Community Handbell Choir, Winchester. Mem. Jaycees, Beta Sigma Phi. Club: Exchange (Winchester). Home: 512 Barr Ave Winchester VA 22601 Office: Rubbermaid Comml Products Valley Ave Winchester VA 22601

KERNAN, BARBARA DESIND, senior government executive; b. N.Y.C., Jan. 11, 1939; d. Philip and Anne (Feuer) Desind; m. Joseph E. Kernan, Feb. 14, 1973. BA cum laude, Smith Coll., 1960; postgrad. Oxford U., 1963; MA, Harvard U., 1963, postgrad. John F. Kennedy Sch. of Govt. Harvard U., 1983; postgrad. in edn. policy George Washington U., 1980. Editor, Harvard Law Sch., 1960-62; tchr. English, Newton High Sch. (Mass.), 1962-63; editor Allyn & Bacon Pubs., Boston, 1963-64; edn. asso. Upward Bound, Edn. Assos., Inc., Washington, 1965-68; edn. program specialist Title I, Elem. and Secondary Edn. Act, U.S. Office Edn., 1969-73; fellow Am. Polit. Sci. Assn., Senator William Proxmire and Congressman Alphonzo Bell, 1973-74; spl. asst. to dep. commr. for elem. and secondary edn. and dir. dissemination sch. finance and analysis, U.S. Office Edn., 1975-77, chief program analysis br. div. edn. for disadvantaged, 1977-79, chief grant program coordination staff Office Dep. Commr. for Ednl. Resources, 1979-80; chief priority concerns staff Office Asst. Sec. Mgmt., U.S. Dept. Edn., Washington, 1980-81, dir. div. orgnl. devel. and analysis Office of Dep. Undersec. for Mgmt., 1981-86; sr. exec. service candidate on spl. project to improve status of women Sec. Transp., Washington, 1983-84; assoc. adminstr. for adminstrn. Nat. Hwy. Traffic Safety Adminstrn., Dept. Transp., 1986—. Recipient awards U.S. Office Edn., 1969, 71, 77, U.S. Dept. Edn., 1981-86; scholarships Smith Coll., 1958-60, Harvard U., 1962-63; Am. Polit. Sci. Assn. fellow, 1973-74; Sr. Exec. fellow John F. Kennedy Sch. Govt. Harvard U., 1983.

KERNEY, EVELYN L., utilities executive; b. Tuscaloosa, Ala., Jan. 28, 1945; d. Robert Lee and Arnetta (Green) Palmer; m. Fulton L. Burns, June 21,1964 (div. Oct., 1971); m. Robert Lee Kerney Jr, May 17, 1985. BA, Canisius Coll., Buffalo, 1983, MS, 1985; doctoral studies, SUNY, Buffalo, 1985—. Lic. realtor. Mailgirl N.Y. Telephone, Buffalo, 1965-85, order typist, 1965-70; supr., acting mgr., trainer N.Y. Telephone, Buffalo, N.Y.C., 1970—; real estate sales rep. Mil-Hil Realty, Buffalo, N.Y.C., 1985—; Exec. advisor N.Y. Telephone Jr. Achievment, 1977. Comm. mem. Rep. Club, Buffalo Urban League Guild. Mem. Women in Communications, Nat. Assn. of Female Execs., AAUW, Alpha Sigma Lambda. Home: 233 Brunswick Blvd Buffalo NY 14208 Office: Canisius Coll Nat Honor Soc Continuing Edn Buffalo NY 14208

KERN-FOXWORTH, MARILYN LOUISE, journalism educator; b. Kosciusko, Miss., Mar. 4, 1954; d. Jimmie and Manella (Dickens) Kern; m. Gregory Lamar Foxworth, July 3, 1982; 1 child, Gregory Lamar II. BS, Jackson State U., 1974; MS, Fla. State U., 1976; PhD, U. Wis., 1982. Pub. relations asst. Sta. WJTV, Jackson, Miss., 1974; communications specialist Fla. State U., Tallahassee, 1974; advt. coordinator City of Tallahassee, 1975-76; coll. relations rep. GTE Automatic Electric, Northlake, Ill., 1977; AM traffic mgr. Sta. WWQM Radio, Madison, Wis., 1978-79; prodn. mgr. Sta. WHA-AM, Madison, 1979-80; columnist, reporter Mid-West Observer, Madison, 1979-80; asst. prof. U. Tenn., Knoxville, 1980-87; prof. Tex. A&M U., College Station, 1987—. Assoc. editor Nashville Banner, 1983; contbr. chpt. to Dictionary Lit. Biography, 1985; contbr. articles to mags. including Black Collegian (Unity award 1985). Co-chair advisory Phyllis Wheatley YWCA, Knoxville, 1983-85. Amon Carter Evans scholar U. Tenn., 1983; recipient Kizzy award Black Women's Hall of Fame, Chgo., 1980; named a Woman of Achievement U. Tenn., 1983; fellow Am. Press Inst., 1988, Poynter Inst., 1988. Mem. Pub. Relations Soc. Am. (Recognition of Excellence 1985), Assn. for Ednl. Journalism (nat. com., Research Award 1980), Nat. Communication Assn. (planning com.), Black Media Assn., Alpha Kappa Alpha. Home: 3417 Parkway Terr Bryan TX 77802 Office: Tex A&M U Dept Journalism 230 Reed McDonald College Station TX 77843-4111

KERNODLE, UNA MAE, educator; b. Jackson, Tenn., Mar. 4, 1947; d. James G. and Mary E. (McLemore) Sikes. B.S. in Home Econs., U. Tenn., 1969; M.Edn., U. Alaska, 1974. Tchr., head dept. vocat. edn. and electives Chugiak High Sch., Anchorage; edn. cons. State of Alaska, Anchorage Talent Bank; presenter Gov.'s Conf. on Child Abuse, Alaska Vocat. Edn. Assn. Conf. Active Women's Resource Ctr.; state officer Alaska Home Econs. Mem. Am. Home Econs. Assn., Anchorage Assn. Edn. Young Children, NEA, Am. Vocat. Assn. Democrat. Baptist. Office: Chugiak High School PO Box 218 Eagle River AK 99577

KERNS, GERTRUDE YVONNE, psychologist; b. Flint, Mich., July 25, 1931; d. Lloyd D. and Mildred C. (Ter Achter) B.; B.A., Olivet Coll., 1953; M.A., Wayne State U., 1958; Ph.D., U. Mich., 1979. Sch. psychologist Roseville (Mich.) Pub. Schs., 1958-68, Grosse Pointe (Mich.) Pub. Schs., 1968-86; pvt. practice psychology, Grosse Pointe, 1980—; instr. psychology Macomb Community Coll., 1959-63. Mem. Mich., Am. psychol. assns., Mich., Nat. socs. sch. psychologists, NEA, Psi Chi. Home: 28820 Grant St Saint Clair Shores MI 48081 Office: 63 Kercheval Suite 205 Grosse Pointe MI 48236

KERPER, MEIKE, family violence and addictions educator, consultant; b. Powell, Wyo., Aug. 13, 1929; d. Wesley George and Hazel (Bowman) K.; m. R.R. Milodragovich, Dec. 25, 1963 (div. 1973); children—Dan, John, Teren, Tina, Stana. B.S., U. Mont., 1973; M.S., U. Ariz., 1975; postgrad. Ariz. State U., 1976-78. Cert. domestic violence counselor, alcoholism and drug abuse counselor Family therapist Cottonwood Hill, Arvada, Colo., 1981; family program developer Turquoise Lodge, Albuquerque, 1982; co-developer abusers program Albuquerque Shelter Domestic Violence, 1984; family therapist Citizens Council Alcoholism and Drug Abuse, Albuquerque, 1984-86; pvt. practice cons. and trainer family violence and treatment, Albuquerque, 1986—; mem. Concerned Citizens for Children, planning com. Ctr. Parenting Excellence, La Grande, Oreg. Co-author: Court Diversion Program, 1985; author Family Treatment, 1982. Lobbyist CCOPF, Santa Fe, 1983-86. Recipient commendation Albuquerque Shelter Domestic Violence, 1984. Mem. Nat. Assn. Prevention of Child Abuse, Nat. Assn. Alcoholism Counselors, N.Mex. Assn. Alcoholism Counselors, Delta Delta Delta. Republican. Episcopalian. Club: PEO. Avocations: Art history; reading; Indian culture; swimming; public speaking. Home: Rt I Box 80A Cove OR 97824

KERR, CATHERINE SPAULDING, environmental advocate; b. Los Angeles, Mar. 22, 1911; d. Charles Edgar and Gertrude Mary (Smith) Spaulding; m. Clark Kerr, Dec. 25, 1934; children: Clark E., Alexander W., Caroline M. AB, Stanford U., 1932. Co-founder, environ. leader Save San Francisco Bay Assn., 1961—, v.p., 1987—. Editor Kensington Outlook, 1947-49. Advisor Mortar Bd., Theta Sigma Phi, Univ. YWCA, 1950-67; founder Fgn. Student Hospitality Program; mem. adv. bd. East Bay Regional Park Dist., 1976-82, 1985-88. Recipient Robert C. Kirkwood award, 1985, Calif. Council Landscape Architects citation, 1982, Sol Feinstone Environ. award, 1981, Carnegie Found. Advancement of Teaching cert. disting. service, 1979, Berkeley Citation award, 1974. Mem. Stanford U. Alumni Assn. (hostess com.). Democrat. Mem. Soc. Friends. Clubs: Town and Gown, Berkeley Fellows. Home and Office: 8300 Buckingham Dr El Cerrito CA 94530

KERR, CHERIE BELLE DEPIETRO, public relations executive; b. Columbus, Ohio, Oct. 20, 1943; d. Charles James and Margaret Irene (Littlewood) DePietro; student Citrus Coll., 1961-63; children: Sean, Shannon Drake. Copywriter for homebuilding co., 1969-71; founding mem. The Groundlings, improvisational comedy group, Los Angeles, 1973-74; with Martin Advt., Tustin, Calif., 1971-74; freelance publicist, writer, 1974-78; founder, pres. Kerr & Assocs., pub. relations, Huntington Beach, Calif., 1978—; founder ExecuProv comedy workshop for bus. profls., 1987—; tchr. improvisational comedy to adults and children; founder Kerr Comedy Co. Winner 1st place Top 40 Lyric Competition in Music City Song Festival, 1985. Mem. Calif. Press Women's Assn. Office: 7755 Center Ave Suite 350 Huntington Beach CA 92647

KERR, CYNTHIA JOAN, controller; b. Evergreen Park, Ill., Sept. 29, 1947; d. Constance Julius and Catherine Josephine (Fennell) Petrauskas; m. John Thomas Kerr, Oct. 16, 1965 (div. Apr. 1973); children: Joan Marie, Kristen Louise. A, Parsons Coll., 1977; BS, Ind. U., South Bend, 1980. Expeditor Simplicity Pattern, Niles, Mich., 1969-77; acct. Midas Wood Products, Union, Mich., 1977-79; controller Midas Van Conversion, Elkhart, Ind., 1979-82, Coachmen Van, Elkhart, 1982-85, Sportscoach Corp., Elkhart, 1985—; loan officer Coachmen Credit Union, Middlebury, Ind., 1986-87. clk. Village of Edwardsburg, Mich., 1977. Mem. Nat. Mgmt. Assn. (bd. dirs. 1983-85), Coachmen Mgmt. Assn., Coachmen Women's Assn., Graph Art Internat. Union (bd. dirs. 1974-75, steward 1969-76). Home: 69005 S Cass St PO Box 355 Edwardsburg MI 49112 Office: Sportscoach of America PO Box 609 Elkhart IN 46515

KERR, DEBORAH MACPHAIL, cluster sales manager; b. Gettysburg, Pa., June 14, 1951; d. John Archie and Jeanne Alma (Spangler) MacPhail; m. Robert Stair Kerr, Jr., May 25, 1974. BS in Music Edn., Gettysburg Coll., 1973. Selection/tng. coordinator Commonwealth Nat. Bank, Harrisburg, Pa., 1978-79; safety tng. mgr. Ralston Purina Co., Mechanicsburg, Pa., 1979-81; data processing edn. coordinator Hamilton Bank, Lancaster, Pa., 1981-82, dir. mgmt. devel., 1982-83; asst. v.p., dir. manpower devel. Hamilton Bank, subs. CoreStates, Lancaster, 1982-85; asst. v.p., dir. corp. devel. CoreStates Fin. Corp., Phila., 1985-86; asst. v.p. personnel, tng. coordinator, Consumer Banking Group Phila. Nat. Bank, 1986—, v.p., personnel and tng. coordinator, Consumer Banking Group, Phila. Nat. Bank, 1987, v.p., cluster sales mgr., 1988—; mem. corp. adv. bd. Lebanon Valley Coll., Annville, Pa., 1985—; instr. Am. Inst. Banking, Lebanon, 1983-84; mem. tng. degree adv. com. Pa. State U., Middletown, Pa., 1983-84; mem. state edn. exec. adv. com. Pa. Am. Inst. Banking, Harrisburg, 1982; lectr. in field. Mem. Am. Soc. Tng. and Devel. (chpt. pres. 1981; Leigh Woehling Meml. award 1985, mem. exec. com. human resource devel. careers 1986-87). Avocations: reading, gardening, hiking, camping.

KERR, ELIZABETH MARGARET, educator, author; b. Sault Ste Marie, Mich., Jan. 25, 1905; d. John Arthur and Katherine Dorothy (Hirth) Kerr. BA, U. Minn., 1926, MA, 1927, PhD, 1941. Instr. English, Tabor Coll., Hillsboro, Kans., 1929-30, U. Minn., Mpls., 1930-37, 38-43, Coll. of St. Catherine, St. Paul, 1937-38; asst. prof. Rockford (Ill.) Coll., 1943-45; instr. Milw. State Coll., 1945-55; assoc. prof. U. Wis., Milw., 1956-59, prof., 1959-70, prof. emeritus English, 1970—. Author: Bibliography of the Sequence Novel, 1950, Yoknapatawpha: Faulkner's Little Postage Stamp of Native Soil, 1969, William Faulkner's Gothic Domain, 1979, William Faulkner's Yoknapatawpha: "A Kind of Keystone in the Universe", 1984. MLA research grantee, 1942, Summer Salary Support grantee U. Wis., Milw., 1959, 1961. Mem. MLA, Dickens Studies, Soc. for Study So. Lit. Democrat. Congregationalist. Home: Fairhaven 435 Starin Rd Whitewater WI 53190

KERR, LESLIE ANN, educator, editor, writer; b. Pitts., Sept. 25, 1949; d. David Richard and Lorna Deane (Grant) K.; m. Joseph Vera-Martinez, Martinez; 1 child, Jon Grant. AA in Journalism, Los Angeles Valley Coll., 1971; BA in Journalism, Calif. State U., Los Angeles, 1977; postgrad., Western State U., 1980; grad. cert. corp. communications, U. So. Calif. Cub reporter Valley News and Green Sheet, Van Nuys, Calif., 1971-72; copy writer Bride's Mag. Conde West Publs., N.Y., 1972-74; editorial asst. Calif. State Bar Jour., Los Angeles, 1974-77; exec. editor Rainbow Publs., Burbank, Calif., 1978-80, Transworld Eshibits, Inc., Chgo., 1980-82; pub. info. officer Santa Barbara (Calif.) City Coll., 1982-84; communications specialist Everest & Jennings, Inc., Camarillo, Calif., 1984-87; educator First Luth. Day Sch., Camarillo, 1987—. Contbr. articles to profl. jours. Mem. Ventura County Symphony League; vol. Rep. Com., Ventura County, 1982. Named an Outstanding Young Woman in Journalism, 1971. Mem. Women in Communications, Internat. Assn. Bus. Communications, Pub. Info. Communicators Assn., Friends Commn. for Women of Ventura County. Republican. Lutheran. Office: Ascension Luth Sch 380 Arneill Rd Camarillo CA 93010

KERR, MABEL DOROTHEA, physician, educator; b. Toronto, Ont., Can. (parents Am. citizens); d. George Houston and Mabel (Wark) Kerr; B.S., Ohio State U., 1944; M.D., Columbia, 1950. Intern dept. medicine St. Luke's Hosp., N.Y.C., 1950-51, resident, 1951-52; psychiat. resident Payne Whitney Clinic, N.Y. Hosp., 1952-57; practice medicine, specializing in psychiatry, N.Y.C., 1954—; assoc. attending psychiatrist N.Y. Hosp., 1979—; clin. asst. prof. psychiatry Cornell U. Med. Coll., 1968-79, clin. assoc. prof., 1979—; asst. med. examiner, officer chief med. examiner City of N.Y., 1957-66. Pres., Elmora Found. Fellow N.Y. Acad. Medicine; mem. AMA, Am. Psychiat. Assn., Women's Med. Soc. N.Y. State, Am. Med. Women's Assn. Address: 20 E 68th St New York NY 10021

KERR, NANCY KAROLYN, pastor, mental health consultant; b. Ottumwa, Iowa, July 10, 1934; d. Owen W. and Iris Irene (Israel) Kerr; student Boston U., 1953; AA, U. Bridgeport, 1966; BA, Hofstra U., 1967; postgrad. in clin. psychology Adelphi U. Inst. Advanced Psychol. Studies, 1968-73; m. Richard Clayton Williams, June 28, 1953 (div.); children—Richard Charles, Donna Louise. Ordained pastor Mennonite Ch., 1987. Pastoral counselor Nat. Council Chs., Jackson, Miss., 1964; dir. teen program Waterbury (Conn.) YWCA, 1966-67; intern in psychology N.Y. Med. Coll., 1971-72; research cons., 1972-73; coordinator home services, psychologist City and County of Denver, 1972-75; cons. Mennonite Mental Health Services, Denver, 1975-78; asst. prof. psychology Messiah Coll., 1978-79; mental health cons., 1979-81; called to ministry Mennonite Ch., 1981, pastor Cin. Mennonite Fellowship, 1981-83, nat. chmn. summer curriculum, coordinator campus peace evangelism, 1981-83, mem. Gen. Conf. Peace and Justice Reference Council, 1983-85; instr. Associated Mennonite Bibl. Sems., 1985; teaching elder Assembly Mennonite Ch., 1985-86; pastor Pulaski Mennonite Ch., 1986—; mem. Tri-County Counseling Clinic, Memphis, Mo., 1980-81; spl. ch. curriculum Nat. Council Chs., 1981; mem. Cen. Dist. Conf. Peace and Justice Com., 1981—. Mem. Waterbury Planned Parenthood Bd., 1964-67; mem. MW Children's Home Bd., 1974-75; bd. dirs. Boulder (Colo.) ARC, 1977-78; mem. Mennonite Disabilities Respite Care Bd., 1981-86. Mem. Am. Psychol. Assn., Soc. Psychologists for Study of Social Issues, Davis County Ministries Assn. (v.p. 1988—). Office: Pulaski Mennonite Ch Box 98 Pulaski IA 52584

KERR, VALERIE ANN, nursing educator; b. Alma, Mich., Jan. 10, 1940; d. Floyd Arther and Martha Ella (Wells) Tomlin; m. Larry Lee Kerr, June 15, 1961; children—Kerry, Kristin, Karmen. Nursing diploma Saginaw Gen. Hosp. Sch. Nursing, 1961; BS, Cen. Mich. U., 1983. Charge nurse Gratiot Community Hosp., Alma, 1961-66, 67-74; clin. nursing instr. Mid-Mich. Community Coll., Harrison, Mich., 1978-82, instr., 1982-86; supr. Mich. Masonic Home, Alma, 1986—; migrant program sch. nurse Montcalm Intermediate Sch. Dist., Stanton, Mich., 1981. Club leader, exchange student hostess Mich. 4-H, Gratiot County, 1975-77; fair dept. supt. Gratiot County Agrl. Soc., 1981-83; mem. Mich. Farm Bur./Gratiot Women's Orgn., 1978. Mem. Saginaw Gen. Hosp. Sch. Nursing Alumni Assn., Phi Kappa Phi. Home: 10838 Pingree Rd Elwell MI 48832

KERRY, PENNY LE, architectural executive; b. Great Falls, Mont., Mar. 1, 1942; d. Percy Orval and Betty (Lawson) Dent; m. Del Swanson, Nov. 12, 1958 (div. 1973); 1 child, Darcy B.; m. William M. Kerry, July 21, 1973 (div. 1987); m. Carl Francis Pompei, Oct. 15, 1988. Jr. clk. Gen. Telephone Co., Spokane, Wash., 1960-63; sec. Am. Sign and Indicator, Spokane, 1963-66, IBM Corp., Spokane, 1966-69; office mgr. Far No. Regional Ctr., Redding, Calif., 1969-70; adminstrv. asst. Bank Bldg. Corp., Burlingame, Calif., 1970-71; v.p. R.M. Merkadeau & Assocs., Burlingame, 1971-78; pres. PNI Omnitects, San Francisco, 1978—; pres. bd. Associated Builders & Contractors, 1983—, Fin. Suppliers Assoc., Madison, Wis., 1985—; bd. dirs. Pvt. Sector Council, Washington, 1987—. Contbr. articles to research books. Co-chairperson Rep. Bush for Pres., San Francico, 1988; del. Rep. Nat. Conv., New Orleans, 1988. Named Woman Entrepreneur of Yr., San Francisco C. of C., 1985. Mem. Pvt. Industry Council, Inst. Bus. Designers (pres. 1979-81). Clubs: City, Chief Exec. Officers. Lodge: Kiwanis. Office: PNI Omnitects 135 Mississippi St San Francisco CA 94107

KERRY, VANESSA TROQUILLE, sales executive; b. Ft. Sill, Okla., June 26, 1959; d. Gilmore Joseph and Annie (Troquille) K. Student, Northwestern State U., Natchitoches, 1977-79; BA in Poli. Sci., U. New Orleans, 1981. Account sales rep. Dun & Bradstreet, New Orleans and Richmond, Va., 1981-85, New Orleans, 1984-85; regional coordinating mgr. feature products Dun & Bradstreet, Houston, 1985-86; div. sales mgr. Dun & Bradstreet, St. Louis, 1986-88; product mgr. Dun & Bradstreet, New Providence, N.J., 1988—. Mem. Nat. Assn. Female Execs. Republican. Roman Catholic. Office: Dun & Bradstreet One Diamond Hill Rd Murray Hill NJ 07974

KERSAVAGE, CAROL JOAN, editor, technical writer; b. Marquette, Mich., Apr. 23, 1934; d. L. John and Jen Evelyn (Peterson) Larson; m. Paul Charles Kersavage, Sept. 13, 1958; children: Jeffrey, Gregory, Bradley, Lisa. BS, Mich. State U., 1956; MA, Pa. State U., 1959. Asst. home econs. editor Coop. Extension Service, University Park, Pa., 1956-58; project assoc. Pa. Forum on Families, University Park, 1979-80; mng. editor Outdoor Writers Assn. of Am., State College, Pa., 1984—; publications editor Outdoor Writers Assn. of Am., State Coll., Pa., 1984—; free-lance writer, editor The Pa. State U., Univ. Park, 1967—, writer, editor audio visual services, 1981-82; copy editor Jour. of Distance Edn. Pa. State U., State Coll., Pa. 1987—. Editor: Outdoors Unltd., 1984—, Annual Membership Directory, 1984—. Bd. dirs. Mental Health/Mental Retardation, Bellefonte, Pa. 1984—. Mem. Outdoor Writers Assn. Am. Luth. Club: Home Economists in Homemaking (pres. 1982-83). Home: 229 Oak Ln State College PA 16801

KERSHUL, KRISTINE KAY, author, publisher; b. Salem, Oreg., Mar. 20, 1951; d. Urban Gregory and Patricia L. K. Student, U. Hartford, 1969-70, Portland State U., 1970-71, Deutsche Sommerschule am Pazifik, Heidelberg, Fed. Republic Germany, 1972; BA, Schiller Coll., 1973; postgrad., Karl-Ruprecht U., Heidelberg, Fed. Republic Germany, 1973-74; MA, U. Calif., 1977; postgrad., U. Wash., 1977-80. Instr. Schiller Coll., Heidelberg, 1975-76; translator U.S. Embassy, Bonn, Fed. Republic Germany, 1975-76; teaching asst. U. Calif., Santa Barbara, 1974-75, 77, U. Wash., Seattle, 1977-80; mgr. program Applied Physics Lab., Seattle, 1980-81; pres. Bilingual Books, Seattle, 1981—; travel guide bilingual Schiller Coll., Heidelberg, 1972-74; translator Berlitz, Seattle, 1977-80. Author: German in 10 Minutes a Day, 1981, French in 10 Minutes a Day, 1981, Spanish in 10 Minutes a Day, 1981, Italian in 10 Minutes a Day, 1981, Chinese in 10 Minutes a Day, 1981, Japanese in 10 Minutes a Day, 1982, Norwegian in 10 Minutes a Day, 1982, Ingles en 10 Minutos al DiA, 1982, Russian in 10 Minutes a Day, 1984, Hebrew in 10 Minutes a Day, 1987. Mem. Modern Lang. Assn., Pacific NW Council Fgn. Lang., Am. Council Tchrs. Fgn. Langs. Office: Bilingual Books 6018 Seaview Ave NW Seattle WA 98107

KESLER, MARY ELIZABETH, educational administrator; b. Gettysburg, Pa., Oct. 12, 1943; d. A. Dean, Sr., and Virginia (Peters) K. AB, Randolph-Macon Woman's Coll., 1965; MusM, Northwestern U., 1966. Music tchr. Foxcroft Sch., Middleburg, Va., 1966-70, dir. admissions, asst. dean, 1969-71; dir. coll. counseling Hockaday Sch., Dallas, 1971-81, asst. headmistress, 1981-86; trustee Coll. Bd., 1982-86; headmistress The Agnes Irwin Sch., 1986—. Mem. Nat. Assn. Coll. Admissions Counselors (cons.), Tex. Assn. Coll. Admissions Counselors (pres. 1980-81), Nat. Assn. Prins. Schs. for Girls. Democrat. Methodist. Office: The Agnes Irwin Sch S Ithan Ave Rosemont PA 19010

KESSLER, JEAN S., executive secretary; b. New Brunswick, N.J., Oct. 20, 1954; d. John S. and Henrietta Margueritte (Pasquier de Lumeau) Kessler; m. Michael P. Gutzan, Sept. 16, 1984; A in Applied Sci. with highest honors, Middlesex County Coll., 1981; postgrad. Edison State Coll., 1984—. Sec. to dir. Carter-Wallace, Inc., Cranbury, N.J., 1977-78, exec. sec. to corp. v.p., 1978-80; exec. sec. to v.p. Continental Ins. Co., Piscataway, N.J., 1981, exec. sec. to sr. v.p., 1981-84, exec. sec. to exec. v.p., 1984—. Recipient Sec. of Yr.

award Profl. Secs. Internat., 1981-82. Cert. profl. sec. Mem. Profl Secs. Internat. (chmn. civic com. New Brunswick chpt. 1980-81, sec. of yr. com. 1981-82; mem. nominating com. 1981, audit com. 1982, ways and means com. 1981-82), Nat. Assn. Female Execs., Nat. Assn. Ins. Women, Mensa, Nu Tau Sigma. Office: One Continental Dr Cranbury NJ 08570

KESSLER, LEONA HANOVER, interior designer; b. Phila., Sept. 15, 1925; d. Herman and Ida (Gleaner) Hanover; B.S. in Textile Engring. (Sara Tyler Wister scholar), Phila. Coll. Textiles and Sci., 1948; m. Sydney Kessler, Aug. 28, 1948; children—Andrew Louis, Todd Hanover. Pvt. practice interior design and cons. Lee Kessler Interiors, Phila., 1957—; textile designer, stylist, color cons.; mem. faculty Moore Coll. Art, 1970-72, Art Inst. Phila., 1973-78, Phila. Coll. Textiles and Sci., 1972-81; juror textile design and interior design; works exhibited designer showcases, local house tours, faculty shows. Named Alumnus of Month, Textile Engr., 1971. Mem. Am. Soc. Interior Designers (dir. Pa. East chpt. 1967-78, chpt. recognition awards 1974, 80). Author: That Which Was Once a Warp, 1971; contbr. articles and photographs to mags. and newspapers. Address: 3421 Warden Dr Philadelphia PA 19129

KESSLER, MARY ELIZABETH, accountant; b. Alexandria, Minn., Oct. 7, 1957; d. Warren L. and Elsie M. (Kalina) Johnson; m. Michael M. Kessler, May 3, 1986. BS, U. Minn., 1983, MBA, 1988. Sales rep. Right Time Internat., Bloomington, Minn., 1978-79; nat. sales coord. Land O Lakes Foods, Arden Hills, Minn., 1979-83; controller, chief fin. officer Jed Johnson, Alan Wanzenberg & Assocs., N.Y.C., 1983-86; acctg. mgr. Farm Credit Services, St. Paul, 1986—. Vol. Big Sister Program, St. Paul, 1976-81.

KESSLER, RIKKI G., education specialist; b. N.Y.C., May 20, 1934; d. Murray and Lea (Lessow) Glasser; m. Jules Yale Kessler, Dec. 26, 1954; children: Barry, Edward, Sharon. BA, Queens Coll., 1955; MS in Edn., Hofstra U., 1970. Cert. tchr. Tchr. N.Y.C. Pub. Schs., 1954-56; pres. Learning Links Inc., Roslyn, N.Y., 1976—; reading specialist Great Neck (N.Y.) Pub. Schs., 1967—. Author various study guides. Pres. coordinating council PTA, Roslyn, 1976-78. Mem. NOW, Internat. Reading Assn., Nat. Council Jewish Women, N.Y. State Reading Assn., Great Neck Tchrs. Assn., Nassau Reading Council. Democrat. Jewish.

KESSLER, SONIA BERER, educator; b. N.Y.C., May 30, 1931; d. Paul Nicholas and Bertha (Sudman) B.; m. Milton Kessler, Aug. 24, 1952; children: David Lawrence, Paula Nan., Daniel Solomon. BA, CUNY, 1952; MS, SUNY, Buffalo, 1956; postgrad., SUNY, Binghamton, 1984—, Inst. for Creative Edn., 1986. Cert. tchr. N.Y., Wash., Ohio. Tchr. faculty The Niagara St. Sch., Niagara Falls, N.Y., 1952-56, Univ. St. Sch., Seattle, 1956-57; editorial assoc. Charles Merrill Pub. Co., Columbus, Ohio, 1959-60; tchr. faculty Columbus Torah Acad., 1960-62; pub. relations dir. North Shore Sch. Dist., Sea Cliff, N.Y., 1964-65; tchr. faculty Jennie F. Snapp Sch., Endicott, N.Y., 1966-68, The MacArthur Sch., Binghamton, N.Y., 1969—; vis. cons. Pedagogical Ctr. Antwerp, 1985.; lectr. gifted edn., Binghamton, Antwerp. Editorial assoc.: Uncle Ben: Skill Text, 1960; editor ednl. brochures North Shore Schs., 1964-65.; presenter in field. Coordinator Project Law-Related Edn. Goals for Am. Leadership Syracuse (N.Y.) U.; mem. Gifted Edn. Com., N.Y., Antwerp, Belgium, 1984—, New Eng. Social Studies Conf., Boston, 1982, Spice of Learning for Gifted and Talented project in gifted edn., Binghamton, N.Y., 1984-86; active Temple Israel Sisterhood, Binghamton, 1977—. Recipient Research Sabbatical award Binghamton Sch. System, 1985. Mem. Hadassah, Univ. Women, N.Y. State Reading Tchrs. Assn., NEA Tchrs. Assn. (rep.), N.Y. State Tchrs. Assn. (rep.), Binghamton Tchrs. Assn. (rep.). Democrat. Home: 25 Lincoln Ave Binghamton NY 13905

KESTEN, HEATHER ANNE, marketing company administrator; b. Toronto, Ontario, Can., Apr. 18, 1946; d. Sidney Norman and Sybil Joy (Pullan) K. BS in Fine & Applied Art, Advt. Journalism, U. Oreg., 1968; MEd in Counseling, Lewis & Clark Coll., 1976. Graphic artist Meier & Frank Dept. Store, Portland, Oreg., 1968-70; asst. exec. dir. Willamette Council Camp Fire Inc., Salem, Oreg., 1970-74; assoc. dir. fin. devel. Nat. Camp Fire Inc, Kansas City, Mo., 1976-79; dir. fin. devel. Oreg. Lung Assn., Portland, 1979-81; registered rep. Portland, 1981-84; v.p. Laughlin Group, Portland, 1984-86; prodn. mgr. Mktg. One Inc., Portland, 1986—; cons. mktg. Kevane & Assocs. Inc., Portland, 1986-87. Mem. Internat. Assn. Fin. Planners, Inst. Cert. Fin. Planners (cert.). Democrat. Home: 2748 SW Moss St Portland OR 97219

KESTER, PATRICIA ANNETTE, clinical psychologist, educator; b. Colorado Springs, Colo., Aug. 9, 1945; d. James Douglas and Lucille Erma (Townley) K.; B.A., U. Tex., Austin, 1967; M.Ed., U. Houston, 1973; Ph.D., U.S. Internat. U., 1978. Social worker Okla. Dept. Public Welfare, Oklahoma City, 1967-68, Tex. Dept. Public Welfare, Houston, 1968-69, Harris County Child Welfare, Houston, 1969-71; tchr. Houston Ind. Sch. Dist., 1971-72; counselor Tex. Research Inst. for Mental Sci., Houston, 1973-74; research assoc. dept. psychiatry SUNY, Stony Brook, 1974-76; psychol. intern Mercy Hosp., San Diego, 1977-78; lectr. dept. psychology U. Calif., San Diego, 1979; postdoctoral fellow Garrard Ctr. for Psychology, La Mesa, Calif., 1979-80; pvt. practice clin. psychology, La Mesa, Calif., 1980-82, Orange, Calif., 1980—, La Jolla, Calif., 1982—; adj. asst. prof. Chapman Coll., Orange, 1979-84. Bd. dirs. Who Cares, community mental health ctr., Houston, 1973-74. NIH fellow, 1974-76; NIMH grantee, 1975-76. Mem. Am. Psychol. Assn., Calif. Psychol. Assn., Calif. Assn. Marriage and Family Therapists, Am. Assn. Sex Educators and Therapists, Acad. San Diego Psychologists, San Diego Soc. Sex Therapy and Edn. (pres. 1986-87), Soc. Scientific Study Sex (local chpt. chair 1985-86, Western Region conf. chair 1986). Contbr. articles to profl. publs. Home: PO Box 278 La Jolla CA 92038 Office: 8950 Villa La Jolla Dr Suite 2200 La Jolla CA 92037 also: 1485 N Tustin St Suite 230 Orange CA 92667

KESTON, JOAN BALBOUL, public relations executive; b. N.Y.C., Feb. 6, 1937; d. Sol and Adele (Gredinger) Balboul; (div. Mar. 1986); children: Lisa, Vicky, Sol. BA, N.Y.U., 1958; MA in Pub. Adminstrn., U. So. Calif., 1981; postgrad., Rutgers U., 1982—. Br. mgr. Social Security Adminstrn., Rockville, Md., 1978-86; exec. dir. Pub. Employees Roundtable, Washington, 1986—. Editor: (book) Hagadah, 1972, (newsletter) Unsung Heroes, 1986. Mem. Federally Employed Women, Nat. Council Social Security Mgrs. Assn. (del. 19976—), Internat. Personnel Mgrs. Assn., Amer. Fgn. Service Assn., Profl. Mgrs. Assn., Dirs. Pub. Adminstrn. Assn. of U. So. Calif. (treas.), Am. Soc. Pub. Adminstrs. Jewish. Home: 330 Lynn Manor Dr Rockville MD 20850

KETOVER, HARRIET A., state legislator, television producer and moderator; b. Portland, Maine, Jan. 5; d. Morris Paul and Lillian A. (Stiman) Lerman; m. J. Miles Ketover; children: Jill M., Kimberly F. Student, Wards Sch. Bus., Boston, U. Farmington, 1981, U. So. Maine, 1982—. Nurse's asst. Osteo. Hosp., Portland, 1971-73; asst. exec. dir. NAACP, Portland, 1976-77; TV producer, moderator Portland, 1970—; mem. Ho. of Reps. State of Maine, 1980-84, 86—. Contbr. producer for "Collage" aired by Maine Pub. Broadcasting Network; produced documentaries. Mem. steering com. R.I.F.F.L.E., Lincoln Mid. Sch. P.T.O., Nat. Assn. Jr. League; chairperson Am. Cancer Residential Crusade, Nat. and Local Pub. Cable Cameraperson, Cumberland County Dem. and City Com., Nat. Gov.'s Conf. Staff, Red Cross Life Saver, Little League #8, Brownies Club, Bands Club; founder Girl's Club; host Dem. Conv. Com.; bd. dirs. Parents of Learning Disabled Children, Portland Area Community TV, 1977-80, Am. Cancer Soc. Recipient Mother and Dau. Yr. award, Swimming award, Meritorious Service award; named Champion Bowler. Mem. NAACP, Nat. Resources Council, World Affairs Council of Maine, New Eng. Women Caucus State Legislators, Nat. Council State Legislators, Sisterhood Club (lif, past pres.). Jewish.

KETSIS, KAY A., international trade executive; b. Athens, Greece, Aug. 31, 1939; came to U.S., 1963; d. Alex I. and Fani (Mais) K.; 1 child, Novi; m. Henry H. Grossman, June 5, 1988. BBS, Pace U. Mgr. export traffic Thomson-CSF, Inc., Harrison, N.Y., 1968-72, Spring Industries Inc. (formerly Spring Mills, Inc.), N.Y.C., 1972-79, GAF Corp., N.Y.C., 1979-81; dir. internat. traffic and transp. AMF, Inc., Stamford, Conn., 1981—. Home and Office: 17 Hughes Rd Somerset NJ 08873

KETTENHOFEN, GRETCHEN MARIA, publishing executive; b. Canaan, Conn., Nov. 4, 1935; d. Leo J. and Celice (Stem) K.; m. Gunther Paul Mittendorf, Apr. 19, 1980. BA cum laude, Barnard Coll., 1957. Ops mgr. Oxtoby-Smith Inc., N.Y.C.; survey field dir. Audits and Surveys, N.Y.C.; exec. v.p. Lee Sluzberg Research, N.Y.C.; adminstrv. asst. Aorett Frece Ginsberg, N.Y.C.; now asst. to publisher Adweek, N.Y.C. Contbr. articles to profl. jours. Chairperson St. Bartholemew's Breakfast Program, N.Y.C., 1987-88. Episcopalian. Home: 153 Dupont St Brooklyn NY 11222

KETTLE, SALLY ANNE, marketing consultant; b. Omaha, Feb. 2, 1938; d. Harry Eugene and Elaine Josephine (Winston) Smiley; m. William Frederick Kettle, July 20, 1968 (div. 1973); children: Christopher, Winston. BS in Edn., U. Nebr., 1960, postgrad. Cert. tchr., S.C., Nebr. Tchr. Dist. 66 Schs., Omaha, 1966-72; owner, mgr. The Rick Rack, Ltd., Lakewood, Colo., 1974-75; coordinator merchandising communications 3M, St. Paul, 1978-80, sr. coordinator internat. corp. communications, 1981-84; corp. dir. communications Intran Corp., St. Paul, 1984; pres. Sally Kettle & Co., Bloomington, Minn., 1985—; tchr. TV, U. Omaha, 1968-69; community faculty Met. State U., Mpls., 1983—; adj. faculty mem. Normandale Community Coll., Bloomington, 1983—; speaker numerous orgns. TV hostess City of Bloomington Cable TV, 1984-86. Chair 13th Precinct, Bloomington, 1978-83; bd. dirs. 41st Sen. Dist., Bloomington, 1982-83; cable TV commr. Bloomington City Council, 1984-85; mem. Better Bus. Bur.; founder Ad Rev. Council; mem. state cen. com. and platform commn. DFL, 1988—; bd. dirs. Fellowship Christian Athletes, 1988—. Mem. Am. Advt. Fedn. (conf. com. 1985-87, pub. service com. 1986—), Advt. Fedn. Minn. (bd. dirs. 1982-86), Nat. Assn. Female Execs., C. of C., Nat. Grad. Women's Honor Soc., Phi Delta Gamma, Kappa Alpha Theta. Mem. Assemblies of God Ch. Club: Minn. Press (newsmaker com.). Home: 10321 Morris Rd Bloomington MN 55437

KETTLEWELL, JEANNE KAY, marketing executive; b. Lafayette, Ind., June 15, 1955; d. John and Norma (Henry) K. BS in Microbiology and Chemistry, Ohio State U., 1977. Sales rep. Sargent-Welch Sci., Dallas, 1977-81, Organon Diagnostics, Dallas, 1979-81, Am. Sci. Products, Dallas, 1981-82; mgr. mktg. Am. Sci. Products, Chgo., 1982-83; mgr. regional sales Am. Sci. Products, Irvine, Calif., 1983-87; v.p. sales and mktg. Pacific Biotech, Inc., San Diego, 1987—. Mem. Clin. Lab. Mgrs. Assn. (pres. 1988-89), Nat. Assn. Female Execs., Nat. Assn. Profl. Saleswomen, Am. Soc. Microbiology, Med. Mktg. Assn., Biomedical Mktg. Assn. Republican. Episcopalian. Office: Pacific Biotech 9050 Camino Santa Fe San Diego CA 92121

KETZ, CHRISTINE MARY, transportation planning and marketing consultant; b. Scranton, Pa., Jan. 10, 1948; d. Edward George and Margaret (Surmaitis) Gruss; m. Gerald Charles Ketz, Oct. 4, 1969; 1 child, Erika, Kristen. B.S., Bloomsburg U., 1969; M.S., U. Louisville, 1973; M.B.A., Tenn. State U., 1981. Dir. current planning Louisville and Jefferson County Planning Commn., Louisville, 1971-79; pres. CK Cons., Nashville, 1979-81; market analyst Kaiser Permanente, Los Angeles, 1981-82; product specialist Computer Sci. Corp., Huntington Beach, Calif., 1982; mgr. cons. services div. Cordoba Corp., Los Angeles, 1984-87; prin. Chris Ketz and Assocs., Manhattan Beach, Calif., 1987—. Recipient Spl. award County Judge/City Mayor Louisville, 1974. Mem. Am. Mktg. Assn., Am. Planning Assn. Republican. Roman Catholic. Avocations: Skiing; tennis. Home: 335 31st St Hermosa Beach CA 90254 Office: 1142 Manhattan Ave Suite CP62 Manhattan Beach CA 90266

KEUCHEN, TOISTER ELAINE, employment agency executive; b. Bklyn., Nov. 5, 1930; d. Murray Toister and Elizabeth Stein; m. Herbert Keuchen; 1 child, Susannah. Student, U. Fla., 1952. Occupational therapist Stony Lodge Hosp., Ossining, N.Y., 1966-75; pres. Crickett Employment Agy., Ossining.

KEULEGAN, EMMA PAULINE, special education educator; b. Washington, Jan. 21, 1930; d. Garbis H. and Nellie Virginia (Moore) K. BA, Dumbarton Coll. of Holy Cross, 1954. Cert. tchr. elem. and spl. edn. Tchr. St. Dominic's Elem. Sch., Washington, 1954-56, Sacred Heart Acad., Washington, 1956-59, Our Lady of Victory, Washington, 1959-63, St. Francis Acad., Vicksburg, Miss., 1963-78, Culkin Acad., Vicksburg, 1978—. Treas. PTA, Vicksburg, 1980. Mem. Internat. Reading Assn. (treas. 1986—), Colonial Dames XVIIC (1st v.p. Miss. chpt. 1987—), Daughters of Am. Colonists (chaplain 1985—), DAR (chpt. regent 1967-69). Republican. Roman Catholic. Home: 215 Buena Vista Dr Vicksburg MS 39180 Office: Culkin Elem Sch Rt 11 Box 63 Vicksburg MS 39180

KEWIN, NANCY ANN, sales/mktg. executive; b. Wyandotte, Mich., June 26, 1953; d. Arthur L. and Virginia M. (Lapham) Kewin; B.Music, U. Ariz., 1975; M.B.A., Pepperdine U., 1984. Keyboard dept. mgr. West Los Angeles Music, 1976-78; electronic merchandising specialist Norlin Corp., Lincolnwood, Ill., 1978-79; Western region sales/mktg. mgr. Moog Music/Norlin Corp., Los Angeles, 1979-84; dir. communications and edn. Roland Corp. U.S., Los Angeles, 1984-88, v.p. communications, edn., 1988—. Gen. Music scholar, 1971-72; Albert A. Haldeman Fine Arts scholar, 1972-75; recipient Moog Music Sales Achievement awards, 1980-82. Mem. Nat. Assn. Female Execs. Republican. Home: 226 Glendora Ave Long Beach CA 90803

KEY, CYNTHIA RAYE, data processing executive; b. Winston-Salem, N.C., Apr. 19, 1958; d. James Edward and Versie Mae (Forrest) K. Cert., Raleigh Sch. Data Processing, 1977. Lab. technician II Bowman Gray Sch. Medicine, Winston-Salem, 1977-78; computer programmer, operator Salem Acad. and Coll., Winston-Salem, 1978-82; coordinator data processing II U. N.C., Chapel Hill, 1983—. Mem. N.C. State Employees Assn., Nat. Assn. for Female Execs. Republican. Baptist. Office: U NC Student Stores CB #1530 Daniels Bldg Chapel Hill NC 27599-1530

KEY, DOROTHY LAUSBERG, financial consultant; b. Arnold, Pa., Oct. 28, 1947; d. Robert Joseph and Alice Mae (Smith) Lausberg; m. Robert Joseph Key, May 10, 1976 (div. 1982). BA in Rehab. Edn., Pa. State U., 1969. CLU; chartered fin. cons., 1986. Social caseworker Harmarville Rehab. Ctr., Pitts., 1969-75; sales rep. Key Bellevilles, Inc., Leechburg, Pa., 1975-82; agt. Prudential Ins. Co., Pitts., 1982-84; assoc. SMA Fin. Services, Pitts., 1984—. Mem. Life Underwriters Polit. Action Com., Pitts., 1985-88; sponsor Pa. Women's Campaign Fund, 1986. Mem. Am. Soc. CLU and Chartered Fin. Cons., Nat. Assn. Life Underwriters, Pitts. Assn. for Fin. Planning., Assn. Life Underwriters (bd. dirs.), State Mut. Agts. Assn., North Hills C. of C. (adv. bd.), North Hills Bus. and Profl. Women. Democrat. Roman Catholic. Club: Zonta. Lodge: Rotary. Avocations: reading, cultural events, continuing education, public speaking, civic activites. Office: SMA Financial Services 2000 Gateway Center Three Pittsburgh PA 15222

KEY, HELEN ELAINE, accounting, consulting company executive; b. Cleve., Jan. 16, 1946; d. Maud and Helen (Key) Vance. B.S., W.Va. State Coll., 1968; M.Ed., Cleve. State U., 1977. Tchr. Cleve. Bd. Edn., 1968—; instr. Cuyahoga Community Coll., Cleve., part-time, 1969-78, Dyke Coll., Cleve., part-time, 1979—; pres. H.E. Key & Assos., Cleve., 1983—; treas. BK4W Inc., Cleve., 1981. Mem. Am. Assn. Notary Pubs., Women Bus. Owners Assn., AAUW, NAACP, Cleve. Area Bus. Tchrs., NEA, Pi Lambda Theta, Alpha Kappa Alpha. Democrat. Baptist. Club: Toastmistress (sec. 1978) (Cleve.). Home: 564 Wilkes Ln Richmond Heights OH 44143

KEY, MARY RITCHIE (MRS. AUDLEY E. PATTON), linguist, author, educator; b. San Diego, Mar. 19, 1924; d. George Lawrence and Iris (Lyons) Ritchie; children: Mary Helen Key Ellis, Harold Hayden Key (dec.), Thomas George Key. Student, U. Chgo., summer 1954, U. Mich., 1959; M.A., U. Tex., 1960, Ph.D., 1963; postgrad., UCLA, 1966. Asst. prof. linguistics Chapman Coll., Orange, Calif., 1963-66; asst. prof. linguistics U. Calif., Irvine, 1966-71; assoc. prof. U. Calif., 1971-78, prof., 1978—, chmn. program linguistics, 1969-71, 75-77, 87—; cons. Am. Indian langs., Spanish, in Mexico, 1946-55, S.Am., 1955-62, English dialects, 1968-74, Easter Island, 1975, Calif. Dept. Edn., 1966, 70-75, Center Applied Linguistics, Washington, 1967, 69; lectr. in field. Author: numerous books including Comparative Tacanan Phonology, 1968; Male/Female Language, 1975, Paralanguage and Kinesics, 1975, Nonverbal Communication, 1977, The Grouping of South American Indian Languages, 1979, The Relationship of Verbal and Nonverbal Communication, 1980, Catherine the Great's Linguistic Contribution, 1980, Polynesian and American Linguistic Connections, 1984, Comparative Linguistics of South American Indian Languages, 1987; founder, editor: newsletter Nonverbal Components of Communication, 1972-76; mem. editorial bd · Forum Linguisticum, 1976—, Lang. Scis., 1978—, La Linguistique, 1979—, Multilingua, 1987—, contbr. articles to profl. jours. Recipient Friends of Library Book award, 1976; U. Calif. Regent's grantee, 1974; Fulbright-Hays grantee, 1975; Faculty Research fellow, 1984-85. Mem. Linguistic Soc. Am., Am. Dialect Soc. (exec. council; regional sec. 1974-83), Internat. Reading Assn. (dir. 1968-72), Delta Kappa Gamma (local pres. 1974-76). Office: Program in Linguistics U Calif Irvine CA 92717

KEY, RAMONA THORNTON, health facility administrator; b. Little Rock, Ark., Dec. 13, 1939; d. J.P. and H. Belle (Jones) T.; m. Charles E. Winters, Jan. 21, 1961 (dec. Dec. 1965); children: Lesa Ingram, Kellie Winters, Dale Winters; m. George Trujillo, May 24, 1970 (dec. July 1977); 1 child, Melinda Trujillo; m. Dennis Russell Key, May 15, 1982 (div. Feb. 1988). BS in Psychology, Southwestern Coll., 1963; cert. coronary intensive care, U. Tenn., 1973; postgrad., Memphis State U., 1979-81. Nurse various hosps., 1961-72; dir. personal adjustment ctr. Mental Health and Retardation Ctr., Oxford, Miss., 1972-75; cons. Interagy. Commn.'s Devel. Disabilities Tng. program State of Miss., 1974-75; coordinator for adult acute psychiat. services, liaison with local mental health ctr. Boulder (Colo.) Psychiat. Inst., 1975-77; head nurse behavior modification VA Hosp., Memphis, 1978-81; hosp. supr. Vista Sandia Psychiat. Hosp., Albuquerque, 1981-85, dir. nursing services, 1985-88; leader health workshops, Miss., 1974; bd. dirs. Nurse Profl. Standards Bd., VA Med. Ctr., Memphis, 1979-81; mem. faculty U. N.Mex. Coll. Nursing, 1986—. Mem. Am. Nurses Assn., N.Mex. Nurses Assn. (CEU com. 1986—), N.Mex. Orgn. Nurse Execs. (program chairperson 1987-88). Democrat. Methodist. Home: 3702 Rose Circle SE Rio Rancho NM 87124 Office: Univ New Mexico Mental Health Ctr Dir Nursing Service 2600 Marble NE Albuquerque NM 87106

KEYES, DARLYNN LADD, real estate executive; b. Denver, Apr. 14, 1948; d. Ernest Victor and Mary Louise (Webb) K. BS, U. Wyo., 1971. Lic. in real estate, Fla.; cert. real estate broker, Colo. Dir. mktg., ski instr., ski patrol Geneva Basin, Grant, Colo., 1972-78; gen. mgr. Tumbling River Guest Ranch, Grant, 1974-76; owner Above Timberline Outfitters, Grant, 1974—, Keyes Real Estate and Investment Co., Vail, Colo., 1979—; comml. and residential real estate salesperson 1977-79; interval owner in real estate Streamside of Vail, 1979-80; project dir. real estate Brewster Green, Cape Cod, Mass., 1981-82, Vallarta Torrs, Puerta Vallarta, Mex., 1983-84; real estate salesperson Clube Praia de Ora, Algarve, Portugal, 1984; project dir. real estate Sandstone Creek Club, Vail, 1985-87; sales dir. Gold Point Condos, Breckenridge, Colo., 1987—; sec., treas. Viking Vacation Internat., Brewster, 1982-83. Mem. Nat. Assn. Exec. Women, Colo. Bd. Realtors, Vail Bd. Realtors, Colo. Cattleman's Assn., Nat. Bd. Realtors, Colo. Wool Growers Assn., Nat. Dude Ranch Assn. (bd. dirs. 1975, Washington rep.), Am. Resort and Residential Devel. Assn., Profl. Assn. Diving Instrs. Clubs: Alpine Garden, Beaver Scuba Divers (Vail); London (Eng.) Gliding. Home and Office: PO Box 1952 Vail CO 81657

KEYES, EMMALOU, director of clinical services, nurse practitioner; b. Hutchinson, Kans., Nov. 13, 1931; d. Ferguson and Vieginia Lucile (Copenhaver) Reynolds; m. Mark B. Cripe, Nov. 13, 1953 (div. 1962); m. William Robert Keyes, Mar. 24, 1967; children: Lee Edward, Jay Scott. BS in Nursing, Pan Am. U., 1984. Cert. family nurse practitioner. Pub. health nurse Hidalgo County Health Dept., Edinburg, Tex., 1952-77; family nurse practitioner Hidalgo County Health Care Corp., Edinburg, 1977-79; title XIX screener Tex. Dept. Health, Austin, 1979-80; sch. nurse Progreso (Tex.) Ind. Sch. Dist., 1980-82; clinic services dir. Planned Parenthood, McAllen, Tex., 1982—; bd. dirs., disaster nurse Am. Red Cross, McAllen. Mem. Am. Nurses Assn., Tex. Nurses Assn. (dist. pres., treas., bd. dirs.), Am. Pub. Health Assn., Nat. Assn. Nurses in Family Planning, Am. Heart Assn. Episcopalian. Home: 21 S 35th McAllen TX 78501 Office: Planned Parenthood 1017 Pecan McAllen TX 78501

KEYES, I(RVONA) MARY, health care facility executive; b. Mason City, Iowa, May 27, 1936; d. Irvin John Witte and Bonnie Marie (Broers) Westphal; m. Thomas Robert Keyes, Oct. 17, 1959 (div. Jan. 1976); children: Teresa, Michael, Kerry, Maureen. RN diploma, St. Mary's Sch. Nursing, Rochester, Minn., 1957. Head nurse neurology St. Mary's Hosp., Rochester, 1957-59; asst. dir. nurses Walker Meth. Health Care, Mpls., 1967-68; dir. nurses Chateau Care Ctr., Mpls., 1968-76; coordinator health care Chanassen (Minn.) Treatment Ctr., 1976-77; staff nurse Abbott-Northwestern Hosp., Mpls., 1977-79; assoc. dir. chem. dependency programs Golden Valley Hosp., Mpls., 1979-83; program dir. Warren Eustis House for Adolescents, Eagan, Minn., 1983-84; chief exec. officer The Gables Extended Treatment Program for Chemically Dependent Women, Rochester, 1984-88, Choices for Women Extended Treatment Program for Women, Palm Springs, CA, 1988—; speaker chem. dependency numerous profl. confs. and community groups, 1985—. Contbr. articles on chem. dependency to profl. jours., 1986—. Mem. Minn. Women's Forum on Chem. Health, Mpls., 1984—; mem. task force Olmsted County Chem. Dependency Planning Com., Rochester, 1986—; officer Human Services adv. Council to Minn. Commr. Health, 1974-81. Recipient Service award Mayor of Rochester, 1986, Women's Forum on Chem. Health, 1986; named Outstanding Mem. Adv. Bd. Minn. Commr. Health, 1979. Mem. Minn. Chem. Dependency Assn. (officer bd. dirs. 1986-87), Inst. Chem. Dependency Profls. Minn. (cert.), St. Mary's Sch. Nursing Alumni Assn. Democrat. Roman Catholic. Office: Gables Extended Treatment Program 604 5th St SW Rochester MN 55901

KEYES, JESSICA ANN, stock exchange executive; b. N.Y.C., Apr. 28, 1950; d. Bernard Seymour and Ruth (Harrison) K.; m. Robert B. Lakser. BA, Queens Coll., Flushing, N.Y., 1971; MBA, N.Y.U., 1981. Tchr. Hirsch Sch., N.Y.C., 1971-74; programmer C.I.T. Fin., N.Y.C., 1974-77; analyst S.I.A.C., N.Y.C., 1977-78, U.S. Trust, N.Y.C., 1978-79; project mgr. Bankers Trust, N.Y.C., 1981-82; cons. N.Y. Stock Exchange, N.Y.C., 1979-81; dir. automation, 1982-87, mng. dir. automation, 1987—; cons. Smalltech, N.Y.C., 1982-83. Contbr. articles to Averbach, Ramis Proc. Mem. IEEE, Assn. Computing Machinery, Beta Gamma Sigma, Kappa Delta Pi. Office: NY Stock Exchange 20 Broad St New York NY 10005

KEYES, MARLENE MACNEAL, software engineering manager; b. N.Y.C., Aug. 4, 1952; d. Paul R. and Pearl H. (Lurie) Weissman; 1 child, Heidi Elizabeth MacNeal. BA in Biol. Sci., U. Calif., Santa Barbara, 1974, postgrad., 1977; postgrad., Calif. State U., 1988—. Lab. technician Udylite Corp., Los Angeles, 1974-75; data entry operator S.B. Cottage Hosp., Santa Barbara, 1976-77; jr. programmer Delco, Goleta, Calif., 1976-77; systems engr. Comptek Research, Santa Barbara, 1977-79; program staff specialist Aerojet Electro Systems, Azusa, Calif., 1979-84; project mgr. Structured Systems and Software, Laguna Hills, Calif., 1984—. Chmn. CALMA GDS User's Group, Los Alamitos, Calif., 1981-82, pres., founder AESC PC User's Club, Azusa, 1983-84; wish coordinator Make-A-Wish Found., Newport Beach, Calif., 1987—. Mem. Nat. Assn. Female Execs., Bus. and Profl. Women (hospitality chmn. Glendora area 1982-84). Republican. Baptist. Office: Structured Systemns & Software 23141 Plaza Pointe Dr Laguna Hills CA 92653

KEYES, STEPHANIE NADYNE, urban planner, real estate developer; b. Bklyn., Sept. 11, 1953; d. Sydney and Lilyan (Feigeles) Schlesser; m. William A. Keyes Jr., Oct. 15, 1983; 1 stepdau., Shannon Colleen. BA, U. Fla., 1975, MA, 1978. Cert. Am. Inst. Cert. Planners. Asst. planner City of Gainesville, Fla., 1975-77; assoc. planner Lee County, Fort Myers, Fla., 1977-79, sr. planner, 1979; regional planner SW Fla. Regional Planning Council, Fort Myers, 1979-82; sr. planner Gee and Jenson, EAP, Inc., Fort Myers, 1982-83; exec. dir. Econ. Devel. Coalition, Fort Myers, 1983-85; owner, prin. Stephanie Keyes, AICP, Inc., Fort Myers, 1985—. Exec. Charles Bigelow for Commr. campaign, Lee County, 1986. Mem. Am. Planning Assn. (hon. mention hurricane evac. plan, 1982), Fla. Planning and Zoning Assn., (pres. SW Fla. chpt. 1986), Econ. Devel. Coalition (bd. dirs. 1985—), Five County Bldrs. and Contractors (bd. dirs. 1985-88, Spike award), Met. Ft. Myer's C. of C. (mem. city com. 1986), Downtown Property Owner's Assn. (exec. dir. 1986—). Republican. Jewish. Home: 110 Pinebrook Dr Fort Myers FL 33907 Office: 1637 Hendry St Fort Myers FL 33901

KEYSER, MARTHA FLORENCE, public relations executive; b. Salt Lake City, Feb. 8, 1943; d. James Farrington and Margaret (Ballard) K. Cert., U. Geneva, 1964; BA, U. Utah, 1965; MBA, U. Colo., 1975. Mgr. mktg. communications Ownes-Corning Fiberglass, Toledo, Ohio, 1974-79; mgr. communications Champion, Stamford, Conn., 1979-82; pres. Keyser Assocs., Rowayton, Conn., 1982-85; mgr. pub. affairs Savin Corp, Stamford, 1985-87; v.p. corporate communications Madison Sq. Garden, N.Y.C., 1988—. Bd. dirs. Bell Island, Rowayton, 1985—, Family Recovery Ctr., New Canaan, Conn., 1987—. Mem. Women in Communications, Pub. Relations Soc. Am., Women in Mgmt. Republican. Episcopalian. Home: 12 E Beach Dr Rowayton CT 06853 Office: Madison Sq Garden 2 Penn Plaza New York NY 10121

KEYSERLING, HARRIET H., state legislator; b. N.Y.C., Apr. 4, 1922; d. Isadore and Pauline Hirschfeld; m. Ben Herbert Keyserling, June 24, 1944; children—Judy, Billy, Paul, Beth. B.A. in Econs., Barnard Coll., 1943. Mem. S.C. Ho. of Reps., 1977—, mem. joint legis. energy com., 1982—, com. for purpose of ofcl. consultation with fed. govt. concerning away-from-reactor storage facility for spent nuclear fuel; mem. adv. panel on nuclear waste disposal office of Tech. Assessment of U.S. Congress, 1979-82; mem. exec. com. Nat. Conf. State Legislatures, 1979-82, vice chmn. com. on energy, 1982, chmn. women's network, 1981-82; mem. adv. com. to U.S. Commn. on Civil Rights. At-large mem. Beaufort County Council, 1975-77; chair, founder S.C. Women in Govt.; chair Legislative Com. Cultural Affairs. Democrat.

KEYSTON, STEPHANI ANN, landscape contractor; b. Baytown, Tex., Aug. 6, 1955; d. Herbert Howard and Janice Faye (Stowe) Cruickshank; m. George Keyston III, Oct. 8, 1983; 1 child, Jeremy George. AA with honors, Merced Coll., Merced, Calif., 1975; BA in Journalism with distinction, San Jose State U., 1976. Reporter, Fresno (Calif.) Bee, 1974-75; reporter, photographer Merced (Calif.) Sun-Star, 1974-77; pub. info. officer Fresno City Coll. (Calif.), 1977-80; dir. communications Aerojet Tactical Systems Co., Sacramento, 1980-83; co-owner, v.p. Keyco Landscape Contractor, Inc., Redwood City, Calif., 1984—. Co.-coordinator Aerojet United Way Campaign, 1981; Aerojet Tactical Systems Co. coordinator West Coast Nat. Derby Rallies, 1981-83. Mem. Internat. Assn. Bus. Communicators (dir. Sacramento chpt. 1983), Citrus Heights C. of C. (v.p. 1983). Republican. Home: 835 Shepard Way Redwood City CA 94062 Office: Keyco Landscape Contractor Inc PO Box 3461 Redwood City CA 94064

KHALSA, GURUMEET KAUR, security company executive; b. Glendale, Calif., June 26, 1948; d. Iver Oley and Erma Maxine (McCune) Hopperstad; m. Qudrat Singh Khalsa; 1 child, Guru Sundri Kaur. AA, Solano Coll., 1968; studied yoga under Dr. Yogi Bhajan, from 1969. From writer to counselor to meditation and yoga instr. 3HO Found., Los Angeles, 1970-81; field officer Akal Security Inc., Santa Fe, N.Mex., 1981-84, tng. instr., 1984-85, ops. mgr., 1985-86, mktg. adminstr., 1986—. Author: (with others) Training Manual for Security Officers, 1987. Mem. Nat. Orgn. for Female Execs. Office: Akal Security Inc PO Box 1197 Santa Cruz NM 87567

KHANI, PATRICIA EBRAHIM, educator, accountant; b. Cambridge, Mass., Mar. 7, 1944; d. Robert Hugh and Edith Mary (Greene) Traill; m. Mohsen Ebrahim Khani, Mar. 4, 1978. BBA, Suffolk U., 1966; MS in Acctg., Northeastern U., 1969. CPA, Mass. Acct. Coopers and Lybrand, Boston, 1969-72; v.p., treas. Boston Fin. Tech. Group, Inc., Boston, 1972-73; asst. prof. Salem (Mass.) State Coll., 1973-79; assoc. prof. Grad. Sch. Bus. New Hampshire Coll., Manchester, 1979—; prin. Khani LaPointe and Torrisi, PC, North Andover, Mass., 1978—; developer Equine Bus. and Tax Seminar, various locations, 1983—; various speaking engagements. Author: Equine Business Plan, 1988; contbr. articles to profl. jours. Named to Hon. Ky. Col. Gov. Y.A. Brown, 1976. Mem. Am. Inst. CPA's, Mass. Soc. CPA's, Am. Horse Council, Internat. Arabian Horse Assn. (treas. 1974-75, commr. U.S. nat. show 1977-79), Beta Alpha Psi. Avocation: Arabian horses. Home: 17 Tiffany Ln Bedford NH 03102 Office: Khani LaPointe and Torrisi 200 Swanton St North Andover MA 01845

KHEEL, ANN SUNSTEIN, civic worker; b. Pitts., Nov. 5, 1915; A.B. with honors, Cornell U., 1936; m. Theodore Woodrow Kheel, July 1, 1937; children—Ellen Margaret (Mrs. Arnold S. Jacobs), Robert Jeffrey, Constance Elizabeth (Mrs. Timothy D. Smith), Martha Louise, Jane Meredith (Mrs. John R. Garrett Stanley), Katherine Emily. Columnist, Ithaca (N.Y.) Jour., assoc. editor Cornell Alumni News, 1936-37; asst. editor Tide Mag., N.Y.C., 1937-39; info. specialist Dept. Agr., Washington, 1939-43, editor Land Policy Rev.; bd. dirs. Play Schs. Assn., 1944-55; bd. dirs. Riverdale Neighborhood Assn., Riverdale/Bronx, N.Y., 1953-65, v.p., 1958-60; del. to President's Com. on Equal Employment Opportunity, Washington, 1963, 64; spl. corr. N.Y. Herald Tribune, 1957; sec., bd. dirs. N.Y. Urban League, 1965—, founder, chmn. ann. Frederick Douglass Awards Dinners, 1966—; corp. mem., trustee Schomburg Center for Research in Black Culture, 1971-86; mem. Mayor's Screening Panel for Bd. of Higher Edn. of N.Y.C., 1964-66; trustee Rand Inst. of N.Y.C., 1973-76; mem. Coop. Edn. Commn., N.Y.C. Bd. Edn., 1968—; appointee Regents Regional Coordinating Council for Post-secondary Edn., N.Y.C., 1974-76; chmn. State Parks and Recreation Commn. for N.Y.C., 1977-86. Home: 407 W 246th St Bronx NY 10471

KHELIL, NAJAT ARAFAT, physicist; b. Nablus, Jordan, July 5, 1942; came to U.S., 1962.; d. Tawfic A. and Shuhra S. Arafat; m. Chakib M. Khelil, Oct. 5, 1964; children: Sina, Khaldoun. BS in Physics and Chemistry, Cairo U., 1960; MS in Nuclear Physics, Ohio State U., 1965; PhD, North Tex. State U., 1974. Assoc. prof. U. Algiers, Algeria, 1974-80, George Washington U., Washington, 1981-84, Shaw U., Raleigh, N.C., 1985; cons. Orgn. Arab Students, Washington, 1984—; researcher Nat. Bur. Standards, Gaithersburg, Md., 1981-82. Vol. Am. Cancer Soc., Heart Fund; bd. dirs. United Holy Land Fund, Chgo., 1986—, Rainbow Coalition, 1987—. Fulbright scholar Am. Info. Service, 1962-63. Mem. Am. Phys. Soc., Union Palestinian Eng., Council Pres.'s Arab-Am. Orgn. (chairperson 1987), Arab Women's Council (pres. 1986—), Moslem Women's Assn. (v.p. 1986—), Sigma Pi Sigma. Moslem. Home: 11209 Hunt Club Dr Potomac MD 20854

KIANG-ULRICH, MARILYN KUO SHUEI, research physiologist; b. Beijing, July 18, 1915; came to U.S., 1949; d. Hua-Peng and Yuen (Sheng) K.; m. George John Ulrich, Mar. 25, 1949 (dec. July 1975); children: Patricia, Lisa. Student, Osaka (Japan) Women's Med. Coll., 1934-37, U. Calif., San Francisco, 1950-51; MA, U. Calif., Santa Barbara, 1973, PhD, 1977. Cert. med. technologist, clin. lab. scientist. Med. technologist Harriman Jones Hosp., Long Beach, Calif., 1951-53; supervising lab. technologist Valley Clin. Lab., Santa Barbara, 1953-73; research physiologist Inst. Environ. Stress, U. Calif., Santa Barbara, 1977—. Contbr. articles to profl. jours. Mem. Am. Assn. for Advancement Sci., Am. Soc. Med. Tech., Calif. Assn. Med. Lab. Tech., Gerontol. Soc. Am., N.Y. Acad. Scis. Office: U Calif Inst Environ Stress Santa Barbara CA 93108

KIBRICK, ANNE, nursing educator, university dean; b. Palmer, Mass., June 1, 1919; d. Martin and Christine (Grigas) Karlon; m. Sidney Kibrick, June 16, 1949; children: Joan, John. R.N., Worcester (Mass.) Hahnemann Hosp., 1941; B.S., Boston U., 1945; M.A., Columbia Tchrs. Coll., 1948; Ed.D., Harvard U., 1958; L.H.D. (hon.), St. Joseph's Coll., Windham, Maine, 1973. Asst. edn. dir. Cushing VA Hosp., Framingham, Mass., 1948-49; asst. prof. nursing Simmons Coll., Boston, 1949-55; dir. grad. div. Boston U. Sch. Nursing, 1958-63, dean, 1963-68, prof., 1968-70; chmn. dept. nursing Boston Coll. Grad. Sch. Arts and Sci, 1970-74; chmn. sch. nursing Boston State Coll., 1974-82; dean Sch. Nursing U. Mass., Boston, 1982—; cons. div. nursing USPHS, 1964-68; cons. Nat. Student Nurses Assn., 1985—; mem. nat. adv. council nurse tng. USPHS, NIH, 1968-73; cons. Hebrew U.-Hadassah Med. Orgn., Jerusalem, 1971—; mem. Inst. Medicine of Nat. Acad. Scis., 1972—, mem. steering com. costs of edn. of health professions, 1972-74; mem. Nat. Med. Audiovisual Tng. Center, 1972-76, Gov.'s Com. and Area Bd. Mental Health and Mental Retardation, Nat. Commn. for Study Nursing and Nursing Edn., 1970-73; mem. faculty com., regent's external degree program in nursing SUNY, 1974-82; mem. hosp. mgmt. bd. U. Hosp., U. Mass., 1976-81; dir. Medic Alert, Am. Jour. Nursing Co.; cons. Cumberland Coll. Health Scis., New South Wales, Australia, 1986, Menoufia U., Shibin El Kom, Egypt, 1987. Mem. editorial bd. Mass. Jour. Community Health. Bd. dirs. Brookline Mental Health Assn., Met. chpt. ARC., Children's Ctr. Brookline and Greater Boston, Inc., 1984—. Fellow Am. Acad. Nursing; mem. Nat. Mass. Leagues Nursing (pres. 1971-73), Am. Nurses Assn., Mass. Nurses Assn. (dir. 1982-86), AIDS Internat. Info. Found. (founding mem. 1985), Mass. Nurses Found. (v.p. 1983-86), Nat. Acads. of Practice, Mass. Med. Soc. (bd. dirs. postgrad. med. inst. 1983—), Blueprint 2000, Sigma Theta Tau, Pi Lambda Theta. Home: 381 Clinton Rd Brookline MA 02146

KICHLINE, SUSAN KAY, marketing professional; b. Bethlehem, Pa., June 15, 1958; d. Stanley Kunsman and Nancy (Bauder) K. Student, Mansfield (Pa.) State Coll., 1976-77, Lesley Coll., 1982-83, Suffolk U., 1984—. Asst. mgr. Allegro Cafe/Adagio Buffet, N.Y.C., 1977-80; mgr. Sheraton-Boston Hotel, 1981-82; asst. to sr. v.p. Robert Jameson Assocs., Boston, 1982-83; systems adminstr. Fidelity Investments Retail Services, Boston, 1983-87; project coordinator facilities devel. dept. Fidelity Brokerage Services, Boston, 1987—. Involved in various civic theater performances, Pa., 1967-76; TV appearances include Al Albert's Showcase, Phila., 1968, Chief Halftown (NBC-TV), 1969, P.M. Magazine (ABC-TV), 1979; other performing arts roles. Mem. Nat. Assn. Female Execs. Home: 114 Old Harbor St #1 South Boston MA 02127 Office: Fidelity Brokerage Services 161 Devonshire St 3d Floor Boston MA 02110

KIDD, CATHY A., controller; b. Lexington, Ky., Oct. 24, 1957; d. Chester Allen and Lois Catherine (Horn) K.; m. Michael W. Stratton, July 8, 1978 (div. 1985); m. Richard M. Rickel Jr. B.A. in Acctg., Georgetown Coll., Ky., 1978, MA in mgmt. U. Phoenix, Tucson, postgrad. in Bus. Staff auditor Commonwealth of Ky., Frankfort, 1978-79; acct. Dept. Local Govt., Frankfort, 1979-80; controller Stouder Meml. Hosp., Troy, Ohio, 1980-82, Woodford Meml. Hosp., Versailles, Ky., 1982-84, Health Am. Corp., Tucson, 1984-86, St. Mary's Hosp., Tucson, 1986—. Mem. Healthcare Fin. Mgmt. Assn., Nat. Assn. Female Execs., Am. Bus. Women's Assn., Phi Mu, Phi Beta Lambda. Democrat. Mem. Disciples of Christ Ch. Avocations: needlepoint; macrame; swimming; bicycling; reading. Office: St Mary's Rd Tucson AZ 85745

KIDD, DEBRA JEAN, communications consultant; b. Chgo., May 13, 1956; d. Fred A. and Jean (Pezzopane) Winchar; m. Kim Joseph Kidd, July 22, 1978; 1 child, Jennifer Marie. A.A. in Bus. with high honors, Wright Jr. Coll., 1977. Legal sec. Sidley & Austin, Chgo., 1977-80; investment adminstr. Golder, Thoma & Co., Chgo., 1980-81, exec. asst., 1981-84; sales rep. Dataspeed, Inc., Chgo., 1984, midwestern regional mgr. Dataspeed, Inc., Chgo., 1985; communications cons. Chgo. Communications, Inc., Chgo., 1986—; owner, founder Captain Kidd's Video, Niles, 1981-84. Vol. Am. Lung Assn., Chgo., 1979; vol. tchr. CCD Our Lady Mother of Ch., Norridge, Ill., 1981-83. Mem. Nat. Assn. Female Execs., Nat. Assn. Bus. Women, Nat. Assn. Profl. Saleswomen, Nat. Network of Women in Sales, Bus. and Profl. Women's Club, Phi Theta Kappa. Roman Catholic. Avocations: camping; snow and water skiing; horseback riding; sailing; reading; needlepoint.

KIDD, NANCY VAN TRIES, psychologist, mediator; b. Huntingdon, Pa., June 5, 1933; d. Samuel Musser and Jesse Pauline (Haupt) Van Tries; m. Joseph Jerome Rowley, Jr., Aug. 4, 1956 (div. 1967); children—Linda Rowley Tawfik, Joseph J. III, Bruce W.; m. 2d Jerome Thomas Kidd, May 23, 1970. B.A. in Journalism and Fine Arts, Pa. State U., 1955, D.Ed. in Counseling and Psychology, 1977; M.Ed. in Elem. Edn. and Ednl. Psychology, Temple U., 1969. Assoc. prof. psychology and counseling Community Coll. R.I., 1973-82; psychologist Child, Adult and Family Psychol. Ctr., State College, Pa., 1981-83; family mediator, counselor Ariz. Counseling Ctr., Phoenix, 1983; psychologist, dir. Psychol. and Counseling Resources, Richmond, 1985—; mediator Greater Richmond Mediation Network, 1984—. Contbr. articles to profl. jours. Trustee Pa. State U., 1984—. Mem. Am. Psychol. Assn., Va. Psychol. Assn., Acad. Family Mediators, R.I. Personnel and Guidance Assn. (exec. bd. 1978-79), Pa State Alumni Club, Phi Delta Kappa, Pi Lambda Theta, Kappa Kappa Gamma. Methodist. Office: Psychol & Counseling Resources Inc 6901 Patterson Ave Richmond VA 23226

KIDD, REBECCA (LOUISE) MONTGOMERY, artist; b. Muncie, Ind., Nov. 29, 1942; d. Joe Bucklyn and Mary Marguerite (Mark) Montgomery; corr. student comml. art, Famous Artists Schs.; cert. of completion corr. course U. Sci. and Philosophy, Waynesboro, Va., 1976; m. Ben Roy Kidd, Apr. 10, 1964; children—Daniel Ben, Diana Piper. Character painter, 1966—; portrait painter and drawer, 1962-81, 83—; painter in oils, pastels; outdoor scene, still life, floral painter, 1969—; children's story illustrator, 1972-74; restorer old houses, 1972-81; adaptor of master's paintings, 1974-82; miniature painter, 1974-82; film illustrator, 1975; Am. Indian painter, 1975-81; trading pin designer, 1977, 78; lithograph printmaker, 1977; monotype printmaker, 1978—; one woman show: Roadside Gallery, Melfa, Va., 1982; group shows include: Roadside Gallery, 1977—, The Gallery, Ct. Plaza, Salisbury, Md., 1977-84, Queens Coll., Cambridge U., 1982. Mem. Quality Edn. Accomack County (Va.), Exec. Com., 1979-80. Mem. Eastern Shore Art League (constn. and bylaws chmn. 1979, dir. 1982), Visual Artists and Galleries Assn., Nat. Mus. Women in Arts (charter), Nat. Trust Historic Preservation (assoc.), Internat. Platform Assn. (merit award and popular choice award 1984 conv.). Subject of articles in several news publs. Address: 9 Lake St Onancock VA 23417

KIDD, VIVIAN GRAVELY, non-profit organization administrator, consultant; b. Cool Ridge, W.Va., Oct. 4, 1947; d. Franklin S. and Zenobia Vivian (Peters) Gravely; m. Victor V. Kidd, Jan. 10, 1970. B.A., W.Va. Inst. Tech., 1969; M.S., W.Va. Coll. Grad. Studies, 1981. Tchr., Staunton (Va.) Pub. Sch., 1970-71; dir. pub. info. Goodwill Industries Kanawha Valley, Charleston, W.Va., 1971-73; dir. pub. info. Black Diamond council Girl Scout U.S.A., Charleston, 1973-76; communications dir. United Way of Kanawha Valley, Charleston, 1976-78; dep. commr. W.Va. Dept. Labor, Charleston, 1978-83; exec. dir. W.Va. Edn. Fund, Inc., Charleston, 1983—; mem. Gov.'s Honors Acad., Charleston, 1984. Bd. dirs. Literacy Vols. W.Va. Mem. W.Va. Indsl. Relations Research Assn. (pres.). Democrat. Methodist. Office: WVa Edn Fund Inc 1126 Kanawha Valley Bldg Charleston WV 25301

KIDDER, MARGOT, actress; b. Yellowknife, Can., Oct. 17, 1948; m. Tom McGuane, 1975 (div.); 1 dau., Maggie; m. John Heard. AttendedU. B.C. Began career in Can. theater and TV; film debut in Gaily, Gaily, 1969; other films include Quackser Fortune Has a Cousin in the Bronx, 1970, Sisters, 1972, Gravy Train, 1974, The Great Waldo Pepper, 1975, The Reincarnation of Peter Proud, 1975, 92 in the Shade, 1977, Superman, 1978, The Amityville Horror, 1979, Superman II, 1981, Some Kind of Hero, 1981, Trenchcoat, 1983, Superman III, 1983, Little Treasure, 1985, Superman IV; starred in TV series Nichols, 1972, TV movie Honky Tonk, 1974; other TV appearances include Mod Squad, Vanishing Act, 1986, Hoax, 1986, Louisiana, The Glitter Dome, Body of Evidence, 1988. Office: Gersh Agy 222 N Canon Dr Beverly Hills CA 90210 •

KIEBALA, SUSAN MARIE, accounting and management educator; b. Bay City, Mich., Aug. 22, 1952; d. Edwin Edward and Ruth May (Jarvela) Bukowski; m. Joseph Kiebala, Oct. 6, 1973; children: James, Adam, Kara. BS, Ferris State Coll., 1973; MBA, Western Mich. U., 1977. Acct. Consumers Power Co., Jackson, Mich., 1973-76, Eaton Corp., Marshall, Mich., 1976-78; instr. acctg. Kellogg Community Coll., Battle Creek, Mich., 1978—. Coordinator Youth Soccer League, Marshall, 1986—; sec./treas. Marshall Soccer Boosters, 1987—; chmn. Marshall Citizens for Quality Schs., 1988. Mem. Nat. Assn. Accts. Home: 527 Sherman Dr Marshall MI 49068 Office: Kellogg Community Coll 450 North Ave Battle Creek MI 49017

KIECOLT-GLASER, JANICE KAY, psychologist; b. Oklahoma City, June 30, 1951; d. Edward Harold and Vergie Mae (Lively) Kiecolt; m. Ronald Glaser, Jan. 18, 1980. BA in Psychology with honors, U. Okla., 1972; PhD in Clin. Psychology, U. Miami, 1976. Lic. psychologist, Ohio. Clin. psychology intern Baylor U. Coll. Medicine, Houston, 1974-75; postdoctoral fellow in adult clin. psychology U. Rochester, N.Y., 1976-78; asst. prof. psychiatry Ohio State U. Coll. Medicine, Columbus, 1978-84, assoc. prof. psychiatry and psychology, 1984—, active various coms.; presenter confs. on various mental health and social behavioral topics; mem. AIDS study sect., NIH, 1988—. Mem. editorial bd. Brain, Behavior and Immunity jour., 1986—, Jour. Behavioral Medicine, 1988—; reviewer Health Psychology jour., Jour. Cons. and Clin. Psychology, Jour. Personality and Social Psychology, Psychiatry Research jour., Psychosomatic Medicine jour.; contbr. articles to profl. jours., also chpts. to books. NIMH grantee, 1985—. Mem. Am. Psychol. Assn., Soc. Behavioral Medicine (program com. 1985, 87, New Investigator award 1984), Acad. Behavioral Medicine Research, Phi Beta Kappa. Office: Ohio State U Coll Medicine Dept Psychiatry 473 W 12th Ave Columus OH 43210

KIEFFER, SUSAN WERNER, geologist; b. Warren, Pa., Nov. 17, 1942. BS in Physics and Math., Allegheny Coll., 1964; MS in Geol. Scis., Calif. Inst. Tech., 1967, PhD in Planetary Scis., 1971; DSc (hon.), Allegheny Coll., 1987. Postdoctoral research geochemist UCLA, 1971-73, asst. prof. geology, 1973-79; geologist U.S. Geol. Survey, Flagstaff, Ariz., 1979—. Co-editor: (with A. Navrotsky) Microscopic to Macroscopic: Atomic Environments to Mineral Thermodynamics, 1985. Alfred P. Sloan Found. fellow, 1977-79; W.H. Mendenhall lectr., U.S. Geol. Survey, 1980; recipient Disting. Alumnus award, Calif. Inst. Tech., 1982; recipient Meritorious Service award Dept. Interior, 1986. Fellow Am. Geophys. Union, Mineral. Soc. Am. (award 1980), Geol. Soc. Am., Meteoritical Soc.; mem. Nat. Acad. Scis., Am. Acad. Arts Scis. Office: US Geol Survey 2255 N Gemini Dr Flagstaff AZ 86001

KIEHL, LEE LEARNED, hospital administrator; b. Dearborn, Mich., May 9, 1954; d. Don Rankin and Ann (Chlipala) Learned; m. Mark Henry Kiehl, Dec. 30, 1977; children: Erich, Paul. BS, U. Mich., 1975, M in Health Service Adminstrn., 1977; MBA, U. Mo., 1979. Planning assoc. Area II Health Systems Agy., Moberly, Mo., 1977-78; dir. planning and devel. Christian Hosp. N.E.-N.W., St. Louis, 1979-82, asst. adminstr., 1982—. Mem. Am. Coll. Healthcare Execs., Greater St. Louis Women in Health Adminstrn. (pres. 1983-84, sec. 1985-86), Greater St. Louis Alliance for Hosp. Planning (sec., treas. 1982-83), U. Mich. Alumni Assn. Home: 12 Terrace Gardens Saint Louis MO 63131

KIEHNE, ANNA MARIE, accountant, educator, systems analyst; b. Preston, Minn., Dec. 15, 1947; d. Alvin H. and Anna M. (Goldsmith) K. B.B.A., Winona State U.; postgrad. Calif. State U.-Los Angeles, 1974-78, cert. in systems analysis UCLA, 1984. Acct. Murray Howard Realty, Los Angeles, 1974-78; staff acct. Bowest Corp., La Jolla, Calif., 1978-79; acctg. supr. Majestic Investment, Denver, 1979-81; adminstrv. acct. ECA/Intercomp. systems analyst Home Savs., 1983-88; tchr. adult edn. Election judge, Denver; del. to primary, county, state Democratic convs., 1980, 82. Mem. Nat. Assn. Accts. (cert. in flexible budgeting and performance reporting), Internat. Platform Assn., Nat. Assn. Female Execs.; Nat. Women's Polit. Caucus. Lutheran. Home: 880 Parkview Ave Saint Paul MN 55117

KIEL-LIGHTLE, PATRICIA HALL, medical equipment sales manager; b. Drexel Hill, Pa., June 14, 1942; d. Robert Coleman and Dorothy (Bidelman) Hall; m. Alan L. Kiel, Feb. 1, 1964; children—Susannah, Jennifer; m. 2d, Kenneth E. Lightle, July 7, 1979. A.A., Centenary Coll., Hackettstown, N.J., 1962; student Delaware Valley Coll., Doylestown, Pa., 1976-77, Calif. State U.-Fullerton, 1978-86. Exec. sec. to product safety dir., nat. sales mgr. and v.p. mktg. Air-Shields, Hatboro, Pa., 1974-77, tech. sales rep., So. Calif., 1978, terr. sales mgr., So. Calif., 1979, area sales mgr., So. Calif., 1980-84, regional trainer, 1983-84, nat. accounts mgr., 1984-87, Western region sales mgr., 1987—. Recipient numerous awards Air-Shields Co. Mem. Nat. Assn. Female Execs. Republican. Episcopalian.

KIELSMEIER, CATHERINE JANE, educational administrator; b. San Jose, Calif; d. Frank Delos and Catherine Doris (Sellar) MacGowan; M.S., U. So. Calif., 1964, Ph.D., 1971; m. Milton Kielsmeier; children—Catherine Louise, Barry Delos. Tchr. pub. schs. Maricopa, Calif.; sch. psychologist Campbell (Calif.) Union Sch Dist., 1961-66; asst. prof. edn. and psychology Western Oreg. State Coll., Monmouth, 1966-67, 70; asst. research prof. Oreg. System Higher Edn., Monmouth, 1967-70; dir. spl. services Pub. Schs., Santa Rosa, Calif., 1972—. Mem. Sonoma County Council Community Services, 1976—, Sonoma County Orgn. for Retarded/Becoming Independent, 1978—. Mem. Council for Exceptional Children. Club: Commonwealth of Calif. Home: 7495 Poplar Dr Forestville CA 95436 Office: 211 Ridgeway Ave Santa Rosa CA 95402

KIELTY, PAMELA JANE, speech pathologist; b. Pitts., Mar. 23, 1947; d. George and Mildred Mary (Bartley) K.; m. Stephen Chase Todd, June 9, 1983; children: Adam Bartley Todd, Eric Chase Todd. BS, Clarion (Pa.) U., 1969; MS, Vanderbilt U., 1971; EdS, U. Ky., 1983. Speech pathologist Lawrence County Soc. for Crippled Children and Adults, New Castle, Pa., 1969; speech and hearing specialist Capital Area Intermediate Unit, Lemoyne, Pa., 1969-74; speech pathologist U. Ky. Med. Ctr., Lexington, 1974-76, Bowling Green (Ky.) Bd. Edn., 1977—; cons. Diagnostic Network, Bowling Green, 1981; mem. Ky. Bd. Examiners for Speech Pathology and Audiology, Frankfort, 1978-82. Mem. Capital Arts Assn., Bowling Green, 1982—, Ky. Mus. Assn., Bowling Green, 1984—, Common Cause, Washington, 1986—. Mem. Am. Speech and Hearing Assn., Ky. Speech and Hearing Assn., Council for Exceptional Children. Democrat. Presbyterian. Home: 813 Villa Ct Bowling Green KY 42101 Office: Bowling Green Bd Edn 1211 Center St Bowling Green KY 42101

KIENBAUM, KAREN SMITH, lawyer; b. Flint, Mich., Aug. 10, 1943; d. George Arnold and Ellen Janice (Wills) Smith; m. Thomas Gerd Kienbaum, June 24, 1966; 1 child, Ursula. BA in History and Edn., U. Mich., 1965; JD, U. Detroit, 1975. Bar: Mich. 1975. Tchr. Donoero High Sch., Royal Oak, Mich., 1966-72; dep. defender Legal Aid and Defender Assn., Detroit, 1975-77; assoc. Blue Cross Blue Shield, Detroit, 1977-78, asst. gen. counsel, 1981—; assoc. Clark, Hardy, Lewis et al, Birmingham, Mich., 1978-80. Mem. Fed. Bar Assn., Mich. Bar Assn. (appointee prepaid legal services 1978-85), Detroit Bar Assn. (chmn. corp. sect. 1985—, Chair person of Yr. labor sect. 1983, bd. dirs.), ACCA (bd. dirs. 1985—), DBA Found. (trustee 1987—). Clubs: Renaissance, Grosse Pointe Hunt (Detroit). Home: 894 Edgemont Park Grosse Pointe Park MI 48230 Office: Blue Cross Blue Shield 600 Lafayette E Detroit MI 48226

KIENHOLZ, LYN SHEARER, arts projects coordinator; b. Chgo.; d. Mitchell W. and Lucille M. (Hock) Shearer; student Sullins Coll., Md. Coll. Women. Assoc. producer Kurt Simon Prodns., Beverly Hills, Calif., 1963-65; owner, mgr. Vuokko Boutique, Beverly Hills, 1969-75; bd. dirs. Los Angeles Inst. Contemporary Art, 1976-79, Fellows of Contemporary Art, 1977-79, Internat. Network for Arts, 1979—, Los Angeles Contemporary Exhbns., 1980-82; exec. sec., bd. dirs. Beaubourg Found. (now George Pompidou Art and Culture Found.), 1977-81; visual arts adv. Performing Arts Council, Los Angeles Music Center, 1980—; bd. govs. Calif. Inst. Tech. Baxter Art Gallery, 1980-85; adv. bd. dirs. Fine Arts Communications, pub. Images & Issues mag., 1981-85; founder, pres. bd. dirs. Calif./Internat. Arts Found., 1981—; bd. dirs., western chmn. ArtTable 1983—; exec. bd. Sovereign Fund, 1981—; exec. bd. dirs. Scandinavia Today, 1982-83, Arts, Inc., 1987—, Art L.A./87, 1987, Art L.A., 1988; mem. adv. bd. Otis/Parsons Sch. Design, 1983-85, U. So. Calif. dept. fine arts, 1983-85; bd. dirs. UK/LA Festival of Britain, 1986-88; hon. bd. dirs. L'Ensemble des Deux Mondes, Paris, 1986—; mem. Comité International pour les Musées d'Art Moderne, 1985—. Bd. dirs. Arts, Inc., 1987—. Co-host radio program ARTS/L.A., 1987—; contbg. editor Calif. mag., 1984—. Address: 2737 Outpost Dr Los Angeles CA 90068

KIESOW, LINDA F., data processing executive; b. Rock Island, Ill., July 5, 1953; d. Oscar R. and Helen F. (Junk) McElroy; m. James Thomas Kiesow, May 26, 1973. B.Bus. in Acctg., Western Ill. U., 1979; M.B.A., U. Iowa, 1985. Cert. data processor. Produce mgr. Carthage Super Valu, Ill., 1974-75; aggregate sample analyst Valley Quarry, St. Augustine, Ill., 1975-76; data processing mgr. Moline Consumers Co., Ill., 1979-87; ops. supr. Alcoa, Davenport, Iowa, 1987—. Fulbright scholar Western Ill. U., Macomb, 1977; Coll. Bus. Scholar, Western Ill. U., 1978; Acctg. Dept. scholar Western Ill. U., 1978. Mem. Acctg. Soc. (mem. banquet com. chmn., v.p. 1977-78), Nat. Assn. Female Execs., Data Processing Mgmt. Assn., Assn. of Inst. for Cert. of Computer Profls., Alpha Lambda Delta, Phi Kappa Phi. Republican.

Baptist. Avocations: reading; sports. Home: 4907 48th Ave Moline IL 61265 Office: Alcoa PO Box 3567 Davenport IA 52808

KIEVMAN, BEVERLY STEIN, marketing, public relations and sales training executive; b. Atlanta, Nov. 21, 1937; d. Jack Clarence and Bess (Segal) Stein; student Rollins Coll., 1954-56; A.B. in Journalism, U. Ga., Athens, 1958; children—Mark, Steve; stepchildren—Chris, Carson, Michele, Corin. Founder, pres. Atlanta Models & Talent, Inc., 1960-71; pres. Beverly Anderson & Assos., Atlanta, 1972-74; dist. mgr. Research Inst. Am., Atlanta, 1975-76, dir. mgmt. services, 1976-77, regional dir., 1977-78; founder, pres. Mktg. Innovations Corp., Atlanta, 1979—; dir. Nat. Bank of Ga., 1981—, Delta Queen Steamboat Co., 1984-86. Pres. Ga. chpt. Leukemia Soc. Am., 1981-82; mem. Martin Luther King Jr. State Holiday Commn., 1985-86. Mem. Women's Forum, Inc. (nat. bd. dir. 1980-82), Women's Commerce Club Am. (dir. 1981-85), Com. of 200, Sales and Mktg. Execs. (dir. 1980-81), Atlanta Advt. Club (dir. 1971-74), Women in Film (dir. 1974-76), Women Bus. Owners (dir. 1980-81), Nat. Speakers Assn. Author: The Complete Success Workbook for Today's Saleswoman, 1982. Home: Adams Rd Rt 14 Box 265 Cumming GA 30130 Office: 5775 Peachtree-Dunwoody Rd Bdlg E Suite 200 Atlanta GA 30342

KIGGINS, MILDRED L., telemarketing firm executive; b. Hempstead, N.Y., Sept. 14, 1927; d. Wolfgang and Hannah Ingeborg (Olsson) Weissmann; m. Andrew Edward Kiggins, Jan. 8, 1962 (div. 1982); children: Daniel Mark, David Bruce. Diploma, Donovan Bus. Coll., Hackensack, N.J., 1945, Luther Coll. Acad., 1947. Exec. sec. Am. Machine & Foundry Inc., Stamford, Conn., 1954-61; telemktg. rep. Adult Independence Devel. Ctr., 1977—, Harry Schoenfeld Ins. Services & Design, Los Gatos, Calif., 1985—, Donald P. Jorgensen, CPA, 1987—; sec. Salois & Parrott, Cert. Shorthand Reporters, 1985—. Tchr. Sunday sch. St. John's Lutheran Ch., Stamford, 1948-50. Mem. Nat. Assn. Female Execs. Republican. Avocations: gardening, music, sports, church activities. Home: 4644 Pinto River Ct San Jose CA 95136

KIKKAWA-WARD, CAROL HIROKO, nursing agency administrator; b. Honolulu, Oct. 29, 1938; d. Raymond Sumito and Marjorie Matsuyo (Kiyota) Okumura; m. Stanley Yoshinori Kikkawa, June 17, 1960 (div. 1978); children: Scott Kanji, Lori Tammie, Kerrie Naomi; m. David Windle Ward, Dec. 26, 1980. BS in Nursing, U. Hawaii, 1960, MPH, 1978. Staff nurse Kuakini Hosp., Honolulu, 1960-61, Kaiser Hosp., Honolulu, 1961-62, Good Samaritan Hosp., Los Angeles, 1962-63, Kaiser-Permanente Med. Group, Honolulu, 1967-69; asst. dir., pub. health nurse Big Sister League Los Angeles, 1963-65; infant coordinator, program dir. Parent and Child Ctr., Kalihi, Hawaii, 1968-70; dir. nursing and health services, disaster health services Pacific ARC, Honolulu, 1974-81; adminstr. Med. Personnel Pool, Honolulu, 1981—; cons., trainer in Am. Samoa and Bethel, Alaska, 1977-80; asst. prof. community nursing Hawaii-Loa Coll., 1984; cons., instr. CareGivers of Hawaii, 1983-86; lectr. U. Hawaii Sch. Nursing, Hawaii State Network on Aging; policy chair Hawaii State Adv. Bd. on Elderly Affairs, 1981-88. Mem. Hawaii Assn. for Home Care (pres. 1986—), Hawaiian League of Nursing (vice-chmn.), Sigma Theta Tau. Democrat. Episcopalian. Home: 7248 Anakua St Honolulu HI 96825 Office: Med Personnel Pool 1441 Kapiolani Blvd Suite 1320 Honolulu HI 96814

KILBANE, ADRIENNE F., small business owner; b. Chgo., Jan. 19, 1933; d. Herbert E. and Edna M.(Qualmann) Seyring; m. Robert H. Kilbane, Feb. 24, 1951 (div. 1974); children: Robbyn Kilbane McFadden, Lawrence H., Gregory A., David J. AA, Lake County Jr. Coll., 1981; BA, Barat Coll., 1984. Lic. real estate Ill. Med. asst. Med. Office, Grayslake, Ill., 1960-70; treas. sch. dist., sec. to supt. Spaulding Sch. Dist. 58, Waukegan, Ill., 1970-74; sec. sch. fin. office Highland Park (Ill.) Dist. #108, 1974-83; asst. to dir. Waukegan Pk. Dist., 1983-84; assoc. real estate Corder Realty, Waukegan, 1978—; pres., owner Ice Cream Harbor Inc., Waukegan, 1984—. Pres. PTO, Waukegan, 1963-64; leader Girl Scouts Am., Waukegan, 1958-63; den mother Boy Scouts Am., 1962-71; active Big Bros./Big Sisters. Mem. Art Inst. Chgo., Lincoln Pk. Zool. Soc., Nat. Assn. Realtors, Nat. Assn. Female Execs., Nat. Assn. Prevention Cruelty Animals, Am. Cancer Inst., World Wildlife Fund, No. Ill. Tourism Council, Ill. Conv. and Tourism Bur., Waukegan Lake County F. of C. (dir.), Phi Theta Kappa. Republican. Lutheran. Clubs: Exchange, Duck's Unltd. Home: 605 Frolic Ave Waukegan IL 60085

KILBORN, BARBARA JEAN, nutrition educator; b. Mpls., Apr. 8, 1945; d. Alan John and LaVonne Mary (Fitzgerald) Brant; m. Michael David Jones, July 2, 1966 (div. Nov. 1971); m. Alan Roger Kilborn, May 27, 1972; children: John Fitzgerald, Alana Merrel. BA, San Diego State U., 1969, MS, 1980. Registered dietitian; cert. home economist. Home economist San Diego Gas and Electric Co., 1969-73; instr. Grossmont Coll., El Cajon, Calif., 1973-84, San Diego State U., 1983-84; nutrition cons. Dairy Council Am., San Diego, 1984—. Mem. Calif. Home Econs. Assn. (v.p. 1987—, pres. San Diego dist. 1985-87, v.p. 1984-85), Am. Dietitic Assn., Soc. for Nutrition Edn., Inter Agy. Council, Soc. Consumer Affairs Profls. Republican. Roman Catholic. Home: 1543 Stalker Ct El Cajon CA 92020

KILCULLEN, MARY ANN, military officer; b. Tucson, Feb. 11, 1956; d. William Joseph and Phyllis (O'Brien) K.; m. John Edward Martin, June 28, 1985; children: Kirstin Meischel Kilcullen-Martin, Monique Alexandria. BS, Ariz. State U., 1981; field artillery student, Alpha Battery Officer Student Bn., Ft. Sill, Okla., 1985-86. Commd. 2d lt. F.A., U.S. Army, 1981, advanced through ranks to capt., 1984; with Tactical Intelligence, Babenhausen, Fed. Republic of Germany, 1984-85; comdr. Hdqrs. and Headqrs. Battery, 212th F.A. Brigade, Ft. Sill, 1986—. Named one of Outstanding Young Women Am., 1987. Mem. Res. Officer Assn., Assn. U.S. Army, Field Artillery Assn. Democrat. Roman Catholic. Avocations: sailing, water skiing, writing poetry, photography. Home: 7204 SW Drakestone Blvd Lawton OK 73505-7446 Office: Hdqrs and Hdqrs Battery 212th Field Artillery Brigade Fort Sill OK 73505

KILDE, SANDRA JEAN, nurse anesthetist, educator, consultant; b. Eau Claire, Wis., June 25, 1938; d. Harry Meylan and Beverly June (Johnson) K. Diploma Luther Hosp. Sch. Nursing, Eau Claire, 1959; grad. anesthesia course Mpls. Sch. Anesthesia, 1967; BA, Met. State U., St. Paul, 1976; MA, Coll. St. Thomas, 1981; EdD, Nova U., 1987. RN, Wis., Minn. Operating room nurse Luther Hosp., Eau Claire, 1959-61, head nurse operating room, 1961-63; supr. operating room Midway Hosp., St. Paul, 1963-66; staff anesthetist North Meml. Med. Ctr., Robbinsdale, Minn., 1967-68; program dir. Mpls. Sch. Anesthia, St. Louis Park, Minn., 1968—; adj. asst. prof. St. Mary's Coll., Winona, Minn., 1982—, program dir. Masters Degree Program, 1984—; ednl. cons. accreditation visitor Council on Accreditation of Nurse Anesthesia Ednl. Programs/Schs., Park Ridge, Ill., 1983—; presentations in field. Recipient Good Neighbor award Sta. WCCO, Mpls., 1980. Mem. Am. Assn. Nurse Anesthetists (pres. 1981-82, pres. and bd. dirs. Edn. and Research Found. 1981-83, cert. profl. excellence 1976), Minn. Assn. Nurse Anesthetists (pres. 1975-76). Lutheran. Avocations: gardening, fishing, photography, choir directing, playing guitar and piano. Home: 11784 Madison St Blaine MN 55434 Office: Mpls Sch Anesthesia 6715 Minnetonka Blvd Saint Louis Park MN 55426

KILGORE, CATHERINE C., economic geologist, researcher; b. Los Angeles, Dec. 25, 1956; d. Donald Evan and Elsie Ellen (Walden) Cook; m. Thomas Jefferson Kilgore, III, Aug. 5, 1978; 1 child, Devin Walden. B.S. in Geology, Fort Lewis Coll., 1978; postgrad. in mineral econs. Colo. Sch. Mines, 1981-82. Geologist U.S. Geol. Survey, Denver, 1979, Colo. Dept. Health, Denver, 1979-80, U.S. Bur. Mines, Denver, 1980—. Author info. circulars, articles. Recipient spl. achievement award U.S. Bur. Mines, 1983, 86. Mem. Soc. Mining Engrs. (session chmn. 1986). Avocations: stained glass art, gourmet cooking. Office: US Bur Mines MAFO Bldg 20 Denver Fed Ctr Denver CO 80225

KILGORE, JUDITH SHAMILLE, municipal project administrator; b. Chattanooga, July 3, 1955; d. Julian Henry and Edith Irene (Harrison) K.; 1 child, Katherine Elizabeth. BA, U. Tenn., Chattanooga, 1977; M in Urban Planning, U. Tenn., 1980. Neighborhood planner Neighborhood Housing Service, Knoxville, Tenn., 1977-80; specialist comml. revitalization City of Ft. Wayne, Ind., 1980-83; mgr. Westlake Ctr. project City of Seattle, 1983—; Advisor market study rev. com. Dept. Employment Security, Seattle, 1986—; mem. Wash. State Task Force on Com. Area Devel., Seattle, 1986—. Bd. dirs. Seattle Emergency Housing Services, 1986—. HUD fellow, 1978. Mem. Am. Planning Assn., 101 Black Women, Assn. Single Adoptive Parents. Office: Dept Community Devel 400 Yesler Way 2d Floor Seattle WA 98104

KILKELLY, MARJORIE LEE, state legislator; b. Hartford, Conn., Dec. 1, 1945; d. Bruce Hamilton and Corlys Lucille (Lux) Brewer; m. Jeffrey Fortier, Sr., Feb. 14, 1972 (div. Feb. 1974); children: Jeffrey Jr., Robert M.; m. Joseph Kilkelly, Feb. 21, 1975 (div. Sept. 1979); 1 child, Sarah A.E. BS in Human Services, N.H. Coll., 1986, MS in Community Econ. Devel., 1986. Asst. to dir. Lincoln County Summer Youth Employment Program, Wiscasset, Maine, 1978; coordinator Community Food & Nutrition Program Coastal Enterprises, Inc., Wiscasset, 1978-79, Coastal Econ. Devel. Corp., Wiscasset, 1979-80; dir. Head Start Program Coastal Econ. Devel. Corp., Bath, Maine, 1980-84; asst. instr. N.H. Coll., Manchester, 1985-86; dir. Jr. Tots Wiscasset Recreation Program, 1985—; dir. food services Boothbay Sch. Dept., Boothbay Harbor, Maine, 1985—; elected mem. 113th Legis. State of Maine, 1986—; treas. Coastal Enterprises Inc., Rundlet Block, Wis., 1981—; rep. to Internat. Conf. on Econ. Devel., New Delhi, 1983—. Former mem. Blaine House Conf. on Families Planning Com., 1979-80; active Maine Human Services Council Sta. 23, Augusta, Maine, 1980—; Sunday sch. tchr. St. Philips Episcopal Ch., Wiscasset, 1984-85; chair coordinating com. St. Philips Food Bank, 1986—; chair Wis. Dem. Com., 1986—; nat. chmn. schs. S.O.S. Nat. Hunger Awareness Program, Denver, 1986—. grantee Maine Welfare Edn. Employment Tng. Program, 1983; named Outstanding Young Woman U.S. Jaycees, 1986. Democrat. Episcopalian. Clubs: B.P.W. (Damariscotta, Maine); CONA (Newcastle, Maine). Home: W Alna Rd PO Box 180 Wiscasset ME 04578 Office: Maine House of Reps State House Sta 2 Augusta ME 04333

KILLEA, LUCY LYTLE, state official; b. San Antonio, July 31, 1922; d. Nelson and Zelime (Pettus) Lytle; B.A., Incarnate Word Coll., San Antonio, 1943; M.A. in History, U. San Diego, 1966; Ph.D. in History, U. Calif., San Diego, 1975; m. John F. Killea, May 11, 1946; children—Paul, Jay. Research analyst for Western Europe, Army Intelligence, Spl. Br., Washington, 1944-48; adminstrv. asst. Dept. State, London, 1946; econ. officer Econ. Coop. Adminstrn., The Hague, Netherlands, 1949; research analyst CIA, Washington, 1948-56; part time book reviewer USIS, 1956-60; teaching and research asst. U. Calif., San Diego, 1967-72; exec. dir., exec. v.p. Fronteras de las Californias, San Diego, 1974-78; mem. City Council, San Diego, 1978-82, dep. mayor, 1982, mem. planning commn., 1978; mem. Calif. State Assembly, 1982—; lectr. socioeconomics of Baja, Calif. and Mex., Southwestern Coll., Chula-Vista, 1976; lectr. dept. history San Diego State U., 1976-77; participant, organizer, panelist, moderator confs. in field, U.S., Mex.; mem. Palm City Sanitation Dist., 1978-82, Met. Transit Devel. Bd., 1978-82. Regional Employment and Tng. Consortium Bd., 1978-80, City-County Reinvestment Task Force, 1978-80. Bd. trustees San Diego Zool. Soc., 1976-78; mem. San Diego County Cultural Heritage Com., 1971-78, vice chmn., 1973-75; mem. Hist. Site Bd., City San Diego, 1968-75, vice chmn., 1971-75; bd. dirs. San Diego Hist. Soc., 1971-77; chmn. Internat. Com. Conv. and Visitors Bur., 1978, host com., 1976-77; adv. bd. Sharp Hosp.; bd. dirs., com. mem. Friends of Library, U. Calif., San Diego; founding mem. Caridad Internacional; mem. James S. Copley Library Adv. Council, U. San Diego, 1981—; active community orgns. including LWV, Fine Arts Soc. San Diego, YWCA, San Diego Mus. Art, San Diego Chpt. ARC, Dimensions, Aardvarks Ltd., Pacific Beach Hist. Soc., San Diego Symphonic Assn. Research grantee, Justice Found., 1965, U. Calif., San Diego, 1971; recipient awards, Conf. Calif. Hist. Socs., 1966, Inst. for Protection of Children, City of Tijuana and Tijuana Com., 1966, Alice Paul Award, Nat. Women's Polit. Caucus, 1982; named one of 12 Women of Valor, Beth Israel Sisterhood of Temple Beth Israel, San Diego, 1966, Woman of Accomplishment, Bus. and Profl. Clubs. San Diego, 1979, Woman of Yr., San Diego Irish Congress, 1981; honored Leukemia Soc., 1980; named alumna of distinction Incarnate Word Coll., San Antonio, 1981. Mem. Nat. Women's Polit. Caucus, Calif., Women in Bus., Mus. Photog. Arts, San Diego Arts Center, Nat. Trust Historic Preservation, San Diego Hist. Soc. (life), San Diego County Congress of History, Travelers Aid Soc., Navy League, Vietnam Vets. Assn. Mid City C. of C., San Diego C. of C., Nat. Assn. State Legislatures, NCCJ, World Affairs Council, Am. Fgn. Service Assn., Incarnate Word Alumnae Assn., U. San Diego Alumni Assn., U. Calif. San Diego Alumni and Friends, Calif. Elected Women's Assn. for Edn. and Research (bd. 1980-85, sec., treas., 1980-81, v.p. 1982-85). Democrat. Roman Catholic. Clubs: Catfish, Army-Navy (Arlington, Va.). Contbr. writings to publs. in field. Office: Calif State Capitol Room 3173 Sacramento CA 95814

KILLEBREW, ELLEN JANE (MRS. EDWARD S. GRAVES), cardiologist; b. Tiffin, Ohio, Oct. 8, 1937; d. Joseph Arthur and Stephanie (Beriont) K.; B.S. in Biology, Bucknell U., 1959; M.D., N.J. Coll. Medicine, 1965; m. Edward S. Graves, Sept. 12, 1970. Intern, U. Colo., 1965-66, resident 1966-68; cardiology fellow Pacific Med. Center, San Francisco, 1968-70; dir. coronary care, Permanent Med. Group, Richmond, Calif., 1970-83; asst. prof. U. Calif. Med. Center, San Francisco, 1970-83, assoc. prof., 1983—. Robert C. Kirkwood Meml. scholar in cardiology, 1970; recipient Physician's Recognition award continuing med. edn. Diplomate in cardiovascular disease Am. Bd. Internal Medicine. Fellow ACP, Am. Coll. Cardiology: mem. Fedn. Clin. Research, Am. Heart Assn. (research chmn. Contra Costa chpt. 1975—, v.p. 1980, pres. chpt. 1981-82, chm. CPR com. Alameda chpt. 1984). Home: 30 Redding Ct Tiburon CA 94920 Office: 280 W MacArthur Blvd Oakland CA 94611

KILLELEA, ELLEN MARIE, construction engineer; b. N.Y.C., Jan. 7, 1952; d. Joseph Richard and Lillian Ruth (Smith) K. BArch, Ga. Inst. Tech., 1974. Draftsman Sy Richards Architect Inc., Atlanta, 1974; layout engr. Westinghouse Elevator Co., Atlanta, 1974-77; asst. project engr. Turner Constrn. Co., Detroit, 1977-79, project engr., 1979-86, sr. project engr., 1986—; arbitrator Am. Arbitration Assn. Nat. Panel of Arbitrators for the Constrn. Industry, Detroit, 1987—. Mem. Sierra Club, 1986—. Mem. Mensa, Greenpeace. Club: Grosse Pointe (Mich.) Hunt.

KILLENS, MARIE THÉRÈSE ROLANDE, member canadian Parliament; b. Trois-Rivieres, Que., Can., June 29, 1927; d. Omer Joseph and Cecile Marie (Thelland) Gauthier; student St. Agele de Laval Convent Boarding Sch.; m. Raymond Lowes Killens, Sept. 3, 1945; children—Francena, Doreen, Joanne, Daniel, Louise. Commnr., mem. exec. com. Montreal Catholic Sch. Commn., 1973-79; bd. dirs. Vanier CEGEP Coll., 1975, mem. exec. com. 1978, vice-pres. 1977-79; M.P., Saint-Michel, 1979—. Mem. Canadian Catholic Sch. Trustees Assn. (bd. govs. 1973-78), Spera Found. for Drug Addicts. Liberal. Roman Catholic. Office: House of Commons, Confederation Bldg, Ottawa, ON Canada K1A 0A6 *

KILLIAN, ELIZABETH ANNE, interior designer; b. Escanaba, Mich., Oct. 2, 1940; d. John Thomas and Ruth Isabell (Morin) Loeffler; m. John William Killian, Dec. 30, 1961; children: Patrick, Michael, Daniel, Amy. BS in Interior Design, U. Wis., 1979. Curator Sun Prairie (Wis.) Hist. Museum, 1977-79; sr. interior designer Flad & Assocs., Madison, Wis., 1979—; guest lectr. U. Wis.; cons. Vista Structures, Sun Prairie, 1978. Mem. Inst. of Bus. Designers (bd. dirs. Wis. chpt. 1984-86, newsletter 1984-86), Illuminating Engrng. Soc. (bd. dirs. Madison chpt. 1984-85), Nat. Council for Interior Design Qualification (cert.). Roman Catholic. Home: 1763 Tam O Shanter Sun Prairie WI 53590

KILLIAN, PATRICIA HALE, communications professional, consultant; b. Washington, May 20, 1942; d. Everett and Betty Virginia (Douglas) Hale; m. Charles Rodney Killian; children: Jaima, Grant. Student, Washington U., St. Louis, 1960-63; BA, U. Nebr., 1966, MA, 1967; PhD, U. Iowa, 1974. Speech clinician Iowa Pub. Schs., 1967-71; grad. asst. Wendell Johnson Speech and Hearing Ctr., Iowa City, 1971-74; vis. asst. prof. Drake U., Des Moines, 1975; asst. prof. U. Colo., Boulder, 1977-81; clin. dir. U. Colo., Denver, 1979-81; pvt. practice speech pathologist Denver, 1981—. Mem. city charter commn., Wheat Ridge, 1976-78; mem. parish council Calvary Episcopal Ch., Golden, Colo., 1987, also lector; mem. State Colo. Women's Econ. Devel. Council (co-chair women's econ. summit 1988); candidate state legislature, 1988. Mem. Am. Speech Lang. Hearing Assn., Colo. Speech Lang. Hearing Assn., Nat. Assn. Women Bus. Owners (bd. dirs. 1986-87, pres., bd. dirs. Colo. chpt. 1984-85, 88), Wheat Ridge C. of C. (small bus. com. 1986-87). Democrat. [illegible] Office: Speech Perfection and Rehab 7330 W Jefferson Suite 219 Denver CO 80235

KILLICK, KATHLEEN ANN, biochemist; b. Chgo., Jan. 22, 1942; d. Orson Smyth and Maori Madeline (Maloney) K.; B.S. in Biology (NSF undergrad. fellow, Pullman scholar), Ill. Inst. Tech., 1964, M.S. in Microbiology, 1966, Ph.D. in Biochemistry, 1969; cert., U. Uppsala, 1977; postgrad. Argonne (Ill.) Nat. Lab., U. Chgo., 1969-70. Postdoctoral fellow Boston Biomed. Research Inst., 1970-76, staff scientist dept. devel. biology, 1976-82; asst., prof., dept. of biol. scis., St. John's Univ., N.Y., 1982—; lectr. dept. microbiology and molecular genetics Harvard U. NSF trainee, 1968-69, spl. fellow, 1972-74, grantee, 1978—; AEC postdoctoral fellow, 1969-70; Selznick fellow Hereditary Disease Found., 1978. Mem. N.Y. Acad. Scis., AAAS, Am. Soc. Microbiology, Northeastern Soc. Microbiology, Am. Chem. Soc., Am. Soc. Biol. Chemistry, Gerontology Soc., Electrophorosis Soc., Carbohydrate Soc., Sigma Xi. Democrat. Roman Catholic. Office: Grand Cen Utopia Parkways New York NY 11439

KILLORAN, ELIZABETH MARY, librarian; b. Worcester, Mass., Mar. 10, 1953; d. Thomas Richard and Malvina Margaret (Gervais) Killoran. B.A. cum laude in English, Worcester State Coll., 1976; M.L.S., Simmons Coll., 1980. Vol. Worcester Art Mus. Library, 1978-80; reference, serials asst. Robert H. Goddard Library, Clark U., Worcester, 1978-80; dir. med. library Milford-Whitinsville Regional Hosp. (Mass.), 1980—. Cert. Med. Library Assn. Mem. Grafton Hist. Soc. (Mass.), 1983; (founding) Friends of the Nat. Library of Medicine; mem. Mass. Audubon Soc., Lincoln, Mass., 1983; foster parent Foster Parents Plan, Inc., Warwick, R.I., 1983; sponsor Maryknoll Fathers and Brothers (N.Y.), 1983. Mem. Worcester County Poetry Assn. (bd. dirs. 1972, poetry award 1972), Central Mass. Consortium of Health Related Libraries (chairperson 1985-86), Mass. Health Scis. Library Network, Med. Library Assn., Soc. Preservation New Eng. Antiquities, Lambda Iota Tau. Roman Catholic. Office: Med Library Milford-Whitinsville Regional Hosp 14 Prospect Milford MA 01757

KILPATRICK, CAROLYN CHEEKS, state representative, educator; b. Detroit, June 25, 1945; d. Marvell and Willa Mae (Henry) Cheeks; divorced; children: Kwame, Ayanna. Student, Ferris State Coll., Big Rapids, Mich., Western Mich. U.; MS in Edn., U. Mich., 1977. Tchr. Murray Wright High Sch., Detroit; mem. Ho. of Reps. State of Mich., 1978—; del. Dem. Convs., 1980-84; majority whip Ho. of Reps.; mem. House Appropriations Com. Rep. Detroit Substance Abuse Advisory Council; participant Mic. African Trade Mission, 1985, UN Internat. Women's Conf., 1986; del., participant Nairobi (Kenya) Internat. Agriculture Show Mich. Dept. of Agriculture; mem. resource com. TV documentary Your Children, Our Children; bd. trustees Henry Ford Hosp. Recipient Anthony Wayne award Wayn State U., Disting. Legislator award Gentlemen of Wall Street, Burton-Abercrombie award 13th Dem. Congl. Dist. Mem. Nat. Orgn. 100 Black Women, Nat. Black Caucus of State Legislators (chairperson Mich. legis. session 1983-84), Nat. Order Women Legislators, Nat. Orgn. Black Elected Legis. Women (treas.). Mem. Pan African Orthodox Christian Ch. Office: Ho of Reps State Capitol 105 Capitol Bldg Lansing MI 48909

KILPATRICK, MELISSA ROSS, computer scientist; b. Henderson, Tenn., May 8, 1960; d. David Tucker and Willie Mae (Johnson) Ross; m. Marlin Elbon Kilpatrick May 22, 1981. BS in Computer Sci., Freed-Hardeman Coll., 1982. Programmer Creative Computer Systems, Memphis, 1982; systems engr. Integrated Bus. Solutions, Memphis, 1982-83; programmer, with customer support Data Concepts, Memphis, 1983, programmer Baddour, Inc., Memphis, 1983-84; programmer Fed. Express Corp., Memphis, 1984-85, sr. programmer, 1985—; mem. team employee investments Fed. Express Corp., Memphis, 1986. Mem. team Handicapped Services, Memphis, 1986-87; mem. Bread for World, Memphis, 1987. Mem. Nat. Assn. Female Exec. Mem. Ch. of Christ. Home: 4461 W Sentinel Rock Terr Larkspur CO 80118

KILTY, LEAOLA ANGELLEANA, small business owner; b. Weatherford, Tex., Apr. 9, 1936; d. Clearance Edward and Angelleana (Miller) Dugan; m. Charles Alexander Kilty, Aug. 9, 1954; 1 child, Deborah Lea. AA in Bus. Adminstrn., Los Angeles Community Coll., 1976; BS in Bus. Adminstrn., Calif. State U., Northridge, 1983; cert. in graphoanalysis, Internat. Graphoanalyst Assn., Chgo., 1986. Office mgr. Vallepac Inc., San Fernando, Calif., 1969-71; bookkeeper Thorn Refrigeration Corp., Pacoima, Calif., 1971-74, exec. asst., 1977—; clk. accounts payable Hope Community Mental Health Ctr., Lakeview Terrace, Calif., 1974-75, fin. counselor, 1975, mgr. acctg. dept., 1975-77; owner Handwriting Revelations, Mission Hills, Calif., 1986—; cons. in field. Mem. Club 100 San Fernando YWCA, 1984—; recording sec. Sylmar (Calif.) Assn., 1986-87. Mem. The Exec. Female, Bus. and Profl. Women San Fernando (recording sec. Tri-Valley dist. 1984-85, v.p., program chair 1985-86, pres. 1986-87, found. chair 1987—, Club Bull. award 1986-87, Coro Track Meml. award 1986-87, North Hollywood Stblzn. award 1986-87, Blood Bank award 1986-87), So. Calif. Graphoanalyst Soc. (life), Calif. State U. Alumni Assn. Republican. Home: 13682 Shablow Ave Sylmar CA 91342 Office: Thorn Refrigeration Corp 13721 Desmond St Pacoima CA 91331

KIM, ARLENE, nurse; b. Brawley, Calif., Oct. 22, 1939; d. Roy Clement and Orpha (Davison) Webber; m. Joseph S. Kim, Dec. 27, 1964 (dec.); children: Angela, Joy, Roy, Joseph. AS in Nursing, Pacific Union Coll., 1960; BS, Calif. State U., 1976, MS, 1979. Office nurse R.E. Gleffe, Yuba City, Calif., 1960-61; charge nurse Sutter County Hosp., Yuba City, 1961-62; float nurse Washington Adventist Ch., Takoma Pk., Md., 1962-65; charge nurse Whittier (Calif.) Hosp., 1965-67; staff nurse White Meml. Hosp., Los Angeles, 1967-68, U.S. Eighth Army, Seoul, 1970-71; chair dept. nursing West Indies Coll., Kingston, Jamaica, 1979-83; supr. Clearlake (Calif.) Home Health, 1984-86; pub. health nurse Calif. State Vets. Home, Yountville, 1986—. Author: Use of Protocols in a Home Health Agency, 1979. Mem. Assn. Seventh Day Adventist Nurses. Republican. Home: 460 Howell Mt Rd Angwin CA 94508 Office: Vets Home Calif Yountville CA 94599

KIM, DONNA MARIE, personnel consultant; b. Honolulu, July 14, 1957; d. Dyoniscio and Theodora Mildred (Scizuki) Ting Cang. BS in Computer Sci., Honolulu U., 1977. Cert. employment specialist. Mgr., recruiter Employment Personnel, Aiea, Hawaii, 1978-82; cons., team mgr. Assoc. Services, Honolulu, 1982-84; pub. relations dir. Internat. Fitness, Honolulu, 1984-86; recruiter, sr. cons. Profl. Career Devel., Irvine, Calif., 1986—. Elected official Waipahu (Hawaii) City Council. Mem. Calif. Assn. Personnel Cons., Women in Sales. Home: 26144 Serrano Ct Eltoro CA 92630 Office: Profl Career Devel 12752 MacArthur Blvd Suite 210 Irvine CA 92715

KIMBALL, MARJORIE GOOCH, health care administrator; b. Winthrop, Mass., Mar. 29, 1933; d. George D. Gooch and Marie A. (Foster) Porter; m. Donald C. Kimball, July 12, 1953; children: Paul C., D. Scott, James B. BS, Rivier Coll., 1977; MS, Northeastern U., 1981. Cert. med. technologist. Lab. supr. Mennonite Hosp., LaJunta, Colo., 1961-65, Ludlow (Mass.) Hosp., 1965-66; technologist Elliot Hosp., Manchester, N.H., 1967-76; supr. blood bank Boston Hosp. for Women, 1979-81; supr. Am. Assn. Blood Banks Reference Lab. Brigham & Women's Hosp., Boston, 1980-81; dir. reference, histocompatibility and edn. services R.I. Blood Ctr., Providence, 1981—; clin. asst. prof. med. tech. Southeastern Mass. U.; adj. prof. med. tech. U. R.I. Pres. LWV, Merrimack, N.H., 1972, editor/pub. Know Your Town, 1972; mem. adv. com. Student Blood Bank program N.E. region ARC, Dedham, Mass.; bd. dirs. R.I. Schs. for Med. Technologists, Providence. Mem. R.I. Blood Bankers Soc. (bd. dirs. 1986—), Mass. Blood Bankers Soc. (bd. dirs. 1979-81), Am. Soc. for Histocompatibility and Immunogenetics, Am. Assn. Blood Banks, Am. Soc. for Med. Tech. Office: RI Blood Ctr 405 Promenade St Providence RI 02908

KIMBALL, MIRIAM PATRICIA, psychology educator, consultant; b. New Rochelle, N.Y., Feb. 8, 1953; d. John Bernard and Miriam Anne (Monsour) Donnellon; m. James Philip Kimball, Apr. 26, 1975; children: Shannon, Cassandra, Leah. BA in Psychology, St. Mary's Coll., Notre Dame, Ind., 1975; MA in Human Devel., U. Md., College Park, 1977. Mktg. coordinator Met. Fed. Savs. and Loan, Washington, 1975-78; instr. psychology Charles County Community Coll., La Plata, Md., 1978—; cons. staff devel. Personnel Assets, La Plata, 1982—; speaker women's advancement week USN, St. Indigoes, 1987, Md. League of Credit Unions, Balt.,

1987. Democrat. Roman Catholic. Home: Rt 4 4035 Mt Carmel Rd La Plata MD 20646

KIMBER, CLARISSA THERESE, educator; b. Merced, Calif., Feb. 1, 1929; d. George Card and Isabelle Marie (Chodat) K. AB, U. Calif., Berkeley, 1949; MS, U. Wis., 1962, PhD, 1969. Elem. tchr. Caleb Greenwood Sch., Sacramento, 1950-59; acting asst. prof.geography U. Calif., Riverside, 1963-67; asst. prof. geography State U. Calif., Hayward, 1967-68; from asst. prof. to prof. geography Tex. A&M U., 1968—. Author: Martinique Revisited: Changing Plant Geographies of a West Indian Island, 1988; contbr. articles to profl. jours. Bd. dirs. Community Singers, 1974-79. Mem. AAAS, Assn. Am. Geographers, Am. Geog. Soc., Caribbean Studies Assn., Ethno Pharmacology Soc. (charter), Soc. Women Geographers, Internat. Assn. for Vegetation Sci., Royal Geog. Soc., Assn. Am. Geographers (nat. councilor 1979-82, chmn. research grants com., program chair 1978), Orgn. Tropical Studies (bd. govs. 1984—), Delta Kappa Gamma, Phi Delta Gamma, Phi Kappa Phi, Sigma Xi. Home: 1208 Berkeley St College Station TX 77840 Office: Tex A&M U Geography Dept College Station TX 77843-3147

KIMBERG, IRIS SANDRA, physical and occupational therapist; b. N.Y.C., Jan. 6, 1955; d. Samuel and Irene (Messer) K.; m. Edward Fritsche. BS in Occupational Therapy, Syracuse U., 1976; MS in Phys. Therapy, Columbia U., 1983. Lic. phys. and occupational therapist, N.Y. Occupational therapist Mayor's Office for the Handicapped, N.Y.C., 1974-76, United Cerebral Palsy, N.Y.C., 1976-78, Inst. Rehab. Medicine, N.Y.C., 1977-81; founder, dir. Home Therapists Assn., N.Y.C., 1979—; adj. prof. LaGuardia Community Coll., N.Y.C., 1978-85; rehab. cons. Multiple Sclerosis Soc., 1980—, Muscular Dystrophy Assn., 1981—, N.Y. Childhood Ctr., 1982—; specialty resource person Am. Occupational Therapy Assn. Author instrn. and info. materials. Recipient Service award Multiple Sclerosis Soc., 1987. Mem. Am. Occupational Therapy Assn., Met. N.Y. Occupational Therapy Assn. (treas. 1986—), Empire State Phys. Therapy Assn., Nat. Home Care Assn., Profl. Rehab Assn., Ins. Women in Claims, Am. Phys. Therapy Assn., Washington Sq. Park Civic Assn. Democrat. Jewish. Clubs: Washington Sq. Tennis, N.Y. Roadrunners, Wall St. Racquet. Home: 310 Greenwich St New York NY 10013 Office: Home Therapists Assn 19-21 Warren St New York NY 10007

KIMBERLIN-HARRIS, CECILIA LOUISE, microbiologist; b. Louisville, Dec. 1, 1947; d. Acel Irving and Evelyn (Quigley) Kimberlin; m. Al R. Harris, June 20, 1973; children: Kevan, Sarah. BS, U. Louisville, 1969; MS, PhD, U. Okla., 1973. Asst. prof. microbiology Jundi Shapor U., Ahwaz, Iran, 1976-79; asst. prof. U. Ky. Med. Sch., Lexington, 1979-82; dir. microbiology Pathology Cytology Labs., Lexington, 1982-85; cons. Lexington, 1985-86; mgr. research and devel. Abbott Labs. Inc., North Chicago, Ill., 1986—; dir. microbiology labs. Kuzistan Province, Ahwaz, 1977-78. Contbr. articles to profl. jours. Named to Hon. Order Ky. Cols., 1972. Mem. Am. Soc. for Microbiology, South Cen. Assn. for Clin. Microbiology (regional rep. 1985, bd. dirs. 1985), Assn. for Clin. Pathology (assoc.), Ill. Assn. for Clin. Microbiology, Sigma Xi. Democrat. Office: Abbott Labs Inc 14th and Sheridan Rd North Chicago IL 60064

KIMBLE, BARBARA ANN, protective services official; b. Toledo, Mar. 21, 1945; d. George Leroy and Elvera Betty (Rose) Kimble. BA, U. Toledo, 1967; grad. Patricia Stevens Modeling and Career Coll., 1967; postgrad. in Computer Sci., N. Tex. State U., 1986—. Modeling instr. Patricia Stevens Modeling and Career Coll., Toledo, 1966, Barbizon Sch. Modeling, Dallas, 1972; operator Nat. Crime Info. Ctr., FBI, Dallas, 1979-83, investigative communications technician, 1983-84, coordinator, 1983-87; gen. police instr., tech. info. specialist, FBI, Dallas, 1987—; Texette and tour guide Dallas Cowboys, 1971-79. Named Miss Amity, Miss Tex. Universe Pageant, 1971; recipient Performance award, FBI, 1981-85. Mem. Nat. Baton Twirling Assn., Nat. Baton Twirling Judges Bur., Nat. Baton Twirling Tchrs. Assn., Tex. Criminal Justice Info. Users Group. Avocations: sewing, dancing, crocheting.

KIMBLE, GLADYS AUGUSTA LEE, nurse, civic worker; b. Niagara Falls, Can., June 28, 1906; d. William and Florence Augusta Baker (Buckton) Lee; RN, Christ Hosp., Jersey City, 1929; BS, Columbia U. Tchrs. Coll., 1938, MA, 1948; m. George Edmond Kimble, Jan. 5, 1952. Nurse, Willard Parker Hosp., N.Y.C., 1931; asst. and supervisory relief nurse Margaret Hague Maternity Hosp., Jersey City, 1931-37; staff nurse, relief supr. Manhattan Eye, Ear and Throat Hosp., 1937-38; sr. staff, asst. nurse supr. Vis. Nurse Service, N.Y.C., 1938-41; sr. public health nurse USPHS, Little Rock, 1941-43; public health supr. Providence Dist. Nursing Assn., 1943-46; edn. dir. Jersey City Public Health Nursing Service, 1946-49, also instr. Seton Hall U., 1947-48; public health nurse cons. U.S. Inst. Inter-Am. Affairs, Brazil, 1949-51; dir. public health dept. Englewood (N.J.) Hosp., 1951-53; nurse coordinator exchange visitor nurse program Overlook Hosp., Summit, N.J., 1964-71. Recipient Appreciation award for service rendered Providence Hosp., 1944; Woman of Yr. award Essex County Bus. and Profl. Women, 1968. Fellow Am. Public Health Assn. (life), mem. Sarasota Geneal. Soc. (charter), AAUW. Episcopalian. Lodges: Daus. of the Nile (charter), Ladies Oriental Shrine of N. Am. (SAR-I Ct. 79), Royal Order of Jesterettes, Eillim Ives #18, Saratoga. Home: 4540 Bee Ridge Rc Villa 12 Sarasota FL 34233

KIMBROUGH, BRENDA ELAINE, computer software specialist; b. Detroit, Feb. 26, 1940; d. Harold Monroe and Raciene Maurice (Ison) Simmons; m. George Nathaniel Kimbrough, June 9, 1962 (div. 1981); children: Craig Harold, Traci Lynn. BS, Wayne State U., 1962, MA, U. Mich., 1967; cert. edn. specialist, Wayne State U., 1984. Cert. tchr. spl edn. K-12 mentally impaired, counseling and guidance K-12. Spl. edn. tchr. Detroit Bd. Edn., 1962-67, elem. tchr., 1967-78, counselor, 1978-1983, computer trainer, 1984-85, microcomputer software coordinator, 1985—; cons. Detroit Fedn. Tchrs., 1979, Mich Assn. Computer Users, 1985, Delta Kappa Gamma, 1986, WDTR Radio, 1985-86. Editor: Detroit Pub. Schs. Software Catalog, 1985—. Tutor TAIOPS, Detroit Pub. Library, 1976-79; bd. govs. Wayne State U. Coll. Edn. Alumni, 1987—. Mem. NAACP, 1975-86, Metro Detroit Reading Council (mem. adv. bd. 1986-87), Detroit Assn. Computer Users (treas. 85—), Metro Detroit Alliance Black Adminstrs., Mich. Assn. Computer Users In Learning, Beta Sigma Phi, Phi Delta Kappa, Delta Sigma Theta, Delta Kappa Gamma (treas. 1986—). Office: Detroit Pub Schs 9345 Lawton Detroit MI 48206

KIMBROUGH, EMILY (EMILY KIMBROUGH WRENCH), writer; b. Muncie, Ind., Oct. 23, 1898; d. Hal Curry and Charlotte Emily (Wiles) K.; m. John Wrench, Dec. 31, 1926; children—Margaret Achsah and Alis Emily (twins). B.A., Bryn Mawr Coll., 1921; student, The Sorbonne, Paris, 1922. Editor: Fashions of the Hour, Marshall Field & Co., Chgo., 1922-27; fashion editor: Ladies' Home Jour, 1927; mng. editor, 1927-29, writer, 1932—; Author: (with Cornelia Otis Skinner) Our Hearts Were Young and Gay, 1942, We Followed Our Hearts to Hollywood, 1943, How Dear to My Heart, 1944, It Gives Me Great Pleasure, 1948, The Innocents from Indiana, 1950, Through Charley's Door, 1952, Forty Plus and Fancy Free, 1954, So Near and Yet So Far, 1955, Water, Water Everywhere, 1956, And a Right Good Crew, 1958, Pleasure by the Busload, 1961, Forever Old, Forever New, 1964, Floating Island, 1968, Now and Then, 1972, Time Enough, 1974, Better Than Oceans, 1976. Home: 11 E 73d St New York NY 10021

KIMBROUGH, EVELYN SUE, environmental engineer; b. Nashville, Aug. 30, 1954; d. George Robert and Irene K.; A.A., Martin Coll., 1974; B.S., Vanderbilt U., 1976. Environ. scientist U.S. EPA, Research Triangle Park, N.C., 1977—. Methodist. Club: Order of Eastern Star. Home: 32 Justin Ct Durham NC 27705 Office: MD-14 Research Triangle Park NC 27711

KIMBROUGH, LAURIE KIM, public relations executive; b. Corinth, Miss., Oct. 10, 1957; d. Billy Carroll and Martha Anne (Young) K. BS, Miss. U. for Women, 1980; MS, U. Southern Miss., 1983; M Specialist, U. London, 1983. Broadcast intern Sta. WCBI-TV, Columbus, Miss., 1977; journalism intern The Clarion Ledger, Jackson, Miss., 1979; journalist The Daily Corinthian, Corinth, 1980-81; journalism instr. U. So. Miss., Hattiesburg, Miss., 1982-83; pub. relations intern Methodist Hosp., Hattiesburg, Miss., 1982-83; pub. info. officer Miss. Power Co., Gulfport, Miss., 1983-84; pub. relations coordinator Allied Signal, Inc. Automotive div., Providence, 1984-87; mgr. advt. and pub. relations Century Telephone Enterprises, Inc., Monroe, La., 1987—. Vol. Miss. Republican Party Campaign U.S. Senator, 1979. Mem. Pub. Relations Soc. Am., Pub. Relations Soc. La., Internat. Assn. Bus. Communicators, Soc. Profl. Journalists, Miss. Press Assn. (1st place investigative writing award 1981). Mem. Ch. of Christ. Home: 9 Old Sterlington Rd #908 Monroe LA 71203 Office: Century Telephone Enterprises Inc PO Box 4065 Monroe LA 71211

KIMBROUGH, VICKY KAY, nurse, educator; b. Anniston, Ala., May 20, 1957; d. William E. and Marguerite (Coleman) K. BS in Nursing, Jacksonville State U., 1978; MS in Nursing, U. Ala., 1982. Cert. emergency nurse. Staff nurse ICU Northeast Ala. Regional Med. Ctr., Anniston, 1978-80; staff nurse critical care Baptist Med. Ctr. Montclair, Birmingham, 1981-84, edn. coordinator ambulatory div., 1984—; instr. basic cardiac life support Am. Heart Assn., Birmingham, 1984—; support instr. affiliate faculty Am. Heart Assn., Birmingham, 1985—. Mem. Emergency Nurses Assn., Ala. Soc. for Healthcare, Edn. and Tng. of the Am. Hosp. Assn., Sigma Theta Tau. Clubs: Toastmasters (pres. 1986), BPW. Office: Bapt Med Ctr Montclair 800 Montclair Rd Birmingham AL 35213

KIMES, BEVERLY RAE, editor, writer; b. Aurora, Ill., Aug. 17, 1939; d. Raymond Lionel and Grace Florence (Perrin) K.; m. James H. Cox, July 6, 1984. B.S., U. Ill., 1961; M.A. in Journalism, Pa. State U., 1963. Dir. publicity Mateer Playhouse, Neff's Mills, Pa., 1962, Pavillion Theatre, University Park, Pa., 1963; asst. editor Automobile Quar. Publs., N.Y.C., Princeton, N.J., 1963-64, assoc. editor, 1965-66, mng. editor, 1967-74, editor, 1975-81; editor The Classic Car, 1981—. Bd. dirs. Auburn-Cord-Duesenberg Mus., Milestone Car Soc.; mem. internat. coordination com. Nat. Automotive History Collection, Detroit Pub. Library. Recipient Cugnot award Soc. Automotive Historians, 1978, 79, 83, 85, 86, Thomas McKean trophy, 1983, 85, 86, Moto award Nat. Assn. Automotive Journalists, 1984, 85, 86. Mem. Internat. Motor Press Assn., Milestone Car Soc. (bd. dirs.), Soc. Automotive Historians (pres. 1987—). Author: The Classic Tradition of the Lincoln Motor Car, 1968; (with R.M. Langworth) Oldsmobile: The First Seventy-Five Years, 1972; The Cars That Henry Ford Built, 1978; (with Rene Dreyfus) My Two Lives, 1983; (with Robert C. Ackerson) Chevrolet: A History from 1911, 1984; The Standard Catalog of American Cars 1805-1942, 1985; The Star and the Laurel: The Centennial History of Daimler, Mercedes and Benz, 1986; editor: Great Cars and Grand Marques, 1976; Packard: History of the Motor Car and the Company, 1979; Automobile Quarterly's Handbook of Automotive Hobbies, 1981.

KIMMANAU, ERNA MARY, health care consultant; b. Apr. 27; d. Ferdinand Henry and Mary Barbara (Lienert) K. BS, Marquette U., 1962; MBA, Xavier U., 1969. Acctg./payroll supr. St. Michael Hosp., Milw., 1962-67; researcher St. Louis U., 1969-70; assoc. adminstr. St. Francis Hosp., Waterloo, Iowa, 1970-75; v.p. St. Joseph Hosp., Milw., 1975-76; v.p. ops. St. Elizabeth Hosp., Appleton, Wis., 1976-78; dir. edn. Sacred Heart Hosp., Eau Claire, Wis., 1978-79; risk mgmt. cons. Alexander and Alexander, Chgo., 1979-80; cons. edn. Hosp. Sisters Health System, Springfield, Ill., 1980-85; cons. ednl. resources SSM Health Care System, St. Louis, 1985-87, bus. mgr. Jewish Hosp., St. Louis, 1987-88; adminstr. Dermatology Specialists, Inc., St. Louis, 1988—; facilitator Mgmt. By Responsibility, Chgo., 1983-87, Quality Mgmt. Skills, Kansas City, Mo., 1987. Mem. scholarship com. Kennedy High Sch., St. Louis, 1986-87. Recipient Achievement award Dale Carnegie Inst., 1974, Best Speech award Dale Carnegie Inst., 1974, Highest Human Relations award Dale Carnegie Inst., 1974. Mem. Am. Soc. Tng. and Devel., Am. Soc. Health Edn. and Tng. Roman Catholic.

KIMMEL, ELLEN BISHOP, psychologist, educator; b. Knoxville, Tenn., Sept. 16, 1939; d. Archer W. and Mary Ellen (Baker) Bishop; B.A., U. Tenn., 1961; M.A., U. Fla., 1962, Ph.D., 1965; div.; children—Elinor, Ann, Jean, Tracy. Asst. prof., research asso. Ohio U., 1965-68; asst. prof. U. South Fla., Tampa, 1968-72, assoc. prof., dir. Univ. Studies Coll., 1972-73, prof. psychology and ednl. psychology, 1975—; disting. vis. prof. psychology Simon Fraser U., Vancouver, B.C., Can., 1980-81; cons. numerous sch. systems, bus. and govt. Mem. Fla. Blue Ribbon Task Force on Juvenile Delinquency, 1976-77; mem. Fla. Gov.'s Commn. on Women, 1979—; mem. adv. bd. Stop Rape, Good Govt., Inc. Recipient Outstanding Teaching award U. South Fla., 1978; Woman of Achievement award U. Tenn., 1983; 12 research grants. Fellow Am. Psychol. Assn. (governing council 1982-85, pres. local div. 1986-88); mem. Am. Ednl. Research Assn., Am.Assn. Counseling and Devel., Assn. Women in Psychology, Women in Edn., Psychonomic Soc., Southeastern Psychol. Assn. (pres. 1978-79), So. Soc. Philosophy and Psychology, Athena Soc., Sigma Xi, Delta Kappa Gamma, Omicron Delta Kappa. Democrat. Contbr. articles to jours., chpts. to books. Office: U South Fla FAO 276 Tampa FL 33620

KIMMEL, MARJORIE ANNE, health care executive; b. Ft. Wayne, Ind., July 11, 1936; d. Edward Henry and Marie Virginia (Woodworth) Ernst; student Ind. State U., Ohio U.; BS, Park Coll., Kansas City, Mo.; m. Kenneth Robert Kimmel, Nov. 24, 1955; children: Kathleen Marie Opdyke, Cynthia Louise Kimmel. Sec. bd. trustees, then acting dir. Recovery Ctr., Inc. (formerly Washington County Council Alcoholism), Marietta, Ohio, 1978-79, exec. dir. 1979—. Chairperson adv. bd. Washington County Dept. Human Services; pres. Employee Assistance Resource Network; treas., trustee Eve, Inc., shelter battered women. Cert. alcoholism counselor, employee assistance profl.; lic. profl. counselor. Bd. dirs. Mid-Ohio Valley Vols. Am., O'Neill Sr. Citizens Ctr. Mem. Assn. Labor, Mgmt., Adminstrs. and Cons. Alcoholism, Ohio Task Force Women and Alcohol, Nat. Council on Alcoholism/Ohio, Nat. Assn. Alcoholism and Drug Abuse Counselors, Ohio Assn. Alcoholism and Drug Abuse Counselors, Nat. Assn. Female Execs. Office: 427 2d St Marietta OH 45750

KINARD, AGNES DODDS, lawyer, historian, author; b. Pitts.; d. Robert James and Agnes Julia Raw; m. Morton Frank, June 4, 1944 (div. 1958); children: Allan Dodds, Michael Robert, Marilyn Morton; m. James Pinckney Kinard, Dec. 27, 1961. BA in History cum laude, U. Pitts., 1936; LLB, U. Pitts, 1939; JD, U. Pitts., 1961; postgrad., Chatham Coll., 1980. Bar: Pa. 1940. Law researcher Reed, Smith, Shaw & McClay, Pitts., 1940-41; exec. sec. Allegheny County War Price and Ration Bd., Pitts., 1941-44; British Colonies section chief, asst. to the deputy adminstr. Lend-Lease Adminstrn., Washington, 1944-46; women's editor, columnist Canton (Ohio) Economist, 1946-58; assoc. broker, sales Kelly Wood Real Estate, Pitts., 1959-72; broker, pres., co-owner Mountain Real Estate Co., Inc., Confluence, Pa., 1973—. Author: Historical Survey of the Landscape Design Society of Western Pennsylvania: 1962-83, 1983, Celebration of Carnegie in Pittsburgh, 1981, The Jane Holmes Residence-A Century of Caring, 1982; commd. symphony by Nikolai Lopatnikoff for the Pitts. Symphony Orch., 1972. Bd. dirs. Pitts. Plan for Art, Sch. Vol. Assn., Pitts. Youth Symphony Orch. Assn., Pitts. Symphony Assn.; founder, mem. Rachel Carson Homestead Assn., Pioneer Crafts Council (founder, pres., co-chmn. Long Range Planning com.). Recipient Award of Merit Pitts. History and Landmark Found. Mem. Pitts. Civ. Garden Ctr. (life), Nat. Council State Garden Clubs (life), landscape design critic, Nat. Soc. Arts & Letters (life), Landscape Design Soc. of We. Pa. (founding bd. mem., past pres., recipient Helen S. Hull Plaque for Lit. Horticultural Interest, 1986), Carnegie Mus. of Art Women's Com., Kappa Kappa Gamma.

KINARD, HELEN MARIE PAWNEE MADISON, corporate executive; b. Washington, July 3, 1943; d. David and Helen (Young) Madison; m. Clark Kinard, June 12, 1963 (div. Feb. 1965); children: Lenise Sharon, Monique Sherine. B in Med. Tech., Washington Sch. of Med. Tech., 1963; BA, Howard U., 1971, MSW, 1973, postgrad., 1976-78; postgrad., Calif. Coast U., 1985—. Asst. to mgr. Cramton Auditorium Howard U., Washington, 1968-70, asst. prof., 1972-73, asst. to adminstrv. asst. to prof., 1973-75; writer, co-star Family Counselor Sta. WJZ-TV, Balt., 1971-73; dir. asst. prof. social work Howard U. Children's Concern Ctr., Washington, 1973-74; conf. coordinator World Peace Through Law Ctr., Washington, 1974-75; chairperson social planning sequence, asst. prof. U. D.C., Washington, 1974-76; sr. assoc. Roy Littlejohn Assocs., Inc., Washington, 1975—; bd. dirs. Caribbean Festivals, Inc., Washington. Author: (poems) To Life-To Love, 1983; editor: (report) Desegregation in Pub. Higher Edn., 1975. Bd. dirs. Washington Parent-Child Ctr., 1983—. Grantee NIMH, 1971-73; recipient EMMY award AFTRA, 1973, Contbr. to Human Rights award UN, N.Y.C., 1974. Mem. Am. Planning Assn. (assoc.), Nat. Assn. Social Workers, Assn. Black Psychologists (bd. dirs.), Howard U. Alumni Assn. (bd. dirs. 1986—), Howard U. Alumni Club of D.C. (pres. 1983—), Freedom Bowl Alumni Com. (bd. dirs. 1986—), Caribbean-Am. Intercultural Orgn. (bd. dirs.), Phi Delta Kappa (charter), Delta Sigma Theta. Home: 305 Webster St NW Washington DC 20011 Office: Roy Littlejohn Assocs Inc 1101 14th St NW 10th floor Washington DC 20005-5601

KINDLE, MARY ETHEL SMYERS (MRS. CECIL HALDANE KINDLE), librarian; b. Aplin, Ark., Sept. 24, 1913; d. Dan Taylor and Ruby Robb (Neale) Smyers; B.S., U. Ark., 1936; M.S. in L.S., Columbia U., 1941, postgrad. Tchrs. Coll., 1941, 54-57, 69-74; postgrad. Fordham U., 1962-63; m. Cecil Haldane Kindle, Jan. 26, 1941; children—Mary Anne (Mrs. Roger Alan Stafford) (dec.), Elizabeth Lee (Mrs. Burke Baker III), Cecil Haldane (Mrs. Magid Abraham), Millicent Robb. Asst. children's and adult depts. Little Rock Public Library, 1930-34; librarian elem. schs., Fort Smith, Ark., 1936-39, Liberty St. Elem. Sch., Nyack, N.Y., 1940-41; librarian young people's dept. Bloomingdale br. N.Y. Public Library, 1954, Nyack High Sch., 1954-57, Hilltop Jr. High Sch., Nyack, N.Y., 1957-68, Valley Cottage Elem. Sch., 1968-75. Cons. Bethlehem (Conn.) Public Library, 1958; sec. bd. dirs. Rockland Fed. Credit Union, Nyack, 1976-77. Mem. Vols. for Internat. Tech. Assistance, 1965-68; mem. search com. for supt. Nyack Public Schs., 1977-78, mem. citizens budget adv. com., 1978-79, mem. facilities com., 1979-80; pres. guild First Reformed Ch., Nyack, 1981-84 ; pres. Rockland/Westchester Classical Union of Ref. Ch. Women, 1981-84 . Recipient Martha Washington medal SAR, 1971. Mem. NEA (co-chmn. membership Rockland County, N.Y. 1967-69), ALA, N.Y. Library Assn., Rockland County Sch. Librarians Assn. (rec. sec. 1963), N.Y. State, Rockland County (rec. sec. 1968-72), Nyack (v.p. 1974-75) tchrs. assns., Am. Security Council, Little Rock Jr. Fedn. Women's Clubs (charter), Kappa Delta Pi, Delta Kappa Gamma (charter mem. Ft. Smith, Ark. chpt. 1940, co-installer Epsilon chpt. N.Y.C. 1944, chmn. publicity and publs. com. Alpha Eta chpt. 1972-75). Editor: Authors of Rockland County, 1960. Deceased. Home: 332 N Midland Ave Upper Nyack NY 10960

KINDRED, JOAN HOVER, actress, civic worker, home economist; b. Poughkeepsie, Nov. 28, 1930; d. Ernest William and Florence (Christiansen) Hover; B.S., U. Md., 1953; m. John Joseph Kindred, III, Aug. 25, 1956 (div. Aug. 1980); 1 dau., Drewry Ann. Promotion and speech writer Sta. WTOP, Washington, 1953-54; producer, star daily TV women's culinary arts show Sta. WRC, Washington, 1955-56; home economist Potomac Electric Power Co., 1956; producer, star indsl. and comml. film for TV, 1956-59; pres. Snark, Ltd., repertory group, N.Y.C., 1969-72. Vice pres., bd. dirs. Twilight Park Assn., 1971-75; bd. dirs. Sheltering Arms Children's Service, 1974-87, treas. aux., 1975-77. Republican. Presbyterian. Address: 1070 Park Ave New York NY 10128

KINER, SUSAN LOUISE, advertising executive; b. Blue Island, Ill., Feb. 9, 1954; d. Donald Raymond and Billie Sue (Adams) Kiner; m. Jack Modzelewski, May 19, 1978. BS in Communications, U. Ill., 1976; MM, Northwestern U., Evanston, Ill., 1986. With Benton & Bowles, Inc., N.Y.C., 1976-78, Chgo., 1978-79, Tatham-Laird & Kudner, Chgo., 1979-80; account supr. D'Arcy-MacManus & Masius, Chgo., 1981-85; pres. Kiner Communications, Inc., 1985—; v.p., sr. acct. supr. Cramer-Krasselt, 1986—; founder Info-Video Internat., 1986; cons. for comedian, Tim Cavanagh, Chgo., 1980-81; producer, co-host, co-founder: (radio show) Coming Attractions, 1987—; judge Addy awards, U.S. TV and Video awards, 1983, 87, Mobius awards 1987. State fundraiser John Anderson Presdl. campaign, 1980; exec. com. Nat. Unity Party, Ill., 1981; bd. dirs. Towers Condominium Assn. Recipient Chgo. YWCA Leadership award, 1981. Mem. Am. Advt. Fedn. (6th dist. conf. chmn. 1982-84, gov. 1982-84, speaker nat. conv. 1986), Chgo. Advt. Club (co-chmn. seminars 1981, social chmn. 1981-82, bd. dirs. 1984-85, roster chmn. 1984, seminar chmn. 1985), Women's Advt. Club (bd. dirs. 1984-86, program chmn. 1984, edn. dir. 1985, v.p. 1986), Women in Film, Northwester U.'s Kellogg Alumni Club (program chmn.). Home and Office: 1221 N Dearborn Pkwy Chicago IL 60610

KING, ANDREA, lawyer; b. Syracuse, N.Y., June 11, 1941; d. John Paul and Bertha Marie (Pedersen) K. Student, Keuka Coll., Keuka Park, N.Y., 1959-61; BS, SUNY, Geneseo, 1964; JD, Syracuse U., 1985. Bar: N.Y., 1986. Tchr. public schs., Syracuse, Liverpool, N.Y., Hilo, Hawaii, 1964-69; clin. sec. Crouse-Irving Meml. Hosp., Syracuse, 1970-77, 80-82; legal sec. Donald K. Martin, Esq., Hilo, 1978-79; assoc. atty. Cherundolo, Bottar & DelDuchetto, Syracuse, 1986; sole practice law Syracuse, 1986—. Lead articles editor Law Review Syracuse U., 1984-85. Mem. ABA, N.Y. State Bar Assn., Onondaga County Bar Assn. Office: 407 S Warren St Syracuse NY 13202

KING, AUDREY, lawyer, communications executive; b. N.Y.C., Jan. 30, 1942. BA, Columbia U., 1968; JD, NYU, 1972. Bar: N.Y. 1973. Atty. Sperry Corp., N.Y.C., 1972-76; atty. GAF Corp., N.Y.C., 1976-78, dir. mktg. services, 1978-84; v.p. Telephonics Corp., Huntington, N.Y., 1984—; adjunct faculty NYU; lectr. on warranties, mktg., govt. regulations, mgmt.; bd. dirs. N.Y. Sch. Law, N.Y.C. Home: 400 E 56th St New York NY 10022 Office: Telephonics Corp 789 Park Ave Huntington NY 11743

KING, BARBARA JEAN, nurse; b. Cape Girardeau, Mo., June 28, 1941; d. Otto Samuel and Goldie Elizabeth (Clover) Fowler; student Weatherford Jr. Coll., 1965; R.N., John Peter Smith Hosp. Sch. Profl. Nursing, 1969. Cert. advanced cardiac life support; m. Charles Basil King, Jr., Sept. 4, 1972; children—Otto Samuel, Christopher Lee. Head nurse pediatrics and isolation County Hosp., also intensive care and coronary care units Small Gen. Hosp., Ft. Worth, 1969-72; dir. nursing service Jarvis Heights Nursing Center, Ft. Worth, 1976-77; dir. nursing services Ft. Worth Rehab. Farm, 1978-80; staff nurse, asst. supr. shift Decatur Community Hosp. (Tex.), 1983-85 ; staff nurse and supr. Burdgeport Hosp., 1986— instr. vocat. nursing Cooke County Coll., Gainesville, Tex., 1981; cons. convalescent centers and hosps. Chmn. child care com. Women of Moose, 1977—; ch. organist Zion Valley Cumberland Presbyterian Ch.; asso. organist St. Matthew Cumberland Presbyn. Ch. Served with M.C., USN, 1962-65. Mem. Dirs. Nursing Homes Assn. Tarrant County (v.p.). Democrat. Home: Route 1 Box 198 Alvord TX 76225

KING, BILLIE JEAN MOFFITT, professional tennis player; b. Long Beach, Calif., Nov. 22, 1943; d. Willard J. Moffitt; m. Larry King, Sept. 17, 1965. Student, Calif. State U. at Los Angeles, 1961-64. Amateur tennis player 1958-67, profl., from 1968; mem. Tennis Challenge Series, 1977, 78; host Colgate women's sports TV spl. The Lady is a Champ, 1975; co-founder, dir. Kingdom, Inc., San Mateo, Calif.; sports commentator ABC-TV, 1975-78; mem. U.S. Team which won Fedn. Cup, 1976; co-founder, pub. WomenSports mag., 1974—. Author: Tennis to Win, 1970, (with Kim Chapin) Billie Jean, 1974. Named Sportsperson of Yr., Sports Illustrated, 1972; Woman Athlete of Yr., A.P., 1967, 73; Top Woman Athlete of Yr., 1972; Woman of Yr., Time mag., 1976; One of 10 Most Powerful Women in Am., Harper's Bazaar, 1977; One of 25 Most Influential Women in Am., World Almanac, 1977. Office: care Chuck Bennett Internat Mgmt Group 22 E 71st St New York NY 10021 *

KING, CAROL LOUISE, city official; b. Detroit, Dec. 10, 1948; d. William Albert and Mary Theresa (Simon) K.; B.A. in English and Speech, Western Mich. U., 1971. Sales rep. Am. Can Co., Detroit, 1973-76; employment counselor, account exec. New Options, In., Detroit, 1976-78; congressional aide, 1978-79; pres. Mich. conf. NOW, 1979-80; placement coordinator Displaced Homemaker Project, Warren, Mich., 1980-82; adminstrv. asst. to Detroit City Councilwoman Maryann Mahaffey, 1982—; legis. liaison, cons. in field. Vice pres. Mich. conf. NOW, 1978-79, pres. Macomb County (Mich.) chpt., 1976-78, nat. chairperson reproductive rights com. 1978-79, nat. bd. dirs., 1980—; bd. dirs. Mich. Welfare Reform Coalition, S.E. Mich. Anti-Rape Network, Sojourner Found.; regional dir. NOW, mem. Mich. Polit. Action Com., nat. bd. dirs. 1980-86; bd. dirs., chairperson pub. affairs Planned Parenthood Detroit, 1980—; founding mem., mem. steering com. Democratic Citizens Caucus, 1980; chmn. Detroit Welfare Reform Coalitions, 1986—; mem. exec. com. People's Campaign for Choice, 1987-88. Mem. ACLU, Nat. Abortion Rights Action League, Voice of Reason, Older

Women's League, Women's Econs. Club Detroit, Detroit Women's Forum. Democrat.

KING, CAROLYN ALLABY, rehabilitation facility administrator; b. Yellowknife, N.W.T., Can., Oct. 30, 1948; came to U.S., 1966; d. J. Kenneth and Marjorie E. (Mills) Allaby; m. Don E. King Jr., Dec. 30, 1971; children: Jeremy, Patrick. BA, U. Western Ontario, 1971; MEd, U. Louisville, 1985. Family caseworker Dept. Human Resources, Louisville, Ky., 1971-76; worker social services, dir. children's services, dir. programs New Hope Services Inc., Jeffersonville, Ind., 1978—; bd. dirs. Highland Community Ministries Day Care Ctr., Louisville, United Crescent Hill Ministries Child Care Ctr., Louisville, Jefferson (Ky.) Human Services Assn.; cons. in field. Mem. Ind. Presch. Adminstrs. Spl. Edn. (sec., treas. 1981), Ind. Assn. Rehab. Facilities, Ind. Preschool Adminstrs., Preschool Interagy. Planning Council, Council Exceptional Children, Council Retarded Citizens. Home: 2934 Riedling Dr Louisville KY 40206 Office: New Hope Services Inc PO Box 486 Jeffersonville IN 47130

KING, CAROLYN DINEEN, U.S. judge; b. Syracuse, N.Y., Jan. 30, 1938; d. Robert E. and Carolyn E. (Bareham) Dineen; children: James Randall, Philip Randall, Stephen Randall; m. John L. King, Jan. 1, 1988. A.B. summa cum laude, Smith Coll., 1959; LL.B., Yale U., 1962. Bar: D.C. 1962, Tex. 1963. Practice law Houston, 1962-79; circuit judge U.S. Ct. Appeals 5th Circuit, Houston, 1979—. Trustee, mem. exec. com., treas. Houston Ballet Found., 1967-70; mem. Houston dist. adv. council SBA, 1972-76; mem. Dallas regional panel President's Commn. White House Fellowships, 1972-76, mem. commn., 1977; bd. dirs. Houston chpt. Am. Heart Assn., 1978-79; nat. trustee Palmer Drug Abuse Program, 1978-79; trustee, sec., treas., chmn. audit com., fin. com., mem. mgmt. com. United Way Tex. Gulf Coast, 1979-85. Mem. ABA, Fed. Bar Assn., State Bar Tex., Houston Bar Assn., Phi Beta Kappa. Roman Catholic. Office: US Ct Appeals 11020 US Courthouse 515 Rusk Ave Houston TX 77002-2694

KING, CAROLYN MAE, educator; b. Fond du Lac, Wis., Oct. 23, 1946; d. John Francis and Adina Elnora (Bahr) K.; BS, Wis. State U., Oshkosh, 1970; MS, Niagara U., 1974. Tchr. phys. edn. Public Schs. Niagara Falls (N.Y.), 1970-83; women's swim coach Niagara (N.Y.) U., 1975-76; substitute tchr., Niagara Falls, 1983-84, tchr. phys. edn., 1984—, elem. dir., 1987—. Water safety instr. ARC; mem. Nat. Ski Patrol. Recipient award Joseph P. Kennedy Jr. Found., 1972. Mem. Niagara Falls Tchrs., N.Y. State United Tchrs., Am. Fedn. Tchrs., Alpha Kappa Delta. Democrat. Lutheran. Club: College. Home: 459 Chicora Rd Lewiston NY 14092

KING, CHERYL WALLER, hospital administrator; b. Atlanta, July 17, 1957; d. Robert D. and Belle (Lindler) Waller. BBA, Berry Coll., 1979. Sales major accounts Kerrigan Datamedia Inc.; fin. analyst Dun & Bradstreet, Greenville and Columbia, S.C.; asst. controller Greater Greenville C. of C.; controller Conch Republic Woodworks, Inc., The Headquarters, Inc., Key Largo, Fla.; dir. pub. relations, adminstrv. asst. Mariners Hosp., Plantation Key, Fla. Active ARC, Keys Hosp. Found., Inc.; bd. dirs. Am. Cancer Soc. Mem. Nat. Assn. Female Execs., Cousteau Soc., Planetary Soc., Am. Soc. Profl. and Exec. Women, Amnesty Internat. USA, Jaycees (bd. dirs.), Alpha Phi Omega. Methodist. Home: PO Box 2095 Key Largo FL 33037 Office: Mariners Hosp 50 High Point Rd Tavernier FL 33070

KING, CHRISTINE LEDESMA, program manager; b. N.Y.C., Dec. 15, 1945; d. Ricardo Ledesma and Julia (Benedicto) Ledesma; m. Kenneth K. King Jr., July 29, 1967; children: Michelle Ariadne, Ronald Edward. BA in French, Beaver Coll., Glenside, Pa., 1967; MBA with distinction, Northeastern U., 1985. Pvt. practice translator, interpreter Boston, 1967-74; adminstrv. aide Communication Systems div. GTE Corp., Needham, Mass., 1974-78, mgr. adminstrv. services Bus. Communication Systems div., 1978-81, program mgr. Atlantic Op., 1981—; lectr. telecommunications Northeastern U., Boston, 1981—. Mem. IEEE, Beta Gamma Sigma. Mem. United Ch. Christ. Office: GTE Atlantic Operation 180 First Ave Needham MA 02194

KING, CHRISTINE PARAN, business analyst, consultant; b. Los Angeles, Aug. 4, 1949; d. Paul Suren and Marjorie Augusta (Jacobs) K. Ed. pub. schs., Fontana, Calif. Sr. engring. technician Atlantic Richfield, Los Angeles, 1973-76; computer coordinator Occidental Petroleum, Irvine, Calif., 1978-79; supr. data processing Stanford Applied Engring., Costa Mesa, Calif., 1979-80; mgr. data processing Chase Manhattan Bank, Heidelberg, Fed. Republic Germany, 1980-81; MIS bus. analyst Apple Computer, Inc., Cupertino, Calif., 1981-85, cons., 1985-87; cons. Keyword Office Tech., San Jose, Calif., 1985; supr. warehouse adminstrn. Nat. Semiconductor, Inc., Sunnyvale, Calif., 1987—. Active abused children, homeless causes. Mem. Assn. Small Systems Users, No. Calif. PICK Users. Republican. Home: 1430 Sunshade Ln San Jose CA 95122

KING, CLAUDETTE YVONNE, educator; b. Cornelius, N.C., May 1, 1938; d. James and Mattie Josephine (Nelson) Caldwell; m. Roland King, Sept. 30, 1962; children: Dorinda, Kiwesa, Karimah. BA, CUNY, 1973; MA, Columbia U., 1974, EdM, 1979. Psychol. counselor Bellevue Hosp., Pub. Sch. 106 Day Hosp., N.Y.C., 1974-79; educator N.Y.C. Bd. Edn., 1974-87; adj. instr. Mercy Coll., Dobbs Ferry, N.Y., 1984—; exec. dir. Leon E. Nelson Found. for Arts and Humanities, N.Y.C., 1983—; reading clinician Columbia U., N.Y.C., 1983-85; sec., treas. World Wide Sprinkler Corp., Bronx, N.Y. V.p. Westchester Black Women's Polit. Caucus, New Rochelle, N.Y., 1984; commuhity relations coordinator New Rochelle High Sch., 1981. Mem. NAACP, Am. Personnel and Guidance Assn., Assn. Minority Enterprises N.Y.C. Democrat. Episcopalian. Club: Jack and Jill Am. (Westchester) (historian 1987-88). Home: 9 Pershing Ave New Rochelle NY 10801

KING, CLAUDIA LOUAN, film producer, lecturer; b. Merced, Calif., May 1, 1940; d. Alvin Cecil and Thelma May (Matthew) K.; m. Douglas McLean, July 10, 1965 (div. 1975); children: Kia Gabrielle, Kendra Sue. BA, U. Calif., 1963; MA, Ind. U., 1969. Lectr. U. Fla., Gainesville, 1969-70; asst. prof. U. Nev., Las Vegas, 1973-79; producer Source 17 Prodns., Santa Monica, Calif., 1979-85; freelance producer Chico, Calif., 1985—; producer Rape is Everybody's Concern, 1978, Los Angeles Personally Yours, 1985; screenplay writer, The Garden of Eden, 1983, My Sisters Keeper, 1986. Carnegie grantee, 1969; Nev. Endowment for Humanities grantee, 1978. Mem. Women in Film, Coll. Art Assn. Democrat. Home: Rt 1 Box 1476 Orland CA 95926

KING, CORETTA SCOTT (MRS. MARTIN LUTHER KING, JR), lecturer, writer, concert singer; b. Marion, Ala., Apr. 27, 1927; d. Obidiah and Bernice (McMurray) Scott; m. Martin Luther King, Jr., June 18, 1953 (dec. Apr. 1968); children: Yolanda Denise, Martin Luther III, Dexter Scott, Bernice Albertine. A.B., Antioch Coll., 1951; Mus.B., New Eng. Conservatory Music, 1954, Mus.D., 1971; L.H.D., Boston U., 1969, Marymount-Manhattan Coll., 1969, Morehouse Coll., 1970; H.H.D., Brandeis U., 1969, Wilberforce U., 1970, Bethune-Cookman Coll., 1970, Princeton U., 1970; LL.D., Bates Coll., 1971. Voice instr. Morris Brown Coll., Atlanta, 1962; commentator Cable News Network, Atlanta, 1980—; lectr., writer. Author: My Life With Martin Luther King, Jr., 1969; contbr. articles to mags.; Concert debut, Springfield, Ohio, 1948, numerous concerts, throughout U.S., concerts, India, 1959, performances, Freedom Concert. Del. to White House Conf. Children and Youth, 1960; sponsor Com. for Sane Nuclear Policy, Com. on Responsibility, Moblzn. to End War in Viet Nam, 1966, 67, Margaret Sanger Meml. Found.; mem. So. Rural Action Project, Inc.; pres. Martin Luther King, Jr. Found.; chmn. Commn. on Econ. Justice for Women; mem. exec. com. Nat. Com. Inquiry; co-chmn. Clergy and Laymen Concerned about Vietnam, Nat. Com. for Full Employment, 1974; pres. Martin Luther King Jr. Center for Nonviolent Social Change; co-chairperson Nat. Com. Full Employment; mem. exec. bd. Nat. Health Ins. Com.; active YWCA; bd. dirs. So. Christian Leadership Conf., Martin Luther King, Jr. Found. Gt. Britain; trustee Robert F. Kennedy Meml. Found., Ebenezer Bapt. Ch. Recipient Outstanding Citizenship award Montgomery (Ala.) Improvement Assn., 1959, Merit award St. Louis Argus, 1960, Distinguished Achievement award Nat. Orgn. Colored Women's Clubs, 1962, Louise Waterman Wise award Am. Jewish Congress Women's Aux., 1963, Myrtle Wreath award Cleve. Hadassah, 1965, award for excellence in field human relations Soc. Family of May, 1968, Universal Love award Premio San Valentine Com., 1968, Wateler Peace prize, 1968, Dag Hammarskjold award, 1969, Pacem in Terris award [illegible] 1969 Leadership for Freedom award Roosevelt U., 1971, Martin Luther King Meml. medal Coll. City N.Y., 1971, Internat. Viareggio award, 1971, numerous others; named Woman of Year Utility Club N.Y.C., 1962, Woman of Year Nat. Assn. Radio and TV Announcers, 1968. Mem. Nat. Council Negro Women (Ann. Brotherhood award 1957), Women Strike for Peace (del. disarmament conf. Geneva, Switzerland 1962, citation for work in peace and freedom 1963), Women's Internat. League for Peace and Freedom, NAACP, United Ch. Women (bd. mgrs.), Alpha Kappa Alpha (hon.). Baptist (mem. choir, guild adviser). Club: Links (Human Dignity and Human Rights award Norfolk chpt. 1964). Address: Martin Luther King Jr Ctr for Nonviolent Social Change 449 Auburn Ave NE Atlanta GA 30312

KING, DEBORAH IRENE, academic administrator; b. Bklyn., Sept. 3, 1952; d. Roland Burlough and Ethel Marianna (Blunt) K. BA, Richmond Coll., 1974; MS, St. John's U., Jamaica, N.Y., 1978, Pace U., 1985. Cert. elem., intermediate, jr. high sch. tchr., adminstr., N.Y. Dir. Wise Meml. Montessori Learning Ctr., St. Albans, N.Y., 1974-78; dir. reading lab. Malcolm-King Coll., N.Y.C., 1979-80; tchr. Pub. Sch. 269, Bklyn., 1978-80; aftersch. ctr. dir. Pub. Sch. 156, Laurelton, N.Y., 1980-81; tchr. Pub. Schs. 95 and 176, Jamaica and Cambria Heights, N.Y., 1981-83; music dir., intern in edn. adminstn. Pub. Sch. 176, Cambria Heights, 1984-85; aftersch. prog. asst. dir. Pub. Sch. 134, St. Albans, 1985—; tchr. Pub. Sch. 176, Cambria Heights, 1983-87; adminstr. Pub. Sch. 156, Laurelton, N.Y., 1987—; tutor N.Y.C. Bd. Edn., Jamaica, 1980—. Mem. parish council, lector St. Pascal Baylon Ch., 1986—; mem. Civics Com., St. Abbans. Mem. Am. Montessori Soc., Assn. Black Educators N.Y., Phi Delta Kappa. Home: 86-47 164 St Apt 3C Jamaica NY 11432

KING, JANET FAYE, nurse; b. Bellefontaine, Ohio, Aug. 11, 1947; d. Robert Lee and Wanda Beatrice (Shields) Swartz; diploma Community Hosp. Sch. Nursing, Springfield, Ohio, 1968; student Southwestern Okla. State U., 1979; m. Dwayne King, Jan. 11, 1969; children: Michael Dwayne, Valerie Lynn, Michelle Renee. Staff nurse Doctors Hosp., Columbus, Ohio, 1968; head nurse Southwestern Meml. Hosp., Weatherford, Okla., 1970-73; substitute clin. instr. Western Okla. Area Vocat. Tech. Sch., Burns Flat, Okla., 1973-77; asst. dir. nursing, inservice dir. Cordell Christian Home (Okla.), 1977-83; vis. nurse Am. Home Health, Cordell, 1983—, dir. patient care, 1984-87; area coordinator Health Care Profls., Woodward, 1987-88; coordinator patient care Health Watch, Weatherford, 1988—. Chmn. med. personnel ARC blood drive, Burns Flat, 1977—, instr., 1979—; chmn. Am. Cancer Soc., Burns Flat; tchr. Sunday Sch., Bapt. Ch., also mem. nursery com. Mem. Young Homemakers (treas. 1975-77). Clubs: New Direction Extension (treas. 1980-81). Home: 203 Potomac St Burns Flat OK 73624 Office: Health Watch Box 762 Elk City OK 73644

KING, JEAN ANNE HUTCHINS, nurse; b. Fords, N.J., June 16, 1938; d. John Richard Jr. and Anne Margaret (Sidnet) Hutchins; m. Peter King III, Nov. 28, 1975. BS in Nursing, Russell Sage Coll., 1959. RN, N.J. From asst. head nurse to head nurse to supr. various hosps., 1959-70; headnurse, supr. San Diego VA Hosp., La Jolla, Calif., 1971-74; supr. Ministry Def. and Aviation Hosp., Jeddah, Saudi Arabia, 1974-77; nursing cons. AMI Internat. Inc., Beverly Hills, Calif., 1978-81; hosp. services advisor King Abdul Aziz Teaching Hosp., Riyadh (Saudi Arabia) U., 1979-80; asst. dir. nursing King Fahad Hosp. AlBaha, Saudi Arabia, 1981-83; nursing cons., office mgr. AMI Saudi Arabia Ltd., Riyadh, 1984-85; locum dir. nursing King Khaled Eye Specialist Hosp., Riyadh, 1986; staff nurse VA Med. Ctr., Lyons, N.J., 1987—. Mem. Nat Assn. for Female Execs. Lutheran. Home and Office: 73 Village Circle Bridgewater NJ 08807

KING, JEANNE SNODGRASS, mus. registrar; b. Muskogee, Okla., Sept. 12, 1927; d. Chester Alba and Mabel Ethel (Etheridge) Owens; student Northeastern State Coll., 1944-46, U. Okla., 1947-49; m. Morris Eugene King, Apr. 16, 1977. Curator, asst. dir. Philbrook Art Center, Tulsa, 1955-68; mng. editor Ednl. Dimensions, Inc., Shaker Heights, Ohio, 1969-71; registrar Thomas Gilcrease Inst. Am. History and Art, Tulsa, 1973—; researcher, lectr. in field; art cons.; juror art competitions. Recipient award Indian Arts and Crafts Bd., Dept. Interior, Washington, 1966. Mem. Am. Assn. Mus., Native Am. Art History Assn. Author: American Indian Painters, A Biographical Directory, 1968; (catalogs) Native American Painting, 1981, Fred Beaver & Solomon McCombs/Meml. Exhibn., 1981; coordinator, author Oscar Howe Retrospective Exhbn. Catalog, 1982; contbr. articles to mags. Home: 3931 S Madison Tulsa OK 74105 Office: 1400 Gilcrease Museum Rd Tulsa OK 74127

KING, JOAN HONE, writer, art dealer, book researcher, editor; b. N.Y.C., Nov. 27, 1929; d. John Hone and Frederica (Stevens) Auerbach; cert. of studies Inst. Polit. Scis., Paris, 1950; B.A. cum laude, Bryn Mawr Coll., 1951; m. Nicholas LeRoy King, Feb. 19, 1955; children—Sarah, Bayard, Ledyard. Ledyard; m. Cass Canfield, Aug. 30, 1984. Cons. J. Walter Thompson, Paris, 1951-52; researcher, librarian Time-Life Inc., Paris, 1952-54; mgr. Ohrbach Dept. Store, N.Y.C., 1956-57; housing locator Am. embassy, Paris, 1963-69; spl. asst. for book and art research to Cass Canfield, Harper & Row, N.Y.C., 1971—; art dealer, N.Y.C., 1973—; cons. in field. Active fund raising Bryn Mawr Coll., 1970-72, Sr. Citizens' Center, Newport, R.I., 1975. Mem. Colonial Dames Am. Club: Byrn Mawr Club (N.Y.C.). Republican. Episcopalian. Illustrator: The Incredible Pierpont Morgan (Cass Canfield), 1974; researcher, illustrator: Sam Adam's Revolution, 1976; Outrageous Fortunes, 1980; author: Passages: The Iron Will of Jefferson Davis, 1978; Noni and Other Stories, 1983; author hist. and fictional works; exhibitor winter antique show, N.Y.C., 1987-88. Home and Office: 960 Park Ave New York NY 10028

KING, JOY LA SHRYELL, music educator; b. Pittsburg, Tex., June 19, 1954; d. Leroy and Mary Jo (Chappell) Jenkins; m. Robert Irvin King, Dec. 16, 1978. B.S. in Music, Bishop Coll., 1978; M.Ed., Prairie View U., 1982. Tchr. music Dallas Ind. Sch. Dist., 1978—; dir. choir Winneka Sch. Dist., Dallas, 1983—. Mem. Gamma Sigma Sigma. Baptist. Home: 2703 Garapan Dr Dallas TX 75224

KING, JOYCE CALISTRI, columnist; b. Charleroi, Pa., May 26, 1927; d. Jeremiah James and Vera Colette (Hurley) Calistri; m. William Louis King, II, Dec. 22, 1951; children: Mari Joyce, William Louis, III, Donald II. BA, U. Pa. Coll. for Women, 1949. Tchr. Romper Room TV, WTPA-TV, Harrisburg, Pa., 1954-55, WGAL-TV, Lancaster, Pa., 1956-57; hostess, producer Joyce King Show, WHP-TV, Harrisburg, Pa., 1959-60; sta. mgr. WSUB-TV Cable, Shillington, Pa., 1969-70; publicity dir. Bavarian Festival, Barnesville, Pa., 1974-76; wine columnist Reading Eagle, Reading, Pa., 1978—; feature writer Reading Eagle, 1978—; freelance columnist newspapers, mags., 1972—; student activities dir. Reading Hosp. Sch. Nursing, Reading, Pa., 1965-69; newsletter editor Young Republicans, Harrisburg, Pa., 1949-50, AAUW, 1955-56; dir. publicity Green Hills Theatre, Reading, Pa., 1963-67; mem. Pres.'s Art Council. Alvernia Coll., Am. Legion, U. Pa., 1945-, Mem. Am. Women Radio and TV (pres. 1960), AAUW (v.p. 1955). Republican. Roman Catholic. Home: 2624 Whittier Ave Sinking Spring PA 19608 Office: Reading Eagle 345 Penn St PO Box 582 Reading PA 19603

KING, KATHLEEN, cooperative finance corporation executive; b. Endicott, N.Y., Sept. 21, 1956; d. Richard Francis and Maureen (Beale) K. Student NYU, 1976-78, Drexel U., 1974-76, George Mason U., 1985—. Data processing adminstr. Amstar Corp., N.Y.C., 1975-78; tech. writer Parsons, Brinckerhoff, Quade & Douglas, N.Y.C., 1978-79; tech. rep. Compuer Usage Co., Sunnyvale, Calif., 1979-81; systems engr. Computer Network Co., Washington, 1981-82; staff systems analyst Satellite Bus. Systems, McLean, Va., 1982-84; mgr. tech. support services C. of C. of U.S., Kensington, Md., 1984-87; mgr. ops. and tech. support services Nat. Rural Utilities Coop. Fin. Corp., 1987— . Mem. Nat. Assn. Female Execs., Nat. Office Adv. Panel. Democrat. Roman Catholic. Avocations: needlepoint; horseback riding; French language. Office: Nat Rural Utilities Coop Fin Corp 1115 30th St NW Washington DC 20007

KING, KATHRYN JACKSON, utility executive; b. Baytown, Tex., Jan. 13, 1932; d. Cecil Alfred and Kathryn Jane (Calloway) Jackson; m. John Richard King, Jan. 5, 1951; children: Kellie, Kimberly. AS, Lee Coll., 1967. Acct. Kilgore's Materials, Baytown, 1950-55; dir. services Exxon Research and Engring., 1955-66; mgr. adminstrv. services San Bernard Electric Cooperative, Bellville, Tex., 1974—. Author: Facts Members Should Know, 1987. Mem. [illegible] for Rural Electrification, Austin, Tex., 1987; steering com. Dist. 14 Dem. candidate for Congress, [illegible] Tex., 1987. Mem. Tex. Electric Cooperatives Admins. and Personnel Mgmt. Assn., Tex. Rural Electric Women's Assn., Nat. Assn. Female Execs. Methodist. Office: San Bernard Electric Coop 309 W Main Bellville TX 77418

KING, LAURA JANE, librarian, genealogist; b. Pemberville, Ohio, Jan. 19, 1947; d. Richard D. and Jessie Florence (Brown) Zepernick; B.A., Bowling Green (Ohio) State U., 1969, M.Ed., 1976; m. Bruce William King, June 17, 1972; 1 son, Christian Andrew. Cert. geneal. lectr.; cert. geneal. record searcher. County extension agt. home econs. Ohio Coop. Extension Service, Paulding County, 1970-77; local and family historian Pemberville Pub. Library; mem. PRIDE com., vocat. home econs. dept. Paulding Exempted Village, 1975—; instr. genealogy Office Continuing Edn. Bowling Green State U., Eastwood Sch. Dist. Community Edn. Mem. Paulding County Bicentennial Commn., 1975-77; organist 1st Presbyn. Ch., Pemberville, ruling elder, ch. historian. Recipient Tenure award Coop. Extension Service, 1975; mem. Wood Counti Citizen's Com. for Bicentennial of U.S. Constn. and NW Ordinance; mem. Pemberville Sch. Adv. Com. Mem. Ohio Geneal. Soc. (pres. Wood County chpt. 1978-80, chmn. public relations chmn. 1982-83, chmn. First Families of Wood County com.), Berks County Geneal. Soc., Palatines to Am., DAR (vice regent chpt. 1975-77, regent chpt. 1979-83, registrar chpt. 1985—, state vice chmn. pages 1978-80, state chmn. lineage research 1980-87, state and div. outstanding jr. mem. 1980, state chmn. membership commn. 1983-87, state chmn. pub. relations 1986—, state recording sec. 1987—), U.S. Daus. of 1812, First Families Ohio, Daus. Union Vets., Nat. Soc. Magna Charta Dames, Colonial Dames 17th Century, Daus. Am. Colonists (chpt. regent 1986—, state chmn. pub. relations, 1987), Bus. and Profl. Women's Club (pres. Paulding 1975-76, v.p. 1974-75), Am. Home Econs. Assn., Council Ohio Genealogists, Colonial Order Crown of Charlemagne, Phi Upsilon Omicron Alumni. Club: Order Eastern Star. Corr. docent DAR Mus., Washington. Home: 14553 N River Rd Pemberville OH 43450

KING, LIS SONDER, writer, public relations executive; b. Roskilde, Denmark; came to U.S., 1956, naturalized, 1961; d. Carl Otto and Gerda Vohnsen (Sonder) Petersen; m. Robert King (div. 1972); 1 dau., Dorte; m. Theodore Allin Pace, 1972; grad. Roskilde Katedralskole, arts degree Sch. Fine Arts, Copenhagen, 1952; Feature writer Berlingske Tidende, Copenhagen, 1956-58; reporter, editor Moreau Pub. Co., Bloomfield, N.J., 1957-59; reporter, editor St. Thomas (V.I.) Daily News, Island Times, San Juan, P.R., 1962-63; editor The Advance, Dover, N.J., 1961-63; pub. relations dir. Fluid Chem. Co., Newark, 1963-64,Keyes, Martin & Co., Springfield, N.J., 1964-69; pres. Lis King Pub. Relations, Mahwah, N.J., 1969—; columnist Harris Pubs., N.Y.C., 1981—, Suburban News, Paramus, N.J., 1986—. Author, editor: St. Thomas Directory, 1962; author: Furniture: Make-Do, Make-Over, Make Your Own, 1977; contbr. articles to various pubs. V.p. Save Our Rights Equally, Mahwah, 1986—. Mem. Nat. Home Fashions League, Taxpayers Assn. Mahwah. Avocations: travel, gardening, reading, breeding Great Danes. Home and Office: 30 Dundee Ct Box 725 Mahwah NJ 07430

KING, LYNDA ANNE WHITLOW, psychologist, educator; b. Danville, Va., Aug. 7, 1947; d. Detlef F. and Doris F. (Van Hook) Whitlow; student Coll. of William and Mary, 1965-67; B.S., U. Md., 1969; M.A., U. Washington, 1975, Ph.D., 1979; m. Daniel Walter King, Nov. 29, 1969. Research asst. Bur. of Sch. Service and Research, U. Washington, Seattle, 1975-76, research asso., 1976-77; instr. City Coll., Seattle, 1976-78; asst. prof. psychology Central Mich. U., Mt. Pleasant, 1979-83, assoc. prof., 1983—. Vol., ARC, 1981—. Served with Nurse Corps, U.S. Army, 1969-72. R.N., Wash. Mem. Am. Ednl. Research Assn., Midwestern Psychol. Assn., Common Cause, Phi Delta Kappa, Sigma Theta Tau, Phi Kappa Phi. Contbr. articles on psychology to profl. jours. Home: 500 Cedar Dr Mount Pleasant MI 48858 Office: Cen Mich U Sloan Hall Mount Pleasant MI 48859

KING, LYNNE MOHRMANN, insurance agent; b. Charleston, S.C., Oct. 6, 1945; d. Edwin Raymond and Kathryn (Wohlers) Mohrmann; m. Thomas J. King Jr., July 20, 1968; children: Thomas J. III, Elizabeth J. BA in German, Coll. Charleston, 1967; postgrad. in German, U. Va., 1967-68. Library asst. Charleston County Library, 1968-70, personnel dir., ops. mgr., 1973-86; agt. Mass. Mut. Life Ins. Co., Charleston, 1986—; chmn. staff devel. com. Charleston County Library, 1982-86; mem. higher edn. consortium, staff devel. com. S.C. Library Assn., 1982-86. Solicitor bus. div. United Way, 1986; vestry St. John's Episcopal Ch., 1982-85, dir. Christian edn., 1986—, mem. search com., 1986-87. Haymaker fellow Coll. Charleston, 1966-67; recipient Supr. award Juvenile Restitution Program, 1983. Mem. Am. Assn. Life Underwriters, Charleston Trident C. of C., Bus. and Profl. Women (sec. 1986-87, career woman of the yr. 1985), LWV, Alpha Kappa Gamma, Phi Mu (nat. pub. relations dir. 1982-86, nat. extension dir. 1986—). Home: 1305 Gilmore Rd Charleston SC 29407 Office: Mass Mut Life Ins Co 151 Meeting Suite 500 Charleston SC 29401

KING, LYNNETTE LEE, banker; b. Oakland, Calif., June 21, 1946; d. Alvin Leo Seward and Vera Lee (Turgeon) Seward Null; m. James Patrick King, June 21, 1968. B, Stanford U., 1968, M, 1969. Cert. tchr. community coll., Calif. Vol. Peace Corps, Ponape, Caroline Islands, 1969-71; educator Kyoto (Japan) YMCA, 1971-73; researcher VA Hosp., Palo Alto, Calif., 1974-76; project dir. Stanford U., Palo Alto, 1976-77; product mgr. Crocker Bank, San Francisco, 1978; v.p. consumer mktg. Wells Fargo Bank, San Francisco, 1978-83; exec. v.p. Security Savs., Scottsdale, Ariz., 1983-85; regional v.p. Citicorp Savs., Oakland, 1985-87, dir. statewide mortgage bus., 1987-88; sr. v.p. Calif. Savs. & Loan, San Francisco, 1988—; speaker deregulation and fin. services. Bd. dirs. Friends of the Scottsdale Symphony Orchestra, 1985, Bus. Vols. for the Arts, East Bay. Republican. Office: Calif Fed Savs & Loan 500 Sansome St San Francisco CA 94111

KING, MARCIA, library director; b. Lewiston, Maine, Aug. 4, 1940; d. Daniel Alden and Clarice Evelyn (Curtis) Barrell; m. Howard P. Lowell, Feb. 15, 1969 (div. 1980); m. Richard G. King Jr., Aug., 1980. BS, U. Maine, 1965; MSLS, Simmons Coll., 1967. Reference, field advisory and bookmobile librarian Maine State Library, Augusta, 1965-69; dir. Lithgow Pub. Library, Augusta, 1969-72; exec. sec. Maine Library Adv. Com., Maine State Library, 1972-73; dir. Wayland (Mass.) Free Pub. Library, 1973-76; state librarian State of Oreg., Salem, 1976-82; dir. Tucson Pub. Library, 1982—. Bd. dirs., chmn.-elect Tucson United Way; mem. adv. bd. com. Sta. KUAT (PBS-TV and Radio); mem. adv. bd. Resources for Women, Inc. Mem. ALA, Pub. Library Assn., Ariz. State Library Assn., AAUW, Assn. Specialized and Coop. Library Agys., Exec. Women's Council So. Ariz., Resources for Women Inc. (adv. bd.). Unitarian. Office: Tucson Pub Library 110 E Pennington PO Box 27470 Tucson AZ 85726

KING, MARCIA JONES, potter, physicist; b. Oak Park, Ill., May 17, 1934; d. Walter Leland Jones and Florence W. (Dull) Anderson; m. James Craig King, Nov., 1953 (div. 1966); 1 child, James Craig King, Jr. BS, Johns Hopkins U., 1960, PhD, 1969. Elec. engr. Electronic Communications, Inc., Timonium, Md., 1959-63; research assoc. theoretical particle physics Syracuse (N.Y.) U., 1969-72; asst. editor The Physical Rev. Brookhaven Nat. Lab., Upton, N.Y., 1972-74; physicist Argonne (Ill.) Nat. Lab., 1974-78; pvt. practice potter and physicist Syracuse, N.Y., 1978—. Contbr. articles to profl. jours.; exhibiter pots throughout cen. N.Y. Mem. Am. Physical Soc., Syracuse Ceramic Guild (pres. 1982-84), Phi Beta Kappa, Sigma Xi. Democrat. Home and Office: 228 Buckingham Ave Syracuse NY 13210

KING, MARJORIE SOMMERLYN, medical photographer; b. Conway, S.C., June 22, 1925; s. Bernard St. Lawrence and Mary Essie (Lupo) Sommerlyn; student Coker Coll., 1943-45; m. John L. King, Jan. 11, 1945; children—John Bernard, William Lawrence, Mary Elizabeth. Photopprinter for editor bus. pages Miami Daily News, 1954; owner, operator King's Portrait Studio, Conway, S.C., 1956-58; clk. bacteriol. lab. Jackson Meml. Hosp., Miami, 1963-65; photo lab. technician biomed. communications dept. U. Miami Med. Sch., 1965-67, photo lab. technician II, 1967-70, photographer III trainee, 1970-72, photographer III, 1973-76, photographer III supr., 1977-80; ret., 1985; owner M.S. King Enterprises, 1985—. Den mother Girl Scouts U.S.A. (OFAM council). Recipient Golden Key award Boy Scouts Am., 1957. Mem. Biol. Photog. Assn., Soroptimist Inst. Miami, DAR, UDC. Democrat. Episcopalian. Clubs: Miami Yacht, Coconut Grove Sailing (C gull pres.), West End Pool Aquatic (pres.). Lodge: Soroptimist. Home: 8035 SW 17th St Miami FL 33155

KING, MARY-CLAIRE, epidemiologist, educator, geneticist; b. Evanston, Ill., Feb. 27, 1946; 1 child, Emily King Colwell. BA in Math., Carleton Coll., 1966; PhD in Genetics, U. Calif., Berkeley, 1973. Asst. prof. U. Calif., Berkeley, 1976-80, assoc. prof., 1980-84, prof., 1984—; mem. bd. sci. counselors Nat. cancer Inst.; cons. Com. for Investigation of Disappearance of Persons, Govt. Argentina, Buenos Aires, 1984—. Contbr. more than 80 articles to profl. jours. Recipient Alumni Achievement award Carleton Coll. Mem. AAAS, Am. Soc. Human Genetics, Soc. Epidemiologic Research, Phi Beta Kappa, Sigma Xi. Office: Univ of California Sch Pub Health Berkeley CA 94720

KING, PATRICIA, training consultant; b. Paterson, N.J., Mar. 17, 1941; d. Salvatore Francesco and Anna Marie (Pisacane) Puglise; A.B., Coll. St. Elizabeth, 1963; m. David Jay Clark, Sept. 7, 1974; 1 child, Kerry Ann King. With Equitable Life Assurance Soc., N.Y.C., 1963-65; personnel officer Bankers Trust Co., N.Y.C., 1965-72; founder, pres. Patricia King Assocs., N.Y.C., 1972—. Mem. Nat. Orgn. Italian-Am. Women (nat. bd. dirs.). Author: Perform-Planning and Appraisal; Mind to Disk to Paper: Business Writing on a Word Processor, Never Work for A Jerk; (with others) The New Secretary: How to Get Respect, Rewards, Recognition; contbg. author: Affirmative Action for Women.

KING, PATRICIA LYNN, community development grant manager; b. Piqua, Ohio, May 8, 1955; d. Wallace Lynn and Nan Ellen (Lantz) Geuy; children: Heather Lynn, James Matthew. AA in Bus., Clark Tech. Sch., 1975. Legal sec. Gorman, Veskauf & Henson, Springfield, Ohio, 1975-76, Jewett, West, Stegner and Lehmkuhl, Springfield, 1976-77, Robert M. Strapp, Urbana, Ohio, 1977-78; personnel asst. Mercy Meml. Hosp., Urbana, 1978-79; grant mgr. City Hall City of Urbana, Ohio, 1983—. Clk. council City of Urbana, 1977—. Republican. Methodist. Office: City Hall 205 S Main St Urbana OH 43078

KING, PATRICIA MILLER, library administrator, historian; b. Bklyn., July 26, 1937; d. Donald Knox and Amy Beatrice (Heyliger) Miller; m. Samuel W. Stein, Jan. 2, 1978 (dec. May 1988); 1 child by previous marriage, Victoria Elizabeth King. A.B., Radcliffe Coll., 1959, A.M., 1961; Ph.D., Harvard U., 1970. Teaching asst. Harvard U., 1965-70; asst. prof. Wellesley Coll., Mass., 1970-71; dir. research Haney Assocs., Concord, Mass., 1971-73; dir. Schlesinger Library, Radcliffe Coll., 1973—, dir. projects. Contbr. articles to profl. jours. Mem. adv. bd. The Women's Resource Ctr., New England Med. Ctr., Tufts U. Sch. Medicine, Boston, 1982-86; mem. sci. and edn. consortium adv. com. Harvard Med. Sch., 1983-85; bd. dirs. Database Task Force, 1986—, treas., 1988—; bd. dirs. Nat. Council for Research on Women, N.Y.C., 1983—. Grantee in field. Mem. Mass. Hist. Soc., Am. Antiquarian Soc. (membership com.), Orgn. Am. Historians, Am. Hist. Assn., Berkshire Conf. of Women Historians. Home: 3 Whittier St Cambridge MA 02140 Office: Schlesinger Library Radcliffe Coll 10 Garden St Cambridge MA 02138

KING, PEGGY, producer; b. N.Y.C., July 5, 1950; d. Philip K.; m. Ronald Victor Garcia, Apr. 29, 1988. BA magna cum laude, Tufts U., 1972; MA, Am. Film Inst., 1978. Producer Sta. WLVI-TV, Boston, 1973-76; story analyst The Ladd Co. and Daniel Melnick's Ind. Co., Los Angeles, 1980-82; story editor ABC Motion Pictures, Los Angeles, 1982-84, dir. creative affairs, 1984-85; v.p. prodn. FilmAccord, Los Angeles, 1986-87; ind. film producer Los Angeles, 1987—. Writer, producer TV comml. Morrison and Schitt Scramble, 1976 (Addy award 1976); producer: (film) Norman and the Killer, 1978. Recipient Life Achievement Scholarship award Am. Film Inst., 1978.

KING, PEGGY HUDSON, nurse administrator; b. Vicksburg, Miss., Jan. 17, 1955; d. James Arthur and Dessie (Hall) Hudson; m. Dennis Ray King, June 5, 1977; 1 child, Devita Rachell. AA, Hinds Jr. Coll., 1975; BSN, U. Miss., 1981; MSN, U. So. Miss., 1983. RN. Staff nurse U. Med. Ctr., Jackson, Miss., 1975-77, St. Dominics Hosp., Jackson, 1977; staff nurse VA Med. Ctr., Jackson, 1977-80, relief nursing coordinator, 1980-84, nigh nursing supr., 1984—. V.p. Nat. Council Negro Women, Jackson, 1984, 85; health and welfare chmn. Pratt United Meth. Ch., Jackson, 1985; mem. community service com. ARC, Jackson, 1987. Brit. studies, hospice grantee NIH, 1983, Oncology Nursing Soc. grantee, New Orleans, 1987. Mem. Am. Nurses Assn., Miss. Nurses Assn. (edn. com. Jackson chpt. 1985—), Dist. 13 Nurses Assn. (v.p. 1985, bylaws com. 1987), Sigma Theta Tau, Alpha Lambda Delta. Democrat. Lodge: Heroines Cyrenes (sec. 1984—). Office: VA Med Ctr 1500 E Woodrow Wilson Jackson MS 39209

KING, REGINA MASON, school system administrator; b. N.Y.C., Feb. 19, 1935; d. Reginald and Georgianna (Simms) Mason; m. Ronald H. King, Nov. 19, 1955 (div.); children: Kevin, Melanie. BS, Columbia U., 1957, MA, 1960. nat. cert. counselor and career counselor. Tchr. Bd. Edn., N.Y.C., 1957-61, guidance counselor, 1966-75, ednl. evaluator, 1975-78, chairperson Commn. on the Handicapped, 1978-83, supr. spl. edn., 1983-86, dir. pupil personnel, 1986-87, supr. career services Adult Edn., 1987—; instr. Coll. New Rochelle, N.Y., 1986; counselor Westchester Lib. System, Elmsford, N.Y., 1986—; career counselor Hudson View Assocs. Vol. United Negro Coll. Fund, N.Y.C., 1980-85; mem. Bd. for Riverdale Community Ctr., 1986, Bronx Women's Network, Riverdale, 1986. Mem. Am. Soc. Tng. Devel., N.Y.C. Assn. Adminstrv. Women in Edn., N.Y. Assn. Personality Types, Am. Assn. Counseling and Devel. Club: Ben Franklin. Home: 4705 Henry Hudson Pkwy Riverdale NY 10471

KING, RHETA BARON, rehabilitation professional; b. Los Angeles, Dec. 15, 1935; d. Albert James and Marietta (Malcomson) Baron; m. Stuart Alan Walling, June, 11, 1956 (div. July 1968); children: S. Alan, Lynne Heather; m. Kenneth Bruce King, Oct. 11, 1968 (div. Apr. 1983). AB cum laude, Occidental Coll., 1957; postgrad., Calif. State U., Los Angeles, 1960-68, Calif. State U., Long Beach, 1963-64. Cert. rehab. counselor, Calif. Rehab. counselor Calif. Dept. Rehab., Burbank, 1972-74; coordinator staff devel. Los Angeles, 1974, program supr., 1975-78; nat. dir. staff devel. Comprehensive Rehab. Services, Inc., Arcadia, Calif., 1978-80; dir. comprehensive rehab. ctr. Daniel Freeman Meml. Hosp., Inglewood, Callif., 1981-83, dir. vocat. programs, 1984-86; pvt. practice rehab. counseling Pasadena, Calif., 1981—; tech. advisor Devel. Disabilities Area Bd., Los Angeles, 1978; cons. Social Security Office Hearings and Appeals, Pasadena and West Los Angeles, Calif., 1981—, Am. Coll. Neurology, 1986, Nat. Multiple Sclerosis Soc., 1986—; ptnr. Inst. for Profl. Competency, Pasadena and Agoura, Calif., 1986—; research scientist Human Interaction Research Inst., Los Angeles, 1986—. Author graphic model, 1980. Mem. Gov.'s Com. for Employment of Handicapped, Calif., 1983—, Los Angeles Long-Term Care Task Force, 1987; friend Huntington Library, San Marino, Calif., 1986-87. Elizabeth Woods fellow, 1964. Mem. Nat. Rehab. Assn., Occidental Coll. Alumni. Republican. Episcopalian. Club: Pasadena Heritage. Home: 515 S Oakland Ave Apt 5 Pasadena CA 91101 Office: Human Interaction Research Inst 1849 Sawtelle Blvd Suite 102 Los Angeles CA 90025

KING, RUBY THOMPSON, educator, civic worker; b. nr. Wrightsville, Ga.; d. Charles D. and Maude (Douglas) Thompson; student S. Ga. Coll.; B.A., Scarritt Coll., M.A.; postgrad. George Peabody Coll. Tchrs., U. Ga., Fla. State U., U. Edinburgh (Scotland); m. Seabron Larry King. Tchr. English, Brunswick, Ga.; tchr. Lowndes County Ga.; tchr. English, Coffee County (Ga.) high schs., 1966—. Conf. sec. missionary personnel Woman's Soc. Christian Service; active numerous local fund drives; coordinator Wesleyan Service Guild; 8th Dist. Sci. Fair committeewoman; sponsor Young Teens; charter mem. Tri-Hi-Y Internat., chmn. convocation; field rep. World Field Research, Inc.; editor Ga. Bull. Dir. Thompson-King Found.; trustee Florence Crittendon Home, Savannah, Ga.; mem. Pub. Library Bd.; White House appointment Nat. Traffic Safety Council, Washington; staff Am. Research Bur., Inc. state news reporter Atlanta Jour.; mem. Macon Music Chorus; mem. Nat. Rep. Party Task Force. Named Star Tchr., Ga. C. of C.; Douglas Citizen of Year for distinguished community service; Albert Schweitzer fellow. Mem. Home Demonstration Council So. Ga., Conf. Hist. Soc., Ga. Edn. Assn. (county chmn. pub. relations), NEA, Am. Soc. Psychical Research, Ga. Assn. Edn., Nat. Assn. English Tchrs., UDC, Internat. Platform Assn., Internat., Am. assns. univ. women, D.A.R., Philharmonic Club, Nat. Heritage Commn. Preservation Hist. Shrines, Nat. Council Tchrs. English, Am. Security Council, Canterbury Cathedral Assn., Canterbury Cathedral Preservation Soc., Nat. Shrine/Hist. Trust Preservation, Thespian Soc., Scarritt Alumni Club. Methodist. Clubs: Order Eastern Star, Garden Study; Fine Arts, Woman's Garden Guild. Author: History of Historic Ebenézer Methodist Church, 1800-1988; author poetry pub. in Am. Anthology of Verse, Nat. Anthology Poetry, Quaderni di Poesia, Anthology of Internat. Poetry; contbr. to poetry jours. in U.S., Scotland, Eng. and Italy. Address: 111 N Gaskin Ave Douglas GA 31533

KING, RUTH ALLEN, management consultant; b. Providence, Oct. 8, 1910; d. Arthur S. and Wilhelmina H. (Harmon) Allen; grad. Tefft Bus. Inst., Providence, 1929; 1 dau., Phyllis King Dunham. Sec. to atty., Providence, 1929; stenographer N.Y. Urban League, N.Y.C., 1929-75; sec. adminstrn., adminstrv. asst., placement officer, asst. dir. Nat. Urban League Skills Bank, to 1975; founder/sec. The Edges Group, Inc., 1969—; Named Affirmative Action Pioneer, Met. N.Y. Project Equality, 1975; Ruth Allen King Scholarship Fund established, 1970; EDGES Ruth Allen King Ann. Excalibur award established, 1978; recipient Ann Tanneyhill award for commitment to Urban League Movement, 1975; Recognition award NCCJ, 1975; spl. citation Gov. of R.I. and Providence Plantations, 1981, citation Medgar Evers Coll., 1983; Ruth Allen King Appreciation Day proclaimed in her honor, Providence, Mar. 9, 1981, N.Y.C., 1975; citation R.I. Ho. of Reps., 1981; plaque Urban League R.I., 1981; Woman of Yr. award Suffolk (N.Y.) chpt. Jack and Jill of Am., 1982; numerous others. Mem. N.Y. Personnel Mgmt. Assn., Council Concerned Black Execs., Julius A. Thomas Soc. (charter), NAACP (life). Home and Office: 185 Hall St Apt 1715 Brooklyn NY 11205

KING, SHERYL JAYNE, educator, counselor; b. East Grand Rapids, Mich., Oct. 29, 1945; d. Thomas Benton III and Bettyann Louise (Mains) K. BS in Family Living, Sociology, Secondary Edn., Cen. Mich. U., 1968, M in Counseling, 1971. Educator Newaygo (Mich.) Pub. Schs., 1968-72; interior decorator Sue King Interiors, Grand Rapids, Mich., 1972-73; dir. girl's unit Dillon Family and Youth Services, Tulsa, 1973-74; mgr. Fellowship Press, Grand Rapids, Minn., 1974-76; educator, counselor Itasca Community Coll., Grand Rapids, 1977-81, dept. head, 1980-81, 85-86, 86-87; educator Dist. 318, Grand Rapids, 1977—; bd. dirs., chairperson program com. Marriage and Family Devel. Ctr., Grand Rapids, 1985—. Contbr. articles to profl. jours. Mem. issues com. No. Minn. Citizens League, Grand Rapids, 1984—, Blandin Found. Study, 1985-86; chairperson Itasca County Women's Consortium, Grand Rapids, 1983-87; Women's Day Conf., Grand Rapids, 1983-87; dir. audio tech. Fellowship of Believers, Grand Rapids, 1974-87, deaconess, 1974—; dir. Camp Dominion, Cass Lake, Minn., 1976-80; mem. Fitness com., chmn. aquatic com., YMCA, Grand Rapids, 1974-87. Recipient Outstanding Service award (10 times) Fellowship of Believers, 1974-79. Mem. Nat. Assn. Female Execs., Alpha Delta Kappa. Republican. Club: Quadna (Hill City, Minn.). Home: 208 NE 3d Ave Grand Rapids MN 55744 Office: Dist 318 902 N Pokegama Ave Grand Rapids MN 55744

KING, SHIRLEY ANN MIELKE, editor; b. Paulding, Ohio, June 5, 1935; d. Edward Michael John and Vanda Steiner (Schultz) Mielke; m. Lowell King, June 6, 1953 (div. Jan. 1977); children—Michael David, David Matthew. Student Ball State U., St. Francis Coll., Fort Wayne Sch. Fine Arts. Bookkeeper, Napoleon Egg Co., Albion, Ind., 1954-56, Noble County REMC, Albion, 1956-61; editor Avilla News (Ind.), 1971—. Recipient awards Avilla Jaycees, 1982, 83. Mem. Avilla C. of C. (chmn. festival 1982). Democrat. Lutheran. Home: 208 N Main Avilla IN 46710 Office: Tri-County Pub Co 209 S Main Churubusco IN 46723

KING, SUSAN BENNETT, manufacturing company executive; b. Sioux City, Iowa, Apr. 29, 1940; d. Francis Moffatt Bennett and Marjorie (Rittenhouse) Sillin; divorced. AB, Duke U., 1962. Legis. asst. U.S. Senate, Washington, 1963-66; dir. Nat. Com. for Effective Congress, Washington, 1967-71, Ctr. Pub. Financing of Election, Washington, 1972-75; exec. asst. to chmn. Fed. Election Commn., Washington, 1975-77; commr. U.S. Consumer Product Safety Commn., Washington, 1978, chmn., 1978-81; dir. consumer affairs Corning (N.Y.) Glass Works, 1982, v.p. corp. communications, 1983-86; pres. Steuben Glass, N.Y.C., 1987—; vice chmn. U.S. Regulatory Council, U.S. Govt., Washington, 1979-80; del. Consumer Affairs Orgn. Econ. Cooperation and Devel., Paris, 1980-81. Chairperson bd. visitors inst. policy and scis. Duke U., Durham, N.C., 1985-87, trustee, 1987—; trustee Keuka Coll., Keuka Park, N.Y., 1983-87. Fellow Inst. Politics Harvard U., 1981. Mem. Nat. Consumers League (pres. 1984-85). Democrat. Office: Steuben Glass 715 Fifth Ave New York NY 10022

KING, VERNA ST. CLAIR, retired school counselor; b. Berwick, La.; d. John Westley and Florence Ellen (Calvin) St. C.; A.B., Wiley Coll., 1937; M.A., San Diego State U., 1977; m. Alonzo Le Roy King, Aug. 27, 1939; children—Alonzo Le Roy (dec.), Joyce Laraine, Verna Lee Eugenia King Bickerstaff, St. Clair A., Reginald Calvin (dec.). Tchr., Morgan City, La., 1939-40; tchr. San Diego Unified Sch. Dist., 1955-67, parent counselor, 1967-78, counselor grades 1-9, 1978-86; cons. Tucson Sch. Dist., 1977—, dir. compensatory edn., 1983—. Mem. Calif. Democratic State Central Com., 1950—, Dem. County Central Com., 1974—, del. nat. conv., 1976, 84, mem. exec. bd. Dem. State Central Com., 1982—; mem. San Diego County Sander Adv. Commn., 1982; hon. life mem. PTA; bd. dirs. YWCA, 1983—, v.p., 1987-88. Recipient Key to City, Mayor C. Dail, 1955, cert. United Negro Coll. Fund dr., 1980, Urban League Pvt. Sector award, 1982, 4th Ann. Conf. on Issues in Ethnicity and Mental Health Participants award, 1982; named Woman of Dedication, Salvation Army, 1985, Citizen of Yr., City Club and Jaycees, 1985, Woman of Achievement, Pres.' Council, 1983; numerous other honors. Mem. NEA (women's council 1980-82), AAUW, Calif. Tchrs. Assn. (state council 1979—, area dir. 1985—), San Diego Tchrs. Assn. (dir. 1958, 64, sec. 1964-67), Nat. Council Negro Women, San Diego County Council Dem. Women (pres. 1986-88), Compensatory Edn. Assn. (area dir. 1982-87), Pres. Women, Inc., Alpha Kappa Alpha (pres. 1978-80), Delta Kappa Gamma. Methodist. Clubs: Women's Inc., Order Eastern Star. Home: 5721 Churchward St San Diego CA 92114 Office: San Diego Unified Sch Dist 2850 Logan Ave San Diego CA 92113

KING, VICTORIA VAN BEUREN, otolaryngologist; b. St. Louis, Jan. 16, 1953; d. Willard Van Beuren and Frances Howell (Lewis) K.; B.A. in Human Biology with honors, Stanford U., 1975; M.D., U. Mo., Columbia, 1979. Diplomate Am. Bd. Otolaryngology. Resident in otolaryngology Stanford U. Hosp., 1980-83, chief resident; practice medicine specializing in head and neck surgery, Palo Alto, Calif. Mem. U.S. Olympic Swimming Team, 1968, U.S. Swimming Teams to Australia, Tahiti, Can. and Eng., 1969-72. U.S. Nat. Swimming Champion, 1969; recipient award for scholastic achievement Am. Med. Women's Assn. Fellow, Am. Coll. Surgeons; mem. AMA, Am. Acad. Facial Plastic and Reconstructive Surgery, Am. Acad. Otolaryngology/Head and Neck Surgery, Alpha Omega Alpha. Office: 770 Welch Rd Suite 370 Palo Alto CA 94304

KING, VIRGINIA, librarian; b. Akron, Ohio, May 12, 1917; d. Wilson Reed and Eunice Mina (White) King. B.S. in Music Edn., Greenville Coll. (Ill.), 1939, B.A., 1941; M.Music, U. So. Calif., 1954, M.S.L.S., 1967. Music tchr. Los Angeles Pacific Coll., 1943-45, 46-65, Greenville Coll. (Ill.), 1945-46; music prof. and librarian Azusa Pacific U. (Calif.), 1965-82, music and periodicals librarian, 1982—. Named Outstanding Tchr., 1975. Mem. ALA, Christian Librarians Assn., Coll. Music Soc., Choral Condrs. Guild, Music Educators Nat. Conf., Calif. Music Educators Assn., NEA, Calif. Tchrs. Assn. Office: Azusa Pacific Univ Citrus and Alosta Sts Azusa CA 91702

KING, YVONNE LEVELLE, insurance company executive; b. N.Y.C., Dec. 18, 1942; d. Granville Oliver and Mayme (Flemming) LeVell; m. Richard Alfredo Kier, Sept. 8, 1962 (div. 1978); children—Richard, Roland; m. Emmett Alonzo King, Oct. 19, 1980; stepchildren—Andre, Jackie. B.A. in Lang. Arts, Calif. State U.-Hayward, 1969; M.A., U. Calif.-Berkeley, 1972. Registered rep. Nat. Securities Dealers Assn. Instr., U. Calif.-Berkeley, 1970-72; ednl. specialist-writer, producer Eastman Kodak, Rochester, N.Y., 1974-76; writer, cons. Hewitt Assocs., Stanford, Conn., 1977-78; planner, product mgr. Avon Products, N.Y.C., 1978-81; dir. investment products, real estate product mgr., pension ops., project control mgr. Individual Fin. Group Equitable Life Assurance Soc. U.S. Life Computer Cntr. div., 1982—. Awards chmn. Westport (Conn.) council Boy Scouts Am., 1981; bd. dirs., v.p. pub. affairs Tri-W-Black Families, Westport, 1981; bd. dirs., Unity Ch. of Christ, Teaneck, N.J., 1984-86, Pres.'s Black Resource Group, Equitable Life Soc. U.S., 1987—. Democrat. Office: Equitable Life Assurance Soc 400 Willow Tree Rd Leonia NJ 07605

KING-BAILEY, VALARIE, civil engineer; b. Chgo., Oct. 24, 1958; d. Leroy and Jeanette Ora (Green) King; m. Vincent Malone Bailey, June 9, 1985. BS in Civil and Environ. Engring., U. Wis., 1981; MBA in Info. Systems, Lake Forest Coll., 1985; postgrad., Keller Grad. Sch. of Mgmt. Registered engr.-in-tng. Design engr. U.S. Steel Corp., Chgo., 1981-83; customer engr. Intergraph Corp., Schaumburg, Ill., 1984-86, account mgr., 1986-88; civil/site application engr. Arlington Heights, Ill., 1988—; speaker U. Wis. Coll. Engring., Madison, 1982-84. Sci. Fair judge Chgo. Pub. Schs., 1981-83; ann. guest speaker Nat. Honor Soc., Chgo., 1981—. Scholar George M. Pullman Found., Chgo., 1976, Wendell Phillips Alumni Found., Chgo., 1976, U. Wis. Coll. Engring., 1980. Mem. ASCE, Nat. Assn. Female Execs., Soc. Women Engrs. Office: Intergraph Corp 85 W Algonquin Rd 6th Floor Arlington Heights IL 60005-4422

KINGDON, HOLLY, small business owner; b. Cleve., Jan. 19, 1960; d. Henry Shannon and MaryLee (Colman) K. BS in Computer Sci. cum laude, Duke U., 1981. Systems programmer Standard Software Systems, Durham, N.C., 1981; systems architect Tseng Info. Systems, Durham, 1982; pvt. practice software engr. Durham, 1983; instr. Rutledge Coll., Durham, 1983-84; co-owner, mgr. Liberated Types, Ltd., Durham, 1984—. Co-chair Durham media com. Coalition for Alternatives to Shearon Harris, 1987. Mem. Nat. Assn. Female Execs. Democrat. Office: Liberated Types Ltd 2904 Hillsborough Rd Durham NC 27705

KING-ETTEMA, ELIZABETH DOROTHY, video and film editor, writer, photographer; b. Morristown, N.J., Sept. 29, 1953; d. James Claude and Martha Helene (Dawson) King; m. Dale Frederic Ettema, Feb. 13, 1982; children—Taylor Braam, Claire Elizabeth. B.A. in Art History, UCLA, 1975; postgrad. U. N.M., 1977-78. Writer, Bettis & Parks Advt., Albuquerque, 1975-76; bus. mgr. N.M. Ballet Co., Albuquerque, 1976-78; asst. editor Dury Assocs., Los Angeles, 1978, Another Editing Pl., Los Angeles, 1978-79, Bullywood Prodn., Los Angeles, 1979, Alan Landsburg Prodn., Los Angeles, 1980-81, Columbia TV, Los Angeles, 1982-83; video editor Am. Film Inst., Los Angeles, 1983-85. Video editor Scenario, 1984, U.S. 49/Calif. 1, 1985. Recipient scholarship UCLA Extension, 1979. Mem. Motion Picture and Videotape Editors Guild, Soc. Children's Book Writers, Internat. Documentary Assn. Democrat. Episcopalian. Club: Embroiderer's Guild of Am. (historian chpt. 1984-85, v.p., program chmn. 1987-88). Avocations: photography, embroidery. Home and Office: 7235 Forbes Ave Van Nuys CA 91406

KING-JEFFERS, SHARON WINDSOR, lawyer; b. Chelsea, Mass., Mar. 17, 1940; d. Edward Windsor King and Mildred Bowman (Bannar) Moldenhauer; m. Leland Roland Jeffers, Apr. 20, 1968; children—Sean Edward, Lance Thomas. B.S.L., Western State U., Fullerton, Calif., 1974, J.D., 1975. Bar: Calif. 1978. Legal research supr. 1st Am. Title Ins. Co., Santa Ana, Calif., 1978-79; sole practice, Norco, Calif., 1979-80, assoc. practice, 1981-82; sole practice, Riverside, Calif., 1982—; selected participant Leadership Am. '88. Editorial staff Western State U. Law Rev., 1973-75. Trustee Chaffey Community Coll., Alta Loma, Calif., 1977-82, sec. 1977-79, v.p., 1979-80, pres., 1980-82; trustee Charter Grove Psychiat. Hosp., Corona, Calif., 1982—, pres., 1984-86; adv. bd. Charter Med. Network, 1983; past pres. Corona Music Theater Assn.; former bd. dirs., pres., charter mem. vol. Aux. Kellogg Psychiat. Hosp., others; mem. Inland Empire Cultural Arts Found., Riverside, San Bernardino, 1983; mem. Child Care Action Task Force, Riverside. Recipient Am. Jurisprudence award in criminal law Bancroft-Whitney Co., 1972; Calif. Legal Secs. scholar, 1973. Mem. State Bar Assn. Calif., Riverside County Bar Assn. (estate planning, probate, trust sect., pub./bar relations, medical/legal liaison and law and media coms., family law sect., chmn. speakers bur., participant Leadership Am. '88, also steering com., liaison), Nu Beta Epsilon. Republican. Roman Catholic. Clubs: Toastmasters Internat., USAF Acad. Parents (Inland Empire) (treas. 1987-88). Lodge: Soroptomists (co-chmn. intercommunity com. Riverside chpt. 1983-84, del. 1984-86, chmn. women helping women com. 1985, chmn. gold key com. 1987-88, v.p. 1988, pres. 1988-89). Office: 4255 Main St Suite 3 Riverside CA 92501

KINGMAN, ELIZABETH YELM, anthropology researcher; b. Lafayette, Ind., Oct. 15, 1911; d. Charles Walter and Mary Irene (Weakley) Yelm; children—Mixie Kingman Eddy, Elizabeth Anne Kingman. BA U. Denver, 1933, MA, 1935. Asst. in anthropology U. Denver, 1932-34; mus. asst. Ranger Naturalist Force, Mesa Verde Nat. Park, Colo., 1934-38; asst. to husband in curatorial work, Indian art exhibits Philbrook Art Ctr., Tulsa, 1939-42, Joslyn Art Mus., Omaha, 1947-69; tutor humanities dept. U. Omaha, 1947-50; asst. to husband in exhibit design mus. of Tex. Tech. U., 1970-75, bibliographer Internat. Ctr. Arid and Semi-Arid Land Studies, 1974-75; librarian Sch. Am. Research, Santa Fe, 1978-86; research assoc., 1986—; v.p. Santa Fe Corral of the Westerners, 1985-86. Mem. Archeol. Inst. Am. (v.p. Santa Fe chpt. 1981-83), LWV, Santa Fe Hist. Soc. (sec. 1981-83). Presbyterian. Home: 604 Sunset St Santa Fe NM 87501-1118 Office: Sch Am Research 660 Garcia St Santa Fe NM 87501

KINGSLEY, CAROL ROGENE, educator, administrator; b. Carlsbad, N.Mex., Jan. 15, 1947; d. Monroe Thurman and Robbye Jean (Miller) K. Student, Baylor U., 1965-68; B in Univ. Studies, U. N.Mex., 1968-70. Ordained to ministry Scientology Ch.; cert. Hubbard Sr. Scientologist. Tchr. Job Corps, Albuquerque, 1969-70; dir. Mission Albuquerque, 1970-74; counselor Am. Saint Hill Orgn., Los Angeles, 1974-76; technician Atlas Minerals, Moab, Utah, 1976-78; counselor M-K Field Ministry, Los Angeles, 1979—; educator Jefferson Hall Acad., Los Angeles, 1982—; lectr. Am. Studies U. N.Mex., 1970-72; cons. Auditor's Assn; rep. Oaks Meadow Sch., 1984-86. Pres. Young Reps., N.Mex., 1965; active citizens com. for human rights, Los Angeles, 1980—; active Religious Freedom Crusade, Los Angeles, 1984—; organizer Way-to-Happiness Found., Los Angeles, 1986—. Recipient Leadership award Elks Club, N.Mex., 1965; Scholar Altrusa Club, N.Mex. 1965, Baylor U., Waco, Tex., 1965-68, Am. Saint Hill, Los Angeles, 1972-78. Mem. Internat. Ecclesiastic League (sr. field auditor, Most Valuable 1985-87), Concerned Bus. Mens Assn Am. (educator 1986—), Flag Service Orgn. (field staff 1979—), Internat. Assn. Scientologists, Applied Scholastics Internat., Los Angeles Dianetic Research Found. (Auditor of Yr. 1986), U. N.Mex. Alumni Assn., Psi Kappa Psi, Phi Sigma Tau. Home: 814 Micheltorena Los Angeles CA 90026

KINGSTON, MAXINE HONG, author; b. Stockton, Calif., Oct. 27, 1940; d. Tom and Ying Lan (Chew) Hong; m. Earll Kingston, Nov. 23, 1963; 1 child, Joseph Lawrence. B.A., U. Calif., Berkeley, 1962. tchr. English, Sunset High Sch., Hayward, Calif., 1965-66, Kahuku (Hawaii) High Sch., 1967, Kahaluu (Hawaii) Drop-In Sch., 1968, Kailua (Hawaii) High Sch., 1969, Honolulu Bus. Coll., 1969, Mid-Pacific Inst., Honolulu, 1970-77; prof. English, vis. writer U. Hawaii, Honolulu, 1977; Thelma McCandless Disting. Prof. Eastern Mich. U., Ypsilanti, 1986. Author: The Woman Warrior: Memoirs of a Girlhood Among Ghosts, 1976 (Nat. Book Critics Circle award for non-fiction; cited by Time mag., N.Y. Times Book Rev. and Asian Mail as one of best books of yr.), China Men, 1981 (Am. Book award; runner up for Pulitzer prize and Nat. Book Critics Circle award nominee 1988), Hawai'i One Summer, 1987, Tripmaster Monkey--His Fake Books, 1989, Through The Black Curtain, 1988; contbr. short stories, articles and poems to mags. and jours., including Iowa Rev., The New Yorker, Ms., Am. Heritage, Redbook. Recipient Mademoiselle Mag. award, 1977, Anisfield-Wolf race relations award, 1978; Stockton (Calif.) Arts Commn. award, 1981; Hawaii award for Lit., 1982; NEA writing fellow, 1980; Guggenheim fellow, 1981; named a Living Treasure of Hawaii, 1980, Asian/Pacific Women's Network Woman of Yr., 1981.

KINKADE, KATE, publishing executive, magazine editor, insurance executive; b. N.Y.C., Jan. 22, 1951; d. Joel M. and Peeta S. (Sherman) Sandleman; m. Patrick Ramsey, June 27, 1981; children: Jamaa Ramsey, Kikanza Ramsey. BS in Speech, Emerson Coll., Boston, 1972; postgrad., Am. Coll., Bryn

Mawr, Pa. CLU. Agt. Equitable Life Ins., Los Angeles, 1973-75, mgr., 1975-77; v.p. Lincoln Nat. Life Ins., Tarzana, Calif., 1977-80; pres. TIME Ins., Encino, Calif., 1980—; mng. editor McGee Pub., Burbank, Calif., 1983—; exec. v.p. Life Underwriters Assn., Encino, 1978-81. Contbr. articles to profl. jours. Mem. steering com. nat. office Beyond War, Palo Alto, Calif., also Los Angeles regional fin. support and chairperson local chpt., Burbank, Calif., 1984—. Recipient Asst. Prodn. awards Equitable Life, 1973, 77, Lincoln Nat. Life, 1978, 80, Pacific Mut. Life, 1983. Mem. Assn. CLU's. Democrat. Jewish. Office: Ramkade Inc 15760 Ventura #1734 Encino CA 91436

KINLEIN, M(ARY) LUCILLE, nurse; b. Ellicott City, Md., Dec. 17, 1921; d. Julius Augustus and Mary Teresa (Plantholt) K.; B.A., Coll. Notre Dame, Balt., 1943; B.S. in Nursing Edn., Catholic U. Am., 1947, M.S., 1953. Asst. prof. nursing Cath. U. Am., 1947-69, dir. masters program in cardiovascular disease nursing, 1962-69; mem. faculty Georgetown U. Sch. Nursing, 1970-74; pres. D.C. Profl. Nurses Exam. Bd., 1955-61, D.C. Practical Nurses Exam. Bd., 1961-67; cons. HEW, 1964-74; ind. general nurse, 1971-79; ptnr. Détente Manor, McLean, Va., 1978-81; vis. prof. U. So. Miss., Hattiesburg, 1975-78, also coordinator Center Nursing Edn., Practice and Research; vis. lectr. univs. Wis., Va., Alaska Pacific U.; mem. Washington Nursing Devel. Conf. Group; founder Nat. Center of Kinlein, 1979, Inst. of Kinlein, 1983. Recipient Alumni Achievement award Coll. Notre Dame, 1973, Cath. U. Am., 1974; Linda Richards award Nat. League Nursing, 1977. Mem. Am. Nurses Assn., Nat. League Nursing, Am. Heart Assn., Sigma Theta Tau, Kappa Gamma Pi. Roman Catholic. Author: Independent Nursing Practice with Clients, 1977; Moving That Power Within, 1983, expanded edit., 1985; Author-editor: Cordising: A New Understanding of Caring, 1986; co-author: Concept Formalization in Nursing, 1973; founder Jour. of Kinlein, 1981. Home: 6700 Belcrest Rd Apt 615 Hyattsville MD 20782 Office: 6525 Belcrest Rd Hyattsville MD 20782

KINNAMON, PENNY LYNN, purchasing services specialist; b. Independence, Kans., Mar. 24, 1955; d. Milford Newell Hinman and Pauline Riola (Bishop) Winkler; children: Bryan Edward, Libbie Suzanne. AA in Acctg., Tulsa Jr. Coll., 1986. Nursing asst. Mercy Hosp., Independence, 1974, technician cen. supply, 1974-79, purchasing asst., 1979-82, dir. purchasing, 1982-83; purchasing agt. Sheraton Kensington Hotel, Tulsa, 1984—. Leader Magic Empire council Girl Scouts U.S., 1984-85. Mem. Phi Theta Kappa. Republican. Home: 2133 S Louisville Tulsa OK 74114 Office: Sheraton Kensington Hotel 1902 E 71st Tulsa OK 74136

KINNAN, JOEN PRITCHARD, free-lance writer, editor, consultant; b. Canton, Ohio, May 21; d. William Davis and Thelma (Gibbs) Pritchard; m. Donald Henry Kinnan, Mar. 8 (div.); children—Glynis Joen, Jason Pritchard. B.A., Denison U.; postgrad. Kent State U., Ohio State U. Cert. elem. and secondary tchr., Ohio, Mich. English, history, geography and social studies tchr. Upper Arlington Schs., Ohio, later John Norup Jr. High Sch., Berkley, Mich.; sketchwriter, editor Marquis Who's Who, Chgo., 1964-74, asst. dept. head, 1966-68, head sketchwriting dept., 1968-74, freelance writer, editor, 1974-86; sr. assoc., writer, workshop facilitator William M. Young & Assocs., Oak Park, Ill., 1978-83; freelance writer, editor, cons., River Forest, Ill., 1983—; freelance newsletter editor Talmis, Inc., Chgo., 1984; intermittantly pvt. adult tutor. Ghostwriter mag. articles in health care and ednl. field. Democratic precinct worker; past publicity chmn. Oak Park-Proviso-Riverside Ind. Dems.; active McCarthy and McGovern presdl. campaigns, Walker gubernatorial campaign, Stevenson and Simon senatorial campaigns; past mgr. River Forest Boys' Little League. Mem. Ind. Writers of Chgo., Chgo. Women in Pub., Greenpeace, Citizens for Better Environment, Smithsonian Instn., Delta Gamma. Avocations: cats; nouvelle and ethnic cooking; travel.

KINNE, FRANCES BARTLETT, university president; b. Story City, Iowa; d. Charles Morton and Bertha (Olson) Bartlett; m. Harry L. Kinne, Jr. (dec.). Student edn., U. No. Iowa; B of Music Edn., Drake U., M. of Music Edn., DFA (hon.), 1981, hon. degree; PhD cum laude, U. Frankfurt, Fed. Republic of Germany, 1957; LHD (hon.), Wagner Coll., N.Y.; LLD (hon.), Lenoir Rhyne Coll. Tchr. music Kelley (Iowa) Consol. Sch., 1936-37; supr. music Boxholm (Iowa) Consol. Sch., Des Moines pub. schs., 1940-43; sr. hostess Camp Crowder, Mo., 1943-46; dir. recreation VA, Wadsworth, Kans., 1946-48; lectr. music, English and Western culture Tsuda Coll., Tokyo, 1949-50; cons. music U.S. Army Gen. Hdqrs., Tokyo, 1950-51; mem. faculty Jacksonville (Fla.) U., 1958—, disting. Univ. prof., 1961-62, prof. music and humanities, 1963—, dean, founder Coll. Fine Arts, 1961-79, interim pres., 1979, pres., 1979—; disting. Univ. prof., 1961-62; chmn. Ind. Colls. and Univs. of Fla.; mem. adv. council Nat. Soc. Arts and Letters; past dir. Barnett Bank of Jacksonville, also mem. salary rev. com. Author: A Comparative Study of British Traditional and American Indigenous Ballads, 1958; contbr. chpt. to book, articles to profl. jours. Bd. dirs., trustee Drake U.; hon. bd. dirs. Jacksonville Symphony Assn.; trustee Greater Jacksonville Com. Found.; bd. dirs., mem. exec. com. Eye Research Found.; bd. govs. Mazda Gator Bowl Assn.; mem. Christopher Columbus Hemisphere Commn.; bd. dirs. Bert Thomas Scholarship Fund, Optic Fedn. Recipient hon. awards Bus. and Profl. Women's Clubs, 1962, Disting. Service award Drake U., 1966, 1st Fla. Gov.'s award for achievement in arts, 1972, EVE award in edn., 1973, Arts Assembly Individual award, 1978-79, Roast award Soc. for Prevention of Blindness, 1980, Brotherhood award NCCJ, 1981, Top Mgmt. award Jacksonville Sales and Mktg. Execs., 1981, Alumni Achievement award U. No. Iowa, Ann. Burton C. Bryan award, Pub. Service award Physicians Edn. Network, Freedom Found. Valley Forge Brotherhood of NCCJ award, Disting. Service award Fla. Soc. Ophthalmology, Women of Achievement award 1st Coast Bus. and Profl. Women's Club Jacksonville; named Eve of Decade, Fla. Women's Hall of Fame, to Fla. Women's Hall of Fame, hon. mem. 3d Armored Div., U.S. Army, day named in her honor Women's Club of Jacksonville and other orgns.; one of six women featured on History Week posters apptd. by Mayor Jacksonville; Paul Harris fellow Rotary Found. Mem. AAUW, Nat. Music Tchrs. Assn., Fla. Music Tchr. Assn., Music Educators Nat. Conf., Fla. Music Edn. Assn. (past bd. dirs.), Assn. Am. Colls. (bd. govs., exec. com.), Friday Musicale, Fla. Coll. Music Edn. Assn. (past pres., v.p.), Delius Assn. of Fla., Fla. Council of 100, Nat. Assn. Schs. Music (past chmn. region 7), Ind. Colls. and Univs. of Fla. (chmn.), Jacksonville C. of C. (mem. com. of 100), Jacksonville Women's Network Internat. Council Fine Arts Deans (past chmn.), Jacksonville Women's Network Inner Wheel (internat.), Nat. Soc. Arts and Letters (adv. council), P.E.O., Green Key (hon.), Ret. Officers Assn. (hon. mem. Mayport chpt.), Alpha Xi Delta, Mu Phi Epsilon (Elizabeth Mathias award, judge internat. music edn. award), Alpha Psi Omega (hon.), Alpha Kappa Pi (hon.), Alpha Kappa Psi (hon.), Beta Gamma Sigma, Omicron Delta Kappa (hon.), Alpha Xi Delta (Woman of Distinction award). Clubs: St. John's Dinner (past pres.), Exchange (Golden Deeds award); River, Seminole. Home: 7304 Arrow Point Trail S Jacksonville FL 32211

KINNE, MARILYN GINGER, oil company executive; b. Evanston, Ill., July 15, 1949; d. Leonard George and Mary Rose (Blasius) Ginger. BS in Biochemistry, U. Wis., 1971; MBA in Mgmt. Sci., Lake Forest Coll., 1978. Chemist Stepan Chem., Chgo., 1971-72, Kraft Inc., Chgo., 1972-76; sales engr. Mobile Oil Corp., Chgo., 1976-83; sales mgr. Mobile Oil Corp., Chgo. and Cin., 1983-86; sales support mgr. Mobile Oil Corp., Chgo., 1986; co-owner, v.p. sales Clark County Oil Co., Springfield, Ohio, 1986—. Republican. Roman Catholic. Home: 9000 Symmes Knoll Ct Cincinnati OH 45140 Office: Clark County Oil Co 1660 S Yellow Springs St Springfield OH 45506

KINNERSLEY, SUSAN VIOLA, health care administrator, nurse; b. Columbus, Wis., May 23, 1951; d. Lester Otto and Lois Viola (Rath) Henning; children: Rebecca Sue, Kenneth Ryan. BS in Nursing, Olivet Nazarene Coll., Kankakee, Ill., 1973; MS, Govs. State U., Park Forest South, Ill., 1977. RN, Ill., Calif., Ind. Nurse Aide Columbus Community Hosp., Wis., 1967-69; nurse aide Riverside Hosp., Kankakee, 1971-73, RN, 1973; RN Palos Community Hosp., Ill., 1973-74; instr. St. Joseph Hosp. Sch. of Nursing, Joliet, Ill., 1974-76; project coordinator Our Lady of Mercy Hosp., Dyer, Ind., 1976-78, asst. dir. nursing, 1978-80, dir. of spl. services, 1980-81; dir. of nursing services Culver Union Hosp., Crawfordsville, Ind., 1981-84, dir. of patient services, 1984, asst. adminstr., 1984-86; dir. nursing, asst. adminstr. AMI-Visalia (Calif.) Community Hosp., 1986—. Adv. bd. Am. Med. Home Care, Crawfordsville, 1984-85, Ivy Tech Assoc. Degree Program, Lafayette, Ind., 1985-86. Mem. Calif. Soc. for Nursing Service Adminstrn., Sigma Theta Tau (Delta Omicron chpt.). Republican. Nazarene. Club: Quota. Avocations: softball, reading. Office: Visalia Community Hosp 1633 S Court St Visalia CA 93277

KINNEY, LISA FRANCES, state senator; b. Laramie, Wyo., Mar. 13, 1951; d. Irvin Wayne and Phyllis (Poe) K.; m. Rodney Philip Lang, Feb. 5, 1971; 1 child, Cambria Helen. BA, U. Wyo., 1973, JD, 1986; MLS, U. Oreg., 1975. Reference librarian U. Wyo. Sci. Library, Laramie, 1975-76; outreach dir. Albany County Library, Laramie, 1975-76, dir., 1977-83; mem. Wyo. State Senate, Laramie, 1985—. Author: (with Rodney Lang) Civil Rights of the Developmentally Disabled, 1986; (with Rodney Lang and Phyllis Kinney) Manual For Families with Emotionally Disturbed and Mentally Ill Realtives, 1988; contbr. articles to profl. jours; editor, compiler pub. relations directory for ALA, 1982. Bd. dirs. Big Bros./Big Sisters, Laramie, 1980-83. Recipient Beginning Young Profl. award Mt. Plains Library Assn., 1980; named Outstanding Wyo. Librarian Wyo. Library Assn., 1977, Outstanding Young Woman State of Wyo., 1980. Mem. ABA, Nat. Confs. of State Legislatures (various coms.), LWV, Am. Bus. Women's Assn., Laramie C. of C. Democrat. Club: Snowy Range Internat. Folk Dance (pres. 1980-87). Lodges: Zonta Internat., Gem City Lioness. Avocations: photography, dance, reading, travel, languages. Home: 603 Spring Creek Laramie WY 82070

KINNEY, MARJORIE SHARON, finance and marketing executive; b. Gary, Ind., Jan. 11, 1940; d. David H. and Florence C. Dunning; student El Camino Coll., 1957, 58; LHD (hon.), West Coast U., 1982, Coll. San Mateo, 1987-88; MBA, Pepperdine U., 1988; m. Daniel D. Kinney, Dec. 31, 1958 (div. 1973); children: Steven Daniel, Michael Alan, Gregory Lincoln, Bradford David; m. Bradley Thomas Jr., Nov. 9, 1985 (div. Apr. 1987). Ptnr., Kinney Advt. Inc., Inglewood, Calif., 1958-68; pres. Greeters of Am., 1967-69; chmn. Person to Person Inc., Cleve., 1969-72; pres. Kinney Mktg. Corp., Encino, Calif., 1972-80; sr. v.p. Beverly Hills (Calif.) Savs. & Loan Assn., 1980-84; chmn., pres. Kinney & Assocs., Laguna Niguel, Calif., 1985—; dir. Safeway Stores, Inc., Chubb/Pacific Indemnity Co.; lectr. Bd. dirs. ARC, 1976-81, United Way, 1979-81; trustee West Coast U.; adv. bd. U.S. Human Resources, Womens Legal Edn. Fund; briefing del. to Pentagon Fed. Res. Dept. and White House, 1986; pres. Santa Fe Rep. Women, 1987—. Presbyterian. Office: 81 Palm Beach Ct Laguna Niguel CA 92677

KINNEY, SUE SUMMERS, social services supervisor; b. Greensboro, N.C., July 17, 1947; d. Bart Hughes and Gladys (Biggs) Summers; m. Stratford Darnell Kinney Sr., Mar. 15, 1969; children: Suzette Danielle, Stratford Darnell Jr. Grad. secretarial, Croft Bus. Coll., 1966. Teletype operator Talon, Inc., Greensboro, 1966; typist I Guilford County Dept. Social Services, Greensboro, 1966-68, clk. II, 1968-69, eligibility specialist I, 1969-72, 74-77, eligibility supr. I, 1977-84, eligibility II, 1984—. Asst. girl scout leader Girl Scouts USA, Greensboro, 1977-78, girl scout leader, 1978-80; precinct chmn. Dem. Party, 1984-85. Mem. N.C. Social Services Assn. Democrat. Methodist. Office: Guilford County Dept Social Services PO Box 3388 Greensboro NC 27405

KINOSIAN, JANET MARIE, journalist; b. Los Angeles, June 20, 1957; d. Kasper John and Carol Grace (Boghosian) K. BA in Psychology, UCLA, 1980; MA in Psychology, Loyola Maramount, 1987. Intern Los Angeles Mag., 1980-81; staff writer Orange County Media Group, Costa Mesa, Calif., 1982-84; contbg. editor Orange Coast Mag., Costa Mesa, Calif., 1984—. Contbr. numerous articles to nat. mags. and newspapers; internationally syndicated by N.Am. Syndicate, Times of London, N.Y. Times Syndicate Sales Corp. Co-founder Campus Coalition for Peace, 1978, INternat. Women's Solidarity Coalition, 1979; mem. Nat. Orgn. Women, 1980-85, Alliance for Survival, 1978-81. Mem. Orange County Press Club, Pacific Coast Press Club, Hollywood Women's Press Club, Calif. Assn. Independent Writers, Am. Psychol. Assn. (assoc.), Pi Beta Phi. Democrat. Presbyterian. Home: 11692 Chenault St Apt 103 Los Angeles CA 90049 Office: Orange Coast Mag 254-D Fischer St Suite 8 Costa Mesa CA 92660

KINSLER, BRENDA KAYE, psychologist; b. Flemington, Fla., Feb. 24, 1954; d. Louis and Lucinda Lanette (Brown) K.; m. Sherman N. Adams III; 1 child, Edward Jamal. BS, Howard U., 1976; MA, Columbia U., 1979; EdM, Harvard U., 1980; postgrad., Vanderbilt U., 1986—. Sch. psychologist D.C. Pub. Sch. System, Washington, 1985—; cons. Progressive Life, Washington, 1986—; presenter various workshops, 1982-87. Contbg. author: Cognitive Education, 1986. Sec. ministries of social concerns First Bapt. Ch. of Capitol Hill, Nashville, 1982-84; adv. com. YWCA Domestic Violence Program-Children's Project, Nashville, 1983-84. Named one of Outstanding Young Women of Am., 1982, 84; NIMH fellow, 1982. Mem. Am. Psychol. Assn., Nat. Assn. Sch. Psychologists, Assn. for Play Therapy, Nat. Black Child Devel. Inst., D.C. Assn. of Sch. Psychologists (treas. 1987—), Nat. Assn. Female Execs., Phi Delta Kappa, Delta Sigma Theta. Democrat. Baptist. Home: 2101 New Hampshire Ave NW #512 Washington DC 20010 Office: Logan Cen Diagnostic and Placement Ctr 3d and G Sts NE Washington DC 20002

KINZEY, OUIDA BLACKERBY, retired mathematics educator, photographer, photojournalist; b. Leeds, Ala., Feb. 6, 1922; d. George W. and Kate (Spruiell) Blackerby; m. William Thomas Kinzey, Feb. 6, 1943. AB, Birmingham So. Coll., 1942, EdM, 1959; advanced profl. diploma, U. Ala., 1964. Tchr. math. Phillips High Sch., Birmingham, Ala., 1942-44, Humes High Sch., Memphis, 1944-45; chmn. math. dept. Woodlawn High Sch., Birmingham, 1945-69; assoc. prof. math. Birmingham So. Coll., 1969-84, prof. emeritus, 1984—, dir. vis. profs. program, 1971-75, also mem. alumni leadership bd.; cons., lectr., speaker and workshop dir. throughout S.E. region. Author: (audio-visual text) Creative Teaching Mathematically, 1973; author, photographer photographic essays; photographs exhibited one man shows including Birmingham So. Coll., 1984, Samford U., 1984, Med. Ctr. East, 1985. Grantee NSF, 1959, 61, 64, 71, Kellogg Found., 1978, Mellon Found., 1980, 81, 84, Title III, 1982; recipient Grand Nat. award NEA/Kodak, 1984; named an Outstanding Educator of Am., 1972. Mem. Ala. Assn. Coll. Tchrs. Math., Ala. Acad. Sci., United Daus. Confederacy, AAUW, Nat. Council Tchrs. Math., Math. Assn. Am., Ala. Edn. Assn., Ala. Poetry Soc. Ala. Writers' Conclave, Am. Math. Soc., Nat. League Am. PEN Women, Phi Beta Kappa, Kappa Delta Pi, Delta Kappa Gamma, Kappa Delta Epsilon, Kappa Mu Epsilon, Theta Sigma Lambda, Delta Phi Alpha, Alpha Lambda Delta. Club: Speech Arts (pres., v.p., sec., treas.). Democrat. Methodist. Avocations: photography, collecting rocks, Indian artifacts and antiques. Home: 1413 Swallow Ln Birmingham AL 35213

KINZIE, JEANNIE JONES, radiation oncologist; b. Great Falls, Mont., Mar. 14, 1940; d. James Wayne and Lillian Alice (Young) Jones; m. Joseph Lee Kinzie, Mar. 26, 1965 (div. Sept. 1982); 1 child, Daniel Joseph. Student, Oreg. State U., 1960; BS, Mont. State U., 1961; MD, Washington U., St. Louis, 1965. Diplomate Am. Bd. Radiology. Intern. in surgery U. N.C., Chapel Hill, 1965-66; resident in therapeutic radiology Washington U., St. Louis, 1968-71, instr. in radiology, 1971-73; asst. prof. in radiology Med. Coll. of Wis., Milw., 1973-75; asst. prof. in radiology U. Chgo., 1975-78, assoc. prof. in radiology, 1978-80; assoc. prof. of radiation oncology Wayne State U., Detroit, 1980-85; prof. radiology U. Colo., Denver, 1985—; dir. radiation oncology U. Hosp., Denver, 1985—; bd. dirs. Rocky Mountain Oncology Soc.; cons. Denver Vets. Hosp., Denver Gen. Hosp., Rose Med. Ctr., FDA Ctr. for Devices and Radiologic Health; sci. adv. bd. Cancer League of Colo.; examiner Am. Bd. Radiology; cons. Food and Drug Adminstrn., 1987—; adv. physician Colo. Med. Found. 1988—. Assoc. editor Internat. Jour. Radiation Oncology Biology and Physics; contbr. articles to profl. jours.; chpts. to books. Bd. dirs. Denver unit Am. Cancer Soc., 1986—. NIH grantee, 1973-75; Am. Coll. Radiology fellow, 1984. Mem. Denver Med. Soc., Colo. Med. Soc., Colo. Radiol. Soc., Rocky Mountain Oncology Soc., Am. Coll Radiology, Soc. Head and Neck Surgeons, AMA, Am. Radium Soc., Am. Soc. Therapeutic Radiologists, Am. Cancer Soc. (bd. dirs. Denver unit). Am. Soc. Clin. Oncology. Republican. Lutheran. Home: PO Box 2585 Evergreen CO 80439 Office: Radiation Oncology Box A031 4200 E 9th Ave Denver CO 80262

KIPER, LYNN MARGARET, nurse; b. New Orleans, July 2, 1963; d. Thomas Joachim and Marilyn Viola (Green) K. BSN, Dillard U., 1985. Occupational therapist Lafon Nursing Home, New Orleans, 1981; nursing technician Mercy Hosp., New Orleans, 1984-85; RN Hotel Dieu Hosp., New Orleans, 1985—. Named one of Outstanding Young Women Am., 1984, 86, 87. Democrat. Roman Catholic. Home: 2928 Cherry St New Orleans LA 70118

KIRBY, DEBORAH MACDONALD, rehabilitation psychologist; b. Washington, May 19, 1948; d. Robert Angus and Margarett Mary (Harrison) MacDonald; B.A., George Washington U., 1970; M.Ed., Am. U., 1972; m. Stephen Edward Kirby, Sept. 6, 1980; 1 dau., Jessica Lynn. Psychiat. asst. Chestnut Lodge Psychiat. Hosp., Rockville, Md., 1969-70; research psychologist Dept. Army, 1970; clin. intern Am. U. Counseling Center, 1972; clin. psychologist Bay County Guidance Clinic, Panama City, Fla., 1972-73; rehab. counselor State of Fla., Panama City, 1974; rehab. psychologist Woodrow Wilson Rehab. Center, Fisherville, Va., 1975-84; dir. Shenandoah Counseling Assos., 1981-88; pres. Shenandoah Ctr. for Mental Health, P.C.; mem. med. staff King's Daus. Hosp., Staunton, Va., 1982—. Mem. Am. Psychol. Assn., Va. Assn. Clin. Counselors, Va. Psychol. Assn., Va. Counselors Assn., Va. Mental Health Counselors Assn., Kappa Alpha Theta. Democrat. Club: Charlottesville-Albemarle Kennel (past dir.). Author papers in field. Office: Shenandoah Ctr for Mental Health PC PO Box 696 Stanton VA 24401

KIRBY, DIANA CATHERINE, nurse, army officer; b. Guttenberg, Iowa, Jan. 22, 1951; d. Albert Edward and Bernadette Lucretia (Berns) Cherne; BS in Nursing, U. Iowa, 1973; MS in Edn., U. So. Calif., 1977; MS in Nursing, U. Md., 1987; lic. pilot; m. Fred W. Kirby, Nov. 24, 1981. Mem. nursing staff Mercy Med. Ctr., Dubuque, Iowa, 1973-74; commd. 1st lt. Nurse Corps, U.S. Army, 1974, advanced through grades to maj., 1984; service in W. Ger.; community health nurse William Beaumont Army Med. Center, 1978-80, Ft. Leonard Wood, Mo., 1980-82, Ft. Meade, Md., 1987; chief community nursing Dewitt Army Community Hosp., Ft. Belvoir, Va., 1987—. Mem. Am. Nurses Assn., Iowa Nurses Assn., Nat. League Nursing, Am. Nurses Found., Assn. Mil. Surgeons U.S., Nat. Trust for Hist. Preservation, Am. Philatelic Soc., Sigma Theta Tau. Roman Catholic. Address: 6833 Silver Ann Dr Lorton VA 22079

KIRBY, JOYCE JENSEN, nursing administrator, consultant; b. Seneca Falls, N.Y., Sept. 21, 1939; d. Harold Lund and Elsie Risa (Larsen) Jensen; m. Peter G. Kirby, June 16, 1962; children: Heather A., Heidi P., Peter L. Diploma in Nursing, Genessee Hosp., Rochester, N.Y., 1960; BS in Nursing, U. South Fla., 1976, MS, 1977. Cert. nurse. Dir. edn. Meml. Hosp., Cumberland, Md., 1965-67; asst. dir. nursing B.W. Martin Meml. Hosp., Mt. Vernon, Ohio, 1970; asst. adminstr. Port Allegheny (Pa.) Community Hosp., 1972-74; assoc. exec. dir. Humana Hosp. Pasco div. Humana Co., Dade City, Fla., 1976-77, Humana Hosp. Brandon (Fla.) div. Humana Co., 1977-82; v.p. Voluntary Hosps. Am. Mgmt. Services, Tampa, Fla., 1982-83; assoc. exec. dir. Human Women's Hosp., San Antonio, 1983-85; dir. patient services H. Lee Moffitt Cancer Ctr. and Research Inst., Tampa, Fla., 1985-86; asst. dir. nursing ops. Citrus Meml. Hosp., Inverness, Fla., 1987—; cons. Delta Consulting, San Antonio, 1983—; instr. emergency med. services local fire dept., Port Allegheny, 1971-73. Chairperson blood pressure screening program McKean County (Pa.) chpt. Am. Heart Assn., 1971-73, also bd. dirs. Mem. Oncology Nurses Assn. (charter, v.p. greater Tampa chpt. 1985-87), U. South Fla. Alumnae Assn. (charter, outstanding achievement in nursing award 1983), Career Woman's Assn., Sigma Theta Tau (charter, pres. Tampa chpt. 1981-83), Phi Kappa Phi. Republican. Presbyterian. Home: 633 Gillette Ave Temple Terrace FL 33617 Office: Citrus Meml Hosp 502 W Highland Blvd Inverness FL 32652

KIRBY, JULIA NUCKOLLS, health services administrator; b. Knoxville, Tenn., July 18, 1948; d. William Knox and Dorothy Wilson (Dobbs) Nuckolls; m. William Mac Gallaher, Aug. 16, 1966 (div. 1981); m. Richard Dale Kirby, Jan. 23, 1982. BA, David Lipscomb Coll., 1971; MEd, Memphis State U., 1974. Sec. Vanderbilt U., Nashville, 1967-71; resource tchr. Waycross (Ga.) Pub. Schs., 1971-72; tchr., counselor Western Mental Health Inst., Bolivar, Tenn., 1972-74, dir. work therapy, 1974-75, dir. adjunctive therapy, 1975-79; asst. residential supt. N.T. Winston Devel. Ctr., Bolivar, 1979-83; exec. dir. Reach Unltd., Inc., Houston, 1983—; cons. to non-profit orgns., Harris County, Tex., 1983—; speaker on handicapped issues, Tex., 1983—. Served with USNR, 1979-88. Mem. Assn. for Retarded Citizens (mem. Exec. Assn., Profl. of Yr. 1986), Nat. Rehab. Assn., Am. Assn. for Mental Disabilities, Nat. Assn. Female Execs., Assn. for Severely Handicapped. Republican. Baptist. Home: 15022 Mulberry Meadows Dr Houston TX 77084 Office: Reach Unlimited Inc 12777 Jones Rd #290 Houston TX 77070

KIRBY, MARY WEEKS, educator, reading specialist; b. Cheverly, Md., Nov. 23, 1947; d. Isaac Ralph and Dorothea (Huppert) Weeks; m. William Charlie Kirby, Feb. 14, 1976; children: Joie, Fatimah, Tariq. Bachelor in Music Edn., James Madison U., 1969; MEd, Va. Commonwealth U., 1976; cert. Writers' Digest Sch., 1988. Cert. tchr. of music, reading and elem., Va. Music instr. Charles City County Schs., Providence Forge, Va., 1969-70, Hanover Learning Ctr., Va., 1970-72; sales cons. Boykins's Music Shop, Richmond, Va., 1972-74; elem. tchr. New Kent Pub. Schs., Va., 1974—, writing cons., 1980—; owner/operator Wacky Timepieces; presentor ednl. and reading workshops, 1980-82. Sponsor Young Authors' Workshop, New Kent, 1985—; co-chmn., presentor Parents Anonymous of Va., 1984—; trustee Islamic Ctr. of Va., 1985—, sec., 1981-85; active Boy Scouts Am., Girl Scouts U.S. Mem. New Kent Edn. Assn. (officer 1977-81), Va. Edn. Assn., NEA, Richmond Area Reading Council (sec. 1982-83), Sigma Alpha Iota (life). Avocations: needlework, reading, swimming. Home: 1309 Bull Run Dr Richmond VA 23231 Office: New Kent Pub Schs Quinton VA 23141

KIRBY, PATRICIA, instructional designer, writer; b. Washington, July 21, 1939; d. Edward Montague and Marjorie (Arnold) K. BA, Trinity Coll., Washington, 1961; MA, Catholic U., Washington, 1964, EdD, 1982. Research asst. Howard U., 1965-66, instr., 1966-68, 71-72, 75-76; instr. Washington Internat. Coll., 1974-81, Washington Tech. Inst., 1972-73; instructional designer Forest Service, USDA, Washington, 1977-82; instr. Trinity Coll., 1971-72, 83—; instructional designer, newsletter co-editor Communications Technol. Applications, Inc., McLean, Va., 1986—; instr. Kingsborough Community Coll., 1968-70; ind. translator, 1962—. Author: (monograph) cognitive, learning and transfer skill acquisition, 1979. Guide Camp Fire Girls, Washington, 1962-63; organizer Spanish speaking social and lang. tng. program, Sacred Heart Ch., 1964-65. Grantee Eastman Kodak, 1984; named one of U.S. learning style experts, 1981. Mem. Nat. Soc. Performance Instrn. (Potomac chpt. program chmn.), Washington Apple Computer Users Group (co-chmn. ednl. spl. interest group), Nat. Soc. Female Execs., Christian Sociologists (co-founder), Am. Life League, Cath. League, Amnesty Internat., Nat. Humane Edn. Soc. Republican. Roman Catholic. Home: PO Box 90227 Washington DC 20090-0227

KIRCHEN, ELAINE DOYLE, corporate executive; b. Utica, Dec. 1, 1942; d. Harold Bingham and Alice (Cunningham) Doyle. BA, Russell Sage Coll., 1964; MA, U. Pa., 1965; MBA, Wharton Sch., 1966. With Morgan Guaranty Trust Co., N.Y.C., 1966-68, asst. v.p., 1968-70, v.p., 1972-78; v.p. Handy Assocs., N.Y.C., 1978-80, Boyden Assocs., N.Y.C., 1980-82, William H. Willis Inc., N.Y.C., 1982—. Mem. YWCA. Mem. Acad. Women Achievers, Avdt. Women N.Y. Home: 400 E 58th St New York NY 10022 Office: William H Willis Inc 445 Park Ave New York NY 10022

KIRK, CARMEN ZETLER, data processing executive; b. Altoona, Pa., May 22, 1941; d. Paul Alan and Mary Evelyn (Pearce) Zetler. BA, Pa. State U., 1959-63; MBA, St. Mary's Coll. Calif., 1977. Cert. in data processing. Pub. sch. tchr. State Ga., 1965-66; systems analyst U.S. Govt. Dept. Army, Oakland, Calif., 1967-70; programmer analyst Contra Costa County, Martinez, Calif., 1970-76; applications mgr. Stanford (Calif.) U., 1976-79; owner Zetler Assocs., Palo Alto, Calif., 1979—; cons. State Calif., Sacramento, 1985—. Author: (tech. manuals) Comparex, 1982-83. Vol. Stanford Med. Ctr. Aux., 1985—. Office: Zetler Assocs PO Box 50395 Palo Alto CA 94303

KIRK, COLLEEN JEAN, conductor, educator; b. Champaign, Ill., Sept. 7, 1918; d. Bonum Lee and Anna Catherine (Hoffert) K. B.S. with high honors, U. Ill., 1940, M.S., 1945; Ed.D., Columbia U., 1953. Tchr. music public schs. Danvers, Ill., 1940-44, Watseka, Ill., 1944-45; instr. Univ. High

Sch., Urbana, Ill., 1945-49; asst. prof. edn. and music U. Ill., 1949-58, asso. prof., 1958-64, prof., 1964-70; prof. Fla. State U., Tallahassee, 1970—; condr. choral union Fla. State U., 1970—; choral clinician, condr., adjudicator. Dir. music Wesley United Meth. Ch., Urbana, 1947-70; dir. jr. chorus, Ill. Summer Youth Music, Urbana, 1963-71; co-dir. Fla. Honors Choral Ensemble, Tallahassee, 1980-81; dir. Fla. Jr. High Sch. Choral Ensemble, Tallahassee, 1983; author: (with others) Modern Methods in Elementary Education, 1959; (with Harold Decker) Choral Conducting: Focus on Communication, 1988; contbr. numerous articles to Choral Jour. Mem. Am. Choral Dirs. Assn. (pres. So. div. 1971-75, nat. pres. 1981-83), Am. Choral Found., Inc., Music Educators Nat. Conf., Assn. Profl. Vocal Ensembles, Fla. Music Educators Assn., Internat. Fedn. Choral Music, AAUP, Coll. Music Soc., Fla. Vocal Assn., Fla. Coll. Music Educators Assn., Sonneck Soc., Pi Kappa Lambda, Kappa Delta Pi, Sigma Alpha Iota. Office: Fla State U Sch Music Tallahassee FL 32306

KIRK, JUDY OBERLINK, writer, educator; b. Grand Rapids, Mich., May 24, 1941; d. Dwight Raymond and Doris Jane (Green) Oberlink; m. James Philip Kirk Jr., Dec. 27, 1961; children: David, Melinda. Student, Beloit Coll., 1959-61; BA, U. Mo., Kansas City, 1964, MS in English Lit., 1986. Tchr. Michigan City (Ind.) Sch. Dist., 1964-65; freelance writer 1972-78; with pub. relations dept. The Learning Exchange, Kansas City, 1978-79; columnist Kansas City Star & Times, 1979—; instr. English Johnson County Community Coll., Shawnee Mission, Kans., 1984—. Contbr: poetry to Number One Mag., 1985, The Mind's Eye, 1987; contbr. articles to Christian Science Monitor, Kansas City Star Sunday Magazine, others. Republican. Epscopalian. Home: 376 W Lakeshore Lake Quivira KS 66106 Office: Johnson County Community Coll Communications Dept 12345 College Blvd Shawnee Mission KS 66210

KIRK, MARILYN KAY FOSTER, fund-raising executive; b. Great Bend, Kans., Apr. 29, 1946; d. Harry Charles and Helen Kathryn (Radenberg) F. B.A., Kans. Wesleyan U., 1968; M.Ed., U. Okla., 1970; postgrad. U. Kans., 1982-84. Asst. dean of students Westmar Coll., LeMars, Iowa, 1970-72, dean of students, 1972-77; assoc. dir. devel. Carroll Coll., Waukesha, Wis., 1977-78; dir. devel. Kans. Wesleyan U., Salina, 1978-79; corp. dir. devel. Kans. State Hist. Soc., Topeka, 1979-84; dir. devel. Garrett-Evang. Theol. Sem., Evanston, Ill., 1984-87; asst. chancellor univ. relations U. Wis. Parkside, Kenosha, 1987—; adviser in higher edn. Congressman Berkley Bedell of Iowa, 1976-77; cons. fund raising, 1980—. Mem. mktg. team Kaw Valley council Girl Scouts U.S.A., 1982-84; bd. dirs. Topeka YWCA, 1982-84, Kans. Com. for Humanities, Topeka, 1983-84, Samaritan Counseling Ctr., Evanston, Ill., 1987—, Kenosha Found. Inc., 1987—; bd. mgrs. Kans. Expocentre, Topeka, 1983-84. Named Outstanding Young Alumna, Kans. Wesleyan U., 1977. Mem. Pub. Relations Soc. Topeka (dir. 1983-84), Nat. Assn. Fund Raising Execs., Topeka Fund Raisers, Nat. Assn. Women Deans, Adminstrs. and Counselors (coll. sect. dir. 1977-82). Democrat. Presbyterian. Club: PEO (treas. 1982-84, v.p. 1984—Topeka). Office: Wood Rd Box 2000 Kenosha WI 53141

KIRK, MARTHA MATHENY, security executive; b. Alexandria, La., Jan. 7, 1947; d. James Jackson Matheny and Gloria Jane (Handley) Holley; m. Guy Douglas Harkness, Nov. 7, 1964 (div. 1978); children: Melissa Lea, Alisa Christine, Amy Louise; m. Ben T. Kirk, Oct. 17, 1980 (div. 1982); 1 child, Christopher Handley Kirk. BS in Criminal Justice, Southeastern U., 1978. Supr. Reynolds Inst., Ponchtoula, La., 1979-82; security mgr. D.H. Holmes, Hammond, Ind., 1982-83; regional security mgr. D.H. Holmes, Baton Rouge, 1983—. Mem. La. Assn. Credit Card Investigators, La. Forgery Investigators, Exec. Female, Greater Baton Rouge C. of C. Republican. Episcopalian. Home: 16737 Ticonderoga Ave Baton Rouge LA 70817 Office: DH Holmes Ltd 7173 Florida Blvd Baton Rouge LA 70806

KIRK, SUSAN SHAW, lawyer; b. San Jose, Calif., Nov. 4, 1940; d. Wallace Garland and Dorothy (Kirk) Shaw; children—Jenifer Kirk Swaringen, Michael Penton Swaringen. A.B. in Communications and Pub. Policy, U. Calif.-Berkeley, 1962; postgrad. Stanford U., 1979, U. Mich., 1981; J.D., U. Santa Clara, 1981. Bar: Mich. 1981. Research asst. Council for Social Planning, Oakland, Calif., 1963; fellow Coro Found. Internship in Pub. Affairs, 1963; office mgr. AFL-CIO Com. on Polit. Edn., Oakland, 1963-64; legal asst. Moran, Lawlor & Rhea, Oakland, 1964-65; spl. asst. to dean of student affairs, planner/analyst Stanford U., 1965-79; extern to William A. Ingram, U.S. Dist. Ct., San Francisco, 1979; law clk. Ruffo, Ferrari & McNeil, San Jose, 1980; atty. Consumers Power Co., Jackson, Mich., 1981—, gen. counsel CMS Capital Corp (subs. of CMS Enterprises and affiliate of Consumers Power Co.), 1987—. Mem. ABA, State Bar Mich., Am. Arbitration Assn. (panel of arbitrators). Episcopalian. Home: 715 W Michigan Ave Jackson MI 49201 Office: Consumers Power Co 212 W Michigan Ave Jackson MI 49201

KIRK, SUSANNE SMITH, editor; b. Washington; d. Harold Clair and Theodora (Varner) Smith; m. Donald Kirk, May 31, 1965 (div. 1985). Student Kaiserin-Theophanu Sch., Cologne, W.Ger., 1958; A.B., Smith Coll., 1963; cert. Goethe Inst., Berlin, 1963; M.S., Columbia U., 1965. Reporter, South China Morning Post, Hong Kong, 1965-67; corr. German News Agy., Saigon, Vietnam, 1968-69; editor Charles Tuttle Pubs., Tokyo, 1972-74; freelance journalist, 1965-74; asst. editor Charles Scribner's Sons (now div. MacMillan Pub.), N.Y.C., 1975, editor, 1976-80, asst. v.p., 1977—, fgn. rights dir., 1978-82, sr. editor, 1980-85, exec. editor, pub., 1985—. Speaker various writers' confs. Contbr. articles to newspapers. Mem. Women's Nat. Book Assn. Clubs: Snarks Ltd. (v.p. 1983-84, pres. 1985-86), Smith Coll. (N.Y.C.). Home: 33 E End Ave New York NY 10028 Office: Charles Scribner's Sons 866 3d Ave New York NY 10022

KIRKHART, KAREN EILEEN, educator; b. Pomona, Calif., Jan. 6, 1948; d. Harry Burdell and Mabel Eileen (Reinhardt) K.; BA, Pomona Coll., 1970; MSW, U. Mich., 1972, PhD, 1979; m. Nick L. Smith, July 21, 1984. Community service worker Community Action Center, Adrian, Mich., 1970-71; therapist Family Service Agy. of Genessee County, Flint, Mich., 1971; therapist Family and Sch. Consultation Project, Ann Arbor, Mich., 1971-72; teaching asst. Psychology Dept., Sch. Social Work, U. Mich., 1974-77; asso. dir. evaluation curriculum devel. project Inst. Labor and Indsl. Relations, U. Mich.-Wayne State U., 1976-78; asst. prof. ednl. psychology U. Tex., Austin, 1979-85; assoc. prof. social work Syracuse U., 1986—; mem. epidemiologic and services research com. NIMH, 1981-84; research product evaluator NSF, 1980-85. Mem. adv. bd. Office of Research and Evaluation, Austin (Tex.) Ind. Sch. Dist., 1980-84. Mem. Am. Psychol. Assn. (chmn. sect. on evaluation div. 18 1986-88), Assn. for Advancement of Behavior Therapy, Evaluation Network (pres. 1981), Evaluation Research Soc. (council 1983-85), Am. Evaluation Assn. (bd. dirs. 1986), Eastern Evaluation Research Soc., Nat. Council Community Mental Health Centers, Am. Ednl. Research Assn., Soc. Psychol. Study of Social Issues, Nat. Orgn. Women. Home: 329 Germania Ave Syracuse NY 13219-1107 Office: Syracuse U Sch Social Work Brockway Hall Syracuse NY 13244-6350

KIRKLAND, BERTHA THERESA (MRS. THORNTON CROWNS KIRKLAND, JR.), engineer; b. San Francisco, May 16, 1916; d. Lawrence and Theresa (Kanzler) Schmelzer; m. Thornton Crowns Kirkland, Jr., Dec. 27, 1937 (dec. July 1971); children: Kathryn Elizabeth, Francis Charles. Supr. hosp. ops. Am. Potash & Chem. Corp., Trona, Calif., 1953-54; office mgr., T.C. Kirkland, elec. contractor, 1954-56; sec.-treas., bd. dirs. T.C. Kirkland, Inc., San Bernardino, Calif., 1958-74; design-install estimator Add-M Electric, Inc., 1972-82, v.p., 1974-82; estimator, engr. Corona Indsl. Electric, Inc. (Calif.), 1982-83; asst. project engr. Fischbach and Moore, Inc., Los Angeles, 1984—. Episcopalian. Club: Arrowhead Country (San Bernardino). Home: 526 E Sonora St San Bernardino CA 92404 Office: Fischbach and Moore Inc 4690 Worth St Los Angeles CA 90063

KIRKLAND, CAROLYN SUE, insurance agency owner; b. Atmore, Ala., Jan. 27, 1949; d. Charles James Cayson and Burnette (White) Prim; m. Jerry Titus Kirkland, June 25, 1966 (div. Oct. 1985); children: Jerry Titus Jr., Janet Lynne. AA in Bus., Pensacola Jr. Coll., 1980; BS in Mktg., U. West Fla., 1982. Agt., owner Sue Kirkland Agy. State Farm Ins. Co., Pensacola, Fla., 1983—. Bd. dirs. Jr. Achievement, 1987-90. Mem. Am. Mktg. Assn. (pres.-elect 1987—, sec. 1985-86, v.p. membership com. 1986-87, N.W. Fla. chpt.), Nat. Assn. Female Execs. Democrat. Episcopalian. Lodge: Order of Eastern Star, Sertoma (sgt. at arms 1987—). Office: 196 E Nine Mile Rd #A Pensacola FL 32514

KIRKLAND, PATTI JEAN BREAZEALE, utilities executive; b. Augsburg, Federal Republic of Germany, June 23, 1956; (parents Am. citizens); d. Horace Eugene and Johnnie Ruth (Yancey) Breazeale; m. Wilburn Earl Kirkland, Jan. 22, 1975; 1 child, Michael Wilburn. BS in Electronic Engring. Tech., U. So. Miss., 1980, postgrad., 1984—. Systems control specialist Miss. Power Co., Gulfport, 1980-82, teleprocessing analyst, 1982-86, supr. teleprocessing, 1986—. Mem. Polit. Action Com., 1986-87. Mem. Assn. Data Communications Users, Nat. Mgmt. Assn., IEEE Computer Soc. Republican. Roman Catholic. Office: Miss Power Co 2992 W Beach Blvd Gulfport MS 39501

KIRKMAN, BETH ALLEN, software executive; b. Key West, Fla., Sept. 4, 1958; d. George Millard and Frances (Jouett) Allen; m. L. Brent McCuiston, May 14, 1982 (div. 1983); m. Kevin William Kirkman, Dec. 20, 1986; 1 child, Kyle Allen. BFA, Tex. Christian U., 1981. Assoc. systems engr. Datapoint Corp., Dallas, 1981-82; mgr. info. services Tex. Christian U., Ft. Worth, 1982-85; sr. acct. mgr. Info. Assocs., Ft. Worth, 1985—; cons. in field. Vol. Ft. Worth Spl. Olympics, 1982-84. Mem. Nat. Assn. Student Fin. Aid Adminstrs., Tex. Assn. Student Fin. Aid Adminstrs., Southwestern Assn. Student Fin. Aid Adminstrs., Am. Assn. Coll Registrar's Admissions Officers, Kappa Delta Alumni. Mem. Disciples of Christ Ch. Home: 9050 Markville St Apt 332 Dallas TX 75243 Office: Info Assocs 840 E Central Pkwy Suite 150 Plano TX 75074

KIRKPATRICK, ANNE SAUNDERS, systems analyst; b. Birmingham, Mich., July 4, 1938; d. Stanley Rathbun and Esther (Casteel) Saunders; m. Robert Armstrong Kirkpatrick, Oct. 5, 1963; children: Elizabeth, Martha, Robert, Sarah. Student, Wellesley Coll., 1956-57, Laval U., Quebec City, Can., 1958, U. Ariz., 1958-59; BA in Philosophy, U. Mich., 1961. Systems engr. IBM, Chgo., 1962-64; systems analyst Commonwealth Edison Co., Chgo., 1981—. Treas. Taproot Reps., DuPage County, Ill., 1977-80; pres. Hinsdale (Ill.) Women's Rep. Club, 1978-81. Club: Wellesley of Chgo. (bd. dirs. 1972-73). Home: 524 N Lincoln Hinsdale IL 60521 Office: Commonwealth Edison Co 72 W Adams Room 1122 Chicago IL 60603

KIRKPATRICK, DIANE MARIE, personnel manager; b. N.Y.C., Dec. 11, 1950; d. Henry and Elinor (Deschler) Sanchez; m. J. Bradley Kirkpatrick, Jan. 23, 1977; children: Scott, Mary. BA in Psychology (honors) and Spanish, Washington Coll., Chestertown, Md., 1972. Pub. relations dir. Maryvale Prep. Sch., Brooklandville, Md., 1972-75; restaurant cons. Colomeco Enterprises, Balt., 1975-80; mgr. restaurant John Eager Howard Room and 13th Fl Lounge in Belvedere Hotel, Balt., 1980-83; interior sales designer The Bombay Co., Balt., 1983-85; sr. personnel supr. Kelly Services, Inc., DeLand, Fla., 1985—. Mem. St. Barnabas Sch. PTO, DeLand, 1985—, McInnis Elem. PTA, DeLand, 1986—, GIFTS Parent of Gifted Children, DeLand, 1986—, bus. edn. adv. com. Deland Sr. High Sch., 1987-88. Mem. DeLand C. of C., Nat. Assn. Female Execs., Zeta Tau Alpha (sec., historian 1985—). Republican. Presbyterian. Home: 1310 Good Earth Dr PO Box 1608 DeLeon Springs FL 32028

KIRKPATRICK, ELEANOR BLAKE, civic worker; b. Mangum, Okla., Mar. 10, 1909; d. Mack Barkley and Kathryn (Talbott) Blake; m. John Elson Kirkpatrick, June 20, 1932; 1 child, Joan Elson. B.A. in French, Smith Coll., 1931; D.Humanities (hon.), Oklahoma City U., 1968. Ptnr. Kirkpatrick Oil Co., Oklahoma City, Kirkpatrick Oil & Gas, Oklahoma City. Bd. dirs. Kirkpatrick Ctr., Oklahoma City; treas. Kirkpatrick Found., Oklahoma City. Named to Okla. Hall of Fame, Okla. Heritage Assn., Oklahoma City, 1975; recipient Evergreen Disting. Service award Nat. Assn. Mature People, Okla., 1982, Bd. Trustees award Omniplex Sci. Mus., Oklahoma City, 1984; co-founder, hon. pres. Alliance Française, Oklahoma City; bd. mem. Oklahoma Art Ctr. Mem. Oklahoma City U. Opera (bd. dirs.), Soc. and Library Soc. (hon.), Oklahoma City U. Library Soc. (bd. dirs.). Avocation: backgammon. Office: Kirkpatrick Oil Co 1300 N Broadway Dr Oklahoma City OK 73103

KIRKPATRICK, JEAN, sociologist; b. Quakertown, Pa., Mar. 2, 1923; d. Peter and Helen (Roberta) Spangler Romig. B.A., Moravian Coll., 1950; M.A., Lehigh U., 1954, postgrad., 1965-67; Ph.D., U. Pa., 1971. Dir. programming Ednl. Computer Corp., King of Prussia, Pa., 1967-73; founder, exec. dir. Women for Sobriety, Inc., Quakertown, Pa., 1974—; lectr., cons. women and alcoholism. Recipient Humanitarian award Moravian Coll., Bethlehem, Pa., 1980; named Woman of Yr. Bus. and Profl. Women's Assn., Quakertown, 1982. Mem. Internat. Commn. on Alcoholism. Republican. Lutheran. Author: Turnabout: Help for Life, 1978; A Fresh Start, 1981; Reflections, 1980; Goodbye Hangovers; Hello Life, 1986.

KIRKPATRICK, JEANE DUANE JORDAN, political scientist, government official; b. Duncan, Okla., Nov. 19, 1926; d. Welcher F. and Leona (Kile) Jordan; m. Evron M. Kirkpatrick, Feb. 20, 1955; children: Douglas Jordan, John Evron, Stuart Alan. A.A., Stephens Coll., 1946; A.B., Barnard Coll., 1948; M.A., Columbia U., 1950, Ph.D., 1968; postgrad. (French govt. fellow), U. Paris Inst. de Sci. Politique, 1952-53; L.H.D. (hon.), Mt. Vernon Coll., 1978, Georgetown U., 1981, U. Pitts., 1981, U. West Fla., 1981, U. Charleston, 1982; L.H.D. hon., St. Anselm's, 1982, Hebrew U., 1982, Betheny Coll., 1983, Colo. Sch. Mines, 1983, St. John's U., 1983; Loyola Coll., 1985; Hebrew Union Coll., 1985; Universidad Francisco Marroquin, Guatemala, 1985; Coll. of William and Mary, 1986. Research analyst Dept. State, 1951-53; research asso. George Washington U., 1954-56, Fund for the Rep., 1956-58; asst. prof. polit. sci. Trinity Coll., 1962-67; assoc. prof. polit. sci. Georgetown U., Washington, 1967-73; prof. Georgetown U., 1973—; Leavey prof. in founds. Am. freedom, 1978—; sr. fellow Am. Enterprise Inst. for Pub. Policy Research, 1977—; mem. cabinet U.S. permanent rep. to UN, 1981-85; co-chmn. task force presdl. election process 20th Century Fund; cons. Am. Council Learned Socs., Dept. State, HEW, Dept. Def., intermittently 1955-72; vice chmn. com. on v.p. selection Democratic Nat. Com., 1972-74, mem. nat. commn. party structure and presdl. nomination, 1975; mem. credentials com. Dem. Nat. Conv., 1976; mem. internat. research council Center for Strategic and Internat. Studies. Author: Foreign Students in the United States: A National Survey, 1966, Mass Behavior in Battle and Captivity, 1968, Leader and Vanguard in Mass Society: The Peronist Movement in Argentina, 1971, Political Woman, 1974, The Presidential Elite, 1976, Dismantling the Parties: Reflections on Party Reform and Party Decomposition, 1978, The Reagan Phenomenon, 1983, Dictatorships and Doublestandards, 1982;Legitimacy and Force (2 vols.), 1988. Editor, contbr.: Elections USA, 1956, Strategy of Deception, 1963, the New Class, 1978, The New American Political System, 1978; Contbr.: articles to Publius; others. Trustee Helen Dwight Reid Ednl. Found., 1972—; trustee Robert A. Taft Inst. Govt., 1978—; mem. bd. curators Stephens Coll. Recipient Disting. Alumna award Stephens Coll., 1978, B'nai B'rith Humanitarian award, 1982, award of the Commonwealth Fund, 1983, Gold medal VFW, 1984, French Prix Politique, 1984, Dept. Defense Disting. Pub. Service medal, 1985, Spl. award from the Mayor N.Y.C., 1985, Presdl. medal of Freedom, 1985, others; Earhart fellow, 1956-57. Mem. Internat. Polit. Sci. Assn. (exec. council), Am. Polit. Sci. Assn., So. Polit. Sci. Assn. Office: Am Enterprise Inst 1150 17th St NW Washington DC 20036

KIRKPATRICK, LINDY MOORSHEAD, health science facility administrator; b. Phila., June 3, 1956; d. Arthur Albert and Nancy (Fox) Moorshead; m. David Eccleston Kirkpatrick, Aug. 28, 1982. BS, U. Del., 1978; MS, Va. Poly. Inst. and State U., 1982; MBA, Old Dominion U., 1986. Clin. dietitian Norfolk (Va.) Gen. Hosp./ARA Foodservices, 1978-79, adminstrv. dietitian, 1979-81; food service dir. Surburban Hosp., Bethesda, Md., 1981-82; supervising mgr. Norfolk Pub. Schs., 1982-83; food service dir. Westminster Canterbury, Virginia Beach, Va., 1983; with workshop faculty Hosp. Corp. Am., Nashville, 1983-86, food service cons., 1983-86; food service dir. Peninsula Hosp. div. Hosp. Corp. Am., Hampton, Va., 1983-86; fin. ops. analyst Ea. Va. Med. Authority, Norfolk, 1986—; cons. dietitian Community Mental Health Ctr., Norfolk, 1978-81, Ghent Psychol. Practice, Norfolk, 1979-81, Coliseum Park Nursing Home, Hampton, 1983-86; instr. Johnson and Wales Coll., Norfolk, 1982—. Mem. Am. Dietetic Assn., Va. Dietetic Assn., Tidewater Nutrition Council (treas. 1982-84), Assn. Hosp. Foodservice Adminstrs. (sec. 1981-82). Republican. Episcopalian. Clubs: Virginia Beach Waterski, Virginia Beach Racquet, Tidewater Windsurfing (Virginia Beach). Home: 4637 Bradston Rd Virginia Beach VA 23455 Office: Ea Va Med Authority PO Box 1980 Norfolk VA 23501

KIRKPATRICK, NANCY FOSTER, museum administrator; b. Aurora, Ill., Aug. 21, 1933; d. Richard Joseph and Helen Irene (McGall) Foster; m. David Allen Kirkpatrick, Nov. 18, 1967 (dec. May 1977). Student Am. U., George Washington U. Budget analyst Smithsonian Instn., Washington, 1962-73, budget officer, 1973-77, exec. officer Hirshhorn Mus. and Sculpture Garden, 1977—. Mem. Am. Assn. Mus. Democrat. Presbyterian. Office: Smithsonian Instn Hirshhorn Mus & Sculpture Garden 8th at Independence Ave Washington DC 20560

KIRKPATRICK, SHARON MINTON, nurse, educator; b. Independence, Mo., Aug. 31, 1943; d. Charles Russell and Minnetta (Brotherton) Minton; m. John P. Kirkpatrick; children: John Brent, Kraig Russell. Grad. in nursing, Ind. Sanitarium and Hosp., Independence, 1965; AA, Graceland Coll., Lamoni, Iowa, 1965; BS, Calif. State U., Sacramento, 1976; M in Nursing, U. Kans., 1981, PhD in Nursing, 1988. RN, Mo., Kans., Iowa. Office coordinator Family Practice Physicians, Cupertino, Calif., 1965-67; head nurse Truman Med. Ctr. East, Kansas City, Mo., 1977-79; tchng. asst. U. Kans. Med. Ctr., Kansas City, 1980; asst. nursing prof. Graceland Coll., Lamoni, 1980-86, div. nursing chairperson, 1986—; proj. dir. Pro-Salud Maternal e Infantil, Dominican Republic, 1986—, health clinics, Haiti, 1986—. Contbr. articles to profl. jours., 1983-86. Bd. trustees Ind. Sanitarium and Hosp., Independence, 1977-86; mem. corp. body Truman Neurol. Ctr., Kansas City, 1979-86; bd. dirs. Health Care Systems, Inc., Independence, 1982—, Devel. Properties, Independence, 1982—, First Kensington Corp., Independence, 1982—. Mem. Am. Nurses Assn. (mem. council on cultural diversity), Mo. Nurses Assn., Profl. Nurses Assn. (pres. 1982-84), Sigma Theta Tau. Republican. Mem. Reorganized Ch. Jesus Christ of Latter Day Saints. Club: Jr. Women's (Cupertino, Calif.) (past pres.). Home: 114 NW Lakewood Blvd Lee's Summit MO 64063 Office: Graceland Coll Lamoni IA 50140

KIRKSEY, TERRIE LYNN, geriatric center administrator, social work consultant; b. Shaw, Miss., Nov. 18, 1958; d. Clarence Clayton and Mary Juanice (King) K. B of Social Work, Delta State U., 1980; MSW, U. Tenn. Ctr. for Health Scis., 1985. Asst. dir. recreational therapy Rosewood Manor, Memphis, 1980, dir. social services, 1981-83; dir. social services Memphis Health Care Ctr., 1980-81, St. Peter Villa, Memphis, 1983-84; asst. dir. Josephine K. Lewis Ctr. for Sr. Citizens, Memphis, 1984—; social work cons. Bapt. Home Plus Home Health Agy., Memphis, 1986—. Bd. dirs. Retired Sr. Vol. Program, sec. 1986-87; bd. dirs. Alzheimer's Day Care Inc., sec. 1987—. Mem. Phi Theta Kappa. Democrat. Home: 4055 Chinaberry Cove Memphis TN 38115 Office: Josephine K Lewis Ctr for Sr Citizens 1188 N Parkway Memphis TN 38105

KIRLEY, MARION RACHEL, psychoanalyst, psychotherapist; b. Winthrop, Mass., Aug. 7, 1934; d. Patrick Francis and Hazel Elizabeth (Cody) K. BS in Nursing, Boston Coll., 1959, MS in Nursing, 1967, EdD, 1980. Cert. psychoanalyst Am. Inst. Psychoanalysis, cert. psychotherapist, clin. nurse specialist. Staff nurse Mass. Gen. Hosp., Boston, 1959-61, supr. operating room, 1961-63, psychiat. nurse clinician, 1969-74; instr. Mt. Auburn Hosp., Cambridge, Mass., 1963-65; nursing care coordinator Danvers (Mass.) State Hosp., 1967-69; inst. Salem (Mass.) State Coll., 1976; nurse clinician San Francisco Gen. Hosp., 1981; asst. psychoanalyst Karen Horney Clinic, N.Y.C., 1981-86; pvt. practice psychoanalysis Boston, 1987—. Served to capt. U.S. Air Force 1969-71. Mem. Assn. Advancement Psychoanalysis, Am. Nursing Assn. (cert.) , Am. Nurses Council Psychiat. Mental Health Nursing, Mass. Nurses Assn. Roman Catholic. Office: 1 Hawthorne Pl Suite 101 Boston MA 02114

KIRMSE, ANNE-MARIE ROSE, O.P., educator, researcher; b. Bklyn., Sept. 23, 1941; d. Frank Joseph Sr. and Anna (Keck) K. BA in English cum laude, St. Francis Coll., 1972; MA in Theology with honors, Providence Coll., 1975; PhD in Theology, Fordham U., 1988. Cert. elem. tchr., N.Y. Tchr. elem. sch. Diocese Bklyn., 1962-73; instr. adult edn. Diocese Rockville Centre, N.Y., 1974—; dir. religious edn. St. Anthony Padua Parish, East Northport, N.Y., 1975-83; dir. spiritual programs Diocese Rockville Centre, 1979—; demonstration tchr. Paulist Press, N.Y.C., 1968-70; cons. Elem. Sch. Catechetical Assocs., Bklyn., 1971-73; mem. adj. faculty grad. program Sem. Immaculate Conception, Huntington, N.Y., 1979-80; adj. instr. Molloy Coll., Rockville Centre, 1985; asst. to Rev. Avery Dulles, Fordham U., Bronx, N.Y., 1988—. Recipient Dominican scholarship Providence (R.I.) Coll., 1973, Kerygma award Diocese Rockville Centre, 1980, Presdl. scholarship Fordham U., 1988; McGinley fellow Fordham U., 1988. Mem. Sisters of St. Dominic, 1960—; Nat. Cath. Edn. Assn.; Long Island Women's Ordination Conf. Democrat. Roman Catholic. Office: Fordham U Dept Theology Bronx NY 10458

KIRSCH, DOROTHY ANN, publisher; b. Rochester, N.Y., Oct. 1, 1936; d. Edward and Sylvia E. (Moskin) Tejw; m. Donald Kirsch, June 6, 1959; children—Mark Adam, Karen Rebecca, Jonathan Bradford. A.B., U. Rochester, 1956. Treas., dir. Wall St. Group, Inc., N.Y.C., 1959—; pub., editor N.Y. Visitor's Reporter, Inc., N.Y.C., 1975—; treas., dir. Wall St. Group/Calif., Los Angeles, 1979—. Mem. N.Y. State Commn. Human Rights, 1972-75. Mem. Women's Orgn. of Brandeis U. (life), Phi Beta Kappa. Clubs: Wall Street, NYU, Citicorp (N.Y.C.). Office: NY Visitor's Reporter 63 Wall St New York NY 10005

KIRSCH, MIERA ROYBAL, civic leader; b. Hollywood, Calif., Feb. 26, 1949; d. Joseph James and Mabel Eleanor (Keenan) Roybal; m. Lon J. Larsen, Mar. 8, 1969 (div. 1972); 1 child, Jennifer Elizabeth; m. Robert Alan Kirsch, Oct. 26, 1979. Grad. high sch., Van Nuys, Calif., 1967. Sec. Capitol Records, Hollywood, 1967-72; adminstrv. asst. Motown Records, Hollywood, 1973-76. Author: Access to Nashville, 1983; Editor: Mastering Multiple Sclerosis, 1986; producer ednl. film The Search Goes On, 1985. Peer counselor Multiple Sclerosis Clinic, UCLA, 1980-82, Multiple Sclerosis Soc., Nashville, 1983—; mem. Mayor's Adv. Com. Handicapped People, Nashville, 1985—, Beyond War Orgn., 1986; sponsor Mission Internat., Bogata, Columbia, 1985—; chmn. bd. dirs. Md., Tenn. Multiple Sclerosis Soc., Nashvill, 1984-85, phone chmn. WCDN-TV Action Auction, Nashville, 1985—. Democrat. Roman Catholic.

KIRSCHSTEIN, RUTH LILLIAN, physician; b. Bklyn., Oct. 12, 1926; d. Julius and Elizabeth (Berm) K.; m. Alan S. Rabson, June 11, 1950; 1 child, Arnold. B.A. magna cum laude, L.I. U., 1947; M.D., Tulane U., 1951; D.Sc. (hon.), Mt. Sinai Sch. Medicine, 1984; LL.D. (hon.), Atlanta U., 1985. Intern Kings County Hosp., Bklyn., 1951-52; resident pathology VA Hosp., Atlanta, Providence Hosp., Detroit, Clin. Center, NIH, Bethesda, Md., 1952-57; fellow Nat. Heart Inst., Tulane U., 1953-54; mem. staff NIH, Bethesda, 1957-72, 74—; asst. dir. div. biologics standards NIH, 1971-72; dep. dir. Bur. Biologics, FDA, 1972-73, dep. asso. commr. sci., 1973-74; dir. Nat. Inst. Gen. Med. Scis., 1974—; bd. dirs. Found. Advanced Edn. Scis.; chmn. grants peer rev. study team NIH; mem. Inst. Medicine, Nat. Acad. Scis., 1982—. Recipient Superior Service award HEW, 1971, 78, Presdl. Meritorious Exec. award, 1980, Presdl. Disting. Exec. Rank award, 1985. Mem. Am. Assn. Immunologists, Am. Assn. Pathologists, Am. Soc. Microbiology. Home: 6 West Dr Bethesda MD 20814 Office: Nat Inst Gen Med Scis Dept Health & Human Services Bldg 31 9000 Rockville Pike Bethesda MD 20892

KIRSHNER, JANET BERGER, public relations executive; b. N.Y.C., Mar. 24, 1933; d. Elmer Steil and Elsie (Feinberg) Berger; student U. Calif.-Berkeley, 1951-53; BS, UCLA, 1956; m. Lester Kirshner, Sept. 8, 1957; children: Elizabeth, Jonathan. Partner, H/K Communications, N.Y.C., 1974-78, pres., owner, 1981—; dir. public relations Branielle Assos., N.Y.C., 1978-79, Delphi Commodities, N.Y.C., 1979-80; v.p. public relations and adminstrn. Fahy Internat. Trading Corp., N.Y.C., 1980-81. Mem. Public Relations Soc. Am. Club: Advt. of N.Y. Office: 244 Madison Ave New York NY 10016

KIRSTEIN, NAOMI WAGMAN, service executive; b. Israel, Mar. 23, 1937; came to U.S., 1939; BS in Pub. Relations and Communications, Boston U., 1958. With H.E. Harris and Co., 1958-61; coop. advt. mgr. Polaroid Corp., 1961-63; office mgr., pub. relations exec. N.Y. State Council on Arts, 1963-65; pub. relations dir. Mass. chpt. Heart Fund Assn., 1965-66; freelance pub. relations dir. Edward A. Finch Co., 1967-69; freelance pub. relations dir., pres. Rima Newmar Inc., 1970-71; owner, mgr. Wagman Travel, 1972-77, Custom Travel, Brookline, Mass., 1977—; owner Custom Spas Worldwide,

1986—; spa cons. Author: Sun and Daughter Signs, 1974; contbr. articles to profl. publs. Mem. Am. Friends of Israel Soldiers (dir. N.E. region), Women in Travel, Food and Travel Writers Assn. (press mem.), Tau Mu Epsilon. Jewish. Office: Custom Travel Custom Spas Worldwide 1308 Beacon St Brookline MA 01923

KIRWAN, KATHARYN GRACE (MRS. GERALD BOURKE KIRWAN, JR.), retail executive; b. Monroe, Wash., Dec. 1, 1913; d. Walter Samuel and Bertha Ella (Shrum) Camp; m. Gerald Bourke Kirwan Jr., Jan. 13, 1945. Student, U. Puget Sound, 1933-34; BA, BS, Tex. Woman's U., 1937; postgrad., U. Wash., 1941. Librarian Brady (Tex.) Sr. High Sch., 1937-38, McCamey (Tex.) Sr. High Sch., 1938-43; mgr. Milady's Frock Shop, Monroe, 1946-62, owner, mgr., 1962—. Meml. chmn. Monroe chpt. Am. Cancer Soc., 1961—; mem. Snohomish County Police Services Action Council, 1971; mem. Monroe Pub. Library Bd., 1950-65, pres. bd., 1964-65; mem. Monroe City Council, 1969-73; mayor City of Monroe, 1974-81; commr. Snohomish County Hosp. dist. 1, 1970—, chmn. bd. commrs., 1980—; mem. East Snohomish County Health Planning Com., 1979—; mem. Snohomish County Law and Justice Planning Com., 1974-78, Snohomish County Econ. Devel. Council, 1975-81, Snohomish County PUD Citizens Adv. Task Force, 1983; sr. warden Ch. of Our Saviour, Monroe, 1976-77. Served with USNR, 1943-46. Mem. AAUW, U.S. Naval Inst., Ret. Officers Assn., Naval Res. Assn., Bus. and Profl. Women's Club (2d v.p. 1980-82, pres. 1983-84), Washington Gens., Snohomish County Pharm. Aux., C. of C. (pres. 1972). Episcopalian. Home: 538 S Blakely St Monroe WA 98272 Office: 108 W Main St Monroe WA 98272

KIRWIN, ROSE MARY, corporate executive; b. Quincy, Mass., June 18, 1941; d. Brantisio Nicholas Carlos and Mary Virginia (Scoledge) Lucci; m. Francis Joseph Kirwin, Oct. 24, 1964; children: Virginia Marie, Laura Ann. BBA, Aquinas Jr. Coll., Milton, Mass., 1961; BA in Sociology summa cum laude, U. Mass., Boston, 1978. Mgr. Youth Resources, Inc., Braintree, Mass., 1971-74, U. Mass., Boston, 1974-78; office mgr., paralegal Atty. Ward and Avery, Boston, 1978-79; research analyst Alcohol Resource Ctr., Newton, Mass., 1980-84; exec. dir. DOVE, Inc., Quincy, 1985-87, dir. community programs div., 1987—; sec. Youth Resources, Inc., Braintree, 1975-79; pres. DOVE, Inc., Quincy, 1980-83; grant writer, cons. in field, Braintree, 1978-81; bd. dirs. St. Thomas More, Braintree, 1979—, Home for Now, Inc., 1987—, Hull (Mass.) Interagency Council, treas., 1988. Mem. curriculum and meger coms., U. Mass., Boston, 1975-78, student rep., bd. trustees, 1978; bd. dirs. Braintree Community Gardens, 1981. Mem. Nat. Assn. Female Execs., Interagency Council of South Shore (v.p. 1985—). Democrat. Roman Catholic. Home: 28 Bushnell Terr Braintree MA 02184 Office: DOVE Inc Confidential Box 287 Quincy MA 02269

KIRZ, STEPHANIE AGER, public relations executive; b. Seattle, Apr. 28, 1946; d. Robert Lee and Jean (Purrington) Ager; B.A. in Art, U. Wash., 1969; m. Howard Lutz Kirz, Mar. 9, 1978. V.P., gen. mgr. Cole & Weber Pub. Relations subs. Ogilvy & Mather; pres. Ager & Assocs., advt. agy.; pres., Chief Exec. Officer Ager/BP&N Pub. Relations, 1986—. Pres., Wash. Panhellenic, 1967-68. Mem. Women in Communications (v.p. fin. 1981), Pub. Relations Soc. Am. (Totem award 1980, 86), Kappa Kappa Gamma. Club: Seattle Tennis, Columbia Tower. Home: 705 McGilvra Blvd E Seattle WA 98112 Office: 1115 1st Ave S Seattle WA 98104

KISCADEN, LAURA LINNÉA, psychologist; b. Mpls., Nov. 3, 1950; d. Robert Albert and Eleanor Esther (Hultman) K.; m. Roger Russell Alm, Oct. 14, 1983. BA in Psychology, Moorhead (Minn.) State U., 1972; MS Counseling & Guidance, U. N.D., 1974; postgrad., Ill. Sch. Profl. Psychology. Licensed psychologist, Minn. Counselor Cen. Tech. Community Coll., Hastings, Nebr., 1974-76; counselor, dir. career ctr. Anoka-Ramsey Community Coll., Coon Rapids, Minn., 1976-77; counselor Normandale Community Coll., Bloomington, Minn., 1979; career devel. specialist State Dept. Edn., St. Paul, 1978, 80-83, sex equity specialist, 1984—; Cons. in field, 1978—. Dept. edn. del. Minn. Women's Consortium; counselor, speaker Washington County Family Violence Network; bd. dirs. Explorer Scouts, St. Paul, 1980-83. N.D. Bd. Higher Edn. scholar, 1973-74; named Outstanding Young Woman of Am., Fuller & Dees, 1976. Mem. Am. Assn. for Career Devel. (regional dir. 1982), NOW (pres. Hastings chpt. 1975-76), St. Paul C. of C. (youth and edn. task force 1981-83). Office: Minn State Dept Edn 550 Cedar St Saint Paul MN 55101

KISCHEL, BEATRICE, cosmetology educator, administrator; b. New London, Conn., Oct. 6, 1920; d. William and Fannie Ida (Lubchansky) Bronitsky; m. Jack Kischel, Mar. 26, 1944; children: Marc, Faye-Elaine Forman, Ilene. Student Mohegan Coll., 1987—. Cert. hairdresser, comestician instr. Instr., New London Acad. (Conn.), 1962-69; dean, instr. Albert-Beatrice Sch., New London, 1970—. Former pres. New London Hebrew Ladies Aid, Ednl. Soc. Yeshiva U. Women's Orgn.; dist. dir. Conn. PTA; neighborhood chmn. Girl Scouts U.S.A., New London. Mem. Conn. Hairdressers and Cosmeticians Assn. (sec. 1963-65, dir. 1973-75, 1st v.p. Shoreline Affiliate #8 1988—), Tchrs. Ednl. Council. Home: 962 Bank St New London CT 06320

KISCO, VIVIENNE MARIE, nurse; b. N.Y.C., May 24, 1960; d. John Henry LaMarre and Constance Mary (Brown) LaMarre Lang; m. Humberto Pareja, Aug. 12, 1978 (div. 1984); m. Stephen William Kisco, Mar. 1, 1985. AS in Nursing, St. Petersburg Jr. Coll., 1988. RN, Fla. Unit sec. St. Petersburg (Fla.) Osteo. Hosp., 1976-77; staff nurse Palms of Pasadena Hosp., South Pasadena, Fla., 1977-83, Morton F. Plant Hosp., Clearwater, Fla., 1983—; instr. CPR, Am. Heart Assn., 1979-82. Flight nurse USAFR, 1982-87, USAR, 1987—. Mem. Am. Nurses Assn., Nat. Assn. Female Execs., Internat. Thespian Soc., Am. Orchid Soc., Fla. West Coast Orchid Soc. Democrat. Roman Catholic. Home: 6531 Emerson Ave S South Pasadena FL 33707 Office: Morton F Plant Hosp 323 Jeffords St Clearwater FL 33517

KISER, NAGIKO SATO, librarian; b. Taipei, Republic of China, Aug. 7, 1923; came to U.S., 1950; d. Takeichi and Kinue (Sooma) Sato; m. Virgil Kiser, Dec. 4, 1979 (dec. Mar. 1981). Secondary teaching credential, Tsuda Coll., Tokyo, 1945; BA in Journalism, Trinity U., 1953; BFA, Ohio State U., 1956, MA in Art History, 1959; MLS, cert. in library media, SUNY, Albany, 1974. Cert. community coll. librarian, Calif., cert. jr. coll. tchr., Calif., cert. secondary edn. tchr., Calif., cert. tchr. library media specialist and art, N.Y. Pub. relations reporter The Mainichi Newspapers, Osaka, Japan, 1945-50; contract interpreter U.S. Dept. State, Washington, 1956-58, 66-67; resource specialist Richmond (Calif.) Unified Sch. Dist., 1968-69; editing supr. CTB/McGraw-Hill, Monterey, Calif., 1969-71; multi-media specialist Monterey Peninsula Unified Sch. Dist., 1975-77; librarian Nishimachi Internat. Sch., Tokyo, 1979-80, Sacramento City Unified Sch. Dist., 1977-79, 81-85; sr. librarian Camarillo (Calif.) State Hosp., 1985—. Editor: Short Form Test of Academic Aptitude, 1970, Prescriptive Mathematics Inventory, 1970, Tests of Basic Experience, 1970. Mem. Calif. State Supt.'s Regional Council on Asian Pacific Affairs, Sacramento, 1984—. Library Media Specialist Tng. Program scholar U.S. Office Edn., 1974. Fellow Internat. Biographical Assn.; mem. ALA, AAUW, Calif. Library Assn., Calif. Media and Library Educators Assn., Asunaro Shoogai Kyooiku Kondankai Lifetime Edn. Promoting Assn. (Japan), The Mus. Soc., Internat. House of Japan, Matsuyama Sacramento Sister City Corp., Japanese Am. Citizens League, UN Assn. U.S., Ikenoboo Ikebana Soc. Am. Mem. Christian Science Ch. Office: Camarillo State Hosp Profl Library 1878 S Lewis Rd Camarillo CA 93011

KISER, SHARON ANN, volunteer service professional; b. Dayton, Ohio, Aug. 2, 1945; d. Charles Russell and Louise Matilda (Baer) Warner; m. Peter Joseph D'Onofrio, Oct. 16, 1971 (div. June 1976); m. Ronald Eugene Kiser, June 14, 1986; 1 stepchild, Rebecca Erin. Degree in secretarial sci., Miami Jacobs Jr. Coll., 1971; AS in Bus. Adminstrn., Sinclair Community Coll., 1986. Cert. dir. volunteer services, Ohio. Exec. sec. NCR Corp., Dayton, 1963-78; dir. vol. services Grandview Hosp. and Med. Ctr., Southview Hosp. and Family Health Ctr., Dayton, 1978—; speaker Nat. Osteo. Guild Assn., Dayton, 1981; nat. speaker Am. Soc. Dirs. Vol. Services Ednl. Conf., Houston, 1983, Cin., 1984, Phila., 1986; mem. tng. com., human resources com. Voluntary Action Ctr. United Way, Dayton, 1983, 86. Contbr. articles to profl. jours. Mem. Dayton Art Inst., Ohio Soc. Dir. Vol. Services (mem. chmn. Southwestern Ohio 1981-85, mem. by-laws com. 1980-81, S.W. Ohio's newspaper rep. 1982-84), Am. Soc. Dir. Vol. Services (Creative Achievement award 1983, 84, 86, mem. innovative programming com. 1987), Pub. Relations in Health Orgns. Methodist. Home: 7230 Charlesworth Dr Huber Heights OH 45424 Office: Grandview Hosp 405 Grand Ave Dayton OH 45405

KISH, CARLA ELENE, consultant, lobbyist; b. Ann Arbor, Mich.; d. Leslie and Rhea (Kuleske) Kish; m. Jonathan S. Stephens, Feb. 1987. B.A., U. Mich., 1970, M.Sc., 1972; M.A., London Sch. Econs., Eng., 1974. Cons., Subcom. on Energy and Environment, Ho. Com. on Interior and Insular Affairs, 1976-80; Western rep. Western Orgn. Resource Councils, 1980; legis. asst. to Sen. Levin of Mich., 1980-84; dep. conservation dir. The Wilderness Soc., 1984-86; cons., lobbyist D&R Internat., 1987—. Office: D&R Internat 962 Wayne Ave Silver Spring MD 20910

KISKOWSKI, ANNA MARIE, nursing administrator; b. South Bend, Ind., Aug. 7, 1928; d. Barnhard D. and Verna K. (Wilkeson) Johnson; m. Robert G. Kiskowski, May 21, 1983 (dec. Sept. 1984). B.S. in Nursing Edn., Ind. U., 1955, M.S. in Health and Safety, 1957. Cert. sch. nurse. Staff nurse Meth. Hosp., Indpls., 1949-51; pediatric supr. Meml. Hosp., South Bend, 1951-53; sch. nurse South Bend Community Sch. Corp., 1955-74, coordinator health services, 1974-88; chmn. Ind. Sch. Nurse Consortium, Indpls., 1977-81; adv. com. Ind. U. Sch. Nursing, South Bend, 1981-84. Adv. com. Project Head Start, South Bend, 1980-88; bd. dirs. Child Abuse and Neglect Orgn., 1982-88, Diabetes Assn. St. Joseph County (Ind.), 1984-88, Meml. Continuing Edn. Inst., 1985-88; mem. Sexual Abuse Consortium, 1981-84. Recipient cert. of appreciation Ind. U. Sch. Nursing, 1982. Mem. Am. Sch. Health Assn., AAUW, Nursing Research Consortium North Central Ind., Delta Kappa Gamma. Lutheran. Home: 51742 Portage Rd South Bend IN 46628 Office: South Bend Community Sch Corp 635 S Main St South Bend IN 46601

KISLAK, JEAN HART, art director; b. Mineola, N.Y.; d. Frank Ernest and Isabelle Tayor (Ellis) Hart; m. William I. Herendeen, Aug. 22; remarried Louis G. Johnson, Jan. 31; 1 child, Jennifer Taylor; remarried Jay Kislak, Apr. 7, 1985. Student Peace Jr. Coll., Raleigh, N.C., Queens Coll., Charlotte, N.C. With Storer Broadcasting Co., Miami, Fla.; with S.E. Banks N.A., Miami, Fla., 1974-84, art dir., 1981-84; mem. Gov. Fla. Panel Visual Arts, 1980, Dade County Art in Pub. Places, 1979-81; art cons., 1974—. Bd. dirs. Viscaya Mus., Miami, 1963, Beaux Arts, U. Miami, 1968, Theatre Art Patrons, Miami, 1965; trustee Dade County Zool. Soc., 1988—; mem. Bacardi Imports Art Bd., 1983—, Kislak Art Found., 1986—, Fla. State Bd. Art in Pub. Places, 1987. Recipient Gov. Fla. award art, 1976, 79, Miami Dade Pub. Library award, 1978, Bus. Com. for Arts award, 1975-79, WPBT Pub. TV award, 1976, 77, 80, Lowe Gallery, U. Miami cert. recognition, 1980, Dade County Art in Pub. Places cert. recognition, 1981, 82. Address: 2 Palm Bay Ct Apt 21W Miami FL 33138

KISSANE, JEAN CHARLOTTE, lawyer; b. Phila., Feb. 6, 1946; d. William C. and Grace A. (McGlade) K. AB, Lycoming Coll., 1968; JD, Widener U., 1986. Tchr. history Colonial Sch. Dist., New Castle, Del., 1968-86; assoc. Skadden, Arps, Slate, Meagher & Flom, Wilmington, Del., 1986—. Recipient Am. Jurisprudence awards, 1986. Mem. ABA, Del. Bar Assn., Phi Delta Phi, Phi Kappa Phi. Democrat. Office: Skadden Arps Slate Meagher & Flom Box 636 One Rodney Sq Wilmington DE 19899-0636

KISSEÉ, LOIS JEAN, sales executive; b. Cleve., Feb. 24, 1937; d. Vaughan George and Grace Marie (Martin) Williams; m. Eldon Lee Kisseé, Dec. 1, 1953 (div. 1979); children: Dana Vaughan, Jeffrey Lee. BS in Acctg., Calif. State U., Northridge, 1973. Div. controller The Newhall Land and Farming Co., Valencia, Calif., 1969-81; fin. cons. Security Pacific Bank, Los Angeles, 1981-82; area mgr. Action Owners Group Service Corp., Sunnyvale, Calif., 1982-84; account rep. Computax Inc., Torrance, Calif., 1984-87; exec. sales mgr. Lex Computer Systems, Santa Ana, Calif., 1987—. Mem. Nat. Assn. Female Execs., Nat. Assn. Accts. Republican. Methodist. Office: Lex Computer Systems 2922 S Daimler Suite 103 Santa Ana CA 92705

KISSLING, RONDA ALSTOTT, educational administrator; b. Indpls., Sept. 8, 1946; d. Glenn Leroy and Marcella (Ruffner) Alstott; m. Michael G. Kissling, Dec. 25, 1971 (div. Nov. 1980). BS, Ind. U., 1969, MS, 1971, EdS, 1983. Tchr. Ctr. Grove Community Sch. Corp., Greenwood, Ind., 1969-79, reading coordinator, 1979-80, gifted program coordinator, 1980-82, curriculum dir., 1982—. Bd. dirs. Campfire Boys and Girls, Indpls., 1987—. Mem. NEA Council for Exceptional Children, Nat. Assn. for Supervision and Curriculum Devel., Ind. Assn. for Supervision and Curriculum Devel., Nat. Sch. Pub. Relations Assn., Ind. U. Alumni Assn., Delta Kappa Gamma, Gamma Phi Beta. Office: Ctr Grove Community Sch Corp 2929 S Morgantown Rd Greenwood IN 46142

KISTIAKOWSKY, VERA, physics researcher and educator; b. Princeton, N.J., Sept. 9, 1928; d. George Bogdan and Hildegard (Moebius) K.; m. Gerhard Emil Fischer, June 16, 1951 (div. 1975); children—Marc Laurenz Fischer, Karen Marie Fischer. A.B., Mt. Holyoke Coll., 1948, Sc.D. (hon.), 1978; Ph.D., U. Calif.-Berkeley, 1952. Staff scientist U.S. Naval Research Def. Lab., San Francisco, 1952-53; fellow U. Calif.-Berkeley, 1953-54; research assoc. Columbia U., N.Y.C., 1954-57, instr., 1957-59; asst. prof. Brandeis U., Waltham, Mass., 1959-62, adj. assoc. prof., 1962-63; staff mem. MIT, Cambridge, 1963-69, sr. research scientist, 1969-72; prof. physics, 1972—; Phi Beta Kappa lectr., Washington, 1983-84. Author: Atomic Energy, 1959; One Way Is Down, 1967; contbr. articles on nuclear and elem. particle physics to profl. jours. Dir. Council for a Liveable World, Boston, 1983—; co-chmn. United Campuses to Prevent Nuclear War, 1987—. Recipient Centennial award Mt. Holyoke Coll., 1972. Fellow AAAS, Am. Phys. Soc. (councilor 1974-77); mem. Assn. for Women in Sci. (pres. 1982-83). Office: MIT 24-522 77 Massachusetts Ave Cambridge MA 02139

KISTLER, TERRI JO, occupational therapist; b. Ortonville, Minn., Aug. 13, 1953; d. Kenneth James and Aletta Louise (Waller) Simonitch; m. John Allen Kistler Jr., Aug. 25, 1979 (div. Mar. 1986). BS in Occupational Therapy, U. Puget Sound, 1975. Sr. occupational therapist Moose Lake State Hosp., 1976-77; occupational therapist Beaufort (S.C.) County Home Health, 1978-83, Creative Rehab., Inc., Minnetonka, Minn., 1983-84; pvt. practice occupational therapy Faribault and Owatoma, Minn., 1984—; emergency dispatcher Sea Pines-Forest Beach Fire Dept., Hilton Head Island, S.C., 1978-80; occupational therapist Bay View Nursing Ctr., Beaufort, 1980-83; mem. Low County Aging Adv. Com., Ridgeland, S.C., 1981-83; guest speaker Courage Ctr. Stroke Network, Golden Valley, Minn., 1985-87; cons. Woodvalve VI Group Home, Owatonna, 1985—. Bd. dirs. Beaufort Heart Assn., 1980-83, St. Mary's Human Devel. Ctr., Ridgeland, 1982; chmn. Skate-For-Heart Am. Heart Assn., Beaufort, 1982; organizer Different Strokes Club, Faribault, 1984, Tonna Stroke Supporters, Owatonna, 1985, Respiratory Conf., Faribault, 1985, Stroke-Busters Club, Owatonna, 1986; mem. planning com. Faribault Health Fair, 1985; mem. Allied Health Profls. Assn. Arthritis Found., 1985—. Mem. Am. Occupational Therapy Assn., Minn. Occupational Therapy Assn. Democrat. Lutheran. Home: 13401 Morgan Ave S #110 Burnsville MN 55337

KITAGAWA, AUDREY EMIKO, lawyer; b. Honolulu, Mar. 31, 1951; s. Yonoichi and Yoshiko (Nagaishi) K. B.A. cum laude, U. So. Calif., 1973; J.D., Boston Coll., 1976. Bar: Hawaii, 1977, U.S. Dist. Ct. Hawaii, 1977. Assoc., Rice, Lee & Wong, Honolulu, 1977-80; sole practice, Honolulu, 1980—. Exec. editor Internat. Law Jour., 1976. Mem. Historic Hawaii Found., 1984. Mem. Hawaii Bar Assn., ABA, Assn. Trial Lawyers Am., Japan-Hawaii Lawyers Assn. (v.p. 1982—), Law Office Mgmt. Discussion Group, Hawaii Lawyers Care, Phi Alpha Delta. Republican. Club: Honolulu. Office: 820 Mililani St Suite 615 Honolulu HI 96813

KITCH, DIANA LEBOSQUET, therapist; b. Wichita, Kans., July 1, 1941; d. John Rude and Florence Edith (Bergstresser) LeBosquet; B.A. in Philosophy and Religion, Southwestern Coll., 1963; M.A. in Psychology, Wichita State U., 1979; m. Paul Richard Kitch, Apr. 1, 1974; children—Mary Suzanne, William Russell Parlette. Staff counselor Wichita State U. Counseling Center, 1976—; cons. to chaplain VA Hosp., Wichita, 1980-81, psychology technician, 1979-80; cons. Developmental Vision Clinic, Wichita, vol. Suicide and Crisis Center, Honolulu, 1971-72. Acting chairperson Wichita Hospice, Inc., 1981-82. Mem. Am. Psychol. Assn., N. Am. Soc. Adlerian Psychology. Club: University. Contbr. articles to profl. jours. and books. Home: 8218 E Douglas Wichita KS 67206 Office: Wichita State U Counseling Ctr PO Box 91 Wichita KS 67208

KITCHELT, MAUREEN THERESE, communications company executive; b. N.Y.C., June 11, 1956; d. Thomas S. and Elaine (Marshall) Mulrenin; m. Kenneth J. Kitchelt. BA in French, Towson State U., 1981. Lead software technician ADAC Labs., Sunnyvale, Calif., 1979-80, Hamel, Park, McCabe, Washington, 1981-82; product cons. ITT Dialcom Inc., Silver Springs, Md., 1983-85, mgr. internat. sales and support, 1985-86; dir. internat. sales Dialcom Services Inc., Rockville, Md., 1986—. Mem. Nat. Assn. Female Execs.

KITCHENER, KAREN STROHM, psychology educator; b. Toledo, Ohio, Sept. 29, 1943; d. Vincent Robert and Miriam (Zulch) Strohm; m. Richard Frank Kitchener, Aug. 21, 1965; children: Gregory David, Brian Thomas. BA, U. Calif., Santa Barbara, 1965; MA, Claremont Grad. Sch., Calif., 1968, U. Minn., Mpls., 1971; PhD, U. Minn., 1977. Lic. psychologist, Colo. Staff psychologist Colo. State U., Ft. Collins, 1971-75; teaching asst. U. Minn., Mpls., 1975-76; staff psychologist Centennial Ctr. for Psychol. Svcs., Ft. Collins, 1976-77; asst./assoc. prof. counseling psychology U. Denver, 1977—. Co-editor: (book) Adult Cognitive Development, 1986; contbr. articles to profl. jours. Recipient Ralph Berdie award for outstanding research on coll. student devel. Am. Assn. for Counseling & Devel., 1983. Fellow Am. Psychol. Assn. (ethics com. chmn. 1987); mem. Am. Coll. Personnel Assn. Office: U Denver Sch Edn GCB109 Denver CO 80208

KITCHENS, STEPHANIE MELISSA, advertising and public relations executive; b. Harrisburg Corners, Ark., Sept. 17, 1952; d. Charles Earl Kitchens and Freda Margaret (Blackwood) Armer. Student, Cerritos Coll., 1969-70, Chaffey Coll., 1970-72; cert. dental assisting, Chaffey Coll., 1970-71. Dental asst. Dr. William s. Arnett, Upland, Calif., 1972-78; office mgr. Dr. Michael P. Blum, Anaheim, Calif., 1978-80; salesperson Merrill-Lynch Real Estate, Fullerton, Calif., 1981-82; chief fin. officer Simms Advt., Inc., Placentia, Calif., 1983—. Mem. Am. Heart Assn. Women's Guild, Orange, Calif., 1982; mem. Rep. Women, Placentia, 1983; mem. St. Jude Hosp., Yorba Linda (Calif.) Women's Task Force, 1986—; del. Govt. in Action, Sacramento, 1987; founder, first pres. Operation Heart Fund. Mem. Bus. and Profl. Women (North Orange county chpt. pres. elect 1985-86, pres. 1986—, membership, recruiting, newsletter, polit. action com. awards, San Orco dist. membership chair 1987—), Calif. Fedn. Bus. and Profl. Women (mem. expansion chair 1988-89). Mem. Ch. of Christ. Home: 158 N Starflower St Brea CA 92621 Office: Simms Advt Inc 187 W Orangethorpe Ave Suite I Placentia CA 92670

KITHCART, LINDA KAY, banker; b. Morristown, N.J., Mar. 1, 1943; d. Ralph and Doris-Lee (Worzel) Nordquest; m. Richard F. Vreeland, Dec. 26, 1964 (div. Oct. 1974); children: Richard R., Randall E.; m. Chalen H. Kithcart, Jr., Nov. 8, 1976 (dec. Feb. 1980). Cert., Katherine Gibbs Sch., N.Y.C., 1962; BS summa cum laude, Caldwell Coll., 1987. Salesperson Tri-County Realty, Inc., Riverdale, N.J., 1974-80; office mgr. C. H. Kithcart, Inc., Riverdale, 1974-80; exec. sec. Prospect Park Nat. Bank, Wayne, N.J., 1980-81; adminstrv. sec. First Nat. Bank N.J., Totowa, 1981-82, commercial lending rep., 1982-83; asst. cashier Citizens First Nat. Bank of N.J., Glen Rock, 1983-85, asst. v.p. corp. banking, 1985—. Mem. Nat. Assn. Bank Women, Nat. Honor Soc. Republican.

KITT, ANNE JANE, social worker; b. Scunthorpe, Lincolnshire, Eng., Mar. 9, 1941; d. Edward Jack and Ellen (O'Dowd) Prince; m. Bernard Michael Kitt, Apr. 20, 1963; children: Bridget Kathryn and Patrick Bernard. BA, Holy Names Coll., Oakland, Calif., 1963; MSW, Calif. State U., Sacramento, 1975. Lic. clin. social worker, marriage, family and child counselor, Calif. Med. lab. technologist Physicians Clin. Lab., Sacramento, 1963-74; social worker Vis. Nurses Assn., Sacramento, 1976-77; social worker, hosp. liaison Alta Calif. Regional Ctr., Sacramento, 1978-84, resource developer, supr., 1984—. Editor newsletter, Sacramento, 1974-80 (nominated best Newsletter, Pulitzer Prize, 1979). Mem. Calif. Assn. Marriage and Family Therapists (life, chair com. on alcoholism 1975, cert. of appreciation 1975-78), Sacramento Assn. for the Retarded (dist. social worker 1986). Democrat. Home: 33 Keel Ct Sacramento CA 95831 Office: Alta Calif Regional Ctr 2031 Howe Ave Sacramento CA 95825

KITTAY, EVA FEDER, philosophy educator; b. Malmo, Sweden, Aug. 13, 1946; came to U.S., 1953, naturalized, 1958; d. Leo and Sara (Golembioski) Feder; B.A., Sarah Lawrence Coll., 1967; M.A., CUNY, 1977, Ph.D., 1978; m. Jeffrey Kittay, June 11, 1967; children—Sesha, Leo. Asst. prof. philosophy, SUNY at Stony Brook, 1979-86, assoc. prof. 1986—; vis. asst. prof. U. Md., College Park, 1978-79; adj. lectr. Lehman Coll., CUNY, fall 1974, 75, John Jay Coll. Criminal Justice, spring 1975. SUNY Awards Program summer fellow, 1982; Exxon Ednl. Found. grantee, 1985-86. Mem. Am. Philos. Assn., Soc. for Women in Philosophy, Philosophy of Sci., Soc. for Philosophy and Public Affairs, Soc. Philosophy and Psychology (exec. com.). Author: Metaphor: Its Cognitive Force and Linguistic Structure; co-editor, Women and Moral Theory; contbr. articles to profl. jours. Office: SUNY Dept Philosophy Stony Brook NY 11794

KITTLITZ, LINDA GALE, small business owner; b. Waco, Tex., Jan. 22, 1949; d. Rudolf Gottlieb and Lena Hulda (Landgraf) K. BA in Art, Tex. Tech. U., 1971. Sales rep. Taylor Pub. Co., San Francisco and Dallas, 1972-73, Internat. Playtex Corp., San Francisco, 1974-76, Faberge Inc., San Francisco, 1976-78, Soflens div. Bausch and Lomb Co., San Francisco, 1978-81, Ben Rickert Inc., San Francisco, 1981-86, Golden West Envelope Co., San Francisco, 1987-88; mfr's. sales rep. Dearing Sales, San Francisco, 1986-87; owner, mgr. Lip Service Telecommunications Co., San Francisco, 1988—. Mem. Nat. Assn. Female Execs. Democrat. Baptist.

KITTRELL, LAURA FRANCES, former employment counselor; b. Dallas, Jan. 12, 1918; d. William Henry and Frances Louise (Wasson) K. B.A. in Sociology, Tex. Women's U., 1939; M.Liberal Arts, So. Meth. U., 1973. Youth counselor Nat. Youth Adminstrn., Dallas, 1939-41; interviewer Tex. Employment Commn., Dallas, 1942-45, interviewer, counselor, 1950-76; mem. nat. staff ARC, Washington, 1945-46. Vol. Dallas County Democratic Com., 1976. Lutheran. Home: 5623 W Hanover Dallas TX 75209

KIVELSON, MARGARET GALLAND, physicist; b. N.Y.C., Oct. 21, 1928; d. Walter Isaac and Madeleine (Wiener) Galland; m. Daniel Kivelson, Aug. 15, 1949; children: Steven Allan, Valerie Ann. AB, Radcliffe Coll., 1950, AM, 1951, PhD, 1957. Cons. Rand Corp., Santa Monica, Calif., 1956-69; asst. to geophysicist UCLA, 1967-83, prof., 1983—, also chmn. dept. earth and space scis., 1984-87; prin. investigator of magnetometer, Galileo Mission, Jet Propulsion Lab., Pasadena, Calif., 1977—; overseer Harvard Coll., 1977-83; mem. adv. council NASA, 1987—; mem. adv. coms. NSF, Dept. of Energy, Com. Solar and Space Physics, 1977-86, com. planetary exploration, 1986-87. Editor: The Solar System: Observations and Interpretations, 1986; contbr. articles to profl. jours. Named Woman of Yr., Los Angeles Mus. Sci. and Industry, 1979, Woman of Sci., UCLA, 1984; recipient Grad. Soc. medal Radcliffe Coll., 1983, 350th Anniversary Alumni medal Harvard U. Mem. Am. Geophysics Union, Am. Phys. Soc., AAAS, Am. Astron. Soc. Office: UCLA Dept Earth & Space Sci 6843 Slichter Los Angeles CA 90024

KIZER, CAROLYN ASHLEY, poet, educator; b. Spokane, Wash., Dec. 10, 1925; d. Benjamin Hamilton and M. (Ashley) K.; m. Stimson Bullitt, Jan., 1948 (div.); children—Ashley Ann, Scott, Jill Hamilton; m. John Marshall Woodbridge, Apr. 11, 1975. B.A., Sarah Lawrence Coll., 1945; postgrad. (Chinese govt. fellow in comparative lit.), Columbia U., 1946-47; studied poetry with, Theodore Roethke U. Wash., 1953-54. Specialist in lit. U.S. Dept. State, Pakistan, 1964-65; first dir. lit. programs Nat. Endowment for Arts, 1966-70; poet-in-residence U. N.C. at Chapel Hill, 1970-74; Hurst Prof. Lit. Washington U., St. Louis, 1971; lectr. Spring Lecture Series Barnard Coll., 1972; acting dir. grad. writing program Columbia, 1972; poet-in-residence Ohio U., 1974; vis. poet Iowa Writer's Workshop, 1975; prof. U. Md., 1976-77; poet-in-residence, disting. vis. lectr. Centre Coll., Ky., 1979; disting. vis. poet East Wash. U., 1980; Elliston prof. poetry U. Cin., 1981;

Bingham disting. prof. U. Louisville, Ky., 1982; disting. vis. poet Bucknell U., Pa., 1982; vis. poet SUNY, Albany, 1982; prof. Columbia U. Sch. Arts, 1982; prof. poetry Stanford U., 1986; participant Internat. Poetry Festivals, London, 1960, 70, Yugoslavia, 1969, 70, Pakistan, 1969, Rotterdam, Netherlands, 1970, Knokke-le-Zut, Belgium, 1970; sr. fellow humanities council Princeton U., 1986. Author: The Ungrateful Garden, 1961, Knock Upon Silence, 1965, Midnight Was My Cry, 1971, Mermaids in the Basement: Poems for Women, 1984, Yin: New Poems, 1984 (Pulitzer prize 1985), The Nearness of You, 1987; translator Carrying Over, 1988; founder, editor: Poetry N.W., 1959-65; contbr. poems, articles to Am. and Brit. jours. Recipient award Am. Acad. & Inst. Arts & Letters, 1985, award in lit. San Francisco Arts Commn., 1986, Gov.'s awards State Wash., 1965, 85, Pulitzer Prize for Poetry, 1985. Mem. ACLU, Amnesty Internat., P.E.N., Poetry Soc. Am., Acad. Am. Poets. Episcopalian. Address: 19772 8th St E Sonoma CA 95476

KIZZEE, MARGARET LEIGH, finance editor, investment representative; b. Huntsville, Tex.; d. Amos Ulishes and Minnie Faye (Watkins) Leigh; m. Matthew Kizzee, June 3, 1978; 1 child, Meryl-Ina Samantha. BS with honors, Sam Houston State U.; postgrad. Houston Baptist U. Registered investment rep., Tex. Page editor Sam Houston State U., Huntsville, 1975-76, assoc. editor, 1976, editor, 1976-77; copy editing intern Roanoke Times & World-News, Va., 1977; fin. writer Bus. & Energy Internat., Inc., Houston, 1978-79; fin. editor Am. Capital Fin. Services, Inc., Houston, 1980—, regional rep., 1985—. Sam Houston State U. Alumni Assn. scholar, 1974; Jesse H. Jones Found. scholar, 1976; recipient Bill Hay Meml. award Bill Hay Found., 1977. Mem. Nat. Assn. Female Execs., Internat. Assn. Bus. Communicators, Sigma Delta Chi. Baptist. Avocations: restoring antiques, collecting rare books, coins and stamps, horticulture. Office: Advantage Capital Corp 2800 Post Oak Blvd Houston TX 77056

KJOS, VICTORIA ANN, lawyer; b. Fargo, N.D., Sept. 17, 1953; d. Orville I. and Annie J. (Tanberg) K. BA, Minot State U., 1974; JD, U. N.D., 1977. Bar: Ariz. 1978. Assoc. Jack E. Evans, Ltd., Phoenix, 1977-78, pension and ins. cons., 1978-79; dep. state treas. State of N.D., Bismarck, 1979-80; freelance cons. Phoenix, 1980-81, Anchorage, 1981-82; asst. v.p., v.p., mgr. trust dept. Great Western Bank, Phoenix, 1982-84; assoc. Robert A. Jensen P.C., Phoenix, 1984-86; ptnr. Jensen & Kjos, P.C., Phoenix, 1986—; lectr. in domestic relations. Author: Employee Stock Ownership Plans: A Unique Concept in Corporate Financing and Employee Benefits, 1976; co-author: Breath Samples Not Required to be Preserved; contbr. articles to profl. jours. Mem. Ariz. Dem. Council, Western Pension Conf.; bd. dirs. Arthritis Found., Phoenix, 1986—, v.p. for chpt. devel., 1988-89. Mem. ABA, Ariz. Bar Assn. (exec. council family law sect.), Maricopa Bar Assn., Assn. Trial Lawyers Am., Ariz. Trial Lawyers Assn., Ariz. Women's Lawyers Assn., NOW, Phi Delta Phi. Office: Jensen & Kjos PC 3246 N 16th St Phoenix AZ 85016

KLAASEN, MARY GREEN, management consultant; b. Dallas, June 18, 1942. BS, U. Houston, 1963; MA, Mich. State U., 1967; postgrad., Tulane U., 1969-70, U. New Orleans, 1979-81. Sales clk. Laufman's Jewelers, Houston, 1959-60; sales person Liberty's, London, 1963-64; instr. Mich. State U., East Lansing, 1966-69; owner, mgr. Logos Bookstore, New Orleans, 1971-81; mgmt. cons. M. Klaasen & Co., New Orleans, 1981—; Mgmt. trainer Mgmt. Tree Systems, Dallas, 1984—; bd. dirs. Galilean Bookstore, Houston, 1986—. Editor The Logos, 1983-84, Mgmt. Tree Systems newsletters, 1986-87. Mem. Am. Soc. Tng. and Devel., Assn. of Logos Bookstores (dir. mktg and advt. 1983-85, bd. dirs. 1977-80, 87—), Women's Bus. Owners of Am., New Orleans-Gulf South Booksellers (sec. 1986-87). Home: 1728 Cadiz New Orleans LA 70115 Office: 1728 Cadiz New Orleans LA 70115

KLAJBOR, DOROTHEA M., lawyer, consultant; b. Dunkirk, N.Y., Dec. 2, 1915; d. Joseph M., Sr., and Susan R. (Schrantz) K.; student George Washington U., 1949-52; J.D., Am. U., Washington, 1956. Admitted to D.C. bar, 1957; successively legal asst., legis. atty., atty., 2d asst. to Chief U.S. Marshal, civil rights compliance officer Dept. of Justice, Washington, 1938-70; supr. Town of Dunkirk, N.Y., 1973-76; mem. N.Y. State Liquor Authority, Buffalo, 1976-82. Bd. dirs. Center for Women Govt., Albany, N.Y., 1978-82, Dunkirk Sr. Citizens Ctr., 1983; mem. Chautauqua County Task Force on Aging, 1972-73, Town of Dunkirk Indsl. Devel. Agy., 1972-76, Chautauqua County Planning Bd., 1973-76, No. Chautauqua County Intermcpl. Planning Bd., 1974-76, Chautauqua County Overall Econ. Devel. Planning Bd., 1974-76, Literacy Vols., 1972-76, West Dunkirk Vol. Fire Dept., 1973—; adv. bd. Dunkirk Sr. Citizens, 1974-76; mem. women's div. N.Y. State Democratic Com. Mem. Am. Bar Assn. (life), Fed. Bar Assn., D.C. Bar, Women's Bar Assn. D.C., AAUW, Nat. Lawyers Club, Cath. Daus. Am., No. Chautauqua Club Assocs. (life), Dunkirk Hist. Soc. (life), Kappa Beta Pi. Democrat. Roman Catholic. Clubs: Chautauqua County Dem. Women's (treas. 1974-76), Zonta Internat. (chmn. com. on status of women; Industry Person of Yr. award 1980, Calista Jones award for advancement rights of women 1984), Town of Dunkirk Dem. Home: 91 Forest Pl Fredonia NY 14063

KLAMERUS, KAREN JEAN, pharmacist, educator; b. Chgo., Aug. 10, 1957; d. Robert Edward and Jane Mary (Nawoj) K.; m. Frederick P. Zeller. BS in Pharmacy, U. Ill., 1980; PharmD, U. Ky., 1981. Registered pharmacist Ky., Ill. Staff pharmacist Haggin Meml. Hosp., Harrodsburg, Ky., 1980-81, Regional Med. Ctr., Madisonville, Ky., 1982; critical care liasion, 1982; clin. pharmacist resident U. Nebr., Omaha, 1983; clin. pharmacist cardiothoracic surgery U. Ill., Chgo., 1983-88, clin. asst. prof. dept. pharmacy practice, 1983-86, asst. prof., 1986-88, departmental affiliate dept. pharmaceutics, 1986-88; cons. Dimensional Mktg. Inst., Chgo., 1983-88, Channing, Weinbergs' Co., Inc., N.Y.C., 1983-88; sr. clin. scientist Wyeth-Ayerst Research, Phila., 1988—. Mem. rev. bd. Am. Jour. Hosp. Pharmacy, Clin. Pharmacy, Drug Intelligence and Clin. Pharmacy. Mem. Heart Assn. DuPage County (bd. dirs.), Am. Soc. Clin. Pharmacol. and Therapists, Assocs. of Clin. Pharmacol., Am. Assn. Colls. Pharmacy, Am. Coll. Clin. Pharmacy, Am. Heart Assn., Am. Soc. Hosp. Pharmacists, No. Ill. Soc. Hosp. Pharmacists, Rho Chi. Avocations: computers, sports, gardening, sewing. Office: Wyeth-Ayerst Research PO Box 8299 Philadelphia PA 19101-1245

KLANIT, VALERIE CHARLOTTE, nurse; b. Shaftsbury, Vt., Dec. 2, 1932; d. William Henry Harrison and Angeline Margaret Stella (Fuller) Hill; m. Edward Joseph Klanit (dec. July 1984); 1 child, Joyce Ellen Klanit Artadi. Grad., The Mount Sinai Hosp. Sch. of Nursing, 1955. RN, N.Y. Staff nurse The Jack Martin Respiratory Ctr. of The Mt. Sinai Hosp., N.Y.C., 1955-57; v.p. Chauffeurs Unlimited, Inc., N.Y.C., 1957-77; staff nurse Rusk Inst., N.Y.C., 1957-58, Beth Israel Med. Ctr., N.Y.C., 1978-79; owner, mgr. Powers Fish Market, Inc., N.Y.C., 1977-84; tchr. Techs. for Creating, Boston, 1983—; staff nurse Doctors Hosp., N.Y.C., 1984-86; pvt. duty nurse Personal Health Care Services, Albany, N.Y., 1987-88; nurse Albany Med. Ctr. Hosp., 1988—; real estate sales assoc. Century 21-Stanley Major Ltd., West Sand Lake, N.Y., 1988—. Author numerous poems. Recipient Outstanding Service to Community award Mayor Koch City of N.Y., 1983. Mem. Alumnae Assn. of Mt. Sinai Hosp. Sch. Nursing (various coms. 1965-77, bd. dirs. 1968), Rensselaer County Bd. Realtors. Democrat. Clubs: Empire State Girls Bowling. Home: 70 Second St Albany NY 12210 Office: Albany Med Ctr Hosp 43 New Scotland Ave Albany NY 12208 also: Century 21-Stanley Major Ltd Main St West Sand Lake NY 12196

KLAPPER, CAROL L., magazine publisher; b. Bklyn., Jan. 20, 1923; d. Jerome Joseph and Frances (Ritter) K. B.A., Bklyn. Coll., 1943. Asst. prodn. mgr. Better Publs., N.Y.C., 1944-46; editor Pines Publs., N.Y.C., 1946-55, editorial dir., 1956-62; v.p., editorial dir. Popular Library, N.Y.C., 1963-71; pub. CBS Mags., N.Y.C., 1972-84, v.p., pub., 1985-87; v.p., pub. Diamandis Communications Inc., 1987—; bd. dirs. Nat. Assn. Visually Handicapped. Elected Acad. Women Achievers, YWCA, 1985. Avocations: gardening; photography. Office: CBS Mags 1515 Broadway New York NY 10036

KLAPPER, NAOMI, manufacturing executive; b. Katovitz, Poland, Nov. 5, 1938; came to U.S., 1961; d. Jacob Klapper and Henia (Thompeter) Shelef; children: Jim Wilon, Nitza Wilon. BA, Bar Ilan U., 1961; MA, N.Y.U., 1963; DHL, The Jewish Theol. Sem., 1974. Prof. Hunters Coll., N.Y.C., 1968-71, Queens Coll., N.Y.C., 1971-72, The Jewish Theol. Sem., N.Y.C., 1972-86; asst. prof. Rutgers U., New Brunswick, N.J., 1972-73; prof. Prince George (Md.) Community Coll., 1973-86; pres. X Factor Assocs., Bethesda, Md., 1986—; dir. tng. Zenith Data Systems, Vienna, Va., 1988—. Assoc. editor Soc. for Tech. Communicators, 1987—; author: SHARP, 1987.

KLARNET, BETTY, magazine editor. Mng. editor Harper's Bazaar, N.Y.C. Office: Harper's Bazaar 1700 Broadway New York NY 10019 *

KLEBANOW, BARBARA ELAINE, educator; b. N.Y.C., Dec. 6, 1936; d. Joseph Herman and Helen (Feldstein) Klebanow. BA, U. Conn., 1958; MS, Yeshiva U., 1960; profl. diploma U. Conn., 1965; MS, Lehman Coll., 1977. Cert. sch. dist. adminstr., N.Y.; cert. reading specialist, N.Y.; cert. spl. edn. tchr., N.Y. Elem. classroom tchr. North Rockland Central Sch. Dist., Stony Point, N.Y., 1960-64, reading specialist elem. level, 1964-69, reading specialist secondary level, 1969—, adminstrv. intern, 1977-78; Internat. Reading Assn. state coordinator for N.Y., 1985—, adv. group chair for Cert. in Reading, 1987—. Recipient "Celebrate Literacy" award Rockland Reading Council, 1987. Fellow Assn. Women Adminstrs. in Westchester, Rockland Reading Council; mem. N.Y. State Reading Assn. (pres. 1983-84, Reading Tchr. award 1987), Phi Delta Kappa. Avocations: travel, reading, handicrafts. Office: North Rockland Cen Sch 117 Main St Stony Point NY 10980

KLEE, MARGARET ANN, software engineer; b. Boston, Feb. 18, 1961; d. James Butt and Lucille Janet (Hollies) Klee. BA, Simon's Rock Coll., 1981. Programmer, Goodyear Atomic Corp., Piketon, Ohio, 1982-84, software engr., 1984-85; software engr. Gen. Dynamics Corp., Fort Worth, 1985-87, sr. software engr., 1987—. Mem. IEEE, Assn. for Computing Machinery, Soc. for Computer Simulation, Tex. Gould Users Group (chmn. Ft.Worth 1985-88, post-chmn. 1988—), Ada Spl. Interest Group-Gould Users Group (chmn. 1985-87), Nat. Mgmt. Assn. (Ft. Worth chpt. 1987—), Nat. Assn. Female Execs. Episcopalian. Avocations: sailing, singing. Home: 209 Covington Dr Benbrook TX 76126

KLEES, EILEEN MARY, marketing executive; b. Lakewood, Ohio, Oct. 16, 1953; d. Bernard John and Kathleen (Monaghan) Dillemuth; m. Richard F. Gang, June 15, 1972 (div. Aug. 1978); m. Charles J. Klees, Oct. 10, 1987. BS, U. Ill., 1981. Telephone and field sales rep. Am. Guild/Metro Readers, Cleve., Chgo., 1971-76; sales exec. Audition div. LTD, Bensenville, Ill., 1976-79; dir. mktg. cons. EM-D Enterprises, Chgo., 1979-83; account supr. Carlyle Mktg., Chgo., 1983—; cons. Klees Direct, Chgo., 1987—; mgr. DMA-Midwest Telemktg. Assn., Chgo., 1987—. Bd. dirs. Lincoln Park Conservation Assn. Mem. Chgo. Assn. Direct Mktg., Telemktg. Council. Democrat. Home: 1840 N Hudson Chicago IL 60614-5202

KLEIN, BEVERLY, insurance agent; b. Cleve., May 16, 1947; d. David and Janice Yetta (Sateman) Bloom; divorced; children: Shawn, Lisa. AA in Nursery Sch. Teaching, Cleve. Community Coll., 1967; AA in Nursery Sch. Edn., Cuyahoga Community Coll. Tchr. Cleve. Music Settlement, 1968-69; clk. United Underwriters Ins. Agy., Inc., Cleve., 1969-70; sec., owner Stone Gold Prodns., University Heights, Ohio, 1970-74, Wednesday Moring Music Pub. Co., University Heights, 1970-74; mgr. office R. Macknin Ins. Agy., Inc., Beachwood, Ohio, 1978-83; agt., v.p. Sterling Ins. Agy., Inc., Cleve., 1983—. Pres. PTA, University Heights, 1978-80. Mem. Ind. Ins. Agts. Assn. of Ohio Inc., Ins. Bd. Gr. Cleve., Ins. Women Cleve. Jewish. Home: 2184 Vernon Rd University Heights OH 44118 Office: Sterling Ins Agy Inc 1001 Euclid Ave #605 Cleveland OH 44115

KLEIN, CHARLOTTE CONRAD, public relations executive; b. Detroit, June 20, 1923; d. Joseph and Bessie (Brown) K. BA, UCLA, 1945. Corr. UPI, Los Angeles, 1945-46; staff writer CBS, Los Angeles, 1946-47; publicist David O. Selznick Studios, Culver City, Calif., 1947-49, Foladare and Assocs., Los Angeles, 1949-51; publicist to v.p. Edward Gottlieb & Assocs., N.Y.C., 1951-62; v.p. to sr. v.p. Harshe Rotman & Druck, N.Y.C., 1962-78; dir. press/govt. affairs Sta. WNET-TV, N.Y.C., 1978-79; pres. Charlotte C. Klein Assocs., N.Y.C., 1979-84; sr. v.p., group supr. Porter Novelli, N.Y.C., 1984—. Contbr. articles to profl. jours. Bd. dirs. Manhattan chpt. Am. Cancer Soc., 1988—. Recipient Cine Golden Eagle, 1977. Mem. Pub. Relations Soc. Am. (accredited, pres. N.Y. chpt. 1985-86, Silver Anvil award 1978), Women's Forum (bd. dirs. N.Y. chpt. 1986-87), Women Execs. in Pub. Relations (pres. 1965). Clubs: Overseas Press, Vertical. Home: 138 E 36th St New York NY 10016 Office: Porter Novelli 1633 Broadway New York NY 10019

KLEIN, DEBORAH RAE, health facility administrator; b. Detroit, Mar. 29, 1951; d. Chester Anthony and E. Jacquelyn (Hollenbeck) Simpson; m. Robert Joseph Klein, Apr. 15, 1977; 1 child, Jeffrey. BS in Nursing, Mich. State U., 1974; MS in Health Adminstrn., U. Houston, 1984. Grad. nurse St. Mary's Hosp., Livonia, Mich., 1974; RN U.S. Army, Ft. Polk, La., 1974-78; dir. nursing Byrd Meml. Hosp., Leesville, La., 1978-79, Alvin (Tex.) Community Hosp., 1979-83; adminstrn. resident Katy (Tex.) Med. Ctr., 1983-84, dir. nursing, 1984-85; chief operating officer, dept. nursing Katy (Tex.) Community Hosp., 1985—; cons. in field. Sec., treas. Sam Houston council Boy Scouts Am., 1984—. Served to cpt. U.S. Army, 1972-78. Mem. Am. Assn. of Critical Care Nurses, Houston Orgn. of Nurse Execs., Am. Coll. Healthcare Execs. Republican. Roman Catholic. Home: 21130 Park Valley Dr Katy TX 77450 Office: AMI Katy Med Ctr 5602 Medical Center Dr Katy TX 77450

KLEIN, DYANN LESLIE, theatre properties company executive; b. Clifton, N.J., June 1, 1951; d. Alfred L. and Florence (Slaff) K.; m. Jason Kasarsky, Sept. 26, 1985. BA, Ohio State U., 1973; postgrad., Rutgers U., 1976, Sch. Visual Arts, 1983-86. Art therapist Jackson Meml. Hosp., Miami, Fla., 1973-74; prodn. asst. Dom Albi Assocs., N.Y.C., 1974-75; freelance prodn. asst. N.Y.C., 1975-76, freelance designer and stylist, 1976-80; pres. Props For Today, Inc., N.Y.C, 1980—; guest speaker Fashion Inst. of Tech., N.Y.C., 1987; bd. dirs. Tipps Directory, N.Y.C. Mem. Am. Film Inst., Nat. Assn. Female Execs., Roundtable for Women in Food Service, Inc., Am. Rental Assn., Internat. Spl. Guests Soc., Nat. Assn. Broadcast Employees and Technicians. Jewish. Office: Props For Today Inc 121 W 19th St 3d Fl New York NY 10011

KLEIN, ERICA HOPE LEVY, writer; b. Santo Domingo, Dominican Republic, Nov. 13, 1956; came to U.S., 1962; d. Robert R. and Mildred (Levy) K.; m. Kenneth Alan Kroll, Apr. 17, 1988; stepchildren: Beth Kroll, Clayton Kroll. BA, Washington U., 1977. Cert. secondary edn. Copywriter St. Louis Post Dispatch, 1978-81, Kerlick, Switzer & Johnson, St. Louis, 1981, SSA Advt., St. Louis, 1981-83; sr. copywriter Direct Mail Corp. Am., St. Louis, 1983—; ind. screenwriter 1978—; travel photojournalist Mo.-Ill. area travel publs., 1979—; instr. advt. copywriting Washington U., St. Louis, 1988—. Recipient Addy Flair award Advt. Fedn., 1982-83. Mem. Direct Mktg. Assn. (Echo Leader award 1987), St. Louis Travel Writers Assn. (pres. 1987—). Jewish. Home: 9035 W Swan Circle Brentwood Forest Saint Louis MO 63144 Office: Direct Mail Corp Am 1533 Washington Ave Saint Louis MO 63103

KLEIN, ESTHER MOYERMAN (MRS. PHILIP KLEIN), publisher; b. Phila., Nov. 3, 1907; d. Louis and Rebecca (Feldman) Moyerman; B.S., Temple U., 1929; student U. London, 1954; m. Philip Klein, Apr. 26, 1930; children—Arthur, Karen Louise Klein Mannes. Reporter, Phila. Jewish Times, 1925, Atlantic City Times, 1927; feature writer Pub. Ledger Syndicate, 1928-29, Pub. Ledger, Evening Bull., Phila. Record, 1929-32; pub. relations counsellor, editor Art Alliance Bull., 1945-49; commentator Sta. WPEN, 1949-53; pub. Phila. Jewish Times, 1953-74; author, hist. researcher, 1974—; lectr. women's clubs, 1951—. Del. Internat. Conf. Residential Adult Edn., Holland, 1957, Germany, 1959; participant in first workshop Residential Adult Edn. for Adult Edn. Assn. U.S., 1954. Mem. Gov.'s Commn. on Charitable Orgns., 1969—; chmn. Rittenhouse Sq. Women's com. for Phila. Orch., 1957; organizer bicentennial women's com. Walnut St. Theatre; adv. com. Friends Nat. Independence Hist. Park; chmn. bicentennial program Beth Zion - Beth Israel Congregation; bd. dirs. Rittenhouse Found., Phila. Jewish Times Inst., also dir. ann. cooking festivals; exec. com. Long Beach Island Found. Arts and Scis., N.J. Named Distinguished Dau. Pa.; recipient Gimbel Phila. award, 1975; awards Alumnae Girls High Sch., Phila. Art Alliance, Temple U., City Council Phila., Colonial Hist. Soc.; Klein Recital Hall at Temple U. named in her honor. Mem. Pa. Newspaper Pubs. Assn., Temple U. Alumni (honored at 80th anniversary, 1964), Phila. High Sch. for Girls Alumnae, Hannah Penn House, Emergency Aid of Pa., Chgo. Art Mus., Mus. Modern Art N.Y., Pan Am. Assn. Club: Print. Author: A Guidebook to Jewish Philadelphia, 1965; International House Celebrity Cookbook, 1965; History and Guidebook of Fairmount Park, 1974. Address: 135 S 18th St Philadelphia PA 19103

KLEIN, FAY MAGID, health administrator; b. Chgo., Jan. 12, 1929; d. Victor and Rose (Begun) Magid; m. Jerome G. Klein, June 27, 1948 (div. 1970); children: Leslie Klein Janik, Debra Lynne. BA in English, UCLA, 1961; MA in Pub. Adminstrn., U. So. Calif., 1971. Cert. health adminstrn. Supr. social workers Los Angeles County, 1961-65; program specialist Econ. and Youth Opportunity Agy., Los Angeles, 1965-69; sr. health planner Model Cities, Los Angeles, 1971-72; dir. prepaid health plan Westland Health Services, Los Angeles, 1972-74; exec. dir. Coastal Region Health Consortium, Los Angeles, 1974-76; grants and legis. cons. Jewish Fed. Council of Los Angeles, 1976-79; planning council Jewish Fed. Councils of So. Fla., Palm Beach to Miami, 1979-82; adminstrv. dir. kidney diseases dept. medicine UCLA, Los Angeles, 1982-84; dir. west coast Israel Cancer Research Fund, Los Angeles, 1984—; cons. Arthritis Found., Los Angeles, 1984, Bus. Action Ctr., Los Angeles, 1982, Vis. Nurses Assn., Los Angeles, 1982. Charter mem. Los Angeles County Mus. of Art, Mus. of Contemporary Art, Los Angeles; cons. Los Angeles Mcpl. Art Gallery, 1979; mem. Art Council Wight Gallery, UCLA. Fellow U.S. Pub. Health, U. So. Calif., 1970-71. Mem. Am. Pub. Health, Lifetime Alunmi Assns. UCLA, USC.

KLEIN, FRANCES ANN WANG, toy co. exec.; b. Bklyn., June 18, 1923; d. Philip and Sarah (Eckstein) Wang; B.S. with high honors, U. Ill., 1945; m. Elvin B. Klein, June 23, 1943 (div.); children—Michael, Bari Klein Freiden, Philip. Pre-sch. tchr. Kansas City (Mo.) Co-op. Pre-Sch., 1952-59; co-founder U.S. Toy Co., Inc., Kansas City, Mo., 1952, exec. v.p., 1952—, founder Constructive Playthings div., 1954; guest lectr. at tchr.-tng. instns., 1959—; mem. adv. council, spl. edn. dept. Shawnee-Mission Sch. Dist., 1972. Mem. Mo. (state sec. 1967-68), Kansas City (v.p. 1956-57) assns. for edn. young children, Johnson County Assn. Children with Learning Disabilities (v.p. 1970-71), Council Jewish Women, Phi Sigma Sigma. Jewish. Clubs: Hadassah, Altrusa (dir.) (Kansas City, Mo.). Home: 8301 Briar Ln Prairie Village KS 66207 Office: 1227 E 119th St Grandview MO 64036

KLEIN, HARRIET FARBER, lawyer; b. Elizabeth, N.J., Apr. 30, 1948; d. Melvin Julius and Frances Mildred (Novit) Farber; m. Paul Martin Klein, Sept. 9, 1973; children—Andrew, Zachary. B.A. with honors, Douglass Coll., New Brunswick, N.J., 1970; J.D., Rutgers U., 1973. Bar: N.J. 1973, U.S. Dist. Ct. N.J. 1973. Jud. clk. chancery div. Superior Ct. N.J., 1973-74; assoc. Budd, Larner, Kent, Gross, Picillo & Rosenbaum, Newark, 1974-78; ptnr. Greenbaum, Rowe, Smith, Ravin, Davis & Bergstein (and predecessor), Woodbridge, N.J., 1979—; mem. N.J. State Bd. Bar Examiners, 1987—, reader, 1977-87; mem. Essex-Newark Legal Services Vol. Project, 1983-84. Pres. Sisterhood of Congregation B'nai Israel, Millburn, N.J., 1985-87. Mem. Essex County Bar Assn., N.J. Bar Assn., ABA, Order of Barristers, Phi Alpha Theta. Home: 45 Ridgewood Terr Maplewood NJ 07040 Office: Greenbaum Rowe et al PO Box 5600 Woodbridge NJ 07095

KLEIN, IRMA FRANCES, career development educator, consultant; b. New Orleans, Jan. 5, 1936; d. Harry Joseph and Gesina Frances (Bauer) Molligan; m. John Vincent Chelena (dec. 1963); 1 child, Joseph William; m. Chris George Klein, Aug. 14, 1965; 1 stepchild, Arnold Conrad. BS in Bus. Augustine Coll., postgrad. Mktg. Inst., Chgo., Loyola U., Chgo., Realtors Inst., Baton Rouge. Mgr. Stan Weber & Assocs., Metairie, La., 1971-75; tng. dir., 1975-81; cons. Coldwell Banker Comml. Co., New Orleans, 1981; dir. career devel. Coldwell Banker Residential Co., New Orleans, 1982-85. Instr. U. New Orleans, Bonnabel High Sch., Realtors Inst., La. Real Estate Commn. Author: Career Development, 1982; Training Manual, 1978, Obtaining Listings, 1986, Participative Marketing, 1986, Marketing & Servicing Listings, 1987, Designing Training Curriculum, 1987. Active Friends of Longue Vue Gardens, La. Hist. Assn. Meml. Hall Found. Mem. La. Realtors Assn. (bd. dirs. 1973-74, grad. Realtors Inst. 1976), Jefferson Bd. Realtors (v.p. 1984), Edn. and Resources (cert., pres. La. chpt.), Research Club of New Orleans (pres. 1984-85), Realtors Nat. Mktg. Inst. (ambassador Tex. and La. 1985—, Outstanding Achievement award 1985, cert. broker 1980, residential specialist 1977), Nat. Assn. Realtors (nat. conv. speaker 1986), CRB (pres. La. chpt. 1982-83, chmn. edn.), CRS (pres. La. chpt. 1988), Forty Scholars Soc. Republican. Roman Catholic. Clubs: Antique Study Group of New Orleans, Confederate Lit. (New Orleans) (pres.), Research (New Orleans). Avocation: antiques.

KLEIN, JO ANN MARTUCCI, office systems consultant, communications officer; b. Mt. Vernon, N.Y., Mar. 4, 1947; d. Joseph Anthony and Ann Gloria Isabell (Paparatto) Martucci; m. Henry Alexander Klein, Oct. 22, 1972. Student in Math., Columbia U., 1965-67; AA, Fairleigh Dickinson U., 1984, BS, 1986. Cert. tchr., spl. edn., N.Y. Exec. asst. Gordon W. White Inc., N.Y.C., 1965-66; asst. editor Columbia U., N.Y.C., 1966-69, mgr. data processing/classified documentation, 1969-72; asst. security officer Riverside Research Inst., N.Y.C., 1972-75; internal cons. Consolidated Edison, N.Y.C., 1975—; cons. and lectr. in field. Contbr. articles to profl. jours. Chairperson major gifts program Juvenile Diabetes Found., N.J. and N.Y. chpt., 1972-86; chairperson publicity and fund raising Am. Diabetes Assn., N.J., 1985-86. Mem. Office Products Exchange Network (founder 1981, pres. 1984-86, dir.-editor OPEN newsletter 1984-85), Am. Mgmt. Assn., Assn. Info. Systems Profls., Assn. Women in Computing, Nat. Assn. Female Execs., Cons. Interface, Am. Soc. Indsl. Security. Avocations: golf, swimming, interior decorating, photography, handicrafts.

KLEIN, JUNE ROBBINS, banker, information services executive; b. N.Y.C., June 5, 1948; d. David D. and Ethel (Kramer) Robbins; m. Ira Paul Klein, Sept. 5, 1970; children: Russell, Jason. BS in Math., Boston U., 1970; MBA in Fin. & Mktg., NYU, 1983. Cert. in Data Processing. Programmer, analyst Fed. Res. Bank of N.Y., N.Y.C., 1970-71; systems mgr. Merrill Lynch, Pierce, Fenner and Smith, N.Y.C., 1971-75; systems engring. specialist IBM, N.Y.C., 1975-83; v.p. product devel. Citicorp., N.Y.C., 1983-86; v.p. mktg. mgr. Chase Manhattan Bank, N.Y.C., 1986—. Contbr. articles to profl. jours. Global bank rep. Chase Polit. Action Com., 1987; bd. dirs. Vols. Am. Mem. Electronic Banking Econs. Soc., Internat. Securities Ops. Assn., Fin. Women's Assn., Info. Industry Assn., Nat. Assn. Corp. Dirs. Home: 444 E 82d St 11M New York City NY 10028

KLEIN, KAREN, human resources officer; b. Detroit, Feb. 3, 1959; d. Henry Morton and Eleanore (Tand) Klein. B.A., Vanderbilt U., 1980. Benefits adminstr. Commerce Union Bank, Nashville, 1980-81; benefits coordinator InterFirst Corp., Dallas, 1981-83, pension analyst, 1984-87; planning adminstr., First Republic Bank Corp, 1987—. Active Washington Workshops, 1976; sponsor 500, Inc., arts support group, 1986—; mem. Dallas Summer Musicals Guild. Named hon Ky. col., 1979. Mem. 500, Inc. (exec., named outstanding mem. 1986-87), Vanderbilt U. Alumni Assn., Alpha Delta Pi. Republican. Home: 9821 Summerwood Circle Apt 2403 Dallas TX 75243 Office: First Republic Bank Corp PO Box 83100 Dallas TX 75283-3100

KLEIN, KAY JANIS, nurse; b. Detroit, Aug. 22, 1942; d. Alexander Michael Corey and Lillian Emiline (Stanley) Kilborn; divorced; children: Tonya Kay, William James, Jason Ronald Somers. Student, C.S. Mott Community Coll., 1960-62, Mich. State U., 1962-64; AA, AS in Nursing, St. Petersburg Jr. Coll., 1978; student, U. South Fla., 1985—. RN; cert. varitypist. Mgr. display Lerner Shops, Flint, Mich., 1960-62; layout artist Abdulla Advt., Flint, 1966-67; varitypist, artist City Hall Print Shop, Flint, 1967-70; nurse Suncoast Hosp., Largo, Fla., 1976-78, Largo Med. Ctr. Hosp., 1978-81, 84—; assoc. dir. nursing Roberts Home Health Service, Pinellas Park, Fla., 1982-84; inservice edn. instr., dir. video edn., team leader oncology dept. Largo Med. Ctr. Hosp., 1980-81. Editor, illustrator: (book) Some Questions and Answers About Chemotherapy, 1981, Thoughts for Today, 1981; illustrator: (cookbooks) Spices and Spoons, 1982, Yom Tov Essen n' Fressen, 1983; various brochures and catalogues; art work in permanent collection of C.S Mott Jr. Coll., Flint, 1962. Historian Am. Businesswomen's Assn., Flint, 1968-73 (scholarship 1976); outreach chmn. Temple B'nai Israel, Clearwater, Fla., 1981-85; regional outreach coordinator Union of Am. Hebrew Congregations, N.Y.C., 1983-85. Mem. Phi Theta

Kappa. Republican. Jewish. Home: 1651 Gulf Blvd Unit 43 Clearwater FL 34630 Office: Largo Med Ctr Hosp 201 14th St SW Largo FL 33540

KLEIN, LORI KATHLEEN, accountant, financial planner; b. Tomball, Tex., Nov. 26, 1954; d. Howard H. and Jeanette (Kleb) K. BS in Acct., U. Houston, Clear Lake, 1977. CPA, Cert. Fin. Planner., lic. security planner. Staff acct. Harriet Herns & Co., Lake Jackson, Tex., 1978-82; CPA. Carmack, Simek and Co., Houston, 1982-83; ptnr. Jackson, Klein and Co., Houston, 1983—; dir. Bank Adv. Bd., Houston, 1986—. Contbr. articles to various newspapers. Bd. dirs. Heart Assn, Houston, 1987. Mem. Tomball C. of C. (bd. dirs., v.p. 1983, chmn. 1988—), Am. Inst. CPA's, Tex. State Soc. CPA's, Houston CPA's, Pea Rev. Div. CPA's, Inst. Cert. Fin. Planners, Am. Ins. CPA's., Bus. and Profl. Women (pres. 1984-85). Lutheran. Office: Jackson Klein and Co 10515 Rodgers Rd Houston TX 77070

KLEIN, NANCY HESS, interior designer; b. Cin., Aug. 31, 1950; d. Stanley Edward and Ruth (Wood) Hess; m. Thomas Michael Klein, July 3, 1987. BS, Syracuse U., 1972. Assoc. interior designer Armstrong World Industries, Lancaster, Pa., 1972-78; dir. interior design Haak, Kaufman, Reese & Beers, Lancaster, 1978-81; assoc. interior designer Janet Schirn Interiors, Chgo., 1981-82; contract mktg. cons. The Wool Bur., Inc., Chgo., 1983—; interior design textiles, instr. Internat. Acad. of Merchandising and Design, Chgo., 1986—. Recipient Citation for Design Excellence Pa. and cen. Pa. State chpt. AIA, 1980; named One of Outstanding Young Women of Am., 1978. Mem. Am. Soc. Interior Designers (cert. by nat. council for interior design qualification examination 1980, profl. mem., industry found. mem.), Internat. Facility Mgmt. Assn., Internat. Furnishings and Design Assn., Nat. Home Fashions League (v.p. ways and means com. 1986-87, v.p. inter-soc. liaison 1987-88), Chgo. Hist. Soc., Chgo. Archtl. Found., Art Inst. of Chgo., Inst. Bus. Designers (friend of chpt.), Landmarks Preservation Council of Ill., Nat. Trust for Hist. Preservation, League of Hist. Am. Theatres, Soc. for Mktg. Profl. Services, Alpha Chi Omega. Home: 10 W Chestnut #4 Chicago IL 60610 Office: The Wool Bureau Inc 11-113A Merchandise Mart Chicago IL 60654

KLEIN, PAULA SCHWARTZ, metals broker, public relations and development executive; b. Chgo., Oct. 16, 1941; d. Arthur A. and Rosalyn (Davidson) Schwartz; student Mich. State U., 1959-60; B.A., Governors State U., 1974, M.A., 1975; m. Sanford David Klein, Dec. 18, 1960 (div. 1981); children—Gregory Scott, Julie Ann. Mem. editorial staff Okinawa Morning Star, Machinato, 1960-63; exec. dir. Bloom Twp. Com. on Youth, Chicago Heights, Ill., 1975-81; dir. fund devel. and pub. relations South Chgo. Community Hosp., 1981-84; v.p. South Chgo. Health Care Found., 1982-84; dir. devel. and pub. relations Chgo. Crime Commn., 1985-88; broker Universal Metals, Chgo., 1988—. Mem. Calumet Area Indsl. Commn. Mem. Nat. Soc. Fund Raising Profls., Nat. Assn. Prevention Profls., So. Suburban Youth Service Alliance, Criminal Def. Consortium, Nat. Assn. Hosp. Devel., Twp. Ofcls. Ill., Youth Network Council, Sierra Club. Jewish. Home: 1908 N Dayton Chicago IL 60614 Office: Universal Metals 2201 W Fulton St Chicago IL 60612

KLEIN, PHYLLIS KATZ, public relations executive; b. Trenton, N.J., Aug. 14, 1945; d. Milton and Frieda (Green) Katz; m. Neil Kleinhandler, 1970 (div. 1978). B.S., Boston U. Sch. Communication, 1967. Adminstrv. asst. Am. Petroleum Inst., N.Y.C., 1967-69; account exec. Irving Straus Assocs., N.Y.C., 1969-70; account exec., supr. Daniel J. Edelman Inc., N.Y.C., 1971-72; dir. publicity-pub. relations Clairol, N.Y.C., 1972—; corporate spokesperson various TV talk shows, 1980—. Mem. Am. Women in Radio and TV, Cosmetic Exec. Women, Women in Communications, Fashion Group. Democrat. Jewish. Office: Max Factor and Co 12100 Wilshire Blvd Los Angeles CA 90025

KLEIN, ROSEMARY, clinical psychologist; b. Aurora, Ill.; d. Arthur H. and Marylou (Allen) K. BS, U. Ill., 1973; MA, U. Ill., Chgo., 1976, PhD, 1982. Intern community, clin. psychologyCommunity Mental Health Ctr. Rutgers U. Med. Sch., Piscataway, N.J., 1980-81; sr. clinician child outreach program South Shore Med. Health Ctr., Quincy, Mass., 1981-83; clin. psychologist, cons., group psychotherapy coordinator Dorchester (Mass.) Counseling Ctr., 1984-86; pvt. practice psychology Boston, 1985—; mem. faculty dept. psychology U. Mass., Boston, 1986—; cons. PMC Substance Abuse Program, Dorchester, 1984-87, Mass. Rehab. Commn., Boston, 1985-87, Dorchester High Sch., 1987; assoc. clin. dir. Danvers State Hosp., Hathorne, Mass., 1987—. Campaign vol. Dukakis Presdl. Race, Mass., 1987; precinct co-capt., Brookline, Mass. Mem. Am. Psychol. Assn., Mass. Psychol. Assn., New Eng. Soc. Group Psychology Therapy. Democrat. Office: Rosemary Klein PhD PO Box 158 Brookline MA 02146

KLEIN, RUTH B., civic worker, packaging co. exec., poet, author; b. Cin., Jan. 31, 1908; d. Samuel and Minnie (Schunke) Becker; student U. Calif. at Los Angeles, 1926-28, San Jose State Coll., 1928-29; m. Charles Henle Klein, Sept. 23, 1938; children—Betsy Klein Schwartz, Charles Henle, Carla Klein Fee III. Sec., Novelart Mfg. Co., Cin., 1960—, dir., 1960—. Vol. Aid to Visually Handicapped program Cin. sect. Nat. Council of Jewish Women, 1951-82, sec., 1954-56, 63-64, bd. dirs., 1952-70; bd. dirs. Civic Garden Center of Greater Cin., 1956-63, chmn. spl. services for aid to visually handicapped, 1952-82. Mem. Nat. Braille Assn., Greater Cin. Writers League, Verse Writers' Guild Ohio. Club: Contemporary Literary. Author: Latitude of Love; Longitude of Lust, 1979; contbr. poems to various anthologies. Home: 6754 Fair Oaks Dr Cincinnati OH 45237

KLEIN-GILLIGAN, BONNEE, advertising executive; b. Pitts., May 27, 1954; d. James J. and Patricia R. (Redrick) Klein; m. James Vincent Gilligan, July 4, 1981. Diploma in graphic arts, York Acad. Arts, 1975. Art. dir. Imaging Systems Corp., Derry, Pa., 1978-81; advt. mgr. Pelikan, Inc., Franklin, Tenn., 1981-84; pres., founder, chief exec. officer Klein Gilligan and Assocs., 1983—. Freelance designer, 1975-85; Recipient plaque Office Mag., 1978, Office World News Mag., 1981; Best Read Ad award Geyers' Dealer Topics Mag., 1982. Mem. Am. Advt. Fedn., Nashville C. of C., Creative Forum, Assn. of Women Entrepreneurs. Office: Klein Gilligan & Assocs 2914 Berry Hill Dr Nashville TN 37204

KLEINKE, JOAN ANN, academic administrator, psychology educator; b. Sacramento, July 23, 1945; d. William Clifford and Dolores Mary (Smith) K. BA in Speech and Sociology, Calif. State U., Sacramento, 1968; MEd in Counseling and Guidance, Brigham Young U., 1975, EdD in Counseling, 1982. Advisor Seattle U. Sch. Edn., 1970-73; vets. counselor Mayday Co., Seattle, 1973; curriculum specialist, grad. student instr. Brigham Young U., Provo, Utah, 1975, advisor student activities, instr. organizational behavior,, 1976-79; grad. asst. to coordinator counselor tng. program, Dept. Ednl. Psychology Brigham Young U., Provo, 1979-81; counselor Utah State U., Logan, 1983-84, asst. dir., counselor, clin. asst. prof. psychology,, 1984-86, asst. v.p. Student Services dept., clin. asst. prof. psychology,, 1986-88, assoc. v.p. Student Services, clin. assoc. prof. psychology, 1988—; tech. writer Quinton Instrument Co., Seattle, 1974; mgr., trainer, curriculum specialist, instr. interpersonal relations and communications lab. Brigham Young U., 1979, mem. numerous coms. including adv. com. on Women's Concerns, 1976-79, Emergency Preparedness com., 1975-79; sem. instr. ch. edn. system Ch. Jesus Christ of Latter-day Saints, 1981-82; vice chairperson Profl. Employees Assn. Utah State U., 1984-86, exec. com., 1984-86; mem. exec. com. Edith Bowen Elem. Sch. Adv. Board Utah State U., 1986—; mem. Accreditation Preparation com. Utah State U., 1986—; mem. Strategic Planning com. Utah State U., 1987—. Active Assn. Mormon Counselors and Psychotherapists, 1985—. Alcohol and Drug Abuse Rehab. Counseling grantee Utah State Dept. Social Services, 1986—, Utah Commn. on Criminal and Juvenile Justice, 1987—; Helpline grantee Bear River Assn. Govts., 1986—, United Way, 1986—; Graduating Student Survey grantee Utah State U., 1986—, Ednl. Plans Survey, 1986—, Student Opinion Survey, 1986—; named one of Outstanding Young Women of Am., 1980, 82. Mem. Am. Psychol. Assn., Am. Assn. Counseling and Devel., Am. Coll. Personnel Assn., Nat. Assn. Student Personnel Adminstrs., Delta Kappa Gamma. Office: Utah State U TSC 220 Logan UT 84322-0175

KLEINLEIN, KATHY LYNN, career counseling executive; b. S.I., N.Y., May 2, 1950; d. Thomas and Helen Mary (O'Reilly) Perricone; m. Kenneth Robert Kleinlein, Oct. 30, 1983. B.A., Wagner Coll., 1971, M.A., 1974; M.B.A., Rutgers U., 1984. Cert. secondary tchr., N.Y., N.J., Fla. Tchr. English, N.Y.C. Bd. Edn., S.I., 1971-74, Matawan (N.J.) Bd. Edn., 1974-79; instr. English, Middlesex County Coll., Edison, N.J., 1978-81; med. sales rep. Pfizer/Roerig, Bklyn., 1979-81, mgr. tng. ops., N.Y.C., 1981-87; dir. sales tng. Winthrop Pharms. div. Sterling Drug, N.Y.C., 1987-88, Reuters Info. Systems, N.Y.C., 1988—; pres. Women in Transition, career counseling firm; personnel mgmt. officer U.S. Army Res., N.J., 1981-86; dir. sales tng. and devel. Sterling Drug, Inc. div. Winthrop Pharms., N.Y.C.; cons. Concepts & Producers, N.Y.C., 1981-85. Trainer United Way, 1982-83, mem. polit. action com., 1982—; mem. Republican Presdl. Task Force, Washington, 1983—. Served to Capt., U.S. Army, 1974-78. First woman in N.Y. Army N.G., 1974; first woman instr. Empire State Mil. Acad., Peekskill, N.Y., 1976. Mem. Nat. Soc. Pharm. Sales Trainers, Sales and Mktg. Execs., Am. Soc. Tng. and Devel., N.J. Assn. Women Bus. Owners, LWV, Matawan C. of C., Alpha Omicron Pi. Republican. Roman Catholic. Club: Atlantis Divers (N.Y.C.). Home: 93 Idolstone Ln Matawan NJ 07747 Office: Reuters Info Systems 1700 Broadway St New York NY 10019

KLEINSCHNITZ, BARBARA JOY, oil company executive, consultant; b. Granite Falls, Minn., Aug. 25, 1944; d. Arthur William and Joy Ardys (Roe) Green; m. Charles Lewis Kleinschnitz, Dec. 28, 1963; 1 child, Katheryn JoAnn Kleinschnitz Hartsock. BBA, U. Denver, 1983; student, Colo. Women's Coll. Leadman Schlumberger Well Services, Denver, 1968-76; supr., log processing Scientific Software-Intercomp, Denver, 1976-82; tech. cons. Tech. Log Analysis, Inc., Lakewood, Colo., 1982-83; customer support mgr. Energy Systems Tech., Inc., Englewood, Colo., 1983-86; cons. technical Littleton, Colo., 1986—; documentation specialist Q.C. Data Collectors, 1987—; cons. Tech. Log Analysis, Inc., Denver, 1982-83, Energy Systems Tech., 1986—. Vol. Denver Police Reserve, 1973-75. Mem. Nat. Organ. Women, Nat. Assn. Female Execs., Assn. Women Geoscientists, Soc. Profl. Well Log Analysts, Denver Well Log Soc. (bd. dirs. 1986-87, v.p. 1987-88, pres. 1988—). Democrat. Roman Catholic. Home and Office: 8692 W Frost Ave Littleton CO 80123

KLEKODA-BAKER, ANTONIA MARIE, forensic specialist, consultant; b. Grand Rapids, Mich., June 30, 1939; d. Anthony Joseph and Adele Elizabeth (Fifelski) Zoppa; m. Raymond Syl Klekoda, Aug. 31, 1957 (div. 1977); children: Cecilia (dec.), Vanessa, Rhonda, Darla, Norman, Yvette, Patrice; m. Frederick John Baker, Dec. 31, 1986. Student, Davenport Coll., Grand Rapids, Mich., 1956, Aquinas Coll., Grand Rapids, Mich., 1957-58, 77. Organist, choir dir. Basilica of St. Adalbert, Grand Rapids, Mich., 1957-62; music instr. Mich. Acad. of Music, Northern Mich., 1962-63; owner Handwriting Analysis Service, Grand Rapids, 1963-87; editor Garfield Park Assn., Grand Rapids, Mich., 1974-76; feature columnist Grand Rapids Press., 1966-76; staff Diocesan Pubs., Grand Rapids, 1977-85; musician, Convs., community theater, Western Mich. Contbr. over 4000 articles to profl. jours. and mags.; delivered over 3500 lectrs. Resource authority Grand Rapids Pub. Library, 1976—; organizer City Neighborhood Assn., Garfield Park, Grand Rapids, 1973, mem. Greater Grand Rapids Convention Bur., 1984-85. Recipient Safety Engrs. award W. Mich. Chpt. Soc. Safety Engrs., 1985, Holland Rotarian award, Holland, Mich. Rotary Club, 1985, Sparta Rotary award, Sparta, Mich. Rotary Club, 1986. Mem. Nat. ASssn. Pastoral Musicians, Nat. Assn. of Document Examiners, Alliance Women Entreprenurs, Grand Rapids Fedn. Musicians, Mich. Graphological Resources (chairperson, woman of the year 1986-87), Data Personnel Mgmt. Assn. Roman Catholic. Home and Office: 325 Aurora SE Grand Rapids MI 49507

KLEMZAK, AUDREY KAY, accounting firm executive; b. Dearborn, Mich., Aug. 23, 1941; d. Thomas B. and Catherine (Palmer) Sweeney; m. Donald Richard Klemzak, Oct. 10, 1963 (dec. 1981). Student, U. Detroit, 1959-61. Supr. retail foods Kroger Co., Livonia, Mich., 1964-77; pres., owner A.K. Klemzak Inc., Stuart, Fla., 1977-81; v.p., controller Myers and Assocs., Inc., Stuart, Fla., 1981-85; firm mgr. Mehlich, Roegiers Goldin and Co., CPAs, Stuart, Fla., 1985—. Dir., treas. Animal Rescue League, Stuart, Fla. Mem. Nat. Assn. Female Execs., Stuart C. of C., Pilot Club, Fla., Inst. CPAs (assoc.). Club: Governor's (Palm Beach). Home: 9900 NE Ocean Blvd Apt 3 Jensen Beach FL 34957

KLEPPER, ELIZABETH LEE, physiologist; b. Memphis, Mar. 8, 1936; d. George Madden and Margaret Elizabeth (Lee) K. BA, Vanderbilt U., 1958; MA, Duke U., 1963, PhD, 1966. Research scientist Commonwealth Sci. and Indsl. Research Orgn., Griffith, Australia, 1966-68, Battelle Northwest Lab., Richland, Wash., 1972-76; asst. prof. Auburn (Ala.) U., 1968-72; Plant physiologist USDA Agrl. Research Service, Pendleton, Oreg., 1976-85, research leader, 1985—. Assoc. editor Crop Sci., 1977-80; mem. editorial bd. Plant Physiology, 1977—; mem. editorial adv. bd. Field Crops Research, 1983—; mem. editorial bd. Irrigation Sci.; contbr. chpts. to books and articles to jours. Marshall scholar British Govt., 1958-59; NSF fellow, 1964-66. Mem. AAAS, Am. Soc. Plant Physiologists, Crop Sci. Soc. Am., Soil Sci. Soc. Am. (Fellows com. 1986—), Am. Soc. Agronomy (monograph com. 1983-86), Sigma Xi. Home: 1454 SW 45th Pendleton OR 98701 Office: USDA Argl Research Service PO Box 370 Pendleton OR 98701

KLEPPICK, MARGARET CATHERINE, hospital administrator; b. Pitts., Sept. 27, 1947; d. Robert James and Mary Elizabeth (Fisher) Williams; divorced; children: Jodi Marie, Roberta Joy. Assoc.'s degree, Robert Morris Coll., 1985. Coordinator med. edn. Mercy Hosp., Pitts., 1975-83; adminstrv. dir. med. edn. Shadyside Hosp., Pitts., 1983—. Mem. Assn. Hosp. Med. Edn., Council of Adminstrv. Dirs. in Med. Edn. of Assn. Hosp. Med. Edn. (pres., founder 1987), Pa. Assn. Med. Edn., Alliance for Continuing Med. Edn., Nat. Assn. Female Execs. Democrat. Roman Catholic. Office: Shadyside Hosp 5230 Centre Ave Pittsburgh PA 15232

KLESPER, NANCY LEE, nurse; b. Bridgeport, Conn., Oct. 7, 1947; d. Frederick William and Philomena Ann (Simmons) K.; m. Russell Bayles, June 14, 1974 (div. Sept. 1978). Student, Sacrad Heart U., 1975-77; BA in Psychology, Bridgeport Nurse Anesthesia Sch.; postgrad., Profl. Sch. Psychol. Studies, 1987. RN anasthetist, N.C.; cert. hypnotist in psychology. Nurse operating room Norwalk (Conn.) Hosp., 1974-77, 79-80; asst. dir. nursing Roncelli Inst., Bridgeport, 1978-79; nurse psychiat. staff Conn. Mental Health, New Haven, 1979; nurse anasthetist St. Mary's Hosp., Waterbury, Conn., 1982-86; freelance anasthetist San Diego, La Jolla, Calif., 1986—. Mem. Am. Assn. Nurse Anasthetist, Calif. Assn. Nurse Anasthetists, Calif. Assn. Marriage and Family Therapists. Republican. Roman Catholic. Club: Sterling House Ski (Stratford, Conn.). Home and Office: 347 Pine Ave Carlsbad CA 92008

KLESPIES, LINDA SUE, company administrator; b. Akron, Ohio, May 12, 1952; d. Nicholas Joseph and Willie Ruth (Bryan) K. MusB, Mt. Union Coll., 1974; Mus.M., Wichita State U., 1976; BMus Edn., Ohio State U., 1979; postgrad. in Musicology, Ind. U., 1977. Tchr. music Bd. Edn. Findlay (Ohio), 1979-80; mgr. trainee Friendly Restaurant, Canton, Ohio, 1980; asst. mgr. Ponderosa Inc., Kent, Ohio, 1980-82, dist. tng. instr., Kansas City, Kans., 1982, mgmt. devel. designer and instr., Dayton, 1982-83, (assigned to E.S.I. Meats) orgn. devel. specialist, Dayton, 1983-85; personnel adminstr. Frito-Lay, Inc., 1985-86; human resource systems mgr. Stone Container Corp., 1986—. Dir. children's choir Ch. of Master, Akron, 1972-73; dir. choir Salem United Meth. Ch., Wichita, 1974-76; mem. bd. advisors hospitality mgmt. program Ohio State U., 1984-85, home study div. Cornell U., 1984-85, guest instr. 1986—, Pensacola Jr. Coll., 1988—. Mem. Am. Soc. Personnel Adminstrn., Internat. Platform Assn., Am. Soc. Tng. and Devel., Nat. Assn. Female Execs., Pensacola Personnel Group, Pensacola C. of C., Mortar Bd., Mu Phi Epsilon, Pi Lambda Theta, Alpha Lambda Delta. Democrat. Methodist. Club: Rainbow Girls (past worthy advisor, capt. drill). Avocations: music, exercise, football, swimming, blown glass and shells collecting. Office: Stone Container Corp 101 Stone Blvd Cantonment FL 32533

KLIEBHAN, M(ARY) CAMILLE, college president; b. Milw., Apr. 4, 1923; d. Alfred Sebastian and Mae Eileen (McNamara) K. Student, Cardinal Stritch Coll., Milw., 1945-48; B.A., Cath. Sisters Coll., Washington, 1949; M.A., Cath. U. Am., 1951, Ph.D., 1955. Joined Sisters of St. Francis of Assisi, Roman Catholic Ch., 1945; legal sec. Spence and Hanley (attys.), Milw., 1941-45; instr. edn. Cardinal Stritch Coll., 1955-62, assoc. prof., 1962-68, prof., 1968—, head dept. edn., 1962-67, dean students, 1962-64, chmn. grad. div., 1964-69, v.p. for acad. and student affairs, 1969-74, pres., 1974—, bd. dirs., 1974—, Bd. dirs. Goals for Milw. 2000, 1980-82, Wis. Sch. Profl. Psychology, 1985-87; mem. coordinating bd. Nat. Council Accreditation Tchr. Edn., 1981-83; treas. Wis. Found. Ind. Colls., 1974-79, 87—, v.p., 1979-81, pres., 1981-83; bd. dirs. DePaul Rehab. Hosp., 1982—, Sacred Heart Sch. Theology, 1983—, Internat. Inst. of Wis., 1984—, Mental Health Assn. Milwaukee County, 1983—, Pub. Policy Forum, 1987—; mem. TEMPO, 1982—, bd. dirs., 1986—. Mem. Am. Psychol. Assn., Wis. Assn. Tchr. Educators, Phi Delta Kappa, Delta Epsilon Sigma, Psi Chi, Delta Kappa Gamma, Kappa Delta Pi. Lodge: Rotary (Milw.).

KLIEWER, PAULINE ANNETTE, nursing educator; b. Tofield, Alta., Can., Jan. 1, 1939; d. Franz Abram and Helena (Konrad) Peters; came to U.S., 1967; m. Henry Kliewer, Aug. 24, 1968; children—John Richard, Laura Jean. B.S. in Nursing, U. B.C., 1961; B.R.E., Mennonite Brethren Bible Coll., Winnipeg, Man., 1963; M.A., U. Wash., 1969, Ph.D. in Speech Communication, 1986. Nursing diplomate. Staff nurse Vancouver Gen. Hosp., 1960-61; vis. nurse Victorian Order of Nurses, Winnipeg, 1962-63; prof. English, Osaka Women's U. (Japan), 1964-67; nursing supr. Snohomish County Health Dept., Everett, Wash., 1970-71; instr. nursing Everett Community Coll., 1974-86, dir. curriculum project nursing div., 1983-86; asst. prof. Pacific Luth. U., 1986-87; assoc. prof. Calif. State U., Fresno, 1987—, chairperson nursing dept., 1987—; cons. nursing curriculum Fresno Pacific Coll. (Calif.), 1980-81. Workshop leader Free Methodist Conf., 1983, Mennonite Bibl. Sem., 1982. Crown Zellerbach Corp. research grantee, 1960; U. Wash. scholar, 1985. Mem. Am. Nurses Assn., Internat. Speech Communication Assn., Western Speech Communication Assn., Nat. League Nursing, Orton Soc. (Seattle). Office: Calif State U Dept Nursing Fresno CA 93740-0025

KLIMA, MARTHA SCANLAN, state legislator; b. Balt., Dec. 3, 1938; d. Thomas Moore and Catherine A. (Stafford) Scanlan; m. James Patrick Klima Jr., Apr. 8, 1961; children: Jennifer, J. Patrick III, Andrew. AA, Villa Julie Coll., 1958. Med. stenographer U. Md. Med. Sch., Balt., 1958-63; legis. Ho. of Dels., Annapolis, Md., 1982—; sec. Cen. Md. Health Systems Agy., 1981-83; commr. State Planning Commn., State of Md., 1983—. Del. Rep. Nat. Conv., Dallas, 1984; trustee The Jenkins Meml., Catonsville, Md., 1984—; bd. dirs. Greater Balt. Med. Ctr., Towson, 1986—, Md. Spl. Olympics, 1987—. Named Freshman of Yr., Ho. of Dels., 1984. Mem. Am. Legis. Exchange Council (state chmn. 1987—), Women Legis. Md. (v.p.), Congress of PTA's (hon. life), Balt. County C. of C. (Award of Merit 1981). Roman Catholic. Clubs: Hampton Sch. Gophers (pres.), Exchange (Balt.). Address: 1403 Newport Pl Lutherville MD 21093 Office: Ho of Dels 308 Lowe House Office Annapolis MD 21401

KLIMAN, SYLVIA MAY STERN, filmmaker, writer, editor, realtor; b. Boston, July 16, 1934; d. Edward I. and Bernice Stern; AB, Vassar Coll., 1956; m. Allan Kliman, June 24, 1956; children: Gilbert Harrow, Douglas Hartley. Editorial asst. Harvard Law Sch. profs., Cambridge, Mass., 1956-58; editor Vassar Miscellany News, Poughkeepsie, N.Y., 1953-56; editor founder Park Parent, Brookline, Mass., 1968-73; pres. Sylvia S. Kliman Real Estate Brokerage, 1971—; pres. Dunewind Films, 1979—, creative cons. for feature films & TV, 1977— . Vol. Mass. ARC Blood program, 1970-73; polit. speechwriter, 1960—; mem. Barn Gallery, Ogunquit Mus. of Art, Friends of Vassar Art Gallery. Trustee Park Sch., Brookline, 1970-73; bd. friends Peter Bent Brigham Hosp., 1970-75; bd. dirs. Spl. Com. to Restore Ogunquit Dunes, 1975—. Mem. Park Sch. Parents Assn. (pres. 1968-70), Norfolk Dist. Med. Soc. Womens Aux., Boston Museum Fine Arts. Unitarian. Club: Vassar (dir.) (Boston). Home: 40 Newton St Brookline MA 02146 Other: Dunewind Ogunquit ME 03907

KLIMKOWSKI, SISTER M. ANN FRANCIS, academic administrator; b. Wyandotte, Mich., Jan. 1, 1931; d. Alexander and Mary (Koncki) K. BSE, Bowling Green (Ohio) State U., 1961, MEd, 1967; PhD, U. Toledo, 1983. Tchr. various schs., 1954-72; prin. elem. sch. Mpls., 1972-76; asst. prin. high sch. Oregon, Ohio, 1976-77; founding dir. Lifelong Learning Ctr. Lourdes Coll., Sylvania, Ohio, 1979-81, acting acad. dean, 1981-83, pres., 1983—; mem. Cen. Cath. High Sch. Adv. Council, Toledo, 1983—; bd. dirs. Mid-Am Bank & Trust Sylvania Br. Bd. dirs. Metro Toledo Chs. United, 1983—. Mem. Am. Assn. Higher Edn., Ohio Assn. Ind. Colls. and Univs., Ohio Coll. Assn. (exec. com. 1986—), Toledo C. of C., Sylvania C. of C. Roman Catholic. Lodge: Zonta (profl. women's group Toledo chpt.). Home: 6855 Convent Blvd Sylvania OH 43560 Office: Lourdes Coll Office of the Pres 6832 Convent Blvd Sylvania OH 43560

KLINCK, PATRICIA EWASCO, state official; b. Albany, N.Y., May 13, 1940; d. Albert C. and Mary Ann (Sopko) Ewasco; m. C. Hoagland Klinck, Jr., Sept. 12, 1970; 1 dau., Natalie Childs. B.A. in History, Smith Coll., 1961; M.S. in L.S, Simmons Coll., Boston, 1963; postgrad. in edn., SUNY, Albany, 1964-67. Young adult worker Boston Pub. Library, 1961-63; library dir. Colonie Central High Sch., Albany, 1963-67; librarian Library/U.S.A., U.S. Pavilion, N.Y. World's Fair, summer 1965; library dir. Simon's Rock Coll., Gt. Barrington, Mass., 1967-70; regional dir. N.W. Regional Library, Vt. Dept. Libraries, Montpelier, 1970-72; dir. extension services div. N.W. Regional Library, Vt. Dept. Libraries, 1972-73, 73-74, acting asst. state librarian, 1973, asst. state librarian, 1974-77, state librarian, 1977—; chmn. New Eng. Library Bd., 1979-81; bd. dirs. Chief Officers State Library Agys., 1978-80, vice chmn., 1978-80, chmn., 1981-82; mem. White House Conf. Preliminary Design Commn., 1985-86. Mem. Vt. Bicentennial Commn., 1986—; bd. dirs. Vt. Hist. Soc., 1977—. Mem. ALA (legislation com. 1986—), Assn. State Library Agys. (bd. dirs. with ALA 1986—), Assn. Specialized and Cooperative Library Agys. of ALA (bd. dirs.), New Eng. Library Assn., Vt. Library Assn., Vt. Council on Humanities. Home: 47 Brewer Pkwy South Burlington VT 05401 Office: Vt Dept Of Libraries 111 State St c/o State Office Bldg PO Montpelier VT 05602

KLINE, COLLEEN MORGAN, broadcast executive; b. Amarillo, Tex., June 9, 1936; d. George Franklin and Mildred (Adams) Gathright; m. Robert Conrad Morgan, Nov. 20, 1958 (div. 1964); 1 child, Michael Conrad; m. Donald E. Kline, Apr. 21, 1970 (div. 1977). Student U. Hawaii, 1955-58; B.S., West Tex. State Coll., 1959. Asst. to v.p. of on-the-air promotion ABC-TV Network, N.Y.C., 1960-63; asst. to local, nat. sales mgr. McLendon Broadcasting, Dallas, 1964-69; owner, cons. Polyhedron, Buffalo, N.Y., 1969-72; city clk. City of Vail, Colo., 1972-83; gen. mgr., part-owner Sta. KRVV, Vail, 1983-88 ; cons. Erie County Dept. Mental Health, Buffalo, 1969-72; cons., trainer jobs to program U.S. Dept. Labor, Buffalo, 1970-71; cons. Taft Broadcasting Co., Sta. WGR-TV, Buffalo, 1971. Developer mktg. course N.Y. State Dept. Continuing Edn., 1969; media cons. KREG-TV, Glenwood Springs, Colo. Mem. Vail City Council, Colo., 1983—; exec. com. Eagle County Democratic Com., Vail, 1983—; county chmn. Dems. for Hart Campaign, Vail, 1984—; bd. dirs. Eagle County Airport Commn., Vail, 1982—. Mem. Vail Resort Chamber Assn., Vail Bus. and Profl. Women (Woman of Yr.). Methodist. Office: Sta KRVV 1000 S Frontage Rd W Suite 100 Vail CO 81657

KLINE, KIM EILEEN, journalist, editor; b. Paterson, N.J.; d. Richard and Ruby (Powe) K. BA in Sociology, Princeton U., 1976. Writer, editor Curriculum Concepts Inc., N.Y.C., 1975-76; research analyst Agy. Exchange, Paterson, 1978-79; bilingual scriptwriter Paterson Area Community Television, 1979; dir. media promotions Amsterdam News, N.Y.C., 1980-82; slot editor, chief copy editor The Paterson News, 1983-86; copy editor The Record, Hackensack, N.J., 1986—. Roman Catholic.

KLINE, KRISTINE JO, utility executive; b. Havre, Mont., Oct. 22, 1957; d. Edwin John and Donna Louise (Purdy) Haugen; m. Donald Ralph Kline, June 24, 1978; children: Cole Edwin, Cortney Dawn. AS in Water, Waste Water Tech., No. Mont. Coll., 1978; BS in Microbiology, Mont. State U., 1980. Supt. waste treatment plant City of Havre, 1980—; part-time instr. No. Mont. Coll., Havre, 1981—; field scout Pollution Technics, 1980. Mem. Water Polution Control Fedn., 1978. Mem. Water Pollution Control Assn. (chmn. edn. com. 1983-85, pres. 1986-87, mem. com. 1987-88, W.D. Hatfield award 1987-88), AAUW, Beta Sigma Phi. Methodist. Home: 1129 Cleveland Ave Havre MT 59501 Office: City of Havre Box 231 Havre MT 59501

KLINE, LINDA, executive search and corporate outplacement consultant; b. Boston, Aug. 8, 1940; d. George and Eva (Weiner) Kline; B.A. in Biology, Boston U., 1962. Personnel dir. Block Engring. Inc., Cambridge, Mass.,

1964-66; brokerage mgr. Eastern Life Ins. Co. N.Y., Boston, 1966-68; mgr. direct placement Lendman Assos., N.Y.C., 1968-72; dir. women-in-mgmt. div. Roberts-Lund, Ltd., N.Y.C., 1972-77; pres. Kline-McKay, Inc., Exec. Search and Outplacement Cons., Maximus Cons., Inc., N.Y.C., 1978—; exec. dir. Majority Money, women's network, 1976-79; tchr. fin. planning for women Marymount-Manhattan Coll., 1977; lectr. and/or cons. women's programs at several colls. and univs. and corps. Bd. dirs. Women Bus. Owners Edn. Fund, 1982-86, Mom's Amazing, 1985—; community bd. dirs. Mt. Sinai Med. Ctr., 1984—. Mem. Women Bus. Owners N.Y. (dir. 1978-84). Co-author: Career Changing: The Worry-Free Guide, 1982. Address: 3 E 48th St #6 New York NY 10017

KLINE, LINDA ROSE, computer software specialist; b. Paterson, N.J., Jan. 15, 1961; d. Stanley Paul and Marilyn Rose (Esposito) K. BS in Math., Montclair (N.J.) State Coll., 1982; MS in Computer Sci., Stevens Inst. Tech., 1986. Software engr. Lear Seigler, Inc., Fairfield, N.J., 1982-83, Bendix Corp., Teterboro, N.J., 1983-84; software programmer Keuffel & Esser, Inc., Whippany, N.J., 1984-85; software engr. Singer Kearfott, Wayne, N.J., 1985-86; software cons. Lear Seigler, Inc., Florham, N.J., 1986-87, Electro-Nucleonics, Inc., Fairfield, 1987, Matlen Silver Group, Parsippany, N.J., 1988—. Mem. Ind. Computer Cons. Assn., Assn. Computing Machinery, Nat. Assn. Female Execs., The Inst. Elec. and Electronics Engrs., Inc. Republican. Roman Catholic. Home: 242 Ridge Rd West Milford NJ 07480 Office: Compusoft Unltd 242 Ridge Rd West Milford NJ 07480

KLINE, MABLE CORNELIA PAGE, educator; b. Memphis, Aug. 20, 1928; d. George M. and Lillie (Davidson) Brown; 1 dau., Gail Angela Page. Student LeMoyne Coll.; B.S.Ed., Wayne State U., 1948, postgrad. Tchr., Flint, Mich., 1950-51, Pontiac, Mich., 1953-62; tchr. 12th grade English, Cass Tech High Sch., Detroit, 1962—; coordinator Summer Sch. High Sch. Proficiency Program. Life mem. YWCA, NAACP. Mem. NEA (life), Assn. Supervision and Curriculum Devl., Am. Fedn. Tchrs., Nat. Council Tchrs. English, Internat. Platform Assn., Wayne State U. Alumni Assn., Delta Sigma Theta. Episcopalian. Home: 1101 Lafayette Towers W Detroit MI 48207 Office: 2421 2d Ave Detroit MI 48207

KLINE, MIRIAM MARIE, educational administrator, township official; b. Hamburg, Pa., Sept. 28, 1934; d. Emanuel James and Mabel Elsie (Heimbach) Wagner; m. Richard Daniel Kline, Mar. 31, 1956; children—Eugene Richard, Ann Marie Kline Womack. Student pub. schs., Hamburg; student Pa. State U., 1988. Supr. Am. Casualty, Reading, Pa., 1952-55; sec. Hamburg Area Sch. Dist., 1961-85, sec., dir. dist. support services, 1985—; sec.-treas. Twp. of Perry, Shoemakersville, Pa., 1973—. Author: (booklet) Effective Educational Secretary, 1983. Mem. Berks County Assn. Ednl. Secs. (v.p. 1985-87), Berks County Assn. Twp. Officials, State Assn. Ednl. Secs., State Assn. Twp. Suprs., State Assn. Mcpl. Secs., Pa. Sch. Bds. Assn., Nat. Assn. Ednl. Office Personnel, Bus. and Profl. Womens Club, Pa. Assn. Notaries. Republican. Lodge: Women of Moose. Avocations: quilting; reading; travel. Home: 681 Ridge Rd Shoemakersville PA 19555 Office: Hamburg Area Sch Dist Windsor St Hamburg PA 19526

KLING, CANDACE M., architectural lighting design consultant; b. Phila., Oct. 30, 1945; d. Harry C. and Rosemary Roberta (McLaughlin) Wilson. Broadway lighting designer Jean Rosenthal, N.Y.C., 1963-68, Howard Brandston Lighting Design, 1968-70; assoc. Jules Horton Lighting Design, N.Y.C., 1970-72; with Marriott Hotel Corp., Washington, 1972-80; owner C.M. Kling & Assocs., Inc., Alexandria, Va., 1980—; guest lectr. Mt. Vernon Coll., Cath. U. Am., U. Md. Design Schs. Recipient award of Merit Chgo. Marriott Hotel Lighting Design. Mem. Illuminating Engrs. Soc., Internat. Assn. Lighting Designers, NOW. Office: 919 King St Alexandria VA 22314

KLINGENSMITH, THELMA HYDE (MRS. DON J. KLINGENSMITH), retired educational administrator; b. Kauville, S.D., May 23, 1904; d. Eber Watson and Ida (Lebert) Hyde; B.A. magna cum laude, John Fletcher Coll., 1928; M.S. in Ed., U. N.D., 1962; m. Don Joseph Klingensmith, Sept. 11, 1930; children—Merle Joseph, Eunice Victoria Klingensmith Evans. Tchr. rural schs., Almont, N.D., 1922-24; exec. sec. Young People's Gospel League, Chgo., 1928-30; asst. supt. Ponca Meth. Indian Mission, Ponca City, Okla., 1936-43; tchr. English, Almont High Sch., 1951-54; supt. schs. Morton County, Mandan, N.D., 1959-73; mem. Am. Assn. Sch. Adminstrs. seminar to Russia, 1969. Bd. dirs. N.D. div. Am. Cancer Soc., 1958-72, chmn. pub. edn. com., 1958-60, sec., 1960-66; sr. v.p. N.D. Young Citizens League, 1959-63, sr. pres., 1963-65; legis. rep. N.D. Council County Supts. Assn., 1963-66; adviser Morton County Library Bd., 1960—, trustee, 1977-83, 84—; sec.-treas. Heart River Gospel Assn., 1950-66, dir., 1950—; dir., treas. N.D. Action Com. for Environ. Edn., 1968-75; bd. dirs. Dickinson Coll. Found. 1969—; v.p. West Wis. Conf., Women's Soc. Christian Service, Methodist Ch., 1945-46; legis. rep. N.D. Woman's Christian Temperance Union, 1978—; Western dist. coordinator Christian Social involvement N.D. Conf., United Meth. Women, 1979-83; Western dist. coordinator Christian Personhood, 1983-85; Dakota area del. Internat. Conf. Christian Heritage in Govt., United Meth. Ch., London, 1981; co-chmn. nat. Conv. Prohibition Party, 1983; treas. N.D. Council on Gambling Problems, 1985-88. Named N.D. Mother of the Yr., 1965; recipient citation for conservation edn. Nat. and N.D. wildlife fedns., 1974, Pres.' citation Vennard Coll., 1984, tribute and statuette N.D. Eagle Forum, 1985. Mem. Mandan Hosp. Aux., Mandan Friends of the Library, N.D. Assn. Sch. Adminstrs., Am. Bible Soc., N.D. Library Assn. (trustee citation award 1980, cert. of appreciation 1982), N.D. Library Trustees Assn. (v.p. 1967-68, 74-76, sec. 1971-73, dir. 1976-82, pres. 1979-81), N.D. Wildlife Fedn. (chmn. essay contest 1973-78), Marquis Library Soc. (adv. mem.). Clubs: Golden Grad of Vennard Coll. (pres. 1981-84) (University Park, Iowa); Zonta (dist. VII chmn. pub. affairs com. 1968-70; del. internat. convs. 1968, 70, 72). Editor: Almont Jubilee History Book, 1956; Morton County Elementary Tchrs. Bull., 1959-73. Home: 206 Collins Ave PO Box 663 Mandan ND 58554

KLINGER, LINDA ANNE, telecommunications administrator; b. Wenatchee, Wash., Apr. 4, 1949; d. Robert Gene and Elizabeth (Talley) Gormley; m. Marvin Klinger, Aug. 23, 1980. A in Applied Arts, Wenatchee Valley Coll., 1969; student, Wash. State U., 1969-72; BBA, City U., Portland, Ore., 1987. English dept. program coordinator Wenatchee Valley Coll., 1972; student activities coordinator Edmonds (Wash.) Community Coll., 1973-76; analytical asst. GTE NW, Everett, Wash., 1976, supply specialist, 1976-78, supply adminstr., 1978-80; supply supr. GTE NW, Beaverton, Oreg., 1980-84; mgr. Phone Mart GTE NW, Gresham, Oreg., 1984-88, supr. bus. control orders and maintenance, 1988—. Mem. GTE Vol. Network, Beaverton, 1987—. Recipient Gov's. Award for Volunteerism, Ore., 1984. Mem. Am. Bus. Women (chair edn. com. 1984—). Democrat. Baptist. Lodge: Soroptimist (treas. NW region 1988—). Home: 17609 NW Rolling Hill LN Beaverton OR 97006

KLINGER, MARILYN SYDNEY, lawyer; b. N.Y.C., Aug. 14, 1953; d. Victor and Lillyan Judith (Hollinger) K. BS, U. Santa Clara, 1975; JD, U. Calif., Hastings, 1978. Bar: Calif. 1978. Assoc. Chickering & Gregory, San Francisco, 1978-81, Steefel, Levitt & Weiss, San Francisco, 1981-82; assoc. Sedgwick, Detert, Moran & Arnold, San Francisco, 1982-87, ptnr., 1988—. Sec. Hastings Dems., San Francisco, 1975-78; vol. atty. Lawyers Commn. on Urban Affairs, San Francisco, 1978-80; atty. Sta. KQED Call-a-Lawyer, San Francisco, 1979—; bd. dirs. Paradise Cay Homeowners Assn., Tiburon, Calif., v.p., 1985-87. Mem. ABA (tort and ins. practice sect., surety and fidelity com.), Surety Forum (lectr.), Northern Calif. Surety Underwriters Assn., Northern Calif. Surety Claims Assn. (lectr.). Democrat. Clubs: Tiburon Yacht (hospitality chmn. 1985-86). Home: 213 Jamaica St Tiburon CA 94920 Office: Sedgwick Detert Moran & Arnold 1 Embarcadero Ctr 16th Floor San Francisco CA 94111

KLINGER, SHERRY NADINE, public relations executive; b. Hollywood, Calif., July 13, 1953; d. David G. and Stella Z. (Sunderland) K. B of Polit. Sci., Calif. State U., Northridge, 1986. Account exec. David Gest and Assocs., Los Angeles, 1972-82; polit. appointee Reagan Adminstrn., Washington, 1982-83; pres. The Klinger Group, Burbank, Calif., 1984—. Contbr. articles to newspapers, mags. Del. to Rep. Nat. Conv., 1980, 84; vol. Rep. election campaigns, 1979-86. Jewish. Office: The Klinger Group 178 S Victory Blvd Suite 106 Burbank CA 91502

KLINGMAN, JILL COLLEEN, educator; b. Imperial, Neb., Sept. 12, 1955; d. Wilferd Duane and Shirley (Carter) Fanning; m. Bradley Harold Klingman, May 31, 1980; children: Jacob William, Joshua James. BA in Edn., U. Neb., 1977; MEd, Kearney (Neb.) State Coll., 1983. Elementary tchr. Centura Pub. Sch., Cairo, Neb., 1977-80, Grand Island (Neb.), 1980—. Mem. Grand Island Edn. Assn., Neb. Edn. Assn. (pres. 1978-79), Alpha Delta Kappa (sec. 1985). Democrat. Lutheran. Home: 1740 Idlewood Grand Island NE 68803 Office: Grand Island Pub Sch 910 E 8th St Grand Island NE 68801

KLINK, KARIN ELIZABETH, medical communications company executive, writer; b. N.Y.C., Nov. 12, 1937; d. Nils Gustaf and Mary Josephine (Crowley) Hernblad; m. Fredric J. Klink, Nov. 28, 1958 (div. Apr. 1979); children: Christopher Frederick, Charles Gustaf. BA in Geology, Barnard Coll., 1958; MFA in Film Making, Columbia U., 1963; MS in Counseling and Art Therapy, U. Bridgeport, 1977; grad. cert. in corp. video Fairfield U., 1983. Film editor, writer Eye Gate House, N.Y.C., 1966-68; sr. editor Starting Tomorrow, N.Y.C., 1968-70; dir. creative therapies Hall-Brooke Hosp., Westport, Conn., 1978-83; mgr. editorial devel. New Eng. Advt. Assn., Norwalk, Conn., 1984-85; editorial dir. Logical Communications, Norwalk, 1985; pres. Creative Word & Image, Rowayton, Conn., 1985—; cons. audio-visual specialist in Wetlands, Norwalk Schs., 1985; free-lance writer, editor for various cos., Conn., 1984—. Artist; exhibited in various shows; author films, filmstrips and videotapes; designer, animator The Stage Evolves, 1964; writer, photographer slide tape, 1985. Sec. bd., aerial photographer Preserve the Wetlands, Rowayton, 1983—; bd. dirs. Arts Inst., Silvermine Guild, New Canaan, Conn., 1984—. Mem. Women in Communications, Inc., Am. Art Therapy Assn. (profl.), Silvermine Guild Artists (artist mem., various awards), Rowayton Art Ctr. (artist mem.), So. Conn. Art Therapy Assn. (art therapist, pres. 1982-83). Democrat. Episcopalian. Avocations: drawing; painting; aerial photography; sailing; painted Easter egg in White House collection at Smithsonian Inst. Home and Office: 13 Sammis St Rowayton CT 06853

KLINK, SHARON MAY, sales executive; b. Whittier, Calif., Feb. 8, 1946; d. Hubert Miller and Garnet May (Prater) Jones; m. Gary Lee Klink, June 18, 1966 (div.); children—Robert Douglas, Jeffrey Loren. Student Pasadena Coll. (scholar), 1963-65; A.A., Rio Hondo Coll., 1978; student Calif. State U.-Fullerton, 1978; B.S.B.A., U. Redlands, 1982. Sec. Armorlite Lens Co., Pasadena, 1963-64, James, Pond & Clark, Pasadena, 1964-65; sales sec. Fiberboard Paper, Commerce, Calif., 1965-67; instr. aide East Whittier Sch. Dist., Calif., 1974-78; sales rep. Gen. Can Co., Montebello, Calif., 1978-86, Brouse-Whited Creative Packaging, Marina del Rey, Calif., 1986; br. mgr. Gen. Can Inc., Hayward, Calif., 1986-88; bus. banking mgr. Wells Fargo Bank, N.A., San Jose, Calif., 1988—. Sec. ch. bd. Ch. of the Nazarene, 1973-76, children's dir., 1965-69; youth dir. Women's Christian Temperance Union, 1965-69; treas. P.T.A., 1977-79; bd. dirs. Bay Area Crisis Nursery, Concord, Calif.; vol. Valley Meml. Hosp. Emergency Room, Livermore, Calif. Mem. Nat. Assn. Female Execs. Republican. Avocations: writing; golfing; snorkling; cooking. Office: Wells Fargo Bank 2170 Tully Rd San Jose CA 94122

KLINMAN, JUDITH POLLOCK, biochemist, educator; b. Phila., Apr. 17, 1941; d. Edward and Sylvia (Fitterman) Pollock; m. Norman R. Klinman, July 3, 1963 (div. 1978); children—Andrew, Douglas. A.B., U. Pa., 1962, Ph.D., 1966. Postdoctoral fellow Weizmann Inst. Sci., Rehovoth, Israel, 1966-67; postdoctoral assoc. Inst. for Cancer Research, Phila., 1968-70, research assoc., 1970-72, asst. mem., 1972-77, assoc. mem., 1977-78; asst. prof. biophysics U. Pa., Phila., 1974-78; assoc. prof. chemistry U. Calif.-Berkeley, 1978-82, prof., 1982—; mem. ad hoc biochemistry and phys. biochemistry study sects. NIH, 1977-84, phys. biochemistry study sect., 1984-88, Guogenheim, 1988—. Mem. editorial bd. Jour. Biol. Chemistry, 1979-84; contbr. numerous articles to profl. jours. Fellow NSF, 1964, NIH, 1964-66. Mem. Am. Chem. Soc. (exec. council biol. div. 1982-85, chmn. nominating com. 1987-88), Am. Soc. Biol. Chemists (membership com. 1984-86, pub. affairs com. 1987—), Sigma Xi. Office: U Calif Dept Chemistry Berkeley CA 94720

KLIPSCH, LEONA KATHERINE, retired newspaper publisher and editor; b. Vancouver, Wash., Feb. 24, 1914; d. Louis John and Marie Rosetta (Debitt) Hinkel; A.B., Smith Coll., 1935; student Sorbonne, Paris, 1934, Columbia U. Grad. Sch. Library Service, summers 1942-44; m. Robert Darius Klipsch, Nov. 25, 1937; children—Phyllis Marie Klipsch Smith, Katharine Klipsch Abbott, Marjorie Klipsch McCracken. Tchr. French and library sci. Marshall U., Huntington, W.Va., 1949-54; br. librarian Albuquerque Public Library, 1955-56; high sch. librarian, Gallup, N.Mex., 1963-65; co-owner, editor Defensor Chieftain, Socorro, N.Mex., 1965-82, pub., 1980-82. Bd. dirs. Socorro Gen. Hosp. Mem. AAUW, PEO, Sigma Delta Chi. Republican. Presbyterian. Author: Treasure Your Love (Librarian prize for jr. novel 1958); (as Jean Kirby) A Very Special Girl, 1963. Home: 1304 Kitt Pl PO Box V Socorro NM 87801

KLOCEK, KATHLEEN ANNE, parent educator; b. Pitts., Nov. 5, 1948; d. Alexander and Frances Florence (Tropeck) Kravec; m. Daniel Leonard Klocek, Dec. 26, 1970; children—Joseph, Timothy, Kara, Matthew. B.S., Duquesne U., 1970. Exec. officer mgr. Kaufmann's, Pitts., 1970-71; nat. parenting trainer Am. Soc. Psychoprophylaxis in Obstets./Lamaze, Washington, 1977-81; exec. dir. Parenting Assocs., Verona, Pa., 1980—; cons. Mom's House, Inc., Pitts., 1986—. Contbr. articles to Childbirth Educator mag., 1982—. Mem. Family Resource Coalition, Am. Soc. Psychoprophylaxis in Obstetrics (bd. dirs. 1975-81), Mothers Are People Too Program. Republican. Byzantine Catholic. Avocations: genealogy; ice skating; swimming; reading; photography. Office: Parenting Assocs 8243 Lincoln Rd Verona PA 15147

KLOCKNER, KAREN MARTHA, book editor; b. Glen Ridge, N.J., Feb. 28, 1952; d. Joseph Steinert and Doris Ellen (Fenton) K.; m. Frederick Alexander, Dec. 30, 1978; 1 child, Sarah Elizabeth. BA, Cornell U., 1975; MA, Simmons Coll., 1980. Editorial asst. Horn Book Mag., Boston, 1975-77, asst. editor, 1977-79; editorial asst. The Atlantic, Boston, 1981-82; asst. editor Little, Brown and Co., Boston, 1982-83, assoc. editor, 1983-85, editor, 1985-86, sr. editor, 1986—. Translator: The Christman Train, 1984, Otto the Bear, 1985, The Black Sheep, 1986; editor Saint George, 1984 (Caldecott Medal), Village of Round and Square Houses, 1987 (Caldecott Honor). Sch. tchr. Old South Ch., Boston 1977-79, Old North Ch., Marblehead, Mass. 1982-83. Mem. Am. Library Assn., New Eng. Library Assn. Office: Little Brown and Co 34 Beacon St Boston MA 02108

KLODOWSKI, AMY MARTHA AUSLANDER, lawyer; b. N.Y.C., Oct. 13, 1952; d. Oscar and Beatrice (Feinberg) Auslander; m. Harry F. Klodowski, Jr., Nov. 12, 1983; children: Deborah Bea, Daniel Francis. BA, Kent State U., 1974; JD, U. Pitts., 1978. Bar: Pa. 1978. Atty., Equitable Resources, Inc., Pitts., 1978—. Mem. ABA, Fed. Energy Bar Assn., Pa. Bar Assn., Allegheny County Bar Assn. Club: Rivers (Pitts.). Office: Equitable Resources Inc 420 Blvd of the Allies Pittsburgh PA 15219

KLOEPFER, MARGUERITE FONNESBECK, writer; b. Logan, Utah, Nov. 13, 1916; d. Leon and Jean (Brown) Fonnesbeck; m. Lynn William Kloepfer, Aug. 6, 1937; children: William Leon, Kenneth Lynn, Kathryn Kloepfer Ellis, Robert Alan. BS, Utah State U., 1937. Legal sec. Lynn W. Kloepfer, Atty., Ontario, Calif., 1958-74; freelance writer, novelist Ontario, 1974—. Author: Bentley, 1979, Singles Survival, 1979, But Where is Love, 1980, The Heart and the Scarab, 1981, Schatten in der Wuste, 1983; contbr. short stories to Seventeen, Women's Day, numerous others; contbr. articles on travel to profl. jours. Pres. Foothill chpt. Nat. Charity League Inc., Ontario, 1965-67, nat. pres., 1968-70; pres. Interfraternity Mother's Clubs council U. So. Calif., Los Angeles, 1971-72, mem. coordinating council, town and gown; pres. Law Aux. San Bernandio County, Calif., 1957-58, Law Aux. Calif., 1974-75. Club: Friday Afternoon (West San Bernandio County) (pres. 1986-87). Home: 306 E Hawthorne St Ontario CA 91764

KLOPFENSTEIN, MELINDA LEE, accountant; b. Lansing, Mich., Oct. 18, 1944; d. George Wayne and Cecil Lorena (Wilcox) Brown; m. Lee David Klopfenstein, May 28, 1966 (div. May 26, 1981); children: Mark Wayne, Susan Gail. BS in Math, Mich. State U., 1965; BBA in Acctg., Saginaw Valley State Coll., 1978. Bookkeeper Ernst and Whinney, Saginaw, Mich., 1977-79; franchise acct. Tuffy Service Ctrs., Inc., Saginaw, 1980-85, Tuffy Assocs. Corp., Saginaw, 1986; acct. R&D, Inc. doing bus. as Tuffy Muffler, Saginaw, 1986—. Editor Civic Newcomers, Saginaw, 1969; dir. Saginaw Jaycees Aux., 1972-75, named Woman of Yr., 1975; co-chair Miss Saginaw County, 1973, Luth. Social Services of Mich. Ambassadors, 1988—, sec. Saginaw County pres.'s council, 1988—; treas. Our Saviour Luth. Ch., Saginaw, 1983-87, fin. sec., 1987—. Mem. Mich. State U. Coll. Nat. Sci. Alumni Assn. (bd. dirs.). Home: #10 Slatestone Dr Saginaw MI 48603

KLOPFLEISCH, STEPHANIE SQUANCE, social services agency administrator; b. Rupert, Idaho, Dec. 21, 1940; d. William Jaynes and Elizabeth (Cunningham) Squance; B.A., Pomona Coll., 1962; M.S.W., UCLA, 1966; m. Randall Klopfleisch, June 27, 1970; children—Elizabeth, Jennifer, Matthew. Social worker, Los Angeles County, 1963-67; program dir. day care, vol. services Los Angeles County, 1968-71; div. chief children's services Dept. Public Social Services, Los Angeles County, 1971-73, dir. bur. of social services, 1973-79; chief dep. dir. Dept. Community Services, Los Angeles County, 1979—; with Area 10 Devel. Disabilities, 1981-82; bd. dirs. Los Angeles Fed. Emergency Mgmt. Act, 1985—, pres., 1987; bd. dirs. Los Angeles Shelter Partnership. Mem. Calif. Commn. on Family Planning, 1976-79; mem. Los Angeles Commn. Children's Instns., 1977-78; bd. dirs. United Way Info., 1978-79; chmn. Los Angeles County Internat. Yr. of Child Commn., 1978-79, Los Angeles Shelter Ptnrship., 1987; bd. govs. Sch. Social Welfare, UCLA, 1981-84. Mem. Nat. Assn. Social Workers, Am. Public Welfare Assn., Am. Soc. Pub. Adminstrn.

KLOS, SUSAN, motion picture company executive; b. East Meadow, N.Y., May 16, 1955; d. Christopher Henry and Agnes Catherine (Hamel) K.; children: Jesse Blue, Rainbow Rachel. Student, SUNY, Stony Brook, 1975. Pres., owner Big Time Picture Co. Inc., Los Angeles, 1978—. Producer, dir. (film) Instant Replay U.S.A., 1970; exec. producer Imagination Boogie, 1987—. Baseball coach Palisades League, Pacific Palisades, Calif., 1982-86; den leader Western Los Angeles council Boy Scouts Am., 1985-86, asst. cubmaster 1986-87; troop leader Girl Scouts U.S., Los Angeles County, 1986—. Mem. Women in Film, Am. Cinema Editors (affiliate), Motion Picture Sound Editors (assoc.), Pacific Palisades C. of C., Am. Film Inst. Alumni Assn. (fellow 1975-76). Office: Big Time Picture Co Inc 12210 1/2 Nebraska Ave Los Angeles CA 90025

KLOSNER, NAOMI CERTNER, psychologist; b. N.Y.C., June 8, 1941; d. Simon and Anne (Beresowsky) Certner; m. Jerome Martin Klosner; children: Michael, Lise, Marc. BA, SUNY, Buffalo, 1962; MA, Columbia U., 1963; PhD, NYU, 1968. Asst. prof. Hofstra U., Hempstead, N.Y., 1968-70; research assoc. Community Service Soc., N.Y.C., 1970; asst. prof. Queensboro (N.Y.) Community Coll., 1970-71; cons. Great Neck (N.Y.) Pub. Schs., 1973-80; psychologist N.Y.C. Bd. Edn., Queens, 1980—; adj. prof. NYU, 1973-80; cons. in field, 1980—. Mem. com. for the gifted PTA, Bayside, 1976. Mem. Am. Psychol. Assn. Home: 27-20 Little Neck Blvd Bayside NY 11360

KLOSTER, CAROL GOOD, book and video cassette distribution company executive; b. Richmond, Va., Aug. 18, 1948; d. David William and Lucy (McDowell) Good; m. John Kenneth Kloster III, Feb. 15, 1975; children—John Kenneth IV, Amanda Aileen. A.B., Coll. William and Mary, 1970. Personnel supr. Charles Levy Circulating Co., Chgo., 1974-75, warehouse supr., 1976-77, warehouse mgr., 1978-80, dir. sales, 1980-83, asst. v.p., dir. mktg., 1984; v.p., gen. mgr. Video Trend of Chgo., 1985-86; v.p. gen. mgr. Computer Book Service div. Charles Levy Circulating Computer Book Service, 1986—. Recipient Algernon Sidney Sullivan award Coll. William and Mary, 1970. Presbyterian. Home: 322 Bonnie Brae Hinsdale IL 60521 Office: Computer Book Service 4201 Raymond Dr Hillside IL 60162

KLOTZMAN, DOROTHY ANN, musical educator, conductor, composer; b. Seattle, Mar. 24, 1937; d. Henry and Irva (Graham) Hill. B.S., Juilliard Sch., 1958, M.S., 1960. Prof., chmn. music Bklyn. Coll., 1971-81; dir. Conservatory Music, 1981—. Condr., Bklyn. Coll. Symphonic Band, 1970-81, Symphony Orch., 1980—, 1st woman condr., Goldman Band, 1973-75, 77, bd. dirs., Goldman Band, 1979, guest condr., Guggenheim Concerts Band, 1980-83, bd. dirs., Guggenheim Concerts Band, 1980—; Composer: symphonic band Good Day Sir Christmas; soprano solo, chorus and instrumental ensemble Divertimento; chamber orch. Concerto; saxophone and orch. Chimera; ballet Variations; orch. Overture for a Dedication; arranger: orch. Slavonic Dance No. 12 (Dvorak); editor: Richard Franko Goldman: Selected Essays and Reviews, 1948-1968. Mem. citizens adv. bd. WNCN, 1976; Bd. dirs. Bklyn. Ctr. for Performing Arts at Bklyn. Coll., 1983—; trustee Bklyn. Coll. Found, 1981—. Recipient N.Y. Philharmonic Young Composers' Contest 1st prize, 1953-54; Benjamin award in composition, 1955, 58; Fromm prize composition Aspen Music Sch., 1960; Danforth Found. E. Harris Harbison award, 1972. Mem. Am. Music Center, Am. Musicol. Soc., Coll. Music Soc., Music Library Assn., Am. Soc. Composers and Performers. Home: 543 E 24th St Brooklyn NY 11210 *

KLOZE, IDA IRIS, lawyer; d. Max and Bertha (Samet) K. A.A., George Washington U., 1944, A.B., 1947; LL.B., U. Md., 1926. Bar: Md. 1927, U.S. Supreme Ct. 1949. Sole practice, Balt., 1927-34; dep. collector IRS, Balt., 1934-39; with GAO, 1943-45, War Assets Adminstrn., 1945-49, Labor Dept., 1950-53, FTC, 1956-71; vol. atty. Pro Bono Law Litigation Div. Pub. Citizen, Washington, 1972—. Mem. Mrs. Rosalyn Carter's Com. Mental Health; exec. sec. Commn. for Prevention Infantile Paralysis, Balt., 1940-42; lobbyist Md. Legislature for Widows and Old Age Pensions, Balt., 1938-40; sec. Citizen's Commn. Md., Balt., 1935-39. Mem. ABA, Women's Bar Assn. (v.p. Balt. 1928-32), Profl. Women's Councils (pres. 1928-33), Nat. Women's Party (lobbyist, legal asst. life mem. 1951—), Fed. Bar Assn. (rec. sec., mem. nat. council, sec. com. gen. counsels 1951-52).

KLUDSIKOFSKY, LAVERNE MARY, health care administrator, nurse; b. Minot, N.D., July 12, 1938; d. Vernon LeRoy and Ada May (Robinson) Reynolds; m. Roy G. Kludsikofsky (div. June 1980); 1 child, Tamera Lee. Diploma, Providence Sch. Nursing, Portland, Ore., 1959; BA, Linfield Coll., 1987. RN. RN Providence Hosp., Portland, 1959-60; RN, office mgr. P. Burgner, R. Gray and J.C. Hoyt M.D., Portland, 1960-69; owner, copr. sec., mgr. Providence Flowers and Gifts Inc., Portland, 1966-73; RN Multnomah County Home Health, Portland, 1973-74; nurse, coordinator Yamhill County Home Health, McMinnville, Oreg., 1975-79; nurse, mgr. Wash. County Dept. Pub. Health, Hillsboro, Oreg., 1979-83; dir. Tuality Home Health (formerly Washington County Home Health Care Assn.), Forest Grove, Oreg., 1983-88; v.p. Jarett Assocs Inc, Los Alamitos, Calif., 1988—; cons. Jarrett and Assocs., Van Nuys, Calif., 1986—; mem. adv. com. Concordia Coll. Health Care Adminstrn., Portland, 1985—. Author: The Nurse Assistant and Home Health Aide, 1983, The Nurse Assistant and Home Health Aide Trainers Manual, 1983. Charter mem. Mary Ann Nimmo Hospice, Forest Grove, 1981—; mem. exec. bd. Oreg. Comprehensive Cancer Program, Portland, 1980-85; charter., bd. dirs. Mid-Willamette Hospice, Salem, Oreg., 1978-79; mem. Oreg. Covenant Camping Program. Mem. Oreg. Assn. Home Care (pres. 1977-79, 86, pres.-elect 1984-86, Hope Runnels's award 1986), Nat. Assn. Home Care. Mem. Evangelical Covenant Ch. Home: 4302 Pickwick Circle #308 Huntington Beach CA 92649 Office: Tuality Home Health 4334 Katella Ave Los Alamitos CA 90720

KLUETER, NANCY LEE, marketing administrator; b. Champaign, Ill., Nov. 30, 1959; d. Herschel Henry and Mavis Jean (Bourgois) K. Grad., Wash. Sch. for Secs., 1978; BS in Mktg., Calif. State U., Los Angeles, 1987. Exec. sec. Am. Iron and Steel Inst., Washington, 1978-81; asst. mgr. AMC Acad. 6 Theatres, Greenbelt, Md., 1981-83; adminstr. nat. advt. AMC Theatres, Los Angeles, 1983—. 2d reader 1st Ch. Christ Scientist, Los Angeles, 1985-88. Mem. Gold Key. Office: AMC Film Mktg 15821 Ventura Blvd Encino CA 91436

KLUK, NADA, insurance company executive; b. Munich, Germany, Oct. 22, 1946; d. Marko and Zorka (Medic) Borkovich; m. Ronald Andrew Kluk, June 1, 1968. Asst. supr. Washington Nat. Ins. Co., Evanston, Ill., 1969-72, supr., 1972-74, gen. supr., 1974-75, asst. mgr., 1975-77, mgr., 1977—, mem. mgmt. adv. council, 1979-81, chmn. group coverages and procedures com., 1985—, sec. group underwriting com., 1985—, mem. 75th anniversary com., 1986. Vol. Am. Cancer Soc., Chgo., 1980-85; capt. vols. bus. div. United Way, Evanston, 1981-84. Nominee YWCA Leader Luncheon, 1979. Mem.

Soc. Group Contract Analysts (host meeting 1985), Nat. Assn. Female Execs. Democrat. Roman Catholic. Avocations: reading, walking. Office: Washington Nat Ins Co 1630 Chicago Ave Evanston IL 60201

KNAAK, JEAN T. HANSON, business executive, consultant; b. Parkers Prairie, Minn., May 9, 1942; d. Milton and Mabel (Eggen) Thompson; m. William C. Knaak; children: Jill, Mark. BS, N.D. State U., 1964, MS, 1970; PhD, U. Minn., 1983. Instr. Oak Grove High Sch., Fargo, S.D., 1963-64, Red Lake Falls (Minn.) Sch., 1964-81; dir. Pine to Prairie Coop. Ctr., Red Lake Falls, 1971-81; pres. Convergent Systems Inc., St. Paul, 1983—, CSI Nanny Profls., 1985—, Bus. Security, Inc., 1986—. Mem. exec. council Agassiz Health Systems Agy., East Grand Forks, 1976-81; pres. Red Lake Falls Day Care Ctr., 1976-81; mem. N.D. Health Coordinating Council, Bismark, 1976-80; exec. council Prince Peace Lutheran Ch. Mem. Nat. Adv. Council Vocat. Edn. (vice chmn. 1982-85), Am. Vocat. Assn. (exec. bd. dirs. 1976-83, v.p. 1976-83, pres. 1981-82), Minn. Vocat. Assn. (pres. 1975-76), Kappa Delta Pi, Phi Delta Kappa, Delta Kappa Gamma, Phi Kappa Phi. Home: 2456 Arkwright Saint Paul MN 55117 Office: Convergent Systems Inc 245 E 6th St Suite 703 Saint Paul MN 55101

KNAPP, CAROL P., lawyer; b. Mishawaka, Ind.; d. Edward James and Virginia (Sorenson) Potocki. BS in Polit. Sci. with distinction, U. Minn., 1974; JD summa cum laude, Woodward Wilson Coll., 1978. Bar: Ga. 1978, U.S. Dist. Ct. (no. dist.) Ga. 1978. Sole practice Atlanta, 1979—. Chmn. Crescendo Ball Cystic Fibrosis, 1986, host com. 1987, Variety Club Cash for Kids Dinner, 1987; ball com. Beaux Art Ball Benefit Atlanta Coll. Art, 1984; polit. writer Andrew Young's Mayor Campaign, 1981; legal asst. Bo Ginn's Governor Campaign, 1982. Recipient Humanitarian Medal Vatican, 1986; named Lady Knights Malta of St. John Jerusalem, Supreme Order Hosp. St. John Jerusalem, 1986. Mem. Ga. Trial Lawyers Assn., Atlanta Bar Assn. Office: 2045 Peachtree Rd Suite 717 Atlanta GA 30309

KNAPP, CAROLYN MARIE, humane society administrator; b. Iowa City, Aug. 28, 1956; d. David Edward and Doris Marie (White) Knapp; m. Richard Ray, Apr. 28, 1984: 1 child, Randi Reneé. BS in Social Work, Iowa State U., 1979. Asst. Paulsen Veterinary Clin., Cedar Rapids, Iowa, 1972-73, Linn County Veterinary Clinic, Marion, Iowa, 1973-74; crew chief Blacks Seec Corn Co., Ames, Iowa, 1975-77; mgr., bartender Am. Legion Hall, Ames, 1976-78; owner Toughskin Hounds Kennels, Ames and Colfax, Iowa, Palmyra, Mo., 1978—; instnl. instr. Mitchellville (Iowa) Tng. Sch., 1979-81; social worker Ill. Dept. Children and Family Services, Quincy, 1981-83; ptnr. Rhinehart Trucking, Palmyra, 1984-87; exec. dir. Quincy Humane Soc., 1984—. Mem., com. chmn., bd. dirs. Quincy Area Network Against Domestic Violence, 1982—; com. chmn., bd. dirs. Woodlawn Ctr., Quincy, 1984—. Named one of Outstanding Young Women Am., 1984, 86. Mem. Am. Humane Soc., Am. Bloodhound Club, Quincy Kennel Club (bd. dirs. 1986—). Home: Rural Rt 1 Box 455 Palmyra MO 63461 Office: Quincy Humane Soc PO Box 1023 Quincy IL 62306

KNAPP, CONSTANCE ANNE, management consultant; b. N.Y.C., Jan. 25, 1948; d. Harold Thomas and Jacqueline (Devine) K. BA, SUNY, New Paltz, 1969; MBA, Fordham U., 1975. Cert. System Profl. Actuarial trainee The Home Ins. Co., N.Y.C., 1969-72; Tech. Rep. Rapidata, Inc., N.Y.C., 1972-74; mgmt. cons. The Equitable Life Ins. Soc., N.Y.C., 1974-79; mgr. fin. info. systems The N.Y. Times, 1979-83; owner C.A. Knapp Enterprises, Bklyn., 1984—; lctr. Pace U., N.Y.C., 1985—; coll. coordinator, The Inst. of Mgmt. Scis, N.Y.C., 1987-88; student liaison, Assn. For Systems Mgmt., N.Y.C., 1987—. Contbr. articles to profl. jours., 1980—. Fellow Life Mgmt. Inst.; mem. The Inst. Mgmt. Scis., The Assn. of Computing Machinery, Assn. for Systems Mgmt., Ind. Computer cons. Assn. Democrat. Mem. United Ch. of Christ.

KNAPP, MILDRED FLORENCE, social worker; b. Detroit, Apr. 15, 1932; d. Edwin Frederick and Florence Josephine (Antaya) K.; B.B.A., U. Mich., 1954, M.A. in Community and Adult Edn. (Mott Found. fellow 1964), 1964, M.S.W. (HEW grantee 1966), 1967. Dist. dir. Girl Scouts Met. Detroit, 1954-63; planning asst. Council Social Agencies Flint and Genessee County, 1965; sch. social worker Detroit public schs., 1967—; field instr. grad. social workers. Mem. alumnae bd. govs. U. Mich., 1972-75, scholarship chmn., 1969-70, 76-80, chmn. spl. com. women's athletics, 1972-75, class agt. fund raising Sch. Bus. Adminstrn., 1978-79; mem. Founders Soc. Detroit Inst. Art, 1969—, Friends Children's Museum Detroit, 1978—, Women's Assn. Detroit Symphony Orch., 1982—; trustee Children's Mus. Recipient various certs. appreciation. Mem. Nat. Assn. Social Workers, Acad. Cert. Social Workers, Nat. Community Edn. Assn. (charter), Outdoor Edn. and Camping Council (charter), Mich. Sch. Social Workers Assn. (pres. 1980-81), Detroit Sch. Social Workers Assn. (past pres.), Detroit Assn. U. Mich. Women (pres. 1980-82), Detroit Fedn. Tchrs. Methodist. Clubs: Detroit Boat, Detroit Women's City. Home: 702 Lakepointe Grosse Pointe Park MI 48230 Office: 4300 Marseilles Detroit MI 48224

KNAPP, ROSALIND ANN, lawyer; b. Washington, Aug. 15, 1945; d. Joseph Burke and Hilary (Eaves) K.; B.A., Stanford U., 1967, J.D., 1973. Admitted to Calif. bar, 1973, D.C. bar, 1980; with Dept. Transp., Washington, 1973—, asst. gen. counsel legislation, 1979-81, dep. gen. counsel, 1981—. Mem. D.C. Bar Assn., Calif. Bar Assn. Office: 400 7th St SW Washington DC 20590

KNAPP, VIRGINIA ESTELLA, retired educator; b. Washington, May 11, 1919; d. Bradford and Stella (White) Knapp; B.A., Tex. Tech. U., 1940; M.A., U. Tex. 1948; postgrad. Sul Ross Coll., 1950, Stephen F. Austin U., 1964-68. Tchr. journalism, high schs., Silverton, Tex., 1940-41, Electra, Tex., 1941-42, Joinerville, Tex., 1942-60, Carthage, Tex., 1961-69; tchr. history and journalism Longview (Tex.) High Sch., 1969-80; instr. Trinity U., San Antonio, summer 1972; fellowship tchr. Wall St. Jour., Tex. A&M U., College Station, summers 1964-67. Chmn., Rusk County (Tex.) Hist. Commn., 1980—. Recipient Wall St. Jour. award Outstanding Journalism Tchrs. of Yr., 1965-66; Trail Blazer award Tex. High Sch. Press Assn., 1980; Woman of Yr. award, 1983. Mem. Tex. State Tchrs. Assn., Classroom Tchrs. Assn., Tex. Assn. Jour. Dirs., Rusk County Heritage Assn., Rusk County Hist. Commn., Women in Communications (pres. Longview chpt. 1972-74, Service award 1975), Tex. Press Women, DAR. Episcopalian. Contbr. hist. writing to Ala. Rev., Progressive Farmer, Rusk County C. of C. Brochure, Rusk County Heritage, numerous others. Home: 321 College Ave Henderson TX 75652 Office: 514 N High Henderson TX 75652

KNAUER, JANIS MARION, dietitian; b. Rockville Centre, N.Y., June 19, 1956; d. Frederick Frances and Rita (Fagan) Lando; m. Stuart Leslie Knauer, May 1, 1980; children: Michael, Leslie. BS in Dietetics, Marywood Coll., 1978. Registered dietitian, N.J. Dietitian Moody Sch. Cerebral Palsied Children, Galveston, Tex., 1979-80; pediatric dietitian Tex. Children's Hosp., Houston, 1980-82; coordinator nutrition edn. and tng. Alief (Tex.) Independent Sch. Dist., 1982-86; dir. food service Service Am., Williamstown, N.J., 1986—; Dial-a-Dietitian So. Tex. Dietetic Assn., Houston, 1984-86. Contbr. articles to various jours. Vol. ambulance squad, Wenonah Fire Dept., N.J. 1986—. Mem. Am. Dietetic Assn., N.J. Dietetic Assn., (licensure chmn. so. dist.), Dietitians Bus. and Industry, Dietitians Sch. Food Service. Republican. Roman Catholic. Home: 8 S Lincoln Ave Wenonah NJ 08090 Office: Service Am Corp Radix Elem Radix Rd Williamstown NJ 08094

KNAUER, VELMA STANFORD, savs. and loan assn. exec.; b. Pottstown, Pa., July 4, 1918; d. Chester Miller and Pearl Fretz (Miller) Stanford; student public schs.; m. Joseph Daniel Knauer, Feb. 17, 1940; children—Joseph Daniel, Susan Velma Knauer Metz. With U.S. Axle Co., Inc., Pottstown, 1936-45; with First Fed. Savs. & Loan Assn., Pottstown, 1953—, controller, 1953—, asst. treas., 1953-62, asst. sec., 1962-75, treas., 1976—. Mem. Am. Soc. Profl. and Exec. Women. Home: 970 Feist Ave Pottstown PA 19464 Office: Box 1 High and Hanover Sts Pottstown PA 19464

KNAUER, VIRGINIA HARRINGTON WRIGHT (MRS. WILHELM F. KNAUER), government official; b. Phila., Mar. 28, 1915; d. Herman Winfield and Helen (Harrington) Wright; m. Wilhelm F. Knauer, Jan. 27, 1940; children: Wilhelm F., Valerie H. (Mrs. I. Townsend Burden III). B.F.A., U. Pa., 1937, LL.D. (hon.); grad., Pa. Acad. Fine Arts, 1937; postgrad., Royal Acad. Fine Arts, Florence, Italy, 1938-39; LL.D., Phila. Coll. Textiles and Sci., Allentown Coll. St. Francis de Sales, Widener Coll., Chester, Pa., Tufts U.; Litt.D., Drexel U.; L.H.D., Russell Sage Coll., Pa. Coll. Podiatric Medicine, Jacksonville U. Dir. Pa. Bur. Consumer Protection, 1968-69; spl. asst. to Pres. for consumer affairs White House, 1969-77; dir. U.S. Office Consumer Affairs, Washington, 1971-77, 81—; spl. adv. to Pres. for consumer affairs White House, 1983—; pres. Virginia Knauer & Assos., Inc., Washington, 1977-81; chmn. Council for Advancement of Consumer Policy, 1979-81; U.S. rep., vice chmn. consumer policy com. OECD, 1970-77, 81—; mem. Council Wage and Price Stability, 1974-77; Councilman-at-large, Phila., 1960-68; vice-chmn. Philadelphia County Rep. Com., 1958-77; pres. Phila. Congress Rep. Women's Councils, 1958-77; dir. Pa. Council Rep. Women, 1963-80; founder N.E. Phila. Council Rep. Women, pres., 1956-68. Bd. dirs. Hannah Penn House, 1956—, v.p., 1971; former trustee Pa. Coll. Podiatric Medicine; co-founder Knauer Found. Historic Preservation. Recipient Gimbel-Phila. award, 1977, Ind. Achievement in Govt. award Soc. Consumer Affairs Profls., 1983; named Disting. Dau. Pa., 1969. Mem. Nat. Trust Historic Preservation, Zeta Tau Alpha, Kappa Delta Epsilon (hon.). Episcopalian. Office: US Office Consumer Affairs 1725 1st St NW Washington DC 20201

KNECHT, JULIA ANN, firefighter, paramedic; b. Bayshore, N.Y., July 3, 1959; d. Thomas Francis and Patricia Adele (Lamberta) K. Student, Suffolk County Community Coll., Selden, N.Y., 1978-79, Daytona (Fla.) Community Coll., 1981-83, Seminole County Community Coll., Sanford, Fla., 1984—. Paramedic Flagler County Ambulance Service, Bunnell, Fla., 1983-84, Herndon Ambulance Service, Orlando, Fla., 1984; firefighter, paramedic Seminole County Fire Dept., Sanford, Fla., 1984—; reserve paramedic Daytona Beach Fire Dept., 1983-85; paramedic part time Rural Metro Ambulance Service, Orlando, 1986—. Firefighter, paramedic Osteen (Fla.) Vol. Fire Dept., 1986—. Republican. Presbyterian. Home: 2499 Tipton Dr Deltona FL 32738

KNEE, JUDITH SEGAL, public relations executive, speechwriter; b. Phila., Nov. 2, 1946; d. Jack Alexander and Claire (Fineman) Segal; m. Daniel Eric Knee, June 4, 1967 (div. Mar. 1973). BA, U. Pa., 1967. Human resources mgr. N.J. Bell Telephone Co., Newark, 1968-76; EEO specialist AT&T, Basking Ridge, N.J., 1977-80; public relations research C&P Telephone, Washington, 1981-83; exec. communications Bell Atlantic Network Services, Inc., Arlington, Va., 1984—. Mem. NOW (pres. N.J. chpt. 1974-76, nat. bd. dirs., regional dir. D.C., N.J., Pa., Del., Va., W. Va., Md. 1977-83, 51st state council 1986—). Democrat. Jewish. Home: 1414 C St SE Washington DC 20003 Office: Bell Atlantic Network Services Inc 1310 N Court House Rd 10th Floor Arlington VA 22201

KNEE, RUTH IRELAN (MRS. JUNIOR K. KNEE), social worker, health care consultant; b. Sapulpa, Okla., Mar. 21, 1920; d. Oren M. and Daisy (Daubin) Irelan; B.A., U. Okla., 1941, cert. social work, 1942; M.A., U. Chgo., 1945; m. Junior K. Knee, May 29, 1943 (dec. Oct. 21, 1981). Psychiat. social worker, asst. supr. Ill. Psychiat. Inst., U. Ill. at Chgo., 1943-44; psychiat. social worker USPHS Employee Health Unit, Washington, 1944-46, chief psychiat. social worker, 1946-49; psychiat. social work asso. Army Med. Center, Walter Reed Army Hosp., Washington, 1949-54; psychiat. social work cons. HEW, Region III, Washington, 1955-56; with NIMH, Chevy Chase, Md., 1956-72; chief mental health care adminstrn. br. USPHS, 1967-72, assoc. dep. adminstr. Health Services and Mental Health Adminstrn., 1972-73, dep. dir. Office of Nursing Home Affairs, 1973-74; long-term mental health care cons.; mem. com. on mental health and illness of elderly HEW, 1976-77; mem. panel on legal and ethical issues Pres.'s Commn. on Mental Health, 1977-78; liaison mem. Nat. Adv. Mental Health Council, 1977-81. Bd. dirs. Hillhaven Found., 1975-86. Fellow Am. Public Health Assn. (sec. mental health sect. 1968-70, chmn. 1971-72), Am. Orthopsychiat. Assn. (life), Gerontol. Soc. Am.; mem. Am. Assn. Psychiat. Social Workers (pres. 1951-53), Nat. Conf. Social Welfare (nat. bd. 1968-71, 2d v.p. 1973-74), Inst. Medicine/Nat. Acad. Sci. (com. study future of pub. health), Council on Social Work Edn., Nat. Assn. Social Workers (sec. 1955-56, nat. dir. 1956-57, 84-86, chmn. competence study com., practice and knowledge com. 1963-71), Acad. Cert. Social Workers, Am. Public Welfare Assn., DAR, Phi Beta Kappa, Psi Chi. Club: Women's Nat. Democratic. Editorial bd. Health & Social Work, 1979-81. Address: 8809 Arlington Blvd Fairfax VA 22031

KNEISSL, HILDE MARI, accountant; b. Fuerstenfeld, Austria, Mar. 30, 1941; came to U.S., 1963; d. Karl and Hildegard (Korty) Flecker; divorced; children: Ursula Susan, Michelle Louise. BS in Accountancy, Bentley Coll., 1980, MS in Taxation, 1988. CPA, Mass.; notary pub., Mass. Acct. Beers & Tisdale, Inc., Sudbury, Mass., 1980-81; sr. acct. Lucas Tucker & Co., Brighton, Mass., 1981-84; ptnr. JM Hughes & Co., P.C., Melrose, Mass., 1984—. Fellow Mass. Soc. CPA's (chairperson mgmt. of an acctg. practice com.); mem. Am. Inst. CPA's. Home: 23 Cider Mill Rd Sudbury MA 01776 Office: JM Hughes & Co PC One W Foster St Melrose MA 02176

KNEPP, JOY LYNN, service executive; b. Connellsville, Pa., Apr. 5, 1957; d. James Vernon and Beverly Ann (Corristan) Coffman; m. Gerald Louis Knepp, Oct. 13, 1984; 1 child, Robert Alan. BS, BA, Pa. State U., 1979. Elem. art tchr. Monaca Sch. Dist., Pa., 1979-80; substitute tchr. Connellsville Sch. Dist., Pa., 1980-82, Somerset (Pa.) Sch. Dist., 1980-82; asst. mgr. Luther P. Miller Convenience Store, Somerset, 1982-83; tour dir. Scholastic Tours Inc., Greensburg, Pa., 1983; conf. planner, mgr. Hidden Valley Conf. Ctr., Somerset, 1983-87; ednl. services mgr. Somerset Newspapers, Inc., 1987—. Mem. Laurel Arts Soc., Nat. Assn. Female Exec. Republican. Home: PO Box 365 Somerset PA 15501 Office: Hidden Valley Conf Ctr One Gorden Craig Head Meml Dr Somerset PA 15501

KNERLY, MARY JOHNSON, service company executive; b. Cleve., Feb. 5, 1925; d. Lawrence Redfield and Margaret (Geltz) Johnson; m. Stephen J. Knerly, Sept. 20, 1944 (div. Dec. 1974); children: Margit Anne Knerly Daley, Stephen J. Jr., Mary Ellen Knerly Kosicki. Student, Lake Erie Coll., Painesville, Ohio, 1942-44; BA, Case Western Res. U., 1946, postgrad., 1948-49. Nursery sch. tchr. Bingham Day Nursery, Cleve., 1945-46; book reviewer Cleve. Press newspaper, 1946-62; ednl. cons. The Lakewood (Ohio) Found., 1957-65; v.p. The Fairmount Theatre of the Deaf, Cleve., 1978-81, pres., 1981-84; pres. Service Service Inc., Cleve., 1984—; owner Beaconhill Ltd., Cleve., 1984-87; part-time counselor Service Corps of Retired Execs., Cleve., 1987—. Columnist The Business Score, Sun Newspapers, Cleve., 1987. Pres. Cleve. Gallery Group, 1960-70; bd. dirs. Cleve. Music Sch. Settlement, 1961-87, Cleve. Ballet, 1977-84; exec. com. The Singing Angels, Cleve., 1967-87. Mem. Am. Womens' Econ. Devel. Corps, Nat. Assn. Female Execs., Women Bus. Owners Assn., Western Res. Archtl. Historians (pres. 1981-83). Republican. Clubs: City, Twentieth Century, Mid-Day. Office: Service Service Inc 11428 Cedar Ave Room C-1 Cleveland OH 44106

KNEZO, GENEVIEVE JOHANNA, science and technology policy researcher; b. Elizabeth, N.J., Aug. 8, 1942; d. John and Genevieve (Sadowski) K.; 1 child, Alexandra M. A.B. in Polit. Sci., Douglass Coll., Rutgers U., 1964; M.A. in Sci., Tech. and Pub. Policy, George Washington U., 1981. With Congl. Research Service, Library of Congress, Washington, 1967—, specialist in sci. and tech., 1979—, head sci., research and tech. sect., 1986—. Author profl. publs. Mem. AAAS, NOW, D.C.-Brasilia Ptnrs. of Ams., Sierra Club, Phi Beta Kappa, Pi Sigma Alpha. Avocations: white-water canoeing; hiking; gymnastics; classical music. Home: 606 Oakley Pl Alexandria VA 22302 Office: Sci Policy Research Div Congl Research Service Library of Congress Washington DC 20540

KNIGHT, ALEXA DAVEY, health care administrator; b. Denver, Aug. 1, 1949; d. F. Norton and Margaret E. (Monaghan) Davey; m. G. Kent Knight Dec. 11, 1971 (div. May 1976). BS in Occupational Therapy with honors, Colo. State U., 1973; MBA, U. Denver, 1979. Lic. adminstr. nursing homes. Geophys. tech. asst. Husky Oil Co., Denver, 1974-77, assoc. landman, 1977-80; tech. sales rep. Eastman Kodak Co., San Francisco, 1980-84, regional bus. and mktg. specialist, 1984; systems sales rep. Control Data Corp., Sunnyvale, Calif., 1984-85; asst. adminstr. The Sequoias, Portola Valley, Calif., 1985-87, San Fransisco, 1987—. Active Calif. Assn. Homes for the Aging, com. mem., 1986-87. Republican. Club: Marina Sailing Soc. (San Fransisco). Home: 395 Catamaran St Foster City CA 94404 Office: The Sequoias 1400 Geary Blvd San Francisco CA 94109

KNIGHT, ALICE D. TIRRELL, state legislator; b. Manchester, N.H., July 14, 1903; d. Nathan Arthur and Clara (Stiles) Tirrell; B.A., U. N.H., 1925, postgrad., 1933; postgrad. Boston U., 1941-42; m. Norman Knight, Nov. 15, 1952. Tchr., Newton Falls (N.Y.) High Sch., 1925-26; prin. Oswegatchie (N.Y.) Union Sch., 1926-27, Bartlett Sch., Goffstown, N.H., 1932-35; home lighting specialist Public Service Co. N.H., Manchester, 1935-39; tchr. merchandising Mt. Ida Jr. Coll., Newton Centre, Mass., 1939-45; home service dir. Boyd Corp., Portland, Maine, 1945-47; dist. home economist Frigidaire Sales Corp., Boston, 1948-64; mem. N.H. Ho. of Reps., 1967-74, 76-78, 80—; rep to N.H. Gen. Ct., 1967—; mem. joint legis. com. on elderly affairs, 1983—; pres. Greater Manchester Community Concert Assn., 1985-87; co-chmn. Goofstown Bicentennial Com. of the Constn., 1986—. Mem. budget com. Town of Goffstown, 1966-72; mem. Gov.'s Adv. Com. Alcoholism, 1972-73, 74-78, Statewide Health Coordinating Council, 1977-78, N.H. Hist. Soc.; past pres. bd. dirs. Hillsborough County North Cancer Soc.; bd. dirs. N.H. Cancer Soc. Recipient award N.H. Program on Alcohol and Drug Abuse, 1971, 75, Gov.'s Recognition award, Hillsborough County, 1986, Pub. Service award Union Pomona Grange, 1987. Mem. Am. Home Econs. Assn., Nat. Home Fashions League (pres. 1957-58), Nat. Order State Legislators, Vis. Nurses Assn. (bd. dirs. Greater Manchester chpt. 1981-87), N.H. Council World Affairs, Nat. Grange, DAR (regent 1974-76), Nat. Order Women Legislators (treas. 1968-71), Manchester Bus. and Profl. Women (pres. 1972-74), Nat. Soc. New Eng. Women. Clubs: Republican. Mem. Unity Ch. Clubs: Order Eastern Star (life), Soroptomist (life) (Boston); Goffstown Unity, Goffstown Garden (pres. 1976-78), Goffstown Shirley (pres. 1977-78).

KNIGHT, BERNICE HELENE, technical sales professional; b. Attleboro, Mass., Aug. 29, 1944; d. William Herbert and Helene Marie (Annis) K. BA, U. Chattanooga, 1965. Tchr. science Catoosa County Bd. Edn., Ringgold, Ga., 1965-67; chemist Crystal Springs Textile, Chickamauga, Ga., 1967-68; tech. dir. Lutex Chem. Corp., Chattanooga, Tenn., 1968-83; tech. sales rep. George A. Goulston Co., Monroe, N.C., 1983—. Instr. water safety ARC, Chattanooga, 1967. Mem. Am. Assn. Textile Chemists & Colorists. Club: St. Bernard. Office: George A Goulston Co 700 N Johnson Monroe NC 28110

KNIGHT, CATHARINE CURRIE, research psychologist; b. Mpls., Oct. 15, 1947; d. Robert Preston and Agnes Tindall (Oleson) Vinall; m. Kirby Charles Knight, Sept. 12, 1971 (dec. Nov. 1981); m. Walter Julius Kuleck, Jan. 2, 1983. BS in Speech Pathology, Audiology, St. Cloud (Minn.) State U., 1969, MA in Speech Pathology, Audiology, 1972; PhD in Ednl. Psychology, Ariz. State U., 1982. Speech and lang. pathologist Anoka-Hennepin (Minn.) Sch. Dist. #11, 1970-71; ednl. dir. Tri-County Action Program, St. Cloud, 1971-73; speech and lang. pathologist Therapy Assocs., St. Paul, 1973-75, Vis. Nurse Service, Phoenix, 1975-78; instr. psychology Mesa (Ariz.) Community Coll., 1978-81; v.p. Cognitive Processing Inc., Cleveland Heights, Ohio, 1983—; pres. The Hennepin Group, Inc., Cleveland Heights, 1985—; cons. in field, 1983—. Contbr. articles to profl. jours. Nat. Inst. of Child Health and Human Devel. postdoctoral fellow, 1983-86; grantee Spencer Found., 1984-87. Mem. Am. Psychol. Assn., Soc. for Research in Child Devel., Am. Edn. Research Assn., Ruger Collectors Assn., Pi Lambda Theta. Lutheran. Club: Cleve. Venture (founder 1983).

KNIGHT, FREIDA H., controller; b. Winder, Ga., Jan. 4, 1943; d. Owen E. and Dorothy (Wilkins) Herndon; m. Howard V. (Jack) Knight, June 7, 1964; children: Vicki, Eddie, Jonathan. BBA, U. Ga., 1965. Co-pres. Knight Enterprises, Carl, Ga., 1964—; cons. Mitchell Kot Personnel, Atlanta, 1979-80; acct. Shibamoto Am. Inc., Norcross, Ga., 1980-84; controller Athens (Ga.) Bandage Inc., 1984—; corp. sec.-treas. West-Barrow Constrn., Carl, 1988—. City clk. Town of Carlsbad, 1979; dir. West Barrow Recreation, 1975-79; mem. PTO, 1970—; dir. publicity Winder-Barrow Acad. Booster Club. Mem. Nat. Assn. Female Execs., Barrow County C. of C. Home: Lakeside Dr Carl GA 30203

KNIGHT, GEORGINE MARIE, medical technologist; b. Hazleton, Pa., Feb. 22, 1954; d. George and Eleanor Marie (Subally) K.; B.S. in Med. Tech., Wilkes Coll., 1977. Med. technologist, asst. crew chief chemistry Nesbitt Meml. Hosp., Kingston, Pa., 1977—. Winner Northeastern Pa. Philharm. Talent Competition, 1971. Mem. Am. Soc. Clin. Pathologists (affiliate, registered med. technologist). Home: 458 Monument Ave Wyoming PA 18644 Office: 562 Wyoming Ave Kingston PA 18704

KNIGHT, GLADYS (GLADYS MARIA KNIGHT), singer; b. Atlanta, May 28, 1944; d. Merald, Sr. and Elizabeth (Woods) K.; m. Barry Hankerson, Oct. 1974; 1 dau., Shanga; children from previous marriage: Kenya, James. Grad. high sch. Author: lyrics Way Back Home, others; first pub. recital, Mt. Mariah Bapt. Ch., Atlanta, 1948; toured with Morris Brown Choir, 1950-53, recitals local chs. and schs., 1950-53; winner grand prize Ted Mack's Amateur Hour 1952; jazz vocalist, Lloyd Terry Jazz Ltd., 1959-61, mem., Gladys Knight and the Pips (formerly Pips Quartet), 1953—, concert appearances in Eng., 1967, 72, 73, 76, Australia, Japan, Hong Kong, Manila, 1976; rec. artist, Brunswick, 1957-61, Fury, 1961-62, Everlast, 1963, Maxx and Bell, 1964-66, Motown, 1966-73, Buddah, Capitol, Columbia, MCA, 1988; TV appearance Charlie & Co., 1985; appeared in HBO film Sisters in the Name of Love, 1986. Winner 6 gold Buddah records, 1 gold, 1 platinum Buddah album; 2 Grammy awards; named Top Female Vocalist, Blues and Soul mag. 1972; spl. award Washington City Council for inspiration to youth in city, 1972; other awards include Clio, AGVA, NAACP Image, Ebony Music, Cashbox, Billboard, Record World, Rolling Stone, Ladies Home Jour., Am. Music award (with Pips), 1984. Address: care Sidney A Seidenberg 1414 Ave of the Americas New York NY 10019 *

KNIGHT, JEANNE ELIZABETH, pharmaceutical sales representative; b. Moline, Ill., Sept. 15, 1956; d. George Emil Henning and Jeannine Alice (Johnson) Johnson; m. James Henry Knight, Apr. 4, 1987. BA, Augustana Coll., Rock Island, Ill., 1978. Sr. profl. sales rep. Merck, Sharp & Dohme Pharmaceutical Labs., West Point, Pa., 1978—. Active Iowans for Tax Relief, Des Moines, 1986—, Concerned Women Am., 1986. Named to Vice Pres.' Club Merck, Sharp & Dohme, 1987. Mem. Eagle Forum. Republican. Mem. Evang. Free Ch. Home and Office: 1039 N 23d Pl Fort Dodge IA 50501

KNIGHT, KATHY, small business owner, writer; b. Oakland, Calif., June 22, 1950; d. William Pell Bruns and Doris Diana (Koofman)Burrell; m. Paul C. LoCascio, Jan. 29, 1967 (div. Jan. 1979). Student, Radio Electronic Tech. Sch., 1965-67, Merrill Computer Sch., 1988—. Owner, dispatcher At Your Service Limousine, N.Y.C., 1979-87; v.p., art dir. Golden Sphinx Records, N.Y.C., 1980—; financier Recording Project- UFO, N.Y.C., 1980; pres., owner Knight Mfg., N.Y.C., 1987—; mgmt. asst. Curtis Knight Mgmt. & Prodn. Co., N.Y.C., 1976—; assoc. producer Cosmic Prodns., N.Y.C., 1987—; cons. Documentary Jimi Hendrix. Artist for various album covers and posters. Vol. Am. Heart Assn.; mem. Rep. Nat. Com., 1987. Mem. Am. Mus. Natural History, Nat. Audubon Soc., Nat. Arbor Day Found., Nat. Assn. Female Exec., Am. Film Inst. Mayan Order, Christian Children's Fund. Mem. Worldwide Ch. God. Office: Curtis Knight Mgmt & Prodn Co 59 Carmine St New York NY 10014

KNIGHT, LILA CUCKSEE, secretary; b. Chattanooga, Apr. 11, 1931; d. William Henry and Anna Leona (Bonine) Cucksee; children: David, Jonathan, Paul, Joel Knight, Sheryl Knight Carlock. Diploma in Sectl. Sci., Edmondson Jr. Coll., 1983; diploma Life Underwriters Tng. Council, Chattanooga, 1986; life ins. lic. Modern Woodmen Sch., 1983. Pre-need sales woman Lakewood Memory Gardens, Rossville, Ga., 1983, Tenn./Ga. Meml. Park, Rossville, 1983; dist. rep. Modern Woodmen of Am., Rossville, 1983-84; ins. agt. United Ins. Co. of Am., Chattanooga, 1984-86; area sales mgr. World Book/Child Craft, Chattanooga, 1986; sr. clk., Gwinnett Mental Health/Mental Retardation/Substance Abuse Ctr., Lawrenceville, Ga., 1986—. Mem. Lakeview Home-Sch. Orgn., Fort Oglethorpe, Ga., 1955-86. Mem. Smithsonian Instn., Modern Woodmen Am., Nat. Assn. Female Execs., Sunbelt Resorts, Buckhorn Landing. Republican. Baptist. Club: Lakeview Happy Healthy Homemakers. Avocations: poetry, hiking, swimming, singing. Home: PO Box 1734 Lawrenceville GA 30246-1734 Office: PO Box 687 Lawrenceville GA 30246

KNIGHT, MARGARETT LEE, lawyer, editor; b. Newtown, Ind., Jan. 3, 1923; d. Charles Oscar and Edna (Pace) Smith; m. Robert Cook Knight, June 20, 1961. LL.B., Ind. U., 1945, J.D., 1965; A.B., Mills Coll., 1953; LL.M., Yale U., 1955. Bar: Ind. 1945. Dep. atty. gen. Ind. Home: 1318 Hoover Ln Indianapolis IN 46260 Office: Atty Gen 219 State House Indianapolis IN 46204

KNIGHT, ROYALTY MARIE, medical marketing representative; b. Chgo., Jan. 4, 1952; d. Thomas James and Annette (Jones) K. BS, St. Louis U., 1976, MA, 1978. Audiologist, researcher St. Louis VA Med. Ctr., 1977-80; clin. audiologist St. Louis U. Hosps., 1980; parent involvement specialist St. Louis Bd. Edn., 1980-82; mktg. coordinator Compton Ednl. Services, Chgo., 1982; med. convention rep. Detroit div. Dupont Critical Care, 1982—; sales cons. Breakout mag., Chgo. Mem. Queen's Community Workers, Detroit, 1986-87, Wayne County (Mich.) Youth at Risk Task Force, 1987. Mem. Dupont Pres.'s Club (achievement award 1986, 87), Nat. Assn. Female Execs., The Blue Army. Home: PO Box 1237 Southgate MI 48195 Office: Dupont Critical Care 1600 Waukegan Rd Waukegan IL 60085

KNIGHT, SARA CHAMBERS, sales executive; b. Memphis, June 17, 1948; d. Macie Marion and Sarah (Hendrix) Chambers; m. Robert Dewey Knight, Aug. 17, 1969 (div. July 1981); children: Macy Marian, Robert Miles. BBA in Banking and Fin. cum laude, U. Miss., 1970; grad., Inst. of Banking, 1972. Mgmt. trainee Deposit Guaranty Nat. Bank, Jackson, Miss., 1970-72, asst. tng. mgr., 1971-72; office mgr. Holiday Inn, Columbus, Miss., 1972-77, Old South Coors, Inc., Columbus, 1981-82; sales rep. J.L. Teel Co., Inc., Columbus, Miss., 1982-85; mgr. sales J.L. Teel Co., Inc., Columbus and Tupelo, Miss., 1985—. Mem. Columbus Jr. Aux., 1978—. Mem. U. Miss. Alumni Assn., Delta Gamma Alumni Assn. (pres. N.E. Miss. chpt. 1980, 81), Phi Kappa Phi, Beta Gamma Sigma, Crewe of Bacchus. Republican. Episcopalian. Clubs: Woodland Garden (Columbus); Northriver Yacht (Tuscaloosa, Ala.); Old Waverly Golf (West Point, Miss.). Home: 522 Huckleberry Hills Columbus MS 39701 Office: J L Teel Co Inc Hwy 45 N Columbus MS 39701 also: 705 Robert E Lee Dr Tupelo MS 38801

KNIGHT, SHIRLEY, actress; b. Goessel, Kans., July 5, 1936; d. Noel Johnson and Virginia (Webster) K.; m. John R. Hopkins; children: Kaitlin, Sophie. D.F.A., Lake Forest Coll., 1978. Actress theatre and films. Active Com. for Handgun Control, nat. civil rights orgns., worker for peace. Recipient various acting honors U.S. and abroad. Office: care Badgley McQueency & Connor 9229 Sunset Blvd Suite 607 Los Angeles CA 90069

KNIGHTEN, KATHERINE WELLS, English language educator; b. Sweetwater, Tex., Dec. 2, 1937; d. James E. and Katherine (Carter) Wells; m. James A. Knighten, Apr. 10, 1960 (div. 1982); children: Kathy J., Jim. BA, North Tex. State U., 1958; MEd, Tex. Tech U., 1968; PhD, So. Ill. U., 1977. Tchr. music Jefferson County R-1, Lakewood, Colo., 1958-61; tchr. Aldine Ind. Sch. Dist., Houston, 1964-66, Humble (Tex.) Ind. Sch. Dist., 1966-67; band dir. Calvert, Tex., 1968-69; tchr. remedial reading Oakwood (Tex.) Ind. Sch. Dist., 1970-71, secondary tchr., 1971; reading specialist Houston Ind. Sch. Dist., 1974; teaching and research asst. So. Ill. U., Carbondale, 1975-77; assoc. prof. English edn. Ball State U., Muncie, Ind., 1977—; with G/T Cadre State of Ind., 1985—; leader Jr. Great Books, 1986—; cons. in field. Author: You're a Poet (And May Not Know It), 1980; poetry. Mem. Nat. Council for the Social Studies (media com.), Nat. Council Tchrs. English, Ind. Council Tchrs. English (pres. 1985-86), Nat. Assn. Lab. Schs. (assoc. editor jour. 1980—), Daus. Am. Colonists (vice regent Muncie chpt.). Office: Burris Lab Sch Ball State U Muncie IN 47306

KNIGHT-GORDON, RENEE MARIE, real estate broker; b. Boston, Aug. 20, 1955; d. Edward Albert and Irene Frances (Ago) Knight; divorced; Christina Marie, Katie Jane, Clifford Edward. AS in Bus., Bunker Hill Community Coll.; BM, Holliston Jr. Coll. Computer operator Met. Credit Union, Chelsea, 1981-82; salesperson Coldwell Banker Real Estate Co., Sdugus, Mass., 1985-86; broker Able Real Estate, Malden, Mass., 1987—. Advocate Fair Share of Mass., Malden, 1978. Home: 4 Shawmut St Malden MA 02148 Office: Able Real Estate 102 Main St Malden MA 02148

KNIPPA, SHARON SCHOOLER, municipal agency director; b. Austin, Tex., July 20, 1942; d. Paul and Elizabeth (Stewart) Schooler; m. Jerry Louis Knippa, Jan. 1959 (div. Jan. 1964); children: Jerry Paul, Gary Louis. Student, San Antonio Coll., 1963. Exec. sec. to city mgr. City of San Antonio, 1963-66; exec. sec. Lone Star Brewing Co., San Antonio, 1966-68; adminstrv. asst. San Antonio Convention and Visitors Bur., 1968-70, City Mgrs. Office, San Antonio, 1970-72; dir. adminstrn. and pub. relations San Antonio Convention and Visitors Bur., 1972-84, exec. asst. dir., 1984-87, acting exec. dir., 1988—. Mem. Internat. Assn. Convention and Visitors Burs., Internat. Travel and Tourism Research Assn., Assn. Film Commissioners (internat.), Tex. Hotel Sales and Mktg. Assn., San Antonio Hotel Sales and Mktg. Assn. Republican. Methodist. Office: San Antonio Convention & Vis' Bur PO Box 2277 121 Alamo Plaza S San Antonio TX 78298

KNIPPSCHILD, ERNESTINE, psychic consultant; b. Sfintu Gheorghe, Transylvania, Romania, July 13, 1932; came to U.S., 1949; d. Adalbert Julius and Elizabeth Emilia (Lichtfuss) Ott; m. William Knippschild, Aug. 29, 1951; children—Clara Elizabeth, William Albert, Robert Bryan. E.S.P. devel. tchr., coordinator Ridley High Sch., Ridley Twp., Pa., 1972—; lectr. Parastudy, Inc., Chester Heights, Pa., 1969-80; lectr., cons. Kiwanis, DeWitt Club, Liverpool, N.Y., 1978-84; pres., owner Rainbow Parasensory Sci. Assocs., Edgemont, Pa., 1980—; psychic cons. Rainbow Parasensory Sci., Edgemont, 1980—; psychic cons. Nat. Assn. Rev. Appraisers and Mortgage Underwriters, Scottsdale, Ariz., 1985—; stress cons. Field Service Assocs., Newtown Square, Pa., 1981—; conductor workshops and seminars on extended metaphysical hypnosis and regression Beaver County Community Coll. Mem. Spiritual Frontiers Fellowship, Nat. Assn. Female Execs. Avocations: writing; traveling; helping people. Home: 1300 Stackhouse Mill Rd Newtown Square PA 19073 Office: Rainbow Parasensory Sci Assocs PO Box 495 Edgemont Township PA 19028

KNISELY, SALLY, psychotherapist; b. Baraga, Mich., Mar. 17, 1917; d. Henry Samuel and Flora (Hagerman) Knisely; A.B., U. Mich., 1944; M.A., U. Chgo., 1946; Ed.D., Columbia U., 1964. Day nursery caseworker Bur. Family Service, Orange, N.J., 1946-49; caseworker to mentally ill vets. VA, N.Y.C., 1949-53; child psychotherapist Inter-Agy. Guidance Center, Yonkers, N.Y., 1953-58; child psychotherapist Monsey (N.Y.) Mental Health Clinic, 1957-58; child psychotherapist New Rochelle (N.Y.) Guidance Center, 1958-59; pvt. practice psychotherapy, Stamford, Conn., 1968—; cons. numerous nursery sch. and presch. programs. Fellow Conn. Soc. Clin. Social Workers; mem. Am. Orthopsychiat. Assn., Council Psychoanalytic Psychotherapists, Nat. Assn. Edn. Young Children, Soc. Health and Human Values, Nat. Assn. Social Workers, Nat. Assn. of Deaf, Am. Deafness and Rehab. Assn., AAUW, Nat. Bd. Examiners in Clin. Social Work. Home and office: 69 Jordan Ln Stamford CT 06903

KNITTLE, DOLORES FLORIO, construction company executive; b. Cleve., Nov. 5, 1937; d. William Florio and Lena (Scaglione) DePaul; m. Feb. 20, 1960; children: Katherine, Alan. AA in Bus. Adminstrn., Bowling Green State U., 1976. Traffic clk. Ea. States Farmers Exchange, Huron, Ohio, 1956-60; asst. office mgr. Bloyer and Gilchist, Inc., Huron, 1960-62; office mgr. Wilkes and Co., Inc., Huron, 1962-67; exec. sec. Glidden Durhee SCM, Huron, 1967-72; v.p. Hubbard Constrn. Inc., Huron, 1972—. Mem. Nat. Assn. Female Execs. Office: Dolores Knittle 740 River Rd Huron OH 44839

KNIZESKI, JUSTINE ESTELLE, insurance company executive; b. Glen Cove, N.Y., June 4, 1954; d. John Martin and Elsie Beatrice (Gozelski) Knizeski. B.A., Conn. Coll., 1976; M. Mgmt., Northwestern U., 1981. Customer service supr. Brunswick Savs., Freeport, Maine, 1977-79; investment analyst Bankers Life and Casualty Co., Chgo., 1980-83, dir. corp. planning and analysis, 1983-87; dir. budgets, cost acctg. Blue Cross/Blue Shield of Ill., 1987—. Chmn. bd. dirs. Alternatives, Inc., Chgo., 1984-87, vice chmn., 1987-88, bd. dirs., 1983-84; mem. Chgo. Council Fgn. Relations, 1984-85. Mem. Planning Forum. Avocations: sailing; bicycling; traveling; painting.

KNOEBEL, SUZANNE BUCKNER, cardiologist, medical educator; b. Ft. Wayne, Ind., Dec. 13, 1926; d. Doster and Marie (Lewis) Buckner. A.B., Goucher Coll., 1948; M.D., Ind. U.-Indpls., 1960. Diplomate: Am. Bd. Internal Medicine. Asst. prof. medicine Ind. U., Indpls., 1966-69, assoc. prof., 1969-72, prof., 1972-77, Krannert prof., 1977—; asst. dean research Ind. U., Indpls., 1975—; assoc. dir. Krannert Inst. Cardiology, Indpls., 1974—; asst. chief cardiology sect. Richard L. Roudebush VA Med. Ctr., Indpls., 1982—. Fellow Am. Coll. Cardiology (v.p. 1980-81, pres. 1982-83); mem. Am. Fedn. Clin. Research, Assn. Univ. Cardiologists. Office: Ind U Sch Medicine 1100 W Michigan St Indianapolis IN 46223

KNOLLE, MARY ANNE ERICSON, human resources company executive; b. Kilgore, Tex., Jan. 7, 1941; d. Evert Eric and Frances Leone (Scott) Ericson; children by previous marriage: Clay Claflin, Sunny Claflin; m. John W. Knolle, Mar. 14, 1980; children: Sara Anne, Evelyn. BA, North Tex. State U., 1962; MA, U. Tex., 1968; postgrad., UCLA, 1964-66, U. Houston, 1974-76. Editor co. publs. Gt. S.W. Life Ins. Co., 1962; prof. U. Balt., 1968, Miami (Fla.) Dade Coll., 1968, Savannah (Ga.) State Coll., 1969, U. Houston, 1972-76; dir. pub. relations Alvin (Tex.) Coll., 1970-72; founder, pres. Panorama Programs, Houston, 1972-76; coordinator mgmt. devel. tng. Brown & Root, Inc., Houston, 1970-79; div. founder, mgr. mgmt. and orgnl. devel. systems Diversified Human Resources Group, Inc., Houston, 1979—; founder, pres. Panorama Mgmt. Inst., Houston, 1979—; founder, pres. Panorama Cons., 1980—; cons. moot ct. U. Tex. Law Sch., 1965—. Judge regional speech contest Houston Jaycees. Recipient Blockbuster award United Way, 1979. Mem. Am. Soc. Tng. and Devel., Houston C. of C. (chmn. edn. com.), Alpha Delta Pi (pres. alumnae). Presbyterian. Club: Houston Indoor Tennis. Office: 12307 Broken Arrow Houston TX 77024

KNOPF, SUSAN, publisher; b. White Plains, N.Y., Mar. 10, 1956; d. Alfred Jr. and Alice (Laine) K. BA, Brown U., 1978; postgrad., NYU, 1979—, Alliance Francaise, 1985—. Asst. dir. children's programs Book of the Month Club, N.Y.C., 1978-81; pres., co-founder Reading Rainbow Gazette, Inc., N.Y.C., 1982—; dir. Aegis Edits., N.Y.C., 1988—; research cons. Stonehenge Press/Time-Life Books, Inc., N.Y.C., 1980-84, editorial cons., 1981-84; cons. story dept. Walt Disney Prodns., N.Y.C., 1982-84. Author: Shape Books for Little Hands, 1985, Caramba! The Book!, 1987; editor: The Wit and Wisdom of Nasraddin Hodja, 1986, Dominique's, 1987, The Barbara Pym Cookbook, 1988. Mem. ALA, Am. Booksellers Assn., The Author's Guild, People for the Am. Way. Office: Aegis Editions 220 W 13th St Apt #2C New York NY 10011

KNORR, BETTY JEWEL BENKERT (MRS. NEIL MCLEAN KNORR), naturalist; b. Summit, N.J., Aug. 10, 1928; d. William R. and Amelia (Kreutzer) Benkert; grad. high sch.; Ph.D. (hon.), Hamilton State U., 1973, Colo. State Christian Coll., 1973; m. Neil McLean Knorr, Dec. 13, 1946. Licensed bird bander Fish and Wildlife Service, U.S. Dept. Interior, 1957—; banded over 50,000 wild birds of 182 different species; spl. ornithol. research on shorebirds, hummingbirds and blackbirds; other varied research in bird banding; established extensive wildflower preserve and rhododendron gardens at home; engaged in propagation rare native wildflowers donating same to public arboretums, preserves and sanctuaries; vol. tchr., cons. on conservation and nature study, 1948—; tchr. Brookdale Coll.; active many local, state, nat. conservation issues; responsible for sav. wilderness area threatened with destruction and now preserved as part of Cheesequake State Park; organizer nation-wide Project S.N.A.P. to salvage threatened native plants and replant them for ednl. and civic purposes. Active Girl Scouts U.S.A., 1938—; counselor, cons. Boy Scouts Am., 1960—. Mem. Amateur Organists Assn. Internat., Monmouth, Shore organ socs., Eastern Bird Banding Assn., Nat., N.J. Audubon socs., Torrey Bot. Club, Am. Fern Soc. Home: Rural Route 2 Box 459 Easy St Howell NJ 07731

KNOTT, TARA DAVIS, evaluation consultant; b. Alexandria, La., Dec. 5, 1943; d. Raoul Lynwood and Ruby Montez (Luneau) Brister; B.A. in Psychology, Memphis State U., 1971, M.A. in Speech Pathology, 1975; B.A. in Speech and Music, La. State U., 1961; Ph.D. in Evaluation Research, Clayton U., 1978; m. David Howard Knott, Aug. 6, 1978. Evaluator family practice dept. U. Tenn. Center for Health Scis., 1976-78; research cons. Deafness Found., 1978, Nat. Hearing Assn., 1978; evaluation cons. Covington Mental Health Center, 1978-79; head data collection Project WOMAN, 1978-79; evaluation cons. Mid South Hosp., 1979—, Jackson Splty. Hosp., 1980—; United Inns, 1981—, Memphis Mental Health Inst., U. Tenn. Center Health Scis., 1979—, Rivendell Corp. Am., 1984—, Hosp. Corp. Am., 1983—, Meharry Med. Sch., 1986—; pres. Evaluation Resources, Inc., 1983—; cons., tchr. hosps., colls. and univs. Grantee in alcoholism and drug abuse. Mem. Am. Evaluation Assn., Soc. Neurosci., Employee Assistance Soc. N.Am., Am. Psychol. Assn., Am. Soc. Tng. and Devel., Am. Edn. Research Assn., Am. Fitness in Industry, Tenn. Evaluation Network. Democrat. Methodist. Contbr. articles to profl. jours. Office: 4646 Poplar Suite 305 Memphis TN 38117

KNOTTS, VALERIE ANN BOWMAN, dietitian; b. Warsaw, Ind., May 4, 1932; d. Kenneth Dixie and Evelyn Louise (Holmes) Bowman; m. Floyd Everitt Knotts, Jr., Mar. 19, 1955 (div. Aug. 1979). BS, U. Ala., 1953; MEd, U. Houston, 1970, EdD, 1975. Dir. food service Sakowitz Store-Post Oak, Houston, 1960-65; clin. dietitian Diagnostic Ctr. Hosp., Houston, 1966-67; ptnr. Gilbert-Knotts Dietary Cons., Houston, 1967-71; assoc. prof., coordinator grad. program in nutrition Tex. Womans' U., Houston, 1973-80; assoc. dir. acad. services U. Tex. Health Sci. Ctr., Houston, 1980-83; pvt. practice dietitian Houston, 1985—; dietary cons. Kingwood (Tex.) Nutrition Cons., 1985-88; asst. prof. in Nutition Cen. State U., Edmond, Okla., 1988—. Editorial bd. Inside Running and Fitness, Houston, 1978—; contbr. articles to profl. jours. Bd. dirs. Am. Diabetes Assn., Houston, 1979-85; mem. wellness adv. bd. Kingwood Country Club, task force Am. Heart Assn. Kingwood, 1986-87. Mem. Am. Dietetic Assn. (Tex. del. 1981-87), Tex. Dietetic Assn., South Tex. Dietetic Assn., Sports and Cardiovascular Nutritionists, Exec. Group, Exec. Womens Network, Alpha Phi. Republican. Episcopalian. Home: 4627 Shetland Ln Houston TX 77027 Office: Central State U Edmond OK 73060

KNOTTS, VALERIE KAY JENSEN, state agency administrator; b. Stoneham, Mass., Apr. 21, 1933; d. Nicklaus and Bertha Frances (Emery) Jensen; m. Franklin Delano Knotts, Sept. 11, 1960; children: Kimberly, Kristen, Katharine, Franklin, Kerri. BS, U. N.H., 1954; MS, Boston U., 1983. Registered occupational therapist, U.S., lic. occupational therapist, Mass. Dir. occupational therapy City of N.Y.C., Coler Hosp., 1955-57; pvt. practice occupational therapy N.Y.C., 1955-59; pivot therapist USPHS, Boston and New Orleans, 1957-58; program dir. U.S. Army Spl. Services, Republic of Korea, Fed. Republic of Germany, 1959-60, 63-64; researcher Easter Seal Soc., Manchester, N.H., 1967-68; co-owner Knotts Assocs., Manchester, N.H., 1969-76; counsel pub. relations N.H. Optometric Assn., Concord, 1973-76; officer pub. info. Commonwealth of Mass. Dept. Pub. Health, Cushing Hosp., Framingham, 1976—; instr. N.Y. Med. Coll., N.Y.C., 1956-57; project dir. Busy Bee Transp. Services, Framingham, 1978-82, Community Health Services Outreach, 1983-86, Framingham; project planner Adult Day Ctr., Inc., Framingham, 1982-83; co-owner Franklin House Foster Care, Ashland, Mass., 1982—. Author tng. manuals, 1984-86; editor 'Round the Square, 1982—; producer videotape workshops (award NE Hosp. Assembly). Mem. exec. bd. Framingham chpt. ARC, 1986—; pres. Performing Arts Ctr. MetroWest, Framingham, 1984-86; mem. Fed. Ch. Choir. Named Woman of Yr., Manchester Jaycettes, 1975. Mem. Am. Assn. Univ. Women (pres. Manchester chpt. 1975-76), New Eng. Pub. Health Assn., Am. Occupational Therapy Assn., Mass. Pub. Health Assn. (chairperson health adminstrn. and planning), Boston Computer Soc., Boston U. Health Alumni Assn., Phi Delta. Democrat. Congregationalist. Club: Framingham Womens (exec. bd. 1985-86). Home: 579 Chestnut St Ashland MA 01721 Office: Cushing Hosp/Dept Pub Health Box 190 Dudley Rd Framingham MA 01701

KNOUSE, JANE BRINKMEYER, mortgage company executive; b. Seward, Neb., Dec. 12, 1953; d. Victor H. and Mildred (Heers) Brinkmeyer; m. Stephen T. Knouse, May 18, 1974. BSBA, U. Neb., Lincoln, 1975; MS in Systems Mgmt., U. So. Calif., 1984. Ops. mgmt. Ajax Fin., San Diego, 1978-84; zone servicing mgr. PMI Corp., Irvine, Calif., 1984-87; ops. analyst GE Capital Mortgage Ins., Anaheim, Calif., 1987—. Mem. Nat. Assn. Bus. Economists (forecast panel 1988), Alpha Lambda Delta, Omicron Delta Epsilon, Phi Chi Theta. Office: GE Mortgage Ins 2390 E Orangewood Ave #300 Anaheim CA 92806

KNOWLES, BARBARA BANG, immunologist; b. N.Y.C., Feb. 27, 1937; d. Christian John and Undine Gaylord (Dodge) Bang; m. John Appleton Knowles, Nov. 28, 1959 (div. 1984); children: Jared Appleton, Amanda Gaylord. AB, Middlebury Coll., 1958; MS, Ariz. State U., 1963, PhD, 1965. Postdoctoral fellow Dept. Genetics, U. Calif., Berkeley, 1965-67; from research assoc. to prof. The Wistar Inst. of Analogy and Biology, Phila., 1967—; prof. pathology and lab. medicine U. Pa. Sch. Medicine, Phila., 1984—; cons. Cancer Info. Dissemination Service, 1979—; vis. prof. Hahnemann Med. Coll., Phila., 1978—; vis. sr. scientist Cold Spring Harbor Labs., 1987-88; adj. prof. U. Penn., Phila., 1978—; mem. cancer research manpower review bd. NIH, 1980-83. Co-author: Biology of Human Teratomes, 1983; mem. edit. bd. Monoclonal Antibody News, 1982—, Molecular Cellular Biology, 1984—, Differentiation, 1988—, Immunogentics, 1976-79; patentee in field; contbr. over 120 articles to profl. jours. Recipient numerous research grants NIH, 1971—, Am. Cancer Inst., 1975—. Mem. AAAS, Genetics Soc. Am., Am. Soc. Human Genetics, Sigma Xi. Democrat. Episcopalian. Office: The Wistar Inst Anatomy and Biology 36th St at Spruce Philadelphia PA 19104

KNOWLES, CONNIE FISHER, banker; b. Delaware, Ohio, Dec. 22, 1916; d. Robert Morgan and Dora L. (Albright) Fisher; m. Jack O. Knowles, Nov. 28, 1939 (div. 1977); children—Donna L. Knowles Born, Jane Ann Knowles Wise. Student Ohio State U., 1933-35; A.B., Depauw U., 1937; B.E., Capital U., 1938. Sec., Miami YWCA, Fla., 1938-39; asst. v.p. Coconut Grove Bank, Miami, 1984—. Founder Guild Mus. and Sci., Miami, 1952, Guilded Lillies for Crippled Children, Miami, 1974; bd. dirs. Miami YWCA. Mem. So. Fla. Hist. Assn., Am. Inst. Banking, Miami Women's Panhellenic Assn. (pres. 1960-61), AAUW (pres. 1940-41); Alpha Chi Omega (pres. 1947-48). Club: Riviera Country. Home: 6810 Tordera St Coral Gables FL 33146 Office: Coconut Grove Bank 2701 S Bayshore Dr Miami FL 33133

KNOWLES, JOCELYN WAGNER, health writer, women's health specialist; b. N.Y.C., Feb. 22, 1918; d. Frederick and Violet Alice (Swain) W.; m. Clive Dorman Knowles, 1950 (div. 1959); 1 child, Katherine Miranda. Student, London Sch. Econs., 1938; BS, Columbia U., 1939, MA, 1940; MPH, UCLA, 1970. Exec. dir. Nat. Physicians Forum, Inc., N.Y.C., 1945-49; West coast editor Nat. Foremen's Inst. Prentice-Hall Co., Los Angeles, 1959-68; writer, editor The Female Patient mag., N.Y.C., 1980-81; dir. Planned Parenthood of S.W., Silver City, N.Mex., 1981-83; freelance writer N.Y.C., 1977—; cons. Calif. State Agy. on Aging, San Francisco, 1976-77. Contbr. articles to med. mags.; staff bookreviewer L.A. Times. First woman organizer Brotherhood of Railway Trainmen, 1945-47; publicist Farmers Union of Iowa, Des Moines, 1951, Golden Gate Arboretum, San Francisco, 1976; bd. dirs. Nat. Womens Health Network, 1981-85. NIH grantee U. Calif., Los Angeles, 1968-70; Va. Ctr. for the Arts fellow, Charlottesville, 1976, Woolrich fellow Columbia U., N.Y.C., 1977, Wurlitzer Found. fellow, Taos, N. Mex., 1981. Mem. Nat. Women Writers Assn., Am. Pub. Health Assn., Nat. Women's Health Network. Jewish.

KNOWLES, MARJORIE FINE, dean, law educator; b. Bklyn., July 4, 1939; d. Jesse J. and Roslyn (Leff) Fine; m. Ralph I. Knowles, Jr., June 3, 1972. BA, Smith Coll., 1960; LLB, Harvard U., 1965. Bar: Ala., N.Y., D.C. Teaching fellow Harvard U., 1963-64; law clk. to judge U.S. Dist. Ct. (so. dist.), N.Y., 1965-66; asst. U.S. atty. U.S. Atty.'s Office, N.Y.C., 1966-67; asst. dist. atty. N.Y. County Dist. Atty., N.Y.C., 1967-70; exec. dir. Joint Found. Support, N.Y.C., 1970-72; asst. gen. counsel HEW, Washington, 1978-79; insp. gen. U.S. Dept. Labor, Washington, 1979-80; assoc. prof. U. Ala. Sch. Law, Tuscaloosa, 1972-75, prof., 1975-86, assoc. dean, 1982-84; law prof., dean Ga. State U. Coll. Law, Atlanta, 1986—; cons. Ford Foundation, N.Y.C., 1973—; trustee Coll. Retirement Equities Fund, N.Y.C., 1983—; mem. exec. com. Conf. on Women and the Constitution, 1986—, Am. Law Inst.-ABA Com. on Continuing Profl. Edn., 1987—. Contbr. articles to profl. jours. Am. Council Edn. fellow, 1976-77, Aspen Inst. fellow, Rockefeller Found., 1976. Mem. ABA (chmn. new deans workshop 1988), Ala. State Bar Assn., N.Y. State Bar Assn., D.C. Bar Assn., Am. Arbitration Assn. (panel arbitrators 1985—). Office: Ga State Univ Coll of Law University Plaza Atlanta GA 30303-3083

KNOWLES, PATRICIA KAIRALLA, dancer, choreographer; b. W. Palm Beach, Fla., May 14, 1942; d. George E. and Mireille Sylvia (Cowan) Kairalla; B.A. in English, Fla. State U., Tallahassee, 1964, M.A. in Dance, 1966; m. Frank L. Knowles, June 26, 1965. Instr., choreographer, dancer U. Ga., Athens, 1966-70, Eastern Mich. U., Ypsilanti, 1970-73; dir. dance, choreographer, performer Brevard (N.C.) Music Center, summers 1968-70; head dept. dance U. Ill., Champaign-Urbana, 1973—; dancer, cons. in field.; mem. panel dance Ill. Arts Council, 1979-80; choreographer Ill. Dance Theatre, univ. and regional dance cos., others. Grantee Mich. Arts Council, Ill. Arts Council, Australian Council; 3 works commd. by Harbinger Dance Co. Mem. Council Dance Adminstrs., Am. Coll. Dance Festival Assn. (bd. dirs.), Nat. Assn. Schs. Dance (treas. 1982—, cons., program accreditor). Democrat. Roman Catholic. Home: 401 W Indiana St Urbana IL 61801 Office: 4-501 Krannert Ctr 500 S Goodwin St Urbana IL 61801

KNOWLES, PHYLLIS BRADFUTE, title insurance company executive; b. Cin., Oct. 16, 1927; d. Fred Lott and Mary (White) Bradfute; m. Harry V. Knowles, Aug. 24, 1950 (div. 1973); children—Pamela A. Fleizach, Debra A. Zakarin. BA, Barnard Coll., 1950. Exec. sec. Carrie Chapman Catt Meml., N.Y.C., 1950-53; pres. Quinbee & Bradfute Internat. Promotions, Eastchester, N.Y., 1957-75; exec. mgr. Urban Developers, Phila., 1975-79; v.p., chief exec. officer Gibraltar Title & Escrow Co. of Boca Raton, Fla., 1979—. Author: Records of the Town of Eastchester, 1969. Pres. LWV, Eastchester, 1954-56, Eastchester Hist. Soc., 1965-76; treas. West County Hist. Soc., 1970-76; treas. Univ. Arts League, Phila., 1977-79. Mem. Nat. Assn. Notaries. Republican. Methodist. Club: Boca West. Avocations: Doll house building; historian; lecturer. Home: 1626 Bridgewood Dr Boca Raton FL 33434 Office: Gibraltar Title & Escrow Co 3200 N Military Trail Boca Raton FL 33431

KNOX, BEVERLY HARTMAN, realtor; b. Nashville, Aug. 28, 1938; d. Cleander C. and Bertie (Bouland) Hartman; m. Warren Dale Knox, Aug. 19, 1936; children: Jeanne, John. Student, U. Tenn., 1973-79, Nashville State Tech., 1980. Lic. real estate broker, Tenn.; cert. profl. sec. Exec. sec. Anchor Wire Corp., Goodlettsville, Tenn., 1965-69; buyer, adminstrn. asst., purchasing agt. Commerce Union Bank, Nashville, 1969-76; affiliate broker Beck & Beck, Nashville, 1977-79; broker Bill Dorris & Assocs., Goodlettsville, Tenn., 1986—. Mem. Nashville Bd. Realtors. Baptist. Home: 3350 Freeman Hollow Rd Goodlettsville TN 37072 Office: Bill Dorris & Assocs 108 Depot St Goodlettsville TN 37072

KNOX, HAVOLYN CROCKER, financial consultant; b. Charlotte, N.C., Oct. 20, 1937; d. Earl Reid and Etta Lorane (Wylie) Crocker; m. Charles Eugene Knox, July 20, 1963 (div. 1981); children: Charles Eugene Jr., Sandra Leigh. Cert. Stenography, U. N.C., Greensboro, 1956. Charted Fin. Cons., CLU. Exec. sec. Stellings-Gossett Theatres, Inc., Charlotte, 1956-57; legal sec. McDougle, Ervin, Horack & Snepp, Charlotte, 1957, Pierce, Wardlow, Knox & Caudle, Charlotte, 1957-63; adminstrv. asst. Charlotte-Mecklenburg Planning Commn., 1980; exec. asst. Conn. Mut. Life Ins. Co., Charlotte, 1981-86; assoc. The Hinrichs Fin. Group, Charlotte, 1986—. Ops. dir. Eddie Knox for Mayor campaign, Charlotte; campaign mgr. Herb Spaugh for City Council, Charlotte, 1981, 83, 85; registration chmn. Kemper Open Golf Tournament, Charlotte, 1976-79; pres. The Legal Aux., Charlotte, 1972-73; bd. dirs. Oratorio Singers of Charlotte, 1986—. Recipient William Danforth Found. award, 1955. Mem. Am. Soc. CLUs, Am. Soc. Chartered Fin. Cons., Nat. Assn. Life Underwriters, Charlotte Assn. Underwriters. Republican. Presbyterian. Club: The Tower (Charlotte). Lodge: Civitan. Home: 2331 Carmel Rd Charlotte NC 28226 Office: The Hinrichs Fin Group 1600 Charlotte Plaza Charlotte NC 28244

KNOX, MARGARET ELLIOTT, newspaper editor; b. Norfolk, Va., Aug. 16, 1919; d. Roy and Mary (Upshur) Elliott; A.B. cum laude, U. Ala., 1941; m. Robert Bost Knox, Jr., Apr. 26, 1944 (dec.). With Raleigh (N.C.) Times, 1941, Raleigh News and Observer, 1942, Richmond (Va.) Times Dispatch, 1942-44, New Orleans States-Item, 1944-46, N.Y. World Telegram & Sun,

N.Y.C., 1946-59, Norfolk Virginian-Pilot, 1962-63; founder, editor Leader, Research Triangle Park, N.C., 1966-81, editor emeritus, 1981-86; editorial bd. adv. Capitol Broadcasting Co., Raleigh, 1981-86, exec. editor, editorial cons. The Village Cos., Chapel Hill, N.C., 1986—. Life mem. bd. dirs. Friends of Library, N.C. State U., 1984—. Recipient Best Series award N.Y.C. Newspaper Women's Club, 1951; Headliner award N.C. Women in Communications, 1981. Mem. N.C. Press Assn., Am. Newcomen Soc. Episcopalian. Lodge: Rotary. Home: 2922 Wycliff Rd Raleigh NC 27607 Office: 20 Park Plaza Research Triangle Park NC 27709

KNOX, MAUDIE MARLIN, small business owner; b. Kinston, N.C., Mar. 31, 1943; d. George William and Sarah Nell Marlin; m. Marlin L. Mosby, 1963 (div. 1978); children: Marlin L. Mosby III, W. Michael Mosby, Amanda M. Mosby; m. Castle Redford Knox, Nov. 8, 1980. BS, Memphis State U., 1965. Travel cons. A&I Travel Agy., Memphis, 1978-79; dir. sales and mktg. Fred's Travel Agy., Memphis, 1979-83; v.p. Leisure Travel Agy., Memphis, 1983—; owner, v.p. Unique Planning Network, Memphis; bd. dirs. Convention and Visitors Bur., Memphis, 1986-87. Bd. dirs. Memphis Prepatory Sch., Memphis, 1978-82. Mem. Memphis Soc. Area Execs., Soc. Sales and Mktg. Execs. (bd. dirs. 1986—), Home Builders Assn. Memphis (bd. dirs. 1980—), Delta Gamma. Methodist. Office: Unique Planning Network 5386 Mendenhall Mall Memphis TN 38115

KNOX, REBECCA HOWLAND, occupational therapy consultant; b. Wilmington, Del., May 5, 1943; d. F. Stratton, Jr. and Elizabeth Hussey (Brown) K.; m. Gerald W. McCollum, June 6, 1964 (div. Apr. 1975). BA, Brown U., 1965; cert. Tufts U., 1968; MA, St. Mary's Coll., Winona, Minn., 1983. Lic. occupational therapist, Mass. Occupational therapist Robert Breck Brigham Hosp., Boston, 1968; research asst. Inst. for Family and Youth, Cambridge, Mass., 1968-73; occupational therapy cons. Wellmet Project, Inc., Cambridge, 1973, Boston Area Nursing Homes, 1973—, Ctr. House, South Boston, Mass., 1976—, Wellsprings, Cambridge, 1985—; cons. Liberty Sch., Cambridge, 1974—, Women's Job Counseling Ctr., Cambridge, 1987—; researcher Tigerlily Research, Cambridge, 1985—. Sponsor 2 children Holy Land Christian Mission Internat. (now Children Internat.), 1983—; mem. Harbor Area Mental Health Human Rights Com., Boston, 1985—. Mem. Am. Occupational Therapy Assn., Mass. Occupational Therapy Assn., Internat. Transactional Analysis Assn., Boston Orthomolecular Soc., Assn. for Psychol. Type, Nat. Assn. for Female Execs., Mensa. Democrat. Buddhist. Avocations: observing cats, drawing psychol. maps. Office: Wellsprings PO Box 175 Cambridge MA 02141

KNOX HASTINGS, KATHERINE, lawyer; b. Erie, Pa., Dec. 7, 1953; d. William Wallace and Agnes (Graham) K.; m. R. Radcliffe Hastings. BS, U. Mich., 1976; JD, U. Pitts., 1980. Bar: Pa. 1980, U.S. Dist. Ct. (ea. dist.) Pa. 1981. Law clk. U.S. Dist. Ct. (ea. dist.) Pa., Phila., 1980-81; assoc. Schnader, Harrison, Segal & Lewis, Phila., 1981-84; sr. atty. IU Internat. Corp., Phila., 1984—. Recipient Coll. All-Am. Swimming award Assn. Intercollegiate Athletics Women, 1974, 75, 76. Mem. ABA, Pa. State Bar Assn., Phila. Bar Assn. Home: 617 Hopkinson House Philadelphia PA 19106 Office: IU Internat Corp 1500 Walnut St Philadelphia PA 19102

KNUDSEN, BETTY ANN, public and governmental relations consultant; b. Kingsport, Tenn., Oct. 10, 1926; d. Lester Bolton and Nelle Virginia (Lloyd) Leonard; m. John Peter Knudsen, Aug. 27, 1949; children: John Erik, Karl Edward, Karen Louise. A.B. in Psychology, U. Ga., 1948. Kindergarten tchr. St. Timothy's Day Sch., Raleigh, N.C., 1963-65; dir. religious edn. Ch. of the Good Shepherd, Raleigh, 1967-70; community coordinator Goals for Raleigh, 1972-75; county commr. Wake County, N.C., 1976-84, chmn. bd. commrs., 1979-80; cons. pub. and govtl. relations, Raleigh, 1985—; extension edn. tchr. Meredith Coll., Raleigh, 1981-82; mem. N.C. Gov.'s Sci. and Tech. Bd., 1978-85; bd. dirs. N.C. Ctr. Pub. Policy Research, Raleigh, 1978—; del. White House Conf. on Small Bus., 1986. Author successful application for Raleigh to be All-Am. City, 1975. Editor booklets on civic issues. Pres. LWV, Wake County, 1973-75; founder, active Women's Polit. Caucus Wake County, 1975—; founder, chmn. N.C. Women's Resource Ctr.; past pres. Women's Forum N.C., Raleigh, 1985—, charter mem. 1976—; candidate for sec. of state N.C., 1984; mem. N.C. Democratic Exec. Com.; dep. campaign dir. for Lt. Gov., 1988. Named Tarheel of Week, Raleigh News and Observer, 1975, Vol. of Yr., City of Raleigh, 1975; recipient Civic award Wake County Opportunities, 1978, Gail Bradley Meml award Women's Forum of N.C., named Woman of the Yr Bus. and Prof. Women. Mem. Raleigh C. of C., Nat. Bus. Women Owners, Triangle Internat. Trade Assn., AAUW, Bus. and Profl. Women, NOW, Phi Beta Kappa, Psi Chi, Alpha Lambda Delta, Phi Kappa Phi. Episcopalian. Avocations: American Indian archeology; lepidoptery; lapidary work. Home and Office: 617 Macon Pl Raleigh NC 27609

KNUDSEN, JEAN ELLEN, insurance company executive; b. Bklyn., Nov. 3, 1948; d. Tingvald John and Ruth Edith (Warring) Knudsen. B.A. in French magna cum laude, Wagner Coll., 1970; cert. in ocean marine ins. with highest distinction, Coll. of Ins.-N.Y.C., 1977. Translator French, Bertschman & Maloy, N.Y.C., 1970-71; asst. v.p., asst. mgr. home office claims Marine Office of Am. Corp., N.Y.C., 1971—; mem. marine mgrs. com., 1976-86. Contbr. articles to profl. jours. Harold Jackson scholar Coll. Ins., 1987. Mem. Maritime Law Assn., Assn. of Average Adjusters in U.S., Soc. Maritime Personal Injury Cons., Nat. Assn. Ins. Women (N.Y.C. chpt.). Republican. Lutheran. Avocations: photography, travel, needlework, bicycling. Home: 192 Lexington Ave Staten Island NY 10302 Office: Marine Office of America Corp 180 Maiden Ln New York NY 10038

KNUDSON, KATHRYN HELEN MALLOY, psychologist, army officer; b. St. Louis, Mar. 19, 1949; d. Albert Joseph and Julia (Kozar) Malloy; B.A. magna cum laude, U. Mo., St. Louis, 1971; M.A., U. Calif., Riverside, 1974, Ph.D. (NIMH fellow), 1978; m. Gregory Blair Knudson, Oct. 21, 1972; children—Todd Christopher, Kimberley Christina. Commd. 2d lt. U.S. Army, 1971, advanced through grades to maj., 1986; research psychologist Walter Reed Army Hosp. Research Inst., Washington, 1979-84; staff officer/research psychologist U.S. Army Med. Research and Devel. Command, Ft. Detrick, Md., 1984-88; research psychologist Letterman Army Inst. Research, Presidio of San Francisco, 1988—. Mem. Am. Psychol. Assn.

KNUDSON-FITZPATRICK, ANNE HOWLAND, physical fitness company executive; b. Camden, N.J., Feb. 5, 1952; d. Harry Edward and Anne (Howland) K.; B.A. in Polit. Sci., English Bucknell U., 1974; m. Brian Fitzpatrick, Aug. 19, 1985; 1 child, Ryan. With Ga. Pacific Corp., Trenton, N.J., 1975-80, lumber sales mgr., 1978-80; founder, pres., dir. Princeton (N.J.) Nautilus Fitness Ctrs. (name changed to The Princeton Fitness Ctr., parent co. Princeton Nautilus ExerDance, Inc., Princeton Nautilus Tanning Ctr., Princeton Massage Group, Princeton Corp. Health Mgmt. Group, Inc., Princeton Nautilus Home Fitness, Inc., Princeton Nautilus Home Massage, Inc.), 1979—; regional rep. Northeastern Citizen Alpine Com. div. U.S. Ski Assn., 1977-79; mem. U.S. Alpine and Nordic Ski Racing Team, 1977-81; bd. dirs., pres. N.J. affiliate Am. Heart Assn., 1985-86; small bus. cons. Mercer County Community Coll. Mem. Am. Soc. Profl. and Exec. Women, Am. Coll. Sports Medicine, Nat. Fedn. Bus. and Profl. Womens Clubs, C. of C. Princeton Area (instr. adult sch. 1980, Entrepreneur of Yr., 1987), Mchts. Assn. Princeton (promotion com., pres. 1984-85, v.p. 1986), Princeton Bus. Assn. (bd. dirs.), Women Sports Found. (area rep. 1980), Princeton Resource Network of Women. Presbyn. Clubs: Flying Dutchmen Ski, Sweet Jersey Athletic. Winner 2d pl. eastern championship Am. Assn. Ski Racing, 1986; represented U.S. internat. Alpine Competition, 1988. 1st alt. USA Ski Team, 1987. Home: 12 Kilmer Dr Belle Mead NJ 08502 Office: Princeton Nautilus Fitness Ctr Princeton Shopping Center Princeton NJ 08540

KNUFF, ALANA MARIE, architectural designer; b. Akron, Ohio, Aug. 7, 1944; d. Edmund George and Mari catherine (Icabucci) Balzano; m. William George Knuff II, july 9, 1966; children: William George III, Kentrina Marie. BA, U. Detroit, 1966; postgrad., Lawrence Inst., Southfield, Mich., 1972-73, Erie Community Coll., Amherst, N.Y., 1973-74; cert., Northeastern U., Boston, 1985-87. Drafter James R. Cronin Assocs., Palos Heights, Ill., 1975; space planner St. James Hosp., Chicago Heights, Ill., 1975-76; drafter Deck House, Acton, Mass., 1977-78, Gifford Pierce, Architect, Groton, Mass., 1978; designer, drafter Structural Engrng. Service, Lunenburg, Mass., 1978-82; customer support personnel Bausch & Lomb, Woburn, Mass., 1983-84; product analyst Computervision, Bedford, Mass., 1984-85; prin. Alana M. Knuff Assocs., Groton, Mass., 1985—. Mem. Groton Planning Bd., Mass., 1979-85, Millhouse Task Force, Groton, 1987. Mem. LWV. Home and Office: 270 Chicopee Row Groton MA 01450

KNUTH, JOANN KEROLA, computer services corporation executive; b. Youngstown, Ohio, Dec. 1, 1931; d. Joseph J. and Mary George K.; student U. Notre Dame Coll., 1949-50; B.A., Youngstown State U., 1952, postgrad., 1970-72; postgrad. Kent State U., 1966-67; m. Richard L. Knuth, July 4, 1957; children—Richard L., Mary Jo. High sch. tchr., Hubbard, Ohio, 1952-54, 56-57; edtorial asst. Catholic Exponent, 1955-56; computer programmer IBM, Kingston, N.Y. and Lexington, Mass., 1956-57; mathematician Boeing Airplane Co., Seattle, 1957-58; instr. Youngstown (Ohio) State U., 1966-80; pres. Knuth Computer Services, Inc., Hubbard, 1978—; corp. sec./treas. P I & I Motor Express, Inc., Grandview Realty & Devel. Co., Inc. Pres. Hubbard High Sch. PTA, 1976, 77. Office: 4 Walnut Pl Hubbard OH 44425

KNUTSON, CATHE S., marketing executive; b. Natick, Mass., Mar. 23, 1958; d. John Francis Sheehan and Marjorie Elizabeth (Werner) Picchi; m. Lawrence R. Knutson, June 29, 1986. B.S. in Econs. and Mgmt., B.A. in Psychology, Franklin Pierce Coll., 1980. Field dir. Media Stats., Inc., Silver Spring, Md., 1980-81; supr. domestic stats. Am. Textile Mfrs. Inst., Washington, 1981-82; dir. stats. Envelope Mfrs. Assn., Arlington, Va., 1982-83; office automation cons. Coopers and Lybrand, Washington, 1983-84; industry mktg. analyst Wang Labs., Lowell, Mass., 1984-86; ptnr. Sofsearch Corp, 1986-87; systems support mgr. Fed Reserve Bank of Phila., 1987. Contbg. author poetry anthology. Home: 825 N 29th St Apt 5D Philadelphia PA 19130

KNUTSON, MARILYN SUE, real estate corporation officer; b. Mpls., Mar. 13, 1938; d. Charles James and Beatrice Elizabeth (Godfrey) Goucher; m. Lavern Anthony Crowe, Feb. 12, 1960 (div. 1973); 1 child, Sharon Dawn Crowe. Grad. high sch., Mpls. Editor Minn. TV Guide, Mpls., 1957-59; personnel dir. Employers Overload, Mpls., 1959-62; realtor Thorpe Bros. Edina Realty, Mpls., 1963-79, Charles Bohannon, Inc., Maui, Hawaii, 1976-79; pres. Knutson & Assocs. Realtors, Kailua-Kona, Hawaii; bd. dirs. Kona Bd. Realtors. Editor West Hawaii Today newspaper, 1983—; real estate editor KKON-KOAST commentary, 1984—; columnist This Week, Big Island, 1988—. Republican. Office: Knutson & Assocs 75-6082 Alii Dr #7 Kailua HI 96740

KNUTSON, SHARON LEE, county government offical; b. Thief Falls River, Minn., May 31, 1942; d. Ernest LeRoy and Lois Faye (Jones) Swanson; m. Royal C. Knutson, Aug. 21, 1965; children: Chadwyn, Christopher. BA in Home Econs. Edn., Augsburg Coll., 1964; MS in Interpersonal Communication, N.D. State U., 1981. County agt. Minn. Extension Service, Ada, 1964—. Chair women's div. Red River Valley Winter Shows, Crookston, Minn., 1986—. Mem. Nat. Assn. Extension Home Economists (sec. Minn. chpt. 1969), Minn. Assn. Extension Agts., Federated Women's Study Club, Epsilon Sigma Phi. Lutheran. Home: 507 Tulip Ln Ada MN 56510 Office: County Extension Service Courthouse Office Bldg Ada MN 56510

KOART, NELLIE HART, real estate investor and executive; b. San Luis Obispo, Calif., Jan. 3, 1930; d. Will Carleton and Nellie Malchen (Cash) Hart; m. William Harold Koart, Jr., June 16, 1951 (dec. 1976); children: Kristen Marie Kittle, Matthew William. Student Whittier Coll., 1947-49, BA, U. Calif.-Santa Barbara, 1952; MA, Los Angeles State Coll., 1957. Life diploma elem. edn., Calif. Farm worker Hart Farms, Montebello, Calif., 1940-48; play leader Los Angeles County Parks and Recreation, East Los Angeles, Rosemead, Calif., 1948-51; elem. tchr. Potrero Heights Sch. Dist., South San Gabriel, Calif., 1951-55, vice prin., 1955-57; real estate salesman William Koart Real Estate, Goleta, Calif., 1963-76, real estate investor KO-ART Enterprises, Goleta, 1976—, pres. Wm. Koart Constrn. Co., Inc., Goleta, 1975—; real estate sales person Joseph McGeever Realty Co., Goleta, 1976—; adv. bd. Bank of Montecito, Santa Barbara, Calif., 1983—. Editor: Reflections, 1972. Treas. Santa Barbara County Fedn. Republican Women, Alamar-Hope Ranch, 1981-82, treas. County Bd., 1983-84; treas. Com. to Recall Hone, Maschke and Shewczyk, Goleta, 1984; treas. Santa Barbara County Lincoln Club, 1983-87; assoc. mem. state central com. Calif. Republican Party, 1985-87. Mem. Santa Barbara Apartment Assn., Antique Automobile Club of Am. (sec. treas. Santa Barbara 1980-84). Club: Cardinal and Gold (Los Angeles). Avocations: swimming, numismatics, college and professional football. Office: KO-ART Enterprises Post Office Box 310 Goleta CA 93116

KOBAR, JOANNE, franchise executive; b. New London, Conn., Nov. 2, 1941; d. Edward B. and Margaret (Reeves) Enright; m. Michael L. Kobar, July 13, 1963; children: Michael, Christopher, Elisabeth, Jennifer, Mark. Grad., Katharine Gibbs, Providence, R.I., 1960. Pvt. sec. Electric Boat div. Gen. Dynamics, Groton, Conn., 1960-64; office mgr. SM Strong Real Estate Agy., Old Lyme, Conn., 1982-84; founder, pres. Thank Goodness I Found, Inc., Old Lyme, 1982—. Coordinator, leader local troop Girl Scouts U.S., Boy Scouts Am., Va. and Conn., 1972-79; pres. Virginia Beach PTA, 1978; founder, organizer Old Lyme Town-wide Meml. Day Fair, 1982—; choir dir. Christ the King Ch. Mem. Am. Bus. Women's Assn., Am. Entrepreneur's Assn., Nat. Alliance Female Execs., Mother's Home Bus. Network. Roman Catholic. Office: TGIF Inc PO Box 828 Old Lyme CT 06371

KOBAYASHI, ANN H., state legislator; b. Honolulu, Apr. 10, 1937; m.; 3 children. Student Pembroke Coll., Northwestern U. Officer family corp.; former legis. aide, adminstrv. asst. Hawaii Senate, now mem. Senate from 14th Dist. Republican. Office: Office of the State Senate State Capitol Honolulu HI 96813 Address: 3657 Waaloa Way Honolulu HI 96822 *

KOBAYASHI, HESTER ATSUKO, environmental scientist; b. Honolulu, Oct. 4, 1938; d. Teruo and Kinuyo (Shinkawa) K. B.A., U. Hawaii, 1960, M.S., 1963; M.S. in Pub. Health, UCLA, 1976, D.P.H., 1981. Mgr. Arctic research U. So. Calif., Los Angeles, 1968-72, research assoc., 1973; marine environmentalist Port of Los Angeles, 1972-73; researcher in environ. sci. UCLA, 1976-81; research assoc. in environ. sci. U. Ill., Urbana, 1980-82; environ. researcher BP Am., Cleve., 1982—; cons. EPA, 1984—. Contbr. articles to profl. jours.; patentee in field. Mem. N.J. Inst. Tech. (indsl. adv. bd. Hazardous Waste Mgmt. Ctr.), Am. Soc. Microbiology, Am. Chem. Soc., Soc. Environ. Toxicology and Chemistry, Water Pollution Control Fedn., Sigma Xi. Office: BP Am 4440 Warrensville Center Rd Cleveland OH 44128

KOBE, LAN, medical physicist; b. Semarang, Indonesia; naturalized; d. O.G. and L.N. (The) Kobe. BS in Physics, IKIP U., Bandung, Indonesia, 1964, MS in Physics, 1967; MS in Med. Physics and Biophysics, U. Calif.-Berkeley, 1975. Physics instr. Sch. Engrng., Tarumanegara U., Jakarta, Indonesia, 1968-72; research fellow dept. radiation oncology U. Calif.-San Francisco, 1975-77; clin. physicist in residence dept. radiation oncology UCLA, 1977-78, asst. hosp. radiation physicist, 1978-80, hosp. radiation physicist, 1980—; instr. radiation oncology physics to resident physicians and med. physics graduate students. Contbr. sci. papers to profl. publs. Newhouse grantee U. Calif.-Berkeley, 1974-75, grantee dean grad. div. U. Calif.-Berkeley, 1975; recipient Pres. Work Study award U. Calif., Berkeley, 1974-75, Employee of Month award UCLA, 1983, Outstanding Service award UCLA, 1986. Mem. Am. Assn. Physicists in Medicine (nat. and So. Calif. chpts.), Am. Assn. Individual Investors (life). Lodge: Rosicrucian Order. Office: UCLA Hosp and Clinics Dept Radiation Oncology Los Angeles CA 90024

KOBER, ARLETTA REFSHAUGE (MRS. KAY L. KOBER), educational administrator; b. Cedar Falls, Iowa, Oct. 31, 1919; d. Edward and Mary (Jensen) Refshauge; B.A., State Coll. Iowa, 1940; M.A., U. No. Iowa; m. Kay Leonard Kober, Feb. 14, 1944; children: Kay Mary, Karilyn Eve. Tchr. high schs., Soldier, Iowa, 1940-41, Montezuma, Iowa, 1941-43, Waterloo, Iowa, 1943-50, 65-67, co-ordinator Office Edn. Waterloo Community Schs., Waterloo, Iowa, 1967-84; head dept. co-op. career edn. West High Sch., Waterloo, 1974-84. Mem. Waterloo Sch. Health Council; nominating com. YWCA, Waterloo; Black Hawk County chmn. Tb Christmas Seals; ward chmn. ARC, Waterloo; co-chmn. Citizen's Com. for Sch. Bond Issue; pres. Waterloo PTA Council, Waterloo Vis. Nursing Assn., 1956-62, 82—; pres. Kingsley Sch. PTA, 1959-60; v.p. Waterloo Women's Club, 1962-63, pres., 1963-64, trustee bd. clubhouse dirs., 1957-58; mem. Gen. Fedn. Women's Clubs, Nat. Congress Parents and Tchrs.; Presbyterial world service chmn. Presbyn. Women's Assn.; bd. dirs. Black Hawk County Republican Women, 1952-53, United Services of Black Hawk County, Broadway Theatre League, St. Francis Hosp. Found. Mem. AAUW (v.p. Cedar Falls 1946-47), NEA, LWV (dir. Waterloo 1951-52), Black Hawk County Hist. Soc. (charter), Delta Pi Epsilon (v.p. 1966-67), Delta Kappa Gamma. Club: Town (dir.) (Waterloo). Home: 1046 Prospect Blvd Waterloo IA 50701 Office: 503 W 4th St Waterloo IA 50701

KOCH, CAREL EVELYNN, designer; b. Lincoln, Nebr., Mar. 23, 1960; d. Robert Carl and Gertrude Evelyn (Kornmuller) K. B.S., Drexel U., 1982. Design asst. Sydney Carvin Milliken, N.Y.C., 1981, 82-83, Jones New York, N.Y.C., 1983-84; sales rep., designer Asymmetry, N.Y.C., 1984-85; designer Rayman/Ridless, N.Y.C., 1985-87; designer, producer, sales rep. Carel Koch Indsl. Design, N.Y.C., 1983, designer Echo Design Group, Albert Nipon Belts, 1987-88; designer Philip Sand Belts, 1988—. Mem. Nat. Assn. Female Execs., Phi Eta Sigma, Phi Kappa Phi, Omicron Nu. Avocations: dance, film, art, making jewelry, travel. Home: 151 Dekalb Ave Apt 1 Brooklyn NY 11217 Office: Philip Sand Belts 243 W 39th St New York NY 10018

KOCH, DIANE LYNN, programmer, analyst; b. Chgo., Aug. 7, 1960; d. Richard John and Anna Mae (Petersen) Fahlstrom. A.A.S. in Bus. Adminstrn., Thornton Community Coll., 1980; B.S. in Computer Sci., North Central Coll., 1986. Programmer Harris Hub Co., Inc., Harvey, Ill., 1977-81; tech. assoc. AT&T Bell Labs., Naperville, Ill., 1981-86; programmer/analyst Arthur Andersen & Co., Chgo., 1986; free-lance data processing cons., 1986—. Mem. Nat. Assn. Female Execs. Avocations: writing; journalism. Home: 3S 567 Lorraine Ave Warrenville IL 60555

KOCH, EDNA MAE, lawyer; b. Terre Haute, Ind., Oct. 12, 1951; d. Leo K. and Lucille E. (Smith) K. BS in Nursing, Ind. State U., 1977; JD, Ind. U., 1980. Bar: Ind. 1980, U.S. Dist. Ct. (so. dist.) Ind. 1980. Assoc. Dillon & Cohen, Indpls., 1980-85; ptnr. Tipton, Cohen & Koch, Indpls., 1985—; leader seminars for nurses Ball State U., Muncie, Ind., St. Vincent Hosp., Indpls., Deaconess Hosp., Evansville, Ind., others; lectr. on med. malpractice Cen. Ind. chpt. Am. Assn. Critical Care Nurses, Indpls. "500" Postgrad. Course in Emergency Medicine, Ind. Assn. Osteo. Physicians and Surgeons State Conv., numerous others. Mem. ABA, Ind. State Bar Assn., Indpls. Bar Assn., Ind. Trial Lawyers Assn., Am. Nurses Assn., Ind. State Nurses Assn. Republican. Office: Tipton Cohen & Koch 47 S Meridian St Suite 200 Indianapolis IN 46204

KOCH, HARRIETT BERGER, company executive, nurse; b. Wilmette, Ill., Mar. 21, 1924; d. Henry A. and Dorothy (Cole) Berger; m. Jerome Louis Koch, Dec. 16, 1969; children: Stephen, James, Robert. Student, Carleton Coll., 1940-42; diploma, St. Luke's Hosp., Chgo., 1945; BS, U. Chgo., 1946, MA, 1958. Instr. U. Ill., Chgo., 1958-60; asst. dir. Evanston (Ill.) Hosp. Sch. Nursing, 1960-65, cons., 1969-72; exec. dir. Video Nursing, Inc., Evanston, 1965-73; v.p. Am. Jour. Nursing Co., N.Y.C., 1973-82; pres. Spectrum, Ltd., Chgo., 1982—; cons. Boston Coll. Sch. Nursing, 1969-71, West Liberty (W.Va.) Sch. Nursing, 1970, Thornton Jr. Coll., Chgo., 1970; project grant reviewr HEW, 1972-79. Author: Militant Angel, 1951; editor: Workbook and Study Guide for Medical-Surgical Nursing, 1965; producer numerous videotapes on nursing, 1965-86; contbr. numerous articles to nursing jours. Bd. dirs. Chgo. Nurses Found., 1986—. USPHS grantee, 1965-72. Mem. Am. Nurses Assn., Ill. Nurses Assn. (bd. dirs. 1971-75, chmn. council on continuing edn. 1973-74). Democrat. Unitarian. Office: Spectrum Ltd 400 E Randolph Suite 2014 Chicago IL 60601

KOCH, MARY ANN P., psychologist; b. Indpls., Jan. 12, 1953; d. Bert Letellier and Marjorie (Raiser) Pearce; m. Michael H. Koch, June 28, 1981. BA in Polit. Sci., Ind. U., 1974; MA in Psychol. Religion, Harvard U., 1978; MS in Clin. Psychol., U. Ky., 1980, PhD in Clin. Psychol., 1982. Psychologist Eastern State Hosp., Lexington, Ky., 1979-80, Fed. Correctional Inst., Lexington, 1980-81, VA Med. Ctr., Salem, 1981-82, Radford (Va.) U. Counseling Ctr., 1982-84, The Counseling Ctr., Roanoke, Va., 1983, Roanoke Meml. Hosp., 1983—, Roanoke Valley Psychiat. Ctr., Salem, 1986-87. Mem. speaker bur. Mental Health Assn.; group leader Am. Diabetes Support Group, Roanoke. Mem. Am. Psychol. Assn., Va. Psychol. Assn., Va. Acad. Clin. Psychologists, Assn. for Advancement of Psychology, Am. Soc. of Group Psychotherapy and Psychodrama, Am. Diabetes Assn. (bd. dirs.). Democrat. Office: The Counseling Ctr 3144 Brambleton Ave Roanoke VA 24018

KOCH, PATRICIA ELLEN, lawyer; b. Hackensack, N.J., Apr. 2, 1947; d. George Frederick and Jane Elizabeth (Kinsella) Koch. B.A., Georgian Ct. Coll., 1969; J.D., Seton Hall U., 1972. Bar: N.J. 1972. Law sec. to judge Morris County Superior Ct. (N.J.), 1972-73; dep. pub. defender State of N.J., Newton-Morristown, 1973-79; atty. N.J. Bell Telephone Co., Newark, 1979—. Counsel Morris County unit Am. Cancer Soc., 1975—; mem. Morristown Town Council, 1982-85, pres. council, 1984; mem. Morris County Democratic Com., 1982, 84, Morristown Planning Bd., 1983, ALFRE, 1981—; mem. N.J. Bd. Architects, 1980—, pres., 1983; trustee St. Thomas Aquinas Coll., Sparkill, N.Y., 1974—; v.p., trustee Morris County Legal Aid Soc., 1979—. Mem. ABA, N.J. Bar Assn., Morris County Bar Assn., Assn. Corp. Counsel, Zonta Internat. (pres. 1980-81 Morristown). Roman Catholic. Home: Two Rona Rd Morristown NJ 07960 Office: NJ Bell Telephone Co 540 Broad St Newark NJ 07101

KOCH, PAULA KAY, small business owner; b. St. Joseph, Mo., Apr. 7, 1948; d. Kenneth Leedy and Harriette Evelyn (Morton) Houston; m. Richard Reid Koch Jr., Nov. 24, 1978 (dec. Oct. 1985). BA, U. Ark., 1981. Med. sec. John H. Gaskins, MD, Kansas City, Mo., 1971-78; sch. editorial asst. Unity Sch. Christianity, Unity Village, Mo., 1982; asst. to pres. Stone Enterprises, Leawood, Kans., 1982-84, v.p. mktg., 1984-86; pres., prin. Koch Communications, Lake Lotawana, Mo., 1986—; adj. instr. advt. Johnson County Community Coll., Overland Park, Kans., 1988; cons. Vi-Cam Video, Sedalia, Mo., 1987, Summit Associated Mktg., Lee's Summit, Mo., 1984—, OURS, Independence, Mo., 1987; bd. dirs. Stone Enterprises, Ltd., 1986—. Bd. dirs. Kansas City Interfaith Peace Alliance, 1987, Heartland Alliance, 1986, also ex officio; active Common Cause. Donald W. Reynolds Found. scholar U. Ark., 1980. Mem. Profls. United Against Cancer, Sierra Club, Sigma Delta Chi. Mem. Unity Ch. Home and Office: C54 Lake Lotowana MO 64063

KOCH, RITA ELIZABETH, computer specialist; b. Middletown, Conn., Mar. 22, 1948; d. Francis Xavier Joseph and Margaret (Whalen) K.; m. Salvatore Sclafani, Dec. 29, 1984; 1 child, Margaret Anne. BA, U. Conn., 1971; postgrad., Calif. State U., Hayward, 1972, New Sch. for Social Research, 1982-83, Baruch Coll., 1983, NYU, 1980. Computer programmer U.S. Dept. HUD, Washington, 1977-79, computer specialist, N.Y.C., 1979-84; computer specialist IRS, Washington, 1984—; mem. Fed. Women's Program, N.Y.C., 1982. Mem. Concord Village Assn.-Communications, Bklyn., 1982-83, Consumer Council Health Ins. Plan, N.Y.C.-Bklyn., 1983-84. Mem. Assn. Computing Machinery, Nat. Assn. Female Execs., Nat. Trust for Hist. Preservation, Capitol Hill Restoration Soc., Poetry Ctr. Avocations: historic preservation, Victorian era, poetry. Home: 535 Second St SE Washington DC 20003

KOCHANOWSKI, VIVIAN FRENCH, nurse; b. Blue Mound, Kans., Mar. 1, 1939; d. Carlton Clyde and Vivian Electa (Squires) French; B.S.N., U. Kans., 1961; M.S. in Adult and Occupational Edn., Kans. State U., 1975; m. Glen Frederick Kochanowski, Nov. 30, 1963; children—Glenda Lynn, Patrick Eugene, Sean Andrew. Staff nurse Hempstead (N.Y.) Gen. Hosp., 1963-66; instr. nursing Asbury Hosp., Salina, Kans., 1966-79, dir. Sch. Nursing, 1979—; chmn. Kans. Assn. Hosp. Schs. of Nursing, 1980-86. Served to lt. (j.g.), USNR, 1961-63. Mem. Am. Nurses Assn., Kans. League Nursing (v.p. 1985-87, sec. 1988), Nat. League Nursing. Office: 400 S 7th St Salina KS 67401

KOCHER, CYNTHIA, real estate developer and agent; b. Lompoc, Calif., May 6, 1954; d. John Wayland and Marjorie (Bartle) K. B.A. in Asian

Studies, U. Oreg., 1976; M.Internat. Mgmt., Am. Grad. Sch. Internat. Mgmt., 1978. Comml. asst., mgr. Far East imports Barber S.S. Lines, N.Y.C., 1978-80; asst. sec. internat. cash mgmt. Mfr.'s Hanover Trust Co., N.Y.C., 1980-84; sales staff Century 21-Gordon Agy., 1984-86; broker, salesperson Forest Hill Realty, 1986—; pres. Restorations Unltd., 1985-86. Recipient 5th pl. award Internat. Speech Contest in Japanese, Asahi Shimbun, 1975. Mem. Japan Soc., Asian Mgmt. Bus. Assn., Assn. M.B.A. Execs., Nat. Assn. Female Execs., DAR (geneal. records chmn. 1985-86, schs. chmn. 1985-86, yearbook co-chmn. 1983-87, rec. sec. 1986-87). Home: Box 3408 Jersey City NJ 07303 Office: 647 Mt Prospect Ave Newark NJ 07104

KOCHER, JO ANN CATHERINE, federal agency supervisor; b. N.Y.C., June 10, 1946; d. Arthur and Helen (Goodridge) K. BS in Edn., St. John's U., Jamaica, N.Y., 1967; MS in Communications Arts, Queens Coll., CUNY, Flushing, 1969. Tchr. pub. schs. N.Y.C., 1967-69; customer service rep. Saturn Airways, N.Y.C., 1969-70, sta. mgr., 1970-72; spl. agt. Bur. Alcohol, Tobacco and Firearms, N.Y.C., 1972-80; ops. officer Bur. Alcohol, Tobacco and Firearms, Washington, 1980-82; resident agt.-in-charge Bur. Alcohol, Tobacco and Firearms, Honolulu, 1982—. Active YWCA. Recipient Mgr.'s award Interagy. com. on Women in Fed. Law Enforcement, Washington, 1984. Mem. Hawaii State Law Enforcement Ofcls. Assn. (sec. 1985-86), Federally Employed Women. Roman Catholic. Club: Honolulu. Office: Bur Alcohol Tobacco and Firearms 300 Ala Moana Blvd Honolulu HI 96850

KOCHTA, RUTH MARTHA, art gallery owner; b. Bklyn., Jan. 5, 1924; d. Harry Joseph and Anna (Braun) Evers; m. Albert Emil Kochta, Nov. 7, 1948; children: Alan, Carol. Student, CUNY, Queens, 1965-68, Art Students League, 1970-75. Artist Queens, N.Y. and Lenox, Mass., 1965—; dir. Imperial Gallery, N.Y.C., 1981; owner, dir. Clark Whitney Gallery, Lenox, 1983—. Work exhibited at Nat. Acad., N.Y.C. 1969, Audubon Artists, N.Y.C. 1971, Guild Gallery, N.Y.C. 1979, other exhibits.

KOCHTITZKY, LYNNE DAWSON, priest; b. Yonkers, N.Y., July 25, 1941; d. Alan Russell and Margaret Victoria (Black) Dawson; m. Rodney Morse Kochtitzky, May 23, 1981. RN, St. Luke's Sch. Nursing, 1962; BA, Marymount Manhattan, 1973; MPH, Columbia U., 1974; MDiv, Gen. Theol. Sem., 1982. RN; ordained to ministry Episcopal Ch. Staff nurse St. Luke's Hosp., N.Y.C., 1962-63; head nurse Roosevelt Hosp., N.Y.C., 1965-66; staff nurse Albert Einstein Med. Ctr., N.Y.C., 1966-68; instr. nursing Misericordia Sch. Nursing, N.Y.C., 1968-71, St. Luke's Sch. Nursing, N.Y.C., 1971-73; asst. prof. N.Y. Hosp. Cornell U., N.Y.C., 1974-79; chaplain St. Barnabas Nursing Home, Chattanooga, Tenn., 1982-83; asst. rector St. Paul's Episc. Ch., Franklin, Tenn., 1983-86; curate Christ Ch., Bronxville, N.Y., 1986—; mem. Episc. women's caucus Diocese of N.Y., chair ad hoc com. to study abortion, 1986-87; bd. dirs. Floating Hosp., N.Y.C., 1976-79, Jansen Meml. Hospice, Tuckahoe, N.Y., 1987—; cons. Concern for Dying, N.Y.C., 1979-82; lab trainer Lead Cons., Inc., Reynoldsburg, Ohio, 1986—. Mem. St. Luke's Sch. Nursing Alumnae (pres. 1979-81). Home and Office: Christ Ch 17 Sagamore Rd Bronxville NY 10708

KOCSIS, FLORA ELIZABETH, marketing executive; b. Ventura, Calif., Nov. 14, 1962; d. Steve Charles and Carol Ann (Sgarlata) Kocsis; m. Jeffrey Allen Brottman, Aug. 2, 1986 (div. Aug. 1987). BA in Telecommunications, Mich. State U., 1984. Research analyst Majers Corp., Lisle, Ill., 1984-86; sr. promotion analyst Majers Corp., Lisle, 1986-87, account exec., 1987-88; sales support supr. Helene Curtis, Chgo., 1988—. Asst. dir. Nat. Hunting and Fishing Day Mich. United Conservation Clubs, Lansing, 1983. Roman Catholic. Home: 1599 Country Lakes Dr #103 Naperville IL 60540

KODA-CALLAN, ELIZABETH, illustrator; b. Stamford, Conn., Sept. 26, 1944; d. Alexander John and Helen (Wojciehowski) Koda; m. J. Michael Callan, Aug. 14, 1971 (div. 1978); 1 dau., Jennifer Kristen. B.A. in Art, U. Dayton, 1966; postgrad Sch. Visual Arts, 1969-70, 72-75. Designer Glamour mag. Condé Nast Publs., N.Y.C., 1967-69; designer, art dir. CBS, N.Y.C., 1969-70; designer, illustrator Mademoiselle mag., N.Y.C., 1970-71; asst. to illustrator Visible Studio, N.Y.C., 1973-75; designer, art editor, assoc. art dir. Scholastic Inc., N.Y.C., 1975-81; illustrator Pushpin Lubalin Peckolick, N.Y.C., 1982—; designer, assoc. art dir. Scholastic's Early Childhood Program Teaching Guides, 1981 (Am. Inst. Graphic Arts book design show award 1982); illustrator 200 Years of American Illustration, 1976. Recipient illustration awards, Soc. Illustrators, 1975; Art Dirs. Show, Art Dirs. Club, 1980, Print Mag. N.Y. Regional Show, 1982; Graphis Annual, Zurich, Switzerland, 1983-84. Mem. Graphic Artists Guild. Democrat. Home and Office: 792 Columbus Ave Apt 6D New York NY 10025

KODIS, MARY CAROLINE, retail and restaurant consultant; b. Chgo., Dec. 17, 1927; d. Anthony John and Callis Ferebee (Old) K.; student San Diego State Coll., 1945-47, Latin Am. Inst., 1948. Controller, div. adminstrv. mgr. Fed. Mart Stores, 1957-65; controller, adminstrv. mgr. Gulf Mart Stores, 1965-67; budget dir., adminstrv. mgr. Diana Stores, 1967-68; founder, treas., controller Handy Dan Stores, 1968-72; founder, v.p., treas. Handy City Stores, 1972-76; sr. v.p., treas. Handy City div. W.R. Grace & Co., Atlanta, 1976-79; founder, pres. Hal's Hardware and Lumber Stores, 1982-84; retail and restaurant cons., 1979—. Treas., bd. dirs. YWCA Watsonville, 1981-84, 85-87; mem. Santa Cruz County Grand Jury, 1984-85. Recipient 1st Tribute to Women in Internat. Industry, 1978; named Woman of the Yr., 1986. Republican. Home and Office: 302 Wheelock Rd Watsonville CA 95076

KOECHLEIN, LOIS JANE ELLIS, compensation administrator; b. Cin., Mar. 27, 1951; d. Naaman Hubert and Verna Ann (Phillips) Ellis; m. Harold David Koechlein, Aug. 4, 1979; 1 child, Timothy Harold. BA, Wilmington (Ohio) Coll., 1973; MBA, U. Dayton, 1981. Tchr. pub. schs. Mansfield, Ohio, 1973-75; supr. benefits Buckeye Union Ins. Co., Columbus, 1975-81; mgr. employee benefits TG&Y Stores Co., Oklahoma City, 1982-84; compensation adminstr. Jack Eckerd Corp., Clearwater, Fla., 1985-87, supr. employee benefits, 1987—. Mem. Am. Assn. Personnel Adminstrs., Personnel Adminstrn. Assn. of Tampa, Am. Bus. and Profl. Women (legis. chair 1986—). Democrat. Home: 4308 Jetton Ave Tampa FL 33629 Office: Jack Eckerd Corp 8333 Bryan Dairy Rd Box 4689 Clearwater FL 33518

KOEHLER, CHARLENE, hearing aid specialist; b. Tyler, Tex., Dec. 13, 1938; d. Charles Potter Brodie and Helen Ruth (Browning) Bassett; m. William Albert Koehler, Feb. 8, 1958 (div. Aug. 1981); children—Nancy M. Koehler Hamilton, Patrick W., Jeannette Lee, Charles M.; m. 2d, LaVerne Samuel Jensen, Sept. 11, 1981. Student pub. schs., Pleasanton, Tex. Lic. hearing aid specialist, Tex. Sec. hearing aid dept. Sears, Dallas, 1974-79, hearing aid sales, 1979-83; owner, operator Charlene Koehler & Assocs., Dallas, 1983—. Pres. Self-Help for Hard of Hearing, Dallas, 1985—; sec. bd. dirs. Music is Forever. Mem. Dallas Assn. Hearing Aid Specialists (sec. 1981-83), Tex. Hearing Aid Assn., Nat. Hearing Aid Soc. Democrat. Roman Catholic. Club: Quota Internat. Home: 2622 Langdon Ave Dallas TX 75235 Office: 10143 Shoreview Dallas TX 75238

KOEHLER-SAPP, JANICE MANCINELLI, deacon; b. Colorado Springs, Colo., Jan. 2, 1948; d. Albert Daniel and Yolanda (Conte) Mancinelli; m. Edward Frank Koehler, Nov. 23, 1968 (div. 1981); 1 dau., Jordan Conte; m. 2d, David Brewer Sapp, May 7, 1983; stepchildren: Lara Elizabeth, Catherine Leigh. BA, U. Md., 1971; MA, George Mason U., 1982; MDiv Wesley Theol. Sem., Am. U., Washington, 1988. Ordained deacon United Meth. Ch., 1986. Tchr. Pub. Sch. Bds., Montgomery County, Md., 1971-76, Stafford County, Va., 1976-78; instr. Quantico Marine Base (Va.), 1978-79; editor CACI, Arlington, Va., 1979-81; proposal mgr. ORI, Arlington, 1982-83; pres., owner Janus Communications, Burke, Va., 1980—; proposal mgr. No. Va. Office Magnavox, Falls Church, 1983—; asst. pastor Mt. Vernon United Meth. Ch., Alexandria, Va., 1985—; assoc. pastor St. Thomas United Meth. Ch., Manassas, Va., 1988—. Author, coordinator promotional mats, 1982; contbr. articles to children's publs. (award Va. Edn. Assn. 1978). Founder, Mothers without Custody, Offspring, Washington, 1980—; cons. Potency Restored, Silver Spring, Md., 1981—, Women's Kaleidoscope, Alexandria, Va., 1982—; ch. educator United Meth. Ch., Fairfax, Va., 1983-84, researcher women's issues, 1983. Recipient letter of commendation. PRI, Inc., Alexandria, 1979-80. Democrat. Clubs: Washington Calligrapher's Guild. Home: 8220 Thornwood Ct Manassas VA 22110 Office: Mt Vernon United Meth Ch 2006 Belleview Rd Alexandria VA 22306

KOEHLY, JUDITH DIANE, educational materials company executive; b. Phila., Oct. 28, 1945; d. Arthur M. and Katherine W. (Furlong) Hucklebridge; m. Kenneth A. Koehly, Aug. 14, 1965; children: Christopher James, Katherine Jeane. BA, Upsala Coll., 1971. Substitute tchr. Wayne (N.J.) Bd. Edn., 1972-76; office mgr. Ctr. for Intellectual Achievement, East Winsdor, N.J., 1979-81; pres. Playing for Knowledge, Inc., East Winsdor, 1981—; cons. Ctr. for Intellectual Achievement, Elizabeth, N.J., 1980—, NL Assocs., Inc., East Windsor, 1981—, Great Ideas, Inc., Poughquag, N.Y., 1981-83. Mem. Bookman's Club N.J. Home: 4 Poplar Run East Windsor NJ 08520 Office: Playing for Knowledge Inc 4 Poplar Run East Winsdor NJ 08520

KOELLER, SHIRLEY, educator; b. Cin.; d. Maurice Lipian; A.B., U. Calif., 1959; M.A., U. Colo., 1971, Ph.D., 1975; 1 son, Kevin. Tchr., San Francisco Public Schs., 1966-67, Jefferson County Public Schs., 1967-69; teaching asso. U. Colo., 1971-74; coordinator elem. Tech. Center Sheridan (Colo.) Public Schs., 1974-75; lectr. Calif. State Coll., San Bernardino, 1975-78; asst. prof. Tex. Tech. U., Lubbock, 1978-83, assoc. prof., 1983—; dir. Caprock Area Writing Project, 1985. Editor Tex. Reading Report, 1983-86. Mem. Am. Ednl. Research Assn., Assn. Childhood Edn., Assn. Supervision and Curriculum Devel., Internat. Reading Assn., Nat. Council Social Studies, Nat. Council Tchrs. English, S.W. Ednl. Research Assn., Kappa Delta Pi, Phi Delta Kappa. Contbr. articles in field to profl. jours. Office: Texas Tech U PO Box 4560 Lubbock TX 79409

KOELMEL, LORNA LEE, data processing executive; b. Denver, May 15, 1936; d. George Bannister and Gladys Lee (Henshall) Steuart; m. Herbert Howard Nelson, Sept. 9, 1956 (div. Mar. 1967); children: Karen Dianne, Phillip Dean, Lois Lynn; m. Robert Darrel Koelmel, May 12, 1981; stepchildren: Kim, Cheryl, Dawn, Debbie. BA in English, U. Colo., 1967. Cert. secondary English tchr. Substitute English tchr. Jefferson County Schs., Lakewood, Colo., 1967-68; sec. specialist IBM Corp., Denver, 1968-75, personnel adminstr., 1975-82, asst. ctr. coordinator, 1982-85, office systems specialist, 1985-87, backup computer operator, 1987—; computer instr. Barnes Bus. Coll., Denver, 1987—; owner, mgr. Lorna's Precision Word Processing and Desktop Pub., Denver, 1987—. Organist Christian Sci. Soc., Buena Vista, Colo., 1963-66, chmn. bd. dirs.,Thornton, Colo., 1979-80. Mem. Nat. Assn. Female Execs., Nat. Secs. Assn. (retirement ctr. chair 1977-78, newsletter chair 1979-80, v.p. 1980-81), U. Colo. Alumni Assn., Alpha Chi Omega (publicity com. 1986—). Republican. Club. Nat. Writers. Lodge: Job's Daus. (recorder 1953-54).

KOENIG, ELIZABETH BARBARA, sculptor; b. N.Y.C., Apr. 20, 1937; d. Hayward and Selma E. (Rosen) Ulman; m. Carl Stuart Koenig, Sept. 10, 1961; children: Katherine Lee, Kenneth Douglas. BA, Wellesley Coll., 1958; MD, Yale U., 1962; postgrad., Art Students League N.Y., 1963-64, Corcoran Sch. Art, 1964-67. Exhibited one-woman shows including St. John's Coll., Annapolis, Md., 1974, also solo retrospectives Lyman Allyn Mus., New London, Conn., 1978, Rotunda of Pan-Am. Health Orgn., Washington, 1978; group shows include Internat. Dedication Nat. Bur. Standards, Gaithersburg, Md., 1966, No. Va. Mus., Alexandria, 1975, Textile Mus., Washington, 1974-75, Meridian House Internat., Washington, 1980; commd. works include: Free Spirit marble carving Washington Hebrew Congregation, 1978, Monumental Torso bronze for grounds George Meany Ctr. for Labor Studies, 1982; represented in many pvt. collections, U.S. and Europe, 1965—. Recipient 1st prize sculpture Tri-State Regional Exhbn., Md., 1970, 2d and 3d prize sculpture, 1971. Mem. Artists Equity Assn. (v.p. Washington 1977-83), Art Students League N.Y. (life), Internat. Sculpture Ctr., New Arts Ctr. Avocations: reading, gardening. Home: 9014 Charred Oak Dr Bethesda MD 20817

KOENIG, JOAN FOSTER, real estate broker; b. Harrisburg, Ill., Feb. 15, 1930; d. William Jennings and Adria May Foster; B.S., Miami U., 1951; M.A., Ariz. State U., 1967; m. Alan Eastman Disbrow, June 26, 1978; children—William R., Theodore J. Airline stewardess Am. Airlines, Inc., 1951-52; research investigator Procter & Gamble Co., Cin., 1952-53; co-owner, v.p. Koenig Aviation, Inc., Casa Grande, Ariz., 1953-69; real estate sales assoc. Ed Post Realty, Scottsdale, Ariz., 1978-79; real estate broker Koenig Real Estate, Casa Grande, 1980—. Bd. govs. Casa Grande Town Hall, 1972-75; bd. dirs. Hoemako Hosp. Aux.; vice-chmn. Pinal County Democratic Com., 1972-76, dist. 6 chmn., 1972-76, mem. state exec. com., 1972-76; pres. West Pinal County Dem. Women's Club, 1975, 84. Recipient Women's Flight Achievement award Internat. Flying Farmers, 1964. Mem. AAUW (pres. Casa Grande br. 1986-88), Women's Council Realtors, Ariz. Fedn. Dem. Women's Clubs (2d v.p. 1987-88, 1st v.p. 1988-89), Casa Grande Valley Cotton Wives, Casa Grande Hist. Soc., Casa Grande Panhellenic (pres. 1970), Mortar Board, Kappa Kappa Gamma. Democrat. Episcopalian. Club: Woman's of Casa Grande (bd. dirs. 1985-87), Desert Woman's (v.p. 1988-89). Home: Route 1 Box 469 Casa Grande AZ 85222 Office: PO Box 432 Casa Grande AZ 85222

KOENIG, SHARON ANN, banker; b. Appleton, Wis., Dec. 2, 1947; d. Joseph A. and Dolores Iva (Bergner) Gregorius; m. Stanley Louis Koenig, Aug. 7, 1971; children: Bryan Louis, Lisa In Hee. Student, Carthage Coll., 1966-68; BA, U. Wis., 1971. Residential mortgage loan processor, underwriter First Wis. Nat. Bank Madison, 1971-80, mgr., officer residential mortgage dept., 1980-83, comml. mortgage loan officer, 1983-86, coordinator, officer mortgage and SBA, 1986—. Officer, rep. Nakoma Neighborhood Assn., Madison, 1984-86; vice chmn. Families by Adoption South Cen. Wis., Madison, 1985-87, chmn. 1987—. Mem. Madison Bd. Realtors, Wis. Mortgage Bankers Assn., Nat. Mortgage Bankers Assn. Home: 4206 Manitou Way Madison WI 53711 Office: First Wis Nat Bank Madison One S Pinckney St Madison WI 53711

KOENIG, SIERRA SUE, accountant; b. Reno, Sept. 23, 1954; d. Raymond Louis and Pearl Ruth (McCann) K.; m. John W. Galarneau, Aug. 2, 1975 (div. Nov. 1977); 1 child, John William. Degree in acctg., U. Calif., Davis, 1976. CPA, Calif. Cert. property mgr., Calif. Property mgr. S&M Capital, Sacramento, 1973-76; CPA Main Hurdman, Sacramento, 1977-84; prin. Sierra Services, San Diego, 1977—; acct. Stock/ALPER, San Diego, 1985-87; cons. Alpine, Calif., 1986—, Sierra Services, El Cajon, Calif., 1984-87. Treas. Mothers Against Drunk Drivers, San Diego, 1984; chairperson membership com. Women Escaping a Violent Environment, San Diego, 1984; vol. March of Dimes, San Diego, 1986; Sacramento Area Economical Opportunity Council; mem. Ch. Luth. of the Good Shepard, Alpine. Mem. Nat. Assn. for Female Execs. (bd. dirs. 1985—), Adam Computer Soc. (sec./treas. 1985-87), Nat. Assn. for Women Accts. Democrat. Office: Sierra Services 868 N 2d St Suite 301 El Cajon CA 92021

KOERING, MARILYN JEAN, anatomy educator, researcher; b. Brainerd, Minn., Jan. 7, 1938; d. Clement J. and Vi K. (Holtkamp) K. B.A., Coll. St. Scholastica, Duluth, 1960; M.S., U. Wis.-Madison, 1963, Ph.D., 1967, postgrad., 1968. Instr. dept. anatomy U. Wis., 1963-64; asst. prof. George Washington U., 1969-73, assoc. prof., 1973-79, prof. anatomy, 1979—; vis. assoc. div. biology Calif. Inst. Tech., 1976; affiliate scientist Wis. Primate Research Ctr., Madison, 1975-78; guest worker Pregnancy Research br. Nat. Inst. Child Health and Devel., 1977-84; vis. prof. Jones Inst. for Reproductive Medicine, Eastern Va. Med. Sch., 1985—. Mem. editorial bd. Biology of Reproduction, 1974-78; contbr. articles to profl. jours. Recipient NIH fellow, 1967-68; NIH grantee, 1969—. Mem. Am. Assn. Anatomists, Soc. Study Reproduction, AAAS, Washington Assn. Electron Microscopists, Sigma Xi. Office: George Washington U Med Ctr Dept Anatomy 2300 I St Washington DC 20037

KOESTENBLATT, MARLENE PHYLIS, psychologist; b. N.Y.C., Aug. 10, 1945; d. Al and Sally (Vogel) Charney; 1 child, Erik David. BA, Hunter Coll., 1967; MA in Clin. Psychology, Fairleigh Dickinson U., 1980; postgrad in sch. psychology, Montclair State Coll., Upper Montclair, N.J., 1986. Cert. sch. psychologist. Counselor community companion program Mental Health Assn. N.J., Madison, 1977-78; cons. Summit Art Ctr. Caravan Kessler Rehab. Ctr., West Orange, N.J., 1979-80, Advs. for Learning Disabled Adults, Verona, N.J., 1982-84; cons., instr. communication disorders demonstration program Montclair State Coll., 1985-86; assoc. Learning Disabilities Cons., Bryn Mawr, Pa., 1984—; mem. adv. bd. Nat. Network for Learning Disabled Adults, Washington, 1982-84, N.J. Dept. Higher Edn., Trenton, 1985—, Applied Concepts Corp., Edinburg, Va., 1986—. Ushkow Found. grantee, Long Island, N.Y., 1984, 85. Mem. Assn. on Handicapped Student Service Programs in Post Secondary Edn., Profl. Service Network for Learning Disabled Adults, Assn. for Children and Adults with Learning Disabilities (Cert. of Recognition), N.Y. Neuropsychology Group, Psi chi. Jewish. Office: Learning Disabilities Cons 30 Summit Grove Ave Bryn Mawr PA 19010

KOESTER, JOANNE E., public official; b. Hartford, Conn., Mar. 7, 1934; d. Harry Joseph and Elsie Pauline (Malcarne) Eustace; m. Roy George Koester, Apr. 23, 1955; children: Gary, Karen. Grad. high sch., Tampa. Sec. Electric Supply Co., Tampa, 1952-55; clk. library Richmond Heights (Ohio) High Sch., 1965-73; registrar Voter Registration Office Bd. County Commrs., Sarasota, Fla., 1973-76; supr. elections Sarasota County, Fla., 1976-77. Mem. Fla. St. Assn. Suprs. Elections. Republican. Roman Catholic. Club: Zonta (pres. 1985-86). Home: 6255 Muriwood Ct Sarasota FL 34243 Office: Supr Elections 101 S Washington Blvd Sarasota FL 34234

KOEWERS, MARY LYNN, lawyer; b. Grand Rapids, Mich., Jan. 1, 1945; d. Charles Henry and Agnes Margaret (Illg) Brudi; m. John Edward Koewers, June 28, 1963 (div. 1970); children—Deanna Lynn, Kimberly Sue, John Edward; m. 2d David H. Cossin, Dec. 10, 1982. B.A. in Polit. Sci., U. Mich., 1978, B.A. in Journalism, 1978; J.D., Thomas M. Cooley Law Sch., 1981. Bar: Mich. 1981. Assembler, Lescoa, Inc., Kentwood, Mich., 1970-72; legal sec. Wheeler, Upham, Bryant & Uhl, Grand Rapids, Mich., 1972-75, Cholette Perkins & Buchanan, Grand Rapids, 1977-78; law clk. firm Dilley & Dilley, Grand Rapids, 1981; sole practice law, Grand Rapids, 1981-87; dir. mktg., bus. mgr. Northland Tool and Die, Inc., Rockford, Mich., 1988—. Mem. ABA, State Bar Mich., Women Lawyers Assn. Mich., Altrusa. Republican. Lutheran. Home: 6777 Rix SE Ada MI 49301 Office: Northland Tool and Die Inc 10399 Northland Dr Rockford MI 49341

KOGA, ELAINE, controller; b. San Francisco, Feb. 8, 1942; d. Harry Takeo and Mitsuko Kaneko K.; m. Tad T. Murano, July 19, 1964 (div. 1981); children: Michael M., Kevin G. BS, U. San Francisco, 1980. Tax acct. Robert H. Mann, CPA, San Francisco, 1971-72; chief acct. H. Shenson, Inc., San Francisco, 1972-78; asst. controller, acctg. mgr. Esprit De Corp, San Francisco, 1978-80; v.p., controller Marsquare Internat., Inc., San Francisco, 1980; controller Peat, Marwick, Mitchell, CPA, San Francisco, 1981, Armstrong, Bastow, Potter, CPA, San Jose, Calif., 1982, Sofabed Conspiracy, Inc., Berkeley, Calif., 1983-84; asst. v.p., controller Montgomery Capital Corp., San Francisco, 1984—. Mem. Nat. Assn. Accts. (bd. dirs. 1981-84). Home: 1007 Arlington Ln Daly City CA 94014 Office: Montgomery Capital Corp 244 California St Suite 700 San Francisco CA 94111

KOGA, MARY, artist, photographer, social worker; b. Sacramento, Aug. 10, 1920; d. Hisakichi Harry and Tsugime (Yoneda) Ishii; m. Albert M. Koga, June 28, 1947. B.A., U. Calif., Berkeley, 1942; M.A. (Sch. Social Service Adminstrn. scholar), U. Chgo., 1947; M.F.A., Art Inst. Chgo., 1973. With Family Service Bur., United Charities of Chgo., 1947-52; chief psychiat. social worker Med. Sch. Northwestern U., 1952-58; asst. prof. clin. social work Sch. Social Service Adminstrn. U. Chgo., 1959-69; adj. prof. photography dept. Columbia Coll., Chgo., 1973—. Contbr. to Women of Photography, 1975, Family of Children, 1977, Chicago: The City & Its Artists, 1945-78, 1978, others; one-woman shows include: Sch. of Art Inst. Chgo., 1971, Evanston Art Center, 1972, Shado Gallery, 1977, Utah State U., 1979, Pitts. Film-makers Gallery, 1983, J.B. Speed Art Mus., 1985, Truman Coll., 1985, Knox Coll. Art Gallery, 1986, Ill. Wesleyan U. Art Gallery, 1988, Rutgers U., 1988; group shows include, Art Inst. Chgo., 1973, 84, 85, Smithsonian Traveling Exhbn., 1975, U. Mich., 1978, San Francisco Mus. Modern Art, 1975, 78, others; represented in permanent collections: San Francisco Mus. Modern Art, Art Inst. Chgo., Mus. Contemporary Photography, Chgo., Exchange Nat. Bank, Seagram Co., Kimberley Clark Corp., Knox Coll. Art Dept.; many pvt. collections. Chmn. publicity com., bd. dirs. Japan Am. Soc. Chgo., Inc., 1967—. Ill. Arts Council grantee, 1975, 79, 84; Nat. Endowment Arts grantee, 1982. Mem. Soc. Photog. Edn., Friends of Photography, Photog. Soc., Nat. Assn. Social Workers. Home and Studio: 1254 Elmdale Ave Chicago IL 60660

KOGA, RUTH KAMURI, retailing executive; b. Honolulu, July 19, 1929; d. Nenichi and Mino (Ozama) Kamuri; B.A., Smith Coll., 1951; m. George Koga, Nov. 22, 1958; 1 dau., Suzanne. With Ritz Dept. Stores, Honolulu, 1951-84, pres., 1975-84; pres. Suzanne at the Royal, 1984-86. Bd. dirs. Am. Cancer Soc., 1972-80, Hawaii Visitors Bur., 1984-86. trustee St. Louis High Sch., 1980—, Hawaii News Agy., Found., 1980—; fund raiser Kuakini Hosp. Aux., 1956-65; active fund raising for charity and scholarships; mem. council Lyon Arboretum, 1987—. Recipient award Am. Cancer Soc., 1976. Mem. Nat. Retail Mchts. Assn., Honolulu C. of C., Honolulu Art Acad. Democrat. Clubs: Smith Alumni, Waialae Country. Home: 1254 Center St Honolulu HI 96816

KOHANKIE, CAROL LANGDON, development consultant; b. New London, Conn., July 15, 1940; d. Wilbur Spencer and Mary (Leather) Langdon; m. Robert Watson Kohankie II, Aug. 26, 1967; 1 child, Robert Watson III. BFA in Textile Design, Moore Coll. of Art, Phila., 1963; MEd, U. Hartford, 1968. Exec. dir. Jr. Achievement, Wooster, Ohio, 1980-81; pres. Kie Creations, Flower Mound, Tex., 1981-86; chmn. Christian Community Action Festival of Trees, Lewisville, Tex., 1986-87; assoc. dir. devel. Dallas Ballet, 1987-88; dir. devel. and communications The Winston Sch., Dallas, 1988; cons. Dancer's Unltd., Inc., Dallas, 1987-88, Christian Community Action, Lewisville, 1982-87. Chmn. Zip Code Task Force, Flower Mound, 1982-86; mem. Planning and Zoning Commn., Flower Mound, 1983-84; mem. Dallas Com. Internat. Visitors. Named Guardian Angel Christian Community Action, 1987; English Speaking Union travel grantee, Phila., 1962. Mem. Nat. Soc. Fund Raising Execs. Dallas and Ft. Worth, Council for Advancement and Support Edn., English Speaking Union (bd. dirs. 1986—), AAUW. Republican. Presbyterian. Clubs: Women of Flower Mound, 500 Inc. Home: 3930 Willow Run Flower Mound TX 75028

KOHL, GRETCHEN MARIE, government official, information systems project manager; b. Oakland, Calif., Nov. 23, 1946; d. William and Vera Leone (Furman) Erks; children: Edward Ryan, Andre Emil, Jessica Leone, Joseph William. B in Pub. Adminstrn., U. San Francisco, 1980. Adminstrv. officer Traffic and Procurement Depts. Naval Supply Ctr., Oakland, 1972-75; dep. dir. Adminstrv. Services div. Dept. Health and Human Services, San Francisco, 1975-85; info. resources mgr. Gen. Services Adminstrn., San Francisco, 1985—; small bus. counselor U.S. Dept. Health and Human Services, San Francisco, 1979-82; cons. Kohl Kompanie, Alameda, Calif., 1982—. Rep. Aid for Adoption of Spl. Kids Am. Calif. Assn. of Adoption Agys., 1981-82, peer counselor, Oakland, 1981—; coach Spl. Olympics, Alameda, 1982—. Served with USCGR, 1976-81. Mem. U. San Francisco Alumni Assn., Diabled Childrens Computer Group, Intergovernmental Council in the Tech. of Info. Processing. Democrat. Presbyterian. Home: 2308 San Antonio Ave Alameda CA 94501 Office: Gen Services Adminstrn 525 Market St 9KT San Francisco CA 94105

KOHL, MARY ANN, publisher, author; b. Seattle, Jan. 23, 1947; d. John Ross Faubion and Bette Louise (Fritzlen) Faubion Clement; m. Michael Ladd Kohl, July 13, 1968; children: Hannah Cathryn and Megan Lindsey. BE, Old Dominion U., 1969. Cert. elem. edn., Wash. Tchr. Ferndale (Wash.) Sch. Dist., 1969-79; early childhood edn. instr. Whatcom Community Coll., Bellingham, Wash., 1985—; publisher Bright Ring Publ., Bellingham, 1985—; tchng. cons. Bright Ring Publ., Bellingham, 1985—. Author: (books) Acting Up, Acting Out, 1983, Scribble Cookies and Other Creative Independent Art Experiences for Children, 1985. Mem. Nat. Assn. Edn. Young Children, Wash. Assn. Edn. Young Children. Home: 1900 North Shore Dr Bellingham WA 98226 Office: Bright Ring Publ PO Box 5768 Bellingham WA 98227

KOHLER, JUDITH ANN, association administrator; b. Cleve., Feb. 12, 1943; d. Joseph John and Victoria R. (Maycheck) Konecsni; m. Fred Eric Kohler, Mar. 20, 1965; 1 dau., Erika. B.Sc., Ohio State U., 1964. Med. social worker Cuyahoga County Welfare, Cleve., 1964-65; social worker Operation Headstart, Columbus, Ohio, 1965-67; exec. sec. Ill. Commn. on Status of Women, 1974-80, exec. dir., 1980-85; assoc. dir. Women Employed, 1985—. Bd. dirs. McDonough County Youth Services Bur., Macomb, Ill., 1978-80; bur. rep. Macomb Youth Guidance Council, Macomb, 1978-80; campaign mgr. for local sch. bd. candidate, 1975, 78, 81; campaign mgr. for legis. candidate, 1980; mem. adult adv. bd. Ill. Dept. Corrections; bd. dirs. Ill. Caucus on Teenage Pregnancy. Mem. NOW, Ill. Citizens Council on Women, Nat. Women's Polit. Caucus (Ill. bd. dirs. 1975), Ill. Women's Lobby Corp. Home: 3130 N Lake Shore Dr Apt 305 Chicago IL 60657 Office: Women Employed 5 S Wabash Ave Suite 415 Chicago IL 60603

KOHLER, PAT JEAN, food products executive, consultant; b. Witchita, Kans., Jan. 8, 1951; d. Kenneth Leroy and Mary Jane (Stroup) K.; m. Steven Anthony Heptner, Sept. 30, 1968 (div. Jan. 1971); children: Michelle Paulene, April Diane; m. RickyDennis Harms, June 26, 1982. AA in Bus., Modesto Jr. Coll., 1976; BA in Bus., Calif. State U., Turlock, 1978; postgrad., N.Y.U. Cert. Mgmt. Acct. Supr. accounting Dist. Attorney's Office, Modesto, Calif., 1974-77; cost acct. Gen. Foods Corp., Modesto, Calif., 1978-80, supr. cost acctg., 1980-82; cons. personal computer Gen. Foods Corp., White Plains, N.Y., 1982-85; cons. computer systems Gen. Foods Corp., Rye Brook, N.Y., 1985—; instr. Calif. State U., Turlock 1980-81. Contbr. articles to profl. jours. Mem. Westchester Corp. Microcomputer Users Group. Republican. Home: 1296 Judy Rd Mohegan Lake NY 10547 Office: Gen Foods Corp 250 North St White Plains NY 10625

KOHN, JAYNE IRENE, utilities executive; b. Chillicothe, Ohio, Feb. 2, 1935; d. Ezra Alfred and Addie Nancy (Hatfield) Nunley; m. Clyde E. Kohn, Sept. 7, 1958; children: Anita Lynn and Tonita Kay (twins). Grad. high sch., Richmondale, Ohio. Telephone operator Gen. Telephone Co., Waverly, Ohio, 1953-54; chief operator Circleville, Ohio and Waverly, 1954-77; supr. service dept. Circleville, 1977-82, mgr. customer service, 1982-86; mgr. operator service Marion, Ohio, 1986—. Bd. dirs. Circleville C. of C., 1982-85. Recipient Pacesetter award Circleville United Way, 1983-86, Gold Key award Circleville Unted Way, 1987; named Exec. of Yr. Profl. Sec. Internat., 1984, Ohio Ho. of Reps., 1984, 87. Mem. Nat. Assn. Female Execs., Ohio Bus. and Profl. Women's Club (pres.-elect 1984-86, 87—, chair membership com., v.p. 1986-87), Circleville Bus. and Profl. Women's Club (v.p. 1987-88, Outstanding Mem. 1985), Pickaway County Harness Horsemans Assn. (pres.-elect 1987-88, pres. 1988-90). Democrat. Lutheran. Clubs: GTE Good Govt. (bd. dirs. Marion chpt. 1984-87). Home: 21306 River Rd Circleville OH 43113 Office: Gen Telephone Co 100 Executive Dr Marion OH 43113

KOHN, JULIEANNE, travel agent; b. Detroit, Apr. 15, 1946; d. Ralph Merwin and Jane Tacke (Meyers) K.; B.A., Heidelberg Coll., Tiffin, Ohio, 1968; postgrad. Eastern Mich. U., 1969-70; diploma Inst. Cert. Travel Agts., 1979. Travel agt. Am. Express Co., Detroit, 1970-73, Thomas Cook Inc., Detroit, 1973-75; mgr. Island Traveller, Grosse Ile, Mich., 1975-76; pres., owner Flying Suitcase, Inc., Grosse Ile, 1976—; ptnr. Tri-Kohn Investments, Grosse Ile, Mich., 1983—. Mem. Am. Soc. Travel Agts., Inst. Cert. Travel Agts. (life). Episcopalian. Club: Grosse Ile Golf and Country. Home: 9781 Hawthorn Glen Dr Grosse Ile MI 48138 Office: 8117 Macomb St Grosse Ile MI 48138

KOHN, KAREN JOSEPHINE, graphic and exhibition designer; b. Muskegon, Mich., Jan. 8, 1951; d. Herbert George and Catherine Elizabeth (Johnson) K.; m. Robert Joseph Duffy Jr. , July 10, 1982; children: Megan Kathleen, Sarah Evelyne. B.F.A., cum laude, U. Mich., 1973; M.F.A., Sch. Art Inst. Chgo., 1975. Free lance designer, Chgo., 1976-77; designer Stevens Exhibits, Chgo., 1977-78; artist-in-residence Chgo. Council on Fine Arts, 1978-79; designer Chgo. Hist. Soc., 1979-81, dir. design, 81-84; prin. Karen Kohn & Assocs., Chgo., 1985—. Designer Chicago History quar. mag., 1979-84 (4 awards Am. Assn. Mus. 1982, 83, 85), poster for Holabird & Root Exhbn., 1980 (award Am. Assn. Mus. 1982), invitation Ill. Toys Exhbn., 1982 (award Am. Assn. Mus. 1983), poster Chgo. Furniture Exhbn., 1984. Mem. Am. Assn. Mus., Nat. Assn. Mus. Exhibitors (Midwest regional rep. 1983-84), Soc. Typog. Arts, Chgo. Mus. Communicators.

KOHN, MARY LOUISE BEATRICE, nurse; b. Yellow Springs, Ohio, Jan. 13, 1920; d. Theophilus John and Mary Katharine (Schmitkons) Gaehr; A.B., Coll. Wooster, 1940; M.Nursing, Case Western Res. U., 1943; m. Howard D. Kohn, 1944; children: Marcia R., Marcia K. Epstein. Nurse, 1943-44, Atlantic City Hosp., 1944, Thomas M. England Gen. Hosp., U.S. Army, Atlantic City, 1945-46, Peter Bent Brigham Hosp., Boston, 1947, Univ. Hosps., Cleve., 1946-48; mem. faculty Frances Payne Bolton Sch. Nursing Case Western Res. U., 1948-52; vol. nurse Blood Service, ARC, 1952-55; office nurse, Cleve., part time 1955—; free-lance writer. Bd. dirs. Aux. Acad. Medicine Cleve., 1970-72, officer, 1976—; mem. Cleve. Health Mus. Aux.; mem. women's com. Cleve. Orch., 1970; women's council WVIZ-TV. Mem. Am., Ohio nurses assns., alumni assns. Wooster Coll., Frances P. Bolton Sch. Nursing (pres. 1974-75), Assn. Operating Rm. Nurses, Antique Automobile Assn. Am., Western Res. Hist. Soc., Am. Heart Assn., Cleve. Playhouse Aux., Internat. Fund for Animal Welfare, Cleve. Animal Protective League, U.S. Humane Soc., Friends of Cleve. Ballet, Smithsonian Instn., Council World Affairs, Orange Community Arts Council. Clubs: Cleve. Racquet, Women's City, Women's of Case-Western Res. U. Sch. Medicine. Author: (with Atkinson) Berry and Kohn's Introduction to Operating Room Technique, 5th edit., 1978, 6th edit., 1986. Asst. editor Cleve. Physician, Acad. Medicine Cleve., 1966-71. Home: 28099 Belcourt Rd Cleveland OH 44124

KOHNKE, ELAINE ESTHER, jewelry store owner; b. Chgo., July 7, 1924; d. Barnard Albert and Grace Agnes (Olson) K. Sec., Nat. Union Fire Ins. Co., Chgo., 1942-45; mgr. jewelry mfg. Marcasite Mono Co., Chgo., 1945-68; owner Elaine's Marcasite Monogram Co.-Warren Jewelers, Chgo., 1968—. Republican. Roman Catholic. Office: Elaine's Marcasite Monogram Co Warren Jewelers 5 N Wabash Ave Chicago IL 60602

KOHRING, DAGMAR LUZIA, fundraiser, consultant; b. Lage, Fed. Republic Germany, Mar. 8, 1951; came to U.S., 1966; d. Wilfried and Luzia W. (Knichel) K.; m. Arthur Gingrande Jr., Dec. 29, 1976 (div. June 1982). BA, Am. U., 1972, MA, 1974. Cert. fundraising exec. Asst. dir. devel. Harvard Art Mus., Cambridge, 1981-83; campaign officer Harvard U., Cambridge, 1983-85; sr. cons., campaign dir. C.H. Benz Assocs., Westfield, N.J., 1985-88; v.p. Brakeley, John Price Jones Inc., Stamford, Conn., 1988—. Nat. Endowment for the Arts fellow, 1983. Mem. Nat. Soc. Fundraising Execs. Club: Harvard (N.Y.C.). Home: 36 Hancock St Apt 7A Boston MA 02114 Office: Brakeley John Price Jones Inc 1600 Summer St Stamford CT 06905

KOKENGE, ANN RENEE, public relations executive; b. Miami Beach, Fla., Aug. 25, 1962; d. Thomas Reid and Annick Renee (Audubon) K. BA summa cum laude, Barry U., 1984; MA in Communications summa cum laude, U. Miami, 1987. Bank officer, mgmt. assoc. Barnett Bank South Fla., North Miami, 1984-86; asst. mgr., pub. and consumer relations Burger King Corp., Miami, 1987-88, mgr. pub. and consumer relations, 1988—. Fellow Nat. Assn. Female Execs.; mem. Pub. Relations Soc. Am., Internat. Assn. Bus. Communicators, Women In Communications. Republican. Roman Catholic. Office: Burger King Corp 17777 Old Cutler Rd Miami FL 33157

KOKKINOS ASHLEY, SOPHIA, engineering program engineer; b. Athens, Greece, Jan. 15, 1943; came to U.S., 1961; d. John Spyro and Efthimia (Panagiotithou) Kokkinos; m. Joseph Lavon Ashley III, May 15, 1965; 1 child, Natalia. BS in Physics, N.E. La. U., 1965, MS in Physics, 1968; MS in Engring., Old Dominion U., 1978; D in Pub. Administrn., U. La Verne, 1988. Registered profl. engr., Calif. Tchr. several states, 1968-77; mech. engr. Navy Atlantic Div., Norfolk, Va., 1978-79; mech. engr. Naval Civil Engring. Lab., Port Hueneme, Calif., 1979-87, mgr. naval advanced base program, 1987—; cons. in field, Camarillo, Calif., 1983—. Contbr. articles to profl. jours. Tchr. Greek, Greek Orthodox Ch., 1982-83. Named Engr. of Yr., Naval Civil Engring. Lab. 1985, Engr. of Yr. Naval Facilities Engring. Comand, 1986, Engr. of Yr. Engring. Council San Fernando Valley, Calif., 1986, Engr. of Yr. Engring. Council Ventura, Calif., 1986; recipient Fed. Engr. of Yr. award NSPE, 1986. Mem. Soc. Women Engrs. (pres. 1985-86, v.p. 1983-85), Soc. Mil. Engrs., Daus. Penelopy (Grand Marshall 1984-85), Sigma Xi. Home: 1461 Brookhaven Ave Camarillo CA 93010

KOKO, PATRICIA CONNERY, social services administrator; b. Chgo., Nov. 6, 1942; d. Thomas Joseph and Ruth Evelyn (Bowers) Connery; m. Paul G. Koko; 1 child, Marie Helene. BA in History, Rosary Coll., 1964. Registered social worker, Ill. With collections dept. Apollo Savs. and Loan, Chgo., 1964-65; asst. to pres. Exec. Airlines, Chgo., 1965-66; assoc. dir. St. Catherine-St. Lucy Parish Parish Community Service, Oak Park, Ill., 1974-78, dir. St. Catherine-St. Lucy Parish, 1978—; assoc. dir. Home Companion Service, Oak Park, 1974-78, exec. dir., 1978—. Producer, dir.: (videotapes) Alzheimers Disease, 1987, Coping with Arthritis, 1985, Helping Confused Clients, 1984. Coordinator Oak Park, River Forest (Ill.) Hunger Task Force/Food Pantry, 1982—; sec. Oak Park, River Forest Community of Chs., 1982-84; v.p. Oak Park, River Forest Community Welfare Council, 1982-84; chmn. Oak Park Twp. Sr. Citizens Com., 1976-78; tng., cons. Met. Chgo. Coalition on Aging-Respite Care Task Force, Chgo., 1984—; liaison on aging Council for Community Services, Oak Park, 1984-86; past pres. Sr. Citizens Services Coordination Council, Oak Park, 1979—. Fellow Nat. Council on Aging, Mid-Am. Congress on Aging. Roman Catholic. Lodge: Zonta (chmn. membership com. 1987—, bd. dirs. 1983-85, v.p., 1987—). Office: Home Companion Service 38 N Austin Blvd Oak Park IL 60302

KOLANSKY, ELSA HARWITZ, journalist; b. Scranton, Pa., May 17, 1927; d. Isaac Harold and Hilda (Heller) Harwitz; B.A. in Journalism, Pa. State U., 1948; postgrad. New Sch. Social Research, 1975, Phila. Writers Sch., 1977, Temple U. Grad. Seminars, 1978-80, Pa. State U. Real Estate Inst., 1978; m. Harold Kolansky, June 8, 1948; children—Jeffrey M., Betta, Daniel M. Lic. real estate, Ill. Freelance writer, editor, 1948—; reporter Phila. weeklies, 1950-54, Beth Sholom Congregation Newsletter, 1970-72, Jenkintown Times Chronicle Bi-Centennial Edition, 1975; feature editor Am. Acad. of Child. Psychiatry Newsletter, 1978—; editor Aux. News-The Phila. Geriatric Ctr., 1985-86. contbg. author chpt. Montgomery County-Second Hundred Years, 1983. Active Pa. State U. fund raising; mem. Beth Sholom Congregation and Sisterhood Bd., co-chmn. Sisterhood Adult Edn., 1982-83; mem. Hadassah, Faculty Wives Jefferson Med. Coll. and Hosp. Mem. Women's Com. Phila. Assn. Psychoanalysis (treas. 1970), AAUW, Phila. Geriatrics Center (bd. dirs.), Phila. Writers Conf. (2d prize interview div. 1981), LWV. Republican. Club: Cheltenham Racquet.

KOLATA, GINA, journalist; b. Balt., Feb. 25, 1948; d. Arthur and Ruth Lillian (Aaronson) Bari; m. William George Kolata; children: Therese Bari, Stefan Matthew. BS, U. Md., 1969, MA, 1973; postgrad., MIT, 1969-70. Copy editor Sci. Mag., Washington, 1973-74, writer, 1974-87; reporter N.Y. Times, N.Y.C., 1987—. Co-author: Combatting the Number One Killer: The Scientific Report on Heart Disease, 1978, The High Blood Pressure Book, 1979 (Blakeslee award 1980); columnist Bild der Wissenschaft, 1984-87, Jour. Investigative Dermatology, 1985-87; contbr. articles to mags., newspapers. Coordinator charity dinners So Others Might Eat program, Washington, 1983-87. Recipient William Harvey award E.R. Squibb and Son, 1982. Mem. Nat. Assn. Sci. Writers. Democrat. Roman Catholic. Office: New York Times Science Times Section 229 W 43rd St New York NY 10036

KOLATA, MARGARET ANN, healthcare services executive; b. Watertown, Wis., May 13, 1955; d. Carl Vincent and Marcella Elizabeth (Maciolek) K. Student, Nat. U., 1986. Adminstrv. asst. Spectrum Emergency Care, Colorado Springs, Colo., 1977-78; asst. regional mgr. Spectrum Emergency Care, Colorado Springs, 1978-81; physician recruiter Spectrum Emergency Care, Dallas, 1983-84; regional mgr. Spectrum Emergency Care, Los Angeles, 1984—; dist. mgr. Spectrum Emergency Care, San Diego, 1985—. Mem. Los Angeles C. of C., Nat. Assn. Female Executives. Office: Spectrum Emergency Care 6150 Lusk Blvd B203 San Diego CA 92121

KOLB, SUSAN ELIZABETH, plastic surgeon; b. Havre de Grace, Md., Nov. 26, 1954; d. Charles Eugene and Doris Helen (McFarland) K. BA, Johns Hopkins U., 1976; MD, Washington U., St. Louis, 1979; postgrad., Wilford Hall Med. Ctr., San Antonio, 1979-84. Chief Plastic Surgery dept. Wright-Patterson Med. Ctr., Wright-Patterson AFB, Ohio, 1984—; asst. prof. Wright State U., Dayton, Ohio, 1985—. Served to maj. USAF, 1979—. Mem. Air Force Clin. Surgeons, Am. Soc. Plastic and Reproductive Surgeons, Am. Coll. Surgeons, Phi Beta Kappa, Alpha Omega Alpha. Office: SGHSR WPMC Wright-Patterson AFB OH 45433

KOLBE, MARGARET ANN, data processing training consultant; b. Chgo., Sept. 19, 1948; d. Walter A. and Catherine M. (Herda) Lisowski; m. Michael Joseph Kolbe, Dec. 8, 1973. B.S. in Psychology magna cum laude, Loyola U., Chgo., 1970; cert. Honeywell Inst. Info. Sci., 1970. Data processing cons. COMSI, Inc., Oak Brook, Ill., 1970-75; v.p. product devel. Deltak, Inc., Naperville, Ill., 1975-84; v.p., ptnr. The Info. Engrs., St. Charles, Ill., 1984—. Author tng. series, also poetry. Ill. Acad. Sci. scholar, 1966. Mem. Ind. Writers Chgo., Soc. Tech. Communication, Assn. Devel. of Computer-based Instructional Systems, Ind. Computer Cons. Assn., Nat. Soc. Performance and Instrn., Nat. Writers Club. Roman Catholic. Avocation: creative writing. Office: Info Engrs 36W290 Crane Rd Saint Charles IL 60175

KOLBESON, MARILYN HOPF, advertising executive; b. Cin., June 9, 1934; d. Henry Dilg and Carolyn Josephine (Brown) Hopf; children—Michael Llen, Kenneth Ray, Patrick James, Pamela Sue Kolbeson Lang, James Allan. Student U. Cin., 1947, 48, 50. Sales and mktg. mgr. Cox Patrick United Van Lines, 1977-80; sales mktg. mgr. Creative Incentives, Houston, 1980-81; pres. Ad Sense, Inc., Houston, 1981-87, M.H. Kolbeson & Assocs., The Phoenix Books, 1987—; cons. N.L.P. Communications; lectr., cons. in field. Mem. adv. bd. Alief Ind. Sch. Dist., 1981-87, pres., 1983-84; bd. dirs. Santa Maria Hostel, 1983-86, v.p., 1983-84; founder, pres. Mind Force, Houston, 1978-87 and Seattle, 1987—. Mem. Greater Houston Conv. and Visitors Council, loaned exec., 1986-87; mem. adv. bd. Am. Inst. Achievement, 1986-87; charter mem. Rep. Task Force. Mem. Houston Advt. Splty. Assn. (bd. dirs. 1984-87, treas. 1985, v.p. 1986-87), Galleria Area C. of C. (bd. dirs. 1986-87). Republican. Christian Scientist. Clubs: Toastmasters (area gov. 1978), Grand (v.p. 1986), Regency. Office: 5247 S Brandon Seattle WA 98118

KOLE, JANET STEPHANIE, lawyer, writer, photographer; b. Washington, Dec. 20, 1946; d. Martin J. and Ruth G. (Goldberg) K. A.B., Bryn Mawr Coll., 1968; M.A., NYU, 1970; J.D., Temple U., 1980. Bar: Pa. 1980. Assoc. editor trade books Simon & Schuster, N.Y.C., 1968-70; publicity dir. Am. Arbitration Assn., N.Y.C., 1970-73; freelance photojournalist, N.Y.C., 1973-76; law clk. Morgan Lewis & Bockius, Phila., 1977-80; assoc. Schnader, Harrison, Segal & Lewis, Phila., 1980-85, Cohen, Shapiro, Polisher, Shiekman & Cohen, Phila., 1985—; author books including: Post Mortem, 1974; contbr. numerous articles to gen. interest publs., profl. jours.; bd. editors New Am. Rev. Mem. Mayor's Task Force on Rape, N.Y.C., 1972-77; adv. Support Ctr. Child Advs., Phila., 1980—; mem. Phila. Vol. Lawyers for the Arts; steering com. Lawyers' Com. Reproductive Rights. Fellow Acad. Advocacy; mem. Assn. Trial Lawyers Am., ABA (former editor Litigation News, now chmn. com. on monographs and unpublished papers, com. spl. pubs.). Democrat. Office: Cohen Shapiro Polisher Shiekman & Cohen 12 S 12th St Philadelphia PA 19107

KOLWYCK, EMILY DIANE, music therapist; b. Humboldt, Tenn., Mar. 27, 1958; d. Bobby Dean and Mary Sunshine (Fly) K. B in Music Therapy/Music Edn. magna cum laude, East Carolina U., 1980; cert. in substance abuse counselor tng. I and II, Amarillo (Tex.) Coll., 1984. Cert. tchr. N.C., Tex.; registered music therapist. Intern in music therapy NW Tex. Hosp., Amarillo, 1981-82, mental health technician, 1982, music therapist, 1982—, dir. clin. tng. in music therapy, 1985-86; speaker conf. Tex. Guidance Counselors Assn., Amarillo, 1984. Vol. Suicide and Crisis Ctr., Amarillo, 1984—, trainer of vols., 1984—, Amarillo chpt. Big Brothers-Big Sisters, 1986-87, Amarillo confs. Panhandle Head Injury Found., 1985, 86. Named one of Outstanding Young Women Am., 1984; A.J. Fletcher scholar, 1978. Mem. Nat. Assn. Music Therapy, Nat. Assn. Female Execs., Phi Kappa Phi. Republican. Baptist. Office: NW Tex Hosp PO Box 1110 Amarillo TX 79175

KOMECHAK, MARILYN GILBERT, psychologist; b. Wabash, Ind., Aug. 28, 1936; d. Russell and Evelyn Georgianna (Snyder) Gilbert; B.S., Purdue U., 1954; B.S., Tex. Christian U., 1966, M.Ed., 1968; Ph.D., North Tex. State U., 1975; m. George J. Komechak, Aug. 23, 1958; children—Kimberly Ann, Gilbert Matthew. Tchr. elem. sch., Huntsville, Ala., 1959-60; counselor clin. staff Child Study Center, Ft. Worth, 1968-74; assoc. dir. behavioral Sch. for Community Service, North Tex. State U., Denton, 1974-77; pvt. practice psychology, Ft. Worth, 1977—; adj. prof. Tex. Christian U., U. Tex., Arlington; dir. Jon Pierce, Inc.; cons. to schs. and mgmt.; mem. adv. bd. Trinity Valley Mental Health/Mental Retardation, Mental Health Assn. Tarrant County, 1980; presenter to profl. groups, 1974—. Mem. Sanger-Harris adv. bd. for Dallas/Ft. Worth, 1983—; hon. trustee World Olympiads of Knowledge; mem. chancellor's alumni adv. com. U. North Tex., 1987. Author: (poetry) The Prairie Tree, 1987; contbr. poetry to prof. jours. Mem. Am. Psychol. Assn., Tex. Psychol. Assn., Tarrant County Psychol. Assn. (officer 1977), Am. Soc. Clin. Hypnosis, Psi Chi, Delta Gamma. Episcopalian. Author: Getting Yourself Together, 1982; contbr. articles on counseling and psychology to profl. jours., poetry to anthologies. Office: 5280 Trail Lake Dr Fort Worth TX 76133

KOMP, BARBARA ANN, technical writer, publications administrator; b. La Porte, Ind., Nov. 3, 1954; d. Gerald Lee and Betty Mae (Schelin) K. B.A. in Elem. Edn., Ball State U., 1977; student Mech. and Elec. Engring. Tech., Purdue U., 1984-86, Ind. Vocat. Tech. Coll., 1986—. Quality control insp. Foreman Mfg. Co., Rolling Prairie, Ind., 1978-80; quality control insp. Weil-McLain Co., Michigan City, Ind., 1980-81, jr. quality control engr., 1981-84, tech. writer, 1984-88, tech. pubs. mgr., 1988—. Advisor Jr. Achievement, Michigan City, 1982—. Mem. Am. Soc. Quality Control (cert., membership chmn. 1981-83, treas. 1984-85), Soc. for Tech. Communication (Tech. Manual Achievement Award 1986). Avocations: writing childrens' stories, jazz aerobics, photography, skin care cons. Office: Weil-McLain A Marley Co Blaine St Michigan City IN 46360

KONDEK, PATRICIA LEE, music copyist, arranger; b. New Kensington, Pa., Apr. 2, 1939; d. Joseph and Mary (Youshock) K.; m. Robert Josslyn Leonard, June 2, 1967 (dec. Dec. 1972). Student, West Liberty State Coll., 1957-58, Ind. State Tchrs., 1959-60; studies with Albert Lee Bryan, New Kensington, 1950-62; diploma, Sherwood Music Conservatory, Chgo., 1961. Owner Knight Music Reproductions, N.Y.C., 1962-69, Pat Kondek Music Service, N.Y.C., 1969—; bd. dirs. True Copy Co. Inc., DuMont, N.J., 1986—; pres. Patco Industries, N.Y.C., 1986—. Music copyist: (albums) Sinatra Trilogy, 1980, Stuck on TV, 1985, (TV show) Maureen McGovern 1982. Republican. Home: 215 W 83rd St Apt 7-F New York NY 10024

KONDRATAS, SKIRMA ANNA, federal agency administrator; b. Vilkaviškis, USSR, Jan. 26, 1944; d. Bronius and Gražina (Starinskas) Makaitis; m. Ramunas Antanas Kondratas, June 27, 1970; children: Vidmas Antanas, Rimga Alena. BA, Harvard U., 1965; MA, Boston U., 1969; MBA, George Mason U., 1981. Dep. dir. research Rep. Nat. Com., Washington, 1981-84; sr. policy analyst Heritage Found., Washington, 1984-86; dir. Office of Analysis & Evaluation Food and Nutrition Service, USDA, Alexandria, Va., 1986-87, adminstr., 1987—. Author: (with Stuart Butler) Out of the Poverty Trap, 1987; contbr. articles to profl. jours. Fulbright fellow, 1965-66, Nat. Def. Fgn. Lang. fellow, 1966-67. Mem. Phi Beta Kappa. Roman Catholic. Office: USDA Food and Nutrition Service 3101 Park Center Dr Alexandria VA 22302

KONEZNY, LORETTE M. SOBOL, publisher, manufacturing company executive; b. N.Y.C., Sept. 5, 1948; d. Jack and Florence (Silver) Sobol; m. Gerald Walter Konezny, June 4, 1972 (div. 1988); 1 child, Scott David. B.S., U. Bridgeport, 1971; postgrad. Adelphi U., 1972-73, Parsons Sch. Design, 1977. Instr., Middle Sch., Malverne, N.Y., 1971-72; pvt. instr. art, Long Island, 1972-76; instr. art, adult art end. programs, Rockville Centre, Oceanside and Lawrence, N.Y., 1976-79; pres. Pen Notes, Inc., Freeport, N.Y., 1979—; art cons. Rockville Centre High Sch., 1976-77; exhibited in group shows Adelphi U., 1973, Hewlett East Rockway Temple, 1976, Moscow Internat. Book Fair, 1987; represented in permanent collection Yeshiva U., Los Angeles; bus. cons. Baldwin C. of C., 1986. Author, pub. Learning to To Tell Time, 1982, Learning to Print, 1984; Learn Handwriting, 1986; Learn to Write Numbers, 1987; patentee calligraphy guide; profiled in Working Women—The Homebased Business Guide and Directory, 1984., Executive Female mag., July/Aug. 1986; exhibited at Moscow Internat. Book Fair, 1987. Mem. L.I. Networking Entrepreneurs (founding pres. 1984-85), Soc. Scribes. Office: 134 Westside Ave Freeport NY 11520

KONIARES, FLORENCE HELEN, federal transportation executive; b. Medford, Mass., Mar. 6, 1926; d. Angelo and Helen (De Benedetto) Cagno; m. Harry Koniares, Nov. 4, 1954 (dec. 1969). Associate's degree, Dell Sch., 1945. Sec. Phoenix Mut. Life Ins. Co., Boston, 1945-47; editor, proofreader Medford Daily Mercury, 1947-48; adminstrv. asst. Sta. WVOM-Radio, Brookline, Mass., 1948-54; adminstrv. sec. MIT Lincoln Lab., Lexington, Mass., 1954-61; exec. sec. Electronic Space Structures Corp., Maynard, Mass., 1961-65, NASA Electronics Research Ctr., Cambridge, Mass., 1965-70; personnel mgmt. asst. transp systems ctr. U.S. Dept. Transp., Cambridge, 1970-72, personnel mgmt. specialist transp. systems ctr., 1972-82, tng. officer transp. systems ctr., 1982—. Instr. Stop Smoking Clinic, Danvers, Mass., 1983-85; notary pub. Commonwealth of Mass., 1979—. Mem. N.E. Regional Tng. Council, Am. Soc. Tng. and Devel., Greater Boston Real Estate Bd. Democrat. Roman Catholic. Home: 34 Hamilton Rd Arlington MA 02174 Office: USDOT Transportation Systems Ctr Kendall Sq Cambridge MA 02142

KONIOR, LYNNE BARTLETT, public relations and advertising executive; b. Paoli, Pa., Feb. 21, 1953; d. John B. and Dorothy F. (Lemon) Willey. B.S. cum laude, U. Mass., Amherst, 1979. Coordinator devel. and spl. projects Nat. Recreation and Parks Assn., Arlington, Va., 1979-81; dir. pub. relations Weight Watchers Eastern Mass. and R.I., Boston, 1981-82; dir. devel. and pub. relations Nat. Kidney Found. Mass., Boston, 1982-84; v.p. pub. relations Arnold & Co., Boston, 1984-85; chmn., chief exec. officer King Konior Inc., Boston, 1985—. Mem. adv. com. Boston for the World, 1985—, devel. com. U.S. Olympic Com.; devel. cons. Summer Solstice Art Festival, 1984. Mem. Publicity Club Boston (Bell Ringer awards 1985, 86, 87, Spl. Merit award 1985), Nat. Assn. Female Execs., Advt. Club Greater Boston. Avocations: ceramics, racquetball. Office: King Konior Inc 87 Summer St Boston MA 02110

KONON, NEENA NICHOLAI, space planner/interior designer; b. Chgo., Dec. 4, 1951; d. Nicholas Alexander and Marie G. (Korotkoff) K. BFA cum laude, Ohio U., 1973. Interior designer Architectonics, Inc., Chgo., 1973-75, sr. interior designer, 1978-82; interior designer Space Mgmt. Assoc., Inc., Chgo., 1975-78; design prin. Borkon & Konon Assoc., Inc., Chgo., 1982-84; dir. interior design Perkins & Will, Inc., Chgo., 1984—. Iason restoration Holy Trinity Russian Orthodox Cathedral, Chgo., 1987, millenium com., 1988. Mem. Internat. Facilities Mgrs. Assn. Republican.

KONOPKA, CHRISTINE ANTOINETTE, quality assurance professional; b. Bielsk-Podlaski, Poland, Mar. 1, 1957; came to U.S., 1968; d. John Karolczuk and Nellie Perini; m. Anthony Konopka, Apr. 17, 1982; children: Daniel, Iwonka and Mark (twins). AS, Sacred Heart U., Bridgeport, Conn., 1978, BS, 1979. Personnel coordinator Avco Lycoming Textron, Stratford, Conn., 1981-83, exec. sec., 1983-86, purchased material quality engring. analyst, 1986—. Mem. Phi Delta Phi. Home: 340 Prayer Spring Rd Stratford CT 06497

KONOPKA, MARIANNE ELIZABETH, health science facility administrator; b. N.Y.C., Nov. 4, 1943; d. Michael Stanley and Lucille Martha (Torbik) K. BS in Nursing, L.I. U., 1971; M of Pub. Adminstrn., NYU, 1978. From staff nurse to head nurse Greenpoint Hosp., Bklyn., 1964-67; asst. supr., instr. Mt. Sinai Hosp., N.Y.C., 1967-75; supr., asst. dir. Meth. Hosp., Bklyn., 1975-81; dir., mgmt. analyst Youngstown (Ohio) Hosp. Assn., 1981-85; adminstr. Vis. Nurse Assn. of Youngstown, 1985—; mgmt. cons. Youngstown, 1985; bd. dirs. Health System Agy., Ohio, 1986-87. Contbr. articles to profl. jours. Mem. Am. Hosp. Assn., Am. Acad. Ambulatory Nursing Adminstrs. (charter), Ambulatory Care Nurses Assn. (founder, pres. 1979-81). Democrat. Roman Catholic. Office: Vis Nurse Assn of Youngstown 518 E Indianola Ave Youngstown OH 44502

KONSTENIUS, DONNA JEAN, sales executive; b. L'Anse, Mich., Aug. 30, 1949; d. William George and Mary J. (Short) K.; m. Robert S. Munday, Feb. 26, 1977 (div. Nov. 1986). Student, Propect Hall, 1968. Sec. legal Quarles, Herriott, Clemons, Milw., 1968-69; various positions Miller Brewing

Co., Milw. and Dallas and Chgo., 1969-76; sec. to pres. Cad-Rich Sales, Chgo., 1976-78; adminstrv. asst. to asst. mktg. mgr. Rubbermaid Applied Products, Statesville, N.C., 1978-80; various positions to mgr. midwest region Mars White Knight Co., Asheville and Indpls., N.C. and Ind., 1980—. Bd. dirs. Emanuel Luth. Sch., Asheville, 1985-87. Mem. Nat. Assn. Female Execs., Beta Sigma Phi. Republican. Home: 9484 Aberdare Dr Indianapolis IN 46250 Office: Mars White Knight PO Box 6874 Asheville NC 28816

KONTZ, MARY MARGARET, nursing administrator; b. St. Paul, Dec. 13, 1955; d. Milo James and Loretta Margaret (Winkler) K. BS in Nursing, U. Miami, Coral Gables, Fla., 1978, MS in Nursing, 1984, postgrad., 1986—. RN. Mem. surg. staff Mercy Hosp., Miami, 1978-79; mem. emergency staff Parkway Hosp., Miami, 1979-80; mem. faculty Jackson Meml. Hosp., Miami, 1980-86, asst. dir. nursing and patient edn., 1986—; cons. community hosps., Miami, 1982—. Mem. N.Am. Nursing Diagnosis Assn., So. Area Nursing Diagnosis Assn. (adv. com., interim editor SANDA News, state rep. 1985—), Am. Nurses Assn., Fla. Nurses Assn., Sigma Theta Tau. Home: 9301 SW 92 Ave Apt 315-B Miami FL 33176 Office: Jackson Meml Hosp 1611 NW 12 Ave Miami FL 33136

KOOL, RHONDA FAY, chemical technologist; b. Edmonton, Alta., Can., Apr. 16, 1959; d. Clarence Ruben and Doris Christine (Tomlin) Plunkie; m. Richard Mitchell Kool, Aug. 24, 1985. Diploma in Chem. Tech., No. Alta. Inst. Tech., Edmonton, 1984. Hairstylist Raymond's Salon, Edmonton, 1978-82; chem. technologist No. Alta. Dairy Pool, Edmonton, 1984—; union lab. rep. Alta. Brotherhood Dairy Employees, Edmonton, 1986-88. Mem. Chem. Tech. Alumni Assn. Office: No Alta Dairy Pool, 16110 116 Ave, Edmonton, AB Canada

KOONIN, MICHELE SUZANNE, social worker; b. Los Angeles, Dec. 11, 1945; d. Herman and Lucile (Torrence) Kupersmith; divorced; children: Nicole, David. BA in Psychology, San Diego State U., 1978, MSW, 1981. Social worker, therapist VA, San Diego, 1980-84; psychiat. social worker San Diego County Mental Health, 1984-88; therapist, cons., dir. of domestic adoption program Resources for Ind. Adoption, Coronado, Calif., 1988—, therapist, dir. domestic adoption program, 1988—; mem. task force San Diego Coll. System, 1986-87. Author: Staying Healthy: A Training Manual for Group Work with Seniors, 1986. Active Pacific Beach Community Council, San Diego, 1986-88. Recipient Nat. Comdrs. award Disabled Am. Veterans, 1986. Fellow Soc. Clin. Social Work; mem. Health Care Providers in Clin. Social Work (diplomat), Nat. Assn. Female Execs. Democrat. Office: Resources 830 Orange Ave Suite B Coronado CA 92118

KOONTZ, EVA ISABELLA, technologist, researcher; b. Jetmore, Kans., Feb. 3, 1935; d. Vernon Ward and Lillian Mae (Bell) K. BS in Natural Scis., Sterling (Kans.) Coll., 1957; cert. in med. tech., U. Kans. Med. Ctr., 1958. Staff technologist St. Lukes Hosp., Kansas City, Mo., 1974-79; clin. lab. mgr. and supr. Quincy Research Ctr., Kansas City, Mo., 1979-80; staff technologist Lakeside Hosp., Kansas City, Mo., 1980-82; med. technologist supr. Midwest Research Inst., Kansas City, Mo., 1982-88; toxicology technologist Clin. Reference Labs., Inc., Lenexa, Kans., 1988—. Mem. Am. Soc. for Med. Tech., Am. Assn. for Clin. Chemistry, Mo. Soc. Med. Technologists. Republican. Presbyterian. Home: 10251 Cedarbrooke Ln Kansas City MO 64131 Office: Clin Reference Labs Inc 11840 W 85th St Lenexa KS 66214

KOONTZ, KATY, journalist; b. Phila., Sept. 26, 1959; d. Donald Ross and Betty Ann (Fyfe) K.; m. Steven Harlan Friedlander, May 18, 1988. BA in Journalism, BA in Anthropology, Pa. State U., 1981. Campus corr. The New York Times, University Park, Pa., 1979-81; editorial sec. Purchasing Mag., Boston, 1981; pub. relations asst. Simmons Coll., Boston, 1981-82; researcher Playboy Guides, N.Y.C., 1982-83; free lance journalist N.Y.C., 1983-84; assoc. editor United Media Enterprises, N.Y.C., 1984; lifestyles editor Success Mag., N.Y.C., 1984-86; travel and features editor McCall's Mag., N.Y.C., 1986-87; free lance journalist N.Y.C., 1987—. Contbr. articles to newspapers and mags., 1978—. Vol. United Neighbors of East Midtown, N.Y.C., 1987. Mem. Am. Soc. Journalists and Authors, Pa. State Alumni Assn., Phi Beta Kappa, Phi Kappa Phi. Democrat. Club: Penn State Club of N.Y. Home: 26 Cheever Pl #2 Brooklyn NY 11231

KOOP, CAROLYN PASCUCCI, accountant; b. Fresno, Calif., Jan. 7, 1953; d. John and Jennie Ann (Tacchino) Pascucci; m. Stuart Mitchell Koop. BS, Millikin U., 1984. CPA, Ill. Branch specialist Security Pacific Nat. Bank, Norwalk, Calif., 1976-77; trust clk. Security Nat. Bank Roswell (N.Mex.), 1978-80; systems analyst POISE Co., Roswell, 1980-82; sr. acct. KMG Main Hurdman, CPA, Decatur, Ill., 1984-85; acctg. officer 1st Nat. Bank Decatur, 1985—. Mem. Nat. Assn. Female Execs., Nat. Assn. Accts. (pres. 1987-88, v.p. edn. 1986-87, dir. programs 1985-86, mem. controllers council, del. to Mid-Am. council), Nat. Assn. for Bank Cost and Mgmt. Club: Millikin Women's Assn. (Decatur) (sec. 1986-87). Office: 1st Nat Bank Decatur 130 N Water Decatur IL 62525

KOOP, TAMARA TERRI, university program specialist; b. Sheboygan, Wis., Sept. 19, 1950; d. Arthur H. and Ruth B. (Laubenstein) K. A. U. Wis., West Bend, 1970; BS, U. Wis., 1972; MS, U. Wis., Platteville, 1978. 4-H and youth agt. U. Wis. Coop. Extension Service, Oconto and Waukesha, 1973-77, 78—; teaching asst. U. Wis., Platteville, 1977-78; Advisor Waukesha County 4-H Leaders' Assn., 1978—, Waukesha County 4-H Council of Teens, 1978—; cons. Waukesha County Fair Assn., 1978—. Author (periodical) Entre Nous, 1984—. Mem. Dept. Youth Devel., Oconto and Waukesha, 1973—, vice-chmn., chmn., 1985-87, Waukesha; office chairperson Waukesha County U. Wis. Extension and Land Conservation Depts., 1987—; bd. dirs. Wis. State Fair Jr. Fair Bd., West Allis, 1985—. Recipient Disting. Service award Nat. Assn. Extension 4-H and Youth Agts., 1984, Disting. Service award Wis. Assn. Extension 4-H and Youth Agts., 1984. Mem. Waukesha County Assn. Vol. Adminstrs. (sec. 1986—), Home Econs. Profl. Council, Epsilon Sigma Phi. Lodge: Rotary. Office: Waukesha County U Wis Extension 500 Riverview Ave Waukesha WI 53188

KOOPMANN PARRISH, RETA COLLENE, retail executive; b. Oklahoma City, Feb. 27, 1944; d. Henry William and Hazel (Rollins) Singleton; m. Fred Koopman, June 1, 1963 (div. 1974); 1 child, Rebecca Dawn; m. Walter J. Parrish, Jan 3, 1987. BA, Calif. Coast U., 1987, postgrad. in bus. adminstrn., 1987—. Front end mgr. Kroger Co., Cleve., 1969-72; accounting Johns Manville, Denison, Tex., 1972-74; bakery/deli merchandiser Kroger Co., Columbia, S.C., 1974-83; v.p. bakery, deli Kash & Karry div. Lucky's Inc., Tampa, Fla., 1983—. Authro tng. manuals, 1984, 86, 87. Vol. Spl. Olympics, Tampa, 1986, 87. Mem. Internat. Deli/Bakery Assn. (exec. bd.), Nat. Assn. for Female Execs. Republican. Mem. Ch. Christ. Lodge: Eagles. Home: 505 Rooks Rd Seffner FL 33584 Office: Kash & Karry div Luckys Stores 6422 Harney Rd Tampa FL 33810

KOPACK, LAURA REYES, lawyer; b. Laredo, Tex., June 23, 1953; d. Jose Lino and Dora Guillermina (Moreno) Reyes; m. Alan Joseph Kopack, Aug. 11, 1973; children: Samantha Terese, Alexandra Frances. BA in Philosophy, Wayne State U., 1975; JD, U. Detroit, 1980. Bar: Mich. 1980, U.S. Dist. Ct. (ea. dist.) Mich. 1980. Corp. counsel City of Detroit, 1979-82; staff atty. Detroit Edison Co., 1982—; bd. dirs. Inner City Bus. Improvement Forum/S.E. Mich. Bus. Devel. Ctr., Detroit, Internat. Inst., Detroit, Legal Aid and Defenders Office; chmn. bd. dirs. Service Employment Redevel., Detroit. Contbr. tax articles to profl. jours. Mem. New Detroit Inc., Pvt. Industry Council, Detroit, United Found. social work allocation com., Detroit, Future of Mich., Detroit; trustee S.W. Detroit Hosp., Westland Med. Clinic. Recipient Most Polit. award Hispanic Leadership Devel. Program, Detroit, 1981. Mem. ABA, Mich. Bar Assn., Detroit Bar Assn., Latin Bar Assn., Mich. Trial Lawyers Assn., Detroit C. of C. (Leadership Detroit VIII). Republican. Roman Catholic. Clubs: Hispanic Econ. (pres.), Edison Athletic (Detroit). Home: 34511 Woodvale Livonia MI 48154 Office: Detroit Edison Co 2000 2d Ave 688 WCB Detroit MI 48226

KOPACK, PAMELA LEE (MACMINN), business services executive; b. Portland, Maine, July 25, 1951; d. Everett John Foye and Lois Florence (Loveland) MacMinn; student Sears, Roebuck Extension Inst., 1969-73, Newspaper Inst. Am., 1979-85; m. Charles Thomas Kopack, Apr. 2, 1971. Sales staff Sears Roebuck & Co., Cleve., 1966-69, credit collector, 1972-75; exec. sec., asst., Cole Nat. Corp., Cleve., 1976-79; various positions as employment counselor, travel cons., bridal cons., model, photographer, advt. aide; pres. Kopack Service Bur., Cleve., 1979—; distbr. Shaklee, 1984—. Author poetry pub. in Poetry-People, 1975, other publs., 1974—, lyrics for songs recorded on single records and albums, 1974-79; author greeting cards, articles, short stories. Mem. Career Guild (New Feature award 1982), Secs. Workshop, P.S. for Profl. Secs. (Bur. Bus. Practice, article award 1979), Internat. Platform Assn., Nat. Assn. Female Execs. Clubs: Homeowners Assn., Women's Opportunity Workshop, Nat. Assn. Notaries. Recipient poetry award for Facets of a Housewife, pub. in Beyond Verse, 1977. Compiler Royal Doulton Manual for Collectors. Address: 16493 Prospect Rd Strongsville OH 44136-5543 Office: PO Box 38171 Olmsted Falls OH 44138

KOPENHAVER, JOSEPHINE YOUNG, painter, educator; b. Seattle, June 9, 1908; d. George Samuel and Blanche Cecilia (Castle) Young; A.B., U. Calif., 1928; M.F.A. (scholar 1936-37), U. So. Calif., 1937; spl. student Claremont Grad. Sch., 1951, 67, Chouinard Art Inst., 1946-47, Otis Art Inst., 1954-55; m. Ralph Witmer Kopenhaver, Apr. 11, 1931. Prof. art Chaffee Jr. Coll., Ontario, Calif., 1946-47, Los Angeles City Coll., 1948-73, Woodbury U., Los Angeles, 1973-76, summer sessions Calif. State U., Los Angeles, 1950, Pasadena City Coll., 1949, Otis Art Inst., Los Angeles, 1959, Pasadena Art Inst., 1948; profl. painter, exhibiting artist, 1933—; work included in exhibits mus. and pvt. galleries U.S. and Mex., 1933—, including Hatfield Galleries, Los Angeles; art juror; represented Archives of Am. Art Oakland (Calif.) Art Mus. Winner first award in oil Los Angeles Art Festival, 1936, various art awards. Mem. Los Angeles Art Assn. (bd. dirs.), Nat. Watercolor Soc. (sec.), Audubon Artists, Artists for Econ. Action, Calif. Tchrs. Assn. Clubs: Los Angeles Athletic, Zeta Tau Alpha. Office: PO Box 10666 Glendale CA 91209 Office: PO Box 10666 Glendale CA 91209

KOPENHAVER, PATRICIA ELLSWORTH, podiatrist. Student, Columbia U., 1950-53; BA, George Washington U., 1954; MA, Columbia U., 1956; Dr. Podiatric Medicine, SUNY, 1963; postgrad., N.Y. Coll. Podiatric Medicine, 1980. Diplomate Nat. Bd. Podiatry Examiners. Practice podiatry Greenwich, Conn., 1964—; mem. staff Laurelton Convalescent Hosp., Greenwich. Publicity dir. Neighbors Club, YWCA, 1968—; Bd. dirs. Monmouth Opera Guild, 1965; trustee Monmouth Opera Festival, 1966, v.p., 1964; mem. Greenwich Arts Council; program chmn. Greenwich Women's Republican Club, 1983-84, 4th dist. rep., 1984-85, 1987—; mem. Greenwich Exchange for Women's Work, 1984; chmn. bd. Greenwich Woman's Club Gardeners, 1986 . Recipient Hosp. Fund award for med. research translations ARC. Mem. Am. Podiatry Assn. (career guidance com.), Conn. Podiatry Assn., Fairfield Podiatry Assn., Am. Woman's Podiatry Assn. (sec.), Am. Assn. Women Podiatrists (charter pres. 1969-78), Acad. Podiatry, Am. Podiatry Council, UN Assn. U.S.A., Acad. Podiatric Medicine, AAUW (chmn. nominating com. 1981, 1st v.p. 1983-84, chmn. fund raising 1984-85, chmn. women's issues 1985), Am. Podiatric Circulatory Soc., NOW, George Washington U., Columbia alumni assns., Fairfield County Alumni Assn. Columbia U., Nat. Fedn. Rep. Women, Bruce Mus., Nature Conservancy, Federated Garden Clubs Conn., Croquet Found. Am., St. Mary Ladies Guild, Greenwich Gardeners Pi Epsilon Chi. Clubs: Soroptimist (vice chmn. program com. 1985—, regional med. scholarship chmn. 1987), Toastmasters, Travel (program com. 1984—, Indian com.), Greenwich Women's (chmn. civic and public affairs com. 1970, program chmn. 1983—, pres. 1985—, scholarship chmn. 1985—). Home: 2 Sutton Pl S New York NY 10022 Office: 8 Deerfield Dr Greenwich CT 06830

KOPF, PATRICIA NICELY, lawyer; b. Rutherford, N.J., Feb. 21, 1950. AB with high honors, Wellesley Coll., 1971; JD, Harvard U., 1974. Bar: N.Y. 1975, Calif. 1980, U.S. Ct. Appeals (2d, 5th, 9th cirs.). Assoc. atty. White & Case, N.Y.C., 1974-80; assoc. atty. Fenwick, Davis & West, Palo Alto, Calif., 1980-81; ptnr., 1982—; exec. bd. mem. Sect. Bus. Litigation and Fed. Cts., Santa Clara (Calif.) Bar Assn. Contbr. articles to profl. jours. Adv. council Wellesley Coll., 1986—. Mem. ABA, N.Y.C. Bar Assn., Phi Beta Kappa. Clubs: West Bay Wellesley, Wellesley Coll. Office: Fenwick Davis & West Two Palo Alto Sq Palo Alto CA 94306

KOPLEY, MARY KATHERINE, legislative consultant/lobbyist; b. Cortland, N.Y., May 13, 1956; d. Andrew Michael and Barbara Ann (Stoker) K.; m. Richard Z. Steinhaus, Sept. 25, 1982. BA in Polit. Sci. with honors, Russell Sage Coll., 1978. Mem. research staff N.Y. State Assembly Banks Com., 1975; legis. analyst Steinhaus & Hochauser, N.Y.C., 1976; legis. cons. Richard Z. Steinhaus Esquire, Tarrytown, N.Y., 1977-80; ptnr. Richard Z. Steinhaus Assocs., Albany, N.Y., 1981—; guest lectr., mem. career network Russell Sage Coll. Co-chair membership com. Urban League, Capital dist. Devel. Com.; bd. dirs. Project Strive. Office: 90 S Swan St Albany NY 12210

KOPLIN, JENNIFER LEE, advertising executive; b. Oklahoma City, June 13, 1956; d. Randall Marion and Melba Lee (Mills) Johnson; m. Brent Robert Koplin, Aug. 22, 1983; 1 child, Steven Brent. AA, Ricks Coll., 1977; BA, Brigham Young U., 1980. Sales rep. S.W. Times Record, Ft. Smith, Ark., 1980-82; gen. mgr. Happy Ads Classified Paper, Salt Lake City, 1982-83; media planner Scopes, Garcia Advt., Salt Lake City, 1983-86; media dir. Dahlin, Smith, White Advt., Salt Lake City, 1986—. Mormon.

KOPLOVITZ, KAY, communication network executive; b. Milw., Apr. 11, 1945; d. William E. and Jane T. Smith; m. William C. Koplovitz Jr., Apr. 17, 1971. BS, U. Wis., 1967; MA in Communications, Mich. State U., 1968. Radio and TV producer, dir. Sta. WTMJ-TV, Milw., 1967; editor Communications Satellite Corp., Washington, 1968-72; dir. community services UA Columbia Cablevision, Oakland, N.J., 1973-75; v.p., exec. dir. UA Columbia Satellite Services Inc., Oakland, 1977-80; pres., chief exec. officer USA Network, N.Y.C., 1980—. Mem. bd. overseers NYU Grad. Sch. Bus., 1984-87; bd. dirs. Nat. Jr. Achievement, 1986—. Recipient Action for Childrens TV award, 1979, Twin award Ridgewood YWCA, 1980, Matrix award Women in Communications, 1983, Outstanding Alumnus award Mich. State U. Grad. Sch. Bus., 1985, Outstanding Corp. Social Responsibility CUNY, 1986, Women Who Run the World award Sara Lee Corp., 1987; Cable Merit scholar, 1968. Mem. Nat. Cable TV Assn. (advt. com. 1979-82, Idell Kaitz award 1979), Women in Cable (founding bd. mem., membership chmn. 1979-80, v.p. 1981-82, pres. 1982-83), Cable Advt. Bur. (bd. dirs., exec. com., treas. 1981-87, Chmn.'s award for Leadership 1987), Nat. Acad. Cable Programming (bd. dirs. 1984-87), Advt. Council Inc. (bd. dirs. 1985-87), Com. of 200, Womens Forum, N.Y.C. Partnership (bd. dirs. 1987—), Mus. Broadcasting (bd. dirs. 1988—). Office: USA Network 1230 Ave of Americas 18th Floor New York NY 10020

KOPMAN, ELIZABETH SUZANNE, health care administrator; b. Phila., Aug. 27, 1950; d. Frederick and Beatrice (Gans) Perlitch; m. Arthur Kopman, June 21, 1970 (div. June 1986); children: Brad, Jaime. Diploma in Nursing, Temple U., 1971; AA, LaSalle Extension U., 1974. Head nurse Phila. Geriatric Ctr., 1971-73; supr. St. Mary's Hosp., Phila., 1974-75; nursing supr. Ashton Hall Rehab. Ctr., Phila., 1975-78; dir. nursing Northwood Nursing Home, Phila., 1978-80, adminstr., 1980-82; asst. dir. Mayo Nursing Ctr., Phila., 1982-84, adminstr., 1986—; owner Popcorn Video, Phila., 1984-86; instr. first aid Loesche Sch., Phila., 1982; buyer movies Popcorn Video, Phila., 1984—; mem. products com. GERI-Med, Phila., 1987—. Contbr. articles to profl. jours. Coach Max Meyers Athletic Club, Phila., 1985—. Mem. Nat. Assn. of Female Execs., Long Term Nursing Adminstrs. Republican. Jewish. Home: 409 Audubon Terr Philadelphia PA 19116 Office: Mayo Nursing Ctr 650 Edison Ave Philadelphia PA 19116

KOPP, JENNIFER LEE, technical illustrator; b. Phoenix, May 30, 1949; d. Leonard Owen and Gloria Belle (Shaffer) Kelly; student Los Angeles Pierce Coll., 1976-78, Moorpark Coll., 1981-83; m. Glenn Robert Kopp, Sept. 7, 1969; children—M. Scott, G. Douglas (dec.). Supr., Volt Tech. Corp., Van Nuys, Calif., 1977-78, project coordinator, El Segundo, Calif., 1979-80; checker in drafting Mainstream Engring., Sherman Oaks, Calif., 1978-79; sr. tech. illustrator Dynaction Resources, Chatsworth, Calif., 1979; sr. tech. illustrator Litton Data Command Systems, Agoura Hills, Calif., 1980-88. Dir. North Shore chpt. Gt. Salton Sea Experience, 1986; dir. Salton Legal Def. Group Systems, Agoura Hills, Calif., 1980-87; sec.-treas. North Shore Vol. Fire Co., 1985-86. Recipient Presdl. Sports award Pres.' Council on Phys. Fitness, 1973, 4 awards of Merit for sports L.A. Pierce Coll., 1977; Sportsmanship award Women's Internat. Motorcycle Assn., 1976, Citizenship award, 1978. Mem. Nat. Abortion Rights Action League, Nat. Women's Polit. Caucus, NOW, Calif. Abortion Rights Action League, Nat. Rifle Assn., Nat. Assn. Female Execs. Club: Litton Data Command Systems Rod and Gun (pres. 1982-83, v.p. 1984-85), North Shore C. of C. (pres., exec. dir. 1987-88). Home: 101760 Sea Breeze Dr North Shore CA 92254 Office: PO Box 3097 North Shore CA 92254

KOPP, NANCY KORNBLITH, state legislator; b. Coral Gables, Fla., Dec. 7, 1943; d. Lester and Barbara M. (Levy) Kornblith; B.A. with honors, Wellesley Coll., 1965; M.A., U. Chgo., 1968; m. Robert E. Kopp, May 3, 1969; children—Emily, Robert E. III. Instr. polit. sci. U. Ill. at Chgo., 1968-69; mem. profl. staff, spl. subcom. on edn. U.S. Ho. of Reps., Washington, 1970-71; legis. staff Md. Gen. Assembly, Annapolis, 1971-74; mem. Md. Ho. of Dels., 1975—, chmn. appropriations Subcom. on edn. and human resources, 1981—; rep. to Nat. Conf. State Legislators; asst. majority leader, 1987—, chmn. NCSL fiscal affairs and oversight com., So. Reg. Edn. Bd. Mem. Am. Polit. Sci. Assn., LWV, AAUW, Common Cause. Democrat. Jewish. Office: Lowe House Office Bldg Room 223 Annapolis MD 21401

KOPPEL, AUDREY FEILER, electrologist, educator; b. N.Y.C., Sept. 25, 1944; d. Jules Eugene and Lee (Gibel) Feiler; m. Mark Alyn Koppel, May 28, 1967; children—Jason, Seth. B.A., Bklyn. Coll., 1972; diploma in electrolysis Hoffman Inst., 1975; postgrad. George Washington U., 1984, Essex Community Coll., 1984, Kree Inst., 1980. Electrologist, Bklyn., 1976, Glemby Internat., N.Y.C., 1976-78, Island Electrolysis, Manhasset, N.Y., 1982-84; registrar, supervising instr. Kree Inst., N.Y.C., 1978-82; pres. North Shore Electrolysis, Manhasset, 1982-84; dir., electrologist Bklyn. Studio, 1982—; pres. Ray Internat., 1986—. Editor, author pamphlet Glossary for Electrolysis, 1985; contbr. articles to profl. jours. Active Greater N.Y. council Boy Scouts Am., 1977-84. Mem. Am. Electrolysis Assn. (v.p. 1984—, edn. chmn. 1984—, continuing edn. coordinator 1985), N.Y. Electrolysis Assn. (corr. sec. 1983-85, pres. 1985—), Internat. Guild of Electrologists (merit award 1978). Democrat. Jewish. Clubs: U.S. Power Squadron, Bklyn. Yacht. Avocations: boating; swimming; music. Office: Bklyn Studio of Electrolysis 2376 E 16th St Suite 1 Brooklyn NY 11229

KOPRIVICA, DOROTHY MARY, management consultant, real estate and insurance broker; b. St. Louis, May 27, 1921; d. Mitar and Fema (Guzina) K. B.S., Washington U., St. Louis, 1962; cert. in def. inventory mgmt. Dept. Def., 1968. Mgmt. analyst Army Transp. Supply and Maintenance Command, St. Louis, 1954-57, Dept. Army Transp. Materiel Command, St. Louis, 1957-62; program analyst Dept. Army Aviation System Command, St. Louis, 1962-74, spl. asst. to comdr., 1974-78; ins. broker D. Koprivica, Ins., St. Louis, 1978—; real estate broker Century 21 KARE Realty, St. Louis, 1978—. Mem. Bus. and Profl. Women (pres. 1974-75). Eastern Orthodox. Lodge: Order Eastern Star.

KORABIK, KAREN SUE, psychology, educator; b. Chgo., May 2, 1949; arrived in Can., 1976; d. Michael John and Helen Louise (Jarecki) K; m. Russell Neckorcuk, Aug. 29, 1969(div. 1974). BA with honors, St. Louis U., 1967, MS, 1971, PhD, 1975. Instr. U. Mo., Rolla, 1974, St. Louis U., 1974; asst. prof. U. Guelph, Ont., Can., 1975-85, assoc. prof., 1985—. Contbr. articles to profl. jours. Research grantee Social Sci. and Humanities Research Council, Ottawa, Ont., Can., 1982-87. Mem. Am. Psychol. Assn., Can. Psychol. Assn. (co-chair program evaluation sect. 1982-83), Acad. Mgmt. Office: U Guelph, Dept Psychology, Guelph, ON Canada N1G 2W1

KORATICH, DOROTHY B., retail company executive; b. Centerville, Pa., Aug. 18, 1834; d. George and Mary (Kresovich) Bellish; widowed; children: George M., Richard M., Stephanie A., Michael P. Student, Cleve. Bus. Sch., 1954-55, Waynesburg Coll., 1984-85, 86-87. Labor relations sec. Eaton Axle Corp., Cleve., 1953-55; overpayment officer Bur. Employment Security, Waynesburg, Pa., 1955-61; owner, operator Koratich's Tavern-Restaurant, Waynesburg, 1961-74; owner, developer Waynesburg Plaza Shopping Ctr., 1971—; owner, mgr. Koratich's Golden Rail, Waynesburg, 1986—. Active mem. adv. com. Greene County Indsl. Devel., Waynesburg, 1987—. Mem. Greater Waynesburg Area C. of C. (exec. bd., sec. 1986—, chmn. Rain Day Com. 1988). Democrat. Serbian Orthodox. Home: RR 2 Box 23 Waynesburg PA 15370 Office: Waynesburg Plaza Shopping Ctr RR 2 Box 23 Waynesburg PA 15370

KORDEK, KATHLEEN ANN, lawyer; b. Norristown, Pa., May 4, 1947; d. Joseph W. and Pauline (Wiskoski) K.; m. Thomas P. Bruderle, Aug. 23, 1969; children: Matthew K., David K. BA, Gwynedd-Mercy Coll., 1969; MA in Teaching, U. Kans., 1972; JD, George Mason U., 1982. Bar: Va. 1983, Md. 1985, D.C. 1985. Adj. prof. No. Va. Community Coll., Alexandria, 1974-81; staff counsel Williams Industries, Inc., Falls Church, Va., 1982-85; asst. gen. counsel First Va. Banks, Inc., Falls Church, 1985—. Editor George Mason U. Law Rev., 1982. Mem. Washington Met. Corp. Counsel Assn., Fairfax County Bar Assn., Phi Delta Phi. Office: First Va Banks Inc 6400 Arlington Blvd Falls Church VA 22046

KOREY, LOIS BALK, advertising executive; b. N.Y.C., May 19, 1933; d. Samuel and Lillian (Rosenblatt) Balk; m. Stanton Korey, Jan. 12, 1958 (div.); children—Susan, Christopher. Jr. partner Jack Tinker & Partners Advt. Co., N.Y.C., 1964-66; jr. partner, copywriter McCann Erickson Advt. Co., N.Y.C., 1967-69; creative dir. Revlon, N.Y.C., 1972; exec. v.p., creative dir. Needham, Harper & Steers Advt., Inc., N.Y.C., 1973-82; pres. Korey, Kay & Ptnrs., Advt., N.Y.C., 1982—. Writer: TV shows including Sunday Night Comedy Hour, Ernie Kovacs Show, Andy Griffith Show, Steve Allen Tonight Show, George Gobel Show, Wide Wide World; (Recipient 18 Clios, Am. TV Comml. Festivals: 8 Andys, Advt. Club N.Y., Cannes Film Festival TV Comml. award 1973, 10 Hollywood Film Festival awards.); Contbr. articles to mags. and profl. jours. Mem. Writers Guild Am., Dramatists Guild, Acad. of TV Arts and Scis. Office: 130 Fifth Ave New York NY 10011

KORN, JUDITH ANN, human relations consultant; b. N.Y.C., Mar. 23, 1947; d. Eugene and Bertha (Magaram) Kron; B.A. cum laude, SUNY, Buffalo, 1968; M.A., Columbia Univ. Tchrs. Coll., 1969; m. Barry Paul Korn, Aug. 2, 1969; children—Lisa Michele, Suzanne Leslie, Amy Beth. Speech, hearing pathologist Long Island Jewish Hillside Med. Center, New Hyde Park, N.Y., 1969-71; dir. Human Relations Inst., White Plains, N.Y., 1979—; adj. prof. Coll. New Rochelle, 1981-86 . Mem. Am. Soc. Tng. and Devel., Am. Assn. for Counseling and Devel., Assn. Humanistic Edn. and Devel., Phi Beta Kappa. Office: 7 Pine Brook Dr White Plains NY 10605

KORNBLEET, LYNDA MAE, insulation contractor; b. Kansas City, Kans., June 15, 1951; d. Seymore Gerald Kornbleet and Jacqueline F. (Hurst) Kornbleet Malka. BA, U. St. Thomas, Houston, 1979. Lic. real estate salesperson. Temporary counselor Lyman's Personnel, Houston, 1974-75; real estate salesperson Coldwell Banker, Houston, 1975-77; sales, office mgr. Acme Insulation, Dallas, also Houston, 1977-79; pres., owner Payless Insulation, Houston, 1979—. Mem. Nat. Assn. Remodeling Industry (bd. dirs. Houston 1982-84), Houston Air Conditioning Council (bd. dirs. 1982-83), Cellulose Insulation Contractors (chmn. Houston 1981-82), Houston Bus. Council, 1987-88. Democrat. Jewish. Avocations: bridge, golf, baseball, basketball. Office: Payless Insulation 207 Reinerman St Houston TX 77007

KORNBLUTH, SANDRA JOAN, transportation company administrator; b. N.Y.C., Oct. 27, 1951; d. Louis and Rose (Rosansky) K. BA magna cum laude, Queens Coll., 1973; MA in Romance Langs., Princeton U., 1975. Instr. French lang. Princeton (N.J.) U., 1973-77; mgr. cargo tariffs Air France, N.Y.C., 1977-82; mgr. internat. pricing Emery Worldwide, Wilton, Conn., 1982-86, dir. pricing, 1986—; mem. adv. bd. Cargo Rate Services, Miami, Fla., 1984—. Bd. dirs. Literacy Vols. Greater Norwalk, 1987. Fullbright-Hayes scholar, 1973. Office: Emery Worldwide Old Danbury Rd Wilton CT 06897

KORNEL, ESTHER, psychologist; b. Basel-Stadt, Switzerland, Dec. 16, 1928; came to U.S., 1958; d. Salomon and Perla (Muehlrad) Mueller; m. Ludwig Kornel, May 27, 1952; children: Ezriel Edward, Amiel Mark. BA, Roosevelt U., 1971, MA, 1973; PhD, Ill. Sch. Profl. Psychology, 1979. Clin. psychologist Luth. Gen. Hosp., Park Ridge, Ill., 1973-74; unit coordinator

Luth. Gen. Hosp., Park Ridge, 1974-82; pvt. practice psychologist Des Plaines, Ill., 1974—; cons. oncology, group leader oncology staff Luth Gen. Hosp., 1975-82, coordinator psychology tng., 1981-82; group leader mastectomy counseling project, Northwestern U. Cancer Ctr., Chgo., 1981-82. Mem. Amnesty Internat., N.Y.C., Women's Am. Orgn. for Rehab. through Tng., N.Y.C., Women's Internat. Zionist Orgn., N.Y.C., Common Cause, Washington. Recipient Experimental Family Therapist award Inst. Juv. Research State of Ill., 1984. Mem. Am. Psychol. Assn., Assn. for Advancement of Psychol., Am. Soc. Clin. and Eperimental Hypnosis (assoc.), Forest Inst. Profl. Psychology (clin. tng. cons. 1985—). Democrat. Jewish. Office: 8780 Golf Rd Suite 202 Des Plaines IL 60016

KORNER, ANN MARGARET, biochemist; b. Bristol, England, Oct. 7, 1947; came to U.S., 1969; d. Stephan and Edith (Laner) K.; m. Sidney Altman, Oct. 8, 1972. BA, MA, Cambridge (England) U., 1969; M of Phil, Yale U., 1972, PhD, 1974. Research assoc. Yale U., New Haven, Conn., 1975-85; dir. Bioscript, Hamden, Conn., 1985—; cons. editor Nat. Inst. Health, Bethesda, Md., 1986—, Alan R. Liss Pubs., N.Y.C., 1986—. Contbr. articles to profl. jours. Mem. Yale U. Women's Orgn. (hon. adv. 1987, chmn. com. spousal issues 1987). Democrat. Jewish.

KORNER, HILDA, personnel executive; b. N.Y.C., June 2, 1931; d. Manuel and Sadie (Brookman) Troob; m. Herbert Korner, Aug. 1, 1953 (div. Feb. 1971); children—David, Peter. B.S. in Personnel Adminstrn, SUNY-Rochester, 1974. Owner, operator Gallery III, Marin County, Calif., 1964-69; supr. personnel services SUNY-Buffalo, 1970-72, dir. recruitment and promotion of women, 1972-75, coordinator human research devel., 1975-77; mgr. employment Stanford Linear Accelerator Ctr., Calif., 1977-83, asst. personnel dir., 1983—; instr. D'Youville Coll., Buffalo, 1973-74, Ohlone Coll., Fremont, Calif., 1982-83; co-owner, ptnr. Korn Kompany, Palo Alto, Calif., 1985—. Workshop leader Resource Ctr. for Women, Palo Alto, 1981-83. Avocations: theater; symphony; chamber music; travel; reading. Home: PO Box 7414 Menlo Park CA 94026 Office: Stanford Linear Accelerator Ctr PO Box 4349 Stanford CA 94309

KORNFELD, ELISE JOY, personnel executive; b. Bklyn., Mar. 28, 1957; d. Arthur Neil and Phyllis Lorraine (Schaum) K. BA, Adelphi U., 1979; cert. in compensation and benefits, NYU, 1986. Asst. mgr. personnel Bonwit Teller, Manhasset and N.Y.C., N.Y., 1979-83; head cashier Saks Fifth Ave., Scottsdale, Ariz., 1984; adminstrv. asst. Motorola Corp., Scottsdale, 1985; adminstrv. asst. Pfizer Co., N.Y.C., 1985-86, compensation and benefits asst., 1986—. Office: Pfizer Co 235 E 42nd St New York City NY 10017

KORNFELD, PHYLLIS LORRAINE SCHAUM, educator; b. Bklyn.; d. Max and Gussie (Goldberg) Schaum; B.A., Bklyn. Coll., M.S.; postgrad. CCNY; Ed.D., Columbia U., 1972; children—Keith D., Elise J. Tchr. public sch., Bklyn.; reading clinician Bklyn. Community Counsel Center, N.Y. Infirmary; sr. lang. disabilities therapist Coney Island (N.Y.) Hosp.; remedial edn. tchr. Children's Aid Soc.; lectr. grad. div. Bklyn. Coll.; asst. prof. lang. arts and reading Paterson Coll., Wayne, N.J., Bklyn. Coll., CUNY; asst. prof., co-dir. Reading Center Ferkauf Grad. Sch. Yeshiva U., N.Y.C.; asst. prof. Coll. New Rochelle; adj. asso. prof. C.W. Post Coll. Fellow Am. Orthopsychiat. Assn.; mem. Manhattan Council Internat. Reading Assn. (pres. 1969-70), Mensa, AAUP, Internat. Reading Assn., Phi Delta Kappa. Office: 16 W 16th St New York NY 10011

KORNHAUS, DEBORAH ANN, savings and loan executive; b. Kansas City, Mo., Nov. 8, 1954; d. Lawrence David and Vera Mae (Rowe) Winsky; m. John Patrick Kornhaus, June 2, 1979; 1 child, Ashley Lynne. BS, Kans. State U., 1976. CPA, Kans. Staff acct. Grant Thornton, Kansas City, 1976-78; supr. Touche Ross & Co., Kansas City, 1978-81; v.p. fin. Colonial Savings, Shawnee Mission, Kans., 1981—. Vol. Campaign to Reelect Bob Dole, Johnson County, Kans., Am. Cancer Soc., Johnson County, Campaign for Excellence Shawnee Mission Sch. Dist., 1987. Recipient Leadership Overland Park award Johnson County Community Coll. and Overland Park C. of C., 1986. Mem. Am. Inst. CPA's, Fin. Mgrs. Soc., Kans. Soc. CPA's, Econ. Devel. Com. for Kans., Overland Park C. of C. (mem. Pres. Club). Republican. Roman Catholic. Office: Colonial Savs 4000 Somerset Shawnee Mission KS 66208

KORNMAYER, ELISE MARION, computer software consultant; b. Fairhope, Ala., Jan. 4, 1954; d. Emil Fred Jr. and Alice Nielsen (Straum) K.; m. Craig L. Roberts, Aug. 1972 (div. Dec. 1974); m. John F. Dooley, June 20, 1981 (div. Aug. 1985). BA, Rice U., 1976, MA, 1981. Programmer, analyst Axxess Info., Mountainside, N.J., 1981-83; software cons., bd. dirs. Watchung Software Group, Plainfield, N.J., 1983—. Episcopalian. Office: Watchung Software Group 861 South Ave Suite 2F Plainfield NJ 07062

KOROTKIN, AUDREY RHONA, communications executive; b. Phila., Aug. 8, 1957; d. Arthur Lewis and Carol Ruth (Ruffner) K. BA in Russian Area Studies magna cum laude, U. Md., 1979. Prodn. asst. NBC Nightly News, Washington, 1978-79; news anchorwoman Sta. WCBM Radio, Balt., 1978-79; news, sports, anchor reporter Sta. WBAL Radio, Balt., 1979-86; exec. dir. Triple Crown Prodns., Inc., Louisville, 1986—. Contbg. writer Md. Horse Mag., 1985. Mem. Nat. Abortion Rights Action League, Balt., 1980—. Mem. AFTRA, NOW, Turf Publicists Am., Md. Racing Writers Assn., Phi Kappa Phi. Democrat. Jewish. Home: 2221 Strathmoor Blvd Louisville KY 40205 Office: Triple Crown Prodns Inc 700 Cen Ave Louisville KY 40208

KORP, PATRICIA ANNE, management analyst; b. Lincoln, Nebr., Nov. 15, 1942; d. Theodore R. and Elizabeth Anne (Olson) Munn; m. Vince L. Korp, Jan. 15, 1965 (div. 1986); children—Kathleen Anne, Karen Lee Korp Martinez. BS in Journalism, U. Wyo., 1967, MA, 1974. Women's editor Sheridan (Wyo.) Press, 1964-66; pub. info. and research asst. Wyo. Dept. Edn., 1967-69; dir. pub. relations and communications Wyo. Edn. Assn., 1969-71; coordinator info. services Mountain Plains Program, Glasgow, Mont., 1972-73; freelance pub. relations, Laramie, Wyo., 1973-74; pub. info. specialist Bur. Land Mgmt., Rawlins, Wyo., 1975-76, Cheyenne, Wyo., 1976-81, chief Office Pub. Affairs, 1981-85, Washington hdqrs. office, 1985—; communications specialist Wyo. Spl. Olympics, 1978-79. Editor: Wyo. Edn. News, 1969-71; asst. editor Wyo. Horizons, 1976-80, editor, 1980-85. Mem. Wyo. Council Children and Youth, 1976-77. Recipient All-Am. award Ednl. Press Assn. Am., 1st place award Nat. Fedn. Press Women, 1980. Mem. Nat. Fedn. Press Women, Capital Press Women, Federally Employed Women, Wyo. Press Women (sec.), Seton Cath. High Sch. Athletic Assn. (sec. 1981-83, pres. 1984), Sigma Delta Chi. Democrat. Roman Catholic. Home: 409 Maple Ct Herndon VA 22070-5458 Office: 18th and C Sts NW Room 5600 Washington DC 20240

KORRICK, GAIL HELENE, social work therapist, educator, consultant; b. Boston, Jan. 26, 1937; d. Louis Abraham and Molly (London) Goldman; m. Ira Korrick, Aug. 3, 1975. A.A., Boston U., 1956; B.S., U. Buffalo, 1958; M.S.S.W., Boston U., 1960. Jr. caseworker Mass. Meml. Hosp., Boston, 1960-63; field work instr. Boston U. Sch. Social Work, 1962-63; clin. social worker dept. social work-medicine and surgery Yale New Haven Hosp., 1963-82; field work instr. U. Conn. Sch. Social Work, Storrs, Conn., 1966-76; clin. instr. social work-medicine Yale U. Sch. Medicine, New Haven, 1965—; social work cons. New Haven Ostomy Assn., 1968-81; field work instr. So. Conn. U., New Haven, 1974-80; social work cons. in-service teaching program Yale New Haven Hosp. Nursing Dept., 1975-82; clin. social work cons. Gastrointestinal Tumor Study Group Project sect. gastroenterology Yale U. Sch. Medicine, New Haven, 1975-86; social work cons. Gen. Oncology Clinic, Yale/New Haven Hosp., 1979-81; mem. recruitment com. undergrad. divs. Boston U., 1978—; co-chmn. Com. to Develop a Social Work Oncology Group in Conn., 1978-79; mem. planning com. Social Work Oncology Group, 1980—; pvt. practice clin. social work, New Haven, 1980—; mem. speakers bur., metro unit Am. Cancer Soc., New Haven, 1980-82. Bd. mem. Nat. Found. Ileitis and Colitis, 1983, Cornerstone Found., 1988. Recipient Plaque, So. Conn. State Coll., 1976. Mem. Nat. Assn. Social Workers (diplomate), Nat. Council Social Welfare (diplomate clin. social work, 1987), Acad. Cert. Social Workers, Acad. Clin. Social Workers, Conn. Cert. Ind. Social Workers, Conn. Social Work Oncology Group, Mass. Social Work Oncology Group, Conn. Oncology Assn. Democrat. Jewish. Office: 111 Park St Suite 1-L New Haven CT 06511

KORSMEYER, MARY DRAKE, lawyer, court officer; b. Portsmouth, Ohio, Oct. 27, 1937; d. James Clinton Drake and Eliza Abigail (Bradford) Mitchell; m. Jerome Daniel Korsmeyer, June 25, 1960; children—Carol, David, Keith. B.A., Cornell U., 1959; J.D., U. Pitts., 1978. Bar: Pa. 1978, U.S. Supreme Ct. 1983. Securities analyst Irving Trust Co., N.Y.C., 1960; sewing instr. Joseph Horne Co., Pitts., 1972-75; law clk. Commonwealth Ct. of Pa., Washington, 1979-80; sole practice law, McMurray, Pa., 1980-81; assoc. firm Peacock, Keller, Yohe, Day & Ecker, Washington, Pa., 1981-86, ptnr., 1987—; standing master in divorce, child custody officer Washington County Ct. Common Pleas, 1983-84. Mem. Internat. Assn. Def. Counsel Zonta Club (sec. 1986-88), Pa. Trial Lawyers Assn., Washington County Bar Assn. (exec. com. 1984-87, treas. law library com. 1981-83, chmn. 1983-84), Allegheny County Bar Assn., Soc. Hosp. Attys. of Western Pa. (pres. 1988—), Am. Acad. Hosp. Attys., Delta Delta Delta (sec. South Suburban Alumnae chpt. 1981-83, treas. 1983-85). Democrat. Roman Catholic. Home: 132 Highland Dr McMurray PA 15317 Office: Peacock Keller Yohe Day & Ecker 70 E Beau St Washington PA 15301

KORTH, CHARLOTTE WILLIAMS, furniture and interior design firm executive; b. Milw.; d. Lewis C. and Marguerite Peil Brooks; student U. Wis., 1941; m. Robert Lee Williams, Jr., Oct. 25, 1944 (dec.); children—Patricia, Melissa Williams O'Rourke, R. Brooks; m. Fred Korth, Aug. 23, 1980. Vice pres., co-owner Charlotte's Inc., El Paso, Tex., 1951-76; pres. Paso del Norte Design, Inc., El Paso, 1978—; chmn. bd., chief exec. officer Charlotte's, Inc., El Paso, 1979—; mem. adv. bd. Mountain Bell Telephone Co., 1976-79; First City Nat. Bank, El Paso, 1981-86. Mem. women's com. El Paso Symphony Orch.; charter mem. Com. of 200, 1982—, Mus. of Women in the Arts, 1985—. Recipient Silver plaque Gifts and Decorative Accessories mag., 1978; named Woman of Year, Women's Polit. Caucus, 1979, Outstanding Woman Entrepreneur El Paso, Am. Bus. Women's Assn., 1979. Mem. Am. Soc. Interior Designers (dir. Tex. 1977—), Inst. Bus. Designers, El Paso C. of C. (dir. 1976—), El Paso Women's C. of C., Delta Gamma. Clubs: Coronado Country, El Paso, International (El Paso); Santa Teresa (N.Mex.) Country. Home: 1054 Torrey Pines El Paso TX 79912 Also: 4200 Massachusetts Ave Washington DC 20016 Office: Charlotte's Fine Furniture Pepper Tree Square 5411 N Mesa St El Paso TX 79912

KORTMAN, JOYCE ELAINE, graphic arts company executive, civic worker; b. Holland, Mich., Dec. 24, 1935; d. Henry John and Jeanette (Van Kampen) De Ridder; m. Harris Jay Kortman, May 15, 1956; children: David, Calvin, Lafon, Renee, Mark. Ed., Davenport Coll., Hope Coll., Western Theol. Sem. Mem. adv. council Nat. Inst. Arthritis, Metabolism and Digestive Disease, NIH, 1973-75; mem. West unit Health Systems' Agy. Bd., HEW, 1972-83; active Mich. affiliate Am. Diabetes Assn., 1970—, vice chair nat. coordinating com. for pub. activities, mem. com. on pub. affairs and Mich. del. co-chmn. work group on nat. resources Nat. Commn. on Diabetes, 1975; cons., speaker, and consumer adv. in health; propr. DaCal Printing Co., Heritage Printing Service, Holland; pres. Galien Travel Inc. Mem. adv. bd. Mich. Dept. Pub. Health, 1974—; mem. Commn. on Handicapped Concerns, Mich. Dept. Labor, Holland Christian Schs. PTA. Recipient cert. of appreciation Am. Diabetes Assn., 1970, citation for outstanding contbn., Am. Diabetes Assn., 1973, Vol. of Yr. award Am. Diabetes Assn., 1976, Meritorious Service award Am. Diabetes Assn., 1976. Mem. Holland C. of C. (1st vice chair bd.), Calvinette Internat. (counselor, co-chair com. on curriculum revision). Office: 16935 Riley St Holland MI 49423

KOSHI, ANNIE KARICKAMPALLY, English language educator; b. Changanacherry, Kerala, India; d. Chacko Varkey Thollairam and Thresia Chacko; m. Mathew Koshi; children: Sarita, Anita, Mathew, Jr. MA, Kerala U., India, 1969, De Paul U., 1970; MEd, Columbia U., 1970, EdD, 1977. Sr. lectr. Assumption Coll., Kerala, India, 1958-69; tchr. Louis Brandeis High Sch., N.Y.C., 1977-82; asst. prof. linguistics Adelphi U., N.Y.C., 1980—; asst. prof. CCNY, 1982—; cons. N.Y.C. Bd. Edn., 1986, Applied Linguistics. Mem. Nat. Council Tchrs. English, Teaching English As A Second Lang., Computer-Using Educators, N.Y. State Tchrs. English (mem. com. 1980—), N.Y. State Tchrs. English to Speakers Other Langs. (chair applied linguistics 1988), Pi Lamda Theta. Home: 101-52 113th St Richmond Hill NY 11419 Office: CCNY 138 St and Convent Ave New York NY 10031

KOSHLAND, MARIAN ELLIOTT, immunologist, educator; b. New Haven, Oct. 25, 1921; d. Waller Watkins and Margaret Ann (Smith) Elliott; m. Daniel Edward Koshland, Jr., May 25, 1945; children—Ellen R., Phyllis A., James M., Gail F., Douglas E. B.A., Vassar Coll., 1942, M.S., 1943; Ph.D., U. Chgo., 1949. Research asst. Manhattan Dist. Atomic Bomb Project, 1945-46; fellow dept. bacteriology Harvard Med. Sch., 1949-51; asso. bacteriologist biology dept. Brookhaven Nat. Lab., 1952-62, bacteriologist, 1963-65; asso. research immunologist virus lab. U. Calif., Berkeley, 1965-69; lectr. dept. molecular biology U. Calif., 1966-70, prof. dept. microbiology and immunology, 1970—, chmn. dept., 1982—; mem. Nat. Sci. Bd., 1976-82; mem. adv. com. to dir. NIH, 1972-75. Contbr. articles to profl. jours. Mem. Nat. Acad. Scis., Am. Acad. Microbiology, Am. Assn. Immunologists (pres. 1982-1983), Am. Soc. Biol. Chemists, Phi Beta Kappa, Sigma Xi. Office: U Calif Dept Microbiology & Immunology Berkeley CA 94720

KOSINSKY, BARBARA TIMM, librarian; b. St. Louis, July 4, 1942; d. Paul E. and Virginia L. (Borcherding) T.; m. John P. Kosinsky, July 25, 1964; children: James Alan, Bethany Anne. BS in Edn., Concordia Coll., River Forest, Ill., 1964; BA in Computer Sci., North Cen. Coll., Naperville, Ill., 1986; MLS, SUNY, Buffalo, 1972. Cert. tchr., Ill., N.Y. Tchr. St. Paul Luth. Sch., North Tonawanda, N.Y., 1964-67; librarian Trinity Luth. Sch., West Seneca, N.Y., 1971-80; free-lance writer West Seneca and Naperville, 1978—; librarian North Cen. Coll., Naperville, 1981—. Contbr. articles to religious mags. Mem. ALA, Am. Soc. Info. Sci., Nat. Writers Club., Libras. Home: 2721 Rolling Meadows Dr Naperville IL 60565 Office: Oesterle Library North Cen Coll 320 E School St Naperville IL 60566

KOSKI, ANN LOUISE, museum director; b. DeKalb, Ill., July 27, 1951; d. Lauri V. and Evelyn J. (Mosher) K. BA in Anthropology, U. Mich., 1973; MA in Anthropology, Northwestern U., 1974; MA in Hist. Preservation, Eastern Ill. U., 1983. Asst. dir. Contract Archeology Program Ctr. for Am. Archeology, Kampsville, Ill., 1977-81; asst. curator Greenwood Sch. Mus./Coles County Hist. Soc., Charleston, Ill., 1981-82; dir. Oswego (N.Y.) County Hist. Soc., 1983-85, Neville Pub. Mus. of Brown County, Green Bay, Wis., 1986—; field cons. Am. Assn. State & Local History, Nashville, Tenn., 1985. Co-author: Massey and Archie: A Study in Two Hopewellian Homesteads in the Western Illinois Uplands, 1985; assoc. editor Voyageur Magazine, 1986—; contbr. mag. articles, book revs., research reports. Mem. Am. Assn. State and Local History, M.W. Mus. Conf., Wis. Fedn. Mus., Ill. Archeol. Survey. Office: Neville Pub Mus of Brown County 210 Museum Pl Green Bay WI 54303

KOSKI-PONTON, ELLEN IRENE, sales executive, management consultant; b. Louisville, June 10, 1947; d. Edward Zacharias and Doris Jean (Speer) Koski; m. George Evan Ponton, Oct. 12, 1985; children by previous marriage—Monica Linette Arnold, Matthew David Arnold, Marcus Aaron Arnold; stepchildren—Yvonne Larae Ponton, Colleen Ruth Ponton. AS in Bus. Adminstrn., Tidewater Community Coll., 1983; BA in Interdisciplinary Studies, U. S.C., Lancaster, 1985, postgrad., 1985—. Adminstrv. asst. Northwestern Mut. Life, Norfolk, Va., 1981-83, asst. dir. mktg., Charlotte, N.C., 1983-84; ind. distbr. Herbalife, Monroe, N.C., 1983—; eligibility specialist Union County Dept. Social Services, 1985-86; mgmt. cons. Dorey Electric, Norfolk, Va., Advanced Marine Enterprises, Virginia Beach, Va., 1982-83; bus. mgr. EOR Monroe Urgent Care and Marshville Med. Ctr., 1986-87; adminstr., South Point Family Practice, P.A., 1987—. Foster parent Ohio Youth Commn., Del, 1976-79, Cath. Family Services, Virginia Beach, 1980-81; pres. Tidewater Assn. Talented and Gifted, Virginia Beach, 1982; vol. Rape Crisis Companion, Monroe, N.C., 1985—. Club: Amateur Trapshooting Assn. (Vandalia, Ohio). Avocations: trapshooting; reading; swimming. Home: 4610 Nesbit Rd Monroe NC 28110

KOSMES, KARA MARIE, accountant; b. Haverhill, Mass., Dec. 29, 1958; d. Theophilos and Mary Josephine (Azzarito) K. BSBA summa cum laude, Merrimack Coll., 1980. Acctg. supr. Haverhill Mcpl. Hosp., 1980-81; acct. John A. Rosatone, P.A., Havehill, 1981-84; office mgr. Stephanotis Flower Shop, Havehill, 1986—; sr. acct. William J.F. Murphy, CPA, Havehill, 1984—; cons. in field. Mem. Winnekenni Found. Lodge: Soroptomist (treas. 1986—) (Haverhill). Home: 35 Westland Ter Haverhill MA 01830 Office: William JF Murphy CPA 396 Main St Haverhill MA 01830

KOSSIN, SUSAN FRANCES, government official, consultant; b. N.Y.C., May 3, 1949; d. Benjamin and Evelyn Peace (Flaks) K. B.A., George Washington U., 1970; M.S., Boston U., 1973. Adminstrv. asst. Rockefeller Found., N.Y.C., 1970-71; writer, reporter, editor WBUR-FM and other radio stas., Boston, N.Y.C., 1971-74; asst. to regional adminstr. U.S. Gen. Services, N.Y.C., 1974-75; mgmt. intern, 1975; exec. dir. N.Y. Fed. Exec. Bd., N.Y.C., 1975—; chmn. bd. Fedkids Inc. Child Care Ctr. Corp. Vol., Planned Parenthood, N.Y.C., 1983. Named Outstanding Greek Woman, Panhellenic Council, George Washington U., 1970; recipient Spl. Achievement awards U.S. FAA, N.Y.C., 1976, 80, 83; Appreciation award U.S. Dept. Labor, N.Y.C., 1984. Mem. Federally Employed Women N.Y. (dir. 1974-85, legis. chmn. 1983-85), Women's City Club of N.Y. Office: NY Fed Exec Bd care GSA 26 Federal Plaza Rm 1713 New York NY 10278

KOSSOW, SUELLEN ELIZABETH, bank executive; b. Milw., July 23, 1953; d. John Frederick and Patricia Jean (Mulvaney) K. B.S., Barry U., 1981; M.B.A. in Internat. Bus., U. Miami, 1983. Writer, reporter The Oracle, Tampa, Fla., 1971-72; tech. writer Southeast Banks, Miami, Fla., 1974-75; tech. writer Bank of Miami, 1975-76, dir. personnel, 1976-79, dir. tng. and tech. writing, systems analyst, 1979-80, dir. mircocomputers, 2d v.p., 1980-84, corp. exec. offices dir. pub. relations and community involvement program, 2d v.p., 1984-87, product mgr. S.E. Banks, N.A., 1987—; sec., dir. Popular Computers, Inc., Miami, 1983-87; product mgr. Community Bank, 1987; adj. lectr. Barry U., Miami, 1984—; pres. Holly Morgan Assocs., Inc., 1985-87. Producer, host, moderator Financial Insights TV show. Docent, Ctr. for Fine Arts, Miami, 1985-89; chmn. com. Miami's for Me, 1986; mem. South Fla. Hist. Soc., Mus. Natural History, N.Y.C., Smithsonian Soc. Mem. Nat. Assn. Bank Women. Office: SE Banks NA 1 SE Fin Ctr Miami FL 33131

KOSTER, DURELE KAY, public relation consultant; b. Rockford, Ill., Dec. 10, 1943; d. Carl Frederick and Margaret Thompson (Gray) Brandquist; m. Frank Jay Koster (div. Jan. 1985); 1 child, Andrew Carl. BA in Journalism, Drake U., 1965. Sec., jr. copywriter Campbell-Mithon Advt., Chgo., 1965-67; account exec. Selz Seaboldt and Assocs., Chgo., 1968-70; office mgr. Geja's Internat., Chgo., 1970-82, Schindler Pub. Relations, Chgo., 1982-85; office mgr., asst. to chmn. bd. Field Devel. Corp., Chgo., 1985-86; cons. asst. Blackman, Kallick, Bartelstein, Chgo., 1986-87, mktg. dir., edn. coordinator, dir. seminars, 1988—. Contbr. articles to newspapers, mags. Bd. dirs. Chgo. City Day Sch., Latin Sch. Chgo., Infant Welfare Soc. Chgo.; mem. Lincoln Park Conservation Assn., Lincoln Park Zool. Assn. Mem. Nat. Assn. Female Execs., Chgo. Council Fgn. Relations, Lincoln Cen. Assn., St. Ignatius Coll. Prep. Club, MidNorth Assn. (bd. dirs. 1973-75), Alumni Mothers Club, (assoc.) Nat. Assn. Women Bus. Owners. Democrat. Methodist. Home: 2206 N Burling Chicago IL 60614 Office: 300 S Riverside Plaza Suite 660 Chicago IL 60606

KOSTICH, SHIRLEY ANN, health services administrator; b. Milw., June 3, 1944; d. Ferdinand and Vetial (Burbey) Homan; m. Nikola Peter Kostich, May 28, 1969; children: Natasha and Aleksandar. BS, U. Wis., 1967. Case worker social services Unicare, Milw., 1967-69; cons. residential care Unicare, Madison, Wis., 1969-70; with after care team Med. Coll. Wis./Milw. County, 1979-80; adminstrv. coordinator med. services Milw. County Mental Health Complex, 1981—; coordinator Am. Bd. Psychiat. and Neurology Oral Exams, Milw. 1986; cons. seminar Alliance Mentally Ill, Milw. 1985-86. Editor: Newsletter Mental Health Complex, 1986-87. Chmn. Shorewood (Wis.) High Sch. Post Prom Com. 1986; pres. adv. council sexual assault treatment ctr. Good Samaritan Med. Ctr. 1987—; coordinator Milw. County Mental Health Complex campaign United Way, 1986-89, Silver award, Chmn.'s award. Mem. Editor's Forum (Nat. Competition award), Nat. Assn. Med. Staff Services, Nat. Assn. Female Execs. Serbian Orthodox. Home: 3715 N Lake Dr Shorewood WI 53211 Office: Milw County Mental Health Complex 9455 Watertown Plank Rd Milwaukee WI 53226

KOSTINKO, GAIL ANN, infosystems specialist; b. Pottsville, Pa., Aug. 10, 1951; d. George and Ann (Withnosky) K. BA in French, Pa. State U., 1973; MLS, U. Md., 1974; postgrad., Howard U., 1984-85. African reference specialist Moorland-Spingaron Research Ctr., Howard U., Washington, 1975-78; pvt. practice cons. in devel. issues, projects and African affairs Washington, 1979—. Contbr. articles to profl. jours. Fgn. Language Study fellowship African Studies Program Howard U., 1984. Mem. Am. Soc. for Info. Sci., African Studies Assn., African Lit. Assn., Nat. Assn. Female Execs. Office: 1684-A Euclid St NW Washington DC 20009

KOSTREVA, ADRIENNE LEE GAAL, retail executive, consultant, director; b. Dearborn, Mich., Nov. 7, 1945; d. Michael Andrew and Beatrice Bennett (Herrman) Gaal; m. Daniel J. Kostreva; divorced. MBA with honors, Roosevelt U., 1980. From asst. buyer to buyer Filene's Basement, Boston, 1967-71; store mgr. Design Research, Boston, 1972-73; store supr. Bargains Unltd., Boston, 1974; dist. mgr. Commonwealth Trading, Inc., Boston, 1975-77; regional mgr. Marshall's Inc., Boston, 1977-78; staff cons. Deloitte Haskins & Sells, Chgo., 1980; dir. mdse. planning The Doody Co., Columbus, Ohio, 1981; pvt. practice cons. Columbus, 1982-83; v.p., dir. stores Charles A. Stevens, Chgo., 1983-85; pres. Adrienne Kostreva & Assocs., Ltd., Chgo., 1985—; instr. Franklin U., Columbus, 1982-83, Capital U., Columbus, 1982-83, Roosevelt U., Chgo., 1984—; project dir. retail program Chgo. City Wide Coll., Chgo., 1986—. Mem. Friends of Chgo. City Ballet, 1983-86; cons. Bd. Devel. Network, Columbus, 1982-83; tutor 4th Presbyn. Ch. Tutoring Program, Chgo., 1983—; chmn. program com., bd. dirs. Roosevelt U. Alumni Assn. Bd. of Govs., Chgo., 1984—. Mem. Fashion Group, Inc. (treas. Boston chpt. 1971-73), Women's Exec. Network of Chgo. Office: Adrienne Kostreva & Assocs Ltd 230 N Michigan Ave Chicago IL 60601

KOTCHER, SHIRLEY J. W., lawyer; b. Bklyn.; d. Irving and Violet (Miller) Weinberg; m. Harry A. Kotcher; children—Leslie Susan, Dana Anne. B.A., NYU; J.D., Columbia U. Bar: N.Y. In-house counsel Booth Meml. Med. Ctr., Flushing, N.Y., 1975-83, gen. counsel, 1983—; advisor health care Borough Pres. Queens, N.Y., 1978. Author: Hidden Gold and Pitfalls in New Tax Law, 1970. Mem. ABA (health law forum com.), Nat. Health Lawyers Assn., Am. Acad. Hosp. Attys., Nassau County Bar Assn., Am. Soc. Law and Medicine, Am. Soc. Risk Mgrs., Greater N.Y. Hosp. Assn. (legal adv. com. 1976—). Office: Booth Meml Med Ctr Main St Flushing NY 11335

KOTCHIAN, SARAH BRUFF, city government health executive; m. Bob Nellums; 1 child, Laura Bruff Nellums. B.A. cum laude, Middlebury Coll., 1975; M.Ed., Harvard U., 1977; M.P.H., U. Wash., 1985. Tchr. English, Cushing Acad., Ashburnham, Mass., 1975-76; staff assoc. Chrysalis, Inc., Cambridge, Mass., Spring 1977; instr. Harvard U., Cambridge, fall 1977; career counselor Roxbury/Harvard Sch. Program, 1977-78; health educator Planned Parenthood, Albuquerque, 1978-79; health edn., tng. counselor N.Mex., Family Planning Council, Albuquerque, 1979-82; adminstrv. asst. Environ. Health Dept., Albuquerque, 1982-83, dep. dir., 1983-86, dir., 1987—; co-founder City Women's Work seminars; mem. Nat. Accrditation Council Environ. Health Curriculum, 1987—; chair Low-Income Families Task Force, 1987-88; assoc. gen. chair Albuquerque United Way Campaign, 1988. Contbr. articles to profl. jours. Co-founder, chmn. Nat. Women's Health Network N.Mex., 1982, publicist, 1983-86; rep. FDA Ob/Gyn Devices Com. Recipient Glamour Outstanding Working Woman award, 1986, Woman on the Move award Albuquerque YMCA, 1985, Gov.'s award for Outstanding N.Mex. Women finalist, 1986; co-chair hazardous waste minimization com. 1987—, mem. action bd. 1986-87, joint policy com., 1988), Leadership Albuquerque Alumni (bd. dirs.), Nat. Environ. Health Assn. Mem. Am. Pub. Health Assn. (chair environ. sect. 1987, chmn. membership com. environ. sect., joint policy com. 1985-86, mem. environment sect. council 1986—), N.Mex. Pub. Health Assn. (chmn. legis. com.), Nat. Conf. Local Environ. Health Adminstrs., N.Mex. Environ. Health

Assn., Phi Delta Kappa. Office: City of Albuquerque 1 Civic Plaza Albuquerque NM 87103

KOTLER, NANCY KELLUM, lawyer; b. Boston, Mar. 27, 1936; s. Ralph and Ethel (Sandler) Kellum; m. Philip Kotler, Jan. 30, 1955; children—Amy, Melissa, Jessica. Student, Radcliffe Coll., 1953-55; B.A., U. Chgo., 1958; M.A., Northwestern U., Evanston, Ill., 1959; J.D., Loyola U.-Chgo., 1977. Bar: Ill. 1977. Instr. English, U. Ill.-Chgo., 1961-62; instr. English and linguistics Northeastern Ill. U., Chgo., 1962-68; instr. English, Nat. Coll. Edn., Evanston, Ill., 1970-71; instr. legal writing Kent Coll. Law, Chgo., 1979-80; assoc. Lurie, Sklar & Simon Ltd., Chgo., 1982-86; sole practice, Chgo., 1987—; adjunct instr. Northeastern Ill. U., 1987—. Woodrow Wilson Fellow, 1958. Mem. Chgo. Bar Assn., ABA.

KOTOWSKI, CHRISTINE ANNE, nurse; b. Buffalo, Feb. 8, 1947; d. Leonard Michael and Irene (Jedrzejewski) Zmozynski; m. David M. Kotowski, Oct. 26, 1968; children—Jeffrey, Jennifer, Kenneth, Gregory. B.S. in Nursing Cum Laude, Daemen Coll., N.Y., 1983. Registered profl. nurse N.Y. Nurse's asst. St. Joseph Inter-Community Hosp., Cheektowaga, N.Y., 1978-80; camp nurse Jewish Ctr., Greater Buffalo, Amherst, 1981; charge nurse Williamsville Suburban Nursing Home, N.Y., 1981, day supr., 1982, asst. dir. nursing, 1982-84; nurse cons. Brown and Kelly Law Offices, Buffalo, 1984—; cons. and lectr. in field. Pre-Cana sponsor Our Lady of Blessed Sacrament Ch., Depew, N.Y., 1985—; supporter Bowmansville Vol. Fire Dept; mem. alumni bd. dirs. Daemen Coll. Nursing. Mem. Nat. Assn. Female Execs., Profl. Nurses Assn. Western N.Y., Western N.Y. Paralegal Assn., Delta Epsilon Sigma. Republican. Roman Catholic. Club: St. Mary's High Sch. Athletic (Lancaster). Avocations: Choir; church projects; tennis; reading. Office: Brown and Kelly Buffalo NY 14202

KOTSIANAS, MARINA, infosystems engineer; b. Athens, Greece, Sept. 27, 1957; came to U.S., 1980; d. Nicholas and Pauline (Amira) Kanellopoulos; m. Panos Kotsianas, Aug. 21, 1982. Diploma in engring., Nat. Tech. U., Athens, 1980; MS, Rensselaer Poly. Inst., 1982; profl. designation in bus. mgmt., UCLA, 1988. Researcher Ctr. Computer Graphics Rensselaer Poly. Inst., Troy, N.Y., 1982-84; software engr., tech. specialist Cadam, subs. Lockheed Corp., Burbank, Calif., 1984-86; cons. Solidtech, Buena Park, Calif., 1986-87; sr. engr. devel. Matra Datavision Inc., Los Angeles, 1987—. Horton fellow, 1981. Mem. IEEE Computer Soc., Nat. Assn. Female Execs., Assn. Computing Machinery. Office: Matra Datavision 11444 W Olympic Blvd Los Angeles CA 90064

KOTUK, ANDREA MIKOTAJUK, public relations firm executive, medical writer; b. New Brunswick, N.J., Oct. 19, 1948; d. Michael and Julia Dorothy (Muka) Mikotajuk. B.A., Douglass Coll., Rutgers U., 1970. Pub. relations asst. Wall St. Jour. Newspaper Fund, Princeton, N.J., 1970; editorial asst. Redbook mag., N.Y.C., 1970-71; asst. pub. relations dir. Children's Aid Soc., N.Y.C., 1971-75; assoc. pub. relations dir. Planned Parenthood, N.Y.C., 1975-80; pres. Andrea & Assocs., N.Y.C., 1980—. Writer publicist ads for newsmags., healthcare corps., for non-profit agys.; contbg. editor Arts Mag., 1970-75. Mem. Healthcare Businesswomen's Assn. (writer 1982—), Nat. Assn. Female Execs., Am. Med. Writers Assn. Office: Andrea & Assocs 36 E 23d St New York NY 10010

KOUBA, LISA MARCO, lawyer; b. Chgo., July 1, 1957; d. Edward Samuel and Phyllis Lavergne (Pincus) Marco; m. Kenneth Edward Kouba, Sept. 24, 1983. BA with honors, U. Ill., 1978; JD cum laude, Loyola U., Chgo., 1981. Bar: Ill. 1981, U.S. Dist. Ct. (no. dist.) Ill. 1981, U.S. Ct. Appeals (6th, 7th, 8th and 10th cirs.) 1982. Ptnr. Clausen, Miller, Gorman, Caffrey & Witous, P.C., Chgo., 1981-87, ptnr., 1987—. Editor Loyola Law Jour., 1981. Bd. dirs. Modine & Co. Dance Troupe, 1988. Mem. Ill. Bar Assn., Chgo. Bar Assn. (chmn. young lawyers sect. on appellate law 1982-83), Appellate Lawyers Assn. (bd. dirs. 1986-88). Office: Clausen Miller et al PC 10 S LaSalle St Chicago IL 60603

KOUKOL-MCGUIRE, SUSAN MARIE, dietitian, marketing executive; b. Chgo., Dec. 26, 1953; d. Earl James and Helen Lillian (Beckstrom) K. B.S., Bradley U., 1975; M.S., No. Ill. U., 1976; M.B.A., Loyola U., Chgo., 1985. Diet therapist Kishwaukee Hosp., De Kalb Ill., 1976; clin. dietitian Palos Hosp., Palos Heights, Ill., 1977-79; mini course instr. DePaul U., Chgo., 1980-82; nutrition cons. Carsten's Health Systems, Chgo., 1983-85; chief dietitian St. Joseph Hosp., Chgo., 1979-85; mktg. mgr. Ekco Products, Wheeling, Ill., 1986—. Editor: Eat Well Guide to Good Dining in Chicago, 1983. Bike-A-Thon chmn. Am. Diabetes Assn., Evanston Route, 1981. Mem. Am. Dietetic Assn. (young dietitian of yr. award 1981), Ill. Dietetic Assn. (chair consumer affairs), Chgo. Heart Assn. (Eat Well Tag chmn. 1983-84), Chgo. Dietetic Assn. (pres. 1982-83, historian 1984, legis. chmn. 1983-84), Dietitians in Bus. and Industry (pres. Ill. chpt. 1987-88), Am. Soc. Hosp. Food Service Adminstrs. (program chair 1987-88), Kappa Omicron Phi, Sigma Kappa. Office: PCA/Ekco Products 2100 N Saunders Rd Northbrook IL 60065

KOUNS, MARJORIE KATHERINE, producer, designer; b. Elmhurst, Ill., Aug. 4, 1957; d. William Cundiff and Joanna (Pappandreou) K. Window designer Bergdorf Goodman Co., N.Y.C., 1979-80, Henri Bendels Co., N.Y.C., 1980-82; studio mgr. Met. Home Mag., N.Y.C., 1980-84; asst. to choreographer World Figure Skating Championships, Ottawa, Ont., Can., 1983-84; prodn. coordinator Pro Skates, N.Y.C., 1983; asst.gen. mgr. Palladium, N.Y.C., 1985-86; sales rep. Gt. Am. Ventures, N.Y.C., 1986; producer M Prodns. and Events, N.Y.C., 1986—, pres., designer Koutons, Inc., N.Y.C., 1987—; corp. events dir. Octagon, on-site mgr. Met. Home Showcase, 1988. Nat. Assn. Female Execs., N.Y.C. C. of C., Bus. Cir. N.Y. Democrat. Episcopalian. Home and Office: 15 Minetta St New York NY 10012

KOUPAL, JOYCE ANN, marketing executive, consultant; b. Sacramento, Mar. 7, 1932; d. Cecil Wallace and Elizabeth Louise (DeRee) Nash; m. Edwin Augustus Koupal (dec. Mar. 1976); children: Cecil Edwin, Christine Ann, Diane Marie. Exec. dir. People's Lobby, Inc., Los Angeles, 1976—, The Printing Press, Los Angeles, 1977-81; ind. polit. cons. San Rafael, Calif., 1980-82; gen. mgr. Assn. for Advanced Tng. in Behavioral Scis., Los Angeles, 1982-83; owner Koupal Enterprises, Sacramento, 1987—. Author: (with Faith Keating) Success Is Failure Analyzed, 1976. Mem., bd. dirs. Women's Clinic, 1975-87; mem. Los Angeles County Energy Commn., 1975-76. Recipient Sylvia Leventhal Ann. award Assn. for Study of Community Orgns., 1974. Mem. Women's Network. Home and Office: 2513 River Plaza Dr #16 Sacramento CA 95833

KOVACHEVICH, ELIZABETH, federal judge; b. Canton, Ill., Dec. 14, 1936; d. Dan and Emilie (Kuchan) Kovachevich. B.B.A. in Fin. magna cum laude, U. Miami; J.D., Stetson U. Bar: Fla. 1961, U.S. Dist. Ct. (mid. and so. dists.) Fla. 1961, U.S. Ct. Appeals (5th cir.) 1961, U.S. Supreme Ct. 1968. Research and adminstrv. aide Pinellas County Legis. Del., Fla., 1961; assoc. DiVito & Speer, St. Petersburg, Fla., 1961-62; house counsel Rieck & Fleece Guilders Supplies, Inc., St. Petersburg, 1962—; sole practice St. Petersburg, 1962-73; judge 6th Jud. Cir., Pinellas and Pasco Counties, Fla., 1973-82, U.S. Dist. Ct. (mid. dist.) Fla., St. Petersburg, 1982—; chmn. St. Petersburg Profl. Legal Project-Days in Court, 1967. Bd. regents State of Fla., 1970-72; legal advisor, bd. dirs. Young Women's Residence Inc., 1968; mem. Fla. Gov.'s Commn. on Status of Women, 1968-71; mem. Pres.'s Commn. on White House Fellowships, 1973-77; mem. def. adv. com. on Women in Service, Dept. Def., 1973-76; Fla. conf. publicity chmn. 18th Nat. Republican Women's Conf., Atlanta, 1971; lifetime mem. Children's Hosp. Guild, YWCA of St. Petersburg; charter mem. Golden Notes, St. Petersburg Symphony; hon. mem. bd. of overseers Stetson U. Coll. of Law, 1986. Recipient Disting. Alumni award Stetson U., 1970, Woman of Yr. award Fla. Fedn. Bus. and Profl. Women, 1981, ann. Ben C. Willard Meml. award, Stetson Lawyers Assn., 1983, numerous others. Mem. ABA, Fla. Bar Assn., Pinellas County Trial Lawyers, Assn. Trial Lawyers Am., Am. Judicature Soc., St. Petersburg Bar Assn. (chmn. bench and bar com., sec. 1969). Office: US Dist Ct 611 US Courthouse Room 310 Tampa FL 33602

KOVACIC, CANDACE SAARI, law educator; b. Washington, Mar. 19, 1947; d. Donald George and Martha Eleanora (Saari) K. AB, Wellesley Coll., 1969; JD, Northeastern U., 1974. Law clk. Judge J. Oakes, U.S. Ct. Appeals, 2d Cir., Brattleboro, Vt., 1974-75, Chief Justice W. Burger, U.S. Supreme Ct., Washington, 1975-76; assoc. Wilmer, Cutler & Pickering, Washington, 1976-80, Cole & Groner, Washington, 1980-81; prof. Am. U. Coll. of Law, Washington, 1981—; vis. prof. UCLA, 1988; del. Faculty Senate, Washington U., 1982-83; mem. ABA Gun Control Com., 1978-81, ABA Evaluating Jud. Performance Com., Washington, 1979-82. Contbr. articles to profl. jours. Officer Eisenhower Found. for Prevention of Violence, 1977-81; mem. D.C. Cir. Com. on the Bicentennial of the Constn., 1986—; moot ct. panelist Nat. Assn. of Attys.Gen., Washington, 1986—. Wellesley Scholar Wellesly Coll., 1968, 69; recipient U. Faculty award for outstanding teaching, Am. U., 1987. Office: Am U Coll of Law 4400 Massachusetts Ave NW Washington DC 20016

KOVACS, ALBERTA ROSE, nurse, consultant; b. West Homestead, Pa.. Diploma, W. Pa. Hosp. Sch. Nursing, 1949; BS in Nursing, U. Pitts., 1957, MLitt, 1958; EdD, Columbia U., 1968. Staff nurse Western Pa. Hosp., Pitts., 1949-52, head nurse, 1952-53; staff nurse VA Hosp., Pitts., 1955-56; research asst. sch. nursing, dept. engring. U. Pitts., 1958-59; dormitory nurse Tchrs. Coll. Columbia U., N.Y.C., 1960-61; instr., dormitory nurse Point Park Jr. Coll., Pitts., 1962-63; clin. instr. sch. nursing South Side Hosp., Pitts., 1963-66, asst. dir. nursing edn., 1966-67; research assoc., prof. U. Pitts., 1968-69, 73-74, research asst., 1972-73; asst. prof. Pa. State U., Pitts., 1969-72, Carlow Coll., Pitts., 1972-82; assoc. prof. W. Va. U., 1983—; cons., editor 1982-83, 86—. Author: The Research Process: Essentials of Skill Develoment and Answer Guide, 1985; contbr. articles to profl. jours. Recipient Disting. Alumna award for clin. practice Western Pa. Hosp. Sch. Nursing, 1988. Mem. Am. Nurses Assn., Am. Assn. Univ. Profs., Council of Nurse Researchers, Nat. League for Nursing, Pa. Nurses Assn., Pa. League for Nursing eidotr newsletter, gov. council), W. Va. Nurses Assn., Soc. for Research in Nursing Edn., Columbia U. Dept. Nursing Alumnae, U. Pa. Sch. Nursing Alumnae, Sigma Theta Tau, Kappa Delta Pi, Pi Lambda Theta, Phi Delta Kappa. Home: 3612 Pinewood Dr West Homestead PA 15120

KOVACS, GAIL LOUISE PATEK, hospital administrator, nurse, biologist; b. Cleve., Feb. 17, 1949; d. Louis Cornelius and Veronica Rose (Skerl) Patek; m. John Joseph Kovacs, June 24, 1972 (div.); 1 child, Jeffrey Joseph. BA in Biology cum laude, Ursuline Coll., 1971; RN, Cleve. Met. Sch. Nursing, 1975; MBA magna cum laude, Cleve. State U., 1982. Med. technologist Cleve. Clinic Found., 1971-72; immunology research asst. Case Western Res. U., Cleve., 1972-73; staff nurse Mt. Sinai Hosp., Cleve., 1975-76, staff nurse Cleve. Met. Gen. Hosp., 1976, infectious disease nurse, 1976-78; assoc. dir. supply services Univ. Hosps of Cleve., 1978-79, asst. dir. material mgmt., 1979, administrv. assoc., 1979-80, assoc. dir. material mgmt., 1980-84, asst. gen. mgr. adminstrn., 1984-87; dir. ops. Meridia Health Ventures, Inc., 1988—; lectr. mgmt., epidemiology and material mgmt. Mem. research bd. advisors Am. Biog. Inst. Recipient Paul Widman Meml. award Ctr. Health Affairs/Greater Cleve. Hosp. Assn., 1985; Cleve. Found. grantee, 1980-81. Mem. Am. Coll. Health Care Execs., Health Care Adminstrs. Assn. N.E. Ohio, Healthcare Fin. Assn., Transplantation Soc. of N.E. Ohio, Health Care Fin. Mgmt. Soc., Health Care Material Mgmt. Soc. (v.p.; Presdl. citation 1985), Internat. Material Mgmt. Soc., Soc. for Hosp. Purchasing and Material Mgmt., N.E. Ohio Soc. for Health Care Material Mgmt., Beta Gamma Sigma. Roman Catholic. Home: 1450 Blossom Park Ave Lakewood OH 44107 Office: Meridia Health Ventures Inc 6700 Beta Dr Mayfield Village OH 44143

KOVAL, YVONNE MARIE, banker; b. Connellsville, Pa., Aug. 10, 1961; d. Bernard Paul and Loretta Bernadette (Fetsko) K. BS, Duquesne U., 1983; postgrad., Carnegie-Mellon U., 1988. Credit analyst Equibank, Pitts., 1983-85, sr. credit analyst, 1985-86, loan recovery officer, 1986—. Mem. Nat. Assn. Female Execs. Democrat. Roman Catholic. Home: 5863 Wallace Ave Bethel Park PA 15102

KOVALIC, JOAN MARIE, lawyer; b. Pitts., Dec. 27, 1948; d. Francis Bernard and Margaret Dolores (Poyma) Kovalic; B.A., Carnegie Mellon U., 1970, M.S., 1972; J.D., George Washington U., 1979; m. Keith Earl Bernard, May 22, 1982. Bar: Pa. 1979, D.C. 1980. Water resources analyst Com. Environment and Public Works, U.S. Senate, Washington, 1971; manpower policy analyst Office Asst. Sec. for Policy and Evaluation, U.S. Dept. of Labor, 1972-73; profl. staff mem. for water resources Com. Public Works and Transp., U.S. Ho. of Reps., 1973-78, asst. counsel for water and environ., 1979-80; dep. dir. Office Water Program Ops., U.S. EPA, 1980-82; asso. firm Taft, Steffinius and Hollister, Washington, 1982-85; gen. counsel, v.p. Weston, Inc., Washington, 1985—; exec. dir., Interstate Conf. Water Problems, 1982—, gen. counsel, 1982-85; sec. Nat. Water Alliance, 1983-87, gen. counsel, 1983-85. Mem. Am. Bar Assn., Pa. Bar Assn., D.C. Bar Assn., Women's Bar Assn., Water Pollution Control Fedn., Am. Public Works Assn., Am. Corp. Counsels Assn., Phi Kappa Phi, Phi Alpha Delta. Office: Weston Inc 955 L'Enfant Plaza SW Suite 600 Washington DC 20024

KOVARIK, COLLEEN ANN, hydrogeologist; b. Flushing, N.Y., Nov. 15, 1958; d. Ernest Alfred and Dorothy Ann (Campbell) Smith; m. Daniel C. Kovarik, July 11, 1981. BS, SUNY, Stony Brook, 1980. Well site geologist Exploration Services, Inc., Midland, Tex., 1981-83; v.p. Well Set, Inc., Midland, 1983-84; ind. geologist Midland, 1984-86, Bohemia, N.Y., 1986-87; hydrogeologist ERM-Northeast, Plainview, N.Y., 1987—. Mem. Am. Assn. Petroleum Geologists.

KOVELESKI, KATHRYN DELANE, educator; b. Detroit, Aug. 12, 1925; d. Edward Albert Vogt and Delane (Bender) Vogt; B.A., Olivet (Mich.) Coll., 1947; M.A., Wayne State U., Detroit, 1955; m. Casper Koveleski, July 18, 1952; children—Martha, Ann. Tchr. schs. in Mich., 1947—; tchr. Garden City Schs., 1955-56, 59—, resource and learning disabilities tchr., 1970—. Mem. NEA, Mich. Edn. Assn., Garden City Edn. Assn., Bus. and Profl. Women (pres. Garden City 1982-83, Woman of Yr. 1983-84). Congregationalist. Clubs: Wayne Lit. (past pres.), Sch. Masters Bowling League (v.p. 1984-88), Odd Couples Bowling League (pres. 82-83). Office: 33411 Marquette St Garden City MI 48135

KOVEN, JOAN FOLLIN HUGHES, designer, special events administrator; b. Washington, Nov. 9, 1937; d. John Rodgers and Viola Brockett (Pugh) Hughes; BS, W.Va. U., 1959; postgrad. Scarritt Coll., 1959, U. Salisbury (Zimbabwe), 1961, Sorbonne, 1962, 63, Am. U., 1973, George Washington U., 1979; m. Ronald Pierre E. Koven, Mar. 29, 1965 (div. 1977); children—Michele Elise Josette, Martine Sarah Aimee. Tchr., dir. home econs. dept., art dept., library Old Umtali Schs., Zimbabwe, 1960-62; adolescent counselor, Dreux High Sch., France, 1962-65; freelance market researcher, Paris, 1965-66; dir. student recreation center, Dreux, 1966; v.p. Koven Freres jewelry, N.Y.C., 1971-75; designer, fabricator jewelry, Washington, 1977—; exec. asst. in spl. events, adminstrv. mgmt. to M.B. Patterson, Washington, 1976—. Mem. zoning comm. Palisades Citizens Assn., 1974; mem. commn. on missions Met. Meml. Methodist Ch., 1984; mem. adv. council Calvert Marine Mus., 1983-84; bd. dirs. Friends of Patterson Park; tech. planning com., mem. adv. council J. Patterson Hist. Park and Mus.; sec., treas., bd. dirs. Marpat Found., 1985—; mem. Earthwatch Research Team, Fiji, 1984, U. Calif. research project, Fiji, 1986. Kroger scholar, 1955; cert. scuba diver. Mem. Am. Malacological Union, Conchologists Am., Hawaiian Shell Club, Am. Litoral Soc., Aircraft Owners and Pilots Assn., Soc. Women Geographers, Omicron Nu, Phi Upsilon Omicron. Club: Nat. Capital Shell. Home: 4812 V St Washington DC 20007

KOWALCZEWSKI, DOREEN MARY THURLOW, communications company executive; b. London, May 5, 1926; came to U.S., 1957, naturalized, 1974; d. George Henry and Jessie Alice (Gray) Thurlow; BA, Clarke Coll., 1947; postgrad. Wayne State U., 1959-62, Roosevelt U., 1968; m. Witold Dionizy Kowalczewski, July 26, 1946; children: Christina Julianna, Janet Alice, Stephen Robin. Agy. supr. MONY, N.Y.C., 1963-67; office mgr. J.B. Carroll Co., Chgo., 1967-68; mng. editor Sawyer Coll. Bus., Evanston, Ill., 1968-71; mgr. policyholder service CNA, Chgo., 1971-73; EDP coordinator Canteen Corp., Chgo., 1973-75; mgr. documentation and standards LRSP, Chgo., 1975-77; data network mgr. Computerized Agy. Mgmt. Info. Services, Chgo., 1977-86; founder, chmn. Tekman Assocs., 1982—; assoc. Austin Cons., 1986—; chpt. sec. Soc. Tech. Communications, 1988—. Pres., Univ. Park Assn., 1980-84. Mem. Nat. Assn. Female Execs., Women in Info. Processing, Chgo. Women in Mgmt., Soc. Tech. Communications, Mensa. Home: 8923 Southview Brookfield IL 60513

KOWGIOS-OLIVUCCI, CATHY, magazine editor, free-lance writer and editor; b. Yonkers, N.Y., Sept. 28, 1960; d. Michael William Sr. and Lula Mae (Kite) Kowgios; m. John Victor Olivucci, Nov. 2, 1984. BA in English and Journalism, Marymount Coll., Tarrytown, N.Y., 1982. Jr. writer publicity CARE Internat., N.Y.C., 1982; editorial asst. Home Mag., Oradell (N.J.) and N.Y.C., 1982-84; new products editor Home Mag., N.Y.C., 1984-86; assoc. articles editor 1001 Home Ideas, N.Y.C., 1986-88, kitchen and bath editor, 1988—. Editor, author: 1987 New Products Guide; contbr. articles to McCall's, Working Mother, HOME mag., (column) Changing Homes, Publications International Consumer Guide. Mem. Women in Communications. Home: 40 Hillside Ave Westwood NJ 07675 Office: 1001 Home Ideas 3 Park Ave New York NY 10016

KOZA, JOAN LORRAINE, fabric mfg. co. exec.; b. Berwyn, Ill., Apr. 28, 1941; d. Frank Louis and Lorraine Frances (Thomas) K.; B.S. in Communications, U. Ill., 1963. Office mgr. Dwan Med. Center, Summit, Ill., 1959-64; law office mgr. firm Gordon, Reicin & West, Chgo., 1964-73; sales mgr. Ambassador Hotels, Chgo., 1973-76; v.p. sales and mktg. MPC Industries, Inc. & subs., indsl. and recreational fabrics, Chgo., 1976—; owner, mgr. JK Advt., 1977—; pres. Chgo. Legal Secs. Assn., 1970-72; v.p. Ill. Assn. Legal Secs., 1970-73. Pres., chmn. bd. Children's Research Found., 1963-66. Named Chgo. Legal Sec. of Yr., 1972, Ill. Legal Sec. of Yr., 1972. Mem. Alpha Lambda Delta, Theta Sigma Pi. Roman Catholic. Home: 546 Banyon Ln LaGrange IL 60525 Office: 4834 S Oakley Pl Chicago IL 60609

KOZAK, MARLENE GALANTE, information and planning services director; b. Oak Park, Ill., Mar. 31, 1952; d. Joseph Angelo and Josephine (Malatia) Galante; m. Lawrence Edward Kozak, Apr. 16, 1977. BA in Chemistry, BS in Biology, U. Ill., Chgo., 1974, MS in Molecular Genetics, 1976; cert. in mgmt., Am. Mgmt. Assn., Chgo., 1984. Research/teaching asst. U. Ill., Chgo., 1974-76; info. scientist G.D. Searle & Co., Skokie, Ill., 1977-78; info. analyst Arnar Stone Labs. div. Am. Hosp. Supply Corp., 1978-79, sr. info. analyst, 1979-81; mgr. info. services Am. Critical Care div. Baxter-Travenol, 1981-85; dir. info. resources and planning DuPont Critical Care subs. El DuPont De Nemours, Waukegan, Ill., 1986—; speaker in field. Contbr. articles to profl. jours. Lay minister Archdiocese of Chgo., 1979—. Mem. Am. Soc. Info. Sci. (sec.-treas. 1982), Drug Info. Assn. (dir. publicity 1979), Digital Equipment Corp. User's Soc., Pharm. Mfrs.'s Assn. (speaker, coordinator), Soc. for Info. Mgmt. Office: Du Pont Critical Care 1600 Waukegan Rd Waukegan IL 60085

KOZAR, JENNIFER LEA, osteopathic physician; b. Mexia, Tex., Mar. 10, 1948; d. James Marlin and Betty Jo (Long) Wrenn; m. Raymond Davis Brendle, Nov. 8, 1968 (div. 1980); m. Bradley Kenneth Kozar, June 19, 1982; 1 child, Hunter Wrenn. B.A., Austin Coll., 1975; D.O., Kirksville Coll. Osteo. Medicine, Mo., 1980. Intern Okla. Osteo. Hosp., Tulsa, 1980-81; gen. practice osteo. medicine, Westside Clinic, Mount Pleasant, Mich., 1981-86, Liberty (Mo.) Family Med. Services Inc., 1986—; chmn. family practice dept., chief staff, trustee Central Mich. Community Hosp. Bd. dirs. Sexual Assault Task Force, Mount Pleasant, 1983-85; physician advisor Hospice Central Mich., Mount Pleasant, 1984-85. Mem. Am. Osteo. Assn. (sec.-treas. West Dist. chpt. 1987-88), Mich. and Mo. Assns. Osteo. Physicians and Surgeons, Mich. State Med. Soc., Mo. Soc. Am. Coll. Gen. Practicioners (v.p. 1988), Mount Pleasant C. of C., Delta Omega. Republican. Episcopalian. Lodge: Zonta. Avocations: travel; swimming. Home: 1333 E Bennett Mount Pleasant MI 48858 also: 11705 Gillette Overland Park KS 66210-3506

KOZBERG, DONNA WALTERS, rehabilitation adminstration executive; b. Milford, Del., Jan. 1, 1952; d. Robert Glyndwr and Gailey Ruth (Bedorf) Walters; m. Ronald Paul Kozberg, June 8, 1974. BA, U. Fla., 1973, M in Rehab. Counseling, 1974; MFA, CUNY, 1979; MBA, Rutgers U., 1986. Cert. rehab. counselor. Rehab. counselor Office Vocat. Rehab., N.Y.C., 1975-81; area dir. Lift, Inc., Staten Island, N.Y., 1981-83; ea. region dir. pub. relations, advt. Lift, Inc., Mountainside, N.J., 1983-85, v.p., 1985—; self-employed writer, editor 1975—. Contbr. articles to profl. jours.; assoc. editor Parachute mag., 1978; editor-in-chief (newsletter) Counselor Adv, 1980. Mem. Nat. Rehab. Assn. (Spl. citation 1974, grantee 1973), Nat. Rehab. Adminstrs. Assn., Nat. Rehab. Counselors Assn., Poets and Writers, Nat. Assn. Female Execs. Home: 714 Woodland Ave Westfield NJ 07090 Office: Lift Inc PO Box 1072 Mountainside NJ 07092

KOZIOL, SUSAN ANN, nurse; b. Hammond, Ind., Sept. 24, 1958; m. Edward Koziol, June 5, 1982. BS in Nursing, St. Xavier Coll., 1980; MS in Nursing, Gov.'s State U., 1985; postgrad., U. Notre Dame, 1986. Nursing supr. Bodimetric Home Health, Chgo., dir. profl. services, adminstr., regional adminstr.; staff nurse St. Margaret Hosp., Hammond, Ind., dir. nursing; cons. Caregivers Coping Support, Hammond. Contbr. articles to profl. jours. and newspapers. Mem. Nat. Assn. Home Care, Ill. Council Home Health Services, Ind. Assn. Home Health Agys., Am. Orgn. Nurse Execs., Ind. Orgn. Nurse Execs., Gov.'s State U. Alumni Assn. (bd. dirs.). Home: 8784 Butterfield Lane Orland Park IL 60462

KOZLOFF, JUDITH BONNIE, lawyer; b. St. Louis, Mar. 4, 1926; d. Isador and Ruth (Gould) Friedman; BS, Northwestern U., 1947; JD, U. Denver, 1968; m. Lloyd M. Kozloff, June 16, 1947; children: James S., Daniel I., Joseph H., Sarah R. Law clk. Mr. Justice Day, Colo. Supreme Ct., Denver, 1969-70; admitted to Colo. bar, 1969, Calif. bar, 1981; asso. Holland & Hart, Denver, 1970-73; sec., gen. counsel Affiliated Bankshares Colo., Boulder, 1973-78; atty. Mountain States Tel. & Tel. Co., Denver, 1979-80, Pacific Bell, San Francisco, 1981-87 . Recipient award Pacific Telephone Employees for Women's Affirmative Action, 1981. Mem. Colo. Bar, Calif. Bar Assn.

KRA, PAULINE SKORNICKI, French educator; b. Lodz, Poland, July 30, 1934; came to U.S., 1950, naturalized, 1955; d. Edward and Nathalie Skornicki; student Radcliffe Coll., 1951-53; B.A., Barnard Coll., 1955; M.A., Columbia U., 1963, Ph.D., 1968; m. Leo Dietrich Kra, Mar. 10, 1955; children—David Theodore, Andrew Jason. Lectr., Queens Coll., City U. N.Y., 1964-65; asst. prof. French, Yeshiva U., N.Y.C., 1968-74, assoc. prof. French, 1974-82, prof., 1982—. Mem. MLA, Am. Assn. Tchrs. French, Am. Soc. 18th Century Studies, Société française d'étude du XVIII siècle, Assn. for Computers and Humanities, Assn. for Literary and Linguistic Computing, Phi Beta Kappa. Author: Religion in Montesquieu's Lettres persanes, 1970; contbr. articles to profl. jours. Home: 109-14 Ascan Ave Forest Hills NY 11375 Office: 500 W 185 St New York NY 10033

KRABISCH, IRENE RIPLEY, medical technologist; b. South Paris, Maine, Nov. 17, 1930; d. Charles Kendall and Ethel Mildred (Young) Ripley; m. Herbert Wilhelm Krabisch, Oct. 31, 1970. Student, Farmington State U., 1949-51, Cen. Maine Gen. Hosp. Sch. Med. Tech., 1951-52. Med. technologist Cen. Maine Gen. Hosp., Lewiston, 1952-54, Albany (N.Y.) Meml. Hosp., 1954, Drs. S. Propp., Wm. Scharfman, Albany, 1954, Albany Med. Cen. Hosp., 1954—. Home: Garage Place Rd Ghent NY 12075 Office: Albany Med Ctr New Scotland Ave Albany NY 12208

KRACH, MARILYN JEAN, airline executive; b. Howell, Mich., Nov. 7, 1943; d. Ervan Robert and Virginia (Harter) Donahoe; m. Clarence E. Krach, Aug. 21, 1971; children—Heidi Virginia, Frederick William Morton, Hansel Clarence. B.A., Spring Arbor Coll., Mich., 1965; M.S., Ind. U., 1971. Elem. sch. tchr. Winfield Twp., Lake County, Ind., 1965-68, Lake Ridge Schs., Lake County, Ind., 1968-69; elem. asst. prin. Lake Ridge Schs., Lake County, 1969-71; pres. ACE Air Cargo Express, Cleve., 1976—. Pres., Montessori Assn., Berea, Ohio, 1978-80; v.p. Middleburg Heights PTA, Ohio, 1981-82. Republican. Lutheran. Avocations: boating, singing, cooking. Home: 15093 Pine Valley Trail Middleburg Heights OH 44130 Office: ACE Air Cargo Express Inc 5300 Riverside Dr Cleveland OH 44135

KRACOFF, ELLEN KAREN, lawyer; b. N.Y.C., May 22, 1950; d. Beatrice (Kaplan) Newman; 1 child, Mark A. B.S. magna cum laude, Barry Coll., 1973; M.S., Fla. Internat. U., 1977; J.D., Nova U., 1980. Bar: Fla. 1981, U.S. Dist. Ct. (so. dist.) Fla. 1981, U.S. Ct. Appeals (5th and 11th dists.) 1982.

Registered securities rep., mortgage broker. Tchr. Madonna Acad., Hollywood, Fla., 1974-78; legal clk., 1978-81; assoc. firm Lawrence Bunin, P.A., Hollywood, 1981-84; ptnr. firm Berman, Kracoff and Sherman, 1985-86, Pioneer Diversified Investments, Inc., 1985-86; ptnr., sec. Providence Title Ins. Corp., 1986—. Staff Law Jour., Nova U., 1978-80; contbr. article. Recipient John F. Kennedy Community Service award Miami-Dade Community Coll., 1971. Mem. ABA, Fla. Bar Assn., Am. Home Econs. Assn. (adv. bd. 1972-73), Attys. Title Ins. Fla., Kappa Omicron Phi, Delta Epsilon Sigma. Republican. Jewish. Home: 5318 SW 86th Way Cooper City FL 33328 Office: 1333 S University Dr Suite 206 Plantation FL 33324

KRADITOR, AILEEN S., historian; b. Bklyn., Apr. 12, 1928; d. Abraham and Henrietta K.; B.A., Bklyn. Coll., 1950; M.A., Columbia U., 1951, Ph.D., 1962. Instr., R.I. Coll., Providence, 1962-63, asst. prof., 1963-67; vis. prof. history Sir George Williams U., Montreal, Que., Can., 1968-69; prof. history Boston U., 1973-80, prof. emerita, 1980—. Author: Jimmy Higgins: The Mental Eorld of the American Rank and File Communist, 1930-1958, 1988. Recipient Ansley award Columbia U., 1963; Nat. Endowment Humanities fellow, 1975-76; Guggenheim fellow, 1976-77; Radcliffe Inst. fellow, 1975-76. Mem. Orgn. Am. Historians, Soc. Am. Historians. Republican. Jewish. Author: The Ideas of the Woman Suffrage Movement, 1890-1917, 1965; Up from the Pedestal, 1968; Means and Ends in American Abolitionism, 1834-1850, 1969; The Radical Persuasion, 1890-1917, 1981. Home: 11 Christina Wayland MA 01778

KRAESZIG-MULCAHY, KARLA MARIA, optometrist; b. Indpls., Oct. 29, 1951; d. Harry E. and Lillian (Lieland) Kraeszig; m. James George Mulcahy, Oct. 11, 1980; 1 child, James Lionel. BS, Ind. U., 1973, OD, 1975. Optometrist Arner & Kraeszig, Rockford, Ill., 1976-82; owner, optometrist Dr. Karla Kraeszig-Mulcahy, Byron, Ill., 1982—; mem. Vol. Optometric Services to Humanity, 1980—. Mem. Am. Optometic Assn. (contact lens sect., Ill. chairperson profl. enhancement program 1984—), Ill. Optometric Assn. (v.p. orgn. 1985—), Phi Beta Kappa, Omega Epsilon Phi.

KRAETZER, MARY C., sociologist, educator, consultant; b. N.Y.C., Sept. 12, 1943; d. Kenneth G. and Adele L. Kraetzer. A.B., Coll. New Rochelle, 1965; M.A., Fordham U., 1967, Ph.D., 1975. Instr. Mercy Coll., Dobbs Ferry, N.Y., 1969-70, asst. prof., 1970-75, assoc. prof., 1975-79, prof., 1979—; research asst. Fordham U., Bronx, N.Y., 1965-67, teaching asst., 1967-68, teaching fellow, 1968-69, adj. instr., 1971-75, adj. asst. prof., 1975-76; adj. assoc. prof. L.I. U. Grad. Br. Campus Mercy Coll., 1976-79, adj. prof., 1979-81, coordinator M.S. in Community Health Program, 1976-81; research cons. elem. schoolbooks Nat. Council of Chs./Church Women United Task Force on Global Consciousness, N.Y.C., 1971; mem. adv. com. edn. and society div. Nat. Council Chs., 1975-78; mem. evaluation team Middle States Assn. Colls. and Secondary Schs. Commn. on Higher Edn., Monmouth, N.J., 1976. Contbr. chpts. to books, articles to profl. jours. Recipient citation Am. Men and Women of Sci., 1978; Bd. Regents scholar, 1961-65, Fordham U. scholar, 1965-68; Fordham U. fellow, 1968-69; grantee Mercy Coll., 1984, 85, 86, 88; NSF summer intern, 1967. Mem. Am. Sociol. Assn., Am. Pub. Health Assn. Office: Mercy Coll 555 Broadway Dobbs Ferry NY 10522

KRAFT, ELAINE JOY, community relations and communications official; b. Seattle, Sept. 1, 1951; d. Harry J. and Leatrice M. (Hanan) K.; m. Lee Somerstein, Aug. 2, 1980; children: Paul Kraft, Leslie Jo. BA, U. Wash., 1973; MPA, U. Puget Sound, 1979. Reporter Jour. Am. Newspaper, Bellevue, Wash., 1972-76; editor Jour./Enterprise Newspapers, Wash. State, 1976; U.S. senator from Wash., 1976-78; mem. staff Wash. Ho. of Reps., 1978-82, public info. officer, 1976-80, mem. leadership staff, asst. to caucus chmn., 1980—; ptnr., pres. Media Kraft Communications; mgr. corp. info., advt. and mktg. communications Weyerhaeuser Co., 1982-85; dir. communications Weyerhaeuser Paper Co., 1985-87; mgr. community relations N.W. region Adolph Coors Co. 1987—. Recipient state and nat. journalism design and advt. awards. Mem. Nat. Fedn. Press Women, Women in Communications, Wash. Press Assn. Home: 14329 SE 63d Bellevue WA 98006 Office: 301 116th Ave #380 Bellevue WA 98004

KRAFT, LISBETH MARTHA, veterinarian, scientist; b. Vienna, Austria, May 16, 1920; came to U.S., 1923, naturalized, 1929; d. Rudolph and Marie F. (Mikota) K. B.S., N.Y. State Coll. of Agr., Cornell U., 1942, D.V.M., N.Y. State Coll. Vet. Medicine, Cornell U., 1945. Diplomate: Am. Coll. of Lab. Animal Medicine (pres. 1966, dir. 1965-67). Research asst. dept. parasitology N.Y. State Vet. Coll., Ithaca, 1945-46, N.Y. State Vet. Coll. (div. of nutrition), Harvard Med. Sch., Boston, 1946; bacteriologist N.Y. State Dept. Health, Albany, 1947-49; research asst. Yale Med. Sch. New Haven, 1949-50, instr. preventive medicine, 1950-52, asst. prof. dept. microbiology, 1952-55, research assoc. dept. of pathology, 1957-61; veterinarian Yale Med. Sch. New Haven (Med. Center), 1960-61; asst. dir. N.Y.C. Dept. of Health (Bur. of Labs.), 1961-65; assoc. mem. dept. lab. diagnosis Pub. Health Research Inst., N.Y.C., 1961-65; assoc. prof. microbiology Sch. Vet. Medicine, U. Pa., Phila., 1965; cons. to Bioquest, div. of Becton Dickinson & Co., Hackensack, N.J., 1965-66; research veterinarian, cons. med. div. of Oak Ridge Asso. Univs., Oak Ridge, Tenn., 1966-67; founder L.M. Kraft Assos. (consultants in lab. animal sci.), Goshen, N.Y., 1968-72; dir. research and devel. Carworth div. of Becton Dickinson & Co., New City, N.Y., 1972-73; also mgr. spl. services Carworth div. of Becton Dickinson & Co., 1972-73; asso. scientist dept. physics U. San Francisco, 1974-77; research scientist, NASA-Ames Research Center, Moffett Field, Calif.; Cons. to Sloan Kettering Ins., Walker Labs., Rye, N.Y., 1958-59, WHO, Azul, Argentina, S. Am., 1965, NASA (Ames Research Center), Moffett Field, Calif., 1972—. Contbr. articles on immunology and diseases of lab. animals and space flight effects to profl. jours. Mem. Am. Assn. for Lab. Animal Sci. (dir. 1960-67, chmn. awards com. 1967, editorial bd. 1964-65, assoc. editor 1966—, Griffin award 1972), AVMA (Charles River prize 1981), Assn. for Applied Gnotobiology, Am. Soc. Microbiology, Am. Soc. Lab. Animal Practitioners, AAAS, Nat. Research Council (adv. council Inst. Lab. Animal Resources 1966-67), N.Y. Acad. Scis., Sigma Xi. Address: PO Box 28 Moffett Field CA 94035

KRAGULAC, OLGA GOLUBOVICH, interior designer; b. St. Louis, Nov. 27, 1937; d. Jovica Todor and Milka (Slijepcevich) Golubovich; A.A., U. Mo., 1958; cert. interior design UCLA, 1979. Interior designer William L. Pereira Assocs., Los Angeles, 1977-80; assoc. Reel/Grobman Assocs., Los Angeles, 1980-81; project mgr. Kaneko/Laff Assocs., Los Angeles, 1982; project mgr. Stuart Laff Assocs., Los Angeles, 1983-85; restaurateur The Edge, St. Louis, 1983-84; pvt. practice comml. interior design, Los Angeles, 1981—. Mem. invitation and ticket com. Calif. Chamber Symphony Soc., 1980-81; vol. Westside Rep. Council, Proposition 1, 1971; asst. inaugural presentation Mus. of Childhood, Los Angeles, 1985. Recipient Carole Eichen design award U. Calif., 1979. Mem. Am. Soc. Interior Designers, Inst. Bus. Designers, Phi Chi Theta, Beta Sigma Phi. Republican. Serbian Orthodox. Home and Office: 700 Levering No 4 Los Angeles CA 90024

KRAINIK, ARDIS, opera company executive; b. Manitowoc, Wis., Mar. 8, 1929; d. Arthur Stephen and Clara (Bracken) K. BS cum laude, Northwestern U., 1951, DFA (hon.), 1984, postgrad., 1953-54; LHD (hon.), DePaul U., 1985, Loyola U., 1986, U. Wis., 1986; DFA (hon.), St. Xavier Coll., 1986, Knox Coll., 1987, Columbia Coll., Chgo., 1988. Tchr. drama, pub. speaking Horlick High Sch., Racine, Wis., 1951-53; exec. sec., office mgr. Lyric Opera, Chgo., 1954-59; asst. mgr. Lyric Opera, 1960-76, artistic administr., 1976-80, gen. mgr., 1981—, gen. dir., 1987—; bd. dirs. No. Trust Co. Mezzo soprano appearing with, Chgo. Lyric Opera, 1955-59, Cameo Opera Co., Chgo.; appeared in: Artists Showcase, NBC-TV, recitals throughout area. Recipient Commendatore Italian Order Merit, 1984, Ill. Order Lincoln, 1985, Alumni Merit award Northwestern U., 1986, Award of Achievement Girl Scouts U.S.A., 1987, Dushkin Service award Music Ctr. of North Shore, 1987; named one of Chicagoans of Yr. Boys and Girls Club, 1987. Mem. Nat. Council on the Arts, Ill. Arts Alliance, Internat. Assn. Opera Dirs., Opera Am. (bd. dirs), Mortar Bd., Phi Kappa Lambda. Christian Scientist. Clubs: Economic (bd. dirs.), Commercial (Chgo.). Office: Lyric Opera of Chgo 20 N Wacker Dr Chicago IL 60606

KRAKOW, AMY GINZIG, advertising executive; b. Bklyn., Feb. 25, 1950; d. Nathan and Iris (Minkowitz) Ginzig; m. Gary Scott Krakow, Nov. 7, 1976. B.A. in Speech and Theatre, Bklyn. Coll., 1971, postgrad. in TV prodn. Promotion mgr Popular Mechanics, N.Y.C., 1976-77; N.Y. copy mgr. U.S. News and World Report, N.Y.C., 1977-80; promotion mgr.Sta. WINS-Radio, N.Y.C., 1980-82, creator, supervising exec. advt. campaign, , 1981-82; promotion dir. CBS Mags., N.Y.C., 1982-84, The Village Voice, N.Y.C., 1984-85, New York Woman (Am. Express Pub.), 1987—; cons. Silverman Collection, Santa Fe, 1985—; sem. leader Radcliffe Pub. Workshop, 1987; producer Festival of Street Entertainers, N.Y.C., 1984, 85, 87, 88, Albuquerque, 1986. Contbr. articles to consumer and trade mags. including New York, Family Circle, Working Woman, others. Bd. dirs. Sideshows by the Seashore, Coney Island, U.S.A., Bklyn., 1985—, Bond Street Theater Coalition, 1985—, City Lore, N.Y.C., 1987—. Recipient Addy award, 1985, BPA award, 1981. Mem. Advt. Women N.Y., Delta Phi Epsilon (exec. bd. 1984-85). Home: 57 Warren St New York NY 10007 Office: NY Woman 1120 6th Ave New York NY 10036

KRAKOWSKI, BLANCHE BELLA, physician; b. Paris, France, Aug. 5, 1936; came to U.S., 1953; naturalized citizen, 1958.; d. Israel Jacques Krakowski and Frieda (Fajerman) Lipski. BA, CUNY, 1958; MD, Med. Coll. Pa., 1962; M in Pub. Adminstrn., NYU, 1981. Diplomate Am. Bd. Pediatrics. Intern Nassau County Hosp. Med. Ctr., 1962-63, resident in pediatrics, 1963-65; pediatrician Cen. Nassau Med. Group, Hempstead, N.Y., 1965-70; assoc. pediatrics, dept. community health, assoc. attending physician dept. pediatrics Brookdale Hosp. Med. Ctr., Bklyn., 1970—; asst. prof. clin. pediatrics SUNY Med. Sch., Bklyn., 1983—. Fellow Am. Acad. Pediatrics. Jewish. Office: Brookdale Hosp Med Ctr Linden Blvd and Rockaway Pkwy Brooklyn NY 11212

KRALJEVIC, SUSAN CURRY, writer, consultant, speaker; b. Covington, Va., Oct. 6, 1946; d. Robert Wilton and Virginia Colaw Curry; m. Vladimir Kraljevic, Oct. 27, 1970; children: Vladimir Brando, Kristian Marko, Virginia Susanna. Student, Concord Coll., 1964-67; BS in Clothing, Textiles, and Related Art (home econs. scholar), Va. Poly. Inst. and State U., 1969. Merchandising/mktg. asst. Glamour mag., N.Y.C., 1969-71, mktg. editor, 1972, press editor, 1973-76, pub. relations dir., 1976-78; publicity supr. Info. Ctr. of Internat. Gold Corp., Ltd., N.Y.C., 1978-84, mktg. cons. precious jewelry, 1984-87; assoc. editor Fashion Galleria mag., N.Y.C., 1986; contbg. writer Apparel News Group, Los Angeles and N.Y.C., 1987—; Sec.-treas. N.Y. Upbeat, 1974-76; spokesperson Creative Writing Week Colonial Sch., Pelham, N.Y., 1987, nutrition instr., 1988; film and restaurant cons. with spouse, 1988. Contbg. editor Fodor's Mid-Atlantic, 1974, Aurum, 1981, 84. Named Outstanding Alumna, Merchandising and Design Soc. of Va. Poly. Inst. and State U., 1982. Mem. Kappa Omicron Phi. Republican. Presbyterian. Home and Office: 110 W 40th St Suite 1405 New York NY 10018

KRAM, SHIRLEY WOHL, federal judge; b. N.Y.C., 1922. Student, Hunter Coll., 1940-41, CUNY, 1940-47; LL.B., Bklyn. Law Sch., 1950. Atty. Legal Aid Soc. N.Y., 1951-53, atty., 1962-71; assoc. Simons & Hardy, 1954-55; sole practice 1955-60; judge Family Ct., N.Y.C., 1971-83, U.S. Dist. Ct. N.Y.(so. dist.), N.Y.C., 1983—. Author: (with Neil A. Frank) The Law of Child Custody, Development of the Substantive Law. Office: US Dist Ct US Courthouse Foley Sq New York NY 10007 *

KRAMER, ANNE PEARCE, writer, communications and film executive, educator, research psychoanalyst; m. Stanley Kramer (div.); children: Larry David, Casey Lise. BA magna cum laude, U. So. Calif., MA, 1965, PhD, 1972. Gen. exec. asst. to producer/dir. Stanley Kramer Prodns., also prodn. exec., assoc. producer, story editor, casting dir., dialogue dir.; sr. lectr. cinema and comparative lit. U. So. Calif., Los Angeles; acting asst. prof. comparative lit. and film Calif. State U., Long Beach; pres. Cathexis 3, Los Angeles; story editor, v.p. creative affairs Castle Hill Prodns., Inc., Los Angeles, 1978-80; story editor Columbia Pictures, 1981-83, exec. story editor, exec. creative dir. 1983-86, creative cons. to the chmn., 1987; free-lance cons. film prodn. and editorial pub., 1986—; creative collaborator Clifton Fadiman, Ency. Brit. Films; judge Focus Award for Screenwriting; cons. communications Sta. KPFK-Radio, govt., others. Author: (with others) Directors at Work, 1970, Neo-Metamorphoses-A Cyclical Study, Comparative Transformations in Ovidian Myth and Modern Literature, 1972, Interview with Elia Kazan, 1974, Focus on Film and Theatre. Bd. dirs. Model UN; expert witness on censorship for Los Angeles Dist. Atty.; nurses aide ARC, Children's Hosp.; former pres. Recovery Found. for Disturbed Children; former ednl. cons., instr. Camarillo State Mental Hosp.; mem. Psychoanalytic Ctr. Calif. (affiliate).a Mem. MLA, AAUP, Women in Film, Delta Kappa Alpha, Phi Kappa Phi, Pi Beta Phi.

KRAMER, BARBARA SUE, mfg. co. exec.; b. N.Y.C., June 15, 1941; d. Sidney I. and Belle Rose Kramer; B.A. in English Lit., Barnard Coll., 1963. Mem. advt. promotion staff McCall's Mag., N.Y.C., 1963-66; account exec. Peter Rothholz Assos., N.Y.C., 1969-72; pres. Bobbie Kramer Assos., N.Y.C., 1972-73; dir. public relations Stiefel/Raymond Advt., N.Y.C., 1974-81, Art Carved div. Lenox China Inc., N.Y.C., 1981—. Mem. LWV (chmn. Ga. chpt. 1967-68), Women in Communications. Club: Publicity (N.Y.). Home: 315 E 56th St New York NY 10022

KRAMER, CAROL GERTRUDE, marriage and family counselor; b. Grand Rapids, Mich., Jan. 14, 1939; d. Wilson John and Katherine Joanne (Wasdyke) Rottschafer; m. Peter William Kramer, July 1, 1960; children: Connie R. Kramer Sattler, Paul Wilson. AB, Calvin Coll., 1960; MA, U. Mich., 1969; PhD, Holy Cross Coll., 1973; MSW, Grand Valley State U., 1985. Diplomate Internat. Acad. Profl. Counseling and Psychotherapy. Elem. tchr. Jenison (Mich.) Pub. Sch., 1960-64; sch. social worker Grand Rapids Pub. Sch., 1964-73; pvt. practice marriage and family counselor Grand Rapids, 1973-83; v.p. Human Resource Assocs., Grand Rapids, 1983—; guest lectr. Calvin Coll., Mich. State U., Grand Valley State U., 1975-85. Ruling elder First Presbyn. Ch., Grand Rapids, 1975-78; mem. Gerald R. Ford Rep. Women, Grand Rapids, 1973—; bd. dirs. March of Dimes, Grand Rapids, 1980-87; mem. Mich. Bd. of Licensing Marriage Counselors, 1985-88. Named one of Outstanding Young Women in Am., 1974. Fellow Am. Marriage and Family Therapists; mem. Kent County Family Life Council . Home: 12622 Park Dr Wayland MI 49348 Office: Human Resource Assocs 300C Waters Bldg Grand Rapids MI 49503

KRAMER, CECILE E., medical librarian; b. N.Y.C., Jan. 6, 1927; d. Marcus and Henrietta (Marks) K. B.S., CCNY, 1956; M.S. in L.S., Columbia U., 1960. Reference asst. Columbia U. Health Scis. Library, N.Y.C., 1957-61, asst. librarian, 1961-75; dir. Med. Library, Northwestern U., Chgo., 1975—; asst. prof. edn. Northwestern U., 1975—; instr. library and info. sci. Rosary Coll., 1981-85 ; cons. Francis A. Countway Library Medicine, Harvard U., 1974. Mem. editorial bd. Revs. in Library and Info. Sci., Sci. and Tech. Libraries. Mem. Med. Library Assn. (chmn. med. sch. libraries group 1975-76, editor newsletter 1975-77, instr. continuing edn. 1966-75), Assn. Acad. Health Scis. Library Dirs., Biomed. Communications Network (chmn. 1979-80), Greater Midwest Regional Med. Library Network. Home: 2626 Lakeview Ave Chicago IL 60614 Office: Northwestern U Med Library 303 E Chicago Ave Chicago IL 60611

KRAMER, ELEANOR, real estate broker; b. N.Y.C., Feb. 18, 1939; d. Herman I. Kramer and Fay (Berger) Kramer-Levy; m. Richard H. FitzGerald III, Dec. 24, 1959 (div.); m. Gregory F. Navarro, Oct. 1, 1975; children: Brad, Cindy. Student, Manhattan Community Coll., 1967-70; BA in Speech and Theater, Bkyln Coll., 1975; MS in Urban Affairs, CUNY, 1976. Tchr. cultural arts Bronx (N.Y.) Bd. Edn., 1966-70; tax preparer H&R Block, Mamaroneck, N.Y., 1977-84; real estate broker, pres. Tritown Realty Corp., Mamaroneck, 1978—; adj. prof. sociology Rcokland Community Coll., Suffern, N.Y., 1979-85, Westchester Community Coll., Valhalla, N.Y., 1979-85; founded dance therapy St. Vincent's Hosp.; lectr., demonstrator N.Y.C. Pub. Schs; co-creator women's ednl. seminar Library of Congress. Mem. pub. relations com. Bicentennial commn. Village of Mamaroneck, 1976; bd. dirs. Community Action Program, Mamaroneck, 1977-79. Mem. NOW (ad hoc chmn. 1970), LWV (bd. dirs. 1977-79), Nat. Soc. Tax Preparers. Office: PO Box 77 Mamaroneck NY 10543

KRAMER, JANE, author; b. Providence, Aug. 7, 1938; d. Louis Irving and Jessie (Shore) K.; m. Vincent Crapanzano, Apr. 30, 1967; 1 dau., Aleksandra. B.A., Vassar Coll., 1959; M.A., Columbia U., 1961. cons. German Marshall Fund; bd. dirs. Internat. Com. of East and Central European Pub. Project. Writer: The Morningsider, 1962, The Village Voice, 1963, New Yorker Mag. 1963—; books include Off Washington Square, 1963, Allen Ginsberg In America, 1969, Honor to the Bride, 1970, The Last Cowboy, 1978, Unsettling Europe, 1980; (Emmy award 1966). Recipient Am. Book award for nonfiction, 1981; Overseas Press Club Am. award, 1979; Front Page award, 1977; named Woman of Yr. Mademoiselle, 1968. Mem. Council Fng. Relations, Com. to Protect Journalists (bd. dirs.), PEN (bd. dirs.), Environ. Def. Fund, Authors Guild and League, Writers Guild, Nat. Book Critics Circle. Office: New Yorker 25 W 43rd St New York NY 10036

KRAMER, JANICE LYNN, leasing associate; b. Queens, N.Y., Oct. 24, 1962; d. Jerold and Rosalind (Mann) K. Assoc. degree in applied sci., Suffolk Community Coll., 1982, AA, 1983; BBA in Mgmt., Hofstra U., 1985, postgrad., 1986—. Mgmt. trainee Chase Manhattan Bank, New Hyde Park, N.Y., 1985-86; mktg. officer Chase Manhattan Bank, N.Y.C., 1986-88, asst. treas., 1987-88; leasing assoc. Newmarket Devel. Corp., Plainview, N.Y., 1988—. Notary pub., Suffolk County, 1982. Mem. Nat. Assn. Female Execs., Soc. Advancement of Mgmt., MBA Assn., Nassau County Republicans, Personal Dynamics Network. Office: Newmarket Devel Corp 1 Dupont St Plainview NY 11803

KRAMER, K. DIANE, special education administrator; b. Atchison County, Kans., June 3, 1949; d. Wilbur Curtis and Jeannette Irene (Domann) Bishop; m. Terrence Leon Kramer, Dec. 19, 1970; children: Kelly Leigh, Kyle Michael. BS in Edn., Emporia State U., 1971, MS, 1975. Cert. tchr., Kans. Instr. spl. edn. Unified Sch. Dist. #253, Emporia, Kans., 1971-75; sch. psychologist Flint Hills Spl. Edn. Cooperative, Emporia, 1975-76; lectr. Emporia State U., 1982. 1986-87; asst. dir. Flint Hills Spl. Edn. Coop., Emporia, 1976-88; dir. personnel Unified Sch. Dist., 1988—; cons. Dept. Edn. St. of Kans., Topeka; speaker various groups, Kans. Bd. dirs. United Way Lyon County, 1986—, div. chmn. 1984-85, 87; mem. adv. bd. Kans. Childrens Service League 1975—; adv. bd. Spl. Olympics 1972—; session presentor Internat. Conv. of the Council for Exceptional Children, Washington, 1971. Recipient numerous grants. Mem. United Sch. Adminstrs. (rep. assembly 1986-87), Kans. Assn. Spl. Edn. Adminstrs. (sec. 1978-79, assoc. bd.), Council Exceptional Children (pres. 1981-82, sec./treas. 1976-77), Nat. Assn. Gifted and Talented, Emporia Adminstrs. Assn. (sec./treas. 1984-85). Republican. Roman Catholic. Office: Unified Sch Dist #253 501 Merchant Emporia KS 66801

KRAMER, KAREN SUE, psychologist; b. Los Angeles, Sept. 6, 1942; d. Frank Pacheco Kramer and Velma Eileen (Devlin) Moore; m. Stewart A. Sterling, Dec. 30, 1965 (div. Sept. 1974); 1 child, Scott Kramer. BA, U. Calif., Berkeley, 1966; MA, U.S. Internat. U., 1976; PhD, Newport Internat. U., 1980. Psychometrist U. Calif. Counseling Ctr., Berkeley, 1966-67; social worker Alameda County Welfare Dept., Oakland, Calif., 1967-69; vol. coordinator San Diego County Probation Dept., 1971-73, officer, 1973-76; coordinator and counselor clin. and outreach programs Western Inst., San Diego, 1976-77; program coordinator and counselor Women's Resource Ctr., Oceanside, Calif., 1977-78; pvt. practice psychology San Diego, 1978-81; prof. psychology Nat. U., San Diego, 1979-81; pres. Health Services, San Diego, 1979-81; pres. North County council, Calif. Dept. Social Services, Emeryville, 1981-83, cons., 1981-83; now affirmative cons. psychologist Calif. Dept. Mental Health; pres. North County Council Social Concerns, Vista, Calif., 1977-78; planner analyst San Diego County Dept. Health Services, San Diego, 1979-81; affirmative action officer State Compensation Ins. Fund, San Francisco, 1983-87; mem. adv. bd. Chinatown Resources and Devel. Ctr., San Francisco, 1984-87, San Francisco Rehab. Ctr., 1984-87. Mem. Personnel Mgmt. Assn. of Aztlan. Office: Dept Mental Health Prevention Br 2340 Irving St Suite 108 San Francisco CA 94122

KRAMER, LYNNE ADAIR, lawyer; b. Oceanside, N.Y., June 25, 1952; d. Paul and Ruth (Kleiner) K.; m. Frederick Eisenbud, Aug. 29, 1976; children—Joshua Kramer-Eisenbud, Benjamin Kramer-Eisenbud. B.A., Smith Coll., 1973; J.D., Hofstra U., 1976. Bar: D.C. 1976, N.Y. 1977, Va. 1977; assoc. firm Thomas Stanton, Alexandria, Va., 1976-77, firm Dominic A. Barbara, Carle Place, N.Y., 1977-78; sole practice, Commack, N.Y., 1979—; lectr. Suffolk Acad. Law (N.Y.), 1981—; guest lectr. Hofstra U. Law, 1983-84, NITA program, 1985—, Toro Sch. Law, 1982-83. Trustee, Temple Beth David, 1981; legal adviser Human Rights Commn. and Women's Equal Rights Congress Com., 1982-84. Mem. Nassau/Suffolk Women's Bar Assn. (bd. dirs., chmn. judiciary 1982-83, sec. 1983-84, pres. 1984-85), Matrimonial Bar Assn. Suffolk (bd. dirs., treas. 1983-84), Assn. Trial Lawyers Am., ABA (matrimonial and family law com.), N.Y. State Bar Assn. (matrimonial and family law sect.), Suffolk County Bar Assn. (lawyers referral com. 1982-84, cts. com. 1983-84, fee disputes com. and judiciary com. 1985—, bd. dirs. 1986—), Suffolk County Womens Bar Assn., Nassau County Bar Assn., Women's Bar Assn. State of N.Y. (bd. dirs. 1984-85, judiciary appeals panel 1984-85), Smith Coll. Club Suffolk County (pres. 1982-83). Republican. Jewish. Home: 7 Bradshaw Ln Fort Salonga NY 11768 Office: Lynne Adair Kramer 6165 Jericho Turnpike Commack NY 11725

KRAMER, MARCIA GAIL, journalist; b. Greenfield, Mass., Dec. 30, 1948; d. Louis Aaron and Blanche Shirley (Weiner) K.; m. Richard Runes. B.A. in Polit. Sci., Boston U., 1970. Reporter Greenfield Recorder Gazette, Mass., 1969; reporter N.Y. Daily News, 1970-82, Albany bur. chief, 1982-86; city hall bur. chief 1986—; adj. prof. journalism Columbia U., 1980, NYU, 1982—. Guest appearances various radio and TV programs; lectr., various N.Y.C. colls. and univs. Mem. Gov.'s Adv. Com. on Drug Abuse, 1978; trustee Day Top Village Found., 1987—. Recipient Pub. Service award Kings County Borough, 1974; recipient Gold Typewriter award and Bobby Spellman Heart of N.Y. award N.Y. Press Club, 1979; Legis. Reform award Patrolman's Benevolent Assn., 1981; Ret. Detectives Ardee award, 1981. Mem. N.Y. Press Women (v.p. 1977-78), N.Y. Press Club (fin. sec. 1979-80, 1st v.p. 1980-81, 2d v.p. 1981-85, pres. 1985-87, bd. govs. 1987—, Byline award 1984, Gold Typewriter award, 1987, Salurians award 1987). Office: NY Daily News 220 E 42d St New York NY 10017

KRAMER, RUTH, accountant; b. N.Y.C., June 20, 1925; d. Isidore and Sarah (Heller) Kleiner; m. Paul Kramer, Oct. 27, 1946; children: Stephen David, Lynne Adair. BA, Bklyn. Coll., 1946. Registered pub. acct., N.Y. Tchr. elem. sch. N.Y.C. Bd. Edn., 1946-50; acct. Lichtenstein & Kramer, N.Y.C., Lynbrook, N.Y., 1954; jr. ptnr. Paul Kramer & Co., Lynbrook, 1954-56, ptnr., 1956-65, mng. ptnr., 1965—; cons. Nassau County (N.Y.) Dist. Attys. Office, 1956-65; expert witness acctg. matters Nassau County Grand Juries, 1956-65; mem. IRS liaison com. Bklyn. Dist., 1965-76; mem. N.Y. State Bd. for Pub. Accountancy, 1982—. Troop leader Girl Scouts U.S., 1947-48; chmn. Tri-Town sect. Anti Defamation League, 1952-53; active Heart Fund; pres. Lynbrook Women's Rep. Club, 1956-58; treas. Assembly Candidates Campaign Com., 1964; mem. Nassau County Fedn. Rep. Women, Syosset Woodbury Rep. Club. Named Woman in Acctg., local TV channel, 1974. Mem. Nat. Soc. Pub. Accts. (del.), Empire State Assn. Pub. Accts. (Meritorious Service award, 2d v.p., 1975-76, 1st v.p. 1977-78, pres. 1978-79, Pres.'s award, 2d past pres. exec. bd. 1979-80, 1st past pres. exec. bd. 1981-82, pres. Nassau County chpt. 1962-63, 75-76, state bd. dirs. 1980—, Woman of Yr. award 1982), Tax Inst. C.W. Post Coll., Acctg. Inst. C.W. Post Coll. Clubs: Sisterhood North Shore Synagogue; Am. Jewish Congress, Lynbrook Pythian Sisters (past chief). Home and Office: 23 Hilltop Dr Syosset NY 11791

KRAMER, SYLVIA MALCMACHER, dentist; b. Cleve., July 14, 1952; d. Morry and Maria Lola (Rolnik) Malcmacher; m. Roger Stephen Kramer, May 24, 1951; children: Lindy Bess, Meryl Stacey, Joshua Lloyd. Cert. dental hygiene, Ohio State U., 1974, BS, 1974; DDS, Case Western Res. U., 1982. Pvt. practice dental hygienist Cleve., 1974-78, gen. practice dentistry, 1982-84; adj. clin. instr. dentistry Case Western Res. U., Cleve., 1985—. Mem. Park Synagogue, Cleveland Heights, Ohio. Mem. Nat. Council Jewish Women, Brandeis U. Nat. Women's Com., Alpha Omega. Republican. Home: 22100 S Woodland Rd Shaker Heights OH 44122 Office: Case Western Res U 2126 Abington Rd Cleveland OH 44106

KRAMPITZ, NORMA CYNTHIA, painter, weaver; b. Big Lake, Minn., June 8, 1911; s. August and Hilda Christina (Gunderson) Peterson; student Macalaster Coll., 1929-31, Western Res. U., 1952-56; m. Lester O. Krampitz, Feb. 21, 1932; 1 dau., Joyce R. Krampitz Hansen. One-man shows: Theatre Cleveland Inc., 1960, Western Res. Sch. Medicine, 1966; group shows include: Jewish Community Center, Cleve., 1963, 64, 66, 67, Cleve. Mus. Art, 1966, Masillon (O.) Mus. 1965, 68, Textile Arts Show, Cleve., 1968, 70. Pres. Western Reserve U. Med. Wives, Cleve., 1950-52; active Hearing and Speech Center, Cleve., 1958. Recipient William C. Grawer Artist award Western Res. U., 1965, Baldwin Purchase award for weaving Massilion Mus., 1968, painting and weaving awards Ohio Art Contest. Mem. Nat. League Am. Pen Women, Cleve. Mus. Art, Textile Arts Club, Am. Craft, Western Res. Hist. Soc., Nova, Orgn. Visual Arts., Nat. Mus. Women in the Arts. Democrat. Presbyterian. Home: 2476 Taylor Rd Cleveland Heights OH 44118

KRANIK, DEBORAH LYNN, field programs coordinator; b. Pitts., Jan. 24, 1954; d. Andrew and Mary (Magera) K. BA, Duquesne U., 1975; MA in Lit., Am. U., 1976. Campaign news sec. Casey for Congress, Pitts., 1976; staff asst. Nat. Rep. Congl. Com., Washington, 1977-78; field dir. Benedict for Congress, Morgantown, W.Va., 1978, 80; dist. rep. for Congressman Benedict, Morgantown, 1980-82; legis. analyst Am. Petroleum Inst., Washington, 1983-87; external liaison assoc., 1987—; fundraising cons. Okla. Redistricting Project, Bartlesville, 1982. Mem. AAUW, Womens Council on Energy and the Environment, Women In Govt. Relations. Republican. Byzantine Catholic. Home: 1221 N Roosevelt St Arlington VA 22205 Office: Am Petroleum Inst 1220 L St NW Washington DC 20005

KRANITZKY, MARY LISA, construction company executive; b. Schenectady, N.Y., July 20, 1955; d. Charles William Kranitzky, and Shirley Ann (Thomas) Ballou. B.S. in Fin., U. Ala., 1982. Fin. specialist Gen. Electric Co., Birmingham, Ala., 1981-83, supv. acctg. adminstrn., Atlanta, 1984-85, corp. auditor, Schenectady, 1985-87; mgr. fin. analysis and auditing Gen. Electric Constrn. Services, Burkville, Ala., 1988—. Bd. dirs. Birmingham Opera Theater, 1980—. Recipient Acad. Excellence medal Fin. Execs. Inst., 1982. Mem. Beta Gamma Sigma, Phi Kappa Phi, Omicron Delta Epsilon. Episcopalian. Avocations: music; water skiing; reading. Home: 2136 N Sutherland Dr Montgomery AL 36116 Office: Gen Electric Constrn Services One Plastics Dr Burkville AL 36752

KRANKING, MARGARET GRAHAM, artist; b. Florence, S.C., Dec. 21, 1930; d. Stephen Wayne and Madge Williams (Dawes) Graham; BA summa cum laude (Clendenin fellow), Am. U., 1952; m. James David Kranking, Aug. 23, 1952; children: James Andrew, Ann Marie Kranking Eggleton, David Wayne. Asst. to head publs. Nat. Gallery Art, Washington, 1952-53; profl. artist, 1966—; tchr. art Woman's Club Chevy Chase (Md.), 1976-88; guest instr. Amherst Coll.; 1985; one-man shows: Spectrum Gallery, Washington, 1974, 76, 78, 79, 83, 85, 87, Gallery Kormendy, Alexandria, Va., 1979, Philip Morris U.S.A., Richmond, Va., 1982, 83, 86; group shows include: Balt. Mus., 1974, 76, Corcoran Gallery Art, Washington, 1952, 72, USIA Traveling Exhibit, C. Am., 1978-79, Am. Assn. Retired Persons Traveling Exhibition, 1986; represented in permanent collection U. Va., 1979, Philip Morris U.S.A., 1982, 83, U.S. Coast Guard, 1986, 87, AT&T, 1986, Freddie Mac, 1987; traveling exhbn. Nat. Watercolor Soc., 1985-86, Watercolor Color U.S.A., 1987, Am. Watercolor Soc., 1988, Am. Artist mag., 1988, Mich. Watercolor Soc., 1985; ofcl. artist U.S. Coast Guard. Mem. Spectrum Gallery Washington, So. Watercolor Soc., Artists Equity, Washington Watercolor Assn., Acad. Artists, Potomac Valley Watercolorists (pres. 1981-83), Am. Watercolor Soc. (assoc.), Nat. Watercolor Soc. Roman Catholic. Home: 3504 Taylor St Chevy Chase MD 20815

KRANYIK, ELIZABETH ANN, educator; b. Bridgeport, Conn., Nov. 15, 1957; d. Andrew Ladislaus and Marion Irene (Slater) K. BS summa cum laude, Western Conn. State U., 1979. Cert. elem. tchr., Conn. Tchr., program coordinator Fairfield (Conn.) Elem. Summer Sch., 1973-85; tchr. St. Maurice Sch., Stamford, Conn., 1980-82, Our Lady of Lourdes Sch., Melbourne, Fla., 1982-85, St. Pius X Sch., Fairfield, 1985-87, Bridgeport Pub. Schs., 1988—; free-lance tutor, Stamford; cons., tchr. Mill River Wetlands Program, Fairfield, 1985-87. Vol., tour guide H.M.S. Rose Found., Bridgeport, Conn., 1985—. Mem. Alliance Francais (Merit award 1979), Nat. Cath. Educators Assn. Roman Catholic. Home: 10 Seahawk Ct Milford CT 06460 Office: Capt's Cove Seaport 1 Bostwick Ave Bridgeport CT 06666

KRASKER, ELAINE S., state legislator; b. Portsmouth, N.H., Apr. 18, 1927; m. Shel Krasker; 3 children. BA, U. N.H., 1949. Mem. N.H. State Senate. Democrat. Jewish. Address: Little Harbor Rd Portsmouth NH 03801 •

KRASNOW, E. JUDITH LEVINE, mental health official; b. Stamford, Conn.; d. Harry Hirsh and Adele Rae (Steinhauer) Levine; A.B., Boston U., 1958; M.S., Sch. Social Work Simmons Coll., 1960; D.S.W., Cath. U. Am., 1969; m. Erwin G. Krasnow, Sept. 4, 1960; children—Michael Andrew, Catherine Beth. Caseworker Boston Children's Services Assn., 1960-61; psychiat. social worker, dep. dir. treatment unit Alexandria (Va.) Community Mental Health Center, 1962-69, dir. preventive services and tng., 1969-77, dir., 1978—; field instr. Cath. U., Howard U., George Washington U.; cons. various social agys. and schs.; examiner Va. Bd. Social Workers. Bd. dirs. Nat. Child Research Center, 1974-76; rep. Parents Assn. steering com. Sidwell Friends Sch., 1981-82, sec., 1984-86; mem. Social Welfare Adv. Com., U.S. Employment Service, 1966-68; mem. Boston U. Reunion com., 1988. NIMH tng. grantee in mental health, 1959-60. Fellow Am. Orthopsychiat. Assn.; mem. Nat. Assn. Social Workers (clin. register bd.), Acad. Cert. Social Workers, Mental Health Assn., Fedn. Clin. Social Workers, Nat. Council Community Mental Health Centers, Mental Health Adminstrs. Assn., Va. Assn. Community Services (bd. mental health council exec. com., member-at-large 1987—). Editorial bd. Social Work Met. Washington, 1976-77; contbr. research articles to profl. publs. Home: 5604 Surrey St Chevy Chase MD 20815 Office: 206 N Washington St Alexandria VA 22314

KRATOFIL, KAREN ANN, public relations executive; b. Braddock, Pa., Jan. 22, 1964; d. Anthony Stephen and Sandra Lee (Hopta) K. BS in Journalism, W.Va. U., 1986. Pub. relations Key Care Home Health Agy., Jeannette, Pa., 1985-86; pub. relations coordinator Leukemia Soc. Am., Pitts., 1986—; freelance pub. relations Blanda Co., Irwin, Pa., 1987—. Mem. Greensburg Rep. Com., Pa., 1986. Mem. Pub. Relations Soc. Am., Delta, Delta, Delta. Roman Catholic. Home: RD 1 Green Hills Rd Irwin PA 15642 Office: Leukemia Society 717 Liberty Ave 1614 Clark Bldg Pittsburgh PA 15222

KRAUK, ELSIE ALEXANDRIA, educator; b. N.Y.C., Oct. 28, 1919; d. Harry and Katherine Huczko Harasym; B.A., Hunter Coll., 1941; M.A., Tchrs. Coll., Columbia U., 1942; postgrad. Johns Hopkins U., 1949-56, Towson State U., 1949-50, U. Md., 1956-59; m. Pembroke Mitchell Krauk, July 18, 1943; 1 son, James Mitchell. Tchr. phys. edn. Thomas Johnson Elem. Sch., Balt., 1942-43; social caseworker Dept. Public Welfare, Balt., 1948-49; tchr. grade 4 and 5 Guilford Ave. Elem. Sch., Balt., 1949-52, Glenmount Elem. Sch., 1952-77, ret., 1977; tutor, vol. work, 1977—. Tchr. rep. exec. bd. PTA, 1956-58, 63-65, area tchr. representing Balt., 1961-63. Mem. Ret. Public Sch. Tchrs. Assn., Md. Ret. Tchrs. Assn., NEA. Home: 6216 Walther Ave Baltimore MD 21206

KRAUS, CYNTHIA JANIS (SAMBOR), logistics analyst; b. Johnstown, Pa., Apr. 12, 1957; d. Frank John Sambor and Janis Louise (Barrou) Sambor Melvin. B.S. in Bus., U. Md.; cert. in fashion merchandising Bradford Sch., 1976. Buyer Glosser Bros., Johnstown, Pa., 1976-77; store mgr. The Ltd., Columbus, Ohio, 1977-82; fin. analyst ASG, Silver Spring, Md., 1982-83; logistic analyst Ketron, Inc., Arlington, Va., 1983—. Co-editor: Small Store Strategy, 1981; author: Logistic Element Manager Plan, 1983, Integrated Logistic Detail Specification, 1986. Bd. dirs. Pa. State Soc., Washington, 1983-85; majorette advisor Connemaugh Twp. Area High Sch., Davidsville, Pa., 1976, 77; teen bd. advisor The Ltd., Wheaton, Md., 1980, 81, 82. Recipient Outstanding Achievement award The Ltd., Greensburg, Pa., 1980. Mem. Soc. Logistic Engrs.

KRAUS, MOZELLE DEWITTE BIGELOW (MRS. RUSSELL WARREN KRAUS), psychologist, educator; b. Vicksburg, Miss., Sept. 29, 1929; d. Raymond Demar and Henrietta (DeWitte) Bigelow; m. Russell Warren Kraus, Sept. 30, 1961. BS, D.C. Tchr's. Coll., 1952; MA, George Washington U., 1954; EdD., Am. U., 1965.Instr., Dept. Def., Washington, 1952-54; tchr. Wheaton (Md.) High Sch., 1954-55; grad. asst. Am. U., 1955-56; research asst., then assoc. to Dr. Leonard Carmichael, former sec. Smithsonian Instn., Washington, v.p. Nat. Geog. Mag., 1956-72; pvt. practice, Washington, 1972—; asso. prof. psychology George Washington U., 1965—; instr. psychology USDA Grad. Sch., 1964—; vis. prof. U.S. Naval Sch. Hosp. Adminstrn., 1968-69; group therapy Salvation Army, Washington, 1980—. Fellow Am. Orthopsychiat. Assn.; mem. AAAS, Am. Psychol. Assn., Va. Psychol. Assn., Nat. Register Health Providers, Internat. Council Psychologists, D.C. Psychol. Assn., DAR, Salvation Army Aux., Phi Delta Gamma, Sigma Xi, Psi Chi, Sigma Kappa, Kappa Delta Epsilon. Episcopalian. Contbr. articles to profl. jours.; author newspaper column Person to Person. Home: 5500 Friendship Blvd 925 N Chevy Chase MD 20815

KRAUS, NORMA JEAN, business executive; b. Pitts., Feb. 11, 1931; d. Edward Karl and Alli Alexandra (Hermanson) K. B.A., U. Pitts., 1954; postgrad. NYU Grad. Sch. Bus. Adminstrn., 1959-61, Cornell U. Grad. Sch. Labor Relations, 1969-70. Personnel mgr. for several cos., 1957-70; corp. dir. personnel TelePrompter Corp., N.Y.C., 1970-73; exec. asst., speech writer to lt. gov. N.Y. State, Office Lt. Gov., Albany, 1974-79; v.p. human resources, labor relations and stockholder relations Volt Info. Scis., Inc., N.Y.C., 1979—. Co-founder, Manhattan Women's Polit. Caucus, 1971, N.Y. State Women's Polit. Caucus, 1972, vice chair N.Y. State Women's Polit. Caucus, 1978; bd. dirs. Ctr. for Women in Govt., 1977-79. Served to lt. (s.g.) USNR, 1954-57. Pa. State Senatorial scholar, 1950-54. Mem. Women's Econ. Roundtable, Indsl. Relations Research Assn., Employment Mgmt. Assn., Am. Compensation Assn. Democrat. Avocations: politics, women's rights, breeding Persian cats. Office: Volt Info Scis Inc 101 Park Ave New York NY 10178

KRAUS, PANSY DAEGLING, gemology consultant, contributing editor; b. Santa Paula, Calif., Sept. 21, 1916; d. Arthur David and Elsie (Pardee) Daegling; m. Charles Frederick Kraus, Mar. 1, 1941 (div. Nov. 1961). AA, San Bernardino Valley Jr. Coll., 1938; student Longmeyer's Bus. Coll., 1940; grad. gemologist diploma Gemological Assn. Gt. Britain, 1960, Gemological Inst. Am., 1966. Clk. Convair, San Diego, 1943-48; clk. San Diego County Schs. Publs., 1948-57; mgr. Rogers and Boblet Art-Craft, San Diego, 1958-64; part-time editorial asst. Lapidary Jour., San Diego, 1963-64, assoc. editor, 1964-69, editor, 1970—, sr. editor, 1984-85; pvt. practice cons., San Diego, 1985—; lectr. gems, gemology local gem, mineral groups; gem & mineral club bull. editor groups. Mem. San Diego Mineral & Gem Soc., Gemol. Soc. San Diego, Gemol. Assn. Great Britain, Mineral. Soc. Am., Epsilon Sigma Alpha. Author: Introduction to Lapidary, 1987; editor, layout dir.: Gem Cutting Shop Helps, 1964, The Fundamentals of Gemstone Carving, 1967, Appalachian Mineral and Gem Trails, 1968, Practical Gem Knowledge for the Amateur, 1969, Southwest Mineral and Gem Trails, 1972, revision editor Gemcraft (Quick and Leiper), 1977; contbr. articles to Lapidary jour., Keystone Mktg. catalog. Home and Office: 6127 Mohler St San Diego CA 92120

KRAUSE, HEATHER DAWN, computer design specialist; b. Kansas City, Kans., May 6, 1956; d. Jack E. Firth and Bonnie Jo (Reeves) Cupps; m. Kerry Murray Krause, May 23, 1981. Cert., Kansas City Skill Ctr., 1980. Cert. drafting tchr., Mo. Assoc. drafter Black & Veatch, Kansas City, Mo., 1980; technician mech. design Wilcox Electric, Kansas City, 1980; coordinator computer-aided design systems Smith & Loveless, Inc., Lenexa, Kans., 1980—; instr. Longview Community Coll., Lee's Summit, Mo., 1987—. Mem. Nat. Computer Graphics Assn., Kansas City Area AutoCAD Computer-Aided-Design User's Group, Kansas City Computer-Aided-Design User's Group, Nat. Assn. for Female Execs. Democrat. Home: PO Box 11314 Kansas City MO 64112

KRAUSE, MARY FAITH, computer sales executive, marketing professional; b. Mt. Clemens, Mich., July 28, 1953; d. Richard Louis and Alyce Jean Boden; m. William Heinrich Krause, Mar. 15, 1980. B.S., Ariz. State U., 1979; M.B.A., City U., Seattle. Recruiter, Search Northwest, Bellevue, Wash., 1979-80; pres. MFK Internat., Kirkland, Wash., 1980-87; dir. global accounts MacIntosh Hardware and Softward Corp., 1987—; pres. Cottage Industries Internat., 1983-84; cons. Custom Clothing Guild, 1983-84. Co-author: China Brief Experience, 1985. Columnist Corp. Corner for MacZone mag.; contbr. articles to various sales, mktg. jours. Bd. dirs. Seattle-Chonging Sister City Assn., 1985. Mem. Kirkland C. of C. (membership com. 1983), Seattle C. of C., Electronic Businesswomen's Assn. (chmn. 1983-84), Forum East (chmn., dir. 1982-83), Am. Mgmt. Assn., Pacific Northwest Personnel Mgmt. Assn., Northwest Consultants Assn. (pub. relations com. 1984-85), Am. Soc. Personnel Adminstrn., Downtown Bus. Users Group. Republican. Roman Catholic. Office: MFK Internat 805 16th Ave W Kirkland WA 98033

KRAUSKOPF, JOAN MIDAY, lawyer, educator; b. Canton, Ohio, Apr. 24, 1932; d. Clement I. and Elizabeth (Bellinger) Miday; m. Charles Joseph Krauskopf, July 4, 1954; children—Timothy Karl, David Andrew. A.B., Ohio U., 1954; J.D., Ohio State U., Columbus, 1957. Bar: Ohio 1958, Colo. 1961, Mo. 1969. Instr. law Ohio State U., Columbus, 1957-59, asst. prof., 1959-60; sole practice, Boulder, Colo., 1961-62; adj. prof. U. Mo., Columbia, 1963-74, prof., 1974-87; prof. Ohio State U., Columbus, 1987—; William Maier, Jr. chair law, W.Va., 1986-87. Author: Advocacy for the Aging, 1983; Law for the Elderly, 3d edit., 1984, Cases on Property Division at Marriage Dissolution, 1984. Mem. Mo. Human Rights Commn., 1976-83; bd. dirs. NOW Legal Def. and Edn. Fund, 1980-87, Mo. Gerontology Inst., Columbia, 1980-87; mem. policy bd. Ctr. Aging Studies, Columbia, 1980-87. Recipient Teaching award U. Mo. Alumnae, 1977; U. Mo.-Columbia Faculty Alumni award, 1985; Medal of Merit, Ohio U., 1979; Research award Sch. Law, 1981; Pres.'s 300th Commencement award Ohio State U., 1987. Mem. ABA, Mo. Bar Assn. (chmn. family law), Am. Trial Lawyers Assn., Am. Law Inst. Democrat. Unitarian. Office: Ohio State U Coll Law Columbus OH 43210

KRAUSS, JOY ELEANOR, advertising executive; b. Newark, Oct. 12, 1931; d. Joseph Mendel and Hermina Carmen (Roth) Kesslinger; m. Mitchell Arnold Krauss, Aug. 31, 1952; children: William Roger, Susan Elizabeth, Caroline Toby. Student, NYU; BA, Smith Coll., 1952. Sec. ACLU, Washington, 1952-53, U.S. Army, Lawton, Okla., 1954-55; from office mgr. to v.p. J.M. Kesslinger & Assocs., Newark, 1956—. Author: (cookbook) The Family Feast, 1986. Bd. dirs. Westfield, N.J. chpt. PTA, 1964-67, Sisterhood Temple, Westfield, 1964-67. Mem. Advt. Club of N.J., Nat. Assn. Female Execs. Democrat. Jewish. Home: 33 Manchester Dr Westfield NJ 07090 Office: J M Kesslinger & Assocs 37 Saybrook Pl Newark NJ 07102

KRAUSS, JUDITH BELLIVEAU, nursing educator; b. Malden, Mass., Apr. 11, 1947; d. Leo F. and Dorothy (Conners) Belliveau; m. Ronald L. Krauss, Sept. 5, 1970; children: Jennifer Leigh, Sarah Elizabeth. BS, Boston Coll., 1968; MS in Nursing, Yale U., 1970. Head nurse Conn. Mental Health Ctr., New Haven, 1970; instr., clin. specialist Conn. Mental Health Ctr. and Yale U., New Haven, 1971-72, unit chief, 1972-73; asst. prof. Yale U., 1973-79, assoc. dean, assoc. prof. nursing, 1979-85, dean, prof. nursing, 1985—; Mem. Congl. Commn. on Am. Youth and Families, New Haven, 1984—, nat. adv. com. Program for Urban Systems of Care for Chronically Mentally Ill, Robert Wood Johnson Found., 1985—, med. adv. com. Hole in the Wall Gang Camp for Seriously Ill Children, Conn., 1986—. Author: The Chronically Ill Psychiatric Patient and the Community, 1982 (Am. Jour. Nursing Book of Yr. 1982); editor Archives of Psychiat. Nursing, 1986—; mem. editorial bd. Image, Issues in Mental Health Nursing, Psycholsocial Rehab., Psychiat. Nursing Forum, Hosp. and Community Psychiatry; contbr. articles to profl. jours. Named Disting. Alumna Yale Sch. Nursing, 1984; Am. Nurses Found. scholar, 1978. Mem. Am. Nurses Assn., New Eng. Orgn. Nursing (exec. bd. 1986—), Conn. Nurses Assn. (chairperson cabinet on practice 1986), Sigma Theta Tau (Disting. Lectr. award 1987), Delta Mu (Founders award 1987). Office: Yale U Sch of Nursing 855 Howard Ave Box 9740 New Haven CT 06536-0740

KRAUT, JOANNE LENORA, computer programmer, analyst; b. Watertown, Wis., Oct. 29, 1949; d. Gilbert Arthur and Dorothy Ann (Gebel) K.; B.A. in Russian, U. Wis., Madison, 1971, M.S. in Computer Sci., 1973. Computer programmer U. Wis. Sch. Bus., Madison, 1969-72, Milw. Ins. Co., 1973-74; tech. coordinator Wis. Dept. Justice, Madison, 1974-83; sr. systems programmer/analyst Benchmark Criminal Justice Systems, Waukesha, Wis., 1983—. Mem. Lakewood Gardens Assn. (dir. 1981-83), Dundee Terrs. Condominium Assn. (officer 1983—), Phi Beta Kappa. Home: 609 Dundee Ln Hartland WI 53029 Office: 17500 Liberty Ln New Berlin WI 53151

KRAVER, DEBORAH, educator; b. N.Y.C., Aug. 12, 1949; d. Henry Norman and Christine (Perry) K. BS, SUNY, Oswego, 1971; MEd, Suffolk U., 1978. Tchr. math. Scituate (Mass.) Pub. Schs., 1971—, dir. intramurals, 1973-77, curriculum leader math., 1980—; pvt. practice cons. in math.; advisor honor soc. Scituate Pub. Schs., 1983—. Mass. Dept. Edn. grantee, 1986-87. Mem. Nat. Council Tchrs. Math. Democrat.

KRAVITCH, PHYLLIS A., judge; b. Savannah, Ga., Aug. 23, 1920; d. Aaron and Ella (Wiseman) K. B.A., Goucher Coll., 1941; LL.B., U. Pa., 1943; LL.D. (hon.), Goucher Coll., 1981. Bar: Ga. 1943, U.S. Dist. Ct. 1944, U.S. Supreme Ct. 1948, U.S. Circuit Ct. Appeals 1962. Practice law Savannah, 1944-76; judge Superior Ct., Eastern Jud. Circuit of Ga., 1977-79, U.S. Ct. Appeals (5th cir.), Atlanta, 1979-81, U.S. Ct. Appeals (11th cir.), 1981—; mem. law sch. council Emory U., Atlanta, 1986. Trustee Inst. Continuing Legal Edn. in Ga., 1979-82; mem. Bd. of Edn., Chatham County, Ga., 1949-55, Law Sch. Council Emory U. Sch. Law, Atlanta, 1986. Recipient Hannah G. Solomon award Nat. Council of Jewish Women, 1978. Fellow Am. Bar Found.; mem. Am. Bar Assn., Savannah Bar Assn. (pres. 1976), State Bar of Ga., Am. Judicature Soc., Am. Law Inst. Office: US Ct Appeals PO Box 8085 Savannah GA 31412

KREAGER, EILEEN DAVIS, bursar; b. Caldwell, Ohio, Mar. 2, 1924; d. Fred Raymond and Esther (Farson) Davis. B.B.A., Ohio State U., 1945. With accounts receivable dept. M & R Dietetic, Columbus, Ohio, 1945-50; complete charge bookkeeper Magic Seal Paper Products, Columbus, 1950-53, A. Walt Runglin Co., Los Angeles, 1953-54; office mgr. Roy C. Haddox and Son, Columbus, 1954-60; bursar Meth. Theol. Sch. Ohio, Delaware, 1961-86; adminstrv. cons. Fin. Ltd., 1986—; ptnr. Coll. Administrv. Sci., Ohio State U., 1975-80; seminar participant Paperwork Systems and Computer Sci., 1965, Computer Systems, 1964, Griffith Found. Seminar Working Women, 1975; pres. Altrusa Club of Delaware, Ohio, 1972-73. Del. Altrusa Internat., Montreal, 1972, Altrusa Regional, Greenbrier, 1973. Assoc. Am. Inst. Mgmt. (exec. council of Inst., 1979); mem. Am. Soc. Profl. Cons., Internat. Platform Assn., Ohio State U. Alumna Assn., AAUW, Kappa Delta. Methodist. Clubs: Ohio State U. Faculty, Delaware Country. Home: PO Box 214 Worthington OH 43085

KREAMER, ANNE ELIZABETH, landscape architect; b. Mpls., Nov. 3, 1956; d. John Joseph Gryboski and Mary Elizabeth Galman; m. John Harold Kreamer, May 23, 1980 (div. July 1982). Student, U. Wis., 1975-80. With sales dept. Electrolux, Lawrence, Mass., 1982—; sales mgr. Electrolux, Amesbury, Mass., 1984-85; landscape architect Frank Todd & Assocs., Rowley, Mass., 1987-88. Baptist. Home: 13 Market St Newburyport MA 01950 Office: Frank Todd & Assocs 116 Main St Rowley MA 01969

KREBS, CAROL MARIE, architect, construction executive; b. St. Louis, May 6, 1958; d. Festus John and Virginia (Klohr) K. B in Environmental Design, U. Kans., 1982. Archtl. intern GSA, Kansas City, Mo., 1980-81, Old Post Office Renovation, St. Louis, 1980-81; free-lance archtl. designer St. Louis, 1981-84; archtl. designer Interior Space, St. Louis, 1984, Gina Ward and Assoc., St. Louis, 1984-85, Michael Fox and Assoc., St. Louis, 1985-86; mgr. facility design and constrn. Southwestern Bell Telephone, St. Louis, 1986—. Big sister Big Bros./Big Sisters of Greater St. Louis, 1986—. Mem. AIA (assoc.). Avocation: historic bldg. rehabs. Home: 1913 Withnell Ave Saint Louis MO 63118 Office: Southwestern Bell Telephone One Bell Ctr 32-G-6 Saint Louis MO 63101

KREBS, LOIS SHEILA, development director; b. Phila., July 3, 1938; d. Leon and Esther (Rader) Ponnock; m. Robert Krebs, Nov. 8, 1959; children: Hope, Abbey K. Myers, Wendy. BA, U. Pa., 1959. Pres. Surfside Motel, Inc., Lake George, N.Y., 1960-78; asst. to dir. Jewish Nat. Fund, Phila., 1979; exec. dir. Boys Town Jerusalem Found. Am., Phila., 1979-87; dir. devel. Albert Einstein Health-Care Found., Inc., Phila., 1987—; cons. in field. Pres. Har Zion Temple Sisterhood, Penn Valley, Pa., 1974-76; bd. dirs. State Israel Bonds, Women's Div., Phila., 1976—; bd. dirs. Har Zion Temple, 1974—, vice chmn. bd. trustees, 1986—. Named one of Outstanding Young Women of Am., 1970. Mem. Nat. Soc. for Fundraising Execs., Nat. Assn. Hosp. Devels., Phi Sigma Sigma (pres. 1958-59). Home: 508 Sabine Circle Wynnewood PA 19096 Office: Albert Einstein Healthcare Found York & Tabor Rd Philadelphia PA 19141

KREBS, MARGARET ELOISE, publishing company executive; b. Clearfield, Pa., Apr. 20, 1927; d. Henry Louis and Delia Louise (Beahan) K.; grad. high sch. With Progressive Pub. Co., Inc., Clearfield, 1945—, bus. office mgr., 1956-60, bus. mgr., 1960-63, asst. to pub., 1963-69, asso. pub., 1981—, dir., exec. v.p., 1969-77, pres., 1977—;v.p./sec. dir. Indiana Broadcasters, Inc. (Pa.), Stas. WDAD-AM and WQMU-FM, 1967—; v.p./sec. Clearfield Broadcasters, Inc., Stas. WCPA-AM and WQYX-FM, 1965—, dir., 1971—. Mem. Pa. Newspaper Women's Assn., Clearfield Bus. and Profl. Women's Club (pres. 1952-53, dist. membership chmn. 1952-53), Sigma Delta Chi. Democrat. Roman Catholic. Club: Lake Glendale Sailing (sec. 1966—). Home: 526 Ogden Ave Clearfield PA 16830 Office: 206 E Locust St Clearfield PA 16830

KREEGER, JEAN ANN, insurance company executive; b. York, Pa., July 16, 1950; d. Frank G. and Ardene (Livingstone) Kopp; 1 child, Michelle L. B.S., York Coll. of Pa., 1972; M.Ed., Millersville U., 1973. Lic. ins. agt., Pa. Juvenile probation officer County of York, Pa., 1974-79; agt. State Farm Ins. Co., Dallastown, Pa., 1979-83, agy. mgr., York, 1983—. Named to Millionaire Club State Farm, 1980-83, 85-87, Legion of Honor, 1982, 83. Mem. Nat. Assn. Life Underwriters (bd. dirs.). Methodist. Lodge: Sertoma (charter). Home: RD 3 Box 439 Dallastown PA 17313 Office: State Farm Ins 2709 S Queen St York PA 17403

KREER, IRENE OVERMAN, meeting management executive; b. McGrawsville, Ind., Nov. 11, 1926; d. Ralph and Laura Edith (Sharp) Overman; m. Henry Blackstone Kreer, Dec. 22, 1946; children: Laurene (dec.), Linda Kreer Witt. BS in Speech Pathology, Northwestern U., 1947. Speech pathologist pub. schs. Chgo., 1947-49; staff asst., lectr. Art Inst. Chgo., 1962—; pres. Irene Overman Kreer & Assocs., Inc., Chgo., 1962—; bd. dirs., officer SKK Inc., Chgo., 1962—; frequent lectr. on art, architecture Chgo. area; TV appearances representing Art Inst. edn. programs. Formerly bd. dirs. Glenview (Ill.) Pub. Library. Mem. Field Mus., Chgo. Architecture Found., Smithsonian Assocs., Nat. Trust for Hist. Preservation, Assoc. Alumnae Northwestern U. (bd. dirs. 1975—). Republican. Mem. Glenview Community Ch.

KREGAR, SHIRLEY A(NN), academic administrator; b. Latrobe, Pa., Mar. 22, 1945; d. David S. Kregar and Ivadeen (Valentine) Pitcairn. AS, Robert Morris Coll., Pitts., 1965; BA in Social Scis., Thomas A. Edison Coll., Princeton, N.J., 1980; MA in Anthropology, U. Pitts., 1983. Vol. The Peace Corps, Cuzco, Peru, 1965-67; sec. Ctr. for Latin Am. Studies, U. Pitts., 1968, sr. sec., 1968-69, adminstrv. sec., 1970, adminstrv. specialist I, 1971-74, adminstrv. specialist II, 1975-76, adminstrv. specialist III, asst. dir., 1976—; panelist Internat. Studies Assn., 1971; cons. residence life program U. Pitts., 1978, mem. screening com. U.S. Office Edn. Tchr. Exchange and Summer Seminar Programs, 1978, 80-81, mem. Greek room scholarship selection com., 1980, mem. U. Fulbright interview com., 1986; registrar, asst. to acad. dean semester at sea program Inst. for Shipboard Edn., Pitts., 1986. Guest editor: (newsletter) CLASicos, 1985; asst. to editor: Estudios Andinos, 1973-74; contbr. articles to profl. jours. U. Pitts. Ctr. for Internat. Studies Travel grantee, 1977, Tinker Found. Field Research grantee, 1983. Mem. Pitts. Peace Inst., Western Pa. Conservancy, Latin Am. Anthropology Assn., Latin Am. Studies Assn., Latin Am. Indian Literatures Assn. Office: U Pitts Latin Am Studies 4E04 Forbes Quadrangle Pittsburgh PA 15260

KREGER, CHRISTINE L., health care administrator; b. Somerset, Pa., May 22, 1947; d. Thomas W. and Genevie (Everhart) K. BA in Psychology, Cleve. State U., 1979; MBA, Case Western Res. U., 1986. Work leader med. secretaries Cleve. Clinic Found., 1976; adminstrv. asst. Cleve. Clinic, 1977-78, divisional adminstr., 1979—. Recipient Woman of Excellence award

YWCA Career Achievement, 1982. Mem. Am. Acad. Med. Adminstrs., Med. Group Mgmt. Assn., N.E. Ohio Hosp. Adminstr. Assn. Home: 3341 Warrensville Center Rd Shaker Heights OH 44122 Office: Cleve Clinic Found 9500 Euclid Ave Cleveland OH 44106

KREGER, PATRICIA ANN, marketing executive; b. Somerset, Pa., Jan. 14, 1959; d. William Barry and Shirley Ann (Miller) Shaffer; m. Mark Alan Kreger, July 1, 1978. Grad. high sch., Somerset, Pa., 1976. Lic. ins. agent, Pa. Asst. mgr., corp. sec., treas. Bituminous Ins. Agy., Somerset, Pa., 1976-84; mktg. mgr. Hidden Valley Resort and Conf. Ctr., Somerset, 1984-86; agy. underwriter, sr. account exec. Navarra Ins. Services, Inc., Mars, Pa., 1987—. Republican. Home: 203 Clearbrook Ct Mars PA 16046 Office: Navarra Ins Services Inc 910 Sheraton Dr Suite 400 Mars PA 16046

KREINDLER, LAURIE, film producer; b. N.Y.C., Nov. 24, 1958; d. Lee Stanley and Ruth (Bilgrei) K.; m. Thomas Laster. BA, U. N.C., 1980. Pres. LKL Prodns. Inc., N.Y.C., 1981—. Producer documentary film Solar Advantage (Council Non-Theatrical Events Golden Eagles award), 1981, Hunger in New York, 1985, motivational film Hands Across America, 1986; producer/dir. I Can Do It (White House screening), 1983. Recipient Family Industry award Nat. Council Family, Los Angeles, 1985. Mem. Edn. Film Library Assn. (Am. Film award 1986), AFTRA. Office: LKL Prodns Inc 60 W 70th St New York NY 10023

KREIS, NELLIE S., media specialist, librarian; b. Omaha, Ill., Apr. 30, 1935; d. John William and Inez Izabel (Harrell) Switzer; m. Hedman Fredrick Kreis, Mar. 5, 1960; children: Alison Kreis Dillon, Erik Frederick. BA, U. Kans., 1967; MEd, U. Miami, 1967; D in Info. Sci., Nova U., 1988. Cert. tchr. and librarian. Librarian Miami Dade Jr. Coll., 1961-63; librarian Dade County Pub. Sch., Miami Springs, Fla., 1958-60; librarian Dade County Pub. Sch., Miami, Fla., 1963-64, edn. specialist media services, 1984—; adj. prof. Nova U., 1985—. Mem. ALA, Fla. Assn. Media Edn. (chmn. intellectual freedom com. 1984-85). Republican. Home: 679 NE 58th St Miami FL 33137 Office: Dade County Pub Schs Library Media Services 172 NE 15 St Miami FL 33132

KREISER, JEAN MARIE, portfolio manager; b. Milw., Aug. 2, 1958; d. Fred A. and Patricia J. (Slagle) Mikkelson. BS summa cum laude, U. Wis., Eau Claire, 1980; MBA, U. Wis., Milw., 1986. Spl. educator Rio (Wis.) Community Sch. Dist., 1980-83; portfolio and office mgr. Robert W. Baird & Co. Inc., Milw., 1984—. Coordinator, coach Spl. Olympics, Rio, 1980-83. Mem. Internat. Assn. Fin. Planning, Beta Gamma Sigma. Roman Catholic. Office: Robert W Baird & Co Inc 777 E Wisconsin Ave Milwaukee WI 53202

KREISER, PEGGY LEE, personnel analyst; b. Harrisburg, Pa., July 4, 1952; d. Robert Lee and Janet Marie (Pugh) Kreiser. B.S. in Elem. Edn., E. Stroudsburg State Coll., 1974; postgrad in computer programming, Pa. State U., 1982-85; cert. in writing for children and teenagers Inst. Children's Lit. Cert. elem. tchr., Pa. Playground instr. Susquehanna Twp. Recreation Assn., Harrisburg, 1972-74; salesperson Young Jrs., Harrisburg, 1974; subs. tchr. Harrisburg, 1974; clk. typist Harrisburg State Hosp., 1974-81, adminstrv. asst., 1981-84, personnel analyst, 1984—, bd. dirs. blood bank, 1983—. Editor HSH Happenings, 1981-84; writer: Children's Lit. mag. Vol. Civil Def., Harrisburg, 1972. Mem. Cen. Pa. Lit. Council (tutor), Nat. Assn. Female Execs., Nat. Edn. Tchrs. Assn. Republican. Presbyterian. Avocations: tennis; reading; writing; stitchery; sports.

KREITMAN, LENORE ROBERTS, lawyer; b. N.Y.C., June 6, 1947; d. Solomon and Mildred R. (Roberts) K. BA, Queens Coll., 1967; MA, U. Pa., 1969, PhD, 1976; JD in Internat. Law with honors, Columbia U., 1976. Bar: N.Y. 1977, U.S. Dist. Ct. (so. and ea. dists.) N.Y. 1977, D.C. 1979, U.S. Ct. Appeals (D.C. cir.), 1979. Assoc. Cravath, Swaine & Moore, N.Y.C., 1976-80, Kaye, Scholer, Fierman, Hays & Handler, N.Y.C., 1980-82, Burrows & Poster, N.Y.C., 1982-84, Loeb and Loeb (formerly Hess, Segall, Guterman, Pelz, Steiner & Barovick), N.Y.C., 1984-88; atty. Credit Lyonnais, N.Y.C., 1988—; exchange lectr. Université de Lyon, France, 1970-71; adj. lectr. French CCNY, 1972-73. Editor Columbia Law Rev., 1974-76. AAUW Ednl. Found. fellow 1975-76; Harlan Fiske Stone scholar. Mem. Internat. Bar Assn., Union Internationale des Avocats, ABA, N.Y. State Bar Assn., D.C. Bar Assn., Assn. Bar of City N.Y., Am. Br. of Internat. Law Assn., Am. Soc. Internat. Law. Home: 16 W 16th St Apt 8-RS New York NY 10011 Office: Credit Lyonnais Legal Dept 95 Wall St New York NY 10005

KREITZBURG, MARILYN JUNE, librarian; b. Rockford, Ill.; d. A.E. and Margaret Louise (Harvey) K.; student Rockford Coll. for Women, 1948-50; A.B. magna cum laude, Knox Coll., 1954; M.A., U. Va., 1956; cert. philosophy U. Edinburgh (Scotland), 1960. Copywriter radio and TV, Black Hawk Broadcasting Co., Waterloo, Iowa, 1956-57; freelance promotion, N.Y.C., 1957; lectr. on Asia, women and fgn. affairs, Ill., Iowa, 1959-60; order librarian, asst. to coll. librarian Knox Coll., Ill., 1960-72; librarian, asst. prof. U. Pitts. at Johnstown, 1972—, reference librarian and head library instructional services, 1977—. Bd. dirs. Prairie Players Civic Theater, 1962-64; rescue vol. Richland Twp. Vol. Fire Dept., 1977, ARC Disaster Inquiry Service; mem. Inter-Service Club Council, 1976-80. Recipient medal DAR, 1948; Helen Lee Wessels fellow, 1954-55; Fulbright fellow at large, 1957-59. Mem. Women's Assn. U. Pitts. at Johnstown (pres. 1978-79, exec. bd.), Assn. Coll. and Research Libraries, ALA, Johnstown Art League, Inter Nos, Phi Beta Kappa, Delta Kappa Gamma (chpt. v.p. 1986—), Pi Sigma Alpha, Sigma Alpha Iota, Pi Beta Phi. Clubs: Soroptimists (pres. 1978-80, exec. bd.), Sr. Citizens Hobby Show (publicity and hospitality com. 1977-78). Office: U Pitts Library Johnstown PA 15904

KREITZER, LOIS BEECHING, insurance company manager; b. Akron, Ohio, Oct. 18, 1949; d. Bradford Joseph and Eunice Lois (Jackson) Beeching; m. J. Karl Kreitzer, Apr. 30, 1983. BS in Fine Arts magna cum laude, U. Cin., 1977. Underwriter Safeco Ins. Co., Cin., 1977-81; area underwriting mgr. Chgo., 1981-83; mgr. ops. Globe Am. Casualty, Milford, Ohio, 1983-85; mgr. underwriting Nat. Gen. Ins., St. Louis, 1985—. Office: Nat Gen Ins Co One National Gen Plaza Saint Louis MO 63045

KREJCSI, CYNTHIA ANN, textbook editor; b. Chgo., Dec. 28, 1948; d. Charles and Dorothea Bertha (Hahn) K.; m. Daniel Neil Ehlebracht, May 16, 1986. B.A., North Park Coll., 1970. Prodn. editor Ency., Brit. Chgo., 1970-71, style editor, 1971-72 ; asst. editor Scott, Foresman & Co., Glenview, Ill., 1972-77, assoc. editor, 1977, editor, 1978-84, sr. editor, 1984—; sr. editor Benefic Press, Westchester, Ill., 1977-78. Mem. Nat. Assn. Female Execs., Chgo. Council on Fgn. Relations, Field Mus. Natural History, Chgo. Women in Pub., Internat. Reading Assn.. Office: Scott Foresman & Co 1900 E Lake Ave Glenview IL 60025

KREMENITZER, JANET PICKARD, educator, child development researcher, consultant; b. Bklyn., Sept. 12, 1949; d. Leonard and Francine (Saltzman) Pickard; B.A., Queens Coll., City U. N.Y., 1971; M.A., Tchrs. Coll. Columbia U., 1972, Ed.M., 1974, Ed.D., 1977; m. Martin William Kremenitzer, Dec. 21, 1974; children—Rebecca Jolie, David Aaron. Instr., Barnard Coll. Columbia U., N.Y.C., 1971-73; tchr. Dalton Sch., N.Y.C., 1972-73; lectr. CCNY, 1973-75; asst. prof. Western Conn. State Coll., Danbury, 1977-79; mem. adj. faculty, 1982; ednl. cons., Newtown, Conn., 1979—, New Haven (Conn.) Hebrew Day Sch.; research cons. Associated Neurologists Danbury, 1982—; research asst. Rose F. Kennedy Center for Research in Mental Retardation and Human Devel., Albert Einstein Coll. Medicine, 1973-74; v.p., founding dir. edn. Maimonides Acad. Western Conn., Inc., 1978-80, bd. dirs., 1978—, coordinator early childhood program, 1983—; dir. aerobic fitness program Maimonides Acad., 1987—. Mem. Am. Psychol. Assn., Soc. Research in Child Devel., Internat. Soc. Devel. Psychobiology, AAPHER, Pi Lambda Theta. Club: Hadassah. Address: Brookwood Dr Newtown CT 06470

KREMENTZ, JILL, photographer, author; b. N.Y.C., Feb. 19, 1940; d. Walter and Virginia (Hyde) K.; m. Kurt Vonnegut, Jr., Nov. 1979; 1 child, Lily. Student, Drew U., 1958-59; attended Art Students League, Columbia U. With Harper's Bazaar mag., 1959-60, Glamour mag., 1960-61; pub. relations staff Indian Industries Fair, New Delhi, 1961; reporter Show mag., 1962-64; staff photographer N.Y. Herald Tribune, 1964-65; staff photographer Vietnam, 1965-66; assoc. editor Status-Diplomat mag., 1966-67; contbg. editor N.Y. mag., 1967-68; corr. Time-Life Inc., 1969-70; contbg. photographer People mag., 1974—. Contbr. photography numerous U.S. and fgn. periodicals.; one-woman photography shows Madison (Wis.) Art Center, 1973, U. Mass., Boston, 1974, Nikon Gallery, N.Y.C., 1974, Del. Art Mus., Wilmington, 1975; represented in permanent collections Mus. Modern Art, Library of Congress; photographer: The Face of South Vietnam (text by Dean Brelis), 1968, Words and Their Masters (text by Israel Shenker), 1974; photographer, author: Sweet Pea: A Black Girl Growing Up in the Rural South (foreword by Margaret Mead), 1969, A Very Young Dancer, 1976, A Very Young Rider, 1977, A Very Young Gymnast, 1978, A Very Young Circus Flyer, 1979, A Very Young Skater, 1979, The Writer's Image, 1980, How It Feels When a Parent Dies, 1981, How It Feels to be Adopted, 1982, How It Feels When Parents Divorce, 1984, The Fun of Cooking, 1985, Lily Goes to the Playground, 1986, Jack Goes to the Beach, 1986, Katherine Goes to Nursery School, 1986, Jamie Goes on an Airplane, 1986, Tanya Goes to the Dentist, 1986, Benjy Goes to a Restaurant, 1986, Holly's Farm Animals, 1986, Zachary Goes to the Zoo, 1986, A Visit to Washington, D.C., 1987. Recipient Nonfiction award Washington Post/Children's Book Guild, 1984. Mem. PEN, Am. Soc. Mag. Photographers (bd. dirs.). Address: care Alfred A Knopf Inc 201 E 50 St New York NY 10022

KREMER, HONOR FRANCES (NOREEN), business executive; b. Ireland, Aug. 9, 1939; came to U.S., 1961; B.S., City U. N.Y., M.S., Baruch Coll.; m. Manny Kremer, May 17, 1963; 1 son, Patrick David. Group sec. Bentalls, Ltd., Kingston-On-Thames, Surrey, Eng., 1954-58, Central Secondary Sch., Hamilton, Ont., Can., 1959-61; office mgr. Aschner Assocs., N.Y.C., 1961-63; public relations asst. McMaster U., Hamilton, 1963-64; office mgr. Packaging Components, N.Y.C., 1965-67; head acctg. Shaller Rubin Assos., N.Y.C., 1967-72, v.p. fin. and adminstrn., 1972-79, sr. v.p., 1979-82, sr. v.p., mem. exec. com., 1982—, sec.-treas. multi-media div., 1972-75 ; pvt. practice bus. cons., 1986—. Mem. Nat. Fedn. Bus. and Profl. Women (dir., v.p.), Advt. Fin. Mgmt. Group. Roman Catholic. Office: 122 E 25th St New York NY 10010

KRENCESKI, MARY ANGELIA, chemist; b. Malone, N.Y., May 18, 1955; d. Edwin Walter and V. Irene (LaPree) K.; m. James J. Tkacik, July 20, 1982. BS in Chemistry, Siena Coll., 1977; MS in Materials Sci., U. Conn., 1981, PhD in Materials Sci., 1983. Chem. technician Gen. Electric Co. Noryl Products, Selkirk, N.Y., 1977-79; research scientist Eastman Kodak Co., Rochester, N.Y., 1984—, group leader, 1986-87. Contbr. articles to profl. jours. Mem. program com. Co-operative Extension 4-H Div., Rochester, 1986—. Doctoral dissertation fellowship Univ. Conn., 1983. Mem. Am. Chem. Soc., Soc. Plastics Engrs., Nat. Assn. Female Execs., Phi Kappa Phi. Roman Catholic. Office: Eastman Kodak Co 1669 Lake Ave Bldg 82 Rochester NY 14650

KRENZER, GAIL CLAIRE (OVERHOLT), pediatric psychologist; b. Omaha, July 27, 1944; d. Donald McLeran and Claire Luella (Abbott) Overholt; m. Vernon William Krenzer, June 18, 1966; children: Douglas William, Jeffrey Donald, Andrew Richard. BS with distinction, U. Nebr., 1966, MEd, 1969, cert. in sch. psychology, 1978, PhD, 1980. Cert. tchr., counselor, sch. psychologist, Nebr.; lic. psychologist, Nebr. Tchr. English Tecumseh (Nebr.) Jr. Sr. High Sch., 1966-67; tchr., guidance counselor Cen. High Sch., Omaha, 1967-71; sub. tchr., tchr. adult edn. Omaha Pub. Schs., 1973-76; sch. psychologist Millard Pub. Schs., Omaha, 1979-85; pvt. practice in pediatric psychology Omaha, 1981—; psychologist Services for Crippled Children, Omaha, 1979-83; instr. U. Nebr., Omaha, 1977-79, 82-83, adj. prof., 1985—. Den mother, com. chmn. Boy Scouts Am.; mem. parent adv. com. Talented and Gifted Edn.; unit orgn. chmn. LWV; mem. Christian edn. bd. Countryside Community Ch.; bd. dirs. Meyer Children's Rehab. Inst., 1980-86, Creche Child Care Ctr., 1984-86, Hattie B. Monroe Home, U. Nebr. Med. Ctr.; trustee Goodwill Industries Nebr., 1984—; cons. Girl's Club of Omaha; mem. Omaha Community Com. on Sch. Desegregation, 1973-74. U. Nebr. career scholar, 1965-66. Mem. Am. Psychol. Assn., Nebr. Psychol. Assn. , Nat. Assn. for Edn. of Young Children, Omaha Assn. for Edn. Young Children, Pi Beta Phi Alumni Assn., Phi Delta Kappa. Democrat. Club: Loveland Community (Omaha). Home and Office: 8305 Hickory St Omaha NE 68124

KREPPS, ETHEL CONSTANCE, lawyer; b. Mountain View, Okla., Oct. 31, 1937; d. Howard Haswell and Pearl (Moore) Goomda; R.N., St. John's Med. Center, 1971; B.S., U. Tulsa, 1974, J.D., 1979; m. George Randolph Krepps, Apr. 10, 1954; children—George Randolph, Edward Howard Moore. Nurse, St. John's Med. Center, Tulsa, 1971-75; admitted to Okla. bar, 1979; individual practice law, Tulsa, 1979—; mem. Indian law alumni com. U. Tulsa COll. Law; atty., dir. Indian Child Welfare Program, 1981—; atty. Native Am. Coalition, Inc., Kiowa Tribe Okla., Tulsa Indian Youth Council, Legal Research Okla. Indian Affairs Commn. Chmn., Okla. Indian Child Welfare Orgn., 1981—; tribal sec. Kiowa Tribe Okla., 1979-81. Mem. ABA, Fed. Bar Assn., Tulsa Women Lawyers Assn., AM. Indian Bar Assn., Okla. Indian Bar Assn., Okla. Bar Assn., Tulsa County Bar Assn., Oklahoma County Bar Assn., Am. Indian Nurses Assn. (v.p.), Nat. Indian Social Workers Assn. (pres. 1984—), Assn. Trial Lawyers Am., Phi Alpha Delta, Nat. Native Am. C. of C. (sec. 1980—), Internat. Indian Child Conf. (founder, chair). Democrat. Baptist. Author: A Strong Medicine Wind, 1979; Oklahoma Memories, 1981. Home: 4425 NW 19th Oklahoma City OK 73107 Office: 4010 N Lincoln Suite 200 Oklahoma City OK 73102

KREPS, JUANITA MORRIS, former secretary commerce; b. Lynch, Ky., Jan. 11, 1921; d. Elmer M. and Cenia (Blair) Morris; m. Clifton H. Kreps, Jr., Aug. 11, 1944; children: Sarah, Laura, Clifton. A.B., Berea Coll., 1942; M.A., Duke U., 1944; Ph.D., 1948; hon. degrees, Bryant Coll., 1972, U. N.C. at Chapel Hill, 1973, Denison U., 1973, Cornell Coll., 1973, U. Ky., 1975, Queens Coll., 1975, St. Lawrence U., 1975, Wheaton Coll., 1976, Claremont Grad. Sch., 1979, Berea Coll., 1979, Tulane U., 1980, Colgate U., 1980, Trinity Coll., 1981, U. Rochester, 1984. Instr. econs. Denison U., 1945-46, asst. prof., 1948-50; mem. faculty Duke U., 1955-77, assoc. prof., 1962-68, prof. econs., 1968-77; James B. Duke prof. Duke, 1972-77; asst. provost Duke U., 1969-72, v.p., 1973-77; U.S. sec. commerce 1977-79; bd. dirs. N.Y. Stock Exchange, 1972-77; dir. Eastman Kodak Co., RJR Nabisco, Inc., Citibank/Citicorp., ARMCO, UAL Corp., J.C. Penney, AT&T, Deere & Co., Zurn Industries, Inc., Chrysler Corp.; Trustee Berea Coll., Duke Endowment, Nat. Humanities Center, 1983-86, HumRRO, 1980-83, Council on Fgn. Relations; trustee Tchrs. Ins. and Annuity Assn.; mem. Coll. Retirement Equities Fund, 1985—; bd. dirs. Nat. Merit Scholarship Corp., 1972-77, Ednl. Testing Service, 1971-77; mem. Nat. Manpower Policy Task Force. Author: (with C.E. Ferguson) Principles of Economics, 2d rev. edit, 1965, Lifetime Allocation of Work and Income, 1971, Sex in the Marketplace: American Women at Work, 1971, Women and the American Economy, 1976; co-author: (with C.E. Ferguson) Contemporary Labor Economics, 1973; Editor: (with C.E. Ferguson) Employment, Income and Retirement Problems of the Aged, 1963, Technology, Manpower and Retirement Policy, 1966, Sex, Age and Work, 1975. named to Presdl. Commn. on Nat. Agenda for the 80's, 1979; recipient N.C. Pub. Service award, 1976; Stephen Wise award, 1978, Woman of Yr. award Ladies Home Jour., 1978, Duke U. Alumni award, 1983, Haskins award Coll. Bus. and Pub. Adminstrn., NYU, 1984, first Corp. Governance award Nat. Assn. Corp. Dirs., 1987, Dir.'s Choice Leadership award Nat. Women's Econ. Alliance Found., 1987, Distinctg. Meritorious Service medal Duke U. Alumni, 1987. Fellow Gerontol. Soc. (v.p. 1971-72); mem. Am. Econ. Assn. (v.p. 1983-84), So. Econ. Assn. (pres. 1975-76), AAUP, AAUW (Achievement award 1981), Indsl. Relations Research Assn. (exec. com.). Office: Duke U 115 E Duke Bldg Durham NC 27708

KRESCH-HAGLER, SANDRA DARYL, communications executive; b. N.Y.C., Sept. 13, 1945; d. Howard Kresch and Jean (Goldsmith) Gleich; B.S., U. Pa., 1966; m. Samuel H. Hagler, Jan. 6, 1973. Research assoc. Simat, Helliesen & Eichner, Inc., N.Y.C., 1966-67; study dir. Nat. Analysts, Inc., Phila., 1968-69; pres. Sandra D. Kresch Cons. Services, Calif., 1969-70; v.p., mgr. market research Nat. Analysts, Inc., Chgo., 1970-75; v.p. Booz, Allen Venture Mgmt., N.Y.C., 1976-78; v.p. corp. devel. Booz Allen Hamilton, Inc., N.Y.C., 1978-80, v.p. mgmt. cons., 1980-83; sr. v.p. mktg. Time Video Info. Services, Inc., 1983-84; dir. strategic planning Mag. Group, Time Inc., 1984-86; dir. internat. devel. Time Mag., 1986—. Bd. dirs. [illegible] of N.Y., personnel com., bd. dirs. Spence-Chapin Services to Families, also chmn. personnel and pension com., exec. com., fin. [illegible] com.; pres. bd. dirs. Jose Limon Dance Found., Inc., chmn. exec. com., mem. nominating com. Recipient Tribute to Women in Internat. Industry award, 1978. mem. Am. Mktg. Assn., Fin. Woman's Assn., Advt. Women N.Y., Pub. Investors Am. (adv. bd.). Democrat. Jewish. Club: Hemisphere. Home: 14 E 75th St New York NY 10021 Office: 1271 Ave of the Americas New York NY 10020

KRESHON, MICHELLE ELIZABETH, bank training coordinator; b. Beaver Falls, Pa., Mar. 14, 1956; d. Michael Joseph and Elizabeth Anna (Pletz) Oros; m. Richard Allen Kreshon, June 21, 1986. BS, Edinboro U., 1978; postgrad., Am. Inst. Banking, 1979-87. Elementary tchr. Blackhawk Sch. Dist., Beaver Falls, 1978-79; teller Century Nat. Bank & Trust, Rochester, Pa., 1979-84, bank trainer, 1984-87, tng. coordinator, 1987—. Tchr. Sunday sch. First Luth. Ch., Beaver Falls, 1983—. Recipient Service award CenturY Nat. Bank & Trust, 1984. Mem. Nat. Assn. Female Execs., Exec. Women's Council. Democrat. Club: Am. Turners (Beaver Falls). Office: Century Nat Bank & Trust 1001 Pennsylvania Ave Monaca PA 15061

KRESS, CHARLEEN EDWARD, retail consultant; b. Lancaster, Pa., Nov. 4, 1949; d. Charles Edward and Marie Nenette (Berit) K. BA, Vassar Coll., 1971. Merchandise mgr., buyer Bloomingdale's, N.Y.C., 1973-80; v.p. retail properties Crown Center Redevelopment Corp. div. Hallmark Cards, Inc., Kansas City, Mo., 1980-84; v.p. real estate and mktg. The Talbots div. Gen. Mills, Hingham, Mass., 1984-86. Bd. dirs. Unicorn Theater, Kansas City, 1982-84; bd. dirs. New Ehrlich Theater, Boston, 1985-87. Home and Office: 132 Amory St #6 Brookline MA 02146

KRESSIN, EILEEN KAY, real estate agent; b. Port Washington, Wis., July 1, 1950; d. Harold Frederick and Emma Helen (Nierode) K. B.S., Central Mo. State U., 1974. Directory rep. Southwestern Bell Tel. Co., Kansas City, Mo., 1975-76, directory sales supr., Houston, 1976-78, staff mgr. directory tng., St. Louis, 1978-80, dist. mgr., directory tel. sales, clerical, Kansas City, Mo., 1980-81, div. sales mgr. yellowpages, Oklahoma City, 1981-85; sales assoc. Apple Realty, Inc., Oklahoma City, 1985—. Organist, Holy Cross Lutheran Ch., Oklahoma City, 1982—. Mem. Am. Mktg. Assn. (v.p. 1980), Sales Mgmt. Exec. Assn., Central Mo. State U. Alumni Assn. Republican. Lutheran. Club: Oklahoma City Ski. Office: Apple Realty Inc 11317 S Western Suite 100 Oklahoma City OK 73170

KRETSCHMER-WEYLAND, KATHRYN ANN, association professional, personnel director; b. Dayton, Ohio, May 21, 1954; d. Charles G. and Mary Lou (Gehring) K.; m. Gregory Donald Weyland, Sept. 29, 1979; 1 child, Julia Kathryn. BA in Sociology, Wheeling Coll., 1976. Staff asst. US Conf. of Mayors, Washington, 1976-79, personnel dir., 1978—, sr. staff assoc., 1984-86, prin. assoc., 1986—. Mem. Washington Personnel Assn., Nat. Assn. Female Execs. Roman Catholic. Office: US Conf of Mayors 1620 Eye St NW Washington DC 20006

KRICH, ANDREA SUSAN, social service agency administrator; b. Newark, Sept. 20, 1945; d. Benjamin and Mary (Raskin) K.; children: Jay, Todd, Eric. BEd, Mich. State U., 1968; MA in Counseling, Oakland U., 1975. Reading specialist Willoughby (Ohio) Sch. Dist., 1968-69; dir. Big Bros./Big Sisters of Oakland County, Pontiac, Mich., 1975-78; CETA trainer City of Pontiac, 1979, vis. lectr. Madonna Coll., Livonia, Mich., 1980; pres. Quality Resume Service, Rochester, Mich., 1979-81; exec. dir. Big Bros./Big Sisters Somerset (N.J.) County, 1984—. Trustee Somerset County Child Assault Prevention Program, 1986—. Jewish. Lodge: Rotary. Home: 26 Crabapple Ln Franklin Park NJ 08823 Office: Big Bros /Big Sisters Somerset County 205 W Main St Somerset NJ 08876

KRICKA, HANNA HALYNA, pharmaceutical company executive; b. Czestochowa, Poland, Jan. 1, 1939; d. Leonid and Helena (Sachnofska) Kryckyj. B.S. in Basic Scis., Drexel Inst. Tech., 1962; M.S. in Info. Scis., Drexel U., 1971; M.Bus. Policy, Columbia U., 1981. Lit. scientist Merck Sharp & Dohme Research Labs., West Point, Pa., 1963-64; sr. lit. and info. scientist Merrell-Nat., Phila., 1964-69; assoc. dir. clin. info. and sr. info. scientist Hoechst Pharm. Inc., N.J., 1970-73; dir. sci. info., internat. div. Bristol Myers Co., N.Y.C., 1973-83, mgr. clin. research and info. ctr. Med. Research Div. Am. Cyanamid Co., Pearl River, N.Y., 1983A— . Mem. Am. Chem. Soc., N.Y. Acad. Scis., Am. Soc. Info. Sci., Assn. Computing Machinery, Drug Info. Assn., Am. Mgmt. Assn., Assn. Info. and Image Mgmt, Pharm. Mfg. Mgrs. Assn., Ukrainian Engrs. Soc. Republican. Byzantine Catholic. Club: Columbia (N.Y.C.). Home: 215 E 80th St PH-J New York NY 10022 Office: Am Cyanamid Co Med Research Div Middletown Rd Pearl River NY 10965

KRIEG, REBECCA JANE, editor; b. Bloomington, Ill., Oct. 7, 1953; d. Russell Edward and Betty Ilena (Clesson) Krieg. BA summa cum laude in Christian Edn., Lincoln Christian Coll., 1977; student U. Ky. Trainer self-help skills for retarded Lincoln Devel Ctr. (Ill.) 1975-76; women's editor Lincoln Courier, 1977-84; campus ministry intern Christian Student Fellowship, U. Ky., Lexington, 1984; copy editor Lexington Herald-Leader, Ky., 1985—. Vol. rep. Cen. Ill. chpt. Cystic Fibrosis Found., 1982-84; a founder Logan County Com. Against Domestic Violence and Sexual Assault, 1983, v.p., bd. dirs., 1983-84; vol. Rape Info. and Counseling Service, Springfield, Ill., 1982-83. Mem. Golden Key, Delta Epsilon Chi. Mem. Christian Ch. Avocations: piano, singing, crocheting, cooking, hiking. Office: Lexington Herald-Leader Main at Midland Lexington KY 40507

KRIEGMAN, JANICE LEE, marketing professional; b. Newark, Mar. 31, 1956; d. Leonard W. and Frances (Pearl) K. BA, Conn. Coll., 1978; MBA, Seton Hall U., 1982. Mktg. mgr. JB Papers, Inc., Union, N.J., 1980-85; mktg. dir. Arthur Andersen & Co., Roseland, N.J., 1985—. Mem. Am. Mktg. Assn., Communications, Advt. & Mktg. Assn., Pub. Relations Soc. Am. Bus. and Profl. Advt. Assn. Office: Arthur Andersen & Co 101 Eisenhower Pkwy Roseland NJ 07068

KRIENKE, CAROL BELLE MANIKOWSKE (MRS. OLIVER KENNETH KRIENKE), realtor, appraiser; b. Oakland, Calif., June 19, 1917; d. George and Ethel (Purdon) Manikowske; student U. Mo., 1937; B.S., U. Minn., 1940; postgrad. UCLA, 1949; m. Oliver Kenneth Krienke, June 4, 1941; children—Diane (Mrs. Robert Denny), Judith (Mrs. Kenneth A. Giss), Debra Louise (Mrs. Ed Paul Davalos). Demonstrator, Gen. Foods Corp., Mpls., 1940; youth leadership State of Minn. Congl. Conf., U. Minn., Mpls. 1940-41; war prodn. worker Airesearch Mfg. Co., Los Angeles, 1944; tchr. Los Angeles City Schs., 1945-49; realtor DBA Ethel Purdon, Manhattan Beach, Calif., 1949; buyer Purdon Furniture & Appliances, Manhattan Beach, 1950-58; realtor O.K. Krienke Realty, Manhattan Beach, 1958—. Manhattan Beach bd. rep. Community Chest for Girl Scouts U.S., 1957; bd. dirs. South Bay council Girl Scouts U.S.A., 1957-62, mem. Manhattan Beach Coordinating Council, 1956-68; mem. Long Beach Area Childrens Home Soc. (v.p., 1967-68, pres. 1979; charter mem. Beach Pixies, 1957—, pres. 1967; chmn. United Way, 1967); sponsor Beach Cities Symphony, 1953—. Mem. DAR (life, citizenship chmn. 1972-73, v.p. 1979, 83—), Colonial Dames XVII Century (charter mem. Jared Eliot chpt. 1977, v.p., pres. 1979-81, 83-84), Friends of Library, Torrance Lomita Bd. of Realtors, South Bay Bd. Realtors, Nat. Soc. New England Women (life, Calif. Poppy Colony), Internat. Platform Assn., Soc. Descs. of Founders of Hartford (life), Friends of Banning Mus., Manhattan Beach Hist. Soc., Manhattan Beach C. of C. (Rose and Scroll award 1985), U. Minn. Alumni (life). Republican. Mem. Community Ch. (pres. Women's Fellowship 1970-71). Home: 924 Highview St Manhattan Beach CA 90266 Office: O K Krienke Realty 1716 Manhattan Beach Blvd Manhattan Beach CA 90266

KRIER, CYNTHIA TAYLOR, state legislator, lawyer; b. Beeville, Tex., July 12, 1950; m. Joseph Krier, 1982. B.J., U. Tex., 1971, J.D., 1975. Bar: Tex. 1975. Of Counsel Matthews & Branscomb, San Antonio; mem. Tex. State Senate from 26th dist., 1985—. Mem. ABA, Tex. Bar Assn., San Antonio Bar Assn., Omicron Delta Kappa, Phi Kappa Phi, Phi Delta Phi. Republican. Office: Tex State Senate State Capitol Austin TX 78711 Other Address: 301 S Frio San Antonio TX 78207

KRIGER, DEBORAH ANNE, artist; b. Phila., Sept. 17, 1953; d. Robert Aaron and Winifred Wanda (Cross) K.; m. Richard Frederick Snyder. Student, Md. Inst. Fine Art, 1974-78, U. Sask., 1977, Del. Water Gap, 1978, N.Y. Studio of Drawing and Painting, 1979. Exhbns. include Hobart Coll., Geneva, N.Y., Smith Coll., Geneva, 1982, Alliance Française, N.Y.C., 1983, Prince St. Gallery, N.Y.C., 1984, Curators Choice, Bklyn., 1985, On The Edge, Bklyn., 1986, Decisions/Divisions, N.Y.C., 1986, Off the Waterfront, N.Y.C., 1986; group shows include Profile Gallery, N.Y.C., 1979, Vals-les-Bains, Arcèche, France, 1980, Permanent Collection of Federated Union of Black Artists, Republic South Africa, 1983, La Roche de Juvinas, Arcèche, 1985. Mem. Artist's Equity N.Y., Bklyn. Waterfront Artist's Coalition. Home and Studio: 216 Plymouth St Brooklyn NY 11201

KRIGSMAN, NAOMI, psychologist, consultant; b. Haifa, Israel; came to U.S., 1953, naturalized, 1961; d. Bezalel and Regina (Yacobi) Goussinsky; m. Ruben Krigsman; children—Michael W., Richard G., Jonathan H. MS, CCNY; PhD, Hofstra U.. Lic. psychologist, N.Y. State. Psychologist Mental Retardation Clinic, Flower-Fifth Avenue Hosp., N.Y.C., Children's Ctr., N.Y.C. Dept. Welfare, Rehab. Clinic, St. Barnabas Hosp., Newark, United Cerebral Palsy Ctr., Roosevelt, N.Y., Burke Rehab. Ctr., White Plains, N.Y., New Rochelle City Sch. Dist., N.Y.; v.p. Devel. Research Assocs. Inc.; cons. on employment selection, career devel., employee relocation, quality circles, U.S. and Israel; feature writer N.Y. Womensweek, 1978-79. Co-author tng. materials for quality circles; also author articles. Fellow N.Y. State Mental Health Dept., 1958-59. Mem. Am. Psychol. Assn., Westchester County Psychol. Assn. (chmn. profl. edn. com. sch. psychology div. 1976-78, founder, past. pres. div. indsl./orgnl. psychology). Home: 13 Dupont Ave White Plains NY 10605

KRINER, SALLY GLADYS PEARL, artist; b. Bradford, Ohio, Jan. 29, 1911; d. Henry Walter and Pearl Rebecca (Brubaker) Brant; m. Leo Louis Kriner, Feb. 28, 1933; children—Patricia Staab, Jane Palombo. Grad. Arsenal Tech. sch. Indpls.; student Ind. U.-Indpls., 1954, Herron Sch. Art, Indpls., 1958. Exhibited in one woman shows Hoosier Salon, Indpls., 1960, Village Art Gallery, Southport, Ind., 1967, 70, 73, Brown County Art Guild, Nashville, Ind., 1970, 74, 77, 80, 83, 87; group shows include South Side Art League, Indpls., 1959-74, Indpls. Art League, 1959-64, Brown County Art Guild, 1974—; represented in permanent collections Riley Hosp., Indpls., others. Founder Southside Women's Symphony Com., Indpls., 1958; treas. Perry Twp. Republican Club, Ind., 1960-65; pres. State Assembly Women's Club, 1965-67; bd. dirs. ARC, Indpls., 1942-45, Southside Civic Orgn., Indpls., 1954, Clowes Hall Women's Com., Indpls., 1963. Recipient citation ARC, 1946; citation Marion County Meritorious Service Award, 1959; citation Greater Southside Civic Orgn., 1961; Art award Kappa Kappa Kappa, 1967, 68, 70, 71. Fellow Indpls. Art League Found. (numerous awards 1960-66); mem. Southside Art League, Inc. (pres. 1964-65, numerous awards 1964-75, founder), Ind. Artists Club, Inc. (Purchases award 1978), Ind. Heritage Arts, Inc., Rutland Art Assn., Brown County Art Guild (pres. 1980-83, v.p. 1983—), Ind. fedn. Arts Clubs (bd. dirs. 1963-73), Ind. Artist (chmn. prize fund 1974-75), Consignment and appraisal of fine arts, Hoosier Salon, Indpls. Mus. Arts, Nat. Soc. Arts and Letters, Nat. Mus. Women in Arts, Hoosier Group Women in Arts. Presbyterian. Avocation: growing flowers. Home and Studio: Rural Route 3 Box 208 Nashville IN 47448

KRINTZMAN, B. J., real estate broker, television show host; b. Worcester, Mass., Dec. 30, 1946; d. Sumner B. and Shirley R. (Sigel) Cotzin; m. Steven Krintzman, Aug. 9, 1969 (div. Jan. 1978); children—Douglas Andrew, Joshua Barrett. A.B., Vassar Coll., 1968; M.B.A., Harvard U., 1970. Lic. real estate broker, Mass. Mng. dir. Boston Shakespeare Co., 1979-82; dir. planning Boston Symphony Orch., 1982-84; talk/game show hostess Newton Continental Cablevision, Mass., 1984-85; real estate broker Hughes Assocs., Newton, 1984—. Mem. adv. bd. WBZ-TV Fund for the Arts, 1982-85; mem. adv. bd. Boston Shakespeare Co., 1982-84, bd. dirs., 1979-82; bd. govs. Harvard Bus. Sch. Alumni Assn., 1983-86; trustee Mass. Cultural Alliance, 1980-84; mem. scholarship com. Worcester County Vassar Club, 1976-82, chairperson, 1982; commr. Human Rights Adv. Bd., Worcester, 1977-78. Named 1 of 10 Outstanding Young Leaders of Greater Boston, Boston Jaycees, 1980. Mem. Greater Boston Real Estate Bd., Harvard Bus. Sch. Assn. (bd. govs. 1983-86). Jewish. Club: New Eng. Backgammon (Boston). Avocations: crossword puzzles; antiques; theatre; tennis. Home: 30 Avalon Rd Waban MA 02168 Office: Hughes Assocs 1631 Beacon St Waban MA 02168

KRIPALANI, LAKSHMI ASSUDOMAL, educator; b. Hydersbad Sindh, Pakistan, Aug. 24, 1920; came to U.S., 1962, naturalized, 1972; d. Assudomal Shewakram and Hari Assudomal (Advani) K.; diploma Montessori Internat., 1946; B.A. with honors, U. Bombay, 1962; M.A., Iowa U. and Seton Hall U., 1966, cert. supr. and prin., 1976. Founder, headmistress New India Sch., 1943-47; founder Pawai Refugee Camp Sch. for Refugees, Bombay, India, 1947; head mistress Garrison Sch., Bombay, 1948-62; dir. Montessori Sch., Iowa City, 1962-64; founder Montessori Sch., Newark, 1964-65; founder. Montessori Center of N.J., 1966, now gen. dir.; internat. examiner Montessori Tchr. Tng. Centers; cons. in field. Mem. Assn. Supervision and Curriculum Devel., N.J. Edn. Assn., Nat. Assn. North Am. Montessori Tchr. Assn., Assn. Montessori Internat., Nat. Council Montessori Tchr. Trainers. Republican. Hindu-Unitarian. Contbr. in field. Home and Office: 340 N Fullerton Ave Upper Montclair NJ 07043

KRISTIAN, FRANCINE ANN-CATHERINE, infosystems company executive; b. Ely, Minn., Dec. 23, 1962; d. Gregory Joseph and Julie Kathryn (Fink) K. AA, Mesabi Community Coll., 1983; BS, Mankato State U., 1985; acct., computer sci., Electronic Data Systems Corp., Dallas, 1985-87; systems engr., Sarasota, Fla., 1987—. Mem. Inst. Cert. Mgmt. Accts., Nat. Assn. Female Execs. Office: Electronic Data Systems Corp 5400 Legacy Dr B4-1A-17 Plano TX 75024

KRISTOF, FAITH MARILYN, banker; b. Tigerton, Wis., Mar. 22, 1951; d. Ralph O. and Violet V. Hermann; B.S. (scholar), U. Wis., Stevens Point, 1973; m. James D. Kristof, May 25, 1974; children—Jill Renee, Paul James. With Citizens State Bank of Wittenberg, Wis., 1973—, asst. v.p., br. mgr., Eland, Wis., 1975—. Pres., Maple Hills Golf Course Women's League, 1977-78. Mem. Am. Women Bankers Assn., Am. Legion. Lutheran. Club: Maple Hills Golf. Home: Rt 2 Box 94A Wittenberg WI 54499 Office: Box A Eland WI 54427

KRIVOY, KATHY LYNN, marketing and finance specialist; b. Euclid, Ohio, Jan. 6, 1956; d. Douglas D. and Dawna (Allen) K.; m. David Eric Rogers, May 29, 1982. BA in Econs, U. Rochester, 1978, MBA in Mktg. and Fin., 1984. Lic. real estate agt., Pa. Internat. market sales forecaster Eastman Kodak, Rochester, N.Y., 1978-79, domestic film market sales forecaster, 1979-81; analyst Mgmt. Services div. Eastman Kodak, Rochester, 1981-83, specialist Consumer Products div., 1983-85; account executive U.S. Sales div., Allentown, Pa. Eastman Kodak, Rochester, P, 1985-87; ptnr. Gemroi Co., Fredericksburg, Va., 1987-88; asst. to v.p. corp. planning Benjamin Moore & Co., Montvale, N.J., 1988—. Vol. Voluntary Action Ctr., Allentown, 1987; mem. adv. bd. to County Commrs., steering com. Community Services for Children. Mem. Nat. Assn. for Female Execs. Republican. Office: Benjamin Moore & Co. 51 Chestnut Ridge Rd Montvale NJ 07645

KRIZANOSKY, MARY SUZANNA, water treatment plant operator; b. Evanston, Ill., July 18, 1958; d. Andrew Michael and Margaret Ellen (Kennedy) K. BA, Calif. State U., Sacramento, 1982. Cert. water treatment operator, Calif. Dept. Health Services. Mgr. Sierra Coll. Recycling Ctr., Rocklin, Calif., 1982-83; conservation aide Nat. Park Service, Moab, Utah, 1983; plant operator 1 City of Sacramento, 1984-86, plant operator 2, 1986—. Mem. Internat. Union Operating Engrs., Audubon Soc., Phi Kappa Phi. Home: 4580 Chapparal Dr Placerville CA 95667 Office: City of Sacramento 101 Bercut Dr Sacramento CA 95814

KROEZE, KAROL ANN, security company executive; b. Denver, Mar. 19, 1945; d. Charles Lockhart and Sarah Elizabeth (Knapp) Michner; m. Robert Harold Kroeze, Mar. 9, 1968; children: Kristina Ann, Sara Elizabeth. BA in Sociology, U. Oreg., 1967. Various clerical positions Eugene, Oreg., 1969-77; sec., treas. Pacific Security & Alarm Systems, Eugene, 1978—; also bd. dirs. Pacific Security & Alarm Systems; bd. dirs. Paideia Sch., Eugene, 1982-84. Adminstrv. asst. Lane Rural Fire Dist. #1, Eugene, 1977—; active Westside Neighborhood Quality Project, Eugene, 1972-74. Mem. Oreg. Mcpl. Fin. Officers, Nat. Burglar and Fire Alarm Assn. Oreg. Assn. Chiefs of Police, Oreg. State Builders Bd., Christian C. of C. Republican. Presbyterian. Home: 2460 York St Eugene OR 97404 Office: Pacific Security and Alarm Systems Box 1742 Eugene CO 97440

KROKENBERGER, LINDA ROSE, chemist, environmental analyst; b. Ridley Park, Pa., July 17, 1954; d. Roy Frank and Rose Marie (Kraffert) K. BS in Chemistry, Syracuse U., 1976. Radiopharm. chemist Upstate Med. Ctr., SUNY, Syracuse, 1976-78; chemist IT Corp. (formerly West Coast Tech. Services), Cerritos, Calif., 1978-80, analytical chemist, 1980-81, sr. chemist, 1981-84, asst. mgr. lab., 1984-85, project mgr. environ. protection agency, 1985-86; mgr. data control Enseco-Cal Lab., West Sacramento, Calif., 1987; asst. mgr. lab. Sci. Applications Internat. Corp., San Diego, 1987—. Recipient Citizenship award DAR, 1972. Mem. Am. Chem. Soc., ASTM, Assn. Official Analytical Chemists, Soc. Environ. Toxicology and Chemistry. Republican. Methodist. Home: 1230 Pebblewood Dr Sacramento CA 95833 Office: Sci Applications Internat Corp 10260 Campus Point Dr San Diego CA 92121

KROLOPP, SHARON MARIA, human resources administrator; b. Chgo., Jan. 15, 1963; d. Rudolph William and Rita Mary (Serafin) K. Cert. in Women's Studies, U. Wis., 1985, BA in Behavioral Sci. and Law, 1985, BA in Sociology, 1985. Adminstrv. asst. U. Wis. Extension, Madison, 1984-85; coordinator human resources and payroll systems Wickes Cos., Wheeling, Ill., 1986-88; recruitment specialist Newark Electronics, Chgo., 1988—. Mem. Nat. Assn. Female Execs. Roman Catholic. Home: 4122 Cove Ln Glenview IL 60025

KROMHOUT, ORA MORLIER, instructional systems designer; b. New Orleans, Nov. 26, 1925; d. Dudley Hypolite and Wilhelmine Louise (Cooper) Morlier; B.A., Newcomb Coll., Tulane U., 1945; M.S., U. Ill., 1951; Ph.D., Fla. State U., 1975; m. Robert Andrew Kromhout, Dec. 21, 1950; children—Sharon, Brian, Ethan. Physicist U.S. Dept. Agr., New Orleans, 1945-50; research physicist Zenith Radio Corp., Chgo., 1952-56; ednl. research asso. Computer Assisted Instrn. Center, Tallahassee, Fla., 1966-72; project mgr. Center for Instructional Devel. and Services, Tallahassee, 1974—. Mem. Tallahassee Mcpl. Code Enforcement Bd., 1981-86; sec. LeMoyne Art Found., 1967-69. Mem. LWV Fla. (v.p., state legis. chmn. 1971-75), LWV Tallahassee (mem. bd. 1958-63, 1980-85), IEEE (exec. bd. 1980—), Am. Ednl. Research Assn., Phi Kappa Phi, Phi Delta Kappa, Pi Mu Epsilon, Sigma Delta Epsilon. Home: 206 Westminster Dr Tallahassee FL 32304 Office: Fla State U Coll Edn Tallahassee FL 32306

KRONE, D. MARIE, small business owner; b. Buffalo, Jan. 13, 1943; d. Kenneth Roland and Geraldine Agnes (Kornprobst) Potter; m. Raymond Patrick Krone (div. Apr. 1972); 1 child, Lea Marie. BS, SUNY, Geneseo, 1964; MS, SUNY, Albany, 1967. Tchr. Lansingburg (N.Y.) Jr. High Sch., 1964-65; admissions counselor SUNY, Delhi, 1967-68; prin. Cabin Hill Boarding House, Delhi, 1968-74; mgr. Archibald's Garage Restaurant, Delhi, 1974-76, Surfcomber Restaurant, Milford, Conn., 1976-78, Torey Pines Resort, Milford, 1978-79; prin. The Inn for All Seasons, Antrim, N.H., 1979-81; salesperson Royal Bus. Machines, San Diego, 1981-83; prin. Uni-Lion Enterprises, Del Mar, Calif., 1983—. Mem. Del Mar C. of C. (pres.'s club 1984—), So. Calif. Race Com., Winners Circle Internat.

KRONE, DEBRA JEAN, marketing professional; b. Knoxville, Tenn., May 3, 1955; d. James William and Ruby A. (Holmes) Floyd; m. Patrick Trainor, Sept. 22, 1973 (div. 1978); 1 child, Amy Michelle; m. Stephen W. Krone, Dec. 23, 1983. BS in Acctg., U. Cin., 1977. Acct. GECC, Cin., 1978-79; sales recruiter Sales Consultants, Cin., 1979-81; area sales mgr. Gorham Textron, Cin., 1981-83; sales rep. Applause, Denver, 1983-84; dist. sales mgr. Waterford Crystal Inc., Denver, 1984-87; freelance trainer sales reps. various cos., Denver, 1987—. Republican. Baptist. Home and Office: 21 Almond Dr Johnston RI 02919

KRONIN, BERNADETTE SMITH, editor, publisher, advertising executive, public relations consultant; b. N.Y.C., Feb. 23, 1948; d. Stanley Allen and Toby (Percak) Smith; children—Amy Bernadette Rose, Karen Edna Wendy. B.A. in History and English, Bucknell U., 1964; M.A. in Liberal Studies, SUNY-Stony Brook, 1971; Ed.M., Columbia U., 1982. Tchr. history N.Y., 1964-69; innovator pre-sch. programs, Shoreham, N.Y., 1975-79; editor, pub. Community Jour., Wading River, N.Y., 1978—, advt. mgr., 1978—; editor Shoreham-Wading River Newsletter, 1978—; profl. breeder, shower A.K.C. golden retriever dogs; cons., workshop leader, 1979—. Editor: C. of C. Directory, Shoreham, 1983, 84; contbr. articles N.Y. Times, Reader's Digest, Psychology Today Mag.; columnist N.Y. Times, 1986-88. Advisor Teen Recreation Adv. Com., Rocky Point, N.Y., 1979-82; mem. Nuclear Emergency Evacuation Com., 1979-82; pres. PTA, Wading River, 1980-83; v.p. Spl. Edn. PTA, Wading River, 1979-80; active Com. Gifted and Talented Children, Wading River, 1979-80, Occupational Edn. Commn., 1979-80; mem. Suffolk County Human Rights Commn. Recipient Disting. Service award Am. Cancer Soc., 1982-83; award of merit N.Y. State Pub. Relations Assn., 1982-83; award of honor Nat. Sch. Pub. Relations Assn., 1981. Mem. Wading River C. of C. (bd. dirs. 1979-80), Suffolk County Bus. and Profl. Women's Assn., Women's Equal Rights Congress, East End Women's Network, Rocky Point C. of C. (bd. dirs.), Sigma Delta Chi, Kappa Kappa Gamma. Roman Catholic. Club: L.I. Press. Home: PO Box 619 Wading River NY 11792 Office: Community Jour PO Box 619 Wading River NY 11792

KRONMAN, CAROL JANE, lawyer; b. Passaic, N.J., Mar. 25, 1944; d. Robert M. and Helen K. (Harris) K.; m. William D. Lipkind, Aug. 15, 1965 (div. 1975); children: Audrey Jane, Heather Sue. AB, Cornell U., 1965; MA, Columbia U., 1966; JD, Yeshiva U., 1980. Bar: N.Y. 1981, N.J. 1981, Fla. 1981, U.S. Dist. Ct. N.J., U.S. Dist. Ct. (so. dist.) N.Y. Asst. prof. William Paterson Coll., Wayne, N.J., 1967-69; treas. Capital Theatre Inc., N.J., 1977-83; coordinator paralegal studies Montclair State Coll., N.J., 1982-83, prof., 1982-85; ptnr. Kronman & Kronman P.A., Totowa, N.J., 1981-85; ptnr. N.J. office Max E. Greenberg, Cantor & Reiss, South Hackensack, N.J., 1986-87; ptnr. Blodnick, Pomeranz, Schultz and Abramowitz, P.C., N.Y. and N.J., 1987—; pvt. investment advisor, N.J., 1977-84. Recipient Certs. of Appreciation, Rotary Club, Caldwell and Parsippany, N.J. Mem. ABA, N.J. Bar Assn., N.Y. Bar Assn., Fla. Bar Assn., Bergen County Bar Assn. Home: 26 Spruce Rd North Caldwell NJ 07006 Office: Blodnick Pomeranz Reiss Schultz & Abramowitz 769 Northfield Ave West Orange NJ 07052 also: 477 Madison Ave New York NY 10022

KROSSNER, RHONDA PARRELLA, psychologist; b. Mt. Vernon, N.Y., Dec. 29, 1951; d. Joseph and Ida (Cornacchia) Parrella; m. William J. Krossner Jr., Sept. 4, 1977; children: Steven, Laura. BS summa cum laude, Fordham U., 1973, MA, 1975, PhD, 1983. V.p. Psy. Minn. Corp., Duluth, 1977—; head neuropsychology div. Neurosci. Inst., Duluth, 1984—. NIMH fellow, 1975. Mem. Nat. Acad. Neuropsychologists, Am. Psychol. Assn., Phi Beta Kappa. Home: PO Box 3047 Duluth MN 55803 Office: 205 W 2d St Duluth MN 55802

KROUSE, ANN WOLK, publishing executive; b. Chgo., Feb. 4, 1945; d. Barnett David and Shirley (Schwartz) Wolk; m. Paul Carl Krouse, Aug. 8, 1964; children: Amy Renee, Beth Diane, Joseph David, Katie Sue. Student, U. Miami, Fla., 1962. Ops. mgr. Playboy Club, Chgo., 1963-64; v.p. Ednl. Communications, Inc., Lake Forest, Ill., 1967—; bd. dirs. URT Industries, Inc., Hialeah Gardens, Fla., Peaches Entertainment Corp., Hialeah Gardens. Pub., co-editor (book) Who's Who Among Black Americans, 1976-88 (Outstanding Reference Book, 1976). Bd. dirs. scholarship found. Ednl. Communications, Inc., 1970—; mem. Jewish United Fund, 1970—, Mothers Against Drunk Driving, 1985—. Mem. Nat. Sch. Pub. Relations Assn., Ednl. Press Assn., Direct Mail Mktg. Assn., Lake Forest Open Lands Assn. Office: Ednl Communications Inc 721 N McKinley Rd Lake Forest IL 60045

KROUSE, DIANE MURRAY, advertising company executive; b. Far Rockaway, N.Y., May 24, 1954; d. Jan and Kathleen (Mann) Murray; m. David Allan Krouse, Oct. 10, 1982; 1 child, Sarah Elizabeth. BA, Stanford U., 1977. Promotion coordinator Beetleboards Internat., Los Angeles, 1977-78; account exec. RAP Communications, Los Angeles, 1978-79; v.p., mgmt. supr. D'Arcy, Masius, Benton and Bowles, N.Y.C., 1979-85, Los Angeles, 1985—. Mem. Phi Beta Kappa. Home: 2256 Linnington Ave Los Angeles CA 90064 Office: D'Arcy Masius Benton and Bowles 6500 Wilshire Blvd Los Angeles CA 90048

KROUSE, SUSAN APPLEGATE, museum curator; b. Detroit, July 1, 1955; d. John D. and Carol Edith (Summers) Applegate; m. Ned Allan Krouse, Aug. 19, 1978. A.B., Ind. U., 1976, M.A., 1981. Acting curator I.U. Museum, Bloomington, Ind., 1978-79; curator New Hanover County Mus., Wilmington, N.C., 1981-86; teaching asst. U. Wis., Milw., 1986—. Mem. Am. Assn. Anthropology. Office: U Wis Dept Anthropology PO Box 413 Milwaukee WI 53201

KROZSER, LINDA JO, marketing executive; b. Cleve., May 29, 1955; d. Joseph James and Elsie Ruth (Boros) K. BA in Psychology, Marietta Coll., 1977; MBA, Ohio State U., 1980. Sales rep. Procter & Gamble, Akron, Ohio, 1977-79; market research asst. Gen. Mills, Inc., Mpls., 1981-82, market research asst. mgr., 1982-85; market research mgr. Tropicana Products, Inc., Bradenton, Fla., 1985, Pillsbury Co., Mpls., 1985—. Chmn. com. bd. mgmt. Downtown YMCA, Mpls., 1983—. Mem. Am. Mktg. Assn., MBA Assn. (pres. 1980). Roman Catholic. Home: 3008 Lake Shore Dr Minneapolis MN 55416 Office: The Pillsbury Co Pillsbury Ctr MS 2178 Minneapolis MN 55402

KRUCKEBERG, VICKY LEE, home economist; b. Alton, Ill., Nov. 13, 1951; d. Kenneth and Hertha May (Brewer) K.; B.S., So. Ill. U., Carbondale, 1974, M.S., 1975. Grad. teaching asst. So. Ill. U., 1974-75; saleswoman Paul Harris Stores, St. Louis, 1975; textile conservator U.S. Cav. Mus., Ft. Riley, Kans., 1979, N.Y. State Parks, Recreation and Hist. Preservation Dept., 1980-85; costume conservator Kent State U. Mus., Ohio, 1985-87; costume curator, conservator Detroit Hist. Mus., 1988—; project dir. Intermus. Services Conservation Project, 1984, conservation project Inst. Mus. Services, 1984; project dir. 1985; instr. clothing and textiles Kans. State U., Manhattan, 1975-80. Recipient Home Econs. Faculty Research award Kans. State U., 1977, Grad. Sch. Faculty Research award, 1978. Mem. Am. Assn. Mus., Am. Assn. State and Local History, Am. Inst. Conservation, Internat. Inst. Conservation, Costume Soc. Am., Assn. Coll. Profs. Textile and Clothing, Am. Home Econs. Assn., Internat. Com. Museums, Embroiderers Guild Am. Republican. Presbyterian. Author papers in field. Office: Detroit Hist Mus 5401 Woodward Ave Detroit MI 48202

KRUEGER, BETTY JANE, telecommunication company executive; b. Indpls., Oct. 4, 1923; d. Forrest Glen and Hazel Luellen (Taylor) Burns; student Butler U., 1948-49; m. Alan Douglas Krueger, Apr. 4, 1975; 1 son by previous marriage—Michael J. Vornehm. Supr., instr. Ind. Bell Telephone Co., Indpls., 1941-54; supr. communications Jones & Laughlin Steel Co., Indpls., 1954-56, Ford Motor Co., Indpls., 1956-64, U.S. Govt., Camp Atterbury, Ind., 1964-66; dir. communications Meth. Hosp. of Ind., Indpls., 1966-79; pres. owner Rent-A-Radio, Inc. of Ind., Indpls., after 1979; sec.-treas. Communications Unltd., Inc. Former pres. Am. Legion Aux.; chmn. for Ind., Girls State U.S.A., 1972-77; probation officer vol., 1973-74; suicide prevention counselor, 1972-73. Recipient award for outstanding community service Ford Motor Co., 1961. Mem. Am. Soc. Hosp. Engring., Am. Hosp. Assn., Nat. Assn. Bus. and Ednl. Radio, Inc., Internat. Teletypewriters for the Deaf, Asso. Public Safety Communications Officers, Inc., Am. Bus. Women. Methodist. Home: Rural Route 2 Box 119 Franklin IN 46131 Office: 4032 Southeastern Ave Indianapolis IN 46203

KRUEGER, BONNIE LEE, editor, writer; b. Chgo., Feb. 3, 1950; d. Harry Bernard and Lillian (Soyak) Krueger; m. James Lawrence Spurlock, Mar. 8, 1972. Student Morraine Valley Coll., 1970. Adminstrv. asst. Carson Pirie Scott & Co., Chgo., 1969-72; traffic coordinator Tatham Laird & Kudner, Chgo., 1973-74; traffic coordinator J. Walter Thompson, Chgo., 1974-76; prodn. coordinator, 1976-78; editor-in-chief Assoc. Pubs., Chgo., 1978—; editor-in-chief Sophisticate's Hairstyle Guide, 1978—, Sophisticates Beauty Guide, 1978—, Complete Woman, 1981—; pub., editorial services dir. Sophisticate's Black Hair Guide, 1983—. Mem. Statue of Liberty Restoration Com., N.Y.C., 1983; campaign worker Cook County State's Atty., Chgo., 1982; poll watcher Cook County Dem. Orgn., 1983. Mem. Soc. Profl. Journalists, Nat. Assn. Female Execs., Am. Health and Beauty Aids Inst. (assoc. mem.), Sigma Delta Chi. Lutheran. Clubs: Sierra, Cousteau Soc. Office: Complete Woman 1165 N Clark St Chicago IL 60610

KRUEGER, CHERYL ANN, accountant; b. Russell, Kans., May 26, 1956; m. Michael R. Einspahr, Jan. 7, 1987. BS in Acctg., U. Denver, 1978. CPA, Colo. Tax sr. Arthur Andersen and Co., Denver, 1978-82; tax supr. Energetics, Inc., Englewood, Colo., 1982-84; tax mgr. Nat. Oil Co., Denver, 1984-85; pres. Cheryl A. Krueger, Englewood, 1985—. Mem. Am. Inst. CPA's, Colo. Soc. CPA's, Denver Women's Soc. CPA's, Alliance of Profl. Women, Petroleum Accts. Soc. Home: 8322 Adams Way Denver CO 80221 Office: 3773 Cherry Creek Dr N Suite 575 Denver CO 80209

KRUEGER, JUDI JO, recreation executive; b. Shawano, Wis., Aug. 22, 1963; d. Gale Willis and Muriel Estelle (Johnson) K. BS, Fla. State U., 1984; postgrad., San Jose State U. Dir. health club Century 21, Jacksonville, Fla., 1985-86; recreation dir. Fair Oaks West, Sunnyvale, Calif., 1986—; publicity, sports and spl. event coordinator FMC Corp., San Jose, Calif., 1985-87. asst. editor Tr-County Indsl. Recreation Newsletter, Sunnyvale. Vol. Crippled Children's Soc., Santa Clara, 1985, Big Bros./Big Sisters, Santa Clara, 1987. Mem. Tri County Indsl. Recreation Council, Nat. Employee Service Recreation Assn. (Outstanding Program Promotion award 1986, Award of Excellance, 1987), Sigma Lambda Sigma, Omega Alpha Rho. Republican. Methodist. Home: 900 Pepper Tree Lane Santa Clara CA 95051 Office: 655 S Fair Oaks Ave Sunnyvale CA 94086

KRUEGER, KATHERINE KAMP, lawyer; b. Chgo., Apr. 7, 1944; d. Rudolph Pollay and Josephine Yvette (Marland) Kamp. Student U. Paris, Sorbonne, 1963-64; B.S. magna cum laude, Tulane U., 1965, M.S., 1968; J.D., Northwestern U., 1980. Bar: Tex. 1980, Ill. 1988. Micropaleontologist, Gulf Oil Corp., New Orleans, 1967-68; custodian collections geology Field Mus., Chgo., 1968-76, lectr., 1975-76; lectr. earth sci. Northeastern Ill. U., Chgo., 1977; atty. oil and gas Gulf Oil Corp., Houston, 1980-81, Amoco Prodn. Co., Houston, 1981-87, atty. environ. law Amoco Corp., Chgo., 1987—; bd. dirs. The Eureka Soc., Escondido, Calif., 1974—; vol. lectr. Desk and Derrick, Houston, 1983. Contbr. articles to profl. jours. Campaign vol., poll watcher Ind. Democratic candidate for Ill. Constl. Conv., Chgo., 1968; poll watcher Ind. Democratic candidate for Ill. Rep., Chgo., 1978; del. Dem. Senatorial Dist. 7 Conv., Tex., 1984. NSF Student grantee microbiol. dept. U. Miami Marine Lab., 1960-64; grantee La. Heart Found., Sophie Newcomb Coll. Botany Dept., 1962-63, Grad. Sch. Tulane U. Scholars and Fellows Orgn., 1965-66; named Steinmayer Best Geol. Student, Tulane U., 1965; Houston Bar Found. fellow, 1982—. Mem. ABA, State Bar Tex., Houston Bar Assn., Chgo. Bar Assn., Phi Beta Kappa, Sigma Gamma Epsilon, Eta Sigma Phi. Home: PO Box 1606 Evanston IL 60204

KRUEGER, PAMELA ANN HICKS, airline pilot; b. Colebrook, N.H., Oct. 26, 1952; d. Parker Alba and Janet Louise (Brakel) Hicks; 1 child, Catherine Ann. BS in Bus. Adminstrn., Hawthorne Coll., Antrim, N.H., 1974. Commd. lt. USN, 1974; served as aviator USN, San Diego, 1974-84; ret. USN, 1984; 1st officer/airline pilot Transam. Airlines, 1985, N.Y. Air, N.Y.C., 1986-87, Continental Airlines, N.Y.C., 1987—. Recipient Amelia Earhart award 99's, N.H., 1975. Mem. Assn. Naval Aviation, Aux. of USAF, Ret. Officers Assn. Office: Continental Airlines PO Box 17228 Washington DC 20041

KRUKOWSKI, MARILYN DENMARK, biology educator and researcher; b. N.Y.C., May 3, 1932; d. Henry and Julia Marian (Lipshitz) Denmark; m. Lucian Krukowski, Jan. 14, 1955; 1 child, Samantha Henriette. B.A., Bklyn. Coll., 1954; M.S., NYU, 1962, Ph.D., 1965. Instr., N.Y. Med. Coll., N.Y.C., 1964-66, asst. prof., 1966-69; asst. prof. Washington U., St. Louis, 1969-75, assoc. prof. 1975-87, prof. biology 1987—. Contbr. sci. articles to profl. jours. Recipient Founders Day award NYU, 1965. Mem. AAAS, Am. Soc. Bone and Mineral Research, Am. Soc. Cell Biology, Sigma Xi. Democrat.

Home: 24 Washington Terr Saint Louis MO 63112 Office: Washington U Dept Biology Saint Louis MO 63130

KRULEWICH, HELEN D., lawyer; b. Paterson, N.J., Apr. 6, 1948; d. George and Kathrine P. (Vanderheide) Dworetzky; m. Leonard M. Krulewich, Sept. 2, 1972; children—Sara Heide, David Samuel. B.S., Syracuse U., 1970; J.D., Suffolk U., 1974. Bar: Mass. 1974, N.J., U.S. Supreme Ct. Clk. Nutter, McClennen & Fish, 1970-74, Rackemann, Sawyer & Brewster, Boston, 1974-75; pvt. practice, Boston, 1975-78, assoc. regional counsel real estate ops. Prudential Ins. Co. Am., Boston, 1978-85; counsel Karger & Arnowitz, Boston, 1985—; mem. Esplanada Citizens Adv. Com., Met. Dist. Commn. Bd. dirs., chmn. edn. and enrollment coms. Govt. Ctr. Childcare Corp.; trustee Hist. Neighborhood Found.; mem. auction com. Big Sisters. Mem. Mus. Fine Arts, Condominium Assn., Beacon Hill Civic Assn., The Children's Mus., Opera Assn., Inst. Contemporary Art, Mus. Modern Art, New Eng. Women in Real Estate, Urban Land Inst., ABA, Mass. Bar Assn., Boston Bar Assn. (daycare com., condo com. corp. lawyers com.), Mass. Conveyancers Assn. (legis. subcom. on timeshare), Mass. Assn. Women Lawyers (scholarship found.), Women's Bar Assn., LWV, Friends Pub. Garden. Office: Karger & Arnowitz 18 Tremont St Boston MA 02108

KRULFELD, RUTH MARILYN, anthropologist, educator; b. N.Y.C., Apr. 15, 1931; d. Leon and Frances (Rosenberg) Pulwers; m. Jacob Mendel Krulfeld, Aug. 28, 1964; 1 child, Michael David. B.A. cum laude, Brandeis U., 1956; Ph.D., Yale U., 1974. Field researcher micro-geographic research farms in Singapore, Malaya, 1951-53; anthropol. research in Jamaica, 1957, Costa Rica, Nicaraugua, Panama, 1958, Lombok, Indonesia, 1960-62; asst. prof. anthropology, dir. grad. students George Washington U., Washington, 1964-72, assoc. prof., 1973-76, prof., 1976—, chmn. dept. anthropology, 1984-87, founder, dir. spl. grad. program in 3d world devel. Contbr. articles to profl. jours. Currier scholar Yale U., 1958; grantee Found. for Study of Man, 1957; Ford fellow, 1960-62; grantee Am. Council Learned Socs. and Social Sci. Research Council, 1963. Mem. Anthrop. Soc. Washington, Am. Anthrop. Assn. Jewish. Home: 4012 N Woodstock St Arlington VA 22207 Office: George Washington U Dept Anthropology Washington DC 20052

KRUPINSKY, JACQUELYN STOWELL, publisher; b. Springfield, Vt., July 2, 1932; d. Lewis Henry and Ethel Nellie (Warren) Stowell; m. Marvin Joseph Krupinsky, June 15, 1954; children: Lisa Ann, Steven Scott. BA, U. Vt., 1954. Library asst. Hallowell-Farmingdale (Maine) Sch. Dist., 1980-84; publisher Woodbury Press, Litchfield, Maine, 1984—. Author: Look Out for Loons, 1983, Henry the Hesitant Heron, 1987. Mem. Soc. of Children's Book Writers, Maine Writers and Publishers Alliance, Maine Media Women. Home amd Office: Box 700 RFD 1 Whippoorwill Rd Litchfield ME 04350

KRUPNIK, VEE M., business executive; b. Chgo.; d. Phillip and Jane (Glickman) K.; m. Melvin Drury, Sept. 24, 1978. B.S., Northwestern U., C.P.A., real estate broker, ins. broker, Ill. Assoc. dir. corp. fin. Weis, Voisin, Cannon, Chgo., 1967-68; pres. PEC Industries Inc., Ft. Lauderdale, Fla., 1969-71; acct., real estate and ins. broker Vee M. Krupnik & Co., Chgo., 1971-73; sales cons. Baird & Warner Inc., Chgo., 1973-81, asst. v.p. comml.-investment div., 1981-85, v.p. corp. group, 1985—. Mem. Internat. Assn. Fin. Planning (bd. dirs. 1985-87), Internat. Council Shopping Ctrs., Nat. Assn. Corp. Real Estate Execs., Nat. Assn. Securities Dealers, Women's Exec. Network, Nat. Assn. Realtors (bd. dirs. 1983-84, comml. investment council), Cert. Comml. Investment Mems. (pres. Ill. chpt. 1983-84), Ill. Assn. Realtors (bd. dirs. 1983-84), Chgo. Bd. Realtors (bd. dirs. 1982-85), Chgo. Assn. Commerce and Industry, Comml. Investment Multiple Listing Service (pres. 1982-84), Comml. Real Estate Orgn., Network of Women Entrepreneurs, Chgo. Real Estate Exec. Women. Home: 5757 N Sheridan Rd Chicago IL 60660 Office: Baird & Warner Inc 200 W Madison St #2500 Chicago IL 60606

KRUPP, BARBARA D., artist; b. Elyria, Ohio, July 1, 1942; d. Edward G. and Wilma Mary Nuhn; m. James L. Krupp, July 27, 1942; children: Rory, Rolf, Rachelle, Rodney. X-ray technician Elyria Meml. Hosp., 1969-74; ptnr. The Rockport (Miss.) Collection, 1983—. Represented in numerous pub. and pvt. collections including the Musee des Duncan, Paris, France, Art Expo, N.Y. and Art Expo Cal in Los Angeles; represented in permanent collection at Barbara Krupp Gallery, Rockport, Mass. Recipient Bronze medal, Salon d'Aout. Mem. Rockport Art Assn., Pitts. Watercolor Soc., Ky. Watercolor Soc. Ohio Watercolor Soc., Baycrafters, Midwest Watercolor Soc., Canton Art Inst., ga. Watercolor Soc., Massillon Mus. Ohio. Roman Catholic. Home and Office: Rural Rt 2 PO Box 277 Wakeman OH 44889

KRUPP, JUDY-ARIN, educational consultant; b. New London, Conn., Feb. 4, 1937; d. Harold and Minnie (Watchinsky) Peck; m. Alan Frederick Krupp, June 15, 1958; children: Peter, Larry, Susan, Karen. BA, Conn. Coll., 1958; MS in Edn., Queens Coll., 1960; PhD, U. Conn., 1980. Tchr. gen. sci. Westbury (N.Y.) Pub. Schs., 1958-60; tchr. biology Roslyn (N.Y.) Pub. Schs., 1960-61; cons. edn. U.S., Can., Norway, Fed. Republic of Germany, 1980—. Author: Adult Development: Implications for Staff Development, 1980, The Adult Learner, A Unique Entity, 1982, When Parents Face the Schools, 1984; contbr. over 30 articles to profl. jours. and chpts. to books. Trustee Home Care/Lutz Jr. Ms., Manchester, Conn., 1970-76; pres. Hosp. Aux., Manchester, 1976; vol. Conn. Arthritis Assn., Newington, 1980—, Ohio Arthritis Assn., Columbus, 1980. Recipient appreciation award Conn. Arthritis Assn., 1985; NSF grantee, 1959. Mem. Am. Assn. for Counseling and Devel., Am. Assn. for Adult and Continuing Edn., Am. Psychol. Assn., Assn. for Supervision and Curriculum Devel., N.Am. Assn. for Counsel and Supervision (rep. adult devel. and aging com. 1985-87), Nat. Staff Devel. Council (trustee 1987—), Conn. Orgn. for Profl. Devel. (pres. 1984-85, Outstanding Leadership award 1984), Phi Delta Kappa, Phi Kappa Phi, Pi Lambda Theta. Home and Office: 40 McDivitt Dr Manchester CT 06040

KRUPSAK, MARY ANNE, lawyer; b. Schenectady, Mar. 26, 1932; d. Ambrose Michael and Mamie (Wytrwal) K.; B.A. in History, U. Rochester, 1953; M.S. in Pub. Communications, Boston U., 1954; JD U. Chgo., 1962; LLD (hon.), 1975; H.H.D. (hon.), Russell Sage Coll., 1973; Litt.D. (hon.), Clarkson Coll., 1975; L.H.D., Mt. Mary Coll., 1977, Alliance Coll., 1977, Keka Coll., 1977; m. Edwin Margolis, June 30, 1969. Program assoc. Gov. Averell Harriman, 1954-58; adminstrv. asst. to Congressman Samuel Stratton, 1958-59; admitted to N.Y. State bar, 1963; pvt. practice; asst. counsel Office of Temp. Pres., N.Y. State Senate; mem. staff Speaker N.Y. Assembly, until 1968; mem. N.Y. State Assembly, 1968-72, N.Y. Senate, 1972-74; lt. gov. N.Y., 1975-79; pvt. practice law, 1979—; bd. dirs. Coleco Industries, Hartford, Conn., Air Ky., Valyte Internat. Ltd. Co-chairperson N.Y. del. Democratic Nat. Conv., 1972. Mem. N.Y. State, Montgomery County bar assns., AAUW, Bus. and Profl. Women, Women's Polit. Caucus, NOW, Nat. Council Women U.S., Kosciusko Found., Assn. Bar City N.Y., Rosary Soc. Roman Catholic. Office: Botein Hays & Sklar The Albany Bldg 146 State Street Albany NY 12207

KRUSE, CHRISTINE G., nurse, poet; b. Denver, May 21, 1952; d. Dean Elwood and Charlotte Grace (Lake) Oglevie; children: Pamela Rouchelle, Gregory Peter. RN, BSN, Olivet Nazarene Coll., 1974. RN, Mo. Charge nurse Trinity Luth. Hosp., Kansas City, Mo., 1974-75, staff nurse surgery, 1975-77; nursing audit coordinator Bethany Med. Ctr., Kansas City, Kans., 1977-79, spl. projects asst., 1978-80, adminstrv. coordinator, 1980-83, PRN, primary nurse, 1984-86; relief charge Valley Hosp. Med. Ctr., Spokane, Wash., 1986-88; patient care coordinator Hospice of N. Idaho, Coeur d'Alene, 1988—; audit cons. Olathe Community Hosp. (Kans.), 1979. Author: Patient-Centered Audit, 1984. Pres., Dist. 512 Kans. Parents Assn. for Hearing-Impaired Children, Shawnee Mission, 1983-84, 79-80; exec. Parent Adv. Council to Sch. Bd., Shawnee Mission, 1983-84. Mem. Mid Am. Romance Authors, Romance Writers Am. Democrat. Home: W 6927 Prairie Post Falls ID 83854

KU, CECILIA CHOU YUAN, analytical chemist, researcher; b. Peking, China, Jan. 9, 1942; came to U.S., 1966; naturalized, 1974; d. Hsiao-Hsing and Chin-Chung (Shih) Yuan; m. James Chen Ku, June 3, 1967; children—Grace, Philip. B.S., Nat. Taiwan Normal U., Taiwan, 1966; M.S., Carnegie-Mellon U., 1968. Cert. tchr., Pa. Chemist U. Pitts., 1969-71, Research Triangle Inst., N.C., 1974-75; chemist, scientist Carnegie-Mellon U., Pitts., 1971-73; analytical chemist, quality control chemist, US Dept. Labor Occupational Safety and Health Adminstrn., Salt Lake City, 1976—, cons., 1982—. Mem. Am. Indsl. Hygiene Assn. Mem. Evangelical Free Ch. Avocations: computers; statistical process control; cooking; piano. Office: US Dept Labor Occupational Safety & Health Adminstrn 1781 S 300 W PO Box 15200 Salt Lake City UT 84115

KUBISTAL, PATRICIA BERNICE, secondary school principal; b. Chgo., Jan. 19, 1938; d. Edward John and Bernice Mildred (Lenz) Kubistal. AB cum laude, Loyola U., Chgo., 1959, AM, 1964, AM, 1965, PhD, 1968; postgrad. Chgo. State Coll., 1962, Ill. Inst. Tech., 1963, State U. Iowa, 1963, Nat. Coll. Edn., 1974-75. With Chgo. Bd. Edn., 1959—, tchr., 1959-63, counselor, 1963-65, adminstrv. intern, 1965-66, asst. to dist. supt., 1968-69, prin. spl. edn. sch., 1969-75, prin. Simpson Sch., 1975-76, Brentano Sch., 1975-87, Roosevelt H.S., 1987; supr. Lake View Evening Sch., 1982—; lectr. Loyola U. Sch. Edn., Nat. Coll. Edn. Grad. Sch., Mundelein Coll.; coordinator Upper Bound Program of U. Ill. Circle Campus, 1966-68. Book rev. editor of Chgo. Prins. Jour., 1970-76, gen. editor, 1982—. Active Crusade of Mercy; mem. com. Ill. Constnl. Conv., 1967-69; mem. Citizens Sch. Com., 1969-71; mem. edn. com. Field Mus., 1971; ednl. advisor North Side Chgo. PTA Region, 1975; gov. Loyola U., 1961-87. Recipient Outstanding Intern award Nat. Assn. Secondary Sch. Prins., 1966, Outstanding Prin. award Citizen's Shc. Com. of Chgo., 1986; named Outstanding History Tchr., Chgo. Pub. Schs., 1963, Outstanding Ill. Educator, 1970, one of Outstanding Women of Ill., 1970, St. Luke's-Logan Sq. Community Person of Yr., 1977; NDEA grantee, 1963, NSF grantee, 1965, HEW Region 5 grantee for drug edn., 1974, Chgo. Bd. Edn. Prins.' grantee for study robotics in elem. schs.; U. Chgo. adminstrv. fellow, 1984. Mem. Ill. Personnel and Guidance Assn., NEA, Ill. Edn. Assn., Chgo. Edn. Assn., Am. Acad. Polit. and Social Sci., Chgo. Prins. Club (pres. aux.), Nat. Council Adminstrv. Women, Chgo. Council Exceptional Children, Chgo. Council Fgn. Relations, Chgo. Urban League, Loyal Christian Benevolent Assn., Kappa Gamma Pi, Pi Gamma Mu, Phi Delta Kappa, Delta Kappa Gamma (parliamentarian 1979-80, Lambda state editor 1982—, mem. internat. communications com.), Delta Sigma Rho, Phi Sigma Tau. Home: 5111 N Oakley Ave Chicago IL 60625 Office: Brentano Sch 2723 N Fairfield Chicago IL 60647

KUBLER-ROSS, ELISABETH, physician; b. Zurich, Switzerland, July 8, 1926; came to U.S., 1958, naturalized, 1961; d. Ernst and Emma (Villiger) K.; children: Kenneth Lawrence, Barbara Lee. M.D., U. Zurich, 1957; D.Sc. (hon.), Albany (N.Y.) Med. Coll., 1974, Smith Coll., 1975, Molloy Coll., Rockville Centre, N.Y., 1976, Regis Coll., Weston, Mass., 1977, Fairleigh Dickinson U., 1979; LL.D., U. Notre Dame, 1974, Hamline U., 1975; hon. degree, Med. Coll. Pa., 1975, Anna Maria Coll., Paxton, Mass., 1978; Litt. D. (hon.), St. Mary's Coll., Notre Dame, Ind., 1975, Hood Coll., 1976; L.H.D. (hon.), Amherst Coll., 1975, Loyola U., Chgo., 1975, Bard Coll., Annandale-on-Hudson, N.Y., 1977, Union Coll., Schenectady, 1978, D'Youville Coll., Buffalo, 1979, U. Miami, Fla., 1976; D.Pedagogy, Keuka Coll., Keuka Park, N.Y., 1976; Litt.D. (hon.), Rosary Coll., River Forest, Ill., 1976. Rotating intern Community Hosp., Glen Cove, N.Y., 1958-59; research fellow Manhattan State Hosp., 1959-62; resident Montefiore Hosp., N.Y.C., 1961-62; fellow psychiatry Psychopathic Hosp., U. Colo. Med. Sch., 1962-63; instr. psychiatry Colo. Gen. Hosp., U. Colo. Med. Sch., 1962-65; mem. staff LaRabida Children's Hosp. and Research Ctr., Chgo., 1965-70; chief cons. and research liaison sect. LaRabida Children's Hosp. and Research Ctr., 1969-70; asst. prof. psychiatry Billings Hosp., U. Chgo., 1965-70; med. dir. Family Service and Mental Health Ctr. S. Cook County, Chicago Heights, Ill., 1970-73; pres. Ross Med. Assos. (S.C.), Flossmoor, Ill., 1973-77; pres., chmn. bd. Shanti Nilaya Growth and Health Ctr., Escondido, Calif., 1977—; mem. numerous adv., cons. bds. in field. Author: On Death and Dying, 1969, Questions and Answers on Death and Dying, 1974, Death-The Final Stages of Growth, 1975, To Live Until We Say Goodbye, 1978, Working It Through, 1981, Living With Death and Dying, 1981, Remember The Secret, 1981, On Children and Death, 1985, AIDS: The Ultimate Challenge, 1988; contbr. chpts. to books, articles to profl. jours. Recipient Teilhard prize Teilhard Found., 1981; Golden Plate award Am. Acad. Achievement, 1980; Modern Samaritan award Elk Grove Village, Ill., 1976; named Woman of the Decade Ladies Home Jour., 1979; numerous others. Mem. AAAS, Am. Holistic Med. Assn. (a founder), Am. Med. Women's Assn., Am. Psychiat. Assn., Am. Psychosomatic Soc., Assn. Cancer Victims and Friends, Ill. Psychiat. Soc., Soc. Swiss Physicians, Soc. Psychophysiol. Research, Second Attempt at Living. *

KUBRICKY, JOAN MONAHAN, financial executive; b. Hudson Falls, N.Y., Apr. 13, 1938; d. Leo F. and Loretta (Reardon) Monahan; m. L. H. Kubricky, May 24, 1958 (div. Dec. 1981); children: John, Thomas, Joanne; m. John C. Mannix, June 6, 1982; stepchildren: John, Elizabeth, Margaret, Patricia, Mark. AA, Adirondack Community Coll., 1970; BS, Skidmore Coll., 1988. Pres. Ridge Enterprises, Inc., Glens Falls, N.Y., 1971-75, 84—; treas. Duke Concrete Products, Inc., Glens Falls, N.Y., 1975-79, pres., chief exec. officer, 1980-82; treas. John Kubricky & Sons, Inc., Glens Falls, N.Y., 1975-79; pres., chief exec. officer Kubricky Constrn. Corp., Glens Falls, N.Y., 1980-83; bd. dirs. Evergreen Bancorp, Glens Falls, 1st Nat. Bank, Glens Falls, bd. dirs. Tri-County United Way, Inc., Glens Falls, 1983—; trustee St. Michael's Coll., Winooski, Vt., 1983—. The Hyde Collection, Glens Falls, 1987—. Mem. Internat. Assn. Fin. Planners, Pvt. Industry Council (bd. dirs. local chpt. 1979-83, vice chmn. Warren, Washington and Saratoga counties chpt. 1983-87), Glens Falls Bd. Realtors, nat. Assn. for Female Execs., Adirondack Regional C. of C. (bd. dirs., sec. 1981-84), LWV (bd. dirs. 1977-80), Every Woman's Council, Women in Network. Democrat. Roman Catholic. Home and Office: Ridge Rd Star Rt Glens Falls NY 12801

KUBY, BARBARA ELEANOR, personnel executive, management consultant; b. Medford, Mass., Sept. 1, 1944; d. Robert William and Eleanor (Frasca) Asdell; m. Thomas Kuby, July 12, 1969. BS in Edn./ Psychology, Kent State U., 1966, MEd, 1987. Tchr. Nordonia/Euclid (Ohio) Pub. Schs., 1966-76; mgr. tng. and devel. United Bldg. Facilities, Manama, Bahrain, 1979-81, Norton Co., Akron, Ohio, 1981-85; v.p. Kuby and Assocs. Inc., Chagrin Falls, Ohio, 1973—; corp. dir. human resource devel. and systems TransOhio Savs. Bank, Cleve., 1985-88; v.p. human resources Leasing Dynamics, Inc., Cleve., 1988—; adj. faculty, cons. Buffalo State U., 1972—, Lake Erie Coll., Cleve., 1985—; lectr., cons. Cleve. State U., 1978—, Inst. for Fin., Chgo., 1986—; program dir. Ctr. Profl. Adv., East Brunswick, N.J., 1978—. cons., lectr. Girls Scouts Am., Cleve., 1981—; cons. Vocat. Info. Program, Cleve., 1970-85, trustee; Colleague of Creative Edn. Found. Mem. Am. Mgmt. Assn., Am. Soc. for Tng. and Devel., Orgnl. Devel. Network, Gestalt Inst. of Cleve., Greenpeace. Club: City (Cleve.). Home: 7236 Chagrin Rd Chagrin Falls OH 44022

KUCHARCHUK, SHERRY ANNE, corporate professional; b. Toronto, Ont., Can., Nov. 20, 1954; d. Stephen and Anne (Bodnar) Zahumeny; m. Kenneth William Kucharchuk. BSc with honors, U.Toronto, 1977. Coordinator traffic Gabriel Can., Toronto, Ont., 1977-78, co-ordinator advt. and sales promotion, 1978-81; office mgr. Mattel Electonics, Toronto, Ont., 1981-84; adminstr. sales planning Campbell Soup Co. Ltd., Toronto, Ont., 1985-86, analyst corp. devel., 1986-87; product mgr. Morris Nat. Inc., Toronto, Ont., 1987—. Roman Catholic. Office: Morris Nat Inc, 1795 Meyerside Dr #9, Mississauga Can L5T 1E3

KUCHENBECKER, RUTH HELEN, constrn., carpet co. exec.; b. Neenah, Wis., Mar. 4, 1937; d. August Herman and Rose E. (Buss) Peapenburg; student public schs., Neenah; m. Alfred Paul Kuchenbecker, Nov. 16, 1957; children—Ann Marie, Mary Kay, Amy Lynn. Sec., bookkeeper Wis. Paper Group, Menasha, 1955-65, Towne, Inc., Mech. Contractors, Appleton, Wis., 1967-69; partner, sec.-treas. Kuchenbecker Builders, Neenah, 1968—; sec.-treas. Wholesale Builders Supply, Inc., 1970—; owner, pres. Kuchenbecker Carpets Inc., Neenah, 1975—; partner D&K Leasing, Neenah, 1979—, Kuchenbecker Custom Woodworking, 1981—. Mem. Nat. Right to Work Com. Mem. Nat. Assn. Women in Constrn. (past pres., bd. dirs. Fox Valley chpt.), Nat. Assn. Home Builders Women's Aux. Republican. Lutheran. Office: 1573 N Deerwood Neenah WI 54956

KUCHNIR, FRANCA TAGLIABUE, physicist, educator; b. Russe, Bulgaria, July 18, 1935; came to U.S., 1960, naturalized, 1973; d. Luigi and Matilde (Perez) Tagliabue; B.S., U. San Paulo, 1958; M.S., U. Ill., 1962, Ph.D., 1965; m. Moyses Kuchnir, Aug. 6, 1960; children—Louis, Deborah. Research asst. U. Ill., 1960-66, asst. prof. 1969-70; fellow nuclear physics Argonne Nat. Lab., 1966-68, asst. physicist, 1970-71; fellow med. physics U Chgo., 1971-73, asst. prof., 1973-74, assoc. prof., 1974—, dir. med. physics, 1980-84. Mem. Am. Phys. Soc., Am. Assn. Physicists in Medicine, Radiol. Soc. North Am. Contbr. articles in field to profl. jours. Office: 5841 S Maryland Ave Chicago IL 60637

KUCK, MARIE ELIZABETH BUKOVSKY, retired pharmacist; b. Milw., Aug. 3, 1910; d. Frank Joseph and Marie (Nozina) Bukovsky; Ph.C., U. Ill., 1933; m. John A. Kuck, Sept. 20, 1945 (div. Nov. 1954). Pharmacist, tchr. Am. Hosp., Chgo., 1936-38, St. Joseph Hosp., Chgo., 1938-40, Ill. Masonic Hosp., Chgo., 1940-45; chief pharmacist St. Vincent Hosp., Los Angeles, 1946-48, St. Joseph Hosp., Santa Fe, 1949-51; dir. pharm. services St. Luke's Hosp., San Francisco, 1951-76; pharmacist Mission Neighborhood Health Center, San Francisco, 1968-72; mem. peer rev. com. Drug Utilization Com., Blue Shield Calif. and Pharm. Soc. San Francisco. Recipient Bowl of Hygeia award Calif. Pharm. Assn., 1966. Mem. No., Calif. (legis. chmn. aux. 1967-69, chmn. fund raising luncheon 1953-71, pres. San Francisco aux. 1974), Nat., Am., No. Calif. (pres. 1955-56, pres. San Francisco aux. 1965-66, editor ofcl. publ. 1967-70), San Francisco (sec. 1977-79, treas. 1979-80, pres. 1982-83; Pharmacist of Yr. award 1978) pharm. socs., Am. Pharm. Assn. (pres. No. Calif. br. 1956-57, nat. sec. women's aux. 1970-72, hon. pres. aux. 1975—), Calif. Council Hosp. Pharmacists (organizer 1962, sec.-treas. 1962-66), Am. Soc. Hosp. Pharmacists, Assn. Western Hosps. (gen. chmn. hosp. pharmacy sect. conv. San Francisco 1958), Internat. Pharmacy Congress (U.S. del. Brussels 1958, Copenhagen 1960), Fedn. Internationale Pharmaceutique, Lambda Kappa Sigma. Home: 2261 33d Ave San Francisco CA 94116

KUCZAK, SOPHIE MARIE, small business owner; b. Wroclaw, Poland, Aug. 18, 1952; came to U.S., 1960; d. Walter and Janina (Pudlo) K. AA, Wright Coll., 1972; student, U. Ill., Chgo., 1972-73. Lab. and radiocardiogram technician N.W. Hosp., Chgo., 1970-73; owner, mgr. Kuczak Sausage Shoppe, Inc., Chgo., 1973—. Mem. Internat. Deli and Cheese Assn., Nat. Assn. for Female Execs., Nat. Assn. Women Bus. Owners, Roundtable for Women, Polish-Am. Congress (Ill. chpt.), Young Polish Women's Alliance (gen. mem.), Norwood Park C. of C. (bd. dirs. 1986). Republican. Roman Catholic.

KUDER, ALICE ANN, religious organization administrator; b. Chehalis, Washington, Dec. 13, 1957; d. Alphonse John and Mary Margaret (Sterns) K. AA, Centralia Community Coll., 1978; BA, Western Wash. U., 1980. Youth minister St. Nicholas Cath. Ch., Gig Harbor, Wash., 1980-84; dir. youth services Bergamo Conf. and Renewal Ctr., Dayton, Ohio, 1984—; cons. Archdiocese of Seattle, 1980-84, Archdiocese of Cin., 1984—. Author: Friends Forever, 1987. Big Sister United Way, Dayton, Ohio, 1985-86; mem. Pax Christi USA, Washington, 1982—, Bread for the World, Washington, 1979—; advocate Rape Relief, Tacoma, 1982-83. Mem. Nat. Assn. Female Execs. Democrat. Roman Catholic. Office: Bergamo Ctr 4400 Shakertown Rd Dayton OH 45430

KUDLA, RUTH MAY, non-profit organization administrator; b. Livonia, Mich., May 13, 1928; d. Earl James and Nellie MaryEllen (Williams) Frantz; m. George Martin Kudla, Feb. 15, 1947; children: Cheryl, George Jr., Vickie, Nancy, John. From bookkeeper to v.p. Rolison pro Hardware, Inc., Brighton, Mich., 1973—; spl. clk. Livingston County Health Dept., Howell, Mich., 1973—. Pres. Livingston County div. Am. Heart Assn., 1977—, mem. state food festival com., 1987. Roman Catholic. Lodge: Elks. Home: 2630 Bowen Howell MI 48843 Office: Am Heart Assn Mich Livingston County Div 204 S Highlander Way Howell MI 48843

KUEHL, NANCY LOUISE, shorthand agency executive; b. Lufkin, Tex., May 22, 1947; d. Vance DeVille Ethridge and Sally Viola (Scale) Loggins; m. Jack B. Ely, Mar. 13, 1966 (div. 1967); 1 child, Robert Sterling; m. William Albert Kuehl Jr., Sept. 23, 1972; children: Kristofer Jason, Kerry Elissa. BA, Stephen F. Austin State U., 1981. Paralegal asst. Harvill & Hardy, Houston, 1976-77; litigation supr. Fenley & Bate, Lufkin, 1976-77; legal asst. Forrest G. Braselton, Nacogdoches, Tex., 1977-78; owner, prin. Letter-Perfect, Nacogdoches, 1980-85, Kuehl Reporting Service Inc., Bryan, Tex., 1987—; ct. reporter Hill & Mace, Nacogdoches, 1982-87. Author: How to Set Up a Successful Typing Service, 1982, The Glass Staircase, 1982, A Seale Anthology, Vols. 1 and 2, 1985. Mem. Nat. Assn. Legal Secs., Tex. Assn. Legal Secs., Houston Assn. Legal Secs., Nat. Shorthand Reporters Assn., Tex. Shorthand Reporters Assn., Nacogdoches Writer's Group, Phi Alpha Theta, Pi Sigma Alpha, Sigma Tau Delta. Democrat. Mem. Christian Church (Disciples of Christ). Office: Kuehl Reporting Service PO Box 4165 Bryan TX 77805-4165

KUEHNE, MARGARET ANN, federal agency administrator; b. Balt., Nov. 12, 1939; d. Milton Woodrow and Marie Anna (Vain) Wilson; divorced; 1 child, Brian Scott Jeznach; m. Charles David Kuehne, Apr. 12, 1975; 1 child, Cheryl Anne. Grad. high sch., Dundalk, Md., 1957. Sec. Social Security Adminstrn. div. Dept. Health, Edn. and Welfare, Balt., 1957-58, asst. budget and reports, 1958-69; computer operator Woodlawn, Md., 1969-81, supervisory computer operator, instr. computer, 1981-82; mgr. computer operators Social Security Adminstrn. div. Dept. Health and Human Services (formerly Dept. Health, Edn. and Welfare), Woodlawn, Md., 1982-85, specialist network control, 1985—. V.p. Episc. Women's Council, Sykesville, Md., 1987; pres. Episcopal Ch. Women, Sykesville, Md., 1988; mem. Alter Guild, St. Barnabas, Sykesville, Md. Mem. Esa Alpha Tau (v.p. Balt. chpt. 1970-71, pres. 1971-72). Democrat. Home: 7313 Brown St Sykesville MD 21784

KUEVER, NANCY JEANNE, photographic finishing company executive; b. Cleve., Feb. 23, 1947; d. John Francis and Antoinette Marie (Nurre) Egan; m. Richard Philip Chepey, Dec. 30, 1967 (div. Feb. 1974); m. Gary William Kuever, Dec. 13, 1981. Student, John Carroll U., Cleve., 1966-67; BA cum laude, Ursuline Coll. for Women, 1968; postgrad., St. Louis U., 1969-71; student in theol., Ch. of Scientology, Clearwater, Fla., 1978-80. Cert. secondary tchr.; ordained to ministry, 1976. Secondary sch. tchr. Augustinian Acad. for Boys, St. Louis, 1968-69, Lindbergh Sr. High Sch., St. Louis, 1969-75; dir. mktg. Rainbo Color Inc., St. Louis, 1981-86, pres., 1986—. Mem. Photo Mktg. Assn., St. Louis Regional Commerce and Growth Assn., St. Louis C. of C. Office: Rainbo Color Inc 1401 S Boyle Saint Louis MO 63110

KUHAR, JUNE CAROLYNN, retired fiberglass manufacturing company executive; b. Chgo., Sept. 20, 1935; d. Kurt Ludwig and Dorothy Julia (Lewand) Stier; m. G. James Kuhar, Feb. 5, 1953; children: Kathleen Lee, Debra Suzanne. Student William Rainey Harper Coll., Chgo. Engaged in fiberglass mfg., 1970—; sec.-treas. Q-R Fiber Glass Industries Inc., Elgin, 1970—. Mem. Multiple Sclerosis Soc., Nat. Fedn. Ileitis and Colitis, Bus. and Profl. Women N.W., Bus. and Profl. Woman's Club (pres. 1984—), Women in the Arts (charter). Home: 2303 Meadow Dr Rolling Meadows IL 60008

KUHL, ALINE, small business owner; b. Cin., Aug. 16, 1961; d. Donald Kuhl and Marcy (Martin) Cavanaugh; m. Robert Harold Craig, June 2, 1984. Clk. New World Foodshop, Cin., 1977-80, mgr., 1980-86; owner, mgr. Clifton Natural Food Store, Cin., 1986—. Office: Clifton Natural Food Store 207 W McMillan Cincinnati OH 45219

KUHL, KATHY, data processing consultant; b. Olney, Ill., Oct. 26, 1956. BS, Eastern Ill. U., 1977. Programmer, analyst John Alden Ins. Co., Coral Gables, Fla., 1979-80, Group Health Inc., 1980, Western Ill. U., Macomb, 1980-85; data processing cons., Ft. Pierce, Fla., 1985—. Programmer, analyst St. Lucie County Sch. Bd., 1986—. Mem. Nat. Assn. Female Execs.

KUHL, MARGARET HELEN CLAYTON (MRS. ALEXIUS M. KUHL), banker; b. Louisville, 1908; d. Joseph Leonard and Maude (Mitzler) Clayton; student Loyola U. Home Study Div., Chgo., 1955—, Buena Vista Coll., Storm Lake, Iowa, summer 1964-65, 66; m. Alexius M. Kuhl, Apr. 21, 1936; children—Carol Lynn Ford Wassmuth, James Michael (adopted). Sales lady, buyer Silverberg, Akron, Iowa, 1924-34; owner dress shop, Fonda, Iowa, 1934-40; librarian, Fonda, 1940-43; bookkeeper, teller First Nat. Bank,

Fonda, 1943-44; tchr. speech and drama, librarian asst. Our Lady Good Counsel Sch., Fonda, 1963-69; pres., chmn. bd. Pomeroy State Bank, 1975-83, also dir. Recipient Adult Leadership award Catholic Youth Orgn., 1967, Pro Deo Juventute award, 1969. Mem. Cath. Daus. Am. (dist. dep. 1964-70, state chmn. ecumenism 1970-72, state treas. 1970-72), Diocesan Council Cath. Women (chmn. orgn. and devel. 1964-65), Nat. Council Cath. Women (diocesan pres. 1968-70, diocesan sec. 1966-67; chmn. Women in Community Service Sioux City Diocesan Bd. 1971-72), Women in Community Service (pres. Iowa bd. 1972-73), Legion of Mary (pres. curia 1964-66, 67-70). Clubs: Sun City (Ariz.) Country, Lakes; Fonda Golf. Home: 4th and Queen Sts Fonda IA 50540

KUHLER, DEBORAH G., state legislator; b. Moorhead, Minn., Oct. 12, 1952; d. Robert Edgar and Beverly Maxine (Buechler) Ecker; m. George Henry Kuhler, Dec. 28, 1973; children: Karen Elizabeth, Ellen Christine. BA, Dakota Wesleyan U., 1974; MA, U. N.D., 1977. Outpatient therapist Ctr. for Human Devel., Grand Forks, N.D., 1975-77; mental health counselor Community Counseling Services, Huron, S.D., 1978-88; owner, dir. community edn. Kuhler Funeral Home, Huron, 1978—; adj. prof. Huron Coll., 1979-83; mem. from dist. 23 S.D. Ho. Reps., Pierre, 1987—, mem. House Edn. com., House Health and Welfare com. and Joint Interim Judiciary com. Active Beadle County Rep. Women, 1st United Meth. Ch. Mem. Am. Mental Health Counselors Assn., Am. Assn. Counseling and Devel., AAUW (Achivement in Politics award 1987), Huron Area C. of C., Phi Kappa Phi, Beta Sigma Phi. Home: 1360 Dakota Ave S Huron SD 57350

KUHLMAN, JOSIE-LEE, social work administrator; b. Malakoff, Tex., Aug. 23, 1917; d. Marvin Ernest and Dora Elizabeth (Andress) Humphrey; m. Harold Herman Kuhlman, Aug. 8, 1938; 1 child, Janice Elizabeth. AB, U. Redlands, 1943; MA, Am. Bapt. Sem., 1944, postgrad., 1977-79; postgrad., Hartford Sem., 1945-46; MSW, U. Denver, 1958; postgrad., NYU, 1961-65. Cert. profl. fund raiser, cert. community coll. instr. (life), Calif.; ordained to ministry Bapt. Ch. Missionary Am. Bapt. Ch., Roxas City, Philippines, 1946-51; exec. dir. Girl Scouts U.S., Benton Harbor, Mich., 1958-61; dir. orgn. commn. Office Mayor of N.Y.C., 1961-65; exec. dir. Camp Fire Girls, San Francisco, 1967-72; program mgr. Childrens Home Soc., Sacramento, 1979-85; exec. dir. Chrysalis Ho., Fresno, Calif., 1985—. Co-chmn. Mayors Status of Women com., San Francisco, 1969-73, forum coordinator, 1973; candidate for mayor City of San Francisco, 1975; mem. mayors community devel. com., San Francisco, 1975-79. Recipient Women Helping Women award Soroptimists, San Francisco, 1979. Mem. Am. Bapt. Ministers Council, Calif. Assn. Adoption Agys. (chmn. no. sect. 1984-86, pres. 1986—), Pvt. Adoption Agy. Coalition, Reach, State and Nat. Rehab. Assn. (pres. 1977-78), Caledonians Clan Donald Scottish. Republicans. Lodges: Zonta (pres. San Francisco chpt. 1972-73, area dir. 1973-74, v.p. Fresno chpt. 1986-87, pres. 1987—). Home and Office: Chrysalis House Inc 2134 W Alluvial Fresno CA 93711

KUHLMANN, HELEN JUANITA, counselor; b. Vicksburg, Miss., July 22, 1926; d. Clarence Baron and Mary Anne (Cunningham) Huff; m. Arthur Henry Kuhlmann, Oct. 11, 1945 (div. Dec. 1973); children: Jeffrey David, Lynn Carol, Jack D'Owen, Casey Richard, Susan Anne, Barbee, Kris. Student La. State U., 1942-44. Owner, mgr. h.k. farm, Leoti, Kans., 1973-76; outpatient dir. Baton Rouge Chem. Dependency Unit, 1977-81; inpatient dir. Cyprus Hosp. alcohol program, Lafayette, La., 1981; pres., counselor Recovery Resources, Baton Rouge, 1981-83; owner, counselor The Recovery Group, Baton Rouge, 1983—; cons. The Turning Point, Baton Rouge, 1985-87, Love Life Workshops, Baton Rouge, 1985—; lectr. Baton Rouge Chem. Dependency unit, 1983-85. Chmn. bd. dirs. Chem. Dependency Funding Found., 1985-87. Mem. La. Assn. Substance Abuse Counselors (mem. oral testing bd.), Nat. Assn. Alcoholism, and Drug Abuse Counselors. Republican. Mem. Unity Ch. Avocations: yoga, stitchery. Office: Recovery Group 9040 Florida Blvd Baton Rouge LA 70815

KUHLMANN, ROBERTA LYND, educator; b. Denver, June 23, 1935; d. Warren Clyde Waters and Ina Blanche (Buffington) Lindsey; m. Roger Carl Kuhlmann, Aug. 30, 1968 (dec. Nov. 1970); 1 child, Carlynd Kay. AA, Los Angeles City Coll., 1959; BA, Calif. State U., Los Angeles, 1961; MBA, Calif. State U., Fullerton, 1969; PhD, Claremont Grad. Sch., 1983. Office clk. Pub. Service Co. of Colo., Denver, 1953-57, Kafton Sales Co., Los Angeles, 1957-62; tchr. Nogales High Sch., LaPuente, Calif., 1962-64; prof. Chaffey Coll., Alta Loma, Calif., 1964—. Republican. Home: 7862 Alta Cuesta Cucamonga CA 91730 Office: Chaffey Coll 5885 Haven Ave Alta Loma CA 91701

KUHN, ANNE NAOMI WICKER (MRS. HAROLD B. KUHN), educator; b. Lynchburg, Va.; d. George Barney and Annie (Hicks) Wicker; m. Harold B. Kuhn. Diploma Malone Coll., 1933, Trinity Coll. Music, London, 1937; A.B., John Fletcher Coll., 1939; M.A., Boston U., 1942, postgrad., 1965-70; postgrad. (fellow) Harvard U., 1942-44, 66-68; hon. grad. Asbury Coll., 1978. Instr., Emmanuel Bible Coll., Birkenhead, Eng., 1936-37; asst. in history John Fletcher Coll., University Park, Iowa, 1938-39; librarian Harvard U., 1939-44; tchr. adult edn. program U.S. Armed Forces, Fuerstenfeldbruck Air Base, Germany, 1951-52; prof. Union Bibl. Sem., Yeotmal, India, 1957-58; lectr. Armenian Bible Inst., Beirut, Lebanon, 1958; prof. German, Asbury Coll., Wilmore, Ky., 1962—, co-dir. coll. study tour to E. Ger. and W. Ger., 1976, 77, 78, co-dir. acad. tours, 1979, 80; dir. acad. tour, Russia, 1981, 85, Scandanavia, 1982, Indonesia, Singapore, 1983, Hong Kong and Thailand, 1983, 85, E.Ger., W.Ger., France and Austria, 1983, Russia and Finland, 1984, 85, Peoples Republic China, 1984, 85, Estonia, Latvia, 1985, Portugal, Spain, France, Ireland, Scotland, Norway, England, 1987; tchr. Seoul Theol. Sem., fall 1978. Author: (pamphlet) The Impact of the Transition to Modern Education Upon Religious Education, 1950; The Influence of Paul Gerhardt upon Wesleyan Hymnody, 1960, Light to Dispel Fear, 1987; transl. German ch. records, poems, letters; contbr. articles to profl. jours. Del. Youth for Christ World Conf., 1948, 50, London Yearly Meeting of Friends, Edinburgh, Scotland, 1948, World Council Chs., Amsterdam, 1948, World Friends Conf., Oxford, Eng., 1952, World Methodist Conf., Oslo, Norway, 1961, Deutscher Kirchentag, Dortmund, Germany, 1963, German Lang. Congress, Bonn, W. Ger., 1974, Internat. Conf. Religion, Amsterdam, Netherlands, Poland, West Berlin, Fed. Republic Germany, 1986, Internat. Missionary Conf., Eng., 1987, Congress on the Bible II, Washington, 1987; participant Internat. Congress World Evangelization, Lausanne, Switzerland, 1974; del., speaker Internat. Conf. on Holocaust and Genocide, Oxford and London, 1988; mem. acad. tour Poland, 1988. Recipient German Consular award, Boston, 1965, Thomas Mann award Boston U., 1967; named Ky. Col., 1978. Fellow Goethe-Institut für Germanisten, Munich, 1966-68, 70-71. Mem. AAUW, Am. Assn. Tchrs. German, NEA, Ky. Ednl. Assn., Lincoln Lit. Soc., Protestant Women of Chapel, Delta Phi Alpha (award 1963, 65). Quaker. Club: Harvard Faculty. Home: 406 Kenyon Ave Wilmore KY 40390

KUHN, KATHLEEN JO, accountant; b. Springfield, Ill., Aug. 9, 1947; d. Henry Elmer and Norma Florene (Niehaus) Burge; m. Gerald L. Kuhn, June 22, 1968; children: Gerald Lynn, Brett Anthony. BS in Bus., Bradley U., 1969. CPA, Ill. Controller Byerly Music Co., Peoria, Ill., 1969-70; staff acct. Clifton Gunderson & Co., Columbus, Ind., 1970-71; acct. Dept. of Transp., State of Ill., Springfield, 1972-76; acct. Gerald L. Kuhn & Assocs., Springfield, 1976-78, ptnr., 1979—. Writer, editor co. policy guideline, 1979-80. Recipient Attendance award Continuing Profl. Edn. for Accts., 1977-79, 82-88. Mem. Am. Inst. CPAs, Ill. Soc. CPAs, Am. Woman's Soc. CPAs. Lutheran. Clubs: Olympic Swim, Metro. Federated Jr. Women's. Home: 2511 Westchester St Springfield IL 62704 Office: 323 S Grand Ave W Springfield IL 62704

KUHN, LUCILLE ROSS, retired naval officer; b. Washington, July 19, 1927; d. Lilburn Joseph and Flora Lee (Perry) K.; A.A. with distinction, George Washington U., 1959, B.A., 1960. Ins. clk. Southwestern Life Ins. Co., Richmond, Va., 1945-48; joined U.S. Navy, 1949, advanced through grades to capt., 1975; woman officer rep. 2d Navy Recruiting Area, Washington, 1963-65; U.S. Naval Security Group, Washington, 1965-68; dir. mil. personnel 12th Naval Dist., San Francisco, 1968-70; mem. staff Office Asst. Sec. Def. for Legis. Affairs, Washington, 1971-74; dir. Officer Candidate Sch., Newport, 1975-77; dir. pay/personnel adminstrv. support system Bur. Naval Personnel, Washington, 1977-79; comdg. officer Recruit Tng. Command, Orlando, Fla., 1979-81; dep. comdr. Navy Recruiting Command, Washington, 1981-84. Aide de camp to Va. govs., 1960—. Decorated Legion of Merit with gold star, Meritorious Service medal with gold star, Nat. Def. Service medal with bronze star. Mem. Am. Sailing Assn., Naval Hist. Found., Naval Inst., Psi Chi. Home: 2302 Kenmore Rd Richmond VA 23228

KUHN, MARGARET (MAGGIE), organization executive; b. Buffalo, 1905; d. Samuel Frederick and Minnie Louise (Kooman) K. B.A., Case-Western Res. U., 1926. Formerly with YWCA, Cleve., Phila.; Gen. Alliance Unitarian Women, Boston; later with United Presbn. Ch. U.S.A., N.Y.C.; editor, writer for ch. mag. Social Progress; alt. observer for Presbyns. at UN; ret. 1970; a founder Gray Panthers, Phila., 1971; now nat. convener; cons. nat. task force on women United Presbyn. Ch., past 3d v.p. health, edn. and welfare assn.; lectr.; mem. nat. adv. bd. Hospice, Inc.; adv. TV series Over Easy; former mem. Fed. Jud. Nominating Com. Pa. Author: Get Out There and Do Something about Injustice, 1972, Maggie Kuhn on Aging, 1977. Recipient 1st ann. award for justice and human devel. Witherspoon Soc., 1974, Disting. Service award in consumer advocacy Am. Speech and Hearing Assn., 1975, Freedom award Women's Scholarship Assn. Roosevelt U., 1976, ann. award Phila. Soc. Clin. Psychologists, 1976, Peaceseeker award United Presbyn. Peace Fellowship, 1977, Humanist of Yr. award Am. Humanist Assn., 1978. Office: Gray Panthers 3635 Chestnut St Philadelphia PA 19104 *

KUHN, NANCY JANE, educator; b. Gettysburg, Pa., Feb. 27, 1946; d. Charles Elbert and Marie Jane (Sterner) K.; m. John P. Richards, Jan. 23, 1982. BA, Roanoke Coll., 1968; MEd, U. Va., 1970. Asst. admissions dir. Roanoke Coll., Salem, Va., 1968-69, Chatham Coll., Pitts., 1970-72; assoc. prof. Community Coll. of Allegheny County, Pitts., 1972-80; sr. trainer Washington Hosp. Ctr., 1980-83; mgmt. tng. coordinator Equibank, Pitts., 1983-84; supr. ednl. devel. Alcoa Labs., Pitts., 1984-87, mgr. edn. and tng., 1987—. Bd. dirs. Hope Ctr., New Kensington, Pa., 1986—, U. Pitts. Mgmt. Program for Execs., 1987—. Gov.'s fellow, 1969-70. Mem. Am. Soc Tng. and Devel. (nat. research com. 1985—), Am. Soc. Engring. Edn., Pa. Fedn. of Tchrs. (exec. bd. 1979-80), Coalition of Labor Union Women (exec. bd. 1979-80). Democrat. Office: Alcoa Labs Alcoa Center PA 15069

KUHN, SARAH, educator, consultant; b. Boston, June 24, 1952; d. Thomas Samuel and Kathryn (Louise) Muhs K.; m. Ralph Edward LaChance, 1987. BA, Harvard U., 1974; PhD, MIT, 1987. Project mgr. Stone Ctr. Wellesley (Mass.) Coll., 1987—; pvt. practice cons., researcher Cambridge, 1984—; instr., researcher MIT, 1980-83; economist, Econ. Lit. Project, Boston, 1979—; mem. High Tech Research Group, Cambridge, 1981—. Author: Computer Manufacturing in New England, 1982, (with others) The Retail Revolution, 1981, Massachusetts High Tech: The Promise and the Reality, 1984. Fellow Harvard-MIT Joint Ctr. Urban Studies, 1982-83; Eastern Women's Rowing Champion, Nat. Women's Rowing Assn., 1974. Mem. Assn. Computing Machinery, Am. Planning Assn. Jewish. Home: 340 Winter St Framingham MA 01701 Office: Wellesley Coll Stone Ctr Wellesley MA 02181

KUHNERT, HELEN LAVON, nurse clinical specialist; b. Wichita Falls, Tex., Sept. 25, 1940; d. Cecil Vaughn and Helen Maurine (Castlebury) Graves; m. Robert Waldon Harmon, June 9, 1962 (div. Feb. 1975); children—Alison, Amy, Laurie, Warren; m. 2d, Robert Morris Kuhnert, July 23, 1976. Diploma in nursing, Meml. Hosp. Sch. Nursing, Houston, 1961; B.S.N., Tex. Women's U., 1974. R.N., Tex. Asst. head nurse Meml. Bapt. Hosp., Houston, 1961-62; staff nurse Highland Gen. Hosp., Pampa, Tex., 1964-69, Presbyn. Hosp., Dallas, 1969-70, 74-75; supr. stresslab Cardiology Assocs., Dallas, 1975-77; research nurse U. Tex. Health Sci. Ctr. at Dallas, 1977-79, clin. specialist, 1979-88; clin. research assoc. E.R. Squibb & Sons, Dallas, 1988—; mem. task force Am. Heart Assn., Dallas, 1977-82, hypertension screening capt., 1978-80. Contbr. articles to med. jours. Mem. Sanctuary Choir, Richardson Heights Baptist Ch. (Tex.), 1979—; mem. Richardson High Sch. Band Club. Mem. Am. Nurses Assn., Tex. Nurses Assn., Nat. Assn. Research Nurses and Dietitians, Assoc. of Clin. Pharmacology, Sigma Theta Tau. Republican. Club: Theta Moms (Richardson). Home and Office: 7131 Townbluff Dallas TX 75248

KUHR, ERNESTINE MICHELLE, mechanical engineer; b. Elkins Park, Pa., Apr. 25, 1959; d. Manuel Irwin and Lois Jean (Grass) K.; m. Donald Ray Anthony, Aug. 29, 1982. BS, Carnegie Mellon U., 1980. Registered profl. engr., N.C., S.C. Asst. engr. Babcock and Wilcox Co., Lynchburg, Va., 1981-82; nuclear prodn. engr. Duke Power Co., Charlotte, N.C., 1982—. Guide Pioneer Girls, Charlotte, N.C., 1984-86; tchr. Calvary Ch. Sunday Sch., Charlotte, 1987-88; vol. Am. Red Cross, 1988. Mem. Am. Soc. Mech. Engrs., Soc. Women Engrs., Profl. Engrs. of N.C., Tau Beta Pi, Pi Tau Sigma. Democrat. Home: 9814 McClendon Ct Matthews NC 28105 Office: Duke Power Co PO Box 33189 Charlotte NC 28242

KUHRT, SHARON LEE, nursing administrator; b. Denver, July 20, 1957; d. John Wilfred and Yoshiko (Ueda) K. BS in Nursing, Loretto Heights Coll., 1982. RN, Colo., Hawaii; cert. sch. nurse, Colo. RN level III Porter Meml. Hosp., Denver, 1981-87; asst. nursing supr. Kapiolani Med. Ctr. for Women & Children, Honolulu, 1987—. Mem. Am. Assn. Critical Care Nurses. Home: 1541 Dominis St #1806 Honolulu HI 96822

KUIK, LAUREN, software vendor company executive; b. Trenton, N.J., Jan. 4, 1947; d. Willard Leslie and M. Evelyn (Mabey) Culver; m. Joseph Paul Kuik, Nov. 29, 1969; children—Jennifer Evelyn, Leslie Rebecca. Assoc. Liberal Arts, Trenton Jr. Coll., 1966. Sec., bookkeeper Kuik Hauling, Titusville, N.J., 1974—; with Applied Data Research, Inc., Princeton, N.J., 1983—, mgr. order and revenue processing, 1986-87, mgr. adminstrv. support and services ADR Internat., 1987—. Pres., Welcome Wagon of Hopewell, N.J., 1979. Mem. Internat. Tng. in Communication Council (pres. Council I, Colonial Region 1984), Nat. Assn. Female Execs. Lutheran. Office: Applied Data Research Inc Route 206 and Orchard Rd CN-8 Princeton NJ 08540

KUKEC, ANNA MARIE, journalist; b. Chgo., Feb. 3, 1958; d. Ernest P. and Angeline Kukec. AA with honors, Moraine Valley Community Coll., Palos Hills, Ill., 1978; BA in Mass Communications and Journalism, St. Xavier Coll., Chgo., 1983. Columnist, editor TV/radio Pulitzer Community Newspapers, Chgo., 1977—; guest lectr. on radio and cable TV various schs.; judge TV contest Chgo. Internat. Film Festival, 1982-83. Vol. telethon March of Dimes, Chgo., 1983, judge AIR awards, 1987; vol. Muscular Dystrophy Assn., 1985-87; mem. college board Mademoiselle mag., 1979. Winner Nat. Piano Playing Auditions, Nat. Guild Piano Tchrs., 1968-78; recipient Paderewski Meml. award, 1978; named Woman of Yr., Village of Evergreen Park and Evergreen Park High Sch., 1985. Mem. Women in Communications, Nat. Fedn. Press Women, Ill. Women's Press Assn., Chgo. Headline Club (bd. dirs.), Suburban Press Club (various awards), Sigma Delta Chi. Office: Daily Southtown Economist 5959 S Harlem Ave Chicago IL 60638

KUKLINSKI, JOAN LINDSEY, librarian; b. Lynn, Mass., Nov. 28, 1950; d. Richard Jay and M. Claire (Murphy) Card; B.A. cum laude, Mass. State Coll., Salem, 1972; M.L.S., U. R.I., 1976; m. Walter S. Kuklinski, June 17, 1972. Classified librarian U. R.I. Extension Div. Library, Providence, 1974-75, U. R.I. Cataloging Dept., Kingston, 1975-79; original cataloger Tex. A&M U. Library, College Station, 1979-82; cataloger Goldfarb Library, Brandeis U., Waltham, Mass., 1982-83; automation coordinator, 1983-85; network coordinator Minuteman Library Network, Framingham, Mass., 1985—. Mem. Town of South Kingstown (R.I.) Women's Adv. Commn., 1977-79. Mem. ALA (resources and tech. services div. 1980—), Library Info. Tech. Assn., Am. Contract Bridge League, Delta Tau Kappa. Office: Minuteman Library Network 49 Lexington St Framingham MA 01701

KULL, BARBARA ANNE, small business owner; b. Cin., Sept. 11, 1946; d. Robert David and Naomi (Hail) Reese; m. Tony M. Horn, June 27, 1964 (div. Mar. 1976); children: Lauren, Scott, Jodi. Student, U. Cin., 1976-80. Sec. JMG Film Co., Cin., 1964-75; with real estate sales Signature Realtors, Cin., 1975-77; legal clk. Office of Hearings and Appeals, Cin., 1976-80; wholesale distbr. Barb's Aviary Supply, Marco, Fla., 1982—. Mem. Marco C. of C., Nat. Assn. Female Execs. Republican. Mem. Dutch Reformed Ch.

KULP, NANCY JANE, comedienne; b. Harrisburg, Pa., Aug. 28, 1921; d. Robert Tilden and Marjorie (Snyder) K.; m. Charles Malcolm Dacus, Apr. 1, 1951. B.A. in Journalism, Fla. State U., 1943; postgrad., U. Miami, 1950. Publicity dir. radio sta. WGBS, 1946-47; continuity dir. radio sta. WIOD, Miami, 1947-49; continuity dir.-performer TV Sta. WTVJ, Miami, 1949-50; prof. TV and motion picture history Juniata Coll., Huntingdon, Pa., 1985, artist in residence, 1985. Began acting career in Hollywood, Calif., 1952; motion pictures include Model and the Marriage Broker, 1952, Star is Born, 1953, Sabrina, 1954, Three Faces of Eve, 1955, The Parent Trap, 1957, A Wilder Summer, 1983; appeared on: TV shows Playhouse 90, 1956, Lux Video, 1955, Lucy Show, 1956, Bob Cummings Show, 1955-60, Beverly Hillbillies, 1961-71, Brian Keith Show, 1973, Sanford and Son, Return of the Beverly Hillbillies, 1981, Scarecrow and Mrs King, 1986, Simon and Simon, 1986; star play: Busbody (Nominated for Emmy award 1967); Broadway play Mornings at Seven, 1982; play Accent on Youth, Long Wharf Theatre, 1983, appeared in Romeo and Juliet, Ga. Shakespeare Festival, 1987, also London retrospective Showboat, Carnegie Hall. Hon. chmn. Humane Soc., 1965—; co-chmn. Roosevelt Coachella Valley March of Dimes, Valley March of Dimes; Dem. candidate for Congress, 9th dist. Pa., 1984. Served to lt. (j.g.) WAVES, USNR, 1943-45. Mem. Acad. Motion Pictures Arts and Scis., Actors and Others for Animals, LWV, Pi Beta Phi. Democrat. Club: Greyhound of Am. (Darien, Conn.).

KUMIN, LIBBY BARBARA, speech pathologist, college administrator; b. Bklyn., Nov. 11, 1945; d. Herbert H. and Berniece (Shuch) K.; m. Martin J. Lazar, Jan. 18, 1969; 1 child, Jonathan Kumin. B.A. summa cum laude, LIU, 1965; M.A., NYU, 1966, Ph.D., 1969. Lic. speech pathologist, Md. Asst. prof. speech pathology U. Md., College Park, 1972-76; cons., 1976-80; adj. prof. Loyola Coll., Balt., 1976-80, assoc. prof., 1980-88, chmn. dept. speech, 1983—, prof., 1988—, dir. Speech and Lang. Ctr. Mem. Speech/Lang./Hearing Commn., Howard County Bd. Edn., Columbia, Md., 1982—; specialist in speech and language in Down Syndrome. Author: Aphasia, 1978; author articles on Down Syndrome, others. Vol. cons. Howard County Office on Aging, 1977-83. Recipient Outstanding Individual of Year award Howard County Assn. Retarded Citizens, Nat. Meritorious Service award Nat. Down Syndrome Congress, 1987. Aaron and Lillie Straus Found. grantee, 1983—; Columbia Found. grantee; recipient summer research award Loyola Coll., 1983. Mem. Am. Speech/Lang./Hearing Assn. (cert.), Md. Speech and Hearing Assn., Nat. Down Syndrome Congress, ARC, Sigma Tau Delta, Pi Lambda Theta. Office: Loyola Coll Dept Speech Pathology 4501 N Charles St Baltimore MD 21210

KUMIN, MAXINE WINOKUR, author, poet; b. Phila., June 6, 1925; d. Peter and Doll (Simon) Winokur; m. Victor Montwid Kumin, June 29, 1946; children—Jane Simon, Judith Montwid, Daniel David. A.B., Radcliffe Coll., 1946, M.A., 1948. Free-lance writer 1953—; Cons. in poetry Library of Congress, 1981-82. Author: poems Halfway, 1961, The Privilege, 1965; novel Through Dooms of Love, 1965, The Passions of Uxport, 1968; poems The Nightmare Factory, 1970; novel The Abduction, 1971; poems Up Country, 1972 (Pulitzer prize for poetry 1973); novel The Designated Heir, 1974; poems House, Bridge, Fountain, Gate, 1975, The Retrieval System, 1978, Our Ground Time Here Will Be Brief, 1982, The Long Approach, 1985, In Deep: Country Essays, 1987; essays To Make A Prairie, 1979; short stories Why Can't We Live Together Like Civilized Human Beings?, 1982; author 20 children's books; contbr. poems to nat. mags. Recipient Am. Acad. and Inst. Arts and Letters award, 1980, Levinson award Poetry Mag., 1987; Woodrow Wilson vis. fellow, 1979-80; Acad. Am. Poets fellow, 1985. Mem. Poetry Soc. Am., PEN Am., Authors Guild. Address: Curtis Brown Assoc 10 Astor Place New York NY 10003-6903

KUMM, DORIS JEAN, state legislator; b. Watertown, S.D., Oct. 27, 1929; d. Earl Edward Lebert and Minnie Augusta (Schwanke) Lebert Richardson; grad. Cosmetology Sch., Watertown, S.D.; m. Vincent Jerald Kumm, May 29, 1949; children—Deborah, Kelly, Roxanne, Marty, Todd, Kathy. Mem. S.D. Ho. of Reps., 1978—, mem. agr. and natural resources, transp. and bonding coms. Mem. S.D. Rep. Com., del. state conv., 1978; del. Rep. Nat. Conv., 1980, 1988—; mem. exec. com. Codington County (S.D.) Rep. Com. Mem. BPW, Women In Mgmt., Roundtable Extension, Rep. Women, Nat. Order Women Legislators (regional dir.). Lodge: Kiwanis. Home: 521 6th St SE Watertown SD 57201 Office: State Capitol Pierre SD 57501

KUMM, LYNN A., medical executive manager; b. Niagara Falls, N.Y., Oct. 17, 1957; d. Kenneth Fredrick and Roberta Lynn (LaCoure) K. Student, Niagara U., N.Y., 1979—. Med. exec. mgr. Edwin W. Gates, M.D., Niagara Falls, N.Y., 1976-87. Deacon Riverside Presby. Ch., Niagara Falls, N.Y., 1986-87. Recipietn Cert. of Achievement, Am. Diabetes Assoc., 1970. Mem. Am. Bus. Women's Assoc. (sec.), Am. Artists Orgn., Am. Forestry Assoc. Republican. Episcopalian. Club: Women of the Woods (Niagara Falls). Home: 230 N. Water St. Lewiston NY 14092 Office: Edwin W Gates MD 621 Tenth St Niagara Falls NY 14302

KUMMER, RUTH MARY ANN, therapist; b. Wyandotte, Mich., July 27, 1930; d. Archibald Jacob and Anna Lucille (Copp) Lambrix; m. Joseph Talbot Kummer, May 17, 1974; children: Frederic Joseph, Mariane, David T., Joseph T. B.S., Siena Heights Coll., 1960, M.A., 1969; student (NFS grantee) Wayne State U., 1965, postgrad in substance abuse. Tchr., Roman Catholic Diocese Chgo., 1948-52, Toledo, 1953-59, Detroit, 1959-67, tchr. jr. high sch. Diocese Lansing, Mich., 1967-68; prin. elem. sch. Archdiocese Detroit, Chelsea, Mich., 1968-69, dir. religious edn., 1970-74; clinic supr. edn. Breast Cancer Detection Ctr., U. Mich., Ann Arbor, 1975-79; chaplain, coordinator lay ministers St. Joseph Hosp., Ann Arbor, 1980-84; pres. Roman Cath. Dominican Laity, Chgo., 1980-84, presentor Buffalo, 1983, del. Bologna, Italy, 1983; counselor Adult Edn., Ypsilanti Publ. Schs., 1986—. Contbr. articles to profl. jours. Vol., Meals on Wheels, Ann Arbor, 1979. Mem. Chi Sigma Iota. Home: 3904 Golfside Rd Ypsilanti MI 48197

KUMRO, SUSAN DOROTHY, protective services offical; b. Buffalo, Feb. 13, 1957; d. Ronald Clarence and Suzanne (Wild) K. AS in Secretarial Sci., Alfred (N.Y.) State Coll., 1977. Sec. Conn. Dept. Transp., Hartford, 1977-80; state trooper Conn. State Police Dept., Colchester, 1980-85; resident trooper Town of Colchester Conn. State Police Dept., 1985-86; instr. Conn. State Police Acad., Meriden, 1986—; instr. Mcpl. Police Acad., Meriden, 1982—. Vol. dir. security and communications Conn. Spl. Olympics, Milfred, 1986—. Mem. Internat. Assn. Women Police, Conn. Assn. Women Police (v.p. 1984-86), New London County Detectives. Methodist.

KUNDERT, ALICE E., school system administrator; b. Java, S.D., July 23, 1920; d. Otto J. and Maria (Rieger) K. Elem. tchr.'s cert., No. State Coll., Aberdeen, S.D., state tchr. cert. Tchr. elem. grades 1939-43, 48-54; clk., mgr., buyer Gates Dept. Store, Beverly Hills, Calif., Clifton Dress Shop, Hollywood, Calif., 1943-48; dep. supt. schs. Campbell County, S.D., 1954; county cts. clk. 1955-60, register deeds, 1955-69; town treas. Mound City, 1965-69; auditor State of S.D., Pierre, 1969-79; sec. of state 1980-87; coordinator sch. programs of S.D. Edn. and Cultural Affairs dept. Bicentennial U.S. Constn. and State Centennial, 1987—. Leader 4-H Club, 1949-53, county project leader in citizenship, 1963-64; sec. Greater Campbell County Assn., 1955-57; organizer, leader Mound City Craft and Recreation Club, 1955-60; chmn. Heart Fund, March Dimes, Red Cross, Mental Health drs.; mem. S.D. Gov.'s Study Commn., 1968—; mem. state and local adv. com. region VIII Office Econ. Opportunity; bd. mem., chmn. Black Hills Recreation Lab., 1956-61; exec. sec. Internat. Leaders Lab., Ireland, 1963; Polit. co. vice chmn. Rep. Com., 1964-69, sec-treas. fin. chmn., 1968; mem. State Rep. Adv. Com., 1966-68; state and nat. counselor Teen Age Rep. Club Campbell County, 1964—. Named Outstanding Teenage Rep. adv. in nation, 1970, 71, 76; Recipient Disting. Alumni award No. State Coll., 1975. Home: 407 N Van Buren St Pierre SD 57501 Office: Office Sec of State State Capitol Bldg Pierre SD 57501

KUNIN, MADELEINE MAY, governor; b. Zurich, Switzerland, Sept. 28, 1933; came to U.S., 1940, naturalized, 1947; d. Ferdinand and Renee (Bloch) May; m. Arthur S. Kunin, June 21, 1959; children—Julia, Peter, Adam, Daniel. B.A., U. Mass., 1956; M.S., Columbia U., 1957; M.A., U. Vt., 1967; several hon. degrees. Newspaper reporter Burlington Free Press, Vt., 1957-

58; guide Brussels World's Fair, Belgium, 1958, TV asst. [illegible] WCAX-TV, Burlington, 1960-61; freelance writer, instr. English Trinity Coll., Burlington, 1969-70; mem. Vt. Ho. of Reps., 1973-78; lt. gov. State of Vt., Montpelier, 1979-82, gov., 1985-87, reelected gov., 1986—; fellow Inst. Politics, Kennedy Sch. Govt., Harvard U., 1983; lectr. Middlebury Coll., St. Michael's Coll., 1984; mem. Vt. Commn. on Adminstrn. of Justice, 1976-77, Vt. Joint Fiscal Com., 1977-78; mem. exec. com. Nat. Conf. Lt. Govs., 1979-80. Author: (with Marilyn Stout) The Big Green Book, 1976; contbr. articles to profl. jours., mags. and newspapers. Mem. exec. com. Dem. Policy Council. Named Outstanding State Legislator, Eagleton Inst. Politics, Rutgers U., 1975. Mem. Nat. Gov.'s Assn. (mem. exec. com.), New England Gov.'s Conf. (chairperson). Democrat. Address: Office of the Gov Pavilion Bldg 5th Floor Montpelier VT 05602

KUNKEL, BARBARA, psychotherapist, consultant; b. Garfield, N.J., Mar. 17, 1945; d. Everett Edward and Florence Hilda (Davidsen) K.; m. Jack E. Decker, Nov. 23, 1966 (div. Nov. 1981); children: Tasha Jade, Lara Ashley. BA in Psychology and Pre-Theology, Elmira Coll., N.Y., 1966; MA in Human Devel., Fairleigh Dickinson U., 1983; postgrad. Union Grad. Sch. Income maintenance supr. Sussex County Welfare, Newton, N.J., 1975-79; dept. supr. Colonial Penn Ins. Co., Phila., 1979-81; administrv. mgr. Velo-Bind, Inc., Mt. Laurel, N.J., 1982-83; mgmt., human relations cons. pvt. practice, N.J. and Maine, 1983—; clk. Supreme Jud. and Superior Cts., York County, Maine, 1985-88; cons. Ctr. for Addictive Behaviors, Inc., Salem, Mass., 1988—; treas., psychotherapist Circle Counseling Assocs., Waltham, Mass., 1988—; mem. faculty Nasson Coll., Springvale, Maine, 1986—. Artist stained glass windows. Teaching fellow Fairleigh Dickinson U., 1983-84. Mem. Mensa. Libertarian. Zen Buddhist. Avocations: canoeing, photography, furniture restoration. Home: PO Box 10 Alfred ME 04002 Office: Circle Counseling Assocs 24 Crescent St Waltham MA 02154

KUNKEL, GEORGIE MYRTIA, retired school counselor; b. Seattle; d. George Riley and Myrtia (McLaughlin) Bright; m. Norman C. Kunkel, June 25, 1946; children—N. Joseph D.C., Stephen Gregory, Susan Ann, Kimberly Jane. B.A. in Edn., Western Wash. U., 1945; M.Ednl. Psychology, U. Wash., 1968. Typist, clk. FHA, Seattle, 1940; tchr. pub. schs. Vadar, Centralia, Wash., Seattle, 1941-67; pvt. cons., Seattle, 1970-85; counselor Highline Pub. Schs., Seattle, 1967-82; sch. counselor rep. State of Art Conf., Balt., 1980; cons. Project Equality, Highline Sch. Dist., Seattle, 1975-76. Editor Women and Girls in Edn., 1972-75. Contbr. articles to profl. jours. Organizer Women and Girls in Edn., Wash. state, 1971; pres. Wash. State NOW, 1973; mem. West Seattle Community Council, 1980. Grantee Women Adminstrs. Wash. State, 1971, Edn. Service Dist., Seattle, 1980. Mem. NEA (sec. pub. relations), Am. Assn. Counseling and Devel. (pres. state br. 1982-83), Am. Sch. Counseling Assn. (pres. state div. 1980-81), Seattle Assn. Counseling and Devel. (organizer), Holmes Harbor Homeowners Assn. (organizer and pres.). Democrat. Unitarian Universalist. Club: Past Presidents (Seattle). Avocations: writing; singing. Home and Office: 3409 SW Trenton St Seattle WA 98126

KUNKLE, SANDRA LEE, brokerage house executive; b. Park Ridge, Ill., June 20, 1960; d. Arland Blaine Kunkle and Judith (Spyrison) Carpenter. BS in Fin., U. Ky., 1982. Cert. fin. planner. Acct. exec. Paine Webber and Co., Chgo., 1982-84; v.p., mut. fund coordinator Bear Stearns and Co., Chgo., 1984—; instr. "Successful Investing" Chgo. Bar Assn., 1985 . Contbr. articles to women's mags., 1985. Mgr. campaign Rep. com., Chgo., 1985-87. Mem. Am. Horse Show Assn. (Chgo. and Ky. chpts.). Home: 145 W Burton Pl Chicago IL 60610 Office: Bear Stearns and Co Inc Three First National Plaza Chicago IL 60602

KUNNANZ, LYNN FRANCES, retail executive; b. Springfield, Mo., Dec. 29, 1961; d. Arthur R. Kunnanz and Emma Jo (Gottbreht) Sugar. Student, Moorhead (Minn.) State U., 1980-81; BA in Mktg. and Mgmt., Minot (N.D.) State U., 1984. Mktg. intern Town and Country Ctr., Minot, 1984; Asst. dept. mgr. May D&F, Denver, 1984-85, dept. mgr., 1985—; free-lance mktg. cons. Denver, 1985—. Vol. Big Sisters Colo., Denver, 1987—. Mem. Nat. Assn. Female Execs., Nat. Fedn. Bus. and Profl. Women. Roman Catholic. Office: May D&F 2700 S Colo Blvd Denver CO 80222

KUNSTADTER, GERALDINE S., foundation executive; b. Boston, Jan. 6, 1928; d. Harry Herman and Nettie Sapolsky; m. John W. Kunstadter, Apr. 23, 1949; children—John W., Lisa, Christopher, Elizabeth. Student MIT, 1945-48. Draftsman, U. Chgo. Cyclotron Project, 1948; engring. asst. Gen. Electric Corp., Lynn, Mass., 1948-49; chmn., dir. A. Kunstadter Family Found., N.Y.C., 1966—; host family program dir. N.Y.C. Commn. for UN, 1971-86; pres. Nat. Inst. Social Scis., 1979-81. Bd. dirs. Ptnrs. of Ams. Found., Washington, Menninger Clin., Topeka, Yale-China Assn., Inst. Current World Affairs, English-Speaking Union, Eliot Feld Ballet, N.Y.C., Ctr. U.S.-China Arts Exchange, N.Y. Regional Assn. Grantmakers, East Side Internat. Community Ctr., Am. Forum; mem. resource council Partners of Ams., Washington, mem. nat. com. U.S.-China relations; mem. Peace Links Leadership Network, Nat. Council of Women (internat. hospitality com.), Overseas Devel. Council, N.Y.-Beijing Friendship City Com.; past mem. coms. MIT; trustee, chmn. bd. Windham Coll., Putney, Vt. Recipient Windham award, 1970, silver medal Nat. Inst. Social Sci., 1981. Club: Am. Women's, Hurlingham, Lansdowne (London).

KUNTZ, MARION LUCILE LEATHERS, classics historian, educator; b. Atlanta, Sept. 6, 1924; d. Otto Asa and Lucile (Parks) Leathers; m. Paul G. Kuntz, Nov. 26, 1970; children by previous marriage: Charles, Otto Alan (Daniels). BA, Agnes Scott Coll., 1945; MA, Emory U., 1964, PhD, 1969. Lectr. Latin Lovett Sch., Atlanta, 1963-66; mem. faculty Ga. State U., 1966—, assoc. prof., 1969-73, prof. Latin and Greek, 1973—, Regents' Prof., 1975, chmn. dept. fgn. langs., 1975-84, research prof., 1984—, Fuller E. Callaway disting. prof., 1985—. Author: Colloquium of the Seven About Secrets of the Sublime of Jean Bodin, 1975, Guillaume Postel, Prophet of the Restitution of All Things: His Life and Thought, 1981, Jacob's Ladder and the Tree of Life: Concepts of Hierarchy and the Great Chain of Being, 1986, Postello, Venezia e Il Suo Mondo, 1987; also scholarly articles; mem. editorial bd. Library of Renaissance Humanism. Named Latin Tchr. of Year State Ga., 1965; Semple scholar, 1965; Am. Classical League scholar, 1966; Am. Council Learned Socs. grantee, 1970, 73, 76, 81, 87; recipient medal for excellence in Renaissance studies, City of Tours, France. Mem. Am. Philol. Assn., Renaissance Soc. Am., Am. Soc. Aesthetics, Am. Cath. Philos. Assn., Soc. Philosophy and Religion, Am. Soc. Ch. History, Am. Histo. Assn., Internat. Soc. Neo-Platonic Studies, Internat. Soc. Neo-Latin Studies, Soc. Christian Philosophers (mem. exec. bd. 1987—), Société des Seiziémistes, Medieval Acad., Soc. Medieval and Renaissance Philosophy, Soc. di Philosophique Medievale, Archaeol. Inst. Am., Classical Assn. Midwest and South (Semple award 1965), Am. Acad. Rome (sec.-treas. 1970-74), Italian Cultural Soc., Nat. Trust Hist. Preservation, DeKalb Hist. Soc. (v.p. 1977-80), Hellenic Study Club (pres. Atlanta 1974), Atlanta Preservation Soc., Ga. Trust for Hist. Preservation, World Monuments Fund, Phi Beta Kappa, Phi Kappa Phi, Omicron Delta Kappa. Roman Catholic. Home: Villa Veneziana 1655 Ponce de Leon Ave Atlanta GA 30307

KUNTZ, MARY M. KOHLS, corporate treasurer; b. Chgo., Nov. 25, 1928; d. George William and Myrtle Hansen K.; m. Earl Jeremy Kuntz, July 28, 1957; children: Karen A., Bradford G. Student, Northwestern U., 1946-50. Pvt. practice acctg. Chgo., 1951-63; owner Chgo. Tax Service, 1954-63; controller Gen. Bus. Services, Chgo., 1960-68; v.p., treas. Gen. Tele-Communications, Inc., Chgo., 1968—. Leader Girl Scouts Am., 1968-71; pres. Wilmette (Ill.) PTA, 1971-75. Mem. Assn. Telemessaging Services Internat., Nat. Soc. Pub. Accts., Chgo. Soc. Clubs. Clubs: Women's Club of Wilmette (bd. dirs. 1975). Office: Gen Tele-Communications Inc 69 W Washington St Chicago IL 60602

KUO, LOUISE RAMONA, management consultant, real estate investor; b. N.Y.C., May 28, 1963; d. Larry Han-Ching and Lilian Li-Cheng (Chou) K. BA in Internat. Relations and French, MA in Internat. Policy Studies, Stanford U., 1985. Cons. Bain and Co., San Francisco, 1986—; gen. ptnr. Vision Investments, San Francisco, 1987—. Scholar Thomas J. Watson Meml. Found.-IBM, 1981-85, Peter N. Teige Meml. Found.-World Affairs Council, 1985. Mem. Phi Beta Kappa, Pi Sigma Alpha. Democrat. Office: Bain & Co One Embarcadero Ctr #3400 San Francisco CA 94111

[illegible] ESSEE SOLOMON, event producer; b. Chgo., Dec. 7; d. Joseph David and Doris (Schoke) Solomon; [illegible] 1937; m. Irv Kupcinet, Feb. 12, 1939; children—Karyn (dec.), Jerry S. Asst. to dir. psychology dept. Michael Reese Hosp., Chgo., 1939-41; exec. producer eight Jefferson Award Shows; producer 1st Literary Arts Ball, Cultural Center, Chgo., 1979; talent coordinator Kup's Show, Chgo., 1964-84; producer for spl. events, 1978—. Mem. adv. bd., bd. dirs. Free St. Theater; prodn. chmn. Acad. Honors, 1984-87; chmn. bd. trustees Acad. Sch. Performing Arts, 1984-86, hon. lifetime chair, 1986—; prodn. chmn. Variety Club Telethon, 1984, 85; bd. dirs. Mus. Broadcasting Commn.; exec. com. Chgo. Tourism Council, 1984—; exec. bd. Internat. Theatre Festival, 1985-86; mem. sponsors com. Chgo. Pub. Library, 1985-86. Decorated Knight of Orange Nassau (Netherlands); recipient Spl. award Jefferson Com., 1976; Cliff Dwellers award, 1975; Emmy award CBS, 1977, 79; Artisan award Acad. Theatre Arts and Friends, 1977; Prime Minister's medal for service to Israel, 1974; Woman of Yr. award Facets Multimedia, 1982, Mass Media award Nat. Conf. Christians and Jews, 1988, others; named (with Irv Kupcinet) Mr. and Mrs. Chgo. by Chgo. Acad. for the Arts, 1988, Woman of Yr. Variety Club #26, 1988. Mem. Nat. Acad. TV Arts and Scis. (governing bd., program chmn. 1982—, Govs. award 1986). Jewish. Club: Arts.

KUPER, DANIELA F., advertising executive; b. Chgo., June 18, 1950; d. Harry W. and Anne F. (Fisher) K.; children—Judah E., Sahra J. B.A., So. Ill. U., 1971. Account exec., copywriter, creative dir. Griff Advt., Boulder, Colo., 1978-82; pres., creative dir. Kuper-Finlon Advt., Boulder, 1982—; speaker in field. Vol. creative writing with children Foothill Sch., Boulder, 1985. Recipient Alfie award Denver Ad Fedn., 1983, 84, 85, 86, Addie award, 1984, 85, 86, Peak award 1985, 86, BPAA award 1984, 85, 86. Mem. Denver Ad Fedn., Boulder C. of C., Art Dirs. Club Denver (award 1985, 86). Office: Kuper-Finlon Advt 2060 Broadway Suite 400 Boulder CO 80302

KUPERMAN, AGOTA MARIA, foreign service officer, librarian; b. Budapest, Hungary, Aug. 8, 1944; came to U.S., 1956; d. Istvan Madaras and Sharlotte (Rottmann) Schiff. BA, Rutgers U., 1966; MLS, Ind. U., 1968. Reference librarian U.S. Naval Acad., Annapolis, 1976-77; regional library cons. USIA, Iran, 1978-79, Islamabad, Pakistan, 1979; East Asia and Near East library specialist USIA, Washington, 1979-81, bibliographic specialist, 1981-83, chief fgn. service nat. personnel, 1983-85; dep. chief fgn. personnel Voice of Am., Washington, 1985-87; regional library cons. USIA, Tunisia, Algeria, Morocco, Egypt, Sudan, Israel, Yemen, Syria, Jordan, 1987—. Mem. ALA. Home and Office: Dept State USIA Washington DC 20520-6360

KUPPER, EMILY LOUISE, real estate broker; b. Beijing, People's Republic of China, Aug. 22, 1923; d. Lucius Bunyan and Nell Blake (Fowler) Olive; m. Thomas J. Kupper; children: Elise Kim Kupper Lovewell, Thomas Tor. AB, Meredith Coll., 1945; student in advt. art, Pratt Inst., 1945-46; lic., U. Conn., 1969. Advt. artist Nat Simons Advt., N.Y.C., 1949-51; free lance artist N.Y.C., 1951-54; art tchr. Brunswick Sch., Greenwich, Conn., 1965-66; assoc. Greenwich Properties, Inc., 1969-72; real estate agt. Alex Taylor Assocs., Greenwich, 1972-74; owner Guide Points Realty Co., Inc., Greenwich, 1974—; advt. dir. Connect, Inc., Conn., 1974-79, pres. 1981-82. Mem. Nat. Bd. Realtors, Conn. Bd. Realtors, Women's Council of Realtors, Greenwich Bd. Realtors, Farm and Land Inst., Greenwich C. of C. (com. 1985-87). Congregationalist. Home: 2 Merry Lane Greenwich CT 06831 Office: Guide Points Realty Co Inc 403 E Putnam Ave Cos Cob CT 06807

KUPPERMAN, HELEN SLOTNICK, lawyer; b. Boston; d. Morris Louis and Minnie (Kaplan) Slotnick; B.A., Smith Coll.; postgrad. Royal Acad. Dramatic Art, London; J.D., Boston Coll., 1966; m. Robert H. Kupperman, Dec. 23, 1967; 1 dau., Tamara. Bar: Mass. 1966, D.C. 1986. Atty., advisor NASA, Washington, 1966-73, sr. atty., 1973-77, asst. gen. counsel for gen. law, 1977-86, assoc. gen. counsel, 1986, spl. asst. gen. counsel space station, 1986-87, chairperson contract adjustment bd., 1974-87, exec. v.p. Robert H. Kupperman & Assocs. Inc., 1987—; adj. fellow space policy study Ctr. Strategic and Internat. Studies, 1987—; rep. on U.S. delegation to legal subcomittee of UN Com. on Peaceful Uses of Outer Space, 1977-87. Recipient NASA Sustained Superior Performance award, 1977, Exceptional Service medal, 1983, NASA Ses Bonus, 1980, 85, Space Station Task Force Group Achivement award NASA, 1984. Mem. U.S. Assn. of Internat. Inst. Space Law (sec. 1981), ABA, Fed., Mass., D.C., Boston bar assns., Internat. Women Lawyers Assn., Internat. Inst. Space Law, Am. Astronautical Assn. (gen. counsel 1986). Jewish. Bus. editor Boston Coll. Indsl. and Comml. Law Rev., 1965-66. Home: 2832 Ellicott St NW Washington DC 20008 Office: 400 Maryland Ave SW Washington DC 20546

KURASCH, TERI JOYCE, lawyer; b. Chgo., Mar. 31, 1956; d. Harold Earl and Eleanor (Cohen) Lieberman; m. Jonathan Kurasch, June 18, 1951; children: Tracy, Kevin. BS in Psychol., U. Ill., 1976; JD, IIT, 1979; postgrad., U. Chgo. Bar: Ill., 7th Dist. Fed. Ct., 6th Circuit Ct. Appeals. Ptnr. Lieberman and Kurasch, Chgo., 1979-81; sr. lawyer Fed. Res. Bank Chgo., 1981-84, asst. counsel, 1984-85, asst. v.p., 1985-87, v.p., assoc. gen. counsel, 1987—; sec. Fed. Res. System Ins. Com., Chgo. 1981—. Com. Chair Freedom Info. Subcom., Kansas City 1986—; chmn. Consolidation Guidelines Task Force, Chgo. 1986; chmn. Northbrook Newcomers, 1985-85. Mem. Women's Bar Assn., Chgo. Bar Assn., U. Chgo. Women's Bus. Group. Office: Fed Res Bank Chgo 230 S LaSalle Chicago IL 60690

KURE, PATRICIA ANN, police social worker; b. Oak Park, Ill., Feb. 28, 1952; d. Fred Matthew and June Dorothy (Malkin) K. BS in Psychology and Sociology, Elmhurst (Ill.) Coll., 1974; MS in Guidance and Counseling, U. Wis., Whitewater, 1975. Police social worker Wheaton (Ill.) Police Dept., 1976-78; social worker Bensenville (Ill.) Home Soc., 1978-79; police social worker New Berlin (Wis.) Police Dept., 1979—; instr. police sci. Waukesha County Tech. Inst., Wis., 1982—, group facilitator, 1983—; hostage negotiator New Berlin Police Dept., 1982—. Bd. dirs. Family Service Waukesha County, 1983—, sec., 1984-86, treas., 1986—. Mem. Wis. Juvenile Officer Assn., Waukesha County Juvenile Officers Assn. Office: New Berlin Police Dept 17165 W Glendale Dr New Berlin WI 53151

KURELOWECH, KATHY MARY, medical technologist; b. Butte, Mont., June 6, 1952; d. Edward Stephen and Dorothy Marie (Klobchar) Mihelich; m. Richard S. Kurelowech, Oct. 11, 1987. BA in Med. Tech., Carroll Coll., 1974; MBA in Mgmt., Western Internat. U., 1986. Med. technologist St. Patrick Hosp., Missoula, Mont., 1974-75, supr. hematology, 1975-78; supr. chemistry John C. Lincoln Hosp., Phoenix, 1978—; cons. in field. Mem. Am. Soc. Clin. Pathologists (cert.), Nat. Cert. Agy. for Med. Lab. Personnel (cert.), Am. Mgmt. Assn., Human Factors Soc., Nat. Assn. for Female Execs.

KURETSKY, SUSAN DONAHUE, art historian; b. Charleston, S.C., Oct. 11, 1941; d. James Kenneth and Esther (Lawshe) Donahue; A.B., Vassar Coll., 1963; M.A. (Woodrow Wilson fellow), Harvard U., 1964, Ph.D. (Bernice Cronkhite fellow), 1971; m. Robert L. Kuretsky, July 17, 1969. Teaching fellow Harvard U., 1965-67; asst. prof. art Boston U., 1969-74; asso. prof. art Vassar Coll., 1975—; cons. pub. programs Nat. Endowment Humanities. Smith fellow in Dutch and Flemish art Nat. Gallery, Washington, 1974-75. Mem. Coll. Art Assn. and Historians Am. Author: The Paintings of Jacob Ochtervelt, 1979; (with others) Gods, Saints and Heroes: Dutch Painting in the Age of Rembrandt, 1980-81; contbr. articles and revs. to profl. jours. Office: Vassar College Box 114 Poughkeepsie NY 12601

KURILCHYK, DEBORAH ANN, government official; b. Lansing, Mich., June 4, 1950; d. Walter and Virginia Adelaide (Travis) K. BA in Polit. Sci., U. Calif., Santa Barbara, 1972; cert. secondary tchr., Calif. State U., Long Beach, 1973; MPA, U. So. Calif., 1983. Substitute tchr. Newport Harbor High Sch., Newport Beach, Calif., 1973-75; intern, research asst. Office of Sec., Dept. of Treasury, Washington, 1975; asst. to city mgr. for community relations City of Brea, Calif., 1976; staff asst. U.S. Rep. Robert Badham, Washington, 1977-80; mgr. pub. affairs com. Fluor Corp., Irvine, Calif., 1980-84; dir. govt. relations Fluor Corp., Irvine, 1984-86; asst. house liaison U.S. Dept. of Energy, Washington, 1987—. Bd. dirs. Orange County Rep. Assocs., 1980-86; sec. St. Vincent de Paul Soc., Orange, 1979; mem. Calif. State Rep. Exec. Com., 1983-84; staff, invitation control com. Presdl. Inaugural, Washington, 1980-81; bd. dirs., mem. Ctr. 500 Orange County Performing Arts [illegible] Learned Ladies chpt. 1978-84). Mem. Nat. Assoc. Bus. Polit. Action Coms. (bd. dirs. 1983 86), [illegible] (founder, coordinator 1982-86), Pi Alpha Alpha, Delta Gamma (Gamma Kappa chpt.). Office: US Dept Energy Office Congl Affairs 1000 Independence Ave SW Washington DC 20585

KURIO, PAMELA RENEE, construction executive; b. Houston, May 1, 1964; d. Bernhard Roy and Ellen Mae (Brodie) K. Student, U. Tex., 1982-84. Ptnr. PamBee Interiors and Design, Houston, 1979—, PamBee Jewelry and Apparel, Houston, 1982—; v.p. Kurio Drywall Co. Inc., Houston, 1984—; owner Fazazz Enterprises, Houston, 1985-86, Dome Capitol Lumber Co. of Nashville, 1986, Kurio Home Builders, Nashville, Tenn., 1986—; pres., owner Kurio Drywall Co. of Tenn., Inc., Nashville, 1986—. Republican. Methodist. Office: Kurio Drywall Co 1585 W Belt North Houston TX 77043 Also: 31A Cleveland Ave Nashville TN 37210

KURISU, GAIL NAOMI, meeting consultant; b. Wailuku, Hawaii, Nov. 6, 1946; d. George Y. and Caroline M. (Miki) Izumi; m. Craig S. Kurisu, June 24, 1967 (div. May 1981); 1 child, Stacy. BA, San Jose (Calif.) State U., 1970. Occupational therapist San Jose Hosp., 1973-77; office mgr., sec. Alfred C.R. Hughes, M.D., Mountain View, Calif., 1977-79; v.p. fin. Pad Travel, Inc., Palo Alto, Calif., 1979-81; sales dir. Ramada Inn, Santa Clara, Calif., 1981-83, Toll House Hotel, Los Gatos, Calif., 1983-84; salesperson West Coast Promotions, Inc., Sunnyvale, Calif., 1984-85; ptnr., founder Reservations Plus, Sunnyvale, 1984—; cons. Maple Tree Inn, Sunnyvale, 1984, Haus Inn, Sunnyvale, 1985. Mem. Hotel Sales and Mktg. Assn. (bd. dirs. 1985-87), Peninsula Corp. Travel Assn., Meeting Planners Internat. Buddhist. Office: Reservations Plus 1141 Merrimac Dr Sunnyvale CA 94087

KURISU, RUTH PATRICIA, small business owner, management consultant; b. Phillipsburg, N.J., May 26, 1950; d. Lawton Hughes and Grace Truell (Banks) Faunce; m. Verne Yoshiki Kurisu, Sept. 5, 1981. BS in Chemistry, Ursinus Coll., 1971; cert. in electric power engring., UCLA, 1981, cert. in mgmt., 1984. Chemist Dynachem div. Morton Thiokol, Tustin, Calif., 1975-78; quality assurance engr. So. Calif. Edison Co., Rosemead, 1978-81, sr. project adminstr., 1981-84, supr. corp. documentation services, 1984-86; owner SolderMask, Inc., Costa Mesa, Calif., 1986—; also bd. dirs. Solder Mask, Inc., Costa Mesa, Calif. Named Woman of Achievement YWCA, 1983. Mem. Employer Adv. Council, Nuclear Info. and Records Mgmt. Assn. (bd. dirs. 1984-86, treas. 1985-86), Am. Soc. Quality Control (cert. quality engr.). Office: SolderMask Inc 118 E 16th St Costa Mesa CA 92627

KURRASCH, TERRIE LEE, hospital administrator, consultant; b. Oakland, Calif., Nov. 16, 1946; d. Chester Harold and Kathryn Verna (Mansfield) Ensign; m. Arthur Allen Kurrasch, June 15, 1969. B.S., Calif. State U.-Hayward, 1969; M.P.H., U. Calif.-Berkeley, 1980. Dir. child life Children's Hosp. Med. Ctr. No. Calif., Oakland, 1970-78; health planner H.O.M. Group, Inc., San Francisco, 1981-83; dir. planning Providence Hosp., Oakland, 1983-87; facilities planning coordinator N.C. region, Kaiser Permanente Health Plan., Inc., 1987; lectr. Calif. State U.-Hayward, 1978-80. Bd. dirs. Alameda Family Service Agy. (Calif.), 1980-83; mem. adv. bd. Alameda council Boy Scouts Am., 1982—. Mem. Am. Hosp. Assn., Soc. Hosp. Planners, Health Care Execs. No. Calif., Am. Coll. Hosp. Adminstrs. (nominee), AAUW. Clubs: Encinal Yacht (Alameda); Sierra. Lodge: Job's Daughters.

KURTZ, BARBARA BRANDON, educational administrator; b. Hillsdale, Mich., Jan. 17, 1941; d. Robert Dale and Dortha May (Bird) Brandon; m. Robert Roger Kurtz, June 20, 1964; children—Kevin, Christopher, Kathryn. B.S. in Music Edn., Western Mich. U., 1963; M.A. in Edn., Mich. State U., 1969; postgrad. John Carroll U., 1979-80; Ph.D. in Early Childhood Edn., Clayton U., 1983. Pres. adminstrn. U. Iowa Coop. Preschool, Iowa City, 1972-75; dir. Coral Nursery, Iowa City, 1975-77; head tchr. Covenant Early Childhood Programs, Cleve., 1977-79, dir., 1979—; supr. practicum Case Western Res. U., Cleve., 1977—; adj. faculty Lakeland Community Coll., Kirtland, Ohio, 1981—; project coordinator Child Day Care Planning Project of Cuyahoga County, Cleve., 1985—. Author: Center-Sponsored Family Day Care Homes, 1984. Editor: (with Brenda Boyd) Student Aide Training Packet, 1978. Contbr. articles to profl. jours. Mem. adv. panel Beginnings jour., 1984—; mem. day care adv. council Ohio Dept. Human Services. Recipient Gov.'s Spl. Recognition award State of Ohio, 1985. Mem. Nat. Assn. for Edn. of Young Children, Nat. Coalition for Campus Child Care, Ohio Assn. for Edn. of Young Children, Cleve. Assn. for Edn. of Young Children (pres., Early Childhood award 1984), Nat. Assn. Hosp. Affiliated Child Care Programs. Democrat. Roman Catholic. Avocations: cross-country skiing; snowshoeing; hiking; travel; reading. Home: 8856 Kirtland-Chardon Rd Kirtland OH 44060 Office: Covenant Early Childhood Programs 11205 Euclid Ave University Circle Cleveland OH 44060

KURTZ, DOLORES MAY, civic worker; b. Reading, Pa., Oct. 27, 1933; d. Harry Claude and Ethel Gertrude (Fields) Filbert; m. William McKillips Kurtz, Oct. 26, 1957. Cert. secretarial program, Pa. State U., 1980. Legal sec. Snyder, Balmer & Kershner, Reading, 1951-53; head teletype operator E.I. duPont de Nemours, Reading, 1953-56; exec. sec. Ford New Holland (Pa.) Inc. (formerly Sperry New Holland div. Sperry Corp.), 1956—. Mem. Lancaster County Rep. Com., 1983-85; pres. New Holland Area Woman's Club, 1982-84; bd. dirs. Lancaster County Fedn. Women's Clubs, 1982—, 2d v.p., 1984-86, 1st v.p., 1986-88, pres. 1988—; founding mem. Summer Arts Festival, New Holland, 1980—, bd. dirs., 1985—; membership chmn. S.E. dist. Pa. Fedn. Women's Clubs, 1984-86; bd. dirs. Community Meml. Park Assn., New Holland, 1957-82; area rep., bd. dirs. Woman's Rep. Club Lancaster County, 1982-84; committeewoman New Holland Boro 1983-85. Recipient Outstanding Vol. for Pa. award Pa. Fedn. Women's Clubs, 1984. Methodist. Avocations: arts and crafts, travel, photography, boating.

KURTZ, KAREN BARBARA, editor, writer; b. Ft. Dodge, Iowa, July 21, 1948; d. Clifford Wenger and Eleanor Marie (Ulrich) Swartzendruber; m. Mark Allen Kurtz, June 25, 1977. AA, Hesston Coll., 1968; BA in Edn., Goshen (Ind.) Coll., 1970; MA in Elem. Edn., Ind. U., 1975. Lifetime cert. elem. tchr. First grade tchr. Fairfield Community Sch., Goshen, 1970-79; asst. editor and advt. copywriter Barth and Assocs., Middlebury, Ind., 1986-87; free-lance writer Kurtz Lens and Pen, Goshen, 1979—; asst. dir.. info. services Goshen (Ind.) Coll.; asst. dir. Info. Services, Goshen Coll., 1987—. Author: Paper Paint and Stuff, 1984; asst. editor: Heritage Country Mag., 1986-87; contbr. articles to various mags. Ch. bd. dirs. Goshen City Ch. of Brethren, 1977, also chmn. stewardship dr., coordinator art in the ch. Mem. NEA, Ind. State Tchr.'s Assn., Fairfield Educators Assn. Republican. Club: Bayview.

KURTZ, MAXINE, personnel services executive, lawyer; b. Mpls., Oct. 17, 1921; d. Jack Isadore and Beatrice (Cohen) K. BA, U. Minn., 1942; BS in Govt. Mgmt., U. Denver, 1945, JD, 1962; postdoctoral student, U. Calif., San Diego, 1978. Bar: Colo. 1962. Analyst Tri-County Regional Planning, Denver, 1945-47; chief research and spl. projects Planning Office, City and County of Denver, 1947-66, dir. tech. and evaluation Model Cities Program, 1966-71; personnel research officer Denver Career Service Authority, 1972-86, dir. personnel services, 1986—; expert witness nat. com. on urban problems U.S. Ho. of Reps., U.S. Senate. Author: Law of Planning and Land Use Regulations in Colorado, 1966; co-author: Care and Feeding of Witnesses, Expert and Otherwise, 1974; bd. editors: Pub. Adminstrn. Rev., Washington, 1980-83, 88—; editorial adv. bd. Internat. Personnel Mgmt. Assn.; prin. investigator: Employment: An American Enigma, 1979. Active Women's Forum of Colo.; Denver Dem. Party; chair Colo. adv. com. to U.S. Civil Rights Commn., 1985—. Sloan fellow, U. Denver, 1944-45; recipient Outstanding Achievement award U. Minn., 1971. Mem. Am. Inst. Planners (sec. treas. 1968-70, bd. govs. 1972-75), Am. Soc. Pub. Adminstrn. (nat. council 1978-81, Donald Stone award), ABA, Colo. Bar Assn., Denver Bar Assn., LWV, Pi Alpha Alpha. Jewish. Lodge: Order of St. Ives. Home: 2361 Monaco Pkwy Denver CO 80207 Office: Denver Career Service Authority 414 14th St Denver CO 80202

KURTZ, PATRICIA ROSE, educator; b. Detroit, Jan. 13, 1944; d. Albert G. and Rose (Jasinski) Kurtz. B.A., Madonna Coll., 1963; postgrad. U. Mich., 1966-67; grad. degree Oakland U., 1986. Cert. elem. tchr., Mich.

Tchr., Livonia Pub. Schs. (Mich.), 1963—; observer elem. classes in Russia, 1967, China, 1971. Vol., Beaumont Hosp., Royal Oak, Mich., 1980—(Silver Pin award for 500 hrs. service 1984); vol. Rep. Conv., Detroit, 1980. Mem. NEA, Mich. Edn. Assn., Livonia Edn. Assn., PTA. Roman Catholic. Club: Cranbrook Acad. Art (Bloomfield Hills, Mich.). Home: 3835 Quarton Rd Bloomfield Hills MI 48013

KURTZIG, SANDRA L., computer software company executive; b. Chgo., Oct. 21, 1946; d. Barney and Marian (Boruck) Brody; children: Andrew Paul, Kenneth Alan; B.S. in Math., UCLA, 1967; M.S.in aeronaut. engring., Stanford U., 1968. Math analyst TRW Systems, 1967-68; mktg. rep., Gen. Electric Co., 1969-72; chmn. bd., chief exec. officer, pres. ASK Computer Systems, Los Altos, Calif., 1972-85, chmn. bd., 1986—. Cited one of 50 most influential bus. people in Am., Bus. Week, 1985. Office: ASK Computer Systems Inc 2440 W El Camino Real Mountain View CA 94039-7640 *

KURZ, KELLI MCDONALD, advertising executive; b. Torrance, Calif., Aug. 30, 1955; d. Henry James and Jimmie Lois (Manning) McDonald; m. Michael Dennis Kurz, Oct. 4, 1986. BJ with honors, Tex. Tech U., 1977. Media buyer Ranck-Ross-Moore Advt., Denver, 1977-79; media planner, buyer Tracy-Locke/BBDO Advt., Denver, 1979-81; media dir. Barnhart & Co. Advt., Denver, 1981-83; v.p., media dir. Evans/Bartholomew Pollack Norman, Denver, 1983—. Media liaison, mem. fund raising com. Excelsior Youth Ctr., Aurora, Colo., 1984—, Am. Lung Assn., Denver, 1984—; media coordinator, mem. mmktg. task force com. ARTREACH, Denver, 1983—. Mem. Denver Advt. Fedn. (social chmn. 1985-86, ad expo chmn. 1985-87, v.p., bd. dirs. 1986—), ADZ (chmn. membership com. 1979-82), Chi Omega, Beta Theta Pi. Republican. Methodist. Home: 8249 S Trenton Way Englewood CO 80112 Office: Evans/Bartholomew Pollack Norman 2128 15th St Denver CO 80202

KUSHNER, GAIL LORI, human resources executive; b. Bronx, N.Y., Nov. 22, 1953; d. Benjamin and Helen (Teitelbaum) Schwartz; m. Larry Jay Kushner, Dec. 22, 1979; children: Marisa Arielle, Danielle Rachel, Kimberly Fawn. BA, Hofstra U., 1974; MA, Columbia U., 1975. Lic. tchr., N.Y. Dir. student services Poly. Inst. N.Y., Bklyn., 1978-80; mgr. adminstrn. and word processing info. services div. Chem. Bank, N.Y.C., 1980-82; mgr. adminstrn., office systems, asst. treas. Chem. Bank, N.Y.C., 1982-84, mgr. adminstrn., office systems, asst. v.p., 1984-85, dir. info. services tng., asst. v.p., 1985-87, mgr. staffing and devel. human resources div., 1987-88, v.p. human resources div., 1988—; arbitrator Am. Arbitration Assn., N.Y.C., 1983—; bd. dirs. Mar-Dan Abstract Corp., Bronx, 1986—. Active Rosedale Neighborhood Assn., White Plains, N.Y., 1983—, Jewish Community Ctr. of Harrison. Mem. Assn. Info. Sytems Profls., Human Factors Soc., InterBank Audit Personnel Group, Hofstra U. Alumni Assn., Hadassah, Phi Epsilon Alumni Assn. Republican. Jewish. Home: 7 Quincy Ln White Plains NY 10605 Office: Chem Bank Corp Support Human Resources 380 Madison Ave New York NY 10017

KUSIAK, VICTORIA MAYDOSZ, physician; b. Honesdale, Pa., Sept. 19, 1950; d. William Liopold and Ruth Lois (Quick) Maydosz; m. Joseph Francis Kusiak, May 3, 1975. BS summa cum laude, Albright Coll., 1971; MD, U. Pa., 1975. Diplomate Am. Bd. Internal Medicine and Cardiovascular Diseases. Intern in medicine Hosp. of U. Pa., Phila., 1975-76, jr. resident in medicine, 1976-77, sr. resident in medicine, 1977-78, cardiology fellow, 1978-80, research fellow in cardiology, 1980-81; co-dir. cardiac catherization lab. Thomas Jefferson U. Hosp., Phila., 1983-85; assoc. dir. clin. investigation Smith Kline and French Labs, Phila., 1985-86, dir. clin. investigation, 1986-88, group dir. clin. investigation, 1988—; adj. asst. prof. pharmacology Temple U. Sch. Med., Phila., 1985—, adj. asst. prof. med., 1985—; adj. asst. prof. med. U. Pa. Sch. Med., 1985—, Jefferson Med. Coll., 1985—. Contbr. chpts. to various med. books; contbr. articles to sci. jours. Mem. Winterthur Guild, Del., 1984—, Whitemarsh Hist. Soc., Ft. Washington, Pa., 1987. Fellow Am. Coll. Cardiology; mem. AMA, Pa. Med. Soc., Phila. County Med. Soc. (emergency room com., 1981-84), Phila. Coll. Cardiology, Soc. Cardiac Angiography, Alpah Omega Alpha. Republican. Roman Catholic. Office: Smith Kline & French 1500 Spring Garden St Philadelphia PA 19130

KUSKA, LORRAINE ELIZABETH, lawyer; b. White Plains, N.Y., Nov. 19, 1961; d. Frank William and Marie Claire (Massicotte) K. DEC, Coll. Lafleche, Trois-Rivieres, Que., Can., 1981; LLL, U. Ottawa, Ont., 1985. Bar: Quebec 1985. Crown atty. Que. Ministry Justice, Hull, 1985-86; asst. counsel IBM Can. Ltd., Markham, Ont., 1986—. adviser Jr. Achievement Metro Toronto, 1988. Mem. Can. Bar Assn., Que. Bar Assn., Can. Mfgr's Assn. (quality com., legal subcom. environ.). Roman Catholic. Office: IBM Can Ltd, 3500 Steeles Ave E, 46/948, Markham, ON Canada L3R 2Z1

KUSMA, KYLLIKKI, lawyer; b. Tartu, Estonia, Dec. 8, 1943; came to U.S., 1951, naturalized, 1958; d. August and Helju (Traat) K.; B.F.A., Ohio U., 1966; M.A. (Vets. Rehab. Adminstrn. fellow), Ohio State U., 1967; J.D., Ohio No. U., 1976; M.L.T., Georgetown U., 1980. Bar: Ohio 1977, D.C. 1978. Speech and hearing therapist Lima (Ohio) Meml. Hosp., 1967-70, Tipp City (Ohio) Schs., 1970-74; atty.-adv. Office Chief Counsel, IRS, Washington, 1977-81; v.p., asso. tax counsel Security Pacific Nat. Bank, Los Angeles, 1981-83; ptnr. Brownstein Zeidman & Schomer, Washington, 1983—; instr. Wright State U., 1972-76. Author: (with others) Mortgage-Backed Securities Special Update: REMICs, 1988. Vol. local civic, polit. activities. Mem. ABA, D.C. Bar Assn., Ohio Bar Assn., D.C. Women's Bar Assn., Phi Kappa Phi. Democrat. Office: Brownstein Zeidman & Schomer 1401 New York Ave #900 Washington DC 20005

KUSMA, TAISSA TURKEVICH, database services manager; b. Lviv, Ukraine, July 17, 1935; came to U.S., 1957; d. Leo and Olga (Gorny) Turkevich; m. Bohdan R. Kusma, May 14, 1960; children: Lydia Maria, Orest Roman. B of Applied Sci. in Chem. Engring., U. Toronto, 1956; MLS, U. R.I., 1976. Indexer, abstractor Hercules Co., Wilmington, Del., 1957-60; chem. librarian Merck, Sharp & Dohme, Rahway, N.J., 1960-61; reference librarian R.I. Jr. Coll., Lincoln, 1979-80; cataloger Pawtucket (R.I.) Pub. Library, 1980-81; reference librarian R.I. Coll., Providence, 1981; mgr. database services Am. Math. Soc., Providence, 1981—; cons. Adv. Com. Coordination Info. Systems UN, Geneva, 1986; adv. com. Grad. Sch. Library and Info. Scis., U. R.I., 1986-88. Editor: Mathfile User's Guide, 1982, MathSci User Guide, 1986. Mem. Assn. Info. and Dissemination Ctrs. (sec., treas. 1983-87), Nat. Fedn. Abstract and Info. Services (chair publs. com. 1986—), Info. Tech. Div. Spl. Library Assn. (chair membership com. 1986—), Assn. Am. Pub. (database com. 1984—), Am. Soc. Info. Sci. (nominating com. 1988, chair exhibits subcommittee 1987), Blackstone Valley Hist. Soc., Ukrainian Engr.'s Soc. Am., Heritage Com. R.I., Beta Phi Mu. Mem. Ukrainian Catholic Ch. Home: 9 Cliffside Dr Lincoln RI 02865 Office: Am Math Soc PO Box 6248 wpl Charles St Providence RI 02940

KUSSMAN, ARDYS ANN, apparel manufacturing company executive; b. Pawnee City, Nebr., Jan. 22, 1948; d. Edmund Fangman and Evelyn Louise (Runnebaum) Lackey; m. Elbert Dale Kussman, Sept. 2, 1967 (div. July 1976); 1 child, Angela. Grad. high sch., Seneca, Kans. Prodn. planning analyst Lee Co., Merriam, Kans., 1972-73, supr. prodn. planning, 1974-75, mgr. prodn. planning, 1976-78, mgr. material control, 1979-80, mgr. forecasting, 1981, dir. forecasting and planning, 1982-84, v.p. ops. planning, 1985; v.p. ops. VF Corp., Wyomissing, Pa., 1986-87; sr. v.p. ops. Lee Co., Merriam, 1988—. Republican. Roman Catholic. Home: 9033 W 101st Terr Overland Park KS 66212 Office: Lee Co 9001 W 67th St Merriam KS 66201

KUSSMAN, BERNADINE LEE, interior designer; b. Toledo, Sept. 13, 1935; d. Bernard Leo and Florence May (Yoxall) Johnson; m. Richard Leroy Kussman, Dec. 29, 1955 (div. Dec. 1981); children: Craig Scott, Richard Lance. Student, Pomona Coll., 1954; AA, Fullerton Jr. Coll., 1957; BA, Calif. State U., Long Beach, 1965; MS in Pub. Health, UCLA, 1967; post-grad., Western State U. of Law, Fullerton, 1983-85. Registered nurse, Calif. RN Long Beach Nurses Assn., 1957-68; instr. health edn. UCLA, 1967, Cal. State U., Long Beach, 1968-70; nurse ICU Lakewood (Calif.) Gen. Hosp., 1968; travel agt. Coastline Community Coll., 1976; travel agy. Montgomery Wards, A & A Travel, A Carousel of Travel, 1975-83; owner An Interior Design by Bunny, Long Beach, 1979—. Author: Health Knowledge Tests, 1967. Bd. dirs. Los Angeles Maritime Mus., San Pedro, Calif., 1981—, 49er Athletic Found., Long Beach, 1965-81, Young Horizons, Long Beach and Garden Grove, Calif., 1987—. Recipient Appreciation cert. Long Beach Drug Abuse Edn. Program, 1970; Commendation cert. Los Angeles County Rep. Cen. Com., 1971, Seal Beach Civic and Bus. Community, 1961. Mem. Long Beach Assistance League (service to youth chair 1971), Calif. State U. Long Beach Pres.'s Affiliates, Fine Arts Affiliates, Long Beach Civic Light Opera, USN League, Friends of Los Angeles Maritime Mus. (bd. dirs. 1979, pres., pilot), San Pedro Womens C. of C., DAR. Republican. Home: 6431 Bixby Hill Rd Long Beach CA 90815

KUTASI, KATALIN ERZSEBET, banker; b. Ann Arbor, Mich., Sept. 7, 1956; d. Karoly and Margaret (Vidonyi) K. BA in Acctg., Mich. State U., East Lansing, 1978; MBA in Fin., DePaul U., 1983. Cost acct. Continental Ill. Nat. Bank and Trust Co. of Chgo., 1978-80, banking officer trade fin., 1980-85, 2d v.p., 1985—. Active Chgo. Council on Fgn. Relations, 1984-85. Mem. Am. Council for the Arts, Mich. State U. Alumni Assn. (bd. dirs. 1978-85), Gamma Phi Beta. Republican. Roman Catholic.

KUTI, OLUFOWORA BOLA, health science facility adminsitrator; b. Lagos, Nigeria, Mar. 27, 1947; came to U.S., 1972; d. Emmanuel Adetutu and Badejoko Yetunde (Akapo) Sotomi; m. Emmanuel Oladeinde Kuti, Aug. 7, 1971; children: Kolawole B., Olasumbo A. Diploma in nursing, U. Lagos, 1970; BS in Nursing, U. Md., Balt., 1977; M in Bus. and Pub. Adminstrn., Southeastern U., 1979; cert. in nursing adminstrn., Villanova U., 1987. Charge nurse D.C. Doctors Hosp., Washington, 1974-79; charge nurse Leland Meml. Hosp., Riverdale, Md., 1979-80, supr. nursing, 1980-84; coordinator for nursing suprs. Suburban Hosp., Bethesda, Md., 1984-87; pres. Stat Med. Services, Inc., Upper Marlboro, Md., 1988—. Mem. Am. Nurses Assn. (cert.), Am. Assn. Critical Care Nurses, Quality Assurance Council, Nat. Assn. for Female Execs. Home and Office: 1008 Dannet Pl Upper Marlboro MD 20772

KUTNI, LINDA KAY, accountant; b. Waco, Tex., July 22, 1954; d. Allen R. and Diana Marie (Levy) Greenstein; m. Michael James Kutni, Dec. 7, 1980. BS in Education, Baylor U., 1976; BBA, U. Tex., 1978. CPA, Tex. Acct. Greenstein, Logan & Co., Waco, 1978-81; sr. acct. Parrish, Greenstein, Moody, & Harelik, Waco, 1981-86, Talbert & Talbert, Waco, 1986-87. Bd. dirs. Waco Girls Club, Waco, 1984—; treas. Waco Civic Ballet, 1986—; active Jr. League, Waco. Mem. Am. Inst. CPA's, Am. Women CPA's, Tex. Soc. CPA's, Cen. Tex. Chpt. CPA's. Lodge: Altrusa. Home: 3604 Brannon Waco TX 76710 Office: Talbert & Talbert 1005 Columbus Ave Waco TX 76701

KUTYLOWSKI, JOAN, mechanical engineer; b. Dearborn, Mich., Jan. 9, 1960; d. Casimer and Bernice (Skrzypek) K. BS in Mech. Engring., U. Mich., 1981. Sec. Cody High Sch., Detroit, 1974-80; drafter Wolverine Tube Co., Dearborn Heights, Mich., 1979-80; gen. engr. Consumers Power Co., Jackson, Mich., 1981-84; project engr. Moylan Engring Assocs., Dearborn, 1984-88; sr. engr. Multiple Dynamics Corp., Southfield, Mich., 1988—. Mem. ASHRAE, Mich. Soc. Profl. Engrs. (pub. relations com. 1987), Engring. Soc. Detroit, Am. Polish Engring. Assn., Pi Tau Sigma. Roman Catholic. Club: Toastmasters (sec. 1985, ednl. v.p. 1987). Office: Multiple Dynamics Corp 29200 Southfield Suite 103 Southfield MI 48076

KUVSHINOFF, BERTHA HORNE, painter, sculptor; b. Dungeness, Wash., Aug. 29, 1915; d. Mellon Tobias and Mariamagdalena (Volnagel) Horne; m. Nicolai V. Kuvshinoff. Represented in numerous mus., pvt. and pub. collections, including Evansville (Ind.) Art Mus., Miami (Fla.) Mus. Modern Art, Seattle Art Mus., World's Fair, Seattle, 1962-63. Recipient Diploma of Merit of Univ. of Arts, Univ. Delle Arti, Rome, Italy. Studio: 121 1/2 Yale Ave N Seattle WA 98109

KUYKENDALL, RUTH JANE, real estate executive; b. Jackson, Mich., Aug. 22, 1908; d. James Elwood and Nellie Bethune (Allen) Bartlett; student Mich. State U., 1927-28, Fla. State Coll. for Women, 1929-31; m. Hubert Paul Kuykendall, June 12, 1945. Mgr., Myakka Hotel, Venice, Fla., 1931-41; corp. sec. J.E. Bartlett & Sons, Inc., 1931-54, pres., 1955-56; owner, mgr. Kuykendall Real Estate Co., 1951-85. Mem. Internat. Platform Assn., Am. Inst. Parliamentarians, Gulf Coast Parliamentarians (past v.p.), DAR, (parlimentarian 1980-86), Am. Legion Aux., Daus. Am. Colonists, (chpt. chmn. hist. landmarks and memls. 1982—, chpt. chmn. patriotic edn. 1983,84, 85), VFW Colonial Dames XVII Century, Descs. Mayflower, Magna Charta Dames (chaplain 1987-88), Plantagenets Soc., La Boutique des Huit Chapeaux et Quarante Femmes. Republican. Methodist. Home: 261 Ponce de Leon Ave Venice FL 34285

KUYPER, JOAN CAROLYN, foundation administrator; b. Balt., Oct. 22, 1941; d. Irving Charles and Ethel Mae (Pritchett) O'Connor; B.A. in Edn., Salisbury State U., 1963; postgrad. Columbia U., 1978; MA in Arts Mgmt. and Bus., NYU, 1988; m. L. William Kuyper, Dec. 20, 1964; children—Susan Carol, Edward Philip. Elem. sch. tchr. Prince Georges County Schs., Md., 1963-68; free lance singer, opera, oratorio, chamber music Amato Opera, N.Y.C., 1977-78, also musical orgns., 1968-80; owner, mgr. Privette Artists' Registry, Placement Service for Singers, Teaneck, N.J., 1969-78; exec. dir. Teaneck Artists Perform-Chamber Music Series, 1975-80; program dir. Vols. in Arts & Humanities, Vol. Bur. Bergen County, N.J., 1978-81; dir. Bergen Mus. Art and Sci., 1981-83; cons. Am. Soc. Prevention Cruelty to Animals, 1984, Am. Council for the Arts, 1987; dir. ops. Isabel O'Neil Found. and Studio, 1984-86. Dir. vol. services March of Dimes Birth Defects Found. of Greater N.Y., 1986-88; bd. dirs Pro Arte Choral and adv. bd. on the arts, Teaneck, 1976-81. Mem. Am. Assn. Mus., Mus. Council N.J., Am. Mktg. Assn., Assn. for Vol. Adminstrn. Democrat. Presbyterian. Clubs: Altrusa (bd. dirs. 1984-86, pres. 1986-88), P.E.O., Phi Alpha Theta. Home: 501 Rutland Ave Teaneck NJ 07666 Office: 233 Park Ave S New York NY 10028

KUZINA, JAN CELESTE, aeronautical engineer; b. Winnipeg, Man., Can., Oct. 30, 1956; d. John and Iris Alice (Huziak) K. BSC in physics with honors, U. Manitoba, 1982; M in Aero. Engring., Carleton U., 1985. Flight instr. Winnipeg Flying Club, 1975-77; charter pilot Aero Trades Western Ltd., Winnipeg, 1977; research officer Nat. Research Council Can., Ottawa, Ont., Can., 1981, Low Speed Aerodyns. Lab., Ottawa, Ont., Can., 1982-83, Nat. Research Council Can. Unsteady Aerodyns. Lab., Ottawa, Ont., 1984-85; aerodyn. flight test coordinator de Havilland Aircraft of Can., A Boeing Co., Toronto, Ont., 1986—; speaker in field. Contbr. articles to profl. jours. Recipient Female Pvt. Pilot of Yr. award Royal Can. Flying Clubs Assn., 1973, Allister R. Gillespie Meml. award, 1975; S.F. Kay scholar in sci., 1980; Amelia Earhart fellowship Zonta Internat., 1984. Mem. Canadian Aeros. and Space Inst., Fedn. Engring. and Scientific Assns. Office: de Havilland Aircraft, Garratt Blvd, Toronto, ON Canada M3K 1Y5

KVAPIL, THERESA FRANCESCA, insurance company underwriter; b. Cin., Oct. 3, 1961; d. Otto Arthur and Diane Lillian (Mannerino) K. BSBA, Xavier U., Cin., 1984, MBA, 1988. Supr. Gano Alley, Cin., 1984-85; mgr. Tyler's, Cin., 1986; supr., clk. Great Am. Ins., Cin., 1986—. Mem. Nat. Assn. for Female Execs., Assn. of MBA Execs. Republican. Roman Catholic. Home: 1214 Louden St Apt #2 Cincinnati OH 95202 Office: Great Am Ins 11353 Reed Hartman Hwy Cincinnati OH 45242

KWAN, NORMA MARGARET, winery art director; b. Hong Kong, Sept. 1, 1955; came to U.S., 1974; d. William and Emily (Wang) K. Profl. cert., Parsons Sch. Design, N.Y.C., 1977. Art dir. Compton Advt. Co., N.Y.C., 1977-79; asst. art dir. Mademoiselle mag., N.Y.C., 1980-82; art dir. Warner-Amex Satellite Entertainment, N.Y.C., 1982-84, Avon Products, N.Y.C., 1984; sr. art dir. Chesebrough Pond's Inc., Greenwich, Conn., 1984-88, Gallo Winery, Modesto, Calif., 1988—. Office: Gallo Winery PO Box 1130 Modesto CA 95353

KWAN, SHIRLEY, writer, producer; b. Madrid, Oct. 2, 1958; d. Hon Cheun and Kazuko (Yoshioka) K.; m. Kazuhiro Kisaichi, 1988. BA, Wash. State U., 1980; MS in Journalism, Columbia U., 1982; student, Columbia U. Internat. Fellows Program, 1982. Acting edn. editor Sta. WNET-TV, N.Y.C., 1980, cons., 1980-81; newswriter Satellite News Channel, Stamford, Conn., 1982-83, Newsday, Melville, N.Y., 1983-84; nat. copyreader Dow Jones & Co., N.Y.C., 1984-85; ind. multi-media writer/producer N.Y.C., 1985—; cover story corr. Cross and Talk mag., Tokyo, 1986—; cons./assoc. producer Sta. WETA-TV, Washington, 1986-87; cons. ALC Press Inc., Tokyo, 1986-88. Producer (feature film) Soho Murder, 1987-88; investigative reporter/production mgr.: Who Killed Vincent Chin, 1985-86 (New Directions Film Festival selection 1988); contbr. to periodicals, films and video prodns.. Mem. Asian Am. Journalist Assn. (treas. 1987—), Asian CineVision (vol. staffer/editor 1982-85, mem. 1988 Asian Am. Internat. Film Festival Com.). Home and Office: 448 State St Brooklyn NY 11217

KWANDT, JOANNE, nursing unit administrator; b. Camden, N.J., Mar. 23, 1944; d. John Joseph and Frances Ann (Robinson) Mahady; m. Dennis Charles Kwandt, May 30, 1969; children: Charann, Dennis Charles II. Student, Woman's Coll. Ga., Milledgeville, 1962-63; diploma in nursing, Grady Meml. Hosp., Atlanta, 1966; student, Ga. State Coll., Atlanta, 1963-67; AA, Merced (Calif.) Jr. Coll., 1972; BS in Social Psychology, Park Coll., 1979; MA in Psychology, U. No. Colo., 1980; cert. secondary sch. tchr., Boise (Idaho) State Coll., 1981; EdS, Coll. William and Mary, 1987, student, 1987—. RN, Ga., Calif., Oreg. Va.; cert. clin. specialist; cert. secondary sch. counselor, Idaho. Grad. nurse Grady Meml. Hosp., Atlanta, 1966-67; staff RN Piedmont Hosp., Atlanta, 1967-68; RN vis. and office Home Health Service Agy., Eugene, Oreg., 1970-71; aide learning disabilities Lajes AFB Elem. Sch., Azores, 1973-77; intern in counseling Boise State Coll., 1980; psychiatric RN child and adolescent units Charter Colonial Inst., Newport News, Va., 1983-85; lectr. Charter Colonial Inst., 1985; supr. nursing Ea. State Hosp., Williamsburg, Va., 1985-87; nurse mgr., clin. specialist Psychiat. Inst. Richmond, Va., 1987—; pvt. duty nurse, instr. pre-natal classes USAF Hosp., Lajes AFB; adj. instr. regional ctr. Park Coll., Mt. Home AFB, Idaho, 1980-82, Boise State Coll., Mt. Home AFB, 1981-82; counselor in field. Vol. children's unit Ea. State Hosp., 1985-87. Served to 1st lt. USAF, 1968-70. Mem. Va. Nursing Assn., Non-Commd. Officers Assn. Aux. (bd. dirs. 1980—, treas. internat. aux. bd. 1981, sec. 1983, 2d v.p. 1984-87, pres. 1987—). Democrat. Home: HCR01 Box 118 West Point VA 23181 Office: Psychiat Inst Richmond 3001 5th Ave Richmond VA 23222

KWASNIK, JEANNE MARIE, marketing professional; b. Columbus, Ohio, Nov. 7, 1961; d. Frederick Francis and Barbara Mary (Seidel) K. BS, SUNY, Albany, 1983. Adj. math instr. Monroe Community Coll., Rochester, N.Y., 1983, mgr. microcomputer labs., 1984-85; microcomputer salesperson Leon's Computer Mart, Rochester, 1983-84; applications instr. Sci. Calculations, Fishers, N.Y., 1985-86, mktg. communications liaison, 1986-87, computer aided engring. specialist, 1987; systems cons. Wang Labs., Inc., Rochester, 1987—; corp. rep. to People's Republic of China, 1986. active speaker Churchville-Chili High Sch., Churchville, N.Y., 1987; coach Catholic Youth Orgn., Rochester, 1983-84. Mem. Nat. Assn. Female Execs., Mfrs. Agent Nat. Assn., Smithsonian Assocs. Democrat. Roman Catholic.

KWIEDOROWICZ, LAURIE ANN, scientist; b. Cleve., Nov. 24, 1957; d. Albert James and Marion Francis (Winkel) Hauch; m. Darius M. Kwiedorowicz, Apr. 11, 1987. BS, Va. Poly. Inst. & State U., 1979; MS, U. Md., 1982. Textile technologist individual protection div. Chem. Research Devel. Engring. Ctr., U.S. Army, Aberdeen Proving Ground, Md., 1982—. Mem. Intersoc. Color Council, Nat. Assn. for Female Execs. Office: US Army CRDEC SMCCR-PPI Aberdeen Proving Ground MD 21010

KWOLEK, STEPHANIE LOUISE, chemist; b. New Kensington, Pa., July 31, 1923; d. John and Nellie (Zajdel) K. B.S., Carnegie-Mellon U., 1946; D.Sc. (hon.), Worcester Poly. Inst., 1981. Chemist, E.I. duPont de Nemours & Co. Inc., Wilmington, Del., 1946-59, research chemist, 1959-67, sr. research chemist, 1967-74, research assoc., 1974-86; cons. in polymer chemistry, 1986—. Contbr. articles to profl. jours.; patentee in field. Recipient award for contbns. to Kevlar, Am. Soc. Metals, 1978, engring./tech. award Soc. Plastics Engrs., 1985; inducted into U. Akron Polymer Processing Hall of Fame, 1985. Mem. Am. Chem. Soc. (award for creative invention 1980), Am. Inst. Chemists (Chem. Pioneer award 1980), Franklin Inst. Phila. (Howard N. Potts medal 1976), Carnegie Mellon U. Alumni Assn. (merit award 1983), Sigma Xi, Phi Kappa Phi. Club: DuPont Country (Wilmington).

KYD, MARILYN GRATTON, writer, editor; b. Wichita, Kans., Jan. 26, 1948; d. Robert and Celia (Goldman) G.; m. Charles W. Kyd, Mar. 25, 1984. AA, Pasadena City Coll., 1967; BA in English and History, UCLA, 1969. Cert. secondary tchr., Calif. Tchr. English Glendora (Calif.) High Sch., 1970-72; tchr. English and creative writing Hueneme High Sch., Oxnard, Calif., 1972-76; employment counselor Snelling & Snelling, Oxnard, 1976-77; ptnr., mgr. MG Personnel Agy., Santa Monica, Calif., 1977-78; tech. writer, editor Stanwick Corp., Ventura, Calif., 1978-80; engring. writer Northrop Corp., Oxnard, 1980; logistics analyst Automation Industries, Vitro Labs., Oxnard, 1980-81; mgr. documentation Computer Data Corp., Westlake Village, Calif., 1981-82; dir. mktg. Kiely Profl. Services, Westlake Village, 1983-84; pres., owner CashMaster Bus. Systems, Inc., Seattle, 1984—; owner, operator profl. resume preparation bus.; free-lance tech. writer and editor. Author: It's A Good Thing I'm Not Married, 1975; contbr. articles to profl. jours. Named Young Careerist, Bus. Profl. Women, 1975; recipient 3d place Nat. Writers Club articles contest, 1976, 2d place for photography, Port Hueneme Harbor Days, 1976, Honorable mention Writer's Digest Articles Contest, 1987. Mem. Nat. Writers Club, Soc. Tech. Communication, UCLA Alumni Assn., Mensa (columnist 1978, proctor Channel Islands area). Office: 12345 Lake City Way NE Suite 220 Seattle WA 98125

KYLE, CORINNE SILVERMAN, management consultant; b. N.Y.C., Jan. 4, 1930; d. Nathan and Janno (Harra) Silverman; m. Alec Kyle, Aug. 29, 1959 (div. Feb. 1969); children: Joshua, Perry (dec.), Julia. BA, Bennington Coll., 1950; MA, Harvard U., 1953. Assoc. editor Inter-Univ. Case Program, N.Y.C., 1956-60; co-founder, chief editor Financial Index, N.Y.C., 1960-63; research analyst McKinsey & Co., N.Y.C., 1963-64; sr. research asso. Mktg. Sci. Inst., Phila., 1964-67; founding partner Phila. Group, 1967-70; sr. asso. Govt. Studies and Systems, Phila., 1970-72, cons. program planning and control, Phila., 1972—, sr. asso. Periodical Studies Service, 1978—; v.p., dir. research Total Research Corp., Princeton, N.J., 1981-82; mgr. social research The Gallup Orgn., Princeton, 1982-86; v.p., Response Analysis Corp., 1986—; lectr. research methods Temple U., 1981—; dir. Verbena Corp., N.Y.C. Contbr. numerous articles to profl. publs. Mem. adv. council to 8th Dist. city councilman, Phila., 1971-79; mem. 22d Ward Democratic Exec. Com., 1971-78, State Dem. Com., 1974-76; mem. Pa. Gov.'s Council on Nutrition, 1974-76; v.p. Miquon Upper Sch. Bd., Phila., 1977-78; trustee Princeton Regional Scholarship Found., 1982—, pres., 1984-85; mem. bd. edn. Princeton Regional Sch. Dist., 1984—, pres. 1987—. Mem. Am. Polit. Sci. Assn., Am. Assn. for Pub. Opinion Research. Home: 156-A Spruce St Princeton NJ 08540

KYLE, DEBORAH ALDERMAN, mechanical engineering technician; b. Parkersburg, W.Va., Sept. 17, 1952; d. Morris Yeager and Zoe Madeline Alderman; m. Roger William Kyle, July 8, 1985. BFA, Ohio U., 1975; AS in Mech. Engring. Tech., Parkersburg Community Coll., 1986. With drafting/purchasing dept., Eastern Electric, Inc., Mineral Wells, W.Va., 1970-83; engr. technician Fenton Art Glass Co., Williamstown, W.Va., 1977-87; engr. technician quality dept., Manville Sales Corp., Parkersburg, 1988—. Recipient Best-of-Show Art award Parkersburg Art Ctr., 1972, 1st prize in Art show W.Va. U., 1973. Mem. Instrument Soc. Am., Nat. Assn. Female Execs. Home: 41 Mt Pleasant Estates Mineral Wells WV 26150

KYLE, NANCY R., financial executive; b. Hazleton, Pa., June 4, 1952; d. Robert H. and Frances M. (Dvorshock) Krensavage; BS, Pa. State U., 1973; MBA, LaSalle U., 1979; m. Joseph B. Ritvalsky, Nov. 29, 1975. Chief evaluator United Cerebral Palsy Assn., Phila., 1973-76; controller United Way of S.E. Delaware County, Chester, Pa., 1976-79; corp. fin. analyst Alco Standard Corp., Valley Forge, Pa., 1979-81, asst. to pres. in charge corp. planning, 1981-84, mergers and acquisitions, 1984—; fin. cons. Bd. dirs. ARC, 1980-82, instr. CPR, advanced first aid, 1975-85; mem. Republican Nat. Com., 1978—; mem. bus. adv. council LaSalle U.; mem. fund raising com. Dressage at Devon. Recipient citation ARC, 1981. Mem. Assn. for Corp. Growth, Planning Forum (bd. dirs.), Phila. Fin. Assn., Pa. State U. Alumni Assn., LaSalle U. Alumni Assn., LaSalle U. Council of Pres.'s Assocs. Republican. Roman Catholic. Contbr. articles to profl. jours. Office: PO Box 834 Valley Forge PA 19482

KYLE, PATRICIA ANN, marketing company executive; b. Hammond, Ind., Apr. 16, 1936. AB, Ind. U., 1957, MA, 1958; MA, Georgetown U., 1976, PhD, 1979. Sec. Esso Mediterranean, Geneva, 1959; adminstrv. asst. UNESCO, Paris, 1960-63, Sen. Ted Kennedy, Washington, 1964-65; asst. prof. Queens Coll., Charlotte, N.C., 1969-72, U. N.C., Charlotte, 1972-80; pres. FacFind, Inc., Charlotte, 1980—. Chmn. bd. dirs. Mecklenburg County Social Services. Recipient DECA award N.C. Assn. Distbg. Edn., Small Bus. Devel. award Charlotte C. of C. Mem. Charlotte Sales and Mktg. (editor), Am. Mktg. Assn., Adminstrv. Women in Edn. (pres. N.C. chpt.). Home and Office: 7113 Lakeside Dr Charlotte NC 28215-9998

KYLE-RENO, SHELIA ANN, lawyer; b. Owensboro, Ky., Sept. 13, 1951; d. Herman William and Evelyn Maxine (Johnson) Kyle; m. Charles Edward Reno, Feb. 7, 1974; 1 child, La Mer Kyle-Reno. B.A., Wright State U., 1978; J.D., U. Dayton, 1983. Bar: Ohio 1983. Computer operator Owensboro Mcpl. Utilities, 1971-73; community organizer City Mgrs. Office, Owensboro, 1972-73; hotline coordinator Ky. Wesleyan U., Owensboro, 1971-73; law extern U.S. Magistrates, Dayton, 1981-82; law clk. Henley Vaugh Becker, Wald, Dayton, Ohio, 1982-83; atty. Legal Aid Soc. of Dayton, 1983—, EEO officer, 1983-86, mng. lawyer, 1985-86, coordinator Contract Atty. Program, 1985—, mng. atty. family law unit, 1985-86, coordinator client services, 1985—, acting exec. dir., 1986—. Pres. Womens Polit. Caucus, Dayton, 1980; mem. People for Am. Way, 1982. Key to City, City of Owensboro, 1971. Mem. ABA, Ohio Bar Assn., Dayton Bar Assn., Am. Acad. Trial Lawyers, Ohio Acad. Trial Lawyers, Miami Valley Assn. Women Attys., ACLU, NOW, Phi Alpha Delta. Democrat. Home: 5565 Hummock Rd PO Box 26425 Dayton OH 45426 Office: Legal Aid Soc Dayton 117 S Main St Suite 515 Dayton OH 45402

KYLE-WHITE, BARBARA LOUISE, real estate executive; b. Gloucester, Mass., July 11, 1945; d. Roland Parsons and Margaret (Stickney) Kyle; m. Asher Abbott White, Jr., Sept. 22, 1979; children: Anna, Andrew. RN, U. Pa., 1966, BSN, 1970; CRNA, U. Wash., 1978. Staff nurse U. Pa., Phila., 1966-69; intensive care nurse to mental health counselor U. Calif., San Francisco, 1969-72; sales assoc. Lord and Taylor, Chgo., 1974-75; anesthetist Group Health Hosp. Valley Gen., Seattle, 1975-79; adminstrv. exec. Am. Corp. Overseas, Oxford, Eng., 1979-84; owner catering company London and Seattle, 1984-85; sales mgr., mdse. mgr. Talbots, Seattle, 1985-87; real estate sales, investment counselor Windermere Real Estate/JL Inc., Bellevue, Wash., 1987—; lectr. in field. Editor Upper Heyford Cookery Book, 1983. Hostess Medina Home and Garden Tour, Wash., 1988; organizer Upper Heyford Arts and Crafts Fair, Oxford, Eng., 1981. U. Pa. Senatorial scholar. Mem. Assn. Cooking Profls., Master Chefs Inst. London, Nat. Assn. Female Execs., Real Estate Bd. of Seattle, Nat. Assn. Nurse Anesthetists. Republican. Episcopalian. Home: PO Box 194 Medina WA 98039 Office: Windermere Real Estate/JL Inc 2955 80th Ave SE Mercer Island WA

KYRIAKOU, LINDA GRACE, diversified manufacturing executive; b. N.Y.C., Dec. 5, 1943; d. Frank Thomas and Dolores Helen (Coscia) LaGamma; B.A., Hunter Coll., 1965; m. Konstantinos Kyriakou, May 7, 1967; 1 dau., Christina Elena. Info. editor Nat. Bur. Econ. Research, N.Y.C., 1967-69; dir. research/account officer Booke & Co., N.Y.C., 1969-75; mgr. communications services C.I.T. Fin. Corp., N.Y.C., 1975-79; dir. corp. communications Sequa Corp., N.Y.C., 1979-87, v.p. communications, 1988—. Mem. Public Relations Soc. Am., Nat. Investor Relations Inst. (dir. N.Y. chpt. 1981-82), Women's Bond Club N.Y. (bd. govs. 1978-80). Home: 300 E 59th St New York NY 10022

KYTLE, CAROLINE ELIZABETH, writer; b. Charleston, S.C., July 25, 1913; d. Alfred Oswald and Anna Belle (Linn) Larisey; m. David Calvin Kytle, Jan. 23, 1946. AB in English, Ga. State Womans Coll., 1935. Clerical position Office of the Pres. Ga. State Womans Coll., Valdosta, 1936-39; clk. materials bur. Nat. Youth Adminstrn., Atlanta, 1939-41; sec. Citizens' Fact Finding Movement of Ga., Atlanta, 1941-42; staff writer pub. relations Bell Aircraft, Marietta, Ga., 1942-45; produced a house organ with no asst. Davison-Paxon Dept. Store, Atlanta, 1945-46. Author: Willie Mae, 1958 (Ohioana Book award 1958), Home on the Canal, 1983, The Voices of Robby Wilde, 1987; author, editor: Time Was: A Cabin John Memory Book, 1976; author, photographer: Four Cats Make One Pride, 1978. Democrat. Unitarian. Home: 6600 81st St Cabin John MD 20818

LABAR, TRACY RUCKERT, marketing professional; b. Pitts., Feb. 26, 1958; d. James Charles and Eileen May (Briggs) R.; m. Woody LBar, Sept. 12, 1987. Student, Bradford U., 1977. Word processor Pocono Mountain Vacation Bur., Stroudburg, Pa., 1983-84; sales rep. Tree Tops, Inc., Bushkill, Pa., 1984-85, referal dir., 1985-87; office adminstr. Daniel W. Keuler Real Estate, Canadensis, Pa., 1987—. Mem. Nat. Assn. Female Execs., Animal Protection Inst., North Shore Animal League. Republican. Roman Catholic. Home: PO Box 154 Rte 191 Mountainhome Canadensis PA 18325 Office: Tree Tops Inc Box 163 Bushkill PA 18324

LABARBERA, ELLEN, editor; b. Passaic, N.J., Oct. 17, 1948; d. Jack Howells, and Mary (Singer) Samson; B.A., Antioch Coll., 1971; m. Michael J. LaBarbera, May 20, 1973; children—Jessica Mary, Julia Anne, Cara Jane. Editor, Marcel Dekker, Inc., N.Y.C., 1971-73, Thomas Bouregy & Co., Inc., N.Y.C., 1973-76; sr. editing supr. McGraw-Hill Book Co., N.Y.C., 1976-78, sponsoring editor, 1978-83; free-lance editorial cons., 1983—.

LABATT-SIMON, JACQUELINE G., market research professional; b. N.Y.C., Oct. 18, 1939; d. Sol and Blanche (Shapiro) Goldman; m. Malcolm R. Labatt-Simon, Nov. 26, 1965 (div. 1978); children: Pamela Leslie, Christopher Harré Marques. BS, Columbia U., 1962; MBA, Pace U., 1985. Research analyst Young and Rubicam, N.Y.C., 1962-65, project mgr. Ogilvy and Mather Inc., N.Y.C., 1965-68; cons. J.G. Labatt-Simon, Rye, N.Y., 1968-78, 79-82; research dir. Compton Advt., N.Y.C., 1978-79; mgr. market research Cahners Exposition Group, Stamford, Conn., 1985—; con. City of Rye, 1986-87. Mem., dir. Rye Sch. bd., 1983-85; mem. Rye Cable TV Com., 1986—; deacon Rye Presbn. Ch., 1987—; bd. dirs. Jr. League, Larchmont, N.Y., 1973-80. Mem. Am. Mktg. Assn. Republican. Office: Cahners Exposition Group 999 Summer St Stamford CT 06905

L'ABBE, MARY-KAY COCO, corporate ecology administrative assistant; b. Reserve, La., Sept. 21, 1933; d. George R. and Mabel (Schmidt) Coco; divorced; children: Monique Fay Coco L'Abbe and Michelle Kay Coco L'Abbe (twins). Student, Loyola U., New Orleans, 1951-52, 54-56; Assoc. in Acctg., U. Southwestern La., 1954. With human resources/treasury dept. Shell Chem. Co., 1954-68; adminstr. environ. and indsl. hygiene dept. chems. div. BASF Corp., 1971—. Chmn. com. Inter-Civic Council Assn., Baton Rouge, 1983—. Mem. Air Pollution Control Assn. (chmn. com. 1982—), Am. Indsl. Hygiene Assn. (chmn. program com. Deep South chpt. 1983—), La. Water Pollution Control Assn. (treas., sec.), La. Air Pollution Control Assn., La. Women In Politics, Women In The Mainstream, Bus. and Profl. Women Assn. (treas., sec., v.p. Baton Rouge chpt. 1982-86, pres.-elect 1987—). Democrat. Roman Catholic. Clubs: Gonzales Country (La.) (chair program com. 1966-67, pres. 1967-68). Home: 382 Fairway Dr Condo 16 Fairway Village LaPlace LA 70068 Office: BASF Corp PO Box 457 River Rd Geismar LA 70034

LABEDZ, BERNICE R., state legislator; b. Omaha, Sept. 19, 1919; m. Stanley J. Labedz, May 9, 1942; children—Terry, Jan, Toni, Frank. Former businesswoman, employee Nebr. State Dept. Revenue, then mayoral, senatorial asst., pub. relations dir.; mem. Nebr. State Legislature, 1976—. Recipient community service awards. Office: Nebr State Capitol Bldg Lincoln NE 68509 also: 4417 S 40th St Omaha NE 68107

LABELLA, ARLEEN ELDA, educator, author, lecturer; b. Rome, N.Y., Mar. 26, 1945; d. Paul Anthony and Elda Marie (Guaspari) LaBella; m. Dennis James O'Brien, Sept. 1, 1979; 1 child, Colin LaBella O'Brien. B.A., SUNY-Oswego, 1967; M.Ed., North Adams State Coll., 1971, U. Buffalo, 1975; Ed.D., U. Mass., 1985. Cert. elem. tchr., N.Y. Pub. sch. tchr. various pub. schs., Vt., N.Y., 1967-74; adj. prof. U. Buffalo, N.Y., 1975-79; psychol. counselor Bennington Coll., 1975-82; co-founder, co-dir. Profl. Resources, Inc., Reston, Va., 1982—; cons./trainer numerous U.S. corps., govt. agys. and orgns., 1975—; nat. seminar leader Rutherford Training Workshops, Boulder, Colo., 1980-82, CareerTrack Seminars, Boulder, 1982-84; chairperson steering com. Women's Resource Ctr., Bennington, Vt., 1977; cons. Women in State Employment, Mpls., 1984-85. Co-author: Personal Power, 1983, Managing Assertively (trainer's manual), 1978, Personal Effectiveness (audio-cassette series). Contbr. numerous articles to profl. jours. Task force mem. Gov.'s Commn. on Status of Women, Burlington, 1975-76. Mem. Am. Soc. Tng. and Devel. Avocations: aerobics, traveling.

LA BELLE, JANE, fashion designer; b. Evanston, Ill., Dec. 5, 1949; d. Robert Edward and Virginia Ann (Ross) Beckwith; m. Richard John Cicero, May 21, 1977 (div. Nov. 1983); 1 child, Nina; m. Gery Thomas Blue, Feb. 16, 1984; children: Levon Ross, Wyatt Robert. Student, Northwestern U., 1967, U. Denver, 1968-69, Stanford U., 1970-72, Calif. Coll. Arts & Crafts, 1972. Owner Bearware, Aspen, Colo., 1973-77; childrens clothing designer Bearware (name now Bearware, Inc.), Aspen, Woodstock (N.Y.), and Davisville (N.H.), 1973-77, 81—; pres. Bearware, Inc., Aspen, Woodstock (N.Y.), and Davisville (N.H.), 1981—; studio mgr. Aspen Recording Studios, 1977-81; cons. in field. Home: Rte 1 Box 321 Contoocook NH 03229 Office: Bearware Inc 321 Dustin Rd Davisville NH 03229

LABENSKI, TERESA FRANCES, health care administrator; b. Norwich, Conn., Dec. 12, 1941; d. Peter Edward and Frances Teresa (Szalkowski) L. RN, St. Francis Hosp. Sch. Nursing, 1962; BA in Psychology cum laude, U. Hartford, Conn., 1977, MPA, 1980. RN, Conn., Mich. Nurse various practices, Hartford, 1962-77; br. mgr. Kelly Health Care, Hartford and Waterbury, Conn., 1977-80; mgr. profl. services Troy, Mich., 1981-85; sales rep. Med-X Co., Newington, Conn., 1980-81; exec. dir. Community Health Services, Port Huron, Mich., 1985—; counselor Oakland U. Continuum Ctr., Rochester, Mich., 1982—. Trustee Fed. Emergency Mgmt. Act Bd., Port Huron, 1985—, Blue Water Hospice, 1985-87. Mem. Alumnae Assn. St. Francis Sch. Nursing, Nat. League for Nursing, Mich. League for Nursing, Vis. Nurses Assn., AAUW, Nat. Assn. Career Women, Blue Water Personnel Assn. of Career Women. Home: 902 La Salle Blvd Port Huron MI 48060

LABOUNTY, RACHAEL, communications executive; b. Davenport, Iowa, Mar. 29, 1958; d. Kenneth Ardel and Esther (Ortman) Thompson; m. David John LaBounty, Jan. 12, 1985; 1 child, Andrew Espy. BA, St. Louis U., 1986; MPA, Park Coll., 1988. Sec. Continental Telephone System, St. Louis, 1977-81, tariffs analyst, 1981-84; mgr. staff tariff implementation Nat. Exchange Carriers Assn. Inc., Whippany, N.J., 1984-85; mgr. toll planning United Telephone System, Overland Park, Kans., 1985—. Coordinator, editor: NECA: Access Charge Handbook, 1985. Mem. Mo. Future Compensation Com. (chmn. contract subcom.), NE Future Compensation Com., Mo. Bus. Week, Info. Exchange, Kappa Delta Pi, Delta Tau Kappa. Republican. Mennonite. Office: United Telephone System Midwest Group 5454 W 110th Overland Park KS 66211

LACEY, JUNE ARMSTRONG, retired educator; b. Windfall, Ind., Dec. 28, 1912; d. Ray and Pearl (Shawhan) Armstrong; m. Dudley Howarth Lacey, Feb. 15, 1936; children—Michael Lacey, Patricia Lacey Woods. Student Central Normal U., 1932; B.S. in Edn., Ball State Tchrs. Coll., 1960; M.A. in Edn., Ball State U., 1966. Cert. elem. tchr., Ind. Tchr. Windfall Elem. Sch., Ind., 1932-35, 44-57, Whitewater Elem. Sch., Richmond, Ind., 1935-36, Jefferson Sch., Tipton, Ind., 1957-60, Kokomo Ctr. Twp. Schs., 1960-77; mem. Govs. Council Children and Youth, Indpls., 1940-50; instr. math lab. Ind. U., Kokomo, 1977. Pres. Windfall PTA, 1940-49; mem. Howard County Hist. Soc., 1975-77; v.p. Methodist Women, 1980-86; pres. Tipton br. Am. Cancer Soc., 1985, co-chmn. Daffodil Days, 1984-85; dep. assessor Wildcat Twp., Tipton County, Ind., 1984—; dep. Windfall Trustees Office, 1984—. Mem. Ind. Retired Tchrs. Assn. Democrat. Methodist. Club: Homemakers. Lodge: Eastern Star. Avocations: Writing poetry; antiques; home decorating. Home: 312 W Sherman Box 265 Windfall IN 46076

LACH, ALMA ELIZABETH, food and cooking writer, consultant; b. Petersburg, Ill.; d. John H. and Clara E. (Boeker) Satorius; diplome de Cordon Bleu, Paris, 1956; m. Donald F. Lach, Mar. 18, 1939; 1 dau., Sandra Judith. Feature writer Children's Activities mag., 1954-55; creator, performer TV show Let's Cook, children's cooking show, 1955; hostess weekly food program on CBS, 1962-66, performer TV show Over Easy, PBS, 1977-78; food editor Chgo. Daily Sun-Times, 1957-65; pres. Alma Lach Kitchens Inc., Chgo., 1966—; dir. Alma Lach Cooking Sch., Chgo.; lectr. U. Chgo. Downtown Coll., Gourmet Inst., U. Md., 1963, Modesto (Calif.) Coll., 1978, U. Chgo., 1981; resident master Shoreland Hall, U. Chgo., 1978-81; food cons. Food Bus. Mag., 1964-66, Chgo.'s New Pump Room, Lettuce Entertain You, Bitter End Resort, Brit. V.I., Midway Airlines, Flying Food Fare, Inc., Berghoff Restaurant, Hans' Bavarian Lodge, Unocal '76, Sweetwater Restaurant; columnist Modern Packaging, 1967-68, Travel & Camera, 1969, Venture, 1970, Chicago mag., 1978, Bon Appetit, 1980, Tribune Syndicate, 1982. Recipient Pillsbury award, 1958; Grocery Mfrs. Am. Trophy award, 1959, certificate of Honor, 1961; Chevalier du Tastevin, 1962; Commanderie de l'Ordre des Anysetiers du Roy, 1963; Confrerie de la Chaine des Rotisseurs, 1964; Les Dames D'Escoffier, 1982. Mem. U. Chgo. Settlement League, Am. Assn. Food Editors (chmn. 1959). Clubs: Tavern, Quadrangle (Chgo.). Author: A Child's First Cookbook, 1950; The Campbell Kids Have a Party, 1953; The Campbell Kids at Home, 1953; Let's Cook, 1956; Candlelight Cookbook, 1959; Cooking a la Cordon Bleu, 1970; Alma's Almanac, 1972; Hows and Whys of French Cooking, 1974, The World and I, 1988. Contbr. to World Book Yearbook, 1961-75, Grolier Soc. Yearbook, 1962. Home and Office: 5750 Kenwood Ave Chicago IL 60637

LACH, CHRISTINE MARIE, real estate appraiser; b. Chgo., June 12, 1956; d. Walter T. and Violet A. (Ranieri) L.; m. Eric W. Hinds. BS in Fin., U. Ill., 1978. Appraisal trainee Home Savs. Assn., Houston, 1978-79; data collector Cole-Layer-Trumble, Houston, 1979; asst. v.p. Real Estate Research Corp., Chgo., 1986—; appraiser Allison-Bullitt-Hutchins, Inc., 1979-86. Mem. AAUW (pres. Montrose br. 1980-81), Am. Inst. Real Estate Appraisers. Home: 5317 Central Western Springs IL 60558 Office: Real Estate Research Corp 72 W Adams St Chicago IL 60603

LACHENBRUCH, TERESA COX, banker; b. Wichita, Kans., Jan. 16, 1956; d. Loren Eugene and Virginia Lee (Hayman) Cox; m. Roger Bennett Lachenbruch, Feb. 11, 1978. B.S. magna cum laude, U. Colo.-Denver, 1981; MBA, U. San Francisco, 1985. Research analyst Ind. Bankshares Corp., San Rafael, Calif., 1981-83; product mgr., asst. v.p. Westamerica Bank, San Rafael, 1983-87, br. group mgr., v.p., 1987—. Mem. Am. Mktg. Assn. (Outstanding Mktg. Student 1981), Phi Chi Theta, Beta Gamma Sigma. Office: Westamerica Bank 1108 5th Ave San Rafael CA 94901

LACHMAN, VICKI DIANE, health care consultant, psychotherapist; b. Norristown, Pa., Feb. 8, 1946; d. James William and Mae K. (Godshall) L.; m. William J. Gall, July 7, 1968 (div. Feb. 1976). Diploma, Phila. Gen. Hosp. Sch. Nursing, 1967; BSN, U. Pa., 1972, MSN, 1974; PhD in Organizational Systems Theory/Devel. Group Process, Temple U., 1983. Cert. Nurse Adminstr., Clin. Specialist in Psychiatric and Mental Health Nursing. Psychiatric staff nurse Phila. Gen. Hosp., 1967-68, intensive care staff nurse, 1971-72; pumonary staff nurse Valley Forge Gen. Hosp., Phoenixville, Pa., 1968-69; intensive care nurse Reynolds Army Hosp., Lawton, Okla., 1969-70; med.-surg. staff nurse St. Francis Hosp., Tulsa, 1970-71; intensive care and emergency room staff nurse JFK Hosp., Stratford, N.J., 1972-74; clin. instr., lectr. St. Agnes Sch. Nursing, Phila., 1974-75; staff assoc. Laurel Inst., Inc., Phila., 1974-78; assoc. Phila. Profl. Assocs., 1978-79; assoc. dir. U. Medicine and Dentistry N.J., 1983-84, dir. nursing mgmt., adj. prof. sch. osteopathic medicine, ctr. for health care mgmt., 1983-85; dir. health services div. Mobix Corp., Cherry Hill, N.J., 1986, distbr., 1986-87; founder V.L. Assocs., Phila., 1979—; with nursing adv. com. Camden County Coll. Nursing Program, 1984, Edison State Coll. Baccalaureate Program, 1984; cons. Medford Leas, 1987—; cons. mgmt. devel. orientation program Children's Hosp. Phila., 1987—; other consultancies; bd. dirs. Community Multi-Health Services Found., Inc., Phila., Phila. Recovering Nurses; presenter various health care tng. sessions; lectr. in field. Author: Stress Management: A Manual for Nurses; contbr. numerous articles to profl. jours.,. Mem. Am. Hosp. Assn., Am. Soc. Health Manpower Edn. and Tng., Am. Orgn. Nurse Execs., Am. Nurses Assn., Am. Soc. Tng. Devel., Del. Valley Hosp. Assn., Hosp. Trustee Assn. Pa., Organizational Devel. Network, Pa. Nurses Assn., Pa. Orgn. Nurse Execs., Sigma Theta Tau. Democrat. Lutheran. Home: 8016 Winston Rd Philadelphia PA 19118 Office: VL Assocs 150 N 2d St Philadelphia PA 19106

LACKAS, SANDRA LEE, pharmaceutical company executive; b. Hartford, Wis., Aug. 19, 1942; d. Alfred Michael and Maxine J. (Cook) L. BS, Mt. Mary Coll., Milw., 1964. Cert. nuclear med. technologist. Research asst. Internal Medicine Clinic, U. Heidelberg, Fed. Republic Germany, 1968-73; supr. radioimmunoassay lab., edn. coordinator Sch. Nuclear Med. Tech., St. Mary's Hosp., Milw., 1973-76; tech. mktg. rep. Nuclear Med. Lab., Dallas, 1976-79, mgr. quality control labs., 1979-81, product mgr., Santurce, P.R., 1981-82, mktg. rep. 1982-83; with Warner-Lambert Co., Morris Plains, N.J., 1976-83, product mgr., 1981-82, mktg. mgr. Key Pharms., Inc., Miami, Fla., 1983-86; dir. mktg. Non-Invasive Monitoring Systems, Miami, 1986-88; brand mgr. prescription products Goldline Labs., Ft. Lauderdale, Fla., 1988—. Developer control serum, 1981; researcher articles on gastrointestinal research, 1969-72; contbr. articles to profl. jours. Mem. Am. Soc. Med. Technologists, Am. Mktg. Assn. Roman Catholic. Home: 2333 Brickell 2814 Miami FL 33129 Office: Goldline Labs 1900 W Commercial Blvd Fort Lauderdale FL 33309

LACKS, CECILIA, photography educator; b. St. Louis, July 21, 1945; d. Louis and Lenore (Gimpelson) L. BA, Washington U., 1967; MS, Boston U., 1971; PhD, St. Louis U., 1987. Tchr. English John Burroughs Sch., St. Louis, 1967-69; tchr. journalism, coordinator gifted program Ferguson-Florissant Sch. Dist., St. Louis, 1972-82, photographer newsletter, pubs., 1983; photographer, writer St. Louis, 1972—; instr. St. Louis U., 1982-84, Webster U., 1985-86; assoc. dir. Internat. Edn. Consortium, St. Louis, 1984-86; cons. Conf. on Edn., St. Louis, 1975-80; pres. Beanie Enterprises, St. Louis, 1978—; coordinator Internat. Culture Ctr., 1987—. One woman shows include Louis Beaumont Gallery, 1985, Univ. City Library Gallery, 1987, Grae Gallery, 1987, CORO Found., St. Louis, 1985; group shows include Messing Gallery, 1986; represented by Grae Gallery, St. Louis; author: Downtown Lady; theatre critic Suburban Jours., St. Louis, 1980-86; contbr. articles to profl. jours. Grantee Experiment in Internat. Living, 1972; recipient Travel and Research award 1982; Am. Dance Festival fellow, 1986. Mem. St. Louis Artists Coalition, NEA, Sponsors of Sch. Pubs. (pres. 1980, scholar 1967, grantee 1972). Home: 7443 Stanford Saint Louis MO 63130

LACKS, PATRICIA EVERETT, clinical psychologist, educator; b. Ontario, Oreg., Feb. 22, 1941; d. Franklin A. and Viola L. (Chamberlain) Everett; B.A., Washington U., St. Louis, 1961, M.A., 1962, Ph.D. (USPHS trainee 1961-66), 1966; m. Paul Gawronik, Apr. 4, 1981; children by previous marriage—Jeffrey, Amy. Staff psychologist Malcolm Bliss Mental Health Center, St. Louis, 1966-70; dir. research Jewish Employment and Vocat. Service, St. Louis, 1970-72; assoc. prof. clin. psychology Washington U., 1972-87, lectr., 1987—. NIH grantee, 1981-85. Fellow Am. Psychol. Assn., Mo. Psychol. Assn. (pres. 1976), assoc. fellow Inst. Rational Emotive Therapy; mem. Assn. Advancement Behavior Therapy. Author papers in field, 2 books. Office: Washington U Psychology Dept Saint Louis MO 63130

LACOMBE, RITA JEANNE, computer sales executive; b. Panama City, Fla., Sept. 28, 1947; d. Robert Rosairio and Virginia May (Mauldin) L. AA, Los Angeles Pierce Coll., 1967; BSBA, Calif. State U., Northridge, 1969; postgrad., Stanford U., 1986. Br. mgr. Security Pacific Nat. Bank, San Fernando Valley, Calif., 1970-78; bankcard compliance officer, asst. v.p. Security Pacific Nat. Bank, Woodland Hills, Calif., 1978-82; sect. mgr., v.p. Security Pacific Nat. Bank, Los Angeles, 1982-87; sr. sales rep. corp. microcomputer sales ComputerLand, Los Angeles, 1987—. Membership chair Sierra Club, Los Angeles, 1982. Mem. Nat. Assn. Female Execs. Democrat. Roman Catholic.

LACROIX, CARLENE, realtor; b. Muskogee, Okla., Sept. 21, 1933; d. Carl William and Clarice Denton (Cantrell) Stoddard; m. Stephen R. LaCroix, May 16, 1952; children—Marc Stephen, Curt Alan. Student William Woods Coll., U. Okla. Sales assoc. Coldwell-Banker Ed Post, Scottsdale, Ariz., 1972-82; sales mgr. City Property Mgmt., Scottsdale, 1982-83; owner, broker LaCroix Realty, Scottsdale, 1983—. Mem. Nat. Assn. Realtors, Ariz. Regional Multiple Listing Service, Scottsdale Bd. Realtors, Scottsdale C. of C. Club: Scottsdale Racquet. Republican. Avocations: tennis; traveling. Office: LaCroix Realty PO Box 4955 Scottsdale AZ 85261

LACROIX, FLORA LUISA, artist, writer; b. Mexico City, Sept. 5, 1911. Student, Acad. Jerome, Paris, 1927-28, Atelier Laurent-Derrieux, Paris, 1928-30, Ecole Nat. Arts Decoratifes, Nice, France, 1928-30, Ecole Nat. Beaux Arts, Paris, 1931-33. Archtl. designer Indian Hill Land Co., 1952-60, Lusk Corp., Tucson, 1961-63; free-lance archtl. designer Tucson, 1962-67; instr. fine arts Tucson Adult Edn. Program, 1967-70; pvt. instr. Lacroix Studio, 1970-78; artist Sonoita, Ariz., 1978—. Represented in collections in Tex., Nev., Mex.; painter Kino Missions Collection (16 paintings); patentee free arm movement sleeve; author: A Biography, Development of Imagination for Adults. Mem. Am. Artists Profl. League, Nat. League Pen Women. Club: Salmagundi (N.Y.C.). Home and Office: PO Box 194 Sonoita AZ 85637

LACROIX, MURIEL CLAIRE, business analyst; b. Woonsocket, R.I., July 20, 1939; d. Rene A. and Regina S. (Recore) L. BEd, Rivier Coll., 1971; BBA, Bryant Coll., 1980, postgrad., 1988—. Tchr. jr. high pvt. and pub. schs., Mass. and R.I., 1964-74; student loan rep. Eastland Savs. Bank, Woonsocket, 1974-78; acct. Data Gen. Corp., Westboro, Mass., 1978-83; bus. analyst support services sect. Data Gen. Corp., Milford, Mass., 1983—; prof. acctg. Newbury Coll., Boston, 1988. Mem. Nat. Assn. for Female Execs., Bryant Coll. Alumni Assn. Roman Catholic. Home: 301 Wrentham Rd Bellingham MA 02019

LACY, CARLENE HAMILTON, convenience store specialist; b. Clovis, N.Mex., July 13, 1942; d. Stephen Montgomery and Annie Iona (Bullock) Hamilton; m. Buck Cowart, July 24, 1960 (div. 1972); children—Suzan Annette, Joseph Buck, Jacquelyn Maurie; m. 2d Billy P. Lacy, Apr. 17, 1976. Student civil engring. N.Mex. State U., 1966-67. Draftsman, Bridgers & Paxton, Albuquerque, 1967-68; mech. draftsman, jr. designer Environ. Engring., Dallas, 1968-71; mech. designer Gaynor & Sirmen Cons. Engring., Dallas, 1971-73; stores planning mgr. Southland Corp., Dallas, 1973-80, 7-Eleven stores equipment devel. mgr., 1980-84; dir. sales devel. projects IMI Cornelius Co., Anoka, Minn., 1984-86 ; pres., owner Associated Planners, 1986—. Del., Tex. Democratic Conv., 1980, 82. Recipient Max award Southland Corp., Dallas, 1983. Mem. Nat. Assn. Convenience Stores, Nat. Adv. Group Petroleum and Convenience Store Operators, Internat. Foodservice Cons. Soc., Nat. Restaurant Assn., Am. Soc. Plumbing Engrs. (treas. 1978-79, pres. 1981), LWV. Home and Office: 1350 E Flamingo Rd #286 Las Vegas NV 89119

LACY, CAROL ANGELA, insurance executive; b. Watford, Eng., July 15, 1943; came to U.S., 1967, naturalized, 1976; d. Thomas and Winifred Joan (Stromberg) Carney; m. Floyd Raymond Lacy, May 25, 1968; children—Susan, Timothy. Claims adjuster Central Mut. Ins. Co., Toronto, Can., 1964-68; exec. sec. TransFresh Corp., Salinas, Calif., 1968-70; claims examiner Monterey Bay Found., Salinas, 1972-78; pres., account mgr. ABC Med. Claims Services, Salinas, 1978—; chmn. bd. dirs. Monterey County Spl. Health Care Authority, Salinas, 1982-85. mem. adv. bd. Natividad Hosp., Salinas, 1979-82, North Monterey County Bd. Edn., Salinas, 1977-83, 101 Bypass com., 1984-88, chmn. 1987-88; treas. Monterey County Bds. Assn., Salinas, 1981-83; mem. Monterey County Grand Jury, Salinas, 1984-85; pres. Prunedale PTA, Salinas, 1976; founding trustee Med. Ctr. Found. Monterey County, 1988. Recipient Honorary Service award Prunedale PTA, 1982. Mem. Monterey Bay Life Underwriters Assn. Republican. Baptist. Avocations: stamp collecting; fishing; gardening.

LADA-BUTTERWORTH, JOAN ELIZABETH, speech-language pathologist; b. Worcester, Mass., Oct. 9, 1953; d. Joseph Jr. and Rita Ann (Holewa) Lada; m. John Butterworth Jr., Aug. 8, 1986. BS, Northeastern U., 1976; MS, Purdue U., 1977. Licensed speech lang. pathologist, Mass. Staff speech lang. pathologist Burbank Hosp., Fitchburg, Mass., 1977-81, clin. dir. speech, lang. and hearing ctr., 1981—; adv. Montachusett voice club Northeastern U., 1981—,. Mem. Am. Speech Lang. Hearing Assn. (cert.),

Mass. Speech-Lang.-Hearing Assn. (regional rep. 1986-87), Alexander Graham Bell Assn. Office: Burbank Hosp Nichols Rd Fitchburg MA 01420

LADD, FRANCES NOLDE, communications and computer documentation executive; b. Reading, Pa., Jan. 26, 1937; d. Hans William and Frances Dean (Wilcox) Nolde; m. Alexander Haven Ladd, June 21, 1958 (div. 1967); children: Laurel Dean, Alexis Arms. BA, Conn. Coll., 1958; MA, Middlebury Coll., 1976; MBA, U. N.H., 1984. Freelance editor McGraw Hill and Houghton Mifflin Pub. Cos., N.Y.C., Boston, 1968-70; tchr. English Abbot Acad., Andover, Mass., 1970-73; dir. co-edn. Middlesex Sch., Concord, Mass., 1973-76; tech. editor Digital Equipment Corp., Maynard, Mass., 1976-79; documentation mgr. Digital Equipment Corp., Merrimack, N.H., 1979-84; communications mgr. Digital Equipment Corp., Concord, 1984—. Counselor and vol. East Boston Drug Clinic, 1969-70, workshop leader, 1984; chairperson Carlisle Youth Commn., 1976-78; hospice vistor Hospice Program Emerson Hosp., Concord, Mass., 1979—; co-leader Cancer Support Group Emerson Hosp., Concord, Mass., 1982—; co-chmn. Carlisle Village Assn., 1982-88; bd. dirs. Carlisle State Park Adv. Bd., 1984-88. Mem. Soc. Tech. Communications (Excellence award 1981), Exec. MBA Alumni Club U. N.H. (bd. dirs.). Democrat. Unitarian. Home: 62 Lowell Rd Carlisle MA 01741

LADD-KIDDER, LISA KATHERINE, clinical psychologist; b. Boston, July 13, 1944; d. Alexander Hackett and Eleanor Mary (Murphy) Ladd; B.A., U. South Fla., 1966; M.Ed. (Office Edn. fellow), U. Ga., 1970; M.S., Hahnemann Med. Coll., 1973; m. James Kidder, 1977. Geog. analyst C.I.A., Washington, 1967-69; dormitory dir., counselor Swarthmore Coll., 1971-72; counselor counseling and psychol. services Kutztown U., 1972-85, dir. acad. advisement dept. acad. services, 1985—, also assoc. prof.; pvt. practice psychology, 1978—; workshop presenter. Recipient 1st prize Fla. Poetry Contest, 1966; lic. tchr. spl. edn., emotionally disturbed, Pa.; lic. for pvt. practice, Pa. Mem. Am. Psychol. Assn., Assn. Pa. State Coll. and Univ. Faculties, Internat. Transactional Analysis Assn. (cert.) Democrat. Author: Cartographic Analysis of Southeast Asia, 1966. Home: 239 Pennsylvania Ave Kutztown PA 19530 Office: 307 Administration Bldg Kutztown U Kutztown PA 19530

LADDUSAW-LANE, LISA ANN-MICHAEL, publisher, editor; b. Remsen, Iowa, July 18, 1954; d. Richard Paul and Doris Marie (Frank) Laddusaw; m. Daniel Joseph Lane, Apr. 12, 1953. BA, Calif. State U. at Fullerton, 1977. Asst. art dir. Wolsey Co., 1972-79; advt. mgr. Holman's Dept. Store, 1979-85; art dir. The Vaughn Orgn., 1985-86; prodn. mgr. Bus. Research and Communications, Monterey, Calif., 1986-87, prodn. dir., 1987-88, mng. editor, 1988—. Democrat. Roman Catholic. Home: 26193 Paseo Del Sur Monterey CA 93940

LADNER-RICHARDSON, DELBRA PETTICE, business consultant; b. Wichita, Kans., Jan. 14, 1957; d. Woodrow Charles Ladner and Geraldine (Yarbrough) Taylor; m. Dennis Richardson, July 3, 1976; children: Dennis Donche, Dakira Chinara. AA, Clark County Community Coll., 1977; AS, Sinclair Coll., 1980; BA in Bus. Mgmt., U. Redlands, 1984. Clk., matron, spl. agt. Police Dept. City of Las Vegas, Nev., 1976-78; resource specialist Harrison Twp., Dayton, Ohio, 1978-81; with Calif. Trade Tech. Coll., Long Beach, 1981-82; redevel. and relocation cons. Port & Flor, Inc., Manhattan Beach, Calif., 1982-88; devel. and mgmt. cons. Ladner-Richardson & Assocs., Carson, Calif., 1986-88; pres. Ladner, Albert and Hall, Los Angeles, 1988—. Newspaper columnist Teen Talk, 1978. Mem. Los Angeles Homeless Task Force, 1986-87, Carson Adv. Bd., 1987; chmn. Carson Relocation Task Force, 1987. Mem. Nat. Assn. Housing and Redevel. Ofcls., Internat. Right of Way Assn., Nat. Assn. Female Execs., Nat. Health Network. Democrat. Club: 100 Black Women (Los Angeles). Lodge: Order of Ea. Star.

LAFACE, CONNIE MARION, school system administrator; b. Pitts., July 16, 1942; d. Constantine Joseph and Mary Theresa (DeRiggi) LaF.; m. James Donald Olson, Feb. 20, 1982. BS, Calif. State U., Northridge, 1964; postgrad., Calif. State U., San Luis Obispo, 1976; MBA, U. So. Calif., 1968. Asst. mgr. traffic ops. Pacific Telephone, Los Angeles, 1964-68; with Los Angeles Unified Sch. Dist., 1968—, coordinator gender equity, 1983-85, dir. Commn. for Sex Equity, 1985—; cons. TIDE Project Calif. Dept. Edn., Sacramento, 1983—; mem. steering com. Forward Looking Strategies Com. to Yr. 2000, Los Angeles, 1986—. Contbr. articles to profl. jours. Chair Los Angeles Marathon Com., 1975; guide Los Angeles Beautiful, 1981—; bd. dirs., leadership and program devel. coms. YWCA, Los Angeles, 1985—. Recipient life service award Calif. Tchrs. Assn., 1975, bd. dirs.' Outstanding Leadership award, 1988, Outstanding Service award Nat. Assn. Women in Constrn., 1984, award United Crusade, 1977-78, award Chevron USA, 1985, cert. of commendation Los Angeles City Council, 1985. Mem. NOW, UN Internat. Research and Tng. Inst. for Advancement of Women, Nat. Assn. Women Execs., Women in Ednl. Leadership, Women Educators (chair publicity com. 1982-85), Bus. and Profl. Women Assn., Delta Kappa Gamma (pres. Xi chpt. 1986—). Home: 12736 Tiara St North Hollywood CA 91607 Office: Commn for Sex Equity 450 N Grand Ave H256 Los Angeles CA 90012

LA FARGE, PHYLLIS, editor; b. N.Y.C., June 10, 1933; d. Thomas Sergeant and Marie (Iselin) La F.; student Radcliffe Coll., 1955; m. Chester H. Johnson, Sept. 13, 1958 (div. 1980); children: Clare, Thomas. Contbg. editor Parents mag., N.Y.C. Mem. PEN, Am. Soc. Mag. Editors. Author: Keeping Going; (with Joan Costello) The Strangelove Legacy: Growing Up American.

LAFAYE, CARY DUPRE, librarian; b. Horry County, S.C., June 22, 1945; d. Moffatt Barmore and Helen Elizabeth (Cappelmann) DuPre; m. Angus Bird Lafaye, Mar. 21, 1970; 1 dau., Helen Cary. B.A. cum laude, U.S.C., 1967, M. Librarianship, 1973. Reading, history tchr. Moultrie Jr. High Sch., Mount Pleasant, S.C., 1967-69; tchr. French, history Irmo High Sch. (S.C.), 1969-71; library asst. U.S.C., Columbia, 1971-72; librarian Richland County Pub. Library-Cooper Br., Columbia, S.C., 1973-74; reference librarian Midlands Tech. Coll., Beltline Library, Columbia, 1975—. Mem. Ala, S.C. Library Assn., Southeastern Library Assn., U. S.C. Coll. Library and Info. Sci. Assn. (v.p. 1987-88), Phi Beta Kappa, Beta Phi Mu (chpt. pres. 1983-84), Kappa Delta. Home: 1412 Haynsworth Rd Columbia SC 29205 Office: Midlands Tech Coll Beltline Library PO Drawer 2408 Columbia SC 29202

LAFFAL, FLORENCE, artist; b. N.J., Jan. 3, 1921; d. Jacob and Sarah (Berman) Schultz; B.S. in Fine Arts Edn., So. Conn. Coll., 1957; M.A. in Fine Arts and Fine Arts Edn., Columbia, 1958; m. Julius Laffal, Aug. 24, 1943; children—Paul David, Kenneth. Tchr. art North Haven Sch. System, 1958-66; free-lance artist 1966-80; owner gallery, 1969-80; editor, pub. Folk Art Finder. Mem. Silvermine Guild Artists, Soc. Conn. Craftsmen (pres., dir. 1968-74). Author: Artist-Craftsmen of Connecticut Datebook, 1971; Breads of Many Lands, 1975. Office: Gallery Press Inc 117 N Main Essex CT 06426

LAFFERTY, SHERALIN STOCKWELL, engineer; b. New Orleans, Feb. 22, 1959; d. Norman David and Helen Wenifred (Shepard) Stockwell; m. Randel Alan Lafferty, Aug. 23, 1986. BS in Bio-engring., U. Calif., San Diego, 1980. Bio-mech. lab aide VA Hosp., La Jolla, Calif., 1979-80; mech. engr. Cubic Western Data, San Diego, 1980-82; instrument research and devel. engr. Cilco, Pomona, Calif., 1983-85; mfg. engr. Am. Dade, Costa Mesa, Calif., 1985-86; air sweeper design engr. Sweeper div. FMC, Pomona, 1986—; chairperson communications team FMC Sweeper, Pomona, 1987—; mentor employee involvement team for assembly line, Pomona, 1987—. Gate and lighting cons. Mountain Meadows Homeowners Assn., Pomona, 1985—. Mem. Nat. Assn. Female Execs. Republican. Clubs: FMC Golf League (treas. 1987—); Sq. Dance (hospitality com. 1987—). Home: 1801 Alicante Pomona CA 91768 Office: FMC Sweeper Div 1201 E Lexington Pomona CA 91766

LAFFOND, LAURA JEAN, therapist, health facility administrator; b. Attleboro, Mass., Sept. 22, 1956; d. WIlliam Russell and Jane Bernice (Kuech) Haid; m. William Terry Laffond, June 25, 1983; 1 child, Jeffrey Richard. BS in Phys. Therapy, Russell Sage Coll., Troy, N.Y., 1978; M Pub. Adminstrn., Northeastern U., 1982. Phys. therapist Meml. Hosp., Albany, 1978-79; phys. therapist Marlboro (Mass.) Hosp., 1979-81, mgmt. intern, 1981; research asst. Morgan, Holland Mgmt. Corp., Boston, 1981-82; dir. phys. therapy, health promotion Fallon Clinic, Inc., Worcester, Mass., 1982—. Worksite Intervention Task Force cons., mem. program council Am. Heart Assn., 1986-87. Mem. Am. Phys. Therapy Assn., Nat. Wellness Assn., Assn. Fitness in Bus., Mass. Pub. Health Assn., Worcester Women's Network. Home: 324 Goodale St West Boylston MA 01583 Office: Fallon Clinic Inc 630 Plantation St Worcester MA 01605

LAFONTANT, JEWEL STRADFORD, lawyer; b. Chgo., Apr. 28, 1922; d. Cornelius Francis and Aida Arabella (Carter) Stradford; 1 son, John W. Rogers III. A.B., Oberlin Coll., 1943; J.D., U. Chgo., 1946. Bar: Ill. bar 1947. Asst. U.S. atty. 1955-58; sr. ptnr. Vedder, Price, Kaufman & Kammholz, Chgo.; dep. solicitor gen. U.S. Washington, 1972-75; dir. Mobil Corp., Continental Bank, Foote, Cone & Belding, Equitable Life Assurance Soc. U.S., Trans World Corp., Revlon, Inc., Ariel-Capital Mgmt., Harte-Hanks Communications, Inc., Pantry Pride, Inc., Revlon Group, Equitable Life, Howard U., Midway Airlines; past mem. U.S. Adv. Commn. Internat. Edn. and Cultural Affairs, Nat. Council Minority Bus. Enterprises, Nat. Council on Ednl. Research; past chmn. adv. bd. Civil Rights Commn.; mem. Pres.'s Pvt. Sector Survey Cost Control; pres. Exec. Exchange; past U.S. rep. to UN. Bd. editors: Am. Bar Assn. Jour. Former trustee Lake Forest (Ill.) Coll., Oberlin Coll., Howard U., Tuskegee Inst.; bd. govs. Ronald Reagan Presdl. Found.; mem. Martin Luther King, Jr., Fed. Holiday Commn. Fellow Internat. Acad. Trial Lawyers; mem. Chgo. Bar Assn. (bd. govs.). Home: 180 E Pearson St Chicago IL 60611 Office: 115 S LaSalle St Chicago IL also: Mobil Corp 150 E 42nd St New York NY 10017

LAFORTUNE, VICTORIA ANNE, television producer; b. Amherst, Mass., Aug. 4, 1944; d. Leon Robert and Julia Marie (Gagne) LaF. BA, So. Conn. Coll., 1968. Prodn. coordinator Lorimar Prodns., Los Angeles, 1977-81, assoc. producer-dir., 1981—. Speaker in field. Vol. fundraiser Los Angeles Dems., 1986-87. Mem. Woman in Film, Acad. TV Arts and Scis. Democrat. Office: Lorimar Prodns 3970 Overland Ave Culver City CA 90232-3783

LAFOUREST, JUDITH ELLEN, editor, publisher, writer, educator; b. Indpls., Jan. 10; d. Edward Elston and Dorothy Jeanette (Parker) LaFourest; B.A., Ind. U.-Purdue U., Indpls., 1972; M.A.T., Ind. U., 1980; m. William E. Lugar; 1 dau., Beth Anne Gruner; 1 son, Paul Christopher Stewart Pitts Lugar LaFourest. Lead pre-vocat. instr., ednl. adminstr. Opportunities Industrialization Center, Indpls., 1972-76; part-time English and human relations instr. Profl. Careers Inst., Indpls., 1975-78; editor, pub. Womankind, Indpls., 1977-83; co-dir. Womankind Center, 1981-82; editor, creative writer, photographer Bio-Feed-Back Bio Dynamics/BMC, Indpls., 1977-80; mem. assoc. faculty, creative writing inst. Ind.U.-Purdue U., Indpls., 1979-86, supr. student tchrs. of English, 1983—; adj. faculty dept. English, Butler U., 1984—; also lectr., free-lance editor. Ind. sec. NOW, 1978-80. Recipient Disting. Alumni award Ind. U.-Indpls., 1980. Mem. Nat. League Am. Pen Women, Nat. Women's Studies Assn., Ind. U.-Indpls. Liberal Arts Alumni Assn. (pres. 1982), Sigma Tau Delta. Office: Butler U Dept English 4600 Sunset Ave Indianapolis IN 46208

LAFRANCE, BRENDA EILEEN TSIONIAON, infosystems specialist, consultant, tribe official; b. Malone, N.Y., Dec. 28, 1950; d. John David and Ruth Dorothy (Lazore) Cook; m. Jake William LaFrance, Apr. 4, 1970; children: Margaret Mary, John Francis. BA in Biology and Chemistry, Potsdam (N.Y.) State U., 1976; MBA, Clarkson U., 1981; MS in Mgmt. Info. Systems, 1985. Cons. St. Regis Mohawk Tribe, Hogansburg, N.Y., 1974-77; quality control technician Kraft, North Lawrence, N.Y., 1976-79; program dir. Planned Parenthood of No. N.Y., Watertown, 1981-82; info. systems analyst Health & Welfare of Can., Ottawa, Ont., 1982-85; band adminstr. St. Regis Band Council, Que., Can., 1985-86; cons. mgmt. Hogansburg, 1986-87; tribal chief St. Regis Mohawk Tribe, Hogansburg, 1986—; cons., trainer St. Regis (Que.) Drug & Alcohol Div., 1984—, Planned Parenthood No. N.Y., Watertown, 1982 . Pres. Mohawk Indian Housing Corp., Hogansburg, 1974; community organizer St. Regis Mohawk Tribe-Health & Alcohol, Hogansburg, 1977-79, Akwesasne Freedom Sch., Hogansburg, 1981. Recipient Research Assistantship, Clarkson U., 1979, Teaching Assistantship, Clarkson U., 1980, Humanitarian award St. Regis Mohawk Tribe, 1985. Mem. Nat. Assn. Female Execs., Am. Indians in Sci. and Engring. Iroquois. Home: PO Box 190 Cook Rd Hogansburg NY 13655 Office: St Regis Mohawk Tribal Council Community Bldg Hogansburg NY 13655

LA FROSCIA, ELIZABETH JEANNE, banker; b. Bklyn., May 24, 1942; d. Philip and Anna (Sirico) Deffina; m. Hannibal Frances La Froscia, July 30, 1966; children: Louis, Christine, Stephanie, Bruce; foster children: Skelly, Donald, Nhu, Nhan, Nghia Nguyen. BA in English, Polit. Sci. cum laude, Queens Coll., 1981; postgrad., St. John's U., 1983-84. Adminstrv. asst. Chem. Bank, L.I., N.Y., 1975-79; project leader, sr. trainer Citibank, Forest Hills, N.Y., 1979-88; dir. tng., officer Dime Savs. Bank, Valley Stream, N.Y., 1986—. Tchr. liaison N.Y.C. Pub. Sch. Bd. Edn., Bklyn., 1968; den leader Boy Scouts Am., Bklyn., 1970; foster parent Cath. Guardian Soc., Bklyn., 1986—, Vietnamese Refugee Program, Bklyn., 1986—. Recipient award Cath. Archdiocese of Bklyn., 1973. Mem. Am. Bus. Womens Assn., Am. Soc. Trainers and Devel., Club for Adoptive Parents (pres. 1978-80). Democrat. Office: Dime Savs Bank Tng Dept Green Acres Mall Valley Stream NY 11582

LAGAN, CONSTANCE HALLINAN, author, lecturer; b. Jamaica, N.Y., Feb. 18, 1947; d. John Francis and Muriel Ellen (Mylett) Hallinan; m. Patrick Andrew Lagan, June 17, 1967; children: Colleen Sharon, Kelly Corinne, Erin Dawn, Kerry Cathleen. A. in Applied Sci., Nassau Community Coll., 1966; student, Hofstra U., 1981-83. Proprietor, mgr. Creations by Connie, North Babylon, N.Y., 1980—; founder, exec. dir. Entrepreneurial Ctr. Small Bus. Devel., 1988—; lectr. Displaced Homemakers, Babylon, N.Y., 1986, Port Washington Sch. Dist., N.Y., 1987. Author: the Marketing Options Report Series for Craftspeople, 1983-88, (with others) Mothers' Money Making Manual, 1987; author, appeared in video Applique: Traditional, Stained, and Shadow, 1988; designer Strip Piece Quilted Vest, 1984 (Design Hall of Fame 1985); contbg. editor Homeworking Mothers mag., 1987—; columnist L.I. Heritage, Mineola, N.Y., 1983-84; contbr. articles to popular mags. and profl. jours. Leader Girl Scouts of Am., North Babylon, 1972-74; coach Patriot Soccer Club, North Babylon, 1980-81; vol. quilter The Ribbon, Denver, 1985-86, Sunbow Quilters for Peace, Auburn, Wash., 1986—. Grantee Staten Island Children's Mus., 1982, Ridgewood Youth Council, 1982, Port Washington Adult Edn., 1987; Newcombe scholar Hofstra U., 1981-83. Fellow Soc. Craft Designers, Nat. Quilting Assn., Am.-Internat. Quilt Assn., Mothers' Home Bus. Network, L.I. Quilter's Soc. Office: Creations by Connie 35 Claremont Ave North Babylon NY 11703

LAGANGA, DONNA BRANDEIS, publishing company sales executive; b. Bklyn., June 27, 1949; d. Sidney L. and Sylvia (Herman) Brandeis; B.S. in Bus. Edn., Central Conn. State Coll., New Britain, 1972, M.S., 1975; m. Thomas LaGanga, Aug. 11, 1974. Various secretarial positions, 1969-72; tchr. bus. Lewis S. Mills Regional High Sch., Burlington, Conn., 1972-78; cons. Southwestern Pub. Co., Pelham Manor, N.Y., 1978-84, dist. sales mgr., 1984—; co-owner Colonial Welding Service; seminar condr., 1980—. Adv. bd. secretarial sci. dept. LaGuardia Community Coll., Long Island City, N.Y., 1982—; adv. bd. Krissler Bus. Inst. EDPA grantee, 1973; cert. profl. sec. Mem. Nat. Assn. Female Execs., Assn. Info./Systems Profls., Am. Mgmt. Assn., Nat. Bus. Edn. Assn., Profl. Secs. Internat., Eastern Bus. Edn. Assn., Conn. Bus. Edn. Assn., New Eng. Bus. Edn. Assn., Profl. Secs. Assn. N.Y., Nat. Assn. Cert. Profl. Secs., U.S. Golf Assn., Delta Pi Epsilon. Avocations: knitting, sewing, reading, bicycling, golfing. Home: 612 S Main St Torrington CT 06790 Office: South Western Pub Co 5101 Madison Rd Cincinnati OH 45227

LAGASSEY, ELIZABETH ALEXANDRA WILKEL, real estate professional; b. New Britain, Conn., Jan. 28, 1955; d. John William and Helen Nadja (Demko) Wilkel; m. Donald Henry Lagassey, Mar. 10, 1978. Student, Hartford (Conn.) Hosp. Sch. Nursing, 1973-75, Manchester (Conn.) Community Coll., 1980-88. Supr. customer service Gen. Electric Corp., East Hartford, Conn., 1980-81; sr. adminstrv. asst. Fotomat Corp., East Hartford, 1981-83; contract adminstr. Nat. Telephone Co., South Windsor, Conn., 1982-84; div. adminstr. Marshall Erdman and Assocs., Inc., East Windsor, Conn., 1984-88; broker River's Edge Realty, Coventry, Conn., 1987-88, Elizabeth W. Lagassey Real Estate, Danville, Vt., 1988—. Author: Computer System Primer, 1986. Mem. Realtors Polit. Action com., Conn., 1975—. Mem. Nat. Soc. Pub. Accts., Nat. Assn. Credit Mgmt., Nat. Assn. Realtors, Am. Soc. Notaries. Republican. Russian Orthodox.

LAGLE, LINDA JOYCE, communications specialist; b. Chgo., May 11, 1949; d. Sidney and Alice (Kasprzyck) Glass; m. William James Lagle, Apr. 1, 1978. BA, Coe Coll., Cedar Rapids, Iowa, 1971. Copywriter Killian Co., Cedar Rapids, 1972-74; program coordinator, copywriter Sta. KQCR-FM, Cedar Rapids, 1974-76; asst. dir. advt. Turner Corp., Cedar Rapids, 1976-78; news bur. dir. Coe Coll., Cedar Rapids, 1978-84; assoc. dir. pub. relations Gettysburg (Pa.) Coll., 1984-86; dir. news services Drew U., Madison, N.J., 1986—; bd. dirs. Advt. Fedn. of Cedar Rapids, 1975-77; chmn. 9th dist. Addy awards competition, Cedar Rapids, 1976. Editor: The 50th Season, 1983; contbr. articles to mags. and jours. Bd. dirs. Olde Barn Players Dinner Theatre, Cedar Rapids, 1975-76, Community Theatre, Cedar Rapids, 1980-83; bd. dirs., mem. pub. relations com. YWCA, Cedar Rapids, 1981-84. Recipient 1st Place award in radio 9th dist. Advt. Fedn., 1976; Merit award Case Orgn., 1979; grantee Gettysburg Coll., 1985. Mem. Women in Communication, Inc., Council for Advancement and Support of Edn. (dist. conf. speaker 1987). Roman Catholic. Lodge: Kiwanis (v.p. 1988—). Office: Drew U Tilghman House Madison NJ 07940

LAGONTERIE, YVETTE MARIE, federal agency administrator; b. Jamaica Queens, N.Y., Jan. 14, 1956; d. Donald Edwin and Marcella Marie (Goode) LaG. BA in Mass Communications, SUNY, Buffalo, 1977; postgrad., CUNY, Bernard Baruch, 1984—. Radio newscaster Sta. WEBR, Buffalo, 1977; researcher Juvenile Diversion, N.Y.C., 1978; immigration insp. U.S. Immigration and Naturalization Service, N.Y.C., 1978-83, immigration examiner, 1983-85, deportation officer, 1985, mgr. N.Y. citizenship, 1986; dir. legalization U.S. Immigration and Naturalization Service, Bklyn. and Queens, N.Y., 1987-88; spl. asst. to dep. commr. U.S. Immigration and Naturalization Service, Washington, 1988—; lectr. Nassau Acad. Law, 1986-87. Recipient Community Service award Korean Seafood Assn., 1987, Service award Nat. Council Ecuadorian Women, 1987; Named Outstanding Young Women Yr., 1987. Mem. Blacks in Govt. (mem. regional exec. council, recording sec.), Immigration Officers Assn., Nat. Assn. Female Execs., Am. Profl. Women, NAACP. Office: US Immigration and Naturalization Service 425 I St NW Washington DC 20536

LAGRONE, LAVENIA WHIDDON, chemist, real estate broker; b. Conroe, Tex., Feb. 27, 1940; d. James Lewis and Cora Lee (DeLuish) Whiddon; A.A., Kilgore Coll., 1960; B.S., North Tex. State U., 1962; grad. med. technology Baylor U. Med. Center, 1962; m. Doyle W. LaGrone, June 26, 1959 (div. Sept. 1965); 1 child, Russell Randal. Sr. technologist in spl. chemistry Baylor U. Med. Center, Dallas, 1962-63; research chemist, supr. labs., cardiovascular surgery Southwestern Med. Sch., Dallas, 1964-69, Upstate Med. Center, SUNY, Syracuse, 1969-70; research assoc., supr. lab., dept. surgery U. Tex. Med. Br., Galveston, 1970-74, research assoc., supr. labs., pediatric nephrology, 1974—, mem. chem. safety com., 1984-87; real estate broker DeLanney & Assocs., realtors, 1979-83; owner La Grone & Assocs., Realtors, 1983—. Chmn. student activities PTA Galveston, Tex., 1976-77. Recipient Top Real Estate Sales award, Top Real Estate Producer award, DeLanney & Assocs., 1979, also Broker's Excellence award and Top Real Estate Commn. award, 1980, also Million Dollar Producer award, 1980-83, Multi-million Dollar producer, 1984-87. Mem. Am. Soc. Clin. Pathologists (registered med. technologist), Nat. Assn. Realtors, Tex. Assn. Realtors, Galveston Bd. Realtors, Multiple Listing Service (budget com.), Phi Theta Kappa. Club: Bus. and Profl. Women's (pub. relations officer 1985-86, Young Careerist award chmn. 1987). Contbr. articles to chemistry and med. jours. Home: 142 San Fernando St Galveston TX 77550 Office: U Tex Med Br 301 University Blvd Galveston TX 77550

LAGUERRE, JOSELLE LOUIS, English language educator; b. Cap-Haitian, Haiti, May 17, 1960; d. Jacques Transtamar and Mercie Pauline (Pierre-Louis) L.; m. Clifford Edgar LaGuerre, Mar. 19, 1978; children: Clifford E. Jr., Joelle Paule. BA in English, History, Atlantic Union Coll., 1981; MA in English Lang., Andrews U., 1982. Cert. ESL tchr. Instr. English Pacific Union Coll., Angwin, Calif., 1982-86, asst. prof., 1986-87, also bd. dirs. English Lang. Program,; tchr. lang. arts Dade County Pub. Schs., Miami, Fla., 1987—. Sec. Agape, South Lancaster, mass., 1979-81. United Fedn. Tchrs. scholar, 1977-81. Mem. Tchrs. English to Speakers of other Langs., Internta. English Program Dir.'s Assn. Democrat. Adventist. Home: 22129 SW 103 Ct Miami FL 33190 Office: Riviera Jr High Sch 10301 SW 48th St Miami FL 33165

LAGUNA, ASELA RODRÍGUEZ, Spanish educator; b. San German, P.R., Dec. 6, 1946; came to U.S., 1968; d. Ramon Rodríguez and Eugenia Seda; B.A. in Humanities, U. P.R., Mayaguéz, 1968; M.A. in Comparative Lit., U. Ill., Champaign-Urbana, 1970, Ph.D., 1973; m. Elpidio Laguna-Díaz, June 21, 1975; children—Asela, Maria E., Alexandra. Teaching asst. U. Ill., 1969-73; mem. faculty Rutgers U., Newark, 1973—, assoc. prof. Spanish, 1979—; organizer, dir. 1st nat. pub. conf. Images and Identities: The Puerto Rican in Literature, 1983. Research grantee Rutgers U., 1977-78, merit award, 1983; N.J. Dept. Higher Edn. grantee, 1985. Mem. Internat. Comparative Lit. Assn., Am. Comparative Lit. Assn., Assn. Tchrs. Spanish and Portuguese, Assn. Latin Am. Studies. Roman Catholic. Author: Shaw in the Hispanic World, 1981; editor: Imagénes e identidades: el puertorigueño en la literatura, 1985; Images and Identities: The Puerto Rican in Two World Contexts, 1986; Puerto Rican Literature: An Introduction, 1986; also articles in field. Home: 283 Newman St Metuchen NJ 08840 Office: Rutgers U Dept Langs Conklin Hall Newark NJ 07102

LAHRMAN, DOLORES MARIE, archivist, retired; b. Indpls., June 11, 1920; d. Walter M. and Helen M. (Kahl) L. B.S. in Edn., St. Francis Coll., Ind., 1941; student Loyola U., Chgo., 1944, 46, 47; M.A. in Library Sci., Ind. U., 1964. Part-time instr. St. Francis Coll., 1941-43; tchr., St. Andrew's Sch., Ft. Wayne, Ind., 1941-44, St. Mary of the Angels Sch., New Orleans, 1944-45, St. John Baptist Sch., Earl Park, Ind., 1945-46, St. Francis High Sch., Lafayette, Ind., 1946-48; asst. archivist Ind. U., Bloomington, 1962-77, archivist, 1977-88. Poet. Hist. preservation advocate Monroe County Hist. Soc., 1970-78; archivist/curator Andrew Wylie Hist. House, 1981-88. Mem. Sisters of St. Francis, Ind., 1935-48, Discalced Carmelites, La., 1948-62. Mem. Soc. Ind. Archivists (charter), Midwest Archives Conf., Soc. Am. Archivists, Nat. Assn. Female Execs., Soc. of Indiana Pioneers, Ind. German Heritage Soc., AAUW, Clover Internat. Poetry Assn., Ind. U. Alumni Assn., Beta Phi Mu. Roman Catholic. Avocations: reading, writing, Imperial Russian history, music, opera. Home: 5470 W Beach Ln Bloomington IN 47401 Office: Ind U Archives Bryan Hall 201 Bloomington IN 47405

LAINE, DOLORES MAE (DEL), city official; b. Vallejo, Calif., Mar. 20, 1930; d. Leslie Merritt and Mabel Ysabel (Paulson) Wright; A.A., City Coll. San Francisco, 1950; B.A., Calif. State U., Berkeley, 1953; M.Sc., Calif. State U., San Francisco, 1960; m. Ed Laine, Mar. 30, 1962; children—Paul, Brooke, Alison, Paige. Dir. Lake Tahoe (Calif.) Recreation Div., 1961-62; co-owner Laine Assocs. Advt. and Pub. Relations, South Lake Tahoe, Calif., 1961-72, Laine Assocs. Photography, South Lake Tahoe, 1962—; pres. Del Laine and Daus., 1985—; owner Laine Assocs. Cons., 1983—; chmn. South Lake Tahoe Parks and Recreation Commn., 1974-76; councilwoman City of South Lake Tahoe, 1976-80, 84—, mem. affirmative action task force, 1978-80, mayor pro-tem, 1976-77, 86-87, mayor, 1977-78, 87-88. Co-founder, producer Lake Tahoe Children's Theatre, 1962-72; chmn. Tahoe Regional Planning Agy. Urban Design Com., 1973-76; chmn. Tahoe Basin Transp. Authority, 1979—; chmn. Tahoe Regional Transp. Dist., 1981—; chair adv. com. to Calif. Dept. Transp., 1983—. Mem. Nat. Women's Polit. Caucus, South Tahoe Women's Ctr. (pres. 1980-81, dir.), Lake Tahoe Hist. Soc. (pres. 1970-74). Presbyterian. Club: Soroptimist Internat. (regional gov. 1976-78, founder, coordinator Calif. legis. workshop). Office: Box 7322 South Lake Tahoe CA 95731

LAING, KAREL ANN, magazine publisher; b. Mpls., July 5, 1939; d. Edward Francis and Elizabeth Jane Karel (Templeton) Hannon; m. G. R. Cheesebrough, Dec. 19, 1959 (div. 1969); 1 child, Jennifer Read; m. Ronald Harris Laing, Jan. 6, 1973; 1 child, Christopher Harris. Grad., U. Minn., 1960. Sales mgr., pub. Guthrie Symphony Opera Program, Mpls., 1969-71; account supr. Colle & McVoy Advt. Agy., Richfield, Minn., 1971-74; owner The Cottage, Edina, Minn., 1974-75; salespromotion rep. Robert Meyers & Assocs., St. Louis Park, Minn., 1975-76; cons. Webb Co., St.Paul, 1976-77, account mgr., pub., 1977—. Contbr. articles to profl. jours. Community vol. Am. Heart Assn., Am. Cancer Soc., Edina PTA; charter sponsor Walk Around Am., St. Paul, 1985. Mem. Bank Mktg. Assn., Fin. Instn. Mktg. Assn., Advt. Fedn. Am., Am. Bankers Assn., Direct Mail Mktg. Assn., St. Andrews Soc. Republican. Presbyterian.

LAIR, HELEN MAY, poet; b. New Castle, Ind., Jan. 3, 1918; d. Harry and Loma D. (Delon) Humphrey; m. Marvin E. Lair, July 2, 1966; children: Michael Lucas, Joan Lucas Krueckegerg, Nancy Lucas (dec.). Student, Anderson Coll., U. Wis., John Herron Sch. Art. Author: (poetry) Lair Of The Four Winds, 1978, Earth Pilgrim, 1981, (column) New Castle Courier Times, 1982—; contbr. numerous poems to anthologies and publs. including Poetry Rev., Our Western World's Greatest Poems, Today's Best Poems, Best Loved Contemporary Poems, Adventures in Poetry. Pres. Henry County (Ind.) Art Guild; mem. Hoosier Salon. Recipient Farnell award, N.Y. Poetry Forum, Richard Miller award, Muncie (Ind.) Star 1st place award, Ind. State Fedn. Poetry 1st place award. Mem. Women in Communication, Acad. Women Poets, Nat. Fedn. Poets, Internat. Poets Achievement, N.Y. Poetry Forum, Acad. Leonardo da Vinci, Internat. Platform Assn., Epsilon Sigma Alpha. Roman Catholic. Office: 1202 Mourer St New Castle IN 47362

LAIRD, ANNE MARIE, personnel director; b. Orange, N.J., June 23, 1941; d. Paul M. and Anne (Byrne) Kelly; m. Daniel A. Laird, Aug. 13, 1960; children: Daniel, Michael, Kelly, Paul. Student, Glassboro State Coll. Employment supr. Continental Can Co., Millville, N.J., 1976-78, human resrouces supr., 1978-81; human resrouces supr. Houston, Tex., 1981-85; complex human resources supr. Santa Ana, Calif., 1985—. Chair N.J. United Way, Millville, 1978, CEDA Program, 1979. Mem. Am. Soc. Personnel Mgrs., Personnel Indsl. Relations Assn., Internat. Mgmt. Council (pres. 1978). Home: 24731 Calle El Toro Grande El Toro CA 92630

LAIRD, DORIS ANNE MARLEY, humanities educator, musician; b. Charlotte, N.C., Jan. 15, 1931; d. Eugene Harris and Coleen (Bethea) Marley; m. William Everette Laird Jr., Mar. 13, 1964; children: William Everette III, Andrew Marley, Glen Howard. MusB, Converse Coll., Spartanburg, S.C., 1951; opera cert. New Eng. Conservatory, Boston, 1956; MusM, Boston U., 1956; PhD, Fla. State U., 1980. Leading soprano roles S.C. Opera Co., Columbia, 1951-53, Plymouth Rock Ctr. of Music and Art, Duxbury, Mass., 1953-56; soprano Pro Musica, Boston, 1956, New Eng. Opera Co., Boston, 1956; instr. Stratford Coll., Danville, Va., 1956-58, Sch. Music Fla. State U., Tallahassee, 1958-60, dept. humanities, 1960-68; asst. prof. Fla. A&M U., Tallahassee, 1979—. Author: Colin Morris: Modern Missionary, 1980; contbr. articles to profl. jours. Soprano Washington St. Meth. Ch., Columbia, S.C., 1951-53, Copley Meth. Ch., Boston, 1953-56, Trinity United Meth. Ch., Tallahassee, 1983—; mem. Saint Andrews Soc., Tallahassee, 1986—; judge Brain Bowl, Tallahassee, 1981-84. Recipient NEH award, 1988; Phi Sigma Tau scholar, 1960, vis. scholar Cornell U., 1988. Mem. AAUP, AAUW, Nat. Art Educators Assn., Tallahassee Music Tchrs. Assn., Tallahassee Music Guild, Am. Guild of Organists, DAR (mus. rep. 1984-85), Colonial Dames of 17th Century (music dir. 1984-85). Democrat. Club: University Wy Women's. Avocations: traveling, dancing. Home: 1125 Mercer Dr Tallahassee FL 32312 Office: Fla A&M U Dept Humanities Tallahassee FL 32307

LAIRD, JEAN ELOUISE RYDESKI (MRS. JACK E. LAIRD), author, educator; b. Wakefield, Mich., Jan. 18, 1930; d. Chester A. and Agnes A. (Petranek) Rydeski; Bus. Edn. degree Duluth (Minn.) Bus. U., 1948; postgrad. U. Minn., 1949-50; m. Jack E. Laird, June 9, 1951; children—John E., Jane E., Joan Ann P., Jerilyn S., Jacquelyn T. Tchr., Oak Lawn (Ill.) High Sch. Adult Evening Sch., 1964-72, St. Xavier Coll., Chgo., 1974—. Writer newspaper column Around The House With Jean, A Woman's Work, 1965-70, Chicagotown News column The World As I See It, 1969, hobby column Modern Maturity mag., travel column Travel/Leisure mag., beauty column Ladycom mag., Time and Money Savers column Lady's Circle mag., consumerism column Ladies' Home Jour. Mem. Canterbury Writers Club Chgo. (past. pres.), Oak Lawn Bus. and Profl. Women's Club (Woman of Yr. award 1987), St. Linus Guild, Mt. Assisi Acad., Marist, Queen of Peace parents clubs. Roman Catholic. Author: Lost in the Department Store, 1964; Around The House Like Magic, 1968; Around The Kitchen Like Magic, 1969; How To Get the Most From Your Appliances, 1967; Hundreds of Hints for Harrassed Homemakers, 1971; The Alphabet Zoo, 1972; The Plump Ballerina, 1971; The Porcupine Story Book, 1974; Fried Marbles and Other Fun Things To Do, 1975; Hundreds of Hints for Harassed Homemakers; The Homemaker's Book of Time and Money Savers, 1979; Homemaker's Book of Energy Savers, 1981; also 298 paperback booklets. Contbr. numerous articles to mags. Home: 10540 S Lockwood Ave Oak Lawn IL 60453 also: Whitewood Ave Grand Beach MI 49118 also: Lake Geneva WI 53147

LAIRD, SHIRLEY EDER, communication company executive; b. Ridley Park, Pa.; d. Charles E. and Wilhelmina F. Eder; married; children: Craig, Holly Alison, Heather Anne. BA, Cedar Crest Coll. Dir. publs. The Kling Ptnrship, 1966-70, 71-77; assoc. Weld Coxe Mgmt. Cons., 1970-71; editor living sect. Today's Post, King of Prussia, Pa., 1970-71; pub. affairs counsel to pres. Hahnemann Med. Coll. and Hosp., Phila., 1977; owner Laird Unltd., Haverford, Pa., 1977—. Columnist Montgomery Pub. Co., 1967-81; contbr. to mags. Chmn. 12:12 Forum YMCA, Phila., 1970, vice chmn., 1978-80; adv. bd. Villanova U. Theatre, 1983-87. Mem. Pub. Relations Soc. Am., Women In Communications, Phila. Pub. Relations Assn., Nat. League Am. Pen Women, Soc. Profl. Journalists. Republican. Episcopalian. Home and Office: 523 Montgomery Ave Haverford PA 19041

LAKAH, JACQUELINE RABBAT, political scientist, educator; b. Cairo, Apr. 14, 1933; came to U.S., 1969, naturalized, 1975; d. Victor Boutros and Alice (Mounayer) Rabbat; m. Antoine K. Lakah, Apr. 8, 1951; children: Micheline, Mireille, Caroline. BA, Am. U. Beirut, 1968; MPh, Columbia U., 1974, cert. Middle East Inst., 1975, PhD, 1978. Asst. prof. polit. sci. and world affairs Fashion Inst. Tech., N.Y.C., 1978—; asst. prof. grad. faculty polit. sci. Columbia U., N.Y.C., summer 1979, vis. scholar, 1982-83, also mem. seminar on Middle East; guest faculty Sarah Lawrence Co., 1981-82; cons. on Middle East; faculty research fellow SUNY, summer 1982. Fellow Columbia Faculty, 1974, NDEA Title IV, 1974, Middle East Inst., 1975; Rockefeller Found. scholar, 1974. Mem. Am. Profs. for Peace in Mid. East, Internat. Studies Assn., Am. Polit. Sci. Assn., Fgn. Policy Assn., Internat. Studies Assn., Internat. Polit. Sci. Assn. Roman Catholic. Home: 41-15 94th St Queens NY 11373 Office: Seventh Ave at 27th St New York NY 10001

LAKE, ANN WINSLOW, lawyer; b. Lowell, Mass., May 14, 1919; d. Frank and Helen Jablonski; B.S., Lowell State Coll., 1940; J.D., U. Detroit, 1946; M.A., Boston State Coll., 1964, Boston U., 1967; m. Thomas E. Lake, Sept. 5, 1942; children—Beverly Wilkes, Douglas, Warren. Tchr. schs. in Maine, Ga. and Detroit, 1940-43; admitted to Mass. bar, 1946; ind. practice, Dedham, Mass., 1946—; prof. law Salem (Mass.) State Coll., 1970—; mem. Mass. Commn. Study Labor Laws, 1972-74, Mass. Mental Health Legal Advisers Com., 1974-79. Mem. Mass. Adv. Commn. Acad. Talented Pupils, 1960-64, Mass. State Coll. Bldg. Authority, 1964-67, Mass. Com. to Recruit and Screen Candidates for Office Atty. Gen., 1974-78, U. Lowell Found., 1977-82. Recipient award Mass. State Coll. Alumni Assn., 1963, 64, 72, Mass. Assn. Mental Health, 1969, 72. Fellow Am. Bar Found., Mass. Bar Found.; mem. Nat. Assn. Women Lawyers (pres. 1980-81), Polish Bus. and Profl. Women's Club Greater Boston (pres. 1977-79), Norfolk Mental Health Assn. (pres. 1972-73), Mass. Assn. Women Lawyers (pres. 1971-72), Assn. Mass. State Colls. Alumni (pres. 1961-64), Riverdale Improvement Assn. (pres. 1959). Republican. Address: 40 Sawyer Dr Dedham MA 02026

LAKE, BARBARA LEE, educator; b. Cleve., Feb. 8, 1934; d. Byron Edwin and Eva Maria Melissa (Kays) Ice; children: Melissa lee, Ellen Maria. Student, Colby Coll., 1952-53; BS in Edn., Wheelock Coll., Boston, 1956; postgrad., Pacific Luth. U., Tacoma, Wash., 1975. Elem. tchr. Oxnard (Calif.) Sch. Dist., 1956-58, Army Am. Sch. System, Heilbronn, Fed. Republic Germany, 1958-59, Wayne (N.J.) Sch. Dist., 1959-61, Cleve. Sch. Dist., 1961-62, Peru (Ind.) Sch. Dist., 1962-64; kindergarten tchr. Puyallup (Wash.) Sch. Dist., 1966-67; asst. dir. Puyallup PlayCare Ctr., 1969; tchr. Tacoma Sch. Dist., 1969-71; day care coordinator Clover Park Vocat. Tech. Inst., Tacoma, 1972—; cons. Dept. of Def., Washington, 1977-79; advisor Child Devel. Assn. Credential, Washington, 1980—; validator Nat. Assn. for Edn. Young Children, Washington, 1985—; mem. exec. bd. Puyallup PlayCare Ctr., 1985—, Lakewood Community Ctr., Tacoma, 1980-83. Named Disting. Educator Clover Park Found., 1984. Mem. Tacoma Assn. for Edn. Young Children (pres. 1983-84), Wash. Assn. Edn. Young Children, Nat. Assn. Edn. Young Children, Am. Vocat. Assn., Wash. Vocat. Assn., Phi Delta Kappa. Office: Clover Park Vocat Tech Inst 4500 Steilacoom Blvd SW Tacoma WA 98499

LAKE, BLAIR MOODY, nursing educator; b. Nashville, June 14, 1932; d. Marlin Sheridan and Sara Alice (Blair) Moody; m. Richard Harrington Lake (dec. May 1987), July 17, 1954; children—Richard Moody, Mary Anne (dec.), William Moody, Sara Blair. Cert., U. Neuchatel, Switzerland, 1950; Diploma, U. Paris (Sorbonne), 1951; B.A., U. Tenn., 1952; A.A.S., No. Va. Community Coll., 1971; M.S.N., Cath. U. Am., 1978; cert. oncology nursing edn. Georgetown U. Sch. Nursing, 1978. Personnel adminstr. U.S. Civil Service, Fort Sheridan, Ill., 1952-53; office mgr. U.S. Navy Exchange, Bangkok, Thailand, 1955-56; staff and charge nurse, Fairfax Hosp., Va., 1971-72; econs. cons. R.H. Lake Assocs., 1970—, Thailand, 1972; primary nurse oncology Arlington Hosp., Va., 1979-80; oncology clin. practitioner Georgetown U. Hosp., Washington, 1980-82; assoc. prof. nursing Brevard Community Coll., Cocoa, Fla., 1982-85. Vol. sch. nurse Fairfax County Public Schs., 1974-76; crisis intervention counselor Haven of No. Va., Annandale, 1977-78; vol., pub. and profl. edn. Am. Cancer Soc., Fairfax County, Va., Brevard County, Fla., 1978-85. Mem. Am. Nurses Assn., Oncology Nursing Soc., Sigma Theta Tau, Alpha Delta Pi. Episcopalian. Clubs: Daus. of U.S. Army; Washington Bangkok Women's Club. Avocations: equitation; swimming; historical research; current affairs. Office: 3098 Landmark Blvd #2102 Palm Harbor FL 34684

LAKEMORE, BARBARA D., magazine editor. Exec. editor Family Circle, N.Y.C. Office: Family Circle 110 5th Ave New York NY 10011 *

LAKE-SMITH, NANCY JOYCE, publishing company executive; b. Chgo., Aug. 25, 1951; d. Donald Kent and Elaine Joyce (Newman) Gedman; m. C.J. Lake-Smith, Nov. 8, 1985. B.A. in Journalism, U. Minn., 1973, J.D., 1977. Asst. dir. U. Minn. Alumni Assn., St. Paul, 1973-74; admitted to Minn. bar, 1977; partner firm Margoles & Gedman, St. Paul, 1978-80; mgr. acquisitions and mktg. Mason Pub. Co., St. Paul, 1980-81; pres. Butterworth Legal Pubs. div. Butterworth (London-established 1818)-Reed Internat. P.L.C., Stoneham, Mass., 1981-85; pres. Butterworth Legal Pubs., St. Paul, 1985—. Office: Butterworth Legal Pubs 289 E Fifth St Saint Paul MN 55101

LAKOS, MARCILLE HARRIS, clinical psychologist; b. Ontario, Oreg., Dec. 10, 1917; d. Marvin and Una Leota (Smith) Hurst; B.S. in Psychology, U. Oreg., 1947, M.S. in Psychology, 1949; m. Eugene A. Lakos, Mar. 3, 1957; 1 son, John Stuart. Co-therapist, Nathan W. Ackerman, Family Inst., N.Y.C., 1955-60, 62-72; pvt. practice clin. psychology, N.Y.C., 1972—. Mem. Am. Psychol. Assn., Fedn. Am. Scientists, AAAS, N.Y. State Psychol. Assn., N.Y. Acad. Scis., Nat. Register Health Service Providers in Psychology (cert., council), Sigma Xi. Home and Office: 201 E 66th St New York NY 10021

LA LIBERTE, ANN GILLIS, graphic designer, arts consultant; b. St. Paul, Nov. 10, 1942; d. Edward Robert and Frances Caroline (Sullivan) Gillis; m. Paul Henry La Liberte, Aug. 22, 1964; children: Paul E., Elizabeth A., Stephen A., Helen C., Peter N., Marc H. Student, Am U., 1963-64, Cardinal Stritch Coll., Milw., 1960-63; BA, Coll. St. Catherine, St. Paul, 1985. Artist, owner Ann La Liberte Papers and Posters, Minnetonka, Minn., 1968-71; artist, operator A.L.L. Graphic Design and Drawings, Minnetonka, Minn., 1983—; vis. artist Arts in the Schs., Mpls., 1985—. Liturgical designer Christian Chs., Mpls., St. Paul, 1977—; paintings and sculptures exhibited Mpls., St. Paul area, 1983-87; sculpture Life Exhibit, Paul VI Inst. for the Arts, Washington, 1988. Del. Minn. Ind. Reps., 1969, v. chair, 1970; promotional artist, Soc. Preservation Human Dignity, Palatine, Ill., 1973, Minn. Citizens Concerned for Life, 1980—, Secular Franciscans, St. Paul, 1985; deanery rep. Pastoral Council Archdiocese of St. Paul, Mpls., 1978-82; chair devel. task force Out-Reach program Resurrection Ch., Mpls., 1980-81, cons. artist 1983—. Mem. Nat. Assn. Liturgical Ministers, Mpls. Soc. Fine Arts, Coll. St. Catherine Alumna Assn., Artists for Life Nat. Slide Registry, Delta Phi Delta. Roman Catholic. Home: 13418 Excelsior Blvd Minnetonka MN 55345

LALKA, JUDITH CANDELOR, lawyer; b. Phila., Dec. 14, 1947; d. Samuel and Helen Margaret (DiVito) Candelor; children: Carolyn, Susan. BS, Drexel U., 1968; MS, Carnegie Mellon U., 1970; JD magna cum laude, Wayne State U., 1973. Bar: Mich. 1973. Assoc. Dickinson, Wright, Moon Van Dusen & Freeman, Detroit, 1973-81, ptnr., 1981-85; gen. counsel, sr. v.p., corp. sec. Comerica Inc., Detroit, 1985—. Mem. ABA (co-chairperson subcoms. secured transactions, com. on Uniform Comml. Code), Mich. Bar. Assn., Detroit Bar Assn., Detroit Bar Found. (trustee 1985—, treas. 1985-87), Am. Corp. Counsel Assn. (bd. dirs. Mich. chpt.). Office: Comerica Inc 211 W Fort St Detroit MI 48275

LALLATIN, CARLA SUE, business executive; b. Casper, Wyo., Apr. 27, 1946; d. Carl Dabney and Dorothy May (Stuart) Moulden; student U. Mo., 1971-72; AA, Met. Jr. Coll., 1971; 1 dau., Natalie. Typesetting mgr. Allen Typesetting Co., Kansas City, Mo., 1967-69; publs. dir. United Computing Systems, Kansas City, Mo., 1969-74; purchasing state adminstr. State Wyo., Cheyenne, 1974-79; dep. commr. mcpl. supplies City of N.Y., 1979-85; v.p. network services Bid Net, 1985-86; pres. Lallatin & Assocs., 1986—; guest lectr. World Trade Inst., Mich. State U., Nat. Inst. Govtl. Purchasing, Nat. Purchasing Inst., NYU, Nat. League of Cities, Nat Assn. Purchasing Mgmt, LIU, U. Tex., 1975—; adv. bd. McGraw-Hill, Gov.'s adv. bd., adv. council on printing, Fed. Surplus Property, U.S. Minority Bus. Devel. Fin. adviser Girl Scouts U.S., 1977-79. Recipient Award of Merit and Award of Excellence, Internat. Assn. Bus. Communicators, 1974. Mem. Nat. Inst. Govt. Purchasing (bd. dirs., cert. of appreciation), Nat. Assn. State Purchasing Ofcls. (cert. of merit Cronin Club), Nat. Contract Mgmt. Assn., Am. Pub. Works Assn., Nat. Assn. Purchasing Mgrs. (nat. testing com., cert. appreciation), Am. Bus. Women's Assn. (pres. 1978-79, Top Ten Bus Women of Year), Purchasing Mgmt. Assn. N.Y. (bd. dirs.). Office: 61-15 97th St Suite 7A Rego Park NY 11374

LALLY, ANN MARIE, retired educational administrator; b. Chgo., Sept. 23, 1914; d. Martin J. and Della (McDonnell) L. AB, Mundelein Coll., 1935; AM, Northwestern U., 1939, PhD, 1950; postgrad., Chgo. Tchrs. Coll., Chgo. Art Inst., 1935-36. Tchr. Amundsen High Sch., 1935, Lindblom and Von Steuben High Schs., Chgo., 1936-38; chmn. art dept. Schurz High Sch., 1938-40; supr. art Chgo. Pub. Elementary Schs., 1940-48, dir. art Chgo. Public Schs., 1948-57; prin. John Marshall High Sch., 1957-63; supt. Dist. 16, Chgo. Pub. Schs., 1963-64, Dist. 5, 1964-80; lectr. Wright Jr. Coll., 1948; instr. creative drawing Chgo. Acad. Fine Art, 1941; instr. interior design Internat. Harvester Co., 1946-48; lectr. in edn. DePaul U., 1952-74; lectr. in edn. and art U. Chgo., 1956-59; lectr. edn. Chgo. Tchrs. Coll., 1960-62; trustee Pub. Sch. Tchrs. Pension and Retirement Fund Chgo., 1957-71, sec.-treas., 1960-65, pres., 1965-70. Contbr. articles to art and ednl. jours. Charter mem. women's bd. Loyola U., Art Inst. Chgo. Mem. Am. Assn. Sch. Adminstrs., Ill. Assn. Sch. Adminstrs., NEA (life), Ill. Edn. Assn., Dist. Supts. Assn. (pres. 1973-75), Ill. Women Adminstrs. Assn. (award 1979), Nat. Council Adminstrv. Women in Edn. (chmn. profl. relations com. 1958-62), Assn. Supervision and Curriculum Devel., Chgo. Area Women Adminstrs. in Edn. (Outstanding Adminstrn. award 1981), Nat. Art Edn. Assn. (mem. council 1956-60), Western Arts Assn. (pres. 1956-58), Internat. Soc. Edn. in Art, Ill. Art Edn. Assn. (pres. 1955), LWV of Chgo., Chgo. Art Educators Assn. (founder, past v.p., sec. and treas), Ill. Club Cath. Women (bd. dirs. 1981—, rec. sec. 1982-86), Chgo. Pub. Sch. Art Soc., Chgo. Hist. Soc., AAUW (Chgo. chmn. elem. and secondary edn. 1966—, dir.-at-large 1962-66, 78-80, mem. Ill. div. promoting individual liberties task force), Chgo. Area Reading Assn. (bd. dirs. 1963-69), Nat. Assn. Secondary Sch. Prins., Ill. Assn. Secondary Sch. Prins., Chgo. Prins. Assn., Artists Equity Assn. of Chgo., Council on Fgn. Relations, Mundelein Coll. Alumnae Assn. (past pres., chmn. bd., Magnificat medal 1964), Pi Lambda Theta, Delta Kappa Gamma (chmn. legis. com. 1985—). Clubs: Chgo. Woman's (chair legacy com. 1987—), Univ. Guild. Home: 307 Trinity Ct Evanston IL 60201

LALLY, NORMA ROSS, federal agency administrator; b. Crawford, Nebr., Aug. 10, 1932; d. Roy Anderson and Alma Leona (Barber) Lively; m. Robert Edward Lally, Dec. 4, 1953 (div. Mar. 1986); children: Robyn Carol Murch, Jeffrey Alan, Gregory Roy. BA, Boise (Idaho) State U., 1974, MA, 1976; postgrad., Columbia Pacific U., 1988—. With grad. admissions Boise State U., 1971-74; with officer programs USN Recruiting, Boise, 1974; pub. affairs officer IRS, Boise and Las Vegas, 1975—; speaker in field, Boise and Las Vegas, 1977—. Contbr. articles to newspapers. Vol. Am. Cancer Soc., Las Vegas; mem. task force Clark County Sch. Dist., Las Vegas. Served as staff sgt., USAF, 1950-54. Mem. Mensa. Club: Toastmasters (Las Vegas). Home: 7303 Coffeyville Las Vegas NV 89117 Office: IRS 300 Las Vegas Blvd S Las Vegas NV 89101

LALONDE, GEORGIA JEAN, lawyer; b. Dallas, July 23, 1950; d. George Bernard and Bettye Jean (McCoy) LaLonde; m. Steven Glen Wilkens. B.A., North Tex. State U., Denton, 1972; J.D., So. Methodist U., 1981. Bar: Tex. 1982. Tchr. Dallas Ind. Sch., 1972-73, Terrell (Tex.) Ind. Sch., 1973-77; legal aide Neiman-Marcus Co., Dallas, 1978-80; compliance specialist InterFirst Bank, Dallas, 1980-82; assoc. firm Hart & Krohn P.C., Houston, 1982-83, McLain, Cage, Hill & Niehaus P.C., Houston, 1983—; dir. Suzanne de Lyon Inc., Houston, 1982-83, SF Internat., Inc., Warren Internat., Inc., Suzanne de Lyon, Inc. Bd. dirs. Sharma Found., Houston, 1983—. Mosbacher Found. scholar, Houston, 1977. Mem. ABA (internat. law com.), Houston Bar Assn., Tex. Bar Assn. (internat. law com.), Houston C. of C. (internat. bus. com.). Chi Omega. Office: McLain Cage Hill & Niehaus PC 6363 Woodway Suite 800 Houston TX 77057

LAM, JULIE JOLEE, province agency administrator; b. Cheng-Du, Peoples Republic China, Apr. 12, 1947; came to Can., 1967.; d. Charles A.Y. and Kwei-Yu (Mao) Chiang; m. Joseph K.J. Lam, Dec. 18, 1971; children: Michael, Jacqueline. BS, Brandon (Man., Can) U., 1970. Programmer N.Am. Life Assurance, Toronto, Ont., Can., 1970-72; programmer, analyst Govt. Ont., Toronto, 1974-77, Bell Can., Toronto, 1977-81; system analyst Can. Imperial Bank Com., Toronto, 1981-82; project leader-billing system AT&T, Piscataway, N.J., 1984; system analyst Min. Environ., Toronto, 1984—. Recreational dir. Mandarin program Toronto Caths., 1985-86; v.p. Toronto Chinese Opera Group, 1986-87, pres., 1988—. Mem. Chineses Can. Info. Processing Profls., Oversea Chinese Women's Assn. (dir. 1986—), Women in Info. Processing (planning com. 1985—). Home: 18 Ardmore Cres, Richmond Hill, ON Canada L4B 2H7 Office: 65 St Clair Ave E, Toronto, ON Canada M4T 2Y3

LAMAR, GLORIA DEAN, infosystems specialist; b. Docena, Ala., Dec. 3, 1949; d. Louis Lawrence and Evelyn (Sudduth) L. BS in Computer Sci., Ala. A&M U., 1972. Keypunch operator USX (name formerly U.S. Steel Corp.), Pitts., 1972-76, programmer, 1976-78; system engr. IBM, Youngstown, Ohio, 1978-80; systems analyst Dollar Bank, Pitts., 1980-82, project leader, 1982-84, project mgr., 1984—; prin. Caribbean Import/Export, Pitts., 1983—. Formerly active Big. Bros./Big Sisters Pitts., 1983, Black Rep. Council, 1985—; pres. Penn Hill Mutli-Purpose Ctr., 1987; mem. Greater Pitts. Literacy Council, 1987; Allegheny County committeewoman, 1988. Mem. Nat. Assn. Female Execs. Methodist. Home: 558 Grove Rd Verona PA 15147 Office: 1041 Allegheny Ave Oakmont PA 15139

LAMAR-MOORE, ELLEN CLAUDETTE, educational administrator; b. Mobile, Ala., Jan. 20, 1951; d. Earl Claude and Irna Ellen (Marshall) L.; m. Fredd L. Moore, Sept. 5, 1987. BS in Edn., Tuskegee Inst., 1973, MEd in Adult Edn., 1976; postgrad., U. Wis., 1978-81; diploma, Air U., Maxwell AFB, 1986. Sec. to dir., coordinator community services Human Resources Devel. Ctr. Tuskegee (Ala.) Inst., 1972-76; adminstrv. asst. to provost-exec. v.p. Tuskegee Inst., 1976-78; adminstrv. asst., relief counselor Attic Halfway House Inc., Madison, Wis., 1983-85; instr. Ala. State U., Montgomery, 1985—, coordinator academic quality control, 1985-88, adminstrv. asst. student personnel services, 1988—; tax preparer H&R Block Inc., Montgomery, 1986—; cons. Mary Kay Cosmetics, Montgomery, 1986—, Jr. Educators Tomorrow, Hurtsboro, Ala. 1976—, Children's Found. Breakfast Campaign, Atlanta, 1977-78; pres., owner Lamar Resource Devel. Inc., Montgomery, 1987—. Bd. dirs. Lee County (Ala.) Council Govts., 1978, Hope Haven Alcoholic Treatment Ctr., Madison, 1982. Mem. Phi Delta Kappa. Home: 806 W Canyon Ct Montgomery AL 36110 Office: Ala St U 235 Councill Hall Montgomery AL 36195

LA MARR, BETTY JEAN, computer company official; b. Pine Bluff, Ark., Sept. 24, 1948; d. Joe Nathan Johnson and Vernestine (Shelton) Aytch; m. Hugh La Marr Jr., Aug. 21, 1966 (div. Jan. 1969); 1 child, Phillip; m. Charles Edward Harris, Aug. 24, 1984. BS, Calif. State U., Los Angeles, 1974; MBA, Pepperdine U., 1979. Account mgr. IBM, Los Angeles, 1974-81; with bus. devel. office Union Bank, Los Angeles, 1981; sales mgr. Digital Equipment Corp., Culver City, Calif., 1981—. Named in "100 Business and Professional Women of America" by Dollars and Sense mag. Mem. Nat. Assn. Female Execs., Nat. Assn. Profl. Saleswomen. Home: 540 W Knoll Dr Apt 2 Los Angeles CA 90048 Office: Digital Equipment Corp 6101 W Centinela Ave Culver City CA 90230

LA MARRE, MILDRED HOLTZ, business executive; b. Phila., May 10, 1917; d. Philip and Dora H.; student George Washington U., 1939-40; B.A., U. Md., 1966; m. Jack Understein, Dec. 25, 1938 (dec.); children—Robert, Norma Lisa, Norman, Gary; m. 2d, John La Marre, Feb. 14, 1981. With Jack Understein Co., Washington, 1960-71; exec. asst. Muskie for Pres., Washington, 1971-72; researcher Carnegie Endowment Internat. Peace, Washington, 1973-76; personal asst., adminstrv. asst. to Under Sec. Lucy Wilson Benson, U.S. Dept. of State, 1977-78; exec. asst. Mike Barnes for Congress, 1978; pres. Internat. Personal Shopping Service, Ltd., N.Y.C., 1980-84; exec. asst. John La Marre Appraisers, 1982—; actress, print model, 1987—. Bd. dirs. Hebrew Home Greater Washington, 1970-83, Internat. Sickle Cell Anemia Research Inst., Washington, 1976-83. Democrat. Address: 880 5th Ave Apt 7A New York NY 10021

LAMARRE, SUSAN LOUISE, foundation administrator; b. Oakland, Calif., June 21, 1943; d. Francis Harold and Frances Mary (Johnson) L. Student, Notre Dame Md. Coll., 1961-62, Am. U., 1963-64; BS, N.D. State U., 1966. Interior designer Chase Furniture, Washington, 1967-71; meeting coordinator Assn. Mgmt., Washington, 1974-76, Am. Cons. Engrs. Council, Washington, 1976-78; v.p. mktg. Constrn. Products Mfrs. Council, Washington, 1978-84; dir. meetings, travel Am. Cancer Soc., Atlanta, 1984—. Mem. Am. Soc. Assn. Execs., Greater Washington Soc. Assn. Execs., Am. Soc. Tng. Devel., Meeting Planners Internat., Profl. Conv. Mgmt. Assn. Republican. Roman Catholic. Home: 2161 Peachtree Rd NE #805 Atlanta GA 30309 Office: Am Cancer Soc 3340 Peachtree Rd NE Atlanta GA 30026

LAMARSH, JEANENNE MARIE, management consultant; b. Two Rivers, Wis., June 19, 1943; d. Gilbert J. and Arlene A. (Urban) L.; m. Karl L. Oestreich, Sept. 4, 1964; children: Karl Lynn, Nicole. BS, U. Wis., 1965; MA, Kent State U., 1968. Gen. mgr. Norden, Inc., Glenview, Ill., 1973-80; assoc. Cheshire, Ltd., Atlanta, 1978-85; pres. LaMarsh & Assocs., Inc., Morton Grove, Ill., 1980—. Co-author: Sexual Harassment (1981 Book award, Am. Soc. Personnel Adminstrn.). Mem. East Maine sch. bd., Niles, Ill., 1976-79, Women Helping Women, Women in Govt. Mem. Mfg. Mgmt. Inst. (bd. dirs. 1985—), LWV, Am. Soc. Tng. and Devel., Nat. Soc. for Performance and Instrn.

LAMB, ANN MARIE, research assistant; b. N.Y.C., Oct. 14, 1938; d. Leonard Joseph Cammalleri and Angela Marie (Mirandi) Stein; m. Jackson L. Lamb, 1964 (div. Sept. 1980); children: Judith Mirandi, Angela Holladay. BS, SUNY, Cortland, 1960; MS in Edn., Miss. State U., University, 1969, postgrad.; certificate, U. Ga. Drug and Alcohol Studies, Athens, 1977.

Cert. psychometrist, tchr., counselor, Miss. Dir. special programs Noxubee County Schs., Macon, Miss., 1968-74; rep. region Div. Alcohol and Drugs Mental Health Agy. St. Miss., Jackson, 1974-76; dir. program Mental Health Services Sch. Age Children Amory (Miss.) Pub. Schs., 1976-78; exec. dir. 3 Rivers Area Health Services Inc., Amory, Miss., 1978-81; grad. asst. Rehabilitation Research and Tng. Ctr. Low Vision Blind Miss. State U., University, 1982-83; counselor student fin. aid Miss. Sate U., University, 1983-87; asst. research Rehabilitation Research and Tng. Ctr. Low Vision/ Blind Miss. State U., University, 1987—; test adminstr. Standardized Testing Program Miss. State U. 1985—. Contbr. articles to profl. jours. Mem. Concerned Citizens Clay County, pres./sec. 1980-84; mem. Democratic Exec. Com. Clay County 3d Dist., 1984—. Mem. Miss. Counselor Assn., Council Exceptional Children, Phi Delta Kappa, Faculty Women Assn. (sec. 1985), Internat. Platform Assn. Roman Catholic. Office: Rehab Research Tng Ctr LOw Vision 48-50 Magruder St University MS 39762

LAMB, ELIZABETH ANNE, lawyer; b. Kingston, N.Y., Nov. 8, 1946; d. John Patrick and Marie Winifred (Delaney) L. B.A., Coll. Mt. St. Vincent, Riverdale, N.Y., 1968; J.D., St. John's U., Jamaica, N.Y., 1975. Bar: N.Y. 1976. Asst. press sec. to Commr. Bess Myerson, N.Y.C., 1969-70; press sec. Congressman Hugh L. Carey, N.Y.C. and Washington, 1970-74; legis. asst. to Gov. Hugh L. Carey, N.Y.C., 1974-75; assoc. gen. counsel N.Y., State Criminal Justice Service, N.Y.C., 1975-80; sr. EEO counsel St. Regis Paper Co., N.Y.C., 1980-82; exec. v.p. Marcon Mgmt. Services, Inc., N.Y.C., 1982-84; sole practice, N.Y.C., 1984—;. legal cons. to Archdiocese of N.Y. for immigration matters. Mem. Assn. Bar City N.Y., N.Y. State Bar Assn., ABA, Met. Mus. Art. Democrat. Roman Catholic. Home: 12 E 86th St New York NY 10028

LAMB, URSULA SCHAEFER, history educator; b. Essen, Germany, Jan. 15, 1914; came to U.S., 1935, naturalized, 1949; d. Waldemar Joachim and Maria Katharina (Hoffman von Fallersleben) Schaefer; m. Willis Eugene Lamb, Jr., June 5, 1939. Student, U. Berlin, 1933-35, Smith Coll., 1935-36, 49; M.A., U. Calif., Berkeley, 1937, Ph.D., 1949. Instr. and asso. Barnard Coll., Columbia U., N.Y.C., 1943-51; tutor Brasenose Coll. and Univ. Lectures, Oxford, Eng., 1958-61; lectr., sr. lectr., advisor to library Yale U., New Haven, 1961-74; prof. history U. Ariz., Tucson, 1974-86, prof. emeritus, 1986—; Eva G. R. Taylor lectr. Royal Inst. Nav., London, 1981. Asso. editor Hispanic Am. Hist. Rev, 1975-86; mem. editorial bd. Terrae Incognitae, 1978—; author: Frey Nicolás de Ovando, 1956, 2d edit., 1977; translator, author: intro. A Navigator's Universe: The Libro de Cosmographia of 1538 (Pedro de Medina), 1972; contbr. articles to profl. jours. Social Sci. Research Council grantee, 1943, Am. Council Learned Socs. travel grantee, 1947; Guggenheim Meml. fellow, 1968; NEH sr. scholar, 1972-73; Am. Philos. Soc. travel grantee, 1975; NSF grantee, 1978-79; Jeannette Black fellow Brown U., spring 1985. Mem. Conf. Latin Am. History, Am. Hist. Assn., Conn. Acad. Arts and Scis., Soc. History of Discovery (pres. 1975-77), Internat. Soc. History of Nautical Sci. and Hydrography (U.S. rep. 1976), Internat. Commn. Maritime History (U.S. rep. 1977-80), Soc. Spanish and Portuguese Hist. Studies, Am. Soc. Renaissance Studies, Instituto de Cultura Hispanica (Caracas). Home: 848 N Norris St Tucson AZ 85719 Office: Univ Ariz Dept History 215 Social Sci Tucson AZ 85721

LAMB, VICTORIA A. ZVONCHECK, administrative recruiter; b. L.I., N.Y., June 24, 1959; d. Juls and Sue Joyce (Davies) Zvoncheck; m. Mark E. Lamb, Apr. 9, 1983 (div. July 1985); 1 child, Elizabeth Victoria. Lic. employment recruiter, N.J. Asst. dept. mgr. Hahne's Dept. Store, Eatontown, N.J., 1977-79; store mgr. The Gen. Store, Washington, 1979-80; area mgr. Marshall's, Inc., Toms River, N.J., Edison, N.J., Shrewsbury, N.J., New London, Ct., 1980-86; mgr., adminstrv. recruiter Terralot div. Diedre Moire Corp., East Brunswick, N.J., 1986—. Mem. Christ Ch. Choir, Shrewsbury, 1973-75, 86—. Mem. Nat. Assn. Female Execs. Democrat. Episcopalian. Club: Episcopal Ch. Women (Shrewsbury). Home: 17 Maple Crest Ln Colts Neck NJ 07722 Office: Terralot 579 Cranbury Rd Suite C East Brunswick NJ 08816

LAMBERG, JOAN BERNICE, purchasing agent; b. St. Paul, July 5, 1935; d. Gustave William and Anna Marie (Steinhilpert) L. Student, U. Mo., Rolla, 1971. Payroll clk. Continental Baking Co., Mpls., 1953-54; with scheduling and inventory control Stewart Paint Mfg. Co., Mpls., 1954-72; purchasing and sales coordinator Horton-Earl Co., South St. Paul, Minn., 1972—. Mem. Northwestern Soc. for Coatings Tech. (treas. 1984-85, sec. 1985-86, v.p. 1986-87, pres. 1987-88, tech. com. 1985—, membership chmn. 1985, 87, Trigg award 1985-86), Fedn. of Socs. for Coatings Tech. (membership com. 1985—, bd. dirs. 1987—), Women in Coatings. Home: 6949 Macbeth Circle Woodbury MN 55125 Office: Horton-Earl Co 949 S Concord St South Saint Paul MN 55075

LAMBERT, BARBARA ROSENBERG, retail executive; b. Bklyn., Feb. 8, 1954; d. Abraham and Bertha (Benson) Rosenberg; children: Justin Keith, Craig Joel. AAS Textile Apparel Mktg., Fashion Buying and Mdsing., Fashion Inst. of Tech., 1973. Exec. mgr. trainee Abraham and Strauss, Hempstead, N.Y., 1972-73; sr. asst. buyer Sanger Harris, Dallas, 1975-77; regional mgr. Cotton Comfort Retail Stores, Boulder, Colo., 1981—. Office: Cotton Comfort Retail Stores Inc 6235 Lookout Boulder CO 80301

LAMBERT, DEBORAH KETCHUM, public relations executive; b. Greenwich, Conn., Jan. 22, 1942; d. Alton Harrington and Robyna (Neilson) Ketchum; m. Harvey R. Lambert, Nov. 23, 1963 (div. 1985); children: Harvey Richard Jr., Eric Harrington. BS, Columbia U., 1965. Researcher, writer The Nowland Orgn., Greenwich, Conn., 1964-67; model Country Fashions, Greenwich, Conn., 1964-67; owner, mgr. Paper Collectables, McLean, Va., 1973—; freelance writer to various newspapers and mags. 1977-82; press sec. Va. Del. Gwen Cody, Annandale, Va., 1981-82; assoc. editor Campus Report, Washington, 1985—; adminstr. asst. Accuracy in Media, Inc., Washington, 1983-84, pub. affairs dir., 1985—; dir. Accuracy in Academia, Washington, 1985—. Columnist: The Eye, The Washington Inquirer, 1984—, Squeaky Chalk, Campus Report, 1985—; contbr. articles to various mags. Co-founder, mem. Va. Rep. Forum, McLean, 1983—. Mem. Pub. Relations Soc. Am., Washington, DAR., World Media Assn. Republican. Presbyterian. Home: 1945 Lorraine Ave McLean VA 22101 Office: Accuracy in Media Inc 1275 K St NW Washington DC 20005

LAMBERT, DEBORAH SUE, data processing professional; b. Dayton, Ohio, Apr. 13, 1952; d. Walter Robert and Charlotte Marie (Rogers) L.; m. Thomas Ray Greer, Sept. 3, 1978 (div. 1980); children: Douglas Allen Byrd, Deborah Lynne Byrd. BA, Sinclair Coll., 1983. Teller Wright-Patt Credit Union, Fairborn, Ohio, 1977; auditor Wright-Patt Credit Union, Fairborn, 1977-78, interviewer sr. loan, 1978, loan officer, 1978-79, from asst. mgr. to mgr. remote mem. services, 1979-82, data coordinator, 1982-84; mgr. system quality assurance Summit Info. Systems Inc., Corvallis, Oreg., 1984-87; dir. product mgmt. Summit Info. Systems Inc., Corvallis, 1988—. Mem. Nat. Credit Union Adminstrn. (cert.), Nat. Assn. Female Execs., Am. Bus. Women's Assn., Ohio Credit Union League (cert. ops.). Home: 572 SE Hathaway Pl Corvallis OR 97333 Office: Summit Info Systems 850 SW 35th St Corvallis OR 97333

LAMBERT, JEAN MARJORIE, health care consultant; b. Bay City, Mich., Mar. 19, 1943; d. Richard William and Fidelis Rena (LeVasseur) L. BA, Madonna Coll., Livonia, Mich., 1967; MA, Eastern Mich. U., 1975. Dir. religious edn. Archdiocese of Detroit, 1970-75, dir. of evaluation, 1975-77; assoc. dir. programming Intermedia Found., Santa Monica, Calif., 1977-78; acad. dean St. John Provincial Sem., Plymouth, Mich., 1978-84; asst. dir. quality mgmt. Sisters of Mercy Health Corp., Farmington Hills, Mich., 1984-87; sr. cons. Mercy Collaborative, Livonia., Mich., 1987—; asst. prof. homiletics St. John Sem., Plymouth, Mich., 1978-85, St. Mary of the Woods Coll., Terre Haute, Ind., summer 1985, St. Meinrad Sem., Ind., summer 1984. Editor Religious Edn., 1975-77. Nat. Cath. Edn. Assn.-Assn. Theol. Schs. for U.S. and Can. grantee, 1983. Mem. Groundwork Network, Internat. Teleconferencing Assn., Nat. Assn. Female Execs., Am. Hosp. Assn., Am. Mgmt. Assn., Nat. Assn. Quality Assurance Profls. Roman Catholic. Avocations: woodcarving, photography, continuing education. Office: Mercy Collaborative 38777 Six Mile Rd #205 Livonia MI 48152

LAMBERT, LORENE COOK, graphic artist, travel writer; b. Nashville, Feb. 8, 1950; d. Smith Foster and Mary Elizabeth (Clark) Cook; m. Fredric Alton Lambert Jr., Sept. 20, 1974; 1 child, Rachel Elizabeth. BA in English, Belmont Coll., 1972. Asst. cashier Mid-South Securities Corp., Nashville, 1972-73; manuscript marker So. Bapt. Sunday Sch. Bd., Nashville, 1973-74, art prodn. asst., 1974-77; supr. taxpayer pubs. Dept. Revenue, State of Tenn., Nashville, 1977-83; graphic artist, travel writer Tenn. Dept. Tourist Devel., Nashville, 1984—; free lance graphic artist, 1985—; art dir.: Tenn. Vacation Guide, 1986; designer logo Scenic River Celebration, 1985, Tourism Logo Type, 1985. Publicity chmn. Tenn. Wild Horses and Burro Days Celebration, Cross Plains, Tenn., 1984—; tchr. Sunday Sch. First Bapt. Ch. of Donelson, Nashville, 1984—. Recipient 1986 Nat. Vols. for Pub. Lands award. Home: Rt 1 Box 109 Greenwood Rd Cross Plains TN 37049 Office: Tenn Tourist Devel PO Box 23170 Nashville TN 37202

LAMBERT, MARIA AURORA, hospital executive; b. Guatemala City, Guatemala, Aug. 2, 1943; came to U.S., 1961; d. J. Enrique and Maria Aurora (Boburg) Polanco; m. Frederick C. Lambert III, Apr. 24, 1965; children: Frederick IV, Elizabeth, Ingrid. Diploma in nursing, St. Mary's Hosp., 1964; B, Thomas More Coll., 1976; MBA, Xavier U., 1979. Registered nurse, Ohio, Va., W.Va. Staff RN St. Mary's Hosp., Huntington, W.Va., 1964-67, head nurse, 1967-70; staff nurse Halifax Community Hosp., South Boston, Va., 1970; staff nurse St. George Hosp., Cin., 1971-72, emergency room supr., 1972-77, dir. nursing, 1977-80; v.p. patient care St. Francis and St. George Hosps., Cin., 1980-81, v.p. ops., 1981-82; v.p. adminstrn. The Jewish Hosp. of Cin., Inc., 1983—. Mem. Am. Coll. Health Care Execs. Club: Zonta (sec. 1987—). Home: 12042 Cedarcreek Dr Cincinnati OH 45240 Office: The Jewish Hosp of Cin Inc 3200 Burnet Ave Cincinnati OH 45229

LAMBERT, PEGGY LYNNE BAILEY, association executive; b. Seattle, Oct. 15, 1948; d. John Thomas and Doris Mae (Lindgren) Bailey; m. Tom Kenneth Newton, May 25, 1975 (div. 1980); m. Allan Gregory Lambert, Aug. 3, 1980; children: Eli Raven, Joshua Alec. BA in Psychology, Beloit Coll., 1970; MS in Counseling Psychology, Ill. Inst. Tech., 1973; JD, Syracuse (N.Y.) U., 1978. Bar: D.C. 1983. Mental health specialist Ill. Dept. Mental Health, Chgo., 1971-72; research faculty Cornell U., Ithaca, N.Y., 1973-75; assoc. O'Connor, Sovocool, Pfann and Greenburg, Ithaca, 1978, Dacy, Richin & Meyers, Silver Springs, Md., 1979-81; ins. adminstr. Nat. Assn. Broadcasters, Washington, 1981-86, dir. ins. programs, 1986—. Mem. ABA, Bar Assn. of D.C., Am. Soc. Assn. Execs., S.E. Bus. and Profl. Women's Club. Democrat. Jewish. Office: Nat Assn Broadcasters 1771 N St NW Washington DC 20036

LAMBERT, REBECCA FOTOUHI, corporation executive; b. Binghamton, N.Y., Jan. 31, 1947; d. Abol Hassan and Eleanor Margaret (Page) Fotouhi; m. John Kendall Lambert, Aug. 30, 1968 (div. May 1975); m. Edward S. Bent, June 20, 1987. Student, Simmons Coll., 1965-68; B.A., Williams Coll., 1969; A.M.P., Harvard Bus. Sch., 1982. Vice-pres., treas. Champlain Properties, Stowe, Vt., 1971-75; adminstrv. asst. Nat. Republican Senatorial Com., 1975-76; strategist Wallop for U.S. Senate Campaign, Washington, 1976-77; chief of staff Senator Malcolm Wallop, Washington, 1977-80; dep. asst. sec. U.S. Dept. Energy, Washington, 1981-82; assoc. dep. sec. U.S. Dept. Commerce, Washington, 1982-83; dir. corp. info. CBS Inc., N.Y.C., 1983; govt. relations cons. law firm Wiley & Rein, 1984-85; pres. Lambert Broadcasting, Inc., N.Y.C., 1985—; mem. Reagan Transition Team, 1980. Trustee St. Stephens Sch., Rome; mem. Am. Council Young Polit. Leaders; pres. Bellevue Hosp. Assn., 1986—. Van Lear fellow, 1978. Episcopalian. Home: 410 E 57th St New York NY 10022

LAMBERT, SHIRLEY ANNE, marketing professional, publisher; b. Dayton, Ohio, Sept. 28, 1945; d. Norman Frank and Muriel Noreen (Atkinson) Best; m. Joseph Calvin Lambert, Apr. 27, 1968 (div. 1986); children: Joseph Calvin III, James Edward, Kristin Carole. BA in Polit. Sci., Wellesley Coll., 1967; degree in French, Universite de Paris, 1966; MLS, Simmons Coll., 1980. Mktg. asst. G.K. Hall and Co., Boston, 1969-73; cons. Info. Dynamics Corp., Reading, Mass., 1973-75, Pergamon Press, Elmsford, N.Y., 1979-82; computer lab. coordinator Cherry Creek Schs., Aurora, Colo., 1983-85; mktg. dir. Libraries Unltd., Littleton, Colo., 1985—. Author: Clip Art and Dynamic Designs for Libraries and Media Centers, vol. 1; reviewer Am. Reference Books Ann., 1987-88, Library and Info. Sci. Ann., 1986-88. Host parent Am. Field Service, N.Y., 1986-87; selection chmn. Ams. Abroad; Returnee, 1962. Mem. ALA, Rocky Mountain (Colo.) Dressage Assn. (local chpt. sec. 1984-85), Colo. Hunter/Jumper Assn., Phi Beta Kappa, Beta Phi Mu. Republican. Congregationalist. Office: Libraries Unltd PO Box 3988 Englewood CO 80155-3988

LAMBIRD, MONA SALYER, lawyer; b. Oklahoma City, July 19, 1938; d. B.M., Jr. and Pauline A. Salyer; m. Perry A. Lambird, July 30, 1960; children: Allison Thayer, Jennifer Salyer, Elizabeth Gard, Susannah Johnson. B.A., Wellesley Coll., 1960; LL.B., U. Md., 1963. Bar: Okla. 1968, Md. Ct. Appeals 1963, U.S. Supreme Ct. 1967. Atty. civil div. Dept. Justice, Washington, 1963-65; sole practice law Balt. and Oklahoma City, 1965-71; mem. firm Andrews Davis Legg Bixler Milsten & Murrah, Inc. and predecessor firm, Oklahoma City, 1971—; cons. World Orgn. China Painters; minority mem. Okla. Election Bd., 1984—; mem. Profl. Responsibility Tribunal Okla. Supreme Ct., 1984—; Master of Bench, sec.-treas., Am. Inn of Ct. XXIII in Oklahoma City, 1986—. Editor: Briefcase, Oklahoma County Bar Assn., 1976. Profl. liaison com. City Oklahoma City, 1974-80; mem. Hist. Preservation of Oklahoma City, Inc., 1970—; del. Oklahoma County and Okla. State Republican Party Conv., 1971—; women's com. Okla. Symphony Orch., legal advisor, 1973—, bd. dirs., 1973—; incorporator, bd. dirs. R.S.V.P. of Oklahoma County, pres., 1982-83; bd. dirs. Congregate Housing for Elderly, 1978—, Vis. Nurses Assn., 1983-86, Oklahoma County Friends of Library, 1980—. Mem. ABA, Okla. Bar Assn. (pres. elect labor and employment law sect.), Oklahoma County Bar Assn. (bd. dirs. 1986—, chmn. 1988), Oklahoma County Bar Found. (pres.), Jr. League Oklahoma City (dir. 1973-76, legal adv.), Oklahoma County and State Med. Assn. Aux. (dir.). Methodist. Clubs: Seven Colls. (pres. 1972-76), Women's Econ. (steering com. 1981-86). Home: 419 NW 14th St Oklahoma City OK 73103 Office: 500 W Main Oklahoma City OK 73102

LAMDEN, EVELYN OLSON, advertising executive; b. Akron, Ohio, Nov. 1, 1950; d. Myrle Mylo Olson and Luz (Talaña) Swartz; m. William Edward Lamden, Aug. 31, 1986. BA in Mass Media Communications magna cum laude, U. Akron, 1980. Sec. Goodyear Tire Co., Akron, 1968-74, field merchandiser, 1975-76, display coordinator, 1976-79, regional advt. mgr., 1979-83; ptnr., dir. Budji Corp., Los Angeles, 1983-85; sr. account exec. Internat. Communications Group, Los Angeles, 1985-87, account dir., 1987-88; ptnr. Lamden Family-Property Mgmt., 1988—. Pres., Goodyear Community Theater, Akron, 1976-79; bd. dirs., Dallas Repertory Theater, 1980-83, Redondo Beach (Calif.) Community Theater, 1987. Recipient Best Speaker award Toastmasters Internat., Akron, 1972. Mem. Women in Communications, Nat. Assn. Female Execs. Democrat. Roman Catholic. Office: Internat Communications Group 8441 Whale Watch Way La Jolla CA 92037

LAMEL, LINDA HELEN, college president, lawyer; b. N.Y.C., Sept. 10, 1943; m. John E. Sands, July 31, 1977; 1 child, Diana Ruth. B.A. magna cum laude, Queens Coll., 1964; M.A., NYU, 1968; J.D., Bklyn. Law Sch., 1976. Bar: N.Y. 1977, U.S. Dist. Ct. (3d dist.) N.Y. 1977. Mgmt. analyst U.S. Navy, Bayonne, N.J., 1964-65; secondary sch. tchr. Farmingdale Pub. Sch., N.Y., 1965-73; curriculum specialist Yonkers Bd. Edn., N.Y., 1973-75; program dir. Office of Lt. Gov., Albany, N.Y., 1975-77; dep. supt. N.Y. State Ins. Dept., N.Y.C., 1977-83; pres., chief exec. officer Coll. of Ins., N.Y.C., 1983—; dir. Seneca (N.Y.) Ins. Co., Fin. Benefit Group, Inc., Boca Raton, Fla. Contbr. articles to profl. jours. Campaign mgr. lt. gov.'s primary race, N.Y. State, 1974. Mem. ABA (tort and ins. sect. com. chmn. 1985-86), N.Y. State Bar Assn. (exec. com. ins. sect. 1984—), Am. Mgmt. Assn. (ins. and risk mgmt. council), Fin. Women's Assn., Phi Beta Kappa, Kappa Delta Pi, Phi Alpha Theta. Office: Coll of Insurance 101 Murray St New York NY 10007

LAMISON, LEATHA MAE, statistician; b. Courtland, Va., May 5, 1953; d. Winget and Beatrice L.; m. Michael Nathan White, May 25, 1985; 1 child, Darren Lamison-White. BA in Sociology, Norfolk Va.) State U., 1974; postgrad., Va. Commonwealth U., 1974-76. Tchr. Richmond (Va.) Pub. Schs., 1974-77; social worker Richmond Dept. Welfare, 1978; tng. specialist Bur. of Census, Washington, 1979; regional technician Bur. of Census, Ft. Walton Beach, Fla., 1980, Mobile, Ala., 1980; survey statistician Bur. of Census, Washington, 1981—; real estate agt., investor Omega Properties, Lanham, 1986—. Researcher poverty sect. World Almanac, 1983-86. Mem. Commerce Com. for Black Concerns, Washington, 1987. Mem. NAACP, Nat. Assn. Female Execs., Alpha Kappa Delta, Washington Investors, Ltd. Democrat. Baptist. Home: 9505 Vermell Pl Largo MD 20772

LAMM, CAROLYN BETH, lawyer; b. Buffalo, Aug. 22, 1948; d. Daniel John and Helen Barbara (Tatakis) L.; m. Peter Edward Halle, Aug. 12, 1972. B.S., SUNY Coll.-Buffalo, 1970; J.D., U. Miami (Fla.), 1973. Bar: Fla., 1973, D.C., 1976, N.Y. 1983. Trial atty. frauds sect. civil div. U.S. Dept. Justice, Washington, 1973-78, asst. chief comml. litigation sect. civil div., 1978, asst. dir., 1978-80; assoc. White & Case, Washington, 1980-84, ptnr., 1984—. Fellow Am. Bar Found.; mem. ABA (chmn. young lawyers div., assembly del., sec., chmn. internat. litigation com., nominating com., com. chmn. sect. internat. law), Fed. Bar Assn. (chmn. sect. on antitrust and trade regulation), Bar Assn. D.C. (bd. dirs., sec.), D.C. Bar (bd. govs. steering com. litigation sect., bd. govs.), Am. Law Inst., Women's Bar Assn. D.C., Am. Soc. Internat. Law, Internat. Bar Assn., Nat. Women's Forum. Democrat. Clubs: City Tavern (Washington); Columbia Country. Contbr. articles to legal publs. Home: 2101 Connecticut Ave NW Washington DC 20008 Office: White & Case 1747 Pennsylvania Ave NW Suite 500 Washington DC 20006

LAMMERT, LOIS JEAN CECELIA, banker; b. Scarsdale, N.Y., Dec. 6, 1963; d. Thomas King and Jean Evon (Turcott) L. AB in English Lit. and Econs., Smith Coll., 1985. Loan officer Bank Boston, 1985—. Mem. Big Sisters Boston, 1987—. Republican. Roman Catholic. Clubs: Boston Smith (bd. dirs., v.p. young alumnae, nominating com.), Community Boating, Links. Home: 17 Claremont Park Boston MA 02118 Office: Bank Boston 3 Cambridge Ctr Cambridge MA 02142

LAMON, GAYLE MORSE, sales administrator; b. Newark, Del., Mar. 2, 1953; d. Richard Alwin and Ina Kathleen (Jones) M.; m. Edgar Lamon Jr., Mar. 27, 1976 (div. Mar. 1983). Student, Catawba Coll., 1971-73; BS in Mktg. with cum laude, U. Del., 1975. With quotations dept. Amfac Electric Co., Pasco, Wash., 1976-77; rep. sales Scott Paper Co., Tri Cities, Wash., 1977-78, Monroe, Mich., 1978-79; sr. rep. sales Toledo, 1979-84; area mgr. sales Lexington, Ky., 1984-86; sr. area mgr. Reading, Pa., 1986-87; pres., gen. ptnr. Sun Valley Diversities, Reading, 1987—. Mem. Nat. Assn. for Female Execs. Republican. Methodist.

LAMON, LILLIAN MCINNIS, banker; b. Quepos, Costa Rica, Feb. 22, 1950; d. William Mansell and Julia (Morice) McInnis; m. Donald Joseph Lamon, Apr. 18, 1968; children: Michael Keith, Dallas Lyn. BA, Pan Am. U., 1972; MA, Tex. A&M U., 1975. Tchr. Harlingen (Tex.) Ind. Schs., 1972-81; sr. v.p. MBank Harlingen, 1981-85; v.p. Harlingen State Bank, 1985—. Bd. dirs. United Way of Harlingen, 1981—, Vol. Services Council, Harlingen, 1985—; bd. dirs., treas. Family Emergency Assistance, Harlingen, 1984—; bd. dirs. state and local chpts. Am. Heart Assn., Harlingen, 1984—; mem. exec. bd., treas. Jr. League of Harlingen, 1982—. Recipient Vol. of Yr. award, Am. Heart Assn., 1983, Presdl. Citation award, 1987. Mem. Am. Bankers Assn. Republican. Club: Algodon (bd. dirs. 1987—). Home: 2322 Riverside Dr Harlingen TX 78550 Office: Harlingen State Bank PO Box 191 Harlingen TX 78550

LAMONT, ALICE, accountant, consultant; b. Houston, July 19; d. Harold and Bessie Bliss (Knight) L. BS, Mont. State U.; MBA in Taxation, Golden Gate U., 1982. Tchr. London Central High Sch., 1971-80; acct. Signetics, Sunnyvale, Calif., 1980-82, Metcalf, Frix & Co., Atlanta, 1983-84; propr. Alice Lamont Ltd., 1985—. Mem. Atlanta Hist. Soc., High Mus. Art. Mem. AAUW (life), Ga. Soc. CPAs (assoc.), EDP Auditors, Inst. Internal Auditors, English Speaking Union. Episcopalian. Club: Atlanta Woman's (co-chair ways and means com. 1985-86, asst. treas. 1986-88).

LAMONT, BARBARA, television executive; b. Pager, Bermuda, Nov. 9, 1939; came to U.S., 1949; d. Theophilus and Muriel (Aird) Alcántara; m. Ludwig Gelubter, Dec. 20, 1959; children: Michel, David, Elisabeth. BA in Internat. Law, Sarah Lawrence Coll., 1960; MBA, Harvard U., 1985. Reporter WINS Radio, N.Y.C., 1971-73; reporter, anchor WNEW TV, N.Y.C., 1973-76; writer, reporter CBS News, N.Y.C., 1976-82; dir. ops. Nigerian TV Authority, Lagos, Nigeria, 1982-84; writer ABC News, N.Y.C., 1986-87; pres., chief exec. officer New Orleans Teleport, 1987—; adj. assoc. prof. journalism Columbia U., N.Y.C., 1980-82, 82-86. Author: City People, 1976; mem. editorial bd. Amsterdam News, N.Y.C., 1986—; contbr. articles to the N.Y. Times. Dist. leader N.Y. County Dem. Com., N.Y.C., 1969-72; mem. Council Elected Black Democrats, N.Y.C., 1969-72; bd. dirs. Planned Parenthood N.Y.C., 1971; mem. Nat. Women's Polit. Caucus, Washington, 1972; mem. exec. council Kennedy Sch. Alumnae Assn., Cambridge, Mass., 1985—; mem. parents com. Williams Coll., Williamstown, Mass., 1986—. Recipient AP award, 1973, Ret. Detectives award N.Y.C. Detectives Assn., 1975. Mem. Nat. Assn. Broadcasters, Urban League (fiscal reform com.). Republican. Club: Harvard. Office: WCCL-TV 620 Desire St New Orleans LA 70117

LAMONT, FRANCES STILES (PEG), state legislator; b. Rapid City, S.D., June 10, 1914; d. Frederick Bailey and Frances (Kenney) Stiles; m. William Mather Lamont, 1937 (dec.); children—William Stiles, Nancy, Peggy, Frederick. B.A., U. Wis., 1935, M.A., 1936. Mem. staff McCalls mag., N.Y.C., 1936-37; vice-chmn. Gov.'s Commn. on Status of Women, 1964-73; chmn. Gov.'s Adv. Council on Aging, 1967-73; mem. S.D. State Senate from 2d Dist., 1975—. Named S.D. Mother of Yr., 1974. Mem. DAR, AAUW, LWV, Phi Beta Kappa, Kappa Alpha Theta. Republican. Episcopalian. Office: SD State Capitol Bldg Pierre SD 57501 also: PO Box 1415 Aberdeen SD 57402 •

LAMONT, ROSETTE CLEMENTINE, foreign language and literature educator, writer, translator; b. Paris; came to U.S., 1941, naturalized, 1946; d. Alexandre and Loudmilla (Lamont) L.; m. Frederick Hyde Farmer, Aug. 9, 1969. B.A., Hunter Coll., 1947; M.A., Yale U., 1948, Ph.D., 1954. Tutor Romance langs. Queens Coll., CUNY, 1950-54, instr., 1954-61, asst. prof., 1961-64, assoc. prof., 1965-67, prof., 1967—; mem. doctoral faculty French and comparative lit. CUNY, 1968—; State Dept. envoy Scholar Exchange Program, USSR, 1974; research fellow, 1976; lectr. Alliance Française, Maison Française of NYU; vis. prof. Sorbonne, Paris, 1985-86. Author: The Life and Works of Boris Pasternak, 1964, De Vive Voix, 1971, Ionesco, 1973, The Two Faces of Ionesco, 1978; also contbr. to various books. mem. editorial bd. Centerpoint; contbg. editor Performing Arts Jour.; contbr. articles to profl. jours., N.Y. Times, Columbia Dictionary of Modern European Literature. Decorated chevalier, then officier des Palmes Academiques, officier des Arts et Lettres (France); Guggenheim fellow, 1973-74; Rockefeller Found. humanities fellow, 1983-84. Mem. MLA, Am. Soc. Theatre Research, Internat. Brecht Soc., PEN, Drama Desk, Phi Beta Kappa, Sigma Tau Delta, Pi Delta Phi. Club: Yale. Home: 260 W 72nd St New York NY 10023 also: 51 W Chester St Nantucket MA 02554 Office: CUNY Queens Coll Dept Romance Langs Flushing NY 11367 also: Grad Center CUNY 33 W 42 St New York NY 10036

LAMONTAGNE, NANCY HARTSHORN, technology research and automotion specialist; b. Gardner, Mass., June 14, 1949; d. Charles and Pauline Flora (Blouin) Hartshorn; B.S. in Math. and Computer Sci., U. Mass., 1971; M.Mgmt., Simmons Coll., 1981; m. Stephen Paul Lamontagne, Mar. 1, 1980. Project evaluation satellite specialist M.I.T. Lincoln Lab., Bedford, Mass., 1972-74; mfg. systems analyst USM Corp., 1974-77; fin. and mfg. systems sr. programmer Digital Equipment Corp., 1977-80; mgmt. info. systems mgr. The Gillette Co., Andover, Mass., 1980-84; corp. mgr. tech. research and planning Sanders Assocs., Inc., Nashua, N.H., 1984—; cons. data processing and office mgmt.; lectr. Simmons Coll., Network for Exempt Women at Sanders. Commr. town dist., 1984-86; vol. N.H. Spl. Olympics, 1986; mem. computer adv. bd. St. Anselm's Coll. Recipient Disting. Woman Leader award Southern N.H., 1984. Mem. Am. Mgmt. Assn., Data Processing Mgmt. Assn. Home: 15 Viau Rd Windham NH 03087 Office: Sanders Assocs Daniel Webster Hwy S Nashua NH 03061

LAMOUREUX, GLORIA KATHLEEN, military nursing administrator; b. Billings, Mont., Nov. 2, 1947; d. Laurits Bungaard and Florence Esther (Nielsen) Nielsen; m. Kenneth Earl Lamoureux, Aug. 31, 1973 (div. Feb. 1979). BS, U. Wyo., 1970; MS, U. Md., 1984. Enrolled USAF, 1970, advanced through grades to lt. col.; staff nurse ob-gyn dept. 57th Tactical Hosp., Nellis AFB, Nev., 1970-71, USAF Hosp., Clark AB, Republic Philipines, 1971-73; charge nurse ob-gyn dept. USAF Rgn. Hosp., Sheppard AFB, Tex., 1973-75; staff nurse ob-gyn dept. USAF Rgn. Hosp., MacDill AFB, Fla., 1976-79; charge nurse ob-gyn dept. USAF Med. Ctr., Andrews AFB, Md., 1979-80, MCH coordinator, 1980-82; chief nurse USAF Clinic, Eielson AFB, Alaska, 1984-86, Air Force Systems Command Hosp., Edwards AFB, Calif., 1986—. Named one of Outstanding Women Am., 1983. Mem. Nurses Assn. of Am. Coll. Obstetricians and Gynecologists (sec.-treas. armed forces dist. 1986—), Air Force Assn., Assn. Mil. Surgeons U.S., Bus. and Profl. Women's Assn., Sigma Theta Tau. Republican. Lutheran. Home: 4500 W Rosamond Blvd Space 5 Rosamond CA 93560 Office: AFSC Hosp Edwards Edwards AFB CA 93523-5300

LAMPARTER, ELLEN, oil company executive; b. Binghamton, N.Y., Oct. 11, 1957; d. William C. and Ann (Martyn) L. BA, Miami U., 1978; MBA, George Washington U., 1980. Spl. asst. HEW, Washington, 1978-80; mgmt. analyst GAO, Washington, 1980; econ. analyst Standard Oil Co., Cleve., 1981-82; bus. planner Standard Oil Co., Houston, 1982-85; wholesale and aviation pricing coordinator Standard Oil Co., Cleve., 1985-87; mgr. planning British Petroleum N.Am., 1987—. Teaching asst. Dale Carnegie, Houston, 1983; Stephen minister Lakewood Presbyn. Ch., Cleve., 1987. Mem. Am. Mktg. Assn. (writer local chpt. jour. 1986-87). Office: British Petroleum NAm 550 Westlake Park Blvd Suite 1800 Houston TX 77079

LAMPE, ANNACAROL, corporate communications specialist; b. Indpls., Sept. 30, 1951; d. William George and Helen Eleanor (Biddle) L.; m. Peter J. Florzak, Dec. 10, 1985; 1 child, Anna Eleanor. Student, Wroxton Coll., St. Mary, Eng., 1972, U. Hawaii, 1973; BS, Ind. U., 1973, MS, 1974; MBA, Rockhurst Coll., 1981. Tchr. speech, drama, English Eastside High Sch., Butler, Ind., 1974-77; dir. student activities Penn Valley Community Coll., Kansas City, Mo., 1977-79; mgr. tech. communications Martin Marietta Co., Oak Ridge, Tenn., 1983-84; assoc. dir. Kaleidoscope Hallmark Cards Inc., Kansas City, 1981-83, communications specialist, 1984—; speaker, presenter workshops stress mgmt., leadership, sex equity, 1977—; leader Midwest Conf. Women Bus., Kansas City, 1980. Mem. Kansas City Jr. League, 1986—; bd. dirs. Oak Ridge Arts Council, 1983, Tenn. Art Ctr., 1984, Westport Ballet, Kansas City, 1985. Recipient Key to City Mayor Love, Johnson City, Tenn., 1981, Young Careerist award Bus. Profl. Women No. Ind., 1977; named Outstanding Young Women Am., 1985, Outstanding Woman, Girl Scouts Am., Kansas City, 1987. Mem. Internat. Assn. Bus. Commnicators (Silver Quill Excellence 1986), Soc. Tech. Communicators. Republican. Lutheran. Home and Office: 5411 NW 84th Ct Kansas City MO 64154

LAMPKIN, BARBARA JO, laboratory administrator, computer analyst; b. Lynn, Mass., Nov. 24, 1947; d. George James and Ella Margaret (Lunsford) L. BS in Med. Tech., Woman's Coll. of Ga., 1969; postgrad. Boston U., 1978-84. Registered med. technologist Am. Soc. Clin. Pathologists. Med. technologist Med. Ctr. of Central Ga., Macon, 1969-71; hematology head tech. Coliseum Park Hosp., Macon, 1971-74; hematology chief tech. Boston City Hosp., 1974-76; satellite lab. supr. Smith-Klein Labs., Waltham, Mass., 1976-77; blood bank technologist ARC, Boston, 1977-78; hematology chief tech. Bioran Med. Labs., Cambridge, Mass., 1978-84; computer analyst and implementation specialist Collaborative Med. Sytems, Newton, Mass., 1984-86; product dir., computer analyst, Blood Bank, 1986—. Campaign vol. Democratic Nat. Com., Mass., 1980-86; bd. dirs. Mass. Choice, Boston, 1985-86, vol., 1983-86; mem. Nat. Abortion Rights Action League, Washington, 1974—. Mem. Am. Soc. Clin. Pathologists (affiliate), Am. Soc. Profl. and Exec. Women. Roman Catholic. Club: Boston Beanstalk Tall (bd. dirs. 1984-86, pub. relations chmn. 1984-86). Avocations: gourmet cuisine, skiing, travel, reading, knitting. Office: Co-Med div Mumps Collaborative 246 Walnut St Newton MA 02160

LAMY, M(ARY) REBECCA, land developer, former government official; b. Ft. Bragg, N.C., Nov. 21, 1929; d. Charles Joseph and Sarah Esther (Koonce) L.; B.A., U. N.C., Greensboro, 1952. Procurement analyst Air Force MIPR Mgmt. Office, Washington, 1958-60, procurement and fiscal officer, 1960-68; budget analyst Naval Air Systems Command, Washington, 1968-69, indsl. specialist, 1969-71; indsl. specialist A.D.T.C., Eglin AFB, Fla., 1971-74, Def. Logistics Agy., Alexandria, Va., 1974-81; logistics mgmt. specialist Strategic Systems Project Office, Dept. Navy, Washington, 1981-82; procurement analyst Hdqrs. Dept. Army, Washington, 1982-85. Recipient Outstanding Performance awards U.S. Air Force, 1956, 65, 72, 73; Quality award Def. Logistics Agy., 1979, Outstanding Performance award, 1978, 79, Exceptional Service award, 1983, 84, 85; Comdr.'s award Hdqrs. Dept. Army, 1985; others. Mem. U. N.C. at Greensboro. Alumni Assn. Home and Office: PO Box 1494 Jacksonville NC 28541

LANCASTER, ELAINE L., banker; b. Hennessey, Okla., July 20, 1935; d. Linley R. Krebs and Violet Elma Krebs Benson; B.S., U. Md., 1963; m. William Duval Lancaster, Apr. 30, 1977; children from previous marriage—Cameron Lakin, Jeffrey Lakin. withCalif. Fed. Savs. and Loan, Los Angeles, 1973-77; consumer loan mgr. Coast Fed. Savs. and Loan, Hawthorne, Calif., 1977-78; regional consumer loan officer Glendale Fed. Savs. & Loan, Riverside, Calif., 1983-86, statewide mgr. student loans, 1986—.Mary Hardin Baylor Coll. scholar, 1955; Ford Found. fellow, 1965-66. Mem. Savs. and Loan League, Am. Inst. Banking, Nat. Notary Assn., AAUW, Nat.Mgmt. Assn., YWCA, NOW. Democrat. Club: Toastmistresses. Office: Glendale Fed Savs & Loan 401 N Brand Ave Glendale CA 91304

LANCASTER, LINDA LEE, management consultant, educator; b. Chgo., July 29, 1947; d. Robert Campbell and Virginia L. (Nelson) Johnson; m. Gary Lancaster, Aug. 31, 1968 (div. Jan. 1970). BA, Elmhurst Coll., 1977; MBA, Rosary Coll., River Forest, Ill., 1983. Asst. to pres. Ill. Structural Steel Corp., Cicero, 1972-74; office mgr. Am. Investement Co., Inc., Chgo., 1974-75; ops. analyst 1st Nat. Bank of Chgo., 1975-76, staff officer, 1976-83; project mgr. Montgomery Ward, Chgo., 1983-87; sr. v.p. Howard Lancaster & Assocs., Oak Park, Ill., 1987—. Treas. Lone Tree council Girl Scouts U.S., Oak Park, Ill., 1983-85, bd. dirs., 1980-83; pres. 333 Condominium Assn., Oak Park, 1987—, bd. dirs., 1979-84. Mem. Nat. Assn. Female Execs. Lutheran. Home and Office: Howard Lancaster & Assocs 333 S East Ave Suite #207 Oak Park IL 60302

LANCASTER, SALLY RHODUS, foundation executive; b. Gladewater, Tex., June 28, 1938; d. George Lee and Milly Maria (Meadows) Rhodus; m. Olin C. Lancaster Jr., Dec. 23, 1960; children: Olin C. III, George Charles, Julie Meadows. BA magna cum laude, So. Methodist U., 1960, MA, 1979; PhD, East Tex. State U., 1983. Tchr. English, Tex. pub. schs., 1960-61, 78-79; exec. v.p., grants adminstr. Meadows Found., Inc., Dallas, 1979—, also trustee; bd. dirs. Trustee So. Meth. U., East Tex. State U. (regent 1987—), Interscholastic League Found., Friends of Fair Park, Partnership for Arts, Culture, Edn.; trustee Nonprofit Loan Ctr. Mem. Am. Personnel and Guidance Assn., Conf. S.W. Founds., Council on Founds. (edn. program com.), So. Meth. U. Alumni (disting. alumni 1986), Philos. Soc. of Tex., Phi Beta Kappa (assoc. pres. 1980-82, nat com. on assns. 1983-85), Am. Assn. Continuing Edn. Presbyterian. Office: 2922 Swiss Ave Dallas TX 75204

LANCASTER, SUZANNE CORBIN, medical technician; b. Washington, Oct. 23, 1947; d. William Boggs and Nadine (Kennedy) Corbin; m. James Harrison Lancaster, June 20, 1969 (div. 1973); 1 child, Martha Elizabeth. AA, DeKalb Community Coll., Clarkston, Ga., 1976, AS, 1982. Cert. advanced emergency med. technologist. Police officer Emory U., Atlanta, 1978-82; paramedic, firefighter DeKalb City Fire Dept., Decatur, Ga., 1982-83, Henry City Fire Dept., McDonough, Ga., 1983-84; physical measurements technician Equifax Services, Atlanta, 1984—. Instr., vol. ARC, Atlanta, 1978—; ski patroller Nat. Ski Patrol, Denver, 1980—, instr. winter emergency care, supr. Dixie Region; instr. advanced life support Am. Heart Assn., 1983-84; v.p. program and edn. bd. Parents Without Ptnrs., Jonesboro, Ga., 1984. Mem. Emergency Med. Technologists Assn., Exec. Womens Assn. Republican. Presbyterian. Club: Atlanta Ski. Home: 281 Northern Ave #1C Avondale Estates GA 30002 Office: Equifax 2536 Century Pkwy Atlanta GA 30345

LANCOUR, KAREN LOUISE, educator; b. Cheboygan, Mich., June 2, 1946; d. Clinton Howard and Dorothy Marie (Passeno) L. AA, Alpena Community Coll., 1966; BA, Ea. Mich. U., 1968, MS, 1970. Teaching asst. Ea. Mich. U., Ypsilanti, 1968-70; tchr. sci. Utica (Mich.) Community Schs., 1970—. Nat. event supr. Sci. Olympiad, 1986—, nat. rules com., 1987—, state event supr., 1986—, regional dir., 1987. Mem. Nat. Assn. Sci. Tchrs., Nat. Biology Tchrs. Assn., Met. Detroit Sci. Tchrs. Assn., Smithsonian Inst., Nat. Wildlife Assn., Nat. Geographic Soc., Edison Inst., Mortar Bd., Phi Theta Kappa, Kappa Delta Phi. Democrat. Roman Catholic. Home: 8378 18 Mile Rd 202 Sterling Heights MI 48078 Office: Henry Ford II High Sch 11911 Clinton River Rd Sterling Heights MI 48078

LAND, JUDY M., land developer and appraiser; b. Phoenix, Oct. 6, 1945; d. Sanford Karl Land and D. Latanne (Hilburn) Land Krauss; divorced; children: Neal McNeil III, Latanne Tahnee. Student, Geneva Sch., 1965; AA in Econs., Merritt Coll., 1967; MBA, Brklyn Bus. Sch., 1984. Cert. real estate developer, broker and appraiser. Gen. mgr. ACE Rent-A-Car, San Francisco, 1967-71; with real estate sales dept. Odmark/Welch Co/Mesa Realty, San Diego, 1971-76; v.p. Brehm Communities, San Diego, 1977; mgr. investment div. Ayers Realty, Encinitas, Calif., 1978-79; asst. v.p. Harry L. Summers Inc., La Jolla, Calif., 1982-85; pres. Land Co., Carlsbad, Calif., 1979—; cons. Broadmoor Homes, San Diego, 1982. Fundraiser Hunger Project, 1979-86, Youth at Risk, 1984-86, Multiple Sclerosis Soc., 1984; mem. exec. com. U.S. Olympics, 1984; bd. dirs. Polit. Policies Com., San Diego, 1986. Mem. Nat. Assn. Real Estate Appraisers, Nat. Assn. Women Execs., Nat. Assn. Home builders, Home Builders Council (pres. 1985), Building Industry Assn. San Diego (bd. dirs. 1985), Econ. Devel. Corp. San Diego (membership com. 1984), Women Comml. Real Estate, Life Spike Club.

LAND, MARGARET F., statistics educator, consultant; b. Norman, Okla., Feb. 20, 1939; m. Hugh C. Land, May 24, 1957 (dec. 1968); children—Peter Colman, David Foster, Stephanie Ruth; m. Richard O. Albert, June 26, 1981. B.S., Northwestern State U. of La., 1963, M.S., 1967; Ph.D., Okla. State U., 1981. Asst. prof. math., N.W. La. State U., Natchitoches, 1967-70; asst. prof. and stats. cons. N.Mex. State U., Las Cruces, 1977-80; teaching assoc. Okla. State U., Stillwater, 1970-77, 80-81; asst. prof., cons. Tex. A&I U., Kingsville, 1981-86, assoc. prof., 1986—; pvt. practice cons. statistician, 1979—; Fulbright vis. fellow, Venezuela, Author jour. articles. State del. Tex. Republican Party, 1984; county del. Tex. Med. Assn. Aux., 1983-85. Mem. Am. Statis. Assn. (subcom. on statis. cons. edn. 1984—), Biometric Soc., Am. Soc. Quality Control. Lutheran. Clubs: Mensa, Intertel, Triple Nine, Audubon Soc. Research or work interests: Consulting, experimental design, quality control, regression, sample surveys. Subspecialties: Statistics; Quality control. Home: 1800 Newell St Alice TX 78332 Office: Tex A&I U Dept Math Box 172 Kingsville TX 78363

LAND, MARY ELIZABETH, author, composer; b. Benton, La., Sept. 28, 1908; d. Thomas T. and Elizabeth (Langford) Land; student Gulf Park Coll., Gulfport, Miss., 1924-25, Cheyney Trent Sch. Poetry, Calif., 1937, U. Chgo., 1938; m. Edward Timothy Kelly, 1925; 1 dau., Patricia Kelly Stevens; m. 2d, George T. Lock, 1931; 1 son, George T. Lock-Land. Mem. staff La. Conservation Rev., La. Dept. Conservation, New Orleans, 1940-41, Miss. Valley Sportsman, 1948, So. Outdoors Mag., Atlanta, 1959, 60, 61, West Bank Guide, New Orleans, 1962, Sportsman's News, Hot Springs, Ark., 1960; author (with Arthur Van Pelt) syndicated column, Outdoors South, for weekly newspapers Miss., La., 1947, 48; feature writer Fisherman Mag., 1954, R X Sports and Travel Mag., 1971, Down South Mag., 1964, Natchitoches Times, 1970. Named Co-Poet Laureate for Tenn., 1941; recipient Blue Ribbon award Gulf Coast br. Nat. League Am. Pen Women, Merit certificate Nash Motor Co., 1953, 1st Pl. award La. Press Assn., 1969-70, Merit certificate and 2 Keys to City Mayor New Orleans, 1954, Outstanding Contbn. certificate La. Soc. Colonial Dames, 1971, certificate Am. Bicentennial Research Inst., 1973. Mem. Nat. League Am. Pen Women (past br. pres.), Nat. Fedn. Am. Press Women, La. Press Women, Outdoor Writers Assn. Am., La. Outdoor Writers Assn. (charter), Fedn. Musicians. Author: Shadows of the Swamp (poetry), 1940, Mary Land's Louisiana Cookery, 1954 (So. Books award 1956), New Orleans Cuisine, 1968 (2d pl. award Fedn. Am. Press Women 1969), Abode (poetry), 1972, Dreams (poetry), 1977; contbr. conservation articles to mags., poetry to anthologies; composer: You Hang In My Heart, 1959, As Strange As You Are, 1959, Drink Deep, 1959, Piano Cho Cho Zarzosa, 1959, Voice-Allehandra Allegra, 1959. Address: 310 Shearwater Dr Ocean Springs MS 39564

LAND, SUSAN KAY, engineering technician; b. Kokomo, Ind., Nov. 29, 1954; d. Thomas Jr. and Judith Ann (McClelland) Barnett; m. James Joseph Copeland, July 16, 1973 (div. 1974); m. Robert Allen Land, Dec. 8, 1978 (dec.); children: Amber Kay, Angela Sue, Richelle Anne. A in Engring., Purdue U., 1985. Office mgr. Hendrickson-Griggs, Russianville, Ind., 1975-77; accts. pub. clk. Baker, McHenry & Welsh, Indpls., 1979, Carnation Co., Kokomo, 1979-80; engring. technician Delco Electronics, Kokomo, 1985-87, A.H.M. Graves Co., Inc., Noblesville, Ind., 1987—; sales assoc. New Homes Mktg. Specialists. Mem. Nat. Bd. Realtors, Ind. Bd. Realtors, Met. Indpls. Bd. Realtors, Hamilton County Bd. Realtors. Democrat. Methodist. Lodges: Order Eastern Star (sec. 1976-79), Rainbow. Home: 738 Dorchester Dr Noblesville IN 46060

LANDAU, DOROTHY RUTH, local government executive; b. S.I., N.Y., Oct. 5, 1957; d. Robert August and Dorothy Faith (Schaut) L. AS in Applied Sci., SUNY-Farmingdale, 1977; BS in Biology, Wagner Coll., 1979. Sci. tchr. Bais Yaakov, S.I., 1979-81; dental asst. Dr. Marvin Freeman, S.I., 1981-82; office mgr. Dr. Bennett C. Fidlow, S.I., 1982-85; polit. aide to S.I. Borough Pres., 1985—. Environ. chmn. S.I. League for Better Govt., 1984—; pres. Tottenville Improvement Council Inc., Staten Island, 1985—; Dem. candidate for N.Y. State Assembly 60th dist., 1986, dist. leader; dir. community bds. S.I. Borough Pres.' Office; founder, pres. environ. group S.I.L.E.N.T., S.I., 1985; 1st v.p. 123d Democratic Club, S.I., 1986; social chmn. S. Shore Democratic Club; founding mem. Friends of Clay Pit Pond Park; mem. Protectors of Pine Oak Woods Inc., Roserio Alliotta Dem. Club, Dem. Orgn. of Richmond; trustee S.I. Bd. Leukemia Soc. Am., 1988—, dir., chair Celebrity Waiters Luncheon. Recipient Community Activist Award Office of Pres. S.I. Borough, 1987. Mem. Nat. Assn. Female Execs., Bus. and Profl. Women (Young Careerist for S.I.). Roman Catholic. Avocations: photography, sports, ceramics, youth programs. Home: 406 Sleight Ave Staten Island NY 10307 Office: S I Borough Pres Office Borough Hall Staten Island NY 10301

LANDAU, EDYTHE, film producer; b. Wilkes-Barre, Pa.; d. Harry and Rose (Zatcoff) Rudolph; B.A., Wilkes Coll.; J.D., U. West Los Angeles, 1981; m. Ely A. Landau; children—Jon, Tina, Kathy. Exec. v.p. Nat. Telefilm Assocs., Inc., 1953-60, Landau Prodns., 1960-70, Am. Film Theatre, 1970-75; producer, v.p. Edie & Ely Landau, Inc., Los Angeles, 1978—; producer films: Hopscotch, Beatlemania, The Chosen, The Holcroft Covenant; for TV, The Deadly Game, Separate Tables, The Christmas Wife, Mr. Johnson and Mr. Halpern; admitted to Calif. bar, 1981; developed award-winning films including: Long Days Journey Into Night, 1962, The Pawnbroker, 1965, King - A Filmed Record, Montgomery to Memphis (Oscar nomination best documentary). 1970; Man in the Glass Booth 1975; The Chosen (best picture Montreal World Film Festival), 1981. Mem. Acad. Motion Pictures Arts and Scis., Women in Film, ABA, Calif. State Bar Assn., Beverly Hills Bar Assn.

LANDAU, IRENE GOLDBLATT, psychology educator; b. Chgo., Aug. 23, 1928; d. Nathan Edward and Betty (Schwarzbach) Goldblatt; m. Melvin M. Landau, Aug. 30, 1959; children: Julie, Michael. PhB, U. Chgo., 1948, MA, 1955, PhD, 1976. Registered psychologist, Ill. Vocat. counselor Chgo. Dept. Welfare, 1951-53; psychologist Inst. Juvenile Research, Chgo., 1955-61, cons. psychologist, 1963; psychologist Community Family Service & Mental Health Ctr., Chgo., 1968-72; asst. prof. Mundelein Coll., Chgo., 1976-82, assoc. prof., 1982—; bd. dirs. Over the Rainbow for Nonambulatory Physically Handicapped, Evanston, Ill., 1985—. Mem. Am. Psychol. Assn., Midwestern Psychol. Assn., Ill. Psychol. Assn., Chgo. Psychol. Assn. (exec. council 1985—), Phi Beta Kappa, Sigma Xi (assoc.). Office: Mundelein Coll 6363 N Sheridan Rd Chicago IL 60660

LANDAU, JACQUELINE CECILE, business educator; b. Queens, N.Y., Jan. 31, 1953; d. Joseph Victor and Ruth (Abrams) L. BA, Hamilton Coll., 1975; MS, Cornell U., 1980, PhD, 1983. Asst. prof. bus. Tulane U., New Orleans, 1983—; cons. in field. Contbr. numerous articles to profl. jours. Mem. Nat. Acad. of Mgmt., Nat. Psychol. Assn., Am. Psychol. Assn., New Orleans Personnel Mgmt. Assn., Internat. Conf. on Women and Orgns. (local chairperson for arrangements 1987—). Office: Tulane U AB Freeman Sch of Bus New Orleans LA 70118

LANDAU, LAURI BETH, accountant, tax consultant; b. Bklyn., July 21, 1952; d. Jac and Audrey Carolyn (Zuckernick) L. BA, Skidmore Coll., 1973; postgrad., Pace. U., 1977-79. CPA, Oreg. Mem. staff Audrey Z. Landau, CPA, Suffern, N.Y., 1976-78; mem. staff Ernst & Whinney, N.Y.C., 1979-80, mem. sr. staff, 1980-82, supr., 1982-84; mgr. Arthur Young & Co., N.Y.C., 1984-87, prin., 1987—; speaker World Trade Inst., N.Y.C., 1987—. Composer songs. Career counselor Skidmore Coll., Saratoga Springs, N.Y., 1977—, mem. leadership com. Class of 1973, 1983-85, pres., 1985—, fund chmn., 1987—. N.Y. State Regents scholar, 1970. Mem. Am. Inst. CPA's, N.Y. State Soc. CPA's. Democrat. Clubs: Skidmore Alumni (N.Y.C.); German Shepherd Dog Am. Office: Arthur Young & Co 277 Park Ave New York NY 10172

LANDAU, SHELLY, screenwriter; b. Englewood, N.J., Dec. 19, 1956; d. Gilbert William and Miriam (Friedman) L. BA in Biology, UCLA, 1978, JD, 1981; MFA in Profl. Writing, U. So. Calif., 1983, MA in Applied Linguistics, 1985. Bar: Calif. 1981. Researcher, aide bur. Consumer Protection FTC, Washington, 1980; teaching asst. freshman writing U. So. Calif., Los Angeles, 1981-85; staff writer TV show Double Trouble, Los Angeles, 1983; story editor TV show Rocky Road, Los Angeles, 1985-86; exec. script cons. TV show Webster, Los Angeles, 1986—. Mem. Writers Guild Am. West. Office: Paramount Studios Clara Bow Bldg 5555 Melrose Ave Los Angeles CA 90038

LANDAZURI, COLLEEN ANN, public health nurse; b. Fond du Lac, Wis., Sept. 8, 1950; d. James Edward and Elizabeth Ann (Masloff) Flood; m. Gabriel Landazuri, Oct. 26, 1974; children: Dario James, Patrick Xavier, Alexander Gabriel. BS in Nursing, Marquette U., 1972, postgrad., 1976-77. Staff nurse Nursing Bur., Milw. Health Dept., 1972-75, Lady Pitts program nurse, 1975-76, dist. supr., 1976-80, dir. prenatal edn. and assessment program, 1980—; fed. nurse trainee, 1976-77, coordinator interdisciplinary dental and nursing student program Marquette U. Sch. Dentistry, 1976-77. Mem. Greater Milw. Com. for Unmarried Parent's Services, 1980—, vice co-chairperson., 1985, chairperson, 1986; mem. critical health problems curriculum adv. com. Milw. Pub. Schs., 1980-86, chmn., 1982-84; mem. adv. com., sch. aged parents program Lady Pitts Ctr., 1980—; mem. health and human services resource bd. Milw. Urban League, 1987—, community services com. March of Dimes, 1988—, Time of Your Life Program network com. Family Service of Milw., mem. adv. com. Family Hosp. Teen Pregnancy Service, 1984-86, nurse adv. com. March of Dimes, 1985-86; choir mem. St. Catherine's Ch. Mem. Southea. Wis. Patern-Child Nursing Orgn. (vice chmn. 1988, mem. conf. 1986—), Urban League (Milw. chpt. health resources com.), Sherman Park Community Assn., Orgn. Twin-Blessed Mothers (sec. 1984), Sigma Theta Tau. Roman Catholic. Club: North Shore Jrs. Woman's. Home: 3368 N 44th St Milwaukee WI 53216 Office: 841 N Broadway Suite 228 Milwaukee WI 53202

LANDBERG, ANN LAUREL, psychotherapist; b. Chgo., June 20, 1926; d. Carl Ryno and Ebba Sadie Elvira (Engstrom) Granlund; m. Harry Morton Landberg, Apr. 1, 1953 (dec. Feb. 1967); stepchildren—Rosabel, Marcene. R.N., Swedish Hosp. Sch. Nursing, Seattle, 1948. Asst. head nurse Halcyon Hosp., Seattle, 1948; doctor's asst. Office of H.M. Landberg, M.D., Seattle, 1948-50, psychotherapist, 1950-67; pvt. practice psychotherapy, Seattle, 1967—; cons. Good Shepherd Sch. for Disturbed Girls, Seattle, 1954—, bd. dirs., 1954-60. Mem. Am. Psychotherapy Assn., King County Med. Aux., Stevens Hosp. Aux. (life), Swedish Hosp. Alumni (pres. 1952-53), Nat. Council Jewish Women, City of Hope, Edmonds Arts Assn. (life patron), Seattle Forensic Inst. (charter). Club: Swedish (Seattle). Home: 16900 Talbot Rd Edmonds WA 98020 Office: 1007 Spring St Seattle WA 98104

LANDER, KATHLEEN GELCHER, writer, editor; b. Los Angeles, Apr. 24, 1923; d. Joseph and Grayce Clara (McCormick) Gelcher; B.A., U. So. Calif., 1944; postgrad. U. Calif.-Irvine, 1972-73, N.Y.U., 1977; m. Robert Frank Lander, Sept. 6, 1947 (div. 1974); children—Jeffrey, Richard, Lisa, Marc. Reporter, editor, San Marino (Calif.) Tribune, Inglewood (Calif.) Daily News, Rodgers-McDonald Newspapers, Los Angeles, 1944-47; owner public relations co., Inglewood, 1947-49; west coast editor High Fidelity Trade News, 1972-74; editor Consumer Electronic Product News, N.Y.C., 1974-77; free-lance writer-editor consumer and trade publs., N.Y.C., 1977—; sr. editor Leisure Time Electronics; editor LTE Reports, 1980-85. Founding mem., pres. LWV, Santa Ana, Calif., 1961-63, chmn. Orange County Council, LWV, 1958; bd. dirs. Orange County Community Action Council, 1964-69. Mem. Women in Communications, Inc., Mortar Bd. Alumnae of So. Calif. (pres. 1945-46), LWV. Home: 144 E 36th St Apt 1-C New York NY 10016

LANDERS, ANN (MRS. ESTHER P. LEDERER), columnist; b. Sioux City, Iowa, July 4, 1918; d. Abraham B. and Rebecca (Rushall) Friedman; m. Jules W. Lederer, July 2, 1939 (div. 1975); 1 dau., Margo Lederer Howard. Student, Morningside Coll., 1936-39, LHD (hon.), 1964; hon. degrees, Wilberforce (Ohio) Coll., 1972, Am. Coll. Greece, 1979, Meharry Med. Coll., 1981, Jacksonville U., 1983, St. Leo Coll., 1984, Fla. Internat. U., 1984, Med. Coll. Pa., 1985, New Eng. Coll., 1985, U. Wis., 1985, Lincoln Coll., 1986, Nat. Coll. Edn., 1986, Southwestern Adventist Coll., 1987; hon. degree, Duke U., 1987. Syndicated columnist Chgo., 1955—; pres. Eppie Co., Inc., Chgo. Author: Since You Asked Me, 1962, Teen-agers and Sex, 1964, Truth is Stranger, 1968, Ann Landers Speaks Out, 1975, The Ann Landers Encyclopedia, 1978; syndicated columnist Los Angeles Times—Creators Syndicates. Chmn. Eau Claire (Wis.) Gray-Lady Corps, ARC, 1947-53; chmn. Minn.-Wis. council Anti-Defamation League, 1945-49; asst. Wis. chmn. Nat. Found. Infantile Paralysis, 1951-53; hon. nat. chmn. 1963 Tb Christmas Seal Campaign; bd. sponsors Mayo Clinic, 1970; mem. sponsors com. Mayo Found.; nat. adv. bd. Dialogue for the Blind, 1972; adv. com. on better health services AMA; county chmn. Democratic Party Eau Claire; bd. dirs. Rehab. Inst. Chgo.; nat. bd. dirs. Am. Cancer Soc., Nat. Cancer Inst.; vis. com. bd. overseers Harvard Med. Sch.; mem. Pres.'s Commn. Drunk Driving; trustee Menninger Found., Nat. Dermatology Found., Am. Coll. Greece, Deree-Pierce Coll., Athens, Meharry Med. Sch., Hereditary Disease Found. Recipient award Nat. Family Service Assn., 1965; Adolf Meyer award Assn. Mental Health N.Y., 1965; Pres.'s Citation and nat. award Nat. Council on Alcoholism, 1966, 2d nat. award, 1975; Golden Stethoscope award Ill. Med. Soc., 1967; Humanitarianism award Internat. Lions Club, 1967; plaque of honor Am. Friends of Hebrew U., 1968; Gold Plate award Acad. Achievement, 1969; Nat. Service award Am. Cancer Soc., 1971; Robert T. Morse award Am. Psychiat. Assn., 1972; plaque recognizing establishment of chair in chem. immunology Weizmann Inst., 1974; Jane Addams Public Service award Hull House, 1977; Health Achievement award Nat. Kidney Found., 1978; Nat. award Epilepsy Found. Am., 1978; James Ewing Layman's award Soc. Surg. Oncologists, 1979; citation for disting. service AMA, 1979; Thomas More medal Thomas More Assn., 1979; NEA award, 1979; Margaret Sanger award, 1979; Stanley G. Kay medal Am. Cancer Soc., 1983; 1st William C. Menninger medal for achievement in mental health, 1984, Albert Lasker pub. service award, 1985. Fellow Chgo. Gynecol. Soc. (citizen hon.); mem. LWV (pres. 1948), Brandeis U. Women (pres. 1960). Clubs: Chgo. Econs. (dir. 1975), Harvard, Sigma Delta Chi. Office: Chgo Tribune 435 N Michigan Ave Chicago IL 60611

LANDERS, VERNETTE TROSPER, educator, author; b. Lawton, Okla., May 3, 1912; d. Fred Gilbert and LaVerne Hamilton (Stevens) Trosper; A.B. with honors, U. Calif. at Los Angeles, 1933, M.A., 1935, Ed.D., 1953; Cultural doctorate (hon.), Lit. World U., Tucson, 1985; m. Paul Albert Lum, Aug. 29, 1952 (dec. May 1955); 1 child, William Tappan; m. 2d, Newlin Landers, May 2, 1959; children: Lawrence, Marlin. Tchr. secondary schs., Montebello, Calif., 1935-45, 48-50, 51-59; prof. Long Beach City Coll., 1946-

47; asst. prof. Los Angeles State Coll., 1950; dean girls Twenty Nine Palms (Calif.) High Sch., 1960-65; dist. counselor Morongo (Calif.) Unified Sch. Dist., 1965-72, coordinator adult edn., 1965-67, guidance project dir., 1967; clk.-in-charge Landers (Calif.) Post Office, 1962-82; ret., 1982. V.p., sec. Landers Assn., 1965—; sec. Landers Vol. Fire Dept., 1972—; life mem. Hi-Desert Playhouse Guild, Hi-Desert Meml. Hosp. Guild; apptd. dep. dir. gen. for Ams. Internat. Biog. Centre, Cambridge, Eng., 1987. Bd. dirs., sec. Desert Emergency Radio Service. Recipient internat. diploma of honor for community service, 1973; Creativity award Internat. Personnel Research Assn., 1972, award Goat Mt. Grange No. 818, 1987; cert. of merit for disting. service to edn., 1973; Order of Rose, Alpha Xi Delta, 1978; poet laureate Center of Internat. Studies and Exchanges, 1981; diploma of merit in letters U. Arts, Parma, Italy, 1982; Golden Yr. Bruin UCLA, 1983; World Culture prize Nat. Ctr. for Studies and Research, Italian Acad., 1984; Golden Palm Diploma of Honor in poetry Leonardo Da Vinci Acad., 1984; Diploma of Merit and titular mem. internat. com. Internat. Ctr. Studies and Exchanges, Rome, 1984; Recognition award San Gorgonio council Girl Scouts U.S., 1984, 85; Cert. of appreciation Morongo Unified Sch. Dist., 1984; plaque for contribution to postal service and community U.S. Postal Service, 1984; Biographee of Yr. award for outstanding achievement in the field of edn. and service to community Hist. Preservations of Am.; named Princess of Poetry of Internat. Ctr. Cultural Studies and Exchange, Italy, 1985; community dinner held in her honor for achievement and service to Community, 1984; Star of Contemporary Poetry Masters of Contemporary Poetry, Internat. Ctr. Cultural Studies and Exchanges, Italy, 1984; named to honor list of leaders of contemporary art and lit. and apptd. titular mem. of Internat. High Com. for World Culture & Arts Leonardo Da Vinci Acad., 1987; other awards and certs. Life fellow Internat. Acad. Poets, World Lit. Acad.; mem. Am. Personnel and Guidance Assn., Internat. Platform Assn., Nat. Ret. Tchrs. Assn., Calif. Assn. for Counseling and Devel., Am. Biog. Research Assn. (life dep. gov.), Nat. Assn. Women Deans and Adminstrs., Montebello Bus. and Profl. Women's Club (pres.), Nat. League Am. Pen Women (sec. 1985-86), Leonardo Da Vinci Acad. Internat. Winged Glory diploma of honor in letters 1982), Landers Area C. of C. (sec. 1985-86, Presdl. award for outstanding service), Desert Nature Mus., Phi Beta Kappa. Clubs: Whitter Toastmistress (Calif.) (pres. 1957); Homestead Valley Women's (Landers). Lodge: Soroptimists (sec. 29 Palms chpt. 1962, life mem., Soroptimist of Yr. local chpt. 1969, Woman of Distinction local chpt. 1987-88). Author: Impy, 1974, Talkie, 1975; Impy's Children, 1975; Nineteen O Four, 1976, Little Brown Bat, 1976; Slo-Go, 1977; Owls Who and Who Who, 1978; Sandy, The Coydog, 1979; The Kit Fox and the Walking Stick, 1980; contbr. articles to profl. jours., poems to anthologies. Home: 632 Landers Ln PO Box 3839 Landers CA 92285

LANDES, SALLY ANN, computer executive; b. Akron, Ohio, Dec. 2, 1940; d. Oran W. and Isabelle (Davis) Shockley; m. George T. Plehn, Nov. 21, 1959 (div. July 1980); children: Elizabeth Moritz, Ted, Mitchell, Matthew; m. Kenneth R. Landes, Oct. 13, 1981. Pres. Loveland Computer Ctr. Bd. dirs. Loveland City Beautification, 1985—; chair task force Bus. Council, Loveland, 1987. Mem. Loveland C. of C. (bd. dirs. 1986—), No. Colo. Better Bus. Bureau (bd. dirs. 1983—), LWV (chair Loveland membership 1978-80). Democrat. Roman Catholic. Home: 947 E 7th St Loveland CO 80537

LANDEY, FAYE HITE, consultant; b. Atlanta, May 12, 1943; d. Irving and Sophia (Held) Hite; m. Benjamin Landey, Aug. 30, 1964; children: Leah, Sharon. Student U. Ill., 1961, Hebrew U., Jerusalem, 1962; BA, Emory U., 1964. Cert. housing mgr. Office mgr. Grolier Interstate, Atlanta, 1969-72; asst. adminstr. Campbell-Stone, Atlanta, 1972-78; owner Cupboard Gift Shop, Atlanta, 1974-78; adminstr. Campbell-Stone North, Atlanta, 1978-81; sales mgr. Apex Supply Co., Atlanta, 1981-83; owner Landey & Assocs., Atlanta, 1983—; chief exec. officer Retirement Dimensions, Atlanta, 1986—; advisor Fulton County Council on Housing, 1982. Treas., charter mem. Sandy Springs (Ga.) Arts and Heritage Soc., 1981; dir. Sandy Springs C. of C., 1982; founder Coalition Fulton County Civic Assns., 1983; mem. bd. com. Sandy Springs Benefit Ball, 1978-83; bd. dirs. Cath. Social Services; state del. Republican Party. Author: The Graying of America, It's Effects on Developers and Land Sales, 1987. Mem. Am. Assn. Homes for Aging (nat. house del. 1981), Ga. Assn. Homes for Aging (pres. elect 1982), Nat. Council on Aging, Am. Soc. on Aging, Ga. Gerontology Soc. Jewish. Club: Woman's Forum (Atlanta). Home and Office: 495 Tahoma Dr NE Atlanta GA 30338

LANDIS, SARA MARGARET SHEPPARD, editorial consultant; b. Badin, N.C., May 20, 1920; d. Thomas Coates and Ouida (Watson) Sheppard; m. Williard Griffith Landis, Dec. 7, 1945; children: Susan Sheppard, Timothy Joseph, Margaret Carol. Student, Flora MacDonald Coll. Women, 1937-38, Rice Bus. Coll., 1939; AB in Journalism, U. N.C., 1942. Editorial asst. Redbook Mag., N.Y.C., 1942-43; with Doubleday and Co., N.Y.C., 1944-46, Eagle Pencil Co., N.Y.C., 1953-54; mgr. personnel Workman Service, N.Y.C., 1955-56, Clay Adams Co., N.Y.C., 1957-58; job analyst Bigelow Carpet Co., N.Y.C., 1959-60; asst. to guidance dir. Childrens Village, Dobbs Ferry, N.Y., 1960-61; dir. promotions, advt. Oceans Publs., Dobbs Ferry, 1961-66; mgr. promotions Reinhold Pub. Co., N.Y.C., 1967-68, Watson Guptil Pub. Co., N.Y.C., 1968, Chilton Book Co., Phila., 1968-69; cons. editorial, promotions Sheppard-Landis Inc., N.Y.C., 1969—. Mem. Woman's Speaking Union, Woman's Nat. book Assn (treas.), Friends Epiphany Br. N.Y. Pub. Library. Home and Office: 271 Ave C Peter Cooper-Stuyvesant Town New York City NY 10009

LANDMAN, BETTE EMELINE, academic administrator; b. Piqua, Ohio, July 18, 1937; d. Wilson Richard and Lois (Wilson) L. BS, Bowling Green State U., 1959; MA, Ohio State U., 1961, PhD, 1972. From instr. to asst. prof. anthropology Springfield (Mass.) Coll., 1962-67; asst. prof. Temple U., 1967-71; asst. prof. anthropology Beaver Coll., Glenside, Pa., 1971-76, dean, 1976-85, v.p. acad. affairs, 1980-85, acting pres., 1982-83, 85, pres., 1985—. Bd. dirs. Abington Meml. Hosp., Pa., 1986—. Recipient Disting. Teaching award Christian R. and Maru F. Lindback Found., 1973; NSF fellow, 1961-63, Wenner-Glen Found. for Anthrop. Research fellow, 1965-66. Mem. Am. Council on Edn. (state coordinator 1980-84), Assn. Am. Coll. (bd. dirs. 1986—), Mid. States Assn. (chmn., team mem. 1985—), Assn. Presbyn. Colls. and Univs. (exec. com. 1988—), Sigma Xi. Office: Beaver Coll Church and Easton Rds Glenside PA 19038

LANDMAN, MARY SUE, small business owner; b. Zeeland, Mich., May 10, 1951; d. Martin Edsel and Geraldine (Sal) Johnson; m. Jack Edwin Landman, Aug. 18, 1973. BS and BA, Aquinas Coll., 1982. Co-owner, controller, sec., treas. Progressive Blasting Systems, Grand Rapids, Mich., 1971-83; co-owner Ten Harmsel Furniture, Holland, Mich., 1983—. Home: 4295 Indian Spring SW Grandville MI 49418

LANDOVSKY, ROSEMARY REID, director figure skating school, coach; b. Chgo., July 26, 1933; d. Samuel Stuart and Audrey Todd (Lyons) Reid; m. John Indulis Landovsky, Feb. 20, 1960; children: David John, Linette. BA in Psychology, Colo. Coll., 1956. Profl. skater Holiday on Ice Touring Show, U.S., Mex., Cuba, 1956-58; skating dir. and coach Paradice Arena, Birmingham, 1958-62, Les Patineurs, Huntsville, Ala., 1960-62; coach competitive (Ice Skating Inst. Am., U.S. Figure Skating Assn.) Michael Kirby and Assocs., River Forest, Chgo., Ill., 1962-63; rink mgr., skating dir. Lake Meadows Ice Arena, Chgo., 1963-68; coach (ISIA, USFSA) Rainbo Arena, Chgo., 1968-73; skating dir. Northwestern U. Skating Sch., Evanston, Ill., 1968-73, Robert Crown Ice Ctr., Evanston, 1973-75; dir. instl. programs Skokie (Ill.) Park Dist., 1975-87; competition dir. ISIA All America Competition, 1985—. Dir., producer, choreographer Ice Show: Nutcracker Ballet, 1973, Ice Extravaganza III, 1985, Ice Lights '86, '87. Election judge, worker, Ind. Dems., Chgo., 1962, 66. Mem. Profl. Skaters Guild, Ice Skating Inst. Am. Office: Skokie Skatium 9300 Bronx Skokie IL 60077

LANDRAM, CHRISTINA LOUELLA, librarian; b. Paragould, Ark., Dec. 10, 1922; d. James Ralph and Bertie Louella (Jordan) Oliver; m. Robert Ellis Landram, Aug. 7, 1948; 1 child, Mark Owen. B.A., Tex. Woman's U., 1945, B.L.S., 1946, M.L.S., 1951. Preliminary cataloger Library of Congress, Washington, 1946-48; cataloger U.S. Info. Ctr., Tokyo, Japan, 1948-50, U.S. Dept. Agr., Washington, 1953-54; librarian Yokota AFB, Yokota, Japan, 1954-55; librarian St. Mary's Hosp., West Palm Beach, Fla., 1957-59; librarian Jacksonville (Ark.) High Sch., 1959-61; coordinator Shelby County Libraries, Memphis, 1961-63; head catalog dept. Ga. State U. Library, 1963-86, librarian, assoc. prof. emeritus, 1986—. Contbr. articles to library jours. Mem. Ga. Library Assn. (chmn. resources and tech. services sect. 1969-71), Metro-Atlanta Library Assn. (pres. 1967-68), ALA (chmn. cataloging norms 1979-80, nominating com. 1977-78), Southeastern Library Assn. (mem. govtl. relations com. 1975-78, intellectual freedom com. 1984-86, mem. Rothrock awards com. 1987—). Presbyterian. Home: 1478 Leafmore Ridge Decatur GA 30033

LANDRENEAU, ELLEN RITA, consultant; b. Ville Platte, La., Jan. 26, 1949; d. Joseph Otis and Clamie (Fusilier) L.; B.S., U. Southwestern La., 1971; M.S., U. So. Miss., 1978; m. A. Dale Thibodeaux, Feb. 21, 1981. Staff nurse Wuesthoff Meml. Hosp., Cocoa, Fla., 1971-72; pub. health nurse Brevard County Health Dept., Melbourne, Fla., 1972-74; day camp nurse Baton Rouge Assn. Retarded Citizens, 1974; staff nurse ICU, Earl K. Long Hosp., Baton Rouge, 1976; lab. asst. Southeastern La. U., 1974-77; instr. nursing Pearl River Jr. Coll., Poplarville, Miss., 1978; edn. cons. Acadiana Mental Health Center, Lafayette, La., 1979; asst. prof. U. Southwestern La., Lafayette, 1978-85; staff nurse Cypress Hosp., 1985-87; nursing standards cons., 1984—; clin. research mgr., Inst. Biol. Research and Devel. Mem. Am. Nurses Assn., La. Nurses Assn., Sierra Club, Alpha Lambda Delta, Phi Kappa Phi, Sigma Theta Tau. Roman Catholic. Home: 100 Edgebrook Circle Lafayette LA 70508

LANDRIEU, MARY, state treasurer; b. Nov. 23, 1955. Real estate agt, La. state rep. from dist. 90, until 1987, La. state treas., 1987—; del., Dem. Nat. Conv., 1980. Address: Office of State Treas PO Box 44154 Baton Rouge LA 70804 *

LANDRUM, THELMA LOUISE, insurance executive; b. Spartanburg, S.C., Sept. 22, 1947; d. Henry Thompson and Juanita Thompson Geter; m. William E. Moragne, Nov. 2, 1964 (div. 1967); 1 child, Troy London; m. Carl Edward Landrum, Sept. 13, 1969; 1 child, Paul Benedict. Student, N.H. Coll. Bus., Salem, 1977-78, Mesa (Ariz.) Community Coll., 1978-81; BS in Nursing, Ariz. State U., 1983. Asst. buyer Gilchrist's Dept. Store, Boston, 1969-73; asst. dir. activities Greenbriar Health Care, Nashua, N.H., 1974-77; purchasing specialist Prudential Property & Casualty, Scottsdale, Ariz., 1979-80; RN Staff Builders Nursing, Phoenix, 1982-84; ins. claim specialist State Farm Ins. Co., Tempe, Ariz, 1984—. Fellow Nat. Assn. of Female Execs.; mem. Sigma Theta Tau. Democrat. Office: State Farm Ins Co 1665 W Alameda Dr Tempe AZ 85289

LANDRY, BRENDA LEE, securities analyst; b. Wolfboro, N.H., June 24, 1942; d. Christopher Lee and Barbara F. (Sullivan) Landry; m. Franklin Winfield McCann, June 28, 1980. B.A., Vassar Coll., 1964. Sales analyst Polaroid Co., Cambridge, Mass., 1966-70; 1st v.p. White Weld, N.Y.C., 1970-78, Merrill Lynch, N.Y.C., 1978-80; prin. Morgan Stanley & Co., Inc., N.Y.C., 1980—. Contbr. articles to profl. jours.; various TV appearances. Mem. N.Y. Soc. Security Analysts, Women's Fin. Assn., Photo Mfrs. Assn. Republican. Club: Vassar. Home: PO Box 10 Water Mill NY 11976 Office: Morgan Stanley 1251 Ave of the Americas New York NY 10020

LANDRY, MONIQUE, Canadian government official; b. Montreal, Que., Can., Dec. 25, 1937; m. Jean-Guy Landry; four children. Grad., U. Montreal. Mem. parliament Govt. Can., 1984—; former parliamentary sec. to Sec. of State and Minister of Internat. Trad; Minister of State for External Relations Govt. Can., 1986—; former mem. Standing Com. on Communications and Culture, Joint Com. on Ofcl. Langs. Policy and Programs, Standing Com. on Fin., Trade and Econ. Affairs. Mem. Can.-Europe, Can.-NATO Parliament Assns., Can.-France Inter-Parliament Assn. Office: Dept External Affairs, Lester B Pearson Bldg, 125 Sussex Dr, Ottawa, ON Canada K1A 0A6 *

LANDSBERGER, BETTY HATCH, human development professional, gerontologist, educator; b. Tampa Aug. 9, 1918; d. Hugh Brenton and Margaret Lauder (Macdonell) Hatch; B.A. in Sociology, Fla. State U., 1939; M.A. Ed., U. Mich., 1940; Ph.D., Cornell U., 1951; m. Henry A. Landsberger, June 10, 1951; children—Margaret Ann Landsberger Thomas, Samuel Ernest, Ruth Elizabeth Landsberger Hazard. . Mem. faculty edn. dept. Fla. State U., Cornell U., Roosevelt U., Chgo., 1941-54; program asso. evaluation research Learning Inst. N.C., Durham, 1969-71; mem. faculty U. N.C. Sch. Nursing, Chapel Hill, 1976—, asst. prof. nursing, 1979-81, asso. prof., 1981—; cons. N.C. Div. Health Services, public schs. Chmn. Orange County Sr. Citizens Bd., 1981—; adv. bd. area agy. on aging, 1985—. Mem. N.C. Assn. Research in Edn. (pres. 1975-76), AAUP (chpt. pres. 1983), Phi Beta Kappa, Phi Kappa Phi, Pi Lambda Theta. Democrat. Author: Long Term Care for the Elderly; contbr. articles to profl. jours. and textbooks. Home: 807 Kings Mill Rd Chapel Hill NC 27514 Office: U NC Sch Nursing Chapel Hill NC 27514

LANDSKE, DOROTHY SUZANNE, state senator; b. Evanston, Ill., Sept. 3, 1937; d. William Gerald and Dorothy Marie (Drewes) Martin; m. William Steve Landske, June 1, 1957; children: Catherine Suzanne, Jacqueline Marie Basilotta, Pamela Florence Landske Snyder, Cheryl Lynn, Eric Thomas. Student St. Joseph's Coll., Ind. U., U. Chgo. Receptionist Cedar Lake Med. Clinic (Ind.) 1959-62; owner, operator Sues Bridal House, 1967-75; dep. clk.-treas., Cedar Lake, 1975; chief dep. twp. assessor Center Twp., Crown Point, Ind., 1976-78, twp. assessor, 1979-84, mem. Ind. Senate, 1984—. Vice chmn. Lake County Republican Central Com., 1978—; Lake County rep. to 5th Congl. Dist. Mem. Council State Govts., Nat. Order Women Legislators, Nat. Council State Legislators (bd. dirs. Midwest Women's Network). Roman Catholic.

LANDSMAN, SANDRA GILBERT, psychologist, transactional analyst; b. Detroit, Jan. 5, 1933; d. Arthur Bernard (dec.) and Ida Myra (Finkelstone) (dec.) G.; BS, Wayne State U., 1966, MA, 1970, PhD, 1984; m. Rodney Glenn Landsman, Apr. 3, 1955; children: Aaron William Landsman, Michael Alan Peterson, Victoria Louise Landsman Peterson, Jonathan Gilbert, Faith Susan, Jill Barbara. Cons., counselor Continuum Center for Women, Oakland U., Rochester, Mich., 1970-77; pvt. practice Transactional Analysis, Farmington Hills, Mich., 1966-87; clin. cons., U.S., Can., Europe, South Am.; Transactional Analysis, clin. supr. North Metro & Dearborn Downriver Growth Centers, Rochester and Allen Park, Mich., 1975-78; mem. faculty Macomb County (Mich.) Community Coll., 1976-79; dir. clin. and edn. services Landsman/Foner & Assocs., West Bloomfield, Mich., 1977-82; disting. lectr. Sch. Social Work, Mich. State U., 1975-78; cons. in field; mem. faculty dept. psychology Columbia Pacific U.; internat. presentor on psychopathology and pre and peri-natal psychology, U.S., Can., Europe, S.Am., 1966—. Cert. social worker, Mich. Mem. Internat. Transactional Analysis Assn. (mem. editorial bd.), U.S. Transactional Analysis Assn. (clin. teaching mem.), European Transactional Analysis Assn., Pre & Peri-Natal Assn. N.AM., Nat. Assn. Social Workers, Am. Assn. for Counseling and Devel., Am. Coll. Personnel Assn., Assn. Specialists in Group Work, Mich. Assn. for Counseling and Devel., Mich. Coll. Personnel Assn., Mich. Assn. Specialist Group Work (past pres.), Mich. Assn. Women Deans, Adminstrs. and Counselors, New Directions in Edn. and Psychotherapy (charter, trustee), Pre and Perinatal Assn. of N.Am. Author: Affective Disorders: The Assessment, Development, and Treatment Strategies of Manic-Depressive Structure; I'm Special: An Experiential Workbook for the Child in Us All, Found: A Place for Me-the Development Diagnosis and Treatment of Manic-Depressive Structure, (with others) Secret Places; contbr. articles to profl. publs. Home: 109 Olympus Way Jupiter FL 33477 Office: PO Box 7134 Jupiter FL 33468-7134

LANDSMANN, LEANNA, editor, publisher; b. Ithaca, N.Y., May 26, 1946; d. George and Katherine (Mehlenbacher) Abraham; m. Guy Landsmann, July 14, 1968. B.A., St. Lawrence U., 1968. Tchr. public schs. Ivory Coast, West Africa, 1968-69, Prattsburg, N.Y., 1969-70; asso. editor Instr. Publs. Inc., N.Y.C., 1971-76; editor-in-chief Instr. Publs. Inc., 1976—, pub., 1978—, also pres.; v.p. Harcourt Brace Jovanovich Inc.; mem. faculty Stanford U. Pub. Course, 1980, 81; sec. Edn.'s Study Group Elem. Edn., 1985-86. Mem. nat. bd. Impact II, Girls Clubs Am.; vol. public schs., vol. public relations work in edn. Mem. EDPRESS, Nat. Assn. Edn. Young Children, Internat. Reading Assn., Assn. Childhood Edn. Internat., Mag. Pubs. Assn., Assn. Supervision and Curriculum Devel. Office: Instr Publs 545 Fifth Ave New York NY 10017

LANE, ALBERTA CANADY, physician assistant; b. Savannah, Ga., Aug. 6, 1945; d. Hoyt Paul Sr. and Annie Alberta (Cobb) Canady; m. Joseph Manning Lane Jr., Sept. 2, 1967 (div. Jan. 1973); children: Joseph III, James Michael. Grad., Candler Sch. Nursing, 1966; student, Ga. State U., 1966, U. Ga., 1967-68. RN, physician asst. ICU staff nurse Dekalb Gen. Hosp., Decatur, Ga., 1966-67, St. Mary's Hosp., Athens, Ga., 1967-68; emergency room supr. Athens Gen. Hosp., 1969-70; operating room staff nurse Candler Gen. Hosp., Savannah, 1970-72; office nurse Drs. David B. and John M. Fillingim, P.C., Savannah, 1972-75; physician asst. John M. Fillingim M.D., Savannah, 1975—. Contbr. articles to profl. jours. Den mother Cub Scouts Am., Savannah, 1976-80; mem. Calvary Bapt. Temple Choir, Savannah, 1978—, dir. 4th grade Sunday sch., 1978-82, 5th grade Sunday sch., 1986—. Mem. Ga. Assn. Physician Assts. Office: John M Fillingim MD 500 Eisenhower Dr Savannah GA 31406

LANE, CHARLOTTE KNOX, association executive; b. Washington, Pa., July 1, 1918; d. Robert Welch and Sarah (Chaney) K.; m. Perry Mehaffey Lane Sr., Apr. 13, 1940; children: Penelope K. Snyder, Sarah Lane Sutherland, Perry Mehaffey Jr., Gregory Scott (dec.). Student, Sweet Briar Coll., 1936-38, Miss Conley's Sch., 1938-39. Sec. Washington County Blind Assn., Pa., 1967; office mgr. Washington County Tourism, Pa., 1967-69, exec. dir., 1969—. V.p. Washington County History and Landmarks, 1983—; sec. Bradford House Assn., Washington, 1985—; mem. Pa. Bd. Hist. Preservation, Harrisburg, 1983-85. Recipient award for significant contbn. Washington County Arts Council, 1987. Mem. Nat. Tour Assn., Travel Pa. Assn. (bd. dirs. 1975—, sec. 1975-80), Pa. Travel Council, Duncan Glass Soc. (bd. dirs. 1984—). Democrat. Presbyterian. Lodge: Zonta (bd. dirs. Washington). Home: RD #7 Box 9 Washington PA 15301 Office: Washington County Tourism 59 N Main St Washington PA 15301

LANE, DONNALEE ANN MUCCIARONE, marketing executive; b. Milford, Mass., Jan. 1, 1945; d. Peter Angelo Mucciarone and Rose Marie (Taddeo) Mandra; m. Francis T. Lane, Sept. 6, 1969 (dec. Mar. 1970); children: Michael J., Stephen F., Susan M. Lane-Penza. BS in Mgmt., Northeastern U. Coll., 1983. Proofreader Factory Mut. Corp., Norwood, Mass., 1964-65; supr., tech. typing group Electronic Systems div. Sylvania, Needham, Mass., 1965-69; cons. communications Norwood, 1969-71; adminstrv. asst. B.D. Electrodyne, Sharon, Mass., 1972-74; office adminstr. Decision Research Corp., Wellesley, Mass., 1975-78; mgr. graphic arts dept. CSA Press, Bedford, Mass., 1978-80; sr. publications engr. RCA Corp., Burlington, Mass., 1980-84, mgr. mktg. communications BBN Laboratories Inc. (now BBN Systems and Techs. Corp.), Cambridge, Mass., 1984—. Leader, council del. Girl Scouts of U.S., Norwood, 1969-74. Mem. Internat. Assn. Bus. Communicators (bd. dirs.), Armed Forces Communications and Electronics Assn., Assn. Retarded Citizens, Sigma Epsilon Rho. Roman Catholic. Home: 19 Manchester Rd Norwood MA 02062 Office: BBN Techs Corp 10 Moulton St Cambridge MA 02238

LANE, GLORIA JULIAN, foundation administrator; b. Chgo., Oct. 6, 1932; d. Coy Berry and Katherine (McDowell) Julian; m. William Gordon Lane (div. Oct. 1958); 1 child, Julie Kay Rosewood. BS in Edn., Cen. Mo. State U., 1958; MA, Bowling Green State U., 1959; PhD, No. Ill. U., 1972. Cert. tchr. Assoc. prof. William Jewell Coll., Liberty, Mo., 1959-60; chair forensic div. Coral Gables (Fla.) High Sch., 1960-64; assoc. prof. No. Ill. U., DeKalb, 1964-70; prof. Elgin (Ill.) Community Coll., 1970-72; owner, pub. Lane and Assocs, Inc., San Diego, 1972-78; prof. Nat. U., San Diego, 1978—; pres., chief exec. officer Women's Internat. Ctr., San Diego, 1982—; founder, dir. Living Legacy Awards, San Diego, 1984—. Author: Project Text for Effective Communications, 1972, Project Text for Executive Communication, 1980, Positive Concepts for Success, 1983; editor Who's WhoAmong San Diego Women, 1984, 85, 86, Systems and Structure, 1984. Bd. dirs. Cen. for Neurologic Studies, San Diego, 1986—; trustee Community Service Cen. for Disabled, San Diego, 1985—. Named Woman of Accomplishment Soroptimist Internat., 1985, Pres.'s Council San Diego, 1986, Ctr. City Assn., 1986, Woman of Yr. Girl's Clubs of San Diego, 1986; recipient Independence award Ctr. for Disabled, 1986. Club: Charter 100 (pres. 1986—) (San Diego). Home and Office: 6202 Friars Rd 311 San Diego CA 92108

LANE, HELEN SCHICK, retired speech and hearing educator, administrator, psychologist; b. Columbus, Ohio, Feb. 24, 1906; d. Adam John and Florence (Erfurt) Schick; m. LeRoy Thomas Lane, June 23, 1936. BA, Ohio State U., 1926, MA, 1928, PhD, 1930. Asst. psychologist Cen. Inst. for the Deaf, St. Louis, 1930-32, psychologist, 1932—, registrar Tchr.'s Tng. Coll., 1932-41, prin., 1941-72, prin. emeritus, 1972—; asst. prof. psychology Washington U., St. Louis, 1931-41, assoc. prof., 1941-61, prof. edn. Grad. Inst. Edn., 1961-72, prof. dept. speech and hearing, 1972-82. Contbr. numerous articles to profl. jours. Vol. history alumni research Cen. Inst. for the Deaf, 1982—; chairperson Christian Outreach Bd. Pilgrim Congl. Ch., St. Louis, 1980-87. Helen S. Lane Endowed Scholarship program named in her honor Cen. Inst. for Deaf, 1972; recipient Silver Fawn award Boy Scouts Am., 1974. Fellow: Am. Psychol. Assn., Am. Speech, Lang. and Hearing Assn.; mem. Alexander Graham Bell Assn. for Deaf (bd. dirs. 1946-68, pres. 1965-69), Am. Assn. Sch. Adminstrs., Sigma Alpha Iota (nat. chairperson Internat. Music Fund 1948-54, Sword and Rose of Honor award 1950-60). Republican. Home: 7290 Greenway Ave Saint Louis MO 63130 Office: Cen Inst for Deaf 818 S Euclid Saint Louis MO 63110

LANE, JANET MALLETT, manager, writer; b. Sioux City, Iowa, May 24, 1950; d. Howard Emil Mallett and Mary Beatrice (Rosecrans) Maffit; m. John Robert Penaligon, June 22, 1985; 1 child, Jessica Noelle. Degree in gen. writing program, Colo. U., 1988. English sec. Taipei (Taiwan) Am. Sch., Republic China, 1973-75; free lance writer Sioux City (Iowa) Journal, 1975-77; dir. promotion and pub. services Sta. KTIV, Sioux City, 1975-77; dir. promotion Sta. KMTV, Omaha, 1977-79; entrepreneur Lane-Tornell Communications, Omaha, 1979; rep. crude oil Murphy Oil U.S.A. Inc., Denver, 1980-86; ptnr. Network, the Magazine for Colo. Women, Denver, 1987—. Contbr. articles to various jours.; songwriter Bow Mar Blackouts, Colo. 1986-87. Vol. Nancy Dick Senate, Denver, 1985.

LANE, JULIA A., nursing educator; b. Chgo., June 29, 1927; d. James and Julia (Ivins) L. BSN, DePaul U., 1956; MSN, Cath. U. Am., 1961; PhD, Loyola U., Chgo., 1974. Cert. midwife. Staff nurse St. Joseph Hosp., 1954-55, Chgo. Bd. of Health, 1955-57; instr. South Chgo. Hosp. Sch. Nursing, 1957-58, dir. edn., 1960-63; assoc. prof. Loyola U. Sch. Nursing, 1963-74, dean, 1974—. Office: Loyola Univ Sch Nursing 820 N Michigan Chicago IL 60611 *

LANE, KATHLEEN MARGARET, optical company administrator; b. Mpls., Oct. 25, 1946; d. Bernard Melvin and Margaret (Beck) Aanerud; m. Kenneth LeRoy Lane, Sept. 1, 1979; 1 child, Dennis Leon. Cost acct. Honeywell, Mpls., 1964-66; bank bookkeeper Columbia Heights State Bank, Minn., 1968-71; inventory control mgr. Hodes Optical Inc., Torrance, Calif., 1972-75, office mgr., 1975-79; lens supr. Coburn Optical Industries, Inc., Carson, Calif., 1979-85, br. mgr., St. Paul, 1985; customer relations Opti Fair, Aneheim, Calif., 1978-83. Mem. Am. Inst. Banking, Nat. Assn. Female Execs. Avocations: restoring old furniture; camping; knitting. Office: Coburn Optical Industries Inc 1471 Brewster St Saint Paul MN 55108

LANE, MARGARET BEYNON TAYLOR, librarian; b. St. Louis, Feb. 6, 1919; d. Archer and Alice (Jones) Taylor; B.A., La. State U., 1939, J.D., 1942; B.S. in L.S., Columbia U., 1941; m. Horace C. Lane, Jan. 6, 1945; children—Margaret Elizabeth, Thomas Archer. Reference and circulation asst. Columbia Law Library, N.Y.C., 1942-44; law librarian, asst. prof. U. Conn. Sch. Law, Hartford, 1944-46; law librarian La. State U. Law Sch., Baton Rouge, 1946-48; recorder documents La. Sec. of State's Office, Baton Rouge, 1949-75; law librarian Lane Fertitta, Lane & Tullos, 1976—. Author: State Publications and Depository Libraries, 1981, Selecting And Organizing State Government Publications, 1987. Mem. depository library council to Pub. Printer, 1972-77; mem. plan devel. com. La. Fed. Depository Library, 1982-83. Treas. Delta Iota House Bd. of Kappa Kappa Gamma, 1965-68. Inducted into La. State U. Hall of Fame, 1987. Mem. ALA (interdivisional com. public documents 1967-74, chmn. 1967-70; govt. documents round table, state and local documents task force 1972—, coordinator 1980-82; James Bennett Childs award 1981), La. Library Assn. (Essae M. Culver Disting. Service award 1976; chmn. documents com. 1982-83, Lucy B. Foote award subject specialist sect. 1986), La., Baton Rouge Bar Assns., Mortar Bd., Phi Delta Delta, Kappa Kappa Gamma. Club: Baton Rouge Library. Home: 7545 Richards Dr Baton Rouge LA 70809 Office: POB 3335 Baton Rouge LA 70821

LANE, NANCY LEE, diagnostic systems company personnel executive; b. Boston, Sept. 3, 1938; d. Samuel M. and Gladys (Pitkins) Lane. Student U. Oslo, 1961; B.S., Boston U., 1962; M.P.A., U. Pitts. Grad. Sch. Pub. and Internat. Affairs, 1967; cert. program for mgmt. devel. Harvard U. Grad. Sch. Bus. Adminstrn., 1975. Project mgr. Westinghouse Broadcasting Co., 1964-66; dep. dir. personnel Nat. Urban League, N.Y.C., 1967-72; 2d v.p. Chase Manhattan Bank, N.Y.C., 1972-73; v.p. personnel Off Track Betting Corp., N.Y.C., 1973-75; v.p. personnel and adminstrn., dir. Ortho-Diagnostic Systems, Inc., Raritan, N.J., 1976—. Recipient Disting. Alumni award Boston U. Coll. Communication, 1987. Home: 37 W 12th St New York NY 10011 Office: Ortho Diagnostic Systems Inc Route 202 Raritan NJ 08869

LANE, PATRICIA MIKHAEL, nurse; b. Colorado Springs, Colo., Nov. 28, 1938; d. Edward Frank and Elaine Patricia (Henry) L.; m. Joseph Melton (div. 1980); children: Raymond Edward, Dorothy Twynette. BS in Nursing, San Diego State U., 1964; postgrad., U. Wis., 1978-80. RN, Calif., Wis., Va. Grad. teaching asst. U. Wis., Green Bay, 1978-79; staff nurse Psychiat. and Alcohol Abuse Unit, Green Bay, Wis., 1979-80; staff nurse Psychiat. Unit, Rockingham Meml. Hosp., Harrisonburg, Va., 1980-81, nursing edn. instr., 1983-87, instr. nursing edn., 1987—; pub. health nurse San Diego County; pub. work leader for stress mgmt., communications, conflict mgmt., assertiveness. Mem. Am. Nurses Assn. (cert. psychiatric nurse), Cen. Va. Council Staff Devel., Am. Soc. Tng. and Devel., Blue Ridge Chpt., San Diego State U. Faculty Wives, Cancer Soc. San Diego. Home: Rt 1 Box 171 Timberville VA 22853 Office: Rockingham Meml Hosp 235 Cantrelle St Harrisonburg VA 22801

LANE, ROBIN R., lawyer; b. Kerrville, Tex., Nov. 28 1947; d. Rowland and Gloria (Benson) Richards; m. Stanley Lane, Aug. 22, 1971 (div. 1979); m. 2d, Anthony W. Cunningham, Nov. 12, 1980; children: Joshua Lane, Alexandra. BA with honors in Econs., U. Fla., 1969; MA, George Washington U., 1971; JD, Stetson Coll. Law, 1978. Bar: Fla. 1979, U.S. Ct. Appeals (11th cir.) 1981, U.S. Supreme Ct. 1986. Mgmt. trainee internat. banking Gulf Western Industries, N.Y.C.; internat. research specialist Ryder Systems, Inc., Miami, Fla., 1973, project mgr., 1974; assoc. Wagner, Cunningham, Vaughan & McLaughlin, Tampa, Fla., 1979-85; sole practice, 1985—; guest lectr. med. jurisprudence Stetson Coll. Law, 1982-87. Contbr. articles to various revs. Recipient Am. Jurisprudence award-torts, Lawyers Co-op. Fla., 1979; Scottish Rite fellow, 1968-69. Mem. Acad. Fla. Trial Lawyers (mem. com. 1983-84), Assn. Trial Lawyers Am., Fla. Bar Assn., ABA, Fla. Women's Network, Omicron Delta Epsilon, Delta Delta Delta. Clubs: Palma Ceia Tampa; Tower. Home: 914 Golf View St Tampa FL 33629 Office: Barnett Plaza 101 E Kennedy Suite 1480 Tampa FL 33602

LANE, SARAH MARIE, newspaper correspondent, freelance writer; b. Conneaut, Ohio, July 27, 1946; d. Robert George and Julia Ellen (Sanford) Clark; m. Ralph Donaldson Lane, May 28, 1977; children: Richard, Laura. Student, Muskingum Coll., 1964-66; BS in Edn., Kent (Ohio) State U., 1977. Cert. tchr., Ohio. Columnist News Herald, Conneaut, 1963-64; tchr. 1st grade Mesopotamia (Ohio) Local Schs., 1968; chpt. one aide Maplewood Local Schs., Cortland, Ohio, 1983-85; corr. Warren (Ohio) Tribune Chronicle, 1986—. George Record scholar, 1964. Mem. Bazetta-Cortland His. Soc. (v.p.1984-87). Republican. Mem. Christian Ch. (Disciples of Christ). Home and Office: 298 Corriedale Dr Cortland OH 44410

LANE, SHARI LEA, distribution company executive; b. Carmel, Calif., Oct. 20, 1950; d. Joseph Reynolds and Joan Martha (McBride) McElrath Lane. B.A., U. Va.-Fairfax, 1972; postgrad., U. Phoenix, 1988—. Notary pub.; real estate broker; grad. Realtors Inst. Asst. dir. personnel Mayflower Hotel, Washington, 1972-73; personnel adminstr. PRC Planning Research Corp., McLean, Va., 1973-75; dir. sales 1928 Jewelry Co., Burbank, Calif., 1975-78; dir. new home sales Sterpa Realty Register, Glendale, Calif., 1978-82; nat. accounts mgr. Bekins Moving & Storage, Glendale, Calif., 1982-83; mgr. Internat. Sales adminstrn. Applause Inc., Woodland Hills, Calif., 1983—. Mem. Nat. Assn. Female Execs. (assoc.), Womens Assn. Realtors (sec. treas. 1980-82), Am. Telemktg. Assn. Republican. Episcopalian. Avocations: swimming (Ala. state champion 1966 breastroke); gourmet cooking; travel. Home: 8633 Oso Ave Canoga Park CA 91306

LANE, SHARON SUZANNE, data processing educator; b. Gainesville, Tex., Dec. 26, 1950; d. Keith Dwight Sr. and Vonna Jean (Woods) Swim; m. Charles Franklin Sebastian Jr., June 15, 1972 (div. Nov. 1978); children: Jennifer, Nikole, Sebastian; m. Larry Eugene Lane; children: Ashley Lauren, Jamie Katrina. Student, Howard Coll. Big Spring, 1969-70; BS in Edn., Abilene (Tex.) Christian U., 1973; postgrad., Tex. Tech U., 1979—. Cert. in elem. edn. Kindergarten tchr. Piggott (Ark.) Ind. Sch. Dist., 1973-75, Corning (Ark.) Ind. Sch. Dist., 1975-76, Big Spring Ind. Sch. Dist., 1976-79; 1st grade tchr. Lubbock (Tex.) Ind. Sch. Dist., 1979-85, data processing instr., staff devel. instr., 1985—, mem. elem. curriculum guidance devel. com., 1988. Mem. Tex. Computer Educators Assn. (co-program com. chairperson for area conf. 1987-88), Tex. Classroom Tchrs. Assn., Internat. Council for Computers in Edn. Mem. Ch. of Christ. Home: 3408 Elmwood Lubbock TX 79407 Office: Whiteside Elem 7508 Albany Lubbock TX 79424

LANES, AVA MARIE, educator; b. Bowman, N.D., May 15, 1952; d. George Oscar and Kathryn Eloise (Davis) Odegaard; m. Paul Robert Lanes, Aug. 20, 1977. B.S. cum laude in Edn., U. N.D., 1974; M.A., Ball State U., 1977. Cert. spl. edn. Speech pathologist Dickinson Pub. Schs., 1974-76, preschool speech pathologist, 1977-78, speech, language, hearing coordinator, 1978-81, asst. dir. spl. edn., 1981-84, adminstrv. asst. for curriculum and instruction, 1984—; adj. prof., U.N.D., Dickinson, 1978; private therapist, Dickinson, 1978-81. Bd. dirs. Dickinson C. of C., 1979-80, Statewide Tchr. Ctr., Grand Forks, N.D., 1980-82, Dickinson Tchr. Ctr., 1979-83, Dickinson Consortium, 1979-80; U. N.D. fund chmn. for Class of 1974; mem. adv. bd. St. Joseph's Hosp.; mem. Dickinson br. N.D. Centennial Commn. Recipient Acad. Achievement award Ball State U., 1977. Mem. N.D. Council for Exceptional Children (rec. sec. 1983-84, pres.-elect 1984-85), Council for Exceptional Children (chpt. pres.-elect 1979-80, pres. 1980-81), AAUW (publicity chmn. 1975-76), Am. Speech/Language/Hearing Assn. (publicity chmn. 1977-78), N.D. Council of Sch. Adminstrs. Republican. Lutheran. Avocations: photography (People's choice award 1984-85), cross country skiing, gardening. Home: 1470 2nd Ave Dickinson ND 58601 Office: Dickinson Pub Schs 444 W 4th St Dickinson ND 58602-1057

LANES, DENISE DEE, international trading company executive; b. Bklyn., Feb. 14, 1951; d. Irving and Sylvia (Maltz) L.; B.A., SUNY, Stony Brook, 1972; M.B.A., St. Johns U., 1977. Sales asst. Mitsui & Co. (U.S.A.), Inc., N.Y.C., 1972-81, asst. gen. mgr., 1981-85; owner, mgr. World Traders (U.S.A.), Inc., Rego Park, N.Y., 1981—. Mem. Nat. Assn. Women Bus. Owners, The Global Bus. Assn. (treas.), Defenders of Wildlife. Office: World Traders (USA) 98-05 67th Ave Rego Park NY 11374

LANES, SELMA GORDON, critic, author, editor; b. Boston, Mar. 13, 1929; d. Jacob and Lily (Whiteman) Gordon; B.A., Smith Coll., 1950; M.S. in Journalism, Columbia, 1954; m. Jerrold B. Lanes, Nov. 21, 1959 (div. Mar. 1970); children—Andrew Oliver, Matthew Gordon. Asst. to publicity dir. Little Brown & Co., Boston, 1950-51; asso. editor Focus Mag., N.Y.C., 1951-53; travel page editor Boston Globe, 1953; spl. editorial asst., researcher Look Mag., 1956-60; children's entertainment editor Show Mag., 1961-63; critic children's books for Book World (N.Y. Herald-Tribune, later World Jour. Tribune, Wash. Post and Chgo. Tribune), 1965-71, N.Y. Times Book Rev., 1966—; articles editor Parents Mag., 1971-74; editor-in-chief Parents Mag. Press, 1974-78; cons. to Penguin Books, 1967, Starstream Books, 1980-81; lectr. New Sch./Parsons Sch. Design, 1975-77, Del. Art Mus., 1979; dir. Schiller-Wapner Galleries, 1983-84; freelance writer, 1984—. Judge, Children's Spring Book Festival, 1970, dir., 1972; judge N.Y. Times Ten Best Illus. Children's Books, 1973, 79, 80. Trustee Fund for Art Investment, N.Y.C. Mem. Phi Beta Kappa. Author (juvenile) Amy Loves Good-byes, 1966; The Curiosity Book, 1968; Down the Rabbit Hole, A critical work for adults on children's literature, 1971, paperback, 1976; The Art of Maurice Sendak, 1980; selector-adapter: A Child's First Book of Nursery Tales, 1983; Lillian Gish: An Actor's Life for Me, 1987. Office: 36 E 81st St New York NY 10128

LANEY, ELIZABETH CARDWELL, free-lance photojournalist; b. Bluefield, W.Va., Aug. 19, 1912; d. Alexander Drake Cardwell and Harriet Louise (Parker) Martin; m. Luther Hubbard Laney, Apr. 6, 1941; 1 son, Charles. Student St. Paul Normal Coll., 1930-31, Franklin U., Ohio State U., Bliss Bus. Sch., Columbus Bus. Coll., St. Mary of the Springs, Ill. Wesleyan Coll., Columbus Tech. Inst., Ohio Dominican Coll., Capital U.; cert. Poro Sch. Cosmetology, 1941. Stenographer, U.S. Govt., Dayton, Ohio, 1941-43; cosmetician, mgr., owner Laney Beauty Salon, Columbus, Ohio, 1945-50; sec., auditor City of Columbus, 1950-75; spl. feature contbg. writer The Ohio State Sentinel, 1960-62, Call and Post Newspaper (syndicated), 1967—, photojournalist, 1977—; editor Ohio Bapt. Jour. Ohio Bapt. Gen. Conv., 1984—. Author: (poetry) Poetry in Prayer, 1977. Editor Centennial Jour., 1969; 100 Years, Shiloh Baptist Church History, 1974. Composer numerous hymns. Ch. sch. tchr., dir. pub. relations Shiloh Bapt. Ch., 1970—, Sunday Sch. sec., treas., founder Gleaners class; dir. pub. relations Eastern Union Missionary Bapt. Assn., Eastern Union Assembly Ground, Eastern Union Bapt. Coll., Ohio Bapt. Gen. Conv., 1983; sec. bd. trustees Eastern Union Bapt. Coll.; mem. Eastern Union Assembly Ground; publicity chmn. Christian Women's Workshop; active mem. Urban League, Urban League Guild, Women's Service Bd. Grant Hosp. (life), Ch. Women United (life), Ohio Bapt. Women's Conv. (life); founder, organizer Triangle Civic Assn., 1945; sec. Eastgate Garden/Civic Assn., 1955-57. Named Woman of Yr., Shiloh Bapt. Ch., 1962, 71, 75; recipient Cert. of Honor, Mayor Tom Moody, 1975, Cert. of Honor, Columbus City Council, 1975; 1st, 2nd, 3rd prize certs. Columbus Writers Guild, 1965-70; 1st, 2nd, 3rd place ribbons Golden Hobby Show, 1979-81; numerous ribbons, prizes Ohio Dominican Coll., 1980-81; selected as guest photojournalist Israel Journalist, Jerusalem Post Newspaper; 1 of 5 selected for Equal Opportunity Day, Columbus Call and Post Newspaper, 1962; recipient Mayor's award for vol. service, 1984; named WCKX Citizen of Week, 1987; cited for Civic and Community service Columbus Urban League Guild, 1987. Mem. Women in Communications, Nat. Assn. Colored Women's Clubs, Eta Phi Beta (named chpt. Black Woman of Yr. 1983). Republican. Lodge: Order Eastern Star. Avocations: music; arts; writing; photography; travel.

LANEY, VICTORIA JOY, computer company manager; b. Silver Spring, Md., July 18, 1951; d. Culbert and Edna (Bryant) L. BA in English and Psychology, Brigham Young U., 1975, MA in Mgmt., 1977; student, Nova U., 1980. Personnel analyst IBM, Armonk, N.Y., 1977-79; coll. recruiter IBM, Boca Raton, Fla., 1979-81, personal computer dealer sales trainer, 1981-83, product developer, 1984-85; product mgr. IBM, Marietta, Ga., 1986—; IBM-loaned mem. faculty U. Utah, Salt Lake City, 1983-84. Editor: Writing to Read with Students of Limited English Proficiency, 1987; also contbr. articles to profl. jours. Mormon missionary, France and Belgium, 1972-74; mem. bd. Relief Soc., N.Y. and Fla., 1977-82; pres. alumni council Brigham Young U. Grad. Sch. Mgmt., Provo, Utah, 1986—, pres. Nat. Laney Family Orgn. Named one of Outstanding Young Women of Am., 1977. Republican. Home: 3351 Lake Crest Ln Roswell GA 30075

LANG, BARBARA BRYANT, management consultant; b. Jacksonville, Fla., Oct. 16, 1943; d. Chester A. and Margaret (Small) Bryant; m. Gerald B. Lang, Apr. 30, 1962; 1 child, Yalanda Maria. B.S. in Bus. Edn., Edward Waters Coll., Jacksonville, Fla., 1965; postgrad. Calif. Research Lab., Sacramento, 1982. Adminstrn. mgr. IBM, Atlanta, 1976-78, mgr. adminstrn. ops., 1978-80, mgr. secretarial services, 1980-84, sr. fin. mgr., 1984-85; pres. GYB Assocs., Atlanta, 1985-86; mgr. plans and controls, IBM Corp. Asset Mgmt., Rockville, Md., 1986-88; corp. program mgr.-govt. and external programs IBM Corp., 1988—. Past chpt. pres. Jack and Jill Am., 1983; co-chair adv. com. Southside High Sch., Atlanta, 1985-86; mem. task force Just Us Theatre, Atlanta, 1986; chair polit. action com. Nat. Coalition of 100 Black Women, 1988—. Mem. Women Bus. Owners, Am. Soc. Tng. and Devel., Nat. Assn. Female Execs., Atlanta C. of C. (women's workshop com. 1985), The Profl. Woman (bd. dirs.). Democrat. Presbyterian. Avocation: interior decorating. Home: 4413 Westover Pl NW Washington DC 20016 Office: 1801 K St NW Suite 1200 Washington DC 20006

LANG, ELAINE, psychologist; b. New Rochelle, N.Y., Mar. 17, 1955; d. William and Sarah (Rosenblum) L. BS, Tufts U., 1977; MA, Temple U., 1981, PhD, 1984. Lic. clin. psychologist, Mass. Intern Mass. Mental Health Ctr., 1982-83; research asst. Ctr. for Applied Social Research, Boston, 1977-79; psychotherapist Psychol. Services Ctr., Phila., 1980-82, Brookline (Mass.) Mental Health Ctr., 1982-84; clin. psychologist Newton (Mass.)-Wellesley Hosp., 1984-85; pvt. practice psychotherapist Brookline, 1983—; program evaluator clin. psychology clinic Temple U., Phila., 1980-81, instr. psychology dept., 1981-82; clin. psychologist So. Jamaica Plain Health Ctr., Jamaica Plain, Mass., 1984—, dir. tng., 1986—; assoc. psychologist Brigham & Women's Hosp., Boston, 1985—; clin. instr. Harvard Med. Sch., Boston, 1985—. Fellow NIMH, 1979, Harvard Med. Sch., 1982. Mem. Am. Psychol. Assn., Mass. Psychol. Assn., Mass. Assn. Psychoanalytic Psychotherapy, Psychologists Social Responsibility. Office: 1776 Beacon St Brookline MA 02146

LANG, GLORIA HELEN, tool engineer; b. N.Y.C., Mar. 15, 1932; d. Michael and Elizebeth (Snyder) L.; student Kent State U., 1957-61, Youngstown State U., 1977; A.A., SUNY, 1982. Retail salesman, 1947-51; owner, operator tax service, Tampa, Fla., 1954-55; tool and die maker Gen. Motors Corp., Warren, Ohio, 1955—; tool and die apprentice Ohio State U., 1972-76; tooling engr., cutting tool cons., pres., chief exec. officer Lang Industries, Inc., Warren, 1977—; lectr. on females in modern machine trades. Served with U.S. Army, 1951-54. Mem. Nat. Assn. Female Execs., Nat. Tool, Die and Precision Machining Assn., Nat. Small Bus. Assn., NOW, Internat. Platform Assn., Am. Soc. Bus. and Profl. Women, Am. Legion (past comdr. post 748 Warren). Home: 4793 Ardmore Ave Youngstown OH 44505 Office: Lang Industries Inc PO Box 8135 Youngstown OH 44505

LANG, JEAN MCKINNEY, editor, educator; b. Cherokee, Iowa, Nov. 6, 1921; d. Roy Clarence and Verna Harvey (Smith) McKinney; BS, Iowa State U., 1945; MA, Ohio State U., 1969; postgrad. U. South Fla., 1972; 1 dau., Barbara Jean (Mrs. Michael L. Wilcox). Merchandiser, jewelry buyer Rike-Kumler Co., Dayton, Ohio, 1952-59, Met. Co., Dayton, 1959-64; tchr. DeVilbiss High Sch., Toledo, 1966-67; chmn. dept. retailing Webber Coll., Babson Park, Fla., 1967-72; asso. editor Wet Set Illustrated, 1972-75; sr. editor Pleasure Boating, Largo, Fla., 1975-84; tchr. bus. adminstrn. St. Petersburg (Fla.) Jr. Coll., 1974—; editor Suncoast Woman, 1986—. Mem. U.S. Senatorial Bus. Adv. Bd.; mem. Nat. Boating Safety Adv. Council, 1979-81; Recipient recognition Nat. Retail Mchts. Assn., 1971, certs. of appreciation U.S. Power Squadron, 1976, Webber Coll., 1972. Mem. AAWU, Fla. Women's Network, Greater Tampa C. of C., Tampa Aux. Power Squadron, USCG Aux., Sales and Mktg. Execs. of Tampa (pres.'s award 1973), Fla. Outdoor Writers Assn., Am. Mktg. Assn., Gulf Coast Symphony, Internat. Platform Assn., Fla. Council Yacht Clubs, Chi Omega. Republican. Presbyterian. Clubs: Toledo Yacht (hon.), Tampa Yacht and Country. First woman to cruise solo from Fla. to Lake Erie in single-engine inboard, 1969, to be accepted into Fla. Council Yacht Clubs; yachting accomplishments published in The Ensign, Lakeland Boating, Yachting, Boote mags. Office: PO Box 402 Largo FL 34649

LANG, KATHERINE ANNE, counseling psychologist; b. Benson, Minn., Jan. 22, 1947; d. Howard James and Barbara Anne (Bennett) L. B.A. in Art History, Smith Coll., Northampton, Mass., 1969; M.A., Bethel Theol. Sem., St. Paul, 1973; M.Ed., U. Mo.-Columbia, 1978, Ph.D., 1982. Lic. psychologist, Calif. Tchr., Am. Sch., Barcelona, Spain, 1970-71; campus ministry Univ. Reformed Ch., East Lansing, Mich., 1973-76; counselor Univ. Counseling Ctr., U. Mo., Rolla, 1978-79; coordinator Ctr. for Student Vols. Action, 1979-81; counseling psychologist U. Calif., Davis, 1982—; pvt. practice counseling psychologist, Sacramento, Calif., 1986—; cons. in field. Mem. Am. Psychol. Assn. Avocations: workshops on prayer; skiing; tennis; racquetball; writing. Office: U Calif Counseling Ctr Davis CA 95864

LANG, MABEL LOUISE, classics educator; b. Utica, N.Y., Nov. 12, 1917; d. Louis Bernard and Katherine (Werdge) L. B.A., Cornell U., 1939; M.A., Bryn Mawr Coll., 1940, Ph.D., 1943; Litt.D., Coll. Holy Cross, 1975, Colgate U., 1978. Mem. faculty Bryn Mawr Coll., 1943—, successively instr., asst. prof., 1943-50, assoc. prof., 1950-59, prof. Greek, 1959-88, chmn. dept., 1960-88, acting dean coll. 2d semester, 1950-59, 60-61; chmn. mng. com. Am. Sch. Classical Studies, Athens, 1975-80; chmn. admissions and fellowship com. Am. Sch. Classical Studies, 1966-72; Blegen disting. research prof. semester I Vassar Coll., 1976-77; Martin classical lectr. Oberlin Coll., 1982. Co-author: Athenian Agora Measures and Tokens; author: Palace of Nestor Frescoes, 1969, Athenian Agora Graffiti and Dipinti, 1976; Herodotean Narrative and Discourse, 1984. Contbr. articles profl. jours. Guggenheim fellow, 1953-54; Fulbright fellow Greece, 1959-60. Mem. Am. Philos. Soc., Am. Acad. Arts and Scis., German Archaeol. Inst., Am. Philol. Assn., Archaeol. Inst. Am., Soc. Promotion Hellenic Studies (Eng.), Classical Assn. (Eng.). Home: 905 New Gulph Rd Bryn Mawr PA 19010

LANGAN, TERRI LYNNE, professional society administrator; b. Phila., Oct. 4, 1947; d. Morton and Claire (Roth) Sultanoff; m. Patrick Albert Langan, Jan. 31, 1976; 1 child, Matthew Jeremy. BS, U. Md., 1969; postgrad., Johns Hopkins U., U. Md., 1971-76, U. Wyo., 1979-80. Tchr. Howard County Dept. Edn., Ellicott City, Md., 1969-76, tchr., team leader, 1974-76; market researcher The Rouse Co., Columbia, Md., 1976-77; adminstr. Columbia Assn., Columbia, 1977-78; asst. dir. Profl. Devel. and Tng., Balt., 1978-81; dir. edn. and communications services Am. Iron and Steel Inst., Washington, 1981-86; dir. tng. and profl. devel. Nat. Assn. Coll. and U. Bus. Officers, Washington, 1987—; cons. ABA, Chgo., 1978-81, U.S. Dept. Edn., Washington, 1974; speaker Md. State Dept. Edn., Balt., 1972. Author: (with others) Becoming Citizens, 1981; contbr. articles to profl. mags. Mem. Am. Soc. Assn. Execs., Am. Soc. Tng. and Devel. Office: Nat Assn Coll and Univ Bus Officers 1 Dupont Circle Washington DC 20036-1178

LANGDON, JULIA MARIE, school administrator; b. Pueblo, Colo., Sept. 22, 1963; d. Clarence Mark and DewAnn Carol (Drout) L. Student, Dartmouth Coll., 1983-85; BA in Art History cum laude, Wellesley (Mass.) Coll., 1985. Asst. to registrar Hood Mus. Art, Hanover, N.H., 1983-84; curatorial asst. The Byer Mus. Arts, Evanston, Ill., 1984; intern dept. paintings Mus. Fine Arts, Boston, 1984-85; intern Mass. Advanced Studies Program, Milton, 1985; teaching fellow The Ethel Walker Sch., Simsbury, Conn., 1985-86; asst. dean students Foxcroft Sch., Middleburg, Va., 1986-87; program asst. office elem. and secondary edn. Smithsonian Inst., Washington, 1988—. Mem. Nat. Assn. Female Execs., Wellesley Friends of Art. Episcopalian. Home: 1732 18th St NW Washington DC 20009 Office: Smithsonian Instn Arts and Industries 1163 Washington DC 20560

LANGDON, MARY, educator, musician; b. Fall River, Mass., Apr. 9, 1919; d. Richard and Mabel Rebecca (Hanscom) Leather; student Hartt Coll. Music, 1952-54; m. Wilbur Spencer Langdon II, Aug. 27, 1938; children—Carol Langdon Kohankie, Wilbur Spencer III. Numerous concert, oratorio, orch. and opera performances, 1952—; pvt. voice tchr., Mystic, Conn., 1952—; faculty U.R.I., Kingston, 1974—, asst. prof. music, 1981-84, assoc. prof., 1984—; adj. instr. in voice Conn. Coll., New London, 1980, adj. assoc. prof. in voice, 1987. Bd. dirs. Music Sch. of Westerly Center for the Arts, 1980—. Mem. Nat. Assn. Tchrs. Singing (regional gov. New Eng. and Can. Provinces), Music Tchrs. Nat. Ass., Internat. Assn. Research in Singing. Republican. Congregationalist. Home: 27 Gravel St Mystic CT 06355 Office: U RI Music Dept Kingston RI 02881

LANGE, CATHERINE L., photographer; b. Chgo., Oct. 18, 1949; d. Frank Michael and Irene Josephine (Kozak) L.; B.A. in Visual Arts, DePaul U., 1982; postgrad. Inst. Design, Chgo., 1982-84; 1 dau., Jennifer C. Schmidt. Circulation and mktg. mgr. Ragan Communications, Inc., Chgo., 1978-80, mng. editor The Ragan Report, 1978-81, editor The Reporter's Report, 1979-81, contbg. editor Speechwriter's Newsletter, 1980-82; dir. Ragan Books, 1980-82; freelance photographer, 1982—; prodn. mgr. ProTypography, 1986—. Home: 5124 S Troy St Chicago IL 60632

LANGE, ELIZABETH ANN, librarian; b. Webster, S.D., Sept. 20, 1938; d. Martin Gustave and Mabelle Emma Lou (Reich) L. BS, No. State Coll., 1960; MA, U. Minn., 1970. Cataloger Iowa State U. Library, Ames, 1961-68, head catalog dept., 1968-72; head catalog div. U. Minn. Libraries, Mpls., 1972-79; asst. dir. tech. services U. S.C. Libraries, Columbia, 1979—. Mem. ALA (chmn. elect catalog norms discussion group 1976), Southeastern Library Assn., S.C. Library Assn. Home: 900 Gregg St 1-B Columbia SC 29201 Office: Thomas Cooper Library Univ SC Columbia SC 29208

LANGE, JESSICA, actress; b. Minn., Apr. 20, 1949; d. Al and Dorothy L.; m. Paco Grande, 1970 (div. 1982); dau. with Mikhail Baryshnikov, Alexandra; children with Sam Shepard: Hannah Jane, Samuel Walker. Student, U. Minn.; student mime, with Etienne DeCroux, Paris. Dancer Opera Comique, Paris; model Wilhelmina Agy., N.Y.C. Films include: King Kong, 1976, All That Jazz, 1979, How to Beat the High Cost of Living, 1980, The Postman Always Rings Twice, 1981, Frances, 1982 (Acad. award nominee for best actress 1982), Tootsie, 1982 (Acad. award for best supporting actress 1982), Country, 1984, Sweet Dreams, 1985, Crimes of the Heart, 1986; Star Showtime TV prodn. Cat on a Hot Tin Roof, 1984; in summer stock prodn. Angel on My Shoulder, N.C., 1980. Office: care Jeff Berg ICM Artists Ltd 8899 Beverly Blvd Los Angeles CA 90048 *

LANGE, KATHERINE JOANN, writer; b. Wyandotte, Mich., Feb. 8, 1957; d. James DiDi and Margaret Ann (Kirk) Putman. Student, Normandale Coll., 1980-82. V.p., artist mgr. The T.S.J. Prodns. Inc., Richfield, Minn., 1975—; mgr., agt. The T.S.J. Booking Agy., Richfield, 1980—; asst. editor, author Songwriter U.S.A. mag., Atlanta, 1986-87; staff writer Music Mgmt. and Internat. Promotion mag., Copenhagen, 1983—. Contbr. articles to Sun Newspapers, Songwriter Connection, Woman's Press. Mem. ASCAP, Nat. Assn. Female Execs., Am. Fedn. Musicians. Democrat. Lutheran. Home and Office: The TSJ Prodns Inc 422 Pierce St NE Minneapolis MN 55413

LANGE, KATHRYN ANN, small business owner; b. Spokane, Wash., June 30, 1941; d. Chester Emil and Marabel (Edmonds) Rodell;. BA in English, U. Ariz., 1965; MA in Applied Behavioral Sci., Whitworth Coll., 1985. Substitute tchr. Eugene, Oreg. and Coeur d'Alene, Idaho, 1970-71; sec. legal Pub. Defender, Coeur d'Alene, 1971-74; sec. Eugene Register-Guard, 1968-70; exec. dir. White Pine Council Camp Fire Girls, Coeur d'Alene, 1974-83; adult educator Certified Volt Trainer AAUW, Coeur d'Alene, 1983-86; owner Career Mgmt. Assocs., Coeur d'Alene, 1986—; cons. personnel and orgns.; freelance writer; coordinator Western Women's Career Mgmt. Forum, 1986; adv. bd. mem. Lewis Clark St. Coll., 1988. Bd. dir. United Way Kootenai County, 1974-80; adv. mem. bd. dirs. Women's Ctr. Inc., 1979-80, also vol. counselor, 1987; co-founder N. Idaho POW-MIA, 1971; advisor Rural Women's Oral History Project, U. Idaho, 1975. Camp Fire scholar, Leadership Inst. Spokane, 1976. Mem. Am. Bus. Women's Assn. (pres. Syringa Charter Chpt. 1979), Kappa Kappa Gamma. Home and Office: 2501 Sherman Ave #258 Coeur d'Alene ID 83814

LANGELETT, MONA LORRAINE, auditor; b. Decatur, Ill., Oct. 2, 1951; d. Max Leon and Lela Lucille (Myers) Fleming; m. Frederick Walter Langelett, Aug. 29, 1971 (div. 1986); 1 child, Stephen Michael. Student, Kankakee (Ill.) Community Coll., 1969-70, Gov.'s State U., University Park, Ill., 1987—. Chartered bank auditor. Sec. Ends Ins. Service, Bourbonnais, Ill., 1965-69; payroll clk. Sears Roebuck and Co., Kankakee, Ill., 1969-71; inventory clk. Wurlitzer Distbg. Co., Dekalb, Ill., 1971-72; sec. to pres. Bank of Carbondale, Ill., 1972-74; sec. Olstens Temp. Services, Kankakee, 1974; trust sec. City Nat. Bank, Kankakee, 1975-77, asst. auditor, 1977-86; auditor Keystone Bancshares Inc., Kankakee, 1987; audit mgr. 1st of Am. Bank Corp., Kalamazoo, 1987—. Treas. Mental Health Ctr. Kankakee County, 1986—. Mem. Working Women's Council. Office: 1st of Am Bank 189 E Court St Kankakee IL 60901

LANGEMO, DIANE KAY, nurse, educator; b. Grand Forks, Nev., Jan. 2, 1947; d. Eric A. and Helyn E. (Olson) Morrison; m. Mark A. Langemo, Aug. 20, 1982; children: Brent, Darrin, Steven. BS of Nursing, U. N.D., 1969; M of Nursing, U. Wash., 1970; PhD, U. Minn., 1987. RN. Staff nurse emergency room United Hosp., Grand Forks, 1969, 70, 75; asst. prof. adult health program U. N.D. Coll. Nursing, Grand Forks, 1970-73, asst. prof., coordinator, 1973-78, assoc. prof., 1978-85, prof., chairperson dept.

nursing, 1987—. Author: Nursing as a Career, 1982. Recipient research award Sigma Theta Tau, 1984, 88. Mem. Am. Nurses Assn. (council nurse researchers), N.D. Nurses Assn. (v.p. 1982—, N.D. nurse of yr. 1982), Midwest Nurse Researchers, Red River Nurses Assn. (pres. 1980-82, nurse of yr. 1982), Diabetes Assn. (bd. dirs. 1976-83), Beta Sigma Phi (pres. 1979, 83). Club: Lincoln Women's Golf (Grand Forks) (v.p. 1985-87, pres. 1987—). Home: 3207 East Elmwood Dr Grand Forks ND 58201

LANGENHEIM, JEAN HARMON, biology educator; b. Homer, La., Sept. 5, 1925; d. Vergil Wilson and Jeanette (Smith) H.; m. Ralph Louis Langenheim, Dec. 1946 (div. Mar. 1961). BS, U. Tulsa, 1946; MS, U. Minn., 1949, PhD, 1953. Research assoc. botany U. Calif., Berkeley, 1954-59; research fellow biology Harvard U., Cambridge, Mass., 1962-66; asst. prof. biology U. Calif., Santa Cruz, 1966-68, assoc. prof. biology, 1968-73, prof. biology, 1973—; academic v.p. Orgn. Tropical Studies, San Jose, Costa Rica, 1975-78; mem. sci.adv. bd. EPA, Washington, 1977-81; chmn. com. on humid tropics U.S. Nat. Acad. Nat. Research Council, 1957-77; mem. com. floral inventory Amazon NSF, Washington, 1975-87. Contbr. articles to profl. jours. Grantee NSF, 1966-88; recipient Disting. Alumni award U. Tulsa, 1979. Fellow AAUW, Calif. Acad. Scis.; mem. Botanical Soc. Am., Internat. Soc. Chem. Ecology (pres. 1986-87), Ecol. Soc. Am. (pres. 1986-87), Assn. Tropical Biology (pres. 1985-86). Home: 191 Palo Verde Terrace Santa Cruz CA 95060 Office: U Calif Thimann Labs Santa Cruz CA 95064

LANGER, DOROTHY, venture capitalist; b. Boston, Aug. 1, 1942; d. Harold Aaron and Goldie (Fineman) Potcherkoff; BS in Chemistry, Simmons Coll., 1964. Tech. librarian Shell Chem. Co., N.Y.C., 1964-65; research chemist Radiation Research Corp., Westbury, L.I., 1965-68; systems engr. IBM, 1968-71, mktg. rep., 1972-73, process industry rep., 1973-74, mktg. mgr., 1974-76, regional mktg. mgr., 1976-77, corp. mktg. cons., 1977-79, br. mgr., 1980-81; v.p. mktg. Gartner Group, Inc., Stamford, Conn. 1982-83; dir. N.E. ops. Businessland, Inc., Stamford, 1983-84; with 3i Ventures, Boston, 1985—; lectr. on women's issues and entrepreneurism; dir. Persoft, Inc.; mem. Sta. WGBH. Trustee Simmons Coll., 1977-82; bd. dirs. Capital Dist. Jr. Achievement, 1980-82; chmn. corp. giving Simmons Coll. Pride II, 1981-86, mem. Boston Mus. Fine arts, Dance Umbrella. Mem. World Affairs Council, Boston Computer Soc., Associated Homeowners Boston, Beacon Hill Civic Assn., Women's Econ. Roundtable, Mensa. Office: 3i Ventures 99 High St Boston MA 02110

LANGER, ELLEN JANE, psychologist, educator; b. N.Y.C.; d. Norman and Sylvia (Tobias) L. BA, NYU, 1970; PhD, Yale U., 1974. Cert. clin. psychologist. Asst. prof. psychology The Grad. Ctr. CUNY, 1974-77; assoc. prof. psychology Harvard U., Cambridge, Mass., 1977-81, prof., 1981—; cons. Nat. Acad. Scis., 1979-81, NASA; mem. Harvard Med. Sch. Div. on Aging, 1979—, Psychiat. Epidemology steering com. 1982—; chair program social psychology Harvard U., 1982—, chair Faculty Arts and Scis. Com. of Women, Harvard U., 1984—. Author: Personal Politics, 1973, Psychology of Control, 1983, Mindfulness, 1988; contbr. articles to profl. and scholarly jours. Guggenheim Fellow, grantee NIMH, NSF, Soc. for Psychol. Study of Social Issues, Milton Fund, Sloan Found., 1982. Fellow Computers and Soc. Inst., Am. Psychol. Assn.; mem. Soc. Expl. Social Psychology, Phi Beta Kappa, Sigma Xi. Democrat. Jewish. Office: Harvard Univ Dept Psychology 33 Kirkland St Cambridge MA 02138

LANGER, SUSANNE M., cosmetologist; b. Red Wing, Minn., Aug. 19, 1955. Diploma Cosmetology, Ritter St. Paul Coll., 1974; grad., Bruno's, 1978. Instr. Ritter's St. Paul Coll., 1974-75; asst. mgr., mgr. Scot Lewis Inc., Bloomington, Minn., 1975-79; edn. dir. My Kind of Place, St. Paul, 1979-80; pres., co-owner Someone's Looking (formerly Charpentier's Inc.), St. Paul, 1980-86, owner, 1986—; co-owner, pres. SuPro, Inc., St. Paul; styles dir. women's sect. Minn. Cosmetology Edn. Com. Fundraiser, chairperson Battered Women's Shelter, St. Paul, 1984, Children's Home Soc., St. Paul, 1985; vol. St. Paul Food Shelves Food Dr., 1985, 88; vol., model United Arts Fashion Show, 1986; vol. fundraiser pub. TV Action Auction, Ronald McDonald House, Food Shelf Drives Someone's Looking, St. Paul, MS Walkathon, 1988. Recipient numerous hairstyling awards. Mem. Nat. Cosmetologists Assn., Minn. Hairdressers and Cosmetologists Assn., St. Paul Cosmetologists Assn. (dir. 1981-83, pres. 1983-85), Hair Am., Minn. Hair Fashion Com. Home: 400 Selby Ave Saint Paul MN 55102 Office: Someone's Looking Inc 151 Endicott Arcade Saint Paul MN 55101

LANGFELD, MARILYN IRENE, creative art company director; b. St. Louis, Apr. 28, 1951; d. Norman Max and Celeste (Brown) L. Student, Vanderbilt U., 1968-70; B.A. cum laude, Sonoma State U., 1978-80. Printer, Sojourner Truth Press, Altanta, 1971-73; carpenter apprentice Housebuilders Union, Atlanta, 1973-74; self employed housebuilder, Perry, Me., 1974-75; graphic artist Cuthberts Printing, San Rafael, Calif., 1976-77; graphic Designer Community Type & Design, Fairfax, Calif., 1977-80; owner, creative dir. Langfeld Assocs., San Francisco, 1980—. Recipient Am. Corp. Identity award, 1986, Type Dirs. Club award, 1987, Desi award, 1987, Simpson Paper Co. award, 1987, Printing Industries of Am. award, 1987. Mem. People Speaking Adv. Bd., 1979-84. Sonoma State scholar, Bank of Sonoma County, 1979-80; Vanderbilt U. scholar, 1968-69, 69-70; bd. dirs. Horizons Found. Mem. San Francisco C. of C., Am. Inst. Graphic Artists, San Francisco Art Dirs. Club, Western Art Dirs. Club. Art Dirs. and Artists of Sacramento, San Francisco Better Bus. Bur. Clubs: San Francisco Ad, City, Advertising (San Francisco). Democrat. Jewish. Office: 381 Clementina St San Francisco CA 94103

LANGFORD, CAROL A., pediatrician; b. Chgo., July 20, 1940; d. Robert Erwin and Beatrice (Hall) Langford; BA, Stanford U., 1962; MD, U. Chgo., 1969; m. Arthur G. Robins, June 14, 1969; children: Sebastian, Jeremy. Vol., Peace Corps, Columbia, 1962-63, pediatrician Roxbury Dental and Med. Group Boston, 1977-82; pediatrician Roxbury Comprehensive Community Health Ctr., 1984-86; instr. psychiat. day hosp., Tufts U, Boston, 1979-81; instr. pediatrics Tufts U., 1979-88, Boston U., 1986-87, New Eng. Sch. Acupuncture, Boston, 1981-82; cons. Langford Resort Hotel; herbal and acupuncture cons. Whole Health Assocs., Watertown, Mass., 1981-83; health book reviewer New Age mag. Den mother Boy Scouts Am.; tour leader, vol. Arnold Arboretum. May C. Willett fellow in child neurology, 1975-77. Diplomate Am. Bd. Pediatrics; mem. Am. Acad. of Pediatrics, Mass. Med. Soc., Fla. Native Plant Soc., Boston Mycological Club, Sierra Club, Audubon Soc., Friends of the Farlow. Mem. United Ch. of Christ. Author booklet: Aloe Vera Queen of Medicinal Plants, 1980. Office: Joseph M Smith Comm Health Ctr 51 Stadium Way Allston MA 02134

LANGFORD, SALLIE FRANCES, legal administrator; b. Helena, Ark., Nov. 12, 1948; d. George Lee and Peggy Gene (Conklin) Cline; m. Clifford Hollis Langford, June 19, 1975; children: Cortney Paige, Benjamin Andrew. BSEd, U. Ark., 1970, MA, 1971. Cert. secondary tchr., Ark. Tchr. Fayetteville (Ark.) High Sch., 1971-72; sec., staff supr. Kendig, Stockwell and Gleason, Beverly Hills, Calif., 1972-78; loan processor S&L Mortgage Co., Sunland, Calif., 1978-79; sec. Wood Law Firm, N. Little Rock, Ark., 1979-80; legal adminstr. House, Wallace and Jewell, P.A., Little Rock, Ark., 1980-87. Exec. couple Nat. Marriage Encounter, Little Rock, 1982-84; career speaker Boy Scouts Am., Little Rock, 1985—. Schenley Wholesaler's Found. scholar, 1966-70. Mem. ABA, Ark. Word Processing Assn., Assn. Legal Adminstrs. (regional v.p. 1987-88, asst. regional v.p. 1986-87, pres. 1982-83), Little Rock Legal Secs. Assn. (instr. 1985). Episcopalian. Home: 6905 Flintrock Dr North Little Rock AR 72116 Office: House Wallace and Jewell PA 425 W Capitol Ave Little Rock AR 72201

LANGHAM, NORMA, educator, author, composer; b. California, Pa.; d. Alfred Scrivener and Mary Edith (Carter) Langham; B.S., Ohio State U., 1942; B. Theatre Arts, Pasadena Playhouse Coll. Theatre Arts, 1944; M.A., Stanford, 1956, postgrad. Summer Radio-TV Inst., 1960; student Pasadena Inst. Radio, 1944-45. Tchr. sci. California High Sch., 1942-43; asst. office pub. info. Denison U., Granville, Ohio, 1955; instr. speech dept. Westminster Coll., New Wilmington, Pa., 1957-58; instr. theatre. California U. of Pa., 1959, asst. prof., 1960-62, assoc. prof., 1962-79, emeritus, 1979—, co-founder, sponsor, dir. Children's Theatre, 1962-79; mem. Calif., Pa. Community Choir; founder, producer, dir. Food Bank Players, 1985, Patriot Players, 1986. Recipient award exceptional acad. service Pa. Dept. Edn., 1975; Appreciation award Bicentennial Commn. Pa., 1976. Henry C. Frick Ednl. Commn. grantee. Mem. Theatre Assn. Pa., Internat. Platform Assn., California U. of Pa. Assn. Women Faculty (founder, pres. 1972-73), AAUW (co-founder California br., 1st v.p. 1971-72, pres. 1972-73; Outstanding Woman of Yr. 1986), Dramatists Guild, DAR, Alpha Psi Omega, Omicron Nu. Presbyn. (elder). Author: (play) Magic in the Sky, 1963; (text) Public Speaking; (play) John Dough (Freedoms Found. award 1968); (plays) Who Am I?, Hippocrates Oath, Gandhi, Clementine of '49, Soul Force, Esther; composer-lyricist (play) Why Me, Lord?; Music in Freedom, The Day the Moon Fell. Home: Box 455 California PA 15419

LANGHOUT-NIX, NELLEKE, artist; b. Utrecht, Netherlands, Mar. 27, 1939; came to U.S., 1968, naturalized, 1978; d. Louis Wilhelm Frederick and Geertruida (Smits) Nix; M.F.A., The Hague, 1958; m. Ernst Langhout, July 26, 1958; 1 son, Klaas-Jan Marnix. Head art dept. Bush Sch., Seattle, 1969-71; dir. creative projects Project Reach, Seattle, 1971-72; artist-in-residence Fairhaven Coll., Bellingham, Wash., 1974, Jefferson Community Center, Seattle, 1978-82, Lennox Sch., N.Y.C., 1982; dir. NN Gallery, Seattle, 1970—; guest curator Holland-U.S.A. Bicentennial show U. Wash., 1982, Birdshow, Chase Gallery, 1983; executed wall hanging for King County Courthouse, Seattle, 1974; one-woman shows: Nat. Art Center, N.Y.C., 1980, Gail Chase Gallery, Bellevue, Wash., 1979, 80, 83, 84, Original Graphics Gallery, Seattle, 1981, Bon Nat. Gallery, Seattle, 1981, Kathleen Ewing Gallery, Washington, 1986; 3-man show Exhbn. Space, N.Y.C., 1982, Lisa Harris Gallery, Seattle, 1985, 87, 88; group shows include: Cheney Cowles Mus., Spokane, 1977, Bellevue Art Mus., 1978, 86, Renwick Gallery, Washington, 1978, Kleinert Gallery, Woodstock, N.Y., 1979, Artcore Meltdown, Sydney, Australia, 1979, Tacoma Art Mus., 1979, 83, 86, 87, Ill. State Mus., Springfield, 1979, Plener Sandomierz, Poland, 1980, Plener Kielce, Poland, 1980, Western Assn. Art Museums traveling show, 1979-80, Madison Square Garden, N.Y.C., 1981; represented in permanent collections Plener Collection, Sandomierz, Poland; Bell Telephone Co. Collection, Seattle, Children's Orthopedic Hosp., Seattle, installations Tacoma Art Mus. Bd. dirs. Wing Luke Mus., Seattle, 1978-81; v.p. Denny Regrade Community Council, 1978-79; mem. Seattle Planning Commn., 1978-84. Recipient Wallhanging award City of Edmonds (Wash.), 1974; Renton 83 merit award, 1984; Merit award Internat. Platform Assn. Art Exhibit, 1984, silver medal 1st place, 1985, 87. Mem. Denny Regrade Arts Council (co-founder). Allied Arts Seattle, Nat. Platform Assn., Wash. State Art Alliance, Nat. Mus. Women in Arts (a founder), Nat. Mus. of Women in Arts (chairperson Wash. state com.), Seattle-King County Community Arts Network (bd. dirs. 1983-85, chmn. 1984-85). Mailing Address: PO Box 375 Mercer Island WA 98040

LANGLEY, CYNTHIA MURRAY, dentist; b. Elgin, Tex., Feb. 10, 1954; d. Robert O. Jr. and Juanita (Briggle) Murray; m. J.D. Langley, Mar. 19, 1978; children: Melissa Sue, Travis James. BS, Tex. A&M U., 1976; DDS, Baylor Coll., 1978. Dental officer Gorgas Hosp. Dental Clinic, Panama Canal Zone, 1978; practicing dentistry Balboa, Panama Canal Zone, 1978-79; assoc. prof. Dept. Gen. Practice U. Tex. Dental Branch, Houston, 1980-81; practicer, asst. adminstr. L.L. Gregory D.D.S. Inc., Houston, 1981-82; assoc. dentist C.C. Sullivan D.D.S., Houston, 1980-82; practicing dentistry Bryan, Tex., 1982—; bd. dirs. Baylor Coll. of Dentistry Century Club, 1988-90, Death, Disability and Retirement Trust, 1988-91. Contbr. articles to profl. jour. Delegate Rep. St. Conv. 1986, 88; co-mgr. J.D. Langley campaign 1985-86; bd. dirs. Opera and Performing Arts Soc., 1984-87, A&M United Methodist Ch., 1986—; bd. dirs., spl. events chmn. Rep. Women of the Brazos Valley, 1988. Mem. ADA, Tex. Dental Assn., Am. Assn. Women Dentists, Brazos Valley Dist. Dental Soc. (judicial com. 1986-87), Acad. Gen. Dentistry, Houston Dist. Dental Soc & Brazos Valley Acad. Gen. Dentistry, Am. Bus. Women Assn. (bd. dirs. 1985—), Brazos Country A&M (bd. dirs. 1985—). Office: 3131 Briarcrest Dr E Bryan TX 77802

LANGLEY, LYNNE SPENCER, newspaper editor, columnist; b. West Palm Beach, Fla., June 4, 1947; d. George Hosmer and Elwa June (Harries) Spencer; B.A. with honors, Coll. of Wooster, 1969; student Glasgow U., Scotland, 1967-68; m. William A. Langley, Oct. 10, 1970. Feature writer, asst. women's editor Palm Beach Times, West Palm Beach, Fla., 1969-70; asst. editor Brunswick (Maine) Times Record, 1971; investigative reporter Maine Times, Topsham, 1971-75; asst. mng. editor York County Coast Star, Kennebunk, Maine, 1976-78; gardening editor, nature columnist, reporter Charleston (S.C.) Post-Courier, 1979—; editor Maine Audubon Soc. News, 1975-76; stringer Newsweek mag., 1971-75; speaker; Author: Nature Watch, 1987; free lance writer. Active Charleston Natural History Soc., Nat. Audubon Soc. Recipient Communicator of Yr. award S.C. Wildlife Fedn., 1983, Writing awards S.C. Press Assn., 1987, S.C. Assn. Mentally Retarded, Charleston Natural History Soc., 1985, Charleston County Parks and Recreation Commn., 1985. Mem. Am. Hort. Soc., Garden Writers Assn. Am., PEO (sec. chpt. D Maine 1975-76, corresponding sec. chpt. J S.C. 1986-88), Charleston Mus., Sigma Delta Chi. Home: PO Box 97 Adams Run SC 29426 Office: 134 Columbus St Charleston SC 29401

LANGLEY, PATRICIA ANN, lobbyist; b. Butler, Pa., Feb. 13, 1938; d. F.J. and Ella (Serafine) Piccola; m. Harold D. Langley, June 12, 1965; children: Erika, David. BA, U. Pitts., 1961; postgrad., Georgetown U., 1967, Cath. U. Am., 1985. Legis. staff U.S. Congress, Washington, 1961-63; dir. social studies Am. Polit. Sci. Assn., Washington, 1963-65; legis. specialist U.S. Congress, Washington, 1965-67, caseworker, 1967-68; polit. staff Dem. Study Group U.S. Congress, Washington, 1969; Washington rep. Family Services Am., 1975-82, dir. Washington hdqrs., 1982—; bd. dirs. Coalition for Children and Youth, Washington, 1977-78; chmn. steering com. for the Coalition on White House Conf. on Families, 1979-80, Ad Hoc Coalition on A.F.D.C., 1981-82. Mem. Donaldson Run Civic Assn., Arlington, Va., 1980—. Recipient Service Recognition U.S. Dept. Health and Human Services, 1980. Mem. Am. Soc. of Assn. Execs., AAUW, Women in Govt. Relations. Roman Catholic. Home: 2515 N Utah St Arlington VA 22207 Office: Family Services Am 1319 F St NW Suite 606 Washington DC 20004

LANGSTON, NANCY CROSS, management consultant; b. Ahoskie, N.C., Nov. 20, 1954; d. H.A. Cross and Frances Ruth (Steen) Johnson; 1 child, Kelly Ann. Student, N.C. State U. extension, Shelby, 1983. Asst. office mgr. Douglass Med., Raleigh, N.C., 1975-77; billing and collection specialist No. Telecom, Research Triangle, N.C., 1977-80; sales service adminstr. Frank Ix and Sons, Inc., Lincolnton, N.C., 1981-84; material control specialist Delmar Window Coverings, Beatrice Gastonia, N.C., 1984-87; cons., pres., owner D/B/A Mgmt., Sarasota, Fla. and Gastonia, 1987—; gen. mgr. West Coast Med. Transfer, Sarasota, 1987—; prin. Tradewinds Co., Sarasota, 1987—. Troop leader, dist. trainer, dist. program com. mem. Pioneer council Girl Scouts of U.S., N.C., 1984-86, county coordinator, 1985-86; sec., treas. PTA, Lincolnton, 1980-83; notary pub., Fla., 1987—. Mem. Nat. Assn. Female Execs., Sarasota County Safety Council, Am. Soc. Notaries. Presbyterian. Clubs: Jr. Women's (Raleigh); New Neighbor's (Lincolnton). Home: 7219 Captain Kidd Ave Sarasota FL 33581

LANGUM, W. SUE, civic worker; b. Kennett, Mo., Jan. 10, 1934; d. Howard S. and Lucille (Hubble) Walker; m. Norman H. Nelson, June 22, 1957 (dec. Sept. 1969); 1 child, Kirby Walker Nelson; m. John K. Langum, Dec. 28, 1972. Student, Northwestern U., 1952-53, Crane Jr. Coll., 1953-54. Service rep. Ill. Bell Telephone Co., Chgo., 1956-57; receptionist Tri-City Animal Hosp., Chgo., 1967-69; research asst. Bus. Econs. Inc., Chgo., 1969-73, dir., 1973—. V.p. Elgin Council PTA, 1969-73; bd. dirs. OEO, 1972-73, Meals on Wheels, Elgin, 1972—, Coloquy Coffee House, 1968-70, Judson Coll. Friends, 1976—, Elgin Hist. Soc., Elgin Symphony Orch. Assn., 1984—, Elgin Symphony League, 1982—, pres., 1984-86; bd. birs. United Meth. Women, 1978—, pres., 1980-84; vol. Fish, 1974-76; bd. dirs., treas. Easter Seal Assn. for Crippled Children, 1977—; mem. Elgin Beautification Commn. Mem. LWV (v.p. Elgin club 1965—). Republican. Clubs: Elgin Women's, Tuesday Morning Bible Study, Current History Forum. Home: 477 Oakhill Rd Elgin IL 60120

LANGWORTHY, AUDREY HANSEN, state legislator; b. Grand Forks, N.D., Apr. 1, 1938; d. Edward H. and Arla (Kuhlman) Hansen; m. Asher C. Langworthy Jr., Sept. 8, 1962; children: Kristin H., Julia H. BS, U. Kans., 1960, MS, 1962. Tchr. jr. high sch. Shawnee Mission Sch. Dist., Johnson County, Kans., 1963-65; councilperson City of Prairie Village, Kans., 1981-85; mem. Kans. State Senate, 1985—; del. Midwestern Conf. State Legislatures, 1988; alt. del. Nat. Conf. State Legislatures, 1985-87, del., 1987—; mem. subcom. Latin Am. com. State/Fed. Assembly. City co-chmn. Kassebaum for U.S. Senate, Prairie Village, 1978; pres. Jr. League Kansas City, Mo., 1977, Kansas City Eye Bank, 1982-85; bd. dirs. Greater Kansas City ARC, 1975—, pres., 1984; nat. bd. govs. ARC, 1987—. Recipient Outstanding Vol. award Community Services Award Found., 1983, Confidence in Edn. award Friends of Edn., 1984. Mem. Nat. Rep. Legislator's Assn., LWV, AAUW, English-Speaking Union, U. Kans. Alumni Assn., Kappa Kappa Gamma. Lutheran. Home: 6324 Ash Prairie Village KS 66208

LANHAM, BETTY BAILEY, anthropologist, educator; b. Statesville, N.C., Aug. 12, 1922; d. Clyde B. and Naomi (Bailey) L. B.S., U. Va., 1944, M.A., 1947; Ph.D., Syracuse U., 1962. Mem. faculty River Falls State Tchrs. Coll., 1948-49, U. Md., 1949-50, Wakayama U., Japan, 1951-52, Randolph Macon Women's Coll., 1954-55, Oswego State Tchrs. Coll., 1956-58, Hamilton Coll., 1961-62, Ind. U., 1962-65, Western Mich. U., 1965-67, Albany Med. Coll., 1967-70, Guyana U., 1969-70; prof. anthropology Indiana U. of Pa., 1970—. Contbr. articles to jours. Wenner-Gren Found. for Anthrop. Research predoctoral fellow, 1951-52; AAUW predoctoral research fellow, 1959-60. Mem. Am. Anthrop. Assn., Assn. Asian Studies, Soc. Psychol. Anthropology, Caribbean Studies Assn. Democrat. Home: 121 Dolores Circle Indiana PA 15701 Office: Ind U Dept of Sociology & Anthropology Indiana PA 15705

LANIER, VIOLA WILSON, educator; b. Lincoln, Ala., Dec. 16, 1927; d. Phillip and Lera B. (Montgomery) Wilson; m. Isiah Williams, July 28, 1945 (div. 1973); children: Curtis L., Quensetta D. Williams Lucas; m. Lavert D. Lanier, June 27, 1974. BS in Edn., Ala. State U., 1952; MS in Edn., Ind. U., 1960. Cert. tchr., Ind. Tchr., prin. Talladega County Schs., Ala., 1947-50; tchr. Montgomery (Ala.) County Schs., 1952-53, Indpls. Pub. Schs., 1959—; supr. instruction Shelby and Autauga Couty Schs., Ala., 1954-59; asst. dir. Nat. Coll. Bus., Indpls., 1977-80; exec. dir. Enrichment Learning Ctr. and Mus., Indpls., 1984—. Adv. com. ERIC Global Issues Project, Indpls., 1986-88, Indpls. Jr. High Improvement Com., 1986-88. Recipient Community Service award Indpls. Mayor's Office, 1982; U.S. Edn. Found. grantee, 1985. Fellow NEA; mem. Hist. Landmarks Found., Ind. Council Social Studies (sec. 1986-87), Freedoms Found. (v.p. Indpls. chpt. 1981—, honor medal 1982), Indpls. C. of C., Delta Sigam Theta, Phi Delta Kappa. Democrat. Mem. Christian Ch. Home: 209 Buckingham Dr Indianapolis IN 46208 Office: Indpls 400 Indianapolis IN 46236

LANKAU, JUDITH LAMPMAN, utility company executive; b. Rochester, N.Y., Apr. 17, 1943; d. Elmer Franklin and Helen Alma (Schroth) Lampman; m. Paul Allan Lankau, July 14, 1962; children—Paul Allan, Jr., Kelly, Kristyn. B.S., Pa. State U., 1977. Paralegal MacCartney Law Offices, Nyack, N.Y., 1963-79; supr. Orange and Rockland Utilities, Spring Valley, N.Y., 1979-80, mgr. consumer affairs, 1980-85, mgr. community relations, Pearl River, N.Y., 1985-86, mgr. community affairs and conservation services, 1986—. Bd. dirs. Rockland County United Way, N.Y., 1985—, Jr. Achievement of Rockland County, 1985-87, Rockland Tchrs. Ctr., Stony Point, N.Y., 1985-86; mem. adv. bd. Impact II, Spring Valley, 1985-86. Recipient Chairman's award Orange and Rockland Utilities, 1984, 85, Tribute to Women in Industry award TWIN Forum, 1985. Mem. Women in Mgmt. (pres. 1986—, Achievement award 1985), Soc. Consumer Affairs Profls., Am. Gas Assn., Electric Edison Inst., Pub. Relations Council. Avocations: tennis; boating; swimming. Home: 46 Jerrys Ave Nanuet NY 10954 Office: Orange and Rockland Utilities Inc 75 West Route 59 Spring Valley NY 10977

LANKFORD, LINDA MARIE, construction executive; b. Lubbock, Tex., Aug. 24, 1947; d. Jimmie and Maryann Florence (Jones) Smyth; m. Bobby Ray Lankford, July 31, 1964 (div. 1974); children: Jimmie, Bobby, Michael. Grad. high sch.; student, Antelope Valley Coll., Lancaster, Calif. Cert. pvt. pilot. Haistylist 1963-75; adminstrv. asst., controller Pagosabode, Inc., Pagosa Springs, Colo., 1975-80; office mgr. Aspen Homes, Pagosa Springs, 1978-80; adminstrv. asst. Teroco Constrn., Pagosa Springs, 1980-85; site supt. Teroco Constrn., Lake Arrowhead, Calif., 1985-86; mgr. Mission Bell Inc., Ventura, Calif., 1986-87; quality control inspector Quality Cons., Inc., Federal Way, Wash., 1987-88; quality control supt. Kaufman and Broad Inc., Los Angeles, 1988—. Pres. PTO, Pagosa Springs, 1983; sec.-treas. Aspen Springs Owners Assn., 1979; founder Ennis Youth Soccer Assn., Ennis and Archuleta County Soccer Assn. Mem. Nat. Assn. Female Execs., Archuleta County Builders Assn. Republican. Baptist. Office: Kaufman and Broad 11601 Wilshire Los Angeles CA

LANNIN, BARBARA J., public relations professional; b. Traverse City, Mich., Jan. 12, 1932; d. Forrest Henry and Fraces Louise (Germaine) L.; m. Armin G. Weng, Dec. 27, 1952 (div. 1981); children: Michael Jon, Michelle Sue Runge. BA, Rockford (Ill.) Coll., 1975. Freelance writer various Ogle County (Ill.) newspapers, 1969-75; exec. dir., founder Yellow Bird Senior Citizens, Oregon, Ill., 1975-79; exec. dir. Ea. Will County Srs., Monee, Ill., 1979-83; pub. relations dir. Combined Communication Services, Lisle, Ill., 1983—. Home: 2215 Crescent Ln Aurora IL 60505 Office: Combined Communication Services 901 Warrenville Rd Suite 206 Lisle IL 60532

LANPHEAR, MARTHA JEAN, lawyer; b. Wichita Falls, Tex., Jan. 28, 1944; d. Clarence Ernest and Kathern Martha (Golden) Eldridge; m. Thomas Joseph Lanphear, Jan. 5, 1974; children—Kathern Eileen, Laura Patricia. A.B., U. Mich., 1965; J.D., George Washington U., 1977. Bar: Va. 1977. Personnel specialist CSC, Washington, 1966-72, appeals officer, 1972-79; appeals officer, atty. Merit Systems Protection Bd., 1979-80, acting regional dir., Washington, 1982, hearing officer, 1980-86, adminstv. judge, 1986—. Recipient Performance award Merit Systems Protection Bd., 1982, 84, 85, 86, 87. Office: Merit Systems Protection Bd 5203 Leesburg Pike Suite 1109 Falls Church VA 22041

LANPHEAR, SHAWNA RAE, computer company professional; b. Bozeman, Mont., July 7, 1957; d. Donald Douglas and Dona Aline (McNeil) L. BA in Bus. Mgmt., Mont. State U., 1979; JD, Calif. Western Sch. Law, 1985. Asst. gen. mgr. Lanphear Ins. Agy., Bozeman, 1969-79; specialist compliance, registrar Gt. Global Assurance Co., Scottsdale, Ariz., 1980-83; adminstr. mktg. Millidyne Inc., San Diego, 1983-86; rep. contracts Computer Scis. Corp., San Diego, 1986-87; mgr. contracts adminstrn. Informaties Legal Systems, Phoenix, 1987—. Mem. ABA, Contracts Mgmt. Assn., Nat. Assn. Female Execs., Alpha Gamma Delta (corr. sec. 1981, asst. rush 1982), Tau Pi Phi. Republican. Home: 6163 N Granite Reef Scottsdale AZ 85253

LANPHERE, BETTY JOANNE, court reporter; b. Indpls., Mar. 26, 1938; d. Paul Sheldon and Doris Mae (Mathis) Furry; student Browning Bus. Coll., Albuquerque, 1967-68; m. James A. Lanphere, June 2, 1962; children—Michael, Lisa, Kristine, Scott, Jamie, Kimberly, Susan, Kevin, Julie, Jill, Kelly. Sec., Sandia Corp., Albuquerque, 1955-62, legal firm Jones, Gallegos, Snead & Wertheim, Santa Fe, 1967-68, firm Stephenson, Campbell & Olmsted, Santa Fe, 1968-69; ct. reporter Nye Reporting Service, Santa Fe, 1969, Lanphere Reporting Service, Santa Fe, 1969—; ofcl. reporter U.S. Dist. Ct., Santa Fe; mem. N.Mex. Ct. Reporting Bd., 1975—; mem. Nat. Audio-Video Com. on Electronic Rec., 1974—. Roman Catholic. Office: PO Box 449 58 S Federal Pl Santa Fe NM 87501

LANS, DEBORAH EISNER, lawyer; b. N.Y.C., Oct. 26, 1949; d. Asher Bob and Barbara (Eisner) L. A.B. magna cum laude, Smith Coll., 1971; J.D.

cum laude, Boston U., 1974. Bar: N.Y. 1975, U.S. Dist. Ct. (so. and ea. dists.) N.Y. 1975, U.S. Ct. Appeals (2d cir.) 1975, U.S. Supreme Ct. 1983. Assoc. Lans Feinberg & Cohen, N.Y.C., 1975-80, ptnr., 1980-84; ptnr. Morrison Cohen & Singer, N.Y.C., 1984—. Mem. Am. Arbitration Assn. (comml. panel arbitrators 1984—), Assn. Bar City N.Y. (chmn. young lawyers com. 1981-83, joint com. fee disputes, 1982, judiciary com. 1984-85, exec. com. 1985—), N.Y. State Bar Assn. (ho. of dels. 1984-87), N.Y. Bar Found. Office: Morrison Cohen & Singer 110 E 59th St New York NY 10022

LANSBURY, ANGELA BRIGID, actress; b. London, Oct. 16, 1925; came to U.S., 1940; d. Edgar and Moyna (Macgill) L.; m. Peter Shaw, Aug. 12, 1949; children: Anthony, Deirdre. Student, Webber-Douglas Sch. Drama, London, 1939-40, Feagin Sch. Drama, N.Y.C., 1940-42. Actress 1943—. Actress with Metro-Goldwyn-Mayer, 1943-50; films include: Gaslight, 1944, National Velvet, 1944, The Picture of Dorian Gray, 1944, The Harvey Girls, 1946, Till the Clouds Roll By, 1946, If Winter Comes, 1947, State of the Union, 1948, Samson and Delilah, 1949, Kind Lady, 1951, The Court Jester, 1956, The Long Hot Summer, 1957, Reluctant Debutante, 1958, Summer of the 17th Doll, 1959, A Breath of Scandal, 1959, Dark at the Top of the Stairs, 1960, Blue Hawaii, 1961, All Fall Down, 1962, Manchurian Candidate, 1963, In the Cool of the Day, 1963, The World of Henry Orient, 1964, Out of Towners, 1964, Something for Everyone, 1969, Bedknobs and Broomsticks, 1970, Death on the Nile, 1978, The Lady Vanishes, 1979, The Mirror Crack'd, 1980, The Pirates of Penzance, 1982; star TV series Murder She Wrote, 1984— (Golden Globe awards 1984, 86); appeared in TV miniseries Little Gloria, Happy at Last, 1982, Lace, 1984, Rage of Angels, pt. II, 1986; appeared in TV movie of the week Gift of Love, 1982; appeared in plays Hotel Paradiso, 1957, A Taste of Honey, 1960, Anyone Can Whistle, 1964, Mame (on Broadway), 1966 (Tony award for Best Mus. Actress 1966), Dear World, 1968 (Tony award for Best Mus. Actress 1969), All Over (London Royal Shakespeare Co.), 1971, Gypsy, 1974 (Tony award for Best Mus. Actress 1975), The King and I, 1978, Sweeney Todd, 1979 (Tony award for Best Mus. Actress 1979), Hamlet, Nat. Theatre, London, 1976 (Sarah Siddons award 1974, 80). Named Woman of Yr., Harvard Hasty Pudding Theatricals, 1968; inducted Theatre Hall of Fame, 1982. Office: care William Morris Agy 151 El Camino Beverly Hills CA 90212

LANSKY, JUDITH, career consultant; b. Boston, July 19, 1946; d. Merton Warren and Ida (Waitzkin) L.; B.A., Barnard Coll., 1968; M.A. (tuition scholar), U. Rochester, 1969; M.B.A. with distinction, DePaul U., 1979. Coordinator acad. programs Reid Hall, Paris, 1969-70; grants adminstr. Inst. Internat. Edn., Chgo., 1974-76; dir. student employment services Columbia Coll., Chgo., 1976-78; mktg. adminstr. W.B. Dolphin & Assos., Chgo., 1978-79; mktg. cons. Technomic Consultants, Chgo., 1980-81; adminstr. pediatric nursing Rush-Presbyn.-St. Luke's Med. Center, Chgo., 1981-82; founder, pres. Lansky Career Cons., Chgo., 1982—. Bd. dirs. Flexible Careers, Chgo., 1975-78, Chgo. Coalition on Women's Employment, 1976-78; steering com. mem. Ill. Women's Agenda, 1976-77. Mem. Women in Mgmt. (chair career devel. 1983-84), Met. Bus. Assn. (bd. dirs.), Profl. Career Counselors Network (founding). Editor: The Job Hunter's Notebook, 1975. Home: 525 W Hawthorne Chicago IL 60657 Office: 676 N St Clair St Suite 1860 Chicago IL 60611

LANTRIP, KAY LYNN, civil engineer; b. Herrin, Ill., Aug. 25, 1953; d. Robert F. and Pauline K. Osowski; student So. Ill. U., 1971-73; B.S. in Civil Engring., U. Ill., 1975; m. Bruce M. Lantrip, Aug. 3, 1974; 1 child, Emily Katherine. Civil engr., Old Ben Coal Co., Benton, Ill., 1975-77, Bechtel Power Corp., Gaithersburg, Md., 1977; civil engr. Ralph M. Parsons Co., Balt. Regional Rapid Transit System, Balt., 1977-80; sr. project mgr. George Hyman Constrn. Co., 1980—. Registered profl. engr. Mem. Chi Epsilon. Home: 5452 Thunder Hill Rd Columbia MD 21045

LANTRY, MARILYN MARTHA, state legislator; b. St. Paul, Oct. 28, 1932; d. Louis Leonard and Josephine (Cermak) Kunz; m. Jerome Horton Lantry, 1953; children: Jacqueline, Kathleen. Grad. high sch. Legislative aide to city councilman Tedesco, Minn., 1973-80; mem. Minn. State Senate, 1981—. Democrat. Roman Catholic. Office: 2169 Beech Saint Paul MN 55119 *

LANZETTA, TERESA ANN, advertising executive; b. Middletown, Conn., Sept. 23, 1958; d. Vincent William and Loretta Theresa (Simons) L. Student, Palomar Coll., 1982. Asst. advt. mgr. Hydro Products, Inc., San Diego, Calif., 1975-81; advt. cons. O'Hara & O'Hara, Houston, 1981-84; dir. advt. merchandising Polaris Vac-Sweep, San Marcos, Calif., 1984-85; owner The Write Words, Cardiff, Calif., 1985—; cons. Career Devel. Corp., San Diego, 1987—; instr. Calif. Aerobic Dance, Inc., San Diego, 1987—. Editor Seahorse mag., Waterlog mag., 1978-81, Aqua, 1982; contbr. articles to profl. jours. Vol. Friends of Leucadia, Calif., 1984—, Lupus Found. Am., Washington, 1985—. Mem. Internat. Assn. Bus. Communicators, No. Bay Pub. Relations Soc., Nat. Assn. Female Execs. Office: The Write Words PO Box 456 Cardiff CA 92007-0456

LAPADOT, SONEE SPINNER, automobile manufacturing company official; b. Sidney, Ohio, Apr. 19, 1936; d. Kenneth Lee and Helyn Kathryn (Hobby) Spinner; m. Jan. 13, 1955 (div. Apr. 1970); 1 son, Douglas Cameron; m. Robert Stephen Lapadot, May 4, 1974. Student U. Cin., 1954-56, U. Akron, 1966. Mgr. engring. change implementation Terex div. Gen. Motors, Hudson, Ohio, 1975-77, mgr. prodn. scheduling, 1977-78, gen. adminstr. product purchasing, 1978-79; sr. staff asst. non-ferrous metals Gen. Motors, Detroit, 1979-80, mgr. tires and wheels, 1980-83, mgr. staff purchasing, 1983-85, mgr. corp. constrn. contracting, 1985-86; mfg. techs. adminstr. Chrysler Motors, Detroit, 1986-87, mgr. mfg. prodn. control adminstrn. and services, 1988—. Active fund-raising Boy Scouts Am., Grosse Pointe, Mich., 1980-82, Detroit, 1985-88, United Fund, Detroit, 1980-88, Jr. Achievement, Detroit, 1984. Mem. Soc. Automotive Engrs., Am. Soc. Profl. and Exec. Women, Am. Prodn. and Inventory Control Soc., Automotive Industry Action Group (schedule process mgmt. com.), Nat. Assn. Female Execs., Mensa. Club: Women's Econ. Detroit. Home: 1941 Squirrel Rd Bloomfield Hills MI 48013 Office: Chrysler Motors Corp 12000 Chrysler Dr Highland Park MI 48288

LAPELLE, DIANE MCDONNELL, banker; b. Chgo., June 22, 1952; d. George F. and Mary M. (Merrick) McDonnell; m. William J. Lapelle, June 19, 1976. BA, U. Notre Dame, 1974. With staff ops. and mgmt. services Continental Ill. Nat. Bank, Chgo., 1974-76, cash position sr. analyst, 1976-79, mgr. cash position, 1979, ops. officer, 1980, mgr. cash position and ops. control, 1981, 2d v.p., 1982-85, relationship mgr. money ctr. banks, 1985-86, v.p., 1986—. Mem. Assocs. St. Joseph Hosp., Chgo., 1979—. Club: Notre Dame (bd. govs. 1986-87). Office: Continental Ill Nat Bank 231 S LaSalle St Chicago IL 60697

LAPHAM, SANDRA LEE, nurse; b. St. Paul, Dec. 1, 1957; d. Donald John and Sally Ann (Bartsch) Hoffman; m. Steven Allen Lapham, Oct. 22, 1983. BS in Nursing, U. Minn., 1981, MS in Childbearing, Childrearing Family Nursing, 1987. Registered Nurse. Staff nurse U. Minn., Mpls., 1981-85; head nurse Mercy Med. Ctr., Coon Rapids, Minn., 1985-87; head nurse antepartum-birthing Abbott Northwestern Hosp., Mpls., 1987—. Mem. Nurses Assn. Am. Coll. of Ob-Gyn. (Minn. state legis. coordinator 1983—), U. Minn. Nursing Alumni Soc. (bd. dirs. 1982-84), Sigma Theta Tau, Phi Kappa Phi, Alpha Tau Delta (pres. 1979-81). Democrat. Methodist. Home: 9510 Quincy St NE Blaine MN 55434 Office: Abbott Northwestern Hosp 800 28th St at Chicago Minneapolis MN 55407

LAPIN, SHARON JOYCE VAUGHN, interior designer; b. Lagrange, Mo., July 28, 1938; d. John Nolan and Wilma Emma (Huebotter) Vaughn; BA summa cum laude, U. Wash., Seattle, 1960; m. Byron Richard Lapin, Oct. 14, 1972. Appeared in various Broadway shows, TV commls. and TV shows, 1962-72; owner Sharon Lapin Designs St. Louis. Bd. dirs. St. Louis conservatory and Schs. for Arts, 1977—, v.p., 1982-87; chmn. bd. Studio Set, 1978-81, pres., 1975-78, bd. dirs., 1975-83; bd. dirs. Friends of Sci. Mus., 1980—, v.p., 1984-85; pres. Assocs. Bd. Dirs., St. Louis Sci. Ctr., Inc., 1986-87; bd. dirs. Jr. Div., St. Louis Symphony Women's Assn., 1973-75. Mem. AFTRA, Screen Actors Guild, Actors Equity Assn., Am. Soc. Interior Designers, Pi Beta Phi.

LAPINSKI, FRANCES CONSTANCE, data processiong systems executive; b. Flushing, N.Y., Sept. 19, 1950; d. Frank Stanley and Frances A. (Gaziano) L. BS in Edn., SUNY, Oswego, 1972, MS in Edn., 1974; PhD in Program Edn. Adminstrn., Syracuse U., 1976; postgrad., NYU, 1983—. Tchr. Mexico (N.Y.) Boces, 1971-72; chancellor's intern SUNY, Oswego, 1972-74; coordinator housing Lemoyne Coll., Syracuse, 1974-76; project coordinator Am. Assn. State Colls. and Univs., Washington, 1976-79; project mgr. Robt Bell & Co., Balt., 1979-81; asst. treas. Chase Manhattan Bank, N.Y., 1981-83; info. ctr. mgr. Depository Trust Co., N.Y., 1983—. Vol. Spl. Olympics, N.J., N.Y., 1984—, Pntrs. in Peacemaking, N.J., 1987—. Mem. Assn. Women in Computing, Microcomputer Mgrs. Assn. (vendor liaison 1986—). Office: Depository Trust Co 11 Broadway (7) New York NY 10004

LAPOTAIRE, JANE ELIZABETH MARIE, actress; b. Ipswich, Suffolk, U.K., Dec. 26, 1944; d. Louise Elise Burgess; 1 child, Rowan Joffe. Student Grammer Sch., 1963. Leading actress Royal Shakespeare Co., Nat. Theatre of Gt. Brit., London, 1967—; free-lance television and film actress BBC-TV, ITV, Paramount Pictures, MGM and United Artists, Broadway, N.Y.C.; mem. com. Women's Playhouse Trust, 1981-84 ; vis. fellow Brighton U., Sussex. Co-author film script Do Us Part, 1982. Pres. Southwark Globe Project Com. CARE. Recipient London Critics award, 1979, S.W.E.T. award, 1980, Variety Club of Gt. Brit. award, 1980, Tony award, 1981. Mem. Gulbenkian Foun. Working Party. Club: Bristol Old Vic Theatre (hon. pres.). Avocations: walking; Cordon Bleu cookery; water colors; gardening.

LAPPANO-COLLETTA, ELEANOR RITA, research, career and educational consultant; b. N.Y.C., Jan. 12, 1930; d. Ernest and Mary Carmella (Spicciato) Lappano; m. Archangelo Colletta, Nov. 18, 1961; children: Mary Elizabeth, John Ernest, Gina Rose. BS in Chemistry, Fordham U., 1951, MS, 1953, PhD in Biology, 1955. Mem. faculty NYU Postgrad. Med. Sch., 1956-58; mem. faculty, research assoc. devel. biology Rockefeller U., N.Y.C., 1958-59; instr. pathology SUNY Downstate Med. Ctr., Bklyn., 1959-60; biochem. cytologist Hosp. for Spl. Surgery, N.Y.C., 1960-62; research assoc. animal behavior Am. Mus. Natural History, N.Y.C., 1962-67; asst. prof. Manhattan Coll., Riverdale, N.Y., 1967-72; assoc. Sloan-Kettering Inst., N.Y.C., 1973-74; asst. prof. pathology N.Y. Med. Coll., Valhalla, 1974-75; analyst mgmt. performance Office Comptroller, City of N.Y., 1977-78; mem. nat. adv. research resources council NIH, 1973-77; devel. scientist personal products div. Lever Bros., Edgewater, N.J., 1979-80; ind. mgmt. cons., Bronx, N.Y., 1980—. Author papers and reports in field. Pres. Pub. Sch. 122 Community Sch. Bd. 10 N.Y.C. Parents' Assn., 1970-72, treas. parents and prins. forum, 1972-73; edn. chmn. Community Coalition for Scatter Site Housing, 1972-74, West Bronx Civic Improvement Assn., 1971-79; bd. dirs. United Owners Assn., Somers, N.Y., 1979-81. NIH grantee, 1957-58; Office of Naval Research fellow 1955. Mem. AAAS, AAUW, Sigma Xi. Home: 3238 Tibbett Ave Riverdale NY 10463 Office: 6035 Broadway Riverdale NY 10471

LAPPE, FRANCES MOORE, author, lecturer; b. Pendleton, Oreg., Feb. 10, 1944; d. John and Ina (Skrifvars) Moore; m. Marc Lappe, Nov. 11, 1967 (div. 1977); children: Anthony, Anna; m. J. Baird Callicott, Dec. 1, 1985. B.A. in History, Earlham Coll., 1966; Ph.D. (hon.), St. Mary's Coll., 1983, Lewis and Clark Coll., 1983, Macalester Coll., 1986, Hamline U., 1987, Earlham Coll., 1988. Co-founder, mem. staff Inst. for Food and Devel. Policy, San Francisco, 1975—. Author: Diet for A Small Planet, 1971, 75, 82, World Hunger: Ten Myths, 1982, Now We Can Speak, 1982, What To Do After You Turn Off the TV: Fresh Ideas for Enjoying Family Time, 1985; co-author: (with Joseph Collins) Nicaragua: What Difference Could a Revolution Make?, Food and Farming in the New Nicaragua, 1982, Aid as Obstacle, 1980, World Hunger: Twelve Myths, 1986, What Can We Do?, 1980, (with William Valentine) Mozambique and Tanzania: Asking the Big Questions, 1980, (with Adele Beccar-Varela) Casting New Molds: First Steps Toward Worker Control in a Mozambique Factory, 1980, (with Peter Sketchley) Food First: Beyond the Myth of Scarcity, 1977, rev. (with Joseph Collins), (with Rachel Schurman and Kevin Danaher) Betraying the National Interest, 1987. Named to Nutrition Hall of Fame Ctr. for Sci. and Pub. Interest, 1981; recipient Mademoiselle Mag. award, 1977; World Hunger Media award, 1982, Right Livelihood award, 1987. Office: Inst for Food and Devel Policy 145 9th St San Francisco CA 94103

LAPPO, ILONA AIJA, software executive; b. Riga, USSR, June 21, 1943; came to U.S., 1959; BA, Case Western Res. U., 1965; MA, Boston U., 1975, PhD, 1982. Asst. to editor Predicasts, Inc., Cleve., 1968-69; instr. Coll. Wooster, Ohio, 1968; teaching asst. Boston U., 1971-74, lectr., 1975-82; instr. Northeastern U., Boston, 1980-82; dir. mktg. Logical Software Inc., Cambridge, Mass., 1983-84, v.p. sales, 1984-85, pres., 1986—; dir. sales Uniworks, Inc., Wellesley, Mass., 1985-86. Bd. dirs. Dance Projects, Inc., Cambridge, 1978—. Boston U. grantee, 1972. Mem. Boston Colloquium for Logic (planning com. 1972-78). Office: Logical Software Inc PO Box 905 Cambridge MA 02238

LAPTAD, MARIA NITA RAMERIEZ, counselor; b. San Pablo, Philippines, Apr. 18, 1947; arrived in U.S., 1975; d. Joaquin Villanueva and Elpidia (Magpantay) Ramirez; m. Raymond Alan Laptad. BA cum laude, St. Theresa's Coll., Manila, 1963, BS in Edn. magna cum laude, 1964; MA in Ednl. Adminstrn., Ateneo de Manila, 1965, MA in Edn. and Counseling, 1966; MA in Sociology, Asian Social Inst., 1972. Asst. prin., head lit. and English dept. St. Theresa's Coll., Manila, 1963-65; dean student affairs, dir. lang. arts Ateneo de Manila Grade Sch., 1967-79; with St. Paul's Coll., Manila, 1967-69; dir. pastoral sociology research, project prof. Research Ctr., Manila, Asian Social Inst. Grad. Sch., Manila, 1969-76; chief exec. officer, counselor Shadow Hills Samaritan, Inc., Lakewood, Calif., 1976—; pres. Power Cube, Inc., Orange, Calif., 1987—; cons. George Basil & Assocs., Montreal, 1983-86; mgr. S.H.S., Inc., Las Vegas, 1986—. Campus counselor Asian-Am. Students Orgn., U. Calif., Davis, 1976-78; cons. Prison Ministries, Las Vegas, 1978-79; cons.internat. del. Vatican II, Rome, 1976—. Mem. Nat. Assn. Female Execs. Republican. Roman Catholic. Club: Commander's. Home: PO Box 1070 Lakewood CA 90711-3249 Office: Shadow Hills Samaritan Inc 4228 Lakewood Blvd Long Beach CA 90808

LARBALESTRIER, DEBORAH ELIZABETH, writer; b. Pitts., July 17, 1934; d. Theron Benjamin and Granetha Elizabeth (Crenshaw) Cowherd; m. Dec. 25, 1969 (div.). AB, Storer Coll., 1954; student, Robert H. Terrell Law Coll., 1954-58, Woodbury Coll., 1959-60; certs., Univ. W. Los Angeles, 1971-73. Cert. legal asst., paralegal specialist. Author Prentice-Hall Inc., Englewood Cliffs, N.J., 1975—; prof. Southland Career Inst., Los Angeles, 1985—; bd. dirs. Am. Paralegal Assn., Los Angeles, 1975-80, exec. dir., 1980—; nat. chmn. Am. Inmate Paralegal Assn., 1984—; cons. Fed. Bur. Prisons, 1983—. Mem. Los Angeles Police Dept. (Wilshire div.) Community Police Council, 1985—, Harbor Human Relations Council, Wilmington, Calif., 1985—; vol., crime prevention specialist Los Angeles Police Dept. (Wilshire div.), 1985—. Recipient gold plaque Am. Paralegal Assn. Chpt. Pres., Los Angeles, 1975, Nat. Notary Assn., Hawaii, 1979, cert. of acknowledgement Los Angeles Police Dept., 1985, Humanitarian Award of Spl. Merit, So. Calif. Motion Picture Council, 1987. Mem. U. of W. Los Angeles (adv. bd. 1980, 88), Am. Paralegal Assn. (exec. dir. 1975), Am. Inmate Assn. (nat. chmn. 1983), U. W. Los Angeles Paralegal Alumni Assn. Republican. Jewish. Home: 1321-1/2S Sycamore Ave Los Angeles CA 90019 Office: Am Paralegal Assn PO Box 35233 Los Angeles CA 90035

LARCH, SARA MARGARET, medical administrator; b. Des Moines, Iowa, Feb. 14, 1956; d. William Arthur and Beverly Frances (Klanjac) L. BA in Pub. Adminstrn., Miami U., Oxford, Ohio, 1978; postgrad., Ind U., 1986—. Personnel clk. City Nat. Bank, Detroit, 1978-79; econ. anlyst asst. Cargill, Inc., Mpls., 1979-81; adminstrv. asst. Ind. U. Med. Ctr., Indpls., 1981-82, ob-gyn. adminstr., 1982-88; adminstr. Georgetown U. Med. Ctr., Washington, 1988—; mem. planning com. Parent Care Conf., Indpls., 1985-86. assoc. editor Ob-Gyn Newsletter, Indpls., 1984-86. Vol. Indpls. Mus. Art, 1982-83, White River Park Commn., Indpls., 1984, Indpls. Zoo, 1987—. Mem. Assn. Mgrs. Gynecology and Obstetricians (pres. 1986-87), Med. Group Mgmt. Assn., Acad. Practice Assembly (council of pres. 1986-87). Office: Georgetown U Med Ctr 3800 Reservoir Rd NW Washington DC 20007

LARD, LINDA J. STEIN, commercial lending officer; b. Ridgewood, N.J., June 1, 1958; d. Herbert William and Dolores Ann (Suenderhauf) S. BS in Bus. Adminstrn., Bucknell U., 1980; MBA in Fin., Pace U., 1983. Lic. ins., investments, securities broker. Internat. operations mgr. Chem. Bank, N.Y.C., 1980-83, departmental controller, 1983-84; divisional controller First Nat. Bank of Md., Balt., 1984-86; comml. lender First Nat. Bank of Md., Rockville, 1986—; fin. planner Lebowitz & Assocs., Ltd., Balt., 1985—. Mem. Internat. Assn. for Fin. Planners, Balt. Chpt. for Fin. Planners, C. of C. of Montgomery County, Md. Clubs: Columbia Athletic Assn. (Md.); Women's Internat. Bowling (Balt.) (team capt. 1986-87). Office: First Nat Bank of Md 25 S Charles St Baltimore MD 21201

LAREAU, CAROL ANN, publishing sales administrator; b. Clayton, N.Mex., June 14, 1950; d. Charles Russell Davis and Vivian Lee (Morrison) Dickson; m. Woodrow B. Anderson, Apr. 2, 1967 (div.); children: Bobby Don Anderson, Kimberly Lynn Anderson; m. Robert A. Lareau, Aug. 30, 1980. Mgr. Pizza Hut, Amarillo, Tex., 1969-72; prodn. supr. Precon Corp., Ludlow, Mass., 1976-81; mgr. sales and adminstrn. Trimco, Inc., Ludlow, 1981-83; sales rep. Pioneer Valley Plastics, Three Rivers, Mass., 1983-87, Union Bookbinding, Medford, Mass., 1987-88; mgr. Met. Looseleaf, Mt. Marion, N.Y., 1988—; account mgr. Met. Looseleaf, Mt. Marion, N.Y., 1987—. Home: 115 S West St Feeding Hills MA 01030

LAREAU, MARYBETH BASS, marketing professional; b. N.Y.C., July 12, 1941; d. James Gordon and Marjorie (Mestell) B.; m. Gerard Arthur Lareau, June 6, 1970 (div. Nov. 1984). AB in Biology, Bucknell U., 1963. V.p., creative group head Dancer Fitzgerald Sample, Inc., N.Y.C., 1966-78; sr. v.p., creative dir. Norman Craig & Kummel, N.Y.C., 1978-79; creative dir., pres. Lareau & Assocs., N.Y.C., 1980—; guest lectr. St. John's U., N.Y.C., 1980-83; adj. instr. Fashion Inst. Tech. SUNY, N.Y.C., 1982-84, 87—. Contbr. articles to mags., jours.; prin. works include L'eggs Pantyhose, 1974-78, corp. advt. campaign Gen. Electric Corp., 1981. Recipient ANDY award Advtg. Club N.Y., 1975, EFFIE award Am. Mktg. Assn., 1976. Mem. Internat. Wine and Food Soc., Advtg. Women N.Y. (chair pub. service com. 1986—). Episcopalian. Home and Office: 140 West End Ave New York NY 10023

LAREDO, RUTH, concert pianist; b. Detroit, Nov. 20, 1937; d. Ben and Miriam (Horowitz) Meckler; m. Jaime Laredo, June 1, 1960 (div. Nov. 1974); 1 dau., Jennifer. Diploma, Curtis Inst. Music, 1960. Asst. prof. Yale U. Sch. Music, 1974-76; mem. faculty Aspen Sch. Music, 1975. N.Y.C. debut with Leopold Stokowski and Am. Symphony, 1962, debut with Boulez and N.Y. Philharmonic, 1974; soloist with major Am. orchs., including those in N.Y.C., Cleve., Detroit, Phila., and Nat. and Am. symphonies, performed at Aspen, Marlboro, Spoleto, Israel and Caramoor festivals, recordings with Columbia Records include piano sonatas of Alexander Scriabin, 1970-71, complete solo piano works of Rachmaninoff, works of Ravel; editor piano music of Rachmaninoff, 1980—. Office: care Shaw Concerts Inc 1995 Broadway New York NY 10023 *

LARGE, DARLENE DINTINO, association executive, art educator; b. New Brunswick, N.J., Mar. 31, 1935; d. Albert William Dintino and Sophia (Terbovich) Terrill; m. Bruce Derr Large, June 16, 1956; children—Dirk, Letti, Todd, Rajakumari. B.S., Pa. State U., 1959; postgrad. Centro Venezuelano Americano, Caracas, Venezuela, 1956-57, Colinas des Bellos Artes, Caracas, 1957-58, Millersville State U., Pa., 1973-75. Cert. art tchr., Pa. Tchr. art Haven Jr. High Sch., Evanston, Ill., 1969-70; founder, pres. Homes of the Indian Nation, South India, 1972—; tchr. art Ephrata Area Sch. Dist., Pa., 1973-78; lectr. Pa. State U.-Grove City Coll., 1979—; tchr. art Dist. of Manheim Twp., Lancaster, Pa., 1984-85. Den mother Boy Scouts Am., Evanston, 1967-69; chmn. programs PTO Clay Elem. Sch., Ephrata, Pa., 1977; coordinator vols. Spanish Ctr., Lancaster, Pa., 1972-73; chmn. Cancer Drive, West Earl Twp., Pa., 1973. Named Woman of the Yr., Soroptomists, Lancaster, Pa., 1979; recipient Disting. Alumna award Pa. State U., 1982, Coll. of Edn. award Pa. State U., 1986. Democrat. Avocations: reading; stitchery; painting; ceramics; batik; writing; walking. Home: 41 N Hershey Ave Box 115 Leola PA 17540 Office: Homes of Indian Nation 41 N Hershey Ave Box 302 Leola PA 17540

LARK, SYLVIA, artist, educator; b. N.Y., Nov. 8, 1947. MFA, U. Wis., 1972. Asst. prof. U. Calif., Berkeley, 1977-81, assoc. prof., 1981-85, prof., 1985—. One woman shows include Mus. Modern Art, N.Y.C., galleries in San Francisco, Los Angeles, Frankfurt, West Germany; exhibited in over 15 major pub. mus., corp. and U. collections. Recipient Humanities Research award U. Calif., 1982, 86; Fulbright Hays fellow, 1977. Mem. Nat. Women's Caucus for Art (nat. adv. bd. 1981-84, 1986-89), Coll. Art Assn., Women's Forum West. Office: U Calif Art Dept 238 Kroeber Hall Berkeley CA 94720

LARKIN, DOLORES MARY, service executive; b. Gloucester, Mass., Sept. 13, 1951; d. Edward H. and Sarah A. (Capillo) L. BS, U. Mass., 1973; MA, Columbia U., 1976; MHA, Duke U., 1980; postgrad., U. Chgo., 1984—. Tchr. Southbridge (Mass.) Pub. Sch., 1973-74; instr., head coach U. Chgo., 1976-78; adminstrv. intern Chgo. Hosp. Council, 1980-81; mgr. mktg. Evang. Health System, Oak Brook, Ill., 1981-85, adminstrv. dir., 1985-86; assoc. Consol. Cath. Health Care, Westchester, Ill., 1986—. Mem. Friends of Oak Park (Ill.) Library, 1984-86. Mem. Am. Mktg. Assn., Chgo. Area Planning and Mktg. (program com. 1987). Home: 1141 S Highland Oak Park IL 60304 Office: Consol Cath Health Care 1 Westbrook Corp Ctr Westchester IL 60153

LARKIN, JACQUELINE LEE, sales manager; b. Framingham, Mass., Aug. 29, 1948; d. Livio Charles and Genevieve (Ward) Costa; m. Jay V. Larkin, Mar. 12, 1971 (div. Aug. 1974). Student Framingham State U., 1966-69, Sch. Practical Arts, Boston, 1969-71. Mgr. adminstrn. TEE, Inc., Boston, 1978-81; telemktg. mgr. Warren Gorham & Lamont, Boston, 1982-85; communications cons. Larkin Communications, Boston, 1985—; telemktg. mgr. R.S. Means, Inc., Kingston, Mass., 1985—. Author: Good Connections: Successful Telephone Selling, 1984; co-author: Telemarketing Operations Handbook, 1985. Mem. Nat. Assn. Female Execs., Nat. Assn. Women in Sales, Profl. Pubs. Mktg. Group (steering com. 1983-85), DMA Telephone Mktg. Council, Am. Telemktg. Assn. Democrat. Unitarian. Avocations: photography; writing. Home: 29 School St Wayland MA 01778 Office: Larkin Communications 7 Oakley St Dorchester MA 02124

LARKIN, JANE RITA, brokerage company executive; b. N.Y.C., May 14, 1917; d. Edward Francis and Catherine Veronica (Keenan) L. B.S. with highest honors, St. John's U., N.Y.C., 1938. Br. office ops. mgr. Merrill Lynch, Bklyn., 1942-59; allied mem. N.Y. Stock Exchange, Hirsch & Co., N.Y.C., 1959-70, mem. N.Y. Stock Exchange, 1970—; allied mem. N.Y. Stock Exchange DuPont Glore Forgan, N.Y.C.; dep. dir. compliance, v.p. Paine Webber, N.Y.C., 1974—; mem. arbitration panel N.Y. Stock Exchange. Republican. Roman Catholic. Office: Paine Webber 120 Broadway New York NY 10271

LARKIN, JOAN KUPERSMITH, lawyer; b. N.Y.C., Jan. 30, 1953; d. Seymour and Ruth (Schechner) K.; m. Christopher Craig Larkin. BA, NYU, 1973; JD, New Eng. Sch. Law, Boston, 1976. Bar: N.Y. 1977, D.C. 1978, Fla. 1978, Calif. 1980. Intern Mass. Attys. Gen. Office, Boston, 1974-75; reporter, cons. Bur. Nat. Affairs, Washington, 1975-76; trademark atty. U.S. Patent and Trademark Office, Washington, 1976-79; assoc. Fulwider, Patton, Rieber, Lee & Utecht, Los Angeles, 1979-84, ptnr., 1984-87, Macdonald, Halsted & Laybourne, Los Angeles, 1987—, ptnr., 1987—; mem. pub. adv. com. for trademark affairs U.S. Dept. Commerce, 1979—. Contbr. articles in field. Recipient spl. achievement awards U.S. Dept. Commerce, 1978. Mem. ABA, Calif. State Bar (exec. com. intellectual property sect. 1986—), U.S. Trademark Assn. (co-chmn. Paralegal Forum 1986, bd. dirs. 1987—), Assn. Bus. Trial Lawyers, Women Lawyers Assn. Los Angeles, Trademark Soc. (pres. 1978-79), Los Angeles Patent Law Assn. (co-editor newsletter 1980), Phi Alpha Delta. Office: Macdonald Halsted & Laybourne 725 S Figueroa St Los Angeles CA 90017

LARKIN, JUNE NOBLE, foundation executive; b. N.Y.C., June 17, 1922; d. Edward John and Ethel Louise (Tinkham) Noble; m. David Shiverick Smith, Dec. 8, 1945 (div. 1968); children: E.J. Noble, David S., Jeremy T.,

Bradford D.; m. Frank Yoakum Larkin, Mar. 4, 1968. B.A., Sarah Lawrence Coll., 1944; L.H.D. (hon.), St. Lawrence U., 1980; D.Mus. (hon.), Mannes Sch. Music, 1984. Trustee Sarah Lawrence Coll., 1964-73, chmn. bd., 1971-73, now hon. trustee; trustee Mus. Modern Art, 1969—, v.p., 1978—; trustee The Juilliard Sch., 1974—, chmn. bd., 1985—; trustee Museums Collaborative, 1973-76, The Eaglebrook Sch., 1974-81, Greenwich Hosp., 1967-82, Cultural Council Found., 1976-79; bd. dirs. Repertory Theatre of Lincoln Center, 1969-72; chmn. bd. trustees Edward John Noble Found., N.Y.C., 1972—; Mem. N.Y.C. Cultural Council, 1971-74, Nat. Parks Centennial Commn., 1972-73, Mayor's Com. Cultural Policy, N.Y.C., 1974, Presdl. Task Force on Arts and Humanities, 1981. Trustee Alliance for the Arts, 1978-86 ; trustee N.Y. Philharm., 1979—, Mus. of Broadcasting, 1982—, Ptnrs. for Livable Place, 1982-85; hon. chmn. bd. trustees North Country Hosps., Gouverneur, N.Y., 1959-78; bd. dirs. Lincoln Ctr. Performing Arts, 1985—, Arts Coalition Empire State, 1984-87, N.Y. Regional Assn. Grantmakers, 1984-87. Mem. Nat. Soc. Colonial Dames State of N.Y., N.Y. Internat. Festival of Arts, Inc. (bd. dirs. 1985—). Clubs: Colony (N.Y.C.); Sulgrave (Washington). Home: 600 Lake Ave Greenwich CT 06830 Office: 32 E 57th St New York NY 10022

LA ROCQUE, MARILYN ROSS ONDERDONK, communications executive; b. Weehawken, N.J., Oct. 14, 1934; d. Chester Douglas and Marion (Ross) Onderdonk; B.A. cum laude, Mt. Holyoke Coll., 1956; postgrad. N.Y. U., 1956-57; M. Journalism, U. Calif. at Berkeley, 1965; m. Bernard Dean Benz, Oct. 5, 1957 (div. Sept. 1971); children: Mark Douglas, Dean Griffith; m. 2d, Rodney C. LaRocque, Feb. 10, 1973. Jr. exec. Bonwit Teller, N.Y.C., 1956; personnel asst. Warner-Lambert Pharm. Co., Morris Plains, N.J., 1957; editorial asst. Silver Burdett Co., Morristown, 1958; self-employed as pub. relations cons., Moraga, Calif., 1963-71, 73-77; pub. relations mgr. Shaklee Corp., Hayward, 1971-73; pub. relations dir. Fidelity Savs., 1977-78; exec. dir. No. Calif. chpt. Nat. Multiple Sclerosis Soc., 1978-80; v.p. public relations Cambridge Plan Internat., Monterey, Calif., 1980-81; sr. account exec. Hoefer-Amidei Assocs., San Francisco, 1981-82; dir. corp. communications, dir. spl. projects, asst. to chmn. Cambridge Plan Internat., Monterey, Calif., 1982-84; dir. communications Buena Vista Winery, Sonoma, Calif., 1984-86, asst. v.p. communications and market support, 1986-87; dir. communications Rutherford Hill Winery, St. Helena, Calif., 1987—; instr. pub. relations U. Calif. Extension, San Francisco, 1977-79. Mem. exec. bd., rep-at-large Oakland (Calif.) Symphony Guild, 1968-69; co-chmn. pub. relations com. Oakland Museum Assn., 1974-75; cabinet mem. Lincoln Child Center, Oakland, 1967-71, pres. membership cabinet, 1970-71, 2d v.p. bd. dirs., 1970-71. Bd. dirs. Calif. Spring Garden and Home Show, 1971-77, Dunsmuir House and Gardens, 1976-77, San Francisco Symphony Assn., 1984— ; mem. Calif. State Republican Central Com., 1964-66; v.p. Piedmont council Boy Scouts Am., 1977. Mem. DAR (chpt. regent 1960-61, 66-68), U. Calif. Alumni Assn., Public Relations Soc. Am. (chpt. dir. 1980-82; accredited), Sonoma Valley Vintners Assn. (dir. 1984-87), Napa Valley Wine Auction (pub. relations com.), Internat. Wine and Food Soc. (Marin chpt.), Calif. Hist. Soc., San Francisco Mus. Soc., Nat. Trust for Historic Preservation, Smithsonian Assocs., Sonoma Valley C. of C. (bd. dirs. 1984-87), Am. Inst. Wine and Food, W.I.N.O. (San Francisco chpt.), Knights of the Vine (master lady 1985—). Clubs: Commonwealth of Calif.; Mount Holyoke Coll. Alumnae. Author: Maestro Baton and His Musical Friends, 1968; Happiness is Breathing Better, 1976.

LAROSA, LINDA (MRS. DANIEL MOSNER), horticulturist, design director; b. Columbia, S.C., Apr. 21, 1952; d. Frank and Virginia (Wilkes) LaR. B.S., Midlands Coll., 1975. Tchr. R. Earl David Elem. Sch., Columbia, 1972-77; asst. horticulturist World Trade Ctr., N.Y.C., 1982; owner-operator Linda LaRosa Interior Plantscapes, N.Y.C., 1982—; designer, dir. theme convs. for various bus. firms, orgns., cultural instns. and photo/video styling, 1984—; owner, operator Plant Care Mobile, N.Y.C., 1986—; Coordinator floral tng. program, tchr. interior plant design, artistic dir. floral guild Cathedral St. John the Divine, N.Y.C., artist in residence; tchr. floral design St. Luke's Ch., N.Y.C.; lectr. N.Y. State Dept. Parks & Recreation, 1987-88, others. Mem. Nat. Trust Hist. Preservation, Am. Hort. Soc., N.Y. Hort. Soc., N.Y. Visitors and Conv. Assn., Am. Woman's Econ. Devel. Corp. Home: 854 W 180th St New York NY 10033

LAROSE, HEATHER MARGARET, controller; b. Weston, Ont., Can., Dec. 6, 1954; d. James Gray and Margaret Aileen (Banks) Watson; m. Norman William LaRose, May 26, 1979. Cert. mgmt. acct., 1985. Accts. payable clk. Watts and Henderson Ltd., Toronto, Ont., Can., 1975-77; payroll supr. Watts and Henderson Ltd., 1977-79, bookkeeper, 1980-81; acct. ITCO Properties, Ltd., Toronto, 1981-84; chief acct. ITCO Properties, Ltd., 1984-86, controller, 1987—. Mem. Soc. Mgmt. Accts. Club: Fitness Inst. (Toronto). Office: Itco Properties Ltd, Royal Bank Plaza, North Tower, Suite 1525, Toronto, ON Canada M5J 2J2

LAROUNIS, MARY GEORGE, psychiatric social worker; b. Cefalonia, Greece, Dec. 21, 1934; came to U.S., 1953, naturalized, 1960; d. George P. and Stamatia O. (Razis) Efthymiatos; m. George P. Larounis, Jan. 13, 1958; 1 child, Daphne H. Student, Pierce Coll., Athens, Greece, 1951-53; BA, Hunter Coll., 1955; MSW, Columbia U., 1957; AESA, U. Paris VII; PhD in Clin. Psychology, U. Paris, 1987. Case worker Community Service N.Y., 1957-60; caseworker Am. Aid Soc., Paris, 1964-66, asst. dir., 1966-79; asst. dir. Am. Student and Family Counselling Service, 1979—; pres. Internat. Counseling Service, Paris, 1979—. Mem. Nat. Assn. Social Workers, Acad. Cert. Social Workers. Clubs: Polo (Paris), Racing (France).

LARRABEE, JANET JOHNS, hotel executive; b. Chgo., Jan. 18, 1951; d. Stanley Walter and Marianne (Losin) Johns; m. Rockwell John Larrabee III, May 26, 1973. BA, Bradley U., 1973; student MBA program, Okla. City U., 1984-85, Drexel U., 1985. Controller Black Hawk Ins., Peoria, Ill., 1973-76, Health Maintenance Life, Agana, Guam, 1976-77, Atkins Kroll Ltd., Agana, 1977-79; staff acct. Kusenberger and Assocs., Del Rio, Tex., 1979-83; controller Hilton Hotel, Oklahoma City, 1983-84, Lincoln Plaza Hotel, Oklahoma City, 1984-85; controller Four Seasons Hotel, Phila., 1985-86, Newport Beach, Calif., 1986, San Antonio, 1987; project controller Ritz-Carlton Hotel, Chgo., 1987-88; controller Whitehall Fremont Hotels, Chgo., 1988—. Mem. Internat. Assn. Hospitality Accts., Tex. Hospitality Accts. Assn. Home: 307 Jewel Saint Charles IL 60174 Office: Whitehall Fremont Hotels 105 E Delaware St Chicago IL 60611

LARRABEE, VIRGINIA ANN STEWART, educator; b. Jacksonville, Fla., Nov. 21, 1923; d. Edwin Homer and Clara Victoria (Anderson) Stewart; student Pine Manor Jr. Coll., 1941-43; B.A., Wellesley Coll., 1945; M.Ed., U. Vt., 1961; Ed.D., Boston U., 1969; m. Wesley Campbell Larrabee, May 4, 1947; children—Susan Ann, Diane Elaine, Linda Jane, Judith Ann. Asst. buyer B. Altman & Co., N.Y.C., 1945-46; tchr. public schs., Forest Dale, Vt., 1955-59, Shoreham, Vt., 1959-62; audiovisual dir., Shoreham, 1959-62; elem. supr., Castleton, Vt., 1962-64; instr., master tchr. Harvard, summers 1963-65; elem. supr. public schs., Rutland, Vt., 1964-66; asst. prof. edn. Castleton State Coll., 1966-68, assoc. prof., 1969-74, prof., 1974—, chmn. dept. edn., 1972—, dir. grad. program in reading, 1974—, dir. Edn. Computer Ctr., 1984—; visiting prof., Harvard U., 1986-87; mem. adv. com. Right to Read, Vt., 1974—; mem. Vt. Edn. Commr.'s Forum, 1981—; owner, operator farm and orchard, 1953—. Sunday Sch. supt. Congregational Ch., Shoreham, 1948-60, choir dir., 1958-64. Mem. New Eng. (past dir.), Vt. (dir., pres. 1978—, editor newsletter 1980—) reading councils, Internat. Reading Assn., Nat., Vt. (past pres.), New Eng. (past dir.) assns. supervision and curriculum devel., Phi Delta Kappa (v.p. Vt. chpt. 1988—), Delta Kappa Gamma, Pi Lambda Theta. Clubs: Vt. Wellesley, Shoreham Hist. Home: RFD Box 56 Shoreham VT 05770 Office: Castleton State Coll Castleton VT 05735

LARRIMORE, PATSY GADD, nurse; b. Knoxville, Tenn., Feb. 18, 1933; d. Harry Collins and Frances (Irwin) Gadd; m. Walter Eugene Larrimore, Jan. 29, 1954; children: Patricia J. Titus, Walter Eugene Jr., Beverly Ann Calderon. BS, Johns Hopkins U., 1976, MEd, 1977. RN. Pediatric supr. Johns Hopkins Hosp., Balt., 1960-68; supr. critical care South Balt. Gen. Hosp., 1968-78; dir. nursing Hosp. for Sick Children, Washington, 1978-84; field rep. Joint Commn. Accreditation Hosp., Chgo., 1984-87; dir. nursing Bon Secours Hosp., Balt., 1987—; asst. prof. nursing, Catonsville Community Coll., 1974-78; cons. Joint Commn. Accreditation Hosp., 1987—. Contbr. articles to profl. jours. Leader Girl Scouts U.S. Mem. Am. Heart Assn. (bd. dirs. Balt. chpt. 1972-84, Md. chpt. 1978-85, Bronze Service award Md. affiliate 1981, Silver Disting. Service Cen. Md. chpt. 1980, Bronze Service Recognition award, 1979), Am. Assn. Critical Care Nurses, Am. Nurses Assn., Advanced Nursing Adminstrn., Assn. Care Children's Health (bd. dirs. 1981-82), Am. Soc. Nursing Service Adminstrs., Phi Delta Kappa. Home: 108 Mountain Rd Linthicum MD 21090

LARSCHAN-WEISS, DEBORAH RAECHADAH, distribution company executive; b. San Francisco, July 17, 1954; d. David and Mildred (Rombouts) Whitehead; m. Philip Charles Larschan, Dec. 10, 1977 (div. 1981); m. Daniel Sanford Weiss, Nov. 30, 1987. BS, Syracuse U., 1978. News reporter Sta. WKTV, Utica, N.Y., 1974-76; asst. dir. TV news Sta. WCNY, Syracuse, N.Y., 1976-78; retailer Video Ctr., Las Vegas, 1978-81; mktg. dir. Video Products Distbrs., Sacramento, 1981-86, v.p. corp. relations, 1986—; corp. v.p. Exec. Publs. Inc., Los Angeles, 1986—, also bd. dirs., 1986—. Bd. dirs. Sacramento Children's Home, 1987, Sacremento Multiple Sclerosis Soc., 1987. Mem. Nat. Assn. Female Execs., Masters of Exec. Excellence, Jewish Bus. and Profl. Women's Orgn., Sacramento Symphony Assn., San Francisco Symphony Assn., Phi Beta Kappa. Republican. Home: 2830 Wrendale Way Sacramento CA 95821 Office: Exec Publs 182 Cadillac Dr Sacramento CA 95825

LARSEN, DEBORAH GAY, accountant; b. Benklemen, Nebr., Apr. 18, 1952; d. Leonard B. and Dorothy M. (Summers) Kokes; m. Eric J. Larsen, June 4, 1977; children: Amanda, Kerry. BS, Oreg. State U., 1975. CPA, Oreg. Staff acct. Haskins and Sells, Portland, Oreg., 1975-77; mgr. tax, staff John F. Forbes and Co., Coos Bay, Oreg., 1977-84; tax mgr. KMG Main Hurdman, Coos Bay, Oreg., 1984-87, Erickson, Donnelly and Co., Coos Bay, Oreg., 1987—. Treas. United Way S.W. Oreg., 1982, bd. dirs. 1981-87. Mem. Am. Inst. CPA's, Oreg. Soc. CPA's, South Coast Chpt. CPA's (pres. 1985-86). Republican. Methodist. Club: PEO (treas. 1981-82). Lodge: Soroptimists (treas. 1981-86, bd. dirs. 1987). Office: Erickson Donnelly and Co PO Box 927 Coos Bay OR 97420

LARSEN, DIANE ELAINE, federal official; b. North Vancouver, B.C., Can., Jan. 8, 1958; d. Lawrence Wayne and Joyce Vivien (Nordby) L. Diploma in Electronic Tech., B.C. Inst. Tech., Vancouver, 1980. Teller Bank of Montreal, Vancouver, 1976-78; radio insp. Fed. Dept. Communications, Vancouver, 1980-86; dist. mgr. Fed. Dept. Communications, Whitehorse, Y.T., 1986—. Home: 70 N Romelagh Ave, North Burnaby, BC Canada V5B 1H6 Office: Dept of Communications, 4133 4th Ave, Suite 201, Whitehorse, YK Canada Y1A 1H8

LARSEN, GRACE HUTCHISON, educator; b. Pomona, Calif., Dec. 4, 1920; d. Forest Glen and Pearl Carrie (Wolfe) Hutchison; B.A., U. Calif., Berkeley, 1942, M.A., 1945; Ph.D., Columbia U., 1955; m. Charles Edward Larsen, Nov. 27, 1943; children—Charles Eric, Douglas Edward. Instr., Rutgers U., Newark, 1947-49, 51-55; lectr. Bryn Mawr (Pa.) Coll., 1949-50; instr. Swarthmore (Pa.) Coll., 1949-51; asst. specialist in agrl. econs. U. Calif., Berkeley, 1955-62, asso. specialist, 1962-66; prof. Emerita history Holy Names Coll., Oakland, Calif., acad. dean, 1970-80; mem. Accreditation Commn. for Sr. Colls. and Univs. Archbishop Riordan fellow in Am. History, 1942-43; Genevieve McEnerney fellow in history, 1945-46; Sigmund Martin Heller travelling fellow, 1946-47; Nat. Endowment for Humanities summer grantee, 1980. Mem. Am. Hist. Assn., West Coast Women Historians, Agrl. History Soc., Phi Beta Kappa. Contbr. articles to profl. jours.; author: (with H.E. Erdman) Revolving Finance in Agricultural Cooperatives, 1965. Home: 4649 Meldon Ave Oakland CA 94619 Office: 3500 Mountain Blvd Oakland CA 94619

LARSEN, JEAN MAYCOCK, educator; b. Provo, Utah, Feb. 23, 1931; d. Lawrence S. and Lorna (Booth) Maycock; B.S., Brigham Young U., Provo, 1953, M.S., 1960; Ph.D., U. Utah, 1972; m. A. Dean Larsen, Feb. 14, 1958; children—David Lawrence, Paul Joseph, Ann, Charlotte. Tchr. schs. in Oreg. and Utah, 1953-55, 57-58; mem. faculty Brigham Young U., 1960—, prof. family scis., 1976—, coordinator early childhood edn. program, 1980—. Mem. Nat. Assn. Edn. Young Children, Assn. Childhood Edn. Internat., Utah Assn. Edn. Young Children (past pres., chmn. adv. bd.), Am. Ednl. Research Assn., Soc. Research Child Devel., Phi Kappa Phi. Republican. Mormon. Author curriculum materials in field; also research. Home: 2678 North 880 East Provo UT 84604 Office: Brigham Young U 1319-A SFLC Provo UT 84602

LARSEN, KAREN MARIE, lawyer; b. Cheyenne Wells, Colo., July 14, 1954; d. Jack D. and Emma (Hermes) L. BA, U. Denver, 1976; JD, Hamline U., 1979. Bar: Colo. 1979, U.S. Dist. Ct. Colo. 1979. Assoc. Law Offices of Norman L. Arends, Cheyenne Wells, 1979-81; sole practice Cheyenne Wells, 1981-83; gen. counsel RPJ Energy Fund Mgmt., Mpls., 1983-87, also bd. dirs. and sec.; fin. planner, investment adviser free-lance, Mpls., 1988—; bd. dirs. AEI Real Estate Funds, Mpls.; bd. dirs., v.p. Kenecreek, Inc., Cheyenne Wells, 1982—; gen. counsel Colo. A.S.A., Denver, 1979-85. Del. State Dem. Conv., Colo., 1982; pres. Sacred Heart Parish Council, Cheyenne Wells, 1980-83; treas., East Cheyenne Bus. Assn., Cheyenne Wells, 1979-83. Named Colo. Woman of the Yr., Colo. Jaycees, 1983. Mem. ABA, Colo. Bar Assn., Sigma Nu Phi. Democrat. Roman Catholic. Home: 1892 Gold Trail Eagan MN 55122 Office: Larsen Fin Services 3601 W 77th St Suite 880 Bloomington MN 55435

LARSEN, PAULINE M., photographer; b. Storm Lake, Iowa, June 11, 1935; d. Leonard and Esther (Rouze) Cole; m. Richard N. Larsen, m. May 25, 1958; children: Chris, Scott. BA, Wheaton Coll., 1958; postgrad., Iowa State U. Cert. elem. and secondary tchr., Iowa; cert. English tchr., Iowa. Tchr. various schs., Iowa, 1958-77; coordinator and cons. media tng. Media Now, Red Oak, Iowa, 1977-82; pvt. practice photography Newell, Iowa, 1980—; cons. media tng. Named one of Top Ten Photographers State of Iowa, 1982-85. Mem. NEA (life), Nat. Council Tchrs. English (life), Profl. Photographers Am., Profl. Photographers Iowa, Wedding Photographers Internat. Club: TTT Soc. (Newell) (sec. 1983—). Home and Office: 521 N Fulton St Newell IA 50568

LARSON, CHERYL L., mathematician, analyst; b. Seattle, Mar. 18, 1948; d. Merle and Elaine Edith (Skersies) Hottenstein; m. Richard Thomas Larson, Mar. 24, 1972. BS, Seattle Pacific U., 1970. Computer aide R.W. Beck and Assocs., Seattle, 1970-71, sr. computer aide, 1971-72, jr. technician, 1972-73, engrng. technician, 1973-76, sr. technician, 1976-78, sr. analyst, 1978—; v.p. the Network of R.W. Beck and Assocs., 1982-85. Mem. Nat. Assn. Female Execs. Republican. Office: RW Beck and Assocs 2121 Fourth Ave Seattle WA 98121

LARSON, ELAINE LUCILLE, nurse researcher, epidemiologist, educator; b. Douglas, Ariz., Apr. 27, 1943; d. John Earl and Jerry Lucille (Hunter) Williamson; m. Steven Mark Larson, June 14, 1965; children: Nathan, Justine. BS, U. Wash., 1965, MA, 1969, PhD, 1981. Registered nurse. Nurse specialist, instr. U. Wash. Hosp., Seattle, 1965-69, hosp. epidemiologist, 1967-70, assoc. dir. nursing., asst. prof., 1976-83; postodoctoral fellow U. Pa., Phila., 1983-85; Nutting chmn. in Clin. Nursing Johns Hopkins U. Sch. Nursing, Balt., Md., 1985—; pres. Cert. Bd. for Infection Control. Contbr. numerous articles to profl. jours. Testified in House and Senate for nursing edn. and research, 1984-85; testified in Joint Econ. Com. for testing of disinfectants. Grantee Johnson & Johnson, 1985. Fellow Am. Acad. Nursing, NSF (inst. of medicine 1986). Presbyterian. Office: Johns Hopkins U Sch Nursing 600 N Wolfe St Baltimore MD 21205

LARSON, EMILIE G., retired educator; b. Northfield, Minn., Apr. 28, 1919; d. Melvin Cornelius and Frieda (Christiansen) L.; A.B., St. Olaf Coll., 1940; M.A., Radcliffe Coll., 1946; student U. Chgo., 1951-52. Tchr. Hanska (Minn.) High Sch., 1940-42, Two Harbors (Minn.) High Sch., 1942-43; tchr. J.W. Weeks Jr. High Sch., Newton, Mass., 1946-56, guidance counselor, 1956-79; counselor Warren Jr. High Sch., Newton, 1979-81. Deacon, Univ. Luth. Ch., 1979; bd. dirs. Bus. History and Econ. Life Program, Inc., Northeastern U. Mem. AAUW (state v.p. for program devel., topic chmn. Mass. div. 1975-76; corp. rep., area rep. for internat. relations Minn. div. 1984-86), Mass., Newton tchrs. assns., St. Olaf Coll. Alumni Assn. (dir. 1982-85), PEO, Virginia Gildersleeve Internat. Fund for Univ. Women Inc. (membership com., bd. dirs.), Pi Lambda Theta. Lutheran. Contbr. articles to profl. jours. Address: 1008 W 1st St Northfield MN 55057

LARSON, JACQUELYNNE BORST (PENNY), real estate auction executive; b. Glens Falls, N.Y., Nov. 3, 1938; d. Jacque Becker and Madeline (Edmunds) Borst; m. Donald F. Larson, Apr. 4, 1957 (div. Feb. 1981); children—Daniel, David, Christy. Student U. Ill., 1956-57. Lic. real estate salesperson. Sole propr. Larson Enterprises, Glenview, Ill., 1960-72; controller Ada S. McKinley Community Services, Chgo., 1973-82; exec. v.p. Kaufman Lasman Assocs., Inc., Chgo., 1982-86; chief exec. officer Fed. Auction Service Corp., 1986-88; chief ops. officer Larry Latham Auctioneers, 1988—. Officer, bd. dirs. LWV, Glenview, 1973-74, North Shore Assn. for Retarded, Evanston, 1969-71; mem. East Maine Dist. 63 Sch. Bd., Des Plaines, Ill., 1974-79; deacon Presby. Ch. of Glenview, 1974. Recipient $25 Million Sales award Kaufman Lasman Assocs., 1985. Mem. Nat. Assn. Realtors, Chgo. Real Estate Bd. (Salesperson of Yr. 1985, 86). Home: 303 W Eugenie St Chicago IL 60614 Office: Fed Auction Service Corp 1759 N Sedgwick Chicago IL 60614

LARSON, JEANNE M., health services executive, consultant, researcher; b. Mpls., May 1, 1949; d. Emlen Kermit and Mildred Evangeline (Gulsvig) L.; m. Arne Eugene Skaalure, May 13, 1972 (div. 1981); m. Dewey A. Johnson, Aug. 24, 1985. B.A., Gustavus Adolphus Coll., 1971; M.B.A., St. Thomas Coll., 1982. Sch. nurse Dept. Defense Overseas Dependents Sch., Okinawa, Japan, 1972-74; staff nurse U.S. Army Camp Kuwae Hosp., Okinawa, 1974-75; instr. diabetes and health edn. Metro. Med. Ctr., Mpls., 1976-79; dir. and mktg. mgr. Competent Nursing Services, Mpls., 1979-81; pres., v.p. Austin Larson Corp., Mpls., 1981-83; pres. Optional Care Systems, St. Paul, 1984—; research cons. U. Minn. Sch. Nursing Mpls., 1982—; cons. Honeywell Corp., Mpls., 1984. Author: Diabetes Manual, 1979; Healthcare Cost Management, 1985; mem. Gov.'s Task Force on Promoting Minn.'s Health Care Resources; del. People to People Health Care and Home Health Program, Republic of China, 1987; mem. Minn. Healthcare Adv. Council, Dept. of Trade and Econs. Devel., 1988. Recipient U.S.A. award for Graphics Design, 1981, Nat. Creative Nurse award Minn. Nurses Assn., 1979, Allene Von Son Nat. award, 1978. Mem. Ind. Bus. Assn. Minn. (v.p., bd. dirs. 1982—, Small Bus. Woman of Yr. 1983), Nat. Assn. Home Care (info. resource com. 1984, nominating com. 1985, Health Maintenance Orgn. and Home-Care com. 1987). Office: Optional Care Systems Inc 2550 University Ave Suite 330N Saint Paul MN 55114

LARSON, JULIA LOUISE FINK, land use planner; b. Bethesda, Md., July 11, 1950; d. James A. and Helen J. (Grubb) Fink; m. Louis C. Larson, May 27, 1978 (div. Dec. 1981). BS, Radford Coll., 1972; MS, Oreg. State U., 1975; postgrad., Ga. State U., 1986—. Geography tchr. Rappahannock County High Sch., Washington, Va., 1972-73; research asst./sec. Oreg. Natural Area Preserves Adv. Com., 1974-75; energy conservation specialist Oreg. Dept. Energy, Salem, 1976-77; mem. Oreg. Fire Protection Master Planning Com., 1978-79, Oreg. State Environ. Edn. Adv. Com., 1977-80; growth mgmt. planner Salem Fire Dept., 1978-79; land use planner Salem Dept. Community Devel., 1979-83; field rep. Data Research & Applications, Inc., Atlanta, 1983-84; land use coordinator Ga. Mfd. Housing Assn., Atlanta, 1984-86; owner, The Planning Edge, Atlanta, 1986-87; land use planner, EDAW, Inc., Atlanta, 1987—; cons. Contbg. editor: 1979 Sun Calendar; co-editor: 1976 Energy Calendar. Vice-pres. Liberty Jaycee Women, Salem, 1981; land use adv. Northside Neighbors, Salem, 1979. Recipient cert. of appreciation City of Salem, 1983. Mem. Am. Inst. Cert. Planners, Ga. Planning Assn. (editor Ga. Planner, 1986-87), Am. Mgmt. Assn., AAUW (group leader 1987-88, newsletter editor 1987-88, bd. dirs. 1987—), Am. Assn. Geographers, Am. Bar Assn. (student mem.), Am. Assn. Women Law Students, Ga. Assn. Zoning Adminstrs. and Bldg. Ofcls., High Mus. Art, Smithsonian Assocs., Ga. Conservancy, Delta Theta Phi. Avocations: backpacking; writing; wine tasting. Home: 4717 Roswell Rd L4 Atlanta GA 30342

LARSON, KARIN LOUISE, financial analyst; b. Mpls., Aug. 8, 1938; d. Walter Carl and Clara Margaret (Nelson) L. BA, U. Minn., 1960; MBA, U. So. Calif., 1971. With Capital Guardian Research Co., Los Angeles, 1961-88, research assoc., 1966-68, fin. analyst, 1968-71, exec. v.p., dir., 1971-88; sr. v.p., dir. Investment Co. Am., Los Angeles, 1980-88; v.p., dir. research Capital Group Research, Los Angeles, 1986—; sr. v.p. Capital Research Internat., Los Angeles, 1987—, also bd. dirs. Baptist. Office: Capital Guardian Research Co 333 S Hope St 52d Floor Los Angeles CA 90071

LARSON, NANCY LORENE, information systems manager; b. N.Y.C., Jan. 24, 1954; d. Norman Oscar and Barbara (Hayes) L. Student, U. Calif., Irvine, 1973-74; BA in Applied Math., U. Calif., Berkeley, 1979. Instr. math, computer Lawrence Hall Sci., Berkeley, 1978-79; programmer, analyst Infomatics Inc., Palo Alto, Calif., 1979; user cons. EDS Nuclear Inc., San Francisco, 1979-81; communications mgr. Echo Energy Cons., Oakland, Calif., 1982-83; info. services mgr. BP Alaska Exploration, San Francisco, 1983—. Mem. Nat. Assn. Female Execs., Assn. Systems Mgmt. Office: BP Alaska Exploration 100 Pine St San Francisco CA 94111

LARSON, NANCY MARIE, research physicist; b. Dickinson, N.D., Sept. 30, 1946; d. Austin George and Margit Dagmar (Lutness) Zander; m. Duane Clark Larson, Sept. 7, 1968; 1 child, Linnea Margit. BS in Math., Mich. State U., 1967, MS in Physics, 1968, PhD in Physics, 1972. Mem. research staff Oak Ridge (Tenn.) Nat. Lab., 1972—. Contbr. articles to profl. jours. Pres. Karns (Tenn.) Community Club, 1987, treas., 1985-86; treas. Karns Primary and Intermediate PTA, 1983-85, pres., 1982-83. Mem. Am. Phys. Soc. Lutheran. Office: Oak Ridge Nat Lab Bldg 6010 PO Box X Oak Ridge TN 37831-6356

LARSON, STEPHANIE SUSAN, marketing professional; b. Denver, May 9, 1951; d. John Joseph and Virginia (Frainer) Blocksom; m. Michael H. Larson, Dec. 30, 1972; 1 child, Tess. AA, Springfield (Ill.) Coll., 1971; BA in English, U. Wis., Milw., 1976. Copywriter James S. Cline Inc., Sheboygan, Wis., 1976-80; dir. pub. relations Lakeland Coll., Sheboygan, 1980-83, St. Nicholas Hosp., Sheboygan, 1983—. chmn. pub. relations com. Sheboygan United Way, 1986, Children's Soc. Service Bd., Sheboygan, 1987. Mem. Wis. Hosp. Pub. Relations and Mktg. Assn. (mem.-at-large 1985-86, dist. rep. 1986-87, sec. 1987-88). Home: 4449 N Evergreen Dr Sheboygan WI 53081 Office: St Nicholas Hosp 1601 N Taylor Dr Sheboygan WI 53081

LARUE, LINDA CUMMINGS, child care center administrator; b. Sanford, N.C., May 22, 1948; d. Charles Lee and Betty Jo (Shinault) Cummings; m. Robert Russell LaRue, Apr. 1, 1966; children—Charles Channing, Rusty Lee, Katherine Cummings. Student public schs. Sanford, N.C. Dir., Mini-Skool Ltd., Winston Salem, N.C., 1973-79; owner, ptnr. Dandy Lion Ltd., Winston Salem, 1980-84, Kelly's Sta., Sanford, N.C., 1981-85; pres. LaRue, Inc., Kernersville, N.C., 1980—, Learning Ctr. Assocs., 1984—, A Brighter Child Learning Ctr., 1984—. Treas. Kernersville Childrens Little Theatre, 1983-84, pres., 1984-85; pres. Kernersville Elem. Sch. PTA, 1986-87; mem. Forsyth County Home Econs. Coop. Edn. (chmn. 1987-88),. Republican. Presbyterian. Clubs: Kernersville Womans (2d v.p. 1985—, 1st v.p. 1986-87, pres. 1987—), East Forsyth Booster Athletic, Glenn Athletic Booster Assn., Northwest Guilford Booster Assn., Kernersville Raiders Booster, Kernersville Garden (1st v.p. 1988). Avocations: sailing, painting, needlecrafts, biking, photography. Home: 222 Vandyke St Kernersville NC 27284 Office: A Brighter Child Learning Ctr 820 Salisbury St Kernersville NC 27284

LARUE, RITA RENEA, musician; b. Houston, Feb. 22, 1957. AA, Cumberland Jr. Coll., Lebanon, Tenn., 1976; MusB, Houston Bapt. U., 1980. Music asst. Baptist Temple Ch., Houston, 1973-77; music assoc. W. U. Bapt. Ch., Houston, 1979-85; minister of music Autumn Creek Bapt. Ch., Houston, 1986-87; exec. asst. GeoQuest Internat., Inc., Houston, 1985—; music coordinator, festival adjudicator, Union Bapt. Assn., Houston, Bapt. Gen. Conv. of Tex.; coordinator Tex. Bapt. All-State Choir Auditions, Houston. Recipient music scholarship, Cumberland Jr. Coll., 1975, Houston Bapt. U., 1976-80, Heights Kiwanis Club scholarship, 1975, Heights Rotary Club scholarship, 1975. Mem. Am. Choral Dirs. Assn., Ch. Music Conf. of the So. Bapt. Conv., Nat. Assn. Female Execs., Sigma Alpha Iota. Home: PO Box 272223 Houston TX 77277 Office: GeoQuest Internat Inc 4605 Post Oak Pl Suite 130 Houston TX 77027

LARWOOD, LAURIE, psychologist; b. N.Y., 1941; Ph.D., Tulane U., 1974. Pres., Davis Instruments Corp., San Leandro, Calif., 1966-71, cons., 1969—; asst. prof. organizational behavior State U. N.Y. at Binghamton, 1974-76; assoc. prof. psychology, chairperson dept., assoc. prof. bus. adminstrn. Claremont (Calif.) McKenna Coll., 1976-83, Claremont Grad. Sch., 1976-85; prof., head dept. mgmt. U. Ill.-Chgo., 1983-87; dean sch. bus. SUNY, Albany, 1987—; mem. western regional advisory council SBA, 1976-81; dir. The Mgmt. Team; pres. Mystic Games, Inc. Mem. Acad. Mgmt. (editorial rev. bd. Rev. 1977-82, past chmn. women in mgmt. div., chmn. research/devel.-tech. innovation div.), Am. Psychol. Assn., Assn. Women in Psychology. Author: (with M.M. Wood) Women in Management, 1977; Organizational Behavior and Management, 1984, Women's Career Development, 1987, Strategies-Successes-Senior Executives Speak Out, 1988; mem. editorial bd. Sex Roles, 1979—, Consultation, 1986—, Occupational Behavior, 1987—, Group and Orgn. Studies, 1982-84, editor, 1986—; founding editor Women and Work, 1983, Jour. Mgmt. Case Studies, 1983—; contbr. numerous articles, papers to profl. jours. Home: Schenectady NY 12309 Office: SUNY Sch Bus Albany NY 12222

LARY, MARILYN SEARSON, librarian; b. Walterboro, S.C., Sept. 3, 1943; d. Charles Baring and Julia Caroline (Rizer) Searson; AB, Newberry Coll., 1964; MLS, U. N.C., 1965; PhD, Fla. State U., 1975; m. Jahangir Lary, Oct. 27, 1975; children: Sara, Heidi. Young adult librarian Greenville County (S.C.) Library, 1965-66; library dir. U. S.C., Sumter, 1966-69; instr. Radford (Va.) U., 1969-70; asst. prof. East Carolina U., Greenville, 1970-72; reference librarian Clemson U., S.C., 1972-73; asst. prof. U. Mich., Ann Arbor, 1975-78, U. South Fla., Tampa, 1978-84; librarian Hillsborough Community Coll.-Brandon Ctr., Tampa, 1984-86; dir. learning resource ctr. Dalton (Ga.) Coll., 1986—. Mem. ALA, Ga. Library Assn. Methodist. Home: 334 W Nance Sp Rd Resaca GA 30735 Office: Dalton Coll Learning Resource Ctr Dalton GA 30720

LASA, MADELAINE IVETTE, dietician, educator; b. Humacao, P.R., Aug. 6, 1954; d. Miguel Angel and Margarita (Silva) Hernandez; m. Ivan Lasa, Jan. 24, 1976; children: Marlene, Astrid. BS in Nutrition and Dietetics, U. P.R., Rio Piedras, 1975. Lic. dietitian, P.R. Intern San Juan VA Med. Ctr., Rio Piedras, 1975-76; chief adminstrv. dietitian P.R. Dept. of Health, Cayey, 1978-79; dir. food and nutrition service P.R. Dept. of Health, Guayma, 1979-81; clin. dietitian VA Med. Ctr., Gainesville, Fla., 1983-84, clin. nutrition specialist, 1984—; clin. dietitian P.R. Health Dept., Humacao, 1977-78; adj. clin. instr. dietetics U. Fla., Gainesville, 1983—; mem. nutrition support team VA Med. Ctr., Gainesville, 1983—, team leader cardiac rehab. teaching program, Gainesville, 1986—. Author: Handbook of Clinical Nutrition, 1986; (with others) Gainesville Veterans Administration Medical Center Diet Manual, 1984, 87. Sec. Partido Nuevo Progresista, Caquas, P.R., Caquas, 1976-80; active Girl Scouts Am. Mem. Am. Dietetic Assn., Fla. Dietetic Assn., Gainesville Dist. Dietetic Assn., Nat. Kidney Found. Council on Renal Nutrition (sec, 1987-88), Coll. of Nutritionists and Dietitians of P.R. Republican. Roman Catholic. Office: VA Med Ctr 1601 SW Archer Rd Gainesville FL 32602

LASCH, JUDITH, television producer, author, lecturer; b. Hudson County, N.J., Feb. 3, 1939; m. (dec. 1962); children—Callie, Amy and Beth (twins). A.A., Brookdale Community Coll.; B.A., Thomas A. Edison Coll. Fashion dir. Talon, N.Y.C., 1972-78; cons. to DuPont Co., N.Y.C., 1978-80, Xerox, N.Y.C., 1980-83; exec. producer Focus on New York, N.Y.C., 1983—, China-Am. Exchange (video show airing in China); lectr. Fashion Inst. Tech., N.Y.C., other ednl. instns. Author: The Teen Model Book, 1986; (workbook) The Teen Guide to Beauty, 1982. Pres. N.J. State Fedn. Women's Clubs, 1964, civics and legis. dist. leader, 1966; leader Girl Scouts U.S.A.; group leader African Safari and student trips to France. Mem. Am. Women Entrepreneurs, Nat. Assn. Female Execs., Victorian Soc. Am. Avocations: travel; crafts; arts; reading; gardening; camping; cooking; nature. Home: 235 E 22d St New York NY 10010

LASCHENSKI, MATHILDA JANE, art educator, sculptor; b. Drexel Hill, Pa., Oct. 3, 1942; d. Joseph Edward and Mathilda Diana (Gates) L. BS, Phila. Coll. of Art, 1964; MEd, Temple U., 1970, Columbia U., 1986; EdD, Columbia U., 1987. Tchr. art Phila. Sch. Dist., 1965—; freelance ceramist Phila., 1965—. One-woman exhibition Columbia U., N.Y.C., 1985; sculptures exhibited at Phila. Art Alliance, Phila. Civic Ctr. Mus., Fleisher Art Meml. at Phila. Mus. Art, Phila. U. of Arts, Tyler Sch. Art at Temple U., Trenton (N.J.) Mus. Art. Mem. Girl Scouts U.S., Phila., 1986—. Mem. Pa. Art Edn. Assn., Women's Caucus for Art, Phila. Fedn. Tchrs., Women in Edn.

LASHER, DONNA MARIA, lawyer; b. N.Y.C., Mar. 1, 1948; d. Thomas Earl and Angela (Canora) Fleming; m. Burton John Lasher, Aug. 21, 1976 (div. May 1982); 1 child, John Thomas. BS in Secondary Edn., Fordham U., 1969; JD, SUNY, Buffalo, 1972. Bar: N.Y. State, 1972. Asst. corp. counsel N.Y.C. Corp. Counsel Office, 1972-79; asst. dist. atty. Office Queens County Dist. Atty., N.Y.C., 1979-83, dep. insp. gen./ dept. advocate N.Y.C. Dept. Correction, 1983-86; prin. law asst. to acting superior ct. judge N.Y. State Ct. System, N.Y.C., 1986—; arbitrator N.Y.C. Small Claims Ct. Bd. dirs. Hilltop Village Coop. No. 4, N.Y.C. Mem. N.Y. State Bar Assn., Queens County Bar Assn. Roman Catholic. Office: N.Y. State Supreme Ct 88-11 Sutphin Blvd Jamaica NY 11435

LASHLEE, JOLYNNE VAN MARSDON, army officer, nurse, administrator; b. Asheville, N.C., May 22, 1948; d. William Reid and Frances (Furey) Van Marsdon. BS in Nursing, U. Fla., 1971; M Health Care Adminstrn., Baylor U., 1982. Team leader surg. specialties Shand Teaching Hosp., Gainesville, Fla., 1971; commd. lt. U.S. Army Nurses Corps, 1971, advanced through grades to lt. col., 1981; asst. head nurse organ transplant service unit Walter Reed Hosp., Washington, 1972; staff nurse surg. ICU, head nurse multi-service nursing unit Nurnberg, W. Ger., 1972-75; head nurse recovery room William Beaumont Army Med. Center, Ft. Bliss, El Paso, Tex., 1975-76, dep. dir. patient care specialist course, 1976-78; ednl. coordinator, project officer U.S. Lyster Hosp., Ft. Rucker, Ala., 1978; adminstrv. resident Madigan Army Med. Center, Tacoma, 1981-82; chief nurse methods div. Walter Reed Hosp., 1982-85; mem. Army Surgeon Gen.'s Task Force on Health Care, 1985-86; pvt. image marketer Color 1 Assocs. div. Frances Denney. Active Boy Scouts Am. Mem. Am. Hosp. Assn., Am. Coll. Healthcare Execs., Assn. Health Care Adminstrs. Nat. Capital Area, Am. Assn. Critical Care Nurses, Baylor U. Healthcare Adminstrs. Alumni. Home: 8555 Laurens Ln #1308 San Antonio TX 78218-6008 Office: HQ HSCIG San Antonio Tex. TX 78234

LASITER, ELEANOR JANET, nurse, director rehabilitation facility; b. Wadena, Sask., Can., Dec. 10, 1934; d. Reginald Clarence and Ellen Mae (Morton) Svedberg; m. Carl William Lasiter, Dec. 16, 1955; children: Tamara Rundle, Kim Cain, Susan Hammer, John Lasiter. RN, Deaconess Sch. Nursing, 1955; BS in Health Sci., Chapman Coll., 1979. RN. Staff nurse Home of Guiding Hands, Lakeside, Calif., 1968-69, coordinator staff devel., 1969-70, dir. residential services, 1970-75, exec. dir., 1982—, also bd. dirs.; nurse clinician San Diego Regional Ctr. Developmentally Disabled, 1977-80, project coordinator, 1980-82; nurse educator Merric Coll., San Diego, 1975-77, mem. adv. com., 1983—, mem profl. adv. com., 1985—. Named Service Provider of Yr., Sen. Ellis Adv. Com., 1985; named one of Women of Accomplishment, Soroptimist Internat., 1986; recipient Clair Burgener Found., 1987. Mem. Am. Assn. Mental Deficiency (sec. region II 1985—), Calif. Assn. Residential Resources (bd. dirs., Adminstr. of Yr. 1985). Democrat. Lutheran. Home: 5359-29 Aztec Dr La Mesa CA 92041 Office: Home of Guiding Hands 10025 Los Ranchitos Rd Lakeside CA 92040

LASON, SANDRA WOOLMAN, English as a second language educator; b. Chgo., July 30, 1934; d. Irwin Robert and Annette (Hassman) Woolman; m. Marvin Mitchell Lason, Feb. 8, 1959 (dec. 1972); children: Caryn Anne, Joel Steven, Scott David. BS with highest distinction, Northwestern U., 1956; MA, Northeastern Ill. U., 1976; postgrad., U. Okla., 1982—. Cert. K-12 tchr. Tchr. Sch. Dist. 69, Skokie, Ill., 1956-60, tchr., dir. gifted, 1972-76; tchr., adminstr. MONACEP, Morton Grove, Ill., 1964-76; freelance writer-editor 1976—; curriculum writer-editor The Economy Co., Oklahoma City, 1978-80; instr., assoc. dir. English dept. U. Okla., Norman, 1980-83; prof., ESL coordinator Oklahoma City Community Coll., 1983—; adj. prof. ESL Austin Coll., Sherman, Tex., 1977; gifted child coordinator for Ill. MENSA, 1973-76; judge Okla. Olympics Mind, Mensokie Essay Contest, 1987; chmn. com. for ESL Okla. State Regents, 1985-86; speaker presentations on writing, ESL and educating the gifted. Writer-editor: K-8 Language Arts Series Expressways, 1980; author (with others) Resource Book, Oklahoma Gifted Galaxy, 1983; editor numerous books; contbr. numerous articles to profl. jours. Officer Karen Brown Chpt. Bobs Roberts Hosp., Skokie, 1964-74, Children's Meml. Hosp., Chgo., 1960-71; bd. dirs. Okla. Hillel Found., 1984-87, Women's Resource Ctr., Norman, 1982-83; officer Kenton PTA. Mem. Nat. Council Tchrs. English, MLA, MENSA, Pi Lambda Theta, Alpha Epsilon Phi(officer alumnae chpt.). Jewish. Lodge: B'nai B'rith. Home: 2103 Melrose Dr Norman OK 73069 Office: Oklahoma City Community Coll 7777 S May Ave Oklahoma City OK 73159

LASS, LESLIE JANE, writer, public relations consultant; b. Bklyn., Sept. 17, 1951; 1 dau., Emily Arden. B.A., U. Calif.-Berkeley, 1974, M.A., 1978. Teaching asst. English dept. U. Calif.-Berkeley, 1975-78; assoc. editor mktg. publs. Bank of Am., San Francisco, 1978-80; owner LL Communications, Oakland, Calif., 1980—; pub. relations specialist Bechtel, San Francisco, 1986-87; dir., mgr. services Peabody Group, San Francisco, 1987-88; outreach dir. The Hayward Hosp., 1988—. Contbr. articles to mags. and newspapers.

LAST, DIANNA LINN, data processing company executive; b. Canton, Ohio, Dec. 29, 1944; d. Ld Mervyn and Veronica Lee Schneider; m. David D. Last, Nov. 29, 1969; 1 child, Jason Holder. BA in German, Ohio State U., 1966. Research asst., programmer trainee high-energy physics dept., Ohio State U., Columbus, 1964-66; mfg. programmer RANCO, Inc., Columbus, 1966-68; sr. edn. rep. Honeywell Info. Systems, Cleve., 1968-72; dist. mgr. Honeywell Info. Systems, Orlando, Fla., 1972-78, telecommunications cons., 1978-79; mgr. networking edn. Honeywell Info. Systems, Phoenix, 1979-81, mgr. distributed systems, 1981-85; account and tech. mgr. Honeywell Info. Systems, Beijing, People's Republic of China, 1985; resident dir., chief rep. Honeywell Bull (formerly Honeywell Info. Systems), Beijing, People's Republic of China, 1985-87; dir. Integrated Info. Architecture programs, Honeywell Bull, Phoenix, 1987—; bd. advisor Internat. Bus. Orgn., Am. Grad. Sch. Internat. Mgmt.; cons., speaker in field. Sunday sch. tchr., mem. bishop's com. St. John Baptist Episc. Ch., Phoenix, 1980-83, lay reader, 1983—; mem. adv. bd. Ariz. Assn. Children and Adults with Learning Disabilities, 1983—; mem. design task force Maricopa Community Colls., 1984—. Mem. IEEE (past vice chmn. programs). Home: 1274 E Marconi Ave Phoenix AZ 85022

LAST, MARIAN HELEN, social services administrator; b. Los Angeles, July 2, 1953; d. Henry and Renee (Kahan) Last. BA, Pitzer Coll., 1975; postgrad., U. So. Calif., 1975-84; MS, Long Beach State U., 1980. Lic. marriage therapist. Coordinator City of El Monte, Calif., 1975-76, project dir., 1976-82; pvt. practice psychotherapist Long Beach, Calif., 1982—; div. mgr. City of El Monte, 1982—; cons. U. So. Calif. Andrus Ctr., Los Angeles, 1977-78; bd. dirs. Coordinating Council, City of El Monte, 1980—, Sr. Pres.'s Council, 1982—, Com. on Aging, 1986—. Co-author rape survival guide, 1971. Dir., founder Rape Response Program, Pomona, San Gabriel, Calif., 1971-80; cons. sexual assault Pitzer Coll., Claremont, Calif., 1975-78; chair Sr. Conf. Com., San Gabriel Valley, 1984—. Recipient Susan B. Anthony award NOW, Pomona, 1976. Mem. Am. Soc. Aging, Calif. Assn. Nutrition Dirs., Calif. Parks and Recreation Soc., Calif. Assn. Marriage and Family Therapists. Democrat. Jewish. Club: Women's. Home: 3372 Rowena Dr Rossmoor CA 90720 Office: City of El Monte 3120 N Tyler Ave El Monte CA 91731

LASTER, CONNIE MCDANIEL, accountant; b. High Point, N.C., Mar. 8, 1960; d. Allen Thomas and M. Donise (Smith) McDaniel; m. Randy Clyde Laster, Jan. 1, 1987. BS in Acctg. magna cum laude, High Point Coll., 1982. CPA, N.C. Staff acct. Sharrard, McGee & Co., P.A., High Point, 1982-84, audit sr. acct., 1984-88, audit mgr., 1988—. Treas. Christ United Meth. Ch., High Point, 1981—; mem. allocations com. United Way of High Point, 1985-87. Named one of Outstanding Young Women Am., 1986. Mem. Am. Inst. CPA's, N.C. Assn. CPA's. Republican. Methodist. Office: Sharrard McGee & Co PA 1813 N Main St High Point NC 27261

LASURE, LINDA LEE, chemical company executive; b. Barlesville, Okla., Nov. 23, 1946; d. Basil Riggs Lasure and Lucille Lavella (White) Lasure-Steward. BS, St. Cloud (Minn.) State U., 1968; PhD, Syracuse U., 1973. Research fellow N.Y. Bot. Garden, Bronx, 1972-74; research scientist Miles Labs., Elkhart, Ind., 1979, sr. research scientist, 1979-80, supr., 1980-84, dir. bioproduct research, 1984—. Editor: (book) Gene Manipulation in Fungi, 1985; contbr. articles to profl. jours. Nat. Def. Edn. Act fellow, 1969-72. Mem. AAAS, N.Y. Acad. Sci., Am. Soc. Microbiology (pres. Ind. br. 1977-78, councilor Ind. bd. 1979-81, governing council), Genetics Soc. Am. Home: 28393 County Rd 16 Elkhart IN 46516 Office: Miles Labs Elkhart IN 46516

LATHAM, ALICE FRANCES PATTERSON, public health nurse; b. Macon, Ga., Dec. 18, 1916; d. Frank Waters and Ruby (Dews) Patterson; R.N., Charity Hosp. Sch. Nursing, New Orleans, 1937; student George Peabody Coll. Tchrs., 1938-39; BS in Pub. Health Nursing, U. N.C., 1954; M.P.H., Johns Hopkins U., 1966; m. William Joseph Latham, July 21, 1940 (dec. Apr. 1981); children: Jo Alice (Mrs. Phillip Schmidt), Marynette (Mrs. Charles Stephens), Lauruby Cathleen; m. Sidney Dumas Herndon, Apr. 26, 1985. Staff pub. health nurse assigned spl. venereal disease study USPHS, Darien, Ga., 1939-40; county pub. health nurse Bacon County, Alma, Ga., 1940-41; USPHS spl. venereal disease project, Glynn County, Brunswick, 1943-47; county pub. health nurse Glynn County, 1949-51, Ware County, Waycross, 1951-52; pub. health nurse supr. Wayne-Long-Brantley-Liberty Counties, Jesup, 1954-56 dist. dir. pub. health nursing Wayne-Long-Appling-Bacon-Pierce Counties, Jesup, 1956-70; dist. chief nursing S.E. Ga. Health Dist., 1970-79, organizer mobile health services, 1973—. Exec. dir. Wayne County Home Health Agy., 1968-80; exec. dir. Ware County Home Health Agy., 1970-79, mem. exec. com., 1978-85; mem. governing bd. S.E. Ga. Health Systems Agy., 1975-82; mem. governing bd. Health Dept. Home Health Agy., 1978—, also author numerous grant proposals. Bd. dirs. Wayne County Mental Health Assn., 1959, 60, 61, 81, 82, Wayne County Tb Assn., 1958-62; a non-alcoholic organizer Jesup group Alcoholics Anonymous, 1962-63; mem. adv. council Ware Meml. Hosp. Sch. Practical Nursing, Waycross, Ga., 1958; mem. Altar Guild, St. Paul's Episcopal Ch., 1979—, vestrywoman, 1981-82. Recipient recognition Gen. Service Bd., Alcoholics Anonymous, Inc. Fellow Am. Pub. Health Assn.; mem. Am., 8th Dist. (pres. 1954-58, sec. 1958-60, dir. 1960-62, 1st v.p. 1962), Ga. (exec. bd. 1954-58, program rev. continuing edn. com. 1980-86) nurses assns., Ga. Pub. Health Assn. (chmn. nursing sect. 1956-57), Ga. Assn. Dist. Chiefs Nursing (pres. 1976). Contbr. to state nursing manuals, cons. to Home Health Service Agys. Home: Route 6 Box 46 Brunswick GA 31520

LATHAM, CAROLINE JANET MACDONALD, retired state official, home economist; b. Raymond, Wash., Jan. 9, 1917; d. John Richard and Alice Alzina (Campbell) MacDonald; m. Charles A. Latham, Nov. 19, 1938 (div. June 1966); 1 son, Richard E. AA, Grays Harbor Coll., 1937; student U. Wash., 1938-39; BS in Home Econs., U. Idaho, 1956; MS in Home Econs. Edn., 1965. Buyer, Fredrick & Nelson, 1938; tchr. Buhl (Idaho) High Sch., 1943-64; grad. asst., vis. prof. U. Idaho, 1964-65; asst. state supr. home econs. Idaho Bd. for Vocat. Edn., Boise, 1965-72, acting state supr., 1972-73, state supr. home econs. edn., 1973-83, ret., 1983; exec. sec. Idaho Vocat. Assn., 1983—. Bd. dirs. Future Homemakers Am., 1966-68, 76-78; circle pres. First Methodist Ch., 1974. Recipient hon. chpt. degree Idaho Assn., Future Homemakers Am., 1955, hon. state degree, 1956; disting. service award, Future Homemakers Am. 1985, Idaho Vocat. Assn., 1985; named Outstanding Buhl Bus. Women, 1958; Iowa State U. fellow, 1967; Mich. State U. fellow, 1969. Mem. Home Econs. Edn. Assn., Am. Vocat. Assn., Am. Home Econs. Assn., Nat. Assn. State Suprs. Home Econs. (pres. 1975), Idaho Home Econs. Assn. (pres. 1974-75), Boise C. of C. (sec. women's div. 1969), Idaho Pub. Employees Assn. (sec. River Run chpt. 1985-88, v.p. 1988-89), Phi Omicron Upsilon, Delta Kappa Gamma. Methodist.

LATHAM, EMILEIGH MAXWELL, communications executive; b. Pink Hill, N.C., Oct. 26, 1923; d. Hugh Edgar and Emily (Turner) M.; m. Herald Rowe Latham, May 26, 1951; children—Lynn Corbell, Diann, Herald Jeffrey Student, U. N.C., 1940-42, BA in Journalism, 1944. News dir. Sta WTAR-AM-FM-TV Norfolk, Va., 1947-51, pub. relations mgr. products div. Holiday Inns, Inc., Memphis, 1972-74; community relations dir. Sta. WKNO-TV-FM, Memphis, 1974-76; project coordinator Auction, Sta. WNET, N.Y.C., 1977; asst. dir. community relations L.I. Coll. Hosp., Bklyn., 1978; asst. dir. public affairs Fairfax Hosp. Assn., Springfield, Va., 1981-83; pub. relations coordinator Inova Home Care, Springfield, Va., 1983—. Editor: Pacesetter, Holiday Inns, Inc., 1973; Healthline, L.I. Coll. Hosp., 1978. Mem. Women in Communications Inc. Methodist. Club: No. Va. Press. Home: 5303 Queensberry Ave Springfield VA 22151 Office: 8003 Forbes Pl Suite 200 Springfield VA 22151

LATHAM, GERDA JEKSTIES, writer; b. Koenigsberg, German Democratic Republic, Aug. 22, 1912; came to U.S., 1923; d. Johannes and Gertrude Maria Augusta (Bender) Jeksties; m. George Henry Latham, Oct. 19, 1944 (dec. 1964); children: George Henry Jr., (step) Dorothy Agnew Latham. Fund raiser Meml. Hosp., Wilmington, Del., 1945—; pres. Ch. Women United Del., 1961-63, Am. Bapt. Chs. Del., 1964-68, Am. Bapt. Women, 1968-71; treas. Delmarva Ecumenical Agy., 1978-82; guide Longwood Gardens, Kennett Sq., Pa., 1964-79. Author: Gardening in Two Worlds, 1986, Legacy from DE Women, 1987. Initiated community transp. service for the elderly, 1981. Mem. Nat. Assn. Am. Pen Women (diamond state chpt. publicity chmn. 1985—), Canterbury Garden Club (pres./treas. 1963-66), Flower Show Judges Council (sec. 1985-86), Del. Valley Writers' Workshop. Home: 2012 Silverside Rd Wilmington DE 19810

LATHAM, MARY ELIZABETH, clergywoman; b. Cin.; d. Lawrence Lorenzo and Eugenia (Peters) Latham; B.A. cum laude, Asbury Coll., 1929. Tchr. math. and Latin, McAfee High Sch., Mercer County, Ky., 1929-32; entered ministry of evangelism Ch. of the Nazarene, 1933, ordained to ministry, 1937; traveled in work of evangelism and Christian edn., 1937-48; internat. dir. vacation Bible schs. Dept. Ch. Schs., Kansas City, Mo., 1948-67; dir. audiovisuals Ch. of the Nazarene, 1962-74; chmn. audiovisual com. Council of Chs. Greater Kansas City, 1955-58, chmn. com. on communications edn., 1966-67; chmn. Latham Communications, 1975—; also lectr. Recipient Albert F. Harper award Adult Ministries, Ch. of Nazarene, 1980. Author: Vacation Bible School, Why, What, and How, 1954, 9th rev. edit., 1968; Adventures with Jesus, 1948, rev. edits., 1951, 54, 57, 60, 63; Teacher, You Are an Evangelist, rev. edit., 1977; contbr. numerous covers and articles to periodicals; dir. prodn. films The Great Transition, motion picture of Nazarene Colls., 1964; Sing His Wonderful Name, 1965; Would You Believe It?, 1967; The Debtors and They Do Not Wait, 1968; The Way Out and God's Word for Today's World, 1969; Moving Ahead, 1970; Just for the Love of It, 1971; To Make a Miracle, 1972; To New Worlds, 1972; The Church of the Nazarene, 1974; The Alabaster Story, 1974; dir. filmstrips with cassettes How Young Is Our Welcome? and What Made the Orange Go Away?, 1976; producer videotape Roy T. Williams-The Man, The Leader, 1983. Address: 10268 Cedarbrooke Ln Kansas City MO 64131

LATHOM, PATRICIA G., advertising and marketing systems executive; b. San Francisco, Oct. 30, 1925; d. A.S. and Ethelyn (Ross) Green; m. J.W. Lathom, Sept. 15, 1945 (div. Nov. 1965); children: Jan W., Christina R. Student, Scripps Coll., 1943-44; BA, Calif. State U., Los Angeles, 1969, postgrad., 1969-71; adult ednl. credential, UCLA, 1972; postgrad., San Francisco Theol. Sem., 1981—. Cert. in consumer sci., home econs., sociology, adult edn., social sci., systems research. Customer service rep. Western Lithograph Co., Los Angeles, 1956-57; west coast office mgr. Revere Corp. Am., Los Angeles, 1957-60; tchr. Glendora (Calif.) Adult Sch., 1973-75; moderator Smokenders, Los Angeles, 1976-80; regional mgr. World Wide Services, San Marino, Calif., 1981-84; franchise owner Successful Living, Inc. div. David C. Cook Pub. Co., Mpls., 1980—; owner, mgr. Lathom Assocs., San Marino, 1967—. Chmn. Community Chest, Monterey Park, Calif., 1953-54; pres. Repetto PTA, Monterey Park, 1955-56; charter mem. Reagan Presdl. Task Force, 1982-88, trustee, 1986-88; sponsor The Ronald Reagan Presdl. Found., 1987-88. Recipient Key Woman award, Inglewood Jr. Chamber Aux, 1953, Monterey Park Jr. Chamber Aux, 1955, Community Chest div. chmn. awards, 1953, 54, fellowship Internat. Biog. Assn., London, Eng., 1975. Mem. Nat. Assn. Female Execs., Mus. Contemporary Arts, Found. for Community Artists, Am. Soc. Profl. and Exec. Women, Soc. for Advancement Mgmt. (v.p. 1964-65, exec. cons. 1965-66ú, Phi Upsilon Omicron, Alpha Kappa Delta. Presbyterian. Home: 1925 Kerns Ave San Marino CA 91108 Office: Lathom Assocs 1613 Chelsea Rd Suite 123 San Marino CA 91108

LATHROP, GERTRUDE ADAMS, chemist, consultant; b. Norwich, Conn., Apr. 28, 1921; d. Williams Barrows and Lena (Adams) L. B.S., U. Conn., 1944; M.A., Tex. Woman's U., 1953, Ph.D., 1955. Devel. chemist on textiles/Alexander Smith & Sons Carpet Co. Yonkers, N.Y., 1944-52; research assoc. textiles Tex. Woman's U., 1952-56; chief chemist Glasgo Finishing Plant div. United Mchts. & Mfrs., Inc., Conn., 1956-57; chief chemist Old Fort Finishing Plant div. United Mchts. & Mfrs., Inc., N.C., 1957-63; research chemist United Mchts. Research Ctr., Langley, S.C., 1963-64; lab. mgr. automotive div. Collins & Aikman Corp., Albemarle, N.C., 1964-78; chief chemist, lab. mgr. Old Fort Finishing Plant div. United Mchts., 1979-82. Treas. First Congregational Ch., Asheville, N.C., 1985-87; tax-aide counselor IRS, Am. Retired People for Elderly, pub. relations com., Swannanoa Valley, N.C., 1984—. Recipient Disting. Alumni award U. Conn. Sch. Home Econs. and Family Studies, 1980-81. Mem. Am. Chem. Soc., Am. Assn. Textile Chemists and Colorists (sect. research chmn., treas., vice chmn. 1962-64; chmn. edn. com. Piedmont sect. 1977-78), ASTM (chmn. transp. fabrics on flammability com. 1973-75), Bus. and Profl. Women's Club (pres. chpt. 1974-76, Woman of Yr. 1979, 80), Iota Sigma Pi. Home: 301 Mountain St Black Mountain NC 28711

LATHROP, LORI, theatrical producer, director, actress. BA in Bus Adminstrn., Western Ill. U. Founder, co-producer, promotion/publicity dir., bus. mgr. Saturday Night Leftovers, Metrolina's Off-Broadway Theatre Co., Concord, N.C., 1986—. Dir., publicity and props, actress A Coupla White Chicks Sitting Around Talking; publicity and props: Rattlesnake in a Cooler, Charlotte, 1986, Glengarry Glen Ross, Seascape with Sharks and Dancer, To Gillian on Her 37th Birthday, Orphans, Ladies at the Alamo, Steambath, Charlotte, 1987; appeared in various regional theater plays including Cactus Flower, Phila., Here I Come, Twelfth Night, Midsummer Night's Dream, Inherit the Wind (1978-85), Mornings at Seven, 1981, Bedroom Farce, 1983, An Ounce of Prevention, 1984, Octette Bridge Club, 1987; playwright: Blithe Shadows in the Nightshade, The Wives of Willobie. Chmn. fundraising com. Golden Circle Theatre, 1985-86, pres. bd. dirs., 1986; bd. dirs. Playwrights Forum, Charlotte, 1981-83. Home and Office: Saturday Night Leftovers 282 S Union St Concord NC 28025

LATHROP, WENDY PAM, surveyor; b. Hollywood, Calif., Feb. 10, 1952; d. Paul Alan and Martha Sheila (Robinson) L. BA in Visual Arts and Spanish, Albion Coll., 1973. Cert. land surveyor, planner, N.J., Pa. With drafting sect. Deleuw-Cather, Phila., 1974-75, Franklin and Lindsey Inc., Phila., 1975-77; with surveying, drafting, inspection sects. Thomas Tyler Moore Assocs., West Trenton, N.J., 1977-81, pres. Ms Tech. Cons. subs., 1983-85; surveyor Nassau Surveying, and affiliate cos. Chyun Assoc., Van Note-Harvey Assocs., Princeton, N.J., 1981-83; coordinator survey dept. Lord, Anderson, Worrell and Barnett, Lumberton, N.J., 1986; office mgr., chief surveyor David E. Goldenbaum Assocs., Lambertville, N.J., 1986-88; assoc. and chief surveyor MAP Surveying, Lebanon, N.J., 1988—. Contbr. articles to profl. jours. Mem. South Trenton Area Residents. Mem. Am. Congress on Surveying and Mapping, Nat. Soc. Profl. Surveyors, Forum for Women in Surveying (co-founder 1983), N.J. Soc. Profl. Land Surveyors (various com. chairs, Profl. of the Month award 1983), Profl. Land Surveyors Assn. of N.J. (recording sec. 1984, 85, pres. 1986, 87), Pa. Soc. Land Surveyors (corresponding mem.), World Tang Soo Do Assn., Nat. Women's Martial Arts Fedn., Phi Beta Kappa. Democrat. Jewish. Home: 974 Lamberton St Trenton NJ 08611

LATIMER, CYNTHIA LESETTE, teacher; b. Chgo., Mar. 14, 1958; d. Harold Augustus and Ina Pearl (Humphrey) L. BE, Ill. State U., 1980; ME, No. Ill. U., 1988. Cert. learning disability, social/emotional disorders, ednl. adminstrn., Ill. Tchr. learning disability East Aurora Sch. Dist 131, Aurora, Ill., 1981, West Aurora Sch. Dist. 129, Aurora, 1981—; cons., evalutator learning disability Wheaton, Ill., 1986—. Ill. Tchr. Spl. Edn. scholar, 1976.

Mem. Ill. Edn. Assn. (lobbyist 1981—, congl. contract team 1987—, vice sectional chmn. 1987—), Aurora Edn. Assn. (sec.. 1985-87, Aurora Edn. Assn.-West (sec. 1985—), Nat. Assn. Female Execs., Kappa Delta Pi. Democrat. Presbyterian. Home: 1228 Downing Ct Wheaton IL 60187 Office: Abraham Lincoln Elem Sch 641 S Lake St Aurora IL 60506

LATIMER, SUZANNE LOUISE, hospital administrator; b. Albany, N.Y., Mar. 3, 1954; d. Olin Kenneth and Madeline Louise (Weeks) Latimer; R.N., Albany Med. Center Sch. Nursing, 1975; B.S.N., Russell Sage Coll., 1981, M.S. in Health Services Adminstrn., 1984. Gen. staff nurse labor and delivery Albany (N.Y.) Med. Center, 1975-81; physician's asst. Bellevue Maternity Hosp., Schenectady, 1979, interim dir. nursing, 1980, adminstrv. asst. to adminstr., 1980-82, quality assurance coordinator, 1980—, dir. patient support services, 1982-88, dir. quality mgmt., 1988—, risk mgr., 1983—. Vol., educator Am. Cancer Soc., 1975—; vol., instr., ARC, 1980—; mem. Anesthesia Patient Safety Found., 1986—; bd. dirs. YWCA, Albany. Mem. Am. Soc. Health Care Risk Mgrs., Nat. Commn. for Certification of Physician's Assts., N.Y. State Assn. Quality Assurance Profls., Nat. Assn. Quality Assurance Profls., Am. Mgmt. Assn., Am. Acad. Physician's Assts., Assn. Hosp.Risk Mgmt. of N.Y., Nat. Assn. Female Execs., Nat. Fire Protection Agy., Am. Pub. Health Assn., N.Y. State Pub. Health Assn. Democrat. Roman Catholic. Home: 902 N Brandywine Ave Schenectady NY 12308 Office: 2210 Troy Rd PO Box 1030 Schenectady NY 12301

LATIOLAIS, MINNIE FITZGERALD, nurse, hospital administrator; b. Vivian, La., Dec. 26, 1921; d. Thomas Ambrose and Mildred Surita (Nagle) Fitzgerald; RN, Touro Infirmary, New Orleans, 1943; m. Joseph C. Latiolais, Jr., July 19, 1947; children—Felisa, Diana, Sylvia, Mary, Amelia, Joseph Clifton, III. Orthopedic surg. nurse Ochsner Clinic, New Orleans, 1943-47, asst. dir. nursing, 1947; supr. Lafayette (La.) Gen. Hosp., 1960-64; adminstrv. asst., supr. operating room Abbeville (La.) Gen. Hosp., 1964-68; gen. mgr., neurol. surg. nurse J. Robert Rivet, neurol. surgeon, Lafayette, 1968-78; hosp. cons. asso. B.J. Landry & Assos., hosps. cons., Lafayette, 1979—; dir. nursing Acadia St. Landry Hosp., Church Point, 1981-82; supr. supplies, processing and distbn. Univ. Med. Ctr., Lafayette, 1982—; bd. dirs. SW La. Rehab. Assn., 1975—, pres., 1979-80; mem. Mid-La. Health Systems Agy., 1977-82, project rev. chmn., 1978-80; vice chmn. Acadica Regional Clearing House, 1984-88; mem. crafts and practical nurse com. Lafayette Regional Vocat.-Tech. Inst., 1980-84, chmn. 1983-84. Mem. Am. Nurses Assn., La. State Nurses Assn., Lafayette Dist. Nurses Assn. (pres. 1967-69). Roman Catholic. Clubs: Lafayette Woman's, Lafayette Garden. Home: 1121 S Washington St Lafayette LA 70501

LATNER, SELMA, psychoanalyst; b. Bronx, N.Y., Aug. 11, 1920; d. Isidore and Jennie (Reisman) Levy; m. Harold Latner, Mar. 23, 1959 (dec. 1972); children—Gail, Karen, Irwin. B.B.A., CCNY, 1942; M.S.W., U. Pitts., 1945; Ph.D. in Psychoanalysis, Heed U., 1984. Bd. cert. psychoanalyst; diplomate in clin. social work. Lic. marriage and family therapist, N.J. Caseworker, Jewish Family Service, N.Y.C., 1949-53, Community Service Soc., Queens, N.Y., 1950's; sr. caseworker Jewish Family Services, Hackensack, N.J., 1965-68; sr. family and marriage therapist Bergen County Family Counseling Service, Hackensack, 1968-83; pvt. practice psychoanalyst, Teaneck, N.J., 1981—; Bd. dirs. Am. Anorexic and Bulimia Assn., Teaneck, 1984-88. Recipient plaque for Outstanding Profl. Human Services, Am. Acad. Human Services, 1974-75. Mem. Nat. Alliance Family Life, Nat. Assn. Social Work (gold card mem.), Am. Anorexia and Bulimia Assn. (v.p.), N.J. Soc. Clin. Social Work, Nat. Assn. Advancement Psychoanalysis, N.J. Inst. Tng. Psychoanalysis. Avocations: tennis; music; dance forms; art. Home: 416 Beatrice St Teaneck NJ 07666

LATTA, DIANA LENNOX, interior designer; b. Lahaina, Maui, Hawaii, Aug. 5, 1936; d. D. Stewart and Jean Marjorie (Anderson) Lennox; grad. the Bishop's Sch., La Jolla, Calif., 1954; student U. Wash., 1954-56; m. Arthur McKee Latta, Jan. 26, 1957 (dec.); children—Mary-Stewart, Marion Mckee (Mrs. Marshall V. Davidson). Dir., Vero Beach (Fla.) br. of Wellington Hall, Ltd., Thomasville, N.C., 1970-72; asst. to chief designer Rablen-West Interiors, Vero Beach, 1972-75; design and adminstrv. asst. to pres. Design Studio Archtl. & Interior Design Concepts, Inc., Vero Beach, 1975-82; owner, designer The Designery, Vero Beach, 1983-87; designer's asst. Frank J. Lincoln Interiors, Inc., Locust Valley and Vero Beach, N.Y., 1987—. Mem. Indian River Meml. Hosp. Women's Aux., Vero Beach, 1957-70, chmn. Charity Ball, 1960, v.p., 1962-64; leading actress in Vero Beach Theatre Guild prodns.: The Laughmaker, 1964, Oklahoma, 1966; model for Holly Fashion Show, Vero Beach, 1962-69; mem. adv. bd. Indian River County 4-H Horsemaster's Club, 1973-76; chmn. fund raising, pub. relations com. McKee Jungle Gardens Preservation Soc., Inc., bd. dirs., Vero Beach Mut. Concert Assn., 1973-76, chmn. hospitality com. 1974; bd. dirs. Vero Beach Theatre Guild, 1964. Mem. Internat. Platform Assn., Republican Women Aware. Kappa Kappa Gamma. Republican. Episcopalian. Club: Riomar Bay Yacht (club tennis champion 1964, 66, chmn. tennis com. 1964-66). Home: 555 Honeysuckle Ln Vero Beach FL 32963 Office: 6160 North A1A Vero Beach FL 32963

LAU, ELIZABETH MARTINEZ, sales, public relations and marketing executive, researcher; b. Bayamo, Oriente, Cuba, Nov. 17, 1951; came to U.S., 1967; d. Jose Ramon and Roselvi Kathy (Lau) M.; m. Jose Ramon Argiz, Aug. 9, 1952 (div.); m. Justo Ernesto Montero, Nov. 7, 1950. Student Miami Dade Jr. Coll., 1973-75, U. Miami, 1985—. Exec. sec. Union Fin., Miami, Fla., 1972-75; export sales mgr. Inter City Auto Stores, Miami, 1975-80; salesman A.G.E. Paper, Miami, 1982—. Mem. Nat. Assn. Female Execs., Pacific Inst. Alumni Assn. Republican. Roman Catholic.

LAUBE-MORGAN, JERRI, university dean, nursing educator; b. Terre Haute, Ind., July 1, 1928; d. George J. and Martell (McBride) DeWald; m. William B. Laube, Aug. 8, 1947 (dec. Feb. 1979); children—Stephen William, Joan Martelle; m. Cecil J. Morgan, Feb. 14, 1983. B.S. in Nursing and Psychology, U. Tenn., 1961; M.S. in Nursing, U. Colo., 1969; Ph.D., Tex. Woman's U., 1974. Instr. St. Joseph Sch. Nursing, Memphis, 1957-62, St. Paul Sch. Nursing, Dallas, 1962-67; asst. and assoc. prof. nursing Baylor U., 1969-74; therapist Indpls. Inst. of T.A., Inc., 1974-80, prof. sch. nursing Ind. U., 1974-80; prof., asst. dean U. So. Miss., Hattiesburg, 1980-81, prof., dean, 1981—. Author: Perspectives of Disaster Recovery, 1985; contbr. articles to profl. jours. Mem. Gov's. commn. Children and Youth, Miss., 1983—; bd. dirs. So. Miss. chpt ARC, Hattiesburg, 1987—. Fellow Am. Acad. Nursing; mem. Am. Nurses' Assn., Council Specialists in Psychiat./Mental Health Nursing, Am. Psychol. Assn., Am. Group Psychotherapy Assn., Am. Assn. Marriage and Family Therapists, Nat. League for Nursing, Sigma Theta Tau. Episcopalian. Club: Altrusa. Home: 710 Edgewood Dr Hattiesburg MS 39401 Office: U So Miss Sch Nursing So Sta Box 5095 Hattiesburg MS 39406

LAUBER, MIGNON DIANE, food processing company executive; b. Detroit, Dec. 21; d. Charles Edmond and Maud Lillian (Foster) Donaker; student Kelsey Jenny U., 1958, Brigham Young U., 1959; m. Richard Brian Lauber, Sept. 13, 1963; 1 dau., Leslie Viane (dec.). Owner, operator Alaska World Travel, Ketchikan, 1964-67; founder, owner, pres. Oosick Soup Co., Juneau, Alaska, 1969—. Treas., Pioneer Alaska Lobbyists Soc., Juneau, 1977—. Mem. Bus. and Profl. Women, Alaska C. of C. Libertarian. Club: Washington Athletic. Author: Down at the Water Works with Jesus, 1982; Failure Through Prayer, 1983. Home: 321 Highland Dr Juneau AK 99801 Office: PO Box 1625 Juneau AK 99802

LAUCKS, EULAH CROSON, educational foundation executive; b. Gold Hill, Nev., Oct. 23, 1909; d. George Edward and Nettie (Lagomarsino) Croson; m. Irving Fink Laucks, Nov. 9, 1942 (dec. Mar. 1981); 1 child, Mary Lisa. A.B. cum laude, U. Wash., 1938; Ph.D., U. Calif.-Santa Barbara, 1978. Promotional writer Laucks Lab., Inc., Seattle, 1938-42; pres. Laucks Found., Inc., Santa Barbara, 1978—. Author: The Meaning of Children, 1981; also articles in mags., chpt. in book. Bd. dirs. Ctr. for Study Democratic Instns., 1965-79. Mem. Women In Communications, Inc. (life).

LAUDER, ESTEE, cosmetics company executive; b. N.Y.C.; m. Joseph Lauder; children: Leonard, Ronald. LLD (hon.), U. Pa., 1986. Chmn. bd. Estee Lauder Inc., 1946—. Author: Estee: A Success Story, 1985. Named One of 100 Women of Achievement Harpers Bazaar, 1967, Top Ten Outstanding Women in Business, 1970; recipient Neiman-Marcus Fashion award, 1962; Spirit of Achievement award Albert Einstein Coll. Medicine, 1968; Kaufmann's Fashion Fortnight award, 1969; Bamberger's Designer's award, 1969; Gimbel's Fashion Forum award, 1969; Internat. Achievement award Frost Bros., 1971; Pogue's Ann. Fashion award, 1975, Golda Meir 90th Anniversary Tribute award, 1988; decorated chevalier Legion of Honor France, 1978; medaille de Vermeil de la Ville de Paris, 9, 1979; 4th Ann. award for Humanitarian Service Girls' Club N.Y., 1979; 25th Anniversary award Greater N.Y. council Boy Scouts Am., 1979; L.S. Ayres award, 1981; Achievement award Girl Scouts U.S.A., 1983; Outstanding Mother award, 1984; Athena award, 1985; honored Lincoln Ctr., World of Style, 1986. Office: Estee Lauder Inc 767 Fifth Ave New York NY 10153

LAUDER, VALARIE ANNE, editor, educator; b. Detroit, Mar. 1, 1926; d. William J. and Murza Valerie (Mann) L.; AA, Stephens Coll., Columbia, Mo., 1944; postgrad. Northwestern U. With Chgo. Daily News, 1944-52, columnist, 1946-52; lectr. Sch. Assembly Service, also Redpath lectr., 1952-55; freelance writer for mags. and newspapers including N.Y. Times, Yankee, Ford Times, Travel & Leisure, Am. Heritage, 1955—; editor-in-chief Scholastic Roto, 1962; editor U. N.C., 1975-80, lectr. Sch. Journalism, 1980—; nat. chmn. student writing project Ford Times, 1981-86; pub. relations dir. Am. Dance Festival, Duke U., 1982-83, lectr., instr. continuing edn. program, 1984; contbg. editor So. Accents mag., 1982-86. Mem. nat. fund raising bd. Kennedy Ctr., 1962-63. Recipient 1st place award Nat. Fedn. Press Women, 1981; 1st place awards Ill. Women's Press Assn., 1950, 1951. Mem. Pub. Relations Soc. Am. (treas. N.C. chpt. 1982, sec. 1983, v.p. 1984, pres. 1986, chmn. council of past pres., chmn. 25th Ann. event 1987, del. Nat. Assembly 1988—), Women in Communications (v.p. matrix N.C. Triangle chpt. 1984-85), N.C. Pub. Relations Hall of Fame Com., DAR, Soc. Mayflower Desc. (dir. Ill. Soc. 1946-52), Chapel Hill Hist. Soc. (dir. 1981-85, chmn. publs. com. 1980-85), Chapel Hill Preservation Soc. Clubs: N.C. Press (2d v.p. 1983-85, pres. 1985, 1st pl. awards 1981, 82, 83, 84), Univ. Woman's, Women's Press N.C. (3d v.p. 1981-83, 1st pl. awards 1981, 82). Office: U NC CB #3365 Chapel Hill NC 27599-3365

LAUDONE, ANITA H., lawyer, business executive; b. 1948; m. Colin E. Harley; children: Clayton T. Harley, Victoria Spencer Harley. B.A., Conn. Coll., 1970; J.D., Columbia U., 1973. Admitted to N.Y. State bar, 1974, practiced in N.Y.C., 1973-79; asst. sec. Phelps Dodge Corp., N.Y.C., 1979-80, sec., 1980-84, v.p., sec., 1984-85. Editor Columbia Law Rev., 1973. Mem. Phi Beta Kappa. Address: 510 North St Greenwich CT 06830

LAUENSTEIN, ANN GAIL, librarian; b. Milw., Nov. 8, 1949; d. Elmer Lester Herbert and Elizabeth Renatta (Bovee) Zaeske. B.A., U. Wis.-Madison, 1971, M.A., 1972. Asst. librarian U. Wis.-Wausau, 1972-73; cataloger, librarian MacMurray Coll., Jacksonville, Ill., 1973-76; corp. librarian Anheuser-Busch Co., Inc., St. Louis, 1976—; facilitator Anheuser-Busch Quality Circle, St. Louis, 1984—; Sec. Friends of Kirkwood Library, 1986—; mem. adv. council Sch. Info. Sci. U. Mo., 1987—. Mem. Spl. Libraries Assn. (network liason 1981-83, chmn. employment com. 1983-84, chmn. hospitality com. 1984-85), St. Louis Regional Library Network (council 1981-83), St. Louis Online Users Group, AAUW (editor jour. 1981-84, publicity chmn. 1985-87, scholar 1984), Women in Bus. Network (adv. panel 1980-82, 86-87, programs planner 1987-88), Ohio Coll. Library Consortium Acquisitions Users Council. Avocation: stamp collecting. Office: Anheuser-Busch Co Inc One Busch Pl Saint Louis MO 63118

LAUFENBERG, TERRE LYNN, insurance company executive; b. Madison, Wis., Dec. 26, 1951; d. Roy Charles and Ruth Marie (McCloskey) Pierstorff; m. Gary Peter Laufenberg, Feb. 15, 1969; children: Amie, Monte, Tawna. Sales agt. Bankers Life and Casualty, Madison, 1977-80, mgr., 1981-84; br. mgr. Bankers Life and Casualty, Peoria, 1984—. Office: Bankers Life and Casualty 4300 N Brandywine Peoria IL 61614

LAUFER, BEATRICE, composer; b. N.Y.C.; d. Samuel and Fanny (Silverman) L.; m. Theodore Lassoff, Oct. 2, 1940 (dec. 1955); 1 child, Samuel; m. Seymour H. Rinzler, Oct. 19, 1969 (dec. 1970). Student Julliard Sch. Music, 1944. Composer: Symphony No. 1 (performed by Eastman-Rochester Symphony Orch., 1945-46, performance Germany and Japan under auspices of State Dept., 1948, performed by Nat. Gallery Orch., Washington, 1982), Dance Festival (performed by Eastman-Rochester Symphony, 1946-47); choral compositions include: Under the Pines, Spring Thunder performed Tanglewood, 1949, Song of the Fountain, inter-racial chorus, UN Freedom celebration, 1952; Small Concerto for Chamber Orch. performed McMillan Theatre, Columbia, 1949-50, Ile, opera, world premiere Royal Opera Co., Stockholm, Sweden, 1958, recorded by Yale U. Orch. 1978, Broadcast Nat. Pub. Radio, 1980, 87; Second Symphony performed by Oklahoma City Orch., 1961; premiere concerto at Donnell Library Ctr., 1962; premiere performance Prelude and Fugue for Orch., Brevard Music Ctr., N.C., 1964, Cry! orchestral prelude, Orch. of Am., Town Hall, 1966, Lyric string trio, Bowdoin Coll. Contemporary Music Festival, 1966, performed with Eastman-Rochester Symphony, 1968, Shreveport Symphony Orch., 1978, Berkshire Symphony Orch., 1981; In the Throes performed Shreveport Symphony, 1980, New Orleans Symphony Orch., 1982, Berkshire Symphony Orch., 1985; Conn. Found. of Arts grantee for performance And Thomas Jefferson Said (symphonic version performed by S.W. Floridan Symphony Orch., 1987), Norwalk Symphony Orch., 1976, 3 excerpts performed by USAF Chamber Players, Washington, 1985, premiere version for concert band baritone solo performed by The Goldman Meml. Band, 1986, also at the Aspen (Colo.) Music Festival, 1987, orchestral performance We Hold These Truths, S.W. Fla. Symphony, Nov. 1987; premiere opera Ile performed by Shanghai (Peoples Republic of China) Opera House, 1988; master ceremonies Young Am. Artists, radio sta. WNYC; hostess The Conductor Speaks series sta. WNYC. Mem. ASCAP, Am. Symphony Orch. League, Am. Music Ctr. Address: PO Box 3 Lenox Hill Sta New York NY 10021

LAUGHLIN, ALICE MARGARET, chemistry educator; b. Malone, N.Y., Feb. 19, 1918; d. John and Rose Ellen (Murray) L. BS, St. Joseph Coll., West Hartford, Conn., 1949; MS, U. Vt., 1954; EdD, Columbia U., 1965; postgrad., Fordham U., 1971-76. Lab. technician S.I. Hosp., 1949-50; teaching asst. U. Vt., 1950-52; asst. biochemist Vt. Agrl. Expt. Sta., 1952-56; research chemist Nat. Biscuit Co., 1956-57; research asst. hematology and chemotherapy Columbia-Presbyn. Med. Ctr., N.Y.C., 1957-61; instr. sci. Sch. Nursing, St. Michael Hosp., Newark, 1961-62; asst. prof. Jersey City State Coll., 1962-67, assoc. prof., 1967-74, chmn. dept., 1969-70, prof. chemistry dept., 1974—; resource mem. cons. meeting on chem. curriculum in jr. coll. NSF, 1969; resource mem. long range planning bd. Sch. Nursing St. Francis Hosp., Jersey City, 1963—. Revisor: Roe's Principles of Chemistry, 12th edit., 1976; mem. editorial panel Mosby's Comprehensive Rev. of Nursing, 8th edit., 1974. Mem. Am. Chem. Soc. (sec. Hudson Bergen br. 1971-72, bd. dirs. 1972-73, 87-88), Am. Microchem. Soc., Am. Assn. Cereal Chemists, Am. Inst. Chemists, Am. Assn. Clin. Chemists, Am. Soc. Med. Techonologists, AAUP, N.J. Soc. Med. Technologists (sci. assembly person biochemistry 1976-78, 79-80), N.Y. Acad. Sci., N.J. Acad. Sci., AAUW (chair Jersey City br. 1987—), Iota Sigma Pi. Home: 1225 76th St North Bergen NJ 07047 Office: Jersey City State Coll Chemistry Dept Jersey City NJ 07305

LAUGHLIN, JUDITH ANN, computer consulting executive; b. Buffalo, Dec. 13, 1947; d. Eugene M. and Catherine L. (Ryan) Larouere; B.S. in Nursing, D'Youville Coll., 1969; M.S. in Community Health Nursing, SUNY, Buffalo, 1972, Ph.D. in Orgnl. Communication and Policy, 1980; m. Daniel E. Laughlin, July 29, 1967. Public health nurse Erie County Health Dept., 1969-70; gen. duty nurse psychiatry E.J. Meyer Hosp., Buffalo, 1971; coordinator lead detection and prevention program Erie County Health Dept., 1972-73; public health nurse cons. Erie County Dept. Mental Health, 1973-75; dir. Erie County Dept. Anti-Rape and Sexual Assault, 1975-77; asst. prof., area dir. health planning and mgmt., nursing SUNY, Buffalo, 1977-81, now clin. assoc. prof.; dir. human resources Am. Precision Industries, Inc., Buffalo, 1981-82; owner Mgmt. Devel. Group, Buffalo, 1982-85; dir. nursing services, dir. ednl. services Upstate N.Y. Mgmt. Cons. Practice, Ernst & Whinney, Buffalo, 1985-87; v.p. Computer Professionals Unltd., Inc., Buffalo, 1987—; mgmt. cons. Chmn. Erie County Victim/Witness Coordination Bd., 1978-85; bd. dirs. Buffalo chpt. ARC, 1978-83, chmn. tng. and devel. com., 1979-83; chmn. Erie County Sexual Assault Task Force, 1974; mem. Erie County Energy Com., 1973; chmn. Image of Nursing Speakers Bur., 1983—; bd. dirs. Niagara Frontier Rehab. Ctr., 1987—; vol. Am. Lung Assn., 1983-87. Recipient awards for county programs, resolution for leadership in victim services Erie County Legislature, 1979, Disting. Alumni award 50th Anniversary SUNY, 1986. Am. Nurses Assn., N.Y. Nurses Assn. (bd. dirs.), Internat. Communications Assn., N.Y. State Public Health Assn., Nat. Orgn. Victim Assistance, Sigma Theta Tau, Pi Lambda Theta. Contbr. articles to profl. jours. Home: PO Box 211 Wales Center NY 14169 Office: Computer Profls Unltd PO Box 102 Springbrook NY 14140

LAUGHLIN, KATHLEEN PATRICIA, public agency administrator; b. Framingham, Mass., Aug. 24, 1957; d. Daniel Richard and Patricia Ann (Hogan) L. BA, Coll. of Holy Cross, 1979; M in Pub. Adminstrn., Columbia U., 1981. Asst. dir. support ops. budget unit N.Y.C. Bd. Edn., 1981-83, exec. asst. div. spl. edn., 1984-85, dep. budget dir. div. spl. edn., 1985-87, exec. asst. div. sch. bldgs., 1987—. Mem. Publicworks Forum, 1983—; women's advisor Mayor's Women's Advisor Program, N.Y.C., 1985-87. U.S. Dept. Edn. fellow, 1979, 80. Mem. Mary Anthony Dance Theatre Found. (treas., bd. dirs. 1986—). Democrat. Roman Catholic. Office: NYC Bd Edn Div Sch Bldgs 28-11 Queens Plaza N Long Island City NY 11101

LAUGHLIN, MARILYN JEAN, financial services company executive; b. Chgo., Mar. 27, 1936; d. Herman William and Alice (Donahue) Bendig; diploma in reins., Coll. Ins., N.Y.C., 1977; m. Terry Laughlin, May 14, 1966. From sec. to reins. adminstr. CNA Ins. Co., 1956—; v.p. Laughlin Assos., Inc., Roselle, Ill., 1972—. Mem. Nat. Assn. Female Execs. Roman Catholic. Home: 56 N Salt Creek Rd Roselle IL 60172 Office: CNA Plaza Chicago IL 60685

LAURENTS, LANI MARY, accountant, small business owner; b. Balt., May 20, 1938; d. Joseph Merrill Keenan and Frances (Dysier) Kay; m. Carl William Lewis, Dec. 4, 1954 (div. Mar. 1985); children: Lynn L. Edwards, Keenan William Lewis, Laura R. Chenault, Carol L. Lewis. Student, Del Mar Jr. Coll., San Jacinto Coll. Sr. clk. Shell Oil Co., Houston, 1974-76, acct. asst. clk., 1976-78, sr. acct. asst. clk., 1978-80, control acct., 1980-81, sect. supr., 1981-87, sr. fin. acct. head office, 1987—. Active Young Rep. Women, Corpus Christi, 1968. Roman Catholic. Home: 5918 San Felipe #4 Houston TX 77057 Office: Shell Oil Co PO Box 4405 Houston TX 77252

LAURICELLA, JANET MAY, executive director, cosmetics consultant; b. Fitchburg, Mass., Dec. 9, 1944; d. Ronald George and Pauline Janet (Perodeau) LeClair; m. David Lauricella, Apr. 3, 1987; children: Thomas II, Kristine, Beth, Robert, Heather, Cheryl. BA in Biology, Fitchburg State Coll., 1974, postgrad., 1974-80. Owner, operator Mrs. Connell's Nursery Sch., Westminster, Mass., 1980-82; assoc. dir. Mental Health Assn. North Cen. Mass., Fitchburg, 1982-83; job specialist Jobs for Bay State Grads., Fitchburg, 1983-84; state dir. student activities Jobs for Bay State Grads., Boston, 1984-87; exec. dir. United Way Greater Gardner, Mass., 1987—; beauty cons. Mary Kay Cosmetics, Westminster, 1987—; pres., bd. dirs. Mental Health Assn. North Cen. Mass., Fitchburg, 1985—. Contbr. articles to profl. jours. Past pres. Oakmont Music Parents Assn., Ashburnham, Mass., mem., 1985—; bd. dirs. Montachusett Girl Scouts Council, Worcester, Mass., 1987. Mem. Nat. Assn. Female Execs., Am. Soc. Tng. and Devel, Bus. and Profl. Women. Lutheran. Office: United Way of Greater Gardner 66 Parker St Gardner MA 01440

LAURIE, PIPER (ROSETTA JACOBS), actress; b. Detroit, Jan. 22, 1932; m. Joseph Morgenstern, 1962; 1 child. Acted in sch. plays; motion picture debut in Louisa; other motion pictures include The Milkman, Francis Goes to the Races, Prince Who Was A Thief, Son of Ali Baba, Has Anybody Seen My Gal, No Room for the Groom, Mississippi Gambler, Kelly and Me, Golden Blade, Dangerous Mission, Johnny Dark, Dawn at Socorro, Smoke Signal, Ain't Misbehavin', Until They Sail, The Hustler, Carrie, 1976, Tim, 1978, Return to Oz, 1985, Children of a Lesser God, 1986; TV appearances include Days of Wine and Roses, Playhouse 90, The Deaf Heart, The Ninth Day, G.E. Theatre, Play of the Week, Hallmark Hall of Fame, Nova: Margaret Sanger, The Woman Rebel, In the Matter of Karen Ann Quinlan, Rainbow, Skag, The Thorn Birds, 1983; TV films include The Bunker, 1981, Love, Mary, 1985, Mae West, 1985, Promise, 1986, Toughlove, 1985; appeared Broadway play Glass Menagerie, 1965, off-Broadway plays Rosemary and The Alligators, 1961. Acad. award nominee for the Hustler, 1962, Carrie, 1976; recipient Emmy award Acad. TV Arts and Scis., 1987. Mem. Acad. Motion Picture Arts and Scis. Address: care Triad Artists Inc 10100 Santa Monica Blvd 16th Floor Los Angeles CA 90067 *

LAURISKI, SUSAN CATHERINE, banker; b. Detroit, Dec. 3, 1945; d. Charles Louis III and Eleanor Marie (Henchel) Roehm; AS, Phoenix Coll., 1981; BA in Mgmt., U. Phoenix, 1986. Data processing specialist Detroit Bank & Trust Co., 1963-66; with First Nat. Bank of Ariz. (name changed to First Interstate Bank of Ariz. 1981), Phoenix, 1970—, br. mgr., 1980—, v.p., asst. div. v.p., 1982-85, v.p., br. loan adminstr., 1985, v.p., dept. head IRA dept., 1985-86, br. mgr., v.p., 1987—. Bd. dirs. Maricopa Camp Fire Council, Phoenix, 1981-84, Phoenix South Community Mental Ctr., 1988—; adv. Jr. Achievement, Phoenix, 1978-81; chmn. March of Dimes Walk-a-Thon, Phoenix, 1977-81. Nat. Assn. Bank Women Western Regional scholar, 1981-82. Mem. Nat. Assn. Bank Women (pres. state council 1984-85, mem. class VII Valley leadership program 1985-86, chmn. nat. conf.). Republican. Roman Catholic. Home: 315 W Edgemont St Phoenix AZ 85003 Office: 6695 W Bell Rd Glendale AZ 85308

LAURO, SHIRLEY MEZVINSKY, playwright, educator; b. Des Moines, Nov. 18, 1933; d. Phillip and Helen Frances (Davidson) Shapiro; m. Norton Mezvinsky, July 22, 1956 (div. 1967); 1 child, Andrea Mezvinsky; m. Louis Paul Lauro, Aug. 18, 1973. B.S. cum laude, Northwestern U., Evanston, Ill., 1955; M.S., U. Wis., 1957; postgrad. Columbia U., 1970-73. Instr. speech and theater CCNY, N.Y.C., 1967-71; instr. speech, theater and playwriting Yeshiva U., N.Y.C., 1971-76; instr. creative writing Manhattan Marymount Coll., N.Y.C., 1978-79; instr. speech and drama Manhattan Community Coll., N.Y.C., 1978-79; lit. cons. Ensemble Studio Theater, N.Y.C., 1975-80, prodn. critic, 1975—, mem. council, 1975—. Author novel: The Edge, 1965; author plays: The Contest (Nat. Found. for Jewish Culture playwright's award 1981), 1975; The Coal Diamond (Heidemann Prize Actors Theater of Louisville's Festival of New Am. Plays 1980, Best Short Plays of 1980), 1979; Open Admissions-one act version (N.Y. Dramatists Guild Hull-Warriner Playwrights award 1981, Samuel French Playwrights award 1979, Ten Best Plays of 1981 N.Y. Times), 1984; Nothing Immediate (Samuel French playwright's award 1979), 1979; Margargaret and Kit (nomination for Susan Blackburn Prize 1980), 1980; I Don't Know Where You're Coming From at All, 1979; In the Garden of Eden, 1984, Sunday Go To Meetin', 1987; Open Admissions-full length version (Tony nominee, Drama Desk nominee, Theater World award), 1984; Pearls on the Moon (Residency Alley Theater, 1987) 1987, A Piece of My Heart, 1988; author screenplay: Open Admissions (CBS-TV Network) 1988. N.Y. Found. Arts Playwright's fellow, 1985; John Guggenheim Playwrights fellow, 1986; NEA Playwrights fellow, 1987. Mem. PEN, Ensemble Studio Theater, League Profl. Theater Women (v.p.), Dramatists Guild, Authors League, Authors Guild, Writer's Guild. Democrat. Jewish. Office: Care Gilbert Parker William Morris Agy 1350 Ave of the Americas New York NY 10019

LAUTIERI, ANTOINETTE SYLVIA, marketing professional; b. Warwick, R.I., July 6, 1955; d. Rosindo and Luigia (DiCarlo) L.; m. Tullio D. Pitassi, July 21, 1985. BA in Math., Econs., R.I. Coll., 1977; MBA, Bryant Coll., 1984. Actuary asst. Amica Mut. Ins. Co., Providence, 1977-79, actuary analyst, 1979-83, mktg. analyst, 1983-85; mktg. dir. Telemarketing Systems, Inc., Quincy, Mass., 1985-86, Janson Pubs., Inc., Providence, 1986-88, Bay Loan and Investment Bank, Providence, 1988—. Designer various advertisements, catalogues, brochures. Mem. Am. Mktg. Assn., Am. Mgmt. Assn., Nat. Assn. Female Execs., Providence Bus. and Profl. Women (treas. 1982-83, 1st v.p. 1984-85, pres. 1983-85), Smithsonian Assocs., Pi Mu Epsilon, Delta Mu Delta. Home: 299 Legion Way Cranston RI 02910 Office: Bay Loan and Investment Bank 610 Manton Ave Providence RI 02909

LAUTZENHISER, NIANN KAY, psychologist, real estate broker; b. Bryan, Ohio, Jan. 29, 1945; d. Kermit Arden and Luella Marie (Keppler) L. Student, Bowling Green (Ohio) State U., summers 1963-65; BS in Edn., Miami U., Oxford, Ohio, 1966; MS in Edn., St. Francis Coll., Ft. Wayne,

Ind., 1971, MS, 1975; postgrad., Purdue U. Extension, Ft. Wayne, 1974, N.W. Tech. Coll., Archbold, Ohio, 1976-78, 80. Lic. sch. psychologist, Ind.; lic. guidance counselor, Ind.; lic. tchr. math., Ind.; nat. cert. counselor. Math. tchr. John F. Kennedy Jr. High Sch., Kettering, Ohio, 1966-69; math. tchr. Angola (Ind.) High Sch., 1969-70, guidance counselor, 1970-75, counseling psychologist, 1975-77; counseling psychologist Angola Middle Sch., 1977—. Bd. dirs. Switchboard, Inc., Angola, 1974-75, Angola Community Service, Inc., 1974-76, Edon (Ohio) Community Pre-Sch., Inc., 1981-85. Recipient Master Sch. Counselor cert. Nat. Assn. Sch. Counselors, 1976. Mem. NEA, Ind. State Tchrs., Assn., Angola Classroom Tchrs. Assn., Nat. Assn. Sch. Psychologists, Am. Assn. for Counseling and Devel., Ind. Assn. for Counseling and Devel., Ohio Assn for Counseling and Devel. Office: Angola Middle School R# 6 Box 415 Angola IN 46703

LAUVER, PATRICIA ELLEN, engineer; b. Elizabeth, N.J., Oct. 22, 1951; d. Milton Renick and Edith Marie (Gedeon) L.; B.S. in Math. with honors, Mich. State U., 1973; M.B.A., Xavier U., 1978. Mem. tech. staff Rockwell Internat., Anaheim, Calif., 1974-75, Columbus, Ohio, 1975-78; dept. head design assurance Teledyne CAE, Toledo, 1978-85; mgr. life cycle cost GTE, Billerica, Mass., 1985-86; dir. cost engring. dept. HAY Systems, Inc., 1986—; instr. U. Toledo Community and Tech. Coll., Owens Tech. Coll. Adviser Jr. Achievement, 1976-77, 78-79; sec. ch. council Luth. Ch. Recipient Twin award City of Toledo YWCA, 1982. Mem. Nat. Mgmt. Assn. (treas Buckeye Council 1980-81, v.p. youth activities Rockwell Internat. Columbus chpt. 1976-77, pres. Teledyne CAE chpt. 1981-82, chairperson bd. chpt. 1982-83, nat. dir. 1984-85), Soc. Women Engrs., Soc. Logistics Engrs., Am. Soc. Quality Control, Joint Tech. Coordinating Group/Aircraft Survivability, AAUW (study group leader 1983-84). Home: 8 Holbrook Dr Nashua NH 03062 Office: One Olde North Rd Chelmsford MA 01824

LAVA, LESLIE MICHELE, lawyer; b. LaGrange, Ill., Mar. 18, 1957; d. James Edward and Ruth Jane (Hadraba) L. BA with honors, Vanderbilt U., 1978; JD with honors, U. Fla., 1981. Bar: Ill. 1981, U.S. Dist. Ct. (no. dist.) Ill. 1981, Fla. 1982, Calif. 1985, U.S. Dist. Ct. (no. dist.) Calif. 1985, D.C. Ct. Appeals 1987. Assoc. Chapman and Cutler, Chgo., 1981-84, Brown & Wood, San Francisco, 1984—. Mem. Edgewood Children's Ctr., San Francisco, 1985—, Calif. Marine Mammal Ctr., San Francisco, 1985—. Mem. ABA, Fla. Bar Assn., Calif. Bar Assn., San Francisco Mcpl. Bond Forum, Nat. Assn. Bond Lawyers, Order of Coif, Phi Beta Kappa, Phi Kappa Phi, Pi Sigma Alpha. Republican. Club: Harbor Point Racquet and Beach (Mill Valley, Calif.). Office: Brown & Wood 555 California St Suite 5060 San Francisco CA 94104

LAVALLE, EDITH, arbitrator, consultant; b. New Haven, Dec. 24, 1919; d. Joseph and Mary Ann (Rapuano) Zuccarelli; m. Francis LaValle, July 1, 1944; children—Fern LaValle Julianelle, Gary R. A.A. in Bus. Adminstrn., Larson Jr. Coll., 1939; B.A. in Human Services, Franconia Coll., 1977. Exec. dir. Conn. Laborers Health and Pension Funds, West Haven, 1961-83; arbitrator Am. Arbitration Assn., Hartford, Conn., 1983—; lectr. U. New Haven, 1980; cons. health and pension fund planning. Contbr. book revs. Bd. dirs. Youth Continuum, New Haven, 1976—(Community Service award 1985); fund raising program dir. Tng. Research Inst. Residential Youth Ctrs., New Haven, 1986—; counselor for aged St. John the Evanelist Ch., New Haven, 1981-84; vol. arbitrator Better Bus. Bur., New Haven, 1982—; pres. Baybrook Arms Housing Corp., West Haven, 1979—. Roman Catholic. Home: 41 Jones Hill Rd Apt 202 West Haven CT 06516

LAVALLEE, DEIRDRE JUSTINE, marketing professional; b. Woonsocket, R.I., June 14, 1962; d. Albert Paul and Margaret Justine (O'Brien) L. BS in Chem. Engring., U. R.I., 1984. Sales engr. NGS Assocs. Inc., Canton, Mass., 1985-87; mgr. dist. sales MKS Instruments Inc., Andover, Mass., 1987—. Mem. Balt. Council Fgn. Affairs. Mem. Am. Inst. Chem. Engrs. (sec. chpt.), Am. Soc. Materials, Am. Inst. Physics, Am. Vacuum Soc. Club: Chesapeake Bay Mates (Annapolis, Md.). Home: 22 Faraday Dr Timonium MD 21093 Office: MKS Instruments Inc 5330 Sterling Dr Boulder CO 80301

LAVELLE, BETTY SULLIVAN DOUGHERTY, legal professional; b. Omaha, Nov. 12, 1941; d. Marvin D. and Marie C. (Sery) Sullivan; children from previous marriage: Clayton B. Dougherty, Lance A. Dougherty; m. James S. LaVelle, 1986; 1 child, Lindsay L. A of Pre-Law, U. Nebr., 1960; student, U. Colo., 1964-66; BA in Philosophy, Metro State Coll., 1979; cert. legal assistant, U. San Diego, 1979. Teaching asst. Metro State Coll., Denver, 1978; paralegal Holland and Hart, Denver, 1979-85; paralegal litigator Rothgerber, Appel, Powers and Johnson, Denver, 1985-88; pres. Vivant, Inc., Boulder, 1988—; owner, mgr. Homestead Group Home for Elderly, Boulder, 1988—; mediator domestic relations 20th Jud. Dist., Boulder, 1984-85. Contbr. articles to profl. jours. Vol. legal aid Thursday Night Bar, Denver Bar Assn., 1979-86, paralegal coordinator, panelist, speaker, 1983-85; mediator landlord/tenant project City of Boulder, 1983-87; coach, trainer Ctr. for Dispute Resolution, Denver and Boulder, 1984-86; vol. Shelter for Homeless, Boulder, 1988—. Recipient cert. U. Denver Coll. Law, 1981, Hoagland award Colo. Bar Assn., 1984. Mem. Colo. Bar Assn., Boulder Bar Assn. (assoc.), Soc. Profls. in Dispute Resolution, Rocky Mountain Legal Assts. (adv. bd. 1980-81, bd. dirs. 1983-85, dir. pro bono services 1984-85). Republican. Home and Office: 1660 Bradley Dr Boulder CO 80303

LAVELLE, GEORGANN W., marketing professional; b. Macon, Ga., Sept. 7, 1940; d. George Bertrum and Florence (Norrie) Wright; m. James P. Lavelle, Sept. 22, 1973 (div. 1980). Lic. X-ray technician, Piedmont Hosp., Atlanta, 1959; student, Marsh Bus. Sch., 1964. Sales asst. Selcom, Inc., Atlanta, 1975-79, sales agt., 1979-80; mgr. Bernard Howard and Co., Atlanta, 1980-83; sales mgr. Hillier, Newmark, Wechsler and Howard, Atlanta, 1983-86; mktg. cons. Sta. WEKS-FM/Trans World Broadcasting, Atlanta, 1986-88, nat. sales mgr., 1988—. Fellow Atlanta Broadcasting Execs. Club. Republican. Methodist. Home: 5700 Kingsport Dr Atlanta GA 30342

LAVERY, BEATRICE CANTERBURY, city official; b. Los Angeles, d. Charles Milton and Bernice Mae (Peacock) Canterbury; A.B., U. So. Calif., 1948; m. Frederic William Wile, Jr., 1952 (dec. 1960); 1 child, Geoffrey; m. Emmet G. Lavery, Sept. 27, 1963, (div.); 1 child, Tracy. Press rep. NBC, Hollywood, 1949-52; fashion dir. Bullocks Dept. Store, Los Angeles, 1960-63; advt. dir. Rose Marie Reid Swimsuits, Los Angeles, 1963-65; merchandising dir. Compton Advt., Los Angeles, 1966-67; freelance advt. and public relations cons., 1967-70; prin. adminstrv. coordinator, chief of protocol to Mayor Tom Bradley of Los Angeles, 1973—; bd. dirs. Stock Exchange/World Trade Club Greater Los Angeles, Internat. Visitors Council Los Angeles. Mem. Internat. Trade Com. Los Angeles Area C. of C., Nat. Com. U.S.-China Relations; adv. bd. Asia Soc. Decorated Order of Orange Nassau (Netherlands), Order of Merit, Fed. Republic of Germany; recipient award Media Women Founder's, 1970, award Los Angeles City Human Relations Bur., 1970; decorated Order of Leopold II King Baudouin I of Belgium, 1987, Lazo de Dama de la expresada Orden de Isabel la Catolica King of Spain, 1988. Mem. Women in Communications (pres. 1949-51), Los Angeles Advt. Women (Lulu award 1965), Fashion Group (dir. 1958-63), Hollywood Women's Press Club, U. So. Calif. Journalism Alumni Assn. (pres. 1972-73), Am. Women for Internat. Understanding (regional dir. 1987-88), Trusteeship for Betterment of Women. Home: The Penthouse Apt G-8 101 Ocean Ave Santa Monica CA 90402 Office: 200 N Spring St Los Angeles CA 90012

LAVIN, BERNICE E., business executive; b. 1925; m. Leonard H. Lavin, Oct. 30, 1947; children—Scott Jay, Carol Marie, Karen Sue. Student, Northwestern U. Sec., v.p., treas. Alberto-Culver Co., 1961—, also dir.; sec.-treas., dir. Alberto-Culver Export, Inc., Leonard H. Lavin & Co., Milani Foods, Inc., Draper Daniels, Inc., Sally Beauty Co.; sec.-treas. Pay-Less Beauty Supply Co., Victory Beauty Systems, Inc., Bee Discount Co., The Beautician's Warehouse. Home: Glencoe IL 60022 Office: Alberto-Culver Co 2525 Armitage Ave Melrose Park IL 60160

LAVIN, MILDRED H., food products company executive, former education educator; b. Boston; married. BEd with high honors, Chgo. Tchr.'s Coll. North, 1964; MA in Teaching in Biology, Northeastern Ill. State Coll., Chgo., 1969; PhD in Ednl. Media and Sci. Edn., U. Iowa, 1971. Cert. elem. tchr., Ill. Co-owner, operator family-owned furniture store, Evanston, Ill., 1956-64; tchr. sci. jr. high sch., Evanston Twp. Sch. Dist., 1965-68; asst. to dir. Office of Research and Devel. Northeastern Ill. State Coll., Chgo., 1968-69; with U. Iowa, Iowa City, 1971—; chmn. adv. com. Continuing Edn. Women U. Iowa, 1971-76; asst. prof. U. Iowa Coll. Edn., 1971—; convenor Interinstl. Com. Bachelor of Liberal Studies Degree for Iowans, 1976-77; asst. dir. U. Iowa Ctr. for Credit Programs, 1978-85; dir. spl. projects Office of Dean U. Iowa, 1985-87; emerita asst. prof., administr. U. Iowa, 1987—; pres. Food Crafters Lab., Iowa City, 1987—; cons. CERLI Regional Lab., Northfield, Ill., 1968; adj. asst. prof. U. Iowa, 1979-87. Contbr. articles to profl. jours. Former mem. Iowa Pub. TV Task Force - Iowa Coordinating Council on Postsecondary Edn., 1977-83; observer, reporter Iowa Caucuses Nat. News Poll Service, 1988; mem. steering com. Iowa City Nat. Issues Forum, 1987; dir. joint U. Iowa/AAUW project, Building Math Confidence, Iowa City and Carroll, 1982. Radio program grantee Iowa Humanities Bd., 1982; recipient Creative Program award for Women Aware Conf. Nat. Univ. Edn. Assn., 1973, 1st place Creative Programming award Nat. Univ. Continuing Edn. Assn., 1985, Outstanding Service Citation Nat. Univ. Continuing Edn. Assn., 1985. Mem. Nat. Assn. Women Bus. Owners, Bus. and Profl. Women (charter mem. 1987—), AAUW (mem.-at-large 1988—), Alpha Sigma Lambda. Democrat. Jewish. Office: Food Crafters Box 1847 Iowa City IA 52244

LAVIN, NANCY JEAN, sales executive; b. Montpelier, Vt., Dec. 27, 1952. BS, U. Vt., 1974. Account exec. Garber Travel, Brookline, Mass., 1978-79; v.p. LND Sales Co., Ashland, Mass., 1979-88, Framingham, Mass., 1988—. Mem. New Eng. Sanitary Supply Assn., Internat. Sanitary Supply Assn. Office: LND Sales PO Box 2931 Framingham MA 01701

LAVINE, MARY ANN, consultant; b. Austin, Minn., June 15, 1935; d. Leslie Ted and Alice Seneva (Erie) Young; m. Lyndon B. Petersen, Aug. 22, 1954 (dec.); children—Elizabeth Hilton (dec.), Penny; m. 2d, Maurice Charles Lavine, Aug. 21, 1969 (dec. 1984); 1 dau., JoAnne. B.A. in Edn., Ariz. State U.-Tempe, 1973, M.A., 1979. Program developer, instructional team leader Washington Elementary Dist. 6, Phoenix, 1973-81; cons. home health care personnel Referral Services, Inc., Phoenix, 198, 1988—.ner Kids Are Spl., 1984-88; planning assoc. Glendale Community Council; pres. Beth Hilton Found., 1986—; sec. YWCA Ctr. Com., Glendale, 1986—; active Glendale Leadership Advancement and Devel. program, 1985. Mem. Disabled Am. Vets. Aux. (past dept. commdr.), Am. Soc. Tng. and Devel., Nat. Council Social Studies, Midtowners Bus. and Profl. Women's Club, Glendale C. of C., Am. Soc. Curriculum and Devel., Nat. Assn. Women Bus. Owners, Ariz. Networking Council, Nat. Assn. Female Execs., Ariz. State U. Alumni Assn., Glendale C. of C. (bd. dirs.), Kappa Delta Pi, Pi Lambda Theta. Republican. Presbyterian. Lodge: Soroptimists. Avocations: hiking, cooking, travel, music. Office: PO Box 1696 Glendale AZ 85311-1696

LAVINGTON, JOI BAUER, real estate executive; b. Wichita Falls, Tex., July 21, 1952; d. Robert Roland Bauer and Sharon (Bornhuetter) Billings; m. Charles Stephen Lavington III, Jan. 21, 1984; children: Kiel Chad, Mikaela Kendra. AA, Orange Coast Coll., 1972; BS, Woodbury U., 1974; postgrad., Coast Line Coll., Rancho Santiago, Santa Ana, Calif. Cert. real estate salesman, Calif. Designer S.O.G. of Calif., Los Angeles, 1975-76, Stuart Mann Calif., Los Angeles, 1976-84; owner, mgr. I-N-JOI Cloze, Garden Grove, Calif., 1979-81; asst. to pres. Bauer Realty & Investments, Irvine, Calif., 1985-86; mgr., v.p. Century 21 Profls., Irvine, Calif., 1986—, instr. tng., 1987—. Mem. Realty Investment Assn. Orange County, East Orange County Bd. Realtors, Irvine Bd. Realtors. Democrat. Unitarian-Universalist. Home: 1209 Willet Circle Anaheim CA 92807 Office: Century 21 Profls 4482 Barranca Pkwy #180 Irvine CA 92714

LAVITT, WENDY ADLER, author; b. N.Y.C., Nov. 28, 1939; d. Ralph M. and Eve Evelyn (Sperling) Adler; B.A., Finch Coll., N.Y.C., 1961; m. Mel S. Lavitt, Sept. 10, 1959; children—Kathy, John, Meredith. Copy editor Holt, Rinehart & Winston, N.Y.C., 1961-63; docent Mus. Am. Folk Art, 1978-79, guest curator Am. Folk Dolls show, N.Y.C., 1983-84; freelance mag. writer, 1979-84; antique dealer, 1978-81; owner Made in America, antiques, N.Y.C., 1981-84; lectr. in field, 1980—. Author: American Folk Dolls, 1982, Dolls: Knopf Collector Guide, 1983, Labors of Love: America's Textiles and Needlework 1650-1930, 1987; also articles. Home: 15 E 91st St New York NY 10028

LAVORGNA, DENISE APRIL, computer systems programmer; b. Phila., Apr. 26, 1952; d. Emanuel and Mafalda (Gentile) Lavorgna. B.S., Drexel U., 1973. Computer programmer Drexel U., Phila., 1972-73, Def. Personnel Support Ctr., Phila., 1973-79, computer systems analyst, 1979-85, computer systems programmer, 1985—. Mem. Nat. Assn. Female Execs., DPSC Mgmt. Club (speakers bur. 1984-85, fed. women's program com.), Nat. Wildlife Found., Phila. Zool. Soc., Fed. Govt. Info. Processing Councils, Phi Kappa Phi, Beta Gamma Sigma. Baptist. Avocations: painting; sculpting; piano; ballet; sewing. Office: Def Personnel Support Ctr 2800 S 20th St Philadelphia PA 19101

LA VOY, DIANE EDWARDS, foundation executive; b. Caracas, Venezuela, Nov. 10, 1948; d. Edward Edwards and Margaret Lucille (Buchheit) Edwards Ross-Jones; B.A., Wellesley Coll., 1970; M.Pub. Affairs, Princeton U., 1977; m. David Wayne La Voy, Apr. 3, 1971; 1 dau., Sarah Edwards. Intern, Friends Com. on Nat. Legis., Washington, 1970-71; assoc. mgr. Quaker House, Washington, 1971-74, art dir., 1973-74; asst. editor Ams. mag. OAS, Washington, 1971-73; founder/dir. Washington Office on Latin Am., 1974; mem. profl. staff U.S. Senate Select Com. To Study Govtl. Activities with Respect to Intelligence, 1974-76; mem. profl. staff Subcom. Evaluation and Oversight of Ho. of Reps. Permanent Select Com. on Intelligence, 1977-83; staff Inter-Am. Found., 1983—, rep. for Chile, 1984—. Founder, 1st pres. E St. Friends, 1979-80; active Am. Friends Service Com., 1971-84; elder Presbyn. Ch., 1982—. Democrat. Author articles and reports in field. Home: 3416 Belleview Ave Cheverly MD 20785

LAW, CAROL JUDITH, medical psychotherapist; b. N.Y.C., May 1, 1940; d. Aldo and Jennie (Feldman) Settimo; m. Perry J. Koll, Dec. 26, 1967 (div. Nov. 1974); 1 son, Perry J.; m. 2d, Edwin B. Law, June 1, 1979. BA, Upsala Coll., 1962; postgrad. Rutgers U., 1964-66; MA, Columbia Pacific, 1982, PhD, 1984. Diplomate Am. Bd. Med. Psychotherapy. Personnel dir. Hotel Manhattan, N.Y.C., 1961; supr. social work Essex County, Newark, 1962-67; exec. dir. USO, Vungtau, South Vietnam, 1967-68; dir. Dept. Health and Rehab. Services, Pensacola, Fla., 1968-79; therapist, tchr. Franciscan Renewal Ctr., Scottsdale, Ariz., 1982—; mem. state adv. bd. Parents Anonymous, Phoenix, 1982; chmn. Gov.'s Adv. Commn. Drugs and the Elderly, Tallahassee, 1978. Pres. Jaycettes, Pensacola, 1969; chmn. social com. United Way Fund, Pensacola, 1977; mem. adv. bd. USO, Pensacola, 1973. Fellow Am. Acad. Polit. and Social Sci.; mem. Am. Assn. Pub. Adminstrs. Republican. Roman Catholic. Club: Phoenix Country, Desert Highlands Country. Home: 8214 E Del Cadena St Scottsdale AZ 85258

LAW, JOYCE ANN, accountant; b. Ft. Worth, Jan. 9, 1950; d. M.C. Hartley and Ruth (Futrelle) Hartley; m. Lowry Lee McKee, Oct. 15, 1969 (div. Mar. 1982); m. Howard Goodrich Law III, July 23, 1983; children: Kristina, Jennifer, David. BBA in Acctg. with highest honors, Ea. Ky. U., 1977. Staff acct. Criswell, Murrell, Hall & MacIntosh, CPA's, Moore, Okla., 1978; accounts receivable supr. Equity Industries Corp., Virginia Beach, Va., 1979-80; staff acct. Hermann Hosp., Houston, 1980-82; acctg. mgr. HCA/Diagnostic Ctr. Hosp., Houston, 1982—. Mem. Hosp. Fin. Mgmt. Assn., Phi Kappa Phi. Republican. Methodist. Office: HCA/Diagnostic Ctr Hosp 6447 Main Houston TX 77030

LAW, MARGARET YUEN-MING, social worker; b. Chungking, People's Republic of China, June 3, 1945. BA in sociology, cultural anthropology, Whittier Coll., 1968; MSW, U. So. Calif., 1975. Lic. clin. social worker, Calif. Children services worker Dept. Pub. Social Services, Los Angeles, 1970-78; med. social worker Calif. Dept. Health Services, Los Angeles, 1978-79; program planner Dept. Health Services, Los Angeles, 1979—; mem. adv. bd. Dept. Mental Health, San Gabriel Valley Services Region, Los Angeles, 1982—, bd. dirs. Asian Health Project, Los Angeles, 1986—, Assn. Chinese Social Workers, Los Angeles, 1986—; chair Chinese Interagy. Council, Los Angeles, 1987. Editor, producer multi-lang. brochures in alcoholism prevention, 1984. Vol. Friends for a Chinatown Library, Los Angeles, 1971—, Asian Pacific Planning Council, Los Angeles, 1972—; Orgn. Chinese Am. Women, 1981—, Assn. for Study of Community Orgn., 1983—. Fellow Coro Found.; mem. Asian Women's Network, Coalition on the Homeless, Asian Am. Employee Assn. (v.p. 1982), Los Amigos de la Humanidad. Democrat.

LAW, SYLVIA HAMLETT, state agency administrator, financial management consultant; b. Balt., Feb. 4, 1946; d. Beatrice and Jerusha (Jones) Hamlett; m. Kenneth H. Law, June 16, 1966 (div. July 1986); children: Steven John, Lisa Virginia. BS in Acctg., U. Balt., 1970; MBA, Morgan State U., 1976. Acct. Naron & Wagner, Balt., 1966-67; asst. legis. auditor State of Md., Balt., 1969-73; dir. internal audits Morgan State U., Balt., 1973-76, dir. fiscal affairs, 1976-80; chief gen. acct. Md. Dept. of Health, Balt., 1982-84, dir. mgmt. services adminstr., 1984-85, dir. fiscal services adminstrn., 1985—; adj. prof. Morgan State U., Balt., 1973-83; cons. in field. Mem. Nat. Assn. of Black Accts., Nat. Assn. of Accts., Md. Pub. Fin. Officers, Delta Sigma Theta. Democrat. Pentecostal. Club: Links. Home: 4130 Buckingham Rd Baltimore MD 21207 Office: Md Dept of Health and Mental Hygiene 201 W Preston St Baltimore MD 21201

LAWDER-WATSON, SUZANNE CLINE, rehabilitation facility executive; b. Harrisonburg, Va., Aug. 14, 1945; d. William Mitchell and Joan Addie (Cline) Robbins; m. Shelby Lawder, June 29, 1968 (div. June 1978); 1 child, Holly. BBA, Ariz. State U., 1968. Acting dir. Voluntary Action Ctr., Tucson, 1972-79; exec. asst. Allure Coll. of Beauty, Tucson, 1979-81; sales mgr. Lovett Realty, Tucson, 1978-81; timeshare coordinator Breckenridge Co., Tucson, 1981-82; coordinator, dir., v.p. Goodwill Industries of Tucson, 1982-87, pres., 1987—. Advisor United Way, Tucson, 1986—; registrar Youth Soccer League, Tuscon. Mem. Am. Soc. Personnel Adminstrn., Tucson Personnel Adminstrn. (com. mem.), Ariz. Affirmative Action Assn., Key Group (membership chmn. 1987). Home: 9121 E 27th St Tucson AZ 85710 Office: Goodwill Industries of Tucson Inc 1940 Silverlake Suite 405 Tucson AZ 85713

LAWHON, TOMMIE COLLINS MONTGOMERY, home economics educator; b. Shelby County, Tex., Mar. 15; d. Marland Walker and Lillian (Tinsley) Collins; m. David Baldwin Montgomery, Mar. 31, 1962 (dec. Aug. 1964); m. John Lawhon, Aug. 27, 1967; 1 child, David Collins. B.S., Baylor U., 1954; M in Home Econs. Edn. in Home Econs., Tex. Woman's U., 1964, Ph.D., 1966. Cert. tchr., Tex., home economist, family life educator. Tchr., Victoria Pub. Schs. (Tex.), 1954-55; stewardess, supr. Am. Airlines, Dallas/Fort Worth, 1955-62; prof. home econs. Ea. Ky. U., Richmond, 1966-67, North Tex. State U., Denton, 1968—; profl. presenter Profl. Devel. Inst., North Tex. State U., 1981—, mem. faculty senate 1984—, chmn. com. on coms., 1987—, com. status of women, 1984-87; bd. dirs. Univ. union, 1985-88, mem. Status of Women Com., 1984-87, mem. Com. on Coms., 1986—, chmn. 1987-88, vice chmn., 1988—. Co-author: Children are Artists, 1971; Hidden Hazards for Children and Families, 1982; editor: What to do with Children, 1974; Field Trips for Children, 1984; contbr. articles to profl. jours. Chmn., United Way North Tex. State U., 1980-81; chmn. crusade Am. Cancer Soc., Denton County, 1982-83; chmn. nominating com. First Bapt. Ch., Denton, 1983-84, 84-85. Recipient Presdl. award Tex. Council on Family Relations, 1979; Fessor Graham award North Tex. State U., 1980; Recipient Service award Am. Cancer Soc., 1983; Outstanding Home Economists Alumni award Baylor U., 1985, named Honor Prof. North Tex. State U., 1975. Mem. Tex. Council on Family Relations (pres. 1977-79, chmn. policy advisor com. 1986-88, nominating com. 1986-88), Denton Assn. for Edn. of Young Children (pres. 1970-72, 84-85, 85-86, v.p. 1986—), Tex. Assn. Coll. Tchrs. (v.p. N. Tex. State U. chpt. 1987—), Tex. Home Econs. Assn. (chmn. nominating com. 1983-84, chmn. child devel. and family relations sect. 1988—), Nat. Council on Family Relations (com. 1982-83), North Tex. Home Econs. Inter-orgnl. Council (adviser 1983-85). Alpha Iota/Phi Upsilon Omicron (advisor 1970-82, chmn. nat. com. 1984-87). Democrat. Clubs: Tri D (v.p. Baylor U. 1953-54); Univ. Grad. (pres. Tex. Woman's U. 1965-66). Office: Coll of Education U North Tex Denton TX 76203

LAWLAH, GLORIA GARY, state legislator, educator; b. Newberry, S.C., Mar. 12, 1939; d. Eugene Calvin and Erline (Guess) Gary; m. John Wesley Lawlah III, 1960; children: John Wesley IV, Gloria Gene, Gary McCarrell. BS, Hampton U., 1960; MA, Trinity Coll., Washington, 1970; postgrad., George Washington U., 1968-81. Mem. Md. Ho. of Dels.; mem. Dem. State Cen. Com., 1982-86; mem. coordinating com. 26th Legis. Dist., Prince Georges, Md., 1982-87; mem. Black Dem. Council, Md. Bd. dirs. Nat. Polit. Congress Black Women, 1984-87, Coalition on Black Affairs, 1980-82, Pub. Access Cable Corp., Prince Georges City, 1980-85, Hillcrest-Marlow Planning Bd., Prince Georges City, 1982-87, Family Crisis Ctr., Prince Georges City, 1982-84; co-chair Rev. Task Force for Pub. Safety, Prince Georges City, 1982; del. Dem. Nat. Conv.; co-chair Prince Georges City Exec. 7th Councilmanic Dist. Campaign, 1982; mem. Ctr. for Aging Greater S.E. Community Found. Mem. Nat. Council Negro Women (life), NAACP (3d v.p. Prince Georges City chpt. 1980-82). Club: Links. Home: 3801 24th Ave Hillcrest Heights MD 20748 Office: Lowe Office House Bldg Room 205 Annapolis MD 21401-1991

LAWLER, PATRICIA CARMELLA, consultant; b. N.Y.C., Jan. 6, 1953; d. John Joseph and Rose A. (DeMarco) Lanigan; m. Michael D. Lawler, Aug. 21, 1982. A.A.S., Manhattan Community Coll., 1972; B.S., St. John's U., Jamaica, N.Y., 1975, M.B.A., 1978. Corporate planning analyst Eastern States Bankcard, Lake Success, N.Y., 1975-79; mgr. planning and devel. Nat. Data Corp., Fairfield, N.J., 1979-82; product mgr. Dun & Bradstreet, Norwalk, Conn., 1982-83; cons., owner Lawler Assocs., Stamford, Conn., 1983—. Bd. dirs. N.Y.C. NASCP, 1980-83. Mem. Info. Industry Assn., Pres.'s Soc. Alumni Assn. (bd. reps.). Office: 185 Ocean Dr E Stamford CT 06902

LAWLEY, JO RODGERS, retail executive; b. Reform, Ala., May 16, 1939; d. Lewis Manley and Lella Maude (Davidson) Rodgers; m. William Davis Lawley, Sr., Mar. 18, 1961; 1 son, William Davis. B.S., U. Ala.-Tuscaloosa, 1960. Buyer, Pizitz, Inc., Birmingham, Ala., 1961-66, mdse. mgr., 1966-70, v.p. sales promotion, 1970-74; v.p. sales promotion Halle's, Cleve., 1974-79; sr. v.p. mktg. M. O'Neil Co., Akron, Ohio, 1979-85, 86—; sr. v.p. Famous-Barr, St. Louis, 1986—; dir. Malone, Inc., Akron and Charlotte, N.C. Dir. Akron Jr. League, 1983-86; adv. bd. U. Akron, 1983—; dir., officer Nat. Retail Mchts. Assn. Mktg. Div., 1974—; mem. parents council Hampden-Sydney Coll.; mem. Founders Club Hampden-Sydney Coll. Mem. U. Ala. Alumni Assn. (Outstanding Alumni award 1984), Alpha Chi Omega. Republican. Methodist. Office: 12679 Spruce Pond Saint Louis MO 63131

LAWLIS, PATRICIA KITE, air force officer, computer consultant; b. Greensburg, Pa., May 5, 1945; d. Joseph Powell, Jr., and Dorothy Theresa (Allshouse) Kite; m. Mark Craig Lawlis, Sept. 17, 1976 (div. 1983); 1 child, Elizabeth Marie. B.S., East Carolina U., 1967; M.S. in Computer Sci., Air Force Inst. Tech., 1982; postgrad. Ariz. State U., 1986—. Cert. secondary math. tchr. Employment counselor Pa. State Employment Service, Washington, Pa., 1967-69; math. tchr. Fort Cherry Sch. Dist., McDonald, Pa., 1969-74; commd. 2d lt. U.S. Air Force, 1974, advanced through grades to maj., 1986, data base mgr. Air Force Space Command, Colorado Springs, Colo., 1974-77, computer systems analyst, USAF in Europe, Birkenfeld, Germany, 1977-80, prof. computer sci. Air Force Inst. Tech., Wright-Patterson AFB, Ohio, 1982-86; computer cons. C.J. Kemp Systems, Inc., Huber Heights, Ohio, 1983—; Ada cons., Ada Joint Program Office, Washington, 1984—. State treas. NOW, Pa., 1973-74. Recipient Mervin E. Gross award Air Force Inst. Tech., 1982, Prof. Ezra Kotcher award, 1985. Mem. Assn. Computing Machinery, Computer Soc. of IEEE, Tau Beta Pi (v.p. 1981-82), Upsilon Pi Epsilon. Office: Ariz State U Dept Computer Sci Tempe AZ 85287

LAWRENCE, DEAN GRAYSON, retired lawyer; b. Oakland, Calif.; d. Henry C. and Myrtle (Grayson) Schmidt; A.B., U. Calif.-Berkeley, 1934, J.D., 1939. Admitted to Calif. bar, 1943, U.S. Dist. Ct., 1944, U.S. Ct. Appeals, 1944, Tax Ct. U.S., 1945, U.S. Treasury Dept., 1945, U.S. Supreme Ct., 1967; asso. Pillsbury, Madison & Sutro, San Francisco, 1944, 45; gen. practice Oakland, 1946-50, San Jose, 1952-60, Grass Valley, 1960-63, 66—; county counsel Nevada County, 1964-65. Nevada County Bd. Suprs., 1969-

73, chmn., 1971. Sec. Nev. County Humane Animal Shelter Bd., 1966-86; state humane officer, 1966-82; pres. Nev. County Humane Soc., 1974-86, mem. Humane Soc. U.S., Fund for Animals; bd. dirs. Nevada County Health Planning Council, Golden Empire Areawide Health Planning Council, 1974, 75. Mem. Bus. and Profl. Women's Club, AAUW, Animal Protection Inst. Am. (Humanitarian of Yr. 1986), Animal Legal Defense Fund, Golden Empire Human Soc. Phi Beta Kappa, Sigma Xi, Kappa Beta Pi, Pi Mu Epsilon, Pi Lambda Theta. Episcopalian. Office: PO Box 66 Grass Valley CA 95945

LAWRENCE, DONNA MARIE, inventory coordinator; b. Paris, Ky., Jan. 31, 1953; d. Thomas Euclid Lawrence Jr. and Nora Frances (Harris) Downey; m. Ronald Dean Bradley, June 12, 1980 (div. Sept. 1984); 1 child, Ronald Dean Bradley II. AA, Midway Jr. Coll., 1973; BA, Morehead (Ky.) State U., 1976. Cert. secondary tchr., Ky. Merchandise mgr. Mile High Girl Scout Council, Denver, 1976-77; admissions legal clk. Health Scis. Ctr. U. Colo., Denver, 1977-80; asst. mgr. Foxmoor Casuals, Kansas City, Mo., 1980-81; tchr. Lincoln Acad., Kansas City, Mo., 1980-81; medico-legal clk. St. Joseph Hosp., Kansas City, 1981-83; field service rep. Am. Express, Inglewood, Colo., 1984-85; inventory coordinator Adolph Coors Co., Golden, Colo., 1985—; tchr. Red Cross Community Ctr., Denver, 1977-78; court rep. St. Joseph Hosp., Kansas City, 1980-83; speaker for release of confidential info. St. Joseph Hosp., Kansas City, 1980-83; sales trainer Am. Express, Inglewood, 1984-85; software trainer Adolph Coors Co., Golden, Colo., 1988—. Mem. Nat. Assn. Female Execs., Alpha Kappa Alpha. Democrat. Baptist. Office: Adolph Coors Co 1221 Ford St Golden CO 80401

LAWRENCE, ERMA JEAN, local agency administrator; b. Hope, Ark., July 12, 1926; d. Clarence Roberson and Emma Lee (Muldrew) Jones; m. Joseph S. Lawrence; children: Ronald, Goristene, Imogene, Michelle, Valerie. Cert., Washington U., St. Louis, 1967, Mo. U., 1969. Practical nurse Firmin Desloge Hosp., St. Louis, 1953-63; tax collector, audit processor Collection of Revenue dept. City of St. Louis, 1963-66; community developer Human Devel. Corp., St. Louis, 1966-72; dir. West End Devel. Corp./Operation Challenge, St. Louis, 1972-78; exec. dir. Northside Preservation Commn., St. Louis, 1978—; pres. Northside Residential Housing Corp., St. Louis, 1983—; mem. Gov.'s Commn. on Neighborhoods, Mo., 1976-80. Co-organizer Poor People's Campaign, St. Louis; coordinator Met. Black Health Caucus; pastor's aid Bapt. Ch. of Good Shepard; mem. Urban League, Magic-108 Radio Community Service, Community Fed., Police Community Relations Commn., St. Louis, Met. Tenant Orgn., Black Women's Community Devel. Found., numerous other community orgns.; bd. dirs. St. Louis Bd. Edn., 1975, Community Housing/Resource Bd., Role-Model Bd. Edn., Dignity Reading Clinic, Alliance for Regional Community Health, Inc., others. Mem. Home Builders Assn. Democrat. Baptist. Club: Art and Culture. Office: Northside Preservation Commn 5647 Delmar Blvd Saint Louis MO 63112

LAWRENCE, ESTELENE YVONNE, transit executive, musician; b. Lynch, Ky., Aug. 10, 1933; d. Samuel Coleridge and Florence Estelle (Gardner) Taylor; m. Otto Lee Lawrence, Sept. 14, 1957; children—Stuart, Neil, Adelbert. Student Fenn Coll., 1953-60, Cleve. Inst. Music, 1955-56, John Carroll U., 1977-78, Northeastern U., 1979-80. Stenographer Cleve. Transit System/Regional Transit Authority, 1951-76, tng. asst., 1976-78, personnel devel. asst., 1978-82, dist. adminstr., 1983—; supr./mgmt. skills instr. RTA, 1976—, dir. tng. and career devel., 1986—; dir. music Friendly United Baptist Ch., 1947—; piano tchr., 1953-73; pianist/organist Nat. Bapt. Conv., 1971, 80. Publicity chmn. Moses Cleve. Sch. PTA, 1965-75; audit chmn. RTA Main Office Credit Union, 1980-83; dist. sec. Boy Scouts Am., 1982-83; chmn. adv. bd. Baldwin Wallace Coll., 1984—; mem. adv. bd. Cleve. Mgmt. Devel. Consortium, 1985—. Mem. Cleve. Mgmt. Seminars (treas. 1979-81, pres. 1981-83), Conf. Minority Transp. Ofcls., Phi Kappa Gamma (pres. 1966-69). Mem. A.M.E. Ch. Clubs: East 153d Street (v.p. 1980—), East Ky. Social. Home: 4066 East 153d St Cleveland OH 44128 Office: Greater Cleve Regional Transit Authority 615 Superior Ave NW Cleveland OH 44113

LAWRENCE, FRANCES ELIZABETH, educator; b. Glendale, Calif., Feb. 26, 1925; d. Felix William and Bessie Marie Powers; m. Vester Blount Lawrence, Apr. 2, 1955; children: Elizabeth Gail, Mark William, Cynthia Sue Cherry. AA, Pasadena Jr. Coll., 1945; BA, Whittier Coll., 1949. Tchr. Victor Sch. Dist., Victorville, Calif., 1949-56, Adelanto (Calif.) Sch. Dist., 1965—; mem. planning bd. San Bernardino County Spelling Connection Com., 1985, Adelanto Dist. Curriculum Com., 1985-86. Served with USNR, 1945-49. Mem. Early Childhood Caucus Calif. Tchrs. Assn., Adelanto Dist. Tchrs. Assn. (rep.). Democrat. Lodges: Job's Daus. (majority mem.), Order Eastern Star. Home: 18258 Symeron Rd Apple Valley CA 92307

LAWRENCE, GAIL ROBINSON, personnel director; b. Harvard, Ill., Aug. 25, 1962; d. Charles Terry and Barbara Jo (Conley) Robinson; m. Jere Kyle Lawrence, June 21, 1986. BS, Eastern Ill. U., 1984. Employment mgr. Hendrick Med. Ctr., Abilene, Tex., 1984-87; personnel dir. Rolling Plains Meml. Hosp., Sweetwater, Tex., 1987—. Mem. choir, edn. com. United Meth. Ch., Sweetwater, 1986—. Mem. Big Country Personnel Assn., Tex. Hosp. Personnel Assn., AAUW, Am. Hosp. Assn., Am. Soc. of Personnel Adminstrs. (treas. 1983-84), Sweetwater C. of C. (women's div. 1987). Republican. Club: Sweetwater Country. Home: 1429 Sunnyvale Sweetwater TX 79556

LAWRENCE, GLORIA EDITH, non-profit organization executive; b. N.Y.C., d. Victor R. and Mamie (Moss) L.; B.S., CCNY, 1956; postgrad. Columbia U., 1959, New Sch. Social Research, 1960-62. Dir. devel. So. Elections Fund, N.Y.C., 1969-70, Harlem Dowling Children's Center, N.Y.C., 1975-77; pub. relations exec. March of Dimes, N.Y.C., 1980-85; with fin. devel. unit Nat. bd. YWCA, N.Y.C., 1982-85; pres. Gloria Lawrence Cons. Firm; dir. Third World Women's Bank. Bd. dirs. Ams. for Democratic Action, 1977-86; Fellow (hon.) John F. Kennedy Library Found.; apptd. mem. Archives and Reference Research for N.Y.C., 1978—; mem. N.Y. County Com., 1973-78; del. Dem. Nat. Conv.; spl. asst. to pres. N.Y.C. Council, 1977; mem. N.Y. State Econ. Devel. Task Force, N.Y.C. Urban Affairs Com. Mem. Nat. Women's Polit. Caucus. Episcopalian. Club: Women's City (bd. dirs.). Home: 165 West End Ave New York NY 10023

LAWRENCE, JACQUELINE BURNS, management company executive, consultant, builder; b. Washington, Dec. 22, 1945; d. Jack and Pauline (Hardie) Burns; m. Charles Edward Lawrence, II, Dec. 31, 1968 (dec. 1973); 1 child: Charles Edward, III. B.A., Emory U., 1967; Tchr. Cert., Ga. State U., 1968. Tchr., Willis High Sch., Marietta, Ga., 1967-69. Slater-Marietta Sch., Greenville, S.C., 1969-70; pres. Southeast Office Mgmt., Lilburn, Ga., 1979—; pres. JBL Investments Inc., 1985—; ptnr. Premier Builders; cons. Homeland Communities, Atlanta, 1979-87, CLS Land Co., Atlanta, 1981-86, Falling Water Investment, Inc., Atlanta, 1983-86, Ortega Bock, 1986-87. Mem. Nat. Assn. Home Builders, Home Builders Assn. Metro Atlanta, Sales and Marketing Council. Republican. Methodist. Advocations: reading; tennis; boating; sports cars. Home: 382 Westminster Ln Lilburn GA 30247 Office: JBL Investment Inc 382 Westminister Ln Lilburn GA 30247

LAWRENCE, JEAN HOPE, writer, public relations consultant; b. Waukegan, Ill., Mar. 5, 1944; d. George Herbert and Hope Delinda (Warren) L.; 1 child, Kelsey Hope. BA, George Washington U., 1966. Tech. editor, Am. Chem. Soc., Washington, 1966; proposal writer Krohn-Rhodes Inst., Washington, 1966-67; legislative counsel Aerospace Industries Assn., Washington, 1967-82; v.p., co-owner Data Specific, Washington, 1985-86; editorial adviser Am. C. of C. Execs., Alexandria, Va., 1983-86, lectr., 1984—. Contbg. editor: Communications Concepts, 1983-86; editor, pub., creator: (newsletter) Get It Done!, 1987—. Contbr. numerous articles to mags. Mem. Washington Edn. Press Assn., Washington Ind. Writers, Women's Direct Response Group. Democrat. Methodist. Avocation: essayist. Address: 3217 Connecticut Ave NW Washington DC 20008

LAWRENCE, JOAN MCEWEN BILLS, recording company executive; b. Hopkinsville, Ky., Oct. 15, 1932; d. Joseph Thomas McEwen and Thelma Irene (Grace) Fox; m. John E. Bills Jr.; children: Jennifer Jones, John E. III, James L., Robert J.; m. Mark M. Lawrence (div.). Student, U. Tenn., Knoxville, 1950-53, U. Tenn., Nashville, 1961-62, Aquinas Jr. Coll., 1962-63. Ballet instr. Nashville, 1960-68; adminstr. Shelby Singleton Records, Nashville, 1968-70; adminstrv. asst. to gen. mgr. Sta. WLAC, Nashville, 1970-73; nat. dir. promotion Mercury Records, Chgo., 1973-76, Pvt. Stock Records, Inc., N.Y.C., 1976-78, Arista Records, Inc., Los Angeles, 1978-87; pres. Joan Lawrence Mktg., Inc., Nashville, 1987—. Mem. Nashville Symphony Assn., Country Music Assn., Cheekwood Arts. Republican. Roman Catholic.

LAWRENCE, KATHLEEN WILSON, government relations advisor; b. N.Y.C., Dec. 7, 1940; d. Jules William and Catherine (Kelly) Wilson; m. James J. Balsdon, Oct. 31, 1959 (div. 1968); children—Julia A. Balsdon Wise, Maryclaire Balsdon Dorough; m. G. Andrew Lawrence, July 6, 1974; 1 child, Andrew W. Student, Queens Coll., 1959, U. Va., 1977, No. Va. Community Coll., 1976-80, Harvard U., 1985. Staff asst. to pres. White House, Washington, 1969-73; exec. dir. Nat. Fedn. Republican Women, Washington, 1974-75; dir. adminstrn. Citizens for Reagan, Washington, 1976; pres. Lawrence Co., Alexandria, Va., 1977-84; dep. undersec. U.S. Dept. Agr., Washington, 1984-87; assoc. Heron, Burchette, Ruckert & Rothwell, Washington, 1987—; dir. Tri Cities Communication, Craig, Colo., Lawrence Co., Rural Telephone Bank, Washington. Mem. exec. com. Am. Cancer Soc., Alexandria, 1983-84, bd. dirs., 1980-85; mem. corp. bd. Alexandria Health Services Corp., 1980—; bd. dirs. Va. Fedn. Republican Women, 1981-82, Olde Belhaven Towne Civic Assn., Alexandria, 1984-85; dir. Pvt. Sector Council, 1987—; mem. Nat. Adv. Council on Rural Devel., 1987—, exec. com. Nat. Adv. Council SBA, 1987—, Nat. Commn. Agrl. Fin., Pvt. Sector Council (bd. dirs. 1987—). Roman Catholic. Avocations: travel; reading; needlework. Office: Heron Burchette Ruckert & Rothwell 1025 Thomas Jefferson St NW Suite 700 Washington DC 20007

LAWRENCE, NANCY ELIZABETH, food service executive; b. Enterprise, Ala., Mar. 25, 1960; d. James Allyn and Nedra Blanche (Brown) Spiers; m. Robert Wayne Lawrence, Feb. 12, 1984; children: Ian, Robin Ann. Student, Austin Peay State U., Clarksville, Tenn., 1978-80. Driver Domino's Pizza, Lexington, Ky., 1982, mgr. trainee, 1982-83; store mgr. Domino's Pizza, Hickory, N.C., 1983-84, dir. ops., 1984—. Author: numerous poems, short stories. Mem. Nat. Assn. Female Execs., Nat. Geog. Soc., Smithsonian Instn., The Franklin Mint Collectors Soc. Office: PO Drawer #5038 Hickory NC 28603-5038

LAWRENCE, PATRICIA ANNE, nurse; b. Worcester, Mass., Nov. 14, 1931; d. Ralph Seavey and Maude Irma (Hayward) L.; A.B., Bates Coll., Lewiston, Maine, 1954; M.A., Columbia U., 1960. Staff nurse Cornell U. Med. Center, 1954-57, Newton (Mass.)-Wellesley Hosp., 1957-58; instr. Cornell U.-N.Y. Hosp. Sch. Nursing, 1958-59, 60-61, Rutgers U. Coll. Nursing, 1961-64; asst. prof. Duke U. Sch. Nursing, 1964-70; ednl. dir. diabetes project N.C. Regional Med. Program, 1969-73; assoc. prof. U. N.C. Sch. Nursing, Chapel Hill, 1973—; site visitor, cons. diabetes research and tng. centers NIH, 1977-78, adv. bd. Nat. Diabetes Clearinghouse, 1978-80; bd. dirs. Am. Assn. Diabetes Educators, 1973-75. Mem. Am. Nurses Assn., N.C. Nurses Assn., Am. Diabetes Assn. (dir. 1974-79, sec. 1976-77, v.p. 1977-79, dir. N.C. affiliate 1973-79, 81-83), Internat. Diabetes Fedn., AAUP, Am. Kennel Club (tracking judge). Co-author: Picture Pages for Diabetic Care, 1973; editor: Diabetes Spectrum, 1987—; also numerous articles, chpts. in books. Co-editor: Educating Diabetic Patients, 1981; editorial bd. Diabetes care, 1977-83. Home: 4711 Easley St Durham NC 27705 Office: U NC CB #7460 Carrington Hall Chapel Hill NC 27599

LAWRENCE, RACHEL REGINA (GINA), sales representative; b. Hattiesburg, Miss., Nov. 13, 1960; d. Wayne Byron and Rachel W. (Sullivan) Lott; m. John Roland Lawrence, Sept. 1, 1984. A.A., Pearl River Jr. Coll., 1980; B.S., U. So. Miss., 1982. Paralegal asst. Ingram, Matthews & Fowler, Hattiesburg, 1982-83; sales rep. ComputerKraft, Hattiesburg, 1983-84, ComputerWorld, Jackson, Miss., 1984-85; mgr. AC3 Computing Products, Jackson, 1985-86; territory mgr., Ross Labs., Jackson, 1987—. Named Top Sales Rep. of Yr., ComputerWorld, 1985. Mem. Am. Bus. Women's Assn., Nat. Assn. Female Execs. Republican. Methodist. Club: Stonegate Ladies. Avocations: tennis; sewing; skiing; swimming. Home: 222 Creekline Dr Madison MS 39110 Office: AC3 Computing Products 805 S Wheatly St Ridgeland MS 39157

LAWRENCE, RUTH BECKER, nurse, contractor; b. Bklyn., June 16, 1925; d. Edward F. and Lillian (Davis) Becker; B.S., nursing diploma Simmons Coll., 1947; m. W. Leland Lawrence, Feb. 8, 1948; children—Stoddard, Thomas, Jeffrey, Leland Davis, Leigh Anne, Richard. Instr. nursing, Simmons Coll., Boston, 1947; staff nurse Nassau Hosp., Mineola, N.Y., 1947-48; staff pediatric nurse Hartford (Conn.) Hosp., 1948-49; dir. nursing service Springfield (Vt.) Hosp., 1977-86; now nurse cons. Choir, tchr. Sunday Sch., Congl. Ch.; den mother Boy Scouts Am.; vol. ARC; bd. dirs. Springfield Sch. Bd., 1962-72. Mem. Am. Nurses Assn., Council Nursing Adminstrs., Vt. Hosp. Assn. Dirs. Nursing.

LAWRENCE, SALLY CLARK, educational administrator; b. San Francisco, Dec. 29, 1930; d. George Dickson and Martha Marie Alice (Smith) Clark; m. Henry Clay Judd, July 1, 1950 (div. Dec. 1972); children—Rebecca, David, Nancy; m. John I. Lawrence, Aug. 12, 1976; stepchildren—Maia, Dylan. Docent Portland Art Mus., Oreg., 1958-68; gallery owner, dir., Sally Judd Gallery, Portland, 1968-75; art ins. appraiser, cons. Portland, 1975-81; interim dir. Mus. Art. Sch., Pacific Northwest Coll. Art, Portland, 1981, asst. dir., 1981-82, acting dir., 1982-84, dir., 1984—; pres. Art Coll. Exchange Nat. Consortium, 1983—. Mem. Nat. Assn. Schs. Art and Design (bd. dirs. 1984-88). Office: Pacific NW Coll of Art 1219 SW Park St Portland OR 97205

LAWRENCE, STELLA, electrical engineer, educator; b. Montreal, Que., Can., Feb. 2, 1918; came to U.S., 1924, naturalized, 1945; d. M. and Fannie (Broide) Hertchikoff; BA magna cum laude, NYU, 1938, MS, 1941; BEE summa cum laude, Poly. Inst. Bklyn., 1949, MEE, 1952. Devel. engr. Control Instrument Co., 1943-47; lectr. physics CCNY, 1958-70; mem. switching systems devel. dept. Bell Telephone Labs., 1947-60; asst. prof. Bronx Community Coll., 1960-65, asso. prof. elec. engring. tech., 1966-80, prof., 1980—; cons. advanced tech. dept. Ampex Corp., 1975—; cons. orbiting systems Aerospace Corp., summer 1978; cons. Jet Propulsion Lab., summer 1980; vis. scientist Lawrence Berkeley Lab., U. Calif., summer 1981, L.B. Johnson Space Center, summer 1982; cons. Air Force Wright Aero. Labs., Ohio, summer 1983. Mem. Community Planning Bd. 7, Bronx, N.Y.C., 1970—. Faculty research fellow Argonne (Ill.) Nat. Lab., 1974, NASA Langley Research Center, summer 1976, NASA Marshall Space Flight Center, summer 1977, NSF fellow, 1977-80, NASA Ames, 1984-85, Navy research fellow Warminister Air Devel. Ctr., 1986, NASA Lewis Research Ctr., summer, 1987. Fellow Bklyn. Engrs. Club; mem. IEEE (sr., exec. com. N.Y. sect. 1956—, regional exec. com. 1975), Soc. Women Engrs. (sr., charter), Am. Soc. for Engring. Edn., N.Y. Acad. Scis., Phi Beta Kappa, Sigma Xi, Pi Mu Epsilon, Sigma Pi Sigma. Home: 3288 Reservoir Oval E Bronx NY 10467 Office: 181st and University Ave Bronx NY 10453

LAWRENCE, SUSAN BUCKMAN, state government official; b. Canandaigua, N.Y., Aug. 16, 1944; d. Lewis Edward and Thelma (Paul) Buckman; m. C. Bruce Lawrence. BA, U. Rochester, 1966. Cert. tchr., N.Y. History tchr. Rochester (N.Y.) Sch. Dist., 1967-78; dir. econ. devel. N.Y. State Econ. Devel., Rochester, 1978—; adj. instr. N.Y. State Sch. Indsl. and Labor Relations at Cornell U., 1979-83. Author: Writing it Right, 1981. Bd. dirs. Rochester Eye Bank, 1984—, Compeer, 1985—, Urban League Econ. Devel. Corp., Rochester, 1985—, Finger Lakes Regional Edn. Ctr., 1985—, Monroe County Local Devel. Corp.; corp. mem. Rochester United Way, 1981—; mem. N.Y. State Econ. Devel. Council, Genesee Regional Transp. Council. Democrat. Home: 276 Crosman Terr Rochester NY 14620 Office: NY State Dept Econ Devel 121 East Ave Rochester NY 14604

LAWRENCE, TELETÉ ZORAYDA, speech and voice pathologist, educator; b. Worcester, Mass., Aug. 5, 1910; d. James Newton and Cora Valeria (Hester) Lester; A.B. cum laude, U. Calif., Berkeley, 1932; M.A., Tex. Christian U., 1963; pvt. study voice with Edgar Schofield, N.Y.C., 1936-41, drama with Enrica Clay Dillon, N.Y.C., 1937-40; m. Ernest Lawrence, Oct. 9, 1939; children—James Lester, Valerie Alma. Lic. speech-lang. pathologist. Mem. Am. Lyric Opera Co., 1939—; instr. speech Sch. Fine Arts, Tex. Christian U., Fort Worth, 1959-66, asst. prof., 1966-71, assoc. prof., 1971-75, prof., 1975-76, emeritus, 1976—, speech pathologist specializing voice disorders Speech and Hearing Clinic, 1959—, faculty research leave, Gt. Britain, Western Europe, Hungary, 1968; pvt. practice speech and voice pathology, 1960—. Mem. bd. Sunshine Haven, home for retarded children, 1957-59; gen. chmn. Ft. Worth and Tarrant County, Nat. Retarded Children's Week, 1954; mem. family and child welfare div. Community Council Ft. Worth and Tarrant County, 1955-57, mem. health and hosp. div., 1959-60; mem. women's com. Ft. Worth chpt. NCCJ, 1956-59; exec. v.p. Fine Arts Found. Guild of Tex. Christian U., 1955-56, past exec. sec., past fin. sec. Recipient Faculty Research grant Tex. Christian U., 1961. Fellow Internat. Soc. Phonetic Scis.; mem. Nat. Council Chs. (bd. joint com. missionary edn. Pacific Coast area, 1952-55), United Ch. Women of Ft. Worth (chmn. Christian world missions dept. 1955-57, pres. 1957-59). Ft. Worth Area Council Chs. (v.p. 1955-57, exec. com. 1957-59, bd. dirs. 1959-60), U. Calif. Alumni Assn. (life), Am. Speech-Lang.-Hearing Assn. (life; cert. clin. competence in speech pathology), Tex. Speech-Lang.-Hearing Assn. (cert.), Ft. Worth Council for Retarded Children, Speech Communication Assn. (sec. speech and hearing disorders interest group 1962-63, mem. com. 1961-64), Am. Dialect Soc., Internat. Assn. Logopodics and Phoniatrics, Phonetic Soc. Japan, AAUP (emeritus), Lambda Ma'ams of Lambda Chi Alpha (pres. Ft. Worth 1962-63), Phi Beta Kappa Assn., Ft. Worth, Phi Beta Kappa (Alpha of Calif. chpt.; charter mem., v.p. Delta of Tex. chpt. 1971-73, pres. 1973-74), Delta Zeta, Psi Chi, Sigma Alpha Eta. Republican. Mem. Christian Ch. Clubs: Woman's of Fort Worth, Women of Rotary. Participant, 13th Congress of Internat. Assn. Logopedics and Phoniatrics, Vienna, 1965, 14th Congress, Paris, 1968, 15th Congress, Buenos Aires, 1971, 16th Congress, Interlaken, Switzerland, 1974, 17th Congress, Copenhagen, 1977, 18th Congress, Washington, 1980, 19th Congress, Edinburgh, Scotland, 1983; participant 10th Internat. Congress of Linguists, Bucharest, 1967; participant 6th Internat. Congress of Phonetic Scis., Prague, 1967, 7th Internat. Congress, Montreal, 1971, 8th Internat. Congress, Leeds, Eng., 1975; participant 1st Congress Internat. Assn. Sci. Study Mental Deficiency, Montpellier, France, 1967, Semmelweis Ann. Week, Budapest Acad. Scis., 1968, 3d World Congress Phoneticians, Tokyo, 1976. Author: Handbook for Instructors of Voice and Diction, 1968; contbr. articles to profl. jours. Home: 3860 South Hills Circle Fort Worth TX 76109

LAWRIK, SUSAN E., financial executive; b. Passaic, N.J., Aug. 31, 1956; d. Alex and Margaret (Eckhoff) L.; m. Brian K. Shields, Sept. 1, 1985. BBA, William Patterson Coll., 1978. Credit clk. Gen. Elec. Credit, Roseland, N.J., 1978-80; researcher U.A. Columbia Cable TV, Oakland, N.J., 1980-82; returns supr. Scribners Book Co., N.Y.C., 1982-84; credit analyst Motorola C & E, Glen Rock, N.J., 1984-85; credit mgr. Seton Co., Norristown, Pa., 1985-88, The Lehigh Group, Allentown, Pa., 1988—. Office: The Lehigh Group Allentown PA 18106

LAWS, JUDITH A., human resources consultant; b. St Louis, July 3, 1937; d. James C. and H. Idell (McIntyre) L. BA, Washington U., St. Louis, 1959; BS in Metaphysics, Claregate Coll., London, 1980. Vol., Peace Corps, Cameroon, 1962-63; personnel generalist HEW, Washington, 1964-66; asst. to dir. 1970 White House Conf. Children and Youth, 1966-68; manpower devel. and tng. cons., Washington, 1969-73; alcohol edn. cons., Washington, 1974—; credential and communications specialist Assn. Labor-Mgmt. Adminstrs. and Cons. on Alcoholism, Arlington, Va., 1984—. Contbg. editor Quarante, 1985-87; contbr. articles to The Beacon, Jour. Esoteric Physhol., 1987—. Mem. adv. council Alcoholism Treatment Ctr. Washington, 1976-78, nat. adv. bd. Peer Plus, 1988—; bd. dirs. Whitman-Walker Clinic, Washington, 1979. Mem. Nat. Writers Club, Inst. Noetic Scis., Nat. Health Fedn. Avocations: playwriting, acting, psychospiritual research. Home: 2800 Woodley Rd NW Washington DC 20008

LAWSON, ANN MARIE MCDONALD, librarian; b. Jersey City; d. William and Mary Agnes (Dolan) McDonald; student Columbia, 1947, N.Y. U., 1949, City Coll. N.Y., 1959, Pratt Inst., 1963; m. Philip James Lawson, Apr. 26, 1952. Methods analyst Rueben H. Donnelley Corp., N.Y.C., 1953-57; librarian chems. div. Union Carbide Corp., N.Y.C., 1957-65, Tatham Laird & Kudner, N.Y.C., 1965-67, Met. Transp. Authority, N.Y.C., 1967-80; cons., 1980—; active library tng. program Ballard Sch. (YWCA), 1949—; cons. WHO, Geneva, Switzerland, 1950; lectr. Pratt Inst. Grad. Library Sch., 1967. Mem. Assn. Records Mgrs. and Adminstrs. (pres. 1948-50); Spl. Libraries Assn. Republican. Contbr. articles to mags. Home and Office: 119 Washington Pl New York NY 10014

LAWSON, BARBARA HOKE, marketing executive; b. Princeton, W.Va., Apr. 17; d. Leonard Iverson and Lucille (Woodson) Hoke; m. Max Wendell Lawson, June 12, 1951; children: Max Wendell, Leonard Blaine. BA in Psychology, W.Va. U., 1951, postgrad., 1967-69; postgrad., Marshall U., 1964. Tchr. Mercer County Schs., Princeton, 1953-55, Kanawha County Schs., Charleston, W.Va., 1962-68; TV tchr. States of Tenn. and W.Va., 1968-76; v.p., sec., treas. Lawson Chevrolet-Mazda, Greeneville, Tenn., 1971—; pres. Lawson Mktg., Inc., Greeneville, 1978—; new math cons. Kanawha County Schs., 1966-67; cons. W.Va. State Dept. Edn., Charleston, 1968-71; media cons. Tusculum Coll., Greeneville, 1973-76. Creator various ednl. products. Pres. Youth Builders, Greeneville, 1978; youth adv. council Asbury United Meth., Greeneville, 1974—, Takoma Adventist Hosp., Greeneville, 1985—; bd. dirs. Nolichucky Mental Health Ctr., Greeneville, 1980, E. Tenn. Regional Organ Procurement Agy., Johnson City, Tenn., 1985-87. Named Outstanding Woman Greene County Jaycees, 1978, Outstanding Educator Bus. and Profl. Women's Club of Greeneville, 1984. Mem. Am. Mgr. Assn., Am. Mktg. Assn. (Acad. Health Care Mktg.), Am. Soc. Tng. and Devel., Nat. Assn. Female Execs., Tri-Cities Metro-Advt., Delta Kappa Gamma, Greeneville C. of C. Republican. Clubs: Link Hills Country, Little Theatre. Home: Rt 5 Box 414 Greeneville TN 37743 Office: Lawson Mktg Inc 401 W Irish St Greeneville TN 37743

LAWSON, BONNIE L., medical group management company executive; b. Chgo., Sept. 26, 1949; d. Steve and Evelyn (Cymbal) Krakowski; m. Timothy P. Lawson, June 13, 1970 (div. 1984); children: Erik Steven, Jason Patrick. Student, Western Ill. U., 1967-70; AS, Fla. Jr. Coll., 1979; student, U. N. Fla., 1986—. Registered profl. nurse, Fla. Psychiatric nurse Bapt. Med. Ctr., Jacksonville, Fla., 1980, Oak Ctr., Jacksonville, 1980-81; community medicine nurse Univ. Hosp., Family Practice Diagnostic Ctr., Jacksonville, 1981-85; nurse mgr. U. Hosp., Park Place Med. Ctr., Jacksonville, 1985-87; program dir. optifast program Humana Hosp., Orange Park, Fla., 1987, exec. dir., 1987-88; mgr. client services Profl. Billing Systems, Inc., Jacksonville, 1988—. Mem. Med. Group Mgmt. Assn., Jacksonville C. of C. Republican. Episcopalian. Home: 7842 Linkside Dr Jacksonville FL 32256 Office: Profl Billing Systems Inc 1833 Boulevard Suite 500 Jacksonville FL 32206

LAWSON, BRENDA MICKLOW, financial adviser; b. Birmingham, Ala., Feb. 19, 1954; d. Andrew William and Geraldine (Cooley) Micklow; B.S., Jacksonville State U., 1976, M.S., 1977; m. James Ronald Lawson, July 24, 1976; children: Lori, Trey. Pres. Lawson & Company, The Fin. Group, 1982—; adj. faculty U. Ala.-Birmingham. Named 1st runner up Miss Ala. U.S.A., 1974; cert. fin. planner. Mem. Internat. Assn. Fin. Planners (past pres., chmn. bd., now dir. Ala. chpt.), Inst. Cert. Fin. Planners, Phi Mu. Rupublican. Author: The Cashless Society, 1976; Value Issues in Counseling, 1978; composer: When, 1978; columnist, Bus. Jour. Home: 1313 Al Seier Ln Birmingham AL 35226

LAWSON, CHARLENE ANN, data processing executive; b. Findlay, Ohio, Dec. 15, 1948; d. Charles Dwight and Geraldine Marie (Blaksley) Shively; m. Terry Michael Lawson, Aug. 9, 1976; children: Shannon Monroe, Wesley Dwight. Diploma, Internat. Bus. Coll., Ft. Wayne, Ind., 1968; degree in real estate, So. Ohio Coll., 1978; AAS in Computer Sci., Sinclair Coll., Dayton, Ohio, 1984. Adminstrv. asst. Marathon Oil Co., Findlay, 1969-74; mktg. analyst Savin Bus. Machines, Irvine, Calif., 1974-75, Systems & Services, Inc., Greenville, S.C., 1975-76; owner, realtor Village Green Realty, Dayton, 1979-84; mgr. word processing MacDonald Creative Mktg., Dayton, 1981-82; mktg. analyst The Computer Shoppe, Louisville, 1984-85; bus. systems analyst Humana, Inc., Louisville, 1986, systems communications mgr., 1986—. Mem. Assn. for Systems Mgmt. (symposium co-chair 1987, sec. 1987-88, bd. dirs. 1987-88), Data Processing Mgmt. Assn. (v.p. awards com. 1986-87, bd. dirs. 1986-88, v.p. programs com. 1987-88), Kentuckiana Data Processing Assn. (chmn. bd. dirs. 1987-88), Dayton Downtown Am. Bus. Women's Assn. (pres. 1982-83, chair ways and means com. 1983-84, nat.

chpt. del. 1982-84), Coffee Trees Am. Bus. Women's Assn. (edn. com. chair 1986-87, bus. assn. com. chair 1986-87, nat. chpt. del. 1986-87, Mem. of Month 1987, Woman of Yr. 1987-88, 88-89), Am. Bus. Women's Assn. (gen. chmn. dist. IV). Republican. Lutheran. Home: 1115 Creekview Circle New Albany IN 47150-2027 Office: Humana Inc 500 W Main St Louisville KY 40201-1438

LAWSON, JOYCE ANNE, real estate specialist; b. Grundy, Va., Sept. 16, 1941; d. Arthur Fleming and America Corinne (Mounts) Lester; m. David Leroy Lawson, June 10, 1961 (div. June 1974); children: David B., Tinamaree. Grad. high sch., Grundy, 1960. Escrow sec., officer Title Ins. & Trust, Ventura, Calif., 1962-74; mgr. escrow Boardwalk Escrow, Thousand Oaks, Calif., 1974-80; pres. Cameo Escrow, Thousand Oaks, Calif., 1980-83; pvt. practice bus. cons. Ventura, 1983-85; salesman real estate, cons. V.C.R.E., Ventura, Calif., 1985—. Republican. Lodge: Soroptimists. Home: 486 Serento Circle Thousand Oaks CA 91360 Office: V C R E 31 N Oak St Ventura CA 93001

LAWSON, KAREN EELLS, management consultant; b. East Liverpool, Ohio, May 12, 1947; d. Byron Rigby and Mildred Josephine (Myler) Eells; m. Robert Donald Lawson, Feb. 24, 1984. BA, Mt. Union Coll., 1969; MA, U. Akron, 1973. Tchr. English Plain Local Sch. Dist., Canton, Ohio, 1969-77; instr. Rochester (N.Y.) Bus. Inst., 1977-78; br. mgr. Monroe Savs. Bank, Rochester, 1978-82; tng. dir. Rochester Community Savs. Bank, 1982-86; cons., pres. K.E. Lawson Assocs., Rochester, 1986—; adj. faculty Rochester Inst. of Tech. Bd. dirs. Vols. of Am., Rochester, 1986—. Mem. Nat. Speakers Assn., Assn. for Bank Trainers and Cons., Nat. Assn. Bank Women (pres. 1985-86), Am. Soc. for Tng. and Devel. (bd. dirs. 1986—). Republican. Methodist. Club: Toastmistress (pres. 1980-81). Home: 50 Squirrels Heath Rd Fairport NY 14450 Office: KE Lawson Assocs PO Box 306 Fairport NY 14450

LAWSON, MELISSA ARCHILLA, elementary educator; b. Ft. Worth, Oct. 22, 1950; d. Eliel and Foye (Jackson) Archilla; m. Billy Granville Lawson, Feb. 26, 1971 (div. 1975). 1 son, Mark Christopher. B.S. in Edn. cum laude, N. Tex. State U., 1978; M.Ed., So. Meth. U., 1981. Cert. elem. tchr., English elem. tchr., bilingual tchr., Tex. Bilingual tchr. Dallas Ind. Sch. Dist., 1978-82, Richardson, Tex., 1982—. Interpreter 1980 Census, Dallas, 1980. Scottish Rite Masons scholar, 1968; Masters Degree grantee, 1978. Mem. Dallas Assn. Bilingual Educators, Tex. Tchrs. ESL, Richardson Edn. Assn., Assn. Adult Educators, Tex. Ret. Tchrs. Assn. Republican. Baptist. Club: Alpha Delta Pi. Office: Richardson Ind Sch Dist 400 S Greenville Ave Richardson TX 75081

LAWSON, ROSA OLIVIA V., banker; b. Mexico City, Mexico, June 17, 1944; d. Roberto and Delia (Martinez) Villa; 1 child, Maria Fernanda. M. Econs., National Autonomous U. Mex., 1965; postgrad. Inst. Social Studies, The Hague, Holland, 1967. Prof. Nat. Autonomous U., Mex., 1968-73; dep. mgr. fin. programming Nacional Financiera, Mexico, 1976-77; chief advisor Treasury Dept., Mexico, 1979-81; chief compensation and benefits div. Inter-Am. Devel. Bank, Washington, 1985—; mem. editoral bd. dirs. Investigación Económica mag., Mexico, 1969-70; mem. presdl. commn. on fin. Pres.'s Office, Mex., 1978-81. Author: Nacional Financiera: Development Bank for the Economic Improvement of Mexico, 1976. Nat. Autonomous U. grantee, 1967; hon. mem. "Juan Loyola Prize", Economists Nat. Assn. Mexico, 1978-81. Avocations: music; reading; movies. Home: 11002 Wickshire Way Rockville MD 20852 Office: Inter-Am Devel Bank 1300 New York Ave Washington DC 20577

LAWSON, SANDRA SUE, personnel executive; b. Chester, Pa., Jan. 26, 1945; d. George William and Kathleen (Burnettee) Lawson; m. Frank Pratt Newton, Jr., Feb. 8, 1969 (div. June 1980). BS, U. Tenn., 1966, postgrad., 1973-75; postgrad U. Va., 1967-68. Personnel asst. U. Tenn., Knoxville, 1973-75; benefits asst. mgr. M.D. Anderson Hosp., Houston, 1975-76; asst. personnel dir. Jefferson Davis Hosp., Houston, 1976-77; co-owner, mgr. 3d St. Souvenir Mart, Las Vegas, 1977-85; owner mgr. T Shirts by Sandra, Las Vegas, 1980-88; employment mgr. EG&G/EM, Las Vegas, 1984—. Bd. dirs. Family Planning, Las Vegas, 1985, Child Find/Nev. Assn. Missing Children, 1984-85; supporting mem. Opportunity Village for Retarded Citizens. Mem. So. Nev. Personnel Assn. (sec. 1985-86), Rocky Mountain Personnel Assn. (conv. com. Las Vegas chpt. 1987), So. Nev. Indsl. Employers, Nat. Asn. Exec. Females. Club: Soroptimists (pres. 1983-85, 87-88, Blanch Edgar award 1985). Avocations: travel, collect clowns and wind chimes, reading, golfing. Home: 6828 E Bonanza Rd Las Vegas NV 89110-4156 Office: EG&G/EM PO Box 1912 Las Vegas NV 89125

LAWSON-KERR, KATHRYN, clinical psychologist, educator; b. St. Louis, Nov. 16, 1954; d. Frederick William and Patricia (Jordan) L.-K.; m. David Franklin Baughn, Dec. 7, 1985. BA in Psychology, Washington U., St. Louis, 1975; MA in Psychology, U. Minn., 1979; PhD in Clin. Psychology, La. State U., 1986. Clin. resident psychology U. Miss. Med. Ctr., Jackson, 1983-84, instr. psychiatry, 1984-86, asst. prof., 1986 ; lectr. in field. Contbr. articles to profl. jours. Vaughn Stroke research grantee, 1984. Mem. Internat. Neuropsychol. Soc., Am. Psychol. Assn., Southeastern Psychol. Assn., Miss. Psychol. Assn., Assn. for Advancement Behavior Therapy, Nat. Head Injury Found. Office: U Miss Med Ctr Dept Psychiatry and Human Behavior 2500 N State St Jackson MS 39216

LAWTON, JACQUELINE AGNES, retired communications company executive, management consultant; b. Bklyn., June 9, 1933; d. Thomas G. and Agnes R. (McLaughlin) Maguire; m. George W. Lawton, Feb. 14, 1954; children—George, Victoria, Thomas. With N.Y. Telephone, 1954-82, mktg. mgr. govt., edn. and med. Mid State, 1978-81, mktg. mgr. health care, N.Y.C., 1981-82; dist. field market mgr. health care and lodging; region 1 N.E. and Region 2 Mid Atlantic, AT&T-Am. Bell, N.Y.C., 1982-83; Eastern region mgr. personnel, mktg. and sales AT&T Info. Systems, Parsippany, N.J., 1983-86, pvt. practice mgmt. cons., Cornish Flat, N.H., 1986—. Mem. Nat. Assn. Female Execs. Republican. Roman Catholic. Home and Office: PO Box 163 Cornish Flat NH 03746

LAWTON, LORILEE ANN, pipeline supply company owner, accountant; b. Morrisville, Vt., July 17, 1947; d. Philip Wyman Sr. and Margaret Elaine (Ather) Noyes; m. Lee Henry Lawton, Dec. 6, 1969; children: Deborah Ann, Jeffrey Lee. BBA, U. Vt., 1969. Sr. acct., staff asst. IBM, Essex Junction, Vt., 1969-72; owner, treas. Red-Hed Supply Inc, Winooski, Vt., 1972—. Apptd. bd. dirs. Colchester (Vt.) Community Devel. Assn., 1987, also treas./sec. Mem. Assoc. Gen. Contractors Am., Assoc. Gen. Contractors Vt., Am. Water Works Assn., Vt. Waterworks Assn., New Eng. Waterworks Assn., No. Vt. Homebuilders Assn., Greater Burlington Computer Users Group, Water and Sewer Distbrs. Am. Republican. Home: 53 Middle Rd Colchester VT 05446

LAWYER, VIVIAN JURY, lawyer; b. Farmington, Iowa, Jan. 7, 1932; d. Jewell Everett Jury and Ruby Mae (Schumaker) Brewer; m. Verne Lawyer, Oct. 25, 1959; children—Michael Jury, Steven Verne. Tchr.'s cert. U. No. Iowa, 1951; B.S. with honors, Iowa State U., 1953; J.D. with honors, Drake U., 1968. Bar: Iowa 1968, U.S. Supreme Ct. 1986. Home econs. tchr. Waukee High Sch. (Iowa), 1953-55; home econs. tchr. jr. high sch. and high sch., Des Moines Pub. Schs., 1955-61; sole practice law, Des Moines, 1972—; bd. dirs. Micah Corp.; chmn. juvenile code tng. sessions Iowa Crime Commn., Des Moines, 1978-79, coordinator workshops, 1980; assoc. Law Offices of Verne Lawyer, Des Moines, 1981—; co-founder, bd. dirs. Youth Law Center, Des Moines, 1977—; mem. com. rules of juvenile procedure Supreme Ct. Iowa, 1981-87, adv. com. on costs of ct. appointed counsel Supreme Ct. Iowa, 1985—; trustee Polk County Legal Aid Services, Des Moines, 1980-82; mem. Iowa Dept. Human Services and Supreme Ct. Juvenile Justice County Base Joint Study Com., 1984—; mem. Iowa Task Force permanent families project Nat. Council Juvenile and Family Ct. Judges, 1984—; mem. substance abuse com. Commn. Children, Youth and Families, 1985—; co-chair Polk County Juvenile Detention Task Force, 1988. Editor: Iowa Juvenile Code Manual, 1979, Iowa Juvenile Code Workshop Manual, 1980; co-editor 1987 Cumulative Supplement, Iowa Academy of Trial Lawyers Trial Handbook; author booklet in field, 1981. Mem. Polk County Citizens Commn. on Corrections, 1977. Iowa Dept. Social Services grantee, 1980. Mem. ABA, Iowa Bar Assn., Polk County Bar Assn., Polk County Women Attys. Assn., Assn. Trial Lawyers Am., Assn. Family Counseling in Juvenile and Family Cts., Purple Arrow, Phi Kappa Phi, Omicron Nu. Republican. Home: 5831 N Waterbury Rd Des Moines IA 50312 Office: 427 Fleming Bldg Des Moines IA 50309

LAXSON, SUSAN JENSEN OURAND, realtor; b. Albuquerque, N.M., Oct. 2, 1949; d. James Robert and La Verna (Jensen) Ourand; m. Daniel Calvin Laxson, Nov. 20, 1982; 1 child, Christopher Daniel. BA, U.S. Internat. U., San Diego, 1982; MEd, U.S. Internat. U., 1982. Escrow officer First Centennial Title Co., San Diego, 1975-78; store owner Kismet Enterprises, Mex. and Calif., 1978-82; tchr. Rancho Santa Fe (Calif.) Sch., 1982-86; real estate sales Merrill Lynch, La Jolla, Calif., 1986—. Author: The Soul Taker, 1982. Mem. San Diego Bd. Realtors, Calif. Bd. Realtors, San Diego Zoological Soc. Republican. Presbyterian. Club: Torrey Pines Women's Golf (La Jolla). Home: 8831 Caminito Sueno La Jolla CA 92037 Office: Merrill Lynch Realty 1227 Prospect St La Jolla CA 92037

LAY, RUTH RYNER, tennis professional; b. Vienna, Ga., Dec. 26, 1925; d. James Buford and Ruth (Lewis) Ryner; m. Joseph Ewell Lay, Sept. 13, 1947; 1 dau., Ruth Lewis. B.A., Agnes Scott Coll. 1946. Profl., mgr. Cumberland Tennis Club, Atlanta, 1968-71; asst. mgr. Tennis Lady, Inc., Atlanta, 1972-76; profl. coach, 1976-84; profl. WCT/Peachtree World of Tennis, Norcross, Ga., 1985—. Recipient Touchstone trophy So. Tennis Assn., 1966; Nat. Service bowl U.S. Tennis Assn., 1971; Jacobs bowl So. Tennis Assn., 1978; named to So. Tennis Hall of Fame, 1982. Mem. U.S. Tennis Assn. (chmn. Jr. Wightman Fedn. Cup 1975-84), Ga. Profl. Tennis Assn., So. Tennis Assn. (officer 1965-78), U.S. Profl. Tennis Assn. Democrat. Presbyterian. Avocations: fishing. Office: WCT/Peachtree World of Tennis 6200 Peachtree Corners W Norcross GA 30092

LAYCOCK, DEANE CLARK, bank officer; b. Lutherville, Md., Apr. 23, 1921; d. Robert Otto and Sadie (Robinson) Clark; student Balt. Coll. Commerce, 1937-38; m. Zane B. Laycock, Dec. 6, 1952. With Fiduciary Trust Co., Boston, 1962-68, 74-86 , trust officer, 1974-86 , v.p., 1981-86; exec. asst. to pres. Yale U., 1969-74; asst. treas. Radcliffe Coll., 1975-83. 1st v.p., chmn. fin. com. Boston YWCA, 1976-79, bd. dirs., 1976-79; exec. com., chmn. planning and evaluation com., trustee United Community Planning Corp., Boston, 1977-83, asst. treas., 1981-82, dir., v.p. fin., 1981-82; bd. dirs. Mass. chpt. Arthritis Found., 1981-83; bd. dirs., mem. council, chmn. research com. YMCA of U.S.A., 1981—, v.p. council, 1984-87, vice chmn. bd. dirs., 1984-87. Mem. Nat. Alliance Profl. and Exec. Women's Networks (founding mem., bd. dirs. 1980—, pres. 1980-83), Boston Luncheon Club Bus. and Profl. Women (founder, pres. 1975-80, exec. com. 1975-84), Clubs: Harvard, Federal (Boston). Office: 175 Federal St Boston MA 02105

LAYTON, KATHLEEN MARGARET, computer company software sales executive, consultant; b. St. Louis, Dec. 20, 1947; d. Paul Thomas and Margaret (Boultinghouse) Dunn; m. Jon J. Layton, July 26, 1968 (div. July 1979); children: J. Thomas, Jennifer M. BS in Math., SE Mo. U., 1971; MBA, Washington U., St. Louis, 1986. Pricing analyst Vico Corp., St. Louis, 1976-78; mgr. fin. analysis LLC Corp., Clayton, Mo., 1978-80; tech. cons. Control Data Corp., St. Louis, 1980-81, account mgr., 1981-82, region mgr., 1982-85, dir. mktg.-emerging markets, 1986; nat. sales mgr., Affinitec Corp., 1986—; speaker to women in bus., 1980-85. Com. chmn. Ethical Soc., Clayton, 1978—; v.p., treas. Francis Howell Sch. Dist., St. Charles, 1982-84; bd. dirs., publicity chmn. RIII Baseball Assn., St. Charles, 1983-84. Curator's scholar Southwest Mo. U., Cape Girardeau, 1967; Control Data Corp. scholar Washington U., 1984-86. Mem. Nat. Assn. Female Execs., NOW (polit. action com.), Am. Ethical Union (rep.). Avocations: racquetball, hiking, canoeing, reading. Home: 3 La Baron Ct Saint Charles MO 63303 Office: Affinitec Corp 2252 Welsch Industrial Ct Saint Louis MO 63146

LAZAR, MARDA GOLDFINE, cosmetics company executive; b. Chgo., Jan. 12, 1956; d. Judd Arnold and Audree (Lazarus) Goldfine; m. Andrew P. Lazar, Apr. 18, 1982; 1 child, Michael Goldfine. B.F.A., Ariz. State U., 1977; student U. Iowa, 1973-75, Hispanic Inst., Burgos, Spain, 1975. Lic., real estate, Ill. Cosmetic, indsl., corp. designer Frederick Vallarta & Assocs., Chgo., 1978; toy, indsl., package designer Playskool, Inc., Chgo., 1978-79; space utilization analyst Baxter Travenol Labs., Inc., Deerfield, Ill., 1979-82, exec. staff asst. to dir., 1982-83; pres. DermaLab Ltd., Bensenville, Ill., 1983-87, design and real estate cons., 1987—, also dir., chmn. publicity Crusade of Mercy, Baxter Travenol, 1981-82; womens bd. dirs. Lambs Farm, Libertyville, 1982—. Mem. Ind. Cosmetic Mfrs. Assn., Gamma Phi Beta. Jewish. Club: Northmoor Country. Lodge: B'nai B'rith. Avocations: running, travel, gourmet cooking, golf, art.

LAZAR, NANCY PADGETT, law librarian; b. Newberry, S.C., June 3, 1932; d. Price J. and Caroline (Weeks) P.; B.S., Northwestern U., 1953; M.L.S., U. Md., 1972; J.D., Georgetown U., 1977; m. David Lazar, Aug. 6, 1953. Bar: D.C. 1977. Asst. librarian U.S. Ct. Appeals for D.C. Circuit, Washington, 1972-74, supervisory librarian, 1974-81, circuit. librarian, 1981—. Mem. D.C. Bar Assn., Am. Assn. Law Libraries, D.C. Law Librarians Soc., Am. Library Assn., D.C. Library Assn. Home: 5301 Duvall Dr Bethesda MD 20816 Office: US Courthouse Washington DC 20001

LAZAR, WENDY PHILLIPS, retail executive, writer; b. Rochester, N.Y., Apr. 8, 1939; d. Sam and Anne Naomi (Koren) Phillips; m. Martin Lazar, June 3, 1967; children: Jodi Alissa, Kim Sheryl. BS, Syracuse U., 1961. Producer, writer and host radio and TV, N.Y.C. and Japan, 1957-70; owner Amerika Yorozu Soodanjo, Norwood, N.J., 1978-80; v.p. Women Working Home, Inc., Norwood, 1980-85; pres. Catalog Marketplace, Inc., 1985—. cons., mem. adv. com. NYU Ctr. for Study of Foodservice Mgmt., 1982-84. Author: The Jewish Holiday Book, 1977; co-author, pub.: Women Working Home, 1981, 2d edit., 1983. Mem. Better Bus. Bur., Nat. Panel Consumer Arbitrators, 1985—. Recipient Top Rated Speaker award Internat. Platform Assn., 1982. Mem. Nat. Alliance of Homebased Businesswomen (co-founder 1980, pres. 1982-84), NE Bergen Indsl. Assn., LWV. Democrat. Avocations: skiing, canoeing, ice skating, swimming, cooking. Office: Catalog Marketplace Inc PO Box 144 Norwood NJ 07648-0144

LAZARIS, PAMELA ADRIANE, municipal agency administrator; b. Dixon, Ill., Oct. 13, 1956; d. Michael Constantine and Ellen Euridice (Eftax) L.; m. Eugene Dale Monson, Oct. 17, 1987. BFA in Fine Arts, U. Wis., Milw., 1978; MS in Urban and Regional Planning, U. Wis., 1982. Analyst planning Wis. Dept. Natural Resources, Madison, 1979-82; asst. city planner City of Albert Lea, Minn., 1982-83; specialist community devel. City of Winona, Minn., 1983-85; coordinator community devel. City of Waseca, Minn., 1985—. Vol. spl. events Farmam.-Minn. Agrl. Interpretive Ctr., Waseca, 1985-86. Named one of Oustanding Young Women of Am., 1986. Mem. Am. Inst. Cert. Planners (cert.), Am. Planning Assn. (bd. dirs. so. dist. Minn. chpt. 1986—), Minn. Planning Assn. (bd. dirs. so. dist. 1985—), Minn. Indsl. Devel. Assn. Club: Toastmasters (Waseca) (sgt.-at-arms 1987, ednl. v.p. 1988). Home: PO Box 325 110 6th Ave NE Waseca MN 56093 Office: City of Waseca 508 S State St Waseca MN 56093

LAZAROF, ELEANORE BERMAN, artist; b. N.Y.C., Sept. 2, 1928; d. Isidor and Elsie (Goldstein) Berman; children: Deborah Nicholas, Jan Nicholas, Anthony Nicholas, David Lazarof. BA, UCLA, 1950. One woman shows include: Kirk De Gooyer Gallery, Los Angeles, 1982, Kouros Gallery, N.Y.C., 1982, Los Angeles City Hall, 1984, Gallery Xt, Brussels, Belgium, 1985, New England Ctr. for Contemporary Art, Mass., 1985, Mcpl. Gallery, Kampen, The Netherlands, 1986, Mcpl. Gallery, Amstelveen, The Netherlands, 1986; exhibited in group shows: LAART, N.Y.C., 1986, U. Hawaii, Hilo, 1986, Elaine Starkman Gallery, N.Y.C., 1982, Los Angeles County Mus. Art, 1981, Boston Ctr. for the Arts, 1981, Wesleyan Coll., 1980, Newport Harbor Mus., 1977; represented in permanent collections: Los Angeles County Mus. Art, Bklyn. Mus., Milw. Art Ctr., Grunwald Graphic Art Ctr., UCLA, others. Mem. N.A.W.A., Artists Equity Assn. (adv. bd.), Los Angeles Printmaking Assn., Nat. Watercolor Soc.

LAZARUS, JOAN HOUSE, dancer, choreographer, educator; b. Urbana, Ill., Feb. 11, 1952; d. Arthur Stephen and Vear Maxine (Simon) H.; m. Peter D. Lazarus, May 14, 1972 (div. 1978); m. Stephen L. McCandless, Sept. 30, 1978 (div. 1984). BA in Psycholinguistics, Ind. U., 1973; MA in Dance, U. Oreg., 1978. Artistic dir. Lazarus Dance Theater, Eugene, Oreg., 1978-81; instr. U. Oreg., Eugene, 1978-81; asst. prof. Mills Coll., Oakland, Calif., 1981-84; sec. Lazarus Prodns., San Francisco, 1984—; artistic dir. Lazarus/Dance, San Francisco, 1984—; artist-in-residence High Sch. of Arts, San Francisco, 1985—; adminstrv. asst. Comunity Relations Dept., San Francisco Ballet, 1986—; asst. producer Nat. Dance Inst. Event of Yr., San Francisco, 1986—; mem. adv. council Dance Calif. Choreographer: Trio Solo, 1978, We're Off, 1978, Limited Editions, 1980, Limited Editions II, 1981, Side-by-Side-by-Sondheim, 1982, Loom, 1982, Re-Opening, 1983, A Zappa Affair, 1984, Syntactic Structures, 1985, Buddies, 1985-86, Grey Matters, 1986, Preface, 1986, Metrix, 1986, Preludion Angelicus, 1986, Retreat, Fall-back, Disguise, 1987; producer dance series New & Nearly New Dances, All Dance/No Tech. Vol. coordinator, field adv. council Bay Area Dance Coalition, San Francisco, 1986—; asst. arts couns. San Francisco Edn. Fund; mem. steering com. Dance Calif. Mem. Bay Area Lawyers for the Arts, In Flight Studios. Home and Office: 1539 Greenwich St Apt 5 San Francisco CA 94123

LAZARUS, ROCHELLE BRAFF, advertising executive; b. N.Y.C., Sept. 1, 1947; d. Lewis L. and Sylvia Ruth (Eisenberg) Braff; m. George M. Lazarus, Mar. 22, 1970; children: Theodore, Samantha, Benjamin. AB, Smith Coll., 1968; MBA, Columbia U., 1970. Product mgr. Clairol, N.Y.C., 1970-71; account exec. Ogilvy & Mather N.Y.C., 1971-73, account supr., 1973-77, mgmt. supr., 1977-84, sr. v.p., 1981—, account group dir., 1984-87; gen. mgr. Ogilvy & Mather Direct, 1987—. Mem. Smith Coll. Career Counseling Bd., Northampton, Mass., 1978—. Recipient YWCA Women Achievers award 1985. Home: 530 E 86th St New York NY 10028 Office: Ogilvy & Mather Direct 450 Park Ave S New York NY 10016

LEA, SUZANNE MOORE, sciences educator; b. Waxahachie, Tex., Jan. 27, 1944; d. Wallace C. and Josephine M. (Lumpkins) Moore; m. Michael David Lea, June 14, 1964; children—Katharine Alexandra, Michael David. B.A. cum laude, Rice U., 1964; M.S. in Physics, Ohio State U., 1966; Ph.D. in Physics, Duke U., 1970; M.S. computer sci. UNC., 1986. Instr. physics Davidson County Community Coll., Lexington, N.C., 1970-77, instr. physics, 1978-79; vis. asst. prof. physics U. N.C.-Greensboro, 1977-78, 83-84, research assoc., 1978-83, adj. assoc. prof., 1984-87, asst. prof. computer sci., 1987—; asst. prof. physics Livingstone Coll., Salisbury, N.C., 1979-82, assoc. prof., 1982-85, chmn. physics dept., 1979-85. Nat. Merit scholar, 1960-64; NSF grantee, 1980-83, 85-87. Mem. Am. Phys. Soc., Am. Assn. Physics Tchrs. (pres. So. Atlantic Coast Sect. 1981-82, mem. exec. com. So. Atlantic Coast sect. 1982-83, sect. rep. 1987—), N.C. Acad. Sci., Am. Astron. Soc., N.C. Assn. Astronomers, Assn. for Computing Machinery (graphics spl. interest group). Democrat. Episcopalian. Contbr. articles to profl. jours. Home: 205 Oakwood Dr Thomasville NC 27360 Office: U NC Math Dept Greensboro NC 27412

LEAB, KATHARINE KYES, publisher; b. Cleve., Mar. 17, 1941; d. Rogers Martin and Helen Gilmore (Jacoby) Kyes; m. Daniel J. Leab, Aug. 17, 1964; children—Abigail, Constance, Marcus. BA, Smith Coll., 1962; postgrad. Columbia U., 1963-64. Sr. editor Columbia U. Press, 1966-72; editor, pub. Am. Book Prices Current, 1972—; creator, mgr. BAMBAM (Bookline Alert: Missing Books and Manuscripts), UTOPIA. Author: (with Daniel J. Leab) The Auction Companion, 1981; contbr. articles to profl. jours., anthologies. Trustee Washington Montessori Sch., 1984—. Mem. ALA (security com. Rare Books and Manuscripts sect.), Bibliog. Soc. Am. (fin. com.). Club: Cosmopolitan. Office: Bancroft Parkman Inc Titus Rd PO Box 1236 Washington CT 06793

LEACH, ELIZABETH A. BIERYLA, consultant, seminar leader; b. Scranton, Pa., July 21, 1949; d. Henry Joseph and Helen Theresa (Switlinski) Bieryla; m. Donald J. Leach, July 16, 1971 (marriage dissolved); 1 child, Michael J. BS in Human Services, U. Scranton (Pa.), 1979, MS in Rehab. Counseling, 1980. Cert. rehab. counselor, ins. rehab. specialist. Adjuster Gallager Bassett Ins. Services, Scranton, Pa., 1975-79; grad. asst. U. Scranton, 1979-80; ptnr. Rehab. Mgmt. Group, Scranton, 1980-83; tng. dir., asst. risk mgr., rehab. counselor Commonwealth Telephone Enterprises, Wilkes-Barre, Pa., 1982-84; eap mgr. Avtex Fibers, Front Royal, Va., 1984-86; pres. Med. Benefits Mgmt. Services, Inc., Phoenixville, Pa., 1986—; guest presentor Bur. of Vocat. Rehab., Phila., 1982 and Mgmt. Edn. Ctr., ASPA chpts., Del. Mfg. Assn; chmn. Profl. Devel. Greater Valley ASPA, 1987-88. Bd. dirs., various com. chairs., Planned Parenthood of Lackawanna County, Scranton, 1977-80, Pa. Power & Electric, Scranton, 1979. Mem. Nat. Rehab. Assn., Nat. Assn. of Rehab. Profls. in the Pvt. Sector, Nat. Rehab. Counseling Assn., Nat. Assn. Female Execs., Am. Assn. Personnel Adminstrs. , Delta Tau Kappa, Alpha Sigma Lambda. Home: 4703 Eland Downe Phoenixville PA 19460 Office: Med Benefits Mgmt Services Inc PO Box 541 Phoenixville PA 19460

LEACH, ERIN DONNELL, tour coordinator; b. Yakima, Wash., Dec. 19, 1956; d. Donald Alfred and Ardelle Elaine (Nelson) L. AA, Shoreline Jr. Coll., 1977; BA, Western Wash. U., 1980; postgrad., NYU. Designer kitchen and office Scan/Line Inc., Honolulu, 1980-81; asst. mgr. Solid Oak Factory, Bellevue, Wash., 1982; sr. supr. Wien Air Alaska, Seattle, 1983-84; mgr. interline reservations Internat. Travel Reps., N.Y.C., 1985; tour coordinator Japan Travle Bur., N.Y.C., 1986—. Author: (poems) My Room, 1986, Mother, 1987.

LEACH, LINDA MCCOY, educational administrator; b. Lumberton, N.C., Oct. 23, 1951; d. Johnny Robinson and Sadie (Howell) Robinson McCoy. AAS, Robeson Tech. Coll., 1979; BS, Fayetteville State U., 1982, postgrad., 1986—; MEd, Campbell U., 1985. Vet. service officer Robeson Tech. Coll., Lumberton, 1973-81; adminstrv. asst. N.C. Gen. Assembly, Raleigh, 1983, N.C. Dem. Party Hdqrs., Raleigh, 1983-84; counselor, recruiter, testing adminstr. Bladen Tech. Coll., Dublin, N.C., 1984—. Campaign sec. Thompson for Alderman, Lumberton, 1978; asst. Farmers for Re-Election of Jimmy Carter, Lumberton, 1980. Mem. N.C. Assn. Women Deans, Adminstrs. and Counselors, Nat. Assn. Accts., Nat. Assn. Female Execs., AAUW, Nu Tau Sigma, Delta Mu Delta, Alpha Kappa Mu, Lumberton Women of Essence (founder, sec. 1976-80). Home: PO Box 275 Lumberton NC 28359

LEACH, MARY JOANN, nurse; b. Dennison, Ohio, Feb. 18, 1957; d. James F. and Ann J. (Vanem) Sullivan; m. Ronald G. Leach, Mar. 23, 1984. AS in Nursing, Kent State U., 1977; BS in Nursing, Akron U., 1985. RN, Ohio. Staff nurse in pediatrics Dr.'s Hosp., Massillon, Ohio, 1977-81; staff nurse in ICU Massillon Community Hosp., 1981-87, head nurse, 1987—; v.p. L.L. Miller Inc., Canton, Ohio, 1986—. Mem. Sigma Theta Tau. Roman Catholic. Home: 3544 Moonlight Bay Dr NW Canton OH 44708 Office: Massillon Community Hosp 875 8th St NE PO Box 805 Massillon OH 44648-9983

LEACHMAN, CLORIS, actress; b. Des Moines, June 30, 1930; m. George England, 1953 (div. 1979); 5 children. Ed., Northwestern U. Actress: (films) including Kiss Me Deadly, 1955, Butch Cassidy and the Sundance Kid, 1969, W.U.S.A., 1970, The Steagle, 1971, The Last Picture Show, 1971 (Acad. award for best supporting actress 1971), Dillinger, 1973, Daisy Miller, 1974, Young Frankenstein, 1974, Crazy Mama, 1975, High Anxiety, 1977, The North Avenue Irregulars, 1979, Scavenger Hunt, 1979, Herbie Goes Bananas, History of the World, Part 1, 1982, Shadow Play, Walk Like a Man, Hansel and Gretel; TV series including Lassie, 1957, Route 66, Laramie, Trials of O'Brien, Mary Tyler Moore Show, Phyllis, 1975-77, Facts of Life, (TV movies) including Silent Night, Lonely Night, 1969, Brand New Life, 1973, The Migrants, 1974, A Girl Named Sooner, 1975, Ladies of the Corridor, The New Original Wonder Woman, 1975, It Happened One Christmas, 1977, Long Journey Back, 1978, Willa, 1979, S.O.S. Titanic, 1979, The Acorn People, 1981, Advice to the Lovelorn, 1981, Miss All-American Beauty, 1982, Dixie: Changing Habits, 1983, The Demon Murder Case, 1983, Ernie Kovacs, Between the Laughter, 1984, Deadly Intentions, 1985, Love is Never Silent, (TV miniseries) Backstairs at the White House, 1979; guest appearance: The Love Boat, 1976. Recipient 6 Emmy awards. Address: McCartt Oreck Barrett 9200 Sunset Blvd Suite 1009 Los Angeles CA 90048

LEACHMAN, CONNIE JEAN KENNEDY, sales executive; b. Elkins, W.Va., Dec. 31, 1957; d. George Bruce and Helen Lucille (Stiles) Kennedy; m. Bradley Leachman, June 6, 1987. Cert. in Mgmt. Effectiveness, U. So.

Calif., 1987. With Topflight Corp., Buena Park, Calif., 1978—, prodn. mgr., 1984-85; gen. mgr. western div. Topflight Corp., Buena Park, 1986-88; sales service mgr. Topflight Corp., York, Pa., 1988—. Assistor Kids' Club-Union Rescue Mission, 1987. Mem. U. So. Calif. Alumni Assn. Republican. Office: Topflight Corp 160 E 9th Ave York PA 17404

LEAHEY, DIANNE MARIE, quality assurance engineer; b. Worcester, Mass., Dec. 17, 1960; d. James Joseph and Annette Marie (L'Heureux) L. BS in Chemistry, Worcester (Mass.) Polytechnic Inst., 1982. Process asst. Kimberly Clark Corp., Fullerton, Calif., 1982-83; auditor quality assurance Galileo Electro-Optics, Sturbridge, Mass., 1983-85; engr. quality assurance Unitrode Corp., Watertown, Mass., 1985-87, asst. mgr. quality assurance, 1987—. Home: 186 Gardner St #2-9 Arlington MA 02174 Office: Unitrode Corp 580 Pleasant St Watertown MA 02172

LEAHY, JEANNETTE (JEANNETTE OLIVER LEAHY TINEN KAEHLER), actress; b. Eau Claire, Wis., Sept. 9, 1927; d. Kenneth A. and Berthe Hortence (Borie) Oliver; student various acting workshops; m. Thomas J. Leahy (dec.); children—Denyse Leahy Karsten Feeney, Thomas J.; m. William J. Tinen, June 15, 1969 (dec.); m. 3d, Wallace W. Kaehler, Jan. 13, 1980. TV personality Jeannette Lee, Sta. WFBM-TV, Indpls., 1950-53; actress Peninsular Players, summer stock theatre, Door County, Wis., 1960—, also radio, TV, stage, film, comml. Vice-pres., Evanston Drama Club, 1961-62; dir. Wilmette Children's Theatre, 1960-65; bd. dirs. Easter Seal Soc., 1970-75. Mem. Actors Equity Union, SAG, AFTRA, Chgo. Unlimited. Republican. Roman Catholic. Clubs: North Shore Country, Michigan Shores, Wilmette-Kenilworth (pres. 1956-57), North Shore Assos. (pres. 1982-83).

LEAHY, MARJORIE ANNE, communications firm executive; b. Jackson, Tenn., Aug. 31, 1938; d. John and Marjorie Elizabeth (Aylor) Solinsky; m. Edward James Leahy, July 2, 1960; children—James Peter, Laura Marjorie, John Edward. B.S., Syracuse U., 1960. Reporter, TV editor Rome Sentinel (N.Y.), 1961-62; free-lance writer, Croton, N.Y., 1967-78; editor Clearwater, Inc., Poughkeepsie, N.Y., 1974-76; reporter news, features Gannett Westchester, Tarrytown, N.Y., 1978-81; pres. Five String Prodns., Croton, 1981—, health fitness pubs., 1985—, production mgr., Croton-Cortlandt Gazette, 1987; cons. publs. Revlon Health Care Group, Tuckahoe, N.Y., 1981-86, Am. Brands, Inc., N.Y.C., 1986—. Mem. Croton Conservation Adv. Council, 1978—; coordinator Clearwater Hudson River Festival, Croton, N.Y., 1978—; bd. dirs. Clearwater Inc., 1984-86, exec. com., 1985-86; vol. instr. ecology Westchester County, 1988—. Mem. Women in Communications (chairperson publicity 1982-83, v.p. 1983-84). Home and Office: 62 Van Wyck St Croton-on-Hudson NY 10520

LEAK, MARGARET ELIZABETH, financial services executive; b. Atlanta, Sept. 9, 1946; d. William Whitehurst and Margaret Elizabeth (Whitsitt) L. BS in Psychology, Okla. State U., 1968; postgrad., U. Okla., 1960-69, Cornell U., 1976-78; grad. advanced mgmt. program, Harvard U., 1983. Editor communications Eastern State Bankcard Assn., N.Y.C., 1969-71; sr. edn. specialist Citibank, N.Y.C., 1971-73; adminstr. orgn. devel. NBC, N.Y.C., 1973-74; mgr. tng. and devel. Atlantic Cos., N.Y.C., 1974-76, sec. human resources, 1976-78, v.p. human resources, 1978-86, v.p. human resources and corp. communications, 1984-86, sr. v.p. adminstrv. services, 1987—. Mem. adv. bd. grad. mgmt. program for women Pace U., 1976-78. Mem. Am. Soc. Personnel Adminstrn. (sr. v.p. adminstrv. services), Ins. Co. Edn. Dirs. Soc. (nat. v.p. 1978), Gamma Phi Beta. Presbyterian. Office: Atlantic Cos 45 Wall St New York NY 10005

LEAKE, BRENDA GAIL, nurse; b. Harriman, Tenn., Aug. 5, 1950; d. James Frank and Pauline Ruby (McGuffey) Judd; m. Lee Leake, Aug. 1, 1970 (div. Apr. 1974). AS in Nursing, U. Nev., Las Vegas, 1971, BN, 1986; cert. enterostomal therapist, U. Calif., San Diego, 1975. RN, Nev. Staff nurse Humana Hosp. Sunrise, Las Vegas, 1971-73, relief charge nurse, 1973-76, enterostomal therapist, 1976—; speaker Hospice Vol. program, Las Vegas, 1982—, I Can Cope program, Las Vegas, 1984—. Author instructional guide. Vol. Am. Cancer Soc., 1983—, mem. program devel. nurse edn. com. Mem. Intenat. Assn. Enterostomal Therapists (cert.), Am. Nurses Assn., So. Nev. Nurses Assn., World Council Enterostomal Therapists, Am. Urol. Assn. (cert.), So. Nev. Ostomy Assn. (med. advisor 1976—), Ileitis & Colitis Assn., Advanced practitioners Nursing (cert., program chmn. 1986—). Republican. Presbyterian. Office: Humana Hosp Sunrise 3186 Maryland Pkwy Las Vegas NV 89109

LEAKE, VILMA LOUISE DEW, education educator; b. Phila., Dec. 12, 1935; d. Ernest and Geneva (Wynn) Dew; m. George J. Leake, Sept. 7, 1952; children: Yollanda G., Dierda J. BA, Livingston Coll., 1957; MEd, U. Buffalo, 1968; postgrad., U. San Francisco, 1987—. Tchr. Charlotte (N.C.) Meak Sch. System, 1954—, Highland High Sch., Gastonia, N.C., 1957-59; dir. adminstrn. Barbara Scotia Coll., Concord, N.C., 1959-60; tchr. Sch. Dist. #31, Buffalo, 1960-64. Founder, pres. Minister's Wives, Charlotte; chair Juvenile Service Bd., Charlotte, 1986—; leader So. Christian Leadership Conf., Charlotte, 1987—; 1st v.p. African Meth. Zion Ch. Mem. NAACP, N.C. Assn. Educators, Charlotte Mecklenburg Assn. Educators, Womens' home and Overseas Missionary Soc., Delta Sigma Theta, Phi Lamda Theta. Home: 10122 Whitethorn Dr Matthews NC 28105

LEARK, JUNE SACHIKO, marketing professional; b. Downey, Calif., Mar. 26, 1953; d. George and Fumiko (Iwai) Okubo; m. William G. Leark, Nov. 22, 1980. BA, Whittier Coll., 1975. Sales clk. Sears Roebuck & Co., Cerritos, Calif., 1971-75; sec. product info. dept. Davison Chem. div. W.R. Grace & Co., South Gate, Calif., 1975-79; dept. clk. Nissan Motor Corp. in USA, Carson, Calif., 1979-81; statistician USA div. Nissan Motor Corp., Carson, Calif., 1981-84, sales asst., 1984-85, sales analyst, 1985—. Mem. Nat. Assn. Female Execs. Office: Nissan Motor Corp in USA 18501 S Figueroa St Carson CA 90248-4504

LEARN, DORIS LYNN, school district purchasing director; b. Long Beach, Calif., May 11, 1949; d. Rowe Francis and Annie Mae (Tunstill) Christopher; m. Thomas Robert Learn, Oct. 17, 1987. Student Foothill Coll., 1966-67, DeAnza Coll., 1969-71. Cashier Navy Exchange, China Lake, Calif., 1965-66, Navy Exchange, Moffett Field, Calif., 1966-67; exec. sec. Varian Assocs., Palo Alto, Calif., 1967-75; salesperson Jorgensen Steel, Langhorne, Pa., 1976; exec. sec. Pennsbury Sch. Dist., Fallsington, Pa., 1976-82, dir. purchasing, 1982—. Mem. Pa. Assn. Sch. Bus. Ofcls. (Pa. registered sch. bus. specialist 1986, mem. conf. com. 1986), Assn. Sch. Bus. Ofcls., Pa. Sch. Bds. Assn., Nat. Assn. Female Execs., Govt. Fin. Officers Assn., Pennsbury Assn. Suprs. and Adminstrs., Nat. Purchasing Assn., Delaware Valley Assn. Sch. Bus. Officials. Republican. Presbyterian. Avocations: needlecrafts, golf, spectator sports. Home: 1365 Brook Ln Jamison PA 18929 Office: Pennsbury Sch Dist 134 Yardley Ave Box 338 Fallsington PA 19054

LEARY, NANCY JANE, marketing professional; b. Natick, Mass., Mar. 25, 1952; d. Norman Leslie and Dorothy (Holmquist) Pidgeon; m. Patrick J. Leary, Sept. 17, 1977 (div. May 1984). AA, Mass Bay Coll., Wellesley, Mass., 1979; BS, Lesley Coll., Cambridge, Mass., 1988. Sec. GTE Corp., Needham, Mass., 1973-78; coordinator edn. Cullinet Software Inc., Westwood, Mass., 1983-84, adminstrv. asst., 1984-85, mgr. adminstrn., 1985-86; specialist product mktg. Cullinet Co., Westwood, Mass., 1986-88; v.p. mktg. and adminstrn. Jonathan's Landscaping, Bradenton Beach, Fla., 1988—.

LEARY, NOREEN ELIZABETH, utility executive; b. Butte, Mont., July 14, 1949; d. Edward T. and Mae H. (Walsh) L. BA in Math., U. Mont., 1971; sloan fellow (grad. bus.), London Bus. Sch., 1984. Math. tchr. South Cen. Jr. High Sch., Butte, 1971-72; power ops. specialist Bonneville Power Adminstrn., Portland, Oreg., 1974-76; pub. utility specialist Bonneville Power Adminstrn., Portland, 1976-79, asst. to dir. power supply, 1979-80; area power mgr. Bonneville Power Adminstrn., Walla Walla, Wash., 1980-82; dir. mktg. Nat. Hydro, Boston, 1982-83; mgr. power contracts engring and research Sierra Pacific Power Co., Reno, 1985—. Volleyball referee Wash. State Athletic Orgn., Vancouver, 1974-80; bd. dirs. United Way, Walla Walla, Wash., 1981-82. Office: Sierra Pacific Power Co PO Box 10100 6100 Neil Rd Reno NV 89520

LEASON, MARIE ELENA, government education technician; b. Canon City, Colo., Aug. 2, 1947; d. Victor and Helen M. (Orecchio) Falgien; m. Karl E. Leason, July 19, 1969. Student, So. Colo. State Coll., 1965-67. Clk.-typist Army Edn. Ctr. U.S. Dept. Def., Ft. Carson, Colo., 1966-69, test adminstr., 1969-74, edn. aid, 1974-81, edn. technician, 1981—. Mem. Bus. and Profl. Women's Assn., Mt. Plains Adult Edn. Assn., Nat. Assn. Female Execs., Federally Employed Women, Fed. Women's Program Com. (v.p. 1985-86). Democrat. Roman Catholic. Home: 3076 Ute St Canon City CO 81212-9368 Office: Army Edn Ctr Bldg 2217 Fort Carson CO 80913-5019

LEATHERBERRY, ANNE KNOX CLARK, manufacturer children's wear, gift designer; b. Geneva, Ill., Jan. 19, 1953; d. Donald William and Margaret Lorraine (Johnson) Clark; m. David Boyd Leatherberry, Aug. 5, 1978; children: Elizabeth Anne, Laura Knox. BS in Bus., Miami U., Oxford, Ohio, 1975. With Carson, Pirie, Scott & Co., Chgo., 1975-77; health care sales specialist Gen. Foods Corp., Northlake, Ill., 1977-78; account mgr. Cin., 1978-79; pres., owner Annie's Originals/Kids Collectables, Ltd., Waukesha, Wis., 1979—; cons. Lamb's Quarters, Hartford, Wis., 1982-83, Ungerwear, West Alexandria, Ohio, 1982-84, Little Bits, Waukesha, 1984—, Evelyn's Creations, East Troy, Wis., 1986—, others. Sec. bd. dirs. Waukesha Area Symphonic Band, 1987—, mem., 1979—, Carroll Coll. Community Orch., Waukesha, 1985-86. Mem. Dir. Mktg. Assn., Soc. Craft Designers, Nat. Assn. Female Execs., Kappa Kappa Gamma. Republican. Lutheran. Lodge: PEO. Home and Office: W255 S6635 Ridge Rd Waukesha WI 53186

LEATHERBERRY, JUANITA BROWN, accounting executive services; b. Buckingham, Va., Mar. 29, 1951; d. Warren G. Harding and Gretchen Hoyt (Jackson) Brown; m. Daniel Henry Leatherberry, Aug. 15, 1970; children: Daniel Maurice, Janice Marie. Bs in Acctg., Va. Commonwealth U., 1973. CPA, Va. Supr. sr. acct. Peat, Marwick, Mitchell & Co., Richmond, Va., 1973-78; acctg. instr. profl. in residence Va. State U., Petersburg, 1977-78; dir. corp. acct. A.H. Robins Co., Inc., Richmond, Va., 1978—; rep. fin. sect. Pharm. Mfr. Assn., Washington, 1986—. Bd. dirs. Bethlehen Ctr., Richmond, 1980; mem. budget and allocations com. United Way of Greater Richmond, 1973-76; active various ch. coms.; vol. tchr. Sunday Sch. Recipient Outstanding Achievement award Laurels Women's Honor Soc., 1972, Outstanding Black Achievement award YMCA, 1985, Leadership Effectiveness Series award Sean-Delaney Leadership Programs, Inc., 1984. Fellow Va. Soc. CPA's (award of achievement 1973), Am. Inst. CPA's; mem. Phi Beta Lambda (named Miss Future Bus. Exec. 1973). Baptist. Home: 8303 Audley Ln Richmond VA 23227 Office: A H Robins Co Inc 1407 Cummings Dr Richmond VA 23220

LEATHERBY, JOANN, lawyer; b. Los Angeles, May 13, 1955; d. Ralph William and Eleanor Augustine (Samson) L. BA, Iowa Wesleyan Coll., 1977; JD, UCLA, 1980. Bar: Calif., 1980. Exec. dir. Women's Legal Clinic, Los Angeles, 1978-81; v.p. adminstrn. UniCare Ins., Irvine, Calif., 1981-82; sole practice Newport Beach, Calif., 1982-84; gen. counsel Ricoh Electronics, Inc., Santa Ana, Calif., 1984—; bd. dirs. UniCare Fin. Corp., Irvine, 1980—. Mem. Calif. Women Lawyers Assn. Home: 3400 Ave of the Arts C-414 Costa Mesa CA 92626 Office: Ricoh Electronics Inc 2320 Red Hill Ave Santa Ana CA 92705

LEATHERS, MARGARET WEIL, foundation administrator; b. Princeton, Ind., Dec. 22, 1949; d. Albert J. and Nora Jewel (Franklin) Weil; m. Charles L. Leathers, June 19, 1971 (div. Dec. 1987); children: Julianna L., Kevin Sean. AB, U. Ill., 1971; MS, Russell Sage Coll., 1979. Cert. tchr., N.Y. Employment counselor Snelling & Snelling, Schenectady, N.Y., 1972-76; substitute tchr. Monahasen High/Jr. High Sch., Schenectady, 1978-79; grant abstractor State of N.Y., Albany, 1979; program coordinator Am. Lung Assn. Santa Clara-San Benito Counties, San Jose, Calif., 1982-84, dir. programs, 1984-87, nat. clinic leader trainer, 1986—, acting exec. dir., 1987-88, exec. dir., 1988—. Author: Camp Superstuff Workbook and Teachers Manual, 1983; contbr. articles to profl. publs. and mags. Bd. dirs., officer Santa Clara Valley Council Parent-Participating Nursery Schs., 1980-81; resource vol. Lyceum Santa Clara Valley, 1983-87; leader Explorer post Boy Scouts Am., San Jose, 1988; mem. adminstrv. bd. council ministries United Meth. Ch. Mem. Am. Pub. Health Assn., Soc. Pub. Health Educators, Am. Sch. Health Assn., Phi Beta Kappa, Phi Kappa Phi, Eta Sigma Gamma, Alpha Xi Delta (pres. Santa Clara Valley 1985-87). Democrat. Home: 341 Springpark Circle San Jose CA 95136 Office: Am Lung Assn 1469 Park Ave San Jose CA 95126

LEATON, MARCELLA KAY, insurance representative, business owner; b. Eugene, Oreg., Oct. 9, 1952; d. Robert A. and Wanda Jo (Garner) Boehm; m. Michael G. Schlegel, Aug. 9, 1975; children: Kaellen June, Krystalynn Michele. Grad. high sch., Springfield, Oreg. Sales rep. The Prudential, Novato, Calif., 1973—; bus. owner Marcella Enterprises, Novato, 1983—. Contbr. articles to profl. jours. Named one of Outstanding Young Women Am., 1979. Mem. Nat. Assn. Life Underwriters (Nat. Quality award 1978, 80, 84), Marin Life Underwriters, Nat. Assn. Profl. Saleswomen (founder Marin chpt. 1982, pres. 1982-85, chmn. 1985-86, nat. v.p. 1985-86, awards and recognition chmn. 1985—, nat. pres. 1987-88), Leading Life Producers No. Calif., Million Dollar Round Table (qualifying). Clubs: President's, Western Star. Office: Marcella Enterprises 901 Reichert Ave Suite #100 Novato CA 94945

LEAVELL, ALMA MALONE, emeritus dean; b. Clay County, Ala., Nov. 15, 1916; d. William Robert and Alice Swillie (Reagan) Ingram; B.S., Jacksonville State U., 1938; M.Ed., Hardin-Simmons U., 1950; Ed.D., George Peabody Coll., 1965; m. Clifton James Malone, May 7, 1941 (dec. 1959); m. 2d, James Berry Leavell, Dec. 22, 1972; children—Mary Carolyn Williams, Judith Anne Finch. Tchr. pub. schs., Clay County, Ala., 1934-41, Abilene, Tex., 1955-60; tchr. pub. edn. Hardin-Simmons U., Abilene, 1961-65; asst. prof. edn. Houston Baptist U., 1965-79, Disting. prof. edn., 1979-84, chmn. dept. edn., 1973-84, dean Coll. Edn. and Behavioral Studies, 1980-84, dean emeritus, 1984—; cons. lang. arts Houston Area Schs. Recipient Ted Booker Outstanding Tex. Educator award, 1983; Outstanding Educator award Religious Heritage of Am., 1983; endowed acad. scholarship established in her honor Houston Bapt. U., 1984. Mem. Am. Assn. Colls. Tchrs. Edn., Tex. Assn. Tchr. Educators, Tex. Assn. Coll. Tchrs. of Edn., Internat. Reading Assn., Delta Kappa Gamma, Kappa Delta Pi. Democrat. Baptist. Home: 8112 Fondren Houston TX 77074 Office: 7502 Fondren Houston TX 77074

LEAVINE, BARBARA ANN, operations executive; b. Galesburg, Ill., Feb. 23, 1959; d. gene T. and Barbara Ann (Ambrose) Kimble; m. W.W. Pepper Leavine, May 24, 1983; 1 child, Anthony Joseph. BA, U. Fla., 1980. Dept. mgr. Robinson's of Fla., Orlando, 1981-85; recruiter Delta Search, Orlando, 1985-87; ops. mgr. Progressive Ins. Co., Tampa, Fla., 1987—. Recipient Top Producer award Fla. Assn. Personnel Cons., 1986. Democrat. Episcopal. Home: 1528 White Oak Houston TX 77009

LEAVITT, AUDREY FAYE COX, TV programming executive; b. Old Hickory, Tenn., June 1, 1932; d. James Aubrey and Bernice (Hudnall) Cox; student David Lipscomb Secondary Sch. and Coll., 1947, Tenn. Sch. Broadcasting, 1949-50, Vanderbilt U., 1948-50; children—Jack, Teresa. Woman commentator, continuity chief radio sta. WGNS, Murfreesboro, Tenn., 1949-50; announcer, continuity chief, traffic dir. Sta. KDWT, Stamford, Tex., 1950-51; sales account exec. Sta. KMAC, San Antonio, 1952; continuity chief, announcer Sta. KEYL-TV, San Antonio, 1952-54, also firm dir.; film buyer, mgr. Sta. WOAI-TV, San Antonio, 1954-68, ops. mgr. film, videotape traffic, continuity, 1968-71; film and videotape operations mgr., film buyer Sta. KENS-TV, San Antonio, 1972-79; exec. v.p. Jim Thomas & Assos., San Antonio, 1979-80; owner Communique Internationalé, TV programming syndication, 1981—, Strategic Planning Services; exec. producer TV series The Lone Star Sportsman Show; writer, exec. producer and dir. TV series Weather or Not; writer, producer gourmet cooking show For Men Only, The Great Age, 1988. Mem. Internat. Platform Assn., San Antonio Conservation Soc., San Antonio Livestock and Rodeo Exposition, Yellow Rose Tex., Nat. Assn. Female Execs., World Affairs Council. Republican. Office: PO Box 6493 San Antonio TX 78209

LEAVITT, JOAN KAZANJIAN, state health official, physician; b. Boston, Jan. 14, 1926; d. Varaztad Hovannes and Marion V. (Hanford) Kazanjian; m. Don K. Leavitt; children—Mark S., Lynda Donn. A.B., Radcliffe Coll., 1947; M.A., Smith Coll., 1949; M.D., Boston U., 1953. Intern in pediatrics Boston City Hosp., 1953-54, resident in pediatrics, 1954-55; resident in pediatrics Mass. Gen. Hosp., Boston, 1955-56, 57-58; pediatrician Comanche County (Okla.) Guidance Center, 1959; practice medicine specializing in pediatrics Altus, Okla., 1959-64; med. dir. Jackson County (Okla.) Health Dept., 1960-67, Kay County (Okla.) Health Dept., 1967-76; chief maternal and child health service Okla. Health Dept., Oklahoma City, 1976; dep. commr. for personal health services Okla. Health Dept., 1976-77, commr. of health, 1977—. Mem. AMA, Okla. State Med. Assn., Okla. Public Health Assn., Oklahoma County Med. Soc., Assn. State and Territorial Health Ofcls. (pres. 1985-86), Sigma Xi. Office: 1000 NE Tenth St PO Box 53551 Oklahoma City OK 73152

LEAVITT, JUDITH ANN, information specialist; b. Washington, Iowa, Nov. 21, 1947; d. David Elwood and Ada Beth (Denison) Kleese; m. David Russell Leavitt, Aug. 30, 1969; children: Joseph, John. BA with honors and distinction, U. Iowa, 1970; MLS, Ind. U., 1977. Periodicals and catalog librarian Ball State U., Muncie, Ind., 1979-81; supr. info. ctr. Collins div. Rockwell Internat., Cedar Rapids, Iowa, 1982—. Author: Women in Management, 1980, 82, Dual Career Families, 1982, American Women Managers & Adminstrators, 1985, Local Area Networks, 1986, Telecommuting, 1986, Women in Management and Administration, 1988. Named Woman of Yr., Cedar Rapids YWCA, 1985. Mem. Spl. Libraries Assn., Women Library Workers Assn., Iowa Library Assn., LWV, Beta Phi Mu. Democrat. Unitarian. Club: Toastmasters (past pres. local chpt.). Home: 1223 38th St NW Cedar Rapids IA 52405 Office: Rockwell Internat 400 Collins Rd NE Cedar Rapids IA 52498

LEAVITT, MARY JANICE DEIMEL, educator, civic worker; b. Washington, Aug. 21, 1924; d. Henry L. and Ruth (Grady) Deimel; B.A., Am. U., Washington, 1946; postgrad. U. Md., 1963-65, U. Va., 1965-67, 72-73, 78-79, George Washington U., 1966-67; m. Robert Walker Leavitt, Mar. 30, 1945; children Michael Deimel, Robert Walker, Caroline Ann Leavitt Snyder. Tchr., Rothery Sch., Arlington, Va., 1947; dir. Sunnyside, Children's House, Washington, 1949; asst. dir. Coop. Sch. for Handicapped Children, Arlington, 1962, dir., Arlington, Springfield, Va., 1963-66; tchr. mentally retarded children Fairfax (Va.) County Pub. Schs., 1966-68; asst. dir. Burgundy Farm Country Day Sch., Alexandria, Va., 1968-69; tchr., substitute tchr. specific learning problem children Accotink Acad., Springfield, Va., 1970-80; substitute tchr. learning disabilities Children's Achievement Center, McLean, Va., 1973-82, Psychiat. Inst., Washington and Rockville, Md., 1976-82, Home-Bound and Substitute Program, Fairfax, Va., 1978-84; asst. info. specialist Ednl. Research Service, Inc., Rosslyn, Va., 1974-76; docent Sully Plantation, Fairfax County (Va.) Park Authority, 1981-87, 88—, vol. Honor Roll, 1987; sec. Widowed Persons Service, 1983-85, mem., 1985—. Mem. edn. subcom. Va. Commn. Children and Youth, 1973-74; Den mother Nat. Capital Area Cub Scouts, Boy Scouts Am., 1962; troop fund raising chmn. Nat. Capitol council Girl Scouts U.S.A., 1968-69; capt. amblyopia team No. Va. chpt. Delta Gamma Alumnae, 1969; vol. Prevention of Blindness, 1980—; fund raiser Martha Movement, 1977-78. Recipient award Nat. Assn. for Retarded Citizens, 1975. Mem. AAUW (co-chmn. met. area mass media com. D.C. chpt. 1973-75, v.p. Alexandria br. 1974-76, fellowship co-chmn. Springfield-Annandale br. 1979-80, name grantee ednl. found. 1980, historian 1980-82, cultural co-chmn. 1983-84), Assn. Part-Time Profls. (co-chmn. Va. local groups, job devel. and membership asst. 1981), Older Women's League, Nat. Trust for Historic Preservation, Nat. Mus. of Women in the Arts (charter mem.), Smithsonian Resident Assoc. Program, Delta Gamma (treas. No. Va. alumnae chpt. 1973-75, pres. 1977-79, found. chmn. 1979-81). Roman Catholic. Club: Arlington Hall Officer's. Home: 7129 Rolling Forest Ave Springfield VA 22152

LEBEAU, JOYCE CHARNAY, psychologist; b. New York, Calif., July 30, 1941; d. David Buckley Charnay and Shirley Renée (Kraft) Miller; m. Christoper R. LeBeau, Aug. 9, 1971; children: Deborah Ann, Joshua Mark. BS, Dominican Coll., San Rafael, Calif., 1972, MS, 1977; PhD, Calif. Grad. Sch., San Rafael, 1984. Prodn. asst. Four Star Prodns., Los Angeles, 1966-70; operator day care Tiburon, Calif., 1970-74; edn. coordinator St. Vincent's Sch., San Rafael, 1974-78; pvt. practice psychology Larkopur, Calif., 1978-84, Ross, Calif., 1984—; cons. Katherine Bransen Sch., Ross, 1979-84, Marin Cath. Sch., Kentfield, Calif., 1979-87, St. Marks Sch., San Rafael, 1980-84. Author: Give Yourself a Hug, 1986, Where do You Go from Up, 1986, Silver Spoon Syndrome, 1986. Mem. Calif. Assn. Marriage and Family Therapy, Marin County Assn. Marriage and Family Therapy, Nat. Alliance Mental Health. Avocations: cooking, gardening, walking, travelling, films. Office: 27 Ross Common PO Box 1563 Ross CA 94987

LEBEDEFF, DIANE ALEXIS, judge; b. Detroit, June 25, 1943; d. Alexis M. and Vera A. Lebedeff; m. Keith Lonesome; 1 child, Angelica Lebedeff. B.A., U. Mich., 1965, J.D., 1968. Admitted to N.Y. bar, 1969, Mich. bar, 1969; asso. appellate counsel Legal Aid Soc., N.Y.C., 1968-71; atty. div. criminal justice services N.Y. State, 1971-73; atty. N.Y.C. Dept. Rent and Housing Maintenance, 1976-80, gen. counsel, 1976-80, also counsel N.Y.C. Rent Guidelines; housing judge N.Y. Civil Ct., 1980-82, judge, 1983-87; acting justice N.Y. State Supreme Ct, 1988—. Mem. Community Bd. 2, N.Y.C., 1979-80. Mem. Assn. Bar City N.Y., Am. Bar Assn., Nat. Assn. Women Judges, N.Y. State Assn. Women Judges (bd. dirs. 1984-86, sec. 1986-88, v.p. 1988—), N.Y. State Bar Assn., N.Y. Women's Bar Assn. Clubs: Women's City, City (N.Y.C.). Address: 111 Centre St New York NY 10013

LEBELL, JANE, radio producer, announcer, writer; b. N.Y.C., Apr. 29, 1944; d. Irving and Harriet (Adler) LeB. Student, Mannes Coll. Music, 1961-63; Diploma in vocal music, U. Hartford, 1965. Mgr. visitor's services Lincoln Ctr., N.Y.C., 1974-76; staff announcer Sta. WQXR-AM & FM, N.Y.C., 1973—, writer, announcer, producer Today in N.Y., 1973—, writer, commentator, producer Program Notes, 1975-77, writer, commentator, producer IBM's Salute to the Arts, 1977—, programmer, announcer C.D. Preview, 1988—. Mem. council N.Y. Philharmonic, N.Y.C., 1978—; pres. Alumni and Friends of LaGuardia High Sch., N.Y.C., 1982-86, v.p. fundraising, 1986—. Recipient Angel award, 1986, 87, Gabriel award, 1987. Mem. Dutch Reformed Ch. Office: WQXR AM & FM 229 W 43d St New York NY 10036

LEBLANC, CAROLINE ANNE, nurse, psychotherapist, educator; b. Worcester, Mass., Dec. 11, 1947; d. Leonard Eugene and Gertrude Rita (Plamondon) LeB.; m. Jon Ralph Hager, May 24, 1969; children: Keith Erik Hager, Brant William Hager. BSN cum laude, Boston Coll., 1969; MS, U.Md., 1978; postgrad. Georgetown U., 1980-83. Pub. health and psychiat. staff nurse, 1969-71; occupational health nurse Def. Supply Agy., Boston, 1971-72; sr. asst. nurse officer USPHS, 1972-74; asst. prof. psychiat. nursing Bloomsburg (Pa.) State Coll., 1978-81; pvt. practice contractural services rural nursing and mental health, clin., ednl. and consultative services, Williamsport, Pa., 1977-82; commd. capt. Nurse Corps, U.S. Army, 1982; nurse/psychotherapist Walson Army Hosp., Ft. Dix, N.J., 1982-86; clin. nurse specialist, asst. clin. prof. psychiatry Med. Coll. of Ga., Augusta, 1986—; pvt. practice nursing, psychotherapy, Augusta, 1987—; faculty adv. Bloomsburg State Coll. Campus Child Care Center, 1980-81. Founding mem. Balt. Nurses NOW Task Force; founding mem. Wellspring Center for Human Potential, Md., 1974-75. Served with USPHS, 1972-74. Cert. specialist in psychiat. and mental health nursing. Mem. Am. Nurses Assn., Am. Orthopsychiat. Assn., Ga. Nurses Assn., Nat. Rural Health Care Assn., Phi Kappa Phi, Sigma Theta Tau, Sigma Xi. Home: 191 Blackstone Camp Rd Martinez GA 30907

LEBLANC, KAREN MARIE, realtor; b. Waltham, Mass., May 29, 1945; d. Moise S. and Mary E. (Murphy) LeB.; student pvt. schs., also various banking courses. With Bank of Watertown, 1964—, asst. v.p. lending div., 1979-80, v.p. mortgage and consumer lending, 1980-86; mgr. Century 21 West Realty, Waltham, 1986—. Mem. Savs. Bank Women Mass. (officer 1981-82), Watertown C. of C. (bd. dirs.), Nat. Assn. Bank Women, Savs. Address: 14 Blackmer Rd Sudbury MA 01776

LEBLANC, MARGARET JUMONVILLE, education service administrator; b. New Orleans, May 4, 1947; d. Harry Nicholas and Dorothy (Hubert) Jumonville; m. Samuel C. LeBlanc, Sept. 5, 1969; 1 child, Tim. BA in Elem. Edn., U. New Orleans, 1969; MEd in Guidance and Counseling, Loyola U., New Orleans, 1988. Cert. tchr., La. Tchr. Orleans Parish Sch. Bd., New Orleans, 1969-72, Discovery Sch., New Orleans, 1974-75; dir. edn. The New

Sch.-St. Mark's Community Ctr., New Orleans, 1975-77; founder, owner, dir. edn. Woodridge Acad., Pearl River, La., 1977—; bus. devel. Elem. Sch. K-8, Woodridge Acad., 1977—, campus devel. Four Bldg./Five Acre Compus, 1977—. Mem. Assn. Supervision and Curriculum Devel., La. Assn. for the Edn. Young Children, Slidell Library, Slidell Symphony, Alpa Sigma Nu, Phi Delta Kappa, Chi Sigma Nu (nat. honor soc.). Republican. Office: Woodridge Acad Route 4 PO Box 199 Pearl River LA 70452

LEBO, MARIE, mortgage broker; b. Newark, Jan. 22, 1941; d. Frank Joseph and Anna (Ferrara) Vumbaca; lic. in real estate Profl. Sch. Bus., Union, N.J., 1973; student NYU, 1973-74; m. Richard Lebo, Apr. 4, 1959; children—Corey Allen, Linda Marie. Sec. to pres. J.I. Kislak Mortgage Co., Newark, 1962-72, mortgage loan originator sales dept., 1973-77, asst. v.p., 1977-81; partner, owner Mortgage Brokerage Services Co., East Orange, N.J., 1984-85; v.p. Supreme Fin. Services, Inc., Somerville, N.J., 1982-83, J.I. Kislak Mortgage Corp., 1984-85, 87—, exec. v.p. Premier Fin. Group, 1985-86; sr. v.p. GAF Fin., 1987—, v.p. J.I. Kislak Co., 1988—. Mem. Nat. Assn. Female Execs., Am. Soc. Profl. and Exec. Women, Nat. Assn. Rev. Appraisers and Mortgage Underwriters. Office: 1000 Rte 9 Woodbridge NJ 07095

LEBOW, JEANNE GREGORY, literature educator; b. Richmond, Va., Jan. 29, 1951; d. Eugene Swift and Beatrice Lawson (Harman) Gregory; m. Howard Marc Lebow (div.); m. Steven Louis Shepard. AB, Coll. William and Mary, 1973; MA, Hollins Coll., 1982; postgrad., U. So. Miss., 1984—. Tchr. English Park View Jr. High Sch., South Hill, Va., 1973-75; tchr. Falling Creek Jr. High Sch., Richmond, 1975-77; with pub. relations dept. Barn Dinner Theatre, Roanoke, Va., 1977-78; with pub. relations dept. photo div. The Kroger Co., Roanoke, Va., 1978-81; instr. Memphis State U., 1982-84; assoc. dir. writing project, teaching asst. U. So. Miss., Hattiesburg, 1984-87; Fulbright lectr. U. Ouagadougou, Burkina Faso, 1987-88; assoc. River City Contemporary Writers Series, Memphis, 1983-84; judge freshman essay contests, Memphis, 1983-84, Wordsmith High Sch. contest, Memphis, 1984; panelist Conf. on Coll. Composition and Communication; supr. judging Scholastic Writing Awards, Hattiesburg, 1987. Author numerous poems; contbr. poetry to So. Fla. Poetry Rev., 1987—, other jours. Organizer Friends of Ragland Hills, Hattiesburg, 1987. Recipient award Ga. State Poetry Soc., 1983; Fulbright scholar, 1987-88. Mem. MLA (chair film com. south cen. region, panelist south Atlantic region 1985), Nat. Council Tchrs. English, Miss. Philol. Assn. (chair poetry com. 1986), South Miss. Writing Project (assoc. dir. 1986-87), Sierra Club, Phi Kappa Phi.

LEBOW, SUSAN M., lawyer; b. Bklyn.; d. Philip Jay and Anne (Benjamin) Weingard; B.A. magna cum laude, Bklyn. Coll., 1959; LL.B. cum laude, Bklyn. Law Sch., 1964; m. Marvin LeBow, Dec. 20, 1959; children—Adam, Douglas, Jacqueline, Philice. Admitted to N.Y. bar, 1964; staff atty. law dept. Port Authority N.Y.-N.J., 1964-70; editor Matthew Bender & Co. Legal Pubs., N.Y.C., 1970-73; partner Sarisohn, Sarisohn, Carner, Steindler, Creditor & LeBow, Esqs., Commack, N.Y., 1973—; former counsel Huntington chpt. NOW; former counsel to N.Y. State Assn. for Gifted and Talented. Trustee Suffolk County council Girl Scouts U.S.A., 1975-81; Suffolk County liaison officer N.Y. State Lt. Gov., 1974-78; mem. adv. bd. Women's Ednl. and Counseling Ctr., SUNY, Farmingdale. Recipient cert. of appreciation Suffolk County, 1977. Mem. Suffolk County Bar Assn., Nassau County Bar Assn., N.Y. State Bar Assn., Nassau-Suffolk Women's Bar Assn., Nat. Acad. TV Arts and Scis., Phi Beta Kappa. Office: 350 Veterans Memorial Hwy Commack NY 11725

LEBOWITZ, CHARLOTTE MEYERSOHN, social worker; b. Germany, Dec. 22, 1924; d. Franz and Magda (Wellisch) Meyersohn; came to U.S., 1938, naturalized, 1943; B.A., Brown U., 1946; M.S.W., Simmons Coll., 1948; m. Marshall Lebowitz, Aug. 7, 1949; children—Wendy Lebowitz Nowak, Marian, Mark (dec.). Psychiat. social worker Jewish Family and Children's Service, Boston, 1948-49, ARC Home Service Dept., Boston, 1949-53, Youth Guidance Center, Framingham, Mass., 1962-69, Brandon Sch., Natick, 1969-74, Natick Pub. Schs., 1975—; adj. clin. instr. Boston Coll. Sch. Social Work, 1981-82; mem. exec. bd. Natick Service Council, 1982—; cons. YWCA, 1970-71. Exec. bd. mem. PTA, 1955-71, chmn. presch. unit, 1955-56, mem. council, 1956-70; trustee council Leonard Morse Hosp., 1976—. Mem. Acad. Cert. Social Workers, Nat. Assn. Social Workers, Sch. Adjustment Counselors Assn., Social Workers Employed Less Than Full Time, Boston Inst. Devel. Infants and Parents, Simmons Coll. Sch. Social Work, Brown U. alumni assns., LWV, Nonesuch Pond Improvement Assn. Jewish. Clubs: Sisterhood of Temple Israel of Natick, Rivers Sch. Tennis. Home: 2 Abbott Rd Natick MA 01760 Office: Natick Sch Dept Natick MA 01760

LEBRASSEUR, KATHRYN VINJE LEROY, personnel director; b. Alexandria, Minn., Mar. 10, 1930; d. James Kellogg and Innis Margaret (Thompson) LeR.; m. Donald John LeBrasseur, Aug. 21, 1954; children: Paul, James. BEd, U. Minn., 1952; postgrad., U. Minn., Duluth, 1952, U. Ariz., 1953, U. Wis., 1969-72, U. Alaska, 1976-77. Tchr. Cloquet (Minn.) High Sch., 1952-53, Mansfeld Jr. High Sch., Tucson, 1953-54, St. Louis Park (Minn.) Jr. High Sch., 1954-60, Willmar (Minn.) Jr. High Sch., 1960-68, Cathedral Jr. High Sch., Superior, Wis., 1972-75, North Star Borough Schs., Fairbanks, Alaska, 1975-78; dir. sr. citizen's programs, personnel dir. Douglas County, Alexandria, 1979—; cons. 12 County Sr. Citizen Clubs, Alexandria, 1979—; coordinator Douglas County Task Force on Aging, 1980—, County Personnel Com.; advisor re-entering student program and sr. citizen program Alexandria Vocat. Tech. Inst., 1985—; del. Assn. Minn. Counties, 1987. Author: (newspaper column) Sr. Citizen News, 1979—. Capt. United Way, 1980—; mem. Supt.'s Community Council, Alexandria, 1987—. Recipient Community Service award Alaska No. Lights Jaycees, 1977, Bicentennial award Alaska Bicentennial Com., 1979; named Outstanding Tchr., U. Minn. Coll. Edn., 1952, Citizen of Yr. Elks, 1985. Mem. Minn. Gerontol. Soc., Minn. Pub. Employees Relations Assn., Minn. Personnel Dirs. Assn., Minn. Orgn. Sr. Citizen Program Coordinators (pres. 1983), Am. Assn. Univ. Women (pres. Willmar chpt. 1966-67), Douglas County Hist. Soc. Club: Alexandria Woman's. Home: 521 W Lincoln Alexandria MN 56308 Office: Sr Citizen and Personnel Office 305 W 8th Alexandria MN 56308

LEBSACK, PHYLLIS JEAN, county clerk; b. McCook, Nebr., July 22, 1921; d. George and Katherine Elizabeth (Kechter) Gettman; m. Samuel Lebsack, Aug. 8, 1942 (dec. Mar. 1981); children—Julie Ann, Christy Jean, Todd Douglas. Court clerk Red Willow County Ct., McCook, 1944-45, 1947-48, deputy county clk., 1970-77, county clk., 1977—; clk. City of McCook, 1948-50; sec. Red Willow County Health Bd., 1977—, Red Willow County Commrs., 1977—; county registrar Bur. Vital Statistics, Red Willow County, 1977-85; dir. Election Registration Bd., McCook, 1952-67; vice chmn. clerks W. Central Dist., Nebr., 1984-85, chmn., 1986-87. Democrat. Avocations: crafts; bridge; golf. Home: 911 E 3d St McCook NE 69001 Office: Court House McCook NE 69001

LECHTMAN, PAMELA JOY, travel writer; b. St. Paul, Apr. 29, 1943; d. Ben L. and Leona Betty (Cell) Price; B.S., U. Minn., 1965; m. Allen Lee Lechtman, June 16, 1967; children—Arthur Thomas, Anthony Grant. Tchr. art St. Paul Ind. Sch. Dist., 1966-67; tchr. Alameda (Calif.) Unified Sch. Dist., 1967-68; with public relations dept. Fitness, Inc., 1976-79; travel writer, 1979—; travel editor Shape mag., Woodland Hills, Calif., 1981—; travel columnist News Chronicle, Thousand Oaks, Calif., 1980-83; instr. tourism Ventura (Calif.) Coll., 1978-80; producer radio program Update, Sta. KVEN-AM, Ventura, 1974-80; spa editor Total Health; contbg. West Coast editor Connections, 1981-84; author broadcasting guide You're On The Air, 1979; travel editor Ventura County Mag.; travel writer Jewish Jour., Los Angeles; contbr. Health and Fitness News Service Los Angeles Times Syndicate; guest lectr. UCLA Extension Travel Journalism; editor (newsletter) Calif. for Nonsmoker's Rights, Westside Br. Cert. travel counselor, Inst. Cert. Travel Agt. Mem. Soc. Am. Travel Writers, AAUW (Grant fellow Ventura County Br. 1976, individual grantee 1980), Internat. Assn. of Food, Wine and Travel Writers. Home: 4261 E Cresthaven Dr Westlake Village CA 91362-4279 Office: Shape Mag 21100 Erwin St Woodland Hills CA 91367

LECKIE, CAROL MAVIS, state government administrator; b. Watertown, Wis., Feb. 25, 1929; d. Arthur Walter Bessel and Effie Vada (Squires) Downs; m. Ralph Junior Judd, Sept. 27, 1947 (div. Dec. 1952); children—Russell Howard, Barbara Rae; m. Leonard John Leckie, Sept. 30, 1977; stepchildren: Leonard John, Gordon Armstrong, Lorna Jean. Grad. high sch. Madison, Wis. Mgr. data processing Dept. Justice, State of Wis., Madison, 1971-79, mgr. Records Mgmt. Program, 1979-83, mgr. Typography Sect., 1983—. Mem. com. State of Wis. Employees Combined Campaign, Madison, 1986, co-chair, 1987. Mem. Assn. Records Mgrs. and Adminstrs. (pres. 1983-84), Nat. Assn. Female Execs., Bus. Forms Mgmt. Assn., Internat. Assn. Printing House Craftsmen. Lutheran. Avocations: travel, aerobics. Home: 1213 Iowa Dr Madison WI 53704 Office: State of Wis 1 W Wilson St Suite B-355 Madison WI 53702

LE COCQ, RHODA PRISCILLA, author, educator; b. Lynden, Wash.; d. Ralph B. and Nellie O. (Straks) Le C.; BA, Wash. State U.; MA in Creative Writing, Stanford U.; MA in Philosophy, U. Calif.-Santa Barbara, 1967; PhD, Calif. Inst. Integral Studies, 1970. Radio writer and actress sta. KHQ, Spokane, sta. KOIN, Portland, Oreg., sta. KIRO, Seattle; owner Le Cocq-Luray, N.Y.C.; lit. scout Farrar, Straus & Cudahy, N.Y.C.; public relations dir. art sch. Honolulu Acad. Arts, 1957-58; owner, propr. public relations counseling firm, Honolulu, 1958-61; info. officer Office CD City and County of Honolulu, 1961-63; info. and legis. officer Sacramento County (Calif.) Dept. Social Welfare, 1969-80; research cons. Integral Sci. Found., Inc., 1981-86; instr. U. Hawaii, 1960-61; asst. prof. philosophy extension dept. U. Calif., Davis, 1970-71; assoc. prof. Calif. Inst. Integral Studies, 1972-81; lectr. Bombay, India, 1973, Cultural Integration Fellowship, 1975-80, Regional Assn. Transpersonal Psychology, 1977. Served to lt. USNR, 1942-46, ret. Res., 1970. Recipient cert. for contbn. to East-West Understanding, Cultural Integration Fellowship, 1969, Author Aiding Internat. Understanding, Cambridge, Eng., 1973, photog. and publs. awards NACID, 1974. Mem. Public Relations Soc. Am., Internat. Platform Assn., Smithsonian Assocs., USNR Assn., Audubon Soc., Wash. State U. Alumni Assn., U. Calif. Santa Barbara Alumni Assn., Stanford Alumni Assn., Mensa, Kappa Alpha Theta, Theta Sigma Phi. Clubs: San Francisco Press; Marines Meml. (life) (San Francisco); Commonwealth Club. Author: Heidegger and Sri Aurobindo, 1972; Vision of Superhumanity, 1973; The Mother/Father Pair, 1977; short story Behold A Pale Horse included in several anthologies, dramatized Nat. Gen. Electric Theatre TV, 1957. Mailing Address: Box 37 Corte Madera CA 94925

LE COUNT, VIRGINIA G., communications company executive; b. Long Island City, N.Y., Nov. 22, 1917; d. Clifford R. and Luella (Meier) LeCount. BA, Barnard Coll., 1937; MA, Columbia U., 1940. Tchr. pub. schs. P.R., 1937-38; supr. HOLC, N.Y.C., 1938-40; translator Guildhall Publs., N.Y.C., 1940-41; office mgr. Sperry Gyroscope Co., Garden City, Lake Success, Bklyn. (all N.Y.), 1941-45; billing mgr. McCann Erickson, Inc., N.Y.C., 1945-56; v.p., bus. mgr., bd. dirs. Infoplan Internat, Inc., N.Y.C., 1956-69; v.p., bus. mgr. Communications Affiliates Ltd., Communications Affiliates (Bahamas) Ltd., N.Y.C., 1968-71; bus. mgr. Jack Tinker & Ptnrs., Inc., N.Y.C., 1969-70; mgr. office services Interpublic Group of Cos., Inc., N.Y.C., 1969-70, corp. records mgr., 1972-83, mktg. intelligence data mgr., 1978-83. Mem. Alumnae Barnard Coll. Mem. Marble Collegiate Ch. Club: Atrium. Home: 136 E 55th St Apt 10Q New York NY 10022

LECUYER, ELLEN DELPHINE, publishing company junior executive; b. Montreal, Que., Can., May 10, 1956; d. Lucien and Doris (Daly) L.; m. Michael S.L. Levesque, Dec. 30, 1983. B in Commerce, Concordia U., Montreal, 1977. Research analyst Reader's Digest, Montreal, 1977-79, asst. mgr. mktg. research, 1979-81, mgr. mktg. research, 1981-87, asst. product mgr., 1987—. Mem. Am. Mktg. Assn., Profl. Market Research Soc. Avocations: cross country skiing, curling. Home: 4554 Royal Ave, Montreal, PQ Canada H4A 2M8 Office: Reader's Digest Assn Can, 215 Redfern Ave, Westmount, PQ Canada H3Z 2V9

LECUYER-COONS, GEORGEIDA CELENE, nurse, small business owner; b. Clifton, Kans., Jan. 4, 1926; d. George and Ida Marie (Savoie) L.; m. Roger James Freeman (div. 1971); children: George W., Kathryn A., Margaret J., John M.; m. Merlyn D. (Tony) Coons (dec. 1985). BA, Park Coll., Parkville, Mo., 1980; RN, Avila Coll., Kansas City, Mo., 1948. RN, Kans. Med.-surg. staff nurse Research Hosp., Kansas City, Mo., 1966-67; anesthetist Oral Surgeons, Inc., Kansas City, 1967-70; instr. practical nursing Kansas City Bd. Edn., Mo., 1972-75; oncology staff nurse U. Kans. Med. Ctr., Kansas City, Kans., 1975-78; mental health staff nurse VA Hosp., Leavenworth, Kans., 1978-82; gerontology staff nurse VA Hosp., Topeka, 1982-85; ret. VA Hosp., 1985; owner Baby Boomer Hdqrs. of Kans., Salina, 1986—; ednl. cons. VA Hosp. In-Service dept., Topeka. 1982-85; conductor workshops on behaviors, team concept, alcoholism and ageism. Local leader Boy Scouts Am., Girl Scouts U.S., Kansas City, Mo., 1962-66. Served with U.S. Cadet Nursing Corps, 1944-47. Recipient Excellent Bedside Caregiver award U. Kans. Med. Ctr., 1977, Spl. Advancement award VA, 1982. Mem. Nat. Assn. Ret. Fed. Employees, Am. Assn. Ret. Persons. Republican. Roman Catholic. Club: Salina (Kans.) Christian Women's. Office: Baby Boomer Hdqrs of Kans PO Box 1454 Salina KS 67402-1454

LEDBETTER, SANDRA GALE SHUMARD, political party administrator; b. Little Rock, Oct. 18, 1948; d. Frank Ney and Mildred Elizabeth (Oldham) Shumard; B.A., U. Ark., 1971; m. Joel Yowell Ledbetter, Jr., Dec. 16, 1971; children—Elizabeth Talbot, Ann Shay, Mildred Myonne Mitzi. Tchr., Pulaski County (Ark.) Spl. Sch. Dist., 1970-72, Miss Selma's Sch., Little Rock, 1972-74, Pulaski Acad., Little Rock, 1976-81; mem. local com. Dem. Party, Pulaski County, 1976-82, mem. state com., 1976-82, campaign coordinator state party, 1978, del. to nat. conv., 1980, co-chmn. state adv. com., 1981—, mem. advance team for Joan Mondale, Mondale for Pres. campaign, 1982, exec. dir. state party, 1984-87; adminstrv. asst. to gov. State of Ark., 1982-84. Mem. Pres.'s Roundtable U. Cen. Ark., mem. advancement com.; trustee U. Ark., 1986—; mem. bd. Forest Heights (Ark.) Jr. High PTA, 1987—. Mem. Assn. Dem. Exec. Dirs. (bd. dirs.), Jr. League Little Rock (dir. 1981-82, 86-87, project chmn. 1982-83). Methodist. Home: 2200 Andover Ct #1305 Little Rock AR 72207

LEDBETTER, SHARON FAYE WELCH, school principal; b. Los Angeles, Jan. 14, 1941; d. James Herbert and Verdie V. (Mattox) Welch; m. Robert A. Ledbetter, Feb. 15, 1964; children—Kimberly Ann, Scott Allen. B.A., U. Tex.-Austin, 1963; learning disabilities cert. Southwestern U., Tex., 1974; M.Ed., Southwest Tex. State U., 1979, prin. cert., 1980, supt. cert., 1984. Speech pathologist Midland Ind. Sch. Dist., Tex., 1963, Austin Ind. Sch. Dist., Tex., 1964-72; speech pathologist, asst. prin. Round Rock Ind. Sch. Dist., Tex., 1972-84 also mem. coms.; prin. Hutto Ind. Sch. Dist., 1984-88 . Pres., Berkman PTA, 1983-84; sponsor Jr. Woman's Club, 1980-82; mistress ceremonies Hutto Beauty Pageant, 1986, 87. Recipient Appreciation awards Round Rock Sch. Dist., 1984, St. Judes Children's Research Hosp., 1985, Soc. Disting. Am. High Sch. Students, 1985. Mem. Nat. Assn. Secondary Sch. Prins., Tex. Assn. Secondary Sch. Prins., Tex. Elem. Prins. and Suprs. Assn., Assn. Supervision and Curriculum Devel., Adminstrv. Women in Edn., Nat. Assn. Female Execs., Tex. Assn. Community Schs., Gen. Fedn. Women's Club, Tex. Fedn. Women's Clubs (com. chair), Round Rock Women's Club (pres.), Hutto C. of C., Phi Delta Kappa, Delta Kappa Gamma. Avocations: horses; spectator sports. Home: Rt 1 Box 8A Hutto TX 78634

LEDBETTER-STRAIGHT, NORA KATHLEEN, insurance company executive; b. Gary, Ind., May 11, 1934; d. Jacob F. and Nora I. (Bollen) Moser; student U. Houston, 1954-58; m. Robert L. Straight, Aug. 9, 1975; 1 dau., Cindy Kathleen Ledbetter Baurax. Vice pres. Hindman Mortgage Co., Inc., Houston, 1960-70, also mng. partner Assocs. Ins. Agy.; corp. sec. N.Am. Mortgage Co., Houston, 1970—; mng. partner N.Am. Ins. Agy., 1970—, now also pres. and mng. officer; ins. counselor Houston Apt. Assn., 1978—, dir. product service council, 1981—; mem. adv. bd. for continuing edn., State Bd. Ins.; v.p., sec. Better Bodies of Tex., Inc. CPCU; cert. Ins. Inst. Am., Soc. Cert. Ins. Counselors. Mem. Ind. Ins. Agts. Am., Soc. Cert. Ins. Counselors, Soc. C.P.C.U.'s, Community Assos. Inst. (dir. 1976-80), Ind. Ins. Agts. Tex., Tex. Assn. Affiliated Agts. (v.p., bd. dirs.), Ind. Ins. Agts. Houston (dir. 1974-78). Republican. Methodist. Author curriculum materials in field. Office: 14825 St Mary's Ln Houston TX 77079

LEDBURY, DIANA GRETCHEN, educator; b. Denver, Mar. 7, 1931; d. Francis Kenneth and Gretchen (Harry) Van Ausdall; m. Chander Parkash Lall, Dec. 26, 1953 (div. Aug. 1973); children—Anne, Neil, Kris; m. Eugene Augustus Ledbury, Sept. 13, 1976; stepchildren—Mark, Cindy, Rob. B.A. in Sociology, Colo. U., 1953. Instr. Home, and family life Community Coll., Seattle, 1957-71; asst. tchr. Renton Sch. Dist., Wash., 1974-83; adult edn. tchr. Mental Health Network, Renton, 1984—; coordinator Inter-Study, Renton, 1985—, program dir. Crossroads Child Care, 1985-86, family services coordinator , 1986-87, program supr. Candyland Too Child Care Ctr., 1987—. Mem. Renton Area Youth Services Bd., Sch. and Community Drug Prevention Program, Renton dist. council PTA, Renton Citizen's Com. on Recreation; vol. Griffin Home for Boys; coordinator Modern Dance Prodn., Carco Theater; adult leader Camp Fire Girls' Horizon Club; mem. bd. Allied Arts of Renton; mem. Bicentennial Com. for a Cultural Arts, Edn. and Recreation Ctr.; PTA rep. Dimmit Jr. High Sch.; mem. Sch. and Community Recreation Com.; founder Handicapped Helping Themselves, Mental Health Network; precinct committeeperson 11th dist. Republican party, Wash., 1976-85. Recipient Golden Acorn award Wash. State Congress PTA, Renton, 1972. Mem. Assn. Social and Health Services (mem. com. 1984-85), AAUW (legis. chair 1983-87). Episcopalian. Club: Campfire Horizon (leader). Avocations: arts; culture; recreation; child and family advocate.

LEDERBERG, VICTORIA, state legislator, lawyer, psychology educator; b. Providence, July 7, 1937; d. Frank and Victoria (Marzilli) Santopietro; m. Seymour Lederberg, 1959; children—Tobias, Sarah. A.B., Pembroke Coll., 1959; A.M., Brown U., 1961, Ph.D., 1966; J.D., Suffolk U., 1976. Mem. R.I. Ho. of Reps., 1975-82, chmn. subcom. on edn., fin. com., 1975-82, subcom. on mental health, retardation and hosps. and health, spl. legis. commns pub. sch. funding and funding handicapped edn. programs; mem. Democratic Nat. Exec. Com.; mem. R.I. State Senate, 1985—, chmn. fin. com. subcom. on social services, 1985—; prof. psychology R.I. Coll., 1978—; atty. Licht & Semonoff, Providence. USPHS fellow physiol. psychology, 1964-66. Mem. New Eng. Bd. Higher Edn.; trustee Brown U., 1983—, Roger Williams Coll., 1980—, Butler Hosp., 1985—, a;so sec. of corp. Mem. New Eng. Psychol. Assn., R.I. Psychol. Assn., Women Educators, New Eng. Edn. Research Orgn., ABA, R.I. Bar Assn., Sigma Xi. Office: RI State Capitol Bldg Providence RI 02903 Address: 190 Slater Ave Providence RI 02906

LEDERER, MARIE A., political campaign official; b. Phila., Oct. 24, 1927; d. Donato and Edith (Vitacolonna) Panosetti; ed. Phila. Public Relations Inst., 1966-67, Temple U., 1973-76; m. William J. Lederer, June 17, 1950; children—Doneda M. Lederer Guyon, William M., Regina M. Instr. polit. sci. Temple U., Phila., 1976-77; exec. dir. Jackson for Pres. Com., 1976; del. Dem. nat. conv., 1976, 84; voter registration chmn. Dem. exec. com., 1978-79; adminstrv. asst. to Congressman Joseph F. Smith, Pa., 1981-82; asst. to Dep. Auditor Gen. of Pa., 1985. Dir. Southeastern Pa. Heart Assn., 1968-71; mem. bd. dirs. Balch Inst., ARC, U.S.S. Cruiser Olympia Ship; mem. Phila. Art Alliance. Recipient Pa. Ho. of Reps., 1974, certs. of merit U.S. Ho. of Reps., 1982. Roman Catholic. Clubs: Am. Legion Ladies Aux., Hist. Ships Assn., Mexican Soc. Home: 1237 Shackamaxon St Philadelphia PA 19125

LEDERHAUS, JULI-ANN MARIE, hotel food and beverage director; b. Oakland, Calif., Mar. 21, 1949; d. Gustav Frederick and Jeanne (Sanna) Glenewinkel; m. Walter Thomas Lederhaus, Jan. 12, 1975. AA, City Coll. San Francisco, 1969. Gen. cashier San Franciscan Hotel, 1970-72; asst. food and beverage controller Fairmont Hotel, San Francisco, 1972-74, head food and beverage cashier, 1974; food and beverage controller Fairmont Hotel, New Orleans, 1975-77; front office mgr. Traveler's Inn, Fairbanks, Alaska, 1977, gen. mgr., 1977-80; exec. chef Marsal's, Anchorage, Alaska, 1981-82; food and beverage dir. Hotel Captain Cook, Anchorage, 1982-85, Clarion Hotel, Anchorage, 1986—; adj. prof. Alaska Pacific U., Anchorage, 1980; co-chmn. Mayor's Adv. Com. Anchorage Mcpl. Health Dept., 1985-87. Mem. Internat. Wine and Food Soc., Anchorage Restaurant and Bar Assn. (bd. dirs. 1986-87, pres. 87-88), Chaine des Rotisseurs (Maitre de Table 1987). Office: Clarion Hotel 4800 Spenard Rd Anchorage AK 99517

LEDERMAN, CINDY SHELLENBERGER, lawyer; b. Phila., Mar. 2, 1954; d. Donald Lee and Dolores Marie (Patton) Shellenberger; m. Robert Elliot Lederman, July 3, 1976. BA, U. Fla., 1976; JD, U. Miami, Fla., 1979. Bar: Fla., 1979, N.Y., 1986. Assoc. Mitchell L. Perlstein P.A., Miami, Fla., 1979-81, Brown, Huysman, Matthews & Singer, Miami, 1981-82; asst. city atty. North Miami Beach, Fla., 1982-84, dep. city atty., 1984—. Vice-chair Dade County Commn. Status Women, 1987—; mem. Coalition Hispanic Am. Women, 1987—, Forum of North Dade; chmn. Mediation Pilot Project Com., 1987-88. Named one of Outstanding Women of Yr. North Dade C. of C., 1988. Mem. ABA, Fla. Bar Assn. (vice chmn. govt. lawyer com. 1987—, chmn. grievance com. 1988), Acad. Fla. Trial Lawyers, Dade County Bar Assn. (bd. dirs. 1987—), Fla. Assn. for Women Lawyers (pres. 1986-87, pres.'s award 1986), Fla. Council of Bar Assn. Presidents, AAUW. Office: City of North Miami Beach 17011 NE 19th Ave North Miami Beach FL 33162

LEDERMAN, MARIE JEAN, English language Educator; b. Bklyn., Dec. 28, 1935; d. Samuel and Gladys (Leeshutz) Candel; m. Theodore Lederman, June 28, 1957 (div. 1963); 1 child, Mark; m. Martin Benis, 1977. B.S. magna cum laude, NYU, 1957, Ph.D., 1966; M.A., Bklyn. Coll., 1963. Tchr. English, N.Y.C. Bd. Edn., 1957-59, cons., 1975-76, 78-79; instr. NYU, 1965-66; asst. prof. N.Y.C. Community Coll., 1966-68; asst. prof. SEEK program CUNY, 1968-69, successively asst. prof., assoc. prof., prof. Baruch Coll., 1969-79, 88—, cons. chancellor's SEEK task force, 1975, univ. dean acad. affairs, 1979-85; dean for freshman skills La Guardia Community Coll., Long Island City, 1985-87; cons. Mohawk Valley Community Coll., Utica, N.Y., 1980, Tex. A&I U., 1984, U. Toronto, 1984, Framingham State Coll., 1987, Woodrow Wilson Fellowship Found., 1985. Contbr. articles to profl. jours. Bd. dirs. Jean Cocteau Repertory Theatre, 1985—, v.p., 1988—. Recipient CUNY faculty research award, 1976-78; Fund for Improvement of Postsecondary Edn. grantee, 1981-87. Mem. N.Y.C. Assn. Tchrs. of English (v.p. 1979-86), Community Coll. Gen. Edn. Assn. (bd. dirs. 1982-87), Coll. Composition and Communication Assn. (minority affairs adv. com. 1982-87), MLA, Nat. Council Tchrs. of English. Democrat. Jewish. Office: Bernard M Baruch Coll CUNY Dept English 17 Lexington Ave New York NY 10010

LEDGERWOOD, HELEN DIANE, accountant; b. Chattanooga, Sept. 24, 1946; d. Howard Brown and Helen Irene (Boettcher) Blakely; m. Larry Ledgerwood, Aug. 12, 1967; children: Jennifer, Cheryl. BS in Acctg., Calif. State U., Long Beach, 1976. Asst. controller Don Roberto Jewelers, El Toro, Calif., 1979-80; staff acct. Nicholas Terpstra, CPA, Santa Ana, Calif., 1980-81; sr. acct. Rusty Pelican Restaurants, Irvine, Calif., 1981-83; acctg. mgr. Adams Fin. Group, Costa Mesa, Calif., 1983-85, cons., 1985—; acct. The Lusk Co., Irvine, 1985-88, sr. acct., 1988—. Republican.

LEDOUX, ERIKA ELEONORA, museum curator; b. Helmstedt, Germany, June 30, 1936; came to U.S., 1956; d. Walter and Eleonora (Schenkelberger) Baum; m. Edmund Gabriel Ledoux, Dec. 21, 1956 (dec. 1981); children: Karl Edmund (dec.), Lorie Ann. Student, U. So. La., 1968-69; cert. in archtl. drafting, Harris Vocat. Sch., Opelousas, La., 1981. Tchr. St. Edmund's Elem. Sch., 1967-70; elect. draftsman Slemco, Lafayette, La., 1981-82; tchr. drafting Lafayette Vocat. Sch., 1982—; curator Eunice (La.) Mus., 1984—. Artist in oils, acrylics, ink, sculpture. Recipient various ribbons for art work. Mem. Southeastern Mus. Conf. Clubs: Eunice Home Demonstration, Eunice Lafter 40. Home: PO Box 428 Eunice LA 70535

LEDUFF, STEPHANIE, marketing director; b. Columbus, Ohio, Apr. 30, 1953; d. Dallas Preston and Esther L. (Gregory) Winkfield; divorced; 1 child, Eric Wallace. BS in Edn., Ohio State U., 1975; postgrad., Harvard U., 1981-82, MIT, 1981-82, U. So. Calif., 1984-85. Pub. relations dir. Monclair (N.J.) Pub. Schs., Mayor's Office, New Orleans; mng. editor Gambit Newspaper, New Orleans, 1983-86; mktg. dir. News-Press, Ft. Myers, Fla., 1986—. Chairwoman Gannett Found. Grant Com., Ft. Myers, 1986—, Constn. Bicentennial Com., Ft. Myers, 1987; bd. dirs. March of Dimes, Ft. Myers, 1987-89, Barbara Mann Performing Arts Ctr., Ft. Myers, 1987-89, Abuse, Counseling, Treatment Ctr., Ft. Myers, 1987-89; mem. Regional Econ. Outlook Steering Com., 1987—. Mem. Fla. Pub. Relations Assn., Internat. Newspaper Mktg. Assn. Lodge: Zonta. Office: News-Press 2442 Anderson Ave Fort Myers FL 33901

LEDWITH, BEVERLY EILEEN, clothing and textiles educator, home economist, consultant; b. San Francisco, Oct. 14, 1938; d. Paul Henry and

Elva (Edwards) L. BA, San Jose (Calif.) State U., 1960, MA, 1964; PhD, Mich. State U., East Lansing, 1985. Cert. home economist, Calif. Tchr. Bellflower (Calif.) High Sch., 1961-63, Novato (Calif.) High Sch., 1964-68; instr. West Valley Coll., Saratoga, Calif., 1968—; cons., tchr. Spl. Needs, Los Gatos, Calif., 1972-80; cons. B2 Cons., Los Gatos, 1981—. Contbr. numerous articles to profl. jours. Radell fellow, 1983. Mem. Am. Home Econs. Calif. Home Econs. Assn. (chair-convention 1971-73, extended edn. grantee 1981), Assn. of Coll. Profs. of Textiles and Clothing, Nat. Council on Family Relations, Am. Sewing Guild (organizing dir. 1986-87), Omicron Nu. Office: West Valley Coll 14000 Fruitvale Ave Saratoga CA 95070

LEE, ALISON ANN, education director; b. Holyoke, Mass., June 30, 1950; d. Robert Keating and Audrey Ethel (Emery) L.; student Russell Sage Coll.; 1968-70; BA, Mt. Holyoke Coll., 1975; MA, Cen. Mich. U., 1985. Lab. technician Holyoke Hosp., 1969-72; research asst. U. Mass. Health Services, Amherst, 1972-73; med. technologist Wesson unit Baystate Med. Center, Springfield, Mass., 1973-78; cons. Tulsa City-County Health Dept., 1979-81, Moton Health Center, Tulsa, 1980-84; lead med. technologist St. Francis Hosp., Tulsa, 1978-86, dir. edn. Springer Clinic, 1986—. Alumnae admissions rep. for Greater Tulsa, Mt. Holyoke Coll.; past public edn. chmn., mem. profl. edn. com., bd. dirs. Am. Cancer Soc.; mem. adv. bd. Am. Heart Assn.; vol. various community activities. Mem. Am. Soc. Clin. Pathologists, Am. Soc. Clin. Chemistry, Nat. Mgmt. Assn., Am. Soc. Med. Tech., Profl. Women Tulsa, Am. Coll. Hosp. Adminstrs., Alumnae Assn. Mt. Holyoke. Home: 6370 H South 80 East Ave Tulsa OK 74133 Office: 6160 S Yale Tulsa OK 74136

LEE, AMY ELAINE, software company administrator; b. Knoxville, Tenn., June 7, 1960; d. Forrest Columbus and Mary Christine (Smith) L. AS, Cumberland Coll., 1979; student, U. Tenn., 1979-81. With Am. Software, Inc., Atlanta, 1982—, project mgr., 1984-87, sr. project coordinator, 1987—; cons., coordinator Faberge/Elizabeth Arden Internat., Acton, Eng., 1988—; analyst, cons. PTT Telecommunications, Hague, The Netherlands, 1987; sr. coordinator Faberge, Inc., Mahwah, N.J., 1986—. Vol. Muscular Dystrophy Assn., 1988. Mem. Nat. Assn. Female Execs., French Elephants. Republican. Baptist. Office: Am Software Inc 470 E Paces Ferry Rd Atlanta GA 30305

LEE, ANNE NATALIE, nurse; b. Bklyn.; d. Taras Pavlovich and Maria (Jukovskaya) Dubovick; B.A., Hunter Coll., 1940; M.A., N.Y.U., 1948; R.N., McLean Hosp. Sch. Nursing, Waverly, Mass., 1946; M.S., Boston U., 1958; m. Henry Lee, Feb. 20, 1945; adopted children—Alice, Jennifer, Philip. Pvt. duty nurse, N.Y.C., 1946-48; staff nurse Vis. Nurse Service, 1947-48; staff nurse health dept. Schoharie Co., N.Y., 1948-51; supervising nurse N.Y. Dept. Health, Syracuse, 1951-53, cons. hosp. nursing, Albany, 1958-63, cons. nurse in service edn., 1963-75, dir. Bur. of Hosp. Nursing Services, 1975-80; cons. nursing services and adminstrn., 1980—; dir., coordinator nursing service instr. program co-sponsored N.Y. State Dept. Health, N.Y. State Hosp. Assn., N.Y. State League Nursing, N.Y. State Nurses Assn., 1954-57; sometimes lectr. Mem. Am. Nurses Assn. (cert. advanced nursing adminstrn.), Sigma Theta Tau. Contbr. articles to profl. jours. Home and Office: 1149 Hillsboro Mile Hillsboro Beach FL 33062

LEE, ANTOINETTE JOSEPHINE, architectural historian, preservationist; b. Berwyn, Ill., July 5, 1948; d. Stephen K.F. and Katharine (Whitworth) Lee; m. Allan Leroy Olson, Aug. 11, 1978. B.A. in History, U. Pa., Phila., 1969; M.Ph. in Am. Civilization, George Washington U., Washington, 1973; Ph.D. in Am. Civilization, 1975. Cons. hist. preservation, Washington, 1972-77, coordinator edn. services Nat. Trust Historic Preservation, Washington, 1977-82; dir., supr. architect project Columbia Hist. Soc., Washington, 1982-87; cons. hist. preservation Office of Planning D.C., Washington, 1982; cons. U.S. com. Internat. Council on Monuments and Sites, Washington, 1985-88, Victorian Soc. in Am., Phila., 1985; cons. historian Archtl. League, N.Y.C., 1985-86; cons. historian archtl. firms and nonprofit assns., 1985—, Washington pub. sch., 1986—; contract historian Nat. Park Service, 1986. Editor: Guide to Undergraduate and Graduate Education in Historic Preservation, 1981, A Biographical Dictionary of American Civil Engineers, 1972; coeditor The American Mosaic: Preserving a Nation's Heritage, 1987; contbr. numerous articles in field to publs. Vice-chmn. Arlington County Hist. Affairs and Landmark Rev. Bd.,1984-87. Winston-Churchill Meml. fellow Washington br. English-Speaking Union, 1976; material culture fellow George Washington U., 1970-71. Mem. Soc. Archtl. Historians (bd. dirs.), Am. Studies Assn., Assn. Preservation Tech., Am. Planning Assn., Hist. Reservation Edn. Found. (treas.), Arts Club of Washington. Home: 4851 N 28th St Arlington VA 22207 Office: 1717 Massachusettes Ave NW Suite 203 Washington DC 20036

LEE, BARBARA MARIE, cattle breeder; b. Beloit, Wis., Oct. 28, 1955; d. James Robert and Agnes Marie (Hanson) L.; m. Ernest J. Miller Jr., Jan. 5, 1985 (div. June 1987); 1 child, Amanda Marie. BS, U. Wis., 1977, MS, 1979. Extension intern Jefferson County (Wis.) Courthouse, 1976; 4-H youth specialist dairy sci. staff U. Wis., Madison, 1978; assoc. editor Brown Swiss Bulletin, Beloit, 1979-80; mktg. specialist Brown Swiss Enterprises, Inc., Beloit, 1980-81, dir. mktg., 1981-86; mgr. dairy progeny testing Am. Breeders Services, DeForest, Wis., 1986—; cons. Hickory Grove Jersey Farm, Clinton, Wis., 1986—; accredited judge dairy cattle shows, 1977—; judge Brown Swiss cattle Nat. Brazil Show, 1982, Nat. Peru Show, 1983, Internat. Expo, 1983, Royal Winter Fair, 1985; mem. Wis. Dept. Agrl. and Trade mission to Mex., 1981, 84, Venezuala, Columbia, 1984. Leader Clinton 4-H, 1973-83; active Jefferson Prairie Lutheran Ch., Poplar Grove, Ill. Dairy Shrine Club scholar, 1977; named to Hon. Order of Ky. Colonels, 1983. Mem. Holstein Assn. (Top Jr. 1974), Brown Swiss Cattle Breeders, Assn. of Women In Agriculture (bd. dirs. 1987—), Dairy Shrine Club (scholar 1977), Livestock Industry Inst. (bd. dirs. 1983—), Wis. Alumni Assn., Wis. Agrl. and Life Sci. Alumni Assn. (bd. dirs. 1980-83). Lutheran. Clubs: Women's Bowling League (v.p. 1980-83), ABS Mixed Bowling League, BS Women's Softball Team. Home: 4493 Golf Rd Windsor WI 53598 Office: Am Breeders Service 6908 River Rd DeForest WI 53532

LEE, BETTY REDDING, architect; b. Shreveport, La., Dec. 6, 1919; d. Joseph Alsop and Mary (Byrd) Redding; student La. State U., 1936-37, 37-38, U. Calif. War Extension Coll., San Diego, 1942-43; student Centenary Coll., 1937; grad. Roofing Industry Ednl. Inst., 1980, 81, 82, 84, 86, 87, 88; m. Frank Cayce Lee, Nov. 22, 1940 (dec. Aug. 1978); children—Cayce Redding, Clifton Monroe, Mary Byrd (Mrs. Kent Ray). Sheetmetal worker Consol.-Vultee, San Diego, 1942; engrng. draftsman, 1943-45; jr. to sr. archtl. draftsman Bodman & Murrell, Baton Rouge, 1945-55; sr. archtl. draftsman to architect Post & Harelson, Baton Rouge, 1955-60; asso. architect G. Ross Murrell, Jr., Baton Rouge, 1960-66; staff architect Charles E. Schwing & Assos., Baton Rouge, 1966-71, Kenneth C. Landry, Baton Rouge, 1971, 73-74; design draftsman Rayner & McKenzie, Baton Rouge, 1972-73; cons. architect and planner, div. engrng. and cons. services, La. Dept. Health and Human Resources, Baton Rouge, 1974-82; architect La. Dept. Facility Planning and Control, 1982—; co-author: Building Owners Guide for Protecting and Maintaining Built-Up Roofing Systems, 1981; designed typical La. country store for La. Arts and Sci. Ctr. Mus. Mem. La. Assn. Children with Learning Disabilities, 1970-71, Multiple Sclerosis Soc., 1963-82, CPA Aux., 1960-69, PTA, 1953-66; troop leader Brownies and Girl Scouts U.S.A., 1959-60; asst. den mother Cub Scouts, 1955-57. Licensed architect, Mem. AIA, La. Architects Assn., Nat. Fire Protection Assn., Constrn. Specifications Inst. (charter mem. Baton Rouge chpt.), Miss. Roofing Contractors Assn. (hon.), ASTM, Nat. Roofing Contractors Assn., So. Bldg. Code Congress Internat., La. Inst. Bldg. Scis. (founding mem. 1980), Architect and Engrng. Performance Info. Ctr., Jr. League Baton Rouge. Baton Rouge Caledonian Soc., DAR, Kappa Delta. Democrat. Episcopalian. Clubs: Fais Do Do, Le Salon du Livre. Home: 1994 Longwood Dr Baton Rouge LA 70808 Office: Capitol Station Box 94095 Baton Rouge LA 70804-9095

LEE, BEVERLY ING, educational administrator; b. Honolulu, Oct. 10, 1932; d. Tim Sheu and Helen (Heu) Ing; m. Daniel David Lee, June 21, 1962; children: Helen Ann, Terence Daniel, Scott David. BA, Coll. of the Pacific, Stockton, Calif., 1954; MA, Columbia U., 1957. Officer Honolulu Police Dept., 1957-61; adminstr. Dept. Edn. State of Hawaii, Honolulu, 1961-88; controller Classic Travel, Honolulu, 1988—; bd. dirs. Hawaii State Employee's Credit Union, Honolulu, 1986—, John Howard Assn., Honolulu, 1985—. Mem. Gov.'s Commn. on Child Abuse, Honolulu, 1985—; bd. dirs. Hawaii Family Stress Ctr., Honolulu, 1975—, Nat. Com. on Child Abuse, Honolulu, 1983—; mem. Casey Family Program Advisory Com. Mem. AAUW, Delta Kappa Gamma, Tri Delta. Office: Dept Edn 801 W Hind Dr Honolulu HI 96821 Also: Classic Travel 1413 S King St Room 201 Honolulu HI 96814

LEE, BOBBIE JEAN, social service administrator; b. Cedar Lane, Tex., Apr. 2, 1947; d. Robert lewis and Lucinda (Williams) Grice; 1 child, Jarvis Lynn. Student, Prairie View A&M Coll., 1965-69, Houston Community Coll., 1985-86. Quality control inspector Tex. Instruments, Houston, 1969-70; supr. food service St. Luke's Hosp. and Tex. Children's Hosp., Houston, 1970-73; interviewer Tex. Employment Commn., Houston, 1973-74; social service worker State Tex. Dept. Human Services, Houston, 1974—. Sponsor Nat. Rep. Congl. Com., Washington, 1984-87; sec. Meredith Mannor Civic Club, Houston, 1985-86; mem. Houston Mus. Fine Arts, Houston Arthritis Found. Mem. Communication Workers Am., Am. Pub. Welfare Assn., Nat. Assn. Female Execs., The Cousteau Soc., Smithsonian Inst. Baptist. Club: Fishing of Am. (Floral Park, N.Y.). Home: PO Box 14582 Houston TX 77021 Office: Tex Dept Human Services 6711 bellort Houston TX 77087

LEE, BRENDA (BRENDA MAE TARPLEY), singer, entertainer; b. Lithonia, Ga., Dec. 11, 1944; m. Ronnie Shacklett; children: Julie, Jolie. First appeared on Red Foley Ozark Jubilee Show, 1956; appeared in film Smokey and the Bandit II, 1980, in cable TV spl. Legendary Ladies, 1986, in PBS spl. Shake Rattle and Roll, 1988; musical recordings include Brenda Lee, 1960, Sincerely, 1961, All Alone Am I, 1962, By Request, 1964, Bye Bye Blues, 1966, 10 Golden Years, 1966, Memphis Portrait, 1970, Now, 1975, and many others. Recipient Gov.'s award Nat. Acad. Recording Arts and Scis., 1984. Address: Brenda Lee Entertainments care Ronnie Shacklett Box 110033 Nashville TN 37202 *

LEE, CHARLENE ELIZABETH, public relations executive; b. Houston, Sept. 14, 1942; d. Preston Windsor Lee and Lois Elberta (Crowder) Lee Perkins; divorced; children: Kelly DeShawn Davis, Colleen Dawn Davis. BA in Speech and Bus. English, Wayland Bapt. U., Plainview, Tex., 1966. Office mgr. Sta. WJDX/WZZQ-FM, Jackson, Miss., 1974-76; exec. asst. Grace Jones, Inc., Salado, Tex., 1976-77; adminstrv. coordinator Scott and White Perinatal Ctr., Temple, Tex., 1977-82; communications specialist Scott and White Pub. Affairs, Temple, 1982—; speaker in field. Mem. Temple Civic Theatre, 1982—; chmn. Leon chpt. March of Dimes, Temple, 1980-82. Mem. Pub. Relations Soc. Am., Tex. Pub. Relations Assn., Tex. Soc. for Hosp. Pub. Relations and Mktg. (Telstar award 1985-86), Bell County Communications Profls. Assn. (membership chairperson 1987—, pres. 1986-87, Bell award 1986), Temple C. of C. (mem. various coms. 1984—), Wayland Bapt. U. Alumni Assn. (assoc.), Altrusa Club of Temple (v.p. 1981-82, 88—, chmn. various comns. 1979-87). Republican. Episcopalian. Office: Scott and White Pub Affairs 2401 S 31st St Temple TX 76508

LEE, CORINNE ADAMS, retired educator; b. Cuba, N.Y., Mar. 18, 1910; d. Duston Emery and Florence Eugenia (Butts) Adams; m. Glenn Max Lee, Oct. 30, 1936 (dec. Feb. 1964). BA, Alfred U., 1931. Cert. tchr., N.Y. Tchr. English Lodi (N.Y.) High Sch., 1931-36, Ovid (N.Y.) Cen. Sch., 1936-67. Author: (light verse) A Little Leeway, 1983, (anecedotes, quips) A Little More Leeway, 1984, (essays, short stories) Still More Leeway, 1986. Mem. Nat. Ret. Tchrs. Assn., N.Y. State Ret. Tchrs. Assn., Schuyler County Ret. Tchrs. Assn., Elmira and Area Ret. Tchrs. Assn., LWV, PTA (life). Avocations: reading, travel, writing.

LEE, CYNTHIA LOUISE, accounting administrator; b. Dayton, Ohio, Nov. 14, 1954; d. Warren E. and Mary C. (Crandall) L. BS in Acctg., Ind. U., 1976, MBA in Acctg., 1976. CPA, Ohio. Sr. auditor Deloitte Haskins & Sells, Dayton, 1976-80; audit supr. Monsanto Research Corp., Miamisburg, Ohio, 1980-85, mgr. acctg., 1985—. Sec. Montgomery County Children Services Bd., Dayton, 1987, vice chmn. 1988—. Fellow Am. Inst. CPA's; mem. Ind. U. Alumni (treas.), Beta Alpha Psi, Beta Gamma Sigma. Club: Mound Golf League (Miamisburg) (sec., treas. 1983-85). Office: Monsanto Research Corp PO Box 32 Miamisburg OH 45342

LEE, DIANA BELINDA, banker; b. Florence, S.C., July 2, 1953; d. Henry Barker and J Jeannine (Berry) L. AB, Coker Coll., 1973; AA, Fashion Inst. Am., 1973; diploma retail banking Am. Inst. Banking, 1983; postgrad Coker Coll. Customer service rep. 1st Nat. Bank S.C., Columbia, 1974-79; with S.C. Nat. Bank, Florence and Columbia, 1979-82; with S.C. Fed., various locations, 1982-87, br. mgr., Columbia, 1983-85, asst. sec., br. mgr., Hartsville, 1985-87, br. mgr. Security Fed. Savs. & Loan Assn., Columbia, 1987—; br. mgr. Security Fed., 1987—. Bd. dirs. Am. Cancer Soc., 1985—, chmn. regional edn. funds crusade, 1985—, regional dir., 1987-88; chmn. Hartscapades parade, 1986; co-chmn. Richland County First Lady Cookbooks. Mem. C. of C. Columbia, Forest Acres Area Council C. of C. (pres. 1985, bdr. dirs. 1987—), Nat. Assn. Bank Women, Am. Bus. Womens Assn. (chmn. fund raising 1984-85), Am. Inst. Banking. Republican. Presbyterian. Avocations: reading, sewing, dance, crafts, designing. Home: 79-H Islay Ln Columbia SC 29210 Office: Security Fed 7001 Garners Ferry Rd Columbia SC 29209

LEE, ELEANOR, state legislator; b. Elgin, Ill., July 17, 1931; d. Earl H. and Catherine (Goldback) S.; m. David H. Lee, 1951; children: Virginia Baylan, Phyllis Kenworthy, Marcia. BA, Evergreen State Coll. Bus. mgr. Fairman B. Lee Co., Inc.; former mem. Wash. Ho. of Reps.; mem. Wash. State Senate. Recipient Women Helping Women Soroptomists; named Woman of Yr. Highline Bus. and Profl. Women, 1986. Office: PO Box 66274 Burien WA 98166 *

LEE, FRANCES HELEN, editor; b. N.Y.C., Jan. 6, 1936; d. Murray and Rose (Rothman) Lee; B.A., Queens Coll., 1957; M.A., NYU, 1962. Editorial asst. Christian Herald Family Bookshelf, N.Y.C., 1957-62; with Gordon and Breach Sci. Pubs., Inc., N.Y.C., 1964-66, Am. Electric Power Service Corp. AEP Operating Ideas, N.Y.C., 1966-69, Indsl. Water Engrng. Mag., N.Y.C., 1969-71; directory editor Photographic div. United Bus. Publs., N.Y.C., 1971-80; editor Am. Druggist Blue Book, Hearst Books/Bus. Publs. Group, 1980-81, spl. projects coordinator motor manuals Hearst Book div., 1981-82, editor New Price Report, 1982-84; editor Am. Druggist Blue Book, 1982-88. Supr. Bronx div. N.Y. State CD, 1953-59. Mem. com. on N.Y.C. charter revision Citizens Union, 1975, com. on city personnel practices, 1975-76, com. on city mgmt., 1977—, bd. dirs., 1978—, co-chmn. com. on N.Y.C. Cultural Concerns, 1979—. Recipient cert. of honor NYU Alumni Fedn., 1985, Meritorious Service award, 1986 . Mem. N.Y. Bus. Press Editors, Women's Equity Action League (chmn. research com.), NYU Alumnae Club (dir. 1976-78, rec. sec. 1978-80, v.p. 1980-82, pres. 1982-84, rep. to bd. dirs. fedn. 1984-86), NYU Alumni Fedn. (dir.-at-large 1986—); N.Y. Bus. Pres. Edirots (bd. dirs. 1988—). Club: NYU (bd. govs. 1987—). Home: 170 2d Ave New York NY 10003

LEE, GERI CYMER, chemical company executive; b. Racine, Wis., Feb. 16, 1951; d. Henry John and Lily Elizabeth (Lewis) Cymer; m. John K. Lee, Aug. 21, 1971 (div. Oct. 1979). BA in Bus. Mgmt., Alverno Coll., 1983. With accounts payable S.C. Johnson & Son Inc., Racine, 1972-78, staff acct. accounts payable, 1978-81, acct., group leader accounts payable, 1981-82, inventory analyst inventory control, 1982-83, sr. inventory analyst inventory control, 1983, sr. cost mgmt. analyst home care fin., 1983-85, project supr. cost mgmt. home care fin., 1985-87, fin. project supr. internat. fin., 1987—. Vol., contbr. Downtown Racine Devel. Com., 1982—; fin. advisor Racine Area United Way, 1983-84; hon. chair Invest in Excellence Campaign Alverno Coll., 1987—; fin. advisor Johnsons Mut. Benefit Assn. bd. dirs., 1984-87. Mem. Nat. Assn. Female Execs. Republican. Lutheran. Home: 4829 Charles St Racine WI 53402 Office: SC Johnson & Son Inc 1525 Howe St Racine WI 53403

LEE, JACQUELENE RAYE, hospital adminstrator; b. Walnut Ridge, Ark., Aug. 10, 1946; d. Arthur Earl and Jessie Christine (Elliot) L. Student, Monticello Coll., 1964-65, George Washington U., 1965-67; BA, New Sch. Social Research, 1974, MA in Human Resources and Manpower Devel., 1978; postgrad., U. La Verne, 1985—. Personnel specialist U.S. Civil Service Commn., Washington, 1968-70, Dept. Army, Bklyn., 1970-72, Dept. Health, Edn., and Welfare, N.Y.C., 1972-75; asst. personnel officer SBA, N.Y.C., 1974-75; classification officer VA Med. Ctr., Bklyn., 1975-80; health systems specialist VA Med. Ctr., Los Angeles, 1980—; bd. dirs. Lee Equipment Co., Visaelia, Calif., 1981—, sec. and treas. 1986—. Vice chair Valley Network, San Fernando Valley, Calif., 1981-82; sec. Bus. and Profl. Women of Santa Monica, Calif., 1983-84; chair bd. mgmt. YWCA, W. Los Angeles, 1984—; bd. dirs. YWCA, Los Angeles, 1985—. Mem. Am. Acad. Med. Adminstrs., Women in Health Adminstrn., Health Care Execs. of So. Calif., Sierra Club (Simi Valley group sec. 1985-86). Office: VA Med Ctr Brentwood Hosp 11301 Wilshire Blvd Los Angeles CA 90073

LEE, JACQUELINE IRIS, community development planner; b. Spokane, Wash., Nov. 18, 1952; d. Reverend Daniel and Ruth Thelma (Clark) L.; m. Reginald M. Burke, Sept. 15, 1973 (div. Dec. 1980). BA, St. Mary's U., San Antonio, 1975, MA, 1978; M of City and Regional Planning, U. Calif., Berkeley, 1982; student, Barbizon Sch. Modeling, 1983. Ct. reporter Dun & Bradstreet, San Antonio, 1972-73; research asst. St. Mary's U., 1973-75; manpower planner City of San Antonio, 1978; planner Spanish Speaking Unity Counil, Oakland, Calif., 1980-83; project adminstr. The John Stewart Co., Sausalito, Calif., 1983-84; housing asst. Jubilee West Inc., Oakland, 1985-86; cons. Naomi Gray and Assocs. and Apape Works, San Francisco, 1984-86; employment monitor County of Bexar, San Antonio, 1986—; cons. Ctr. for Black Concern, Oakland, 1984—, Beckman Image Devel., Oakland, 1984—, Naomi Gray & Assocs., San Francisco, 1984—, East Oakland Youth Devel. Ctr., 1984-87. Mem., leader Topeka and San Antonio chpts. Girl Scouts U.S., 1958-71; coordinator Voter Registration and Awareness Project, San Antonio, 1978; activist S. African Apartheid, Black Student Union, 1970-73; mem. G. Givens Voices of Zion, San Antonio, 1986-87; mem. Allen Temple Bapt. Ch., Oakland, 1980-86, Second Bapt. Ch., 1986—. Mem. Nat. Assn. Planners. Baptist. Home: 901 W Silver Sands Dr #2801 San Antonio TX 78216 Office: County Bexar Dept Community Resources 203 W Nueva Suite 304 San Antonio TX 78207

LEE, JESSICA LYNN, film executive; b. N.Y.C., Dec. 8, 1960; d. Manfred and Roberta (Baschnagel) L. BA, Wheaton Coll., Norton, Mass., 1982; postgrad., NYU, 1986. Research assoc. E.F. Hutton Co., N.Y.C., 1982-83; trading liaison specialist Forstmann-Leff Co., N.Y.C., 1983-84; jr. analyst, liaison specialist James D. Wolfensohn, Inc., N.Y.C., 1984-85; adminstr. mktg. and distbn. Paramount Pictures, Inc., Los Angeles, 1985—. Mem. Citizens for Trudy Mason, N.Y.C., 1985-86. Mem. Assn. Ind. Video/Filmmakers, Ind. Feature Prodns., N.Y. Women in Film. Democrat. Home: The Palms 1959 Grace Ave Hollywood CA 90068 Office: Paramount Pictures 5555 Melrose Ave Hollywood CA 90038

LEE, JULIA T., librarian. came to U.S., 1957; d. Y.C. and K.C. (Yang) Tang; m. Wei-Ming Lee. BA, Nat. Taiwan U., Taipei, 1956; MLS, U. Ill., 1963. Librarian St. Theresa High Sch., Decatur, Ill., 1963-64; bibliographer U. Calif. Library, Santa Barbara, 1964-65; tech. librarian Dow Chem. Co. Tech. Library, Midland, Mich., 1965-71; librarian Mich. Molecular Inst., Midland, 1971—. Mem. Mich. Library Consortium (trustee 1983—). Office: Mich Molecular Inst 1910 W Saint Andrews Rd Midland MI 48640

LEE, LILY KIANG, scientific research company executive; b. Shanghai, China, Nov. 23, 1946; came to U.S., 1967, naturalized, 1974; d. Chi-Wu and An-Teh (Shih) Kiang; B.S., Nat. Cheng-Chi U., 1967; M.B.A. (scholar), Golden Gate U., San Francisco, 1969; m. Robert Edward Lee; children—Jeffrey Anthony, Michelle Adrienne, Stephanie Amanda, Christina Alison. Acct., then acctg. supr. Am. Data Systems, Inc., Canoga Park, Calif., 1969-73; sr. acct. Pertec Peripheral Equipment div. Pertec Corp., Chatsworth, Calif., 1973-76; mgr. fin. planning and acctg., then mgr. fin. planning and program control Sci. Center div. Rockwell Internat. Corp., Thousand Oaks, Calif., 1976—. Mem. Am. Mgmt. Assn., Nat. Mgmt. Assn., Nat. Property Mgrs. Assn., Nat. Assn. Female Execs. Republican. Baptist. Office: Rockwell Internat Corp PO Box 1085 1049 Camino Dos Rios Thousand Oaks CA 91360

LEE, MARGARET, psychologist. PhD, Columbia U., 1969. Psychologist Pomona, N.Y. Office: Summit Profl Bldg Rt 45 Pomona Rd Pomona NY 10970

LEE, MARGARET ANNE, psychotherapist; b. Scribner, Nebr., Nov. 23, 1930; d. William Christian and Caroline Bertha (Benner) Joens; m. Robert Kelly Lee, May 21, 1950 (div. 1971); children: Lawrence Robert, James Kelly, Daniel Richard. AA, Napa Coll., 1949; student, U. Calif., Berkeley, 1949-50; BA, Calif. State Coll., Sonoma, 1975; MSW, Calif. State U., Sacramento, 1977. Lic. clin. social worker, marriage and family counselor, Calif.; tchr. Columnist/stringer Napa (Calif.) Register, 1946-50; eligibility worker, supr. Napa County Dept. Social Services, 1968-75; instr. Napa Valley Community Coll., 1978-83; practice psychotherapy Napa, 1977—; bd. dirs. Project Access, 1978-79. Trustee Napa Valley Community Coll., 1983—, v.p. bd. trustees, 1984-85, pres. bd. trustees, 1986, clk., 1988; bd. dirs. Napa County Council Econ. Opportunity, 1984-85, Napa Chpt. March of Dimes, 1957-71, vice chair edn. com. 1987—; trustee Calif. Community Coll., also legis. com. 1985-87, edn. com. 1987-88. Recipient Fresh Start award Self mag., Mental Health Assn. Napa, 1983, award Congl. Caucuson Women's Issues, 1984. Mem. Nat. Assn. Social Workers, Mental Health Assn. Napa County, Calif. Assn. Physically and Handicapped, Women's Polit. Caucus. Democrat. Lutheran. Lodge: Soroptimists. Home: 15 Camilla Dr Napa CA 94558 Office: 1100 Trancas PO Box 2099 Napa CA 94558

LEE, MARGARET NORMA, artist; b. Kansas City, Mo., July 7, 1928; d. James W. and Margaret W. (Farin) Lee; PhB, U. Chgo., 1948; MA, Art Inst. Chgo., 1952. Lectr., U. Kansas City, 1957-61; cons. Kansas City Bd. Edn., Kansas City, Mo., 1968-86; guest lectr. U.Mo.-Columbia, 1983, 85, 87; one-woman shows Univ. Women's Club, Kansas City, 1966, Friends of Art, Kansas City, 1969, Fine Arts Gallery U. Mo. at Columbia, 1972, All Souls Unitarian Ch. Kansas City, Mo., 1978; two-Woman show Rockhurst Coll., Kansas City, Mo., 1981 exhibited in group shows U. Kans., Lawrence, 1958, Chgo. Art Inst., 1963, Nelson Art Gallery, Kansas City, Mo., 1968, 74, Mo. Art Show, 1976, Fine Arts Gallery, Davenport, Iowa, 1977; represented in permanent collections Amarillo (Tex.) Art Center, Kansas City (Mo.) Pub. Library, Park Coll., Parkville, Mo. Mem. Coll. Art Assn. Roman Catholic. Contbr. art to profl. jours.; author booklet. Home and studio: 4109 Holmes St Kansas City MO 64110

LEE, MARVA JEAN, counselor, physical education educator, consultant; b. Cleveland, Miss., Feb. 16, 1938; d. Henry Davis and Willie Mae (Caver) Hardy. B.S., George Williams Coll., 1960; M.A., Northeastern Ill. U., Chgo., 1972; M.Edn., Loyola U., Chgo., 1978. Child care worker Inst. Juvenile Research, Chgo., 1960-61; phys. educator Chgo. Bd. Edn., 1961-69; instr. George Williams Coll., Downers Grove, Ill., 1969-73; phys. educator Chgo. Bd. Edn., 1973-86, counselor, 1986—, workshop leader family life edn., 1983—. Chmn. Chgo. Pub. Sch. campaign United Negro Coll. Fund, Chgo., 1981, 82, chmn. profl. women's aux., 1983—; bd. dirs. Chgo. com. NAACP Legal Defense and Edn. Fund, 1980—; sec. bd. dirs. Treshan Youth Found., Chgo., 1977—; mem. Com. to Elect/Re-elect Roland Burris State Comptroller, 1978—, Com. to Elect Harold Washington Mayor Chgo., 1982-83. Named Outstanding Vol., Mid-Am. chpt. ARC, Chgo., 1976, Outstanding Vol., United Negro Coll. Fund, N.Y.C., 1982; recipient Image award Fred Hampton Found., 1979. Mem. AAHPER and Dance, Ill. Assn. Health, Phys. Edn. and Recreation (mem. exec. com. Chgo. dist.), Ill. Council Family Relations, Am. Assn. Counseling and Devel., Chgo. Guidance and Personnel Assn. Inc., Council Coll. Attendance, Secondary Sch. Counselors Council, Alpha Kappa Alpha. Avocations: community vol.; community fundraiser; travel. Home: 8300 S Peoria St Chicago IL 60620 Office: Percy L Julian High Sch 10330 S Elizabeth Chicago IL 60643

LEE, MAYA, clinical psychologist, educator; b. Chgo., Sept. 30, 1937; d. Philip Bruno and Renee (Roll) Dispensa; children—Barbara Pauline, Elizabeth Renee, Renee Marie Foss, Kelly Anne. B.A., Gov.'s State U., 1974, M.A., 1975; Ph.D., U.S. Internat. U., 1978. Lic. psychologist, Calif. Intern, San Bernardino County Mental Health (Calif.), 1977-78, psychologist, 1978-80; pvt. practice psychology, San Bernardino, 1980—. Gov.'s State U. grantee, 1973, 74. Mem. Am. Psychol. Assn., Inland Empire Psychol.

Assn., NOW. Democrat. Jewish. Home: 1797 N Arrowhead San Bernardino CA 92405

LEE, MICHELE, actress; b. Los Angeles, June 24, 1942; d. Jack and Sylvia Helen (Silverstein) Dusick; m. James Farentino, Feb. 20, 1966 (div. 1983); 1 son, David Michael; m. Fred Rappoport, Sept. 27, 1987. Appeared in: Broadway play How To Succeed in Business Without Really Trying, 1962-64; Broadway play Seesaw, 1973; appeared in: movie How To Succeed in Business Without Really Trying, 1967, The Love Bug, 1969; TV series Knots Landing, 1979—. Recipient Top Star of Tomorrow award Motion Picture Exhibitors of U.S. and Can., 1967; recipient Drama Desk award Broadway Critics, 1973, Outer Critics Circle award, 1973; nominated for Antoinette Perry award, 1973-74, Emmy for Knots Landing, 1981-82.

LEE, MICHELLE MINOR, grocery stores area manager; b. Dallas, Feb. 23, 1962; d. James Joseph Minor and Emma Louis (Willingham) King; m. Mitchell Houser Lee, Feb. 23, 1985. BBA, North Tex. State U., 1980-84. Store clk. 7-Eleven Stores Southland Corp., Dallas, 1978-84, store mgr., 1984-85, supr., area manager, 1985—. Events coordinator for 7-Eleven stores Muscular Dystrophy, Dallas, 1986-87; mem. dist. charitable com. March of Dimes, Dallas, 1985. Mem. Nat. Assn. Female Execs. Republican. Mem. Assembly of God Ch. Office: 7-Eleven Stores Dist 1602 575 W Arapaho Richardson TX 75080

LEE, NELDA S., art appraiser and dealer, film producer; b. Gorman, Tex., July 3, 1941; d. Olan C. and Onis L.; A.S. (Franklin Lindsay Found. grantee), Tarleton State U., Tex., 1961; B.A. in Fine Arts, N. Tex. State U., 1963; postgrad. Tex. Tech. U., 1964, San Miguel de Allende Art Inst., Mexico, 1965; 1 dau., Jeanna Lea Pool. Head dept. art Ector High Sch., Odessa, Tex., 1963-68. Bd. dirs. Odessa YMCA, 1970, bd. dirs. Am. Heart Assn., Odessa, 1975; fund raiser Easter Seal Telethon, Odessa, 1978-79; bd. dirs. Ector County (Tex.) Cultural Center, 1979—, Tex. Bus. Hall of Fame, 1980-85; bd. dirs., mem. acquisition com. Permian Basin Presdl. Mus., Odessa, 1978; bd. dirs., chairperson acquisition com. Odessa Art Mus., 1979—; pres. Mega-Tex. Prodns., TV and movie producers; pres. Ector County Democratic Women's Club, 1975. Recipient Designer-Craftsman award El Paso Mus. Fine Arts, 1964. Mem. Am. Soc. Appraisers, Appraisers Assn. Am., Appraisers of Fine Arts Soc., Nat. Soc. Lit. and the Arts, Tex. Assn. Art Dealers (pres. 1978-79), Odessa C. of C. Contbr. articles to profl. jours. Office: Nelda Lee Inc 2610 E 21st St Odessa TX 79761

LEE, PAMELA ANNE, corporate accounting manager; b. San Francisco, May 30, 1960; d. Larry D. and Alice Mary (Reece) L. BS in Bus., San Francisco State U., 1981. CPA, Calif. Typist, bookkeeper, tax acct. James G. Woo, CPA, San Francisco, 1979-85; tutor bus. math. and statistics San Francisco State U., 1979-80; teller to ops. officer Gibraltar Savs. and Loan, San Francisco, 1978-81; sr. acct. Price Waterhouse, San Francisco, 1981-86; corp. acctg. mgr. First Nationwide Bank, Daly City, Calif., 1986—; acctg. cons. New Performance Gallery, San Francisco, 1985, San Francisco Chamber Orch., 1986. Founding mem., chair bd. trustees Asian Acctg. Students Career Day, 1988. Mem. Am. Inst. CPA's, Calif. Soc. CPA's, Nat. Assn. Female Execs., Nat. Assn. Asian-Am. CPA's (bd. dirs. 1986, news editor 1987, pres. 1988). Republican. Avocations: reading, music, travel, personal computing. Office: First Nationwide Bank 455 Hickey Blvd Daly City CA 94015

LEE, PATRICIA TAYLOR, music educator; b. Portland, Oreg., Aug. 22, 1936; d. James Russell and Helen A. (Sherman) Taylor; m. Richard Diebold Lee, June 17, 1957; children: Elizabeth, Deborah, David. BA, Mills Coll., 1957; MA, Yale U., 1959; D in Mus. Arts, Temple U., 1979. Instr. piano U. Calif., Davis, 1969-75; prof. music West Chester (Pa.) U., 1978-88, dean grad. studies, 1984-85, dean of faculty of profl. studies, 1986-87, assoc. v.p. acad. affairs, 1987-88; prof. music, chair music dept. San Francisco State U., 1988—; pianist Sacramento Symphony, 1963-75. Contbr. articles to Clavier mag., 1981-87; pianist (rec.) Stanley Weiner Trio for Violin, Clarinet and Piano, 1975. V.p. Sacramento Regional Arts Council, 1969-71; pres. Sacramento Symphony League, 1962-64; pres. Jr. League of Sacramento, 1972-73. Mem. Music Tchrs. Nat. Assn., Coll. Music. Soc., Pa. Music Tchrs. Assn. (bd. dirs.), Nat. Assn. of Women Deans, Adminstrs. and Counselors, Sacramento Symphony Assn. (sec. 1962-67), Phi Beta Kappa, Sigma Alpha Iota (hon.). Democrat. Episcopalian. Home: 2001 Sacramento St #4 San Francisco CA 94109 Office: San Francisco State U Music Dept San Francisco CA 94132

LEE, QWIHEE PARK, plant physiologist; b. Republic of Korea, Mar. 1, 1941; d. Yong-sik and Soon-duk (Paik) Park; m. Ick-whan Lee, May 20, 1965; children: Tina, Amy, Benjamin. MS, Seoul Nat. U., Republic of Korea, 1965; PhD, U. Minn., 1973. Head dept. plant physiology Korea Ginseng and Tobacco Inst., Seoul, 1980-82; instr. Sogang U., Seoul, 1981, Seoul Women's U., 1981; research assoc. U. Wash., Seattle, 1975-79, 86—. Exec. dir. Korean Community Couseling Ctr., Seattle, 1983-86. Named one of 20 Prominent Asian Women in Wash. State, Chinese Post Seattle, 1986. Mem. AAAS. Buddhist. Home: 10723 Bartlett Ave NE Seattle WA 98125 Office: U Wash Ctr Bioengring RJ-30 1959 Northeast Pacific Seattle WA 98195

LEE, REBECCA ANNE, physician, surgeon; b. Long Island City, N.Y., Apr. 7, 1951; d. Kenneth Addison and Rose Marie (Deves) L.; 1 child, Rachel Marie Nandi. BS, CCNY, 1973; MD, Rutgers U., Piscataway, N.J., 1977. Lic. physician, Md., N.Y. Resident in surgery Howard U. Hosp., Washington, 1977-82; surg. fellow trauma and intensive care Lincoln Med. and Mental Health Ctrs., Bronx, N.Y., 1982-84; attending surgeon, trauma chief St. Barnabas Hosp., Bronx, 1983-84; minor Brookdale Hosp., Bklyn., 1985; surg. house physician Provident Hosp., Balt., 1985-86; surg. fellow Bayley Seton Hosp., Staten Island, N.Y., 1986-88. Mem. AMA, Am. Med. Women's Assn., Nat. Med. Assn., NAACP, Alpha Kappa Alpha. Democrat. Home: 62 Vanderbilt Ave Staten Island NY 10304 Office: Bayley Seton Hosp Vanderbilt Ave and Bay Sts Staten Island NY 10304

LEE, REDENA JOYCE, manufacturing company executive; b. Ada, Okla., Oct. 12, 1947; d. Homer Reese and Bessie Dean (Harlin) Scott; m. John Edward Lee, June 29, 1964; children: Kimberly Joyce Bowker, Misty Dawn. Grad. high sch., Sulphur, Okla., 1965; student, E. Cen. U., Ada, Okla., 1973. Sec. Okla. Dept. Pub. Welfare, Oklahoma City, 1966-67; clk. stenographer U.S. Govt.-Kerr Research Lab., Ada, 1970-74; bookkeeper Scott Mfg. Co., Inc., Ada, 1974-80, adminstrv. asst., 1980-85, v.p., gen. mgr., 1985—. Mem. Ada C. of C. Democrat. Mem. Ch. of Christ. Home: Rt 4 Box 422 Ada OK 74820 Office: Scott Mfg Co Inc PO Box 1650 Ada OK 74820

LEE, SANDRA MARGARET, oil company executive; b. Springfield, Mass., Oct. 16, 1957; d. Reginald C. and Barbara A. (DeMuzie) L. BS in Mgmt. and Mktg., Okla. State U., 1979. Credit analyst Del State Bank, Del City, Okla., 1979-80; div. order analyst Phillips Petroleum Co., Bartlesville, Okla., 1980-83, systems and procedure specialist, 1983-85; supr. div. order sect. Phillips 66 Natural Gas Co., Bartlesville, 1985—; participant seminars Phillips 66 Nat. Gas Co., 1980-87, co. recruiter coll. campuses, 1985, 86. Active St. Christopher Episcopal Ch., Del City, 1968—; solicitor United Fund Dr., Bartlesville, 1985, 86; mem. Okla. State U. Varsity Bowling Team, 1976-79. Named one of Outstanding Young Women of Am., 1986. Mem. AAUW (culinary arts com. 1986—), Nat. Assn. Div. Order Analysts (balloting and counting com. 1986), Sooner Assn. Div. Order Analysts, Okla. State U. Alumni Assn. (life), Jane Phillips Sorority, Alpha Kappa Psi (life). Democrat. Home: 1535 Kings Dr Apt 1026 Bartlesville OK 74006

LEEBOV, WENDY, consulting company executive; b. Pitts., Aug. 13, 1944; d. Mike and Florence (Labovitz) L.; 1 child, Nikki. BA, Oberlin Coll., 1966; MEd, Harvard U., 1970, EdD, 1971. Founder, tchr. Cambridge (Mass.) Pilot Sch., 1966-70; tchr., trainer, adminstr. Sch. Dist. Phila., 1970-78; dir. tng. Family Planning Council, Phila., 1978-82; dir. human resource devel. Albert Einstein Med. Ctr., Phila., 1982-85; v.p., gen. mgr. The Einstein Cons. Group, Phila., 1985—. Author: Service Excellence, 1988; editor: nat. newsletter Guest Relations in Practice, 1986—; contbr. articles to profl. jours. Pres. Women's Bail Fund, Phila., 1987; founder Pa. Women's Campaign Fund, Phila., 1985—; mem. Mayors Commn. for Women. Recipient Instl. Hospitality award Hosp. Assn. of Pa., 1983. Mem. Am. Soc. Healthcare Edn. and Tng., Am. Soc. Tng. and Devel. Democrat. Jewish. Home: 321 Queen St Philadelphia PA 19147 Office: The Einstein Consulting Group York and Tabor Rds Philadelphia PA 19141

LEEDER, ELLEN LISMORE, language and literature educator; b. Vedado, Havana, Cuba, July 8, 1931; came to U.S., 1959; d. Thomas and Josefina (Jorge) Lismore; m. Robert Henry Leeder, Dec. 20, 1957; 1 child, Thomas Henry. Doctora en Pedagogía, U. Havana, Cuba, 1955; MA, U. Miami, 1966, PhD, 1973. Lang. tchr. Emilia Azcárate Sch., Havana, 1950-52, St. George's Sch., Havana, 1952-59; tchr. The Cushman Sch., Miami, Fla., 1960-62; from instr. to prof. Spanish Barry U., Miami Shores, Fla., 1960—, now chmn. and coordinator fgn. langs.; prof. Miami-Dade Community Coll., Fla., 1974-75, vis. prof. U. Madrid, Spain, 1982; cons. NEH, Miami, 1981-83; judge, Asociación Criticos y Comentaristas del Arte, Miami, 1985-87; oral examiner, juror Dade County Pub. Schs., Miami, 1986-87. Author: El Desarraigo en Las Novelas de Angel Maria de Lera, 1978, Justo Sierra y el Mar, 1979. Mem. MLA, South Atlantic MLA, Am. Council Teaching Fgn. Lang., Am. Assn. Tchrs. of Spanish and Portuguese (v.p. southeastern Fla. chpt. 1984-87), Visiting Nurse Assn. (bd. dirs. 1978-80), Phi Alpha Theta, Kappa Delta Pi, Sigma Delta Pi, Alpha Mu Gamma. Club: Coral Gables Country. Home: 830 SW 101 Ave Miami FL 33174 Office: Barry Univ 11300 NE 2 Ave Miami Shores FL 33161

LEEDS, CANDACE, public relations executive; b. N.Y.C., July 28, 1947; d. Lawrence and Phyllis (Friedman) L.; m. Robert Jones, May 5, 1975 (div. 1977). B.S., Skidmore Coll., 1969; M.A., NYU, 1971. Assoc. dir. Town Hall, N.Y.C., 1972-76; account exec. Grey & Davis, N.Y.C., 1976-77, v.p., 1977-78, sr. v.p., 1978-80; sr. v.p. The Rowland Co., N.Y.C., 1980—. Nat. bd. dirs. Young Audiences, N.Y.C., 1982—, N.Y. Lyric Opera, N.Y.C., 1980-87; exec. v.p. Frank Barth, Inc., N.Y.C., 1987—, Ronald McDonald House. Spl. scholar Juilliard Sch. Music, N.Y.C., 1959-65; recipient Cert. of Achievement, Fontainebleau Ecole d'Art Am., 1968. Mem. Women in Communication. Club: Liberty (N.Y.C.).

LEEDS, ELIZABETH LOUISE, miniature collectibles executive; b. Los Angeles, July 24, 1925; d. Charles Furnival and Etta Louise (Jackson) Mayes; m. Walter Albert Leeds, Jan. 20, 1973 (dec.); children—Pam Ravey Lewis, Linda Ravey McCallam, Diane Ravey Lathrop, Tom Ravey. Student pub. sch., Prescott, Ariz. Lic. real estate agt., Ariz., cert. motel mgr. Real estate agt., Prescott, Ariz., 1962-64; sec. to mgr. Kon Tiki Hotel, Phoenix, 1964-65; draftsman Goleta Water Dist., Calif., 1965-68; asst. to vp research and design House of Mosaics, Santa Barbara, Calif., 1968-69; exec. chmn. poster design, dept. music U. Calif.-Santa Barbara, 1969-74; v.p. Colorform West, Inc., Santa Barbara, 1974-75; pres. Leeds Miniatures, Inc., Lincoln City, Oreg., 1975-86; cert. instr. Technologies for Creating, DMA, Inc., 1986—; lamp and silk screen designer Colorform West, Inc. Illustrator: Just A Story by Gustav Coenod, 1964. Mem. Hobby Industry Am., Miniatures Industry Assn. Am., Nat. Assn. Female Execs., Eugene C. of C., Eugene Bus. and Profl. Women. Republican. Clubs: Assn. Humanistic Psychology, Internat. New Thought Alliance, Assn. Transpersonal Psychology. Home: 2290 Arthur Ct Eugene City OR 97405

LEEDS, NANCY BRECKER, sculptor, lyricist; b. N.Y.C., Dec. 22, 1924; d. Louis Julius and Dorothy (Faggen) Brecker; m. Richard Henry Leeds, May 9, 1945; children—Douglas Brecker, Constance Leeds Bennett. Student Pine Manor Jr. Coll. Pres. Roseland Ballroom, N.Y.C., 1977-81. One-woman shows: Andrew Crispo Gallery, N.Y.C., 1979, Jeannette McIntyre Gallery Fine Arts, Palm Springs, Calif., 1987-88; exhibited in group shows at Bond Street Gallery, Great Neck, N.Y., Gallery Ranieri, N.Y.C., 1978, Country Art Gallery, 1984, Nature Conservatory Show, Country Art Gallery, 1985, Bonwit Teller, Manhasset, N.Y., 1985, Jeanette C. McIntyre Gallery, Palm Springs, Calif., 1987. Writer lyrics for musical Great Scot, 1965; lyricist for popular music. Trustee The Floating Hosp., N.Y.C., 1975—, v.p. Mem. ASCAP, The Dramatist Guild, The Songwriters Guild. Avocations: tennis; skiing.

LEEDY, EMILY L. FOSTER (MRS. WILLIAM N. LEEDY), consultant; b. Jackson, Ohio, Sept. 24, 1921; d. Raymond S. and Grace (Garrett) Foster; B.S., Rio Grande Coll., 1949; M.Ed., Ohio U., 1957; postgrad. Ohio State U., 1956, Mich. State U., 1958-59, Case Western Res. U., 1963-65; m. William N. Leedy, Jan. 1, 1943; 1 son. Dwight A. Tchr., Frankfort (Ohio) schs., 1941-46, Ross County Schs., Chillicothe, Ohio, 1948-53; elementary and supervising tchr. Chillicothe City Schs., 1953-56; dean of girls, secondary tchr. Berea City Schs., 1956-57; vis. tchr. Parma City Schs., 1957-59; counselor Homewood-Flossmoor High Sch., Flossmoor, Ill., 1959-60; teaching fellow Ohio U., 1960-62; asst. prof. edn., 1962-64; assoc. prof., counselor Cuyahoga Community Coll., 1964-66; dean of women Cleve. State U., 1966-67, assoc. dean student affairs, 1967-69; guidance dir. Cathedral Latin Sch., 1969-71; dir. women's service div. Ohio Bur. Employment Services, 1971-83; cons. in edn., 1983—. Mem. adv. com. S.W. Community Info. Service, 1959-60; youth com. S.W. YWCA, 1963-70, chmn., 1964-70, bd. mgmt., 1964-70; group services council Cleve. Welfare Fedn., 1964-66; chmn. Met. YWCA Youth Program study com., 1966, bd. dirs., 1966-72, v.p., 1967-68; chmn. adv. council Ohio State U. Sch. Home Econs., 1977-80; trustee Rio Grande Coll., 1988—. Named Cleve. area Woman of Achievement, 1969; named to Ohio Women's Hall of Fame, 1979; recipient Outstanding Contbn. special award Nat. Assn. Commns. for Women, 1983, Meritouious Service award Nat. Assn. Women Deans, Adminstrs. and Counselors, 1984. Mem. AAUW, Am., Northeastern Ohio (sec. 1958-59, exec. com. 1963-64, public relations chmn. 1962-64, newsletter chmn., editor 1963-64, del. nat. assembly 1959-63) personnel and guidance assns., LWV, Am. Assn. Retired Persons (Ohio women's initiative spokesperson 1987—), Nat. (publs. com. 1967-69, profl. employment practices com. 1980-82, Meritorious Service award 1984), Ohio (program chmn. 1967, editor Newsletter 1968-71) assns. women deans and counselors, Cleve. Counselors Assn. (pres. 1966), Women's Equity Action League, Zonta Internat. (exec. bd. 1968-70, treas. 1970-72, chmn. dist. V Status of Women 1980-81), Nat. Assn. Commns. for Women (dir. 1980-81, sec. 1981-83), Rio Grande Coll. Alumni Assn. (Atwood Achievement award 1975), Bus. and Profl. Women's Club (Nike award 1973), Am. Assn. Retired Persons, Ohio Retired Tchrs. Assn., Service Corps of Retired Execs. Delta Kappa Gamma. Club: Women's City (Cleve.). Home: 580 Lindberg Blvd Berea OH 44017 Office: 699 Rocky Rd Chillicothe OH 45601

LEEPER, MYRA JEAN, telecommunications executive; b. Orrville, Ohio, Feb. 5, 1954; d. Homer James and Alma Nadine (Haun) Lowe; m. Joseph P. Leeper, Sept. 7, 1974; 1 child, Ryan Matthew. Student, Coll. Wooster, 1972-74, Ohio State U., 1975-76; BFA, U. Akron, 1984. Clk. accounts payable Rubbermaid Inc., Wooster, Ohio, 1978, credit correspondent, 1978-82, supr., office services, 1982-84, corp. telecommunications specialist, 1984—. Choir dir. Fredericksburg (Ohio) Presbyn. Ch., 1987. Mem. Mich.-Ohio Telecommunications Assn. (chmn. membership 1987—). Home: Box 72 Fredericksburg OH 44627

LEEPER, REBECCA SUSAN, systems analyst, consultant; b. Leesburg, Va., Oct. 2, 1952; d. Loren Leon and Lilyan Ruth (Barbour) L. BS, Coll. of William and Mary, 1977; MBA, George Washington U., 1986. Mgmt. analyst U.S. Dept. of Treasury, Washington, 1980-83, project mgr., 1983-86; systems analyst, cons. Systemhouse, Inc., Arlington, Va., 1986—. Mem. Beta Gamma Sigma.

LEER, MARY KELLEY, performing arts producer; b. Mpls., Feb. 4, 1950; d. George Harold and Doris Lillian (Sjostrand) Kelley; m. Charles William Leer Jr., June 24, 1972; children: Maxwell Kelley, William Joseph. BA in Art History, U. Minn., 1974. Tchr. Salisbury (Conn.) Summer Sch., 1972-74; program dir. Urban Arts Program, Minn. Pub. Schs., 1974-75, Mpls. Arts Commn., 1975-76; coordinator dance touring program Nat. Endowment for the Arts, N.Y.C. and Washington, 1976-79; program analyst N.Y. State Council on the Arts, N.Y.C., 1978-79; exec. dir., producer N.Y. Dance Festival and Dance Umbrella, N.Y.C., 1979-80; exec. asst. to producer N.Y. Shakespeare Festival, N.Y.C., 1981-84; exec. dir. World Theater, St. Paul, 1985-86; producer, owner Ruby's Cabaret for the Performance Arts, Mpls., 1986-87; dir. Ballet of the Dolls, Mpls., Theatre De La Jeune Lune, Mpls.; cons. Lake Placid (N.Y.) Olympic Orgn. Commn., 1979-80; cons. Natonal Endowment for the Arts, Washington, 1979-83. Organizer George Latimer for Gov., Minn., 1986. Named Best of the Twin Cities Twin Cities Reader, 1986. Democrat. Home: 2401 Irving Ave S Minneapolis MN 55405

LEES, MICHELLE, dancer, educator; b. Quantico, Va., Mar. 18, 1947; d. Urban August and Marilyn Rose (Wolf) Lees; m. Emmons Oslar Larson, May 29, 1972; children: Torva Christiana, Peer Jakob. Prin. dancer Nat. Ballet, Washington, 1964-72, Chgo. Ballet, 1972-74; assoc. dir. Md. Youth Ballet, Bethesda, 1974—; choreographer Md. Youth Ballet, Bethesda, 1985—. Contbr. articles to profl. jours. Recipient medal Internat. Ballet Competition, 1972. Office: Md Youth Ballet 7649 Old Georgetown Rd Bethesda MD 20814

LEESON, JANET CAROLINE TOLLEFSON, cake specialties company executive; b. L'Anse, Mich., May 23, 1933; d. Harold Arnold and Sylvia Aino (Makikangas) Tollefson; student Prairie State Coll., 1970-76; master decorator degree Wilton Sch. Cake Decorating, 1974; grad. Cosmopolitan Sch. Bus., 1980; m. Raymond Harry Leeson, May 20, 1961; 1 son, Barry Raymond; children by previous marriage—Warren Scott, Debra Delores. Mgr., Peak Service Cleaners, Chgo., 1959; co-owner Ra-Ja-Lee TV, Harvey, Ill., 1961-66; founder and head fgn. trade dept. Wilton Enterprises, Inc., Chgo., 1969-75; tchr. cake decorating J.C. Penney Co., Matteson, Ill., 1975; office mgr. Pat Carpenter Assocs., Highland, Ind., 1975; pres. Leeson's Party Cakes, Inc., cake supplies and cake sculpture, Tinley Park, Ill., 1975—; lectr. and demonstrator cake sculpture and decorating; lectr. small bus. and govt. Sec., Luth. Ch. Women; active worker Boy Scouts Am. and Girl Scouts U.S., 1957-63; bd. dirs. Whittier PTA, 1962-70; active Bremen Twp. Republican party. Recipient numerous awards for cake sculpture and decorating, 1970—. Mem. Internat. Cake Exploration Soc. (charter, Outstanding Mem. Ill. 1984), Retail Bakers Am., Chgo. Area Retail Bakers Assn. (1st pl. in regional midwest wedding cake competition 1978, 80, 1st pl. nat. 1982, others), Am. Bus. Women's Assn. (chpt. publicity chmn., hospitality chmn. 1982-83, chmn. membership com. 1988, named Woman of Yr. 1986), Ingalls Meml. Hosp. Aux., Lupus Found. Am. Lutheran (hot line girl tuesdays Ill. chpt.). Home and Office: 6713 W 163d Pl Tinley Park IL 60477

LEET, MILDRED ROBBINS, consultant; b. N.Y.C., Aug. 9, 1922; d. Samuel Milton and Isabella (Zeitz) Elowsky; m. Louis J. Robbins, Feb. 23, 1941 (dec. 1970); children: Jane, Aileen; m. Glen Leet, Aug. 9, 1974. B.A., N.Y. U., 1942. Pres. women's div. United Cerebral Palsy, N.Y.C., 1951-52; bd. dirs. United Cerebral Palsy, 1953—, chmn. bd., 1953-55; rep. Nat. Council Women U.S. at UN, 1957-64, 1st v.p., 1959-64, pres., 1964-68, hon. pres., 1968-70; sec., v.p. conf. group U.S. Nat. Orgns. at UN, 1961-64, 76-78, vice chmn., sec., 1962-64, mem. exec. com., 1961-65, 75—, chmn. hospitality info. service, 1960-66; vice chmn. exec. com. NGO's UN Office Public Info., 1976-78, chmn. ann. conf., 1977; chmn. com. on water, desertification, habitat and environment Conf. NGO's with consultative status with UN/ECOSOC, 1976—; mem. exec. com. Internat. Council Women, 1960-73, v.p., 1970-73; chmn. program planning com., women's com. OEO, 1967-72; chmn. com. on natural disasters N.Am. Com. on Environment, 1973-77; N.Y. State chmn. UN Day, 1975; partner Leet & Leet (cons. women in devel.), 1978—; dir. Trickle Up Program, 1979—. Author articles; editor: UN Calendar & Digest, 1959-64, Measure of Mankind, 1963; editorial bd.: Peace & Change. Co-chmn. Vols. for Stevenson, N.Y.C., 1956; vice chmn. task force Nat. Democratic Com., 1969-72; commr. N.Y. State Commn. on Powers Local Govt., 1970-73; chmn. Coll. for Human Services, 1985—; former mem. bd. dirs. Am. Arbitration Assn., New Directions, Inst. for Mediation and Conflict Resolution, Spirit of Stockholm; bd. dirs. Hotline Internat., v.p. Save the Children Fedn., 1986—; rep. Internat. Peace Acad. at UN, 1974-77, Internat. Soc. Community Devel., 1977—; del. at large 1st Nat. Women's Conf., Houston, 1977; chmn. task force on internat. interdependence N.Y. State Women's Meeting, 1977; mem. Task Force on Poverty, 1977—; chmn. Task Force on Women, Sci. and Tech. for Devel., 1978; U.S. del. UN Status of Women Commn., 1978, UN Conf. Sci. and Tech. for Devel., 1979, co-dir. Trickle Up Program, Inc, 1979—; Brazzaville Centennial Celebration, 1980; mem. global adv. bd. Internat. Expn. Rural Devel., 1981—; mem. Council Internat. Fellows U. Bridgeport, 1982—; trustee overseas edn. fund LWV, 1983—; v.p. U.S. Com. UN Devel. Fund for Women, 1983—; mem. Nat. Consultative Com. Planning for Nairobi, 1984-85; co-chmn. women in devel. com. Interaction, 1985—; mem. com. of cooperation Interam. Commn. of Women, 1986; bd. dirs. Nat. Women's Conf. Com., 1986-87; adv. com. Am. Assn. Internat. Aging, 1986—. Recipient Crystal award Coll. for Human Services, 1983, ann. award Inst. for Mediation and Conflict Resolution, 1985, Woman of Conscience award Nat. Council Women, 1986, Temple award Inst. of Noetic Scis., 1987, Presdl. End Hunger award, 1987, Giraffe award Giraffe Project, 1987; co-recipient Rose award World Media Inst., 1987, Human Rights award UNIFEM, 1987, Pres.' Medal Marymount Manhattan Coll., 1988, Leadership award Peace Corps, 1988. mem. AAAS, Women's Nat. Dem. Club. Clubs: Cosmopolitan, NYU. Home: 54 Riverside Dr New York NY 10024 also: 2 Briar Oak Dr Weston CT 06883 Office: 790 Madison Ave New York NY 10021

LEFEBVRE, DIANE L., telephone company supervisor; b. Lowell, Mass., June 5, 1961; d. Marc E. and Priscilla G. (Garnache) Lefebvre; m. Kenneth R. Dias, June 13, 1981. BS, U. Lowell, 1983. Asst. staff mgr. NYNEX Service Co., Boston, 1983-86; cen. officer supr. New Eng. Telephone, Malden, Mass., 1986—. Chmn. Fifth Congl. Republican Council, Lowell, 1985-86; pres. Big Brother-Big Sister of Greater Lowell Inc., 1983-84. Named Big Sister of Yr., Lowell, 1980. Republican. Roman Catholic. Home: 53 Taylor Dr Franklin Park NJ 08823 Office: Bellcore Piscataway NJ 08854

LEFEVRE, CAROL BAUMANN, psychologist; b. Pierron, Ill., Nov. 26, 1924; d. Berhard Robert and Eunice Leone Hoyt (Heston) Baumann; m. Perry Deyo LeFevre, Sept. 14, 1946; children: Susan LeFevre Hook, Judith Ann LeFevre-Levy, Peter Gerret. AA, Stephens Coll., 1944; MA in Sociology, U. Chgo., 1948, MST, 1965, PhD in Human Devel., 1971. Registered psychologist, Ill. Tchr. Chgo. Theol. Sem. Nursery Sch., 1962-63, U. Chgo., Lab. Sch., 1965-66; asst. prof. psychology St. Xavier Coll., Chgo., 1970-74, assoc. prof., 1974-86, acting chmn. dept. psychology, 1970-71, chmn. dept. psychology, 1971-77, asst. dir. Inst. Family Studies, 1973-82, dir., 1982-85; intern in clin. psychology with Adlerian pvt. practitioner, Chgo., 1973-75; pvt. practice clin. psychology, Chgo., 1975—; mem. staff Logos Inst. Chgo. Theol. Sem., 1973-76; speaker in field. Author, researcher on subjects including returning women grad. students' changing self-conceptions, women's roles, inner city children's perceptions of sch., aging and religion. Pub. Health Service tng. grantee NIMH, 1969. Mem. Am. Psychol. Assn., Ill. Psychol. Assn., Gerontol. Soc., N.Am. Soc. Adlerian Psychology, Phi Beta Kappa. Mem. United Ch. of Christ. Home: 1376 E 58th St Chicago IL 60637 Office: 400 Ravinia Pl Orland Park IL 60462

LEFFLER, NELL FOUST, associate realtor, retired librarian; b. Humboldt, Tenn., Dec. 25, 1922; d. Asa Burnette and Lucille (Sinclair) Foust; student Vanderbilt U., 1942-43; B.A., Lambuth Coll., 1944; M.A., Fla. State U., 1951; m. John Edward Leffler, Nov. 26, 1952. Asst. librarian Fla. State U. Library, 1952, 65-72, head serials cataloging, 1970-74, univ. librarian, head dept. cataloging, 1974-79, univ. cataloging librarian, 1979-84, reference libarian sci. div., 1984-85, ret., 1985; real estate salesman, 1986—; asst. librarian Colquitt-Thomas County Regional Library, Moultrie, Ga., 1952; reference librarian Fla. Legis. Reference Bur., Tallahassee, 1954-63; research librarian Fla. Bd. Regents, Tallahassee, 1963-65. Mem. ALA, Southeastern Library Assn., Audubon Club, Beta Phi Mu, Pi Beta Phi. Democrat. Methodist. Club: Apalachee Yacht. Home: 2413 Miranda Ave Tallahassee FL 32304 Office: Fla State U 165 Library Tallahassee FL 32306

LEFKOWITZ, JOAN MUCHNICK, food products executive; b. Hartford, Conn., Jan. 4, 1949; d. Samuel Yarver and Dorothy Helen (Kasdan) Muchnick; m. Paul Lefkowitz, Nov. 1, 1970; children: Jeffrey Peter, Samuel Adam. BA in Econs., Emory U., 1970. Asst. buyer Scarborough's, Austin, Tex., 1970-72; recruiter, mgr. human resources Burdine's, Miami, Fla., 1972-78; search cons. Corp. Advisors, Miami, 1978-80; mgr. human resource Burger King Corp., Miami, 1980-83, dir. human resource, 1983—. Mem. So. Coll. Placement Assn., Leadership Miami Alumni Assn. Office: Burger King Corp PO Box 520783 Miami FL 33152

LEFKOWITZ, ROSE FRANCES, medical records administrator, educator, author; b. Detroit, July 24, 1954; d. Charles and Miriam (Pollack) L.; m.

Harold Greenberger, Nov. 6, 1983; 1 child, David Jay. BA cum laude, Bklyn. Coll., 1975; BS cum laude, Downstate Med. Ctr., 1977; M in Pub. Adminstrn., NYU, 1981, postgrad., 1987—. Dir. med. records sect., Trafalgar Hosp., N.Y.C., 1977-78; asst. dir. med. records sect., Maimonides Med. Ctr., Bklyn., 1978-80; instr. Downstate Med. Ctr., Bklyn., 1981-83, asst. prof., 1983—; cons. Jr. Coll. Health Sci., Daejeon, Republic of Korea, 1983-85, St. Mary's Hosp., Bklyn., 1984-86, Mary Immaculate Hosp., Queens, N.Y., 1984-86, Woodhull Med. Ctr., Bklyn., 1986—, Parkway Hosp., Queens, 1986—; bd. dirs. Bklyn. Hospice Program; mem. clin. preceptors com. Downstate Med. Ctr., 1978—, mem. adv. com., 1981—, clin. site coordinator, 1982—; preceptor Borough of Manhattan Community Coll. Med. Record Tech. Program, 1977-80, Downstate Med. Ctr.-SUNY Med. Record Adminstrn. Program, 1978-80. Author: (with I. Topor) Comparative Health Recordkeeping Systems in Nontraditional Settings, 1988; developed videotape presentation Examination Before Trial: Guide for Health Care Professionals, 1987; contbr. articles to profl. jours. Mem. numerous SUNY governing coms., 1981-87. Mem. Am. Soc. of Law and Medicine (mem. speaker's bur. 1986—), Health Care Fin. Mgmt. Assn., Nat. Assn. Female Execs., Am. Med. Record Assn., Med. Record Assn. of N.Y. State (mem. speaker's bur. 1986—, mem. cons.'s listing 1986—, mem. edn. com. 1986, coding arbitration subcom. 1985-86, pub. relations com. 1982-83), Greater N.Y. Med. Record Assn. (bd. dirs., exec. council 1982—, chmn. publicity com. 1982-83, editor newsletter 1984-85, subcom. on edn. Bklyn. and S.I. chpt. 1986-87, editor jour. 1984-87, scholarship and ednl. fund com. 1986), Met. N.Y. Tumor Registrars Assn. (v.p. 1986-87, co-dir. edn. com.). Office: Downstate Med Ctr 450 Clarkson Ave Box 105 Brooklyn NY 11203

LEFLER, SALLY GENE, association executive, management consultant, director; b. St. Louis, Apr. 8, 1936; d. James I. Lefler and Gene (Heitman) Tripodi. B.A., Lindenwood Coll., St. Charles, Mo., 1957; postgrad. honors program, Am. U., Case Western Res. U., Harvard U. Trainee U.S. Dept. State, 1957-58; tchr., counselor Fairfax Hall Coll. Prep., Waynesboro, Va., 1958-60; buying exec. Famous-Barr, May Co., St. Louis, 1960-63; exec. dir. St. Louis Carondelet YWCA, 1966-70; fin. and devel. cons. Nat. Bd. YWCA, Atlanta, San Francisco and N.Y.C., 1970-73; real estate broker Holiday Builders, St. Simons Isle, Ga., 1973-74; freelance cons., Chgo., Conn., 1975-79; mgmt. cons., N.Y.C., 1979—; dir. Asusa, 1988—; dep. support coordinator world conf. World Assn. of Girl Guides/Girl Scouts, London, Eng., 1984; dir. Office Nat. Bd. dirs., Girl Scouts U.S.; mem. Internat. Tng. Inst. World YWCA, nat. bd., 1969—; lectr. in field. Author, organizer: A Social History of Art in Missouri, 1969; asst. editor: Administration Manual, Nat. Bd. YWCA, 1974-75. Republican. Mem. Christian Scientist Ch. Club: Press (Brunswick, Ga.). Lodge: Zonta (treas., bd. dirs., sec. St. Louis County chpt.). Avocations: international travel, exploration of cultures through music and the arts. Home: 5 Orchard Hills New Canaan CT 06840

LEFRANÇOIS, REJEANNE BERNIER, state agency official; b. Bristol, Conn., Nov. 13, 1931; d. Wilfred Henry and Mary Angel (Poulin) B.; m. Joseph Lucien Edgar, Jan. 6, 1951 (dec. 1971); children: Stephen David, Terese Denise, Richard Daniel, Suzanne Dianne, Thomas Donald. BA, Shaw U., 1969; MEd, N.C. State U., 1972. Fgn. lang. instr. Kittrell (N.C.) Jr. Coll., 1969-70; fgn. lang. cons. N.C. Dept. Pub. Instrn., Raleigh, 1972-73; licensing cons. N.C. Office Child Dare Care Licensing, Raleigh, 1973-74; human relations cons., social research assoc. N.C. Human Relations Council, Raleigh, 1974-76; dir. Internat. Women's Yr. Council, Raleigh, 1976-77; dir. family life office Cath. Diocese of Raleigh, 1978-80; dir. Hospice Wake County, Raleigh, 1980-81; dir. edn. Cen. Carolina Hosp., Sanford, N.C., 1982-83; adminstrv. asst. gov.'s office State of N.C., Raleigh, 1984-85; personnel analyst N.C. Employment Security Commn., Raleigh, 1985—; ptnr. geneal. research concern Carolina Abstractors, 1985—. Author: France's Annual Travel Log, 1985, (with others) Abstracts of Wayne County Wills, vol. I (1780-1868), 1986, Compiled Index to Wayne County (1780-1868), 1988; contbr. articles to spl. interest publs.; also patentee. Mem. nat. supervisory com. for cert. of instr. trainer's ARC, 1988. Mem. Internat. Assn. Personnel in Employment Security (chmn. blood program 1987, 88). Republican. Roman Catholic. Home: 2910 Poole Rd Raleigh NC 27610 Office: Employment Security Commn 700 St Mary's St Raleigh NC 27605

LE GALLIENNE, EVA, actress; b. London, Jan. 11, 1899; d. Richard and Julie (Norregaard) Le G. Ed., Collège Sévigne, Paris; M.A. (hon.), Tufts Coll., 1927; D.H.L., Smith Coll., 1930, Ohio Wesleyan U., 1959, Goucher Coll., 1960, U. N.C., 1964, Bard Coll., 1965, Fairfield U., 1966; Litt.D., Russell Sage Coll., 1930, Brown U., 1933, Mount Holyoke Coll., 1937. Founder, dir. Civic Repertory Theatre, N.Y.C., opening October 25, 1926. Debut in: The Laughter of Fools, Prince of Wales Theatre, London, 1915; New York debut in: The Melody of Youth, 1916; appeared, in New York and on tour in Mr. Lazarus, 1916-17, (with Ethel Barrymore in) The Off Chance, 1917-18, Not So Long Ago, 1920-21, Liliom, 1921-22, The Swan, 1923; Hannele in: The Assumption of Hanele, by Hauptmann, 1923, Jeanne d'Arc, by Mercedes de Acosta, 1925, The Call of Life, by Schnitzler, 1925, The Master Builder, by Ibsen, 1925-26; presented: Allison's House (Pulitzer prize), Alice in Wonderland, others; co-founder (with Margaret Webster of) over 30 plays in 7 years including, Am. Repertory Theatre, which produced Henry VIII, Ibsens' John Gabriel Brokman; Ibsen's Hedda Gabler and Ghosts, 1948, Allison's House; toured in: The Corn Is Green, 1949-50; on Broadway in The Southwest Corner, 1955; as Queen Elizabeth in: on Broadway in Schiller's Mary Stuart, N.Y.C., 1957, on tour, 1959-60; in, Maxwell Anderson's Elizabeth the Queen, 1961-62; toured in: Sea Gull, Nat. Repertory Theatre, 1963-64; in: The Trojan Women; appeared with, APA Repertory Theatre, N.Y.C.; as Marguerite in: Exit The King; also directed: Chekov's The Cherry Orchard, 1967-68, Doll's House, Seattle Repertory, 1975; appeared as Countess in: All's Well That Ends Well, Shakespeare Festival Theatre, Stratford, Conn., 1970; in: Dream-Watcher, White Barn Theatre, 1975, The Royal Family, Helen Hayes Theatre, N.Y.C., 1976, nat. tour, 1976-77; To Grandmother's House We Go, Biltmore Theatre, N.Y.C., 1980-81; appeared: in movie The Resurrection, 1979; (Spl. Tony award Am. Theatre Wing 1964, Emmy award 1978); Author: autobiography At 33, 1934, Flossie and Bossie, 1949 (London edit. 1950), With a Quiet Heart, 1953, The Mystic in the Theatre, a study of Eleonora Duse, 1966; Translator many works of Henrik Ibsen, Hans Christian Anderson; dir. Alice in Wonderland, Virginia Theatre, N.Y.C., 1982-83. Recipient Brandeis U. award for drama, 1966; winner of Pictoral Rev. Achievement award, 1926; gold medal Soc. Arts and Town Hall Club award, 1934; Am. Acad. Arts and Letters medal for good diction on the stage, 1945; Outstanding Woman of Year award Women's Nat. Press Club, 1947; spl. award ANTA, 1964; award, 1977; Handel medallion City N.Y., 1976; Nat. Medal of Arts award, 1986; decorated cross Royal Order St. Olaf, 1961. Mem. Actors' Equity Assn., AFTRA, Screen Actors Guild, Dramatists Guild.

LEGG, ROSE M., municipal government official; b. Dearborn, Mich., July 25, 1930; d. George A. and Ann (Sherman) Allore; m. Gerald Richard Legg, Jan. 28, 1950; children: Judy, JoAnn, Justine, Jerry. Student, Oakland (Mich.) Community Coll., 1970, Wayne County Community Coll., Detroit, 1975-76; Cert. mcpl. clk., Mich. State U., 1979. Clerk Charter Twp. of Brownstown, Mich., 1966—; mem. adv. bd. clk.'s program Mich. State U.; mem. election scheduling com. Wayne County; former mem. tax allocation bd. Author: (video) Our Town Brownstown, 1986. Bd. dirs. Huron Valley Pub. Library, 1972-85, Sr. Citizen Adv. Com., 1975-87, Mich. Twp. Assn., 1972-74; sec. Huron Valley Dem. Club, 1972-82; active Project Pulchritude, 1985. Named Clerk Yr. Mich. Twp. Assn., 1987; recipient Grass Roots Govt. award, Mich. Twp. Assn., 1987. Mem. Wayne County Mcpl. Clerks Assn., Tri County Clerk Assn., IIMC. Roman Catholic. Office: Charter Township of Brownstown 21313 Telegraph Brownstown MI 48183

LEGRANDE, MARGARET ESTELLA, school system administrator; b. Richmond, Va., May 28, 1931; d. Samuel Patrick LeGrande and Lula Estella LeGrande (Coxe) Groome; m. Floyd Posby, Aug. 20, 1960 (div. 1987); children: Floyd, Margaret LeGrande. Student, Va. Union U., 1952-54, 56; BS in Nursing, Va. Commonwealth U., 1957; postgrad., Columbia U., 1972, Pace U., 1974, Yeshiva U., 1985; MS, New Sch. Social Research, 1987. RN., N.Y.; cert. tchr., N.Y. Supr. Mt. Sinai Hosp., N.Y.C., 1958; pvt. duty nurse Hosp. for Joint Diseases, N.Y.C., 1959-65; head nurse Dept. Health, N.Y.C., 1965-66; dir. staff devel. Coll. View Nursing Home, N.Y.C., 1966-72; supr. Jewish Home and Hosp. for Aged, N.Y.C., 1972-77; supr. Concord Nursing Home, Bklyn., 1977-78, dir. nursing, 1978-80; tchr., clin. instr. N.Y.C. Bd. Edn., 1982-85, tchr., coordinator, 1985—; health planner Health Systems Agy., N.Y.C., 1974-76; adj. prof. physical/health edn. Borough of Manhattan Community Coll., N.Y.C., 1988; lectr. in field. Bd. dirs. Citizen Care Day Care, N.Y.C., 1986—, Citizen Care Com., N.Y.C., 1986—, N. Manhattan Credit Union, N.Y.C., 1987—; chmn. program com. Harlem Teams for Self Help Inc., N.Y.C., 1987—; mem. task force Harlem Hosp. Community Bd., N.Y.C. Recipient Sojourner Truth award Harlem Women's Com. New Future Found., 1988, Spl. Mother Yr. award ABG Cable TV, 1988, Recognition award Med-Manhattan Soc. Practical Nursing., 1988. Mem. Am. Coll. Health Care Adminstrs., Assn. Supv. and Curriculum Devel., Am. Mgmt. Assn., Nat. Assn. Female Execs., Chi Eta Phi, Alpha Kappa Alpha. Democrat. Episcopalian. Home: 626 Riverside Dr #24G New York NY 10031

LEGRANGE, JANE DEBORAH, industrial physicist; b. N.Y.C., Sept. 21, 1953; d. Herbert Alfred and Celia (Nooger) LeG.; m. Doron Zeilberger, June 3, 1979; children: Celia, Tamar. BA, U. Pa., 1975; MS, U. Ill., Urbana, 1977, PhD, 1980. Fellow Weizmann Inst., Rehovot, Israel, 1980-82; vis. fellow Princeton (N.J.) U., 1982-84; mem. tech. staff ATT Engring. Research Ctr., Princeton, 1984—. Contbr. articles to profl. jours. Mem. Am. Physical Soc. Office: ATT Engring Research Ctr Box 900 Princeton NJ 08540

LEGROS, SUSAN LEBLANC, bank executive; b. Lake Charles, La., Jan. 9, 1952; d. John Ozeme and Lila Mae (Thomas) LeBlanc; m. Andy Joseph Legros Jr., Mar. 6, 1976. Student, La. State U., 1970-72, McNeese State U., 1972-74; diploma real estate fin., Am. Bankers Assn. and Ohio State U., 1981. Sales assoc. Reinauer Real Estate, Lake Charles, 1976-77; note clk. Am. Bank of Commerce, Lake Charles, 1977-79, mgr. real estate, 1979-81, officer personal banking, 1981-83, asst. v.p., 1983-85, v.p., 1985-87; spl. assets officer Farm Credit Bank, Jennings, La., 1988—. Treas. opposition com. F.E.M.A., Calcasieu Parish, 1984-87; v.p. Southwest La. chpt. ARC, Lake Charles, 1986—, bd. dirs., 1984-87. Mem. Nat. Assn. Bank Women (treas. Lake Charles chpt. 1982-83, v.p. 1983-84, pres. 1984-85, program chmn. state conv. 1987), Home Builder Assn. Southwest La. (bd. dirs. 1983-87), La. Farm Bur. Democrat. Roman Catholic. Office: Farm Credit Bank PO Box 318 Jennings LA 70546

LE GUIN, URSULA KROEBER, author; b. Berkeley, Calif., Oct. 21, 1929; d. Alfred Louis and Theodora (Kracaw) Kroeber; m. Charles A. Le Guin, Dec. 22, 1953; children: Elisabeth, Caroline, Theodore. B.A., Radcliffe Coll., 1951; M.A., Columbia, 1952. Vis. lectr. or writer in residence numerous workshops and univs., U.S. and abroad. Author: Rocannon's World, 1966, Planet of Exile, 1967, City of Illusion, 1967, A Wizard of Earthsea, 1968, The Left Hand of Darkness, 1969, The Tombs of Atuan, 1971, The Lathe of Heaven, 1971, The Farthest Shore, 1972, The Dispossessed, 1974, The Wind's Twelve Quarters, 1975, A Very Long Way from Anywhere Else, 1976, Orsinian Tales, 1976, The Language of the Night, 1978, Leese Webster, 1979, Malafrena, 1979, The Beginning Place, 1980, Hard Words, 1981, The Eye of the Heron, 1981, The Compass Rose, 1982, King Dog, 1985, Always Coming Home, 1985, Buffalo Gals, 1987, Wild Oats and Fireweed, 1988, A Visit from Dr. Katz, 1988, Catwings, 1988; also numerous short stories, poems, criticism, screenplays. Recipient Boston Globe-Hornbook award for excellence in juvenile fiction, 1968; Nebula award, 1969, 75; Hugo award for best novel, 1969, 75; Gandalf award, 1979; Kafka award, 1986; best novella, 1973; best short story, 1974; Newbery honor medal, 1971; Nat. Book award, 1973; Fulbright fellow France, 1953-54. Mem. Sci. Fiction Research Assn., Sci. Fiction Writers Assn., Authors League, PEN, Writers Guild West, NOW, Phi Beta Kappa.

LEHBERGER, LOIS MARIE, accountant; b. Boston, July 3, 1956; d. Thomas Edward, Jr. and Dorothea Ann (Norton) Palmer; m. Reinhold Helmuth Lehberger, May 27, 1979; children: Kimberly Gabriella, Katrina Theresa. BA in Econs., Acctg., Coll. Holy Cross, 1978. Acct. Cambex Corp., Waltham, Mass., 1978-80, mgr. acctg., 1980-85, controller, 1985-87, mgr. treasury ops., 1987—. Mem. Phi Beta Kappa, Alpha Sigma Nu, Omicron Delta Epsilon. Democrat. Roman Catholic. Home: 8 Holly Ln Ashland MA 01721 Office: Cambex Corp 360 Second Ave Waltham MA 02154

LEHMAN, CLARA MAY HILEMAN, physician; b. Sharon, Pa., Oct. 30, 1901; d. Mayberry and Clara May (Keasey) Hileman; B.S., Pa. State U., 1924; postgrad. Columbia, 1927-28, Marine Biol. Lab., 1930-31; M.D., Woman's Med. Coll., Pa., 1935; m. Robert N. Lehman, Apr. 24, 1938; 1 dau., Mary Dorcas. Intern Lancaster (Pa.) Hosp., 1935-36, resident, 1936-37; practice gen. medicine, Pa., 1936-47; practice staff geriatrics U.S. Army Hosp., Ft. Meyer, Va., 1948-51, VA Hosp., Aspinwall, Pa., 1955-57, Woodville State Hosp., Carnegie, Pa., 1957-68. Mem. AMA, Pa., Allegheny County med. socs., Royal Soc. Health, Alpha Omega Alpha, Alpha Epsilon Iota. Address: 801 Washington Ave Tyrone PA 16686

LEHMAN, EVELYN JEANNE, lawyer; b. Ann Arbor, Mich., June 13, 1930; d. Arthur Conrad and Mildred Georgianna (Pearce) L.; B.A., Mt. Holyoke Coll., 1951; LL.B., U. Mich., 1954; m. Apr. 4, 1959; 1 son, Arthur Scott Long. Admitted to N.Y. State bar; assoc., then partner firm Gifford, Woody, Palmer & Serles, N.Y.C., 1957-85, Townley & Updike, 1985—. Pres., YWCA of City of N.Y., 1982-86, mem. bd. trustees, 1982—. Mem. Am. Bar Assn. Office: 405 Lexington Ave New York NY 10147

LEHMAN, JAN MARIE, elementary educator; b. Lebanon, Pa., Oct. 2, 1957; d. Richard Jacob and Helen Mae (Zartman) L. BS magna cum laude, Millersville (Pa.) U., 1979; MeD, Pa. State U., State College, 1986. Cert. elem. and early childhood tchr., Pa. Tchr. kindergarten Lebanon Sch. Dist., 1979—; cooperating tchr. Pa. State U., University Park, 1983, Millersville U., 1983-85, 87—. Mem. Assn. for Childhood Edn. Internat., Nat. Assn. for the Edn. Young Children, Lebanon Edn. Assn., Lebanon Edn. Rep. Council, NEA. Democrat. Home: 621 Noble St Lebanon PA 17042 Office: Lebanon Sch Dist 1000 S 8th St Lebanon PA 17042

LEHMAN, JANELL PATRICE, insurance sales professional; b. Lowville, N.Y., Jan. 13, 1958; d. Myron Martin and LaJune Marie (Lyndaker) L. AAS in Bus. Adminstrn., Jefferson Community Coll., 1978, AS in Data Processing, 1978. Lic. ins. agt.; cert. health cons. Asst. bookkeeper Walter H. Bisnett, Inc., Watertown, N.Y., 1978-79; switchboard operator Lewis County Gen. Hosp., Lowville, 1979-80; asst. mgr. Thom McAn Shoe Store, Fayetteville, N.Y., 1981-82; sales and service rep. Blue Cross of Watertown, 1982—. Chmn. pulpit com. Lowville Bapt. Ch., 1986, chmn. Christian edn. com., 1987. Mem. Nat. Assn. Female Execs. Democrat. Home: 7774 Summit Ave Lowville NY 13367

LEHMAN, LINDA LEE, ecological and environmental specialist; b. Doylestown, Pa., Sept. 5, 1945; d. William Arthur and Anna (Kennedy) L.; m. George Dane Vose, Feb. 19, 1980; children: Aaron Dane, Mackenzie Ann. BS in Geology, Fla. Atlantic U., 1975; MS in Hydrogeology, U. South Fla., 1978; postgrad., U. Minn. Research asst. U. South Fla., St. Petersburg, 1975-76; hydrogeologist Parson's, Brinckerhoff, Quade & Douglas, McLean, Va., 1977-79, U.S. Nuclear Regulatory Commn., Washington, 1979-82; research asst. U. Minn., Mpls., 1982; fellow in research Minn. Geol. Survey, St. Paul, 1982-83; cons. in field Savage, Minn., 1983-85; pres. L. Lehman & Assocs., Inc., Burnsville, Minn., 1985—; cons. to issues regarding nuclear waste State of Nev., Carson City, 1983—, Yakima Indian nation, Toppenish, Wash., 1983-86, State of Minn., St. Paul, 1983-86, Upper and Lower Sioux Communities, So. Minn., 1986. ; participant in Internat. Ground Water Flow and Transport Modeling Validation sponsored by Swedish Nuclear Inspectorate. Mem. Nat. Water Well Assn., Internat. Assn. Hydrogeologist, Am. Geophysical Union, Am. Inst. of Hydrology, Minn. Safety Council, Minn. Ground Water Assn. (pres. 1988—), Environ. Quality Bd., Adv. Bd. on Ground Water Protection, Engineer's Club of Mpls. Office: L Lehman & Assocs Inc 1103 W Burnsville Pkwy #209 Burnsville MN 55337

LEHMAN, MARY JULIA, chemical company executive; b. Racine, Wis., Jan. 17, 1943; d. Bernard Joseph and Velma Dorothy (Schowalter) Wynhoff; m. Kermit A. Lehman, Aug. 22, 1964; children: Steven, Kate. BS, U. Wis., 1965. Cert. med. tech. Med. tech. in biochemistry Milw. County Hosp., Wis., 1965-66; med. tech. specialist The Harwood Clinic, Wauwatosa, Wis., 1966-68; med. tech. in chemistry The Valley Hosp., Ridgewood, N.J., 1968-70; med. tech. in hematology Providence Hosp., Seattle, 1972-76; sales rep. Biosci. Enterprises, Van Nuys, Calif., 1976-78, Dow Chem. Co., Seattle, 1978-80; communications specialist Dow Chem. Co., Midland, Mich., 1980-81, product market mgr., 1981-85, mgr. tng., devel., 1985—; bd. dirs. Adult Edn. Adv. Council, Midland; mem. Valley Coll. Consortium, Midland, 1985—. Bd. dirs. United Way, Midland, 1987—. Mem. Am. Soc. Tng. and Devel., Delta Zeta Alumni (fin. adv. 1986—). Office: Dow Chemical Co 2020 W H Dow Ctr Midland MI 48674

LEHMAN, SANDRA KAY, association executive; b. Johnstown, Pa., Dec. 29, 1940; d. William O. and Helen M. (Blough) L.; B.S., Pa. State U., 1962; postgrad. U. So. Calif., Rensselaer Poly. Inst., spl. corp. courses. Procurement agt. Def. Fuels Supply Center, Alexandria, Va., 1964-67; programmer, analyst Def. Supply Ag., Alexandria, 1967-69; mgr. OCR services and ops. SDA Corp., Cheverly, Md., 1969-73; chief program devel. unit Assn. State and Territorial Health Ofcls., Washington, 1973-74; dir. composition and OCR services Informatics, Inc., Riverdale, Md., 1974-77; assoc. dir. student services Assn. Am. Med. Colls., Washington, 1977-79, assoc. dir. computer services, 1979-88, dir. computer services, 1988—; cons. Hewlett Packard laser printer, treas. Regional Users Group, 1981-83; mgmt. cons. Maine Dept. Health, 1979, MCI Corp., 1983—. Treas., fund raiser Alexandria Choral Soc., 1978-84, rep. to Alexandria Performing Arts Council, 1978-84. Mem. Mu Phi Epsilon, Gamma Phi Beta, Mensa. Home: 815 Church St Alexandria VA 22314 Office: 1 Dupont Circle NW Washington DC 20036

LEHMAN, SHERELYNN, psychotherapist; b. Cleve., June 27, 1941; d. Marvin and Esther (Morgenstern) Friedman; m. Theodore Gary Falcon, Aug. 19, 1962 (div. Apr. 1971); 1 child, Michael Aaron Falcon; m. Paul James Lehman, Apr. 21, 1974 (div. Nov. 1984); 1 child, Jonathan Paul. BS, Ohio U., 1963; postgrad., UCLA, 1970-72; MA, Loyola U., Los Angeles, 1974. Cert. sex therapist; lic. marriage, family and child counselor. Instr. psychology Cuyahoga Community Coll., Cleve., 1977-82; pvt. practice marriage, family and sex therapy Cleve., 1978—; instr. psychology St. Thomas of Villanova, Miami, Fla., 1980-81; clin. mem. Gender Team Case Western Res. U., Cleve., 1983—. Author: Love Me, Love Me Not: How to Survive Infidelty, 1985; TV personality A.M. Cleve., Sta. WKYC (NBC), 1981—; talk show host sta. WJW, Cleve., 1983-85. Fellow Internat. Council of Sex Edn. and Parenthood; mem. Am. Assn. for Marriage and Family Therapy (clin.), Nat. Com. on Values and Sexuality (v.p.), Am. Assn. Sex Educators, Counselors and Therapists (adv. bd., nat. pub. relations com.), Am. Assn. TV and Recording Artists, Assn. for Retarded Citizens, Assn. for Children with Learning Disabilities, Phi Beta Kappa, Pi Gamma Mu, Kappa Delta Pi, Alpha Lambda Delta. Office: 3619 Park E Suite 213 S Beachwood OH 44122

LEHMANN, ESTHER STRAUSS, investment company executive; b. Binghamton, N.Y., Apr. 19, 1944; d. Julius and Betty (Lind) Strauss; m. Aaron Lehmann, Feb. 27, 1966; children: Shanna, Shira, Marc, David. BS, Cornell U., 1966; cert. in vol. and non-profit orgn. mgmt., U. Conn., 1976; cert. employee benefits specialist, U. Pa., 1983. V.p. Fairway Mgmt., West Hartford, Conn., 1976-80; investment exec. Herzfeld & Stern, Paramus, N.J., 1980-86, Gruntal & Co., Inc., Paramus, 1988—. Home: 1632 Dover Ct Teaneck NJ 07666

LEHMANN-CARSSOW, NANCY BETH, educator, coach; b. Kingsville, Tex., Sept. 9, 1949; d. Valgene William and Ella Mae (Zajicek) Lehmann; m. William Benton Carssow, Aug. 1, 1981. B.S., U. Tex., 1971, M.A., 1979. Free-lance photographer, Austin, Tex., 1971—; geography tchr., tennis coach Austin Ind. Sch. Dist., Tex., 1971-78, 79—; salesperson, mgr. What's Going On-Clothing, Austin, 1972-78; area adminstr. Am. Inst. Fgn. Study, Austin, 1974-81; area rep. World Encounters, Austin, 1981—, tour guide, Egypt, Kenya, 1977, 79, 81, 87; participant 1st summer inst. Nat. Geog. Soc., Washington, 1986. Author curriculum materials. Photographer for book: Bobwhites, 1984. Recipient Merit award Nat. Council Geog. Edn., 1975, Creative Teaching award Austin Assn. Tchrs., 1978, Teaching Excellence award U. Tex. Ex-Student's Assn., 1987; Fulbright scholar, Israel, 1983. Mem. Nat. Council Social Studies, NEA, Nat. Council Geog. Edn., East African Wildlife, Earthwatch (participant archaeol. dig. in Swaziland 1984), Delta Kappa Gamma (pres. 1986-88), Phi Kappa Phi. Democrat. Roman Catholic. Avocations: stained glass; photography; tennis; gardening; needlepoint. Home: 1025 Quail Park Dr Austin TX 78758 Office: Lanier High Sch 1201 Peyton Gin Rd Austin TX 78758

LEHMKUHL, MICHELE, military officer; b. Marshalltown, Iowa, Feb. 5, 1953; d. William Charles and Colette (Hoffmann) Nagle; m. Lee James Lehmkuhl, Mar. 22, 1982; children: Anjanette Marie, Elizabeth Michele. AA, Miss. Gulf Coast Jr. Coll., 1979; BBA, U. Iowa, 1982; postgrad., Cen. Mich. U., Dayton, Ohio, 1987—. Enlisted USAF, 1974; law enforcement specialist USAF, Biloxi, Miss., 1974-76; asst. dir. Deaf Ctr., Gulfport, Miss., 1977-79; mgmt. engring. officer Deaf Ctr., Kelly AFB, Tex., 1982-85; maj. command wartime manpower requirements officer Wright-Patterson AFB, Ohio, 1985-86; maj. command manpower requirements analyst Wright-Patterson AFB, 1986—. Safety chmn. Northwest Crossing PTA, San Antonio, 1984; chmn. fundraising com. Mt. Olive United Ch. of Christ, Dayton, Ohio, 1987. Mem. Air Force Assn., 2750th Air Base Wing Co. Grade Officers Council (recorder), Am. Bus. Women's Assn. Home: 6030 Honeygate Dr Huber Heights OH 45424 Office: HQ AFLC/XRMQ Wright-Patterson AFB OH 45433

LEHNER, EDITH ANNE, bldgs. mfg. co. exec.; b. Raleigh N.D., May 5, 1932; d. Daniel D. and Scholastica (Volk) Dirk; student Minot (N.D.) State Coll., 1949-50, Mt. Marty Coll., 1950-51, St. John's U., Summer 1959, B.A., Coll. St. Benedict, 1960; postgrad. State U. N.D., 1965, Marquette U., 1967, U. Pa., 1976; m. George F. Lehner, Feb. 17, 1975. Tchr. Bismarck (N.D.) Parochial Schs., 1949-55, 56-64; tchr. drama, speech Minot (N.D.) Public Schs., 1964-66; tchr. English, speech Upper Merion Sr. High Sch., King of Prussia, Pa., 1966-70; tchr. pvt. voice, piano, Minot, N.D., 1960-66; v.p. in charge field constrn., office mgmt. and fin. Bldg. Concepts, Inc., Douglassville, Pa., 1975—. Mem. Internat. Platform Assn., Nat. Real Estate Assn., Pa. Real Estate Assn., Pa. Manufactured Housing Assn., Bldg. Industries Exchange. Democrat. Roman Catholic. Home: 140 N Wall St Spring City PA 19475 Office: 236 Benjamin Franklin Hwy Douglassville PA 19518

LEHR, JANET, photographic art dealer; b. N.Y.C., June 7, 1937; d. Herbert Davis and Florence (Lustig) Cooperman; children: Florence, Michael, Samuel. BS, NYU, 1955; JD, Bklyn. Law Sch., 1958. Pvt. practice art dealer, photographer N.Y.C. Home and Office: 891 Park Ave New York NY 10021

LEHTO, ARLENE IONE, educator, former state legislator; b. Duluth, Minn., Sept. 14, 1939; B.A. Speech, U. Minn.-Duluth; M.P.A., Harvard U., 1984. Beauty salon mgr., hairstylist 1961-67; pres. ops. Lehto's Printing, Inc. 1970-82; editor, Lake Superior News, 1969-74; mem. Minn. Ho. of Reps., St. Paul, 1976-82, tchr. social studies Westford Pub. Schs., 1986—. Bd. dirs. United Devel. Achievement Ctr. Duluth, 1974-82. Recipient Citizen award EPA Minn., 1974, Albert J. Chesley award Minn. Pub. Health Assn.; named among Women Who Made a Difference ABC-TV, 1981; Bush fellow, 1983. Mem. Save Lake Superior Assn. Editor: Ahoy, Charles River Power Squadron. Mem. adminstrv. council, chmn. Calvary United Methodist Ch., Arlington, Mass. Home: 35 Mott St Arlington MA 02174

LEIBEL, SHELLEY JOY, lawyer; b. Bklyn., Jan. 24, 1957; d. Sol and Lee (Kornbluth) L.; m. Ben J. Szwalbenest, Nov. 8, 1981. BA summa cum laude, Queens Coll., Flushing, N.Y., 1978; JD, Temple U., 1981. Bar: Pa. 1981. Law clk. to presiding judge Pa. Ct. Common Pleas, Phila., 1980; assoc. Law offices of Elaine Smith, Phila., 1980-82; ptnr. Smith and Leibel, Phila., 1982—; instr. Inst. Paralegal Tng., Phila., 1986—. Vol., advisor United Way Southeastern Pa., 1985—. Mem. Pa. Bar Assn., Phila. Bar Assn., Phi Beta Kappa. Home: 1107 Bryn Mawr Ave Bala Cynwyd PA 19004 Office: Smith & Leibel 1420 Locust St Suite 110 Acad House Philadelphia PA 19102

LEIBUNDGUTH, SUZANNE JEAN, writer, editor; b. Chgo., June 10, 1953; d. Peter Emerick and Jean Denise (Curtis) L. BA, Ind. U., 1974; cert. in teaching, Loyola U., Chgo., 1976; MEd, U. N.Mex., 1979. Cert. elem. and high sch. English as a 2d lang., spl. edn., Ill., Calif., N.Mex. Editorial asst. BJ Martin Publs., Chgo., 1974-76; freelance newscaster Sta. KUNM-

Radio, Albuquerque, 1977-78; writer, instr. Ctr. for the Handicapped City Colls. Chgo., 1979-81; adminstrv. asst., abstracter McDermott, Will & Emery, Chgo., 1982-85; tng. writer, editor Chgo. Fire Dept., 1985-87; writer The Presbyn. Nursing Home Disaster Plan, Evanston, Ill., 1988—; reporter, writer news/feature articles Lerner Newspapers, Chgo., Evanston, 1981—, reporter, writer feature articles Chgo. Tribune, 1983-85; writer pub. info. office U. N.Mex., Albuquerque, 1977-78; tchr. spl edn., bi-lingual edn. St. Mary of the Lake reading program Loyola U., Chgo., 1976, U. N.Mex. 1976. Vol. Peace Corps, Mali, 1979; canvass organizer McGovern for Pres., Los Angeles, 1972; respite worker, mgr. Esperanza Adult Group Home, Albuquerque, 1978-79; writer Chgo. Nuclear Freeze Com., 1985; active Paul Simon for Senator 1984. Mem. Soc. Prof. Journalists, Nat. Writers Union. Democrat. Unitarian. Club: Forest Trails Hiking Group (Chgo.), Am. Youth Hostels.

LEIDIGH, LAURA FRANCES, insurance executive; b. Miami Beach, Fla., July 12, 1944; d. Charles Henry Jr. and Frances Willowdean (Tulk) Routh; m. Tomas Denver Leidigh, Feb. 11, 1961 (div. 1978); 1 child, Gregory Tomas. AA in Bus., Valencia Coll., 1969; BS in Bus., Fin., Rollins Coll., 1973; postgrad., U. South Fla. CPCU. Underwriter Continental Casualty Co., Orlando, Fla., 1971-73; mgr. underwriting Ins. Time Ga., Orlando, 1973-75, Gordon B. Phillips and Co., Orlando, 1975-77; sr. v.p. E.H. Crump (Crump/Loveless), Atlanta, 1977-84; asst. v.p. Fred S. James (New Amsterdam Excess), Atlanta, 1984-87; exec. v.p. Interfin. Ins. Cons., Atlanta, 1987—. Mem. Atlanta Ballet, Atlanta Symphony, Soc. Chartered Property and Casualty Underwriters. Republican. Baptist. Office: Interfin Ins Cons 400 Perimeter Cen Terr Suite 135 Atlanta GA 30346

LEIDNER, SUSAN YOUNGMAN, educational specialist; b. Coral Gables, Fla., Jan. 9, 1947; d. Thomas Jr. and Alice Stole (Lore) Youngman; m. H. Robert Leidner, Aug. 11, 1974; 1 child, Leah Marie. AA, Orlando (Fla.) Jr. Coll., 1968; BA, Fla. Tech. U., 1970; MEd, U. Cen. Fla., 1974. Cert. elem. tchr., Fla. Tchr. English English Estate Elem. Sch., Fern Park, Fla., 1969-70; tchr. primary Pinecrest Elem. Sch., Sanford, Fla., 1970-72; tchr. intermediate grades Red Bug Elem. Sch., Casselberry, Fla., 1972-79, specialist primary grades, 1979—; staff developer Seminole County Schs., Sanford, 1984—; speaker Fla. State Reading Council, Orlando, 1986, Rainbows of Reading Fla. Conv., 1986; sch. readiness facilitator Parent Edn. Workshop, 1986. Developer Eager Readers Program, 1985, Perceptual Motor Playgrounds, 1985. Mem. Frontier-Civitan Internat., Orlando, 1974-75, Seminole Educators Pol. Action Com., Sanford, 1983-84; program chair Luth. Ch. Women's Club, Winter Park, Fla., 1985-86; adv. bd. local PTA, liaison rep., 1983-85. Recipient Golden Apple award Seminole News, Longwood, Fla., 1985. Mem. Fla. Tching. Profession Assn., Seminole Edn. Assn. (faculty rep., outstanding contbr. 1973, 76), Assn. Curriculum and Devel., Phi Delta Kappa, Kappa Kappa Iota (project dir. 1987). Democrat. Home: 3343 Ellwood Ct Winter Park FL 32792 Office: Seminole County Schs 4000 Red Bug Rd Casselberry FL 32707

LEIFERMAN, SILVIA WEINER (MRS. IRWIN H. LEIFERMAN), artist, civic worker, sculptor; b. Chgo.; d. Morris and Annah (Kaplan) Weiner; m. Irwin H. Leiferman, Apr. 20, 1947. Student, U. Chgo., 1960-61; studied design and painting, Provincetown, Mass. Organizer, charter mem. women's div. Hebrew U. Chgo., 1947; Head Pres. Accessories by Silvia, Chgo., 1964; organizer women's div. Edgewater Hosp., 1954; chmn. bd. Leiferman Investment Corp.; chairwoman spl. sales and spl. events greater Chgo. Com. for State of Israel; originator, organizer Ambassador's Ball, 1956, Presentation Ball, 1963; met. chmn. numerous spl. events Nat. Council Jewish Women, Nathan Goldblatt Soc. Cancer Research, Chgo.; now life mem., trustee; chmn. numerous spl. events North Shore (Ill.) Combined Jewish Appeal; chmn. women's com. Salute to Med. Research City of Hope, 1959; founder Ballet Soc. of Miami; Bd. dirs. Jewish Children's Bur., North Shore Women's Aux., Mt. Sinai Hosp., George and Ann Portes Cancer Prevention Center Chgo., Nat. Council Jewish Women, Fox River (Ill.) Sanitorium, Edgewater Hosp., Greater Chgo. Bonds for Israel, Orgn. of Rehab. and Tng. Exhibited one-woman shows, Schram Galleries, Ft. Lauderdale, Fla., 1966, 67, D'Arcy Galleries, N.Y.C., 1964, Stevens Annex Bldg., Chgo., 1965, Miami (Fla.) Mus. Modern Art, 1966, 72, Contemporary Gallery, Palm Beach, Fla., 1966, Westview Country Club, 1968, Gallery 99, 1969; exhibited group shows, Ricardo Restaurant Gallery, Chgo., 1961, 62, Bryn Mawr (Chgo.) Country Club, 1961, 62, Covenant Club Ill., Chgo., 1963, D'Arcy Galleries, 1965, Internat. Platform Assn., 1967, Miami Mus. Modern Art, 1967, Bacardi Gallery, 1967, Hollywood Mus. Art, 1968, Gallery 99, Miami, Lowe Art Mus., Crystal Ho. Gallery, Miami Beach, 1968; represented in numerous pvt. collections. Bd. dirs. Brandeis U., Art Inst. Chgo., Miami Mus. Modern Art; co-founder, v.p. Silvia and Irwin Leiferman Found.; donor Leiferman award auspices City of Hope; internat. co-chairwoman Ball Masque; mem. pacesetter/trustee com. Greater Miami Jewish Fedn., 1976-77; founder Mt. Sinai Hosp. Greater Miami, Fla.; donor Michael Reese Hosp., 1978; benefactress Miami Heart Inst., 1979, St. Joseph Hosp., 1979, Mt. Sinai Med. Center, 1979. Recipient citations for def. bond sales U.S. Govt., for Presentation Ball State of Israel, 1965; Pro Mundi Beneficio Gold medal Brazilian Acad. Humanities, 1976; numerous awards Bonds for Israel; numerous awards Combined Jewish Appeal North Shore Spl. Gifts; Keys to cities Met. Miami area; named Woman of Valor State of Israel, 1963; donor award Miami Heart Inst. Fellow Royal Soc. Arts and Scis.; mem. Internat. Council Mus., 1st Ann. Cultural Conf. Chgo., Am. Fedn. Arts, Artist's Equity Assn., Fla. Poetry Soc., Miami Art Center, Miami Beach Opera Guild Com., Greater Miami Cultural Art Center, Guild Com. Greater Miami Cultural Art Center, Sculptors of Fla., Royal Acad. Arts, Internat. Platform Assn., Lowe Art Mus., Am. Contract Bridge League, Friends of U. Haifa. Jewish (mem. bd.). Clubs: Standard, Bryn Mawr Country, Covenant, Green Acres, International, Boye, Whitehall, Key (Chgo.); Jockey, Westview Country, Tower (Miami Beach, Fla.); Brickell Bay. Home: 10155 Collins Ave Bal Harbour FL 33154

LEIGHTON, GERTRUDE CATHERINE KERR, lawyer, educator; b. Belfast, Ireland, Dec. 9, 1914; came to U.S., 1915, naturalized, 1918; d. Archibald O. and Gertrude (Hamilton) L. A.B., Bryn Mawr Coll., 1938; LL.B., J.D., Yale U., 1945, postgrad. fellow in law, 1947-48. Bar: N.Y. 1947. Lectr., Barnard Coll., N.Y.C., 1940-42; with Carter, Ledyard & Milburn, N.Y.C., 1945-47; asst. in research Yale U., 1947-48; vis. lectr. law Yale U., 1949-50; asst. prof. polit. sci. Bryn Mawr Coll. (Pa.), 1950-55, assoc. prof., 1955-64, prof., 1964-82, emeritus prof. 1982, vis. McBride prof., 1982-85, sec. faculty, 1975-82, chmn. dept., 1963-65, 68-71; lectr. law U. Pa., Phila., 1959-61; vis. assoc. research prof. law and psychiatry, 1961-65. Contbr. articles to legal jours. Fund for Advancement Edn. fellow, 1953-54, Rockefeller Found. fellow, 1957-58. Mem. ABA, Am. Soc. Internat. Law.

LEIGHTON, MIRIAM, artist, consultant; b. N.Y.C., Nov. 7, 1913; d. Nathan and Rose (Unger) Kaback; m. Bruce Leighton, Feb. 22, 1965 (dec.); children: Elayne Joyce, Jo-Ann Helene. Student, NYU, 1934, 45. Cons. Saks Fifth Ave., N.Y.C., 1954-56; free lance cons. Ft. Lee, N.J., 1973-80; cons. in field; rep. Artists and Sculptors, N.J., 1984—. Democrat. Jewish.

LEIGL, KATHLEEN ANN, human resource administrator; b. Mayville, Wis., Oct. 26, 1952; d. Philip Alphonse and Mary Jane (Caine) L. BS, U. Wis., Oshkosh, 1975, MS in Indsl. Relations, 1984. Corp. personnel supr. Siecor Corp., Hickory, N.C., 1984-87; sr. human resources adminstr. govt. systems sector Harris Corp., Melbourne, Fla., 1987—. Mem. Am. Soc. Personnel Adminstrs., South Brevard County Personnel Assn., Indsl. Relations Research Assn., Hickory C. of C., Nat. Assn. Female Execs. Roamn Catholic. Home: 2416 Malabar Lakes Dr NE Palm Bay FL 32905 Office: PO Box 94000 Melbourne FL 32905

LEINER, MELISSA GAYLE, fin. planner and cons.; b. Salinas, Calif., Feb. 20, 1953; d. Fred B. and Helen G. (Gertner) L.; B.A., Skidmore Coll., 1975. Sales asst. Paine Webber Jackson & Curtis, N.Y.C., 1976, Kidder Peabody, Washington, 1977-78; v.p., fin. cons., fin. planner Shearson Lehman Bros., McLean, Va., 1978-87; v.p. sales Exec. Career Mgmt. Services, Tysons Corner, Va., 1987—. Active United Jewish Appeal, Nat. Council Jewish Women. Cert. fin. planner. Mem. Internat. Assn. Fin. Planners, Stockbrokers Soc., Skidmore Coll. Alumni Assn. Club: Skidmore Coll. Alumni (pres. Washington area), Pres's. Home: 1021 Arlington Blvd Apt E-1213 Arlington VA 22209 Office: Exec Career Mgmt Services 2070 Chain Bridge Rd Tysons Corner VA 22180

LEINO, DEANNA ROSE, educator; b. Leadville, Colo., Dec. 15, 1937; d. Arvo Ensio Leino and Edith Mary (Bonan) Leino Malenck. B.S. in Bus. Adminstrn., U. Denver, 1959, M.S. in Bus. Adminstrn., 1967; postgrad. Community Coll. Denver, U. No. Colo., Colo. State U., U. Colo., Met. State Coll. Cert. tchr., vocat. tchr., Colo. Tchr. Jefferson County Adult Edn., Lakewood, Colo., 1963-67; tchr. bus., coordinator coop. office edn., Jefferson High Sch., Edgewater, Colo., 1959—; instr. Community Coll. Denver, Red Rocks, 1967-81, U. Colo. Denver, 1976-79, Parks Coll. Bus. (name now Parks Jr. Coll.), 1983—; dist. adviser Future Bus. Leaders Am. Active City of Edgewater Sister City Project Student Exchange Com.; pres. Career Women's Symphony Guild; treas. Phantoms of Opera, 1982—; active Opera Colo. Assocs. & Guild, I Pagliacci; ex-officio trustee Denver Symphony Assn., 1980-82. Recipient disting. service award Jefferson County Sch. Bd. 1980; Jefferson High Sch. Wall of Fame 1981. Mem. NEA (life), Colo. Edn. Assn., Jefferson County Edn. Assn., Colo. Vocat. Assn., Am. Vocat. Assn., Colo. Educators for and about Bus., Profl. Secs. Internat., Career Women's Symphony Guild, Profl. Panhellenic Assn., Colo. Congress Fgn. Lang. Tchrs., Wheat Ridge C. of C. (edn. and scholarship com.), Delta Pi Epsilon, Phi Chi Theta, Beta Gamma Sigma, Alpha Lambda Delta. Republican. Roman Catholic. Club: Tyrolean Soc. Denver. Avocations: decorating wedding cakes, crocheting, sewing, music. Home: 3712 Allison St Wheat Ridge CO 80033

LEIPPRANDT, KATHLEEN MARIE BALDWIN, finance company executive; b. Iwakuni, Japan, June 28, 1962; came to U.S., 1964; d. Benjamin George Jr. and Maureen Margaret (McGuigan) Baldwin; m. Douglas John Leipprandt, Aug. 31, 1985. BA in Econs., DePauw U., Greencastle, Ind., 1984. Cert. fin. planner. Mortgage analyst Balcor Co. subs. Am. Express Corp., Skokie, Ill., 1984-86; registered rep. Equitable Fin. Services Co., Northbrook, Ill., 1986—; bd. dirs. Baldwin Fin. Systems, Inc., Northbrook. Mem. Nat. Assn. for Female Execs., Fin. Planning Network, Alpha Chi Alumni Assn. Republican. Mem. Christian Ch. Office: Equitable Fin Services Co 5 Revere Dr Suite 500 Northbrook IL 60062

LEIPZIG, LIBBY BLACK (MRS. FRED LEIPZIG), state official, automotive products company executive; b. Easton, Pa.; d. Benjamin and Mary (Bizar) Black; student Paterson Normal Sch., N.J., 1928, Rutgers U., 1943-44, Fairleigh Dickinson U., 1962; m. Fred Leipzig, Apr. 12, 1940; 1 dau., Marta Beth Leipzig Berman; 1 stepson, Howard A. Leipzig. With N.J. State Employment Service, Passaic, 1941—, supr. profl. comml. dept., Paterson, N.J., 1962-69, supr. indsl. services dept., Passaic, 1969-72; v.p. Major Automotive Products Co., Inc., Clifton, N.J. 1945-69, sec.-treas., 1969—. Home: The Promenade 5225 Pooks Hill Rd Bethesda MD 20814

LEIS, MARGARET DONNA SULLIVAN, dental hygienist; b. Fairfax, Okla., Mar. 4, 1957; d. Robert Joseph and Mary (Hutsko) S.; m. Angel Arturo Leis. AA, Dental Sch., U. Tex. Houston, 1977. Cert. dental hygienist, Tex. Dental hygienist M.D. Anderson Cancer Hosp. and Tumor Inst., Houston, 1977-87; clin. inst. Dental br. U. Tex., Houston, 1977-87; lectr. in field. Recipient Clinic award Dallas County Dental Soc., 1978; Table Clinic award Houston Dist. Dental Soc., 1978; Cert. of Merit, Am. Prosthodontic Soc., 1979; Outstanding Employee award M.D. Anderson Hosp. and Tumor Inst., 1980; Jack Winston award for grad. hygienist, 1984. Mem. Jr. Dental Hygienist Assn., Am. Dental Hygienist Assn. Roman Catholic. Office: MD Anderson Hosp & Tumor Inst 6723 Bertner Ave Houston TX 77030

LEIS, WINOGENE B. (MRS. HENRY PATRICK LEIS, JR.), nurse association executive; b. Clay, W.Va., Feb. 27, 1919; d. Gruder L. and Daisy M. (Young) Barnette; R.N. cum laude, Kanawha Valley Hosp., 1939; m. Henry Patrick Leis, Jr., Jan. 8, 1944; children: Henry Patrick III, Thomas Federick. Nurse, Kanawha Valley Hosp., 1939-43. Decorated lady comdr. Equestrian Order Holy Sepulchre Jerusalem. Mem. Woman's Aux. Internat. Coll. Surgeons (corr. sec. N.Y. State surg. div. 1955-57, v.p. 1961-63, pres. 1963-67; pres. U.S. sect. 1970, dir. 1970—, pres. Internat. Body 1977-78, bd. govs. 1978—), Flower Fifth Avenue Hosp. Woman's Aux. (dir. 1956-59, 69—), Woman's Aux. N.Y. Acad. Scis., Woman's Aux. N.Y. State Med. Soc., Woman's Aux. Internat. Coll. Surgeons (corr. sec. 1972-74, pres. 1977-78, dir. 1978—), Woman's Aux. Cabrini Med. Ctr., Woman's Aux. Westchester County Med. Ctr., Woman's Aux. Lenox Hill Hosp., Woman's Aux. So. Med. Assn. Republican. Roman Catholic. Home: The Pines 113 11 Ave N North Myrtle Beach SC 29582

LEISER, LENORE AVERIL, educator; b. N.Y.C., Oct. 13, 1936; d. George Edward and Eleanor E. (Egan) L. AB, Coll. of Mt. St. Vincent, 1958; MA, NYU, 1960. Cert. secondary tchr., N.Y. Tchr., chairperson depts. math, phys. edn. Maria Regina High Sch., Hartsdale, N.Y., 1960—. Mem. Pi Lambda Theta. Roman Catholic. Home: 837 Webster Ave New Rochelle NY 10804 Office: Maria Regina High Sch 500 Hartsdale Ave Hartsdale NY 10530

LEITCH, ALMA MAY, city official; b. Fredericksburg, Va., Nov. 24, 1924; d. Maurice Andrew Doggett and Nora May (Spicer) L.; grad. James Monroe High Sch., Fredericksburg; various specialized courses U. Va., Va. Poly. Inst. Dep. commnr. revenue City of Fredericksburg, 1946-69, commr. revenue, 1970—; mem. Va. Adv. Legis. Council, 1977-78; mem. subcom. Commonwealth Va. Revenue Resources and Econ. Commn., 1978. Bd. dirs. Fredericksburg, Stafford and Spotsylvania area chpt. ARC, 1960—, chmn., 1969, treas.; sec. Democratic Com. Fredericksburg, 1964; pres., bd. dirs. Rappahannock United Way for Fredericksburg, Spotsylvania, and Stafford counties, 1979; mem. Our Town Fredericksburg, Fredericksburg area mus. Recipient various service awards; Outstanding Citizenship award Fredericksburg Area C. of C., 1979. Mem. Commrs. Revenue Assn. Va. (pres. 1979-80), Va. Govtl. Employees Assn. (dir.-at-large 1979-80), League No. Va. Commrs. Revenue (pres. 1972), Va. Assn. Local Exec. Constl. Officers (exec. com.), Internat. Assn. Assessing Officers, Va. Assn. Assessing Officers, Hist. Fredericksburg Found., Bus. and Profl. Women's Club. Club: Ann Page Garden (pres. 1980-82, Mary B. Benoit award 1977), Altrusa. Home: 511 Hanover St Fredericksburg VA 22401 Office: City Hall Box 644 Fredericksburg VA 22401

LEITER, BEULAH G. (MRS. ROBERT PAUL LEITER), lawyer; b. Chgo.; d. Jehiel D. and Rose (Rossman) Liebling; J.D., John Marshall U., 1945, LL.M., 1946; student U. Chgo., U. Ga., Emory U.; m. Robert Paul Leiter, May 10, 1936; children—Darryl J., Paula S. Admitted to Ga. bar, 1945, U.S. Dist. Ct. (5th and 11th dists.) Ga., U.S. Ct. Appeals (5th cir.), U.S. Supreme Ct.; since practiced in Atlanta; mem. firm Leiter & Leiter, 1946—; dep. sheriff, 1958—. Mem. Iota Tau Tau, 1951—, So. chancellor, 1955-57, Internat. supreme chancellor, 1955-59, mem. supreme council, 1955-63, supreme asso. dean, 1959-61, internat. supreme dean, 1961-63. Mem. nat. women's com. Brandeis U., 1961—. Mem. Internat. Fedn. Women Lawyers (legal edn. com. 1958, penal law, outer space law, UN com. coms. 1959-60), Nat. Assn Women Lawyers (mental health com.), Am. Trial Lawyers Assn., Internat. Platform Assn., Am. Judicature Soc., Com. Women in Pub. Service, Ga. Assn. Women Lawyers (past v.p., rec. sec., exec. com.), U. Ga. Alumni Soc., Nat. Sheriffs Assn., Ga. Bar Assn., Fulton County Lawyers Assn. (charter, trustee 1952, rec. sec. 1956—), Nat. Assn. Claimant Attys., Am. Bus. Women's Assn., PTA, Atlanta Art Assn., Phi Kappa Delta. Clubs: Equity (publicity com. 1959-60, 62—), Old War Horse Lawyers, Nat. Travel, Smithsonian Assos. Am. Mus. Natural History. Home: 1265 Poplar Grove Dr NE Atlanta GA 30306 Office: PO Box 1492 Atlanta GA 30301

LEITH, PRISCILLA TREMPER, consultant; b. Utica, N.Y., Jan. 17, 1935; d. John Schrader and Gertrude Marie (Walsh) Tremper; A.B., Vassar Coll., 1956; M.B.A., Babson Coll., 1982; m. John Douglas Leith, Aug. 4, 1957; children—Jennifer, Margery. Engring. asst. Atomic Power Equipment div. Gen. Electric Co., San Jose, Calif., 1956-57; engring. aide U.S. Geol. Survey Office, Honolulu, 1958; instr. U. Wis. Extension div., Madison, 1962-64; contbg. editor Newton (Mass.) Times, 1973-74; free-lance corr. Newton Graphic, 1976-77. Steering com. mem. Campaign for Choice, 1985-87; state coordinator Mass. NOW, 1977-78; legis. coordinator, 1985-87; mem. steering com. Mass. Women's Polit. Caucus, 1973-75; co-founder Newton Women's Polit. Caucus, 1973; 2d v.p. Newton League of Women Voters, 1972-73, treas. 1986—; pres. Oshkosh (Wis.) League of Women Voters, 1967-69; 2d vice chmn. Winnebago County (Wis.) Democratic Party, 1969-71. Mem. New Eng. Women's Press Assn., Women's Equity Action League, NOW. Club: Vassar (Boston). Contbg. author, editor: (booklet) Politics Is for Women, 1973; editor: Solid Waste in Newton, 1972. Contbr. numerous articles to newspapers. Office: 162 Islington Rd Newton MA 02166

LEITHWOOD, DOREEN MARJORY, personnel director; b. North Battleford, Sask., Can., Aug. 25, 1930; d. Hugh Scott and Maude Christina (Ficken) Loudfoot; m. Robert Parker Leithwood, Mar. 27, 1948; children: David Robert, Brian Richard. Cert. Personnel Mgmt., Humber Coll., 1976. Cashier T. Eaton Co. Ltd., Toronto, 1948-49; cashier Dominion Stores, Toronto, 1955-57, bookkeper, personnel dir., 1957-60; sales, area mgr. Beauty Counselor, Brampton, Ont., 1961-65; with payroll, personnel dept. A.J. Jackson Constrn., Toronto, 1965-67, Kenting Aviation, Toronto, 1967-69; tng., sales mgr. Ashton Promotions, Toronto, 1969-72; sales, customer services Cameo Careers, Toronto, 1972-76; chief exec. officer Bramalea Personnel Inc., Brampton, 1976—. Bd. dirs. YMCA, Brampton, 1983-84, Peel Children's Found., Mississauga, Ont., 1984-86; exec. Brampton Liberal Assn., 1978-79; del. Liberal COnvention, Ottawa, Ont., 1978-79. Mem. Fedn. Temporary Help Services (bd. dirs. 1985-88, pres. Toronto chpt. 1985-87, Leadership award 1986), Personnel Assn. of Peel (sec., treas. 1987—), Assn. Profl. Placement Agencies and Cons., Brampton Indsl. Assn. (pres. 1981-82),Toronto Ad and Sales Club (chmn. sales courses, 1969-74), Brampton Bd. Trade (bd. dirs. 1978-86). Progressive Conservative. Anglican. Lodge: Zonta (v.p. 1987). Office: Bramalea Personnel Inc, 73B Bramalea Rd, Brampton, ON Canada L6T 2W9

LEITZINGER, SANDRA MAYES, artist, journalist; b. Philipsburg, Pa., Feb. 29, 1936; d. Kenneth Frank and Louise (Kirby) Mayes; m. Charles T. Kurtz III, June 4, 1960 (dec. 1964); children—Karen Elizabeth, Charles Kenneth; m. Robert Frederick Leitzinger, July 8, 1967; 1 child, Robert Franklin. B.S. in Home Econs. and Journalism, Pa. State U., 1957. Home economist Pa. Power and Light Co., Williamsport, Pa., 1957-60; auto racing columnist Clearfield Progress, Pa., 1963-67, Centre Daily Times, State College, Pa., 1982—; freelance automotive artist, 1972—. One-woman shows include: Pa. State U., 1981, Interlaken Inn, Lakeville, Conn., 1987, 88; exhibited in group shows at l'art et l'automobile, N.Y.C., 1980, 88, Painters of Central Pa., Pa. State U., 1983, Alleghenies Mus. Art, Loretto, Pa., 1987, 88; represented in permanent collection at Mus. of Our Nat. Heritage, Lexington, Mass., also in pvt. and corp. collections U.S. and Europe; artist poster, program covers Watkins Glen Internat., 1984-85. Recipient Merit award Strathmore Paper Co., 1980, Bronze award for art display Am. Orchid Soc., 1977, Outstanding Regional Pub. award Antique Automobile Club Am., 1959. Mem. Pa. Soc. Watercolor Painters, Internat. Motor Press Assn., Sports Car Club Am., Antique Automobile Club Am., Internat. Motor Sports Assn. Republican. Avocations: travel; gardening; photography. Home: 130 West Outer Dr State College PA 16801 Office: Leitzinger Imports Inc 3220 W College Ave State College PA 16801

LEIWANT, JOAN DIAMOND, advertising agency executive; b. Newark, Aug. 20, 1945; d. Morris David and Sue Harriet (Kastner) Diamond; m. Bruce Harlan Leiwant, July 1, 1982. BA, U. Miami, 1968. Advt. asst. Suburban Pub. Corp., Union, N.J., 1969; assoc. dir. recruitment advt. div. Keyes, Martin & Co., Springfield, N.J., 1969-81; v.p., dir. recruitment advt. div. David H. Block Advt., Inc., Montclair, N.J., 1982—; classified advt. symposium speaker N.J. Press Assn., 1981; recruitment advt. speaker N.J. Employers Assn., 1982. Office: David H Block Advt Inc 33 S Fullerton Ave Montclair NJ 07042

LEKAREW, GLADYS, college administrator; b. Yonkers, N.Y.; m. Gerald Lekarew, July 14, 1958; children: Carol, Mark. BS, NYU, 1952. Buyer Arkwright, N.Y.C., 1952-56, Kirby-Block, N.Y.C., 1956-58; personnel staff Abraham and Straus, Hempstead, N.Y., 1970-75; placement dir. Berkeley Sch., Hicksville, N.Y., 1975-78, White Plains, N.Y., 1978-80; dir. Berkeley Sch., Hicksville, 1980-82; sr. v.p. career devel. Berkeley Sch., Garrett Mountain, 1982—. Mem. Am. Soc. Personnel Adminstrs., Am. Soc. Tng. and Devel., Fashion Group. Office: The Berkeley Schs Box F Little Falls NJ 07424

LELAIDIER-JAMES, PAULA CLAIRE, educator; b. N.Y.C., Mar. 22, 1947; d. Joseph Walfried and Pauline Ann (Butz) LeLaidier; m. Alan William James, Apr. 29, 1978; children: Sean Lawrence Smith, Adam Lawrence Smith. BS in Elem. Edn., St. John's U., 1968; postgrad., various univs. Cert. elem. tchr., N.Y., Ind. Tchr. New Hyde Park (N.Y.) Pub. Schs., 1970-71, Taylor Community Schs., Kokomo, Ind., 1971-75; tchr. Emanuel Lutheran Early Childhood Program, Patchogue, N.Y., 1979-83, dir., 1981-83; tchr. Emanuel Lutheran Day Sch., Patchogue, 1983-86; dir. Emanuel Lutheran After-Sch. Program, Patchogue, 1985-86; tchr. South Country Cen Schs, Brookhaven, N.Y., 1986—; instr. Suffolk County Coordinated Council for Gifted and Talented, Oakdale, N.Y., 1978-79; mem. staff devel. day planning com. South County Cen. Schs., 1988, policy bd. Tchr. Ctr., 1988. Author Hist. Time Capsule elem. sch. play, 1985; directorial asst. Playcrafters Children's Theatre, 1981; editor Cub Scout Pack newsletter, 1978-81. Mem. exec. bd. PTA, Bellport, N.Y., 1978-79; mem. adv. bd. Brookhaven (N.Y.) Elem. Sch., 1987—, social studies textbook com., 1988, staff devel. day planning com, 1988, mem. Tchr. Ctr. Policy Bd., 1988. Mem. N.Y. State United Tchrs. Clubs: Bellport Yacht (exec. bd. 1986—), Bellport Garden (house tour, flower show chair 1983-86). Lodge: Soroptomists. Office: South Country Sch Dist Dunton Ave East Patchogue NY 11772

LELAND, ALISON WALTON, investment banker; b. Boston, Sept. 7, 1958; d. Gerald Clark and Helen (Seth) Walton; m. Mickey Leland, Nov. 27, 1944; 1 child, Jarrett David. BA, Spelman Coll., 1980; JD, Georgetown U., 1985. Acct. exec. Atlanta Jour. Constitution, 1980-82; investment banker Shearson Lehman Hutton, INc., Houston, 1986—. Mem. adv. com. Houston Ballet, 1987; bd. dirs. Houston Met. Ministries, 1987, Congl. Black Caucus, Washington, 1983, Houston Met. YWCA, Midtown Arts Ctr., Homeless in Am. Park People. Mem. Houston C. of C. (mem. com. 1986), Spelman Alumnae Assn. Democrat. Episcopalian. Office: Shearson Lehman Hutton Inc 6350 Texas Commerce Tower Houston TX 77006

LELAND-YOUNG, JANET KAYE, psychiatric social worker; b. Saginaw, Mich., Dec. 6, 1954; d. Ward Coville and Betty Jane (Browne) Leland; m. Paul R. Stuhmer, Mar. 22, 1977 (div. Dec. 1980); m. Loren J. Leland-Young, June 5, 1982; 1 child, Amanda Robin. BA, Mich. State U., 1977, MSW, 1981. Cert. social worker, Mich. Assoc. prof. Mich. State U., Lansing, 1976-77; instr. Lansing Community Coll., 1979—; therapist Sanctuary, Royal Oak, Mich., 1981-82, Cath. Social Services, Pontiac, Mich., 1982-84; residential dir. Battered Women's Shelter, Pontiac, 1984; pvt. practice psychiat. social work Detroit, 1986; cons. Mich. State U., 1977-81, Ingham County (Mich.) Women's Commn., 1979, Council for Children at Risk, Detroit, 1981; expert witness Ingham County Prosecutor, 1981. Author: Rape Research and Analysis, 1977. Bd. dirs. Listening Ear Crisis Ctr., East Lansing, Mich., 1979. Recipient Cert. Appreciation, NOW, 1979, Cert. Appreciation, Council Against Domestic Assault, 1979. Mem. Nat. Assn. Social Workers, Acad. Cert. Social Workers. Office: Cath Social Services 93 Franklin Blvd Pontiac MI 48053

LEMA, GRETCHEN BLECH, business manager; b. Mich., Sept. 20, 1953; d. Reinhold and Anita Helene (Betat) Blech; m. Albert Lee Lema; 1 child, Jennifer Nicole. Student, Pacific Union Coll., 1972, Stanislaus State Coll., 1974. Mgr. bus. Turlock (Calif.) Orthopedic Ctr., 1973—. Mem. Med. Group Mgmt. Assn. Republican. Office: Turlock Orthpedic CTr 1199 Delban Ave Turlock CA 95380

LEMASTER, SAUNDRA FORD, advertising executive; b. Louisville, Sept. 3, 1956; d. James Duiguid and Arlene Audrey (Abbs) Ford; m. Joseph William Lemaster, May 24, 1980; 1 child, Blake Alan. BA, U. Ky., 1978. Advt. salesperson Lexington (Ky.) Herald-Leader, 1980-83, N.W. Cable Interconnect, Seattle, Wash., 1983-84, Sta. WRDU-FM, Raleigh, N.C., 1985—. Named Dist. Salesperson Raleigh Sales and Mktg. Exec., 1986. Mem. Raleigh Advt. Club. Republican. Lutheran. Home: 11953 Straight A Way Raleigh NC 27612 Office: WRDU-FM 4700 Six Forks Rd Suite 106 Raleigh NC 27709

LEMASTER, SHERRY RENEE, fund raising administrator; b. Lexington, Ky., June 25, 1953; d. John William and Mary Charles (Thompson) LeM. BS, U. Ky., 1975, MS, 1984. Cert. fund raising exec.; cert. real estate agt. Lab. technician in virology, serology Cen. Ky. Animal Disease Diagnostic Lab., Lexington, 1975-76; grant coordinator, environ. specialist Commonwealth Ky. Dept. for Natural Resources and Environ. Protection, Frankfurt, 1976-78; coordinator residence hall program Murray (Ky.) State U., 1978-80; dean students Midway (Ky.) Coll., 1980-81, v.p. devel., alumnae affairs, 1981-86; dir. devel. Wilderness Road Council Girl Scouts U.S., Lexington, 1986—. Ambassador, U. Ky. Coll. Agr.; career cons. acad. support services U. Ky.; field reader U.S. Dept. Edn., 1987—; chmn. Midway chpt. Am. Heart Assn., 1981, Woodford County chpt., 1983; mem. adminstrv. bd. First United Meth. Ch., Lexington, 1982-84, 87; mem. Council for Advancement and Support Edn., 1981-86, chmn. Ky. conf., 1982; planning com. Nat. Disciples Devel. Execs. Conf., 1984; active East Ky. First Quality of Life Com. Recipient Young Career Woman award Bus. and Profl. Women's Club, Frankfort, 1981; named Ky. col., 1977, hon. sec. state, 1984. Mem. Am. Council on Edn., Nat. Soc. Fund Raising Execs. (bd. dirs. Lexington chpt. 1986), Greater Lexington Area C. of C. (accreditation com. 1982), Advancement Women in Higher Edn. Adminstrn. (former state planning com.), Ky. Assn. Women Deans Adminstrs. and Counselors (editor Newsletter 1981), U. Ky. Alumni Assn. (life), Gen. Fedn. Womens Clubs, P.E.O. (charter), Ninety-Nines Internat. Assn. Women Pilots (vice chmn. Ky. Bluegrass chpt. 1986-87, chmn. and chmn. bd. 1987-88), Lexington Jaycees, N.Y. Found. Ky. Women, Kentuckians N.Y., Pi Beta Phi Nat. Alumnae Assn. (alumnae province pres. 1980-81, sec. bd. dirs. Ky. Beta chpt. 1982-84), Alpha Kappa Psi Alumnae Assn. (charter Murray chpt.). Avocations: pvt. pilot, needlecrafts, swimming, equitation, racquetball. Home: 104 Highview Dr PO Box 4127 Midway KY 40347-4127 Office: Wilderness Rd Girl Scout Council 2277 Executive Dr Lexington KY 40505

LEMASTER, SUSAN M., freelance writer, marketing consultant; b. Cody, Wyo., May 9, 1953; d. Floyd Morris and Virginia Kristena (Renner) LeM.; B.A., U. Wyo., Casper, 1979; A.A., Casper Coll., 1977. Reporter, night editor Casper Star Tribune, 1972-76; copy editor, editor In Wyo. mag., Casper, 1979; info. dir. Wyo. Rural Electric Assn., Casper, 1980-81; story editor Wyo. Horizons mag., Casper, 1981-82; asst., instr. English lab. Casper Coll., 1982-84; mktg. mgr. Chen & Assocs., Inc., 1984-87; freelance writer, 1982—; night sch. instr. Casper Coll., 1983-84, summer sch. instr., 1984; editor Casper Jour., summers 1983-84. Recipient First Place News Story, Wyo. Press Assn., 1973; First Place Editing award Wyo. Press Women, 1980. Mem. Soc. for Mktg. Profl. Services (co-chair membership com. 1986, sec. Colo. chpt. 1987), Network for Archtl. and Engring. Proflls. (bd. dirs. 1985-87). Democrat. Club: Denver Press. Home: 21 S Sherman St Denver CO 80209

LEMAY, MICHELE LYNNE, bank manager; b. Washington, Oct. 18, 1962; d. Michael F. and Maxine J. (Lewek) LeM. BS in psychology, U. Richmond, 1983; MBA in mktg., mgmt., Marymount U., 1987; postgrad., Coll for Fin. Planning, 1987—. Mgmt. intern Cen. Fidelity Bank, Vienna, Va., 1984-85; asst. bank mgr. Cen. Fidelity Bank, Alexandria, Va., 1985-86; br. mgr. II Perpetual Savings Bank, Reston, Va., 1986—. Lodge: Rotary. Home: 11559 Rolling Green Ct #200 Reston VA 22091 Office: Perpetual Savs Bank 11180 S Lakes Dr Reston VA 22091

LEMBERGER, NORMA, financial executive; b. Monticello, N.Y., July 21, 1944; d. Joe J. and Ellen Ann (Rosman) L. BS summa cum laude, Bklyn. Coll., 1965. With IBM, 1965—, treas. Americas Group, 1988—. Mem. Econ. Women's Round Table. Home: 34 Limestone Rd Armonk NY 10504

LEMKE, CORRINE LARUE, university grants official; b. Sabin, Minn., May 25, 1934; d. Oswald Edward and Ida M. (Krabbenhoft) L. B.A. in Philosophy, Moorhead State U., 1952. Notary pub., Minn. With WDAY radio and TV sta., Fargo, N.D., 1953-67; fin. aid grant coordinator Moorhead State U., 1967—, mem. task force study of changing student mix, 1983-84. Vol. Comstock Hist. House, Moorhead. Recipient cert. Gov. Minn., 1976, 10 yr. service award Moorhead State U., 1980, letter of commendation U.S. Dept. Edn., 1983. Mem. Minn. Assn. Fin. Aid Adminstrs., Midwest Assn. Student Fin. Aid Adminstrs., Minn. Hist. Soc., State Hist. Soc. North Dakota, State Hist. Soc. Wis., Concordia Hist. Inst. of St. Louis, Phoenix Soc. of Moorhead, Concordia Coll. Alumni Assn., Moorhead State U. Alumni Assn. Lutheran. Author pvt. family history publs. Home: 3209 Village Green Dr East Moorhead MN 56560 Office: Moorhead State U Moorhead MN 56560

LEMMONS, PATRICIA KATHERINE, public relations executive; b. Decatur, Ill., Dec. 4, 1957; d. Lowell Maynard and Lou Ellen (Cox) L. B.A. (James Millikin scholar), Millikin U., 1980; M.S., Northwestern U., 1981. Promotions asst. Herald and Review, Decatur, 1977; asst. dir. pub. relations Nat. Coll. Edn., Evanston, Ill., 1981-85, dir. pub. relations, 1985-86; account exec. Ruth Rashman Assocs., 1986—; publicity dir. Theatre 7, Decatur, 1980; pub. relations coordinator Trinity Theatre, Evanston, 1983-85. Recipient Dr. and Mrs. W. J. Darby prize Millikin U., 1980. Mem. Women in Communications Inc. (bd. dirs. North Shore chpt. 1984-86, pres. North Shore chpt. 1986-88, v.p. internal publs. Chgo. chpt. 1988—), Ill. Theatre Assn., Sigma Delta Chi-Soc. Profl. Journalists, Phi Kappa Phi. Home: 1121 Church St Apt 406 Evanston IL 60201

LEMON, BERNICE THORSON, nurse; b. Houston, Minn., Mar. 6, 1926; d. Theodore O. and Bertha Olivia (Karlsbraten) Thorson; m. George Lawton Lemon, Dec. 31, 1950; children: Ted Charles, Bernice Krin, Susan Jo, Laura Thorson, Barbara Anne. RN. Head nurse operating room U. Minn., Mpls., 1947-50; nursery nurse Midway Hosp., St. Paul, 1947-48; office nurse Dr. Lemon, Lewisburg, W.Va. and self-employed pvt. duty nurse, intermittently, 1959-68; nurse, 1968—; nurse vol. to World Conf. at Caux, Switzerland, 1974, 80-81, 84, 86-87. Founder, mem. Sing Out Roanoke Valley, 1973-78, Gymn-Sing Roanoke Valley Inc., 1978-81; participant cultural exchanges, including HEW and Kennedy Found. Arts Exchange to Poland, 1977, Am. Friendship Alumni to Mainland China and Romania, 1980; counselor Offender Aid Restoration, Inc., Roanoke, Va., 1979-81; initiated and promoted Drug Dependency Alert, Roanoke Valley, 1981; chaplain Roanoke Dem. Club, 1980-81; active Bible Study Fellowship; hostess planning com. for Internat. Confs., Emory U., Atlanta, 1987. Served with USPHS, 1942-43. Recipient Roanoke Valley Outstanding Service award Roanoke Bicentennial Commn., 1976, recognition for artistic presentation on 2d Polish Am. Symposium of Music, Krakow Conservatory, Poland, 1977. Lutheran. Avocations: sports, reading, music appreciation, needlework, gardening. Home: 6924 River Ridge Dr Nashville TN 37221

LEMON, JOAN RAQUELLE, day care director; b. Independence, Kans., Mar. 15, 1950; d. Clarence Russell and Kodosha Irene (Parsons) L.; m. Darrell Stephen Mullinax, Oct. 11, 1975 (div. Sept. 1987); 1 child, Jonathan. BA, Evangel Coll., Springfield, Mo., 1971; MA, Kans. State U., 1973. Speech pathologist Kans. Neurol. Inst., Topeka, 1971-75, dir. speech and hearing clinic, 1975-79; pvt. practice cons. Topeka, 1979; assoc., registered rep. The Franz Co. (div. New Eng. Life Ins. Co.), Topeka, 1979-81; speech pathologist Topeka Assn. for Retarded Citizens, 1982-84; prin., dir. Granny's House Child Care, Topeka, 1984—. Mem. Child Care Providers Assn., Kans. Assn. for Edn. of Young Children. Office: Granny's House Child Care 1216 Mulvane Topeka KS 66604

LEMONDS, KATHRYN JOYCE, technology company executive; b. Oroville, Calif., June 9, 1948; d. Homer Bertus Daily and Betty Louise (Owens) Daily Owens; m. Thomas Andrew Lemonds, Apr. 1, 1967 (div. Aug. 1972); 1 child, Laura Marie. Student Wash. State U., 1966-67; A.A., Diablo Valley Coll., 1985; student J.F. Kennedy U., 1985—. Engring. asst. Pacific Gas & Electric Co. Research Lab., San Ramon, Calif., 1972-82, sr. tech. specialist, 1982—; chief software designer LeMonde Designer Software, San Ramon, 1986—. Supr. host com. Democratic Nat. Conv., San Francisco, 1984. Mem. Software Entrepreneurs Forum, NOW, Summit Orgn. Club: Lafayette Orinda Presbyterian Ch. Shipmates (Calif.). Avocations: studying ballet, tap and jazz dancing, skiing, traveling, reading. Home: 2604 Shadow Mountain Dr San Ramon CA 94583

LENEHAN, PAMELA FARRELL, investment banker; b. Stamford, Conn., May 19, 1952; d. John R. and Elsie M. (White) Farrell; children: Sarah, Paul. BA in Math. Econs. magna cum laude, Brown U., 1974, MA in Econs. with honors, 1974. V.p. electronics div. corp. banking Chase Manhattan, N.Y.C., 1974-81; dir. investment banking tech. group First Boston Corp., N.Y.C., 1981—. Republican. Roman Catholic. Club: Field. Home: 90 Boulder Trail Bronxville NY 10708 Office: The First Boston Corp Park Ave Plaza New York NY 10055

LENGEL, ELIZABETH HILSCHER, behavior specialist; b. Ripon, Wis., Dec. 19, 1953; d. Frederick Albert and Patricia Ann (Westbrook) Hilscher; m. David Wayne Lengel, Nov. 18, 1978; children: John David, James Thomas. BA, Tift Coll., Forsyth, Ga., 1976; postgrad., Ga. Coll., 1977-80. Behavior disorders tchr. Bibb County Pub. Schs., Macon, Ga., 1976-81; sr. behavior specialist State of Ga. Dept. Youth Services, Macon, 1984—; cons. pvt. and pub. hosps. Macon, 1984—. Active Troubled Children Council, Bibb County, Twiggs County, Jones County, Ga., 1985—. Mem. Ga. Coalition on Consultation, Edn., and Prevention, Ga. Juvenile Services Assn., Mid. Ga. Council for Children and Youth. Baptist. Home: 6725 Moseley Dixon Rd Macon GA 31210 Office: DYS Services 1818 Forsyth St Box 4903 Macon GA 31208

L'ENGLE, MADELEINE (MRS. HUGH FRANKLIN), author; b. N.Y.C., Nov. 29, 1918; d. Charles Wadsworth and Madeleine (Barnett) Camp; m. Hugh Franklin, Jan. 26, 1946; children: Josephine Franklin Jones, Maria Franklin Rooney, Bion. A.B., Smith Coll., 1941; postgrad., New Sch., 1941-42, Columbia U., 1960-61. Tchr. St. Hilda's and St. Hugh's Sch., 1960—; mem. faculty U. Ind., 1965-66, 71; writer-in-residence Ohio State U., 1970, U. Rochester, 1972, Wheaton Coll., 1976—, Cathedral St. John the Divine, N.Y.C., 1965—. Author: The Small Rain, 1945, Ilsa, 1946, Camilla Dickinson, 1951, A Winter's Love, 1957, And Both Were Young, 1949, Meet the Austins, 1960, A Wrinkle in Time, 1962, The Moon by Night, 1963, The 24 Days Before Christmas, 1964, The Arm of the Starfish, 1965, The Love Letters, 1966, The Journey with Jonah, 1967, The Young Unicorns, 1968, Dance in The Desert, 1969, Lines Scribbled on an Envelope, 1969, The Other Side of the Sun, 1971, A Circle of Quiet, 1972, A Wind in the Door, 1973, The Summer of the Great-grandmother, 1974, Dragons in the Waters, 1976, The Irrational Season, 1977, A Swiftly Tilting Planet, 1978, The Weather of the Heart, 1978, Ladder of Angels, 1979, A Ring of Endless Light, 1980, Walking on Water, 1981, A Severed Wasp, 1982, And it was Good, 1983, A House Like a Lotus, 1985, Trailing Clouds of Glory, 1985, A Stone for a Pillow, 1986, Many Waters, 1986, A Cry Like a Bell, 1987. Pres. Crosswicks Found. Recipient Newbery medal, 1963; Sequoyah award, 1965; runner-up award Hans Christian Andersen Internat. award, 1965; Lewis Carroll Shelf award, 1965; Austrian State Lit. award, 1969; Bishop's Cross, 1970; U. South Miss. medal, 1978; Regina medal, 1984; Alan award Nat. Council Tchrs. English, 1986; collection of papers at Wheaton Coll. Mem. Authors Guild (pres., mem. council, mem. membership com.), Authors League (mem. council), Writers Guild Am., Colonial Dames. Episcopalian. Home: Crosswicks Goshen CT 06756 Office: care Farrar Straus & Giroux Inc 19 Union Sq W New York NY 10003

LENICK-OLIVIER, SANDRA HELEN, marketing executive; b. Coaldale, Pa., Aug. 26, 1957; d. John Joseph and Helen (Koshuta) Lenick; m. Timothy James Olivier, Oct. 10, 1987. BS, Pa. State U., 1979; MBA, U. Ariz., 1986. Conv. coordinator Marriot's Camelback Inn, Scottsdale, Ariz., 1979-81; catering sales mgr. Tucson Doubletree Hotel, 1983-84; account exec. JLTC & Assocs., Tucson, 1984-85; v.p. mktg. D.L. West Mfg., Inc., Tucson, 1986—; owner catering bus., Tucson, 1981-83; cons. in field, Tucson, 1986—; speaker in field, Tucson, 1986—. Recipient 1st prize U. Ariz. Bus. Plan Competition, 1986. Mem. Assn. Collegiate Entrepreneurs, Nat. Assn. Female Execs., Mfrs. Agents Nat. Assn., Pa. State Alumni Assn. Roman Catholic. Home: 3602 Schaefer St Culver City CA 90232 Office: DL West Mfg Inc 5170 S Julian Suite 318 Tucson AZ 85706

LENKE, JOANNE MARIE, publishing executive; b. Chgo., Aug. 27, 1938; d. August Julian and Dorothy Anna (Gold) L.; B.S., Purdue U., 1960; M.S., Syracuse U., 1964, Ph.D., 1968. Tchr. pub. schs., Evanston, Ill., 1960-63; editor Test Dept., Harcourt, Brace & World, Inc., N.Y.C., 1967-70; research psychologist Harcourt Brace Jovanovich, Inc., N.Y.C., 1970-73, exec. editor, 1973-75; asst. dir. ednl. measurement div. The Psychol. Corp., N.Y.C., 1975-83, dir. ednl. measurement and psychometrics, Cleve., 1983-85, San Antonio, 1986, v.p., dir. Measurement div., 1986—; field reader U.S. Office Edn., 1972, NSF grantee, 1963-64. Mem. Nat. Council on Measurement in Edn., Am. Psychol. Assn., Internat. Reading Assn., Am. Ednl. Research Assn. Adv. editor Jour. of Ednl. Measurement, 1974-78. Home: 1311 Vista del Monte San Antonio TX 78216 Office: The Psychol Corp 555 Academic Ct San Antonio TX 78204

LENKER, SALLY ALBRIGHT, mortgage company executive; b. Bellefonte, Pa., Sept. 13, 1944; d. Ralph W. and Marjorie (Sellers) Albright; m. Robert K. Lenker, June 22, 1963 (div. Feb. 1971); children: Robert B., Scott. Student, Pa. State U., 1962-63; Grad., Pa. Bankers Sch. of Banking, Bucknell, Lewisburg, Pa., 1977, U. Va, Charlottesville, 1985. Lic. real estate broker, Pa. Teller State Coll. (Pa.) Fed. Savs. and Loan, 1964-67, mortgage dept. asst., 1969-73; office mgr. Falk Realty, State College, 1967-69; from mortgage specialist to mortgage dept. head Mellon Bank (formerly Central Counties), State College, 1973-86; co-owner, v.p. Mortgage Placement Services, Inc., State College, 1986—; instr. Am. Inst. of Banking, Central, Pa., 1976-84; guest lectr. fin. workshop Juniata Coll., Huntingdon, Pa., 1979; guest lectr. fin. courses Pa. State U., University Park, 1987. Mem. Centre County Bd. of Realtors, Home Builders Assn. Cen. Pa. (bd. dirs. 1986—, chmn. tng. and edn. 1987—), Bus. and Profl. Womens Club (2d v.p., membership chmn. 1986-87, v.p. 1987-88, pres. 1988-89), State College High Sch. Alumni Assn. (trustee 1987—). Republican. Home: 158 W South Hills Ave State College PA 16801 Office: Mortgage Placement Services Inc 126 E Foster Ave State College PA 16801

LENNOX, ARLENE JUDITH, physicist; b. Cleve.; d. Richard Theodore and Mary Rose (Felber) L.; m. David Paul Eartly. BS in Math, Notre Dame Coll., Cleve., 1963; MS in Physics, U. Notre Dame, 1972, PhD in Physics, 1974. Staff physicist Fermilab, Batavia, Ill., 1974-86, dept. head Neutron Therapy Facility, 1986—. Contbr. articles to profl. jours. Coordinator summer jobs program Ill. Research Council, DuPage and Kane Counties, Ill., 1984—; bd. dirs. Ill. Cancer Council, Chgo., 1986—; mem. Kishwaukee Symphony, DeKalb. Named an Outstanding Woman Leader in Sci. and Medicine, Dupage County, Ill., 1986. Mem. Am. Assn. of Physicists in Medicine, Am. Physical Soc. Office: Fermilab Neutron Therapy Facility PO Box 500 MS 301 Batavia IL 60510

LENNOX, SHIRLEY ANN, artist, educator, consultant; b. San Francisco, Nov. 8, 1931; d. James Joseph and Mildred Mae (Hall) Amos; m. Arthur James Lennox, Jan. 6, 1951; children: Sharron Kay, Kathleen Melanie, Bonnie Marie, Colleen Leta. Student pub. schs., South Glens Falls, N.Y. Window display artist Fowlers' Inc., Glens Falls, 1948-51; owner, operator Discovery House Gallery, Palo Alto, Calif., 1969-71; owner, operator, tchr. porcelain painting Lennox Art Sutdio, Santa Maria, Calif., 1972—; cons. art, Santa Maria, 1985—; owner, operator Gallerie 272, Morton, N.Y., 1979-81; resident artist, gallery mgr. Options Gallery, Shell Beach, Calif., 1985. Exhibited paintings in one-woman shows: Village Gallery, Hilton, N.Y., Lake George Inst. History and Art, N.Y., 1974, Swan Gallery, Albion, N.Y., 1979, Options Gallery, Shell Beach, Calif., 1984, Morro Bay Mus. Natural History, 1985; group shows include: The Calif. Scene (with Ansel Adams and others), Foothill Coll., Los Altos, Calif., 1970, Suburban Rochester Art Group shows, N.Y., 1976-80, Santa Ynez Art Shows, Calif., 1983-84, Los Padres Artists Guild Shows, 1983-86, Faulkner Gallery, 1985, Gallery 113, Santa Barbara, 1987, Sheldon Swope Art Gallery, Terre Haute, Ind., 1987; represented in permanent collections: Old Courthouse Mus., Lake George, N.Y., Shelter Cove Lodge, Pismo Beach, Calif; represented by The Sandpiper, Pismo Beach, Calif., Visions Fine Art Gallery, Morro Bay, Calif. Active Santa Maria Arts Council, 1988—. Mem. Internat. Porcelain Arts Tchrs., Internat. Soc. Marine Painters Inc. (juried profl. mem.), Nat. Soc. Painters in Casein and Acrylic (assoc.), Santa Maria Women's Network, Santa Barbara Art Assn. (juried), Cen. Coast Watercolor Soc., San Luis Obispo Art Assn., Artists Guild of Santa Ynez Valley, Porcelain Portrait Soc., Nat. Mus. Women in the Arts (charter mem.), Nat. Assn. Female Execs. Republican. Mem. Unity Ch. Avocations: photography, camping.

LENNOX (FISCH), CAROL JEANINE, advertising agency executive; b. Wichita Falls, Tex., Sept. 13, 1952; d. Johnny Melvin and Betty Joy (Chastain) Cole; m. Scott Michael Lennox, Mar. 25, 1972 (div. Oct. 1979); m. Elliot Ronald Fisch, Apr. 26, 1986; stepchildren: Julie Ellen, Kendra Elissa. BS, Tex. Christian U., 1975; postgrad. Tex. Wesleyan Coll., 1979, 80. Cert. tchr., Tex. Tchr. learning disabled Ft. Worth Ind. Sch. Dist., 1975-78; fundraiser, editor, coll. relations Tex. Wesleyan Coll., Ft. Worth, 1978-81; account exec., account supr. DBG & H, Inc., Ft. Worth, 1981-84, mgmt. supr., 1984-85; pres. The Lennox Group, Arlington, Tex., 1985-87; v.p. Synergy Works, 1984-87, pres., 1987—; v.p. Synergy Works, Arlington, 1984—, Diversified Media Reps., Arlington, 1985—; lectr. local univs.; instr. Continuing Health Edn. Ctr., Ft. Worth, 1985-86; cons. Ft. Worth Opera, 1986, mem. mktg. com., 1986—; Contbr. articles to local mag. Vol. People for Am. Way, Windstar Found. Recipient Council for Advancement and Support of Edn. award, 1981, Addy award, 1988. Mem. Network of Exec. Women, Advt. Club Ft. Worth (bd. dirs. 1983-85), Internat. Platform Assn. Democrat. Mem. Christian Ch. (Disciples of Christ). Avocations: reading, writing, dancing, aikido, windjammer cruises, metaphysics.

LENNSTROM, NANCY, librarian; b. Hood River, Oreg., June 15, 1931; d. George Minshall and Elsie Winnifred (McLucas) Knox; m. Charles Owen Lennstrom, Nov. 26, 1952; children—Kathleen Marie Mason, Diane Louise, Peter Charles, Heidi Annette. B.A. in English, U. Wash., 1974, M.L.S., 1975. Readers service librarian Highline Coll. Library, Midway, Wash., 1975—. Bd. dirs. Child Hearing League, Seattle, 1960-62; leader Camp Fire Girls, Seattle, 1961-64, bd. dirs. PTA, elem. and jr. high schs., Seattle, 1958-65; advisor liberal religious youth Unitarian Universalist Ch., Seattle, 1969-74; mem. adv. com. Seattle Internat. U. Library; exec. bd. Washington Coalition Against Censorship. Mem. Assn. Coll. and Research Libraries (sec. 1982-84, nat. conf. 1984 com.), Community Coll. Librarians and Media Specialists. Democrat. Unitarian. Home: 1915 SW 170th St Seattle WA 98166 Office: Highline Community Coll Library PO Box 98000 Des Moines WA 98198-9800

LENOIR, GLORIA CISNEROS, small business owner, business manager; b. Monterrey, Nuevo Leon, Mex., Aug. 18, 1951; came to U.S., 1956, naturalized, 1974; d. Juan Antonio and Maria Gloria (Flores) Cisneros; m. Walter Frank Lenoir, June 6, 1975; children: Lucy Gloria, Katherine Judith. Student, Inst. Am. Univs., 1971-72; BA in French Art, Austin Coll., 1973, MA in French Art, 1974; MBA in Fin., U. Tex., 1979. French tchr. Sherman (Tex.) High Sch., 1973-74; French/Spanish tchr. dept. chmn. Lyndon Baines Johnson High Sch., Austin, 1974-77; legis. aide Tex. State Capitol, Austin, Tex., 1977-81; stock broker Merrill Lynch, Austin, 1981-83, Schneider, Bernet and Hickman, Austin, 1983-84; bus. mgr. Holleman Photographic Labs., Inc., Austin, 1984—; group counselor, organizer Inst. Fgn. Studies, U. Strasbourg, France, summer 1976; mktg. intern IBM, Austin, summer 1978; mktg. cons. Creative Ednl. Enterprises, Austin, 1980-81; hon. speaker Mex.-Am. U. of Tex., Austin, 1984; speaker various orgns., bus. classes, Austin, 1981-84; speaker, coordinator small bus. workshops, 1985. Photos published in Women in Space, 1979; photos exhibited throughout Tex., 1979. Neighborhood capt. Am. Cancer Soc., Austin, 1982-86; hospitality chmn., first grade coordinator PTA, Austin, 1986; vol. liaison leads program Austin Coll., Austin, 1983—. Recipient Night on the Town award IBM, 1978. Mem. Photo Mktg. Assn., Nat. Fedn. Ind. Businessmen, Austin C. of C., Hispanic C. of C. (Vol. award 1986). Republican. Presbyterian. Home: 1202 W 29th St Austin TX 78703 Office: Holleman Photographic Labs Inc 919 W 12th St Austin TX 78701

LENOIR, MARIA ANNETTE, management consultant; b. St. Louis, June 11, 1950; d. Jack and Beatrice (Brown) Doyle; m. Howard L. Williams, Sept. 29, 1969 (div. Aug. 1981); 1 child, Howard L. Jr.; m. Aguinaldo Alphonse Lenoir Jr., June 28, 1985; 1 stepchild, Aguinaldo Alphonse III. Student, Florissant (Mo.) Valley Community Coll., 1974-76, Webster U., 1979-80. Stenographer Internat. Shoe Co., St. Louis, 1968-69; office mgr. Chemplastics Inc., St. Louis, 1969-71; advt./media coordinator Ralston Purina Co., St. Louis, 1971-73, sec., 1973-76, adminstrv. asst., 1976-79, sales/mktg. adminstr., 1979-84; pres., chief exec. officer, owner Corp. Image, Inc., St. Louis, 1984—; instr. St. Louis Univ., 1987, St. Louis Community Coll.; pub. relations advisor Mo. White House Conf. Small Bus., St. Louis, 1986; mem. adv. panel Omni Internat. Hotel, St. Louis, 1986. Contbr. articles to profl. jours. Mktg. advisor Jr. Achievement of Miss. Valley, Hazelwood, Mo., 1983—; mem. Women's Assn. St. Louis Symphony, 1984—, ACE (div. of SCORE), St. Louis, 1985—; role model St. Louis Pub. Sch., 1987. Named Outstanding Young Women Am., 1987. Mem. Meeting Planners Internat., Nat. Assn. Women Bus. Owners, St. Louis Conv. and Visitors Commn., Assn. Ind. Meeting Planners (adv. com., bd. dirs.), Women in Bus. (chmn. spl. com. 1983), Florissant Valley Community Coll. Alumni Assn. (v.p. 1985-86, sec./treas. 1987, Alumna of Yr. award 1986 Hall of Fame), Women in Leadership Alumni, Nat. Assn. Female Execs., St. Louis Regional Commerce & Growth Assn. Democrat. Pentecostal. Club: Boulder Yacht (Carlyle, Ill.). Office: Corp Image Inc 4825 Lockwig Saint Louis MO 63033

LENOX, MARY FRANCES, university dean; b. Chgo., July 19, 1944; d. Eleazar and Truesillia (Bryson) L. B.S., Chgo. State U., 1966; M.A., Rosary Coll., 1968; Ed.D., U. Mass., 1975. Tchr., librarian Chgo. pub. schs., 1967-71; asst. reference librarian Ctr. for Inner City Studies, Northeastern Ill. U., Chgo., 1971-72; dir. ednl. materials ctr. Chgo. State U., 1971-72; mgr. circulation dept. learning resource ctr., faculty mem. Governors State U., Park Forest South, Ill., 1973-75; media specialist Chgo. Pub. Schs., 1973-78; mem. faculty Nat. Coll. Edn. Urban Campus, Chgo., 1977-78; assoc. prof. Sch. Library and Info. Sci., U. Mo.-Columbia, 1978-84, dean, 1984—; vis. prof. U. Denver, 1979, Stephens Coll., Columbia, 1980, 81; faculty-in-residence Chgo. Pub. Library, 1981; cons., speaker in field. Contbr. articles to profl. jours. Bd. dirs. Halfway House Com., Inc., Chgo., 1977, New Wave Corp., Columbia, 1981-85; mem. adv. bd. The Legal Inst., Burbank, Calif., 1977—; mem. bd. cons. The High-Low Report, N.Y.C., 1979-83; producer, moderator Black Women: African Past to Columbia Present Sta. KOPN-FM, Columbia, 1979; mem. editorial bd. Jour. of Youth Services. Named Outstanding Educator, Dist. II Chgo. Pub. Schs., 1977; Kellogg Nat. fellow, 1982-85. Mem. ALA (Grolier awards com. 1980), Am. Assn. Sch. Librarians (sch. media program of yr. awards com. 1979-80), Mo. Library Assn. (chmn. library educators 1978-82, outreach roundtable 1980-81), AAUW, Assn. Study Afro-Am. Life and History, Assn. Library and Info. Sci. Educators (chmn. Council of Deans and Dirs. 1987-88), Pi Lambda Theta, Delta Kappa Gamma, Kappa Delta Pi. Avocations: hiking, photography, floral designs, rock collecting, travel, environmental preservation. Office: U Mo-Columbia Sch Library & Info Sci 104 Stewart Hall Columbia MO 65211

LENSMITH, BETTY, business executive; b. Oconomowoc, Wis., Oct. 3, 1928; d. Alex F. and Vera (Zeiters) Henschel; m. Eugene A. Lensmith, Nov. 14, 1949; children—Lissa Kathleen, Larry Eugene. Receptionist, Schrader Studio, Milw., 1947; mgr. Tooley Myron Studios chain, 1948-49; owner, mgr. Country Studio, Oconomowoc, 1950—, Town and Country Studio, 1957—; founder, pres., treas. Photographers Specialized Services, Inc., Oconomowoc, 1968—; founder, pres. Ret. Persons Specialized Services, 1981—, Golden World Products, 1982—, Photo-Treasures, 1984—; instr. Winona Sch. Photography, 1975—, Miami and Traingle Inst. (Pa.), 1977, No. Ga. Sch. Photography, 1978. Recipient awards Kodak Co. Mem. Profl. Photographers Am. (cert. photographic craftsman, recipient various awards), Am. Soc. Photographers, Am. Mgmt. Assn., Studio Suppliers Assn., Female Execs., 700 Club, Presidents Club. Author: The Guide to Lighting, Posing and Composing, 1971, rev. edit., 1986; Selling, The Name of the Game, 1976; Profitable Promotions and Merchandising Techniques, 1977; The Basic Guide to Commercial Photography, 1979. Home: 423 N Lake Rd Oconomowoc WI 53066 Office: 650 Armour Rd Oconomowoc WI 53066

LENTINI, COLLEEN GAIL SHERWOOD, government official; b. Middleboro, Mass., Oct. 22, 1944; d. Robert Bridge and Jeanette Louise (Letendre) Sargent; A.A., Montgomery Coll., 1983; m. Joseph Charles Lentini, Dec. 5, 1983; children—Stephen, Suzanne, Richard. Personnel asst. Nat. Cancer Inst., Bethesda, Md., 1974-76, adminstrv. asst., 1976-79, adminstrv. officer, 1979-81; spl. asst. program planning and evaluation Nat. Inst. Arthritis, Diabetes and Digestive and Kidney Diseases, Bethesda, Md., 1981-82, spl. asst. program analysis, 1982-83; adminstrv. officer Office of Insp. Gen., EPA, Washington, 1984-87, chief tech. and program services Office Research and Devel., EPA, Washington, 1987—. Recipient Superior Performance awards , 1970, 72, 77, 79, 87, Spl. Act award, 1987. Mem. Nat. Assn. Female Execs., Phi Theta Kappa. Democrat. Roman Catholic. Home: 18420 Tranquil Ln Olney MD 20832 Office: Office of Research Program Mgmt ORD EPA 401 M St SW Washington DC 20460

LENTS, ANN, lawyer; b. Houston, Sept. 4, 1949; d. Max Richey and Mary Frances (Hunsicker) L.; m. James David Heaney II, Aug. 11, 1973; children: J. David, Mary Elizabeth. BA, Wellesley Coll., 1971; JD, U. Tex., 1974. Bar: Tex. 1974, U.S. Dist. Ct. (so. dist.) Tex. 1975, U.S. Ct. Appeals (5th, 10th and 11th cirs.) 1981, U.S. Supreme Ct. 1982. Assoc. Vinson & Elkins, Houston, 1974-81, ptnr., 1981—. Bd. dirs. Houston Child Guidance Ctr., 1988—, Houston Bus. Forum, 1982. Fellow Tex. Bar Found., Houston Bar Found.; mem. ABA, Tex. Bar Assn., Houston Bar Assn. (bd. dirs. antitrust sect. 1977-79), Ex-editors Assn. Tex. Law Rev., U. Tex. Law Sch. Assn. (bd. dirs. 1981-82), Fed. Energy Bar Assn. (antitrust com. 1987-88). Presbyterian. Office: Vinson & Elkins 1001 Fannin 3300 First City Tower Houston TX 77002

LENTZ, CHRISTINE MARIE ANDERSON, university administrator; b. Madison, Wis., Nov. 17, 1958; d. Wilbur R. and Lorraine K. (Schufletowski) Wiessinger. BSBA, U. Wis., 1980; MBA, Boston U., 1983. Mgr. mgmt. info. systems Econ. Devel. and Indsl. Corp., Boston, 1981-82; asst. dir. info. resources Boston U., 1983-84, dir. info. resources, 1985—; cons. City of Boston, 1984; instr. MBA program Boston U., 1987—. Tchr. Sunday sch. 1st Luth. Ch., Boston, 1983-85. Mem. Soc. for Info. Mgmt., Data Processing Mgmt. Assn. Republican. Office: Boston U 685 Commonwealth Ave Boston MA 02215

LENTZ, DEBRA LEE, airline executive; b. Racine, Wis., Nov. 2, 1962; d. Robert Joseph and Carol Ann (Gross) L. Student, Scottsdale Community Coll.; grad., McConnell Travel Sch., Mpls., 1981. Flight sch. dispatcher Scottsdale (Ariz.) Air Ctr., 1981-82; charter supr. Air Scottsdale, 1982-83; receptionist Cutter Aviation Co., Phoenix, 1983; gen. mgr. Ariz. Air Co., Scottsdale, 1983-87; dir. flight ops. Cutter Aviation, Inc., Phoenix, 1988—. Vol. Scottsdale Ctr. for Arts, 1986—. Mem. Nat. Assn. Female Execs., Rio Salado Gun Club, Phi Theta Kappa. Home: 3202 N 67th Pl Apt B Scottsdale AZ 85251 Office: Cutter Aviation Inc 2802 Old Tower Rd Phoenix AZ 85034

LENTZ, ROBIN JO, credit union executive; b. Los Angeles, Oct. 27, 1947; d. Joseph Vincent and Nellie Nancy (Tennenblum) Incorvaia; m. Bob Monte Hannah, Feb. 1, 1969 (div. 1973); children—Kimberly, David; m. 2d, Robert George Lentz, Mar. 15, 1975. Student Nat. U., San Diego, 1983-85; grad. Western Regional Sch. Credit Union Execs., 1975, Advanced Mgmt. Inst., 1982. Mrg., chief exec. officer Whittier (Calif.) Gentelco Fed. Credit Union, 1966-75; account rep. Members Ins. Co., Irvine, Calif., 1975-78; chief exec. officer Van Camp Fed. Credit Union, San Diego, Calif., 1978-79; pres., chief exec. officer Cabrillo Fed. Credit Union, San Diego, 1979—; treas. San Diego Regional Ad Council, 1983. Mem. Credit Union Execs. Soc., San Diego Mgrs. Assn. (pres. 1984), Nat. Assn. Fed. Credit Unions, Calif. Credit Union League (pres. San Diego chpt. 1982-83, 88—), San Diego C. of C. Democrat. Roman Catholic. Home: 13802 Paseo Cardiel San Diego CA 92129 Office: Cabrillo Fed Credit Union 1450 Frazee Rd #406 San Diego CA 92108

LEO, KAREN ANN, library administrator; b. Akron, Ohio, June 5, 1945; d. Ellsworth John and Flonnie Ada (Dykes) Hunter; m. Louis J. Leo, May 23, 1970. B.A., Baldwin-Wallace Coll., 1967; A.M. in Library Sci., U. Mich., 1968. Fiction librarian Cleve. Pub. Library, 1968-69; reference librarian San Jose State Coll., Calif., 1969-70; head reference librarian, asst. to county librarian Stanislaus County Free Library, Modesto, Calif., 1970-77; asst. city librarian Pomona Pub. Library, Calif., 1977-81; head central library Riverside City and County Pub. Library, Calif., 1981-85; library dir Orange (Calif.) Pub. Library, 1985—. Community adviser Jr. League of Riverside, 1982-85. Mem. community video adv. bd., Orange, 1985—. Mem. AAUW, Calif. Library Assn. (community relations com.), ALA. Democrat. Methodist. Office: Orange Pub Library 101 N Center St Orange CA 92666

LEON, MARGARET ADELE, financial service marketing company executive; b. Boston, Mar. 19, 1948; d. Richard and Florence (Hattub) L. B.S., Boston State Coll., 1969; M.A. in Counseling, Salem State Coll., 1977. Tchr. Chelsea Schs., Mass., 1969-76, guidance counselor, 1977-82; group therapist Behavioral Assocs., Brookline, Mass., 1977-79; real estate agt. Gen. Devel., Peabody, Mass., 1979-81; ins. and securities agt. A.L. Williams, Lynn, Mass., 1981-83, regional v.p., 1983-87, sr. v.p., 1987—. Avocations: photography, sewing, cooking, skiing, martial arts. Office: A L Williams Corp 679 Western Ave Suite 4 Lynn MA 01905

LEON, MARIA ELBA, savings and loan executive; b. Cananea, Sonora, Mex., Mar. 17, 1948; d. Ramon and Victoria (Acosta) Leon; came to U.S., 1949, naturalized, 1964. Student U. Ariz., 1962-64, 66-70, 70-71, Pima Community Coll., 1971—. Bilingual sec., adminstrv. asst. So. Ariz. Bank & Trust Co., 1964-71; asst. v.p., security officer Banco de las Am., 1971-74; asst. v.p., branch mgr. Home Fed. Savs. & Loan Assn., Tucson, 1974-75, v.p., regional mgr., 1979, v.p. community relations, bus. devel. mktg. div., 1980—; owner, pres. J. Elba Corp. Inc., 1984-87; trust devel. officer Valley Nat. Bank, 1988—. Chmn. bd. trustees El Dorado Hosp. & Med. Ctr.; past pres. Soroptimist Internat. Desert Tucson; mem. Ariz.-Mex. Commn. Office of Gov., 1978; bd. dirs. 88-Crime; chmn. fin. adv. com. Pima Community Coll., 1981; del. Ariz. Acad. Town Hall, 1979; mem. Tucson Airport Authority, 1980. Named Outstanding Civic Leader LULAC, 1975; Outstanding Young Hispanic Woman, Adolph Coors Co., 1980, Outstanding Citizen, 1981. Mem. Ariz. Bus. and Profl. Women's Club, Exec. Women Internat., Exec. Women's Council So. Ariz., Exec. Women's Council. Democrat. Roman Catholic. Home: 1150 N El Dorado Pl #213 Tucson AZ 85715

LEON, TANIA JUSTINA, composer, music director, pianist; b. Havana, Cuba, May 14, 1943; came to U.S., 1967; d. Oscar and Dora (Ferran) L. BA in Piano and Theory, Peyrellade Conservatory Music, Havana, 1963; MA in Music Edn., Nat. Conservatory Music, Havana, 1965; BA in Acctg., U. Havana, 1965; BS in Composition, NYU, 1971, BS in Music Edn., 1973, MA in Composition, 1973. resident composer Lincoln Ctr. Inst., 1985, teaching artist, 1982—; founder Dance Theatre Harlem Music Dept. Orch.; panelist N.Y. State Council on the Arts, 1980, 81, 86, Nat. Endowment for the Arts composing program, 1980-82, recording program, 1985—; mem. adv. bd. Bklyn. Coll. Conservatory, 1982-84, Meet the Composer, 1983—, Children TV Workshop; artistic dir. Composers Forum Inc., N.Y.C., 1987; assoc. prof. composition Bklyn. Coll., 1987; bd. dirs. Am. Music Ctr. Piano soloist, Cuba, 1964-67; music dir. TV, Havana, 1965-66; piano soloist, N.Y. Coll. of Music Orch., N.Y.C., 1967, NYU Orch., N.Y.C., 1969, Buffalo Symphony Orch., 1973; staff pianist, condr., Dance Theatre of Harlem, N.Y.C., 1968—, assoc. condr., 1983—, music dir., 1968-79; founder, Dance Theatre of Harlem Orch., 1975; concert series Meet the Performer, 1977; music dir.: concert series Dance in Am. Spl, Sta. WNET-TV; guest condr. concert series, Genova (Italy) Symphony Orch., 1972, Juilliard Orch., Festival Two Worlds, Spoleto, Italy, Symphony New World, 1974, Royal Ballet Orch., 1974, 76, BBC Orch., 1974, 76, Halle Orch., 1974, Buffalo Philharm. Orch., 1975, Concert Orch. of L.I., 1979, Sadler's Wells Orch., 1979, London Universal Symphony, 1979, Composer's Forum, 1979, Lincoln Ctr. Outdoor Festival, 1980, Bklyn. Coll. Symphony, 1981, J. F. Kennedy Ctr. Opera House Orch., 1981, 82, Radio City Music Hall, 1982, Spoleto Festival, Charleston, 1983, Orch. of Our Time, N.Y., N.Y. Grand Opera, Colonne Orch., Paris, Mich. Opera, Human Comedy Royale Theatre, Broadway, Pasadena Orch., P.R. Symphony, Met. Opera Orch., Phoenix Symphony, Columbus Symphony Orch., Fund. Latinoamericana Musica Contemporanea P.R., Am. Women Condr./Composer Symposium, Eugene, Oreg., New Music Am., Houston, numerous others; royal command performer concert series, London Palladium, 1974, 76, Concert Orch. L.I., 1976, concert pianist, Sta. WNYC-FM, 1968-70; conductor coordinator: concert series Music by Black Composers Series, Bklyn. Philharmonia, 1978-79; music dir., condr., Bklyn. Philharm. Community Concert Series, 1977—; mus. dir.: concert series The Wiz, 1978, Death, Destruction and Detroit, 1979, Alvin Ailey Am. Dance Theatre, 1983—, Whitney Mus. Contemporary Music Concert Series, 1986—; mus. dir., composer: Maggie Magalita, 1980, The Golden Windows, 1982; apptd. music dir. concert series, Intar Theatre, N.Y.C.; condr., mus. dir.: concert series Godspell, NYU, 1978, Carmencita, 1978, The Wiz, 1978; composer: ballet music Haiku, 1974, Tonos; piano concerto, 1970, Sailor's Boat; score for musical, 1974, Dougla; African ballet, 1974, La Ramera de la Cueva; score for musical, 1974, Namiac Poems; voice, chorus and orch., 1975, Spiritual Suite; 2 sopranos, chorus and mixed ensemble with narrator, 1976, Concerto Criollo; concerto for piano, 8 timpanies and orch., 1976, Pet's Suite, 1980; for flute and piano I Got Ovah; for soprano, piano and percussion, based on poems by Carolyn M. Rodgers, Concerto Criollo, 1980, Four Pieces for Cello, 1981, De-Orishas, 1982, Ascend, Fanfarre for Brass and Percussion, 1983, for solo piano Momentum, 1984, Bata, 1985, Permutation Seven, 1985, A La Par, 1986, Ritual, 1987, Pueblo Mulato, 1987; records on Opus One. Recipient Young Composers prize Nat. Council Arts, Havana, 1966; recipient Alvin Johnson award Am. Council Emigres in the Profession, 1971, Cintas award in composition, 1974-75, 78-79, Nat. Council Women of U.S. Achievement award, 1980, Byrd Hoffman Found. award, 1981, Key to City of Detroit, 1982, Queens Council on Arts award, 1983, Manhattan Arts award, 1985, Dean Dixon Achievement award, 1985, Meomposer award 1978-87; Nat. Endowment for Arts fellow, 1975. Mem. ASCAP (Composers award 1978-87), French Soc. Composers, Am. Fedn. Musicians, Ctr. New Music, Am. Music Ctr. (bd. dirs. 1985—), Internat. Artists Alliance, Am. Women Composers, AFL-CIO. Home: 35-20 Leverick St Apt B430 New York NY 11372

LEONARD, DEBI LYNN (DELYN KYNTA), manufacturing company marketing executive; b. Dodge City, Kans., May 6, 1955; d. Harold Duane and Kynta Lov (Kennedy) L. Student, Marymount Coll., 1972-76, Vo-Tech. U., Salina, Kans. 1976-78. Comml. art sales rep. Shoppers Guide, Salina, 1977-81; sales rep. Sta. KYEZ-AM, Salina, 1981-82, Freedom News, Denver, 1982-83; designer Delyns Fashions, Denver, 1983-86; mktg. mgr. Lenko Enterprises, Cripple Creek, Colo., 1981—, Cellular One Mobile Communications, 1988—. Vol. Annual Bridal Show, Salina, 1985; active Am. Cancer Soc., membership drive YMCA. Mem. Life Underwriters Assn., Am. Bus. Womens Assn. Midwest Corvette Assn., Nat. Assn. Female Execs.; Denver Advt. Assn. Avocations: windsurfing; skiing; swimming; hot air ballooning. Office: Lenko Enterprises PO Box 16 Cripple Creek CO 80818

LEONARD, DONNA KAY SNIDER, lawyer; b. Cin., Aug. 24, 1945; d. James Benjamen and Ruby (Crowley) Battles; AA, Coll. Mt. St. Joseph of Ohio, 1979, BA magna cum laude, 1980; JD, No. Ky. U., 1984; children: Michelle Lynn, Lorrie Danielle. With Kroger Co., Cin., 1970—, legal adminstr. and asst. corp. sec. law dept., 1975—, asst. corp. sec., 1982-87; assoc. Frost & Jacobs, Cin., 1987—. Mem. mgmt. com. YMCA. Mem. ABA, Greater Cin. Women Lawyers, Ohio Bar Assn., Cin. Bar Assn., Alpha Chi, Kappa Gamma Pi. Republican. Methodist. Club: Toastmasters. Home: 7341 Riverby Rd Cincinnati OH 45255 Office: Frost & Jabocs 2500 Cen Trustee Ctr Cincinnati OH 45201

LEONARD, DOROTHY LOUISE, environmental analyst; b. Newark, Aug. 30, 1932; d. Joseph Peter and Charlotte Mary (Dinkel) L.; m. Gary Lawrence Fellows, Sept. 4, 1954 (div. Mar. 1978); children: Mark Leonard, Paige Charlotte Wright, Scott Lawrence, Joy Dorothy. BA, Syracuse U., 1954; postgrad., SUNY, Brockport, 1976, George Washington U., 1982-84. Asst. planner Monroe County Dept. Planning, Rochester, N.Y., 1975-77; specialist coastal resources N.Y. Dept. State, Albany, 1977-80; program analyst Office Coastal Zone Mgmt. Nat. Oceanic & Atmospheric Adminstrn. div. U.S. Dept. Commerce, Washington, 1980-83, specialist fisheries devel. Nat. Marine Fisheries Service, 1983-86, environ. analyst Nat. Ocean Service, 1986 ; pres. Dorothy Leonard Assocs., Washington, 1985—. Mem. com. N.Y. Legis. Com. on Women, Albany, 1975-77; pres. Washington Area Waterfront Action Group, Washington, 1986—. Mem. Am. Fisheries Soc., Am. Soc. Limnology and Oceanography, AIA (urban design com. 1986—), Chesapeake Bay Citizen Adv. Com., Waterfront Washington Assn., Survival of the Sea Soc. (bd. advisors 1987—), LWV, Phi Kappa Phi. Republican. Presbyterian. Home and Office: 14337 Long Green Dr Silver Spring MD 20906

LEONARD, EILEEN ANN, motion picture trust fund executive; b. N.Y.C., Oct. 4, 1941; d. Errol Thomas and Marjorie (Cleary) Connelly; m. Wayne Leonard, Jan. 28, 1967 (div. Mar. 1975); 1 dau., Kimberly Anne; m. 2d Kenneth Paul Vensel, Sept. 6, 1980. B.A., Fairleigh Dickinson U., 1963. French sec. French Railroads, N.Y.C., 1964-65; legal sec. W.R. Grace Co., N.Y.C., 1965-67; exec. sec. Internat. Industries, Los Angeles, 1968-70; adminstr. Contract Services Adminstr. Trust Fund, Los Angeles, 1974-76, dir., 1976—. Pub. relations chairperson Los Angeles Basin Equal Opportunity League, 1975-84; bd. dirs. Internat. Inst., Los Angeles, 1983-86, Inroads, Los Angeles. Mem. Dir. Guild Am., Women in Film. Roman Catholic. Home: 12431 Landale St Studio City CA 91604 Office: Contract Services Adminstr Trust Fund 14144 Ventura Blvd Sherman Oaks CA 91604

LEONARD, FLORENCE IRENE, educator; b. Trenton, Apr. 12, 1934; d. Esau and Alverine (Arnold) Courtney; B.A., Trenton State Coll., 1968, M.Ed., 1979, supr./prin. cert., m. Henry L. Leonard, Feb. 21, 1953; children—Guy Anthony, Carl Henry, Celeste Alverine, Troy Courtney. Librarian asst. dept. edn. N.J. State Library, 1960 64; tchr. Harrison Elem. Sch., Trenton, 1968—, supr., 1981—, also part-time acting prin. Deaconess local ch. Chs. of God in Christ, Trenton. Mem. NEA, N.J. Edn. Assn., Trenton Edn. Assn., Mercer County Edn. Assn. Author: The Xerox Intermediate Dictionary, 1973; designer mural of the Crucifixion, Holy Trinity Ch. of God in Christ. Trenton, 1954, girls' dormitory for Chs. of God in Christ, Monrovia, Liberia, 1959. Home: 9 James Cubberly Ct Trenton NJ 08610 Office: Harrison Sch Genesee St Trenton NJ 08611 also: Trenton Bd Edn N Clinton Ave Trenton NJ 08609

LEONARD, KATHLEEN LIVEZEY, foundation administrator; b. Norman, Okla., July 6, 1939; d. William Edmund and Martha (Taylor) Livezey; m. William Lake Leonard, June 26, 1962 (div. 1976); children: W. David, Elizabeth Lake; m. David Yanis, July 24, 1982; stepchildren: Elaine Yanis Bennett, Steven Robert. BA in English with honors, Bryn Mawr Coll., 1961; MA in English Lit., Yale U., 1962. Editorial asst. Folger Shakespeare Library, Washington, 1963-65; asst. to pres. The Feminist Press SUNY, Old Westbury, 1974-76; program dir. N. Shore Community Arts Ctr., Great Neck, N.Y., 1976-79; assoc. adminstr. The McGraw-Hill Found., N.Y.C., 1980-86, adminstr., 1987—. Bd. dirs. Creative Arts Workshop, Port Washington, N.Y., 1972, co-pres., 1973-74; bd. dirs. Career Services for Women Inc., Port Washington, N.Y., 1972-74. Mem. Corp. Vols. N.Y. (v.p. 1985-86, pres. 1986-87, Pres.'s Vol. Action award 1987). Home: 38 Rogers Rd Kings Point NY 11024 Office: The McGraw-Hill Found Inc 1221 Avenue of the Americas New York NY 10020

LEONARD, LEIGH LAURENS, lawyer; b. Durham, N.C., June 17, 1960; d. Raleigh Webster Leonard and Betty Lou (McGee) Molnar. BA magna cum laude, Simon's Rock Coll., 1980; JD, Am. U., 1984. Bar: N.C. 1985, U.S. Dist. Ct. (ea. and we. dists.) N.C. Assoc. Marshall & Solomon, Raleigh, N.C., 1984-87, Howard, From, Stallings and Hutson, Raleigh, N.C., 1987—. Blodgett scholar, 1978-79, Simon's Rock Coll. Faculty scholar, 1979-80. Mem. ABA, N.C. Bar Assn., Wake County Bar Assn., Assn. Women Attys. Democrat. Home: 1428 Fairway Ridge Dr Raleigh NC 27606 Office: Howard From Stallings & Hutson 1407 Hillsborough St Raleigh NC 27605

LEONARD, MARIE THÉRÈSE PIERRETTE, communications executive; b. Hull, Que., Sept. 13, 1949; d. Wilfred Paul and Cécile Lucile (Schafer) Cloutier; m. William Frederick Leonard, Sept. 1, 1973; children: Marie Geneviève, Dominique. BS in Social Scis., Carleton U., Ottawa, Ont., Can., 1972. Office asst. to dist. officer Nat. Parole Service Govt. Can., Ottawa, 1966-69; task force researcher Solicitor Gen.'s Dept. Got. Can., Ottawa, 1972; dean women, lectr. in psychology Ontario Ministry Agriculture and Food, Centralia, Ont., Can., 1972-73; elem. sch. tchr. Bahamian Govt., Andros, 1973; job placement officer, restoration counsellor Ont. Ministry Community and Social Services, Barrie, Ont., 1974-75; pub. relations, info. dir. Can. Cancer Soc. Nova Scotia Div., Halifax, Can., 1975-77; head communications sect. The Royal Coll. Physicians and Surgeons of Can., Ottawa, 1982—, mng. editor, Annals, 1985—. Com. mem. Quebec City Unit, Que., 1979-80; mem. edn. com. Can. Cancer Soc.; vol. Ottawa Montessori Sch., 1982—. Mem. Can. Pub. Relations Soc. (bd. dirs. 1988—). Office: The Royal Coll Physicians & Surgeons Can, 74 Stanley Ave, Ottawa, ON Canada K1M 1P4

LEONARD, MARTA LYNN, academic administrator; b. Ft. Bragg, Calif., May 7, 1951; d. David August and Lena Zaira (Tavelli) Lazzarini; m. Robert Edward Leonard, Jr., Apr. 12, 1975. AA, Santa Rosa (Calif.) Jr. Coll., 1971; BA, Calif. State U., San Jose, 1974; MA, U. San Francisco, 1985; postgrad., U. Calif., Sacramento, 1987—. Cert. elem. tchr., Calif.; cert. in adminstrv. service. Legal sec. Ryerson & Comstock, Santa Rosa, 1971; consumer cons. Better Bus. Bur., San Jose, 1973; waitress Lyons Restaurant, Santa Rosa, 1975; tchr. Santa Rosa Unified Sch. Dist., 1975-79; tchr., job counselor Fairfield (Calif.)-Suisun Unified Sch. Dist., 1979-84, project dir., 1984-86, program mgr., 1986, asst. prin., 1986—; profl. race car driver, 1976—. Columnist Car Watch, 1984. Mem. Nat. Assn. for Stock Car Auto Racing, Sports Car Club Am. (championship 1980-81), Internat. Motor Sports Assn. Republican. Roman Catholic. Office: Leonard Co Racing 96 Railroad Ave Suite G Suisun City CA 94585

LEONARD, MARTHA REED, educational administrator; b. Mpls., May 1, 1938; d. William Chester and Elizabeth (Martin) Reed; m. William E. Hostettler, Dec. 19, 1959 (div. Apr. 1975); children: Jane Elizabeth, Paul Andrew, Julie Marie; m. Frederic E. Leonard, July 18, 1975 (div. Apr. 1987). BA, U. Minn., 1960; MBA, Rutgers U., 1982. Jr. scientist U. Minn., Mpls., 1960-61, asst. to dean grad. sch., 1961-65, asst. to dean biol. scis., 1965-66; asst. to dean nursing Seton Hall U., South Orange, N.J., 1976-79, v.p. student affairs, 1980; asst. to pres. Poly. U., Bklyn., 1982-85, v.p. univ. relations, 1985—. Mem. Am. Assn. Univ. Adminstrs. (profl. standards arbitrator), U. Minn. Alumni Assn., Rutgers U. Alumni Assn. Office: Poly U 333 Jay St Brooklyn NY 11201

LEONARD, PATRICIA LYNN, university administrator; b. Rockville, Centre, N.Y., May 28, 1955; d. John Thomas and Grace Lillian (Foster) L.; B.A. in Social Work and Secondary Edn. in Social Studies, Coll. Misericordia, 1977; M.A. in Coll. Student Personnel Adminstrn., Mich. State U., 1979. Grad. resident adviser Mich. State U., 1977-79; residence coordinator U. N.C., Charlotte, 1979-80; area coordinator Miami U., Oxford, Ohio, 1980-83, instr. in personnel and guidance, 1980-83; assoc. dean students U. N.C.-Wilmington, 1983-87, dean students, 1987—; cons. to student affair staff Coll. Misericordia. Mem. Am. Assn. Counseling and Devel., Nat. Assn. Fgn. Student Advisors, So. Assn. Coll. Student Affairs, Am. Coll. Personnel Assn., Ohio Coll. Personnel Adminstrs., Phi Delta Kappa, Alpha Delta Mu. Office: U NC Wilmington NC 28403-3297

LEONARD, SPRING BIXBY, financial consultant; b. Brookline, Mass., Mar. 30, 1953; d. Robert Johnson and Barbara (Bixby) L. BSBA in Fin. with honors, Northeastern U., 1983. Registered investment adv. Fin. analyst Crosby Valve Co., Wrentham, Mass., 1975-79, USAF, Bedford, Mass., 1980-81; fin. planning and systems dataCon, Inc., Burlington, Mass., 1983-84; assoc. Duffield Fin. Group, Norfolk, Mass., 1985-86; owner SBL Fin. Enterprise, Norfolk, Mass., 1986—; lectr. local groups, 1986—; tchr. Franklin (Mass.) Pub. Schs., 1987—; bd. dirs. Fed. Credit Union. Chmn. Personnel Bd., Norfolk, 1984—; bd. trustees, chmn. planned giving and legacy com., mem. exec. com. Am. Cancer Soc., Neponset Valley Unit, 1986—, bd. dirs. Mass. div., 1988—. Mem. Internat. Assn. Fin. Planners.

LEONARD, VIRGINIA KATHRYN, budget officer; b. Street, Md., Aug. 31, 1944; d. Elbert Monroe and Mildred Rudolph (Patrick) Joines; m. James Richard Leonard, Aug. 31, 1963; children: James Richard II, Raymun Bradley. Student, Ea. Nazarene Coll., 1962-63; AA, Harford Community Coll., 1976; BS in Bus. Mgmt., U. Md., 1983. Sec. with U.S. Army, Aberdeen, Md., 1965-75; program analyst Facilities Engring., Aberdeen, Md., 1976-79; budget analyst Aberdeen Proving Ground Command, 1980; program analyst officer Facilities Engring., Aberdeen, Md., 1981; budget analyst Test and Evaluation Command, Aberdeen, Md., 1982-83, budget officer, 1985—; budget analyst Dept. of Army, Washington, 1984. Mem. Am. Soc. Mil. Comptrollers. Office: Aberdeen Proving Ground Test and Evaluation Command AMSTE-RM-B Aberdeen MD 21005

LEONARDIS, MARGIE MAY, commercial service corporation executive; b. Newark, Nov. 6, 1962; d. Thomas Anthony and Anna May (Nagle) L. Student, Seton Hall U., 1983—. Sec. Comml. Service Corp., Newark, 1980-82, acctg. adminstr., 1982-85, gen. mgr., 1985—; model Haynes and Co., Newark, 1981-83; cons. Venture Service Systems, Union, N.J., 1982—, VinTrac, Inc., Newark, 1987—; cons. United Lenders Service, Newark and Denver, 1988, sec. 1988—. Editor computer software Auto Recovery System, 1985. Campaign asst. Michael P. Buttone Assn., Newark, 1978; mem. com. Love Newark Com., 1988. Mem. Nat. Assn. Female Execs., Greater Newark C. of C. Roman Catholic. Club: J/B Travel (Union) (sec. 1987-88). Home: 37 Snyder Rd Fords NJ 08863 Office: Comml Service Corp 361 Grove St Newark NJ 07103

LEONARD-MCCONNELL, FLORENCE MULLINS, legal association administrator; b. Callaway, Va., Mar. 19, 1931; d. William Marshall and Fannie Lera (Prillaman) Mullins; m. Robert W. Leonard, June 24, 1950 (div. Mar. 1983); children: Susan Gail Leonard Little, William Ralph, Molly Marie; m. Edward B. McConnell, Oct. 21, 1984; stepchildren: Annalee, Marilyn, Edward B. Jr., Barbara, William. Grad high sch., Newport News, Va. Ednl. sec. guidance office James City County Oub. Schs., Williamsburg, 1975-77; asst. sec. to bd. dirs. Nat. Ctr. for State Cts., 1979-80, sec. to bd. dirs., 1980—, exec. sec. to exec. dir., 1977-79, adminstrv. asst. to exec. dir., 1979-88, asst. to pres., 1988—. Past bd. dirs. Newport News Operatic Soc., mem. exec. com. Presbyterian. Clubs: Kingsmill Women's Social, Kingsmill Book, Wednesday Morning Music (past bd. dirs., mem. exec. com.). Home: Mile Course Williamsburg VA 23185 Office: Nat Ctr for State Cts 300 Newport Ave Williamsburg VA 23187-8798

LEONARDO, ANN ADAMSON, marketing and sales executive, consultant; b. Hamilton, Lanark, Scotland, Jan. 4, 1944; d. James Walker and Margaret Patterson (Burnside) Adamson; m. John Constantine Leonardo, Jr., Mar. 29, 1975; 1 child, Elizabeth Margaret. BS in Mktg. and Bus., Ryerson Coll., 1970. Market research mgr. MacLaren Advt., Toronto, Can., 1965-70; group product mgr. Menley & James, Montreal, 1970-74; mktg. mgr. Maybelline Div.-Plough, Toronto, 1974-75; v.p. mktg. Van De Kamp's Bakery, Glendale, Calif., 1976-80; v.p. mktg. and sales Cal West Periodicals, Oakland, 1980-84; mktg. cons., Novato, Calif., 1984—; dir., pres. Family House Inc., San Francisco; dir. Marin Services for Women, Larkspur, Calif. Mem. Am. Mktg. Assn., Smithsonian Inst. Home: 102 La Merida Ct Novato CA 94945

LEONDAR, BARBARA, academic administrator; b. N.Y.C., Jan. 19, 1928; d. Marcy and Pauline (Spiwack) L.; m. Aaron Reuben Cohn, Dec. 21, 1947 (div. 1962); children: D'Vera, Daniel Charles, Joel Jacob. BA, NYU, 1947; MA, Calif. State U., Northridge, 1964; EdD, Harvard U., 1968. English tchr. Taft High Sch., Woodland Hills, Calif., 1960-64; asst. prof. Harvard U., Cambridge, 1967-68, 1969-72, U. Mass., Boston, 1968-69; asst. dean, assoc. prof. Rutgers U., New Brunswick, N.J., 1972-74; assoc. dean Boston U., 1974-80; v.p. acad. affairs Worcester (Mass.) State Coll., 1980-86; pres. U. Maine, Ft. Kent, Maine, 1986—. Editor: The Arts and Cognition, 1977; contbr. articles to prof. jours. Kent fellow Danforth Found., 1966-68, Fulbright fellow, 1984. Mem. Modern Lang. Assn., Am. Soc. for Aesthetics, Nat. Council Tchrs. of English, New England Assn. Schs. and Colls. (mem. various accreditation teams 1978-84). Office: U Maine Fort Kent Pleasant St Fort Kent ME 04743-1292

LEONE, JUDITH GIBSON, educational media specialist, video production company executive; b. Toms River, N.J., Sept. 27, 1945; d. James Delaney and Louise Gertrude (Eberhardt) Gibson; m. Stephan Robert Leone, Nov. 27, 1971; stepchildren: Cheryl, Debra. BA, Kean Coll., 1970; MLS, Rutgers U., 1980. Cert. edn. media specialist. Tchr. Toms River Sch., 1970-84, media specialist, 1984—; v.p., owner Prodn. House, Toms River, 1985—; mem. region 5 book eval. com. N.J. State Library System, 1986—. Sec., bd. dirs. The Shelter, Inc., Bricktown, N.J., 1979—. Mem. N.J. Ednl. Assn., Ednl. Media Assn. N.J., Ocean County Library Assn., Internat. TV Assn., Internat. Assn. Sch. Librarianship. Democrat. Club: Toms River Country. Home: 143 Cranmoor Dr Toms River NJ 08753 Office: Prodn House 46 Cranmoor Dr Toms River NJ 08753

LEONESIO-MONS, CLAUDIA CARRUTH, theater director, actress; b. Dinuba, Calif., Feb. 19, 1952; d. Harold Rhead and Ferne Carole (Hensley) Carruth; m. Carl Andrew Mons, Dec. 28, 1985. Cert., Santa Clara Valley Med. Ctr. Sch. Radiol. Tech., San Jose, Calif., 1973; student, W. Valley Coll., 1975-76; BA with honors, U. Calif., Santa Barbara, 1980. Coordinator performing arts Hutchinson (Kans.) Repertory Theatre, 1980-82; dir. Sunflower Puppeteers Recreation Services for Handicapped, Hutchinson, 1980-82; puppeteer Stony Creek Critters Puppet Theatre, Santa Cruz, Calif., 1982—; producing dir., v.p. Tri-Crown Family Theatre, Escondido, Calif. and Sterling, Kans., 1984; speaker, workshop leader Kans. Assn. Retarded Citizens, Topeka, 1980-82, Puppeteers of Am. Nat. Festival, Atlanta, 1982; guest speaker Profl. Businesswoman's Assn., Hutchinson, Kans., 1981; instr. Hutchinson Community Coll., 1981, Performing Arts Theatre of Handicapped, Carlsbad, Calif., 1985, bd. dirs. 1986-87; puppeteer Puppet Studio Theatre, Palo Alto and San Francisco, 1983; artistic dir. Starmakers Theatre Co., Carlsbad, 1984—, coll. artist in residence, Vista (Calif.) Unified Sch. Dist., Calif. Arts Council, 1986-87. Co-author: (play) A Candle for Everyman, 1980, (radio drama) Madre Theresa, 1982. Grants advisor Kans. Arts Commn., Topeka, 1981; vol. Concert for Spl. People Oceanside (Calif.) Jaycees, 1987. Named one of Outstanding Young Women of Am., 1981; recipient Cert. Assn. Kans. Theatre, 1982, Human Rights award Bahai Communities of North San Diego, 1987. Mem. Calif. Theatre Council, Assn. Theatre and Disability, Puppeteers of Am., San Diego Puppetry Guild. Democrat. Roman Catholic. Home: Rt 3 Box 330-C Escondido CA 92025 Office: Assn Retarded Citizens NC 550 W Vista Way Suite 200 Vista CA 92083

LEONG, CAROL JEAN, electrologist; b. Sacramento, Jan. 9, 1942; d. Walter Richard and Edith (Bond) Bloss; m. Oliver Arthur Fisk III, Apr. 12, 1964 (div. 1973); 1 child, Victoria Kay. BA in Sociology, San Jose (Calif.) State Coll., 1963; degree, Western Bus. Coll., 1964; cert. in electrolysis, Bay Area Coll. Electrolysis, 1978. Registered and cert. clin. profl. electrologist, Calif. Model various orgns., Calif., 1951-64; employment counselor Businessmen's Clearinghouse, Cin., 1966-67; dir. personnel Kroger Food Corp., Cin., 1967-68; prin. Carol Leong Electrolysis, San Mateo, Calif., 1978—; prin. Designs by Carol, San Mateo, 1987—. Contbr. articles to profl. publs. Recipient Cert. of Appreciation San Francisco Lighthouse for the Blind, 1981-82, 83. Mem. Internat. Guild Profl. Electrologists (mem. continuing edn. com.), Nat. Assn. Female Execs., Peninsula Humane Soc., San Francisco Zool. Soc., Friends of Filoli, AM. Electrologists Assn., Electrologists Assn. Calif., Chi Omega. Republican. Methodist. Home: 3339 Glendora Dr San Mateo CA 94403 Office: Carol Leong Electrolysis Suite 205 36 S El Camino Real San Mateo CA 94401

LEONIDOW, NATASHA MATRINA, nursing administrator; b. Nyack, N.Y., June 12, 1958; d. Paul and Matrina (Butich) L. AAS, Rockland Community Coll., 1979; BS in Nursing cum laude, SUNY Coll. Technology, Utica, 1982; MS in Nursing magna cum laude, Syracuse U., 1985. RN, N.Y.; cert. nurse adminstr. Staff nurse Englewood Hosp., N.J., 1979-80; charge nurse Mary Imogene Bassett Hosp., Cooperstown, N.Y., 1980-82, nursing service coordinator, 1983-86, asst. dir. systems devel., 1986-87; assoc. nursing practice coordinator Strong Meml. Hosp.-U. Rochester, N.Y., 1987—. Translator: Excellence in Russian Language, 1976 (Otrada award). Served as 1st lt. USAR, 1987—. Mem. Nat. League of Nursing, Sigma Theta Tau. Office: Strong Meml Hosp Elmwood Ave Rochester NY 14620

LEPERE, GENE HARRIET, home furnishings industry consultant; b. N.Y.C., Oct. 16, 1926; d. Joseph Herman and Jennie (Berman) Hirshhorn; A.B., U. So. Calif., 1949; M.B.A. with honors, Pace U., 1977; m. Edward M. Kelley, Sept. 11, 1955; m. 2d James E. LePere, Mar. 15, 1963. Mgr., Los Angeles County Probation Dept., 1955-63; v.p., gen. mgr. LePere, Inc., antiques and fine arts, N.Y.C., 1966-75; mgr. mktg. info. Furniture div. Sperry & Hutchinson Co., N.Y.C., 1976-79; owner, pres. Gene LePere Assos., Mt. Kisco, N.Y., 1979-83. Mem. Nat. Assn. Exec. Women, Internat. Women Writers Guild, The Authors Guild, Inc. Jewish. Author: Never Pass This Way Again, 1988; contbr. articles to profl. publs.

LEPOME, PENELOPE MARIE, rehabilitation counselor, educator; b. Buffalo, Dec. 17, 1945; d. Raymond Arthur and Mildred Evelyn (Johnson) Kramer; m. Robert Charles LePome, May 26, 1966 (div. Jan. 1982); children: Lisa Anne, Kathryn Jane, Robert Charles II. BA in Biology, SUNY, Buffalo, 1967; MS in Vocat. Rehab., U. Nev., Las Vegas, 1984. Cert. rehab. counselor; cert. substitute tchr., Nev. Co-owner, salesman Flamingo Realty, Las Vegas, Nev., 1974-76; substitute tchr. Clark County Sch. Dist., Las Vegas, 1969-74, 1982-84; adj. faculty Clark County Community Coll., Las Vegas, 1984-86, Truckee Meadows Community Coll., Reno, 1987; bus. and industry field specialist, Tng. Inst. Clark County Community Coll., 1985-86; probation officer on call Clark County Juvenile Services, Las Vegas, 1984; counselor Nike House, Las Vegas, 1984; mental health techician III, State of Nev., 1984-86 ; rehab. coordinator I, Nev. Bur. Vocat. Rehab., Reno, 1986—; pvt. practice rehab. counseling, 1984-86. Active Nev. Womens Polit. Caucus, Las Vegas, 1983-85 ; carnival chmn. Rex Bell PTA, Las Vegas, 1974-75, treas., 1975-76; leader Frontier Area Girl Scouts, Las Vegas, 1975-76, cookie sale chmn., 1980; treas., bd. dirs. Young Audiences, Las Vegas, 1979-80. N.Y. State Regents scholar, 1963. Mem. Am. Assn. Counseling & Devel., AAUW (div. officer Nev. 1983-85, pres. 1982-83, v.p. programming 1981-82, v.p. membership 1980-81, life mem.), Assn. Part-time Profls. (bd. dirs.), Nat. Rehabilitation Assn. Republican. Lodge: Toastmasters. Office: 1050 Matley Ln Reno NV 89502

LERCH, JUSTINE FREDERICKS, school principal; b. Wilmington, N.C., Nov. 8, 1948; d. Christine Fredericks L. BA, Lynchburg Coll., 1970; MEd, Duke U., 1975. Tchr. Peabody Sch., Wilmington, 1970-71, Pine Valley Sch., Wilmington, 1971-79; asst. prin. Sunset Park Jr. High Sch., Wilmington, 1979-80; prin. Edwin A. Alderman, Wilmington, 1980—. Pres. New Hanover County chpt. N.C. Symphony, 1988. Named Adminstr. of Yr. New Hanover County Bd. Edn., 1986, Adminstr. of Yr. First Union Nat. Bank, 1986, Prin of Yr. Wachovia Bank and Trust, 1986, 87, EOP Boss of Yr., 1988. Mem. Assn. Supervision and Curriculum Devel., N.C. Assn. Sch. Adminstrs., Phi Delta Kappa (sec. 1986-87, pres. 1987-88). Presbyterian. Office: Edwin A Alderman 2025 Independence Blvd Wilmington NC 28403

LERMAN, EILEEN R., lawyer; b. N.Y.C., May 6, 1947; d. Alex and Beatrice (Kline) L.; B.A., Syracuse U., 1969; J.D., Rutgers U., 1972; M.B.A., U. Denver, 1983. Admitted to N.Y. State bar, 1973, Colo. bar, 1976; atty. FTC, N.Y.C., 1972-74; corp. atty. RCA, N.Y.C., 1974-76; corp. atty. Samsonite Corp. and consumer products div. Beatrice Foods Co., Denver, 1976-78, assoc. gen. counsel, 1978—, asst. sec., 1979-85; ptnr. Davis, Lerman, & Weinstein, Denver, 1985—; dir. Legal Aid Soc. of Met. Denver, 1979-80. Bd. dirs., vice chmn. Colo. Postsecondary Ednl. Facilities Authority, 1981—; bd. dirs., treas. Am. Jewish Com., also v.p.; mem. Leadership Denver, 1983. Mem. Colo. Women's Bar Assn. (dir. 1980-81), ABA, Colo. Bar Assn. (bd. govs.), Denver Bar Assn., N.Y. State Bar Assn., Rutgers U. Alumni Assn. Lodge: Soroptimists. Home: 1018 Fillmore St Denver CO 80206 Office: Davis Lerman & Weinstein 50 S Steele St Suite 420 Denver CO 80209

LERMONDE, VIVIAN CLAIRE, communications consultant; b. Niagara Falls, N.Y., Mar. 14, 1949; d. Rufus Joseph and Marion Catherine (Ryan) L. BA in English, Ursuline Coll., Cleve., 1970; MA in English, John Carroll U., 1972. Legis aide Ohio Ho. of Reps., Columbus, 1973-79; sales mgr. Sheraton-Columbus, 1980-81; media person Ohio Senate, Columbus, 1981-83; cons. Lermonde Communications, Columbus, 1983—; tchr. pub. speaking communications skills dept. ColumbusState Community Coll., 1977—. Bd. dirs. Columbus Theater Ballet, 1979-81; mem. publicity com. Ohio Democratic Com., 1980; pres., co-founder Columbus Irish Feis, 1981. Roman Catholic. Club: Press (Columbus). Lodge: Ancient Order Hibernians (pres. Franklin County 1981-84, Ohio publicity chmn. 1987—, outstanding service award Franklin County 1985).

LERNER, BARBARA, public policy consultant, researcher, writer; b. Chgo., Mar. 31, 1935; d. Jacob Israel and Mary (Turen) L. BA with honors, U. Ill., 1956; MA, U. Chgo., 1961, PhD, 1965, JD, 1977. Bar: Ill. 1977; registered psychologist, Ill. Clin. psychologist Ill. Mental Health Ctr., Chgo., 1965-68; assoc. prof. Ohio U., Athens, 1968-70; pvt. practice clin. psychologist Chgo., 1970-78; assoc. prof. Roosevelt U., Chgo., 1972-74; study dir. Nat. Acad. Scis., Washington, 1977-78; pres. Lerner Assocs., Princeton, N.J., 1981—; assoc. editor U. Chgo. Law Rev., 1975-77; vis. scholar Ednl. Testing Service, Princeton, 1978-79, sr. research scientist, 1980-81; expert witness fed. cts. Debra P. vs. Turlington, Tampa, Fla., Marshall vs. Ga., 1983. Contbr. articles to profl. jours. Pres. nominee U.S. Dept. Edn., Washington, 1986; mem. adv. com. U.S. Commn. Civil Rights, N.J., 1985-87. Recipient Cert. of Appreciation award for outstanding service U.S. Dept. Edn., 1985. Mem. Am. Psychol. Assn., ABA, Nat. Council Measurement in Edn., Am. Ednl. Research Assn., Phi Beta Kappa, Sigma Xi. Jewish.

LERNER, GERDA M., historian, educator, author; b. Vienna, Austria, Apr. 30, 1920; came to U.S., 1939, naturalized, 1943; d. Robert and Ilona (Neumann) Kronstein; m. Carl Lerner, Oct. 6, 1941 (dec.); children: Stephanie, Daniel. B.A., New Sch. Social Research, 1963; M.A. (faculty scholar), Columbia U., 1965, Ph.D., 1966. Lectr. New Sch. Social Research, N.Y.C., 1963-65; asst. prof. L.I. U., 1965-67, assoc. prof., 1967-68; mem. faculty Sarah Lawrence Coll., Bronxville, N.Y., 1968-80; dir. Master's Program in Women's History, 1972-76, 78-79; ednl. dir. Summer Inst. in Women's History, 1976, 79; scholar-in-residence Rockefeller Found. Conf. Center, Bellagio, Italy, 1975; Robinson-Edwards prof. history U. Wis., Madison, 1980—, Wis. Alumni Research Found. sr. disting. research prof., 1984; co-dir. FIPSE grant for Promoting Black Women's History, 1980-83. Author: screenplay Black Like Me, 1964; novel No Farewell, 1955, The Grimke Sisters from South Carolina: Rebels Against Slavery, 1967; The Woman in American History, 1971, Black Women in White America: A Documentary History, 1972, The Female Experience: Documents in American History, 1976, A Death of One's Own, 1978, The Majority Finds its Past: Placing Women in History, 1979, Teaching Women's History, 1981, The Creation of Patriarchy, 1986. Social Sci. Research Council research fellow, 1970-71; Ford Found. grantee, 1978-79; Guggenheim fellow, 1980-81; Ednl. Found. Achievement award AAUW, 1986. Mem. Am. Hist. Assn., Orgn. Am. Historians (pres. 1981-82), AAUP, Authors League, Am. Studies Assn., PEN. Office: Univ Wisconsin Dept History 5123 Humanities Bldg 455 N Park St Madison WI 53706

LERNER, SUSAN A., psychologist; b. N.Y.C., Sept. 6, 1946; d. Harry and Annette (Ober) Herbst; B.A. cum laude, Queens Coll., CUNY, 1973; M.A., St. John's U., 1975; Ph.D., Howard U., 1980; m. Daniel J. Lerner, June 2, 1974; 1 son, Scott Paget. Prisoner liaison Queens House of Detention, Forest Hills, N.Y., 1972-73; grad. asst. dept. psychology Howard U., Washington, 1976-78; research asst. Human Resources Research Orgn., Alexandria, Va., 1978; staff psychologist, coordinator student tng. Gt. Oaks Ctr., Silver Spring, Md., 1978-82; staff psychologist Patuxent Instn., Jessup, Md., 1982-83; assoc. clin. dir. for mental health services PSI Assocs., Inc., Washington, 1983-84; dir. clin. services PSI Services Inc., Landover, Md., 1984-85; clin. adminstr. div. forensic programs St. Elizabeth's Hosp., Washington, 1986—; cons. Montgomery County Dept. Addictions, Victims, and Mental Health Services, Rockville, Md., 1986—, Montgomery County Pre-Release Ctr., Rockville, 1986—; cons. KHI Services Inc., Rockville; instr. dept. psychology Prince George's Community Coll., Largo, Md. NSF trainee, 1978-79. Mem. Am. Psychol. Assn., Md. Psychol. Assn., Eastern Psychol. Assn., Southeastern Psychol. Assn., D.C. Psychology Assn., Nat. Honor Soc. in Psychology. Contbr. to microfilms in field. Home: 12621 Red Pepper Ct Germantown MD 20874

LERNER, SUZAN BARBARA, catering company executive; b. N.Y.C., May 7, 1944; d. Jack Michael and Sophie (Nachman) L. BA in Sociology, Marymount Coll., 1988. Ptnr. Elegant Evening, Inc., Bklyn., 1980—; owner, mgr. Creative Kitchens, Ltd., Bklyn., 1988—. Editor: Hypotensive Surgery, 1970. Sec.-treas. Roosevelt Reform Dems., Bklyn., 1964; dir. Citizens for Robert F. Kennedy, Bklyn., 1964. Mem. Soc. for Advancement Food Research in Am., Soc. for Am. Cuisine, Roundtable for Women, Nat. Assn. Female Execs. Jewish. Office: Creative Kitchens Ltd 1801 Stillwell Ave Brooklyn NY 11229

LERSCH, DELYNDEN RIFE, engineering manager; b. Grundy, Va., Mar. 22, 1949; d. Woodrow and Eunice Louise (Atwell) Rife; B.S. in E.E., Va. Poly. Inst. and State U., 1970; postgrad. Boston U., 1975—; m. John Robert Lersch, May 9, 1976; children—Desmond, Kristofer. With Stone & Webster Engrng. Corp., 1970—, elec. engr., supr. computer applications, Boston, 1978-80, mgr. computer graphics, 1980-84, mgr. engrng. systems and computer graphics, 1984-87, div. chief info. techs., 1987—. Named Stone and Webster's Woman Engr. of Yr., 1976, 79; Mass. Solar Energy Research grantee, 1978; honored by Engrng. News Record mag. for contbns. to constrn. industry, 1983. Mem. Assn. Women in Sci., Soc. Women Engrs. (sr.), IEEE (sr.), Women in Sci. and Engring., Energy Communicators, Nat. Computer Graphics Assn., Profl. Council New Eng., Nuclear Energy Women (dir. Mass. chpt. 1978, New Eng. region 1979), LWV. Congregationalist. Club: Boston Bus. and Profl. Women's. Author: Cable Schedule Information Systems As Used in Power Plant Construction, 1973, 2d edit., 1975; Information Systems Available for Use by Electrical Engineers, 1976; contbr. articles in field of computer aided design and engring. Home: 6 Blue Skye Dr Hingham MA 02043 Office: 245 Summer St Boston MA 02101

LESAC, CAROLYN JO, surgery educator; b. Milw., May 17, 1955; d. Joseph F. and Carolyn (Hightower) LeS. BS, Miss. Coll., 1977; postgrad., Va. Commonwealth U., 1987—. Critical Care RN, registered Emergency Med. Technician, paramedic. Staff nurse Elmbrook Meml. Hosp., Brookfield, Wis., 1977-79; coordinator cardiovascular services Milw. Regional Med. Ctr., 1979-83; coordinator critical care edn. Med. Coll. Va., Richmond, 1983-85, asst. prof Surgery, dir. Advanced Life Support Ctr., 1985—; cons. advanced life support Richmond area, 1983—. Contbr. articles to profl. jours. Paramedic Tuckahoe Vol. Rescue Squad, Richmond, 1986—. Research grantee Smith, Kline, and French Pharms., Richmond, 1987. Mem. Am. Assn. Critical Care Nurses (local pres. 1986-87), Nat. Assn. Female Execs. Mailing Address: NCV Station Box 44 Richmond VA 23298

LESCH, ANN MOSELY, political scientist, educator; b. Washington, Feb. 1, 1944; d. Philip Edward and Ruth (Bissell) Mosely; B.A., Swarthmore Coll., 1966; Ph.D., Columbia U., 1973. Research asso. Fgn. Policy Research Inst., Phila., 1972-74; asso. Middle East rep. Am. Friends Service Com, Jerusalem, 1974-77; Middle East program officer Ford Found., N.Y.C., 1977-80, program officer, Cairo, 1980-84; assoc. Univs. Field Staff Internat., 1984-87; assoc. prof. Villanova U., 1987—. Bd. dirs. Am. Near East Refugee Aid, 1980-86; mem. Quaker UN Com., 1979-80; mem. U.S. adv. com. Interns for Peace, 1978-82. Fellow Catherwood Found., 1965; NDFL fellow, 1967-71. Mem. Middle East Studies Assn., Middle East Inst., Am. Polit. Sci. Assn. Unitarian. Author: Political Perceptions of the Palestinians on the West Bank and Gaza, 1980; Arab Politics in Palestine, 1979; The Politics of Palestinian Nationalism, 1973; contbr. articles to profl. jours. Office: Villanova Univ Polit Sci Dept Villanova PA 19085

LESH, ANGELA DAWN, marketing executive; b. Altadena, Calif., Dec. 23, 1947; d. Olin Eugene and Betty Jean (Carroll) Lesh; m. Michael James Cussen, Nov. 20, 1974 (div. July 1981); m. John A. Czepiel. B.A. in Rhetoric, U. Calif.-Davis, 1970; M.A. in Communications, Calif. State U.-Sacramento, 1971. Jr. research analyst Doremus, San Francisco, 1971-73; market research analyst Med. Care Found., Sacramento, 1973; dir. market research Wells Fargo Bank, San Francisco, 1973-78; sr. project mgr. Shaklee Corp., San Francisco, 1978-79; pres. A. Dawn Lesh & Assocs., Kensington, Calif., 1979-81; dir. market research Bank of Am., San Francisco, 1981-86; v.p. strategic planning and mktg. research N.Y. Stock Exchange, 1986—, v.p. strategic planning, mktg. research. Mem. Am. Mktg. Assn. (dir. 1983-84), Women in Communication Fields (founder), Advt. Research Found. Fin. Research Council (co-chmn. fin. workshop 1984), Mktg. Sci. Inst., Fin. Women's Assn., Calif. Aggie Alumni Assn. Democrat. Home: 110 Bleecker St Apt 12 New York NY 10012 Office: The NY Stock Exchange 11 Wall St 17th Floor New York NY 10005

LESHANE, PATRICIA ROLAND, lobbyist; b. Binghamton, N.Y., July 19, 1954; d. Ralph M. and Cecelia M. (Gearon) R.; m. Patrick J. Sullivan, Sept. 5, 1986. BS in Urban Planning, Springfield (Mass.) Coll., 1976; M. in Health Care Adminstrn., Hartford (Conn.) Grad. Ctr., 1983. Youth dir. Middlesex YMCA, Middletown, Conn., 1975-77; extension 4-H agt. U. Conn., Storrs, 1977-79; dir. planning Easter Seal Soc. of Conn., Hebron, 1979-83; ptnr. Sullivan & LeShane, Hartford, 1983—; corporator Springfield (Mass.) Coll. Mem. Hartford Rehab. Ctr., 1986. Recipient Young Alumni award Springfield Coll., 1986; named one of Women of the Time, Hartford Advocate, Women to Watch Hartford Women, 1988. Mem. Assn. of Entrepreneurial Women, 1985—. Democrat. Roman Catholic. Home: 14 Essex Ct Farmington CT 06032 Office: Sullivan & LeShane 287 Capitol Ave Hartford CT 06106

LESLIE, ELOISE MYRETTA, municipal administrator; b. Ruston, La., Sept. 10, 1943; d. Sammie and Velma (Bunch) Williams; m. Peyton Hawkins Leslie, Sr.; children: LaSandra Patrice Bartee, Phylisa Carlette, Eric Lamont, Peyton Hawkins Jr. AA, Grambling (La.) State, 1966, KCK Community Coll., Kansas City, Kans., 1987. Office mgr. Jones & Willis, D.D.S. Inc., Kansas City, 1975-76; bookkeeper DRAG, Alcohol Treatment Ctr., Kansas City, 1979; intake analyst City of Kansas City, 1979-83, employment supr., 1983—; Sec. Human Relations Commn., Kansas City, 1979-81. Active Dem. Women's Fedn., Kansas City, 1986—; bd. dirs. Democracy, Inc., Kansas City, 1983—. Mem. IMPA, Personnel Mgrs. Roundtable, Kans. Rehab. Services Employers Council, Kansas City Community Coll. Placement, Women's C. of C., Grambling Alumni Assn., Am. Soc. for Pub. Adminstrn. Democrat. Baptist. Club: Young Matrons. Home: 5720 Georgia Kansas City KS 66104 Office: Mcpl Office Bldg 701 N 7th St Kansas City KS 66101

LESLIE, INGELIN LØNØ, nursing administrator; b. Horten, Vestfold, Norway, Jan. 6, 1953; came to U.S., 1976; d. Thor Lønø and Randi (Kroken) Johansen; m. John Franklin Leslie, Jan. 10, 1976; children: Timothy Franklin, Inger Joyce. Diploma, Fredrikstad Realskole, Norway, 1970; postgrad., Møre Folkehøyskole Ålesund, Norway, 1970-71; diploma, Østfold Sykepleierskole, Norway, 1975; postgrad., Kans. State U., 1986—. RN, Calif., Ind., Kans., Wis. Staff nurse Rikshospitalet, Oslo, 1975-76, U. Wis. Hosps. and Clinics, Madison, 1976-79; staff nurse, asst. head nurse Alexian Bros. Hosp., San Jose, Calif., 1979-81; staff nurse Union Hosp., Terre Haute, Ind., 1981-82, Terre Haute Regional Hosp., 1983-84; supr. nursing The St. Mary Hosp., Manhattan, Kans., 1984—. Mem. Am. Nurses Assn. Presbyterian. Home: 2921 Hickory Ct Manhattan KS 66502-3115 Office: The St Mary Hosp 1823 College Ave Manhattan KS 66502

LESSE, ETTA GORDON (MRS. S. MICHAEL LESSE), psychiatric social worker; b. Trenton, N.J.; d. H. Charles and Rose (Miers) Gordon; B.A., Beaver Coll.; M.Social Sci., Smith Coll.; postgrad. Bryn Mawr Coll. Sch. Social Economy; U. Pa. Sch. Social Work; m. S. Michael Lesse; children—Toni Gordon and Cathy Ross (twins). Exec. sec. Clinic for Child Psychiatry, Temple U. Med. Sch., Phila.; psychiat. social worker Bur. Family Service, Orange, N.J., Family Welfare Soc., Newport, R.I.; intake worker Bur. Family Service, Orange, N.J.; case supr., asst. to chief social worker VA, Phila.; consultant for social agys. and ct. Social and health counsellor to Draft Bd., Orange, N.J.; organizer steering com. for establishment case work sect. Council Social Agys., Newport, R.I.; chmn. Workshop for Profl. Social Workers Lehigh Valley; group chmn. regional conf. pub. edn. Gov.'s Commn. Pub. Edn., Pa. Gov.'s Commn. on Aging; cons. foster home devel. Northampton County Children's Aid Soc.; profl. participant in religion and psychiatry seminars, Easton, Pa.; interviewer Easton-Phillipsburg (Pa.) Commn. Human Relations; mem. adv. bd. Northeastern region Pa. Dept. Pub. Welfare. Lectr. to child study group PTA, Easton, Pa. Bd. dirs. Lehigh Valley Center Performing Arts Assn., v.p.; bd. dirs. Lehigh Valley Community Council, 1975—, Planned Parenthood of Northampton County; exec. bd. Am. Heart Assn., 1978—; mem. adv. bd. Jr. League of Lehigh Valley. Mem. Nat. Assn. Social Workers, Acad. Certified Social Workers, AAUW (past br. pres., dir. Eastern br., chmn. career advancement loan fund, named Outstanding Woman of Yr. 1981-82, founder, chair meml. fund 1987—), Lehigh Valley Mental Health Assn. (dir., chmn. com. on personnel and nominating), Allentown Art Mus., Women's Com. Phila. Assn. Psychoanalysis, Northampton County Med. Soc. Aux., (dir. 1980—, v.p., pres., chmn. scholarships, chmn. med. and profl. nursing students loan fund), Phila. Orch. Assn., Met. Opera Assn., Smith Coll. Alumni Assn. Contbg. author Two Hundred Years of Life in Northampton County, Pa. Home: 2768 Stephens St Easton PA 18042

LESSENDEN, EDITH ANN FLEMING, writer, monologist; b. Garden City, Kans., Jan. 21, 1922; d. Arthur Milo and Edith Ann (Hambleton) Fleming; m. Chester Merral Lessenden, June 1, 1943; children—Sandra L. Lessenden; Marged L. Amend, Eve L. Supica, Mark Charles. A.B., Kans. U., 1946, M.A., 1952. Editor-writer Med. Aux. News, Kans., 1958-60, Allegro, Topeka Symphony, 1970-86; writer, dir. musical revues; contbr. articles to various publs. Organizer, chmn. Symphony League, Topeka, 1966-70, bd. dirs., 1966—; bd. dirs. Kans. Med. Aux., 1958—, pres., 1964-65; bd. dirs. AMA Aux., 1970-77, fund-raiser, 1973-75, regional v.p. 1975-77. Recipient Charles Marling award Topeka Symphony Soc., 1984. Mem. Nat. League Am. Pen Women (Roller award 1985, pres. Topeka br. 1986-88, pres. Kans. chpt. 1988—), Kans. Authors Club, P.E.O. (chpt. pres. 1959-60, coop. bd. pres. 1961-62), Mortar Bd. Republican. Methodist. Clubs: Minerva (pres. 1963-64), Western sorosis (pres. 1980-81). Avocations: French conversation; sewing; needlepoint; reading.

LESTCH, MAXINE ELLEN, psychologist; b. N.Y.C., June 21, 1952; d. Murray H. and Dorothy (Kapelner) L. Student, U. Vienna, 1970, U. Nicaragua, 1971; BS, Wilmington Coll., 1972; MS, U. Chgo., 1974; PhD, Fordham U., 1984. Licensed psychologist N.Y. Psychologist Mens Prison Hosp. Rikers Island, N.Y.C., 1974-75, Puerto Rican Inst. Family Services, N.Y.C., 1975-76, Rusk Inst. Rehab. Med., N.Y.C., 1977-78, Com. Handicapped Bd. Edn. N.Y.C., 1979—; therapist Met. Ctr. for Mental Health. Mem. Am. Psychol. Assn., Clin. Guidance Bd. Edn. Office: Clin Guidance 347 Baltic St Brooklyn NY 11201

LESTER, CYNTHIA JO, dean of students, counselor; b. Terrell, Tex., Nov. 30, 1947; d. Joe Edward and Zelma Mae (Cathey) Moffitt; m. William Lee Ray Lester, Aug. 10, 1970 (div. Dec. 1983); 1 child, Cinda Lee. BA, East Tex. State U., 1971, postgrad., 1988—; MEd, SW Tex. State U., 1973; postgrad., Wichita State U., 1982. Cert. elem. tchr. Tchr. reading and lang. arts San Antonio Ind. Sch. Dist., 1971-74; reading specialist Kingman (Kans.) Jr. High, 1974-80, Riley Jr. High Sch., Great Bend, Kans., 1980-81; tchr. Plainville (Kans.) Elem. Sch., 1981; dir. Chickasia Handicapped Pre-Sch., Kingman, 1982; dir., adminstr. Kingman County Girls Home, 1982-83; tchr. Quinlan (Tex.) Ins. Sch. Dist., 1983-87, adminstrv. asst., 1985—, dean of students, 1987—; tutor, counselor, foster parent Kingman County Girls Home, 1981-83. Election judge Quinlan Mayoral Elections, 1985, election clk., 1987; co-chmn. St. Jude's Bike-A-Thon, Quinlan, 1987; spl. adv., vol. Foster Child Adv. Services, Dallas, 1987—. 21st Annual Petroleum Inst. fellow U. Houston, 1984. Mem. Quinlan Classroom Tchrs. Assn. (pres. 1985-86, sec. 1984-85), Tex. Classroom Tchrs. Assn., Tex. Computer Educators Assn., Nat. Assn. for Female Execs., Nat. Assn. Student Activity Advisors, Phi Delta Kappa, Epsilon Sigma Alpha. Democrat. Baptist. Home: 1613 Amesbury Rockwall TX 75087 Office: Quinlan Mid Sch 401 N Kuykendall Rural Rt 3 PO Box 18 Quinlan TX 75474

LESUEUR, JOAN KAVANAUGH, librarian; b. Mt. Sterling, Ky., Nov. 16, 1929; d. Joe Miller and Nancy Hall (Clay) Kavanaugh; m. Alexander Armand Lesueur, Sept. 7, 1960; 1 child, Alexander Armand Jr. AB in Edn., U. Ky., 1951, MA in Spanish, 1954, MS in Library Sci., 1971. Tchr. Douglas County High Sch., Douglasville, Ga., 1951-52, Pinkerton High Sch. and Midway (Ky.) Jr. Coll., 1953-55, 1956-59; tchr. Coll. High Sch., Bartlesville, Okla., 1955-56; asst. prof. Spanish Morehead (Ky.) State U., 1959-61, 62-63, 64-65; inst. library sci. Western Carolina U., Cullowhee, N.C., 1968-78; librarian Canton (N.C.) Jr. High Sch., 1978—. Pres. Jackson County and Haywood County Cancer Soc., Sylva and Waynesville, N.C., 1982-83, 85-86; bd. dirs. N.C. div. Am. Cancer Soc., Raleigh, 1982-86. Named Tchr. of Yr. Haywood County N.C. Educators, 1984. Mem. Am. Assn. Sch. Librarians, N.C. Assn. Sch. Librarians (presenter media program 1986), N.C. Assn. Educators (state pres. support personnel div. 1982-83, bd. dirs. 1982-83, Outstanding Mem. award 1987), Nat. Cathedral Assn. Diocese Western N.C. (co-chmn. 1978-81), Phi Delta Kappa (sec.-treas. Western Carolina chpt., Outstanding Tchr. award Western Carolina chpt. 1981), Delta Kappa Gamma, Beta Phi Mu, Blue Grass Soc. Colonial Daughters of 17th Century, Kappa Kappa Gamma, Daughters of 1812 Ky., DAR. Episcopalian (vestryman, lay reader). Home: 209 Pigeon St Waynesville NC 28786 Office: Canton Jr High Sch 60 S Penland Canton NC 28716

LETRENT-JONES, TONY GUPTON, marketing professional; b. Rocky Mount, N.C., June 24, 1950; d. Talmadge Louis and Evelyn Hortense (Farmer) Gupton; m. Santo Anthony LeTrent, Sept. 9, 1972 (div Apr. 1976); m. Alfred Earle Jones, Mar. 21, 1981. BA in Psychology, Sociology, U. N.C., 1972. Instr. Bus. Career Inst., Fayetteville, N.C., 1973; prodn. planner Blue Bell, Inc., Wilson, N.C., 1973-75; mfg. mgmt. trainee Blue Bell, Inc., Lillington, N.C., 1975-76, office mgr., sr. planner, 1976-78; product mgr. Blue Bell, Inc., Greensboro, N.C., 1978-82, mdse. mgr., 1982-84; mdse. mgr. H.H. Cutler, Grand Rapids, Mich., 1984-85; dir. merchandising, design Ithaca Industries, Inc., Wilkesboro, N.C., 1985-86; pres. TLJ Enterprises, Greensboro, 1987—; cons. Hanes Knitware, Winston-Salem, N.C., 1987. Vol. Commn. Status of Women, Greensboro. Mem. Preservation Soc., Nat. Assn. Female Execs. Democrat. Baptist. Home and Office: 304-C N Lindell Rd Greensboro NC 27403

LETZIG, BETTY JEAN, association executive; b. Hardin, Mo., Feb. 18, 1926; d. Robert H. and Alina Violet (Mayes) L. B.A., Scarritt Coll., 1950, M.A., 1968. Ednl. staff The Methodist Ch., Ark., Okla. Tex., 1953-60; staff exec. Nat. Div. United Meth. Ch., N.Y.C., 1960—; coordinator Mission Personnel Support Services, 1984—. Contbr. articles to profl. jours. Bd. dirs. Internat. Services Assn. for Health, Inc., Atlanta, 1974—, Vellore Christian Med. Coll., N.Y.C., 1984—; mem. U.S. com. Internat. Council Social Welfare, Washington, 1983—; active Nat. Interfaith Coalition on Aging, Athens, Ga., 1972—, pres., 1981-85. Recipient Deaconess Exchange award Commn. Deaconess Work, 1961-62. Mem. Nat. Council Aging, Nat. Voluntary Orgns. Ind. Living for Aging (exec. com. 1978-84), Nat. Council Social Welfare, Older Women's League. Methodist. Avocations: travel; beachcombing; photography; needlework. Home: 235 E 22d St Apt 1U New York NY 10010 Office: Nat Program Div Gen Bd Global Ministries 475 Riverside Dr Room 300 New York NY 10115

LEUNG, BETTY BRIGID, nurse; b. Shanghai, People's Rep. China, Oct. 28, 1949; d. Chek Sang and Si Iun (Vong) L. Diploma, St. James Sch. Nursing, 1974; BSN, Hunter-Bellevue Sch. Nursing, 1985, postgrad., 1986—. Nurse ICU St. James Mercy Hosp., Hornell, N.Y., 1974-80; sr. staff ICU NYU Med. Ctr., N.Y.C., 1980-81, nurse clinician, 1981-85, asst. clin. coordinator, 1985—. St. James Sch. Nursing scholar, 1972-74. Mem. Am. Assn. Critical Care Nurses. Roman Catholic. Office: NYU Med Ctr 560 First Ave New York NY 10016

LEUNG, LINA LEE, real estate developer; b. Macau, July 5, 1932; came to U.S., 1956; d. Chu Ho and Fok Yee (Leung) Lee; m. Kamman Francis Leung, July 26, 1959; children: Eileen, Elaine, Wing, Wesley. BA in Lit., U. Hong Kong, 1954; degree in home econs., Glendale Coll., 1959, Calif. State U., 1962. Cons. Li Chung Shing Tong Patent Medicine Manufactury, Hong Kong, 1950—, internat. mktg. cons., 1956—; owner, pres. Kam Co., Los Angeles, 1952—, Chang Shu-Chi Art Studio, Los Angeles, 1963—; owner, founder South Sea Investment and Mgmt., Los Angeles, 1978—; chmn., chief exec. officer Golden Capital Enterprise, Los Angeles, 1982—; founder Ea. Savs. Bank, Alhambra, Calif., 1984—; chmn. Golden Summit Enterprises, Inc., Los Angeles, 1986—; ptnr., treas. Seven Star Investment Group, Los Angeles, 1973—. Bd. dirs. Leong Family Assn. So. Calif., Los Angeles, 1984. Mem. Hong Kong Assn. So. Calif., Apt. Owners Assn. So. Calif., Apt. Assn. Greater Los Angeles, Chinese C. of C. Los Angeles. Democrat. Buddhist. Home: 1260 Mill Ln San Marino CA 91108 Office: South Sea Investment and Mgmt Co 767 N Hill St Suite 304 Los Angeles CA 90012

LEUS MCFARLEN, PATRICIA CHERYL, water chemist; b. San Antonio, Mar. 12, 1954; d. Norman W. and Jacqueline S. (Deason) Leus; m. Randy N. McFarlen, June 28, 1986. AA, Highline Community Coll., 1974; BS in Chemistry, Eastern Wash. U., 1980. Lab. technician, oil analyst D.A. Lubricant, Vancouver, Wash., 1982-83; plant chemist Navajo Generating Sta., Page, Ariz., 1983—. Sci. judge Page Schs. Sci. Project Fair, 1985; chemist Navajo Generating Sta./Page Sch. Career Day, 1986. Mem. Am. Chem. Soc., Sigma Kappa (treas. 1976-78). Methodist. Office: Navajo Generating Sta Chem Dept PO Box W Page AZ 86040

LEVACK, ANN MARIE, producer, talent consultant; b. N.Y.C., Sept. 11, 1940; d. Arthur Paul and Helen G. (O'Brien) L. B.A., Marymount Coll., 1962. Dir. spl. promotions Muscular Dystrophy Assn., N.Y.C., 1974-81, N.Y. assoc. producer Jerry Lewis Telethon, 1978-81; adminstrv. dir. Actors & Dirs. Lab., N.Y.C., 1982-83; producer Salute to Corp. Stars, Leukemia Soc., N.Y.C., 1984, 85, 86, Gospel According to Della, N.Y.C., 1985; talent cons. CBS-TV, N.Y.C., 1985—; bd. dirs. 42nd St. Theatre Row, N.Y.C., 1982-83. Alt. del. Democratic 1st Jud. Dist. Conv., N.Y.C., 1984; Mem. N.Y. County com. 63d Dem. Assembly, 1985; mem. exec. com. Mid-Manhattan-New Dem. Club, N.Y.C., 1985—. Roman Catholic. Club: Can. Women's of N.Y. (N.Y.C.). Home: 951 1st Ave New York NY 10022

LEVALLEY, JOAN CATHERINE, accountant; b. Decatur, Ill., Nov. 27, 1931; d. Clarence and Pearl Mae (McClure) Krall; m. Charles R. LeValley, Apr. 13, 1958 (div.); children—Curtis Ray, Cara Marie. B.A. in Bus., Manchester Coll., 1957. Acct. with various firms, 1960-76; pvt. practice acctg., Park Ridge, Ill., 1964-79; pres., dir. LeValley & Assocs., Inc., Park Ridge, 1979—. Mem. Nat. Assn. Pub. Accts., Ind. Acct. Assn. Ill. (2d woman pres. 1987-88), Bus. and Profl. Women Park Ridge (pres. 1974-75, Bus. Woman of Yr. 1983), Park Ridge C. of C. (treas. 1985-87). Baptist. Avocations: baking; sewing; gardening. Home: 1215 Linden Ave Park Ridge IL 60068 Office: LeValley & Assocs Inc 841 W Touhy Ave Park Ridge IL 60068

LEVBARG, DIANE, fashion industry executive; b. Mar. 18, 1950; d. Morrison Levbarg and Ann-Louise Lewis; m. Martin I. Klein, May 23, 1974. Cert. in retail studies Coll. for Distributive Trades, London; student Vassar Coll., 1972. Exec. Trainee Harrods, London, 1970-71; exec. trainee, asst. dept. mgr., asst. buyer Saks Fifth Ave, N.Y.C., 1971-73; asst. buyer, buyer Bonwit Teller, N.Y.C., 1973-75; merchandise mgr. Bloomingdale's, N.Y.C., 1975-82; pres., fashion cons. Diane Levbarg & Assocs. Inc., N.Y.C., 1982—; exec. v.p. Missoni U.S.A.; v.p. Nina Ricci; cons. Daniel Hechter, Christian Dior U.S.A., Bogner U.S.A.; adv. bd. Lab Inst. of Mdsing. V.P., James Beard Affiliate, City Meals-on-Wheels. Named One of 100 Women of Promise, Good Housekeeping. Address: 200 E 72d St New York NY 10021

LEVE, TERESA LISA, auditor; b. Phila., Oct. 28, 1962; d. Richard Charles and Therese (Dowling) L. BBA, Shippensburg U., 1984; postgrad., Loyola Coll., Balt., 1985-86. CPA, Md. Fin. adminstr. for B-1 Bomber program Westinghouse Def. and Electric Ctr., Balt., 1984-86; internal auditor Westinghouse Electric Ctr., Balt., 1986-87, sr. auditor, 1987—, co-capt. Md. spl. Olympic team, 1985-86, co-capt. cystic fybrosis team, 1985-87. Mem. Inst. Internal Auditors, Nat. Assn. Female Execs., Columbia Assn. Roman Catholic. Office: Westinghouse DOC PO Box 746 MS 1706 Baltimore MD 20206

LE VECQUE, CHARLOTTE ROSE, clinical social worker, psychotherapist; b. Darby, Pa., Nov. 11, 1944; d. George Alfred and Charlotte Vivian (Bungart) Le V.; B.S., Western Mich. U., 1966; M.S.W., Adelphi U., 1968. Diplomat clin. social work. Psychiat. social worker Patton State Hosp., Patton, Calif., 1968-71; sr. psychiat. social worker mental health unit San Bernardino (Calif.) County Hosp., 1971-74; licensed clin. social worker dept. psychiatry So. Calif. Permanente Med. Group, Fontana, Calif., 1974-86, dir. social services, 1986—. Lic. clin. social worker; cert. social worker, N.Y. Mem. Acad. Cert. Social Workers, Soc. Clin. Social Work, Soc. Hosp. Social Workers, Nat. Assn. Social Workers, Nat. Registry Health Care Providers, Alpha Omicron Pi. Democrat. Clubs: American Fox Terrier, Western Fox Terrier Breeders Assn. (bd. govs. 1973, 78, 84, editor Kliptails 1984, 85, v.p. 1987), Orange Empire Terrier Group (v.p. 1984, bd. dirs. 1987, chmn. show com. 1987—), San Bernardino Humane Soc., Kennel Club of Palm Springs (v.p. terrier group 1985, corr. sec. 1986). Office: 9985 Sierra Ave Bldg 7 Fontana CA 92336

LEVELL, ROSEMOND HULL, disability analyst; b. N.Y.C., Mar. 15, 1939; d. Roseman and Eva Adela (Wright) Hull; m. David S. Levell, June 20, 1959; 1 child, Marsha Levell-Braggs. B.A., Queens Coll., 1976; M.Profl. Studies in Disability Determination, NYU, 1984. Tchr. Bd. Edn., N.Y.C., 1977-79; social service disability analyst Office of Disability Determinations, N.Y.C., 1979—; social service disability analyst-liaison to Social Security Adminstrn. Dist. Office 120, Jamaica, N.Y., 1984—. Own Cambria Heights Sports Com., N.Y., 1978, 232 Block Assn., Cambria Heights, 1975-84. Seek Ace scholar Queens Coll.; N.Y. State Dept. Social Services grantee NYU. Mem. Nat. Assn. U. Women (chpt. sec. 1983—), Nat. Assn. Disability Examiners, Pub. Employees Fedn. (sec. black caucus Office Disability Determinations div. 1983-85). Episcopalian. Club: NYU (N.Y.C.). Home: 116-48 232d St Cambria Heights NY 11411 Office: 92-31 Union Hall St Jamaica NY 11433

LEVENSON, INA, dermatologist; b. Bklyn., Feb. 21, 1939; d. Hyman Al and Jeanne (Samilowitz) Gilbert; m. Ernest Levenson, Jan. 1962; children: Adam, Nathan. BA, NYU, 1960; MD, SUNY, Bklyn., 1964. Intern pediatrics Univ. Hosp. and Hillman Clinic, Ala., 1964-65; resident in dermatology Marquette U. Affiliated Program, Milw., 1965-69; dermatologist Med.-Surg. Clinic, Milw., 1969-71, Assocs. in Dermatology, Milw., 1971-81; practice medicine specializing in dermatology Milw., 1981—; cons. in field. Contbr. articles to profl. jours. Fellow Am. Acad. Dermatology; mem. Am. Soc. Dermatol. Surgeons, Wis. Dermatol. Soc., Wis. Women Entrepreneurs, Phi Beta Kappa. Jewish. Home: 12247 W Verona Ct West Allis WI 53227 Office: 2011 10th Ave South Milwaukee WI 53172 also: 9200 W Loomis Rd Franklin WI 53132

LEVENTHAL, SHEILA SMITH, educator; b. Raymondville, Tex., May 4, 1941; d. M. C. and Jessie Mae (Sansom) Smith; m. Ira Yale Leventhal, Aug. 5, 1966; 1 child, Adam Yale. B.S., N. Tex. State U., 1963, M.Ed., 1965; postgrad. Nova U., 1972, MIT, 1979. Elem. tchr. Grapevine Pub. Schs. (Tex.), 1963-65; tchr., team leader Lamplighter Sch., Dallas, 1965—, mem. steering com., computer staff, 1979-84. Staff mem. Episcopal Sch. of Spirituality, Dallas, 1983. Mem. NEA, Tex. Tchrs. Assn., Women of St. Francis (v.p. Dallas 1983), Phi Delta Kappa. Home: 2947 Talisman Dr Dallas TX 75229 Office: Lamplighter Sch 11611 Inwood Rd Dallas TX 75229

LEVENTHAL, TERI V., communications executive; b. N.Y.C., Feb. 23, 1932; d. Solomon Edward and Lillian Francis (Taub) Feldman; m. Herbert Leventhal, May 29, 1957; children: Lawrence Richard, Sheryl Ann, Neil Richard. BS, Bridgeport U., 1953; postgrad., CCNY, 1979-82. Dental hygienist Dept. Health, N.Y.C., 1953-59; market researcher Market Research Inc., N.Y.C., 1971-73; tchr. Bd. Cooperative Edn., N.Y.C., 1973-82; pres. All Media Communication Corp., N.Y.C., 1982-84, TVL Media Assocs. Inc., N.Y.C., 1984—; telemktg. cons. Saslow, N.Y.C., 1983-86, Econodent, N.Y.C., 1984-86, Island Dental, N.Y.C., 1986—, Met. Life, L.I. Pres. chpt. Hadassah, Baldwin, N.Y., 1971-73; rep. Civic Assn., Baldwin, Freeport, N.Y., 1981-85; bd. dirs. YMHA, Baldwin, 1978-82. Named Woman of Yr. Hadassah, N.Y.C., 1969; recipient Pres.' award Hadassah, N.Y.C., 1973, Service awards, 1964-84. Mem. Nat. Assn. Female Execs., Am. Soc. Tng. Devel. (advt. com.), Long Island Assn. Republican. Jewish. Club: Presidents. Office: TVL Media Assocs 223 Jericho Turnpike Mineola NY 11501

LEVERS, LISA LOPEZ, health science facility administrator; b. Massillon, Ohio, Jan. 24, 1952; d. Robert Elwood and Gloria Isabella (Lopez) L. BA in English Lit., Kent (Ohio) State U., 1974, MEd in Rehab. Counseling, 1975, PhD in Counseling and Human Development, 1987—. Lic. profl. clin. counselor, social worker, Ohio. Trainer, counselor drug abuse Town Hall II, Kent, 1974-76; counselor, adv. client's rights Western Res. Psychiat., Northfield, Ohio, 1976; counselor mental health Western Res. Human Services, Akron, Ohio, 1976-86; dir. case mgmt. services The Counseling Ctr. Wayne and Holmes Counties, Wooster, Ohio, 1986-87; coordinator tng. Blick Clinic, Inc., Akron, 1987—. Producer, photographer: (video film) Safety Counts, 1981, (slide/tape show) Helping People Help Themselves, 1982; compiler: (catalog) Films and Video Cassettes on Rehabilitation, 1985; editor: (newsletter) Access, 1986-87. Bd. dirs. Rape Crisis Ctr., Akron, 1977-79, YWCA, Akron, 1978-81, Parents Anonymous, Akron, 1981-82; Am. del. Internat. Tribunal on Crimes Against Women, Brussels, 1976. Grantee Ohio Dept. Health, Akron, 1979-80. Mem. Am. Assn. Counseling and Devel., Ohio Assn. Counseling and Devel., Am. Mental Health Counselors Assn. (tng. govt. relations 1987), Ohio Mental Health Counselors Assn. (bd. dirs. 1986—, pres. elect), Inst. for Studies of Everyday Life, Mensa. Democrat. Home: 96 Dick Ave Akron OH 44302 Office: Blick Clinic Inc 640 W Market St Akron OH 44303

LEVI, SUZANNE EVANS, business forms company executive; b. Gainesville, Tex., Oct. 28, 1938; d. Gilbert Warren and Jessica Earlyne (Lowe) Evans; m. William C. Thurston; 1 child, Steven L.; m. Richard Joseph Levi, Nov. 4, 1967; 1 child, James Stanford. Student, Barnard Coll., 1956, Columbia U., 1957-60, U. Ill., Chgo., 1970. Asst. banquet dept. Waldorf Astoria, N.Y.C., 1957-60; exec. asst. Hewitt Assocs., Libertyville, Ill., 1963-70; supr. Washington Nat. Ins. Co., Evanston, Ill., 1970-81; supr. office info. systems Moore Bus. Forms and Systems Div. Moore Corp. Ltd., Glenview, Ill., 1981—. Contbr. articles to profl. jours. Mem. office systems adv. bd. Triton Coll., River Grove, Ill. Mem. Assn. Info. Systems Profls., Internat. Soc. Wang Users, Women Mgmt. Unitarian. Home: 25 Fox Trail Lincolnshire IL 60015

LEVICK, MYRA FRIEDMAN, art psychotherapist, educator; b. Phila., Aug. 20, 1924; d. Louis and Ida (Segal) Friedman; B.F.A., Moore Coll. Art, 1963; M.Ed., Temple U., 1967; Ph.D., Bryn Mawr Coll., 1982; m. Leonard J. Levick, Dec. 26, 1943; children—Bonnie, Karen, Marsha. Lic. psychologist and cert. med. psychotherapist. Art psychotherapist Albert Einstein Med. Center, Phila., 1963-67; dir. adjunctive therapies and dir. grad. tng. program in art therapy, Hahnemann Med. Coll. and Hosp., Phila., 1967-73, dir. masters creative arts in therapy tng. program, 1973-86, prof., cons. mental health scis. dept. Hahnemann U., 1977—; cons. affiliated clinics and instns. Recipient Outstanding Alumni award Moore Coll. Art, 1975; Humanitarian award Ronald Bruce Nippon Assn., 1976; NIMH grantee, 1975-78. Mem. Am. Art Therapy Assn. (founder, 1st pres. hon. life mem.), Family Inst. Phila. (exec. bd. 1982-84), Am. Psychol. Assn., Pa. Psychol. Assn., Am. Ortho-Psychiat. Assn., Internat. Soc. Psychopathology of Expression, Am. Soc. Psychopathology of Expression. Author: They Could Not Talk and So They Drew, Children's Styles of Coping and Thinking, 1983; Mommy, Daddy, Look What I'm Saying: What Children Are Telling You Through Their Art, 1986; contbg. author: Current Psychotherapies, 1975; Handbook of Innovative Psychotherapies, 1981, The Psychiatric Therapies, 1984; sr. editor The Arts in Psychotherapy, 1975-81, editor-in-chief, 1982-86, emeritus, 1986—; contbr. articles to profl. lit. Home and Office: 21710 Palm Circle Boca Raton FL 33433

LEVIN, AMY BETH, magazine editor; b. Bklyn., Jan. 11, 1942; d. Herbert Daniel Suesholtz and Shirley (Burrows) Alter; m. Robert J. Levin, May 10, 1967 (dec. May 1976); m. 2d Arthur M. Cooper, June 9, 1979. B.A., Syracuse U., 1963. Asst. editor Redbook Mag., N.Y.C., 1964-65, assoc. editor, 1966-70, sr. editor, 1971-76, assoc. articles editor, 1976-78; articles editor Ladies Home Jour., N.Y.C., 1978-80; editor-in-chief Mademoiselle Mag., N.Y.C., 1978—. Recipient citation for gen. excellence Am. Soc. Journalists and Authors, 1982. Mem. Am. Soc. Mag. Editors, Media Women. Jewish. Office: Mademoiselle Magazine 350 Madison Ave New York NY 10017

LEVIN, AMY ELIZABETH, librarian; b. Salt Lake City, Aug. 1, 1943; d. Robert Leonard and Frances Janet (Bentley) Evans; m. Harold Bumberg, May 28, 1969 (dec. Oct. 1971); m. Stanford Malcolm Levin, May 26, 1974 (dec. Nov. 1983); children: Rena Frances, Joseph Irvin. Student, U. Minn., 1963; BS in Natural Sci., U. Wis., 1965; M in Library and Info. Scis., U. Pitts., 1969. Asst. tech. librarian Research Lab. J&L Steel Corp., Pitts., 1965-68; med. library trainee VA Hosp., Pitts., 1968-69; head geology library U. Minn., Mpls., 1969-70; researcher Harvard U. Med. Sch., Cambridge, Mass., 1971-72; reference librarian U.S. Geol. Survey, Washington, 1972-74; asst. chief access services Smithsonian Instn., Washington, 1974-83; librarian, online specialist Smithsonian Nat. Air and Space Mus., Washington, 1983—; mem. spl. edn. adv. com. Arlington City (Va.) Schs., 1982—. Author: Bibliography of Part-Time Work, 1982, 2d edit., 1985; contbr. book revs. and articles to profl. jours. Chair sch. bd., bd. dirs. Agudas Achim Cong., Alexandria, Va., 1985—. Mem. ALA, Spl. Libraries Assn., Med. Library Assn., Geosci. Info. Soc. (newsletter editor 1972-74), D.C. Online Users Group, Assn. Part-Time Profls. (nat. bd. dirs. 1982—). Jewish. Home: 916 S 20th St Arlington VA 22202 Office: Smithsonian Instn Libraries 3106 Nat Air and Space Mus Washington DC 20560

LEVIN, BETSY, lawyer, university dean; b. Balt., Dec. 25, 1935; d. M. Jastrow and Alexandra (Lee) L. A.B., Bryn Mawr (Pa.) Coll., 1956; LL.B., Yale U., 1966. Bar: D.C. 1967, Colo. 1982. Research geologist U.S. Geol. Survey, Washington, 1956-63; law clk. to presiding justice U.S. Ct. Appeals (4th cir.), Balt., 1966-67; spl. asst. to U.S. Ambassador Arthur J. Goldberg, N.Y.C., 1967-68; dir. edn. studies Urban Inst., Washington, 1968-73; prof. law Duke U., Durham, N.C., 1973-80; gen. counsel U.S. Dept. Edn., Washington, 1980-81; dean, prof. law U. Colo., Boulder, 1981-87; exec. dir. Assn. Am. Law Schs., Washington, 1987—; mem. Nat. Council Ednl. Research, 1978-79; mem. civil rights reviewing authority HEW, 1979-80; mem. task force Tng. the Adv., 1985—. Co-author: Educational Policy and the Law, 1982; editor: Future Directions for School Finance Reform, 1975; co-editor: The Courts, Social Science and School Desegregation, 1977, School Desegregation: Lessons of the First 25 Years, 1979. White House fellow, 1967-68. Fellow Am. Bar Found., Colo. Bar Found.; mem. ABA (adv. com. on coll. and univ. nonprofl. legal edn. 1986—), Nat. Assn. Women Judges (program com. 1985—), Am. Law Inst. (council), Soc. Am. Law Tchrs., Order of Coif. Office: Assn Am Law Schs 1 DuPont Circle NW Washington DC 20036 also: U of Colo Sch of Law Office of the Dean Boulder CO 80309

LEVIN, CAROL ARLENE, educator; b. Los Angeles, Apr. 4, 1945; d. Harold Allen and Sally (Salter) L. AA, Santa Monica Coll., 1965; BA, UCLA, 1967. Cert. tchr., 1969, bilingual tchr., 1977. Tchr. Los Angeles Unified Schs., 1969—, bilingual tchr., 1977—; master tchr. U. Calif., Los Angeles, 1985—; pres., v.p. Calif. Assn. Childhood Edn., Los Angeles, 1977-81; chmn. workshop Calif. State Assn. for Childhood Edn. Internat. Conf., Universal City, 1979; invited observer Assn. for Childhood Edn. Internat. White House Conf.-Families, Los Angeles, 1980; tchr., adviser elem. news Sta. KTTV, Los Angeles, 1980-82. Editor: (with others) Our Los Angeles, 1976; contbr. articles to profl. jours. Treas. Dickens Towers Homeowners Assn., Sherman Oaks, Calif., 1978-80; sec. Sherman Villas Homeowners Assn, Sherman Oaks, 1981-83; mem. Sherman Oaks Homeowners Assn., 1986—, Palm Springs (Calif.) Tennis Club Owners Assn., 1981—; mem. Los Angeles Music Ctr. Theatre Group Vols., 1987—. Recipient P.I.E. award Los Angeles Schs., 1978, 79, 80, 81. Mem. Nat. Edn. Assn., Calif. Tchrs. Assn., United Tchrs. Los Angeles. Republican. Jewish. Office: Huntington Dr Sch 4435 N Huntington Dr Los Angeles CA 90032

LEVIN, DEANNA LYNN, accountant; b. Hammond, Ind., Aug. 8, 1963; m. Steven J. Levin, May 25, 1986. BS in Commerce, DePaul U., Chgo., 1985. CPA. Auditor Grant Thornton, CPA's, Chgo., 1985-88; internal auditor Continental Bank, Chgo., 1988—. Am. Inst. CPA's, Ill. CPA Soc., Am. Women's Soc. CPA's.

LEVIN, DEBBE ANN, lawyer; b. Cin., Mar. 11, 1954; d. Abram Asher and Selma Ruth (Herlands) L. BA, Washington U., St. Louis, 1976; JD, U. Cin., 1979; LLM, NYU, 1983. Bar: Ohio 1979. Staff atty. U.S. Ct. Appeals 6th Circuit, Cin., 1979-82; assoc. Schwartz, Manes & Ruby Co., LPA, Cin., 1983—; lectr. tax conf. U. Cin., 1984-86, adj. prof. coll. of bus., 1987-88. Editor: U. Cin. Law Review, 1972-79. Recipient Judge Alfred Mack prize U. Cin., 1979. Mem. ABA, Ohio Bar Assn., Cin. Bar Assn., Cin. Bus. & Profl. Women's Club, Order of Coif. Jewish. Office: Schwartz Manes & Ruby Co LPA 2900 Carew Tower Cincinnati OH 45202

LEVIN, GAIL, author, photographer, educator; b. Atlanta, Feb. 19, 1948; d. Barron and Shirley (Sunshine) Levin. B.A., Simmons Coll., 1969; M.A., Tufts U., 1970; Ph.D., Rutgers U., 1976. Instr. New Sch. for Social Research, N.Y.C., 1973-75, Bernard Baruch Coll., CUNY, 1974; asst. prof. art history Conn. Coll., New London, 1975-76; vis. prof. art history Grad. Center CUNY, 1979-80; curator Whitney Mus. Am. Art, N.Y.C., 1976-84; vis. prof. Nesbit Coll. Design, Drexel U., 1985-86; asst. prof. art Baruch Coll. CUNY, 1987, assoc. prof. art, 1988—; Will and Ariel Durant prof. humanities St. Peter's Coll., Jersey City, 1987-88; producer, host Art at Issue, Manhattan Cable TV, 1985-86. Author: Abstract expressionism: The Formative Years 1978, Synchromism and American Color Abstraction, 1910-25, 1978, Edward Hopper: The Complete Prints, 1979, Edward Hopper as Illustrator, 1979, Edward Hopper: The Art and the Artist, 1980, Edward Hopper, 1984, Twentieth Century American Painting The Thyssen-Bornemisza Collection, 1987; author, photographer: Hoppers Places, 1985; film: Edward Hopper, 1981; contbr. articles to profl. jours.; one-person shows: Kingston Artists Group, Gallery Rondout, 1984; Kennedy Galleries, Inc., N.Y.C., 1985, Jane Voorhees Zimmerli Art Mus., 1985, Meml. Art Gallery, U. Rochester, 1985, Fay Gold Gallery, Atlanta, Barridoff Gallery, Portland, 1986, Cedar Rapids Art Mus., 1986, Hopper House Art Ctr., Nyack, N.Y., 1986, Hilton Head Art League, S.C., 1986, U. Iowa Art Mus., 1987, St. Peter's Coll. Art Gallery, Jersey City, 1987, Pa. Acad. of Fine Arts, 1987; group shows Catskill Ctr. for Photography in Woodstock, N.Y., 1985, A.I.R. Gallery, N.Y.C., 1985, The 9th Precinct Gallery, N.Y.C., 1986, Baruch Coll. Art Gallery, 1987, A.I.R. Gallery, N.Y.C., 1985, 86, 87. Recipient Alumnae Achievement award Simmons Coll., 1986; NEH research grantee, 1984, Am. Council Learned Socs. research grantee, 1988. Mem. Coll. Art Assn., Pen Freedom to Write, Internat. Assn. Art Critics. Address: 125 E 84th St New York NY 10028

LEVIN, IRENE STAUB, librarian; b. Bklyn., Sept. 30, 1928; d. Harry and Regina (Klein) Staub; B.A., Hunter Coll., CUNY, 1949; M.L.S., L.I.U., 1969; m. Harold E. Levin, Nov. 19, 1950; children—Alan, Leslie, Kim, Paula. Reference librarian and young adults Henry Waldinger Library, Valley Stream, N.Y., 1969-87, program coordinator public relations, 1976-87; free-lance info. specialist, Boynton Beach, Fla., 1988—; cons. on Jewish books and libraries; lectr. books with Judiac themes. Trustee, Sisterhood Temple B'nai Israel of Elmont, 1969-71, 87, Temple B'nai Israel of Elmont, 1982. Recipient Library Public Relations Council award, 1973. Mem. Nassau County Library Assn., Assn. Jewish Libraries (editor Bull., 1973-83, Newsletter, 1978—), Am. Mizrachi Women, Hadassah. Contbr. to Contemporary Literary Criticism, Vol. 13, 1979.

LEVIN, JEANETTE BROOKS, market researcher, travel agent, property management executive; b. Buffalo, Aug. 5, 1930; d. Morris Jacob and Anna Pearl (Orzech) Brooks; m. Frank Levin, July 11, 1954; children: Arnold, Robert, David Susan. Student U. Buffalo, 1950-58, SUNY, Buffalo, 1965-70; lic. real estate agt.; cert. Guided Observation Tchr. Program, Cheektowaga (N.Y.) Schs., 1968. Adult edn. tchr. Cleveland Hill Sch., Cheektowaga, 1965-68; founder, owner, prin. Buffalo Survey & Research, Inc., 1965—; property mgmt. agt. Jackson Sq. Assocs., Buffalo, 1978—; pres., mgr. Buffalo Survey Travel Tours, 1978—; cons. politics, image-making for candidates, 1974—. Columnist Buffalo Jewish Rev., 1976-80; media pollster Buffalo newspaper and TV; survey on U.S. tourism, 1973. Pres., Temple Shaarey Zedek Sisterhood, Buffalo, 1977-78, Past Pres.'s Council, 1981-83. Honoree Temple Shaarey Zedek Ann. Ball, 1977; recipient citation for ch. worker of week Amherst Bee, 1978, citations for high degree of accuracy in polling Buffalo News, 1971-87, 85-87. Mem. Mktg. Research Assn., Am. Assn. Pub. Opinion Research, Am. Mktg. Assn., Am. Contract Bridge League. Home: 324 Crosby Blvd Eggertsville NY 14226 Office: 1255 Eggert Rd Buffalo NY 14226

LEVIN, LUBBE, university administrator; b. Wels, Austria; came to U.S., 1949, naturalized, 1955; d. Charles S. and Sonia Levin; student U. Nantes (France), 1966; A.B. with gt. distinction, Stanford U., 1967; M.A., U. Calif., Berkeley, 1968, Ph.D. in French, 1973; m. David Medlinsky. Asst. prof. French, Washington U., St. Louis, 1973-75; mem. staff systemwide adminstrn. U. Calif., 1976—, dir. policy devel., spl. asst. to v.p., 1979—, dir. acad. and staff employee relations, 1982-83, asst. v.p. acad. and staff employee relations, 1983—; lectr. French, U. Calif., Berkeley, 1980—. Calif. State scholar, 1965-66; NDEA fellow, 1971-72; faculty Research grantee Washington U., 1974. Mem. Acad. Academic Personnel Adminstrn., Indsl. Relations Research Assn., NOW, MLA, Calif. Women in Govt., Phi Beta Kappa. Author articles in field. Office: U Calif Systemwide Adminstrn 191 University Hall Berkeley CA 94720

LEVIN, MARLENE, human resource agency executive, educator; b. Detroit, Oct. 7, 1934; d. Louis and Cele (Drapkin) Bertman; m. Jerome J. Goodman, Apr. 4, 1954 (dec. Mar. 1962); children—Bennett J., Marc R.; m.

Herbert R. Levin, June 7, 1967. Student U. Miami, 1952-53; B.A., Coll. of New Rochelle, 1975; M.P.A., NYU, 1978. Cert. human resource mgr. Asst. administr. Richmond Children Ctr., Yonkers, N.Y., 1973-74; research assoc. Westchester Country Dept. Mental Health, N.Y., 1975-80, clinic adminstr., 1980-82; founder, pres. The Phoenix Group, Armonk, N.Y., 1982—; adj. prof. Iona Coll., New Rochelle, N.Y., 1978—; cons. Social Area Research, Scarsdale, N.Y., 1983-84; lectr./trainer Volvo of Am., Inc., Rockleigh, N.J., 1983-84, Lederle Labs., Spring Valley, N.Y., 1984—. Contbr. articles on sociol. subjects to profl. jours. Mem. Mental Health Council, Mount Kisco, N.Y., 1981-83, Council for Youth, Armonk, 1984-85; mem. legis. adv. com. N.Y. State 37th Dist., 1984. Mem. Nat. Staff Devel. Council, NOW (v.p. White Plains 1978-80). Democrat. Jewish. Avocation: stamp collecting. Home: 14 Day Rd Armonk NY 10504 Office: Phoenix Group Ltd 14 Day Rd Armonk NY 10504

LEVIN, PAMELA JEAN, nurse counsellor; b. Rockford, Ill., Oct. 26, 1942; d. Clifton Elgin and Zola Brenice (Griffith) Backus; children: Eric Daniel, Jennifer Jean Levin-Landheer. BS, U. Ill., 1964. RN. Staff nurse, med. nursing Boston VA Hosp., 1964-65; chief nursing dept. Washington Hosp., Boston, 1965-66; staff nurse Highland, Cowell and Alta Bates Hosps., Oakland and Berkeley, Calif., 1967-70; asst. dir. Day Treatment Ctr. Gladman Hosp., Oakland, 1970; pvt. practice transactional analysis San Francisco Bay Area and No. Calif., 1971—; internat. lectr. transactional analysis and devel.; assoc. Transactional Analysis Community Services, San Francisco, 1977; co-pres., v.p. Eric Berne Seminars of San Fransisco, 1977-78; cons. Family Forum Los Angeles, 1971; co-founder Group House Inc., Berkeley, 1971; coodinator N.W. Fla. Alcoholic Rehab. Clinic, 1966; co-founder Orr's Hot Springs Healing Retreat Community, Ukiah, Calif., 1974-79. Author: Becoming The Way We Are, A Transactional Guide to Development, 1974, (children's book) The Fuzzy Frequency, 1978, Cycles of Power, A Guidebook for the Seven Stages of Life, 1981, French transl., 1986, How to Develop Your Personal Powers, A Workbook for your Life's Time, 1982, Health Communications, 1988; author, founder Experiencing Enough, human potential tng. course, 1984; founding mem., editorial bd. quar. jour. Women & Therapy, 1982-86; contbr. numerous articles to profl. jours.; developer instructional aids including blocks, cymbals, devel. cycle and deviations chart, growth and devel. chart, series of comparative charts of psychol. theory; featured commentator/analyst in film Hello Up There, Eric!, Rogers Prodns., Inc., 1979. Recipient Eric Berne Sci. award for article The Cycle of Development, 1984. Mem. Internat. Transactional Analysis Assn. (cert. Level I and II, 1st woman teaching and clin. mem., co-founder women's caucus 1970, bd. trustees 1973, 74, 75, chmn. pub. info. and profl. relations com. 1987—, press screeing com. 1976-78, women's editorial bd. jour. 1977, editor Script, internat. newsletter 1983-85, co-editor 1986), Can. Assn. for Transactional Analysis, Am. Assn. Counselling & Devel., Inst. Devel. Edn. and Psychotherapy, Nat. Assn. Female Execs., AAUW, New Directions in Edn. & Psychotherapy, Internat. Soc. for Study of Innovative Psychotherapies, Media Alliance, Feminist Writer's Guild, Author's Guild, Author's League. Home: Box 1429 Ukiah CA 95482

LEVINE, BARBARA ROSEN, acquisition/development manager; b. Rutland, Vt., Mar. 14, 1934; d. David Solomon and Pearl (Seff) Rosen; m. Robert I. Levine, June 12 1955; children—Marc, Gary. B.S. in Occupational Therapy, Columbia U., 1955. Registered occupational therapist, N.Y., N.J. Dir. pub. relations U.S. Navy Ship's Stores, Yokosuka, Japan, 1956-58; dir. occupational therapy Roosevelt Hosp., Edison, N.J., 1964-66; editor in chief Am. Jour. Occupational Therapy, N.Y.C., 1966-68; cons. N.Y. Occupational Therapy Assn., N.J. Occupational Therapy Assn., West Bergen Mental Health Assn., Hackensack Hosp. (N.J.), others, 1969-79; acquisition devel. mgr. Xerox Learning Systems, Stamford, Conn., 1980—; cons. Family Counseling, Jr. League/ARC, Infant Devel. Pilot Program, Ridgewood, N.J., 1975-78. Bd. dirs. LWV, Metuchen, N.J., Ridgewood, N.J.; bd. dirs. Family Counseling Service, Ridgewood, 1974-78. Mem. Am. Soc. Tng. Devel., Nat. Soc. Performance Instrn. Republican. Clubs: Upper Ridgewood Tennis, Innis Arden Country. Editor-in-chief: Am. Jour. of Occupational Therapy, 1966-68. Office: Xerox Learning Systems 1600 Summer St Stamford CT 06904

LEVINE, BERYL JOYCE, state supreme court justice; b. Winnipeg, Man., Can., Nov. 9, 1935; came to U.S., 1955; d. Maurice Jacob and Bella (Gutnik) Choslovsky; m. Leonard Levine, June 7, 1955; children: Susan Brauna, Marc Joseph, Sari Ruth, William Noah, David Karl. BA, U. Man., Winnipeg, 1965; JD with distinction, U. N.D., 1974. Assoc. Vogel, Branther, Kelly, Knutson, Weir & Bye, Ltd., Fargo, N.D., 1974-85; justice N.D. Supreme Ct., Bismarck, 1985—, chmn. jud. planning com. Bd. dirs. Fargo Youth Commn., 1974-77, Hospice of Red River Valley, Fargo; chmn. Gov.'s Commn. on Children at Risk, 1985. Named Outstanding Woman in N.D. Law, U. N.D. Law Women's Caucus, 1985. Mem. Cass County Bar Assn. (pres. 1984-85), N.D. State Bar Assn., Burleigh County Bar Assn., Order of Coif. Office: ND Supreme Ct State Capitol Bismarck ND 58504 *

LEVINE, BRENDA EILEEN, small business owner, educator; b. Norfolk, Va., Aug. 22, 1940; d. Michael and Edith Minnie (Nevias) Brown; m. Joel H. Levine, Dec. 27, 1969; 1 child, Marci Ellen. BA, William and Mary Coll., 1962; MA, Columbia U., 1965. Cert. secondary tchr. English tchr. Azalea Jr. High Sch., Norfolk, 1962-64; English tchr., dir. sch. shows Fairlawn (N.J.) High Sch., 1965-70; English tchr. Readington (N.J.) Sch., 1970-72, Mariah Acad., Highland Park, N.J., 1972-74; owner, mgr. Bren-Joe Kennels, Freehold, N.J., 1972—. Brownie co-leader Girl Scouts U.S., Freehold, N.J., 1987. Named Outstanding Mother of Yr. Heritage Masonic Lodge, N.Y.C., 1979. Mem. Sand and Sea Kennel Club, Belgian Sheepdog Club Am., Raritan Belgian Sheepdog Club (pres. 1977-78, trophy chmn. 1978-82, bd. dirs. 1987, show chmn. 1975-76), Phi Theta Kappa, Kappa Delta Pi. Republican. Jewish. Lodge: Masons. Home and Office: 471 Jackson's Mill Rd Freehold NJ 07728

LEVINE, CLAIRE LOTITO, manufacturing company executive; b. Passaic, N.J., Aug. 7, 1957; d. Michael Joseph and Jean Claire (Benecchi) Lotito; m. Robert Stern Levine, Apr. 16, 1955. BBA, William Paterson Coll., N.J., 1980; MBA in Mktg., Fairleigh Dickinson U., 1987. Mktg. analyst Schmid Products, Little Falls, N.J., 1980-81; sales analyst Becton Dickinson Consumer Products Co., Franklin Lakes, N.J., 1981-83; asst. product mgr. Becton Dickinson Consumer Products Co., 1983-84, product mgr., 1984—. Office: Becton Dickinson Consumer Products One Becton Dr Franklin Lakes NJ 07417-1883

LEVINE, DONNA KAY, advertising sales representative; b. Detroit, Nov. 3, 1955; d. Daniel Martin and Sophie (Blatt) L. BS, U. Mich., 1977; MA in Advt., Mich. State U., 1978. Sales rep. CASS Student Advt., Evanston, Ill., 1978-79, Webb Co., Chgo., 1979-84, Reynes and Assocs., Chgo., 1984-85; pres. Donna Levine Assocs., Chgo., 1985—. Office: Donna Levine Assocs 750 N Orleans Chicago IL 60610

LEVINE, ELLEN R., magazine editor; b. N.Y.C., Feb. 19, 1943; d. Eugene Jack and Jean (Zuckman) Jacobson; m. Richard U. Levine, Dec. 21, 1964; children—Daniel, Peter. Student in polit. sci., Wellesley Coll. Reporter The Record, Hackensack, N.J., 1964-70; food and decorating editor Cosmopolitan, N.Y.C., 1976-82; editor-in-chief Cosmopolitan Living, N.Y.C., 1980-81, Woman's Day, N.Y.C., 1982—; dir. N.J. Bell, Newark; trustee Elisabeth Morrow, Englewood, N.J., 1983—; commr. U.S. Atty. Gen.'s Commn. on Pornography, 1985-86. Author: Planning your Wedding, Waiting for Baby, Rooms That Grow With Your Child. Mem. exec. com. Senator Bill Bradley, 1984. Named to Writers Hall of Fame, 1981, Acad. Women Achievers, YWCA, 1982; recipient Outstanding Profl. Achievement award N.J. council Girl Scouts U.S., 1984, Woman of Achievement award N.J. Fedn. Women's Clubs, 1984. Home: 470 Highview Rd Englewood NJ 07631 Office: Woman's Day 1515 Broadway New York NY 10036

LEVINE, FAITH LAUREL, educational director; b. Richmond Hill, N.Y., May 10, 1939; d. Henry and Pearl (Freedman) Brofman; children: Debra Sue Goldberg, Heidi Beth Levine. BA, Queens Coll., 1960; MS in Early Childhood Edn., Bklyn. Coll., 1965; postgrad., Bklyn. Coll., St. John's U., NYU, Pace U., 1965-80. Lic. tchr., elem. sch. prin., dir. early childhood edn., N.Y. Tchr. early childhood N.Y.C. Bd. Edn., Bklyn., 1960-79; head tchr. Headstart, Bklyn., 1965; tchr. English as second lang. Hato Rey, P.R., 1966-67; coordinator early childhood N.Y.C. Bd. Edn., Bklyn., 1979—; dir. nursery unit Jewish Community House, Bklyn., 1985-86. Contbr. to manuals. N.Y. State grantee, 1978. Mem. Flatlands Civic Assn. (recording sec.), N.Y. Pub. Sch. Early Childhood Assn. (v.p. 1984—), United Fedn. Tchrs. (chpt. leader 1967-69), Nat. Assn. Adminstrv. Women Edn., Brownsville Boys Alumni Assn. (chpt. pres. 1975-79). Democrat. Jewish. Clubs: Hadassah (program chmn. 1968-70), Kings Sq. Dance (recording sec. 1987-88). Home: 1355 E 80th St Brooklyn NY 11236 Office: Pub Sch 73 241 McDougal St Brooklyn NY 11233

LEVINE, GWENN KAREL, hospital administrator; b. Jersey City, Mar. 11, 1945; d. Milton and Mildred (Cohen) Karel; m. Ronald W. Levine, Jan. 28, 1967 (div. Nov. 1979); children: David Trevor, Joshua Loren. BA in Politics with honors, Brandeis U., 1966; postgrad. in pub. adminstrn., NYU, 1966-67; MA in Polit. Sci., Fordham U., 1975, postgrad. doctoral degree, 1973-77. Intern U.S. Congress, Washington, summer 1965; planning assoc. Bergen-Passaic Health Systems Agy., Hackensack, N.J., 1977-81; dir. program devel. Bergen-Passaic Hosp. and Physician Council, Totowa, N.J., 1981; dir. program planning St. Joseph's Hosp. and Med. Ctr., Paterson, N.J., 1981—; mem. Policy and Plan Devel. Com. N.J. Statewide Health Coordinating Council, Trenton, N.J., 1987—; chmn. N.J. Comprehensive Rehab. Adv. Com., 1988. Trustee Ramat Shalom Synagogue, Spring Valley, N.Y. Recipient Silver award Health Services Div. Am. Mktg. Assn., 1986. Mem. Soc. for Hosp. Planning and Mktg. of Am. Hosp. Assn., Hosp. Planning and Mktg. Soc. N.J. (sec.-treas. 1984, v.p. 1985, pres. 1986). Democrat. Office: St Joseph's Hosp and Med Ctr Dir Program Planning 703 Main St Paterson NJ 07503

LEVINE, HELEN SAXON (MRS. NORMAN D. LEVINE), medical technologist; b. San Francisco; d. Ernest M. Saxon and Ann S. Dippel; m. Norman D. Levine, Mar. 2, 1935. AB, U. Ill., 1939. Supr. lab. San Francisco Dept. Pub. Health Tb Sanatorium, 1944-46, U. Ill. Health Services, Urbana, 1952-65; research assoc. in immunobiology, zoology dept. U. Ill., Urbana, 1965—. Mem. Pres.'s Council U. Ill. Kranner Art Mus.-Docent. Mem. AAUP, AAAS, Am. Heart Assn., Ill. Acad. Sci., Ill. Pub. Health Assn., Am. Soc. Med. Technologists, Am. Soc. Clin. Pathologists, Sigma Delta Epsilon. Home: 702 LaSell Dr Champaign IL 61822 Office: Morrill Hall U Ill Urbana IL 61801

LEVINE, JANIS E., financial analyst; b. Akron, Ohio, Apr. 7, 1953; d. Paul and Sarah (Levin) L.; student U. Cin., 1971-73; B.S. in Acctg., U. Akron, 1975; M.B.A., Xavier U., 1978. Acctg. intern Price Waterhouse & Co., Cleve., 1974-75; systems acct. Mead Corp., Cin., 1975-77; internal auditor, sr. capital expenditures analyst Champion Internat. Corp., Stamford, Conn., 1977 . Vol., Headstart and ARC; adv. Jr. Achievement; mem. Young Republicans. Recipient Young Citizens Achievement award for Headstart, 1969. Mem. Women in Mgmt., Bus. and Profl. Women, Young Leadership Council, Nat. Assn. Female Execs., Stamford Forum for World Affairs, Westport-Weston Arts Council, Assn. M.B.A. Execs., Nat. Assn. Accts. (community programs dir.), AAUW, Am. Jewish Congress, B'nai B'rith Women, Beta Alpha Psi (sec.). Office: Champion Internat Corp 1 Champion Plaza Stamford CT 06921

LEVINE, JOANN, civic organization executive; b. Cin., Apr. 5, 1945; d. Jerome and Molly (Lucas) Apseloff; m. Marc Samuel Levine, Jan. 29, 1965; children: Ami Jennifer, Shelley, Benjamin. Student Ohio State U., 1963-66, U. Houston, 1984. Sec. Ohio State U., Columbus, 1966-67; sec., treas. United DC Inc., Houston, 1981—. Pres. Sisterhood Agudat Achim, 1972-73, advisor, 1974-81; bd. dirs. Synagogue Agudat Achim, 1972-73; organizer Lead Blood Testing Program Women's Ctr. of Leominster, Mass., 1979-81. Mem. Nat. Assn. Female Execs., Orgn. Rehab. and Tng. Jewish. Club: Hadassah (Houston). Avocations: reading, tennis, swimming. Home: 6235 Queensloch Houston TX 77096 Office: United DC Inc 8947 Market St Houston TX 77029

LEVINE, JUDITH DEE, lawyer; b. N.Y.C., Sept. 2, 1950; d. Joshua and Selene Beverly (Davidson) L. BA, Kirkland Coll., 1972; JD, U. Denver, 1975. Bar: Colo. 1975, U.S. Dist. Ct. Colo. 1975, Ohio 1979, U.S. Ct. Appeals (9th cir.) 1979, N.Y. 1982. Assoc. Brownstein Hyatt Farber & Madden, Denver, 1975-78, Krupman, Fromson, Bownas & Selcer, Columbus, Ohio, 1979-80; assoc. Guren, Merritt, Feibel, Sogg & Cohen, Columbus, 1980-82, ptnr., 1982-84; ptnr. Benesch, Friedlander, Coplan & Aronoff, Columbus, 1984—. Speaker, steering com. mem. The Entrepreneurship Inst. Columbus, 1984-85,; vol. Sta. WOSU Auction, Columbus, 1984—; acct. exec. Franklin County United Way, 1985; pres. Columbus Comml. Real Estate Women, 1988—; trustee Franklin County Unit Am. Cancer Soc., 1988—. Mem. ABA (chmn. subcom. on mortgage loan commitments for lenders and borrowers 1985—), Colo. Bar Assn., Ohio Bar Assn., Columbus Bar Assn., Women Lawyers of Franklin County, Order of St. Ives. Democrat. Club: Capital. Office: Benesch Friendlander et al 88 E Broad St Columbus OH 43215

LEVINE, KAREN ROBIN, municipal administrator; b. Hartford, June 23, 1956; d. Harry Saul and Joyce Ann (Berman) L. BA in History, U. Conn., 1978, MPA, 1980. Playground supr. Meriden (Conn.) Parks and Recreation Dept., 1974-79; research asst. Affirmative Action Office U. Conn., Hartford, 1979-80; planning analyst Office of Policy and Mgmt., Hartford, 1980-82; adminstrv. asst. bd. selectmen Town of Bolton, Conn., 1982—. Mem. Conn. Town and City Mgmt. Assn., Pub. Risk and Ins. Mgmt. Assn., Capital Region Council of Govt., Council of Small Towns, Conn. Conf. Municipalities. Jewish. Office: Selectmen's Office 222 Bolton Ctr Rd Bolton CT 06043

LEVINE, LAURA AMY, project manager; b. N.Y.C., May 3, 1959; d. Aaron and Florence (Chaiter) L. AS, Temple U., 1980, BA magna cum laude, 1981; MBA, Georgetown U., 1983. Project mgr. Small Bus. Adminstrn., Washington, 1982-83; fin. analyst R.H. Macys Inc., Newark, 1983-85; cons., analyst Computer Horizons Corp., Parsippany, N.J., 1985-87; corporate fin. mgr. Citicorp Investment Bank, N.Y.C., 1987—. Mem. Nat. Assn. Female Execs. Jewish.

LEVINE, MARILYN MARKOVICH, lawyer, arbitrator; b. Bklyn., Aug. 9, 1930; d. Harry P. and Fannie L. (Hymowitz) Markovich; m. Louis L. Levine. June 24, 1950; children: Steven R., Ronald J., Linda J. Morgenstern. BS summa cum laude, Columbia U., 1950; MA, Adelphi U., 1967; JD, Hofstra U., 1977. Bar: N.Y. 1978, U.S. Dist. Ct. (so and ea. dists.) N.Y. 1978, D.C. 1979, U.S. Supreme Ct. 1982. Sole practice Valley Stream, N.Y., 1978—; contract arbitrator Bldg. Service Industry, N.Y.C., 1982—; panel arbitrator Retail Food Industry, N.Y.C., 1980—; arbitrator N.Y. Dist. Cts., Nassau County, 1981—. Panel arbitrator Suffolk County Pub. Employee Relations Bd., 1979—, Nassau County Pub. Employee Relations Bd., 1980—, Nat. Mediation Bd., 1986—, N.Y. State Pub. Employee Relations Bd., 1984—; mem. adv. council Ctr. Labor and Industrial Relations, N.Y. Inst. Tech., N.Y., 1985—; counsel Nassau Civic Club, 1978—. Mem. ABA, N.Y. State Bar Assn., D.C. Bar Assn., Nassau County Bar Assn., N.J. Bd. Mediation (panel arbitrator), Am. Arbitration Assn. (arbitrator 1979—), Fed. Mediation Bd. (arbitrator 1980—). Home and Office: 1057 Linden St Valley Stream NY 11580

LE VINE, NATHALIE CHRISTIAN, performing arts administrator, choreographer, ballerina; b. Las Animas, Colo., July 21, 1929; d. Fleming Vincent and Juanita J. (Jobe) Christian; m. Victor Theodore Le Vine, July 19, 1958; children: Theodore Vincent, Nicole Jeanette Le Vine Vizcarra. BA in Polit. Sci., UCLA, 1958; student Royal Ballet Sch., London, 1959-60; studies with Michel Panaieff, Los Angeles, 1945-48, Mia Slavenska, Los Angeles, 1948-53, Rozelle Frey, Los Angeles, and others. Tchr. Wilcoxon Sch. Dance, Los Angeles, 1946-48, Sutro-Seyler Studio, Los Angeles, 1949-51, Brown Gables Conservatory of the Arts, Los Angeles, 1952-61, Ecole de Danse, Cameroun, West Africa, 1961-62, Dawn Quist Sch. Dance, Accra, Ghana, West Africa, 1969-70; pvt. tchr. ballet and dance, St. Louis, 1963-67; mem. faculty dance Washington U., St. Louis, 1967-69, 70-71; founder, dir. Met. Ballet St. Louis, 1974; prin. tchr. Le Vine Acad. of Ballet, St. Louis, 1964-86; guest tchr. master classes, 1971—, U. Hawaii, South Hold Dance Theater, South Bend, Ind., M. Tracy Sch. Ballet, Kailua, Hawaii; co-artistic dir. St. Louis Dance Theater, 1966-72, choreographer, 1966-72; prin. tchr. Met. Ballet of St. Louis, 1974—, also bd. dirs.; participant planning dance performances, St. Louis, 1964— ; cons. to Phelps County Dance Assn., 1978-79, Roila (Mo.) Bd. of Parks and Recreation, 1978-79; guest tchr. various dance schs. and theaters, 1964—; soloist Ballet de Los Angeles, 1948-49, Radio City Music Hall, N.Y.C., 1952-53; appeared in various TV and stage prodns., Los Angeles, 1946-48, Santa Monica, Calif., 1945-50, Laguna Beach, Calif., 1946-51; appeared in Greatest Show on Earth, other motion pictures, 1950-52. Mem. Nat. Soc. Arts and Letters, Phi Beta Kappa. Democrat. Office: Met Ballet of St Louis 524 Trinity Ave Saint Louis MO 63130-4321

LEVINE, REBECCA-SUE, lawyer; b. N.Y.C., July 1, 1946; d. Isaac and Jeanette (Katz) Kurash; m. Paul Edward Levine, Dec. 22, 1968 (dec. Sept. 1976). BS in Journalism, Ohio U., 1967; JD, Bklyn. Law Sch., 1982. Bar: N.Y. 1983. Sr. editor Women's Wear Daily, N.Y.C., 1972-75; editor-in-chief Men's Wear Mag., N.Y.C., 1975-78; editor Booke and Co., N.Y.C., 1983-85; sole practice, N.Y.C., 1985—; adj. instr. journalism Fashion Inst. Tech., N.Y.C., 1972—. Pres. Quality-Ruskin Tenants Fedn., Forest Hills, N.Y., 1974, 75; fundraiser Mental Health Assn. Greater N.Y., 1976—; vol. Humane Soc. N.Y., 1978-79; mem. Older Women's League, N.Y.C., 1985—; v.p. 27 Victoria Owners Coop., N.Y.C., 1985-86; active Bronx Zoo, Mus. Natural History. Mem. ABA, N.Y. State Bar Assn., Bklyn. Bar Assn., Bklyn. Women's Bar Assn., Women in Communications, Networks Unlimited, Mortar Bd., Chimes. Avocations: photography, travel, wildlife study. Home and Office: 200 E 27th St New York NY 10016

LEVINE, SANDRA MARY, marketing agency executive, lecturer, author; b. Newark, May 30, 1935; d. Samuel P. and Josephine E. (Sinisgalli) Marzano; student, Rutgers U.; m. Sidney I. Levine, Apr. 5, 1973 (div.); children—Joseph B. Martinez, Samuel A. Martinez. Exec. v.p. Staflex Co., N.Y.C., 1968-83; prin. SML Levine Enterprises, Inc., N.Y.C., 1983-86; owner, mgr. Sinisgalli's, Ocean City, N.J., 1986—. Mem. Internat. Assn. Clothing Designers (exec. dir.), Women's Bus. Club. N.Y. (founder, pres.), Women in Apparel Related Industries (founder, pub.), B'nai B'rith, Hadassah. Office: Central Sq Suite 202 Linwood NJ 08403

LEVINE, SUZANNE BRAUN, magazine editor; b. N.Y.C., June 21, 1941; d. Imre and Esther (Bernson) Braun; m. Robert F. Levine, Apr. 2, 1967; children: Joshua, Joanna. B.A. with honors, Radcliffe Coll., 1963. Reporter Seattle mag., 1963-65; reporter, researcher Time/Life Books, N.Y.C., 1965-67; features editor Mademoiselle, N.Y.C., 1967-68, McCalls mag., N.Y.C., 1968-69; free-lance writer 1970; mng. editor Sexual Behavior mag., 1971-72, MS. mag., N.Y.C., 1972—; screener nat. mag. awards WICI Clarior awards. Co-editor: The Decade of Women, A Ms History of the Seventies, 1980; exec. producer: Ms TV spl, 1981, She's Nobody's Baby, TV documentary, 1981 (Peabody award). Bd. dirs. Women's Action Alliance; Woodrow Wilson Guest Lectr. Coordinator, Chautauqua Conf. on Families. Mem. Am. Soc. Mag. Editors (exec. com.), Women's Media Group. Office: 1 Times Square New York NY 10036

LEVINE, YARI, artist, jewelry designer; b. Minsk, Russia; came to U.S. 1927; d. Samuel and Lillian (Lapidus) Turboff; m. Samuel S. Levine, June 10, 1945; children—Steven Robert, Mark Eric. Cert. in Fine Arts, Pratt Inst., 1939; student Am. Artists Sch., 1941, New Sch. Social Research, 1942-43. One-woman shows at: Ward Egleston Galleries, 1964, Washington Hebrew Congregation, N.Y.C., 1959, Brandeis U., 1966, U. Wis., 1969, Union of Am. Hebrew Congregations, 1953, 66, Nassau Community Coll., 1970, Art and Design Atelier, 1980, Hebrew Tabernacle, 1981; exhibited in group shows at: Creative Gallery, John Myers Gallery, 1952, A.C.A. Gallery, 1954, 55, 56, Nat. Acad. Galleries, 1953-78, Internat. Jewish Conf. Exhibit, Los Angeles, 1955, Suffolk Mus., 1957, 300th Houston Commemorative Exhibit, 1957, Art League of L.I., 1957, Heckscher Mus., 1962, Lido Gallery, 1970, Harbor Gallery, 1974, Hudson Guild Gallery, 1980, Artists Equity of N.Y., 1980, Lever House, 1983, Jacob K. Javits Fed. Bldg., 1984, 85; works represented in permanent collections at House of Living Judaism of Union of Am. Hebrew Congregations, N.Y.C., Westchester Reform Temple, Temple Sinai of Washington, U. Wis., others. Named Artist of Jewish Yr., Union of Am. Hebrew Congregations, 1966. Fellow Internat. Inst. Arts and Letters; mem. Artists Equity of N.Y., Nat. Assn. Women Artists, Jewish Visual Artists Assn. of Nat. Council on Arts in Jewish Life, Internat. Platform Assn. Address: 63 Hamlet Rd Levittown NY 11756 Studio: 24 Fifth Ave Suite 214 New York NY 10011

LEVINE-SHNEIDMAN, CONALEE, psychologist; b. N.Y.C., Feb. 22, 1930; d. Robert and Lillian (Kurlander) Levine; m. J. Lee Shneidman, Sept. 3, 1961; children—Philip, Jack. Student Black Mountain Coll. (N.C.); Ph.D., NYU, 1959. Cert. in psychoanalysis and psychotherapy. Pvt. practice psychoanalysis and psychotherapy, N.Y.C., 1961—; assoc. prof. psychology NYU, 1965-70; adj. assoc. prof. Yeshiva U., 1970-73. USPHS grantee, 1958. Mem. Am. Psychol. Assn., Am. Orthopsychiat. Assn., N.Y. State Psychol. Assn., Psychoanalytic Soc. of Postdoctoral Program for Tng. and Research. Office: 27 W 86th St New York NY 10024

LEVINO-JONES, ALISON, interior designer; b. Schenectady, N.Y., May 26, 1956; d. Theodore Prussing and Anne (Laycock) LeVino; m. R. Scott Jones, May 2, 1981. Student in sociology, Lynchburg Coll., 1977; BA in Interior Design, U. Conn., 1979. Project designer Gresham, Smith & Ptnrs., Nashville, 1979-81; project dir. Quantrell Mullins, Atlanta, 1981-83; prin. Godwin & Assocs./Atlanta, 1983-88; pres. Godwin Procurement Corp., Atlanta, 1985-88; owner LeVino-Jones Health Facility Design Interiors, 1988—; lectr. in field. Contbr. design work to profl. mags. Vol. Children's Wish Found., Atlanta, 1986—; fundraiser Am. Heart Assn., Atlanta, 1984-86; mem. vol. fundraising program Ga. Alliance for Children, Atlanta, 1985-86; mem. Peachtree Hills Civic Assn., Atlanta, 1983—. Mem. Am. Soc. Interior Designers (bd. dirs. 1985-87, chmn. programs com. 1985-86, chmn. awards com. 1987, chmn. community services spl. project 1986-87), Inst. Bus. Designers, Atlanta Women's Network, Buckhead Bus. Assn. Republican. Episcopalian. Home: 2335 Virginia Place Atlanta GA 30305

LEVINSON, DOROTHY JANICE, educator; b. Laurel, Miss., Feb. 1, 1918; s. Solomon Louis and Bessie Marian (Mindel) Wisenberg; B.A., Rice Inst., Houston, 1937; M.A., Northeastern Ill. U., Chgo., 1970, Northwestern U., 1974; m. Nathan Levinson, Jan. 11, 1945 (dec.); children—Irving Walter, Robert David. Tchr., Houston public schs., 1938-44, Edgewood Jr. High Sch., Highland Park, Ill., 1967-88. Pres. Volta PTA, Chgo., 1959-61. Served with WAVES, 1944-45. Mem. Nat. Council Tchrs. English, NEA, Ill. Congress Parents and Tchrs. (dist. publs. chmn. 1961-62), Hadassah, Phi Beta Kappa. Jewish. Home: 8000 Foster Ln Niles IL 60648

LEVINSON, ROCHELLE FOX, cleaning company executive; b. Chattanooga, May 30, 1949; d. Isaac Israel and Bertha (Klempner) Fox; m. Morton Allen Levinson, July 12, 1970 (dec. 1982); children—Jason Franklin, Lori Anne. Student Memphis State U., 1967-68, Draughon's Bus. Coll., 1968-69. Pres. Clean Team, Inc., Arlington, Tex, 1978—. Active Arlington Women's Shelter Aux., Mid-Cities Jewish Community Ctr.; mem. nat. panel consumer arbitrators Better Bus. Bur. Mem. Arlington C. of C., Fort Worth C. of C., Nat. Assn. Female Execs., Network for Exec. Women, . Clubs: Altrusa (info. chmn. 1985-87, yearbook editor 1984-86, editor 1984-86), The Arlington Girls Club (Wildflower aux.). Lodge: B'nai Brith (charter pres. Mid-Cities Couples). Avocations: dancing; traveling; photography. Office: Clean Team Inc 3630 Pioneer Pkwy Suite 116 Arlington TX 76013

LEVINSON, SUNNI ROBERTA, health education consultant; b. Bklyn., Feb. 28, 1949. R.N., St. Johns Episcopal Sch. Nursing, 1968; B.S., St. Joseph's Coll., North Windham, Maine, 1984. Asst. head nurse emergency services St. John's Episcopal Hosp., Bklyn., 1968-69; psychiat nurse Interboro Gen. Hosp., Bklyn., 1969-70; team leader medicine/surgery/orthopedics and gynecology N.Y. Med. Coll., Flower Fifth Ave Hosp., N.Y.C., 1970-72; head nurse communications N.Y.C. Health and Hosp. Corp. Emergency Med. Services, 1972-73, supr. nurses emergency med. services tng. div., Maspeth, N.Y., 1973-80, dir. edn. program emergency med. services tng. div., Queens Hosp. Ctr., N.Y.C., 1980-81, exec. adminstr. Emergency Med. Services Acad., Queens Hosp. Ctr., 1981-86; co-founder, exec. dir. Wagler Assocs., health edn. cons., 1986—; cons. health services div. N.Y.C. Emergency Med. Service, Maspeth, 1983-85; cons. med. systems devel. St. Joseph Children's Services, Bklyn., 1985—, asst. med. dir., 1988—; liaison from emergency med. service to Bur. Emergency Health Services, N.Y. State Dept. Health, Albany, 1981-85. Mem. N.Y. State Nurses Assn., Nat. Assn. Emergency Med. Technicians, N.Y. Acad. Scis., N.Y.C. Regional Emergency Med. Services Council. Democrat.

LEVIT, EDITHE JUDITH, physician, medical association administrator; b. Wilkes-Barre, Pa., Nov. 29, 1926; m. Samuel M. Levit, Mar. 2, 1952; children: Harry M., David B. B.S. in Biology, Bucknell U., 1946; M.D., Woman's Med. Coll. of Pa., 1951; D.M.S., Med. Coll. Pa., 1978. Grad. asst. in psychology Bucknell U., 1946-47; intern Phila. Gen. Hosp., 1951-52, fellow in endocrinology, 1952-53, clin. instr., asso. in endocrinology, 1953-57, dir. med. edn., 1957-61, cons. med. edn., 1961-65; asst. dir. Nat. Bd. Med. Examiners, Phila., 1961-67; assoc. dir., sec. bd. Nat. Bd. Med. Examiners, 1967-75, v.p., sec. bd., 1975-77, pres., chief exec. officer, 1977-86, pres. emeritus, life mem. bd., 1987—; cons. in field, 1964—; council Coll. Physicians of Phila., 1986—; dir. Phila. Electric Co.; bd. mgrs. Germantown Savs. Bank, Phila. Contbr. articles to profl. jours. Bd. dirs. Phila. Gen. Hosp. Found., 1964-70; bd. dirs. Phila. Council for Internat. Visitors, 1966-72; bd. sci. counselors Nat. Library Medicine, 1981-85. Recipient award for outstanding contbns. in field of med. edn. Commonwealth Com. of Woman's Med. Coll., 1970; Alumni award Bucknell U., 1978; Disting. Dau. of Pa. award, 1981; Spl. Recognition award Assn. Am. Med. Colls., 1986; Disting. Service award Fedn. State Med. Bds., 1987; Master A.C.P. Fellow Coll. Physicians of Phila.; mem. Inst. Medicine of Nat. Acad. Scis., AMA, Pa., Phila. County med. socs., Assn. Am. Med. Colls., Phi Beta Kappa, Alpha Omega Alpha, Phi Sigma. Home: 1910 Spruce St Philadelphia PA 19103 Office: 3930 Chestnut St Philadelphia PA 19104

LEVITAS, MIRIAM C. STRICKMAN, educational center administrator; b. Phila., Aug. 3, 1936; d. Morris and Bella (Barsky) Cherrin; m. Bernard Strickman, June 3, 1956 (dec. 1975); children—Andrew, Brian, Craig, Deron; m. Theodore Clinton Levitas, Apr. 25, 1976; children—Steven, Leslie, Anthony. Student Temple U., 1953-56, LaSalle U., Chgo., 1968. V.p. programming interior design Nat. Home Fashions League, Atlanta, 1974-75; salesman Ga. Bd. Realtors, 1971; adminstr. Stanley H. Kaplan Ednl. Ctr., Atlanta, 1974-84; owner, pres. Levitas Services, Inc. (Internat. Destinations), Atlanta, 1984—; owner, v.p. Nat. Travel Services and Internat. Destinations, Atlanta, 1984-85; realtor Sotheby's Internat. Realty, 1985—. Exec. producer, host local TV programs, Atlanta, 1988; solo pianist Paul Whiteman TV, Phila. Youth Orch., Frankford Symphony Orch., 1950. Pres. Ahavath Achim Sisterhood, Atlanta, 1977-79; chmn. High Tea at the Ritz Scottish Rite Children's Hosp., women's div. Israel Bond, Atlanta; mem. Young Women of the Arts Atlanta, Atlanta Symphony, High Mus. Art, Nat. Mus. of Women in Arts (charter), Alliance Theater Atlanta. Phila. Bd. Edn. scholar, 1952. Mem. Nat. Assn. Health Professions, Atlanta Bd. Realtors, Nat. Home Fashions League, Nat. Com. for Prevention of Child Abuse, Brandeis Nat. Women (life), Hadassah (life), Nat. Council Jewish Women (life), B'nai Brith (life).

LEVY, BARBARA MINA WEXNER, writer, publisher, editor; b. Hot Springs, Ark., Jan. 30, 1927; d. Henry David and Helen Ruth (Loeb) Wexner; A.A., Lindenwood Coll., 1945; student U. Houston, 1958-59; m. Herbert E. Levy, July 25, 1945; children—Barbara Dian, Richard H., Lauren. Feature writer Houston Town, 1957-58; regional editor Boot & Shoe Recorder, Houston, 1958-65; with customer service Scholastic Mag., Englewood Cliffs, N.J., 1966-67; fashion shoe editor Window Shopping World, N.Y.C., 1967-68; women's fashion editor Boot & Shoe Recorder, N.Y.C., 1968-74; pub., editor Barbara's Report/Shoes and. . . , Miami, Fla., 1974—; lectr. in field. Mem. alumnae bd. Lindenwood Coll., 1967-68, v.p., 1969. Mem. Footwear and Accessories Council N.Y.C. (pres. 1973, chmn. bd. 1974, honored for creative contbn. to industry 1982), Fashion Group, Women in Communications. Contbr. articles to profl. jours. Address: 1236 NE 92nd St Miami FL 33138

LEVY, CAROL, editor; b. Lynn, Mass., Apr. 13, 1931; d. Samuel and Helen (Alpers) L. B.A., Syracuse U., 1952. Mem. staff The Reporter mag., 1952-53, True mag., 1953-54; with spl. services U.S. Army, 1954-56; mem. staff Forbes mag., 1957-61; research editor Dun's Rev. (now Business Month), N.Y.C., 1961-62; sr. editor Dun's Rev. (now Business Month), 1963-69, asst. mng. editor, 1969-71, mng. editor, 1971—. Home: 10 Downing St New York City NY 10014 Office: Bus Month 488 Madison Ave New York NY 10022

LEVY, CHARLOTTE LOIS, law librarian, educator, consultant, lawyer; b. Cin., Aug. 31, 1944; d. Samuel M. and Helen (Lowitz) L.; m. Herbert Regenstreif, Dec. 11, 1980; 1 dau., Cara Rachael Regenstreif. B.A., U. Ky., 1966; M.S., Columbia U., 1969; J.D., No. Ky. U., 1975. Bar: Colo. 1979. Law librarian No. Ky. U., 1971-75; law librarian, assoc. prof. law Pace U., 1975-77; mgr. Fred B. Rothman & Co., Littleton, Colo., 1977-79; law librarian, assoc. prof. Bklyn. Law Sch., 1979-85; adj. prof. Pratt Inst. Grad. Sch. Library and Info. Sci., 1982-85; atty. Cabinet for Human Resources, Frankfort, Ky., 1985—; cons. to various libraries, pubs. Mem. Am. Assn. Law Libraries (cert. law librarian), Law Library Assn. Greater N.Y., ABA, Bklyn. Bar Assn. Democrat. Jewish. Author: The Human Body and the Law (Am. Jurisprudence Book award in domestic relations 1974, in trusts 1975), 1974, 2d edit., 1983; Computer-Assisted Litigation Support, 1984; mem. editorial bd. No. Ky. U. Law Rev., 1974-75. Home: 3147 High Ridge Dr Lexington KY 40502 Office: Cabinet for Human Resources Office of the Counsel 275 E Main St Frankfort KY 40621

LEVY, JOANNA SUE, voice educator; b. N.Y.C., Sept. 14, 1951; d. Leonard Saul and Geraldine (Plush) L. BS, Ithacha Coll., 1972; MFA, Hofstra U., 1974. Cert. music tchr., N.Y. Prin. solo artist N.Y.C. Opera, Washington Opera, Pitts. Opera, St. Louis Opera, 1978-85; also numerous appearances throughout U.S; pvt. voice tchr. N.Y.C., 1984; bd. edn. officer N.Y.C., 1985—; instr. voice SUNY, Purchase, 1986—. Mem. Nat. Assn. Tchrs. Singing, Am. Guild Music, Sigma Alpha Iota. Jewish. Office: NYC Bd Edn 131 Livingston St Brooklyn NY 11201

LEVY, JULIA, immunology educator, researcher; b. Singapore, May 15, 1935; came to Can. 1940; d. Guillaume Albert and Dorothy Frances (Brown) Coppens; m. Howard Bernard Gerwing, Oct. 8, 1955 (div. 1962); children—Nicholas, Benjamin; m. Edwin Levy, June 13, 1969; 1 child, Jennifer. B.A. with honors, U. B.C., 1955; Ph.D., U. London, 1958. Asst. prof. U. B.C., Vancouver, 1959-65, assoc. prof., 1965-72, prof. immunology, 1972—; dir., v.p. research and devel. Quadra Logic Technologies, Vancouver, 1980—; cons. Monsanto Chems., Mo., 1978-80; mem. Prime Minister's Nat. Adv. Bd. on Sci. and Tech., 1987—. Fellow Royal Soc. Can.; mem. Am. Soc. Immunology, Can. Soc. Immunology (pres. 1983-85), Can. Fedn. Biol. Sci. (pres. 1983-84). Home: 2034 W 36th Ave, Vancouver, BC Canada V6M 1K9 Office: U BC, 300-6174 University Blvd, Vancouver, BC Canada V6T 1W5

LEVY, ROCHELLE FELDMAN, artist; b. N.Y.C., Aug. 4, 1937; d. S. Harry and Eva (Krause) Feldman; m. Robert Paley Levy, June 4, 1955; children—Kathryn Tracey, Wendy Paige, Robert Paley, Angela Brooke, Michael Tyler. Student Barnard Coll., 1954-55, U. Pa., 1955-56; B.F.A., Moore Coll. Art, 1979. Mgmt. cons. Woodlyne Sch., Rosemont, Pa., 1983-84; sr. ptnr. DRT Interiors, Phila., 1983—; ptnr. Phila. Phillies, 1981—. One-woman shows: Watson Gallery, Wheaton Coll., Norton, Mass., 1977, U. Pa., 1977, Med. Coll. Pa., Phila., 1982, Aqueduct Race Track, Long Island, N.Y., 1982, 68, Phila. Art Alliance, 1983, Moore Coll. Art, Phila., 1984. Pres., League of Children's Hosp., Phila., 1969-70. Recipient G. Allen Smith Prize, Woodmere Art Gallery, Chestnut Hill, Pa., 1979. Trustee Moore Coll. Art, 1988—; mem. selections and acquisitions com. Pa. Acad. Fine Arts, 1979—; bd. mgrs., 1975—, chmn. exec. com., 1982—. Mem. Allied Artists Am., Artist's Equity, Phila. Art Alliance, Phila. Print Club.

LEVY, (ALEXANDRA) SUSAN, construction company executive; b. Rockville Centre, N.Y., Apr. 26, 1949; d. Alexander Stanley and Anna Charlotte (Galasieski) Jankoski; m. William Mack Levy, Aug. 12, 1977. Student, Suffolk Community Coll., Brentwood, N.Y., 1976. Cert. constrn. assoc. Supr. N.Y. Telephone Co., Babylon, 1970-74; v.p. Aabbacco Equipment Leasing Corp., Lindenhurst, N.Y., 1974-81; pres., owner Femi-9 Contracting Corp., Lindenhurst, 1981—. Mem. affirmative action adv. council N.Y. State Dept. Transp., Albany, 1984—, human resources adv. panel Long Island Project 2000; mem. Presdl. Task Force, Washington, 1982—. Served with U.S. Army, 1967-69. Recipient Henri Dunant Corp. award ARC Suffolk County, 1986. Mem. Nat. Assn. Women in Constrn. (founder L.I. chpt., pres. 1983—, regional chmn. woman-owned bus. enterprise com., nat. chmn. pub. relations and mktg. com., nat. dir. Region 1 1988—, Mem. of Yr. L.I. chpt. 1987), Nassau Suffolk Contractors Assn. (sec. 1984-87, sec.-treas. 1987—, bd. dirs.), Women Constrn. Owners and Execs., Nat. Assn. Women Bus. Owners (charter), Am. Platform Assn. Republican. Roman Catholic. Avocations: reading, writing, golf. Home: 131 Hollins Ln East Islip NY 11730 Office: Femi-9 Contracting Corp 305 E Sunrise Hwy Lindenhurst NY 11757

LEW, GINGER, lawyer; b. San Mateo, Calif., Nov. 3, 1948; d. Bing and Suey Bow (Ng) L.; m. Carl Lennart Ehn, Feb. 2, 1984; children: Melissa, Jeremy. BS, UCLA, 1970; JD, U. Calif.-Berkeley, 1974. Bar: Calif. 1974, D.C. 1980. Dep. city atty. City of Los Angeles, 1974-75; asst. regional counsel Dept. Energy, San Francisco, 1975-77, dep. regional counsel, 1977-78, chief counsel, 1978-80, dep. asst. sec. of state for East Asia, Dept. of State, Washington, 1980-81, spl. adviser, 1981-82; ptnr. Stovall, Spradlin, Armstrong & Israel, Washington, 1983-86, Arthur Young Co., Washington, 1986—. Recipient Outstanding Achievement award Dept. of State, 1980, Meritorious Service award, 1981. Mem. ABA, Asian Pacific Am. Bar Assn. (bd. dirs. 1981-83), Women's Bar Assn., Orgn. of Chinese-Americans, Pi Sigma Alpha. Clubs: Commonwealth (San Francisco); Nat. Lawyers. Office: Stovall & Spradlin 2600 Virginia Ave NW Suite 820 Washington DC 20037

LEW, KAREN LESLIE, writer; b. Washington, Feb. 19, 1942; d. Lyman Littlefield and Betsy Mae (Dekema) Woodman; student San Francisco State Coll., 1960-61, El Camino Jr. Coll., 1966, UCLA, 1967, U. Alaska, Anchorage, 1971, 75, 77, Sheldon Jackson Coll., 1979, Anchorage Community Coll., 1980, 81, 82, 83; m. Dan Wing Lew, Jan. 12, 1962 (div. 1970); children—Kent Charles, Danika Leslie, Mark Daren. Info. specialist ITT Arctic Services, Inc., Anchorage, Alaska, 1969-71; adminstrv. asst., Mike Ellis Advt., Anchorage, 1971; copywriter, continuity dir. sta. KYAK, Anchorage, 1971-72; copywriter, media buyer Graphix West, Anchorage, 1972-73; classified advt. mgr. Anchorage Daily News, 1973-74; media specialist Alaska Native Commn. on Alcoholism/Drug Abuse, 1974-75; copywriter, continuity dir. Sta. KYAK/KGOT, Anchorage, 1976-77; advt. mgr. Alaska Advocate, Anchorage, 1977-78; advt. rep., writer Alaskafest mag., Anchorage, 1979; info. officer Dept. Natural Resources, State of Alaska, Anchorage, 1979-83, Dept. Fish and Game, 1983-85; freelance writer, 1969—; adj. lectr. composition Anchorage Community Coll., 1982; speaker in field ednl. and community groups. First v.p. Anchorage Council on Alcoholism, 1976-77; vol. arts writer; adv. bd. Independence Mine State Historic Park, 1984-85. Recipient various state and nat. awards for writing, 1969-86. Mem. Nat. Fedn. Press Women, Alaska Press Women (v.p., 1973, 85, rec. sec. 1982), Public Relations Soc. Am., Fireweed Mountaineers Ltd. (pres. 1983-84). Unitarian-Universalist. Clubs: Anchorage Chess, U.S. Chess Fedn., Theatre Guild, Anchorage Community Theatre, Audubon Soc., Anchorage Community Chorus. Editor newsletter Alaska State Council on the Arts, 1979-82; arts columnist Alaskafest Mag., 1979-84. Home: Kripalu Ctr for Yoga & Health PO Box 793 Lenox MA 01240

LEWANDOWSKI, DOROTHY J., educator; b. Chgo., June 16, 1934; d. Stephen Frank and Susan Eleanor (Lassa) L. BS in Edn., Mt. Mary Coll., Milw., 1962; MA in Reading, Cardinal Stritch Coll., Milw., 1977. Cert. tchr., Wis. Tchr. St. Mary's Sch., Port Washington, Wis., 1956-61, St. Frances Cabrini Sch., West Bend, Wis., 1961-68, St. William Sch., Waukesha, Wis., 1971-74; rep. World Book-Childcraft Inc., Milw., 1971—; tchr. chpt. I resource extended day kindergarten Durkee Sch., Kenosha, Wis., 1974—; lectr. in field. Editor: (children's poetry) Resource Rhymes and Reasons, 1985. Mem. Internat. Reading Assn., Bus. Profl. Women (found. chair 1984), Wis. State Reading Assn., Delta Kappa Gamma (2d v.p. 1984). Democrat. Roman Catholic. Home: 2092 S 102d St #309 West Allis WI 53227 Office: Durkee Sch 839 62d St Kenosha WI 53180

LEWIN, ELIZABETH SAMELSON, financial planner; b. Bridgeport, Conn., Feb. 26, 1938; d. Lester and Edith Hecht Samelson; B.A., N.Y. U., 1959; A.S., Sacred Heart U., 1977; cert. fin. planner, Adelphi U., 1980; children—Valerie, Eric. With Hirsch Travel, 1974-76; founder, dir. Budget Adv. Service, Westport, Conn., 1977-84; sr. v.p. Black & Nash Assocs., Wilton, Conn., Mineola, N.Y. and N.Y.C., 1984-86; fin. planning officer, Soc. for savs., Hartford, Conn., 1985—; lectr. on money mgmt., fin. planning. Mem. Internat. Assn. Fin. Planners (v.p. 1980-83, pres. 1983-84), Women's Place, Author's Guild, Nat. Assn. Female Execs. Author: Your Personal Financial Fitness Program, 1983; Financial Fitness for Newlyweds, 1984, Financial Fitness Through Divorce, 1987. Contbr. articles to money mgmt. publs.

LEWIS, ANN FRANK, political analyst, commentator; b. Jersey City, Dec. 19, 1937; d. Samuel and Elsie (Golush) Frank; student Radcliffe Coll., 1954-55; children—Patricia Fay, Beth Ellen, Susan Jane. Asst. to mayor of Boston, 1968-75; dep. campaign mgr. Bayh for President, 1975-76; congl. adminstrv. asst., 1976-81; adminstrv. asst. to Congresswoman Barbara Mikulski, 1978-81; polit. dir. Democratic Nat. Com., 1981-85; co-leader Mass. Women's Polit. Caucus, 1972-74, co-chmn. polit. planning, 1985-87; recorder Nat. Women's Polit. Caucus, 1972-75, chmn. dem. task force; mem. Newton (Mass.) Dem. City Com., 1972-75; mem. nat. bd., exec. com. Americans for Dem. Action, from 1975, nat. dir., 1985-87; mem. nat. bd. Jewish Hist. Soc.; bd. dirs. Am. Jewish Histo. Soc. Mem. Women's Equity Action League, NOW. Jewish. Office: 1074 Thomas Jefferson Washington DC 20007

LEWIS, BARBARA ANN, writer, public relations consultant; b. Buffalo, July 8, 1945; d. Earl and Rose (Galante) Spellburg; m. Knoxie Henry Lewis, Sept. 6, 1975 (div. 1982). B.S., Daemen Coll., 1966; postgrad. SUNY, 1967-69. Exec. sec., sci. instr. Erie Community Coll., Buffalo, 1966-69; beauty and fashion dir., v.p. U.S. Universal, 1971-73; originator, pres. Magic of Venus Internat., Inc., Chgo., 1971-73; writer, producer, narrator The Beauty of It All radio show (nationwide), 1973-75; writer charm curriculum Erie Community Coll., 1968-69; author, producer charity benefit play: The City of Hope, 1972; pub. relations cons. Chgo., 1974-76, Houston, 1982—. Syndicated newspaper columnist The Beauty of It All, 1970-73; contbr. articles to profl. jours. Adoptive parent World Vision, Nairobi, Kenya, 1980—; campaigner Whale Protection Fund, 1978—; mem. Middlebrook Community Assn., Houston, 1978—; charter mem. Statue of Liberty-Ellis Island Commn. Named Student Tchr. of Yr., Nat. Bus. Edn. Assn., 1966; recipient Outstanding Achievement in Bus. Edn. award Nat. Assn. Bus. Tchr. Edn., 1966. Mem. Nat. Bus. Edn. Assn., AAUP, N.Y. Assn. Jr. Coll. Tchrs., Am. Fedn. Tchrs., Faculty Senate of Erie Community Coll., Tex. Mariners Cruising Assn., Alumni Assn. Daemen Coll. Roman Catholic. Club: Clear Lake Rowing. Office: 15815 Stonehaven Dr Houston TX 77059

LEWIS, BARBARA JIMMIE, artist; b. El Paso, Tex., Mar. 14, 1932; d. Frederick Howard and Mildred (Neilson) Cushing; m. Rollin C. Lewis, Oct. 27, 1951; children—Lynn, Bradley, David. Student, U. Tex.-El Paso, 1950-70, U. Nev., 1982—. Tchr., El Paso Pub. Schs., 1954-69; condr. various art classes, workshops; represented by Gallery " 20" , Farmington, N.Mex., Artistic License, Farmington. Exhibited in group shows in Salt Lake City, Las Vegas, Nev., Farmington, N.Mex.; nat. and regional shows in Calif., Utah, Tex., Nev., N.Mex. (first prize watercolor 1982) Mem. N.Mex. Watercolor Soc., Nev. Watercolor Soc., Am. Watercolor Assn. (assoc.), Nat. League Am. Penwomen, Watercolor West Assn. (assoc.), So. Ariz. Watercolor Guild.

LEWIS, BETTY ANN, writer, historian, researcher; b. Fresno, Calif., June 1, 1925; s. Roy William and Dorothy Fredricka (Porter) Bagby; student Hartnell Coll.; m. Monte Randall Lewis, Jan. 11, 1946; children—Christine, Marci, Mike, Kelly. Author: Victorian Homes of Watsonville, 1974; Walking and Driving Tour of Historic Watsonville, 1975; Highlights in the History of Watsonville, 1975; Watsonville Memories That Linger, 1976; Monterey Bay Yesterday, 1977; Watsonville Yesterday, 1978; Watsonville Memories That Linger, Vol. II, 1980; W.H. Weeks, Architect, 1985; speaker, cons. research radio programs. Mem. Watsonville Library Bd., 1982—; mem. Santa Cruz County Hist. Resource Commn., 1985—. Recipient SCOPE awards, 1977, 78; San Jose State U.-Sourisseau Acad. research grantee; named Watsonville Woman of Yr., 1987. Mem. Nat. League Am. Pen Women, Theatre Historians, Calif. Hist. Soc., Calif. Conf. Hist. Socs., (v.p. 1982), Pajaro Valley Hist. Assn. (pres. 1980-81, Hubert Wyckoff Meml. award 1979), Santa Cruz Soc. for Hist. Preservation (award for book on W.H. Weeks 1986). Republican. Presbyterian (elder). Office: Mansion House 420 Main St Suite 204 Watsonville CA 95076

LEWIS, BEULAH ANN GRAY, accountant, consultant; b. Starr, S.C., July 31, 1938; d. Charles Carlton and Margaret Noami (Busby) G.; m. Henry Y. Lewis, Sept. 7, 1957 (div. Mar. 1980); 1 child, Paul Anthony. Course in bookkeeping, Forrest Coll., 1957, 71. Bookkeeper First Nat. Bank, Anderson, S.C., 1957, 1959-60, R.I. Hosp. Trust Co., Newport, 1957-58, Br. Banking and Trust Co., Fayetteville, N.C., 1960; teller First Citizens Bank and Trust Co., Ft. Bragg, S.C., 1960-62; clk. S.C. State Hwy. Dept., Anderson, 1965-67, Dow Badische Co., Anderson, 1968-71; staff acct. Nat. Soc. Engr. Exam., Seneca, S.C., 1971-73, J. B. Watson, CPA, Wadesboro, N.C., 1973-87; pvt. practice accting. 1987—; accredited practitioner Accreditation Council Accountancy, Alexandria, Va., 1985. Mem. Nat. Soc. Pub. Accts. Presbyterian. Home: PO Box 937 Wadesboro NC 28170

LEWIS, BRENDA ANNETTE, computer system specialist; b. Nashville, July 3, 1953; d. Charles H. and Dorothy F. Lewis. BS, Fisk U., 1975; M of Pub. Health, U. Tenn., 1977. Health planner Okla. Health Systems Agy., Tulsa, 1977-79; systems engr. IBM Corp., Tulsa, 1979-83; mktg. support rep. IBM Corp., Irving, Tex., 1983-86; adv. systems rep. IBM Corp., Houston, 1986-87, Ft. Worth, 1987—. Mem. Jr. Black Acad., Dallas, 1987—. Mem. NAACP, Minority Leaders and Citizens Council, Nat. Assn. Female Execs., Alpha Kappa Alpha (chpt. pres. 1981-83, nat. nominating com. 1986—). Democrat. Episcopalian.

LEWIS, CAROLYN ANNE, investment executive; b. Austin, Tex., Oct. 25, 1954; d. R.B. and Margaret (Sibley) Lewis. B.A., Duke U., 1976; M.B.A., Harvard U., 1982. V.p. corp. planning Distbn. Systems, Inc., Houston, 1982-84; pres. Houston Trailer, Inc., 1984-86, Peachtree Land Co., 1986—.

LEWIS, CHARLENE, data processing executive; b. Manson, Ark.; d. Robert Leo and Dorothy Donibee (Kidd) Lewis. BS in Acctg., San Diego State U., 1971; MBA, Nat. U., 1980. Gen. acct. Anacomp, Inc. (formerly Datagraphix, Inc.), San Diego, 1970-73, adminstrv. acct., 1973-76, acctg. group leader, 1976-77, supr. acctg., 1977-79, sr. fin. analyst, 1979-84, mgmt. info. systems specialist, 1984-87, specialist data processing, 1987—. Mem. Mgmt. Club. Clubs: Walkabout, International. Home: 12719 La Tortola San Diego CA 92129 Office: Anacomp Inc PO Box 82449 San Diego CA 92138

LEWIS, DIANE PATRICIA, finance executive; b. Elizabeth, N.J., Oct. 9, 1956; d. Walter Charles and Ethel Alida (Worth) L. Assocs. of Bus., Union Coll., 1976; B of Psychology, Rutgers Coll., 1979. Br. mgr. Household Fin. Corp., Wayne, N.J., 1979-85; budget coordinator comml. sector Chase Manhatten Bank, N.Y.C., 1985—; dir. seminars, workshops, classes Eckankar, Rahway, N.J., 1979—; freelance computer cons., N.Y.C., 1986—. Mem. Phi Theta Kappa. Office: 2350 Broadway Suite 1225 New York NY 10024

LEWIS, EDITH JO AN DIETRICH, nurse, educator; b. New Albany, Ind., Aug. 15, 1951; d. Walter Riddle and Peggy JoAn (Byers) D.; m. Stefan Joseph Lewis, Feb. 14, 1987. AA in Nursing, Ind. U. SE, 1971; BS in Nursing, Ind. U., 1975; MS in Counseling, Ind. U. SE, 1984. Cert. RN, Ind., Ky. Clin. instr. Spalding U., Louisville, Ky., 1978-79; dir. edn. North Clark Community Hosp., Charlestown, Ind., 1979-88; exec. dir. CommuniCare Cons., Inc., New Albany, Ind., 1985—; instr. Personal Dynamics Inc., 1986—. Bd. dirs. Hospice So. Ind., New Albany, 1983—, Am. Heart Assn. So. Ind., New Albany, 1984—, Louisville chpt. Am. Diabetes Assn., 1986. Recipient Dr. Thomas Frist Humanitarian award Hosp. Corp. Am., 1984. Mem. Am. Assn. for Counseling and Devel., Nat. Assn. for Female Execs., Nat. Speakers Assn. of Ky., Ind. Assn. for Specialists in Group Work, Ky. Assn. for Specialists in Group Work. Home and Office: CommuniCare Cons Inc Rural Rt 3 Box 230 Borden IN 47106

LEWIS, ELEANOR ROBERTS, lawyer; b. Detroit, Jan. 5, 1944; d. David Edward and Patricia Mary (Easterbrook) Roberts; m. Roger Kutnow Lewis, June 24, 1967; 1 child, Kevin Michael. B.A., Wellesley Coll., 1965; M.A.T., Harvard U., 1966; J.D., Georgetown U., 1974. Bar: D.C. 1975, U.S. Dist. Ct. D.C. 1975, U.S. Ct. Appeals (D.C. cir.) 1975, U.S. Ct. Appeals (10th cir.) 1976, U.S. Supreme Ct. 1980. cert. tchr. Tchr., Waltham (Mass.) High Sch., 1966-67, Holton-Arms Sch., Bethesda, Md., 1967-71; atty. HUD, Washington, 1974-76, asst. gen. counsel, 1979-82; atty. Brownstein Zeidman & Schomer, Washington, 1976-79; asst. gen. counsel U.S. Dept. Commerce, Washington, 1982—. Author, editor (with others) Street Law, 1975. Contbr. chpts. to books, articles to legal and fin. jours. Bd. dirs. Dana Place Condominium, Washington. Wellesley Coll. scholar, 1963-65. Mem. ABA, D.C. Bar Assn., Women's Bar Assn. D.C., Women in Housing and Fin. Home: 5034 1/2 Dana Pl NW Washington DC 20016 Office: US Dept Commerce 14th & Constitution Ave NW Washington DC 20230

LEWIS, ELIZABETH NANCY, hospital administrator; b. St. Paul, Aug. 23; d. Clyde E. and Elsie I. (Larson) Hegman; RN, St. Barnabas Hosp. Sch. Nursing, 1968; BS, U. Minn., 1976; MS, PhD, Columbia Pacific U. Staff nurse Mpls. St. Paul area hosps., 1968-74; asst. coordinator staff devel. and inservice edn. Midway Hosp., St. Paul, 1974-77; adminstrv. asst., dir. nursing NW Gen. Hosp., Milw., 1977-78; dir. nursing adminstrn. San Dimas Community Hosp., Calif. 1978-79; asst. adminstr. Dr.'s Hosp., Pinole, Calif., 1979-84; cons. research and devel. Nat. Med. Enterprises, Los Angeles, 1984-85; assoc. adminstr. Ross Gen. Hosp., Republic Health Corp., Ross, Calif., 1985-88; v.p. patient care services St. Luke's Hosp., San Francisco, 1988—. Co-author: Nurse Staffing and Patient Classification; Strategies for Success, 1984, Manual of Patient Classification, 1988. Bd. govs. St. Paul div. Minn. affiliate Am. Heart Assn.; mem. senate and student bd. U. Minn. Mem. East Bay Nursing Adminstrs. Council, Am. Orgn. Nurse Execs., Flying Samaritans Internat., Calif. Soc. Nursing Service Adminstrs., Sigma Theta Tau. Home: 15 Mt Burney Ct San Rafael CA 94903 Office: St Luke's Hosp 3555 Army St San Francisco CA 94110

LEWIS, EVELYN, communications and public relations executive; b. Goslar, Germany, Sept. 19, 1946; came to U.S. 1952, naturalized 1957; d. Gerson Emanuel and Sala (Mendlowicz) L. B.A., U. Ill.-Chgo., 1968; M.A., Ball State U., 1973, Ph.D., 1976. Research analyst Comptroller, State Ill., Chgo., 1977-78; lectr. polit. sci. dept. Loyola U., Chgo., 1977; asst. to commr. Dept. Human Services, Chgo., 1978-81; group mgr. communications Arthur Anderson & Co., Chgo., 1981-84; dir. communications and pub. relations Heidrick and Struggles, Inc., Chgo., 1984—; adj. faculty Roosevelt U. Sch. Bus. Adminstrn., 1988. Mem. Children of the Holocaust, Chgo., 1982; mem. venture grants com. United Way of Chgo.; bd. dirs. Parental Stress Services. Mem. Internat. Assn. Bus. Communicators, Publicity Club Chgo., Council of Communication Mgmt, Nat. Assn. Female Execs., B'nai Brith. Jewish. Club: Metropolitan (Chgo.). Avocations: writing, poetry, bicycling, hiking. Office: Heidrick and Struggles Inc 125 S Wacker Dr Chicago IL 60606

LEWIS, FLORA, journalist; b. Los Angeles; d. Benjamin and Pauline (Kallin) L.; m. Sydney Gruson, Aug. 17, 1945 (div.); children—Kerry, Sheila, Lindsey. B.A., UCLA, 1941; M.S., Columbia U., 1942, LHD (hon.), 1984; LL.D., Princeton U., 1981; hon. doctorate, Mt. Holyoke Coll., Bucknell U., Muhlenberg Coll., Manhattan Marymount. Reporter Los Angeles Times, 1941, A.P., N.Y., Washington, London, 1942-46; free lance or contract for Observer, Economist, Financial Times, France-soir, Time Mag.; free lance or contract for N.Y. Times Mag., London, Warsaw, Berlin, Hague, Mexico City, Tel Aviv, 1946-54, Prague, Warsaw, 1956-58; editor McGraw-Hill, N.Y.C., 1955; bur. chief Washington Post, Bonn, London, N.Y.C., 1958-66; syndicated columnist Newsday, Paris, N.Y.C., 1967-72; bur. chief N.Y. Times, Paris, 1972-80; European diplomatic corr. N.Y. Times, 1976-80, fgn. affairs columnist, 1980—. Author: Case History of Hope, 1958, Red Pawn, 1964, One of Our H-Bombs is Missing, 1967, Europe: A Tapestry of Nations, 1987; contbr. to anthologies, books, mags. Mem. council Internat. Inst. for Strategic Studies, London; bd. dirs. Inst. for East-West Security Studies, N.Y.C. Arthur D. Morse fellow in communications and society Aspen Inst. for Humanistic Studies, 1977; decorated chevalier Legion d'Honneur; recipient awards for best interpretation fgn. affairs, 1956, best reporting fgn. affairs, 1960; Overseas Press Club award; Columbia Journalism Sch. 50th Anniversary Honor award, 1963; award for disting. diplomatic reporting George Washington U. Sch. Fgn. Service, 1978, Carr Van Anda award Ohio State U. Sch. Communications, 1982, Fourth Estate award Nat. Press Club, 1985, Matrix award for Newspapers N.Y. Women in Communications Inc., 1985, Elmer Holmes Bobst award in Arts and Letters

NYU, 1987; named hon. fellow UCLA Coll. Arts and Scis. Mem. Council on Fgn. Relations, Internat. Inst. for Strategic Studies (council), Inst. for East-West Security Studies (bd. dirs.), Phi Beta Kappa. Office: NY Times Foreign News Desk 229 W 43d St New York NY 10036 also: NY Times, 3 Rue Scribe, Paris 9e France

LEWIS, GLADYS SHERMAN, nurse, educator; b. Wynnewood, Okla., Mar. 20, 1933; d. Andrew and Minnie Elva (Halsey) Sherman; R.N., St. Anthony's Sch. Nursing, 1953; student Okla. Bapt. U., 1953-55; A.B., Tex. Christian U., 1956; postgrad. Southwestern Bapt. Theol. Sem., 1959-60, Escuela de Idiomas, San Jose, Costa Rica, 1960-61; M.A. in Creative Writing, Central (Okla.) State U., 1985; m. Wilbur Curtis Lewis, Jan. 28, 1955; children—Karen, David, Leanne, Cristen. Mem. nursing staff various facilities, Okla., 1953-57; instr. nursing, med. missionary Bapt. mission and hosp., Paraguay, 1961-70; vice-chmn. edn. commn. Paraguay Bapt. Conv., 1962-65; sec. bd. trustees Bapt. Hosp., Paraguay, 1962-65; chmn. personnel com., handbook and policy book officer Bapt. Mission in Paraguay, 1967-70; trustee Southwestern Bapt. Theol. Sem., 1974-84, chmn. student affairs com., 1976-78, vice-chmn. bd. 1978-80; ptnr. Las Amigas Tours, 1978-80; writer, conference leader, campus lectr., 1959—. Active Democratic party; leader Girl Scouts U.S.A., 1965-75; Okla. co-chmn. Nat. Religious Com. for Equal Rights Amendment, 1977-79; tour host Meier Internat. Study League, 1978-81. Mem. AAUW, Internat. and Am. colls. surgeons women's auxiliaries, Okla. State, Okla. County med. auxiliaries. Author: On Earth As It Is, 1983; Two Dreams and a Promise, 1984; also religious instructional texts in English and Spanish; editor Sooner Physician's Heartbeat, 1979-82; contbr. articles to So. Bapt. and secular periodicals. Home: 14501 N Western Ave Edmond OK 73013

LEWIS, HELEN PHELPS HOYT, association executive; b. Lakewood, N.J., Dec. 27, 1902; d. John Sherman and Ethel Phelps (Stokes) Hoyt; m. Byron Stookey, May 11, 1929 (dec. Oct. 20, 1966); children: John Hoyt, Lyman Brumbaugh, Byron; m. Robert James Lewis, Aug. 5, 1971. A.B., Bryn Mawr Coll., Pa.) Coll., 1923; M.A., Union Theol. Sem. of Columbia U., 1925. Bd. mgrs. Christodora Settlement House, N.Y.C., 1927-38; 1st v.p. Christodora Settlement House, 1929-38; nat. bd. YWCA, 1927-30; mem. women's adv. council N.Y. Bot. Garden, 1952—; mem. nursing com. Columbia Presbyn. Med. Center, N.Y.C., 1944-54; trustee Columbia Presbyn. Med. Center, 1969-78, hon. trustee, 1978—; mem. women's aux. Neurol. Inst., N.Y.C., 1939—, chmn., 1949-54; mem. women's exec. com., chmn. com. hosp. auxs. United Hosp. Fund, 1951-64, vice chmn. women's campaign com., 1961-62, chmn. women's subcom. distbn., 1963-65, vice chmn. women's exec. com., 1963-64. Mem. Colonial Dames Am. (dir. 1951-56, chmn. scholarship com. 1949-51, pres.-gen. 1953-56), Daus. Cincinnati. Republican. Presbyterian. Clubs: Darien (Conn.); Garden (pres. 1935-38), Millbrook Garden (past pres.), Garden Club Am; Colony (N.Y.C.) (gov. 1954-76, sec. 1956-59, sec., v.p. 1969-71, pres. 1972-76, chmn. membership com. 1956-71). Address: 580 Park Ave New York NY 10021

LEWIS, HONEY A., lawyer, reserve police officer; b. Los Angeles, July 10, 1942; d. Joseph and Esther (Lebenson) L. BA in Polit. Sci., UCLA, 1964; JD, U. San Fernando, 1968; MA in Polit. Sci., Calif. State U., East Los Angeles, 1973. Bar: Calif. 1969, U.S. Dist. Ct. (so. dist.) 1969, U.S. Supreme Ct. 1981. Sole practice Los Angeles, 1969-70; dep. city atty. City of Los Angeles, 1970—; res. officer Los Angeles Police Dept., 1980—. Former rep. 43d assembly dist. Dem. Cen. Com. Mem. ABA, Los Angeles County Bar Assn., Am. Judicature Soc. Clubs: San Fernando, Valley (Calif.) Track.

LEWIS, JEANNETTE KAY, academic administrator; b. Columbus, Ohio, Sept. 11, 1952; d. William Joseph and Luella (Sanders) L. BS, Ohio Wesleyan U., 1973; MA, Ohio State U., 1978. Cert. tchr., supr., adminstr., Ohio. Tchr. Columbus Pub. Schs., 1973-79, reading specialist, 1979-81, community liaison, 1981-82, instr. arts impact dance, 1982-83; assoc. dir. instrn. and tng. N.J. Edn. Assn., Trenton, 1983-86; dir. profl. devel. Ohio Edn. Assn., Columbus, 1986—; leadership cons. Conn. Edn. Assn., Hartford, 1986-87; trainer N.J. Edn. Assn., 1986—. Mem. NEA, Nat. Assn. Improvement Instrn. (regional v.p. 1987), Am. Soc. for Tng. and Devel., Assn. Supervision and Curriculum Devel., Am. Mgmt. Assn., Nat. Sch. Vols, Phi Delta Kappan. Democrat. Methodist. Office: Ohio Edn Assn 225 E Broad St Columbus OH 43216

LEWIS, JUDITH ANN, personnel executive; b. Pitts., July 23, 1947; d. George T. and Madeleine Paustenbach; m. Gary S. Lewis, May 26, 1984. Personnel asst. White Motor Corp., Cleve., 1969-76; personnel mgr. St. Regis Paper Co., Cleve., 1976-79; mgr. indsl. relations Lever Bros., Balt., 1979-82; dir. human relations McCormick and Co., Inc., Balt., 1982—; bd. dirs. McCormic-Stange Flavor div., Balt., 1987—. Pres. Exec. Women's Network, Balt., 1980—. Mem. Am. Soc. Personnel Adminstrs. (sr. profl.). Office: McCormick and Co Inc 230 Schilling Circle S Hunt Valley MD 21031

LEWIS, KAREN CALLIS, accountant; b. Batesville, Ark., Aug. 13, 1951; d. Tommy Lee Callis and Alloween (Bradley) Turner; m. H. Bert Lewis, Feb. 26, 1972; children: Margaret Allison, Zachary Bert. BSE summa cum laude, U. Ark., 1979. CPA, Ark. Bus. tchr. Decatur (Ark.) High Sch., 1979-80; dir. acctg. Sparks Regional Med. Ctr., Ft. Smith, Ark., 1980—; mem. adv. com. Westark Community Coll., Ft. Smith, Ark. Pres. Sparks Good Neighbor Found., Ft. Smith, 1986—. Mem. Am.Inst. CPA's, Ark. Soc. CPA's, Healthcare Fin. Mgmt. Assn., Beta Sigma Pi (treas. 1986—), Phi Beta Lambda (Phi Xi chpt. historian 1978), Kappa Delta Pi. Republican. Methodist. Home: 6811 South V St Fort Smith AR 72903 Office: Sparks Regional Med Ctr 1311 South I St Fort Smith AR 72901

LEWIS, KATHRYN MONICA, nurse educator; b. Youngstown, Ohio, Sept. 20, 1936; d. Peter Paul and Mary (Slosar) Janic; m. Charles Edward Lewis, Aug. 23, 1969; children: Michelle Marie, Mark Paul. Diploma in nursing, St. Elizabeth Hosp., Youngstown, 1957; B in Nursing, Ariz. State U., 1972, MEd, 1975. RN, Ohio, Ariz., Calif.; cert. tchr., Ariz. Charge nurse polio ward St. Elizabeth Hosp., Youngstown, 1957-59, surg. staff nurse, 1959-60; office nurse Leonard Caccamo, MD, Youngstown, 1959-60; staff nurse Alta Bates Hosp., Berkley, Calif., 1960; charge nurse med., surg. Good Samaritan Hosp., Phoenix, 1960-69, coordinator surg. nursing care, 1969-74, instr. critical care, 1974-85; ind. instr. nursing, paramedicine, cardiovascular and electrocardiography, critical care nursing Am. Heart Assn. Ariz., Samaritan Health Services, Phoenix Fire Dept. Paramedic Tng.; parttime clin. instr. Mesa Community Hosp., 1985—. Contbr. articles to profl. jours; author pre-operative instructional mans.; producer numerous ednl. videotapes. Active various coms. Am. Heart Assn. Maricopa County, Ariz., 1984—. Recipient Merit award City of Phoenix and Phoenix Fire Dept., 1984. Mem. Am. Trauma Soc., Am. Nurses Found., Am. Nurses Assn., Am. Assn. Critical Care Nurses (cert., past mem. cert. com., past pres. Phoenix chpt., past bull. chairperson, past edn. com. chairperson, recording sec.), Nat. Critical Care Inst. Edn., Ariz. State Nurses Assn. (mem. continuing edn. com.), Assn. Advancement Instrumentation, St. Elizabeth Hosp. Alumni Assn., Sigma Theta Tau, Phi Kappa Phi. Roman Catholic. Home: 5801 E Windsor Scottsdale AZ 85257 Office: Kacel Inc PO Box 8627 Scottsdale AZ 85252 also: Phoenix Coll 1202 W Thomas Rd Phoenix AZ 85013

LEWIS, LINDA DONELLE, neurologist, educator; b. Columbus, Ohio, Nov. 27, 1939; d. Donald Peter and Ann Elizabeth (Karn) Lewis; B.S., Bethany Coll., 1961, D.Sc. (hon.), 1981; M.D., W.Va. U., 1965; m. Gary Gambuti, Oct. 6, 1979. Practice medicine specializing in neurology, N.Y.C., 1971—; asst. prof. neurology Coll. Physicians and Surgeons, Columbia U., N.Y.C., from 1971, now clin. prof., assoc. dean student affairs, 1979—; cons. in field; mem. N.Y. State Bd. for Profl. Med. Conduct, 1979—. Recipient Outstanding Teaching award Columbia U., 1977. Mem. AMA (nat. com. on med. edn.), N.Y. State Med. Soc. (del.), New York County Med. Soc., Am. Assn. Med. Colls., Am. Acad. Neurology, AAAS. Contbr. articles to sci. jours. Home: 320 Central Park W New York NY 10025 Office: 710 W 168th St New York NY 10032

LEWIS, LINDA ELLEN, venture capitalist; b. Norwich, Conn., Oct. 30, 1958; d. Richard Forrest and Frances Amelia (Stankewicz) L. BS, Purdue U., 1980; MBA, U. Chgo., 1984. Med. technologist Assocs. in Internal Medicine, Chgo., 1980-82; mktg. analyst Joint Commn. on the Accreditation of Hosps., Chgo., 1983; cons. Laventhol & Horwath, Phila., 1984-85; assoc. Cain Bros., Shattuck & Co., N.Y.C., 1985-88; asst. v.p. Elf Technologies, Inc., Stamford, Conn., 1988—. Mem. U. Chgo. Women's Bus. Group, Nat. Assn. Female Execs. Club: Chgo. Bus. Sch. (N.Y.C.). Office: Elf Technologies Inc High Ridge Park PO Box 10037 Stamford CT 06904

LEWIS, LINDA F., cosmetics executive; b. Pensacola, Fla., Dec. 27, 1944; d. Herman Estess and Ruth (Hidgon) Godwin; m. Robert Chris Lewis, Aug. 12, 1961; children: Tammy Lynn Brunner, Christie Leigh. Sales dir. Mary Kay Cosmetics, Dallas, 1974—. Republican. Baptist. Home: 7157 Belgium Rd Pensacola FL 32506

LEWIS, LINDA LOUISE, educator; b. Kalispell, Mont., Aug. 21, 1947; d. Neil Forrester and Mildred (Britzman) Chidley; m. Russell Frederick Lewis, June 28, 1969; 1 child, Katie Jeannine. BA with honors, U. Mont., 1968; postgrad., Mont. State U., 1969-70. Cert. tchr., Calif. Tchr. Vallejo (Calif.) City Unified Sch. Dist., 1970-86, instructional assoc., 1986—. Sec. adv. council Highland Sch., Vallejo, 1979-86; mem. adv. council Davidson Sch., Vallejo, 1986-87; mem. Solano County Apt. Owners Assn., Vallejo, 1983-87, Solano County Reading Assn. Grantee State of Calif., 1985, 86. Mem. NEA, Calif. Tchrs. Assn., Vallejo Edn. Assn., Calif. Assn. Compensatory Edn., Delta Kappa Gamma. Republican. Presbyterian. Office: Davidson Sch 436 Del Sur St Vallejo CA 94591

LEWIS, LINDA WARD, editor; b. River, Ky., Aug. 20, 1945; d. Carl and Sarah Jane (Preston) Ward; m. W. Lavon Lewis, July 8, 1967; 1 child, Stacy Annette. BA in English, Eastern Ky. U., 1966, MA in English, 1967. Publs. dir. Internat. Fertility and Research Program, Research Triangle Pk., N.C., 1973-78; editor Fancy Pubs., Los Angeles, 1978—. Office: Fancy Publs Box 6050 Mission Viejo CA 92690

LEWIS, LUCINDA LEE, nursing administrator; b. Alma, Ark., May 10, 1956; d. Warren Darrell and Violet Ruth Blaylock; m. Gary Dale Lewis, July 29, 1975 (div. May 1988); children: Jared Scott, Audra Morgan. AA, Westark Community Coll., Ft. Smith, Ark., 1977; BS, Coll. of Ozarks, Clarksville, Ark., 1985. RN. Nurse Sparks Regional Med. Ctr., Ft. Smith, 1977; epidemiologist St. Edward Mercy Med. Ctr., Ft. Smith, 1978-85, CPR instr., 1981—, ambulatory services dir., 1985-87; adminstrv. dir. Mercy Med. Services, Ft. Smith, 1988—. Mem. United Meth. Ch. adminstrv. bd., Alma, 1977—; advisor Westark Community Coll., Ft. Smith, 1986-87. Named One of Outstanding Young Women of Am., 1986. Mem. Nat. Assn. Female Execs., Pilot Club Internat. Home: 122 Meadors Dr Alma AR 72921 Office: Saint Edward Mercy Med Ctr 7301 Rogers Ave Fort Smith AR 72903

LEWIS, SR. MARGARET MARY, medical facility administrator; b. Phila., Apr. 2, 1929; d. John Francis and Julia Mary (Creary) L. Student, St. Francis Med. Ctr., Trenton, N.J., 1951-53; BS, Villanova U., 1961; MA, Trenton State Coll., 1971; ArtsD, Cath. U., 1976. Joined Sisters of St. Francis, 1946. Elem. tchr. St. Bernadette Sch., Silver Spring, Md., 1949-51; lab. supr. St. Francis Hosp., Wilmington, Del., 1953-64, v.p., 1985—; med. technician edn. coordinator St. Francis Med. Ctr., Trenton, 1964-71; program dir. med. tech. Neumann Coll ., Aston, Pa., 1971-84; adminstrv. asst. Pa. Hosp., Phila., 1984-85. Author: Clinical Parasitology, 1975; contbr. numerous articles to profl. jours. Chairperson Delchester Health Edn. Consortium, Chester, Pa., 1981-84; bd. dirs. Delaware County chpt. ARC, Media, Pa., 1974-81. Recipient Benjamin Rush award Delaware County Med. Soc., 1973, Allied Health Edn. award NIH, Bethesda, Md., 1974. Mem. Am. Soc. Clin. Pathologists (assoc., program surveyor 1966-71), Am. Soc. Med. Technologists, Am. Soc. Healthcare Execs. (nominee), Nat. Accredidation Agy. for Clin. Lab. Scis. (survey team chmn. 1980-85). Republican. Roman Catholic. Home: 905 Milltown Rd Wilmington DE 19808 Office: St Francis Hosp 7th and Clayton Sts Wilmington DE 19805

LEWIS, MARGARET ONEIDA, health science company director; b. Nashville, June 4, 1944; d. Emmett Leon and Myra Frances (Thompson) Still; m. Donald Edward Lewis, Aug. 29, 1965. Diploma in nursing, Met. Gen. Hosp. Sch. Nursing, Nashville, 1965. RN, Tenn. Coordinator staff devel. Bapt. Hosp., Nashville, 1972-76; supr. audit EDS Fed., Nashville, 1976; supr. rev. coordinator Tenn. Found. for Med. Care, Nashville, 1976-79; from discharge planner to coordinator utilization rev. So. Hills Hosp., Nashville, 1979-84; dir. quality assurance Transmed-HCA, Nashville, 1984-85; dir. utilization mgmt. Health Net, Inc., Nashville, 1985—; cons., com. mem. Georgetown U., Washington, 1985-86. Mem. Nat. Assn Quality Assurance Profls., Nat. Assn. Female Execs., Tenn. Fedn. Bus. Profl. Women's Clubs, Bus. and Profl. Women's Club Nashville (recording sec. 1986-87, 2d v.p. 1987—, pres. elect 1988—). Republican. Baptist. Home: 3332 Old Franklin Rd Antioch TN 37013 Office: Health-Net Inc 4525 Harding Rd Suite 100 Nashville TN 37205

LEWIS, MARGARET SHIVELY, librarian; b. Indpls., Sept. 27, 1925; d. William E. and Florence (Knox) Shively; m. Phillip Fenton Lewis, Sept. 10, 1948; children—David William, Catharine, Fredrick, Thomas. B.A., Oberlin Coll., 1947; M.L.S., St. John's U., Jamaica, N.Y., 1971. Librarian Optometric Ctr. N.Y., N.Y.C., 1971; head librarian Coll. Optometry, SUNY, N.Y.C., 1971—; mem. exec. com. SUNY Council Head Librarians, Albany, 1977-79; chairperson Faculty Orgn., SUNY Coll. Optometry, N.Y.C., 1980-82; mem. SUNY/OCLC Network Adv. Com., 1986—. library fellow St. John's U., Jamaica, N.Y., 1969. Fellow Am. Acad. Optometry; mem. ALA, Assn. Vision Sci. Librarians (chairperson 1977-78), N.Y. Regional Med Librarians, Phi Beta Kappa. Democrat. Episcopalian. Home: 44-09 244th St Douglaston NY 11363 Office: SUNY Coll Optometry 100 E 24th St New York NY 10010-3677

LEWIS, MARTHA WELLS, economist; b. Madison, Wis., Mar. 1, 1922; d. Sidney Deeds and Hope Blanche (Shank) Wells; m. Robert George Lewis, June 6, 1942; children: Eric, Sarah, M. Dustin, Peter. BA, U. Wis., 1945. Asst. to dir. Nat. Council of Agrl. Life and Labor, Washington, 1958-59; selection staff U.S. Peace Corps, Washington, 1962-64; treas., asst. sec. Kickapoo Canyon, Inc., Wauzeka, Wis., 1972-82; research dir. Flashmaps, Inc., Washington, 1974-77; cons. econ. devel. Washington, 1977-82; dir. women in devel. program Ptnrs. of the Ams., Washington, 1982—; cons. women's ednl. programs Nat. Adv. Council, 1976, Conf. on Women and Food U. Ariz., Tucson, 1978. Pres. Nat. Capital Chpt. Women's Equity Action League, 1974-76. Mem. Assn. for Women in Devel. (sec. 1986—), Women and Food Info. Network, Inc. (sec. 1985—), Nat. Farmers Union. Home: 3512 Porter St NW Washington DC 20016 Office: Ptnrs of the Americas 1424 K St NW Washington DC 20005

LEWIS, MARY ELLEN, psychotherapist; b. Green Bay, Wis., Nov. 17, 1948; d. Lawrence Edward, Jr., and Irene Marie (Mumm) L.; B.A. in Sociology, U. Wis., Madison, 1970, M.S.S.W., 1972. Psychotherapist Central Comprehensive Mental Health Center, Centralia, Ill., 1972-75, clin. dir., 1975-76; psychotherapist Family Counseling, Aurora, Ill., 1977-80, dir. individual and family counseling div., 1980-83; pvt. practice psychotherapy, counseling, 1983—. Program chmn. Kane County NOW; adv. bd. YWCA, Aurora. Cert. sch. social worker, parent effectiveness tng. instr., Ill. Mem. Women in Mgmt., Women in Networking (adv. bd.), Nat. Assn. Social Workers, Acad. Cert. Social Workers, Am. Assn. Ethical Hypnotists, Am. Assn. Sex Educators, Counselors and Therapists (cert. sex counselor). Office: 411 W Galena Blvd Aurora IL 60506

LEWIS, MARY THERESE, artist; b. Blue Island, Ill., June 21, 1951; d. Christian Henry and Marie Anne (Corcoran) Berns; B.S. in Math. with highest honors, U. Ill., 1974; M.S. in Physics, U. Chgo., 1978; m. Richard W. Lewis, Feb. 16, 1979. Lead engr. research and devel. robotics and artificial intelligence Boeing Mil. Airplane Co., Wichita, Kans., 1978-84; self-employed artificial intelligence engr., 1984-85; artist, 1985—. Mem. Am. Assn. Artificial Intelligence, Internat. Platform Assn., Phi Kappa Phi. Avocation: classical piano. Home and Office: 2221 Inwood Dr Wilmington DE 19810

LEWIS, MELINDA ANNE, corporate safety administrator; b. Arlington, Va., Oct. 25, 1958; d. Jack Collins and Jacqueline Lucille (Allen) L. Grad., Largo Sr. High, 1973-76. Policy typist Marsh & McLennan Ins. Agy., Washington, 1977-79; account rep. Frank B. Hall & Co., San Antonio, 1979-80, regional mgr., 1980-81; account exec. Charles R. Myers Ins. Agy., San Antonio, 1981-84; risk mgr. James E. Strates Shows, Inc., Orlando, Fla., 1984-85, Reithoffer Shows, Inc., Coral Springs, Fla., 1985—; ins. cons. various outdoor amusement bus., 1984—; pub. relations Boys and Girls Clubs of Am. Mem. Miami Showmen's Ladies Auxilary. Office: Reithoffer Shows Inc 5332 NW 77th Terr Coral Springs FL 33067

LEWIS, NANCY ANN, nurse; b. Zanesville, Ohio, Apr. 1, 1950; d. David Griff and Barbara Ann (Hoy) L. Diploma, Albany (N.Y.) Med. Ctr. Hosp., 1972; BS in Nursing, Pa. State U., 1981; MS in Nursing, U. Pitts., 1985. Registered Nurse. Staff nurse Albany Med. Ctr. Hosp., 1972-75; team leader Harmarville Rehab. Ctr., Pitts., 1975-76, patient care coordinator, 1976-82, nursing supr., 1982—. Contbr. articles to profl. jours. Mem. Am. Nurses Assn., Am. Assn. Neurosci. Nurses, Assn. Rehab. Nurses (S.W. Pa. chpt. pres. 1985-86), Assn. Clin. Nursing Specialists,. Republican. Methodist. Office: Harmarville Rehab Ctr P O Box 11460 Pittsburgh PA 15238

LEWIS, PAMELA ANDERSON, banker; b. Wise, Va., June 23, 1954; d. Billy Eugene and Wanda (Flanary) Anderson; m. Keith Ward, Nov. 13, 1972 (div. Mar. 1977); 1 child, Billy Keith; m. George Mack Lewis Jr., June 4, 1982. Cert., Johnson City (Tenn.) Vocat. Sch. With catalog dept. Sears, Johnson City, 1977-79, exec. sec. mgrs. office, 1979-80; br. sec. 1st Tenn. Bank, Johnson City, 1980-81, exec. asst. to regional pres., 1981—. Vol. Salvation Army/Adopt an Angle, Johnson City, 1985, 86; asst. for ann. art show Johnson City Area Arts Council, 1981—; mem. adv. bd. secretarial sci. Tri-Cities State Tech., Johnson City, 1986—. Named one of Outstanding Young Women of Am., 1985. Mem. Profl. Secs. Internat. (treas. 1986-88, pres.-elect 1988—, bd. dirs. Tri-Cities chpt. 1984—). Office: 1st Tenn Bank NA 1919 N Roan St Johnson City TN 37601

LEWIS, PAMELA LYNNE, marketing professional, consultant; b. Nashville, Nov. 23, 1958; d. John Joseph and Joan Muriel (Warren) L. BA in Econs. and Mktg., Wells Coll., 1980. Nat. publicist Warner Amex Satellite Entertainment, N.Y.C., 1980-84; nat. media mgr. RCA Records, Nashville, 1984-85; pres. Pamela Lewis & Assocs., Nashville, 1985—; nat. publicist WASEC-MTV: Music Television, The Movie Channel, Nickelodeon. Contbr. articles to mags. Mem. Cheekwood Botanical Garden and Fine Arts Ctr., Nashville, 1984-87, Nashvillians for a Nuclear Arms Freeze, Planet Earth Project. Named Best Entertainment Publicist Nashville Scene Mag., 1987. Mem. Nat. Entertainment Journalists, Nat. Assn. Female Execs., Nashville Entertainment Assn. (music com.), Country Music Assn., Nat. Assn. Recording Arts and Scis. (voting), Acad. Country Music (voting), Alliance Française, Nashville C. of C. Democrat. Club: Unity Singers. Home: 225 Chapel Ave Nashville TN 37206 Office: Pamela Lewis Media Relations Mktg 10 Music Circle S Nashville TN 37203

LEWIS, PATRICIA SUE, public relations executive; b. Milw., May 11, 1952; d. Nonald Jack and Ruth Lavern (Pedersen) L. Diploma with honors, Institut D'Etudes Politiques, Paris, 1973; BA, Ripon Coll., 1974; MS in Journalism, Northwestern U., 1975. Assoc. writer, editor Gen. Dynamics Corp., St. Louis, 1975-76, news and info. specialist, 1976-78; mgr., pub. affairs Gen. Dynamics Corp., Tampa, Fla., 1978-80; acct. exec. Pub. Communications, Tampa, 1980-81, Roberts & Hice, Tampa, 1983-84; dir. pub. relations The Mktg. Ctr., St. Petersburg, Fla., 1984-85; prin. Lewis Pub. Relations, Tampa, 1985—; instr. U. So. Fla., Tampa, 1980-81; registered lobbyist State of Fla., 1981—. Editor Mother Goose in Stitches, 1975; contbr. articles to profl. jours. Cons. Bicentennial Horizon's of Am. Music, St. Louis, 1976; cons. Internat. Council SHopping Ctrs. Kids Say No To Drugs pub. service program, 1987; bd. dirs. Hospice Care, Inc., Pinellas County, Fla., 1986—;pub. relations com. Met. Ministries, Tampa, 1987. Mem. Pub. Relations Soc. Am. (accredited mem.), Fla. Free-lance Writer's Assn., Nat. Assn. Female Execs., Humane Soc. U.S., Alliance Francaise. Republican. Home: 3315 W Horatio St #114 Tampa FL 33609 Office: Lewis Pub Relations Services 3314 Henderson Blvd Tampa FL 33609

LEWIS, PATTY J., communications company executive; b. Omaha, Oct. 1, 1952; d. Harlan Gale and Mildred Olive (Noyes) Lewis; m. James Morgan Holden, Apr. 15, 1974 (div. 1977); m. Leonard Val Pollreis, Dec. 8, 1978. B.A. in Psychology, Bellevue Coll., 1984. Sales rep. Northwestern Bell Telephone Co., Omaha, 1976-78, account exec. industry cons., 1978-82, 84-85, mgr. real estate design and constrn., 1985—; account exec. industry cons. AT&T Info. Systems, Omaha, 1982-83. Trustee Sanitary Improvement Dist. 1, Union Nebr., 1984-86. Mem. Nat. Assn. Female Execs. Democrat. Mem. Christian Ch. (Disciples of Christ). Avocations: skiing; water skiing; snowmobiling; reading. Office: Northwestern Bell 100 S 19th-Izard Omaha NE 68102

LEWIS, RITA HOFFMAN, plastic products manufacturing company executive; b. Phila., Aug. 6, 1947; d. Robert John and Helen Anna (Dugan) Hoffman; 1 child, Stephanie Blake. Student Jefferson Med. Coll. Sch. Nursing, 1965-67; Gen. mgr. Sheets & Co., Inc. (now Flower World, Inc.), Woodbury, N.J., 1968-72; dir., exec. v.p., treas. Hoffman Precision Plastics, Inc., Blackwood, N.J., 1973—; ptnr. Timber Assocs.; guest speaker various civic groups, 1974—. Author: That Part of Me I Never Really Meant to Share, 1979; In Retrospect: Caught Between Running and Loving. Mem. Com. for Citizens of Glen Oaks (N.J.), 1979—, Gloucester Twp. Econ. Devel. Com., 1981—, Gloucester Twp. Day Scholarship Com., 1984—; chairperson Gloucester Twp. Day Scholarship Found., 1985—; bd. dirs. Diane Hull Dance Co. Recipient Winning Edge award, 1982, Mayor's award for Womens' Achievement, 1987, Outstanding Community Service award Mayor, Council and Com., 1987. Mem. Sales Assn. Chem. Industry, Blackwood Businessmen's Assn. Roman Catholic.

LEWIS, ROSALIND, software engineer; b. Phila., Nov. 8, 1962; d. Richard Eugene and Daisy Mae (Lewis) Guy. BS, U. So. Calif., 1983; MS, Poly. Inst. N.Y., 1985. Programmer/analyst Alcoa labs., Alcoa Ctr., Pa., 1983, 84; asst. office mgr. NASA Indsl. Application Ctr., Los Angeles, 1983-84; software engr. Litton Guidance and Control Systems, Woodland Hills, Calif., 1985-87; mem. tech. staff The Aerospace Corp., Los Angeles, 1987—. Recipient fellowship Nat. Consortium Minorities in Engring., 1983. Mem. Los Angeles Council Black Profl. Engrs. (instr. 1987—, recipient Valuable Service award 1987), Litton Women Engring. Orgn. Home: 4210 W 63rd St Los Angeles CA 90043

LEWIS, SAMELLA SANDERS, artist, educator; b. New Orleans, Feb. 27, 1924; d. Samuel and Rachel (Taylor) Sanders; m. Paul Gad Lewis, Dec. 22, 1948; children—Alan Stephen, Claude Anthony. Student, Dillard U., 1941-43; B.S., Hampton Inst., 1945; M.A., Ohio State U., 1947, Ph.D., 1951; postgrad., U. So. Calif., 1964-66; L.H.D. (hon.), Chapman Coll., 1976. Asst. prof. Hampton (Va.) Inst., 1945-47; asso. prof. art Morgan State Coll., 1950-52; chmn. dept. art, prof. Fla. A&M U., 1953-58; prof. SUNY, Plattsburgh, 1958-67; coordinator edn. Los Angeles County Mus. Art, 1968-69; prof. Asian, African, Afro-Am. Art History Scripps Coll., Claremont, Calif., 1970-84; prof. emerita Scripps Coll., 1984—; artistic cons.; curator Richard Hunt: Sculptures and Drawings (8 countries in Africa), USIA, Arts Am., 1986-87, Jacob Lawrence: Paintings and Drawings for Africa and the Caribbean , USIA, Arts Am., 1988-89. Author: Art, Afarican American Textbook, 1978, The Art of Elizabeth Catlett, 1984; producer five films on Black Am. artists; founder Mus. African Am. Art, Los Angeles, 1976; founder, dir., The Gallery, Los Angeles, 1969-79, Asanti Gallery, Pomona, Calif., 1980; Art editor Internat. Rev. African Am. Art, 1976—; One woman shows, Clark Mus., Claremont, Calif., 1979, Univ. Union Gallery, 1980, group shows include, Huntsville (Ala.) Mus., 1979, Smithsonion Instn. travelling exhbn., 1980-81; represented in permanent collections, Balt. Mus. Art, Oakland Mus. Art, High Mus., Atlanta, Palm Springs Mus., Va. Mus. Art. Fulbright fellow, 1962; NDEA post doctoral fellow, 1964-66; Ford Found. grantee, 1965, 81. Mem. Assn. Asian Studies, Nat. Conf. Artists, So. Calif. Art History Assn., Coll. Art Assn. Am. Home: 1237 S Masselin Ave Los Angeles CA 90019

LEWIS, SHIRLEY ANN REDD, academic fund director, educational consultant; b. Winding Gulf, W.Va., June 11, 1937; d. Robert Fountain and Thelma Danese (Biggers) Redd; m. Ronal McGhee Lewis, Aug. 17, 1963; 1 child, Mendi Dessalines Shirley. BA, U. Calif., Berkeley, 1960, MSW, 1970; PhD, Stanford U., 1979; cert., U. London, U. Ghana, 1971. Tchr. Ravenswood City Schs., East Palo Alto, Calif., 1962-63, N.Y.C. Schs., 1964-65; counselor coordinator U. Calif., Berkeley, 1967-71; college instr. Los Altos

(Calif.) Community Coll., 1970-72; researcher Stanford (Calif.) Sch. Edn., 1972-79; prof. Peabody Coll., Vanderbilt U., Nashville, Tenn., 1980-81; prof., assoc. dean Meharry Med. Coll., Nashville, 1982-85; exec. dir. The Black Coll. Fund, Nashville, 1986—; cons. Vanderbilt Sch. Divinity, Nashville, 1987, Urban League, N.Y.C., 1987. Co-author: The Nairobi Method, 1972, The 1-2-3 Method, 1985. Trustee Rust Coll., Holly Springs, Miss., 1986—, Philander Smith Coll., Little Rock, 1986—; mem. adv. com. Black Family Com. of Nashville, 1987; mem. program com. Domestic Violence YWCA, 1987; mem. United Way Appropriations Com., 1987. Recipient Carnegie fellow, 1968-70; named Outstanding Contributor, Meharry Med. Coll. Pre Alumni Assn., 1986. Mem. Internat. Reading Assn., Jack and Jill of Am. (pres. 1986-88). Democrat. Methodist. Office: The United Meth Ch Bd Higher Edn and Ministry PO Box 871 Nashville TN 37202

LEWIS, SUE BLASINGAME, real estate broker; b. Miami, Fla., Dec. 3, 1933; d. Earnest LeRoy and Clara Louise (Collins) Blasingame; student public schs.; grad. Realtors Inst., 1973; m. James C. Lewis, Apr. 5, 1952; children—Susan C., James C. III, Douglas C. Saleswoman Claytons' Realty, Winter Park, Fla., 1972-76; polit. aide, 1976, 78, 79, 80; pres. Sue Lewis Cons., Inc., Winter Park, 1980—; speaker in field. Chmn. Seminole County Planning and Zoning Commn., 1980—, Seminole County Land Planning Agy., 1981—. Mem. Cultural Alliance Cen. Fla. Republican. Home: 2532 Long Iron Ct Longwood FL 32779 Office: 2251 Lucien Way Suite 130 Maitland FL 32751

LEWIS, THERESA P., sales executive; b. Buffalo, May 26, 1956; d. Esley Earle Lewis and Patricia (Lucas) Fuller. BBA, U. Ga., 1977. Mktg. services mgr. Interface Flooring Systems, LaGrange, Ga., 1977-82; terr. mgr. Interface Flooring Systems, Tampa, Fla., 1983—. Mem. Inst. Bus. Designers (bd. dirs. North Fla. chpt., 1986—), Internat. Facility Mgrs. Assn. (programs co-chairperson Suncoast chpt., 1986—). Republican. Methodist. Home and Office: 4012 Pinelimb Ct Tampa FL 33614

LEWIS, THOMASINE ELIZABETH, magazine editor-in-chief; b. Manila, Phillipines, Sept. 20, 1958; d. Thomas Donald and Elizabeth Jane (Munson) L. Student, Broward Community Coll., 1977, Universidad de las Americas, Mexico City, 1977, U. Fla., Los Angeles Valley Coll., 1979, UCLA, 1984. Copy editor, reporter Mexico City News, 1979-80; mng. editor LF Pub., Los Angeles, 1980-82; editor Eton Pub., Hollywood, Calif., 1982-83; editor in chief Playgirl Mag., Santa Monica, Calif., 1983-86; exec. editor mag. devel. Petersen Pub., Hollywood, Calif., 1986-87; exec. editor Japan Jour. Mag., Marina del Rey, Calif., 1987—. Bd. dirs. Santa Monica Red Cross; mem. League of Women Voters, NOW, People for the Am. Way. Home: 3004-A Grand Canal Venice CA 90291

LEWIS, VERNITA ANN WICKLIFFE, beauty culturist, fast food restaurant executive; b. Chgo., Apr. 6, 1955; d. Kernett Henry and Clara Lillian (Wells) Robinson; m. Lloyd Maurice Wickliffe, Sr., Jan. 31, 1976 (dec. 1982); children—Calvin Earl, Nicole Latrice, Lloyd Maurice Jr.; m. Kenneth Lewis, Feb. 17, 1985. Student William Jones Comml. Bus. Sch., 1971-72; degree Pivot Point Inst., 1982-83; student Prairie State Coll., 1987-88. Lic. cosmetology tchr. Clerk Typist I & II State Dept. Pub. Aid., Chgo., 1972-74, caseworker I, 1975-77, med. caseworker II, 1978-79, med. caseworker III, 1979-83; cosmetology student instr. Lyndon Beauty Acad., Steger, Ill., 1985—; owner Kenny's for Ribs and Pizza, Chgo., 1985—, MS VE's Profl. Skin Care Salon, Park Forest, Ill.; lectr., cons. Huth Jr. High Sch., Matteson, Ill., 1985—; with child devel. pre-school program Prairie State Jr. Coll., 1988—; underwriter drug abuse program Jesse James Lloyd Wickliffe Meml. Scholarship Fund. Recipient 2d and 3rd place trophies Unique Beauty Sch. Competition, 1982, Morris Acad., 1982; 4th and 3rd place trophies Pivot Point Beauty Sch., 1983; Creative Service award Environ. Conservation Commn., 1984. Mem. Nat. Assn. Female Execs., Nat. Hair Dressers and Cosmetologists Assn., Nat. Cosmetology Assn. (educator esthetics div. 1986—), Ill. Cosmetology Assn. (educator aesthetics div. 1986), Nat. Assn. Nail Artists. Democrat. Club: Sno Goffers Ski. Avocations: music; bowling; gardening.

LEWIS, VICTORIA, educator, marriage, family and child counselor; b. Jacksonville, Fla., Aug. 16, 1945; d. Gaudencio and Mary Magdalene (Barcelona) Somera; m. Rodney G. Lewis, Jan. 5, 1976; children: Joseph, Rita, Anthony, Celine, Michael. AA, Los Angeles Valley Coll., 1975; BA, Immaculate Heart Coll., Los Angeles, 1977; MS in Edn., Mt. St. Mary's Coll., Los Angeles, 1982; postgrad., Calif. State U., Northridge, 1984-86. Cert. in secondary teaching, community coll. counseling. Computer operator, programmer Pixie of Calif., Los Angeles, 1964-71; research analyst, counselor, adminstr., grant writer Learning Skills Lab., Van Nuys, Calif., 1978-81; marriage, family and child counselor intern Pasadena (Calif.) Counseling Group, 1981-84, lectr. women's careers, 1982-84; tchr. English secondary lang., reading specialist, bilingual studies ednl. counselor Los Angeles Unified Sch. Dist., 1984—; lectr. on parenting, 1983-84. Mem. parent com. Teen Ctr., Van Nuys, 1979-81. Ford Found. scholar, 1975. Mem. NEA, Nat. Council Tchrs. English, Calif. Assn. for Marriage and Family Therapists, Calif. Sch. Counseling Assn., Calif. Personnel and Guidance Assn. Mailing Address: PO Box 2094 Van Nuys CA 91404

LEWIS, VIRGINIA ELNORA, museum director; b. Sault Ste. Marie, Ont., Can., Apr. 7, 1907; d. Dan and Katherine (Barres) L. A.B., U. Pitts., 1931, M.A., 1935; postgrad., Carnegie Inst. Tech., 1932-33. Proofreader Carnegie Inst. Tech. Press, 1931-33; mem. faculty U. Pitts., 1934—, prof. fine arts, 1957-67, prof. emeritus, 1967—, acting head dept., 1954, 57-58, summers 1940-63; curator exhbns. Henry Clay Frick fine arts dept., 1946-85; head librarian Henry Clay Frick fine arts library, 1963-65; asst. dir. Henry Clay Frick fine arts bldg., 1965-67; dir. Frick Art Mus., Pitts., 1969-85; researcher Helen C. Frick Found., 1967-69; dir. Dennis (Mass.) Art Gallery, 1953; cons., dir. Westmoreland County Mus. Art, 1954-56; adv. group, 1981. Author: Andrey Avinoff: The Man, 1953, Russell Smith: Romantic Realist, 1956; also articles, exhbn. catalogues, revs.; contbr.: New Cath. Ency. Served as ensign USNR, 1941. Recipient disting. performance awards Chatham Coll. Com., Pitts., salute Kaufmann's Dept. Store, Pitts., 1974; named Woman of Year Pitts. Post Gazette, 1956, Disting. Dau. of Pa., 1977. Mem. Soc. Archtl. Historians (dir., chmn. Pitts. chpt. 1956), Coll. Art Assn. Am., Am. Assn. Museums, Pa. Hist. Soc., 100 Friends Pitts. Art (exec. bd.), Nat. Trust Hist. Preservation (chmn. session 14th ann. meeting), Print Council Am., Pitts. Plan Arts, Internat. Council Museums, Arts and Crafts Center Pitts., Pitts. Bibliophile Soc., Spl. Libraries Assn., Xylon. Clubs: Women's Press, Zonta, Monday Luncheon (pres. 1970—), Women's City (Pitts.).

LEWIS, VIRGINIA GAYLE, purchasing officer; b. Crockett, Tex., Apr. 7, 1946; d. Gail and Leda Mae (Keels) Cook; m. Billy Joe Lewis, Mar. 10, 1940; 1 child, Billy Mark. Asst. mgr. J.O. Lewis Lumber Co., Crockett, Tex., 1965-69; acctg. supr. Tex. Youth Commn. div. Crockett State Sch., Crockett, 1973, warehouse supr., 1975, purchasing and supply officer, 1976—. Pres. Crockett Band Boosters, 1984, also established band scholarship, 1983; leader Youth Share Group, Crockett, 1985-87; mem. scholarship com. Wal Mart, Crockett, 1982-83. Recipient Recognition for Dedicated Service, Crockett State Sch., 1985, 86. Mem. Nat. Assn. Govt. Purchasers, Tex. Assn. Pub. Purchasers, Davy Crockett Pilot Club, Nat. Assn. Female Execs., Tex. Pub. Employees Assn. (pres. Crockett chpt. 1980-86). Democrat. Baptist. Office: Tex Youth Commn Crockett State Sch PO Box 411 Crockett TX 75835

LEWIS, WANDA ELLA, nurse; b Portsmouth, Ohio, June 12, 1927; d. George Frank and Emma Abigail (Rice) Jarrell; R.N., Christ Hosp. Sch. Nursing, 1951; m. Ramon Lamar Lewis, May 2, 1960; children—Kris, Gail Jean. Supr. nurses Clinton Meml. Hosp., Wilmington, Ohio, 1951-53; staff nurse Pima County Hosp., Tucson, 1953-55; field nurse Bur. Indian Affairs-Alaska Native Service, Bethel, 1955-58; stewardess Wien Airlines, Fairbanks, Alaska, 1958-61; admissions supr. Providence Hosp., Anchorage, 1972-75; staff nurse, charge nurse Spring View Center, Springfield, Ohio 1975-80; dir. nurses Good Shepherd Nursing Home, 1980-81; supr. St. John's Nursing Home, Springfield, 1981-82; staff nurse Community Hosp., 1982-85; gen. supr. Ohio Masonic Home, Springfield, Ohio, 1985—. Active with mentally retarded, 1975-80; vol. instr. English, Udornthani, Thailand and Vientiene, Laos, 1965-67. Republican. Home: 2650 E High St Springfield OH 45505

LEWIS JOHNSON, BARBARA ANN, lawyer; b. N.Y.C., Feb. 20, 1949; d. Charles Edward and Mary Phyllis (Frisby) Lewis; m. James Michael Johnson, Oct. 15, 1971 (div. July 1979); 1 child, Michael C.; m. Henderson (Bo) Walker, Apr. 1, 1984 (dec. July 1986); 1 child, Panya. BA, NYU, 1970, MSW, 1972; JD, Columbia U., 1984. Bar: N.Y. 1985. Social worker The Wiltwyck Sch., Bklyn., 1973-76; dir. clin. services, Queens group homes The Children's Village, Dobbs Ferry, N.Y., 1976-79; asst. dir. admissions, asst. prof. social work NYU Sch. Social Work, 1979-81; assoc. atty. Cadwalader, Wickersham & Taft, N.Y.C., 1984—; psychotherapist Dept. Mental Health State N.Y., 1981—; bd. dirs. Blind Beggar Press, Bronx, N.Y. Producer Black Heritage Dancers, 1975. Mem. adv. bd. Citiarts Workshop, N.Y.C., 1983-85; mem. Bklyn. Regional Adv. Council N.Y. Div. Human Rights, 1983-86; bd. dirs. Cinque Art Gallery, N.Y.C., 1987; vol. Vol. Lawyers for the Arts, N.Y.C., 1984. Mem. ABA, Met. Bar Assn., Assn. Black Social Workers.

LEWITAS, HOLLY LYNN, health science facility administrator; b. Bay Shore, N.Y., May 5, 1949; d. Wilmur Murl and Kathyrn Lee (Craven) McCown; m. Alvin R. Lewitas; chidren: David, Alison. BS in Nursing, SUNY, 1971. RN. Supr., clinical psychiat. nurse Ypsilanti (Mich.) St. Hosp., 1971-74; dir. nursing Children's Inst. Devel. Disabilities, Chgo., 1974-78; dir. staff devel. Chgo. Lakeshore Hosp., 1978-79; supr. nursing Northside Home Health Care, Chgo., 1979-83; dir. profl. services Total Home Health Care, Chgo., 1984-85, adminstr., owner, 1985—; cons. Irish Found. Human Devel., Dublin 1979-80, Psychiat. Care Plan Systems, Chgo. 1983-85; dir. Med. Fin. Corp., Chgo. 1986—. Mem. Nat. Assn. Home Care, Am. Fed. Home Care, Nat. Assn. Female Exec. Office: Total Home Health Care 1050 N State St Chicago IL 60610

LEWITZKY, BELLA, choreographer; b. Los Angeles, Jan. 13, 1916; d. Joseph and Nina (Ossman) L.; m. Newell Taylor Reynolds, June 22, 1940; 1 dau., Nora Elizabeth. Student, San Bernardino Valley (Calif.) Jr. Coll., 1933-34; hon. doctorate, Calif. Inst. Arts, 1981, Occidental Coll., 1984. Chmn. contemporary dance dept. U. So. Calif., Idyllwild, 1956-72; adv. panel U. So. Calif., 1972—; founder Sch. Dance, Calif. Inst. Arts, 1969, dean, 1969-72; vice chmn. dance adv. panel Nat. Endowment Arts, 1974-77, mem. artists-in-schs. adv. panel, 1974-75; mem. Nat. Adv. Bd. Young Audiences, 1974—, Joint Commn. Dance and Theater Accreditation, 1979—; com. mem. Am. chpt. Internat. Dance Council of UNESCO, 1974—; bd. dirs. Am. Arts Alliance, 1977-82, Arts, Edn. and Americans, 1978—; trustee Nat. Found. Advancement Arts, 1982—, Lake Placid Ctr. for Arts, 1982-84, Calif. Arts Council, 1983-86, Calif. Assn. Dance Cos., 1976-81, Nat. Found. Advancement in Arts; trustee Idyllwild Sch. Music and the Arts, 1986—. Co-founder, co-dir., Dance Theatre, Los Angeles, 1946-50; founder, dir., Dance Assocs., Los Angeles, 1951-55; founder 1966, since artistic dir., Lewitzky Dance Co., Los Angeles; choreographer, 1948—; founder, artistic dir. The Dance Gallery, Los Angeles; contbr. articles in field. Mem. adv. com. Actors' Fund of Am., 1986—, Women's Bldg. Adv. Council. 1985—, Calif. Arts Council, 1983-86, City of Los Angeles Task Force on the Arts, 1986. Recipient ann. award Dance mag., 1978; Dir.'s award Calif. Dance Educators Assn., 1978; recipient YWCA achievement award, 1982; Mellon Found. grantee, 1975, 81, 86; Guggenheim Found. grantee, 1977-78; Nat. Endowments for Arts grantee, 1969-86. Mem. Am. Arts Alliance (bd. dirs. 1977), Internat. Dance Alliance (adv. council 1984—), Dance/USA (bd. dirs. 1988).

LEWRIGHT, WILMA LEE, interior designer, consultant; b. Lafayette, Ind., Sept. 15, 1923; d. Paul Oscar and Dora (Coy Kamstra) Johnson; m. William Kenneth Lewright, Feb. 18, 1951; children: David and Robert (twins), Dora Lee. Student, St. Francis Coll. for Women, Lafayette, 1941-43, Purdue U., 1943-46, Ind. U., 1946-47, Lafayette Bus. Coll., 1947. Interior decorator Colonial Furniture, Indpls., 1947-50; freelance designer, cons. Tulsa, 1951-52, archtl. designer, 1951-52; freelance designer, cons. Houston, 1953-54; pres. Wilhelmina's Interiors, Northridge, Pasadena, Calif., 1967—; cons. in field. Mem. Internat. Clock and Watch Assn., Am. Inst. Fine Arts, Internat. Assn. Fine Arts. Republican. Presbyterian. Home: 1141 S Oak Knoll Pasadena CA 91106 Office: 435 Vecino Dr Covina CA 91723

LEWTON, KATHLEEN LAREY, public relations executive; b. Bloomington, Ill., Feb. 27, 1948; d. Fred Jr. and Frances White Larey; m. John C. Lewton, Aug. 1970. BA, Ill. Wesleyan U., 1970; MS in Journalism, Northwestern U., 1977; postgrad., U. Minn., 1985—. Asst. dir. pub. relations Bowling Green (Ohio) State U., 1971-76; dir. pub. relations, exec. asst. to pres. Flower Hosp., Sylvania, Ohio, 1977-82; v.p. pub. relations St. Vincent Med. Ctr., Toledo, 1982-87, v.p. mktg. com., 1987—. Mem. bd. student publs. Bowling Green State U., 1979-83; trustee Met. YMCA Greater Toledo, 1980—, chmn. strategic planning com., 1986—; chmn. communications com. Toledo Festival, 1983, vice chmn., 1984; active Sta. WGTE-TV Auction Bd., 1982—, chmn. auctioneers, 1985-86, chmn. telephones com., 1987—; mem. communications com. United Way Greater Toledo, 1985, chmn. tng., mem. campaign cabinet and exec. com., 1987—; chmn. spl. projects com. Toledo Sesquicentennial Commn., 1986—; chmn. mktg. com. Ohio Commn. for Bicentennial of U.S. Constn. and N.W. Ordinance, 1986—. Hosp. recipient MacEachren award Acad. Hosp. Pub. Relations, 1978, 82, 84, 85, 87, Gold Quill award Internat. Assn. Bus. Communicators, 1983, 84, 85, Addy award Am. Advt. Fedn., 1982, 85, others; named one of Toledo's Ten Outstanding Young Women Toledo Women Jaycees, 1979; named one of Outstanding Toledo Women Toledo Women Jaycees, 1984; named one of Top Ten Working Women Glamour mag., 1984; named Disting. Lectr. U. Miami, 1982; honored YWCA Tribute to Women and Industry Program, 1983. Mem. Am. Assn. Med. Colls. (group on pub. affairs), Am. Soc. for Hosp. Mktg. and Pub. Relations (Touchstone awards com., Touchstone award 1986, 87), Pub. Relations Soc. Am. (bd. dirs. health sect. 1984—, chmn. 1988—), Soc. for Hosp. Planning and Mktg. (nat. edn. com.), Ohio Soc. for Hosp. Pub. Relations (bd. dirs. 1979-81, treas. 1982), Women in Communications, Inc. (bd. dirs. 1975-81, v.p. 1975-79, pres. 1980-81), Pub. Relations Dirs. Council (chmn. n.w. Ohio council 1978-79), Sigma Kappa (Colby award). Democrat. Roman Catholic. Office: St Vincent Med Ctr 2213 Cherry St Toledo OH 43614

LEYLAND, MARY FRANCIS CAHILL, government official; b. Bennington, Vt., Aug. 20, 1936; d. John Francis and Mary Agnes (Wilson) Cahill; m. George Pearce Leyland. BA, Newton Coll. Sacred Heart, 1958; MEd, U. Mass., 1967. Systems analyst IBM, 1967-69; exec. officer EPA, Washington, 1972-77; asst. dir. ACTION/Peace Corps, Washington, 1977-79; asst. dir. Internat. Devel. Cooperation Agy., Washington, 1979-82; dep. dir. Dept. Vets. Benefits VA, Washington, 1982—. Mem. Citizens Assn. Georgetown, Washington, 1980—. Mem. Sr. Execs. Assn. (bd. dirs. 1985—), Exec. Women in Govt. Roman Catholic. Club: Hay Harbor. Home: 1213 30th St NW Washington DC 20007

L'HEUREUX-DUBÉ, CLAIRE, judge; b. Quebec City, Que., Can., Sept. 7, 1927; d. Paul H. and Marguerite (Dion) L'H.; m. Arthur Dubé (dec. 1978); children: Louise Dubé, Pierre Dubé. BA magna cum laude, Coll. Notre-Dame de Bellevue, Que., 1946; LLL cum laude, Laval U., Que., 1951, LLD (hon.), 1984; LLD (hon.), Dalhousie U., 1981, Montreal U., 1983. Bar: Que. 1952. Ptnr. Bard, L'Heureux & Philippon, 1952-73; sr. ptnr. L'Heureux, Philippon, Garneau, Tourigny, St.Arnaud & Assocs., from 1969; Puisne judge Superior Ct. Que., 1973-79, Ct. Appeal of Que., 1979-87, Supreme Ct. Can., Ottawa, 1987—; commr. Part II Inquiries Act Dept. Manpower and Immigration, Montreal, 1973; del. Gen. Council Bar of Que., 1968-70, com. on adminstrn. justice, 1968-73, others; pres. family law com., Family Ct. com. Que. Civil Code Revision Office, 1972-76; pres. Can. sect. Internat. Commn. Jurists, 1981-83; participant Internat. Invitational Conf. on Matrimonial and Child Support, Inst. Law Research and Reform, Edmonton, Alta., 1981; adminstr., mem. Que. founding com. of Judges' Conf., 1982-83, lectr. in family law. Editor: (with Rosalie S. Abella) Family Law - Dimensions of Justice, 1983; chmn. editorial bd. Can. Bar Rev., 1985—; author articles, conf. proc., book chpt. Bd. dirs. YWCA, Que., 1969-73, Ctr. des Loisirs St. Sacrement, 1969-73, Ctr. Jeunesse de Tilly-Ctr. des Jeunes, 1971-77; v.p. Can. Consumers Council, 1970-73; v.p. Vanier Inst. of the Family, 1972-73; lifetime gov. Fondation Univ. Laval, 1980, bd. dirs., 1984-85; mem. Comité des grandes orientations de l'Univ. Laval, 1971-72; mem. nat. council Can. Human Rights Found., 1980-82, 82-84; mem. Can. del. to Peoples Republic China on Status of Women, 1981. Apptd. Queen's Counsel, 1969; recipient Medal of the Alumni, U. Laval, 1986. Mem. Can. Bar Assn., Can. Inst. Adminstrn. Justice, Internat. Soc. Family Law (bd. dirs. 1977—, v.p. 1981—), Internat. Fedn. Woman Lawyers, Fedn. Internat. des Femme Juristes, L'Assn. des Femmes Diplômées d'Univ., Assn. Québécoise pour l'Étude Comparative du Droit (pres. 1984—), Phi Delta Phi. Roman Catholic. Office: Supreme Ct of Can, Supreme Court Bldg, Wellington St, Ottawa, ON Canada K1A 0J1

LI, TU LEUNG, management executive; b. N.Y.C., Nov. 10, 1948; d. Gum Ming and Toa Moy (Wong) Lee; m. Ta M. Li, Dec. 31, 1969; 1 child, Ta Ming. B.S., U. Utah, 1977. Sr. cons. Aetna Ins. Co., Salt Lake City, 1977-78; advt. mgr. Assn. Surg. Technologist, Littleton, Colo., 1978-80; research mgr. MET-Research Co., Lakewood, Colo., 1980-82; pres., chief exec. officer Tatum & Assocs., Littleton, 1982-85; sr. acct. Martin Marietta Data Systems, Colo., 1985—; dir. Asian X-M Ltd, Loveland, Colo. Contbr. articles on computer mgmt. techniques to publs. Sec., Friends of Littleton Library, 1984. Mem. AAUW (bd. dirs. 1983-84). Club: Argonauts Investment (pres. 1982-83) (Littleton).

LIAN, NANCY WINTSCH, association executive; b. Waterbury, Conn., Nov. 8, 1935; d. Harry and Enid Hildegard (Steig) Wintsch; m. Edvin B. Lian, Apr. 29, 1961; children: H. Tanja, Heidi E. BA, Carleton Coll., 1957; postgrad. Tchrs. Coll. Columbia U., 1964. Cert. assn. exec. Tchr. ESL, Doshisha High Sch., Kyoto, Japan, 1957-59; pub. relations asst. Takashimaya, Inc., N.Y.C., 1959-60; research MLA, N.Y.C., 1960-65; asst. sec.-treas. N.E. Conf. on Teaching Fgn. Langs., N.Y.C., 1965-76; dir. adminstrn. and meetings Nat. Home Improvement Council, N.Y.C., 1976-81; exec. dir. N.Y. Library Assn., N.Y.C., 1981—; bd. regents Inst. for Orgn. Mgmt. U.S. C. of C., Washington, 1983—, chmn. N.E. bd. regents, 1986; mem. N.Y. State Continuing Library Edn. Com., 1981-84. Co-author; Foreign Language Offerings and Enrollments in Secondary Schools, 1961-62, 1962. Dir. Carleton Coll. Alumni Bd., 1982-85; coordinator Carleton Alumni Admissions Met. N.Y., 1978-82; leader Experiment in Internat. Living, Ulm, Germany, 1960. Recipient Assn. Exec. of Yr. award N.Y. State Assn. Conv. Burs., 1984. Mem. Am. Soc. Assn. Execs. (nominating com. 1983, ann. conf. adv. com. 1987, 88). N.Y. Soc. Assn. Execs. (dir. 1982-85, chmn. coms., 1979-80, 82, 86), Internat. Assn. Library Execs. (1st v.p. 1983-84, pres. 1985). Congregationalist. Office: NY Library Assn 15 Park Row New York NY 10038

LIANG, VERA BEH-YUIN TSAI, psychiatrist; b. Shanghai, China, July 29, 1946; came to U.S., 1970, naturalized, 1978; d. Ming Sang and Mea Ling Chu Tsai; m. Hanson Liang, Nov. 6, 1971; children—Eric G., Jason G. M.B.B.S., U. Hong Kong, 1969. Diplomate Am. Bd. Psychiatry and Neurology. Intern, Cambridge Hosp. (Mass.), 1970-71; resident Hillside div. L.I. Jewish Med. Ctr., New Hyde Park, N.Y., 1971-73; fellow Albert Einstein Coll. Medicine, Bronx, N.Y., 1973-75; instr. SUNY-Downstate Med. Ctr., Bklyn., 1975-79; asst. prof. SUNY-Stony Brook, 1979—; med. dir. Hillside Eastern Queens Ctr., Queens Village, N.Y., 1978—; vis. lectr. Jamaica Hosp., Queens, N.Y., 1980; cons. in field. Mem. Am. Psychiat. Assn., Am. Acad. Child Psychiatry, N.Y. Council Child Psychiatry. Contbr. articles to profl. jours. Office: HEQ Center 96-09 Springfield Blvd Queens Village NY 11429

LIAPAKIS, PAMELA ANAGNOS, lawyer; b. Queens, N.Y., Jan. 26, 1947; d. Charles G. and Mary (Andriakos) Anagnos; m. John Liapakis, Nov. 9, 1969 (div. 1981). B.A., Bklyn. Coll., 1967; J.D., St. John's U. Sch. of Law, 1970. Bar: N.Y., U.S. Supreme Ct. Assoc., Harry H. Lipsig, P.C., N.Y.C., 1969-72, Berman & Frost, N.Y.C., 1972-75; pvt. practice law, Bklyn., 1975-76; sr. ptnr. Lipsig, Sullivan & Liapakis, P.C. N.Y.C., 1976—. Author: Appellate Advocacy, Trial Diplomacy Jour., Sept. 1987, Feb. 1988. Recipient Freedom award Inst. Jewish Humanities, 1988. Mem. ABA, N.Y. Women's Bar Assn. (rec. sec. 1974-75, 3rd v.p. 1976-77, treas. 1975-76), Assn. Trial Lawyers Am. (bd. govs. 1986-88), Assn. of City Trial Lawyers (bd. dirs. 1987—), N.Y. State Trial Lawyers Assn. (bd. dirs. 1985-86, dep. treas. 1987-88, liaison to Alliance for Consumer Affairs), Assn. of Bar of City of N.Y (ad hoc com. on med. malpractice). Greek Orthodox. Home: 515 E 79th St Apt 14D New York NY 10021 Office: Lipsig Sullivan & Liapakis 100 Church St New York NY 10007

LIBASSI, PATRICIA CAMPBELL, writer; b. Mason City, Iowa, Sept. 29, 1929; d. David Lawrence and Mary Beatrice Campbell (dec.); R.N., St. Joseph Hosp. Sch. Nursing, South Bend, Ind., 1949; student Ind. U., U. Buffalo; m. Paul Joseph LiBassi, Aug. 12, 1950; children—Michael, Mark, David, J. Douglas, Patricia Ann, Suzanne Marie. Staff nurse, then night supr. William Coleman Hosp. for Women, 1952; staff nurse, pvt. duty nurse Ft. Leavenworth Army Hosp., 1954, Buffalo Gen. Hosp., Childrens' Hosp., St. Joseph Intercommunity Hosp., 1956, 57, 60; with Call for Action, Sta. WIVB-TV, Buffalo, 1976—, co-dir., 1979—, nat. bd. dirs., 1980-83, N.E. regional dir., 1980; tchr. great books elem. sch., 1967, 68. Contbr. Buffalo Evening News, Youngstown Yacht Club paper. Bd. dirs. Call for Action, Inc., 1980-83; participant Western N.Y. Telethon for Children's Hosp., Buffalo; mem. bd. advisors Am. Biog. Inst., Inc.; active Western N.Y. Telethon Children's Hosp., 1972—. Mem. Nat. Writers Club, Action Line Reporters Assn., Am. Film Inst., Notre Dame Alumni Wives, Nat. Geog. Soc. Clubs: Youngstown Yacht, Niagara on the Lake Sailing. Home and Office: 4990 Pine Ledge Dr W Clarence NY 14031

LIBBIN, ANNE E., lawyer; b. Phila., Aug. 25, 1950; d. Edwin M. and Marianne (Herz) L.; m. Christopher J. Cannon, July 20, 1985. A.B., Radcliffe Coll., 1971; J.D., Harvard U., 1975. Appellate atty. NLRB, Washington, 1975-78; assoc. Pillsbury, Madison & Sutro, San Francisco, 1978-83, mem., 1984—. Mem. ABA (labor and employment sect.), State Bar Calif. (labor law sect.), Bar Assn. San Francisco, Nat. Women's Health Network, No. Calif. Field Hockey Assn. Club: Radcliffe (San Francisco). Office: Pillsbury Madison & Sutro 225 Bush St San Francisco CA 94104-2105

LIBBY, JULIANNA, naval architect; b. Westbrook, Maine, Mar. 10, 1956; d. Clifford Emery and Elizabeth Phipps (Bennett) L. BCE, U. N.H., 1978; MS in Ocean & Marine Engring., George Washington U., Washington, 1982. Naval architect David Taylor Reasearch Ctr., Bethesda, Md., 1978-88; with Bath (Me.) Iron Works Corp., 1988—. Assoc. mem. Am Soc. Naval Engrs., Am. Soc. Civil Engrs. Republican. Mem. United Ch. of Christ. Office: Bath Iron Works Corp Bath ME 04530

LIBBY, SANDRA CHIAVARAS, educator; b. Clinton, Mass., Apr. 8, 1949; B.S. in Spl. Edn., Fitchburg (Mass.) State Coll., 1970, M.Ed. in Reading, 1976; postgrad. (fellow) Clark U., 1981-83; 2 children. Tchr. spl. class Webster (Mass.) Schs., 1970-73, asst. coordinator program materials, resource room, 1974, tchr./coordinator primary spl. needs program, 1975-78, tchr. jr. high English, 1978-79, reading tchr. jr. high, 1979-80 adminstrv. asst. intern Shepherd Hill Regional Sch., Dudley, Mass., 1980-81; dir., owner Teddy Bear Day Care Ctr., Dudley, Mass., 1983-85; developmental specialist Ft. Devens Post Learning Ctr., Shirley, Mass., 1985-86; resource room tchr. Murdock High Sch., Winchendon, Mass., 1986; coordinator, tchr. gifted and talented Lancaster Pub. Schs., Lancaster, Mass.; tchr. behavioral modification Middle Sch., Winchendon, 1986-87; coordinator, tchr. gifted and talented Lancaster Pub. Schs. Mem. Nat. Edn. Assn., Mass. Tchrs. Assn., Lancaster Tchrs. Assn., Nat. Council Tchrs. English. Club: Webster Emblem (pres. 1984-85). Cert. in elem. and spl. edn., reading, reading supervision, learning disabilities, English (secondary), Mass. Home: 54 Green St Leominster MA 01453

LIBERATI, SHARI LYNN, television producer; b. Pitts., May 30, 1961; d. Joseph James and Margaret (Laird) L. BA, Dickinson Coll., Carlisle, Pa., 1983. Pub. relations assoc. Metro-Arts, Harrisburg, Pa., 1982-83; prodn. asst. Pa. Ho. Reps., Harrisburg, Pa., 1983; TV producer WHTM-TV, Harrisburg, Pa., 1983-86; continuity dir., producer WHP-TV, Harrisburg, Pa., 1986—; advt. cons., free-lance writer cen. Pa. area businesses, 1983—; producer corp. videos. Recipient Alumni award, Dickinson Coll., 1983. Cen. Pa. Advt. Fedn., Nat. Assn. Exec. Women. Home: 623 State St #4 Lemoyne PA 17043 Office: WHP-TV 3300 North Sixth St Harrisburg PA 17110

LIBERATI CHRISTIE, BARBARA LINETTE, lawyer; b. Phila., Sept. 28, 1947; d. James Snyder and Ingrid Wanda (Sommer) C. B.S., Chatham Coll., Pitts., 1969; J.D., Villanova U., 1972. Bar. Pa. 1972, U.S. Dist. Ct. (ea. dist.) Pa. 1973, U.S. Ct. Appeals (3d cir.) 1973, U.S. Supreme Ct. 1976. Asst. dist. atty. Phila. Dist. Atty.'s Office, 1972—, sr. trial asst. in homicide div., dist. atty., 1974—. Office: 1421 Arch St 7th Floor Philadelphia PA 19107

LIBERATORE-PACKER, MARCIA ANTOINETTE, emergency medicine physician; b. Buffalo, N.Y., Jan. 7, 1954; d. Donato F. and Liese L. (Medele) Liberatore; m. Louis M. Packer, Apr. 21, 1987. BA in Molecular, Cellular and Devel. Biology, Psychology magna cum laude, U. Colo., 1977; MD, U. Colo., Denver, 1981. Cert. in emergency medicine. Intern Marshall U. Sch. Medicine, Huntington, W.Va., 1982-83; resident U. Okla. Health Sci. Ctr., Oklahoma City, 1983-85; attending physician South Suburban Hosp., Hazel Crest, Ill., 1985-87; mem. emergency com. South Suburban Hosp., Hazel Crest, 1986-87; attending physician Resurrection Hosp., Chgo., 1985-87; physician emergency medicine Alaska, 1987—. Contbr. articles to profl. jours., 1978—. Mem. Am. Coll. Emergency Physicians (Ill. chpt.), AMA. Club: 99's (Chgo.).

LIBERTY, LINDA A., tanning center executive; b. Albany, N.Y., Jan. 20, 1949; d. Roland and Gladys Ruth (Palmateer) Roberts; m. Harold Leon Waite III, Nov. 25, 1966 (div. Oct. 1974); children: Harold Leon IV, Christopher Roland; m. Robert Raymond Liberty, Dec. 27, 1974; children: Jason, Shane, Robert Raymond Jr. Lic. real estate broker. Long distance operator N.Y. Telephone, Schenectady, 1964-67; sales mgr. Wallace Co., Schenectady, 1967-68; office mgr. Allied Pub., Ballston Spa, N.Y., 1968-71; inventory and prodn. specialist Environment/One, Ballston Lake, N.Y., 1971-75; gen. mgr. Tan & Trim Inc., Clifton Park, N.Y., 1982-85; v.p. Sun Maker Tanning Ctrs./Health Wave Industries, Hudson Falls, N.Y., 1985—. Contbr. articles to mags. Mem. Northeast Network Exec. Women (pres.), Nat. Assn. Female Execs. (bd. dirs. Schenectady), Adirondack Regional C. of C. (presdl. com.). Republican. Roman Catholic. Home: 74 Rt 146 Mechanicville NY 12118 Office: Health Wave Industries PO Box 230 Hudson Falls NY 12839

LIBET, ALICE QUANTE, clinical psychologist; b. Savannah, Ga., Feb. 7, 1949; d. Albert Herman and Anita (Mahany) Quante; m. Julian Mayer Libet, Nov. 27, 1976; children: Jared Quante, Ariel Quante. BA cum laude with gen. honors, U. Ga., 1971, MS, 1974, PhD, 1977. Instr. Ga. Retardation Ctr., Athens, 1974-75; research psychologist VA Med. Ctr., Charleston, S.C., 1978-81; clin. psychologist dept. pediatrics Med. U. S.C., Charleston, 1977-83; adminstr. community program S.C. Dept. Mental Retardation, 1983-86; adj. faculty Coll. Charleston, 1985—; dir. residential programs Charleston County Mental Retardation Bd. Contbr. articles to profl. jours. Mem. Psi Chi. Home: 28 Hillcreek Blvd Charleston SC 29412 Office: Charleston County Mental Retardation Bd 200 Coming St Charleston SC 29403

LIBRIZZI, MARIE ANN, art consultant; b. Phila., May 21, 1950; d. Moses Sebastian and Adeline (Dettore) L.; 1 child, Mark. BA in Arts, Architecture, Pa. State U., 1973. Gen. ptnr. Old Main Frame Shop & Gallery, State College, Pa., 1973—, Triangle Enterprise, State College, Pa., 1980—, Gallery 136, State College, Pa., 1985—. Author: Arts In The Home, 1983. Mem. Am. Artists Soc., Assn. Antique Dealers (cons. 1982—), Downtown Bus. Assn., Women In Bus. (cons. 1983-84, bd. dirs.), Profl. Picture Framers Assn., Nat. Pilots Assn., U.S. C. of C. (spl. projects com. State College chpt. 1986-87). Republican. Roman Catholic. Club: Radio Control (State College). Home: RD #2 Box 279 Pennsylvania Furnace PA 16865

LICATA, MARCY, health care administrator; b. Manhattan, N.Y., June 21, 1949; d. Vincent James and Angelina (Pugliani) Mannino; m. Dominick Licata, Feb. 4, 1967 (div. Sept. 1976); children: Lisa, Vincent. AA, Suffolk Community Coll., 1976; BA, Dowling Coll., 1978; postgrad., Pilgrim Psychiatric Ctr., Brentwood, N.Y., 1985—. Social worker Outreach Services YMCA, Bayshore, N.Y., 1978-79; counselor Women's Pavilion, Deer Park, N.Y., 1978-79; counselor Bill Baird Inst., Hauppauge, N.Y., 1979-82, asst. adminstr., 1982-85, adminstr., 1985—; lectr. various schs. Women's Health Care Issues; TV talk show guest Point of View, N.Y.C., 1987. Mem. Nat. Assn. Female Execs., Nat. Abortion Rights Action League, Mothers Against Drunk Drivers. Democrat. Roman Catholic. Office: Bill Baird Inst 1324 Motor Pkwy Hauppauge NY 11788

LICENCE, DIANNE E., heating and cooling company executive; b. Danbury, Conn., Apr. 21, 1941; d. George Edward and Florence Lillian (Tarrant) Watson; m. Edward Albert Licence, Sept. 30, 1961; 1 child, Davin Edward. Cert., Small Bus. Coll., Danbury, Conn., 1976; cert. interior design and interior decorating, West Conn. State Coll., 1987. Lab. tech. Barden Corp., Danbury, Conn., 1959-62; co-owner World of Fabrics, Danbury, 1964-65; office mgr. Sperry Controls, Corp., Brookfield, 1965-67; bus. mgr. E.A. Licence Heating & Cooling, Brookfield, 1973—; bus. mgr. Newtown (Conn.) Color Ctr., Inc., 1979-87, store mgr., 1987—; cons. Newtown Color Ctr., Inc., 1979-87. Chmn., Brookfield Youth Commn., 1988—, vice chmn., 1987-88; v.p. Art League, Bethel, Conn., 1983-85. Mem. Brookfield C. of C. (pub. service dir. 1987, fund raising organizer for charitable family). Episcopalian. Home: 11 Powder Horn Hill Brookfield Center CT 06805 Office: Newtown Color Center Inc 5 Queen St Newtown CT 06804

LICHTER-HEATH, LAURIE JEAN, lawyer; b. Bklyn., Mar. 13, 1951; d. Irving and Beatrice (Gelber) Lichter; m. Donald Wayne Heath, Feb. 28, 1981; children: Michele Samuel, Adam Ryan. BS with honors, U. Tenn., Knoxville, 1972; JD, John Marshall Law Sch., 1975; postgrad. NYU, 1978; LLM, Georgetown U., 1979. Bar: Ill. 1975, D.C. 1977, N.Y. 1980, Nev. 1981. Law clk. D.C. Ct. Appeals, Washington, 1975-77; atty. enforcement div. SEC, Washington, 1977-78; lectr. NYU Sch. Continuing Edn. in Law and Taxation, 1980-81; atty. govt. relations asst. Met. Life Ins. Co., N.Y.C., 1978-81; assoc. atty. Miller & Daar, Reno, Nev. 1981; legal cons. Stockton, Calif., 1981-84; asst. prof. U. Pacific, Stockton, 1984—. Instr., YMCA, Knoxville, 1969-72; leader Concerned Parents, Stockton, Calif., 1984. Mem. Coalition to Stop Food Irradiation; guest lectr. on Ethics U. Pacific Alumni Assn. U. Ill. fellow, 1972; presenter seminar Starting a New Bus. City of Stockton Bus. Devel. Program, 1985-88. Contbr. papers to Am. Bus. Law Jour.; presenter in field. Mem. Nev. Bar Assn., N.Y. Bar Assn. D.C. Bar Assn., Ill. Bar Assn., ABA, AAUW, Western Bus. Law Assn. (exec. sec.), Sierra Club.

LICHTI, BARBARA JEAN, accountant; b. Corydon, Ind., Jan. 14, 1942; d. Lester and Evelyn Rose Ferguson; diploma acctg. Bryant and Stratton Bus. Coll., Louisville, 1962; enrolled to practice before IRS; m. Marvin Lichti, Dec. 20, 1963; 1 dau., Diana. Acct., Sta. WLKY, Louisville, 1962-64; head dept. grain storage Dept. Agr., Champaign, Ill., 1964-68; acct. Larry Buhrmester, Champaign, 1968-73, Armstrong & Acord, C.P.A.s, Champaign, 1973-75; self-employed acct., Champaign, 1976—. Mem. Twin Cities Bus. and Profl. Women's Club, Nat. Assn. Tax Practioners, Assn. Bus. Accts., Nat. Assn. Enrolled Agts., Nat. Soc. Pub. Accts., Ill. Ind. Accts. Assn. Address: 909 Devonshire St Champaign IL 61820

LICHTY, PATRICIA ANN, playwright/director, transportation executive; b. Mpls., Dec. 12, 1952; d. Kenneth Frank Jr. and Gwendolyn Margaret (Nelson) L. BS in Drama, Radio and TV, East Tex. State U., 1975; postgrad., U. Minn., Mpls., 1973, 1980-82, New Sch. Social Research, 1978-80, Manhattan Sch. Music, 1979. Lighting tech. East Tex. State U. Playhouse, Commerce, 1973-75; disc jockey, dir. promotion Sta. KETR-FM Radio, Commerce, Tex., 1975-76; asst. studio mgr. A&R Recording Inc., N.Y.C., 1976-78; with coll. promotion Lifesong Records (CBS Associated), N.Y.C., 1978, mgr. A&R, 1978-79; asst. traffic and claims Lane Bryant Inc., N.Y.C., 1979-80; coordinator transp. Pillsbury Co., Mpls., 1980-84, specialist transp., 1984-88; bd. dirs. W. Bank Sch. Music, 1987-88; mem. leadership com. Pillsbury Poppin' Joy Singers, 1984-88; dir. Abundant Life Players, 1987—. Author, dir.: (play) The Champion, 1987, Operation Messiah, 1987, Yellow Brick Road, 1988. Vol. United Way, Mpls., 1980-86, Sta. KETR-TV (PBS) Action Auction, St. Paul, 1985; liason for Pillsbury USA for Africa, Mpls., Los Angeles, 1985-86. Mem. Nat. Acad. Recording Arts and Sci., Minn. Music Acad., Nat. Assn. Female Exec, Alpha Phi Social Sorority, (chaplain 1970-71), Am. Film Inst. Home: 3720 Minnehaha Ave Apt 17 Minneapolis MN 55406

LIDDELL, CYNTHIA ANN, corporate administrator, psychologist; b. San Rafael, Calif., Nov. 11, 1951; d. James Nelson and Bettyjane (Hambridge) Liddell; children: Danielle René, Justin Bryan. B.S. cum laude, U. Calif.-Davis, 1973; M.A. summa cum laude, Calif. State U.-Sacramento, 1975. Cert. psychologist, community coll. tchr., Calif.; lic. contractor, Calif. Asst. prof. Calif. State U.-Sacramento, 1972-74; adminstr. State of Calif., Sacramento, 1974-79; mng. ptnr. Liddell & Assocs., 1979-81; chmn. bd. Carefree Greens, Inc. Mem. Calif. Gov.'s Roundtable, Sacramento, 1975. Calif. State scholar 1969. Mem. Internat. Erosion Control Assn. (program mgr., pres. 1974-76), AAUW, Psi Chi, Mu Alpha Theta, Calif. Women in State Service North Calif. Democrat.

LIDDELL, JANE HAWLEY HAWKES, civic worker; b. Newark, Dec. 8, 1907; d. Edward Zeh and Mary Everett (Hawley) Hawkes; A.B., Smith Coll., 1931; postgrad. in art history, Harvard U., 1933-35; M.A., Columbia U., 1940; Carnegie fellow Sorbonne, Paris, 1937; m. Donald M. Liddell, Jr., Mar. 30, 1940; children: Jane Boyer, D. Roger Brooke. Pres., Planned Parenthood Essex County (N.J.), 1947-50; trustee Prospect Hill Sch. Girls, Newark, 1946-50; mem. adv. bd., publicity and public relations chmn. N.J. State Mus., Trenton, 1952-60; sec., then v.p. women's br. N.J. Hist. Soc.; women's aux. prodn. chmn. Englewood (N.J.) Hosp., 1959-61; pres. Dwight Sch. Girls Parents Assn., 1955-57; v.p. Englewood Sch. Boys Parents Assn., 1958-60; mem. Altar Guild, women's aux. bd., rector's adv. council St. Paul's Episcopal Ch., Englewood, 1954-59; bd. dir. N.Y. State Soc. of Nat. Soc. Colonial Dames, 1961-67, rep. conf. Patriotic and Hist. Socs., 1964—; bd. dirs. Huguenot Soc. Am., 1979-86, regional v.p., 1979-82, historian, 1983-84, co-chmn. Tercentennial Book, 1983-85; bd. dirs. Soc. Daus. Holland Dames, 1965-82; nat. jr. v.p. Dames of Loyal Legion, USA; bd. dirs., mem. publs. com. Daus. Cin., 1966-72; bd. dirs. Ch. Women's League Patriotic Service, 1962—, pres., 1968-70, 72-74; bd. dirs., chmn. grants com. Youth Found., N.Y.C., 1974—; chmn. for Newark, Smith Coll. 75th Ann. Fund, 1948-50; pres. North N.J. Smith Club, 1956-58; pres. Smith Coll. Class 1931, 1946-51, 76-81, editor 50th anniversary book, 1980-81. Author: (with others) Huguenot Refugees in the Settling of Colonial America, 1985. Recipient various commendation awards. Republican. Mem. Colonial Dames Am. (N.Y.C. chpt.). Clubs: Colony, City Gardens, Church (N.Y.C.); Jr. League Bergen County; Needle and Bobbin, Nat. Farm and Garden; Englewood Woman's, Englewood Field; Hillsboro (Pompano Beach, Fla.). Editor: Maine Echoes, 1961; research and editor asst., Wartime Writings of American Revolution Officers, 1972-75.

LIDDELL, MARLANE ADAIR, magazine editor; b. San Diego, Feb. 11, 1944; d. Robert Randall and Beatrice Sylvia (Waite) L.; m. C. Gregory Gay, Apr. 21, 1979; stepchildren—Merrill, Brian. B.A. in English Lit., San Diego State U., 1965. Pub. affairs writer EEOC, Washington, 1965-67; text editor Topic Mag., USIA, Washington, 1967-68, photo editor, 1968-70; asst. editor Smithsonian Mag., Washington, 1970-74, articles editor, 1974-87, bd. editors, 1987—; photo editor Acad. Press, Orlando, Fla., 1983. Editor: (textbook) Introduction to Criminal Justice. Mem. Chi Omega (bd. dirs. 1962-65). Democrat. Episcopalian. Mem. Nat. Press Club, Washington Press Club (sec. 1982-83, v.p. 1983-84, pres. Found. 1984-87, bd. dirs.). Avocations: swimming; tennis. Office: Smithsonian Mag 900 Jefferson Dr Washington DC 20002

LIDDY, MARIE THERESE, career cons. co. exec.; b. Newark, July 27, 1932; d. Joseph A. and Veronica Cecelia (Beston) L.; B.A. in English and Music, Chestnut Hill Coll., Phila., 1967; M.A. in English and Drama, St. Bonaventure U., Olean, N.Y., 1972, M.A. in Theology and Psychology, 1977. Tchr., counselor John Carroll High Sch., Bel Air, Md., 1968-70; instr. English, asso. in counseling St. Bonaventure U., 1970-72; lectr., career adv. Temple U., Phila., 1972-76; co-dir. campus community, counselor, adminstr. LaSalle Coll., Phila., 1977-78; research and devel. Am. Inst. Property and Liability Underwriters, 1978-80; pres., exec. dir. Mainstream Access, Inc., Phila., 1980-83; prin. Mainstream Access Inc., N.Y., 1983—; seminar leader, 1968—. Mem. Interreligious Task Force Soviet Jewry, 1976-81, Phila. Human Relations Commn., 1972-76; co-sponsor Women's Inter Faith Dialogue on Middle East, 1976-78. Mem. Nat. Assn. Female Execs., Am. Soc. Tng. and Devel., Forum of Exec. Women. Contbr., Insurance (Job Finder series), 1981; contbr. articles to profl. jours. Home: 64 Southgate Rd Mount Laurel NJ 08054 Office: One Commerce Square Philadelphia PA 19103

LIDE, NEOMA JEWELL LAWHON (MRS. MARTIN JAMES LIDE, JR.), poet; b. Levelland, Tex., Apr. 1, 1926; d. Charles Samuel and Juel (Yeager) Lawhon; Secretarial cert. Draughon's Bus. Coll., 1943; student U. Tex., 1944-46; R.N., Jefferson-Hillman Sch. Nursing, 1950; m. Martin James Lide, Jr., Nov. 12, 1950; children—Martin James, III, Brooks Nathaniel, Gardner Lawhon. Writer column Baldwin Times, Bay Minette, Ala., 1964-68, Shades Valley Sun newspapers, Birmingham, Ala., 1974-75; v.p., sec. Martin J. Lide Assocs., Inc., Birmingham, 1977-81; R.N. supr. St. Martin's in the Pines, 1984. Mem. def. adv. com. Women in Services, for Ala., 1961-63; coordinator women's activities Nat. Vets. Day, Birmingham, 1961-68; mem. exec. com., 1968-70; exec. bd. Women's Com. of 100 for Birmingham, 1964-65. Mem. Gorgas bd. U. Ala., Tuscaloosa, 1959. Recipient citation Merit, Muscular Dystrophy Assn. Am., 1961. Author: (poetry) Instead of Sunset, 1973; (fiction) Life of Service-These are My Jewels, 1979; Music in the Wind - The Story of Lady Arlington, 1980; Brother James Bryan-Hope Lives Eternal, 1981; Music of the Soul, 1982; The Past and Psyche of Arlington, 1983, The Light Side of Life in the American Colonies, 1988. Home: 3536 Brookwood Rd Mountain Brook Birmingham AL 35223

LIDSKY, ELLA, librarian; b. Wilno, Poland; came to U.S. 1962; d. Leib and Sheina (Izygzon) Cwik; m. Alexander Lidsky, Feb. 20, 1963; 1 son, David Abraham. B.A., Pedagogical Inst. Odessa, USSR; M.S., Columbia U., 1966; M.A., 1973. Cert. Russian and Hebrew lang. tchr. Tchr. high sch., USSR, Poland, 1944-46, Poland, 1948-1951, elem. sch. Israel, 1961-62; catalog librarian Tchrs. Coll., Columbia U., N.Y.C., 1966-68; cataloger librarian Fairleigh Dickenson U., Teaneck, N.J., 1968-69, asst. dir. tech. services, Madison, N.J., 1973-84; asst. librarian U.S. Ct. Internat. Trade Law Library, 1985—; cataloger librarian Ramapo Coll., Mahwah, N.J., 1971-73. Mem. ALA, AALL. Law Assoc. of Greater N.Y., Tech. Services Librarians. Democrat. Jewish. Office: US Ct Internat Trade One Federal Plaza New York NY 10007

LIEBELER, SUSAN WITTENBERG, government official, lawyer, educator; b. New Castle, Pa., July 3, 1942; d. Sherman K. and Eleanor (Klivans) Levine; B.A., U. Mich., 1963, postgrad. Law Sch., 1963-64; LL.B. (Stein scholar), UCLA, 1966; m. Wesley J. Liebeler, Oct. 21, 1971; 1 dau., Jennifer. Bar: Calif. 1967, Vt. 1972. Law clk. Hon. Gordon L. Files, Calif. Ct. of Appeals, 1966-67; assoc. firm Gang, Tyre & Brown, 1967-68, firm Greenberg, Bernhard, Weiss & Karma, Los Angeles, 1968-70; asso. gen. counsel Republic Corp., Los Angeles, 1970-72; gen. counsel Verit Industries, Los Angeles, 1972-73; prof. of law Loyola Law Sch., Los Angeles, 1973-84; spl. counsel, chmn. John S. R. Shad, SEC, Washington, 1981-82; vis. prof. U. Tex., summer 1982; Commr. U.S. Internat. Trade Commn. Washington, 1984—, vice chmn., 1984-86, chmn., 1986—; cons. Office of Policy Coordination, office of Pres.-elect, 1981-82; cons. U.S. Ry. Assn., 1975, U.S. EPA, 1974, U.S. Price Commn., 1972. Mem. State Bar Calif., Los Angeles County Bar Assn., Adminstrv. Conf. U.S., Order of Coif. Independent. Jewish. Sr. editor UCLA Law Review, 1965-66; contbr. articles to legal publ.

LIEBELER, VIRGINIA MARY MAYER, writer; b. Great Falls, Mont., May 23, 1900; d. John Henry and Sophia Julia (Sosnick) Mayer; m. Rae E. Liebeler, 1922 (dec. 1976); children: Yvonne, Natalie, John Rae. BA in Edn., U. Minn., 1922, MA, 1950. With pub. relations Mpls. Soc. Fine Arts and Mpls. Symphony Orchestra, 1928-35, Minn. Hosp. Service Assn. (Blue Cross of Minn.), 1935-44; co-dir. NW Hosp. Service Plan (Portland Oreg. Blue Cross), 1944-45; tchr. evening div. Minn. Voc. Sch. Adults, 1945-54; tchr. tng. specialist U. Minn., 1946-68; writer Hosp. Mgmt. Mag., 1942-54. Author: (novel and radio program) Kid Galahad, 1936; (novel) You, the Jury, 1944; also wrote 12 tng. manuals for tchrs., numerous textbooks; numerous articles, poetry and shortstories; writer, editor, state dir. enrollment Blue Cross News. Campaigner Hubert Humphrey for Mayor, 1940's. Mem. Writers' Workshop (pres. 1938-40), Novel Workshop (pres. 1946-48), U. Minn. Alumni Assn., Nat. League Am. Penwomen (numerous positions) (recipient numerous awards 1968-80), Internat. Poetry Soc. (honorary), Beta Sigma Phi (honorary). Roman Catholic. Home: 4805 NW 47th Terr (Tamarac) Fort Lauderdale FL 33319 also (summer): 1758 Highlands Rd Franklin NC 28734

LIEBELT, ANNABEL GLOCKLER, biologist; b. Washington, June 27, 1926; d. Otto Gottlieb and Henley Florentina (Hallberg) Glockler; divorced; children: Ralph Arthur, Laurie Ann Marunich, Erica Lynn, Nancy Louise Guthrie. BA, Western Md. Coll., 1948; MS, U. Ill. Coll. Medicine, Chgo., 1955; PhD, Baylor U., 1960. Biologist Nat. Cancer Inst., NIH, Bethesda, Md., 1949-52; from research asst. to assoc. prof. Baylor Coll. Medicine, Houston, 1954-71; assoc. prof. cell and molecular biology Med. Coll. of Ga., Augusta, 1971-74; prof. anatomy, chair microscopic anatomy Northeastern Ohio Univ., Rootstown, 1974-86; guest researcher, biologist Nat. Cancer Inst., NIH, Bethesda, 1986-87, expert, 1987—; cons. biol. com. breast cancer task force, 1976-80. Contbr. articles to profl. jours. and books. Past pres. Am. Cancer Soc., Kent, Ohio, 1974-78; co-leader Girl Scouts U.S.; vestry rep. Diocesan Convs. I.P.A. fellow Nat. Cancer Inst., NIH, Bethesda, 1982-86; partial merit scholar Western Md. Coll. Mem. Am. Assn. Anatomy, Am. Assn. Cancer Research, Internat. Acad. Pathology, Am. Assn. Exptl. Pathologists, Fed. Am. Soc. Exptl. Biology, Am. Assn. Lab. Animal Sci., N.Y. Acad. of Sci., Soc. for Toxicological Pathologists, Assn. Women in Sci., Sigma Xi, Beta Beta Beta. Democrat. Episcopal. Home: 830 Quince Orch Blvd #202 Gaithersburg MD 20878 Office: NIH Nat Cancer Inst Registry Exptl Cancers Bethesda MD 20892

LIEBEL-WECKOWICZ, HELEN PAULINE GRIT, historian, educator, political analyst; b. N.Y.C., June 17, 1930; d. Emil Frederick and Anna Wilhelmina Johanna (Bonk) Liebel; m. Thaddeus E. Weckowicz, July 11, 1966. B.A. summa cum laude, Bklyn. Coll., 1952; M.A., Northwestern U., 1953, Ph.D., 1959. Assoc. editor Chgo. Consol. Ency., 1954-55; mem. Am. Hist. Assn. microfilming project of captured German war documents, 1958-59; Sessl lectr. Bklyn. Coll., 1959-62; mem. faculty U. Alta, Edmonton, Can., 1962—, prof. history, 1972—; mem. Can. nat. com. Internat. Congress, 1967-70, 77-80; research dir. Can. Council grants, 1969-71, 73-74; cons. in field. Author books, articles in field; mem. editorial bd. Can. Jour. History, Austrian Hist. Yearbook; research editorial bd. Am. Biog. Inst., 1986—. Recipient Commemorative Gold medal Am. Biog. Inst., 1986; Fulbright grantee, W. Ger., 1955; AAUW scholar, 1956-57; grantee Carnegie Fund., 1957-58, U. Alta., 1962-82, Am. Com. Promotion of Habsburg Studies, 1984—. Mem. Am. Hist. Assn., Am. 19th Century Studies Assn., Can. 18th Century Studies Assn., Can. Hist. Soc., German Studies Assn., Conf. Group Central European History, Internat. Econ. Hist. Soc., Internat. Soc. 18th Century Studies, Bicentaire French Rev. U. Rene Descartes. Democrat. Club: U. Alta. Faculty. Office: Dept History U Alta, Edmonton, AB Canada T6G 2H4

LIEBEN, EILEEN BROOKS, university administrator; b N.Y.C., Jan. 23, 1916; d. Thomas and Margaret (Culkin) Brooks; B.A., Manhattanville Coll., 1937; M.A., Creighton U., 1962; m. Theodore J. Lieben, Dec. 13, 1941; children—Peter, John, Thomas Geoffrey. Asst. dean of women Creighton U., Omaha, 1962, instr. English, 1963-64, dean of women, assoc. dean students, 1963—, acting v.p. student personnel, 1982-84, assoc. v.p. Student services, 1984—, coordinator fall honors program, 1978—. Bd. dirs. Performing Artists Omaha, 1981-85, dir. spl. projects univ. relations, 1985—. Recipient Creighton Disting. Adminstr. Service award, 1973, Mary Lucretia Creighton award for Advancement of Women, 1981, Girl Scout Women Achievement award, 1987, Jesuit Colls. and Univs. award, Nat. Assn. Student Personnel, 1988; Sperry Hutchinson, Nebr. Com. Humanities grantee; Nebr. Arts Council grantee; Musicians Union grantee. Mem. Joslyn Mus. Women's Assn. Am. Assn. Higher Edn., Nat. Assn. Women Deans, Adminstrs. and Counselors, Assn. Am. Colls., AAUW. Roman Catholic. Home: 514 S 57th St Omaha NE 68106 Office: 2500 California St Omaha NE 68178

LIEBER, ANNA, graphic designer, art director; b. Germany, Aug. 13, 1947; came to U.S., 1949; d. Sol and Miriam (Scher) L. B.A., CUNY, 1969; postgrad. NYU, 1972-73; postgrad. in design Sch. Visual Arts, 1981-83. Lic. tchr., N.Y. Asst. art dir. Archie Comics, N.Y.C., 1969-70; asst. prodn. mgr. Appleton-Century-Crofts Pub., N.Y.C., 1970-71; tchr. art and English Beha Jr. High Sch., N.Y.C., 1971-76; coordinator After-Sch. Workshops, Bd. Edn. N.Y.C., 1971-76; prodn. dir. Nat. Rev. mag., N.Y.C., 1976-86, art dir. 1986-87; prin. Lieber Design, N.Y.C., 1983—. Designer Egglectric Light, 1983. Mem. Women in Prodn. (charter, bd. mem. 1982-83, newsletter editor 1982-83), Graphic Artists Guild (spl. projects coordinator, steering com. officer 1983—), Women in Design, Am. Inst. Graphic Arts.

LIEBER, MIMI LEVIN, sociologist; b. Detroit, Mar. 22, 1928; d. Theodore and Rhoda (Katzin) Levin; B.A., U. Chgo., 1949, M.A., 1951; postgrad. Harvard U., 1959-60; m. Charles D. Lieber, July 17, 1960; children—John Nathan, James Edmund, George Theodore, Anne Gabrielle. With Columbia Bur. Applied Social Research, Internat. Research Assocs., N.Y.C., 1951-53; with Research Services Ltd., London, 1953-55; assoc. creative research dir. Tatham-Laird, Chgo., 1955-59; pres. Lieber Attitude Research, N.Y.C., 1960-86; v.p. Temple Barker & Sloane Inc., N.Y.C., 1987—. Trustee Jewish Bd. Guardians, 1968-75; mem. Community Planning Bd., N.Y.C., 1975-82; trustee Soc. Advancement Judaism, 1971-73; mem. N.Y. State Bd. Regents, 1981—. Mem. Am. Sociol. Assn., Am. Mktg. Assn. Club: Harvard. Office: 425 Park Ave Suite 2200 New York NY 10022

LIEBERMAN, HELEN OKEN, educator; b. N.Y.C.; d. Charles and Bertha (Posner) Oken; m. Herbert A. Lieberman, Aug. 21, 1949; children: Bruce A., Robert A. BA, Hunter Coll., 1945; MA magna cum laude, Fairleigh Dickinson U., 1976. Tchr. N.Y.C. Dept. Pub. Edn., 1947-50, West Lafayette (Ind.) Pub. Schs., 1951-53; tchr., learning specialist Livingston (N.J.) Schs., 1964-69, reading therapist, 1969-70, asst. prin., learning cons., learning disabilities teaching cons., 1970—, mem. supt. council, 1986—. Liaison mem. Livingston Schs. PTA, 1977—; mem. exec. bd. council PTA, supt., mem. climate assessment com. local sch. bd. Home: 4 Browning Dr Livingston NJ 07039

LIEBERMAN, NANCY ANN, lawyer; b. N.Y.C., Dec. 30, 1956; d. Elias and Elayne Hildegarde (Fox) L. B.A. summa cum laude, U. Rochester, 1977; J.D., U. Chgo., 1979; LL.M. in Taxation, NYU, 1981. Bar: N.Y. 1980. White House intern, 1975; law clk. to presiding justice U.S. Ct. Appeals 5th Cir., Shreveport, La., 1979-80; ptnr. Skadden Arps Slate Meagher & Flom, N.Y.C., 1981—. Recipient McGill prize, 1977; N.Y. State Regents' scholar, 1973. Mem. ABA, Assn. Bar City N.Y., Phi Beta Kappa. Republican. Jewish. Home: 145 E 84th St Apt 5D New York NY 10028 Office: Skadden Arps Slate Meagher & Flom 919 3rd Ave New York NY 10022

LIEBES, RAQUEL, import/export company executive; b. San Salvador, El Salvador, Aug. 28, 1938; came to the U.S., 1952; d. Ernesto Martin and Alice Bella Juliane (Philip) L.; m. Richard Paisley Kinkade (div. 1977); children: Kathleen Paisley, Richard Paisley Jr., Scott Philip. BA, Sarah Lawrence Coll., 1960; MEd, Harvard U., 1961; MA, Yale U., 1962; postgrad., Yale, 1961-65. Instr. Spanish Sarah Lawrence Coll., Bronxville, N.Y., 1958-60, admissions rep., 1963-68; instr. spanish Yale U., New Haven, 1964-66; exec. stockholder Import Export Co., San Salvador, 1968—, also bd. dirs. Contbr. glossary of Spanish med. terms. Hon. consul Govt. of El Salvador, 1977-80; docent High Mus. of Art, Atlanta, 1972-77; vol. Grady Hosp., Atlanta, 1966-71; instr. Spanish for med. drs. Tucson Med. Ctr., 1966-71; chmn. Atlanta Council for Internat. Visitors, 1966-71; mem. Outreach Group on Latin Am., Washington, 1982-86; founding mem. John Kennedy Ctr. for Art; lay leader Jewish Community of El Salvador, 1980-88. Mem. Empresa Prirada of El Salvador, Agape of El Salvador, Jr. League of Washington. Republican. Clubs: Harvard (Washington and N.Y.C.), Yale. Home: 700 New Hampshire Ave Washington DC 20037

LIEBIG, PHOEBE S., educator; b. Cambridge, Mass., Dec. 28, 1933; d. Marshall Harvey Stone and Emmy (Portmann) Allen; m.Anthony E. Liebig, June 19, 1954 (div. 1961); 1 child, Steuert. Cert. tchr. Dept. asst. Classics Dept. UCLA, 1956-62; tchr. Los Angeles Unified Sch. Dist., 1961-70; specialist info. Ancom Systems, Los Angeles, 1970-71; specialist grants Gerontology Cen. U. So. Calif., Los Angeles, 1971-75; lctr., sr. adminitrv. analyst and coordinator Gerontology Ctr. U. So. Calif., Los Angeles, 1976-80, dir. planning, 1980-86; research asst. prof. Sch. Gerontology U. So. Calif., Los Angeles, 1983-86; dir. geriatric edn. cen. Sch. Med. U. So. Calif., Los Angeles, 1984-86; sr. policy analyst Am. Assn. Retired Persons, Washington, 1986-88, asst. prof. gerontology, acting dir. program of Policy and Services Research, 1988—; cons. UCLA 1980—. Author: 50 State Teachers Retirement Systems: A Comparative Analysis, 1987; contbr. articles to profl. jours. Subproject dir. Alzheimer's Disease Research Cen., 1984-86, Nat. Inst. Health, Dept. Health and Human Services; project dir. Geriatric Edn. Cen., Health Resource and Service Adminstn., Dept. Health and Human Services 1984-86. Mem. Gerontological Soc. Am. (exec. com. sec., sec. study group econs. 1986—), Am. soc. Aging (sec. 1985-86), Am. Soc. Pub. Adminstn., Assn. Pub. Policy and Mgmt. Analysis (reviewer), Internat. Soc. Preretirement Planners (editorial bd. 1986—), Los Angeles County Mus. Art, Early Music Ensemble. Democrat. Home: 7404 Cedar Ave Takoma Park MD 20912 also: 8932 Gibson St Los Angeles CA 90034 Office: Am Assn Retired Persons 1909 K St NW Washington DC 20049

LIEBL, CATHERINE JEAN, petroleum company executive; b. Portland, Oreg., Apr. 22, 1946; d. Charles and Iris Pauline (Mortimer) Liebig; m. Hans Liebl, Feb. 19, 1967. BBA, CCNY, 1967. From staff acct. to audit mgr. Arthur Young & Co., CPA's, N.Y.C., 1967-75; mgr. fin. reports and consol. Mobil Corp., N.Y.C., 1975-77, mgr. fin. analysis, 1977-80, controller films div. Mobil Chem. Co., Pittsford, N.Y., 1981-83, asst. controller Mobil Chem. Co., N.Y.C., 1983-85; mgr. computer systems and computer services, Mobil Oil Corp U.S. Mktg and Refining, Fairfax, Va., 1985-86; mgr. applications devel. Mobil Corp., N.Y.C., 1986—. Mem. Am. Inst. CPA's, Am. Mgmt. Assn. Home: 263 Queens Grant Rd Fairfield CT 06430 Office: Mobil Corp 150 E 42d St New York City NY 10017

LIEBMAN, JUDITH T., advertising executive; b. N.Y.C., July 21, 1945; d. Jesse and Shirley (Breiter) L.; m. Charles Hyman, June 22, 1980; children: Jake Caleb, Max Abraham. BA, Am. U.; MBA, Fordham U. Account supr., v.p. Wunderman, Ricotta & Kline, N.Y.C., 1972-81; v.p., mgmt. supr. N.W. Ayer, N.Y.C., 1981-86; sr. v.p., mng. dir. Bozell, Jacobs, Kenyon & Eckhardt Direct, N.Y.C., 1986—. Mem. Direct Mktg. Assn., Assn. MBA's, Pubs. Ad Club. Jewish. Office: Bozell Jacobs Kenyon & Eckhardt 40 W 23d St New York NY 10010

LIEBOW, JOANNE ELISABETH, college public information specialist; b. Cleve., May 15, 1926; d. Arnold S. and Rhea Eunice (Levy) King; m. Irving M. Liebow, June 30, 1947 (div. Jan. 1972); children—Katherine Ann Liebow Frank, Peter. Student (Sophia Smith scholar 1946), Smith Coll., 1944-47; B.A., Case Western Res. U., 1948. Cleve. reporter Fairchild Publs., N.Y.C., 1950-51; free-lance pub. relations, Cleve., 1972-78; pub. info. specialist Cuyahoga Community Coll., Cleve., 1979—. Founder, pres. Mt. Sinai Hosp. Jr. Women's Aux., Cleve., 1948-50; pres. PTA, Bryden Elem. Sch., Beachwood, Ohio, 1964; mem. bd., pres. Beachwood Bd. Edn., 1968-76. Recipient Exceptional Achievement award Council for Advance Edn., 1982, Citation award, 1982, Grand Prize, 1983. Mem. Women in Communications, Inc. (Cleve. Communicator's award 1982). Home: 23511 Chagrin Blvd Apt 211 Cleveland OH 44122 Office: Cuyahoga Community Coll Ea Campus 4250 Richmond Rd Warrensville Twp OH 44122

LIEBSCHUTZ, SARAH FISHER, political scientist, educator; b. Honesdale, Pa., Nov. 24, 1934; d. J. Harold and Goldye (Kurlancheek) Fisher; m. Sanford J. Liebschutz, Aug. 26, 1956; children—David Samuel, Jane Margaret. B.A., Mt. Holyoke Coll., 1956; Ph.D., U. Rochester, 1971. Asst. prof. polit. sci., SUNY-Brockport, 1970-75, assoc. prof., 1977-81, prof., 1981—; research assoc. The Brookings Instn., Washington, 1975-77, field assoc., 1973-77; field assoc. Princeton U., 1980-85. Chmn. Rehovot, Israel Sisters cities Com., Rochester, N.Y., 1977—; mem. Region II Nat. Archives Adv. Council, 1972-75; mem. SUNY Research Found. Joint Award Council, 1980-81; bd. dirs. Rochester Gen. Hosp., United Way Greater Rochester. Sr. fellow Rockefeller Inst. of Govt., Albany, N.Y., 1985, faculty fellow, 1985-1990. Mem. Am. Polit. Sci. Assn., Am. Soc. Pub. Adminstrn., Phi Beta Kappa. Jewish. Co-author Brookings reports on community devel. block grants (4), 1976-83; Author: Federal Aid to Rochester, 1984; contbr. articles to profl. jours. Home: 6 S Pittsford Hill Ln Pittsford NY 14534 Office: SUNY Coll at Brockport Dept Polit Sci Brockport NY 14534

LIEDER, MARY ANDREA, sales and marketing consulting company executive; b. Mpls., Sept. 6, 1938; d. William H. and Anne J. (Gamradt) Berney; m. James Edward Lieder; children—Timothy, Jon, William, Kristin. A. Liberal Arts, U. Minn., 1958; B.A., Met. State U., 1976. Lic. real estate broker, Minn. Property mgr. Sage Co., Madsen Constrn. Co., Mpls., 1967-69; cons. Coult Mortgage Co., St. Paul, 1969-77; social worker Courage Ctr., Mpls., 1977-78; dir. sales and mktg. Swanson Abbott Devel. Co., Mpls., 1978-81; dir. condominium and townhouse div. Edina Realty, Mpls., 1981-83; pres., owner Lieder Corp., Mpls., 1983—; mem. examining bd. Truth in Housing, City of Mpls., 1984—; bd. dirs. Project for Pride in Living, Mpls. Mem. Minn. Multi-Housing Assn. Republican. Roman Catholic. Avocation: painting in oils and mixed media. Home: 2460 Kyle Ave N Minneapolis MN 55422 Office: Lieder Corp 3100 W Lake St Minneapolis MN 55416

LIEF, INEZ, real estate executive; b. Newark, Sept. 19, 1926; d. Jacob and Sophie (Levin) Hyatt; student public schs.; grad. Grad. Realtors Inst., 1974; m. Teddy Lief, Oct. 20, 1946; children—Linda, Barry (dec.), Scott. Cert. residential specialist, real estate brokerage mgr., residential specialist, residential broker mgmt. Engaged in real estate, 1967—; mgr. Burgdorff Realtors, Mendham, N.J.; mgr. property mgmt. dept. Weichert Co., Realtors, Morristown, N.J., 1980—; partner Bernard Shub Real Estate; owner Century 21 Arbor House; mem. condemnation commn. Superior Ct. N.J., 1980—. Recipient Harry L. Schwarz award Morris County Bd. Realtors, 1975, named Realtor of Yr., 1983. Mem. Morris County Bd. Realtors (pres. 1981, 82), N.J. Assn. Realtors (3d dist. v.p. 1983-85), Nat. Assn. Realtors (cert. trainer in ethics and arbitration), Somerset County Bd. Realtors, Nat. Assn. Exec. Women, Nat. Mktg. Inst. Home: 15 Humphrey Rd Convent Station NJ 07961 Office: 4 E Main St Mendham NJ 07945

LIEFF, ANN SPECTOR, music company executive; b. Miami, Fla., Jan. 16, 1952; d. Martin Wilson and Dorothy (Miller) Spector; m. William Allen Lieff, Aug. 24, 1975; 1 child, Laura Rebecca. BA in Sociology, U. Denver, 1974. V.p. Spec's Music, Miami, Fla., 1974-80, pres., chief exec. officer, 1980—. Mem. nat. alumni bd. U. Denver, 1983-86; mem. Jewish Community Ctrs., Miami, 1983—. Mem. Nat. Assn. Retail Merchandisers, Am. Technician Soc., Hadassah. Democrat. Jewish. Home: 9965 SW 131st ST Miami FL 33176 Office: Spec's Music PO Box 652009 Miami FL 33265

LIEM, ANNIE, pediatrician; b. Kluang, Johore, Malaysia, May 26, 1941; d. Daniel and Ellen (Phuah) L. BA, Union Coll., 1966; MD, Loma Linda U., 1970. Diplomate Am. Bd. Pediatrics. Intern Glendale (Calif.) Adventist Hosp., 1970-71; resident in pediatrics Children's Hosp. of Los Angeles, 1971-73; pediatrician Children's Med. Group, Anaheim, Calif., 1973-75, Anaheim Pediatric Med. Group, 1975-79; practice medicine specializing in pediatrics Anaheim, 1979—. Fellow Am. Acad. Pediatrics; mem. Los Angeles Pediatric Soc., Orange County Pediatric Soc. Office: 1741 W Romneya #D Anaheim CA 92801

LIEURANCE, ELIZABETH ELLEN, personnel director; b. Chgo., Dec. 25, 1951; d. Charles Harry and Georgia Elaine (Swanson) L.; m. Richard Ruehs, July 4, 1976 (div. Jan. 1978). BS, Kearney State Coll., 1973. Counselor vocat. rehab. State of Nebr., Kearney, 1973-74; personnel asst. FotoMat Corp. Offices, LaJolla, Calif., 1975-76, MicRo-Rel, Inc., Phoenix, 1976-78; dist. personnel rep. La Belles Dist. Office, Phoenix, 1978-79; asst. dir. personnel Phoenix Gen. Hosp., 1979-81; mgr. employment/employee relations Sacred Heart Gen. Hosp., Eugene, Oreg., 1981—; cons. labor relations, Eugene, 1984—; instr. adult edn. Lane Community Coll., Eugene, 1986—. Bd. dirs. ARC, Eugene, 1986—; counselor Student Crisis Ctr., Kearney State Coll., 1973. Mem. Am. Soc. Personnel Adminstrs., Pacific Northwest Personnel Mgrs. Assn., Oreg. Hosp. Soc. Personnel Adminstrs. Republican. Office: Sacred Heart Gen Hosp 1255 Hilyard St Eugene OR 97401

LIGENZA, ANDREA, nurse; b. Lansford, Pa., Apr. 7, 1952; d. Stanley Walter and Mary (Porambo) L. Diploma in Nursing, Hosp. of U. Pa., 1973; BS in Nursing, U. Pa., 1976. RN; cert. nurse practitioner, Pa. Staff nurse Hosp. of U. Pa., Phila., 1973-79, nurse practitioner cardio-thoracic surgery sect., 1979-88; pvt. practice nurse practitioner, 1988—; preceptor nursing students U. Pa., 1985—; founder, group leader Self Esteem Workshops, 1986—; nurse practitioner Cardiothoracic Surg. Assocs. Pa. Hosp., 1988—. Vol. Gary Hart for Pres. campaign, Phila., 1984. Mem. People for Am. Way, Puccini Inst., Sigma Theta Tau. Democrat. Roman Catholic. Club: Center City Running. Avocations: classical music, tennis, travel, writing poetry. Office: 301 S 8th St Suite 3F Philadelphia PA 19107

LIGHT, DOROTHY KAPLAN, lawyer, insurance executive; b. Alden, Iowa, May 20, 1937; d. Edward T. and Bessie (Nachazel) Kaplan; m. Ernest Isaac Light, Dec. 28, 1959; children—Christina, William, Samuel, David (twins). B.A., U. Iowa, 1959, J.D., 1961. Bar: Iowa 1961, N.J. 1973; C.P.C.U. Sole practice, Marshalltown, Iowa, 1962-63, Iowa City, 1963-71; with U.S. Army, N.J., 1972-74; asst. gen. counsel Prudential Property & Casualty Ins. Co., Holmdel, N.J., 1974-75, assoc. gen. counsel, 1975-77, dir. corp. services, 1977-79, dir. pub. affairs mktg. dept., 1979-82, dir. pub. affairs, 1982-83, v.p. govt. affairs, 1982-87; v.p., corp. sec. The Prudential Ins. Co. Am., Newark, 1987—; bd. dirs. N.J. Natural Gas Co. Pres. Monmouth Ocean Devel. Council N.J., 1986-87; trustee Monmouth Conservation Found., 1982—; mem. Airport Adv. Study Com. Monmouth County, 1984; exec. adv. com. Family and Children's Services. Recipient Silver Gull award for Service, 1988, Policymaker of N.J. award Exec. Women N.J., 1986. Mem. Iowa Bar Assn., N.J. Bar Assn., Am. Soc. Corp. Secs. Republican. Roman Catholic. Office: Prudential Ins Co Am Prudential Plaza 23 Pl Newark NJ 07101

LIGHT, MARGARET COE, controller, accountant; b. Waterbury, Conn., July 16, 1947; d. John Allen and Margaret (Connick) Coe. Student U. Calif.-Davis, 1965-67; B.A., UCLA, 1969, M.B.A., 1975. C.P.A., Calif. Cert. mgmt. acct. Trust adminstr. Hong Kong and Shanghai Bank, Beverly Hills, Calif., 1969-71; jr. acct. George P. Madok, C.P.A., Los Angeles, 1972-75; sr. acct. Ernst & Whinney, Trenton, N.J., 1976-78; staff acct. Dart Industries, Inc., Los Angeles, 1978-82, audit mgr. Dart & Kraft, Inc., Atlanta, 1982-84; sr. fin. analyst Kraft, Inc., 1984-85, asst. controller fin. planning and analysis Food Service Group, 1985-87; mgr. bus. analysis Kraft-Rosenblum, 1987-88, controller, 1988—; speaker Inst. Internal Auditors, N.Y.C., 1983. Mem. Calif. State Soc. C.P.A.s, N.J. State Soc. C.P.A.s, Nat. Assn. Accts. (dir. N.J. chpt. 1977, Los Angeles chpt. 1980), Am. Inst. C.P.A.s, Ill. Racquetball Assn. (bd. dirs.), Beta Gamma Sigma. Episcopalian. Office: Kraft-Rosenblum 2101 91st St North Bergen NJ 07047

LIGHT, PAMELA DELAMAIDE, interior designer; b. Pittsburg, Kans., Sept. 16, 1950; d. Jack Riley and Pearl Darlene (Nelson) Delamaide; m. Kenneth Layne Light, July 25, 1970 (div. Apr. 1974); m. I Dennie Pimental, Nov. 2, 1985. Student Ohio U., 1968-70; B.S. in Art, Ball State U., 1973. Interior design apprentice Jon Wilding Studio, Anderson, 1970-71; interior designer Suniland Office Furniture, Houston, 1973-83; furniture rep. Reeves, Rice & Light, Houston, 1983-84; interior designer H.O.K., San Francisco, 1986-87; sr. project designer Interior Architects, San Francisco, 1987—; cons. Front to Back, Houston, 1982-84. Mem. Inst. Bus. Designers (v.p. programs Houston 1983, pres. south Tex. chpt. 1985, pres. No. Calif. chpt. 1987), Citizens for Animal Protection, Houston Humane Soc. Republican. Methodist.

LIGHTE, MONNA KLINE, entrepreneur, jewelry company president; b. Boston, Aug. 23, 1930; d. Bernard and Myrtle (Caro) Troub; m. Fred Juster Lighte, 1964; children: Jan Alexis, Jack Lawrence. BA, U. Chgo., 1944; MA, New Sch. for Social Research, N.Y.C., 1967. Content analyst Commn. on Freedom of Press, N.Y.C., 1944-45; assoc. editor Calling All Girls mag., 1945-48, Adventure mag., Black Mask mag., 1948-50; exec. dir. Hemispheric Cong. for Women, Inc., N.Y.C., 1971-76; asst. to dean Coll. for Human Services, Ft. Lauderdale, Fla., 1977-79; owner, pres. The Little Jack Co., Miami, 1979—; lectr. in field. Author: Jesus Freaks, Jews on the Left and Utopia, 1977, Politics as a Sexual Experience, 1978; contbr. book reviews and articles to profl. jours. Bd. dirs., v.p. Children's Psychiat. Ctr., Miami; chairperson Dade County Commn. on Status of Women, 1979-81; mem. Fla. Gov.'s Commn. on Status of Women, 1974-78; trustee Third Century U.S.A.; bd. advisors New World Sch. Arts, Met. Dade County Performing Arts Ctr., Fla. Internat. U. Women's Inst.; founding mem. Friends of Art, Lowe Mus., U. Miami; mem. U. Miami Women's Guild; Fla. state rep. to steering com. Nat. Women's Polit. Caucus; Dem. nominee, Fla. Ho. of Reps., 1974. Mem. AAUW, Am. Sociol. Assn., Fedn. of Orgns. for Profl. Women, Nat. Fedn. Bus. and Profl. Women, Soc. for Internat. Devel., Soc. for Psychol. Study of Social Issues, Soc. for Women in Sociology, Nat. Assn. Commns. for Women (regional dir.), Inter-Am. Commn. on Women of OAS (nat. del.), Metro-Dade Mayor's Adv. Com. on the Performing Arts Complex. Home: 1429 Venetian Way Miami FL 33139

LIGHTFOOT, JAN LINDA, artist, photographer; b. Middletown, Conn., Dec. 3, 1949; d. Francis St. Martin and Isabella Carta-Fairfield Me. AS, U. Maine at Orono, 1977. Freelance artist, photographer Maine, 1978-83; bd. coordinator Hospitality House Inc., Fairfield, Maine, 1982—; program coordinator Hospitality House Inc., Hickley, Maine, 1986—; speaker in field. Impressionistic artist; photographer wildlife. Office: Hospitality House Inc PO Box 62 Hinckley ME 04944

LIGHTNER, CANDY LYNNE, advocate, consultant, author; b. Pasadena, Calif., May 30, 1946; d. Dykes Charles and Katherine (Karrib) Doddridge; children: Serena, Travis. Student pub. schs., Fairfield, Calif.; hon. D.Humanities, St. Francis Coll., Johnstown, Pa., 1984; D in Pub. Service (hon.), Kutztown U., Johnstown, Pa., 1987; HHD (hon.), Marymount Coll., Johnstown, Pa., 1987. Dental asst., various pvt. offices 1964-70; real estate salesperson Calif., 1972-80; founder, pres., chmn. bd. Mothers Against Drunk Driving, Hurst, Tex., 1980-85; cons. Mothers Against Drunk Driving, Arlington, Tex., 1985-87. Contbr. articles to profl. jours. Mem. Sacramento County Task Force on Drunk Driving, Presdl. Commn. on Drunk and Drugged Driving; bd. dirs. Nat. Commn. on Drunk Driving, 1984—, Nat. Partnership for Drug Free Use, Nat. Hwy. Safety Adv. Com., Love is Feeding Everyone (LIFE), 1988—, Found. Mideast Communication, 1988, others. Named to Good Housekeeping's Most Admired Women's Poll, 1986; ranked in top 25 of Am. Most Influential Women World Almanac and Book of Facts, 1986; recipient Pres.'s Vol. Action award, 1983, Jefferson award Am. Inst. Pub. Service, 1983, Testimonial award Civitan Internat., 1984, Epilepsy Found. award, 1984, Woman of Year award Mortar Bd. Soc., Baylor U., 1985, Anti-discrimination award, 1985, YWCA Woman of Year award, 1986, Commonwealth award U. Del., 1986, Black and Blue award Thomas Jefferson U. Hosp. Emergency Medicine Soc., Human Dignity award Kessler Inst. for Rehab., Woman of Distinction award Third Nat. Congress Coll. Women Student Leaders and Woman of Achievement, 1987, Disting. Leadership award World Congress of Victimology, 1987, Living Legacy award Women's Internat. Ctr., 1988, Friends of Children award Assn. Childhood Edn. Internat., 1988; selected by Johns Hopkins U. to participate in Anglo-Am. Successor Generation program, 1985; honored as one of Seven Who Succeeded, Time Mag., 1985; honored by Esquire mag. as mem. Am.'s New Leadership Class, 1985, others. Office: 22653 Pacific Coast Hwy Suite 1-289 Malibu CA 90265

LIGHTSTONE, JUDY KAREN, psychotherapist; b. N.Y.C., Sept. 13, 1954; d. Alan Clifford and Renee (Goldschmidt) L.; m. Joel Thomas Hildebrandt, July 11, 1981; children: Sandra Lightstone-Hildebrandt. BA, Antioch Coll., 1976; MA, NYU, 1981; post grad. tng., Women's Therapy Centre Inst., 1984—. Cert. nationally certified counselor, N.Y., elem. tchr., N.Y. Counselor Eastern Women's Ctr., N.Y.C., 1973; asst. counselor Exceptional Student Services, Greenvale, N.Y., 1974-75; counselor Berkeley (Calif.) Women's Refuge, 1976; outreach coordinator Temenos Counseling Ctr., San Rafael, Calif., 1977; co-dir. Marin Women's Health Ctr., San Rafael, 1978; workshop facilitator Children's Creative Response to Conflict, Nyack, N.Y., 1979-81; asst. dir. Career Directions for Homemakers, Bronx, N.Y., 1981-83; parent coordinator, family worker Nyack Head Start, 1983-84; pvt. practice psychotherapist Nyack, 1984—; cons. to various orgns., N.Y. and N.J., 1984—; cons., trainer Children's Creative Response, N.Y.C., 1979-81; coordinator Feminist Therapy Study Group, Rockland, N.Y., 1984—. bd. dirs. Nyack Consumers Coop. Market, 1982-84, Rockland County Women's Network, 1983—, liason, 1986—; vol., organizer Fellowship of Reconciliation, Nyack, 1982—. Mem. Am. Assn. for Counseling and Devel., Am. Orthopsychiatric Assn., Assn. for Specialists in Group Work. Home and Office: 112 School St Nyack NY 10960

LIGON, HELEN HAILEY, computer information systems educator; b. Lott, Tex., Feb. 7, 1921; d. Rolla Will and Bobbye (Ruble) Hailey; m. William Grady Ligon, July 26, 1941; 1 son, William Grady III. B.S., Tex. Women's U., 1942, M.A., 1945; Ph.D., Tex. A&M U., 1976. Cert. data processor. Tchr. Lott Public Schs., 1948-52, Marlin (Tex.) Ind. Sch. Dist., 1952-55; exec. sec. Gen. Tire Co., Waco, Tex., 1956-58; contracting officer, sec. Phillips 66, McGregor, Tex., 1955-56; asst. prof. Baylor U., Waco, 1958-60; assoc. prof. Baylor U., 1960-61, prof. stats. and info. systems, 1976—; dir. Casey Computer Center, 1962-84. Author: Successful Management Information Systems, 1978, Changing Concepts in Management Information Systems, 1979, Successful Management Information Systems, 2d edit., 1986: contbr. articles to profl. jours. Mem. Am. Statis. Assn., Data Processing Mgmt. Assn., Assn. for Computing Machinery, Inst. Mgmt. Scis., Assn. Inst. Decision Sci., Soc. Info. Mgmt., Delta Kappa Gamma, Beta Gamma Sigma, Sigma Iota Epsilon. Democrat. Presbyterian. Office: Baylor Univ Info Systems Dept 5th and Speight Sts Waco TX 76798

LIGON, PATTI-LOU ELSIE, real estate investor, educator; b. Riverside, Calif., Feb. 28, 1953; d. Munford Ernest and Patsy Hazel (Bynum) L. BS, San Diego State U., 1976; BBA, Nat. U., San Diego, 1983, MA in Bus. Adminstrn., 1984; Clear Profl. Credential, Nat. U., 1986. Cert. profl. counselor. Escrow asst. Cajon Valley Escrow, El Cajon, Calif., 1978-79; escrow asst. Summit Escrow, San Diego, 1979-81; escrow officer Fidelity Nat. Title, San Diego, 1982-84, Dawson Escrow, San Diego, 1984; owner, property mgr., investment adviser Ligon Enterprises., San Diego, 1980—, cons., 1982—. Chmn. com., alumnae and assocs. San Diego State U., 1983, 84, 85; com. chmn. San Diego Zool. soc., 1985; pres. Friends of Symphony, Riverside, Calif., 1978. Recipient commendation City and County of Honolulu, 1981. Mem. Nat. Notary Assn., Calif. Escrow Assn., Am. Home Econs. Assn., Nat. Assn. Female Execs, Internat. Platform Assn., Calif. Bus. Edn. Assn., Jr. League of San Diego, Sigma Kappa (pres. 1974, v.p. sorority corp. 1976—). Republican. Methodist. Club: Spinster (pres. 1981), Univ. (San Diego). Avocations: racquetball; clothing design; photography; travel. Home: 4545 Collwood Blvd Unit 12 San Diego CA 92115 Office: Ligon Enterprises 4545 Collwood Blvd San Diego CA 92115

LILAGAN-SCHAEDEL, MARIA NIEVES, educator, consultant; b. Pangasinan, Philippines, June 28, 1944; came to U.S., 1967; d. Ignacio Rodrigo and Ester (Bumanlag) Lilagan; m. James A. Heinrich, Sept. 11, 1971 (div. Mar. 1985); children: Rena M. Heinrich, Aaron J. Heinrich; m. William John Schaedel, Apr. 4, 1985. BS in Edn., Santa Isabel Coll., Manila, 1964, BA, 1965; MA in Teaching, Bilingual/Multicultural Edn., Alaska Pacific U., 1984. Cert. tchr., Alaska. Scriptwriter G. Miranda & Sons Pub. Co., Manila, 1961-62; instr., tchr. Santa Isabel Coll., 1964-66; tng. instr. Cen. Tng. Inst. U.S. Army, Saigon, Vietnam, 1966-67; tchr. St. Mary's High Sch., Salem, S.D., 1967-69; math tchr. T.B. Livaudais Mid. Sch., Gretna, La., 1969-70, St. Joseph's Indian Sch., Chamberlain, S.D., 1970-71; math lab. tchr. Anchorage Sch. Dist., 1971-72, bilingual tutor, 1977-79, bilingual resource tchr., 1979-81, multicultural tchr. expert, ESL/bilingual resource tchr., 1982-85, math tchr., 1985-86; sr. program specialist N.W. Regional Ednl. Lab., Anchorage, 1987—; mem. multicultural edn. program adv. com. Anchorage Sch. Dist., 1982—. Mem. St. Elizabeth A. Seton Sch. Bd., Anchorage, 1981-82; v.p. Filipino Community of Anchorage, Inc., 1986—. NSF grantee, 1968, 71. Roman Catholic. Office: NW Regional Ednl Lab 650 International Airport Rd Anchorage AK 99518

LILES, ROBIN RENEE, agricultural statistician; b. Fayetteville, N.C., Apr. 1, 1957; d. Robert James and Marlene (Hinze) Kasper; m. James Patton Liles, June 15, 1983; 1 child, Christopher Patton. BS in Agrl. Econs., Tex. A&M U., 1978. Agrl. statistician Nat. Agriculture Stats. Service USDA, Little Rock, 1979-82, Nashville, 1982-87; agrl. statistician Washington, 1987—. Mem. Nat. Assn. Female Execs. Roman Catholic. Home: 13816 Fulmer Dr Chantilly VA 22021 Office: USDA Nat Agr Stats Service Room 5912 S Bldg Washington DC 20250

LILJESTRAND, KATHRYN EILEEN, marketing professional; b. Chgo., Sept. 27, 1956; d. Henry A. McCormack and Kathryn Barry Dobbs; m. Bengt Anders Liljestrand, Sept. 13, 1980; 1 child, Kristin Eileen. BA, Siena Coll., Loudonville, N.Y., 1979; student, J. Hagen Sch. Bus., New Rochelle, N.Y., 1979-82. Ops. mgr. Motif Designs, Inc., New Rochelle, 1979-82; sales rep. U.S. Surgical Corp., Norwalk, Conn., 1982-84, product mgr., 1984-85; internat. market specialist mgr. Med. Device Div. Davis and Geck Internat., Wayne, N.J., 1985—. Mem. Am. Mktg. Assn., Nat. Assn. Working Women, Nat. Assn. Female Execs. Democrat. Roman Catholic. Home: 39 Sagamore Trail Sparta NJ 07871 Office: Am Cyanamid Corp 1 Cyanamid Plaza Wayne NJ 07470

LILLEY, DIXIE FRASIER, audiologist, speech pathologist; b. Kalispell, Mont., July 13, 1951; d. Lee ALexander Stewart and Minnie Alice (Steadman) Frasier; m. Charles Albert Lilley, July 4, 1982. BA, U. Mont., 1972, MA, 1975. Cert. speech pathologist and audiologist, Mont. Speech pathologist U. Mont., Missoula, 1975, chief speech pathologist Aphasiology Program, 1976-77; speech pathologist Polson (Mont.) Sch. System, 1975-76; audiologist Whitaker Rehab. Unit, Winston-Salem, N.C., 1977-79, chief audiologist, 1978-79; chief audiologist New Hanover Meml. Hosp., Wilmington, N.C., 1979-84; ptnr. speech and lang. assn. Wilmington, 1980—; owner Hearing and Speech Services, Wilmington, 1984—; cons. Sertoma, Winston-Salem, 1978-79, Wilmington, 1982-84. Mem. Am. Speech Hearing and Lang. Assn., N.C. Speach Hearing and Lang. Assn. Home: 4437 Windtree Rd Wilmington NC 28403 Office: Hearing and Speech Services 2462 Delaney Ave Wilmington NC 59803

LILLIE, MILDRED LOREE, judge; b. Ida Grove, Iowa, Jan. 25, 1915; d. Ottmar August and Florence Elizabeth (Martin) Kluckhohn; m. Cameron Leo Lillie, Mar. 18, 1947 (dec. April 1959); m. A.V. Falcone, Aug. 27, 1966. AB, U. Calif., Berkeley, 1935, JD, 1938; LLD (hon.), Pepperdine U., 1981, Western States U., 1966. Sole practice Fresno, Calif., 1938-42; asst. U.S. atty. U.S. Dept. Justice, Los Angeles, 1942-46; practice law with Charles Carr Los Angeles, 1946-47; judge Mcpl. Ct., Los Angeles, 1947-49, County of Los Angeles Superior Ct., Los Angeles, 1949-58; assoc. justice Calif. Ct. of Appeal, Los Angeles, 1958-84, presiding justice, 1984-88, adminstrv. presiding justice, 1988—; justice protem Calif. Supreme Ct., Los Angeles, 1960, 77, 79, 81-88, mem. Jud. Council State of Calif., San Francisco, 1961-63, 87—. Adv. bd. Western States U. Coll. Law, Fullerton, 1966; bd. dirs. Los Angeles Pops Orchestra, 1984—; bd. dirs. Nat. Conf. Christian and Jews, Los Angeles, 1985—; adv. com. Town Hall, Los Angeles, 1985—; bd. visitors Pepperdine U. Sch. Law, Malibu, Calif., 1985—; trustee Boalthall Fund, U. Calif., Berkeley, 1986—. Recipient award Mademoiselle Mag., 1947, Vol. Activist award, 1976, Cardinal McIntyre award Catholic Press Club, 1981; named Woman of Yr. Los Angeles Times, 1952, Woman of Yr. Mus. of Science and Industry, Los Angeles, 1980. Mem. ABA, Federal Bar Assn., Los Angeles County Bar Assn., Calif. Judges Assn. (com. chmn.), Women Lawyers Assn. (Ernestine Stahlhut award 1969), Los Angeles Trial Lawyers Assn. (Appellate Justice of Yr. 1986), Los Angeles Area C. of C. (bd. dkris. 1975-83), Boalt Hall Alumni Assn. (Citation award 1985), Nat. Assn. Women Judges, Nat. Bus. and Profl. Women of Los Angeles. Democrat. Roman Catholic. Clubs: Ebell, Los Angeles Athletic. Lodge: Soroptimist. Office: 3580 Wilshire Blvd Los Angeles CA 90010

LILLIS, MARY LOUISE, writer, media specialist; b. Kansas City, Mo., Nov. 13, 1927; d. Frederick Charles and Rosella Marie (O'Flaherty) McConnell; m. James Patrick Lillis, Nov. 24, 1949 (dec. Aug. 1982); children: James P., Jr., Kevin T., Timothy D., Charles J., Mary Rose Edwards, Molly Lillis Cahill, Margaret Mary. AB, Avila Coll., 1948. Tchr. English lang., speech Louisburg (Kans.) High Sch., 1948-49; with Midwest Research Inst., Kansas City, 1967—. Editor MRI Quarterly, 1969-80, Viewpoint, 1981-84. Mem. Avila Coll. Bd. Counselors, 1970—, Kansas City Metro Hunger Network, 1985—, Amnesty Internat., Bread for the World, Caths. for Justice. Recipient Disting. Service award Sci. Pioneers, 1979. Mem. Internat. Assn. Bus. Communicators (cert., editor ann. report 1981, Bronze Quill award 1982, 83, 84, bd. dirs., com. chmn. Kansas City br. 1986-87, internat. planning com. 1986, Commendation), Pub. Relations Soc. Am. (bd. dirs., com. chmn. 1975, 87), World Future Soc. (bd. dirs. Kansas City chpt. 1980, 85). Roman Catholic. Home: 431 W 59th St Kansas City MO 64113 Office: Midwest Research Inst 425 Volker Blvd Kansas City MO 64110

LILLY, DIANE PALMER, business executive; b. Mpls.; d. Leroy Sheldon and Irene Palmer; m. David Lilly Jr.; 1 child, Irene Grace. Student Newton Coll. of Sacred Heart. Dir. research adminstrn. Fed. Res. Bank, Mpls., 1972-75, dir. data services, 1975-77, spl. asst. to pres., 1977-78; fed. govt. relations officer Norwest Corp., Mpls., 1978-81, v.p. govt. relations, 1981-87, v.p. corp. relations, 1987—, pres., Norwest Found., 1987—. Downtown area chairperson gen. bus. div. campaign United Way, Mpls., 1978; bd. dirs. Guthrie Theater, 1978-84, Mpls. Inst. of Arts, 1987—, Hennepin Ctr. for Arts, 1978-86, YWCA, Minn. Citizens for Arts, 1983-85, Planned Parenthood of Minn., 1984—; active Minn. Women's Econ. Roundtable, 1981—; participant Leadership Mpls., 1982-83; active Minn. Bus. Partnership,1982-87, Nat. Conf. Fin. Services, Washington. Mem. Am. Bankers Assn., 1983-86 (exec. com., chmn. legis. liaison adv. com. 1984-86). Club: Nat. Economists. Office: Norwest Corp 1200 Peavey Bldg Minneapolis MN 55479

LILLY, LUELLA JEAN, university administrator; b. Newberg, Oreg., Aug. 23, 1937; d. David Hardy and Edith (Coleman) L. BS, Lewis and Clark Coll., 1959; postgrad., Portland State U., 1959-61; MS, U. Oreg., 1961; PhD, Tex. Woman's U., 1971; postgrad., various univs., 1959-72. Tchr. phys. edn. and health, dean girls Cen. Linn Jr.-Sr. High Sch., Halsey, Oreg., 1959-60; tchr. phys. edn. and health, swimming, tennis, golf coach Lake Oswego (Oreg.) High Sch., 1960-63; instr., intramural coach Oreg. State U., Corvallis, 1963-64; instr., intercollegiate coach Am. River Coll., Sacramento, 1964-69; dir. women's phys. edn., athletics U. Nev., Reno, 1969-73, dir. women's athletics, 1973-75, assoc. dir. athletics, 1975-76, assoc. prof. phys. edn., 1971-76; dir. women's intercollegiate athletics U. Calif., Berkeley, 1976—; organizer, coach Lue's Aquatic Club, 1962-64. Author: An Overview of Body Mechanics, 1966, 3d rev. edit., 1969. Vol. instr. ARC, 1951; vol. Heart Fund and Easter Seal, 1974-76; ofcl. Spl. Olympics, 1975; mem. Los Angeles Citizens Olympic Com., 1984. Mem. AAHPER (life), AAUW, Nat. Soc. Profs., Women's Athletic Caucus, Council Collegiate Women Athletics Adminstrs., Western Soc. Phys. Edn. Coll. Women (membership com. 1971-74, program adv. com. 1972, exec. bd. 1972-75), Western Assn. Intercollegiate Athletics for Women (exec. bd. dirs. 1973-75, 79-82), Oreg. Girls' Swimming Coaches Assn. (pres. 1960, 63), Cen. Calif. Bd. Women Ofcls. (basketball chmn. 1968-69), Calif. Assn. Health, Phys. Edn. and Recreation (chmn.-elect jur. coll. sect. 1970), Nev. Bd. Women Ofcls. (chmn. bd., chmn. volleyball sect., chmn. basketball sect. 1969), No. Calif. Women's Intercollegiate Conf. (sec. 1970-71, basketball coordinator 1970-71), No. Calif. Intercollegiate Athletic Conf. (volleyball coordinator 1971-72), Nev. Assn. Health, Phys. Edn. and Recreation (state chmn. 1974—), No. Calif. Athletic Conf. (pres. 1979-82), Phi Kappa Phi, Theta Kappa. Mem. Soc. Friends. Lodge. Soroptimists. Home: 60 Margrave Ct Walnut Creek CA 94596 Office: U Calif 177 Hearst Gym Berkeley CA 94720

LILLY, SHERRIL LYNNE, chemistry instructor; b. Beckley, W. Va., June 17, 1946; d. Arthur and Juanita (Simpson) Herron; m. Ronald Earl Lilly, Dec. 28, 1968 (div. 1975); 1 child, Tonya. BS, Marshall U., 1969; MS, U. Md. Instr. Cabell County Bd. Edn., Huntington, W. Va., 1969-70, 72-73; clin. chemist Cabell Huntington Hosp., Huntington, 1971-72; instr. Prince George County Bd. Edn., Upper Marlboro, Md., 1974-88; program coordinator Gwynn Park Sci., Math. and Tech. Magnet Middle Sch., Brandywine, Md., 1988—; coordinator Laurel High Sch. Sci. Fair, 1983-84; cons. Summer Ctr. for Space Md. State Dept. of Edn., Balt., 1986, dir. 1987; chair chemistry dept. H.B. Owens Sci. Ctr., Lanham, 1986-87; presenter Sci. Trek '87 Children's Sci and Tech., Conf., 1987. Parent vol. Lanham (Md.) Boys and Girls Club, 1984; hostess Talented and Gifted Art Exhibit Md. Summer Ctrs., Annapolis, 1987. Recipient Outstanding Sci. Tchr. award Potomac Electric Power Co., 1987. Fellow Nat. Sci. Techrs. Assn., Md. Assn. Sci. Tchrs. (Sci. Tchr. of the Yr., 1987); mem. Prince George's County Edn. Assn. (cons. homework hot line, 1984—). Republican. Home: 13 Y Hillside Rd Greenbelt MD 20770 Office: Gwynn Park Sci Math and Tech Magnet Middle Sch 8000 Dyson Rd Brandywine MD 20613-7822

LILORE, DOREEN MARY, librarian, labor union official; b. Newark; d. Alfred and Jane Elizabeth (Dodd) Lilore. B.A., Newark State Coll., 1971; M.L.S., Pratt Inst., 1972; D.L.S., Columbia U., 1982. Cert. profl. librarian, tchr., N.J. Reference librarian Paterson Pub. Library (N.J.), 1971-78; teaching asst. Columbia U., N.Y.C., 1979; staff rep. council 52 Am. Fedn. State, County and Mcpl. Employees, AFL-CIO, Jersey City, 1979-84; chief info. officer at program planners, Inc., 1984—. Author: Public Librarian Local Unions, 1984. Mem. ALA (sec. staff orgns. round table), Indsl. Relations Research Assn., Beta Phi Mu, Alpha Sigma Lambda. Roman Catholic. Home: 51 Menzel Ave Maplewood NJ 07040

LILYQUIST, BETTY JEAN, pest control company executive; b. Canova, S.D., Mar. 29, 1942; d. Edwin Arthur and Ann May (Macovets) Ritzman; m. Darrel Alan Lilyquist, Dec. 29, 1940; children: Jodi Lynn, David Alan, Richard Lee. Cert., West L.A. Law Sch., 1986. Clk. Western Power and Gas, Co., Sioux Falls, S.D., 1965; owner, operator Party Sales, Monterey Park, Calif., 1972-74; receptionist Phostoxin Sales, Inc., Alhambra, Calif., 1974, adminstrv. asst.; corp. sec. Pestcon Systems, Inc., Alhambra, dir. regulatory and environ. affairs; technical dir. Sunxon Internat. Sunzon, Inc., Pasadena, Calif. Mem. Grain Elevator and Processing Soc. (mem. registration com. 1987, speaker 1987), Western Agrl. Chem. Assn. (mem. registration com. 1985-87). Home: 1044 Bradshawe Monterey Park CA 91754 Office: Sunzon Internat Inc Braily Bldg 39 Raymond Ave Pasadena CA 91802

LIM, JACQUELINE TY, finance executive; b. Manila, Luzon, Philippines, Jan. 18, 1961; came to U.S. 1979, naturalized, 1985; d. Peter Y.C. and Conchita (Ty) Lim. BS, DePaul U., Chgo., 1983; MM, Northwestern U., Evanston, Ill, 1987. Savs. counselor Talman Home Fed. Savs. and Loan, Arlington Heights, Ill., 1981-83; acct. Beatrice Export Sales Co., Chgo., 1985-86; staff acct. Beatrice U.S. Food Corp., Chgo., 1985-86; sr. acct. Beatrice Internat. Food Co., Chgo., 1986-87; sr. fin. analyst Kraft, Inc., Glenview, Ill., 1987—. Mem. Assn. MBA Execs., Am. Mgmt. Assn. (assoc.), Nat. Assn, Female Execs., Beta Alpha Psi. Roman Catholic. Home: One Kraft Ct Glenview IL 60025

LIN, ALICE LEE LAN, physicist, researcher, educator; b. Shanghai, China, Oct. 28, 1937; came to U.S., 1960, naturalized, 1974; d. Yee and Tsing Tsing (Wang) L.; m. A. Marcus, Dec. 19, 1962 (div. Feb. 1972); 1 child, Peter A. Lin-Marcus. AB in Physics, U. Calif.-Berkeley, 1963; MA in Physics, George Washington U., 1974; postgrad. Rensselaer Poly. Inst. Research asst. in radiation damage Cavendish Lab., Cambridge U., Eng., 1965-66; statis. asst. dept. math. U. Calif.-Berkeley, 1962-63; info. analysis specialist Nat. Acad. Scis., Washington, 1970-71; teaching fellow, research asst. George Washington U., Catholic U. Am., Washington, 1971-75; physicist NASA/Goddard Space Flight Ctr., Greenbelt, Md., 1975-80, Army Materials Tech. Lab., Watertown, Mass., 1980—. Contbr. articles to profl. jours. Mencius Ednl. Found. grantee, 1959-60. Mem. N.Y. Acad. Scis., AAAS, Am. Phys. Soc., Am. Ceramics Soc., Am. Acoustical Soc., Am. Men and Women of Sci., Optical Soc. Am. Democrat. Avocations: rare stamp and coin collecting, art collectibles, home computers, opera, ballet. Home: 28 Hallett Hill Rd Weston MA 02193 Office: Army Materials Tech Lab Mail Stop MS R-SM Bldg 39 Watertown MA 02172

LIN, CARMEN GO, pediatrician; b. Manila, Feb. 11, 1944; came to U.S., 1969; d. George Go and Juana Leesuy; m. Thomas K. Lin, June 3, 1972; 1 child, Christopher. BS, U. Santo Tomas, Philippines, 1960, MD, 1969. Diplomate Am. Bd. Pediatrics. Intern D.C. Gen. Hosp.-Howard U., Washington, 1970-71; resident in pediatrics Newark Children's Hosp., 1971-72, Wyler Children's Hosp.-U. Chgo., 1973-74; practice medicine specializing in pediatrics Hamilton County Bd. Health, Cin., 1978-81, Loveland, Ohio, 1981—; mem. staff Children's Hosp. Med. Ctr., Cin., Our Lady of Mercy Hosp., Cin., Bethesda Hosps., Cin., The Christ Hosp., Cin., Good Samaritan Hosp., Cin.; mem. Women's Faculty Assn. Children's Hosp. Med. Ctr., Cin., 1986—. Mem. AMA, Cin. Acad. Medicine. Roman Catholic. Office: 1608 State Rt 28 Loveland OH 45140

LINCH, ESTRELLA VINZON, insurance underwriter, small business owner; b. Cavite, Philippines, June 18, 1944; came to U.S., 1961; d. Isidro and Filomena (Dragon) Vinzon. BSEE, Philippine Normal Coll., Manila, 1961; MA, U. Nebr., 1964; student, U. Mex., Mexico City, 1964-65; BA, Calif. State U., Long Beach, 1969; MBA, Loyola Marymount U., 1976. Tchr. Spanish Neligh (Nebr.) Pub. Sch., 1962-63, Linda Vista High Sch., San Diego, 1965-66; budget analyst TRW. Redondo Beach, Calif., 1970-72; fin. analyst Rockwell Internat., El Segundo, Calif., 1972-73; asst. controller Crydom Control, El Segundo, 1973-74; asst. to trustee Beverly Hills (Calif.) Bancorp, 1974-76; owner Sage Fin. and Managerial Co., Los Angeles, 1976—; ins. agt., securities rep. Prudential Ins., Santa Monica, Calif., 1976—. Author: Guidelines for Prospective Entrepreneurs in Small Service Oriented Business, 1976. Mem. Million Dollar Round Table, Top Table, Pilipino for Progress (pres. 1982-86), Gen Trias and Philippine Assn. (pres. 1982). Office: Prudential Ins Co Am 624 S Wilton Pl Los Angeles CA 90005

LINCOLN, CATHERINE RUTH, direct marketing company executive; b. Fulmer, Bucks, Eng., Apr. 29, 1941; came to U.S., 1975; d. Geoffrey Morris and Marjorie Elizabeth (Harrison) Allen; m. Robert Adams Lincoln, Feb. 19, 1968; children—Henry Allen, Thomas Adams. B.A. in Modern History with honors, Oxford U., 1962, M.A. in Modern History, 1972; cert. with distinction in contract and criminal law Coll. Law, London, 1975. Researcher, Brit. Diplomatic Service, London, 1962-64, jr. attaché Brit. High Commn., Delhi, Calcutta and Madras, India, 1964-67, 3d sec., Ankara, Turkey, 1967-68; dir. capital campaign St. Paul's Episc. Coll., Lawrenceville, Va., 1977-79; account exec. The Viguerie Co., Falls Church, Va., 1979-82, supr., until 1982, v.p. creative div., 1982-87, regional sales mgr. Ed Burnett Cons, 1987—. Del. county, dist., state convs. Va. Republican. Party, 1977—; block capt., precinct rep., mem. Fairfax County Rep. Com. (Va.), 1979-86; mem. nat. membership com., mem. devel. com. English Speaking Union U.S.A., 1980—; bd. dirs. Indo-Chinese Refugees Social Services, Inc., Washington, 1980-82; bd. assocs. St. Paul's Episc. Coll., 1981—; lay reader Holy Comforter Ch., Vienna, 1982—; treas. Campaign Va. Polit. Action Com., 1984-87. Mem. Direct Mktg. Assn. Washington (dir. 1981-86, pres. 1986), One Hundred Million Club (1980-82). Home: 1052 Douglass Dr McLean VA 22101-2146 Office: Ed Burnett Cons 99 W Sheffield Ave Englewood NJ 07631

LIND, MARILYN MARLENE, artist, writer, genealogist; b. New Ulm, Minn., Aug. 15, 1934; d. Fred S. and Emma L. (Steinke) Thiem; student pub. schs., Aitkin, Minn.; m. Charles R. Lind, Aug. 22, 1952; children—Michael, Bonnie, Vickie. Photographic asst., Aitkin, 1951-52; bookkeeper, office mgr. Rural Electric Assn., Aitkin, 1953-54; office mgr. N.E. Minn. Edn. Assn., Cloquet, 1970-77; pres. The Linden Tree, Cloquet, 1981—; exhibited in one-woman shows: Lake Superior Art Center, Duluth, 1972, Old Towne Gallery, Duluth, 1983; group shows include: Lutheran Brotherhood Ctr. Gallery, Mpls., 1977, Centre Internationale d'Art Contemporain de Paris, 1983. Precinct chmn. Ind. Republicans Minn., 1976-77, co-chmn. Carlton County/Senate Dist. 14, 1977-80, vice-chmn. Carlton County, 1984-85, 8th Congl. Dist. Com., 1977-80, mem. Minn. state central com., 1977-82, county, dist. and state conv. del., 1976-87. Recipient Gallery awards, Duluth, 1972, Mpls., 1977. Mem. Geneal. Soc. Carlton County (founding mem., bd. dirs. 1977-87, v.p. 1980-81, sec. 1982-84, pres. 1986-88). Lutheran. Author: Christoph and August, A Dream and a Promise, 1981; various publs. in field of genealogy research, including: Beginning Genealogy, 1984, Using Maps and Aerial Photography in your Genealogical Research, 1984, Researching and Finding Your German Heritage, 1986; Immigration, Migration and Settlement in the United States, 1985; Printing and Publishing Your Family History, 1986; Looking Backward to Sweden and The Lind-Bure Family 1000-1986, 1986. Home and Office: 1204 W Prospect St Cloquet MN 55720

LINDEGREN, CECILE KEYSER, music educator; b. DeFuniak Springs, Fla., July 1, 1946; d. Charles Renshaw and Ouida (Higdon) Keyser; m. John Emory Lindegren, Feb. 14, 1981; children: Erica Kristen, Jason, Jeremy. AA, Pensacola (Fla.) Jr. Coll., 1967; B in Mus. Edn., Fla. State U., 1969; M in Mus. Edn., U. South Miss., 1979. Cert. elem. and secondary tchr., Fla. Choral dir. Pryor Jr. High Sch., Ft. Walton Beach, Fla., 1969-77, 86—; dir. music and youth Mary Esther (Fla.) United Meth. Ch., 1977-81; owner, instr. Lindegren Music Studio, Ft. Walton Beach, 1981—; children's choir dir. Trinity United Meth. Ch., 1983-87. Dir. Ft. Walton Beach Community Chorus, 1976—. Mem. Okaloosa County Music Tchrs. Assn. (pres. 1981-83), Fla. Vocal Assn. (chmn. local dist. 1973-74, 76-77), Fla. State Music Tchrs. Assn., AAUW (chmn. fine arts com. 1978-80), Kelly Fine Arts Council (arts festival co-chmn. 1986), Playground Mutual Concert Assn. (sec. 1984-86, bd. dirs.), Music Educators Nat. Conf., Am. Coll. Musicians. Democrat. Methodist. Clubs: Ft. Walton Beach Woman's (music dir. 1984-87, 2d v.p. 1984-86), Choctaw Bay Music (pres. 1985-86). Home: 206 Vicki Leigh Ave Fort Walton Beach FL 32548

LINDELL, ANDREA REGINA, college dean, nurse; b. Warren, Pa., Aug., 21, 1943; d. Andrew D. and Irene M. (Fabry) Lefik; m. Warner E. Lindell, May 7, 1966; children—Jennifer L., Jason M. B.S., Villa Maria Coll., 1970; M.S.N. Catholic U., 1975, D.N.Sc., 1975; diploma R.N., St. Vincent's Hosp., Erie, Pa. Instr. St. Vincent Hosp. Sch. Nursing, 1964-66; dir. Rouse Hosp., Youngsville, Pa., 1966-69; supr. Vis. Nurses Assn., Warren, Pa., 1969-70; dir. grad. program Cath. U., Washington, 1975-77; chmn., assoc. dean U. N.H., Durham, 1977-81; dean, prof. Oakland U., Rochester, Mich., 1981—; cons. Moorehead U., Ky., 1983. Editor; Jour. Profl. Nursing, 1985; contbr. articles to profl. jours. Mem. sch. bd. Strafford Sch. Dist., N.H., 1977-80; Gov.'s Blue Ribbon Commn. Direct Health Policies, Concord, N.H., 1979-81; vice chmn. New England Commn. Higher Edn. in Nursing, 1977-81; mem. Mich. Assn. Colls. Nursing, 1981—. Named Outstanding Young Woman Am., 1980. Mem. Nat. League Nursing, Am. Assn. Colls. Nursing, Sigma Theta Tau. Democrat. Roman Catholic. Avocations: water skiing; roller skating; reading; fishing; camping; Office: Oakland U 428 O Dowd Hall Rochester MI 48309

LINDEMAN, CHERYL ANN, educational administrator; b. Cleve., July 16, 1949; d. Glen A. and Marie (Gyuran) DeWyer; m. L. Dean Lindeman, Sept. 4, 1971; children: Sarah, Kristen, Allison. BA in Biology, Wittenberg U., 1971; MS in Biology, U. Akron, 1973; EdD, U. Va., 1984. Cert. tchr., Va. Grad. asst. U. Akron, Ohio, 1971-72; intern in higher edn. Cen. Va. Community Coll., Lynchburg, 1983; sci. tchr. Amherst (Va.) County Pub. Schs., 1973-77, coordinator environ. edn., 1975-77; lectr. in biology Cen. Va. Community Coll., Lynchburg, 1975—, coordinator Pathfinder's Coll., 1984-85; instr., advisor Cen. Va. Gov's. Magnet Sch. for Sci. and Technology, Lynchburg, 1985—. Pres. Women of the Ch., St. Andrew's Presbyn. Ch., Lynchburg, 1984-86. Mem. Va. Acad. Scis., Va. Assn. Biol. Educators, Am. Inst. Biol. Scis., Am. Assn. Gifted Children, Electron Microscopy Soc. Am., Phi Delta Kappa. Home: 109 Yale St Lynchburg VA 24502 Office: Cen Va Magnet Sch 3020 Wards Ferry Rd Lynchburg VA 24502

LINDEN, JUDITH MARSHA, urban planner; b. Bklyn., Nov. 17, 1951; d. Morton and Selma Samilow; m. Jay Linden, Sept. 2, 1973; children: Jessica Nicole, Daniel Elliot. BA cum laude, Ithaca Coll., 1973; postgrad., Rensselaer Poly. Inst., 1976-78. Placement dir. Mass. Med. Soc., 1973-74; pub. relations dir. Albany (N.Y.) Regional Med. Program, 1974-76; assoc. dir. alumni relations Renssalear Poly. Inst., Troy, N.Y., 1976-78; exec. dir. Queens Symphony Orch., Rego Park, N.Y., 1978-83; fundraising cons. Carnegie Hall, New Community Cinema, N.Y.C., 1984-85; cons. Greater Jamaica Devel. Corp., 1987—. Bd. dirs. Open Door Parenting Ctr. Mem. Am. Symphony Orch. League, Bus. and Profl. Women's Assn. Home and Office: 170 Hillpark Ave Great Neck NY 11021

LINDEN, MARGARET JOANNE, librarian, administrator; b. Berkeley, Calif., Nov. 20, 1938; d. Arthur William and Johanna Gesina (Zuydhoek) Dickie; m. Roy Joseph Linden, Jan. 6, 1965. BA, Swarthmore (Pa.) Coll., 1960; MLS, U. Calif., Berkeley, 1962. Librarian Grad. Social Scis. library U. Calif., Berkeley, 1961-65, librarian Giannini Found. for Agrl. Econs., 1965-70; social scis. librarian Idaho State U., Pocatello, 1970-71; head cataloguer Chevron Corp. (formerly Standard Oil Co. of Calif.), San Francisco, 1971-74, asst. chief librarian, 1974-77, chief librarian, 1978-81, mgr. corp. library, 1981—. Mem. Calif. Library Assn., Spl. Libraries Assn. (editor chpt. bull. 1972-73). Office: Chevron Corp 225 Bush St San Francisco CA 94104

LINDER, KATE, actress, flight attendant; b. Pasadena, Calif., Nov. 2; d. Ralph Morris and Molly (Sokoloff) Wolveck; m. Ronald Leonard Linder, Feb. 14, 1976; stepchildren: Jay, Jon, Karyn. BA in Theater, San Francisco State U., 1975. Flight attendant Trans Am. Airlines, San Francisco, 1974-78, United Airlines, Los Angeles, 1978—; actress The Young and The Restless, CBS-TV, 1982—. Spokesperson Love Is Feeding Everyone, Los Angeles, 1985—; hon. chair Child Abuse And Neglect, Ventura, Calif., 1987—. Recipient Bronze Halo award So. Calif. Motion Picture Council, 1985. Mem. Screen Actors Guild, AFTRA, Actors Equity Assn., Airline Flight Attendants Assn. Democrat. Jewish. Office: Brenda Feldman 6922 Hollywood Blvd Suite 407 Los Angeles CA 90028

LINDERSMITH, WRAY BEAL, service executive; b. Lincolnton, N.C., June 6, 1926; d. Lester Ray and Mattie (Abernathy) Beal. Student, Miami U., 1953, Houston U., 1964. Exec. receptionist Woodward & Lothrop, Washington, 1946-51; property mgmt. rep. Fred A. Smith Real Estate, Washington, 1951-53; office mgr. Ken Auto Rental, Miami Beach, Fla., 1953-56; co-owner Ken Buick, Inc., Keystone Auto Rental, Pitts., 1956-62; sales and pub. relations rep. Baker Hotel, Dallas, 1962-67; dir. mktg. and pub. relations Hotel Washington, 1968—; mem. def. adv. com. Women in the Armed Services, Washington, 1969-72; mem. career adv. bd. Sanger Harris store, Dallas, 1966-67. Mem. Advt. Club Washington, Pub. Relations Roundtable, Women's Econ. Alliance Found., Greater Wash. Soc. Assn. Execs., Hotel Sales Mgmt. Assn. (bd. dirs. 1971-72). Republican. Methodist. Clubs: Bal Harbor (Miami), Pitts. Athletic, Tex. State Soc., Tex. Breakfast. Lodge: Soroptimist. Office: South Shore Harbour Resort and Conf Ctr 2500 South Shore Blvd League City TX 77573

LINDGREN, LEAH ANN JANSEN, academic administrator; b. Mpls., Aug. 31, 1962; d. Constance Louise (Raisler) Pope; m. Jay Randolph Lindgren, Nov. 16, 1985. BA cum laude, Concordia Coll., Moorhead, Minn., 1984. Freight dispatcher Continental Grain Co., Fargo, N.D., 1982-83; writer, adminstrv. asst. to alumni dir. office devel. Concordia Coll., 1984, asst. to alumni dir., 1985-86, mgr. catering, confs. dining service, 1986—; Rep. St. Luke's Assn., Fargo, 1986—. Mem. pub. relations bd. Faith Luth. Ch., West Fargo, 1987; asst. com. person Rep. precinct dist. 13, West Fargo, 1986 . Mem. Am. Hosp. Assn., Assn. Conf. Events Dirs. Internat., Nat. Assn. Coll. Univ. Food Services (1st pl. catering spl. events category 1986), Pi Gamma Mu. Club: Toastmasters (Moorhead). Home: 601 9th Ave W West Fargo ND 58078 Office: Concordia Coll Moorhead MN 58078

LINDH, PATRICIA SULLIVAN, banker, former government official; b. Toledo, Oct. 2, 1928; d. Lawrence Walsh and Lillian Winifred (Devlin) Sullivan; m. H. Robert Lindh, Jr., Nov. 12, 1955; children: Sheila, Deborah, Robert. B.A., Trinity Coll., Washington, 1950, LL.D., 1975; LL.D., Walsh Coll., Canton, Ohio, 1975, U. Jacksonville, 1975. Adoption case worker Cath. Charities, Chgo., 1954-55; editor Singapore Am. Newspaper, 1957-62; spl. asst. to counsellor to Pres. 1974, spl. asst. to Pres., 1975-76; dep. asst. sec. state for ednl. and cultural affairs Dept. State, 1976-77; v.p., dir. corp. communications Bank Am., Los Angeles, 1978-84, World Banking P.R. Bank Am., San Francisco, 1985—. Trustee La. Arts and Sci. Center, 1970-73, Calif. Hosp. Med. Ctr.; bd. dirs. Jr. League of Baton Rouge, 1969, Children's Bur. Los Angeles, 1979, 84; Rep. state vice chairwoman La., 1970-74; Rep. nat. committeewoman, La., 1974; mem. adv. bd. Jr. League Los Angeles, 1980-84; bd. visitors Southwestern U. Sch. Law. Roman Catholic. Home: 850 Powell St San Francisco CA 94108

LINDHOLM, SUE CAREY, lawyer; b. Atlanta, Jan. 4, 1944; d. William Oscar and Sue Carey (Rooney) Lindholm; children—Gregory de Torony, Sue Carey de Torony. A.A., Gulf Park Coll., 1962; A.B.J., U. Ga., 1964, J.D. cum laude, 1982. Bar: Ga. 1982. Asst. editor Briefings Dean Rusk Ctr., Athens, Ga., 1982-83; sole practice, Athens, 1983-84; law clk. for Justice George T. Smith, Ga. Supreme Ct., 1984—. Mem. ABA, Ga. Bar Assn. Address: 4230 Bingham Ct Stone Mountain GA 30083

LINDLEY-DOMINGUEZ, PATRICIA J., lawyer; b. Sapulpa, Okla., Mar. 13, 1940; d. Allen L. and Cornelia Madelyn (Brown) Monroe; m. Clyde E. Lindley, June 8, 1958 (div. 1970); children: Kenton K., Rafaella D.; m. Oscar Dominguez, July 21, 1979. AA, Kansas City Jr. Coll., 1961; BA, Avila Coll., 1968, JD, U. Mo., 1974. Bar: Mo. 1974, C.Z. 1974, U.S. Ct. Appeals (5th cir.) 1976, U.S. Ct. Claims 1979, U.S. Supreme Ct. 1979. Social worker, supr. Mo. Div. Welfare, 1961-69; asst. coordinator U. Mo., Kansas City, 1969-70; dir. social work Project Headstart, Kansas City, 1970-71; intern pvt. law firm and Legal Aid, Kansas City, Mo., 1971-74; staff atty. Panama Canal Commn., 1974—, asst. gen. counsel, 1983—, dep. gen. counsel, 1988—, mem. women's adv. council, 1975-84; legal advisor Panama Canal Coll. Charter Commn., 1978; adj. prof. Nova U., Panama Regional Ctr., 1978-79. Vol. legal advisor U.S.A. Girl Scouts-Panama, 1975—; vol. Balboa Youth Recreation Council, 1974-79, Joint Com. Infant and Child Protection, 1974-79, Foster Home Com., 1974-79. Mem. C.Z. Bar Assn. (sec., v.p., pres. 1977-79), Mo. Bar Assn., Fed. Bar Assn. (v.p. Panama chpt. 1980). Democrat. Home: 610 Calle Mindi, Balboa Heights Panama Office: Office of Gen Counsel Panama Canal Commn APO Miami FL 34011

LINDNER, CHARLOTTE K., librarian; b. N.Y.C., Feb. 28, 1922; d. Louis B. and Ada (Kreitman) Fisch; B.A., N.Y.U., 1942; M.L.S., Columbia U., 1959; children—Carol, Gregory, Amy. Asst. cataloger D. Samuel Gottesman Library, Albert Einstein Coll. Medicine, Bronx, N.Y., 1958-63, cataloger, 1963-76, asst. librarian, 1974-76, acting dir. library, 1976-78, dir. library, 1978—. Mem. Med. Library Assn.

LINDNER, ERNA CAPLOW, educator, choreographer, movement therapist; b. N.Y.C., May 26, 1928; d. Abraham Murray and Mildred T. (Farb) Caplow; A.B., Bklyn Coll., 1948; M.S., Smith Coll., 1950; Ph.D., Columbia Pacific U., 1986; m. Norman Lindner, June 18, 1950 (dec. Sept. 1981); 1 dau., Amy Beth. Instr. dance Brown U., 1950-54, Rutgers U., 1954-55; dance specialist Samuel Field YM—YWHA, Queens, N.Y., 1962-68; dance specialist N.Y.C. Bd. Edn., 1963-69; asst. dance dir., choreographer Martin de Porres Center, Queens, 1967-70; dir. Saturday Cultural Program, Rochdale Village Nursery Sch., Queens, 1964-73; dir.-choreographer Danceabouts Co., N.Y.C., 1966-80; prof. health, phys. edn. and recreation Nassau Community Coll. SUNY, L.I., 1968—; adj. prof. phys. edn. and dance Adelphi U., 1979—; lectr. and tng. cons. on dance for spl. populations. Charter mem. Queens Council on Arts, exec. bd. dirs., 1970-74; sec., mem. exec. com. Nat. Ednl. Council Creative Therapies. Mem. Am. Dance Guild (charter mem., past nat. pres., nat. exec. bd.), Am. Dance Therapy Assn., Am. Assn. Sex Educators, Counselors and Therapists (cert. sex educator, sex counselor), Heritage Com. Nat. Dance Assn., Council of Services Ea. Dist. Contbr. chpts on dance to Fun for Fitness; interviewer on dance Sta. WHPC-FM; (with others) selected music and wrote manual for Special Music for Special People, Ednl. Act Rec. Co., 1977; Special Dancing on Your Feet and in Your Seat, 1982; Come Dance Again, 1987. Author: (with others) Therapeutic Dance/Movement, 1979; (monograph) Use of Dance in Sex Education and Counseling, 1974; also articles on geriatric dance therapy. Home: PO Box 993 Woodside NY 11377 Office: Nassau Community Coll Stewart Ave Garden City NY 11530

LINDQUIST, EDITH LORRAINE, physical education educator; b. Duluth, Minn., Aug. 2, 1931; d. Andrew H. and Edith Margaret (Nordmark) Lindquist; B.S. (Calif. State scholar 1952), U. Calif., Santa Barbara, 1953; M.S., U. So. Calif., 1955; Ph.D. (teaching asst. 1962, 65), U. Mich., 1968. Instr. phys. edn. Los Angeles city schs., 1953-65; research grantee Horace R. Rackham Sch. Grad. Studies, U. Mich., 1968; prof. phys. edn. San Jose (Calif.) State U., 1966—, coordinator undergrad. maj. program; research chmn. Western Soc. Phys. Edn. Coll. Women, 1975-78, spl. projects chmn., 1975; cons. in field. Grantee HEW, 1971; spl. projects grantee Western Soc. for Phys. Edn. Coll. Women, 1977-78; Calif. State Dept. Edn. grantee, 1979-80. Mem. AAPHERD (fellow Research Consortium on Completed Research), Calif. Assn. Health, Phys. Edn. and Recreation, Calif. Tchrs. Assn., N.Am. Soc. Psychology of Sport and Phys. Activity, Alpha Delta Pi. Democrat. Author papers in field. Asso. editor Motor Skills: Theory into Practice, 1976—. Home: 17269 James Lex Ln Morgan Hill CA 95037 Office: San Jose State Univ San Jose CA 95192

LINDQUIST, JUDITH DOWDLE, lawyer; b. Elmhurst, Ill., Sept. 30, 1949; d. John Axel and Ethel Linea (Johnson) Lindquist; m. John Anthony Dowdle, June 26, 1970; children—John Erick, Andrew Ryden, Lindsay Julia, Claire Linea. B.S., U. Ill., 1971; J.D., U. Chgo., 1974. Bar: Minn. 1974; cert. math. tchr., Ill. Atty., researcher Ill. Legis. Investigating Commn., Chgo., summer 1972; atty., shareholder Fredrikson & Byron Law Firm, Mpls.,

1974-84; of counsel firm Gray, Plant, Mooty, Mooty & Bennett, P.A., Mpls., 1985-88; lectr. for Am. Law Inst., ABA, Minn. Continuing Legal Edn. Program, NYU Tax Inst., 1986, So. Fed. Tax Inst., 1986-87, Notre Dame U. Estate Planning Inst., 1985, 87; adj. faculty William Mitchell Coll. Law, 1985—. Legal cons. Mpls. Mayor's Task Force on City Employee Pensions, 1976-77; cons., advisor, mem. Gov.'s Small Bus. Innovation Research Grant Commn., Mpls., 1983-84; cons., advisor, mem. Gov.'s Council on Entrepreneurship and Innovation, 1984. Bd. dirs., v.p. Southside Family Nurturing Center, Mpls., 1978-85; trustee Minn. Pub. Employees Retirement Assn., 1985—; mem. tax adv. group for U.S. Rep. Bill Frenzel, Minn., 1987—. Mem. ABA (com. on continuing profl. edn., adv. group on pensions), Am. Law Inst., Minn. Bar Assn. (chairperson employee benefits sect. 1983-84), ABA (tax sect.), Mpls. Pension Council, Midwest Pension Conf., Nat. Assn. Women Bus. Owners, Order Coif, Phi Beta Kappa, Phi Kappa Phi. Home: 295 Woodlawn Ave Saint Paul MN 55105 Office: Gray Plant Mooty et al 3400 City Ctr 33 S 6th St Minneapolis MN 55402

LINDSAY, DEBRA SUSAN, health information services administrator; b. Hammond, Ind., Oct. 22, 1952; d. Leroy Dewey and Armeda May (Atteberry) L.; divorced; children: Lisa. AS, Ind. U., Gary, 1986. Med. transcriptionist Munster (Ind.) Community Hosp., 1980-85; acting dir. med. records dept. Meml. Hosp. Tampa, Fla., 1986-87, asst. dir. med. records, 1987—. Mem. Am. Med. Record Assn., Gulf Coast Med. Record Assn. Home: 202 Columbia Ave Apt 4 Tampa FL 33606

LINDSAY, KATHERINE ANN, principal; b. Decatur, Ill., Apr. 18, 1946; d. Frank Merrill and Margery (Crawford) L. BS, Millikin U., Decatur, 1968; MEd, U. Ill., 1969. Cert. ednl. adminstr., guidance counselor, Ill. Tchr. Decatur Pub. Sch. Dist., 1969-75, adminstrv. intern, 1975-76, prin. Pershing Sch., 1976-82, prin. South Shores Elem. Sch., 1982—; ednl. adv. com. Millikin U., Decatur, 1976—. Co-author, illustrator: (book) Decatur, Today and Yesterday, 1979. Pres. Mental Health Assn. of Macon County, Decatur, 1972; bd. dirs. ARC, Macon County chpt., Decatur, 1981-84, 85—, YWCA, Decatur, 1986—, Am. Cancer Soc., Macon County chpt., Decatur, 1988—; deacon, elder Cen. Christian Ch., Decatur, 1986—. Named Outstanding Young Educator award Decatur Jaycees, 1972, Young Alumnus of Yr. Millikin U., 1973, Outstanding Educator Alpha Delta Kappa, 1982, Adminstr. of Yr. Decatur Assn. Ednl. Office Personnel, 1983; recipient Those Who Excel award Ill. Bd. Edn., 1985. Mem. Assn. Supervision and Curriculum Devel., Decatur Assn. Bldg. Adminstrs. (pres.), Delta Kappa Gamma, Phi Delta Kappa. Lodge: Zonta. Home: 1580 Lynnwood Dr Decatur IL 62521 Office: South Shores Elem Sch 2500 S Franklin St Decatur IL 62521

LINDSAY, VIRGINIA ELENA, county government official; b. San Francisco, Oct. 20, 1947; d. Robert Joseph and Elda (Rodoni) Carney; m. Mark Lovett Lindsay, Feb. 1, 1969 (div.); children: Kelly Maureen, Molly Elena. AA, San Francisco City Coll., 1967; BA, Sacramento State Coll., 1969. Booking officer Jefferson County Corrections Dept., Louisville, 1975, correction aide, 1975-78, mental inquest officer, 1976-78, diversion and intervention interviewer, 1978-79, acting classification officer, 1979, correctional services mgr., 1979-82, asst. community corrections ctr. mgr., 1982-84, correctional services mgr., 1984-85, asst. community corrections ctr. mgr., 1982-84, correctional services mgr., 1984-85; mgr. Community Corrections Ctr., Louisville, 1985—, mgr. correctional services, 1985-86; mgr. correctional services Jefferson County Corrections Dept., 1975—; cons. classifications Nat. Inst. Corrections, Boulder, Colo., 1985—; mem. tng. adv. com., corrections rev. com. Mem. Am. Correctional Assn., Am. Jail Assn. Republican. Lutheran. Office: Jefferson County Corrections Dept 600 W Jefferson St Louisville KY 40202

LINDSETH, VIRGINIA MACDONALD, educational psychologist; b. Ithaca, N.Y., Apr. 17, 1935; d. John Winchester and Mary Elizabeth (Browne) MacDonald; m. Jon Andrew Lindseth; children—Andrew, Steven, Karen, Peter. B.A., Cornell U., 1956; M.A., John Carroll U., 1975; Ph.D., Case Western Res. U., 1980, MBA, 1987. Cert. sch. counselor, Ohio. Dean of students Hathaway Brown Sch., Shaker Heights, Ohio, 1970-75, head Upper Sch., 1974-75; dir. studies Univ. Sch. Upper Sch., Hunting Valley, Ohio, 1975-79; asst. dir., dir. studies Lower Sch., Shaker Heights, 1979-86, ednl. cons., 1986—; dir. Ctr. for Profl. Devel. John Carroll U., University Heights, Ohio, 1986-87, adj. prof. 1984—; pres. bd. trustees Resource: Careers, Cleve., 1987—. Trustee Ursuline Coll., Pepper Pike, Ohio, 1986—. Mem. Am. Psychol. Assn. Republican. Roman Catholic.

LINDSEY, APRIL RENEE, academic administrator, library director; b. New Castle, Pa., Jan. 9, 1953; d. John Francis and Phebe Gay (Mears) Donley; m. John Lawrence Lindsey, Nov. 30, 1974; 1 child, Jared Trevor. BA in Social Work, Asbury Coll., Wilmore, Ky., 1974; MLS, U. N.C., 1988. Bus. asst. John Wesley Coll., Greensboro, N.C., 1977-81; library asst. John Wesley Coll., High Point, N.C., 1981-86, dir. library services, 1986—. Mem. ALA, Intellectual Freedom Round Table of ALA, Library Research Round Table of ALA. Home: Rt 2 Box 320 Asheboro NC 27203 Office: John Wesley Coll Library 2314 N Centennial High Point NC 27260

LINDSEY, BONNIE JOAN, vocational educator; b. Oklahoma City, May 4, 1935; d. David DeWitt and Genevieve Catherine (Rucinski) Bevans; m. Donald G. Lindsey, Apr. 3, 1963 (div. 1974): 1 child, Jon Erik. AS, Mt. San Jacinto Coll., 1973; BA Vocat. Edn., Long Beach State U., 1975, MA Vocat. Edn., 1977. Tchr. Riverside (Calif.) Regional Occupation program, 1972-74, mem. adv. com., 1983-85; supr. Colton-Redlands-Yucaipa Regional Occupation Program, Redlands, Calif., 1974-75; assoc. prof. Riverside Community Coll., 1975—. Author: Medical Assisting, 1974, 75. Mem. Am. Assn. Med. Transcription (pres. Orange Empire chpt. 1985-88), Am. Assn. Med. Assts., Calif. Assn. Med. Assisting Instrs., Vocat. Indsl. Clubs of Am. (named Advisor of Yr. 1974), Epsilon Pi Tau. Democrat. Roman Catholic. Home: 13360 Gold Pl Moreno Valley CA 92388 Office: Riverside Community Coll 4800 Magnolia Ave Riverside CA 92506

LINDSEY, DOTTYE JEAN, educator; b. Temple Hill, Ky., Nov. 4, 1929; d. Jesse D. and Ethel Ellen (Bailey) Nuckols; B.S., Western Ky. U., 1953, M.A., 1959; m. Willard W. Lindsey, June 14, 1952 (div.). Owner, Bonanza Restaurant, Charleston, W.Va., 1965; tchr. remedial reading Alice Waller Elem. Sch., Louisville, 1967-75, tchr., 1953-67, 1975—, contact person for remedial reading, 1968—; profl. model Cosmo/Casablancas Modeling Agy., Louisville, 1984—. Bn. sponsor ROTC Western Ky. U., 1950; local precinct capt., 1987—; election officer, 1984—. Named Miss Ky., 1951. Mem. NEA, Ky. Edn. Assn., Jefferson County Tchrs. Assn., various polit. action coms., Internat. Reading Assn., Am. Childhood Edn. Assn., Met. Louisville Women's Polit. Caucus (treas. 1980—). Democrat. Baptist. Office: 7410 LaGrange Rd Suite 104 Louisville KY 40222

LINDSEY, RIKI SUE, real estate agent; b. Longview, Wash., Apr. 11, 1953; d. Ralph Virgil and Clara Ferol (Loper) L.; m. Kurt Michael Thoma, May 13, 1978 (Feb. 1986). AA, Chamberlyne Coll. Jr. Coll., 1973; BFA, Roger Williams Coll., 1976. Retail mgr. Apogee, Boston, 1973; retail buyer T. Edwards, Atlanta, 1974; retail mgr. T. Edwards, Chgo., 1976; dist. mgr. Jaeger Internat., Chgo. and Hartford, N.J., 1976-78; retail mdse. mgr. Peter Wittman, Wellesley, Mass., 1978; pres. Confetti Inc., Newport, R.I., 1978—, Riki Jewelers, Boston, 1984—; real estate The Kaplan Group, Newton, Mass., 1986—; cons. in field. Bd. dirs. Tifobet Theatre Co., Newport, 1979-83; pres. Downtown Mchts., Newport, 1981; mem. R.I. State Commn. on Arts, Newport, 1982-84. Mem. NOW, Nat. Assn. Female Execs., Bus. and Profl. Women. Home: 84 Prospect St Wellesley MA 02181 Office: Riki Jewelers Copley Pl Boston MA 02116

LINDSEY, VICTORIA ELIZABETH, brokerage house executive; b. Atlanta, Dec. 17, 1951; d. Jack William Lindsey and Dorothy Marie (Cates) Doyle. BS, Ariz. State U., 1973; postgrad., Oxford U., 1973; MEd, Ga. State U., 1976. Tchr. Ch. Eng. sch. Wantage, England, 1973; specialist early childhood Young World, Atlanta, 1973-74, Canterbury Sch., Atlanta, 1974-76, Gwinett County Pub. Sch., Lawrenceville, Ga., 1976-77; exec. trade sales Scholastic, Inc., Atlanta and Washington, 1978-81; exec. European sales Scholastic, Inc., Heidelberg, Fed. Republic of Germany, 1981-82; account trader, sr. trader Richardson Greenshields Securities, N.Y.C., 1983-84, Clayton Brokerage Co., N.Y.C., 1984-85; pres., treas. Pelham Trading Co. Inc., N.Y.C., 1985—, bd. dirs. Mem. Nat. Futures Assn. (cert.), Futures Industry Assn., Wall St. Women's Network Group, Nat. Female Execs. Assn. Democrat. Roman Catholic. Office: Pelham Trading Co Inc 373 South End Ave Suite 24S New York NY 10252

LINDSKOG, MARJORIE OTILDA, educator; b. Rochester, Minn., Oct. 13, 1937; d. Miles Emery and Otilda Elvina (Hagre) L. BA, Colo. Coll., 1959, MA in Teaching, 1972. Field advisor/camp dir. Columbine council Girl Scouts U.S., Pueblo, Colo., 1959-65; staff mem. Wyo. Girl Scout Camp, Casper, 1966, dir., 1967; tchr. Sch. Dist. 60, Pueblo, 1966—; asst. dir. camp Pacific Peaks Girl Scouts U.S., Olympia, Wash., 1968, dir., 1969; instr. Jr. Gt. Books Program, 1981—; chmn. credit com. Pueblo Tchr.'s Credit Union. Author: (series of math. lessons) Bronco Mathmania, 1987, 88; area co-chair Channel 8 Pub. TV Auction, Pueblo, 1983-87; contbr. articles to profl. jours. Bd. dirs. Columbine Girl Scout Council, 1983-85, Dist. #60 Blood Bank, 1985—; mem. Pueblo Greenway and Nature Ctr., 1981—. Recipient Thanks badge Girl Scouts U.S. Mem. Colo. Archeol. Soc., Assn. for Supervision and Curriculum Devel., Colo. Assn. for Gifted and Talented, Nat. Council for Tchrs. Math., Intertel, Mensa, Phi Delta Kappa (editor newsletter), Alpha Phi. Lutheran. Club: Pueblo Country. Lodge: Sons of Norway. Home: 2810 7th Ave Pueblo CO 81003 Office: Sunset Park Sch 110 Univ Circle Pueblo CO 81005

LINDSKOG, MARY ELIZABETH, retired school administrator, consultant; b. Toungoo, Burma, Dec. 11, 1926; came to U.S., 1931; d. James Lee and Betty (Ryden) Lewis; m. Paul W. Lindskog, June 7, 1949; children—Eric Woodrow, Jon Lewis. B.A., Macalester Coll., 1949. Tchr. pub. schs., Pequot Lakes, Minn., 1949-50, Duluth, Minn., 1950-51; tchr. Robbinsdale Sch. Dist., Minn., 1958-63, dir. publs. and pub. relations, 1963-85; cons., lectr. in field. Contbr. articles to profl. jours.; editor various curriculum guides. Mem. Nat. Sch. Pub. Relations Assn. (chpt. pres., nat. v.p. 1976-81). Home: 2485 Regent Ave N Minneapolis MN 55422

LINDSTEDT-SIVA, (KAREN) JUNE, marine biologist, oil company executive; b. Mpls., Sept. 24, 1941; d. Stanley L. and Lila (Mills) Lindstedt; m. Ernest Howard Siva, Dec. 20, 1969. Student, U. Calif.-Santa Barbara, 1959-60, U. Calif.-Davis, 1960-62; B.A., U. So. Calif., 1963, M.S., 1967, Ph.D., 1971. Asst. coordinator Office Sea Grant Programs U. So. Calif., 1971; environ. specialist So. Calif. Edison Co., Rosemead, 1971-72; asst. prof. biology Calif. Luth. U., 1972-73; sci. advisor Atlantic Richfield Co., Los Angeles, 1973-77, sr. sci. advisor, 1977-81, mgr. environ. scis., 1981-86, mgr. environ. protection, 1986—; mem. Nat. Sci. Bd., 1984—; mem. biology adv. council Calif. State U.-Long Beach; bd. dirs. So. Calif. Acad. Scis., 1983—; mem. Marine Scis. adv. council Univ. So. Calif. Inst. Coastal and Marine Scis.; trustee Bermuda Biol. Sta. for Research. Contbr. articles to profl. jours. Bd. dirs. Irene McCulloch Found., Los Angeles Devel. Com. Internat. Med. Corps. Recipient Calif. Mus. Sci. and Industry Achievement award, 1976, Trident award for Marine Scis., 11th Ann. Rev. Underwater Activites, Italy, 1970, Achievement award for Advancing Career Opportunities for Women, Career Planning Council, 1978; research grantee; distg. scholar biology Calif. Lut. U. Colloquim Scholars, 1988. Mem. Soc. Petroleum Industry Biologists (pres. 1976-80), AAAS, Marine Tech. Soc., U. So. Calif. Oceanographic Assocs. (bd. dirs.), Conejo Valley Audubon Soc., Calif. Native Plant Soc., Am. Inst. Biol. Sci., Western Soc. Naturalists, Phi Beta Kappa, Sigma Xi, Phi Kappa Phi. Office: Atlantic Richfield Co 515 S Flower St Los Angeles CA 90071

LINDSTROM, ADELINE LILLEY, travel agency owner; b. Cleve., Mar. 8, 1937; d. Ralph I. Lilley and Marjorie Armstrong; children: Eric, Jeff, Brad, Kurt. Student, Brigham Young U., 1955-58, U. Oregon, 1960-61; AA, Mt. Hood Community Coll., 1970. Cert. travel counselor, Inst. Cert. Travel Agts., 1984. Exec. sec., county clk. Riverside County, Calif., 1957-59; switchboard operator, sec., pub. facilities mgr. West coast Champion Internat., Roseburg, Eugene, and Portland, Oregon, 1959-80; owner Addie's You and I Travel Service, Portland, Ore., 1980—, Addie's Tips on Travel Tanning, Portland, 1983—, Addie's Treasures, Portland, 1987—. Author (pamphlet): Women Traveling Alone, 1985, Why Not You and I?, 1987. Mem. Access to the Skies, 1985—; bd. dirs., Shared Outdoor Recreation, for Handicapped, Portland, 1984—; bd. dirs., East Side Bus., Alliance, 1987—; pres., Upper Sandy Bus., Dist., 1987; bd. dirs., Riverside YMCA, Portland, 1986-87. Recipient Overcoming Handicap award U.S. News & World Report, 1983; named Woman of the Yr. Oergon's Women of Excellence, 1984, British Airways, 1984. Mem. Am. Soc. Travel Agts. (treas. 1985-87), Am. Retail Travel Assn., Caribbean Travel Assn., Cruise Lines Internat. Assn., Am. Bus. Women's Assn. (speaker's chmn.), Inst. Managerial and Profl. Women(bd. dirs.), Speakers Bur., Am. Soc. Travel Show (chmn 1988). Office: Addie's You and I Travel 7545 NE Sandy Blvd Portland OR 97213

LINDSTROM, CHERYL ANN, interventional radiologist; b. Milw., Nov. 7, 1956; d. Clarence Sterling and Anna Louise (Tillman) Lindstrom. BS, U. Wis., 1978, MD, 1982. Diplomate Am. Bd. Radiology. Intern in surg. Brown U./R.I. Hosp., Providence, 1982-83; resident in radiology Loyola U. Med. Ctr., Maywood, Ill., 1983-86; interventional radiology fellowship U. Ill. Med. Ctr., Chgo., 1986-87; staff radiologist Oak Lawn (S.C.) Radiologists, 1987—, Christ Hosp. and Med. Ctr., Oak Lawn, Ill., 1987—; assoc. staff Community Meml. Hosp., LaGrange, Ill., 1984-86, Radiology Cons. Ltd. div. Oak Park Hosp., Ill., 1986-87. March of Dimes grantee Mass. Gen. Hosp., Harvard U., 1978; grantee Am. Cancer Soc., 1979; NSF fellow, 1977. Mem. Am. Coll. Radiology, Soc. Cardiovascular and Interventional Radiologists, Radiologic Soc. N.Am., Am. Roentger Ray Soc., AMA, Ill. State Med. Soc., Chgo. Med. Soc., Chgo. Radiologic Soc., Am. Assn. Women Radiologists. Home: 8557 Archer Ave Willow Springs IL 60480 Office: Christ Hosp Dept Radiology 4440 W 95th St Oak Lawn IL 60453

LINDSTROM, NINA LUCILLE, school administrator, director; b. Cleveland, Tenn., Dec. 9, 1940; d. Noah Haskins Jones and Grace (Mae) Burke; m. Larry Lance Lindstrom, June 26, 1966; children: Anton Lee, Kristina Mae. BS in Edn., Biology, U. Tenn., 1963; MS in Edn., Portland (Oreg.) State U., 1970. Cert. tchr., Oreg., Calif. Tchr. sci. Hudson Sch. Dist., LaPuente, Calif., 1963-64, Baldwin (Calif.) Park Dist., 1964-67; tchr. biology Beaverton Sch. Dist. 48, Portland, 1968-70; stud. tchr. supr. Portland State U., 1971; tchr. Portland Community Coll., 1971-72; prin., dir., founder Belmont Sch., Portland, 1973—; co-owner Riverview Properties, Portland, 1973—; v.p. Mt. Park Vet. Clinic, Lake Oswego, 1978—. Chmn. Sunnyside Neighborhood, Portland, 1987; childcare advisor Portland Pub. Schs., 1976-87. Mem. Portland C. of C. (distinquished service award 1985), Belmont Bus. (treas. 1985-86, sec. 1986-87), Oreg. Fedn. Pvt. Schs. (pre-sch. com. 1986-87). Republican. Baptist. Office: Belmont Sch 3841 SE Belmont Portland OR 97219

LINDVIG, ELISE KAY, educational psychologist; b. Sidney, Mont., Feb. 10, 1952; d. William F. and Katheryn E. (Taylor) L. Student Carroll Coll., Mont., 1970-71; BA in Psychology with honors, U. Mont., 1974; MS in Clin. Psychology with high honors, U. Idaho, 1979. Assoc. coordinator Dept. Community Affairs, State of Mont., Glendive, 1974-75; teaching asst. U. Idaho, Moscow, 1975-79; sch. psychologist Hamilton, Mont., 1979-82, diagnostician, cons. in field; bookkeeper, musician, 1975-79. Mem. Am. Psychol. Assn. (assoc.), Mont. Assn. Sch. Psychologists (cons.), Idaho Mental Health Assn., Am. Quarter Horse Assn., Am. Kennel Club, Nat. Hot Rod Assn. Republican. Roman Catholic. Clubs: Eagles Aux., Moose Aux. Condr. research on malnutrition in primates; author: Nutrition and Mental Health, 1979; Grade Retention: Evolving Expectations and Individual Differences, 1982. Home: 119 Santa Cruz Madera CA 93637

LINEBERGER, MARILYN HAZZARD, psychologist; b. Abbeville, S.C., Dec. 10, 1952; d. Sanders and Louise (Lomax) Hazzard; B.A., U. S.C., 1975; M.S., U. Ga., 1977, Ph.D., 1979; m. Frank James Lineberger, Jr., Sept. 1, 1979; 1 child, Winsheket Nicole. Lic. clin. psychologist, Ga. Counselor, Gleams Community Action Agy., Greenwood, S.C., summers 1973-75; asst. prof. psychology Kent (Ohio) State U., 1979-80; asst. prof. psychology and clin. psychologist Emory U., Atlanta, 1980-85, adj. asst.prof. psychology, 1985—; ind. clin. and cons. practice, Atlanta, 1985—. Vol. various polit. campaigns; active Big Bro. and Big Sister orgns. Mem. Am. Psychol. Assn., Assn. Advancement Behavior Therapy, Assn. Black Psychologists, Council on Children, AAAS, Southeastern Psychol. Assn., Mortar Bd., Nat. Honor Soc., Phi Beta Kappa, Psi Chi. Democrat. Methodist. Club: Pre-Profl. Psychology (adviser). Contbr. research articles to profl. lit. Home: 3668 Crossvale Rd Lithonia GA 30058 Office: Piedmont Devel Bldg 1706 NE Expwy Atlanta GA 30329

LINEHAN, HELEN M., sales administrator; b. N.Y.C., Sept. 4, 1939; d. Timothy Finbar and Emma Louise (deLuis) O'Callaghan; m. William Linehan, Nov. 14, 1958 (div. 1979); children—M.E. Linehan, Sarah L. Linehan. Student, Fordham U., 1976-79. Asst. adminstr. Rudolf Steiner, N.Y.C., 1972-76; dir. sales adminstrn. Boris Kroll Fabrics Inc., N.Y.C., 1976—, asst. v.p., 1986-87; edn. com. ACT, N.Y.C., 1986-87; office mgr. Horwitz & Assocs., N.Y.C., 1988—. Democrat. Roman Catholic. Avocations: Marine life; communications with mammals; swimming; writing. Office: Horwitz & Assocs 276 Fifth Ave New York NY 10001

LINFORD, MARY SUZANNE (SUE), food distibrution executive; b. Indpls., Apr. 15, 1935; d. Robert William and Mary Catherine (Madden) Schmutte; widowed; children: Christopher, Douglas, Mark, Paul, Julie. Student, U. Alaska, 1959-80. Lic. real estate agt., Alaska. Various positions Indpls. and Anchorage, 1949-1973; acct., treas., gen. mgr., pres. Linford of Alaska Wholesale Food Distbr., Anchorage, 1973-83; pres., gen. mgr. Linford of Alaska, Anchorage, 1985—; with sales dept. Mercantile Ltd., Anchorage, 1983-85; exec. dir. Common Sense for Alaska, Anchorage, 1984-86; property mgr. Sue Linford Investments, Anchorage, 1983—; pvt. practice real estate, Anchorage, 1985—. Editor State PTA Bulletin, 1969-71. Mem. Alaska State Blue Ribbon Commn., 1979-80, various city commns. City of Anchorage, 1979—, budget commr., 1988—; chmn. library bds. City of Anchorage/Greater Anchorage Borough/Municipality of Anchorage, 1969-77; founding mem., officer Anchorage Arts Council, 1971-74; pres. Anchorage Sch. Bd., 1974-77; active Anchorage PTA. Mem. Alaska State C. of C., Anchorage C. of C. (sec.-treas., v.p., bd. dirs. 1977-81, Outstanding Community Service Gold Pan award 1981), Anchorage Bd. Realtors, Ruralcap (Cert. of Appreciation 1981, Outstanding Contbn. award 1985), Chaîne Des Rôtisseurs, Bailliage of U.S.A. Roman Catholic. Clubs: Petroleum of Anchorage, Anchorage Aquanaut Swim (pres. 1980-81), Alaska-Anchorage U.S. Swimming (publicity com. 1977-78, vice-chairperson tech. com. 1980-81); San Francisco Tennis (life), Capt. Cook Athletic. Lodge: Zonta (bd. dirs. 1968-80), Rotary. Office: Linford of Alaska Inc 4551 Fairbanks St Suite D Anchorage AK 99503

LING, KATHRYN WROLSTAD, health association administrator; b. Watertown, Wis., Aug. 3, 1943; d. Jeffery Harold and Constance Devina (Egre) Wrolstad; m. Cyril Curtis Ling; step-children: Renee Rainey, Roz Harper. BS in History, Polit. Sci., U. Wis., 1965. Supr. recreation ARC, DaNang, Cam Ran Bay, VietNam, 1968; assoc. exec. dir. Am. Cancer Soc., Evanston, Ill., 1968-71, exec. dir., 1971-73; exec. dir. Montgomery County Unit Am. Cancer Soc., Md., 1973-76, cons. income devel., 1976, dir., profl. edn. cancer incidence and end results, 1976-78, dir. income devel., 1978-82; exec. dir. Am. Cancer Soc., Chgo., 1982-84; assoc. exec. dir. Alzheimer's Disease and Related Disorder Assn., Chgo., 1985—, v.p. community service; cons. Nat. Aphasia Assn. Home: Rt 1 Box 900 Lake Geneva WI 54901 Office: Alzheimers Disease and Related Disorders Assn 70 E Lake St Chicago IL 60601

LINGENFELSER, CATHERINE THERESA, computer operator, auditor; b. Savannah, Ga., June 30, 1952; d. William Francis Jr. and Catherine Elizabeth (Moore) L. AA, Armstrong State Coll., 1983. Bookkeeper, asst. office mgr. Valenti Volkswagen Inc. (formerly Terry Motors), Savannah, 1970-74; cost acctg. clk. Great Dane Trailers, Savannah, 1974-81; acctg. clk. Savannah Foods and Industries, 1981-82; computer operator, auditing clk. U.S. Postal Service, Savannah, 1982—. Contbg. author: History of Fayette County, Tennessee, 1986, Moore Family Register, 1986; editor: (quar. newspaper) The Flashback, 1980-83, (monthly computer newspaper) Byts and Bytes, 1987—. Rec. sec. Women's Adv. Council for So. Region Postal Service, Savannah, 1987—; bd. dirs. St. Vincent's Acad., Savannah, 1980-85, v.p. alumnae assn., 1980-82; vol. tour guide Historic Savannah Found., 1980—. Recipient Community Service award La Sertoma Orgn., 1970, Community Service award Historic Savannah Found., 1984. Mem. Savannah Commodore User's Group (pres. 1987—), Ga. Hist. Soc., Savannah Area Geneal. Assn. (lectr. 1987—), Monroe County (Ohio) Hist. Soc., DAR (rec. sec. Lachlan McIntosh chpt. 1986—), United Daus. Confederacy. Democrat. Roman Catholic. Lodges: Order of Crown Charlemagne, Daus. of Ireland (bd. dirs. 1987—). Home: 26 Broadmoor Circle Savannah GA 31406-2268 Office: US Postal Service 532 Indian St Savannah GA 31402-9321

LINGENFELTER, SHARON MARIE, data processing company executive; b. Nyssa, Oreg., June 17, 1947; d. Floyd LeRoy and Ruth Irene (Bale) Martin; (div.); children: Brian James Lingenfelter, Kevin James Lingenfelter. Student George Fox Coll., 1966, Portland State U., 1968. Vice pres. adminstrn. Century Data, Inc., Portland, 1982—; dir. mktg. and adminstrn. Bus. Prospector, San Francisco Bay Area, 1986—. Editing cons. Century Direct Mktg., Inc., 1983—; office systems analyst C.I. NorCal, San Francisco, 1985—. Mem. Nat. Assn. Female Execs., Am. Mgmt. Assn. Republican. Avocations: skiing, writing, travel, painting, reading. Office: Century Data Inc 2355 NW Quimby St Portland OR 97210

LINGHAM, MARCELLA ERMA, community health center administrator; b. Phila., Jan. 15, 1942; d. Harry Boyd and Gladys Marcella Lawson; student Temple U., 1960-62; B.S. in edn., Cheyney State Coll., 1965; M.Ed., Temple U., 1970; Ed.D., Rutgers U., 1980. Tchr., Sch. Dist. Phila., 1965-70; curriculum devel. specialist, reading specialist RCA Service Co., Cherry Hill, N.J., 1970-72; project dir., curriculum developer, ednl. cons. Research for Better Schs., Inc., Phila., 1972-79; asst. prof. Rutgers U. Newark Coll. Arts and Scis., 1980-83; exec. dir. Primary Community Health Ctr. of Mantua, Inc., 1983-84; project dir. Mantua Community Devel. Corp., 1984-85; learning specialist Rutgers U. Coll. Nursing, 1985-86; exec. dir. 2501 Primary Community Health Care Ctr., Inc., 1986—. Vice chairperson bd. dirs. 2501 Health Care Corp., Phila., 1980—, bd. dirs. Black Family Services. Mem. Am. Ednl. Research Assn., Internat. Reading Assn., AAUW, Am. Pub. Health Assn., Assn. Supervision and Curriculum Devel. Democrat. Baptist. Home: 2708 S 86 St Philadelphia PA 19153 Office: 2501 Primary Community Health Care Ctr Inc 2501 W Lehigh Ave Philadelphia PA 19132

LINGLE, KATHLEEN MCCALL, marketing professional; b. Berea, Ohio, Aug. 24, 1944; d. Arthur Vivian McCall and Mary M. (Maxwell) Miller; m. John Hunter Lingle, Sept. 3, 1968; 1 child, Michael Cameron. BA, Occidental Coll., 1966; MS, Ohio State U., 1977. Research assoc. Ednl. Testing Service, Princeton, N.J., 1978-82; mgr. mktg. services Gulton Industries, Princeton, 1982-85; dir. mktg. research services Applied Data Research, Princeton, 1985—. V.p. ops. Unitarian Ch. of New Brunswick, N.J., 1983-84. Mem. Am. Mktg. Assn., Am. Mgmt. Assn. Democrat. Home: 988 Princeton Kingston Rd Princeton NJ 08540 Office: Applied Data Research Rt 206 and Orchard Rd Princeton NJ 08540

LINGLE, MARILYN FELKEL (LYN), freelance writer, small business owner; b. Hillsboro, Ill., Aug. 16, 1932; d. Clarence Frederick and Anna Cecelia (Stank) Felkel; m. Ivan L. Lingle, Oct. 4, 1950; children: Ivan Dale, Aimee Lee Lingle Galligan, Clarence Craig. Sec. Ill. State Police, 1950; with welfare dept. Ill. Pub. Aid, Hillsboro, 1951-52; researcher Small Homes Council, Champaign, 1952-53; sec. Hillsboro Schs., 1954; office, payroll clk. Eagle Picher Zinc, Hillsboro, 1955-56; continuity dir. Sta. WSMI, Litchfield, Hillsboro, 1966-87; ptnr. Church Street Pub/Restaurant; adv. bd. Am. Savs. Bank/Eagles Club, 1986-87. Contbr. poetry to profl. jours. Fin. chmn. Hillsboro Hosp. Aux., 1972; literacy lifeline vol. Graham Correctional Ctr., Hillsboro, 1986—; pres., bd. dirs. Montgomery Players and Encore Play Theatre, 1954-70; child sponsor through World Vision; active PTA, Girl Scouts, Cub Scouts, ch. youth activities. Mem. Cousteau Soc. Democrat. Lutheran. Club: Hillsboro Country. Avocations: bridge, golf, gardening, travel, reading.

LINK, MAE MILLS (MRS. S. GORDDEN LINK), space medicine historian and consultant; b. Corbin, Ky., May 14, 1915; d. William Speed and Florence (Estes) Mills; m. S. Gordden Link, Jan. 11, 1936. B.S., George Peabody Coll. for Tchrs., Vanderbilt U., 1936; M.A., Vanderbilt U., 1937; Ph.D., Am. U., 1951; grad., Air War Coll., 1965. Instr. social sci. Oglethorpe U., 1938-39; instr. English Drury Coll., 1940-41; asso. dir. edn. Ga. Warm Springs Found., 1941-42; mil. historian Hdqrs. Army Air Forces,

1943-45, Office Mil. History, Dept. of Army, 1945-51; spl. asst. to surgeon gen., sr. med. historian U.S. Air Force, Washington, 1951-62; cons. in documentation and space medicine historian NASA, Washington, 1962-64; coordinator documentation, life scis. historian NASA, 1964-70; research asso. Ohio State U. Found., 1970-72; Mem. exec. com. Orgn. for Advancement Coll. Teaching; mem. nat. adv. bd. Am. Security Council. Author: Medical Support of the Army Air Forces in World War II, 1955, Annual Reports of the U.S. Air Force Medical Service, 1949-62, Space Medicine in Project Mercury, 1965; (with others) USA/USSR Joint Publ. Foundations of Space Biology and Medicine, 1976; Editor: U.S. Air Force Med. Service Digest, 1957-62; Contbr. to profl. jours.; Collier's Ency., Ency. Brit.; Contbr. to.: Funk and Wagnall's New Ency. Trustee, dir. history fellows Amos R. Koontz Meml. Found. Recipient Meritorious Service award U.S. Air Force, 1955, Ann. Outstanding Performance awards, 1956-62, Outstanding Alumna award Sue Bennett Coll., 1977. Fellow Am. Med. Writers Assn. (past pres. Middle Atlantic region); mem. Aerospace Med. Assn., Air Force Hist. Found. (charter), Internat. Congress History Medicine, Societe International d'Histoire de la Medecine, Planetary Soc. (charter). Republican. Episcopalian. Clubs: Garden of Va.; Army-Navy (Washington).

LINK, NINA BETH, publisher; b. Bklyn., Sept. 19, 1943; d. Robert R. and Helen (Cohen) Levine; children—David Jon, Gregory Adam. B.A., Beaver Coll., 1965. Sec. WCBS TV, N.Y.C., 1965-66; ednl. systems analyst edn. div. Xerox, N.Y.C., 1966-68; cons. The Link Group, Inc., N.Y.C., 1968-78; v.p., publisher Children's TV Workshop, N.Y.C., 1978—; cons. publishing, communication cos. Named to YWCA Acad. Women Achievers, 1985. Mem. Direct Mail Mktg. Assn., Writer's Guild, Dramatist's Guild, Internat. Reading Assn., Mag. Pubs. Assn. Home: 222 W 83d St New York NY 10024

LINK, PHOEBE FORREST, educator, author; b. Palmerton, Pa., Feb. 20, 1926; d. John Nevins and Phoebe Eleanor (Lewis) Forrest; m. Robert H. Link, July 13, 1962; children—David Forrest, Anne Harris. BA in Psychology, Pa. State U., 1947, MS in Child Devel. and Family Relationships, 1952; postgrad. U. Rochester, 1957-59, Harvard U., 1958. Dir. teen age program YWCA, Lansing, Mich., 1947-50, Rochester, N.Y., 1952-56; research asst. Pa. State U., State College, 1950-52; tchr. Rochester, 1956-60, William Antheil Sch., Trenton, N.J., 1960-63; mem. faculty Trenton State Coll., 1960-63; tchr. State College area schs., 1971—; lectr. Am. Home Econs. Assn. Conv.; cons. family studies, leader continuing edn. workshops Pa. State U., 1977, others; mem. staff dean women Harvard U., Cambridge, Mass., summer 1958; dir. Children's Program for Pa. Dist. Attys. Author: Small? Tall? Not At All, 1973; staff writer Horizon, 1985-87; author, creator Hearthrob series, Pa. State U., 1987; contbr. articles to profl. jours. Trustee Schlow Pub. Library, State College, Pa., 1980-83; founder, first chmn. poetry com. Cen. Pa. Festival Arts. AAUW Simmons grantee, 1984. Mem. NEA, Pa. Edn. Assn., State Coll. Area Edn. Assn., AAUW, Mortar Board Alumni (founder, 1st pres.), Pa. State U. Coll. Human Devel. Alumni (bd. dirs.). Phi Delta Kappa, Omicron Nu Alumni (founder), Tau Phi Sigma. Home: 22 Cricklewood Circle State College PA 16803

LINK, SUSAN DENISE, entrepreneur, photographer; b. Cin., Jan. 3, 1958; d. Edward George and Hazel Rooks (Blalock) L. BBA, U. Cin., 1985. Owner R&B Custom Labs., Cin., 1975-80; mgr. Ohio Valley Photo Supply, Cin., 1976-77; owner LInks Photo and Video, Cin., 1977—, Rainbows Unltd., Cin., 1980—. Still photographer motion picture Lost, 1982. Fellow Nat. Assn. Female Execs., Small Bus. Adminstrn., Photo Mktg. Assn. Republican. Mem. Christian Ch. Office: Links Photo and Video/ Rainbow Unltd 3093 Glenmore Ave Cincinnati OH 45238

LINKE, RUTH ANNA, home economist; b. N.Y.C., Aug. 26, 1926; d. George and Elsie (Schmidt) Renz; B.S., N.Y.U., 1946, Ph.D., 1957; M.A., Columbia U., 1947; m. William F. Linke, Apr. 14, 1949; children—William, Robert Christopher, Jennifer Ann. Instr. part time N.Y. U., Tchrs. Coll., Columbia U., Hunter Coll., Lehman Coll., 1950-64; asst. prof. dept. home econs. and nutrition N.Y. U., 1973-76, assoc. prof., 1976—, acting chmn. dept., 1974-75, dep. chmn., 1979—. Mem. Bd. Edn. Stamford (Conn.), 1962-71, pres., 1964-65, 68-69; mem. urban edn. com. Conn. Assn. Bds. of Edn., 1966-70; mem. Conn. State Advisory Com. for Edn. Profl. Devel. Act, 1966-70. Mem. Am., N.Y. State (dir., v.p. 1982-84, treas. dist. 5 1977-79, dist. pres. 1980-81) home econs. assns., Coll. Tchrs. Household Equipment (membership com. 1979-80), Assn. Home Econs. Tchrs. N.Y.C., Elec. Women's Round Table, Am. Assn. Housing Educators, Am. Vocat. Assn., N.Y. State Home Econs. Tchrs. Assn., AAUW, Omicron Nu, Pi Lambda Theta. Contbr. articles to profl. jours. Home: 75 Ridgecrest Rd Stamford CT 06903 Office: NYU Dept Home Econs and Nutrition Washington Sq New York NY 10003

LINLEY, MARILYN WILLIAMS, television producer; b. Waukesha, Wis., Oct. 26, 1922; d. Arthur Joseph and Vivian Jeanette Marie (LaHaie) Williams; B.A., Carroll Coll., 1944; M.A., Marquette U., 1969; m. Herbert Laflin Linley, 1945 (div. 1963); children—Marilyn Margaret, Elizabeth Anne, Jane Milton. Tchr., Fort Atkinson (Wis.) High Sch., 1944-45; substitute tchr. Accelerated High Sch., Balt., 1945-46; tchr. public schs. Rahway, Long Branch, Eatontown and Oceanport, N.J., 1946-60; columnist Long Branch (N.J.) Daily Record, 1960; tchr. Long Branch Schs., 1960-61; tchr. Mukwonago (Wis.) Union High Sch., 1962-70, team tchr., 1970-71; cons., tchr. English Houston High Sch. for Performing and Visual Arts, 1971-73; tchr. Tng. Center Human Resources Devel. and Edn. Renewal, 1973-74; media staff devel. tchr. Continuing Careers Devel. Center, MacGregor, 1973-74; instr. TV specialist Instructional Media Services, Houston, 1974; instructional TV producer, Houston, 1977—. Former bd. dirs. Episcopal Churchwomen Diocese N.J., Rahway Service League (N.J.), Jr. League, Monmouth, N.J., Welfare Council, Monmouth, Long Branch (N.J.) Public Health Nursing Assn., PTA, Long Branch, N.J., Waukesha, Wis., Waukesha Symphony Orch., 1969; pres. Waukesha Symphony Aux., 1970, Friends U. Wis., Waukesha, 1963-71; mem. devel. adv. council KUHF Pub. Radio. Named Girl of Year, Monmouth Jr. League, 1959; recipient award of achievement Gulf Region Ednl. TV Affiliates, 1980. Mem. Women in Communications, Inc. (Headliner award 1980), Internat. TV Assn. (chmn. bd. Houston), Am. Women in Radio and TV (chmn. bd. Houston), NEA (del. 1973), Cable TV Task Force (exec. bd. 1970-74), Tex. Assn. Ednl. Technologists, Tex. State Tchrs. Assn. (chmn. publicity 1973), Tex. Classroom Tchrs. Assn. (del. 1973, 74), Houston Tchrs. Assn. (faculty rep. 1972—), Tex. Ednl. TV Assn., Houston Area Sch. Librarians, Broadcast Pioneers. Home: 5206 Memorial Dr Houston TX 77007 Office: 3830 Richmond Ave Houston TX 77027

LINN, CAROLE ANNE, dietitian; b. Portland, Oreg., Mar. 3, 1945; d. James Leslie and Alice Mae (Thorburn) L. Intern, U. Minn., 1967-68; BS, Oreg. State U., 1963-67. Nutrition cons. licensing and cert. sect. Oreg. State Bd. Health, Portland, 1968-70; chief clin. dietitian Rogue Valley Med. Ctr., Medford, Oreg., 1970—; cons. Hillhaven Health Care Ctr., Medford, 1971-83; lectr. Local Speakers Bur., Medford. Mem. Am. Dietetic Assn., Am. Diebetic Assn., Oreg. Dietetic Assn. (sec. 1973-75, nominating com. 1974-75, young dietitian of yr. 1976), Oreg. diabetic Assn., Alpha Lambda Delta, Omicron Nu. Democrat. Office: Rogue Valley Med Ctr 2825 Barnett Rd Medford OR 97504

LINN, MARCIA CYROG, educator; b. Milw., May 27, 1943; d. George W. and Frances (Vanderhoof) Cyrog; m. Stuart Michael Linn, 1967 (div. 1979); children: Matthew, Allison; m. Curtis Bruce Tarter, 1987. BA in Psychology and Stats., Stanford U., 1965, MA in Ednl. Psychology, 1967, PhD in Ednl. Psychology, 1970. Prin. investigator Lawrence Hall Sci. U. Calif., 1970-87, prin. investigator Sch. Edn., 1985—, asst. dean Sch. Edn., 1983-85; adj. prof. Sch. Edn. U. Calif., 1985—; Fulbright Prof. Weizmann Inst., Israel, 1983; exec. dir. seminars U. Calif., 1985-86; acting. dir. Instl. Tech. Program, U. Calif., 1986—; cons. Apple Computer U. Calif., 1983—; mem. adv. com. NSF-Sci. Edn. U. Calif., 1978—, Ednl. Testing Service, 1986—, Smithsonian Instn., 1986—, Fulbright Program, 1983-86. Author: Education and the Challenge of Technology, 1987; co-author: The Psychology of Gender - Advances Through Meta Analysis, 1986—; contbr. articles and papers in field. Sci. advisor Parents Club, Lafayette, Calif., 1984-87. Mem. Nat. Assn. Research in Sci. and Teaching (bd. dirs. 1983-86, most outstanding paper, 1978, outstanding jour. article, 1975, 83), Am. Ednl. Research Assn. (chair research on women and edn., 1983-85, women educators research award, 1982, 88), Soc. Research Child Devel. (mem. editorial bd. 1984—), Am. Psychol. Assn., Sierra Club. Office: U Calif Sch Edn 4611 Tolman Hall Berkeley CA 94720

LINNANSALO, VERA, engineer; b. Helsinki, Finland, Oct. 9, 1950; came to U.S., 1960, naturalized, 1969; d. Boris and Vera (Schkurat-Schkuropatsky) L. BS in Computer and Info. Sci., Cleve. State U., 1974, BME, 1974; MBA, U. Akron, 1983. Engring. assoc. B.F. Goodrich Co., Akron, Ohio, 1974-75, assoc. product engr., 1975-77, tire devel. engr., 1977-79, advanced tire devel. engr., 1979-84, quality devel. engr., 1984-85, sr. quality devel. engr., 1985-86; coordinator GM-10 Uniroyal Goodrich Tire Co., Akron, 1986—. Mem. ASME, Am. Soc. Quality Control (sr., cert. quality engr.). Home: 1262 Culpepper Dr Akron OH 44313 Office: Uniroyal Goodrich Tire Co D/0547 UHB-4 600 S Main St Akron OH 44397

LINNELL, KAREN MAE, home health agency executive; b. St. Paul, Dec. 9, 1941; d. Daniel Nelson and Laura Mae (Miller) Rice; m. Richard Phillip Linnell, Dec. 21, 1963; children: Richard Daniel, Matthew Phillip. BS, U. Minn., 1963; student U. Detroit, 1983-85. Tchr. Roseville Pub. Schs., Minn., 1963-64, Birmingham Pub. Schs., Mich., 1964-70; pres., adminstr. Renaissance Health Care, Detroit, 1976—; bd. dirs. Wayne State U. Med. Sch. Adv. Bd., Detroit, 1984—; founder Am. Fed. Home Health Agencies, Washington, 1980; rep. intermediary adv. bd., Milw. 1986—. Recipient Tchr. of Yr. award Detroit Free Press, 1968. Mem. Am. Acad. Med. Adminstrs., Am. Fed. Home Health Agys., (pres. 1982-83, v.p. 1980-82), Am. Fed. Home Health Agys. (pres. 1982-83, regional dir. 1985—), Mich. Home Health Agy. (vice pres. 1983-85, bd. dirs. 1981-82, 85—). Democrat. Presbyterian. Office: Renaissance Health Care 20700 Greenfield Suite 320 Detroit MI 48237

LINNELL, LISA P., editor, promotion specialist, journalist; b. Elizabeth, N.J., Aug. 23, 1958; d. Anthony J. and Dorothy J. (Madonia) Prezioso. B.A. in Journalism and Urban Communication, Rutgers U., 1980; postgrad. Seton Hall U., 1984—. Advt. sales, staff writer The Chronicle, Fairfield, N.J., 1979; corr. The Star Ledger, Newark, 1979; staff writer The Daily Jour., Elizabeth, 1980-83; publs. editor and promotion specialist Dun & Bradstreet Credit Services, N.J., 1983—; intern U.S. Senator Bill Bradley, 1979. Co-host TV program N.J. Press Conference, 1981. Vol. The Lighthouse, N.Y. Assn. Blind, N.Y.C., 1981-84. Mem. Internat. Assn. Bus. Communicators (Iris award of merit in video tape), N.J. Press Women, Kean Coll. Profl. Women's Assn. Roman Catholic.

LINNEN, MARY LOU, entrepreneur; b. Akron, Ohio, Nov. 9, 1932; d. Frank H. and Dorothy Jane (O'Connor) Schellin; m. William P. Linnen, Aug. 28, 1954 (dec. 1980); children: Beth Marie, Margaret Mary, Joseph Christopher. BA, U. Akron, 1954; postgrad., Northwestern U., 1981-84. Elem. tchr. Akron, 1954-55; legal asst. Kenefick, Kilmore & Bergerson, Michigan City, Ind., 1976-81; owner, mgr. Creekwood Inn, Michigan City, 1984—; gen. ptnr. shopping ctr. Lighthouse Pl., Michigan City, 1986—. Sec., bd. dirs. LaLumiere Sch., La Porte, Ind., 1981-87; bd. dirs. Notre Dame Sch. Found., Michigan City, 1986-87; mem. fin. com. Diocese of Gary, Ind., 1987. mem. Harris Fin. Network, Chgo. Area Meeting Planners Assn., Dunes Art Found., Festival Players Guild, Community Ctr. for Arts. Office: Creekwood Inn Rt 20-35 at I-94 Michigan City IN 46360

LINTA, KATHLEEN THORNTON, pharmaceutical marketing professional; b. Fairview Park, Ohio, Jan. 25, 1958; d. Thomas William and Colleen Marie (Burns) Thornton; m. Joseph Michael Linta. BS in Mgmt., Purdue U., 1981. Sales rep. Searle Labs., Madison, Wis., 1981-83; hosp. sales rep. Miles Pharms., Madison, 1983-84; mktg. intern West haven, Conn., 1984-86, asst. product mgr., 1986-87, product mgr., 1987—. Mem. Pharm. Mfg. Assn., Healthcare Businesswomens Assn. Republican. Roman Catholic. Home: 31 Jerimoth Dr Branford CT 06405 Office: Miles Pharms 400 Morgan Ln West Haven CT 06516

LINTON, CYNTHIA CARPENTER, newspaper editor; b. Bronxville, N.Y., Aug. 17, 1938; d. Ralph Emerson and Cynthia (Ramsey) Carpenter; m. John Marshall Linton, June 8, 1963; children—Terrence M., Robert C. B.A., Boston U., 1968. Staff writer Lerner Newspapers, 1972-78, mng. editor, 1978-80, sr. editor, Chgo., 1980-87, exec. editor, 1987—. Recipient awards for writing excellence Suburban Press Club Chgo., 1980, 81, Ill. Press Assn., 1982, Suburban Newspapers Am., 1979, Nat. Newspaper Assn., 1976, N. Ill. Newspapers, 1986, Peter Lisagor award, 1983, 84. Mem. Chgo. Headline Club (v.p.), Chgo. Press Club, Sigma Delta Chi. also: 7519 N Ashland Ave Chicago IL 60626

LINTZ, CONNIE SUE, telecommunications manager, educator; b. Three Rivers, Mich., Feb. 17, 1951; d. Bert Eldon and Hazel Louise (Ulrich) L.; m. John Robert Murphy, Aug. 20, 1983. BS, Western Mich. U., 1972; MBA, Marymount Coll. Va., 1984. Police officer Adams County Sheriff Dept., Brighton, Colo., 1978; operator services Mountain Bell, Denver, 1978-80, strategic planning mgr., 1985-86; pricing and costing mgr. Mountain Bell, 1986-87; instr. Columbia Coll., Aurora, Colo., 1986—; market cons. NeuroFibromotosis Inst., Houston, 1987—; new venture mgr. U.S. West Diversified, Denver, 1987—; lectr. Armed Forces Staff Coll., Langley, Va., 1982-84; tech.-mkt. liaison U.S. West Advanced Techs., 1987—. Chmn. Mountain Bell U.S. Saving Bond Drive, Denver, 1985; chmn. United Way Drive, Denver, 1986. Served with USAF, 1980-84, with ANG, 1985—. Named Outstanding Recruit Denver Police Dept., 1977, Outstanding Res. Intelligence Officer, 1986. Mem. USNG Assn., Colo. Air N.G. Assn. (legis. com. chmn. 1986—, state conv. publicity chmn. 1987), U.S. West Women, Buckley Officers Assn. Republican. Lutheran. Home: 1603 S Flanders Way Aurora CO 80017

LINZALONE, MARY JANE, pianist, educator; b. Somerville, N.J., Feb. 6, 1928; d. Einar Christensen and Marie (Andersen) Börnick; m. Ceasar Anthony Linzalone, Jan. 15, 1955 (dec.); 1 son, Gary Brooks. Student Julliard Sch. Music, 1940-46, Reifling Conservatory, Oslo, Norway, 1948-49. Concert pianist, N.Y., N.J., 1949-51; pianist, entertainer, U.S.A. and Can., 1951-57; mgr., buyer Town and Tweed, Rutherford, N.J., 1957-60; owner, mgr., tchr. Baldwin Piano, Passaic, Rutherford, Ridgewood, N.J., 1961-76, exec. dir. Williams Ctr. Performing Arts, Rutherford, 1978-83, cons., tchr., 1983—, trustee. Dir. Williams Ctr. Artist's Adv. Bd., Rutherford, 1979-84; bd. dirs. Pinellas County chpt. Am. Diabetes Assn. Recipient Citizen of Yr. award Meadowlands C. of C. (N.J.), 1982. Republican. Presbyterian. Home: 316 Orangewood Ln Harbor Bluffs Largo FL 34640

LIONBERGER, ERLE TALBOT LUND, Republican committeewomen; b. St. Louis, Apr. 29, 1933; d. Joel Y. and Erle (Harsh) Lund; m. John S. Lionberger, Jr., June 23, 1956; children—Erle Talbot, Louise Shepley. Student Mary Inst., 1951; A.B., Vassar Coll., 1955. Republican committeewoman Hadley Twp., St. Louis County, 1965—; mem. St. Louis County Rep. Central Com., 1965—; mem. Rep. State Com., 1966-78, 84—; del. Rep. Nat. Conv., 1972, 76, 80, 84, 88, alt. del., 1968; Mo. rep. Rep. Nat. Platform Com., 1988; Mo. chmn. Women for Reagan-Bush, 1984. Bd. dirs. Landmarks Assn. St. Louis, Inc., 1973-76, counselor, 1982—, coordinator Historic Preservation Pilgrimage, 1974; bd. dirs. Friends of Winston Churchill Meml., 1975-76, Save Grant's White Haven, Inc., 1985—; mem. women's exec. bd. Mo. Bot. Garden, 1977-80; mem. St. Louis County Hist. Bldg. Commn., 1976—, Capitol Complex Commn. on Fine Arts, 1983—; chmn. Mo. 7th Senatorial Dist. Com., 1978-84; chmn. Mo. Adv. Council on Hist. Preservation, 1982—; Mo. rep. Lewis and Clark Nat. Hist. Trail Adv. Council, 1984—; bd. dirs. Mo. Heritage Trust, 1982—, Mo. Parks Assn., 1982—Mem. Jr. League St. Louis, Mo. Fedn. Republican Women (bd. dirs. 1980-84), Nat. Soc. Colonial Dames Am. (Mo. bd. dirs. 1976-80, hist. properties chmn. 1975-81, pub. chmn. 1987—), St. Louis Christmas Carols Assn. (area co-chmn. 1979-85). Address: 21 Dartford St Saint Louis MO 63105

LIPARI, JOANNA, actress, author; b. N.Y.C.; d. Edward S. and Ethel Jean (Jahoda) L.; m. Jacques Remi Aubuchon, Apr. 10, 1987. Cert., Harvard U., 1970; AB in English, Manhattanville Coll., 1971; grad., Neighborhood Playhouse, N.Y.C., 1973. moderator workshop Basehart Theatre, Van Nuys, Calif. Author: (with others) The Actor: A Practical Guide to a Professional Career, 1987; contbr. articles to profl. jours.; appeared in films Jo Jo Dancer, Laserblast; TV shows General Hospital, Eischied, Rockford Files, Santa Barbara, Loving, Fatman McCabe; plays Noises Off, Cracked Tokens, Lifetimes10, Wally's Cafe, Father's Day, Golden Boy, Young! I'll Never Be That Again, The Green Cockatoo; assoc. producer 3 Plays of Love and Hate. Mem. Theatre West (past bd. dirs.), Women In Film.

LIPE, LINDA BON, lawyer; b. Clarksdale, Miss., Jan. 10, 1948; s. William Ray and Gwendolyn (Strickland) Lipe; m. Larry L. Gleghorn, Feb. 15, 1983 (div. Feb. 1988). BBA in Accountancy, U. Miss., 1970, JD, 1971. Bar: Miss. 1971, Ark. 1976, U.S. Dist. Ct. (no. dist.) Miss. 1971, U.S. Dist. Ct. (ea. dist.) Ark. 1976, U.S. Ct. Appeals (8th cir.) 1985. Sr. tax acct. Arthur Young & Co., San Jose, Calif., 1971-74, A.M. Pullen & Co., Knoxville, Tenn., 1975; legal counsel to gov. State of Ark., Little Rock, 1975-79; dep. pros. atty. 6th Jud. Dist. Ark., Little Rock, 1979-80; chief counsel Ark. Public Service Commn., Little Rock, 1980-83; asst. U.S. atty. Eastern Dist. Ark., Dept. Justice, Little Rock, 1983—. Mem. ABA, Miss. State Bar, Ark. State Bar Assn. Episcopalian. Office: US Atty's Office 600 W Capitol PO Box 1229 Little Rock AR 72203

LIPHAM, MARY CATHERINE, infosytems specialist; b. Bowdon, Ga., Sept. 16, 1947; d. James Cliff and Mildred Elizabeth (Garrett) L.;. BA, W. Ga. Coll., 1969; MA, U. Ga., 1971. Archivist Md. Hall of Records, Annapolis, 1972-79; residential assessor Md. State Dept. of Assessments and Taxation, Annapolis, 1978-84; mem. task force Md. State Dept. of Assessments and Taxation, 1983-84; comml. indsl. trainee Md. State Dept. of Assessments and Taxation, Upper Marlboro, 1984-86; instr. telecommunications procedures Md. State Dept. of Assessments and Taxation, 1986-87; comml. indsl. assessor Md. State Dept. of Assessments and Taxation, Annapolis, 1986. Mem. Condominium Covenants Com., 1980-82, bd. dirs. 1982-83. Ford Found. fellow, 1969-70. Mem. Internat. Assn. Assessing Officers, Md. Assn. Assessing Officers (parliamentarian). Clubs: Bay County Ramblers Sq. Dance (treas. 1982-84), Davidsonville Ballroom Dance. Home: 1567 Ritchie Lane Annapolis MD 21401 Office: Md Dept Assessments and Taxation 301 W Preston St Baltimore MD 21201

LIPIN, JOAN CAROL, association executive; b. Denver, Aug. 25, 1947; d. Theodore and Kathe (Pardo) Lipin. B.A., NYU, 1969; postgrad. MIT, 1973-74; M.B.A., Boston U., 1977. Adminstrv. staff MIT, Boston, 1969-74; adminstr. Mass. Gen. Hosp., Boston, 1975-76, mgmt. cons., 1976; dept. head N.Y. Hosp., N.Y.C., 1977-80; exec. v.p. Gordon-Keeble, N.Y.C., 1980-83; pres. Thor Scientific, N.Y.C., 1983-86; sr. mgr. health services ARC in Greater N.Y., 1986—; cons.; mem. rev. bd. Ind. Testing Lab., N.Y.C., 1981-85. mem. Forum Corporate Responsibility. Mem. Pharm. Mktg. Assn., N.Y. Acad. Sci., Am. Soc. Zoologists, Am. Mgmt. Assn., Union Concerned Scientists, Am. Pub. Health Assn., N.Y. Com. Occupational Safety and Health, Amnesty Internat., Planning Forum, Audubon Soc., World Wildlife Fund, Thanantology Found. (steering com.). Home: 45 E 89th st Apt 14G New York NY 10128 Office: ARC in Greater NY 150 Amsterdam Ave New York NY 10023

LIPINSKI, JANE LYNN, medical-surgical equipment sales representative; b. Columbia City, Ind., Aug. 20, 1953; d. Wilbur Demoines and Ruth Lucille (Cordill) Bennett; m. James Martin Lipinski, Oct. 26, 1983. B.A. in Bus., Purdue U., 1976. Orthopedic sales rep. Zimmer Co., Mpls., 1978-81; asst. to orthopedic physician, Clearwater, Fla., 1981-82; asst. dir. materials mgmt., Mease Hosp., Dunedin, Fla., 1982-84, sterile processing supr., 1982-84; med./surg. sales rep., surg. instrument specialist Edward Weck & Co., Inc., Research Triangle Park, N.C., 1984—. Mem. Nat. Assn. Female Execs., Assn. Operating Room Nurses, Assn. Hosp. Central Supply Mgrs. Republican. Avocations: scuba diving; underwater photography; tennis. Home: 12525 56th Pl N Royal Palm Beach FL 33411 Office: PO Box 16539 West Palm Beach FL 33416

LIPKA, RUTH PLANTE, educational consultant; b. Woonsocket, R.I., Dec. 30, 1937; d. Philias Leo Plante and Olida Mathilda (Riendeau) Plante Michaud; m. Stephen Lipka, Sept. 1, 1958; children—Craig Stephen, Deanne Ruth. A.A.S. in Secretarial Sci., Bergen Community Coll., 1972; B.A. in Bus. Edn., Montclair State Coll., 1974, M.A. in Bus. Edn., 1977. Tchr. Teaneck Bd. Edn. (N.J.), 1974-75; placement dir. Sawyer Sch., Clifton, N.J., 1976-77; dir., owner Berdan Inst., Totowa, N.J., 1977-87. Mem. Pvt. Career Sch. Assn. N.J. (bd. dirs. 1982—, sec. 1984-86, v.p. 1986-87, pres. 1988—), Nat. Bus. Edn. Assn., N.J. Bus. Edn. Assn., Nat. Assn. Fin. Aid Adminstrs., N.J. Assn. Fin. Aid Adminstrs., Word Processing Info. Assn., Delta Pi Epsilon. Roman Catholic. Home and Office: 13 Jonquil Ct Paramus NJ 07652

LIPKIN, MARY CASTLEMAN DAVIS (MRS. ARTHUR BENNETT LIPKIN), retired psychiatric social worker; b. Germantown, Pa., Mar. 4, 1907; d. Henry L. and Willie (Webb) Davis; student grad. sch. social work U. Wash., 1946-48; m. William F. Cavenaugh, Nov. 8, 1930 (div.); children—Molly C. (Mrs. Gary Oberbillig), William A.; m. 2d, Arthur Bennett Lipkin, Sept. 15, 1961 (dec. June 1974). Nursery sch. tchr. Miquon (Pa.) Sch., 1940-45; caseworker Family Soc. Seattle, 1948-49, Jewish Family and Child Service, Seattle, 1951-56; psychiat. social worker Stockton (Calif.) State Hosp., 1957-58; supr. social service Mental Health Research Inst., Fort Steilacoom, Wash., 1958-59; engaged in pvt. practice, Bellevue, Wash., 1959-61. Former mem. Phila. Com. on City Policy. Former diplomate and bd. mem. Conf. Advancement of Pvt. Practice in Social Work. Mem. Acad. Cert. Social Workers, Nat. Assn. Social Workers, Linus Paul Inst. Sci. and Medicine, Menninger Found., Union Concerned Scientists, Physicians for Social Responsibility, Center for Sci. in Pub. Interest, Jr. League, Seattle Art Mus., Asian Art Council, Wing Luke Mus., Bellevue Art Mus., Pacific Sci. Center, Western Wash. Solar Energy Assn., Nature Conservancy, Wilderness Soc., Sierra Club, Common Cause, ACLU, Pa. Acad. Fine Arts. Clubs: Cosmopolitan, Cricket (Phila.); Women's University (Seattle); Nassau (Princeton, N.J.), Friday Harbor Yacht (Washington). Home: 10022 Meydenbauer Way SE #202 Bellevue WA 98004

LIPMAN, WYNONA M., state legislator; b. Ga.; children—Karen Anne, William (dec.). BA, Talladega Coll.; MA, Atlanta U.; Ph.D., Columbia U.; LL.D. (hon.), Kean Coll., Bloomfield Coll. Former high sch. tchr., lectr. Seton Hall U., Assoc. prof. Essex Community Coll.; mem. N.J. State Senate, 1971—, chmn. state govt. com., mem. joint appropriations com., revenue, fin. and appropriations com. Chmn., Commn. on Sex Discrimination in the Statutes. Recipient Outstanding Woman award Assn. Women Bus Owners, 1983. Office: State Senate Office Sate Capitol Trenton NJ 08625 *

LIPP, NORMA, insurance company executive; b. Ottawa, Ont., Can., Dec. 7, 1938; d. Isadore and Mary (Magalnick) Klaman; m. Lawrence D. Meno, Feb. 1, 1964 (div. 1969); m. Jules Lipp; children—Michael, Traci, A.J. B.A., Mansfield Finishing Sch., 1959; grad. Sch. Design, Miami, Fla., 1978. Asst., Dept. Nat. Revenue, Ottawa, Ont., 1956-58; supr. info. services Can. Broadcast Corp., Ottawa, 1961-63; mgr., comptroller Metr Petroleum Co., Miami, Fla., 1968-69; asst. to pres. Gabor & Co., Inc., Miami, 1969-82; treas., dir. Fin. Planning Assocs., Miami, 1982—; chmn., dir. Fin. Planning Realty, Miami, 1985—. Assoc. Com. to Elect the Pres., Miami, 1984; assoc. mem. Rep. Nat. Com., Miami, 1984. Club: Westview Country (Miami); Williams Island Club. Home: 20251 NE 25th Ave Miami FL 33180 Office: Fin Planning Assocs 15105 NW 77 Ave Miami Lakes FL 33014

LIPPA, BARBARA JEAN, planning ofcl.; b. Rochester, N.Y., Sept. 3, 1952; d. Frank and Joan Patricia (Vitello) Lippa; B.S., SUNY, Brockport, 1974; M.A., George Washington U., 1977, M.S.A., 1982. Legis. intern Com. on Human Resources, U.S. Senate, Washington, 1974; edn. cons., 1974; cons. Nat. Adv. Council on Indian Edn., 1974; staff Nat. Adv. Council on Edn. of Disadvantaged Children, Washington, 1974-77; planning aide Fairfax County (Va.) Planning Commn., 1978-79; dep. exec. dir. Fairfax County Planning Commn., 1979—. Religious edn. tchr. Roman Cath. Ch., Alexandria, 1974-80, coordinator Bible sch., 1977. Recipient award for excellence HEW, 1975, unusual ability increment award, 1982. Mem. Am. Planning Assn., Nat. Assn. Exec. Women, Zonta Internat. Home: 14436 Manassas Gap Ct Centreville VA 22020 Office: 4100 Chain Bridge Rd 7th Fl Fairfax VA 22030

LIPPE, PAMELA TOWEN, political consultant; b. N.Y.C., Mar. 28, 1952; d. Vincent Stuyvesant and Barbara (Crane) Lippe. BA, Hampshire Coll., 1977. Legis. assoc. Friends of the Earth, Washington, 1976-79; found. dir.

MUSE Found., N.Y.C., 1979-81; creative dir. Nat. Com. for an Effective Congress, N.Y.C., 1981-87; exec. dir., N.Y. State Democrat. Assembly Campaign Com., 1987-88; New Eng. regional fin. dir. U.S. Dem. Senate Campaign Com., 1988—; sec., dir. Citizens Vote, Inc., N.Y.C., 1982-86. Celebrity liaison Mondale-Ferraro campaign, 1984. Democrat. Office: Dem Senate Campaign Com 105 E 16th St Suite 7S New York NY 10003

LIPPERT, H. ANNE, banker; b. Berlin; came to Can., 1962; d. Wilhelm G. and Lore S. (Schampert) Kolle; divorced; 1 child, Frank T. Cert. in comml. translation, Alliance Francaise, Paris, 1960; Fellow Inst. of Can. Bankers, U. B.C., Vancouver, Can., 1980. Comml. translator Mercedes-Benz, Stuttgart, Fed. Republic Germany, 1960-62; area mgr. Royal Bank of Can., Vancouver, 1965—, area mgr. Vancouver Downtown br., mgr. Hastings and Granville br., 1987—. Campaign chmn. Salvation Army, Vancouver, 1986—; bd. dirs. Can. Diabetes Assn., Vancouver, 1986—; bd. dirs. fin. com. Can. Mental Health Assn., Vancouver, 1986—; nominee Women of Distinction awards com. YWCA, Vancouver, 1987. Mem. Bd. of Trade (mem. com. 1987). Lutheran. Club: Western Indoor Tennis (Vancouver). Office: Royal Bank, 1497 W Broadway, Vancouver, BC Canada V6H 1H7

LIPPI, LAURA ANNE, journalist; b. Bronx, N.Y., Dec. 14, 1952; d. Attilio and Esther (Cacchione) L. Student, U. Colo., 1970-73; BA in Journalism, CCNY, 1975. Feature writer Local Profile Mag., Eastchester, N.Y., 1976-77, Majority Report Newspaper, N.Y.C., 1977-80; asst. editor Solid Wastes Mgmt. Mag., N.Y.C., 1980-82; reporter The Bergen Times, Hackensack, N.J., 1983-84, Manteca (Calif.) News, 1984-85; free-lance writer 1985—. Vol. Bella Abzug congl. campaign, White Plains, N.Y., 1986-87, Logos Resources Ctr., Bronx, 1978. Mem. Inst. Genetic Psychiatry, Majority Report, NOW, Sierra Club. Democrat. Roman Catholic. Home and Office: 300 1st St Yonkers NY 10704

LIPPITT, ELIZABETH CHARLOTTE, writer; b. San Francisco; d. Sidney Grant and Stella Lippitt; student Mills Coll., U. Calif.-Berkeley. Writer, performer own satirical monologues; contbr. articles to 85 newspapers including N.Y. Post, Los Angeles Examiner, Orlando Sentinel, Phoenix Republic, also advt. Recipient Congress of Freedom award, 1959, 71-73, 77, 78; writer on nat. and polit. affairs for 85 newspapers including Muncie Star, St. Louis Globe-Democrat, Washington Times, Utah Ind., Jackson News. Mem. Commn. for Free China, Conservative Caucus. Mem. Nat. Assn. R.R. Passengers, Nat. Trust for Hist. Preservation, Am. Security Council, Internat. Platform Assn., Am. Conservative Union, Nat. Antivivisection Soc., High Frontier, For Our Children, Childhelp U.S.A., Free Afghanistan Com., Humane Soc. U.S., Young Ams. for Freedom, 8 antivivisection orgns. Clubs: Metropolitan, Olympic, Commonwealth. Pop singer, recorder song album Songs From the Heart. Home: 2414 Pacific Ave San Francisco CA 94115

LIPPY, MARY ELIZABETH, retail company executive; b. Harrisonburg, Va., Mar. 21, 1955; d. William Henry Jr. and Joan Lois (Reid) Brown; m. William Guy Lippy Jr., Sept. 17, 1983. BE, Longwood Coll., 1977. Field rep. Southland Corp., Balt., 1978-83, area tng. mgr., 1983-86, area personnel mgr., 1986-87; personnel adminstr. Southland Corp., Alexandria, Va., 1987—. Mem. Washington Bd. Trade. Mem. Am. Soc. Personnel Adminstrs., Am. Soc. Tng. Devel., Nat. Assn. for Female Execs. Office: Southland Corp 5300 Shawnee Rd Alexandria VA 22312

LIPSCHUTZ, ILSE HEMPEL, French and Franco-Spanish relations, painting and literature educator; b. Boennigheim, Wurttemberg, Fed. Republic Germany, Aug. 19, 1923; came to U.S., 1946; d. Joseph Martin Paul and Fanny (Wurzburger) Hempel; m. Lewis D. Lipschutz, Feb. 6, 1952; children: Elizabeth, Marion, Marc Hempel, Margaret Hempel. Diplôme Institut des Professeurs de Français à l'Etranger, Sorbonne U., Paris, 1942, Licence ès Lettres, 1943, Diplôme d'Etudes Supérieures Lettres, 1944; Diploma de Estudios Hispánicos, U. Madrid, 1945; MA, Harvard U., 1949, PhD, 1958. Teaching fellow Radcliffe Coll.-Harvard U., 1947-50; instr. Vassar Coll., Poughkeepsie, N.Y., 1951-58, asst. prof., 1958-63, assoc. prof., 1963-72, prof., 1972—, Andrew W. Mellon prof. humanities, 1981—; chmn. dept. Vassar Coll., 1975-82; cons., collaborator Spanish Ministry of Culture, Madrid, 1979—; lectr. Prado Mus., Madrid, 1983. Author: Spanish Painting and the French Romantics, 1972, Spanish edit., 1981, (with others) La Imagen romántica de España, 1981, Goya, nuevas visiones, 1987, Viajeros románticos a Audalucía, 1987; contbr. articles to profl. jours. Spanish Govt. fellow U. Madrid, 1945; N.Y. state fellow AAUW, 1950-51; Anne Radcliffe fellow Radcliffe Coll.-Harvard U., 1950-51; faculty fellow Vassar Coll., 1960-61, 67-68; research scholar U.S.-Spain Commn. on Edn., 1979-80; sr. research fellow Fulbright-Hays Commn., 1983-84 (nat. fellowship com. 1972-75, 84—); chevalier Palmes académiques, 1984. Mem. AAUP, AAUW (nat. fellowship com. 1961-67), Soc. Théophile Gautier (bd. dirs. 1986—), Soc. Etudes romantiques. Home: 11 Park Ave Poughkeepsie NY 12603 Office: Vassar Coll Dept French Box 394 Poughkeepsie NY 12601

LIPSCOMB, ANNA ROSE FEENY, hotel executive; b. Greensboro, N.C., Oct. 29, 1945; d. Nathan and Matilda (Carotenuto) L. B.A. in English and French summa cum laude, Queens Coll., 1977. Reservations agt. Am. Airlines, St. Louis, 1968-69, ticket agt., 1969-71; coll. rep. CBS, Holt Rinehart Winston, Providence, 1977-79, sr. acquisitions editor Dryden Press, Chgo., 1979-81; owner, mgr. Taos Inn, N.Mex., 1981—; bd. dirs. N.Mex. Hotel and Motel Assn., 1986—. Editor: Intermediate Accounting, 1980; Business Law, 1981. Contbr. articles to profl. jours. Bd. dirs., 1st v.p. Taos Arts Assn., 1982-85; founder, bd. dirs. Taos Spring Arts Celebration, 1983—; founder, dir. Meet-the-Artist Series, 1983—; bd. dirs. and co-founder Spring Arts N.Mex., 1986; founding mem. Assn. Hist. Hotels, Boulder, 1983—; organizer Internat. Symposium on Arts, 1985; bd. dirs. Arts in Taos, 1983, Taoschool, Inc., 1985—. Recipient Outstanding English Student of Yr. award Queens Coll., 1977; named Single Outstanding Contributor to the Arts in Taos, 1986. Mem. Millicent Rogers Mus. Assn., Taos Lodgers and Restaurant Assn., Taos County C. of C. (1st v.p., bd. dirs. 1988-89). Internat. Platform Assn., Phi Beta Kappa. Democrat. Home: Talpa Route Taos NM 87571 Office: Taos Inn PO Drawer N Taos NM 87571

LIPSKY, JESSICA, small business owner; b. Bklyn., Aug. 24, 1939; d. Morris and Anna (Podolsky) L.; divorced; 1 child, Amanda Nelson. A in Arts and Scis., N.Y.C. Community Coll., 1959; student, New Sch. for Social Research, 1963-69, Bklyn. Mus. Art Sch., 1963-65. Lic. realtor. Adminstrv. asst. Adelphi Coll. Hosp., Bklyn., 1959-61, Hosp. Jaques Loeme Found., Bklyn., 1961-63; exec. sec. L.I. Coll. Hosp., Bklyn., 1963-65; adminstrv. asst. Red Hook Neighborhood Health Ctr., Bklyn., 1965-69, Phoenix House, N.Y.C., 1969-71; prin. addiction specialist counselor ASA, N.Y.C., 1971-72; dir. CRU Addiction Services Agy., Bklyn., 1972-74; pres. The Fabric Alternative, Inc., Bklyn., 1975—. Mem. N.Y. Open Ctr., Park Slope Civic Council, Bklyn., 1985; vol. Asia Soc. Mem. Bklyn. C. of C. Office: 78 7th Ave Brooklyn NY 11217

LIPSKY, JOY-ELLEN, software engineer, company administrator; b. St. Louis, Mar. 5, 1952; d. William and Pauline (Aldridge) L. BA in Math., San Jose (Calif.) State U., 1974, MS in Computer and Info. Sci., 1979. Asst. systems engr. Santa Clara Valley Water Dist., San Jose, 1974-80; sr. systems programmer Mohawk Data Services, Los Gatos, Calif., 1980-82; sr. software engr., assoc. Applied Engring. Assocs., Los Gatos, Calif., 1982-83; program mgr. DB/Access, Cupertino, Calif., 1983—; cons. Images By Suzie, San Francisco, 1986—, Personnel Impressions, San Francisco, 1987—. Named one of Outstanding Young Women Am., 1985. Mem. Assn. for Computing Machinery (chmn. San Francisco Peninsula chpt. 1984-85, mem.-at-large com. on chpts. 1985—), Am. Bus. Women's Assn. (pres. Los Gatos chpt. 1985-86), Phi Kappa Phi, Upsilon Pi Epsilon. Democrat. Office: DB/Access 20111 Stevens Creek Cupertino CA 95014

LIPSKY, LINDA ETHEL, business executive; b. Bklyn., June 2, 1939; d. Irving Julius and Florence (Stern) Ellman; m. Warren Lipsky, June 12, 1960 (div. Sept. 1968); 1 child, Phillip Bruce; m. Jerome Friedman, Jan. 17, 1988. BA in Psychology, Hofstra U., 1960; MPS in Health Care Adminstrn., Long Island U., 1979. Child welfare social worker Nassau County Dept. Social Service, N.Y., 1960-64; adminstr. La Guardia Med. Group of Health Ins. Plan of Greater N.Y., Queens, 1969-72; cons. Neighborhood Service Ctr., Bronx, N.Y., 1973-78; dir. ODA Health Ctr., Bklyn., 1978-82; pres. Millin Assocs., Inc., Nassau, N.Y., 1982—. Mem. Health Care Fin. Mgmt. Assn., Nat. Assn. Community Health Ctrs., Nat. Assn. Female Execs., Hofstra U. Alumni Assn. (mem. senate 1984—, chairperson membership com. 1985—), Pi Alpha Alpha. Republican. Jewish. Avocations: cooking, writing, reading. Office: Millin Assocs Inc 521 Chestnut St Cedarhurst NY 11516

LIPSON, RENEE SUE, organization development consultant; b. Cleve.; d. Louis and Celia (Switky) Rosenfield; m. Leon Lipson, June 24, 1952; (div. Oct. 1964); children—Sheri Ellen Lipson Bidwell, Jodi Faith. B.S., Case Western Res. U., 1952; B.S., Youngstown U., 1963; M.A., John Carroll U., 1968; Ph.D., Mich. State U., 1976; postgrad. Kent State U., 1968-72. Mem. staff Am. Arbitration Assn., Cleve., 1951-52; hostess Welcome Wagon, Youngstown, Ohio, 1952-55; tchr. elem. grades Cleveland Heights-University Heights Bd. Edn., 1963-67; tchr. Hanna Pavilion, Univ. Hosps., Cleve., 1967-68; guidance counselor Warrensville Heights Bd. Edn., Ohio, 1968-70; dir. Drug Edn. Ctr., Cleve. Health Mus. and Edn. Ctr., 1970-72; pres. Living Dynamics, Cleve., 1972-73; cons. Mich. Dept. Edn. Substance Abuse Prevention Edn. Program, Lansing, 1973-789; adminstr., Mich. Senate Edn. Com., Lansing, 1980; cons. Prevention Services Mich. Dept. Civil Rights, Lansing, 1979-80, 80-84; pres. Profl. Cons. Services, Lansing 1984—; adj. prof. Mich. State U., East Lansing, 1979—, Wayne State U., Detroit, 1979—, Cen. Mich. U., 1987—; cons. Ohio State Dept. Edn., 1971-73, Am. Social Health Assn., 1971-73, NSF, Washington, 1971-73. Edn. Research Council Am., Cleve., 1965-70. Co-founder Cuyahoga County Health Coalition, Cleve., 1966-72; 1st chair Ingham County Democratic Womens Caucus, 1983-84; mem. East Lansing Fine Arts Commn., 1980-82; fundraiser Democratic activities, 1980—. Mem. Am. Soc. Tng. and Devel., Lansing Regional C. of C. (com. chmn.), Women Bus. Owners, Mich. Orgn. Devel. Network (founder 1986), Women in Mgmt. Network (founder 1982), ACLU, Common Cause, Women in State Govt. (co founder 1979), Mich. Council for Women in Ednl. Adminstrn. (com. chair), Am. Humanist Assn., Captitol Area Womens Network, Women in Mgmt. Inst. (founder, exec. dir. 1988). Jewish. Avocations: Travel; theater; music; crafts. Office: Profl Cons Services 121 E Allegan Lansing MI 48933

LIPSTATE, JO ANN, cemetery executive, public relations consultant; b. San Antonio, Aug. 4, 1930; d. Herbert and Beatrice (Adelman) Davis; m. Eugene J. Lipstate, Feb. 26, 1950; children—James Mitchell, Betsy Ann Lipstate Horner. Student in fine arts and English, U. Tex., 1947-49. Copywriter Sta.-KATC-TV, Lafayette, La., 1970-73; pres. Lipstate Creative Services, Lafayette, 1973-80; pub. relations cons. N.W. Oil Co., Lafayette, 1979—; v.p. Eugene J. Lipstate, Inc., 1979; pres. Eterna, Inc., doing bus. as Fountain Meml. Gardens and Mausoleum, Lafayette, 1983—; bd. dirs. Mid La. Health Systems Agy., Lafayette, 1980-83, chmn. project, 1982-83; found. mem. Women's Hosp. Acadiana, Lafayette, 1982—; trustee Women's and Children Hosp., Lafayette, 1987. Bd. dirs. Lafayette Juvenile and Young Adult Program, 1969, art therapist, 1970. Mem. Ad Club Acadiana (pres. 1978-79, 3 TV comml. awards 1972). Republican. Jewish. Clubs: City, Oakbourne Country (Lafayette). Avocations: golf; tennis; fishing; painting; gardening. Home: 401 Shelly Dr Lafayette LA 70503 Office: Bldg 12 Oil Center Dr at Heyman Blvd PO Box 52421 Lafayette LA 70505

LIPTAY, LYNNE MIRIAM, pediatrician; b. Panama, C.Z., Nov. 3, 1947; d. Thomas Emil and Lea Miriam (Maki) Oakland; m. John Stephen Liptay, Dec. 30, 1972; children—Thomas John, Steven Robert. B.A., Swarthmore Coll., 1969; M.D., Yale U., 1973. Diplomate Am. Bd. Pediatrics. Intern in pediatrics Montefiore Hosp. and Med. Ctr., N.Y.C., 1973-74, resident in pediatrics, 1974-76; practice medicine specializing in pediatrics, Hyde Park, N.Y., 1976—; mem. staff No. Dutchess Hosp., Rhinebeck, N.Y., 1976—. Co-author: Talk & Toddle, 1983. Fellow Am. Acad. Pediatrics. Office: 7 Pine Woods Rd Hyde Park NY 12538

LIPTON, JOAN ELAINE, advertising executive; b. N.Y.C., July 12; 1 child, David Dean. B.A., Barnard Coll. With Young & Rubicam, Inc., N.Y.C., 1949-52, Robert W. Orr & Assocs., N.Y.C., 1952-57, Benton & Bowles, Inc., N.Y.C., 1957-64; asso. dir. Benton & Bowles, Ltd., London, Eng., 1964-68; with McCann-Erickson, Inc. (advt. agy.), N.Y.C., 1968-85; v.p. McCann-Erickson, Inc. (advt. agy.), 1970-79, sr. v.p., creative dir., 1979-85; pres. Martin & Lipton Advt. Inc., 1985—. Bd. dirs. Advt. Women N.Y. Found., Inc, Women's Forum, 1988; trustee Film/Video Arts, Inc., 1983—; mem. Bus. Council for the UN Decade for Women, 1977-78; bd. visitors Ph.D. program in bus. CUNY, 1986—. Named Woman of Yr. Am. Advt. Fedn., 1974; recipient Honors award Ohio U. Sch. Journalism, 1976, Matrix award, 1979; YWCA award for women achievers, 1979; named Advt. Woman of Yr., 1984. Mem. Advt. Women N.Y. (v.p. 1975-76, v.p. Found. 1977-78), Women in Communications (pres. N.Y. chpt. 1974-76, named Nat. Headliner 1976). Office: 128 E 56th St New York NY 10022

LIPTON, MILDRED CERES, child psychologist; b. Bklyn., May 21, 1921; d. Salvatore and Josephine (Nicotra) Ceres; m. Edmond Lipton, Aug. 2, 1963; stepchildren: Richard Lipton, Judith Hodson. BA, Douglass Coll., 1943; MA, State U. Iowa, 1946. Clin. psychology intern Rockland State Hosp., Orangeburg, N.Y., 1943-44, clin. psychologist children's unit, 1945-48; clin. psychologist VA Mental Health Clinic, Bklyn., 1948-50, Erie (Pa.) Guidance Ctr., 1950-51; chief clin. psychologist Westchester Guidance Ctr., White Plains, N.Y., 1951-63; instr. psychology Mills Coll. of Edn., N.Y.C., 1963-67; pvt. practice clin. child psychology Bklyn., 1967—; instr. psychology St. John U., Jamaica, N.Y., 1983; Ikenobo instr. of Ikebana Bklyn. Botanic Gardens, 1984—. Mem. Am. Psychol. Assn., Bkyln. Mental Health Assn. (bd. dirs., chair com. for emotionally disturbed children, 1967-71), Ikenobo Soc. of Eastern Seaboard (pres. 1986—). Home: 132 Argyle Rd Brooklyn NY 11218 Office: 132 Argyle Rd Brooklyn NY 11218

LIPTON, ZELDA, insurance company executive; b. N.Y.C., Mar. 11, 1923; d. Jacob and Sadie (Bell) Simon; m. Louis Lipton, Mar. 9, 1947; children—Judith Lipton Binstock, Jay. B.A., Hunter Coll., 1943; M.A., NYU, 1945. Tchr., N.Y.C. high schs., 1945-47; with Conn. Gen. Life, Hartford, 1964-79, dir. product devel., 1977-79; 2nd v.p. life/med. product Union Mut. Life Ins. Co., Portland, Maine, 1979-83, 2nd v.p. flexible compensation, 1983-87, v.p. mktg., Columbia Free State Health System, Columbia, Md., 1987—. Contbg. author: Group Life and Health Insurance, A, B and C, 1974-87; Handbook of Employee Benefits, 1983, revised edit., 1988; coauthor: Health Insurance Answer Book, 1986. Mem. Gov.'s Certificate of Need adv. com., Maine, 1983-87. Fellow Life Mgmt. Inst.; mem. Health Ins. Assn. Am., Ins. Acctg. and Systems Assn. Office: Columbia Free State Health System Two Knoll North Drive Columbia MD 21045

LIPTOW, B. J., developer, director; b. Ripon, Wis., July 10, 1956; d. Herman Christian and Lucille (Malzhan) Beier; m. Thomas Frederick Wiles, Oct. 4, 1975 (div. Oct. 1979); m. Randy Lynn Liptow, Apr. 20, 1985. Cert. in real estate, Moriane Park Tech. Bookkeeper Fred Wilkes Exclusive, Inc., Ripon, 1974-88; salesperson Ripon Modular Homes, 1974-88; owner Custom Housing of Distinction, Ripon, 1988—; bd. dirs. Didders and Contractors Wis. Power & Light Co., Ripon, 1984—. Mem. Nat. Assn. Female Execs. Democrat. Lutheran. Home: Rural Rt 2 Ridgeview Estates Ripon WI 54971 Office: Custom Housing Distinction Aspen St Ripon WI 54971

LISA, CATHERINE MARY, educator; b. Hackensack, N.J., Dec. 28, 1955; d. Ralph Nicholas and Catherine H. (Balkenende) L. AA in Edn. and Art, Bergen Community Coll., 1977; BA in Edn. and Humanities cum laude, Felician Coll., 1983. Cert. tchr., N.J. Salesperson Valley Rair Corp., Little Ferry, N.J., 1974-85; reporter, stringer The Independent, 1979-80; tchr. St. Margaret of Cortona Sch., Little Ferry, 1983-86, Englewood (N.J.) Pub. Schs., 1987—. Councilwoman Borough of Moonachie, N.J., 1985-87. Mem. N.J. Edn. Assn., Conf. Rep. Elected Ofcls. Home: 6 Jackson Place Moonachie NJ 07074

LISKOV, BARBARA H., software engineering educator; b. Los Angeles, Nov. 7, 1939. BA in Math., U. Calif., Berkeley, 1961; MS in Computer Sci., Stanford U., 1965, PhD, 1968. With applications programming sect. Mitre Corp., Bedford, Mass., 1961-62, mem. tech. staff, 1968-72; with Harvard U., Cambridge, Mass., 1962-63; grad. research asst. dept. computer sci. Stanford U., Palo Alto, Calif., 1963-68; prof. computer sci. and engring. MIT, Cambridge, 1972—, NEC prof. software sci. and engring. Author: (with others) Lecture Notes in Computer Science 114, 1981; (with J. Guttag) Abstraction and Specification in Program Development, 1986; reference manual; assoc. editor TOPLAS; contbr. articles to profl. jours. Mem. IEEE (tech. coms. on operating systems, software engring., assoc. editor IEEE-TSE), Assn. Computing Machinery (spl. interest groups on microprogramming, exec. com. spl. interest group on programming langs., tech. coms. on operating systems and software engring.), Nat. Acad. Engring. Office: MIT 77 Massachusetts Ave Cambridge MA 02139

LISONI, GAIL MARIE LANDTBOM, lawyer; b. San Francisco, Mar. 11, 1949; d. William A. and Patricia Ann (Cruden) Landtbom; m. Joseph Louis Lisoni, Mar. 24, 1984. B.A., Dominican Coll., Calif., 1971; J.D., U. West Los Angeles, 1978, cert. paralegal, 1974. Bar: Calif. 1979. Campaign treas. Calif. for Lisoni, Arcadia, 1979-81; assoc. Joseph Lisoni, Esq., Los Angeles, 1981, Arnold S. Malter, Esq., Los Angeles, 1982; ptnr. Lisoni & Lisoni, Los Angeles, 1983—. Mem. Assn. Trial Lawyers Am., Calif. Trial Lawyers Assn., Los Angles Trial Lawyers Assn., ABA, Italian Am. Lawyers Assn. Democrat. Roman Catholic. Lodge: Sons of Italy. Office: 3701 Wilshire Blvd Suite 700 Los Angeles CA 90010

LISTA, BETHANNE, publishing executive; b. Willingboro, N.J., Oct. 23, 1962; d. Joseph Charles and Arlene Ellen L. Student, James Madison U., Harrisonburg, Va. V.p. Gunny Assocs., Waynesboro, Va., 1985—; sales exec., Mil. Press Assoc., Waynesboro, 1985—. Vol. YMCA, Waynesboro, 1986. Served in USN, 1981-85. Recipient numerous weighlifting awards. Republican. Roman Catholic. Clubs: DECA (Waynesboro), 4-H (Waynesboro). Lodges: Moose, Eagles. Home: P.O.Box 1044 Waynesboro VA 22980

LISTER, STEPHANIE ANN, nurse; b. New Kinsington, Pa., July 6, 1947; d. Peter and Stephanie Paulette (Dembinski) Smolak; m. Ronald Jay Lister, June 22, 1968; 1 child, Hillary Ann. Student, Calif. State U., Fullerton, 1965-66; AA, East Los Angeles Coll., 1967, RN, 1968; BS in Health Scis., Chapman Coll., 1978. RN burn ward vascular surgery unit Los Angeles County-U. So. Calif. Med. Ctr., 1968-71; RN, ICU Queen of Angels Hosp., Los Angeles, 1971-73; charge RN recovery room So. Coast Med. Ctr., South Laguna, Calif., 1973—. Chairperson ways and means Barry Mores chpt. Orange County Performing Arts Ctr., Costa Mesa, Calif., 1983—; founder Opera Pacific, Costa Mesa, 1987; mem. Orange County Philharm., Costa Mesa, 1987; vol. Providence Speech and Hearing Ctr., Orange, 1986—; co-chairperson Orange County Imagination Celebration in the Park-Laguna Niguel Regional Park, 1987-88. Mem. Am. Assn. Post Anesthesia Nurses, AAUW. Republican. Roman Catholic. Home: 22632 Barlovento Mission Viejo CA 92692

LISTWAN, MARION BARBARA, senior citizen activities director; b. East Newark, N.J., Nov. 18, 1928; d. Walter and Mary (Gorski) Wasowski; m. Frederick Joseph Listwan, Apr. 30, 1949; children: Judith , Eugene, Joseph, Kenneth. AAS in Bus. Adminstrn., Essex County Coll., Newark, 1976; BA in Urban Studies, St. Peter's Coll., Jersey City, 1981; cert. Gerontology, Kean Coll., Union, N.J., 1983. With acctg. dept. N.J. Bell Telephone Co., Newark, 1946-50; with exec. dining services Amerada-Hess Oil Co., N.Y.C., 1968-75; mgr. No. Hudson Sr. Nutrition Project, Harrison, N.J., 1976-81; dir. sr. citizen activities Town of Harrison, N.J., 1981—. Mem. bd. trustees Harrison Pub. Library, 1964—, pres. 1984, 88; mem. Harrison Bd. Elections, 1985—. Recipient Woman of Achievement award Jersey (City) Jrnl., 1981. Mem. Gerontology Inst. N.J. Democrat. Roman Catholic. Lodges: Polish Am. Heritage League, Polish Women's Alliance Am. (pres. 1986—). Home: 43 Searing Ave Harrison NJ 07029

LITLE, MARIANNE MILLER, radiologic technologist, educator; b. Amarillo, Tex., Oct. 4, 1936; d. William Fredrick and Ethel Bowen (Thompson) Miller; m. William E. Litle, Nov. 16, 1963 (div.); children—Kruger E., Midge Smith, William B., Marc S. B.S., U. Tex.-Dallas, 1979; M.S., East Tex. State U., 1983. Cert. radiol. technologist; Radiol. technologist to Dr. Brooks, Dallas, 1961-62, nuclear medicine technologist Parkland Hosp., Dallas, 1962-64; clin. coordinator El Centro Coll., Dallas, 1979—. Contbr. chpt. in book. Mem. Dallas Soc. Crippled Children, 1972—, The Auction for Cultural Arts, 1973. Mem. Tex. Soc. Radiol. Technologists, Am. Soc. Radiol. Technologists, Tex. Soc. Allied Health Profls., Tex. Jr. Coll. Tchr. Assn., Phi Theta Kappa. Republican. Episcopalian. Office: El Centro Coll Main St and Lamar Dallas TX 75201

LITMAN, ROSLYN MARGOLIS, lawyer, educator; b. N.Y.C., Sept. 30, 1928; d. Harry and Dorothy (Perlow) Margolis; m. S. David Litman, Nov. 22, 1950; children: Jessica, Hannah, Harry. B.A., U. Pitts., 1949, J.D., 1952. Bar: Pa. 1952. Practiced in Pitts. 1952—; partner firm Litman, Litman Harris Brown & Watzman, P.A., 1952—; adj. prof. U. Pitts. Law Sch., 1958—; permanent del. Conf. U.S. Circuit Ct. Appeals for 3d Circuit; mem. Allegheny County Judiciary Com. Chmn., Pitts. Pub. Parking Authority, 1970-74; mem. curriculum com Pa. Bar Inst., 1986—; bd. dirs. Pa. Bar Inst. 1972-82. Mem. ABA (del., litigation sect., anti-trust health care com.), ACLU (nat. bd. dirs.), Pa. Bar Assn. (bd. govs. 1976-79), Allegheny County Bar Assn. (bd. govs. 1972-74, pres. 1975), Allegheny County Acad. Trial Lawyers (charter), ACLU of Western Pa. (former counsel, bd. dirs.), United Jewish Fedn. (community relations com.). Home: 1047 Negley Ave S Pittsburgh PA 15217 Office: 1701 Grant Bldg Pittsburgh PA 15219

LITTELL, PATRICIA L., contracting corporation executive; b. Albuquerque, May 28, 1954; d. Birnie Glenn and Eleanor Marie (Maloney) Hammock; student U. N.Mex., 1972-73, Coll. Santa Fe, 1984—; m. E. Austin Littell, Nov. 19, 1979; 4 stepchildren. Exec. sec. to v.p. systems integration BDM Corp., Albuquerque, 1976-80; pres., treas., co-founder Littell and Assocs., Albuquerque, 1979—; civil rights specialist legal dept. City of Albuquerque, 1987—. cons. small bus. firms. Recipient Corp. safety award Associated Gen. Contractors Am., 1980. Mem. Nat. Assn. Female Execs. Rebuplican. Methodist. Home: 1605 Camino Rosario NW Albuquerque NM 87107 Office: Kirtland AFB PO Box 5596 Albuquerque NM 87185

LITTLE, ANNA DENISE, marketing professional; b. Montclair, N.J., May 2, 1954; d. Jethro Craven and Verneader (Wright) L. BA, Fla. State U., 1980. Researcher, tech. asst. Sta. WFSU-TV, Tallahassee, 1979-80; with editorial staff Burrelle's Press Clipping Service, Livington, N.J., 1981-82; customer service and sales rep. Funk and Wagnalls, Inc., L.I., 1982-84; editor, media coordinator Murdoch Mags., N.Y.C., 1984-86; promotional and editorial mgr. Direct Response Group div. Hearst Mags., N.Y.C., 1986—. Mem. Nat. Assn. Female Execs., Acad. TV Arts and Scis. (mem. Blue Ribbon Panel). Democrat. Mem. Pentecostal Ch. Home: 8 Mission St Montclair NJ 07042-4518 Office: Direct Response Group c/o Hearst Mags 1775 Broadway 3d Floor New York NY 10019

LITTLE, DAINTY MARGO, government administrator; b. Richmond, Va., May 22, 1942; d. Lester Franklin and Ester Mae (Edwards) Richardson; m. Charles Perry Little, Oct. 6, 1961. AA, U. Fla., 1968; BS, U. Md., 1974, MA, 1976; postgrad., U. So. Calif., Washington, 1977—. Career counselor U.S. Dept. Agriculture, Washington, 1975-76, chief career devel. br., 1978-84; career counselor Office of Asst. Sec. Adminstrn. and Mgmt. U.S. Dept. Labor, Washington, 1976-78; instr. George Washington U., 1977-79; program officer U.S. Dept. Treasury, Washington, 1984—; owner Little Nostalgia Antique Shop, Brookeville, Md., 1973-78; cons. Mgmt. Inst., Largo, Md., 1979-81; adv. bd. USDA Grad. Sch., Washington, 1980—, George Washington U., 1988—, Doctoral Profl. Assn., U. So. Calif., 1988—. Author: Handbook of Free Services in the Washington Metropolitan Area, 1976, 84, 85, 86; contbr. articles to profl. jours. Chmn. Greenbrier Civic Assn., Fairfax, Va., 1974; com. chmn. Women's Action Task Force, Washington, 1983. Recipient Disting. Service award Tng. Officers Conf., 1986. Mem. AAUW, Am. Assn. Tng. and Devel., Treasury Career Network, Howard County Sheepbreeders Assn., Phi Chi Theta (nat. pres. 1984-86, chmn. bd. 1986—, nat. v.p. internal affairs 1982-84, past pres.'s award 1986). Clubs: Spinning, Herb (Md.). Home: 16601 Batchellor Forest Rd Olney MD 20832 Office: Dept Treasury Fed Exec Inst 12th and Pennsylvania Ave Washington DC 20220

LITTLE, FLORENCE ELIZABETH HERBERT, educator; b. Streator, Ill., July 7, 1911; d. Charles Arthur and Bertha (Schlachter) Herbert; B.A., Mich. State U., 1932; M.S.E., Drake U., 1962; m. Alfred Lamond Little, July 26, 1933 (dec.); children—Alan Rush, Barbara Jean Little Bell. Accompanist, Mich. State U., 1930-32, 33-36, mem. faculty, 1930-32; tchr., pub. schs., Bridgeport, Ill., 1945, Holt, Mich., 1945-46, Hanover, Mich., 1949-50, Pittsford, Mich., 1950-53, Des Moines, 1953-73; now substitute tchr., tutor, public schs., La Place, La.; pvt. tchr. piano and voice, 1932-56. Active CD, Crime Watch, Am. Fedn. Police Nat. CB Posse; mem. Tri-Parish Republican Women's Club. NSF grantee, 1963-64. Mem. Am. Bus. Women's Assn., Smithsonian Instn., NEA, Iowa Edn. Assn., Des Moines Edn. Assn., Orchid Soc. Jefferson, Kappa Kappa Iota, Mu Phi Epsilon. Presbyterian. Club: CB. Instituted elem. music programs, various schs.; hon. mem. editorial adv. bd. Am. Biog. Inst., 1980-83. Home: 130 Tudor Ave River Ridge LA 70123

LITTLE, KAREN MICHELE, educator; b. Buffalo, Oct. 27, 1949; d. Robert Graham and Vivian (Sedore) Little; m. Robert McFarlane Mann, July 10, 1971 (Apr. 1986). BA in English and French, Potsdam Coll., 1971; MA in Humanities, Manhattanville Coll., 1975; MS in Counseling, U. Bridgeport, 1980. Cert. tchr., N.Y. Tchr. various schs., N.Y., 1971-82; coll. adminstrn. intern Marymount Coll., Tarrytown, N.Y., 1977; computer operator IBM, White Plains, N.Y., 1982-85; sr. communications specialist IBM, Buffalo, 1985-86; tchr. Iroquois Sch. Dist., Elma, N.Y., 1986, Lancaster (N.Y.) Schs., 1986-87; guidance counselor Ken-Ton Schs., Kenmore, N.Y., 1987; computer operator info. services Millard Fillmore Hosp., 1988—. Mem. Am. Soc. Tng. and Devel. Democrat. Roman Catholic. Home: 15 Muskingum St Depew NY 14043

LITTLE, KATHRYN MARY, non-profit management and development officer; b. Dallas, Dec. 9, 1954; d. George B. Jr. and Shirley J. (Hawton) L. Student, Converse Coll., 1973-75; BS in Edn., U. Ga., 1977. Ind. polit. cons. various Rep. campaigns Mo., Tex., Washington, N.Mex., Ariz., 1977-79; exec. dir. polit. action com. Tex. Med. Assn., Austin, 1979-80; polit. cons. Reagan-Bush campaign, numerous local elections, Austin, 1980-81; dir. devel., asst. v.p. U.S. C. of C. (Nat. Chamber Found.), Washington, 1981-84; fundraising and mgmt. cons. Washington, 1985-87; dir. devel. Roosevelt Ctr. for Am. Policy Studies, Washington, 1987—; coordinator Tex. Inaugural com., 1970-80; dir. speakers bur. and voter edn. Mo. Freedom to Work com., 1977-78; dir. Citizen's Trust of Citizen's Choice, 1982-84; mem. U.S. C. of C. Pub. Affairs Council, 1979-80. Author articles and manuals on nonprofit mgmt. and fundraising. Bd. dirs., chmn. resources devel. com. Social Ctr. for Psychiat. Rehab., 1987-88; advisor Mercy Med. Airlift Found., Inc., 1987-88, Presdl. Yacht Trust, 1984-88; past mem. Commonwealth Rep. Women's Club. Named one of Outstanding Young Women of Am., 1981. Mem. Nat. Assn. Female Execs., Tex. State Soc., Nat. Soc. Fundraising Execs., AAUW, Am. Assn. Polit. Cons. Presbyterian. Office: Roosevelt Ctr for Am Policy Studies 316 Pennsylvania Ave SE Suite 500 Washington DC 20003

LITTLE, LINDA VIVIAN, nurse; b. Syracuse, N.Y., Apr. 28, 1949; d. Howard Joseph and Alice Evelyn (Wicks) L. Diploma, Crouse Irving Sch. Nursing, 1972; BS in Health Care, East Tex. State U., 1981, MS in Psychology, 1985; postgrad., U. Okla., 1985—. RN, Tex. Staff nurse Oneida (N.Y.) City Hosp., 1972-73; staff nurse, head nurse Rome (N.Y.) Devel. Ctr., 1973-76; staff nurse Southwestern Dialysis Ctr., Dallas, 1976-77; nurse III Terrell (Tex.) State Hosp., 1977-80; charge nurse Children's Med. Ctr., Dallas, 1980-84; team leader Timberlawn Psychiat. Hosp., Dallas, 1981-82; staff, charge nurse McCuistian Regional Med. Ctr., Paris, Tex., 1983; charge nurse, supr. Sam Rayburn VA Ctr., Bonham, Tex., 1983-87; nurse neonatal intensive care unit Gorgas Army Hosp., Panama, 1987—; Ombudsman Texoma Regional Ctr. on Aging, Sherman, Tex., 1986-89. Sponsored child Maria Delfina Guzman, Mex. Mem. Am. Assn. Critical Care Nurses, Nat. Assn. Female Execs., Bus. and Profl. Women, Smithsonian Assocs. Home: PSC Box 282 APO Miami FL 34002

LITTLE, PAULA LYNNE, corporate administrator; b. Holton, Buckinghamshire, Eng., Nov. 28, 1961; d. John Alfred and Kay (Liston) Little; m. Jeff Paul Nedderman, July 21, 1982 (div.). Sec. Birkart Transport Ltd., London, 1977-78; mgr. copy bur. Rank Xerox, London, 1978-80; recruiting officer Prime Appointments, London, 1980-81; rep. account support Wordplex Ltd., London, 1981-82; rep. systems support NBI Inc., Houston, 1983-86, engr. regional systems, 1986-87, mgr. product mktg., 1987—. Roman Catholic. Office: NBI Inc 3451 Mitchell Ln PO Box 9001 Boulder CO 80301

LITTLE, SALLY ANN, engineer; b. Zanesville, Ohio, Aug. 23, 1953; d. Paul E. and Sue M. (Stanchina) L.; D. Vaughan Warner, Aug. 23, 1986. AS in Engring., Cleveland (Tenn.) State Community Coll., 1974; BS in Engring. Sci., U. Tenn., 1977; BA in Psychology, U. Ala., 1983; MPA, Harvard U. Coop. engring. NASA Marshall Space Flight Ctr., Huntsville, Ala., 1975-77, profl. intern., 1978-81, engr. physicist, 1981-87, exec. asst. to dir., 1987-88, tech. mgr., 1988—; engr. flight experiments NASA. Contbr. articles and papers to profl. jours.; speaker in field, 1978—. Mem. Psi Chi, Pi Tau Sigma, Phi Kappa Phi, Tau Beta Pi. Office: Marshall Space Flight Ctr NASA code SA45 Huntsville AL 35812

LITTLE, SHERRY BURGUS, writing educator; b. Osceola, Iowa, July 31, 1937; d. Harold Corbin and Frances Elouise (Dodd) Burgus; m. Richard Lee Little, Sept. 1, 1956; children: David, Benjamin, Megan, Spenser. BA, Ariz. State U., 1959, MA, 1962, PhD, 1971. Instr. Tempe (Ariz.) Union High Sch., 1959-62, Mesa (Ariz.) Community Coll., 1962-64; lectr. Calif. State U., Chico, 1964-68, Fresno, 1968-71; instr. Cen. Ariz. State U., Coolidge, 1971-73; lectr. San Diego State U., 1978-83, asst. prof., 1983—; cons. in field. Co-Author: Technical Mathematics, 1976, Basic Book of Metalworking, 1979; Editor: Welding and Welding Technology, 1973, Metalworking Technology, 1977, Diesel Mechanics, 1982, Mitchell Automechanics, 1986; contbr. numerous articles to profl. jours.; peer reviewer IEEE Transactions in Professional Communication jour., 1986—; book reviewer Wadsworth Pub. Co., 1981. Vice chmn. planning adv. council of San Diego Regional Employment and Tng. Consortium, 1978-83. Mem. Soc. for Tech. Communication (sr.) (v.p. San Diego chpt. 1982-84), Nat. Council Tchrs. English, Conf. on Coll. Composition and Communication, MLA, Calif. Assn. Faculty in Tech. and Profl. Writing (exec. com. 1982-86), Assn. Tchrs. Tech. Writing (bibliography com.), Am. Bus. Communication Assn., Rhetoric Soc. Am., Council for Programs in Tech. and Sci. Communication, Calif. Assn. Tchrs. English, Profl. Communication Soc. of IEEE, Rocky Mountain MLA, Pacific Philol. Assn. Home: 2482 Valley Mill Rd El Cajon CA 92020 Office: San Diego State U Dept English and Comparative Lit San Diego CA 92182-0295

LITTLEDALE, FREYA LOTA BROWN, writer, editor; b. N.Y.C., d. David Milton and Dorothy (Passloff) Brown; B.S., Ithaca Coll., 1951; postgrad. N.Y. U., 1952; 1 son, Glenn David. Tchr. English, Public Schs. Willsboro (N.Y.), 1952-53; editor South Shore Record, L.I., N.Y., 1953-55; asso. editor Maco Mag. Corp., N.Y.C., 1960-61, Rutledge Books and Ridge Press, N.Y.C., 1961-62; juvenile book editor Parents' Mag. Press, N.Y.C., 1962-65; free-lance writer-editor, 1965—; writer Silver Burdett div. Time-Life Corp., 1965; editor, anthologist Arrow Book Club div. Scholastic Book Services; adj. prof. Fairfield U., 1984, 86, 87, 88. Author: The Magic Fish, 1967; (with Harold Littledale) Timothy's Forest, 1969; King Fox and Other Old Tales, 1971; The Magic Tablecloth, The Magic Goat, and The Hitting Stick, 1972; The Boy Who Cried Wolf, 1975; The Elves and the Shoemaker, 1975; Seven at One Blow, 1976; The Snow Child, 1978; The Magic Plum Tree, 1981, The Farmer in the Soup, 1987, Peter and the North Wind; editor: A Treasure Chest of Poetry, 1964; Fairy Tales by Hans Christian Andersen, 1964; Aesop's Fables, 1964; Grimm's Fairy Tales, 1964; 13 Ghostly Tales, 1966; Ghosts and Spirits of Many Lands, 1970; Ghosts, Witches, and Demons, 1971; Strange Tales from Many Lands, 1975; (poetry) I Was Thinking, 1979; (plays) The King and Queen Who Wouldn't Speak, 1975; Stop That Pancake, 1975; The Giant's Garden, 1975; The Magic Piper, 1978; adapter: Pinnochio, 1979; Snow White and the Seven Dwarfs, 1981; The Wizard of Oz, 1982; Frankenstein, 1983; The Sleeping Beauty, 1984; The Little Mermaid, 1986; contbr. to Scribner's Anthology for Young People, 1976; A New Treasury of Children's Poetry, 1984. Mem. Soc. Children's Book Writers, Authors Guild, PEN. Office: care Curtis Brown Ltd 10 Astor Pl New York NY 10003

LITTLEFIELD, VIVIAN M., nursing educator, administrator; b. Princeton, Ky., Jan. 24, 1938; d. Willard Anson and Hester V. (Haydon) Moore; children—Darrell, Virginia. B.S. magna cum laude, Tex. Christian U., 1960; M.S., U. Colo., 1964; Ph.D., U. Denver, 1979. Staff nurse USPHS Hosp., Ft. Worth, Tex., 1960-61; instr. nursing Tex. Christian U., Ft. Worth, 1961-62; nursing supr. Colo. Gen. Hosp., Denver, 1964-65, pvt. patient practitioner, 1974-78; asst. prof. nursing U. Colo., Denver, 1965-69, asst. prof., clin. instr., 1971-74, asst. prof., 1974-76, acting asst. dean, assoc. prof. continuing edn., regional perinatal project, 1976-78; assoc. prof., chair dept. women's health care nursing U. Rochester Sch. Nursing, N.Y., 1979-84; clin. chief ob-gyn., nursing U. Rochester Strong Meml. Hosp., N.Y., 1979-84; prof., dean U. Wis. Sch. Nursing, Madison, 1984—; cons. and lectr. in field. Author: Maternity Nursing Today, 1973, 76; Health Education for Women: A guide for Nurses and Other Health Professionals, 1986. Contbr. articles to profl. jours. Bur. Health Professions Fed. trainee, 1963-64; Nat. Sci. Service award, 1976-79. Mem. Am. Nurses Assn., Health Care for Women Internat. (editorial bd. 1984—), Midwest Nursing Research Soc., Sigma Theta Tau (v.p.). Avocations: golf; tennis. Office: Univ of Wis Sch Nursing 600 Highland Ave H6/150 Madison WI 53792

LITTLEJOHN, GRACE MCMULLEN, information specialist, educator; b. Salisbury, N.C., Sept. 13, 1917; d. Clanton Eugene and Alice (Ellis) Henderson; m. Richard Franklin McMullen (dec. 1964); 1 child, Alice LaFrieta; m. James Edward Littlejohn (dec. 1973). BS, Livingstone Coll., 1938; MLS, N.C. Coll., 1956. Tchr. math. Catawba (N.C.) Bd. Edn., 1942-43, Iredell County Bd. Edn., Statesville, N.C., 1944-50; librarian Currituck (N.C.) County Bd. Edn., 1953-55, Orange County Bd. Edn., Hillsboro, N.C., 1955-59; tchr. math. D.C. Bd. Edn., 1959-66, librarian, 1966—. Chairperson jour. Thirty-ninth Boulé, 1982. V.p. South Manor Civic Assn., Washington, 1987—, pres., 1985-87; bd. dirs. Phyllis Wheatley YWCA, Washington, 1985—. Mem. Nat. Assn. U. Women (v.p., Outstanding Woman Yr. D.C. chpt. 1978), Nat. Council Negro Women (life, pres. Bethune chpt.), D.C. Assn. Sch. Librarians (pres. 1974-77, archivist 1977-87), Phi Delta Kappa, Zeta Tau Sigma, Sigma Gamma Rho (charter). Home: 41 Kennedy St NE Washington DC 20011

LITTMAN, LYNNE, film director; b. N.Y.C., June 26, 1941; d. Carl and Yetta (Abler) L.; m. Taylor Hackford, May 7, 1977; 1 child, Alexander Littman; 1 stepson Rio Hackford. B.A., Sarah Lawrence Coll., 1962; student The Sorbonne, Paris, 1960-61. Researcher for CBS News, 1965; assoc. producer Nat. Ednl. TV, 1966-69; dir. NIMH film series on drug abuse UCLA Media Center, 1970; producer, dir. documentary films, news and pub. affairs series KCET Community TV So. Calif., 1971-77; dir. WNET Ind. Filmmakers Series, 1979; co-producer, dir. TV spl. Rick Nelson, It's All Right Now, 1978, (documentary) In Her Own Time, 1985; films include: Till Death Do Us Part (CPB award), 1976, In The Matter of Kenneth (Los Angeles Emmy award), 1974, Wanted: Operadoras (Los Angeles Emmy award), 1974, Women in Waiting, 1975; dir. film Testament, 1983, short films, Number Our Days (1977 Academy award, best short documentary), Once a Daughter, 1979, Running My Way, (1982 Cine Golden Eagle award). Recipient numerous awards including Los Angeles Press Club award, 1977, San Francisco Internat. Film Festival award, 1977, Corp. for Public Broadcasting award, 1977, Los Angeles Emmy award, 1972, 73, 74, 77; Columbia/Dupont Journalism award, 1977; Ford Found. grantee, 1978. Mem. Dirs. Guild Am. Address: 6620 Cahuenga Terr Los Angeles CA 90068 *

LITWACK, ARLENE DEBRA, psychotherapist, psychoanalyst, consultant, educator; b. Brookline, Mass., July 18, 1945; d. Hyman and Bessie Litwack. B.A. cum laude, Boston U., 1967; M.S., Columbia U., 1969; postgrad. Ctr. for Mental Health, N.Y.C., 1981, Inst. for Psychoanalytic Tng. and Research, 1980—. Caseworker, Pride Treatment Ctr., Douglaston, N.Y., 1969-73, supr., 1973-78, sr. worker, 1978-80; pvt. practice psychotherapy and psychoanalyst, N.Y.C., 1980—; mem. faculty Inst. for Mental Health Edn., Englewood, N.J., 1983—; dir. child therapy dept. L.I. Consultation Ctr., Rego Park, N.Y., 1980-85; faculty workshop leader Human Services Workshops, N.Y.C.; adj. faculty Columbia U., 1977—. Contbr. articles to profl. jours. Mem. Psychoanalytic Study Ctr. Home: 115 4th Ave Apt 3E New York NY 10003

LITWOK, EVELYN, psychologist, financial consultant; b. N.Y.C., July 30, 1951; d. Zygmunt and Genia (Kohn) L.; B.A. in Psychology, U. Buffalo, 1969; M.A. in Psychology (research fellow 1973-75), Temple U., 1975. Dir. Child Devel. Research Lab., Temple U., Phila., 1973-75; dir. evaluation and research W. Phila. Community Mental Health Ctr., 1975-78; co-dir. Women's Resources, Inc., Phila., 1978-84; exec. dir. Women's Resources Distbn. Co., 1981-84; corp. fin. cons. Merrill Lynch Pierce Fenner & Smith, Inc., 1984-87; v.p., fin. cons. Shearson Lehman Bros., 1984—; cons. in mgmt., fiscal planning, comprehensive fund-raising. Named one of the women to watch in '82, Phila. Mag. Mem. Am. Psychol. Assn., Assn. Women in Psychology. Jewish. Contbr. articles to profl. publs. Home: 690 Greenwich St Apt 5C New York NY 10014

LIU, KATHERINE CHANG, artist, art educator; b. Kiang-si, Peoples Republic of China; came to U.S., 1963; d. Ming-fan and Ying (Yuan) Chang; m. Yet-zen Liu; children: Alan S., Laura Y. MS, U. Calif., Berkeley, 1965. lectr. N.J. Watercolor Soc., Pitts. Watercolor Soc., Oreg. Watercolor Soc., Tex. Watercolor Soc., Ohio Watercolor Soc., Ariz. Watercolor Assn., Rocky Mountain Watercolor Workshop, U. Va. extension, Longwood. Coll., Va. One-man shows include Harrison Mus., Utah State U., Riverside (Calif.) Art Mus., Ventura (Calif.) Coll., Roanoke (Va.) Mus. Fine Arts, Fla. A&M U., Louis Newman Galleries, Los Angeles, Lung-Men Gallery, Taipei, Republic of China; sole juror Watercolor State Open Competitions, N.J., Oreg., Pa. 1988; Western Fedn. Exhibition, Houston, 1986, San Diego Internat. Watercolor Exhbn., 1986, Ohio Watercolor Soc., 1986. Recipient Rex Brandt award San Diego Watercolor Internat., 1985, Purchase Selection award Watercolor USA and Springfield (Mo.) Art Mus., 1981, Gold Medal and Mary Lou Fitzgerald Meml. awards Allied Arts Am. Nat. Arts Club, N.Y.C., 1987; NEA grantee, 1979-80. Mem. Nat. Watercolor Soc. (life, chmn. jury 1985, pres. 1983, Top award 1984, cash awards 1979, 87.), Watercolor USA Honor Soc., Nat. Soc. Painters in Case in and Acrylic (2d award 1985), Rocky Mountain Nat. Watermedia Soc. (juror 1984, awardee 1978, 80, 86), West Coast Watercolor Soc.

LIVENGOOD, CANDICE CROCKER, law librarian, genealogist; b. Pitts., Dec. 8, 1946; d. Darwin William and Marian Ida (Rearick) Crocker; m. John Robert Livengood, Aug. 19, 1967; children: Bryan Patrick, Kelly Lynn, John Travis, Justin William. BA in Psychology and Sociology, Grove City Coll., 1968; MLS, U. Pitts., 1987. Dept. mgr. Joseph Horne Co., Natrona Heights, Pa., 1968-69; law librarian Butler County, Pa., 1987—; profl. genealogist, Sarver, Pa., 1976—; free-lance pub. speaker, Pa., 1980—. Compiler: Abstracts from the Kittanning Gazette, 1985, (registry) Family Bible Registry, 1985—. Treas. ABC Gymworks, Natrona Heights, 1980-82, Freeport (Pa.) Area Swim and Dive Team, 1982-84. Mem. DAR, Pa. Sch. Librarians Assn., Western Pa. Geneal. Soc. (rec. sec. 1987—, corr. sec. 1986-87, editor newsletter Brit. interest group 1987—), Devon Family History Soc., Palatines to Am., Cornwall Family History Soc., Western Pa. Law Librarians Assn., Am. Assn. Law Librarians, Butler Area Librarians Assn., Indiana County Hist. and Geneal. Soc., Beta Phi Mu. Republican. Presbyterian. Home: 106 Scenic View Dr Sarver PA 16055 Office: Butler County Law Library Court House Butler PA 16001

LIVERANT, ROBERTA LOIS, small business owner; b. Norwich, Conn., May 2, 1934; d. Robert Henry and Pauline Pearl (Rader) Russell; m. Philip Liverant, Aug. 10, 1963 (div. Aug. 1983); 1 child, Robyn Cindy. Student, Mitchell Coll., 1952-53, U. Conn., 1953-54. Sec. NBC, Chgo.; exec. sec. NBC, N.Y.C., 1959; exec. sec., office mgr. Sta. WPOP, Hartford, Conn., 1959-63; mgr. radio traffic dept. Sta. WTIC, Hartford, 1963-83; instr., owner Oriental and Persian Rug, Hartford, 1983—. Vol. Rep. campaigns; pres., Sisterhood; youth group advisor, sec., bd. trustees Temple Sinai, Newington. Mem. Nat. Assn. Female Execs., Glastonbury Art Guild. Jewish. Home and Office: 42 Cider Mill Rd Glastonbury CT 06033

LIVINGSTON, MARGARET MORROW GRESHAM, civic leader; b. Birmingham, Ala., Aug. 16, 1924; d. Owen Garside and Katherine Molton (Morrow) Gresham; grad. The Baldwin Sch., Phila., 1942; A.B., Vassar Coll., 1945; M.A., U. Ala., 1946; m. James Archibald Livingston, Jr., July 16, 1947; children—Mary Margaret, James Archibald, Katherine Wiley, Elizabeth Gresham. Tutor in math., 1949-55; judge arts and crafts shows, founder edn. program Birmingham Mus. Art, 1962, acting dir., 1978-79, 81, chmn. bd. dirs., 1978-86, sec. bd. dirs. 1978-86, co-editor bulletin, 1970-75, chmn. bd. Birmingham Mus. Art Edn. Council, 1968-70; bd. dirs., past pres. Children's Aid Soc., 1959-81 ; mem. Birmingham Civic Center Authority, 1970-87, bd. dirs. 1987; bd. dirs. U. Ala. Art Gallery, Birmingham, 1978—; bd. dirs. Altamont Sch., Birmingham, 1959—, chmn. bd. 1986. Named Woman of Yr., Birmingham, 1986. Mem. Am. Assn. Mus. (trustees com., edn. com., public relations com.), Internat. Com. of Mus. (edn. com. 1981—). Episcopalian. Clubs: Jr. League, English Speaking Union, Colonial Dames of Commonwealth of Va., Linly Heflin Unit, Ala. State Tennis Assn. Home: 12 Country Club Rd Birmingham AL 35213

LIVINGSTON, MARION GASKILL, civic worker; b. Phila., June 28, 1924; d. Joseph Franklin and Marion Elizabeth (Cook) Gaskill; m. N.B. Livingston, Jr., Jan. 9, 1946; children—John M., Peter G., William. C. Mem. Franklin County Bd. Elections, 1982—. Mem. Franklin County Republican Exec. Com.; del. Rep. Nat. Conv., 1984; committeeman Upper Arlington Ward 6; mem. women's bd. March of Dimes; trustee Martha Kinney Cooper Ohioana Library, Community Shelter Bd.; mem. County Bd. Visitors; mem. Mayor's Adv. Council on Voluntary Service. Mem. Navy League U.S. (dir. Columbus council), Republican.

LIVINGSTON, MOLLIE P., designer; b. N.Y.C.; d. Abraham and Sarah Parnis; m. Leon Jay Livingston; 1 child, Robert Lewis. Sec.-treas. Parnis Livingston Inc.; pres. Mollie Parnis Co., Mollie Parnis Boutique, Mollie Parnis at Home. Designer cadet nurses uniforms. Founder, Dress Up Your Neighborhood awards, Jerusalem, 1967—, N.Y.C., 1972—; founder Livingston Awards for Young Journalists, 1980—; founder Mollie Parnis Sch. Program for Keeping Surroundings Clean, 1975—; overseer Parsons Sch. Design, 1983—. Named Woman of Yr., Einstein Coll. Medicine, 1985—. Home: 812 Park Ave New York NY 10021 Office: 135 Madison Ave New York NY 10016

LIVINGSTON, MYRA COHN, poet, writer, educator; b. Omaha, Nebr., Aug. 17, 1926; d. Mayer L. and Gertrude (Marks) Cohn; m. Richard Roland Livingston, Apr. 14, 1952; children: Joshua, Jonas Cohn, Jennie Marks. B.A., Sarah Lawrence Coll., 1948. Profl. horn player 1941-48; book reviewer Los Angeles Daily News, 1948-49, Los Angeles Mirror, 1949-50; asst. editor Campus Mag., 1949-50; various public relations positions and pvt. sec. to Hollywood (Calif.) personalities 1950-52; tchr. creative writing Dallas (Tex.) public library and schs., 1958-63; poet-in-residence Beverly Hills (Calif.) Unified Sch. Dist., 1966-84; sr. instr. UCLA Extension, 1973—; cons. to various sch. dists., 1966-84, cons. poetry to publishers children's lit., 1975—. Author: Whispers and Other Poems, 1958, Wide Awake and Other Poems, 1959, I'm Hiding, 1961, See What I Found, 1962, I Talk to Elephants, 1962, I'm Not Me, 1963, Happy Birthday, 1964, The Moon and a Star and Other Poems, 1965, I'm Waiting, 1966, Old Mrs. Twindlytart and Other Rhymes, 1967, A Crazy Flight and Other Poems, 1968, The Malibu and Other Poems, 1972, When You Are Alone/It Keeps You Capone: An Approach to Creative Writing with Children, 1973, Come Away, 1974, The Way Things Are and Other Poems, 1974, 4-Way Stop and Other Poems, 1976, A Lollygag of Limericks, 1978, O Sliver of Liver and Other Poems, 1979, No Way of Knowing: Dallas Poems, 1980, A Circle of Seasons, 1982, How Pleasant to Know Mr. Lear!, 1982, Sky Songs, 1984, A Song I Sang to You, 1984, Monkey Puzzle, 1984, The Child as Poet: Myth or Reality?, 1984, Celebrations, 1985, Worlds I Know and Other Poems, 1985, Sea Songs, 1986, Earth Songs, 1986, 1987, Higgledy-Piggledy, 1986, Space Songs, 1988, others; co-editor: The Scott-Foresman Anthology, 1984; Author: The Writing of Poetry; film strips; editor 21 anthologies of poetry; contbr. articles on children's lit. to ednl. publs., contbr., essays on lit. and reading in edn. to various books. Officer Beverly Hills PTA Council, 1966-75; pres. Friends of Beverly Hills Public Library, 1979-81; bd. dirs. Poetry Therapy Inst., 1975—, Reading is Fundamental of So. Calif., 1981—. Recipient Honor award N.Y. Herald Tribune Spring Book Festival, 1958, Excellence in Poetry award Nat. Council Tchrs. of English, 1980, Commonwealth Club award, 1984, Nat. Jewish Book award, 1987. Mem. Authors Guild, Internat. Reading Assn., Soc. Children's Book Writers (honor award 1975), Tex. Inst. Letters (awards 1961, 80), So. Calif. Council on Lit. for Children and Young People (Comprehensive Contribution award 1968, Notable Book award 1972), PEN. Address: 9308 Readcrest Dr Beverly Hills CA 90210

LIVINGSTON, PAMELA ANNA, corporate image consultant communications and marketing management consultant; b. Richmond Hill, N.Y., Nov. 21, 1930; d. Paul Yount and Anna Margaret (Altland) L.; B.A., Adelphi U., 1951; postgrad. NYU, 1952, Columbia U., 1959, Am. Acad. Dramatic Art, 1954, IBM Systems and Mktg. Schs., 1967-70, Brandon Sch. Electronic Data Processing, 1973. Personnel and public relations depts. Am. Can Co., N.Y.C., 1951-60; exec. sec. to pres. York (Pa.) div. Borg-Warner Corp., 1962-65; freelance writer, 1965-67; mktg. ofcl. IBM Corp., 1967-70; research analyst, dir. new EDP bus. Ins. Co. N. Am., 1971-74; asst. to v.p. corp. affairs IU Internt., Phila., 1974-75; communications and mktg. mgmt. cons. specializing in corp. identity, 1975—; corp. image cons., 1984—. Recipient various journalism awards, award in mktg. and sales IBM, 1969-70, award for innovative product application, 1969. Mem. Sales/Mktg. Execs. Internat., Art Alliance, Public Relations Soc. Am., Econs. Club of York C. of C., Phila. Club Advt. Women, AAUW, Phila. Acad. Fine Arts, World Affairs Council, English-Speaking Union, Kappa Kappa Gamma. Contbr. articles to tech. jours. Home and Office: 108 S Rockburn St York PA 17402-3467

LIVINGSTON, PATRICIA ANN, manufacturing company executive; b. Manila, July 30, 1934; d. Marion Michelin and Phoebe (Nelson) Karolchuck; m. Johnston R. Livingston, Sept. 4, 1965; adopted children: Henry, Ann, Jane, David. BA, Reed Coll., 1955. With Office Human Resources Research, George Washington U., 1955-58; asst. sec.-treas. Bus. Equipment Mfg. Assn., N.Y.C., 1958-60; fin. writer N.Y. Post, 1961-62, Chgo. Daily News, 1962-66; fin. columnist Dallas Morning News, 1966-71, also syndicated by Newsday, 1968-69; v.p. fin. Enmark Corp., Denver, 1971-86; pres. Constrn. Tech., Inc., 1986—, also bd. dirs. Trustee Colo. Women's Coll., 1979—, U. Denver, 1982—. Episcopalian. Club: Denver. Home: 869 Vine St Denver CO 80206 Office: 5070 Oakland St Denver CO 80239

LIVINGSTON-ROTH, MARY FRANCES, health services executive; b. Kansas City, Mo., Oct. 6, 1944; d. Carl Emanuel and Frances (Livingston) Roth; m. Kenneth Reeve Sly, Aug. 31, 1963 (div. 1970); children—Kenneth Reeve Jr., Cynthia Denise. Student Green Mountain Coll., 1962-63; nursing edn. Middlesex Meml. Hosp./Vinal Tech., Middletown, Conn., 1980-81. Lic. practical nurse, Conn. Staff nurse Middlesex Meml. Hosp., 1981-82, Talmadge Park Health, East Haven, Conn., 1982-86; founder, owner, pres. South Central Homemaker Agy., Inc., Guilford, Conn., 1983-87; founder, owner, pres. South Central Nursing Agy., Guilford, 1987—; founder, owner, pres. South Cen. Nursing Agy., Inc., Guilford, Conn., 1987—; supporter competitive employment Marrakech, New Haven, 1985—; developer bedmaking program, marketer, instr. Easter Seal Rehab. Ctr., New Haven, 1985—; mem. Guilford Community Mobilization Team; cons. Dept. Vocat. Rehab. New Haven, 1985—. Writer instructional manuals for nurse aid programs. Mem. Nat. Small Bus. Assn., Conn. Assn. Licensee Practical Nurses, Guilford C. of C., Nat. Assn. Female Execs., Ladies Aux. VFW, Am. Legion Aux. Republican. Roman Catholic. Avocations: walking, swimming, gardening, reading, traveling. Home: 137 Water St Guilford CT 06437 Office: South Central Nursing Agy Inc 10 Griswold on the Green Guilford CT 06451

LIVSEY, CONNIE FRANCES, marketing professional; b. Garland, Tex., Oct. 22, 1958; d. Watterson Eins Jr. and Dorthy Frances (Barber) Thigpen. BS in Advt., U. Tex., 1981. Sales rep. Scripps-Howard Bus. Jours., Houston, 1981-83; sales mgr. Scripps-Howard Bus. Jours., N.Y.C., 1983-85; acct. exec. Stillinger-Rapkin Assn., N.Y.C., 1985-86; advt. account mgr. Victoria Mag./Hearst, N.Y.C., 1986—. Assoc. chair NY Addy awards, N.Y. Advt. Club. Named one of Outstanding Young Women Am., 1987. Mem. Advt. Women N.Y. Office: Hearst Mags 1790 Broadway 11th Floor New York NY 10019

LIZOTTE, SHIRLEY GUICE, insurance sales agent, underwriter; b. Carpenter, Miss., Oct. 2, 1935; d. Malcolm Gilchrist and Emma Audrey (Linton) Guice; m. Charles Joel Lizotte, Oct. 8, 1961. Student U. Tex.-Arlington 1982-83. CLU Sec. First Nat. Bank, Jackson, Miss., 1954-61; office mgr., trainee, supr. MONY, Dallas, Ft. Worth, Jackson, 1961-84; adminstrv. asst. Thomas M. Dunning Ins., Dallas, 1984-85; ins. salesman Gen. Am., Ft. Worth, 1986-87, MONY, Ft. Worth, 1987—. Sec. bd. edn. Most Blessed Sacrament Ch., Arlington, Tex., 1985. Mem. Am. Soc. C.L.U., Nat. Assn. Female Execs., Beta Sigma Phi, Life Ins. Co. Office Mgrs. Assn.

(sec. 1982-84), Am. Bus. Women's Assn. (pres. 1961), DAR, First Families of Miss. Roman Catholic. Club: Altrusa PM (Arlington); CLU (Ft. Worth). Avocations: reading, knitting, travel. Home: 2015 Elmridge Dr Arlington TX 76012 Office: Mony Fort Worth TX

LIZUT, NONA MOORE PRICE, retired state health official; b. Quay, N.Mex., Aug. 8, 1923; d. Charley W. and Alba Moore; student N.Mex. State U., 1941-42; m. Charles P. Price, Jr., 1944; 1 son, Charles P. III; m. 2d, William J. Lizut, May 27, 1970. Sec., N.Mex. Health Dept., Santa Fe, 1942-44: sec. environ. div., 1951-68; adminstrv. sec. environ. div. N.Mex. Health and Social Services Dept., Santa Fe, 1968-74, adminstrv. asst. to dep. dir., 1974-78; adminstrv. asst. to dep. sec. N.Mex. Health and Environ. Dept., Santa Fe, 1978-82, adminstr. office of dir. health services div., 1982-84; owner, mgr. Secretarial Services, Santa Fe, 1984-87. Mem. N.Mex. Water Pollution Control Assn. (life, adminstrv. officer 1956-71), N.Mex. Public Health Assn. (sec.-treas. 1962-68, pres. elect 1969), Nat. Secs. Assn. (v.p., program chmn. rec. sec., corr. sec.), Santa Fe C. of C. (women's div.), Santa Fe Women's Club and Library Assn., 1987—, N.Mex. Round Dance Assn. (co-pres. 1981-82, newsletter editor 1979-82), Retired Pub. Employees of N.Mex. (bd. dirs.). Club: Capitol City Bus. and Profl. Women's (v.p., program chmn.). Home: 1408 Santa Rosa Dr Santa Fe NM 87501

LJUNG, GRETA MARIANNE, statistician, educator; b. Jakobstad, Finland; d. Paul Johannes and Ellen Alina L. M.S. in Psychology, Abo Acad., Turku, Finland, 1968; M.S. in Stats., U. Wis., 1972, Ph.D. in Stats., 1976. Instr. in stats. Abo Acad., 1967-69; research and teaching asst. U. Wis., Madison, 1970-74, research assoc. Math. Research Ctr., 1975-77; asst. prof. stats. U. Denver, 1977-79; asst. prof. quantitative methods Boston U. Sch. Mgmt., 1979-86; vis. assoc. prof. applied math. MIT, 1986—; cons. in field; presentations at nat. confs. Research, numerous articles, tech. revs. and reports in time series analysis and forecasting; assoc. editor Jour. Forecasting, Internat. Jour. Forecasting. Research grantee U. Uppsala (Sweden), 1968. Mem. Am. Statis. Assn., Inst. Math. Stats., Internat. Inst. Forecasters. Office: MIT Dept Math 2-332 Cambridge MA 02139

LLANEZA, ANN MARIE, marketing professional; b. N.Y.C., June 26, 1956; d. Raul and Caridad (Chavez) Pallet; divorced; children: Joan and Joseph (twins). BA in Psychology magna cum laude, Fairleigh Dickinson U., 1985; postgrad. in counseling psychology, Nova U. From sec. to v.p. Hudson County Vocat. Sch., 1974-76; adminstr. asst. Bergenline Med. Ctr., 1976-77; asst. to v.p. sales Union Labor Life Ins. Co., 1977-78; exec. asst. New Am. Library, N.Y.C., 1978-79; office mgr., research asst. Jerome E. Driesen, M.D., N.Y.C., 1982-85; dir. mktg. adminstrn. Internat. Med. Ctrs., Inc. (now Humana Med. Plans), Miami, Fla., 1985—; pub. relations coordinator Park Theatre Musical Theatre Assn., Union City, N.J., 1984; mktg. cons., bd. dirs. New Theatre, Inc., Coral Gables, Fla., 1986—. Author, editor corp. newsletter, 1986. Mem. Nat. Assn. Female Execs., Phi Zeta Kappa, Phi Omega Epsilon. Home: 11905 NE 2d Ave C201 North Miami FL 33161 Office: Humana Med Plans 1505 NW 167th St Suite 410 Miami FL 33169

LLEWELLYN, BETTY HALFF, archivist; b. Midland, Tex., June 12, 1911; d. Henry Mayer and Rose (Wechsler) Barnet; m. Martin Zinn, Jr., Nov. 12, 1935 (div. 1947); children: Martin III, Henry Harold, Mary Elizabeth Zinn Stewart; m. 2d, George W. Llewellyn, Nov. 9, 1948 (div. 1966). B.A., So. Meth. U., 1934; grad. Gemological Inst. Am., Santa Monica, Calif., 1968. Dir., New Theater, Dallas, 1936-40; exec. dir. McCord Theater Collection, Dallas, 1968—; ptnr. Halff Interests, Dallas, 1934—; pub. Walnut Hill Pub., Dallas, 1983—; contbr. to numerous schs. and museums, 1978—. Author: (with A.C. Greene) I Can't Forget, 1984. Officer, Lake Charles (La.) LWV, 1946-47; bd. dirs. Lake Charles ARC, 1941-45. Recipient James Smithson Bronze medal Smithsonian Instn., 1978, James Smithson Silver medal, 1980. Mem. So. Meth. U. Alumni Assn., Circus Fans Am., Circus Hist. Assn., Clowns of Am., Mineral. Assn. Dallas, Lone Star Showmans Club, James Smithson Soc., Dallas Gem and Mineral Soc., B'nai B'rith Women, Zeta Phi Eta. Jewish. Club: Pleasant Oaks Gem & Mineral (Tex.).

LLOYD, ARLEEN MARTIN, business educator, account executive, marketing consultant; b. N.Y.C., May 18, 1957; d. David Paul and Ligia (Zeledon-Masis) L.; m. Leonardo Napoles. A.A., Miami Dade Community Coll., 1976; B.B.A., Fla. Internat. U., 1979, M.A. in Internat. Bus., 1983. Cert. tchr., Fla. Sales mgr. Jordan Marsh, Miami, Fla., 1979-80, asst. dir. selling services, 1980-81, asst. buyer, 1981-82; tchr. Miami Springs Sr. High Sch. (Fla.), 1981—; v.p. sales Expediter, Inc., Miami, 1983; bus. instr. Internat. Fine Arts Coll., Miami 1983—; pvt. practice mktg. cons., Miami, 1983-84; account exec. Avanti, Miami, 1984-86; dir. mktg. Paul Mitchell Systems, 1986—. Recipient fund raising award United Way Dade County, 1979. Mem. Dade County Tchrs. Assn., Nat. Assn. Female Execs., Bus. and Profl. Womens Assn., Nat. Assn. Women Bus. Owners, Internat. Platform Assn., Delta Epsilon Chi (advisor 1983). Republican. Roman Catholic. Home and Office: 73 Ludlum Dr Miami Springs FL 33166

LLOYD, CAMILLE, clinical psychologist; b. Albuquerque, June 8, 1951; d. David I. and Cherril (Snow) L. BS summa cum laude, Brigham Young U., 1973; MA, U. Ariz., 1974, PhD, 1977. Lic. psychologist, Tex. Clin. psychology intern U. Wis. Med. Sch., Madison, 1976-77; asst. prof. psychiatry and behavioral scis. U. Tex. Med. Sch., Houston, 1977-83, assoc. prof. clin. psychiatry, behavioral scis., 1983—; dir. student counseling service U. Tex. Health Sci. Ctr., Houston, 1981—, mem. com. for the protection of human subjects, student services com., 1981—, chair com. on status of women, 1983-85; cons. Tex. Internat. Airlines, Houston, 1979; adj. asst. prof. psychology U. Houston; bd. dirs., v.p. Inst. for Research on Women's Health; lectr. in field. Reviewer Archives of Gen. Psychiatry, 1980—, Jour. Abnormal Psychology, 1981—, Jour. of Nervous and Mental Disease, 1983—; contbr. articles to profl. jours. NIMH fellow, 1973-75. Mem. Am. Psychol. Assn. (gen. psychology, psychotherapy divs.), Mental Health Assn. Houston, Mental Health Assn. Houston and Harris County (pub. affairs com.), Phi Kappa Phi, Phi Beta Kappa, Sigma Xi. Home: 7575 Cambridge #1802 Houston TX 77054 Office: U Tex Health Sci Ctr 1100 Holcombe Blvd 16 168 Houston TX 77054

LLOYD, ELIZABETH JEANINE, insurance rehabilitation specialist; b. Terre Haute, Ind., Sept. 17, 1936; d. Raymond Eugene Vaughn and Evelyn Huston (Neel) O'Dell; m. John Edward Mullen, Dec. 5, 1959 (dec. June 1960); 1 child, Shawna Marie; m. Harold Chester Lloyd, Sept. 4, 1964; 1 child, Jeffrey Roger. Cert. nurse, Leominster (Mass.) Hosp., 1958; BS in Health Studies, Anna Maria Coll., 1978; MA in Rehab. Counseling, Assumption Coll., 1980; MS in Nursing, Anne Maria Coll., 1986. RN, cert. ins. rehab. specialist. Pediatric staff nurse Worcester (Mass.) City Hosp., 1958-59; camp nurse Boy Scouts Am., ME, N.H., 1960-62; med., surg. staff and head nurse Clinton (Mass.) Hosp., 1960-70; pub. health nurse Clinton Health Dept., 1965-66; pvt. duty nurse various hosps., Central, Mass., 1970-71; head nurse Quaboag Nursing Home, West Brookfield, Mass., 1971-73; indsl. nurse William E. Wright Com., West Warren, Mass., 1973-74; rehab. coordinator Travelers Ins. Co., Worcester, Mass., 1974—; speaker various colls., med. programs, Mass., 1980-85, Gov.'s Council Mass. Rehab. Com., Boxboro, 1983; coordinator Workers Compensation Job Fair, Worcester, 1982. Author: Rehabilitation: Nursing Management Model, 1986. Mem. Lake Lashaway Assn., North Brookfield, Mass., 1987. Mem. Insurance Rehab. (coordinator nurses 1978—, continuing edn. coordinator 1978—), Nat. Rehab. Assn., Occupational Heatlh Nurses Assn. (program developer 1973-75), Nat. Exec. Female Assn., Assumption Coll. Alumni Assn., Anna Maria Coll. Alumni Assn., Leominster Hosp. Alumni Assn. Congregationalist. Clubs: Worcester Mineral; Southeast Fedn. Home: 30 Silvania Grove North Brookfield MA 01535 Office: Travelers Ins Co 120 Front St Worcester MA 01608

LLOYD, HORTENSE COLLINS, English language educator; b. Houston; d. Jephtha D. and Sallie (Shepherd) Collins; m. Raymond G. Lloyd, Sept. 18, 1943; 1 child, Jacqueline Michele. AB, Prairie View Coll., 1942; MA, Columbia U., 1946. English tchr. Pub. Sch. #42, N.Y.C., 1944-46; instr. English Wiley Coll., Marshall, Tex., 1947, Agrl. and Tech. Coll., Greensboro, N.C., 1947-48, Orangeburg (S.C.) State Coll., 1951-52; English tchr. Alfred Beach High Sch., Savannah, Ga., 1953-58; asst. prof. Tenn. State U., Nashville, 1958-72; asst. prof. Edward Waters Coll., Jacksonville, Fla., 1972-77, prof., dir. honors program, 1977—; field-tested essays for Ednl. Testing Service, Princeton, N.J. Book rev. editor Negro Ednl. Review, 1950—. Pres. Clara White Mission, Jacksonville, 1986—; bd. dirs. Northeast Fla. Camp Fire Girls. Named a Disting. Faculty Mem. Edward Waters Coll., 1988; Danforth fellow, 1970. Mem. AAUW, Nat. Council Tchrs. English, Conf. of College Composition and Communication, Alpha Kappa Alpha. Presbyterian. Home: 5006 Andrew Robinson Dr Jacksonville FL 32209 Office: Edward Waters Coll PO Box 73 1658 Kings Rd Jacksonville FL 32209

LLOYD, JILL, public relations and advertising executive; b. Los Angeles, Oct. 11, 1956; d. A. Thomas and Gloria Irma (Striplin) L.; m. Timothy Steven Bowers, July 8, 1978 (Sept. 1984); 1 child, Steven. B.S. in Communication Arts, Calif. Poly. State U.-Pomona, 1978. Asst. pub. relations dir. Orange County Fair, Costa Mesa, Calif., 1975—, media and pub. relations dir., 1984—; v.p. pub. relations specializing in campaigns for fairs and festivals Profl. Media Services, Del Mar, Calif., 1984-87; mem. adv. com. awards Internat. Assn. Fairs and Expositions, 1984—. Vol. Hospice-Orange County; mem. adv. bd. Fullerton Sch. Dist. Vocat. Agr. Bd., Calif.; leader 4-H, Fullerton, 1975-80, 83-84. Mem. Women in Communications (Clarion award 1986), Internat. Assn. Fairs and Expos (service mem., Best Pub. Relations program award 1979, 1st place awards 1984, 85, 86, 87, 88), Western Fairs Assn. (Merrill award 1986), Nat. Assn. Female Execs. Clubs: Press of So. Calif., Orange County Press. Avocations: photography; tennis; travel. Home: 165 Cornell Irvine CA 92715

LLOYD, KATE RAND, magazine editor; b. Mpls., Dec. 25, 1923; d. Rufus Randall and Helen Starkweather (Chase) Rand; m. John Davis Lloyd, Feb. 25, 1950; children—Kate Angeline Lloyd Traverse, Ann Elizabeth Lloyd Ingrasci, John Rand. B.A. cum laude, Bryn Mawr Coll., 1945. Mem. staff, feature writer Vogue Mag., N.Y.C., 1945-54, sr. feature editor, 1963-74, mng. editor, 1974-77; mng. editor Glamour Mag., N.Y.C., 1974-77; editor-in-chief Working Woman Mag. div. HAL Publs., N.Y.C., 1977-83, editor-at-large, 1983—, also mem. speaker's bur.; adj. lectr. Columbia U. Sch. Journalism, N.Y.C., 1975—, NYU Sch. Continuing Edn., 1982-83. Editor: Glamour Magazine Party Book, 1965, Vogue Beauty and Health Guide, 1975, 76; editorial supr.: Vogue's Book of Etiquette, rev. edit., 1969. Commr. Nat. Commn. on Working Women, Washington, 1979—, N.Y. State Job-Tng. Ptnrship Council, 1986—, N.Y.C. Commn. on Status of Women, 1982—; bd. dirs. Planned Parenthood Fedn. Am., 1978-84, bd. advocates, 1984—; mem. adv. bd. Nat. Women's Polit. Caucus, Inst. for Women and Work, Cornell U.; bd. dirs. Alan Guttmacher Inst., N.Y.C., 1984—, Child-Care Action Campaign, 1984—, Council on Econ. Priorities, 1986—, Women's Equity Action League, 1986—; trustee OEF Internat.; mem. Conf. Bd. Work and Family Research Council. Recipient Prix de Paris, Vogue, 1945, Women of Achievement award YWCA, 1978, Econ. award Women's Equity Action League, 1983, Outstanding Woman in Mag. Pub. award March of Dimes, 1983, Dr. Louis M. Spadaro award Fordham U. Sch. Bus. Mem. AAUW, Am. Soc. Mag. Editors, Women in Communications, Advt. Women N.Y. (bd. dirs. 1982-84, Advt. Women of Yr. award 1987), Fin. Women's Assn., Women's Econ. Round Table, Nat. Council Women. Clubs: Internat. Women's Forum (v.p. 1987-89), Women's Forum (N.Y.C.) (v.p. 1984-85), Colony. Office: Working Woman/McCall's Group 230 Park Ave New York NY 10169

LLOYD, MARGARET ANN, psychologist, educator; b. Weiser, Idaho, Sept. 14, 1942; d. Laurance Henry and Margaret Jane (Patch) L.; B.A., U. Denver, 1964; M.S. in Edn., Ind. U., 1966; M.A., U. Ariz., 1972, Ph.D., 1973. Asst. dean of women Carroll (Wis.) Coll., 1966-68, instr. psychology, 1972-73; asst. prof. psychology Suffolk U., Boston, 1973-76, assoc. prof., 1976-79, prof., 1979-88 , chairperson dept., 1981-88; prof., dept. head Ga. So. Coll., 1988— . Author: Adolescence, 1985; contbr. articles to profl. jours. Mem. AAUP, Am. Psychol. Assn. (commn. on undergrad. edn. 1985-87), New Eng. Psychol. Assn. (steering com. 1984-86), Mass. Psychol. Assn. (sec. 1979-81, chairperson bd. acad. and sci. affairs 1981-82). Home: 111 Elliswood Dr Statesboro GA 30458 Office: Ga So Coll Statesboro GA 30460-8041

LLOYD, MARILYN, congresswoman; b. Ft. Smith, Ark.; d. James Edgar and Iva Mae (Higginbotham) Laird; m. Joseph P. Bouquard (div.); children: Nancy Lloyd Smithson, Mari, Mort II, Deborah Lloyd Riley. Grad., Shorter Coll., 1963. Mem. 94th-100th Congresses from 3d Tenn. dist., Washington, 1975—. Office: US Ho Reps Office of Postmaster Washington DC 20510 *

LLOYD, MARLENE IONE, college administrator, consultant; b. Evansville, Minn., Jan. 1, 1935; d. Clarence Melvin and Pearl Irene (Peterson) Sumstad; m. Edmond Lloyd, Dec. 24, 1961; children: Marla Dawn Fowler, Jaris Andrea. AA, Columbia (Calif.) Coll., 1976; BA, Calif. State U., Fresno, 1979; MS, U. San Francisco, 1983, EdD, 1987. Caterer, cook U. Pacific, Columbia, 1978; computer op. Internal Revenue Service Ctr., Fresno, 1978-79; food cons. Saga Corp., Menlo Park, Calif., 1979-80; instr., supr. Assn. for Retarded Citizens, Fresno, 1980-83; instr. U. San Diego, 1983-84, Calif. State U., Fresno, 1983-86, ABC Colls., Fresno, 1983-85, Westland Coll., Fresno, 1986; dept. coordinator Nat. Coll., Fresno, 1986—; computer cons. Home Econs. Devel. Com., 1985-86. Author: Computer Use in Home Economics in Colleges and Universities, 1981, Community Acceptance of Trained Handicapped Workers, 1980. Scholar, Tamarack Women's Club, 1980. Mem. Am. Home Econs. Assn., Am. Soc. for Tng. and Devel., Phi Delta Kappa (found. chmn. 1986—). Republican. Lutheran. Home: 4289 N Anna Fresno CA 93726 Office: Nat Coll 390 W Fir Clovis CA 93612

LLOYD-JONES, JEAN, state legislator; b. Washington, Oct. 14, 1929; m. Richard Lloyd-Jones, 1951; children: Richard A., Mary, John D., Jeffrey. Student, U. N.Mex., 1946-49; BA, Northwestern U., 1951; MA, U. Iowa, 1970. Formerly mem. Iowa Ho. of Reps.; now mem. Iowa Senate. Mem. LWV (pres. Iowa state league 1972-76). Democrat. Address: 160 Oakridge Ave Iowa City IA 52240 *

LLOYD-MCCAIN, GLORIA LORETTA, insurance company executive; b. Bolton, Miss., Jan. 4, 1956; d. Willie and Alice Jeannette (Thompson) Lloyd. B.S., Jackson State U., 1977. Reporter TV news Sta. WAPT-TV, Jackson, Miss., 1977-81; mktg. rep. United Liberty Life, Houston, 1982—, asst. tng. mgr., family counseling, fin. planning, 1982—. Recipient awards Million Dollar Producers Club, United Liberty Life, 1982. Mem. Project Media, Nat. Assn. Exec. Women, Jackson State U. Alumni. Democrat.

LLOYD-MURIE, ROSEMARIE, graphic arts equipment executive; b. Trenton, Mich., Aug. 23, 1960; d. Edward Robert and Cynthia Mary (Christie) Lloyd; m. John Thomas Murie, Oct. 20, 1984. BBA in Mgmt., Ea. Mich. U., 1988. Sec. Finazzo Constrn. Co., Wyandotte, Mich., 1977-79; payroll clk. Babcock and Wilcox, Wyandotte, 1979; sec. Kelly Services, Trenton, 1980; sec. Heidelberg Ea., Inc., Taylor, Mich., 1981-82, adminstrv. asst., 1982-84, regional adminstrv. mgr., 1984—. Mem. Nat. Assn. Female Execs., Beta Gamma Sigma, Golden Key Hon. Soc. Democrat. Roman Catholic. Home: 10201 Cherokee Taylor MI 48180 Office: Heidelberg Ea Inc 24500 Northline Rd Taylor MI 48180

LOBENE, JOYCE ANNE, real estate corporation executive; b. Rochester, N.Y., Oct. 17, 1939; d. James John and Flora (Anasimele) Nuccitelli; m. Thomas Robert Lobene, May 6, 1961; children: James, Mary, Michael, Thomas J. Lic. real estate broker, N.Y. Sec. Stromberg Carlson, Rochester, N.Y., 1958-59; sec. Xerox Corp., Rochester, 1959-61, customer relations rep., 1961-62; sales assoc. John T. Nothnagle, Inc., North Chili, N.Y., 1978-83, br. mgr., 1983—; cons. in field. Active Ogden Rep. Club, Spencerport, N.Y., 1982—, Bd. Assessment & Rev., 1983—. Recipient numerous profl. awards. Mem. Nat. Realtors Assn., Women's Council Realtors (pres. 1983-85), N.Y. State Bd. Realtors, Real Bd. Rochester. Republican. Roman Catholic. Home: 28 Kresswood Dr Rochester NY 14624 Office: 4156 Buffalo Rd Rochester NY 14624

LOBER, IRENE MOSS, educator; b. N.Y.C., Aug. 1, 1927; d. David and Beckie Moss; BS in Edn., CCNY, 1948; MA, George Washington U., 1967; EdD, Va. Poly. Inst. and State U., 1974; m. Solomon William Lober, Oct. 25, 1947; children—Clifford Warren, Richard Wayne, Lori Ann. Formerly tchr., librarian; prin. staff devel. Fairfax County (Va.) Pub. Schs., 1965-77; supt. University City (Mo.) Pub. Schs., 1977-81, Danbury (Conn.) Pub. Schs., 1981-85; prof. SUNY Coll. at New Paltz, 1985—; guest lectr. Washington U., George Washington U., Va. Poly. Inst., U. Va., Fordham U., C.W. Post Coll., L.I. U.; mem. bus. adv. council Datahr, Inc., 1982-85; cons. in field; founding incorporator Sci. Horizons Inc., Danbury, 1984-85; designated disting. expert and peer reviewer Asst. Sec. End. Chester finn, 1987—. Speaker/presentor various nat. and state confs. and convs. Chairperson Mo. Instructional TV Council, 1981; mem. legal and govt. studies group Nat. Inst. Edn. Dept HEW, nat. adv. bd. U. Wis. Research and Devel. Ctr., 1978-80, lay adv. bd. St. Louis Met. Med. Soc., 1980-81; bd. advisors St. Josephs Inst. for the Deaf, 1980-81; pres. adv. cabinet Greater St. Louis Council Girl Scouts U.S., 1980-81, bd. dirs. Southwestern Conn. Council, 1981-85; bd. dirs. Fairfield council Boy Scouts Am., Danbury region Jr. Achievement, 1981-86, Regional Hospice, Danbury, 1984-86, Danbury Council Am. Heart Assn., 1985-86; apptd. supt. in residence, Western Conn. State U., 1984; exec. bd., trustee United Way No. Fairfield County; div. chairperson United Way campaign, 1982-86; trustee, bd. dirs. United Way, Danbury, 1982-85. Recipient Townsend Harris medal CCNY Alumni Assn.; IDEA fellow; Ford Found. grantee, 1977-78. Mem. Am. Assn. Sch. Adminstrs. (higher edn com. 1987—), Am. Mgmt. Assn., Sch. Adminstrs. Assn. N.Y. State, Ednl. Research Service, N.Y. State Council Sch. Supts., N.Y. State Assn. Sch. Bus. Ofcls., Assn. Sch. Bus. Ofcls. Internat. (nat. chmn. maintenance and ops. research com. 1985—), Nat. Assn. Secondary Sch. Prins., Assn. Supervision and Curriculum Devel., NEA, Authors Guild, Authors League, Nat. Sci. Tchrs. Assn., Internat. Platform Assn., Phi Delta Kappa, Phi Kappa Phi, Pi Lambda Theta (publs. adv. bd. 1981-84). Contbr. articles to profl. jours. Office: SUNY-New Paltz 101F Old Main Bldg New Paltz NY 12561

LOBIG, JANIE HOWELL, special education educator; b. Peoria, Ill., June 10, 1945; d. Thomas Edwin and Elizabeth Jane (Higdon) Howell; m. James Frederick Lobig, Aug. 16, 1970; 1 child, Jill Christina. BS in Elem. Edn., So. Ill. U., 1969; postgrad., San Jose State U., 1983—. Cert. elem. tchr., Calif., Mo., Ill., handicapped edn., Calif., Mo.; ordained to ministry Presbyn. Ch. as deacon, 1984. Tchr. trainable mentally retarded children Spl. Luth. Sch., St. Louis, 1967-68; tchr. trainable mentally retarded and severly handicapped children Spl. Sch. Dist. St. Louis, 1969-80, head tchr., 1980-83; tchr. severly handicapped children San Jose (calif.) Unifed Sch. Dist., 1983-86; tchr. multihandicapped students Santa Clara County Office Edn., San Jose, 1986—. Vol. Am. Cancer Soc., San Jose, 1986-88, Am. Heart Assn., San Jose, 1986-88, St. Louis Reps., 1976-82; troop leader Camp Fire, San Jose, 1984-85; moderator of bd. deacons Evergreen Presbyn. Ch., 1988. Mem. Council for Exceptional Children, Assn. for Severly Handicapped, Nat. Edn. Assn., Calif. Tchrs. Assn. Republican. Home: 3131 Creekmore Way San Jose CA 95148 Office: Fred Marten Spl Sch 14265B Story Rd San Jose CA 95127

LOCICERO, LORETTA JOYCE, management analyst; b. Bklyn., Mar. 11, 1950; d. Armando and Mary Rose (Insolera) L. BS, Fordham U., 1971. Corr. Am. Inst. Physics, N.Y.C., 1972-74; pub. health sanitarian Dept. Health State of N.Y., N.Y.C., 1974-76; cons. Transit Authority City of N.Y., Bklyn., 1976-80, mgr. sect., 1980-84, mgr. system application, 1984-88, mgr. subdivision office program, 1988—. Mem. Bklyn. Botanic Garden. Mem. Nat. Assn. Female Execs., Am. Soc. Profl. Exec. Women, Inst. Indsl. Engrs. (treas. N.Y.C. chpt. 1980-84), Am. Astron. Soc. Roman Catholic. Club: Am. Orchid Soc. (S.I., N.Y.). Home: 4 Third St Brooklyn NY 11231

LOCKE, EDITH RAYMOND, editor; b. Vienna, Austria, Aug. 3, 1921; came to U.S., 1939, naturalized, 1944; d. Herman and Dora (Hochberg) Laub; student Bklyn. Coll., 1940-42, CCNY, 1942-45; m. A. Ralph Locke, Jr., May 29, 1963; 1 dau., Katherine Dee. Asst. to advt. dir. Harper's Bazaar, N.Y.C., 1945-46, asso. mdse. editor Jr. Bazaar, 1946-48; fashion dir. Abbott Kimball Advt. Agy., N.Y.C., 1948-49; asso. fashion editor Mademoiselle mag., N.Y.C., 1949-59, fashion editor, 1959-67, exec. editor, 1967-72, editor-in-chief, 1971-80; editor/producer/host weekly cable TV show for women You Magazine, 1981—; fashion segment producer, Attitudes, 1986—; fashion and TV cons.; mem. Coty award jury Am. Fashion Critics, 1950—. Bd. dirs. Am. Women's Econ. Devel. Mem. Am. Soc. Mag. Editors, Fashion Group (pres. 1972-73). Author: The Red Door, 1965. Office: 230 E 44th St 3E New York NY 10017

LOCKE, LYNDA K., magazine publishing executive; b. Los Angeles, Mar. 26, 1960; d. James Norman and Betty Mae (Sams) L. BA, Mont. State U., 1982. Graphic artist Atari Inc., Sunnyvale, Calif., 1983; asst. art dir. Women's Sports and Fitness Mag., Palo Alto, Calif., 1983-85; prodn. mgr. Women's Sports and Fitness Mag., San Francisco, 1985—; cons. Discover Mag., Palo Alto, 1985—. Mem. Print Buyer's Assn. Home: 678 Lyon St San Francisco CA 94117 Office: Women's Sports Mag 501 2d St Suite 400 San Francisco CA 94107

LOCKETT, ELIZABETH RUTH, educational administrator; b. Orange, N.J., Aug. 22, 1929; d. Waverly and Theresa Fernandez (Da Cruz) Lockett. B.S., Pratt Inst, 1954; M.S. in Nutrition, Hunter Coll., 1959; sch. adminstrn. cert. Pace U., 1972; cert. continuing edn. Notre Dame U. Dietitian St. Anthony's Hosp., Queens, N.Y., 1954-55; adminstrv. dietitian Meml.-Sloan Kettering Hosp., N.Y.C., 1955-57; secondary tchr. N.Y.C. Bd. Edn., 1957-68, sch. adminstr., 1968—; mem. textbook rev. com. N.Y.C. Bd. Edn., 1988. Vol. Vannguard Polit. Club, Bklyn., 1984—; bd. dirs. Alternative Visions for Children and Families, Bklyn., 1988. Recipient John F. Kennedy Community Service award C Sch. Dist. 16-Jr. High Sch. 57, Bklyn., 1978. Mem. N.Y.C. Adminstrv. Women in Edn., Secondary Sch. Adminstrs., Assn. Curriculum Devel. and Supervision, Council Supvrs. and Adminstrs. (rep. exec. bd. 1973—, Service award 1985), Assn. Asst. Prins. (v.p. 1977—), Lambda Kappa Mu (nat. Disting. Service Key award 1976, past nat. officer). Roman Catholic. Avocations: travel; reading; painting on glass; handicrafts. Office: NYC Bd Edn Jr High Sch 324 800 Gates Ave Brooklyn NY 11221

LOCKETT, SANDRA A. JOHNSON BOKAMBA, librarian; b. Hutchinson, Kans., Nov. 18, 1946; d. Herbert Wales and Dorothy Bernice (Harrison) Johnson; B.S., U. Kans., 1968; M.L.S., Ind. U., 1973; children—Eyenga Marthe Bérnice Bokamba, Madeline Bernice. Spl. assignments librarian Gary (Ind.) Public Library, 1973-74, Alcott br. librarian, 1974-76, asst. dir. public relations and programming, 1976-78, head extension services and public relations, 1978-79; head govt. documents dept. U. Iowa Law Library, Iowa City, 1979-84; librarian-in-charge Center Street Library, Milw. Pub. Library, 1984-88, extension services coordinator, 1988—. Pres., Iowa City Community Sch. Dist. Equity Com., 1980-81; mem. Iowa City Com. Community Needs, 1981-83; mem. Assn. Study Afro-Am. Life and History, 1976-78. Gary Public Library grantee, 1978, Agy. Community Devel. Block Grant Fund; named Librarian of the Year Milw. Public Library, 1986; recipient Milw. Mgmt. Merit award, 1988. Mem. NAACP (sec. 1980-81), ALA, Am. Assn. Law Librarians, Mid-Am. Law Library Assn., Iowa Library Assn. (vice-chmn., chmn. elect govt. documents div. 1980-83), Am. Library Assn., Wis. Library Assn., Wis. Black Librarians Network, Alpha Kappa Alpha. Democrat. Roman Catholic. Home: 10213 W Fond du Lac Ave #234 Milwaukee WI 53224 Office: Milwaukee Pub Library Extension Services 814 W Wisconsin Milwaukee WI 53206

LOCKETT-EGAN, MARIAN W., advertising executive; b. Murray, Ky., May 5, 1931; d. Otis H. Workman and Myrtle A. (Jones) Workman-Jordan; m. Barker Lockett, Oct. 11, 1963 (div.); m. 2d, Douglas S. Egan Jr., Feb. 14, 1981; children—Reed Nasser, Jennifer Stephens, George M. Potts, Cynthia Klenk, Stephen R.W. Lockett. Student Murray State U., 1962. Asst. media dir. Noble-Dury & Assocs., Nashville, 1963; asst. research dir. Triangle Broadcast Div., Phila., 1964-68; assoc. Media dir. Lewis & Gilman, Phila., 1968-72; v.p. advt. media, Scott Paper Co., Phila., 1972-83; pres. DMS Communications Inc., Ardmore, Pa., 1983—; faculty adviser The Media Sch., N.Y.C., 1983-85, 87—, exec. dir. Mktg. and Media Edn., 1985-87; mem. TV com. Assn. Nat. Advertisers, N.Y.C., 1977-83; guest lectr. Wharton U., Phila., 1981-82; Gannet vis. prof. U. Fla. Sch. Journalism, Gainesville, 1982. Guest editor Media Decisions, 1981. Trustee Meth. Hosp. Found., Phila., 1974-87. Mem. TV and Radio Advt. Club (pres. 1974). Republican. Episcopalian. Home: 45 Llanfair Circle Ardmore PA 19033 Office: PO Box 110 Ardmore PA 19033

LOCKETT-POWELL, FRANKIE ANN, personnel executive; b. Feb. 27, 1942; d. Dave and Wealthie Lee (Scales) Lockett; student Coll. of DuPage,

1971-72; A.A.S., Florissant Valley Community Coll., 1980; B.S., St. Mary-of-the-Woods Coll., 1984; children—Andre Fernandez, Debra Yvette, Avery Cortez. Postal clk., U.S. Govt., E. St. Louis, Ill., 1965-68; clk. Sch. Dist. 189, E. St. Louis, 1969-70; personnel sec. Atlantic Cos., Chgo., 1970-72; sec. Honeywell Inc., St. Louis, 1972-73; sr. personnel clk. ACF Industries, St. Charles, Mo., 1973-76; personnel and tng. asst. Church's Fried Chicken, Inc., St. Louis, 1976; personnel specialist Prudential Savs. & Loan Assn., Clayton, Mo., 1977-80; personnel dir., office services adminstr. S.W. Truck Body Co., St. Louis, 1980-82; mgr. employee benefits ITT Comml. Fin. Corp., 1982-87; benefits mgr. Citicorp Mortgage, Inc., 1987—; adv. student placement State Community Coll., E. St. Louis, 1977—; mem. com. United Negro Coll. Fund., 1979—; sec. Parker Rd. Baptist Ch., 1978—, mem. long range planning com., 1979—; active Practical Edn. Now program, 1979-80. Recipient Urban League St. Louis Sentinel "Yes I Can" award, 1977; State Community Coll. Certificate of Appointment, 1977. Mem. Greater St. Louis. Am. Bus. Women's Assn. Home: 7274 N Hanley Rd Hazelwood MO 63042 Office: Citicorp Mortgage Inc 670 Mason Ridge Ctr Dr Saint Louis MO 63141

LOCKHART, DEBORAH ANN, computer programmer; b. Mineral Wells, Tex., Feb. 20, 1945; d. Joe Royce and Billie Louise (Crow) Williams; B.S., Tex. Christian U., 1967; postgrad. U. Tex., Arlington, 1971; m. Scott Charles Lockhart, June 17, 1976 (div. 1983); children—Amy Louise, Adam Conan. Programmer aid Ling Temco Vought, Grand Prairie, Tex., 1966-67, 68-69; programmer analyst Trinity U., San Antonio, 1967-68; programmer analyst Info. Systems Tech., Dallas, 1969-71; systems engr. Optimum Systems Inc., Dallas, 1972-75; sr. programmer analyst Univ. Computing Co., Dallas, 1971-72, 75-81; mgr. CIF project Banking Systems, Inc., Dallas, 1981-83; project mgr. Shared Fin. Systems, Dallas, 1983—. Pres. Chapel Downs Community Ctr., 1986-87. Mem. Mensa. Presbyterian.

LOCKHART, KORALJKA, opera magazine editor, public relations consultant; b. Dubrovnik, Yugoslavia, May 30, 1932; came to U.S., 1965, naturalized, 1971; d. Zvonimir Peter and Lina (Kukuljica) Krstic; m. Keith M., Lockhart, July 26, 1966 (div. 1979). Student Music Sch., Dubrovnik, 1941-51, U. Zagreb (Yugoslavia), 1951-55. Music dir. Sta. KKHI-AM-FM, San Francisco, 1965-70; press rep. San Francisco Opera, 1970-74, mag. editor, pub. relations cons., 1981—; acting pub. relations dir. San Francisco Symphony, 1979-80; dir. promotion Com. for Arts and Lectures, U. Calif., Berkeley, 1974-78; cons. in field. Author: San Francisco Opera: The Adler Years, 1953-81, 1981; Opera Calendar, 1980-81. Home: 289 Lexington Rd Kensington CA 94707 Office: War Meml Opera House San Francisco CA 94102

LOCKHART, MADGE CLEMENTS, educator; b. Soddy, Tenn., May 22, 1920; d. James Arlie and Ollie (Sparks) Clements; m. Andre J. Lockhart, Apr. 24, 1942 (div. 1973); children: Jacqueline, Andrew, Janice, Jill. Student, East Tenn. U., 1938-39; BS, U. Tenn., Chattanooga and Knoxville, 1955, MEd, 1962. Elem. tchr. Tenn. and Ga., 1947-60, Brainerd High Sch., Chattanooga, 1960-64, Cleveland (Tenn.) City Schs., 1966-88; owner, operator Lockhart's Learning Ctr., Inc., Cleveland and Chattanooga, 1975—; co-founder, pres. Hermes, Inc., 1973-79; co-founder Dawn Ctr., Hamilton County, Tenn., 1974; apptd. mem. Tenn. Gov.'s Acad. for Writers. AuthAor poetry, short stories and fiction; contbr. articles to profl. jours. and newspapers. Pres. Cleveland Assn. Retarded Citizens, 1970, state v.p., 1976; pres. Cherokee Easter Seal Soc., 1973-76, Cleveland Creative Arts Guild, 1980; bd. dirs. Tenn. Easter Seal Soc., 1974-77, 80-83; chair Bradley County Internat. Yr. of Child. Recipient Service to Mankind award Sertoma, 1978, Gov.'s award for service to handicapped, 1979; mental health home named in her honor, Tenn., 1987. Mem. NEA (life), Tenn. Edn. Assn., Am. Assn. Rehab. Therapy, Cleveland Edn. Assn. (Service to Humanity award 1987). Mem. Ch. of Christ. Clubs: Byliners, Fantastiks. Home: 3007 Oakland Dr Cleveland TN 37312

LOCKMAN, MARCIA ANN, commercial real estate consultant; b. Louisville, July 26, 1951; d. George John and Jean Norman (Hamilton) Korfhage; m. James Richard Lockman, May 25, 1974. BA, Miami U., Ohio, 1973; MS, U. Wis.-Milw., 1974; MBA, U. Minn., 1984. Project dir. NFO Research, Toledo, 1974-76; sales assoc. Welles Bowen, Toledo, 1976-78; research analyst Green Giant, Mpls., 1978-79; market research mgr. Fingerhut, Mpls., 1979-83; self-employed market research cons., Mpls., 1983-85; dir. mktg. Keewaydin, Mpls., 1985-86; instr. U. Toledo, 1977. Commr. Eden Prairie Human Rights and Services, 1978-84; chmn. Eden Prairie Human Service Needs Com., 1980-83; chmn. spl. projects 1983 U.S. Sr. Open Golf Tournament, Chaska, Minn., 1982-83, mktg. com. 1991 USGA Men's Open Golf Tournament; auctioneer KTCA Pub. TV, St. Paul, 1982; mem. mktg. com. USGA Men's Open Golf Tournament, 1991. Mem. Pi Beta Phi (Service award 1973). Republican. Methodist. Clubs: Flagship Athletic, Hazletine Nat. Golf. Avocation: golf. Address: 6561 Beach Rd Eden Prairie MN 55344

LOCKWOOD, LORA LEE, aerospace company executive; b. Takoma Park, Md., Sept. 11, 1941; d. Elden Nelson and Evelyn May (Johnson) L.; m. Eduardo Ruibal Lujambio, Dec. 17, 1960; children: Elizabeth L., Edward J., Rebecca E., Carina E. Student interior design, U. Wash., 1959-60. With Prudential Ins. Co., Seattle, 1960-63; mem. staff computer ctr. Seattle 1st Nat. Bank, 1963-65; mem. staff ops. dept. Bank of West, Bellevue, Wash., 1966-70; adminstrv. asst. mortgage Calif. Fed. Savs. and Loan, Torrance, 1979-81; office mgr. MRP Computer Systems, Torrance, 1982; v.p. adminstrn. Commonwealth Bank, Torrance, 1982-87; sr. v.p. Spotted Elk Corp., Long Beach, Calif., 1987—; chmn. bd. Sixels Corp., Rolling Hills Estates, Calif., 1986—. Republican. Office: Spotted Elk Corp 3205 N Lakewood Blvd Long Beach CA 90808

LODEN, KAREN CLARK, nurse; b. Perth Amboy, N.J., Aug. 23, 1946; d. Francis Anthony and Mary (Cupsie) Clark; m. Michael Loden, May 1, 1969; 1 child, Jonathan. BS in Nursing, Loretto Heights Coll., Denver, 1968; MN in Nursing, La. State U. Med. Ctr., New Orleans, 1983. Staff nurse St. Anthony Hosp., Denver, 1968; charge nurse prince William Hosp., Manassas, Va., 1969; staff nurse, charge nurse ICU-CCU Meml. Gen. Hosp., Las Cruces, N.Mex., 1970-71; staff nurse, charge nurse ICU-CCU Lee County Hosp., Opelika, Ala., 1972-73; charge nurse, acting head nurse pediatrics Jackson County Schneck Hosp., Seymour, Ind., 1974-75; head nurse med.-surg. Drs. Meml. Hosp., Baton Rouge, 1975-77, inservice dir., 1977-79, asst. dir. nursing service, 1979-81; asst. unit dir. E. Jefferson Gen. Hosp., Metairie, La., 1981; staff nurse Lakeside Hosp., Metairie, La., 1982-83; asst. dir. nursing Hôtel Dieu Hosp., New Orleans, 1983—; clin. preceptor Children's Hosp., New Orleans, 1984-85; clin. instr. nursing Our Lady of Holy Cross Coll., New Orleans, 1986-88; CPR instr., trainer Am. Heart Assn. Mem. Am. Assn. Critical Care Nurses, Am. Heart Assn., Sigma Theta Tau. Roman Catholic. Home: 917 Trudeau Dr Metairie LA 70003

LODESTRO, VALERIE CATHERINE, marketing services manager, travel agent, medical assistant; b. Bayshore, N.Y., Apr. 29, 1955; d. William and Marie Roseanne (Chiocco) Logios; m. Charles Vincent Lodestro, Oct. 2, 1982. AAS, Nassau Community Coll., 1975; BBA, Hofstra U., 1983. Med. unit asst. Lydia Hall Hosp., Freeport, N.Y., 1976-83; mktg. service mgr. Arrow Electronics, Melville, N.Y., 1983-84; mktg. com. mgr. Computerland, Syosset, N.Y., 1984-85; mktg. mgr. Prestige Univ., Deer Park, N.Y., 1985—; travel agt. Travel Partners, Bellmore, N.Y., part-time, 1985—. Vol. ARC, Lynbrook, 1972, Head Start, Hempstead, N.Y., 1972; tchr. religious edn. Our Lady of Peace, Lynbrook, 1969-73. Scholar, Hofstra U., 1976-83, nominated spl. honors, Sch. Bus., 1982. Fellow Internat. Assn. Travel Agts., Nat. Assn. Female Execs. Republican. Roman Catholic. Avocations: writing poetry, dancing, reading, aerobics, skating. Home: 312 Ferndale Dr Spartanburg SC 29303

LODGE, PATRICIA GRACE, substance abuse prevention company executive; b. Wilmington, Del., Mar. 16, 1934; d. James Francis and Grace Lyda (Veazey) Kearney; m. Joseph Howard Lodge, Dec. 31, 1970; children: Susan Lynn Proth, Linda Kay Delp, Deborah Gail Wright, William Craig Fisher. Student, Ann Arundel Community Coll., 1976-80, Willsey Inst. Art, Miami, Fla., 1980-81, Fla. Internat. U., 1986-88. Mktg. and pub. relations rep. Minn. Mining and Mfg. Co., Wilmington, 1964-66, Miami, 1966-68; account exec. Wometco, Inc., Miami, 1986-70; photographer Visitor Pub. co., Miami Beach, Fla., 1980-82; co-founder, exec. v.p. Corp. Security Advisors, Inc. (merged Bus. Risks Internat., Inc.), Miami Beach, 1982-87; founder, pres. PGL Enterprises, Miami Beach, 1987—; pub. relations cons. Photographer for various mags. Mem. Nat. Assn. Female Execs. (network dir.), Friends Japanese Garden (bd. dirs., pub. relations and publicity chmn., tour guide), Am. Soc. Mag. Photographers, Zoolog. Soc. Fla. Club: Miami Beach Garden, Jockey of Miami. Home: 1601 W 28th St Sunset Island #1 Miami Beach FL 33140 Office: PGL Enterprises PO Box 402891 Miami Beach FL 33140

LODOWSKI, RUTH ELLEN, physician; b. Dallas, Feb. 15, 1951; s. Charles Harry and Genevieve (Gowaty) L. BS, U. Tex., 1972, MD, 1986; MBA, North Tex. State U., Denton, 1976. Resident asst., then head resident Castilian Dormitory, Austin, Tex., 1971-73; singer self-employed band, Austin, 1972-74; teller Greenville Ave. Bank, Dallas, 1974-75; employment interviewer Tex. Employment Commn., Grand Prairie, 1975-76; personnel intern U.S. Dept. Justice, Seagoville, Tex., 1976-77; personnel asst. Army and Air Force Exchange Service, San Antonio, 1977-78; staffing adminstr., personnel adminstr. Tex. Instruments Inc., Dallas, 1978-81, U. Tex. Med. Sch. of San Antonio, 1982-86; intern, then resident Parkland Meml. Hosp., Dallas, 1986—. Active, YWCA, ARC. Recipient Top 10 Medal of Honor Kiwanis Internat., 1969. Mem. AMA, Tex. Med. Assn., Dallas Area Women Psychiatrist. Club: Tex. Execs.

LODWICK, KATHLEEN LORRAINE, historian, educator; b. St. Louis, Feb. 7, 1944; d. Algha Claire and Kathryn Elizabeth (Worthington) L. BS with honors, Ohio U., 1964, MA, 1965; PhD, U. Ariz., 1976; postgrad. U. Hawaii, 1966-67, Nat. Taiwan Normal U., 1967-68. Asst. prof. history U. No. Colo., 1976-77; asst. prof. history Ind. State U., 1977-78; research assoc. John King Fairbank Ctr. for East Asian Research, Harvard U., 1978-79; asst. prof. history S.W. Mo. State U., Springfield, 1979-82, assoc. prof., 1982-87. prof., 1987-88, dir. acad. affairs, assoc. prof. Pa. State U., Mont Alto, 1988— ; dir. index/biog. guide to Chinese Recorder and Missionary Jour. project, 1977-86. Author: The Chinese Recorder Index: A Guide to Christian Missions in Asia, 1867-1941, 1986. Mem. AAUW, Am. Assn. Univ. Profs., Am. Hist. Assn., Assn. Asian Studies, Nat. Assn. Fgn. Student Affairs, UN Assn., Soc. of Friends, Phi Alpha Theta. Democrat. Home: 1522 Grant Ridge Ln Saint Louis MO 63126 Office: Pa State U Office Acad Affairs Mont Alto PA 17237

LOEB, DOROTHY PEARL, lawyer; b. N.Y.C., Mar. 2, 1935; d. Victor Joseph and Jean (Albert) Caesar; m. Frank David Loeb, June 26, 1955 (dec. Oct. 1972); children: Matthew Stuart, Eric Victor. Student, Bates Coll., 1952-55; BA, Boston U., 1956; JD, Columbia U., 1971. Bar: N.Y. 1972, U.S. Dist. Ct. (ea. and so. dists.) N.Y. 1975, U.S. Supreme Ct. 1976. Asst. dist. atty. Rockland County, New City, N.Y., 1972-75; counsel to commr. dept. social services Rockland County, West Nyack, N.Y., 1975-77; asst. counsel litigation dept. social services N.Y. State, Albany, 1977-78, asst. dir. child support enforcement dept. social services, 1978-80; dep. asst. gen. counsel Dept. Air Force, 1980—. Counsel 1st Unitarian Ch. Rockland County, Pomona, N.Y., 1973-75; legal advisor, bd. dirs. Nyack (N.Y.) Child Care Ctr., McLean Civic Assn., 1988—; chmn. ad hoc com. on legal affairs The Rotanda Condominium, McLean, Va., 1985—. Mem. ABA, Fed. Bar Assn., N.Y. State Bar Assn., Assn. Trial Lawyers Am., Nat. Dist. Attys. Assn., Am. Judicature Soc., League of Women Voters (pres. Rockland, N.Y. br. 1965-67, membership chairperson, Fairfax, Va. dinner unit 1986-87), Am. Assn. Univ. Women (sec. McLean, Va. br. 1986-87). Club: University (Washington) (asst. sec. 1987—). Office: USAF Office of Gen Counsel Pentagon Washington DC 20330

LOEB, FRANCES LEHMAN (MRS. JOHN L. LOEB), civic leader; b. N.Y.C., Sept. 25, 1906; d. Arthur and Adele (Lewisohn) Lehman; student Vassar Coll., 1924-26; L.H.D. (hon.), NYU, 1977; m. John L. Loeb, Nov. 18, 1926; children—Judith Loeb Chiara, John L., Ann Loeb Bronfman, Arthur Lehman, Deborah Loeb Brice. N.Y.C. commr. for UN and Consular Corps, 1966-78. Exec. com. Population Crisis Com., Washington; life mem. bd. Children of Bellevue, Inc., 1974—; bd. dirs. Bellevue Assn., Internat. Presch., Inc., N.Y. Landmarks Conservancy; chmn. bd. East Side Internat. Community Center, Inc.; mem. UN Devel. Corp., 1972—; mem. Women's Nat. Republican Club; life trustee Collegiate Sch. for Boys, N.Y.C.; trustee Cornell U., 1979-88, trustee emeritus, 1988—, trustee Vassar Coll., 1988—; bd. overseers Cornell U. Med. Coll., 1983-88 (life mem. 1988—), Inst. Internat. Edn. (life). Mem. UN Assn. (dir.). Clubs: Cosmopolitan, Vassar, Women's City (N.Y.C.). Home: 730 Park Ave New York NY 10021 Other: Anderson Hill Rd Purchase NY 10577

LOEB, JEANETTE WINTER, investment banker; b. N.Y.C., June 18, 1952; d. Leon and Fay (Rotenberg) Winter; m. Peter Kenneth Loeb, Nov. 1, 1980. BA, Wellesley Coll., 1974; MBA, Harvard U., 1977. Assoc. Goldman, Sachs & Co., N.Y.C., 1977-81, v.p., 1981—, ptnr. 1986—. Wellesley Coll. Devel. Fund chmn. for N.Y. Mem. Phi Beta Kappa. Club: India House. Office: Goldman Sachs & Co 85 Broad St New York NY 10004

LOEB, JOYCE LICHTGARN, interior designer, civic worker; b. Portland, Oreg., May 20, 1936; d. Elias Lichtgarn and Sylvia Amy (Margulies) Freedman; m. Stanley Robinson Loeb, Aug. 14, 1960; children: Carl Eli, Eric Adam. Student U. Calif.-Berkeley, 1954-56; B.S., Lewis and Clark Coll., 1958; postgrad. art and architecture, Portland State U., 1976. Tchr. art David Douglas Sch. Dist., Portland, 1958-59, 61-64; tchr., chmn. art dept. Grant Union High Sch. Dist., Sacramento, 1959-60; designer, pres. Joyce Loeb Interior Design, Inc., Portland, 1976—, cons. designer to various developers of health care facilities. Chairperson fundraisers for civic orgns. and Jewish orgns.; mem. women's com. Reed Coll.; bd. dirs. Met. Family Services, Portland, 1968-71, Young Audiences, Inc., Portland, 1970-76, 78-80, Portland Opera Assn., 1978-84, Arts Celebration, Inc., Portland, 1984—, Congregation Beth Israel, 1986—; chmn. Artquake Festival, 1985, Operaball, 1987; v.p. Beth Israel Sisterhood, 1981-83; trustee Congregation Beth Israel, 1986—, chmn. art interior design com. Mem. Soc. Interior Designers, Nat. Council Jewish Women. Democrat. Club: Multnomah Athletic. Home: 1546 SW Upland Dr Portland OR 97221

LOEB, NACKEY SCRIPPS, publisher; b. Los Angeles, Feb. 24, 1924; d. Robert Paine and Margaret (Culbertson) Scripps; m. William Loeb, July 15, 1952 (dec. 1981); children—Nackey Loeb Scagliotti, Edith Loeb DuBuc. Student, Scripps Coll. Pub. Union-Leader Corp., Manchester, N.H., 1981—. Republican. Baptist. Home: Paige Hill Rd Goffstown NH 03045 Office: Union Leader Corp Amherst St Manchester NH 03105

LOEBLICH, HELEN NINA TAPPAN, paleontologist, educator; b. Norman, Okla., Oct. 12, 1917; d. Frank Girard and Mary (Jenks) Tappan; m. Alfred Richard Loeblich, Jr., June 18, 1939; children—Alfred Richard III, Karen Elizabeth Loeblich McClelland, Judith Anne Loeblich Covey, Daryl Louise Loeblich Valenzuela. B.S., U. Okla., 1937, M.S., 1939; Ph.D., U. Chgo., 1942. Instr. geology Tulane U., 1942-43; geologist U.S. Geol. Survey, 1943-45, 47-59; mem. faculty UCLA, 1958—, prof. geology, 1966-84, prof. emeritus, 1985—, vice chmn. dept. geology, 1973-75; research assoc. Smithsonian Instn., 1954-57; assoc. editor Cushman Found. Foraminiferal Research, 1950-51, incorporator, hon. dir., 1950—. Author: (with A.R. Loeblich, Jr.) Treatise on Invertebrate Paleontology, part C, Protista 2, Foraminiferida, 2 vols., 1964, Foraminiferal Genera and Their Classification, 2 vols., 1987; author: The Paleobiology of Plant Protists, 1980, also articles profl. jours., govt. publs., encys.; editorial bd.: Palaeoecology, 1972-82, Paleobiology, 1975-81. Guggenheim fellow, 1953-54; named Woman of Yr. in Sci. Palm Springs Desert Mus., 1987. Fellow Geol. Soc. Am. (councilor 1979-81); mem. Paleontol. Soc. (pres. 1984-85, medal), UCLA Med. Ctr. Aux. (Woman of Yr. medal), AAUP, Soc. Econ. Paleontologists and Mineralogists (councilor for paleontology 1975-77, hon. mem. 1978—, R.C. Moore medal), Internat. Paleontological Assn., Paleontol. Research Inst., Am. Microscopical Soc., Am. Inst. Biol. Scis., Phi Beta Kappa, Sigma Xi. Home: 11427 Albata St Los Angeles CA 90049 Office: UCLA Dept Earth and Space Scis Los Angeles CA 90024

LOEHRKE, CHRISTINE CAROL, rehabilitation facility administrator; b. Dayton, Ohio, June 9, 1950; d. Eugene Max and Carol Jean (Showalter) L. BA in Psychology, Wittenberg U., 1973. Psychology asst. Vocat. Guidance & Rehab. Services, Cleve., 1973-76, program mgr., 1976-79, tng. specialist, 1979-81; dir. rehab. and planning Goodwill Industries Inc., Dayton, Ohio, 1981-84; assoc. dir. Youth Enrichment Services Inc., Cleve., 1984-87, Epilepsy Found. N.E. Ohio, Cleve., 1987—; instr. Cuyahoga Community Coll., Parma, Ohio, 1979-81; co-founder Westside Guidance Ctr., Lakewood, Ohio, 1974-76; vol. counselor Third Legacy Alcoholism Ctr. Inc., Lakewood, 1974-76. Co-author: (bus. plan) Implementation of a Prime Manufacturing subsidiary in a Sheltered Workshop, 1985. Recipient cert. appreciation Council Exceptional Children, 1977, cert. appreciation, Kiwanis, 1978; named Disting. Rehab. Profl., Nat. Disting. Service Registry Med. and Vocat. Rehab. Div., 1987. Mem. Nat. Rehab. Assn., Nat. Rehab. Adminstrs. Assn., Ohio Rehab. Adminstrs. Assn. (bd. dirs. 1982-84), N.E. Ohio Rehab. Assn. (bd. dirs.), Nat. Assn. Female Execs. Democrat. Lutheran. Home: 1034 E 171st St Cleveland OH 44119 Office: Epilepsy Foundation of Northeast Ohio 2800 Euclid Ave #450 Cleveland OH 44115

LOENING, SARAH LARKIN, author; b. Nutley, N.J., Dec. 9, 1896; d. Adrian H. and Katherine (Satterthwaite) Larkin; student Miss Chapin's Sch., Madame Marty's Sch., Paris, 1913; m. Albert P. Loening, Nov. 28, 1922; 1 son, Albert Palmer. Author: Three Rivers, 1934; The Trevals, a Tale of Quebec, 1936; Radisson, 1938; Dimo (in French), 1940, 79, (in English), 1978; Joan of Arc, 1951; The Old Master, 1958; Zulli, 1954; The Old Master and other Tails, 1968; Mountain in the Field, 1972; The Gift of Life, 1978; Vignettes of a Life, 1983. Past chmn. arts and skill corp. ARC, Camp Upton, past chmn. Hampton chpt.; past pres. Cathedral guild, St. John the Divine, past chmn. Gardeners of St. John's, now chmn. Bibl. Garden; past chmn. Hampton chpt. Am. Red Cross. Recipient Recognition award Govt. of France, 1920; Horticultural award Garden Club Am., Zone III, 1981; citation Layman's Nat. Bible Com. Mem. Am., Order St. John of Jerusalem (dame), St. Luke The Physician. Clubs: Colony, Hroswitha, Southampton Garden (past pres.), St. John's 1st Monday (chmn.). Home: PO Box 905 38 Harvest Lane Southampton NY 11968

LOEVINGER, JANE, psychologist, educator; b. St. Paul, Feb. 6, 1918; d. Gustavus and Millie (Strouse) L.; m. Samuel I. Weissman, July 13, 1943; children: Judith, Michael B. BA in Psychology, U. Minn., 1937, MS in Psychometrics, 1938; PhD. in Psychology, U. Calif., Berkeley, 1944. Instr. psychology and edn. Stanford (Calif.) U., 1941-42; lectr. psychology U. Calif., Berkeley, 1942-43; part-time instr. in stats. and sociology Washington U., St. Louis, 1946-47, research psychologist and cons. air force projects, 1950-53, research assoc. prof. child psychiatry, 1960-64, research assoc. prof., Grad. Inst. Edn., 1964-71, research assoc., Social Sci. Inst., 1964-84, research prof., 1971-74, prof., 1974—, Stuckenberg prof. human values and moral devel., 1984—; research assoc. Jewish Hosp., St. Louis, 1954-60; mem. personality and cognition research rev. com. NIMH, 1970-74; ad hoc reviewer U. Witwatersrand, Johannesburg, Republic of South Africa, 1985, NSF, NIMH, various other orgns.; mem. various coms. Washington U.; lectr. in field. Author: (with R. Wessler) Measuring Ego Development 1: Construction and Use of a Sentence Completion Test, 1970, (with R. Wessler and C. Redmore) Measuring Ego Development 2: Scoring Manual for Women and Girls, 1970, Ego Development: Conceptions and Theories, 1976, Scientific Ways in the Study of Ego Development, 1979, Paradigms of Personality, 1987; cons. editor: Psychol. Rev., 1983—, Jour. Personality and Social Psychology, 1984—, Jour. Personality Assessment 1987—; contbr. articles to profl. jours., book revs., letters and abstracts. Recipient Research Sci. award NIMH, 1968-73, 74-79; Ednl. Testing Service Disting. Vis. scholar, 1969; Margaret M. Justin fellow, 1955-56, NIMH grantee, 1956-79. Fellow Am. Psychol. Assn. (pres. Div. 5 1962-63, mem. com. on tests, mem. polict and planning bd. 1969-72, mem. policy task force on psychologists in criminal justice system 1976-77, pres. Div. 24 1982-83, com. on early career award in personality 1985), Phi Beta Kappa, Sigma Xi (assoc.). Democrat. Home: 6 Princeton Ave Saint Louis MO 63130 Office: Washington U Dept of Psychology Saint Louis MO 63130

LOEW, PATRICIA ANN, small business owner; b. Farmville, Va., Aug. 28, 1943; d. Joseph Leo and Delores (McGurk) Dooley; m. Hubert Victor Loew; children: Moritz, Franz. BA, Clarke Coll., Dubuque, Iowa, 1965; MA, Pius XII Inst. Fine Arts, Florence, Italy, 1966. Chmn. fine arts dept. Little Flower High Sch., Chgo., 1966-68; staff painter Otto Galleries, Vienna, Austria, 1968-71; retail store owner Austrian Ski & Sports Haus, Country Club Hills, Ill., 1971—; fashion coordinator Marhall Field & Co., Chgo., 1966-67; recreational therapistmental health ctr. State of Ill., Tinley Park, 1966-68; asst. translator Richard Neutra Architect, Vienna, 1971; wholesale importer Franz Klammer USA, Ltd., 1986-87. Active Frankfort Ill. chpt. PTA; mem. Friends of the Library, Frankfort. Asst. Art Award scholar Pius XII Inst. Grad. Studies, 1966. Mem. Nat. Sporting Goods Am., Ski Industries Am. Democrat. Roman Catholic. Clubs: Prestwick Country, Women's (Frankfort). Home: 567 Aberdeen Rd Frankfort IL 60423 Office: The Austrian Ski & Sport Haus 19001 S Cicero Ave Country Club Hills IL 60477

LOEWALD, ELIZABETH LONGSHORE, psychiatrist; b. San Francisco, Dec. 23, 1923; d. Isaac Holcomb and Edna (O'Connor) Longshore; m. Hans Walter Loewald, Jan. 4, 1954; children—Katherine, Caroline. A.B., U. Calif.-Berkeley, 1944; M.D., Johns Hopkins Sch. Medicine, 1948. Intern Doctor's Hosp., Washington, 1950-51; resident in psychiatry Sheppard & Enoch Pratt Hosp., Towson, Md., 1951; physician Balt. Health Dept., 1953-55, New Haven Health Dept. (Conn.), 1955-61; resident in psychiatry Yale Sch. Medicine, New Haven, 1975-77, child psychiatry fellow Yale Child Study Ctr., 1977-79, asst. clin. prof. psychiatry Yale Med. Sch., 1979—; practice medicine specializing in child, adult psychiatry, 1979—. Mem. St. Elizabeth's Hosp. Med. Assn., Am. Psychiat. Assn., Conn. Council Child Psychiatrists, Phi Beta Kappa, Alpha Omega Alpha. Contbr. articles to profl. jours. Office: 63 Trumbull St New Haven CT 06510

LOEWY, OLIVIA ROCHELLE, personnel trainer, consultant; b. Calif., Nov. 14, 1946; d. Peter and Annette (Cohen) Markin; m. Aaron David Loewy, June 14, 1970; children: Monika Haley., Alexandra Louise. B.A., UCLA, 1969; M.A. in Ednl. Psychology, Calif. State U.-Northridge; Ph.D., U. So. Calif. Cert. marriage, family and child counselor, Calif. Dir. Full Circle Guidance Clinic, Glendale, Calif., 1977-80; cons., trainer Western region U.S. Dept. Labor, 1980—, U.S. Office Personnel Mgmt., 1982—; co-founder Personal Dimensions, Glendale, Calif.; hon. academic appointee Calif. Sch. Profl. Psychology. Mem. Am. Soc. Tng. and Devel., Calif. Assn. Marriage and Family Therapists. Writer numerous fed. funded grant proposals. Home and Office: 3128 Brookdale Rd Studio City CA 91604

LOFARO, MARIJUDE ANN, mortician; b. N.Y.C., Feb. 1, 1963; d. Angelo S. and Trudy (Vosper) Zotto. AS in Mortuary Sci., SUNY, 1983. Apprenticed Weber Funeral Home, Lake Ronkonkoma, N.Y., 1983; mortician I.J. Morris, Deer Park, N.Y., 1981-82; apprentice Branch Funeral Home, Smithtown, N.Y., 1982-83; mortician Weber Funeral Home, Bonkow Rona, N.Y., 1983-84; mgr., mortician Guidetti Funeral Home, N.Y.C., 1983-84, Coram (N.Y.) Meml. Chapel, 1985-88; owner, mortician, mgr. Emque Chapels: L.I. Funeral Services, Coram, 1986—. Author: An Inexpensive Guide to Burials and Cremations, 1986. Mem. Decisions Womens Orgn., Met. Funeral Dir. Assn., Am. Heart Assn. Republican. Roman Catholic. Lodge: Order of Eastern Star. Home: 7 Awixa Pl Seldon NY 11784 Office: Emque Chapels & LI Funeral Services 3640 Rt 112 PO Box 646 Coram NY 11735

LOFTUS, LINDA MARY, travel agency manager; b. St. Louis, Mar. 6, 1950; d. William Joseph and Doris (Goellner) Kitchin; m. Thomas J. Ownen, Oct. 13, 1973 (div. Mar. 1983); children: Jennifer, Benjamin; m. Patrick Loftus, Aug. 24, 1985. Grad., Inst. Cert. Travel Agts., 1985. Cert. travel cons. Internat. travel cons. Turner Travel, Cranford, N.J., 1980-83; travel mgr. Gelco Travel Services, Iselin, N.J., 1983—. Mem. Travel Industry Profl. Soc. Democrat. Roman Catholic. Home: 27 Long Hill Rd Colonia NJ 07067 Office: Gelco Travel 485 US Rt 1 Iselin NJ 08830

LOGAN, GRACE ELEANOR MILLER (MRS. HENRY WHITTINGTON LOGAN), educator; b. Valencia, Pa., June 22, 1908; d. Alvah John and Lillian (Gibson) Miller; B.S., Temple U., 1930, M.S., 1931; postgrad., 1955-56; m. Henry Whittington Logan, Mar. 16, 1940; 1 son, Henry Whittington III. English instr. Temple U., 1930-33; asst. prof. to dept. head Moravian Coll., Bethlehem, Pa., 1933-42; assoc. prof. edn. and philosophy Widener U., Chester, Pa., 1956-67, prof. English, 1967-85, prof. emeritus, adj. prof. 1985—; dir. Coll. Reading Services, 1958-85; dir. Fed. Office of Edn. Equal Opportunities Tng. Br. Insts., 1965—; bd. dirs. 1683 Caleb Pusey

House, Upland, Pa., dir. bd. of friends, 1986—; cons., lectr. in biblical studies, 1985—; only woman on faculty any mil. coll. U.S. for 8 yrs. Elder, Presbyn. Ch.; mem. adv. bd. Pa. Inst. Tech. Mem. AAUP, Delaware County Hist. Soc. (dir.), Nat. Council Tchrs. English, Coll. English Assn., Coll. Reading Assn., Internat. Reading Assn., Pa. Council of Tchrs., Am. Acad. Religion, Questers Potpourri, Kappa Delta Epsilon, Pi Delta Epsilon. Home: 201 Sykes Ln Wallingford PA 19086 Office: Widener Univ Chester PA 19013

LOGAN, LELIA CHARLOTTE, real estate developer; b. Tampa, Fla., May 31, 1956; d. Claude Duval and Charlotte Patricia (Jordan) L. BS in Fin., U. Fla., 1978; MBA in Fin., U. South Fla., 1984. Mgt. sales Founders LifeIns. Co., Tampa, 1978-80; mgr. policy holder service Met. Life Ins. Co., Tampa, 1980-81; broker Mfrs. Life Ins. Co., Tampa, 1981-82; mgr. devel. Logan Cos., Tampa, 1982—. Mem. Health Human Services Research Unit, 1986-88, Tampa Jr. League, 1979—, Sunshine Players, 1980-83; adv. bd. Gasparilla Distance Classic, Tampa, 1983—, chmn. host, 1983. Photographer Sandspur mag., 1983-86. Mem. Nat. Assn. Indl. Office Parks, Builders Owners Mgrs. Assn., Tampa C. of C., Delta Theta, Kappa Alpha Theta. Republican. Episcopalian. Clubs: Tri-fed (Calif.), Tampa Bay Cycle, Two Rivers Hounds (Tampa). Office: Logan Cos 1200 W Cass St Tampa FL 33606

LOGAN, LINDA ANN, manufacturing executive; b. Cin., Aug. 7, 1950; d. Harold John and Amelia Edna (Scurry) L. BS in Bus. Adminstrn. and Econs., Fisk U., 1972; MBA, Xavier U., 1975. Mktg. analyst Frigidaire subs. Gen. Motors, Dayton, Ohio, 1972-75; mktg. rep. IBM Corp., Dayton, 1975-76; assoc. proj. dir. The Drackett Co. div. Bristol-Myers, Cin., 1977-79; sr. analyst consumer research The Drackett Co., Cin., 1979-82, mgr. consumer research, 1982-84, sr. mgr. consumer research, 1984—; vis. prof. Black Exec. Exchange Program Nat. Urban League, 1978—. Chairperson youth program YMCA Black Achievers, Cin., 1983-84, mem. steering com., 1983-85; bd. dirs. Gross Br. YMCA, Cin., 1984-86 (Black Achiever 1981, Alumni Black Achiever 1982); bd. dirs. Cin. Scholarship Found., exec. sec., 1985-86, v.p., 1987—. Mem. Nat. Black MBA Orgn., Am. Mktg. Assn. (v.p. membership 1985-86, mem. exec. adv. council 1986—), Alpha Kappa Alpha. Democrat. Episcopalian. Home: 7624 Castleton Pl Cincinnati OH 45237 Office: The Drackett Co Bristol-Myers 201 E 4th St Cincinnati OH 45201

LOGAN, MAXINE CORKI, talent agent; b. Chgo., June 23, 1946; d. Joe and Sara (Levine) Nadler; m. Lee Robert Logan; children: Chad Jamie, Casie Blake. Interior decorator Maxine's Interior's, Encino, Calif., 1966-72; real estate sales Masterpiece Properties, Encino, 1965—; owner Am. Black Chronicle, Encino, 1973-74; tchr. Maxine's Ceramics, Encino, 1975-80; owner Maxine's, Encino, 1981-85, Maxine's Talent Agy., Encino, 1985—, Logan's Music Co., Encino, 1986—. Mem. Screen Actor's Guild, AFTRA.

LOGAN, SHARON BROOKS, lawyer; b. Easton, Md., Nov. 19, 1945; d. Blake Elmer and Esther N. (Statum) Brooks; children: John W. III, Troy Blake. BS in Econs., U. Md., 1967, MBA in Mktg., 1969; JD, U. Fla., 1979. Bar: Fla. 1979. Ptnr. Raymond Wilson, Esq., Ormond Beach, Fla., 1980, Landis, Graham & French, Daytona Beach, Fla., 1981, Watson & Assocs., Daytona Beach, 1982-84; prin. Sharon B. Logan, Esq., Ormond Beach, 1984—; legal advisor to paralegal program Daytona Beach Community Coll., 1984—, Jon Hall Chevrolet, Daytona Beach, 1984—, Jon Hall Honda, Daytona Beach, 1984—, Holly Hill Heritage, Inc., Fla., 1984—. Trustee Ocean Pointe Pro, Dayton Beach Shores, Fla., 1984—; sponsor Ea. Surfing Assn., Daytona Beach, 1983—, Nat. Scholastic Surfing Assn., 1987—. Recipient Citizenship award Rotary Club, 1962-63; Woodrow Wilson fellow U. Md., 1967. Mem. ABA, Fla. Bar Assn. (real property and probate sect.), Volusia County Bar Assn. (bd. dirs.), Fla. Real Property Council (bd. dirs., founder, v.p.), Real Property Council Volusia County (v.p. 1987-88), Fla. Assn. Women Lawyers, Volusia County Estate Planning Council, AAUW, Daytona Beach Area Bd. Realtors, Ormond Beach C. of C., Beta Gamma Sigma, Alpha Lamba Delta, Phi Kappa Phi, Omicron Delta Epsilon, Delta Delta Delta (Scholarship award 1964), Sigma Alpha Epsilon. Democrat. Episcopalian. Clubs: Indigo Lakes, Gator. Avocations: cooking, sewing, golf, tennis, aerobics. Office: Sharon B Logan Esq 400 S Atlantic Suite 110 Ormond Beach FL 32074

LOGAN, VERYLE JEAN, retail executive, realtor; b. St. Louis, Oct. 24; d. Benjamin Bishop and Eddie Mae (Williams) Logan. B.S., Mo. U., 1968; postgrad. Wayne State U., 1974, 76, U. Mich.-Detroit, 1978, 80. With Hudson Dept. Store, Detroit, 1968-84, Dayton Hudson, Mpls., 1984-86, div. mdse. mgr., 1983-84, retail exec. div. mdse. mgr. Coats and Dresses, 1984-86; pres. Ultimate Connection, Inc., Mpls., 1987—. Mem. Pilgrim Bapt. Ch.; trustee Harry Davis Found., 1988. Named Woman of Yr., Am. Bus. Women, 1984. Mem. Am. Bus. Womens Assn. (v.p. 1983-84), Minn. Black Networking (exec. bd. 1985—), Delta Sigma Theta Mpls.-St. Paul Alumnae Assn. (life mem., recording sec. 1985-87, chmn. arts and letters, corresponding sec. 1987-88, named Delta of the Yr., 1988). Club: M.L. King Tennis Buffs. Office: PO Box 16438 Minneapolis MN 55416

LOGAN, VICKI, advertising executive; b. Oakland, Calif., Aug. 3, 1954; d. Robert Lee and Freida Elizabeth (Luckett) L. BS in Bus. Adminstrn. magna cum laude, Pepperdine U., 1976; M in Internat. Mgmt. with honors, Am. Grad. Sch. Internat. Mgmt., 1979. Asst. to dep. dir. HUD, Washington, 1978; account exec. Doyle Dane Bernbach Advt., Inc., N.Y.C., 1979-81; sr. v.p., creative dir. Jordan, McGrath, Case, Taylor & McGrath Advt., N.Y.C., 1981—. Office: 445 Park Ave New York NY 10022

LOGEMANN, JERILYN ANN, speech pathologist; b. Berwyn, Ill., May 21, 1942; d. Warren F. and Natalie M. (Killmer) L.; BS, Northwestern U., 1963; MA, 1964, PhD, 1968. Grad. asst. dept. communicative disorders Northwestern U., 1963-68; instr. speech and audiology DePaul U., 1964-65; instr. dept. communicative disorders Mundelein Coll., 1967-71; research assoc. depts. neurology and otolaryngology and maxillofacial surgery Northwestern U. Med. Sch., Chgo., 1970-74, asst. prof., 1974-78, dir. clin. and research activities of speech and lang., 1975—, assoc. prof. dept. neurology, otolaryngology and maxillofacial disorders, communicative disorders, 1978-83, prof. dept. neurology, otolaryngology and maxiofacial disorders, communicative disorders, 1983—, chmn. dept. communicative disorders, 1982—; mem. assoc. staff Northwestern Meml. Hosp., 1976—; assoc. dir. cancer control. Ill. Comprehensive Cancer Council, Chgo., 1980-82. Mem. rehab. com. Ill. div. Am. Cancer Soc., 1975-79, chmn., 1979—. Nat. Inst. Neurologic Disease, Communicative Disorders and Stroke postdoctoral fellow Northwestern U., 1968-70; Inst. Medicine Chgo. fellow, 1981—, Nat. Cancer Inst. grantee, 1975—, Am. Cancer Soc. grantee, 1981-82. Fellow Am. Speech, Lang. and Hearing Assn.; mem. Internat. Assn. Logopedics and Phoniatrics, AAUP, Acoustic Soc. Am. (program com. Chgo. regional chpt.), Linguistic Soc. Am., Speech Communication Assn., Am. Cleft Palate Assn., Ill. Speech and Hearing Assn., Chgo. Heart Assn., Chgo. Speech Therapy and Auditory Soc. Author: The Fisher-Logemann Test of Articulation Competence, 1971, Evaluation and Treatment of Swallowing Disorders, 1983; Manual for the Videofluorographic Evaluation of Swallowing, 1985, Videofluoroscopic Evaluation of Swallowing, 1986; assoc. editor Jour. Speech and Hearing Disorders, Jour. Head Trauma Rehab., Dysphagia Jour., 1978-82. Office: Northwestern U Med Sch 303 E Chicago Ave Chicago IL 60611

LOGIUDICE, ROSEMARY JOANNE, veterinarian; b. Albany, N.Y., Feb. 5, 1955; d. Frank Joseph and Mafalda Rosalie (DeVirgilio) LoGiudice. BS in Agriculture with honors, U. Ill., 1977, BS in Vet. Medicine, 1979, DVM, 1981. Lic. veterinarian. Student vet. asst. Oak Knoll Animal Hosp., Ltd., Moline, Ill., 1974-81; vet. Plato Computer Programmer Coll. Vet. Medicine, U. Ill., Urbana, 1978-81; student vet. asst. Quad City Downs and Friendship Farms, East Moline, Ill., 1974-79, Dr. David M. Rash, Geneseo, Ill., 1970-73; staff veterinarian Ingmire Large Animal Clinic, Joliet, Ill., 1981-83, staff v.p., corp. ptnr., 1983—; Dept. Agriculture meat inspector Illini Beef Packers, Inc., Geneseo, and Wilson Foods, Monmouth, Ill., 1979. Editor U. Ill. Coll. Vet. Medicine Yearbook, 1980. Choir dir. St. John's Cath. Chapel, Champaign, Ill., 1974-79; mem. Peoria Cath. Diocese Liturgical Music Commn., 1975-77; coach nat. champion team Ill. Arabian Horse Assn. Youth Horse Judging Team, 1978, also mem. nat. res. champion team, 1972; mem. U. Ill. Women's Glee Club, 1973-79, pres., 1975-76, tour mgr., 1973-74; mem. U. Ill. Horse Judging Team, 1975-77; coach youth horse judging team Will County 4-H Clubs, Joliet, Ill., 1981-82; alto soloist Joliet Community Chorale, 1982-84; asst. dir., soloist, guitarist St. Jude Cath. Ch.'s Glory and Praise Singers, New Lenox, Ill. Recipient U. Ill. Mother's Assn. award, 1973. Mem. Am. Assn. Equine Practitioners, Ill. State Vet. Med. Assn. (equine practitioners com. 1981-85, CVM worksop com. 1985, 88, human animal bond/animal welfare com. 1988, office relocation com. 1988, chmn. equine practitioner's mktg. and pub. relations com. 1985-86), Ill. Coll. Vet. Medicine Alumni Assn. (bd. dirs. 1987—), Kankakee Valley Vet. Med. Assn. (program chmn. 1983-84, pres. 1984-86), AVMA (Outstanding Service award U. Ill. Student chpt.), Mortar Bd. (pres. 1977), Omega Tau Sigma (pres. 1980, charter mem. Theta chpt. alumni assn., bd. dirs. 1985—, Outstanding Sr. award 1981), Gamma Sigma Delta, Alpha Zeta, Atius, Alpha Lambda Delta. Roman Catholic. Club: Upper Midwest Competitive and Endurance Ride Assn. (ride veterinarian 1981-85). Office: Ingmire Large Animal Clinic Ltd 1410 Mills Rd Joliet IL 60433

LOGUE, LOIS JOAN, medical technologist, association executive; b. Mt. Pleasant, Mich., June 28, 1936; d. Daniel Edward and Thelma Margaret (Hanke) Hughes; student U. Tex., 1954-56; B.S., Incarnate World Coll., 1958; m. William J. Logue, Jr., Oct. 12, 1957; children—Kathleen Sue, William Joseph. Hematology supr. Meml. Hosp. of Chester County, West Chester, Pa., 1967-68; adminstrv. technologist Paoli (Pa.) Meml. Hosp., 1968-78; adminstrv. dir. Nat. Com. for Clin. Lab. Standards, Villanova, Pa., 1979-84; exec. dir. Clin. Lab. Mgmt. Assn., Paoli, Pa., 1984—; v.p. Health Systems Concepts Inc., 1985—; key man State of Pa. for Am. Soc. Med. Technologists, 1977-82. Recipient Chi Omega award for outstanding service to the Profession, Am. Soc. Med. Technologists, 1980, 81. Mem. Am. Soc. Clin. Pathologists, Am. Soc. Med. Technologists, Clin. Lab. Mgmt. Assn. (nat. pres. 1978-79, dir. 1977—, pres. Del. Valley chpt. 1977-80), Clin. Ligand Assay Soc., Chi Omega. Republican. Roman Catholic. Mem. editorial bd. Lab. World, 1978-82. Home: 601 Waynesfield Dr Newtown Square PA 19073 Office: 195 W Lancaster Ave Paoli PA 19301

LOGUE, PEGGY KING, accounting manager; b. Washington, Oct. 30, 1958; d. Lloyd Lee and Barbara (Allen) King; m. Stephen Andrew Logue, Aug. 28, 1982 (separated Dec. 1985); 1 child, Travis Stephen. BS in Acctg., Tenn. Tech. U., 1981; MBA with hons. Southeastern U., Washington, 1987. Asst. fin. mgr. Associated Real Estate Mgmt., McLean, Va., 1981-84; collection adminstr. Rolm Corp., Vienna, 1984; jr. acct. Verdix Corp., Chantilly, Va., 1984-85, acctg. supr., 1985-86, fin. acct. Airbus Service Co., Herndon, Va., customer acct. adminstr., 1988—. Mem. NOW, Nat. Assn. Female Execs. Avocations: running, bicycling, softball, swimming. Home: 713 Brethour Ct Sterling VA 22170 Office: Airbus Service Co Inc 593 Herndon Pkwy Herndon VA 22070

LOHR, JOANN KREFTMEYER, human resource executive; b. Alton, Ill., July 26, 1952; d. Oswald Arthur and Evelyn Lorraine (Shewmaker) Kreftmeyer; m. Douglas Alan Lohr, Dec. 1, 1984. BBA, So. Ill. U., Edwardsville, 1974; postgrad. in law, Washington U., St. Louis, 1974-75. Ops. mgr. Chelsea Industries, Inc., St. Louis, 1973-80; employee relations mgr. Union Carbide Corp., Alamo, Nev., 1981-82, Riverton, Wyo., 1982-83; employee relations mgr. Union Carbide-Viskase Corp., Kentland, Ind., 1984-88; corp. mgr. human resources Viskase Corp., Chgo., 1988—. Editorial bd. Viskase Family mag., 1986—. Founder, pres. Human Resource Council, Kentland, 1986—; charter mem. Park Station Removal and Relocation, Inc., Kentland, 1986—. Mem. Am. Bus. Womens Assn., Am. Soc. Personnel Adminstrs., Kentland Area C. of C. Democrat. Jewish. Office: Viskase Corp 6855 W 65th St Chicago IL 60638

LOHR, KRISTINE MARIE, medical educator, researcher; b. Buffalo, Oct. 29, 1949; d. Leonard Joseph and Lucille Elizabeth (Reger) L. BA in Biochemistry, Canisius Coll., 1971; MD, U. Rochester, 1975. Diplomate Am. Bd. Internal Medicine, Am. Bd. Rheumatology. Resident Ohio State U. Hosps., Columbus, 1975-78; research fellow Duke U. Med. Ctr., Durham, N.C., 1978-81; asst. prof. medicine Med. Coll. of Wis., Milw., 1981-87, chmn. housestaff assistance com., 1983-87; assoc. prof. medicine Univ. Tenn., Memphis, 1987—. Grantee Wis. Arthritis Found., 1982-84, NIH, 1983, 86—, VA Merit Rev. Bd., 1982—. Fellow ACP, Am. Rheumatism Assn.; mem. Am. Fedn. Clin. Research, Am. Med. Women's Assn., Assn. Research in Vision and Ophthalmology, AAUW (bd. dirs. 1986-87). Office: Univ Tenn Memphis Box 3A 956 Court Ave Memphis TN 38163

LOHRY, JANET SUE, accountant; b. Paonia, Colo., May 15, 1941; d. Dana Norman and Helen Anita (Davison) Petersen; m. Charles S. Lohry, Oct. 5, 1959 (div. May 1967); children: Christine Ann, Gary Charles. Grad. high sch., Ft. Collins, Colo., 1959. Receptionist, operator PBX Forney Industries, Ft. Collins, 1959-60; sec. Hooper & Assocs., Ft. Collins, 1967-68; sec., bookkeeper Barker & Collins, P.A., Sheridan, Wyo., 1968-69; bookkeeper Kenneth Cox, CPA, Sheridan, Wyo., 1969-70; adminstr. fin. Burroughs Corp., Casper, Wyo., 1970-80, Stuart Shop, Ltd., Casper, Wyo., 1980-81; controller Sta. KCWY-TV subs. Chrysostom Corp., Casper, Wyo., 1981-84; data operator, accountant Cyclone Well Service, West Winds Trucking, Triple J Oil Resources, Casper, Wyo., 1984—; also sec. bd. dirs. Cyclone Well Service, Casper, Wyo.; cons. Sandy Cordoba Advt., Casper, 1978-82; pres. Burnett Livestock, Buffalo, Wyo., 1987—; sec., bd. dirs. Triple J. Oil Resources. Den mother Boy Scouts Am., Casper, 1972-75; vol. mgr. Zipay for Sheriff, Casper, 1982; campaign mgr. Simmons for State House, 1986; vol. Literacy Vols. of Am., 1987, Spl. Olympics, 1986-87. Republican. Lutheran. Home: 419 W 13th St Casper WY 82601 Office: Cyclone Well Service Ltd 100 N Center #205 Casper WY 82601

LOHSE, PHYLLIS THEDE, data processing executive; b. Salem, Oreg., Oct. 15, 1946; d. Ralph Winn and Dorothy E. (Bower) Thede; m. Richard A.H. Davison, Dec. 28, 1968 (div. 1975); m. Bruce Warren Lohse, Mar. 26, 1979; children: Morgan, Derek. BSc in Math., U. Oreg., 1968; postgrad., U. Toronto, 1972-73; MBA, U. Portland, 1985. Systems programmer Dept. Motor Vehicles St. Oreg., Salem, 1968-69; programmer analyst British Columbia Telephone Co., Vancouver, Can., 1969-71; systems analyst Ryerson Polytech. Inst., Toronto, 1971-73; project leader T. Eaton Co. Ltd., Toronto, 1973-75; mgr. project Braegen Corp., Sunnyvale, Calif., 1975; rep. mktg. IBM, Arlington, Va., 1975-76; systems mgr., mgr. dealer computer services Freightliner Corp., Portland, Oreg., 1976-83; gen. mgr. Ultimate ROADS Inc. (subs. Ultimate Corp.), Grand Prairie, Tex., 1983-88. Sec. bd. ministers Willamette Christian Ch., West Linn, 1986-87; treas., 1987—; program developer Inst. for Managerial and Profl. Women. Mem. Nat. Assn. Female Execs., Kappa Alpha Theta. Republican. Club: City Portland. Home: 2123 SW Greene West Linn OR 97068

LOMBARDO, BONNIE JANE, film company executive; b. Akron, Ohio, Jan. 25, 1941; d. George Mayfield Reed and Grace Jane (Gercevic) Morrison; m. Joseph Stanley Wrobel, Jan. 28, 1959 (div. July 1971); children—Vicki Leopold, Eric Wrobel, Teri Jo Huston; m. Richard Lombardo. A.A. in Bus. Law, Los Angeles Valley Coll., 1974; B.A. in Bus. Adminstrn., U. Akron, 1964. Sec. Los Angeles Valley Coll. Businesswomen's Assn., 1973-74; ops. mgr. TV bus. affairs dept. Columbia Pictures Industries, Burbank, Calif., 1981—. Recipient award of Merit Columbia Pictures Industries, 1977, 87. Mem. Women in Film, Women of Motion Picture Industry, Nat. Assn. Female Execs., Kappa Kappa Gamma (sec. 1962-64). Democrat. Roman Catholic. Avocation: interior design. Home: 20838 Satinwood Dr Saugus CA 91350 Office: Columbia Pictures Industries 3300 Riverside Dr #307-B Burbank CA 91505

LOMBARDO, LISA KERSTIN, small business owner; b. Wilkes-Barre, Pa., May 29, 1955; d. Joseph L. and Normajean G. (Kozicki) Wroblewski; m. John L. Lombardo, June 10, 1978 (div. Jan. 1984). BS, Sch. of Hotel Adminstrn., Cornell U., Ithaca, N.Y., 1978. Various mgmt. positions Rock Resorts Inc., Jackson Hole, Wyo. and Kapalua, Maui, Hawaii, 1978-80; account exec. Hallmark Cards Inc., Kansas City, Mo., 1980-84; dir. of licensing King World Prodns., N.Y.C., 1984-85; v.p. merchandising and promotion LBS Communications, N.Y.C., 1985-86; pres. Desktop Designs, Darien, Conn., 1986—, Brandy Arts Inc., Darien, 1986—; owner Movieland Video Store, Stamford, Conn., 1987—. Mem. Nat. Assn. Female Execs., LWV. Republican. Roman Catholic. Office: Movieland Video Sta 579 Newfield Ave Stamford CT 06905

LOMBARI, LEAANN, financial consultant, credit manager; b. Providence, Mar. 18, 1948; d. Pacifico Ralph and Lesa M. (Giannattassio) Lombari; 1 child, Charles Sabin Burr; m. Donald Jones. Cert. mus. curatorship, R.I. Sch. Design, 1965; BS, R.I. Coll., 1969. Divisional controller Stewart Myers & Co., Manchester, N.H., 1976-78; credit mgr. U. N.H., Durham, 1979—; treas., owner MPAS, Inc., Durham, 1982—; leader workshops in field, 1982—; treas. Ocean Service & Maintenance, Concord, N.H., 1985—; U.S. del. to joint China/U.S. session on trade, industry and econs., 1988. Mem. N.H. Women's Lobby, Concord, 1983-86. Bulova Watch Co. scholar, 1967. Mem. AAUW (topic chairperson 1981-84), BPW (local orgn. pres. 1982-85, treas. 1986-87, chair fin. and investment com. 1986-88, 88—, Woman of Yr. 1985), Nat. Assn. Female Execs., N.H. Women in Higher Edn., Seacoast Women's Network. Lodge: Zonta. Home: N Pembroke Rd Pembroke NH 03275 Office: Univ N H 304 Thompson Hall Durham NH 03824

LOMONTE, LANECE POPE, health administrator; b. Trinity County, Tex., Sept. 4, 1934; d. Alton Lee and Bonnie Irene (Lawrence) Pope; B.S., Sam Houston State U., 1954, postgrad. 1961; M.Ed., U. Md., 1967; 1 dau., Emily Chandler. Asst. to dir. food services Dow Chem., Freeport, Tex., 1954-59; instr. Georgetown Visitation Coll., Washington, 1962-63; tchr. Anne Arundel County (Md.) public schs., 1963-70; asst. to dir. admissions St. John's Coll., Md., 1970-72; owner S:HE, Annapolis and Dallas, 1972-78; adminstrv. aide Hubbard & Assos., Dallas, 1977-80; contracts coordinator Community Health Computing, Houston, 1980-81; tchr. Spring Branch (Tex.) Public Schs., 1981-86; asst. to the pres. Community Health Computing, Houston, 1986—; cons. U. Md., 1964-70. Active, Nottingham W. Civic Assn., Houston, 1980—. Democrat. Methodist. Home: 14007 Myrtlea Houston TX 77079

LONDO, MARLENE JEAN (MAR), therapist, counselor; b. Norway, Mich., July 23, 1931; d. Frank Wilhelm and Alma Olive (Rigotti) Beitel; m. Richard William Londo, Oct. 4, 1952; children: Michael, Robert, Sandra, Jo(Anne). Grad. high sch., Norway, 1949. Therapist, alcohol counselor Am. Found. Counseling Services, Inc., Green Bay, Wis., 1974—. Tchr. religion Diocese of Green Bay, 1967-72, dir. of religious edn. program, 1969-71; pres. parents club Premontre High Sch., 1970-72. Mem. Internat. Transactional Analysis Assn. (rules, ethics com. 1974—). Office: Am Found Counseling Services Inc 130 E Walnut Green Bay WI 54301

LONDON, CHARLOTTE ISABELLA, reading specialist; b. Guyana, S.Am., June 11, 1946; came to U.S., 1966, naturalized, 1980; d. Samuel Alphonso and Diana Dallett (Daniels) Edwards; m. David Timothy London, May 26, 1968 (div. May 1983); children: David Tshombe, Douglas Tshaka. BS, Fort Hays State U., 1971; MS, Pa. State U., 1974, PhD, 1977. Elem. sch. tch., Guyana, 1962-66, secondary sch. tchr., 1971-72; instr. lang. arts Pa. State U., University Park, 1973-74; reading specialist/ednl. cons. N.Y.C. Community Coll., 1975; dir. skills acquisition and devel. center Stockton (N.J.) State Coll., 1975-77; reading specialist Pleasantville (N.J.) Public Schs., 1977—; v.p. Atlantic County PTA, 1980-82; del. N.J. Gov.'s Conf. Future Edn. N.J., 1981. Sec. Atlantic County Minority Polit. Women's Caucus. Mem. Internat. Reading Assn., Nat. Council Tchrs. English, Assn. Supervision and Curriculum Devel., NEA, N.J. Ednl. Assn., AAUW, Pi Lambda Theta, Phi Delta Kappa (sec.). Mem. African Methodist Episcopal Ch. Home: 1419 Cedar Dr Mays Landing NJ 08330 Office: Pleasantville Pub Schs W Decatur Ave Pleasantville NJ 08232

LONDON, CHERYL ANN, communications executive; b. Albuquerque, Apr. 14, 1957; d. Roger William and Barbara Jean (Olendorf) Greer; m. Kim Brian London, June 24, 1978. BA in Biology with honors, U. Calif., Santa Cruz, 1979. Teller, loan processor Monterey Savs. and Loan Co., Watsonville, Calif., 1979-80; data processing acct. rep. Monterey Savs. and Loan Co., Calif., 1980-82; mktg. tech. specialist Tymshare, Inc., Cupertino, Calif., 1982-83; acct. rep. Tymnet, Inc., Irvine, Calif., 1983, assoc. communications cons., 1984; communications cons. Tymnet-McDonnell Douglas, Inc., Irvine, 1984-85, sr. communications cons., 1985, tech. mgr., 1985—. Mem. Nat. Assn. Female Execs. Office: Tymnet-McDonnell Douglas Inc 18881 Von Karmen Ave Suite 450 Irvine CA 92715

LONDON, MARY ELLEN, educational coordinator, consultant; b. Hutchinson, Kans., Apr. 3, 1927; d. Chester Iaasic and Edna Louise (Anderson) Lewis; grad. in Fine Arts/Edn., Kans. U., 1949; M.A. in Early Childhood Edn., Goddard Coll., 1973; postgrad. Froebel Inst., London, 1972; Ph.D., Golden State U.; m. Lewis London, Sept. 30, 1967; 1 son by previous marriage, Richard Norman Batie. Design engr. Boeing, Wichita, Kans., 1952-59; supr., trainer Parent Child Guidance Center Head Start, Los Angeles, 1968-74, Fedn. Head Start trainer, supr., 1974-78; exec. dir. Assistance League Day Nursery-Kindergarten, 1982—; pvt. practice cons. early childhood edn., Los Angeles, 1971—; exec. dir. Assistance League Day Nursery-Kindergarten; dir. Creative Environment Learning Center, Los Angeles, 1971-73; cons. Early Childhood Edn. Study, Newton, Mass., 1970; instr., asst. prof. Long Beach (Calif.) State U., 1975-77; asst. prof. early childhood edn. Pepperdine U., Los Angeles, 1975-78, Calif. State U.-Los Angeles, 1980—, Pacific Oaks Coll., 1981—, LaVerne (Calif.) U., 1975—; field coordinator state pre-sch. career incentive program Inst. for Profl. Devel.; Child Devel. Consortium rep., Washington, 1976—; adv. bd. on follow through Graham Elem. Sch.; advisory bds. on early childhood edn. S.W. Coll., Valley City Coll., Compton Coll., Los Angeles City Coll., Dominguez Hills U., Calif. State U. Long Beach; adv. bds. Harbor Coll., El Camino Coll.; cons. assessor Urban Inst., Region IX ACYF-HEW, 1979—. Recipient awards Kans. Regional Art Exhibit, 1944, Head Start, 1968, 75, efficiency economy award Lockheed, 1962; tchr. tng. cert. OEO, 1966; supervision of year trophy Head Start, 1974, 78. Mem. So. Calif. Assn. for Edn. Young Children (Los Angeles v.p., 1976-78, 83-85), Calif. Assn. for Edn. Young Children (chmn. Internat. Yr. of Child, 1978-79), Nat. Assn. for Edn. Young Children (governing bd., public policy task group, Washington, 1977—, local coordinator conf., Anaheim, 1976), Alpha Kappa Alpha (Black Heritage chmn., 1977-79, 25 year medalion, 1979, community service award, 1979, exhibit award, 1979, Care of Children award Los Angeles City Council 1986), Black Women's Forum Los Angeles, Exec. Female. Methodist. Club: Hollywood Wilshire Soroptimist (v.p., 1987, pres. 1987-88). Artist, organist, dress designer; participant art exhibit, Oakland, Calif., 1965; author: Creative Environment Learning Center, 1973. Home and Office: 1235 Stearns Dr Los Angeles CA 90035

LONDON, SHERI FAITH, finance and securities executive, financial planner; b. Hackensack, N.J., Dec. 6, 1955; d. Julius and Millie (Dier) L. BA, Rutgers U., 1977; postgrad., Emory U., 1978-80. Research asst. grad. sch. Emory U., Atlanta, 1978-79; registered rep. Donald & Co. Securities Inc., Jersey City, 1980—, v.p., registered options prin., 1984—, gen. prin., 1986—; researcher, office mgr. Pub. Citizen's Congress Watch, Washington, 1982-83; pres. S.F.L. Fin. Planning, Inc., Hackensack, 1985—; life, health ins. rep. Berger Agy., Neptune, N.J., 1987—; fin. planner seminars for orgns. and high schs.; cons. in field, 1986—. Contbr. articles to profl. jours. Bd. dirs. Bergen County chpt. ACLU, N.J., 1983—. Emory U. Grad. Sch. grantee, 1978. Mem. Inst. Cert. Fin. Planners (cert.). Home and Office: SFL Fin Planning Inc 15 F Coles Ave Hackensack NJ 07601

LONDRAVILLE, JANIS SWAN, drama and speech educator; b. Albany, N.Y., Sept. 24, 1949; d. Roland John and Clara Eugenia (Swan) Huddleston; m. Clark Aimoku Slayter, May 31, 1974 (div. Apr. 1987); m. Richard John Londraville, Oct. 10, 1987. BA in English cum laude, Keuka Coll., 1971; M in English, Coll. St. Rose, 1973. Researcher Union Coll. Character Research Project, Schenectady, N.Y., 1973-74; lectr. Chaminade U., Honolulu, 1976-78; tchr. English Hawaii Sch. for Girls, Honolulu, 1978-79; tchr., dir. drama and speech The Hawaii Prep. Acad., Kamuela, Hawaii, 1979—. Fellow NEH, 1986, Council for Basic Edn., 1987. Mem. Nat. Forensic League, Hawaii Speech League (chair dist. IV 1985-88), Pi Delta Epsilon, Sigma Tau Delta. Republican. Methodist. Address: 6 Harrington Ct Potsdam NY 13676

LONDRÉ, FELICIA MAE HARDISON, theatre educator; b. Ft. Lewis, Wash., Apr. 1, 1941; d. Felix M. and Priscilla Mae (Graham) Hardison; m. Venne-Richard Londré, Dec. 16, 1967; children: Tristan Graham, Georgianna Rose. BA with high honors, U. Mont., 1962; MA, U. Wash., 1964; PhD, U. Wis., 1969. Asst. prof. U. Wis. at Rock County, Janesville, 1969-75; asst. prof., head theatre program U. Tex. at Dallas, Richardson, 1975-78; assoc. prof. U. Mo., Kansas City, 1978-82, prof. theatre, 1982-87, also mem. various coms., curator's prof., 1987—; dramaturg Mo. Repertory Theatre, Kansas City, 1978—; mem. Folly Theatre Archives Task Force, 1982-83;

artistic advisor New Directions Theatre Co., 1983—; hon. lectr. Mid.-Am. State Univs. Assn., 1986-87; mem. humanitites adv. panel for romantic period Actors Theatre of Louisville, 1986-87. Author: Tennessee Williams, 1979, Tom Stoppard, 1981, Federico Garcia Lorca, 1984, (play) Miss Millay Was Right, 1982 (John Gassner Meml. Playwriting award 1982), (opera libretto) Duse and D'Annunzio, 1987; book rev. editor: Theatre Jour., 1984-86; assoc. editor: Shakespeare Around the Globe: A Guide to Notable Postwar Revivals, Jour. Dramatic Theory and Criticism, 1986—; mem. editorial bd.: Theatre History Studies Jour., 1984-86, Studies in Am. Drama, 1945-present, 1984—, 19th Century Theatre Jour., 1984—, Bookmark Press, Tennessee Williams Rev., 1985—; contbr. articles and book and theatre revs. to profl. publs. Université de Caen Fulbright study grantee, Normandy, France, 1962-63, U. Mo. faculty research grantee, 1985, 86; U. Wis. Grad. fellow, 1966-67; HKC Trustees fellow, 1987-88. Mem. Am. Soc. for Theatre Research (mem. exec. com. 1984—, mem. conv. program com. 1985), Internat. Fedn. for Theatre Research (gen. assembly del. 1985), Am. Theatre Assn. (mem. commn. on theatre research 1981-87, chmn. 1984-86), Theatre Library Assn., The Dramatists Guild, Literary Mgrs. and Dramaturgs Am., MLA, Midwest Chpt. MLA, Mid-Am. Theatre Conf. (chair grad. research paper competition 1985), Internat. Pamorama and Diorama Soc. Republican. Roman Catholic. Home: 528 E 56th St Kansas City MO 64110 Office: Mo Repertory Theatre 4949 Cherry St Kansas City MO 64110

LONERGAN, JOYCE, county official; b. Benton County, Iowa, Mar. 5, 1934; d. Robert and Fannie Mary (Duda) Jacobi; student public schs.; m. Paul J. Lonergan (dec.); children—Patrick Joseph, Peter Thomas, Kathleen Ann, Staci Marie. Mem. Iowa Ho. of Reps. from 87th Dist., 1975-86. Mem. Am. Bus. Women's Assn. Democrat. Roman Catholic. Office: US Courthouse Boones IA 50036

LONG, ALICE FREEMAN, education educator; b. Savannah, Ga., Mar. 12, 1928; d. John Morrison and Sallie Louise (Sandridge) Freeman; m. Charles Houston Long, June 21, 1952; children: John, Carolyn, Christopher, David. AB, Talladega (Ala.) Coll., 1949; MA, U. Chgo., 1952; cert., Erikson Inst., Chgo., 1967. Dir. edn. Ch. of the Good Shepherd, Chgo., 1949-54; tchr. Chgo. Pub. Schs., 1954-55; dir. headstart program Hilliard Homes Housing Project, Chgo., 1967-68; dir. diagnostic nursery U. Chgo. Clinics, 1969-74; instr. child devel. Durham Child Guidance Clinic, Duke U., Durham, N.C., 1974—; past pres., cons. mental health Durham Headstart Program, 1974—; bd. dirs. Durham Day Care Council, 1977—. Recipient Headstart award Durham Headstart Program, 1986. Mem. Assn. for Edn. Young Children, N.C. Day Care Assn., N.C. Headstart Assn., Dirs. State Early Intervention Programs Assn. Home: 405 Wesley Dr Chapel Hill NC 27514

LONG, ANNA MARIBETH, electrical engineer; b. Nashville, Aug. 18, 1960; d. George William and Martha Elizabeth (Love) Long; m. Arvind M. Parikh, June 11, 1988. BS in Applied Sci., U. Louisville, 1982, M in Elec. Engring., 1983. Policy analyst intern U.S. Govt., Washington, 1980-81; master control programmer Sta. WKPC-TV, Louisville, 1982-83; system devel. engr., network analyst IBM, Gaithersburg, Md., 1983—; del. Internat. Student Pugwash Conf., Ann Arbor, Mich., 1983; instr. Montgomery Coll., Germantown, Md., 1984-86, U. Md., College Park, 1986—. Counselor Montgomery County Fin. Counseling Service, 1986-87. Mem. IEEE, NSPE, Omicron Delta Kappa, Tau Beta Pi, Eta Kappa Nu. Office: IBM Systems Div 18100 Frederick Pike Gaithersburg MD 20879

LONG, BONNIE SINE, company executive; b. New Market, Va., Sept. 28, 1950; d. James Lester Sine and Doris Try (Wilkinson) Grim; m. Louis Franklin Southerd, Sept. 12, 1969 (div. 1974); 1 child, Tiage A.D.; m. James Monroe Long, Apr. 1, 1982. AS magna cum laude, Piedmont Va. Coll., 1976; BS magna cum laude, U. Md., 1986. Asst. ednl. resource mgr. Assn. Trial Lawyers Am., Washington, 1977-79; sales mgr. Skyline Inn, Washington, 1979-80; membership services dir. Gen. Fedn. Women's Clubs, Washington, 1980-81; fin. program analyst Advance Tech., Inc., Crystal City, Va., 1981-83; pres. Body Connections, Inc., Gaithersburg, Md., 1983—; sec./treas., bd. dirs. Corp. Systems Tech., Indian Head, Md., 1982—. Editor, designer artwork for flyers and programs ATLA, 1977-79; designer logos for tee shirts, 1976-78; designer advt., 1983—. Researcher on pay discrimination U. Md., 1985; bd. dirs., sec. Meth. Ch., New Carrollton, Md., 1977-78. Mem. Nat. Assn. Female Execs., Gold Key Honor Soc., Mensa. Avocations: reading and writing science fiction, art, piano, travel, makeup artistry. Home: 4910 Hollywood Rd College Park MD 20740

LONG, CYNTHIA GRBA, educator; b. Midland, Tex., Feb. 17, 1960; d. Nick and Wyona (Tyson) G.; m. Gerald Glen Long, May 29, 1980 (dec. 1983); 1 child, Christopher Jason. B in Bus., Tarleton State U., 1985, M in Bus., 1986. Instr. Star (Tex.) Indep. Sch., 1986—; lectr. Tarleton State U., Stephenville, Tex., 1986—; researcher Waco, Tex., 1985. Vol. sec. Abundant Life Assembly of God, Hamilton, Tex., 1985—, dir., tchr. vacation Bible sch., 1987—, children's ch., 1987, Sunday sch. tchr., 1988—. Mem. Nat. Assn. Female Execs., Dublin (Tex.) C. of C. Home: Chapman Lane PO Box 23 Evant TX 76525 Office: Tarleton State U Stephenville TX 76402

LONG, DOROTHY VALJEAN, personnel management company executive; b. Paducah, Ky., Mar. 10, 1928; d. Athel Sr. and Lora Bea (Vaughn) Shepherd; m. Earl Wallace Long; children: Robert Earl and Stephen Howard. Grad. high sch., Chgo.; various certificates in acctg., computing and control data mgmt. Keypunch supr. IBM Corp., Houston, 1950-54; terminal service mgr. SW region Control Data Corp., Houston, 1966-80; pres., chief exec. officer Keypeople Resources, Inc., Houston, 1980—. Pres. PTA, Houston, 1962-63; cons. Mission Bend UMC, 1986; social service vol. Sheltering Arms, 1986-87; mem. Temporary Help Services of Tex., Houston Bus. Council, City of Houston Certification; life mem. Women's Soc. of Christian Service, PTA State of Tex. Mem. Tex. Assn. Personnel Cons. Democrat. Office: Keypeople Resources Inc 2000 W Loop St #1620 Houston TX 77027

LONG, ELLENMAE QUAN, marketing, communication professional; b. Chgo., Oct. 30, 1927; d. Albert Daniel and Alice Elizabeth (Moloney) Quan; m. John Martin Long, May 1, 1954; children: Catherine E., John D., Patrick M. BA cum laude, Mundelein Coll., 1948; MA, Loyola U., Chgo., 1959. Faculty Mundelein Coll., Chgo., 1948-49; specialist, asst. mgr. sales promotions WGN, Inc., Chgo., 1949-56; pres., owner A.D. Quan and Co., Chgo., 1961-78; mgr. mktg. com. Creative Establishment Inc., Chgo., 1979-83, dir. mktg., v.p., 1985-87; v.p. Stark Prodn. Assocs. Ltd., Chgo., 1988—; mem. pub. info. com., mktg. adv. com. Chgo. Access Corp., 1986—; spkr. profl. meetings and seminars in U.S. and abroad. Judging chair U.S. Indsl. Film Festival, 1981—; contbr. articles to profl. jours. Mem. Pub. Relations Soc. Am. (program chmn. Chgo. chpt. 1986-87), Internat. Assn. Multi-Image (bd. dirs. Chgo. chpt. 1987—, 89), Internat. Assn. Bus. Communicators, Women in Communication, Inc. Club: Glenola. Office: Stark Prodn Assocs Ltd 311 N Des Plaines St #608 Chicago IL 60606

LONG, ERNESTINE MARTHA JOULLIAN, educator; b. St. Louis, Nov. 14, 1906; d. Ernest Cameron and Alice (Joullian) Long; A.B., U. Wis., 1927; M.S., U. Chgo., 1932; Ph.D., St. Louis U., 1976; postgrad. Washington U., St. Louis, 1932-68, Eastman Sch. Music, 1956, (NSF fellow) So. Ill. U., 1969-70. Tchr. scis. pub. schs. Normandy dist., St. Louis, 1927-66, Red Bud, Ill., 1966-70, St. Louis, 1970-75; coordinator continuing edn. U. Mo., St. Louis, 1976-79; ednl. cons. Area IV, St. Louis Pub. Schs.; dir. Project Think, Mo. and Ill., 1976-88. Recipient Community Service award St. Louis Newspaper Guild, 1978-79. Mem. AAAS, Am. Physics Tchrs. Assn., Am. Personnel and Guidance Assn. (treas. St. Louis br. 1954), Am. Chem. Soc., Cen. Assn. Sch. Sci. Math. Tchrs. (chmn. chemistry sect.), Am. Soc. for Microbiology, LWV, St. Louis Symphony Soc. (women's div., docent), Am. Guild Organists, NEA, Nat. Sci. Tchrs. Assn. Home: 245 N Price Rd Ladue MO 63124

LONG, KELLY ANN, transportation company executive; b. Detroit, Nov. 25, 1960; d. Gary Dean and Barbara Phyliss (Winstead) Alger; m. George Frederick Long, Feb. 9, 1985. BS in Acctg., Ferris State Coll., Big Rapids, Mich., 1982. Lic. Cosmetologist. Acct. Oxygen Unltd., Inc., Petoskey, Mich., 1982-83, Long Leasing Corp., East Jordan, Mich., 1983-84; pres., owner K.A.L. Truck Ctr., Inc., Kalkaska, Mich., 1984-85, B & B Transp., Inc., Gaylord, Mich., 1985—. Mem. Nat. Assn. Female Execs., U.S. C. of C. Methodist. Home: 918 Woodcrest Dr Gaylord MI 49735 Office: B&B Transp Inc PO Box 4012 627 Alpine St Gaylord MI 49735

LONG, KERRY JEAN, pharmaceutical company executive; b. Joliet, Ill., Oct. 28, 1948; d. Robert Armand and Marilyn Jean (Burt) L. BS in Chemistry, St. Mary's Coll., Notre Dame, Ind., 1970; MBA, U. Chgo., 1978. Analytical chemist Gillette Co., Chgo., 1970-74, Cen. Soya Co., Chgo., 1974-75; analytical chemist G. D. Searle, Skokie, Ill., 1975-78, supr. quality control, 1978-81; mgr. quality control Skokie and San Juan, P.R., 1981-82, University Park, Ill., 1982-84; dir. quality assurance Skokie, 1984-87, sr. dir. quality assurance, 1987—. Mem. St. Mary's Coll. Alumnae (v.p. 1984-87), U. Chgo. Women's Bus. Group. Democrat. Roman Catholic. Office: G D Searle & Co 5200 Old Orchard Rd Skokie IL 60077

LONG, MARY COLE, retired English language educator, author; b. Dallas, Oct. 1, 1922; d. Ernest E. and Sadie Flynn (Boone) Farrow; B.A., Baylor U., 1944; M.A., 1965; m. William Bowman Long, June 3, 1944; children—William Farrow, Daryl Elizabeth, Robert John, Linda Sue. Instr. English. Mary Hardin-Baylor U., Belton, Tex., 1965-72, asst. prof. English, 1972-83; v.p. Bearttollow Pubs. Pres., Leon Heights PTA, 1956, City Council PTA, 1957. Author: Stranger in a Strange Land, 1986. Mem. Central Tex. Poetry Soc. (pres. 1972-77), Poetry Soc. Tex. Home: 415 Downing St Belton TX 76513

LONG, MARY KAY, sales executive; b. Oak Park, Ill., Apr. 24, 1960; d. Thomas Patrick and Joann Elizabeth (Rogers) L. AA, Ferris State Coll., 1980, BA, 1983. Dist. service mgr. Buick Motor Div., Middletown, N.Y., 1984-85; dist. service mgr. Buick Motor Div., Newark, 1985-86, dist. sales mgr., 1986; dist. sales mgr. Buick Motor Div., Los Angeles, 1986—. Office: Buick Motor Div 515 Marin St Suite 205 Thousand Oaks CA 91360

LONG, NICHOLA Y., technical writer; b. Walnut Creek, Calif., Jan. 4, 1955; d. Shogo and Elizabeth (Hughes) Yamaguchi. BS in Indsl. Tech./Electronics, Tuskegee U., 1978. From spl. tech. asst. to tech. writing specialist Western Electric Corp., Winston-Salem, N.C., 1977-86; sr. tech. documentation specialist AT&T Network Systems, Winston-Salem, 1986—. Friend, The Arts Council, Inc., Winston-Salem, 1984-86. Mem. Am. Mgmt. Assn., Am. Soc. Profl. Execs., Tuskegee Nat. Alumni Assn. (pres. Winston-Salem chpt. 1984-86), Alpha Kappa Mu. Home: 168 Carrisbrooke Ln Winston-Salem NC 27104 Office: AT&T Network Systems 2400 Reynolda Rd Winston-Salem NC 27106

LONG, PHYLLIS WILLETTS, lawyer; b. Whiteville, N.C., Feb. 15, 1951; d. Adrian Larnell and Lois Jane (Sasser) Willetts; m. Atwood Edward Long, III, June 19, 1976. B.A. in Edn., U. N.C.-Chapel Hill, 1973; J.D., Washington and Lee U., Lexington, Va., 1980. Bar: N.C. 1980, S.C. Tchr., Fairmont City Schs. (N.C.), 1973-74; adminstrv. asst. N.C. Dept. Transp., Raleigh, 1974-76; atty. Springs Industries, Inc., Ft. Mill, S.C., 1980—. Mem. ABA, N.C. Bar Assn., Mecklenburg County Bar Assn. Republican. Methodist. Office: Springs Industries Inc 205 N White St Fort Mill SC 29715

LONG, ROSE ELLA, bank executive; b. Clay County, Ky, June 10, 1941; d. Robert C. and Edna E. (Murray) Greer; m. Ronald Lee Gray, Feb. 21, 1969 (dec. Apr. 1986); children: Billi Rose, Gwendolyn, Lisa, Ronald, Richard; m. Robert Bruce Long, Dec. 19, 1987; stepchildren: Terry, Jeffrey, Robin. Student, Am. Inst. Banking, Lafayette, Ind. Teller Lafayette Bank and Trust Co., 1979, supr. tellers, 1980, asst. treas., 1981, mgr.savs. and certs. of deposit, 1984, asst. v.p., 1986, br. mgr., asst. v.p., 1987. Active local chpt. YWCA, St. Elizabeth Ladies Aux., Lafayette; co-founder Blended Support Group Lafayette. Mem. Nat. Assn. Bank Women. Republican. Home: 4106 Trees Dr Lafayette IN 47905 Office: Lafayette Bank and Trust Co P O Box 1130 Lafayette IN 47902

LONG, SARAH ANN, librarian; b. Atlanta, May 20, 1943; d. Jones Lloyd and Lelia Maria (Mitchell) Sanders; m. James Allen Long, 1961 (div. 1985); children: Andrew C., James Allen IV; m. Donald J. Sager, May 23, 1987. BA, Oglethorpe U., 1966; M in Librarianship, Emory U., 1967. Asst. librarian Coll. of St. Matthias, Bristol, Eng., 1970-74; cons. State Library of Ohio, Columbus, 1975-77; coordinator Franklin County Pub. Library, Columbus, 1977-79, dir. Fairfield County Dist. Library, Lancaster, Ohio, 1979-82, Dauphin County Library System, Harrisburg, Pa., 1982-85, Multnomah County Library, Portland, Oreg., 1985—; chmn. Portland State U. Library Adv. Council. Contbr. articles to profl. jours. Bd. dirs. Dauphin County Hist. Soc., Harrisburg, 1983-85, 1984-87, ARC, Harrisburg, 1984-85; pres. Lancaster-Fairfield County YWCA, Lancaster, 1981-82; vice-chmn. govt. and edn. div. Lancaster-Fairfield County United Way, Lancaster, 1981-82; sec. Fairfield County Arts Council, 1981-82; adv. bd. Portland State U.. Recipient Dir.'s award Ohio Program in Humanities, Columbus, 1982; Sarah Long Day Fairfield County, Lancaster, Bd. Commrs., 1982. Mem. Oreg. Library Assn. (chmn. legis. com. 1987), Pacific N.W. Library Assn., Pub. Library Assn. (bd. dirs.)., ALA, Western Library Network (network services council). Club: City (Portland). Office: Multnomah County Library 205 NE Russell St Portland OR 97212

LONG, SHELLEY, actress; b. Fort Wayne, Ind., Aug. 23, 1949; m. Bruce Tyson; 1 child, Juliana. Student, Northwestern U. Writer, assoc. producer, co-host Chicago TV program Sorting It Out, 1970's; mem. Second City, Chgo.; guest TV appearances various shows; regular TV series Cheers, 1982-87; motion pictures include A Small Circle of Friends, 1980, Caveman, 1981, Night Shift, 1982, Losin' It, 1983, Irreconciliable Differences, 1984, The Money Pit, 1986, Outrageous Fortune, 1987, Hello Again, 1987; TV films include The Cracker Factory, 1979, The Promise of Love, 1980, The Princess and the Cabbie, 1981. Recipient Emmy award Outstanding Actress in a Comedy Series for Cheers, 1983. Office: care William Morris Agy 151 El Camino Beverly Hills CA 90212 *

LONG, SHIRLEY JEAN, paralegal; b. Alexandria, La., Aug. 5, 1951; d. Troy Leland and Marie (Laird) Tuneberg; m. Kenneth Woodrow Long, Jan. 30, 1971; children—Kayla Marie, Kenneth Blake. Assoc., B.A., La. State U., 1971; paralegal degree Northwestern State U., 1982-85. Legal sec. Gravel, Roy & Burnes, Alexandria, La., 1969-71, William E. Skye, Alexandria, 1972-74; paralegal Provosty, Sadler & deLaunay, Alexandria, 1975—, law office adminstr., 1983-86; advisor Northwestern State U., Natchitoches, La., 1982-83. Mem. Nat. Assn. Female Execs., Nat. Assn. Legal Assts., Central La. Personnel Assn., La. State Paralegal Assn. (charter, dist. dir.). Republican. Club: Order Flying Orchid. Avocations: fresh and salt water fishing; reading. Home: 9281 Hwy 165 S Woodworth LA 71485 Office: Provosty Sadler & deLaunay Law Firm PO Drawer 1791 934 3d St Suite 903 Alexandria LA 71309-1791

LONG, SUSAN VICTORIA, information systems manager; b. Honolulu, Aug. 25, 1948; d. William Henry and Emma Marie Vernon. BS in Mgmt., Rutgers U., 1977; MBA, Momouth Coll., 1982. Exec. sec. Merck & Co., Inc., Rahway, N.J., 1974-76, programmer trainee, then programmer, 1976-78, programmer analyst, then sr. programmer analyst, 1978-80, systems analyst, then sr. systems analyst, 1980-85; project leader Nabisco Brands, Inc., East Hanover, N.J., 1984-85, progect. mgr., 1985—. Committeewoman Middletown/Democratic Assn., 1982-84. Mem. Nat. Assn. Female Execs., Assn. Systems Mgmt., Cherry Tree Village Condominium Assn. (pres. 1982-84). Office: Nabisco Brands Inc PO Box 312 Parsippany NJ 07054-0312

LONG, SUZANNE LYNN, silk screening company executive; b. Stockton, Calif., May 27, 1957; d. H. Donald and Nancy J. (Foosaner) L. B.A., Calif. State U.-Sacramento, 1980. Labor relations investigator State of Calif., Sacramento, 1980; ptnr. Pacific Silk Screening, Laguna Beach, Calif., 1980—. Mem. Friends of Sea Lions. Avocations: yachting; languages; scuba diving. Office: Pacific Silk Screening PO Box 2751 Newport Beach CA 92663

LONGO, DIANE, business administrator; b. Bklyn., June 18, 1957; d. Ralph Francis and Teresa Marie (Scotto) Longo. Cert. grad. Katharine Gibbs Sch., 1976. Exec. sec. Allstate Ins. Co., Farmingville, N.Y., 1977-80, Torrance, Calif., 1980-81; adminstrv. asst. Pepperdine U. Sch. Law, Malibu, Calif., 1981-83, asst. to dean, 1984-86; sales ops. mgr. Herman Miller, Inc., Dallas, 1986—; cons. Law Offices Ronald R. Helm, Oakland, Calif., 1986—. Mem. Meeting Planners Internat., Nat. Assn. Female Execs. Republican. Roman Catholic. Club: Jr. Women's (Woodland Hills, Calif.). Avocations: skiing; tennis; cooking. Office: Herman Miller Inc 300 Crescent Ct Suite 1750 Dallas TX 75201

LONGO, KATHRYN MILANI, pension consultant; b. Jersey City, N.J., July 22, 1946; d. Joseph John Baptiste and Kathryn (Sacco) Milani; BA, Adelphi U., 1969; postgrad. N.Y. U., 1968-69, Hunter Coll., 1969-70; m. John Carmine Longo, Mar. 15, 1970 (div. June 1984). Pension cons. Laiken, Siegel & Co., N.Y.C., 1967-84, ptnr., 1977-84; mng. ptnr. Laventhol & Horwath Retirement and Employee Benefit Cons. Div., 1984-88; cons., 1988—; pres., creative cons. Pinch-Hitters, Inc., North Bergen, N.J., 1978-82. Co-founder, co-chmn. Greater N.Y. Pension Cons. Workshop, 1974-88; jazz dance tchr. Kay Marie Sch. Dance Arts, Hammonton, N.J., 1976-83; guest choreographer Regis Drama Soc., Regis High Sch., N.Y.C., 1978-79. Bd. dirs. Phila. Chamber Orch., 1988. Adelphi U. scholar, 1964-68. Mem. Am. Soc. Pension Actuaries (assoc.), N.J. Assn. Women Bus. Owners, Nat. Assn. Female Execs., Am. Soc. Profl. and Exec. Women, Women Entrepreneurs of N.J., Women Bus. Ownership Ednl. Coalition, Inc. (bd. dirs. 1988). Roman Catholic.

LONGSTREET, LORETTA, services executive; b. E. St. Louis, Ill., Dec. 10, 1955; d. Lucille (Paige) Brock; m. George Longstreet, Feb. 14, 1980; 1 child, Trevon Pierre. Student, So. Ill. U., Edwardsville, 1984—, State Community Coll., 1985—. Dictating machine transcriber U.S. Civil Service, St. Louis, 1973-74; mgr. A & B Lounge and Restaurant, E. St. Louis, 1975-78, Page Confectionery, E. St. Louis, 1978-80; part-time sec. Irvine (Calif.) Coll. Bus., 1981-82; adminstrv. asst. Hickey Mitchell Ins., St. Louis, 1982-84; pres. Profl. Bus. Service, E. St. Louis, 1984—. V.p. Khoury League Baseball Parents, E. St. Louis, 1987; coordinator Khoury League Cheerleaders, E. St. Louis, 1987; mem. Neighborhood Watch, E. St. Louis, 1987. Mem. Pi Omega Pi (pres. Mar-Mar), Phi Theta Kappa. Democrat. Baptist. Home: 723 N 25th East Saint Louis IL 62205

LONGSTRETH, HELEN E., civic worker; b. N.Y.C., Dec. 8, 1935; d. Clyde Marion and Elizabeth (Rudolph) L.; m. Norman H. Asbjornson, March 1963 (div. 1988); children: Elizabeth Erica, Scott Marion. BA, State U. Iowa, 1957, JD, 1959, postgrad., 1960; MEd, Mont. State Coll., 1961; postgrad., U. Minn., 1961-62, U. Okla., 1987-88. Mem. bus. adminstrn. staff Northwestern Bell Telephone Co., Omaha, 1959-60; bus. adminstrn. mgr. Diversified Equities, Mpls., 1961; research asst. U. Nebr., Mpls., 1962; instr. Elkhorn (Nebr.) public schs., Mpls., 1963-64. Vol. worker Children's Hosp.; active Omaha Symphony Guild, Women's Assn. of Joslyn Art Mus., Omaha Civic Music Assn. Mem. Am. Council Christian Ch., Amvets Aux., C. of C., Am. Legion Aux., State U. Iowa Alumni Assn., AAUW (legis. chmn.), Soc. Liberal Arts, Nat. Vocat. Guidance Assn., Inc., Am. Personnel and Guidance Assn., Inc., Nat. socs. profl. engrs. auxs., Omaha Montessori Soc., Neb. Hist. Soc., Airplane Owners' and Pilots' Assns., Am. Citizens' Forum, Mont. Guidance Assn., DAR (bd. dirs.), Mensa (highest group, Intertel), NOW, Minn. Fencing Assn., Les Amis du Vin, Bacchus Wine Soc., Psi Chi, Kappa Beta Pi (pres. chpt. 1957-58, del. Province conv. 1958). Republican. Address: 8401 E 60th St #2817 Tulsa OK 74145

LONGTIN, MAMYE RUTH, school librarian; b. Bradshaw, Tex., Dec. 21, 1925; d. Thomas Alcon and Cora Mae (Cooke) Lewis; m. F. Thomas Longtin, June 8, 1946; children—Linda Longtin Payne, Tomi Longtin Spence. Student State Tchrs. Coll., Ala., 1942-43, Hardin Simmons U., 1956; B.S. in Elem. Edn., Tex. Tech U., 1966, M.Edn., 1972, Supervision Cert., 1980; Sch. Library Cert., Tex. Women's U., 1972. Tchr. pvt. kindergarten, Slaton, Tex., 1958-66; tchr. elem. sch. Slaton Ind. Sch. Dist., 1966-77, elem. librarian, 1978—; mem. Gen. Adv. Bd. Edn., Service Ctr. Region XVII, Lubbock, Tex., 1982—. Mem. Friends of Library, Slaton, 1983—; sponsor Tex. Classroom Tchrs.' Legis. Program, Austin, 1966—, Tex. Library Assn. Legis. Program, Austin, 1982-83; mem. Staton Library Bd., 1984—. Recipient Grand Cross of Color, Supreme Assembly Internat. Order Rainbow for Girls, McAlister, Okla., 1964; named Tex. Tchr. of Yr., VFW Aux., 1983; Freedom Found. Seminar scholar, summer 1984. Mem. Slaton Classroom Tchrs. (Outstanding Service award 1978-79, pres. 1978-79), Tex. Classroom Tchrs. (del. 1978-79, Outstanding Service award 1978-79) Tex. Library Assn., Tex. Assn. Sch. Librarians (dist. chmn. 1979-80), Tex. State Tchrs. Assn. (dist. rep. to county 1976), Lubbock Area Library Assn., West Tex. Assn. Supervision and Curriculum Devel., Ladies Aux. VFW. Mem. Disciples of Christ Ch. Lodge: Order of Eastern Star, Home: 725 W Division St Slaton TX 79364 Office: Slaton Ind Sch Dist 300 S 9th St Slaton TX 97364

LONGWORTH, NANCY JEANNE COVAULT, police officer, attorney; b. Madison, Wis., Feb. 24, 1954; d. Donald Orville and Donna Maria (Hendrickson) Covault; m. Richard Charles Longworth, June 25, 1983; children: Adam Samuel, Faith Analise. BS in Criminal Justice, Ga. State U., 1975; JD, Ind. U., 1985. Bar: Ind. Police officer Indpls. Police Dept., 1976—; sole practice atty. Indpls., 1985—; pres. Button Graphics, Ltd., Inc., Indpls., 1986-88. Active Right to Life of Ind., 1980—. Mem. ABA, Ind. Bar. Assn., Indpls. Bar Assn., Christian Legal Soc., Fraternal ORder of Police (editor Siren 1981-82). Republican. Mem. Assembly of God. Office: Indpls Police Dept 50 N Alabama St Indianapolis IN 46204

LONGYEAR, MARIE MARCIA, publishing company executive, writer; b. N.Y.C., Apr. 26, 1928; d. Benno Alexander and Marcie B. (Trczcka) Bernstein; m. Peter R. Longyear, July 2, 1949 (dec. Apr. 1959); 1 child, John Robert; m. Robert J. Dunphy, June 13, 1983. BA cum laude, Radcliffe U., 1949. Supr. editorial tng. McGraw-Hill Book Co., N.Y.C., 1960-66, dir. pub. services, 1966-85, dir. communications, 1986—; fgn. expert Fgn. Langs. Press, Beijing, Peoples Republic of China, 1985-86; v.p. Vladimir Dedijer Lit. Trust., 1985—. Author, editor: The McGraw-Hill Style Manual, 1983; editor Symposium, 1987. Mem. Author's Guild, Linnaean Soc. Office: McGraw Hill Pub Co 1221 Ave Americas New York NY 10020

LONSFORD, FLORENCE ELIZABETH HUTCHINSON, artist, designer, writer; b. Lebanon, Ind., Jan. 7, 1914; d. Frank Edwin and Jennie Cecelia (Pugh) Hutchinson; B.S. in Sci., Purdue U., 1936; student Nat. Acad. Fine Arts, 1956-58; M.A., Hunter Coll., 1963; student Art Students League, John Herron Art Inst., Barnard-NBC Inst. Radio-TV; m. Graydon Lee Lonsford, Dec. 18, 1938 (dec. Sept. 1958). Owner, operator greeting card design bus., 1966-69; tchr. fine arts N.Y. Public Schs., 1960-80; freelance artist and designer; freelance artist, copywriter Harper's Pub. House; illustrator Morningstar Prodns.; greeting card artist Curzart, Rust Craft Pubs., Dedham, Mass., Nat. Artcrafts, Detroit; paintings sold in decorating dept. Lord & Taylor; illustrator ch. publs.; art editor The Key of Kappa Kappa Gamma, 1947—; paintings shown nat. and regional shows including: Hoosier Salon (Indpls.), Cooperstown, N.Y., Brockton, Mass., Mystic, Conn., Ind. State Fair, Jackson, Miss., N.Y., Ky., Ohio and Mich.; graphics rev. in Revue Moderne, Paris, 1967; writer Artists Equity; contbr. to Woman's Home Companion, Christian Sci. Monitor, Saturday Rev., N.Y. Times, Woman's Day, small verse and lit. mags. Recipient art prizes Ind. State Fair, Nat. Art League, Salmagundi, Hoosier Salon; named Outstanding Educator, Met. Mus. and N.Y. Center Arts and Humanities, 1977; recipient Prix de Honneur, Monaco, 1966; finalist Deauville and Cannes Grand Prix, 1973; elected to Watercolor Soc. Ind. Mem. Nat. Council Tchrs. of English, Women's Aux. N.Y. Acad. Scis., Am. Artists Profl. League, Nat. Art League, Cooperstown Art Assn., Artists Equity, Met. Portrait Soc. (formerly Portrait Club N.Y., Am. Portrait Soc.), Nat. Opera Club Am. (dir.), Oil Pastel Soc. Am., N.Y. Art Tchrs. Assn. (exec. bd.), Greensward Found., Wilderness Soc., Kappa Kappa Gamma (nat. officer), Mortar Bd., Alpha Lambda Delta. Republican. Presbyterian. Home and Office: 311 E 72d St New York NY 10021

LOO, CHARLENE, business executive; b. Foochow, Fukien, China, Oct. 21, 1935; d. Chin Chun and Jen Yu (Chen) Chow; m. Jack Loo; children—Christine, Jerry, Wayne, B.A., Coll. Law and Commerce, Taipei, Taiwan, 1960. Owner Ying's Restaurant, N.Y.C., 1967-85; pres. Ever Ready Blue Print Corp., N.Y.C., 1977—. Office: Ever Ready Blue Print Corp 200 Park Ave S Suite 1316 New York NY 10003

LOOK, CHRISTIE SUE, sales executive; b. Cin., Oct. 3, 1952; d. Harold W. Jr. and C. Sue (Brother) L. BS, U. Maine, 1974. RN. Charge nurse Westbrook (Maine) Community Hosp., 1974-76; staff nurse Stanford U. Hosp., Palo Alto, Calif., 1976-79, Bay Nurses Inc. Registry, Walnut Creek,

Calif., 1979-82; sales rep. UHI-Clinitron, Emeryville, Calif., 1982-83, Franciscan Med. Sales, San Rafael, Calif., 1983-85; sales rep. The Mediscus Group, Hayward, Calif., 1985, dist. dir., 1985-87, regional mgr. No. Calif., 1987—. Mem. Nat. Assn. Female Execs., Calif. Assn. Health Facilities. Democrat. Office: The Mediscus Group 531 Getty Suite D Benicia CA 94510

LOOMIS, JACQUELINE CHALMERS, photographer; b. Hong Kong, Mar. 9, 1930 (parents Am. citizens); d. Earl John and Jennie Bell (Sherwood) Chalmers; m. Charles Judson Williams III, Dec. 2, 1950 (div. Aug. 1973); children: Charles Judson IV, John C., David F., Robert W.; m. Henry Loomis, Jan. 19, 1974; stepchildren: Henry S., Mary Loomis Hankinson, Lucy F., Gordon M. Student, U. Oreg., 1948-50, Nat. Geog. Soc., 1978-79, Winona Sch. Profl. Photography, 1979, Sch. Photo Journalism, U. Mo., 1979. Pres. J. Sherwood Chalmers Photographer, Jacksonville, Fla., 1979—; pres. Windward Corp., Washington, 1984—. Contbr. photos to Nat. Geog. books and mag., Fortune mag., Ducks Unltd., Living Bird Quar., Orvis News, Frontiers Internat., others, also calendars; one-woman show Woodbury-Blair Mansion, Washington, 1980; rep. in pub. and pvt. collections. Trustee Sta.-WJCT-TV, Jacksonville, Fla., 1965-73, mem. exec. com., chmn., 1965-66; co-chmn. Arts Festival, Jacksonville, 1970, chmn., 1971; bd. dirs., mem. exec. com. Nat. Friends Pub. Broadcasting, N.Y.C., 1970-73; bd. dirs. Washington Opera, 1976—, Pub. Broadcasting Service, Washington, 1972-73, Planned Parenthood of North Fla., 1968-70; bd. dirs. Jacksonville Art Mus., 1968-70, treas., 1968; bd. dirs. Jacksonville Symphony Assn., 1988—. Recipient Cultural Arts award Jacksonville Council Arts, 1971, award Easton Waterfowl Festival, 1982, 1st and 2d prizes, 1984. Mem. Profl. Photographers Am. (Merit award 1982), Photog. Soc. Am., Am. Soc. Picture Profls., Jr. League Jacksonville Inc. Republican. Presbyterian. Clubs: Fla. Yacht (Jacksonville); Amelia Island Plantation (Fla.); Ctr. Harbour Yacht (Brooklin, Maine). Avocations: travel, golf, sailing, skiing, riding. Home and Office: 4141 Ortega Blvd Jacksonville FL 32210

LOOMIS, LINDA, lawyer; b. Phoenixville, Pa., Dec. 8, 1955; d. Fred Jesse Hill and Mary Jonice (Osborn) Oblander; m. Larry W. Loomis, May 16, 1981; 1 child, Zachary W. BS, Kans. State U., 1977; JD, Washburn U., Topeka, 1980. Bar: Kans., U.S. Dist. Ct. Kans., 1980. Assoc. Rogers & Reed, Winfield, Kans., 1980-81; ptnr. Rogers & Loomis, Winfield, 1981-83; sole practice Winfield, 1983—. Mem. Kans. Bar. Assn., Cowley County Bar Assn. (pres. 1987). Office: PO Box 286 Suite 306 First Nat Bank Bldg Winfield KS 67156

LOOMIS, MARY JEANETTE, editor-in-chief; b. Houston, July 21; d. Richard William and Mary Evelyn (Richards) Roby; m. Robert Lindsey Loomis, Feb. 10, 1965; children: Robert Duncan, Richard Roby. BA in Fine Art, Scripps Coll., 1966. Pres. Santa Monica (Calif.) Bay Printing and Pub. Co., 1983—; editor-in-chief L.A. West Mag., Santa Monica, 1985—. Editor, designer (datebooks) Datebook for Westsiders, 1982, Yesterday Tripping, 1984; contbr. articles to profl. jours.; fiber artist banners Corpus Christi Ch., Pacific Palisades, 1980; speaker in field. Mem. Civic Action Com., Pacific Palisades, Calif., 1983-85. Mem. Mag. Pubs. Assn., Western Pubs. Assn., Prodn. Club. Los Angeles. Republican. Roman Catholic. Office: Santa Monica Bay Printing & Pub 919 Santa Monica Blvd #245 Santa Monica CA 90272

LOOSE, MARY ELLEN, musician; b. Santa Monica, Calif., May 23, 1954; d. Robert John and Beverly Elvina (Baker) Reese; m. Timothy Neil Loose, Feb. 9, 1980; children: Leslie Alane, Laura Christine, Steven Timothy. Student, Brigham Young U., 1972, Coll. of the Canyons, 1973, Valley Coll., 1975. Music copyist Embryo Music Co., Studio City, Calif., 1978; profl. accompanist so. Calif., 1978—; ptnr. Reese-Loose Music Co., North Hollywood, Calif., 1982—; composer, arranger so. Calif., 1982—; pianist Bob Hope USO Club, Hollywood, Calif., 1979, Embryo Music Co., Studio City, Calif., 1975-76; mus. arranger Grand Land Singers, Cerritos, Calif., 1974-79, Maryann Mendenhall Women's Chorale, Granada Hills, Calif., 1981—. Composer vocal duets, piano solos; mus. arranger (record) Sweet Hour of Prayer, 1984. Mem. ASCAP, Associated Latter-day Media Artists, Ariz. Mormon Songwriters Assn. Republican. Mormon. Home: 907 E Harmony St Mesa AZ 85204

LOPATE, KATHLEEN MARY, medical writer; b. Watsonville, Calif., Sept. 13, 1948; d. Hugh Wagner and Mary Josephine (Stefl) Etteldorf; m. Steven Dale Lopate, July 25, 1971 (div. Nov. 1974); 1 child, Leonard Hugh Alexander. Student, Loyola Marymount U., 1968-69; BA, Marquette U., 1975. Intern pub. relations Mt. Sinai Med. Ctr., Milw., 1974; writer Post Newspapers, Milw., 1975-77; editor Metric News mag., Milw., 1977, Program mag., Waukesha, Wis., 1978; processor dental ins. Hartford, Wis., 1980-84; free-lance med. writer Waukesha, 1984—. Author: Lennie's Story, 1977, Prevention and Protection of Abused Children (newsletter). Mem. pub. info. com. Kidney Found. Wis., Milw., 1973-78; mem. pub. relations com. United Way Waukesha County, 1975. Recipient first place communications contest Stuart Pharms., 1987. Mem. Am. Med. Writers Assn. (completed med. communications core curriculum program 1985), Health Care Pub. Relations Soc. (southeastern Wis. chpt.), Nat. Assn. for Female Execs., Children's Hospice Internat., Alexandria, Va. Home and Office: 216 Tenny Ave Waukesha WI 53186

LOPATIN, FLORENCE, comptroller, financial management executive; b. Detroit, May 28, 1928; d. Leo and Edith (Atkins) Grossman; m. Lawrence Harold LoPatin, Dec. 3, 1950; children—Mark Bruce, Norman Stuart. B.A., U. Mich., 1949; postgrad. Wayne U., 1949-50; B.Acctg., Walsh Coll., Troy, Mich., 1978. Mng. ptnr., Trade Markets, catalogue bus., Southfield, Mich., 1976-78; comptroller Bagel Nosh of Mich., Southfield and Detroit, 1978-85; comptroller L.H. LoPatin & Co., Southfield, 1978—; gen. ptnr., chief operating officer Trees of Life Mgmt. Co., Southfield, Mich., 1978—; comptroller, v.p., treas. River Crest Properties, Inc.; comptroller Westpoint Manor Mobile Home Park, Westridge Mobile Home Park; comptroller, mgr. Willow Oak Profl. Bldg. Brichwood Profl. Bldg.; ptnr., cons. Westpoint Manor Devel. Co., Nottingham Estates, W.R. Southfield Assocs., Birchwood Med. Ctr., Willow Oak Med. Ctr. Chmn. United Fund, Southfield, 1970; bd. dirs. Nat. Council Jewish Women, 1974-78; mem. Women's Assn. Detroit Symphony, 1975—. Mem. Southfield C. of C., Walsh Coll. Alumni Assn. Office: 3000 Town Ctr Suite 1000 Southfield MI 48075

LOPDRUP, KATHLEEN BOSWORTH, community service administrator; b. Northbridge, Mass., May 4, 1960; d. Watson Lincoln and Martha Anne (Burgess) B. BS, Babson Coll., 1982; postgrad., Harvard U., 1985. Bus. mgr. Martha's Vineyard Community Services, Tisbury, Mass., 1982-83; dir. fin. Mystic Valley Mental Health Ctr. Assn. Inc., Lexington, Mass., 1983—. Tchr. Grace Chapel Sunday Sch., Lexington, 1986—, Hopkinton (Mass.) Conglist. Ch., 1984, also Bible study leader 1984. Mem. Zeta Alpha, Kappa Kappa Gamma (corresponding sec. Babson Coll. chpt. 1980-81).

LOPER, CANDICE KAY, computer analyst; b. Sublette, Kans., Oct. 29, 1953; d. Robert Franklin and Marion Joyce (Sooby) L. Student, McPherson (Kans.) Coll., 1971-72; lic. in cosmetology, Crums Beauty Sch., Manhattan, Kans., 1974; student, Garden City (Kans.) Community Coll., 1975-76. Owner, operator Candi's For Beautiful Hair, Garden City, 1974-78; systems project librarian Bank of Am., San Francisco, 1980, analyst, 1981, systems analyst, 1981-82, sr. systems analyst, 1982-83, cons., 1983-84, systems cons., team leader, 1984; project mgr. Wells Fargo Bank, Concord, Calif., 1984-86; systems analyst 1st Nationwide Bank, San Francisco, 1986-88; adv. systems engr. Bank Am., Concord, Calif., 1988—; owner Loper Comp-U-Pix, Concord, 1988—. Home: PO Box 5927 Concord CA 94524 Office: Bank Am 1655 Grant St Concord CA 94520-2468

LOPER, JANET SWANSON, data processing executive; b. Dunkirk, N.Y., Sept. 17, 1934; d. Ralph Edwin and Isabel Spencer (Emerson) Swanson; B.S. in Sales Mgmt., Syracuse U., 1956; m. Lyle C. Loper, Oct. 15, 1971. Systems engr. IBM, Rochester, N.Y., 1956-58, tech. writer, product planner, Endicott, N.Y., 1959-66, planner instruction systems devel. dept., Los Gatos, Calif., 1966-70, mem. R.B. Johnson fellow program, 1970-72, communications analyst, gen. systems div., 1972-79, application devel. cons., 1975-79; v.p., dir. communications Citibank, N.Y.C., 1979-84; pres. Info. Integrators, Inc., 1984—; cons. U.S. Office Edn., 1970. Recipient Outstanding Contbn. award IBM, 1975. Mem. Am. Bus. Women's Assn. (pres. Binghamton chpt. 1964-66), Soc. Tech. Communications (past program dir.), Data Processing Mgmt. Assn. (past internat. dir.).

LOPEZ, CARMEN LUISA, lawyer; b. Isabela, P.R., Nov. 9, 1951; d. Angel L. and Gladys (Rodriguez) L. BSBA, Sacred Heart U., 1973; JD, Suffolk U., 1976. Asst. city atty. City of Bridgeport, Conn., 1977-81; sole practice Bridgeport, 1977—; commr. Atty. Gen. Blue Ribbon Commn., Hartford, Conn., Jud. Selection Com., Hartford, 1986—. Del. Nat. Dem. Credential Com., Conn., 1980; commr. Bridgeport Conv. and Visitor Ctr., 1986; bd. dirs. Barnum Festival, Bridgeport Area Found., 1986. Recipient Am. Juris Prudence award in Trusts, 1975, YWCA Salute to Women award, 1981; named one of Outstanding Young Women Am., 1978. Mem. ABA, Conn. Bar Assn., Bridgeport Bar Assn. Democrat.

LOPEZ, KATHRYN PHILLIPS, school librarian; b. Hale Center, Tex., July 7, 1922; d. Clyde C. and Ada Erma (Stutzman) Phillips; m. Theodore Lewis Lopez, June 27, 1948; children—Stephen William, Ralph Antonio. B.S., West Tex. State Coll., 1943; postgrad. U. Utah, part-time 1962-73, U. N.Mex., part-time 1978-80. Tchr. homemaking Lockney Pub. Schs. (Tex.), 1943, Hale Center Pub. Sch. (Tex.), 1943-44, Springer Pub. Sch. (N.Mex.), 1944-48; teller Bank of N.Mex., Albuquerque, 1948-56; head tchr. Casa Solano Kindergarten, Santa Fe, 1963-68; jr. high sch. librarian Santa Fe Pub. Schs., 1968—, chmn. secondary sch. librarians, 1980—. Trustee, St. John's Meth. Ch., Albuquerque, 1955-57; rec. sec. St. John's Meth. Ch., Santa Fe, 1984-86. Mem. ALA, Am. Assn. Sch. Librarians, N.Mex. Library Assn., N.Mex. Media Assn. (co-editor Books on Rev. for N. Mex. 1987—), Delta Kappa Gamma. Democrat. Home: 210 Sereno Dr Santa Fe NM 87501

LOPEZ, LINDA SINGLETON, mortgage banking administrator; b. Paris, Tex., Sept. 11, 1946; d. Charles Bennett and Floy Evelyn (Ryan) Singleton; m. Phillip D. Lopez de Esquevar, Apr. 19, 1969 (dec. Aug. 1974); 1 child, Charles Robert Thomas. BA, Brigham Young U., 1969; Cert. ct. reporter/paralegal Chapman Ct. Reporting Coll., 1973. Exec. asst. to chief exec. officer Am. Inst. Mortgage, Grand Prairie, Tex., 1974-76; office mgr., cons. The Exception, Dallas, 1976-79; office mgr., bookkeeper Heatilator, Inc., Carrollton, Tex., 1979-80; office mgr., title officer Wood Investments, Houston, 1980-83; escrow adminstr Consol. Capital Co., Emeryville, Calif., 1983-86, title adminstr., sr. paralegal, 1986-87; sr. legal asst., Clorox Co., 1987—; cons. L. Lopez Acctg. Service, Houston, 1980-83, Lopez Enterprises, Novato, Calif., 1985—. Author: Mortgage Banking Terms, 1985; also articles on title and land law. Sec. Daus. of Bilitis, Dallas, 1975-76; founder, pres. N. Dallas chpt. NOW, 1979-80, state del., 1980; social chmn. The Other Side, San Rafael, Calif., 1985-86; vol. acct. Westheimer Art Colony, Houston, 1980-83; vol. clown, entertaining at Spl. Olympics, other events, 1985—. Mem. Mensa (area sec. 1986-87), Bay Area Career Women (vice chair social 1987-88, chair 1988), Alliance Local Orgns. for Women (editor 1985—). Democrat. Avocations: art, astrology, sewing, needlework, volunteer work with children's groups. Office: Clorox Co 1221 Broadway Oakland CA 94612-1888

LOPEZ, MICHELINE BRIERRE, artist, designer; b. Jeremie, Haiti, June 9, 1943; came to U.S., 1981; d. Luc H. and Simone (Lataillade) Brierre; divorced; children: Charles, Lisa. Studied at Nehemie-Jean Art Acad., Haiti, Ramponeau Art Sch., Haiti, Miraflores Art Ctr., Lima, Peru. Owner All Things Beautiful, Miami, Fla., 1985—. Numerous exhibits of paintings, jewelry and drawings include Haiti, P.R., Colombia, Miami; author: Soy Eva; contbr. articles to mags., profl. jours. Regional dir. Inner Peace Program, Haiti, 1976-80. Address: PO Box 570-577 Miami FL 33257

LOPEZ, NANCY, professional golfer; b. Torrance, Calif., Jan. 6, 1957; d. Domingo and Marina (Griego) L.; m. Ray Knight, Oct. 25, 1982; children: Ashley Marie, Erinn Shea. Student, U. Tulsa, 1976-78. Profl. golfer 1978—. Author: The Education of a Woman Golfer, 1979. Named AP Athlete for 1978; admitted to Ladies Profl. Golf Assn. Hall of Fame, 1987. Mem. Ladies Profl. Golf Assn. (Player and Rookie of Yr. 1978). Republican. Baptist. Office: 1 Erieview Plaza Cleveland OH 44114

LOPEZ, SARA ISABEL, chemical and industrial engineer; b. Ocotal, Nicaragua, May 1, 1951; came to U.S., Dec. 4, 1978; d. Ricardo Andres and Emilia Mercedes (Barrios) Lopez; diploma chem. and indsl. engr. U. Centro Americana, 1975; M.B.A. in Fin. and Banking, U. San Francisco, 1984; m. John Kemink, Nov. 6, 1978 (div. 1982); 1 son, Ricardo; m. David Mata, Dec. 2, 1982. Plant engr. Polimeros Centroamericanos S.A., Managua, Nicaragua, 1975-76; mixing and baking supt. Nabisco Cristal S.A., Managua, 1976-77; prodn. and quality control mgr. Jaboneria Prego, S.A., Granada, Nicaragua, 1977-78; indsl. cons. tech. dept. Central Bank of Nicaragua, 1978; indsl. engr. Shaklee Corp., Hayward, Calif., 1979-80; chem. engr. system design Bechtel Petroleum, Inc., San Francisco, 1979-82, progress monitoring engr., indsl. engr. Def. Contract Adminstrn. Services, 1984—; Mem. Nat. Contract Mgmt. Assn., Calif. Alumni Assn., Assn. M.B.A. Execs., Fgn. Affairs Council. Republican. Roman Catholic. Lodge: Soroptimist Internat. Home: 819 Masson Ave San Bruno CA 94066

LOPEZ, WILMA IDA, employment agency executive; b. Santurce, P.R., June 9, 1938; d. Angel Luis and Verania (Morales) L.; B.A. in Psychology, U. P.R., 1959; children—Rene Luis Aviles, Angel Luis Aviles. Sales mgr. Empresas Diaz, Rio Piedras, P.R., 1964-67; real estate broker Mackle Bros., Daytona, Fla., 1967-70; record mgr. San Juan (P.R.) City Hall, 1970-73; mgr. P.R., Kelly Services, Inc., Hato Rey, 1973—, v.p. regional offices, 1988—. Mem. Am. Soc. Personnel Adminstrs., P.R. C. of C., P.R. Mfrs. Assn., Sales and Mktg. Execs. Assn., Am. Bus. Women Assn., Zonta Internat. Republican. Roman Catholic. Office: Kelly Services Inc Scotiabank Plaza Suite 701 Hato Rey PR 00917

LOPEZ-MUNOZ, MARIA ROSA P., land development company executive; b. Havana, Cuba, Jan. 28, 1938; came to U.S., 1960; d. Eleuterio Perfecto and Bertha (Carmenati Colon) Perez Rodriguez; m. Gustavo Lopez-Munoz, Sept. 9, 1973. Student, Candler Coll., Havana, 1951-53; Sch. Langs., U. Jose Marti, Havana, 1954-55. Lic. interior designer. Pres. Fantasy World Acres, Inc., Coral Gables, Fla., 1970-84, pres., dir., 1984—; sec. Sandhills Corp., Coral Gables, Fla., 1978-85, dir., 1978—. Treas. Am. Cancer Soc., Miami, Fla., 1981, also sec. Hispanic Bd., 1987, and bd. dirs. aux. treas.; bd. dirs. Am. Heart Assn., Miami, 1985, also chmn. Hispanic div.; bd. dirs. YMCA, Young Patronesses of Opera, Miami, 1985, Lowe Mus. of U. Miami, 1986—. Recipient Merit award Am. Cancer Soc., 1980, 81, 82, 83, 84; Woman with Heart Award, Am. Heart Assn., 1985, Merit awards, 1980-84, Women of Yr., 1986; named to Gt. Order of José Marti, 1988. Mem. Real Estate Commn. Republican. Roman Catholic. Clubs: Ocean Reef (Key Largo, Fla.); Opera Guild (Miami); Key Biscayne Yacht; Regine's International (Paris), Jockey. Avocations: yachting, snow skiing, scuba diving, guitar. Office: Fantasy World Acres Inc 147 Alhambra Circle Suites 220-21 Coral Gables FL 33134

LOPEZ-ROMANO, SYLVIA SILVA, educational program executive; b. Las Vegas, Nev., Dec. 11, 1937; d. Enrique A. Silva and Faustina Flores; m. 2d, Aldo Romano, Apr. 30, 1977; children: Peter John, Marie, Henry, Vincent, Renee. BA in Social Welfare, Calif. State U., Chico, 1973, BA cum laude in Spanish, 1973, MA in Edn., 1981; postgrad., U. San Francisco, Chico, 1981. Migrant edn. community aide 1968-70; case aide counselor Mental Retardation Service, Chico, Calif., 1970-72, elem. sch. tchr., 1973-75; instr., lectr. Calif. State U., Chico, Calif., 1975-78; coordinator Upward Bound project, Chico, Calif., 1976-80, dir. ednl. equity services programs, dir. student affirmative action, 1980—; adminstrv. fellow Calif. State U.-Chico, 1982-83; lectr. cross cultural awareness for counseling program Laverne U., 1984—; distbr. Success Motivation programs, 1985—; mem. adv. bd. Western Assn. Ednl. Opportunity Programs. Chairperson Student Affirmative Action Adv. Bd., Calif. Acad. Partnership Program, Chico Steering Com.; co-founder Hispanic Profl. Group. Mem. AAUW, NAACP, Hispanic Assn. Community and Edn. (bd. dirs.), Greater Chico C. of C., Delta Phi Upsilon, Delta Kappa Gamma. Democrat. Roman Catholic. Home: 555 Vallombrosa #14 Chico CA 95926 Office: Ednl Equity Services Bldg Retention 2d & Ivy Chico CA 95929

LORANGE, JOANNE, college administrator; b. Southbridge, Mass., Jan. 2, 1946; d. Albert Lucien and Lorraine Marguerite (Briere) Lorange; B.A., St. Elizabeth Coll., 1968; M.A., Columbia U., 1971, M.A. in Higher and Adult Edn., 1972; m. Ronald Davis Herron, May 18, 1974; 1 dau., Jocelyn Lorange-Herron. Dir. residential programming, adminstrv. asst. for housing Tchrs. Coll., Columbia U., 1969-72; dir. fin. aid Richmond Coll., CUNY, S.I., 1972-76; asso. dean students Barnard Coll., Columbia U., 1975-77; dir. admissions/external relations Antioch/New Eng. Grad. Sch., Keene, N.H., 1978—; ptnr. Marketplace Gourmet, Keene, 1985—; instr. New Eng. Coll., Henniker, N.H., 1977-78, Sch. for Lifelong Learning, N.H., 1982-84; cons. Upward Bound, Keene State Coll., N.H., 1982—. Advisor, Women's Center, Richmond Coll., S.I., 1972-75; judge N.H. Jr. Miss Contest, 1980; fund-raising trainer United Way; bd. dirs. Grand Monadnock Arts Council, Keene Summer Theatre, Family Planning Services Southwestern N.H.; asst. Campaign chmn. Monadnock United Way. Mem. N.H. C. of C., N.H. Women in Higher Edn. (pres.), Nat. Assn. Women Deans, Counselors and Adminstrs., Nat. Assn. Student Personnel Adminstrs. Club: Kiwanis. Jour. reviewer Nat. Assn. Student Personnel Adminstrs. Region I, 1980. Home: 105 Bradford Rd Keene NH 03431 Office: Antioch NE Roxbury St Keene NH 03431

LORBER, CHARLOTTE LAURA, publisher; b. Bklyn, Apr. 11, 1952; d. Morris and Libby (Slatsky) L. BBA in Fin., U. Miami, 1975. Dir. special events Third Century U.S.A. Dade County Bicentenial Orgn., Miami, Fla., 1975-76; promotion dir. Donato Advt. Co., Coral Gables, Fla., 1977-78; pres. Towne Pub. & Advt. Co., Inc., Coral Gables, Fla., 1979—. Publisher: (directories) View of our City, 1985-86 (Excellence award), Greater Miami Chamber, 1986-87 (Merit award), (brochure) Big Does Mean Better, 1986-87 (Merit award). Recipient Merit award City of Hialeah, 1977. Mem. Am. C. of C. Execs., Greater Miami C. of C. (trustee), Coral Gables C. of C., Miami Beach C. of C. (trustee), South Miami C. of C., North Dade C. of C., World Trade Ctr. Lodge: Rotary. Office: Towne Pub & Advt 4203 Salzedo St Coral Gables FL 33146

LORCH, BARBARA RUTH DAY, educator; b. Pendleton, Oreg., Sept. 30, 1924; d. George Washington and Ruth Irene (Spangler) Day; B.S., Wash. State U., 1946, M.A., 1947; Ph.D., U. Wash., 1956; m. Robert Stuart Lorch, Dec. 19, 1964; 1 son, John Day. Instr. sociology Ariz. State U., Tempe, 1947-48, Bowling Green (Ohio) State U., 1948-50; asst. prof. U. Ariz., Tucson, 1952-53; acting instr. U. Wash., Seattle, 1953-56; asst. prof. U. Mont., Missoula, 1956-57, assoc. prof., 1957-59; asst. prof. to prof. Calif. State U., Long Beach, 1959-69; prof. U. Colo., Colorado Springs, 1969—. Mem. Am. Sociol. Assn., Western Social Sci. Assn., Phi Beta Kappa, Delta Delta Delta, Phi Kappa Phi, Pi Lambda Theta, Alpha Kappa Delta, Psi Chi. Episcopalian. Contbr. articles to profl. jours. Office: U of Colo Austin Bluffs Pkwy Colorado Springs CO 80907

LORCH, MARY HELEN, computer graphics specialist; b. Orlando, Fla., Jan. 7, 1952; d. A. Thomas and Helen Mary (O'Robko) Bonneville; children: Stacey Lynn Pierce, Clinton Dale Pierce. AA, Valencia Community Coll., 1987; postgrad., Fla. So. Coll., 1987—. Prodn. artist, designer Art Services Orlando; prodn. artist Akins The Artist, Orlando; free-lance artist Orlando; designer, prodn. artist Tupperware Home Parties, Orlando, 1980—, specialist computer graphics, 1984—. Mem. 5-yr. planning com. City of Orlando, 1979. Home: 8428 Mattituck Circle Orlando FL 32829 Office: Tupperware Home Parties PO Box 2353 Orlando FL 32802

LORD, BARBARA JOANNI, public official, lawyer; b. Bay Shore, N.Y., Aug. 7, 1939; d. Theodore and Doris Aileen (Smith) Joanni; m. Robert Wilder Lord, June 24, 1967. B.A., U. Miami, 1961; LL.B., NYU, 1966. Bar: N.Y. 1967, Fla. 1978. Asst. editor A.M. Best Co., N.Y.C., 1961-64; contract analyst Guardian Life Ins. Co., N.Y.C., 1964-66; legal trainee N.Y. State Liquor Authority, 1966-67, atty., 1967-70, sr. atty., 1970-80, assoc. atty., 1980—, sec., 1979—. Mem. ABA, N.Y. State Bar Assn., Fla. Bar Assn. Office: N Y State Liquor Authority 250 Broadway New York NY 10007

LORD, BETTE BAO, writer; b. Shanghai, China, Nov. 3, 1938; came to U.S., 1946, naturalized, 1964; d. Sandys and Dora (Fang) Bao; B.A., Tufts U., 1959, M.A., 1960, hon. doctorate, 1982; hon. doctorate, U. Notre Dame, 1985; m. Winston Lord, May 4, 1963; children—Elizabeth Pillsbury, Winston Bao. Asst. to dir. East-West Cultural Center, Honolulu, 1961-62; program officer Fulbright Exchange Program for Sr. Scholars, 1962-63; dancer, tchr. modern dance, Geneva and Washington, 1964-73; conf. dir. Assoc. Councils of the Arts, N.Y.C., 1970-71; writer, lectr., 1982—; author: (non-fiction) Eighth Moon , 1964 (Readers' Digest Condensed Books), (novel) Spring Moon, a novel of China (Lit. Guild selection), 1981, In the Year of the Boar and Jackie Robinson (named one of best books for children AIH), 1984. Mem. selection bd. White House Fellows, 1979-81; bd. dirs. Nat. Com. U.S.-China Relations, Inc., N.Y.C., 1982. Named Woman of Yr., Chinatown Planning Council, 1982; recipient Nat. Geographic Art prize, 1975, Disting. Ams. Fgn. Birth award, 1984. Mem. Asia Soc. (Pres.'s council), Asia Found., Council on Fgn. Relations. Address: Am Embassy, Beijing Peoples Republic of China

LORD, JACQUELINE WARD, accountant, photographer, artist; b. Andalusia, Ala., May 16, 1936; d. Marron J. and Minnie V. (Owen) Ward; m. Curtis Gaynor, Nov. 23, 1968. Student U. Ala., 1966, Auburn U., 1977, Huntingdon Coll., 1980, Troy State U., 1980; B.A. in Bus. Adminstrn., Dallas Bapt. U., 1985. News photographer corr. Andalusia (Ala.) Star-News, 1954-59, Sta. WSFA-TV, Montgomery, Ala., 1954-60; acct., bus. mgr. Reihardt Motors, Inc., Montgomery, 1962-69; office mgr., acct. Cen. Ala. Supply, Montgomery, 1969-71; acct. Chambers Constrn. Co., Montgomery, 1972-75; pres. Foxy Lady Apparel, Inc., Montgomery, 1973-76; acct. Rushton, Stakely, Johnston & Garrett, attys., Montgomery, 1975-81; acctg. supr. Arthur Andersen & Co., Dallas, 1981-82; staff acct. Burgess Co., C.P.A.s, Dallas, 1983; owner Lord & Assocs. Acctg. Service, Dallas, 1983—; tax acct. John Hasse, C.P.A., Dallas, 1984-86; Dallas Bapt. Assn., 1986—. Vol. election law commr. Sec. of State of Ala. Don Siegelman, Montgomery, 1979-80; mem. Montgomery Art Guild, 1964-65, Ala. Art League, 1964-65, Montgomery Little Theatre, 1963-65, Montgomery Choral Soc., 1965. Recipient Outstanding Achievement Bus. Mgmt. award Am. Motors, 1968. Mem. Am. Soc. Women Accts. (pres. Montgomery chpt. 1976-77, area day chmn. 1978, del. ann. meeting 1975-78). Home: 11029 Watterson Dr Dallas TX 75228

LORD, SALLY ANN, business consultant; b. Pitts., Nov. 25, 1966; d. Winston William and Georgetta Ann (Oravec) L. Grad. high sch., Gibsonia, Pa. Personnel mgmt. cons. Vincent J. Marsico Co., Valencia, Pa., 1984—; sec. Fin. Analysis Group, Valencia, 1985—; treas. Affiliated Leasing Personnel, Gibsonia, 1986—. Mem. Nat. Soc. Female Execs., Pitts. Life Underwriters. Republican. Roman Catholic. Home: Rte 4 Box 242 Valencia PA 16059 Office: Vincent J Marsico Co RD #3 Box 84B Valencia PA 16059

LORDI, KATHERINE M., lawyer; b. Jersey City, Mar. 24, 1949; d. Peter G. and Hilde E. (Illy) L. A.B., Trinity Coll., Washington, 1971; J.D., Fordham U., 1975. Bar: N.J. 1975, U.S. Supreme Ct. 1983. Law clk. Friedman & D'Alessandro, East Orange, N.J., 1974-75, assoc., 1975-76; sole practice, Bloomfield, N.J., 1976—; adj. instr. Coll. St. Elizabeth, Convent Station, N.J., 1978-87, adj. prof., 1986—; legal adviser Mcpl. Ct. Clks. Assn., 1977-84. Trustee, Cath. Family and Community Services, 1980—; adv. bd. Acad. St. Elizabeth, Convent Station, N.J., 1980-84; vice chmn. Essex County Adv. Bd. Status of Women, 1983-85, chmn., 1985-88; trustee New Sch. for Arts, 1988—. Mem. ABA, N.J. Bar Assn., Essex County Bar Assn., Bloomfield Lawyers Club (pres. 1983-84), Bloomfield C. of C. (bd. dirs., trustee, chmn. 1985-88). Roman Catholic. Club: N.J. Profl. Women.

LORENDO, LEAH CAMPBELL, educator, clinical supervisor; b. Auburn, Ala., Apr. 16, 1954; d. Eugene Lionel and Jane Thompson (Campbell) L. BA, Auburn U., 1976, MA, 1978; PhD in Health Care Adminstrn., U. Miss., 1988. Cert. speech lang. pathologist. Grad. asst. Auburn (Ala.) U., 1976-78; faculty assoc. Our Lady of Lake U., San Antonio, 1978-79; instr., clin. supr. U. Miss., Oxford, 1979—; cons. Nat. Student Speech-Lang.-Hearing Assn. Contbr. articles to profl. jours. Vol. exercise instr. U. Miss., Oxford, 1985-88. Mem. Am. Speech-Lang.-Hearing Assn. (com. ednl. tech. 1987-88), Am. Coll. Healthcare Execs., Nat. Assn. Female Execs., Computer Users Speech and Hearing. Office: Univ Miss Dept Communicative Disorders University MS 38677

LORENTSON, HOLLY JEAN, hospice executive; b. Mpls., Nov. 27, 1956; d. Leslie Arnold and Mary Ann Jean (Anderson) L. BA in Nursing, Coll. St. Catherine, St. Paul, 1978; MPH, U. Minn., 1986. RN, Minn.; registered pub. health nurse. RN Abbott/Northwestern Hosp., Mpls., 1978-79; acting dir. community nursing services Ebenezer Soc., Mpls., 1979-81, pub. health nurse supr., 1981-82; charge nurse Ebenezer Hall nursing Home, Mpls., 1982-84; patient services coordinator San Diego Hospice Corp., 1984-85, exec. dir., 1985—; mem. fiscal intermediary provider task force Region X Health Care Financing Adminstrn., 1984-88. Mem. Nat. Hospice Orgn., Calif. State Hospice Assn. (v.p. 1985-88), Calif. Assn. Health Services at Home (com. mem.), Sierra Club. Lodge: Soroptimists (San Diego). Office: San Diego Hospice Corp 3840 Calle Fortunada San Diego CA 92123

LORENTZEN, MARIANNE LOUISE, television executive; b. Mpls., June 10, 1949; d. Anthony Joseph and Marcella (Myszka) Bury; m. Robert Roy Lorentzen, Sept. 21, 1973; children: Brian, Kristin. AA, North Hennepin Coll., Mpls., 1971. Sec. treas. Interlachen, Inc., Brainerd, Minn., 1973—, Video Techniques, Inc., Bradenton, Fla., 1980—. Mem. adv. bd. King Mid. Sch., Bradenton, 1986, 87. Recipient Marie Abel award for best show Fla. State Fair, 1986. Mem. Bunka Art Assn. (corr. sec. 1984-86, 2d v.p. 1986-88, first place award Am. Japanese chpt. 1986). Roman Catholic. Office: Video Techniques Inc 600 US 301 Blvd W Suite 188 Bradenton FL 34205

LORENZ, KATHERINE MARY, banker; b. Elgin, Ill., May 1, 1946; d. David George and Mary (Hogan) L. BA cum laude, Trinity Coll., 1968; MBA, Northwestern U., 1971; grad., Bank Adminstrn. Inst., 1977. Ops. analyst Continental Ill. Nat. Bank & Trust Co., Chgo., 1968-69, supr. ops. analysis, 1969-71, asst. mgr. customer profitability analysis, 1971-73, acctg. officer, mgr. customer profitability analysis, 1973-77, 2d v.p., 1976, asst. gen. mgr. controller's dept., 1977-80, v.p., 1980, controller ops. and mgmt. services dept., 1981-84, v.p., sector controller retail banking, corp. staff and ops. depts., 1984-87, v.p., sr. sector controller pvt. banking, centralized ops. and corp. staff, 1987—. Mem. Nat. Assn. for Bank Cost and Mgmt. Acctg., Nat. Assn. Bank Women. Roman Catholic. Office: Continental Ill Nat Bank & Trust 231 S LaSalle St Chicago IL 60697

LORENZ, VALERIE CLAIRE, psychotherapist; b. Bremerhaven, Federal Republic of Germany, Oct. 9, 1936; d. Heinrich Friedrich and June Alice (Lofland) L.; (div.); children: Patrice, Pamela, Robert. BS, Penn. State U., 1975, MS, 1978; PhD, U. Pa., 1983; postgrad., Inst. Cognitive Therapy Md. Psychol. Assn., 1985. Cert. psychotherapist. Liaison, mental health counselor, research asst. Gov.'s Action Ctr. Penn. St. U., Middletown, 1978; dir. research Gambling Treatment Program Taylor Manor Hosp., Ellicott City, Md., 1983; dir. clin. Md. Treatment Ctr. of Nat. Found. Study and Treatment Path. Gambling, Balt., 1984; dir. Forensic Ctr. Compulsive Gambling, Balt., 1984—; exec. dir. Nat. Ctr. Path. Gambling Inc., Balt., 1986—; mem. adv. bd. Nat. Council Compulsive Gambling, N.Y.C., 1976—; pres. bd. dirs. Alternatives Inc., Pa., 1973-76, Women in Crisis, Harrisburg, Pa., 1973-75; Fla. Council on Compulsive Gambling; qualified expert witness on compulsive gambling in mil., st. and fed. cts. Mem. Editorial bd. Journal of Gambling Behavior, 1982—; contbr. articles to profl. jours., books and mags.; editor annotated bibliography on compulsive gambling; co-editor: Compulsive Gambling and the Law. Lobbyist mentally ill, compulsive gamblers, st. legislature, White House, Congress, 1973—. Mem. Am. Psychol. Assn., Am. Mental Health Counselors Assn., Md. Psychol. Assn. (coordinator legis. dist. 1985—), Ea. Psychol. Assn., Nat. Forensic Ctr., Jr. League Balt., GamAnon, Delta Tau Kappa, Phi Delta Kappa. Office: Nat Ctr Pathological Gambling 651 Washington Blvd Baltimore MD 21230

LORENZ, VIRGINIA MARY, civil engineer; b. Chgo., May 17, 1947; d. Francis Stanley and Teresa Martine (Wendell) L. BSCE, U. Dayton, 1970; MSCE, U. N.Mex., 1983. Lic profl. engr., Ill., N.Mex. Engr., designer Ill. Dept. trans., Ottawa, 1970-73, engr. planning, 1973-77, materials, planning engr., 1977, constrn. engr., 1978; tech. service safety engr. N.Mex. State Hwy. Dept., Santa Fe, 1978-81; material labs. spl. projects engr. N.Mex. State Dept. Hwy., Santa Fe, 1981-84, constrn. support engr., 1984-87, traffic safety engr., 1987—; bd. dirs. N.Mex. Bd. Profl. Engrs. and Surveyors, Santa Fe, 1986—. patentee in field. Mem. Assn. Women in Sci., Inst. Trans. Engrs., Nat. Assn. Female Execs., N.Mex. Profl. Engrs. Office: NMex State Hwy Dept PO Box 1149 Santa Fe NM 87504-1149

LORENZI, NANCY M., university official; d. Louis L. and Mary A. Lorenzi; A.B., Youngstown (Ohio) State U., 1966; M.S., Case Western Res. U., 1968; M.A., U. Louisville, 1975; Ph.D., U. Cin., 1980; m. Robert T. Riley. Dir. med. library Saint Elizabeth's Hosp., Youngstown, 1963-67; reference librarian, head info. services U. Louisville Med. Center, 1968-71; dir. med. center libraries U. Cin., 1972-84; assoc. sr. v.p. U. Cin. Med. Ctr., 1984—. Mem. Med. Library Assn. (pres. 1982-83), Am. Soc. Personnel Adminstrs., Cin. Personnel Assn., Ohio Acad. Scis. Contbr. articles to profl. jours. Office: U Cin 231 Bethesda Ave Cincinnati OH 45267

LORENZON, TERRI ANNE, lawyer; b. Rock Springs, Wyo., Nov. 26, 1950; d. Ray A. and Thelma (Oikari) L. B.A., U. Wyo., 1972, J.D., 1976. Bar: Wyo. 1976, U.S. Dist. Ct. Wyo. 1976. Staff atty. Wyo. Supreme Ct., Cheyenne, 1977-80; adminstrv. aide Environ. Quality Council, Cheyenne, Wyo., 1980—; faculty advisor Nat. Jud. Coll., Reno, 1983, 85, 86. Mem. arts and sci. adv. council U. Wyo., 1980-81; bd. dirs. Cheyenne Planned Parenthood Assn., 1982—. Mem. ABA, Wyo. Bar Assn. Democrat. Roman Catholic. Office: Environ Quality Council 2301 Central Ave Barrett Bldg Room 307 Cheyenne WY 82002

LORING, MEREDITH, communications system sales executive; b. Charleston, S.C., Dec. 24, 1945; d. Elliott Legare Loring and Lillian Marsha (Rosman) Loring Selby; m. Eugene William Goffin, June 7, 1966 (div. Aug. 1976). BA, Stanford U., 1968; MA, NYU, 1967, PhD, 1973. Researcher U.S. State Dept., Rio de Janeiro, 1972-75; mgr. Dushkin Pub. Group, Guilford, Conn., 1975-77; acquisitions editor CBS Coll. Pub., Phila., 1977-79; editorial dir., sr. editor Acad. Press Coll. Dept., N.Y.C. and Orlando, Fla., 1979-84; dir. sales Ea. Phone Corp., Hackensack, N.J., 1984-88; area sales mgr. TSI, Montgomery, N.Y., 1988—; freelance consulting editor 1984—. Committeewoman Buffalo Dem. Com., 1972-73; del. Dem. Nat. Convention, Miami, 1972. Grantee NDEA, 1965-68. Mem. Am. Soc. Criminology, Am. Econ. Assn. Democrat. Episcopalian. Office: TSI 175 Neelytown Rd Montgomery NY 12549

LORIO, KATHRYN VENTURATOS, law educator; b. Pitts., Feb. 15, 1949; d. George Stellios and Aphrodite (Bon) Venturatos; m. Philip D. Lorio III, Nov. 16, 1974; children: Elisabeth Bon, Philip D. IV. BA magna cum laude, Tulane U., 1970; JD, Loyola U., New Orleans, 1973. Bar: La., 1973. Atty. Deutsch, Kerrigan & Stiles, New Orleans, 1973-76; asst. prof. law Loyola U. Law Sch., New Orleans, 1976-79, assoc. prof., 1979-83, prof., 1983—; instr. New Orleans Bar Rev., 1978—; mem. adv. com. joint legis. com. on Forced Heirship and Illegitimate Children State of La., Baton Rouge, 1981. Author: (with others) Louisiana Successions and Donations, 1985; contbr. articles to profl. jours. Bd. dirs. Mental Health Advocacy Bd., New Orleans and Baton Rouge, 1984—. Mem. Am. Assn. Law Schs. (sec. sect. on women and law 1987), Assn. for Women Attys., La. Law Inst. (family law com. 1982—), Phi Beta Kappa, Phi Delta Phi. Greek Orthodox. Home: 23 Richmond Pl New Orleans LA 70115 Office: Loyola U Law Sch 7214 St Charles Ave New Orleans LA 70118

LORMAN, BARBARA K., state senator; b. Madison, Wis., July 31, 1932; 3 children. Student U. Wis., Whitewater and Madison. Pres. Lorman Iron and Metal Co., 1979—; mem. Wis. State Senate from 13th Dist., 1980—, mem. coms. on Agriculture, Health and Human Services, Senate Judiciary and Consumer Affairs, Joint Retirement Systems, Edn. and Govt. Ops., numerous others. Bd. dirs., mem. exec. com. Forward Wis.; mem. Retirement Research Com., Transpn. Projects. Commn.; past pres. Ft. Atkinson Devel. Council, Wis. Mem. Jefferson County Bus. and Profl. Women, New Rep. Conf., Dodge County Fedn. Rep. Women. Office: Wis State Capitol Bldg Madison WI 53702 also: 712 Frederick Ave Fort Atkinson WI 53538

LOTAS, JUDITH PATTON, advertising agency executive; b. Iowa City, Apr. 23, 1942; d. John Henry and Jane (Vandike) Patton; children: Amanda Bell, Alexandra Vandike. BA, Fla. State U., 1964. Copywriter Liller, Neal, Battle and Lindsey Advt., Atlanta, 1964-67, Grey Advt., N.Y.C., 1967-72; creative group head SSC&B Advt., N.Y.C., 1972-74; asso. creative dir. SSC&B Advt., 1974-79, v.p., 1975-79, sr. v.p., 1979-82, exec. creative dir., 1982-86; founding ptnr. Lotas Minard Patton McIver, Inc., N.Y.C., 1986—. Active scholarship fund raising.; bd. dirs. Samuel Waxman Cancer Research Found. Recipient Clio award, Venice Film Festival award, Graphics award Am. Inst. Graphic Artists, 1970, Effie award; named Woman of Achievement, YWCA. Mem. Kappa Alpha Theta. Democrat. Home: 45 E 89th St New York NY 10028

LOTEMPIO, JULIA MATILD, accountant; b. Budapest, Hungary, Oct. 14, 1934; came to U.S., 1958, naturalized 1962; d. Istvan and Irma (Sandor) Fejos; m. Anthony Joseph, Mar. 11, 1958. AAS in Lab. Tech. summa cum laude, Niagara County Community Coll., Sanborn, N.Y., 1967; BS in Tech. and Vocat. Edn. summa cum laude, SUNY, Buffalo, 1970; MEd in Guidance and Counseling, Niagara U., 1973, BBA in Acctg. summa cum laude, 1983. Sr. analyst, researcher Great Lakes Carbon Co., Niagara Falls, N.Y., 1967-71; tchr. sci. Niagara Falls Schools, 1973-75; tchr. sci. and English Starpoint Sch. System, Lockport, N.Y., 1975-77; instr. applied chem. Niagara County Community Coll., Sanborn, 1979; club adminstr., acct. Twinlo Racquetball, Inc., Niagara Falls, 1979-81; bus. cons. Twinlo Beverage, Inc., Niagara Falls, 1981-85; staff acct. J.D. Elliott & Co. PC, CPAs, Buffalo, 1986-87; acct. Wiggle, Semanchin, Wetter and Co., Amherst, N.Y., 1988—; bd. dirs. Niagara Frontier Meth. Home Inc., Niagara Frontier Nursing Home Inc., The Blocher Homes Inc., Buffalo. Mem. faculty continuing edn. United Meth. Ch., Dickersonville, N.Y., 1985—; guest speaker, counselor, tchr. Beechwood Service Guild, Buffalo, 1987—. Mem. Nat. Assn. Accts., Nat. Assn. Female Execs., Nat. Fedn. Bus. and Profl. Women's Club, Internat. Platform Assn., Niagara U. Alumni Assn., SUNY Coll. at Buffalo Alumni Assn., Niagara County Community Coll. Alumni Assn. Office: Wiggle Semanchin Wetter Co 10 John James Audubon Pkwy Amherst NY 14228-1186

LOTH, RENEE, news writer; b. Port Chester, N.Y., Dec. 26, 1952; d. Howard and Irene (Maio) L. BS, Boston U., 1974. Editor East Boston (Mass.) Community News, 1977-79; staff writer Boston Phoenix, 1979-84; assoc. editor New Eng. Monthly, Haydenville, Mass., 1984-85; staff writer Boston Glode, 1985—; mem. emeritus East Boston Community Communications, Inc., 1979—. Contbr. articles to profl. jours. Recipient Excellence in Media award Nat. Women's Polit. Caucus, 1986. Office: Boston Globe 135 Morrissey Blvd Boston MA 02107

LOTLIKAR, SAROJINI DATTARAM, university librarian; b. Bombay, Hindu, India, Apr. 26, 1930; came to U.S. 1969; d. Dattaram V. and Laxmibai D. Lotlikar. B.A. with honors, Bombay U., 1951; diploma in library sci. Bombay Library Assn., 1966; M.S.L.S., Villanova (Pa.) U., 1970; student Internat. Grad. Summer Sch., Aberystwyth, Wales, U.K., 1985. Asst. librarian Khalsa Coll., Bombay, 1966-69; catalog librarian Ganser Library, Millersville (Pa.) U., 1971—; cons. Balodyan, Sch. libraries, Bombay, 1966—. Grantee Millersville U. Trust Fund, 1979. Mem. ALA, Assn. Coll. and Research Libraries, Assn. Pa. Coll. and Univ. Profs. Office: Helen Ganser Library N George St Millersville PA 17551

LOTMAN, ARLINE JOLLES, lawyer, writer; b. Phila., Feb. 5, 1937; d. Samuel and Sarah (Schiffrin) Jolles; m. Maurice Lotman, Sept. 27, 1959 (dec.); 1 child, Maurice. BA, Temple U., 1960, JD with honors, 1977, MA in Communications, 1984. Bar: Pa. 1977, D.C. 1980, U.S. Dist. Ct. (ea. dist.) Pa. 1983, U.S. Ct. Appeals (3d cir.) 1987. Pres. Gen. Models, Bala Cynwyd, Pa., 1969-74; exec. dir. Pa. Gov.'s Commn. on Status of Women, Harrisburg, 1972-74; policy expert HEW, Washington, 1978; sole practice, Phila., 1977—; lectr. law Temple U., Phila., 1983, Villanova U., 1985. Author: (nostalgia column) Jewish Exponent, 1971-74; contbr. articles to profl. jours. Bd. dirs. Jewish Community Relations Council, 1979—, Anne Frank Inst., 1982—, Ams. for Dem. Action, 1977-80; mem. Pa. Dem. State Com., 1986-88, Am. Jewish Congress, 1980—, Com. to Elect Women Judges, 1983—; exec. bd. Com. of 70, 1969— ; chair Jewish Law Day, 1986-87, Montgomery County Dem. Com., 1977-78. Recipient Legion of Honor award Chapel of the Four Chaplains, 1980, Outstanding Service award North Atlantic region Soroptimist Internat., 1975, Louise Waterman Wise award Am. Jewish Congress, Phila., 1974, Editorial citation Phila. Inquirer, Main Line Times; co-recipient award Pa. LWV, 1973; named Outstanding Young Woman of Pa., 1972. Fellow ABA, Pa. Bar Assn.; mem. Phila. Bar Assn. (bd. govs. 1983-84, jud. selection and retention commn. 1983, chmn. pub. sch. edn. com. 1982, assoc. editor The Shingle 1978-79, chmn. com. jud. appointments 1979-81, qualified judges hon. trustee 1986—), Assn. Bond Lawyers, Lawyers Against Apartheid, Women in Communications (Outstanding Communicator of Yr. 1984), NOW (1st hon. mem.), Temple U. Sch. Law Alumni Assn. (exec. com. 1979—, Spl. Achievement award 1987), Temple U. Alumni Assn. (bd. dirs. 1983—). Office: 1608 Walnut St Philadelphia PA 19103

LOTTERHOS, SUZANNE FAIRBROTHER, psychologist; b. Framingham, Mass., May 29, 1942; d. Thomas and Florence Jennette (Hyson) Fairbrother; m. Robert Louis Lotterhos; 1 child, Peter Daniel. BS, East Carolina U., 1965, MA, 1967; PhD, Fordham U., 1980. Lic. psychologist, N.Y. Instr. psychology Wayne Community Coll., Goldsboro, N.C., 1966-68; psychologist counseling CUNY, Queens, 1968-73, William Patterson (N.J.) Coll., 1973-75, Mercer County Community Coll., West Windsor, N.J., 1977-79; adj. prof. Mercer County Community Coll., Wayne, N.J., 1986; sr. clin. psychologist Yardville (N.J.) Youth Correctional Reception Ctr., 1979-84; dir. Psychol. Health Assocs., Lawrenceville, N.J., 1984—; Guest speaker Princeton Unitarian Ch., 1980, 83, 86, 87, Nat. Assn. Bus. Profl. Women, Trenton, N.J., 1985; panelist Cable TV, Phila., 1986, 87; presenter workshops, 1982-83, 85. Coordinator group individual growth program Youth Correction, 1982; active LWV, 1986—; mem. N.J. Prison Project, 1982-86. Mem. Am. Psychology Assn., N.J. Psychology Assn. (Mercer County chpt.). Democrat. Unitarian. Home and Office: Psychol Health Assocs 284 Glenn Ave Lawrenceville NJ 08648

LOTTNER, JOYCE EVELYN, community volunteer; b. Denver, Oct. 9, 1944; d. Stewart L. Herman and Elaine (Segal) Silverman; m. Alan B. Lottner, June 22, 1969; children: Jyll, Craig. BA, Colo. State U., 1966; postgrad., Ariz. State U., 1966, SUNY, Albany, 1970. Unit dir. ARC, Seoul, South Korea, 1967-68; tchr. Phoenix Union Pub. Schs., 1966-67, Englewood (Colo.) High Sch., 1968-69, Voorheesville (N.Y.) Jr./Sr. High Sch., 1969-71, Gen. Equivalency Diploma Program, Englewood, 1971-72; ptnr. Things Unique, Englewood, 1983-85. Mem. Arapahoe County Planning Commn., 1984—; chairperson ways and means com. Cottonwood Creek Elementary PTO, 1984; head room mother Cottonwood Creek Elementary Sch., 1985; mem. strategic planning group Arapahoe Community Coll., 1985; dir. Castlewood Fire Protection Dist., 1985; bd. dirs., legisl. affairs com., chairperson by-laws com., recording sec. Nat. Council Jewish Women; pres. trustees Arapahoe Library Dist., 1984—; orgn. dir. Bill Owens for House Dist. 49, 1982; mem. exec. com. Arapahoe County Reps., 1980-82, dist. capt. 1982-84; chairperson com. to re-elect Bob Brooks, 1986; v.p. House Dist. 40, 1984, chairperson, 1985-87; chairperson Senate Dist. 27, 1985—; chairperson Citizen's Adv. Group for Jewish Concerns, 1984; vol. Paul Powers for Senate, 1984; mem. steering com., hon. bd. mem. Rep. Jewish Coalition, 1984. Mem. ALA (trustee edn. com., vice chmn. conf. program and edn. com.), Colo. Library Assn. (pres. trustee div. 1985). Republican. Jewish. Home: 5359 S Geneva St Englewood CO 80111

LOTZE, BARBARA, physicist; b. Mezokovesd, Hungary, Jan. 4, 1924; d. Matyas and Borbala (Toth) Kalo; came to U.S., 1961, naturalized, 1967; Applied Mathematician Diploma with honors, Eotvos Lorand U. Scis., Budapest, Hungary, 1956; Ph.D., Innsbruck (Austria) U., 1961; m. Dieter P. Lotze, Oct. 6, 1958. Mathematician, Hungarian Central Statis. Bur., Budapest, 1955-56; tchr. math., Iselsberg, Austria, 1959-60; asst. prof. physics Allegheny Coll., 1963-69, assoc. prof., 1969-77, prof., 1977—, chmn. dept., 1981-84; lectr. in history of physics; speaker to civic groups. Mem. Am. Phys. Soc., Am. Assn. Physics Tchrs. (sect. rep. Western Pa., chmn. nat. com. on women in physics 1983-84, Disting. Service award 1986, cert. of appreciation 1988), AAUP, AAUW, N.Y. Acad. Scis., Am. Hungarian Educators Assn. (pres. 1980-82), Wilhelm Busch Gesellschaft (Hanover, Fed. Republic Germany). Editor: Making Contributions: An Historical Overview of Women's Role in Physics, 1984; co-editor The First War Between Socialist States: The Hungarian Revolution of 1956 and Its Impact, 1984; contbr. articles to profl. jours.; research in theoretical physics. Home: 462 Hartz Ave Meadville PA 16335 Office: Allegheny Coll Dept Physics Meadville PA 16335

LOUDEN, FLORENCE MORLEY, research and development company executive; b. N.Y.C., May 21, 1925; d. George Bennett and Dora Huntington (Spencer) Morley; B.A., Smith Coll., 1946; m. William Gordon Louden, Apr. 10, 1948; children—Katherine, Stuart, David, Ann. Fgn. traffic dept. McCann Errickson, N.Y.C., 1946-47; production dept. N.W. Ayer, Phila., 1948-49; owner, treas. Tinicum Research Co., Frenchtown, N.J., 1968—. Bd. dirs. ARC, SE Pa. chpt., 1965-66; sch. dir Palisader Sch. Dist., Kintnersville, Pa., 1976-82, v.p., 1976-77; Democratic Committeewoman Tinicum Twp., 1981-84; mem. Tinicum Twp. Planning Commn., 1982-88; Bucks County Council on Alcoholism, 1983-87. Home: Roaring Rocks Erwinna PA 18920 Office: Box 241 Frenchtown NJ 08825

LOUGHMAN, BARBARA ELLEN, immunologist researcher; b. Frankfurt, Ind., Oct. 26, 1940; d. Jimmie Jewel and Ruth Eileen (Hoyer) Evers; m. Terry B. Loughman, June 28, 1962; children: Lance Evers Loughman, Chad Elliott Loughman. BS, U. Ill., 1962; PhD, Notre Dame U., 1972. Research scientist Ames Research Labs., Elkhart, Ind., 1962-72; staff fellow NIH, Balt., 1972-74; from research assoc. to research mgr. The Upjohn Co., Kalamazoo, Mich., 1974-84; dir. immunology research Monsanto Co., St. Louis, 1984-85; sr. dir. immunology diseases research G.D. Searle/Monsanto Co., St. Louis, 1986-88; dir. project mgmt. Rorer Cen. Research, Horsham, Pa., 1988—. Contbr. over 20 articles to profl. jours. Mem. AAAS, AMA, AWIS, Am. Assn. Immunology. Home: 1522 Timber Point Ct Chesterfield MO 63017 Office: GD Searle R&D Monsanto Life Sci Ctr 700 Chesterfield Village Pkwy Saint Louis MO 63198

LOUIE, ALEXINA DIANE, composer; b. Vancouver, B.C., Can., July 30, 1949. MusB, U. B.C.; MA, U. Calif., San Diego. Profl. solo pianist Vancouver, 1966-71, profl. music copyist, 1970-73; instr. music Pasadena (Calif.) City Coll., from 1974. Compositions include Lamentation for the Canadian Tragedy, 1970, Molly, 1972, Bringing the Tiger Down From the Mountain, 1973, Piece for 9 Flutes, 1975, O Magnum Mysterium: In Memoriam Glenn Gould, 1982, Songs of Paradise, Music for a Thousand Autumns, Concerto for Piano and Orchestra. Named Composer of Yr. Can. Music Council, 1986; composition grantee Can. Council for the Arts, 1974. Address: care Can League Composers, 20 Saint Joseph St, Toronto, ON Canada M4Y 1J9 *

LOUIE, FANNIE, manufacturing company executive; b. Boise, Idaho, Sept. 3, 1948; d. Dick and Helen (Eng) L.; m. Samuel K. Yee, May 30, 1976 (div. Apr. 1986). BS, Oreg. State U., 1970, MBA, 1974. Sec. CIA, Langley, Va., 1970-71; data control specialist Boise (Idaho) Cascade Corp., 1974-76, systems-processing analyst, 1976-81, sr. programmer-analyst, 1981-83, user support lead cons., 1984—. Mem. steering com. Boise Cascade Vols., 1987, chmn. March of Dimes Walk, 1987. Mem. Assn. MBA Execs., Boise C. of C. Lodge: Soroptimists (chmn. orientation and leadership com. Greater Boise chpt.).

LOUIE, MARCIA FUJIMOTO, estate planning lawyer; b. Papaaloa, Hawaii, July 10, 1951; d. Frank Shigeo and Shizue (Inomoto) Fujimoto; m. Martin Louie, June 2, 1978; 1 dau., Beth. B.B.A., U. Mich., 1973; J.D., 1978. Bar: Wash. 1978; C.P.A., Wash., Mich. Sr. auditor, Coopers & Lybrand, Detroit, 1973-78; EDP auditor State of Wash., Seattle, 1979-81; tax mgr. Deloitte Haskins & Sells, Seattle, 1981-84; pvt. practice, 1984—. Bd. dirs. Asian Mgmt. and Bus. Assn., Seattle, 1983-86, Women & Bus., Asian Counseling and Referral Service, Seattle, 1984-86. Mem. Wash. Soc. C.P.A.s, Wash. State Bar Assn., Wash. Women in Tax, Estate Planning Council, Seattle-King County Bar Assn.

LOUW, BEVERLY JUNE, high school dean; b. Springs, Transvaal, South Africa, June 29, 1942; d. Izak Charl and Mavis (Futter) L. BS, Brigham Young U., 1963; MA, Calif. State U., Northridge, 1977; postgrad., Brigham Young U. Art tchr. Clayton Jr. High Sch., Salt Lake City, 1964-67; art dir. advt. Betty Shops, Calgary, 1967-68; art tchr. Ogden (Utah)-Washington Jr. High Sch., 1968-69; art tchr., special edn. Hueneme High Sch., Oxnard, Calif., 1969-76; dean students Tracy (Calif.) High Sch., 1976-79; adminstr. counseling ctr. Brigham Young U., Provo, Utah, 1979-80; graphics design coordinator U. Calif., Livermore, 1980-86; dean students Antelope Valley High Sch. Dist., Lancaster, Calif., 1987—; cons. aquatics Oxnard Recreation Dept., 1969-76; cons. Veep Corp., Livermore, 1983-84; poster designer Sauvignon Wines Concannon Industries, 1983. Author: Check-Pawn, 1986; designer business image Logo Olympia Dry Wall, 1985; designer book cover Safety/Doe, 1984. Fellow Nat. Orgn.Female Execs., Nat. Edn. Assn., Calif. Edn. Assn. Republican. Mormon. Clubs: Hueneme Swim (Oxnard) (coach, mgr.), Bea Bees Swim (Hueneme) (coach, mgr.). Home: 430-20 W J5 Lancaster CA 93534 Office: Desert Winds High Sch Lancaster CA 93534

LOVAAS (BECK), CONSTANCE WINNIFRED, publishing executive; b. Fort Dauphin, Madagascar, July 28, 1927; came to U.S., 1931; d. David and Emma (Hogie) Lovaas; m. Victor William Beck, Sept. 4, 1981. B.A., St. Olaf Coll., 1949. Parish worker St. Timothy Lutheran Ch., Chgo., 1949-51; parish missionary Am. Luth. Ch., Bekily, Madagascar, 1952-58; curriculum writer Malagasy Luth. Ch., Madagascar, 1959-67, 1974-75; audience relations mgr. Radio Voice of Gospel, Antsirabe, Madagascar, 1968-73; assoc. editor Augsburg Pub. House, Mpls., 1977-79, Am. Luth. Ch. Women SCOPE editor, 1979-87. Author, editor 13 enl. booklets in Malagasy lang., 1968-75. Contbr. articles to profl. jours. Ch. sch. workshop tchr. Malagasy Luth. Ch., 1961-75, nat. exec. sec., Sunday schs., 1961-64. Avocation: golf. Office: Augsburg Fortress 426 S 5th St Box 1209 Minneapolis MN 55440

LOVE, EMMA LOUISE, educational administrator; b. Minden, La., Apr. 15, 1944; d. Henry and Annie (Johnson) Allums; divorced; 1 child, Bryan Earl. BA, Calif. State U., Long Beach, 1966, MA, 1976; postgrad., U. So. Calif., 1985. Cert. secondary tchr., counselor, adminstr., Calif. Tchr. secondary schs. Los Angeles Unified Sch. Dist., 1967-74, secondary counselor, 1974-80, asst. prin. secondary counseling services, 1980-84, adviser integration compliance, 1984—; cons. English Med-Core, U. So. Calif., 1980. Dean's Acad. Leadership scholar U. So. Calif., 1985, Verna B. Dauterive scholar, 1986, Educare scholar, 1988. Mem. NAACP, Assn. for Supervision and Curriculum Devel., Calif. Assn. for Supervision and Curriculum Devel., Assn. Adminstrs. Los Angeles, Council Black Adminstrs., Black Women's Forum, Urban League, Calif. Afro-Am. Mus. Found., Phi Delta Kappa. Democrat. Baptist.

LOVE, MICHAEL, design company executive, facilities management consultant; b. Summit, N.J., May 21, 1925; d. Michael and Ethel (Sears) Slifer; m. Edwin P. Love (div.); children—Pamela, Michele. Student Traphagen Sch. Design, 1943-45, U. Miami (Fla.), 1946, Pratt Inst., 1949-50, Parsons Sch. Design, 1980-82. Pres. Quadric Inc., N.Y.C., 1970-78, 82—; v.p. design and constrn. Bankers Trust, N.Y.C., 1978-82; dir. Crestview of Am., Scotch Plains, N.J., 1980—. Lamp designer Am. Soc. Interior Designers; editor articles on interior design Home Mag. Mem. Met. Mus. Art., N.Y.C. Mem. Chief Exec. Officers Club, Am. Soc. Interior Designers (dir.), Constrn. Specifications Inst., Assn. Real Estate Women, Internat. Facilities Mgmt. Assn., Art Deco Soc. N.Y. (pres. 1984—), Profl. Women in Constrn. Club: City (N.Y.C.). Home: 215 E 24th St New York NY 10010 Office: Quadric Inc 686 Lexington Ave New York NY 10022

LOVE, MILDRED LOIS (JAN), public relations executive; b. Iowa City, July 9, 1928; d. Joseph R. and Gladys M. (Parsons) Casey; B.S. in Bus. Adminstrn., U. Iowa, 1951; m. Gerald Dean Love, Apr. 4, 1952; children—Laura Anne Love Parris, Cynthia Love-Hazel, Gregory Alan, Linda Love Mesler, Geoffrey Dare. Vocal soloist Sta. KXEL, Waterloo, Iowa, 1944-46; sec. to lawyer, La Porte City, Iowa, 1944-46; adminstrv. aide Office of Supt., La Porte City High Sch., 1947-48; office mgr. Minn. Valley Canning Co., Iowa div. offices, LaPorte City, 1947-48; sec. dept. mktg. U. Iowa, 1948-51; asst. dept. public relations Chgo. Bd. Trade, 1949-51; exec. sec. patent dept. Collins Radio Co., Cedar Rapids, 1951-52; vol. VA Hosp., Albany, N.Y., 1965-73; adminstrv. dir. Tri-Village Nursery Sch., Delmar, N.Y., 1960-61; participant Internat. Lang. Teaching Exchange, Cambodia, 1961; vol. hosps. in Concord, N.H., 1963-64; vol. Chgo. Maternity Center,

1973-74, mgr. Wolf Trap Assos. Gift Shop, Vienna, Va., 1975-80; gen. mgr. Travelhost of Washington, 1980-81; cons. mgmt., 1980—; chair Nat. Cherry Blossom Festival, Washington. Participant community pageants on local and dist. levels, Iowa, 1950-51; Sunday sch. tchr. Meth. Ch., 1941-61; mem. Flossmoor (Ill.) Planning and Zoning Commn., 1973-74, McLean (Va.) Planning and Zoning Commn., 1975—; precinct worker in Iowa, 1946-52, N.Y., 1956-61, N.H., 1963-64, Va., 1979—; pres. I.O.W.A. Inc., Washington, 1980-81; active various community fund raising drives; mem. Ladies Aux., McCosh Infirmary, Princeton, N.J. Mem. AAUW, Am. Mkgt. Assn., Nat. Assn. Female Execs., Nat. Conf. State Socs. (pres. 1983); LWV, Ariz. Opera League, Delta Zeta. Republican. Clubs: Princeton, Canadian (Washington); Normanside Country, Olympia Fields Winter, Kenilworth. Home: 6102 E Charter Oak Rd Scottsdale AZ 85254

LOVE, SANDRA RAE, info specialist; b. San Francisco, Feb. 20, 1947; d. Benjamin Raymond and Charlotte C. Martin; B.A. in English, Calif. State U., Hayward, 1968; M.S. in L.S., U. So. Calif., 1969; m. Michael D. Love, Feb. 14, 1971. Tech. info. specialist Lawrence Livermore (Calif.) Nat. Lab., 1969—. Mem. Spl. Libraries Assn. (sec. nuclear sci. div. 1980-82, chmn. 1983-84), Beta Sigma Phi. Democrat. Episcopalian. Office: Lawrence Livermore Nat Lab PO Box 808 L-389 Livermore CA 94550

LOVE, SUE, volunteer services coordinator; b. Love Valley, Tenn., Dec. 1, 1943; d. Herbert Richie and Ruby (Walker) L.; 1 child, Melody. BS, Mid. Tenn. State U., 1965; MS, U. Tenn.; PhD, Vanderbilt U. Owner Sweet Sue's Bakery, Nashville, 1978-79; v.p. Buffalo Valley Music, Nashville, 1980-86; asst. to warden De Berry Correctional Inst., Nashville, 1980-85; coordinator of vol. services Spencer Youth Ctr., Nashville, 1985—; tchr. Internat. Secs. Assn., Nashville, 1970-76. Tchr. Sunday Sch. Assn., Nashville, 1960—; coordinator of vols. Jim Sasser for U.S. Senate Campaign, 1975-76, Albert Gore for U.S. Senate, 1983-84. Mem. Nat. Assn. of Vols. in Criminal Justice (Tenn. rep. 1986—), Tenn. Assn. of Vols. in Criminal Justice, Met. Dirs. Vols., Tenn. Network Vol. Dirs., Bus. and Profl. Women (pres. 1978-79), Internat. Profl. Secs. (pres.). Democrat. Baptist. Home: 120 McGavock Pike Nashville TN 37214 Office: Spencer Youth Ctr 4011 Stewarts Ln Nashville TN 37218

LOVE, SUSAN DENISE, accountant, consultant, small business owner; b. Portland, Oreg., Aug. 5, 1954; d. Charles Richard and Betty Lou (Reynolds) Beck; m. Daniel G. Oliveros, Dec. 21, 1979 (div. Nov. 1983); m. Michael Dean Love, Aug. 24, 1984. BA in Graphic Design, Portland State U., 1976. Exec. sec. Creighton Shirtmakers, N.Y.C., 1977-80; dir. adminstrn. Henry Grethel div. Manhattan Industries, N.Y.C., 1980-81; exec. asst. S.B. Tanger and Assocs., N.Y.C., 1981-83; exec. asst., bookkeeper M Life Ins. Co., Portland, 1983-84; acct. cons., owner Office Assistance, Portland, 1984—; owner WE LOVE KIDS Clothing Store, Portland, 1985—; sec./treas. Designers' Roundtable, Portland, 1985—. Mem. Oreg. State Pub. Interest Research Group, Portland, 1985-87, Oreg. Fair Share, Salem, 1987. Democrat. Home: 8321 SE Cornwell Portland OR 97266 Office: Office Assistance PO Box 66234 Portland OR 97266

LOVEJOY, BEVERLY HARRIS, plumbing company and restaurant executive; b. Devils Lake, N.D., Oct. 8, 1935; d. Franklin E. and Frances Marion (Schneider) Harris; m. Floyd M. Lovejoy, June 8, 1952; children—Floyd M. II, Sonja, Marcia, Daniel, Herbert. Vice-pres., Yellowstone Plumbing Co., Inc., 1963—, JSA Corp., Billings, Mont., 1978—. Counselor youth groups Apostle Lutheran Ch., Billings, 1976-77, 79-82. Democrat. Lutheran. Avocations: writing novels; dress designing; skiing; camping. Home: 5040 Rimrock Rd Billing MT 59106

LOVEJOY, R(OYA) LYNN, lawyer, consultant, nurse; b. Wheatland, Wyo., Sept. 4, 1946; d. Cecil R. and Vonda Laura (Mick) Bolich; m. Duane Cecil Lovejoy, July 2, 1965; children: Christine, Wendy, Brenda. BA, Calif. State U., Sacramento, 1979; JD, McGeorge Sch. of Law, 1983. Bar: Fla. 1983; RN, Fla., Calif. Various positions Sacramento, 1979-83; assoc. Kocha & Houston, P.A., West Palm Beach, Fla., 1985, Burton E. Burdick, P.A., Ft. Lauderdale, Fla., 1985-86; sole practice Boca Raton, Fla., 1986—; cons. in field; lectr. in field. Mem. ABA, Fla. Bar Assn., Palm Beach County Bar Assn., Fla. Assn. of Women Lawyers. Republican. Presbyterian. Home: 9943 Three Lakes Circle Boca Raton FL 33428 Office: 370 W Camino Gardens Blvd Plaza 7 Suite 343 Boca Raton FL 33432

LOVELAND, HOLLY STANDISH, information systems executive; b. Slater, S.C., Aug. 28, 1947; d. Albert C. and Lucille E. (Standish) L. AA, Macomb Coll., 1974; BA Siena Heights Coll.,1985. Applications analyst Burroughs Corp., Detroit, 1977-79; programmer analyst Ford Hosp., Detroit, 1979-80, project leader applications support, 1980, project mgr. applications support, 1980-82, mgr. systems services, 1982-84; dept. exec. VI, info. services Wayne County, Detroit, 1984-86, dir. data services City of Milw., 1986—; computer cons. Mem. Soc. for Info. Mgmt. Home: 2549 S Shore Dr Milwaukee WI 53207 Office: 809 N Broadway Rm 400 Milwaukee WI 53202

LOVELAND, KATHERINE ANNE, psychologist; b. Atlanta, June 30, 1955; d. Edward Henry and Olga Helen (Christie) L.; m. James Voorhis Temple, June 2, 1979. BA, U. Va., 1975; PhD, Cornell U., 1980; postdoctoral, U. Houston, 1985. Lic. psychologist, Tex. Vis. asst. prof. psychology Rice U., Houston, 1979-82; research specialist Tex. Research Inst. Mental Scis., Houston, 1982-85; asst. prof. clin. psychiatry and pediatrics U. Tex. Med. Sch., Houston, 1985—; adj. asst. prof. linguistics Rice U., Houston, 1982-86, psychology, 1982—. Contbr. articles to profl. jours. Recipient NIH Research award, 1982-84; NIMH fellow, 1979-80; grantee NIH, 1985—, Mathers Charitable Found., 1987—. Mem. Am. Psychol. Assn., AAAS, N.Y. Acad. Scis., Soc. for Research in Child Devel., Am. Women in Sci., Internat. Soc. for Ecol. Psychology. Office: U Tex Mental Scis Inst 1300 Moursund Houston TX 77030

LOVELESS, ELLIN MCDOUGALL, hearing specialist; b. Goshen, Ind., May 7, 1939; d. Herbert Allen and Esther (Engman) McDougall; m. Mark Edwin Loveless, Apr. 20, 1963; children: Christopher, Timothy. BA, Monmouth (Ill.) Coll., 1961. Lic. hearing specialist, Calif. Owner McCoy Miracle Ear Ctr., Yucca Valley, Calif., 1983—. Officer Tops, Yucca Valley, 1971-87; mem. Prince of Peace council Evang. Luth. Ch. Am., 29 Palms, Calif. 1987. Mem. Hearing Aid Assn. Calif., Nat. Hearing Aid Soc., Am. Bus. Women Assn. Democrat. Office: McCoy Miracle Ear Ctr 7319 Acoma Trail Yucca Valley CA 92284

LOVELL, EMILY KALLED, journalist; b. Grand Rapids, Mich., Feb. 25, 1920; d. Abdo Rham and Louise (Claussen) Kalled; student Grand Rapids Jr. Coll., 1937-39; B.A., Mich. State U., 1944; M.A., U. Ariz., 1971; m. Robert Edmund Lovell, July 4, 1947. Copywriter, asst. traffic mgr. Sta. WOOD, Grand Rapids, 1944-46; traffic mgr. KOPO, Tucson, 1946-47; reporter, city editor Alamogordo (N.Mex.) News, 1948-51; Alamogordo corr., feature writer Internat. News Service, Denver, 1950-54; Alamogordo corr., feature writer El Paso Herald-Post, 1954-65; Alamogordo news dir., feature writer Tularosa (N.Mex.) Basin Times, 1957-59; co-founder, editor, pub. Otero County Star, Alamogordo, 1961-65; newscaster KALG, Alamogordo, 1964-65; free lance feature writer Denver Post, N.Mex. Mag., 1949-69; corr. Electronics News, N.Y.C., 1959-63, 65-69; Sierra Vista (Ariz.) corr. Ariz. Republic, 1966; free lance editor N.Mex. Pioneer Interviews, 1967-69; asst. dir. English skills program Ariz. State U., 1976; free-lance editor, writer, 1977—; part-time tchr., lectr. U. Pacific, 1981-86; part-time interpreter Calif., 1983—, Interpreters Unlimited, Oakland, 1985—; sec., dir. Star Pub. Co., Inc., 1961-64, pres., 1964-65. 3d v.p., publicity chmn. Otero County Community Concert Assn., 1950-65; mem. Alamogordo Zoning Commn., 1955-57; mem. founding com. Alamogordo Central Youth Activities Com., 1957; vice chmn. Otero County chpt. Nat. Found. Infantile Paralysis, 1958-61; charter mem. N.M. Citizens Council for Traffic Safety, 1959-61; pres. Sierra Vista Hosp. Aux., 1966; pub. relations chmn. Ft. Huachuca chpt. ARC, 1966. Mem. nat. bd. Hospitalized Vets. Writing Project, 1972—. Recipient 1st Pl. awards N.Mex. Press Assn., 1961, 62. Pub. Interest award Nat. Safety Council, 1962. 1st Pl. award Nat. Fedn. Press Women, 1960, 62; named Woman of Year Alamogordo, 1960. Editor of Week Pubs. Aux., 1962, adm. N.Mex. Navy, 1962, col. a.d.c. Staff Gov. N.Mex., 1963, Woman of Yr., Ariz. Press Women, 1973. Mem. N.Mex. (past sec.), Ariz. (past pres.) press women, N.Mex. Fedn. Womens Clubs (past dist. pub. relations chmn.), N.Mex. Hist. Soc. (life), N.Mex. Fedn. Bus. and Profl. Womens Clubs (past pres.), Pan Am. Round Table Alamogordo, Theta Sigma Phi (past nat. 3d v.p.), Phi Kappa Phi. Democrat. Moslem. Author: A Personalized History of Otero County, New Mexico, 1963; Weekend Away, 1964; Lebanese Cooking, Streamlined, 1972; A Reference Handbook for Arabic Grammar, 1974, 77; contbg. author: The Muslim Community in North America, 1983. Home: PO Box 7152 Stockton CA 95207

LOVELL, JO ANN, hospitality industry executive, consultant; b. Ithaca, N.Y., Aug. 22, 1937; d. Everett Maransa and Carrie Arlone (Skinner) Odell; m. James G. Lovell, June 21, 1958 (div. 1978); children: Douglas C., David J. BS, Cornell U., 1958; postgrad., U. Calif., 1968; MBA, Case Western Res. U., 1977. Dept. head home econs. Oakmont Regional High Sch., Ashburnham, Mass., 1968-69; dir. research and devel. diet dept. Cleve. Met. Gen. Hosp., 1969-73; account mgr. Stouffer Mgmt. Food Services, Cleve., 1973-76; systems mgr. Stouffer Corp. Hotel Div., Cleve., 1976-79; dir. mgmt. services Cini-Little Internat., Chagrin Falls, Ohio, 1979-82; sr. assoc. Cini-Little Internat., Potomac, Md., 1982-86; sr. assoc., program dir. Robert Barrie and Ptnrs., Ltd., Vienna, Va., 1986—. Contbr. articles to profl. jours. Bd. dirs. Office Econ. Opportunity, Fitchburg, Mass., 1967-69. Fellow Soc. Advancement Food Service Research (bd. dirs. 1978-84); mem. Roundtable for Women (1st v.p. 1986—, pacesetter 1985), Cornell Soc. Hotelmen D.C., Am. Dietic Assn. Democrat. Home: 8180 Inverness Ridge Rd Potomac MD 20854

LOVELL, KAREN DENISE, image consultant; b. Brookhaven, Miss., Aug. 15, 1953; d. Ollie Denson Jr. and Maureen (Catha) L. BA in Radio/TV Journalism, N.E. La. U., 1975, postgrad., 1977-78. Nat. cons. Phi Mu, Memphis, 1975-76; from dir. orientation to coordinator student activities N.E. La. U., Monroe, 1976-79; rep. sales West Pub. Co., St. Paul, 1979-81, Jostens, Inc., Mpls., 1981-85; mgr. regional sales Hayden Pub. Co., Hasbrouck Heights, N.J., 1985; pvt. practice cons. image K. D. Lovell, Dallas, 1985—; trainer nat. sales Your Season Accessories, Dallas, 1986—; cons. BeautiControl Cosmetics, Dallas, 1986—. Editor Women In Exec. Leadership, 1986; contbr. articles to profl. jours. Vol. Spl. Olympics, Dallas, 1982—; vol., com. chmn. Children's Cancer Fund, Dallas, 1982—; fund raiser Wednesday's Child, Dallas, 1985—, Children's Miracle network, Dallas. Named one of The Women of '85 Two Byrds Pub., 1985. Mem. Direct Jewelers Assn. (bd. advisors 1987), North Dallas Network Career Women (past bd. mem.), Women in Exec. Leadership (publicity dir. 1986-87), Mortar Bd., Phi Beta Kappa, Phi Mu (dir. nat. pledge com. 1986—, pres. 1986—). Republican. Baptist. Club: P.E.O. Home and Office: 5626 Preston Oaks Rd #9D Dallas TX 75240

LOVELY, HELEN TENNYSON, nursing care executive; b. Thomastown, Ireland, Apr. 16, 1939; came to U.S., 1963, naturalized 1963; d. James Gerald and Helena Sarah (Carr) Tennyson; m. Warren L. Lovely, July 13, 1963; children—James Warren, Helen Elizabeth, David Patrick. R.N., Bedford Gen. Hosp.-Eng., 1961; cert. midwife, Gables Maternity Hosp.-Eng., 1962; B.S. in Health Services Adminstrn. with honors, Fla. Internat. U., 1979, M.S. in Edn. with honors, 1981. Instr. Dade County Sch. System, Miami, Fla., 1981-82; dir. nursing services Nursefinders of Miami, 1982-84; cons. Miami Springs Sr. Ctr., 1983—; devel. coordinator preferred provider orgn. Gulf Life Ins., 1984-85; founder, chief exec. officer Nat. Council Licensure Examination Rev., 1983—; pres. Profl. Pvt. Nursing Care, Miami, 1983—, dir. nursing services, 1983—; cons. Mactown-Miami Facility for adult mentally retarded and Sunrise Sch. Retarded Children, 1975-84; cons. Miami Springs Sr. Ctr., 1983—; mem. profl. adv. bd. Advanced Human Studies Inst., Coral Gables. Vol., Am. Heart Assn., 1980—; mem. adv. bd. Advanced Human Studies Inst., Coral Gables, 1985-86; mem. Harvard Med. Survey Research Team, 1976—. Mem. Nat. Assn. Female Execs., Mental Health Assn. Greater Miami, Center Fine Arts Miami, Pi Lambda Pi, Kappa Delta Pi. Roman Catholic. Home: 18555 SW 94th Ave Miami FL 33157

LOVELY, MARY RUTH, chemist; b. Bridgeport, Conn., May 4, 1961; d. Edward Coughlin and Nancy Ann (Michalka) L. BS in Chemistry, St. Joseph Coll., 1983; postgrad., U. R.I., 1983-84; MBA in Mgmt., Indsl. Relations, U. Bridgeport, 1988. Grad. asst. chemistry dept. U. R.I., Kingston, 1983-84; quality assurance asst. chemist Clairol, Inc., Stamford, Conn., 1984-85, package devel. sr. chemist, 1985-87; quality services hdqrs. assoc. quality specialist PepsiCo, Inc., Valhalla, N.Y., 1987-88, quality services hdqrs. supr., 1988—. Recipient research fellowship Hartford Hosp., 1982. Mem. Am. Chem. Soc., Nat. Assn. Female Execs., Soc. Soft Drink Technologists, St. Joseph College Alumnae (sec. Fairfield County Club, 1986—). Roman Catholic. Club: Ambassador. Home: 8 Newton Ln Trumbull CT 06611-1020 Office: PepsiCo Inc 350 Columbus Ave Valhalla NY 10595

LOVETRI, JEANNETTE LOUISE, voice educator; b. Southampton, N.Y., Apr. 2, 1949; d. James John and Aline Rita (Zimmer) Lovetri; student Manhattan Sch. Music, 1967-68, Juilliard Sch., 1971-72; pvt. dance, piano and vocal study. Singer opera, cabaret, summer stock, oratorios, jazz, 1966-80; owner voice studio, Greenwich, Conn., 1970-75, N.Y.C., 1975—; tchr. voice music dept. Upsala Coll., East Orange, N.J., 1976-81; founder, dir. The Voice Workshop, pub. speaking seminar, 1983—; guest lectr. Boston Conservatory, 1987; lectr., workshop leader, various U.S. cities, Amsterdam, and Copenhagen; numerous appearances with Bklyn. Contemporary Chorus, Chapman Roberts Singers, Mid-Hudson Opera, others; former chmn. Music Theatre Com. Ann. Symposium. Mem. N.Y. Singing Tchrs. Assn. (dir., pres.), Nat. Assn. Tchrs. Singing.

LOVETT, CLARA MARIA, university provost, historian; b. Trieste, Italy, Aug. 4, 1939; came to U.S., 1962; m. Benjamin F. Brown. B.A. equivalent, U. Trieste, 1962; M.A., U. Tex.-Austin, 1967, Ph.D., 1970. Prof. history Baruch Coll., CUNY, N.Y.C., 1971-82, asst. provost, 1980-82; chief European div. Library of Congress, Washington, 1982-84; dean Coll. Arts and Scis., George Washington U., Washington, 1984-88; provost, v.p. academic affairs, George Mason U., Fairfax, Va., 1988—; vis. lectr. Fgn. Service Inst., Washington, 1979-85; bd. dirs. Inst. for Research in History, N.Y.C., 1981-82; exec. council Conf. Group on Italian Politics, 1980-83, others; lectr., cons. Fgn. Service Inst. State Dept., 1979—; adv. bd. European program Wilson Ctr., 1986—. Author: The Democratic Movement in Italy 1830-1876, 1982 (H.R. Marraro Prize, Soc. Italian Hist. Studies); Giuseppe Ferrari and the Italian Revolution, 1979 (Phi Alpha Theta book award); Carlo Cattaneo and the Politics of Risorgimento, 1972 (Soc. for Italian Hist. Studies Dissertation award), (bibliography) Contemporary Italy, 1985; co-editor: Women, War, and Revolution, 1980, (essays) State of Western European Studies, 1984; contbr. sects. to publs. U.S., Italy. Organizer Dem. clubs Bklyn., 1972-76; exec. com. Palisades Citizens Assn., Washington, 1985-87; vestry mem. St. David's Episc. Ch., Washington, 1986—. Fellow Guggenheim Found., 1978-79, Woodrow Wilson Internat. Ctr. for Scholars, 1979 (adv. bd. West European program), Am. Council Learned Socs., 1976, Bunting Inst. of Radcliffe Coll., 1975-76, others. Mem. Am. Hist. Assn. (officer 1984-87), Am. Assn. Higher Edn. (cons. 1979—), Council for European Studies, Soc. for Italian Hist. Studies, Conf. Group on Italian Politics, others. Avocations: hiking, fishing, swimming. Office: George Mason U/Finley Bldg 4400 University Dr Fairfax VA 22030

LOVETT, JUANITA PELLETIER, clinical psychologist; b. Youngstown, Ohio, Mar. 9, 1937; d. Joseph Acadia and Alice Beatrice (Davis) Pelletier; B.A. with honors in Psychology summa cum laude, Fairleigh Dickinson U., 1975; M. Phil. Tchrs. Coll., Columbia U., 1978, M.A., 1979; Ph.D., Columbia U., 1980; m. James Emmett Lovett, Jr., Aug. 9, 1958; children—Laura Ann, James Emmett. Free lance fashion cons., 1958-70; psychology fellow Westchester Div. N.Y. Hosp.-Cornell Med. Center, White Plains, 1977-80; program dir. inpatient service Fair Oaks Hosp., Summit, N.J., 1980-82; pvt. practice, 1980—; asst. dir. med. research CIBA-GEIGY Pharms., Summit, 1982-83; cons. AT&T Bell Labs., Murray Hill, N.J., 1983; adj. asst. prof. psychology and edn., dept. psychology, Tchrs. Coll., Columbia U., N.Y.C., 1980—; field supr. grad. sch. applied profession psychology Rutgers U., 1981—. Union County Mental Health Bd. mem., 1974-76; coll. companion Overbrook Hosp., Cedar Grove, N.J., 1972-75. Mennen scholar, 1975; recipient Laurie Shavel award, 1975. Mem. Am. Psychol. Assn., N.Y. State Psychol. Assn., Soc. Personality Assessment, N.J. Acad. Psychology, N.Y. Acad. Scis., N.J. Psychol. Assn., Sigma Xi, Phi Omega Epsilon. Contbr. articles to profl. publs. Home: 15 Norwood Ave Apt 5B Summit NJ 07901 Office: 19 Prospect St Summit NJ 07901

LOVETT, PAULA ELIZABETH, state government agency official; b. Tiptonville, Tenn., Apr. 3, 1955; d. Russell Howard and Margie Mildred (Smith) L. BS, U. Tenn., Martin, 1976; MPA, Middle Tenn. State U., 1980. Research analyst Tenn. Dept. Econ. and Community Devel., Nashville, 1976-77, project control officer, 1977-81, grants analyst, 1981-83, grants program mgr., 1983—. Mem. Nat. Assn. Female Execs. Mem. Ch. of Christ. Office: Dept Econ and Community Devel 620 6th Ave N Nashville TN 37219

LOVINS, SHARRON JOYCE, program manager, education planning consultant; b. Malden, Mass., Mar. 8, 1946; d. Max and Gladys (Singer) L. BA, U. Mass., 1967; postgrad., Boston Coll., 1969-70, Boston U., 1970-72. Tchr. English Malden (Mass.) Pub. Schs., 1967-80; ednl. mktg. specialist, customer edn. mgr. Honeywell Info. Systems, Waltham, Mass., 1980-84; sr. ednl. planning specialist Wang Labs., Inc., Burlington, Mass., 1984-86; edn. design cons. Wang Labs., Inc., Lowell, Mass., 1986-88, program mgr., 1988—; mktg. cons. edn., writing, media, 1981—. Contbr. articles to high tech. jours. Fundraiser WGBH Pub. TV, Boston, 1970, 71, Mondale-Ferraro election com., Brookline, Mass., 1984; Tanglewood Festival Chorus singer, Boston Symphony Orch., 1974-81. Mem. Am. Soc. Tng. and Devel., Nat. Assn. Female Execs., Am. Jewish Congress, Combined Jewish Philanthropies. Democrat. Home: 200 Bedford Rd 21A Glenbrook Estates Woburn MA 01801 Office: Wang Labs Inc One Industrial Ave Lowell MA 01852-1901

LOVVORN, JOELLA, newspaper editor; b. Pep, Tex., Mar. 20, 1934; d. Alford Marion and Emma (Daniel) L. B.S., Wayland Bapt. Coll., 1969. Ch. news editor Plainview (Tex.) Daily Herald, 1957-60, typesetter, proofreader, 1965-67; offset printer, photographer Muleshoe (Tex.) Jours., 1960-64; asst. editor Ariz. Bapt. Beacon, Phoenix, 1964-65; society editor Lamb County Leader-News Littlefield, Tex., 1967-69, editor, 1969—. Bd. dirs. United Way Fund, 1979-88, Salvation Army, 1976—; dir. Lamb County Spelling Bee, Littlefield, 1980—; judge Regional Spelling Bee, Lubbock, 1980—; chmn. public info. Am. Cancer Soc., 1968—, Am. Heart Assn., 1976-79; chmn. publicity county chpt. ARC, 1976, retail trade com., 1987—. Recipient appreciation cert. Am. Cancer Soc., 1974, 80, 83, 86-88, Am. Heart Assn., 1974, appreciation plaque Distributive Edn. Classes Am., 1983-85, appreciation plaque Future Farmers Am., 1985. Mem. Soc. Profl. Journalists, Nat. Press Photographers Assn., Tex. Press Assn., West Tex. Press Assn. (contest chmn. 1970), West Tex. Competitive Shooters, Nat. Rifle Assn., Littlefield C. of C. (chmn. publicity). Republican. Lodge: Woodmen of World. Office: Lamb County Leader-News 313 W 4th St Littlefield TX 79339

LOW, KAREN ELIZABETH, travel service executive; b. St. Catharines, Ont., Can., Mar. 6, 1956; d. Norman Bell and Margaret McIntosh (Mowatt) L. Diploma in Hispanic studies, U. Madrid, 1977; BA in Spanish Lang. and Lit. cum laude, McGill U., 1978. Overseas rep. Mex., Fla. Sunflight Holidays, Toronto, Can., 1978-79, sr. overseas rep. Mex., Caribbean, 1979-82; resort supr. Mex. Thomson Vacations, Chgo., 1982-83, resort area mgr. Mex., 1984-85, regional mgr. Mex., The Bahamas, Hawaii, 1985-86, hotel contracts mgr. Mex., Hawaii, Dominican Republic, 1986—. Presbyterian. Office: Thomson Vacations 100 Northwest Point Blvd Elk Grove Village IL 60007

LOW, LUCINDA ANN, lawyer; b. Denver, Nov. 30, 1951; d. John Wayland and Marian Elizabeth (Roth) Low; m. Daniel B. Magraw, Jr., Jan. 3, 1981; children—Kendra Elizabeth Low Magraw, Caitlin Barstow Low Magraw. B.A., Pomona Coll., 1973; J.D., UCLA, 1977. Bar: Calif. 1977, D.C. 1979, Colo. 1984. Assoc. Covington & Burling, Washington, 1977-83; legal cons., Boulder, Colo., 1983-84; ptnr. Sherman & Howard, Denver, 1984—; adj. prof. Am. U. Sch. Law, 1983, U. Colo. Sch. Law, 1987—; lectr. U. Va. Law Sch., 1981, 82. Am. Field Service scholar, 1968-69. Editor in chief UCLA Law Rev., 1977; assoc. editor, 1976-77. Mem. ABA (co-chair inter-am. law com., Sch. Internat. Law and Practice), Colo. Bar Assn. (chair internat. law com. 1985-87), Internat. Law Inst. (lectr. 1982, exec. bd. Procedural Aspects), Am. Soc. Internat. Law, Internat. Trade Assn. Colo. (pres. 1987-88). Democrat. Congregationalist. Home: 728 10th St Boulder CO 80302 Office: Sherman & Howard 633 17th St Suite 3000 Denver CO 80302

LOWE, ADELE VIRGINIA (MRS. ALBERT ST. CLAIR LOWE), pharmacist; b. Indpls., June 27, 1919; d. Michael Angelo and Ivy Opal (Wilson) Lobraico; B.S. Indpls. Coll. Pharmacy, 1941; m. Albert St. Clair Lowe, Dec. 10, 1942; 1 dau., Judith A. (Mrs. Robert Frank Campbell). Chemist, E.I. duPont de Nemours & Co., Pryor, Okla., 1942-43; registered pharmacist Lobraico's Broad Ripple Pharmacy, Indpls., 1943—. Mem. Nat. Assn. Retail Druggists, Womens Orgn. Nat. Assn. Retail Druggists (pres. chpt. 20, 1977-79, chmn. legis. com.) Indpls. Assn. Pharmacists, Broad Ripple Bus. and Profl. Womens Club, Lambda Kappa Sigma (mem. grand council, supr. Midwest region 1948-50, 66-68, supr. So. region 1958-60, 4th v.p. 1950-54, grand v.p. 1968-70, grand pres. 1970-74, mem.-at-large 1974-78, chmn. ednl. trust com. 1975—, hon. adv. 1978-84, Disting. Service citation 1982). Clubs: Order Eastern Star, Daus. of Nile. Home: 12610 Brookshire Pkwy Carmel IN 46032 Office: 902 E Westfield Blvd Indianapolis IN 46220

LOWE, CAROL HILL, social services director; b. Washington, Sept. 12, 1943; d. Lawrence Alexander and Corine (Thorne) Hill; m. John W. Lowe, Nov., 1968 (div. 1981); 1 child, Paul Alejandro. BA cum laude, Albright Coll., 1965; MSW summa cum laude, Howard U., 1967; cert., John F. Kennedy Sch. of Govt., 1986. Caseworker Child Welfare Dept., City of Washington, 1966-67; caseworker welfare U.S. Dept. Pub. Welfare, Washington, 1967-68, Child Welfare Dept., City of Washington, 1968-70; sr. worker, supr. Social Rehab. Agy., 1970-78; assoc. chief Office of Maternal and Child Health, 1978-82; spl. asst. Office of City Adminstr., 1982-85; exec. dir. DC Commn. for Women, 1985—; mem. council Washington Woman Mag. Mem. Task Force on Pay Equity, Older Adult Learning Com., Child Devel. Coordinating Council, Employment and Tng. Coalition, Washington, 1985—, D.C. Child Support Advocacy Coalition and Adv. Com., Instl. Appeals Bd.; bd. dirs. Washington Urban League, 1968—, chairperson, 1983-85; bd. dirs. DC United Way, 1984—, D.C. Choral Arts Soc.; grad. Leadership Washington Bd. Trade/Jr. League Program, 1987. Fellow Nat. Assn. Social Workers (cert.); mem. DC Mental Health Assn., Nat. Assn. Commns. for Women, NOW, Black Women's Agenda, Nat. Council Negro Women, Assn. Black Women Attys., D.C. Urban Mgmt. Assn., Am. Assn. Pub. Adminstrs., Nat. Assn. Black Pub. Adminstrs. Democrat. Episcopalian. Office: DC Commn for Women 2000 14th St NW Washington DC 20011

LOWE, ETHEL BLACK, artist; b. Kiowa County, Okla., Jan. 30, 1904; d. Benjamin Alonzo and Harriet Ann (Heaton) Black; B.A., Central State U., Okla., 1926; M.A., U. Tulsa, 1937; postgrad. U. Okla., U. Colo., Columbia, U. Hawaii; m. William Glenn Lowe, June 5, 1939 (dec. 1942). Tchr. pub. schs., Okla., 1922-39, N.Y., 1942-49, 50-68, ret.; teaching prin. Dragon Sch., Sasebo, Kyushu, Japan, 1949-50; works exhibited 1945—; exhibits include Nat. Assn. Women Artists, 1953, 55, 71, 75, 77, Terry Nat. Art Exhibit, 1952, Provincetown Art Assn., 1952-53, Nassau Community Coll., 1971. Reproductions of works in newspapers, mags. Mem. N.Y. State Ret. Tchrs. Assn., Nat. Assn. Women Artists, Am. Watercolor Soc., Nat. Ret. Tchrs. Assn., Delta Kappa Gamma. Home: 48-50 44th St Woodside NY 11377

LOWE, FLORENCE SEGAL, public relations executive; b. N.Y.C.; d. Samuel I. and Rose (Cantor) Segal; B.S. in Edn., U. Pa., 1930; postgrad. Sch. Social Service, 1935-36; m. Herman Albert Lowe, June 27, 1935; children—Lesley Ellen Lowe Israel, Roger Bernard. Guidance counsellor Phila. Public Schs., 1935-41; Washington corr. Variety and Daily Variety, Phila. Daily News, Manchester Union Leader, TV Guide, 1942-58; spl. public relations Radio Sta. WIP, Phila. and Metromedia, 1958-60; coordinator spl. projects Metromedia, 1960-70; spl. asst. to chmn. pub. affairs Nat. Endowment for Arts, Washington, 1970-86; sr. cons. arts and cultural communications Kamber Group, 1986—. Mem. public relations and advt. com. Nat. Symphony, 1952-56; mem. Sec. State's Commn. on Travel, 1970-71; mem. Coordinating Com. for Ellis Island, 1982-87; mem. Com. for Nancy Hanks Endowment for Arts, Duke Univ. Recipient All-Army Entertainment Contest award, 1958; spl. achievement award Nat. Endowment for Arts Chmn., 1983; Spl. Merit award Fed. Govt., 1981, Spl. Achievement award, 1983, Disting. Service award, 1985. Mem. Am. Women in Radio and TV (founder, pres. 1954-55), Council Jewish Women, Women in Communications (citation for meritorious reporting 1962), Nat. Press Club (bd. dirs. 1981-84), Women's Nat. Press Club (treas. 1954, v.p. 1956, Washington Press Club (bd. dirs. 1983-84), Am. News Women's Club (v.p. 1969-70). Republican. Home: 2801 New Mexico Ave NW Washington DC 20007 Office: The Kamber Group 1920 L St NW Washington DC 20037

LOWE, MARY FRANCES, federal government official; b. Ft. Meade, Md., Apr. 15, 1952; d. Benno Powers and Peggy Catherine (Moore) L. B.A., Coll. William and Mary, 1972; M.A., Fletcher Sch. Law and Diplomacy, 1974, M.A. Law and Diplomacy in, 1975; diplome, Grad. Inst. Internat. Studies U. Geneva, Switzerland, 1975; M.P.H. in epidemiology, Johns Hopkins Sch. Hygiene and Pub. Health, 1986. External collaborator ILO, Geneva, 1974; legis. asst. to U.S. Senator Richard S. Schweiker Washington, 1975-76; profl. staff mem. health and sci. research subcom. U.S. Senate Com. Labor and Human Resources, Washington, 1976-81; exec. sec. U.S. Dept. HHS, Washington, 1981-85; sr. asst. to commr. program policy FDA, 1985—; rep. U.S. delegations 34th and 35th World Health Assemblies, Geneva, 1981, 82; alt. trustee Woodrow Wilson Internat. Ctr. Scholars. Mem. AAAS, Am. Assn. World Health, Exec. Women in Govt., Soc. Risk Analysis, Washington World Affairs Council, Delta Omega. Republican. Home: 7920 Spotswood Dr Alexandria VA 22308 Office: US FDA 5600 Fishers Ln Rockville MD 20857

LOWE, MARY JOHNSON, federal judge; b. N.Y.C., June 10, 1924; children by previous marriage: Edward H., Leslie H.; m. Ivan A. Michael, Nov. 4, 1961; 1 child, Bess J. Michael. BA, Hunter Coll., 1952; JD, Bklyn. Law Sch., 1954; LLM, Columbia U., 1955. Bar: N.Y. 1955. Sole practice N.Y.C., 1955-71; judge N.Y.C. Criminal Ct., 1971-73; acting justice N.Y. State Supreme Ct., 1973-74, justice, 1977-78; judge Bronx County Supreme Ct., 1975-76; justice 1st Jud. Dist., 1978; judge U.S. Dist. Ct. (so. dist.) N.Y., 1978—. Recipient award for outstanding service to criminal justice system Bronx County Criminal Cts. Bar Assn., 1974, award for work on narcotics cases Asst. Dist. Attys., 1974. Mem. Women in Criminal Justice, Harlem Lawyers Assn., Bronx Criminal Lawyers Assn., N.Y. County Lawyers Assn., Bronx County Bar Assn., N.Y. State Bar Assn. (award for outstanding jud. contbn. to criminal justice Sect. Criminal Justice 1978), NAACP, Nat. Urban League, Nat. Council Negro Women, NOW. Office: US Dist Ct US Courthouse Foley Sq New York NY 10007 *

LOWE, RUTH REEVE, librarian; b. Provo, Utah, June 27, 1929; d. Fenton West and Rhea Luthenia (Dixon) Reeve; m. Howard D. Lowe, Sept. 4, 1951; children—Kevin Howard, Linda Ann Lowe Weaver, David Jordan, Alan, Mark. B.S., Brigham Young U., 1951; M.L.S., U. Hawaii, 1969, M.Ed., 1970. Exec. sec. Geneva Steel Co., Orem, Utah, 1949, Bell Telephone Co., Provo, 1951, Gen. Foods Co., Chgo., 1951-52, Abadan Inst. (Iran), 1961-63; sch. librarian Univ. Lab., Honolulu, 1968-69, Blanche Pope Sch., Waimanalo, Hawaii, 1970—; participant Waimanalo Country TV Program, 1983; librarian Latter-Day Saints Ch., Kaneohe, Hawaii, 1970-74, Kailua, Hawaii, 1973-74. Author: A Penny Earned, 1964; artist oil paintings. Active PTA, Utah, Ariz., Hawaii, 1958—; coordinator Multiple Sclerosis, Waimanalo, 1978—; vol. Am. Cancer Soc., Kailua, 1976-78; leader Boy Scouts Am. Fed. Govt. grantee U. Hawaii, 1967-68. Mem. AAUW, ALA, Hawaii Sch. Library Assn. (chmn. 1974-75), Windward Library Assn. (chmn. 1976-78). Republican. Mormon. Clubs: Faculty, Tamaris (Provo). Home: 192 Alala Rd Kailua HI 96734 Office: Lanikai Elem Sch 140 Alala Rd Kailua HI 96734

LOWE, VALERIE CLAIRE, pharmacologist; b. Balt., Jan. 14, 1956; d. Robert Wylie and Doris Ann (Woods) L. BS in Biochemistry, U. Md., 1978. Chemist Md. Dept. Agr., College Park, 1978-79; sr. research technician Johns Hopkins U. Sch. Medicine, Balt., 1979-80; technician gastrointestinal dept. U. Md. Sch. Medicine, Balt., 1980-87; chemist Nat. Inst. Aging div. NIH, Balt., 1981-84; sr. research pharmacologist NOVA Pharm. Corp., Balt., 1984-88, sr. technical assoc., 1988—; tutor chemistry Ctr. for Intensive Ednl. Devel., College Park, 1977-79. Mem. Alpha Chi Sigma (vice master alchemist 1977-78). Democrat. Presbyterian. Home: 9208 Swiven Pl apt 3B Baltimore MD 21237 Office: NOVA Pharm Corp 6200 Freeport Ctr Baltimore MD 21224

LOWELL, SHIRLEE ELAINE, wholesale lighting business owner; b. Denver, May 2, 1927; d. Walter Austin and Gladys Evelyn (DeCastle) L.; m. Hal S. McMurrough, June 1952 (div. 1964); children: Carolyn V., Leslie E., Lowell S., Scott N. Student, Denver, 1944-45, Colo. U., 1948-49, Colo. U., 1958-60. Corr. Internat. div. Time, Inc., Denver, 1946-57; tech. writer Thermovac, Inc., Stockton, Calif., 1959-60; color coordinator R.E. div. Sunset Internat. Petroleum, Rocklin, Calif., 1960-65; mgr. World of Lighting, Carmichael, Calif., 1966-71, Valley Lighthouse, Sacramento, 1971-86; owner Lighting div. Masters Wholesale, Rancho Cordova, Calif., 1987—. Vol. Californians for Drug Free Youth, Sacramento; various civic activities Presbyn. Ch., Carmichael. Democrat. Lodge: Soroptmists. Home: 5110 Kipp Way Carmichael CA 95608 Office: Lighting div Masters Wholesale Rancho Cordova CA 95670

LOWEN, SANDRA SCOTT, journal editor; b. Washington, Nov. 27, 1945; d. Henry Wiley Jr. and Susan Helen (Scott) Singleton; m. John Lowen, Mar. 28, 1987; 1 child, Aliso Emmanuel. BA in English Lit., U. D.C., 1968; BS in Secondary Edn., D.C. Tchrs. Coll., 1968. Proofreader Bur. Nat. Affairs, Washington, 1968; reporter The Washington Daily News, Washington, 1968-69; adminstrv. editor Edufax Early Learning Ctrs., Washington, 1970-72; mgr., co-owner Omega Office Services, Washington, 1971-73; vocalist, songwriter Sunburst & Co., Boulder, Colo., 1973-80; adminstrv. sec. The Washington Times, 1982-84; lectr., editor The Common Suffering Fellowship, Washington, 1984-85; pub. media relations officer Causa Internat., N.Y.C., 1984-86; publications editor Internat. Security Council, N.Y.C., 1986—; lectr. Am. Leadership Confs., Washington, 1984—, Minority Alliance Internat., N.Y.C., 1985-86. Lyricist, composer over 15 songs, 1968—; contbr. articles and short stories to profl. publs. Childbirth cons., Washington and N.Y.C., 1983—; vol. Harlem in Action, The Punch Found.; cosponsor minority art project The Living Wall. Mem. Nat. Assn. Female Execs., Religious Pub. Relations Corps, DAR. Republican. Mem. Unification Ch. Office: Internat Security Council 393 Fifth Ave Suite 400 New York NY 10016

LOWENTHAL, JUDITH NELSON, psychologist; b. Phila., Nov. 15, 1945; d. Sidney David and Pauline (Taksey) Nelson; m. Rodger Lowenthal; m. Alan Robert Morgenstein; children: Jessica, Eric, Ariel. BA, Penn State U., 1966; MA, Temple U., 1969; PhD, U. Pa., 1974. Cert. psychologist. Psychologist Diagnostic & Rehab. Ctr., Phila., 1967-69, Phila. Gen. Hosp., 1969-70, Cope Ctrs., Ambler, Pa., 1972-75; pvt. practice psychotherapy Elkins Park, 1975—; lectr. U. Pa., Phila., 1981—, Community Coll. Phila., 1985—; cons. in field. Pres. Del. Valley AHP, Phila., 1978-80. Mem. Am. Psychol. Assn., Assn. Humanistic Psychology (pres. Phila. chpt. 1978-80). Democrat. Jewish. Home and Office: 530 Elkins Ave Elkins Park PA 19117

LOWERY, KATHLEEN ROLAND, foundation administrator; b. Binghamton, N.Y., June 17, 1953; d. Ralph Mayo and Cecelia Marie (Gearon) R.; m. Mark J. Lowery, Aug. 17, 1974. BS, U. N.C., Greensboro, 1975; MA, U. Conn., 1977. Cert. home economist. Agt. coop. extension Coll. Agr. U. Conn., Bethel, 1977-80; specialist consumer service Price Chopper Supermarkets subs. Golub Corp., Schenectady, N.Y., 1980-83; cons. K.R.L. Cons., Hixson, Tenn., 1984—; community planner Met. Council for Community Services, Chattanooga, 1986088; v.p. gen. bus. markets United Way Bergen County, 1988—; adj. faculty U. Tenn., Chattanooga, 1986—. Bd. dirs. U. Conn. 4H Devel. Fund, Hartford, 1975-77, Growth Opportunities for Gifted and Talented; mem. Danbury (Conn.) Youth Commn., 1976, Chattanooga Venture Adolescent Pregnancy Commn., 1986—, Jr. League of Chattanooga, Jr. League of Schenectady, N.Y.; chair pub. relations Chattanooga Venture Child Care Task Force, 1986-88; mem. Chattanooga Venture Gang Task Force. 1986-88. Recipient Profl. Improvement award AAUP, 1976-77. Mem. Am. Home Econs. Assn. (nat. com. 1985-87), Home Economists in Bus., Tenn. Home Econs. Assn. (regional membership com. 1986-87, dist. pub. relations 1986—), Am. Conf. on Young Children (treas. Tenn. chpt. 1987), Sex Info. Educators Council Conn. Clubs: Investment (Hixson) (v.p. investments 1986-87, pres. 1987—), Chattanooga Women's, Newcomers. Home: 505 Franklin Turnpike #4 Allendale NJ 07401

LOWMAN, MARY BETHENA HEMPHILL (MRS. ZELVIN D. LOWMAN), civic worker, realtor; b. Lewis, Kans., Feb. 10, 1922; d. Frederick William and Gladys (Follin) Hemphill; A.B., Western State Coll., Colo., 1945; m. Zelvin D. Lowman, Oct. 24, 1943; children—Freda Ruth (Mrs. Neal Frink), James Fredrick, William Martin, Elizabeth June (Mrs. Joseph Herbst) (dec.). Tchr., Stout Creek Sch., Colo., 1942-43, San Diego City Sch. Dist., 1944-45, Los Angeles City Sch. Dist., 1948-50; pvt. sch. tchr. So. Inst. Music, 1956-57. Troop leader Frontier council Girl Scouts U.S.A., 1957-70, mem. exec. bd., 1961-73, 2d v.p., 1962-63, pres., 1968-71, recipient Thanks Badge, 1964, chmn. established camp com., 1963-67, dir. Camp Foxtail, 1965, 67, chmn. Gold award com., 1986-87; mem. Calico Task Group, 1986—, chmn., 1988—; mem. Girl Scouts U.S.A. Region VI Com., 1973-75, chmn. Region VI Com., mem. nat. bd., mem. exec. com. and councils com., 1975-78; mem. Am. Field Service Exchange Student Bd. So. Nev., 1961. Parliamentarian, West Charleston PTA, 1957-59, Nev. Congress, 1960-61; chmn. Christian Edn. Commn., 1964-65; chmn. Commn. on Mission of Church, 1966; chmn. exec. com. Clark County Bicentennial Commn., 1974-76; chmn. bd. First Presbyterian Pre-Sch. Day Care Ctr., 1982-85. Family chosen as Nev. All-Am. Family, 1960. Mem. Gen. Fedn. Women's Clubs (dir. 1958-60, 62-64, 72-78, chmn. scholarships and student aid 1974-76, chmn. family living div., 1976-78; treas. Western States Conf. 1968-70, sec. 1970-72, pres. 1972-74), Nev. Fedn. Women's, Clubs, (past pres.), Md. fedn. women's Clubs (past jr. dir.), Clark County Pan-Hellenic Assn., So. Nev. Alumni Club (pres. 1961-62), Internat. Platform Assn. Presbyterian (elder), dir. capital stewarship canvas program, 1987-88, Las Vegas Bd. Realtors (chmn. membership com. 1988—). Clubs: Las Vegas Mesquite (past pres.); Jr. Women's (past pres.) (College Park, Md.); Newcomers (past pres.), Nat. Presbyterian Mariners; (past pres.), Nevada-Sierra District Mariners; Las Vegas Nautilus Mariners. Home: 1713 Rambla Ct Las Vegas NV 89102

LOWRANCE, MURIEL EDWARDS, program specialist; b. Ada, Okla., Dec. 28, 1922; d. Warren E. and Mayme E. (Barrick) Edwards; B.S. in Edn., East Central State U., Ada, 1954; 1 dau., Kathy Lynn Lowrance Gutierrez. Accountant, adminstrv. asst. to bus. mgr. East Central State U., 1950-68; grants and contracts specialist U. N.Mex. Sch. Medicine, Albuquerque, 1968-72, program specialist IV, dept. orthopaedics, 1975-86; asst. adminstrv. officer N.Mex. Regional Med. Program, 1972-75. Bd. dirs. Vocat. Rehab. Center, 1980-84. Cert. profl. contract mgr. Nat. Contract Assn. Mem. Am. Bus. Women's Assn. (past pres. El Segundo chpt., Woman of Yr. 1974), AAUW, Amigos de las Americas (dir.). Democrat. Methodist. Club: Pilot (Albuquerque) (pres. 1979-80, dir. 1983-84, dist. treas. 1984-86, treas. S.W. dist., 1984-86, gov.-elect S.W. dist. 1986-87, gov. S.W. dist. 1987-88). Home: 3028 Mackland Ave NE Albuquerque NM 87106

LOWRIE, KATHRYN YANACEK, recruiting service executive; b. Midland, Mich., Nov. 23, 1958; d. Frank Joseph and Jacqueline Ann (Sipko) Yanacek; m. David Bruce Lowrie, Mar. 14, 1987. BA in Psychology, Northeastern U., 1980. Psychology tech. Research Inst. of Environ. Medicine, U.S. Army, Natick, Mass., 1980-81, computer programmer, 1981-83; assoc. recruiter Mgmt. Adv. Services, Burlington, Mass., 1983-85, v.p. mgmt. info. systems, 1985-86; exec. v.p. Mgmt. Adv. Services, Burlington, 1986—. Mem. Assn. Women in Computing. Roman Catholic. Office: Mgmt Adv Services 16 New England Exec Park Burlington MA 01803

LOWRIE, MIRIAM ELISE, home economist; b. Warren, Minn., June 27, 1946; d. Walter Evald and Jeanette Evelyn (Nelson) Carlson; m. Daniel Howard Lowrie, Apr. 21, 1979; 1 child, Jed. BS in Home Econs., N.D. State U., 1968, MS in Textiles and Clothing, 1971. Home economist Oreg. State Univ. Extension, Hood River, 1971-79; from instr. to asst. prof. Oreg. State Univ. Extension, 1975; 4-H and youth agent Oreg. State Univ. Extension, McMinnville, Oreg., 1979-82; assoc. prof. Oreg. State Univ. Extension, 1981; 4-H and youth agent Oreg. State Univ. Extension, Dallas, 1979—; bd. dirs. L'Amistad, Independence, 1986-87. Mem. YMCA, Salem, Oreg., 1982—; Sunday sch. tchr. St. Mark Lutheran Ch., Salem, 1984—. Mem. Oreg. State Univ. Extension Assn. (pres. 1987), Nat. Assn. Ext. 4-H Agents, Polk County Women in Agriculture, Kappa Delta (pres. 1967-68). Lutheran. Lodge: Soroptimist. Office: Oreg State Univ Extension 288 E Ellendale PO Box 640 Dallas OR 97338

LOWRY, BARBARA JEAN, nursing educator; b. Rockford, Ill., Apr. 14, 1938; d. Albert Rudolph and Barbara Jean (Slater) Isoz; m. Clark Graydon Lowry, Dec. 16, 1961; 1 son, Andrew Karl. B.S., Rockford Coll., 1976, M.A. in Teaching with distinction, 1980. R.N., Ill. Staff nurse Rockford Meml. Hosp. (Ill.), 1960-61, nursing instr., 1964—, lectr., 1981—, curriculum chmn., 1983; staff nurse Copley Meml. Hosp., Aurora, Ill., 1961-62, asst. head nurse, 1962-64; lectr. Rockford Coll., 1983; moderator Alzheimer's Program. Student coordinator Am. Field Service, Rockford, 1983, Keith Sch., 1986-88. Named Am. Field Service Mother, 1982, 84. Mem. Am. Nurses Assn., Nat. League Nursing (accreditation visitor 1986, visitor 1987-88), Am. Assn. Critical Care Nursing, Alzheimers and Related Disease Assn., Ill. Nurses Assn. (pres. 3d Dist. 1987-88), Rockford Meml. Nurses Alumni Assn. (meml. chmn. 1980—). Baptist. Club: Charter of Rockford Coll. Home: 2902 E State St Rockford IL 61108 Office: Rockford Meml Sch Nursing 2400 N Rockton Ave Rockford IL 61101

LOWRY, ETHEL JOYCE, educational administrator; b. Crandon, Wis., Mar. 4, 1933; d. Frank Ames and Leila Emma (Feight) Butler; m. Thomas Franklin Lowry, Dec. 27, 1952; children—Genice Ann, Cheryl Lea, Dwight Thomas. M.S., Bemidji State U., 1969; postgrad., U. N.D., 1970-73, 77-84, N.D. State U., 1978-81, No. State Coll., 1984. Teaching asst. U. N.D., Grand Forks, 1970-73; reading cons. Devils Lake Pub. Sch., N.D., 1973-76; right to read coordinator N.D. Dept. Pub. Instrn., Bismarck, 1976-81, asst. dir. elem. edn., 1981-84, state dir. chpt. I, 1984—. Editor: Reading In the Content Areas, 1980; The Answer Book: A Guide to Teaching Basic Skills K-12, 1988; Your Child and Reading, 1979. Mem. N.D. Reading Assn. (pres. 1981-83, Leadership award 1983). Avocations: reading, cross country skiing, fishing, baking. Home: 1330 Valencia Loop Chula Vista CA 92010 Office: ND Dept Pub Instrn State Capitol Bismarck ND 58505

LOWRY, JOAN MARIE DONDREA, broadcaster; b. Weirton, W.Va., June 8, 1935; d. Rudolph and Mary (Telmanik) Dondrea; m. Robert William Lowry, June 15, 1957; 1 child, Christopher Scott. B.S. in Edn., Baldwin-Wallace Coll., 1956; student Ohio Sch. Broadcasting, 1977-79. Gen. mgr., news dir. Sta. WLRO, Lorain, Ohio, 1980-82; host 35 Live, Cinemavidio TV, Elyria, Ohio, 1980-83; TV show host Continental Cable, Cleve., 1983—; pub. relations dir. Sta. WZLE, Lorain, 1982-83; broadcaster, community relations dir. Sta. WRKG, Lorain, 1983—; performer commls.; speaker in field. Appeared in motion pictures: Those Lips Those Eyes, 1982, One Trick Pony, 1982. Mem. nat. steering com. Better Hearing and Speech, 1985-86; nat. philanthropy chair Delta Zeta Sorority and Found., 1980—, trustee, 1980—; mem. Lorain Litter Control Bd., 1981-83; bd. dirs. Lorain County Sr. Citizens Assn., 1982-85, Lorain Consumers Council, 1980—; v.p. Bay Village PTA Council, 1973-75; nat. pres. Delta Zeta Found., 1987—; mem. Martin Luther King Steering Com., 1987—; chmn. adv. bd. Lorain County Heart Assn., 1988; active Multiple Sclerosis Soc., Am. Cancer Soc., Muscular Dystrophy Assn., Founders Meml. Found, Lorain County Mothers March of Dimes, others; grand marshal numerous parades. Named Woman of Achievement, Nat. YWCA and Lorain County Bus. and Industry Assn., 1983, Ohio Delta Zeta Alumnae Woman of Yr.; recipient U.S. Air Force award, 1982, U.S. Navy award, 1981, Media award Am. Cancer Soc., 1982, Communication award Easter Seals Soc., 1981, Community Service award Lorain County chpt. Am. Heart Assn., 1981, Service to Mankind award Sertoma Internat., 1988; ofcl. hostess for U.S. Army in Lorain County, 1980-83; Mayor's Proclamation, 1982; hon. recruiter award U.S. Army, 1981; recognition award Ohio House Reps. Mem. Lorain County Arts Council, Baldwin-Wallace Alumni Assn. (nat. pres. 1979-81), LWV (chpt. pres. 1966-67), Cleve. Amateur Fencers (pres. 1965-67), Internat. Platform Assn. Byzantine Catholic. Home: 578 Yarmouth Ln Bay Village OH 44140

LOWRY, LOU ELLEN, data processing executive, small business owner; b. Ft. Scott, Kans., Oct. 17, 1953; d. Albert Warren and Ruth Rosamond (Johnson) L.; 1 child Marshal Warren. AA in Liberal Arts, Cottey Coll., 1979; BS, Pittsburg (Kans.) State U., 1981. Various secretarial positions 1972-76; exec. sec. Mid-Continental Waterproofing, Ft. Scott, 1976-78; supr. Southwestern Bell Telephone, Wichita, Kans., 1981-82; asst. mgr. Southwestern Bell Telephone, Wichita, 1982-86; sr. systems programmer Cessna Aircraft, Wichita, 1986-87, mgr. data adminstrn., 1987—. Vol. Children's Miracle Network telethon, 1985. Baptist. Home: PO Box 20567 Wichita KS 67208 Office: Cessna Aircraft 5800 E Pawnee Dept 866 Wichita KS 67218

LOY, MYRNA, actress; b. Helena, Mont., Aug. 2, 1905; d. David Franklin and Della Williams. Grad., Venice (Calif.) High Sch., Westlake Sch. Girls. Appeared in numerous motion pictures, including Best Years of Our Lives (award World Film Festival, Brussels), The Bachelor and the Bobby Soxer, Mr. Blanding Builds His Dream House, If This Be Sin, Cheaper by the Dozen, Airport 75, The End, Just Tell Me What You Want, others; appeared in stage plays Relative Speaking; TV appearances in Death Takes a Holiday, also, Do Not Fold, Spindle or Mutilate, Indict and Convict, Columbo, Ironsides, Family Affair, The Virginian, The Couple Takes a Wife, It Happened at Lakewood Manor, Summer Solstice. Organizer Hollywood Film com. U.S. Nat. Commn. for UNESCO, 1948, mem. commn., 1950-54; asst. head welfare activities ARC, N.Y. area, 1941-45; Mem. Am. Assn. UN, Nat. Commn. Against Discrimination in Housing. Recipient Kennedy Ctr. Honor, 1988. Address: 229 S Orange Dr Los Angeles CA 90036

LOZANO, SUZANNE VILLARREAL, director of center for occupational medicine; b. San Antonio, Oct. 27, 1958; d. Oscar and Carolina (Berlanga) V.; m. Robert Flores Lozano, April 9, 1983. BS in Nursing, U. Tex., Austin, 1981; MS in Health Care Adminstrn., Southwest Tex. State U., 1986. RN, Tex. Staff nurse Audie Murphy VA Hosp., San Antonio, 1982-83, VA Meml. Hosp., Waco, Tex., 1983; cardiac and pulmonary rehab. coordinator Hillcrest Bapt. Med. Ctr., Waco, 1983-86, acting dir. of rehab., 1985-87; dir. occupational medicine Hillcrest Baptist Med. Ctr., Waco, 1987—. Pres. Am. Heart Assn., Waco, 1987— (pres. elect 1986-87, sec., treas. 1985-86); active Am. Cancer Soc. Mem. Am. Nurses Assn., Tex. Nurses Assn. (v.p. dist. 10 1988—). Roman Catholic. Home: 409 O'Campo Ct Waco TX 76708 Office: Hillcrest Bapt Med Ctr 3000 Herring Waco TX 76708

LOZIER, CYNTHIA WOOLEY, physician; b. Mobile, Ala., Sept. 10, 1948; d. Samuel Oliphant and Mary Emma (Chambers) Wooley; m. Phillip Blocker, Feb. 18, 1966 (div. June 1972); m. Mark Davis Lozier, Dec. 15, 1978; children—Darren, Nancy, Joshua. B.S. in Chemistry, U. South Ala., 1974, M.D., 1979. Intern in surgery U. South Ala., Mobile, 1979-80; physician, med. dir. Mostellar Med. Clinic, Bayou La Batre, Ala., 1980-83; practice gen. medicine, Mobile, 1983—; assoc. dir. Famlicare Med. Ctr., Jan. to June, 1986; med. dir. Downtowner Med. Ctr., 1987-88, North Mobile Med. Clinic, Eight Mile, Ala., 1988—; mem. staff Knollwood Park Hosp., Springhill Meml. Hosp., Mobile Infirmary, Doctors Hosp., Providence Hosp., Mobile Community Hosp., U. South Ala. Med. Ctr.; mem. staff dept. community medicine U. Ala.-Birmingham; med. dir. Grandbay Nursing Home, Midsouth Home Health Assn., 1983-87. Served with USPHS, 1980-83. Recipient Commd. Officer award USPHS, 1982, Outstanding Career Woman award, 1984. Mem. AMA, Med. Assn. State Ala., Mobile County Med. Soc., So. Med. Assn., Am. Med. Women's Assn., Mobile C. of C. Roman Catholic. Club: Zonta.

LUBBERS, PHYLLIS RYBINSKI, contract specialist; b. Lakeland, Fla., Sept. 3, 1953; d. Marion Michael and Estelle Barbara (Ogorzelec) Rybinski; m. Edward John Lubbers, Feb. 14, 1987. B.A. in Internat. Affairs, Fla. State U., 1975; M.P.A., U. West Fla., 1986. Mem. adminstrv. staff Ga. Inst. Tech., Atlanta, 1975-82, contracting officer, 1979-81, asst. to dir. Sch. Chemistry, 1981-82; sr. contract adminstr. Metric Systems Corp., Fort Walton Beach, Fla., 1982-87. Mem. AAUW, Atlanta Friendship Force Club, Nat. Contract Mgmt. Assn. Republican. Roman Catholic. Office: 736 N Beal St Fort Walton Beach FL 32548

LUBIC, RUTH WATSON, association executive, nurse, midwife; b. Bucks County, Pa., Jan. 18, 1927; d. John Russell and Lillian (Kraft) Watson; m. William James Lubic, May 28, 1955; 1 son, Douglas Watson. R.N., Sch. Nursing Hosp. U. Pa., 1955; B.S., Columbia U., 1959, M.A., 1961, Ed.D. in Applied Anthropology, 1979; C.N.M., SUNY, Bklyn., 1962; LL.D. (hon.), U. Pa., 1985; D.Sc. (hon.), U. Medicine and Dentistry, N.J., 1986. Mem. faculty Sch. Nursing, N.Y. Med. Coll., Maternity Center Assn., SUNY Sch. Nurse-Midwifery, Downstate Med. Center; staff nurse through head nurse Meml. Hosp. for Cancer and Allied Disease, N.Y.C., 1955-58; clin. assoc. Grad. Sch. Nursing N.Y. Med. Coll., N.Y.C., 1962-63; parent educator, cons. Maternity Center Assn., N.Y.C., 1963-67, gen. dir., 1970—; bd. dirs., v.p. Am. Assn. for World Health U.S. Com. for WHO, 1975—, pres., 1980-81; mem. bd. maternal child and family health research NRC, 1974-80; mem. Commn. on Grads. Fgn. Nursing Schs., 1979-83, v.p., 1980-81, treas., 1982-83; bd. govs. Frontier Nursing Service, 1982—. Author: (with Gene Hawes) Childbearing: A Book of Choices, 1987; contbr. articles to profl. jours. Recipient Letitia White award, Florence Nightingale medal, 1955, Alumnae award Sch. Nursing U. Pa., 1986, Rockefeller Public Service award, 1981, Hattie Hemschemeyer award, 1983; named Maternal-Child Health Nurse of Yr., Am. Nurses Assn., 1985. Fellow Am. Acad. Nursing, AAAS, N.Y. Acad. Medicine (assoc.); mem. Am. Coll. Nurse-Midwives (v.p. 1964-66, pres. elect 1969-70), Am. Pub. Health Assn. (mem. com. internat. health, mem. MCH council, sec. 1982, mem. Governing Council 1986-87, nominating com. 1987, action bd. 1988), Nat. Acad. Sci., Soc. Applied Anthropology, Inst. of Medicine of Nat. Acad. Sci., Nat. Assn. Childbearing Ctrs. (pres. 1983—), Herman Biggs Soc., Am. Assn. World Health., Sigma Theta Tau. Club: Cosmopolitan. Office: 48 E 92d St New York NY 10128

LUBIN, JOY KATHLEEN, human resources executive; b. Elizabeth, N.J., July 20, 1943; d. Joseph Andrew and Mary Elizabeth (Hajicek) Silvoy; children: James David, Dawn Marie. Grad. high sch., Clark, N.J. Asst. to personnel mgr. Boyle-Midway div. Am. Home Products Corp., Cranford, N.J., 1961-68; sales rep. Avon Products, Inc., N.Y.C., 1976-81; supr. human resources Glass Products, Inc. subs. AFG Industries, Carbondale, Pa., 1981—; rep. AFG Employee's Credit Union, Kingsport, Tenn., 1986—. Recipient Outstanding Personal and Profl. Achievement plaque Lackawanna County Pvt. Industry Council, 1986. Mem. Nat. Fedn. Bus. and Profl. Women's Club. Democrat. Roman Catholic. Office: Glass Products Inc Clidco Dr PO Box 313 Carbondale PA 18407

LUBKIN, GLORIA BECKER, physicist; b. Phila., May 16, 1933; d. Samuel Albert and Anne (Gorrin) B.; m. Yale Jay Lubkin, June 14, 1953 (div. Apr. 1968); children: David Craig, Sharon Rebecca. AB, Temple U., 1953; MA, Boston U., 1957; postgrad., Harvard U., 1974-75. Mathematician Fairchild Stratos Co., Hagerstown, Md., 1954, Letterkenny Ordnance Depot, Chambersburg, Pa., 1955-56; physicist TRG Inc., N.Y.C., 1956-58; acting chmn. dept. physics Sarah Lawrence Coll., Bronxville, N.Y., 1961-62; v.p. Lubkin Assocs., electronic cons., Port Washington, N.Y., 1962-68; assoc. editor Physics Today, Am. Inst. Physics, N.Y.C., 1963-69; sr. editor Physics Today, Am. Inst. Physics, 1970-84, editor, 1985—; cons. in field; mem. Nieman adv. com. Harvard U., 1978-82; co-chmn. search/adv. com. Theoretical Physics Inst., U. Minn., 1987—. Contbr. articles to profl. publs. Nieman fellow, 1974-75. Fellow AAAS (mem. nominating com. for sect. B physics 1987—), Am. Phys. Soc. (exec. com. history of physics div. 1983-86, exec. com. forum on physics and society 1977-78); mem. Nat. Assn. Sci. Writers, Sigma Pi Sigma. Jewish. Office: Am Inst Physics 335 E 45th St New York NY 10017

LUBY, ELLEN L., lawyer; b. Alice, Tex., May 21, 1949; d. James O. and Lillian (Hoffman) L.; divorced; 1 child, Winnie Jessica Macklin. BA, U. Tex., 1973; JD, South Tex. Coll. of Law, Houston, 1977. Bar: Tex. 1977. Assoc. Vinson & Elkins, Houston, 1977-85, ptnr., 1985—; bd. dirs. South Tex. Law Rev., Houston, 1984—, pres. 1987—. Contbr. articles to profl. jours. Mem. State Bar Assn. of Tex., Houston Bar Assn. Office: Vinson & Elkins 3500 First City Tower 1001 Fannin Houston TX 77002-6760

LUCAS, ELIZABETH COUGHLIN, educator, counselor; b. Youngstown, Ohio, May 5, 1918; d. Joseph Anthony and Gertrude Elizabeth (Handel) Coughlin; m. Charles Edward Lucas, Apr. 7, 1945. BS magna cum laude, Notre Dame Coll. of Ohio, 1940; Diploma, Harvard U., 1944; MA in Edn., Calif. State Poly U., 1980. Cert. tchr. math, physics, biol. sci., phys. sci., Calif. (life), secondary Pa., Ohio. Tech. sec. for v.p. engring and purchasing

Patterson Foundry and Machine Co., East Liverpool, Ohio, 1941-42; tchr. chemistry Point Marion (Pa.) High Sch., 1942, Lincoln High Sch., Midland, Pa., 1942-44; radar specialist Thunderstorm Project U.S. Weather Bureau, St. Cloud, Fla., 1946, Wilmington, Ohio, 1947; substitute tchr. math, sci. Chaffey (Calif.) Union High Schs., 1971-75; tchr. math Claremont (Calif.) High Sch., 1975-80; tchr., counselor, head sci. dept. San Antonio High Sch., Claremont, 1980—; dist. adv. com., math, sci., Claremont, 1983-85. Author, editor: A Descriptive Study of the Effects of the New Math Syndrome on the Average High School Student, 1980. Served to lt. (j.g.) USNR, 1944-48. Mem. Nat. Council of Tchrs. of Math., Nat. Sci. Tchrs. Assn., Assn. for Supervision and Curriculum Devel., Calif. Math. Council, Nat. Assn. for Exec. Females. Republican. Roman Catholic. Lodge: Cath. Daus. of the Ams. (regent 1975-77, diocesan chmn. 1979-81). Home: 9185 Regency Way Alta Loma CA 91701 Office: San Antonio High Sch 125 W San Jose Claremont CA 91711

LUCAS, ELIZABETH HELENE, artist, calligrapher, educator; b. Pasadena, Calif., Aug. 21, 1936; d. Edward A. and Anona Marie (Snyder) Buse; m. Justice Campbell M. Lucas, Dec. 17, 1960; children—Scott, Stephen, Lisanne. A.A., Long Beach City Coll., 1956; B.A., Whittier Coll., 1958, M.A., 1984. Cert. gen. secondary tchr., Calif. Chmn. dept. sci. Bolsa Grande High Sch., Garden Grove, Calif., 1960-65; ind. tchr. calligraphy Long Beach, Calif., 1976—; instr. Sch. for Adults, Long Beach, 1978-80; assoc. prof. calligraphy Calif. State U.-Long Beach, 1979—, coordinator cert. in calligraphy program, 1982—; instr. calligraphy and bookbinding U. Calif.-Riverside, 1982—; instr. calligraphy Whittier Coll., Calif., 1984-85; free-lance calligrapher and graphic designer, 1976—; designer, pub. line of calligraphy notecards, 1978—, owner Elizabeth Lucas Designs. Author: Calligraphy, The Art of Beautiful Writing, 1984; one-Woman calligraphy shows Long Beach Mus. Art Bookshop/Gallery, 1981, 84, Sr. Eye Gallery, Long Beach, 1982, 85, Gt. Western Savs. and Loan, Long Beach, 1983, David Scott Meier Gallery, Mendocino, Calif., 1983, Whittier Coll. Mendenhall Gallery, 1983; also group shows. Active, past mem. bd. dirs. Long Beach Law Aux., 1960—, Jr. League, Long Beach, 1968—; pres. Lowell Sch. PTA, Long Beach, 1972. Named Sci. Tchr. of Yr., So. Calif. Edison Co., 1963; recipient art awards, including First Place award Calif. State Lawyers' Wives, 1984. Mem. Soc. for Calligraphy (pres. 1982-83), Soc. Scribes and Illuminators, Friends of Calligraphy, Soc. Scribes, Profl. Writers League, Calif. State PTA (hon. life 1973—), Long Beach Mus. Art Found. (co-chairperson dir.'s circle 1985), Long Beach Art Assn., Pub. Corp. for Arts, Fine Art Affiliates of Calif. State U. at Long Beach. Republican. Lodge: Soroptimists (com. chairperson local club 1981—). Home: 518 Monrovia Ave Long Beach CA 90814 Office: Elizabeth Lucas Designs 2501 E 28th St Ste 110 Signal Hill CA 90806

LUCAS, GEORGETTA MARIE SNELL, retired educator, artist; b. Harmony, Ind., July 25, 1920; d. Ernest Clermont and Sarah Ann (McIntyre) Snell; m. Joseph William Lucas, Jan. 29, 1943; children—Carleen Anita Lucas Underwood-Scrougham, Thomas Joseph, Joetta Jeanne Lucas Allgood. BS, Ind. State U., 1942; MS in Edn., Butler U., 1964; postgrad. Herron Sch. of Art, Indpls., 1961-65, Ind. U., Indpls. and Bloomington, 1960, 61, 62, 65. Music, art tchr. Jasonville City Schs., Ind., 1942-43, Van Buren High Sch., Brazil, Ind., 1943-46, Plainfield City Schs., Ind., 1946-52, Met. Sch. Dist. Wayne Twp., Indpls., 1952-56, 1959-68; art tchr. Met. Sch. Dist. Perry Twp., Indpls., 1968-81; chmn. of artists Internat. Platform Assn., 1987; Ind. State U. art chmn. for Nat. League of Am. PEN Women, 1984-88. Illustrator: (book) Why So Sad, Little Rag Doll, 1963; artist (painting) Ethereal Season, 1966, (lithograph) Bird of Time, 1965-66: represented in permanent collections Ind. State U., Ind.-Purdue U.-Indlps.; lectr. Art Educators Assn. Ind., Ind. U.-Bloomington, 1976, Internat. Platform Assn., Washington, 1975, 77, 78, 82, 84 (Recipient Silver award 1978, appointed gov. 1983—). Named Best of Show, Nat. League Am. Pen Women State Show, 1983. Mem. Nat. Assn. Women Artist, Ind. Artist-Craftsmen, Inc. (pres. 1979-85, 87—), Ind. Fedn. Art Clubs (pres. 1986-87), Hoosier Salon, NEA, Art Edn. Assn. Ind., Nat. League Am. Pen Women (state art chmn. 1984—), Fine Art for State Ind. (Internat. Women's Yr. fine art chmn. 1977), Internat. Platform Assn. (bd. dirs. 1983—, chmn. art com. 1987—), Cen. Ind. Artists (hon.), Alpha Delta Kappa (Ind. state chmn. of art 1973-77, pres. 1972-74). Republican. Methodist. Lodge: Eastern Star. Avocations: genealogy, travel, numismatics. Home and Office: 9702 W Washington St Indianapolis IN 46231

LUCAS, LINDA DIANNE, skin care products manufacturing executive; b. Mpls., Nov. 1, 1942; d. Earl Winton and Shirley Grace (Holmgren) Skoog; B.S., Calif. Western U., 1981, M.B.A. candidate; m. Allen Joseph Lucas, Feb. 9, 1963; children—Teresa, Hollyanne, Scott (dec.), Jaime. Cons., Coppercraft Guild, Taunton, Mass., 1963-66; cons. Princess House, Inc., North Dighton, Mass., 1966-75, unit organizer, 1968-72, area dir., 1972-76; br. mgr. Leisure Home Parties, Inc., Racine, Wis., 1976-79, regional dir., 1976-79; dir. sales devel. Act II Jewelry, Inc., Bensenville, Ill., 1979-81; nat. mktg./sales mgr. Life Style Art, Inc., Kenyon, Minn., 1981-83; exec. v.p. Skin Care Internat., Peau Soin d'Amour, Sandy, Utah, 1983—; profl. instr. adult edn., St. Louis Park, Minn. Mem. Nat. Assn. Female Execs., Am. Soc. Profl. and Exec. Women. Lutheran. Author various co. publs. Home: 4730 Barbara Dr Minnetonka MN 55343 Office: 223 Cottage Ave Sandy UT 84070

LUCAS, LURENA GAIL, scientific research company administrator; b. Washington, May 3, 1958; d. Leon Carr and Edna May (Streets) L. AA, No. Va. Community Coll., 1987. Clk.-typist Dept. Navy, Washington, 1977-78; sec. with Dept. Navy, 1978-80, adminstrv. asst., 1980-82, program asst., 1982-83; exec. staff sec., asst. to directorate for Def. Tech. Study Team Inst. Def. Analysis, Alexandria, Va., 1983-84; sr. staff sec. W.J. Schafer Assocs. Inc., Rosslyn, Va., 1984-87; site adminstr. Sci. Applications Internat. Corp., McLean, Va., 1987—. Coordinator Arlington (Va.) Walk-a-Thon Nat. Cerebral Palsy Assn., 1976. Mem. Nat. Assn. Female Execs., DAR. Methodist. Home: 8727 Pebble Ln Manassas VA 22111 Office: Sci Applications Internat Corp 1710 Goodridge Dr Room T-93 McLean VA 22102

LUCAS, SUZANNE, statistician; b. Baxter Springs, Kans., Jan. 16, 1939; d. Ralph Beaver and Marguerite (Sansocie) L.; B.A. in Math., Calif. State U., Fresno, 1967, M.A. in Edml. Theory, 1969; M.S. in Stats., U. So. Calif., 1979; children—Patricia Sue Jennings, Neil Patric Jennings. Asst. to dir. NSF Inst., Calif. State U., Fresno, 1968; Tchr. secondary math. Fresno city schs., 1968-78; statistician corp. indsl. relations Hughes Aircraft Co., Los Angeles, 1979-80; personnel adminstr. Hughes Aircraft Co. Space and Communications Group, Los Angeles, 1981-82, mem. tech. staff in math., 1982-85, staff engr., 1986-87; mem. tech. staff cost analysis The Aerospace Corp., 1987—; lectr. in biostats. U. So. Calif., 1979. Kiwanis scholar, 1958. Mem. Internat. Assn. Parametric Analysts, Inst. Cost Analysis, Air Force Assn., Armed Forces Communications and Electronics Assn., U. So. Calif. Alumni Assn. (life), Kappa Mu Epsilon. Home: 13430 Isis Ave Hawthorne CA 90250 Office: The Aerospace Corp 2350 E El Segundo Blvd M5-632 El Segundo CA 90245

LUCCHETTI, LYNN, advertising manager, military officer, government executive; b. San Francisco, Calif., Aug. 21, 1939; d. Dante and Lillian (Bergeron) L. AB, San Jose State U., 1961; MS, San Francisco State U., 1967; grad. U.S. Army Basic Officer's Course, 1971, U.S. Army Advanced Officer Course, 1976, grad. U.S. Air Force Command and Staff Coll., 1982, U.S. Air Force War Coll., 1983, Sr. Pub. Affairs Officer Course, 1984. Media buyer Batten, Barton, Durstine & Osborn, Inc., San Francisco, 1961-67; producer-dir. Sta. KTVA-TV, Anchorage, 1967-68; media supr. Bennett, Luke and Teawell Advt., Phoenix, 1968-71; commd. 1st lt. U.S. Army, 1971; advanced through ranks to lt. col., 1985; officer U.S. Army, 1971-74, D.C. N.G., , 1974-78, U.S. Air Force Res., 1978—, program advt. mgr. U.S. Navy Recruiting Command, 1974-76; exec. coordinator for the Joint Advt. Dirs. of Recruiting (JADOR), 1976-79; dir. U.S. Armed Forces Joint Recruiting Advt. Program (JRAP), Dept. Def., Washington, 1979—. Author: Broadcasting in Alaska, 1924-1966. Decorated U.S. Army Meritorious Service medal, Nat. Def. medal, U.S. Air Force Longevity Ribbon, U.S. Navy Meritorious Unit Commendation, Dept. Def. Joint Achievement medal, 1984. Sigma Delta Chi journalism scholar, 1960. Mem. Women in Defense, Nat. Council Career Women, Dept. Def. Sr. Profl. Women's Assn., Va. Real Estate Bd. Home: 5416 Barrister Pl Alexandria VA 22304 Office: Dir US Armed Forces JRAP Dept of Defense 1600 Wilson Blvd Suite 400 Arlington VA 22209-2593

LUCENTE, ROSEMARY DOLORES, educational administrator; b. Renton, Wash., Jan. 11, 1935; d. Joseph Anthony and Erminia Antoinette (Argano) Lucente; B.A., Mt. St. Mary's Coll., 1956, M.S., 1963. Tchr. pub. schs., Los Angeles, 1956-65, supr. tchr., 1958-65, asst. prin., 1965-69, prin. elem. sch., 1969-85, 86—, dir. instrn., 1985-86; nat. cons., lectr. Dr. William Glasser's Educator Tng. Ctr., 1968—; nat. workshop leader Nat. Acad. for Sch. Execs.-Am. Assn. Sch. Adminstrs., 1980; Los Angeles Unified Sch. Dist. rep. for nat. pilot of Getty Inst. for Visual Arts, 1983-85, site coordinator, 1983-86. Recipient Golden Apple award Stanford Ave. Sch. PTA, Faculty and Community Adv. Council, 1976, resolution for outstanding service South Gate City Council, 1976. Mem. Nat. Assn. Elem. Sch. Prins., Los Angeles Elem. Prins. Orgn. (v.p. 1979-80), Assn. Calif. Sch. Adminstrs. (charter mem.), Assn. Elem. Sch. Adminstrs. (vice-chmn. chpt. 1972-75, city-wide exec. bd., steering com. 1972-75, 79-80), Asso. Adminstrs. Los Angeles (charter), Pi Theta Mu, Kappa Delta Pi (v.p. 1982-84), Delta Kappa Gamma. Democrat. Roman Catholic. Home: 6501 Lindenhurst Ave Los Angeles CA 90048 Office: Roscomare Rd Sch 2425 Roscomare Rd Los Angeles CA 90077

LUCHT, SONDRA MOORE, state senator; b. Stumptown, W. Va., Dec. 12, 1942; d. Arthur Jackson and Lucille (Cain) Moore; m. William Lucht; 1 child, Carl Joseph. B.A., Glenville State Coll., M.A., Marshall U.; postgrad. James Madison U. Cert. sch. psychologist. Mem. W. Va. State Senate from Dist. 16, 1982—, re-elected, 1986; speaker, lectr. on women in politics, other women's issues, child abuse, other youth issues. Co-founder Shenandoah Women's Ctr. Mem. W.Va. Orgn. Women (pres. 1977-82, chair task force on pay equity 1983—, chair commn. on juvenile law 1985—). Democrat. Address: 1013 Mill Race Dr Martinsburg WV 25401 *

LUCKEY, IRENE, social worker, educator; b. N.Y.C., May 29, 1949; d. Miles Calvin and Ollie Faye (Brevard) L.; m. Robert Lewis Cook, June 23, 1973 (div. Dec. 1983). BA, N.C. A&T State U., 1971; MA, U. Chgo., 1973; D Social Work, CUNY Grad. Sch. and Univ. Ctr., 1982. Med. social worker Met. Hosp., N.Y.C., 1973-76; asst. prof. social work N.C. Agrl. and Tech. State U., Greensboro, 1976-78; dir. ednl. programs Brookdale Ctr. on Aging of Hunter Coll., N.Y.C., 1979-81; vis. prof. social work, gerontology LeMoyne-Owen Coll., Memphis, 1981-82; asst. prof. social work Clark Coll., Atlanta, 1982-84; assoc. dir. Ctr. on Aging U. West Fla., Pensacola, 1985—, asst. prof. social work, 1985—; Nat. Inst. on Aging postdoctoral fellow U. MIch., Ann Arbor, 1987—; cons. Regional Adminstrn. on Aging, N.Y.C., 1981; cons. Atlanta Regional Commn. on Aging, 1984; bd. dirs. Geriatric Residential Treatment Services Inc., Fla., 1986—; mem. State of Fla. Long-Term Care Dist. I Ombudsman council, 1986—; chairperson Ednl. Programs Assn. of Black Social Workers, Pensacola, 1985—; adv. council cons. Mental Health Assn. of Escambia County 1985—; trainer, workshop developer Escambia County Council on Aging, 1986—, (adv. council mem. 1987); organizer, coordinator Black Family in Rural Am. symposium, 1987; mem. Social Research Planning and Practice Task Force on Minority Issues subcom. on Policy and Service/Practice, Gerontological Soc., 1987—. Bd. dirs. N.W. Fla. Area Agy. on Aging, 1985-86; mem. Escambia County Coalition of the Homeless, 1986—. Mem. Council of Social Work Edn., Gerontol. Soc., Assn. for Gerontology and Human Devel. in Hist. Black Univs. and Colls., Alpha Kappa Alpha, Phi Alpha, Alpha Kappa Mu. Home: PO Box 4226 Ann Arbor MI 48106-4226 Office: U Mich Sch Social Work 1065 Frieze Bldg Ann Arbor MI 48109-1285

LUCZ, CAROLYN ANN, communications company executive; b. Oskaloosa, Iowa, Apr. 12, 1936; d. Joseph A. and Marguerite M. (Votroubek) Abrahamson; m. Edward Francis Lucz, Nov. 25, 1955; children—Linda, Joanne Kay, Judy, Patricia, Diana. Student U. Ariz., 1965-82. Reporter, columnist Ariz. Cath. Diocesan Newspaper, Tucson, 1966-69; instr. Pima Community Coll., Tucson, 1980-81; v.p. Communications Skills, Inc., Washington, 1981—; dir. info. services Tucson Med. Ctr., 1969-75; exec. dir. Sunday Evening Forum, Tucson, 1976-83; coordinator career lifestyle dept. Levy's Dept. Store, Tucson, 1983-85; owner, pres. World Geog. Soc., Inc. Mem. Ariz. Adv. Council on Tourism, 1980-87; active Ariz. Town Hall., Phoenix, 1981-85, Tucson Com. Fgn. Relations, 1981-82, Tucson Tomorrow, Inc., 1981—; bd. dirs. Tucson Trade Bur., 1980-83, Tucson Assn. for Blind, 1978-83. Mem. Profl. Travel Film Lecture Assn. (v.p. 1979-81), Internat. Platform Assn., Ariz. Press Women, Exec. Women's Council So. Ariz. (founder 1979, pres. 1979-81), Nat. Alliance for Profl. and Exec. Women's Network (dir. 1981-83). Democrat. Roman Catholic.

LUDEKE, SHERYL ANN, gerontologist; b. Hamilton, Ohio, Dec. 2, 1948; d. Jonas and Ella (Logsdon) Blanton; Gary Cox, Sept. 13, 1971 (div. July 1976); m. Martin Glen Ludeke, Jan. 31, 1986. BA in Psychology of Aging, Antioch Coll., Yellow Springs, Ohio, 1979, M of Adult Devel. and Aging, 1984. Therapeutic recreation specialist. Instr. curriculum development therapeutic recreation vocat. tng. Colerain High Sch., Cin., 1976-78; chmn., pogamming for older adults Villa Julie Coll., Balt., 1979-83; owner cons. Environ. Therapies Cons. Services, Balt., 1978-83; dir. social rehab. Beverly Enterprises, Virgnia Beach, Va., 1983—. Named Big Sister of Yr. Big Bros., Ashtabula, Ohio, 1976; recipient Nat. County award Nat. Assn. Counties, Ashtabula, 1976. Mem. Nat. Therapeutic Recreation Soc., Nat. Assn. Action Profls. Democrat. Unitarian. Office: Beverly Enterprises 101 N Lynn Haven Rd Virginia Beach VA 23454

LUDENIA, KRISTA, psychologist, health facility administrator; b. Alexandria, Minn., Dec. 20, 1942; d. Dell John and Ethel Agnes (Balder) L.; children—Peter Jonathan, John Thomas, Kristin Ashley. B.A., B.S., Quincy Coll., 1967; M.S., Ind. U., 1969; Ph.D., U. Mo., 1972. Asst. chief alcohol and drug unit VA Med. Ctr., Danville, Ill., 1972-74; clin. psychologist VA Med. Ctr., St. Cloud, Minn., 1974-76, coordinator mental hygiene clinic, 1976-78; chief psychology service VA Med. Ctr., Wichita, Kans., 1978-80; chief psychology service, VA Med. Ctr., Bay Pines, Fla., 1980-82; health systems adminstr. VA Med. Ctr., St. Louis, 1982-84; assoc. med. ctr. dir. VA Med. Ctr., Danville, Ill., 1984-86, Boston, 1986—. Recipient Dir.'s Commendation for EEO, 1978, Leadership award VA, 1978, 1979, VA Dir.'s Commendation, 1981, 1982. Mem. Am. Psychol. Assn., Nat. Register Health Care Providers. Home and Office: 150 S Huntington Ave Building 2 Boston MA 02130

LUDMAN, DIANNE MARIE, public relations executive; b. Providence, Sept. 11, 1953; d. Nathan and Sally Lucille (Topal) L. BA, Hofstra U., 1975; postgrad., Hunter Coll., 1975-76; MFA in Museology, Syracuse U., 1978. Communications assocs. Murphy/Jahn, Chgo., 1978-80; mktg. mgr. King & King Architects, Syracuse, 1980-82; mktg. dir. ADD Inc., Cambridge, Mass., 1982-84; dir. pub. relations The Stubbins Assocs., Inc., Cambridge, Mass., 1984—. Author: Hugh Stubbins and His Associates: The First Fifty Years, 1986. Recipient Hatch award The Ad Club Boston, 1983. Mem. Soc. for Mktg. Profl. Services (pres. Boston chpt. 1985-86, bd. dirs. 1982-87, chair Nat. editorial 1981-86, Communication award 1981, 84), Am. Mktg. Assn. (nat. program com., speaker), Boston Soc. Architects (affiliate), Syracuse C. of C. (chair communications 1980-81). Jewish. Office: The Stubbins Assocs Inc 1033 Massachusetts Ave Cambridge MA 02138

LUDVIGSON, GAIL ROSENBERG, investment company executive; b. Cambridge, Mass., Dec. 10, 1942; d. Joel and Ida Florence (Berenson) Rosenberg; m. Max Morris Ludvigson, Oct. 24, 1971; children—Laura, Deborah. B.A. in Econs. with honors, Conn. Coll., 1964; M.A. in Econs., Columbia U., 1965. Chartered fin. analyst. Arbitrageur, Smithers & Co., N.Y.C., 1971-72; sr. investment analyst Ticor, Los Angeles, 1972-79, sr. portfolio mgr., 1979-84; asst. v.p. Trust Services Am., Los Angeles, 1984-86, v.p., 1986; v.p. Bankers Trust Co. Calif. N.A., Los Angeles, 1986—. Fellow Fin. Analysts Fedn., Los Angeles Soc. Fin. Analysts; mem. Women's Bus. and Profl. Group of South Bay (membership chmn. 1985-86, program chmn. 1986-87), Los Angeles Assn. Investment Women (pres. 1985-86). Avocation: music.

LUDWIG, MARGARET G., state legislator. m. Leland Ludwig; 3 children. BA, Colby Coll. Mem. Maine State Senate. Mem. Maine State Sch. Bd. Assn. Address: 3 Rogers Rd Houlton ME 04730 Office: State Senate Office State Capitol Augusta ME 04333 *

LUDWIG, MARSHA MCMAHON, program manager; b. St. Louis, May 29, 1945; d. William Blake and Lydia (Hart) McMahon; m. Gerald E. Ludwig, Aug. 31 1966 (div. Aug 1980); children: Gerald E. Jr., Robert Lawrence. Student, Macalester Coll., 1963-64; AB in History magna cum laude, U. Mo., St. Louis, 1967; MEd in Adminstrn. and supervision, Stetson U., 1980. Cert. mgr., Va., 1987. Adminstrv. asst. Library, U. Mo., St. Louis, 1964-69; mem. mktg. staff then tchr., writer Brevard County Schs., Cocoa Beach, Fla., 1971-80; programmer anslyst proposal mgmt. Rockwell Launch Ops., Kennedy Space Ctr., Fla., 1971-81, safety rep., 1981-84; indsl. engr. Rockwell North Am., El Segundo, Calif., 1984-85; project adminstr. Rockwell Autonetics, Anaheim, Calif., 1985-87, program mgr., 1987—. Author numerous curriculum guides, 1972-80. Active Cape Canaveral Citizens Com., Silver Kellogg/ Calif. Poltech U. Mem. Am. Soc. for Quality control, Nat. Mgmt. Assn. Anaheim/Newport (v.p. 1987-88), Los Angeles chpts. Republican. Presbyterian. Club: Snowbounders (Anaheim). Home: 3030 E Jackson Anaheim CA 92806 Office: Rockwell-Autonetics Sensors & Aircraft Systems Div 3370 Miraloma Ave Anaheim CA 92803

LUDWIG, SUSAN ANDREA, insurance company executive; b. Hartford, Conn., Aug. 24, 1951; d. Andrew and Elsie Irma Ida (Vedder) Le Shay; m. Robert Allyn Ludwig, May 1, 1976. BA in English and Drama, Lenoir Rhyne Coll., Hickory, N.C., 1973. Asst. pension analyst Travelers Ins. Co., Hartford, 1975-76, pension analyst, 1976-78, sr. pension analyst, 1978-80, asst. chief pension analyst, 1980-82, assoc. chief pension analyst, 1982-85, chief pension analyst, 1985-88, asst. dir., 1988—. Arbitrator automobile dispute settlement program Dept. Consumer Protection State of Conn., Hartford, 1984-86; mem. World Affairs Ctr., Hartford. Mem. Bus. and Profl. Women's Club of Hartford, Inc. (chair ways and means com. 1982-83, 2d v.p. 1982-83, 1st v.p. 1983-84, pres. 1984-85, membership chair 1987-88).

LUEBKEMANN, JANNA ROSE, auditor; b. Stuttgart, Ark., Oct. 23, 1960; d. Edward James and Theresa Frances (Sandor) L. BS in Agri-Bus., U. Ark., 1983; postgrad., Ohio State U., 1985-86; MS in Agrl. Econs., U. Ark., 1986. Team leader, inventory auditor RGIS Inventory Specialists, Fayetteville, Ark., 1982-85; inventory auditor RGIS Inventory Specialists, Columbus, Ohio, 1986; asst. team leader, inventory auditor RGIS Inventory Specialists, Memphis, 1986-87; asst. mgr. bakery Seessel's Supermarket, Memphis, 1987—. Den mother, dist. com. Boy Scouts Am., Fayetteville, 1982-85 (Disting. Service award 1985). Recipient Disting. Service award Kiwanis, 1985. Mem. Am. Agrl. Econs. Assn., Alpha Zeta, Alpha Phi Omega. Democrat. Roman Catholic. Home: PO Box 237 Arlington TN 38002 Office: Seessel's Supermarket #1 1761 Union Ave Memphis TN 38103

LUEDKE, JOAN EMILY, small business owner; b. Milw., May 16, 1929; d. Emil (Carmelo) Enrica Mary (Beatrice) Regano; m. Walter Pahl Luedke, Aug. 27, 1949; children: Craig Robert, Jeffrey Scott, Jan Pahl Stevenson. Student, U. Wis., 1947, Layton Sch. Art, 1947-48, Marquette U., 1948-49, U. Wis., 1947. Artist Hixons, Milw., 1948-50; free lance artist, model Gimbels, Milw., 1950-52; coordinator, head of display D.J. Stewarts, Rockford, Ill., 1964-68; buyer, store mgr. D.J. Stewarts, Rockford, 1968-79; owner Joan Luedke Fashions, Rockford, 1979—. Dir. Childrens Theatre, Megoun, Wis. 1957-59, Jr. League Childrens Theatre, Rockford 1963-66, Womens Art Bd. Puppets, 1966-69; vol. Childrens Devel., 1962-64. Republican. Roman Catholic. Office: Joan Luedke Fashions 4223 E State St Rockford IL 61108

LUELLEN, MARGARET ALICE, computer consulting company executive; b. Findlay, Ohio, Aug. 4, 1956; d. Charles Jesse and Jo Sidney (Riddle) L. BA in English, Transylvania U., 1977. Land systems analyst Ashland Exploration Inc., Houston, 1977-79; landman Terra Resources Co., Houston, 1979-81; land systems supr. Elf Aquitaine Petroleum, Houston, 1981-83; pres. Computer Literacy Workshop, Bellaire, Tex., 1983—; cons. Continental Airlines, Houston, 1984—, Citicorp, Houston, 1986—, The Houston Ballet, 1986—. Editor Computer Literacy Newsletter, 1985—. Lectr. Houston Pub. Library Speakers Bur., 1986. Mem. Houston Area League Personal Computer Users, Nat. Assn. Female Execs. Republican. Office: Computer Literacy Workshop 4710 Bellaire Blvd Suite 340 Bellaire TX 77401

LUEPKE, GRETCHEN, geologist; b. Tucson, Nov. 10, 1943; d. Gordon Maas and Janice (Campbell) Luepke; B.S., U. Ariz., 1965, M.S., 1967; U. Colo., summer, 1962. Geol. field asst. U.S. Geol. Survey, Flagstaff, Ariz., 1964; with U.S. Geol. Survey, Menlo Park, Calif., 1967—, geologist, Pacific Br. of Marine Geology, 1976—. Registered geologist, Ore. Mem. U.S. Congress Office Tech. Assessment Workshop, Mining and Processing Placers of EEZ, 1986. Mem. Soc. Econ. Paleontologists and Mineralogists (chmn. com. libraries in developing countries 1988—), Geol. Soc. Am., Ariz. Geol. Soc., Peninsula Geol. Soc., Bay Area Mineralogists (chmn. 1979-80), History of the Earth Scis. Soc., Internat. Assn. Sedimentologists, Sigma Xi. Editor: Stability of Heavy Minerals in Sediments; Econ. Analysis of Heavy Minerals in Sediments. Contbr. articles on heavy-mineral analysis to profl. jours. Office: 345 Middlefield Rd Menlo Park CA 94025

LUHABE, WENDY, marketing executive, researcher; b. Johannesburg, Republic South Africa, May 29, 1957; d. Stanley and Adelaide (Bulana) L.; 1 child, Lumko. BCom, U. Leshotho, So. Africa, 1981; postgrad. in bus., U. Witswatersrand, Johannesburg, 1984. Market devel. mgr. Vanda Cosmetics, Johannesburg, 1981-83; mktg. research mgr. BMW AG, Johannesburg, 1983-86; mktg. trainee mgr. BMW AG, Munich, 1986, BMW N.A. Inc., Montvale, N.J., 1986-87; asst. regional mktg. mgr. BMW N.A., Inc., 1987—; intl. dir. Inst. for Advancement of Women, Johannesburg, 1985. Author: Black Professional Career Women in South Africa, 1985. Mem. Am. Mgmt. Assn.

LUIS, MARGARITA, sales professional; b. Havana, Cuba, Feb. 22, 1959; d. Fuen Yen and Yen (Wong) Gee; m. Brian M. Heneghan, Oct. 25, 1986. BA, Goucher Coll., 1981. Chem. lab. analyst Pall Corp., Glen Cove, N.Y., 1981-82, supr. gen. lab., 1982-86, sr. lab. supr., 1986-87; sales specialist Pall Process Filtration Co. subs. Pall Corp., East Hills, N.Y., 1987—. Mem. Am. Chem. Soc., Nat. Assn. Women Execs. Office: Pall Process Filtration Co 2200 Northern Blvd East Hills NY 11548

LUKAS, ELLEN, author, editor; b. Shenandoah, Pa.; d. Alexander J. and Margaret (McGuire) L.; A.B. in History, Coll. New Rochelle; student Pa. State U., Fordham U. UN corr. Newsweek mag., 1961-65; UN bur. chief Hearst Newspapers, 1965-67; with Harper's Mag., 1969; UNICEF press cons., 1971; press analyst to Sec. Gen. of UN, N.Y.C., 1977-81; editor, UN Dept. Info., 1982-87, UN Human Rights Project, 1987—. Mem. PEN, Authors Guild. Author: (with Mary Lukas) (biography) Teilhard de Chardin, 1977; contbr. Antiquity Mag., Cambridge U. Office: United Nations New York NY 10017

LUKE, MARY E., land resource consultant; b. Racine, Wis., Nov. 22, 1954; d. Walter Puchinsky and Evelyn Marie (Richtmyre) Rogers; m. David Donald Luke, Nov. 2, 1974 (div. 1987); children: Timothy Donald, Trisha Marie. Student, Internat. Correspondence Sch., 1977; AA in Engring., Manatee Community Coll., 1985. Cert. in wastewater collection systems, water disbn. systems. Draftsperson J.W. Peters & Sons, Inc., Burlington, Wis., 1974-80; engring. tech. Craven Thompson & Assocs., Inc., Punta Gorda, Fla., 1980-82; engr., exec. v.p. Morse Engring., Inc., Englewood, Fla., 1982-87; gen. ptnr. Landmark Land Cons., Englewood, 1987—; pres. Luke Design & Land Resources, Inc., Englewood, 1987—. Chairperson com. reps., Port Charlotte, Fla., 1986. Recipient Image award Manatee Community Coll., Brandenton, Fla., 1985, Dinner Speaker award, Venice, Fla., 1985. Mem. Econ. Devel. Council, Charlotte County C. of C. Republican. Roman Catholic. Office: Landmark Land Cons 4212 Access Rd Englewood FL 34224

LUKER, KRISTIN, sociology educator; b. San Francisco, Aug. 5, 1946; d. James Wester and Bess (Littlefield) L. BA, U. Calif., Berkeley, 1968; PhD, Yale U., 1975. Postdoctoral fellow U. Calif., Berkeley, 1974-75, asst. prof. sociology, San Diego, 1975-81, assoc. prof., 1981-85, prof., 1985-86, co-dir. women's studies program, 1984-85, prof. jurisprudence and social policy, sociology, Berkeley, 1986—. Author: Taking Chances: Abortion and the Decision Not to Contracept, 1976 (hon. mention Jessie Bernard award), Abortion and the Politics of Motherhood, 1984 (Charles Horton Cooley award 1985). Bd. dirs. Ctr. for Women's Studies and Services, San Diego,

Ctr. for Population Options, Washington. Recipient Disting. Teaching award U. San Diego, 1984; Guggenheim Found. grantee, 1985. Mem. Am. Sociol. Assn., Sociologists for Women in Soc. Office: U Calif Berkeley Jurisprudence & Social Policy 2240 Piedmont Ave Berkeley CA 94720

LULAY, DICKI, food products executive; b. Portland, Oreg., Sept. 16, 1951; d. Richard Earl and Carolyn Ellen (Stiger) Singleton; m. Terrence Robert Lulay, Oct. 20, 1973; children: Adam Richard, John Christopher. BS, Oreg. State U., 1973; MBA with honors, St. Mary's Coll., 1982. Dir. quality assurance Flavorland Foods, Inc., Salem, Oreg., 1973-74; asst. dir. quality assurance Castle and Cooke Foods, Inc., Salem, 1974-77, dir. quality assurance, 1977-80; mktg. and sales mgr. indsl. food service Castle and Cooke Foods, Inc., San Francisco, 1980-82; mktg. and sales mgr. nat. food service The McKesson Corp., San Francisco, 1982-84, program mgr. contract research, 1984; product mgr. Basic Am. Foods, San Francisco, 1984-87, mgr. bus. devel., 1987—. Fundraiser Cancer Soc., Salem, 1978-79, Mothers March of Dimes, Walnut Creek, Calif., 1983—. Mem. Inst. Food Technologists (exec. com. Oreg. 1978-80, nat. chmn. profl. affairs 1982-83, nat. arrangements chmn. 50th anniversary com. 1986—), Soc. Advancement Food Service Research (bd. dirs. 1988—), Foodsters. Republican. Roman Catholic. Office: Basic Am Foods 550 Kearney St Suite 1000 San Francisco CA 94108

LULAY, GAIL C., human resources executive, consultant; b. Evanston, Ill., Feb. 13, 1938; d. Earl Albert and Helen Marie (Blackwell) Minnich; m. Wayne L. Lulay, Aug. 15, 1959; children: Michael Brent, Catherine Marie. BS, Elmhurst Coll., 1970; MS, Roosevelt U., 1972. Cert. counselor, Ill. Instr. Dist. #181, Hinsdale, Ill., 1970-74; corp. bus. devel. Continental Bank, Chgo., 1974-79; pres., owner Lulay & Assocs., Inc., Lombard, Ill., 1979—; counselor Crisis Counseling Practice, Hinsdale, 1972-79; instr. Elmhurst Coll. Adult Edn., 1982, Coll. of DuPage, Glen Ellyn, Ill., 1983-86; lectr., consultant in field, 1980—. Contbr. articles to profl. jours. Bd. dirs. Crisis Homes, Des Plaines, Ill., 1984-86. Mem. Am. Assn. Counseling and Devel., Am. Soc. Personnel Adminstrn., Assn. Outplacement Cons. Firms, Inc., Human Resources Mgmt. Assn. of Chgo., Roosevelt U. Alumni Assn., Chi Omega. Office: Lulay & Assocs Inc 477 E Butterfield Rd Lombard IL 60148

LULIC, MARGARET ANN, marketing professional; b. St. Paul, Minn., Oct. 20, 1950; d. Thomas and Mary Ann (Reid) L.; m. Robert Joseph Timpane, June 19, 1976; 1 child, Laura. BA cum laude, Marquette U., 1973; MA, U. Chgo., 1974. Tchr., coach Park Ctr. High Sch., Brooklyn Park, Minn., 1974-78; sole cons. Mpls., 1978-79; dir. pub. affairs U. Minn. Inst. Tech., Mpls., 1979-81; mkt. research analyst ADC Telecommunications, Mpls., 1981-82, mkt. research mgr., 1982-83, mgr. mkt. strategy, 1983-85, Original Equipment Mfrs. mkt. mgr., 1986-88, mgr. pub. network mkt., 1988—. Editor state newsletter, 1976; wcontbr. articles to profl. jours. Bd. dirs., com. mem., Citizen's League, 1979-83; campaign coordinator, Minn.; pres., State Advisor's Orgn., Minn., 1975; mem., gov.'s Task Force on Tech., Mpls., 1980; del. State and County Convs. Recipient Pres.'s Citation for Excellence; grantee U. Chgo., 1974. Mem. Women in Telecommunications.

LUM, JEAN LOUI JIN, nurse educator; b. Honolulu, Sept. 5, 1938; d. Yee Nung and Pui Ki (Young) L. BS, U. Hawaii, Manoa, 1960; MS in Nursing, U. Calif., San Francisco, 1961; MA, U. Wash., 1969, PhD in Sociology, 1972. Registered nurse, Hawaii. From instr. to prof. Sch. Nursing U. Hawaii-Manoa, Honolulu, 1961—, acting dean, 1982, dean, 1982—; project coordinator Analysis and Planning Personnel Services, Western Interstate Commn. Higher Edn., 1977; extramural assoc. div. Research Grants NIH, 1978-79; mem. mgmt. adv. com. Honolulu County Hosp., 1982—; mem. exec. bd. Pacific Health Research Inst., 1980-88; mem. health planning com. East Honolulu, 1978-81. Contbr. articles to profl. jours. Recipient Nurse of Yr. award Hawaii Nurses Assn., 1982; USPHS grantee, 1967-72. Fellow Am. Acad. Nursing; mem. Am. Nurses Assn., Am. Pacific Nursing Leaders Conf. (pres. 1983-87), Council Nurse Researchers, Nat. League for Nursing (bd. rev. 1981-87), Western Council Higher Edn. for Nurses (chmn. 1984-85), Western Soc. for Research in Nursing, Am. Sociol. Assn., Pacific Sociol. Assn., Assn. for Women in Sci., Hawaii Pub. Health Assn., Hawaii Med. Services Assn. (bd. dirs. 1985—), Mortar Bd., Phi Kappa Phi, Sigma Theta Tau, Alpha Kappa Delta, Delta Kappa Gamma. Episcopalian. Office: U Hawaii at Manoa Sch Nursing Webster 416 2528 The Mall Honolulu HI 96822

LUMADUE, JOYCE ANN, hobby company executive; b. New London, Conn., Oct. 21, 1941; d. James E. and Camilla (Romeo) Hayes; student U. Conn.; m. Donald Dean Lumadue, June 28, 1958; children—Dawnia Jean, Donald Dean, Robert Ryan, Ronald Jeffrey. Partner, Joydon's Coin Shop, New London, 1958—, House of Leisure, New London, 1967—, Hobby Crafts, New London, 1969—; v.p. New Eng. Internat. Inc., New London, 1969-85, Lumadue Inc., New London, 1978—. Mem. Hobby Industry Assn. Am., Internat. Mgmt. Council, Nat. Assn. Female Execs., NOW. Methodist. Contbr. articles to profl. jours. Office: 78-88 Captains Walk New London CT 06320

LUMMIS, CYNTHIA MARIE, lawyer, rancher; b. Cheyenne, Wyo., Sept. 10, 1954; d. Doran Arp and Enid (Bennett) L.; m. Alvin L. Wiederspahn, May 28, 1983; children: Annaliese Alex. BS, U. Wyo., 1976, U. Wyo., 1978; JD, U. Wyo., 1985. Bar: Wyo. 1985. Rancher Lummis Livestock Co., Cheyenne, 1972—; law clk. Wyo. Supreme Ct., Cheyenne, 1985-86; assoc. Wiederspahn, Lummis & Liepas, Cheyenne, 1986—; mem. Wyo. Ho. Judiciary Com., 1979-86, Ho. Agriculture, Pub. Lands & Water Resources Com., 1985-86; chmn. Ho. Rev. Com., 1987-88; chmn. Joint Revenue Interim Com., 1988-89; chmn. County Ct. Planning Com., Wyo., 1986-88. Sec. Meals on Wheels, Cheyenne, 1985-87; mem. Agrl. Crisis Support Group, Laramie County, Wyo., 1985-87; mem. adv. com. U. Wyo. Sch. Nursing, 1988-90; mem. steering com. Wyo. Heritage Soc., 1986-89. Republican. Lutheran. Club: Rep. Women's (Cheyenne) (legis. chmn. 1982). Office: Wiederspahn Lummis & Liepas 2020 Carey Suite 704 Cheyenne WY 82001

LUMPKIN, PEGGY ANN LANZA, human resources executive; b. Lancing, Tenn., Jan. 22, 1948; d. K.R. and Shirley Elaine (Van Der Aue) Le Croy; m. Joseph A. Lanza, Dec. 21, 1968 (div. July 1982); children: Mario, Dei; m. F. Dale Lumpkin, July 19, 1986. Student, Lewis and Clark Coll., 1966-68; BA in English Lit., Secondary Edn., Portland State U., 1970. V.p. personnel First State Bank Oreg., Portland, 1970-79; personnel mgr. Dept. Environ. Quality State of Oreg., Portland, 1982-83; dir. human resources Oreg. Mut. Ins., McMinnville, 1983—. Bd. dirs. United Way, Yamhill County, Oreg., 1985—; mem. State of Oreg. Fair Dismissals Appeals Bd., Salem, 1977-81. Mem. Bank Adminstrn. Inst. (pres. Portland chpt. 1976), Oreg. Bankers Assn. (chmn. personnel com. 1977-78), Am. soc. Personnel Adminstrs. Republican. Home: 4938 SW Northwood Portland OR 97201 Office: Oreg Mut Ins 4th and Davis McMinnville OR 97128

LUMPKIN, PENNY PALMER, wholesale periodicals company executive; b. Topeka, Aug. 20; d. William H. and Vivian J. Palmer; student U. Ariz., 1957-59, U. Kans., 1959-60; m. Joseph Henry Lumpkin, Nov. 26, 1960; children—William Henry, Kelley Kathleen. Buyer, merchandiser City News & Gift Shop, Topeka, 1954-57; mgr., buyer Vivian's Gift Shop, Topeka, 1961-76; book buyer Palmer News, Inc., Topeka, 1976-79, book buyer, personnel dir., 1979-80, dir. retail ops., treas., 1980—, also dir.; sec., dir. Palmer Cos., Inc., 1983—, treas., 1984—; dir. Ultra Fund-Security Benefit Life. Bd. dirs. Mulvane Art Center, Topeka, 1968-80, Seven Step Found., Topeka, 1969-72, Topeka Civic Theatre, 1984-86; v.p. opeka Pub. Schs. Edn. Found., 1986-87, pres., 1987-88, Stormost Vail Hosp. Found., 1986— ; bd. dirs., charter mem. Mulvane Women, Topeka, 1969; div. chmn. United Way, Topeka, 1969; chmn. King of Hills Pro/Celebrity Tennis Benefit, 1977-79; spl. events chmn. Shawnee County unit Am. Cancer Soc., Topeka, 1976-78, v.p. bd. dirs., 1977, pres. bd. dirs., 1979; mem. exec. bd. Jayhawk Area council Boy Scouts Am.; hon. chmn. holiday treasures Shawnee Country Day Sch., 1985; bd. dirs. Stormont Vail Hosp. Found., 1986—, Mt. Hope Cemetery Bd., 1987-88, sec., 1988—. Named an Outstanding Woman Am., Jr. League of Topeka, 1975; recipient Outstanding Service award Am. Cancer Soc., 1976, Kans. div., 1978. Mem. Central States Periodicals Distbrs. Assn., Am. Booksellers Assn., Mid-Am. Periodicals Distbrs. Assn., Ind. Periodicals Distbrs. Assn., Topeka Friends of Zoo, Am. Heritage Assn., Kappa Kappa Gamma Alums. Republican. Episcopalian. Club: Jr. League (pres. Topeka 1971). Researcher, pub. fund-raising manual Assn. Jr. Leagues, 1974. Home: 3616 SW Canterbury Town Rd Topeka KS 66610-1503 Office: Palmer News Inc 1050 Republican Topeka KS 66604

LUMSDEN, LYNNE ANN, publishing company executive; b. Battlecreek, Mich., July 30, 1947; d. Arthur James and Ruth Julia (Pandy) L.; m. Jon B. Harden, May 3, 1986. Student, U. Paris, 1967-69; B.A., Sarah Lawrence Coll., 1969; postgrad., City Grad. Ctr., 1979-81, NYU, 1980-81; cert. of mgmt., Am. Mgmt. Assn., 1982. Copy editor Harcourt, Brace, Jovanovich, N.Y.C., 1970-71; editor Appleton-Century Crofts, N.Y.C., 1971-73, Coll. div. Prentice-Hall, Englewood Cliffs, N.J., 1974-78; sr. editor Coll. div. Prentice-Hall, 1978-81; asst. v.p., editor-in chief Spectrum Books, 1981-82; v.p. editorial dir., gen. pub. div., 1982-85; exec. v.p., publ., co-owner Dodd, Mead & Co., Inc., 1985—; ptnr., prin. Gamut Publ. Co., 1985—. Chmn. annual fund Sarah Lawrence Coll., Bronxville, N.Y., 1979-81, chmn. nominating com., bd. dirs., 1984-86; mem. N.Y. Jr. League, N.Y.C. Mem. Am. Assn. Pubs. (co-chmn. stats. com., gen. pub. div. 1984—), Am. Book Council (chmn. ethics com.). Episcopalian. Clubs: St. Barts; Sandbar (N.Y.C.). Office: Dodd Mead 71 Fifth Ave New York NY 10003

LUNA, CATHY LEIGH, accountant; b. Pulaski, Tenn., Feb. 13, 1957; d. Charles N. Luna Jr. and Earlene (McClure) Harwell; m. John Joseph Lenahan, Sept. 23, 1985; 1 child, Amanda Leigh Lenahan. BBA, Mid. Tenn. State U., 1978. CPA, Tenn. Audit asst. Blankenship Summar & Assocs., Nashville, 1979-82; audit supr. Touche Ross & Co., Nashville, 1982-84; sr. analyst fin. planning and analysis dept. No. Telecom Inc., Nashville, 1984-85, supr. statutory reporting, 1985-86, mgr. statutory reporting, 1986—. Mem. Nat. Assn. Accts., Am. Soc. CPA's, Tenn. Soc. CPA's. Methodist. Office: No Telecom Inc 200 Athens Way Nashville TN 37228-1803

LUNA, OLIVIA, educator, consultant; b. Los Angeles, May 21, 1932; d. Guadalupe Flores and Lorenza (Saenz) Velarde; m. Ralph Moreno Luna, June 24, 1951 (div.); children—Larry, Samuel, Leno. A.A., East Los Angeles Coll., 1960; B.A., Calif. State U.-Los Angeles, 1962; M.A., La Verne U., 1980, M.S., 1981. Tchr., prin., counselor El Rancho Unified Sch. Dist., Pico Rivera, Calif., 1968—; bilingual specialist, 1972-81; owner, pres. Unlimited Potential Co., Whittier, Calif., 1980—; presenter workshops; ednl. cons., 1972-83. Author handbook. Co-founder Downey chpt. Failures Anonymous Internat., 1985. Recipient Fine Arts award Pico Rivera City Council, 1968. Mem. Calif. Council Adult Edn. (pres. 1980-82), Am. Fedn. Tchrs. (v.p. 1977-80), Calif. Assn. Bilingual Edn., ACLU (sec. Whittier chpt. 1981-83), Los Angeles Racewalkers, Whittier Democratic Club. Unitarian. Avocations: oil painting, writing, racewalking. Home: 1009 Guinea Dr Whittier CA 90601 Office: El Rancho Unified Sch Dist 9333 Loch Lomond Pico Rivera CA 90660

LUNA, PATRICIA ADELE, food manufacturing company executive; b. Charleston, S.C., July 22, 1956; d. Benjamin Curtis and Clara Elizabeth (McCrory) L. BS in History, Auburn U., 1978, MEd in History, 1980; MA in Adminstrn., U. Ala., 1981, EdS in Adminstrn., 1984, PhD in Adminstrn., 1986. Cert. tchr., Ga., Ala. History tchr. Harris County Middle Sch., Ga., 1978-79, head dept., 1979-81; residence hall dir. univ. housing U. Ala., 1981-83, asst. dir. residence life, 1983-85; intern Cornell U., Ithaca, N.Y., 1983; dir. of mktg. Golden Flake Snack Foods, Inc., Birmingham, Ala., 1985—; cons., lectr. in field. Author: Specialization: A Learning Module, 1979, Grantsmanship, 1981, Alcohol Awareness Programs, 1984; University Programming, 1984; Marketing Residential Life, 1985; The History of Golden Flakes Snack Foods, 1986; Golden Flake Snack Foods, Inc., A Case Study, 1987. Fundraiser, U. Ala. Alumni Scholarship Fund, Tuscaloosa, 1983, Am. Diabetes Assn., Tuscaloosa, 1984, Urban Ministries, Birmingham, 1985-88; fundraiser com. chmn. Spl. Olympics, Tuscaloosa, 1985, Am. Cinema Soc., 1987-88; chmn. Greene County Relief Project, 1982-88; bd. dirs. Cerebral Palsy Found., Tuscaloosa, 1985-86; lay rector and com. chmn. Kairos Prison Ministry, Tutwiler State Prison, Ala., 1986-88; lobbyist and mem. task force Justice Fellowship; Rep. com. chmn. Recipient Dir. of Yr. award U. Ala., 1982, 83; Skeets Simonis award for Outstanding Contbns., U. Ala., 1984, nat. award Joint Council on Econ. Edn., 1979, research award NSF, 1979; named to Hon. Order Ky. Cols. Commonwealth of Ky., Rep. Senatorial Inner Circle, 1986; Mem. Sales and Mktg. Execs. (chmn. com. 1985-86), Leadership Ala. (pres. 1982-83, disting. leadership award 1987, commemorative medal of honor 1988), Am. Mktg. Assn., Assn. Coll. and Univ. Housing Officers (com. chmn. 1983-85), Nat. Assn. Student Personnel Officers, Commerce Execs. Soc., Snack Food Assn. (mem. mktg. com. and conf. presenter), Commerce Exec. Soc., Omega Rho Sigma (pres. 1983-84), Omicron Delta Kappa, Phi Delta Kappa, Kappa Delta Pi, Phi Alpha Theta. Methodist. Clubs: Emmaus (chmn. com. 1985-88); Sailing (Tuscaloosa). Avocations: skiing, racquetball, community work, public speaking. Home: 11 Vestavia Hills Northport AL 35476 Office: Golden Flake Snack Foods Inc 110 6th St S Birmingham AL 35201

LUNA-RAINES, MARCIA L., clinical nurse; b. Saginaw, Mich., Mar. 18, 1947; d. George and Bernice (Tomaszewski) Riska; m. Leonard H. Raines; 1 child, Marcus. B in Nursing, UCLA, 1970, M in Nursing, 1977, postgrad., 1987—. Clin. staff nurse Neuropsychiat. Hosp. and Clin., UCLA, Los Angeles, 1972-75; research asst. psychology dept. UCLA, 1977, mental health clin. nurse spl. med. Ctr.,, 1977—; adj. asst. clin. prof. UCLA Sch. Nursing, 1977—; lectr. nursing nation-wide, 1977—. Author (with Linda Gorman and Donna Sultan) Psychosocial Nursing Manual, 1988; contbr. articles to profl. jours. Mem. UCLA Sch. Nursing Alumni Assn. (sec. 1986—). Home: 1646 Bryn Mawr Ave Santa Monica CA 90405 Office: UCLA Med Ctr 10833 Le Conte Ave Rm 14-176 Los Angeles CA 90405

LUND, SISTER CANDIDA, college chancellor; b. Chgo.; d. Fred S. Lund and Katharine (Murray) Lund Heck. B.A., Rosary Coll., River Forest, Ill.; M.A., Catholic U. Am.; Ph.D., U. Chgo., 1963; D.Litt. (hon.), Lincoln Coll., 1968; LL.D. (hon.), John Marshall Law Sch., 1979. Pres. Rosary Coll., 1964-81, chancellor, 1981—. Author: Moments to Remember, 1980; editor: The Days and the Nights: Prayers for Today's Woman, In Joy and in Sorrow, 1984, Coming of Age, 1982, Nunsuch, 1982; author, editor: If I Were Pope, 1987; contbr.: Why Catholic. Mem. Ill. Humanities Council, 1982—. Recipient Profl. Achievement award U. Chgo. Alumni, 1974, U.S. Catholic award, 1984. Fellow Royal Soc. Arts; mem. Am. Polit. Sci. Assn., Thomas Moore Assn. (dir. 1975—). Club: The Arts (bd. dirs. 1987). Home and Office: Rosary Coll 7900 Division St River Forest IL 60305

LUNDBERG, LOIS ANN, public relations professional; b. Tulsa, Sept. 21, 1928; d. John T. and Anna M. (Patterson) McQuay; m. Ted W. Lundberg, Sept. 30, 1954; children: Linda Ann, Sharon Lynn. Student, Long Beach City Coll. With Pacific Telephone, 1950-65; gen. ptnr. McLund Co. Property Mgmt., 1972—; realtor Morgan Realty, 1974—; with Nason, Lundberg and Assoc., Orange, Calif., 1983-85, pres., campaign cons., 1985—. Bd. dirs. Luth. Ch. of the Master, La Habra, Calif., 1970-75, v.p. of congregation, 1986-87; mem. bd. trustees Nixon Law Office Preservation, Inc., 1972-75, Regional Ctr. of Orange County, 1982; bd. dirs. UCI Med. Ctr./Burn Ctr., 1982; apptd. Council on Criminal Justice Com., 1983—; mem. adv. bd. KOCE-TV, 1976—, La Habra Children's Mus., 1985—. Recipient Gov. Ronald Reagan award, 1967, Woman of Achievement award City of La Habra, 1979; named Outstanding Rep. of Orange County, 1978. Lutheran. Home: 1341 Carmela Ln La Habra CA 90631 Office: Nason Lundberg and Assocs 777 S Main St Suite 206 Orange CA 92668

LUNDEBERG, CATHARINA LOUISE, radio station executive; b. Sneek, Friesland, The Netherlands, July 31, 1955; came to U.S., 1962; naturalized, 1967; d. Sietze Nmn and Ban Nio (Lee) Veldhuis; m. John Douglas Osborn, Nov. 20, 1976 (div. Apr. 1981); 1 child, Ryan Douglas; m. Erik Lundeberg, May 21, 1988. Student Chico State U., Calif., 1973-75. Account exec. Sta. KFYE, Fresno, Calif., 1979-80, Sta. KOSO, Inc., Modesto, Calif., 1980-83; gen. sales mgr. Sta. KBEE/KHYV Modesto Broadcasting Inc., 1983-84, sta. mgr., 1984-86; gen. sales mgr. Sta. KDJK, Goldrush Broadcasting Inc., Oakdale, Calif., 1986—. Calif. State scholar, 1973. Mem. Soroptimist Internat. Republican. Methodist. Home: 2420 Killarney Modesto CA 95355 Office: Sta KDJK Goldrush Broadcasting Inc 570 Armstrong Way Oakdale CA 95361

LUNDEN, JOAN, television personality; b. Sept. 19, 1950; m. Michael Krauss; children—Jamie Beryl, Lindsay Leigh, Sarah Emily. Student, Universidad de Las Americas, Mexico City, U. Calif., Calif. State U., Am. River Coll., Sacramento, Calif. Began broadcasting career KCRA-TV and Radio, Sacramento; with WABC-TV, N.Y.C., 1975-80, co-anchor, 1976-80; co-host Good Morning America, ABC TV, 1980—; spokesperson pre-sch. ednl. div. Hasbro, Care for Kids products Revlon. Recipient Outstanding Mother of Yr. award, Nat. Mother's Day Com., 1982. Office: ABC-TV Good Morning America 1965 Broadway New York NY 10023

LUNDGREN, CLARA ELOISE, public affairs officer, journalist; b. Temple, Tex., Mar. 7, 1951; d. Claude Elton and Klara (Csirmaz) L. AA, Temple Jr. Coll., 1971; BJ, U. Tex., 1973; MA, Columbia Pacific U., 1986. Reporter Temple Daily Telegram, 1970-72; news editor Austin (Tex.) Am.-Statesman, 1972-75; mng. editor Stillhouse Hollow Pubs., Inc., Belton, 1975-77; pub. affairs officer Darnall Army Community Hosp., Ft. Hood, Tex., 1978-80; editor Ft. Hood Sentinel III Corps, 1980-85; command info. officer Pub. Affairs Office III Corps, Ft. Hood, 1985-87, community relations officer, 1987-88, dep. pub. affairs officer, 1988—. Recipient Nat. Observer Journalistic Achievement award Dow Jones and Co., 1971. Mem. NOW, Tex. Press Women, Fed. Women's Program, Assn. of U.S. Army, Jaycees. Home: 1305 S 13th Temple TX 76504 Office: III Corps Pub Affairs Office Fort Hood TX 76544-5056

LUNDGREN, GAIL MARIE, lawyer; b. Tacoma, June 14, 1955; d. Arthur Dean and Vera Martha (Grimm) L. A.B. cum laude, Vassar Coll., 1977; J.D. cum laude, U. Puget Sound., 1980. Bar: Wash. 1981. Legal intern Reed, McClure, Moceri & Thonn, Seattle, 1979, Burgess & Kennedy, Tacoma, 1979-80; legal intern Lee, Smart, Cook, Martin & Patterson, P.S., Inc., Seattle, 1980-81, assoc., 1981—. Vestry com. Queen Anne Lutheran Ch., 1983-86, v.p. of congregation, 1988, mem. worship and music com., 1982-83, 84-86, parish cdn. com., 1983-84, v.p., 1988. Recipient Am. Jurisprudence Book awards, 1980. Mem. ABA, Fed. Bar Assn., Wash. State Bar Assn., Seattle-King County Bar Assn., Wash. Assn. Def. Counsel, Order of Barristers. Democrat. Lutheran. Club: Wash. State Vassar (chmn. alumni admissions 1983-85, rep. 1986—).

LUNDGREN, KATHY J., marketing professional; b. Haddonfield, N.J., Feb. 7, 1955; d. Don L. and Margaret L. (Joyce) L. BA in Environ. Biology, Rutgers U., 1977; MS in Biology, William and Mary Coll., 1980; MBA in Mktg., Fairleigh Dickinson U., 1984. Mktg. specialist Econs. Lab.-Apollo Techs., Whippany, N.J., 1980-82; product mgr. Lehn & Fink Nat. Labs., Montvale, N.J., 1982-84; bus. mgr. Cyro Industries, Mt. Arlington, N.J., 1985—. Active Big Sister, Rutgers Community Action, New Brunswick, 1974-77. Mem. Am. Mgmt. Assn., Soc. Plastics Industry, Nat. Assn. Female Execs., Phi Sigma. Office: CYRO Industries 100 Valley Rd Mount Arlington NJ 07856

LUNDGREN, RUTH (MRS. W.F. WILLIAMSON), writer, public relations executive; b. Bklyn.; d. William and Hanna (Carlson) L.; m. W.F. Williamson, Dec. 17, 1949 (dec.); children: John Ross (dec.), Mark Ward. Student, Bklyn. Coll., 1936-41, Columbia U., 1942. Assoc. editor Everywoman's mag., 1940-42; pub. relations staff exec. J.M. Mathes Advt. Agy., 1942-45; dir. pub. relations Pan-Am. Coffee Bur., 1945-48; pres. Ruth Lundgren Ltd., N.Y.C., 1948—. Pub. Ruth Lundgren Newsletter, 1950-58; writer daily column St. Petersburg (Fla.) Times, 1956-60; contbg. editor, writer monthly column Motor Boating and Sailing mag., 1962-80; contbr. to popular profl. publs. Home: 3319 Bay Front Dr Baldwin Harbor NY 11510 Office: Box 184 Baldwin NY 11510

LUNDGREN, SUSAN ELAINE, social science educator, college program director, counselor; b. Martinez, Calif., May 31, 1949; d. Elmer Alfred and Shirley (Bright) L.; 1 child, Alicia Hadiya. AA, Diablo Valley Coll., 1969; BA in English, San Francisco State U., 1971, MA in Counseling, 1975; EdD, U. San Francisco, 1983. Instr., counselor Diablo Valley Coll., Pleasant Hill, Calif., 1976—, coordinator, 1986—, dir. faculty women's ctr., 1983-85; lectr. dept. grad. career devel. John F. Kennedy U., Orinda, Calif., 1982—. Sec., bd. dirs. Rape Crisis Ctr., Concord, Calif., 1985. Named participant in leadership devel. inst. AAUW and Nat. Assn. Community Colls., 1985. Mem. NOW (pres. East Bay chpt. 1982-84, bd. dirs. Calif. chpt.), Calif. Advs. for Re-entry Edn. (conf. speaker 1984, 86), I-Pride, Eureka Consortium (conf. speaker 1986—). Home: 2015 Cedar Berkeley CA 94709 Office: Diablo Valley Coll 321 Golf Club Rd Pleasant Hill CA 94523

LUNDIE, LOUISE MARIE, marketing professional; b. Meeme Twp., Wis., Mar. 2, 1940; d. Henry Joseph and Irene Theresa (Salm) Schwartz; AA, Milw. Area Tech. Coll., 1978; BS, Carroll Coll., 1982; m. Mel A. Lundie, Oct. 2, 1976; 1 dau. by previous marriage, Ann Louise Mathews. Sec. to gen. mgr. St. Regis Paper Co., Milw., 1961-65; asst. to pres. Wells Badger Corp., Milw., 1966-74; sec. to v.p. mktg. Everbrite Electric Signs, South Milwaukee, Wis., 1975, nat. sales adminstr., 1976-81, mgr. mktg. adminstrn., 1981, mgr. corp. planning, advt. and market research, 1981-84, dir. customer service, 1984-87, dir. sales services, 1987—. Pres., 1986, Adult AFS, Cudahy, Wis., 1982—. Mem. Nat. Secs. Assn. (pres. Milw. chpt. 1971-73), Adminstrv. Mgmt. Soc., Friends of Cudahy Library. Home: 5938 S Pennsylvania Ave Cudahy WI 53110 Office: Everbrite Electric Signs 4949 S 110th StS Greenfield WI 53220

LUNDQUIST, JUDITH GAIL, banker; b. Stockton, Calif., Oct. 27, 1938; d. Robert Wesley and Ruth W. (Mowat) Arnett; m. Dean Carl Lundquist, Nov. 15, 1958; children: Pamala, Carl, Brenda. Student in real estate, Delta Jr. Coll., 1979. Owner V.I.P. Realty, Stockton, 1979-81; asst. v.p. State Savs. and Loan, Stockton, 1981-82, procedures supr., 1982-83; v.p., mgr. methods and procedures Am. Savs. and Loan, Stockton, 1983—. Mem. Nat. Assn. Female Execs. Republican. Office: Am Savs and Loan 4651 Quail Lakes Dr Stockton CA 95207

LUNDQUIST, LINDA ANN JOHNSON, marketing executive; b. Iowa City, Iowa, Aug. 15, 1945; d. Elmer Clinton and Georgia Joan (Molloy) L.; m. Scott Arthur Johnson, Sept. 26, 1981. BA, U. Iowa, 1968. Civil engring. drafter firm Shive-Hattery & Assocs., Iowa City, 1968-78; dir. drafting services firm Shoemaker & Haaland, Profl. Engrs., Coralville, Iowa, 1978-82; mktg. rep. Veenstra & Kimm, Inc., Engineers and Planners, Iowa City and West Des Moines, 1982-86; head mktg. support dept. Stanley Cons. Inc., Muscatine, Iowa, 1986-87; office mgr., mktg. coordinator Pace Labs., Inc. Iowa div., Coralville, 1987-88, age. State Farm Ins. Cos., 1988—. mem. spl. appointments Urban Environment Ad Hoc Com., Iowa City, 1985-86, groundwater protection ad hoc adv. com. State Iowa, 1987—. Recipient Spl. Merit award Cedar Rapids Mus. Art, Iowa, 1979. Mem. Greater Iowa City Area C. of C. (mem. environ. concerns com. 1982-87, chair 1984-86, mem. govt. affairs com. 1988—), Soc. Mktg. Profl. Services, Iowa Groundwater Assn. (bd. dirs. 1986—), Nat. Wildlife Fedn., Iowa Wildlife Fedn. (mem. conservation issues com. 1987—), Internat. Fund Animal Welfare, Wilderness Soc., World Wildlife Fund, Alpha Gamma Delta (bd. dirs. house assn. 1986—). Avocations: drawing, watercolors, dance. Office: 407 K-Plaza Hwy 1 W Iowa City IA 52246

LUNDQUIST, MARY ELIZABETH, insurance agency principal; b. Detroit, Dec. 28, 1954; d. Benjamin Albert and Loretta Rose (Dyki) Purcott; m. Dennis Ray Lundquist, July 28, 1978; 1 child, Mark Ryan. AA in Criminal Justice, BA in Music Edn., Madonna Coll., 1976. Cert. ins. counselor; lic. resident agt., Mich. Mktg. clk. John Thomas Agy., Birmingham, Mich., 1970-76; mktg. rep. Nickel Agy. Inc., Birmingham, 1976-78, Republic-Hogg-Robinson, Inc., Southfield, Mich., 1978-80; corp. officer Ins. Guaranty Internat., Southfield, 1980-83, Able/Atlantic Ins., Inc., Southfield, 1983-85; pres., owner Atlantic Ins. Assoc., Inc., West Bloomfield, Mich., 1983—. Mem. Mothers Against Drunk Drivers/Substance Abuse & Chem. Dependency; cons. Mich. Cheerleading Coaches Assn., Lansing, 1987—. Mem. Gt. Am. Agts. Adv. Council, Profl. Ins. Agts. of Am., Nat. Assn. of Life Underwriters, Metro Detroit Ins. Club, Lamaze Childbirth Assn. of Mich. Office: Atlantic Ins Assocs Inc 6346 Orchard Lake Rd Suite 202 West Bloomfield MI 48322

LUNDQUIST, VIOLET ELVIRA, agency administrator; b. Bristol, Conn., Jan. 28, 1912; d. Otto Nimrod and Mabel Elvira (Lindeen) Ebb; diploma music Augustana Coll., Rock Island, Ill., 1932; postgrad. mgmt. systems U. Mo., 1969; m. Vernon Arthur Lundquist, May 14, 1935; children—Karen Ebb, Jane Christine. Tchr. music, public schs., Olds, Iowa, 1932-35; editor Warsaw (Mo.) Times, 1935-45, Anthon (Iowa) Herald, 1945-57; field dir. Iowa Heart Assn., Des Moines, 1957-66; exec. dir. S.E. Iowa Community Action Program, Burlington, 1966-74; adminstrn. dir. S.E. Ariz. Govts. Orgn. Community Services, Bisbee, Ariz., 1975-77; statewide advocate developmentally disabled adults, 1977—; adminstr. Arizona City Med. Ctr., part-time, 1979-80; adminstr. Dist. V Council on Devel. Disabilities, 1980-87. Bd. dirs. Cen. Ariz. Health Systems Agy., 1979—, chmn., 1986—; chmn. Arizona City Home and Property Owners Assn., 1979-82; bd. dirs. Ariz. State Health Planning Council, 1986—; mem. Ariz. Statewide Health Coordinating Council, 1986—, Ariz. Dist. V Human Rights Com., 1986—; pres. Pinal County Assn. for Retarded Citizens, 1987—, v.p., vice chmn. state assn. Recipient Carol Lane award Nat. Safety Council, 1956, 1st place award Nat. Fedn. Press Women, 1952, 53, 55, 57; USPHS scholar, Columbia U., summers 1963, 64; cert. vocat. rehab. adminstr. Mem. Nat. Soc. Community Action Program Dirs. (dir. 1966-75), Ariz. Fedn. Press Women. Lutheran. Clubs: Zonta (area dir. 1984-86), Women of Moose. Home and Office: 609 W Cochise St PO Box 2265 Arizona City AZ 85223

LUNDSTED, BETTY MARGARET, publishing executive; b. Port Jefferson, N.Y., Apr. 7, 1941; d. John and Birgit (Hauger) L. Student, U. Vt., 1958-60. Freelance writer, tchr. N.Y.C., 1973-80; mgr. prodn. Samuel Weiser Inc., York Beach, Maine, 1982-83, v.p., 1983—; bd. dirs. Nicolas-Hays Inc., York Beach. Author: Astrological Insights Into Personality, 1980, Transits: Time of Your Life, 1980, Planetary Cycles, 1984; contbr. articles to profl. jours. Mem. Am. Fedn. Astrologers, Nat. Council Geocosmic Research (chmn. edn. N.Y.C. chpt. 1977-79, nat. conf. coordinator 1978-80). Office: Samuel Weiser Inc Box 612 York Beach ME 03910

LUNDY, JANET CECILE, histotechnologist; b. Laverty, Okla., May 20, 1942; d. Cecil LeRoy and Grace (Arnold) Parish; student pub. schs., Chickasha, Okla.; m. J.W. Lundy, Oct. 20, 1963. Histology technician Presbyterian Hosp., Oklahoma City, 1960-68; supr. histotech. Okla. Health Scis. Center, Oklahoma City, 1968-71; supr. histotech. Hillcrest Osteo. Hosp., Oklahoma City, 1972-75; supr., histotechnologist Bapt. Med. Center Okla., Oklahoma City, 1975-83; founder, operator Precision Histology Lab, 1983—; mem. adj. faculty Oscar Rose Jr. Coll., 1978-83. Mem. steering com. Linwood Pl. Neighborhood Assn., 1980-82. Mem. Okla. Soc. Histotechnologists, Nat. Soc. Histotech. Mem. Ch. Nazarene. Home: 3132 NW 22d St Oklahoma City OK 73107

LUNDY, MARILYNN FRANCES, interior designer; b. Washington, June 16, 1939; d. Kenneth Merle and Julia (Tassey) L. BA, Pa. State U., 1961. Asst. buyer Abraham & Straus, Bklyn., 1961-63; buyer J.C. Penney Co., Inc., N.Y.C., 1963-73; merchandise man Family Fashions by Avon, N.Y.C., 1973-74; product merchandise Federated Dept. Stores, N.Y.C., 1975-80; prin. Lundy Ltd., N.Y.C., 1981-82; dir. mktg. Lincoln Ctr. Performing Arts, N.Y.C., 1982-83; prin. Environ. Images, N.Y.C., 1984—; instr. New Sch. Social Research, N.Y.C., 1979-81. Club: City. Office: Environ Images Suite 30 S One Lincoln Plaza New York NY 10023-7136

LUNDY, SADIE ALLEN, small business owner; b. Milton, Fla., Mar. 29, 1918; d. Stephen Grover and Martha Ellen (Harter) Allen; m. Wilson Tate Lundy, May 17, 1939 (dec. 1962); children: Wilson Tate Jr., Houston Allen, Michael David, Robert Douglas, Martha Jo-Ellen. Degree in acctg., Graceland Coll., 1938. Acct. Powers Furniture Co., Milton, Fla., 1939-40, Lundy Oil Co., Milton, 1941-52; controller First Fed. Savs. & Loan, Kansas City, Mo., 1953-55, Herald Pub. Co., Indepenence, Mo., 1956-58; mgr. Baird & Son Toy Co., Kansas City, Mo., 1959-62; regional mgr. Emmons Jewelers of N.Y., Kansas City, 1963-65; owner, pres. Lundy Tax Service, Independence, 1965-85; acct. Optimation, Inc., Independence, 1974-85, mgr., 1985—; v.p. Lundy Oil Co., Milton, 1941-52. Contbr. articles to profl. jours. Mem. com. Neighborhood Council, Independence, 1985. Mem. Am. Bus. Women's Assn., Independence C. of C. (mem. com. 1965-85). Republican. Mem. Reorganized Ch. of Jesus Christ of Latter Day Saints. Club: Independence Women's. Home: PO Box 520238 Independence MO 64052 Office: Optimation Inc 645 N Powell Rd Independence MO 64050

LUNNEY, NANCY KAYE, non-profit organization executive; b. N.Y.C., June 25, 1940; d. Eugene and Muriel Kaye; m. David John Lunney, Aug. 26, 1963 (div. 1983); children: Elizabeth Andrea, Jennifer Alexandra. BA, NYU, 1962; MA, Pepperdine U., 1976. Free lance musical dir., vocal coach N.Y.C. and Los Angeles, 1962-77; psychotherapist Esalen Inst., Big Sur, Calif., 1977—, program dir., trustee, 1981—, pres., 1982-86; guest faculty Cornell U., Ithaca, N.Y., 1985—. Home and Office: Esalen Inst Big Sur CA 93920

LUONGO, LUCILLE FRANCESCO, communications company executive; b. N.Y.C., May 29, 1948; d. Carmine and Jean (Gubitosi) Ariniello. BA in English and Speech, Hofstra U., 1970, MA in Communications, 1975. Tchr. Roosevelt (N.Y.) High Sch.; exec. sec. Katz Communications, Inc., N.Y.C., 1978-79, asst. dir. corp. communications, 1979-81, dir. communication services, 1981-85, dir. corp. relations, 1982-85, v.p. corp. relations, 1985—. Mem. Internat. Radio and TV Soc., Am. Women in Radio and TV, Nat. Assn. Female Execs., Broadcast Promotion and Mktg. Execs. Office: Katz Communications Co 1 Dag Hammarskjold Plaza New York NY 10017

LUOTO, BETTY J., investments counselor; b. Grand Rapids, Mich., Dec. 15, 1936; d. Lyle M. DeHart and Esther Nell (Moxon) DeHart-Tucker; m. David L. Trembley, June 24, 1955 (div. June 1984); m. Donald E. Luoto, July 17, 1985; children: Carla Sosanya, Brian D. Trembley, Andrew J. Trembley. A in Nursing, Clark Coll., 1979; student, Lower Columbia Coll., Colo. State U., Seattle Securities Sch. RN; registered securities rep., ins. rep.; cert. instr./trainer CPR. RN Monticello Med. Ctr., Longview, Wash., 1970-81; co-owner Luoto's Battle Ground (Wash.) Home Furnishings, 1985—; rep. Interpacific Investors Services, Longview. Monthly columnist The Sr. Newspaper, 1985—. Choir mem. Emmanuel Luth. Ch., Longview, 1983-87. Mem. Bus. and Profl. Women's Assn. (chairperson membership com. 1987, sec. 1988—), Epsilon Sigma Alpha (past office holder). Office: Interpacific Investors Services 212 Park Plaza Longview WA 98632

LUPIN, FREDA MERLIN, civic leader; b. New Orleans, Aug. 19, 1932; d. Jacob and Molly (Friedman) Merlin; m. E. Ralph Lupin, Mar. 18, 1951; children: Jay Stephen, Michael. Grad. high sch., New Orleans. Chmn. numerous coms. Children's Hosp., New Orleans, 1973-82, mem. hon. bd. 1976, 84—; co.-chmn. numerous coms. Sta. WYES-TV, 1973—, trustee, 1986—, WYES-PBS, 1987—, New Orleans Mus. Art, 1988—; chmn. tour of homes Ladies Leukemia League, 1974, co-chmn. LLL luncheon, 1978-79, v.p., 1979-80, pres., 1981, mem. adv. bd., 1982-84; chmn. big gifts luncheon Jewish Welfare Fund Campaign, 1976, mem. new gifts div., 1984; bd. dirs. women's com. New Orleans Symphony, 1977-80; chmn. gourmet gala March of Dimes, New Orleans, 1983, mem. gourmet gala com., 1987; mem. adv. bd. Ridgewood Prep. Sch., 1983—; mem. Sun King Nat. Com. La. State Mus., 1983-84; mem. mayor's host com. La. World Expn., 1984; bd. dirs. Speech and Hearing Ctr., 1984—; mem. Odyssey Ball com. New Orleans Mus. Art, 1985-87, mem. bd. advisors 1986—; v.p. New Orleans City Ballet, 1986—; mem. Vieux Carre Property Owners, Mayor's Bicentennial Constn. Commn., 1987, Gov.'s Commn. on Internat. Trade, Industry and Tourism, 1987; chmn. Overture to the Cultural Season, 1979. Named one of Women in Forefront, 1985; recipient Living Giving award Juvenile Diabetes Found., 1988, Vol. Activist award, 1988. Mem. Nat. Trust for Hist. Preservation, Aux. Tulane Med. Ctr. (charter mem.), New Orleans Mus. Art (women's aux.), Met. Mus. Art, The Smithsonian, La. Hist. Soc., La. Heart Assn. (wine and cheese festival 1970), Contemporary Arts Ctr., Preservation Resource Ctr. New Orleans, Council of Jewish Women (chmn. com. 1971), Am. Israel Cultural Found. (chmn. reservations 1974, bd. dirs. 1974-76), New Orleans C. of C. (women's aux.). Democrat. Clubs: Patio Planters, Pirouttе. Lodge: Sertoma (Service to Mankind award New Orleans chpt. 1984).

LUPONE, PATTI, actress; b. Northport, L.I., N.Y., Apr. 21, 1949; d. Orlando Joseph and Angela Louise (Patti) DuP. B.F.A., The Juilliard Sch., 1972. Off-Broadway prodns. include: The Woods, School for Scandal, The Lower Depths, Stage Directions; appeared in Broadway prodns.: Next Time I'll Sing to You, The Time of Your Life, The Three Sisters, The Robber Bridegroom (Tony award nominee), The Water Engine, The Beggar's Opera, Edward II, The Baker's Wife, 1976, The Woods, 1977, Working, 1978; Catchpenny Twist, 1979, As You Like It, 1981, The Cradle Will Rock, 1982, Stars of Broadway, 1983, Edmond, 1983, Oliver, 1984 star Broadway play Evita, 1979—, Anything Goes, 1987; London prodn. Les Miserables, 1987; films include: King of the Gypsies, 1978, 1941, 1980, Striking Back, 1981, Fighting Back, 1982; TV Appearances include: Kitty, The Time of Your Life. Recipient Antoinette Perry award, 1980. Office: care The Gersh Agy Inc 130 W 42d St Suite 1804 New York NY 10036

LUPTON, MARY HOSMER, owner, retired operator rare book search service; b. Olympia, Wash., Jan. 2, 1914; d. Kenneth Winthrop and Mary Louise (Wheeler) Hosmer; student Gunston Hall Jr. Coll., 1932-33; B.S. in Edn., U. Va., 1940; m. Keith Brahe Wiley, Oct. 12, 1940 (dec. Apr. 1955); children—Sarah Hosmer Wiley Guise, Victoria Brahe Wiley; m. Thomas George Lupton, Nov. 27, 1965; 1 stepson, Andrew Henshaw. Ptnr., Wakefield Press, Earlysville, Va., 1940-55; owner, operator Wakefield Forest Bookshop, Earlysville, 1955-65, Forest Bookshop, Charlottesville, 1965-85, Wakefield Forest Tree Farm, 1955-85. Contbr. articles to profl. mags. Corr. sec. Charlottesville-Albemarle Civic League, 1963-64; sec. Instructive Vis. Nurses Assn., Charlottesville, 1961-62; chmn. pub. info. Charlottesville chpt. Va. Mus. Fine Arts, 1970-77; mem. writers' adv. panel Va. Center for Creative Arts, 1973-75, chmn. pub. info., 1976-77; mem. Albemarle County Forestry Com., 1961-62; bd. dirs. Charlottesville-Albemarle Mental Health Assn., 1980-82. Mem. AAUW, DAR (Am. Heritage com. chmn. 1983-85), Nat. Trust for Hist. Preservation, Assocs. of U. Va. Library, Nat. Mus. Women on Arts, New Eng. Hist. Geneal. Soc., Conn. Soc. Genealogists, Geneal. Soc. Vt., Va., Vt., Albemarle County hist. socs., Va. Soc. Mayflower Descs. (asst. state historian 1979-82), LWV, Soc. Mayflower Descs., Am. Soc. Psychical Research, Brit. Soc. Psychical Research, Nature Conservancy, Va. Forestry Assn., Chi Omega. Unitarian. Address: La Casita Blanca PO Box 5206 Charlottesville VA 22905-0206

LURIE, ALISON, author; b. Chgo., Sept. 3, 1926; children: John, Jeremy, Joshua. AB, Radcliffe Coll., 1947. Lectr. English Cornell U., 1969-73; adj. assoc. prof. English Cornell U., Ithaca, N.Y., 1973-76, assoc. prof., 1976-79, prof., 1979—. Author: V.R. Lang: A Memoir, 1959, Love and Friendship, 1962, The Nowhere City, 1965, Imaginary Friends, 1967, Real People, 1969, The War Between the Tates, 1974, Only Children, 1979, The Language of Clothes, 1981, Foreign Affairs, 1984, The Man With a Shattered World, 1987. Recipient award in lit. Am. Acad. Arts and Letters, 1978, Pulitzer prize in fiction, 1985; fellow Yaddo Found., 1963-64, 66, Guggenheim Found., 1965, Rockefeller Found., 1967. Address: Cornell Univ Dept English Ithaca NY 14850

LURIE, DEBORAH GAIL, nutritionist; b. Flushing, N.Y., Apr. 1, 1957; d. Walter and Barbara Estelle (Behrman) L. BS in Dietetics, U. Md., 1980; MS in Human Nutrition, Foods, Va. Poly. Inst., 1983. Registered dietitian. Diet technician Howard County Hosp., Columbia, Md., 1980-81; lab. technician dept. human nutrition and foods Va. Poly. Inst. & State U., Blacksburg, 1981-83, programmer Coll. Human Resources, 1983; dietician, supr. human study facility Human Nutrition Research Ctr., USDA, Beltsville, Md., 1984, nutritionist nutrient composition lab., 1984—. Mem. Am. Dietetic Assn. (co-chairperson career devel. com., D.C. chpt. 1986-87), Soc. Nutrition Edn., Phi Sigma, Omicron Nu. Office: Nutrient Composition Lab BARC East Bldg 161 Beltsville MD 20705

LURIE, MURIEL, psychiatric social worker; b. N.Y.C., June 16, 1915; d. Arthur and Celia (Nochimson) L.; B.A., SUNY, Albany, 1967, M.S.W., 1972; children—Daniel, Carolyn. Sec., fund raiser, fund-raising concerns, 1937-39; researcher/editor U.S. Senate Com. Investigating R.R.s, 1939-42; newswriter/editor OWI, London, 1942-45; mgr. advt. agy., N.Y.C., 1946-49; dir. social services depts. Childs Nursing Home and University Heights Health Center, Albany, 1973-79; legis./policy asso. N.Y. State chpt. Nat. Assn. Social Workers, 1979-83; dir. Cons. and Counseling Service to Older Adults and Their Families, 1983—; pvt. practice counseling and psychotherapy, Albany, 1978—; cons. area nursing homes, 1972—. Alt. del. White House Conf. on Aging, 1981; chmn. Long-Term Care Task Force, Health Systems Agy. N.E. N.Y., 1976—, chmn. Albany Sub-Area Council, 1985—. Mem. Nat. Assn. Social Workers, Long-Term Care Social Workers N.E. N.Y. (co-founder 1974), Acad. Cert. Social Workers, Urban League, LWV, Health Edn. and Welfare Club Albany (dir. 1978—). Home and Office: 21 Park Ln S Menands NY 12204

LURIE, NANCY OESTREICH, anthropologist; b. Milw., Jan. 29, 1924; d. Carl Ralph and Rayline (Danielson) Oestreich; m. Edward Lurie, 1951 (div. 1963). B.A., U. Wis., 1945; M.A., U. Chgo., 1947; Ph.D., Northwestern U., 1952; LL.D., Northland Coll., 1976. Instr. U. Wis.-Milw., 1947-49, 51-53, asst. prof., 1961-63, prof., 1963-72, chmn. anthropology dept., 1967-70; curator anthropology Milw. Pub. Museum, 1972—; lectr. U. Mich., 1956-61; cons. expert witness for attys. representing tribal clients before U.S. Indian Claims Commn., 1957-64; Fulbright lectr. U. Aarhus, Denmark, 1965-66. Editor, translator: Mountain Wolf Woman: The Autobiography of a Winnebago Woman, 1961; author: A Special Style: The Milwaukee Public Museum 1882-1982, 1983 (Award of Merit Wis. State Hist. Soc. 1984). Recipient (with co-editor) Anisfield-Wolf award for best scholarly book in intergroup relations, The American Indian Today, 1968. Fellow AAAS, Am. Anthrop. Assn. (exec. bd. 1977-80, pres. elect 1983, pres. 1984-85); mem. Am. Ethnol. Soc., Soc. Applied Anthropology, Central States Anthrop. Soc. (pres. 1967), Sigma Xi. Home: 3342 N Gordon Pl Milwaukee WI 53212

LUROS, ELLYN CAROLE, nutritionist, computer software company executive; b. Bronx, N.Y., Jan. 15, 1947; d. Samuel Joseph and Ruth (Feld) Green; m. Richard Marc Luros, Nov. 28, 1968; children: Hilary, Jodi, Jason, Stephanie. BS in Food and Nutrition, U. Ala., 1968. Dietitian Holy Cross Hosp., Mission Hills, Calif., 1968-70, FSC Mgmt. Co., Chatsworth, Calif., 1970-80; pres., chief exec. officer Computrition, Inc., Chatsworth, 1980—. Author: How to Consult-A Guide to Success, 1979, Successfully Marketing and Selling to Nursing Homes, 1985; editorial adv. bd. Health Care Mag.; contbr. articles to profl. jours. Bd. dirs. Heschel Day Sch., Northridge, Calif., 1984-85, chief fin. officer, 1985-87. Bd. dirs. Jewish Fedn. Council. Recipient Outstanding Alumni award U. Ala., 1985. Mem. Am. Dietetic Assn. (Outstanding Young Dietitian award 1976), Dietitians in Bus. and Industry, Am. Sch. Foodservice Assn. (bd. dirs. 1987—), Assn. Hosp. Food Service Adminstrs. (1987—), Roundtable for Women in Foodservice (Pacesetter award 1985), Home Econs. Soc., Cons. Dietitians in Health Care Facilities (chmn. 1976-82, bd. dirs., treas., nat. chmn. 1979-81). Avocations: cooking, travel. Office: Computrition Inc 21049 Devonshire St Chatsworth CA 91311

LUSK, GLENNA RAE KNIGHT (MRS. EDWIN BRUCE LUSK), librarian; b. Franklinton, La., Aug. 16, 1935; d. Otis Harvey and Lou Zelle (Bahm) Knight; B.S., La. State U., 1956, M.S., 1963; m. John Earle Uhler, Jr., May 26, 1956; children—Anne Knight, Camille Allana; m. 2d, Edwin Bruce Lusk, Nov. 28, 1970. Asst. librarian Iberville Parish Library, Plaquemine, La., 1956-57, 1962-68; tchr. Iberville Parish Pub. Schs., Plaquemine, 1957-59, Plaquemines Parish Pub. Schs., Buras, La., 1959-61; dir. Iberville Parish Library, Plaquemine, 1969—; chmn. La. State Bd. Library Examiners, 1979—. Mem. Iberville Parish Econ. Devel. Council, Plaquemine, 1970-71; sec. Iberville Parish Bicentennial Commn., 1973—; mem. La. Bicentennial Commn., 1974. Named Outstanding Young Woman Plaquemine, La. Jr. C. of C., 1970. Mem. La. (sect. chmn. 1967-68), Riverland (sec. 1973-74) library assns., Capital Area Libraries (chmn. com. 1972-74). Democrat. Episcopalian. Author: (with John E. Uhler, Jr.) Cajun Country Cookin' 1966; Rochester Clarke Bibliography of Louisiana Cookery, 1966; Royal Recipes from the Cajun Country, 1969; Iberville Parish, 1970. Home: 206 Pecan Tree Ln Plaquemine LA 70764 Office: 1501 J Gerald Berret Blvd Plaquemine LA 70764

LUSSIER, BARBARA MILLER, architectural services company executive; b. Phila., June 21, 1956; d. Ronald E. and Barbara (Brennan) Miller; m. Grant P. Lussier, Aug. 8, 1981. B.S., Sch. Mgmt., Boston Coll., 1978. Asst. buyer designer sportswear Lord & Taylor, N.Y.C., 1978-81; v.p. mktg., co-owner 3XM Inc., Houston, 1981—; co-owner 3XM Inc., Phila., 1987—. Mem. Urban Land Inst (assoc.), Houston C. of C., Boston Coll. Alumni Club. Home: 136 N Bread St Suite 322 Philadelphia PA 19106 Office: 3XM Inc 18 S Strawberry St Philadelphia PA 19106

LUSTER, ARLENE LEONG, library director; b. Honolulu, Jan. 11, 1936; d. Henry Hung Yun and Sadie Mee Yee (Chun) Leong; m. Gilbert Norman, Mar. 15,1960 (div. July 1980); children: Eugene Norman, Deanna Mee Yee. BA, Tex. Woman's U., 1957; MLS, Western Reserve U., 1958; EdD, U. So. Calif., 1977. Hosp. med. librarian Harbor Gen. Hosp., Torrance, Calif., 1958-59; asst. order librarian U. Hawaii, Honolulu, 1961-63; base librarian Fuchu (Japan) Air Station, 1959-61, Hickam (Hawaii) AFB, 1963-68, Wheeler (Hawaii) AFB, 1968-73; lectr. Leeward Community Coll., Honolulu, 1973-75; naval regional librarian NAVEDTRASUP Det., Pearl Harbor, Hawaii, 1973-79; library dir., command librarian Hdqr. Pacific Air Forces, Hickam AFB, 1979—; Chmn. library adv. com. Leeward Community Coll., 1975-83; proprietor Innovative Mgmt., Honolulu, 1978—. Contbr. articles to profl. jours. Mem. Hawaii Gov.'s Conf. on Libraries, Honolulu, 1978-79, Lt. Gov. Council on Literacy, Honolulu, 1985—. Recipient Superior Performance Cash awards U.S. Civil Service, 1963, 70, 73, 86, 87, Outstanding awards, 1974-78, Air Force Library Publicity awards USAF, 1970-73, 82-83, George Washington Honor medals, Freedoms Found., 1971-72. Mem. ALA (John Cotton Dana Pub. Relations awards 1970-73, Armed Forces Librarians Citation 1980), Hawaii Library Assn. (Disting. Librarian award 1985), Federally Employed Women, Fuzhou Library Soc., Hawaii Chinese History Ctr., Delta Kappa Gamma. Home: 3501 Kepuhi St Honolulu HI 96815 Office: Hdqr Pacific Air Forces Hickam AFB HI 96853-5001

LUSTER, SHERI KAY, advertising executive; b. St. Louis, Jan. 1, 1960; d. Noel Thomas and Joann (McCrackin) L. BS in Advt. and Pub. Relations, Tex. Christian U., 1982. Media buyer Gardner Advt., St. Louis, 1982-83; media dir. Stolz Advt., St. Louis, 1983—; pres. The Media Mix, St. Louis, 1984—; bd. dirs. Glenridge Inc., St. Louis. Mem. St. Louis Advt. Club. Christian Scientist. Office: The Media Mix 2354 Hidden Meadows Ballwin MO 63021

LUTEN, CLAIRE KOVACH, circuit judge; b. Pitts., May 6, 1940; d. Charles Rudolf and Irene (Leistinger) Kovach; m. Michael H. Cates, Mar. 11, 1961 (div.); children: Keir Kayleen, Michelle Irene, Michael James; m. William C. Luten Jr., Aug. 30, 1974; 1 child, William C. III. BS, Valparaiso U., 1961; JD, U. Wash., 1964. Bar: Wash. Bar Assn. 1964, Fla. Bar Assn. 1966. Atty. Cates & Cates, Sarasota, Fla., 1967-69, Crabtree, Brush, Sypett et. al., Sarasota, 1969-70; asst. pub. defender 16th Jud. Cir., Key West, Fla., 1970-71; atty. Nixon & Farnell, Clearwater, Fla., 1971-73; asst. state atty. 6th Jud. Cir., Clearwater, 1973-74, county ct. judge, 1977-84, cir. ct. judge, 1985—; asst. pub. defender 9th Jud. Cir., Orlando, Fla., 1974-75; atty. Webster, Caltagirone & Luten, Clearwater, 1975-76; mem. adv. bd. Pinellas Emergency Mental Health, Clearwater, 1983-87. Mem. editorial bd. Fla. Judges Manual, 1985—. Recipient Disting. Leadership award Fla. Conf. County Ct. Judges, 1977, 79, Pinellas Applauds Community Endeavor award Emergency Mental Health Services, 1984, Torch award Nat. Safety Council, 1987-88. Mem. Fla. Assn. Women Lawyers (pres.), Clearwater Bar Assn. Lutheran. Lodge: Soroptimists Internat. (Women Honoring Women award 1980). Office: Pinellas County Courthouse 5100 144th Ave N Clearwater FL 34620

LUTERNOW, BONNIE ALDEA, financial executive; b. Frankfurt, Fed. Republic of Germany, Aug. 31, 1948. BA, Radcliffe Coll., 1969; MBA, Harvard U., 1978. Dir. overseas fin. analysis Gen. Motors Corp., N.Y.C., 1978-84; mgr. program analysis Gen. Motors Corp., Warren, Mich., 1984—. Advisor Handicapped Scouting, Detroit, 1987; mem. fin. com. Luth. Social Services of Mich., Detroit, 1987, Commn. for Luth. Ch., 1987. Club: Harvard, Radcliffe Alumni (Mich.). Home: 8027 Sugarloaf Trail Clarkston MI 48016 Office: Gen Motors Corp 30009 Van Dyke Warren MI 48090

LUTHER, DIANE JACKSON, periodical publisher, advertising consultant; b. Ft. Worth, Oct. 3, 1934; d. Virgil Everett and Miriam (Dunn) Jackson; children: Colin, Christopher, Clay. BS in Radio and TV Prodn., U. Tex., Arlington, 1954; B in Gen. Studies, Tex. Christian U., 1981. Adminstrv. asst. Ft. Worth Opera Assn., 1972-79, Jerre R. Todd & Assocs., Ft. Worth, 1979-80; dir pub. relations Stevenson Strategies and Tactics, Dallas, 1980-82; pvt. practice advt., pub. relations and mktg. cons. Ft. Worth, 1982—; pub. Women's Yellow Pages, Dallas/Ft. Worth, 1982—; founding mem., then v.p. nat. assn. Arlington, 1985—; also bd. dirs.; regional advt. dir. The Guide Group, Lexington, Ky., 1987—. Named Tex. Media Adv. of Yr. Small Bus. Adminstrn., 1987, Dallas Dist. Media Adv. of Yr. Small Bus. Adminstrn., 1987. Mem. Nat. Assn. Women Bus. Owners, Assn. Women Entrepreneurs of Dallas, Women's Consortium, Women's Coalition, Dallas/Ft. Worth Minority Bus. Devel. Council. Mem. Ch. Christ. Office: Women's Yellow Pages PO Box 110574 Arlington TX 76007

LUTHER, FLORENCE JOAN (MRS. CHARLES W. LUTHER), lawyer; b. N.Y.C. June 28, 1928; d. John Phillip and Catherine Elizabeth (Duffy) Thomas ; J.D. magna cum laude, U. Pacific, 1963; m. William J. Regan (dec.); children—Kevin P., Brian T.; m. 2d, Charles W. Luther, June 11, 1961. Admitted to Calif. bar; mem. firm Luther, Luther, O'Connor & Johnson, Sacramento, 1964—. Mem. faculty McGeorge Sch. Law, U. Pacific, Sacramento, 1966—, prof., 1968—. Judge Bank Am. Achievement awards, 1969-71. Bd. dirs. Sacramento Suicide Prevention League, 1969-70. Mem. ABA, Calif., Sacramento County bar assns., AAUP, Womens Legal Groups, Am. Judicature Soc., Order of Coif, Iota Tau Tau. Mem. bd. advisors Community Property Jour., 1974—, state decision editor, 1974—. Home: 11101 Fair Oaks Blvd Fair Oaks CA 95628 Office: PO Box 1030 Fair Oaks CA 95628

LUTKENHOUSE, ANNE, administrator; b. S.I., N.Y., Feb. 18, 1957; d. Emile Anthony and Jane Anne Lutkenhouse. BA magna cum laude, Wagner Coll., 1979; cert. Goethe Inst., N.Y.C., 1981. Supr. Credit Suisse, N.Y.C., 1979-85; dist. office adminstr. N.Y. City Council, 1985-86; asst. dir., Appalachian Trail Field asst., N.Y.-N.J. Trail Conf., N.Y.C., 1986—; contbg. cons. Wagner Coll. Study Program, Bregenz, Austria, 1978—. Photographer, producer photography show, 1984. Swimming instr. ARC, S.I., 1977; campaign aide council member Fossella, N.Y. City Council, S.I., 1985; pres., bd. dirs. S.I. Chamber Music Players, 1984-86; co-chmn. Flag Day Parade, Tottenville Improvement Council, Inc., 1986; producer Appalachian Trail 50th Anniversary celebration, 1987. Contbr. travel articles to mags; contbg. writer Appalachian Trailway News, 1987—. Mem. Nat. Assn. Female Execs., Norwegian-Am. C. of C. Democrat. Roman Catholic. Avocations: needlecrafts, ballet, skiing, travel. Home: 399 Yetman Ave Staten Island NY 10307 Office: N Y -N J Trail Conf 232 Madison Ave New York NY 10016

LUTON, BARBARA LEWIN, management consultant; b. Chgo., Feb. 14, 1938; d. Thurber and Mary (Vaughan) LeWin; m. Robert Richard Luton, Aug. 26, 1961; children: Elizabeth, Robert, James. BA, Wellesley Coll., 1959; M of Pub. and Pvt. Mgmt., Yale U., 1978. Securities analyst Eaton & Howard, Inc., Boston, 1959-61; prin. Thunder Bay Assocs., Darien, Conn., 1962-88; dir. devel. and alumni affairs Yale Sch. of Orgn. and Mgmt., New Haven, Conn., 1978-80; corp. sec. Donaldson Enterprises, Inc., N.Y.C., 1981-82; v.p. East View Co., N.Y.C., 1983-85. Ruling elder Noroton Presbyn. Ch., Darien, 1970-76. Mem. Wellesley Coll. Alumnae Assn. (pres. 1988-91).

LUTZKER, EDYTHE, historian, writer, researcher; b. Berlin, Germany, June 25, 1904; d. Solomon and Sophia (Katz) Levine m. Philip Lutzker, June 14, 1924; children—Michael Arnold, Arthur Samuel, Paul William B.A., City Coll. N.Y., 1954; M.A., Columbia U., 1959. Bookkeeper, sec., exec. for bus. cos., N.Y.C., 1922-49; research asst. to Prof. Edward Rosen, City Coll. N.Y., 1951-54; author: Women Gain a Place in Medicine, 1969; Edith Pechey-Phipson M.D., Story of England's and India's Foremost Pioneering Woman Doctor, 1973. Pres. Child Care Center Parents Assn., 1943-51. Grantee Am. Philos. Soc., 1964, 65, Nat. Library of Medicine, 1966, 68-71, 72-74. Fellow Royal Soc. Medicine; mem. Am. Assn. History of Medicine, Am. Soc. for Microbiology, Soc. Internat. History Medicine, History of Sci. Soc., Am. Hist. Assn., Jewish Acad. Arts and Scis., Fawcett Soc. Democrat. Contbr. articles profl. publs., lectr. profl. orgns. Founder, v.p. Waldermar M.

Haffkine Internat. Meml. Com. Home and Office: 201 W 89th St New York NY 10024

LUYSTER, VERONICA JULIA, account executive; b. Paterson, N.J., Dec. 25, 1960; d. Peter and Veronica (McArdle) L. Student, Georgian Ct. Coll., 1980; BA, SUNY, Oswego, 1982; MA, U. S. Fla., 1984. Account exec. Advo-System, Fla., 1984—. Vol. speaker Planned Parenthood, Tampa, Fla., 1983-84. Mem. Nat. Direct Mail Assn., Nat. Assn. Female Execs., Palm Beach Ad. Republican. Roman Catholic. Home: 1992 SW Erwin Rd Port Saint Lucie FL 33452 Office: Advo-System Inc 2032 Elmhurst Ct 34952 Miami Lakes FL 33014

LUZZO, KAREN ANN, newspaper publishing administrator; b. Mt. Pleasant, Mich., Feb. 23, 1944; d. Theodore Roosevelt and Wilma Ireta (Terwilliger) Wallington; m. Donald Randall McCoy, June 20, 1964 (div. July 1970); m. Francis Lee Couey (dec. 1985); children: Steven, Deborah Leeann, Joanna Lee, Francis Lee; m. Phillip D. Luzzo, Nov. 21, 1987. AA, Saddleback Jr. Coll., 1970; BS, San Diego State U., 1971. Lic. tchr., Calif. Distbr. Los Angeles Herald Examiner, 1972-77, 77-78, 86—, sr. br. mgr., 1978-81; office mgr. Tranpac Enterprises, Santa Ana, Calif., 1977; asst. zone mgr. The Register Newspaper, Mission Viejo, Calif., 1981-85; ins. agt., fin. cons. A.L. Williams, Laguna Hills, Calif., 1984—. Co-moderator bd. deacons San Clemente (Calif.) Presbyn. Ch., 1986, treas., 1987. Republican. Lodge: Job's Daus. (past honored queen, past chpt. sweetheart-DeMolay). Office: Los Angeles Herald Examiner 1111 S Broadway Los Angeles CA 92670

LYBARGER, ADRIENNE REYNOLDS (MRS. LEE FRANCIS), college administrator; b. Boston, Mar. 8, 1926; d. Joseph Anthony and Albertine (Mouton Drevet) Reynolds; B.A., Mills Coll., Calif., 1947; cert. Katharine Gibbs Sch., 1948; m. Lee Francis Lybarger, Jr., Sept. 15, 1955 (dec); children: Linda, Lauretta, James (dec.), Lisa, Leslie (dec.), Jeffrey (dec.), Lucia, Lana. Asst. to dir. Mid-Century convocation M.I.T. Cambridge, 1949, asst. to dir. West Coast regional office Mid-Century devel. program, 1949-50, asst. dir. So. regional office, 1950-51; asst. to dir. convocation devel. program Ithaca (N.Y.) Coll., 1951; asst. to dir., devel. program U. Buffalo, 1951-52; asst. to dir. Diamond Jubilee program Case Inst. Tech., Cleve., 1952-54; asst. to dir., expansion and improvement program John D. Archbold Hosp., Thomasville, Ga., 1955-61; ptnr. Lybarger Prodns., comml. films, N.Y.C.; asst. dir., dir. regional campaigns, Ohio, Boston, Mass., N.Y.C., also supr. all other nat. regional campaigns Mount Holyoke Coll. Fund for Future, South Hadley, Mass., 1961-63; fund-raising cons. to capital programs, Vocation Service Center and Bronx-Westchester YMCA, YMCA Greater N.Y., 1963-65; dir. devel. and public relations Bank St. Coll. Edn., N.Y.C., 1965-79; cons. S. Bronx Overall Econ. Devel. Corp., 1978-79; v.p. devel. Wells Coll., 1979—, dir. Wells Capital campaign; cons. capital campaign Borough of Manhattan Community Coll., 1979-80; Realtor assoc./mktg. cons. Century 21, Clinton, N.J. Pres., Birch Island (Maine) Corp., 1979; trustee Nat. Women's Hall of Fame, 1987. Author: (with L.F. Lybarger) Proven Guides to Effective Soliciting (slide film), 1950, rev., 1960, 81; exec. producer, Scriptwriter Now More than Ever, Wells Coll. Home: Kings Manor Pittstown NJ 08867 Office: Wells Coll Aurora NY 13026

LYLE, MARY FRANCES, lawyer, lobbyist; b. Texarkana, Tex., Feb. 22, 1936; d. Robert Lewis and Frances Dillahunty (DePrato) Hodges; m. Michael Charles Lyle, July 12, 1954; children—Elizabeth Anne Lyle Miller, Stephen Michael, Mary Carol Lyle Hollis, David Robert. B.A., U. Louisville, 1966; J.D., Vanderbilt U., 1979. Bar: Tenn. 1979. Elem. tchr. Jefferson County Bd. Edn., Louisville, 1966-69, Warren County Bd. Edn., McMinnville, Tenn., 1969-76; assoc. firm Bruce, Weathers, Dughman & Lyle, Nashville, 1984—; lobbyist for women in state legislature Tenn. Women's Polit. Caucus, 1982—. Columnist; contbr. articles to legal pubs. Bd. dirs. Planned Parenthood, Nashville, 1983-87, pres., 1985-87; mem. Met. Transit Authority Adv. Council, Nashville, 1983, Fed. Regulatory Flexibility Act Task Force, Washington, 1981; mem. Project to End Abuse through Counseling and Edn. (bd. dirs.); mem. adv. bd. Madison Hosp. Women's Health Ctr., 1987-88. Mem. ABA, Tenn. Bar Assn., Nashville Bar Assn., Lawyers Assn. for Women, Tenn. Trial Lawyers Assn., C. of C. (pres. com.), Women in Bus. Inc. (pres.), YWCA, LWV, Small Bus. Adminstn., Women Bus. (Advocate Yr. for State of Tenn. 1988), Ct. Appointed Spl. Advocates (bd. dirs.), Leadership Nashville. Democrat. Episcopalian. Clubs: Altrusa, Cable (dir. Nashville 1982-83). Home: 6626 Holt Rd Nashville TN 37211 Office: Bruce Weathers Dughman & Lyle 1610 Parkway Towers Nashville TN 37219

LYLES, JEAN ELIZABETH CAFFEY, journalist; b. Abilene, Tex., Mar. 2, 1942; d. Wiley Luther and Pauline Linn (Marlin) Caffey; m. James Vernon Lyles, Aug. 23, 1969 (div. Aug. 1987). Student, McMurry Coll., 1960-61; BA with honors, U. Tex., 1964. Copy editor Christian Century mag., Chgo., 1972-74, assoc. editor, 1974-84, editor at large, 1984—; assoc. editor Religious News Service, N.Y.C., 1984-87; new editor The Lutheran, Chgo., 1987—. Author: A Practical Vision of Christian Unity, 1982; contbg. author: The First Amendment in a Free Society, 1979; contbg. editor Wittenburg Door, 1982-87; columnist Inside the Am. Religion Scene, 1985-87; contbr. numerous articles to religious and scholarly jours. Mem. Religion Newswriters Assn., Am. Guild Organists, Hymn Soc. Am., United Meth. Assn. Communicators. Democrat. Episcopalian. Office: The Lutheran 8765 W Higgins Rd Chicago IL 60631

LYLES, MARJORIE APPLEMAN, educator; b. New York, Sept. 1, 1946; 1 child, Richard Brent. BS, Carnegie-Mellon U., 1969; MLS, U. Pitts., 1971, PhD in Bus. Adminstrn., 1977. Info. sci. specialist U. Pitts., 1974; instr. Carnegie-Mellon U., Pitts., 1976-77; asst. prof. Ind. U., 1977-82, U. Ill., Champaign, 1982-87; assoc. prof. Ball State U., Muncie, Ind., 1987—; vis. prof. INSEAD, France, 1984; leadership and mgmt. seminars U. Ill., 1984; cons. long range planning Eli Lilly & Co., Indpls., 1979. Contbr. articles to profl. jours. Mem. program com. Greater Indpls., 1980-81; bd. dirs. Christamore House, 1979-82, Ind. Bus. Devel. Found., 1980-82; advisor Upward Mobility Project, Ind., 1978-79. Named one of Outstanding Young Women Am., 1980. Mem. Acad. Mgmt. (exec. policy com. 1982-85, co-chair doctor student consortium 1984), Am. Inst. Decision Scis., Sigma Iota Epsilon. Home: 4401 N Pennsylvania Indianapolis IN 46205 Office: Ball State U Coll Bus Dept Mgmt Sci Muncie IN 47306

LYLES, SARA SUTHERLAND, small business owner; b. Union, S.C., Jan. 3, 1951; d. H. Lloyd and Sara (McLendon) Sutherland; m. John C. West Jr., June 24, 1971 (div. Nov. 1982); m. Robert Thomas Lyles, May 9, 1987. BA, Winthrop Coll., 1972. Cert. tchr. Asst. prof. U. S.C., Columbia, 1972-74; instr. German U.S. Army, Ft. Lewis, Wash., 1974-75; dir. Christian Edn. Bethesda Pres. Ch., Camden, S.C., 1976-78; interior decorator U.S. Capital Corp., Columbia, S.C., 1982-83; owner, mgr. Bones Restaurant, Columbia, S.C., 1984—. Mem. Nat. Restaurant Assn., S.C. Restaurant Assn. Presbyterian. Office: Bones 2011 Devine St Columbia SC 29205

LYLES-ANDERSON, BARBARA DUNBAR, civil engineer; b. Columbia, S.C., June 2, 1954; d. Thomas McDonald and Barbara Ann (Dukes) L. BCE magna cum laude, Clemson (S.C.) U., 1976. Registered profl. engr., S.C. Engr. Davis & Floyd Engrs., Inc., Greenwood, S.C., 1976-80; project mgr. Life Cycle Engring., Inc., Charleston, S.C., 1980—. V.P. Greenwood Ballet Guild, 1978. Mem. ASCE (Charleston chpt. co-chmn. Mathcounts 1986), NSPE (bd. dirs.), S.C. Soc. Profl. Engrs. (Charleston chpt. bd. dirs. 1986-87), Soc. Women Engrs., Am. Waterworks Assn. (com. 1980—), Water Pollution Control Fedn. (com. 1980—), Lords Proprietors Soc., Jr. League of Charleston. Republican. Presbyterian. Home: 4111 N Stratford Rd Atlanta GA 30342 Office: Life Cycle Engring PO Box 300001 Charleston SC 29417

LYMAN, ELISABETH REED, educator; b. Bklyn., Sept. 13, 1912; d. Carl Sweetland and Florence Irene (Bemis) Reed; B.A., Smith Coll., 1933; postgrad. U. Calif.-Berkeley, 1933-38; m. Ernest McIntosh Lyman, June 12, 1934; children—Nancy Lyman Repp, Elisabeth Lyman Rachal, Richard, Jerome, Carl. Instr., Smith Coll., 1941; research asst. Mass. Inst. Tech., 1941, staff mem. Radiation Lab., 1942-46; research asst. prof. Computer-based Edn. Research Lab., U. Ill., Urbana-Champaign, 1962-84, emerita, 1984—. Mem. Urbana Bd. Edn., 1950-65, pres., 1955-60; chmn. Dist.-Wide Sch. Com., Urbana, 1969-70; mem. Urbana Park Dist. Adv. Com., 1971-73, chmn., 1972-73; mem. Urbana Park Bd. Commrs., 1973-79; mem. Boneyard Creek Commn., 1976-87, pres., 1978-81; treas., exec. bd. Univ. YWCA, 1964-77, endowment com., 1987—; bd. dirs. Champaign County United Way, 1974-78. Named Mother of Year, Champaign News Gazette, 1962. Mem. Am. Soc. for Engring. Edn., LWV, Soc. Women Engrs., Ill. Assn. Sch. Bds., U. Ill. Athletic Assn. (bd. dirs. 1976-79, sec. 1977-78, vice chmn. 1978-79), Assn. Devel. Computer-Based Instructional Systems, Assn. for Women in Sci., Crystal Lakeshore Assn. (pres. 1986—, bd. dirs. 1983—), Urbana C. of C. (Women's Bus. Council), Phi Beta Kappa, Sigma Delta Epsilon, Alpha Lambda Delta. Republican. Congregationalist. Contbr. numerous articles to profl. jours. Home: 1009 S Orchard St Urbana IL 61801 Office: U Ill Engring Research Lab 103 S Mathews Urbana IL 61801

LYNCH, BEVERLY PFEIFER, librarian; b. Moorhead, Minn., Dec. 27, 1935; d. Joseph B. and Nellie K. (Bailey) Pfeifer; m. John A. Lynch, Aug. 24, 1968. B.S., N.D. State U., 1957, L.H.D. (hon.); M.S., U. Ill., 1959; Ph.D., U. Wis., 1972. Librarian Marquette U., 1959-60, 62-63; exchange librarian Plymouth (Eng.) Pub. Library, 1960-61; asst. head serials div. Yale U. Library, 1963-65, head, 1965-68; vis. lectr. U. Wis., Madison, 1970-71, U. Chgo., 1975; exec. sec. Assn. Coll. and Research Libraries, 1972-76; univ. librarian U. Ill.-Chgo., 1977—; vis. prof. U. Tex., Austin, 1978; sr. fellow UCLA Grad. Sch. Library and Info. Sci., 1982. Author: Management Strategies for Libraries, 1985, (with Thomas J. Galvin) Priorities for Academic Libraries, 1982. Named Acad. Librarian of Yr., 1981. Mem. Acad. Mgmt., ALA (pres. 1985-86), Am. Sociol. Assn., Bibliog. Soc. Am., Ctr. for Research Libraries (chmn. 1980-81, bd. dirs.), Phi Kappa Phi. Clubs: Caxton, Grolier, Arts (Chgo.). Home: 1859 N 68th St Milwaukee WI 53213 Office: U Ill Chgo Univ Library 801 S Morgan St PO Box 8198 Chicago IL 60680

LYNCH, BRENDA EILEEN, public relations executive; b. Santa Monica, Calif., Aug. 16, 1960; d. Kevin Gary and Edwinia (Martin) L.; m. Vince Silvestri, Oct. 6, 1984. Student, Gonzaga U. extension, Florence, Italy, 1980-81; BA, Loyola Marymount U., 1982. Dir. pub. relations Incolay Studios Inc., San Fernando, Calif., 1982-86; account exec. James Agy., Los Angeles, 1986—. Mem. NOW, Alpha Sigma Nu. Clubs: Los Angeles Publicity, UCLA Publicity. Office: The James Agy 7455 Beverly Blvd Los Angeles CA 90036

LYNCH, CAROLINE HIRTH, medical consultant; b. Hartford, Conn., Feb. 15, 1935; d. Richard William and Emilie (Kaleta) Hirth; m. John Clement Lynch, June 1, 1957; children—Richard John, Allison Emilie. Student Hillyer Coll., 1953-54, 55-58, U. Conn., Storrs, 1954-55. Office mgr. various physicians' offices, Tex., Conn., Ill., 1960-77; cons. MAC Mgmt. and Consulting Services, Vernon, Conn., 1977-79; owner, pres. A Doctor's Service Ctr., Bountiful, Utah, 1979-88; prin. CMTS div. Meditech, Bountiful, 1988— . Author tng. manuals, guides, Instr. water safety ARC, Dallas, 1963-75, instr. disaster services, Salt Lake City, 1983—, vol. caseworker. Mem. Nat. Assn. Female Execs. Mormon. Lodge: Order Amaranth. Avocations: music, travel. Home: 620 E 400 N Bountiful UT 84010 Office: Meditech PO Box 75 Bountiful UT 84010

LYNCH, CATHERINE GORES, social work administrator; b. Waynesboro, Pa., Nov. 23, 1943; d. Landis and Pamela (Whitmarsh) Gores; B.A. magna cum laude and honors, Bryn Mawr Coll., 1965; Fulbright scholar, Universidad Central de Venezuela, Caracas, 1965-66; postgrad. (Lehman fellow), Cornell U., 1966-67; m. Joseph C. Keefe, Nov. 29, 1981; children—Shannon Maria, Lisa Alison, Gregory T. Keefe, Michael D. Keefe. Mayor's intern, Human Resources Adminstrn., N.Y.C., 1967; research asst. Orgn. for Social and Tech. Innovation, Cambridge, Mass., 1967-69; cons. Ford Found., Bogota, Colombia, 1970; staff Nat. Housing Census, Nat. Bur. Statistics, Bogotá, 1971; evaluator Foster Parent Plan, Bogotá, 1973; research staff FEDESARROLLO, Bogotá, 1973-74; dir. Dade County Advocates for Victims, Miami, Fla., 1974-86; asst. to dep. dir. Dept. Human Resources, Miami, 1986-87, computer liaison, 1987—; guest lectr. local univs. Participant, co-chmn. various task forces rape, child abuse, incest, family violence, elderly victims of crime, nat., state, local levels, 1974-86; developer workshops in field; mem. gov.'s task force on victims and witnesses, gov.'s task force on sex offenders and their victims; cert. expert witness on battered women syndrome in civil and criminal cts. Recipient various public service awards including WINZ Citizen of Day, 1979; Outstanding Achievement award Fla. Network Victim Witness Services, 1982; cert. police instr. Mem. Nat. Orgn. of Victim Assistance Programs (bd. dirs. 1977-83; Outstanding Program award 1984). Fla. Network of Victim/Witness Programs (bd. dirs., treas., 1980-81), Nat. Assn. Social Workers, Am. Soc. Public Adminstrs., Dade County Fedn. Health and Welfare Workers, Fla. Assn. Health and Social Services (Dade County chpt., treas., 1979-80). Contbr. writings in field to publs. Office: Dept Human Resources 111 NW 1 St Suite 2210 Miami FL 33128

LYNCH, KATHLEEN ALETA, psychologist; b. Kansas City, Mo.; d. James and Louella (Dowaly) L. BA, U. Mo., Kansas City, 1964; MA, U. Mo., 1969, PhD, 1974. Researcher U. Kans. Med. Ctr., Kansas City, 1964-66; vocat. rehabilitator Mo. State Vocat. Rehab., Kansas City, 1966-69; supervising psychologist U.S. Army, St. Louis, 1974-75; psychologist VA Med. Ctr., West Haven, Conn., 1975-76; chief psychology dept. VA Med. Ctr., West Roxbury, Mass., 1976-85; lectr. Harvard U. Med. Sch., Boston, 1976-85; prin. Lynch Resources, Boston; Cons. Am. Labor Mgmt. Alcoholism Cons. Assn., Washington, 1974-79, Alcohol, Drug Abuse, Mental Health, Washington, 1974-76, U.S. Pub. HealthDept., Boston, 1976-78, Thompson Group, Milwaukee, 1984-86. Contbr. articles to profl. jours. Recipient 10 outstanding woman awards Glamour mag., 1979. Fellow, Mass. Psychological Assn. Home and Office: 6 Whittier Pl Boston MA 02114

LYNCH, LINDA ZANETTI, market research firm executive; b. N.Y.C., Mar. 21, 1933; d. Giacomo and Elise (Linfert) Zanetti; m. David D. Lynch, Oct. 8, 1955 (div. 1984); children—Catherine, Jeffrey, Jonathan, Jennifer. Asst. editor Good Housekeeping, N.Y.C., 1954-57; freelance editor, 1965-75; asst. to dir. Ridgefield Library, Conn., 1975-80; bus. researcher Mktg. Corp. Am., Westport, Conn., 1980-82, mgr. bus. research group, 1982—. Mem. Am. Mgmt. Assn., Am. Mktg. Assn., Assn. Info. Mgrs., Soc. Competitor Intelligence Profls. (founding). Club: Brown. Office: Mktg Corp Am 325 Riverside Ave Westport CT 06880

LYNCH, SISTER MARY DENNIS, librarian; b. Phila., Apr. 23, 1920; d. J. Raymond and Ida A. (Teal) L.; A.B., Temple U., 1941; B.S. in L.S., Drexel U., 1942; M.S. in L.S., Catholic U., 1956; M.A., Villanova U., 1970, St. Charles Sem., 1980. Joined Soc. Holy Child Jesus, 1942; tchr., librarian Sch. Holy Child Jesus, Sharon Hill, Pa., 1942-45, 53-62, Summit, N.J., 1945-47; tchr. social studies West Phila. Cath. Girls High Sch., 1947-53; librarian Rosemont (Pa.) Coll., 1962—, lectr. methods of social studies, 1963-71, chmn. Am. studies com., 1970-73, lectr. polit. sci., 1973-87, lectr. New Testament, 1987—; instr. library sci. dept. Villanova U., summers 1964-65; mem. ednl. adv. bd. St. Charles Borromeo Sem., 1968-76, 78-87; bd. dirs. Tri-State Coll. Library Coop., 1967—, pres., 1980-81, exec. sec., 1967-70; trustee PALINET, 1978-81, 83-86, 88—, v.p., 1986; mem. Pa. State Library Bibliog. Access Study Adv. Com., 1977-78. Mem. Am. Cath. (nat. exec. council 1975-79, 81-87, pres. 1983-85), Pa. (chairperson coll. and research sect. 1975-76, parliamentarian 1977-83) library assns., Assn. Coll. and Research Libraries (pres. Del. Valley chpt. 1987-88), Cath. Library Assn. (v.p. Newman chpt. 1987—), OCLC Users Council (del. 1978-83, exec. com. 1982-83), Am. Acad. Polit. and Social Scis., Acad. Polit. Sci., Am. Studies Assn., Nat. Cath. Ednl. Assn., Nat. Council Social Studies, Beta Phi Mu. Office: Rosemont Coll Library Rosemont PA 19010-1699

LYNCH, NANCY ANN, computer science educator; b. Bklyn., Jan. 19, 1948; d. Roland David and Marie Catherine (Adinolfi) Evraets; m. Dennis Christopher Lynch, June 14, 1969; children: Patrick, Kathleen (dec.), Mary. BS, Bklyn. Coll., 1968; PhD, MIT, 1972. Asst. prof. math. Tufts U., Medford, Mass., 1972-73, U. So. Calif., Los Angeles, 1973-76, Fla. Internat. U., Miami, 1976-77; assoc. prof. computer sci. Ga. Tech. U., Atlanta, 1977-82; assoc. prof. computer sci. MIT, Cambridge, 1982-86, prof. computer sci., 1986—; Ellen Swallow Richards chair MIT, 1982-87; cons. Computer Corp. Am., Cambridge, 1984-86, Apollo Computer, Chelmsford, Mass., 1986—, AT&T Bell Labs, Murray Hill, N.J., 1986—. Contbr. numerous articles to profl. jours. Mem. Assn. Computing Machinery. Roman Catholic. Office: MIT NE43-525 Cambridge MA 02139

LYNCH, PATRICIA ANNE, real estate corporate officer, consultant; b. Blythe, Calif., Dec. 22, 1941; d. Russell Roe and Hazel Elizabeth (Gibson) Travis; m. Lloyd Raymond Beadle, Aug. 26, 1962 (div. 1982); children: Amber, Tiffany. BA, San Jose U., 1963. Licensed real estate broker, Ky.; cert. elem., secondary tchr. Tchr. Calif. Tchrs. Assn., Santa Clara, 1963-69; pres. Creative Activities Pub. Co., San Jose, Calif., 1969-77; real estate sales assoc. Gatewood Gallery of Homes, Los Gatos, Calif., 1978-82; v.p. Lynch Mktg. Internat. Inc., Lexington, Ky., 1983-86; pres. Patricia Lynch Properties, Lexington, 1986—, Prosperity Unlimited, Lexington, 1986—. Author: Investing in the Eighties, 1981. Mem. Calif. Tchrs. Assn., Nat. Tchrs. Assn., Calif. Realtors Assn., Profl. Women's Forum, Lexington Women's Network, Kentucky Real Estate Assn., Inst. Cert. Fin. Planners, Internat. Assn. Fin. Planning, Phoenix Inst. Republican. Episcopalian. Home: 333 Lakeshore Dr Lexington KY 40502 Office: Prosperity Unlimited 2050 Idle Hour Ctr Suite 107 Lexington KY 40502

LYNCH, PATRICIA GATES, ambassador; b. Newark, N.J., Apr. 20, 1926; d. William Charles and Mary Frances (McNamee) Lawrence; m. Mahlon Eugene Gates, Dec. 19, 1942 (div. 1972); children: Pamela Townley Gates Sprague, Lawrence Alan; m. William Dennis Lynch. Student, Dartmouth Inst., 1975. Broadcaster Sta. WFAX-Radio, Falls Ch., Va., 1958-68; pub. TV host Sta. WETA, Washington, 1967-68; broadcaster NBC-Radio, Europe, Iran, USSR, 1960-61; internat. broadcaster, producer Voice of Am., Washington, 1962-69; staff asst. to First Lady The White House, Washington, 1969-70; host Breakfast Show, Morning show, 1970-86; U.S. ambassador to Madagascar and the Comoros 1986—; worldwide lectr., 196-86; adv. com. Ind. Fed. Savs. and Loan Assn., Washington, 1970-86. Author stories on Am. for English teaching dept. Radio Sweden, 1967-68, others on internat. broadcasting. Chairperson internat. service com. Washington chpt. ARC, 1979-68. Grantee USIA, 1983; recipient Pub. Service award U.S. Army, 1960. Mem. Council Am. Ambassadors, Am. Women in Radio and TV (pres. 1966-67), Am. News Women's Club. Republican. Epsicopalian. Clubs: Sulgrave (Washington). Office: care Dept State Antananarivo Madagascar Washington DC 20520-2040

LYNCH, PEGGY PIDCOCK, human resources executive; b. Chandler, Okla., Feb. 2, 1938; d. Que C. and Flora Caroline (Hutchison) Pidcock; m. Thomas Patrick Murphy, Aug. 25, 1965 (div. 1967); m. Arthur Theodore Lynch, Feb. 19, 1971. BA in Psychology magna cum laude, Queens Coll., 1977; MBA, Fordham U., 1983. Supr. customer service Braniff Internat. Airlines, Chgo., N.Y.C., Dallas, 1957-71; adminstrv. asst. Hayden Stone Brokerage, N.Y.C., 1973; mgr. personnel Polygram Corp., N.Y.C., 1977-81; benefit authorizer Social Security Adminstrn., Flushing, N.Y., 1981-83; dir. human resources, office adminstrn. Direct Mktg. Assn. Inc., N.Y.C., 1983-88; dir. personnel Thruway Food Mkts. and Shopping Ctr., Walden, N.Y., 1988—. Mem. Am. Soc. Personnel Adminstrs. Democrat. Office: Direct Mktg Assn 6 E 43d St New York NY 10017

LYNCH, SHERRY KAY, counselor; b. Topeka, Kans., Nov. 20, 1957; d. Robert Emmett and Norma Lea Lynch. BA, Randolph-Macon Woman's Coll., 1979; MS, Emporia State U., 1980; PhD, Kans. State U., 1987. Vocat. rehab. counselor Rehab. Services, Topeka, 1980-81, community program cons., 1981-860 Mem. exec. com. Sexual Assault Counseling Program, Topeka, 1983-86, recruitment coordinator, 1983-86, counselor, 1981-86, Cchemical Abuse and Awareness Adv. Com., Ripon, Wis., 1987—, Nat. Singles Conf. Planning Com., Green Lake, Wis., 1987—; area admissions rep. Randolph-Macon Woman's Coll., Lynchburg, Va., 1981-87; counseling intern, Winthrop Coll., Rock Hill, S.C., 1986-87; counselor Ripon (Wis.) Coll., 1987—; bd. dirs., sec.-treas. Ripon Chem. Abuse and Awareness program, 1987—. Recipient Kans. 4-H Key award Extension Service of Kans. State U., 1974; named Internat. 4-H Youth Exchange Ambassador to France, 1977. Mem. Nat. Rehab. Counseling Assn. (bd. dirs. 1982-88, chairperson br. devel. subcouncil 1982-87, chairperson policy and program council 1987-88), Gt. Plains Rehab. Counseling Assn. (newsletter editor 1982-85, bd. dirs. 1983-87, pres. 1984-85, sec. 1986-87), Gt. Plains Rehab. Assn. (bd. dirs. 1983-85, awards chairperson 1984-85), Kans. Rehab. Counseling Assn. (bd. dirs. 1983-86, pres. 1984-85), Kans. Rehab. Assn. (bd. dirs. 1982-85, advt. chairperson 1983-85), Topeka Rehab. Assn. (bd. dirs. 1982-85, sec. 1982-83, pres. 1983-84), Am. Assn. Counseling and Devel., Am. Coll. Personnel Assn., Wis. Coll. Personnel Assn., Assn. for Specialists in Group Work, Wis. Assn. of Profl. Counselors in Higher Edn. Republican. Methodist. Avocation: tennis. Home: 799 Hillside Terrace #9 Ripon WI 54971 Office: Ripon Coll Counseling Ctr PO Box 248 Ripon WI 54971

LYNCH, SONIA, data processing consultant; b. N.Y.C., Sept. 17, 1938; d. Espriela and Sadie Beatrice (Scales) Sarreals; m. Waldro Lynch, Sept. 18, 1981 (div. Oct. 1983). BA in Langs., CCNY, 1960; cert. in French, Sorbonne, 1961. Systems engr. IBM, N.Y.C., 1963-69; cons. Babbage Systems, N.Y.C., 1969-70; project leader Touche Ross, N.Y.C., 1970-73; sr. programmer McGraw-Hill, Inc., Hightstown, N.J., 1973-78; staff data processing cons. Auxton Computer Enterprises, Piscataway, N.J., 1978—. Mem. bd. fellowship St. Andrew Luth. Ch., Silver Spring, 1987—. Downer scholar CUNY, 1960, Dickman Inst. fellow Columbia U., 1960-61. Mem. Assn. for Computing Machinery. Democrat. Home: 13705 Beret Pl Silver Spring MD 20906 Office: Auxton Computer Enterprises 1100 Wayne Ave Silver Spring MD 20910

LYNCH, SUZANNE HARVEY, lawyer; b. Hornell, N.Y., June 30, 1934; d. Leo Bernard and Eleanor (Leahy) Harvey; m. Daniel F. Lynch, Feb. 14, 1958 (div. Dec. 1980); children: Ann Lynch Steinfort, Daniel F. Jr., Eleanor H., John C. AB, Trinity Coll., 1955; JD, Georgetown U., 1958. Bar: Colo. 1960. Assoc. Martin & Johnson, Boulder, Colo., 1963-64; ptnr. Lynch, MacIntosh & Lynch, Denver, 1965-72; dep. dist. atty. City of Denver, 1973-75; trial atty. EEOC, Denver, 1976-78; dir. div. hearing officers State of Colo., Denver, 1979-82; sole practice Denver, 1982—. editor, co-pub. First Report, 1983—. Chmn. Colo. Com. Workmen's Compensation Procedures, 1981. Mem. Colo. Bar Assn., Colo. Women's Bar Assn. (bd. dirs. 1982-83), Am. Assn. Adminstrv. Law Judges. Democrat. Roman Catholic. Office: 950 S Cherry #915 Denver CO 80222

LYNCH, VIVIAN ELIZABETH, lawyer; b. Detroit, June 17, 1940; d. Edward Winemac and Winifred (Grant) L.; m. Robert L. Rubin, Sept. 18, 1963 (div. Aug. 1973); children: David B., Edward A., Ruth L. BA, Wayne State U., 1960, JD, 1962. Bar: Nev. 1985, U.S. Dist. Ct. Nev. 1985, U.S. Ct. Appeals (9th cir.) 1986. Ptnr., exec. dir. Club Tahoe, Incline Village, Nev., 1978-81; exec. adminstr. Harbor/Depoe Bay, Oreg., 1982; ptnr. Hamilton and Lynch, Reno, 1985—; cons. Oreg. Real Estate Div., Salem, 1982-83; conv. speaker Western Regional Assn. Regulatory Agys., Incline Village, 1983. Editor Survey/Mich. Law Rev., 1961. Wayne State U. scholar, 1961-62. Mem. Washoe County Bar Assn., Am. Trial Lawyers Assn., Nev. Trial Lawyers Assn. (assoc. editor Advocate jour., mem. Amicus Curiae com., Judiciary com., lectr.). Republican. Roman Catholic. Office: Hamilton and Lynch 321 S Arlington Ave Reno NV 89501

LYNCH STEINFORT, ANN SUTHERLAND, marketing and sales executive; b. Washington, Nov. 14, 1957; d. Daniel Frances and Suzanne (Harvey) L.; m. Friedrich W. Steinfort, June 9, 1984. Student, U. Colo., 1977-79. Instr. recreation High Country Inn, Winter Park, Colo., 1977-79; mgr. Ski Depot Sports, Winter Park, Colo., 1979-81; dir. sales SilverCreek Resort, Granby, Colo., 1982-83; v.p. mktg./sales Alpine Peaks Inc., Winter Park, 1983—. Mem. Denver Conv. and Visitors Bur., 1983—; mem. mktg. com. Winter Park Resort Chamber, 1987—. Democrat. Roman Catholic. Home: PO Box 174 Winter Park CO 80482 Office: Alpine Peaks Inc 55 GCR #705 Winter Park CO 80482

LYND, NANCY HELLMAN, editor; b. Bklyn., Nov. 10, 1944; d. Al and Esther Deborah (Kleinspiec) Hellman; B.S., N.Y. U., 1965; M.A., Calif. State U., Northridge, 1973, postgrad., Fullerton, 1978-79, Dominguez Hills, 1977-78; m. William Lynd, July 3, 1973; children—Allyn David Lynd, Barry Howard Lynd. Secondary sch. tchr., N.Y., La., Calif., 1965-67; free lance writer, 1968-72; tchr. Calif. State U., Northridge, 1972-73; programmer/tech. writer Logicon/Intercomp, Inc., Torrance, Calif., 1974-76; pres. Lynd Assos., Santa Ana, Calif., 1976-80; pres. Tech. Text, Inc., 1980-83; mng. editor

Liberty Street Chronicle, 1984-85, UNISYS Corp., 1985—; asst. sec. Mfrs. Resources and Planning, Inc., Santa Ana, 1977-78; cons. Bauer's Mus., 1979—. Active Women for Polit. Action, Orange County Music Center, Inc., South Coast Repetorary Theater. Mem. NOW, Am. Bus. Women's Assn., Nat. Women's Network. Jewish.

LYNN, ADRIAN CLAIRE, retail buyer; b. Jamaica, N.Y., June 30, 1953; d. John and Ruthe Elizabeth (Hughes) L. BS in Clothing and Textiles, Mich. State U., 1975. Mgmt. trainee Montgomery Ward & Co., Inc., Laurel, Md., 1975-76; dept. mgr. Montgomery Ward & Co., Inc., Falls Church, Va., 1976-78; regional merchandiser Montgomery Ward & Co., Inc., Catonsville, Md., 1978-83; asst. replenishment mgr. Montgomery Ward & Co., N.Y.C., 1983-85, asst. jr. sportswear buyer, 1985-87, buyer jr. casual & career sportswear & swimwear, 1987—; advisor Retail Checklist and Adv. Com., N.Y.C., 1979-81. Editor: Fashion Merchandising Systems Tng. Manual, 1984. Active Big Sisters Am., East Lansing, Mich., 1973. Mem. Have a Heart Found. Inc., Delta Sigma Theta. Democrat. Roman Catholic. Home: 5445 N Sheridan Rd #402 Chicago IL 60640

LYNN, DONNA MARIA, public relations executive, small business owner, writer; b. Hollywood, Calif., Oct. 4, 1945; d. Kane Wallace Lynn and Rita (Piazza) Maxwell; m. Dennis D. Schreffler, 1965 (div. 1973); children: Scott G. Schreffler, Susan M. Schreffler. Student, UCLA, 1963-65, U. Utah, 1965-68; BA, U. Ark., 1970; postgrad. in law, U. Balt., 1973-74. Lobbyist, dir. UniServe div. NEA, Washington, 1970-77; pres., chief exec. officer Lynn Assocs., Inc., Westport, Conn., 1977—; mgr. media relations Perrier/Great Waters of France, N.Y.C., 1978-79; sr. cons. The Nestle Co., Washington and White Plains, N.Y., 1979-83; dep. dir. sports div. Hill & Knowlton, N.Y.C., 1983-85; mgr. pub. relations Avon Products, Inc., N.Y.C., 1985-86; supr. account group Daniel J. Edelman, N.Y.C., 1979-81. Features editor: Flight Attendant mag., 1986-87; contbr. numerous articles to newspapers and mags. Founder, dir. Earth Day in Ark., 1970; apptd. del. White House Conf. on Children and Youth, Washington, 1970; liaison White House Press Office, Dem. Nat. Conv., N.Y., 1979; apptd. commr. Md. Commn. for Women, Annapolis, 1976-77; pres. Annapolis Summer Garden Theatre, 1976-78; mem. bus. adv. bd. Nat Down Syndrome Soc., N.Y., 1985—. Mem. Am. Mgmt. Assn., The Fashion Group, Pub. Relations Soc. Am., NEA (life; legis. chair Ark. chpt. 1970-73), Phi Alpha Theta. Office: 2 Burnham Hill Westport CT 06880

LYNN, EVADNA SAYWELL, investment analyst; b. Oakland, Calif., June 1935; d. Lawrence G. Saywell; m. Richard Keppie Lynn, Dec. 28, 1962; children—Douglas, Lisa. B.A., U. Calif.-Berkeley, M.A. in Econs. Chartered fin. analyst. Vice pres. Paine Webber, N.Y.C., 1974-77, Wainwright Securities, N.Y.C., 1977-78, Merrill Lynch Capital Markets, N.Y.C., 1978—. Mem. N.Y. Soc. Security Analysts, San Francisco Security Analysts (treas. 1973-74). Club: Fin. Women's of San Francisco (pres. 1967). Office: Merrill Lynch Capital Markets N Tower World Fin Ctr New York NY 10281

LYNN, GERI DUNLAP, educator; b. Odessa, Tex., Sept. 30, 1954; d. Jerry Cecil and Laquita Adelia (Whisenhunt) Dunlap; m. A. Dale Lynn, June 18, 1983. Student, Odessa Coll., 1972-74; BS in Edn., U. Tex., 1982, MEd, 1987. Lic. tchr., Tex. Child care worker emotionally disturbed adolescents Mary Lee Sch., Austin, Tex., 1979-81; homebound tchr. Balcones Coop., Austin, 1982; tchr. severe and profound unit Round Rock (Tex.) High Sch., 1982-84; tchr. trainable mentally retarded, 1984—; tchr., developer severe and profoundly handicapped unit Westwood High Sch. Annex, Austin, 1987—; tchr. sign lang. Vol., Tex. Spl. Olympics, 1982—, coach, mem. planning com., 1983—, head coach bowling, basketball and gymnastics, 1983—, head coach soccer, track and field, 1984—. Vol. deaf and blind children Tex. Lions, 1981—. Hattie Hewlitt Found. scholar, 1979-81. Mem. Tex. Soc. Autistic Citizens, Kappa Delta Pi. Address: 18504 Lakeview Dr E Jonestown TX 78641

LYNN, LOIS ANN, lawyer; b. Butler, Mo., July 25, 1953; d. George William Lynn and Lois Isabel (Donalson) Davidson. B.A. in Polit. Sci., Wichita State U., 1979; J.D., Washburn Law Sch., 1981. Bar: Kans. 1983. Staff atty. child support enforcement div. State of Kans. Social Rehab. Services, Wichita, 1984—. Campaign organizer Jack Williams for Congress, Wichita, 1976. Mem. Wichita Bar Assn., Kans. Bar Assn., ABA, Assn. Trial Lawyers Am., Am. Judicature Soc., Young Democrats. Home: 7032 Farmview St Wichita KS 67207 Office: State of Kans Dept Social Rehab Services PO Box 1620 Wichita KS 67201

LYNN, LORETTA WEBB (MRS. OLIVER LYNN, JR.), singer; b. Butcher Hollow, Ky., Apr. 14, 1935; d. Ted and Clara (Butcher) Webb; m. Oliver V. Lynn, Jr., Jan. 10, 1948; children—Betty Sue Lynn Markworth, Jack Benny (dec.), Clara Lynn Lyell, Ernest Ray, Peggy, Patsy. Student pub. schs. Sec.-treas. Loretta Lynn Enterprises; v.p. United Talent, Inc.; hon. chmn. bd. Loretta Lynn Western Stores. Country vocalist with MCA records, 1961—(numerous gold albums); most recent album Just a Woman, 1985. Author: Coal Miner's Daughter, 1976. Hon. rep. United Giver's Fund, 1971. Named Country Music Assn. Female Vocalist of Year 1967, 72, 73, Entertainer of Year, 1972, named Top Duet of 1972, 73, 74, 75; recipient Grammy award 1971, Am. Music award 1978, named Entertainer of Decade, Acad. Country Music 1980. Office: care United Talent Inc PO Box 23470 Nashville TN 37202 also: care MCA Records Inc 70 Universal City Plaza Universal City CA 91608 *

LYNN, NANNE JOYCE, educator; b. Muncie, Ind., Sept. 27, 1938; d. Hal Paul and Rose Mary (Femyer) Duffey; divorced;children: Joel Robert, Michael Charles, Lorry Rose. BA, Ball State U., 1960, MA, 1974. Cert. secondary tchr. Dir. child welfare Del. County Dept. of Welfare, Muncie, 1958-63; tchr. Coachella Valley Unified Sch. Dist., Thermal, Calif., 1978—; freelance reporter Desert Sun, Palm Springs, Calif., Palm Desert Post, Palm Desert, Calif., 1978-80. Vol. Birch Bayh for Pres. campaign, Ind., 1970-71. Mem. Palm Desert C. of C. (pub. relations 1980-83), Bus. Profls. Women (ednl. chmn. 1973-74), Phi Delta Kappa, Alpha Phi Gamma. Office: Coachella Valley HIgh Sch 83-800 Airport Blvd Thermal CA 92274

LYNN, PAULINE JUDITH WARDLOW, lawyer; b. Columbus, Ohio, Nov. 14, 1920; d. Charles and Helen P. (Christman) Wardlow; student Wellesley Coll., 1938-40; B.A., Ohio State U., 1942, J.D., 1948; m. Arthur D. Lynn, Jr., Dec. 29, 1943; children—Pamela Wardlow, Constance Karen, Deborah Joanne, Patricia Diane. Admitted to Ohio bar, 1948; practiced in Columbus, 1948-49. Troop leader Girl Scouts U.S.A., 1969-71. Mem. ABA, Columbus Bar Assn., Phi Beta Kappa, Kappa Kappa Gamma (mem. research com. Heritage mus. 1981-87), Pi Sigma Alpha. Republican. Episcopalian. Home: 2679 Wexford Rd Columbus OH 43221

LYNN, SHEILAH ANN, director college program, consultant; b. Anderson, Ind., Jan. 28, 1947; d. John Benton and Kathleen (Taylor) Bussabarger; m. John Hoftyzer, Dec. 21, 1968 (div. June 1982); children: Melanie Kay, John Theo; m. Guy C. Lynn, May 20, 1984. BS, Ind. U., 1969; postgrad., U. N.C., Greensboro, 1972-74; diploma, Data Processing Inst., Tampa, Fla., 1983. Lic. in real estate. Bookkeeper John Hancock Life Ins. Co., Greensboro, 1970-72; freelance seminar leader and devel. Dhahran, Saudi Arabia, 1978-82; dir. programming Fla. Tech. Inst., Jacksonville, 1983-84, instr. in computer sci., 1984-85; real estate sales assoc. Fla. Recreational Ranches, Gainesville, 1985; coordinator informational program Fal. Community Coll., Jacksonville, 1986—; cons. programmer, analyst Postmasters Co., Jacksonville, Fla., 1986—; pres. Acad. Options Cons., Jacksonville, 1986—. Mem. Jacksonville Community Council, Inc., 1986-87, Fla. Literacy Coalition, 1986-87. Mem. Nat. Assn. Female Execs., Fla. Assn. Ednl. Data Systems, Bus. and Profl. Women, Jacksonville C. of C. (bd. dirs. South Council, 1987, internat. devel. bd., 1987). Democrat.

LYON, BERENICE IOLA CLARK, civic worker; b. Westfield, Pa., June 4, 1920; d. Stephen Artemus and Ruth Gertrude (Tubbs) Clark; m. Robert Louis Lyon, May 28, 1944. Pres., Twin Tiers Geneal. Soc., N.Y. and Pa., 1976-88, pub. jour. Gemini; Pa. state pres. Colonial Dames XVII Century, 1981-83, state chmn. heraldry, 1977-79, hon. state pres., 1983—, organizer-pres. Tyoga Gateway chpt., 1973-75, Treaty Elm chpt., 1975-77, state yearbook-directory compiler, 1979-81, Pa. state chmn. 1988—; N.Y. state chmn. DAR, 1968-71, pres. N.Y. council of regents, 1968-71, regent Corning (N.Y.) chpt. 1965-68, Wellsboro (Pa.) chpt., 1977-80, Pa. state vice chmn., 1980-83, Pa. dist. dir., 1983-88, Pa. state chmn., 1987—; N.Y. state chmn. Daus. Am. Colonists, 1965—, Atlantic Coast chmn., 1970-79, organizer-regent Forbidden Trail chpt., 1967-76, regent, 1974-76, 83-88, Pa. state chmn. 1987—; condr. geneal. seminars; speaker to convs., meetings, TV, radio; contbr. articles on heraldry to 17th Century Rev., 1978-79. Recipient medal of appreciation SAR, 1966. Mem. Ams. of Royal Descent, Descs. Knights of Garter, Magna Carta Dames, Old Plymouth Colony Descs., Order of Crown, Order of Washington, Plantagenet Soc., Mansfield Friends of Library (pres. 1980-81). Clubs: Kiwanis Ladies, Clionian Circle (Corning); Mansfield (Pa.) Garden (pres. 1979-80), N.Y. Fedn. Garden Clubs (sect. chmn. 1969-73). Home: Lowenhof 168A Bailey Creek Rd Millerton PA 16936

LYON, MARTHA SUE, naval officer, research engineer; b. Louisville, Oct. 3, 1935; d. Harry Bowman and Erma Louise (Moreland) Lyon. B.A. in Chemistry, U. Louisville, 1959; M.Ed. in Math., Northeastern Ill. U., 1974. Cert. tchr. Ill., Ky. Research assoc. U. Louisville Med. Sch., 1959-61, 62-63; commd. ensign, USNR, 1965, advanced through grades to comdr., 1983; instr. instrumentation chemistry Northwestern U., Evanston, Ill., 1968-70; tchr. sci., chemistry, gifted math. Waukegan (Ill.) pub. schs., 1970-75; phys. scientist Library of Congress, Washington, 1975-76; research engr. Lockheed Missiles & Space Co., Sunnyvale, Calif., 1976-77; instr., assoc. chmn. dept. physics U.S. Naval Acad., Annapolis, Md., 1977-80; analyst Systems Analysis Div., Office of Chief of Naval Ops. Staff, Washington, 1980-81; comdg. officer Naval Res. Ctr., Stockton, Calif., 1981-83; mem. faculty Def. Intelligence Coll., 1983-85; program mgr. Space and Naval Warfare Systems Command, 1985-86, commanding officer PERSUPPACT Memphis, 1986-88; program mgr. Space and Naval Warfare Systems Command, 1988—. Grantee Am. Heart Assn., 1960-62, NSF, 1971, 72. Mem. Soc. Women Engrs., Am. Statis. Assn., Am. Soc. Photogrammetry, Internat. Conf. Women in Sci. Engring. (protocol chair), Mensa, Zeta Tau Alpha, Delta Phi Alpha. Club: Order of Ea. Star. Developer processes used in archival photography, carbon-14 analyses; presenter of papers at profl. cons. Mailing Address: PO Box 845 Millington TN 38053

LYON-RODMAN, SYLVIA, television executive; b. Santiago, Chile, June 25, 1946; came to U.S., 1971, naturalized, 1983; d. Arturo A. and Julie (Valverde) Lyon; student UCLA, 1971-73; m. John S. Rodman, June 6, 1980; children—Lindsay Lyon, Bryan Lyon, Arielle Lyon. Copywriter Eastman Advt., Chile, 1968-70, J. Walter Thompson Advt., Brazil, 1970-71; receptionist KMEX-TV, 1974, public relations exec., 1974-75; dir. advt. and public relations Spanish Internat. Network, Inc., N.Y.C., 1977, asst. to pres., 1978, dir. programming Galavision, 1979—. Trustee Burden Center for the Aged, N.Y.C., 1981—; pres. Cygnus Internat., Inc. Mem. Women in Cable, Parents League of N.Y. (program dir.). Home: 19 E 72d St New York NY 10021

LYONS, CHERIE ANN, educational administrator, author; b. Denver, Dec. 15, 1948; d. Clair Leroy and Mary Margaret (Benner) Case; m. David Greer Lyons, Aug. 22, 1970; children—Michael Greer, Andrea Christine. B.S., U. Colo., 1971, M.A., 1975. Prof. tchr. cert., adminstr. cert. Colo. Dept. Edn. Tchr. English, Cherry Creek Schs., 1971-76; tchr. English, health edn. Jefferson County Schs., Lakewood, Colo., 1971-76, curriculum writer, 1975-78, project dir. career edn., 1976-81, staff devel. specialist, 1981-87, jr. high sch. principal, 1987-88, coordinator prevention programs, 1988—; cons. Region VII Tng. Ctr., U.S. Dept. Edn.; dir. Sch. Team Approach to Substance Abuse Prevention, Jefferson County. Coordinator Jefferson County Prevention Task Force; mem. Lakeshore Homeowners Assn. Mem. Jefferson County Edn. Assn., Colo. Edn. Assn., NEA, Colo. Lang. Arts Soc., Nat. Council Tchrs. English, Nat. Staff Devel. Council, Assn. Supervision and Curriculum Devel., Nat. Soc. for Study of Edn., Internat. Platform Assn., Phi Delta Kappa. Democrat. Episcopalian. Author: The Writing Process: A Program of Composition and Applied Grammar, Book 12, 1982. Home: 8041 Lamar St Arvada CO 80003 Office: Jefferson County Schs 1829 Denver West Dr Bldg 27 Golden CO 80401

LYONS, CYNTHIA LOUISE, airline maintenance manager, free-lance writer; b. Ishpeming, Mich., Aug. 21, 1960; d. Charles Robert and Clarice Virginia (DeVold) L. Student, U. Md., Sigonella, Sicily, Italy, 1981-82. Enlisted USN, 1978; supply logistician Navy Fleet Staff, San Diego, 1979-81; rotable pool mgr. Navy Base Supply, Sigonella, Italy, 1981-82; resigned 1982; materials mgr. maintenance div. Simmons Airlines, Freeland, Mich., 1983-85; asst. purchasing mgr. Simmons Airlines, Negaunee, Mich., 1985-86, sr. mgr. materials, 1986-87; dir. materials maintenance div. Ea. Express/Bar Harbor Airlines, Bangor, Maine, 1987—; mem. material rev. bd., modification approval bd., quality control com. Simmons Airlines, 1986-87; sec. internat. exec. bd. Shorts Aircraft Operators, Belfast, Northern Ireland, 1987—. Contbr. lit. mags. Recipient Cert. of Appreciation Planned Parenthood Fedn., 1987—. Mem. Nat. Assn. Female Execs., Upper Mich. Writers Assn., NOW. Democrat. Lutheran. Home: 420 S Main St Apt 1 Brewer ME 04412 Office: Ea Express/Bar Harbor Airlines Bangor Internat Airport Maintenance Div Bldg 463 Bangor ME 04401

LYONS, EMILY BRADLEY, vision therapist; b. Fresno, Calif.; d. Rollen Ellsworth and Emma Hazel (Bradley) Stump; m. Cecil Venard Lyons, Oct. 30, 1939 (dec. 1968); m. Robert Barnes Monroe, Jan. 19, 1917. Artist, designer Art Studio, Berkeley, Calif., 1928-36; vision therapist Office C. Venard Lyons, O.D., San Francisco, 1937-66, Office Wayne Musser, O.D., Petaluma, Calif., 1966-84; visual cons. Jane Brown Found. for Dance and Related Studies, Oakland, Calif., 1970—; assoc. dir. optometric asst. Optometric Extension Program Found., Santa Ana, Calif., 1969—; lectr., instr. Lyons Visualization Seminars, 1965—. Author: How to Use Your Power of Visualization, 1980; contbr. articles to profl. jours. Recipient award N.W. Congress of Optometry, 1963, Calif. Optometric Assn., 1968, Pres. award Coll. of Optometrists in Vision Devel., 1976. Republican. Office: Lyons Visualization Series 19065 Saint Croy Rd Red Bluff CA 96080

LYOU, KEITH WEEKS (KAY), editor; b. Los Angeles, Aug. 2, 1930; d. Howard Keith Weeks and Ruth Manson (Day) Wood; m. Joseph Lyou, Mar. 26, 1955 (div. 1972); children: Tracy Ann, Joseph Keith. BS, Lindenwood Coll., 1977, MA, 1979. Cert. community coll. instr., Calif. Editorial asst. Annals of Biomed. Engring., Culver City, Calif., 1971-76; exec. asst. Biomed. Engring. Soc., Culver City, 1974-81; editor Inkslingers, Culver City, 1974—; editor biotechnology lab. UCLA, 1974-81, campus advisor theses and dissertations , 1983-86; exec. asst. Biomed. Engring. Soc., Culver City, 1974-81; instr. adult sch. Culver City Unified Sch. Dist., 1979-81. mng. editor Am. Intra-Ocular Implant Soc. Jour., Santa Monica, 1982-83. Trustee Culver City Bd. Edn., 1981—, pres. bd., 1987; counselor Adv. Ctr. for Edn. and Career Counseling, Santa Monica, Calif., 1981-82; vice chair project area com. Project and Redevel., Culver City, 1975-77, 85, chair 1979-82; bd. dirs. Culver City Foster Children's Assn., 1981—. Recipient Citizen Recognition award Culver City C. of C. Mem. Bus. and Profl. Women, Biomed. Engring. Soc., Calif. Elected Women's Assn. for Edn. and Research, LWV. Democrat. Office: Inkslingers PO Box 2160 Culver City CA 90230

LYSTAD, MARY HANEMANN (MRS. ROBERT LYSTAD), sociologist, author; b. New Orleans, Apr. 11, 1928; d. James and Mary (Douglass) Hanemann; m. Robert Lystad, June 20, 1953; children: Lisa Douglass, Anne Hanemann, Mary Lunde, Robert Douglass, James Hanemann. A.B. cum laude, Newcomb Coll., 1949; M.A., Columbia U., 1951; Ph.D., Tulane U., 1955. Postdoctoral fellow social psychology S.E. La. Hosp., Mandeville, 1955-57; field research social psychology Ghana, 1957-58, South Africa, Swaziland, and People's Republic of China, 1968; chief sociologist Collaborative Child Devel. Project, Charity Hosp. La., New Orleans, 1958-61; feature writer African div. Voice Am., Washington, 1964-73; program analyst NIMH, Washington, 1968-78; asso. dir. for planning and coordination div. spl. mental health programs NIMH, 1978-80; chief Nat. Center for Prevention and Control of Rape, 1980-83, Center Mental Health Studies of Emergencies, 1983—; cons. on youth Nat. Goals Research Staff, White House, Washington, 1969-70. Author: Millicent the Monster, 1968, Social Aspects of Alienation, 1969, Jennifer Takes Over P.S. 94, 1972, James the Jaguar, 1972, As They See It: Changing Values of College Youth, 1972, That New Boy, 1973, Halloween Parade, 1973, Violence at Home, 1974, A Child's World As Seen in His Stories and Drawings, 1974, From Dr. Mather to Dr. Seuss: 200 Years of American Books for Children, 1980, At Home in America, 1983; editor: Innovations in Mental Health Services to Disaster Victims, 1985, Violence in the Home: Interdisciplinary Perspectives, 1986, Mental Health Response to Mass Emergencies: Theory and Practice, 1988. Recipient Spl. Recognition award USPHS, 1983, Alumna Centennial award Newcomb Coll., 1986. Home: 4900 Scarsdale Rd Washington DC 20016 Office: 5600 Fishers Ln Rockville MD 20852

MA, JING HENG, East Asian languages educator; b. Beijing, Mar. 15, 1932; came to U.S., 1963; d. Xue Shu and Guo Ying (Yin) Sheng; m. Wei-Yi Ma, Sept. 28, 1958; children: Lyou-fu, Syau-fu. BEd, Taiwan Normal U., 1958; MA, Philippine Women's U., 1963; MA in Applied Linguistics, U. Mich., 1971, PhD in Linguistics, 1983. Instr. Chinese Cornell U. Extension Program, Taipei, Taiwan, 1959-62; lectr. Chinese U. Mich., Ann Arbor, 1963-84; assoc. prof., chairperson dept. East Asian langs. Williams Coll., Williamstown, Mass., 1984—; vis. prof. Chinese Dept., Wellesley Coll., 1988-89. Author: Chinese Language Patterns, 1985, A Study of the Mandarin Chinese Verb Suffix Zhe, 1986. Mem. Chinese Lang. Tchr.'s Assn., Assn. for Asian Studies. Home: 3175 Dolph Dr Ann Arbor MI 48103 Office: Williams Coll Stetson Hall Williamstown MA 01267

MAARBJERG, MARY PENZOLD, office equipment company executive; b. Norfolk, Va., Oct. 2, 1943; d. Edmund Theodore and Lucy Adelaide (Singleton) Penzold; m. John Peder Maarbjerg, Oct. 20, 1966; 1 son, Martin Peder. A.B., Hollins Coll., 1965; M.B.A., Wharton Sch., Pa., 1969. Cons. bus. and fin., Stamford, Conn., 1977-78; corp. staff analyst Pitney Bowes, Inc., Stamford, Conn., 1978-80, mgr. pension and benefit fin. 1980-81, dir. investor relations, 1981-85; v.p. planning and devel. Pitney Bowes Credit Corp., Norwalk, Conn., 1985-86; treas., v.p. planning Pitney Bowes Credit Corp., 1986—. Mem. adv. com. City of Stamford Mcpl. Employees Retirement Fund, 1980-85; mem. fin. adv. com. YWCA, Stamford, 1982-86; bd. dirs. Stamford Symphony, 1985—, Vis. Nurses Assn., 1984-86, Am. Recorder Soc., 1986—. Fellow Royal Statis. Soc.; mem. Fin. Execs. Inst., Phi Beta Kappa. Congregationalist. Office: Pitney Bowes Credit Corp 201 Merritt Seven Norwalk CT 06856

MAARTMAN-MOE, ESTELLE PLATIN, nurse, nursing administrator; b. Oslo, Norway; came to U.S., 1948; d. Ragnvald and Constance Estelle (Platin) M.; m. Thomas J. Trabucco, Mar. 29, 1969 (div. May 1978). AA in Nursing, Northeastern U., 1968; student, SUNY, 1976; BS in Nursing, U. Mass., 1981. RN. Staff nurse Mass. Gen. Hosp., Boston, 1968-69, head nurse, 1969-70; staff nurse Holyoke (Mass.) Hosp., 1970-71; supr. Health Services U. Mass., Amherst, 1971-74, nurse practitioner, 1974-76, nurse practitioner family and pediatrics, 1976—, dir. nursing, 1983—. Recipient Ross award Ross Pharmaceuticals, 1976. Office: U Mass Health Services Amherst MA 01003

MAAS, JANE A., development executive; b. Newark, Ohio, Oct. 8, 1943; d. Donald Louis and B. Lucille Elliott; children: Michelle, Eliot. Exec. asst. acct. Arthur Young & Co., Birmingham, Ala., 1977-79; dir. devel. Northside Christian Schs., St. Petersburg, Fla., 1983-86, Mental Health Service of So. Pinellas, St. Petersburg, 1986—. Active Sertoma Charities, 1973-76, Gulf Coast Symphony Guild, 1974-78, League to Aid Retarded Children, 1974—; bd. dirs. YWCA , 1977, Maas Bros. Consumer Adv. Bd., 1976-77, Friends of Research U. South Fla., Jr. League St. Petersburg; campaign treas. Judge Richard Luce; active various Republican campaigns. Mem. Nat. Soc. Fund Raising Execs. (v.p. 1984—), St. Petersburg C. of C., Nat. Assn. Female Execs., Seminole C. of C. Republican. Mem. Christian Ch. Office: USF Psychiatry Ctr 3515 E Fletcher Tampa FL 33613

MAASS, VERA SONJA, psychologist; b. Berlin, Germany, July 6, 1931; came to U.S., 1958; d. Willy Ernst and Wally Elizabeth (Reinke) Keck; m. Joachim Adolf Maass, Dec. 24, 1954 (div.). BA, Monmouth Coll., 1971; MA, Lehigh U., 1974; PhD, U. Mo., 1978. Tutor in adult basic edn. Teaching Asst. Edn., Kansas City, Mo., 1973-74; clin. intern U. Ky. Med. Sch., Lexington, 1975-76; psychologist, therapist Dunn Mental Health Ctr., Richmond, Ind., 1976-80; psychology br. dir. Dunn Mental Health Ctr., Winchester, Ind., 1980-83; psychology outpatient clin. supr. Tri-County Mental Health Ctr., Indpls., 1983-85; psychology cons. Disability Determination Div., Indpls., 1985—; pres. clin. dir. Living Skills Inst., Inc., Indpls., 1982—; lectr. internat. confs., 1973—. Mem. adv. bd. Sta. WXTZ, Indpls., Indpls. Mus. Art, Indpls. Art League. Mem. Am. Psychol. Assn., Am. Assn. Counseling Devel., Am. Assn. Sex Educators, Counselors and Therapists (cert.), Internat. Acad. Profl. Counseling and Psychotherapy, Ind. Psychol. Assn., League of Aging Service Providers (bd. dirs.). Home: 8204 Westfield Blvd Indianapolis IN 46240 Office: Living Skills Inst Inc 8204 Westfield Blvd Indianapolis IN 46240

MABIE, RUTH MARIE, realtor; b. Pueblo, Colo., Feb. 7; d. Newton Everett and Florence Ellen Allen; M.B.A., La Jolla U., 1980, Ph.D., 1981; m. Richard O. Mabie, Nov. 29, 1946; 1 son, Ward A. Mgr., LaMont Modeling Sch., San Diego, 1962; tchr. Am. Bus. Coll., San Diego, 1964-66; fashion modeling, 1960-72; owner, broker Ruth Mabile Realty, San Diego, 1972—; asst. v.p. Skil-Bilt, Inc., 1976—; dir. Mabie & Mintz, Inc. Bd. dirs. Multiple Sclerosis Dr., 1971—. Mem. San Diego Bd. Realtors, Nat. Assn. Female Execs. Republican. Office: 2231 Camino del Rio So #302 San Diego CA 92108-3605

MACALUSO, MARY LINA, construction company executive; b. N.Y.C., June 14, 1923; d. Gaetano and Rosaria (LaSpina) Cristaldi; widowed; children: William V., Richard W. BS in Bus. Mgmt., Fairleigh Dickinson U., 1971. Pres. Macaluso Builders, Hasbrouck Heights, N.J., 1961—. Advisor Hasbrouck Heights Housing Project, 1986-87. Home and Office: 624 Summit Ave Hackensack NJ 07601

MACAULAY, ALICE ITTNER, physician; b. Bklyn.; d. William and Anna (Holzman) Ittner; B.A. cum laude, Barnard Coll., postgrad., 1944-46; M.D., N.Y. Med. Coll., 1950; postgrad. N.Y. U., 1952-53; M.Sc., L.I. U. at Mercy Coll., 1982, cert. in gerontology, 1983; m. David Harvard Macaulay, July 10, 1936 (dec. 1971). Tchr. N.Y.C. high schs., until 1946; actress Columbia Lab. Players, 1928—, Summer Stock, Roxbury, Conn., 1932-34, Old Vic, London, 1934-35; intern and resident Grasslands Hosp., Valhalla, N.Y., 1950-56, hosp. practice internal medicine Grasslands Hosp., 1956-74, dir. outpatient services, 1956-74, asso. attending internal medicine, 1958-76, chmn. pharmacy and therapeutics com., 1967-74, mem. adminstrv. team, 1961-74, named to Nat. Disting. Service Registry for Med. and Vocat. Rehab., 1987—; hon. attending in internal medicine Westchester County Med. Center, 1976-84, attending emeritus, 1984—; liaison hosp. officer for devel. of Neighborhood Health Centers; chmn. med. adv. bd. Westchester County Public Health Nursing; med. cons., dir. med. affairs Westchester Community Coll.; cons. Office of Vocat. Rehab. and State Med. Programs; cons. hypertension, 1956—; med. adv. bd. Westchester Heart Assn., chmn. com. on hypertension, 1973-75; prof. medicine Pace U. Grad. Sch. Nursing, 1974-77; vocat. rehab. specialist, 1975—; adv. bd. Columbia U. Ctr. for Geriatrics. Bd. dirs., med. cons. Donald Reed Speech Center, 1976—. Mem. AMA, Westchester Acad. Medicine, N.Y. State Med. Soc., Westchester, Am. heart assns., AAAS Cor et Manus, Contin, Am. Lung Assn., N.Y. Trudeau Soc., Alpha Epsilon Iota, Sigma Phi Omega (award 1984). Clubs: Soroptimists; Ardsley Country. Address: Hudson House Ardsley-on-Hudson NY 10503

MACBAIN, MARY RAPP, accountant, consultant; b. Williamson, W.Va., Jan. 8, 1951; d. Roy Thomas and Lucille (Middendorf) Rapp; m. Bruce Douglas MacBain, Nov. 3, 1974; children: Timothy Roy, Michelle Terese. BA, Western Ill. U., 1980; MS in Acctg., Wichita State U., 1983. CPA, Kans. Adminstrv. asst. Northwestern U. Med. Ctr., Chgo., 1970-78; staff acct. Baird, Kurtz & Dobson, Wichita, Kans., 1983; budget specialist St. Francis Regional Med. Ctr., Wichita, 1983-84; owner Mary MacBain and Co., Wichita, 1984—; adj. instr. Wichita State U., 1984-85, Webster U., St. Louis, 1986-87. Vol. Am. Cancer Soc., Wichita, 1984-85. Mem. Am. Inst. CPA's (speaker microcomputer conf. 1985-86, 88, steering com. 1988—), Kans. Soc. CPA's (pres., treas. sec. Wichita chpt. micro users group 1985-88), Nat. Assn. CPA's (bd. dirs. Wichita chpt. 1983-85). Roman Catholic. Club: Wichita Running (bd. dirs. 1983-85). Home and Office: 142 N Dellrose Wichita KS 67208

MACCABEE, JOYCE BARBARA, citizens advocate; b. Queens, N.Y., Dec. 19, 1932; d. Gustave and Charlotte (Michalowski) Fisher; m. Alfred R. Maccabee, June 4, 1955; children: Kevin, Ronald, Susan. Diploma in Adminstrv.-Secretarial, Wood Secretarial Finishing Sch., 1952. V.p. Logus Realty Corp., Bklyn., 1960-73; owner A & M Catering, East Patchogue, N.Y., 1962-79; with S.C. Police Dept., 1969-79; citizens adv. Town of Brookhaven, Medford, N.Y., 1980—. Mem. Nat. Fedn. Rep. Women, Ronald Reagan Pres.'s Trust, Washington, 1985—; com.person Town of Brookhaven, Farmingdale, N.Y., 1975—; pres., v.p., sec. Louis A. Fuoco Rep. Club, East Patochogue, 1977-82. Mem. Profl. Women in Govt. Roman Catholic. Lodge: Lions (v.p. 1985, pres. 1987). Home: 164 Roseland Ln East Patchogue NY 11772 Office: Town of Brookhaven Dept Housing 3233 Rt 112 Medford NY 11763

MACCALLUM, ANNE WHICHARD, nurse, educator, administrator; b. Portsmouth, Va., Nov. 29, 1944; d. Murray P. and Ida Lee (Allen) Whichard; m. M. Reid MacCallum, Sept. 12, 1964; 1 child, Bruce. Student Va. Commonwealth U., 1962-64, M.S., 1978; B.S. in Nursing, Old Dominion U., 1969. Registered nurse, Va. Nursing instr. Norfolk Tech. Vocat. Ctr., Va., 1969-71, Chesapeake Tech. Ctr., Va., 1971-73, Norfolk Gen. Hosp., 1973-76, 1978-81; coordinator patient edn. and discharge planning Children's Hosp. of King's Daughters, Norfolk, 1981-83, assoc. dir. nursing, 1983-85, dir. edn. and profl. devel., 1985—. Mem. Assn. for Care Children's Health, Va. Nurses Assn. (dist. bd. dirs. 1980-83, dist. pres. 1984-87, pres. elect 1987, chmn. council dist. presidents 1986), Va. Nurses Assn. Maternal Health Profl. Practice Group (chmn. dist. 1979-80, state nominating chmn. 1981), Soc. for Health Edn. Tng., Sigma Theta Tau. Methodist. Avocation: sailing. Office: Children's Hosp of King's Daus 800 W Olney Rd Norfolk VA 23507

MACCALLUM, (EDYTHE) LORENE, pharmacist, consultant; b. Monte Vista, Colo., Nov. 29, 1928; d. Francis Whittier and Bernice Viola (Martin) Scott; m. David Robertson MacCallum, June 12, 1952; children: Suzanne Rae MacCallum Homiak and Roxanne Kay MacCallum Batezel (twins), Tracy Scott, Tamara Lee MacCallum Johnson, Shauna Marie MacCallum Bost. BS in Pharmacy U. Colo., 1950. Registered pharmacist, Colo. Pharmacist Presbyn. Hosp., Denver, 1950, Corner Pharmacy, Lamar, Colo., 1950-53; research pharmacist Nat. Chlorophyll Co., Lamar, 1953; relief pharmacist, various stores, Delta, Colo., 1957-59, Farmington, N.Mex., 1960-62, 71-79, Aztec, N.Mex., 1971-79; mgr. Med. Arts Pharmacy, Farmington, 1966-67; cons. pharmacist Navajo Hosp., Brethren in Christ Mission, Farmington, 1967-77; sales agt. Norris Realty, Farmington, 1977-78; pharmacist, owner, mgr. Lorene's Pharmacy, Farmington, 1979—; tax cons. H&R Block, Farmington, 1968; cons. Pub. Service Co., N.Mex. Intermediate Clinic, Planned Parenthood, Farmington. Advisor Order Rainbow for Girls, Farmington, 1975-78. Mem. Nat. Assn. Bds. Pharmacy (com. on internship tng., com. edn., treas. local dist. 1987—, mem. impaired pharmacists adv. com., chmn. impaired pharmacists program N.Mex., 1987—), N.Mex. Bd. Pharmacy (first woman pres. 1987—), Nat. Assn. Retail Druggists, N.Mex. Pharm. Assn. (mem. exec. council 1977-81). Methodist. Lodge: Order Eastern Star (Farmington). Home: 1301 Camino Sol Farmington NM 87401 Office: 901 W Apache Farmington NM 87401

MACCARRONE, RENEE BENNETT, communications company executive; b. Alexandria, La., June 6, 1943; d. William James and Amy Armintha (Jackson) Bennett; B.S., La. Poly. Inst., 1964; postgrad. N.Y. U., 1966-76, Adelphi U., 1977-78; m. Anthony Maccarrone, Nov. 9, 1968; 1 son, Joseph Anthony. With Davis Publs., N.Y.C., 1964-68; with Scholastic Inc., N.Y.C., 1968-83, editorial and advt. adminstr. publ. div., 1980-83; pres. Bennett Communications, Inc., 1983—; cons. in field. Nat. dir. Turn OFF!, Teenagers United to Resist Narcotics in Ourselves, Families and Friends, 1984—. Recipient Crystal Prism award 2d dist. Am. Advt. Fedn., 1983, New Am. Woman award Esquire mag., 1984. Mem. Advt. Women N.Y. (bd. dirs.). Editor: Co-ed's Guide to Getting Married, 1982, 83. Office: 118 Madison Ave New York NY 10016

MACCINI, MARGARET AGATHA, county official; b. N.Y.C., Dec. 6, 1931; d. Camillo and Mary (Varca) Vergano; m. Arthur Maccini, Sept. 25, 1955; children—Mark Robert, Alan Arthur, Deirdre Rose. Student NYU, 1949-51, CCNY, 1952. Cert. mcpl. clk. Exec. sec. Universal Pictures Inc., N.Y.C., 1952-55, Chipman Chem. Co., Bound Brook, N.J., 1956-57; corp. treas. Pyramid Bindery Inc., N.Y.C., 1957-73, pres., 1979-82; adminstrv. asst. Somerset County Bd. Chosen Freeholders, Somerville, N.J., 1973-75, dep. clk. of bd., 1975-76, clk. of bd., 1976—; co-adj. instr., mem. edn. com. Rutgers U. Dept. of Govt. Services, New Brunswick, N.J., 1983—. Bd. dirs. Voluntary Action Ctr., Somerville, 1977-80, N.J. Ctr. for the Performing Arts, Somerville, 1980-83, Camp Okee Sunokee, Bridgewater, N.J., 1980—; dir. Adult Day Care Ctr., Finderne, N.J., sec., 1977-84, commr., sec., treas. Somerset County Cultural and Heritage Commn., Somerville, 1983—, sec. 1983, treas. 1987-88; del. N.J. Counties Cultural and Heritage Assn., 1981—; co-founder, chmn. Van Wickle Dames, Somerset, 1977—; trustee Meadows Found., Inc., Somerset, 1977—, fin. chmn., grantsman, 1982—, pres. 1983-84, v.p. 1987, initiator, supporter Vergano Nature Conservancy; dep. registration clk. Franklin Township Election Bd., Somerset, 1970-75; mem. Somerset County Office on Aging Adv. Council, Raritan, N.J., 1978-83, LWV, 1970-71, St. Matthias Rosary Altar Soc., Somerset, 1975-83, Franklin Township Republican Club, Somerset, 1970-84, Hillsborough Township Rep. Club., Somerville, 1985-88; campaign sec. N.J. Assembly Candidate B. Williams, 1973. Mem. N.J. Assn., Somerset County Governing Officials Assn. (legis. com. 1987-88), Freeholder Bd. Clks. (sec. 1977-78, v.p. 1979-80, pres. 1981-82), Somerset County Mcpl. Clks. Assn. (treas. 1980-81, sec. 1982, v.p. 1983, pres. 1984), Mcpl. Clks. Assn. of N.J. (county rep., alternate 1984—, county membership chmn. 1985, consn. com. 1988), Internat. Inst. Mcpl. Clks. (mem. records mgmt. com. 1984, vice chmn. records mgmt. com. 1985), N.J. Assn. Counties (legis., pub. works and environ. coms. 1982—), Internat. Platform Assn. Somerset County 4-H Assn. (established and funds Vergano Agriculture Scholarship). Roman Catholic. Club: Zonta Internat. (sec. 1977-78). Avocations: cooking, traveling, gardening, farming. Home: 38 Murrary Dr Neshanic NJ 08853 Office: Somerset County North Bridge and High Sts PO Box 3000 Somerville NJ 08876

MACCOBY, ELEANOR EMMONS, psychology educator; b. Tacoma, May 15, 1917; d. Harry Eugene and Viva May (Johnson) Emmons; m. Nathan Maccoby; Sept. 16, 1938; children: Janice Maccoby Carmichael, Sarah Maccoby Bellina, Mark. BS, U Wash., 1939; MA, U. Mich., 1949, PhD, 1950. Study dir. div. program surveys USDA, Washington, 1942-46; study dir. Survey Research Ctr. U. Mich., Ann Arbor, 1946-48; lectr., research assoc. dept. social relations Harvard U., Cambridge, Mass., 1950-58; from assoc. to full prof. Stanford (Calif.) U., 1958-87, chmn. dept. psychology, 1973-76, prof. emeritus, 1987—. Author: (with R. Sears and H. Levin) Patterns of Child-Rearing, 1957, (with Carol Jacklin) Psychology of Sex Differences, 1974, Social Development, 1980; editor: (with Newcomb & Hartley) Readings in Social Psychology, 1957. Recipient Gores award for Excellence in Teaching Stanford U., 1981, Disting. Contbn. to Ednl. Research award Am. Ednl. Research Assn., 1984, Disting. Sci. Contbn. to Child Devel. award Soc. for Research in Child Devel., 1987; named to Barbar Kimball Browning professorship Stanford U., 1979—. Fellow Soc. for Research in Child Devel. (pres. 1981-83, mem. governing council 1963-66), Am. Psychol. Assn. (div. 7 pres. 1971-72, G. Stanley Hall award 1982), Ctr. for Youth Studies; mem. Western Psychol. Assn. (pres. 1974-75), Inst. for Research on Women and Gender (mem. policy bd.), Social Sci. Research Council (chmn. 1984-85). Democrat. Home: 729 Mayfield Stanford CA 94305 Office: Stanford U Dept Psychology Stanford CA 94305

MAC CONKEY, DOROTHY I., academic administrator; b. New Brunswick, N.J., June 5, 1925; d. Donald Thurston and Dorothy Bennett (Hill) Ingling; m. Joseph W. MacConkey, June 19, 1949 (dec. Aug. 1975); children: Donald Franklin, Diane Margaret, Dorothy Frances BA, Beaver Coll., 1947; MA, Wichita State U., 1953; PhD, U. Md., 1974. Lectr. Wichita (Kans.) State U., 1950-51; research-campaign assoc. United Fund and Council, Wichita, 1951-62; research-com. coordination Health and Welfare Council of Nat. Capital Area, Washington, 1963-65; exec. dir. multi-program agy. Prince Georges County Assn. for Retarded Children, Hyattsville, Md., 1965-66; prof. George Mason U., Fairfax, Va., 1966-76, asst. vice pres., acting dean, 1976-82; v.p., dean of coll. Hiram (Ohio) Coll., 1982-85; pres. Davis & Elkins (W.Va.) Coll., 1985—; bd. dirs. Davis Trust Co., Elkins, 1987—; adv. bd. George Mason U. Fdn., Fairfax, 1976—; trustee Beaver Coll., Glenside, Pa., 1971-87; cons., evaluator North Cen. Assn., Chgo., 1985—. Recipient Citizen award for service to handicapped, Fairfax County, 1981, Goddin Women Alumni award, 1985, Woman of Yr. in Edn. award W.Va. Fedn. Women's Clubs, 1986. Mem. Am. Sociol. Assn., Va. Social Sci. Assn., Acad. Affairs Adminstrs., Nat. Assn. Women Deans, Adminstrs. and Counselors. Home: PO Box 2628 Elkins WV 26241 Office: Davis & Elkins Coll 100 Sycamore St Elkins WV 26241

MACCRACKEN, SUSAN JANE, corporate executive, consultant; b. Ashland, Oreg., May 13, 1957; d. Elliott Bolte and Flora Jane (Schuster) Mac. AB in Urban Studies Planning, Wellesley (Mass.) Coll., 1979; M in City Planning, SM in Transp. Systems, MIT, 1982. V.p. analysis Cognetics, Inc., Cambridge, Mass., 1983—. Mem. MIT Alumnae Assn. Office: Cognetics Inc 125 Cambridge Park Dr Cambridge MA 02140

MACDONALD, ANNA KAY, nurse, air force officer; b. Grahn, Ky., Dec. 18, 1950; d. Eaph and Cleo (Nolen) Lowe; m. Ronald Jerry MacDonald, Sept. 3, 1977 (div. 1982). B.S. in Nursing and Behavioral Sci., Loretto Heights Coll., 1983. Staff nurse intensive care unit and cardiac care unit King's Daus. Hosp., Ashland, Ky., 1971-73; commd. officer USAF, 1973, advanced through ranks to maj., 1984; med. surg. staff nurse Rickenbacker AFB Hosp., Ohio, 1973-74; charge nurse intensive care unit and cardiac care unit USAF Hosp., Colo., 1974-78, USAF Med. Ctr., Wright-Patterson AFB, Ohio, 1978-80, cardiac catheterization lab. and rehab. coordinator, 1980-82; chief nurse internal medicine br. USAF Sch. Aerospace Medicine, Brooks AFB, Tex., 1984-87; charge nurse intensive care and spl. care units USAF Med. Ctr., Keesler AFB, Miss., 1987—; instr. Am. Heart Assn., San Antonio, 1983—. Vol. United Way, San Antonio, 1985, UNICEF, Muscular Dystrophy Assn., 1985—. Mem. Am. Assn. Critical Care Nurses, Sigma Theta Tau. Democrat. Baptist. Club: Barry's San Antonio Very Strange Manifans (pres. 1985—). Avocations: piano; macrame. Home: 421 Inverness Ct Ocean Springs MS 39564 Office: USAF Med Ctr Keesler/SGHNI Keesler AFB MS 39534

MACDONALD, CECILIA (CESE), psychotherapist; b. Haileybury, Ont., Can., Oct. 22, 1951; children: Matthew Wachsman, Gordon MacDonald. BA, Coll. New Rochelle, 1973, MA, 1975. Lic. sch. psychologist, N.Y. Pvt. practice psychotherapy N.Y.C. and Westchester, N.Y., 1975; adj. faculty Coll. New Rochelle, N.Y.C., 1977—; profl. dir. Westchester Regional Theatre, Mamaroneck, N.Y., 1976, profl. actress Phoenix Theater, 1960-70; comml., TV actress, N.Y.C., 1960—; trainer Hot-Line Community Sex Info. Agy.; discussant Payne-Whitney Clinic on Incest, N.Y.C., 1985. Author: Shake Hands with your Dragon; contbr. articles to profl. jours. Bd. dirs. Emelin Theater, Mamaroneck, 1972-75; leader, dir. Community Action Program, Mamaroneck, 1974. Fellow Am. Orthopsychiatric Assn.; mem. AAUP, Mental Health Assn. Westchester. Home and Office: 333 W 56th St #61 New York NY 10019

MACDONALD, ELIZABETH HELEN, bassoonist, educator; b. Lancaster, Pa., July 5, 1942; d. Joseph Harold and Verna Elizabeth (Schaeffer) Bishop; B.Mus. in Music Edn., Eastman Sch. Music, Rochester, N.Y., 1964, M.Mus. in Music Lit. and Performance, 1966; m. William Dallas MacDonald, Aug. 17, 1968. Bassoonist, Music in Maine Woodwind Quintet, Bangor, 1966-67; dir. jr. high sch. band and elem. instrumental music, Brewer, Maine, 1967-69; instr. music history, woodwind class and bassoon No. Conservatory Music, Bangor, 1967-69; tchr. jr. high sch. gen. and instrumental music, Orono, Maine, 1969-72; tutor bassoon and oboe Colby Coll., Waterville, Maine, 1972-75; instr. bassoon, woodwind ensemble coach U. Maine, Orono, 1977—; prin. bassoonist Portland (Maine) Symphony Orch., 1967—; pvt. woodwind instr., 1972—; recitalist, soloist, music adjudicator, 1966—. Mem. Music Educators Nat. Conf., Internat. Double Reed Soc., Maine Music Educators Assn. Republican. Methodist. Home: 48 Dillingham St Bangor ME 04401 Office: U Maine Lord Hall Orono ME 04473

MACDONALD, FLORA ISABEL, Canadian government official; b. North Sydney, N.S., Can., June 3, 1926; d. George Frederick and Mary Isabel (Royle) MacD. Attended Empire Bus. Coll.; grad., Nat. Def. Coll., 1972; D.H.L. (hon.), Mt. St. Vincent U., 1979. Formerly in various secretarial positions; with Progressive Conservative Party Hdqrs., Ottawa, Ont., Can., 1956-65, exec. dir., 1960-65; adminstrv. officer, tutor dept. polit. studies Queen's U., 1966-72; also adv. Student Vocat. Bur.; mem. Can. Parliament for Kingston and the Islands, Ont., 1972—; Progressive Conservative spokesman for Indian affairs and no. devel. Can. Parliament, 1972; for housing and urban devel. 1974; chmn. Progressive Conservative Caucus Com. on Fed.-Provincial Relations, 1976; sec. of state for external affairs 1979-80, for external affairs and nat. def., 1980, minister employment and immigration, 1984-86, minister of communications, 1986—; Vice pres. Kingston and Islands Progressive Conservative Assn, 1962-72; nat. sec. Progressive Conservative Assn. of Can., 1966-69; exec. dir. Com. for Ind. Can., 1971; pres. Elizabeth Fry Soc. of Kingston, 1968-70. Mem. Can. Inst. Fgn. Affairs (dir. 1969-73), Can. Polit. Sci. Assn. (dir. 1972-75), Can. Inst. Internat. Affairs, Can. Civil Liberties Assn. Mem. United Ch. of Canada. Office: Minister of Communications, House of Commons, Ottawa, ON Canada K1A 0A6 •

MACDONALD, KAREN CRANE, occupational therapist, geriatric counselor; b. Denville, N.J., Feb. 24, 1955; d. Robert William and Jeanette Wilcox (Crane) M. B.S., Quinnipiac Coll., 1977; M.S., U. Bridgeport, 1982; postgrad. NYU, 1983—. Cert. occupational therapist; instr. NYU, 1985-88, Quinnipiac Coll., 1986—. occupational therapist, coordinator of special care unit Jewish Home for the Elderly, Fairfield, Conn., 1987—, N.Y. Inst., N.Y.C., 1984-86; pvt. practice, Fairfield County, Conn., 1977-88; lectr., cons. in field. Contbr. articles to profl. jours. Youth leader, deacon Union Meml. Ch., Stamford, Conn., 1980—. Teaching fellow NYU, 1983-86. Mem. Am. Occupational Therapy Assn. (scholar 1985, council edn.), Conn. Occupational Therapy Assn. (gerontology liaison 1980-83). Avocations: photography; poetry writing; painting. Home: 56 Pepperbush Ln Fairfield CT 06430 Office: Jewish Home for Elderly 175 Jefferson St Fairfield CT 06430

MACDONALD, KATHARINE MARCH, reporter; b. Los Angeles, Nov. 12, 1949; d. Ian G. and Eve (March) M. Grad. high sch., Beverly Hills, Calif.; student, Santa Monica Coll., 1971-73, Whittier Law Sch., Los Angeles, 1975-76. Scheduling asst. Jess Unruh for Gov., Los Angeles, 1969-70; dep. press. sec. Jess Unruh for Mayor, Los Angeles, 1973; polit. cons. various local campaigns, Los Angeles, 1973-78; researcher Washington Post-Los Angeles Bur., 1978-86; spl. corr. Washington Post-Los Angeles Bur., Washington, 1980-86; reporter State Capitol Bur. San Francisco Examiner, 1986—; guest lectr. journalism and polit. sci. various colleges and universities, 1984—. Mem. Sacramento Press Club, Capitol Corrs. Assn. Office: San Francisco Examiner 925 L St Suite 320 A Sacramento CA 95814

MACDONALD, LENORE LONIGRO, lawyer; b. Chgo., Aug. 21, 1956; d. Jerry Francis and Antonet Joane (Zomparelli) L; m. William S. Macdonald, June 28, 1986. B.A. magna cum laude, Tufts U., 1978; J.D. with honors, Marquette U., 1981. Bar: Ill. 1981, Wis. 1981, U.S. Ct. Appeals (7th cir.) 1982, U.S. Dist. Ct (cen. and so. dist.) Calif., U.S. Dist. Ct. (no. dist.) Ill. 1981, U.S. Dist. Ct. (ea. and we. dists.) Wis. 1981, U.S. Dist. Ct. (so. and cen. dists.) Calif. 1985. Legal intern U.S. atty., Milw., 1979-81, antitrust div. U.S. Dept. Justice, Chgo., 1980; atty.-at-law Burke and Smith, Chgo., 1981-83, McDermott, Will & Emery, Chgo., 1983-85, O'Melveny & Myers, Los Angeles, 1985-86, Chapman & Cutler, 1986-87; asst. state's atty. Cook County Ill., Chgo., 1987—; chmn. law day Justinian Soc., Chgo., 1983; pres. Women and Law, Milw., 1979-81. Author: (with Ramon Klitzke) Patents and Antitrust, 1981. Benefactor Chgo. Council on Fgn. Relations, 1981—; chmn. alumni admissions council Tufts U., Chgo., 1981—; mem. Art Inst. Chgo., 1982—, Jr. League of Evanston, Ill., 1988—. Recipient Am. Jurisprudence awards Marquette Law Sch., Milw., 1981; Outstanding Young Am. award, 1984; Meserve scholar Tufts U., 1974-75; Portia scholar Marquette Law Sch., Milw., 1979-80. Mem. ABA, Ill. State Bar Assn. (mem. assembly 1983-86), Chgo. Bar Assn. (legis. com. 1982—), Tufts U. Alumni Alliance (Outstanding Student award 1975-78).

MACDONALD, LINDA GAIL, personnel director; b. Charleston, S.C., Nov. 2, 1954; d. Robert Harold and Gloria Eleanor (Mulvaney) M. AA in Gen. Edn., Rio Hondo Coll., Whittier, Calif., 1977; BA in Psychology, Pitzer Coll., 1979. Mental health counselor The Firehouse, Montclair, Calif., 1979-80; mgr. employee relations Dolco Packaging, Commerce, Calif., 1980-81; mgr. personnel services BJ Titan Services (formerly BJ Hughes, Long Beach, Calif.), Houston, 1981—. Co-rep. United Way Campaign, Long Beach, Houston, 1982—, U.S. Dept. Treasury Savs. Bond Program, Long Beach, Houston, 1982—; team capt. March of Dimes Ann. Walkathon, Houston, 1983—; participant Jr. Achievement Bowl-a-Thon, Houston, 1986; mem. St. John Vianney Cath. Ch. Haynes Found. scholar, 1978, Calif. State scholar, 1977-79. Mem. Houston Personnel Assn., Internat. Assn. Personnel Women (v.p. 1984-85). Democrat. Roman Catholic. Office: BJ Titan Services Co 5500 NW Central Dr PO Box 4442 Houston TX 77210

MACDONALD, LINDA STEFANIK, lawyer; b. Perth Amboy, N.J., Sept. 29, 1955; d. John and Anna (Janocko) Stefanik; m. John Arch MacDonald, Sept. 17, 1983 (dec. Feb. 1984); m. Kim C. Glenn, Dec. 31, 1987. A.B., Rutgers U., 1977; J.D., Western New Eng. Law Sch., 1981. Assoc. Manning, West Santianiello and Pari, Providence, 1981-82; spl. asst. atty. gen. Atty. Gen.'s Office, Providence, 1982-87; ptnr. Saunders, Dumas & Fleury, East Greenwich, R.I., 1987—; legal counsel R.I. House Com. on Spl. Legislation; sr. trial atty., civil div. Motor Vehicles Dealers Licensing Commn., 1982-83; mem. Bd. Med. Examiners, Providence, 1982-83; chmn. Auto Body Repair Shop Com., 1982-83; legal counsel Auto Wrecking and Sales of Commn., 1982-83. Bd. dirs. YWCA, R.I., 1983, Leukemia Soc. R.I., 1983-85; mem. Cancer Support Group R.I., 1983-85. Named Outstanding Woman, YWCA, R.I., 1983; Outstanding Bd. Mem., Leukemia Soc. R.I., 1984. Mem. ABA, Am. Trial Lawyers Assn., R.I. Bar Assn., R.I. Women's Network, LWV, Warwick Bus. and Profl. Women. Greek Catholic. Home: 26 Corey Ave Warwick RI 02818 Office: Saunders Dumas & Fleury 130 Main St East Greenwich RI 02818

MAC DONALD, SISTER MATTHEW ANITA, college president; b. N.Y.C., June 15, 1938; d. Matthew John and Jean (Ottobre) MacDonald. A.B., Chestnut Hill Coll., Phila., 1960; M.A., U. Pa., 1970, Ph.D., 1973. Cert. tchr. in English and social studies, Pa. Joined Sisters of St. Joseph of Chestnut Hill, Roman Catholic Ch., 1962; fellow in acad. adminstrn. Bryn Mawr Coll., 1974-75; assoc. prof. Chestnut Hill Coll., Phila., 1974—, dir. continuing edn., 1975-80, pres., 1980—; cons.; mem. Phila. Archdiocesan Speakers Bur., 1977—; evaluator Middle States Assn.; chairperson exec. com. Sisters of St. Joseph Coll. Consortium, 1986-88. Bd. dirs. Chestnut Hill Community Assn., 1980—; mem. Mayor's Commn. on Women, Phila., 1981—; dir. NCCJ, 1980-82; nat. adv. bd. commn. social justice Order Sons of Italy; vice chair Pa. Commn. for Women. Fellow Philosophy of Edn. Soc., Am. Council Edn.; mem. Am. Inst. Italian Culture, Commn. Ind. Colls. and Univs. (exec. com.), Nat. Cath. Edn. Soc., Teilhard de Chardin Soc., Assn. Continuing Higher Edn., Found. for Ind. Colls. (exec. com. 1986—). Democrat. Home and Office: Chestnut Hill Coll Philadelphia PA 19118

MACDONALD, THERESA PELLEGRINO, advertising agency executive; b. Port Reading, N.J., Nov. 10, 1927; d. Matthew and Maria (DePalma) Pellegrino; m. Edward B. MacDonald, Aug. 14, 1975. BA, Bucknell U., 1949. Research asst., supr. sampling Young & Rubicam Inc., N.Y.C., 1949-59, supr. media analysis, 1959-64, asst. to media dir., 1964-70, v.p., dir. plan. devel., 1970-74, v.p., mgr. communications services, 1974-81, v.p., dir. communications devel., 1978-81, sr. v.p., 1981—; adminstrv. mgr. Young & Rubicam Inc., N.Y., 1983—. Named Woman Achiever in Bus. YWCA, 1979. Mem. Acad. Women Achievers in Bus., Cath. Assn. Radio and TV Advt. (co-chmn., dir. exec. com.), Advt. Info Services (dir., exec. com. 1975—, v.p. 1978), Am. Assn. Advt. Agys. (chmn. newspaper com.). Republican. Roman Catholic. Home: 350 W 57th St New York NY Office: Young & Rubicam 285 Madison Ave New York NY 10017 •

MACDONALD, VIRGINIA B., state senator; b. El Paso, Tex.; d. Wendell Holmes and Dorothy (White) Blue; student U. N.Mex.; m. Alan Hunter Macdonald, 1941; children—Susan Macdonald, Alan H. Mem. Ill. Ho. Reps., sec. Ho. Republican Caucus in Gen. Assembly, 1972; mem. Ill. Senate, 1980—. Del. 6th Ill. Constl. Conv., 1970; pres. Ill. Fedn. Republican Women; chairwoman Cook County Republican Com., 1964-68; committeewoman Wheeling Twp. Rep. Com.; chmn. Statewide Women's div. Everett McKinley Dirksen's Campaign, 1968; mem. adv. council Community Counciling Center, Suburban Br. Salvation Army; mem. citizens' adv. com. Northwest Suburban Mental Health Assn.; mem. Altrusa; pres. Ill. Fedn. Republican Women, 1972-74. Mem. Mt. Prospect Bus. and Profl. Women. Episcopalian. also: 120 W Eastman St Suite 102 Arlington Heights IL 60004-0593 •

MACDOUGALL, GENEVIEVE ROCKWOOD, journalist, educator; b. Springfield, Ill., Nov. 29, 1914; d. Grover Cleveland and Flora Maurine (Fowler) Rockwood; m. Curtis D. MacDougall, June 20, 1942; children: Priscilla Ruth, Bonnie MacDougall Cottrell. BS, Northwestern U., 1936, MA, 1956, postgrad., 1963—. Reporter, Evanston (Ill.) Daily News Index, 1936-37; assoc. editor Nat. Almanac & Yearbook, Chgo., 1937-38, News Map of Week, Chgo., 1938-39; editor Springfield (Ill.) Citizens' Tribune, also area supr. Ill. Writers Project, 1940-41; reporter Chgo. City News Bur., 1942; tchr. English, social studies Skokie Jr. High Sch., Winnetka, Ill., 1956-68, coordinator TV, 1964-68; tchr. English Washburne Sch., Winnetka, 1968-81; editor Winnetka Public Schs. Staff Newsletter, 1981-87; dir. Winnetka Jr. High Archeology Field Sch., 1971-83; cons., lectr. in field. Author: Grammar Book VII, 1963, 68; (with others) 7th Grade Language Usage, 1963, rev. 1968; also articles. Winnetka Tchrs. Centennial Fund scholar, 1964, 68; named Tchr. of Year, Winnetka, 1976, Educator of Decade Northwestern U. and Found. Ill. Archeology, 1981. Mem. Winnetka Tchrs. Council (pres. 1971-72), NEA, Ill. Edn. Assn., Ill. Assn. Advancement Archeology, Women in Communications (pres. N. Shore alumni chpt. 1949-53), Pi Lambda Theta. Home: 537 Judson Ave Evanston IL 60202

MACE, GEORGIA MAE, insurance company administrator; b. Pisgah, Iowa, June 7, 1949; d. George and Lois Mae (Rife) Stevens; m. Ronald Eugene Mace, May 14, 1971; children: Brandi Lynn, Dana Lynn. AA, Iowa Western Community Coll., 1987. Acctg. clk. U.S. Fidelity & Guaranty, Omaha, 1967-72; supr. Cornhusker Casualty Co. (subs. Berkshire-Hathaway Group), Omaha, 1973-77, treas., 1977-79; asst. comptroller Drum Fin. Corp., Omaha, 1979-80; treas. Acceptance Ins. Holding Inc., Omaha, 1980—. Mem. Ins. Acctg. and Systems Assn. Home: 706 East Maple Missouri Valley IA 51555 Office: Acceptance Ins Holding Inc 105 S 17th Omaha NE 68102

MACE, MARY ALICE, coal company administrator; b. Charleston, W.Va., Nov. 21, 1949; d. John Robert Leake and Georgia Alice (Wilhelm) Crist; m. Charles Michael Mace, May 20, 1968; 1 child, Christina Michelle. Grad. high sch., East Bank, W.Va., 1967. Sec. Capitol Paper Supply, Inc., Charleston, 1967-68, Persingers, Inc., Charleston, 1968-77; benefits coordinator Elk Run Coal Co., Inc., Sylvester, W.Va., 1981—. Sec. PTA, Pettus, W.Va., 1981-83, pres. 1983-85. Mem. Cannelton Benefits Group. Democrat. Home: 4502 Staunton Ave Charleston WV 25304 Office: Elk Run Coal Co Inc PO Box 497 Sylvester WV 25193

MACE, SHARON ELIZABETH, physician; b. Syracuse, N.Y., Oct. 30, 1949; d. James Henry and Leona Helen (Bednarski) M.; B.S., Syracuse U., 1971; M.D., SUNY, 1975. Intern and resident in pediatrics Case-Western Res. U. Hosps., Cleve., 1975-77, fellow in cardiology, 1977-79, instr. dept. emergency medicine, 1980—; research assoc. div. investigative medicine Mt. Sinai Med. Center, Cleve., 1979-80, staff physician depts. emergency medicine and investigative medicine, 1980-86, coordinator emergency medicine residency program; asst. dir. dept. emergency medicine Mt. Sinai Med. Ctr.; dir. emergency dept. Saratoga Hosp., Saratoga Sprongs, N.Y., 1986-88, St. Mary's Hosp., Rochester, N.Y., 1988—; former instr. Case Western Res. U. Sch. Medicine; helicopter flight physician; lectr. Lakeland Community Coll.; instr. Advanced Cardiac Life Support. Contbr. articles to med. jours. Mem. Am. Coll. Emergency Physicians (edn. com., dir. Ohio chpt., bd. dirs. N.Y. chpt.), Soc. Tchrs. Emergency Medicine, Univ. Assn. for Emergency Medicine. Congregationalist. Home: 68 Waterview Circle Rochester NY 14625 Office: St. Mary's Hosp 89 Genesee St Rochester NY 14611

MACE, SUSAN LYNNETTE, nurse, psychotherapist; b. Joplin, Mo., Aug. 8, 1961; d. Leslie J. and Virginia S. (Dunaway) M. BS in Nursing, William Jewell Coll., Liberty, Mo., 1983; MS in Nursing, Tex. Women's U., 1984-86. RN St. John's Regional Health Ctr., Springfield, Mo., 1983; case mgr. Upjohn Home Health Agy., Springfield, 1983-84; clin. nurse specialist VA Med. Ctr., Dallas, 1985; area mgr.-psychiatry St. Joseph's Hosp., Ft. Worth, 1985-86; unit coordinator Green Oaks Psychiat. Hosp., Dallas, 1986-88; pvt. practice psychotherapy Grand Prairie, Tex., 1988—. Mem. Nat. Assn. Female Execs., Sigma Theta Tau. Home: PO Box 330691 Fort Worth TX 76163-0691

MACEDONIA, MARGARET ANNE, teacher; b. Dayton, Ohio, Apr. 21, 1955; d. James William and Sarah Wyatt (Clement) Tisdale; m. David Louis Macedonia, Feb. 18, 1984; children: David Michael, Nicholas James. B of Psychology, Coll. of William and Mary, 1977, M of Edn., 1979. Cert. tchr., Va. Spl. edn. tchr. Arlington (Va.) County Pub. Schs., 1979—, tchr. summer sch., 1980-83, 85, 87; tchr. coordinator Oakridge Sch., Arlington, 1980—, workshop presenter, 1982, ednl. diagnostician, 1983—; mem. evaluation team Arlington County Spl. Edn. State Procedures Check, 1981-82; sec. Spl. Edn. Coordinating Com., Arlington, 1981-83; tchr. rep. Kennedy Ctr. Workshop, Washington, 1982; Arlington Schs. rep. Nat. Assn. Children with Learning Disabilities Conv., 1983; mem. PTA, 1979—. Co-author: Testing Resources for Special Education Teachers, 1982. Music minister New Creation Cath. Community, Newport News, Va., 1977-79, tchr. Sunday sch., 1977-79; interpretive dancer St. Bede's Cath. Ch., Williamsburg, 1978-79; parent coordinator, coach, athletic trainer Oakridge Spl. Olympics, Arlington, 1980-85; election day campaigner Rep. Party, Arlington, 1980-83; coordinator, tchr. Lamb of God Cath. Community, Arlington, 1980-83, Christ House Food Provider, 1981-84, lectr., 1982-83; campaign worker Tribble for Senator, Arlington, 1982. Recipient Excellence in Edn. award U.S. Dept. Edn., 1986, Cert. of Appreciation Spl. Edn. Adv. Com., 1987. Mem. Nat. Edn. Assn., Arlington Edn. Assn., Arlington County Assn. of Adults and Children with Learning Disabilities, William and Mary Alumnae Assn., Kappa Kappa Gamma Alumnae Assn. Home: 5960 Wilson Blvd Arlington VA 22205

MACER-STORY, EUGENIA ANN, writer, artist; b. Mpls., Jan. 20, 1945; d. Dan Johnstone and Eugenia Loretta (Andrews) Macer; divorced; 1 child, Ezra Arthur Story. BS in Speech, Northwestern U., 1965; MFA, Columbia U., 1968. Writing instr. Polyarts, Boston, 1970-72; theater instr. Joy of Movement, Boston, 1972-75; artistic dir. Magik Mirror, Salem, Mass., 1975-76; artistic dir. Magick Mirror Communications, Woodstock, N.Y., 1977—. Author: Congratulations: The UFO Reality, 1978, Angels of Time, 1982, Project Midas, 1986; (plays) Fetching the Tree, Archeological Politics, Strange Inquiries, others; philosophy writer; contbr. articles to profl. jours.; author poetry in Woodstock Times, Manhattan Poetry Rev., others; feature writer, editorial cons. Body, Mind, Spirit mag. Shubert fellow, 1968. Mem. Dramatists Guild, AAAS, N.Y. Acad. Sci., U.S. Psychotronics Assn., Center for UFO Studies. Democrat. Avocations: swimming, outdoor activities, hiking. Office: Magick Mirror Communications Box 854 Woodstock NY 12498

MAC FADDIN, JEAN FRANCES, microbiologist, writer; b. Dover, Del., Oct. 20, 1931; d. John Willis and Dorothy (Roe) Mac F. AA, Hartnell Jr. Coll., 1953, BA in Med. Tech., San Jose State U., 1967, MS in Microbiology, Incarnate Word Coll., 1970. Enlisted U.S. Army, 1955, advanced through grades to sgt. 1st class, 1968; med. lab. technologist U.S. Army Hosps., Ft. McClellan, Ala. and Landstuhl, Fed. Republic Germany, 1955-68; instr. microbiology Acad. Health Scis, U.S. Army, Ft. Sam Houston, Tex., 1968-75; ret. U.S. Army, 1975; free-lance scientific writer microbiology San Antonio, 1975—. Author: Biochemical Tests for Identification of Medical Bacteria, 1975, 2d rev. edit., 1980, Media for Isolation-Cultivation Identification-Maintenance of Medical Bacteria, 1985. Mem. Registry of Med. Technologists Am. Soc. Clin. Pathologists (lic.), Nat. Registry Microbiologists Specialists Microbiologists (lic.), Clin. Lab. Technologists Calif. (lic.), Am. Soc. Microbiology. Republican. Lutheran. Home: 7667 Callaghan Rd Apt 405 San Antonio TX 78229

MACGILLIVRAY, LOIS ANN, academic administrator; b. Phila., July 8, 1937; d. Alexander and Mary Ethel (Crosby) MacG. BA in History, Holy Names Coll., 1966; MA in Sociology, U. N.C., 1971, PhD in Sociology, 1973. Joined Sisters of Holy Names of Jesus and Mary, 1955. Research asst. U. N.C., Chapel Hill, 1969-70, 71-72, instr. sociology, 1970-71; sr. sociologist Research Triangle Inst., Chapel Hill, 1973-81, dir. Ctr. for Population and Urban-Rural Studies,, 1976-81; pres. Holy Names Coll., Oakland, Calif., 1982—; mem. steering com. Symposium for Bus. Leaders Holy Names Coll., 1982—. Bd. dirs. Oakland Council Econ. Devel., 1984-86. Mem. Am. Sociol. Assn., Assn. Ind. Calif. Colls. and Univs. (bd. dirs. 1985—, exec. com. 1985—), Regional Assn. East Bay Colls. and Univs. (past pres., bd. dirs. 1982—). Home: 3500 Mountain Blvd Oakland CA 94619-9989 Office: Holy Names Coll Office of Pres 3500 Mountain Blvd Oakland CA 94619-9989

MAC GILLIVRAY, MARYANN LEVERONE, marketing consultant; b. Mpls., Oct. 18, 1947; d. Joseph Paul and Genevieve Gertrude (Ozark) Leverone; B.S., Coll. of St. Catherine, St. Paul, 1969; Med. Technologist, Hennepin County Gen. Hosp., 1970; M.B.A., Pepperdine U., 1976; m. Duncan MacGillivray, Apr. 28, 1973; children—Duncan Michael, Catherine Mary and Monica Mary (twins), Andrew John. Med. technologist Mercy Hosp., San Diego, 1970-72; with Diagnostics div. Abbott Labs., South Pasadena, Calif., 1972-79, tech. service rep., 1972-74, sr. tech. service rep., 1974-75, product coordinator, mktg., 1975-77, mktg. product mgr., 1977-79; clin. diagnostic mktg. cons., Sierra Madre, Calif., 1979—. Recipient Pres.'s award Abbott Diagnostics Div., 1975. Mem. Biomed. Mktg. Assn., Am. Assn. Clin. Chemistry, Am. Assn. Clin. Pathologists, Am. Soc. Med. Tech., Calif. Assn. Med. Lab. Technologists. Roman Catholic. Home: 608 Elm Ave Sierra Madre CA 91024

MACGREGOR, MELISSA ANN, telecommunications specialist; b. Orange, N.J., Feb. 9, 1959; d. Robert John and Marie Adele (Malone) MacG. BS, Lynchburg Coll., 1981. Project analyst Merrill Lynch, N.Y.C., 1981-83, cons., 1983-85, project mgr., telecommunications, 1985—. Mem. Nat. Assn. Female Execs., Lynchburg Coll. Alumni Club (pres. 1987—). Democrat. Roman Catholic. Office: Merrill Lynch World Fin Ctr New York NY 10080-0515

MACHAMER, LAURIE ELIZABETH, marketing representative; b. Hartford, Conn., Sept. 26, 1957; d. Dean Elliott and Diane Paula (Magee) Machamer. Student U. N.H., 1975-77, Central Conn. State U, 1979-81. Engring. computist Pratt & Whitney Aircraft, East Hartford, Conn., 1978-80; office mgr. G. Fox & Co., Hartford, 1980-82; direct import coordinator Hollywood Accessories, Carson, Calif., 1982-84; mgr. arch./engring. adminstrn. The Elliott Group, Los Alamitos, Calif., 1984-86; exec. recruiter E & M Search Services, Torrance, Calif., 1984-86; ind. mktg. rep., Santa Ana, Calif., 1986—. Mem. Bus. Devel. Assn. of Orange County, Calif., Soc. Mktg. Profl. Services. Avocations: water skiing, tennis, voice. Home: 69 61st Pl #B Long Beach CA 90803 Office: 360 Brookhollow Dr Suite 5356 Santa Ana CA 92705

MACHISAK-HERNDON, MAUREEN DOROTHY, writer, editor; b. Passaic, N.J.; d. John Christian and Dorothy Catherine (Donahue) Machisak. BA in Polit. Sci., Chestnut Hill Coll.; M in Pub. Adminstrn., Notre Dame U. Legal editor Office Adminstrv. Law, State of N.J., Newark, 1980-81; editor Prentice-Hall, Inc., Paramus, N.J., 1982-84; communication and edn. assoc. Employee Benefit Research Inst., Washington, 1984; program analyst GAO, Washington, 1984—; reporter Work in Am. Inst., White Plains, N.Y., 1984; free-lance cons., 1977—; writer, editor BioProbe newsletter BioClin. Systems, Inc., Columbia, Md., 1986—. Recipient merit scholarships Chestnut Hill Coll., Notre Dame U. Mem. Notre Dame Alumnae Assn.

MACHT, BETSY JEAN, environmental consultant; b. Abington, Pa., Feb. 23, 1957; d. Walter Alfred and Jeanette Ruth (Skeirik) M.; m. Steven Richard Senderling. BS, Pa. State U., 1979. Environ. engr. Stearns-Catalytic, Phila., 1979-80; project engr. Ethicon Inc., Somerville, N.J., 1980-81, environ. engr., 1981-83; project engr. Johnson & Johnson Baby Products Co., Skillman, N.J., 1983-86; sr. project mgr. Fred C. Hart Assocs. Inc., Cherry Hill, N.J., 1986—. Mem. Am. Inst. Chem. Engrs., Soc. Women Engrs., Nat. Assn. for Female Execs. (network dir. 1981—). Republican. Mem. Reformed Ch. Am. Office: Fred C Hart Assocs 6981 N Park Dr Suite 401 Pennsauken NJ 08109

MACHTIGER, HARRIET GORDON, psychoanalyst; b. N.Y.C., July 27, 1927; d. Michael J. and Miriam D. (Rand) Gordon; B.A., Bklyn. Coll., 1947; dipl. with distinction, U. London, 1966, Ph.D., 1974; m. Sidney Machtiger, Feb. 7, 1948; children—Avram Coleman, Marcia Gordon, Bennett Rand. Tchr., Phila. Public Schs., 1962-64; ednl. therapist Child Guidance Tng. Center, London, 1966-68; ednl. therapist Sch. Psychol. Service, Inner London Edn. Authority, 1968-70; therapist Paddington Day Hosp., London, 1970-71, London Centre for Psychotherapy, 1971-74, Staunton Clinic, U. Pitts., 1974-78; pvt. practice psychoanalysis, Pitts., 1976—; pres. C.G. Jung Center, Pitts., 1976-81; cons. in field. Mem. SW Pitts. Community Mental Health, 1976-78. Recipient award for Disting. Contributions to Advancement in Edn., Pa. Dept. Edn., 1962; Social Sci. Research Council award, 1973; cert. psychologist, Pa. Fellow Am. Orthopsychiat. Assn.; mem. Inter-Regional Soc. Jungian Analysts. (dir. Pitts. program 1975-85), Am. Acad. Psychotherapists, Am. Psychol. Assn., N.Y. Assn. Analytical Psychologists, Internat. Assn. Group Psychotherapists, Pa. Psychol. Assn., Brit. Psychol. Soc., Brit. Assn. Psychotherapists, Assn. Child Psychology and Child Psychiatry, Western Pa. Group Psychotherapy Assn., Nat. Assn. for Advancement Psychoanalysis, NOW. Home: 207 Tennyson Ave Pittsburgh PA 15213 Office: 110 The Fairfax 4614 Fifth Ave Pittsburgh PA 15213

MACHUZAK, KATHLEEN LOUISE, sales representative; b. Elizabeth, N.J., Jan. 6, 1958; d. John and Rose Anne (Dulemba) M. BS, Rutgers U., 1980, MBA, 1983. Distbn. planning analyst Johnson & Johnson Hosp. Services, New Brunswick, N.J., 1983-84, customer service supr., 1984-86; sales rep. Codman and Shurtleff, Inc. div. Johnson & Johnson, Hartford, Conn., 1986—. Violinist Manchester Symphony Orch., 1986—. Mem. Nat. Assn. Female Execs. Office: Codman and Shurtleff Inc Pacella Park Dr Randolph MA 02368

MACINNES, CATHLEEN FOLEY, health care manager; b. Nyack, N.Y., Nov. 10, 1951; d. Paul Arthur and Willadell (Allen) Foley. BA, Wells Coll., Aurora, N.Y., 1972. Admitting officer Myers Community Hosp., Sodus, N.Y., 1972-78, bus. office mgr., 1978-81, bus. mgr., 1981-84; bus. mgr. Westside Health Services, Rochester, N.Y., 1984-86; mgr. acctg. St. Mary's Hosp., Rochester, 1986-87, accounts mgr. physician services, 1987-88. Dep. mayor Village of Sodus, 1986—. Mem. Healthcare Fin. Mgmt. Assn., Mid-York Med. Accounts Mgmt. Assn, Am. Legion Aux. (7th dist. chmn. 1986-87, Empire Girl's state chmn. 1987). Republican. Home: 15 Carlton St Sodus NY 14551

MACINTYRE, CHRISTINE MELBA, magazine editor, publisher; b. Los Angeles, June 13, 1939; d. George Lewis and Grayce (Parker) Shehady; m. Donald MacIntyre; children—Jeff, Megan. B.S., UCLA, 1962, M.S., 1965, postgrad. Prof. health Pasadena City Coll., Calif., 1969-80; lectr. kinesiology UCLA, 1964-69; weight control therapist Pasadena City Coll., Calif., 1972-80; editor-in-chief Shape Mag., Woodland Hills, Calif., 1980—; cons. Pres.'s Council on Phys. Fitness, Washington, Weider Health Fitness, Woodland Hills, Calif., Jack LaLanne Saps, Greater Los Angeles Nutrition Council, Los Angeles, Calif. Dept. Health Recreation and Phys. Fitness. Author: Fitness: Teacher's Guide; Body Conturing/Conditioning, 1970, 77; contbr. articles to profl. jours. Mem. Soc. Bariatric Physicians, Am. Coll. Sports Medicine. Republican. Club: Malibu Women's. Home: 30188 Morning View Dr Malibu CA 90265 Office: Shape Mag Inc 21100 Erwin St Woodland Hills CA 91367 *Died Sept. 16, 1987.*

MACK, BRENDA LEE, sociologist, public relations consulting company executive; b. Peoria, Ill., Mar. 24; d. William James and Virginia Julia (Pickett) Palmer; A.A., Los Angeles City Coll.; B.A. in Sociology, Calif. State U., Los Angeles, 1980; m. Rozene Mack, Jan. 13 (div.); 1 child, Kevin Anthony. Ct. clk. City of Blythe, Calif.; partner Mack Trucking Co., Blythe; ombudsman, sec. bus facilities So. Calif. Rapid Transit Dist., Los Angeles, 1974-81; owner Brenda Mack Enterprises, Los Angeles, 1981—; lectr., writer, radio and TV personality; co-originator advt. concept Vee/Dee Project; pub. News from the United States newsletter through U.S. and Europe. Past bd. dirs. Narcotic Symposium, Los Angeles. Served with U.S. WAC. Mem. Women For, Calif. State U. Los Angeles Alumni. Home: 8749 Cattaraugus Ave Los Angeles CA 90034 Office: Brenda Mack Enterprises PO Box 5942 Los Angeles CA 90055

MACK, CRISTINA IANNONE, accountant; b. Olean, N.Y., Sept. 25, 1940; d. Angelo M. and Rose M. (Sirianni) Iannone; m. John O. Mack, Nov. 19, 1967; children—Elizabeth, Andrew. B.A. in Math., U. Calif.-Santa Barbara, 1962; postgrad. U. San Francisco, 1978—, Golden Gate U., 1983. Exec. dir. Bar Assn. San Francisco, 1966-68; owner, acct. CIM Assocs., San Francisco, 1978—; pres. LAST Temporary Services, Inc., 1987—. Treas. Mothers Milk Bank, 1977—; bd. dirs. Am. Paralysis Assn. Aux., 1984; precinct adminstr. Rep. County Central Com., 1964-66; Coro Found. fellow, 1963. Mem. Calif. Agrl. Assn. (bd. dirs. dist. 1-A 1986—), Chi Omega Sorority (pres. 1962, treas. 1984—), Calif. Dist. 1-A Agrl. Assn. (bd. dirs.). Roman Catholic. Club: San Francisco Lawyers Wives (pres. 1974, auditor 1978—). Lodge: Little Sisters of Poor Aux. Avocations: hunting; tennis. Home: 2963 23d Ave San Francisco CA 94132 Office: 114 Sansome St Suite 1205 San Francisco CA 94104

MACK, EVELYN WALKER, insurance company executive; b. Westbrook, Maine, 1930. Student Colby Coll., 1952. Second v.p. The New Eng., Boston. Address: The New Eng 501 Boylston St Boston MA 02117

MACK, HAZEL ARLENE, social services administrator; b. Darfur, Minn., Oct. 6, 1914; d. John Aldin and Petra Kaspara (Erickson) Haffey; m. Laurence Peter Mack (dec. Nov. 1978); children: Laurence H., Judy Mack Hennen, Patricia Mack Loyson. Grad. high sch., Lamberton, Minn., 1932. Buyer, bookkeeper Rexall Drug, Marshall, Minn., 1947-49; mgr. Montgomery Ward, Marshall, Minn., 1949-56; dental asst. Dr. Carrow DDS, Marshall, Minn., 1953-56; office mgr. S & L Stores, Marshall, Minn., 1956-58; mealsite mgr. Western Community Action, Marshall, Minn., 1974-87. Mem. Countryside Council, Marshall, 1984-87, task force sr. citizens, Marshall, 1984-87. Democrat Farm Labor. Roman Catholic. Club: Mainstay. Home: 631 River St Lynd Mine MN 56157

MACK, JULIA COOPER, judge; b. Fayetteville, N.C., July 17, 1920; d. Dallas L. and Emily (McKay) Perry; m. Jerry S. Cooper, July 30, 1943; 1 dau., Cheryl; m. Clifford S. Mack, Nov. 21, 1957. B.S., Hampton Inst., 1940; LL.B., Howard U., 1951. Bar: D.C. 1952. Legal cons. OPS, Washington, 1952-53; atty.-advisor office gen. counsel Gen. Services Adminstrn., 1953-54; trial appellate atty. criminal div. Dept. Justice, 1954-68; civil rights atty. Office Gen. Counsel, Equal Employment Opportunity Commn., Washington, 1968-75; judge Ct. Appeals, Washington, 1975—. Mem. Am., Fed., Washington, Nat. Bar Assns., Nat. Assn. Women Judges. Home: 1610 Varnum St NW Washington DC 20011 Office: DC Ct of Appeals 500 Indiana Ave NW Washington DC 20001

MACK, LYNNE MARIE, insurance company executive; b. Phila., Dec. 22, 1952; d. Walter Hutton and Dorothy Marie (Jones) Slockett; m. G. John Mack III, Aug. 19, 1972; 1 child, Lauren Marie. AA with high honors, Burlington County Coll., 1979; BA with high honors, Rutgers U., 1981; postgrad., U. Pa. Adminstrv. asst. Penn Mut. Life Ins. Co., Phila., 1970-74, policy forms analyst, tng. cons., 1984-87; mgr. policy service Northwestern Mut. Life Ins. co., Phila., 1974-76; asst. to pres., sales mgr. Tech Tran Inductotherm Industries, Rancocas, N.J., 1976-77; info. analyst Cigna Corp., Phila., 1981-83; policy forms and compliance specialist Provident Mut. Life Ins. Co., Phila., 1987—. Mem. Am. Soc. CLU'S, Phila. Soc. CLU'S, Nat. Assn. Female Execs., Phi Theta Kappa. Republican. Episcopalian. Club: Atheneum. Home: 17 Churchill St Mount Holly NJ 08060 Office: Provident Mut Life Ins Co 16th and Market Sts Philadelphia PA 19103

MACK, SUZANNE THERESE, transportation planner; b. Jersey City; d. Frank J. and Veronica Patricia (McHugh) M.; m. Robert G. Magro, July 25, 1982; 1 child, Kerry Francis. BS, St. Peter's Coll., Jersey City, 1984. Intern Action—Peace Corps, Jersey City, 1974; asst. planner City of Jersey City, 1975-76, sr. planner, 1976-78, prin. planner, 1978-83, sub-regional transp. planning coordinator, 1976-87, asst. dir. div. of traffic transp., 1987—; mem. exec. com. N.J. Transit Adv. Com., Newark, 1980—; transp. cons. Hudson County Transcend Program, Jersey City, 1984—. Mem. urban enterprise com. Jersey City Econ. Devel. Corp., 1985—. Mem. Inst. Traffic Engrs. Democrat. Roman Catholic. Office: Div Traffic Engring 575 Rt 440 Jersey City NJ 07305

MACK, WILHELMENA, hospital executive; b. Miami, Fla., Oct. 1, 1951; d. Eugene and Gladys (Terry) Brown; 1 dau., Shannon Lynnette. B.A., U. Miami, 1972, M.Ed., 1973; Ed.S., Fla. Atlantic U., 1983, EdD, 1988. Personnel officer Dade County Personnel, Miami, Fla., 1973-74; personnel officer Jackson Meml. Hosp., Miami, 1974-76, edn. coordinator, 1976-79; asst. dir. dept. edn. Meml. Hosp., Hollywood, Fla., 1979, dir. training and devel. dept., 1979—; dir. Traintex Mgmt. Services, Miami, 1978-85; adj. faculty Broward Community Coll., Nova U.; founder Comprehensive Tng. Inst. Bd. dirs. Lincoln Meml. Nursing Home, Goulds, Fla., 1977, Ptnrs. in Excellence, Ft. Lauderdale, Fla., 1983, Outreach Broward; dir.-at-large bd. dirs. Fla. chpt. Am. Lung Assn., mem. exec. com., trustee, pres. Broward-Glades-Hendry chpt. Mem. Fla. Adult Edn. Assn., Nat. Assn. Female Execs., Am. Soc. Tng. and Devel., (v.p. 1977), South Fla. Nurse Educators (pres. 1983), Dania (Fla.) C. of C. (bd. dirs. 1988). Democrat. Baptist. Office: Meml Hosp 3501 Johnson St Hollywood FL 33021

MACKAY, LINDA JUNE, oil company executive; b. Calgary, Alta., Can., June 13, 1956; d. Adolf and Alma (Ergang) Schmidt; m. Thomas James MacKay, Aug. 18, 1979. BA in Econs. with honors, U. Calgary, 1978. Sr. economist Petro Can., Calgary, 1978-82; sr. corp. planner Norcen Energy Resources, Calgary, 1982—. Vol. aquafit instr. YWCA, 1987—, United Way campaign, 1988-89; zone leader Salvation Army, Calgary, 1987. Mem. Internat. Assn. Energy Economists, Can. Assn. Bus. Econs. (pres., bd. dirs. 1981-90), Nat. Assn. Bus. Econs., Calgary Soc. Fin. Analysts, Planning Forum (bd. dirs. Calgary chpt. 1983-88), Econs. Soc. Calgary (bd. dirs. 1980-88), Bus. Womens and Profl. Club. Office: Norcen Energy Resources Ltd, 715 5th Ave SW, Calgary, AB Canada T2P 2X7

MACKAY, PATRICIA MCINTOSH, counselor; b. San Francisco, Sept. 12, 1922; d. William Carroll and Louise Edgerton (Keen) McIntosh; A.B. in Psychology, U. Calif., Berkeley, 1944, elem. teaching credential, 1951; M.A. in Psychology, John F. Kennedy U., Orinda, Calif., 1979; Ph.D. in Nutrition, Donsbach U., Huntington Beach, Calif., 1981; m. Alden Thorndike Mackay, Dec. 15, 1945; children—Patricia Louise, James McIntosh, Donald Sage. Elem. tchr. Mt. Diablo Unified Sch. Dist., Concord, Calif., 1950-60; exec. supr. No. Calif. Welcome Wagon Internat., 1960-67; wedding cons. Mackay Creative Services, Walnut Creek, Calif., 1969-70; co-owner Courtesy Calls, Greeters and Concord Welcoming Services, Walnut Creek, 1971—; marriage, family and child counselor, nutrition cons., Walnut Creek, 1979—; coordinator Alameda and Contra Costa County chpts. Parents United, 1985—; bd. dirs. New Directions Counseling Center, Inc., 1975—, founder, pres. aux., 1977—. Bd. dirs. Ministry in the Marketplace, Inc.; founder, dir. Turning Point Counseling. Recipient Individual award New Directions Counseling Center, 1978, awards Neo-Life Co. Am. Prestige Club, yearly, 1977-86. Mem. Christian Assn. Psychol. Studies, Calif. Assn. Marriage and Family Therapists, C. of C., Prytanean Alumnae, Delta Gamma. Republican. Mem. Zion Fellowship. Club: Soroptomist (dir. 1976, 86) (Walnut Creek). Home: 1101 Scots Ln Walnut Creek CA 94596 Office: 1399 Ygnacio Valley Rd Suite 12 Walnut Creek CA 94598

MACKENZIE, DIANNE VERONICA, computer programmer, systems analyst; b. Providence, Mar. 3, 1947; d. John Domenic and Angelina Loretta (Di Pasquali) Lombardi; m. David Mackenzie, July 4, 1968 (div. Oct. 1981); children: Heather Nicole, Joshua Morgan. BS, Boston U., 1969. Programmer Media Records, N.Y.C., 1981; programmer, analyst Savs. Bank Trust Co., N.Y.C., 1981-82, Guardian Life Ins. Co., N.Y.C., 1982-83; sr. programmer, analyst Chase Manhattan Bank, New Hyde Park, N.Y., 1983-85; programming mgr. Doubleday Book Clubs, Garden City, N.Y., 1985-86; cons. in field N.Y.C., 1986-87; tech. officer Chem. Bank, N.Y.C., 1987-88; cons. in field East Northport, N.Y., 1988—; cons. Teltech Inc., N.Y.C., 1988—; cons. Merrill Lynch, N.Y.C., 1986—; bd. dirs. Katrina Trask Nursery Sch., Saratoga Springs, N.Y., 1976-78; sec. Northport/East Northport Youth Ctr. Soccer Club, 1981-85. Mem. Ind. Computer Cons. Assn. Home: 281 Laurel Rd East Northport NY 11731 Office: Teltech Inc 39 Broadway New York NY 10006-3099

MACKENZIE, JILL ANNE, public relations executive; b. New Brunswick, N.J., May 28, 1957; d. William H. and Helen R. (Rotkewicz) Mac K. BA in Communications, U. Del., 1979. Writer, Rollins Cablevision, Wilmington, Del., 1979-80; pub. relations asst. Del. Art Mus., Wilmington, 1980-81; pub. relations officer Shipley Advt., Wilmington, 1981-82, Hagley Mus. and Library, Wilmington, 1982-86, mgr. pub. affairs, 1986—. Mem. Am. Assn. Mus. (pub. relations com., treas.), Discover Brandywine Pub. Relations Assn. (chmn. advt. 1982—), Internat. Assn. Bus. Communicators, Advt. Club Del., Del. Press Women. Roman Catholic. Office: Hagley Mus and Library PO Box 3630 Wilmington DE 19807

MACKENZIE, LINDA ALICE, computer company executive, consultant telecommunications; b. Bronx, N.Y., June 24, 1949; d. Gino Joseph and Mary J. (Damon) Arale; m. John Michael Lassourreille, Aug. 7, 1968 (div. 1975); 1 child, Lisa Marie Lassourreille; m. Donald John Mackenzie, July 2, 1978 (div. 1982). Student Richmond Coll., 1967-68, West Los Angeles Community Coll., 1978-81. Spl. rep. N.Y. Telephone Co., White Plains, 1968-71; asst. mgr. Paul Holmes Real Estate Inc., Richmond, N.Y., 1974-77; telcom applications specialist engring. Continental Airlines, Los Angeles, 1977-83; data transmission specialist Western Airlines, Los Angeles, 1983-87; owner Computers on Consignment, El Segundo, Calif., 1984—; cons. Farwest Brokers, Los Angeles, 1984-85, Caleb Fed. Credit Union, Las Vegas, Nev., 1985, Nat. Dissemenators, Las Vegas, 1985, Vega & Assocs. Prodn. Div., 1987, Uptech/Downtech, 1986, Dollar Rent-a-Car, 1987, Pomona Sch. Dist., 1987, Advanced Digital Networks, 1987; mktg. cons. AT&T, Los Angeles, 1984-85. Author: The World Within, 1983. Active Calif. Lobbyists for Conservation, 1986. Contbr.: Am. Anthology Poetry, 1987, 88. Am.Recipient Alexander award Met. Mus. Art, N.Y., 1967. Mem. Nat. Assn. Female Execs., El Segundo C. of C.; assoc. mem. Mgmt. Assocs. Republican. Clubs: Marina City, Manhattan Beach Women's. Avocations: painting; creative writing; aerobic dance; skiing; travel. Office: Computers on Consignment 531 Main St Suite 426 El Segundo CA 90245

MACKENZIE, MARY HAWKINS, hospitality placement company executive; b. St. Louis, July 27, 1936; d. Henry Goodheart and Elizabeth Cummings (Collins) Hawkins; m. Robert S. McGregor, Sept. 3, 1956 (div. May 1973); children—Robert B., Mary Catherine McGregor Ryan, Susan Leigh; m. Kenneth W. MacKenzie, Jr., Apr. 24, 1976; 1 son, Kenneth W. III. B.A., So. Methodist U., 1957. Ctr. dir. YWCA, Dallas, 1966-67; profl. cons. in personnel M. David Lowe, Houston, 1973-75; employment mgr. St. Joseph Hosp., Houston, 1976-78; personnel dir. Greater Houston Hosp. Council, 1978; personnel dir. exec. com. Dunfey Hotel, Houston, 1978-81; pres. The Hotelier Inc., Houston, 1981—; industry adv. bd. High Sch. for Restaurant and Travel Careers, 1986-87; guest columnist The Houston Chronicle and The Houston Post, 1987. Chmn. bd. dirs. Houston Jazz Ballet, 1979; mem. vestry Ch. of the Epiphany, Houston, 1979-82; judge Houston Women on the Move, 1987; mem. adv. bd. hotel restaurant mgmt. div., Houston Community Coll., 1988—, mem. 8 for '88 bd. Am. Lung Assn. Mem. Houston Hotel Motel Assn. (assoc.), Tex. Assn. Personnel Cons., Tex. Exec. Women (pres. 1984-85), Houston Women on the Move (chmn. 1985), Houston Hotel Personnel Dirs. (founder, exec. 1980-81), Houston Area Assn. Personnel Cons. (chmn. 1985—), Delta Gamma. Episcopalian. Avocation: Running. Office: Hotelier Inc 6776 Southwest Freeway Suite 150 Houston TX 77074

MACKETY, CAROLYN JEAN, nurse, consultant; b. Chgo., Feb. 27, 1932; d. Gerald James and Minnette (Buis) Kruyf; m. Robert J. Martin, Oct. 3, 1952 (div. 1959); children—Daniel, David, Steven, Laura. Diploma, Hackley Hosp. Sch. Nursing, 1969; B.S., Coll. St. Francis, 1977; M.B.A., Columbia Pacific U., 1987. Nursing coordinator operating room Grant Hosp., Columbus, Ohio, 1981-84, dir. operating room services, 1984-86; pres., owner Laser Cons., Inc., 1986—; v.p. ops. Laser Ctrs. of Am; laser nurse specialist. Mem. Assn. Operating Room Nurses, Am. Soc. Laser Medicine and Surgery (chmn.). Republican. Mem. editorial bd. Indsl. Laser Rev.; editor Laser Nursing; author: Perioperative Laser Nursing.

MACKIE, SUSAN LYNN, accountant; b. West Point, N.Y., Apr. 21, 1958; d. Thomas C. Jr. and Elizabeth (Barbour) M. BS magna cum laude, U. Md., 1979. CPA, Md. Mem. sr. audit staff Thomas Havey and Co., Washington, 1979-85, mgr. audit, 1985—. Contbr. newsletter articles Kapitol Dome, 1983-87. Bd. dirs. Lake VIllage Manor Homeowners Assn., Bowie, Md., 1985-87. Mem. Nat. Assn. Accts. (yr. book dir. 1983-84, manuscript dir. 1986-87, bd. dirs., named Mem. of Yr. Washington chpt. 1982), Am. Assn. CPA's, Md. Assn. CPA's, Am. Soc. Women Accts. Democrat. Methodist. Office: Thomas Havey & Co 4301 Connecticut Ave NW Washington DC 20008

MACKINNON, MARION ELIZABETH, broadcasting advertising executive; b. Providence, Sept. 9, 1952; d. Gordon Henry and Marion Joanna (Taylor) MacK. BA, Emerson Coll., 1972; cert. in teaching, Mass. Maritime Acad., 1973; postgrad., Hyannis (Mass.) Coll., 1972-73. Salesperson Sta. WJAR subs. Outlet Broadcasting Co., Providence, 1974-80, Sta. 91X, Xtra subs. Noble Multimedia Extra, San Diego, 1980-81; sales mgr. Sta. KLAU subs. Corngold Broadcasting, Las Vegas, 1981-82, gen. sales mgr., 1982-84; cons. direct mktg. response Sta. KABC, Los Angeles, 1982—; tchr. Smithfield (R.I.) High Sch., 1978-84; gen. sales mgr. Kottcon Broadcasting, San Bernardino, Calif., 1981-82; freelance sales trainer. Chairwoman: The Scoop Freelancers Directory, 1979. Youth dir. Girls Friendly Soc., Providence, 1970-74; dir. Falmouth (Mass.) Theatrical Dept., 1972-74, Episcopal Diocese Youth Group; asst. dir. Smithfield Theatrical Group; youth dir. Girls Friendly Soc., Providence, 1970; supporter YMCA, Los Angeles, 1982—; creative cons. Jewish Community Ctr. Hope High Sch., Providence. Recipient Honorary Plaque YMCA, Los Angeles, 1985, Commendation award Fairfax Relations Council, Los Angeles, 1987. Mem. So. Calif. Broadcasting Assn., Los Angeles Ad Club, Long Beach C. of C. (com. 1985—); chairwoman R.I. Women Advt. Home: 11511 Rochester Ave #19 Los Angeles CA 90025 Office: Sta KABC 3321 S LaCiemega Blvd Los Angeles CA 90016

MACKINTOSH, PAMELA ANNE, computer software executive; b. Denver, May 27, 1957; d. Salvador Ruben and Carole Anne (Wilson) M. Student, U. No. Colo., 1975-78; BA in Psychology, Colo. Women's Coll., 1980. Mgr. La Hacienda Restaurant, Denver, 1975-80; account rep. Mountain Bell, Denver, 1980-82; v.p. Computer Ins. Systems, Denver, 1982-87, Trion corp., Denver, 1984—; cons. Tosh's Hacienda, 1986-88; bd. dirs. Trion Automated Systems, Vancouver, B.C., Can. Mem. Nat. Assn. Female Execs. Democrat. Roman Catholic.

MACLAINE, SHIRLEY, actress; b. Richmond, Va., Apr. 24, 1934; d. Ira O. and Kathlyn (MacLean) Beaty; m. Steve Parker, Sept. 17, 1954; 1 dau., Stephanie Sachiko. Ed. high sch. Broadway plays include Me and Juliet, 1953, Pajama Game, 1954; actress: movies The Touble With Harry, 1954, Artists and Models, 1954, Around the World in 80 Days, 1955-56, Hot Spell, 1957, The Matchmaker, 1957, The Sheepman, 1957, Some Came Running, 1958 (Fgn. Press award 1959), Ask Any Girl, 1959 (Silver Bear award as best actress Internat. Berlin Film Festival), Career, 1959, Can-Can, 1959, The Apartment, 1959 (Best Actress prize Venice Film Festival), Children's Hour, 1960, The Apartment, 1960, Two for the Seesaw, 1962, Irma La Douce, 1963, What A Way to Go and The Yellow Rolls Royce, 1964, John Goldfarb Please Come Home, 1965, Gambit and Woman Times Seven, 1967, The Bliss of Mrs. Blossom, Sweet Charity, 1969, Two Mules for Sister Sara, 1969, Desperate Characters, 1971, The Possession of Joel Delaney, 1972, The Other Half of the Sky: A China Memoir, 1975, The Turning Point, 1977, Being There, 1979, A Change of Seasons, 1980, Loving Couples, 1980, Terms of Endearment, 1983 (Acad. award 1984); TV shows Shirley's World, 1971-72, Shirley MacLaine: If They Could See Me Now, 1974-75, Gypsy in My Soul, 1975-76, Where Do We Go From Here?, 1976-77, Shirley MacLaine at the Lido, 1979, Shirley MacLaine . . . Every Little Movement, 1980; producer, co-dir.: documentary on China The Other Half of the Sky; author: Don't Fall Off the Mountain, 1970, The New Celebrity Cookbook, 1973, You Can Get There From Here, 1975, Out on a Limb, 1983, Dancing in the Light, 1985, It's All in the Playing, 1987; editor: McGovern: The Man and His Beliefs, 1972. Office: care Internat Creative Mgmt 8899 Beverly Blvd Los Angeles CA 90048 *

MACLEAN, BARBARA BARONDESS, actress, writer, designer; b. N.Y.C., July 4, 1907; d. Benjamin Gregor and Stella (Sirkis) Barondess; m. Douglas MacLean, June 1936 (dec.); m. Leonard J. Knaster, Aug. 22, 1955 (div. Aug. 1974). student NYU, 1925-26, UCLA, 1936-40, Art Sch., Paris, 1952-54; DFA (hon.) Mercy Coll., 1988. Featured in Broadway stage plays including Gay Paree, 1926, Crime, 1927, Riddle Me This, Garden of Eden, (ingenue lead) Topaze, 1929-31, A Thousand Summers, 1932, Death Takes a Holiday, 1932, Faithfully Yours, 1951; motion pictures from 1932-38 include: Rasputin, Hold Your Man, Merry Widow, Tale of Two Cities, Plot Thickens, Easy Money, Queen Christina, Soldiers of the Storm, When Strangers Marry; appeared in TV film The Open Cage, 1982; interior and textile designer, Beverly Hills, Calif. and N.Y., 1938-78; pres. Barbara Barondess MacLean Ltd., Inc. , 1947-73, Discovery Unltd., Palm Beach, Fla., 1973—; designed and manufactured clothes, 1947-52; founder, pres. cosmetics co., Barondess Inc., N.Y.C.; founder Barbara Barondess Theatre Lab., 1982; Columnist Morning Telegraph, 1929-31; created column Little Bo Peep on Broadway; contbr. articles to Hollywood (Calif.) Reporter , N.Y. Jour., Herald-Tribune, Woman's Day, 1962-63; author: Cooking on the Run, One Life Is Not Enough, 1986, Timing, 1986; producer Medea and her Dolls, N.Y.C., 1984, autobiographical documentary film to Statue of Liberty and Ellis Island Mus.; painting and sculpture exhibited in galleries in Beverly Hills and N.Y.C., 1949—. Tchr. 1st aid ARC, 1941-46. Mem. AFTRA, Screen Actors' Guild, Actors Equity, Am. Soc. Interior Designers. Office: Theatre Lab 630 Park Ave New York NY 10021

MACLEOD, DEBBIE EDWARDS, real estate executive; b. Gainesville, Fla., Feb. 26, 1951; d. Hugh Coleman Edwards and Lillian (Harden) Zucha; m. Darrelle C. Stewart, Dec. 31, 1970 (div. 1973); 1 child, Sonia Jo Stewart; m. Peter J. MacLeod, Oct. 27, 1979. Grad. Bert Rodgers Sch. Real Estate, 1972. Real estate broker, Fla. Property mgr. Ray E. Haufler & Co., Gainesville, Fla., 1973-78; pres. Contemporary Mgmt. Concepts, Inc., Gainesville, 1978—, Contemporary Concepts & Investments, Inc., Gainesville, 1983—, Fla. Container Rental Inc., Gainesville, 1986—. Sponsor Ducks Unlimited, Gainesville, 1984. Mem. Gainesville Bd. Realtors (Million Dollar Club 1984), Gainesville Homebuilders, Gainesville C. of C. Republican. Baptist. Avocations: sailing, fishing, interior decorating. Office: 6910 W University Ave Suite 2 Gainesville FL 32607

MACLEOD, JENNIFER SELFRIDGE, psychologist; b. London, Nov. 26, 1929; came to U.S., 1940; d. Harry Gordon Jr. and Charlotte Elsie (Dennis) Selfridge; m. John Alexander Macleod, June 30 (div. 1972); children: Pamela Jennifer, Scott Gordon. BA magna cum laude, Radcliffe Coll., 1949; MA, Columbia U., 1952, PhD, 1958. Asst. research account exec. McCann-Erickson, N.Y.C., 1952-55; asst. dir. research Ogilvie Benson & Mather, N.Y.C., 1955-58; chief psychologist Opinion Research Corp., Princeton, N.J., 1958-71; dir. Eagleton Ctr. for the Am. Woman & Politics Rutgers U., New Brunswick, N.J., 1971; pres. Jennifer Macleod Assocs., Princeton Junction, N.J., 1971—; v.p., dir. personnel Fidelity Bank, Phila., 1976-78; v.p. human resources cons. and research Fidelco Assocs., Phila., 1978; cons. Minority Opportunities Skills Program N.J. State Govt., Trenton, 1986—. Author: You Won't Do: What Textbooks on U.S. Government Teach High School Girls, 1971; contbr. articles to profl. jours. Founding pres. cen. N.J. chpt. NOW, 1969-71, chmn. bd. Univ. Day Nursery, Princeton, 1971; trustee N.J. ACLU, 1973-75; trustee Phila. Bus. Acad., Phila., 1976-78; vol. Beyond War Movement, N.J., 1985—. Mem. Am. Assn. Pub. Opinion Research (cen. N.J. chpt. pres. 1986-87), Am. Psychol. Assn., OD Network, Princeton Research Forum, Assn. Humanistic Psychology, Mensa, Intertel, World Future Soc. Home and Office: 4 Canoe Brook Dr Princeton Junction NJ 08550

MACMACKIN, CINDI LOU, legal consultant; b. Shawsville, Va., May 27, 1957; d. Marvin Via and Geralyn (Keith) M. BS in Human Resources, Va. Polytechnic Inst. & State U., 1981, MA in Coll. Adminstrn., Counseling, 1982. Dist. sales mgr. Avon Products, N.Y.C., 1981-83; dir. sales Guest Quarters Hotels, Washington, 1983-85; legal cons. Trak Legal Services, Washington, 1985—; Judge Teenage Va. Pageant, Staunton, 1984; vol. YMCA, Washington, 1987—. Mem. Nat. Assn. Female Execs. Baptist. Office: Trak Legal Services 1615 L St Suite 930 Washington DC 20036

MACMILLAN, CATHERINE COPE, restaurant owner; b. Sacramento, Mar. 3, 1947; d. Newton A. Cope and Marilyn (Jacobs) Combrink; m. Thomas C. MacMillan, Dec. 18, 1967 (div. Jan. 1984); children: Corey Jacobs, Andrew Cope. BA, U. Calif., 1969; MBA, Calif. State U., Sacramento, 1978. Pub. health microbiologist County of Sacramento, 1969-74; pres., gen. mgr. The Firehouse Restaurant, Sacramento, 1980—; bd. dirs. Westamerica Bank, San Rafael, Calif., Am. Recreation Ctrs., Sacramento. CHmn. Sacramento Conv. and Visitors Bur.; pres. Old Sacramento Propery Owners Council. Mem. Calif. Restaurant Assn. (bd. dirs.), Sacramento Restaurant Assn. (Restaurant of Yr. 1983), Old Sacramento Citizen's and Mchts. Assn. (chmn. bd. 1984), Sacramento Met. C. of C. (bd. dirs.). Office: The Firehouse Restaurant 1112 Second St Sacramento CA 95814

MACMILLAN, MARGARET LAURIE, aerospace company executive; b. Los Angeles, Nov. 28, 1960; d. Donald Bather and Olaug Margrethe (Myhr) M. Student, U. Calif.-San Diego, 1978-80; B.B.A., Calif. State U.-Chico, 1982; M.B.A., U. So. Calif., Los Angeles, 1988. Sr. project control adminstr. Hughes Aircraft Co., Torrance, Calif., 1983—; aerobics instr., 1984-85; cons. Macola Record Co., Hollywood, Calif., 1984, Baby'O Recorders, Hollywood, 1985-86; Pres., co-founder Palos Verdes (Calif.) Girl's Club, 1971-75; participant Los Angeles Olympics Opening Ceremony Internat. Parade. Mem. Phi Chi Theta (v.p. 1982), Phi Kappa Phi, Beta Gamma Sigma, Sigma Iota Epsilon. Avocations: skiing, reading, sky diving, jogging, yoga. Home: 162 Hermosa Ave Hermosa Beach CA 90254 Office: Hughes Aircraft Co 3100 W Lomita Blvd Torrance CA 90509

MACON, IRENE ELIZABETH, designer, consultant; b. East St. Louis, Ill., May 11, 1935; d. David and Thelma (Eastlen) Dunn; m. Robert Teco Macon, Feb. 12, 1954; children—Leland Sean, Walter Edwin, Gary Keith, Jill Renee Macon Martin, Robin Jeffrey, Lamont. Student Forest Park Coll., Washington U., St. Louis, 1970, Bailey Tech. Coll., 1975, Lindenwood Coll., 1981. Office mgr. Cardinal Glennon Hosp., St. Louis, 1965-72; interior designer J.C. Penney Co., Jennings, Mo., 1972-73; entrepreneur Irene Designs Unltd., St. Louis, 1974—; vol. liaison Pub. Sch. System, St. Louis, 1980-82; cons. in field. Inventor venetian blinds for autos, 1981, T-blouse and diaper wrap, 1986; author 26th Word newsletter, 1986. Committeewoman Republican party, St. Louis, 1984; vice chair 4th Senatorial Dist. of Mo., 1984, vol. St. Louis Assn. Community Orgns., 1983; instr. first aid Bi-State chpt. ARC, St. Louis, 1984; block capt. Operation Brightside, St. Louis, 1984; co-chair Status and Role of Women, Union Meml. United Meth. Ch., 1986—. Named one of Top Ladies of Distinction, St. Louis, 1983. Mem. Am. Soc. Interior Designers (assoc.), NAACP, Nat. Mus. Women in the Arts (charter), Internat. Platform Assn., Nat. Council Negro Women (1st v.p. 1984), Invention Assn. of St. Louis (subcom. head 1985), Coalition of 100 Black Women, St. Louis Assn. Fashion Designers. Methodist. Club: Presidents, (Washington). Avocations: reading; designing personal wardrobe; modeling; horseback riding; boating. Home and Office: 5469 Maple St Saint Louis MO 63112

MACON, JANE HAUN, lawyer; b. Corpus Christi, Tex., Sept. 26, 1946; d. E.H. and Johnnie Mae (De Mauri) Haun; m. R. Laurence Macon, Sept. 6, 1969. B in Internat. Studies, U. Tex., 1967, JD, 1970. Bar: Tex. 1971, Ga. 1971, U.S. Dist. Ct. (we. dist.) Tex. 1973, U.S. Ct. Appeals (5th and 11th cirs.) 1973. Legal staff Office Econ. Oppurtunity, Atlanta, 1970-71; trial atty. City of San Antonio, 1972-77, city atty., 1977-83; ptnr. Fulbright & Jaworski, San Antonio, 1983—; pres. Internat. Women's Forum, Washington, 1987—; bd. dirs. Thousand Oaks Nat. Bank, San Antonio. Legal counsel Nat. Women's Polit. Caucus, 1981—; bd. dirs. Alamo council Boy Scouts Am., San Antonio, 1977—. Named to San Antonio Hall of Fame, 1984; named one of Rising Stars, 1984. Fellow Tex. Bar Found., Tex. Bar Assn. (chmn. women and the law 1984-85, client security fund com.), Southwest Research Found.; mem. San Antonio Young Lawyers Assn., Women Lawyers Tex. (pres. 1984-85). Democrat. Baptist. Office: Fulbright & Jaworski 300 Convent Suite 2200 San Antonio TX 78205 Home: 230 W Elsmere San Antonio TX 78212

MACRORIE, CAROL ANN, manufacturing company official; b. Little Falls, N.Y., Feb. 14, 1946; d. Harold D. and Lena Irene (Grassel) MacR.; student Northeastern U., 1973-76, Holyoke Community Coll., 1977—; children—Francis Gulla, Christopher Pasquale. Inventory control clk. Salada Foods, Inc., Woburn, Mass., 1964-69; distbn. supr. Addison Wesley Publ. Co., Reading, Mass., 1969-73; with Digital Equipment Corp., Maynard, Mass., 1973-84, inventory and prodn. control supr., Westfield, Mass., 1979-80, distibn. mgr., 1980-84; corp distbn. mgr. Masscomp, Westford, Mass., 1984-86; plant mfg. mgr Hadco Corp., Derry, N.H., 1986—. Mem. Am. Mgmt. Assn., Am. Prodn. and Inventory Control Soc., Nat. Assn. Female Execs., Delta Nu Alpha. Home: 19 Fairway Dr Apt #24 Derry NH 03038 Office: Hadco Corp Manchester Rd Derry NH 03038

MACROWSKI, JUDITH ANN, educator; b. Waukegan, Ill., Mar. 7, 1949; d. Walter J. and Emily A. (Rygiel) M. BA, Nazareth Coll., Kalamazoo, 1971; MEd, Loyola U., Chgo., 1986. Cert. tchr., Ill. Adminstr., tchr. Woodland Sch., Cages Lake, Ill., 1971-85; tchr. for the gifted Waukegan Pub. Schs., 1986—; reading workshop leader, cons. Lake Edn. Service Ctr., Grayslake, Ill., 1986—. Mem. Am. Fedn. Tchrs., Delta Kappa Gamma. Roman Catholic. Home: 1148 Victoria St North Chicago IL 60064 Office: Waukegan Pub Schs Washington ST Waukegan IL 60085

MACUR, PATRICIA A., computer programmer, analyst; b. Chgo.; d. Alexander J. and Alice Mary (Styburski) Mackiewicz; m. George J. Macur, 1960; children: Alexander, Cindy Macur Conti. BS, SUNY, 1978; MS, Thomas J. Watson Sch. of Engring., 1984. System control analyst IBM Corp., Endicott, N.Y., 1977; programmer trainee intelligent systems NCR, Ithaca, N.Y., 1978-79, assoc. programmer software integration, 1980, assoc. programmer I gen. purpose systems, 1980-81, programmer, analyst terminal software div., 1981-84; applications analyst material mgmt. systems Eastman Kodak Co., Rochester, N.Y., 1984-85, applications analyst planning and control systems, 1985-86; sr. programmer, analyst mfg. systems Ingersoll-Rand Systems, Athens, Pa., 1986—. Mem. IMC. Club: Randettes (Athens). Home: 713 Catalina Blvd Endwell NY 13760 Office: Ingersoll Rand Systems 101 Main St Athens PA 18810

MACUT, SHARON NICKOLENE, newspaper art director; b. Toledo, Ohio, Nov. 10, 1951; d. Nick M. and Nancy (Macut) Petkovich; m. Donald Fredrick Green, July 10, 1981 (div. May 2, 1985). Student, Eastern Mich. U., 1971-73. Dept. sec. Eastern Mich. U., Ypsilanti, 1974-75; fin. mgr. Domestic Violence Project, Ann Arbor, Mich., 1976-81; personal sec. Can.-Am. Investments, Inc., Key Largo, Fla., 1982-83; sales rep. Islamorada (Fla.) Trolley Co., 1984—; art dir. The Reporter, Tavernier, Fla., 1984—; exec. bd. Transp. Planning Adv. Com., Monroe County, Fla., 1985—. Fundraiser Key Largo Pub. Library Bldg., 1985—, Florida Keys Children Shelter, Monroe County, 1985—, Domestic Abuse Shelter, Monroe County, 1986—; mem. Monroe County Commn. on the Status of Women, 1987—. Mem. NOW (pres. Upper Keys chpt. 1984-86, fundraiser Fla. chpt. 1983—), jaycees, NARAL. Democrat. Serbian Orthodox. Office: The Reporter PO Box 1197 Tavernier FL 33070

MAC VICAR, MARGARET LOVE AGNES, materials physicist, educator; b. Hamilton, Ont., Can., Nov. 20, 1943; came to U.S., 1946, naturalized, 1953; d. George Francis and Elizabeth Margaret (Thompson) MacV. SB in Physics, MIT, 1964, DSc in Metallurgy and Materials Sci, 1967; DSc (hon.), Clarkson U., 1985. Postdoctoral NATO, Marie Curie fellow Cavendish Lab., U. Cambridge, Eng., 1967-69; instr. physics MIT, Cambridge, Mass., 1969-70, asst. prof., 1970-74, assoc. prof. physics, 1974-79, Class of 1922 Career Devel. prof., 1973-75, assoc. prof. phys. sci., 1979-83, prof. phys. sci., 1983—, Cecil and Ida Green prof. edn., 1980—, dean undergrad. edn., 1985—; v.p. Carnegie Instn., Washington, 1983-87; Chancellor's Disting. prof. U. Calif., Berkeley, 1979; cons. to univs., industry, non-profit orgns.; mem. corp. C.S. Draper Lab., Cambridge; dir. W.H. Brady Co., Exxon Corp., Research Corp.; co-chair project 2061; vice chmn. adv. com. to directorat of sci. and engring. edn. NSF; mem. Adv. Council on Edn., Sci., Tech., and the Economy, Carnegie Corp.; co-chmn. Nat. Council for Sci., Tech. Edn.; vice chair working group on sci. and engring. talent Govt.-Univ.-Industry Roundtable Nat. Acad. Scis. Mem. editorial adv. bd. World Book Sci. Yr.; patentee in field. Past trustee Carnegie Found. for Advancement Teaching; trustee Boston Mus. Sci.; past mem. Carnegie Council on Policy Studies in Higher Edn. Recipient Most Significant Contribution to Edn. award M.I.T., 1977, Charles A. Dana awards for Pioneering Achievements in Higher Edn., 1986; Young Faculty Research award Gen. Electric Found., 1976-79; Danforth Found. assoc. 1972—. Mem. Am. Women in Sci., Am. Phys. Soc., Am. Assn. of Higher Edn. Club: Boston Women's City. Office: Dean Undergrad Edn Mass Inst Tech Cambridge MA 02139

MACY, JANET KUSKA, radio and television educator; b. Omaha, Nov. 9, 1935; d. Val and Marie (Letovsky) Kuska; BS, U. Nebr., 1957; MS, Kans. State U., 1961; MEd, S.D. State U., 1970. With Fed. Extension Service, U.S. Dept. Agr., Washington, 1956; specialist Kans. State U. Sta. KSAC, 1957-61; home econs. editor U. Nebr. Sta. KUON, 1961-62; specialist Iowa State U. Sta. WOI-TV, 1962-67, S.D. State U. Sta. KESD-TV, 1967-71; radio/TV specialist U. Minn. Sta. KUOM, Mpls., 1971—; travelling field editor Better Homes & Gardens, 1972-73; TV cons. U.S. Consumer Product Safety Commn., 1978-79; media freelancer Gen. Foods, Mpls., 1983; archivist Groves Conf. on Marriage and Family, 1986—. Producer: (TV documentary) Building Blocks for Learning, 1965 (ACE award), (radio programs) Nutrition Award, 1977 (AWRT award), School Bell Awards, (MEA award 1979, 80, 82). Mem. Agrl. Communicators in Edn. (Superior award 1966, 69, 81), Am. Soc. Tng. and Devel., Minn. Intergovtl. Tng. Council, Minn. Edn. Assn., NEA, Epsilon Sigma Phi. Home: 122 Demont Ave #362 Saint Paul MN 55117 Office: U Minn 282 McNeal Hall Saint Paul MN 55108

MACY MARCY, SUZANNE KAY, behavioral ecologist, educator, consultant; b. Seattle, Oct. 24, 1951; d. Marshall Eugene Macy and Kathleen Mae (Lobb) Macy Costello; m. Scott Colson Marcy, May 2, 1981. A.A., Shoreline Community Coll., 1971; B.S., U. Wash., 1974, Ph.D., 1981; postgrad. Sangamon State U., 1984-85. Research asst. dept. psychology U. Wash., Seattle, 1974-75, teaching asst. dept. psychology, 1976-79, instr. psychology, 1979-81, also instructional cons. Ctr. for Instructional Devel. and Research, 1979-81; biol. technician Nat. Marine Fisheries Service, Seattle and Pribilof Islands, Alaska, 1975-77; dir. graphic arts Leisure Press, Highland Falls, N.Y., 1982; writer, editor West Point Mus., N.Y., 1983; mem. vis. faculty in biology Vassar Coll., Poughkeepsie, N.Y., 1984; sci. researcher, sci. office Ill. Legis. Research Unit, Springfield, 1984-85; mem. adj. faculty biology Northwestern State U. of La. Fort Polk Ctr., Leesville, 1986; legis. sci. intern Sangamon State U., Springfield, 1984-85; mem. sr. faculty, leader Sch. for Field Studies, affiliate Northeastern U., Cambridge, Mass., 1985— First author booklet: Alzheimer's Disease: Activity of the 84th Illinois General Assembly and appendix, 1985. Rep., Nat. Mil. Family Assn., Washington, 1986. Nat. Marine Fisheries Service dissertation grantee, 1976, 77. Mem. AAAS, Am. Inst. Biol. Scis. (congl. liaison 1985-87), Animal Behavior Soc., N.Y. Acad. Scis., Phi Beta Kappa, Sigma Xi, Phi Theta Kappa. Clubs: PEO (chpt. corr. sec. and ednl. loan fund chairperson 1983-84) (New City, N.Y.). Avocations: reading; book collecting; painting; drawing; crafts. Home and Office: 9011 Golden Leaf Ct Springfield VA 22153

MACZULSKI, MARGARET LOUISE, association executive; b. Detroit, Apr. 1, 1949; d. Bohdan Alexander and Olga Louise (Martinuick) M. BS, Mich. State U., 1972. Mgr. meetings Nat. Assn. Realtors, Mktg. Inst., Chgo., 1977-82, mgr. mktg., 1982-83; regional sales mgr. Fairmont Hotels, Chgo., 1982; dir., mgr. trade shows and confs. Am. Broadcasting Co./Pub. Div., Wheaton, Ill., 1983-85; mgr. meeting and conf. planning Am. Soc. Personnel Adminstrn., Alexandria, Va., 1985—. Mem. Meeting Planners Internat., Greater Washington Soc. Assn. Execs. (chmn. sire inspection com.), Am. Soc. Assn. Execs., Nat. Assn. Exposition Execs., Mich. State U. Alumni Assn. (treas. D.C. chpt. 1987-88). Republican. Roman Catholic. Avocations: piano, swimming. Home: 5340 Holmes Run Pkwy #219 Alexandria VA 22304 Office: Am Soc Personnel Adminstrn 606 N Washington Alexandria VA 22314

MADDALENA, LUCILLE ANN, management executive; b. Plainfield, N.J., Nov. 8, 1948; d. Mario Anthony and Josephine Dorothy (Longo) M.; m. James Samonte Hohn, Sept. 7, 1975; children: Vincent, Nicholas, Mitchell. AA, Rider Coll., 1968; BS, Monmouth Coll., West Long Branch, N.J., 1971; EdD, Rutgers U., 1978. Newscaster, dir. pub. relations Sta. WBRW, Bridgewater, N.J., 1971-73; editor-in-chief Commerce mag., New Brunswick, N.J., 1973-74; dir. pub. relations Raritan Valley Regional C. of C., New Brunswick, N.J., 1973-74; aide pub. relations to mayor City of New Brunswick, 1974; dir. communications United Way Cen. Jersey, New Brunswick, 1974-77; mgmt. cons. United Way Am., Alexandria, Va., 1977-78; pres., owner Maddalena Assocs., Chester, N.J., 1978—; sr. cons. United Research Co., Morristown, N.J., 1980-81; dir. communications and devel. Xicom Inc., Parsippany, N.J., 1987—; chmn. bd. dirs. OCD Group subs. Xicom Inc., Tuxedo, N.Y., 1984—; also treas. bd. dirs. OCD Group, Parsippany, N.J.; adj. faculty Somerset County Coll., Bridgewater, N.J., 1970; guest lectr. Rutgers U., New Brunswick, N.J., 1975-80. Author: A Communications Manual for Non-Profit Organizations, 1980; editor New Directions for Instl. Advancement, 1980-81. Mem. Chester Borough Council, 1984-87. Recipient Mayor's Commendation City of New Brunswick, 1973. Mem. AAUW, LWV, Nat. Assn. Press Women, N.J. Elected Women Officials, Kappa Delta Pi. Republican. Rqman Catholic. Club: N.J. Sled Dog. Home: 7 Wheeler Rd Chester NJ 07930 Office: OCD Group 1280 Rt 46 Parsippany NJ 07054

MADDEN, BETTY CAMPBELL, media company executive, lawyer; b. Clinton, Iowa, Oct. 13, 1942; d. Merrill J. and Clarice M. (Hanson) Campbell; m. Joseph R. Wolf, June 10, 1965 (div. 1972); 1 dau., Kari M.; m. Lauren R. Madden, Nov. 21, 1976. B.A., Cornell Coll., Mt. Vernon, Iowa, 1965; J.D., Ill. Inst. Tech., 1970; M.B.A., U. Iowa, 1982. Bar: Ill. 1970, Iowa 1974. Sole practice, Antioch, Ill., 1970-74; atty. Meredith Corp., Des Moines, 1974-79, asst. sec., 1979-80, corp. sec., 1980-88. Contbr. articles to profl. jours. Bd. dirs. Des Moines Pastoral Counseling Service, 1983—, Des Moines Symphony, Des Moines Ballet. Mem. Iowa Bar Assn., Polk County Bar Assn., Polk County Women's Bar Assn., Des Moines C. of C. (2000 com.). Baha'i. Club: Des Moines. Office: Meredith Corp 1716 Locust St Des Moines IA 50336

MADDEN, DIANE SLOANE, public information officer; b. N.Y.C., Sept. 6, 1945; d. Mortimer Schachter and Betty (Jessel) Lewis; m. John William Madden, July 4, 1981 (div. Sept. 1985); children: Victoria, Melanie, Ashleigh. BA, Goddard Coll., 1974; EdM, U. Ariz., 1976. With exec. sales dept. House Beautiful mag., N.Y.C., 1971-72; gen. mgr. Stas. KWFM-KEVT Radio, Tucson, 1973-74; interventionist, counselor Suicide Prevention Crisis Ctr., Tucson, 1976-77; pres., therapist Advs. in Counseling., Tucson, 1977-78; dir. fellowships Hand Surgery, Ltd., Tucson, 1978-84; dir. community relations Pima County Dept. Transp. and Flood Control Dist., Tucson, 1984—, also bd. dirs. Commr. Tucson Women's Commn., 1984-86; precinct person Pima County Reps., Tucson, 1984-85, bd. dirs. Pima Coll. Pub. Relations Group. Recipient Copper Letter award City of Tucson, 1986, cert. recognition YWCA Women on the Move, Tucson, 1985, cert. appreciation U. Ariz. Pres. club, 1986. Mem. AAUW, Pima County Med. Soc. (bd. dirs. 1984-85), Tucson C. of C. (mem. leadership team 1984), Leadership Alumni Assn. Home: 260 E Limberlost Rd Tucson AZ 85705 Office: Pima County Dept Transp 1313 S Mission Rd Tucson AZ 85713

MADDEN, KATHRYN RUTH, resource specialist, consultant; b. San Diego, Feb. 25, 1948; d. John Kenneth and Ruth (Pauly) M.; m. Steven Makeig, Mar. 29, 1980 (div. Sept. 1983). BA in English, Calif. State U., Los Angeles, 1974. Cert. multiple subjects specialist, specialist learning handicapped, resource specialist, state sch. program quality reviewer. Profl. expert Los Angeles Community Coll., 1976; resource specialist Alhambra (Calif.) High Sch., 1977-81; dir. learning ctr. Our Lady of Lourdes, Tujunga, Calif., 1982-83, mem. children's liturgy com., 1981-83, mem. team outreach program, 1983-85, coordinator religion outreach program, 1984-85; dir.-on-bd. Pauly Corp., Manitowac, Wis., 1979-84; resource specialist Los Nietos Sch., Whittier, Calif., 1983-84; resource specialist Alhambra City Schs., 1984—, mem. procedural guide spl. edn. com., 1984—, chmn. math. sect., mem. modification com., 1985; cons. Cath. Schs. Los Angeles Archdiocese, 1984—, mem. spl. edn. com., 1985-87. Mem. St. Joseph's Devel. Council, S..D., 1984—; facilitator Renew Group, Tujunga, 1986—. Mem. Nat. Tchrs. Assn., Council Exceptional Children, Nat. Assn. Female Execs., Calif. Assn. Resource Specialists, Calif. Tchrs. Assn., Alhambra Tchrs. Assn. Democrat. Roman Catholic.

MADDICKS, NONA MIHR, production planning administrator; b. Rochester, N.Y., July 20, 1942; d. Norman Carl and Geraldine Helen (Hoffman) Mihr; divorced; 1 child, Shana L. AAS, Rochester Inst. Tech., 1962; BS in Psychology, U. Rochester, 1974. Prodn. asst. Eastman Kodak Co., Rochester, 1969-76, prodn. specialist, 1976-83, supervising prodn. specialist, 1983-86, supr. estimating, scheduling, planning and monitoring, 1986—. Mem. Rochester Club of Printing House Craftsmen (club printer 1983-85, dinner chairperson 1976-78, treas. 1987—). Home: 54 Larkwood Dr Rochester NY 14626 Office: Eastman Kodak Co 343 State St Rochester NY 14650

MADDOCKS-WILBUR, REBECCA LOU, social services administrator; b. Ellsworth, Maine, June 27, 1961; d. Irving Raymond and Joyce Althea (Barker) Maddocks; m. Roland Austin Wilbur Jr., Feb. 14, 1987. AS, U. Maine, 1982, BS, 1984. Cert. elem. sch. tchr. Acad. skills programmer U. Maine and Bangor Community Coll., Bangor, 1982-83; asst. tchr. Ellsworth Devel. Ctr., 1984, tchr., 1984-85, program dir., 1985—. mem. Day Program Providers Group, Millinocket, Maine, 1986—. Mem. Assn. Retarded Citizens, Nat. Assn. Female Execs., Am. Assn. Mental Deficiency, Kappa Delta Pi, Phi Kappa Phi. Republican. Home: RFD #4 Box 82 North St Ellsworth ME 04605 Office: Ellsworth Devel Ctr Box 77 Union St Ellsworth ME 04605

MADDOX, PATRICIA ANN WATSON, sales and marketing executive; b. Bklyn., Dec. 3, 1956; d. William Gerard and Josephine T. (Merulla) Watson; m. John Thomas Martin Jr., Jan. 10, 1975 (div. 1982); children: John Thomas Martin III, Misty Dawn Martin; m. Stephen James Maddox, Mar. 22, 1986. Student, Cen. Ariz. Coll., 1979-81, Rio Salado Community Coll.; AA in Bus. Mgmt., Western Internat. U., 1988. Adminstrv. asst. USAF, McGuire AFB, 1974-77; VA asst. Cen. Ariz. Coll., Coolidge, 1979-81; adminstrv. asst. Ariz. Army N.G., Phoenix, 1981-83; office mgr. sales Accuracy Systems, Inc., Phoenix, 1984—. Leader Girl Scouts U.S., 1978-79; active Phoenix PTA, 1985—; state sec. Am. Def. Preparedness Assn., 1983—; foster parent. Served with Ariz. N.G., 1983-86, with USAR, 1986—. Decorated Good Conduct medal, 1977, Airmen of Month medal, 1976, Army Achievement medal. Mem. Nat. Assn. Female Execs., N.G. Assn., Quartermasters Officers Assn. Democrat. Roman Catholic. Avocations: needlepoint, reading, camping. Home: 2853 E Siesta Ln Phoenix AZ 85024 Office: Accuracy Systems Inc 15205 N Cave Creek Rd Phoenix AZ 85032

MADDOX, PATRICIA JEAN, trucking company executive; b. Wichita, Kans., July 28, 1939; d. Paul Joseph Massey and Mabel Genevieve (Ford) Massey Malcom; m. Paul L. Hutchison, Jan. 14, 1956 (div. Apr. 1961); 1 child, William Hale; m. Dennis W. Maddox (div.); children—John Kevin, Crystal Rene'. Student pub. schs., Wichita. Billing clk. Associated Cartage, Wichita, 1959-63, Transcon Lines, Wichita, 1963-65, Royal Transp., Montebello, Calif., 1965-67; freight rate clk. ONC, Los Angeles, 1967; rate clk., supr. Russell Truck Co., Los Angeles, 1967-83; pres., mgr. RPM Trucking Co. Ltd., Santa Fe Springs, Calif., 1983—. Democrat. Avocation: needlework. Home: 17350 E Temple Sp 236 La Puente CA 91744 Office: RPM Trucking Co Ltd 11753 E Slauson Suite 9 Santa Fe Springs CA 90670

MADEJ, IRENE MARIA JANE, consulting company executive; b. Miami, Fla., Feb. 5, 1943; d. Bernard Joseph and Elenor (Nogaj) Kostrzewski; m. Ronald Arthur Marshall, July 21, 1962 (div. July 1972); children: Constance Marie, Michael Richard; m. Ronald Joseph Madej, May 17, 1975 (dec.). Student, Washtenaw Community Coll., 1976, Bus. Women's Tng. Inst., 1986. Legal sec. Law Office, Jackson, Mich., 1963-70; adminstrv. asst. Educator Sales, Jackson, 1970-72; exec. sec. Rheem Mfg., Jackson, 1972-73; test driver, mechanic Chrysler Corp., Chelsea, Mich., 1973-75; mgr. Health Mgmt. Advisors, Ann Arbor, Mich., 1977-79; sec., treas. Maybury Office Support, Inc., Ann Arbor, 1979-83; chief exec. officer Project III, Ltd., Ann Arbor, 1983-85; pres. The Profl. Group, Ltd., Ann Arbor, 1985—; cons. Beaumont Mgmt. Assn., Ann Arbor, 1983-85, cons. various small bus., Ann Arbor, 1985—; lectr. coll. seminars, Ann Arbor, 1985—. Mem. Civitan, Ypsilanti, Mich., 1981; mem. Chamber Small Bus. Council, Ann Arbor, 1986; mem. E.C.U.S., Ann Arbor, 1984—. Mem. Am. Bus. Women's Assn., Profl. Office Services Assn. (pres. 1981-82), Ann Arbor C. of C., South Univ. Merchants Assn., Nat. Assn. Female Execs. Club: WSME. Office: The Profl Group Ltd 610 Church St Ann Arbor MI 48104

MADER, PAMELA BEILE, fitness administrator; b. Chgo., Dec. 15, 1939; d. Walter Carl and marjorie Eveline (Gasprich) Beile; m. Ronald Edward Mader, Spr. 4, 1964 (div. 1980); children: Todd Anthony, Tammy Ann; m. Frank Allen Roberts, June 20, 1987. BA, Butler U., 1962. Cert. exercise tchr. Choreographer Russell Sch. Ballet, Falls Church, Va., 1975-86; master tchr. Jazzercise, U.S., Falls Church, 1983—; instr. Jazzercise, U.S., Fairfax, Va., 1980—; N.E. regional adminstr. Jazzercise, U.S., Fairfax, 1985—. Choreographer numerous jazz ballets and routines. Home and Office: 10702 Zion Dr Fairfax VA 22032

MADERA, MARIE LOUISE, magazine publishing executive; b. Los Angeles, June 11, 1955; d. Leroy James and Helen Jean (Clark) M. BA, Calif. State U., Long Beach, 1978. Art dir. Keyboard World mag., Downey, Calif., 1978-79, Popular Ceramics mag., Glendale, Calif., 1980; mgr. prodn. Creative Age Pubs., Van Nuys, Calif., 1980-86; dir. prodn. High Tech Pubs., Torrance, Calif., 1986; dir. pubs. So. Calif. Family Living mag., Buena Park, Calif., 1986—; cons. Affluent Target Mktg., La Mirada, Calif., 1986—. Choreographer community theatres, 1981—. Mem. Nat. Assn. Female Execs., Western Pubs. Assn., Advt. Prodn. Assn. So. Calif. Roman Catholic. Office: Affluent Target Mktg 6280 Manchester Blvd #219 Buena Park CA 90621

MADISON, VIVIAN YVONNE, occupational therapist, social services administrator; b. Birmingham, Ala., Dec. 30, 1950; d. Jack Master and Vivian Louise (Nelson) Thomas; m. Robert Earl Madison Jr., June 23, 1972. BS in Occupational Therapy, U. Ala., Birmingham, 1973, MEd, 1977, MS in Criminal Justice, 1986. Dir. adolescent projects United Cerebral Palsy Greater Birmingham, 1973-75; dir. occupational therapy Dept. Family and Child Services, Birmingham, 1975—; clin. prof. occupational therapy U. Ala.-Birmingham, 1974—, lectr. and cons., 1980—; invited clin. prof. Tuskegee (Ala.) U., 1980—; spl. presenter Gt. So. Occupational Therapy Confs., Atlanta, 1983-85. Author research reports in field. Chairperson library com. at Bapt. Ch., Birmingham, 1982-84. Mem. Am. Occupational Therapy Assn. (clin. researcher, resource person in mental health), Ala. Occupational Therapy Assn. (Ala. mental health liaison 1978-83, sec. 1978-82, alumni del. commn. on edn. 1980-86, licensure com. 1979-84), Delta Sigma Theta (mem. com. 1974-83); charter mem. Inst. Profl. Health Service Adminstrs. Democrat. Baptist. Office: Ala Family and Child Services 5201 Airport Hwy Birmingham AL 35212

MADONNA, MARGARET JOSEPHINE, television executive; b. Bklyn., Sept. 24, 1959; d. Anthony Pasquale and Rose (Battista) M. A in Bus., LaGuardia Community Coll., 1978; BS in Bus. Mgmt., St. John's U., 1987. Asst. to mgr. of employee benefits Am. Broadcasting Cos., Inc., N.Y.C., 1978-79, asst. to dir. prime time programming, mgr. cassette library, 1979-83, exec. asst. to v.p. ABC Entertainment, 1984-86; coordinator of affilaite relations Hearst-ABC Viacom Entertainment Services, N.Y.C., 1987, coordinator daytime sales proposals, 1987—. Mem. Internat. Radio and TV Soc., Am. Mgmt. Assn., Omicron Delta Epsilon. Roman Catholic. Home: 132-14 81st St Ozone Park NY 11417

MADORE, SISTER BERNADETTE, college president; b. Barnston, Que., Can., Jan. 24, 1918; came to U.S., 1920, naturalized; d. Joseph George and Mina Marie (Fontaine) M.; A.B., U. Montreal, 1942, B.Ed., 1943; M.S., Cath. U. Am., 1949, Ph.D., 1951. Instr. math. and English, Marie Anne Coll., Montreal, Que., 1943-44; prof. biology, dean of coll. Anna Maria Coll., Paxton, Mass., 1952-76, v.p., 1975-77, pres., 1977—; fund-raising cons.; corporator YMCA. Bd. dirs. Central Mass. chpt. ARC; bd. dirs. Worcester Coll. Consortium; trustee Worcester Boys Club. Mem. AAAS, Am. Soc. Microbiology, Nat. Assn. Biology Tchrs., AAUW, Am. Assn. Higher Edn., Worcester C. of C. Roman Catholic. Lodge: Soroptimist. Home and Office: Anna Maria Coll Sunset Ln Paxton MA 01612

MADORSKY, MARSHA GERRE, lawyer; b. Detroit, June 12, 1951; d. Max and Anne Ruth (Korash) Madorsky; m. Jeffrey Rothstein; 1 child, Whitney Rebecca. BA, U. Fla., 1972, JD, 1975; LLM, U. Miami, 1983. Bar Fla. 1975. Asst. atty. gen. State of Fla., West Palm Beach, 1975-77; assoc. atty. Sandstrom & Haddad, Ft. Lauderdale, Fla., 1977-80; med. fraud atty. Auditor Gen.'s Office, State of Fla., Miami, 1980-81; asst. state's atty., Miami, 1981; assoc. Bercuson, Cahan, Weksler & Lasky, Miami, 1983-84; ptnr. Bercuson, Cahan, Tarr & Madorsky, Miami, 1985-87; of counsel Weinstein & Garvin, PA, 1987. Consumer mem. State of Fla. Ombudsman and Long Term Care Com., 1981—; bd. dirs. Miami Film Festival. Mem. Fla. Assn. Women Lawyers (program chmn.), Democrat. Home: 145 SE 25th Rd #1101 Miami FL 33129 Office: 2250 SW 3d Ave 5th Floor Miami FL 33129

MADRID, DONNA KAY, personnel executive; b. Mt. Ayr, Iowa, May 29, 1937; d. Clete Hewitt and Murice Margery (Cornwall) Madison; married; children: Murice Elaina Scanlon, Cathy Lynne Kolb. AA, Interior Designers Guild, Sherman Oaks, Calif., 1987. Owner Home Cleaning Service, Canoga Park, Calif., 1970-79; designer Beam Interiors, Northridge, Calif., 1979-80; owner, mgr. Innovative Interiors, Chatsworth, Calif., 1980-81; office mgr. Jardine Emett & Chandler, Los Angeles, 1981—, asst. v.p., 1988—. Mem. Personnel and Indsl. Relations Assn., Nat. Assn. Female Execs. Office: Jardine Emett & Chandler 11835 W Olympic Blvd Los Angeles CA 90021

MADSEN, DOROTHY LOUISE (MEG), career counseling executive; b. Rochester, N.Y.; d. Charles Robert and Louise Anna Agnes Meyer; B.A., Mundelein Coll., Chgo., 1968; m Frederick George Madsen, Feb. 17, 1945. Public relations rep. Rochester Telephone Corp., 1941-42; feature writer Rochester Democrat & Chronicle, 1939-41; exec. dir. LaPorte (Ind.) chpt. ARC, 1964; dir. adminstrv. services Bank Mktg. Assn., Chgo., 1971-74; exec. dir. Eleanor Assn., Chgo., 1974-84; founder Meg Madsen Assocs., Chgo., 1984—; women's career counselor; founder, Clearinghouse Internat. Newsletter; founder Eleanor Women's Forum, Clearinghouse Internat., Eleanor Intern Program Coll. Students and Returning Women. Served to lt. col. WAC, 1942-47, 67-70. Decorated Legion of Merit, Meritorious Service award. Mem. Res. Officers Assn., Mundelein Alumnae Assn., Central Eleanor Club, Phi Sigma Tau (charter mem. Ill. Kappa chpt.). Home and Office: 1030 N State St Chicago IL 60610

MADSEN, MILA CORDERO, business executive; b. Lucena, Quezon, Philippines, Feb. 28, 1930; came to U.S., 1952, naturalized, 1956; d. Pablo and Maria Epifania (Arrieta) Cordero; m. Erik Kjaer Madsen, Jan. 30, 1954; children: Kenneth, Kirk, Lizbeth, Jeannine. BA, Far Eastern U., Philippines, 1951; cert. in grad. studies, Smith Coll., 1953, MA, 1954. Pres. Mila Corp., Nassau, Bahamas, 1969-71, Manila, 1971-75; mgr. Brooks Fashions, Merrillville, Ind., 1977-78; pres. Mila Internat. Travel, Merrillville, 1981—, Mila Internat., Inc., Valparaiso, Ind., 1981—; gen. ptnr. Mila Internat. Pacific Resorts, Merrillville, 1984—; pres. Mila Internat. Resort Mgmt. Inc., Tahiti, French Polynesia, 1984—. Author: Technique and Style of James Boswell, 1954; contbr. articles to profl. jours. Founder., bd. dirs. Am. Theater Co., Brussels, Belgium, 1968-71; bd. dirs. Mich. Cancer Found., Detroit, 1975-76. Smith Coll. fellow, 1952-54, Far Eastern U. scholar, 1947-52. Fellow Epsilon Gamma Pi; mem. Philippines Profl. Assn., Lakeshore Bus. and Profl. Women's Club. Roman Catholic. Club: Am. Women (Brussels), (bd. dirs. 1969-70). Home: 75-305 Hoene St Kailua Kona HI 96740 Office: care of Mila Internat Inc 8300 Mississippi Suite D Merrillville IN 46410

MAEDA, JOYCE AKIKO, data processing executive; b. Mansfield, Ohio, Aug. 24, 1940; d. James Shunso and Doris Lucille (Moore) M.; m. Robert Lee Hayes (div. May 1970); 1 child, Brian Sentaro Hayes. BS in Math., Purdue U., 1962, postgrad., 1962-63; postgrad., Calif. State U., Northridge, 1968-75; cert. profl. designation in tech. of computer operating systems and tech. of info. processing, UCLA, 1972. Cons., research asst. Computer Ctr. Purdue U., West Lafayette, Ind., 1962-63; computer operator, sr. tab operator, mem. faculty Calif. State U., Northridge, 1969, programmer cons., tech. asst. II, 1969-70, supr. acad. applicatons, EDP supr. II, 1970-72, mem. spl. project timesharing tech. support, programmer II, 1972-73, supr. statewide timesharing tech. support, programmer II, 1973-74, acad. coordinator, supr. instrn., computer cons. III, 1974-83; coordinator user services Info. Ctr., mem. tech. staff CADAM INC subs. Lockheed Corp., Burbank, Calif., 1983-86, coordinator end user services, tech. specialist computing dept., 1986—; v.p., bd. dirs. Rainbow Computing, Inc., Northridge, 1976-85; pres. Akiko Maeda Tech./Design Cons., Northridge, 1980—; mktg. mgr. thaumaturge Taro Quipu Tech./Design Cons., Northridge, 1987; tech. cons. Digital Computer Cons., Chatsworth Calif., 1988. Author 50 user publs., 1969-83, 98 computer user publs., 1983-87, basic computer programming language; contbr. articles and papers to profl. jours. Mem. IEEE, SHARE, Digital Equipment Computer Users Soc. (author papers and presentations 1977-81, ednl. spl. interest group 1977-83, steering com. Resource Sharing Timesharing System/Extended (RSTS/E), 1979-82). Home: 18257 Shepley Pl Northridge CA 91326 Office: CADAM INC 1935 N Buena Vista St Burbank CA 91504

MAEL, BOBBIE LOUISE, hospital pharmaceutical sales representative; b. Lockport, N.Y., Dec. 12, 1955; d. Robert U. and Margaret L. (Heath) M. AA, U. South Fla., 1976; BS in Bus. Adminstrn., East Carolina U., 1978. Sales rep. Sandoz Pharm. Co., Wilmington, N.C., 1978-83, USV Labs., Buffalo, 1983-85, Purdue Frederick Co., Buffalo, 1985-86, O'Brien Pharms., Buffalo, 1986-88, Kendall McGaw Labs., Inc., Buffalo, 1988—. Contbr. photographs to regional newspapers and mags. Active Emmanuel Meth. Ch., Amherst Women's Suburban Softball League. Mem. Bus. Women's Assn. Republican. Clubs: Amherst Bus. and Profl. Women's; Up Downtown of Buffalo, Bali Matrix Health and Fitness. Home: 19 Robin Rd West Amherst NY 14228

MAES, JEANNE DELONEY, management science educator; b. Montgomery, Ala., May 1, 1951; d. John Elbert and Thyra (Riley) Deloney; m. Fred Maes, May 21, 1977. BS, SUNY, Albany, 1983; MBA, U. South Ala., 1985. Social work supr. I.B.S., Inc., Bklyn., 1975-80; research asst. Coll. Bus., U. South Ala., Mobile, 1983-85, instr., 1985—; v.p., cons. Synergistic Cons. Group, Mobile, 1986—. Author (with others): Budgeting Simplified, 1987. Vol. cons. Mobile C. of C., 1986—. Fellow So. Mgmt. Assn., Am. Mgmt. Assn. (assoc.), Mensa, Gulf Coast Herb Soc. (newsletter editor 1986); mem. Organizational Devel. Inst. Home: 126 Wild Oak Dr Daphne AL 36526 Office: U South Ala Coll Bus Mobile AL 36688

MAGAFAN, ETHEL, artist; b. Chgo., Aug. 10, 1916; d. Peter J. and Julie (Bronick) M.; m. Bruce Currie, June 30, 1946; 1 dau., Jenne Magafan. Student, Colorado Springs Fine Arts Center. guest artist-in-residence Syracuse U., 1976. Painter of: 8 murals including Social Security Bldg (now HEW bldg.), Washington; Recorder of Deeds Bldg., Washington, Fredericksburg (Va.) Nat. Mil. Park, 1978; paintings exhibited, Carnegie Inst., Corcoran Gallery, Pa. Acad. Fine Arts, NAD, Met. Mus., Denver Art Mus., San Francisco Mus., N.Y. Exhbn., 1950-51, 53, 55, 56, 59, 61, 63, 66, 69, 70, 73, 79, 81, Art Gallery, SUNY, Albany, 1981, Midtown Galleries, N.Y.C., 1984; represented in permanent collections, including, Springfield (Mo.) Art Mus., Provincetown Art Assn., Met. Mus. Art, Denver Art Mus., Del. Soc. Fine Arts, Des Moines Art Center, Norfolk Mus., Columbia Mus., Butler (Ind.) Inst. Art, Nat. Mus. Women in the Arts, 1987; one-man show Midtown Galleries, N.Y.C., 1987, others; also pvt. collections. John Stacey scholar, 1947; Tiffany fellow, 1949; Fulbright grantee, 1951; Recipient Collectors Am. Art award, 1947, 48; Adele Hyde Morrison prize San Francisco Mus., 1950; hon. mention Am. Painting Today exhbn., Met Mus. Art, 1950; 1st Hallgarten prize NAD, 1951; Ida Wells Stroud award, Am. Watercolor Soc., 1955; purchase prize Nat. Exhbn. Contemporary Arts, 1956; Altman prize for landscape NAD, 1956; Hallmark Art award, 1952; Purchase award, Ball State Tchrs. Coll. Art Gallery, 1958; Columbia (S.C.) Mus., 1959; Portland (Maine) Mus., 1959; 1st award Albany Inst. Art, 1962; Benjamin Altman award NAD, 1964, 73; Andrew Carnegie prize, 1977; award Conn. Acad. Fine Arts, 1965; purchase award Watercolor, U.S.A., Springfield Mus., 1966; Kirk Meml. award NAD, 1967; Berkshire Art Assn. award, 1966, 67, 68, 75; jurors prize Albany Inst. Art, 1969; Grumbacher award, 1970, 75; Hassam Fund purchase, 1970; Arches Paper award Am. Watercolor Soc., 1973; Zimmerman award Phila. Watercolor Soc., 1973; Pres.'s award Audubon Artists, 1974; Emily Lowe award, 1979; Stefan Hirsch Meml. award Audubon Artists Ann., 1976; award Rocky Mountain Nat. Watermedia Exhbn., 1976; Condec award Silvermine Guild Artists, 1978; award, 1979; Silver medal Audubon Artists, 1983; Cooperstown Art Assn. award, 1978, 83; Highwinds award and medal Am. Watercolor Soc., 1983; drawing award Ball State U., 1981; Art of Northeast USA exhibit award Silvermine Guild, 1984; John W. Taylor award Woodstock Artist's Assn. for Drawing, 1985, Harrison Cady award Am. Water Color Soc., 1987. Mem. NAD (2d v.p. 1975, Benjamin Altman award 1980).

MAGALLANES, DEBORAH JEAN, business consulting company executive; b. Gary, Ind., May 22, 1951; d. Ray Daniel and Courtney Ann (Manders) M.; m. Gary Allen DeBardi, 1975. Student pub. schs., Crown Point, Ind. Adminstrv. asst. Fasfax Corp., Nashua, N.H., 1971-75; mgr. adminstrn. Advanced Tech. Labs., Bellevue, Wash., 1975, part-time, 1975-77; sales asst. VMC Corp., Woodinville, Wash., 1975-76; cons. personnel Bus. Men's Clearing House, Bellevue, 1976-79; salesperson, gen. mgr. Cypress Steel, Inc., Bellevue, 1979, part-time, 1979-80; pres. Magallanes, Inc., Bellevue, 1979—; cons., project mgr. in field. Author: (with others) Guide to Better Relationships Through Dealmaking, 1985. Mem. Up With People, 1969—, Seattle-King County Conv. and Visitors Bur.; bd. dirs. Friends of Youth, Renton, Wash., 1984—, v.p., 1986—; vol. Save the Elephants Campaign, Seattle, 1984—; bd. dirs. Bellevue Leaders, pres., 1982—. Mem. Women's Bus. Exchange (bd. dirs. 1981-85, Networker of Yr. 1983), MIT Alumni Assn. (hon. nat. officer 1984). Club: Briefcase Brigade (Bellevue), Hetty Green Partnership (pres. 1987—). Lodge: Soroptimists (bd. dirs. 1986, 88). Avocations: investments, canoeing, fishing, drill team. Office: 405 114th Ave SE #300 Bellevue WA 98004

MAGANZINI, TERESA AVERSA, lawyer; b. Phila., Dec. 8, 1951; d. Mario Salvatore and Teresa Elena (Sava) Aversa; m. Paul John Maganzini, May 22, 1976. BA, Notre Dame U., 1973; JD, Villanova U., 1976. Assoc. Law Office of Paul Maganzini, Chgo., 1976; asst. state's atty. State's Atty. Office of Cook County, Chgo., 1977—. Mem. ABA, Ill. State Bar Assn., Chgo. Bar Assn. (v.p., bd. dirs. 1984—), Nat. Dist. Attys. Assn. Roman Catholic. Home: 1146 N Kenilworth Oak Park IL 60302 Office: States Atty's Office Cook County 2650 S California Ave Chicago IL 60608

MAGEE, CATHERINE LOUISE, marketing executive; b. Richmond, Va., July 13, 1954; d. Stanley Earl and Louise (Allman) Magee. B.A. in History, Westhampton Coll., 1976. Govt. bond trader Wheat First Securities Inc., Richmond, Va., 1977-78; mcpl. bond retail trader Wheat First Securities, 1978-80; mcpl. bond retail sales Dean Witter Reynolds, Inc., N.Y.C., 1980-81; dir. retail mcpl. bond mktg. Moseley, Hallgarten, Estabrook & Weeden Inc., N.Y.C., 1981-82; account exec. Dean Witter Reynolds, Inc., Richmond, Va., 1984; mktg. rep. HCW, Inc., Boston, 1985; mktg. rep. Liberty Securities Corp., Boston, 1986, mktg. mgr. Liberty Real Estate Corp., 1986—; key career cons. U. Richmond, Va., 1978-80. Recipient Key award, U. Richmond, 1980. Mem. Nat. Assn. Securities Dealers, Nat. Honor Soc., Phi Alpha Theta. Republican. Baptist. Clubs: Richmond Municipal Bond, Municipal Bond of N.Y. Avocations: photography; painting; jazz dance; racquetball; tennis. Home: 11 Exeter St Apt 1 Boston MA 02116 Office: Liberty Real Estate Corp 600 Atlantic Ave Boston MA 02210

MAGEE, JENNIFER KEATING, advertising executive; b. Augusta, Ga., Sept. 27, 1951; d. Robert Eric and martha Corrie (Hadden) Hawkins; m. Donald Alvin Magee, Jr. BBA in Acctg., Ga. State U., 1975. Asst. to dean Sch. Bus. Ga. State U., Atlanta, 1976-78; rep. advt. sales Times Picayune/States Item, New Orleans, 1978-80, advt. mgr., 1980-81; pres. Keating Magee & Assocs., New Orleans, 1981—. Bd. dirs. U. New Orleans Metro Council for Lifelong Learning, 1986; mem. mktg. com. Hospice New Orleans, 1987; mem. policy issues task force United Way for Greater New Orleans, 1987. Advertisements recipient Gold Addy award 1983, 86, 88, Tops award, 1988, Telly award, 1988; listed as one of 83 People to Watch in '83, New Orleans mag., 1983, 15 Women to Watch in S.W. Advt., Adweek Mag., 1984, Women In The Forefront, 1986. Mem. Nat. Assn. for Female Execs., Women's Profl. Council (chmn. mktg. com. 1987), LWV. Office: Keating Magee & Assocs 2223 Magazine St New Orleans LA 70130

MAGGARD, SARAH ELIZABETH, educator, lawyer; b. Whittier, Calif., Nov. 17, 1948; d. William Alexander and Laura (Redford) M. B.A., Whittier Coll., 1970, M.A. in Ed., 1971; J.D., Western State U., Fullerton, Calif., 1981. Bar: Calif. 1982. Tchr., Rowland Unified Sch. Dist., Rowland Heights, Calif., 1971—, also sole practice, Whittier, 1982—. Recipient Am. Jurisprudence awards Bancroft-Whitney Co., 1979, 80. Mem. State Bar Calif., ABA, Los Angeles County Bar Assn., Lawyers Club Los Angeles. Republican. Presbyterian. Assoc. editor Western State U. Law Rev., 1980. Home: 10319 Tigrina Ave Whittier CA 90603 Office: Rowland Unified Sch Dist 1830 Nogales St Rowland Heights CA 91748

MAGGIO, VICTORIA LYNN, infosystems specialist; b. Paterson, N.J., Feb. 2, 1957; d. Robert Wesley Maggio and Rosalie Ann (Benvenuta) Attenasio. Student, U. Tex, 1983. Installation programmer CBM, San Antonio, 1982—. Served with USAR, 1981-87. Mem. Nat. Assn. Female Execs. Roman Catholic. Home: 10127 Rainbow Bend San Antonio TX 78250 Office: 100 NE Loop 410 San Antonio TX 78216

MAGGIORE, SUSAN, geophysical oceanographer; b. Newark, Mar. 14, 1957; d. John James and Marietta Nancy (Testa) M. BS in Geosci., Montclair State Coll., 1978; postgrad., U. So. Miss., 1981-84. Supr. research and communications The Cousteau Soc., N.Y., 1979-81; geophysicist Naval Oceanographic Office, Bay St. Louis, Miss., 1981-85, NE Consortium Oceanographic Research, Narragansett, R.I., 1985-86; mem. tech. staff AT&T Bell Labs., Whippany, N.J., 1986—; writer, creative cons. The Cousteau Soc., Los Angeles, 1981—. Researcher book The Cousteau Almanac of the Environment, 1981; contbr. articles to profl. jours. Vol. Dover (N.J.) Gen. Hosp., 1987. Mem. Am. Geophys. Union, Marine Tech. Soc., Nat. Assn. Female Execs. Roman Catholic. Clubs: Cath. Young Adults (Randolph, N.J.), Amateur Radio (Whippany). Office: AT&T Bell Labs 1 Whippany Rd Whippany NJ 07981

MAGLALANG, FLOR DALOCANOG, educational administrator; b. Cebu City, Philippines, Sept. 22, 1942; came to U.S., 1978, naturalized, 1984; d. Daniel Peras and Fructuosa (Jerusalem) Dalocanog; m. Demetrio Mendoza Maglalang, July 3, 1965; children—Herman, Alfred Kevin, Dmitri, Maurice. B.S.B.A. summa cum laude, U. St. Charles, Cebu City; M.B.A., Ind. U., M.B.A., M.A. in Econs., Ind. U. Fin. analyst Presdl. Econ. Staff, Manila, 1965-68; chief economist Dept. Industry, Manila, 1968-72; gen. mgr. Afra Trade Export-Import, Manila, 1973-78; dir. fin. aid St. Meinrad Coll., Ind., 1979-86; dir. fin. aid Ivy Tech Coll., Columbus, Ind., 1986—; tchr. Vincennes U., Jasper, Ind., 1980—. Mem. fin. com., v.p. St. Nicholas Parish, Santa Claus, Ind., 1985-86. Recipient Good Citizen award DAR, 1985. Mem. Nat. Assn. Student Fin. Aid Adminstrs., Midwest Assn. Student Fin. Aid Adminstrs., Ind. Student Fin. Aid Assn., Ind. U. Alumni Assn. Republican. Roman Catholic. Clubs: Christmas Lake Village Golf and Tennis, CLV Assn. Avocations: reading; movies; dancing; real estate; counseling. Home: 131 Silver Bell Terr Christmas Lake Santa Claus IN 47579 Office: Ivy Tech Coll 4475 Central Ave Columbus IN 47203 also: Ivy Tech Coll Canterbury St Bloomington IN 47401

MAGNER, RACHEL HARRIS, banker; b. Lamar, S.C., Aug. 5, 1951; d. Garner Greer and Catherine Alice (Cloaninger) Harris; B.S. in Fin., U. S.C., 1972; postgrad. UCLA, 1974, Calif. State U., 1975; m. Fredric Michael Magner, May 14, 1972. Mgmt. trainee Union Bank, Los Angeles, 1972-75, comml. loan officer, 1975-77; asst. v.p. comml. fin. Crocker Bank, Los Angeles, 1978, asst. v.p., factoring account exec. subs. Crocker United Factors, Inc., 1978-81; v.p. comml. services div. Crocker Bank, 1981-82, v.p., sr. account mgr. bus. banking div., 1982-83; v.p. corporate banking Office of Pres., Sumitomo Bank Calif., 1983—. Home: 2200 Pine Ave Manhattan Beach CA 90266 Office: Sumitomo Bank of Calif 101 S San Pedro Suite 500 Los Angeles CA 90012

MAGNI, DEBRA KAY, public relations executive; b. Sunbury, Pa., Nov. 5, 1954; d. Wallace Theodore and Florence Dolores (Hendricks) Townsend; m. Anthony Michael Magni, July 2, 1982; 1 dau., Kelly Ann. B.S., York Coll.

Pa., 1978, A.S., 1977. Office mgr. York Coll. Pa., 1973-78; ter. mgr. bus. mgmt. systems Burroughs Corp., Hunt Valley, Md., 1978-80; dir. pub. relations York Coll. Pa., 1980—. Bd. dirs. Am. Cancer Soc., York, 1981-87, S. Central Pa. chpt. Am. Heart Assn., also chmn. pub. relations com., York Alcohol and Drug Services, also v.p., 1982-87, pres., 1987 —, Rape Crisis Ctr. York, 1982-84; mem. programming com. Strand Capitol Performing Arts Ctr., York, 1981-84; mem. York YWCA Mktg. Task Force, 1985, mem. Hanover YWCA mktg. com., 1985—. Council Advancement and Support Edn. scholar, 1981. Mem. Council Advancement and Support Edn., Coll. and Univ. Pub. Relations Assn. Pa., York Coll. Pa. Alumni Assn. Republican. Lutheran. Home: RD 2 Box 851 E Berlin Rd Thomasville PA 17364 Office: York Coll Pa Country Club Rd York PA 17403

MAGNUS, MARGARET MANNION, nursing educator; b. Anthenry, Galway, Ireland; came to U.S., 1954; d. Michael and Mary (Lynskey) Mannion; m. Joseph Magnus, Aug. 7, 1970; 1 dau., Tayna Marie. B.S. in Nursing, Incarnate Word Coll., 1961; M.S. in Nursing, Cath. U., Washington, 1965, Ph.D., 1969. Unit supr. Santa Rosa Children's Hosp., San Antonio, 1961-63; asst. prof. Incarnate Word Coll., San Antonio, 1965-66; asst. prof. New Rochelle (N.Y.) Hosp. Sch. Nursing, 1969-70; mem. faculty Hunter-Bellevue Sch. Nursing, N.Y.C., 1970—, prof. nursing, 1979—, dir. grad. program, 1975-80, dir. undergrad. progrm, 1981-82, assoc. dean, 1983-84; vis. prof. Tchrs. Coll., Columbia U., summer 1986. Author: Fundamentals of Nursing, 1972, Computer Technology and Nursing, 1987. Editor: Blood Groups, 1970. Mem. exec. bd. Ctr. to Promote Health Care Studies N.Y., 1975. Mem. Nat. Assn. Female Execs., Am. Nurses Assn., Sigma Theta Tau, Phi Beta Kappa. Democrat. Roman Catholic. Office: Hunter-Bellevue Sch Nursing 425 E 25th St New York NY 10010

MAGNUSON, CONSTANCE FOSTER, banker; b. Madison, Wis., Mar. 29, 1952; d. Howard Clinton and Mertice Ethel (Johnston) Foster; m. Michael Swan Magnuson, Oct. 22, 1977; children: Karen Marie, Anne Marie. B.A., Northwestern U., 1974, M.B.A., 1978. Trust officer No. Trust Co., Chgo., 1974-78, 2d v.p., 1980, v.p., 1983—; speaker nat. confs. Mem. Northwestern Profl. Womens Assn. (exec. v.p. 1980, sec. 1981), Kappa Kappa Gamma Alumni Assn. (sec. 1981). Office: Northern Trust Co 50 S LaSalle St Chicago IL 60675

MAGNUSSON, MADELINE FRANCES, nonprofessional athletics coach, realtor; b. Woodbridge, N.J., Aug. 19, 1955; d. Frank S. and Lillian M. (Horvath) Gienieczko; m. Drew Robert Magnusson, May 25, 1987. BS in Bus. Adminstrn. and Mktg., Montclair State Coll., 1980. Mgr. Essex Racquet and Health Club, West Orange, N.J., 1980-82; asst. coach Met. YMHA, West Orange, 1980-82; head coach Ridgewood (N.J.) YMCA, 1982-87; age group coach Somerset Hills YMCA, Basking Ridge, N.J., 1987—; realtor Schlott Basking Ridge office, 1987—. Mem. Nat. Assn. Female Execs., Nat. YMCA Coaches Assn. (mem. exec. bd. 1986-87), Am. Swim Coaches Assn., Nat. Realtors Assn., Morris County Bd. Realtors, Somerset County Bd. Realtors. Home: 14 Parry Ct Parsippany NJ 07054 Office: Rt 202 & N Maple Ave Basking Ridge NJ 07920

MAGUIRE, EILEEN, magazine editor; b. Birmingham, Eng., May 30, 1951; came to U.S., 1974; d. Patrick and Kathleen Louisa (Moore) M. Student, NYU, 1985—. Editors' asst. N.Y. mag., N.Y.C., 1976-78; asst. editor Parents mag., N.Y.C., 1978-80, asst. mng. editor, 1980-82, sr. editor, 1982-84, mng. editor, 1984—. Mem. Am. Soc. Mag. Editors. Democrat. Office: Parents Mag 685 Third Ave New York NY 10017

MAGUIRE, SUSAN ANN, broker; b. Bklyn., Sept. 3, 1957; d. Joseph Francis and Ruth (Larsen) McAllister; m. James M. Maguire, June 24, 1983. BBA, Pace U., 1982; MBA, Loyola U., Chgo., 1987. Actuary clk. Home Life Ins. Co., N.Y.C., 1975-77; internal audit, compliance Goldman Sachs & Co., N.Y.C., 1977-79, futures exec. supr., 1979-81; futures exec. supr. Goldman Sachs & Co., Chgo., 1981-85, floor broker, 1985—. Mem. Pace U. Alumni Assn. Roman Catholic. Club: East Bank (Chgo.). Home: 3816 N Greenview Chicago IL 60613 Office: Goldman Sachs & Co 4900 Sears Tower Chicago IL 60606

MAGUIRE-KRUPP, MARJORIE ANNE, real estate developer; b. Stamford, Conn., Apr. 29, 1955; d. Walter Reeves and Jean Elisabeth (Cook) M.; m. Joseph Michael Krupp, Jr., Nov. 26, 1983; children: Parnell Joseph, Maguire Krupp; stepchildren: Theresa Margaret, Donna Marie, Maura Elizabeth. BA in Acctg. cum laude, Franklin and Marshall Coll., 1976; MBA in Fin. with distinction, NYU, 1983, postgrad., 1988—, cert. in real estate, 1986; cert. in French, U. Strasbourg, France, 1971. CPA, Conn.; lic. real estate sales agt., N.J. Supervisory auditor Arthur Young & Co., Stamford, Conn., 1976-80; mgr. fin. planning Combustion Engring., Stamford, 1980-84; asst. v.p., mgr. fin. planning and analysis Kidder Peabody & Co., N.Y.C., 1984-87; pres. Parnell Devel. Corp., 1987—; v.p. fin. Jeremiah Devel. Co., 1987—. Advisor, Jr. Achievement, Stamford, 1979-80; mem. Met. Opera Guild, N.Y.C., 1985-86, Met. Mus. Art, N.Y.C., 1983—, Mus. Modern Art, N.Y.C., 1983—; treas., dir. Cliffhouse Condo Assn., Cliffside Park, N.J., 1983-85. Mem. Am. Inst. CPA's, Nat. Assn. Female Execs., Phi Beta Kappa, Beta Gamma Sigma. Club: Stamford Jaycee Women (pres. 1980-81, chmn. bd. 1981-82, Stamford Disting. Service award, Outstanding Young Woman of Yr. award, 1980). Republican. Presbyterian. Avocations: travel, skiing, sailing, gourmet cooking, piano. Home: 107 Shearwater Ct Port Liberte Jersey City NJ 07305

MAGUIRE-ZINNI, DEIRDRE, federal community development representative; b. Bklyn., Oct. 21, 1954; d. James Michael and Dorothy Ursula (Gronske) Maguire; m. Nicholas A. Zinni, Aug. 27, 1977. BA with honors, SUNY, Stony Brook, 1976; MS, Fla. State U., 1981. Housing specialist Suffolk Community Devel. Corp., Coram, N.Y., 1977-78; planner Palm Beach County Housing and Community Devel., West Palm Beach, Fla., 1980-83, sr. planner, 1983-84, mgr. adminstrn. and ops., 1984-87; fed. community planning and devel. rep. HUD, Jacksonville, Fla., 1987—; staff liaison Affordable Housing Task Force, West Palm Beach, 1985-86, Fla. Community Devel. Assn., Tallahassee, 1985-87. Named one of Outstanding Young Women of Am., 1985. Mem. Palm Beach County Planning Congress, Am. Planning Assn. (planning and women div.). Democrat. Roman Catholic.

MAGYAR, DEBORAH VALELA, motion picture production professional; b. Chgo., Jan. 29, 1957; d. Frank Joseph and Patricia Therese (Madera) Valela; m. Joseph David Magyar, Aug. 13, 1983. BA with honors, Columbia Coll., 1985. Prodn. asst. DDB Needham Worldwide, Chgo., 1977-84; producer Test Spot, Inc., Chgo., 1984-85; set prodn. asst. Columbia Pictures, Chgo., 1986; set coordinator, script supr. Free-lance, Chgo., 1986-87; producer Bayer Bess Vanderwarker & Flynn, Chgo., 1987—; vol. Chgo. Internat. Film Festival, Chgo., 1982. Photographer events Velika Gospa, 1986; contbr. articles to profl. jours. Vol. Jane Byrne Campaign for Re-election, Chgo., 1987. Mem. Women in Film (com. 1986), Women in the Director's Chair (festival vol. 1986, 87). Roman Catholic. Club: TOPS (v.p. 1987-88).

MAHAFFEY, MARCIA JEANNE HIXSON, school administrator; b. Scoby, Mont.; d. Edward Goodell and Olga Marie (Frederickson) Hixson; m. Donald Harry Mahaffey (div. Aug. 1976); 1 child, Marcia Anne. BA in English History, U. Wash.; MA in Secondary Edn., U. Hawaii, 1967. Cert. secondary and elem. tchr. and adminstr. Tchr. San Lorenzo (Calif.) Sch. Dist., 1958-59; tchr. Castro Valley (Calif.) Sch. Dist., 1959-63, vice prin., 1963-67; vice prin. Sequoia Union High Sch. Dist., Redwood City, Calif., 1967-77, asst. prin., 1977—; tchr. trainer Project Impact Sequoia Union Sch. Dist., Redwood City, 1986—, mem. supr.'s task force for dropout prevention, 1987—, mentor tchr. selection com., 1987—, vocat. ednl. master plan com., 1987—; chairperson gifted and talented Castro Valley Sch. Dist.; mem. family services bd., San Leandro, Calif. Vol. Am. Cancer Soc., San Mateo, Calif., 1967, Castro Valley, 1965; sunday sch. tchr. Hope Luth. Ch., San Mateo, 1970-76; chair Carlmont High Sch. Site Council, Belmont, Calif., 1977—. Recipient Life Mem. award Parent, Tchr., Student Assn., Belmont, 1984; named Woman of the Week, Castro Valley, 1967. Mem. Assn. Calif. Sch. Adminstrs. (Project Leadership plaque 1985), Sequoia Dist. Mgmt. Assn. (pres. 1975, treas. 1984, 85), Sequoia Dist. Goals Commn. (chair subcom. staff devel. 1988), Met. Mus. Art, Smithsonian Inst., AAUW, DAR, Animal Welfare Advocacy. Delta Kappa Gamma, Alpha Xi Delta. Club: Carlmont Social.

MAHAFFEY, MARTHA PLUMMER, government official; b. Bryn Mawr, Pa., June 1, 1946; d. John Lewis Plummer and Gloria Joan (Donatelli) Richards; m. Wilton Larron Mahaffey, Nov. 29, 1974; children—Melinda Kathleen, Matthew Timothy. A.B., cum laude, Bryn Mawr Coll., 1968, M.B.A., U. Va., 1970. Mgmt. cons. Booz, Allen & Hamilton, Washington, 1970-72; self-employed cons., Washington, 1972-73; mgmt. cons. Arthur Young & Co., Washington, 1973; program analyst. Exec. Office of President of U.S., Washington, 1973-74; exec. officer Health Care Financing Adminstrn., Dallas, 1974-83, dep. regional adminstr., Boston, 1983-85; dir. Health and Human Services, 1985-87; dir. govt. relations Mgmt. Data Communications Corp., 1988—. Bd. dirs. Montessori Sch. Park Cities, 1981-82; Christian edn. counselor, tchr. St. Michael and All Angels Ch., 1979—. Recipient Administr.'s citation Health Care Financing Adminstrn., 1979-81; Sr. Exec. Service Candidate Selection award HHS, 1983. Mem. Lychnds Honor Soc. Republican. Episcopalian. Home: 10121 Daria Dr Dallas TX 75229 Office: 9701 W Higgins Rosemont IL 60018

MAHAIRAS, EVELYN PHILLIPINE, educator, clinical social worker, psychotherapist, researcher; b. N.Y.C., Sept. 25, 1933; d. Otto and Henrietta (Dolman) Poestges; B.A. in Clin. Psychiatry, Queens Coll., 1954; tchr. cert. Eastern Nazarene Coll., 1972; M.S.W., Ohio State U., 1976; PhD Bryn Mawr Coll., 1986; m. C. Gus Mahairas, June 27, 1954; children—Pamela Linda, Janet Susan, Karen Lee, Evelyn Jean. Diplomate Am. Bd. Clin. Social Work. Psychiat. social worker N.Y. State Dept. Mental Hygiene, 1954-56; bus. rep. N.Y. Telephone Co., Jackson Heights, N.Y., 1956-57; substitute tchr. public schs., Mass., Conn., 1970-74; dir. social services Wives Self Help/City Police and Fire Counselling Service, Phila., 1976-81; research specialist social work service Coatesville (Pa.) V.A. Med. Center, 1981—, adminstrv. asst. geriatric research, edn. com., 1984-85; program dir. Interdisciplinary Team Tng. in Geriatrics, 1986—; coordinator, family therapy residency tng. program psychiatry Thomas Jefferson U. Med. Sch.; Sec., Social Action Com., 1968-70; coordinator Headstart, W. Springfield, Mass., 1968-70; elder, trustee Trinity Presbyn. Ch., Berwyn, Pa., 1987—; mem. Lake Champlain Com., Vt., 1968—. Mem. Nat. Assn. Social Workers (bd. dirs., chmn. com. Profl. Standards Pa. chpt. 1987—, exec. com., fin. com., program chmn., v.p. 1979-81, exec. bd., pres. Brandywine div. 1978-79, co-chmn. continuing edn. 1978-80, mem. social action com., legis. com., chmn. profl. standards 1987—), Acad. Cert. Social Workers, Nat. Register Clin. Social Workers, Mental Health Assn. of Southeastern Pa. Presbyn. (youth fellowship adv., chmn. adult edn.). Co-editor: The Aging Veteran: Interorganizational Relations, Team Training and Staff Development in Geriatrics, Gerontology and Health Care Team Development; contbr. articles to profl. jours. Home: 650 W Wind Dr Berwyn PA 19312 also: Thompson's Point Charlotte VT 19312 Office: Coatesville VA Med Ctr Coatesville PA 19320

MAHAK, FRANCINE TIMOTHY, communications consultant; b. Paris, Sept. 28, 1950; d. James Simmons and Francine (Evans) Timothy; m. Vali Mahak, Aug. 4, 1976; 1 child, Nima. Baccalauréat Philosophie, Cours Victor Hugo, Paris, 1968; BA in Russian, Wellesley Coll., 1972; MA in Linguistics, U. Tehran, Iran, 1976; PhD in Mid. East and Persian Studies, U. Utah, 1986. Instr. Coll. Jeanne D'Arc, Tehran, 1974-75; translator Scetiran Cons. Co., Tehran, 1976-77; vis. instr. Persian U. Utah, Salt Lake City, 1978-81; translator French Found. for Evolutionary Research, N.Y.C., 1982-84; cons. Shipley Assocs., Bountiful, Utah, 1985—; editor, translator Internat. Inst. for Adult Literacy Methods div. UNESCO, Tehran, 1974-77; instr. ESL U. Utah, Salt Lake City, 1982-83. Panel mem. United Way, Salt Lake City, 1980-85. Mem. Nat. Assn. for Female Execs. Club: Wellesley. Home: 621 Grand St Salt Lake City UT 84102 Office: Shipley Assocs 400 N Main Bountiful UT 84010

MAHAN, LORETTA BOSSO, chemical company marketing services coordinator, consultant; b. Phila., Aug. 15, 1948; d. Joseph Vincent and Antoinette Josephine (Teti) Bosso; children—Shawn Adam, Patrick Glenn. Pub. relations writer Spiro & Assocs., Phila., 1966-70; reading aide Octorara High Sch., Atglen, Pa., 1978-79; project mgr., cons. engineered services E.I. DuPont & Co., Wilmington, Del., 1980—. Mem. recreation com. Borough Council, Parkesburg, Pa., 1979-81, Steel Structures Painting Council. Mem. Nat. Assn. Female Execs., Nat. Assn. Corrosion Engrs., Structural Steel Painting Council. Democrat. Roman Catholic. Avocations: music, guitar, racquetball, tennis, swimming. Home: 530 W 2d Ave Parkesburg PA 19365 Office: E I DuPont de Nemours Co Inc Concord Plaza Wilmington DE 19898

MAHER, JEAN ELIZABETH, middle school counselor; b. Cortland, N.Y., Aug. 13, 1953; d. Russell Edgar and Frances Mae (MacGregor) Owen; m. Kevin John Maher, Aug. 6, 1983. BA, Houghton Coll., 1975; MS, SUNY, Oneonta, 1979, cert. of advanced study, 1980. Tchr. English Monticello (N.Y.) High Sch., 1975-80, dir. gifted program, Sr. Hon. Soc. advisor, 1978-79; sch. counselor Lounsberry Hollow Middle Sch., Vernon, N.J., 1980—, coordinator spl. services, 1982—; tchr. Gen. Equivalency Diploma program Port Jervis (N.Y.) High Sch., 1985-86. Leader Youth Group, Port Jervis, 1982; editor ch. newsletter Port Jervis, 1986—. Mem. NEA, Am. Assn. Counseling and Devel., N.J. Edn. Assn., Sussex County Sch. Counselors Assn. (sec. 1983-85, treas. 1985-87, pres. 1987—). Home: RD 5 Box 720 Montague NJ 07827 Office: Lounsberry Hollow Middle Sch PO Box 219 Sammis Rd Vernon NJ 07462

MAHER, KIM LEVERTON, museum administrator; b. Washington, Feb. 25, 1946; d. Joseph Wilson and Helen Elizabeth (Bell) Leverton; m. William Fredrick Maher, June 12, 1965 (div. 1980); 1 child, Lauren Robinson. Student Duke U., 1963-65, George Washington U., 1966; B.A. in English, U. Fla., 1969. Social worker Fla. Health and Rehab. Service, Gainesville, 1969-71, Delray Beach, 1972-74, fraud unit supr., West Palm Beach, 1974-76, direct service supr., 1977-78; ctr. dir. Palm Beach County Employment and Tng. Adminstrn., West Palm Beach, 1979-81; exec. dir. Discovery Ctr., Inc., Ft. Lauderdale, Fla., 1981—. Bd. dirs. Singing Pines Mus., Boca Raton, Fla., 1984—, Broward Art Guild, Ft. Lauderdale, 1985—; mem. Leadership Broward II, Ft. Lauderdale, 1983-84. Recipient Cultural Arts award Broward Cultural Arts Found., 1985. Mem. Am. Assn. Museums, Assn. Sci. and Tech. Ctrs., Southeastern Museums Conf., Leadership Broward Alumnae (curriculum com. 1984—), Fort Lauderdale Downtown Council, Ft. Lauderdale C. of C. (cultural affairs task force 1983—), Women's Exec. Club, Phi Kappa Phi. Republican. Methodist. Avocations: scuba diving; piano; creative writing; collecting art and antiques; painting. Office: Discovery Ctr Inc 231 SW 2nd Ave Fort Lauderdale FL 33301

MAHLENDORF, URSULA RENATE, language educator; b. Strehlen, Silesia, Germany, Oct. 24, 1929; came to U.S., 1969; Student, Oberschule an der Hamburgerstrase, Bremen, Fed. Republic Germany, 1950, U. Tübingen, Fed. Republic Germany, 1950-52, Brown U., 1952-53; MA in English Lit., Brown U., 1956, PhD in German Lit., 1958; student, Bonn (Fed. Republic Germany) U., 1953, London U., 1953-57. Teaching asst. Brown U., Providence, 1953-57; from acting instr. to prof. German U. Calif., Santa Barbara, 1957—, chairperson tutorial program, 1967-68, chmn. dept. Germanic and Slavic langs. and lits., 1980-83, assoc. dean Coll. Letters and Sci.; chmn. western meeting Am. Soc. Aesthetics, 1966, symposium in honor of Harry Slochower, 1977; campus coordinator Edn. Abroad program U. Calif., 1967-69, assoc. dir., 1969-72; co-chair Nietzsche symposium Dept. Germanic and Slavic Langs. and Lits., U. Calif., Santa Barbara, 1981; cons. Philosophy and Lit. jour.; lectr. in field. Editor: (with John L. Carleton) Man for Man: A Multi-Disciplinary Workshop on Affecting Man's Social and Psychological Nature Through Community Action (Charles C. Thomas), 1973, Dimensions of Social Psychiatry, 1979; assoc. editor Am. Imago, Am. Jour. Social Psychiatry, Jour. Evolutionary Psychology; contbr. articles to profl. jours. Recipient Alumni award, 1981; U. Calif. grantee, 1974, 77, 78, 80, 85; Fulbright fellow, 1951-52. Mem. MLA, Am. Assn. for Aesthetics and Art Criticism (past pres. Calif. div.), Assn. for applied Psychoanalysis (profl. mem.), Am. Assn. Social Psychiatry (councillor 1977-81), Internat. Assn. Social Psychiatry (treas. 1978-83). Address: 1919 Santa Barbara St Santa Barbara CA 93101

MAHLUM-HENEGAR, RHONDA LYNN, accountant, realty sales person; b. Crookston, Minn., Apr. 25, 1959; d. Werner Conway and Darlene Harriet (Benson) M. B.S. in Acctg., Moorhead State U., 1981. C.P.A., N.D. Resident asst. Moorhead State U., 1979-81; cons. Small Bus. Inst., Moorhead, 1980-81; auditor Tax Dept. State of N.D., Bismarck, 1981-84; Realtor Bianco Realty, Bismarck, 1984—; acct. Puklich & Eckroth, P.C., Bismarck, 1985-87; controller, N.D. State Treas. Office, 1987—. Officer Heart Butte Water Ski Shows, Lake Tschide, 1982-84. Mem. N.D. Soc. C.P.A.s, Nat. Assn. Realtors, N.D. Assn. Realtors (chmn. edn. 1985-86), Bismarck-Mandan Bd. Realtors (chmn. edn. 1985-86), N.D. Pub. Employees Assn. Club: Supreme Court Racquet & Fitness (Bismarck). Home: PO Box 1812 Bismarck ND 58502 Office: ND Treas Office Capitol Bldg Bismarck ND 58505

MAHON, MARGARET MARY, manufacturing company executive; b. Crossmolina, Ireland, Nov. 19, 1928; came to U.S., 1951, naturalized, 1970; d. Patrick John and Mary Christina (McNamara) M.; B.S., Fordham U., 1974, M.B.A., 1977. Sec., NCR Corp., N.Y.C., 1951-54, 63-74, adminstrv. specialist, 1974-77, dist. sect. mgr., 1977-78, N.Y. dist. adminstrv. mgr., 1978—; mgr. family bus., 1954-63. Mem. Assn. M.B.A. Execs., Grad. Bus. Alumni Assn. Fordham U., N.Y. C. of C. and Industry. Roman Catholic. Club: Lake Isle Country. Home: 12 Yonkers Ave Tuckahoe NY 10707 Office: 50 Rockefeller Plaza New York NY 10020

MAHONE, BARBARA JEAN, automotive company executive; b. Notasulga, Ala., Apr. 19, 1946; d. Freddie Douglas M. and Sarah Lou (Simpson). BS., Ohio State U., 1968; M.B.A., U. Mich., 1972; P.M.D., Harvard U. Bus. Sch., 1981. Systems analyst Gen. Motors Corp., Detroit, 1968-71, sr. staff asst., 1972-74, mgr. career planning, 1975-78; dir. personnel adminstrn. Gen. Motors Corp., Rochester, N.Y., 1979-81; mgr. indsl. relations Gen. Motors Corp., Warren, Ohio, 1982-83; dir. human resources mgmt. Chevrolet-Pontiac-Can. group Gen. Motors Corp., 1984-86; dir. gen. personnel and pub. affairs Inland div. Gen. Motors Corp., Dayton, Ohio, 1986—; chmn. Fed. Labor Relations Authority, Washington, 1983-84; chmn. Spl. Panel on Appeals; dir. Metro Youth; mem. bd. govs. U. Mich. Alumni. Bd. dirs. ARC, Rochester, 1979-82; bd. dirs. Urban League of Rochester, 1979-82; mem. human resorces com YMCA, Rochester, 1980-82; mem. exec. bd. Nat. Council Negro Women; mem. allocations com. United Way of Greater Rochester; bd. dirs. Rochester Area Multiple Sclerosis. Recipient public relations award Nat. Assn. Bus. and Profl. Women, 1976; recipient award for excellence Gen. Motors. Corp., 1978, Mary McLeod Bethune award Nat. Council Negro Women, 1977, Senate Resolution Mich. State Legislature, 1980; named Outstanding Woman Mich. Chronicle, 1975, Woman of Yr. Nat. Assn. Bus. and Profl. Women, 1978, Disting. Bus. Person U. Mich., 1978, 1 of 11 Mich. Women Redbook Mag., 1978. Mem. Nat. Black M.B.A. Assn. (bd. dirs., nat. pres. Disting. Service award, bd. dirs., nat. pres. Outstanding M.B.A.), Women Econ. Club. (bd. dirs.), Indsl. Relations Research Assn., Internat. Assn. for Personnel Women, Engring. Soc. Detroit. Republican. Home: 1475 Ridge Gate Rd Kettering OH 45429 Office: Inland div Gen Motors Corp PO Box 1224 Dayton OH 45401

MAHONEY, SISTER COLETTE, college president, biologist; b. Jamaica, N.Y., July 19, 1926; d. Timothy and Lillian (Boylan) M. B.S., Marymount Coll., 1949, LL.D. (hon.), 1973; M.S., Fordham U., 1952, Ph.D., 1961; H.H.D. (hon.), St. Francis de Sales, 1974; L.L.D. (hon.), Manhattan Coll., 1982, Fordham U., 1987. Joined Religious of Sacred Heart of Mary, 1945; tchr. biology Acad. Sacred Heart of Mary, N.Y.C., 1947-57; prin. Acad. Sacred Heart of Mary, 1965-67; instr. biology Marymount Coll., Arlington, Va., 1957-61; also chmn. sci. dept.; assoc. prof. biology Marymount Coll., Tarrytown, N.Y., 1961-65; pres., trustee Marymount Manhattan Coll., N.Y.C., 1967—; bd. dirs. com. on econ. devel. Council of Ind. Colls., Higher Edn. Service Corp., Manhattan Life Ins. Co., Jack Lenor Larsen, Inc.; mem. nominating com. Am. Stock Exchange., 1980-82. Contbr. articles on biology to sci. publs. Mem. Pres.'s Adv. Com. on Econ. Role of Women, 1973-74; bd. dirs., pres. Middle States Assn.; commr. Women's Coll. Coalition; bd. advisers China Inst. in Am., Inc.; bd. dirs. Inst. for Mediation and Conflict Resolution, N.Y. Council Higher Edn., Council Higher Edn. N.Y.C., Yorkville Civic Council, Council for Career Planning, Inc., Com. for Econ. Devel.; pres. Women's Forum, 1979; trustee Coll. Boca Raton; mem. David Rockefeller's N.C.Y. Partnership Task Force for Youth Employment, 1980-83. Recipient Extraordinary Woman of Achievement award NCCJ, 1978; Brotherhood award NAACP, 1980; Pres.'s award Malcolm-King: Harlem Coll. Extension, 1980; Pres.'s medal Hunter Coll., 1983; Hoey award for interracial justice Hunter Coll., 1983; Women Helping Women award Soroptomist Internat. of N.Y., 1984; named Woman of Yr. East Side C. of C., 1986; decorated cavaliere Order of Merit Italy, 1978. Fellow AAUW; mem. Commn. on Status of Women, Am. Assn. Higher Edn. (bd. dirs.), Am. Inst. Biol. Scis., N.Y. Acad. Scis., N.Y. Bus. and Profl. Women's Assn., N.Y. State Legis. Inst.

MAHONEY, HEIDI LYON, State higher education administrator; b. Buffalo, N.Y., Nov. 14, 1930; d. James Henry and Mary Dorothy (Kaiser) Lyon; m. David John Mahoney, Feb. 19, 1955; children—David, Neal, John. B.S. in Edn., SUNY Coll. at Buffalo, 1952; M.L.S., SUNY-Geneseo, 1968; Ph.D., SUNY-Buffalo, 1978. Librarian, SUNY Coll. at Buffalo, 1970-74, adminstr., 1974-83; asst. commr. postsec. edn. policy analysis Dept. Edn. State N.Y., Albany, 1983—; N.Y. state coordinator Am. Council on Edn. Nat. Indentification Program for Women Adminstrs., Albany, 1981—; panelist, seminars and confs. Contbr. articles to profl. jours. Bd. dirs. Blind Assn., Western N.Y., 1982. Mem. Am. Assn. Higher Edn., Assn. Instl. Research, Assn. for Study of Higher Edn. Roman Catholic. Office: N Y State Edn Dept Rm 5B44 CEC Albany NY 12234

MAHONEY, JANE LAURA, real estate executive; b. Danville, Ill., May 21, 1942; d. Niels Christian and Jane Ellen (Mellick) Nielsen; children: Tamara Jane, Michael Timothy. AA, Monticello Coll., 1962; postgrad. U. Colo., 1962-63, U. Real Estate Inst., Denver, 1973-82. Cert. residential specialist. Sales, fashion show coordinator Neusteters, Boulder, Colo., 1963-64; saleswoman, buyer Elli of Aspen, Colo., 1964-66; owner, broker Mahoney & Co. Realtors, Denver, 1973-83; pres., broker, founder,owner Preferred Properties, Inc., Denver, 1983—; 2d v.p. exec. bd. Denver Bd. Realtor, 1987. Active East Washington Park Neighborhood Orgn., Denver, 1970-76; originator Washington Park Early Learning Ctr., 1972; fund raiser, co-chmn. city life com. Denver Pub. Schs., 1983—; fund raiser Denver Symphony Marathon, 1984. Mem. Denver Bd. Realtors (co-chmn. city life com. 1983, chmn. 1984, bd. dirs.1984-87, 2d v.p. exec. bd. 1987, Salesperson of Yr. 1985), Nat. Assn. Realtors, Colo. Assn. Realtors. Republican. Avocations: gardening, cooking, biking, dancing. Office: Preferred Properties Inc 1041 S Gaylord Denver CO 80209

MAHONEY, JERRI ANN, sales professional; b. Niagara Falls, N.Y., Jan. 14, 1959; d. Leslie James McMonagle and Braunda June (MacSporan) Becker; m. Mark Dennis Mahoney, Sept. 8, 1984; 1 child, Caitlin Elizabeth. Student, Niagara U., 1981-82. Inventory control clk. Olin Corp., Niagara Falls, 1980-82; traffic mgr. Niacet Corp., Niagara Falls, 1983; sales rep. Stott & Davis Motor Express, Buffalo, 1983-87, Transcon Lines, Buffalo, 1987—. Mem. Niagara Falls Traffic Club (pres. 1988, bd. dirs. 1983—), Traffic Club Buffalo. Episcopalian. Office: Transcon Lines 2740 Walden Ave Buffalo NY 14225

MAHONEY, MARGARET ANN, judge; b. Alliance, Nebr., Apr. 22, 1949; d. John Charles and Grace Margaret (Hoban) M.; B.A. (Nat. Merit scholar), Coll. of St. Catherine, 1971; J.D. cum laude, U. Minn., 1974; m. Peter B. Ogren, June 28, 1980. Admitted to Minn. bar, 1974, Fla. bar, 1975; shareholder firm Stringer, Courtney & Rohleder, Ltd., St. Paul, 1974-84; U.S. bankruptcy judge Dist. Minn., Mpls., 1984-87, So. Dist. Tex., Houston, 1987—. Mem. State Bar of Tex., Houston Bar Assn., Houston Bankruptcy Conf., Nat. Conf. Bankruptcy Judges, Minn. Bar Assn., Fla. Bar Assn., Sigma Delta Phi, Phi Beta Kappa. Office: US Dist Ct 8623 US Courthouse 515 Rusk Houston TX 77002

MAHONEY, MARGARET ELLERBE, foundation executive; b. Nashville, Oct. 24, 1924; d. Charles Hallam and Leslie Nelson (Savage) M.; B.A. magna cum laude, Vanderbilt U., 1946; L.H.D. (hon.), Meharry Med. Coll., 1977, U. Fla., 1980, Med. Coll. Pa., 1982. Williams Coll., 1983, Smith Coll., 1985, Beaver Coll., 1985. Fgn. affairs officer State Dept., Washington, 1946-53; exec. assoc., assoc. sec. Carnegie Corp., N.Y.C., 1953-72; v.p. Robert Wood Johnson Found., Princeton, N.J., 1972-80; pres. Commonwealth Fund, N.Y.C., 1980—; trustee John D. and Catherine T. Mac Arthur

Found., 1985—, Hosp. Research and Ednl. Trust, 1983-87, Dole Found., 1984—; vis. fellow Sch. Architecture and Urban Planning, Princeton U., 1973-80. bd. dirs. Council on Found., 1982—; mem. N.Y.C. Commn. on the Yr. 2000, 1985-87, MIT Corp., 1984—; bd. govs. Am. Stock Exchange, 1987—; adv. com. The Robert Wood Johnson Found. Minority Med. Edn. Program, 1987—; adv. bd. Office of the Chief Med. Examiner, N.Y.C., 1987—, Barnard Coll, Inst. Med. Research, 1986—; bd. dirs. Alliance for Aging Research, 1987—; vestrywoman Parish of Trinity Ch., 1982—. Recipient Frank H. Lahey Meml. award, 1984. Mem. AAAS, Inst. Medicine, Council Fgn. Relations, Fin. Women's Assn. N.Y., N.Y. Acad. Medicine, Alpha Omega Alpha (award 1985). Contbr. articles to profl. publs. Office: Commonwealth Fund 1 E 75th St New York NY 10021

MAHONEY, MARGARET ELLIS, advertising exective; b. Detroit, Mar. 17, 1929; d. Seth WIley and Mildred Elizabeth (Hill) Ellis; m. Stephen Bedell Smith, Mar. 15, 1956 (div. Oct. 1962); 1 child, Laura Elizbeth; m. Patrick John Mahoney, Sept. 1, 1972 (dec.). BA, Butler U., 1953. Copywriter Hook Drugs Inc., Indpls., 1953; continuity dir. Sta. WXLW, Indpls., 1954-57; ptnr. Steve Smith and Assocs. Advt., Indpls., 1956-62; account mgr. Sive Advt., Cin., 1963-64, Associated Advt., Cin., 1964-65; copywriter SupeRX Drugs Inc., Cin., 1965-72; promotion writer U.S. News and World Report, Washington, 1974; asst. mgr. advt. Drug Fair, Alexandria, Va., 1975-82; dir. advt. Cosmetic and Fragrance Concepts Inc., Beltsville, Md., 1982—. Hosp. chairperson Sleepy Hollow Citizens Assn., Falls Church, Va., 1973; vestry mem. St. Matthews Episc. Ch., Cin., 1969-71. Mem. Potomac Valley Aquarium Soc. (past treas., past sec., editor jour.), Am. Cichlid Assn. (nat. pub. relations chair 1985—), Delta Delta Delta. Republican. Home: 3011 Aspen Ln Falls Church VA 22042 Office: Cosmetic and Fragrance Concepts Inc 10551 Ewing Rd Beltsville MD 20705

MAHONEY, MARY JEAN, health care administrator; b. Danbury, Conn., June 18, 1929; d. John H. and Esther (Farrell) McGoldrick; m. John A. Mahoney, June 13, 1953 (dec.); children: John, Brian, Noreen, Peter, Mary. BSN, St. Joseph Coll., Hartford, Conn., 1951; MA in Nursing Adminstrn., Columbia U., 1973. Registered nurse. Instr. St. Francis Hosp., Harford, 1951-52; instr., supr. Danbury (Conn.) Hosp., 1952-55, nurse ICU, 1957-59; nurse pub. health Danbury Vis. Nurse Assn., 1965-67, supr., 1967-71, dir., 1971—; acting dir. health City of Danbury, 1980-81; appointee Gov.'s Council on Tb Control, Hosp. Care and Rehab., Hartford, 1977-79; profl. advisor Hospice of Western Conn., Danbury, 1985-87. Trustee Danbury Hosp., 1980—; mem. adv. bd. Danbury Head Start, 1970-80; bd. dirs. Danbury Youth Services, 1982-87. Mem. Sigma Theta Tau. Roman Catholic. Office: Danbury Vis Nurse Assn 198 Main St Danbury CT 06810

MAHONEY, SHERI BURGESS, chemist; b. Flora, Ill., Oct. 14, 1960; d. Betty Jean (McBride) and Olaf Levon Burgess; m. Michael Hunter Mahoney. BS in Chemistry, Miss. State U., 1982. Radiochemist III Grand Gulf Nuclear Sta., Miss. Power & Light Co., Pt. Gibson, Miss., 1983-84, radiochemist II, 1984-85, radiochemist I, 1985-86, chemistry tng. coordinator, 1986-87; chemistry tng. specialist Grand Gulf Nuclear Sta., System Energy Resources, Inc., Pt. Gibson, 1987—. Mem. Am. Chem. Soc., Nat. Assn. Female Execs., Miss. State Alumni Assn., Kappa Kappa Gamma. Home: 1017 Victoria Square Madison MS 39110 Office: System Energy Resources Inc PO Box 756 Waterloo Rd Port Gibson MS 39150

MAHOWALD, JANE FRANCES, civic association adminstrator; b. Bessemer, Mich., July 27, 1932; d. Frederick Russell and Lila Linnea (Johnson) Trevarthen; m. David Martin Mahowald, July 28, 1956; children: Wayne, Terri, Ross. Diploma, St. Luke's Hosp. Sch. Nursing, Marquette, Mich., 1954; BS in Nursing, Wayne State U., 1958; MEd, No. Mich. U., 1967; postgrad., Kent State U., 1987. RN, Mich. Staff nurse, asst. instr. St. Luke's Hosp., Marquette, 1954-56; staff nurse Harper Hosp., Detroit, 1957; instr. med. surg. nursing St. Luke's Hosp. Sch. Nursing, Marquette, 1958-63, edn. dir., 1963-67, dir. sch. nursing, 1967-71; dir. nursing edn. St. Lukes Hosp., Marquette Gen., 1971-74, Luth. Med. Ctr. Sch. Nursing, Cleve., 1974-84; program dir. resources mgmt. Luth. Med. Ctr., Cleve., 1984-86; exec. dir. Ohio Citizens League for Nursing, Cleve., 1986—. Active Ohio Council on Nursing, Columbus, 1984—; mem. commn. health concerns Fedn. Community Planning Cleve., 1986—; pres. bd. dirs. Cleve. League for Nursing, 1979-83; rep. Planning for Rural Nursing, Mpls., 1971-74; sec., pres. comprehensive health planning zone III Upper Peninsula Assn., 1971-74; bd. dirs. Marquette County Heart Assn., Marquette, 1964-67, Marquette-Alger chpt. ARC, 1963-67; chmn. Greater Cleve. Nursing Roundtable 1984-86. Mem. Ohio Nurses Assn., Nat. League for Nursing, Coalition for Revision Nurse Practice Art, Mich. Nurses Assn. (bd. dirs. 1965-69, 2d v.p. 1969-71). Office: Ohio Citizens League for Nursing 2800 Euclid Ave Suite 235 Cleveland OH 44115

MAIELLO, LAURA ANNE, architectural planner, programmer; b. Summit, N.J., Sept. 27, 1956; d. Pasquale Anthony and Joan Marie (Bencduce) M. B in Social Work, Kean Coll., Union, N.J., 1978; MA, Rutgers U., 1982, postgrad., 1982—. Social worker Union County Jail, Elizabeth, N.J., 1978-80, classification officer, 1980-81; research assoc. Rutgers U., Newark, 1981-84; assoc. planning mgr. The Ehrenkrantz Group & Eckstut, N.Y.C, 1984—; adj. prof. Nat. Inst. of Corrections, Washington, 1983; cons. in field. Contbr. articles to profl. jours. Mem. Am. Correctional Assn., Acad. Criminal Justice Scis., Criminal Justice Statistic Assn., Nat. Assn. Female Execs. Home: 95 G Beverly Hill Terr Woodbridge NJ 07095 Office: The Ehrenkrantz Group & Eckstut 399 Lafayette St New York NY 10003

MAIER, NANCY HOPPING, personnel administrator; b. Washington, Mar. 5, 1955; d. Andrew B. and Evelyn (Steed) Hopping; m. Robert A. Maier, Oct. 3, 1981. AS, SUNY, Delhi, 1975; BS, Fairfield U., 1986. Sec. PepsiCo., Purchase, N.Y., 1977-78, Ga.-Pacific Corp., Darien, Conn., 1978-80; exec. sec. Kennecott Corp., Stamford, Conn., 1980-82; adminstrv. asst. Emery Worldwide, Wilton, Conn., 1982-83; benefits adminstr. Am. Maize-Products Co., Stamford, 1983—. Campaign coordinator United Way of Stamford, 1985-88. Mem. Nat. Assn. Female Execs., Stamford Personnel Roundtable. Republican. Episcopalian. Office: American Maize-Products Co 250 Harbor Dr Stamford CT 06904

MAIER, NATALIE DIANE, advertising executive; b. Bklyn., Aug. 3, 1943; d. Joseph Jay and Hilda (Tetenbaum) J.; m. Richard Joseph Maier, Dec. 19, 1964 (div. May 1980); children: Gary Edward, Jody Ellen. BS cum laude, Fairleigh Dickinson U., 1965, MS in Bus. Adminstrn., 1975. Cert. elem. tchr., N.J.; cert. travel agt. Tchr. River Edge (N.J.) Pub. Schs., 1965-66; advt. dir. Florence Shop Dept. Store, Bergenfield, N.J., 1971-77, Twin Boro News, Bergenfield, N.J., 1976-80; advt./mktg. dir. Community Publs., Westwood, N.J., 1980—; travel cons. Travel Port of Bergen County, Park Ridge, N.J., 1983—; advt. cons. Westwood C. of C., 1980—, Westwood Plaza Assn., 1984—. Vol. River Dell High Sch. Band Parents Assn., Oradell, N.J., 1985—, Ctr. for Help in Time of Loss, River Vale, N.J., 1986—. Recipient 1st place advt. award Print Media Services, 1977. Mem. Am. Soc. Travel Agts., Suburban Newspapers Am., N.J. Press Assn., Advt. Club North Jersey, Fairleigh Dickinson Alumni Assn. (planning bd. 1985—), N.J. Metaphysical Soc., Phi Omega Epsilon. Jewish. Club: Garden State Ski (Maywood, N.J.). Lodge: Optimists. Home: 357 Oradell Ave Oradell NJ 07649 Office: Community Publs 369 Fairview Ave Westwood NJ 07675

MAIER, PAULINE, history educator; b. St. Paul, Apr. 27, 1938; d. Irvin Louis and Charlotte (Winterer) Rubbelke; A.B., Radcliffe Coll., 1960; postgrad. London Sch. Econs., 1960-61; Ph.D. in History, Harvard U., 1968, L.L.D. (hon.), Regis Coll., 1987; m. Charles Steven Maier, June 17, 1961; children—Andrea Nicole, Nicholas Winterer, Jessica Elizabeth Heine. Asst. prof., then assoc. prof. history U. Mass., Boston, 1968-77; Robinson-Edwards prof. history U. Wis., Madison, 1977-78; prof. history MIT, Cambridge, 1978—, dept. head, 1979-87; mem. council Inst. Early Am. History, 1982-84; trustee Regis Coll., 1988—. Recipient Douglass Adair award Claremont Grad. Sch.-Inst. Early Am. History, 1976, Kidger award New Eng. History Tchrs. Assn., 1981; fellow Nat. Endowment Humanities, 1974-75, 88—; Charles Warren fellow, 1974-75. Mem. Orgn. Am. Historians (exec. bd. 1978-82), Am. Hist. Assn. (nominations com. 1983-85, chmn. 1985), Soc. Am. Historians, Am. Antiquarian Soc. (exec. council 1984—), Colonial Soc. Mass., Mass. Hist. Soc. Author: From Resistance to Revolution: Colonial Radicals and the Development of American Opposition to Britain, 1765-1766, 1972; The Old Revolutionaries: Political Lives in the Age of Samuel Adams, 1980; The American People: A History, 1986. Home: 60 Larchwood Dr Cambridge MA 02138 Office: MIT E51-216 Cambridge MA 02139

MAILLY, CLAUDY, Canadian legislator; b. Nov. 30, 1938; 1 child. Grad., McGill U. Previously mgr. info. services Domtar Ltd., spl. asst. to pres. Can. Post Corp., corp. affairs advisor Royal Bank Can, mem. Can. House of Commons, 1984—. Author: Le Cortège. Progressive Conservative. Office: House of Commons, Parliament Bldgs, Ottawa, ON Canada K1A 0A6 *

MAIN, EDNA DEWEY, educator; b. Hyannis, Mass., Sept. 1, 1940; d. Seth Bradford and Edna Wilhelmina (Wright) Dewey; m. Donald John Main, Sept. 9, 1961; children—Alison Teresa, Susan Christine, Steven Donald. Degree in Merchandising, Tobe-Coburn Sch., 1960; BA in Edn., U. North Fla., 1974, MA in Edn., 1979, M in Adminstrn. and Supervision, 1983; postgrad. U. Fla., 1986—. Asst. buyer Abraham & Straus, Bklyn., 1960-61; asst. mdse. mgr. Interstate Dept. Stores, N.Y.C., 1962-63; tchr. Holiday Hill Elem. Sch., Jacksonville, Fla., 1974-86; mem. adv. council Coll. Edn., U. North Fla., 1982—, instr. summer sci. inst., 1984—; instr. U. South Fla., 1981, U. Fla., 1987—. Rep., United Way, 1981-86; tchr. rep., chpt. leader White House Young Astronaut Program, 1984-85; mem. supervisory com. Ednl. Community Credit Union. Mem. Nat. Sci. Tchrs. Assn. (sci. tchrs. achievement recognition award 1983), Assn. Supervision and Curriculum Devel., Council Elem. Sci. Internat., Fla. Assn. Sci. Tchrs., Phi Kappa Phi, Phi Delta Kappa, Delta Kappa Gamma, Kappa Delta Pi. Republican. Episcopalian. Office: U Fla 303 Norman Hall Gainesville FL 32611

MAINI, SUSAN JANE, computer software executive; b. Quincy, Ill., Oct. 9, 1949; d. Seldon Dean and Mary Jane (Speckhart) Sims; m. Gino Louis Maini, June 6, 1977. BA, U. Ill., 1971. Asst. dir. Northwest Community Orgn., Chgo., 1972-73; exec. dir. People Acting Through Community Effort, Providence, 1974-76; devel. mgr. Neighborhood Reinvestment Corp., Washington, 1977-84; prin. The Software Library, Providence, 1984—; cons. in field. Mem. Delta Delta Delta. Republican. Methodist. Office: The Software Library 171 Waterman St Providence RI 02906

MAINS, CHRISTINE ROBIN, communications executive; b. Bozeman, Mont., Mar. 30, 1954; d. James J. Mains and Polly McHenry Langhart. BA, San Francisco State U., 1976; BFA, Acad. Art, 1978. Illustrator San Francisco Examiner, 1983-84; asst. production mgr. Chronicle Videotex, San Francisco, 1984-86; production mgr. Dolphin Multi-Media, San Francisco, 1986-88; tradeshow and events coordinator Apple Computers Inc., Cupertino, Calif., 1988—; pvt. practice graphic design, San Francisco, 1978-84; entrepreneur stationery products, San Francisco, 1981-84. Mem. Spl. Interest Group Computer Graphics, Nat. Computer Graphics Assn., YLEM, Nat. Assn. Female Execs. Home: 1233 Arguello #7 San Francisco CA 94122 Office: Apple Computers Inc 10455 Bandley MS/2P Cupertino CA 95014

MAIRS, CANDYCE WENBORG, manufacturing and import company executive; b. Mpls., June 29, 1958; d. Glen Roger and Mary Ann (Bishop) Wenborg; m. Todd Partridge Mairs, Mar. 22, 1980; children: Tealina Partridge, Bryant Wenborg. BA, U. Minn., 1980. Profl. tchr. figure skating Mpls. and St. Paul, 1977-80; import and traffic clk. George S. Bush, Seattle, 1982; import mgr., v.p. Far Ea. Marine Transp., Oakland, Calif., 1982-87; owner, pres. Candyce and Co., Alameda, Calif., 1985-88, Mpls., 1988—. Patentee CoziCarrier infant carrier. Recipient Gold medals Am. Gold Figure and Free Style, 1977, Can. Gold Figure and Free Style, 1977, European Gold Figure and Free Style, 1977, numerous Silver medals, 1973. Mem. Nat. Assn. Female Execs. Episcopal. Club: Dungeness Divers (Bremerton, Washington) (v.p. 1982).

MAISSEL, RAINA EVE, lawyer; b. London, Apr. 12, 1931; came to U.S., 1956; d. Louis and Golde Pearl (Crowne) Corren; m. Leon Israel Maissel, Jan. 22, 1956; children—Simon Joseph, Gerda Sharon, Joseph Saul. LL.B., Univ. Coll. London, 1952. Barrister-at-law Eng. 1953; bar: N.Y. 1977, U.S. Dist. Ct. (so. dist.) N.Y. 1979, U.S. Dist. Ct. (ea. dist.) N.Y. 1979, U.S. Supreme Ct. 1982. Pupil to Hon. S.C. Silkin, London, 1953-54; sole practice, Bournemough, Eng., 1954-56; research assoc. Ballard, Spahr et al, Phila., 1956-58; counsel Moran, Spiegel, et al, Poughkeepsie, N.Y., 1977-80; sole practice, Wappingers Falls, N.Y., 1980-86; assoc. Gellert & Cutler P.C., Poughkeepsie, 1986—. Vice pres. Dutchess County Players, Poughkeepsie, 1962-64; pres. Merrywood Civic Assn., 1972-74; mem. 1st ward com. Democratic party, Poughkeepsie, 1973-74; mem. Poughkeepsie Zoning Bd. Appeals, 1982-83. Mem. ABA, N.Y. State Bar Assn., N.Y. State Bar (com. on mental and phys. disabilities, 9th jud. dist. grievance com.). Jewish. Home: 16 Smoke Rise Ln Wappingers Falls NY 12590 Office: Gellert & Cutler PC 54 Market St Poughkeepsie NY 12601

MAIXNER, NANCY W(HEELWRIGHT), rehabilitation coordinator; b. Washington, July 4, 1952; d. David Page and Arabelle (Leonard) Wheelwright; m. Richard Charles Maixner, Jan. 7, 1976 (div. 1980); 1 child, Sara Elizabeth. BFA in Journalism, So. Meth. U., Dallas, 1974; MS in Rehab. Counseling, U. of North Tex., 1988. Tennis profl. Bent Tree Country Club, Dallas, 1974-77; dir. advt. Nardis of Dallas, 1977-80; account exec. DBG & H Advt., Dallas, 1980-82; asst. mktg. Network Security, Dallas, 1982; rehab. coordinator Richard S. Gold, Dallas; case mgr. Greencry Rehab. Ctr., Dallas, 1988; facilitator Dallas Head Injury Found. Bd. dirs., sec. Freedom Ride Found., Southlake, Tex. Mem. Internat. Assn. Logopaedics and Phoniatrics, Nat. Rehab. Assn., Am. Assn. Counseling and Devel., Rho Chi Sigma, Phi Kappa Phi. Republican. Presbyterian. Home: 6740 Town Bluff Dallas TX 75240

MAIZES, MARION RUTH, special education administrator; b. N.Y.C., June 26, 1936; d. Philip and Bella (Pearly) Krugman; B.A., CCNY, 1957; M.S., Fordham U., 1979; M.S., Coll. of New Rochelle, 1982; m. S. Raymond Maizes, Mar. 19, 1961; children—Paul, Jay. Tchr. English jr. and sr. high sch., N.Y.C., 1957-62; adminstrv. asst. Blythedale Union Free Sch. Dist., Valhalla, N.Y., 1978-79; spl. edn. placement officer Com. on the Handicapped Sch. Dist. 12, N.Y.C. Bd. Edn., 1981-85, asst. chair Com. on the Handicapped, 1985-87, dir. support services and spl. edn. Community Sch. Dist. 12, N.Y.C., 1987—. Chmn., White Plains (N.Y.) women's div. United Jewish Appeal, Fedn. Jewish Philanthropies, 1978-80; v.p. Brandeis U. Nat. Women's Com., Central Westchester chpt., 1971-75. Mem. Council Exceptional Children, Assn. Supervision and Curriculum Devel., Assn. Women Adminstrs. in Westchester, Phi Delta Kappa. Office: Community Sch Dist 12 1000 Jennings St Bronx NY 10460

MAJCHER, KATHY ANNE, health science facility administrator; b. Chgo., Nov. 14, 1949; d. Daniel John and Anne Sabina (Flannery) Mortell; divorced; 1 child, Dylan Jacob. Grad. high sch., Chgo. Proof operator Lake View Trust and Savs., Chgo., 1968-70; lab. clk. Damon Clin. Lab., Chgo., 1973-75, customer service rep., 1975-79, sales rep., 1979-86, sales mgr., 1986—. Mem. Am. Assn. Clin. Chemistry. Roman Catholic. Office: Damon Clin Lab 3231 S Euclid Berwyn IL 60402

MAJEWSKI, MICHELLE ELIZABETH, psychotherapist; b. Marin County, Calif., Dec. 31, 1951; d. H. James and Helen E. (Weber) Radtke; divorced; 1 child, Adam Joseph. BS in Spl. Edn., U. Wis., Oshkosh, 1974, MS in Spl. Edn., 1977, MS in Guidance Counseling, 1980; cert. sch. psychology, Marquette U., 1983. Tchr. spl. edn. Fond du Lac (Wis.) Pub. Schs., 1975; ednl. cons. Ctr. Child and Adolescent Devel., Manitowoc, Wis., 1977; child treatment specialist Inst. Human Services, Fond du Lac, 1979-81; psychotherapist Discovery Mental Health Assocs., West Bend, Wis., 1982—; coordinator child services Fond du Lac County Health Care Ctr., 1976-83; mem. adj. faculty edn. dept. Ripon (Wis.) Coll., 1984-88, dir. coll. bound program, 1986—; dir. Ripon Coll. Learning Disability Program, 1986-88; asst. prof. Marian Coll., Fond du lac, 1988—. Contbr. numerous articles to ednl. jours. V.p. PTO, Fond du Lac, 1986-87. Mem. Orton-Gillingham Soc., Wis. Sch. Psychologists Assn., Kappa Delta Pi (mem. honor soc. in edn.). Home: 320 Taft St Fond du Lac WI 54935 Office: Discovery Mental Health Assocs 123 S 6th Ave West Bend WI 53095

MAJOR, RITA ANNE, arts administrator; b. Long Beach, Calif., Oct. 20, 1942; d. Richard Samuel and Anne Bell (Givens) Walker; m. Albert William Van Patten (div. 1968); children: Richard William Van Patten, Michael Thomas Van Patten, Edward Albert Van Patten; m. Norman Stephen Major Jr., June 22, 1969; 1 child, Norman Stephen III. Grad. high sch., Santa Ana, Calif. Bus. mgr. Pacific Chorale, Santa Ana, 1977-86, adminstrv. mgr., 1987—. Democrat. Office: Pacific Chorale 1020 N Broadway St Suite 302 Santa Ana CA 92701

MAJORS, JUDITH SOLEY, writer, health educator; b. Portland, Oreg., June 17, 1946; d. Alford H. and Leora L. (Carpenter) Soley; B.A., Marylhurst Coll., 1980; A.A., Mt. Hood Community Coll., 1970; m. Jack B. Majors, Mar. 18, 1967; 1 dau., Carrie. Sr. editor Apple Press, Milwaukie, Oreg., 1978—; local TV personality; author; works include: Sugar Free—That's Me, 1978; Sugar Free—Kid's Cookery, 1979; Sugar Free—Microwavery, 1980; Diet Out—Oregon, 1981; Meatless Wonder, 1982; Sugar Free ... Sweets and Treats, 1983. Bd. dirs. Oreg. Diabetes Assn.; adv. bd. North Clackamas Sch. Dist.; mem. Milwaukie Citizens Adv. Com.; bd. dirs. Milwaukie Festival Daze. Mem. Am. Assn. Diabetes Educators, Am. Diabetes Assn. (profl.), Nat. Fedn. Presswomen, Women in Communications, Willamette Writers, Oreg. Community Edn. Assn. Democrat. Home and Office: 5536 SE Harlow St Milwaukie OR 97222

MAJORS, NELDA FAYE, physical therapist; b. Houston, Aug. 3, 1938; d. Columbus Edward and Mary (Mills) M. Cert. in Phys. Therapy, Hermann Sch. Phys. Therapy, Houston, 1960; BS, U. Houston, 1963. Lic. phys. therapist, Tex. Staff therapist Tex. Med. Ctr. Hermann Hosp., Houston, 1960-61; phys. therapist Chelsea Orthopedic Clinic, Houston, 1961-63; dir. phys. therapy Meml. Hosp. Southwest, Houston, 1963-75; owner, pres. Nelda Majors, Inc., Houston, 1975—; profl. adv. bd. Logos Home Health Agy., Houston, 1985-86, AMI Home Care Plus Agy., Houston, 1985-86. Active with Meml. Dr. Meth. Ch., Houston, 1983—; ptnr. Houston Proud Ptnr., 1986—; mem. steering com. Larkin Community Ctr., Houston, 1985-86. Named All Am. Softball Pitcher, Amateur Softball Assn., 1964, All-Regional and All-State Pitcher, Tex. Amateur Softball Assn., 1954-70. Mem. Am. Phys. Therapy Assn. (pvt. practice sect.), Tex. Phys. Therapy Assn., U. Houston Alumni Assn. Republican. Club: U. Houston Cougar. Home: 2 Windermere Ln Houston TX 77063 Office: Nelda Majors Inc 800 Gessner PO Box 19487 Houston TX 77224

MAKAROVA, NATALIA, ballerina; b. Leningrad, Russia, Nov. 21, 1940; m. Edward Karkar, 1976; 1 child, Andrei Michel. Grad., Vaganova Ballet Sch., Leningrad Choreographic Sch., 1959. assoc. artist London Festival Ballet, 1985—. Formerly ballerina with Leningrad Kirov Ballet, performed at Royal Opera House, Covent Garden, London, 1961; toured U.S., 1961, 64; roles include Giselle, Swan Lake, Les Sylphides, Sleeping Beauty, Cinderella, Raymonda, La Bayadere, Onegin (London Evening Standard award 1985), others; joined Am. Ballet Theatre, 1970; guest appearances in U.S. and Europe, 1972—; presented Makarova & Co., 1980 (one season); staged full-length prodn. of La Bayadere for Am. Ballet Theatre, 1980; appeared in Broadway prodn. On Your Toes, 1983 (Tony award 1984, Olivier award); appeared in TV and film prodns.: Makarova: Class of her Own, Channel 4, 1984, Natasha Special, BBC, 1985, (4-part documentary) Ballerina, BBC, 1987; author: A Dance Autobiography, 1979. Recipient Gold medal 2d Internat. Ballet Competition, Varna, Bulgaria 1965. Office: London Festival Ballet, 39 Jay Mews, London SW7 2ES, England also: Am Ballet Theatre 888 7th Ave New York NY 10019 *

MAKER, JANET ANNE, author, lecturer; b. Woburn, Mass., Feb. 13, 1942; d. George Walter and Margaret Anna (Kopasz) M.; children: Thomas Walter, Jane McKinley. BA, UCLA, 1963; MS, Columbia U., 1967; PhD, U. So. Calif., 1978. lectr. in psychology and edn., 1979—. Author: Get It All Together, vol. I & II, 1978, The Word Works, 1979, Interpretive Reading Comprehension, 1984, Keys to a Powerful Vocabulary, Level I, 1982, 88, Keys to a Powerful Vocabulary, Level II, 1983, Keys to College Success, 1980, 85, College Reading, Book 1, 1984, 88, College Reading, Book 3, 1984, 85, 88College Reading, Book 2, 1982, 86. Home and Office: 925 Malcolm Ave Los Angeles CA 90024

MAKER, LYNNE DIANE, communications specialist; b. St. Paul, Mar. 30, 1960; d. Julius Warren and Jeannette June (Topel) M. BA summa cum laude, Coll. of St. Thomas, 1982, M in Bus. Communications, 1987. Intern pub. relations St. Paul Council Camp Fire, 1982; publs. writer , editor Deluxe Corp., St. Paul, 1982-86, specialist corp. communications, 1986—. Participant U.S. Figure Skating Assn. Meml. Fund Benefit Shows, Bloomington, Minn., 1976-77; mem. North Starlettes Precision Team, St. Paul, 1979. Luth. Brotherhood scholar, 1979-80, St. Thomas Disting. scholar, 1978-82. Mem. Internat. Assn. Bus. Communicators, The Loft: A Place for Writing and Lit., Delta Epsilon Sigma. Mem. United Ch. of Christ. Clubs: Roseville Figure Skating of Mpls., Mpls. Figure Skating.

MAKRANSKY, VICTORIA HOOPER, state agency administrator; b. Woodbury, N.J., Sept. 24, 1960; d. Thomas Paul and Anita Marie (Ganley) Hooper; m. Michael Francis Makransky, Apr. 16, 1983. BA in Polit. Sci., Douglass Coll., 1982. Cons. rental village of Deerfield, Maple Shade, N.J., 1982-83; bookkeeper Barbara-George Inc., Edison, N.J., 1983-84; mgr. office Rubaine Co., New Brunswick, N.J., 1984 85; rep. field Div. Motor Vehicles N.J., Trenton, 1985—. Com. person S. Amboy (N.J.) Rep. Party, 1985—. Mem. LWV, Nat. Assn. Female Execs., Douglass Coll. Alumni Assn. (treas. 1987—). Roman Catholic. Home: 265 David St South Amboy NJ 08879 Office: NJ Div Motor Vechicle 481 Rt #46 W Wayne NJ 07470

MAKUPSON, AMYRE PORTER, television executive; b. River Rouge, Mich., Sept. 30, 1947; d. Rudolph Hannibal and Amyre Ann (Porche) Porter; m. Walter H. Makupson, Nov. 1, 1975; children: Rudolph Porter, Amyre Nisi. BA, Fisk U., 1970; MA, Am. U., Washington, 1972. Asst. dir. news Sta. WGPR-TV, Detroit, 1975-76; dir. pub. relations Mich. Health Maintenance Orgn., Detroit, 1974-76, Kirwood Gen. Hosp., Detroit, 1976-77; mgr. news and pub. affairs Sta. WKBD-TV, Southfield, Mich., 1977—. Mem. adv. com. Mich. Arthritis Found., Co-Ette Club, Inc., Met. Detroit Teen Conf. Coalition, Cystic Fibrosis Soc., Alzheimers Disease and Related Disorders Assn.; mem. exec. com. March of Dimes; pres. bd. dirs. Detroit Wheelchair Athletic Assn.; bd. dirs. Barat House, Kids In Need of Direction, Drop-out Prevention Collaborative. Recipient numerous service awards including Arthritis Found. Mich., Mich. Mchts. Assn., DAV, Jr. Achievement, City of Detroit, Salvation Army. Mem. Pub. Relations Soc. Am., Am. Women in Radio and TV (Outstanding Achievement award 1981), Women in Communications, Nat. Acad. TV Arts and Scis., Detroit Press Club, Ad-Craft. Roman Catholic. Office: 26955 W 11 Mile Rd Southfield MI 48034

MALACHI-WHITE, CYNTHIA FENNELL, customer education consultant; b. Phila., Sept. 15, 1956; d. Ralph Wesley and Sarah Perzell (Bagby) M.; m. Andrew White Jr. BS in Music Edn., West Chester (Pa.) State Coll., 1977. Music instr. Downingtown (Pa.) I&A Sch., 1977-78, Phila. Bd. Edn., 1978; cons. McCann Assoc., Inc., Phila., 1978-80; photographer Photo Corp. Am., Phila., 1980-81; service rep. Bell of Pa., Phila., 1981-84; account exec. Bala Cynwyd, Pa., 1984-86, communications cons., 1986-87, customer edn. cons., 1987—. Hon. councilwoman Parrish East Baton Rougue, 1987. Recipient Legion of Honor, Chapel of Four Chaplains, Phila., 1982. Mem. NAACP, Nat. Assn. Female Execs., Alliance Bus. Assn., Phila. Bapt. Assn. (bd. dirs. 1984), Congress Christian Edn. (bd. dirs. eastern dist. 1984—), Alpha Kappa Alpha. Democrat. Home: 334 E Montana St Philadelphia PA 19119 Office: Bell of Pa 1 Parkway 9-D Philadelphia PA 19102

MALACHOWSKI, CARLA, investment company executive; b. Southington, Conn., Nov. 26, 1953; d. Carl Raymond and Jeanette Ann (Zoni) Malachowski; m. Frank J. Csencsits, Mar. 20, 1982 (div. 1986); A.A., Endicott Jr. Coll., 1973; B.A. in History, Newton Coll./Boston Coll., 1975. Admissions rep. Katharine Gibbs Sch., Boston, 1977-79, cons., 1981; mgr. sales tng. and devel. Katharine Gibbs Sch. subs. Macmillan Inc., N.Y.C., 1979-81; mgr. mgmt. info. systems Fidelity Investments, Boston, 1982-85, dir. market mgmt., 1985-86, asst. v.p. 1986-88, v.p., 1988—; speaker, panelist profl. assn. Mem. Am. Soc. Tng. and Devel., Nat. Assn. Securities Dealers. Office: Fidelity Investments 82 Devonshire St L12A Boston MA 02109

MALCHON, JEANNE K(ELLER), state senator; b. Newark, June 17, 1923; d. Leslie Stafford and Edith Katherine (Marcelle) Keller; m. Richard Malchon, 1946; 1 child, Richard Jr. A.A., Va. Intermont Coll., 1943.

Draftsman, Curtis-Wright Propeller div., Caldwell, N.J., 1943-44; civilian employee U.S. Army, Hickam Field, Hawaii, 1944-45; merchandising rep. L. Bamberger & Co., Newark, 1946-49; with Office of Tech. Assessment Task Force, 1971; mem. Gov.'s Commn. on Criminal Justice Standards and Goals, 1981-82, Fla. Jud. Council, 1972-82; commr. Pinellas County (Fla.), 1975-82; mem. Supreme Ct. Dispute Resolution Alternatives Com., Nat. Com. and Nat. Air Quality Commn., 1978-82; mem. Fla. State Senate from Dist. 18, 1982—, chmn. Senate Select Com. on Aging, vice chmn. Senate Health and Rehab. Services Com., 1985-86, Mem. exec. com. Am. Lung Assn., 1977-85, nat. pres., 1982-84; chmn. Nat. Air Conservation Com. 1978-83, mem. Fla. Cancer Control and Research Adv. Bd., 1986—, bd. dirs. Ctr. for Govtl. Responsibility. Recipient women in govt. award Soroptimists, 1979, outstanding equal opportunity efforts award Pinellas County Urban League, 1980, most effective sen. for law enforcement Fla. Sheriff's Assn., 1983, environment award, Fla. Sierra Club, 1984, outstanding legislator of the yr. Fla. Nurses Assn., 1985, legislator of the yr. Fla. Psychol. Assn., 1985, disting. service award Pinellas County Assn. Respiratory Care Mgrs., 1985, Human Service award United Way Pinellas County, 1986, Legislator of Yr. Fla. Consumer Fedn., 1986. Mem. State Assn. Coun-y Commrs. (dir. 1975-80, chmn. urban affairs com. 1979-80), Nat. Assn.-County (criminal justice steering com. 1975-80 , chmn. law enforcement subcom. 1979-80). Democrat. Address: 2400 Pinellas Point Dr S Saint Petersburg FL 33712 Address: 424 Central Ave Suite 804 Saint Petersburg FL 33701

MALDEN, JOAN WILLIAMS, physical therapist; b. Bayshore, N.Y., Apr. 14; d. Sidney S. and Myrtle L. (Williams) Siegel; B.S., N.Y. U., 1957; m. Alan A. Chasnov, Jan. 20, 1951; children—Marc, Robin, Debra and David (twins); m. 2d, Miroslav Mladenovic, Sept. 14, 1967; 1 dau., Kristine. Phys. therapist hosps. and orgns. in N.Y.C. area, 1956-57; phys. therapist Brunswick Hosp. Center, Amityville, N.Y., 1968-69; pvt. practice phys. therapy, Wantagh, N.Y., 1968—; licensure examiner, N.Y. State; cons., tchr. in field. Contbr. articles to profl. jours. Pres. internat. scholarships com. Massapequa chpt. Am. Field Service, 1962-64. Mem. Am. Acad. Cerebral Palsy, Am. Phys. Therapy Assn. (chmn. polit. action com. N.Y. chpt., chmn. L.I. dist.), AAUW (pres. Massapequa chpt. 1962-64), N.Y. State Soc. Continuing Edn. in Phys. Therapy, Airplane Owners and Pilots Assn., Ninety-Nines, Exptl. Aviation Assn., Farmingdale Flyers (officer). Democrat. Unitarian. Home: 35 S Bay Ave Massapequa NY 11758 Office: Wantagh Med Bldg 1228 Wantagh Ave Wantagh NY 11793 also: 158 E Main St Huntington NY 11743

MALDONADO, ELIZABETH MARA, television producer, media consultant; b. Detroit, May 12, 1954; d. Alvin Victor and Mara (Staicri) Plonka; m. Michael Henry Lesiak, July 20, 1979 (div. Apr. 1983); 1 child, Michael Alexander; m. Jesus Enrique Maldonado, Dec. 27, 1984; 1 child, Charles Benjamin. BA, Wayne State U., 1980. Producer Post-Newsweek Sta. WDIV-TV, Detroit, 1980—; prin. Maldonado and Assocs., Grosse Pointe, Mich., 1987; cons. Mich. Cancer Found., Detroit, 1986-87. Producer TV shows Sonya, 1981-83 (Emmy 1982), Free 4 All, GOP Senatorial Debate, 1984; talent coordinator The Tony Orlando Show, 1986. Club: Variety (Southfield, Mich.). Home and Office: 758 Rivard Grosse Pointe MI 48230

MALDONADO-BEAR, RITA MARINITA, economist, educator; b. Vega Alta, P.R., June 14, 1938; d. Victor and Marina (Davila) Maldonado; B.A., Auburn U., 1960; Ph.D., N.Y.U., 1969; m. Larry Alan Bear, Mar. 29, 1975. With Min. Wage Bd. & Econ. Devel. Adminstrn., Govt. of P.R., 1960-64; asso. prof. fin. U. P.R., 1969-70; asst. prof. econs. Manhattan Coll., 1970-72; assoc. prof. econs. Bklyn. Coll., 1972-75; vis. assoc. prof. fin. Stanford (Calif.) Grad. Bus. Sch., 1973-74; assoc. prof. fin. and econs. Grad. Sch. Bus. Adminstrn., N.Y.U., N.Y.C., 1975-81, prof., 1981—; cons. Morgan Guaranty Trust Co., N.Y.C., 1972-77, Bank of Am., N.Y.C., 1982-84, Res. City Bankers, N.Y.C., 1978-87, Swedish Inst. Mgmt., Stockholm, 1982—, Empresas Master of Puerto Rico, 1985— ; dir. Medallion Funding Corp., 1985-87. P.R. Econ. Devel. Adminstrn. fellow, 1960-65; Marcus Nadler fellow, N.Y.U., 1966-67, Phillip Lods Dissertation fellow, 1967-68. Mem. Am. Econs. Assn., Am. Fin. Assn., Metro. Econ. Assn. N.Y., Assn. for Social Econs. Author: Role of the Financial Sector in the Economic Development of Puerto Rico, 1970; contbr. articles to profl. jours. Home: 95 Tam O'Shanter Dr Mahwah NJ 07430 Office: 100 Trinity Pl New York NY 10006

MALDONADO-COLON, ELBA C., school system administrator, state consultant; b. Ponce, P.R., June 1, 1946; d. Arcelio and Celia (Colon) Maldonado. BA cum laude, U. P.R., 1967; MEd, U. Mass., 1980, EdD, 1984. Cert. tchr., Mass., Conn.; cert. supr., Conn. Bilingual tchr. Springfield (Mass.) Pub. Schs., 1972-80; team leader U. Mass./Tchr. Corps Project, Worcester, 1980-81; lectr. U. Tex., Austin, 1981-85; asst. coordinator Hartford (Conn.) Bd. Edn., 1985—; head tchr. Mass. Migrant Edn. Program, Holyoke, 1973-81; bilingual special edn. cons. schs., state agys. Calif., Conn., Fla, Mass., N.H., N.Mex., N.Y., Tex.; instr. Tchrs.' Coll. Columbia U., N.Y.C., 1987. Author: Profiles of Hispanic Children, 1984; (newsletter) Awareness, 1986. Vol. Shriners' Hosp., Springfield, 1978; cons. Community Council-Tchr. Corps Project, Worcester, 1979-80; speaker ALPA Valley Residents for Improvement, Worcester, 1980; tutor, Hartford, 1985-86. Mem. Am. Ednl. Research, Nat. Assn. for Bilingual Edn. (co-chair bilingual spl. edn. 1985-87), Council for Exceptional Children (chairperson Hispanic Caucus 1985-87, mem. commn. on ethnic and multicultural concerns 1985—), Internat. Reading Assn., Conn. Bilingual-Bicultural Edn. Assn. (treas. 1986—). Office: Hartford Bd Edn Bilingual Dept 249 High St Hartford CT 06133

MALEC, JUDITH MARY, sales executive, consultant; b. Jersey City, June 21, 1955; d. Frank and Irene (Bilan) M. Student, Pa. State U., 1976-78; BS in Econs., U. Pitts., 1980. Asst. buyer Joseph Horne Co., Pitts., 1980-81; sales rep. Budget Uniform, Pitts., 1981-83, Allnet, Pitts., 1983-84; sales rep. Dictaphone Co., Pitts., 1984, sr. sales rep., 1985-86; nat. acct. mgr. Lizardy Assocs., Pitts., 1986; nat. sales dir. Lizardy Assocs., San Diego, Calif., 1986—; cons. Southwestern Bell Corp., St. Louis, Mo., 1987—. Mem. Am. Soc. for Tng. and Devel. (cons.-on-call 1987—), Vectors of Pitts. (pres. pioneer 1987), Greater Pitts. C. of C., 1987—. Roman Catholic. Club: Toastmasters. Home: PO Box 15251 Pittsburgh PA 15237 Office: Lizardy Assocs 3825 Liberty Ave Suite 2 Pittsburgh PA 15201

MALEK, MARLENE ANNE, nurse, foundation executive; b. Oakland, Calif., June 22, 1939; d. William Alexander and Yolanda Katherine (Stella) McArthur; m. Frederic Vincent Malek, Aug. 5, 1961; children: Frederic William, Michelle Ann. AA, Armstrong U., 1959; AS in Nursing, Marymount U., 1979; cert. in hospice tng., Arlington, Va., 1980. Dir. Psychiat. Inst. Found., Washington, 1982—; women's bd. Am. Heart Assn., 1973—, bd. treas., 1983—, chmn. ann. luncheon, 1988. Bd. dirs. Nat. Fed. Rep. Women, Washington, 1972-74, Marymount U. Va., Arlington, 1974— ; chmn. Eisenhower Meml. Found., Washington, 1972-74; cons. hospitality Presdl. Inaugural Com., Washington, 1984; mem. adv. bd. Second Genesis Drug Rehab. Program, Bethesda, Md., 1983—, chmn. Second Genesis Benefit, 1968, 84-85; founding mem. Arena Stage Guild, Washington; bd. dirs. Nat. Mus. Women in Arts, 1987, Claude Moore Colonial Farm, 1986. Episcopalian. Avocations: skiing, collecting antiques, painting, running.

MALES-MADRID, SANDRA KAY, medical facility administrator; b. South Gate, Calif., Aug. 1, 1942; d. Albert Odus and Evelyn Louise (Corbett) Males; m. James O. Spurbeck, Apr. 15, 1963 (div. Nov. 1967); m. Miguel Madrid Jr., Feb. 9, 1980; stepchildren: Priscilla, Betty, Dru, Rachel. BA, U. Redlands, Calif., 1987. Payroll clk. Lever Bros. Co., Los Angeles, 1961-69; med. asst. William Stafford, M.D., Fullerton, Calif., 1969-71; mgr. office David H. Armstrong, M.D., Inc., Fullerton, 1971-79; mgr. office Med. Ctr. for Women, Fullerton, 1977-79, adminstr., 1986—; owner Sandy's Discount Boutique, Hemet, Sun City, Calif., 1979-83; asst. adminstr. Fullerton Cardiovascular Med. Group, 1983-86; cons., tchr. Riverside (Calif.) Community Coll., 1984—; bd. dirs. No. Orange County Regional Occupational Ctr., Anaheim, Calif., 1985—. Vol. Riverside Rape Crisis Ctr., 1984—. Republican. Club: Fullerton. Lodge: Soroptimist (Sun City) (sec. 1982-83, Women Helping Women award 1985). Office: Med Ctr for Women 2720 N Harbor Blvd #130 Fullerton CA 91720

MALEY, PATRICIA ANN, director planning and development; b. Wilmington, Del., Dec. 25, 1955; d. James Alfred and Frances Louise (Fenimore) M. AA, Cecil Community Coll., 1973; BA, U. Del., 1975, MA, 1981. Cert. secondary tchr., Del. Analyst econ. devel. City of Wilmington, 1977-78, evaluation specialist, 1978-80, planner II mayor's office, 1980-86, cons. preservation, 1986-87; dir. Belle Meade Mansion, Nashville, 1987-88; dir. planning, devel. Children's Bur. of Del., Wilmington, 1988—; cons. cultural resources M.A.A.R. Inc., Newark, Del., 1987, ITC Cons., Wilmington, 1985-86. Contbg. photographer America's City Halls, 1984; author numerous Nat. Register nominations, 1980-86. Pres., founder Haynes Park Civic Assn., Wilmington, 1977-80; photographer Biden U.S. Senate campaign, New Castle County, Del., 1984; sec. parish council Our Lady Fatima Roman Cath. Ch., 1985-86, choir dir., 1983-87; bd. dirs. Del. Children's Theatre. U. Del. fellow, 1976-77. Mem. Nat. Trust Hist. Preservation, Nat. Assn. Pastoral Musicians, Del. Soc. Architects, Del. Archeol. Soc., Del. Hist. Soc., Pi Sigma Alpha. Democrat. Office: Children's Bur of Del 2005 Baynard Blvd Wilmington DE 19802

MALIK, HELEN THERESA, corporate officer; b. Owosso, Mich., Jan. 23, 1943; d. Anthony Joseph and Helen Ann (Kleinedler) Sovis; m. Frederick Malik, May 22, 1965; 1 child: Frederick Fabian. Student, Charles Stewart Mott Community Coll., Flint, Mich., 1975, Gen. Motors Inst., Flint, Mich., 1985, Lansing (Mich.) Community Coll., 1988. Clk. accts receivable Mitchell Corp. of Owosso, Mich., 1964-67, sec. purchasing dept., 1967-70, clk. payroll dept., 1970-72, sr. clk. payroll and ins. benefits, 1972-82, asst. corp. sec., adminstr. pension, benefits, payroll, 1982—. Mem. Am. Compensation Assn., Am. Payroll Assn., Bar Code User's Group. Roman Catholic. Home: 1425 New Lothrop Rd Lennon MI 48449 Office: Mitchell Corp of Owosso 123 N Chipman St Owosso MI 48867

MALKIEL, NANCY WEISS, college dean, history educator; b. Newark, Feb. 14, 1944; d. William and Ruth Sylvia (Puder) W. BA summa cum laude, Smith Coll., 1965; MA, Harvard U., 1966, PhD, 1970. Asst. prof. history Princeton (N.J.) U., 1969-75, assoc. prof., 1975-82, prof., 1982—, master Dean Mathey Coll., 1982-86, dean of coll., 1987—. Author (as Nancy J. Weiss): Charles Francis Murphy, 1858-1924: Respectability and Responsibility in Tammany Politics, 1968, Blacks in America: Bibliographical Essays, 1971, The National Urban League, 1910-1940, 1974, Farewell to the Party of Lincoln: Black Politics in the Age of FDR, 1983 (Berkshire Conf. of Women Historians prize 1984). Trustee Smith Coll., Northampton, Mass., 1984—, Woodrow Wilson Nat. Fellowship Found., 1975—. Fellow Woodrow Wilson Found., 1965, Charles Warren Ctr. for Studies in Am. History, 1976-77, Radcliffe Inst., 1976-77, Ctr. for Advanced Study in Behavioral Scis., 1986-87. Mem. Am. Hist. Assn., Orgn. Am. Historians (chmn. status women hist. profession 1972-75), So. Hist. Assn., Phi Beta Kappa. Democrat. Jewish. Office: Princeton U Office of Dean Princeton NJ 08544

MALKIN, WENDY B., quality control professional; b. Phila., Oct. 17, 1956; d. Herman and Pauline (Wexler) Silverman; m. Kenneth Malkin. Student Douglas Coll., 1974-76; B.A., William Paterson Coll., 1979. Methods and procedures analyst, personal methods and procedures analyst to v.p. real estate Prentice Hall, Englewood Cliffs, N.J., 1979-81; cost analyst Gen. Bearing, West Nyack, N.Y., 1981-82; cons. ins. systems, 1982-83; cons. GEISCO, Piscataway, N.J., 1983-85; tech. writer On-Line Software Internat., Fort Lee, N.J., 1985-87; mgr. quality control, CCMI/McGraw-Hill, Ramsey, N.J., 1987—. Mem. Nat. Assn. Female Execs. Democrat. Jewish. Avocations: piano; recorder; nutrition and homeopathy; weight training; swimming. Home: 147 B Tierney Dr Cedar Grove NJ 07009 Office: 50 S Franklin Turnpike Ramsey NJ 07446

MALKOFF, EILEEN WEIDER, small business owner; b. Beachwood, Ohio, Feb. 2, 1954; d. Benjamin and Bertha (Yaeger) Weider; m. Robert Jules Malkoff, Nov. 4, 1982. Student, Ohio State U., Cleve., 1972-74; grad., Cleve. Fashion Inst., 1974. Sales rep. Donna Lee Shop, Beachwood, 1969-76; mgr. Hahn Shoes, Beachwood, 1976-79; sales rep. Boris Shoes, Beachwood, 1979-80; fin. advisor Ohio Savs. & Loan, Pepper Pike, 1980-82; owner Goldmasters Jewelers, Inc., Cleve., 1982—. Fund raiser F.O.P.; mem. Cleve. Better Bus. Bur., Cleve. Growth Assn. Mem. Consumers Union, Nat. Fedn. Ind. Bus., Ind. Jewelers Orgn. Democrat. Jewish. Office: Goldmasters Jewelers Inc 1747 Randall Park Mall Cleveland OH 44128

MALLARY, GERTRUDE ROBINSON, civic worker; b. Springfield, Mass., Aug. 19, 1902; d. George Edward and Jennie (Slater) Robinson; student, Bennett Coll., 1921-22, U. Conn., 1941-42; m. R. DeWitt Mallary, Sept. 15, 1923; children—R. DeWitt, Richard Walker. Co-owner, ptnr. Mallary Farm, Bradford, Vt., 1936—; mem. Vt. Ho. of Reps., 1953-56, sec. agr. com., 1953, mem. appropriations com., 1955; mem. Vt. Senate, 1957-58, mem. appropriations com., clk. pub. health com., vice chmn. edn. com., mem. interim legis. com. for study nursing, 1958-59. Pres., Jr. League, Springfield, 1931-33; chmn. Springfield Council Social Agys., 1938-40; mem. Mass. Commn. Pub. Safety, 1941-42; mem. Vt. Bd. Recreation, 1959-65; trustee Fairlee (Vt.) Public Library, 1953-84, Asa Bloomer Found., 1963-71, Orange County 4-H Found., 1969-71; trustee Justin Smith Morrill Found., 1964-71, pres., 1968-71; pres. Vt. Holstein Club, 1951-53; mem. Vt. Gov.'s Commn. for Library Services, 1966; Vt. chmn. Nat. Library Week, 1973; chmn. Fairlee Bicentennial Com., 1974-77; mem. Com. for New Eng. Bibliography, 1971-84, vice chmn. for Vt., 1977; trustee Wesson Meml. Hosp., Springfield, 1937-42, chmn. nursing services, 1939-42; Orange County Chmn. Vt. Achievement Ctr., 1985—. Recipient Theresa R. Brungardt award, 1979. Mem. Vt. Library Trustees Assn. (pres. 1965-67), Vt., Bradford (pres. 1965-69), Fairlee hist. socs., Am. Antiquarian Soc. Editor New Eng. Holstein Bull., 1947-50. Address: Mallary Farm Bradford VT 05033

MALLEN, JOAN CALAGUAS, city government administrator, accountant; b. Caloocan City, Rizal, Philippines, Apr. 28, 1947; d. Vincent Randy Mallen and Gloria (Calaguas) Enriquez; children by previous marriage: Kevin, Vincent, Michelle. AS in Secretarial Sci., St. Louis U., Philippines, 1964, cert. as Statis. Aide, 1968; BS in Acctg., U. Baguio, Philippines, 1968. Acct. aide Govt. Service Ins. System, Philippines, 1964-69; jr. acct. Aaron and Rousen, CPA's, Newport News, 1970; bookkeeper Cen. Wholesale Supply, Norfolk, Va., 1970, Armour Oil Co., Newport News, Va., 1971, Hoffler Med. Clinic, Norfolk, 1972-74; head bus. lic. auditing div. City of Virginia Beach, Va., 1974—; cons. taxes, Virginia Beach, 1974—. Vice chmn. Council United Filipinos of Tidewater, 1985; bd. dirs. Philippine-Am. Chamber Orch., 1987—. Mem. Nat. Assn. Female Execs., Cultural Tour Soc., Mrs. Philippines Soc. Roman Catholic. Club: Filipino Women's of Tidewater (pres. 1982-84, bd. dirs. 1982—). Home: 2425 Entrada Dr Virginia Beach VA 23456 Office: Fin Dept Bus Lic Audit Executive Park Bldg 2 Virginia Beach VA 23456

MALLER, DANNA, manufacturing company executive; b. Champaign, Ill., Dec. 2, 1958; d. Donald and Sandra Joy (Fralick) M. BS, U.S. Mil. Acad., 1980. Commd. 2d lt. U.S. Army, 1980, advanced through grades to capt., 1982; from aviation exec. officer to bn. flight ops. officer U.S. Army, Fort Ord, Calif., 1981-85; sales rep. Container Corp. Am., Santa Clara, Calif., 1985—. Mem. West Point Assn. Grads. Republican. Jewish. Home: 2331 Falling Water Ct Santa Clara CA 95054 Office: Container Corp Am 2500 de la Cruz Blvd Santa Clara CA 95050

MALLEY, DIANE FRANCES, scientist, ecotoxicologist; b. Ottawa, Ont., Can., June 14, 1943; d. John Malley and Marcia Dora (Smith) M.; m. John Anthony Mathias, Aug. 13, 1966; children: Karin Lynn, Lisa Gail, Laura Anne. BS with honors, U. B.C., Vancouver, 1964, MS, 1967; PhD, U. Mich., 1972. Asst. research scientist U. Mich., Ann Arbor, 1972-75; biologist Can. Dept. Fisheries and Environment, Winnipeg, Man., 1976-78; research scientist Can. Dept. Fisheries and Oceans, Winnipeg, 1978-87, mgr. ecotoxicolgy sect., 1987—; mem. adv. com. for natural resources mgmt. Keewatin Community Coll., The Pas, Man., 1984—; vis. asst. prof. U. Victoria, B.C., 1975-76; vis. lectr. U. Sains Malaysia, Penang, 1972-75. Contbr. numerous articles to profl. jours. Vice-chmn. Man. Environ. Council, Winnipeg, 1983-85, chmn. 1985-87; chmn. environment com. Nat. Council Women Can., Ottawa ,1982-85; v.p. Provincial Council Women Can., Winnipeg, 1984-85. Ford Found. grantee, 1972-75. Mem. Am. Soc. Limnology and Oceanography, N.Am. Benthological Soc., Profl. Inst. Pub. Service Can., Soc. Can. Limnologists (sec., treas. 1983-87, pres. 1987—), Soc. Internat. Limnologiae, Can. Soc. Zoologists, Am. Soc. Zoologists, Sigma Xi. Club: Toastmistress (Winnipeg). Office: Freshwater Inst, 501 University Crescent, Winnipeg, MB Canada R3T 2N6

MALLIA, CATHERINE A., real estate executive; b. Galveston, Tex., Aug. 10, 1947; d. Simon Aloysius Mallia, Jr. and Aleta Jo (Wooten) Mallia Benson; m. Kenneth Anthony Van Nostrand, Feb. 5, 1966 (div. Aug. 1979); 1 son, Scott Anthony. Student Galveston Coll., 1971-73, Houston Community Coll., 1975-78. Office sec. Am. Nat. Ins. Co., Galveston, 1965-67, U.S. Army C.E., Galveston, 1967-69; legal sec. Royston, Rayzor, Cook & Vickery, Galveston, 1969-74; adminstrv. asst. Moody House, Inc., Galveston, 1974-75; real estate broker with various firms, Houston, 1975-81; mktg. dir. Spectrum Devel., Houston, 1981-84; owner CML Ventures, Inc. 1984—. Pres., Tallowood Homeowners Assn., Houston, 1980; v.p. bd. dirs. Dad's Club, YMCA, Houston, 1979. Mem. Women in Comml. Real Estate. Home: 1524-E Nantucket Houston TX 77057 Office: CML Ventures Inc PO Box 690692 Houston TX 77269

MALLIN, THERESA MAUREEN, advertising and promotions executive; b. Vallejo, Calif., Mar. 2, 1955; d. Patrick Eugene and Mary Bernice (Cunningham) M. Student, Calif. State U., Sacramento, 1973-77, Utah Tech. Coll., 1983, U. Utah, 1986—. Legis. sec., creative dir. Calif. Trials Lawyers Assn., Sacramento, 1974-79; adminstrv. asst. Samon's Inc., North Salt Lake, Utah, 1979-80; mgr. advt. and promotions Utah Transit Authority; owner Landscaping Services, Salt Lake City, 1979-81, producer audio visual presentations, 1980-87. Illustrator: Cycling for the Serious Cyclist, 1976; singer, songwriter Utah Songwriter's Showcase, 1987. Coach softball teams, Sacramento and Salt Lake City, 1974—; mem. allocations panel United Way, Salt Lake City, 1982-83; bd. dirs. YWCA, Salt Lake City, 1983-85. Recipient Gold and Silver Adwheel Am. Pub. Transit Assn., 1984; 1st Place Sta. KSL-TV Talent Showcase, 1985. Mem. Nat. Assn. Female Execs., Internat. Graphoanalysis Soc., Women in Communications, Utah Songwriters Assn., Utah Ad Fedn. (Silver and Bronze awards 1985, 86). Home: 3624 S Oldham Circle West Valley City UT 84120 Office: 3600 S 700 W Salt Lake City UT 84130

MALLIS, STEPHANIE, architect; b. Bklyn., Sept. 14, 1945; d. Maxwell and Vera Victoria (Levy) Mallis; m. Douglas Kahn, Dec. 30, 1967 (div. 1974). BFA with honors Pratt Inst., 1967; MArch, Harvard U., 1978. Lic. architect, N.Y. Designer, Ward Bennett, N.Y.C., 1967, Skidmore, Owings & Merrill, N.Y.C., 1967-70, Robert Gersin, N.Y.C., 1970-71; prin. Kahn & Mallis Assocs., N.Y.C., 1971-75; assoc. Rogers Butler & Burgun, N.Y.C., 1972-76; assoc. dir. interiors I.M. Pei & Ptnrs., N.Y.C., 1979-86; prin. Stephanie Mallis, Inc., 1986—; cons. Kallmann McKinnell & Wood Architects, Boston, MA of New Hynes Conv. Ctr., Boston U.S. Chancery, Dhaka, Bangladesh, Donald & Liisa Slare Architects, Planned Parenthood N.Y.C. Fulbright scholar, India, 1978-79, 87—; AIA award of merit, 1978; NSID award of excellence, 1967. Mem. Mcpl. Art Soc., Asia Soc., Fulbright Alumni Soc., AIA, Am. Soc. Interior Designers. Club: Harvard. Home: 300 E 33 St New York NY 10016 Office: Stephanie Mallis Inc 405 Lexington Ave New York NY 10174

MALLON, BETH KOHLMEYER, college administrator; b. Oakland, Calif., Feb. 13, 1959; d. Leland James and Mary Ann (Peschka) Kohlmeyer; m. Kevin Frederick Mallon, July 19, 1980. BA, Oreg. Coll. Edn., 1982; postgrad., U. Nebr., Lincoln, 1985—. Cert. elem. tchr., Oreg., Nebr. Tchr. elem. sch. Cen. Sch. Dist. 13J, Independence, Oreg., 1982-84; artist, typesetter United Phone Book Advertisers, Lincoln, 1984-85, contract mgr., 1985, advt. sales coordinator, 1986; chief grad. advisor U. Nebr., Lincoln, 1987—. Frank H. Gore fellow Coll. Bus. Adminstrn., 1985-87. Mem. Nat. Assn. Female Execs., Phi Delta Gamma. Democrat. Roman Catholic. Home: 405 Laramie Trail Lincoln NE 68521-3230

MALLOY, KATHLEEN SHARON, lawyer; b. Evergreen Park, Ill., Apr. 7, 1948, d. Clarence Edmund and Ruth Elizabeth (Petrini) M.; m. Randall Kleinman, Aug. 5, 1978; children: Brighid, Ellena, Grant. BA in Psychology, St. Louis U., 1970; JD, Loyola U., Chgo., 1976. Bar: Ill. 1976, Calif. 1977. Account exec. Complete Equity Mkts., Wheeling, Ill., 1970-76, corp. counsel 1976-80, v.p., gen. counsel, 1980-83, exec. v.p., gen. counsel, 1983, chief operating officer, gen. counsel, 1984-85, vice chmn. bd., gen. counsel, 1986—; founding ptnr. firm Malloy & Kleinman, P.C., Des Plaines, Ill., 1985—. Vol. atty. legal aid orgns., Calif., 1976-79. Mem. ABA, Calif. State Bar Assn., Mensa, Women's Bar Assn., Northwest Suburban Bar Assn., Nat. Legal Aid and Defender Assn. (ex-officio mem. ins. com. 1986—). Office: Malloy & Kleinman PC 640 Pearson St Suite 206 Des Plaines IL 60016

MALLOY, PHEOBE SMALLS, teacher; b. Charleston, S.C., Oct. 9, 1954; d. James and Evelina (Jenkins) Singleton; m. Edward Lamar Smalls, July 9, 1977 (div. Dec. 1983); 1 child, Ashanti Lamar; m. Frank Walter Malloy Jr., Mar. 10, 1984. BA, Johnson C. Smith U., Charlotte, N.C., 1976; MEd, The Citadel, 1979. Cert. tchr. educable mentally handicapped. Intern Ctr. for Human Devel., Charlotte, 1975-76; tchr. for educable mentally handicapped Bapt. Hill High Sch., Charleston, 1976-81; resource tchr. for students with learning disabilities, corr. pub. relations Burke High Sch., Charleston, 1981—, chair exceptional children's month, 1982-86, chair black history month, 1982-86, co-chair sch. based mgmt. team, 1985—, co-chair self-study team for So. Assn. Accreditation, 1986—; est. Spanish program James Simmons Elem. Sch., Charleston, 1985. Liaison editorial staff Handbook for Tchrs., 1982; contbr. articles to profl. jours. Mem. pub. relations com. Burke PTA, 1985-87, co-chair ways and means com., 1986-87; sec. dist. 20 City Council PTA, Charleston, 1986-87. Named Disting. Corr., Burke High Sch., 1986-87, Disting. Vol., Charleston County Schs., 1987, Disting. Vol., James Simons Elem. Sch., 1987. Mem. Council for Exceptional Children, Div. for Learning Disabilities, Cath. Women Orgn., Eta Phi Beta (sec. 1983-84, 1st v.p. 1984-86). Home: 804 Sprague St Charleston SC 29412 Office: Burke High Sch 244 President St Charleston SC 29403

MALMGREN, RENÉ LOUISE, academic arts administrator; b. Mpls., Nov. 14, 1938; d. Albert William and Hildegarde Ann (Topel) Erickson; m. Donald Elwin Malmgren, Dec. 27, 1958; D. Gustaf, Ericka Susan, Tavus Val, Beret Kristina. BA in Theatre, Speech and English, Colo. Women's Coll., 1966; MA in Ednl. Adminstrn and Curriculum Devel., U. Colo., 1981. Cert. supt., Ariz.; cert. type D adminstr., Colo. Cons. creative drama Cultural Arts Program Denver Pub. Schs., 1970-72; tchr. APS Crawford Elem. Sch., Aurora, Colo., 1972-78; instr. Colo. Women's Coll., Denver, 1974-75; tchr. English Hinkley High Sch., Aurora; ednl. dir. Colo. Children's Theatre Co., Denver, 1977-86; adminstrv. intern Aurora Pub. Schs., 1981-82, coordinator curriculum, 1982-85; asst. dir. instrn. fine arts Tucson Unified Sch. Dist., 1985—; external auditor lang. arts Jefferson County Pub. Schs., Littleton, Colo., 1984; curriculum evaluator North Cen. Assn., Grand Junction, Colo., 1984-85; editor theater curriculum Ariz. Dept. Edn., Phoenix, 1986-87; rev. panelist Ariz. Commn. on Arts, Phoenix, 1986-87. Author satellite TV curriculum, 1987; appeared in play The Only Woman Awake, 1984. Del. Colo. Dem. Conv., Denver, 1980; peacekeeper Take Back the Night March-Rape Assistance and Awareness Program, Denver, 1982-84; mem. policy com. Tucson Cable Arts Channel, 1986-87; mem. arts edn. task force Tucson/Pima Arts Council, 1987. Colo. Council on Arts and Humanities grantee, 1978. Mem. Nat. Art Edn. Assn., Assn. for Supervision and Curriculum Devel., Arts in Edn. Council, Nat. Adminstrv. Women in Edn., Ariz. Arts Supervisory Coalition (bd. dirs. 1985—), Ariz. Theatre Educators Assn. (bd. dirs., sec. 1985-86, v.p. 1986-87, pres. elect 1987-88), Phi Delta Kappa. Home: 2612 E La Cienega Dr Tucson AZ 85716 Office: Tucson Unified Sch Dist 2025 E Winsett St Tucson AZ 85719

MALONE, BETTE JUNE, real estate broker, interior designer; b. Seattle, June 29, 1950; d. Harry Louis and Emma (Jeske) Cohn; m. Jon L. Malone, Mar. 13, 1980, (div. Nov. 1981); children: Christine Lynn, Robert Lee. AA in Arts, U. Md. Extension, Naples, Italy, 1977. Cert. broker Realtors Inst. Paralegal JAG, Naples, 1974-76; mktg. rep. Polaroid Corp., Timex Corp., Naples, 1976-78; broker Norwood Group Inc., Nashua, N.H., 1978-81; pres. G. Ea. Properties Corp., Nashua, N.H., 1981—. Dir. United Way, Nashua, 1985; chmn., vip panelist, Easter Seal Soc., Manchester, 1982-87. Named Disting. Woman Leader YWCA, Nashua, 1982. Mem. Greater Nashua Bd. Realtors, (pres. 1986-87, v.p. 1985 Realtor Yr.), New Eng. Chpt. Cert. Real Estate Brokerage Mgrs., Sales and Mktg. Council, Nashua Jaycee Women (chmn. project yr. 1980-81, Outstanding Chmn. Yr. 1980-82), Mensa, Profl. Assn. Diving Instrs. Clubs: MENSA, Profl. Assn. Diving Instrs. Home: 45

Parrish Hill Dr Nashua NH 03063 Office: Great Ea Properties Corp 6 Manchester St Nashua NH 03060

MALONE, CAMILLE, mathematics educator; b. Tulsa, Feb. 22, 1947; d. Oscar Howard and Faydelle (Scott) Shields; m. Hal Dennis Wilkerson; 1 son, Jay David. B.A., North Tex. State U., 1969; M.A., U. Tex.-Dallas, Richardson, 1981. Tchr. math. Dallas Ind. Sch. Dist., 1968-71, 75—, Skyline High Sch., 1984-87, chmn. math. dept., 1987—; instr. math. Eastfield Coll. Campus, Dallas County Community Coll. Dist., Dallas, 1982-86; chmn. supt.'s oversight com. on incentive pay plan Dallas Ind. Sch. Dist., 1983-84; forum panelist Exec. Devel. Seminar, U. Tex., 1984; presentation speaker at doctoral seminar East Tex. State U., 1984, at Nat. Conf. on Ednl. Excellence and Econ. Growth, 1984. Mem. Nat. Council Tchrs. Math. (rep. 1968-69, state conv. 1970-71, presenter Southwestern Regional Conf. 1986—, Jim Collins Outstanding Tchr. award 1986), Nat. Congress Parents and Tchrs., Greenpeace U.S.A., Internat. Fund for Animal Welfare. Mem. Ch. of Christ. Home: 6123 Symphony Ln Dallas TX 75227 Office: Skyline High Sch 7777 Forney Rd Dallas TX 75227

MALONE, CAROL CROSS, university program director; b. Winona, Miss., Feb. 4, 1941; d. Lonnie Letau and Willie Grace (Kemp) Cross; m. Billy F. Malone, Apr. 10, 1960; children: Frank, Anthony. BS, Athens Coll., 1975; MA in Higher Edn. Adminstrn., U. Ala., 1982. Research asst. psychology Athens (Ala.) Coll., 1976; continuing edn. asst. U. Ala., Huntsville, 1976-82, continuing edn. coordinator, 1982-84, dir. continuing med. edn., 1984—; adminstrv. cons. Tenn. Valley Family Physicians, Huntsville, 1978—, dir. Resident Alumni Assn. U. Ala., 1986—, dir. Speakers Bur., 1984—. Consumer arbitrator Better Bus. Bur., Huntsville, 1982—; bd. dirs. Huntsville chpt. Pub. Relations Council Ala., 1983—. Mem. Soc. of Med. Coll. Dirs. of Continuing Med. Edn. (program com. 1987—), So. Pub. Relations Fedn., U. Ala. Resident Alumni Assn. (bd. dirs. speakers bur. 1984—, adminstrv. cons. 1986—). Republican. Baptist. Clubs: Press (Huntsville); Toastmasters (lt. gov. no. div. 1983-84, Outstanding Lt. Gov. award). Home: 1403 Hayden St Athens AL 35611 Office: U Ala Sch Primary Med Care 109 Governors Dr Huntsville AL 35801

MALONE, CLAUDINE BERKELEY, financial and management consultant; b. Louisville, May 9, 1936; d. Claude McDowell and Mary Katharine (Smith) M.; B.A., Wellesley Coll., 1963; M.B.A., Harvard U., 1972. Systems engr. IBM Corp., Washington, 1964; sr. systems analyst Crane Co., Chgo., 1966; controller, mgr. data processing Raleigh Stores, Washington, 1967-70; asst. prof. Harvard U., 1972-76, assoc. prof., 1977-81; fin. and mgmt. cons., Bethesda, Md., 1981—; dir. Scott Paper Co., Houghton Mifflin Co., Campbell Soup Co., Boston Co., Dart Group Inc., Limited Stores; trustee Penn Mut. Life Ins. Co. Chmn. Bus. for Reagan-Bush Com. Mass., 1980; trustee Wellesley Coll., 1982—. Recipient Candace award, 1982. C.P.A., Md. Mem. Assn. Women C.P.A.s, UN Assn., Wellesley Coll. Alumnae Assn. Episcopalian. Club: Washington Wellesley.

MALONE, DOROTHY ANN, insurance agent, marketing executive, consultant, lecturer; b. Logansport, Ind., June 19, 1931; d. Harry and Lena Estella Malone. BBA, McKendree Coll., Radcliff, Ky., 1981; postgrad. in humanities Webster Coll., 1981-84; M. Pub. Service Adminstrn., Western Ky. U., 1984, M. Pub. Counseling, 1985. Lic. life and health agt. Joined U.S. Army, 1952, advanced through grades to master sgt., 1972, ret., 1975; ind. life underwriter, Elizabethtown, Ky., 1977—; dir. mktg. and sales Dixie Rabbit, Inc., Ekron, Ky., 1981—; sr. counselor, tchr. Southeastern Tng. Corp., Elizabethtown, 1987—; cons., lectr. minority and women's subjects. First v.p. Hardin County (Ky.) chpt. NAACP, 1975; mem. Hardin County Human Relations Com., 1977-78; chairperson Hardin County Blue Ribbon Com., 1977; trustee Embry Chapel AME Ch., Elizabethtown, 1983—; mem. Ky. Gov.'s Council on Volunteerism. Decorated Army Commendation medal with 5 oak leaf clusters; recipient numerous letters of commendation and appreciation and awards, including cert. of appreciation NAACP, 1976, others. Mem. Federally Employed Women (chairperson program Ft. Knox Area chpt. 1978-79, v.p. Ft. Knox Area chpt. 1978-79), Ky. Assn. Ret. Mil., Nat. Assn. Exec. Women, Ky. Cen. Assn. Life Underwriters, Life Investors' Pacer Club, Am. Defender Life Ins. Co., NAACP (life), Am. Soc. Profl. and Exec. Women. Lodge: Order Eastern Star.

MALONE, GEORGIA JOAN, lawyer; b. Bklyn., May 3, 1953; d. Joseph F. and Emma (Guistra) Abbate; m. Peter Dechar, Dec. 21, 1985. BS with honors, Boston U., 1975; JD, New Eng. Law Sch., 1978. Bar: N.Y. 1979. Counsel Arlen Realty Devel. Corp., N.Y.C., 1979-80; assoc. Finkelstein, Borah, Schwartz, Altschuler & Goldstein, P.C., N.Y.C., 1980-83, ptnr., 1986—; counsel Rent Stabilization Assn., N.Y.C., 1983-85; adj. prof. NYU, 1984—. Author: Rent Stabilization Digest, 1983, Rent Registration, Tenant Challenges, 1985. Mem. ABA, N.Y. State Bar Assn. (landlord and tenant com.). Office: Finkelstein Borah Schwartz et al 377 Broadway New York NY 10013

MALONE, JEAN HAMBIDGE, educational administrator; b. South Bend, Ind., Nov. 23, 1954; d. Craig Ellis and Dorothy Jane (Piechorowski) Hambidge; m. James Kevill Malone, July 8, 1978; children: Julia Mae, James Kevill. BS in Edn., Butler U., 1976, MS in Edn., 1977. Tchr. Indpls. Pub. Schs., 1977-78; dir. student center and activities Butler U., Indpls., 1978-87. Trustee Eisenhower Meml. scholarship, 1977-80; bd. dirs. Heritage Place of Indpls., 1983-84, Ind. Office Campus Ministries, Intercollegiate YMCA Indpls., 1985-87, Campfire of Cen. Ind. 1980-84, 86-87, Ind. Office Campus Ministries State Bd., 1985—. Recipient Outstanding Faculty award, Butler U., 1980. Mem. Ind. Assn. Women Deans (v.p. bd. dirs. 1987-88), Adminstrs. and Counselors (bd. dirs. 1982-83), Ind. Assn. Coll. Personnel Adminstrs., Nat. Assn. Women Deans, Adminstrs. and Counselors, Kappa Delta Pi, Phi Kappa Phi, Alpha Lambda Delta, Kappa Kappa Gamma. Roman Catholic.

MALONE, LINDA SUE, nurse; b. Shelby, N.C., Sept. 19, 1944; d. Garther Albert and Lucille (Smith) Whisnant; m. Gary P. Malone, Jan. 7, 1965; children: Mark Patrick, Gary Michael, Christopher Matthew. Diploma in nursing Charlotte Presbyn., N.C., 1965; BS, St. Joseph's Coll., 1986. RN, N.C., N.J., Hawaii. Nurse Heilbronn Elem. Sch., Germany, 1967-68; nurse pvt. duty Long Branch Nurses Registry, N.J., 1972-73; staff nurse Cape Fear Valley Med. Ctr., Fayetteville, N.C., 1975-78, coordinator quality assurance, 1978-85, dir. quality assurance, 1985—; cons., lectr. quality assurance. Vol. nurse Westover Jr. High Sch., Fayetteville, 1979; pres. Paramed. Service, Fayetteville, 1982-85. Republican. Methodist. Avocations: crafts, gourmet cooking, water sports. Home: 426 Dunmore Rd Fayetteville NC 28303 Office: Cape Fear Valley Med Ctr Fayetteville NC 28302

MALONE, LUCY WAGGONER, conference coordinating executive; b. Nashville, Oct. 17, 1947; d. Melburn James and Thelma Louise (Yates) Waggoner; m. Michael Blair Malone, Feb. 10, 1963 (div. Jan. 1983); children: Lisa Ann, Mary Elizabeth. AS in Bus. Edn., Vol. State (Tenn.) Coll., 1976, AS in Bus. Mktg., 1988. Motor carrier registration coordinator Tenn. Pub. Service Commn., Nashville, 1969-74; adminstrv. asst. Ted Wynne & Assocs., Nashville, 1976-79; office mgr. Malones Market, Nashville, 1980; exec. asst. Blevins Home Parts Distributor, Nashville, 1981; adminstr. tech. transfer Aladdin Industries, Nashville, 1982-87; exec. dir., bd. dirs. Tech. Transfer Confs., Nashville, 1984—. Tchr. 8th grade girls Baptist Ch., Goodlettsville, Tenn., 1980-82, 7th and 8th grade dept. head, 1983-84; coach girls softball and basketball, 1975-78; newletter editor Pathfinders Class, Brentwood, Tenn., 1986-87. Mem. Licensing Exec. Soc., Tech. Transfer Soc., Meeting Planners Internat. Baptist. Home: 2001 Sunnyslope Ln Goodlettsville TN 37072 Office: Tech Transfer Confs 325 Plus Park Blvd #108 Nashville TN 37217

MALONE, PERRILLAH (PAT) ATKINSON, state official; b. Montgomery, Ala., Mar. 17, 1922; d. Odolph Edgar and Myrtle (Fondren) Atkinson. BS, Oglethorpe U., 1956; MAT, Emory U., 1962. Asst. editor, then acting editor Emory U., 1958-64; asst. project officer Ga. Dept. Pub. Health, Atlanta, 1965-68; asst. project dir. Ga. Ednl. Improvement Council, 1968-69; assoc. dir. Ga. Edn. Improvement Council, 1970-71; dir. career services State Scholarship Commn., Atlanta, 1971-74; rev. coordinator Div. Phys. Health, Ga. Dept. Human Resources, Atlanta, 1974-79; project dir. So. Regional Edn. Bd., 1979-81; specialist Div. Family and Children Services, Atlanta, 1982—; mem. Gov.'s Commn. on Nursing Edn. and Nursing Practice, 1972-75, aging services adv. group Atlanta Regional Commn.; book reviewer Atlanta Jour.-Constn., 1962-79. Recipient Recognition award Ga. Nursing Assn., 1976, Korsell award Ga. Nursing Assn., 1974, Alumni Honor award Emory U., 1964. Mem. Am. Pub. Health Assn., Am. Pub. Welfare Assn., N.Y. Acad. Scis. Methodist. Club: Atlanta Press. Home: 1146 Oxford Rd NE Atlanta GA 30306 Office: 878 Peachtree St Suite 503 Atlanta GA 30309

MALONE, SHERRY, financial planner; b. Oakland, Calif., Aug. 15, 1948; d. Clyde T. and Bonnie (Mandel) Stuhlmacher; m. Roger Malone (div. Jan. 1983); m. Michael Fetzer, April 7, 1957. BS in Polit. Sci., Colo. State U., 1970, postgrad., 1979-82. Legal sec. Harden and Napheys, Attys., Ft. Collins, Colo., 1977-78; paralegal Arnand Newton, Atty., Ft. Collins, 1978-80; instr. dept. econs. Colo. State U., Ft. Collins, 1979-81; fin. analyst The Schierholz Co., Colorado Springs, Colo., 1981-83; fin. planner Fin. Mgmt. Cons., Colorado Springs, 1983—. Volunteer Domestic Violence Prevention Ctr., Colorado Springs, 1986—. Mem. Nat. Assn. Securities Dealers, Phi Beta Kappa, Gamma Phi Beta (scholarship chair. 1968-69). Office: Fin Mgmt Cons 5585 Erindale Dr Suite 106 Colorado Springs CO 80918

MALONEY, CHRISTA DARLENE, manufacturing executive; b. Ashland, Kans., Aug. 27, 1959; d. Ernest Lewis and Wanda Leota (Norton) Ashlock; m. Gregg Maloney, Feb. 18, 1978; children: Nichelle Lei, Natasha DeAnn, Adam Ross. Student, Tabor Coll., 1977-78; course study in social service design, Pratt (Kans.) Coll., 1979. Lic. ins. and security agt. Social service designer Protection (Kans.) Valley Manor, 1979-80; office mgr. Lane Myers Co., Protection, 1980—; sales agt. Leadership Mgmt., Inc., Waco, Tex., 1984-86; ins. agt. Ozark Nat. Life Ins. Co., Kansas City, 1985-88; security broker, dealer, rep. NIS Fin. Services, Kansas City, 1985-88. Mem. Bus. and Profl. Women's Club (Young Careerist 1987). Republican. Club: Friends Library (Protection) (pres. 1986-87). Home: 501 E Main Protection KS 67127

MALONEY, CHRISTINE CAROLYNE, development company executive; b. Albany, Ga., Aug. 27, 1950; d. Wilfred James and Elsbeth M. (Hartmann) Poggi; 1 child, Kristin Lindsey Vance; m. Joseph J. Maloney, July 28, 1976 (div. 1982). B.S., Central Mo. State U., 1972; student Regional Police Acad., Kansas City, Mo., 1980. Parole officer Mo. State Parole, Kansas City, 1973-74; probation officer Jackson County Juvenile Ct., Kansas City, 1974-79; officer Kansas City Police Dept., 1979-82; pres. Poggi Devel. Co., Independence, Mo., 1982—; vol. tchr. Mo. State Parole, 1973; officer Res. Unit Kansas City Police Dept., 1979. Bd. dirs. Community Alcohol Program, Kansas City, 1979-80; mem. Interagy. Council Child Abuse, Kansas City, 1976-80. Recipient 2 Commendation Certs. Kansas City Police Dept., 1980, 81. Mem. Alpha Sigma Alpha. Lutheran. Office: Poggi Devel Co Inc 2661 A Hub Dr Independence MO 64055

MALONEY, LUCILLE TINKER, civic worker; b. Twin Falls, Idaho, Mar. 13, 1920; d. Edward Milo and Lillian (Schaefer) Tinker; tchr.'s cert. Idaho State U., 1940; student U. Wash., 1941; m. Frank E. Maloney, Feb. 20, 1943 (dec.); children—Frank E., JoAnn Maloney Smallwood, Elizabeth Maloney Hurst. Pres., U. Fla. Women's Club, 1960-61, Gainesville Women's Club, 1974-75, Friends of Five Sta. WUFT-TV, Public Broadcasting, 1976-77; chmn., organizer Gainesville Spring Pilgrimage, 1976; founder, pres. Thomas Center Assos., 1978-80; v.p. U. Fla. Art Gallery Guild, 1981, pres., 1982-84; mem. Fla. Gov.'s Challenge Program Com., 1981; trustee Fla. House, Washington; patron, organizer, trustee Hippodrome State Theatre; chmn. Santa Fe Regional Library Bd., 1980-81; pres. Gainesville Women's Forum, 1984-85; mem. Exec. Commn. Fla. for Statue of Liberty-Ellis Island Centennial; trustee Displaced Homemakers, Santa Fe Community Coll.; bd. dirs. Friends of Payne's Prairie, Inc. Recipient Fla. Leadership pin Gov. LeRoy Collins, 1961; Disting. Service award Women in Communication, Inc., 1975, Appreciation plaque Sta. WUFT-TV, 1977, Community Service award Gainesville Sun, 1979, Appreciation cert. Rotary Club Gainesville, 1980, Paul Harris fellowship Rotary Club, 1986, Gainesville Area Woman of Distinction award Sante Fe Community Coll., 1987, Outstanding Service award Jr. League, 1980, Bicentennial plaque Alachua County Bicentennial Com., 1976. Mem. Friends of Library, Fla. State Mus. Assocs. (pres. 1985-87), Friends of Music, Hist. Gainesville, Inc., Found. for Promotion Music, Civic Chorus, Fla. Trust for Hist. Preservation, Fla. League Conservation Voters (bd. dirs. 1983—), Gainesville C. of C. (pub. affairs com. 1983-84), Altrusa Internat., Internat. Platform Assn., Fla. Women's Network. Clubs: Gainesville Garden, Heritage (bd. govs.), Designer, Christmas Wreath So. Living mag., 1982. Home: 1823 N W 10th Ave Gainesville FL 32605

MALONEY, THERESE ADELE, insurance company executive; b. Quincy, Mass., Sept. 15, 1929; d. James Henry and F. Adele (Powers) M.; B.A. in Econs., Coll. St. Elizabeth, Convent Station, N.J., 1951; A.M.P., Harvard U. Bus. Sch., 1981. With Liberty Mut. Ins. Co., Boston, 1951—, asst. v.p., asst. mgr. nat. risks, 1974-77, v.p., mgr. nat. risks, 1977-79, v.p., mgr. nat. risks, 1979-86, sr. v.p. underwriting mktg. and adminstrn. 1986-87, exec. v.p. underwriting, policy decision, 1987—; also bd. dirs.; pres. and bd. dirs. subs. Liberty Mut. (Bermuda) Ltd., 1981—, LEXCO Ltd.; bd. dirs., dep. chmn. Liberty Mut. (Mass.) Ltd., London; bd. dirs. Liberty Mut. Fire Ins. Co.; mem. faculty Inst. Inst., Northeastern U., Boston, 1969-74; mem. adv. bd., risk mgmt. studies Ins. Inst. Am., 1977-83; mem. adv. council Suffolk U. Sch. Mgmt., 1984—; mem. adv. council to program in internat. bus. relations Fletcher Sch. Law and Diplomacy, 1985—. C.P.C.U. Mem. Soc. C.P.C.U.s (past pres. Boston chpt.). Club: University, Algonquin (Boston). Office: Liberty Mut Ins Co 175 Berkeley St Boston MA 02117

MALOTT, ADELE RENEE, editor; b. St. Paul, July 19, 1935; d. Clarence R. and Julia Anne (Christensen) Lindgren; m. Gene E. Malott, Oct. 25, 1957. B.S., Northwestern U., 1957. Coordinator news KGB Radio, San Diego, 1958-60; asst. pub. relations dir. St. Paul C. of C., 1961-63; night editor Daily Local News, West Chester, Pa., 1963-65; editor, co-pub. Boutique and Villager, Burlingame, Calif., 1966-76; sr. editor mag. The Webb Co., St. Paul, 1978-84; editor GEM Pub. Group, Reno, 1985—; co-pub. The Mature Traveler, 1987—; mem. faculty Reader's Digest workshop. Recipient numerous awards Nat. Fedn. Press Women, Calif. Newspaper Pubs. Assn., San Francisco Press Club, Calif. Taxpayers Assn., White House Citations. Mem. Internat. Assn. Bus. Communicators (Merit award 1984), Press Women Minn. (numerous awards).

MALOTT, ANNETTE, media professional, educator; b. Kingsville, Can., May 27, 1941; d. George and Ann (Mayzik) Gerencser; divorced, Feb. 1973, 1 child, Tasha Elana. BA in Communications, U. of Windsor, Ont., 1986. Dir. Personal Devel. Sch., Chatham, Ont., 1969-70; with mktg. dept. Union Gas Ltd., Chatham, 1972-75, regulatory librarian, 1975-79, editor, asst. ed., 1979-84, with systems support dept., 1984-88; editor London (Ont., Can.) Life Insce Co., 1988—; adj. instr. St. Clair Coll., Chatham, 1974—; TV host Chatham Cable TV, 1976—. Host: (TV talk shows) Here's To You, Chatham, 1975, Rogers Cable TV, London. Chmn. pub. relations Chatham Provincial election, 1984; chmn. manpower com. Chatham Fed. election, 1985; pres. Red Cross Soc., Chatham; 1984-85, mem. Chatham City Planning Bd., 1984, spl. projects team, Chatham, 1986; bd. dirs. United Way, 1985—. Mem. Opimian Soc., Internat. Assn. Bus. Communicators. Home: 88-911 Wonderland Rd S, London, ON Canada N6K 2Y7 Office: London Life Insce Co, 255 Dufferin Ave, London, ON Canada N6A 4K1

MALOUF, PAMELA BONNIE, visual arts editor; b. Reseda, Calif., July 9, 1956; d. Jubert George and Marguerite I. (Llido) M. AA in Cinema with honors, Valley Community Coll., 1976. Asst. film editor various film studios including Paramount, 20th Fox, CBS MTM, and others, 1976-80; post prodn. coordinator, supr. David Gerber Co., Culver City, Calif., 1981-82; post prodn. coordinator Paramount TV, Los Angeles, 1982-84; sole proprietor Trailers, Etc., North Hollywood, Calif., 1984-85; film and video editor Paramount Pictures, Los Angeles, 1985-86; film editor Universal Studios, Universal City, Calif., 1986—. Film editor (TV) A Year in the Life, MacGyver, Family Ties on Vacation, Call to Glory, The Making of Shogun, others, (movies) That Was Then, This Now, All in the Family, others; asst. film editor (movies) King of the Gypsies, Star Wars, others. Mem. Internat. Alliance of Theatrical Stage Employees and Moving Picture Machine Operators of the U.S. and Can., Tri-Network (pres. 1979-80), Acad. Magical Arts, Inc. Democrat. Roman Catholic.

MALSON, VERNA LEE, educator; b. Buffalo, Wyo., Mar. 29, 1937; d. Guy James and Vera Pearl (Curtis) Mayer; m. Jack Lee Malson, Apr. 20, 1955; children: Daniel Lee, Thomas James, Mark David, Scott Allen. BA in Elem. Edn. and Spl. Edn. magna cum laude, Met. State Coll., Denver, 1975; MA in Learning Disabilities, U. No. Colo., 1977. Cert. tchr., Colo. Tchr.-aide Wyo. State Tng. Sch., Lander, 1967-69; spl. edn. tchr. Bennett Sch. 29J, Colo., 1975-79, chmn. health, sci., social studies, 1977-79; spl. edn. tchr. Deer Trail Sch., Colo., 1979—, chmn. careers, gifted and talented, 1979-87; mem. spl. edn. parent adv. com. East Central Bd. Coop. Ednl. Services, Limon, Colo. Colo. scholar Met. State Coll., 1974; Colo. Dept. Edn. grantee, 1979, 81. Mem. Council Exceptional Children, Bennett Tchrs. Club (treas. 1977-79), Internat. Biographical Assn., Kappa Delta Pi. Republican. Presbyterian. Avocations: coin collecting; reading; sports. Home: PO Box 403 Deer Trail CO 80105 Office: Deer Trail Pub Schs 26J PO Box 129 Deer Trail CO 80105

MALTBY, TERESA ANN, health science facility administrator, educator, minister; b. Beloit, Wis., Dec. 25, 1943; d. Charles Louis and Wanda Edith (Williams) M. BA in English, St. Xavier Coll., Chgo., 1967; MA in Religious Studies, Mundelein Coll., 1974; D in Ministry, U. Chgo., 1983. Tchr. Little Flower Sch., Chgo., 1967-71; religious ednl. coordinator Little Flower Parish, Chgo., 1968-71; dir. residence halls St. Xavier Coll., Chgo., 1971-72, faculty, 1975-79; edn. coordinator Southwest Cluster of Parishs, Chgo., 1972-76; faculty Ill. Benedictine Coll., Lisle, 1979-80; faculty, pastoral theology St. Mary-of-the-Woods Coll., Terre Haute, Ind., 1980-86; dir. pastora care Mercy Health Care & Rehab. Ctr., Homewood, Ill., 1980-84; dir. mission effectiveness Our Lady of Mercy Hosp., Dyer, Ind., 1985—; bd. govs. Our Lady of Mercy Hosp, 1983—, cons./ethics, 1983-84, Mother McAuley High Sch., 1988—, Warde Corp., 1988—; cons. Dubuque Franciscans Retirement Ctr. 1987; faculty lay ministry program Archdiocese Chgo., 1984—. Contbr. articles to profl. jours. Recipient James A. Rhind award U. Chgo., 1982, Madonna award, Cath. Women's Club Beloit, 1962. Mem. Nat. Liturgical Conf., Acad. Health Care Leadership, Sisters of Mercy. Club: Chgo. Health Tennis. Office: Our Lady of Mercy Hosp Rt 30 Dyer IN 46311

MALTZ, PATRICIA ANN, management consultant; b. New Ulm, Minn., June 20, 1947; d. Neil and Dorothy Francis (Pree) Case; m. Maynard Marvin Maltz, May 20, 1967 (div. 1981); children: Christopher, Katherine. Grad. high sch., Sleepy Eye, Minn. Chief exec. officer Quality Child Care, Inc., Plymouth, Minn., 1973-85, Day Care Fair, Inc., Mound, Minn., 1981-85; cons. Bottom Line Resources, Mound, 1986—; pres. TTI Success and Performance Ctr., Sacramento, Calif., 1986—; owner, operator Family Day Care Resources, Mound, 1985—, Quality Family Foods, Mound, 1986. Mem. Sacramento Women's Network, Greater Sacramento C. of C. Democrat. Lutheran. Home: 3625 Gettyberg Ave S #40 Saint Louis Park MN 55426

MALVEAUX, JULIANNE MARIE, economist; b. San Francisco, Sept. 22, 1953; d. Paul and Proteone Marie (Alexandria) M. BA, Boston Coll., 1974, MA, 1975; PhD, MIT, 1980. Jr. staff economist Council Econ. Advisor The White House, Washington, 1977-78; research fellow Rockefeller Found., N.Y.C., 1978-80; asst. prof. New Sch. Social Research, N.Y.C., 1980-81, San Francisco State U., 1981-85; vis. scholar U. Calif., Berkeley, 1985—, Stanford U., 1987—; cons. women's issues, labor, edn. devel., 1981—. Contbg. editor: Essence mag., 1984—; co-editor Slipping Through the Cracks: Status of Black Women; contbr. articles to profl. jours. Founder, chmn. San Francisco Anti-Apartheid com., 1985-86; bd. dirs. Coleman Advs. Children Youth, San Francisco, 1985—, Nat. Rainbow Coalition, Washington, 1986—, NAACP, San Francisco, 1984, Dem. Women's Forum, San Francisco, 1983; pres. San Francisco Bus. and Profl. Women's Club, 1987—. Named one of Am.'s Top 100 Black Bus. and Profl. Women, Dollar and Sense Mag., 1985, one of 5 Black Women Who Make it Happen, Nat. Council Negro Women and Frito-Lay, 1987; postdoctoral fellow NRC, 1985-86. Roman Catholic. Home: 220 Kingston St San Francisco CA 94110 Office: U Calif Inst Indsl Relations 2521 Channing Way Berkeley CA 94570

MAMALAKIS, MARIE JOHN, public relations educator, writer; b. Shreveport, La., Sept. 15, 1913; d. John Emanuel and Demetria (Passadakis) M. BA, U. Southwestern La., 1933; MLS, La. State U., Baton Rouge, 1941. Tchr. St. Landry Parish, Opelousas, La., 1934-41; tchr. U. S.W. La., Lafayette, La., 1941-65, prof. and dir. pubs. and news, 1965-75, prof. pub. relations, 1975—; cons. pub. relations U. Southwestern La., Lafayette, 1976—. Author: If They Could Talk, 1983; free lance writer, 1942—; editor Lafayette Progress Weekly Paper, 1952-62; author weekly feature Daily Advertiser, 1979—; contbr. articles to numerous jours. Mem. Acadiana Arts Council, Cajun Dome Commn., Planning and Zoning Commn. 1974-84, Regional Planning Com., 1974-84; chmn. Lafayette Civil Service Commn., 1974-83. Recipient Found. Recognition U. Southwestern La. Found., 1987, Civic Cup award YMBC, 1984. Mem. U. Southwestern La. Alumni Assn. (Outstanding Alumna 1985), Lafayette C. of C. (pub. relations com. 1975-77). Republican. Greek Orthodox. Home: 1018 Auburn Ave Lafayette LA 70503 Office: U Southwestern La University Ave Lafayette LA 70504

MAMLOK, URSULA, composer, educator; b. Berlin, Feb. 1, 1928; d. John and Dorothy Lewis; m. Dwight G. Mamlok, Nov. 27, 1947. Student, Mannes Coll. Music, 1942-45; B.Mus., Manhattan Sch. Music, 1955, M.Mus., 1958. Mem. faculty dept. music NYU, 1967-74, CUNY, 1971-74; prof. composition Manhattan Sch. Music, N.Y.C., 1974—. Composer: numerous works including Variations and Interludes for 4 percussionists, 1973, Sextet, 1977, Festive Sounds, 1978, When Summer Sang, 1980, piano trio Panta rhei, 1981, 5 recital pieces for young pianists, 1983, From My Garden for solo viola or solo violin, 1983, Concertino for wind quintet, Strings and percussion, 1984, Der Andreas Garten for voice and harpsichord, flute and harp, 1986, 3 Bagatelles for harpsichord, 1987. Nat. Endowment Arts grantee, 1974; Am. Inst. Acad. Arts and Letters grantee, 1981; Martha Baird Rockefeller grantee, 1982. Mem. Am. Composers Alliance (dir.), Am. Soc. Univ. Composers, Am. Women Composers, Internat. League Women Composers, Music Theory Soc. N.Y., Am. Music Center., Internat. Soc. Contemporary Music (bd. dirs.). Address: 315 E 86th St New York NY 10028

MAMON, DORIS ELAINE, laboratory administrator; b. Chgo., Jan. 31, 1943; d. Julius S. and Helen M. Bonk; B.S., Mundelein Coll., 1976; M.B.A., Marquette U., 1981; M.T., St. Mary of Nazareth Sch. Med. Tech., 1964; children—Deborah, Vincent. Sect. head immunohematology Alexian Bros. Med. Center, Elk Grove Village, Ill., 1969-78; supr. implementation Medistat, Milw., 1978-80; supr. product analyst Tymshare Med. Systems, Brookfield, Wis., 1980-81; sr. mgmt. cons. The Kennedy Group, Menlo Park, Calif., 1981-83; lab. mgr. Sherman Hosp., Elgin, Ill., 1984—. Mem. Am. Hosp. Assn., Am. Soc. Clin. Pathologists, Clin. Lab. Mgmt. Assn., Am. Assn. Blood Banks.

MANASC, VIVIAN, architect, consultant; b. Bucharest, Romania, May 19, 1956; d. Bercu and Bianca (Smetterling) M.; m. William A. Dushenski, Feb. 25, 1984; 1 child, Peter Gabriel. BS in Architecture, McGill U., Montreal, Que., Can., 1977, BArch, 1979; MBA, U. Alta., Edmonton, 1982. Architectural insp. Transport Can., Edmonton, 1977-79; project architect Bell Spotowski Architects, Edmonton, 1980-82; asst. dir. design constrn. Edmonton Pub. Schs., 1982-84; mgr., prin. Ferguson, Simek, Clark Architects Ltd., Edmonton, 1985—. Contbr. articles to profl. jours. Advisor YMCA, Edmonton, 1980-82; mentor RAIC Syllabus Program, Edmonton, 1982-87; bd. dirs. Design Workshop, Edmonton, 1983. Scholar McGill U., 1974. Mem. Alberta Assn. Architects, Royal Architectural Inst. Can., Council Edn. Facility Planners. Office: Ferguson Simek Clark, 11133-124th St, Edmonton, AB Canada TSM OJ2

MANCALL, JACQUELINE COOPER, library and information science educator; b. Phila., Mar. 31, 1932; d. Morris and Bertha Cooper; 1953; m. Elliott Lee Mancall, Dec. 27, 1953; children—Andrew Cooper, Peter Cooper. B.A., U. Pa., 1954; M.S., Drexel U. Sch. Library and Info. Sci., 1970, Ph.D., 1979. Adminstr., Miquon (Pa.) Sch., 1966-67, librarian, 1967-76; teaching asst. Drexel U., Phila., 1976-78, research assoc., 1979, asst. prof., 1979-85, assoc. prof., 1985—; chair Phila. Children's Reading Round Table, 1982-84, faculty council, 1987—; mem. steering com., 1984—mem. sch. library survey com. State Library Pa., 1983; cons. Author: (with M. Carl Drott) Measuring Student Information Use: A Guide for Sch. Library Media Specialists 1983;

research editor Sch. Library Media quar., 1982—; editorial bd. Jour. Library and Info. Sci. Edn., 1981-86; contbg. editor Catholic Library World, 1981-85; contbr. chpts. to books, articles to profl. jours. Bd. dirs. Friends of William Jeannes Meml. Library, Plymouth Meeting, Pa., 1976-79; pres. bd. dirs. Miquon Sch., 1964-66. Mem. ALA (chair research com. 1983-85), Pa. Sch. Librarians Assn. (bd. dirs. 1984-87, chmn. profl. standard com. 1980-82, tech. com. 1982-84), Assn. Am. Library Schs. Democrat. Jewish. Home: Harts Ln Miquon PA 19452 Office: Drexel U Coll Info Studies Philadelphia PA 19104

MANCHESTER, MELISSA TONI, singer, song writer; b. Bronx, N.Y., Feb. 15, 1951; d. David and Ruth M.; m. Kevin DeRemer, May 1, 1982; 1 child, Nathan. Grad., High Sch. Performing Arts, N.Y.C., 1969. Pres., owner Rumanian Pickleworks Music. Singer with Bette Midler, 1971-72, rec. artist Bell and Arista records; recordings include Melissa (Gold Album award), For the Working Girl, Mathematics, 1985; co-writer: Midnite Blue, Come in from the Rain, Whenever I Call You Friend; appeared in play: Song and Dance, 1987. Recipient Best New Female Vocalist of Year award Cashbox mag., 1974; New Female Vocalist of Year award Billboard mag., 1975; Wright award for Midnight Blue, Broadcast Music Inc., 1975; Grammy award for best female vocal, 1982. Mem. Broadcast Music Inc., AFTRA, Screen Actors Guild, Am. Fedn. Musicians. Address: care Triad Artists Inc 10100 Santa Monica Blvd 16th Fl Los Angeles CA 90067 *

MANCHESTER, ROSEMARY, finance company executive; b. Newton, Kans., May 7, 1928; d. Walter Theodore and Lora Margaret (Hutchison) Ingold; children: Timothy, Peter, Mary Elizabeth, Martha. BA, College of Emporia, Kans., 1949; MBA, Pace U., 1979. Lic. securities broker. Adult program dir. White Plains (N.Y.) YMCA, 1973-76; research assoc. Life Office Mgmt. Assn., N.Y.C., 1977-78; registered rep. Waddell and Reed, Inc., Woodbridge, Conn., 1980-81; asst. v.p. Union Trust Co., New Haven, Conn., 1981-84; v.p. Soc. for Savings, Hartford, Conn., 1984-87; cert. fin. planner Blakeslee and Blakeslee, San Luis Obispo, Calif., 1987—; mem. adv. bd. N.Y.C. Private Banking Council, 1985—. Mem. Inst. Cert. Fin. Planners, Internat. Assn. for Fin. Planning (v.p. Conn. chpt. 1985-86), Nat. Assn. Bus. Economists (bd. dirs. Hartford chpt. 1987), Investors Strategy Inst. (pres. 1985-86), Hartford Womens Network. Democrat. Club: Graduates (New Haven). Home: 2660 Spyglass Dr Apt D Shell Beach CA 93449 Office: Blakeslee and Blakeslee 1110 California Blvd San Luis Obispo CA 93401

MANCINI, LINDA, sales executive; b. San Jose, Calif.; d. John and Anne (Dubcich) Ivancovich; divorced; children: Anthony, Cari, Julie, Shelly. BS in Mktg., San Jose State U., 1972. Adminstrv. asst. Verbatim Corp., Sunnyvale, Calif., 1976-78, sales support mgr., 1978-80, communications mgr., 1980-82, sales mgr. office products div., 1985—. Mem. Nat. Office Products Assn., Wholesale Stationers Assn., Nat. Office Machines Assn., 49er's Travelers Club, Golden State Travelers Club. Republican. Roman Catholic. Office: Verbatim Corp 323 Soquel Way Sunnyvale CA 94086

MANDEL, CAROLA PANERAI (MRS. LEON MANDEL), foundation trustee; b. Havana, Cuba; d. Camilo and Elvira (Bertini) Panerai; ed. pvt. schs., Havana and Europe; m. Leon Mandel, Apr. 9, 1938. Mem. women's bd. Northwestern Meml. Hosp., Chgo. Trustee Carola and Leon Mandel Fund Loyola U., Chgo. Life mem. Chgo. Hist. Soc., Guild of Chgo. Hist. Soc., Smithsonian Assos., Nat. Skeet Shooting Assn. Frequently named among Ten Best Dressed Women in U.S.; chevalier Confrerie des Chevaliers du Tastevin. Capt. All-Am. Women's Skeet Team, 1952, 53, 54, 55, 56; only woman to win a men's nat. championship, 20 gauge, 1954, also high average in world over men, 1956, in 12 gauge with 99.4 per cent; European women's live bird shooting championship, Venice, Italy, 1957, Porto, Portugal, 1961; European woman's target championship, Torino, Italy, 1958; woman's world champion live-bird shooting, Sevilla, Spain, 1959, Am. Contract Bridge League Life Master, 1987. Named to Nat. Skeet Shooting Assn. Hall of Fame, 1970. Mem. Soc. Four Arts. Club: Everglades (Palm Beach, Fla.), The Beach. Home: 324 Barton Ave Palm Beach FL 33480

MANDEL, ELLEN DEBORAH, hospital administrator, nutritionist, consultant; b. Newark, Feb. 26, 1957; d. Morris and Ida (Schindel) M.; m. Mitchell Bruce Germansky, Mar. 22, 1979; 1 child, Shayna Mandel Germansky. BS in Foods and Nutrition, Montclair State Coll., 1979; MPA, Seton Hall U., 1985. Registered dietitian, N.J., cert. diabetes educator. Dietetic intern Univ. Medicine and Dentistry N.J., Newark, 1979-80, clin. instr., 1980-84, clin. dietitian Univ. Hosp., 1980-81; asst. dir. food services United Hosps., Newark, 1981-84; dir. food services Raritan Bay Med. Ctr., Perth Amboy, N.J., 1984-86; program mgr. diabetes treatment ctr. Newark Beth Israel Med. Ctr., 1986—; assoc. prof., U. Med. and Dentistry., Newark, 1986—; pvt. practice nutritionist, N.J. Co-editor state dietetic newsletter, 1986—. Bd. dirs. No. N.J. Community Relations Com., 1979-82. Mem. Am. Dietetic Assn., N.J. Dietetic Assn. (ann. meeting program bd. 1986, 87, speakers com. 1985—, advt. chair 1986—, Young Dietitian of Yr. 1986-87), Am. Assn. Diabetes Educators, N.J. Met. Dist. Dietetic Assn. (chair legis. com. 1983-85, chair nominating com. 1985-86). Avocations: sports, needlework, gardening, gourmet cooking, public speaking. Home: 131 River Bend Rd Berkeley Heights NJ 07922

MANDEL, KARYL LYNN, accountant; b. Chgo., Dec. 14, 1935; d. Isador J. and Eve (Gellar) Karzen; m. Fredric H. Mandel, Sept. 29, 1956; children: David Scott, Douglas Jay, Jennifer Ann. Student, U. Mich., 1954-56, Roosevelt U., 1956-57; AA summa cum laude, Oakton Community Coll., 1979. CPA, Ill. Pres., nat. bd. mem. Women's Am. Orgn. for Rehab. through Tng., 1961-77; pres. Excel Transp. Service Co., Elk Grove, Ill., 1958-78; tax mgr. Chunowitz, Teitelbaum & Baerson, CPA's, Elk Grove, Ill., 1958-78; tax mgr. Chunowitz, Teitelbaum & Baerson, CPA's, Northbrook, Ill., 1981-83, tax ptnr., 1984—; sec-treas. Lednam, Inc.; mem. acctg. curriculum adv. bd. Oakton Community Coll., Des Plaines, Ill., 1987—. Contbg. author: Ill. CPA's News Jour. Recipient State of Israel Solidarity award, 1976. Mem. Am. Inst. CPA's, Am. Soc. Women CPA's, Women's Am. ORT, Ill. CPA Soc. (vice chmn. estate and gift tax com. 1985-87, chmn. estate and gift tax com., 1987—, mem. legis. contact com. 1981-82, pres. North Shore chpt., award for Excellence in Acctg. Edn.), Chgo. Soc. Women CPA's, Chgo. Estate Planning Council, Nat. Assn. Women Bus. Owners. Office: 401 Huehl Rd Northbrook IL 60062

MANDEL, LESLIE ANN, financial advisor; b. Washington, July 29, 1945; d. Seymour and Majorie Syble (Perlman) M. BA in Art History, U. Minn., 1967; cert., N.Y. Sch. Interior Design, 1969. Pres. Leslie Mandel Enterprises, Inc., N.Y.C., 1972—; fin. advisor Osmed Inc., Mpls., 1986—, Devine Communication/Allen & Co., N.Y., Del., Utah, N.Mex., 1984—, Am. Kefir Corp., N.Y., 1983—, Sta. KVBC-TV, Los Vegas, 1983—; owner 11 nationwide catalogues, fundraising lists. Photographer: Vogue, 1978; braille transcriber: The Prophet (Kalil Gibran), 1967, Getting Ready for Battle (R. Prawe Jhabuala), 1967; exec. producer film: Hospital Audiences, 1975 (award at Cannes 1976). Fin. advisor Correctional Assn., Osborn Soc., 1977—; founder, treas. Prisoners Family Transportation and Assistance Fund, N.Y., 1972-77; judge Emmy awards of Acad. TV Arts and Scis., N.Y.C., 1970. Recipient Inst. for the Creative and Performing Arts fellowship, N.Y.C., 1966, Appreciation cert. Presdl. Inaugural Com., Washington, 1981. Fellow N.Y. Women in Real Estate; mem. Com. on Am. and Internat. Fgn. Affairs, Sigma Delta Tau, Sigma Epsilon Sigma. Democrat. Jewish. Club: Venture Capital Breakfast (fellow). Home: 4 East 81st St-Penthouse New York NY 10028 Office: Leslie Mandel Enterprises IJL Realty Inc 310 Madison Ave New York NY 10017

MANDELBAUM, DOROTHY ROSENTHAL, psychologist; b. N.Y.C., May 18, 1935; d. Benjamin Daniel and Rachael (Osofsky) Rosenthal; A.B. cum laude, Hunter Coll., 1956; Ph.D., Bryn Mawr Coll., 1975; m. Seymour Jacob Mandelbaum, Aug. 19, 1956; children—David Gideon, Judah Michael, Betsy Daniella. Tchr., Valley Road Sch., Princeton, N.J., 1956-59; instr. ednl. psychology dept. Temple U., Phila., summer 1970; asst. prof. dept. edn. Rutgers, The State U., Camden, N.J., 1974-80, asso. prof., 1980—, dir. women's studies, 1981-86, chair edn. dept., 1986—. AAUW predoctoral fellow, 1973-74. Mem. Am. Psychol. Assn., AAUP, Soc. Research in Child Devel. Contbr. articles on psychology of women and med. edn. to profl. publs. Author: Work, Marriage, and Motherhood: The Career Persistence of Female Physicians, 1981. Home: 2290 N 53d St Philadelphia PA 19131 Office: Rutgers U Camden NJ 08102

MANDELBAUM, JUDITH, consulting firm executive; b. Newark, May 2, 1940; d. Morris and Millicent (Piper) Solomon; m. Barry Richard Mandelbaum, June 13, 1960 (div. Jan. 1980); children—Kenneth, Lisa. B.A., Barnard Coll., 1961; M.A., NYU, 1973. Tchr. English, Chatham Jr. High Sch. (N.J.), 1961-62; adj. prof. English, Morris County Coll., Denville, N.J., 1979-80; asst. dir. Anti-Defamation League, Livingston, N.J., 1980-84; dir. research and communications Louis Hoffman Assocs., Randolph, N.J., 1984-87; research assoc. Skott-Edwards Cons., Rutherford, N.J., 1987—. Author poem: Christmas Special, 1974 (Acad. Am. Poets award 1976). Mem. MLA. Home: 454-209 Prospect Ave West Orange NJ 07052

MANDELL, ARLENE LINDA, public relations executive; b. Bklyn., Feb. 19, 1941; d. George and Esther Kostick; m. Lawrence W. Mandell, May 23, 1982; children by previous marriage: Bruce R. Rosenblum, Tracey B. Rosenblum. BA magna cum laude, William Paterson Coll., 1973. Newspaper reporter Suburban Trends, Riverdale, N.J., 1972-73; writer Good Housekeeping mag., N.Y.C., 1976-78; account exec. Carl Byoir & Assocs., N.Y.C., 1978-86; v.p. Porter/Novelli, N.Y.C., 1986—. Contbr. articles to profl. jours. and newspapers. Recipient 1st place women's interest writing N.J. Press Assn., 1973; named John W. Stahr Writer of Yr., Carl Byoir & Assocs., N.Y.C., 1981. Mem. Women in Communications, Roundtable for Women in Foodservice. Club: Newswomen's. Office: Porter Novelli 1633 Broadway New York NY 10019

MANDIBERG, MYRTLE, psychologist; b. N.Y.C., July 1, 1918; d. Samuel and Sadie (Friedman) M.; B.A., Bklyn. Coll., 1938; M.A., U. Pa., 1940. Intern Wayne County Gen. Hosp., Eloise, Mich., 1940-41, staff psychologist, 1941-42; tchr. nursery sch. Detroit Bd. Edn., 1942-44; staff psychologist Detroit Recorders Ct. Psychopathic Clinic, 1944-49; psychotherapist Devereux Ranch Sch., Santa Barbara, Calif., 1949-51; supr. Reiss-Davis Child Guidance Clinic, Los Angeles, 1959-62; cons., coordinator profl. services Los Angeles Child Devel. Center, 1979-86, v.p., dir. clin. service, 1986-88, exec. dir., 1988—; also pvt. practice child psychology, 1951—; assoc. in psychology UCLA, 1978—. Mem. Am. Psychol. Assn., Calif. State Psychol. Assn., Los Angeles County Psychol. Assn., Assn. Child Psychoanalysis. Home and Office: 1470 Glendon Ave Los Angeles CA 90024

MANDICOTT, GRACE MARIE, healthcare center executive; b. Reading, Pa., Aug. 31, 1942; d. Dominick Adam and Angeline Grace (Carabino) M. Grad., Binghamton Gen. Hosp., 1963; BS, SUNY, Binghamton, 1976; MA, Cen. Mich. U., 1981. RN, N.Y.; cert. nurse practitioner, Pa. Nurse various hosps., 1963-65, St. Peter's Hosp., Albany, N.Y., 1967-68, Gen. Electric Co., 1968, Dr. Janith S. Kice, Garden City, N.Y., 1968-69, Ehtitchner & Co., Binghamton, 1970-72, Family Health Ctr., Johnson City, N.Y., 1972-74; adminstr./mgr., nurse practitioner, physician's asst. internists pvt. offices, Pa., 1975-83; dir., owner Health and Wellness Ctr., Binghamton, 1984—; asst. coordinator med. student clkship., SUNY, Binghamton, 1979-82, asst. instr. Sch. Nursing, 1980; health care cons., Binghamton, 1981—; dir. med. services sales-mktg. mgr. Adelaide Environ. Health Assocs., Binghamton, 1983—; adj. profl. New Sch. for Social Research, N.Y.C., 1985—; speaker in field. Coordinator walkathon Am. Cancer Soc., 1976. Republican. Roman Catholic. Home: 1 Christopher St Binghamton NY 13903 Office: Health and Wellness Ctr Riverhouse 40 Front St Binghamton NY 13903

MANDRAVELIS, PATRICIA JEAN, nursing administrator; b. Hanover, N.H., May 7, 1938; d. William J. and Ruth E. (Darling) Bartis; m. Anthony M. Mandravelis, Nov. 8, 1959; children: Michael A., Tracy J. Diploma in nursing, Nashua (N.H.) Meml. Hosp. Sch. Nursing; BS in Psychology, Sociology, New Eng. Coll.; postgrad., N.H. Coll., 1988. Cert. nursing adminstr. Staff nurse Nashua Meml. Hosp., 1959-60, obstet. nurse, 1962-65, charge nurse, 1969-71, supr., 1971-76, assoc. dir. nursing, 1976-81, dir. nursing, 1981-83, asst. exec. dir. nursing, 1983-87, v.p. nursing, 1987—. Bd. dirs. deNicola Women's Ctr., Nashua, 1987—, Nashua Vis. Nurse program, 1986—; v.p. Nashua chpt. ARC, 1985—. Mem. Nat. League of Nursing, Am. Nurses Assn., Am. Orgn. Nurse Execs., N.H. Nurses Assn., N.H. Orgn. Nurse Execs., Sigma Theta Tau. Office: Nashua Meml Hosp 8 Prospect St Nashua NH 03061

MANDRELL, BARBARA ANN, singer, entertainer; b. Houston, Dec. 25, 1948; d. Irby Matthew and Mary Ellen (McGill) M.; m. Kenneth Lee Dudney, May 28, 1967; children: Kenneth Matthew, Jaime Nicole, Nathaniel. Grad. high sch. Country music singer and entertainer, 1959—, performed throughout U.S. and in various fgn. countries; mem., Grand Ole Opry, Nashville, 1972—; star TV series Barbara Mandrell and the Mandrell Sisters, 1980-82, Barbara Mandrell: Get to the Heart, 1987; albums include Midnight Oil, Treat Him Right, This Time I Almost Made It, This is Barbara Mandrell, Midnight Angel, Barbara Mandrell's Greatest Hits. Named Miss Oceanside, Calif., 1965; Named Most Promising Female Singer, Acad. Country and Western Music, 1971; Female Vocalist of Yr., 1978; Female Vocalist of Yr., Music City News Cover Awards, 1979; Female Vocalist of Yr., Country Music Assn., 1979; Entertainer of Yr., 1980, 81; People's Choice awards (6), 1982-84. Mem. Musicians Union, Screen Actors Guild, AFTRA, Country Music Assn. (v.p.). Mem. Order Eastern Star. Office: care World Class Talent 1522 Demonbreux Nashville TN 37203 *

MANDRELL, REGINA ANGELA MORENO, genealogist; b. Mobile, Ala., Mar. 10, 1906; d. Cameron Anderson and Seana Barkley (Crary) Moreno; A.B., Birmingham-So. Coll., 1926, postgrad., 1960; postgrad. U. Ky., 1964, Smith Coll., Northampton, Mass., 1965; m. George F. Kirchoff, Oct. 4, 1930 (dec.); children—George F., Margaret A. Kirchoff Pennington; m. 2d, William F. Mandrell, Oct. 20, 1971 (dec.). Tchr., attendance supr. Birmingham (Ala.) Public Schs., 1926-71; adminstrv. asst. Jefferson County Mental Health Assn., Birmingham, 1956-59; mem. Ala. Devel. Bd. for Health Survey, 1930; writing and geneal. research compiling family history, 1932—. Recipient George Washington medal Freedom Found., 1961. Mem. Ala. Hist. Soc., Baldwin County (Ala.) Hist. Soc. (officer), Writers Group, Baldwin County Writers Club, Pensacola (Fla.) Hist. Soc., DAR, Magna Charta Dames, Nat. Soc. Colonial Dames XVII Century, Alpha Chi Omega, Kappa Delta Epsilon, Pi Gamma Mu, Chi Delta Phi. Methodist. Author: Reminiscences of the Old South 1834-1866 (3 vols.), 1985, Moreno-Byrne Genealogy, 1988, Crary-Pritchett Genealogy, 1988. Contbr. articles to profl. jours., story to anthology Women of the South. Home: PO Drawer 1466 Fairhope AL 36532

MANERO, VICTORIA, language educator; b. Las Tunas, Cuba, Mar. 23, 1942; came to U.S., 1966; d. Victoriano and Renee (Urquiola) M.; divorced; 1 child, Victoria A. Hernandez. Diploma in Music Edn., Internat. Conservatory of Music, Havana, Cuba, 1958; BA, Mercy Coll., 1970; MA, NYU, 1973; MS, Hunter Coll., 1977. Clk. Am. Express Co., N.Y.C., 1966-69; investigator internat. ops. The Chase Manhattan Bank, N.Y.C., 1969-72; tchr. N.Y.C. Bd. Edn., 1972-77, bilingual program coordinator, 1977-81, supr. bilingual and second lang. edn., 1981—; editor CUNY, 1975, freelance editorial cons., 1975-77, adj. prof., CCNY, 1979. Mem. Assn. for Supervision and Instrn., Nat. Assn. for Bilingual Edn., Tchrs. English to Speakers of Other Langs., N.Y. State Assn. for Bilingual Edn. Home: 711 W 190th St New York NY 10040 Office: Community Sch Dist #5 433 W 123d St New York NY 10040

MANES, EUNICE CONDITT, insurance company executive; b. Durant, Okla., Mar. 12, 1941; d. James Bennett and Johnie Eva Rilla (Laxton) Conditt; divorced; 1 child, Jason. BA in Acctg., U. Tex., Arlington, 1974; MBA, So. Meth. U., 1979. Corp. officer Owen Labs, Inc., Dallas, 1964-72; cons. Irving, Tex., 1972-74; personnel mgr. Alcon Labs, Inc., Ft. Worth, 1974-77, Austin Industries, Dallas, 1977-80; v.p. Blue Cross & Blue Shield of Tex., Dallas, 1980—. Chmn, sub-com. Dallas County Pvt. Industry Council, 1981-85. Mem. Am. Mgmt. Assn., S.W. Pension Conf. (bd. dirs., treas. 1978-80). Office: Blue Cross & Blue Shield of Tex Inc 901 S Central Expressway Richardson TX 75081

MANESCALCHI, LYNE PLAMONDON, advertising and public relations specialist, writer, consultant; b. Montreal, Que., Can., Dec. 11, 1958; d. Gabriel Pierre and Therese Ann (Trudel) Plamondon; m. Filippo Alesi Manescalchi, Feb. 14, 1983; children: Nicolette Lyne, Bearnardo Gabriel. AA, Palomar Coll., 1980; BS in Radio, TV and Film with distinction, Calif. State U., San Diego, 1982. Advt. copywriter Walker Scott Co., San Diego, 1982-84; v.p. Telesis Concepts, Vista, Calif., 1984—; mgr. advt. and pub. relations Mail Boxes Etc., USA, Carlsbad, Calif., 1984-85; asst. dir. advt. Fox Advt./Alopex Industries, San Marcos, Calif., 1985—; entertainer Mus. Ams., Whittier, Calif., 1975. Actress film Hardcore, 1978, TV feature The Return of Frank Cannon, 1980; author, producer: Advertising Recipe Book, 1984; contbr. numerous articles to profl. jours. Democrat. Roman Catholic. Office: Telesis Concepts 1425 Philmar Ln Vista CA 92083-7123

MANFORD, BARBARA ANN, contralto; b. St. Augustine, Fla., Nov. 13, 1929; d. William Floyd and Margaret (Kemper) Manford; Mus.B. in Voice, Fla. State U., 1951, Mus.M., 1970; studied with L. Palazzini, A. Strano, Japelli, E. Nikolaidi, E. Joseph. Appearances in Europe, performing major roles in 12 leading opera houses, 1951-68, with condrs. including Alfred Strano, Felice Cilario, Robert Shaw, Arnold Gamson, Guiseppe Patané, Ottavio Ziino, also numerous concerts and recitals in Paris and throughout Italy and Belgium; performed in world premiere Fugitives (C. Floyd), Fla. State U., Tallahassee, 1950; chosen by Gian Carlo Menotti for leading role in world premiere The Leper, Fla. State U., 1970; numerous radio, TV, and concert appearances, U.S., 1968—; artist-in-residence, asso. prof. voice Ball State U., Muncie, Ind., 1970—; numerous recs. Semi-finalist vocal contest, Parma, Italy, 1964; winner contest, Lonigo, Italy, 1965. Mem. Nat. Assn. Tchrs. Singing, Chgo. Artists Assn., Am. Tchrs. Nat. Assn., Sigma Alpha Iota, Pi Kappa Lambda. Christian Scientist. Home: 104 Colonial Crest Apts Muncie IN 47304 Office: Ball State Univ Muncie IN 47306

MANFREDI, JACQUELINE, automotive magazine executive; b. Los Angeles, Aug. 28, 1944; d. Francis William and Christine (Delgado) Manfredi; m. James Kevin Jaskol, May 5, 1985. Student, Santa Monica Coll., Calif., 1962-64, S.I. Coll., Richmond Coll., CUNY, 1972-73, UCLA, 1973-74. Copy editor Motor Trend Mag., Los Angeles, 1979-81, mng. editor, 1981—. Mem. Internat. Motor Press of Am., Western Pubs. Assn. Democrat. Roman Catholic. Office: Motor Trend Mag 8490 Sunset Blvd Los Angeles CA 90069

MANGAN, JUDITH LAUCK, nursing administrator; b. Luverne, Minn., Nov. 17, 1934; d. Clarence W. and Tillie J. (Elzenga) Lauck; m. Thomas W. Mangan, July 11, 1959; children: Troy, Erin. BA, Met. State U., St. Paul, 1981. Cert. gerontol. nurse. Evening supr. Presbyn. Homes Minn., St. Paul, 1978-80; community services nurse Jewish Family Services, Mpls., 1980-82; edn. coordinator Pkwy. Manor Health Care Facility, St. Paul, 1983; head nurse Cath. Eldercare, Mpls., 1985; asst. dir. nursing, staff devel. coordinator Yorkshire Manor Health Care Facility, Mpls., 1985—. Mem. Am. Soc. Aging, Minn. Gerontological Soc. Democrat. Presbyterian. Home: 1812 Venus Ave Saint Paul MN 55112

MANGAN, PATRICIA ANN PRITCHETT, research statistician; b. Hammond, Ind., Feb. 4, 1953; d. Edward Clayton and Helen Josephine (Mills) Pritchett; m. William Paul Mangan, Aug. 30, 1980; 1 child, Ryan Christopher. BS in Maths. and Stats., Purdue U., 1975, MS in Applied Stats., 1977. Tobacco devel. statistician R.J. Reynolds Tobacco Co., Winston-Salem, N.C., 1978-82, research and devel. statistician, 1982-86, sr. research and devel. statistician, 1986—; cons. Lab. for Application of Remote Sensing, West Lafayette, Ind., 1976-77; statis. engr. Corning Glass Works, Harrodsburg, Ky., 1977. Contbr. articles to sci. jours. Rep. United Way, Winston-Salem, 1985. Mem. Am. Statis. Assn., Wash. Statis. Soc., Nat. Assn. Female Execs., Smithsonian Assocs., Purdue Alumni Assn. Office: RJ Reynolds Tobacco Co BGTC 611-12/104A Winston-Salem NC 27102

MANGE, JUDITH, physical therapist, hospice administrator; b. St. Louis, July 8, 1946; d. Willard Lesman and Bernice (Quicksilver) M.; student Ind. U., 1964-66; B.S., Washington U. Med. Sch., St. Louis, 1968; M.B.A. (grantee), U. Mo., St. Louis, 1980. Staff phys. therapist Jewish Hosp., St. Louis, 1968-71, supr. phys. therapy, 1971-78; housing coordinator Convenant House, St. Louis, 1980; dir. phys. therapy services Irene Walter Johnson Inst. Rehab., St. Louis, 1980-82; hospice cons., St. Louis, 1982—; pres., dir., adminstr. Community Hospice Care, Inc., St. Louis; mem. admissions com., phys. therapy program Washington U., 1979-82, lectr., 1979—. Bd. dirs. Am. Cancer Soc. Mem. Mo. Hospice Orgn. (pres., treas.), Nat. Hosp. Organ. (chmn. planning ann. meeting), Am. Phys. Therapy Assn. (treas. Mo., chmn. St. Louis), Mo. Phys. Therapy Assn., Gerontological Soc., Jewish.

MANGINO, KRISTIN MIKALSON, teacher; b. Spokane, Wash., July 7, 1939; d. Norman Lillard and Mabel Mae (Lewis) Mikalson; m. Paul Angelo Mangino, Aug. 15, 1965; children: Kyle Aaron, Lisan Kristin. Student, Cottey Coll., 1957-58, E.W.C.E., 1958-61; BS in Psychology, Wash. State U., 1961; student, Calif. State U., Fullerton, 1961-66; postgrad., U. Calif.Irvine, 1966; MS in Spl. Edn., Portland State U., 1983. Cert. elem. and secondary tchr., Calif., Wash., Oreg. Tchr. English and reading Jr. High Sch., Anaheim and Monterey, Calif., 1961-68; substitute tchr. Elma (Wash.) Sch. Dist., 1970-71, Evergreen Sch. Dist., Vancouver, Wash., 1974-75; tutor Evergreen Sch. Dist., Vancouver, 1975-84; tutor, substitute tchr. Vancouver and Evergreen Sch. Dists., 1984-88, tutor, 1988—; hostess with service sales City Welcome Service, 1986-87; co-pres. Spl. Edn. Adv. Council, Vancouver, 1986-87. Officer P.E.O., Vancouver, 1984-86. Mem. Nat. Assn. Exec. Females. Republican. Presbyterian. Home and Office: 8506 NE 12th St Vancouver WA 98664

MANGUS, DEBBIE DEE, marketing executive; b. Fort Wayne, Ind., May, 1955; d. Kenneth R. and M. Irene Miller; m. Charles D. Lewis; children—David R., Carrie A.; m. John T. Mangus, Dec., 1981; stepchildren—John T. III, April L., Brandon M., Ryan E. Store activities rep. McDonald's Systems, Newport News, Va., Fort Wayne, Ind., 1978, community relations rep. Fort Wayne, Columbus, Ohio, 1979-81; regional mktg. mgr. Arby's, Inc., Columbus, 1982-83; mktg. dir. McNeill Enterprises, Inc., Chillicothe, Ohio, 1984-86; project mgr. mktg. dept. Mid-Am. Fed., Columbus, 1987—; trainer regional mktg. mgrs. Arby's, Columbus, 1982-83; mktg. cons. MEI Franchisees, Inc. Franchisees, Ohio, Ill., Ky., 1984-86 Fund raiser Ronald McDonald House, Columbus, Indpls., 1980-81 Recipient Best Bets awards McDonald's-Indpls. region, 1980, 81. Mem. Nat. Assn. Female Execs. Methodist. Avocations: reading; softball; bicycling; crafts. Office: Mid-Am Fed 4181 ArlinGate Plaza Columbus OH 43228-4115

MANHART, MARCIA Y(OCKEY), art museum director; b. Wichita, Kans., Jan. 14, 1943; d. Everett W. and Ruth C. (Correll) Yockey; m. Thomas Arthur Manhart; children: Caroline Amanda, Emily Alexandrea. BA in Art, U. Tulsa, 1965, MA in Ceramics, 1971. Dir. edn. Philbrook Art Ctr., Tulsa, 1972-77, exec. v.p., asst. dir., 1977-83, acting dir., 1983-84; exec. dir. Philbrook Mus. of Art (formerly Philbrook Art Ctr.), Tulsa, 1984—; instr. Philbrook Art Ctr. Mus. Sch., Tulsa, 1963-72; gallery dir. Alexandre Hogue Gallery, Tulsa U., 1967-69. Vis. com. Smithsonian Instn./Renwick Gallery, Washington, 1986; cultural negotiator Gov. George Nigh's World Trade Mission (Okla.), China., 1985; com. mem. State Art Coll. of Okla., 1985—; mem. Assocs. of Hillcrest Med. Ctr., 1983—, exec. com., 1985—; com. mem. Neighborhood Housing Services, 1985—; mem. Mapleridge Hist. Dist. Assn., 1982—; steering com. Harwelden Isnt. for Aesthetic Edn., 1983; com. mem. River Parks Authority, 1976; mem. Jr. League of Tulsa Inc., 1974-78; adv. panel mem. Nat. Craft Planning Project, NEA, Washington, 1978-81; regional rep. Art Mus. Assn. Am., 1978—; craft adv. panel mem. Okla. Arts and Humanities Council, 1974-76; juror numerous art festivals, competitions, programs; reviewer Inst. Mus. Services, Washington, 1985; auditor Symposium on Language & Scholarship of Modern Crafts, NEA and NEH, Washington, 1981. Mem. Internat. Council Mus., Assn. Am. Mus., Assn. Art Mus. Dirs., Art. Mus. Assn. Am., Mountain Plains Assn. Mus., Nat. Council Edn. Ceramic Arts, Am. Craft Council, Okla. Mus. Assn. Office: Philbrook Mus Art 2727 S Rockford Rd Tulsa OK 74114

MANIACI, ELIZABETH HOFFER, bank executive; b. Muncie, Ind., July 23, 1955; d. Robert Morrison and Martha Cathern (Quirk) Hoffer; m. Thomas Vincent Maniaci, June 21, 1980. BS in Math., Econs., Tufts U., 1977; postgrad., U. Ariz., 1978-79. Internal auditor Wis. Telephone Co.,

Milw., 1979-80; tax acct. Arthur Andersen and Co., Detroit, 1980-83; assoc. v.p. Fireman's Fund Mortgage Corp., Farmington Hills, Mich., 1983—. Author (with others) (trade pub.) Tax Bibliography for Mortgage Bankers, 1986. Bd. dirs. Pontiac (Mich.) Art Ctr., 1980-82. Mem. Nat. Assn. Accts., Jr. League of Birmingham (Mich.) (pub. relations chmn. 1987-88). Club: Women's Econ. Home: 1751 Villa Birmingham MI 48009 Office: Firemans Fund Mortgage Corp 27555 Farmington Rd Farmington Hills MI 48018

MANIERO, BETH ANN, marketing professional; b. Pitts., Feb. 18, 1958; d. Daniel Albert and Mary Louise (Stabile) M. A in Bus., Wheeler Sch. of Merchandising, 1977. Sr. service asst. Hoffman-York, Inc., Milw., 1977-80; travel agt. AAA World-Wide Travel Agy., Milw., 1980-81; spl. events asst. The Boston Store, Milw., 1981-82; mktg. asst. Southridge Shopping Ctr., Greendale, Wis., 1982-83; mktg. dir. Huntington (W.Va.) Mall/The Cafaro Co., 1984, Crossgates Mall/The Pyramid Co., Albany, N.Y., 1984-86; mktg. mgr. The RREEF Funds/Baybrook Mall, Friendswood, Tex., 1986—. Mem. Nat. Assn. Female Execs., Internat. Council of Shopping Ctrs. (cert. mktg. dir.), Women's Resource Network, Clear Lake Area C. of C. Democrat. Roman Catholic. Club: Ad II (Milw.) (sec. treas. 1978-79). Home: 15534 Zabolio #118 Webster TX 77598 Office: The RREEF Funds/Baybrook Mall 500 Baybrook Mall Friendswood TX 77546

MANILLA, TESS, artist. Student, Bklyn. Mus. Art Sch., Arts Student League, Willimantic Tchr's. Coll.; studied with Leo Manso and Victor Candell, Provincetown Work Shop; studied with Morris Davidson, Pratt Graphic Workshop. pvt. tchr., 1962-83. One-woman shows include Village Art Ctr., N.Y. Long Island U., 1965, Contemporary Arts, Inc., N.Y., 1966, Lincoln Savs. Banks, 1976, Statesman's Club, N.Y., 1977; exhibited in group shows at Art U.S.A., N.Y., A.C.A. Gallery, N.Y., Audubon Artists, N.Y., Bklyn. Mus., Bklyn. Coll., Donnell Library, N.Y., Gallery #35, N.Y., Silvermine Guild of Artists, Conn., Prospect Park Centennial, Lever House, N.Y., Union Carbide, Nat. Arts Club, N.Y., Marist Coll., N.Y., Rockust Coll., Mo., Branden Art Gallery, Iowa, Aames Gallery, N.Y.; represented in private collections Long Island U., Butler Inst., Ohio, and various others. Recipient Merit Scholarship award Art Students League, 1987. Mem. Artists Equity Assn. of N.Y., League of Present Day Artists (Medal of Merit 1974), Bklyn. Arts Council (chmn. exhibits), N.Y. Soc. Women Artists (chmn. nominating com.), Nat. Assn. Women Artists (pub. relations chmn., award for painting 1972, 87), Met. Painters and Sculptors (hon. pres. 1984). Home: 140 Ocean Pkwy Brooklyn NY 11218

MANKILLER, WILMA PEARL, principal chief Indian tribe; b. Stilwell, Okla., Nov. 18, 1945; d. Charley and Clara Irene (Sitton) M.; m. Hector N. Olaya, Nov. 13, 1963 (div. 1975); children—Felicia Marie Olaya, Gina Irene Olaya. Student Skyline Coll., San Bruno College, Calif., 1973, San Francisco State Coll., 1973-75; B.A. in Social Sci., Flaming Rainbow Coll., Okla., 1977; postgrad. U. Ark., 1979. Community devel. dir. Cherokee Nation, Tahlequah, Okla., 1977-83, dep. chief, 1983-85, prin. chief, 1985-87; pres. Inter-Tribal Council Okla.; mem. exec. bd. Council Energy Resource Tribes; bd. dirs. Okla. Indsl. Devel. Commn. Bd. dirs. Okla. Acad. for State Goals, 1985—. Recipient Donna Nigh First Lady award Okla. Commn. for Status of Women, 1985, Am. Leadership award, Harvard U., 1986; inducted Okla. Women's Hall of Fame, 1986. Mem. Cherokee County Democratic Women's Club, Nat. Tribal Chairmen's Assn., Nat. Congress Am. Indians. Avocations: reading; writing. Office: Cherokee Prin Chief PO Box 948 Tahlequah OK 74465

MANLEY, AUDREY FORBES, physician; b. Jackson, Miss., Mar. 25, 1934; d. Jesse Lee and Ora Lee (Buckhalter) Forbes; m. Albert Edward Manley, Apr. 3, 1970. A.B. with honors (tuition scholar), Spelman Coll., Atlanta, 1955; M.D. (Jesse Smith Noyes Found. scholar), Meharry Med. Coll., 1959; MPH, Johns Hopkins U.-USPHS traineeship, 1987. Diplomate: Am. Bd. Pediatrics. Intern St. Mary Mercy Hosp., Gary, Ind., 1960; from jr. to chief resident in pediatrics Cook County Children's Hosp., Chgo., 1960-62; NIH fellow neonatology U. Ill. Research and Ednl. Hosp., Chgo., 1963-65; staff pediatrician Chgo. Bd. Health, 1963-66; practice medicine specializing in pediatrics Chgo., 1963-66; assoc. Lawndale Neighborhood Health Center North, 1966-67; asst. med. dir. 1967-69; asst. prof. Chgo. Med. Coll., 1966-67; instr. Pritzker Sch. Medicine, U. Chgo., 1967-69; asst. dir. ambulatory pediatrics, asst. dir. pediatrics Mt. Zion Hosp. and Med. Center, San Francisco, 1969-70; med. cons. Spelman Coll., 1970-71, med. dir. family planning program, chmn. health careers adv. com., 1972-76; med. dir. Grady Meml. Hosp. Family Planning Clinic, 1972-76; with Health Services Adminstrs., Dept. Health and Human Services, 1976—; commd. officer USPHS, 1976—; chief genetic diseases services br. Office Maternal and Child Health, Bur. Community Health Services, Rockville, Md., 1976-81; acting assoc. adminstr. clin. affairs Office of Adminstr. Health Resources and Services Adminstrn., 1981-83, chief med. officer, dep. assoc. adminstr. planning, evaluation and legis., 1983-85; sabbatical leave USPHS Johns Hopkins Sch. Hygiene and Pub. Health, 1986-87; dir. Nat. Health Service Corps., 1987—. Author numerous articles, reports in field. Trustee Spelman Coll., 1966-70. Recipient Meritorious Service award USPHS, 1981, Mary McLeod Bethune award Nat. Council Negro Women, 1979; also numerous service and achievement awards. Fellow Am. Acad. Pediatrics; mem. Nat. Inst. Medicine of Nat. Acad. Sci., Nat. Med. Assn., Am. Public Health Assn., AAUW, AAAS, Spelman Coll. Alumnae Assn., Meharry Alumni Assn., Operation Crossroads Africa Alumni Assn. Home: 2807 18th St NW Washington DC 20009 Office: Health Services Adminstrs HHS 5600 Fishers Ln Rockville MD 20857

MANLEY, BARBARA LEE DEAN, nurse, hospital administrator, consultant; b. Washington, Nov. 5, 1946; d. Robert L. Dean and Mary L. (Jenkins) Smallwood; m. Major Otis Manley, Nov. 16, 1969; 1 child, Laura Selena. B.S., St. Mary-of-the-Woods, Terre Haute, Ind., 1973; M.A., Central Mich. U., 1981. Indsl. nurse Ford Motor Co., Indpls., 1973-80; employee health nurse Starplex, Inc., Washington, 1981-84, Doctor's Hosp., Lanham, Md., 1984-85; regional occupational health nurse coordinator Naval Hosp., Long Beach, Calif., 1985—; project mgr. Health Care Network, Inc., Washington, 1980-84; cons. Health and Human Services, Washington, 1980-84; pvt. practice contract nurse specialist, Washington, 1980-84; part-time lectr. Compton (Calif.) Coll. Vol. ARC, Ft. Lewis, Wash., 1974-76, Ft. Harrison, Ind., 1978-80; counselor Crisis Hot-Line, Laurel, Md., 1981-83, Laurel Boy's and Girls Club, 1981-84. Fellow Acad. Ambulatory Nursing Adminstrs. (Honor plaque 1981); mem. Assn. Exec. Females, Am. Pub. Health Assn., Am. Nurses Assn., Am. Assn. Occupational Health Nurses, Assn. Hosp. Employee Health Profls. (sec. 1986—, conf. chairperson 1988, Outstanding Nurse of Yr. 1987), Fed. Occupational Safety and Health Council, Fed. Mgrs. Assn., Blacks in Govt., Cen. Mich. U. Alumni Assn. (sec. 1985—), Chi Eta Phi. Presbyterian. Avocations: reading; crocheting; traveling; roller skating. Office: Regional OHN Coordinator Br Med Clinic Naval Sta Long Beach CA 90822

MANLEY, CATHEY NERACKER, interior design executive; b. Rochester, N.Y., Feb. 10, 1951; d. Albert John and Eleanor (Roberts) Neracker; m. Keith Howard Manley, Dec. 2, 1972 (div. Sept. 1977). AS, Endicott Jr. Coll., Beverly, Mass., 1971. Interior designer Bayles Furniture Co., Rochester, 1971-78, dir. mktg. and design, 1978-81; pres. Fabric PROTECTION Rochester, 1982—; bus. cons. Susanne Wiener & Assocs., Stamford, Conn., 1981—; owner Cathey Manley Assocs., Rochester, 1981—; cons. Womens' Career Ctr., Rochester, 1976—. Contbr. to book: What Do You Say To A Naked Room, 1981. Mem. bldg. com. Rochester Health Assn., 1978-83; dir. Family Service of Rochester at Greece (N.Y.), 1973-76, Town of Greece Youth Bd., 1973-77; founder "The Point", Greece, 1971. Fellow Interior Design Soc. (pres. Rochester chpt. 1977-78, nat. bd. dirs. 1977—, nat. pres. at Chgo. 1983-85). Home: 1154 Edgemere Dr Rochester NY 14612

MANLEY, EDITH WALSH, business owner; b. St. Louis, Dec. 30, 1925; d. Daniel Edward and Katherine (Tierney) Walsh; m. Glenn J. Manley, Nov. 22, 1951; children: Moira, Deirdre, Megan. AA, Harris Tchrs. Coll., 1946; BS, St. Louis U., 1948; MPA, Calif. State U., 1980. Social services worker Oakland, Calif., 1970-82; owner Winicorp, San Leandro, Calif., 1982—; pres. Winitax, Inc., San Leandro, 1985—; tchr. San Leandro (Calif.) Schs., 1986-87; speech cons., San Francisco, 1986-87. Author: Layoff, Your Lucky Stars. Bd. dirs. Project Eden, Hayward, Calif., 1977, pres. 1979. Mem. San Leandro (Calif.) C. of C. Roman Catholic. Clubs: Toastmasters (pres. Skywest chpt. 1985-86, leader seminars 1985-87, dir. publicity 1986-87). Office: Winicorp PO Box 3314 San Leandro CA 94578

MANLEY, JOAN A(DELE) DANIELS, retired publisher; b. San Luis Obispo, Calif., Sept. 23, 1932; d. Carl and Della (Weinmann) Daniels; m. Jeremy C. Lanning, Mar. 17, 1956 (div. Sept. 1963); m. Donald H. Manley, Sept. 12, 1964 (div. 1985). B.A., U. Calif. at Berkeley, 1954; D.B.A. (hon.), U. New Haven, 1974; LL.D. (hon.), Babson Coll., 1978. Sec. Doubleday & Co., Inc., N.Y.C., 1954-60; sales exec. Time Inc., 1960-66, v.p., 1971-75, group v.p., 1975-84, also dir.; circulation dir. Time-Life Books, 1966-68, dir. sales, 1968-70, pub., 1970-76; chmn. bd. Time-Life Books Inc., 1976-80; vice chmn. bd. Book-of-the-Month Club, Inc., N.Y.C., until 1984; supervising dir. Time-Life Internat. (Nederland) B.V., Amsterdam, until 1984; bd. dirs. Scholastic Inc., Lehigh Press Inc., AON Corp., Sara Lee Corp. Trustee Mayo Found., Rochester, Minn., Friends of Photography, Carmel, Calif., Keystone Ctr., William Benton Found.; adv. council Stanford U. Bus. Sch., Harvard Divinity Sch., Berkeley Bus. Sch., Yosemite Nat. Insts. Mem. Assn. Am. Pubs. (past chmn.).

MANLEY, NANCY JANE, civil engineer; b. Ft. Smith, Ark., Sept. 13, 1951; d. Eugene Hailey and Mary Adele (Chave) M. BSE, Purdue U., 1974; MSE, U. Wash., 1976; postgrad., U. Minn., 1976-77. Lic. profl. engr., Ga. Sanitary engr. Minn. Dept. Health, Mpls., 1976-77; sanitary engr. water supply EPA, Chgo., 1977; leader primacy unit water supply EPA, Atlanta, 1977-79, leader tech. assistance team, 1979-82; chief environ. and contract planning USAF, Moody AFB, Ga., 1982-84; dep. base civil engr. USAF, Carswell AFB, Tex., 1984-86; dep. base civil engrs. USAF, Scott AFB, Ill., 1986—; mem. tech. adv. com. Scott AFB master plan study Belleville, Ill., 1986—; mem. Fla. Tech. Adv. Com. for Injection Wells, Tallahassee, 1980-82, Nat. Implementation Team for Underground Injection Control Program, Washington, 1979-82; judge Internat. Sci. and Engring. Fair, 1986. Vol. Meals-on Wheels, Girls Scouts, others, various towns, 1982—; crisis intervention counselor Midwest Alliance, West Lafayette, Ind., 1970-74. Recipient Disting. Govt. Service award Dallas/Ft. Worth Fed. Exec. Bd., 1986. Mem. NSPE, Soc. Women Engrs. (local offices 1979-82, 84-86), ASCE, Am. Women in Sci. Office: USAF Civil Engring 375 ABG/DED Scott AFB IL 62225-5045

MANLEY, RHONDA RAMSEYER, construction company executive; b. Detroit, July 11, 1956; d. Kenneth Ralph Ramseyer and Lila Mae Lee; m. Jeffrey Paul Manley, Mar. 3, 1979. Grad. high sch., Ft. Meyers, Fla. Bookkeeper Gyarmathy Enterprises, Inc., Ft. Meyers, 1979; bookkeeper full charge Housing Collaborative, Inc., Phoenix, 1979-81, Phoenix Physical Med. Ctr., 1981-82; comptroller Marko Painting, Inc., Phoenix, 1982—; cons. Michael L. Riddle, Inc., 1983-86; mgr. ops. Monroe L. Riddle, Inc., Phoenix, 1983—; pres., v.p. J&R Enterprises, Inc., 1983—; cons. B&D Painting, 1986. Author numerous poems. Recipient World of Poetry award, 1985, Silver Poet award, 1986, Golden Poet award, 1987. Mem. Nat. Assn. Female Execs. Office: J&R Enterprises Inc 13236 N 7th St 4-212 Phoenix AZ 85022

MANLY, CAROL ANN, speech and language pathologist; b. Canton, Ohio, Nov. 21, 1947; d. William George and Florence (Parrish) M.; m. Martin Tindel, 1987. B.S. in Edn. (PTA scholar, 1965, Penhellenic scholar, 1965), Kent State U., 1969; M.A. (VA fellow), U. Cin., 1970; PhD NYU, 1988. Instr., U. Cin. Med. Center, 1970-72; staff speech pathologist, NYU Med. Center, Goldwater Meml. Hosp., N.Y.C., 1972-75, sr. speech pathologist, 1975-78, supr., 1978-81, asst. dir., 1981-83; pvt. practice, 1983—; cons. speech pathologist Mary Manning Walsh Nursing Home, 1974-85, Drs. Hosp., 1983—; speaker profl. convs. Contbr. articles to profl. jours. Mem. Am. Speech-Lang.-Hearing Assn., N.Y. State Speech-Lang.-Hearing Assn. (com. communication problems of aging), N.Y.C. Speech-Lang.-Hearing Assn., N.Y. Acad. Sci.

MANN, ANGELA BIGGS, educational administrator; b. Atlanta, Apr. 4, 1951; d. Homer Daniel and Jewel (McCoy) Biggs; m. Justin S. Mann, Sept. 21, 1971; children—Justina, Alexis, Rahman. Degree in psychology and edn. Fisk U., 1968-72; postgrad. U. Minn., 1984—. Dir. edn. U. Islam, Nashville, 1973-75; math. instr. U.L. St. Acad., St. Paul, 1975; edn. coordinator Head Start, St. Paul, 1976; dir. child care Phyllis Wheatley Sch., Mpls., 1978-79; pub. relations mgr. Town Square, St. Paul, 1980-82; dir. Head Start, Ramsey Action Program, St. Paul, 1983—; resource access rep. Portage Project, Wis., 1984—. Bd. dirs. Minn. Assn. for Edn. Young Children, St. Paul, 1988—; rules rev. mem. Dept. Human Services State Child Care Rules Rev., St. Paul, 1985—; chmn. arts enrichment St. Anthony Park Sch. Assn., St. Paul, 1984-85; mem. youth allocations com. United Way, 1987—, youth day planning com. C. of C. Leadership, 1986-87; mem. St. Paul Pub. Schs. Early Childhood Family Edn. Adv. Council. Recipient Outstanding Service award Child Care Council, 1977. Mem. Nat. Assn. Edn. Young Children, Resources for Child Caring (v.p. 1977), Nat. Head Start Assn., Minn. Head Start Dirs. Assn. (v.p. 1986—), Nat. Black Child Devel. Inst. C. of C. (child care task force 1986-87), Nat. Assn. Female Execs., Fisk U. Alumni Assn. (sec. 1981—), Delta Sigma Theta (fin. sec. 1987-88). Democrat. Baptist. Home: 1291 Thomas Ave Saint Paul MN 55104 Office: Ramsey Action Program Head Start 586 Fuller Ave Saint Paul MN 55103

MANN, ELVA JAMES, dietitian, educator; b. Truxno, La., June 20, 1904; d. Abner and Lavada (Tugwell) James; m. John F. Kahrs, Jan. 11, 1934 (dec. 1953); m. Gus G. Kindervater, Dec. 14, 1955 (dec. 1963); m. Curt F. Mann, Oct. 10, 1968 (dec. 1973). BS, La. Poly. Inst., 1927. Dietetic intern Johns Hopkins Hosp., Balt., 1927-28, dietitian, 1928-29; dietitian Girl Scout Camp, Annapolis, Md., summer 1928-29; staff dietitian Touro Infirmary, New Orleans, 1929-35, dir. dietary dept., 1935-40, 42-49, dir. dietetic intern program, 1945-49; dir. dietetics Dept. Instns. State of La., Baton Rouge, 1940-42; dietitian Morrison Food Service, Bapt. Hosp. No. La., Crippled Children's Hosp., 1954. Bd. dirs. Silver Cross Nursing Home, 1973-76, King's Daus. Hosp., 1977-80; elder Presbyn. Ch., 1977—. Mem. Am. Dietetic Assn., Brookhaven C. of C., DAR, King's Daus. Aux. Republican. Clubs: Little Theater, Garden (pres. 1981-82). Avocations: gardening, theater, reading, gourmet cooking. Home: 631 S Church St Brookhaven MS 39601

MANN, GRACE CARROL, ballerina, choreographer, educator; b. Berkeley, Calif, Nov. 30; d. Robert H. and Nell Jeanette (Curry) M.; B.A., U. Calif., Berkeley, 1941; student Theodore Kosloff. Dancer, San Francisco Ballet and Opera, 1940, 41, Kosloff Ballet, Hollywood, Calif., 1942-46, film Spectre of the Rose for Ben Hecht, 1945; prin. dancer Original Ballet Russe of Col. de Basil including season Covent Garden, 1947-48; founder Studio of Dance Art, 1951; dir. Ballet Center, Oakland, Calif., 1971—; co-founder Ballet Valmann also choreography; instr. master classes; judge regional ballet auditions; choreography includes: Concerto in D (Poulenc), Concerto (Mendelssohn), Mikrocosmos (Bartok). Mem. Delta Epsilon. Republican. Avocations: reading, collecting paintings. Home: 5960 Margarido Dr Oakland CA 94618 Office: Ballet Ctr 452 Santa Clara Ave Oakland CA 94610

MANN, KAREN, consultant, educator; b. Kansas City, Mo., Oct. 9, 1942; d. Charles and Letha (Anderson) M. BA, U. Calif.-Santa Barbara, 1964; MPA, Golden Gate U., 1975, PhD, 1988. Cert. lay minister Order of Buddhist Contemplatives. Tchr. Sisters of Immaculate Heart, Los Angeles, 1964-68; group counselor San Francisco and Marin County Probation Depts., parole agt. Calif. Dept. Corrections, Sacramento and San Francisco, 1970-86; researcher and cons. Non-profit Orgnl. Devel., 1986—, Computer Applications for Persons with Disabilities, 1986—; adj. faculty Grad. Theol. Union, Berkeley, 1984—. Co-author: Prison Overcrowding, 1979; Community Corrections: A Plan for California, 1980. Active Buddhists Concerned for Animals, San Francisco, 1983—, Fellowship of Reconciliation, N.Y., 1970—; co-founder Network Ctr. for Study of Ministry, San Francisco, 1982; pres. San Francisco Network Ministries, 1980-82; mem. Disabled Children's Computer Resource Group, 1988—, Springwater Ctr. for Meditative Inquiry and Retreats, 1986—. Office: PO Box 377 Lagunitas CA 94938

MANN, KAREN NANCY, cosmetic company executive; b. Queens, N.Y., June 3, 1957; d. Paul and Anni (Eckenberger) M.; m. Robert L. Attride, Sept. 28, 1985. AS in Acctg. cum laude, Nassau Community Coll., 1977; BS in Acctg., U. Fla., 1980. CPA, N.Y. Sr. internal auditor Colt Industries, Inc., N.Y.C., 1980-82, div. laiason, 1982-84; dir. fin. Colt Industries Credit Corp., N.Y.C., 1984-85; internal mgmt. cons. Estee Lauder, Inc., N.Y.C., 1985-87, dir. fin. and Adminstrn., 1987—. Mem. Am. Inst. CPA's, Inst. Internal Auditors, Delta Sigma Pi. Roman Catholic. Home: 25 Pickwick Hill Dr Huntington NY 11746 Office: Estee Lauder Inc 767 Fifth Ave New York NY 10153

MANN, MARYLEN, foundation administrator; b. St. Louis, Mar. 13, 1937; d. Morris and Ruth (Sobel) Lipkind; (widowed); children: Robert Gordon, John Douglas. PhB, Wash. U., 1957, MA in Edn., 1959. Tchr. St. Louis Pub. Schs., 1961-62; supr. student tchrs. Dept. Edn. Wash. Metos U., St. Louis, 1969; instr. edn. U. Mo., St. Louis, 1972-74; instr. curriculum devel. Webster U., St. Louis, 1977-78; dir. various programs CEMREL Inc., St. Louis, 1974-82; dir. Older Adult Service and Info. System, fellow Ctr. Metro Studies, lctr. Dept. Edn. U. Mo., St. Louis, 1983-84; dir. Older Adults Services and Info. Systems Jewish Hosp., St. Louis, 1984—; research instr. Med. Sch. Wash. U., St. Louis, 1984—; bd. dirs. Gerontology Cencentration Adv. Com. Washington U. 1987—, Jewish Hosp. Women's Adv. Council Women's Health Resources 1986—, Jewish Hosp. Home Care Adv. Com. 1982—. Contbr. articles to profl. jours. Bd. dirs. Jewish Ctr. Aged, 1984-87, St. Louis Psychoanalytic Inst., 1983—, Arts and Edn. Council St. Louis, v.p., 1986, chmn. program com., 1986, Gov.'s Advy. Council Aging, Mo. exec. com., 1984-86, Gov.'s Task Force Alternative Care Elderly, 1982, Clayton (Mo.) Sch. Bd., 1970-84, pres., 1979-81, v.p., 1976, sec., 1975. Recipient numerous grants on care of the elderly; named Woman Yr., City Clayton, 1981, Woman of Achievement, St. Louis Globe Democrat, 1980. Mem. Nat. Council Aging Inc., Am. Soc. Aging, Western Gerontol. Assn., Sigma Phi Omega. Home: 900 Audubon Dr Clayton MO 63105 Office: Older Adult Service and Info System 4511 Forest Park Blvd Saint Louis MO 63108

MANN, SHERYL ANN, computer company executive; b. Wichita, Kans., July 11, 1955; d. Charles Edward Trump and Nancy Ann (Dunlap) Littlejohn; m. John Joseph Mann, Sept. 3, 1977; 1 child, Whitney Taylor. BS, Kans. State U., 1977. Asst. mgr. Fashion Conspiracy, Shreveport, La., 1978, mgr., 1979; from assoc. support rep. to support rep. Lanier Bus. Products, Oklahoma City, 1980, support supr., 1980-81; regional support mgr. Harris/Lanier Co., Dallas, 1982—; mem. Harris/Lanier Customer Service User Group, Dallas, 1984—. Mem. Dallas Mus. Art, 1985—. Mem. Nat. Assn. Female Execs., Alpha Chi Omega. Democrat. Roman Catholic. Home: 2410 Pebblebrook Ct Grand Prarie TX 75050 Office: Harris/Lanier Co 2777 Stemmons Suite 1188 Dallas TX 75207

MANNELLY, KATHY OLSON, associate dean, consultant, lecturer; b. Lawrence, Mich., Jan. 24, 1945; d. William Edward and Marjorie Ellen Olson; m. Patrick Kevin Mannelly, Apr. 9, 1980; stepchildren—Brian, Michael. A.B., Grand Rapids Jr. Coll., 1971; B.S. in Psychology, Grand Valley State Coll., 1973; postgrad. Pacific Luth. U., 1982. Lic. social worker, Mich. Coordinator edn., coordinator Sunrise Program, Project REHAB, Grand Rapids, Mich., 1974-75, supr. employee assistance resource, 1975-77, v.p. personnel and mktg., 1977-78; program analyst Dept. Mgmt. and Budget, State of Mich., Lansing, 1978-80; dir. coop. edn., govtl. grants officer Pacific Luth. U., Tacoma, 1980-83, assoc. dean for student life, 1983—; trainer, cons. Dymaxion Corp., Lansing, Profl. Update, Seahurst, Wash., 1975-82; lectr. in hiring practices. Recipient various awards. Mem. Am. Soc. Tng. and Devel., Coop. Edn. Assn., Nat. Assn. Student Personnel Adminstrs., Nat. Assn. Women Deans, Adminstrs. and Counselors, Nat. Orientation Dirs. Assn. (bd. dirs. 1986—), Office: Pacific Luth Univ Tacoma WA 98447

MANNERS, MARILYN KAY FEMI, accountant; b. Washington, Sept. 25, 1954; d. Nathaniel Richards and Odessa M. (Ross) M.; m. Richard Sanders, May 4, 1984 (div. Jan. 1985). BS, Bowie (Md.) State Coll., 1978. Systems acct. USN Dept., Alexandria, Va., 1976-79; auditor Pension Benefit Guaranty Corp., Washington, 1979-80, Calif. Dept. Health and Human Services, Sacramento, 1980-81, Def. Contract Audit Agy., San Jose, Calif., 1981; dir. fin. systems USN Acad., Annapolis, Md., 1981-83; lead auditor Army Audit Agy., Ft. Hood, Tex., 1983; dir. internal rev. Naval Air Sta., Key West, Fla., 1983-85; fin. auditor Adminstrv. Office-U.S. Cts., Washington, 1985; auditor Naval Audit Service, Arlington, Va., 1985-87; operating acct. Naval Data Automation Command, Washington, 1987—. Nominee Md. Commn. for Women, Balt., 1987. Named one of Outstanding Young Women in Am., 1982. Mem. Assn. of Govt. Accts., Am. Soc. of Mil. Comptrollers, Nat. Assn. of Female Execs., Womens Internat. Religious Fellowship, Alpha Kappa Alpha. Democrat. Baptist. Home: 109-69th St Seat Pleasant MD 20743 Office: Washington Navy Yard Naval Data Automation Command Bldg 166 Washington DC 20374-1662

MANNES, ELENA SABIN, television news and public affairs producer; b. N.Y.C., Dec. 3, 1943; d. Leopold Damrosch and Evelyn (Sabin) M. BA, Smith Coll., 1965; MA, Johns Hopkins U., 1967. Researcher Pub. Broadcast Lab. Nat. Edml. TV, N.Y.C., 1968-70; writer Sta. WPIX-TV, N.Y.C., 1970-73; assignment editor Sta. ABC-TB, N.Y.C., 1973-76; producer, writer Sta. WCBS-TV, N.Y.C., 1976-80; producer CBS News, N.Y.C., 1980-87, Pub. Affairs TV/Bill Moyers PBS Documentaries, N.Y.C., 1987—. Recipient Emmy awards Nat. Acad. TV Arts & Scis., 1984, 1985 (2), Peabody award 1985. Mem. Writers Guild Am., Dirs. Guild Am.

MANNING, CYNTHIA ANN, construction engineer; b. Selma, Ala., Dec. 23, 1956; d. Robert Eugene and Elizabeth (Brannan) M. BS in Bldg. Constrn., U. Fla., 1983. Project engr. Fed. Constrn. Co., St. Petersburg, Fla., 1984—. Mem. Alpha Xi Delta. Home: 12256 Country Walk Ln Jacksonville FL 32223 Office: Fed Constrn Co 800 2d Ave S Saint Petersburg FL 33731

MANNING, JOAN ELIZABETH, health service director; b. Davenport, Iowa, July 7, 1953; d. George John and Eugenie Joan (Thomas) Stolze; m. Michael Anthony Manning, July 30, 1977. BA, U. No. Iowa, 1975; postgrad., U. Minn., 1986—. Traveling collegiate sec. Alpha Delta Pi Nat. Sorority, Atlanta, 1975-76; recreational therapist Americana Healthcare Ctr., Mason City, Iowa, 1976-81; communication coordinator Area Agy. on Aging, Mason City, 1981-83; exec. dir. United Way Cerro Gordo County, Mason City, 1983-85, Health Fair of the Midlands, Omaha, 1985-87; dir. health services ARC, Omaha, 1987—. Author Health Notes monthly news column, Omaha, 1986-87. Bd. dirs. YMCA of U.S.A., Chgo., 1981-83, Mason City YMCA, 1980-84, Mason City Parks and Recreation Bd., 1983-85; mem. spl. adv. bd. Cerro Gordo County Human Services Bd., 1983-85; mem. spl. activities com. Omaha Wellness Council of Midlands, 1986—; chmn. wider opportunity task force Great Plains (Neb.) Girl Scouts U.S., 1986—. Mem. Nat. Assn. Female Execs., U. Minn. Alumnae Assn., Alpha Delta Pi. Republican. Roman Catholic. Office: ARC 3838 Dewey Omaha NE 68105

MANNING, MARGUERITE, university dean, clergywoman; b. Phoenix; d. Walter Jerald and Elizabeth (Smith) Manning; A.B., Scarritt Coll., 1942; M.A., Boston, 1943; M.Div., Union Theol. Sem., 1957; M.A., Columbia Tchrs. Coll., 1966, Ed.D., 1975. Ordained to ministry Congregationalist Ch.; dir. student activities U. Tenn., 1943-46; ednl. asst. Riverside Ch., N.Y.C., 1947-55; parish worker East Harlem Protestant Parish, 1955-57; minister East Congl. Ch. and Waits River Meth. Ch., Vt., 1958-61; tchr. English and phys. edn. Baghdad (Iraq) High Sch., 1961-62; adminstrv. asst. dept. guidance and student personnel adminstrn. Columbia Tchrs. Coll., 1962-66; research asso. Bank St. Coll. Edn., N.Y.C., 1966-68; with Bur. Research, N.Y.C. Bd. Edn., 1968-69; sec. personnel United Bd. Christian Higher Edn. in Asia, 1969-71; dean student affairs Rutgers U., Newark, 1971—. Active Red Feather drive; social worker ARC, Camp Shanks, N.Y., World War II; moderator Grafton-Orange Assn. Congl. Chs.; mem. minister's assn. Vt. Congl. Conf., 1958; pres. Women of Grace Ch., Newark; bd. dirs. YWCA. Mem. Nat. Assn. Women Deans and Counselors, Am. Assn. Ednl. Research, Am. Personnel and Guidance Assn., NEA, Am. Assn. Higher Edn., Am. Assn. U. Adminstrs., Bus. and Profl. Women's Club, Pi Lambda Theta (pres. Alpha Epsilon chpt. 1966-68, treas., 1969-72, chmn. nat. nominating com. 1966-67), Kappa Delta Pi, Phi Delta Kappa. Home: 351 Broad St Apt 1009 Newark NJ 07104

MANNING, MARLOU, psychotherapist; b. Tucson, June 2, 1956; d. William Herman and Carole Eleanor (Musgrove) McBratney. BA U. Ariz.,

1981; MA Calif. Grad. Inst., 1983, PhD, 1987. Lic. marriage, family and child counselor. Asst. to pres. Western Psychol. Services, Los Angeles, 1978-81; crisis counselor Cedars-Sinai Med. Ctr., Los Angeles, 1980-84; counselor South Bay Therapeutic Clinic, Hawthorne, Calif., 1982-84; psychotherapist PMC Treatment Systems, Los Angeles, 1984-85, Beverly Hills Counseling Ctr., 1984-85, Comprehensive Care Corp., Los Angeles, 1985-86; pvt. practice, Los Angeles, 1986—; counselor Brotman Med. Ctr., Los Angeles, 1982-83, Julia Ann Singer Ctr., Los Angeles, 1984; bd. dirs. Los Angeles Commn. Assualts Against Women. Mem. AAUW, Am. Orthopsychiat. Assn., Assn. Profls. Treating Eating Disorders, Women in Health, Am. Anorexia-Bulimia Assn., Nat. Assn. Female Execs., Calif. State Psychol. Assn., Calif. Assn. Marriage and Family Therapists. Democrat. Office: 9911 W Pico Blvd Suite 670 Los Angeles CA 90035

MANNING, SHERRY FISCHER, college president emerita, business executive; b. Washington, Apr. 28, 1943; d. Fred W. and Eleanor A. (Mertz) Fischer; B.A. cum laude, Western Md. Coll., 1965, L.H.D., 1980; M.A., William and Mary Coll., 1967; D.B.A., U. Colo. 1973; m. Charles W. Manning, Dec. 23, 1966; children—Shannon Marie, Charles Fischer, Kelly Eleanor. Mktg. rep., systems engr. IBM, 1967-71; staff assoc. Nat. Center for Higher Edn. Mgmt. Systems, 1971-72; exec. asst. to exec. dir. Nat. Commn. of the Financing of Postsecondary Edn., 1972-73; adj. prof. U. Colo., 1973-74; asst. prof. U. Kans., 1975-77; cons. to pres. for acad. planning Universidade Fed. de Ceara, 1976-77; exec. v.p. Colo. Women's Coll., 1977-78, pres., 1978-81, pres. emerita, 1981—; chief operating officer John Madden Co., Englewood, Colo., bd. dirs. 1984—; bd dirs. Solar Energy Research Inst., 1987—, Regis Coll., 1987—, Univ. So. Colo. Found., 1987—, United Bank Services Co., 1978-81, Imperial Am. Energy Inc., Adopt-A-School 1979-82, Denver Symphony 1979-82, Colo. Council on Econ. Edn., 1984-87, Colo. Assn. Commerce and Industry Ednl. Found., 1984-87, Colo. Assn. Commerce and Industry, 1985—; Recipient DAR Outstanding Citizen award, 1961, Faculty Devel. award U. Kans., 1976, Soroptimists Women Helping Women award, 1980. Mem. Nat. Women's Coalition, Women's Forum, Zonta, Altrusa. Republican. Presbyterian. Club: Com. of 200, Newcomen Soc. of U.S., Denver Met. Host: Community Affairs program Sta. KHOW 1979-80; contbr. articles in field. Office: John Madden Co 6312 S Fiddler's Green Circle Suite 150-E Englewood CO 80111

MANNING, SYLVIA, English studies educator; b. Montreal, Que., Can., Dec. 2, 1943; came to U.S., 1967; d. Bruno and Lea Bank; m. Peter J. Manning, Aug. 20, 1967; children—Bruce David, Jason Maurice. B.A., McGill U., 1963; M.A., Yale U., 1964, Ph.D. in English, 1967. Asst. prof. English Calif. State U.-Hayward, 1967-71, assoc. prof., 1971-75, assoc. dean, 1972-75; assoc. prof. U. So. Calif., from 1975, now prof., assoc. dir. Ctr. for Humanities, 1975-77, chmn. freshman writing, 1977-80, chmn. dept. English, 1980-83, vice provost, from 1984, now exec. v.p. Author: Dickens as Satirist, 1971; Hard Times: An Annotated Bibliography, 1984. Contbr. essays to mags. Woodrow Wilson fellow, 1963-64, 66-67. Mem. MLA, Dickens Soc. Office: Univ So Calif Dept English Los Angeles CA 90089 *

MANNION, ELIZABETH, music educator, mezzo-soprano; b. Seattle. BA, BS, U. Wash., 1950; postgrad., The Cornish Inst. Asst. prof. U. Mich., Ann Arbor, 1966-68; assoc. prof. Ind. U., Bloomington, 1968-73, prof., 1973-77; prof. Fla. State U., Tallahassee, 1977-78; Doty Disting. prof. U. Tex., Austin, 1978-84; vis. prof. U. Calif., Santa Barbara, 1984-85, prof., 1985—, dir. Summer Inst. for Vocal Research and Performance Practice, 1987; head voice dept. Aspen (Colo.) Music Festival, 1980-86. Debut at Town Hall, N.Y.C., 1961; leading roles in Carmen, Don Carlos, Il Trovatore, Die Walkure, Parsifal, Cosi fan Tutte, Don Giovanni; soloist command performance White House, Washington, Carnegie Hall, N.Y.C., Eastman Sch. Music, Nat. Gallery Art, Washington, Nat. Arts Found., N.Y.C., Atlanta Symphony, Aspen Festival Orch., Balt. Symphony, Boston Symphony, Cin. Symphony, Dallas Symphony, Detroit Symphony, Interlochen Arts Acad. Orch., Louisville Symphony, Nashville Symphony, NBC Symphony, Phila. Orch., Pitts. Symphony, Richmond Symphony, Seattle Symphony, Singapore Symphony; appeared with N.Y.C. Opera, NBC TV Opera, Bonn (Fed. Republic Germany) Opera, Chgo. Lyric Opera, Ind. Opera Theater, Houston Grand Opera, others. Recipient Excellence in Teaching award Nat. Fedn. Music Clubs, 1973, Sullivan Found. award, Nat. Arts award, Young Artist award Nat. Fedn. Music Clubs; Fulbright scholar, Kathryn Long Sch. Opera scholar; Martha Baird Rockefeller grantee. Office: U Calif Santa Barbara Santa Barbara CA 93106

MANNION PEER, GAIL MARGARET, small business owner; b. Passiac, N.J., Mar. 7, 1953; d. John Francis and Margaret Ellen (Brennan) Mannion; m. Warren Franklin Peer, Dec. 6, 1986. BA, William Paterson Coll., 1975. Apprentice Community Opticians, Paramus and Elizabeth, N.J., 1975-80, optician, 1980-84; mgr. Anspach Bros. Opticians, Sea Girt, N.J., 1984-86; prin. Gail's Optical Shoppe, Sea Girt, 1986—. Mem. Soc. Dispensing Opticians, Nat. Assn. Self Employed, Nat. Acad. Opticianry, Women's Sports Found., Wall Twp. C. of C. Democrat. Roman Catholic.

MANNIS, VALERIE SKLAR, lawyer; b. Green Bay, Wis., May 26, 1939; d. Phillip and Rose (Aaron) Sklar; m. Kent Simon Mannis, Dec. 28, 1958; children: Andrea, Marci. BS, U. Wis., 1970; JD, 1974. Bar: Wis. 1974. Staff atty. Legis. Council, Madison, Wis., 1974-75; sole practice, Madison, 1975-84; asst. to pres. Bank of Shorewood Hills (Wis.), 1984-86; trust officer First Wis. Nat. Bank, Madison, 1986—; founding mem. Legal Assn. for Women, Madison, 1975—. Pres. Nat. Women's Polit. Caucus Dane County, Madison, 1984; bd. dirs. Madison Estate Planning Council, 1980-84, Madison Jewish Community Council, 1975-79, 82-84. Mem. ABA, Dane County Bar Assn. (chmn. property com. 1978-84), State Bar. Wis. (gov. 1980-86), Nat. Assn. Banking Women. Lodge: Rotary. Office: First Wis Nat Bank PO Box 7900 Madison WI 53707

MANNS, SCOTTE HARRIS, newspaper executive; b. Phillippi, W.Va., Jan. 25, 1937; d. William Alvin and Gracelyn Anna (Reed) Harris; grad. Elizabeth (Pa.) High Sch., 1953; m. Don Franklin Manns, Sept. 23, 1961. Adminstr. classified advt. Des Moines Register & Tribune, 1962-63; adminstr. classified advt. Washington Post, 1963-65, supr., 1965-71, asst. mgr., 1971-73, mgr., 1973-76, asst. to v.p. sales, 1976—, advt. mgr., 1976—, dir. advt. sales, 1985—. Mem. Washington Bd. Trade, Advt. Club Washington. Home: 4203 38th Rd N Arlington VA 22207 Office: 1150 15th St NW Washington DC 20071

MANOFF, DINAH BETH, actress; b. N.Y.C.; d. Arnold and Lyova (Rosenthal) (Lee Grant) M. Student public schs., N.Y. and Calif. Appeared in: TV series Soap, 1977-78; TV movie appearances include Raid on Entebbe, 1977, High Terror, 1977, The Possessed, 1977, For Ladies Only, 1981, A Matter of Sex, 1984, The Seduction of Gina, 1984, Celebrity, 1984, Flight #90, 1984, Classified Love, 1986; stage performances include I Ought To Be In Pictures (Tony award), 1980 (Theatre World award); films include Grease, 1977, Ordinary People, 1979, I Ought To Be in Pictures, 1981, Gifted Children, 1983, Leader of the Pack, 1984-85, Alfred and Victoria: A Life, Los Angeles Theatre Ctr., 1986-87. Mem. Screen Actors Guild, Actors Equity, AFTRA. Jewish. Home: New York NY Office: care The Gersh Agy Inc 130 W 42nd St Suite 1804 New York NY 10036 *

MANSEAU, MELISSA MARIE, infosystems specialist; b. Exeter, N.H., Mar. 24, 1962; d. Stuart Wayne and Dorothy Edith (Follis) Cady; m. Gerald Vincent Manseau. AS in Electronic Engring. Tech., N.H. Tech. Inst., Concord, 1982; BS in Computer Sci., U. So. Maine, 1988. Assoc. system technician Nat. Semiconductor Corp. (formerly Fairchild Semiconductor), South Portland, Maine, 1982-83, system technician, 1983-85, sr. system technician, 1985, assoc. computer system engr., 1985-88, software engr., 1988—. Mem. IEEE, IEEE Computer Soc., Nat. Assn. Female Execs. Congregationalist. Home: 10 Pinecrest Dr Hollis Center ME 04042

MANSFIELD, KAREN LEE, nurse; b. Chgo., Feb. 25, 1944; d. Marshall Ness and Leona (Grimsley) Sorenson; m. James B. Mansfield, Feb. 22, 1980; children: Kristin, Anthony, Robert, Jon. AS, Elgin Community Coll., 1970-74. RN, Ill. Staff nurse, surgery Sherman Hosp., Elgin, Ill., 1974-78; clin. instr. surgery Sherman Hosp., Elgin, 1978-80; pres. KLM Neurol. Assistance, Dundee, Ill., 1980—; office mgr. Neurol. and Spinal Surgery, Ltd., Elgin, 1985—. Active Elgin Symphony Auxillary. Mem. Assn. Operating Registered Nurses Aux., Kane County Med. Soc. Aux., Am. Med. Soc., Ill. State Med. Soc. Aux. Office: Neurol & Spinal Surgery Ltd 901 Center St Suite 107 Elgin IL 60120

MANSFIELD, LOIS EDNA, mathematics educator, researcher; b. Portland, Maine, Jan. 2, 1941; d. R. Carleton and Mary (Bowdish) M. BS, U. Mich., 1962; MS, U. Utah, 1966, PhD, 1969. Vis. asst. prof. computer sci. Purdue U., 1969-70; asst. prof. computer Sci. U. Kans., Lawrence, 1970-74, assoc. prof., 1974-78; assoc. prof. math. N.C. State U., Raleigh, 1978-79; assoc. prof. applied math. U. Va., Charlottesville, 1979-83, prof., 1983—; mem. adv. panel computer sci. NSF, 1975-78; cons., vis. scientist Inst. Computer Applications in Sci. and Engring., Hampton, Va., 1976-78. Mem. editorial bd. Jour. Sci. Statis. Computing, 1979—; contbr. articles to profl. jours. Grantee NSF and DOE. Mem. Am. Math. Soc., Soc. Indsl. and Applied Math., Assn. Computing Machinery (bd. dirs. SIGNUM 1980-83). Office: U Va Dept Applied Math Thornton Hall Charlottesville VA 22901

MANSI, MARY P., financial analyst; b. N.Y.C., Oct. 25, 1938; d. Vincent F. and Marie (Del Guidice) Fusco; m. Joseph A. Mansi, Aug. 1, 1959; children: Karen Marie, Jeanine. Student, Douglass Coll., Rutgers U.; BS, SUNY. Cert. fin. planner Adelphi Coll. Tchr. Holy Redeemer Sch., Kensington, Mo., 1958-60; with fin. pub. relations dept. Corp. Relations Network Inc., N.Y.C., 1976-80; reg. rep. First Investors Corp., Melville, N.Y., 1980-83; fin. planner, reg. rep. IDS-Am. Express Co., Melville, 1983-85; fin. planner Cornwall/Matrix Inc., Great Neck, N.Y. Mem. Nat. Assn. Female Execs. Home: 10 Beatrice Ln Glen Cove NY 11542 Office: Cornwall/Matrix Inc Great Neck NY 11021

MANSMANN, CAROL LOS, judge; b. Pitts., Aug. 7, 1942; d. Walter Joseph and Regina Mary (Pilarski) Los; m. J. Jerome Mansmann, June 27, 1970; children: Michael, Casey, Megan, Patrick. B.A., J.D., Duquesne U.; LL.D., Seton Hill Coll., Greensburg, Pa., 1985. Asst. dist. atty. Allegheny County, Pitts., 1968-72; assoc. McVerry Baxter & Mansmann, Pitts., 1973-79; assoc. prof. law Duquesne U., Pitts., 1973-82; judge U.S. Dist. Ct. Pa., Pitts., 1982-85, U.S. Ct. Appeals, Phila., 1985—; mem. Pa. Criminal Procedural Rules Com., Pitts., 1972-77; spl. asst. atty. gen. Commonwealth of Pa., 1974-79; bd. dirs. Pa. Bar Inst., Harrisburg, 1984—. Mem. adv. bd. Villanova U. Law Sch., 1985—. Recipient St. Thomas More award, 1983. Mem. Nat. Assn. Women Judges, ABA, Pa. Bar Assn., Fed. Judges Assn., Am. Judicature Soc., Allegheny County Bar Assn., Phi Alpha Delta. Republican. Roman Catholic. Office: US Ct Appeals 402 US PO and Courthouse 7th & Grant Sts Pittsburgh PA 15219 *

MANSUR, JULIANE LOUISE, urban planner; b. Detroit, June 17, 1957; d. George Alexander and Rachel Eloise (Anthony) Mansur. BA in Geography, U. Calif., Santa Barbara, 1979; MA in Urban & Regional Planning, U. Hawaii, 1985. Environ. reviewer State of Hawaii Environ. Ctr., Honolulu, 1984-85; urban planner City & County of Honolulu Dept. Land Utilization, 1984-85, Research Corp./Sea Grant Extension, Honolulu, 1985; environ. planner R.M. Parsons Co., Honolulu, 1985—. Mem. Am. Planning Assn. (exec. com. 1985-87). Home: 61-732 Papailoa Rd Haleiwa HI 96712 Office: RM Parsons Co 567 S King St Honolulu HI 96813

MANTELL, JOANNE ELLEN, public health researcher; b. Phila., June 9, 1942; d. Nate Margolin and Pearl (Malis) Benoliel; m. Lester Jay Mantell, Dec. 5, 1970. AB, Temple U., 1964; MS, Columbia U., 1966; MS in Pub. Health, UCLA, 1978, PhD, 1982. Dir. service and rehab. cen. Los Angeles unit Am. Cancer Soc., Los Angeles, 1972-75; vis. lectr. Sch. Social Welfare UCLA, 1980-83; prin. investigator AIDS prevention research program Gay Men's Health Crisis, N.Y.C., 1986—; interagy. research coordinator div. AIDS program services N.Y.C. Dept. Health, 1987—; cons. Met. Hosp. Ctr., N.Y.C., 1986, Ohio State Dept. Health, Columbus, 1987. Author jours., contbr. chpts. to books. Pres., bd. dirs. 830-832/34 Broadway Owners Assn., N.Y.C., 1984-87. Grantee Am. Cancer Soc. Calif. div., 1982-87, Commonwealth Fund, 1985-86, Ctrs. Disease Control, 1986-88. Mem. Am. Pub. Health Assn., Am. Sociol. Assn., Soc. Behavioral Medicine, The Gerontol. Soc. Am. Home: 832 Broadway New York NY 10003 Office: NYC Dept Health Div of AIDs Program Services 125 Worth St Box A/I New York NY 10014

MANTHEY, MERRILY RUTH, psychotherapist, educator, consultant; b. Seattle, Mar. 25, 1943; d. Russell S. and Ruth B. Kolemaine; B.A., Evergreen State Coll., 1976. Lic. therapist, Washington; postgrad. m. Arnold E. Manthey, Mar. 29, 1962 (dec.); 1 son, Scott. Research publs. supr. Stanford Research Inst., Huntsville, Ala., 1965-67; communications dir. Marine Constrn. & Design Co., Seattle, 1967-71; pvt. practice therapy, 1971—; instr., public affairs dir. Seattle Acad., 1971-72; owner, dir., tchr. Kent (Wash.) Montessori Sch., 1972-76; instr. Green River Coll., 1974—; dir., therapist Inst. Exec. Stress Mgmt., Inc., Kent, 1976—; cons. human relations; legis. aide to Wash. senator Kent Pullen, 1977-79, lic. cons., 1977—. Ednl. div. chmn., communications dir. Wash. Taxpayers Assn., Citizens Taxpayers Assn.; supr. King Tut Exhbn., Seattle Art Museum, 1978; mem. Kent Arts Commn., 1985—; singer The Rainier Chorale. Recipient Torch award Nat. Honor Soc., 1961; cert. Internat. Found. Human Relations, Amsterdam, Holland, 1980. Mem. Am. Soc. Group Psychotherapy and Psychodrama, Internat. Stress and Tension Control Assn., Assn. Transpersonal Psychology, Internat. Assn. Progressive Montessorians (cert. 1971), Am. Assn. Counseling and Devel., Club: Psychodrama of Wash. Author: Editorial Standards Guide, 1965; How to Promote Your Cause, 1975; editor: The Sou'Wester, 1961; research on stress, human sexuality. Nov. 10, 1986 proclaimed Merrily Manthey Day, Mayor, City of Kent, Wash. Home: PO Box 873 Kent WA 98035 Office: 317A W Meeker St Suite E Kent WA 98032

MANTHORNE, JACKIE ANN, writer, adminstrator; b. Halifax, N.S., Can., Dec. 3, 1946; d. Ralph Eugene and Mildred Freda (Rhuland) M.; BA, Dalhousie U., 1968, BE, 1970. Teaching asst. Miriam Sch. for the Exceptional, Montreal, Que., Can., 1972-73; tchr. Peter Hall Sch. for the Exceptional, Montreal, 1973-75; info. officer Women's Ctr. of Montreal, 1975-78, asst. dir., 1978-86, dir. adminstrv. services, 1986—; pub., editor Les Editions Communiqu' Elles, 1981—. Mem. Internat. Women's Writing Guild, Women's Centre of Montréal, Federation des femmes du Quebec, Centre Investigative Journalism. Editor Communiqu' Elles. (French and English), 1975—, Montreal Women's Directory (French and English), 1977, 80, 82, 85, Canadian Women's Directory (French and English), 1987, Newcomer's Handbook (French, English, Greek, Portuguese, Hindi), 1979. Office: 3585 St-Urbain, Montreal, PQ Canada H2X 2N6

MANTICA, PAMELA ANN, nurse, consultant; b. Albany, N.Y., Nov. 12, 1956; d. Joseph Richard and Patricia Ann (Nunnally) M. ASin Bus. Adminstrn., Hudson Valley Community Coll., 1984; BBA, SUNY, 1987. Cert. in nursing, Albany Med. Ctr., 1977; RN, N.Y. Nurse St. Clare's Hosp., Schenectady, N.Y., 1978-81; critical care nurse Meml. Hosp., Albany, N.Y., 1981-88; nurse cons. Nounan, Trone, Gutermuth & O'Connor, Troy, N.Y., 1987—; profl. services rep. Upstate Imaging and So. Tier Imaging, Latham and Johnson City, N.Y., 1988—. Mem. Nat. Assn. Female Execs., Beta Gamma Sigma, Phi Gamma Nu (recipient scholarship key). Home: 1260 New Loudon Rd Apt. B3 Cohoes NY 12047 Office: 7 Century Hill Dr Latham NY 12110

MANTON, DEBORAH JEAN, chemist; b. Phila., Feb. 16, 1955; d. Russell Frederick and Lois Eileen (Lord) M.; B.A., Franklin and Marshall Coll., 1976; B.S. in Engring. Physics, Washington U. 1978; postgrad. Rochester Inst. Tech., 1981—. Devel. engr. Corning Glass Works, Erwin, N.Y., 1978-80; mfg. devel. engr. Xerox Corp., Webster, N.Y., 1980-82; project mgr. Schlegel Corp., Rochester, N.Y., 1982-83; chief chemist Delco Products div. Gen. Motors, 1983—. Chmn. Rochester area alumni admissions asst. program Franklin and Marshall Coll., 1981-82; treas. Rochester Against Intoxicated Drivers, 1986—. NSF fellow, 1976. Mem. Soc. Women Engrs., Nat. Soc. Profl. Engrs., Assn. Finishing Profls., Soc. Mfg. Engrs., Am. Electroplating Soc. Democrat. Episcopalian. Home: 110 Southland Dr Rochester NY 14623 Office: 1555 Lyell Ave Rochester NY 14606

MANTOVANI, JUANITA MARIE, university dean, educator; b. Chgo., Sept. 18, 1943; d. Norman Bert and Marie Frances (Byczkowski) Watson; A.B. summa cum laude, Marymount Coll., 1965; A.M., UCLA, 1966; Ph.D. in English, U. So. Calif., 1974; m. Robert Albert Mantovani, June 6, 1970. Acting chmn. freshman English program U. So. Calif., 1972-73, asst. dean student affairs, 1973-75, asst. dean humanities, 1975-81, chmn. ethnic studies program, 1980-81, mem. English faculty, 1966-75, mem. adj. faculty, program for study women and men in society, 1975-81; dean undergrad. studies, assoc. prof. English, Calif. State U., Los Angeles, 1981-87, prof., 1987—; mem. English faculty Long Beach City Coll., 1974-77, Pepperdine U. Liberal Studies Program, 1975-77; lectr., condr. workshops on profl. devel. for women, career devel. and liberal arts edn., images of women and ethnic minorities in lit. and media; video and lecture presentations in field. panelist Nat. Endowment for Humanities Research Seminar on Feminism, 1979. Mem. U. So. Calif. Women in Mgmt. (founder 1979—). Office: Calif State U ADM 707 5151 State University Dr Los Angeles CA 90032

MANTYLA, KAREN, sales executive; b. Bronx, N.Y., Dec. 31, 1944; d. Milton and Sylvia (Diamond) Fischer; m. John A Mantyla, May 30, 1970 (div. 1980); 1 child, Michael Alan. Student, Rockland Community Coll., Suffern, N.Y., 1962, NYU, 1967, Mercer U., 1981. Mktg. coordinator Credit Bur., Inc., Miami, Fla., 1973-79; dist. mgr. The Research Inst. Am., N.Y.C., 1979-80, regional dir., 1980-85, field sales mgr., 1985-86, nat. sales mgr., 1986-87; dir. mktg. TempsAmerica, N.Y.C., 1987—. Mem. Sales and Mktg. Execs. of N.Y. (bd. dirs., v.p. Ft. Lauderdale chpt. 1979), Nat. Assn. Female Execs. Home: 3 Rockledge Dr Suffern NY 10901 Office: TempsAmerica 41 E 42d St New York NY 10017

MANUEL, KAREN LEE, educator; b. Boston, Oct. 7, 1947; d. Paul William and Joyce Anderson (Jones) Kind; m. Thomas G. Manuel, Dec. 21, 1968 (div. June 1981); children: Scott, Keith, Todd. BS in Edn., Baldwin Wallace Coll., 1969; MS in Edn., Adelphi U., 1974. Cert. tchr. N.Y., Va., Conn. Tchr. Lauderdale (Mich.) Pub. Schs., 1969-70, Virginia Beach (Va.) Pub. Schs., 1970-72, Garden City (N.Y.) Pub. Schs., 1972-76, New Canaan (Conn.) Pub. Schs., 1976-80; owner, pres. Toddler Time Nursery Sch., Inc., New Canaan, 1980—, also bd. dirs. V.p. Teen Ctr. of New Canaan, 1987; bd. dirs. New Canaan YMCA, 1982-86. Mem. Nat. Assn. Edn. of Young Children, Conn. Assn. Edn. of Young Children, Conn. Assn. of Children with Learning Disabilities. Republican. Home: 36 Rilling Ridge New Canaan CT 06840 Office: Toddler Time Nursery Sch Inc 23 Park St New Canaan CT 06840

MANUELL, LYNN MARIE, cultural administrator, singer, actress; b. Grand Rapids, Mich., Apr. 17, 1961; d. Richard James and Barbara Ann (Reeves) M. AA, Prairie State Coll., Chicago Heights, Ill., 1983; BA with honors, Columbia Coll., Chgo., 1985; student, Am. Acad. Dramatic Arts, N.Y.C., 1985-86, Wavendon Allmusic Plan, U.K., 1987-88. Singer, actress Ill. Theatre Ctr., Park Forest, Ill., 1975-83; singer Whaler/Madison Towers, N.Y.C., 1986; pub. relations photographer Columbia Coll., Chgo., 1983-84, Connie Zonka and Assocs., Chgo., 1984; mgr. Raymond Annlisa Promotional, N.Y.C., 1985; office coordinator Nat. Shakespeare Co., N.Y.C., 1985-86; promotional sales agt. Cliff Steward & Assocs., N.Y.C., 1985, various Broadway shows, N.Y.C., 1985-87; spl. events coordinator Cultural Council Found., N.Y.C., 1986—; asst. coordinator Minority Arts Mgmt., N.Y.C., 1987; events coordinator Soho Booking, N.Y.C., 1987, Community Literacy Research Project, N.Y.C., 1987; singer in N.Y., London and Chgo. Clubs, Spirit of N.Y. Cruise Ship. Author: (poetry) Unicorns and Golden Traces, 1981; contbr. articles to profl. jours. Friend, Community Literacy Research Project, N.Y.C., 1986-87; polit. worker NOW, Chgo., 1978-80; assoc. Am. Theatre Wing, N.Y.C., 1986; mem. Com. to Save Times Sq. Mem. Nat. Orgn. Female Execs., Theatre Devel. Fund, Am. Friends of Royal Shakespeare Co., Dickens Fellowship of N.Y. Home: 110 Post Ave #507 New York NY 10034 Office: Spirit of N Y Cruise Line Pier 11 New York NY 10034

MANUSZAK, CAROLYN, college president. Pres. Villa Julie Coll., Stevenson, Md. Office: Villa Julia Coll Green Spring Valley Rd Stevenson MD 21153 *

MANUTI, ANNABELLE THERESA, advertising agency financial executive; b. Bklyn., Sept. 11, 1928; d. Decio Dan and Anna Michelle (Vanacore) Assorto; m. John Thomas Manuti, Dec. 31, 1958. Student, Hunter Coll., 1950, postgrad. in real estate sch. Continuing Edn., 1980-82. Lic. real estate broker, N.Y. Statis. auditor Am. Fore Ins. Group, N.Y.C., 1950-55; bookkeeper Picard Advt., N.Y.C., 1955-60; supr. dept. acctg. Moquel Williams & Saylor Advt., N.Y.C., 1960-65; comptroller's asst. Frolich Advt., N.Y.C., 1965-70; supr. accounts payable Miller Advt., N.Y.C., 1970-80; v.p. fin. Jaffe Communications, N.Y.C., 1980—; real estate sales mgr. Gen. Devel. Corp., 1980-85. Roman Catholic. Home: 65-70 Booth St Rego Park NY 11374 Office: Jaffe Communications 122 E 42d St New York NY 10168

MANYEN, SUSAN MARY GAGER, automotive executive; b. Rochester, N.Y., Feb. 14, 1956; d. D. Jerome and Carol (Brady) Gager; m. Douglas Paul Manyen, Jan. 20, 1979; 1 child, Paul Douglas. B in Indsl. Adminstrn., Gen. Motors Inst., 1979; MBA, Saginaw (Mich.) Valley State Coll., 1982. Employee benefits rep. Gen. Motors Corp., Saginaw, 1980-83, supr. tech. services Cen. Foundry Div., 1983-86, gen. supr. engring. adminstrv. services, 1986—. Advisor Jr. Achievement, Saginaw, 1982—. Mem. Am. Foundrymen's Soc. (Saginaw Valley chpt. vice chmn. 1985-86, chmn. 1987—). Roman Catholic. Club: Gen. Motors Women's. Home: 4442 Shattuck Rd Saginaw MI 48603

MANZ, BETTY ANN, nurse administrator; b. Paterson, N.J., Nov. 30, 1935; d. James Albert and Elsie (Basse) Brown; diploma Newark Beth Israel Hosp. Sch. Nursing, 1955; B.S.N., Seton Hall U., 1964; m. Roger A. Johnson, Feb. 1988; children—Laura, Richard, Garry. Staff nurse operating room Newark Beth Israel Hosp., 1955-56, recovery room head nurse, 1956-57, operating room head nurse, 1957-58, supr. operating room, 1958-60; substitute tchr. pub. schs. Harding Twp., 1966-70; charge nurse St. Barnabas Med. Center, Livingston, N.J., 1965-70, head nurse emergency room, 1970-72; operating room supr. St. Clares Hosp., Denville, N.J., 1972-77; asst. dir. for operating rooms and post anesthesia rooms Newark Beth Israel Med. Center, 1977-82; asst. dir. nursing operating room care program Thomas Jefferson U. Hosp., Phila., 1982-84; asst. dir./assoc. nursing dir. operating room, anesthesia ICU, ambulatory surgery Univ. Hosp., SUNY-Stony Brook, 1984-87 dir. OR/PACU Amb surgery Med. Ctr. Del., Wilmington and Christiana, Del., 1987—; faculty mem. postgrad. course in microsurg for Am. Coll. Obstetricians and Gynecologists, Newark, 1982; profl. cons. operating room products, also health cons. Henry E. Wessel Assos., Moraga, Calif.; profl. tech. cons., lectr. Surgicot, Inc., Smithtown, N.Y. Dep. dir. Harding Twp. CD, 1967-75. Recipient Service award Essex County Med. Soc., 1979. Mem. AAMI, Am. Nurses Assn., N.Y. State Nurses Assn., Assn. Operating Room Nurses, Am. Soc. Post Anesthesia Nurses, Newark Beth Israel Hosp. Nursing Alumnae Assn., Seton Hall U. Alumnae Assn., Harding Twp. Civic Assn., Am. Field Service. Republican. Club: Mt. Kemble Lake Community. Editor operating room sect. SCORE mag. Home: 2620 Lamper Ln Wilmington DE 19808 Office: PO Box 1668 Wilmington DE 19899

MANZO, VALERIE SUSAN, lawyer; b. Bklyn., Dec. 6, 1951; d. Fred Vincent and Aurelia Regina (DeDomenico) M. BA, SUNY, Stony Brook, 1973; JD, St. John's Law Sch., Jamaica, N.Y., 1979. Bar: N.Y. 1980, U.S. Ct. Appeals (2nd cir.) 1980, U.S. Dist. Ct. (ea. and so. dists.) N.Y. 1984, U.S. Supreme Ct. 1984. Caseworker Suffolk Social Services, Hauppauge, N.Y., 1976-80; asst. dist. atty. Suffolk County, 1980-83; asst. town atty. Town of Smithtown, N.Y., 1983-84; mgr. govt. relations Viacom Cablevision, Hauppauge, 1984—. Mem. Suffolk County Women's Bar Assn. (pres. 1984-85, bd. dirs. 1985—), Suffolk County Bar Assn., N.Y. Cable T.V. Assn., Columbian Lawyers Assn. (treas., sec., v.p., pres. 1987-88). Republican. Home: 49-3A Richmond Blvd Ronkonkoma NY 11779 Office: Viacom Cablevision Box 1600 Motor Pkwy Hauppauge NY 11788

MAPLE, MARILYN JEAN, educational media coordinator; b. Turtle Creek, Pa., Jan. 16, 1931; d. Harry Chester and Agnes (Dobbie) Kelley; B.A., U. Fla., 1972, M.A., 1975, Ph.D., 1985; 1 dau., Sandra Maple. Journalist various newspapers, including Mountain Eagle, Jasper, Ala., Boise (Idaho) Statesman, Daytona Beach (Fla.) Jour., Lorain (Ohio) Jour.; account exec. Frederides & Co., N.Y.C.; producer hist. films Fla. State Mus., Gainesville, 1967-69; writer, dir., producer med. and sci. films and TV prodns. for six medically related colls. U. Fla., Gainesville, 1969—; pres.

Media Modes, Inc., Gainesville. Recipient Blakslee award, 1969, spl. award, 1979, Monsour Lectureship award, 1979. Mem. Health Edn. Media Assn. (dir., awards, 1977, 79), Phi Delta Kappa, Kappa Tau Alpha. Columnist: Health Care Edn. mag.; contbr. Fla. Hist. Quar. Home: 6722 SW 53d Ave Gainesville FL 32608 Office: U Fla Box J-16 Gainesville FL 32610

MAPLES, GLORIA JEAN, artist; b. Memphis, May 18, 1949; d. Hassel Dixon and Ruby Gwendolyn (Garner) Rudd; m. Thomas Roy Maples, July 22, 1973. B.F.A., U. Houston, 1981. Respiratory therapist, various med. instns. and physicians, Dallas, 1970-74; dental asst., Houston, 1975-78; efficiency organizer Harper Oil Tool Co., Houston, 1978-80; artist in clay and fiber, 1978—; propr. G.J.R.M. Designs, Houston, 1983—. Exhibited one-woman retrospective of weavings Mancuso Houston Library, 1983, Loomworks Gallery, San Antonio, 1986; group shows including Sarah Campbell Gallery, Houston, 1980, 82, Glassell Sch. Art, 1982, Lawndale Art Annex Gallery, Houston, 1982; pvt. commns.: sculpture clay mural Spring, 1986, Earth/Wind, 1987, Fire/Rain, 1988, sculpture clay flooring Ocean Spray, 1988. Mem. Tex. Fine Arts Assn., Ceramic Assn. (pres. Houston 1981-82, promoter, coordinator juried exhibit 1982), Am. Craft Council. Office: G J R M Designs 7507 Hereford St Houston TX 77087

MAPP, RAMONA HARTLEY, educator; b. Hartleys Corners, Ala., Jan. 18; d. Smith Culp and Annie Bess (Owens) Hartley; student Ind. U., 1956-57, City Lit. Inst., London, 1959-61, Huntingdon Coll., 1961-62; BA, Old Dominion U., 1965, MA, 1966; EdD, Va. Poly. Inst. and State U., 1980; m. Malcolm Conner Hamby, June 26, 1949 (dec. Jan. 1967); children—Gregory Stuart, Geoffrey Alan; m. 2d, Alf Johnson Mapp, Jr., Aug. 1, 1971. Instr. English, Old Dominion U., Norfolk, Va., 1966-69, 70-71; instr. English, Tidewater Community Coll., Portsmouth, Va., 1971-73, English coordinator, 1973-74, chmn. div. humanities and social scis., 1974-87, prof. English, 1988—; judge internat. essay contest Nat. Assn. Tchrs. of English, 1974; profl. devel. coordinator Southeastern Conf. English in Two-Year Coll., 1981, state rep., 1977-82, asst. program chmn., 1983, program chmn., 1984. Mem. Portsmouth Pub. Library Bd., 1978-81, chmn., 1978-80; bd. dirs. Tidewater Child Care Assn., 1974-81, pres., 1975-77; v.p. Tidewater Literacy Council, 1971-72; corr. sec. Poetry Soc. Va., 1975-76; bd. dirs. Va. Opera Guild, 1980-86, Met. Arts Congress, 1980-82, Cultural Alliance Hampton Roads, 1984-86, Young Audiences Va., Tidewater Assembly Family Life. Recipient Nat. Service award Family Found. Am., 1980; named Outstanding Profl. Woman of Hampton Roads, 1984. Mem. AAUW (v.p. Portsmouth chpt. 1983-85), South Atlantic MLA (sec. two-yr. coll. sect. 1982, program chmn. 1983, chmn. nominating com. 1986), Am. Assn. Colls. and Jr. Colls. (nat. com. internationalizing the curriculum 1976-80), South Atlantic Assn. Depts. English (adminstrv. com. 1983—, v.p. and pres.-elect 1986-87, pres. 1987—), Internat. Intercultural Consortium, Old Dominion U. Friends of Women's Studies (bd. dirs.), Nat. Women's Polit. Caucus (program chmn. 4th congl. dist. Va.1984-87), Phi Kappa Phi, Phi Theta Kappa (hon.), Delta Kappa Gamma. Home: Willow Oaks 2901 Tanbark Ln Portsmouth VA 23703 Office: Tidewater Community Coll Portsmouth VA 23703

MAPPS, PATRICIA JEANNE, management consultant; b. Elizabeth, N.J., June 25, 1948; d. Forrest Grant and Muriel (Munkel) M. BA, U. Mass., 1970; EdM, Harvard U., 1977. Group mgr. Digital Equipment Corp., Maynard, Mass., 1972-83; v.p. Franklin Computer Corp., Cherry Hill, N.J., 1983-84; pres. Mapps & Co., Merion, Pa., 1984—; program dir. MIT Enterprise Forum, Phila., 1985—; adv. bd. Wharton Small Bus. Devel. Ctr., Phila., 1986—, Pa. Innovation Network, Phila., 1986—; bd. dirs. Kensington Hosp., Phila. Presbyterian. Club: Harvard (Phila.).

MARAVICH, MARY LOUISE, realtor; b. Fort Knox, Ky., Jan. 4, 1951; d. John and Bonnie (Balandzic) M. A.A. in Office Adminstrn., U. Nev., Las Vegas, 1970; B.A. in Sociology and Psychology, U. So. Calif., 1972; grad. Realtors Inst. Cert. residential specialist. Adminstrv. asst. dept. history U. So. Calif., Los Angeles, 1972-73; asst. personnel supr. Corral Coin Co., Las Vegas, 1973-80; Realtor, Americana Group div. Better Homes and Gardens, Las Vegas, 1980-85, Jack Matthews and Co., 1985—. Mem. Nev. Assn. Realtors (cert. realtors inst.), Las Vegas Bd. Realtors, Nat. Assn. Realtors, Women's Council of Realtors, Am. Bus. Women's Assn., Nat. Assn. Female Execs. Club: Million Dollar, Pres.'s. Office: 3100 S Valley View Blvd Las Vegas NV 89102

MARCALI, JEAN GREGORY, chemist; b. Jermyn, Pa., May 29, 1926; d. John Robert and Anna Marie Gregory; student U. Pa., 1948-52, U. Del., 1971-72; m. Kalman Marcali, Oct. 6, 1956; children—Coleman, Frederick. Microanalyst E. I. du Pont de Nemours & Co., Deepwater, N.J., 1943-60, tech. info. analyst, Jackson Lab., Deepwater, N.J. also Wilmington, Del., 1960-67, sr. adviser tech. info., Wilmington, 1967-70, supr. tech. info., 1970-82, 85—, supr. adminstrv. services, 1982-85. Sec., Alfred I. DuPont Elem. PTA, 1971, pres., 1972; pres. PTA of Brandywine Sch. Dist., 1973; mem. Wilmington Dist. Republican Com., 1976—. Mem. Am. Chem. Soc. (treas. div. chem. info. 1976-81, chmn.-elect 1981, chmn. 1982, 83, div. councilor 1983—), Am. Chem. Soc. (com. on chem. abstracts service 1983-85, 87—). Lutheran. Clubs: Order Eastern Star, Du Pont Country, United Health. Home: 312 Waycross Rd Wilmington DE 19803 Office: E I du Pont de Nemours & Co Cen Research & Devel Dept Barley Mill Plaza P141212 Wilmington DE 19898

MARCH, JACQUELINE FRONT, chemist; b. Wheeling, W.Va. B.S., Case Western Res. U., 1937, M.A., 1939; Wyeth fellow med. research U. Chgo., 1940-42; postgrad. U. Pitts., 1945, Ohio State U., 1967, Wright State U., 1970-76; m. Abraham W. Marcovich, Oct. 7, 1945 (dec. 1969); children—Wayne Front, Gail Ann March Cohen. Chemist, Mt. Sinai Hosp., Cleve., 1934-40; med. research chemist U. Chgo., 1940-42; research analyst Koppers Co., also info. scientist Union Carbide Corp., Mellon Inst., Pitts., 1942-45; propr. March. Med. Research Lab., etiology of diabetes, Dayton, Ohio, 1950-70; guest scientist Kettering Found., Yellow Springs, Ohio, 1953; Dayton Found. fellow Miami Valley Hosp. Research Inst., 1956. mem. chemistry faculty U. Dayton, 1959-69, info. scientist Research Inst., 1968-79; prin. investigator Air Force Wright Aero. Labs., Wright-Patterson AFB Tech. Info. Center, 1970-79; chem. info. specialist, div. tech. services Nat. Inst. Occupational Safety and Health, HHS, Cin., 1979—; propr. JFM Cons., 1980—; designer info. systems, speaker in field. Recipient Recognition cert. U. Dayton, 1980. Mem. Am. Soc. Info. Sci. (treas. South Ohio 1973-75), Am. Chem. Soc. (pres. Dayton 1977), Soc. Advancement Materials and Process Engring. (pres. Midwest chpt. 1977-78), Affiliated Tech. Socs. (Outstanding Scientist and Engr. award 1978), Am. Congress Govtl. Indsl. Hygienists (rev. com. toxic chemicals 1983—), AAUP (exec. bd.), Sigma Xi (treas. Dayton 1976-79, Conrad P. Straub lectr. 1982, pres. Cin. Fed. Environ. chpt. 1986-87, del. nat. meeting 1987—). Contbr. articles to profl. publs. Home: 154 Stillmeadow Dr Cincinnati OH 45245 Office: 4676 Columbia Pkwy Cincinnati OH 45226

MARCH, SALLY ELAINE COOPER, art educator; b. York, Pa., Sept. 22, 1953; d. Harry Franklin and Ruth Elaine (Withers) Cooper; m. James Orville March, July 22, 1974. BA, U. Del., 1975, cert. Art Edn., 1978. Art tchr. Cecil County Pub. Schs., Elkton, Md., 1979—; mem. fine arts com. Newark Community Days, 1986—. work exhibited at Del. Ctr. for Contemporary Arts, 1984 (Best of Show), Three Rivers Arts Festival, 1986, U. Del., Del. Art Mus., Ctr. for the Creative Arts, L.B. Jones Gallery, Station Gallery, Helio Galleries, N.Y.C., 1988. Mem. revenue sharing screening com. City of Newark, 1984—. Mem. AAUW.

MARCHAND, NANCY, actress; b. Buffalo, June 19, 1928; d. Raymond L. and Marjorie F. M.; m. Paul Sparer, July 7, 1951; children: David, Kathryn, Rachel. B.F.A., Carnegie Inst. Tech., 1949. Vol. actress, Am. Theater Wing, N.Y.C.; TV appearances include A Touch of the Poet; series regular on: Lou Grant, 1977-82; theater engagements at, Circle in the Sq., N.Y.C., Los Angeles Music Center, Lincoln Center, N.Y.C., Am. Shakespeare Festival, Goodman Theater, Chgo., Ahmanson Theatre, Los Angeles; appeared on Broadway in: Mornings at Seven; in: Off Broadway plays Children, Sister Mary Ignatius; films include The Rise and Rise of Michael Rimmer, Promise at Dawn, Goodbye Mr. Chips, Tell Me That You Love Me Junie Moon, Some Kind of Miracle, Sparkling Cyanide, North and South Book II, The Golden Moment--An Olympic Love Story, From the Hip, 1987. Recipient Obie award, 1960; Emmy awards, 1978, 80, 81, 82. Office: William Morris Agy c/o Katie Rothacker 1350 Ave of the Americas New York NY 10019 *

MARCHESANO, CAROLE VIRGINIA, advertising company executive; b. Des Moines, July 30, 1940; d. Samuel Thomas and Geneva Carol (Horner) Mazza; ed. Catholic U.; m. Martin R. Marchesano, Aug. 7, 1956 (div. July 1963); children—Michele, Richard, Russell. Office mgr. Kieffer Assos., Des Moines, 1963-65; comptroller W.A. Lemer Advt., Inc., Washington, 1966-69; owner Goldberg, Marchesano & Assos., Inc., Washington, 1970—, pres., 1978—; cons. advt. office systems. Bd. dirs. draft com. Robertson for Pres.; mem. Bishop's Pastoral Council. Mem. Met. Washington Bd. Trade, Advt. Club Met. Washington, League Advt. Agys., Nat. Acad. TV Arts and Scis., Women in Advt./Mktg. Home: Rt 2 Box 98 Palmyra VA 22963 Office: 927 15th St NW Washington DC 20005

MARCHIONE, MARGHERITA FRANCES, Italian history educator, writer; b. Little Ferry, N.J., Feb. 19, 1922; d. Crescenzo and Felicia (Schettino) M. BA, Georgian Ct., 1943; MA, Columbia U., 1949, PhD, 1960. Instr. Walsh Jr. Coll., Morristown, N.J., 1949-63; lectr. Seton Hall U., South Orange, N.J., 1963-65; tenured prof. Fairleigh Dickinson U., Madison, N.J., 1965-84; pres. Walsh Coll., Morristown, 1966-71; dir. Italian Insts. Abroad, Italy, 1972-74, Salvatori Ctr. for Mazzei Studies, Morristown, 1978—, Corfinio Coll., Italy, 1983—; treas. Religious Tchrs. Filippini, Morristown, 1984—; cons. Philip Mazzei TV Miniseries, Los Angeles, 1987. Author: Twentieth-Century Italian Poetry: A Bilingual Anthology, 1974, From the Land of The Etruscans, 1986, L'Imagine Tesa: Life and Works of Clemente Rebora, 1960, 74; editor: Philip Mazzei: Selected Writings and Correspondence (6 vols.), 1983-84; contbr. numerous articles to profl. jours. Active N.J. Hist. Commn., Trenton, 1977, N.J. Cath. Hist. Commn., South Orange, N.J., 1976. Garibaldi scholar Columbia U., 1957, Fulbright scholar Inst. Internat. Edn., 1964; NDEA grantee Dept. Edn., 1962, 68, NHPRC grantee Nat. Archives, 1978-79, NEH grantee, 1980, 81; recipient Star of Solidarity of the Republic of Italy award, 1977, Nat. Italian American Found. award, 1984, Amita award, Rizzuto award. Mem. Am. Inst. Italian Studies (pres. 1976—), Am. Italian Hist. Assn. (exec. bd. mem. 1977—). Republican. Roman Catholic. Home: Villa Walsh Morristown NJ 07960 Office: Fairleigh Dickinson U Madison Ave Madison NJ 07940

MARCIN, MARIETTA, writer; b. Chgo., Aug. 4, 1932; d. William August and Marietta (Calderini) Marshall; m. Anthony A. Marcin, 1953 (div. 1986); 1 dau., Marietta; m. 2d, Jules Steinberg. B.A., U. Wis., 1953. Editor, Cuneo Topics, Cuneo Press, Chgo., 1953-55, NARDA News, Nat. Appliance Assn., 1956-62, Internat. Design Conf. in Aspen (Colo.), 1963-67; writer Walker Report Rights in Conflict, 1968; cons. Nash Realty, Winnetka, Ill., 1969-85; Midwest editor Kasmar Publs., 1985—. Author: A Zoo in Her Bed, 1963; Profitable Rental Merchandising, 1982; Complete Book of Herbal Teas, 1983. Editor: Great American Short Stories: 1954; Stories of America's Past, 1955. Contbr. articles to profl. jours. and mags. Bd. dirs. Chamber Music Chgo., 1964—, v.p., 1981-83, pres., 1987-88; bd. dirs. Contemporary Concerts Inc., 1976—, sec., 1978-82. Mem. Women in Communications, Midwest Writers Assn., Soc. Midland Authors (dir. 1982—), Chgo. Press Club. Home: 425 Sunset Rd Winnetka IL 60093

MARCINEK, JOYCE E., business executive; b. Nevada, Ohio, July 28, 1930; d. W. Frank and Bernice Marie McCallister; student Newark Coll. Engring., 1952-53, Sinclair Community Coll., 1968-69. With sales, service, public relations depts. Standard Oil Co., Canton and Akron, Ohio, 1957-63; with TRW Supermet, Dayton, Ohio, 1966-70, sales engr., 1972-75; acct. Texaco Inc., Atlanta, 1970-72; asst. to pres. Hot Sam div. Gen. Host, Troy, Mich., 1975-76; accounts rep. Kelly Services, Lexington, Ky., 1976-77, br. mgr., 1977-80; v.p. Career Mgmt., Inc., Lexington, 1980-82; dir. personnel EBS Inc., subs. Traveler's Ins. Co., Lexington, 1982-83; pres. Kelleher Wholesale Div., and Joymar Corp., Orlando, Fla., 1983-86, gen. mgr. Joymar Corp. Temp. Resources, Inc., Southfield, Mich., 1986-87, cons., personnel, 1987—. Active Urban League, Todd Trease Teddy Bear Fund; bd. dirs. Jr. Achievement, program chmn., 1981-82, also contest judge; sponsor, coordinator secretarial scis. Explorer troop Bluegrass council Boy Scouts Am.; team capt. United Way, 1978-81; mem. Better Bus. Bur. Recipient Distributive Edn. award Lexington Edn.-Work Council, 1978; adv. bd. Ken. Jr. Coll., 1982-83. Mem. Sales Mktg. Execs. (dir., coordinator seminar 1979), Adminstrv. Mgmt. Assn. (dir.), Lexington C. of C. (dir., mem. pres.'s council). Club: Zonta (regional dir. public relations). Home and Office: 46675 N Hills Dr Apt 53F Northville MI 48167

MARCOTTE, DEE LORIS, child care center administrator; b. Chgo., Feb. 2, 1951; d. Vincent Marcotte and Sylvia (Wesley) Wall. BS, Blackburn Coll., 1973; MS, Iowa State U., 1975. Program mgr. Head Start Tng. Iowa State U., Ames, Iowa, 1975-76; instr. U. Wis.-Stout, Menomonie, Wis., 1976-77; dir. Children's World, Palatine and Vernon Hills, Ill., 1977-81; office mgr. Grand Lake (Colo.) C. of C., 1981-82; mgr. Winter Park (Colo.)/Grand County Econ. Devel. Com., 1982-83; dir. Child Motivation Ctr., Lakewood, Colo., 1983-85, area adminstr., 1985—; Chair Warren Tech. Adv. Com., Denver, 1987; cons. in field, Denver, 1987. Grantee Home Econs. Research Inst, Ames, 1976. Mem. Nat. Assn. Edn. of Young Children, Colo. Assn. Edn. of Young Children, Applewood Bus. Assn., Lakewood/South Jeffo C. of C. Office: Child Motivation Ctr 441 Wadsworth Suite 102 Lakewood CO 80226

MARCOTTE, MICHELINE LOUISE, real estate associate; b. Sherbrooke, Que., Can., Apr. 21, 1946; came to U.S., 1983; d. Rene Maurice and Bella-Kathleen (Roberts) Begin; m. Gilles Henri Marcotte, Oct. 21, 1967; children: William, Daniel. BSc in Med. Tech., Universite De Montreal, Que., Can., 1966. Registered technologist, Can.; lic. realtor, Va., Calif. Med. technologist Hopital Du Sacre Coeur, Montreal, 1966-73; lab. mgr. Rosemere Regional High Sch., Montreal, 1973-76; med. technologist Peel Meml. Hosp., Toronto, Ont., Can., 1978-82; technologist reference lab. Richmond (Va.) Met. Blood Service, 1983-85; realtor Century 21 Old Richmond Realty, 1985-87, Century 21 Today Realty, Mission Viejo, Calif., 1987—. Mem. Am. Soc. Med. Tech., Am. Assn. Blood Banks, Nat. Assn. Female Execs., Nat. Assn. Realtors, Calif. Assn. Realtors, Century 21 Investment Soc. Club: Walton Park Women's (Richmond) (chairperson hospitality 1984-87).

MARCOTTE, MICHELLE LOUISE, federal agency administrator; b. Windsor, Ont., Can., July 30, 1954; d. David Leo and Patricia (Marentette) M.; m. David Stanley Reade, Aug. 27, 1977; children: Clare, Nathan. BA in Home Econs. with honors, U. Windsor, Ont., 1978. Nutrition columnist Ottawa (Ont.) Jour., 1979-80; mkt. development specialist in food irradition Atomic Energy of Can., Ltd., The Radiochemical Co., Kanata, Ont., 1987—; media food cons. Agriculture Can., Ottawa, 1978-87. Author: Canadian Home Economics Journal, 1979, 80, 88. Mem. Ottawa Home Econs. Assn. (pres. 1982-83), Inst. Food Technology, Can. Inst. Technology, Sci. Writers Can., Canadian Home Econs. Assn., Can. Inst. Food Sci. and Technology. Office: Atomic Energy Can Ltd, Radiochemical Co, 413 March Rd, Kanata, ON Canada K2E 1X8

MARCOU, ANN CLAIRE, counseling administrator; b. Ft. Wayne, Ind., Aug. 12, 1932; d. Juan and Carolyn Lydia (Holliday) Rodriguez; m. William John Marcou, Jan. 15, 1955; children: Patrick, Linda, Michelle, Christopher. BA in English Lit., U. Mich., 1954; MA in Therapeutic Communications, Gov.'s State U., 1978. Research asst. NIMH, Chgo., 1976-80; community prof. health edn. series Gov.'s State U., University Park, Ill., 1978—, cable TV prof. in health edn. dept., 1980—; co-founder, dir. counseling Y-ME Breast Cancer Support Program, Chgo., 1978—; cons. Michael Reese Hosp., Chgo., 1978-81, Am. Cancer Soc., Chgo., 1978; bd. dirs. Plastic Surgery Info. Service, Chgo., 1985—; lectr. AMA, U. Ill., Northwestern U., 1984-86; mem. adv. bd. Ill. Cancer Council, Chgo., 1986—, South Suburban Hosp., Hazel Crest, Ill., 1986—. Co-author breast reconstrn. booklet. Recipient Jefferson award Chicago Sun Times, 1982, Gov. Thompson award State Ill., 1982, Vol. Action award Chgo. Community Trust, 1982; named Citizen of Yr., Chgo. South Suburban C. of C., 1984. Mem. Am. Psychol. Assn., Ill. Psychol. Assn., Soc. Oncology Social Workers. Office: Y-ME Breast Cancer Support Program 18220 Harwood Ave Homewood IL 60430

MARCUS, CONSTANCE WASHBURN, marketing professional, nurse; b. Saugerties, N.Y., May 10, 1951; d. John George and Fay (Zibella) Washburn; m. Lawrence Irwin Marcus, Aug. 18, 1974; 1 child, Brett Jordan. Assoc. in Applied Sci., Ulster County Community Coll., 1974 Registered nurse. Staff nurse Greene County Meml. Hosp., Catskill, N.Y., 1974-78; occupational coordinator Gateway Community Industries, Kingston, N.Y., 1978-80; immunization nurse Am. Inst. in Taiwan, Taipei, Republic of China, 1980-81; utilization review specialist Meml. Hosp. and Nursing Home, Catskill, 1982-83; designed-care coordinator Empire Blue Cross & Blue Shield, Albany, N.Y., 1984-85, education/marketing coordinator, 1985—; guest lectr. Chung Gung Meml. Hosp., Taipei, 1980. Capt. Am. Heart Assn., Kingston, 1986—. Mem. League of Women Voters. Roman Catholic. Club: Community (Saugerties) (pres. 1983-84). Home: 54 W Bridge St Saugerties NY 12477 Office: Empire Blue Cross & Blue Shield PO Box 8650 Albany NY 12208

MARCUS, HELEN MOLLIE, photographer; b. N.Y.C., Oct. 28; d. Joseph M. and Augusta (Hittleman) M. BA, Smith Coll., 1947. With casting CBS-TV, N.Y.C., 1951; in charge subs. rights MCA, N.Y.C., 1952-54; with Goodson Todman Prodns., N.Y.C., 1955-75, assoc. producer Beat the Clock, 1958-61, asst. producer Number Please, 1961, casting dir. To Tell the Truth, 1962-68, assoc. producer What's My Line, 1968-75; freelance photographer N.Y.C., 1975—; mem. adv. bd. Maine Photographic Workshop Congress, Rockport, 1986-87, exec. dir. 3d annual Internat. Photography Congress, 1988; bd. dirs. Photographic Adminstrs. Inc.; lectr. exec. portraiture, bus. practices in photography. Exhibited at N.Y. Pub. Library, Asia Soc., Parents Mag. Gallery. Pres. council Phoenix Theatre, N.Y., 1969-72; mem. adv. bd. Catskill Ctr. Photography; nat. planning com. on the originating artist Am. Council for the Arts, chiar media and the arts com.; bd. dirs. Theatre Adv. Dept. Smith Coll., Northampton, Mass., 1965-80. Mem. Overseas Press Club, Graphic Artists Guild, Am. Soc. Mag. Photographers (pres. 1985-88, pres. N.Y. chpt. 1981-83, v.p. 1983-85), Advt. Photographers Am., Soc. of Illustrators, Maine Photog. Workshops (exec. dir. Third Internat. Congress). Home and Office: 120 E 75th St New York NY 10021

MARCUS, RUTH BARCAN, philosopher, educator, author, lecturer; b. N.Y.C.; d. Samuel and Rose (Post) Barcan; divorced; children: James Spencer, Peter Webb, Katherine Hollister, Elizabeth Post. BA, NYU, 1941; MA, Yale U., 1942, PhD, 1946. Research assoc. in anthropology Inst. for Human Relations Yale U., New Haven, Conn., 1945-47; AAUW fellow 1947-48; vis. prof. Northwestern U., 1950-57, Guggenheim fellow, 1953-54; asst. prof., assoc. prof. Roosevelt U., Chgo., 1957-63; NSF fellow 1963-64; prof. philosophy U. Ill. at Chgo., 1964-70, head philosophy dept., 1963-69; fellow U. Ill. Center for Advanced Study, 1968-69; prof. philosophy Northwestern U., 1970-73; Reuben Post Halleck prof. philosophy Yale U., 1973—; fellow Center Advanced Study in Behavioral Sci., Stanford, Calif., 1979; vis. fellow Inst. Advanced Study, U. Edinburgh, 1983; vis. fellow Wolfson Coll., Oxford U., 1985, 86, Clare Hall, Cambridge; mem. and chmn. adv. com. Princeton U., MIT, Calif. Inst. Tech., Cornell U. Humanities Ctr., among others. Editor: The Logical Enterprise, Logic Methodology and Philosophy of Science VII; mem. editorial bd.: Past or Present, Metaphilosophy, Monist, Philos. Studies; Editor and contbr. to books and profl. jours. Recipient Machette prize for contbn. to profession; Medal, College de France, 1986. Fellow Am. Acad. Arts and Scis.; mem. Council on Philos. Studies (pres. 1988—), Assn. for Symbolic Logic (past exec. council, exec. com. 1973—, v.p. 1980-82, pres. 1981-83, council 1983—), Am. Philos. Assn. (past sec.-treas., nat. dir. 1967-83, pres. central div. 1975-76, chmn. nat. bd. officer 1977-83), Philosophy of Sci. Assn., Institut International de Philosophie (past exec. com., v.p. 1983—), Fédération Internationale Sociétés de Philosophie (exec. com., steering com.), Phi Beta Kappa. Club: Elizabethan of Yale (v.p. 1988—). Office: Yale U Dept Philosophy Box 3650 New Haven CT 06520

MARCUS, SUZANNE GAIL, film producer, screenwriter; b. Jamaica, N.Y., Oct. 26, 1959; d. William B. Marcus and Beverly Sarah (Miller) M. B.F.A., NYU, 1981. Prodn. coordinator Hurrah Prodns., N.Y.C., 1981-82; post-prodn. adminstr. Devlin Video, N.Y.C., 1982-83; ops. and prodn. adminstr. Showtime Entertainment, N.Y.C., 1983-84; founder, chief exec. officer Electric Images Ltd., N.Y.C., 1984—; cons. and lectr. in field. Dir. theater prodn. Shade/Acad. of Desire, 1980; producer, screenwriter film Empress of the Blues: The Bessie Smith Story, 1987. Recipient Stella and Charles Guttman Found. awards, 1985, 86, 87, Haas Found. award, 1986, 87; grantee in field from numerous profl. orgns. Fellow Nat. Assn. Female Execs., Am. Film Inst., Assn. Ind. Video and Film Makers, NYU Tisch Sch. Arts Alumni Assn. Jewish. Avocations: running, swimming, cooking, photography, writing poetry. Home: 33 Gold St Apt 607 New York NY 10038

MARÉ, GINA, banker; b. Washington, Oct. 27, 1952; d. Nenad Dusan and Tanya Vladan (Popovic) Popovic; divorced. BA with honors, Syracuse U., 1972; MA, Harvard U., 1978. Exec. dir. Newton (Mass.) Arts Ctr., 1978-80; investment broker Kidder, Peabody and Co., N.Y.C., 1983-85; asst. office mgr., treas. W.P. Carey and Co., N.Y.C., 1985-87; mgr. U.S. News and World Report, N.Y.C., 1987—; head tutor folklore, mythology, Harvard Coll., 1978; officer Corp. Property Assocs., N.Y.C., 1985-87; mem. adv. bd. New England Bancorp, 1980-83. Editor jour. The Arts Spectrum, 1976; translator mag. The Harvard Advocate, 1982; contbr. pamphlet Crime at Harvard, 1974, 75. Chmn. Sutton Pl. Hist. Preservation com., N.Y.C., 1985—; bd. dirs. Hicks House Theodore Roosevelt Meml., Cambridge, Mass., 1974-78, Mass. Cultural Alliance, 1979-80. Harvard Coll. teaching fellow, 1975-78. Mem. Kirkland House (assoc. Sr. Common Room 1974-83, chmn. Golden Jubilee 1980). Club: Harvard (N.Y.C.).

MARECEK, JEANNE ANN, psychologist, educator; b. Berwyn, Ill., May 28, 1946; d. Frank J. and Josephine (Serio) M. BS, Loyola U., Chgo., 1968; MS, Yale U., 1971, PhD, 1973. From asst. to assoc. prof. psychology Swarthmore (Pa.) Coll., 1972-86, prof., chair psychology dept., 1986—. Contbr. numerous articles to profl. jours. and chpts. to books. Bd. dirs. Women in Transition, Phila., 1980-86. Various fed. research grants. Mem. Am. Psychol. Assn., Ea. Psychol. Assn. Office: Swarthmore Coll Dept Psychology Swarthmore PA 19081

MAREK, ANN ARMSTRONG, marketing and public relations executive; b. N.Y.C., Feb. 20, 1935; d. Andrew F.H. Armstrong and Florence Elizabeth (White) Bowen; A.A.S., N.Mex. State U., 1956; B.A., U. Tex., Arlington, 1975; postgrad. U. Dallas, 1977; m. Gabriel Robert Marek, July 28, 1956; children—Andrew Vincent, Elizabeth Marek West, Melissa Marek Wheeler. Sales rep. Parker Bros., Ft. Worth, 1979, George Farha Toy Distbr. Co., Oklahoma City, 1980; area mgr. retail merchandising Mattel Sales Corp., Dallas, 1980-81; dir. community affairs Family Service Inc., Ft. Worth, 1981-84; dir. mktg./pub. relations Circle T Council Girl Scouts USA, Ft. Worth, 1984—; lectr. U. Tex., Arlington, 1973—. Chmn., Tarrant County Study Commn. on Children and Youth, 1973; vice chmn. Ft. Worth Utility Bd., 1976; mem. task panel on the family Pres.'s Commn. on Mental Health, 1977. Recipient Newsmaker of Yr. award Ft. Worth Press Club, 1973, Child Advocacy award Ft. Worth Mayor's Council on Youth Opportunity, Potter award for outstanding communication program, 1983, 87. Mem. Network Exec. Women, Assn. Girl Scout Execs., Pub. Relations Soc. Am., Women's Policy Forum, Ad Club. Episcopalian. Author report: The Enhancement of Parenting Skills, 1977. Home: 2324 Edwin St Fort Worth TX 76110 Office: 4901 Briarhaven Fort Worth TX 76109

MAREK, MARYBETH, county government official; b. Alexandria, Va., Apr. 4, 1956; d. John Thomas and Phillis Eleanor (Hardie) M. BA, Waynesburg (Pa.) Coll., 1978; M of Pub. Adminstrn., Va. Commonwealth U., 1987. Adminstr. Town of Harpers Ferry, W.Va., 1978-79; dir. community devel. Borough of Sayre, Pa., 1979-80; project coordinator Region I Planning Dist. Commn., Princeton, W.Va., 1980-82; dir. community devel. Town of Ashland, Va., 1982-85; dir. planning and community devel. Caroline County, Bowling Green, Va., 1986—. Leader Girl Scouts U.S., Sayre and Ashland, 1980, 82-84. Mem. Rural Planning Caucus Va. (sec.-treas. 1982-86, chmn. 1987), Am. Planning Assn., Am. Soc. Pub. Adminstrn. Democrat. Roman Catholic. Home: 620 Abbey Dr Ruther Glen VA 22546 Office: Caroline County PO Box 424 Bowling Green VA 22427

MARESCA, DEBORAH KAREN, radiologic technologist; b. Queens, N.Y., June 18, 1957; d. Seymour and Doris (Elkin) Gitt; m. James Peter Maresca, Aug. 22, 1982. AS, Fairleigh Dickinson U., 1979; BS, St. Josephs Coll., 1985. Radiologic technologist St. John's Hosp., Smithtown, N.Y., 1979-82, ultrasound technologist, 1982—; also instr. ultrasound St. John's Hosp., Smithtown, 1982—; radiologic technologist Dr. Katz, Commack, N.Y., 1980-82; ultrasound technologist Dr. Ganguly, Smithtown, 1982-83. Mem.

L.I. Soc. of Diagnostic Med. Sonographers (recording sec. 1983-86), Soc. Diagnostic Med. Sonographers, Am. Soc. of Radiologic Techs. Republican. Home: 1 Gladys St Selden NY 11784 Office: St John's Hosp Rt 25A Smithtown NY 11784

MARESCA, ROSALIA LORETTA, opera company director; b. N.Y.C., Aug. 16, 1923; d. Salvatore and Elizabeth Maresca; hon. grad. Cin. Conservatory of Music, 1958; studied voice with Carmen du Belier and Mario Laurenti; 1 child, Rena. Operatic debut as Adalgisa in Norma, Acad. Music, N.Y.C., 1944; performances with opera cos. throughout U.S. including those of Cin., Phila., Hartford, Chautauqua, New Orleans, Bklyn., Tampa, Rochester, Washington and Syracuse; appearances in theatres throughout U.S., Europe, Japan; prof. voice Manhattan Sch. Music, 1967-73; mgr., dir. San Carlo Opera, Fla. Lyric Opera, Matinee Opera Theatre, Clearwater, Fla., 1973—; voice tchr., head voice faculty Fla. Performing Arts Studio, St. Petersburg; organizer Fla. Artists Mgmt. Enterprise (FAME). Dir. music Pilgrim Congl. Ch. St. Petersburg, 1988. Recipient Pinellas Arts Council award. Mem. Am. Guild Mus. Artists, Am. Guild Radio and TV Artists. Home: 8360E 12 St N St Petersburg FL 33702 Office: 1183D 85 Terrace N Saint Petersburg FL 33702

MARESH, NANCY, marketing professional; b. Iowa City, June 27, 1946; d. Gerald Stanley and Ethel (Nelson) M. Grad. high sch., Denver. Dir. mktg. Doing Bus., Los Angeles, 1979-80; managing dir. Human Factors Cast, Burlington, Vt., 1980-83; exec. dir. Quantum Edn. Discoveries, Burlington, 1983—. Pantee acctg. game, 1982. Recipient grant St. of Vt., 1978. Home: 42 Latham Ct Burlington VT 05401 Office: Quantum Edn Discoveries 1 Mill St Burlington VT 05401

MARGOLIES, ALLISON, clinical psychologist; b. N.Y.C., Feb. 11, 1953; d. Sol and Bunny (Wertans) M.; M.A., Hofstra U., 1976, Ph.D., 1979. Psychologist, Bernard Fineson Developmental Ctr., Queens Village, N.Y., 1979-82; cons. psychologist Aurora Concept, Flushing, N.Y., 1981-84; assoc. psychologist Queens Children's Psychiat. Hosp., Bellerose, N.Y., 1982-85; assoc. psychologist Creedmoor Psychiat. Ctr., Queens Village, 1985—; pvt. practice clin. psychology, Lawrence, N.Y., 1982—. Lic. psychologist N.Y. State; cert. sch. psychologist N.Y. State. Mem. Am. Psychol. Assn., N.Y. State Psychol. Assn., Nassau County Psychol. Assn., Phi Beta Kappa. Qualified expert witness, N.Y. Supreme Ct. Home: 611 Arbucke Ave Woodmere NY 11598 Office: 360 Central Ave Lawrence NY 11559

MARGOLIS, CLORINDA GOLTRA, psychologist; b. Cin., June 2, 1930; m. Joseph Margolis; children—Lovegrove, Jennifer. B.A., U. Cin., 1963, M.A., 1966, Ph.D., 1968. Diplomate Am. Bd. Psychol. Hypnosis. Asst. prof. Jefferson Med. Coll., Phila., 1970-74, assoc. prof., 1976-80, chief consultation and engring., 1970-78, clin. prof., chief psychologist, 1978-82; pres. Clorinda G. Margolis and Assocs., P.C., Phila., 1982—. Author: Manual of Stress Management, 1982. Contbr. articles to profl. jours., chpt. in book. Recipient Milton H. Erickson award Am. Jour. Clin. Hypnosis, 1984. Fellow Am. Psychol. Assn. (newsletter editor div. 30, 1985-87), Pa. Psychol. Assn.; mem. Inst. for Advancement of Health, Am. Pain Soc., Am. Soc. Clin. Hypnosis, Soc. for Clin. and Exptl. Hypnosis, Phila. Soc. Clin. Hypnosis (pres. 1985—). Office: 1015 Chestnut St Suite 1500 Philadelphia PA 19107

MARGOLIS, ESTHER LUTERMAN, court administrator; b. Pitts., Jan. 12, 1939; d. Nathan and Belle (Fogel) Luterman; B.S., Ariz. State U., 1976, M.S., 1978; m. Herbert Marvin Margolis, Apr. 15, 1962; children: Ruth Lys, Judith Lyn. Statistician, court planners office Ariz. Supreme Ct., 1976-77; planner Ariz. Dept. Corrections, 1979; adminstrv. asst. planning and research bur. Phoenix Police Dept., 1979-82, police research analyst, 1982-83; ct. mgmt. analyst Calif. Jud. Council, Adminstrv. Office of Cts., San Francisco, 1983-84; asst. ct. adminstr., jury commr. Contra Costa County Superior Ct., 1984—; instr. Phoenix Community Coll., 1980-82; presenter paper ann. meeting Acad. Criminal Justice Scis., Phila., 1981. Mem. textbook selection com. Roosevelt Sch. Dist., Phoenix, 1975; chmn. bd. YMCA, South Mountain br., 1977-81; bd. mgrs. Phoenix and Valley of the Sun YMCA, 1978-81; pres. bd. dirs. Do it Now Found., 1978-80; bd. dirs. Boys' Clubs Phoenix, 1982-83; fin. officer Pinole Ridge Homeowners Assn., 1986—, pres., 1987—. Mem. Am. Soc. Public Adminstrn. (program com., panel coordinator regional conf. 1983; panel discussant ann. meeting N.Y.C. 1983), Am. Soc. Criminology, Nat. Council Crime and Delinquency, Nat. Assn. Women in Criminal Justice, Profl. Women for Kennedy. Editor ann. report Phoenix Police Dept., 1979-82. Home: 1417 Greenfield Circle Pinole CA 94564 Office: 725 Court St Room 124 Martinez CA 94553

MARGOLIS, GWEN LIEDMAN (MRS. ALLAN B. MARGOLIS), state senator, developer; b. Phila., Oct. 4, 1934; d. Joseph and Rose Liedman; m. Allan Block Margolis, 1953; children—Edward, Ira, Karen, Robin. Student Temple U., 1951-54; A.A. (hon.), Miami Dade U., 1983. Owner, broker Gwen Margolis Real Estate, North Miami Beach, 1965—; mem. Fla. Ho. of Reps., Tallahassee, 1974-80; mem. Fla. Senate, 1980—; dir. Lincoln Savs. and Loan Assn.; realtor, appraiser. Bd. dirs. Anti-Defamation League of B'nai Brith. Recipient Outstanding Woman in Politics award Bus. and Profl. Women's Assn.; Woman of Yr. award North Miami Beach C. of C.; awards Women in Communication, Fla. Women's Polit. Caucus, Profl. Firefighters of Fla.; Legis. Friend of Arts award Gov.'s Arts Com., 1982; Spirit of Life Humanitarian award City of Hope, 1974, 79, established Margolis Cancer Research fellowship. Mem. North Miami C. of C. (dir.). Office: Fla Senate State Capitol Tallahassee FL 32301 Other Address: 13899 Biscayne Blvd North Miami Beach FL 33181

MARGOLIS, MARILYN, nurse; b. Coatesville, Pa., Apr. 15, 1954; d. Milton S. and Betty (Jaskulek) M. BS in Biology, Albright Coll., 1976, BS in Nursing, 1979; MS in Nursing Adminstrn., Emory U. Staff nurse Reading (Pa.) Hosp., 1979-81; staff and charge nurse Emory U., Atlanta, 1981—; supr. nursing Ga. Bapt. Hosp., Atlanta, 1985-86. Active Homeless Women, Atlanta, 1986—. Mem. Am. Nurses Assn., Am. Assn. Critical Care Nurses, Ga. Nurses Assn., Sigma Theta Tau. Democrat. Jewish. Home: 1162 Weatherstone Dr Atlanta GA 30324 Office: Emory U 1364 Clifton Rd Atlanta GA 30322

MARGOLIS, NANCY KROLL, marketing and advertising executive; b. N.Y.C., Sept. 12, 1947; d. Herman and Florence (Yondorf) Kroll; m. Paul D. Margolis, Nov. 12, 1972; children: Kara, Seth. Student Parsons Sch. Design, 1964-65; BA, Ohio State U., 1969. Traffic coordinator Wells, Rich, Greene, N.Y.C., 1970-72; asst. producer Nadler & Larimer, N.Y.C., 1972-73; pres. Nancy Britton Agy., Greenwich, Conn., 1973-75; v.p. Joseph Jacobs Orgn., N.Y.C., 1976-84; assoc. pub. advt. dir. Hadassah Mag., N.Y.C., 1984-86; prin. Margolis & Kroll Mktg. Publisher: The Jewish Traveler, 1987. Recipient 4 advt. awards The Advt. Club of Westchester, 1987. Bd. dirs., N.Y. Jewish Week. Democrat. Jewish.

MARGOSIAN, LUCILLE K. MANOUGIAN (MRS. ERVIN M. MARGOSIAN), artist, educator; b. Highland Park, Mich.; d. George Krikor and Vera Varsenig (Jernukian) Manougian; B.F.A., Wayne State U., 1957, M.A., 1958; postgrad. Calif. State U., Fresno, 1959-60, U. Calif. at Berkeley, 1960-61; m. Ervin M. Margosian, Oct. 28, 1960; children—Rebecca L., Rachel L. One-man show at Jackson's Gallery, Berkeley, Calif., 1961; exhibited in group shows at Detroit Art Inst., 1958, Oakland (Calif.) Art Museum, 1961, Wayne State U. Community Arts Center, Detroit, 1965, San Francisco Ann. Art Festivals, 1967, 68, 69, Jack London Square Arts Festival, Oakland, 1969, 70, Judah L. Magnes Meml. Mus., Berkeley, 1970, Kaiser Center Gallery, Oakland, 1970, Oakland Mus. Changing Gallery, 1969, Olive Hyde Art Center, Fremont, 1971, 73, Richmond (Calif.) Art Center, 1972, Villa Montalvo Galleries at Phelan Estate, Saratoga, Calif., 1976, others; faculty Peralta Community Colls., Laney campus, Oakland, 1967—, prof. art, 1970—, chmn. dept., 1982—. Charter mem. univ. art mus. council U. Calif. at Berkeley, 1965—. Recipient Certificate of Distinguished Achievement, Am. Legion, 1950; Best of Show 1st prize 5th Ann. Textile Exhbn., Fremont, Calif., 1973; Merit award City of Fremont, 1973, Zellerbach Bldg. Gallery, San Francisco, 1975. Mem. Calif. Art Edn. Assn., Oakland Museum Assn., Richmond Art Center, Women of Wayne, Wayne State U. Alumni Assn., East Bay Watercolor Soc., Internat. Platform Assn., Am. Fedn. Tchrs., Peralta Fedn. Tchrs. Office: Laney Coll Art Dept 900 Fallon St Oakland CA 94607

MARGULES, GABRIELE ELLA, publishing company executive; b. Tachov, Czechoslovakia, May 30, 1927; d. David Samuel and Rosa Zerlina (Leinwand) Margules; came to U.S., 1954. Student Cambridge Sch. Art (Eng.), 1944-47; diploma in fine art Royal Acad. Sch., London, 1950; postgrad. New Sch., N.Y.C., 1961-62. Direct mail asst. Harper's mag., 1959-67; direct mail mgr. Forbes mag., 1967-73; promotion mgr. Cath. Digest, 1973-79; circulation dir. Gernsback Publs., N.Y.C., 1979-81, Criminal Justice Publs., N.Y.C., 1981-83, Archaeology Mag., 1983—. Illustrator: Out of the Ark, 1968; Bird Song, 1970; also for Harper's mag. Painting exhibited, 1957-81. One man show (paintings and drawings): Garrison Art Ctr., N.Y., 1985. Recipient 1st prize life drawing Royal Acad., 1949; Meyers Art scholar, 1948, 61. Mem. Artists Equity, Women's Direct Response Group, Direct Mail Mktg. Assn., Mag. Pubs. Assn., Putnam Hist. Assn., Garrison Art Ctr., Barrett House. Democrat. Jewish. Home: 7 High St Cold Spring NY 10516 Office: 15 Park Row New York NY 10038

MARGULIS, LYNN ALEXANDER, biologist; b. Chgo., Mar. 5, 1938; d. Morris and Leone (Wise) Alexander; m. Carl Sagan, June 16, 1957; m. Thomas N. Margulis, Jan. 18, 1967; children: Dorion Sagan, Jeremy Sagan, Zachary Margulis, Jennifer Margulis. A.B., U. Chgo., 1957; A.M., U. Wis., 1960; Ph.D., U. Calif., Berkeley, 1965. Mem. faculty Boston U., 1966-88, asst. prof. biology, 1967-71, assoc. prof., 1971-77, prof., 1977—, Univ. prof., 1986-88; disting. prof. U. Mass., Amherst, 1988—; Sherman Fairchild disting. scholar Calif. Inst. Tech., 1976-77; vis. prof. dept. microbiology U. Autónoma de Barcelona, Spain, 1986. Author: Origin of Eukaryotic Cells, 1970, Symbiosis in Cell Evolution, 1981, Early Life, 1982; (with K.V. Schwartz) Five Kingdoms, 1982; (with Dorion Sagan) Microcosmos, 1986, Origins of Sex, 1986, Garden of Microbial Delights, 1988; contbr. articles to profl. jours. Guggenheim fellow, 1979. Fellow AAAS; mem. Nat. Acad. Sci. (chmn. com. planetary biology and chem. evolution 1977-81). Office: Univ of Mass Dept of Botany Amherst MA 01003

MARGUS, PAULA JEAN, writer, consultant; b. Takoma Park, Md., Nov. 15, 1957; d. Peter Anthony and Helen Arlene (Culbert) M. BS of Health Edn., U. Md., 1982, postgrad., 1987—. Med. interviewer Westat Research Firm and USPHS, Md., 1980-83; prodn. asst. Nat. Sci. Tchrs. Assn., Washington, 1982-84; writing cons. Profl. Resumé and Writing Service, Rockville, Md., 1984-85; tech. writer Prospect Assocs., Rockville, 1985-86; writing cons. Washington and Md., 1986—; free-lance photographer, Washington, 1984—; cons. in field; grant project coordinator Am. Assn. Counseling and Devel. at Coll. Counseling Ctrs., Md. and Washington, 1987. Vol. Community for Creative Non-Violence, Washington, 1987. Mem. Writers' Inc., Nat. Assn. Female Execs., World of Poetry. Home and Office: 12330 Herrington Manor Dr Silver Spring MD 20904

MARIAKIS, JAN IRENE, ins., estate and fin. co. exec.; b. Portland, Oreg., May 28, 1951; d. Lyle Henry and Juanita Jean Vandercook; student Ga. So. Coll., 1971-72; B.S. in Adminstrn. of Justice/Sociology, Portland State U., 1975. C.L.U.; chartered fin. cons. J. Nick Mariakis, Oct. 5, 1985; children—Jennifer Spring, Katherine Nichole. Saleswoman, Lincoln Nat. Life Ins. Co., San Mateo, Calif., 1975-81; owner, mgr. Fiscal Design, Redwood City, Calif., 1981—; corp. treas. Material Handling Corp.; pres. Profl. Fin. Group, Inc., 1987—; dir. Oreg. Handling Equipment Co., Inc., speaker in field. Charter mem. Friendly Acreas Neighborhood Bd.; past local chairwoman Life Underwriters Polit. Action Com. C.L.U. Mem. Nat. Assn. Life Underwriters, Peninsula Assn. Life Underwriters (past pres.), Calif. Assn. Life Underwriters , Internat. Assn. Fin. Planners. Christian Scientist. Club: Friends of Winemakers (Santa Clara). Office: Box 2399 Redwood City CA 94064

MARIE, GERALDINE, writer; b. Kew Gardens, N.Y., Sept. 9, 1949; d. Salvatore Astor and Louise Annette (Ingargiola) Lettieri; m. Alan Julian Marcus, 1984; children—Pamela Stacey, Elizabeth Kara. B.A., Queens Coll., 1971; M.S. in Edn., C.W. Post Coll., 1976. Cert. tchr., N.Y. Tchr. St. Patrick's Sch., Bay Shore, N.Y., 1971-81, Gt. Neck (N.Y.) Sch. Dist., 1981-83; author books including: The Magic Box (named Children's Choice for 1982), 1981; adaptation of The Hound of the Baskervilles (Arthur Conan Doyle), 1980; writer short stories; author cassettes: Children's Fairy Tales, 1979; author reading comprehension games. Mem. Soc. Children's Book Writers. Address: 873 Manor Ln Bay Shore NY 11706

MARIE, KATHY LOUISE, data systems executive; b. Denver, July 24, 1953; d. Johnny Santos and Anna Louise (Martinez) Vigil; m. Philip Randall Marie, Feb. 13, 1971; children: Lisa Jean, Danni Rae. Student, Colo. Women's Coll., 1980-81. Computer operator Western Electric, Aurora, Colo., 1971-75; sr. operator Samsonite Corp., Denver, 1975-77; supr., mgr. of ops. Sterns Roger, Denver, 1977-79; prodn. services mgr. Citicorp, Englewood, Colo., 1979-80; applications mgr. Citicorp, Englewood, 1980-81; computer ops. mgr. CIGNA, Thornton, Colo., 1981-83; sr. ops. mgr. CIGNA, Thornton, 1983-84, ops. section mgr., 1984-85, ops. asst. dir., 1985-87; owner, cons. SYSTEK, Aurora, Colo., 1986—. Mem. Soc. Info. Mgmt., Data Processing Mgmt. Assn., Nat. Orgn. Female Execs., Beta Sigma Phi. Democrat. Roman Catholic. Home: 5776 S Kittredge Ct Aurora CO 80015 Office: CIGNA 12396 Grant St Thornton CO 80241

MARIEN, GAIL DOLORES, printing distributor sales executive; b. N.Y.C., July 29, 1942; d. Vito E. and Ann (Casdia) Ingoglia; m. Albert J. Marien, Jr., Jan. 15, 1966; children—Angela, Natalie. R.N., St. Vincent's Hosp., 1963; B.A. in Psychology summa cum laude, Marymount Coll., 1978; M.S.W., Adelphi U., 1980; cert. Creedmoor Family Therapy Inst., 1983. R.N., Fla., N.Y., N.J.; cert. social worker, N.Y. Indsl. nurse United Airlines, N.Y.C., 1966-71; salesperson Covedata Inc., N.Y.C., 1980-81; EAP dir. Creedmoor Hosp., N.Y.C., 1981-84; sales dir. Human Concepts, Union, N.J., 1984; v.p. sales Covedata, Inc., N.Y.C., 1984—; EAP cons., Franklin Lakes, N.J., 1983—. Adv. Parents for a Better Edn., Glen Cove, N.Y., 1976-78; mem. Parents Adv. Council for Spl. Children, Franklin Lakes, 1986. Mem. Acad. Cert. Social Workers, Assn. of Labor-Mgmt. Adminstrs. and Cons. on Alcoholism, Nat. Assn. Social Workers (cert.), Employee Assistance Soc. of N.Am., Alpha Chi. Avocations: dancing; singing. Home: 812 Linden Way Franklin Lakes NJ 07417 Office: Covedata Inc 230 W 41 St New York NY 10036

MARIENAU, MARY E. SHIRK, nurse, anesthetist; b. Waterloo, Iowa, July 8, 1950; d. Harold Harlin and Mary Jane (Smith) Shirk; divorced; 1 child, Jennifer Sue Marienau. Diploma in Nursing, Allen Meml. Sch. of Nursing, 1971; BA in Sci., U. No. Iowa, 1976; cert. in nurse anesthesia, Mayo Sch. Health Related Scis., 1979; MS, Winona State U., 1986. Office nurse Med. Assn. of Cedar Falls, Iowa, 1970-71; charge RN in med. surg. specialties Sartori Hosp., Cedar Falls, Iowa, 1971-72; asst. head nurse acute care Allen Meml. Hosp., Waterloo, 1972-75, staff RN ICU/Critical Care Unit, 1975-76; staff anesthetist Mayo Clinic, Rochester, Minn., 1979-81; asst. anesthesia supr. Mayo Clinic, Rochester, 1981—, intern in counselor edn., 1984-85; mem. masters program com. Mayo Clinic Nurse Anesthesia Sch. Health Related Scis. , 1984, edn. com., 1984—, student selection com., 1984—; chmn. student and faculty evaluation subcom., 1984—; mem. St. Mary's anesthesia section's communicatin com., 1984-86; on-site visitor Nat. Council on Accreditation of Nurse Anesthesia Programs, 1988—. Author, editor, narrator instructional video for St. Mary's Oseointegrations. Mem. Rochester Civic Music Guild. Mem. Am. Assn. Nurse Anesthetists, Minn. Assn. Nurse Anesthetists. Republican. Baptist. Lodge: Masons (worthy adv. 1968). Office: Mayo Clinic 200 First St SW Rochester MN 55905

MARILAO, ROSELLA QUERUBIN, personnel director; b. Manila, Philippines, Mar. 10, 1939; came to U.S., 1969; d. Anastacio and Pelagia (EspirituSanto) Querabin; (div.); children—George, Willk, Frank, Mary Rose. A.B.A., St. Theresa's Coll., 1957; B.S.B.A., Calif. State U.-Hayward, 1976, M.P.A., 1979. Sales cicrulation mgr. Philippines Internat. Pub. Co., Manila, 1959-66; personnel analyst City of Oakland (Calif.), 1972-76; asst. to dean Chabot Coll., Hayward, 1976-79; personnel adminstr. Claffey Coll., Alta Lana, Calif., 1979-82; dir. personnel Lakeland Community Coll., Mentor, Ohio, 1982—; cons. Peralta Community Coll. Dist., Oakland, 1976-79. Trustee, Lake County Mental Health Center, Mentor, 1982, Community Housing Resource Bd.; bd. dirs. Family Tutcrial Services, 1978; trustee, treas. Lake County Community Services Council, Mentor, 1983; vol. tutor Project LEARN. Mem. Am. Soc. Personnel Adminstrs., Internat. Personnel Mgmt. Assn., Am. Assn. U. Adminstrs., Internat. Assn. Quality Circles, Colls. Univ. Personnel Assn. Roman Catholic. Clubs: Altrusa of Lake (Mentor), Philippine Am. Soc. Ohio. Lodge: Legionarios del Trabajo in Am. Office: Lakeland Community Coll Mentor OH 44060

MARIN, ROSA CELESTE, research consultant, social work educator; b. Arecibo, P.R., June 1, 1912; d. Angel M. and Justa (Marin) Marin; B.S., U. P.R., 1933; M.S., U. Pitts., 1944, D.S.W., 1953. Social welfare officer, acting dist. dir., supr. Fed. Emergency Relief Adminstrn., 1933-36; social worker, gen. supr. in charge of research P.R. Reconstrn. Adminstrn., 1936-40; supr. spl. projects and head research sect. Div. of Pub. Welfare P.R., 1940-44; asst. prof. U. P.R. Sch. Social Work, 1944-59, assoc. prof., 1959-67, dir. Grad. Sch. Social Work, 1967-74, dir. research unit, 1955-74, prof., 1967-74, prof. emeritus, 1980—; cons. on research to supr. ednl. council cons. VA, Dept. Services Against Addiction, Coll. Pharmacy, Municipal Govt. San Juan; chmn. Welfare Devel. Corp.; arts and humanities adv. bd. CSUF; mem. Council Human Resources. Decorated Bicentennial Medallion of Distinction, U. Pitts, 1987. Mem. Assn. Tchrs. P.R., Nat. Assn. Social Workers, Nat. Conf. on Social Welfare, Coll. Social Workers, Soc. Newspaperwomen, Am. Acad. Polit. and Social Scis., Am. Assn. Statisticians, Assn. Research Centers Adminstrn. Editor: Revista Servicio Social, 1949-50, 52-65. Author: Compilation of Adminstrative Cases: Study of dependent Multiproblem Families in Puerto Rico, The Female Drug Addict in Puerto Rico, Fraudulent Medical Prescriptions of Controlled Substances in Puerto Rico; co-author: Manpower Resources and Projections; Effectiveness of the Rehabilitation of Drug Addicts in Puerto Rico. Editor Jour. Humanidad. Contbr. articles to profl. jours. Home: PO Box 6679 Santurce PR 00914 Office: 2153 Teniente Lavergne St Santurce PR 00913

MARINCOLA, DIAN ANGELA, data processing executive; b. Norristown, Pa., May 26, 1954; d. Dominic Peter and Mafalda Monica (D'Amore) M. BA, Shippensburg St. Coll., 1976; MS in Info. Resource Mgmt., Syracuse U., 1983. Info. specialist Regional Resource Ctr. Pa. Info. Ctr. for Spl. Edn., King of Prussia, 1977-81; project supr. Informatics Gen. Corp., Rockville, Md., 1983-84, legal services mgr., 1984-85; user support supr. RMS Assocs. at NASA STI Facility, Balt.-Washington Internat. Airport, Md., 1985—; documentation cons. BRS, Latham, N.Y., 1981. Editor: (newsletter) Prise Wise, 1980-81; author: (newsletter) STI Bulletin, 1985—. Mem. Am. Soc. for Info Sci., Soc. of Profl. Journalists, Soc. for Advanced Learning Technology. Office: NASA STI Facility Balt-Washington Internat Airport Box 8757 Baltimore MD 21240

MARINELLI, ADA SANTI, government official, real estate company official; b. Borgo a Mozzano, Italy, July 27, 1942; came to U.S., 1953; d. Attilio and Maria Josephine (Biondi) Santi; m. Rudolph Marinelli, July 12, 1964; children: Gina Marie, Marisa Bianca. Student, Rivier Coll., 1962-63, George Washington U., 1963; AA with high honors, Prince Georges Community Coll., 1980. Sec. U.S. Post Office, Washington, 1963-70; adminstrv. sec. U.S. Postal Service, Washington, 1970-80, real estate specialist trainee, 1980-82, realty mgmt. and acquisition analyst, 1982-84, real estate specialist, 1984—, prin., 1986—; assoc. broker Larry Eul Realty, Inc., Camp Springs, Md., 1977-83, Alvin Turner Real Estate Upper Marlboro, Md., 1988—. Recipient spl. achievement award U.S. Postal Service, 1987. Mem. Fed. Real Property Assn., Alumnae Assn. Rivier Coll. Democrat. Roman Catholic. Club: Orsogna (Washington) (pres. 1965-66). Home: 7006 Sheffield Dr Camp Springs MD 20748

MARINKO, MONICA MARIE, psychologist; b. Cleve., Feb. 26, 1948; d. Fred Joseph and and Sophia Frances (Gornik) M. BA, U. Detroit, 1970; MA, John Carroll U., 1975. Cert. and lic. sch. psychologist, Ohio. Psychologist Ashtabula (Ohio) Area City Schs., 1975—; pvt. practice sch. psychology Chesterland, Ohio, 1985—. Mem. Nat. Assn. Sch. Psychologists, Ohio Sch. Psychologists Assn., Soc. for Personality Assessment (assoc.). Home: 12321 Norton Dr Chesterland OH 44026 Office: Ashtabula Area City Schs 401 W 44th St Ashtabula OH 44004

MARINO, JOANNE MARIE, psychotherapist, consultant; b. Greenwich, Conn., Feb. 15, 1951; d. Frank Dominic and Matilda (Salvatore) M. B.A., U. Conn., 1973, M.A. in Ednl. Psychology/Rehab. Counseling, 1975. Cert. clin. mental health counselor. Counselor Ea. Ct. Drug Action Program, Inc., Willimantic Conn., 1974-77; sr. counselor Liberation Programs, Inc., Stamford, Conn., 1977-79, program dir. 1980-83, quality assurance coordinator, 1982-83; gen. practice psychotherapy, cons., The Learning Exchange, Cos Cob, Conn., 1983—. Contbr. articles to counseling jours. Mem. Am. Assn. Counseling and Devel., Am. Mental Health Counselors Assn., Assn. of Specialists in Group Work. Avocations: films, traveling, computers, gardening. Office: The Learning Exchange 21 Strickland Rd Cos Cob CT 06807

MARINOFF, ELAINE S., artist, educator; b. Los Angeles, Sept. 24, 1934; d. George Lawrence and Lena (Brown) M.; m. Robert Glen Good, June 9, 1957 (div. 1980); children: Cynthia Ellen, Glendon Robert, Bradley Lawrence. Student, Chouinard Art Inst., Los Angeles, 1950, U. Calif., Berkeley, 1953-55; BA, U. Calif., Los Angeles, 1957; student, Ecole Guerre Lavigene, Paris, 1955-56. Interior designer, pres. Elaine Good Interiors, Los Angeles, 1960-72; instr. the seriographic process U. Calif., Los Angeles, 1986—. One woman exhibitions include Bolen Gallery, Venice, Calif., 1979, Brand Library Gallery, Glendale, Calif., 1979, Downey (Calif.) Mus. Art, 1981, Heritage Gallery, Los Angeles, 1982, Galerie Das Bilderhaus, Frankfurt Fed. Republic Germany, 1983, Galerie Woeller Paquet, Frankfurt, 1984, Criteria Inc. Gallery, Denver, 1985, Waterfront Theater Gallery San Francisco, 1988; selected group exhibitions include Laguna Beach (Calif.) Mus. Art, 1974, Geneis Galleries, Ltd., N.Y.C., 1977, Los Angeles County Mus. Art, 1979, 80, Calif. Mus. Sci. and Industry, 1980, 81, Satyra Galeria fur Erotische Kunst, Kronberg, Fed. Republic Germany, 1981, Jack Gallery, N.Y.C., 1984, Criteria Inc., Denver, 1984. Active with Artists for Econ. Action, Los Angeles, 1976—, Women's Caucus for Arts, Los Angeles, 1984—, UCLA Arts Council, 1986, 87. Mem. Artists Equity (bd. dirs. Los Angeles chpt. 1980), Contemporary Arts Council, Bus. and Profl. Women. Democrat. Jewish. Studio: 1429 W Washington Blvd Venice CA 90291

MARISOL (MARISOL ESCOBAR), sculptor; b. Paris, May 22, 1930. Ed., Ecole des Beaux-Arts, Paris, 1949, Art Students League, N.Y.C., 1950, New Sch. for Social Research, 1951-54, Hans Hofmann Sch., N.Y.C., 1951-54. One-man shows at Sidney Janis Gallery, N.Y.C., 1966, 67, 73, 75, 81, 84 Hanover Gallery, London, 1967, Boymans-van Beuningen Mus., Rotterdam, Netherlands, 1968, Moore Coll. Art, Phila., 1970, Worcester (Mass.) Art Mus., 1971, N.Y. Cultural Center, 1973, Columbus (Ohio) Gallery of Fine Arts, 1974, Makler Gallery, Phila., 1982, Hershhorn Mus. and Sculpture Garden, 1984, Boca Raton Mus. Art, Fla., 1988, numerous others; exhibited in group shows including Painting of a Decade, Tate Gallery, London, 1964, New Realism, Municipal Mus., The Hague, 1964, Carnegie Internat., Pitts., 1964, Art of the U.S.A, 1670-1966, Whitney Mus. Am. Art, N.Y.C., 1966, American Sculpture of the Sixties, Mus. of Art, Los Angeles, 1967, Biennale, Venice, 1968, Art Inst. Chgo., 1968, Image of Man Today, Inst. Contemporary Arts, London, 1968, Bronx Mus., 1976, Bklyn. Mus., 1977; represented in permanent collections at Mus. Modern Art, N.Y.C., Whitney Mus. Am. Art, Albright-Knox Gallery, Buffalo, Hakone Open Air Mus., Tokyo, Nat. Portrait Gallery, Washington, Harry N. Abrams Collection, N.Y.C., Yale U. Art Gallery, Art Inst. Chgo., numerous others. Mem. Am. Acad. and Inst. Arts and Letters (v.p. art 1984-87). Address: care Sidney Janis Gallery 110 W 57th St New York NY 10019 *

MARK, LILLIAN GEE, school founder and official; b. Berkeley, Calif., Mar. 18, 1932; d. Pon Gordon and Sun Kum (Wong) Gee; m. Richard Muin Mark, June 20, 1954; children: Dean, Kim, Faye, Glenn, Lynne. AB in Psychology, U. Calif., Berkeley, 1954; MS in Christian Sch. Adminstrn., Pensacola Coll., 1987. Sec., Western Life Ins. Co., San Francisco, 1944-54; child care tchr. San Diego Child Care Ctr., 1954-55; dir. pre-sch. ABC Nursery, San Mateo, Calif., 1969-76; founder, prin. Alpha Beacon Christian Sch., San Carlos, Calif., 1976—; pres. Alpha Beacon Christian Ministries. Author: Handbook for Parents and Students, 1983, How to Encourage Your Staff. Mem. Assn. Christian Ministries Mgmt. Assn., Christian Schs. Internat. Republican. Mem. Pentacostal Ch. Avocations: tennis, piano, Bible study. Home: 182 Exbourne Ave San Carlos CA 94070 Office: Alpha Beacon Christian Ministries 750 Dartmouth Ave San Carlos CA 94070

MARK, MARILYN, artist; b. Bklyn., Aug. 7; d. Michael Nathan and Loving Henrietta (Valensky) Sabetsky; m. Herbert Murray Mark, May 17, 1953. Painter, N.Y.C.; bd. dirs. Burr Artists, N.Y.C., 1974; writer, contbr. Artists Equity Assn., N.Y.C., 1985; pub. relations dir. and coordinator exhibitions, pres. Visual Individualists United, Bklyn., 1976—; with Stuhr Mus. of Prairie Pioneer, Grand Island, Nebr., 1986—; assoc. trustee Nat. Art Mus. of Sport, U. New Haven, Ct.,1984— . Exhibits include Nat. Mus. Sport; three person show Madison Sq. Garden Ctr., N.Y.C., 1973; collections include Stuhr Mus. Prairie Pioneer, 1983, 86, 88, Am. Arts Sports Mus., U.S. Sports Acad., Mobile, 1987, Nat. Art Sports Mus., U. New Haven, West Haven, Conn., 1977, 86, 87, Ville De Montbard (France) Du Musee Des Beaux Arts, 1974, 86; rep. by Tatem Gallery, Ft. Lauderdale, Fla., Rental Gallery, Des Moines Art Ctr. Recipient Merit award Mus. Soc. Illustrators, 1983, Citation, Gold medal Republic Santo Domingo and Belgo-Hispanica Assn., Belgium, 1977. Mem. Nat. Mus. Women Artists, Nat. Assn. Female Execs. (network dir. 1985—). Avocations: writing; playing electric organ; dancing; walking; travel. Home: 2261 Ocean Ave Brooklyn NY 11229

MARK, RONNIE JOAN, medical librarian; b. Bklyn., Mar. 10, 1941; d. Morris and Sylvia (Moskowitz) Horowitz; m. Steven Mark, June 1, 1969. BS in Biology, Fairleigh Dickinson U., 1963; MS in Library Info. Scis. summa cum laude, Palmer Grad. Library Sch. C.W. Post U., 1978. Med. librarian Ayerst Labs., N.Y.C., 1964-67; head librarian Med. World News, N.Y.C., 1967-77; librarian health scis., asst. prof. L.I. U., Bklyn., 1977-80; dir. med. library Coney Island Hosp., Bklyn., 1980—. Mem. Med. Library Assn., N.Y.-N.J. chpt. Med. Library Assn., Bklyn., Queens, Staten Island Health Scis. Librarians (pres. 1985—), Beta Phi Mu, Beta Mu. Jewish. Office: Coney Island Hosp 2601 Ocean Pkwy Brooklyn NY 11235

MARKEL, DEBRA MARGARET, insurance company executive; b. Richmond, Va., July 15, 1953; d. Lewis C. Markel and Zelda Ellen (Kingoff) Nordlinger; m. Douglas B. Murphy, Mar. 10, 1973 (div. Oct. 1979); children: Matthew A. Murphy, Seth P. Murphy. Student, U. N.C., Greensboro, 1971-72, Va. Commonwealth U., 1976-77. Comml. rater Aetna Ins. Co., Richmond, 1973-74; part-time service rep. Sirco Ins. Agy., Richmond, 1974-78; asst. underwriter Kemper Ins. Co., Richmond, 1978-80; underwriter Reliance Ins. Co., Richmond, 1980-81; comml. mgr. Ames Assurance Co., Norfolk, Va., 1981-83; comml. supr. H-R-H of Tidewater, Chesapeake, Va., 1983-85; mng. portfolio underwriter Royal Ins. Co., Richmond, 1985—; instr. U. Richmond, 1986—, Ins. Women of Richmond, 1978—; mem. exec. bd., newsletter editor Ins. Women of Norfolk, 1983-84. Vol. Chippenham Hosp., Richmond, 1974. Mem. Greater Richmond Chartered Property Casualty Underwriters Assn. (new designee bd. mem. 1986-87, sec.-treas. Va. I-Day 1988), Ins. Edn. Com., NOW. Mem. Unitarian Ch. Office: Royal Ins Co 101 Buford Rd Richmond VA 23235

MARKEY, ELIZABETH HELEN, federal agency administrator; b. Teaneck, N.J., Apr. 27, 1956; d. Thomas Francis and Catherine A. (Dillon) M.; m. James Francis Kelly, May 5, 1984; children: Katherine Angela, Erin Susan. BA in Polit. Sci., U. Fla., 1978; degree in econs., Adam Mickiewicz, Poznan, Poland, 1978; MA in Pub. Adminstrn., Am. U., 1983. Staff asst. U.S. Senator Durkin, Washington, 1979, U.S. Ho. of Reps., Washington, 1979-81; sr. asst. to v.p. Am. U., Washington, 1981-83; presdl. mgmt. intern U.S. Dept. of Treasury, Washington, 1983-84; chief policy and tng. div. info. systems security U.S. Dept. of State, Washington, 1984—; cons. Systems Communications, Washington, 1987—; mem. Congl. Woman's Polit. Caucus, Washington, 1979-81; com. on Post Office and Civil Service U.S. Ho. Reps. Mem. Christian Children's Fund, 1979-83; campaign aide U.S. Congressman Harris, Washington, 1982, Gov. Graham, Fla., 1979. Recipient Civil Service Disting. Honor award U.S. Dept. State, Washington, 1986. Mem. Nat. Assn. Female Execs., Nat. Honor Soc. for Pub. Affairs and Adminstrn., NOW, Predl. Mgmt. Intern Alumni Group, Nat. Soc. for Pub. Adminstrn. Democrat. Home: 3824 Warner St Kensington MD 20895 Office: US Dept State 3301 C St NW Washington DC 20520

MARKEY, JOANNE ZINK, computer consultant; b. Phila., June 7, 1941; d. Albert Barnes and Mildred (Gerhab) Zink; 1 child from previous marriage, James A. Kenney; m. Owen Charles Markey Jr., Aug. 2, 1975; children: Stephen James, Janice M., Michael James. Cons. computer Ambler, Pa., 1978-83; owner, cons. computer Z-Mark Assocs., Ambler, 1983—. Home and Office: 112 Stout Rd Ambler PA 19002

MARKHAM, JUDITH ELLENE, editor; b. Niagara Falls, N.Y., Sept. 21, 1941; d. Edward W. and Edith J. (Weimer) Errick; m. Robert L. Markham, Sept. 19, 1970. BA, Houghton Coll., 1963. Curriculum editor Union Gospel Press, Cleve., 1963-65; asst. editor Child Evangelism mag., Grand Rapids, Mich., 1965-68; asst. book editor Zondervan Pub. House, Grand Rapids, 1968-73, project editor, 1973-78, gen. editor trade books, 1978-80; editor-at-large, 1980-83, editor Zondervan Books, 1983-87; editor Markham Books, 1982-87, editor trade books, 1986-87; ptnr.-owner, Blue Water Ink, 1987—; mem. faculty Sch. Christian Writing, Mpls., 1981, 82; vis. lectr. Houghton Coll., 1986. Author short stories. Named Houghton Coll. Alumna of Yr., 1985. Mem. Grand Rapids Symphonic Choir, 1968-78. Mem. Women's Nat. Book Assn. (chpt. dir. 1975-76), Profl. Women's Network, Alliance of Women Entrepreneurs. Presbyterian. Office: Blue Water Ink PO Box 8877 Grand Rapids MI 49518

MARKHAM, LORI, systems specialist; b. Los Angeles, July 9, 1934; d. Orval Ernest and Delphine (Cano) Paulson; m. David Lawrence Markham, May 1, 1965 (div. Mar. 1967); 1 child, Deborah Louise. AA in Computer Sci., Criss Coll., 1983. Supr. loan account Lincoln Savs., Los Angeles, 1955-58, Imperial Savs., Pasadena, Calif., 1958-61; owner Lori's Holiday Shop, Los Angeles, 1961-64; office mgr. Paulson's Flowers, Los Angeles, 1965-77; corp. sec., treas. Far West Brokers Corp., Brea, Calif., 1978-81; owner Fin. Services, Covina, Calif., 1982—; systems adminstr. Metmor Financial, Los Angeles, 1985—; computing cons. Equity Mortgage, Hacienda Heights, Calif., 1986—. Mem. Inland Soc. Tax Cons., Mortgage Line Users Group, Nat. Assn. Female Execs., China Painters Assn., Delta Theta Tau. Republican. Religious Scientist. Office: Metmor Fin 4050 Wilshire Blvd Los Angeles CA 90010

MARKHAM, ROSEMARY, lawyer; b. Pitts., June 12, 1946; d. Chester James and Elizabeth Helen (Seger) Markham; m. Wayne Joseph Pfrimmer, Sept. 11, 1965 (div. 1975); 1 dau., Adriene. B.A., U. Pitts., 1968; J.D., Duquesne U., 1978. Bar: Pa. 1978; adminstrv. asst. West Pa. Conservancy, Pitts., 1969-70; law clk. Girman & DelSole, 1975-76, Watzman & DeAngelis, 1976-78; serious injury rep. Travelors Ins., 1978-79; assoc. Manifesto & Doherty, 1979-81; individual practice law, 1981—. Mem. ABA, Assn. Trial Lawyers Am., Pa. Bar Assn., Pa. Trial Lawyers Assn., Allegheny County Bar Assn., Mensa. Democrat. Roman Catholic. Club: Rivers. Office: 320 Allegheny Bldg 429 Forbes Ave Pittsburgh PA 15219

MARKLE, CHERI VIRGINIA CUMMINS, nurse; b. N.Y.C., Nov. 22, 1936; d. Brainard Lyle and Mildred (Schwab) Cummins; m. John Markle, Aug. 26, 1961 (dec. 1962); 1 child, Kellianne. RN, Ind. State U., 1959; BS in Rehab. Edn., Wright State U., 1975; BSN, Capital U., 1987; postgrad. in Nursing Adminstrn., Wright State U., 1987—. Coordinator Dayton (Ohio) Children's Psychiat. Hosp., 1962-75; dir. nursing Stillwater Health Ctr., Dayton, 1975-76; sr. supr. VA, Dayton, 1977-85, alcohol rehab. nurse coordinator, 1985-86; dir. nursing Odd Fellows, Springfield, Ohio, 1987—; rehab. cons., Fairborn, Ohio, 1976—. rehab. cons., Fairborn, Ohio, 1976—; newspaper columnist Golden Times, Clark County. Served to 1st lt., USAF, 1959-61. Mem. Am. Nurses Assn. (cert. adminstrn. 1983, cert. gerontology 1984), Ohio Nurses Assn., Dist. 10 Nurses Assn., Nurse Mgrs. Assembly, Gerontological Nurse Assembly, Nat. Assn. Female Execs., Rehab. Soc., Wright State U. Alumni Assn., Am. Legion, Alpha Sigma Alpha, Sigma Theta Tau. Democrat. Roman Catholic. Home: 539 South St Fairborn OH 45324 Office: Odd Fellows 404 E McCreight Ave Springfield OH 45503

MARKLEY, LINDA PAYNE, Spanish educator; b. Ithaca, N.Y., Apr. 29, 1955; d. Damon Aubra and Ruth Hazel (Fish) Payne; m. Michael Lynn Markley, July 19, 1975; children: Laura Michèle, Christa Diane. AA summa cum laude, Fla. Jr. Coll., 1974; BA magna cum laude, Jacksonville U., 1976; postgrad., U. No. Fla., 1978-79. Cert. tchr., N.Y., Fla. Spanish tchr. Oakdale Sch., Hempstead, N.Y., 1976-78; bilingual tng. instr. HRS Dept. of Health and Rehab. Services, 1981-83; Spanish tchr. St. Paul Episc. Sch., Jacksonville, Fla., 1983-84; instr. Fla. Jr. Coll., Jacksonville, 1981-84; Spanish tchr. Duval County Sch. System, Fla., 1978-80, 84-85, Brunswick Jr. Coll., Brunswick, Ga., 1985-86, Frederica Acad., St. Simons, Fla., 1986—. Interpreter City of Jacksonville Beach, 1981-83. Faculty scholar Jacksonville U., 1974-76. Republican. Methodist. Home: 412 Couper Ave Saint Simons Island GA 31522 Office: Frederica Academy 200 Hamilton Rd Saint Simons Island GA 31522

MARKOVICH, OLGA, magazine editor; b. Toronto, Ont., Can., Feb. 24, 1940; d. Bozidar Marinko and Milica (Trumich) M. Diploma in Journalism, Ryerson Poly. Inst., 1965, B in Applied Arts in Journalism, 1973. Asst. editor Shoe and Leather Jour. Southam Communications Ltd., Don Mills, Ont., 1965-72, assoc. editor, 1972; editor Southam Bldg. Guide, Don Mills, 1972-82; mng. editor Can. Indsl. Equipment News, 1975-77, editor, 1977—. Recipient Thomas Turner Meml. award Southam Communications Ltd., 1973, Mktg. award Southam Communications, 1977, Queen Elizabeth's Can. Silver Jubilee medal, 1977. Mem. Bus. Press Editors Assn., Am. Bus. Press, Soc. Serbian Writers and Artists Abroad (London), Serbian Nat. Shield Soc. Can., Serbian Nat. Fedn. (Person of Yr. award 1986). Progressive Conservative. Eastern Orthodox. Home: 254 Chine Dr, Scarborough, ON Canada M1M 2L8 Office: 1450 Don Mills Rd, Don Mills, ON Canada M3B 2X7

MARKOVICH-TREECE, PATRICIA HELEN, economist; b. Oakland, Calif.; s. Patrick Joseph and Helen Emily (Prydz) Markovich; B.A. in Econs.; M.S. in Econs., U. Calif.-Berkeley, postgrad. (Lilly Found. grantee) Stanford U., (NSF grantee) Oreg. Grad. Research Center, DD World Christian Ministries; children—Michael Sean, Bryan Jeffry, Tiffany Helene. With public relations dept. Pettler Advt., Inc.; pvt. practice polit. and econs. cons.; aide to majority whip Oreg. Ho. of Reps.; lectr., instr., various Calif. instns., Chemeketa (Oreg.) Coll., Portland (Oreg.) State U. Commr., City of Oakland (Calif.), 1970-74; coordinator City of Piedmont, Calif. Gen. Planning Commn. Mem. Mensa, Bay Area Artists Assn. (coordinator, founding mem.), Piedmont Civic Assn., CFRTP (bd. dirs.).

MARKOWITZ, GAIL EUNICE, corporate sales, real estate and marketing executive; b. N.Y.C., 1937; d. Morris and Barbara (Schwartz) Schechter; children: Matt, Jami. B.A., Queens Coll., 1959. Account exec. Mark III Advt., 1962-72; v.p. sales Fla. Atlantic Devel. Corp., Forest Hills, N.Y., 1973-75; v.p. Fla. Atlantic Advt., Inc., Forest Hills, 1972-75, Webb Realty, Inc., Forest Hills, 1973-75; pres., owner GM Mktg., Jericho, N.Y., 1975, Fla., 1985—; v.p. sales and mktg. Minieri Communities of Fla., Inc., 1975-78, Met-Com Mktg., Inc., Hicksville, N.Y., 1975-78 ; v.p., cons. advt., advt. and sales promotion cons. Jamaica Estates, N.Y., 1959—; sales mgr. Gen. Devel. Corp., N.Y., 1979-81, Deltona Corp., N.Y., 1982; br. mgr. Better Homes & Gardens Realtors Assocs., Fla., 1983; salesperson, Arvida Corp., Fla., 1984; dir. sales & mktg., Grenadier Investments, 1984-85. Lic. real estate broker, N.Y., Fla.; lic. mortgage broker, Fla. Past pres. PTA; former v.p. Orgn. for Retarded Children; former v.p. Sisterhood Hillcrest Jewish Ctr.; past chairperson Queens State of Israel Bond Program. Mem. Inst. Residential Mktg., Advt. Women N.Y., Com. 100, Nat. Assn. Female Execs. (asst. dir.); Fla. Atlantic Builder's Assn. (program chairperson, bd. dirs., past dir. sales & mktg. council); Women's Exec. Council Broward County. Club: Tiger Bay (Miami, Fla.). Home and Office: 410 NW 65th Terr Margate FL 33063

MARKS, BARBARA HANNAH, magazine publisher; b. Carrollton, Ga., Dec. 23, 1956; d. Marshall Harrison Hannah and Pauline Ruth (Honadel) Chou; m. Henry William Marks, Dec. 18, 1981 (div. Jan. 1987). BS in Mktg., St. John's U., N.Y.C., 1978; postgrad., NYU, 1980-82. Promotion mgr. Playboy mag., N.Y.C., 1978-79; pub. TeenAge Mag., N.Y.C., 1982-84, 86-88, advt. dir., 1986-88, v.p., 1986-88; assoc. pub. Success! Mag., N.Y.C., 1984-86; v.p. pub. CPS, Inc., Bedford, Mass., 1986-88; sr. v.p. group pub. Macfadden Holdings, Inc., N.Y.C., 1988—. Home: 2 Horatio St New York NY 10014 Office: Macfadden Holdings 215 Lexington Ave New York NY 10016

MARKS, BEVERLY ADAMS, data processing personnel executive; b. Atlanta, Dec. 27, 1955; d. Norman Phillip and Joan (Crout) Adams; m. David Paul Marks, July 11, 1981. Student, Berry Coll., Rome, Ga., 1974, DeKalb Community Coll., Atlanta, 1975; AA, El Centro Coll., Dallas, 1976. Computer technician U.S. Gen. Acctg. Office, Dallas, 1977-79; sr. programmer-analyst Dallas Times-Herald, 1979-83; mgr. Nat. FSI Co., Dallas, 1983-87, ind. cons., 1987—; region system support coordinator Internat. Paper Co., 1987—. Mem. Nat. Assn. Female Execs., Women in Computing. Republican. Home: 3520 Big Horn Plano TX 75075 Office: Internat Paper Co 6600 Stemmans Freeway 2d Floor Dallas TX 75380

MARKS, CICELY PHIPPEN, publishing company administrator; b. Boston, May 24, 1947; d. Robert J. and Anne (Peterson) Phippen; m. Franklin D. Marks, June 23, 1974; children: Cynthia Ann, David Maxwell. BA, Trinity Coll., 1969; MLS, U. Md., 1970. Librarian VA, Washington, 1970-85, regional dir. Am. Overseas Book Co., Norwood, N.J., 1986—. Chair liturgy com. Ch. of Christ the King, Silver Spring, Md., 1982—, chair pool com. Americana Finnmark Condominium, Silver Spring, 1984—. Mem. ALA, Spl. Libraries Assn., Med. Library Assn. Home: 2016 Coleridge Dr #201 Silver Spring MD 20902 Office: Am Overseas Book Co 10620 Georgia Ave #101 Silver Spring MD 20902

MARKS, DOROTHY LIND, mathematics tutor; b. N.Y.C., Apr. 30, 1900; d. Alfred Daniel and Martha (Herzog) Lind; m. Norman Lincoln Marks, May 29, 1923 (dec. 1959); 1 son, Alfred Lind (dec. 1980). B.A., Barnard Coll., 1921. Substitute tchr. N.Y. high schs., 1921-28; math tutor The Brearley Sch., N.Y.C., 1953-62, The Marlborough Sch., Los Angeles, 1973—, pvt. and pub. secondary schs., Los Angeles, 1973—, NYU, 1965-72; chmn. math dept. The Lenox Sch., N.Y.C., 1960-70. Bd. dirs. women's orgn. Temple Rodeph Sholem, N.Y.C., 1925-50, fin. sec., 1925-47. Mem. Phi Beta Kappa (recipient Kohn Math. Prize 1921, sec.-treas. Barnard chpt. 1925-50, chartermem. alumnae in N.Y.). Republican. Jewish. Avocations: reading, music, theatre, concerts, ballet.

MARKS, ELAINE, French language educator; b. N.Y.C., Nov. 13, 1930; d. Harry and Ruth (Elin) Marks. B.A., Bryn Mawr Coll., 1952; M.A., U. Pa., 1953; Ph.D., NYU, 1958. Asst. prof. French NYU, N.Y.C., 1958-60; assoc. prof. U. Wis.-Milw., 1963-65; prof. U. Wis., Madison, 1967-68, prof. French, Italian and women's studies, 1980—; prof. French U. Mass., Amherst, 1965-66; dir. Women's Studies Research Ctr., 1977-85. Author: Colette, 1960, 2d edit., 1981, Simone de Beauvoir: Encounters with Death, 1973; co-editor Homosexualities and French Literature, 1979, New French Feminisms, 1980, 81; editor Critical Essays on Simone de Beauvoir, 1987. Recipient Fulbright award NYU, France, 1958. Mem. MLA, Midwest Modern Lang. Assn., Am. Assn. Tchrs. French, Nat. Women's Studies Assn. Home: 2040 Field St Madison WI 53713

MARKS, HELENA LIN, medical technologist; b. Peking, China, Oct. 6, 1935; came to U.S., 1955, naturalized, 1961; d. Kung and Shu-Fan (Lee) Lin; BA in Math. and Physics, Hunter Coll., N.Y.C., 1972; m. John S. Marks, Nov. 28, 1958 (dec. 1973); children: John Lin, Paul Lee; m. 2d J.B. Celleri 1977. Supr. chemistry lab. Tompkins County Hosp., Ithaca, N.Y., 1962-64; supr. labs. Calvary Hosp., Bronx, N.Y., 1964-67; med. technologist N. Cen. Hosp., Bronx, N.Y., 1977-86, Nyack (N.Y.) Hosp., 1986—; real estate saleswoman. Mem. Am. Soc. Clin. Pathologists, N.Y.C. Med. Lab. Suprs. Home: 4 Raleigh Dr New City NY 10956

MARKS, JOAN HARRIET, educator; b. Portland, Maine, Feb. 4, 1929; d. Maurice Edward Rosen and Lillian (Morrison) Silton; m. Paul A. Marks, Nov. 28, 1953; children: Andrew, Elizabeth, Matthew. AB, Sarah Lawrence Coll., 1951; MS, Simmons Coll., 1953. Med. caseworker Mt. Sinai Hosp., N.Y.C., 1953-55, Presbyn. Hosp., N.Y.C., 1955-57; psychiat. caseworker N.Y. Hosp.-Cornell, White Plains, 1959-71; dir. human genetic program Sarah Lawrence Coll., Bronxville, N.Y., 1972—, dir. health advocacy program, 1979—; adv. Am. Bd. Internal Medicine, 1988—. Author: The Genetic Connection, 1978, Advocacy in Health Care, 1985. Trustee Blythedale Children's Hosp., Valhalla, N.Y., 1980—; mem. adv. com. N.Y. State Genetic Diseases Program, 1980-86. Mem. Maternity Ctr. Assn. (bd. dirs. 1979-85), Am. Soc. Human Genetics (social issues com. 1982—), Am. Pub. Health Assn., Am. Soc. Patient Reps., Soc. for Study of Social Biology. Office: Sarah Lawrence Coll Bronxville NY 10708

MARKS, JUANELL SAVAGE, business writing consultant; b. Oakdale, La., May 11, 1945; d. Earl Cleveland and Louella (Ryland) Savage; m. Clinton Reed Marks, Dec. 20, 1966; 1 child, Karyn Melea. BA, Northwestern State U., Natchitoches, La., 1966; MLS, Sam Houston State U., 1975, MEd, 1978. Cert. secondary tchr., adminstr. and supr., Tex. Tchr. English Calcasieu Parish Pub. Schs., Lake Charles, La., 1966-67; librarian Muscogee County Sch. Dist., Houston, 1968-69, 1971-80; supr. resource ctr., communications specialist Litwin Engrs. and Constrn. Inc., Houston, 1980-81; documentation coordinator Metier Mgmt. Systems Inc., Houston, 1981-83; sr. tech. writer CRS Sirrine Inc., Houston, 1983-85; pres., owner Profl. Writing Ideas, Houston, 1984—; sr. developer sales edn. Compaq Computer Corp., Houston, 1987—; grad. instr. U. Houston, Clearlake, Tex., 1979; documentation cons. Exxon Co., Houston, 1985—, Multiple Techs. Inc., Houston, 1985—; sr. developer Compaq Computer Corp., Houston, 1987—. Contbr. articles to profl. jours. Chmn. new mems. com. Tallowood Bapt. Ch., Houston, 1986—, v.p. choir, 1987. Named Outstanding Educator, Spring Branch Ind. Sch. Dist., Houston, 1975-79. Mem. Tex. Assn. Sch. Librarians (chmn. 1979-80, vice chmn. 1978-79, Outstanding Leadership award 1979), Tex. Library Assn. (chmn. awards com. 1977-78), Soc. Tech. Communication, Nat. Assn. Female Execs., Am. Soc. Tng. and Devel. Home and Office: 3023 Kevin Ln Houston TX 77043

MARKS, LILLIAN SHAPIRO, educator; b. Bklyn., Mar. 16, 1907; d. Hayman and Celia (Merowitz) Shapiro; B.S., N.Y. U., 1928; m. Joseph Marks, Feb. 21, 1932; children—Daniel, Sheila Blake, Jonathan. High sch. tchr., N.Y.C., 1929-30; tchr. Evalina de Rothschild Sch., Jerusalem, Palestine, 1930-31; social worker United Jewish Aid, Bklyn., 1931-32; tchr. Richmond Hill High Sch., 1932-40, Andrew Jackson High Sch., Cambria Heights, N.Y., 1940-71; mem. faculty New Sch. Social Research, N.Y.C., 1977-87 ; staff Vassar Summer Inst., 1946. Mem. Am. Fedn. Tchrs., English-Speaking Union, Inst. Ret. Profls. Democrat. Am. editor: Teeline, A System of Fast Writing, 1970; author: College Teeline, 1977; College Teeline Self-Taught, 1983; Touch Typing Made Simple, 1985. Home and Office: 117-16 Park Lane S Kew Gardens NY 11418

MARKS, RENEE LEE, educator; b. Chgo., Nov. 20, 1936; d. Sol and Celia (Freund) Kaplan; m. Donald NOrman Marks, June 22, 1958; children: Robin Debra Marks Dombeck, Steven Michael, Jody Ilene. BSJ, Northwestern U., 1958, postgrad. (Chgo. Bd. Edn. scholar), summer 1978; BJS, Spertus Coll., 1972; MA, Mundelein Coll., 1975; MEd with distinction, De Paul U., 1981; postgrad. in ednl. adminstrn. Northeastern Ill. U., 1980-81; cert. in adminstrn. and supervision Nat. Coll. Edn., Evanston, Ill., 1982, PhD cand., 1984—; cert. in computer sci. U. Ill.-Chgo., 1982-85.Tchr. Chgo. Bd. Edn., 1976—; lectr. on Holocaust. Mem. Nat. Council for Social Studies, Chgo. Council for Social Studies, Assn. for Supervision and Curriculum Devel., Am. Ednl. Research Assn., Nat. Soc. for Study of Edn., Phi Delta Kappa. Jewish. Author, Holocaust curriculum for Chgo. Bd. Edn., 1980. Home and Office: 9036 N Menard Morton Grove IL 60053

MARKS, ROBERTA BARBARA, artist, educator; b. Savannah, Ga.; d. Philip W. and Eleanore (Margolis) Dilner; children—Jeffery Allen, Steven Craig. B.F.A., U. Miami, Coral Gables, Fla., 1980; M.F.A., U. S. Fla., 1981. Instr., lectr. multi-media, lectr., vis. artist to numerous art schs., including U. S. Fla., Tampa, Chgo. Art Inst., Valparaiso U., Ind., Rochester Inst. Tech. Am. Sch. of Crafts, N.Y., Galerie de Koull, Murten, Switzerland, Santa Fe Community Coll., Gainesville, Brookfield Craft Ctr., Conn., U. Wis.-Milw., Parson Sch. Design; juror Riverside Avondale Preservation Art Festival, Jacksonville, Fla., 1981, Ybor Square Art Festival, Tampa, 1980, Miami Lakes Art Festival, Fla., 1975. One woman shows include Brevard Community Coll., Melbourne, Fla., 1982, Cocoa, Fla., 1982, Coventry Galleries, Ltd., Tampa, 1983, Barbara Gillman Gallery, Miami, 1984, 87, Tennessee Williams Fine Arts Ctr., Key West, 1985, Garth Clark Gallery, N.Y.C., 1985, Fred Gros Gallery, Key West, 1985, Key West Art and Historical Soc. East Martello Mus. and Gallery, 1985, U. Miami New Gallery, Fla., 1987, Katie Gingrass Gallery, Milw., 1987, Zimmerman Saturn Gallery, Nashville, 1987, Bern, Zurich Switzerland, 1988, many others; exhibited in group shows at Netsky Gallery, Miami, 1982, The Craftsman's Gallery, Scarsdale, N.Y., 1982, Garth Clark Gallery, Los Angeles, 1983, Nelson-Atkins Mus. Art, Kansas City, Mo., 1983, Am. Craft Mus., N.Y.C., 1984, N. Miami Mus. and Art Ctr., 1985, Joanne Lyon Gallery, Aspen, Colo., 1984, Key West Art and Hist. Soc. East Martello Mus. and Gallery, 1985, Garth Clark Gallery, N.Y.C. and Los Angeles, 1985, 24X24, Ruth Siegel Ltd., N.Y.C., 1987, Artforms Gallery, Louisville, 1986, The Pvt. Collection Women Artists, Ohio, 1987, many others; represented in permanent collections Smithsonian Instn., Renwick Gallery, Rochester Inst. Tech. Fine Arts Dept., U. Utah Mus., U. South Fla. Fine Arts Dept., Galerie du Manoir, La Chaux-de-Fonds, Switzerland, Valencia Community Coll., Okum Gallery, Victoria and Albert Mus., London, IBM, Jacksonville, Fla., AT&T, N.Y.C. , others. Recipient numerous awards. Mem. World Craft Council, Artists Equity Assn., Internat. Sculpture Ctr.

MARKS, TAMARA ELIZABETH, project coordinator; b. San Jose, Costa Rica, Dec. 12, 1962; came to U.S., 1968; d. Russell Edward and Patricia (Hunt) M. Student, Wheaton Coll., Norton, Mass., 1981-83; BA in Hispanic Lang. and Lit., Boston U., 1985. Research analyst Coopers & Lybrand, N.Y.C., 1985-87; project coordinator Helathcare Communications, Inc., Princeton, N.J., 1987—. Pres. Boston U. South Campus Govt., 1984-85; mem. June Opera Festival N.J., Princeton, 1986—. Mem. Am Mus. of Natural History, Boston U. Alumni Assn., Wheaton Coll. Alumni. Republican. Episcopalian. Home: 52 Constitution Hill W Princeton NJ 08540

MARKS, VIRGINIA PANCOAST, music educator; b. Phila., Feb. 9, 1940; d. Ace and Catherine (Regensberger) Pancoast; m. Edward J. Marks, 1961 (div. 1987); children: Brian Charles, Jennifer Anne. BS in Music, Temple U., 1961; MA in Music, American U., 1965. Instr. Settlement Music Sch., Phila., 1957-62, Cornell U., Ithaca, N.Y., 1966-67, Temple U., Phila., 1968-69; prof., coordinator of keyboard studies Bowling Green (Ohio) State U., 1972—; concert pianist Recitals in major cities throughout U.S., 1964—, guest artist Spoleto Festival Spoleto, Italy. Recording Artist Educo Records. Martha Baird Rockefeller grantee; recipient Disting. Teaching award Bowling Green State U., 1980-82, 1st Prize Concert Artists Guild, N.Y.C., 1st Prize Mu Phi Epsilon Internat. Competition. Mem. Music Tchrs. Nat. Assn., Ohio Music Tchrs. Assn. (2d v.p. 1985-88). Office: Bowling Green State U Coll of Mus Arts Bowling Green OH 43403

MARKT, MAUREEN FRANCES, speech and language clinician; b. Brockton, Mass., Jan. 19, 1948; d. Francis Joseph and Marjorie Agnes (White) M.; m. James Clement Bovin, Nov. 6, 1970 (div. June 1973). BA in Speech Pathology and Audiology, U. Mass., 1970; MA in Ednl. Psychology, Am. Internat. Coll., Springfield, Mass. Speech and lang. clinician Holyoke (Mass.) Pub. Schs., 1970—. Chmn. Holyoke Cancer Crusade, 1985; voter registration chmn. Holyoke Dem. Com., 1987; mem. Hist. Deerfield (Mass.); chmn. deaconesses 2d Congregational Ch. Holyoke. Mem. Hampden County Tchrs. Assn. (treas. 1980-81, pres. 1981, sec. 1982, v.p. 1984-86), Holyoke Tchrs. Assn., Am. Speech, Hearing and Langs. Assn. (continuing edn. adv. bd. 1980—), Mass. Tchrs. Assn., Mass. Speech, Hearing and Langs. Assn., New England Hist. and Geneal. Soc., Western Geneal. Soc., Mass. Genealogical Soc., Assn. for Gravestone Studies. Congregationalist. Club: Friends Quadrangle. Home: 257 Franklin St Holyoke MA 01040 Office: Holyoke Pub Schs 98 Suffolk St Holyoke MA 01040

MARKUM, ARLENE, banker; b. N.Y.C., June 15, 1942; d. John Thomas and Mary Louise McAllister; student Pace U., 1975—; m. Onzelo Markum Jr., July 28, 1960; children—Onzelo III, Andrea Gail. Credit adminstrn. clk. Franklin Simon, N.Y.C., 1963; supr. Lord & Taylors, N.Y.C., 1963-68; with Citibank N.Y., N.Y.C., 1969—, asst. mgr., 1974-81, mgr., 1981-85, asst. v.p., 1986—. Mem. Nat. Assn. Female Execs., Nat. Spkty. Mdse. Assn., Am. Soc. Profl. & Exec. Women, Urban Banking Coalition (N.Y. chpt.). Republican. Home: 8400 Shore Front Pkwy Rockaway Beach NY 11693

MARKUS, SHARYN KATHRYN, educator. BA, Eastern Ill. U., 1971; MA, U. Colo., Colorado Springs, 1982. Tchr. Sacred Heart and Ursuline

Acad., Springfield, Ill., 1972-75, Colo. Pub. Sch. Dist. 20, Colorado Springs, 1977—; adj. instr. Colorado Springs Bus. Coll., 1977-78; exec. dir. Colorado Springs Dental Soc., 1976—; asst. dir. yearbook workshop Eastern Ill. U., Charleston, 1983; presenter various workshops and profl. meetings, 1980—; bd. dirs. Southeastern Colo. Health Systems Agy., 1983-86. Author: (booklet) 10-Minute Writing Assignments, 1980 (Ednl. Resources Info. Ctr. award 1980), others; editor jour. Colo Reading Assn., 1982-83; editor newspaper The Vol. Lawman, 1986-88. Youth group leader St. Patrick's Ch., Colorado Springs, 1981; res. police officer, Colorado Springs Police Dept., 1984—, active Neighborhood Watch program, 1986—. Mem. Res. Law Officers Am., Colo. Lang. Arts Soc., Nat. Council Tchrs. English, Am. Soc. Dental Execs., Phi Delta Kappa. Republican. Roman Catholic. Address: Colorado Springs Dental Soc 1304 N Academy Blvd #203 Colorado Springs CO 80909

MARLER, LINDA SUSAN, microbiologist; b. Bloomington, Ind., May 28, 1951; d. Lynne Lionel and Lucille Elizabeth (Widman) Merritt; B.S. in Med. Tech., Ind. U., 1973, M.S. in Allied Health Edn., 1978; m. David William Marler, May 21, 1977 (div.); children—Brian David, Brittney Lynne. Med. technologist, then sr. med. technologist Ind. U. Med. Center, Indpls., 1973—, edn. coordinator dept. microbiology, 1974—, asst. prof. div. allied health Sch. Medicine, 1978-84, assoc. prof., 1984—; speaker in field. Mem. Am. Soc. Microbiology, Am. Soc. Med. Tech., South Central Assn. Clin. Microbiologists (area dir., assn. dir.). Methodist. Office: Fesler 416 1120 South Dr Indianapolis IN 46223

MARLEY, MARY LOUISE, psychologist; b. Columbia, Pa., Apr. 18, 1923; d. William Edward and Carrie Cook (Lockard) M. BS in Edn., Millersville (Pa.) State U., 1944; MEd in Psychology and Audiology, Franklin & Marshall Coll., 1952. Lic. psychologist, Pa., pathologist, audiologist. Cons. remedial reading Dearborn (Mich.) Elem. Schs., 1944-49; tchr. spl. edn. Hershey (Pa.) Elem. Sch., 1949-52; speech pathologist York (Pa.) County Schs. Office, 1952-55, asst. psychologist, 1955-68; clin. psychologist stroke unit York Hosp., 1968-74; pvt. practice clin. psychology York, 1974—; cons. York City, York Twp. and West York Police Depts., 1983—. Author: Organic Brain Pathology and the Bender Gestalt Test, 1982. Pres., cons. Loving Care Inc., York, 1984—. Mem. Pa. Psychol. Assn., Nat. Assn. Neuropsychology, Nat. Register Clin. Psychology, York County Psychol. Assn. Republican. Methodist. Home: 926 McKenzie St York PA 17403 Office: 1620 S Queen St York PA 17403

MARLOW, AUDREY SWANSON, artist, designer; b. N.Y.C., Mar. 3, 1929; d. Sven and Rita (Porter) Swanson; student (scholarships) Art Students League, 1950-55; spl. courses SUNY (Stony Brook), L'Alliance Française m. Roy Marlow, Nov. 30, 1968. With Cohn-Hall-Marx Textile Studio, 1961-65, R.S. Assos. Textile Studio, 1965-73; freelance designer, illustrator Prince Matchabelli, Lester Harrison Agy., J. Walter Thompson Agy., 1957-78; portrait and fine artist, Wading River, N.Y., 1973—; instr. Phoenix Sch. Design (N.Y.C.); exhibits include: Nat. Arts Club, NAD, Parish Art Mus., South Hampton, N.Y., Guild Hall, East Hampton, N.Y., Portraits Inc., Lincoln Ctr., Chung-Cheng Art Gallery, St. John's U., Mystic (Conn.) Art Assn., Harbour Gallery, St. Thomas, V.I. Trustee, Middle Island Public Library, 1972-76. Recipient John W. Alexander medal, 1976, award Council on Arts, 1978, award of excellence Cork Gallery, Lincoln Center, 1982; Grumbacher Bronze medal, 1983; Grumbacher Silver medal 1986; Best in Show award N.Y. Arts Council, 1986. Mem. Pastel Soc. Am. (award 1977, 80), Am. Artists Profl. League (2 1st prize awards), Hudson Valley Art Assn. (award), Knickerbocker Artists (2 awards), Catharine Lorillard Wolfe Art Club (award 1982), Salmagundi Club (5 awards), Nat. League Am. Pen Women (Gold award, Gold medal of Honor). Works represented at N.Y. U., pvt. collections; one-woman show Salmagundi Club, 1982. Home: 76 Northside Rd Wading River NY 11792

MARLOW, DOROTHY RUTH, nurse, educator; b. Phila.; d. William and Lillian (Shisler) M.; diploma Children's Hosp., Phila., 1942; B.S., U. Pa., 1948, M.S., 1956; Ed.D., Columbia U., 1958. Various nursing edn. and nursing service positions Children's Hosp., Phila., 1943-45; supr. pediatric dept., instr. pediatric nursing Hosp. U. Pa., 1945-53; instr. pediatric nursing Sch. Nursing, U. Pa., 1953-56, asst. prof., 1958-61, asso. prof., 1961-65, chmn. grad. program, 1962-64; prof. pediatric nursing, asst. dean. Coll. Nursing, Villanova (Pa.) U., 1965-68, dean Coll. Nursing, 1968-76; cons. curriculum in nursing to various schs. nursing. Mem. Nat. League Nursing, Am. Nurses Assn., Kappa Delta Pi, Sigma Theta Tau, Pi Lambda Theta. Author: Textbook of Pediatric Nursing (best book in coll. textbook group Phila. Book Show, 1962), 1961; Textbook of Pediatric Nursing, 2d edit., 1965 (certificate of award, coll. textbook group Phila. Book Show 1966), 3d edit., 1969, 4th edit., 1973, 5th edit., 1977, 6th edit., 1988. Home: 106 E Sylvan Ave Rutledge PA 19070

MARMER, ELLEN LUCILLE, pediatrician; b. Bronx, N.Y., June 29, 1939; d. Benjamin and Diane (Goldstein) M.; m. Harold O. Shapiro, June 5, 1960; children: Cheri, Brenda. BS in Chemistry, U. Ala., 1960; MD, U. Ala., Birmingham, 1964. Cert. Nat. Bd. Med. Examiners, 1965; Diplomate Bd. Pediatrics, 1969, Bd. Qualified and Eligible Pediatric Cardiology, 1969. Intern Upstate Med. Ctr., Syracuse, N.Y., 1964-65, resident, 1965-66; fellow in pediatric cardiology Columbia Presbyn. Med. Ctr.-Babies Hosp., N.Y.C., 1967-69; pvt. practice Hartford, Vernon, Conn., 1969—; examining pediatrician child devel. program Columbia Presbyn. Med. Ctr.-Babies Hosp., N.Y.C., 1967, instr. pediatrics, 1967-69; dir. pediatric cardiology clinic St. Francis Hosp., Hartford, 1970-80; asst. state med. examiner, Tolland County, Conn., 1974-79; sports physician Rockville (Conn.) High Sch., 1976—; advisor Cardiac Rehab. com., Rockville, 1984—. Councilwoman Vernon Town Council, 1985—; bd. dirs. Child Guidance Clinic, Manchester, Conn., 1970—; life mem. Tolland County chpt. Hadassah, v.p., 1969-70, pres. 1970-72, bd. dirs. 1973-74; mem. B'Nai Israel Congregation and Sisterhood, Vernon, 1969—, chmn. youth commn., 1970-72. Recipient Outstanding Service award Indian Valley YMCA, 1985. Fellow Am. Acad. Pediatrics, Am. Coll. Cardiology; mem. Am. Heart Assn. (council cardiovascular disease in the young 1969—), Conn. Med. Soc., Conn. Heart Assn. (bd. dirs. 1974-75, 83-84, v.p. 1984-86, pres. 1986-88), Heart Assn. Greater Hartford (bd. dirs. 1970—, exec. com. bd. dirs. 1972-73, 79—, sec. 1978-79, 79-80, v.p. 1980-82, pres. 1982-84), Tolland County Med. Assn. (sec. 1971-72), Rockville Pub. Health Nursing Assn., LWV (state program chmn. Vernon chpt. 1971-73). Democrat. Jewish. Office: 351 Merline Rd Vernon CT 06066

MAROIS, HARRIET SUKONECK, psychologist, computer scientist; b. Newark, Jan. 30, 1945; d. Edward and Mae S.; m. George Marois, Oct. 18, 1986. B.A., Rutgers U., 1966; M.A., U. So. Calif., 1968, Ph.D. (NIMH fellow), 1971. NIMH clin. postdoctoral fellow, div. psychiatry Children's Hosp. of Los Angeles, 1971-73; lectr. Calif. State U., Los Angeles, 1971-76; core faculty research series Calif. Sch. Profl. Psychology, Los Angeles, 1973-78, clin. psychologist in pvt. practice, Santa Monica, Calif., 1973-78; vis. asst. prof. Loyola Marymount U., Los Angeles, 1976-78; research assoc. Neuropsychiat. Inst., UCLA, 1978-79, adminstrv. analyst office of vice chancellor UCLA, 1979; sr. mem. tech. staff, project leader Computer Scis. Corp., El Segundo, Calif., 1979-81; systems cons./project administr. First Interstate Services Co., El Segundo, Calif., 1981-83; dir. research and product planning Data Line Service Co., 1983-84; project mgr. Xerox Corp., El Segundo, 1984—; founder, bd. dirs. Brainstorms, Los Angeles, 1985—.Lic. psychologist, Calif. Mem. Assn. Computing Machinery, Am. Psychol. Assn., AAAS. Contbr. articles to profl. jours. Editor et al, social sci. jour., 1971-76. Bd. dirs. So. Calif. Hot Jazz Soc. Los Angeles, 1988.

MARON-SZUCS, SUSAN MARIE, jeweler; b. Los Angeles, Jan. 29, 1954; d. Theodore Edwin and Rosina Frances (Helganz) Harding; m. Dale Maron, Feb. 14, 1975 (div. 1980); m. Alexander Geza Szucs, May 29, 1983; 1 child, Samantha Elizabeth. BS, U. So. Calif., 1975. Cert. gemologist appraiser. Lab. sec. Gemological Inst. Am., Santa Monica, Calif., 1975-77; mgr. Morton Jewelers Inc., San Jose, Calif., 1977—. Mem. Small Bus. Council, San Jose, 1987—. Mem. Women in Bus., Am. Gem Soc. (state chmn. mem. devel. 1985—). Roman Catholic. Clubs: Toastmaster (Toastmaster of Yr. award 1981), San Jose State Quarterback. Office: Morton Jewelers Inc 625 Town and Country Village San Jose CA 95128

MAROON, LORAINE GERTRUDE, real estate developer; b. Winnipeg, Man., Can., Mar. 15, 1938; came to U.S., 1958; d. Edmund J. and Josephine (Payette) Beaudry; m. James W. Maroon, Mar. 15, 1980. BA in Edn., U. Man., 1957. Chief exec. officer, exec. v.p. Manor Park Realty and Devel. Co., Northwestern Constrn. Co., Bloomingdale, Ill., 1963-77; exec. v.p., gen. mgr Vistana Resort, Lake Buena Vista, Fla., 1977-83; exec. v.p. Marquis Hotels and Resorts, Ft. Myers, Fla., 1983-85; exec. v.p., chief operating officer New Seabury (Mass.) Corp.-Cape Cod, 1985—. Chmn. edn. com. ARRADA, Washington, com. tax. legis., mktg., 1986—; sec., bd. dirs. Leukemia Soc., Orlando, Fla., 1979-82. Mem. Am. Hotel Motel Assn., Mass. Hotel Motel Assn. (bd. dirs. 1987-88), Nat. Assn. Home Builders (bd. dirs. Cape Cod chpt. 1987-88). Office: New Seabury-Cape Cod 1 Mallway New Seabury MA 02649

MAROSCHER, BETTY JEAN, librarian; b. Ashland, Ky., Aug. 12, 1934; d. Raymond and Virginia Dell (Staten) Boggs; student Columbus Coll. (Ga.), 1963-64; B.S., Hardin-Simmons U., 1967; M.S. in L.S., Our Lady of Lake U., San Antonio, 1970; M.Ed., Trinity U., 1975; m. Albert G. Maroscher Mar. 21, 1955 (dec.). Tchr., McAllen (Tex.) Ind. Sch. Dist., 1967-68; tchr. Northside Ind. Sch. Dist., San Antonio, 1968-69, librarian, 1969-71; reference ednl. media Trinity U., San Antonio, 1971-76; reference librarian St. Philip's Coll., San Antonio, 1976, audiovisual librarian, mgr. audiovisual dept., 1977-86; librarian, coordinator Learning Resources Ctr., 1986—; lectr., cons. in field; chmn. subcom. programming and scheduling Univ. and Fine Arts Cable TV Com., 1980-81, sec. 1984—. Active ARC; sec., trustee Compañia de Arte Español, 1982-84; sec. Council of Research and Academic Libraries, 1988—. Recipient Minter/Medal Hardin-Simmons U., 1965, 66. Mem. Tex. Library Assn., Bexar County Library Assn., ALA, Tex. Jr. Coll. Tchrs. Assn., Tex. Assn. Chicanos in Higher Edn. (sec. St. Philip's chpt. 1982-84), Instructional Media Services Group, Council Research and Acad. Libraries Coop. Circulation Group (sec.-treas. 1977-79), Pi Gamma Mu (sec. chpt. 1965-67), Alpha Chi (historian 1965-67), other orgns. Republican. Home: 5230 Galahad Dr San Antonio TX 78218 Office: 2111 Nevada St San Antonio TX 78203

MAROT, LOLA, expense control administrator; b. Providence, Oct. 6; d. Frank and Iola (Lombardi) Ansuini; m. Joseph Marot (div. 1973); 1 child, David Joseph. B.A. with distinction, U. R.I., 1973; postgrad. Bryant Coll. Bookkeeper, Diamond Paper Box Co., Providence, 1958-69; export sales adminstr. Brite Industries, Providence, 1973-77; property services asst. Met. Property and Liability Ins. Co., Warwick, R.I., 1977-79, buyer, 1979-83, sr. buyer, 1983-86, supr. printing adminstrn., 1986-87, expense control; adminstr., 1987—. Mem. Univ. Soc. Providence (pres. 1978). Office: 700 Quaker Ln Warwick RI 02886

MARQUARDT, CHRISTEL ELISABETH, lawyer; b. Chgo., Aug. 26, 1935; d. Herman Albert and Christine Marie (Geringer) Trolenberg; children: Eric, Philip, Andrew, Joel. BS in Edn., Mo. Western Coll., 1970; JD with honors, Washburn U., 1974. Bar: Kans. 1974, U.S. Dist. Ct. Kans. 1974, U.S. Supreme Ct. 1979, U.S. Ct. Appeals (10th cir.) 1980. Tchr. St. John's Ch., Tigerton, Wis., 1955-56; personnel asst. Columbia Records, Los Angeles, 1958-59; ptnr. Cosgrove, Webb & Oman, Topeka, 1974-86, Palmer, Marquardt & Snyder, Topeka, 1986—; mem. atty. bd. discipline Kans. Supreme Ct., 1984-86; lectr. in field. Contbr. articles to legal jours. Asst. treas., mem. exec. Rep. com., Kansas, 1983-87; dist. bd. adjudication Mo. Synod Luth. Ch., Kans., 1982—; bd. dirs. Topeka Civic Symphony, 1983—, Kans. Bus. Hall of Fame, 1988—; hearing examiner Human Relations Com., Topeka, 1974-76; local advisor Boy Scouts Am., 1973-74; bd. dirs., nominating com. YWCA, Topeka, 1979-81; trustee Washburn U. Law Sch., 1987—. Named Women of Yr., Topeka Mayor, 1982; Mabee scholar Washburn U., 1972-74. Mem. ABA (house of dels. 1988—, specialization com. 1987—, labor law, family sects.), Kans. Bar Assn. (sec., treas. 1981-82, 83-85, v.p. 1985-86, pres. elect 1986-87, pres. 1987-88, lectr. 1974—, Disting. Service award 1980), Kans. Trial Lawyers Assn. (bd. govs. 1982-86, lectr.), Topeka Bar Assn., Am. Bus. Women's Assn. (lectr., corr. sec. 1983-84, pres. 1986-87, one of Top Ten Bus. Women of Yr, 1985), Golden City Forum, Greater Topeka C. of C. (v.p., bd. dirs. 1983-87). Home: 3121 Briarwood Circle Topeka KS 66611 Office: Palmer Marquardt Snyder 112 SW 6th St Topeka KS 66603

MARQUARDT, KATHLEEN P., business executive; b. Kalispell, Mont., June 6, 1944; d. Dean King and Lorraine Camille (Buckmaster) Marquardt; m. William Wewer, Dec. 6, 1987children—Shane Elizabeth, Montana Quinn. Purser, Pan Am. World Airways, Washington, 1968-75; info. specialist Capital Systems Group, Kensington, Md., 1979-81; dir. pub. affairs Subscription TV Assn., Washington, 1981-83, exec. dir., 1983-86 ; pres. Internat. Policy Studies Orgn., 1983—, pres., designer Elizabeth Quinn Couture, 1986—. Bd. dirs. Am. Tax Reduction Movement, 1983—; chmn. bd. Friends of Freedom, 1982—. Mem. Nat. Women's Polit. Caucus, NOW, Women in Communications, Nat. Assn. Women Bus. Owners. Home: 11 E Irving St Chevy Chase MD 20815 Office: 7201 Wisconsin Ave Suite 705 Bethesda MD 20814

MARQUISS, SUSAN MICHELE, public relations professional; b. Indpls., June 7, 1955; d. Bernard Paul and Charlene Elizabeth (Brown) M. BS, Ball State U., 1976; MS, Butler U., 1985. Sec. Cranfill Advt. Agy., Indpls., 1976-79; pub. relations asst. Ind. Farmers Mut. Ins. Group, Indpls., 1979-86, communications mgr., 1986—; free-lance cons. Sunrise Video Prodns., Indpls., 1985—. Vol. Indpls. Civic Theatre, 1978—, United Way Cen. Ind., Indpls., 1984. Mem. Internat. Assn. Bus. Communicators (historian 1984-85), Profl. Ins. Communicators Am. (Outstanding Achievement award 1985). Republican. Presbyterian. Office: Ind Farmers Mut Ins Group 10 W 106th St Indianapolis IN 46290

MARRIE-WORMAN, PAULA ANN, veterinarian; b. Youngstown, Ohio, Jan. 22, 1956; d. Patrick Joseph and Laura Jean (Lewis) Marrie; m. John Ludwig Worman, Sept. 26, 1981. D.V.M., Ohio State U., 1981. Veterinarian, Greenacres Animal Hosp., Canton, Ohio, 1981-82; owner, veterinarian Gahanna Animal Hosp. (Ohio), 1982—. Sec. Scholarship House Alumnae, Columbus, Ohio, 1984—. Mem. Am. Animal Hosp. Assn., AVMA, Ohio Vet. Med. Assn., Columbus Acad. Vet. Medicine (v.p. 1984-85), Ohio State U. Alumni Assn. (bd. dirs. scholarship program), Am. Fedn. Aviculture, Pilot Dogs Inc., Capital Area Humane Soc., Phi Kappa Phi. Democrat. Roman Catholic. Clubs: Columbus All Breed Tng., Canton All Breed Tng. Home: 4639 Shull Rd Gahanna OH 43230 Office: Gahanna Animal Hosp 144 Johnstown Rd Gahanna OH 43230

MARRIOTT, ALICE SHEETS (MRS. JOHN WILLARD MARRIOTT), restaurant chain executive; b. Salt Lake City, Oct. 19, 1907; d. Edwin Spencer and Alice (Taylor) Sheets; m. John Willard Marriott, June 9, 1927; children—John Willard, Richard Edwin. A.B., U. Utah, 1927, L.H.D. (hon.), 1974; L.H.D. (hon.), Mt. Vernon Coll., 1980. Partner Marriott Corp. (formerly Marriott-Hot Shoppes, Inc.), Washington, 1927—, v.p., dir., 1929—; Mem. Republican Nat. Com., 1959-76, vice chmn., 1965-76, mem. exec. com., 1965-76; mem. D.C. Republican Com., 1959-76; treas. Republican Nat. Conv., 1964, 68, 72, mem. arrangements com., 1960, 64, 68, 72; vice chmn. inaugural com. 1969, hon. chmn., 1973, mem., 1981; mem. Women's Nat. Rep. Club, Rep. Coordinating Com., 1965-69, 73-76. Chmn. adv. com. on arts John F. Kennedy Center For Performing Arts, 1970-76; mem. adv. com. Nat. Com. Child Abuse, 1976—; mem. adv. council Nat. Arthritis and Musculoskeletal and Skin Diseases NIH, 1987—; bd. dirs. Washington Ballet Guild, Washington Home Rule Com., Arthritis and Rheumatism Found. of Met. Washington; trustee John F. Kennedy Center, 1972—; hon. trustee Nat. Arthritis Found., 1987—. Recipient 1st ann. Marriott Lifetime Achievement award Arthritis Found. Met. Washington Area, 1987. Mem. League Republican Women D.C. (treas. 1955-57, v.p. 1957-59), Nat. Symphony Orch. Assn., Am. Newspaper Womens Club (asso. mem.), Capitol Speakers Club (membership chmn.), Welcome to Washington Internat. Clubs (treas., dir.), Chi Omega, Phi Kappa Phi. Mem. Ch. of Jesus Christ of Latter-Day Saints. Clubs: Washington, Capitol Hill, 1925 F Street. Home: 4500 Garfield St Washington DC 20007 Office: Marriott Dr Washington DC 20058

MARRON, DARLENE LORRAINE, real estate development executive, financial and marketing consultant; b. Auburn, N.Y., July 20, 1946; d. William Chester and Elizabeth Barbara (Gervaise) Kulakowski; m. Edward W. Marron, Jr., Apr. 28, 1973. BS cum laude, Rider Coll., 1968; MBA, NYU, 1970. Lic. securities broker. Dir. mktg. Am. Airlines, N.Y.C., 1970-79; asst. v.p. Merrill Lynch, N.Y.C., 1979-83; v.p. Kidder, Peabody & Co., N.Y.C., 1983-86; owner, principal, Marron Cos., Upper Saddle River, N.J., 1986—; fin. and mktg. cons. to real estate devel. industry. Avocations: pianist, flutist, skiing, fly fishing. Home: 743 W Saddle River Rd Ho-Ho-Kus NJ 07423 Office: Marron Cos 118 Hwy 17 Upper Saddle River NJ 07458

MARROUM-KARDOUS, MARIE-CLAIRE, pathologist, researcher; b. Jerusalem, May 24, 1940; came to U.S., 1973; d. Fritz Fadlallah and Pauline May (Merguerian) M.; m. Kal Elie Kardous, Jan. 4, 1975; 1 child, Paul Elie. BS, St. Josephs U., Beirut, 1967; MD, St. Joseph's U., Beirut, 1968. Diplomate Am. Bd. Pathology. Intern Hosp. Broca, Paris, 1967-68; resident in pathology Am. U. Hosp., Beirut, 1969-73; sr. resident in pathology Charlotte (N.C.) Meml. Hosp., 1973-74; fellow, chief resident Meml.-Sloan Kettering Cancer Ctr., N.Y.C., 1974-76; staff pathologist Mercy Hosp., Charlotte, 1976—; sr. attending pathologist Meml. Hosp. & Med. Ctr., Charlotte, 1977—; clin. asst. prof. U. N.C., Chapel Hill, 1980—; med. dir. Pathology Assocs. Services, P.A., Charlotte, 1983—; researcher Heineman Found., Charlotte, 1984—; v.p. Charlotte Pathology Group, P.A., 1985—. Fellow Internat. Acad. Pathology; mem. AMA, N.C. Soc. Pathology, Meml. Sloan Kettering Alumni. Republican. Office: Charlotte Meml Hosp 1000 Blythe Blvd Charlotte NC 28232

MARSDEN, MELISSA CARLSON, communication designer; b. Rockford, Ill., June 10, 1951; d. G. Albert and Bonnie Eileen Carlson; m. Bradd Weber Marsden, Apr. 29, 1979. B.A. in Edn. with honors, U. Ill., 1973. Tchr. Lutheran High Sch., Rockford, 1974-75; adminstr. repairwoman Sundstrand Corp., Rockford, 1976-78, adminstr. contracts, 1978-80, supr. contract group, 1980-83, communication designer, 1983, sr. communication designer, 1984—. Bd. dirs. YWCA, Rockford, 1977-79; corp. campaign chmn. United Way Services. Rockford, 1982. Recipient Gold Plaque award United Way Services, 1982, Award for Excellence Soc. for Tech. Communication, 1987. Mem. Nat. Contract Mgmt. Assn. (1981-83). Internat. Assn. Bus. Communicators. Republican. Lutheran. Club: Quota (dir. 1981-84). Home: 5836 Shelford Ln Rockford IL 61107 Office: Sundstrand Corp 4747 Harrison Ave PO Box 7002 Rockford IL 61125-7002

MARSH, CHARMAYNE, press secretary; b. Dallas, Aug. 14, 1942; d. Earl Lee and Odell Smith M. B in Journalism, U. Tex , 1963. Pub. info. officer U.S. Postal Service, Washington, 1972-76; corr. Washington bur. Dallas Morning News, Reuters Internat. News Service, 1976-81; press sec. to speaker U.S. Ho. of Reps., Washington, 1981—. Mem. Nat. Dem. Club, Washington. Mem. Nat. Press Club. Office: US House Reps Speakers Rooms US Capitol H 204 Washington DC 20515

MARSH, CLARE TEITGEN, school psychologist; b. Manitowoc, Wis., July 7, 1934; d. Clarence Emil and Dorothy (Napiezinski) Teitgen; m. Robert Irving Marsh, Jan. 30, 1955; children: David, Wendy Marsh Tootle, Julie, Laura Marsh Beltrame. MS in Ednl. Psychology, U. Wis., Milw., 1968. Sch. psychologist Milw. Pub. Schs., 1975-76, West Allis (Wis.)-West Milw. Pub. Schs., 1968—. NDEA fellow, 1966-68. Mem. Nat. Assn. Sch. Psychologists, Suburban Assn. Sch. Psychologists (pres. 1976-77, 86-87), Wis. Assn. Sch. Psychologists (chmn. membership com. 1980-84, sec. 85—, chmn. conv. 1987), Phi Kappa Phi, Pi Lambda Theta, Kappa Delta Pi, Sigma Tau Delta, Alpha Chi Omega. Home: 14140 W Honey Ln New Berlin WI 53151 Office: West Allis Sch System 9333 W Lincoln Ave West Allis WI 53227

MARSH, DORIS ELAINE, ballet school owner; b. Saginaw, Mich., Sept. 14, 1931; d. William Henry and Elizabeth Ann (Bates) M. BA, U. Mich., 1953, MA, 1956; postgrad., U. Toronto, Ont., Can., 1954-55, Mich. State U., 1968. Owner, tchr. Doris Marsh Sch. Ballet, Saginaw, 1956—; tchr. Saginaw Pub. Schs., 1956-70; dir. summer dance program Delta Coll., University Ctr., Mich., 1964-83, assoc. prof. dance, 1970-71; instr. Saginaw Valley State U., University Ctr., 1971-81; dir., pres. Saginaw Valley Dancers, 1975—; choreographer Fischer Opera Haus, Frankenmuth, Mich., 1973-74; dance critic Saginaw News, 1986—. Choreographer, costume designer: (ballets) The Nutcracker, 1980, All In Fun, 1980, Clair de Lune, 1980, Summer, 1983; contbr. articles to profl. jours. Pres. Saginaw Valley Dance Council, 1972-73; mem. program com. Temple Theater Arts Assn., Saginaw, 1982-87; bd. dirs. Saginaw Community Concerts, 1960-80. Mem. Mich. Dance Assn., Imperial Soc. Tchrs. of Dancing (assoc.). Home: 2701 Willard Saginaw MI 48602 Office: 6410 Normandy Saginaw MI 48603

MARSH, ELLA JEAN, pediatrician; b. Chgo., Dec. 16, 1941; d. Charles and Eleanor (Canfield) M.; B.A., St. Mary of Woods (Ind.) Coll., 1963; D.O., Chgo. Coll. Osteo. Medicine, 1971. Intern, Doctor's Hosp., Columbus, Ohio, 1971-72; resident in pediatrics, then asst. prof. Chgo. Coll. Osteo. Medicine, 1972-78, assoc. prof. pediatrics, 1978-82; assoc. prof. W.Va. Coll. Osteo. Medicine, 1975—; now chmn. pediatric and newborn nursery, assoc. dir. med. edn. Orlando (Fla.) Gen. Hosp.; mem. staff Orlando Regional Hosp., Fla. Hosp.; pediatric cons. Nat. Bd. Osteo. Examiners; lectr., cons. in field. Donald Bucknar Moore scholar, 1963; diplomate Am. Coll. Osteo. Pediatricians (chmn. evaluating com. 1981—), Nat. Osteo. Bds. Fellow Am. Coll. Osteo. Pediatrics (v.p. 1986, pres. 1988); mem. Am. Osteo. Assn., Fla. Osteo. Assn., AMA, Women's Med. Assn., Chgo. Coll. Osteo. Medicine Alumni Assn., Orlando C. of C., Delta Omega. Roman Catholic. Home: 8210 Imber St Orlando FL 32825 Office: 7824 Lake Underhill Rd Orlando FL 32822

MARSH, JOAN KNIGHT, educational film, video and computer software company executive; b. Butler, Mo., Apr. 8, 1934; d. E. Lyle and Ruth (Hopkins) Knight; m. Alan Reid Marsh, Sept. 27, 1958; children—Alan Reid, Clayton Knight. BA, Tex. Tech. U., 1956. Owner, pres. MarshMedia, Kansas City, Mo., 1969—; dir. Mark Twain Plaza Bank, Kansas City. Bd. dirs., Crittenton Ctr., Kansas City, 1983-88; mem. council Family Study Ctr., U. Mo., Kansas City, 1983—, Children's Relief Assn. Mercy Hosp., Kansas City, 1984—. Mem. Gamma Phi Beta. Republican. Presbyterian. Club: Jr. League (sustaining chmn. 1982-84). Avocation: Egyptology.

MARSH, RITA M., linguist, educator, researcher; b. Muncie, Ind., June 10, 1945; d. Edward M. and Edith M. (Swaim) Marsh; m. Wade G. Birch, Dec. 23, 1976; stepchildren—Dean W. Birch, Cynthia C. Birch. A.B., Ind. U., 1966; student Universidad Nacional Mayor de San Marcos, Lima, Peru, 1965; M.A., Ball State U., 1972; postgrad. U. Hawaii, 1967, NYU Ctr., Paris, summer 1980, Tex. A&M U., 1983; postgrad. Russian Lang. Workshop, Ind. U., summer 1984. Tchr. Spanish, French Crown Point, Ind., 1966-67, Honolulu Pub. Schs., 1968, Benton Central Schs. (Ind.), 1969-70, Leo High Sch. (Ind.), 1971-74; translator, interpreter, Hawaii, 1967-68, Dana World Trade, Ft. Wayne, Ind., 1970; supr. govt. export sales Stewart & Stevenson Services, Inc., Houston, 1974-77; adminstr., asst. treas. Tex. A&M Research Found., College Station, 1977-83; ptnr. B&M Cons., Bryan, Tex., 1981—; lectr. English Lang. Inst., Tex. A&M U., 1983—. Mem. Parks and Recreation Adv. Bd. City of Bryan, 1982—; v.p., 1983—; bd. dirs. LWV, Brazos County, Tex., 1981-83; mem. steering com. Award for Outstanding Woman of Brazos County, 1977—; mem. Brazos County Sesquicentennial Com., 1983—. Mem. Am. Assn. Tchrs. Spanish and Portuguese, Nat. Recreation and Park Assn., Am. Council Tchrs. Fgn. Langs., Tchrs. of English to Speakers of Other Langs., AAUW (bd. dirs.), Com. for Study Cognitive Sci., Phi Delta Gamma (Alpha Alpha chpt. pres. 1982-83), Kappa Alpha Theta (chpt. fin. advisor, mem. house corp. bd.). Home: 3109 Rolling Glen Bryan TX 77801 Office: Tex A&M Univ Mod Lang/ELI College Station TX 77843

MARSH, SHIRLEY M., state senator; b. Benton, Ill., June 22, 1925; d. Dwight Sidney and Margaret Reese (Hager) McVicker; m. Frank Irving Marsh, Mar. 5, 1943; children: Sherry Anne Marsh Tupper, Stephen Alan, Dory Michael, Corwin Frank, Mitchell Edward, Melissa Lou. BA in Social Welfare, U. Nebr., 1972, MBA, 1978; Diploma (hon.), Lincoln (Nebr.) Sch. Commerce, 1975. Placement asst. U. Nebr., Lincoln, 1966-70; caseworker practicum Lancaster County Welfare Dept., Lincoln, 1971-72; mem. Nebr. Legislature, Lincoln, 1973—; vis. instr. Nebr. Wesleyan U., Lincoln, 1978, Doane Coll., Crete, Nebr., 1979. Mem. Lincoln Community Playhouse Guild, 1975—, panel Nat. ID Program for Advancement of Women in Higher Edn., 1983—, adv. com. Am. Coll. Ob-Gyn, Washington, 1981-86;

trustee Nebr. Wesleyan U., Lincoln, 1984—, student affairs com. of bd. govs., 1983-86; bd. dirs. Nebr. Chamber Orch. Guild, Lincoln, 1985-86. Recipient Woman of Yr. award Capitol Bus. and Profl. Women's Club, 1982, Hwy. Safety award Gov. of Nebr., 1984, Ptnr. in Prevention award Nat. Soc. to Prevent Blindness, 1985. Mem. Nat. Order Women Legislators (pres. 1977-78), Nat. Conf. State Legislatures (exec. com. 1982-86), Nat. Fedn. Bus. and Profl. Women, AAUW (grantee 1976), Internat. Women's Orgn. (P.E.O. IA chpt. 1987-88), Delta Kappa Gamma. United Methodist. Home: 2701 S 34th St Lincoln NE 68506 Office: Nebr Legislature Dist #29 State Capitol Bldg Lincoln NE 68509

MARSHAL, NELLIE JEAN, financial executive; b. Pulaski, Tenn., Jan. 30, 1933; d. William Vernon and Elsie Beatrice (Glover) DeRamus; student Baxter Sem.; children—Jerami A., Roberta M. Goldstein. Owner, Trailestate Realty, Reno, 1957-60; v.p. Bank Mortgage Loan Co., Los Angeles, 1960-66; mgr. first trust deed dept. Union Home Loans, Los Angeles, 1966-69; owner Marshal Plan, Inc., Santa Monica, Calif., 1969—; chmn. bd. Golden State Holding Co., Inc., 1980—; speaker in field. Named to Hon. Order of Ky. Cols. Gov. Commonwealth of Ky. Mem. Internat. Platform Assn., Santa Monica Bd. Realtors, Nat. Assn. Review Appraisers and Mortgage Underwriters (sr.), Women in Business, Nat. Assn. Female Execs., Santa Monica C. of C. Democrat. Club: Presidents. Lodge: Thalians. Office: c/o Marshal Plan Inc 2701 Ocean Park Blvd Suite 131 Santa Monica CA 90405

MARSHALL, ALICE MARY, pharmaceutical company executive; b. Welland, Ont., Can., Mar. 16, 1950; d. Thomas Robert and Doris (Hilton) M. BS magna cum laude in Biology, McMaster U., 1973; PhD in Pharmacology, U. Western Ont., 1978; postgrad., York U., 1988—. Postdoctoral fellow Med. Research Council of Can. McMaster U., Hamilton, Ont., 1978-81; research fellow Ont. Mental Health Found. McMaster U., Hamilton, 1981; clin. research assoc. Wyeth Ltd. div. Am. Home Products, Toronto, 1981—; mgr. med. dept. Wyeth Ltd., Toronto, 1981—. Contbr. articles to profl. jours. Mem. Shaw Festival Theatre Found. Research scholar Alcoholism and Drug Addiction Research Found., 1975-78. Mem. Can. Fertility and Andrology Soc., Can. Soc. for Clin. Pharmacology, Drug Info. Assn., Pharm. Mfrs. Assn. of Can. (med. research and devel. sect. 1981—), Soc. for Clin. Trials, Shaw Festival Theatre Found. Anglican. Office: Wyeth Ltd, 1120 Finch Ave W 7th Floor, North York, ON Canada M3J 3H7

MARSHALL, ANNE BRADLEY, lawyer; b. Hartford, Conn., May 29, 1952; d. George A. and Anne Elizabeth (Bradley) M.; m. Bruce Rea Elworthy, Aug. 25, 1979. BA, Wellesley Coll., 1974; JD, Yale U., 1977. Bar: Calif., Tex.; cert. tax specialist. Assoc. Bracewell and Patterson, Houston, 1977-79; assoc. Pettit and Martin, San Francisco, 1981-82, Bronson, Bronson & McKinnon, San Francisco, 1982-83; ptnr. Elworthy and Marshall, Tahoe City, Calif., 1983—; lectr. World Trade Inst., N.Y.C., 1978-80, Am. Mgmt. Assn., 1979, Calif. Continuing Edn. of Bar, Berkeley, 1982. Durant scholar, Wellesley Coll., 1974, Trustee scholar, 1974. Mem. ABA, Bar Assn. San Francisco, Monterey County Bar Assn., State Bar Calif. (estate planning sect.), Placer County Bar Assn., Greater Carmel Valley C. of C. (past bd. dirs.), Phi Beta Kappa. Clubs: Elizabethan (New Haven); Monterey Peninsula Country; Yale of Monterey (past bd. dirs.); Yale (Sacramento); Monterey Bay Wellesley. Office: Elworthy and Marshall Profl Corp 740 N Lake Blvd P O Box 7044 Tahoe City CA 95730-7044

MARSHALL, BONNIE, language professional; b. Concord, N.H., June 9, 1941; d. Sumner Eugene and Agnes Ora (McNeil) M.; m. John Joseph Carey, Aug. 26, 1962 (div. Dec. 17, 1980); children: Lorrie Jean, Peter Dean Carey; m. Stephen Michael Kraemer (div. Aug. 1988), May 25, 1984. BA summa cum laude, Boston U., 1962; MA, Assumption Coll., Worcester, Mass., 1966; Cert., Moscow State U., 1975; PhD, U. N.C., 1983; Cert., Leningrad State U., 1985. Cert. tchr., N.H. Ind. researcher, author; coordinator fgn. languages Hale High Sch., 1982; vis. instr. Wake Forest U., Winston-Salem, N.C., 1981-82, U. Mont., Missoula, 1983-84, 85-86, vis. asst. prof., 1985-86, asst. placement chmn. Randolph-Macon Woman's Coll., Lynchburg, Va., 1982; vis. asst. prof. Coll. of Holy Cross, Worcester, Mass., 1984-85, U. So. Ala., Mobile, 1987-88; asst. prof. Davidson (N.C.) Coll., 1988—; cons. Anaconda Minerals, Missoula, 1982. Author, editor, translator, contbr. numerous articles and revs. to profl. jours. Recipient Outstanding Secondary Educator of Am. award, 1982. Mem. MLA, Am. Assn. Tchrs. Slavic and East European Langs. (pres., v.p. Carlina chpt., treas. Carolinas chpt., Pacific NW Council on Fgn. Langs., N.E. Slavic Assn., N.E. Women Studies Assn. Assn., Am. Folklore Soc., Am. Assn. for Advancement of Slavic Studies. Home: 10 Eastbluff Village PO Box 1447 Meredith NH 03253

MARSHALL, CAK (CATHERINE ELAINE MARSHALL), music educator, composer; b. Nashville, Nov. 24, 1943; d. Dean Byron and Petula Iris (Bodie) M. BS in Music Edn., Ind. U. Pa., 1965; cert., Hamline U., 1981, 82, 83, Memphis State U., 1985. Cert. vocal music tchr., Pa. Tchr. music Mars (Pa.) Area Sch. Dist., 1965-66; music specialist Fox Chapel (Pa.) Area Sch. Dist., 1966—; specialist Chatham Coll., Pitts., 1977—; instrn. rep. elem. curriculum Dist. I, Pitts., 1986—; arts curriculum project Pa. Dept. Edn., 1988. Composer, author: play Pittsburgh-The City With a Smile on Her Face, 1986, holiday mus. The Dove That Could Not Fly, 1986, book Seasons in Song, 1987. Actor North Star Players, Pitts., 1975-80; soloist Landmark Bapt. Ch., Penn Hills, Pa., 1981-86, Bible Bapt. Ch., 1987; performer Pitts. Camerata, 1977—; group leader Pitts. Recorder Soc., Pitts., 1985-86. Mem. NEA, Am. ORFF-Schulwerk Assn., Pitts. Golden Triangle Chpt. (pres. 1985—), Music Educators Nat. Confl., Pa. Music Educators Assn. (elem. jour. 1986—), Am. Recorder Assn., Delta Omicron. Baptist. Home: 1707 Kirk Dr Verona PA 15147 Office: O'Hara Elem Sch 115 Cabin Ln Pittsburgh PA 15238

MARSHALL, CHRISTINA ADELE, social services director; b. Ridgewood, N.J., June 18, 1952; d. Elroy Clifford and Hazel Adele (Vreudenburg) Stark; m. John Arthur Marshall, May 25, 1984. BA in Elem. Edn., William Paterson Coll., 1974. Dir. activities, asst. adminstr. Milford Manor Nursing Home, West Milford, N.J., 1979-82; dir. activities, vol. coordinator, cons. adult day care St. Mary's Nursing Ctr., Leonardtown, Md., 1983—; cons. adult day care Calvert County Adult Day Care, Prince Frederick, Md., 1987—. Author, editor booklet, 1986. Bd. dirs. Freedom Landing, Leonardtown, 1987, pres. bd. dirs., 1988—. Mem. Nat. Assn. Activities Profls., Nat. Vol. Ctr., Md. Activities Coordinators Soc., Helath Facilities Assn. Md., So. Md. Nursing Home Activities Dirs. Assn. (cert., coordinator 1987—). Home: North Star Manor 202 Dent Dr Lexington Park MD 20653 Office: St Mary's Nursing Ctr PO Box 518 Peabody St Leonardtown MD 20650

MARSHALL, CONSUELO BLAND, U.S. district judge; b. Knoxville, Tenn., Sept. 28, 1936; d. Clyde Theodore and Annie (Brown) Arnold; m. George Edward Marshall, Aug. 30, 1959; children: Michael Edward, Laurie Ann. A.A., Los Angeles City Coll., 1956; B.A., Howard U., 1958, LL.B., 1961. Bar: Calif. 1962. Dep. atty. City of Los Angeles, 1962-67; assoc. Cochran & Atkins, Los Angeles, 1968-70; commr. Los Angeles Superior Ct., 1971-76; judge Inglewood Mcpl. Ct., 1976-77, Los Angeles Superior Ct., 1977-80, U.S. Dist. Ct. Central Dist. Calif., Los Angeles, 1980—. Contbr. articles to profl. jours.; notes editor Law Jour. Howard U. Mem. adv. bd. Richstone Child Abuse Center. Research fellow Howard U. Law Sch., 1959-60. Mem. State Bar Calif., Calif. Women Lawyers Assn., Calif. Assn. Black Lawyers, Calif. Judges Assn., Black Women Lawyers Assn., Los Angeles County Bar Assn., Nat. Assn. Women Judges, NAACP, Urban League, Beta Phi Sigma. Mem. Ch. Religious Science. Office: US Dist Ct 312 N Spring St Los Angeles CA 90012 *

MARSHALL, HOLLY RICHBURG, data processing executive; b. Chgo., Sept. 28, 1945; d. Welton E. and Ferne Louise (Templeton) Richburg; student Macalester Coll., 1963-65. Various positions, data processing and sales Hartford, Conn. and Chgo., 1965-75; regional v.p. sales Advanced Systems Inc., Elk Grove, Ill., 1975-77, v.p. mktg., 1977-78; pres. Merit Assos., Schaumburg, Ill., 1978-81; chief exec. officer Universal Bus. Computing, Schaumburg, 1981-87; chmn., pres. AIT, 1986; chief exec. officer Bright Pearl Devel. Corp., 1987; pres., To Be Continued, Inc., Barrington, 1988—; dir. Keys to the City, Los Angeles; bd. dirs. Ken Garen Inc., Skokie, Ill. Regular chorister Lyric Opera Chgo., 1967-69; founding mem. Chi-[illegible] 1987. Office: PO Box 1527 Barrington IL 60011

MARSHALL, JEANIE, organization consultant; b. Cambridge, Mass., Jan. 21, 1944; d. Wilfred James and Mary (Cadwallader) Combellack; B.A. in Sociology, Boston U., 1966; M.S. in Human Resource Devel., am. U., 1982; m. Donald W. Marshall, Aug. 8, 1970. Owner, Marshall House, Inc., pres., human resource devel. cons., Reston, Va., 1975—; human relations trainer continuing edn. program Sch. Social Welfare, SUNY, Albany, 1979-81; tchr. parliamentary procedures Schenectady County Community Coll., 1980; tchr. career devel., presentation techniques Union Coll., Schenectady, 1980-82. Mem. AAUW (pres. Schenectady br. 1977-78, grantee Ednl. Found. 1978-79), Am. Soc. Tng. and Devel., Orgn. Devel. Network, Assn. Creative Change, Assn. Psychol. Type, Nat. Assn. Female Execs. Author articles, tng. manuals, modules, cassette/workbook Am. Mgmt. Assn. Home: 11982 Sentinel Point Reston VA 22091 Office: PO Box 3613 Reston VA 22090

MARSHALL, LINDA RAE, cosmetic company executive; b. Provo, Utah, Aug. 1, 1940; d. Arvid O. and Tola V. (Broderick) Newman; children—James, John. Student Brigham Young U., 1958-59, U. Utah, 1960-61. Buyer, Boston Store, 1961-62; sec. Milw. Gas & Light Co., 1962-64; mktg. rep. Elysee Cosmetics, Madison, Wis., 1971-75, pres., 1975-87; v.p., Dionne, Inc., 1987—; ptnr. Pres. Falk Sch. PTA, Madison. Mem. Aestheticians Internat. Assn. (adv. bd.), Cosmetic, Toiletry and Fragrance Assn. (exec. com., bd. dirs., chmn. voluntary program, chmn. small cosmetic com., membership com. task force). Club: Dental Wives. Author: Discover the Other Woman in You; monthly beauty columnist Beauty Fashion Mag.; contbg. author Cosmetic Industry Sci. and Regulatory Found., 1984. Address: Box 4084 Madison WI 53711

MARSHALL, LYNNOR BEVERLEY, biotechnology company executive; b. Melbourne, Victoria, Australia, Mar. 11, 1943; came to U.S., 1971; d. John A. and Evelyn M. (Post) Gilmore; m. Noel Marshall, 1965 (div. 1977); children: Neil D., David. K. BS with honors, U. Melbourne, Australia, 1963; BEd, U. Melbourne, 1967; PhD, Monash U., Melbourne, 1971. Sr. biochemist, mgr. product, mktg. Beckman Instruments, Palo Alto, Calif., 1972-79; pres. Calif. Medicinal Chemistry Corp., South San Francisco, 1979-83; v.p. corp. devel. Creative Biomolecules, South San Francisco, 1983; v.p. research Advanced Polymer Systems, Redwood City, Calif., 1984-85; exec. v.p. Agen USA Inc., Mt. View, Calif., 1985-86; pres. Alta Biomed., Los Altos, Calif., 1987—; bd. dirs. Chromatochem, Missoula, Mont., Yellowstone Diagnostics, Palo Alto. Mem. Am. Chem. Soc., AAAS.

MARSHALL, MARIE LYNNETTE, technical writer, photographer; b. Canton, Ohio, Sept. 12, 1954; d. Samuel Frederick and Glenda Mae (Spencer) Marshall; m. Thomas Mario Messana, Aug. 4, 1984. BS in Polit. Sci., Journalism, U. Md., 1980. Asst. editor, asst. dir. labor relations Nat. Rural Letter Carriers Assn., Washington, 1975-77; writer S/S Communications Inc., Washington, 1979-80; reporter, asst. editor The Diamondback, College Park, Md., 1979-80; asst. editor, reporter United Indsl. Workers and Seafarers Internat. Union newspaper, Camp Springs, Md., 1982-86; writer Taft Philanthropic Assn., Washington, 1987—; cons., editor Versar, Springfield, Va., 1987. Producer film for labor orgn. America, 1981; contbr. numerous photographic essays to labor pubs; contbr. numerous articles to profl. jours. Mem. Internat. Labor Communications Assn. (feature writing award 1983), Washington Ind. Writers. Democrat. Roman Catholic. Home: 3339 Tea Garden Circle 303 Silver Spring MD 20904

MARSHALL, MARY AYDELOTTE, state legislator; b. Cook County, Ill., June 14, 1921; d. John A. and Nell. A. Rice; B.A. with highest honors, Swarthmore Coll., 1942; m. Roger Duryea Marshall, Mar. 3, 1944; children: Nell Aydelotte, Jenny Winslow Marshall Davies, Alice Marie. Economist anti-trust div. Dept. Justice, Washington, 1942-46; mem. Va. Ho. of Dels., 1966-70, 72—, mem. privileges and elections com., rds. and internal nav. com., chmn. counties, cities and towns com., chmn. health, welfare and instns. com.; chmn. Legis. Study Commn. on Needs Elderly Virginians, 1973-78; chmn. Legis. Commn. Monitoring Long Term Care, 1983-86; mem. No. Va. Transp. Commn., 1974-80; mem. exec. com. Nat. Conf. State Legislators, 1981—, also chmn. long term care task force; chmn. Task Force on Social Security for Women, Fed. Council on Aging, 1978-81; bd. dirs. Washington Met. Council Govts., 1978, 80, 87, 88. Pres., Va. Assn. Mental Health, 1970-73, Va. Fedn. Democratic Women's Clubs, 1971-72; bd. dirs. Nat. Assn. Mental Health, 1972-78; mem. Dem. Central Com. Va., 1976-78. Recipient Achievement award Va. Assn. Mental Health, No. Va. Assn. Mental Health, Va. Fedn. Bus. and Profl. Women's Clubs, Va. Assn. Ind. Retail Gasoline Dealers, No. Va. Altrusa, No. Va. Retarded Citizens Assn.; named WETA Disting. Woman. Mem. AAUW, LWV. Congregationalist. Clubs: Bus. and Profl. Women's, Home Demonstration, No. Va. Dem., Downtown.

MARSHALL, MARY ELLEN, information systems consultant; b. Washington, Apr. 17, 1946; d. George John and Evangelica (Stratigakis) Mantzuranis, m. Bruce Lambert Marshall, Dec. 8, 1969; children: Christopher George, Robert Ambler. BS in Biol. Scis., Fla. State U., 1969, MA in Counseling, Chapman Coll., 1978; MA in Bus., Cen. Mich. U., 1981. Mgr. adminstrv. services The Dayton (Ohio) Power and Light Co., 1975-81; dir. adminstrn. Nimslo Corp., Atlanta, 1981-82; mgr. corp. markets Bell South Corp., Atlanta, 1982-84; dist. mktg. mgr. Wang Labs., Inc., Atlanta, 1984; east regional dir. Arthur Young and Co., Atlanta, 1985-87; practice dir. Booz, Allen and Hamilton, Inc., Bethesda, Md., 1987—; educator Kepner-Tregoe, Dayton, 1978-81. Mem. Data Processing Mgmt. Assn., Nat. Office Automation Conf. (advisor program com. 1986—), Internat. Word Processing Assn. (v.p. program com. 1981-82). Eastern Orthodox. Office: Booz Allen and Hamilton Inc 4330 East West Hwy Bethesda MD 20814-4455

MARSHALL, MERYL CORINBLIT, broadcast production executive, lawyer; b. Los Angeles, Oct. 16, 1949; d. Jack and Nita (Green) Corinblit; B.A., UCLA, 1971; J.D., Loyola Marymount U., Los Angeles, 1974. Bar: Calif. 1974. Dep. pub. defender County of Los Angeles, 1975-77; sole practice, Los Angeles, 1977-78; ptnr. Markman and Marshall, Los Angeles, 1978-79; sr. atty. NBC, Burbank, Calif., 1979-80, dir. programs, talent contracts bus. affairs, 1980, asst. gen. atty., N.Y.C., 1980-82, v.p., compliance and practicies, Burbank, 1982—, v.p. prgram affairs, Group W Prodns., 1987—. Treas. Acad. T.V. Arts and Scis., 1985-87; chmn., Nat. Women's Polit. Caucus, Westside, Calif., 1978-80; mem. Calif. Democratic Central Com., 1978-79; mem. Hollywood Women's Polit. Com., 1988. Mem. Acad. TV Arts and Scis. (treas. 1985), Women in Film. Democrat. Jewish. Office: Group W Productions Co One Lakeside Plaza 3801 Barham Blvd. Los Angeles CA 90068

MARSHALL, MIRA NAN, lawyer; b. Long Branch, N.J., Nov. 26, 1951; d. Donald Stanley and Shirley (Morrow) M. BA magna cum laude, U. Mass., Amherst, 1975; JD, Stanford U., 1982. Bar: D.C. 1982. Housing specialist Ednl. Fund LWV, Washington, 1976-77, project dir., 1978-79; assoc. dir. Equal Housing Opportunity, Met. Washington Planning and Housing Assocs., 1977-78; research asst. Stanford Law Sch. (Calif.), 1980-82; pvt. practice cons., Washington, 1982-83; assoc. Hewes, Morella, Gelband & Lamberton, P.C., Washington, 1984; counsel Nat. Com. against Discrimination in Housing, 1985; assoc. Fried, Frank, Harris, Shriver & Jacobson, Washington, 1986—; cons. community relations div. Am. Friends Service Com., Phila., 1983. Assoc. editor Stanford Jour. Internat. Law, 1981-82; author pamphlet, 1977. Commonwealth scholar, U. Mass., 1971-75; summer intern Stanford Pub. Interest Law Found., 1980. Mem. ABA, Women's Bar Assn. D.C., Phi Kappa Phi. Office: Fried Frank et al 1001 Pennsylvania Ave NW Suite 800 Washington DC 20004

MARSHALL, NANCY HAIG, research library administrator; b. Stamford, Conn., Nov. 3, 1932; d. Harry Percival and Dorothy Charlotte (Price) Haig; m. William Hubert Marshall, Dec. 28, 1953; children—Bruce Davis, Gregg Price, Lisa Reynolds, Jeanine Haig. B.A., Ohio Wesleyan U., 1953; M.A.L.S., U. Wis., 1972. Reference librarian U. Wis., Madison, 1972, assoc. dir. univ. libraries, 1979-86; univ. librarian Coll. William & Mary, Williamsburg, Va., 1986—; dir. Wis. Inter Library Services, Madison, 1972-79; mem. adv. com. Copyright Office, Washington, 1978-82; dir. USBE, Inc., Washington, 1983-86; trustee OCLC, Inc., Dublin, Ohio, 1982-88. Mem. bd. editors Jour. Acad. Librarianship, Va. Librarian; contbr. articles to profl. jours. Mem. ALA (council 1980-88), Wis. Library Assn. (Librarian of Yr. [illegible]), [illegible] Library Assn., Beta Phi Mu. Office: E G Swem Library Coll William & Mary Williamsburg VA [illegible]

MARSHALL, NATALIE JUNEMANN, college administrator; b. Milw., June 13, 1929; d. Harold E. and Myrtle (Findlay) Junemann; m. Howard D. Marshall, Aug. 7, 1954 (dec. 1972); children: Frederick S., Alison B. A.B., Vassar Coll., 1951; M.A., Columbia U., 1952, Ph.D., 1963. Instr. Vassar Coll., Poughkeepsie, N.Y., 1952-54, 59, 59-60, 63, dean studies, prof. econs., 1973-75, v.p. for student affairs, 1975-80, v.p. for adminstrn. and student services and prof. econs., 1980—; teaching fellow Wesleyan U., Middletown, Conn., 1955-56; from asst. prof. to prof. SUNY, New Paltz, 1964-73. Editor: (with Howard Marshall) The History of Economic Thought, 1968; Keynes, Updated or Outdated, 1970; author: (with Howard Marshall) Collective Bargaining, 1971. V.p. N.Y. State div. AAUW, 1964-66; pres. Poughkeepsie Vassar Club, 1965-67; trustee St. Francis Hosp., 1979—, Area Fund of Dutchess County, 1982-87, Hudson Valley Philharm., 1985—. Mem. AAUP, Am. Assn. Higher Edn., Am. Econ. Assn. Home: Box 2467 Poughkeepsie NY 12603 Office: Vassar Coll PO Box 3 Poughkeepsie NY 12601

MARSHALL, PHYLLIS, marketing and public relations executive; b. Phila., Aug. 26, 1933; d. Joseph Moses and Hannah (Schneider) Pulin; m. Edwin Howard Mernyk, Aug. 10, 1952 (div. Aug. 1972); children: Carolyn Anne Mustopa, Jonathan David, Paul Andrew, Suzanne Leigh. Student, Hunter Coll., 1954-55; AA, Am. Acad. Dramatic Art, N.Y., 1968; student, The New Sch., 1973-74. Asst. pub. relations specialist Health Facilities Corp., N.Y.C., 1970-73; freelance pub. relations and writing Wisdom's Child, N.Y.C., 1973-75; pub. relations specialist Ideal Mut. Ins. Co., N.Y.C., 1977-85; dir. corp. communications N.Y. Ins. Exchange, Inc., 1985-87; pres. Marshall Communication Group, Inc., N.Y.C., 1987—. Editor U.S. Reinsurance Report; contbr. articles to Jour. of Commerce, others. Mem. Nat. Ins. Industry Assn., Internat. Assn. Bus. Communicators (bd. govs. U.S. Dist. I, asst. dir. 1986-88, dist. dir. 1988—), N.Y. Internat. Assn. Bus. Communicators (pres. 1984-85, bd. govs. 1983—). Democrat. Jewish. Home: 875 W End Ave Suite 1F New York NY 10025

MARSHALL, PHYLLIS ELLINWOOD, mental health system executive, consultant; b. Kansas City, Mo., Dec. 20, 1929; d. Herbert Dwight and Mildred (Gillham) Ellinwood; m. John D. Reich, July 1, 1950 (div. 1964); children—Martha Reich Millican, Michael David, Donald Martin; m. C. Randolph Marshall, Nov. 27, 1969. B.A., Washington U., St. Louis, 1951, M.S.W., 1969. Adult program dir. St. Louis YWCA, 1962-64, dir. decentralized programs, 1964-67; alcoholism caseworker Malcolm Bliss Mental Health Ctr., St. Louis, 1968; exec. dir. Cobb County YWCA, Ga., 1969-72; dir. Coastal Area Community Mental Health Ctr., Brunswick, Ga., 1973-77; dir. Mental Health Services, Ga. Dept. Human Resources, Atlanta, 1977-84; exec. dir. Integrated Mental Health, Inc., Rochester, N.Y., 1984—; cons. NIMH, Washington, 1979-84, So. Regional Ednl. Bd., Atlanta, 1979-84, N.Y. State Office Mental Health, Albany, 1980-84; co-chair Metro Atlanta Deinstitutionalization Task Force, 1983-85; bd. dirs. Children Have All Rights, Legal, Ednl. and Emotional, Menninger Found. project, Atlanta, 1983-84; mem. council Fingerlakes Health Systems Agy., Rochester, 1985. Contbg. author: Perspectives in Mental Health, 1980, New Directions for Mental Health Services, 1988. Contbr. articles to profl. publs. Bd. dirs. Human Resources Credit Union, Atlanta, 1982-84. Recipient Boss of Yr. award Brunswick Jaycees, 1977, Good Friend award Brunswick Mental Health Assn., 1977, Community Mental Health award Atlanta U., 1980. Mem. AAUW (chpt. pres. 1978), Assn. Mental Health Adminstrs., Ga. Assn. Community Mental Health Ctrs. (pres. 1975-77), Rochester Women's Network. Club: Midtown Tennis (Rochester). Avocations: ocean sailing; music; tennis. Office: Integrated Mental Health Inc Monroe Sq 259 Monroe Ave Rochester NY 14607

MARSHALL, SALLY JEAN, biomaterials scientist; b. Racine, Wis., Jan. 8, 1949; d. Charles and Adele Ruth Rimkus; B.S. with distinction in sci. engring., Northwestern U., 1970, Ph.D. in Materials Sci. and Engring., 1975; m. Grayson William Marshall, Jr., July 4, 1970; children—Grayson William III, Jonathan Charles. Instr. biol. materials Northwestern U., Chgo., 1974-75, asst. prof., 1975-80, assoc. prof., 1980-86, prof., 1986-87, prof. restorative dentistry U. Calif., San Francisco, 1987—, vice chair research, 1988—; varsity swimming coach Northwestern U., Evanston, Ill., 1970-81; vis. fellow U. Melbourne (Australia), 1981. Recipient spl. dental research award Nat. Inst. Dental Research, 1977. Fellow Acad. Dental Materials (treas. 1983-85, v.p. 1985-87, pres. 1987—, bd. dirs. 1983—); mem. Am. Soc. Metals, AIME, Assn. Women in Sci., Am. Swimming Coaches Assn., Ill. Swimming Assn. (Women's Collegiate Coach of Year 1978-79), Internat. Assn. Dental Research, Am. Assn. Dental Research (1st place research award Chgo. sect.), N.Y. Acad. Scis., Am. Coll. Sports Medicine, Soc. Biomaterials, Sigma Xi, Tau Beta Pi, Omicron Kappa Upsilon. Contbr. articles to sci. jours. Home: 45 Wiltshire Ave Larkspur CA 94939 Office: U Calif Restorative Dentistry 707 Parnassus Ave Box 758 San Francisco CA 94143-0758

MARSHALL, SUSAN, lawyer; b. Ellsworth, Kans., July 8, 1950; d. Daniel Benjamin and Elizabeth Jean (Bailey) M. B.A., U. Kans., 1972; J.D. with honors, Washburn U., 1976. Bar: Kans. 1976. Summer legal intern, Campbell, Erickson, Cottingham, Morgan & Gibson, Kansas City, Mo., 1975; research asst., lobbyist Kans. County and Dist. Attys. Assn., Topeka, 1975-76; assoc. Metz & Metz, Lincoln, Kans., 1977-83; county atty. Lincoln County, Kans., Lincoln, 1980-85; sole practice law, Lincoln, 1983—; atty. position Kans. Commn. on Civil Rights, Topeka, 1978-86. Pres. Lincoln Carnegie Library, 1982-88. Mem. ABA, Kans. Bar Assn., Kans. County and Dist. Attys. Assn., Nat. Dist. Attys. Assn., Nat. History Soc. Republican. Office: 113 S 4th St Lincoln KS 67455

MARSHALL, SUSAN LOCKWOOD, civic worker; b. Orange, N.J., Dec. 2, 1939; d. Richard Douglas and Helen Lockwood (Stratford) Nelson; B.E., Wheelock Coll., 1961; m. William Pendleton Marshall, Aug. 20, 1960; children—Jill, James. Vol., Newton-Wellesley (Mass.) Hosp., 1962-63, New Eyes for the Needy, Inc., 1963-64, amblyopia screening program, Short Hills, N.J., 1969-71; bd. dirs. Jr. League of Oranges and Short Hills, Inc., 1967-69, 70-72, corr. sec., 1970-72; fund raising vol. Children's Aid and Adoption Soc. N.J., 1969-73, dir., 1970-73, asst. sec., 1970-72, 1st v.p., 1972-73; bd. dirs. Jr. League Stamford-Norwalk (Conn.), 1974-78, asst. treas., 1976-77, treas., 1977-78; bd. dirs. Program One to One, Inc., 1975-76, also treas.; vol. Voluntary Action Center 1975-76; bd. dirs. Episcopal Churchwomen of St. Luke's Parish, 1974-75, 76-80, 2d v.p., 1976-77, asst. treas., 1977-78, treas., 1978-80, pres., 1980-81; bd. dirs. Lockwood Mathews Mansion Mus., 1979-88, vol., 1979, treas., 1979-88, v.p., 1983-88; mem. council Darien Sch. Parent Bd., 1978-83, recording sec. 1981-83; bd. dirs. Middlesex Jr. High Parents Assn., 1979-83, treas., 1982-83; mem. vol. mgmt. assistance program adv. comm. Darien Chpt. Am. Field Service, 1984-87; Darien High Sch. Parents Assn., 1982-85, chmn., 1984-85; bd. dirs. Darien United Way, 1984—; mem. vol. mgmt. assistance program adv. com. Darien chpt. Am. Field Service, 1984—. Address: 358 Hollow Tree Ridge Rd Darien CT 06820

MARSHALL, VALERIE ANN, lawyer; b. Evansville, Ind., Aug. 26, 1954; d. Arthur E. and Jacqueline J. (Maixner) M. BBA, Stetson U., 1976, JD, 1979. Bar: Fla. 1979. Assoc. Clayton & Landis, Orlando, Fla., 1980-81; in-house counsel Walt Disney World Co., Lake Buena Vista, Fla., 1981-83; assoc. Haas, Boehm, Brown, Rigdon & Seacrest, Orlando, 1983-84; jr. ptnr., workers compensation supr. Haas, Boehm, Brown, Rigdon, Seacrest & Fischer, Orlando, 1984-87; supr. worker's compensation Jeffrey & Thomas, P.A., Maitland, Fla., 1987—. Mem. ABA, Orange County Bar (vice chmn. worker's compensation com. 1984—), Fla. Bar (workers compensation rules com. 1985—), Fla. Assn. for Women Lawyers (sec. 1982-84), Cen. Fla. Corp. Counsel Assn. (sec./treas. 1982-83), NOW, Alpha Chi Omega (v.p. 1974-76). Methodist. Office: Jeffery & Thomas PA 2301 Maitland Ctr Pkwy Suite 206 Maitland FL 32751

MARSHALL-NADEL, NATHALIE, artist, writer, educator; b. Pitts., Nov. 10, 1932; d. Clifford Benjamin and Clarice (Stille) Marshall; m. Robert Alfred Van Buren, May 1, 1952 (div. June 1965); children—Christine Van Buren Popovic, Clifford Marshall, Jennifer Van Buren Lake; m. David Arthur Nadel, Dec. 30, 1976. A.F.A., Silvermine Coll. Art, New Canaan, Conn., 1967; B.F.A., U. Miami, Coral Gables, 1977, M.A., 1982, Ph.D. in

English and Fine Art, 1982. Instr. humanities Miami Ednl. Consortium, Miami Shores, Fla., 1977-79, Barry U., Miami Shores, 1979-81, U. Miami, Coral Gables, 1977-81; sr. lectr. Nova U., Ft. Lauderdale, Fla., 1981-84, assoc. prof. humanities, 1985-86; prof. art, chair dept. art. Old Coll., Reno, Nev., 1986-88; chief artist Rockefeller U., N.Y.C., 1973-75; asst. registrar Lowe Art Mus., Coral Gables, 1976-78; co-founder, dir. The Bakehouse Art Complex, Miami, 1984—; mem. adv. bd. New World Sch. Arts, Miami, 1985—. One-woman shows: Silvermine Coll. Art, New Canaan, Conn., 1968, Ingber Gallery, Greenwich, 1969, Capricorn Gallery, N.Y.C., 1969, Pierson Coll. at Yale U., New Haven, 1970, The Art Barn, Greenwich, 1972, Art Unltd., N.Y.C., 1973, Benevy Gallery, N.Y.C., 1974, Richter Library, U. Miami, 1985, Nova U., Ft. Lauderdale, 1985, Ward Nasse Gallery, N.Y.C., 1985, Old Coll., Reno, 1986, Washoe County Library, Reno, 1987; group shows include: Capricorn Gallery, N.Y.C., 1968, Ingber Gallery, Greenwich, 1968, Compass Gallery, N.Y.C., 1970, Optimums Gallery, Westport, Conn., 1970, Finch Coll. Mus., N.Y.C., 1971, Town Hall Art Gallery, Stamford, Conn., 1973, 74, Jewish Community Ctr., Miami Beach, 1981, Continuum Gallery, Miami Beach, 1982, South Fla. Art Inst., Hollywood, Fla., 1984, Met. Mus., Coral Gables, Fla., 1985, Ward Nasse Gallery, N.Y.C., 1985, Brunner Mus., Iowa State U., Ames, 1986. Author, artist: Vibrations on Revelations, 1973, The Firebird, 1982, numerous artist books, 1968—. Author: Be Organized for College, 1980. Artist: (children's book) The Desert: What Lives There?, 1972. Editor, designer: Court Theaters of Europe, 1982. Contbr. poems to poetry mags., articles to profl. jours. Recipient Sponsor's award for Painting Greenwich Art Soc., 1967; Steven Buffton Meml. award Am. Bus. Women's Assn., 1980. Mem. Coll. Art Assn., MLA, Nat. Women's Studies Assn., Women's Caucus for Art (nat. adv. bd. 1983-88, pres. Miami chpt. 1984-86, southeast regional v.p. 1986). Office: Nova Univ 3301 College Ave Fort Lauderdale FL 33314

MARSHALL-REED, DIANE, psychologist, educator; b. Wyandotte, Mich., Feb. 28, 1950; d. Thomas Edward Mullett and Etta Mae (Morris) McCormick; m. Thomas O. Marshall, Jan. 3, 1968 (div. Nov. 1981); children: Michael, Jonathan; m. Edmond L. Reed III, Sept. 17, 1985. BS, Wayne State U., 1972, MEd, 1976, postgrad. Cert. psychologist, social worker. Counselor for family of terminally ill 1972-82; tchr. homebound and hospitalized Wyandotte Pub. Schs., 1972-81, tchr. learning disabled, 1981, tchr. mentally retarded, 1981-84, ednl. therapist, 1984-87; pvt. practice psychology Riverside Psychol. Services, Trenton, Mich., 1982-88; prin. Hillsdale County Intermediate Sch. Dist., Mich., 1987—; therapist for abusive parents DSS Contract, 1984—; cons. family matters Hillside, Wayne and Oakland Counties, Mich. Cts., 1984—; instr. English for Adult Edn.; speaker in field. Tchr. Sunday Sch. St. Thomas Luth. Ch., Grosse Ile, Mich. Dept. Social Services grantee, 1984-89; named Mother of Yr., News Herald, 1986. Mem. Am. Psychol. Assn., Women in Ednl. Adminstrn. (treas. 1978-80), Mich. Assn. Psychologists, Wayne County Homebound Assn. (past chmn.), Save the Whales, Gorilla Found., Mensa, Phi Delta Kappa, Pi Lambda Theta. Home: 6340 Hudson Rd Osseo MI 49266 Office: Riverside Psychol Services 2171 W Jefferson Suite 102 Trenton MI 48183

MARSTON, LOIS JO ANNE, insurance agent; b. Mountain Lake, Minn., Nov. 8, 1936; d. John P. and Mildred L. (Hagglund) Jungas; m. James B. Marston, June 15, 1958; children: Jamie Marston Kovacs, Holly Marston Ashton, Thomas, Scott, John. BA, Gustavus Adolphus, 1958. CLU, Chartered Fin. Cons. Policewoman, detective Police Dept. City of St. Paul, 1958-60; social worker Watoman County, St. James, Minn., 1963-67; life ins. agt. N.Y. Life, Mt. Lake, 1974—. Leader Camp Fire Girls, Mt. Lake, 1965-75. Mem. S.W. Minn. Assn. CLU, Gen. Fedn. Women's Clubs (past pres.). Mennonite. Home: 12th St Mountain Lake MN 56159 Office: NY Life 1006 3d Ave Mountain Lake MN 56159

MARTELL, RUTH, educational administrator; b. Cologne, Germany; came to U.S., 1939; d. Samuel and Elise (Silberberg) Rubinstein; m. Raymond Martell, June 24, 1953 (div. 1986); children—Erica Ellen, Madeline Ann. B.A. cum laude, Bklyn. Coll., 1951; M.S. in Edn., Queens Coll., 1967; M.S. in Adminstrn., Pace U., 1980. Co-chmn. Nat. Tay Sachs Fund Raising, 1963-67; kindergarten tchr. N.Y.C. Bd. Edn., 1970-78, head tchr. early childhood, 1978, test liaison, 1979—. Asst. to candidate Bess Myerson Senate Campaign, N.Y.C., 1980; vol. Guggenheim Mus., Nat. Tay-Sachs Assn., N.Y.C., English-in-Action, Doctors Hosp., N.Y.C. Mem. Nat. Council Adminstrv. Women in Edn., N.Y.C. Assn. Tchrs. English, Phi Beta Kappa. Jewish. Home: 505 E 14th St New York NY 10009 Office: Sch Dist 10 3961 Hillman Ave New York NY 10009

MARTENEY, LOIRE, international sales executive; b. Phoenix, May 30, 1959; d. Conn Marteney West. Cert. in sales and mktg., U. So. Calif., 1985; postgrad. in law, Western State U., Fullerton, Calif., 1985—. Internat. sales Indo-Atlantic, U.S.A., Los Angeles, 1980-83; area sales mgr. Meadows Airfreight, U.S.A., Los Angeles, 1983-86; account exec. DHL Airways, Los Angeles, 1986—; dir. mktg. OPIS, Inc., Los Angeles, 1985—; owner Reach for Success Publs., 1985—. Author: Your Personal Sales Guide, 1984, Dare to Discipline, 1987. Fundraiser Sr. Action Care Network, Los Angeles, 1983; fundraiser, chairperson Human Rights Awards Banquet, Newport Beach, Calif., 1983. Mem. Internat. Law Soc. (sec. 1985-86), U. So. Calif. Alumni Assn., Delta Theta Phi, Delta Nu Alpha. Democrat. Presbyterian. Clubs: Winston Polo (Anaheim, Calif.); John Wayne Tennis (Newport Beach, Calif.). Home: 195 Claremont Belmont Shores CA 90803

MARTIKAINEN, A(UNE) HELEN, retired health education specialist; b. Harrison, Maine, May 11, 1916; d. Sylvester and Emma (Heikkinen) M.; A.B., Bates Coll., 1939, D.Sc. (hon.), 1957; M.P.H., Yale, 1941; D.Sc., Harvard U., 1964, Smith Coll., 1969. Health edn. sec. Hartford Tb and Public Health Assn., 1941-42; cons. USPHS, 1942-49; chief health edn. WHO, Geneva, 1949-74, now mem. expert adv. panel. Trustee, Bridgton Acad., North Bridgton, Maine; mem program adv. bd., also membership com. U.S. Assn. Club of Rome; citizen councillor Atlantic Council U.S.A., 1987—; mem. N.C. Citizens Council Pub. Health; chmn. Internat. Relations N.C. div. AAUW, N.C. Center of Laws Affecting Women, Inc.; mem. adv. bd. Sch. Pub. Health, U. N.C., Chapel Hill; cons. Commn. on Women's Issues of Episcopal Diocese of N.C., N.C. Women's Resource Ctr., 1987—; bd. dirs. Orange and Durham Counties chpt. U.N. Assn.; citizen councillor Atlantic Council U.S.A., 1987—. Recipient Delta Omega award Yale; Nat. Adminstrv. award Am. Acad. Phys. Edn.; Bates Key award; Internat. Service award, France, 1953; Prentiss medal, 1956; spl. medal, certificate for internat. health edn. service Nat. Acad. Medicine for France, 1959; profl. award Soc. Public Health Educators, 1963. Fellow Am. Public Health Assn. (chmn. health edn. sect., Excellence award 1969); mem. AAUW (rep. to N.C. Council Social Legis.), U.S. Soc. Pub. Health Educators, Internat. Union Health Edn. (Parisot medal, tech. adviser), Acad. Phys. Edn. (asso.), Phi Beta Kappa. Episcopalian. Home: PO Box 3059 Chapel Hill NC 27514

MARTIN, ALISON CADY, interior designer; b. N.Y.C., May 12, 1949; d. Everett Ware Jr. and Ruth Anne (Payan) Cady; m. Robin Bradley Martin, Jan. 29, 1972 (div. 1979). BA, Middlebury (Vt.) Coll., 1971. Pres. Alison Martin Interiors, Ltd., Washington, 1976—. Sec. Great Falls (Va.) Concert Series, 1983—. Republican. Episcopalian. Office: 923 F St NW Washington DC 20004

MARTIN, ANITA ELLEN, nurse; b. Chgo., Aug. 5, 1925; d. Cornelius James and Sophie Ann (Bruczyk) M.; diploma DePaul Hosp. Coll. Nursing, St. Louis, 1949; B.S.N., Mt. St. Mary's Coll., Los Angeles, 1955; postgrad. UCLA, 1955-56, Rutgers U., 1969. Supr. pediatrics St. Mary's Hosp., Evansville, Ind., 1950-52; supr. medicine St. Vincent's Hosp., Los Angeles, 1952-56; supr. pediatrics Hotel Dieu Hosp., El Paso, 1956-60; head nurse Hanson's Disease, USPHS Hosp., Carville, La., 1960-62; head nurse, night supr. gen. surgery Hines (VA) Hosp., 1962-65, head nurse oncolgy, 1965-68, head nurse Restoration Center, 1968-72, community health nurse hosp.-based home care, 1972-74, coordinator hosp.-based health care, 1974-85, counselor alcoholic treatment program Restoration Center, 1968-72, cons. palliative care com., 1979-85; Alzheimer's disease nurse Family Alliance Adult Day Care Ctr., Woodstock, Ill.; lectr. high schs., civic orgns. Mem. Am. Nurses Assn., Nat. Orgn. VA Nurses, Am. Assn. Rehab. Nurses, Ill. State Hospice Assn. (charter). Roman Catholic. Contbr. articles to profl. jours. Home: 3419 W John St McHenry IL 60050 Office: Family Alliance 248 N Throop St Woodstock IL 60098

MARTIN, BARBARA A., sales executive; b. N. Brunswick, N.J., Jan. 24, 1942; d. John Joseph and Stella (Florek) Kociolak; m. Raymond A. Mioduszeuski, Feb. 9, 1963 (div. 1980); 1 child, Sandra Ann. Student, Kean Coll.; A in Mgmt. Sci., Middlesex Co. Coll.; Degree in Sectl. Sci., Berkeley Sectl. Sch., 1961; Cert. Paralegal, Am. Paralegal Inst., S. Orange, N.J. Adminstrv. sec. Benson and Benson, Princeton, N.J., 1961-62; mgr. customer svc. Middlesex Container Co., Inc., Milltown, N.J., 1962-65; mgr. purchasing East Side Hair Co., E. Brunswick, N.J., 1971-78; gen. mgr. Middlesex Container Co., Inc., 1978-87; v.p. ops., sales Rampac Industries, Livingston, N.J., 1987—. Active S. River Dem. Orgn., N.J., 1972; pres. St. Mary's PTA, S. River, 1974-76, 1st v.p., 1976-78; treas. Trenton (N.J.) Reg. PTA, 1976-77. Named Advisor of Yr., St. Peters Athletic Assn., 1974. Mem. Nat. Assn. Female Execs. Clubs: S. River Women's (publicity com. 1978-79), CYO. Home: 106 Griggs Pl East Brunswick NJ 08816 Office: Rampac Industries 513 W Mount Pleasant Ave Livingston NJ 07039

MARTIN, BARBARA VINEYARD, educator; b. Knoxville, Tenn., June 17, 1928; d. Roderick Random and Anna (Nance) Vineyard; m. Robert Harmon Martin, Oct. 27, 1968. BS, Carson-Newman Coll., 1950; MS, U. Tenn., 1964. Cert. Home Economist. Tchr. home economics Grainger County Bd. Edn., Washburn, Tenn., 1950-51, Jefferson County Bd. Edn., Dandridge, Tenn., 1951-58; extension home economist U. Tenn. Agrtl. Extension, Rutledge, 1958-63, Murfreesboro, 1964—. CXert. Appreciation Mayor City of Murfreesboro, 1978. Mem. Nat. Assn. Extension Home Economist (Disting. Service award 1973), Tenn. Assn. Extension Home Economist, Dist. II Assn. Extension Home Economist (pres.), Am. Home Econs. Assn., Tenn. Home Econs. Assn., Nashville and Murfreesboro Area Home Econs. Assn. (reporter), Epsilon Sigma Phi. Baptist. Clubs: Murfreesboro Art League, Rutherford County Hist. Soc. Home: 1811 Avon Rd Murfreesboro TN 37130 Office: Rutherford County Agrl Extension Office County Courthouse Rm 301 Murfreesboro TN 37130

MARTIN, BEVERLY ANN, music educator; b. Clarksville, Ark., Sept. 30, 1951; d. Paul Samuel and Marcella Marie (Matthews) M. BA in Music Edn. magna cum laude, Harding Coll., 1973; M in Music Edn., U. Ark., 1975; postgrad., Oklahoma City U., 1977-82, S. Oklahoma City Jr. Coll., 1979; PhD in Music Edn., U. Okla., Norman, 1987. Tchr. music Lincoln (Ark.) Consolidated Schs., 1975-76; capital campaign coordinator Okla. Med. Research Found., Oklahoma City, 1977-78; adminstrv. sec. Xerox Corp., Oklahoma City, 1978-79; tchr. music Overholser Elem. Sch., Bethany, Okla., 1979—; singer in chorus Memphis Opera Theatre, 1973; actor Boar's Head Players, Fayetteville, Ark., 1976, Lyric Theatre, Oklahoma City, 1978; dir. elem. chorus Sooner State Games, Oklahoma City, 1987. Top fundraiser Cancer Drive Overholser Elem. Sch., Bethany, 1980-83; bd. dirs. Overholser PTA, Bethany, 1981-83; tchr. Mayfair Ch. Christ, Oklahoma City, 1981-85; docent Okla. Art Ctr., Oklahoma City, 1982-83; active Memphis State U. Children's Opera, 1973. Named one of Outstanding Young Women of Am., 1983. Mem. NEA, Okla. Edn. Assn., Music Educators Nat. Conf., Okla. Music Edn. Assn., Canterbury Choral Soc., Pi Kappa Lambda. Republican. Home: 4316 NW 22d Oklahoma City OK 73107 Office: Overholser Elem Sch 7900 NW 36th Bethany OK 73008

MARTIN, BEVERLY ANN, publishing company official; b. Detroit, Dec. 13, 1954; d. Alfred Lemoin and Mary Ann (Sanders) Allen; divorced; 1 child, Corey Shane. Grad. high sch., Walker, La. Proof runner State Times/Morning Adv., Baton Rouge, 1972-73; account rep. Drackett Products Co., Baton Rouge, 1973-74, L'eggs Panty Hose, Baton Rouge, 1974-75; owner, mgr. B&B Sales, Baton Rouge, 1975-78, Type Co., Ink Inc., Lafayette, La., 1978-84, TBC Inc., Lafayette, La., 1981-86; dir. prodn. ops. Times Western Pub. Co., San Diego, 1986—. Mem. Nat. Assn. Female Execs. Democrat. Baptist. Home: 5949 Mildred St Apt 7 San Diego CA 92110 Office: Trans Western Pub Co 8328 Clairmont Mesa Blvd San Diego CA 92111

MARTIN, BRENDA MARIE, small business owner, consultant; b. Buffalo, July 13, 1947; d. James and Etta (Foster) Wilson; m. William Frank Martin; 1 child, Tiffany Marie. Grad. high sch., Buffalo; student, State Tchrs. Coll., Buffalo, 1967-69, U. Ala., 1979-81, Calif. Coast U. Employment adminstrn. mgr. Xerox Corp., Greenwich, Conn., 1969-79; owner, dir. Tiffany's Acad. Personal Devel., Huntsville, Ala., 1980—; producer, hostess TV Talk Shows WAAY-TV, Huntsville, Ala., 1981-83; dir. news, pub. relations WZDX-TV, Huntsville, Ala., 1985-87; instr. So. Bus. Inst., Huntsville, Ala., 1985—. Bd. dirs. United Cerebral Palsy, Huntsville, 1981, Better Bus. Bur., 1984, Huntsville Boys Club, 1986, ARC, 1985; mem. communications com. United Way of Madison County, 1986; mem. Girl Scouts U.S., 1980; v.p. Huntsville Council PTAs, 1986-87, pres., 1987—; mem. Huntsville Madison City Community Clean, 1986-87, Madison County Polit. Caucus, 1987—; chair policy com. Huntsville City Schs., 1986-87. Named one of Outstanding Young Women Am. Gen. Fedn. Women's Clubs, Montgomery, Ala., 1982, Outstanding Community Leader, Ala. A&M U., 1987, Small Bus. Exec. of Yr. Huntsville-Madison County C. of C., 1988; recipient Outstanding Small Bus., Small Bus. Adminstrn., Huntsville, 1987; honored for contributions to elderly in Buffalo, First Lady Pat Nixon, 1972. Mem. Am. Bus. Women's Assn. (v.p. N.Y. chpt. 1976-77, Ways and Means chmn. 1976, corr. sec. Ala. chpt. 1981-82, Woman of the Yr. 1977), Network, Am. Soc. Personnel Adminstrn., Pub. Relations Council Ala., Am. Lung Assn. (bd. dirs. 1983), Am. Inst. Psychotherapy (bd. dirs. 1984). Democrat. Methodist. Home: 2107 Bideford Dr Huntsville AL 35803 Office: Tiffany's Acad Personal Devel and Modeling Inc 9034 G Memorial Pky s Huntsville AL 35802

MARTIN, CAROLANN FRANCES, educator, conductor, cellist; b. Woodward, Okla., Nov. 20, 1935; d. John C. Martin and Leah Mae (Heaston) Shilling; B.Mus.Edn., Oklahoma City U., 1957; M.A. (fellow), Ohio State U., 1964; D.M.A., U. Ariz., 1979. Tchr. music, pub. schs., Okla., 1957-58; asst. prof. Wilson br. Chgo. City Coll., 1964-67; assoc. prof. Morningside Coll., Sioux City, Iowa, 1969-76; dir. opera theater, cellist Oklahoma City Symphony, 1954-58, 67-69, Norfolk Symphony, 1958-59, Columbus (Ohio) Symphony, 1962-64; prin. cellist Chgo. Chamber Orch., 1965-67, Chgo. Civic Orch., 1966-67; prin. cellist Sioux City Symphony; condr. Siouxland Youth Symphony; asst. prin. cellist Tucson Symphony and Ariz. Opera Co., 1976-77; assoc. prof. Pittsburg State U., 1977—; condr., music dir. S.E. Kans. Symphony, Pittsburg State U. Opera Theater, Mid-Am. Youth Symphony, 1977—; asst. condr. Eastern Music Festival, 1983-84; guest condr. Bournemouth Sinfonietta, Eng., Victoria Symphony, Tex.; compact disc recording Journeys: Orch. Music by Am. Women, 1988. Served to 1st lt. USMCR, 1958-61. Winner Nat. Conducting Competition, 1980. Mem. Am. String Tchrs. Assn., Music Educators Nat. Conf., Condrs. Guild (exec. bd.), Kans. Music Tchrs. Assn., Am. Legion, Delta Zeta. Sigma Alpha Iota. Roman Catholic. Home: 107 E Carlton Pittsburg KS 66762 Office: Pitts State U Dept Music Pittsburg KS 66762

MARTIN, CECILIA ANN, educator; b. Broken Bow, Okla., Nov. 10, 1934; d. Cecil C. and Faye (Burks) Martin; B.S., Baylor U., 1955; M.Ed., North Tex. State U., 1962; Ed.D., U. No. Colo., 1975. Instr. phys. edn. Stripling Jr. High Sch., Ft. Worth, 1955-65; cons. in phys. edn. Ft. Worth Ind. Sch. Dist., 1965-74; dir. profl. preparation dept. phys. edn. Colo. State U., Fort Collins, 1974—, asst. dean Coll. Profl. Studies, 1979-80. Mem. Tex. Tchrs. Assn., Am., Tex. (asso. conv. mgr. 1970-71), Colo. (sec. elect) assns. health, phys. edn. and recreation, Nat., Central (membership chmn.) assns. phys. edn. in higher edn., Colo. Assn. Health, Phys. Edn., Recreation and Dance (sec., pres.), Phi Delta Kappa, Kappa Delta Pi, Delta Psi Kappa. Home: 1977 17th Ave Greeley CO 80631 Office: Colo State U Moby Gymnasium Fort Collins CO 80523

MARTIN, CHERI CHRISTIAN, health services administrator; b. Nashville, Mar. 9, 1956; d. Jesse Thomas and Eloise (McClain) Christian; m. George A. Martin, June 25, 1977; 1 child, Matthew Alexander. BS in Family Resources and Consumer Scis., U. Wis., 1977. Asst. buyer Dayton Hudson, Mpls., 1978-79, assoc. buyer, 1979-81; instr. Nat. Coll., Mpls., 1981-82; mgr. store Connco Shoes, Inc., Mpls, 1982-83; patient services rep. Group Health, Inc., Mpls., 1984—. Facilitator seminar Non-Verbal Communication, 1986. Mem. Nat. Assn. Patient Reps., Minn/Dakota Assn. Patient Reps. (bd. dirs.), U. Wis. Alumni Assn. Club: Group Health Social (Mpls.) (pres. 1987—). Home: 4640 Nevada Ave N Crystal MN 55428

MARTIN, CHIPPA, counseling psychologist; b. Bronx, N.Y., Sept. 6, 1942; d. Murray and Rose (Kaplan) Riback; B.A., Queens Coll., 1964; M.A., Goddard Coll., 1978; children—Tara, Beth. Tchr., Manhasset (N.Y.) High Sch., 1964-65; tchr., humanities cons. Millbrook (N.Y.) High Sch., 1972-74; certifier Cambridge (Mass.) Govt. Housing, 1975-77; dir., counselor Aradia Counseling, Boston, 1978—; ptnr. real estate investment co., 1982—. Vice-pres., League Preservation of Hudson Valley, 1972. Lic. social worker, Mass.; nat. cert. counselor art. Mem. Nat. Assn. Social Workers, Am. Personnel and Guidance Assn., Assn. Specialists in Group Work, Assn. Women in Psychology, Boston Visual Artists' Union, Cape Cod Art Assn., Falmouth Artists' Guild, Provincetown Art Assn. Recipient numerous art awards at one-woman and group exhbns.; work included in pvt. collections. Home: 251 Mill St Newtonville MA 02668

MARTIN, CLAIRE PATRICIA, foundation administrator; b. Georgetown, Guyana, S.Am., Aug. 10, 1936; came to U.S., 1956; naturalized, 1975; d. A.A.D. and Ruby Edith (Pollard) M. BS in Biology, Howard U., 1960; MS, Columbia U., 1970; HMO mgrs. tng., Wharton Sch., 1975. Cert. in phys. therapy, N.Y., 1961. Sr. phys. therapist Cornell Med. Ctr., N.Y. Hosp., N.Y.C., 1961-68; assoc. adminstr. NENA Health Ctr., N.Y.C., 1969-72; assoc. dir., ambulatory care Health & Hosps. Corp., N.Y.C., 1972-75; dir., mktg. and enrollment Newark Comprehensive Health Services Plan, 1975-76; exec. dir. Buckeye Health Plan Inc., Cleve., 1976-78; adminstr. ARC Blood Services, Detroit, 1978-84; exec. dir. Albany Area chpt. ARC, N.Y., 1984—; bd. dirs. Vis. Nurse Assn., Albany; trustee Meml. Hosp., Albany; com. mem. Am. Nat. Red Cross Corp. Communications Adv. Council, Nat. Red Cross Black Adv. Com., Washington. Mem. NAACP, Albany, 1985—, Tri-Centennial Com. of Albany, 1986-87; bd. dirs. Urban League of Albany Area Inc., 1985. Mem. Howard U. Alumni Assn., N.Y. State Pub. Health Assn. (bd. dirs. N.E. affiliate 1985—), Health Systems Agy. Northeastern N.Y. Inc. (bd. dirs. subarea council 1985—). Office: American Red Cross Albany Area Chpt Hackett Blvd & Clara Barton Dr Albany NY 12208

MARTIN, CLEO EILEEN, educator; b. Goldfield, Iowa, Aug. 5, 1925; d. Roy Bertram and Fannie Grace (Zinser) Martin; BA, U. No. Iowa, 1946, MA, 1954; postgrad. U. Iowa, 1961. Tchr. English, high schs., New Hampton and E. Waterloo, Iowa, 1946-53; teaching asst., instr., asst. prof., writing supr. freshman rhetoric program U. Iowa, Iowa City, 1954—, dir. summer writing workshops Iowa Writing Project, 1978—; cons. high sch. and coll. writing programs; dir. Writing Workshop Iowa Inst. on Writing, 1979, 80. Mem. Iowa Council of Tchrs. of English (Disting. Service award 1986), Nat. Council of Tchrs. of English, Coll. Conf. on Composition and Communication. Democrat. Home: 405 Crestview Ave Iowa City IA 52240 Office: 72 English-Philosophy Bldg Iowa City IA 52242

MARTIN, CONSTANCE R(IGLER), biology educator; b. Bklyn., Dec. 31, 1923; d. Bernard and Sophie (Robins) Rigler; m. Michael A. Martin, Oct. 6, 1943 (div. 1965); children: April Carol, Brenda Joy; m. Henning R. Norbom, Sept. 3, 1971. BS, L.I. U., 1944; PhD, State U. Iowa, 1951. Research asst. State U. Iowa, Iowa City, 1948-50; research assoc. N.Y. Med. Coll., N.Y.C., 1951-52; sr. physiologist Creedmoor State Hosp., Queens, N.Y., 1953-55; asst. prof. physiology, pharmacology N.Y. Med. Coll., N.Y.C., 1956-57; assoc. prof. L.I. U., Bklyn., 1959-62; asst. prof. physiology C.U.N.Y., N.Y.C., 1963-64; assoc. prof. physiology CUNY, N.Y.C., 1965-66, assoc. prof. biol. scis., 1967-74, prof. biol. scis., 1975—; mem. med. info. com. ASTM, Phila., 1985—. Author: Endocrine Physiology, 1986, Textbook of Endocrine Physiology, 1976. Contbr. articles to profl. jours. Mem. The Endocrine Soc. (chmn. edn. com. 1984-88), Am. Physiol. Soc., Soc. for Study of Reproduction, Am. Soc. for Bone and Mineral Research, N.Y. Acad. Scis., AAAS. Office: CUNY Hunter Coll Dept Biol Scis 695 Park Ave New York NY 10021

MARTIN, DALE, vocational rehabilitation executive; b. N.Y.C., May 10, 1935; m. Robert A. Wishart, Dec. 13, 1985; children by previous marriage: Elizabeth, Devon. BS, U. Conn., 1957. RN, cert. ins. rehab. specialist. Dental asst. Hempstead, N.Y., 1951; with Wesson Maternity Hosp., Springfield, Mass., 1957-58, Huntington Hartford Meml. Hosp., Pasadena, 1958-59; office mgr. Indsl. By Products Inc., Kalamazoo, 1969-72; controller Indsl. By Products Inc., Chgo., 1970-74; cons. Mgmt. Resources Inc., Broomall, Pa., 1978-81; cons., owner Martin-Collard Assn., Inc., Monmouth Beach, N.J., 1980-84; cons., owner, chmn. bd. dirs. MCA, Inc., Boston, 1984—; cons. Viewfinder, Old Chatham, N.Y., 1987—. Contbr. articles to profl. jours.; painter, sculptor. Mem. Nat. Assn. Rehab. Profls. in Pvt. Sector, Sigma Theta Tau. Clubs: Town (v.p.), Ski (Mountain Lakes, N.J.) (founder), Jr. Women's, Jr. League. Office: MCA Inc PO Box 5438 Boston MA 02102

MARTIN, DARLEEN TERASHA, investment company executive; b. Denver, Oct. 4, 1947; d. Joseph Madison and Ora Ophelia (Cobb) M.; m. Wayne Allen Carr, Oct. 4, 1985. Student, Colo. State U., 1965-70. Lic. securities dealer. Project expeditor Priorities Investment Corp., Newark, 1970-74; project mgr. D.C. Devel. Corp., Washington, 1974-80; assoc. v.p. 1st Investors Corp., Austin, Tex., 1981-88, v.p., 1988—. Active Big Brother/Big Sister, Austin, 1984—. Democrat. Baptist. Office: 1st Investors Corp 6448 Hwy 290 E #E104 Austin TX 78723

MARTIN, DONNA CHASTAIN, health service administrator; b. Mitchell, Ind., Mar. 27, 1936; d. Maurice Anthony and Lorena (Caniff) Chastain; m. Franklin E. Martin Jr., Aug. 2, 1958; children: Natalie A. Matthews, Candace Rae, Jennifer Thorlton. RN, St. Vincent's Sch. Nursing, Indpls., 1957; student, Ball State U., 1969, Northwood Inst., French Lick, Ind., 1970, Vincennes U., 1984. RN, Ind., Colo., Tex.; lic. health care adminstr. Ind., Idaho, Ariz. Staff nurse Dunn Meml. Hosp., Bedford, Ind., 1957-58, dir. nurses, 1968-71; office nurse M.G. Van Der Schouw, Ft. Collins, Colo., 1958-60; staff nurse, supr. Larimer County Hosp., Trinidad, Colo., 1960-62; staff nurse, dir. nurses Orange County Hosp., Paoli, Ind., 1962-67; dir. nurses Medco Ctr., French Lick, 1971-77; dist. dir. nursing Am. Med. Mgmt. Inc., Indpls., 1977-85; mgr. quality assurance Forum Group, Inc., Indpls., 1985-86; dir. health services Basic Am. Retirement Communities, Inc., Indpls., 1986—; cons. in field. Mem. Ind. Health Care Assn. Home: Rural Rt. 3 Box 500 Paoli IN 47454 Office: Basic Am Retirement Communities 4000 E Southport Rd Indianapolis IN 46227

MARTIN, DOROTHY ANNE, military officer, consultant; b. Bklyn., July 21, 1938; d. Chester Edward and Sophia Ann (Homontowski) Machulski. AA, Nassau County Community Coll., 1967; BBA, Hofstra U., 1969; MS, Jacksonville State U., 1974. Commd. 1st lt. U.S. Army, 1970, advanced through grades to maj., 1980, ret., 1988; chief mil. police investigations 24th Inf. Div. U.S. Army, Fort Stewart, Ga., 1974-75; staff advisor to comdg. gen. 24th Inf. Div. U.S. Army, Fort Stewart, 1975-77; chief security police Tripler Med. Ctr., Honolulu, 1977-80; Dep. Dir. Indsl. Security Def. Investigative Service, Boston, 1980-82; orgnl. effectiveness cons. 3d Support Command U.S. Army, Frankfurt, Fed. Republic Germany, 1983-86; personnel war planner U.S. Army, New Orleans, 1986-87; staff officer Office of Dir. Personnel and Community Activities U.S. Army, Fort Polk, La., 1987-88; ind. cons., corp. trainer. Contbr. articles to profl. jours. Mem. Women Marines Assn. (pres. 1987—), Nat. Assn. Female Execs., Assn. U.S. Army, Res. Officers Assn., Nat. Assn. Neurolinguistic Programming, Internat. Fedn. Bus. and Profl. Women's Clubs. Democrat. Home: 4701 Robin Hood Dr New Orleans LA 70128 Office: CDR 5th Infantry Div AFZX-PA Fort Polk LA 71459-5000

MARTIN, DOROTHY EVERETT, social work educator, consultant; b. Verona, N.J., Aug. 5, 1919; d. Frank Norton and Edith Sarah (Baker) Everett; m. Donald Darrow Matson, Sept. 11, 1943 (dec. May 1969); children—Martha, Donald E., James Edward, Barbara B.; m. Samuel Preston Martin, III, Sept. 5, 1970. B.S., St. Lawrence U., 1940; M.S.W., Case Western Res. U., Cleveland, 1946. Field dir. Planned Parenthood League Mass., 1966-70; dir. counseling Phila. Family Planning, 1971-72; supr. social work Daroff Hosp.-Albert Einstein Med. Ctr., Phila., 1973-76; supr. social work, sch. age parents program Phila. Sch. Dist., 1976-77; lectr. Sch. Social Work, U. Pa., Phila., 1977—; sex edn. cons., 1975—. Mem. Nat. Assn. Social Workers, Acad. Cert. Social Workers, Am. Assn. Sex Educators, Counselors and Therapists (cert.), Soc. Sci. Study of Sex, NOW, LWV. Democrat. Office: U Pa Sch Social Work 3701 Locust Walk Philadelphia PA 19143

MARTIN, EDITH KINGDON GOULD (MRS. GUY MARTIN), pianist, civic worker; b. N.Y.C., Aug. 20, 1920; d. Kingdon and Annunziata (Lucci) Gould; student Barnard Coll., N.Y.C., 1939-40; pvt. study piano; m. Guy Martin, Oct. 12, 1946; children—Isaiah Guyman III, Jason Gould, Christopher Kingdon, Edith Maria Theodosia Burr. Actress, Barter Theater, 1941, Summer Stock, Nyack, 1942, A Young American, 1946, Louis Bromfield's West of the Moon, 1946, Agatha Christie's Hidden Horizons, 1946; guest pianist Werner Lywen Quartet, 1965—. Bd. dirs. Paul VI Inst. for Arts, 1979—; trustee, past pres. Washington Opera. Served with USNR, 1942-46. Decorated Navy Expert Pistol medal. Clubs: City Tavern, Sulgrave (Washington). Author: Poems, 1934. Composer: Song Cycle on Poems of Lenau and Schiller, 1968. Home: 3300 O St NW Washington DC 20007

MARTIN, EDITH WAISBROT, computer scientist, electronics company executive; b. Chgo., June 25, 1945; d. Alexander Joseph and Helen Mae (Hance) Waisbrot; m. Charles Samuel Martin, Dec. 16, 1967 (div. Jan.,1982); children: William McNutt, Christine Katherine; m. Douglas Carter Montgomery, Sept. 2, 1982. B.A., Lake Forest Coll., 1967; postgrad., Universitat Karlsruhe, W. Ger., 1971-72; M.S. in Info. and Computer Sci., Ga. Inst. Tech., 1975-76, Ph.D., 1980. Dir. computer sci. tech. lab. Ga. Inst. Tech., Atlanta, 1976-80; corp. exec. dir. Control Data Corp., Atlanta, 1980-82; pres. EWM & Assocs., Inc., Atlanta, from 1982; dep. under sec. Dept. Def. for research and advanced tech., Washington, from 1982; U.S. prin. Non-Atomic Research and Devel. Com., from 1982, NATO Def. Research Group, Brussels, Belgium, from 1982; v.p., high tech. ctr. Boeing Electronics, Seattle. Contbr. articles to profl. jours.; editorial reviewer: Mil. Electronics Countermeasures, 1976-80; mem. editorial bd.: IEEE Software, 1983—. Bd. dirs. Ga. Inst. Tech., Atlanta, 1983. Recipient numerous awards Dept. Def., 1982—. Mem. IEEE (exec. bd.dirs. tech. com. on software Computer Soc. 1982—, award of appreciation-recognition 1983), Assn. Computing Machinery, Electronics Industries Assn. (subcom. chmn. 1981 recognition award), Sigma Xi (award of appreciation-recognition from Pres. Ronald Reagan 1983). Republican. Presbyterian. Club: Army-Navy Country (Washington). Office: Boeing Electronics PO Box 24346 Mail Stop 7J-20 Seattle WA 98124 *

MARTIN, GAIL INGRID, brokerage house executive, lawyer; b. Chgo., July 2, 1959; d. Edward Anthony and Barbara Catherine (Payne) M. Premiere degree, U. Paris, France, 1981; BA, U. Ill., 1982; JD, Georgetown U., 1986. Clk. Georgetown U. Law Ctr., Washington, 1984-86; market maker Bear Stearns, San Francisco, 1987—. Mem. Phi Delta Phi. Home: 634 Cabrillo San Francisco CA 94118

MARTIN, HELEN ELIZABETH, educator; b. West Chester, Pa., Feb. 19, 1945; d. Thomas Edwin and Elizabeth Temple (Walker) M.; B.A., The King's Coll., Briarcliff Manor, N.Y., 1967; M.Ed., West Chester U., 1970; postgrad. Goethe Inst., Freiberg, Fed. Republic Germany, 1979, Oxford U., 1979. Tchr. math. and sci. Unionville (Pa.) High Sch., 1967—; mem. Carnegie Forum on Edn. and the Economy. Mem. Pa. Republican State Com., Rep. Com. of Chester County, 1987—. Named Alumna of the Yr. The King's Coll., 1987. Fellow Am. Sci. Affiliation; mem. AAAS, Nat. Sci. Tchrs. Assn., Nat. Council Tchrs. Math., History Sci. Soc., So. Chester County Rep. Women's Council (pres.), Nat. Bd. Profl. Teaching Standards, Red Clay Valley Assn., Brandywine Valley Assn. Clubs: Delaware Camera, Women's Rep. of Chester County, Nat. Sci. Tchrs. Assn. (internat. lectr. 1987), Assn. for Sci. Edn. in U.K. Home: 329 Lambortown Rd West Grove PA 19390 Office: Unionville High Sch Unionville PA 19375

MARTIN, JAN ROGERS, nursery school educator; b. Mt. Vernon, N.Y., Jan. 24, 1947; d. George Arnold and Alta (Snyder) Rogers; m. Joseph Martin, June 26, 1981; 1 child, David. BS in Elem. Edn., Seton Hall U., 1969. Cert. elem. tchr., N.J. Adminstr. Young World Day Sch., Mahwah, N.J., 1974-78; mgr. Thom McAn, Nanuet, N.Y., 1978-80, Macys/ Stride Rite, Nanuet, 1980-81, Marty Schooes, Carlstaff, N.J., 1981-82; realtor Joan Quigg, Saddle River, N.J., 1983—; dir. All Saints Pre Sch., Glen Rock, N.J., 1984—; mem. adv. council Ramapo Coll., Mahwah, 1972-74, Bergen Community Coll., Parmarus, N.J., 1972-74. Mem. Nat. Assn. Edn. Young Children, N.J. Assn. Early Yrs. Children, N.J. Assn. Realtors. Republican. Roman Catholic. Home: 53 Waldwick Ave Waldwick NJ 07463

MARTIN, JEANNE MARIE, computer company administrator; b. Balt., Nov. 7, 1958; d. John Donald and Beverly Ann (Beatty) M. BS, Towson (Md.) State U., 1980. Tchr. Archdiocese Balt., 1980-83; with retail sales The Logical Choice, Inc., Ellicott City, Md., 1983-84; mgr. store The Logical Choice, Inc., Ellicott City, 1984-86; div. mgr. Columbia, Md., 1986-87; asst. to v.p. Dos Computer Ctr. (formerly The Logical Choice, Inc.), Balt., 1987, asst. sales, personnel mgr., advt. mgr., 1987—. Mem. Nat. Assn. for Female Execs., Smithsonian. Democrat. Roman Catholic. Home: 7827 Butterfield Dr Elkridge MD 21227

MARTIN, JERRI WHAN, public relations executive; b. Aurora, Ill., Oct. 21, 1931; d. Forest Livings and Geraldeane Jeanette (Cutler) Whan; m. Charles L. Martin (div.); children: Vicki, Bill, Erica, Kevin. BMus, Wichita State U., 1952. Co-owner Sta. KCNY, San Marcos, Tex., 1957-70; correspondent Austin Am.-Statesman, 1959-85; co-owner Sta. KWFT, Wichita Falls, Kans., 1965—; cons. U.S. Office Econ. Opportunity, Austin, 1966-68, Tex. Ednl. Found., Inc., San Marcos, 1975—, State Bank and Trust Co., San Marcos, 1985—. Mem. ethics com. Hays Meml. Hosp., 1985—; pres. Hays County Women's Polit. Caucus, Tex., 1985—; del. State Dem. Convs., Dallas, Houston, 1982, 84; bd. dirs. Cen. Tex. Higher Edn. Authority, San Marcos, 1982—, Scheib Opportunity Ctr., San Marcos, 1983—, Edwards Underground Water Dist., San Antonio, 1985—, sec. Named Outstanding Reporter in Tex., Tex. Legis., 1960. Mem. Bus. and Profl. Women, Jr. Service League (sustaining), San Marcos C. of C. Office: Tex Ednl Found Inc PO Box 1108 San Marcos TX 78666

MARTIN, JOANNE, utility company executive; b. Akron, Ohio, Feb. 2, 1941; d. John and Ann M. (Capp) Martin; A.Secretarial Sci., U. Akron, 1968. Stenographer, Gen. Tire & Rubber Co., Akron, 1958-61; with Ohio Edison Co., Akron, 1961—, sec. to corp. sec., 1968-72, asst. corp. sec., 1972—. Cert. profl. sec., 1972. Mem. LWV of Akron, Women's Network Akron, U. Akron Alumni Assn., U. Akron John R. Buchtel Soc., Nat. Council Career Women, Nat. Assn. Female Execs., Bus. and Profl. Women's Club. Home: 520 Meredith Ln Apt 305 Cuyahoga Falls OH 44223 Office: 76 S Main St Akron OH 44308

MARTIN, JOSEPHINE WALKER, educator; b. Charleston, S.C., Jan. 15, 1927; d. George Archibald and Josephine Isabel (Walker) M.; A.B., U. S.C., 1946, M.Ed., 1950, Ph.D. (Stoddard fellow), Coll. Edn., 1971; M.A., Columbia U. Union Theol. Sem., 1952; postgrad. C.G. Jung Inst., Zurich, Switzerland, 1954-56. Nat. cert. counselor. Tchr., St. Andrew's Parish High Sch., Charleston, 1947-50; dir. Christian edn. Ch. of St. Edward the Martyr Episcopal, N.Y.C., 1952-54, 56-57; tchr., guidance counselor Crayton Jr. High Sch., Richland County (S.C.) Public Schs., 1957-67; instr. Coll. Edn., U. S.C., Columbia, 1968-71, asst. prof., 1971-77, asso. prof. ednl. founds., 1977-84, prof. emerita, 1984. Mem. vestry Trinity Episcopal Cathedral, Columbia, 1976-79. Mem. AAUP, AAUW, Am. Ednl. Studies Assn., S.C. Hist. Soc., South Caroliniana Soc., LWV, Common Cause, Phi Delta Kappa, Delta Kappa Gamma (pres. chpt. 1980-82). Club: Analytical Psychology of N.Y. Editor: Dear Sister Letters Written on Hilton Head Island 1867, 1977. Home: 1403 Haynsworth Rd Columbia SC 29205

MARTIN, JUDITH CAROL MORAN, lawyer; b. Ann Arbor, Mich., Feb. 10, 1943; d. D. Lawrence and Donna E. (Webb) Moran; children: Laura C., Paul M., A. Lindsay; m. Daniel B. Ventres Jr., Dec. 27, 1984. BA, U. Mich., 1963; postgrad., Universite de Jean Moulin, Institut du Droit, Lyon, France, 1982; JD, U. Minn., 1982; cert., Am. Coll., 1986. Bar: Minn. 1982; CLU, chartered fin. analyst. Tax supr., dir. fin. planning, asst. nat. dir. Coopers & Lybrand, Mpls., 1981-84; dir. fin. planning Investors Diversified Services subs. Am. Express, Mpls. and N.Y.C., 1984-85; sr. tax mgr., dir. fin. planning KPMG Peat Marwick Main & Co., Mpls., 1985—. Author contg. edn. materials on taxation and income and estate planning. Mem. Mpls. C. of C. campaign, Downtown Council Coms., Mpls., 1982-84, Metro Tax Planning Group, 1984-86, Mpl. Estate Planning Council, 1985—; class chmn. fundraising campaign U. Minn. Law Sch., Mpls., 1985; usher Christ Presbyn. Ch., Edina, Minn., 1983—; mem. adv. council on planned giving ARC. Mem. ABA (task force on legal fin. planning), Minn. Bar Assn., Hennepin County Bar Assn., Minn. Soc. CPA's (instr. continuing legal edn. 1983-84, continuing profl. edn. 1986, individual trust and estate provisions 1986 tax reform act 1983-86), Am. Assn. Independent Investors (speaker), Am. Soc. CLU's, Minn. Soc. CLU's (spl. interest groups), Minn. Women Lawyers, Lex Alumnae, U. Mich. Alumni Assn., U. Minn. Alumni Assn. (council govs. 1988—), Minn. World Trade Assn., Internat. Assn. Fin. Planners, Twin Cities Assn. Fin. Planners, U. Minn. Alumni Club (council govs.), Kappa Kappa Gamma. Clubs: Interlachen, Athletic, Lafayette (Mpls.). Home: 1355 Vine Place Orono MN 55364 Office: KPMG Peat Marwick Main & Co IDS Tower Suite 1700 Minneapolis MN 55402

MARTIN, JULIE ROSE, information systems consultant; b. Watervliet, Mich., Oct. 2, 1962; d. Robert Allen Martin and Hildegard Theresa (Schiele) Molter. BS in Pub. Adminstrn., Ferris State U., 1984. Mgr. Paw Paw River Campground, Watervliet, 1980-82; intern Senator Phil Arthurhultz, Lansing, Mich., 1983; receptionist Coloma (Mich.) Computer Co., 1984; field cons. mgmt. info. systems All-Phase Electric, Benton Harbor, Mich., 1985-87; customer service supr. All-Phase Electric, Benton Harbor, 1987—. Mem. Nat. Assn. Female Execs. Republican. Roman Catholic. Home: 2700 Lakeshore Dr Saint Joseph MI 49085 Office: All-Phase Electric 875 Riverview Dr Benton Harbor MI 49022

MARTIN, JUNE JOHNSON CALDWELL, journalist; b. Toledo, Oct. 6; d. John Franklin and Eunice Imogene (Fish) Johnson; A.A., Phoenix Jr. Coll., 1939-41; B.A., U. Ariz., 1941-43, 53-59; student Ariz. State U., 1939, 40; m. Erskine Caldwell, Dec. 21, 1942 (div. Dec. 1955); 1 son, Jay Erskine; m. 2d, Keith Martin, May 5, 1966. Free-lance writer, 1944—; columnist Ariz. Daily Star, 1956-59; editor Ariz. Alumnus mag., Tucson, 1959-70; book editor, gen. feature writer Ariz. Daily Star, Tucson, 1970—; panelist, co-producer TV news show Tucson Press Club, 1954-55, pres., 1958; mem. editorial bd. Clarion, women's issues newspaper. Contbg. author: Rocky Mountain Cities, 1949; contbr. articles to World Book Ency., and various mags. Mem. Tucson CD Com., 1961; vol. campaigns of Samuel Goddard, U.S. Rep. Morris Udall, U.S. ambassador and Ariz. gov. Raul Castro. Recipient award Nat. Headliners Club, 1959, Ariz. Press Club award, 1957-59, Am. Alumni Council, 1966, 70. Mem. Jr. League of Tucson, Tucson Urban League, Pi Beta Phi. Democrat. Methodist. Club: Tucson Press. Home: PO Box 2631 Tucson AZ 85702 Office: PO Box 26807 Tucson AZ 85726

MARTIN, KAREN KRAUSCHE, social services administrator, clinical social worker; b. N.Y.C., Sept. 2, 1947; d. John Francis and Gladys Rose (Cure) K.; m. John Charles Martin, Oct. 16, 1977; children: Stacey Elizabeth, Sean Patrick. BA, Sacred Heart U., 1984; MSW, Fordham U., 1985; postgrad., Smith Coll. Cert. social worker, N.Y. Social worker United Cerebral Palsy, Bridgeport, Conn., 1983, Norwalk Sch. System, Norwalk, Conn., 1983-84, Cath. Family Services, Bridgeport, 1984—; pvt. practice social work Ctr. Family Guidance, Stratford, Conn., 1986—. Bd. dirs. Trumbull (Conn.) Counseling Ctr., 1984—. Mem. Nat. Assn. Social Workers. Roman Catholic. Home: 50 Friar Ln Trumbull CT 06611 Office: Ctr Family Guidance 33 King St Stratford CT 06497

MARTIN, KATHLEEN ANNE, information management consultant; b. Rochester, N.Y., Aug. 19, 1942; d. Edwin Wilkins and Hilda Ellen (Hartell) Martin; B.A., Marygrove Coll., Detroit, 1964; M.A. in L.S. (Josenhans scholar 1965), U. Mich., 1965; advanced online tng. cert. Nat. Library Medicine, 1979; m. Oliver Kalman Peterdy, Oct. 15, 1971 (div. 1981); children—Elizabeth, Matthew. Librarian, Detroit Public Library, 1964-66; bibliographer, then asst. tech. services librarian Edward G. Miner Med. Library, U. Rochester, 1969-72; librarian lab. indsl. medicine Eastman Kodak Co., Rochester, 1966-69, librarian health, safety and human factors lab., 1972-78, tech. info. analyst, 1978-84, health and environment lab., 1978-86; pres. Info Edge, Inc., 1987—. Mem. AAUW (treas. Rochester br. 1979-80), Spl. Libraries Assn., Med. Library Assn., Nat. Assn. Female Execs. Home and Office: 4 Belmont Rd Rochester NY 14612

MARTIN, LAURA BELLE, real estate and farm land manager, retired teacher; b. Jackson County, Minn., Nov. 3, 1915; d. Eugene Wellington and Mary Christina (Hanson) M. BS, Mankato State U., 1968. Tchr. rural schs., Renville County, Minn., 1937-41, 45-50, Wabasso (Minn.) Pub. Sch., 1963-81; pres. Renville Farms and Feed Lots, 1982—. Pres., Wabasso Minn. Edn. Assn., 1974-75, publicity chmn., 1968-74; sec. Hist. Renville Preservation Com., 1978-86, Town and Country Boosters, Renville, 1982-83, publicity chmn., 1988—; pub. chmn. Renville Mus., 1978—. Mem. Genealogy Soc. Renville County, Am. Legion Aux. Democrat. Lutheran. Home and Office: Box 567 Renville MN 56284

MARTIN, LAURA PAEZ REED, clinical psychologist; b. Los Angeles, May 18, 1935; d. Howard Richard and Laura (Paez) Reed; B.A., UCLA, 1958; M.A. (NIMH fellow), U. So. Calif., 1974, Ph.D., 1974; m. Warren Leicester Martin, Aug. 24, 1957; children: Laura, Susan, Warren. Pres. Laura Martin, Ph.D., Inc., 1977—; psychotherapist Psychiat. Assocs. Med. Group, Covina, Calif., 1976—; chief psychologist (adolescence) Sierra Royale Hosp., Azusa, Calif., 1976—; hosp. cons. nursing edn.; lectr. women's issues. Mem. Am. Psychol. Assn., Assn. Mex.-Am. Psychologists, Assn. Women in Sci. Republican. Roman Catholic. Club: U. So. Calif. Golden Circle. Home: 4172 Forest Hill Dr La Cañada CA 91011 Office: Psychiat Assocs Med Group 750 Terrado Plaza Suite 245 Covina CA 91723

MARTIN, LUCY Z(IMMERMAN), public relations executive; b. Alton, Ill., July 8, 1941. BA, Northwestern U., 1963. Adminstrv. asst., copywriter Batz-Hodgson-Neuwoehner, Inc., St. Louis, 1963-64; news reporter, Midwest fashion editor Fairchild Publs., St. Louis, 1964-66; account exec. Milici Advt. Agy., Honolulu, 1967; publs. dir. Barnes Med. Ctr., St. Louis, 1968-69; communications cons. Fleishman-Hillard, St. Louis, 1970-74, Portland, Oreg., 1974-86; pres.and chief exec. officer Lucy Z. Martin & Assocs., Inc., Portland, 1987—. Chmn. women's adv. com. Reed Coll., Portland, 1977-79; mem. Oreg. Commn. for Women, 1984-87; bd. dirs. Ronald McDonald House Oreg., 1986, Oreg. Sch. Arts & Crafts, 1988-90. Recipient MacEachern Citation Acad. Hosp. Pub. Relations, 1978, Rosey awards Portland Advt. Fedn., 1979, Achievement award Soc. Tech. Communications, 1982, Disting. Tech. Communication award, 1982, Exceptional Achievement award Council for Advancement and Support Edn., 1983, Monsoon award Internat. Graphics, Inc., 1984; named Woman of Achievement Daily Jour. Commerce, 1980. Mem. Pub. Relations Soc. Am. (pres. Columbia River chpt. 1984, chmn. bd. 1980-84, Oreg. del. 1984-86, judicial panel N. Pacific dist 1985-86, exec. bd. health care sect. 1986-87, mem. Counselors Acad., Spotlight awards 1985, 86, 87), Portland Pub. Relations Roundtable (chmn. 1985, bd. dirs. 1983-85), Assn. Western Hosps. (editorial adv. bd. 1984-85), Best of West awards 1978, 80, 83, 87), Oreg. Hosp. Pub. Relations Orgn. (pres. 1981, chmn. bd. 1982), Acad. Health Service Mktg., Am. Hosp. Assn., Am. Mktg. Assn., Am. Soc. Hosp. Mktg. & Pub. Relations, Healthcare Communicators Oreg., Internat. Assn. Bus. Communicators (18 awards 1981-87), Oreg. Assn. Hosps. Oreg. Press Women, Nat. and Oreg. Soc. Healthcare Planning & Mktg., Women in Communications (Matrix award 1977). Office: 4380 SW Macadam Ave #285 Portland OR 97201

MARTIN, LYNN MORLEY, congresswoman; b. Evanston, Ill., Dec. 26, 1939; d. Lawrence William and Helen Catherine (Hall) Morley; children from a previous marriage: Julia Catherine, Caroline; m. Harry D. Leinenweber, Jan. 1987. B.A., U. Ill., 1960. Former tchr. pub. schs.; mem. Ill. Ho. of Reps., 1977-79, Ill. Senate, 1979-81; mem. 97th-100th Congresses from 16th Ill. Dist., 1981—. Named to Outstanding Young Women Am. U.S. Jaycees. Mem. AAUW, C. of C. of Rockford, Jr. League. Republican. Office: US House of Reps 1208 Longworth Office Bldg Washington DC 20515

MARTIN, MARSHA ANN, social work educator; b. Iowa City, May 22, 1952; d. Fred Jr. and Helen (Paige) M. BA in Psychology, U. Iowa, 1974, MSW, 1975; DSW, Columbia U., 1982. Program specialist Willkie House Inc., Des Moines, 1976-77; cons. research Clark, Phipps, Clark and Harris Inc., N.Y.C., 1979-81; dir. Midtown Outreach Program, N.Y.C., 1981-86; asst. prof. Sch. Social Work Hunter Coll., N.Y.C., 1986—; cons. Port Authority N.Y. and N.J., 1982—, NIMH, 1985—. Contbr. articles to profl. jours. Cons. U.S. Conf. Mayors, Five City Project 1986; co-chair, bd. dirs. Women Need Inc., 1984—, vice-chair, bd. dirs. N.Y. Coalition Homeless, 1982—, advisor Office Mayor Homeless Services, N.Y.C. 1987—; com. mem. N.Y. State Hands Across Am. 1987—; com. chair, bd. dir. N.Y.C. Coalition Mental Health, 1986—. Nat. Assn. Social Workers, Internat. Conf. Social Welfare, Council Social Work Edn. Democrat. Mem. United Ch. Christ. Office: Hunter Coll Sch Social Work 129 E 79th St New York NY 10021

MARTIN, MARTHA BELL, educator, principal; b. York, Ala., Dec. 27, 1941; d. John Hanson and Stella (Boyd) Bell; m. Paul Wayne Martin, Aug. 12, 1962, Cheryl, Paul, Pamela. Student, Queens Coll., 1960-62; BS, U. Montevallo, 1964. Tchr. Morgan County Sch. Systems, Hartselle, Ala., 1964-65, Wake County Bd. Edu., Raleigh, N.C., 1965-67; tchr., prin. Eastmont Kindergarten, Montgomery, Ala., 1982-87. Baptist. Home: 431 Patlynn Dr Fairhope AL 36532

MARTIN, MARY EVELYN, advertising executive; b. Lexington, Ky., Dec. 23, 1958; d. George Clarke and Georgann Elizabeth (Bovis) M. BA magna cum laude, Lindenwood Coll., 1980; postgrad, U. Ky., 1987—. Asst. to pres. The Hamlets, Ltd/Park Place Country Homes, Louisville, 1984-85; advt. designer, copywriter Park Place Country Homes, 1985-86, 1985-86; creative dir. of advt., mktg., v.p., treas. Park Place Country Homes/Park Place Properties, 1985-86, 1986—; founder, pres. Good Help Consulting Service, Louisville, Lexington, Ky. Editor: (poetry mag.) The Griffin, 1979-80; Author: (one-act plays) XYZ, 1980, The Pipeline, 1978 (Spahmer Creative Writing award 1979). Mem. People for the Am. Way, Greenpeace. Recipient Haggin fellow, U. Ky., 1987. Mem. Am. Film Inst., Nat. Assn. Female Execs., Nat. Assn. Home Builders (affiliate). Democrat. Home: PO Box 23282 Anchorage KY 40223 Office: Park Place Country Homes PO Box 23226 Anchorage KY 40223

MARTIN, MARY JILL LOCKWOOD, accounting educator; b. Wichita, Kans., Jan. 10, 1948; d. Raymond Max and Yolanda (Gigliotti) Lockwood; m. Ronald Douglas Martin, June 29, 1969; 1 child, Jared Lockwood. BA, U. Fla., Gainesville, 1969; JD, Emory U., Atlanta, 1974, LLM in Taxation, 1979. Bar: Ga. 1976; CPA. Sole practice, Atlanta, 1979-81; asst. prof. acctg. Ga. State U., Atlanta, 1981-84; assoc. prof., coordinator tax program Ga. So. Coll., Statesboro, 1984—; cons. Tax Research Inc., Atlanta, 1983—; bd. dirs. Chatham Acad.; mem. Hist. Savannah Found. Contbr. articles to profl. jours. Mem. ABA, Ga. Bar Assn., Ga. Soc. CPAs, Am. Soc. of Women CPAs, Am. Bus. Law Assn. Democrat. Episcopalian. Home: 632 Washington Ave Savannah GA 31405

MARTIN, MARY LOU, manufacturing company specialist; b. New Hampton, Iowa, June 4, 1953; d. Henry Herman and Elsie Alice (Thieman) Harnisch; m. Merl James Martin, May 10, 1980. Student, Gates Bus. Sch., 1973, U. No. Iowa, 1974-85; BS in Mgmt., Mktg., Upper Iowa U., 1987; postgrad. MBA program, U. Iowa, 1987—. Sec. Law Offices John M. Warren, Waterloo, Iowa, 1973; sec. registrar's office, asst. recorder Upper Iowa U., Fayette, Iowa, 1973-74; mfg. systems planning specialist John Deere Tractor Works, Waterloo, 1974-80, mem MRP task force, 1980-81, supr. prodn. control, 1981-84, forecast analyst, master scheduler, 1984—. mem. appropriations com. United Way, Waterloo, 1986. Mem. Am. Prodn. and Inventory Control Soc., Nat. Assn. for Female Execs. Lutheran. Home: 4104 Ansborough Waterloo IA 50701

MARTIN, MONA, database specialist; b. N.Y.C., Mar. 20, 1950; d. Sidney Rivman and Gladyce (Goodrich) Chesloff; m. Robert Dawson Martin, June 8, 1975 (div. Jan. 1986). BA, CUNY, 1973, postgrad., 1974-76; MS, Fairleigh Dickenson U., 1983. Dept. mgr. Abraham and Straus, Hempstead, N.Y., 1978-79; asst. buyer Lord & Taylor, N.Y.C., 1979-81; dept. mgr. Macy's, Eatontown, N.J., 1981-82; info. systems designer AT&T-Bell Labs, Short Hills, N.J., 1983-84; tech. support specialist Relational Tech. Inc., Clifton, N.J., 1984-87; sr. applications cons. Oracle Corp., Iselin, N.J., 1987—. Mem. Am. Assn. Computing Machines, AM/FM Internat., Usenix, NOW. Democrat. Club: Garden State Ski (Maywood, N.J.). Office: Oracle Corp 120 Wood Ave S Iselin NJ 08830

MARTIN, MONA HELEN, university administrator; b. Corning, N.Y., June 24, 1951; d. Clayton Arlinton II and Ramona Louise (Herbert) Teator; student Alfred U., 1981—; m. Thomas J. Martin, Dec. 21, 1968; children—James H., Tina M. Univ. relations records clk. Alfred U., 1974-75, supr. records, 1975-76, records clk., 1976-78, assoc. for devel. research, 1978, supr. research and records, 1979-84, dir. devel. services, 1984—. Vol., CD Disaster Preparedness, Steuben County, United Way, Am. Heart Fund; instr. religious edn. program St. Ignatius Loyola Ch.; bd. dirs. Alfred/Allegany Ednl. Fed. Credit Union. Mem. Alpha Kappa Omicron. Republican. Roman Catholic. Home: 263 Grand St Hornell NY 14843 Office: PO Box 1165 Alfred NY 14802

MARTIN, NANCY JEAN VAN DERVOORT, financial consultant; b. Mpls., Mar. 18, 1928; d. Harvey H. and Edith L. (Coleman) Van Dervoort; children: Bruce, Linda, Steven, Judith. BA, U. Minn., 1949, postgrad. With market researcher Pillsbury Mills, Mpls., 1965-68; mgr. data services Gen. Mills, Mpls., 1968-70; mgr. operational sales GTE Sylvania, Mpls., 1970-73; registered rep. IDS, Mpls., 1973-75; spl. agt. John Hancock Ins., Mpls.; owner, pres. Advisors Assocs., Mpls., 1975-79, Nancy Martin Assocs., Mpls., 1979—; del. White House Conf. on Ins., Washington, 1978; conferee Inst. Devel. Profl. Women at Spring Hill, Mpls. Mem. Internat. Assn. Fin. Planning (past bd. dirs. Twin Cities chpt.), Minn. Entrepreneurs Club, Nat. Assn. Security Dealers. Office: 5775 Wayzata Blvd Suite 815 Minneapolis MN 55416

MARTIN, PAMELA CHRISTINE, data processing executive; b. Englewood, N.J., May 30, 1953; d. Douglas Harry and Christine (Jacob) M.; m. Walter Joseph Paskey, Oct. 30, 1976. BS, Penn. State U., 1975; MBA, Old Dominion U., 1979. Instr., curriculum developer Elwyn (Pa.) Inst., 1975-76; mgr. bus. Patriot Press, Va. Beach, 1977-78; analyst operations research CACI Inc. Fed., Mechanicsburg, Pa., 1979-80, mgr. group, 1980-81, mgr. dept., 1981-83, mgr. dept. group, 1983-86, dir. project mgmt., 1986—; advisor CDS-Tech., Allentown, Pa. 1985—; speaker on systems implementation SCAN-TECH '88. Contbr. articles to profl. jours. Sec., bd. dirs. White Rock Acres Civic Assn., Boiling Springs, Pa. 1986. Mem. Nat. Assn. Female Exec., AAUW (chair scholarship com., 1984-85). Republican. Home: 1358 Horick Dr Boiling Springs PA 17007 Office: CACI Inc-Fed 2401 B N Walnut St Bloomington IN 47401

MARTIN, ROSE, government law information specialist; b. Pozsony, Hungary, Aug. 25, 1928; came to U.S., 1949, naturalized, 1954; d. Ferenc and Zsuzsanna (Nehai Szabo) Kocsis; m. Donald L. Martin, Aug. 23, 1961; 1 child, Virginia Kim. Student Seton Hall U., 1960-61; B.B.A., Kensington U., Glendale, Calif., 1968-69; cert. Cath. U. Am. 1981, George Washington U., 1982. Documents librarian Seton Hall U., South Orange, N.J., 1958-61; mem. office staff Dept. Def., Washington, 1962-63, Dept. Agr., Washington, 1963-67; info. specialist-law Office Adminstrv. Law Judges, Dept. Labor, Washington, 1976—. Active Republican Club, Great Falls, Va., 1986—. Recipient Meritorious award Dept. Agr., 1966, Outstanding award Dept. Labor, 1977. Mem. Am. Assn. Law Libraries, Gt. Falls Woman's Club. Roman Catholic. Club: River Bend Golf and Country (Great Falls). Avocations: travel; tennis; reading; swimming; cooking. Home: PO Box 513 The Plains VA 22171

MARTIN, SALLY NAN, nursing administrator; b. Potsdam, N.Y., Dec. 8, 1947; d. Arthur Ellsworth and Blanche Maryland (Henderson) M. Diploma in nursing, St. Luke's Hosp., N.Y.C., 1968; BS in Sociology, Marymount Manhattan Coll., 1973; EdM in Adult Edn., Columbia U., N.Y.C., 1976; M in Pub. Adminstrn., NYU, 1988. Asst. dir. critical care St. Luke's Roosevelt Hosp. Ctr., N.Y.C., 1980-85; asst. dir. operating room Maimonides Med. Ctr., Bklyn., 1985-86; assoc. dir. nursing The Meth. Hosp., Bklyn., 1986—; chmn. critical care policy and procedure com. nursing dept. St. Luke's/ Roosevelt Hosp.; co-chmn. critical care adminstrv. com. nursing and med. dept.; chmn. ambience com.,also lectr., first line mgr., chmn. evaluation revision com., nursing care plan com.; preceptor for grad. students in nursing adminstrn., NYU; chmn. research on utilization of nursing knowledge workshop Woman's Hosp., N.Y.C. Home: 910 President St Brooklyn NY 11215 Office: The Meth Hosp 506 7th Ave Brooklyn NY 11215

MARTIN, SALLY SYKES, systems analyst, editor, audio-visual producer; b. St. Louis, Feb. 4, 1953; d. William Graham III and Winifred Estelle (Hamilton) M.; m. David Carlton Williams, May 15, 1977. B.A. in English Lit., Washington U., St. Louis, 1975; postgrad. U. Mo.-St. Louis, 1982-85, Washington U., St. Louis, 1987—. Data processing editor Emerson Electric Co., St. Louis, 1976-77; asst. editor Facts and Comparisons, St. Louis, 1977-78; procedures writer/analyst McDonnell Douglas, St. Louis, 1978-82; tech. writer Ralston Purina, St. Louis, 1982-84; supr. communications-product assurance McDonnell Douglas Astronautics Co., St. Louis, 1984-86; long range planning systems and procedures, 1987— ; editor Catalyst newsletter Women in Bus., St. Louis, 1983. Mem. Lafayette Sq. Restoration Com., St. Louis, 1983—, editor Marquis newsletter, 1983-84; treas., mem. vestry, mem. worship com. St. Stephen's Episcopal Ch., St. Louis, 1984-86. Recipient 2d Place award Assn. for Multi-Image Festival, 1983, Elizabeth Cook award Lafayette Sq. Restoration Com., 1984. Mem. IEEE (assoc.), Soc. Tech. Communications (Achievement award for brochure 1984, achievement award for newsletter 1986), KETC, Zoo Friends. Avocation: piano (classical music). Home: 1526 Mississippi Saint Louis MO 63104 Office: McDonnell Douglas Astronautics Co PO Box 516 Saint Louis MO 63166

MARTIN, SHARON JAFFE, waterproofing company executive; b. Elyria, Ohio, June 20, 1944; d. Edward Gilbert and Sylvia Sophia (Werner) Jaffe; m. David Richard Martin, May 8, 1965; 1 child, Jeffrey Ross. Student Miami U., Oxford, Ohio, 1962-64, Lorain Community Coll., 1966, 73-74. Cashier Elyria Meml. Hosp., 1964-67; asst. tchr. Westshore Montessori Sch., North Ridgeville, Ohio, 1973-75, Montessori Cooperative of Vienna, Va., 1975-76; v.p., sec., treas. Reston Pressure Seal, Inc., Va., 1977—; pres. Dave Martin & Son, Inc., 1987—; vol. fin. advisor Fairfax County Fin. Edu. Ctr., 1986—. Mem. Reston Community Players, Inc., treas., 1981-84. Nominated Reston Woman of Yr., 1983. Mem. No. Va. Builders Assn. Jewish. Avocations: dancing; acting, antiques, reading. Home: 11281 Spyglass Cove Ln Reston VA 22091 Office: Reston Pressure Seal Inc PO Box 2292 Reston VA 22090

MARTIN, SHERRY ANN, advertising executive; b. Winchester, Ind., Jan. 17, 1951; came to Can., 1982; d. Jack David and Martha Ann (Burris) M. BA, Purdue U., 1972; MA, Ohio State U., 1976. Product mgr. Montgomery Ward Ins. Co., Chgo., 1976-79; account exec. Stone & Adler Direct Mktg., Chgo., 1979-82; account supr. Stone & Adler Ltd., Toronto, 1982-85; gen. mgr. Foote, Cone & Belding Direct, Toronto, 1985-86; v.p., mng. dir. J. Walter Thompson Direct Response, Toronto, 1986—. Mem. Can. Direct Mktg. Assn., Direct Mktg. Assn. Toronto, Assn. Direct Mktg. Agys. Office: J Walter Thompson Agy, 160 Bloor St E, Toronto, ON Canada M4W 3P7

MARTIN, SHIRLEY, Canadian legislator; b. Nov. 20, 1932; m. Jack Martin; children: John, Christopher. Previously bus. service mgr. for Bell Can, mem. Can. House of Commons, 1984—, prin. del. U.N. 40th Gen. Assembly, vice chair Progressive Conservative Nat. Caucus. Mem. United Ch. Canada. Address: 44 King St East, Unit 9, Stoney Creek, ON Canada L8G 1K1 *

MARTIN, SHIRLEY MARIE, insurance company executive; b. Tekamah, Nebr., Apr. 15, 1944; d. J. Clinton Martin and N. Marie (McKain) Grant; m. Michael P. Burnett, Apr. 19, 1963 (div. Oct. 1980); children: Todd Burnett, Tara Burnett. Student, Everett (Wash.) Jr. Coll., 1962-64; grad., Bell and Howell Sch. Acctg., Chgo., 1974. Fin. coordinator, collection mgr. The Continental Ins. Co., Seattle, 1963-70; audit reviewer The Home Ins. Co., Seattle, 1970-75, premium field auditor, 1975-80; owner Martin & Assocs., Bellingham, Wash., 1980—; author, pub. S.M. Martin Co., Bellingham, 1986—. Mem. Nat. Assn. Premium Auditors, Nat. Assn. Life Underwriters, Nat. Assn. Female Execs., Whatcom C. of C. Democrat. Roman Catholic. Home and Office: PO Box 5523 Bellingham WA 98227

MARTIN, STACEY LYNN, tax specialist; b. Dallas, Dec. 5, 1951; d. Orval Calvin and Della (Morgan) M.; m. Bryan Keith Ellis, Jan. 31, 1987. BA, Austin Coll., 1973; MBA, So. Meth. U., 1974. CPA, Tex. Jr. acct. MacIver & Bell, CPAs, Dallas, 1974-76; staff acct. Steak and Ale Restaurants, Dallas, 1976; internal auditor Columbia Gen. Corp., Dallas, 1976-80; asst. controller M/A/R/C Inc., Dallas, 1981-86, tax specialist, 1986—. Mem. Greenland Hills Neighborhood Assn., Dallas, 1983—. Mem. Am. Inst. CPA's, Tex. Soc. CPA's, Dallas Heritage Soc., Dallas Arboretum Soc., DAR. Presbyterian. Office: M/A/R/C Inc 7850 N Beltline Rd Irving TX 75063

MARTIN, SUSAN KATHERINE, librarian; b. Cambridge, Eng., Nov. 14, 1942; came to U.S., 1950, naturalized, 1961; d. Egon and Jolan (Schonfeld) Orowan; m. David S. Martin, June 30, 1962. B.A. with honors, Tufts U., 1963; M.S., Simmons Coll., 1965; Ph.D., U. Calif.-Berkeley, 1983. Intern Harvard U. Library, Cambridge, Mass., 1963-65, systems librarian, 1965-73; head systems office Gen. Library, U. Calif., Berkeley, 1973-79; dir. Milton S. Eisenhower Library, Johns Hopkins U., Balt., 1979-88, exec. dir. Nat. Commn. on Libraries and Info. Sci., 1988—; instr. U. Md., College Park, 1981; mem. library adv. com. Princeton (N.J.) U., 1987—; mem. vis. com. Harvard U. Library, 1987—. Author: Library Networks: Libraries in Partnership, 1986-87; editor: Jour. Library Automation, 1973-77; mem. editorial bd. Jour. Library Adminstrn., 1986—; contbr. articles to profl. jours. Trustee Phila. Area Library Network, 1980-81; bd. dirs. Universal Serials and Book Exchange, 1981-82, v.p., 1983, pres., 1984. Recipient Simmons Coll. Disting. Alumni award, 1977; Council on Library Resources fellow, 1973. Mem. ALA, Research Libraries Group (gov., exec. com. 1985-87), Library and Info. Tech. Assn. (pres. 1978-79), Assn. Research Libraries, Library of Congress Optical Disk Pilot Project Adv. Com., 1985—, Phi Beta Kappa. Home: 3518 Garrett Ct Ellicott City MD 21043 Office: Johns Hopkins Univ Libraries Milton S Eisenhower Library Baltimore MD 21218

MARTIN, SYLVIA COOKE, human resources professional; b. Balt., May 2, 1938; d. Emanuel Levi and Clara Marie (Evans) Cook; m. Donald W.K. Martin, Sept. 8, 1957; div., Nov. 1970; children: Donald Eugene Kemp Martin, Marcia Lauren Martin. BA, U. Md., 1972; Cert. Execs. at Mid Career, U. Va., 1975; M of Policy Sci., U. Md., Baltimore County, 1978; postgrad., U. Md.; Cert. Human Resource Devel., Bowie (Md.) State Coll., 1987. File clk. Social Security Adminstrs., Balt., 1963-66; intern health ins. Social Security Adminstrn., Balt., 1966-68, mgmt. intern, 1968-70; sr. career devel. specialist Social Security Adminstrn., Health Care Financing Adminstrn., Balt., 1970-78; faculty mem. Antioch Coll., Columbia, Md., 1975-79, cons., 1969—; chief staff tng. and devel. Library of Congress, Washington, 1978—; instr. human resources devel. Bowie State Coll., 1975—. Active United Negro Coll. Fund Job Fair, Washington, 1987, Md. Hist. Soc. Mem. NAACP, Oral History in Mid-Atlantic Region, Md. Genealogical Soc., Nat. Assn. Negro Bus. and Profl. Women's Clubs, Afro-Am. Hist. and Geneal. Soc. (historian 1984-86, parliamentarian 1986-88, pres. 1988-90), Nat. Council Negro Women, The Pierians (parliamentarian 1985-87), Daniel Murray Afro-Am. Culture Assn. (pres. 1988). Democrat. Baptist. Clubs: The Pierians (Columbia) (Parliamentarian 1985-87). Office: Library of Congress 100 Independence Ave Washington DC 20540

MARTIN, TINA LYNNE, retaurant owner; b. Wichita, Kans., Nov. 17, 1961; d. James Emmett and Betty Louise (Somers) M. Grad. high sch., Candler, N.C. Asst. chef Biltmore Village Inn, Asheville, N.C., 1980-81; snack bar cook Pisgah Inn, Waynesville, N.C., 1981; sous chef Point Restaurant, Sheffield, Ala., 1984-85; cook, asst. to owner Court 9 Restaurant, Florence, Ala., 1985-86; cook Pizza Hut, Florence, 1986; owner Four Seasons Bistro, Florence, 1986-87; mgr. Catherine's Chocolates, Florence, 1987; with food bar Bonanza Restaurant, Florence, 1988—. Seventh Day Adventist. Home: 2215 N Wood Ave Florence AL 35630

MARTIN BLAIR, MARY KATHLEEN, psychotherapist; b. Salinas, Calif., Nov. 6, 1947; d. Cal Leonard and Jean (Swanson) Martin; m. Ronald Henry Muszalski, Apr. 1, 1971, (div.); 1 child, Aaron Martin; m. John A. Blair, Aug. 29, 1981. BA in English Lit., San Francisco State U., 1970; MS in Clin. Psychology, John F. Kennedy U., 1980. Lic. psychotherapist; cert. hypnotherapist, Calif. Dir. La Leche League Internat., Chicago, 1971-75; instr. Parent Effectiveness Tng., San Francisco, 1976—; counselor Birthways, Oakland, Calif., 1979, Community Counseling Ctr., Concord, Calif., 1979-80; dir. Comprehensive Enrichment Program, San Leandro (Calif.) Girls Club, 1980-81; sponsor Parents Anonymous Family Stress Ctr., Concord, 1981; pres. MK Assocs., Pleasant Hill, Calif., 1984—; pvt. practice psychotherapy Berkeley and Pleasant Hill, Calif., 1980—; lectr. various cities throughout Calif. Mem. Am. Psychol. Assn., Calif. Assn. Marriage Family Therapists, Am. Orthopsychiat. Assn., Am. Assn. Marriage Family Therapy, Berkeley Psychotherapy Inst., Assn. Psychol. Type, Contra Costa Child Abuse Prevention Council, Nat. Family Life Network, Nat. Assn. Children Alcoholics, Am. Assn. Profl. Hypnotherapists. Office: 2244 Morello Ave Pleasant Hill CA 94523

MARTINEAU, DENISE COREY, physical chemist; b. Oakland, Calif., Mar. 27, 1954; d. Carl Pierre Martineau and Lucille (Cefalu) Swanson. AS in Chemistry, DeAnza Coll., 1985; BA in Chemistry, U. Calif., Santa Cruz, 1987. Free-lance tech. writer San Jose, Calif., 1978-84; tech. coordinator Energy System Planning, Palo Alto, Calif., 1976-78; tech. intern NASA, Moffett Field, Calif., 1984-85; cons. research asst. Stanford (Calif.) U., 1986-87; Ill. Consortium for Ednl. Opportunity Program fellow U. Ill., Urbana, 1986—; student rep. U. Calif. Faculty Commn., Santa Cruz, 1985-86. Editor: Voices: Women in Science, 1987. Chair fundraising student leadership panel YWCA, Urbana, 1987; bd. dirs. Urbana Girl's Club. Recipient scholarship Am. Bus. Women's Assn., 1985-88, merit grad. hon. mention NSF, 1987; Ford Found. alt. Nat. Research Council, 1987-88. Mem. Soc. of Women Engrs. (Excellence award 1985, 86, 87, 88), AAAS, Grad. Women in Sci., Assn. for Women in Sci., Am. Chem. Soc., Am. Phys. Soc. Democrat. Mem. Unity Ch. Office: Univ of Ill Dept Chemistry 505 S Mathews Urbana IL 61801

MARTINEZ, ALICE CONDE, association executive; b. Havana, Cuba, Jan. 4, 1946; came to U.S. 1961; d. Augusto F. and Catalina deSena (Ramos) Conde; m. Jose L. Martinez, Sept. 3, 1966. B.A., George Washington U., 1968, postgrad., 1968-70. Registrar univ. div. George Washington U., Washington, 1968-69; programs coordinator Am. Psychiat. Assn., Washington, 1969-83; exec. dir. Am. Coll. Psychiatrists, Greenbelt, Md., 1983—; cons. Group for Advancement of Psychiatry, 1981—, Am. Acad. Psychiatrists in Alcoholism and Addictions, 1985—, Am. Assn. Geriatric Psychiatry, 1987—. Vol. Greenbelt Mus. Com. Recipient Fellowship Appreciation, Mead Johnson Pharm. Div. and Am. Psychiat. Assn., 1983. Mem. Meeting Planners Internat., Greater Washington Soc. Assn. Execs., Profl. Conv. Mgmt. Assn., Nat. Assn. Female Execs., Pan Am. Soc., Nat. Assn. Cuban-Am. Women in U.S.A. Republican. Roman Catholic. Home: 4 Olivewood Ct Greenbelt MD 20770 Office: Am Coll Psychiatrists PO Box 365 Greenbelt MD 20770

MARTINEZ, BETTY ELNORA, chemical company executive; b. Oklahoma City, Jan. 7, 1947; d. Jim and Jewell Frances Smith; B.S., Oklahoma City U., 1974, M.B.A., 1975; divorced. Pvt. booking agt. and bus. mgr. local rock and roll bands, Okla., Colo., 1960-67; with Kerr McGee Corp., Oklahoma City, 1965-81, acct., 1974-76, solvent sales rep., from 1975, assoc. sales rep. until 1981; petrochems. sales rep. No. Petrochem. Co., Ramsey, N.J., 1981-85; Southern area sales rep. AC Polyethylene Allied/Signal Corp., Morristown, N.J., 1985—. Del. Okla. Democratic Conv., 1972; vol. Grady Hosp., Atlanta, Ga. Rape Crisis Ctr. Mem. M.B.A. Club Oklahoma City U. (pres. 1975), ACLU, Soc. Plastic Engrs. (bd. dirs. 1987-88), Toastmasters (adminstrv. v.p., 1988). Home and Office: PO Box 70426 Marietta GA 30007

MARTINEZ, ESPERANZA G., television director; b. Savannah, Ga., Dec. 8, 1948; d. Victor P. Martinez and Valdena (Pinkney) Hilton. Student, NET TV Tng. Sch., 1970, RCA TV Sch., 1972, New Sch. for Social Research, 1981. Asst. dir. 20 West Theater, N.Y.C., 1981—; bd. dirs. Nzingha Soc. Inc., N.Y.C. Mem. Dirs. Guild Am. (mem. 3 major networks negotiating com.). Democrat. Roman Catholic. Home: 77 Englewood Ave Teaneck NJ 07666 Office: WABC-TV 7 Lincoln Sq New York NY 07666

MARTINEZ, HERMINIA S., banker, economist; b. Havana, Cuba; came to U.S., 1961, naturalized, 1972; d. Carlos and Amelia (Santana) Martinez Sanchez; B.A. in Econs. cum laude, Am. U., 1965; M.S. in Fgn. Service (Univ. fellow), M.S. in Econs., Georgetown U., 1967; postgrad. Nat. U. Mex. Instr. econs. George Mason Coll., U. Va., Fairfax, 1967-68; researcher World Bank, 1967-69, indsl. economist, industrialization div., 1969-71, loan officer, Central Am., 1971-79, loan officer, economist, Mex., 1973-74, Venezuela and Ecuador, 1973-77, sr. loan officer in charge of Panama and Dominican Republic, Washington, 1977-81, sr. loan officer for Middle East and North Africa, 1981-84, sr. loan officer for Western Africa region, 1985-87, sr. economist Africa Region, 1988—. Mid-Career fellow Princeton U., 1988. Mem. Am. Econ. Assn., Soc. Internat. Devel., Brookings Inst. Latin Am. Study Group. Roman Catholic. Contbg. author: The Economic Growth of Colombia: Problems and Prospects, 1973. Home and Office: 4734 Massachusetts Ave NW Washington DC 20016

MARTINEZ, JANET LORANE, sales representative; b. Raton, N.Mex., Nov. 21, 1957; d. Hilario Gilbert and Gladys Mildred (Fresquez) M. AA, U. N.Mex. Service rep. Assoc. Fin. Co., Albuquerque, 1979-80; operator Mountain Bell, Albuquerque, 1980-81; sales rep. US West Communications (formerly Mountain Bell), Albuquerque, 1981—. Democrat. Roman Catholic. Home: 1100 Alvarado Suite 103 Albuquerque NM 87108

MARTINEZ, MARIA ELENA, accountant; b. Laredo, Tex., Aug. 11, 1935; d. Blas and Elvira (Gonzalez) M. AA, Laredo Jr. Coll., 1955. Credit mgr. Hachar's, Inc., Laredo, 1955-58; teletype setter Laredo Morning Times, 1959-60; sec. to v.p. DeLlano's Mexican Products Co., Laredo, 1960-83; acct. Wilkinson Bros. Iron and Metal, Laredo, 1983-86; owner, acct. Martinez Tax and Bookkeeping Service, Laredo, 1986—. Mem. Laredo Women's Bowling Assn. (pres. 1978-79), Tex. Assn. Pub. Advisors (treas. 1987-88). Republican. Roman Catholic. Home and Office: 1606 Garfield St Laredo TX 78040

MARTINEZ, MARY JACQUELIN, dentist; b. Santo Domingo, Dominican Republic, July 17, 1957; came to U.S., 1961; d. Felix Ricardo and Maria (Nuñez) M. BS in Biology, Fordham U., 1978; DDS, NYU, 1982. Gen. practice dentisty Bklyn., 1982—. Sec. Coop. Bd. Sea Isle Owners, Inc., Bklyn., 1986—. Mem. ADA, Acad. Gen. Dentistry. 1st Dental Soc., Bay Ridge Dental Soc., Bay Ridge Dental Soc. Republican. Roman Catholic.

MARTINEZ, SUSANNE, lawyer; b. San Francisco, Mar. 3, 1945; d. Floyd W. and Mary Katherine (Grier) Sitton; B.A., U. Calif., Davis, 1967; J.D., U. Calif., San Francisco, 1970; 1 dau., Jennifer Sue. Admitted to Calif. bar, 1971, U.S. Supreme Ct. bar, 1976; legal asst. San Francisco Neighborhood Legal Assistance Found., 1968-70; staff atty. Youth Law Center, 1970-77; counsel Subcom. on Child and Human Devel., Com. Labor and Human Resources, U.S. Senate, Washington, 1977-80; legis. asst. Senator Alan Cranston, 1980—. Mem. ACLU, San Francisco Bar Assn., Order of the Coif. Democrat. Office: Senate Office Bldg 112 Hart Washington DC 20510

MARTINEZ, VILMA SOCORRO, lawyer; b. San Antonio, Oct. 17, 1943; d. Salvador and Marina (Pina) M.; m. Stuart R. Singer, Nov. 1968; children—Carlos, Ricardo. B.A., U. Tex., 1964; LL.B., Columbia U., 1967. Bar: N.Y. 1968, Calif. 1975. Staff atty. gen. civil rights litigation NAACP Legal Defense and Edn. Fund, 1967-70; EEO counsel N.Y. State Div. Human Rights, 1970-71; litigation assoc. Cahill, Gordon & Reindel, 1971-73; pres., gen. counsel Mexican-Am. Legal Defense and Ednl. Fund, Inc., 1973-82; ptnr. Munger, Tolles & Olson, Los Angeles, 1982—; dir. Anheuser-Busch Cos., Inc.; cons. U.S. Commn. on Civil Rights, 1969-74, U.S. Census Bur., 1975-81, U.S. Treasury Dept., 1976, Calif. Fed. Jud. Selection Com., 1977-80, Presidential Adv. Bd. on Ambassadorial Appointments, 1977-81, U.S. Hispanic-Mexican Govt. Internat. Commn., 1980-82. Regent U. Calif., 1976—, chmn. 1984—; dir. Southwestern Voter Registration and Edn. Project; trustee Edward W. Hazen Found. Recipient Lex award Mexican-Am. Bar Assn., 1983, Jefferson award Am. Idst. Pub. Service, 1976, John D. Rockefeller III Youth award Rockefeller Found., 1977, univ. medal of excellence, Columbia U., 1978, Valerie Kantor award Mex. Am. Legal Defense Edn. Fund, Inc., 1982; John Hay Whitney fellow, 1964, Samuel Rubin fellow Columbia U. Sch. Law, 1983. Office: Munger Tolles & Olson 355 S Grand 35th Floor Los Angeles CA 90071

MARTÍNEZ, YOLANDA R., social services administrator; b. San Bernardino, Calif., Feb. 11, 1936; d. Eduardo R. and Consuelo (Rincon) M.; A.A., San Bernardino Valley Coll., 1959; B.A., U. Wash., 1974; m. William Edward Hawkins, Mar. 27, 1963 (div. Mar. 1983); children—Ricardo, Eduardo, William T. Tchr. public schs., Calif., 1958-59; parole adviser, project dir., counselor Active Mexicanos, Seattle, 1972-76; instr. Everett Community Coll., Everett, Wash., 1975 76; research, translator Wash. State Council Crime and Delinquency, Seattle, 1977; program asst., minority affairs Seattle Central Community Coll., cons. to community offenders programs 1977-81; sr. community service rep. Seattle Dept. Human Resources, 1981—; cons. Chicano mental health. Democratic precinct committeeman, 1968, 70; vol. worker various local and state polit. campaigns; translator Am. Red Cross Lang. Bank, 1975—; chmn. Region 10 Chicano Task Force on Drug Abuse, 1977-79; mem. Seattle Women's Commn., 1977-81; mem. Seattle Cable Citizens Adv. Bd., 1988—; v.p. Concilio for Spanish Speaking; state dir., mem. nat. exec. bd. League United Latin Am. Citizens, 1980-82; chmn. Hispanic adv. bd. Seattle Community Coll. Dist. 6, 1981-83, chair Seattle/Mazatlan Sister City Assn., 1981-83; v.p. Neighborhoods U.S.A., 1987, bd. dirs. 1986; bd. dirs. United Way of King County; dist. adv. com. group health Northgate Clinic; del. White House Conf. on Families, Los Angeles, 1980. Recipient Gov.'s citation, 1974, award for committment to higher edn. Seattle Community Coll. Dist., 1983; award as One of 10 Unsung Heroes in Seattle, Radical Women, 1983; Community Service award Am. G.I. Forum, 1984; named assoc. mem. Eastern Washington U. Found., One of 100 Women Role Models for Pub. Schs., State Office Pub. Instrn. Mem. MUJER Hispanic Woman's Orgn. Author: Usted y La Ley, 1977. Home: 12018 17th Ave NE Seattle WA 98125

MARTING, LEEDA POLLOCK, management consultant; b. Birmingham, Ala., June 28, 1945; d. Lester Euler and Edytha (Chastain) Pollock; m. Rodger A. Marting, July 24, 1971 (div. Dec. 1976); 1 dau., Kristin Roselle. B.S., U. Ala.-Tuscaloosa, 1967, M.A., 1970; Ph.D., Ohio State U., Columbus, 1973; P.M.D., Harvard U., 1983. Asst. dir. Columbus Found., 1973-76; dir. Needmor Fund, Toledo, 1976-79; mgr. Levi Straus & Co., San Francisco, 1979-80; exec. dir. John Hay Whitney Found., N.Y.C., 1980-83; pvt. practice mgmt. cons., N.Y.C., 1983—; bd. dirs. PBS Enterprises, Washington. Mem. exec. com., bd. dirs. Pub. Broadcasting Service, Washington, 1979—; sec. Bank St. Coll., N.Y.C., 1979-83, chmn. bd. dirs., 1983-86; trustee Enterprise Found., Columbia, Md., 1983—. Named Disting. Alumnus in Communications U. Ala., 1978. Democrat. Club: Harvard (N.Y.C.).

MARTINITZ, MELANIE LYNN, civil engineer; b. Salina, Kans, Mar. 26, 1962; d. Dale L. and Nadine L. (Mehl) M. BCE, Kans. State U., 1985. Civil engr. Howard, Needles, Tammen & Bergendoff, Dallas, 1985—. Mem. Assn. Civil Engrs., Nat. Assn. Female Execs. Republican. Baptist. Office: Howard Needles Tammen & Bergendoff 9200 Ward Pkwy Kansas City MO 64131

MARTINSON, CONSTANCE FRYE, television program hostess, producer; b. Boston, Apr. 11, 1932; d. Edward and Rosalind Helen (Sperber) Frye; m. Leslie Herbert Martinson, Sept. 24, 1955; 1 child, Julianna Martinson Carner. BA in English Lit., Wellesley Coll., 1953. Dir. pub. relations Coro Found., Los Angeles, 1974-79; producer/host KHJ Dimensions, Los Angeles, 1979-81, Connie Martinson Talks Books, Los Angeles, 1981—; instr. dept. humanities UCLA, 1981—; celebrity advisor Book Fair-Music Ctr., Los Angeles, 1986. Author Dramatization of Wellesley After Images, 1974; book editor, columnist Calif. Press Bur. Syndicate, 1986—. Pres. Mayor's adv. council on volunteerism, Los Angeles, 1981-82; chmn. community affairs dept. Town Hall of Calif., Los Angeles, 1981-85; bd. dirs. legal def. fund NAACP, Los Angeles, 1981-84. Mem. Women in Cable, Am. Film Inst., Jewish TV Network (bd. dirs. 1985-87). Democrat. Jewish. Clubs: Wellesley Coll. (pres. 1979-81), Mulholland Tennis. Home and Office: 2288 Coldwater Canyon Beverly Hills CA 90210

MARTINSON, HELEN DELABAR, insurance agency executive; b. Van Lear, Ky., Dec. 18, 1939; d. Morris Martin and Carrie Beatrice (Holbrook) McCormick; m. Carl Bernard Delabar, Feb. 2, 1957 (div. June 1970); children: Carl Martin, Gregory Michael, Steven Edward, James Thomas; m. Warren Charles Martinson III, June 7, 1975 (div. May 1982); m. Yancy Bailey Spencer Jr., Apr. 9, 1988. Student, U. Ky., 1963. Cert. ins. counselor. Cashier, sec. So. Life Ins. Co., Lexington, Ky., 1965-66; service rep. Carpenter Warren Ins., Lexington, 1966-69; ins. agt., pres. Delmac Ins. Inc., Lexington, 1969-72; agt., office mgr. O'Leary Ins. Agy., Boyton Beach, Fla., 1972-75, Hayes & Assocs. Inc., Boyton Beach, 1975-77; prodn. mgr. Normandin Ins. Agy. Inc., West Palm Beach, Fla., 1977-80; sec., treas. Normandin-Martinson Ins., West Palm Beach, 1980-85; v.p., mgr. Raymond/Patterson Agy. Inc., West Palm Beach, 1985—. Bd. dirs. Palm Beach County Fire Code and Appeals, West Palm Beach, 1985—. Fellow Profl. Ins. Agts. Fla. (bd. dirs. 1987—, Chmn. award 1982, Leadership award 1985, Agt. of Yr. 1986), Ind. Agts. the Palm Beaches (bd. dirs. 1979-86, 2d v.p. 1982-83, 1st v.p. 1983-84, pres. 1984-85, Chmn. award 1982, Agt. of Yr. 1985). Republican. Baptist. Home: 4956 Sable Pine Circle #B-2 West Palm Beach FL 33417 Office: Raymond/Patterson Agy Inc 2827 Exchange Ct West Palm Beach FL 33409

MARTINSON, IDA MARIE, nurse, physiologist, educator; b. Mentor, Minn., Nov. 8, 1936; d. Oscar and Marvel (Nelson) Sather; m. Paul Varo Martinson, Mar. 31, 1962; children—Anna Marie, Peter. Diploma, St. Luke's Hosp. Sch. Nursing, 1957; B.S., U. Minn., 1960, M.N.A., 1962; Ph.D., U. Ill., Chgo., 1972. Instr. Coll. St. Scholastica and St. Luke's Sch. Nursing, 1957-58, Thornton Jr. Coll., 1967-69; lab. asst. U. Ill. at Med. Center, 1970-72; lectr. dept. physiology U. Minn., St. Paul, 1972—; asst. prof. Sch. Nursing U. Minn., 1972-74, asso. prof., research, 1974-77, prof., dir. research, 1977-82; vis. research prof. Nat. Taiwan U. Def. Med. Ctr., 1981, also prof., chmn. family health care nursing U. Calif., San Francisco, 1982—. Author: Mathematics for the Health Science Student, 1977; editor: Home Care for the Dying Child, 1976, Women in Stress, 1979, Women in Health and Illness, 1986, The Child and Family Facing Life Threatening Illness, 1987; contbr. chpts. to books, articles to profl. jours. Active Am. Cancer Soc. Recipient Am. Bus. Press award, 1977; recipient various grants. Mem. Council Nurse Researchers, Nat. League for Nursing, Am. Acad. Nursing, Am. Nurses Assn., Inst. Medicine, Sigma Xi, Sigma Theta Tau. Lutheran. Office: U Calif Dept Family Health Care Nursing San Francisco CA 94135

MARTONE, ELAINE LEE, music executive; b. Rochester, N.Y., July 10, 1957; d. William Edward and Sylvia (Levine) M. BS in Music cum laude, Ithaca Coll., 1979. Quality control Telarc Internat., Cleve., 1980-82, prodn. mgr., 1982-86, dir. prodn., artist relations, 1986—; music editor over 100 recs.; musician Canton (Ohio) Symphony Orch., 1980—. Mem. Nat. Acad. Recording Arts and Scis. Office: Telarc Internat 23307 Commerce Park Rd Beachwood OH 44122

MARTONE, JOANNE, accountant; b. Yonkers, N.Y., Mar. 3, 1951; d. August Jerome and Winnie (Rudolf) M.; BA in History, Centre Coll. Ky., 1973; postgrad. Ariz. State U., 1979-81. Cert. tchr., Ky., Ariz.; CPA, Ariz. Tchr., basketball coach Junction City (Ky.) Elem. Sch., 1973-77; staff analyst Met. Life Ins. Co., 1975-77; tchr. Glendale Elem. Sch., 1977-78, Camelback Desert Sch., 1978-79; C.P.A., De Marcus & Assos. P.C., Phoenix, 1979-82; individual practice, 1982—; ptnr. Investment Co. Acres, 1976—, The Lucky Leopard, 1977-88; dir. Adaman Mut. Water Co., 1981-82, sec.-treas., 1981-82. Bd. dirs. Impact...for Enterprising Women, 1983-87, North Star, 1985-86; bd. dirs. North Community Behavioral Health Center, Inc., 1984-88, treas., 1986-88. Mem. Am. Inst. CPAs, Ariz. Soc. CPAs . Clubs: Metro Bus. Network (treas. 1986-88), Terns. Home: 5800 W Glenn Dr Suite 250 Glendale AZ 85301 Office: 7112 N 55th Ave Suite B Glendale AZ 85301

MARTONE, PATRICIA ANN, lawyer; b. Bklyn., Apr. 28, 1947; d. David Andrew and Rita Mary (Dullmeyer) M. B.A. in Chemistry, NYU, 1968, J.D., 1973; M.A. in Phys. Chemistry, Johns Hopkins U., 1969. Bar: N.Y. 1974, U.S. Dist. Ct. (so. and ea. dists.) N.Y. 1975, U.S. Ct. Appeals (2d cir.) 1975, U.S. Ct. Appeals (1st cir.) 1981, U.S. Ct. Appeals (fed. cir.) 1984, U.S. Patent and Trademark Office 1983, U.S. Supreme Ct. 1984, U.S. Dist. Ct. (ea. dist.) Mich. 1985. Tech. rep. computer timesharing On-Line Systems, Inc., N.Y.C., 1969-70; assoc. Kelley Drye & Warren, N.Y.C., 1973-77; assoc. Fish & Neave, N.Y.C., 1977-82, ptnr., 1983—; participating atty. Community Law Offices, N.Y.C., 1974-78; atty. Pro Bono Panel U.S. Dist. Ct. (so. dist.) N.Y., 1982-84; lectr. Practising Law Inst., N.Y.C., 1984; dir. N.Y.

Lawyers for the Pub. Interest, 1987—. Mng. editor NYU Law Sch. Rev. Law and Social Change, 1972-73. Contbr. articles to profl. jours. Recipient Founder's Day award NYU Sch. Law, 1973; NSF grad. trainee John Hopkins U., 1968-69; NYU scholar, 1964-68. Mem. ABA, Assn. Bar City N.Y. (mem. environ. law com. 1978-83, trademarks, unfair competition com. 1983-86), Am. Chem. Soc., N.Y. Patent, Trademark and Copyright Law Assn. Club: The Club at Citicorp Ctr. (N.Y.C.). Office: Fish & Neave 875 Third Ave New York NY 10022

MARUMOTO, BARBARA CHIZUKO, state legislator; b. San Francisco, July 21, 1939; d. Takeo and Kathleen (Tsuchiya) Okamoto; B.A., U. Hawaii, 1971; student U. Calif., 1957-60, UCLA, 1957; children—Marshall, Jay, Wendy, Megan. Legis. aide, researcher, Honolulu, 1972-78; mem. Hawaii Ho. of Reps., 1978—, minority floor leader, 1981; elected del. to Constl. Conv., 1978; real estate agt., 1979—. Mem. exec. bd. Hist. Hawaii Found.; bd. dirs. Pacific council Girl Scouts U.S.A.; active Rep. Party, Common Cause, LWV, PTA, Ripon Soc. Clubs: Honolulu, Jr. League Honolulu. Contbr. various news columns to publs. Office: Capitol Room 322 Honolulu HI 96813

MARVEL, FRANCES JEAN, librarian, travel consultant, real estate manager; b. Ferndale, Calif., July 12, 1933; d. Shirley Allison and Meriam Grace (Soule) Boyd; m. Lee Marvel, Aug. 30, 1953; children—Cheryl Kathleen, Donna Lee, John Emery. B.A. in Bus. Edn., Humboldt State U., 1967, M.A., 1976; postgrad. San Francisco State U., U. So. Oreg.; MLS Brigham Young U., 1987. Tchr. Arcata High Sch., Calif., 1968-83; librarian McKinleyville High Sch., Calif., 1983-84; pres. Marvel Mgmt. Co., Bayside, Calif., 1980—; travel cons. Sunsets Unltd., Arcata, Calif., 1982—; div. sec. Humboldt State U., 1958-64; sec. Presidio, San Francisco, State Bd. Equalization, Cal Trans div. hwys. Stephen Bufton Meml grantee, 1967. Mem. No. Humboldt Unified Faculty Assn., Am. Bus. Women's Assn. (Woman of Yr. 1981), ALA, Nat. Bus. Edn. Assn., Humboldt Hist. Soc., Calif. Scholarship Fedn. (life), Calif. Bus. Educators Assn., Calif. Parent Tchrs. Assn., Humboldt State U. Alumni Assn., NEA, Calif. Media and Library Educators Assn. Democrat. Clubs: Exchangettes, Soroptimists. Home: 1380 Clipper Ln Bayside CA 95524 Office: Marvel Mgmt Co PO Box 112 Bayside CA 95524

MARVIN, HELEN RHYNE, state senator; b. Gastonia, N.C., Nov. 30, 1917; d. Dane S. and Tessie (Hastings) Rhyne; B.A. magna cum laude, Furman U., 1938; M.A., La. State U., 1938; postgrad. Winthrop Coll., U. N.C.-Chapel Hill, U. N.C.-Charlotte, U. Colo., U. Vt., U. Oslo; m. Ned Marvin, Nov. 21, 1941; children—Kathryn Nisbet, Richard Morris, David Rhyne. Part-time instr. polit. sci. Gaston Coll.; pres. Gaston County Democratic Women, 1973-75; mem. Gaston County Dem. Exec. Com., 1973-76; mem. N.C. State Dem. Exec. Com., 1973-76; del. Nat. Dem. Conv., 1972, 84; mem. N.C. Senate, 1977—, vice chairperson edn. com., 1979-82, vice-chairperson law enforcement and crime control com., 1981-82, appropriations com., 1981—, chmn. congl. redistricting com., 1981-82, constl. amendment com., 1983-84, chmn. legis. study com. on social, econ. and legal needs of women, 1981-86, chmn. pensions and retirement com., 1985-87, vice chmn. children and youth com., 1985-87, chmn. appropriations com. on jusitce and pub. safety, 1987—, vice chmn. P&R com., 1987—. Bd. dirs. N.C. Equity, Inc., Gaston County Mental Health Assn., Gaston County Family Planning Council, Gaston County Council for Children with Spl. Needs, Gaston County Children's Council; past mem., sec. So. Piedmont Health Services Agy.; past mem. N.C. State Health Coordinating Council, N.C. State Textbook Commn.; past chairperson N.C. Council on Status of Women, N.C. State Social Services Commn., N.C. Day Care Adv. Council; mem. N.C. Commn. on Yr. 2000; former mem. Gov.'s Advocacy Council on Children and Youth; former mem. N.C. Apprenticeship Council; trustee Vagabond Sch. Drama, Sacred Heart Coll., Flat Rock Playhouse; mem. bd. N.C. Child Advocacy Inst., N.C. Child Support Council; elder 1st Presbyterian Ch., 1983—. Recipient N.C. Disting. Woman award, 1987, Valued award, 1980, N.C. Health Dir.'s award, 1988. Mem. So. Polit. Sci. Assn., N.C. Polit. Sci. Assn., Delta Kappa Gamma. Club: Altrusa. Office: NC State Legislature Bldg Raleigh NC 27611 Other Address: 119 Ridge Ln Gastonia NC 28054

MARX, CYNTHIA LOIS, national club executive; b. Kenosha, Wis., Aug. 2, 1947; d. Frank Ralph and Gladys Ann (Hallagher) Valentine; m. Guenther Martin Marx, Sept. 28, 1963; children: David Thomas, Heidi Marie. Diploma in interior decorating, Home Interiors, Inc., Kenosha, Wis., 1985; postgrad., Gateway Tech., Kenosha, Wis. Co-owner Stein N' Teller Restaurant, Kenosha, 1971-76; rep. Avon Products, Niles, Ill., 1983-85; pres. The Higher We Fly Club, Kenosha, 1984—; interior decorator Home Interiors, Inc., Dallas, 1985-86. Rep. UNICEF, Kenosha, 1984-86; sponsor Kenosha Cares Campaign, 1985. Democrat. Lutheran.

MARX, GILDA, fashion designer and manufacturer, aerobic exercise studio owner/president, fitness products producer and distributor;b. Pitts., Nov. 25, 1935; d. Herman and Ruth (Small) Wilstein; m. Leo N. Guzik, 1955 (div.); children—Laura Lynn, Mitchell Allan; m. Robert Stuart Marx, June 30, 1973. Student Los Angeles City Coll., 1953-55. Founder, owner Body Design by Gilda Exercise Studios N.Y.C., Washington, Stamford, Conn., 1960—; founder, v.p., head designer Gilda Marx Industries, Flexatard, Inc., Los Angeles, 1976—, Gilda Marx Swimwear, 1984—, Gilda Marx BODY, 1985—, Gilda Marx Stars of Tomorrow, 1986—, Gilda Marx Sport, 1987—. Trustee, City of Hope, Scripps Clinic. Author: Body Design By Gilda Studios, Inc. Training Manual, 1979; Body by Gilda—Redesign Every Line, 1984; featured in and contbr. numerous articles to Elle, Family Circle, Vogue, Glamour, Mademoiselle, People, N.Y. Times, Cosmopolitan, others. Carried torch Los Angeles Olympics games, 1984; named Woman of Yr., City of Hope, 1984, Top 60 U.S. Corps. Run by a Woman, 1984-87; nominee Am. Fashion award, 1987; recipient Legend of Aerobics award, 1985. Mem. Fitness Found. of Am. (bd. dirs.), Music Ctr. (blue ribbon mem.), Joffrey Ballet. Office: Flexatard Inc 11755 Exposition Blvd Los Angeles CA 90064

MARX, SALLY, insurance agent; b. Bklyn., July 17, 1941; d. Arthur and Anne R. (Schmugler) Miller; m. Ralph J. Marx, Aug. 20, 1961; 1 child, Lee Harris. AA in Bus., Valley Coll., 1967. Typist Prudential Life Ins. Co., Los Angeles, 1959-1967, operator data entry, 1967-73; ins. agt., field mgr. Am. Guaranty Co., Glendale, Calif., 1973—. Pres. El Camino Orgn. Rehab. Tng., Canoga Park, Calif., 1986-87, Woodland Hills (Calif.) Hadassah, 1981-87, Woman Yr., 1983; v.p. bd. dirs. Temple Aliyaa, Woodland Hills, 1962—. Named Woman Yr. Nat. Hadassah, 1983. Democrat. Jewish. Clubs: numerous numismatic (founder). Office: Am Guaranty Co 1930 W Glenoaks Blvd Suite 7 Glendale CA 91201

MARXER, DONNA, graphic design company executive; b. Miami, Fla., Apr. 15, 1934; d. Robert William and Kathryn Alice (Schmidt) M.; m. John David Rafferty, May 30, 1981; stepchildren—David, Colin, Brendan, Brian. B.Design, U. Fla., 1954; M.A., Tchrs. Coll., Columbia U., 1958; grad. Am. Women's Econ. Devel. Corp., 1983. Asst. art dir. Ruder & Finn Graphics, 1960-63; art dir. Zeneth Eidel Assocs., 1964-66; free-lance art dir., designer, N.Y.C., 1966-81; founder, pres. On Paper, N.Y.C., 1981—; lectr. on art, design to colls., univs., profl. orgns. Clients include Life, Money and People mags., N.Y. Times Book Rev., Internat. Paper Co., Renault Corp., McGraw-Hill, Celanese, ABC, CBS; exhibited paintings in one-woman shows, including: York Gallery, N.Y.C., 1967, 20th Century Gallery, Williamsburg, Va., 1976, Marden Fine Arts, N.Y.C., 1979; group shows include: Bklyn. Mus., 1975, Summit Gallery, N.Y.C., 1977; represented in permanent collections. Author, illustrator: The Boatcook, 1983; contbr. to Arts, S.W. Art, Sail, Crusing World; designer and contbr. to Arthritis Today. Mem. Women in Design (pres. N.Y. chpt. 1982-83), Soc. Illustrators, Type Dirs. Office: On Paper 579 Broadway New York NY 10012

MASCOLO, DONNA MARIE, fast food chain executive; b. Lakewood, N.J., Jan. 13, 1955; d. James Vincent and Marilynn Ann (Gutzler) M. BA in Math and Econs., Susquehanna U., 1976; MBA in Mgmt. and Fin., Lehigh U., 1979. Credit mgr. comml. loans Midlantic Banks, Inc., West Orange, N.J., 1976-78; ops. research analyst Air Products & Chems., Trexlertown, Pa., 1978-79; teaching ass. in econs. Lehigh U., Bethlehem, Pa., 1979; systems engr. Bell Labs., Holmdel, N.J., 1979-81; bus. planning advisor Exxon Corp., Coral Gables, Fla., 1981-85; dir. planning and reporting Burger King Corp. subs. Pillsbury Co., Miami, Fla., 1985—. Dir. community devel. com. United Way, Miami, 1987—. Mem. Nat. Assn. Female Execs., Miami C. of C. (dir. strategic planning com. 1987). Home: 6920 SW 109th Pl Miami FL 33173 Office: Burger King Corp 17777 Old Cutler Rd Miami FL 33157

MASELLI, FORTUNE CLAIRE, property management administrator; b. Cambridge, Mass., July 16, 1922; d. Paul Joseph and Stefana (Zullo) Tavilla; m. Aldo G. Maselli, June 4, 1950; children: Ralph, Stefany, Sylvia, Lisa, Paul. A in Bus., Burdett Bus. Coll., 1940; student, Boston U., Rutgers U., Georgetown U., Pepperdine U. Bookkeeper West Disinfecting Co., Boston, 1941-42; jr. acct. Brown Burnhoff and Stevens, Boston, 1942-44; acct. P. Tavilla Co., Boston, 1945-50, Charles Sheet Metal, Camden, N.J., 1967-68; acct. Leisure World of N.J. Trust, Jamesburg, 1968-74, controller, 1968-83; controller Rossmoor Community Assn., Inc., Jamesburg, 1983-87, gen. mgr., 1987—. Active Assemblies of God Ch. Mem. Nat. Assn. Accts. Republican. Office: Rossmoor Community Assn Inc 2 Rossmoor Dr Jamesburg NJ 08831

MASENG, MARI, public affairs consultant; b. Chgo., Mar. 15, 1954; d. Leif Eric and Betty (Hagen) M. B.A., U. S.C., 1975. Reporter Charleston Evening Post, S.C., 1976-78; press sec. Re-elect Thurmond Com., Columbia, S.C., 1978; staff dir. Dole for Pres. Com., Alexandria, Va., 1979-80; spl. asst. to chmn. Reagan-Bush Com., Arlington, Va., 1980; press officer Office of Pres.-Elect, Washington, 1980-81; presdl. speechwriter The White House, Washington, 1981-83; asst. sec. for pub. affairs Dept. Transp., Washington, 1983-85; v.p., dir. corp. affairs Beatrice Cos. Inc., Chgo., 1985-86; dep. asst to the pres., dir. Office of Public Liason The White House, Washington, 1986-87; press sec. Dole for Pres. Campaign, Washington, 1987-88; pub. affairs cons. Washington, 1988—. Recipient Alumna Achievement award U. S.C., Columbia, 1984. Mem. Women's Transp. Seminar, Internat. Aviation Club, Soc. Profl. Journalists, Univ. S.C. Alumni Assn., Chi Omega. Republican. Presbyterian. Club: Monroe (Chgo.). Home: 3101 New Mexico Ave NW Washington DC 20016

MASHINI, DIANA SOCORRO, sales executive; b. Barranquilla, Colombia, June 29, 1945; came to U.S., 1962; d. Mario Rafael and Berta Lucia (Martinez) De La Rosa; m. Samir Abdalla Mashini, Apr. 14, 1962; children: Samir Alexandre, Alexander Anthony. Student, Nortre Dame U. Ground hostess KLM and Peruvian Airlines, Barranquilla, 1960-61; adminstrv. asst. Caterpillar, div. Gen. Electric S.A., Barranquilla, 1961-62; personnel cons. Champion Personnel Systems, Cleve., 1976-83, div. mgr. sales, 1983—; speaker profl. confs. Mem. Nat. Assn. Investment Clubs, Nat. Assn. Personnel Cons., Pan Am. Cultural Soc., Ohio Assn. Personnel Cons., Greater Cleve. Assn. Personnel Cons., Women's City Club Cleve. Republican. Roman Catholic. Office: Champion Personnel System 668 Euclid Ave Suite 300A Cleveland OH 44114

MASI, JANE VIRGINIA, marketing and sales consultant; b. N.Y.C., June 6, 1947; d. Vincent Joseph and Virginia Marie (Beddow) Masi; m. Charles Walter Friedman, Feb. 14, 1976. BA in Communications and Psychology, Mercy Coll., N.Y., 1969; MA, New Sch. Social Research, 1979, now PhD candidate. Asst. sales mgr. Chevron Chem., N.Y.C., 1969-71; writer, 1973-75; ptnr. Masi-D'Angelo Constrn. and Devel. Assocs., N.Y.C., 1979-83; pres., founder Beddow Mills Inc., N.Y.C., 1982-85, Beddow Mfg. Ind., 1983-85; co-pres. TRS Mktg. Inc., N.Y.C., 1985—; founder Energy Works, 1985; founder, dir. TRS Inc. Profl. Suite, 1986—. Author 38 novellas. N.Y. Regents scholar, 1965-69. Mem., Trans-Species Unltd., Soc. Ethical Treatment of Animals. Avocations: woodworking, carpentry, advocating animal rights, design psychology. Office: TRS Mktg Inc 7 E 30th St New York NY 10016

MASLOW, MELANIE JANE, physician; b. N.Y.C., Mar. 11, 1952; d. Morris and Rosalie (Kaufman) Schwartz; m. James Edward Maslow, June 17, 1973 (div. 1977); m. David Tice, Sept. 12, 1985. B.A., Barnard Coll., 1973; M.D., NYU, 1977. Diplomate Am. Bd. Internal Medicine. Intern NYU Med. Ctr.-Manhattan VA Hosp., N.Y.C., 1977-78, resident, chief resident, 1978-81, fellow, 1981-83; co-physician-in-charge infectious disease L.I. Coll. Hosp., Bklyn., 1983-87, co-chief infectious diseases, 1987—; asst. prof. medicine SUNY-Downstate Med. Ctr. Fellow ACP; mem. Am. Soc. for Microbiology, Infectious Diseases Soc. Am., N.Y. Acad. Sci. Democrat. Jewish. Office: Long Island Coll Hosp 340 Henry St Brooklyn NY 11201

MASON, AIMEE HUNNICUTT ROMBERGER, retired educator; b. Atlanta, Nov. 3, 1918; d. Edwin William and Aimee Greenleaf (Hunnicutt) Romberger; B.A., Conn. Coll., 1940; postgrad. Emory U., 1946-48; M.A., U. Fla., 1979, Ph.D., 1980; M.A., Stetson U., 1968; m. Samuel Venable Mason, Aug. 16, 1941; children—Olivia Elizabeth (Mrs. Mason Butcher), Christopher Leeds. Jr. exec., merchandising G. Fox & Co., Hartford, Conn., 1940-41; air traffic controller CAA, Atlanta, 1942; partner Coronado Concrete Products, New Smyrna Beach, Fla., 1953-81; adj. faculty Valencia Jr. Coll., Orlando, Fla., 1969; instr. philosophy and humanities Seminole Community Coll., Sanford, from 1969, now ret. Area cons. ARC, 1947-50; del. Nat. Red Cross, Washington, 1949; founding mem. St. Joseph Hosp. Aux., Atlanta, 1950-53; v.p., treas. New Smyrna Beach PTA 1955-60. Bd. dirs. Atlanta Symphony Orch., Fla. Symphony Orch., 1954-59. Served to lt. USCGR, 1943-46. Recipient award in graphics Nat. Assn. Women Artists, 1939, 41, Golden Hatter award Stetson U., 1973, 74. Mem. Am. Philos. Assn., AAUP, AAUW (founding mem. New Smyrna Beach, exec. bd. 1984-85, chmn. scholarship com. 1984-87, coll./univ. liaison, 1987—), Fla. Philos. Assn. (exec. council 1978-79), Collegium Phenomenologicum, Soc. Existential and Phenomenological Philosophy, Soc. Phenomenology in Human Scis., Merleau-Ponty Circle, Fla. Assn. Community Colls. Home: 2103 Ocean Dr New Smyrna Beach FL 32069

MASON, BARBARA MENTZER, environmental specialist; b. Atlanta, Jan. 2, 1937; d. Maxwell Richardson and Martha Jean (Osborne) Mentzer; m. John Augustus Lee (div. 1978); children: George A., Martha J.A., Sara Lee Fernandez, Maxwell R.M., Rebecca D.C.; m. Edward Augustus Mason, Sept. 22, 1979. BS, Fla. State U., 1959. Tchr. sci. Atlanta Pub. Sch. System, 1959-60, tchr. home econs., 1960-62, 1967-70; specialist mktg. Ga. Egg Commn., Atlanta, 1976-77, coordinator consumer program, 1977-78; state dir. Ga. Clean and Beautiful Dept. Community Affairs State of Ga., Atlanta, 1978—. Tchr. Sunday sch., vacation Bible sch. St. Philips Episc. Cathedral, 1962-67; chmn. com. orgn. Atlanta Clean City Commn, 1976; pres. Peachtree Battle Alliance Civic Assn., 1974-76, v.p., 1975, chmn. beautification, 1977; mem. Council Vol. Adminstrs., Ga. Assn. Vol. Adminstrn., 1986—, Ga. Conservency, 1980—, Ga. Environ. Council, 1986—. Named Outstanding Citizen Fultop County Bd. Commrs., 1986, Outstanding Citizen State Cobb County Clean Commn., Ga., 1987; recipient Profl. Leadership award Keep Am. Beautiful Inc., 1983. Mem. NEA (Ga. chpt.), Am. Home Econs. Assn. (Ga. chpt.), Nat. Assn. Female Execs., Atlanta Womens' Network, DAR Jr. Com. (pres. 1963), Delta Gamma Alumnae (pres. 1963, chmn. recommendations 1959). Home: 975 Vistavia Cr Decatur GA 30033

MASON, BOBBIE ANN, novelist, short story writer; b. Mayfield, Ky., 1940; married. BA, U. Ky.; MA, SUNY-Binghamton; PhD, U. Conn. Author: Nabokov's Garden, 1974; The Girl Sleuth, 1976; Shiloh and Other Stories, 1982 (Ernest Hemingway award, Nat. Book Critic's Circle award nominee, Am. Book award nominee, PEN Faulkner award nominee), In Country, 1985, Spence plus Lila, 1988. Contbr. regularly: The New Yorker, 1980—. Contbr. fiction to: The Atlantic, Redbook, Paris Review, Mother Jones, Harpers, N.Am. Rev., Va. Quar. Rev.,; contbr. works: Best American Short Stories, 1981; The Pushcart Prize: Best of the Small Presses, 1983; Best American Short Stories, 1983 (O. Henry awards, 1986, 88). Grantee Pa. Arts Council, 1983, Nat. Endowment Arts, 1983, Am. Acad. and Inst., 1984; Guggenheim fellow, 1984. Address: care Amanda Urban Internat Creative Mgmt 40 W 57th St New York NY 10019

MASON, CAROLYN, automobile club executive, psychotherapist, consultant; b. Buffalo, July 1, 1927; children—Gilbert D. Sylva, Nickolas A. Sylva, Christopher D. Mason. B.A., George Williams Coll., 1976, M.S.W., 1978; Ph.D., Southeastern U., 1980. Cert. clin. social worker. Pvt. practice psychotherapist, Oakbrook Terrace, Ill., 1973-79; v.p. human resources AAA/Chgo. Motor Club, Chgo., 1980-86, sr. v.p. corp. services, 1986—; cons. Chgo., Milw., 1975—. Author: Synthesis of Physiology and Psychology: Toward Wholism, 1978; artist retrospective aquatints (1st place Ill. Sesquicentennial, 1976). Co-founder All the Way House, Lombard, 1970. AAUW scholar, 1978, Hinsdale Bus. and Profl. Womens Assn. scholar, 1978; winner 1st place Oakbrook Artists Invitational, 1977. Mem. Am. Mgmt. Assn., Am. Assn. Tng. and Devel., AAUP. Democrat. Roman Catholic. Office: AAA Chicago Motor Club 999 E Touhy Ave Des Plaines IL 60018

MASON, CHARLOTTE ALLEN, tax consultant; b. Waynesboro, Va., Oct. 14, 1950; d. Carter Randolph and Helen (Coley) Allen; m. Ronald W. Mason, Aug. 3, 1945 (div. Dec. 1983); children: Jonathan Scott, Mary Carter. Student, Radford U., 1968-70, Roanoke Coll., 1983-84. Teller Sovran Bank, Waynesboro, Va., 1970-73; tax. cons. M.L. Kirby, Accountant, Bedford, Va., 1978-80; gen. ptnr. Kirby & Mason Accounting Office, Bedford, 1980—. Mem. Cen. Va. Adv. Commn., Lynchburg, 1980-86, Bedford City Council, 1980—, chair fin. com., 1986—; bd. dirs. Bedford Centertown, Inc., 1987—. Named one of Outstanding Young Woman of Am., 1982. Mem. Nat. Assn. Enrolled Agents, Nat. Assn. Pub. Accts. Democrat. Presbyterian. Office: Kirby and Mason 101 N Bridge St Bedford VA 24523

MASON, CHARLOTTE JANE, magazine publisher, writer; b. Salem, Mo., Oct. 15, 1947; d. Everett Earnest and Effie Caroline (Bell) M. BA, Webster U., 1980, postgrad., 1983. Editor Meramec Jour., High Ridge, Mo., 1970-77; pub. info. officer Northwest Sch. Dist., House Springs, Mo., 1977-80; mktg. coordinator Webster U., St. Louis, 1980-82; pres. Mason-Totten & Assocs., High Ridge, 1983-85; pub. PRIDE Mag., High Ridge, 1985—; cons. pub. relations, 1981—. Editor St. Louis Poetry Ctr. Newsletter; contbr. articles to mags. Sec., v.p. Community Library Assn., Northwest Community, 1975; del. Gov.'s Conf. on Libraries, Mo., 1976; mem. exec. bd. dirs. Sheltered Workshop, Jefferson County, 1978; v.p. Commn. for Handicapped, Jefferson County, 1979-80, Outstanding Service award, 1980; juror Cir. Ct. Grand Jury, Jefferson County, 1984. Recipient Disting. Service award Boy Scouts Am., Jefferson County, 1975, Responsible Press award Community Tchrs. Assn. Northwest Sch. Dist., 1976. Mem. Nat. Assn. Female Execs., Regional Commerce and Growth Assn., Twin City C. of C., Mo. Writers Guild. Democrat. Office: PRIDE Magazine PO Box 1487 High Ridge MO 63049

MASON, CLAIRE LYNN, rehabilitation consultant, occupational therapist; b. East Stroudsburg, Pa., Sept. 14, 1952; d. David Julius and Frances Lillian (Zacher) Mason; 1 child, Michelle Lyn. BS with honors, U. Fla., 1974. Lic. occupational therapist, Tex., Fla. Occupational therapist Infant Stimulation and Children's Programs, United Cerebral Palsey Ctr. Miami, Fla., 1974-75; dir. occupational therapy Baytown (Tex.) Cerebral Palsy Ctr., 1976-77; dir. occupational therapy/hosp. risk mgr. Rosewood Gen. Hosp., Houston, 1977-83; pres., dir. Mason Health Services, Inc., 1984-87; v.p. Health Focus, 1988—; adj. faculty U. Tex. Med. Br., 1977-84; ins. Liaison for Tex. Occupational Therapists, 1979—; founder Am. HoC for sexually abused children, 1987—. Contbr. articles to profl. jours. Mem. Nat. Assn. Female Execs., Am. Occupational Therapy Assn., Tex. Occupational Therapy Assn. (bd. dirs. 1979-87), Tex. Soc. Allied Health Professions, Tex. Hosp. Safety Assn., Nat. Assn. Scuba Divers. Democrat. Jewish. Mailing Address: 13707 FM 149 Suite 276 Houston TX 77086

MASON, DEBORAH DEITCH, computer programmer, nurse; b. Gettysburg, PA, Jan. 20, 1956; d. Druid Cassatt and Betty Jane (Ridinger) Deitch; m. Jeffrey William Mason. BS in Nursing, U. Md., 1977; postgrad., U. Tenn., 1981; diploma in computer programming, Computer Learning Ctr., 1985. RN, Md. Staff nurse, asst. head operating room nurse U.S. Army Nurse Corps., Ft. Meade, Md., 1977-80; operating room staff nurse Ft. Sanders Med. Ctr., Knoxville, Tenn., 1982, Doctors' Hosp. P.G. Co., Lanham, Md., 1982-84; system trainee, asst. Acacia Mut. Life Ins. Co., Washington, 1985-86; system engr. Citizens & So. Systems, Columbia, S.C., 1986—. Mem. Humane Soc. U.S., 1977-80. Served to capt. U.S. Army, 1977-80, capt. Res. ret. Mem. Nat. Assn. Female Execs., Phi Kappa Phi, Sigma Theta Tau, Columbia Chorale Soc. Republican. Presbyterian. Office: Citizens & So Systems 2951/2 Greystone Blvd 2d floor Control Ctr Columbia SC 29210

MASON, ELIZABETH, health care company executive; b. Camden, N.J., July 27, 1944; d. Anthony J. and Violet J. (Baker) DiIelsi; m. Lucio R. Severino, Sept. 14, 1968 (div. 1975); 1 child, Antonio R.; m. Edwin J. Mason, Dec. 23, 1985; stepchildren: Alma, Edwin J. Jr. BS in Biology, U. Pa., 1967; MSW in Planning, Adminstrn., Rutgers U., 1978; postgrad., Temple U., 1968. Activity therapist Camden County Psychiat. Hosp., Camden, 1962-67; instr. biology Temple U., Phila., 1968-69; tchr. sci. Forrest Sherman John F. Kennedy High Sch., Naples, Italy, 1971-73; dir. therapy services Camden County Health Services Ctr., 1973-78; dir. profl. services AID Health Care Ctrs., Wayne, Pa., 1979-81, Western Div. Beverly Enterprises, Fresno, Calif., 1981-82; v.p. ops. Health Group Care Ctrs. Inc., Chadds Ford, Pa., 1982-85; v.p., gen. mgr. Eastern Div. Health Care Retirement Corp., Chadds Ford, 1985; pres. Concord Healthcare Corp., Wilmington, Del., 1985—; mem. editorial bd. D.O.N. Mag.; bd. dirs. Concord Healthcare Corp., Camden County Health Services System. Vol. tutorial program for Hispanic and Black children. Mem. Nat. Assn. Social Workers (cert.), Gerontol Soc. Roman Catholic. Home: 1301 N Harrison St #1205 Wilmington DE 19806 Office: Concord Healthcare Corp 501 Silverside Rd Suite 30 Wilmington DE 19809

MASON, ELIZABETH, historian, consultant; b. Washington, Jan. 1, 1919; d. Hilarion Noel and Ella Augusta (Moler) Branch; m. John Thomas Mason, Jr., May 8, 1954. BA, Mt. Holyoke Coll., 1940; MA, Columbia U., 1941. Press officer Brit. Embassy, Mexico City, Mex., 1941-47; analyst Office of Naval Intelligence, Washington, 1948-54; instr. U. Maine, Orono, 1955-57; asst. dir.oral history research office Columbia U., N.Y.C., 1959-68, assoc. dir., 1968-84, acting dir., 1980-82; lectr. sch. of library service Columbia U., N.Y.C., 1973-82, Barnard Coll., N.Y., 1978-79, Mt. Holyoke Coll., South Hadley, Mass., 1983; cons. oral history research office Columbia U., N.Y.C., 1985—. Editor: The Oral History Collection of Columbia University, 1979. Nat. officer exec. council Episc. Ch., N.Y.C., 1961-67. Mem. Oral History Assn. (council mem. 1978-81, 1983-84, v.p., pres. elect 1981-82, pres. 1982-83), Mt. Holyoke Coll. Alumnae Assn. (Sesquicentennial award 1988). Home: Amenia Union Rd Sharon CT 06069 Office: Columbia U Oral History Research Office Box 20 Butler Library New York NY 10027

MASON, ELIZABETH JANE, nursing consultant; b. Uniontown, Pa., Aug. 22, 1935; d. William Sherman and Margaret Catherine (Luman) M. Diploma in nursing, Presbyn. U. Hosp., Pitts., 1956; BS in Nursing, U. Pitts., 1959; MS in Nursing, Wayne State U., 1962; PhD in Edn., U. Wis., 1972. Instr. anatomy and physiology, clin. instr. med.-surg. nursing Presbyn. U. Hosp. Sch. Nursing, 1959-61; instr. nursing U. Pitts., 1962-66; asst. prof. med. and surg. nursing U. Wis., Madison, 1966-70; assoc. prof. med.-surg. nursing Va. Commonwealth U., Richmond, 1972-76, assoc. prof. for ednl. planning and devel., 1975-76; asst. dir. undergrad. edn., asst. prof. Ohio State U., Columbus, 1976-80; dir. grad. program nursing adminstrn. and edn., assoc. prof. U. Pitts. Sch. Nursing, 1980-85; cons. nursing standards, quality assurance and productivity, Verona, Pa., 1985—. Author: How to Write Meaningful Nursing Standards, 1978, 2d edit. 1984; mem. editorial bd. Jour. of Nursing Quality Assurance.; patentee software, Excelcare, nursing decision support system. USPHS pre-doctoral fellow, 1970-72. Mem. Am. Nurses Assn., Council Nurse Researchers, Nat. League for Nursing, Computer Applications in Nursing, Am. Ednl. Researchers Assn., Pi Lambda Theta, Sigma Theta Tau.

MASON, JEANNE, entrepreneur; b. Washington, July 17, 1943; d. John Clarke and Germaine (Bernard) M.; m. James Fielder Cook, Jan. 15, 1983; 1 child, David John Posner. Cert., UCLA Sch. Radiologic Tech., 1967. X-ray technologist various hosps., doctors Los Angeles, 1967-75, construction exec., 1975-78; mgr. radiology Sherwood-Trimble Med. Ctr., Los Angeles, 1978-80; mgr. sales and service VARI-X, Inc., Hawthorne, Calif., 1980-82; v.p. mktg. Allied Imaging Co., Los Angeles, 1984-86; owner Mktg. Diversified, Los Angeles, 1982—; pres. Heilig-Heilig & Mason Ltd., Los Angeles, 1986—; owner, pres. Restaurant Placement Group Ltd., Santa Monica, Calif., 1987—; cons. Jason Mktg. Inc., Los Angeles, 1982-83, Calif. Design Assocs., Los Angeles, 1985-86. Advisor AIDS Project, Los Angeles, 1987, mem. AIDS Interfaith Council; vol. Kellogg Tng. Ctr., Los Angeles, 1987.

Mem. Calif. Soc. Radiologic Technologists, Nat. Assn. Women Bus. Owners (bd. dirs. Los Angeles 1987—), Calif. Restaurant Assn. (bd. dirs. Santa Monica chpt. 1988). Democrat. Office: Restaurant Placement Group Ltd 309 Santa Monica Blvd Suite 205 Santa Monica CA 90401

MASON, JOANNE ELISSA, corporate events coordinator, realtor, consultant; b. Troy, N.Y., May 10, 1952; d. William Charles and Veronica Laverna (Harris) Whitney; m. Thomas August Zink, July 17, 1970 (div. 1971); m. Robert L. Mason, May 4, 1974; 1 child, Alecia Lindsay. Diploma, Albany Inst. Banking, 1977, Jim Russell Internat. Sch. Racing, Can., 1978. Accredited by Rensselaer County Bd. Realtors, N.Y. Operator, N.Y. Telephone, Albany, 1970-71; acting mgr. Bankers Trust Co., Albany, 1971-79; owner, mgr. Bob Mason Enterprises, East Greenbush, N.Y., 1973-85; salesperson Gillespie Real Estate, East Greenbush, 1978-85; events coordinator Surplus Freight, Inc., Albany, 1985-87, office mgr., 1987—; pres. JEM Enterprises of Upstate N.Y. Inc., 1985—, Apricot Ct. Realty Inc., 1978—; pres., chief exec. officer Twilight Limousines & Coaches Inc., 1985—; cons. Gasoline Retailers Assn., 1981-84. Contbr. articles to popular mags. Registrar Nassau Women's Rep. Club, 1968-69. Recipient Pyramid Club award Bankers Trust Co., 1971. Share the Spirit award Bankers Trust Co., 1976, numerous 1st pl. racing awards from racing orgns., 1973—. Mem. Nat. Council Corvette Clubs (regional competition dir. 1983-86, founder, chmn. Interclub Assn. 1984-87, hold nat. drag race records and regional competition awards), Tri-Vettes, Ltd. (social dir. 1976-80, gov. 1979-86, editor Corvette Courier 1979-85, author East Region Corvette Jubilee Program 1984-85, Corvette Jubilee award 1984). Methodist. Home: 3 Apricot Ct Clifton Park NY 12065

MASON, JUDITH ANN, administrative aide; b. Newark, Dec. 27, 1945; d. Richard Algie and Mary Ann (Beneck) M. Diploma in legal sci., Spencerian Bus. Coll., 1965; BA, Northeastern Ill. U., 1984. Legal sec. Harney B. Stover, Atty., Milw., 1967-69, Robert P. O'Meara, Atty., Waukegan, Ill., 1969-70; sec. to pres. First Midwest Bank, Waukegan, 1970-72, asst. cashier, 1972-76; legal sec. Eugene M. Snarski, Atty., Waukegan, 1976-81; adminstrv. aide Lake County Forest Preserve Dist., Libertyville, Ill., 1981—; travel rep. Antioch (Ill.) Travel Agy., 1980—, Advance Travel Agy., Zion, Ill., 1980—; pub. speaker for various orgns., Lake County, Ill., 1984—. Author: Why I Remember Yesterday, 1979, Haggadah (play), 1982; editor poetry column: Bank Man Magazine, 1972-75. Tchr. Confraternity Christian Doctrine St. Patrick's Ch., Wadsworth, Ill., 1980-85; lector, eucharistic minister Prince of Peace Ch., Lake Villa, Ill., 1980—; hospice vol. St. Therese Hosp., Waukegan, 1984; speech writer Grace Mary Stern lt. gubernatorial campaign, Lake County, 1984, voter registrar County of Lake, Ill., 1986—; cons. pub. relations Lake County Cir. Ct. Judge campaign, 1988, Presdl. Campaign Paul Simon. Recipient Brian F. Shehanhan Creative Writing award Am. Inst. Banking, 1972, 1st Place pub. speaking, 1974. Mem. AAUW (pub. relations chair 1986, pres. Chain O'Lakes br., 1988—, Ill. pub. info. award 1987), Northeastern Ill. U. Alumni Assn., Nat. Assn. Female Execs., Pi Rho Zeta (pres. 1964-65). Democrat. Roman Catholic. Home: 36377 N Hwy 45 Lake Villa IL 60046 Office: Lake County Forest Preserve 2000 N Milwaukee Ave Libertyville IL 60048

MASON, JUNE-COLLIER, automotive parts company executive. m. Bobby Greenwood (div.); m. Ben Collier (div. 1985); m. Roy Mason, Jan. 1, 1987; 5 children. Grad. high sch., East Prairie, Mo. Receptionist, then bookkeeper Mid-South Elec. Fabricators (name changed to Nat. Industries Inc.), Miss., from 1961; pres., chief exec. officer Nat. Industries Inc., Montgomery, Ala., 1964—. Founder Citizens Against Fgn. Control of Am., 1982. Named to Working Woman mag. Hall of Fame, 1987. Office: National Industries Inc PO Box 3528 Montgomery AL 36109 *

MASON, LINDA ANN, health company executive; b. Columbus, Ohio, Mar. 31, 1947; d. Lloyd Walter and Ann Elizabeth (Seely) M.; m. Clifford A. Bridges, Sept. 14, 1968 (div. Dec. 1982); 1 child, David Lloyd Bridges. BA summa cum laude, Ohio U., 1969; MA, Kutztown (Pa.) U., 1985. Asst. dir. Thomas S. Brownback, Allentown, Pa., 1982—; cons. Kutztown Crisis Pregnancy Ctr. Bd. dirs. Lehigh Valley Nursing Mothers. Mem. Internat. Soc. of Multiple Personality and Dissociation (co-presentor 1985, 86), Christian Assn. Psychological Studies, Lehigh Valley Psychological Assn., Internat. Soc. Profl. Hypnosis, Mortar Bd., Phi Beta Kappa. Home: 3420 Oxford Circle N Allentown PA 18104 Office: Thomas S Brownback 1251 S Cedar Crest Blvd Suite 211A Allentown PA 18103

MASON, LUCILE GERTRUDE, fund raiser, consultant; b. Montclair, N.J., Aug. 1, 1925; d. Mayne Seguine and Rachel (Entorf) M. AB, Smith Coll., 1947; MA, NYU, 1968, 76. Editor ABC, N.Y.C., 1947-51; asst. casting dir. Compton Advt., Inc., N.Y.C., 1951-55, dir. and head casting, 1955-65; conf. mgr. Camp Fire Girls, Inc., N.Y.C., 1965-66; exec. dir. Assn. of Jr. Leagues of Am. Inc., N.Y.C., 1966-68; dir. div. pub. affairs Girl Scouts U.S., N.Y.C., 1969-71; dir. pub. relations YWCA of City of N.Y., 1971-73; dir. community relations and devel. Girl Scout Council of Greater N.Y., N.Y.C., 1973-76; dir. devel. Montclair Kimberley Acad., Montclair, N.J., 1976-78, Ethical Culture Schs., N.Y.C. and Riverdale, N.Y., 1978-80; pres. Lucile Mason & Assocs., Montclair, 1980-83; devel. officer founds. and corps. Fairleigh Dickinson U., Rutherford, N.J., 1983-85; dir. devel. Whole Theatre, Inc., Montclair, N.J., 1985-86, YMWCA of Newark & Vicinity, 1986-88; v.p. adminstrn. The Insts. of Religion and Health, N.Y.C., 1988—; v.p. The Neighborhood Council, Inc., Montclair, 1987—. Bd. counselors Smith Coll., 1964-74, bd. dirs., 1986—, chmn. theatre com., 1969-74, exec. com. bd. counselors, 1969-74; mem. citizens com. Presby Meml. Iris Gardens, 1980—. Mem. Am. Women in Radio and TV (pres. N.Y.C. chpt. 1955-56), Community Agys. Pub. Relations Assn. (membership chmn. 1973-76), Nat. Soc. Fund Raising Execs. (bd. dirs. N.J. chpt. 1983-86). Avocations: collecting pewter, gardening, concerts, plays. Home: 142 N Mountain Ave Montclair NJ 07042 Office: The Insts of Religion and Health 3 W 29th St New York NY 10001

MASON, MARILYN GELL, library administrator, writer, consultant; b. Chickasha, Okla., Aug. 23, 1944; d. Emmett D. and Dorothy (O'Bar) Kilbrew; m. Carl L. Gell, Dec. 29 1965 (div. Oct. 1978); 1 son, Charles E.; m. Robert M. Mason, July 17, 1981. B.A., U. Dallas, 1966; M.L.S., N. Tex. State U., Denton, 1968; M.P.A., Harvard U., 1978. Librarian N.J. State Library, Trenton, 1968-69; head dept. Arlington County Pub. Library, Va., 1969-73; chief library program Metro Washington Council of Govts., 1973-77; dir. White House Conf. on Libraries and Info. Services, Washington, 1979-80; exec. v.p. Metrics Research Corp., Atlanta, 1981-82; dir. Atlanta-Fulton Pub. Library, Atlanta, 1982-86, Cleve. Pub. Library, 1986—; trustee Online Computer Library Ctr., 1984—; Evalene Parsons Jackson lectr. div. librarianship Emory U., 1981. Author: The Federal Role in Library and Information Services, 1983; editor: Survey of Library Automation in the Washington Area, 1977; project dir.: book Information for the 1980's, 1980. Bd. visitors Sch. Info. Studies, Syracuse U., 1981—, Sch. of Library and Info. Sci., U. Tenn.-Knoxville, 1983-85. Recipient Disting. Alumna award N. Tex. State U., 1979. Mem. ALA (mem. council 1986—), Am. Assn. Info. Sci., Ohio Library Assn., D.C. Library Assn. (pres. 1976-77). Home: 2888 Morley Rd Shaker Heights OH 44122 Office: Cleve Pub Library 325 Superior Ave Cleveland OH 44114-1271

MASON, MARSHA, actress; b. St. Louis, Apr. 3, 1942; d. James and Jacqueline M.; m. Gary Campbell, 1965 (div.); m. Neil Simon, Oct. 25, 1973 (div.). Grad., Webster (Mo.) Coll. Mem.: cast Broadway and nat. tour Cactus Flower, 1968; other stage appearances include The Deer Park, 1967, The Indian Wants the Bronx, 1968, Happy Birthday, Wanda June, 1970, Private Lives, 1971, You Can't Take It With You, 1972, Cyrano de Bergerac, 1972, A Doll's House, 1972, The Crucible, 1972, The Good Doctor, 1973, King Richard III, 1974, The Heiress, 1975, Mary Stuart, 1982; film appearances include Blume in Love, 1973, Cinderella Liberty, 1973 (recipient Golden Globe award 1974, Acad. award nominee), Audrey Rose, 1977, The Goodbye Girl, 1977 (recipient Golden Globe award 1978, Acad. award nominee), The Cheap Detective, 1978, Promises in the Dark, 1979, Chapter Two, 1979 (Acad. award nominee), Only When I Laugh, 1981 (Acad. award nominee), Max Dugan Returns, 1982, Heartbreak Ridge, 1986; TV appearances include PBS series Cyrano de Bergerac, 1974, The Good Doctor, 1978, Lois Gibbs and the Love Canal, 1981, Surviving, 1985, Trapped in Silence, 1986, The Clinic, 1987.

MASQUELETTE, MELISSA FANCHER, self-employed; b. Canton, Miss., Sept. 29, 1955; d. Joseph Roderick, Jr., and Elsie (Robinson) Fancher; m. Philip Edward Masquelette, Nov. 25, 1978; child, Grace Fancher. B.B.A., U. Miss., 1977. C.P.A., Tex., Miss. Sr. auditor Arthur Andersen & Co., Houston, 1977-81; sect. supr. Superior Oil Co., Houston, 1981-85. Active Republican pollt. campaigns. Mem. Tex. Soc. C.P.A.s, DAR, Beta Alpha Psi, Beta Gamma Sigma, Phi Kappa Phi, Alpha Lambda Delta, Chi Omega. Episcopalian. Home: 4027 Branard St Houston TX 77027

MASSA, PATRICIA TRACY, social worker; b. Memphis, Aug. 16, 1943; d. Albert A. and Doris (Newman) T.; m. William S. Massa Jr., July 27, 1963 (div. 1976); children: William S. III, Philip Tracy. BS, U. Tenn., 1967, MSW, 1975. Lic. social worker, Tenn. Welfare worker II State of Tenn. Dept. Human Services, Knoxville, 1967-71; social worker Knoxville City Schs., 1971-73; clinician Helen Ross McNabb Mental Health Ctr., Knoxville, 1973-75, Child and Family Services, Knoxville, 1975-82; clin. social worker, psychotherapist, counselor Affiliated Profl. Service, Knoxville, 1977—. bd. dirs., exec. steering com. Greater Knoxville Council on Childcare, 1970; sec., v.p. PTA Ft. Sanders Sch., Knoxville, 1971; mem. childcare bd. Ch. St. Meth. Ch., Knoxville, 1969;. Named Social Worker of Yr. State of Tenn., 1987, Knox County, 1987. Mem. Nat. Assn. Social Workers (diplomate, cert. cons. clin. issues com. 1986—, chair, 1982-86, Tenn. Social Worker of Yr. 1986, Knoxville 1986).

MASSENGILL, ELLEN WEBB, librarian; b. Littlefield, Tex., Mar. 6, 1932; d. Lester L. and Bessie (Webb) M.; BS, Tex. Tech U., 1953, MS, 1959; MLS, North Tex. State U., 1969. Homemaking tchr., Floyd, N.M., 1953-55, Crane, Tex., 1955-56, Seminole, Tex., 1956-68, Littlefield, Tex., 1971-73; librarian Odessa (Tex.) High Sch., 1969-71, Littlefield Jr. High Sch., 1973-82, Littlefield Ind. Sch. Dist., 1982-83, Littlefield High Sch. and Jr. High Sch., 1983-84, Littlefield High Sch., 1984—; dist., area, state adv. bd. mem. Future Homemakers Am., N.Mex., Tex., 1954-68, adv. mem. nat. exec. council, 1954-55; adv. Young Homemakers Tex., 1958-73; co-leader Girl Scouts U.S.A., 1948-49; del. Nat. Citizenship Council, 1954. Recipient Home Econs. Scholarship award Borden Co., 1953, Panhellenic award Lubbock (Tex.) Panhellenic Soc., 1953; Forum award Tex. Tech. U., 1953. Mem. AAUW (reporter, historian, sec., parliamentarian 1956-68), Sch. Library and Info. Sci. Assn., NEA, Am. Home Econs. Assn., Am. Vocat. Assn., PTA, Tex. State Tchrs. Assn. (life), ALA, Tex. Library Assn. (life; sec. dist. 9), Tex. Classroom Tchrs. Assn., Vocat. Homemaking Tchrs. Assn. Tex., Tex. Home Econs. Assn., Lamb County Tchrs. Assn. (treas.), Littlefield Classroom Tchrs. Assn. (treas.), Phi Kappa Phi, Phi Upsilon Omicron, Alpha Lambda Delta, Alpha Chi, Alpha Lambda Sigma, Beta Phi Mu, Delta Kappa Gamma (sec., charter mem. Iota Eta chpt., 2d v.p. 1987—). Democrat. Baptist. Home: 510 E 6th St Littlefield TX 79339 Office: 1100 W 10th St Littlefield TX 79339

MASSEY, DORIS EUNICE, real estate executive; b. New Smyrna, Fla., Dec. 1, 1930; d. George Charles and Dora V. (Waters) Burch; m. John Max Massey, Dec. 12, 1956 (dec. Mar. 1976); children: Dale Max, Dorian Max. Cert., Warlow Real Estate Inst., 1957, 59, Extension Course Inst., 1967, 70, Daytona Beach (Fla.) Community Coll., 1974, 82. Teller, acting sec.-treas. First Fed. Savs. & Loan Assn., New Smyrna Beach, 1948-57; real estate salesperson Edgewater, Fla., 1957-58; owner Edgewater Loan Service, 1957-70; sec. pub. works dept. City of New Smyrna Beach, 1972-77; owner, mgr. Massey Ranch Airpark, New Smyrna Beach, 1950—; mng. ptnr. Massey Enterprises, Edgewater, 1981—; broker-owner Doris E. Massey Real Estate, Edgewater, 1959—; chmn. indsl. devel. bd. City of Edgewater, 1979-86; dir., sec. Cert. Devel. Corp. of S.E. Volusia, New Smyrna, 1983;. Mem. Volusia Coastal Area Met. Planning Orgn. Citizens Adv. Com., 1988—, Volusia County Assn. for Responsible Devel. Named Woman of Yr., Am. Bus. Women, 1976, 87. Mem. Am. Bus. Women (recording sec. 1987-88), New Smyrna Beach Bd. of Realtors (bd. sec. 1988), New Smyrna Beach C. of C. (bd. dirs. 1979-80, 87—, chmn. econ. devel. com. 1983-85, chmn. transp. com. 1987-88). Methodist. Club: Oceanside Women's. Office: 400-402 N Ridgewood Ave Edgewater FL 32032

MASSEY, DOROTHY BUTLER (MRS. GUY M. MASSEY), accountant; b. LaFayette, Ga.; d. R. Maihue and Cora (Sisemore) Butler; student U. Chattanooga, 1949; LL.B., Atlanta Law Sch., 1957, LL.M., 1958; B.B.A., Ga. State Coll., 1966; m. Guy M. Massey, Feb. 21, 1953. Accountant Gulf Oil Corp., Chattanooga, 1944-53, Crawford and Porter, Atlanta, 1953-54; accountant Baker Audio Assos., 1955-70, sec.-treas., 1955-70, also dir.; accountant Glenkaron Assos., Inc., 1955-68, sec.-treas., 1957-68; pres. Massey Co., 1971—, also dir.; pres. Profl. Credit Bur., Inc., 1977—; real estate agt. Shotz Assos. Mem. Am. Soc. Women Accountants (dir.), Ga. Soc. C.P.A.'s, Notaries Pub. Assn., Bus. and Profl. Women, Kappa Delta. Home: 1534 Peachtree Battle Ave NW Atlanta GA 30327

MASSEY, ELEANOR NELSON, school librarian, media specialist; b. Providence, Apr. 1, 1930; d. Walter K. and Jeanette (Perlman) Nelson; m. Marvin Donald Massey, June 29, 1952; children—Henry, David, Michael, Jonathan. B.A., Douglass Coll., New Brunswick, N.J., 1952; postgrad. Rutgers U. Cert. ednl. media specialist. Children's librarian Westfield (N.J.) Pub. Library, 1952-55; librarian Franklin Jr. High Sch., Metuchen, N.J., 1959-61; media specialist Campbell Sch., Metuchen, 1962—; coordinator libraries Metuchen Pub. Schs., 1982—; dir. Woodbridge-East Brunswick Area Coordination Council, 1982-85; mem. interim planning com. N.J. Library Network, 1984-85; cooperating tchr. Kean Coll. and Rutgers U., 1975—; speaker; bibliographer. Author Vice pres. Sisterhood Neve Shalom, Metuchen, 1960; dir. Neve Shalom, 1959-60; bd. dirs. Union-Middlesex Regional Library Cooperative, Region IV, Inc., 1985—. Title II Demonstration Library grantee State of N.J., 1974-76. Mem. Ednl. Media Assn. N.J. (exec. bd. 1976-78), ALA, N.J., Library Assn., Ednl. Media Assn. Middlesex County (treas. 1982-83). Office: Campbell Sch Talmadge Ave Metuchen NJ 08840

MASSEY, PEGGY YVONNE, lawyer; b. Rock Hill, S.C., May 4, 1951; d. Nelson and Nannie (Lytle) Massey. B.S. in Polit. Sci. and English, Xavier U., 1973; J.D., Boston Coll., 1977. Bar: S.C., D.C. Instr. research and writing Council Legal Ednl. Opportunities Program, N.C. Central U. Sch. Law, Durham, summer 1977; instr. bus. dept. Central Piedmont Community Coll., Charlotte, N.C., spring 1977; atty. Palmetto Legal Services, Columbia, S.C., 1977-79; atty.-adviser U.S. Commn. Civil Rights, Washington, 1979-86, D.C. Dept. Human Services, 1987—. Co-author reports on legal system in area of domestic violence. Reginald Heber Smith fellow, 1977. Mem. S.C. Bar Assn., Nat. Conf. Black Lawyers, Washington Bar Assn., Xavier U. Alumni Assn. Democrat. Roman Catholic. Office: DC Dept Human Services 801 N Capitol St NE Washington DC 20002

MASSY, PATRICIA GRAHAM BIBBS (MRS. RICHARD OUTRAM MASSY), social worker, author; b. Newbury, Eng., Mar. 21, 1918; came to U.S., 1963, naturalized, 1969; d. Oswald Graham and Dorothy (French) Bibbs; m. Richard Outram Massy, July 22, 1944 (dec. Aug. 1986); children: Patricia Lynn Massy Holmes, Julie Suzanne, Shaun Adele Massy Brink. BA, U. B.C., 1941, MSW, 1962. With B.C. Welfare Field Service, Vancouver, Kamloops, Abbottsford, 1942-44; social worker Brandon Welfare Dept., Man., Can., 1945; with Children's Aid Soc., Vancouver, 1948-62; supr. Dept. Pub. Social Service, Los Angeles, 1963-70, staff devel. specialist-mgmt., 1970-77; lectr. colls. and seminars; author, publisher: A Study Guide for a Course in Miracles, 1984; One, 1985. Mem. AAUW (treas. 1970), Nat. Assn. Social Workers, Alpha Phi. Mem. Religious Sci. Ch. Home: 18936 Upper Cow Creek Rd Azalea OR 97410

MASTAGLIO, LINDA RUTH, public relations executive; b. Grand Rapids, Mich., Jan. 26, 1954; d. Joseph Young and Ruth Alice (Bush) Donald; m. Michael Carl Mastaglio, Aug. 16, 1973 (div. Mar. 1979); 1 child, Matthew. Student, Alma Coll., 1973-74, Western Mich. U., 1974-78, Kendall Sch. Design, 1980. Coordinator research Starr Commonwealth, Albion, Mich., 1977-78; dir. mktg. Square Real Estate, Grand Rapids, Mich., 1978-81; owner P.R. Firm, Grand Rapids, 1981-83; dir. mktg. services Daveman, Grand Rapids, 1983-86; dir. corp. communications Greiner Engring., Irving, Tex., 1986—. Editor: Am. Legion Regional newsletter, Grand Rapids, 1976; contbr. articles to profl. jours. Bd. dirs. Climbing Tree Alternative Sch., Grand Rapids, 1984-85. Mem. Internat. Assn. Bus. Communicators, Nat. Assn. Female Execs., Grand Rapids C. of C. (pub. relations com. 1979-86, program com. 1984—), Mich. C. of C., Irving C. of C. Office: Greiner Engring Inc 300 E Carpenter Freeway Ste 1210 Irving TX 75062-2726

MASTER, LORI ELIZABETH, financial analyst; b. Camden, N.J., Apr. 30, 1962; d. Alan Harold and Barbara (Berezow) M. BA in Speech Communication and Internat. Politics, Pa. State U., 1984; postgrad., Fordham U., 1988—. Floor mgr. Lord and Taylor, N.Y.C., 1984-85; group coordinator Radio Page Am., N.Y.C., 1985-86; program coordinator Private Satellite Network, N.Y.C., 1986; cons. Goshow Assocs., N.Y.C., 1986—; portfolio asst. Equitable Capital Mgmt. Corp., N.Y.C., 1987-88, asst. stat. research, 1988—. City chmn. Pa. State Alumni Admissions Com., N.Y.C., 1986—. Mem. Nat. Assn. Female Execs., Alpha Phi Omega, Beta Sigma Beta. Republican. Jewish. Club: Pa. State of N.Y.C. Home: 325 E 54th St Apt 4D New York NY 10022 Office: Equitable Capital Mgmt Corp 1221 Ave of the Americas Floor 32 New York NY 10020

MASTERS, ELAINE THERESE, audio-video business owner; b. Columbia, S.C., Sept. 8, 1951; d. Edward John and Emilie Therese (Nawrocki) M. AA in Psychology, Morris County Coll., 1971; BS in Bus. Mgmt., Union for Experimenting Colls. and Univs., 1988. Fin. asst. J.J. Newberry and Co., Dover, N.J., 1966-69; dept. rep. Dept. Drug Abuse Morris County, Morristown, N.J., 1970-71; asst. to head ednl. psychology dept. Ariz. State U., Tempe, 1971; supr. quality control Gen. Semiconductor, Tempe, 1972; mgr. personnel Los Compadres Restaurant, San Diego, 1973-80; office mgr. W.C. Matz Inc., Escondido, Calif., 1980-82; exec. asst. to pres. Gold Medal Pools Inc., Escondido, 1982-86; co-owner, mgr. Masters Video, San Diego, 1987-88; spl. projects coordinator Constrn. Specifications Inst., 1988—; adminstrv. asst. Union for Experimenting Colls. and Univs., San Diego, 1988; coordinator spl. projects San Diego Constrn. Specifications Inst., author, originator Fair Procedures Manual. Mem. Zool. Soc. San Diego, 1980, Greenpeace, Washington, 1982, Cousteau Soc., Norfolk, Va., 1985, Amnesty Internat., N.Y.C., 1986. Recipient Record of Performance cert. San Diego County, 1983. Mem. Nat. Assn. Women Constrn. (cert.), Nat. Assn. Female Execs. Republican. Roman Catholic. Office: Masters Video 10491 Glenellen Ave San Diego CA 92126

MASTERS, PATSY K., health services facility administrator; b. Indpls., Aug. 11, 1941; d. Wayne Clinton and Freida Violet (Sever) Barber; m. Kelly R. Masters Jr., Feb. 28, 1965; 1 child, Valerie Jean. BBA, Pacific Western U., 1983; MHA, Columbia Pacific U., 1986, D in Health Services Adminstrn., 1987. Lic. nursing home adminstr. Document control coordinator Gen. Precision Systems, Inc., Glendale, Calif., 1965-67; exec. sec. Marine Acoustical Services, Miami, Fla., 1967-68; lectr. Internat. Lectrs., Inc., Independence, Mo., 1968-69; sec. to pres. Quipco Assocs., Hialeah, Fla., 1969-71; asst. v.p., loan officer Chaves County Savs. & Loan Assn., Roswell, N.Mex., 1971-78; v.p., branch mgr. Sandia Savs. & Loan Assn., Roswell, 1978-80; adminstrv. asst. N.Mex. Rehab. Ctr., Roswell, 1981-83, assoc. exec. dir., 1983—. Author: manual for bldg. and operating a small community skilled nursing facility. Active Legis. Forum Roswell Area Com. Employment of the Handicapped, 1984-87, Roswell Indsl. Air Ctr. Assn., 1985-86. Recipient Exemplary Performance award Dept. Edn. div. Vocat. Rehab., 1982. Mem. Assn. Western Hosps., Nat. Assn. Female Execs. Home: PO Box 514 Roswell NM 88202 Office: N Mex Rehab Ctr 31 Gail Harris Ave RIAC Roswell NM 88201

MASTERSON, PATRICIA O'MALLEY, publications editor, writer; b. Worcester, Mass., May 15, 1952; d. Paul Francis and Dorothy M. (O'Malley) M. BFA, Emerson Coll., 1974; MA, Goddard Coll., 1980. Reporter, photographer Patriot Newspaper, Webster, Mass., 1975-78; pub. relations dir. Mt. Pleasant Hosp., Lynn, Mass., 1980-84; pubs. editor Ocean Spray Cranberries, Inc., Plymouth, Mass., 1984—; Freelance writer newspaper, mag. articles, 1974—. Contbr. numerous articles to newspapers, mags. Bd. dirs., Cambridge (Mass.) YWCA; publicity com., United Way, 1987, Healthworks; player Abington, Weymouth Mass., Softball Leagues. Recipient Amy England award YWCA, 1986, numerous writing awards; named One of Outstanding Young Women in Am. Jaycees, 1983. Mem. South Shore Ad Club (publicity com. mem.), Women in Communications, Inc., Cooperative Communicators Assn. Home: 132 Union St Rockland MA 02370 Office: Ocean Spray Cranberries Inc 225 Water St Plymouth MA 02360

MASTERSON, PEGGY BELL, advertising executive; b. N.Y.C., Mar. 25, 1943; d. Richard Francis and Frances Dolores (Manning) Bell; grad. cum laude Dominican Coll. of Blauvelt, 1964; m. Patrick Masterson, May 20, 1972. Tchr. jr. high sch. history and art, 1965-69; copywriter Foote, Cone and Belding, 1969-74; with Ted Bates Advt., N.Y.C., 1974-75, creative supr., 1975-76, v.p., 1976-79, sr. v.p., creative dir., 1979-81; sr. v.p., creative dir. Benton & Bowles Advt., N.Y.C., 1981—; tchr. copywriting Tobe Coburn Sch., N.Y.C. Winner copywriting awards. Mem. Nat. Assn. Female Execs., Am. Soc. Profl. and Exec. Women. Office: D'Arcy Masius Benton & Bowles 909 3d Ave New York NY 10022

MASTROBERTE, VIOLET MARIE, nursing administrator; b. Englewood, N.J., Jan. 26, 1932; d. Dominick John and Alsista Viola (Krone) M. BS in Nursing, Fairleigh Dickinson U., 1961, MS in Pub. Adminstrn., 1983; postgrad., N.Y.U., 1979. RN, N.J., N.Y. Various positions Columbia Presby. Med. Ctr., N.Y.C., 1954-71, assoc. dir. nursing, 1971-84, coordinator nursing systems, instr., 1974-79; staff builder supplemental agys., Hackensack and Paramus, N.J., 1979-80; asst. dir. nursing Bergen Pines County Hosp., Paramus, 1980-86, assoc. dir. nursing, 1987-88, interim asst. exec. dir. nursing, 1988, also bd. dirs.; adj. instr. Grad. Sch. Nursing Seaton Hall U. Mem. Am. Nurses Assn., Am. Soc. Profl. Adminstrs., Internat. Personnel Mgmt. Assn., Nat. Assn. Female Execs., Soc. Nursing Profls., N.Y. Acad. Scis., N.J. Profl. Women Inc., Sigma Theta Tau, Phi Alpha Alpha. Home: 43 Brook St Bergenfield NJ 07621 Office: Bergen Pines County Hosp East Ridge Paramus NJ 07662

MASTROCOLA, KATHERINE, educational and health care administrator; b. East McKeesport, Pa., Sept. 12, 1929; d. Charles and Nichol (DiCecco) M. BS, U. Pitts., 1951, MPH, 1970, PhD, 1985. Dir. placement services Point Park Coll., Pitts., 1963-67; staff adminstr. St. Francis Gen. Hosp., Pitts., 1969-72, McKeesport (Pa.) Hosp., 1973-75; staff student personnel services U. Pitts., 1985—; program coordinator, sec.-council grad. students in edn., Pitts., 1983; dir. vols. McKeesport Hosp., 1973-75. Provost Research scholar, 1979; U. Pitts. research grantee, 1985. Office: U Pitts Office Student Personnel Services 5L03 Forbes Quadrangle Pittsburgh PA 15260

MASUCCI, MADELINE ELIZABETH, marketing professional; b. Newton, Mass., Apr. 12, 1958; d. Arthur L. and Madeline A. (Jackson) M. BS, Northeastern U., Boston, 1982. Mem. pub. relations staff Arandel Pub. co., Newton and Wellesley, Mass., 1976-77; with Martin Sales Assocs., Framingham, Mass., 1977-82, head retail force and competetive analysis, 1980-82; v.p., treas. Golden Mile Sales Assocs., Framingham, 1982—. Mem. Nat. Assn. Female Execs., Nat. Assn. Gen. Mdse. Reps., Health and Beauty Aids Club New Eng. Roman Catholic. Office: Golden Mile Sales Assn Inc 225 Worcester Rd Framingham MA 01701

MASZDZEN, BEVERLY JOAN, speech pathologist; b. Schenectady, N.Y., Aug. 13, 1956; d. William Anthony and Joan Mary (Kott) M. AA, Schenectady County Community Coll., 1976; BS in Speech Pathology magna cum laude, Coll. of St. Rose, 1979, MS in Edn., 1981. Lic. speech pathologist, N.Y. Pub. relations rep. Clover Patch Ctr., Schenectady, 1974; pub. relations rep. asst. Schenectady County Community Coll., Schenectady, 1975; petroleum rationing case rev. officer N.Y. State Dept. Energy, Albany, N.Y., 1979-80; speech pathologist United Cerebral Palsy Assn., Albany, 1981—; cons. in microtech. Ctr. for Disabled, Albany, 1986—, asst. tech. coordinator, 1987—. Mem. cultural and community events com. Schenectady County Community Coll., 1975. Mem. Capital Area Speech and Hearing Assn. Home: 5 Crown Terr Albany NY 12209 Office: United Cerebral Palsy Assn 314 S Manning Blvd Albany NY 12208

MATA, ZOILA, chemist; b. Galveston, Tex., Aug. 8, 1837; d. Francisco Zuniga and Leonarda (Sustaita) M. BS in Biology, Chemistry, Tex. A&I U., 1975. Office asst. Galveston Pub. Health Nursing Service, 1959-63; draftswoman Wilson Real Estate Index and Pub, Houston, 1964-65; bookkeeper City Products Corp, Galveston, 1966-67; research asst. U. Tex. Med. Br., Galveston, 1967-70; clk. State Dept. Pub. Welfare, Houston, 1971-72, Quinby Temporary, Houston, 1972-76; research technician Baylor Coll. Medicine, Houston, 1976; sr. chemist Nalco Chemical Co., Sugarland, Tex., 1976—. Mem. Rep. Nat. Hispanic Assembly of Tex. (chair membership credentials 1986—), Rep. Nat. Hispanic Assembly of Harris (vice chair 1986). Named one of Notable Woman of Tex., 1984-85. Mem. Am. Chem. Soc. (rubber div.), Amigas de las Americas, Nat. Chicano Health Orgn. Home: 5980 Laurel Ln #2221 Willowbrook IL 60514 Office: Nalco Chemical Co 6216 W 66th Pl Chicago IL 60638

MATALAMAKI, MARGARET MARIE, educator, consultant; b. Hampton, Iowa, May 10, 1921; d. Byron Jacob and Vera Margaret (Wheaton) Myers; m. William Matalamaki, Sept. 11, 1942 (dec. 1978); children—Judith Marie Gerlinger-Thiem, William Micheal. A.A., Itasca Community Coll., 1941; student U. Minn., 1941-42, 72. High sch. instr. Sch. Dist. 1, Bigfork, Minn., 1942-45, U. Minn. Sch. Agr., Grand Rapids, Minn., 1955-58; high sch. substitute Sch. Dist. 318, Grand Rapids, 1967-69; vocat. instr. Itasca Community Coll., Grand Rapids, 1970-78. bd. dirs. Blandin Found., Grand Rapids, trustee, 1981—, v.p., 1985-87, chmn. 1988—; bd. dirs. Christus Home, Grand Rapids; cons. to Keewatin Community Devel. Corp., Grand Rapids, 1985; mem. consumer adv. bd. Land of Lakes Inc., St. Paul, 1984-87, chmn. 1986-87; pres. Kooch-Itasca Action Council, Grand Rapids, 1981-84; adv. council mem. Women's Econ. Devel. Corp., Mpls., 1984-87; bd. dirs. Itasca Meml. Hosp., 1975-85, Itasca County Nursing Home, 1975-85, No. Itasca Nursing Home, 1982-85, Itasca County Social Services, 1975-85; county commr. Itasca County, 1981-85; legis. coordinator Luth. Ch. Am., 1983-86, staff, advocacy coordinator Minn. Synod, 1983-86; mem. adv. council Inst. Agr., Forestry and Home Econ. U. Minn., 1981—; 4-H club leader, Esko, Minn., 1945-49, Grand Rapids, Minn., 1949-63; home extension leader, Esko, 1945-49, Grand Rapids, 1949-63; county fair judge No. Minn., 1950-84; bd. dirs. United Way Grand Rapids, 1980-84; mem. Grand Rapids Citizen's League, 1980—, Minn. Women for Agr., 1982—, Joint Religious Legis. Coalition, Mpls., 1977-78, U. Minn. Nat. Alumni bd. dirs., 1987—, U. Minn. 4H Found. bd. dirs., 1987—, U. Minn. North Cen., Research Station Found./Fund, 1987— ; bd. dirs. Luth. Social Serives Minn., 1986—, vice chair, mem. adv. bd. Luth. Social Services North Eastern Minn., 1986-87 ; mem. Minn. Child Abuse Team, 1986-87; pres. Luth. Ch. Women, 1959-62, Luth. Ch. Women Synodical Bd., 1972-76, dist. chmn., 1964-65; com. mem. Commn. for a New Luth. Ch., 1985, chmn. transition team, 1986-87 , mem. exec. com. Synod Council, 1976-79; trustee Gustavus Adolphus Coll. Bd., 1988—. Recipient Good Govt. award Grand Rapids Jr. C. of C., 1977, Good Neighbor award WCCO Radio, 1976. Mem. Grand Rapids C. of C. (life). Mem. LWV. Club: PEO (pres., sec. 1964—). Avocations: cross country skiing, canoing, traveling. Home and Office: 5734 Sunny Beach Rd Grand Rapids MN 55744

MATARAZZO, IRENE RAUCH, personnel specialist; b. Neptune, N.J., Oct. 10, 1958; d. Karl Alfred and Maxine Ann (Tark) Rauch; m. Eugene Paul Matarazzo, Oct. 5, 1985. BA in Human Communications, Rutgers U., 1981; postgrad., Fairleigh Dickinson U. Cert. in gen. insurance, Ins. Inst. of Am. With personnel/tng. dept. Six Flags Inc., Jackson, N.J., 1979-81; claims rep. Crum & Forster Ins. Co., Parsippany, N.J., 1981-84; adminstrv. supr. Crume, Forster Ins., Parsippany, N.J., 1985-86; tng. specialist Basking Ridge, N.J., 1986—; mgr. Pillsbury Co., Alexandria, Va., 1984-85. Mem. Nat. Assn. Female Execs., Nat. Assn. Ins. Women, Soc. Ins. Trainers and Educators. Office: Crum & Forster Ins Co 211 Mt Airy Rd Basking Ridge NJ 07920

MATASOVIC, MARILYN ESTELLE, business executive; b. Chgo., Jan. 7, 1946; d. John Lewis and Stella (Butkauskas) M. Student, U. Colo. Sch. Bus., 1963-69. Owner, pres. UTE Trail Ranch, Ridgway, Colo., 1967—; pres. MEM Equipment Co., Mokena, Ill., 1979—; v.p., treas. Marilin Corp., Ridgway, 1968—, Linmar Corp., Mokena, 1976—; ptnr. Universal Welding Supply Co., New Lenox, Ill., 1964—; v.p. OXO Welding Equipment Co, Inc., New Lenox, 1964—. Co-editor newsletters. U.S. rep. World Hereford Conf., 1964, 68, 76, 80, 84. Mem. Am. Hereford Aux. (charter), Am. Hereford Assn., Colo. Hereford Assn., Ill. Hereford Aux. (v.p. 1969-70), Internat. Hereford Orgn., U. Colo. Alumni Assn.

MATCHETTE, PHYLLIS LEE, editor; b. Dodge City, Kans., Dec. 24, 1921; d. James Edward and Rose Mae (McMillan) Collier; A.B. in Journalism, U. Kans., 1943; m. Robert Clarke Matchette, Dec. 4, 1943; children: Marta Susan, James Michael. Reporter, Dodge City Daily Globe, 1944; tchr. English, Dodge City Jr. High Sch., 1944-45; asst. instr. Coll. Liberal Arts, U. Kans., Lawrence, 1945-47; dir. Christian edn. Southminster United Presbyn. Ch., Prairie Village, Kans., 1963-65; editor publs., dir. communications, supr. in-plant printing Village United Presbyn. Ch., Prairie Village, 1965-86 ; freelance journalist, 1987—. Hon. mem. Commn. of Ecumenical Mission and Relations, hon. mem. Program Agy., Presbyn. Ch., U.S.A.; ordained elder Village Presbyn. Ch., 1964, elected elder, 1988—. Mem. Women in Communications, Kans. U. Dames (pres. 1946), Kansas City Young Matrons, P.E.O., Alpha Chi Omega (pres. edn. found. Phi chpt. 1951). Republican. Club: Order of Eastern Star. Home: 7405 El Monte Rd Prairie Village KS 66208

MATECHAK-BLACK, TESSIE, nursing administrator, educator; b. Peckville, Pa., Mar. 19, 1926; d. Wasil and Anna (Horbal) Matechak; A.A. (scholarship), Keystone Jr. Coll., 1947; diploma nursing (scholarship) Sinai Hosp., Md., 1953; B.S. in Nursing, Johns Hopkins U., 1962; M.S. in Nursing, U. Md., 1970; m. James Franklin Black, Jan. 27, 1974. Staff nurse Sinai Hosp., Balt., 1953-54, instr. med.-surg. nursing, 1959-67, asst. dir. inservice edn., 1967-70; head nurse Johns Hopkins Hosp., Balt., 1954-59, asst. instr. emergency service, 1956-56; asso. dir. patient care services Balt. City Hosp., 1970-71; dir. nursing services Bon Secours Hosp., Balt., 1971-73; asso. prof. nursing U. Md., Balt., 1971-73; dir. nursing service Taylor Manor Hosp., Ellicott City, Md., 1974-75; asso. dir. nursing service King Faisal Specialist Hosp., Saudia Arabia, 1975, asst. adminstr. nursing, 1975-77; med. surg. clin. specialist Md. Gen. Hosp., Balt., 1977; asst. dir. nursing service Balt. City Hosps., 1978-79, dir. nursing services, 1981—; asst. prof. nursing Community Coll., Balt., 1981—, asst. chmn. nursing dept., 1985—; cons. Nurses' Med. Deck, 1988—. Sec., VFW Ladies Aux., 1947-48; fund raiser Jewish Charities, 1970-74. Recognition award King Faisal Hosp., 1977. Mem. Am. Nurses Assn., Md. Nurses Assn. (pres. dist. 2 1978-82), Cancer Soc. Md., Am. Bus. Women's Profl. Orgn., Johns Hopkins U. Alumni Assn., Sinai Nurses Alumni (pres. 1973-75), Keystone Jr. Coll. Alumni. Democrat. Greek Catholic. Home: 3619 Lochearn Dr Baltimore MD 21207 Office: Community Coll Balt Baltimore MD 21215

MATERIA, KATHLEEN PATRICIA AYLING, nurse; b. Jersey City, Nov. 7, 1954; d. Donald Anthony and Muriel Cecilia (Joyce) Ayling; m. Francis Peter Materia, June 5, 1983. B.S. in Nursing, Fairleigh Dickinson U., 1976. R.N., N.J. Critical care nurse Palisades Gen. Hosp., North Bergen, N.J., 1976—, grad. nurse, 1976-77; nurse CCU, North Hudson Hosp., Weehawken, N.J., 1977-78. Mem. Alpha Sigma Tau. Democrat. Roman Catholic. Avocations: bowling; dancing.

MATESE, ANGELINA MARIE, service executive, account executive; b. Camden, N.J., June 13, 1960; d. Thomas Henry Sr. and Pauline Marie (Terzian) M. Student, U. Friburg, Switzerland, 1981; BA, La Salle U., Phila., 1982. Internat. receptionist City of Phila., 1979-82; salesperson La Salle U. bookstore, 1978-82; corp. reservations agt. Rosenbluth Travel, Phila., 1982-83, account exec., 1983-85, sr. account exec., 1985-87, account mgr., 1987—. Roman Catholic. Office: Rosenbluth Travel 310 Grant St Suite 530 Pittsburgh PA 15219

MATHENY, MARY JANE, lawyer; b. Wauchula, Fla., May 29, 1953; d. George W. and Anna Lee (Scarborough) Marsh; m. Charles W. Matheny III, Mar. 30, 1974. BA, Fla. State U., 1974, JD with honors, 1978. Personnel aide Office of Gov. State of Fla., Tallahassee, 1974-75; sole practice Sebring, Fla., 1978—; travel agt. Ridge Travel Agy., Sebring, 1985—. Named Outstanding Young Woman of Am., 1980-81. Mem. Fla. Bar Assn. (vice chmn. travel com. 1986-87), Highlands County Bar Assn. (pres. 1983-84), Fla. Fedn. Bus. and Profl. Women (dist. dir. 1985-86, state resolutions chmn. 1986-87), Young Career Woman 1979), Phi Delta Phi. Republican. Baptist. Club: Sebring Bus. and Profl. Women's.

MATHER, SUSAN HOWARD, physician; b. Salisbury, Md., Feb. 6, 1940; d. Dalton Bailey and Jenny Louise (Whaley) Howard; B.S. with honors, U. Md., 1961, M.D., 1965; M.P.H., Johns Hopkins U., 1978; m. John H. Mather, June 17, 1967; children—Stephen, Alexandra. Instr. ambulatory medicine/student health physician U. Md., 1971-75; dir. adult health and epidemiology Prince George's County, Md., 1975-79; program chief pulmonary and infectious diseases VA, Washington, 1979-87; dir. VA AIDS Program Office, Washington, 1987—. Pres. Am. Lung Assn. Md., 1978-80, Am. Lung Assn. So. Md., 1980-82. Mem. Am. Pub. Health Assn., Am. Thoracic Soc. Presbyterian. Home: 12144 Long Ridge Ln Bowie MD 20715 Office: VACO 810 Vermont Ave Washington DC 20420

MATHERS, MARGARET, charitable agency administrator, consultant; b. Ada, Okla., Feb. 16, 1929; d. Robert Lee and Josephine Margaret (Reed) Erwin; m. Coleman F. Moss, Sept. 1956 (div. 1966); children—Carol Lee Doria, Marilyn Frances; m. Boyd Leroy Mathers, Apr. 10, 1967. B.S. in Music, Tex. U., 1950. Service rep. Gen. Telephone Co., Santa Monica, Calif., 1955-58; tchr. pvt. sch., Santa Monica, 1958-60; computer program and data analyst System Devel. Corp., Santa Monica, 1961-66; computer programmer Inst. Def. Analyses, Arlington, Va., 1966-70; typist, transcriber, Edgewater, Md., 1971-80; dir. San Juan Catholic Charities, Farmington N.Mex., 1984—; pres. San Juan Council Community Agys., 1986-87, treas., 1987—; pres. Davidsonville-Mayo Health Assn., Edgewater, 1973-76, 77-80; cons. in field, 1983—. Chmn. county libertarian Party of N.Mex., San Juan County, 1985; asst. sec. Our Lady of Perpetual Health, Parish Council, Edgewater, 1979-82, Parish Council Sacred Heart, Farmington, 1987—; sec. River Club Community Assn., Edgewater, 1975-82. Roman Catholic. Avocations: nature study; birdwatching; reading; music. Office: San Juan Cath Charities 119 W Broadway Farmington NM 87401

MATHES, ANITA SUE, 120; b. Port Lyautey, Morocco, Aug. 19, 1955. Grad. high sch., Spotsylvania, Va. Quality control Stone & Webster Engring. Corp., Boston, 1975-76, technician fed. quality control, 1976-77, data reviewer quality control, 1977-78, insp. quality control, 1978-79, insp. II quality control, 1979-80, data supr. quality Control, 1980, sr. insp. quality control, 1980-82, engr. quality control, 1982-84, sr. engr. quality control, 1984—. Mem. Kappa Delta. Clubs: Thespian (Spotsylvania); PADI (Ft. Worth). Home: 6355 Ridge Crest Trail #1512 Fort Worth TX 76132

MATHESON, LINDA, clinical social worker; b. Martna, Estonia, Dec. 29, 1918; came to U.S., 1962, naturalized, 1969; d. Endrek and Leena Endrekson; Diploma, Inst. for Social Scis., Tallinn, Estonia, 1944; M.S., Columbia U., 1966, Diplomate Clin. Social Work; m. Charles McLaren Matheson, Feb. 5, 1955. Social work officer UN Rehab. and Resettlement Assn., Germany, 1946-48; social worker Victorian Mental Hygiene, Australia, 1955-62; research assoc., social work project dir. Arthritis Midway Ho., N.Y.C., 1966-68; researcher Columbia Presbyn. Med. Center, N.Y.C., 1971-75, now social worker; field instr. Columbia U. Sch. Social Work, 1977-79. Family Found. fellow, 1966; NIMH grantee, 1969-72. Mem. Nat. Assn. Social Workers, Am. Security Council, Nat. Wildlife Fedn., Center for Study of Presidency, Smithsonian Assn., English Speaking Union, Alliance Francaise, Columbia U. Alumni Assn., Internat. Platform Assn., Nat. Trust Historic Preservation, Met. Mus. of N.Y. Lutheran. Home: 30-95 29th St Astoria NY 11102

MATHESON, SALLY JANE, marketing professional; b. Newton, Iowa, Apr. 2, 1962; d. Robert Russell and Joan Marie (Van Gronigan) M. BBA, Iowa State U., 1984. Mktg. asst. The Maytag Co., Newton, Iowa and Marlton, N.J., 1984-85; regional rep. The Maytag Co., Charlottesville, Va., 1985-86; regional rep. The Maytag Co., Frederick, Md., 1986-88, regional mgr., 1988—. Mem. Nat. Assn. Female Execs., Iowa State U. Alumni Assn., Pi Sigma Epsilon, Kappa Kappa Gamma (chair membership 1982-83). Democrat. Roman Catholic. Home: 5806 G Shadbush Ct Frederick MD 21701

MATHEWS, BARBARA EDITH, gynecologist; b. Santa Barbara, Calif., Oct. 5, 1946; d. Joseph Chesley and Pearl (Cieri) Mathews; A.B., U. Calif., 1969; M.D., Tufts U., 1972. Intern, Cottage Hosp., Santa Barbara, 1972-73, Santa Barbara Gen. Hosp., 1972-73; resident in ob-gyn Beth Israel Hosp., Boston, 1973-77; clin. fellow in ob-gyn Harvard U., 1973-76, instr., 1976-77, gynecologist Sansum Med. Clinic, Santa Barbara, 1977—. Bd. dirs. Meml. Rehab. Found., Santa Barbara, Channel City Women's Forum, Santa Barbara, Music Acad. of West, Santa Barbara; mem. citizen's continuing edn. adv. council Santa Barbara Community Coll. Diplomate Am. Bd. Ob-Gyn. Fellow ACS, Am. Coll. Obstetricians and Gynecologists; mem. AMA, Am. Soc. Colposcopy and Cervical Pathology (dir. 1982-84), Harvard U. Alumni Assn., Tri-counties Obstet. and Gynecol. Soc. (pres. 1981-82), Phi Beta Kappa. Clubs: Birnam Wood Golf (Santa Barbara). Author: (with L. Burke) Colposcopy in Clinical Practice, 1977; contbg. author Manual of Ambulatory Surgery, 1982. Home: 2105 Anacapa St Santa Barbara CA 93105 Office: 317 W Pueblo St Santa Barbara CA 93102

MATHEWS, JEAN ANN H., state legislator; b. Ogden, Utah, Oct. 17, 1941; d. Walter H. and Connie Laverne (Jorgenson) Holbrook; m. John Phillip Mathews, Sept. 8, 1960; children—Michael, Mark, Nanette. Student, Weber Coll., Ogden, Utah, 1959-61; A.A., Florissant Community Coll., 1973; BS in Edn. magna cum laude, U. Mo.-St. Louis, 1980; MPA, U. Mo.-Columbia, 1988. Cert. tchr., Mo. Tchr., Mathews Vocal Studio, Florissant, 1964-80; profl. sales evaluator Edison Bros., Inc., St. Louis, 1971-73; mem. Mo. Ho. of Reps., 1981—. Author: Letting Go Is the Hardest, 1972; Repeat Drunken Driver Slips Through the System, 1982. Vice chmn. Florissant Bd. Appeals, 1976-80; committeewoman Florissant Twp., 1979—; sec. Mo. State Republican Party, Jefferson City, 1982—; mem. Gov.'s Commn. on Crime, 1984—. Recipient Golden Gleaner award Ch. Jesus Christ Latter-day Saints, 1969; Rookie Legislator of Yr. award Capitol City Press Corp., Jefferson City, 1981; Eagle award Eagle Forum, 1982; Americanism award VFW, 1983; YWCA Women in Govt. award, 1988; inducted Alumni Hall of Fame, St. Louid Community Coll., Florissant Valley, 1987; named one of Outstanding Young Women of Am., 1974. Mem. Nat. Order Women Legislators, Am. Legis. Exchange Council (state chmn., Outstanding State Legislator 1984), Nat. Fedn. Republican Women, Kappa Delta Pi. Club: Rep. Women North St. Louis County (pres. 1978-82).

MATHEWS, MARY KATHRYN, federal agency administrator; b. Washington, Apr. 20, 1948; d. T. Odon and Kathryn (Augustine) M. Student, Pa. State U., 1966-68; BBA, Am. U., 1970, MBA, 1975. Personnel mgmt. specialist, coordinator coll. recruitment program, GSA, Washington, 1971-75, adminstrv. officer, 1975-78; personnel mgmt. specialist Office of Personnel Mgmt., Washington, 1978; employee devel. specialist Office Sec. Transp., Washington, 1978-80, dep. chief departmental services and spl. programs div., 1980-81; asst. dir. adminstrv. div. Farm Credit Adminstrn., Washington, 1981-84; dir. adminstrv. div. Farm Credit Adminstrn., McLean, Va., 1984-86; chief adminstrv. services div. Farm Credit Adminstrn., McLean, 1987-88; dep. staff dir. Commn. on Civil Rights, Washington, 1988—; chief spl. programs staff and Homebound Handicapped Employment Program GSA, Washington, 1973-74; mem. task force Presdl. Mgmt. Intern Program, Washington, 1977-78; coordinator women's program Mgmt. Devel. Program for Women, Washington, 1979-81 Office of the Sec. of Transp. Mem. Assn. Adminstrv. Mgrs. of Fed. Fin. Regulatory Agencies (charter mem.), Nat. Assn. Mus. of Women in the Arts, Am. Soc. Profl. and Exec. Women, Nat. Trust Hist. Preservation, Delta Gamma (pres. ho. corp. bd. local chpt. 1972-73, rush adv. 1971-73). Home: 6420 Franconia Ct Springfield VA 22150 Office: Commn on Civil Rights 1121 Vermont Ave NW Washington DC 20425

MATHEWS, MONIKA, professional association executive; b. Flensburg, Fed. Republic Germany, Aug. 3, 1941; arrived in Can., 1952; d. Hans Peter and Tuti (Boock) Mohrmann; divorced; children: Kacey Andrea, Tanya Rebekah. Student, UCLA, 1970-73, Los Angeles Valley Coll., 1973-74, Calif. State U., Northridge, 1974-75, Lumbleau Real Estate Sch., Glendale, Calif., 1979-80. Adminstrv. asst. So. Calif. Symphony/Hollywood Bowl Assn., Los Angeles, 1967-68; sec., office mgr. Aspen Airways, Burbank, Calif., 1976-77; cargo sales rep. Saudi Arabian Airlines, Century City, Calif., 1977-79; sales cons. Pechiney World Trade, Torrance, Calif., 1979-82; dir. activities Acad. TV Arts and Scis., Burbank, 1982-87; pvt. practice real estate financing 1988—. Mem. Greater Los Angeles Bar Assn.; bd. dirs. Olive View Med. Ctr. Found. Recipient letter of appreciation The White House, award of appreciation Rancho Los Amigos Med. Ctr. Mem. Women in Film, Nat. Assn. Female Execs., Am. Film Inst., Writers Guild Theater Film Soc., Can./Calif. C. of C. Home and Office: 12155 Blix St North Hollywood CA 91607

MATHEWS, PATRICIA ANN, food and beverage company executive; b. North Tonawanda, N.Y., Oct. 20, 1945; d. Daniel and Elizabeth Marian (Kassay) Por; m. Gregory Robert Mathews, Nov. 20, 1966; 1 child, Christopher Robert. B.A., SUNY-Fredonia, 1967; MBA, SUNY-Buffalo, 1982. Tchr., Wheelock Sch., Fredonia, 1967-68; library intern SUNY-Binghamton, 1968-73; office mgr. Bell and Howell, Buffalo, 1973-76; mgr. college relations Occidental Chem. Co., Niagara Falls, N.Y., 1977-82; mgr. recruitment and devel. Rochester Telephone Co., N.Y., 1982-83; sr. career devel. specialist Anheuser-Busch Co., St. Louis, 1983-87, mgr. employee relations, 1987—. Cons. in human resources, St. Louis, 1983—; coordinator Women in Bus. Network at Anheuser-Busch. Chmn. spl. awards YWCA Leader Lunch, St. Louis, 1985-86. Mem. Personnel Assn. St. Louis (v.p. 1985-86). Internat. Assn. Personnel Women, Am. Soc. Personnel Adminstrs. Lutheran. Avocations: exercise; reading; women's issues. Home: 1013 Hollybend Dr Ballwin MO 63021 Office: Anheuser-Busch Co Inc 12855 Flushing Meadow Dr Saint Louis MO 63131

MATHEWS, ROSEMARIE KAY, quality assurance manager; b. Ottawa, Ill., Jan. 24, 1959; d. Homer Franklin and Violet Patricia (Winn) M. Student, Loraine Bus. Coll., 1983. Quality control inspector Peltier Glass Co., Ottawa, Ill., 1978-80, Tech Sil Corp., Seneca, Ill., 1980; quality control supr. Brand Indsl. Services, Inc., Susquehanna Steam Electric Sta., Berwick, Pa., 1981-82; mgr. quality assurance Brand Indsl. Services, Inc., Susquehanna Steam Electric Sta., Berwick, 1987-88; quality control supr. Brand Indsl. Services, Inc., Davis Besse Nuclear Plant, Oak Harbor, Ohio, 1982-83, Brand Indsl. Services, Inc., Peach Bottom Atomic Power Plant, Delta, Pa., 1983-84; quality assurance mgr. Brand Indsl. Services, Inc., Clinton Power Sta., Clinton, Ill., 1984-87. Mem. fund raising com. AHA, Cancer Soc. Mem. Am. Soc. for Quality Control, Nat. Assn. Female Execs., Smithsonian Inst., Internat. Assn. of Heat and Frost Insulators and Asbestos Workers (quality control div.). Office: Bisco 1420 Renaissance Dr Park Ridge IL 60068

MATHEWS, SHARON WALKER, ballet educator, artistic director; b. Shreveport, La., Feb. 1, 1947; d. Arthur Delmar and Nona (Frye) Walker; m. John William (Bill) Mathews, Aug. 14, 1971; children—Rebecca, Elizabeth, Anna. B.S., La. State U., 1969, M.S., 1971. Dance grad. asst. La. State U., Baton Rouge, 1969-71; 6th grade tchr. East Baton Rouge Parish, 1971-72, health phys. edn. tchr., 1972-74; dance instr. Magnet High Sch., Baton Rouge, 1975—; artistic dir. Baton Rouge Ballet Theatre, 1975—; dance dir. Dancers' Workshop, Baton Rouge, 1971—. Named Dance Educator of Yr., La. Alliance for Health, Physical Edn., Recreation and Dance, 1986-87. Mem. Southwestern Regional Ballet Assn. (bd. dirs. 1981—). Republican. Baptist. Office: Baton Rouge Ballet Theater PO Box 64937 Baton Rouge LA 70896

MATHEWS, SUSAN MCKIERNAN, health care executive; b. N.Y.C., May 28, 1946; d. Thomas Joseph and Eileen Ann (Looschen) McK.; m. robert Emmett Mathews, June 17, 1967; children: Colin Robert, Brendan Robert, Devin Robert, Kiernan Robert. Diploma in nursing, St. Francis Sch. Nursing, 1966; BS in Health Adminstrn., St. Joseph's Coll., 1979; MS in Pub. Service Adminstrn., Russell Sage Coll., 1983; PhD in Health Adminstrn., Columbia Pacific U., 1985. RN, N.Y. Utilization rev. analyst N.Y. State Office Mental Retardation and Devel. Disabilities, Albany, 1980-83; med. rev. analyst Empire Blue Cross & Blue Shield, Albany, 1983-84, mgr. cost containment programs, 1984-85, dir. instl. utilization rev., 1985-86, cons. in field, 1986-88; exec. v.p. Geriatric Health Resources, Troy, N.Y., 1988—; chief operating officer Geriatric Health Resources, Troy, 1988—; sec. bd. dirs. Corp. Health Dimensions. Contbr. articles to profl. jours. Mem. exec. bd. New Scotland Neighborhood Assn., Albany, 1986—. Mem. Am. Assn. Preferred Provider Orgns. Roman Catholic. Home: 63 Crescent Dr S Albany NY 12208 Office: Geriatric Health Resources 2001 Fifth Ave Troy NY 12180

MATHEWS, VIRGINIA TREVOR, food service executive; b. Rochester, N.Y., Sept. 23, 1943; d. Trevor Bruce Burns and Camille (Pavia) Hansen; m. William Thomas Mathews, Sept. 26, 1959; children: Daniel Thomas, Dawn Therese, Dean Timothy, Duane Terrance. Clk. North Brothers Ford, Garden City, Mich., 1964-65; exec. trainee J.L. Hudsons, Detroit, 1965-67; program coordinator Warrendale Community Ch., Dearborn, Mich., 1968-71, 75-76; missionary Word of Life, Nairobi, Kenya, East Africa, 1972-75; prin. DTM Food Mgmt. Service, Dearborn, 1976-80; pres. Cadillac Custom Catering Inc., Dearborn, 1980—; cons. City of Westland, Mich., 1979-81; speaker in field. E. Dearborn Merchants Assn. (mem. com. 1986-87), Nat. Assn. Female Executives (sec. 1986-87), Nat. Assn. Coll. Women (sec. 1973-75), Dearborn C. of C. Republican. Office: 5320 Schacter Dearborn MI 48126

MATHEWS, WILMA, public relations manager; b. Danville, Va., Dec. 23, 1945; d. Clarence Blanchard and Tina Collins (Powell) Kendrick; A.A., Stratford Coll., 1966, B.A., 1970; student East Carolina U., 1966-67, U. Md., European div., 1967-68, Guilford Coll., 1978-80. Asst. editor The Commonwealth Mag., Richmond, Va., 1970-72; news editor The Comml. Appeal, Danville, Va., 1972-73; pub. relations mgr. Danville C. of C., 1973-74; publs. officer Bowman Gray Bapt. Hosp. Med. Center, Winston-Salem, N.C., 1974-78; sr. pub. relations specialist Western Electric, 1978-82; mgr. pub. relations AT&T Internat., Basking Ridge, N.J., 1982-84; media relations mgr. AT&T Network Systems, 1985-87, mgr. pub. relations field support, 1987—; sr. pub. relations adv. N.C. Epilepsy Info. Service, 1979-80. Co-author: On Deadline: Managing Media Relations, 1985; Inside Organizational Communications, 2d edit., 1985, Marketing Communications, 1987; Mem. Danville Bicentennial Commn., 1972-74; bd. dirs. Nat. Tobacco-Textile Mus., 1973-74; mem. Danville City Beautiful Com., 1973-74, Maplewood Cultural Comm., 1986-87. Fellow Internat. Assn. Bus. Communicators (dir. 1978-81, pres. N.C. chpt. 1977, 78, dir. Found. 1984-87, chmn. Found. 1987—, accreditation bd. 1984—); mem. Danville Hist. Soc. (dir. 1973-74), N.C. Zool. Soc., Smithsonian Instn., Internat. TV Assn. (sec. N.C. chpt. 1979-80), Internat. Pub. Relations Assn., Council for Communications Mgmt. (bd. dirs. 1987—), Friends of Maplewood Library (pres. 1985-86), Stratford Coll. Alumni Assn. Republican. Baptist. Lodge: Internat. Order Job's Daus. Home: 65 Hudson Ave Maplewood NJ 07040 Office: 475 South St Morristown NJ 07960

MATHIAS, ALICE IRENE, health plan company executive; b. N.Y.C., Mar 2, 1949; d. Murray and Charlotte (Kottle) M. B.S. in Math., Western New Eng. Coll., 1972. Programmer, Carnation Co., Los Angeles, 1973-78; programmer/analyst Cedars-Sinai Med. Ctr., Los Angeles, 1978-79, Union Bank, Los Angeles, 1979-81; group leader Kaiser Found. Health Plan, Pasadena, Calif., 1981—. Mem. Nat. Assn. Female Execs., Am. Mgmt. Assn., Kaiser Mgmt. Assn., Kaiser Women in Mgmt., Los Angeles County Mus. Art (patron), Los Angeles Philharm. Assn., Soc. Preservation Variety Arts. Home: 4210 Via Arbolada Unit 311 Los Angeles CA 90042 Office: Kaiser Found Health Plan Info Services Dept 393 E Walnut St Pasadena CA 91188

MATHIAS, BETTY JANE, communications and community affairs consultant, writer, editor, lecturer; b. East Ely, Nev., Oct. 22, 1923; d. Royal F. and Dollie B. (Bowman) M.; student Merritt Bus. Sch., 1941, 42, San Francisco State U., 1941-42; 1 dau., Dona Bett. Asst. publicity dir. Oakland (Calif.) Area War Chest and Community Chest, 1943-46; pub. relations Am. Legion, Oakland, 1946-47; asst. to pub. relations dir. Cen. Bank of Oakland, 1947-49; pub. relations dir. East Bay chpt. of Nat. Safety Council, 1949-51; propr., mgr. Mathias Public Relations Agy., Oakland, 1951-60; gen. assignment reporter and teen news editor Daily Rev., Hayward, Calif., 1960-62; freelance pub. relations and writing, Oakland, 1962-66, 67-69; dir. corp. communications Systech Fin. Corp., Walnut Creek, Calif., 1969-71; v.p. corp. communications Consol. Capital companies, Oakland, 1972-79, v.p. community affairs, Emeryville, Calif., 1981-84, v.p. spl. projects, 1984-85, v.p., dir. Consol. Capital Realty Services, Inc., Oakland, 1973-77; v.p., dir. Centennial Adv. Corp., Oakland, 1976-77; communications cons., 1979—; cons. Mountainair Realty, Cameron Park, Calif., 1986—; lectr. in field; bd. dirs. Oakland YWCA, 1944-45, ARC, Oakland, So. Alameda County chpt., 1967-69, Family Ctr., Children's Hosp. Med. Ctr. No. Calif., 1982-85, also mem. adv. bd., 1986—, March of Dimes, 1983-85, Equestrian Ctr. of Walnut Creek, Calif., 1983-84, also sec.; adult and publs. adv. Internat. Order of the Rainbow for Girls, 1953-78; communications arts adv. com. Ohlone (Calif.) Coll., 1979-85, chmn., 1982-84; mem. adv. bd. dept. mass communications Calif. State U.-Hayward, 1985; pres. San Francisco Bay Area chpt. Nat. Reyes Syndrome Found., 1981-86; vol. staff Columbia Actors' Repertory, Columbia, Calif., 1986-87; mem. exec. bd., editor newsletter Tuolumne County Dem. Club, 1987—. Recipient Grand Cross of Color award Internat. Order of Rainbow for Girls, 1955. Order Eastern Star (publicity chmn. Calif. state 1955). Editor East Bay Mag., 1966-67, TIA Traveler, 1969, Concepts, 1979-83. Home: 20575 Gopher Dr Sonora CA 95370

MATHIEU-HARRIS, MICHELE SUZANNE, association executive; b. Chgo., Mar. 24, 1950; d. Joseph Edward Mathieu and Mary Ellen (Knapp) Fisher; m. Robert Steven Harris, May 1, 1988. Student DePaul U., 1971, 74-76, Regents Coll., Albany, N.Y., 1987—. Broadcast coordinator Grey-North Advt., Chgo., 1967-71; head drama dept. Patricia Stevens Coll., Chgo., 1972; instr. beginning acting Ted Liss Sch. of Performing Arts, Chgo., 1973-75; project coordinator grants and contracts Am. Dietetic Assn., Chgo., 1974-81, adminstr. govt. affairs, 1981-86, mgr. licensure communications, 1986—; grant proposal cons. various performance arts, Chgo., 1978—. Editor Legis. Newsletter, 1981-86; contbg. editor Nutrition Forum, 1986, Courier, 1987—; contbr. articles to profl. jours., mags., newspapers. Treas. Am. Dietetic Assn. polit. action com., Washington, 1981-86; adv. bd. Rejoice Repertory Theatre Company, Inc., Chgo. Ill. Arts Council grantee, 1981. Mem. Nat. Assn. Female Execs. Roman Catholic. Avocations: reading, jazzercise. Office: Am Dietetic Assn 208 S LaSalle St Chicago IL 60604

MATHIS, BETTY, public relations counsel; b. Atlanta, Oct. 5, 1918; d. Walter Rylander and Evelyn Battle (Epting) M.; student Agnes Scott Coll., 1934-36. Sports writer, columnist Atlanta Constitution, 1936-39; gen. news and feature writer, then editor spl. supplements, 1939-40; dir. public relations Atlanta Housing Authority, 1940; feature writer, asst. city editor, daily by-line columnist Atlanta Constitution, 1941-43; asst. regional info. exec. OPA, 1943-45; partner Mathis, Murphey & Bondurant public relations counsel, Atlanta, 1945-50; editor Sun Colony Mag., Fort Lauderdale, Fla., 1950-53; partner Mathis & Bondurant public relations, Ft. Lauderdale, 1953-82, owner, 1982—. Bd. dirs. ARC; mem. coms. United Way; sec. vestry All Saints Episcopal Ch., 1974-76, mem. vestry, 1978-80, 85-87, treas., 1979, sr. warden, 1980, del. Diocesan Conv., 1975, 79, 80. Nominee, Pulitzer prize, 1937. Mem. Public Relations Soc. Am., Am. Soc. Hosp. Public Relations (profl. advancement com. 1980), Public Relations Council Fla. Hosp. Assn. (dir. 1977-79, pres. 1977-78), Women in Communications (pres. county 1968, 69, Atlantic Fla. chpt. 1979, named Woman of Yr. 1979), Gold Coast Hosp. Public Relations Council (founding, pres. 1981-82), Am. Hosp. Assn. Democrat. Club: Tower. Home and Office: 1628 NE 15th Ave Fort Lauderdale FL 33305

MATHIS, LAURELLE SHEEDY, entrepreneur, volunteer; b. Southampton, N.Y., Aug. 29, 1948; d. Edmund Sheedy and Tatiana (Widrin) Brooks; m. Robert Trimble Mathis, Oct. 20, 1979; children—Liliana Sheedy, Bronwyn Trimble, Kane Timberlake. B.A., Stephens Coll., Columbia, Mo., 1970; M.B.A., Harvard U., 1977. Spl. asst. Congressman Ed Foreman, Washington, 1970; staff asst. Senator James L. Buckley, Washington, 1971-72; staff asst. to pres. U.S., Washington, 1973-75; v.p. Blyth Eastman Paine Webber, N.Y.C., 1977-81; v.p. Merrill Lynch Capital Markets, N.Y.C., 1981-84. Bd. curators Stephens Coll., 1981-83; bd. curators Putnam Indian Field Sch., Greenwich, Conn., 1986—, chmn. auction, 1987; chmn. Christ Ch. Antiques Show, 1987, 88. Recipient Alumni Achievement award Stephens Coll., 1980. Republican. Episcopalian. Home: 22 Pecksland Rd Greenwich CT 06831

MATHIS, MARSHA DEBRA, computer software company executive; b. Detroit, Dec. 22, 1953; d. Marshall Junior and Anita Willene (Biggers) M. BS, Fla. State U., 1978; MBA, Miss. Coll., 1982. With telecommunications dept. Fla. State Dept. Safety, Tallahassee, 1973-76; asst. to chmn. Tallahassee Savs. and Loan Assn., 1976-78; sales engr. Prehler, Inc., Jackson, Miss., 1978-82; mktg. mgr. Norand Corp., Arlington, Tex., 1982-87; v.p. mktg., sales Profl. Datasolutions, Inc., Irving, Tex., 1987—. Contbr. articles in industry trade jours. Advisor Am. Diabetes Assn., Jackson, 1983—. Mem. Nat. Adv. Group, Nat. Assn. Convenience Stores (Industry Task Force 1987-88). Republican. Roman Catholic. Home: 600 Eagle Nest Irving TX 75063 Office: Profl Datasolutions Inc 5340 Knickerbocker Rd San Angelo TX 76904

MATHIS, THELMA ATWOOD, artist; b. Creal Springs, Ill.; d. Hubert L. and Mima (Hutchison) Atwood; B.S., So. Ill. U., 1955, M.F.A., 1957; student Art Students League, 1957-59; m. John A. Mathis, Sept. 1, 1928 (div. 1950); children—John Atwood, Shirley (Mrs. Frank Woosley), James Stevens. One-man shows So. Ill. U., 1957, 59, Sparta (Ill.) Pub. Library, 1960, Art Mart, Inc., St. Louis, 1961, St. Louis Artists Guild, 1962, Midwestern Coll. (Iowa), 1967; two-man show Madison Galleries, N.Y.C., 1963; juried N.Y.C. Center, 1958, 59, Madison Sq. Garden, N.Y.C., 1958, Nat. Old Testament, St. Louis, 1961, 62, Mo. Art Show, St. Louis City Art Mus., 1954, 55, Nat. Arts & Crafts, Wichita, Kans., 1953, 55; instr., asst. prof. art dept. Midwestern Coll., Denison, Iowa, 1965-70. Recipient Grand prize oil and drawing DuQuoin State Fair, 1955, 56, 58, 59. Mem. St. Louis Artists Guild, AAUW, Pi Lambda Theta. Baptist. Home: Box 13 Pinckneyville IL 62274

MATHISEN, LILLIAN ALICE, TV station executive; b. Bronx, N.Y., Nov. 16, 1941; d. Johann Nordell Bang and Alice (Kostka) M.; m. Thomas Joseph Conroy, July 3, 1965 (div. 1986); children: Christian, Eric, Brian. BA, Fairleigh Dickinson U., 1963. Instr. Fairleigh Dickinson U., Teaneck, N.J., 1963-64; market research field supr. W.R. Simmons Assocs., N.Y.C., 1964-65; assoc. library dir. NYU, Tuxedo, N.Y., 1968-70; computer operator IBM Corp., East Fishkill, N.Y., 1978-79; sys. analyst Texaco, Inc., White Plains, N.Y., 1980-84; adminstrv. asst. Jacobowitz & Gubits, Walden, N.Y., 1985-86; bus. mgr. Sta. WTZA-TV, Kingston, N.Y., 1986—. Mem. Broadcast Fin. Mgmt. Assn. Democrat. Lutheran. Home: RD 1 Box 180 DeLancey NY 13752 Office: Sta WTZA-TV 721 Broadway Kingston NY 12401

MATHISEN, RHODA SHARON, communications consultant; b. Portland, Oreg., June 25, 1942; d. Daniel and Mildred Elizabeth Annette (Peterson) Hager; m. James Albert Mathisen, July 17, 1964 (div. 1977). B.A. in Edn., Moody Bible Coll., 1964. Community Relations officer Gary-Wheaton Bank, Wheaton, Ill., 1971-75; br. mgr. Stivers Temporary Personnel, Chgo., 1975-79; v.p. sales Exec. Technique, Chgo., 1980-83; prin. Mathisen Assocs., Downers Grove, Ill., 1983—; presenter seminars; featured speaker Women in Mgmt. Oak Brook Chpt., 1988.; cons. Haggai Inst., Atlanta; adv. mem. Nat. Bd. Success Group, 1986. Pres. chancel choir Christ Ch. of Oak Brook, 1985-87. Mem. Bus. and Profl. Women (charter mem. Woodfield chpt.), Execs. Club Oak Brook, Internat. Platform Assn., Nat. Assn. Female Execs., Sales & Mktg. Execs. Chgo., Chgo. Council Fgn. Relations, Chgo. Assn. Commerce and Industry (named Ambassador of Month N.W. suburban chpt. 1979), Oak Brook Assn. Commerce and Industry (mem. membership com.), Women Entrepreneurs of DuPage County (membership chmn., featured speaker Jan. 1988), Art Inst. Chgo., Internat. Platform Assn. Republican. Office: Mathisen Assocs Box 9208 Downers Grove IL 60515

MATHISON, LINDA (LOU), forest products company executive; b. Wichita, Kans., Sept. 28, 1941; d. Lewis E. and Lela K. (Kaufman) M. BBS, U. Calif., Berkeley, 1963. Corp. mgr. group benefits Formost-McKesson, Inc., San Francisco, 1968-81; corp. dir. employee benefits Crown Zellerbach Corp., San Francisco, 1981—. Mem. Council on Employee Benefits (trustee 1983—), Nat. Industry Council for HMO Devel., Nat. Assn. Employees on HMO's (pres. 1980—), San Francisco Bus. Group on Health (co-founder). Club: Metropolitan. Office: Crown Zellerbach Corp 1 Bush St San Francisco CA 94104

MATHUS, NINA DAMEREL, marketing executive; b. N.Y.C., July 31, 1941; d. George Sarles and Nina (Tetamo) Damerel; m. John F. Mathus, Apr. 26, 1958; children: David Lackey, Diane Kristi. Student, Fairleigh Dickinson U., 1966-67, County Coll., Morris, 1968-70. Tchr. remedial math., substitute tchr., N.Y. and N.J., 1967-75; with Salisbury Research and Info. System, Conn., 1975, mgr., 1976; project dir. Market Probe Internat., Inc., N.Y.C., 1977; mng. dir. Cen. Telephone Interviewing System, 1978, pres., 1978-80, exec. v.p., 1980—; v.p. Audits & Surveys, Inc., N.Y.C., 1980—. Bd. dirs. Sharon Creative Arts Found., 1976-77; active Boy Scouts Am., Girl Scouts U.S.A., 1965-72. Mem. Am. Mktg. Assn., Market Research Assn., Bus. and Profl. Women's Club. Republican. Clubs: Twin Lakes Beach, Snarks. Office: 650 Ave of Americas New York City NY 10011

MATJASICH, CAROL ANN, marketing executive; b. Chgo., Mar. 27, 1955; d. Walter Arthur and Joan Mary (Sullivan) M. BFA in Visual Communication, No. Ill. U., 1977. Designer Design Investigation Group, Chgo., 1977-80, exec. v.p., 1980-81; owner, exec. v.p. Porter/Matjasich & Assoc., Chgo., 1981—. Mem. Nat. Assn. Women Bus. Owners, Soc. Typographical Arts, Women in Design Assn. of Profl. Design Firms, Chgo. Assn. Commerce and Industry. Office: 154 W Hubbard #404 Chicago IL 60610

MATLACK, ARDENA LAVONNE, state legislator; b. Carlton, Kans., Dec. 20, 1930; d. Walter D. and Bessie B. (Major) Williams; student Kans. Wesleyan U., 1948, Kans. State U., 1949-51, Washburn U., 1955; BA cum laude, Wichita State U., 1969; m. Don Matlack, June 10, 1951; children: Lucinda Donn, Roxanne, Terry Clyde, Rex William, Timothy Alan. Tchr., Carlton Grade Sch., 1948-49; substitute tchr. Clearwater (Kans.) Schs., 1969-74; part-time music tchr., 1960-72; mem. Kans. Ho. of Reps., 1974-84; arts council mem. Kans. Arts Commn., 1985—. Dem. precinct committeewoman, 1966-68, 1986—, mem. Dem. State Com., 1974-78; pres. Kans. State Dem. Club, 1978; chmn. Clearwater March of Dimes, 1980, Clearwater Area United Fund, 1980, 83; choir dir. United Meth. Ch., 1984-87, bell choir dir., 1987—; project leader 4-H, 1962-71. Recipient Gold Star Legis. award Assn. for legis. action by Rural Mayors, 1981. Mem. Clearwater United Methodist Women (hon. life; pres. 1972), Dist. United Meth. Women (hon. life, dist. coordinator social involvement 1975-76), Kans. Press Women's Assn. (hon.), Gold Key, Alpha Xi Delta, Mu Phi Epsilon. Clubs: Clearwater Federated Women's Study (pres. 1966-67); Kans. Fedn. Women's Dem. Clubs (Disting. Achievement award 1977, chair 4th dist. 1987—), Clearwater Bus. and Profl. Women's (pres. 1985-86), West Side Dem., South Side Dem., Sedgwick County Federated Women's Dem. (pres. 1985-88). Home and Office: 615 Elaine St Clearwater KS 67026

MATLAGA-KRIEGER, CAROL, color consulting executive; b. Elizabeth, N.J., May 22, 1952; d. Michael and Agnes Lilian (Bruder) Matlaga; m. Jeffrey Allen Krieger, Sept. 2, 1982. BA in Psychology, U. Denver, 1977. Sales rep. Spectrum, Inc., Denver, 1976-78, Am. Color Corp., Denver, 1978-84; v.p. VisiColor, Inc., Denver, 1984—. Vol. Rocky Mt. Adoption Exchange, Denver, 1984—, Denver Internat. Film Festival, 1984—. Recipient Alfie award Denver Art Fedn., 1985, Award of Excellence for color seperations Monadnock Paper Mills, 1985. Mem. Art Dirs. Club (pres. 1981-82, v.p. 1980-81, Supplier of Yr. 1984-85). Office: VisiColor Inc 5040 E 41st Ave Denver CO 80216

MATLOW, LINDA MONIQUE, photographic agency executive; b. Chgo., July 24, 1955; d. Charles and Milly (Labioso) M. Grad. high sch., Chgo.; student, Sch. Modern Photography, N.Y.C., 1977-79. Promotions and pub. relations staff Jaydee Enterprises, Chgo., 1971-73; mgr. First Venture, Inc., Chgo., 1973-77; photographer, pub. relations staff Bands & Mags., Chgo., 1977—; pres., photographer Pix Internat., Chgo., 1982—. Contbr. photographs to publs. including N.Y. Times, Chgo. Tribune, Boston Globe. Vol. telethon Variety Club of Chgo., 1986, Spl. Childrens' Charities. Named Rock Photographer Night Rock newspaper, Chgo., 1980, 81. Mem. Nat. Press Assn., Nat. Acad. Rec. Arts and Scis. Roman Catholic.

MATOS, MILAGROS ANTONIA, lawyer; b. Santo Domingo, Dominican Republic, May 12, 1950, came to U.S., 1959; d. Miguel Antonio and Leah (Gomez) M.; divorced; 1 child, Alexander Feliz. BS, CCNY, 1972; MS, Hunter Coll., 1977; JD, Bklyn. Law Sch., 1982. Supr. clin. lab. Columbia U./Harlem Hosp., N.Y.C., 1972-79; asst. corp. counsel Office Corp. Counsel, City of N.Y.C., 1982-85; assoc. Wilson, Wiser, Maskowitz, Edelman & Dicker, N.Y.C., 1985—. Mem. ABA, Assn. Trial Lawyers Am., N.Y. Trial Lawyers Assn. Democrat. Roman Catholic. Office: Wilson Elser Maskowitz Edelman & Dicker 420 Lexington Ave New York NY 10170

MATROSS, JEANNE KUKURA, lawyer; b. N.Y.C., Dec. 29, 1946; d. Emmett and Helen (Grekulinski) Kukura; m. Ronald Philip Matross, Aug. 14, 1971; children: Robin, Daniel. BA, Barnard Coll., 1968; JD, NYU, 1971. Bar: Minn. 1972, D.C. 1978. Atty. HUD, Mpls., 1972-86; assoc. gen. counsel Met. Waste Control Commn., 1986—; instr. U. Minn., 1978—; mem. Mayor's Blue-Ribbon Personnel Issues Task Force, St. Paul, 1983—; mem. jud. liaison Minn. Women's Polit. Caucus, 1976-78. Freelance columnist on legal issues Minn. Women's Press, 1985—. Pres. St. Paul LWV, 1982-83, 2d v.p., 1982, chairperson action com., 1979-82; mem. com. to develop Minn. real estate licensure exam. Minn. Dept. Commerce, 1986. N.Y. State Regents scholar, 1964-71. Mem. ABA, Minn. Bar Assn., Ramsey County Bar Assn., Nat. Assn. Women Lawyers, Minn. Women Lawyers Assn., Am. Arbitration Assn. (comml. arbitrator 1983—), Phi Beta Kappa. Roman Catholic. Home: 486 Frontenac Pl Saint Paul MN 55104 Office: 350 Metro Sq Bldg Saint Paul MN 55101

MATSA, LOULA ZACHAROULA, social services adminstr.; b. Piraeus, Greece, Apr. 16, 1935; came to U.S., 1952, naturalized 1962; d. Eleftherios Georgiou and Ourania E. (Fraguiskopoulou) Papoulias; student Pierce Coll., Athens, Greece, 1948-52; B.A., Rockford Coll., 1953; M.A., U. Chgo., 1955; m. Ilco S. Matsa, Nov. 27, 1953; 1 son, Aristotle Ricky. Marital counselor Family Soc. Cambridge, Mass., 1955-56; chief unit II, social service Queen's (N.Y.) Children's Psychiat. Center, 1961-74; dir. social services, supr.-coordinator family care program Hudson River Psychiat. Center, Poughkeepsie, N.Y., 1974—; field instr. Adelphi, Albany and Fordham univs., 1969—. Fulbright Exchange student, 1952-53; Talcott scholar, 1953-55. Mem. Internat. Platform Assn., Internat. Council on Social Welfare, Nat. Assn. Social Workers, Assn. Cert. Social Workers, Civil Service Employees Assn., Pierce Coll. Alumni Assn. Democrat. Greek Orthodox. Contbr. articles to profl. jours.; instrumental in state policy changes in treatment and court representation of emtionally disturbed and mentally ill. Home: 81-11 45th Ave Elmhurst NY 11373 Office: Hudson River Psychiat Ctr Br B Poughkeepsie NY 12601

MATSON, FRANCES SHOBER, social worker; b. Cin., Mar. 21, 1921; d. Frank Lyford and Florence Leone (Bridgeford) Shober; student U. Cin., 1939-41, B.A., 1951, postgrad., 1951-52; M.S.W., U. Calif., 1956; Nat. Registry of Clin. Social Work; m. John Alan Matson, Dec. 2, 1942 (dec.). Councillor, County of San Mateo, 1956-57; therapist, supr. Center for Treatment and Edn. on Alcoholism, Oakland, Calif., 1957-63; pvt. practice social worker, Berkeley, Calif., 1960-64; supr. dept. social service County of Marin, Calif., 1966; psychotherapist Marin Inst., 1966-70, Oaknoll Naval Hosp., 1969; public health social worker Dept. Health County of Contra Costa (Calif.), 1972; psychotherapist Day Care Center for Schizophrenics, Contra Costa County Med. Services, 1972-74; dir. Martinez Mental Health Clinic, Contra Costa County Med. Services, 1974-81; coordinator adult outpatient services, edn., group therapy Contra Costa County Mental Health Center, 1981—. Lic. clin. social worker. Mem. Nat. Assn. Social Workers, Acad. Cert. Social Workers, Internat. Transactional Analysis Assn., Marin Assn. Mental Health, Contra Costa County Mental Health Assn., Soc. Clin. Social Work. Home: Box 2073 Martinez CA 94553 Office: 2025 Port Chicago Hwy Concord CA 94520

MATSUI, DOROTHY NOBUKO, educator; b. Honolulu, Jan. 9, 1954; d. Katsura and Tamiko (Sakai) M. Student, U. Hawaii, Honolulu, 1972-76, postgrad., 1982; BEd, U. Alaska, Anchorage, 1979, MEd in Special Edn., 1986. Clerical asst. U. Hawaii Manoa Disbursing Office, Anchorage, 1974-76; passenger service agt. Japan Air Lines, Anchorage, 1980; bilingual tutor Anchorage Sch. Dist., 1980, elem. sch. tchr., 1980—. Vol. Providence Hosp., Anchorage, 1986, Humama Hosp., Anchorage, 1984, Spl. Olympics, Anchorage, 1981, Municipality Anchorage, 1978, Easter Seal Soc. Hawaii, 1975. Mem. NEA, Alaska Edn. Assn., Smithsonian Nat. Assoc. Program, Smithsonian Air and Space Assn., Nat. Assn. Female Exec., World Aerospace Edn. Orgn., U. Alaska Alumni Assn., Alpha Delta Kappa. Office: Anchorage Sch Dist 7001 Cranberry Anchorage AK 99502

MATSUMURA, VERA YOSHI, pianist; b. Oakland, Calif.; d. Naojiro and Aguri Tanaka; B.A. in Piano Pedagogy, Coll. of Holy Names, Oakland, 1938; pvt. studies with F. Moss, M. Shapiro, L. Kreutzer, P. Jarrett; m. Jiro Matsumura, Aug. 8, 1942; 1 son, Kenneth N. Staff mem., pianist Radio Sta. KROW, Oakland, 1938-39; numerous concert performances in Far East (Japan, Thailand), 1940—; numerous teaching appointments, 1940—; dir. Internat. Music Council, Berkeley, Calif., 1969—. Named to Hall of Fame, Piano Guild, 1968. Mem. Music Tchrs. Nat. Assn., Music Tchrs. Assn. Calif., Internat. Platform Assn., Alpha Phi Mu. Methodist. Home: 2 Claremont Crescent Berkeley CA 94705

MATTARELLA, ANNE, editor; b. N.Y.C., May 12, 1952; d. Leonard and Jean (La Rocca) M.; m. Eric Van. BS, SUNY, Oneonta, 1974; postgrad., Syracuse U., 1975-76. Editorial asst. Syracuse (N.Y.) U. Press, 1976-77; asst. editor Illustrated World Ency., Woodbury, N.Y., 1977-79; asst. editor Romaine Pierson Pubs., Port Washington, N.Y., 1979-80, mng. editor, 1980-85, exec. editor Resident & Staff Physician, Med. Times, 1985—. Mem. Am. Med. Writers Assn., Internat. Assn. Bus. Communicators. Office: Romaine Pierson Pubs 80 Shore Rd Port Washington NY 11050

MATTEI, HELGA DEL CARMEN, corporate professional, communications consultant; b. Aguadilla, P.R., Aug. 6, 1951; d. Max and Maria del Carmen (Castanos) M.; m. Ulises Caraballo (div.); 1 child, Helga del Carmen; m. Gregory Milton Booker, Dec. 1977. Lic. in Journalism, Mass Communication, Nat. Autonomous U. of Mex., 1974, postgrad., 1976-77. Asst. editor Inter-Am. U. Press, San Juan, P.R., 1975; radio producer, press officer Patronato Jornada Casals, Mexico City, 1976; producer Sta. XEEP Radio, Mexico City, 1977; communications dir. Houston Met. Ministries, 1978-79; owner, operator Internat. Communication Cons., Houston, 1979—; v.p., sec. Home Improvement Cons., Inc., Houston, 1979—. Tutor, v.p., corp. sec. Vols. in Pub. Schs. Program; vol. pub. relations/mktg. coordinator Houston Internat. U., producer coordinator parents and children workshops; active Hispanic Scouting com. Friends Scouting; bd. dirs. Houston Met. Ministries. Office: Home Improvement Cons Inc PO Box 30072 Houston TX 77249

MATTES, KITTY, writer; b. Washington, Sept. 22, 1936; d. Samuel Hutchinson and Roberta (Reed) Beer; m. Max H. Mattes; children: Duncan Campbell, Amelia Campbell. BA, Harvard U., 1963; MA, Cornell U., 1971. Previously assoc. dir. Western Socs. Program at Cornell U., Ithaca, N.Y.; now copy editor Cornell U. Press, Ithaca. Author: In Your Hands, A Citizen's Guide to the Arms Race, 1981; contbr. numerous articles to mags., newspapers. Active polit. campaigns and events. Home: 101 Irving Pl Ithaca NY 14850

MATTESON, THERESA DRINE (RIZA), graphic artist, small business owner; b. Ashland, Oreg., Sept. 28, 1964; d. James Gene and Nancy Ellen (Grow) M. Grad. high sch., Hillsboro, Oreg., 1984; diploma, Northwestern Coll. Bus., Portland, Oreg., 1985; student, Portland Community Coll. Advt. artist The Comfort Gallery, Hillsboro, 1984-85, Brodersen's Inc., Forest Grove, Oreg., 1984-85; seamstress, knitter Portland, 1985-86; data entry/newsletter artist Nat. Chronic Epstein Barr Virus Syndrome Assn., Portland, 1986—; sweater designs, fibre artist Hillsboro, 1987—. Recipient cert. appreciation Art Show for the Deaf, 1983. Mem. Nat. Assn. for Female Execs. Roman Catholic.

MATTEUCIG, IOLE LOUISE, library consultant; b. San Francisco, Mar. 1, 1926; d. Anselmo and Rosminda (Stefanini) Cagnoni; m. Giacinto Matteucig, June 26, 1948, children—Catherine, Michael, Laurence. B.A., U. Calif.-Berkeley, 1947, B.L.S., 1948. Instr. library sci., U. San Francisco, 1968-69; instr., librarian City Coll. of San Francisco, 1968-72, dean Library Services, 1972-83, dean, emeritus, 1983—; ind. cons. library mgmt., San Francisco, 1983—; cons. San Francisco Community Coll. Dist., 1983—. HEW grantee, 1970. Mem. ALA (mem. legis. network Washington, 1980-83), Calif. Library Assn., Spl. Library Assn., Assn. Calif. Community Coll. Adminstrs. Home: 55 Aerial Way San Francisco CA 94116

MATTHEW, LYN, art marketing consultant and educator; b. Long Beach, Calif., Dec. 15, 1936; d. Harold G. and Beatrice (Hunt) M.; m. Wayne Thomas Castleberry, Aug. 12, 1961 (div. Jan. 1976); children—Melanie, Cheryl, Nicole, Matthew. BS, U. Calif.-Davis, 1958; MA, Ariz. State U., 1979. Pres., Davlyn Cons. Found., Scottsdale, Ariz., 1979-82; cons., vis. prof. The Art Bus., Scottsdale, 1982—; vis. prof. Maricopa Community Coll., Phoenix, 1979—, Ariz. State U., Tempe, 1980-83; cons. Women's Caucus for Art, Phoenix, 1983—. Bd. dirs. Rossom House and Heritage Square Found., Phoenix, 1987-88. Author: The Business Aspects of Art, Book I, 1979, Book II, 1979; Marketing Strategies for the Creative Artist, 1985. Mem. Women Image Now (Achievement and Contbn. in Visual Arts award 1983), Women in Higher Edn., Nat. Women's Caucus for Art (v.p. 1981-83), Ariz. Women's Caucus for Art (pres. 1980-82, hon. advisor 1986-87), Vocat. Edn. Assn. (sec. 1978-80), Ariz. Visionary Artists (treas. 1987—), Ariz. Acad. Performing Arts (v.p. bd. dirs. 1987—).

MATTHEWS, AGNES CYNTHIA, state senator; b. Washington, Pa., Feb. 1, 1924; d. Spero and Harriet Kosmas; m. Phathon James Matthews, Dec. 5, 1946; children—Denise, Spero. B.S., Barnard Coll., 1946. Dep. mayor (1 term) Wethersfield, Conn., mayor (2 terms), council woman, 1973-81; mem. Conn. Senate (representing 9th dist.), 1982—; v.p., dir. Pie-O-Neer Corp., East Hardford, Conn., 1980—, Sargent's Head Realty Corp., East Lyme, Conn., 1959—, The Stonington Co. Mem. Ch. Women United (nat. bd. dirs. 1977-80), LWV (former pres. Wethersfield/Rocky Hill chpt.), Civitans. Greek Orthodox. Office: Office of the State Senator State Capitol Bldg Hartford CT 06106 *

MATTHEWS, ANNE LAMB, educational administrator, state official; b. Florence County, S.C., Nov. 3, 1942; d. Alex B. and Mettie (Nettles) L.; B.S. in Bus. Edn., Coker Coll., 1964; M.A. in Econs., Appalachian State U., 1968; Ed.D. in Ednl. Adminstrn., U. S.C., 1975; m. Glenny Jeff Matthews, Sept. 2, 1967. Tchr. bus. edn. dept. Hannah-Pamplico High Sch., Pamplico, S.C., 1964-67; instr. dept. bus. adminstrn. and secretarial sci. Florence-Darlington Tech. Edn. Coll., Florence, S.C., 1967-69; tchr.-counselor Youth Study Center, Greenville, S.C., 1970-71; dist. cons. Office Occupations Edn., Anderson (S.C.) Dist. Office, 1971-73; adj. prof. Coll. Bus. Adminstrn. U. S.C., Columbia, 1975-78; state supr. bus. and office edn. S.C. Dept. Edn., Columbia, 1973-80, chief supr. program planning and devel., 1980—, mem. various coms., 1975—; mem. Nat. Adv. Council for Career Edn., Nat. Commn. Employment Policy, Practitioners Task Force; nat. speaker over 300 confs. Vol. Vets Hosp., Columbia, 1978—; trustee Coker Coll., Hartsville, S.C.; bd. dirs. Richland County Am. Cancer Soc. Recipient Hulda Erath award, 1978, 79. Mem. Nat. Bus. Edn. Assn. (chmn. policies com. on bus. and econ. edn. 1979-80, pres. elect 1984, pres. 1985-86), So. Bus. Edn. Assn. (pres. 1984-85), Nat. Assn. State Suprs. of Bus. and Office Edn. (pres. 1977-79), S.C. Office Occupations Assn. (mem. exec. bd. 1973-76), Internat. Soc. for Bus. Edn., Am. Vocat. Assn. (mem. policy and planning com. 1977—), Adminstrv. Mgmt. Soc., S.C. Vocat. Dirs. Assn., S.C. Bus. Edn. Assn. (pres. 1969-70, mem. exec. bd. 1965-77), S.C. Vocat. Assn. (mem. program com. 1975-76), S.C. State Employees Assn., Internat. Word Processing Assn., S.C. Council for Adminstrv. Women in Edn., Nat. Speakers Assn., S.C. Hist. Soc., Friends of State Mus., Delta Kappa Gamma, Phi Delta Kappa. Baptist. Contbr. numerous articles to profl. jours.; author word processing materials; editor and reviewer various manuals and instructional guides on bus. and office occupations programs. Office: 904 Rutledge Bldg State Dept Education Columbia SC 29201

MATTHEWS, CARYL EVE, radio station executive; b. Grand Rapids, Mich., Jan. 20, 1937; d. Walter Ray and Mary Elizabeth (Grant) Matthews. B.Music, Ind. U., 1958, M.Music, 1959. Vis. instr. Ark. State Coll., Conway, 1959-61; instr. Drury Coll., Springfield, Mo., 1961-65; pvt. tchr. piano, 1968—; program producer WBAA-Radio, West Lafayette, Ind., 1969-70, music supr., 1970-77, program dir., music supr., 1977—. instr. piano,

1969—. Soloist, collaborative artist harpsichord and piano; producer, organizer 3 multiple piano festivals, Monster Concerts, Lafayette, 1979-82. Artistic cons. Bach Chorale Singers, 1982-85; bd. dirs. Tippecanoe Arts Fedn., Lafayette, 1982-86; mem. Worship and Music Commn., Episc. Diocese of Indpls., 1985—. Mem. Nat. Guild Piano Tchrs., Sigma Alpha Iota, Pi Kappa Lambda, Alpha Lambda Delta. Episcopalian. Office: Purdue U Radio WBAA West Lafayette IN 47907

MATTHEWS, JEANNE PEARSON, logistic support analyst, company executive; b. Marietta, Ga., July 2, 1941; d. Silas Leon and Edith Mae (Rich) Pearson; m. William Dean Bottoms, Apr. 2, 1960 (div. 1973); 1 child, William Dave; m. William Glenn Matthews, Sept. 4, 1976. Typist, stenographer, sec. Lockheed-Ga. Co., Marietta, 1962-82, gen. acct., price estimator, 1982-84, logistic support analyst, 1984—; pres. J&B Office Service, Inc., Villa Rica, Ga., 1984-87. Mem. Nat. Platform Com. Named Hon. Lt. Col. Aide-de-Camp Ala. State Militia, 1976; named Ms. Lockheed, Lockheed-Ga. Co., 1972, 74. Mem. Nat. Assn. Female Execs., Nat. Film Inst., Nat. Assn. Mature People, Paulding County C. of C., AFL-CIO (recording sec. Lodge 709 1973-79). Democrat. Baptist. Clubs: Kennesaw Mountain Beagle (sec.-treas. Dallas, Ga. 1980—), Atlanta Braves Fan. Lodge: Order Eastern Star. Avocations: Beagles; baseball; swimming. Home: Route 2 Box 519 Villa Rica GA 30180

MATTHEWS, LINDA LLEWELLYN FINK, profl. assn. adminstr.; b. LaPort, Ind., Oct. 29, 1950; d. Omar Ray and Marianne Denham (Smith) Fink, Jr.; student U. N.C., Greensboro, 1968-70; B.A., George Washington U., 1973; m. Daniel G. Matthews, Oct. 25, 1975; children—Strelka Jamila, Francesca Alina. Admnstrv. asst. African Bibliog. Center, Washington, 1974-75, adminstrv. editor, 1975-79, adminstrv. dir., 1979—; adminstrv. dir. African Devel. Info. Assn. U.S.A., 1981-84; fin. analyst Martin Marietta Info. and Communications Systems, 1985—; treas., bd. dirs. African Communications Liaison Services, Washington, 1978-84. Asso. mem. Women's Inst. for Freedom of Press, Washington, 1977-80; coordinator communications liaison com. Washington Task Force on African Affairs, 1975-78; cons. article on Rhodesia, Nat. Geog. Mag., 1975. Mem. African-Am. Women's Assn. Editorial bd. and reviewer A Current Bibliography on African Affairs, 1974—; editor AMA: Women in African & American Worlds, An Outlook, 1975-80, HABARI Special Reports, 1978-84; asso. producer Film Leopold Sedar Senghor, 1975; cons., writer Changing Africa, NBC/WRC-TV, 1976; asst. editor Am-South African Relations: Bibliographic Essays, 1975; compiler, co-author: Burundi: A Selected Bibliography & Resource Guide, 1975. Pres. Operation Santa Claus East, Mich., 1988—. Mem. Am. Mgmt. Assn., Internat. Platform Assn., African Studies Assn., I.D.E.A. Home: 1921 S St NW Washington DC 20009 also: PO Box 53398 Temple Heights Station Washington DC 20009

MATTHEWS, LORRAINE FUNNEMARK, food service executive; b. Algona, Iowa, Apr. 20, 1946; d. Howard Olaf and Frances Elizabeth (Leicher) F.; m. Samuel Leston Matthews, Aug. 23, 1969; children: Kristen, Brian, Eric. BS in Food Sci., Iowa State U., 1968; MS in Nutrition Sci., Drexel U., 1979. Registered Dietitian. Home economist Campbell Soup Co., Camden, N.J., 1968-69; dietetic trainee Phila. Gen. Hosp., 1970-73, clin. dietitian I, 1973-74, clin. dietitian II, 1974-77; clin. dietitian II City of Phila. Nursing Home, 1977-78; adminstrv. dietitian III City of Phila. Dept. Pub. Health, 1978-82; instl. food services dir. City of Phila. Instns., 1982—; instr. Pa. State Univ., Abington, 1983—. contbg. editor Journal of Nutrition for the Elderly, 1981—; contbr. articles to profl. jours. Recipient Phila. Nursing Home award, 1978, 86. Mem. Pa. Dietetic Assn. (pres. 1985-86, Keystone award 1987), Phila. Dietetic Assn. (pres. 1982-83, Outstanding Profl. 1984), Am. Dietetic Assn., Am. Soc. Hosp. Food Service Adminstrn., Nat. Assn. Female Execs., Omicron Nu. Office: City of Phila Nursing Home Girard and Corinthian Aves Philadelphia PA 19130

MATTHEWS, NANCY LOU, librarian; b. Texarkana, Ark., July 8, 1931; d. Edgar and Wilhelmina (Mulhearn) Matthews. B.A., U. Ark.-Fayetteville, 1953; M.S., UCLA, 1984. Research assoc. Baylor U. Hosp., Dallas, 1953-55, Wadley Research Inst., Dallas, 1955-57, Rockefeller Inst., N.Y.C., 1957-60, UCLA Med. Sch., 1960-74; freelance writer, Los Angeles, 1974-82; info. specialist Arco Petroleum, Los Angeles, 1983-84; staff writer Los Angeles Community Coll. Dist., 1979-80, Research Assistance Inc., 1977-79; assoc. librarian Los Angeles Times, 1984-87; owner Matthews Indexing Services, Hot Springs, Ark., 1988—. Contbr. articles to profl. jours. Mem. NOW, ALA, Am. Soc. Info. Sci. Democrat. Ishtarian. Home: 822 Shady Grove Rd Hot Springs AR 71901

MATTHEWS, VALERIE JO, development company executive; b. Omaha, June 6, 1947; d. Blaine Leroy and Betty Rae (Peterson) Rish; m. L. D. Matthews (div. 1975); children: Amy Lynne, Timothy Bryan. Grad. high sch., Omaha, 1965. Acct. various firms, Fremont, Nebr., 1967-78; sales assoc. Sunrise Home, Lincoln, Nebr., 1979-81, Lamb Realty, Thousand Oaks, Calif., 1981-82; rep. and mgr. sales Centex Homes, Oklahoma City, 1982-85; div. pres. Oklahoma City and Denver, 1985-87; ptnr. Lamb Realty, Thousand Oaks, Calif., 1988, C.R. Wood Devel. Inc., Thousand Oaks, 1988—; pvt. practice tax and fin. cons. Vol. YMCA, Fremont, 1972, Vols. in the Arts, Oklahoma City, 1985; active Boy Scouts Am., Thousand Oaks, 1981-82. Mem. Calif. Assn. Realtors, Nat. Assn. Home Builders, Bldg. Industry Assn.

MATTHIES, MARY CONSTANCE T., lawyer; b. Baton Rouge, Mar. 22, 1948; d. Allen Douglas and Mazie (Poche) Tillman. B.S., Okla. State U., 1969; J.D., U. Tulsa, 1972. Bar: Okla. 1973, U.S. Ct. Appeals (10th cir.) 1974, U.S. Ct. Appeals (8th and D.C. cirs.) 1975, U.S. Supreme Ct. 1976. Assoc., ptnr. Kothe, Nichols & Wolfe, Inc., Tulsa, 1972-78; pres. sr. prin. Matthies Law Firm, P.C., Tulsa, 1978—; guest lectr. U. Tulsa Coll. Law, U. Okla. Sch. Law, Oral Roberts U. Sch. Law. Mem. Women's Task Force, Tulsa Community Relations Commn., 1972-73; Recipient Tom Brett Criminal Law award, 1971; Am. Jurisprudence awards, 1971. Mem. ABA (mem. spl. subcom. for liaison with EEOC, 1974—, spl. subcom. for liaison with OFCCP, 1979—, mgmt. co-chmn. equal employment law subcoms. on nat. origin discrimination 1974-75, class actions and remedies 1975-80), Okla. Bar Assn. (council mem. labor law sect. 1974-80, chmn. 1978-79), Women's Law Caucus, Phi Delta Phi. Presbyterian. Contbr. articles on law to profl. jours.; mem. staff Tulsa Law Jour., 1971-72. Office: Reunion Ctr Suite 300 Tulsa OK 74103

MATTHIES, PATRICIA SUE, advertising executive; b. Hinsdale, Ill., Dec. 6, 1959; d. Robert Thorman and Suzanne (Dicke) M. BSBA in Mktg., Valparaiso U., 1985. Creative asst. Ogilvy and Mather Direct Response Advt., Chgo., 1985-86, traffic coordinator, 1986-87, asst. account exec., 1987-88, account exec., 1988—. Mem. Nat. Assn. Female Execs., Chgo. Assn. Direct Mktg. (Cert. Achievement 1985), Direct Mktg. Assn. N.Y., Printers Industry Inst. (Cert. Achievement 1986, 87). Republican. Episcopalian. Clubs: Lakeshore Ski, Chgo. Met. Ski Council. Office: Ogilvy & Mather Direct Response Advt 520 N Michigan Ave Chicago IL 60611

MATTHIS, MELANEY JOY, marketing professional; b. Louisville, July 10, 1963; d. Richard James and Janice Ilene (Davies) McCourt. Student, Broward Community Coll., 1988—. Bookkeeper Lindsley Stores, Inc., Oakland Park, Fla., 1981-83; v.p. merchandising Mr. H.O.W. Wharehouse, Margate, Fla., 1983-85; v.p. internat. mktg. Homer Products Internat. Corp., Ft. Lauderdale, Fla., 1985—; cons. Fortune Group Industries, Miami, 1986—, Choice Group Industries, Ft. Lauderdale, 1986—, Dickinson Dynamics, Madison, Conn., 1986—. Republican. Home: 3505 W Atlantic Blvd #911 Pompano Beach FL 33069 Office: Homer Products Internat Corp 2666 SW 23 Terr Fort Lauderdale FL 33312

MATTHYS, ELIZABETH KLEIN, educator; b. Stamford, Conn., Sept. 10, 1927; d. Henry and Emily Catherine (Weir) Klein; B.S., Simmons Coll., 1949; M.A., Framingham State Coll., 1978; m. Leon T. Matthys, Aug. 29, 1949; children—Lynne, Donna, Beth. Asst. buyer Jordan Marsh Co., Boston, 1949-51; asst. sales mgr. Curity Nursery Products, 1951-52; dir. comml. continuity Gen. Electric Co., Sta. WGY, Schenectady, 1952-53; retail mgmt. program coordinator Henry O. Peabody Sch., Norwood, Mass., 1970-86, New Eng. tour guide Tourco, Hyannis, Mass., 1987—; advisor Tri-County Regional Vocat. Tech. Sch., 1975-86. Leader, Girl Scouts Am., Walpole, Mass., 1951-52, Acton, Mass., Norfolk, Mass., 1960-70; chmn. study group LWV, Acton, Mass., 1962-88, Mem. Fashion Group, NEA, Am. Vocat. Assn., Mass. Vocat. Assn., Norfolk County Tchrs. Assn., Nat. Assn. Distributive Edn. Tchrs., Distributive Edn. Clubs Am. Republican Baptist. Home: 19 Fox Run Circle East Dennis MA 02641

MATTINGLY, PHYLLIS ROSABONHEUR GREENE, handwriting analyst, questioned document examiner; b. Chgo., Mar. 9, 1913; d. Chester Holt and Helen Mary (Jones) Greene; m. John Waller Mattingly, Aug. 28, 1944; children: John Chester, James Robert, David Bruce. A.B., U. Chgo., 1938; M.S., Ill. Inst. Tech., 1940; cert. graphoanalyst Internat. Graphoanalysis Soc., 1975, master cert., 1977. Adminstrv. sec. Gen. Electric X-ray, Chgo., 1938-40; personnel mgr. Progressive Hotels, Chgo., 1940-44; tchr., dean girls Pensacola High Sch., Fla., 1945-48; owner Ft. Collins Welcome Lady, Colo., 1949-70; talk host KCOL Koffee Klub, Ft. Collins, 1950-60; owner Phyllis Mattingly Handwriting Services, Ft. Collins and Malibu, Calif., 1976—; instr. Colo. State U., Ft. Collins, 1980—. Pres. Friends of Ft. Collins Library, 1980-83, Internat. Ctr., Colo. State U., 1977-79; chmn. Council on Aging, Ft. Collins, 1975-76; rep. precinct committeeman, pres. Republican Women's Forum, Ft. Collins, 1965-74; exec. bd. dirs. Planned Parenthood, Denver, 1960-62; pres. Parents without Ptnrs., Ft. Collins, 1980-84. Named to 9 Who Care, Channel 9 television, 1982; U.S. Nat. Ballroom Dance champion, 1985; 1985 Roastee Ft. Collins Found., 1985. Mem. Internat. Graphoanalysis Soc. (instr. ann. congress 1983—, Internat. Graphoanalyst of Yr. 1986), Colo. Graphoanalysis Soc. (Colo. Graphoanalyst of Yr. 1981, pres. 1984-86), So. Calif. Graphoanalysis Soc. (exec. bd. dirs. 1980—, So Calif. Graphoanalyst of Yr. 1984), World Assn. Document Examiners, Nat. Assn. Document Examiners (sec. 1980-83, v.p. 1988—), Internat. Platform Assn. Republican. Christian Scientist. Avocations: dancing, bicycling, theatre, swimming, reading. Home and Office: 1113 Parkwood Dr Fort Collins CO 80525

MATTISON, PRISCILLA JANE, film company executive; b. Phila., July 28, 1960. Cert., Tech. U. Berlin, 1983; BA, Yale U., 1982; cert., Am. Film Inst., 1987. Coordinator prodn. office Eyris Prodns., Inc., N.Y.C., 1983-84; asst. producer LKL Prodns. Inc., N.Y.C., 1984-85; distbn. dir. Michael Blackwood Prodns. Inc., N.Y.C., 1985-86; asst. to pres. New Horizons Picture Corp., Los Angeles, 1987-88; dir. acquisitions, exec.-in-charge devel. Concorde/New Horizons, Los Angeles, 1987—; free-lance assoc. producer, pub. relations, N.Y.C., 1985-86. Dir., editor music video, 1986; composer various songs, 1985—; asst. producer films and videos, 1985—. Fundraiser Cystic Fibrosis Found., Narberth, pa., 1976-78; English tutor Internat. Ctr., N.Y.C., 1985. Recipient Eunice Pond Meml. award Pa. Poetry Soc., 1978; Fulbright scholar Inst. Internat. Edn., 1982. Mem. Greenpeace, Calif. Abortion Rights Action League, Zero Population growth, Assn. Ind. Video and Filmakers, Nat. Assn. Female Execs., Nat. Acad. Songwriters, Fulbright Alumni Assn., Mensa. Democrat. Home: 1440 Barry Ave #6 Los Angeles CA 90025 Office: Concorde/New Horizons 11600 San Vicente Blvd Los Angeles CA 90049

MATTOON, ANDREA SUE, banker; b. Lakewood, Ohio, May 18, 1956; d. Robert Alden and Dorothy (Figgie) M. BA in Psychology, Northwestern U., 1978. Programmer traineethen analyst Bank of Boston, 1978-86, systems analyst, sr. systems analyst, asst. v.p.; sr. sect. mgr. New England Info. Systems Div., 1986; v.p. electronic banking First Interstate Bancorp, Los Angeles, 1986—. Home: 14010 Captains Row #348 Marina del Rey CA 90292 Office: First Interstate Bancorp 707 Wilshire Blvd W 18-37 Los Angeles CA 90017

MATTSON, CAROL LINNETTE, social services administrator; b. Frederic, Wis., Oct. 3, 1946; d. Clarence Waldemar and Lucille Anna Mathilda (Bengtson) Hedlund; m. Wesley Harlan Mattson, June 24, 1967; 1 child, Aaron Ray. BS, U. Wis., Menomonie, 1968. Home econs. tchr. Luck (Wis.) High Sch., 1968-72; township clk. Daniels Township, Siren, Wis., 1973-75; family living instr. Wis. Indianhead Tech. Inst., New Richmond, 1974-77; aging program dir. Polk County, Balsam Lake, Wis., 1977—; sec., bd. dirs. Polk County Transp. for the Disabled and Elderly, Inc., Balsam Lake, 1978—; sec., mem. com. Long Term Support Com., Balsam Lake, 1985—. Mem. Wis. Assn. Nutrition Dirs., Wis. Assn. Aging and Unit Dirs. Lutheran. Home: Route 1 Box 1040 Siren WI 54872 Office: Polk County Aging Programs Courthouse Box 281 Balsam Lake WI 54810

MATTSON, ESTHER JOAN, chemical company personnell executive, b. Worcester, Mass., Mar. 5, 1935; d. John Arthur and Mary Ann (Falcone) Santomenno; A.S., Becker Jr. Coll., Worcester, Mass., 1954; B.S., Pace U., 1977. Personnel programs adminstr. Crompton & Knowles, N.Y.C., 1969-70, mgr. employee benefits, 1970-73, mgr. benefits and compensation, 1973-78, dir. compensation, benefits and career planning, 1978-84, dir. human resources, 1984—. Mem. Am. Soc. Personnel Adminstrn., Am. Soc. Tng. and Devel., N.Y. Personnel Mgmt. Assn. (treas.), Am. Compensation Assn., Am. Arbitration Assn. Home: 3 Canterbury Green Stamford CT 06901 Office: 1 Station Pl Metro Center Stamford CT 06902

MATTSON, KARLA RUTH, home economist, b. Beach, N.D., Mar 9, 1959; d. Walter Donald and Ardyn Ardyl (Thurn) M. BS in Textiles and Clothing and Home Econs. Edn., N.D. State U., 1981. Extension home economist at large N.D. Coop. Extension Service, Park River, Williston and Valley City, 1981-82; extension home economist Bottineau (N.D.) County N.D. Coop. Extension Service, 1982—; N.D. del. to Nat. 4-H Leaders Forum N.D. Coop. Extension Service, Washington, 1986; speaker in field. Author: (slide tape program) Feeling Comfortable, 1981, weekly news column, 1982—, radio spots Sta. KBTO-FM, 1982—; presenter Noon Day Show, Minot, N.D., 1985-87. Coordinator 4-H Club and homemaker activities, N.D., 1982—; participant walk-a-thon March of Dimes, Minot, N.D., 1983; helper Spl. Olympics Program, Lake Metigoshe, N.D., 1983-87; provider story hour Bottineau County Library, 1987; funds collector Am. Cancer Soc., Bottineau, 1987. Mem. Am. Home Econs. Assn. (cert.), N.D. Home Econs. Assn. (2d v.p. 1985-87), Dist. II Home Econs. Assn. (chmn. 1985-87), Nat. Assn. Extension Home Economists, N.D. Assn. Extension Home Economists (treas. 1983-85, various coms.). Lutheran. Home: 715 E 8th St Bottineau ND 58318 Office: Bottineau County Extension Service Courthouse Bottineau ND 58318

MATURA, PAMELA KAY, health science executive, consultant; b. Gallipolis, Ohio, May 22, 1952; d. Virgil Dee Black and Fannie Marie (Newman) Murray; m. Raymond Carl Matura, June 7, 1975; children: Meagan Elise, Ryan Matthew. BS, Rio Grand Coll., 1974; M of Health Sci., U. Fla., 1981. Lic. social worker, Ohio, lic. profl. counselor, Ohio. Protective service specialist Ohio Dept. Mental Retardation, Columbus, 1974-77; project dir. Jackson (Ohio) County Mental Retardation, 1977-78; research asst. U. Fla., Gainesville, 1979; client adviser, guardian Guardian Services, Ltd., Columbus, 1981-83; asst. supt. Gallipolis (Ohio) Devel. Ctr., 1984-85, chief exec. officer, supt., 1985—. Mem. adv. bd. Rio Grande Coll., 1985—, bd. dirs. Named Woman of Yr., Gallia County Bus. and Profl. Women, 1986, Grand Marshall, Gallia County Christmas Parade, 1987. Mem. Nat. Assn. Supts. Pub. Residential Facilities for Mentally Retarded, Assn. for Adult Aging and Devel., Am. Assn. for Counseling and Devel., Nat. Assn. for Female Execs., Gerontological Soc. Am., Gallipolis C. of C., Faculty Women's Assn., Chi Omega Alpha (adviser), Rho Chi Sigma. Democrat. Roman Catholic. Home: 637 Kristi Dr Rt 2 Bidwell OH 45614 Office: Gallipolis Devel Ctr 2500 Ohio Ave Gallipolis OH 45631

MATURIN, THERESA POIRIER, nurse; b. St. Martinville, La., Apr. 21, 1932; d. Leopold and Emilie (Poche) Poirier; Cosmetician, Lafayette (La.) Beauty Sch., 1963; diploma Teche Area Nursing Sch., New Iberia, La., 1975; m. Joseph Newby Maturin, Aug. 23, 1953; 1 son, Roland Joseph. Staff nurse Lafayette Gen. Hosp., 1974, Oakwood Village Nursing Care Center, Lafayette, 1975-80; pvt. duty nurse, Lafayette, 1980—. Pres. La. chpt. Nat. Fedn. Democratic Women, 1979-83; mem. La. Dem. Fin. Council, 1982; pres. St. Mary's Guild, Lafayette. Mem. Lafayette Town House, Am. Bus. Women's Assn. (chmn. local membership 1964), La. Hist. Soc., Smithsonian Assos., Nat. Trust Hist. Preservation, Right to Life, Attakapas Hist. Assn., Am. Security Council, U.S. Capitol Hist. Soc., Nat. Hist. Soc., L'Heure de Musique, France Amerique de la Louisiane (v.p. 1982-83), DAR, Soc. Dames Ct. of Honor, Lafayette Ballet Assn., Soc. Confederacy, Beta Sigma Phi. Roman Catholic. Clubs: Catholic Daus. Ams. (ct. regent 1975-79), UDC (corr. sec. chpt. 1982-83). Home: 2710 Pinhook Rd Lafayette LA 70508

MATZ, KAY ELAINE, savings and loan executive; b. Warren, Ohio, Apr. 18, 1946; d. Nick M. and Julia H. (Petruluk) Kevin; m. Howard C. Matz, Jr., Oct. 11, 1969. grad. bus. mgmt. Hiram Coll., 1987. Staff acct. R.M. Robbins & Assocs., Warren, 1964-73; with 1st Fed. Savs. & Loan Assn. Warren, 1973—, asst. treas., 1980-81, controller, 1982—; ann. fin. auditor Children's Rehab. Ctr., Warren, 1970-74. Mem. Am. Soc. Women Accts. (pres. Youngstown chpt. 1975-76), Fin. Mgrs. Soc. (pres. Pa.-Ohio chpt. 1983-84), Warren Area C. of C., Exec. Link of Warren. Democrat. Clubs: Emblem, Warren Women's Networking. Lodge: Lions (Warren). Avocation: travel. Home: 1558 Atlantic NE Warren OH 44483 Office: 1st Fed Savs & Loan Assn Warren 185 E Market St PO Box 551 Warren OH 44481

MATZ, SHEILA, research pharmacist; b. Sandusky, Ohio, Nov. 28, 1955; d. Jerome G. and Phyllis (Frankel) M. BS in Pharmacy, Ohio State U., 1978. Lic. pharmacist. Synthetic chemist Diamond Shamrock Corp., Painesville, Ohio, 1978-80, formulations chemist, 1980-82; group leader Key Pharms., Miami, 1982-85; mgr. Hercon Labs., South Plainfield, N.J., 1985—. Instr. water safety ARC, 1971—, CPR, 1977-80. Mem. Am. Assn. Pharm. Scientists, Sierra Club. Democrat. Clubs: Appalachian Mountain, Kayak and Canoe Club of N.Y., Franklin Greens Ski. Office: Hercon Labs 200 B Corp Ct South Plainfield NJ 07080

MATZNER, SUSAN CHAPMAN, government and policy researcher; b. N.Y.C., May 17, 1951; d. Leo and Molly (Serok) Chapman; m. N. David Matzner, Mar. 28, 1972; children: Solomon, Isaac, Joseph. BA, Bklyn. Coll., 1972; MS, St. John's U., 1973; postgrad., SUNY, Albany. Cert. elem. tchr., N.Y. Tchr. N.Y.C. Bd. Edn., Bklyn., 1972-74; teaching asst. SUNY, Albany, 1975-78; cons. State Edn. Dept., Albany, 1977-78; research sci. II Div. for Youth, Albany, 1978-80; instr. Coll. St. Rose, Albany, 1977-85; cons. tech. writer Gen. Electric Co., Schenectady, N.Y., 1981; tng. cons. N.Y. state agys., others, various cities, 1981—; research assoc. Inst. Govt. and Policy Studies, Albany, 1986-88; research assoc. Inst. Govt. and Policy Studies, 1986-88. Author: Sets, 1973, Finding Directions, 1973. Pres. sisterhood Temple Israel, Albany, 1986—, bd. dirs. Temple Israel, 1984—. Recipient Regent's Scholarship award N.Y. State Bd. Regents, 1968. Democrat. Jewish.

MAUEL, LORA JEAN, computer center director, graphics artist; b. Chehalis, Wash., June 17, 1959; d. George Alden and Leora May (Diesburg) M. AA, Centralia Community Coll., 1979; BS in Acctg., U. Washington, Seattle, 1981. Cert. data entry operator. Computer ctr. dir. Bowen, Hafey & Pennington, CPA's, Centralia, 1982—. Vol. Centralia Main Street Assn., 1987, United Way Lewis County, 1987. Club: Toastmasters (sec./treas. Chehalis chpt. 1987—, pres. 1988—). Lodge: Order of Eastern Star. Office: Bowen Hafey & Pennington CPA's 120 W Magnolia Centralia WA 98531

MAUGER, PATRICIA ANN, television producer; b. Allentown, Pa., Dec. 21, 1937; d. Von Edgar and Ruth Hannah (Kreitz) M. Grad., Berkeley Sch., East Orange, N.J., 1957. TV producer NBC, N.Y.C., 1964-86; freelance producer N.Y.C., 1986—. Mem. Nat. Acad. TV Arts and Scis., Women in Radio and TV, Mensa. Presbyterian. Home and Office: 5 Tudor City Pl New York NY 10017

MAUL, CAROL ANGSTMAN, public relations executive; b. Princeton, Minn., Jan. 5, 1942; d. Ezra H. and Edna Irene (Balfanz) Angstman; m. Kenneth A. Maul, Aug. 17, 1974. BA, Concordia Coll., Moorhead, Minn., 1963. Tchr. English Minn., 1963-66; owner CAMI Prodns., Beaverton, Oreg., 1977-87; sec., med. staff Fresno (Calif.) Community Hosp., 1987—. Mem. Council City of Beaverton, 1983-86; bd. dirs. Beaverton Sister Cities Found., 1986, Emanuel Hosp. Burn Ctr., Portland, 1986, Met. Area Communication Commn., Beaverton, 1985-86; goal-setting task force City of Fresno, 1987—. Mem. Am. Soc. for Pub. Adminstrn. (pres. 1984-85, bd. dirs. 1983-86), SBA (adv. council 1981-87), Beaverton Area C. of C. (chair com. 1980, 81). Democrat. Lutheran.

MAUL, CAROL ELAINE, small business owner; b. Joliet, Ill., Feb. 28, 1953; d. Donald James and Virginia Olive (Wilson) Johnson; m. Richard Kester Maul, June 16, 1979. Student, Met. State Coll., 1971-76. Mgr. So-Fro Fabrics, Elgin, 1976-79; owner, operator Port Arthur Pie Co., Denver, 1985-87; maker custom infant clothing, freelance musician Denver, 1987—. Prin. flutist Elgin Symphony Orch., 1976-79. Mem. Nat. Assn. Female Execs. Democrat. Baptist. Lodge: Job's Daughters (Honored Queen 1970-71). Home: 1517 S Bellaire Denver CO 80222

MAULDIN, ANNA MARIE MARINO, design company executive, financial consultant; b. Dallas, Oct. 15, 1945; d. Samuel and Marie Rita (Petta) Marino; m. H.R. Mauldin, Dec. 18, 1964 (div. apr. 1972). B.B.A., North Tex. State U., Denton, 1968. Treas., controller Web Thomas Aircraft, Dallas, 1971-75, Dahlgren Mfg. Co., Dallas, 1975-77, Jack Day Constrn. Co., Dallas, 1977-81; controller Southwestern Gage, Dallas, 1981-82; sec., controller Joyce K. Wynn, Inc., Dallas, 1982—; treas. Web Thomas Aircraft Sales, Dallas, 1975—; fin. cons. Dean Property, Dallas, 1981—, Shettle & Assocs.-Attys., Dallas, 1979—; comml. research and analysis fin. cons. Mem. Park Cities League. Republican. Roman Catholic. Office: Joyce K Wynn Inc 2211 N Lamar Suite 200 Dallas TX 75202

MAUN, MARY ELLEN, communications company analyst; b. N.Y.C., Dec. 18, 1951; d. Emmet Joseph and Mary Alice (McMahon) M. BA, CUNY, 1977, MBA, 1988. Sales rep. N.Y. Telephone Co., N.Y.C., 1970-76, comml. rep., 1977-83, programmer, 1984-86; systems analyst Nynex Service Co., N.Y.C., 1987—. Corp. chmn. United Way of Tri-State Area, N.Y.C., 1985; recreation activities vol. Pioneers Am., N.Y.C., 1982—. Recipient Outstanding Community Service award, Calvary Hosp., Bronx, N.Y., 1984. Democrat. Club: N.Y. Road Runners. Home: 3 Farrington Ave Philipse Manor NY 10591-1302 Office: Nynex Service Co 1166 Ave of the Americas New York NY 10036

MAUNSBACH, KAY BENEDICTA, financial analyst, consultant; b. N.Y.C., Apr. 25, 1933; d. Eric and Katherine M. BA, Hunter Coll., 1961; postgrad., NYU, 1961-64. CLU. Jr. fin. analyst Vilas and Hickey, N.Y.C., 1960-62; v.p. investment services Shearson Loeb, Rhoades and Co. Inc., N.Y.C., 1962-73; v.p., dir. corp. communications Manhattan Life Ins. Co., N.Y.C., 1974-80; pres. Atrium Group Ltd., 1980—; gen. ptnr. Prospero Properties, 1982—; chmn. Pegasus Constrn. Corp.; bd. dirs. Regis Camp Devel.; pres. Atrium Holding Corp., 1982—, Prospero Prop. II & of N.Y., 1985-86, Pegasus Asset Mgmt. Corp., 1985—, Pegasus at Water Mill Inc., 1986—, Pegasus at Fishkill Inc., Pegasus at Pleasant Valley Inc., 1987; gen. ptnr. Pegasus at Amenia Partnership, pres. Pegasus at Middletown Ltd. and Pegasus at Bloomingburg Ltd., 1988; v.p. Eaton State Assn. of Fla., 1986—; pres. Olympia Devel. Group Builders, 1988—; ptnr. Riverseage Assn., Huntsville, Ala., 1986—. Trustee Art Festival of Continents, Key West, Fla. Fellow Fin. Analysts Fedn.; mem. Life Advertisers Assn., Nat. Assn. Bus. Economists, Pub. Relations Council, Am. Council Life Ins., Internat. Assn. Bus. Communicators, Fin. Communications Soc., Pub. Affairs Council, Women's Econ. Roundtable, Ins. Women N.Y., Life Ins. Council N.Y., N.Y. Soc. Security Analysts, Chartered Life Underwriters, Life Underwriters Assn. N.Y., N.Y. Bd. Realtors, N.Y. Bus. Communicators, World Futurists Soc. Office: Cordwood Ln Box WWW East Hampton NY 11937 Office: 1433 Reynolds St PO Box 1777 Key West FL 33040

MAUPIN, CAROL GRINSTEAD, food consultant; b. Pawhuska, Okla., Jan. 31, 1936; d. Randolph Henry and Mildred Asilee (Pfaff) Grinstead; B.A., U. Okla., 1958. Asst. to food dir. Neiman Marcus, Dallas, 1958-62; asst. to food dir. So. Meth. U., Dallas, 1963-64; asso. dir. food ops. Mut. of Omaha, 1964-69; dir. tearoom, parties and spl. events Denver Dry Goods, 1970-74; dir. food and party services Jr. League of Houston, 1974-81; partner Jackson and Co., catering service, 1981-83; head food research and devel. Neiman Marcus, Dallas, 1983—; Entertaining columnist Dallas Morning News; food cons. Mus. Food Arts; cooking instr. Batterie de Cuisine Cooking Sch., Foleys, Gourmet Kitchens; food lectr.; food and party cons. protocol office City of Houston; food service cons., bd. dirs. Alley Theatre of Houston. Mem. Am. Home Econs. Assn., Nat. Assn. Cooking Schs., Internat. Food and Wine Soc., Houston Culinary Guild. Republican. Episcopalian. Home: 4423 Westway Ave Dallas TX 75205 Office: Neiman Marcus Dallas TX 75201

MAUPIN, VIRGINIA LEE, religious organization administrator; b. Los Angeles, Apr. 2, 1924; d. Sam Guy and Phyllis Evelyn (Ford) Snyder; m. Willis Preston (Jack) Maupin, July 23, 1944; children: Andrea, Thomas, Shirley. Student, San Diego State U., 1942-44. Sec. Comml. Refrigeration, San Diego, 1944-45; sec. fin. First Presbyn. Ch., Richardson, Tex., 1961-64, sec. fin., Pastor's, 1964-70; adminstr. First Presbyn. Ch., Richardson, 1970—. Mem. Nat. Assn. Ch. Bus. Adminstrs., Network (bd. dirs., sec., treas. 1985-86). Club: Richardson Woman's (pres. 1961-62). Home: 404 Inglewood Dr Richardson TX 75080

MAURER, ELEANOR JOHNSON, oil company executive; b. Milan, Mo., Jan. 23, 1914; d. Harvey Clifton and Bertha Delaney (Wilkerson) Miller; m. Darwin T. Maurer, Aug. 5, 1968 (dec. 1978); 1 child, Jacqueline Eleanor Maroof. Student, Stephens Coll., 1930-31, Southwestern State U., Weatherford, Okla., 1932, Draughons Bus. Coll., 1934. Sec. Kirkpatrick Oil Co., Oklahoma City, 1951-66, asst. to pres., 1966-80, chief exec. officer, 1980—; bd. dirs. Union Bank and Trust Co., S.W. Title and Trust, Kirkpatrick Found., Oklahoma City. Treas. Oklahoma City Community Fedn., 1987—. Named Corp. Woman Yr. Oklahoma City Jour. Record/Woman's Forum, 1984. Mem. Exec. Women Internat. (pres. Oklahoma City chpt. 1964), Com. of 200. Republican. Home: 7900 Lakehurst Dr Oklahoma City OK 73120 Office: Kirkpatrick Oil Co 1300 N Broadway Dr Oklahoma City OK 73103

MAURER, JOANN DENICE, health science facility administrator; b. Bay City, Mich., Dec. 18, 1951; d. Phillip C. Maurer and Elsie (Etherington) McGowan. AS, Eas. Mich. U., 1979; BS in Pharmacy, Mercer U., 1982, PharmD, 1983. Registered Pharmacist, Ga., Fla. Pharmacy intern Drs. Meml. Hosp., Atlanta, 1979-82; pharmacist Egleston Hosp., Atlanta, 1982-84; Clin. specialist Lee Meml. Hosp., Ft. Myers, Fla., 1984—. Lectr. Arthritis Found., Ft. Myers, 1984—. Mem. So. Gulf Soc. Hosp. Pharmacists (pres. 1988—), Am. Soc. Parenteral Enteral Nutrition, Fla. Soc. Hosp. Pharmacists, Phi Theta Kappa. Republican. Episcopalian. Home: 1910 Viginia Ave Apt 502B Fort Myers FL 33901

MAURER, LUCILLE DARVIN, state treasurer; b. N.Y.C., Nov. 21, 1922; d. Joseph Jay and Evelyn (Levine) Darvin; student U. N.C.-Greensboro 1938-40; B.A., U. N.C.-Chapel Hill, 1942; M.A., Yale U., 1945; H.L.D. (hon.), Hood Coll., 1984; m. Ely Maurer, Apr. 29, 1945; children—Stephen Bennett, Russell Alexander, Edward Nestor. Economist, U.S. Tariff Commn., 1942-43; econ. and market research for pvt. firms, 1957-60; cons. Nat. Center for Ednl. Stats., 1969-70; mem. Md. House of Dels., 1969-87 , mem. ways and means com., 1971-87, chmn. joint com. on fed. relations, 1983-87; mem. intergovtl. adv. council U.S. Dept. Edn., 1980-82. Del., Md. Constl. Conv., 1967-68; mem. Montgomery County Bd. Edn., 1960-68; trustee Montgomery Community Coll., 1960-68; vice chmn. nat. planning com., advanced leadership program of seminars on edn. and ednl. policy for state legislators Edn. Commn. of States, 1979-81; mem. exec. com. of edn. com. Nat. Conf. of State Legislatures, 1975-84, chmn., 1978-79, chmn. com. on taxes, trade and econ. devel., 1985-86; mem. adv. com. Servicemems. Opportunity Colls., 1978-82; mem. nat. adv. bd. Inst. for Ednl. Leadership, 1979-81; co-chmn. Md. Commn. on Intergovernmental Cooperation, 1976-82; mem. Nat. Com. on Postsecondary Accreditation, 1974-1979; bd. dirs. Montgomery United Way, 1971-76, 84—; mem. Commn. Higher Edn. of Middle States Assn., 1982-85; mem. Gov.'s Employment and Tng. Council, 1983—. Recipient Legislator of Yr. award Md. Assn. for Retarded Children, 1972; John Dewey award Montgomery County Fedn. Tchrs., 1972; Hornbook award Montgomery County Edn. Assn., 1972; Legislator of Yr. award Md. Assn. Counties, 1984; Willis award for outstanding service Md. Assn. Bds. Edn., 1984. Mem. LWV (past dir. Montgomery County, past dir. Md.), AAUW (Internat. Women's Yr. award Silver Spring 1975), Bus. and Profl. Women's Club (Woman of Yr. 1984), NOW (Legis. Excellence award 1981), Women's Equity Action League, Women's Polit. Caucus, Montgomery County Hist. Soc., Order Women Legislators, Delta Kappa Gamma. Jewish. Office: Goldstein Treasury Bdlg Annapolis MD 21401

MAURER, VICKIE SUE, foundation administrator; b. Lansing, Mich., June 12, 1942; d. Gerald Lee and Margaret Ellen (Washer) M. BS, Eastern Mich. U., 1964. Tchr. phys. edn., civics Dundee (Mich.) High Sch., 1964-65; tchr. phys. edn. Manistee (Mich.) Pub. Schs., 1965-69; camp dir. Girl Scouts of Southwestern Mich., St. Joseph, 1969-72; camp adminstr. Girl Scouts of Singing Sands, South Bend, Ind., 1972-74; program dir., camp adminstr. No. Oakland County Girl Scouts, Pontiac, Mich., 1974-78; program dir. Saharo Girl Scout Council, Tucson, Ariz., 1978-79; exec. dir. Crooked Tree Girl Scout Council, Traverse City, Mich., 1979-85; assoc. dir. Grand Traverse Area United Way, 1985—. Mem. Nat. Assn. Female Execs. Lodge: Zonta. Home: 4553 Goldenrod Dr Traverse City MI 49684 Office: Grand Traverse Area United Way PO Box 423 Traverse City MI 49685-0423

MAURER, VIRGINIA GALLAHER, law educator; b. Shawnee, Okla., Nov. 7, 1946; d. Paul Clark Gallaher and Virginia Ruth (Watson) Abernathy; m. Ralph Gerald Maurer, July 31, 1971; children—Ralph Emmett, William Edward. B.A., Northwestern U., 1968; M.A., Stanford U., 1969, J.D., 1975. Bar: Iowa 1976. Tchr. social studies San Mateo (Calif.) High Sch. Dist., 1969-71; spl. asst. to pres. U. Iowa, Iowa City, 1976-80, adj. asst. prof. law, 1979-80; affiliate asst. prof. law U. Fla., Gainesville, 1981, asst. prof. bus. law, 1980-85, assoc. prof., 1985—, interim dir. MBA Program, 1987—; cons. Gov.'s Com. on Iowa 2000, Iowa City, 1976-77, Fla. Banker's Assn., Gainesville, 1982. Contbr. articles to profl. jours. Mem. fundraising com. Pro Arte Musica, Gainesville, 1980-84. Mem. ABA, Am. Bus. Law Assn., Southeastern Bus. Law Assn. (Proc. editor 1984-87, treas. 1985-86, v.p. 1986-87, pres.-elect 1987-88), Iowa Bar Assn., LWV, U. Fla. Athletic Assn. (bd. dirs. 1982—; v.p., chmn. fin. com.), Gainesville Womens' Forum, Fla. Women' Network, Beta Gamma Sigma, Kappa Alpha Theta, Delta Sigma Pi. Club: Univ. Women's (Gainesville, Fla.). Lodge: Rotary (Gainnesville). Home: 2210 NW 6th Pl Gainesville FL 32603 Office: U Fla Grad Sch Bus Gainesville FL 32603

MAU-SHIMIZU, PATRICIA ANN, lawyer; b. Honolulu, Jan. 17, 1953; d. Herbert G.K. ad Leilani (Yuen) Mau; m. John B. Shimizu, Aug. 15, 1981; 1 child, Melissa Rose. B.S., U. San Francisco, 1975; J.D., Golden Gate U., 1979. Bar: Hawaii 1979. Law clk. State Supreme Ct., Honolulu, 1979-80; atty. Bendet, Fidell & Sakai, Honolulu, 1980-81; legis. atty. Honolulu City Council, 1981-83; legis. atty. House Majority Research Office, Honolulu, 1983-84, dir., 1984—. Mem. Hawaii State Bar Assn., Hawaii Young Lawyers, Hawaii Women Lawyers. Democrat. Roman Catholic. Home: 7187 Hawaii Kai Dr Honolulu HI 96825 Office: State House Reps House Majority Research Office State Capitol Room 308A Honolulu HI 96813

MAUZÉ, ANN COLLINS, public relations executive; b. Dayton, Ohio, Jan. 28, 1940; d. James Kenneth and Leona Hunt (Laurence) Collins; m. George Mauzé III, Oct. 2, 1959; children: Michael Laurence and William Harman. AA, William Woods Coll., 1957-59. New accounts mgr. Brentwood Bank, St. Louis, 1960-62; account exec. Edward C. Haggerty and Assocs., Summit, N.J., 1978-81, account mgr., 1981-84, v.p., 1984—; cons. Leanna Brown Senatorial Campaign, N.J., 1987—. Contbr. articles to profl. jours. Pres. Jr. League of Summit, Inc., 1979-80; trustee N.J. Ctr. for Visual Arts, Summit, 1986—, SAGE, Summit, 1987—, N.J. Youth Symphony, Summit, 1984-86. Mem. Pub. Relations Soc. Am. Republican. Presbyterian. Home: 54 Murray Hill Sq Murray Hill NJ 07974 Office: Edward C Haggerty and Assoc 387 Springfield Ave Summit NJ 07901

MAVILLE, PAULINE BRIGGS, industrial engineer; b. Lebanon, N.H., Jan. 29, 1924; d. Clifton Charles and Grace Francis (Lovering) Briggs; student U.S. Naval Aviation Tech. Tng. Sch., 1944; grad. Plus Sch. Bus., 1968; student Stonehill Coll., 1975-76, Massasoitt Community Coll., 1978-79; m. Feb. 24, 1945 (div.); 1 son, Thomas Briggs. Machinist, various cos., Lebanon, N.H. and Waltham, Mass., 1946-68; jr. indsl. engr. Compo Industries, Inc., Waltham, 1968-70; scheduling coordinator Heath Cons., Inc., Stoughton, Mass., 1971-72; cost estimator Metal Bellows Co., Sharon, Mass., 1972-75; sr. cost estimator Bird-Johnson Co., Walpole, Mass., 1975-79; sr. cost estimator MAPO div. Disney Prodns., Glendale, Calif., 1980-81, indsl. engr. WED div., Glendale, 1981-84; sr. indsl. engr. Electrodynamics div. Allied Signal, North Hollywood, Calif., 1984—. Served with USN, 1944-45. Mem. Am. Inst. Indsl. Engrs., Nat. Property Mgmt. Assn., Am. Legion. Democrat. Club: Bus. and Profl. Women's. Home: 1231 N Verdugo Rd Glendale CA 91206 Office: Allied Signal Inc 1600 Sherman Way North Hollywood CA 91605

MAVIS, DEBORAH KAYE, dietitian; b. Galveston, Tex., June 13, 1953; d. Alonzo Jr. and Billie Kathryn (Frye) M. BS in Food Nutrition and Instl. Adminstrn. magna cum laude, Prairie View (Tex) A&M U., 1975. Cert. secondary vocat. home econs. tchr., Tex.; registered dietitian. Dietetic intern VA Med. Ctr., Hines, Ill., 1975-76; clin. dietitian, edn. and staff devel. dietitian VA Med. Ctr., Dallas, 1976-81; chief dietetic service VA Med. Ctr., Grand Island, Nebr., 1981-83, Shreveport, La., 1983-87, New Orleans, 1987—; mem. Vocat. Tech. Culinary Arts, Shreveport, 1985-86. Mem. Nat. Council Negro Women, New Orleans, 1987. Mem. Am. Dietetic Assn., La. Dietetic Assn., Fed. Exec. Assn., Nat. Assn. Female Execs. Democrat. Baptist. Office: VA Med Ctr 1601 Perdido New Orleans LA 70146

MAVRONIKOLAS, RUTH THORP HARVEY, educator; b. Phila., July 3, 1931; d. Cyril Hingston and Ruth Sharpless (Thorp) Harvey; B.F.A. in Art Edn., Phila. Coll. Art, 1956; M.S. in Edn., U. Pa., 1964; m. Christopher George Mavronikolas, Nov. 27, 1958; children—Elia Ruth, George Christopher. Tchr., Baldwin Sch., Bryn Mawr, Pa., 1957-66, chmn. art dept., 1960-66; assoc. prof. art edn. Phila. Coll. Art, 1966-74, registrar, 1956-57; tchr. Moorestown (N.J.) Friends Sch., 1974-76, chmn. art dept., 1974-76; tchr. Franklin Learning Center, Phila., 1976-82; tchr. Ludlow Elem. Sch., Phila., 1986—. T. Wistar Brown Fund Endl. grantee, 1952-64; Mary Jeannes Fund Ednl. grantee, 1952-53; Anne Townsend Fund grantee, 1952-53. Republican. Home: 208 West End Ave Haddonfield NJ 08033

MAXEY, CATHERINE ANNETTE, human resource executive, consultant, trainer; b. Carbondale, Ill., Dec. 12, 1938; d. J. Ellsworth and Catherine (Crossno) Tucker; m. James H. Maxey, Aug. 20, 1961; 1 son, Gregory Scott. B.A., Ill. Wesleyan U., Bloomington, 1960; M.A., U. Chgo., 1962. Dir. Gwinnett-Rockdale Mental Health Mental Retardation Services, Lawrenceville, Ga., 1973-76; supt. Ga. Regional Hosp., Decatur, 1977-82; exec. dir. Nat. Assn. Social Workers, Silver Springs, Md., 1982-83; instr. U. Ga., Athens from 1984; mem. exec. bd. Health Systems Agy., Atlanta, 1980-82; dir. Health Planning Agy., State of Ga., 1984—; mem. task panel Pres. Commn. on Mental Health, Washington, 1978; del. Internat. Fedn. Social Workers, 1982. Recipient Disting. Alumnus award Ill. Wesleyan U., 1978. Mem. Nat. Assn. Social Workers, Mental Health Assn., Assn. for Retarded Citizens, NOW, Acad. Cert. Social Workers. Democrat. Club: Ansly Golf (Atlanta). Office: Health Planning Agy 4 Executive Park Dr NE Suite 2100 Atlanta GA 30329

MAXEY, JILL RAICHERT, printing company executive; b. Mpls., Aug. 5, 1943; d. Charles Lincoln and DeLoris Alice (Borseth) Raichert; m. Daniel Patrick Maxey, July 31, 1952; children: Douglas Charles, Paul Douglas. Grad. high sch., Robbinsdale, Minn. Office mgr. Dr. N.E. Neslund, Robbinsdale, Minn., 1959-62; v.p. Agner's Litho Service, Edina, Minn., 1965-79; pres. The Printery, Inc., Edina, Minn., 1974—; cons. Minn. Citizens Concerned for Life, Mpls., 1985—. Mem. Berean League, St. Paul, 1983—. Republican. Baptist. Office: The Printery Inc 4640 W 77th St Suite 161 Edina MN 55435

MAXFIELD, ROBIN ROBERTS, television and feature film developer, creative producer; b. Jacksonville, Fla., Nov. 24, 1954; d. Louis Edward and Vivian Lorraine (Musgrove) R.; m. Robert Keldon Maxfield, Feb. 14, 1987. Grad. in x-ray tech., U. Hosp., Jacksonville, 1974; student, Fla. Jr. Coll., 1974-75. Various positions St. Luke's Hosp., U. Hosp. Jacksonville, 1974-76; clown Circus World, Haines City, Fla., 1976; mem. sales staff Chromalloy Photographics, St. Louis, 1977-79; x-ray technician Beaches Hosp., Jacksonville Beach, Fla., 1980-82; model, actress Denise Carol Models, Jacksonville, 1979-82; prin. Resource Network, Jacksonville, 1980-88; participant, vol. Insight Seminars, Internat. Integrity Program. Mem. Am. Film Inst., Nat. Assn. Female Execs., Fla. Motion Picture and TV Assn. (pres. N.E. chpt. 1984-86, bd. dirs. N.E. chpt. 1984-87). Democrat. Methodist.

MAXMAN, SUSAN ABEL, architect; b. Columbus, Ohio, Dec. 30, 1938; d. Richard Jack Abel and Gussie (Brenner) Seiden; children: Andrew Frankel, Thomas Frankel, Elizabeth Frankel; m. William H. Maxman; children: Melissa, Abby, William Jr. Student, Smith Coll., 1960; MArch., U. Pa., 1977. Registered profl. architect, Pa., Ohio, N.J. Project designer Kopple Sheward & Day, Phila., 1978-80; ptnr. Maxman & Sutphin, Phila., 1980-83; prin. Susan Maxman Architects, Phila., 1984—. Works include restoration Vernon House, Germantown, Robert Lewis House (recipient McArthur award 1985), Phila., interior architecture Criminal Justice Ctr., Phila. Participant community leadership seminars, Phila., 1986-87. Recipient Benjamin Franklin Bridge Lighting honor award, Phila., 1986. Mem. AIA (Phila. chpt. bd. dirs. 1980-87, nat. bd. dirs. 1988—), Pa. Soc. Architects (bd. dirs. 1983-87, exec. com., sec. 1984-85, v.p., 1986, pres. 1987). Office: 123 S 22nd St Philadelphia PA 19103

MAXWELL, BARBARA SUE, educator, consultant; b. Bklyn., Feb. 22, 1950; d. Vincent and Esther Alice (Hansen) M. BA in Math Edn., Rider Coll., 1972; postgrad., Montclair State U., 1973. Cert. secondary tchr., N.J. Math tchr. Westwood (N.J.) High Sch., 1973-80; programmer Prudential Ins. Co., Roseland, N.J., 1980-81; programmer, analyst Grand Union, Paramus, N.J., 1981-82; project mgr. Info. Sci., Montvale, N.J., 1982-84; cons. Five Techs., Montvale, N.J., 1985-87; cons., project mgr. Implementation Support Assocs., Orangeburg, N.Y., 1987—; cons. in field, 1984-87; guest speaker Info. Sci. Contbr. articles to profl. jours. Mem. Nat. Assn. Female Execs., N.J. Users of Payroll Personnel, Inform, Am. Payroll Assn. Republican. Lutheran. Office: Implementation Support Assocs 100 Dutch Hill Rd Orangeburg NJ 10962

MAXWELL, FLORENCE HINSHAW, civic worker; b. Nora, Ind., July 14, 1914; d. Asa Benton and Gertrude (Randall) Hinshaw; B.A. cum laude, Butler U., 1935; m. John Williamson Maxwell, June 5, 1936; children—Marilyn, William Douglas. Coordinator, bd. dirs. Sight Conservation and Aid to Blind, 1962-73, nat. chmn., 1969-73; active various fund drives; chmn. jamboree, hostess coms. North Central High Sch., 1959, 64; Girl Scouts U.S.A., 1937-38, 54-56; mus. chmn. Sr. Girl Scout Regional Council, 1956-57; scorekeeper Little League, 1955-57; bd. dirs. Nora Sch. Parents' Club, 1958-59, Eastwood Jr. High Sch. Triangle Club, 1959-62, Ind. State Symphony Soc. Women's Com., 1965-67, 76-79, Symphoguide chmn., 1976-79; vision screening Indpls. innercity pub. sch. kindergartens, pre-schs., 1962-69, also Headstart, 1967—; asst. Glaucoma screening clinics Gen. Hosp., Glendale Shopping Center, City County Bldg., Am. Legion Nat. Hdqrs., Ind. Health Assn. Conf., 1962-73; chmn. sight conservation and aid to blind Nat. Delta Gamma Found., Indpls., Columbus, Ohio, 1969-73; mem. telethon team Butler U. Fund, 1964; symphoguide hostess Internat. Conf. on Cities, 1971, Nat. League of Cities, 1972; mem. health adv. com. Headstart, 1976—, sec., 1980—, mem. social services com., 1987—, assessment team of compliance steering com., 1978-79, 84, 86, 87, appreciation award, 1983; founder People of Vision Aux., 1981, bd. dirs., 1981—. Recipient Cable award Delta Gamma, 1969, Outstanding Alumna award, 1973, scholarship honoree, 1981; Key to City of Indpls., 1972, those Spl. People award Women in Communication, 1980. Mem. Nat., Ind. (dir. 1962—, exec. com. 1971—, v.p. 1983-86, sec., 1971-83, Ind. del. to nat. 3-yr. program planning conf. 1985, internal analysis task force for services 1987, Sight Saving award 1974, life hon. v.p. 1983—) socs. to prevent blindness, Delta Gamma (chpt. golden anniversary celebration decade and communication chmn. 1975, treas. Alpha Tau house corp. 1975-78, nat. chmn. Parent Club Study Com. 1976-77; Service Recognition award 1977, Shield award 1981, Stellar award 1986). Republican. Address: 1502 E 80th St Indianapolis IN 46240

MAXWELL, JUDITH, economist; b. Kingston, Ont., Can., July 21, 1943; d. James Ruffee and Marguerite Jane (Spanner) McMahon; m. Anthony Stirling Maxwell, May 8, 1970; children: David, Elizabeth Jane. B in Commerce, Dalhousie U., 1963; postgrad., London Sch. Econs., 1965-66. Researcher Combines Investigation Br. Consumer and Corp. Affairs, Ottawa, Can., 1963-65; econs. writer Financial Times of Can., Montreal, Que., 1966-72; dir. policy studies C.D. Howe Inst., Montreal, Que., 1972-80; cons. Esso Europe Inc., London, Eng., 1980-82, Coopers & Lybrand, Montreal, Que., 1982-85; chmn. Econ. Council Can., Ottawa, Ont., 1985—; dir. Can. Found. for Econ. Edn., 1985-88, Inst. for Research on Pub. Policy, 1987-88. Author: Energy From the Arctic, 1973; (with C. Pestieau) Economic Realities of Contemporary Confederation, 1980; (with S. Currie) Partnership for Growth, 1984. Mem. Nfld. and Labrador Sci. and Tech. Adv. Council, 1988—. Mem. Can. Assn. Bus. Econs. (pres. 1976-77), Montreal Econs. Assn. (pres. 1975-76), Can. Found. for Econ. Edn. (dir. 1985-87), Newfoundland and Labrador Sci. and Tech. Adv. Council. Office: Econ Council Can, PO Box 527, Ottawa, ON Canada K1P 5V6

MAXWELL, KATHERINE GANT, school psychologist, educational consultant; b. El Paso, Tex., Nov. 27, 1931; d. Leslie and Lillian (Beard) Gant; B.S., Abilene Christian U., 1955; M.S., Miss. State U., 1967, Ph.D., 1974; m. Fowden Gene Maxwell, July 14, 1955; children—Steve, Becky Harvey, Randy. Teaching asst. Miss. State U., Starkville, 1969-72, practicum in sch. psychology, 1973-74; adminstr. psychol. tests Starkville Pub. Schs., 1974-75; sch. psychologist Dixie & Gilchrist (Fla.) County Schs., 1977-79; instr. continuing edn. dept. U. LaVerne (Calif.), 1979-80; sch. psychologist Bryan (Tex.) Ind. Sch. Dist., 1979-80; owner, dir. Reading Improvement Center, College Station, Tex., 1979-80, Assn. Interpersonal Devel., Inc., 1982—; sch. psychologist, ednl. diagnostician Temple (Tex.) Ind. Sch. Dist., 1980-81; sch. psychologist Franklin (Tex.) Ind. Sch. Dist., 1981-82; ednl. cons., College Station, Tex., 1982—; treas. Humana Sunshine Hosp. Aux., 1987-88; newsletter editor Friends Assn. of Symphony Orch., 1987-88, corr. sec., 1988—. Author: What Makes Bosses Tick, 1986. Cub Scout leader Boy Scouts Am., Starkville, 1960; Brownie leader Girl Scouts U.S.A., Starkville, 1961-64; pres. Starkville Overstreet PTA, 1962; sec. Starkville Civic League, 1962-65; vol. Crestview Retirement Home and Brazos Food Bank; active Mental Health Assn. Alachua County (Fla.), 1976-77; treas. Citizens Com. for Mental Health in Bryan, 1979-80, Humana Sunshine Hosp. Aux.; editor newsletter Friends Assn. Symphony Orch., 1987-88; sec.-treas. Am. Cancer Soc. Brazos Valley, 1988—; vol. Crestview Retirement Home, Brazos Food Bank. Mem. Nat. Assn. Female Execs., Mid-South Ednl. Research Assn., Miss. Psychol. Assn., AAAS, Am. Psychol. Assn., Tex. Psychol. Assn., Brazos Valley Psychol. Assn., Council for Exceptional Children, AAUW (women's com. 1984—), Bryan-College Station C. of C. (OPAS gala program chmn. 1988), Bus. and Profl. Women's Club (Bryan/College Station br. newsletter editor, award com. mem.), Opera and Performing Arts Soc. (College Station/Bryan OPAS Gala Program chmn. 1988—, yearbook chmn. 1988—), Arts Council Brazos Valley, Nat. Edn. Honor Soc., LWV, Am. Pen Women (assoc.), Phi Delta Kappa. Clubs: Sorosis (sec. 1962-65, beginning bridge chmn. 1987-88), Tex. A&M Faculty Wives (beginning bridge chmn. 1987-88, sec. 1987-88), Tex. A&M Newcomers, Altrusa, Extension Service (1st v.p. 1984, sec. 1987-88, pres. 1988—), Exec. Wives, Campus Study (pres. 1988—), Book Rev., Brazos Beautiful, Tex. A&M U. Social (pres. fine arts sect. 1988—, 3d v.p. 1988—). Address: Redmond Terr Sta PO Box 10027 College Station TX 77840

MAXWELL, KATHERINE LUMPKIN, financial planner; b. N.Y.C., Oct. 13, 1943; d. John H. and Margaret (Harper) Lumpkin; (div.); 1 dau., Jennifer Lee. B.A., Kans. U.-Lawrence, 1965, B.S., 1967; M.A., Tex. A&I U.-Kingsville, 1971. Cert. fin. planner; lic. stockbroker and prin. Asst. dept. mgr. Vandervoorts, St. Louis, 1965-66; tchr. Topeka, Kans. also Corpus Christi, 1967-69, 70-71; spl. edn. tchr. Dallas Ind. Sch. Dist., 1972-78, sch. counselor, 1978-81; self-employed ins. sales and fin. planner, Dallas, 1981—; fin. planner Asset Mgmt., Dallas, 1983-84; adj. faculty Coll. Fin. Planning, Denver, 1983—; instr. Dallas Community Colls., 1980—; pres., owner Maxwell Fin. Services. Mem. adv. bd. Multiple Careers Magnet Ctr., Dallas Ind. Sch. Dist., 1981—. Mem. Internat. Assn. Fin. Planners (chairperson membership 1986-87, sec., editor newsletter 1987-88, bd.dirs. 1983-84), Am. Bus. Womens Assn., Inst. Cert. Fin. Planners, Nat. Assn. Female Execs. Office: 5025 Arapaho #400 Dallas TX 75248

MAXWELL, LINNEA, marketing communications professional; b. Calgary, Alta., Can., Aug. 15, 1956; d. Edwin Samuel and Violet (Bloomquist) Arnold; m. Curtis R. Maxwell, Nov. 24, 1978. BS in Bus. Adminstrn., Ariz. State U., 1978. Sales rep. Burroughs Corp., Bettendorf, Iowa, 1979-81; advt. copywriter Sta. KWPC/KFMH, Muscatine, Iowa, 1981-83; advt. copywriter MicroAge Computer Stores Inc., Tempe, Ariz., 1984-85, mgr. pub. relations, 1985—; mng. editor MicroAge Quar. Mag., Tempe, 1985—. Mem. Internat. Assn. Bus. Communicators (awards com. 1987), Kappa Delta (alumnae assn. editor, adv. bd.). Office: MicroAge Inc Box 1920 2308 S 55th St Tempe AZ 85281-0460

MAXWELL, MADALYN, lawyer; b. Nashville, Ill., Jan. 9, 1926; d. Ralph Lester and Beulah Madalyne (House) M.; m. Thomas H. McGary, July 4, 1968. AA, Whitworth Coll., Brookhaven, Miss., 1945; BS in Law, U. Ill., 1948, MA in History, 1949. Bar: U.S. Supreme Ct., U.S. Ct. Appeals, (5th and 7th cir. ct.), U.S. Cen. Dist. Ill. Supreme Ct. Law clk. Ill. Supreme Ct., Nashville, 1951-53; asst. atty. gen. State Ill., Springfield, 1953-55, 56—; asst. to treas. Sangamo Electric Co., Springfield, 1955-56. Bd. dirs. Sojourn Women's Ctr., Springfield, 1980-87, chmn., 1982-83; bd. dirs. Springfield Symphony Orch., 1979—. Mem. ABA, Ill. State Bar Assn., Cen. Ill. Women's Bar Assn. (pres. 1986—). Episcopalian. Office: Ill Atty Gen 500 S 2d St Springfield IL 62704

MAXWELL, MARCIA GAIL, insurance company executive; b. Polk County, Ga., Aug. 15, 1948; d. Morris Lee and Mildred Ruth (Head) Martin, Sr.; m. Larry O. Maxwell, July 31, 1970; 1 child, Mischelle D. Sec., Ga. Income Tax Unit, Atlanta, 1969-72; sr. sales rep. Fed. Nat. Mortgage Assn., Atlanta, 1972-83; secondary mktg. acct. exec. Gen. Electric Mortgage Ins. Co., Atlanta, 1983—; rep. GECC Capital Markets Group, Atlanta, 1985—. Recipient #2 Secondary Trader award Gen. Electric Credit Corp., 1984, Winner's Circle award Gen. Electric Credit Corp., 1985, Outstanding Achievement award Gen. Electric Mortgage Ins. Co., 1985, 86. Mem. Nat. Assn. Female Execs., Am. Mgmt. Assn., Nat. Assn. Profl. Mortgage Women (mem. publicity com. 1985—), Nat. Assn. Securities Dealers (registered rep.), SEC (registered rep.). Democrat. Baptist. Clubs: Toastmasters Internat. (pres. 1976-77), Fed. Nat. Mortgage Assn. Recreation (pres. 1980-81), Summit. Avocations: camping; boating; flower arranging. Home: 652 Stillwaters Dr Marietta GA 30064 Office: Gen Electric Mortgage Ins Co 400 Perimeter Ctr Terr Atlanta GA 30346

MAXWELL, PAMELA ANN, school director; b. San Mateo, Calif., Sept. 22, 1950; d. Howard Hugh and Maynell (Milton) M. AA, Cañada Coll., 1971; BS in Human Devel., Calif. State U., Hayward, 1973; M in Early Childhood Elem., Calif. State U., Fresno, 1983. Lic. early childhood edn., Calif. Pre-sch. dir. Kiddie Garden, Redwood City, Calif., 1976-78; tchr. kindergarten Peninsula Christian Schs., Redwood City, Calif., 1973-76, co-dir. schs., 1978-79, exec. dir. schs., 1979—. Author science curriculum books. Mem. creative ministries Peninsula Christian Ch., Redwood City, 1973—; vol. Valley Children's Hosp., Fresno, Calif., 1983. Named Outstanding Tchr. Elem. Edn., 1976. Mem. Assn. Christian Schs. Internat. (chair dirs.), Child Care Co-ordinating Council. Club: Rainbow Girls.

MAXWELL, RUBY HOOTS, county official; b. Hendersonville, N.C., July 4, 1924; d. James Few and Nora Adlaide (Capps) Hoots; m. Foy Judson Maxwell, Apr. 24, 1944; 1 child, Terry Chandler. Supr. Spinning Wheel Rugs, Hendersonville, 1943-48; nurse aid ARC, Hendersonville, 1954-55; asst. Optician, Hendersonville, 1963-64; dep. register of deeds Henderson County, N.C., 1964-78, registrar, 1978—; instr. notary pub. edn. Blue Ridge Tech. Coll., Flat Rock, N.C., 1978—. Active Women's Dem. Club, Hendersonville, 1978—. Recipient award for disting. service to people of Henderson County, 1987. Mem. N.C. Register of Deeds Assn., Am. Soc. Notaries. Avocations: art, music. Office: Register of Deeds Courthouse Hendersonville NC 28739

MAXWELL, SHARON LEE REYNOLDS, government official, consultant; b. Taft, Calif., Mar. 2, 1939; d. Theodore Roosevelt Reynolds and Adelaide Velma (Johnson) Reynolds Sikola; B.A., U. Ariz., 1966, M.A., 1969; divorced; children—Maurynne Ruth, Edward Stuart. Asst. cataloger Tucson Public Schs., 1966-68, tchr., librarian, 1968-72; teaching asst. U. Ariz., 1969-70; with City of Tucson, 1972—, citizen participation dir., 1978—. Mem. Pima area adv. group Health Systems Agy. So. Ariz., 1978-80, mem. governing body, 1979-84; mem. adv. com. Community Mediation Program, 1985-87. Mem. NEA, AAUW, Ariz. Edn. Assn., Nat. Assn. Female Execs., Exec. Women's Council of So. Ariz., Pi Lambda Theta. Avocations: music;

reading; counseling. Home: PO Box 13388 Tucson AZ 85732 Office: City of Tucson PO Box 27210 Tucson AZ 85726

MAXWELL-BROGDON, FLORENCE MORENCY, school administrator; b. Spring Park, Minn., Nov. 11, 1929; d. William Frederick and Florence Ruth (LaBrie) Maxwell; m. John Carl Brogdon, Mar. 13, 1957; children—Carole Alexandra, Cecily Ann, Daphne Diana. B.A., Calif. State U.-Los Angeles, 1955; M.S., U. So. Calif., 1957; postgrad. Columbia Pacific U., San Rafael, Calif., 1982-86. Cert. tchr., Calif. Dir. Rodeo Sch., Los Angeles, 1961-64; lectr. Media Features, Culver City, Calif., 1964—; dir. La Playa Sch., Culver City, 1968-75; founding dir. Venture Sch., Culver City, 1974—, also chmn. bd.; bd. dirs., v.p. Parent Coop. Preschools, Baie d'Urfe Quebec, Calif., 1964—. Author: Let Me Tell You, 1973; Wet 'n Squishy; 1973; Balancing Act, 1977; (as Morency Maxwell) Framed in Silver, 1985; (column) What Parents Want to Know, 1961—. Editor: Calif. Preschooler, 1961-74. Contbr. articles to profl. jours. Treas. Democrat Congl. Primary, Culver City, 1972. Mem. Calif. Council Parent Schs. (bd. dirs. 1961-74), Parent Coop. Preschools Internat. (advisor 1975—), Mystery Writers of Am. (affiliate), Internat. Platform Assn. Libertarian. Home: 10814 Molony Rd Culver City CA 90230 Office: Venture Sch 5333 S Sepulveda Blvd Culver City CA 90230

MAXWELL-WILLIAMS, GWEN, nurse; b. Starkville, Miss., July 4, 1947; d. Charlie Will and Annie Bell (Cannon) Maxwell; m. C.E. Williams, Mar. 19, 1976 (dec. Mar. 25, 1985); 1 child, David Keith. AA in Nursing, Union U., Jackson, Tenn., 1971; BSN, Seattle Pacific U., 1976; MA in Nursing Adminstrn., U. Wash., 1977. Cert. interior designer, operating room nurse, nursing adminstr. Nurse operating room Pub. Health Hosp., Seattle, 1973-76; supr. operating room U. Wash. Hosp., Seattle, 1977-79; dir. operating room Stanford (Calif.) U. Med. Ctr., 1979-82; div. dir. nursing Good Samaritan Hosp., Puyallup, Wash., 1982-84; supr. nursing adminstrn. Harborview Med. Ctr., Seattle, 1985—; pres., owner Distinctive Images Boutique, Inc., Kirkland, Wash., 1986-87; project coordinator Cabrini Hosp., Seattle, 1987—; nurse/order communication analyst Phamis, Inc., Seattle, 1987—; cons. Kimberly Clark Corp., Atlanta, 1980-82. Contbg. editor: Medical Surgical Nursing, A Psychophysiological Approach, 1980; contbr. articles to profl. jours. Bd. dirs. 101 Black Women, Seattle, 1986—, Cen. Area Mental Health Ctr., 1983-85. Mem. Nat. Assn. Female Execs., Women's Bus. Exchange, Delta Sigma Theta. Democrat. Baptist. Club: Mary Mahoney RN's. Lodge: Soroptimist (sec., bd. dirs.). Avocations: reading, gourmet cooking, travel. Home and Office: 14134 110th NE Kirkland WA 98034

MAY, ANN MARIE, nurse; b. Chester, Pa.; d. Thomas W. and Martha (Wells) Lewis; m. John May; children: Donna-Marie Lyons, Robert Carl Lyons. RN, Chester (Pa.) Hosp.; BS, Wilmington Coll. Cert. Occupational Health Nurse. Staff nurse Chester (Pa.) Hosp.; supr. nurse Sacred Heart Hosp., Chester; safety and health specialist Gen. Chem., Claymont, Del. Chmn. bd. Chester-Wallingford chpt. ARC, 1987. Mem. Pa. Occupational Health Nurses (pres. 1986—), N.E. Regional Assn. Occupational Health Nurses (bd. dirs. 1986—), Del. Valley Occupational Health Nurses (pres. 1983-87), Am. Assn. Occupational Health Nurses (coordinator nat. conf. sessions 1987), Am. Indsl. Hygiene Assn. Republican. Episcopalian. Office: Gen Chem Corp 6300 Philadelphia Pike Claymont DE 19703

MAY, AVIVA, educator; b. Tel-Aviv; naturalized Am. citizen, 1958; d. Samuel and Paula (Gordon) Rabinowitz; B.A., in Piano Pedgogy, Northeastern Ill. U., 1979; married (div. 1986); children: Rochelle, Alan, Risa, Ellanna. Tchr., pianist, 1948—; tchr. adult B'nai Mitzva, 1973; tchr. music, dir. McCormick Health Centers, Chgo., 1978-79, Cove Sch. Perceptually Handicapped Children, Chgo., 1978-79; prof. Hebrew and Yiddish, Spertus Coll. Judaica, Chgo., 1980—; tchr. continuing edn. Northeastern Ill. U., 1978-80, also Jewish Community Centers. folksinger, guitarist, 1962—; composer classical music for piano, choral work, folk songs. Recipient Magen David Adom Public Service award, 1973; Ill. State grantee, 1975-79; Ill. State Congressman Woody Bowman grantee, 1978-79. Mem. Music Tchrs. Nat. Assn., North Shore Music Tchrs. Assn. (a founder, charter mem., sec.), Ill. Music Tchrs. Assn., Organ and Piano Tchrs. Assn., Am. Coll. Musicians, Ill. Assn. Learning Disabilities, Sherwood Sch. Music, Yivo Inst. Yiddish. Democrat. Contbr. articles to profl. jours. Home: 3600 North Lake Shore Dr Chicago IL 60613 Studio: Fine Arts Bldg 410 S Michigan Ave Chicago IL 60605

MAY, CHARLENE ROSE, state agency administrator; b. Elyria, Ohio, June 9, 1939; d. Joseph and Lois Rosetta (Shingledecker) Lake; children: J. Matthew, Christine Rose. BA, Ea. Mich. U., 1967; MA, Kans. U., 1977, PhD, 1986. Asst. dir. Nat. Safety Council, Kansas City, Mo., 1965-67; asst. to dir. MPA program Kans. U., Lawrence, 1975-78, research assoc. Ctr. for Pub. Affairs, 1978-80, dir. programs Human Resource Inst., 1980-82; dir. human resource devel. State of Kans., Topeka, 1986—; pres. Cons. Mgrs. Associated, Lawrence, 1982-86. Mem. Am. Soc. Pub. Adminstrn. (v.p. Kans. chpt. 1987-88, pres. 1988—). Office: Div Personnel Services 951 South Landon State Office Topeka KS 66612

MAY, DOROTHY GRACE, biologist, educator; b. Kansas City, Mo., Oct. 5, 1942; d. Ralph Harold and Adelaida Gertrude (Elbe) Kelly; m. J. Russell May Jr., Aug. 10, 1963; children: Charles Nephi, Ruth Frances. BA in Zoology and Chemistry, U. Kans., 1964, BS in Edn., 1965, PhD in Entomology, 1970. Instr. in biology Longview Community Coll., Lees Summit, Mo., 1971-77; vis. asst. prof. biology Rockhurst Coll., Kansas City, 1977-78; lectr. in biology Avila Coll., Kansas City, 1979-82; adj. instr. biology Park Coll., Parkville, Mo., 1983-86, asst. prof., 1986—. Author: Dulcimer Songbag, 1978, Dulcimer Songbag for Christmas, 1978, Dulcimer Classics, 1980, Dulcimer à la Mode, 1983; contbr. articles on biology to sci. jours. Leader Mid-Continent council Girl Scouts U.S., Kansas City, 1977-87, music instr., 1984-86; singer Fine Arts Chorale, Independence, Mo., 1983-87; cellist Northland Philharmonia, Parkville, 1987, Med. Arts Symphony, Kansas City, Kans., 1970-83. Mem. Assn. Midwest Coll. Biology Tchrs., Sigma Xi, Sigma Delta Epsilon (chpt. pres. 1971-72). Mem. Reorganized Ch. Jesus Christ of Latter-day Sts. Club: Prairie Dulcimer (Overland Park, Kans.) (pres. 1983-84, sec. 1985-86). Office: Park Coll Dept Biology Parkville MO 64152

MAY, ELAINE, entertainer, director; b. Phila., 1932; d. Jack Berlin; m. Marvin May (div.); 1 child, Jeannie Berlin; m. Sheldon Harnick. Ed. high sch.; studied Stanislavsky method of acting with, Marie Ouspenskaya. Stage and radio appearances as child actor; performed Playwright's Theatre, Chgo.; appeared in student performance Miss Julie, U. Chgo., (with Mike Nichols); others; appeared with improvisational theatre group in night club The Compass, Chgo., to, 1957, (with Mike Nichols) appeared N.Y. supper clubs, Village Vanguard, Blue Angel, also night clubs other cities; TV debut on Jack Paar Show; also appeared: in Omnibus, 1958, Dinah Shore Show, Perry Como Show, TV spls.; TV debut on Laugh Line, NBC, 1959; recording spoken comedy Improvisations to Music, Mercury Records; weekly appearance NBC radio show Nightline; appeared (with Mike Nichols) NBC radio show, N.Y. Town Hall, 1959, An Evening with Mike Nichols and Elaine May, Golden Theatre, N.Y.C., 1960-61; dir. films A New Leaf, 1972, The Heartbreak Kid, 1973, Mikey and Nicky, 1976 (writer, dir. remake 1985), Ishtar, 1987 (also writer); appeared in film Luv, 1967, California Suite, 1978 (Acad. award Best Supporting Actress 1978); co-author screenplay Heaven Can Wait, 1978; author play Better Part of Valor, Hotline, 1983; stage revue: (with Mike Nichols) Telephone, 1984. Office: Dirs Guild Am 7950 W Sunset Blvd Los Angeles CA 90046 *

MAY, JOSEPHINE, banker; b. Cologne, Germany, Mar. 21, 1922; came to U.S., 1926, naturalized, 1939; d. Curt and Eva M. (Bungartz) Hartog; m. Herman E. May, Nov. 8, 1942; children—Linda J., James E. B.A., George Williams Coll., 1982; postgrad., 1982—. Asst. v.p. Bank of Yorktown, A Cole-Taylor Bank, Lombard, Ill., 1954-56, v.p., cashier, 1957-83, sr. v.p., 1983; pres., 1984-86, also bd. dirs., vice chmn. bd., 1987—; bd. dirs. fin. com. Good Samaritan Hosp., Downers Grove, Ill., 1984-85; mem. task force DuPage Pvt. Indsl. Council, 1985; charter mem. West Suburban Council, Downers Grove, 1984-85. Mem. Internat. Orgn. Women in Real Estate (1st v.p. 1986—), Oak Brook C. of C., Lombard C. of C., Women in Mgmt. (treas. Oak Brook chpt. 1980), DuPage Bank Adminstrn. Inst. (bd. dirs. 1981), Yorktown Mchts. Assn. (bd. dirs. 1983—). Clubs: Oak Brook Breakfast; DuPage (bd. govs. 1985). Avocations: gardening; reading. Office: Cole Taylor Bank/Yorktown 1 Yorktown Ctr Lombard IL 60148

MAY, PHYLLIS JEAN, businesswoman; b. Flint, Mich., May 31, 1932; d. Bert A. and Alice C. (Rushton) Irvine; grad. Dorsey Sch. Bus., 1957; cert. Internat. Corr. Schs., 1959, Nat. Tax Inst., 1978; M.B.A., Mich. U., 1970; m. John May, Apr. 24, 1971; children—Phillip, Perry, Paul. Office mgr. Comml. Constrn. Co., Flint, 1962-68; bus. mgr. new and used car dealership, Flint, 1968-70; controller 6 corps., Flint, 1970-75; fiscal dir. Rubicon Odyssey Inc., Detroit, 1976—; acad. cons. acctg. Detroit Inst. Commerce, 1980-81; pres. small bus. specializing in adminstrv. cons. and acctg., 1982—; supr. mobile service sta., upholstery and home improvement businesses; owner retail bus. Pieces and Things; notary public, 1968—; also real estate broker. Pres. PTA Westwood Heights Schs., 1972, vol. Fedn. of Blind, 1974-76, Probate Ct., 1974-76, mem. citizens adv. bd. Northville Regional Psychiat. Hosp., 1988; Recipient Meritorious Service award Genesee County for Youth, 1976, Excellent Performance and High Achievement award Odyssey Inc., 1981; mem. adv. council Northville Psychiat. Reg. Hosp., 1987-88. Mem. Am. Bus. Women's Assn. (treas. 1981, rec. sec. 1982, v.p. 1982-83, Woman of Yr. 1982), Nat. Assn. Profl. Female Execs. (bd. dirs.), Internat. Platform Assn., Pi Omicron (officer 1984-85). Baptist. Home: 12050 Barlow St Detroit MI 48205 Office: Rubicon Odyssey Inc 7441 Brush St Detroit MI 48202

MAYBERRY, PATRICIA MARIE, lawyer; b. St. Louis, Aug. 25, 1951; d. Samuel G. Mayberry and Shirley (Mayberry) Hawkins. B.A., U. Mo., 1973; M.S.W., U. Houston, 1976; J.D., Thurgood Marshall Law Sch., 1979. Bar: Tex. 1979, Colo. Outreach counselor Juvenile Justice, Houston, 1978-79; sr. law intern Community Legal Services, Houston, 1978-80; law clk. Shell Oil, Houston, 1979-80; commd. capt. U.S. Air Force, 1980; asst. staff judge adv., Denver, 1980-84, resigned, 1984; assoc. Alvin Dillings, P.C., Denver, 1984—. Friend, Denver Girls, Inc., 1981—; usher Chapel One Lowry AFB, Denver, Shorter AME Ch.; mem. Protestant Chapel Council, Denver; bd. dirs. Black Am. West Mus., 1987. Decorated Commendation medal with cluster USAF. Mem. ABA, State Bar Tex. Assn., State Bar Colo. Assn., Assn., Sam Carey Bar Assn., Nat. Assn. Black Women Lawyers, Assn. Trial Lawyers Am., Air Force Assn., Phi Alpha Delta, Delta Sigma Theta. Democrat. Methodist. Home: 3412 S Eagle Apt 102 Aurora CO 80014 Office: 820 16th St Suite 720 Denver CO 80202

MAYBERRY, WANDA LUCILLE, occupational therapy educator; b. Brighton, Colo., Feb. 5, 1934; d. Homer Wagley and Frances Velma (Sutton) M. BS, Colo. State U., 1956; MA, U. So. Calif., 1960; PhD, U. Denver, 1986. Cert. neurodevel. therapist. Staff occupational therapist Matheny Sch. for Cerebral Paisied Children, Peapack, N.J., 1957-59, coordinator therapeutics services, 1961-65; head occupational therapy dept. Denver Gen. Hosp., 1968-73; asst. prof. Colo. State U., Ft. Collins, 1973—, acting head occupational therapy dept., 1980-81; mem. adv. bd. Sewall Rehab. Ctr., Denver, 1981—; mem. adv. com. Colo. Early Childhood Interagy. Initiative, Denver, 1986—. Author, editor edn1. videotapes; contbr. articles to profl. jours. Vol. Peace Corps, 1966-68, 70. Fellow Am. Occupational Therapy Assn. (cert., regional coordinator research Rocky Mountain region 1981-87, rep. commn. on edn. 1985—, roster of accrediation evaluators 1988—); mem. Occupational Therapy Assn. Colo. (v.p. 1971-73, Marjorie Ball award 1975-76), World Fedn. Occupational Therapy, Sensory Integration Internat., Phi Kappa Phi. Office: Colo State U Occupational Therapy Dept Occupational Therapy Bldg Fort Collins CO 80523

MAYBURY, MARY-ELLEN LIVERMORE, state senator; b. Portland, Maine, Nov. 28, 1943; d. Hervey Claflyn and Barbara (Tuttle) Livermore; m. Michael William Maybury, 1965 (div. 1986); children—Mark, Penny; m. David B. Randall, 1988. Student Gorham State Tchrs. Coll., 1962-64, U. Maine, 1972, 84, 85, 86, 87, 88. Mem. Brewer Bd. Appeals, Maine, 1977-79, Maine Ho. of Reps. from Dist. 74, 1982-84, Maine Senate from Dist. 11, 1984—. Pres., Bangor-Brewer LWV, 1975-77, Maine LWV, 1978-79; chmn. Brewer Community Action Group Against Drug and Alcohol Abuse, 1982-83. Mem. Bangor Bus. and Profl. Women (1st v.p. 1984-86). Congregationalist. Club: Brewer City. Republican. Office: Maine State Capitol Bldg Augusta ME 04333

MAYCOCK, RONNIE LEE, computer software company executive; b. Seoul, South Korea, Mar. 25, 1953; came to U.S., 1973, naturalized, 1979; d. Sang-Hoon and Keum-Nock (Hong) Lee; m. Roger Maxwell Maycock, July 1, 1984. Student, Sogang U., Seoul, 1973; BA, UCLA, 1976. Instr. Northrop U., Inglewood, Calif., 1977-78; tech. staff adviser Summation, Los Angeles, 1978-80, dir. tech. services, 1980-83, project mgr., 1983-84, mgr. spl. projects, 1984—, also bd. dirs. Developer various software packages. Mem. Nat. Assn. Female Execs. Avocations: classical guitar, piano. Office: Summation 5801 E Slauson Ave Suite 220 Los Angeles CA 90040

MAYDEW, MARY JO, treasury manager; b. Kansas City, Mo., May 13, 1949; d. Bernard Eugene and Thelma Louise (Beardslee) M. BBA, U. Denver, 1970; MBA, Cornell U., 1986. Sr. EDP auditor Fed. Reserve Bank, Chgo., 1973-74; sr. auditor Argonne (Ill.) Nat. Lab, 1974-75; budget mgr. PBS, Washington, 1975-78; sr. fin. analyst Communications Satellite Corp., Washington, 1978-79; asst. to controller Cornell U., Ithaca, N.Y., 1979-84, asst. treas., 1984-87; treas. Mount Holyoke Coll., South Hadley, Mass., 1987—. V.p. United Way of Tompkins County, Ithaca, 1983-87; mem. fin. com. Holyoke-Chicopee Area Health Resources, Inc./Holyoke Hosp.; bd. dirs. Diabetes Control Found., 1986—. Mem. Nat. Assn. Coll. and Univ. Bus. Officers. Home: 20 Ashfield Ln South Hadley MA 01075 Office: Mount Holyoke Coll 16 Skinner Hall South Hadley MA 01075

MAYER, BEATRICE CUMMINGS, civic worker; b. Montreal, P.Q., Can., Aug. 15, 1921; came to U.S., 1939, naturalized, 1944; d. Nathan and Ruth (Kellert) Cummings; B.A. in Chemistry, U. N.C., 1943; postgrad. U. Chgo., 1946; L.H.D. (hon.), Spertus Coll. Judaica, 1983, Kenyon Coll., 1987; m. Robert Bloom Mayer, Dec. 11, 1947 (dec.); children—Robert N., Mrs. Ruth M. Durchslag. Mem. vis. com. Sch. Social Service Adminstrn. U. Chgo., 1964—, dept. art, 1972; dir. women's bd., 1973—, Art Inst. Chgo. (life trustee) 1984—; bd. dirs. Michael Reese Hosp. Corp., Chgo., 1982—, bd. dirs. Spoleto Festival, 1980; trustee Kenyon Coll., Gambier, Ohio, 1976—, mem. adv. com. to bd. trustees, 1987—; bd. fellows Brandeis U., Waltham, Mass., 1977—; mem. womens bd. Northwestern U., 1978—; trustee Anshe Emet Synagogue, Chgo., 1974—; trustee Mus. Contemporary Art, Chgo., 1974—; mem. adv. com. N.C. Sch. of Arts U. NC., 1983—. Recipient Brandeis U. Disting. Community Service award, 1972, medallion Am. Jewish Com. Human Rights, 1976, Outstanding Achievement award in the Arts, YWCA Met. Chgo., 1979, Centennial Gold Medal for Disting. Community Service Jewish Theol. Sem., 1986, Alumni Laureate award Loyola Coll. Balt., 1984; named to Hall of Fame, Jewish Community Ctrs. Adult Services, 1987. Clubs: Tavern, Standard (Chgo.); Lake Shore Country (Glencoe, Ill.). Home: Hancock Apts 175 E Delaware Pl Apt 7403 Chicago IL 60611

MAYER, ELIZABETH BILLMIRE, educational administrator; B.Ed., Nat. Coll. Edn., Evanston, Ill., 1953; M.A. in Liberal Studies, Wesleyan U., 1979. Teaching asst. Hull House, Chgo., 1950-51; teaching scholar Nat. Coll. Edn. Demonstration Sch., 1952-53; pre-sch. tchr. St. Matthew's Sch., Pacific Palisades, Calif., 1959-63, tchr. 2d grade, 1963-67; librarian Chandler Sch., Pasadena, Calif., 1971-72, tchr. 4th grade, 1972-80, curriculum coordinator 1st-8th grades, 1979-80; tchr. 4th-6th grades Inst. for Experimentation in Tchr. Edn., SUNY-Cortland, 1980; asst. prof. edn. SUNY-Cortland, 1980-82; founder, headmistress The Mayer Sch., Ithaca, N.Y., 1982—. Mem. Nat. Council Tchrs. Math., Nat. Council Tchrs. English, Nat. Sci. Tchrs. Assn., Calif. Assn. Ind. Schs., N.Y. State Assn. Ind. Schs., Phi Delta Kappa (officer 1980-81). Office: The Mayer Sch 1251 Trumansburg Rd Ithaca NY 14850

MAYER, KAY, writer; b. Chgo.; d. Frank J. and Harriet (Schnell) Magnor; m. Kenneth W. Mayer, May 2, 1943; children—Michael J., Patricia A., Mark T. Student Northwestern U., 1938-43. News reporter Tampa Times, 1943; advt. copywriter Marshall Field & Co., Chgo., Earle Ludgin & Co., Chgo., Henri, Hurst & McDonald, Chgo., 1944-58; spl. editor, writer Scott, Foresman & Co., Glenview, Ill., 1966-71; freelance writer Art West, Ariz. Hwys., Southwest Art, Am. Artist, Am. Way, 1971—. Recipient Nat. and State Press Women's 1st place awards, 1983, 84, 85. Mem. Nat. Fedn. Press Women, Ariz. Press Women, Nat. Council Social Studies, Western History Assn., Soc. Southwestern Authors (dir. 1981-83). Home: 1855 C Tanglewood Dr Glenview IL 60025

MAYER, MARIA VIOLET, accountant; b. Budapest, Hungary, Apr. 19, 1936; came to U.S., 1961.; d. David and Julia (Farkas) Okros; m. Franz F. Mayer, Aug. 18, 1960; 1 child, David F. BA, Dobo Viatalin Bus. Coll., 1956. Acct. to dept. head. N.Y.C. Mus., 1961-72; asst. controller, fin. analyst Chase Manhattan Bank, White Plains, N.Y., 1972-82; v.p., acct. Twin City Fed. Savs. and Loan Bank, N.Y.C., 1982—. Republican. Roman Catholic. Club: Feszek. Home: 2 Whitman Rd Yonkers NY 10710

MAYER, MARILYN GOODER, steel company executive; b. Chgo.; d. Seth MacDonald and Jean (McMullen) Gooder; m. William Anthony Mayer, Nov. 14, 1959; children—William Anthony Jr., Robert MacDonald. grad. Career Inst. Chgo., 1941; student Lake Forest Coll., Ill., 1942. Adminstrv. asst. Needham, Louis & Brorby, Chgo., 1949-53; v.p. RMB Corp., Chgo., 1963-71, Mayer Motors, Ft. Lauderdale, Fla., 1965-74, Gooder-Henrichsen, Chicago Heights, Ill., 1975—; dir. Barnett Bank, West Palm Beach, Fla. Trustee Gulf Stream (Fla.) Sch., St. Andrew's Sch., Boca Raton, Fla.; bd. dirs. Bethesda Hosp. Assn., Boynton Beach, Fla., pres. 1981-82; bd. dirs. Gulf Stream Civic Assn. Mem. Soc. Four Arts. Republican. Episcopalian. Clubs: Little, Gulf Stream Bath and Tennis. Avocation: travel. Home: 2925 Polo Dr Gulf Stream FL 33483

MAYER, MYRA LOU, banker; b. Cleve., Oct. 24, 1944; d. Louis E. and Marie (Klein) M. Student, Bard Coll., 1961-62, Am. Coll. in Paris, 1962, Sorbonne, Paris, 1962; BBA, U. Ariz., 1965; MBA, Am. U., 1972. Chartered fin. analyst. Security analyst First Nat. Bank, Chgo., 1965-68; trust investment officer First Am. Bank, N.A., Washington, 1969-77, v.p., head trust investments, 1977-82, v.p. funds mgmt., 1982-84; sr. v.p., treas. Gibraltar Savs. Assn., Houston, 1984—; Vice chmn. membership com. Greater Washington Bd. Trade, 1978-80; guest lectr. portfolio mgmt. Am. U., 1979-82; bd. dirs. Houston Govt. Bond Club, 1985-86, Houston Bus. Forum, 1988—. Mem. Inst. Chartered Fin. Analysts, Houston Soc. Fin. Analysts, Nat. Assn. Bank Women, Forum Club, Houston Bus. Forum (bd. dirs. 1988-89), Houston Bond Club, The Profl. Group. Home: 14 Greenway Plaza Apt 14R Houston TX 77046 Office: Gibraltar Savs Assn 13401 N Freeway Houston TX 77060

MAYER, NANCY ANN, environmental engineer; b. Port Jefferson, N.Y., June 18, 1955; d. John Charles and Dorothy Mildred (Levine) M.; m. David Ira Salman, Jan. 14, 1979; children: Joseph Morris Mayer-Salman, Lon Jeffrey Mayer-Salman. BS in Engring., Cornell U., 1977; MBA, Duke U., 1982. Environ. engr. EPA, Durham, N.C., 1977—. Treas. Durham NOW, 1984-86, N.C. GASP, 1986—; bd. dirs. Eno River Unitarian Universalists, Durham, 1986—; treas. N.C. GASP, 1986—. Mem. Soc. Women Engrs., Air Pollution Control Assn., Triangle Women's Network. Democrat. Office: USEPA MD-15 Research Triangle Park NC 27711

MAYER, PATRICIA HATFIELD, personal assistant to former governor; b. Schenectady, Feb. 23, 1933; d. G. Elliott and Lucille Ropiequet (Goedde) Hatfield; m. Donald Franklin Mayer, Feb. 26, 1955; children—Kathleen Patricia, Leslie Susan, Elliott Hatfield. B.S. in Chemistry, Mary Washington Coll., U. Va.-Fredericksburg, 1954. Dept. mgr., asst. buyer Woodward & Lothrop, Washington, 1968-77; confidential sec. Gov. Va. Charles S. Robb, Fairfax, Va., 1977—; mem. Washington Adv. Bd. Corp. Level. Mem. Mary Washington Coll. Alumni Assn. (2d v.p. 1981-83), Achievement Rewards for Coll. Scientists Inc. (bd. dirs. Met. Washington chpt.). Presbyterian. Clubs: Jr. Women's of Fairfax County (Fairfax, Va.); DAR (state chmn. 1983—, regent Freedom Hill chpt. 1988—). Office: Hunton & Williams PO Box 1147 Fairfax VA 22030

MAYER, PATRICIA JAYNE, finance executive; b. Chgo., Apr. 27, 1950; d. Arthur and Ruth (Greenberger) Hersh; m. William A. Mayer Jr., Apr. 30, 1971. AA, Diablo Valley Coll., 1970; BSBA in Acctg., Calif. State U., Hayward, 1975. Staff acct., auditor Elmer Fox Westheimer and Co., Oakland, Calif., 1976; supervising auditor Auditor's Office County of Alameda, Oakland, 1976-78; asst. acctg. mgr. CBS Retail Stores doing bus. as Pacific Stereo, Emeryville, Calif., 1978-79; controller Oakland Unified Sch. Dist., 1979-84; v.p., controller YMCA of San Francisco, 1984—; instr. acctg. to staff YMCA, San Francisco, 1984—, CBS Retail Stores, 1978-79. Draft counselor Mt. Diablo Peace Ctr., Walnut Creek, Calif., 1970-72; dep. registrar of voters Contra Costa County Registrar's Office, Martinez, Calif., 1972-77. Mem. Nat. Assn. Accts. Democrat. Jewish. Club: Dalmatian of No. Calif. (Roseville). Home: 2395 Lake Meadow Circle Martinez CA 94553 Office: YMCA of San Francisco 220 Golden Gate Ave 3d Floor San Francisco CA 94102

MAYER, SUSAN LEE, nurse; b. N.Y.C., Feb. 10, 1946; d. Hans and Frieda (Schein) Abramson; BSN, Hunter Coll., 1968; MA, NYU, 1974, postgrad., 1974; cert. in gerontology Yeshiva U.; cert. tchr. Adelphi U., 1987. m. Steven Mayer, June 24, 1973; children: Jason, Stuart, Richard, Deborah. Staff nurse ICU-CCU, Montefiore Hosp., Bronx, N.Y., 1968; organizer CCU, Jewish Meml. Hosp., N.Y.C., 1968; supr., adminstr. Morrisania City Hosp., N.Y.C., 1969-76; instr. Adelphi Univ., Garden City, N.Y., 1977-78; substitute nurse Great Neck (N.Y.) Pub. Schs., 1980—; adj. instr. Queensborough Community Coll.; 1987—; tchr. CPR, 1972—, 85—; lectr. PTA groups, 1981-82; research asst. to dean Sch. Nursing Adelphi U., 1987—; part-time staff nurse Winthrop U. Hosp., Mineola, N.Y., 1987—, Bd. dirs. Great Neck Synagogue, 1981—, v.p. Sisterhood, 1978-79, pres., 1979-81; former bd. dirs. Russell Gardens Assn.; founder Work for Share, Zedek Hosp., 1977—. N.Y. State Regents scholar, 1963. Mem. Am. Nurses Assn., Assn. Orthodox Jewish Scientists, Nat. League Nursing, N.Y. Counties Registered Nurses Assn., Nat. Assn. Sch. Nurses, N.Y. Heart Assn., Sigma Theta Tau. Democrat. Home: 28 Laurel Dr Great Neck NY 11021

MAYERSON, SANDRA ELAINE, lawyer; b. Dayton, Ohio, Feb. 8, 1952; d. Manuel David and Florence Louise (Tepper) M.; m. Scott Burns, May 29, 1977 (div. Oct. 1978). BA cum laude, Yale U., 1973; JD, Northwestern U., 1976. Bar: Ill. 1976, U.S. Ct. Appeals (7th cir.) 1976, U.S. Dist. Ct. (no. dist.) Ill. 1977. Assoc. gen. counsel JMB Realty Corp., Chgo., 1979-80; assoc. Chatz, Sugarman, Abrams et al, Chgo., 1980-81; ptnr. Pollack, Mayerson & Berman, Chgo., 1981-83; dep. gen. counsel AM Internat., Inc., Chgo., 1983-85; ptnr. Kirkland & Ellis, Chgo., from 1985, Kelley Drye & Warren, N.Y.C., 1987—. Bd. dirs. Jr. Med. Research Inst. Council of Michael Reese Hosp., Chgo., 1981—. Mem. ABA (bus. bankruptcy com. 1976—), Ill. State Bar Assn. (governing council corp. and securities sect. 1983-86), Chgo. Bar Assn. (current events chmn. corp. sect. 1980-81), 7th Cir. Bar Assn. Democrat. Jewish. Clubs: Yale (N.Y.C.), Metropolitan, Eastbank (Chgo.). Office: Kelley Drye & Warren 101 Park Ave New York NY 10178 *

MAYES, BERNICE ELIZABETH, dietitian; b. Oxford, N.C., Feb. 5, 1937; d. Garland Sherwood and Maggie (Richards) Mayes. Student Va. State Coll., 1954-58; B.S., Fairleigh Dickinson U., 1982. Staff dietitian Clara Maass Hosp., Belleville, N.J., 1960-62, therapeutic dietitian, 1962-68, tng. dietitian, 1965-66; cafeteria mgr. Newark Bd. Edn., 1968-72, asst. dir., 1972-76, dir., 1976—; weekend dietitian St. Barnabas Hosp., Livingston, N.J., 1970-72, project supr., summer 1971; commr. East Orange Bd. Health. Author handbook for employees and food-service tng. manual. Past pres. Essex County (N.J.) Adv. Bd. on Status of Women, 1983; mem. concerned set TLC Day Care Ctr., East Orange, N.J., 1983; mem. Women in Support Essex County Coll. Adv. Bd., Newark, 1983; bd. dirs. Carver Youth and Family Ctr., Trenton, 1983. Mem. U.S. Dept. Agr. Commodity Adv. Bd. (chmn. major cities sect.), Assn. Sch. Bus. Ofcls., Nat. Assn. Colored Women's Clubs (life mem., chmn.), NAACP (life), Essex County Nutrition Council, AAUW, Va. State Alumni Assn., Fairleigh Dickinson Alumni Assn., Roundtable for Women in Foodservice, N.J. Sch. Food Service Assn. (life mem., legis. chmn., pres.), Nat. Assn. Female Execs. Democrat. Episcopalian. Clubs: Garnetts (Plainfield, N.J.); St. Ann's Guild (Newark). Office: Newark Bd Edn 2 Cedar St Newark NJ 07102

MAYES, SHARI TEPPER, interior design firm owner, artist; b. Chgo., Sept. 25, 1942, d. Robert and Mae Plotkin (Gollin) P.; m. Michael Dawe Tepper, July 4, 1961 (div. 1977); children: David Michael, Samuel Robert; m.

John A. Mayes; stepchildren: Diedre Mayes Koik, Warren Shawn Mayes. Student, U. Mich., 1960-61, U. of Rome, Italy, 1963-65; student in art, Italian lit., interior design, Rome, 1965-71. V.p., sec. Teppolli Farms, Aprilia, Italy, 1961-70; owner, oil-painting tchr. art studio, Detroit, 1971-73, Milan, 1973-76; v.p. Gates Assocs., Chgo., 1977-83; pres. Shari Tepper Interior Design, Chgo., 1978—, Mayes-Vostal Interior Design, Glen Ellyn, Ill., 1985—. Head membership and scholarship coms. Am. Women's Assn. Rome, 1961-71; head 4th of July and spl. activities coms. Am. Club Milan, 1973-76. Recipient Honorable mention for oil painting Milan Trade Fair, 1976. Home: 100 E Bellevue Pl Chicago IL 60611 Office: Mayes-Vostal Interiors 799 Roosevelt Rd Bldg 2 Suite 204 Glen Ellyn IL 60137

MAYES, TRICIA GARNER, marketing professional; b. Myrtle Beach, S.C., Sept. 7, 1960; d. Clyde H. and Leila (R. Garner; m. Kent Mayes, Aug. 17, 1985. BS in Speech Communications, U. Tex., 1983. Fax specialist Xerox Corp., Houston, 1983-85, personal computer coordinator, 1985-86, sr. mktg. rep., 1986-87, major account mgr., 1987—, dealer sales mgr., 1988—. Mem. Houston Mus. Fine Arts, 1986-87; fund raiser Sen. Lloyd Bentsen's Fin. Council, Austin, 1983; council vol. George Bush election campaign, 1988. Mem. Stars and Crescent, Delta Delta Delta. Office: Xerox Corp 5151 San Felipe Suite 1200 Houston TX 77056

MAYESKI, FRAN ELIZABETH, educational consultant; b. Rolla, Mo., Nov. 6, 1941; d. Charles Emil and Katherine Dorothy (Parker) Gelven; B.S. in English, St. Louis U., 1964; postgrad. U. Wash., Seattle, 1974; M.B.A., City U., Seattle, 1980; m. John Kent Mayeski, May 21, 1966; 1 son, Mark Edward. Publs. asst. St. Louis U., 1965-66; tchr. St. Charles Schs., Spokane, Wash., 1967-68, Holmes Jr. High Sch., Colorado Springs, 1969, Sacred Heart Sch., Bellevue Wash., 1971-74, Interlake High Sch., Bellevue, 1974-76, area chairperson social studies, 1976-77; tchr., project leader Bellevue Public Schs., 1979-80; dir. staff devel. and spl. projects Ednl. Service Unit 10, Kearney, Nebr., 1980-83; dir. curriculum and instrn. Holdredge City Schs. (Nebr.), 1983-85; ednl. cons.; pres. Promoting Effective Growth, Inc., 1985—; adj. instr. Seattle Pacific U., Kearney State Coll., U. Wyo. Mem. Assn. Supervision and Curriculum Devel., Nebr. Assn. Supervision and Curriculum Devel., Nat. Staff Devel. Council, Am. Ednl. Research Assn., Am. Assn. Sch. Adminstrs., Nat. Assn. Female Execs., Nat. Speakers Assn., Phi Delta Kappa. Club: Kearney State Coll. Faculty Wives. Home: 11 Skyline Dr Kearney NE 68847

MAYFIELD, LORI JAYNE, sales representative; b. Newport Beach, Calif., Sept. 11, 1955; d. John Vincent and Marilyn Jane (Huish) M. Student Linn-Benton Community Coll., 1973-75, N.W. Coll., 1975-76. Gen. ins. cert. Ins. Inst. Am. Cashier Auto Club So. Calif., Anaheim, 1977-80, ins. clk., sec., Fullerton, 1980-81, ins. rep., 1981, field coordinator, Costa Mesa, Calif., 1981-86; auto. club sales rep; pres. LJM Enterprises. Recipient Outstanding Citizenship award YMCA, Santa Ana, Calif., 1984. Mem. Nat. Assn. Female Execs. Office: Auto Club So Calif 18642 S Gridley Rd Artesia CA 90701

MAY-FOWLER, CONSTANCE ANITA, writer, educator; b. Raleigh, N.C., Jan. 3, 1958; d. Henry Jefferson and Lenore Monita (Looney) May; m. Mika Alan Fowler, July 19, 1987. BA, U. Tampa, 1983; postgrad., U. Kans. Asst. to pres. Chambers Internat., Boca Raton, Fla., 1983-84; managing editor Megamedia, St. Petersburg, Fla., 1984-86; instr. Tampa (Fla.) Coll.; screenwriter Skyway Prodns., Tampa; free-lance writer various mags. guest art ciritic Lawrence World Jour. Grantee NEH, 1982, 83. Mem. Screenwriters Guild Am. Democrat. Roman Catholic.

MAYHEW, KATHLEEN ANN, small business owner; b. Corpus Christi, Nov. 12, 1948; d. James T. and Shirley (Strangward) Maher; m. Lewis Baltzell Mayhew, Jr., July 15, 1972. B.A. in Psychology, Santa Clara U., 1970; M.A., San Jose State U., 1973. Cert. counselor community coll., Calif. Instr., Modesto Jr. Coll., 1975-80; social worker asst. Omnicare, Modesto, 1978; social service worker Drs. Med. Ctr., Modesto, 1979; exec. dir. Via, supporting those living with death and life-threatening illness, Modesto, 1980-86, owner Page Creations, 1987—, coordinator mktg./production Modesto Psychiat. Ctr., 1987; counselor Family Service Agy., Modesto, 1974-75; mem. steering com., trainer, bd. dirs. Community Hospice, Modesto, 1979-81; mem. Dirs. of Vols. in Agys., 1981-83; cons., lectr. Bd. dirs. Stanislaus County chpt. Am. Cancer Soc., 1978-83; trustee Stanislaus Meml. Soc., 1979-83, pres., 1983; mem. Title IX Leadership Com., 1976; v.p., rec. sec. Stanislaus County Commn. for Women, 1982-84. Bd. dirs., mem. editorial bd., contbr. Woman's Compendium, 1985. Rotary Club scholar, 1966. Mem. Women's Network, Modesto C. of C. (Leadership Modesto). Democrat. Avocations: photography; cross-country skiing; weaving; mountain climbing.

MAYNARD, LAURIE JEANNE, management consultant; b. Portchester, N.Y., Nov. 3, 1955; d. William H. Jr. and Marilyn G. (Goewey) M.; m. George Oommen, Aug. 9, 1985; 1 child Sarah Maynard Oommen. BA, Union Coll., 1977; MBA, Boston U., 1983. Analyst Data Gen., Milford, Mass., 1983-86; pvt. practice as mgmt. cons. Arlington, Mass., 1986—. Mem. Nat. Assn. Female Execs., Nat. Orgn. Women. Home and Office: 34 Oxford St Arlington MA 02174

MAYNARD, VIRGINIA MADDEN, association executive; b. New London, Conn., Jan. 29, 1924; d. Raymond and Edna Sarah (Madden) Maynard; B.S., U. Conn., 1945; postgrad. Am. Inst. Banking, 1964-66, Cornell U., 1975. With Nat. City Bank (now Citibank), N.Y.C., 1954-79, asst. cashier, 1965-69, asst. v.p., 1969-74, v.p. internat. banking group, 1974-76, comptroller's div., 1976-79; v.p. First Women's Bank, N.Y.C., 1979-80; Internat. Fedn. Univ. Women rep. UN, 1982—; cons. in field. Trustee fellowships endowment fund AAUW Ednl. Found., Washington, 1977-80, Va. Gildersleeve Internat. Fund Univ. Women, Inc. (pres., 1987—). Mem. AAUW (fin. chmn. N.Y.C. br. 1976-79, bylaws chmn. 1979-83, adminstr. Meml. Fund 1983—, Woman of Achievement 1976). Republican. Congregationalist. Home: 601 E 20th St New York NY 10010

MAYNE, LUCILLE STRINGER, finance educator; b. Washington, June 6, 1924; d. Henry Edmond and Hattie Benham (Benson) Stringer; children: Patricia Anne, Christine Gail, Barbara Marie. B.S., U. Md., 1946; M.B.A. (grad. scholar), Ohio State U., 1949; Ph.D. (fellow), Northwestern U., 1966. Instr. fin. Utica Coll., 1949-50; lectr. fin. Roosevelt U., 1961-64; lectr. fin. Pa. State U., 1965-66, asst. prof., 1966-69, assoc. prof., 1969-70; assoc. prof. banking and fin. Case-Western Res. U., 1971-76, prof., 1976—, grad. dean Sch. Grad. Studies, 1980-84; sr. economist, cons. FDIC, 1977-78; cons. Nat. Commn. Electronic Fund Transfer Systems, 1976; research cons. Am. Bankers Assn., 1975, Fed. Res. Bank of Cleve., 1973, 68-70; cons. Pres.'s Commn. Fin. Structure and Regulation, 1971, staff economist, 1970-71; analytical statistician Air Materiel Command, Dayton, Ohio, 1950-52; asst. to promotion mgr. NBC, Washington, 1946-48; expert witness cases involving fin. instns.; dir. Cleve. Citywide Devel. Corp., 1981—, Horizon Savs., 1983—. Assoc. editor: Jour. Money, Credit and Banking, 1980-83, Bus. Econs., 1980-85; contbr. articles to profl. jours. Vol. Cleve. Soc. for Blind, 1979—; mem. TIAA/CREF Policyholders Nominating Com., 1982-84, chair, 1984. Mem. Am. Fin. Assn., Eastern Fin. Assn. (v.p. 1969-72), Fin. Mgmt. Assn. (dir. 1982-83, 2d v.p. 1988—), Midwest Fin. Assn. (dir. 1975-79), Phi Kappa Phi, Beta Gamma Sigma. Episcopalian. Home: 3723 Normandy Rd Shaker Heights OH 44120 Office: Case Western Res U Weatherhead Sch Mgmt U Circle Cleveland OH 44106

MAYO, CORA LOUISE, educator; b. Chgo., Oct. 31, 1925; d. Charles Amos and Mary (Elder) Scott; m. Marion Wesley Mayo, July 21, 1948; children—Lynne, Janice, Jo Ann, Thomas. B.S., U. Ill.-Urbana, 1949, advanced degree in adminstrn. and supervision, 1973; M.A., U. Chgo., 1961; Ph.D., Heed U., Fla., 1981. Program facilitator Chgo. Bd. Edn., 1955—; owner/pres. From the Black Experience, Inc., Chgo., 1979—; dir. pub. relations Afro-Am. Pub. Co., Chgo., 1972-73; ednl. cons. Ednl. Leadership Inst., Chgo., 1976-78; community prof. Govs. State U., Park Forest, Ill., 1975—. Author: Developmental Skills Activities Guide, 1982; columnist Teaching Black Positively; editor Human Relations Digest; author/pub.: (early childhood learning kit) Mwenzi Companeros, 1982. Bd. dirs. Woodson Delany Ednl. Fund, Chgo., 1975—, House of the Black Madonna, Chgo., 1978—; cons. Head Start, St. Stephen's Ch., Chgo., 1982-83; organizer Women for Washington, 1982-83, Women for Jackson, 1984; vol. instr. parenting House of the Black Madonna; proposals cons. Du Sable Mus. Afro-Am. History, Chgo. Recipient Leadership award Boy Scouts Am., 1971; named Outstanding Educator of Yr., Woodson-Delany Ednl. Fund, 1976; others. Mem. Nat. Assn. Media Women (fin. sec. 1983—, sec. chpt. 1982—, v.p. 1973), Women in Communications, Phi Delta Kappa. Democrat. Congregationalist. Club: Debonnettes (pres. 1984) (Chgo.). Home: 1618 E 85th Pl Chicago IL 60617

MAYO, FAYE NUELL, theatrical personal manager; b. Albany, N.Y., Mar. 3, 1936; d. Barney and Estelle Harriet (Potashnick) N.; m. Nick Mayo, Dec. 18, 1981 (dec. 1983). Student, U. So. Calif., 1953-55, Neighborhood Playhouse, N.Y.C., 1956-57. Actress Los Angeles, 1954-64; assoc. producer Valley Music Theatre, Los Angeles, 1964-67; v.p. devel. Computicket div. Computer Scis. Corp., Los Angeles, 1967-70; adminstrv. asst. Shubert Theatre, Century City, Calif., 1971-72; personal mgr. Faye Nuell Mgmt., Beverly Hills, Calif., 1977-80; prodn. exec. MGM Studios, Culver City, Calif., 1980-83; personal mgr. Mayo Mgmt., Los Angeles, 1984—. Ind. producer: Odyssey of Runyon Jones, Los Angeles, 1972, Hollywood Freeway, Los Angeles, 1975; assoc. producer I Do! I Do!. Bd. dirs. Am. Civil Liberties Found., Los Angeles, 1980—; chairperson, co-ordinator charitable and polit. fund raising events in Los Angeles. Mem. Women in Film, Conf. of Personal Mgrs. (treas. 1985-87). Democrat. Office: Mayo Mgmt 1818 Thayer Ave Los Angeles CA 90025

MAYOR, HEATHER DONALD, medical educator; b. Melbourne, Victoria, Australia, July 6, 1930; came to U.S., 1956, naturalized, 1959; d. Joseph Arthur Lindsay and Elizabeth Emily (Boyd) Donald; m. Richard Blair Mayor, May 28, 1956; children: Diana Boyd Hawkins, Philip Hastings. BS, U. Melbourne, 1950, DSc, 1971; PhD, U. London, 1954. Research assoc. virology Walter and Eliza Hall Inst. Med. Research, Melbourne, 1954-55; postdoctoral fellow in immunology Harvard Med. Sch., Cambridge, Mass., 1956-59; mem. faculty Baylor Coll. Medicine, Houston, 1960-75, prof. microbiology, immunology and experimental medicine, 1975—; vis. prof. dept. microbiology U. Melbourne, 1965; vis. lectr. Med. Sch. U. Tex., Houston, 1980—; vis. lectr. Rice U., Houston, 1985—; scholar-in-residence Centro Culturule Della Foundazione Rockefeller, Bellagio, Italy, 1983. Contbr. more than 150 articles to profl. jours.; co-organizer exhbn. Life Shapes, Contemporary Arts Mus., Houston, 1974. Bd. dirs. Tex. Sesquicentennial Com., 1986, Tex./South Australia Jubilee 150 Found., 1986, New Music Forum, Houston, 1986. Recipient Disting. award Ctr. Interaction Man Sci. and Culture, Houston, 1970; grantee Nat. Cancer Inst., Damon Runyon, Robert A. Welch. Mem. Am. Assn. Immunologists, Soc. Cell Biology, Biophysical Soc., Am. Soc. Microbiology, Virology, Am. Assn. Cancer Research. Clubs: Doctors (Houston), Houstonian. Home: 226 Pine Hollow Ln Houston TX 77056 Office: Baylor Coll Medicine 1 Baylor Plaza Houston TX 77030

MAYR, KAY FAYSTINE, radio station executive; b. Lansdale, Pa., June 17, 1939; d. Russell Myers and Frances M. (Stauffer) Swartley, m. Ronald Batson, 1961 (div. 1963); 1 child, John Tracy; m. William Fred Mayr, July 28, 1965; children: Tiffany Lynn, Christina Noelle. BA magna cum laude, Western Conn. State U., 1976. Reservation ticket agent Trans World Airlines, Phila., 1960-65; head tchr. Hamilton Nursery Sch., Conn., 1970-73; with Sta. WLAD/WDAQ, 1977—; asst. sales mgr. Berkshire Broadcasting, Danbury, Conn., 1979-81, sales mgr., 1981-83, gen. sales mgr., 1983-88; gen. sales mgr. Sta. WICC Tribune Broadcasting, Bridgeport, Conn., 1988—; cons. advt., spl. promotions, pub. relations KAY, Inc. (name formerly Danbury Hilton Inn and Conf. Ctr.), 1985—. Pres. Vol. Bur. Greater Danbury, 1983—, Ridgefield Civic Ballet Bd., 1984—; v.p. Ridgefield Workshop, 1984—; trustee United Way of No. Fairfield County, 1983—. Recipient Sales Breakthrough award Radio Advt. Bur., 1979. Mem. AAUW, Am. Women in Radio and TV (pres. New Eng. chpt. 1983-84, found. chmn. 1984-85, state broadcasting chmn. 1985—), Danbury C. of C. (task force on women on the move 1982—). Republican. Avocations: singing, acting, writing, travel. Office: WICC Radio 177 State St Bridgeport CT 06604 also: Danbury Hilton 18 Old Ridgebury Rd Danbury CT 06810

MAYS, CLARA FLORENCE, insurance agent; b. Morenci, Ariz., Dec. 31, 1944; d. William Kilgo and Clara Edna (Hutson) Pryor; m. Herschel Raymond Mays, Oct. 26, 1963; children: Herschel D., Mark S., Kevin W. Student, Missoula Tech. Ctr., 1975. Cert. ins. counselor. Retail salesman East Gate Drug, Missoula, Mont., 1963-64; ins. underwriter, exec. sec. to pres. Glacier Gen. Assurance Co., Missoula, 1964-67; salesman Avon, Missoula, 1967-68; retail salesman Singer Co., Missoula, 1968-70; v.p. ops. Bishop Ins. Service, Polson, Mont., 1977-88; sr. customer service rep. Terry Payne & Co., Missoula, 1988—. Den mother Boy Scouts Am., Arlee, Mont., 1972-73; vice-rector, speaker Cursillo, Missoula, Ronan, Mont., 1975-84; scorekeeper, bracketer Amateur Athletic Union, Wrestling Program, Ronan, 1973-80; scholarship judge Soroptomist Internat., Polson chpt., 1984-85; instr. baton twirling YMCA, Missoula, 1974. Named Disting. Achiever Safeco Ins. Co. Edn. Dept., Seattle, 1979. Mem. Soc. CPCU, Soc. Cert. Ins. Counselors, Nat. Assn. Ins. Women (legis. com. Missoula chpt. 1985), Ins. Inst. Am. (coordinator, instr. 1987-88), Ind. Ins. Agts. Mont. Roman Catholic. Office: Terry Payne & Co Inc PO Box 8747 Missoula MT 59807

MAYSE, MCEVA BRADSHAW, interior decorator; b. Columbia, Ky., Dec. 23, 1926; d. Benjamin Harrison and Malllie (Blakey) B.; m. Arnold Mayse, Feb. 23, 1945; children: William Richard, Nancy Carroyl Mayse Mann. Cert., Lindsey Wilson Coll., Columbia, Ky., 1971, U. Ky., 1979, U. Louisville, 1981. Prodn. supr. Barrett, Inc., Columbia, 1956-58, Lion Uniform, Inc., Columbia, 1958-63, Osh Kosh B'Gosh, Inc., Columbia, 1963-68; office mgr. Summit Manor Nursing Home, Inc., Columbia, 1968-74; personnel supr. TransAm. Delaval, Inc., Columbia, 1974-86; sales rep. and interior decorator The Galleries, Columbia, 1987—; mem. adv. com. Lake Cumberland Region 14 Vocat. Edn., Somerset, 1968—; mem. steering com. Russell Springs (Ky.) Vocat. Sch., 1973—. Active fund-raising com. Lindsey Wilson Coll., Columbia, 1978-86, Adair County Arts Council, Columbia, 1986—. Recipient plaque and cert. Columbia chpt. Am. Cancer Soc., 1982, 84, 85, plaque and cert. Columbia chpt. Am. Heart Assn., 1982, 84, 85, trophies Columbia Golf Assn., 1973, 83, plaque Louisville Old Ky. Home council Boy Scouts Am., 1984; named to Hon. Order Ky. Cols., 1978. Mem. Nat. Personnel Assn., Columbia C. of C. Republican. Presbyterian. Club: Pinewood Country (pres., bd. dirs.). Home: Star Route Box 50 Glens Fork KY 42741 Office: Box 50 Glensfork KY 42741

MAYSON, BETTY ANNE PEEPLES, medical consultant; b. Aiken, S.C., Dec. 23, 1943; d. Junius Black Peeples and Edna Earle (Sandifer) Peeples McKnight; m. Richard Grey Mayson, Sept. 23, 1959 (div. Sept. 1968); children—Richard Grey, Elizabeth Boatwright. Cert. operating room technician Adjust Edn., Augusta, Ga., 1973; Assoc. degree in Nursing with high honors, U. S.C., 1975, B.S. in Nursing cum laude, 1978. R.N., Ga., S.C. Mgr. car rental co., Augusta, Ga., 1966-70; ward clk. Plantation Gen. Hosp., Fla., 1970-72; staff nurse St. Joseph Hosp., Augusta, Ga., 1975-76; teaching assoc. U. S.C., Columbia, 1978; cons. O.F. Furr, Esquire, Columbia, 1977-82; med. cons. Solomon, Kahn, Smith & Baumil, attys., Charleston, S.C., 1982—; cons. Westinghouse Health System, Atlanta, 1977-80, Kirschner Assocs., Atlanta, 1979-80. Vol. Med. U. S.C., Charleston, 1985, Hospice, Charleston, 1986, Friends of Library, 1986. Panhellenic scholar, 1975; Bus. and Profl. Women's Found. Lady Clairol scholar, 1976-78; Lettie Mae Whitehead Meml. scholar U. S.C., 1976-78. Mem. Charleston C. of C., Sigma Theta Tau. Methodist. Home: 851C Sandlake Mount Pleasant SC 29464 Office: Solomon Kahn Smith & Baumil 39 Broad St Charleston SC 29401

MAYSTEAD, SUZANNE RAE, optometrist; b. Hillsdale, Mich., Sept. 30, 1955; d. Marvin Charles and Helen Alberta (Glendenning) Patrick; m. Ivan Karl Maystead, III, June 4, 1977. OD, Ferris State Coll. Optometry, 1979. Research asst. to optometrist, Big Rapids, Mich., 1979-80; clin. assoc. Ferris State Coll. Optometry, Big Rapids, 1979-84; pvt. practice optometry, Portland, Mich., 1980—. Recipient Contact Lens Achievement award Bausch & Lomb, 1979. Mem. Mich. Optometric Assn., Portland C. of C. (Optometric Extension program, Am. Optometric Assn. contact lens sect.). Avocations: indoor gardening, piano. Club: Am. Chesapeake. Home: 7667 Peckins Rd Lyons MI 48851 Office: 1311 E Bridge St Portland MI 48875

MAZER, NORMA FOX, writer; b. N.Y.C., May 15, 1931; d. Michael and Jean (Garlen) Fox; m. Harry Mazer, Feb. 12, 1950; children—Anne E., Joseph D., Susan R., Gina B. Author: I, Trissy, 1971, A Figure of Speech, 1973 (Nat. Book award nominee 1974); Saturday, the Twelfth of October, 1975 (Lewis Carroll Shelf award 1976); Dear Bill, Remember Me? and Other Stories, 1976 (N.Y. Times Notable Book 1976, ALA Notable Book 1976, Sch. Library Jour. Best Books of Yr. 1976, Christopher award 1976, Lewis Carroll Shelf award 1977); (with Harry Mazer) The Solid Gold Kid, 1978 (ALA Best Books for Young Adults 1978, Best of the Best award 1978); Up in Seth's Room, 1979 (ALA Best Books for Young Adults 1979); Mrs. Fish, Ape and Me, The Dump Queen, 1980 (German Children's Literature prize 1982, List of Honor Austrian Children's Books 1983); Taking Terri Mueller, 1981 (Edgar award 1982, Calif. Young Readers' Medal 1985), Summer Girls, Love Boys and Other Short Stories, 1982, When We First Met, 1982 (Iowa Teen award 1985); Someone to Love, 1983 (ALA Best Books for Young Adults 1983), Downtown, 1984 (ALA Best Books for Young Adults 1984, N.Y. Times Notable Book 1984), Supergirl, 1984, Three Sisters, 1986, A, My Name Is Ami (Internat. Reading Assn. Children's Choice, 1987), 1986, B, My Name is Bunny, 1987, After the Rain, 1987 (Sch. Library Jour. Best Books 1987). Home: Brown Gulf Rd Jamesville NY 13078

MAZIA, JUDITH ANN, lawyer; b. Boise, Nov. 21, 1943; d. Daniel and Gertrude Mazia. BA, U. Calif., Berkeley, 1966; postgrad. in urban planning, Columbia U. and Hunter Coll., 1966-67; JD, Hastings Coll. Law, 1974. Bar: Calif. 1974, U.S. Dist. Ct. (no. dist.) Calif. 1974, U.S. Tax Ct. 1987, U.S. Ct. Appeals (9th cir.) 1981, U.S. Ct. Appeals (fed. cir.) 1987. Law clk. Office of Zaide Kirtley, San Francisco, 1972-74; ptnr. Kirtley, Levinson & Mazia, San Francisco, 1975-77; sole practice, San Francisco, 1977—. Pres. bd. dirs. North of Market Child Devel. Ctr. (formerly Hastings Child Care Ctr.), San Francisco, 1982—; mem. Internat. Visitors Ctr., 1985—. Recipient Commendation San Francisco Bd. Suprs., 1984; Rosentiel Found. fellow, 1966-67. Mem. Phi Beta Kappa. Office: 1188 Franklin St Suite 201 San Francisco CA 94109-6839

MAZUR, STELLA MARY, former organization administrator; b. Lowell, Mass.; d. Stanley and Katherine (Cichowicz) M.; B.S. in Edn., U. Lowell; student ARC Mgmt. Tng. Sch., 1962, Nat. Tng. Lab. for Applied Behavioral Sci., 1963. USO club dir., Windsor Locks, Conn., 1942; gen. field rep. ARC, 1944, exec. dir., Waltham, Mass., 1944-79. Spl. assignment State Dept. USIA Graphic Arts Cultural Exchange Program, Eastern Europe, Poland, 1965. Mem. Pres.' Circle, Lowell U. Recipient Waltham Rotary Club spl. citation, 1952; Waltham Community 25 Year Service award, 1969; Recognition award Waltham chpt. ARC, 1971; Outstanding Woman, Waltham News Tribune, 1974; Woman of Today, Waltham Bus. and Profl. Women's Club, 1976; Outstanding Service award ARC New Eng., 1979; Disting. Alumni award U. Lowell, 1979. Mem. Internat. Platform Assn., ARC Retiree Assn., Am. Assn. Ret. Persons, Smithsonian Assos., Lowell U. Alumni Assn. (hon. life). Seton Guild Lowell, Lowell Hist. Soc., Lowell Mus. Corp. Clubs: Vesper Country (Tyngsboro, Mass.); Longmeadow Golf, Country, Lowell U. Pres.' Univ. Circle (Lowell). Author, pub.: Roots and Heritage of Polish People in Lowell, 1976. Home: 170 Andover St Lowell MA 01852

MAZZA, TERILYN MCGOVERN, association executive; b. Troy, N.Y., Apr. 25, 1952; d. Edward Joseph and Mary Elizabeth (Ryan) McGovern; student Royal Acad. Dramatic Art, London, and U. London Westfield Coll., 1972-73; B.A. with honors, Marymount Coll., 1974; M.A., SUNY, Albany, 1976; m. Mario G. Mazza, Oct. 6, 1978. Teaching fellow SUNY, Albany, 1974-76; co. mgr. Cohoes (N.Y.) Music Hall, 1976-78; pub. relations dir. Lake George (N.Y.) Opera Festival, 1978; promotion/research dir. Capital Newspaper Group, Albany, N.Y., 1979-81; promotion dir., columnist Editor & Pub., N.Y.C., 1981-83; v.p., dir. pub. relations, editor, columnist Assn. Bus. Press. Recipient Weyerhauser Craftmanship award Weyerhauser Paper Co., 1980, Design award Strathmore Paper Co., 1980, Telly award Local/Regional TV Comml. Festival, 1982. Mem. Bus./Profl. Advt. Assn., Nat. Assn. for Female Execs., Nat. Bus. Circulation Assn., Women's Direct Response Group, Advt. Women N.Y., N.Y. State Soc. Assn. Execs. Club: Overseas Press. Ann. contbr. Internat. Newspaper Promotion Assn. Yearbook, 1981. Home: 1085 Warburton Ave Yonkers NY 10701 Office: Assn Bus Pubs 205 E 42d St New York NY 10017

MAZZAFERRO, DEBORAH MARIE, sales executive; b. Rochester, N.Y., Sept. 5, 1955; d. Angelo Vincenzo and Anna (Ange) M.; m. James N. Dalesandro, Sept. 3, 1983. AAS, Rochester Inst. Tech., 1974, BS, 1978. Buyer Kaufmann's Dept. Store, Pitts., 1976-80; rep. sales Richter Bros., Inc., Carlstadt, N.J., 1980-85, mgr. dist. sales, 1985-88; assoc. realtor Schlott Inc. Realtors, Bradenton, Fla., 1988—. Mem. Nat. Assn. Female Execs., Manatee County Bd. Realtors, Phila. Women's Culinary Guild. Home: 351 Magellan Dr Sarasota FL 34243

MAZZANTI, KATHY BRYSON, employment company administrator; b. Memphis, July 15, 1953; d. Paul Eugene and Frances L. (Carson) Bryson; m. Paul Anthony Mazzanti, July 22, 1981. BS, Memphis State U., 1978. Tchr. Memphis Bd. Edn., 1978-79; adminstr. advt. dept. ITT Outdoor Lighting subs. ITT Corp., Southaven, Miss., 1979-81; coordinator tng. ITT Outdoor Lighting subs. IIT Corp., Southaven, Miss., 1981-82; rep. sales Todd Corp., St. Louis, 1982-83; br. mgr. Cen. Tech. Services, Inc., Memphis, 1986—. Contbr. articles to profl. jours. Mem. Nat. Assn. Female Execs., Memphis Network. Republican. Presbyterian. Club: Racquet of Memphis. Home: 7973 Farmington Blvd Germantown TN 38138

MAZZEI, DOREEN CHERYL, service executive; b. N.Y., June 28, 1956; d. James Q. and Sylvia E. (Holappa) M. A, Sullivan Community Coll., 1978; BA, N.Y. Inst. Tech., 1987; postgrad., Adelphi U., 1987—. Paraprofl. Nassau Ctr. for Disabled, Woodbury, N.Y., 1978-80; kitchen mgr., gen. mgr. Pointview Inn, Pt. Lookout, N.Y., 1980—. Reporter Community Outlook, Pt. Lookout, 1987. Trustee Pt. Lookout, 1987; sexton Community Ch., Pt. Lookout, 1987. Mem. Research Inst. for the Exec., Nat. Assn. for Female Execs., Smithsonian Inst. Home: 60 Freeport Ave Point Lookout NY 11569

MAZZEO-CAPUTO, STEPHANIE ELVIRA, health educator, nutrition and wellness consultant; b. Bklyn., Oct. 21, 1957; d. Anthony Joseph and Elvira (Morelli) M.; m. Thomas L. Caputo, Nov. 15, 1981. BS in Biology, Bklyn. Coll., 1979; MS in Nutrition, Pa. State U., 1981. Registered dietitian. Nutritionist, health counselor Life Extension Inst., N.Y.C., 1981-83; adminstr. employee health edn. program (Staywell Program) Control Data Corp., N.Y., 1983—; adj. lectr. Bklyn. Coll., 1981-84; instr. Techs. for Creating, N.Y., 1987; nutrition cons. in field, N.Y., 1981—; workshop leader goal setting and counseling skills various non-profit orgns. including Heart Assn. Affiliates. Contbr. articles to profl. jours. Mem. Am. Dietetic Assn., Assn. Fitness In Bus., Am. Soc. Tng. and Devel. (wellness spl. interest group N.Y. metro chpt.), N.Y. Heart Assn. (nutrition counseling subcom.). Office: Control Data Corp Staywell Program 142 W 57th St New York NY 10019

MCADEN, MARY CATHERINE OVERFELT, educator; b. Franklin County, Va., Oct. 22, 1931; d. Walter Madison and Lizzie Aberson (Angell) Overfelt; A.A., Ferrum Coll., 1951; B.A., High Point Coll., 1953; postgrad. Scarritt Coll., 1956; M.A. (Phi Epsilon Omega grantee), U. Va., 1977; m. Robinson H. McAden, Aug. 21, 1954; children—Marcella, James, Ellen, John, Robert. Dir. Christian edn. Mt. Vernon Meth. Ch., Danville, Va., 1953-54, First Meth. Ch., Gainsville, Ga., 1955-56; ednl. missionary Meth. Ch., Bolivia, 1957-67; reading tchr. Callaway (Va.) Elem. Sch., 1974-76, Sandhills Youth Center, McCain, N.C., 1976-79; resource tchr. Samarkand Manor, Eagle Springs, N.C., 1979-81; learning disabilities resource tchr. Western Albemarle High Sch., Crozet, Va., 1981-86; resource tchr. Candor Elem. Sch., N.C., 1986—. Trustee, Ferrum Coll., 1974-75. Named Outstanding Leader in Elem.-Secondary Edn., Callaway Elem. Sch., 1976; recipient Disting. Alumni award Gerrum Coll., 1968, Trustees award, Ferrum Coll., 1976. Mem. NEA. Methodist. Contbr. religious writings to mags., youth publs. Home: 140 Williams Rd Southern Pines NC 28387 Office: Candor Elem Sch Candor NC 27229

MCAFEE, ANN SMITH, foundation developer; b. Gadsden, Ala., Oct. 10, 1946; d. William Loran and Ella Maurene (Grigsby) Smith; m. David Leonard Crain, Dec. 26, 1965 (div. Apr. 1974); children: Mark, Melissa; m. Larry Eugene McAfee, Nov. 22, 1979. Student, Jacksonville State U., 1964-65, George Wallace Jr. Coll., 1966-68, Galveston Coll., 1985-86. Office mgr. Creative Displays, Inc., Gadsden, Ala., 1974-78, Tuscaloosa, Ala., 1978; cons. Outdoor West, Inc., Galveston, Tex., 1979; adminstrn. asst. Galveston

Hist. Found., 1984-86, devel. dir., 1986—. Mem. Mardi Gras com. Galveston, 1985-86; bd. dirs. Leadership Galveston Alumni, 1986-87; mem. steering com. Galvestonians Against Casinos, 1987. Mem. Nat. Soc. Fundraising Execs., Nat. Assn. Female Execs., C. of C. (grad. leadership of Galveston). Home: 67 Wood Villa Tuscaloosa AL 35406 Office: Galveston Hist Found 2016 Strand Galveston TX 77550

MCALESTER, VIRGINIA SAVAGE, historic preservationist; b. Dallas, May 13, 1943; d. Wallace Hamilton and Dorothy Minnie (Harris) Savage; m. Clement McCarty Talkington, Nov. 25, 1965 (div. 1976); children—Clement McCarty Jr., Amy Virginia; m. A. Lee McAlester, July 11, 1977. B.A., Harvard U., 1965. Founding mem. Historic Preservation League, Dallas, 1972—, pres., 1975-76; founder, trustee, pres. Friends of Fair Park, Dallas, 1984-86; bd. dirs. Ctr. for Hist. Resources, Tex. A&M U., 1986—. Author: The Making of an Historic District, 1974, A Field Guide to American Houses, 1984 (Nat. Trust Honor award 1986), Discover Dallas-Fort Worth, 1988. Founding mem. 500, Inc., Dallas, 1965; bd. dirs. Dallas Central Bus. Dist. Assn., 1976-78, East Dallas Design Com., 1973-78; mem. Jr. League, Dallas; pres. Friend of Friar Park, 1984-86. Recipient Janus award Historic Preservation League, 1980, 84, Humanities award Dallas Hist. Soc., 1984, Honor award San Antonio Conservation Soc., 1984, John Neely Bryan award Dallas County Hist. Commn., 1986. Mem. Nat. Trust for Hist. Preservation (bd. advisor 1974-83, Honor award 1986), Soc. Archtl. Historians, Tex. Soc. Architects (hon. 1987). Episcopalian. Clubs: Dallas Country, Harvard (Dallas) (pres. 1987—). Office: 240 Boll St Dallas TX 75204

MC ALISTER, LINDA LOPEZ, university administrator, educator, philosopher; b. Long Beach, Calif., Oct. 10, 1939; d. Manuel Lee and Elena Maria (Sherwood) McAlister; AB, Barnard Coll., 1962; postgrad. Coll. City N.Y., 1963-64; PhD, Cornell U., 1969. Mem. faculty, adminstr. Bklyn. Coll., 1968-77, CUNY. Grad. Center, 1970-77; prof. humanities, dean campus Imperial Valley campus San Diego State U., 1977-82; prof. philosophy, campus dean U. South Fla., Ft. Myers, 1982-85; spl. asst. to vice chancellor for acad. programs State Univ. System Fla., 1985-87; prof. Women's Studies and Philosophy U. South Fla., Tampa, 1987—; Fla. state coordinator Am. Council Edn. Nat. Identification Project, 1983-86. Franz Brentano Found. grantee, 1968-72; Fulbright-Hays research grantee, 1973-74. Mem. Am. Philos. Assn., Nat. Women's Studies Assn., Soc. Women in Philosophy, Assn. von Philosophinen in Deutschland (founding) Author: The Development of Franz Brentano's Ethics, 1982. Contbr. articles to profl. jours. Editor and translator: Psychology From an Empirical Standpoint (Franz Brentano), 1973; Sensory and Noetic Consciousness (Franz Brentano), 1980; editor: The Philosophy of Brentano, 1976; translator: On Colour (Ludwig Wittgenstein), 1977. Office: Univ of South Fla Soc 107 4202 E Fowler Ave Tampa FL 33620

MCALLISTER, JILL, real estate broker; b. Allentown, Pa., Sept. 2, 1938; d. John Raymond and Helen (Hartzell) Fuehrer; m. Willis Eugene McAllister, July 4, 1959; children—John Willis, David Ray, Stephen Charles. Student Cedar Crest Coll., 1956-58, Mt. San Antonio Coll., 1969-71; grad. Realtors Inst., 1973, CCIM, 1985, CRB, 1986, CRS, 1987. Sec., Ivar Lovret, Pomona, Calif., 1962-64; salesperson LaVerne Realty (Calif.), 1965-69, Wheeler/Steffen Real Estate Claremont, Calif., 1969-72; pres. Jill McAllister, Inc., Realtor, , Claremont, Calif., 1972—. Bd. dirs. Boy Scouts Am., 1978—, Foothill Philharmonic, 1977—, Pilgrim Place, 1979—, Curtain Raisers, 1975—, Scripps Fine Arts, 1980—. Mem. Pomona Valley Bd. Realtors (dir. 1981—, pres. 1986), Calif. Assn. Realtors (state dir. 1982—), Nat. Assn. Realtors (nat. dir. 1985—, edn. com.). Republican. Presbyterian. Home: 508 W 11th St Claremont CA 91711 Office: Jill McAllister Inc Realtor 508 W 11th St Claremont CA 91711

MCANDREW-ACKER, KAREN LEE, employment service manager; b. Allentown, Pa., Sept. 30, 1954; d. Thomas Vincent and Pauline Vivian (Lambert) McAndrew; m. Dennis C. Acker, May 30, 1981. Cert. in bus., Lehigh County Community Coll., 1975. Account clk. Gen. Electric Credit Corp., Allentown, 1973-75; adminstrv. asst. AVCO Fin. Services, Bethlehem, Pa., 1975-77; service rep. Manpower Temporary Service, Allentown, 1977-79, service supr., 1979-83, office mgr., 1983-85, br. mgr., 1985—. Mem. Nat. Assn. Profl. Saleswomen (membership com. 1986, 87), Exec. Women Internat. (dir. membership com. 1983-85, pub. relations dir. 1987, 88), Assn. for Info. Systems Profls., Beta Sigma Phi (past office holder). Office: Manpower Temp Services 60 W Broad St Bethlehem PA 18018

MC ANULTY, MARY CATHERINE CRAMER (MRS. CHARLES GILBERT MCANULTY), retired educator; b. Braddock, Pa., June 26, 1908; d. Albert R. and Sara (Kelly) Cramer; A.B., Fla. So. Coll., 1929; M.A., Tchrs. Coll. Columbia, 1937; postgrad. Fla. State U., 1946-50; m. Charles Gilbert McAnulty, Dec. 25, 1937. Elem. tchr. Lake Ann Sch., Lake Garfield, Fla., 1930-31, elem. prin., 1932-34; prin. South Winter Haven Elem. Sch., Winter Haven, Fla., 1935-55; adminstrv. asst. to supervising prin. Winter Haven Area Schs., 1956-60; prin. Fred Garner Elem. Sch., Winter Haven, 1961-68, Lake Alfred Elem. Sch., 1969-70. Asst. chmn. vols., asst. tng. chmn., local chpt. ARC, 1967-68, 2d v.p., also chmn. vols., 1969-70, bd. mem., chmn. service to mil. families, 1970-71, chmn. coll. youth, 1971-72; treas. Imperial Harbours Condominium, 1980-82, pres., 1984; v.p. Beymer United Methodist Women, 1973, 74, 75, pres., 1976, 77; lay del. ann. conf. Meth. Ch., 1978, 79; pres. Lake Region Extension Homemaker's Club, 1974, 75; bd. dirs. Winter Haven Hosp. Aux., rec. sec., 1985-86, corr. sec., 1986-88. Mem. Am. Assn. Supervision and Curriculum Devel., Internat. Reading Assn. (pres., Polk County chmn.), NEA, Fla. Edn. Assn. (dir. dept. elem. sch. prins. 1965-67), Polk County Elem. Prins. Assn. (sec.), LWV (local dir. 1962), AAUW (local br. chmn. status women com. 1963), DAR (chpt. treas. 1967-68, historian 1969-70, regent 1970-72, state chmn. jr. Am. citizens 1972—, dir. dist. VI 1973-74, parliamentarian 1986-89), Fla. So. Coll. Alumni Assn. (sec.), Internat. Platform Assn., P.E.O. (chpt. treas. 1970-74, 80—, chaplain 1976, 77, chpt. pres. 1978-79), Ch. Women United (v.p. 1977—, chmn. adv. bd. 1980-81), Pi Gamma Mu, Delta Kappa Gamma (State Achievement award 1964, Fla. pres. 1962-63, chpt. parliamentarian 1968-73, 87, 88, 89, 90, pres., v.p., treas.). Methodist (choir mem., chmn. commn. edn. 1959-60, supt. study program 1969-70, organist 1970-77, pres. Wesley fellowship class 1972-73, chmn. adminstrv. bd. 1980, 81, 83-85 trustee 1983-88, pres. bd. 1987-88), lay leader 1985, 86, fin. com., workshop com. Clubs: Pilot (charter, pres. 1954-55, 61-62), Poinsettia Garden (pres. 1984-85). Lodge: Order Eastern Star (fin. chair 1987-89), Winter Haven Woman's (edn. chmn. 1967-68, v.p. 1983-84, pres. 1984-85, parliamentarian 1986-90). Home: 333 W Lake Howard Dr Apt 104D Winter Haven FL 33880

MCATEER, DEBORAH GRACE, travel executive; b. N.Y.C., Nov. 3, 1950; d. Edward John and Ann Marie (Cassidy) McA.; m. William A. Helms, Feb. 5, 1948; 1 child, Elizabeth Grace. Student, Montgomery Coll., 1969. Sec. Polinger Co., Chevy Chase, Md., 1969-72, Loews Hotels, Washington, 1972-73; adminstr. asst. Am. Gas Assn., Arlington, Va., 1973-75; mgr. Birch Jermain Horton Bittner, Washington, 1975-77; asst. mgr. Travel Services, McLean, Va., 1977-79; founder, pres. Travel Temps, Washington, Atlanta and Phila., 1979—; tchr. Montgomery Coll., Rockville, Md., 1980-84. Mem. Christ Child Soc., Washington, 1975—. Mem. Internat. Travel Soc. (pres. 1983-84), Pacific Area Travel Assn., Inst. Cert. Travel Cons. (cert.), Nat. Assn. Women Bus. Owners (chair membership com. 1983-84), Women's Commerce Club, PROST. Republican. Roman Catholic. Home: 47 Delta Pl Atlanta GA 30307 Office: Travel Temps 375 Pharr Rd #219 Atlanta GA 30305

MCBATH, AUDREY MARTINA, electronics company executive; b. Cleve., Aug. 4, 1954; d. Harry and Lelia (Smith) McB.; BS in Engring. (Nat. Achievement scholar 1972), Duke U., 1976; MBA U. So. Calif., 1987. Engrs. aid Woodruff, Inc., Beachwood, Ohio, 1975; cost engr. Arthur G. McKee & Co., Cleve., 1976; constrn. project engr. Gt. Lakes Constrn. Co., Cleve., 1976-77; environ. engr. EPA, Durham, N.C., 1977-79, Cin., 1979-83, program mgr. fed. women's program, Cin., 1981-83; cost engr. U.S. Army C.E., Los Angeles, 1983-85; Consortium for Grad. Study in Mgmt. fellow U. So. Calif., 1985-87; bus. adminstr. TRW, Redondo Beach, Calif., 1987—. Mem. Nat. Tech. Assn. (v.p. Cleve. chpt. 1977, Cin. chpt. 1981), Blacks in Govt. (del. 1982), Nat. Black MBA Assn., Los Angeles Council Black Profl. Engrs., MENSA. Home: 3613 Kalsman Dr Los Angeles CA 90016

MCBEE, SUSANNA BARNES, journalist; b. Santa Fe, Mar. 28, 1935; d. Jess Stephen and Sybil Elizabeth (Barnes) McBee; m. Paul H. Recer, July 2, 1983. A.B., U. So. Calif., 1956; M.A., U. Chgo., 1962. Staff writer Washington Post, 1957-65, 73-74, 77-79, asst. nat. editor, 1974-77; asst. sec. for public affairs HEW, 1979; articles editor Washingtonian mag., 1980-81; assoc. editor U.S. News & World Report, 1981-86; news editor, Washington Bur. of Hearst Newspapers, 1987—; Washington corr. Life mag., 1965-69; Washington editor McCall's mag., 1970-72. Recipient Penney-Missouri mag. award, 1969; Sigma Delta Chi Public Service award, 1969. Club: Nat. Press. Home: 5190 Watson St NW Washington DC 20016 Office: 1701 Pennsylvania Ave NW Washington DC 20006

MCBRIDE, BETTY JEAN, county government official; b. Pittsburg, Kans., Sept. 21, 1936; d. Santo and Filomena (Torchia) Sandella; m. Ray Earnest McBride, Apr. 24, 1954; children—Ruth Ann McBride Hall, Wesley Ray. Student pub. schs. Sec., Barker Ins. Co., Columbus, Kans., 1965-66; receptionist, bookkeeper to physician, Columbus, 1966-68; treas. Cherokee County, Columbus, 1968—. Appointed Gov. John Carlin St. Mcpl. Acctg. bd., 1986—, St. Human Resources Bd., 1986—, mem. St. Vehicle Info . processing com. 1984—, St. Re-appraisal adv. bd., 1987—, Kans. County Treas. Legis. Com., 1988—, precinct committeewoman Cherokee County Democratic party, 1966-71, 83—, sec. Cherokee County Dem. Central Com., 1968—. Mem. Kans. County Treas. Assn. (pres. 1984-85), S.E. Kans. County Ofcls. Assn. (pres. 1979, 83), S.E. Kans. County Treas. Assn. (pres. 1972, 76, 82), Am. Legion Aux. Roman Catholic. Home: 429 S Delaware Columbus KS 66725

MCBRIDE, DONNA JANNEAN, publisher; b. Kansas City, Kans., July 3, 1940; d. Donald Merle and Hazel Frances (Williams) McBride. A.B., Central Coll., 1962; M.L.S., U. Mo.-Columbia, 1969. Tchr., Pilot Grove High Sch. (Mo.), 1961-62; corr. Bus. Men's Assurance Co., Kansas City, Mo., 1962-66; acctg. clk. Prudential of Eng., Sydney, Australia, 1966-67; head tech. processes Kansas City Pub. Library (Mo.), 1967-77; customer rep. C.L. Systems, Inc., Newtonville, Mass., 1977-80; dir. support services Leon County Pub. Library, Tallahassee, 1980-82; dir. ops. The Naiad Press, Inc., Tallahassee, 1982—; dir. The Naiad Press, 1976—, Sappho's Library, 1983—. Mem. ALA, Nat. Gay Task Force, Am. Booksellers Assn., Nat. Women's Studies Assn. Home: Rt 1 PO Box 3319 Havana FL 32333 Office: The Naiad Press Inc PO Box 10543 Tallahassee FL 32302

MCBRIDE, EMMA PEARL, civic worker, educator; b. Abbyville, Kans., Feb. 23, 1927; d. Perry Claude and Eva Pearl (Benson) Bachus; m. Frank J. McBride, June 4, 1950; children—Steven F., Susan D., Scott M., Mark D. B.S., Kans. U., 1948, postgrad., 1949. Cert. tchr. Instr. Adela Hale Bus. Coll., Hutchinson, Kans., summers 1947-48, Clay Ctr. High Sch., Kans., 1948-50, Brown-Mackie Bus. Coll., Salina, Kans., 1950-52. Tchr., 1st Methodist Ch., Salina, 1955-70; bd. dirs. YWCA, Salina, 1973-79, fin. chmn., 1976; treas. Jr. High PTA, Salina, 1976; registrar United Methodist Women Kans. W. Conf. Sch. Missions, Salina, 1981; vol. Asbury Hosp., Salina, 1985—; docent Salina Art Gallery, 1985—. Mem. AAUW (corr. sec. 1971-72, exec. bd. 1983-84; named Outstanding Br. Mem. 1985). Republican. Club: Helianthus (pres. 1972-73). Avocations: foreign and domestic travel, arts, crafts, quilting, sewing.

MCBRIDE, JANE FRANCES, aircraft firm executive; b. Boston, Mar. 22, 1959; d. Hugh Robert and Dorothy Ann (Conway) McB. BA, Wesleyan U., 1981. Chief exec. officer FLIGHT TIME Corp., Chestnut Hill, Mass., 1985—. Editor: (with others) Air Charter Guide, 1987. Recipient fieldwork (Kathmandu, Nepal) grant Wesleyan U. 1980. Democrat. Home: 199 Coolidge Ave Watertown MA 02172 Office: FLIGHT TIME Corp 200 Boylston St Chestnut Hill MA 02167

MCBRIDE, JOYCE BROWNING, accountant; b. Ga., May 28, 1927; d. Eph and Zula (Harden) Browning; grad. So. Bus. U., 1947; children—Jan Burge, Gary McBride, Kandie Lysse. Asst. controller Hampton Court Knits, Los Angeles, 1967-78; owner, mgr. McBride & Assocs. Bookkeeping Service, 1978—. Address: 15344 Bambi Ct Moorpark CA 93021

MCBROOM, NANCY LEE, insurance executive; b. Tulsa, Nov. 7, 1925; d. Lee Webster and Dora Irene (Londigan) Adams; m. Robert B. McBroom, Jan. 22, 1945 (dec. Aug. 1969); children: Dacia Adams, Rene McBroom, Robert McBroom. Student, John Brown U., 1941-42, Little Rock Bus. Coll., 1941-42. Profl. horse trainer, judge, breeder N.C., Va. and Calif., 1955-75; owner Stombock's West, Inc., Del Mar, Calif., 1968-74; agt. Mut. Omaha Ins. Co., San Diego, 1978-84; owner, broker McBroom Ins. Services, San Diego, 1984—; dir. Dependent's Riding Program, USMC, Camp LeJeune, Va., 1963-66. Author: Handbook for Riding Instructors, 1963. Mem. com. Civitan Fund Raiser for Spl. Olympics, 1986. Mem. Nat. Assn. Securities Dealers, Rancho Bernardo C. of C. (com. 1986). Republican. Lodge: Soroptimist Internat. (mem. com. Women Helping Women 1985-86). Home: 11906-150 Paseo Lucido San Diego CA 92128 Office: McBroom Ins Services 16776 Bernardo Ctr Dr Suite 110B San Diego CA 92128

MCBURNEY, LINDA LEE, health facility administrator; b. Denver, June 10, 1942; d. Maurice J. and Dorothy Mae (Whitman) Mooney; m. Kenneth Robert McBurney, June 16, 1962 (div. 1980); children: Scott Robert, Laura Lynn, Brenda Sue, Valerie Kaye. BS in Bus. Adminstrn., Regis Coll., 1985. Office mgr. electrical company, Lakewood, Colo., 1980; sec. Safeco Ins. Co., Lakewood, 1980-82; office mgr. oil company, Golden, Colo., 1982; from clerical specialist to exec. sec. Cobe Labs., Lakewood, 1982-86, adminstrv. mgr., 1986—; beauty cons. Mary Kay Cosmetics, Lakewood, 1986—. Mem. Golden Area Sch. Adv. Com., 1974-80, Jefferson County Sr. High Curriculum Council, 1980; room mother Kyffin Elem. Sch., Golden, numerous years; vol. Luth. Hosp. Med. Ctr., Wheatridge, Colo., 1976—; pres. Women's Assn. Arvada (Colo.) Presbyn. Ch., 1979. Mem. Assn. Field Service Mgrs., Gamma Phi Beta. Republican. Home: 5 Paramount Pkwy Lakewood CO 80215 Office: Cobe Labs Inc 1185 Oak St Lakewood CO 80215

MCCABE, ANN ELIZABETH, psychologist, educator; b. Green Bay, Wis., Feb. 13, 1942; d. Paul Edward and Elizabeth Jane (Jacobs) Miskella; B.S., St. Norbert Coll., 1964; M.S., Iowa State U., 1966; Ph.D., U. Wis., Madison, 1973; m. Bernard Oliver McCabe, Nov. 26, 1966 (dec.); 1 son, Brian. Asst. prof. Trinity Coll., Dublin U., 1967-69; asst. prof. U. Windsor (Ont., Can.), 1973-77, assoc. prof. devel. psychology, 1977-87, prof. devel. psychology, 1987—; vis. assoc. prof. U. Toronto, 1979-81; vis. research assoc. Clarke Inst. of Psychiatry, 1985—. Bd. dirs. Childrens Achievement Centre, 1978-80. Recipient grant Royal Commn. Study Violence in Communications Industry, 1976, Gerontology Research Council of Ont., 1983. Mem. Am. Psychol. Assn., Soc. Research in Child Devel., Can. Psychol. Assn. Clubs: U. Windsor Faculty, U. Windsor Faculty Women's. Asso. editor Can. Jour. Early Childhood Edn., 1980-86, Toronto Ski Club; contbr. articles to profl. jours. Home: 7 Elderfield Crescent, Etobicoke, ON Canada M9C 3K6 Office: U Windsor Dept Psychology, Windsor, ON Canada N9B 3P4

MCCABE, CATHERINE CONE, film production manager; b. Portsmouth, Va., Oct. 1, 1942; d. Spencer Burtis and Nancy (Howard) Cone; m. James McCabe, Oct. 13, 1973 (div. 1975); m. Steven Douglas Helm, Mar. 11, 1981; 1 stepchild, Roxanne. Student, Barnard Coll., 1960-62, Columbia Sch. Gen. Studies, 1963-65. Coll. competitions editor Mademoiselle mag., N.Y.C., 1965-66; script supr. various films Los Angeles, 1966-68; prodn. asst. Filmways/MGM, Los Angeles, 1968-70; 2nd asst.. 1st asst. dir. numerous films Chgo., Los Angeles, Mex., 1970-78; prodn. mgr. over 50 films U.S., 1978—. Prodn. asst. Ice Station Zebra, 1968; 1st asst. dir. Bound for Glory, 1976, Raid On Entebbe, 1978; 1st asst. dir. and assoc. producer Mr. Horn, 1980; prodn. mgr. Eleanor, First Lady of The World, 1981. Mem. Dirs. Guild Am., DAR.

MCCABE, KATHRYN JOAN, financial analyst; b. Washington, Dec. 23, 1941; d. William John Jr. and Kathryn Marie (Sears) McC.; m. Stanley John Wilson, Feb. 23, 1963 (div. Nov. 1977); children: Anne Sears, Michael Heath; m. Rex W. Featherston, Sept. 19, 1984. BSBA, Am. U., 1980; MBA, George Washington U., 1982. Ins. underwriter Aetna Life and Casualty Co., Chevy Chase, Md., 1975-76; loan adminstr. Allied Capital Corp., Washington, 1976-78; contracts mgr. Am. U., Washington, 1982-83; credit supr. GTE Corp., Reston Va., 1983-84; head of pub. services Library of Congress, Washington, 1984-86; asst. to pres., chmn. bd. Oxford Industries, Inc., Atlanta, 1987—. Mem. Nat. Fedn. of Bus. and Profl. Women's Clubs, Nat. Assn. of Women Bus. Owners. Democrat. Roman Catholic. Home: 1080 Dogwood Forest Dr Marietta GA 30068

MCCABE-SCHMIDT, CARROLL LOUISE, lawyer; b. Washington, Oct. 27, 1953; d. Eugene Anthony and Louisa Carroll (Wright) McCabe; m. Bruce Edward Schmidt, Jan. 21, 1983; children: Kyle Edward Schmidt, Lauren Nicole Schmidt. B.A. in Social Scis. and Edn., U. No. Colo., 1976; J.D., U. Balt., 1982. Bar: Md. Tchr. Lareine High Sch., Suitland, Md., 1977-78, St. Peter's Sch., Waldorf, Md., 1978-79; law clk. Robert Ades & Assocs., P.C., Landover, Md., 1980-82, assoc., 1982-85; sole practice, 1985—; asst. pub. defender, Md., 1986—; guest lectr. U. Md., College Park, 1983—. Contbr. articles to newspapers. Democrat. Roman Catholic. Office: PO Box 492 Seabrook MD 20706

MCCAFFERTY, BARBARA JEAN, sales executive; b. Lincoln, Nebr., Dec. 6, 1940; d. Russell Rowley and Ruth Alice (Williams) Wightman; m. Eriks Zeltins, Dec. 29, 1962 (div. Oct. 1976); 1 child, Brian K. Zeltins; m. Charles F. McCafferty Jr., Oct. 3, 1981. BS magna cum laude, Del. Valley Coll. Sci. and Agri., Doylestown, Pa., 1984; student, Drexel U., 1958-61. Dept. mgr. Strawbridge & Clothier, Neshaminy, Pa., 1968-73; asst. buyer Strawbridge & Clothier, Phila., 1973-76; office adminstr. Am. Protein Products, Croydon, Pa., 1976-78; tech. librarian Honeywell Power Sources Ctr., Horsham, Pa., 1978-85; sales dir. Colonial Life and Accident Ins., Wayne, Pa., 1985-86; adminstrn. mgr. Mobi Systems, Inc., Ft. Washington, Pa., 1986—. Mem. Nat. Assn. for Female Execs., Nat. Assn. for Profl. Saleswomen, Options, Inc. Republican. Presbyterian. Club: Shawnee-at-Highpoint Racquet (Chalfont, Pa.). Home: 224 Hastings Ct Doylestown PA 18901

MCCAFFERTY, BELINDA SUE, accountant; b. Columbia, S.C., Dec. 24, 1951; d. Edward Earle and Dorothy (Devaney) McCafferty. B.B.A., Delta State U., 1973. Auditor IRS, Jackson, Miss., 1973-77. 78-79, revenue agt., Clarksdale, Miss., 1977, tax auditor, group mgr., Lafayette, La., 1979-80, regional analyst, Dallas, 1980-83, revenue agt., Dallas, 1983-85, revenue agt. group mgr., 1985-87, sect. chief quality rev. staff, 1986-87, chief examination br., 1987—, mem. EEO com., Dallas, 1981-82. Mem. Assn. Govt. Accts. (pres. 1975). Baptist.

MCCAIN, BETTY LANDON RAY (MRS. JOHN LEWIS MCCAIN), political party official, civic leader; b. Faison, N.C., Feb. 23, 1931; d. Horace Truman and Mary Howell (Perrett) Ray; student St. Marys Jr. Coll., 1948-50; A.B. in Music, U. N.C., Chapel Hill, 1952; M.A., Columbia U., 1953; m. John Lewis McCain, Nov. 19, 1955; children—Paul Pressly III, Mary Eloise. Courier, European tour guide Ednl. Travel Assocs., Plainfield, N.J., 1952-54; asst. dir. YWCA, U. N.C., Chapel Hill, 1953-55; chmn. N.C. Democratic Exec. Com., 1976-79 (1st woman); mem. Dem. Nat. Com., 1971-72, 76-79, 80-85, mem. com. on Presdl. nominations (Hunt Commn.), 1981-82, mem. rules com., 1982-85; mem. Winograd Commn., 1977-78; pres. Dem. Women of N.C., 1971-72, dist. dir., 1969-72; pres. Wilson County Dem. Women, 1966-67; precinct chmn., 1972-76; del. Dem. Nat. Conv., 1972, 88; mem. Dem. Mid-term Confs., 1974, 78, mem. judicial council Den. Nat. Com., 1984—; dir. Carolina Tel. & Tel. Co. (1st woman). Sunday sch. tchr. First Presbyn. Ch., Wilson, 1970-71, mem. chancel choir, 1985—; mem. Council on State Goals and Policy, 1970-72, Gov.'s Task Force on Child Advocacy, 1969-71, Wilson Human Relations Commn., 1975-78; mem. career and personal counseling service adv. bd. St. Andrews Coll.; charter mem. Wilson Edn. Devel. Council; active Arts Council of Wilson, Inc., N.C. Art Soc., N.C. Lit. and Hist. Assn.; regional v.p., bd. dirs. N.C. Mental Health Assn.; pres., bd. dirs., legis. chmn. Wilson County Mental Health Assn.; bd. dirs. Friends of U. N.C.-TV, Country Doctor Mus., 1968—, Wilson United Fund; bd. govs., sec. personnel and tenure com. U. N.C., sec. budgets and fin. com. 1987—; bd. regents Barium Springs Home for Children; bd. dirs., pres. N.C. Mus. History Assocs., 1982-83, membership chair, 1987-88; co-chmn. Com. to Elect Jim Hunt Gov., 1976, 80, co-chmn. senatorial campaign, 1984; mem. N.C. Adv. Budget Com., 1981-85 (1st woman); bd. visitors Peace Coll., Wake Forest U. Sch. Law, U. N.C., Chapel Hill; co-chmn. fund drive Wilson Community Theatre; state bd. dirs. N.C., Am. Lung Assn., 1985-88. Recipient state awards N.C. Heart Assn., 1967, Easter Seal Soc., 1967, Community Service award Downtown Bus. Assocs., 1977, award N.C. Jaycettes, 1979, 85, Women in Govt. award N.C. and U.S. Jaycettes, 1985; named to Order of Old Well and Valkyries, U. N.C., 1952; named Dem. Woman of Yr., N.C., 1976. Mem. U. N.C. Chapel Hill Alumni Assn. (dir.), St. Marys Alumni Assn. (regional v.p.), AMA Aux. (dir., nat. vol. health services chmn., aux. liaison rep. Council on Mental Health, aux. rep. Council on Vol. Health Orgns.), N.C. (pres., dir., parliamentarian) med. auxs., UDC (historian John W. Dunham chpt.), DAR, N.C. Soc. Internal Medicine Aux. (pres.), Pi Beta Phi. Contbg. editor History of N.C. Med. Soc. Clubs: Book (pres.); Little Book; Wilson Country. Home: 1134 Woodland Dr Wilson NC 27893

MCCAIN, ELIZABETH DALE, senior benefits coordinator; b. Schenectady, N.Y., June 20, 1963; d. Arthur Williamson McCain and Margaret (Dale) Bain. Student, U. Edinburgh, Scotland, 1983-84; BA in English, Hamilton Coll., 1985. Benefits communications specialist The Singer Co. Hdqrs., Stamford, Conn., 1985-87; sr. benefits coordinator Singer Electronic Systems, Wayne, N.J., 1987—. Vol. Appalachian Service Project, Ky., 1979, 80; exec. advisor Jr. Achievement, Stamford, 1985-86; active Jr. League Stamford, Norwalk, Conn., 1987, Montclair, N.J., 1987—. Mem. Internat. Assn. Personnel Women, Internat. Found. of Employee Benefits, Nat. Assn. Female Execs., Am. Soc. Personnel Adminstrs. Home: 18 Osborne St Bloomfield NJ 07003 Office: Singer Electronic Systems 164 Totowa Rd Wayne NJ 07474-0975

MCCAIN, SARAH SULLIVAN, banker; b. Reading, Pa., July 1, 1938; d. Robert J. and Caroline H. (Horst) S.; B.A., Vassar Coll., 1960; children—Anna Tobin, Robert Sullivan. Programmer/analyst Bankers Trust Co., N.Y.C., 1960-65; v.p. Morgan Guaranty Trust Co. N.Y., N.Y.C., 1974—; ptnr. Sheerlund Properties, Reading, Pa. Home: 40 E 10th St New York NY 10003 Office: 23 Wall St New York NY 10015

MCCALL, DOROTHY KAY, psychotherapist; b. Houston, July 18, 1948; d. Sherwood Pelton and Kathryn Rose (Gassen) McC. BA, Calif. State U., Fullerton, 1973; MS in Edn., U. Kans., 1978; postgrad., U. Pitts., 1981-89. Counselor/intern Ctr. for Behavioral Devel., Overland Park, Kans., 1976-77; rehab. counselor Niagra Frontier Voc. Rehab. Ctr., Buffalo, 1978-79; counselor/instr. dept. motor vehicles Driving While Impaired Program N.Y. State, 1979-80; alcoholism counselor Bry Lin Hosp., Buffalo, 1979-81; instr. sch. social work U. Pitts., 1984; alcohol drug counselor The Whale's Tale, Pitts., 1984-86; sole practice drug and alcohol therapy Pitts., 1986—; faculty Chem. People Inst., Pitts., 1987—; guest lectr. sch. social work U. Pitts., 1982-87; educator/trainer Community Mental Health Ctr., W.Va., 1986-87, Tenn., 1986; tchr. Tri-Community Sch. System, Western Pa., 1984-87; cons. Battered Women's Shelter, Buffalo, 1980, Buffalo Youth and Alcoholism Abuse program, 1980; lectr. in field. Mem. Spl. Adv. Com. on Addiction, 1981-83; bd. dirs. Chem. People, Task Force Adv. Com., 1984-86; bd. dirs. Drug Connection Hot Line, 1984-86; mem. Coalition of Addictive Diseases, 1984-87; co-founder Greater Pitts. Adult Children of Alcoholics Network, 1984; mem. adv. bd. Chem. Awareness Referral and Evaluation System Duquesne U., 1988. Nat. Inst. Alcohol Abuse Tng. grantee, 1981; U. Pitts. fellow, 1983. Mem. Pa. Assn. for Children of Alcoholics (dir. 1987), Assn. of Labor Mgmt. Adminstrs. and Cons. on Alcoholism, Nat. Assn. for Children of Alcoholics, Nat. Assn. Social Workers. Democrat. Office: 673 Washington Rd Pittsburgh PA 15228

MCCALL, POLLY, accountant; b. Ottawa, Kans., Apr. 9, 1962; d. Keith Charles and Bettie Sue (White) Shumway; m. John Daryl McCall, Apr. 16, 1983. BA, Ottawa U., 1984; MS in Bus., U. Kans., 1986. CPA, Kans. Bookkeeper McCall's Electric, Ottawa, 1981-84; treas., chief fin. officer McCall's Electric Motor Service, Inc., Ottawa, 1984-85; tax staff intern KMG/Main Hurdman, Topeka, 1984, tax researcher, 1986; staff acct. Peimann and Greenfield, CPA's, Topeka, 1986-87; subs. acct. Franklin Savs. Assn., Topeka, 1988—; instr. Neosho County Community Coll., 1987—. Sec. Franklin County Dem. Party, 1986—, precinct committeewoman, 1986—; treas. Shumway for Rep. com., Ottawa, 1986; v.p. Ottawa Civic

Theatre, 1987—. Mem. Ottawa Bus. and Profl. Women (treas. 1987—), Am. Soc. Women CPA's, Nat. Fedn. Women Execs. Democrat. Baptist. Home: 813 S Locust St Ottawa KS 66067

MCCALL, SUSAN ELIZABETH, small business owner; b. Ogden, Utah, Nov. 21, 1945; d. Edward George and Virginia Alene (Davis) Mester; m. Gerald Devereaux, APr. 14, 1974 (div. Jan. 1975); m. M. Gary Purse, Mar. 9, 1976; 1 child, Melissa M. BFA, Utah State U., 1975. Office mgr. Sewing DIst., Phoenix, Ariz., 1969-70; art tchr. North Ogden City Schs., 1970-71; graphic arts Permaloy Corp., Ogden, 1972-74; regional purchasing agt. USDA Forest Service, Ogden, 1976; owner, mgr. The Flower Co., Albuquerque, 1976—. Recipient First Place award Utah Soc. Art, 1964. Mem. West Tex. Florist Assn., N.Mex. Floral Assn., Albuquerque Vis.'s Conv. (mktg. com. 1986—), Profl. Women in Bus. Office: The Flower Co 11004 Montgomery Blvd NE Albuquerque NM 87111

MCCALLA, SANDRA ANN, principal; b. Shreveport, La., Nov. 6, 1939; d. Earl Gray and Dorothy Edna (Adams) McC. BS, Northwestern La. State U., 1960; MS, U. No. Colo., 1968; EdD, Tex. A&M U., 1987. With Caddo Parish Sch. Bd., Shreveport, 1960—; asst. prin. Capt. Shreve High Sch., 1977-79, prin., 1979—; instr. math La. State U., evenings 1979-81. Named Educator of Yr., Shreveport Times-Caddo Tchrs. Assn., 1966, La. High Sch. Prin. of Yr., 1985, 87; recipient Excellence in Edn. award Capt. Shreve High Sch., 1982-83; Danforth fellow, 1982-83. Mem. adv. bd. Sta. KDAQ Pub. Radio, 1985—. Active Shreveport Women's Commn., 1983—. Mem. Nat. Assn. Secondary Sch. Prins., La. Assn. Prins. (Prin. of Yr. 1985), La. Assn. Sch. Execs. (Disting. Service award 1983), NEA, La. Educators Assn., Times-Caddo Educators Assn. (Educator of Yr. 1984), Phi Delta Kappa. Democrat. Club: Altrusa.

MCCALLION, HAZEL, mayor; b. Port Daniel, Can.; m. Samuel McCallion; children—Peter, Linda, Paul. Formerly office mgr. Can. Kellogg Co.; mayor City of Mississauga, Ont., Can., 1978—; mem. com. on transp. of dangerous goods Minister of Transport. Dep. reeve City of Streetsville, 1968, mayor, 1970-73; chmn. Mississauga Taxicab Authority, Mississauga Planning com., Mississauga Sign Com.; vice chmn. adv. com. on local govt. mgmt.; chmn. provincial mcpl. subcom. on transp. of dangerous goods; bd. dirs. Credit Valley Hosp. Paul Harris fellow Rotary Internat., 1983. Mem. Streetsville C. of C. (former pres.), Assn. Municipalities Ont. (past pres.), Can. Fedn. Municipalities (bd. dirs.), Can. Jaycees (gov.); hon. mem. Polish Alliance Can., Mississauga Real Estate Bd. (hon.), Alpha Delta Kappa. Club: Mississauga Kinsmen (hon. mem.). Office: City of Mississauga, 300 City Centre Dr, Mississauga, ON Canada L5B 3C1

MCCALLUM, DONNA MARIE, medical technology association administrator; b. Natchez, Miss., Oct. 30, 1949; d. Willie James and Hannah Virginia (Smith) Wimberly; m. Ventress McCallum, Oct. 24, 1971; children: Ventress LaMont, Ashanti Ali. BS, Jackson State U., 1971; postgrad., Calif. State U., Dominguez Hills, 1976, 82, 83. Cons. dist. IV Calif. Assn. Med. Lab. Tech., San Francisco, 1984—. Fundraiser Brotherhood Crusade, Los Angeles, 1981-82. Mem. Nat. Cert. Assn. Lab. Personnel, Nat. Assn. Female Execs., Med. Tech. Assn., Smithsonian Inst. Democrat. Baptist. Home: 1648 Edom St Carson CA 90746

MCCALLUM, PATRICIA ANN, public relations specialist, consultant; b. Cleve., Apr. 25, 1944; d. Jacob and Ruth (Eckert) Palomaki; BSJ., Northwestern U., 1966, postgrad., 1966; m. James S. McCallum, July 2, 1966; children—Julie Lynn, David James. Reporter, New Brunswick (N.J.) Daily Home News, 1966-68; mng. editor Cen. Post, Kendall Park, N.J., 1969-70; govt. reporter Stewart Citizen, Walden, N.Y., 1972-75; editor Army Community Services Bull., Schweinfurt, Ger., 1976; pub. info. officer No. Va. Community Coll., Woodbridge campus, 1978-81; pub. affairs specialist, vol. cons. Directorate of Personnel and Community Activities, Ft. Sill, Okla., 1982-87. Mem. Lawton-Ft. Sill Community Edn. Adv. Council, 1981-87. Recipient 1st place award govt. news feature N.J. Press Assn., 1970; Community Achievement award Schweinfurt Mil. Community, 1976, 77, hon. mention Nat. Sch. Pub. Relations Assn., 1980, cert. of achievement Dept. of Army, 1983, 86, Sec. of the Army award , 1985, Commander's award for Civilian Service, 1987, others. Mem. Women in Communications, Internat. Assn. Bus. Communicators, European Council Parents and Tchrs. (life mem.). Home: 124 Payson Rd Belmont MA 02178

MCCALMAN, MARY ELIZABETH, personnel manager; b. Conway, S.C., June 2, 1938; d. Henry Kemper and Fronie Elizabeth (Ray) Tyler; m. John Calvin Martin, Jan. 11, 1954; children: Anitta E., John C. Martin Jr.; m. Felix McCalman, Nov. 25, 1984. BS, Meth. Coll., 1975; MA, Cen. Mich. U., 1977. Mgr. personnel Hanes Hosiery, Bennettsville, S.C., 1977-80, Wolverine, Shawnee, Okla., 1980-82, L'eggs Products, Florence, S.C., 1982—; bd. dirs. Am. Mgmt. Coll. Bd. dirs. United Way, Florence, S.C., Heart to Heart, March of Dimes; adv. bd. Indsl. Relations, Florence. Mem. Am. Soc. Personnel Adminstrn. Club: Leadership Florence Alumni (pres. 1987-88). Lodge: Civitan (v.p. 1984-85). Home: 1407 Poinsett Dr Florence SC 29501 Office: L'eggs Products 1901 N Irby Florence SC 29501

MC CANDLESS, ANNA LOOMIS, club woman; b. Aspinwall, Pa., July 21, 1897; d. George Wilberforce and Estella (Loomis) McC.; B.S., Carnegie-Mellon U., 1919. Pres., Vis. Nurses Assn. of Allegheny County, 1955-57; mem. vis. com. Margaret Morrison Carnegie Coll., 1962-66; v.p. Alumni Fedn. Carnegie Inst. Tech., 1963-66. Trustee Carnegie-Mellon U., 1966—. Mem. AAUW. Clubs: Coll., Univ., Twentieth Century (pres. 1956-58) (Pitts.); Appalachian Mountain. Home: Park Plaza Apts Craig St Pittsburgh PA 15213

MCCANDLESS, BARBARA J., tax and home economics consultant; b. Cottonwood Falls, Kans., Oct. 25, 1931; d. Arch G. and Grace (Kittle) McCandless; B.S., Kans. State U., 1953; M.S., Cornell U., 1959; postgrad. U. Minn., 1962-66, U. Calif., Berkeley, 1971-72; cert. home economist. m. Allyn O. Lockner, 1969. Enrolled agt. IRS. Home demonstration agt. Kans. State U., 1953-57; teaching asst. Cornell U., 1957-58, asst. extension home economist in marketing, 1958-59; consumer mktg. specialist, asst. prof. Oreg. State U., 1959-62; instr. home econs. U. Minn., 1962-63, research asst. agrl. econs., 1963-66; asst. prof. U. R.I., 1966-67; asso. prof. family econs., mgmt., housing, equipment dept. head S.D. State U., 1967-73; asst. to sec. Dept. Commerce and Consumer Affairs, S.D., 1973-79; now cons. Mem. Nat. Council Occupational Licensing, dir., 1973-75, v.p., 1975-79. Mem. Am. Mktg. Assn., Am. Agrl. Econs. Assn., Am. Home Econs. Assn., Nat. Council on Family Relations, Am. Council Consumer Interests, LWV, Kans. State U. Alumni Assn., Pi Gamma Mu. Club: Brookings (S.D.) Country. Research on profl. and occupational licensing bds. Address: 2114 Potomac Dr Topeka KS 66611

MCCANDLESS, CAROLYN KELLER, publishing company executive; b. Patuxent River, Md., June 6, 1945; d. Stevens Henry and Betty Jane (Bethune) Keller; m. Stephen Porter McCandless, Apr. 22, 1972; children: Peter Keller, Deborah Marion. BA, Stanford U., 1967; MBA, Harvard U., 1969. Fin. analyst Time Inc., N.Y.C., 1969-72, mgr. budgets and fin. analysis, 1972-78, asst. sec., dir. internal adminstrn., 1978-85, v.p., dir. employee benefits, 1985—; voting mem. Empire Blue Cross-Blue Shield. Mem. Erisa Industry Council. Republican. Mem. Unitarian Ch. Office: Time Inc Rockefeller Ctr New York NY 10020

MCCANN, CAROL COLE, banker; b. Detroit, Dec. 7, 1945; d. John Fremont and Doris Adele (Vehmeyer) C.; m. Lee S. Friedman, June 12, 1968 (div. 1972); m. Donald Roger McCann, Nov. 19, 1980. BS, Skidmore Coll., 1968; MSW, U. Conn., 1972. Med. social worker Yale-New Haven Hosp., 1968-70; social work supr. Klingberg Family Ctrs., New Britain, Conn., 1973-75; personal banker Con.. Bank & Trust, Hartford, 1978-80; dir. tng. and devel. Barnett Bank, West Palm Beach, Fla., 1980—, br. mgr., 1981, dir. tng. and devel., 1981—; seminar leader Atlantic High Sch., Boynton Beach, Fla., 1987, Catholic Family Services, Delray Beach, Fla., 1987. Mem. Am. Soc. Tng. and Devel. (pres. 1986-87), Am. Inst. Banking (v.p. edn. 1986-87, pres. 1987—). Home: 3802 Quail Ridge Dr Boynton Beach FL 33436 Office: Barnett Bank of Palm Beach 7320 S Dixie Hwy West Palm Beach FL 33405

MCCANN, JEAN JUANITA, journalist; b. Chgo., Feb. 6, 1923; d. John Gilbert and Hazel Lillian (Anderson) Wilson; m. George F. McCann; children: Cora Liderbach, Ellen Redd, Michael, Mary Jean Stinson, Brian, Margaret, Andrew, Barbara, Gregory, Kathryn. Student, Northwestern U., 1940-44; BA, SUNY, 1985. N.Y. bur. chief Chgo. Jour. Commerce, N.Y.C., 1944-48; corr. Cleve. Plain Dealer, 1968-74; assoc. editor Biomed. News, Falls Church, Va., 1971-72; nat. news editor Oncology Times, N.Y.C., 1979-86, Emergency Medicine and Ambulatory Care News, N.Y.C., 1972—; internat. corr. Physicians Radio Network, Stamford, Conn., 1972—; oncology news editor Cope mag., Denver, 1986—; pres. Med. News, Inc., Cleve., 1979—. Fellow Am. Med. Writers Assn. (sect. head 1983); mem. Nat. Assn. Sci. Writers, Internat. Assn. Sci. Writers, Overseas Press Club, Soc. Profl. Journalists, AAAS. Office: Med News Inc PO Box 18600 Cleveland OH 44118

MCCANN, JOAN CELIA, school administrator; b. Malden, Mass., Jan. 23, 1936; d. Vincent Jacob and Helen Lorraine (Pontone) Celia; A.B. cum laude, Tufts U., 1957; M.A., U. Mich., 1968; Ed.D., Fordham U. 1986; m. William J. McCann, Aug. 23, 1958; children—Susan, Peter. Tchr. 1st grade Gleason Sch., Medford, Mass., 1957-58, Hutchinson Sch., Pelham, N.Y., 1958-61; tchr. 1st grade Siwanoy Sch., Pelham, 1968-69, reading cons., 1969-71, prin., 1971-75; prin. Fox Meadow Sch., Scarsdale, N.Y., 1975—; mem. adminstrv. adv. com. internship St. John's U., 1973—. Mem. Pelham Bicentennial Com., 1974—, sch. cons. Between the Lines publ., 1975; mem. adv. bd. Scarsdale Hist. Soc., 1975—; chmn. Pelham Bicentennial Ball, 1976; adv. com. Westchester County Office of Aging; adv. bd. Prins. Forum at Fordham U. Recipient award in appreciation for cooperation Pelham Manor Fire Dept., 1974; IDEA fellow Charles Kettering Found., 1976, 77. Mem. Internat. Reading Assn., N.Y. State Adminstrs. Assn., Nat. Assn. Elementary Sch. Prins., Nat. Congress Parents and Tchrs. (life), Am. Assn. sch. Adminstrs., Beatrix Potter Soc., Jean Piaget Soc., Jackson Coll. Alumnae Assn., U. Mich. Alumni Assn., Phi Delta Kappa, Chi Omega. Club: Internat. Garden. Home: 242 Eastland Ave Pelham NY 10803 Office: Fox Meadow Sch Brewster Rd Scarsdale NY 10583

MCCANN, MARY CHERI, medical technologist, horse breeder and trainer; b. Pensacola, Fla., July 29, 1956; d. Joseph Maxwell and Cora Marie (Underwood) McC.; m. Robert Lee Spencer, July 20, 1977 (div. Nov. 1983). AA, Pensacola Jr. Coll., 1975; student, U. Md., 1977-78; BS in Biology, Troy State U., 1979; postgrad., U. Fla., 1979. Med. technologist Cape Fear Valley Med. Ctr., Fayetteville, N.C., 1981-85, Doctors Diagnostic Ctr., Fayetteville, 1985-86; sales rep. Waddell & Reed, Fayetteville, 1985-86; med. technologist Roche Biomed. Lab., Burlington, N.C., 1986-87; lab. mgr. Cumberland Hosp., Fayetteville, 1987—. Served with U.S. Army, 1976-77. Mem. Am. Soc. Clin. Pathologists (registrant), Nat. Assn. Female Execs., Am. Quarter Horse Assn., Appaloosa Horse Club, Pinto Horse Assn. Am. Republican. Avocations: horses, karate, guns, oil painting. Home: Route 2 Box 571 Hope Mills NC 28348 Office: Cumberland Hosp Roche Lab PO Box 42308 Fayetteville NC 28309

MCCANN, MARY COLLEEN, food service executive; b. Johnstown, Pa., Oct. 8, 1934; d. Patrick Joseph and Hilda Marie (Ott) McC. BS, Seton Coll., 1956; MPH, U. Pitts., 1964. Dir. dietary dept. Lawrence F. Flick State Hosp., Cresson, Pa., 1957-63; dir. dietetic internship Pa. State U., University Park, 1964-67, dir. inst. food research and service project, 1967-77, asst. prof., 1967-77; dir. Bur. Foodservice Mgmt. Commonwealth of Pa., Harrisburg, 1977-80; pres. McCann-Cannard and Assocs., Inc., Harrisburg, 1980—; mem. competency assurance panel Commn. on Dietetic Registration, Chgo., 1979—, chmn. 1980-81. Cons. editor Pa. Medicine, 1982; contbr. articles to profl. jours. Mem. Pa. Dietetic Assn. (pres. 1970, chair adv. com. on legis. and pub. policy 1976, licensure task force, 1983—, Keystone award 1981, Disting. Service award 1987), Am. Dietetic Assn., Am. Mgmt. Assn., Am. Correctional Food Service Assn., Irish Heritage Soc. Democrat. Roman Catholic. Office: McCann Cannard and Assocs PO Box 1931 Harrisburg PA 17105

MCCANN, VIVIAN CHAMBERS, nurse; b. Pine Bluff, Ark., Feb. 19, 1958; d. Odell and Dollie M. (Johnson) C.; m. Joseph B. McCann Jr. (div.). BS in Nursing, U. Ark., Pine Bluff, 1980; basic coronary care course, Jefferson Regional Med. Ctr., 1981; postgrad., U. Cen. Ark., 1985—. RN, Ark. Treas. Nursing Student Dept. U. Ark., Pine Bluff, 1979-80; nurse Jefferson Regional Med. Ctr., Pine Bluff, 1980-88; advocate of nursing, lectr. Basic Cornary Care Course, Pine Bluff, 1984-85; pane/judge Med.-Surg. Nurse Cert. Exam., 1985. Contbr. articles to profl. jours. Mem. Council on Cardiovascular Nursing Am. Heart Assn., 1984—. Named one of Outstanding Young Women in Am., 1985. Mem. Am. Assn. Critical Care Nurses, Jefferson Regional Med. Ctr. Policy and Procedures, Jefferson Regional Med. Ctr. Wellness Com., Nat. Assn. Female Execs. Home: PO Box 8043 Pine Bluff AR 71611

MCCARN, ELLEN DAHLENE, needle arts company president; b. Montgomery, Ala., Sept. 25, 1946; d. Oscar Jr. and Ellen (Harris) Dahlene; m. Charles John McCarn, May 18, 1968 (div. Mar. 1984); 1 child, Ellen; m. Larry Ray Skipper, Nov. 21, 1987. BS in Home Econs., U. Ala., 1968. Pres. McCarn Enterprises, Inc., Birmingham, 1979—; cons. designer Creative Ideas Mag., Birmingham, 1979—, Oxmoor House Books, Birmingham, 1983—, Southern Living Mag., Birmingham, 1983—, Craft and Needlework Age, Englishtown, N.J., 1984—. Inventor in field; author, editor: Ellen McCarn on English Smocking, 1986; designer, publ. various instructional leaflets; featured in crafts mags. Mem. Birmingham Symphony Women's Orgn., 1972-80, Ballet Guild of Birmingham, 1972—, Service Guild of Birmingham, 1973—, St. Mary's Guild, Birmingham, Valentine Mus. Needlework, Richmond, 1985. Named Designer of Month Decorating and Crafts Ideas Mag., 1979. Mem. Nat. Needlework Assn., Smocking Arts Guild of Am. (sec. 1981), Hobby Industries of Am., DAR, Am. Quarter Horse Assn., Am. Palomino Horse Assn., Delta Gamma. Baptist. Club: Village Garden (pres. 1973-75). Office: McCarn Enterprises Inc 12 Office Park Circle #104 Birmingham AL 35223

MCCARTER, KATHERINE SAUTER, association executive; b. Nyack, N.Y., Nov. 12, 1942; d. William Charles and Josephine Rosina (Schoenle) Sauter; B.A. in Biology, Cedar Crest Coll., Allentown, Pa., 1964; M.H.S. (EPA trainee), Johns Hopkins U., 1973; m. Robert James McCarter, Dec. 6, 1969; 1 dau., Emily Katherine. Chmn. sci. dept. Arundel (Md.) Jr. High Sch., 1964-68; program asso. career devel. program Am. Lung Assn., N.Y.C., 1968; air conservation cons. Mass. Lung Assn., 1968-69; exec. dir. Met. Boston Citizen's Coalition Clean Air, 1968-69; community health educator Environ. Health Adminstrn., Md. Dept. Health, 1971-76; dir. govt. relations Am. Public Health Assn., Washington, 1976-80, asst. exec. dir., 1980-83, assoc. exec. dir., 1984—; bd. dirs. Nat. Coalition Health and Environ., 1980-82; bd. dirs. Coalition for Health Funding, 1983—, treas., 1983-86 , v.p. 1987— ; mem. nat. air pollution manpower devel. adv. com. EPA, 1973-76. Editorial adv. bd., The AIDS Reference Guide, 1987. Mem. Nat. Environ. Health Assn., Am. Public Health Assn., Health on Wednesday. Home: 9027 Billow Row Columbia MD 21045 Office: 1015 15th St NW Washington DC 20005

MCCARTER, LOIS HANSON RATHVON, dance educator, administrator, choreographer; b. Tacoma, Wash., Aug. 24, 1925; d. Carl Arthur and Signe Cecelia (Fries) Hanson; m. Hal Campbell Rathvon, Jan. 22, 1945 (dec. 1978); children—Katherine Rathvon Deitz, Hal C. Jr., Richard, William. Student Central Wash. State U., 1944-45, Eastern Wash. State U., 1968-69, SUNY-Buffalo, 1972, UCLA, 1972-73; B.F.A. in Dance, Cornish Inst., 1977. Cert. Labanotation tchr. Owner, dir. Rathvon Sch. Dance, Richland, Wash., 1950-71, Rathvon Concert Dancers, 1950-71; dance instr. Company of Man, Buffalo, 1972; choreographer, lectr. Everett Community Coll., Bellevue Civic Ballet, Richland Allied Arts, Buffalo U. Opera Co., 1972-77; dance instr. Black Arts West, Ewajo, Seattle, 1973; arts cons. King County Arts Commn., Seattle, 1974-75; dir. Hearing Impaired Arts Program, Seattle, 1975-79; dance instr. Cornish Inst., Seattle, 1978-84, recruiting officer, 1978-79, chmn. dance dept., 1979-86, co-dir. Cornish Dance Theater, 1981-86. Choreographer: Nutcracker Suite, 1969-70; Concert Waltz, 1969; Carnival of Animals, 1967, 83; Slippery When Wet, 1982; Alone/Together, 1981; Love Is the Thing, 1984; author: Chronology of Dance Development in U.S., 1975. Mem. King County Arts Commn., 1978-81; dance advisor Wash. State Cultural Enrichment Program, 1969-72; bd. mem. NW Sch. Arts, Humanities and Environ., Seattle, 1979-81, Dance Notation Bur. Nat. Profl. Adv. Bd., N.Y.C., 1980-84; bd. dirs. Am. Coll. Dance Festival Assn., 1986-88. Wash. State Arts Commn. grantee, 1969-70; recipient Cultural Achievement award, Seattle Music and Arts Found., 1977, Allied Arts Council Mid-Columbia Region award, Richland, 1971, Community Achievement award Altrusa Club, Richland, 1970. Mem. Dance Notation Bur., Conf. on Research in Dance. Clubs: PEO, Soroptomist (Seattle-Met.). Home: 14051 Hill Top Ln NW Seattle WA 98177 Office: Dance Dept Cornish Inst 710 E Roy St Seattle WA 98102

MCCARTHY, ANN LOREE, marketing administrator; b. Cherokee, Iowa, Sept. 6, 1951; d. Philip Daniel and Ruth (Johnson) McC.; m. Joseph Milton Strout, June 12, 1982; children: Mark McCarthy, Megan McCarthy. BS, Iowa State U., 1973; MBA, U. Wis., Oshkosh, 1983. CPA, Iowa, Tex. Auditor Peat Marwick Mitchell & Co., Des Moines, 1973-74; mgr. promotion Kimberly Clark Corp., Neenah, Wis., 1974-84; owner McCarthy Cons., San Antonio, 1984-85; mgr. group promotion Ralston Purina Co., St. Louis, 1985—. Named Corp. Woman of Yr. Women in Mgmt., 1983. Mem. NOW, Am. Soc. Women CPA's. Office: Ralston Purina Co Checkerboard Sq Saint Louis MO 63164

MCCARTHY, ANNA-MARIE FRANCES, federal agency administrator; b. Albany, N.Y., Oct. 21, 1946; d. Daniel Joseph and Tomasina (Fallone) Kilmade; m. Robert Allen McCarthy, Sept. 3, 1967; children: Daniel Kilmade, Kevin Michael. BA, Coll. of St. Rose, 1970. Positions in staff support HUD, Washington, 1976-79, mgmt. analyst, 1979-81, staff budget analyst, 1981-83, chief budget and legislation coordination br., 1983—. Mem. Alumni Assn. Coll. of St. Rose. Democrat. Roman Catholic. Home: 6109 Glen Oaks Ct Springfield VA 22152 Office: HUD 4517th St SW Room 10160 Washington DC 20410

MCCARTHY, CATHERINE FRANCES, lawyer; b. N.Y.C., Feb. 13, 1921; d. Joseph J. and Eva E. (Berger) McC.; m. Peter Donald Andreoli, Aug. 25, 1945; children—Peter, Brian, Catherine, Christine, Francine. B.S., St. John's U., 1941, LL.B., 1943; Bar.: N.Y. 1943, U.S. Supreme Ct. 1966. Assoc., Spencer, Ordway & Wierum, 1942-50; sole practice, N.Y.C. and Pelham, N.Y., 1950-67; real estate atty. Gen. Foods Corp., White Plains, N.Y., 1967-68, trademark atty., 1968-73, chief trademark counsel, 1973-81, dir. legal services-trademarks, 1981-88, sole practice, Pelham, N.Y., 1988— . Recent decisions editor St. John's Law Rev., 1942-43. Mem. ABA, Assn. Bar City N.Y., N.Y. State Bar Assn., Westchester County Bar Assn., Westchester-Fairfield Corp. Counsel Assn., U.S. Trademark Assn. (dir. 1976-80, trademark rev. commn.). Home and Office: 134 Harmon Ave Pelham NY 10803

MCCARTHY, GRACE MARY, Canadian provincial government official; b. Vancouver, B.C., Can., Oct. 14, 1927; d. George and Allrietta (McCloy) Winterbottom; m. Raymond McCarthy, June 23, 1948; children—Mary, Calvin. Pres. Grayce Florists, Vancouver; mem. legis. assembly province of B.C., Victoria, 1966—, dep. premier, provincial sec., minister of recreation and travel industry, 1976-78, dep. premier, minister of human resources, 1978-83, minister human resources, B.C. transit, 1983-86; provincial sec. and and Minister of Govt. Services, 1986, dep. premier and minister of Econ. Devel., 1986—; commr. Bd. Parks and Pub. Recreation, 1961-66. Past pres. Vancouver Credit Women's Bus. Club, B.C. Social Credit Party; chmn. Capt. Cook Bicentennial Com., 1978, Yr. of Child, 1979; mem. nat. adv. bd. Salvation Army; bd. dirs. Can. Assn. Christians and Jews. Recipient Pres.'s award Greater Victoria Tourist Assn., Medal of Distinction Internat. Assn. Lions Clubs, H.J. Merilees award of Yr., Greater Vancouver Conv. and Visitors Assn., Marketer of Yr. award Internat. Sales and Mktg. Execs.; Silver medal Can. Govt. Fellow Coll. Fellows Royal Archtl. Inst. Can. (hon.); mem. Hastings C. of C. (1st women pres.); hon. mem. Vancouver Aquarium Assn., Florists' Transworld Delivery Service, Northwest Florist Assn., Vancouver Tourist Assn., B.C. Chefs Assn., B.C. Motels, Resorts and Trailer Parks Assn., Victoria Acadamie of Chefs de Cuisine, Van Dusen Bot. Gardens Assn. Anglican. Club: Variety Internat. (first woman mem.). Lodge: Daus. of Nile. Office: Parliament Bldgs, Victoria, BC Canada

MCCARTHY, HANNAH M., college president. Pres. Daniel Webster Coll., Nashua, N.H. Office: Daniel Webster Coll University Dr Nashua NH 03063 *

MCCARTHY, JEAN CATHERINE, parks and recreation official; b. Fitchburg, Mass., Jan. 3, 1925; d. Charles H. and Catherine I. (Beer) McC. Grad. mgmt. course, U. Mass. Inst. Govtl. Services, 1980. Clk.-typist Fitchburg Park-Recreation-Forestry Dept., 1948-53, prin. clk., 1953-70, adminstrv. asst., 1970-76, supt. parks and playgrounds, city forester, 1976-82, adminstrv. asst. and city forester, 1982—. Founder, 1st pres. MonT. unit Am. Cancer Soc., 1970—, chmn. pub. info., 1976-77, mem. cancer crusade com., 1981—, bd. dirs., 1970-84, pres., 1987-88; chmn. MonT. Unit Cancer Prevention Study II, 1982—; bd. dirs. Micah Housing Rehab. Program, 1974-76; mem. adv. com. for adult and occupational edn. Fitchburg Pub. Sch. System, 1979-82; rep. U.S. Nat. Council, World-Wide Consultation of Cath. Laity, Rome, 1975; bd. dirs. founding assembly Nat. Council Cath. Laity, 1971-82, sec. exec. bd., 1974-78; bd. dirs. U.S. Cath. Mission Council, 1980-82; mem. Worcester Diocesan Council, Worcester, Mass., 1966-76, pres., 1968-74; mem. Worcester Diocesan Pastoral Council, 1972-74; internat. conv. clk. Daus. of Isabella, 1970, 74, sec. Mass. Circle, 1961-62, regent Jeanne d'Arc Circle, 1959-60, trustee Jeanne d'Arc Circle, 1979-82, chmn. liturgy Jeanne d'Arc Circle, 1979-84; lay dir. Worcester Diocesan Cursillo Secretariat and Leaders' Sch., 1983—, mem. Team for Women's Weekends; mem. adv. bd. Gov.'s Commn. on Women's Issues, 1984—. Recipient State award Am. Cancer Soc., 1972, 77, state cert. appreciation, 1976, award for 25 yrs. of service, 1985; cert. for advancement public service in Commonwealth Mass., U. Mass. Inst. Govtl. Services, 1980; cert. appreciation United Neighbors of Cleghorn Inc., 1980, Brain Injured Children Softball Marathon Com., 1980. Home: 294 Madison St Fitchburg MA 01420 Office: Park and Recreation-Forestry Dept City Hall 718 Main S t Fitchburg MA 01420

MCCARTHY, JOANNE ELIZABETH, educator, consultant; b. Allentown, Pa., May 6, 1943; d. Robert Franklin and Sarah Elizabeth (Knauss) Schall; m. William James McCarthy, June 21, 1969. B.A., UCLA, 1968; M.Ed., U. Rochester, 1974; M.S., U. LaVerne, 1981; M.A., Mills Coll., 1983. Elem. tchr. Centralia Sch. Dist., Buena Park, Calif., 1968-70; reading specialist elem. sch. Spencerport (N.Y.) Sch. Dist., 1973-74, Wayne Central Sch. Dist., Ontario, N.Y., 1974-75; tchr. State Demonstration Project, Pittsburg (Calif.) Unified Sch. Dist., 1977-78; English and reading tchr. Vallejo (Calif.) City Unified Sch. Dist., 1978—; staff devel. cons. Profl. Devel. Ctr. Mem. NEA, Assn. Supervision and Curriculum Devel., Calif. Assn. Tchrs. English, Nat. Council Tchrs. English, Phi Delta Kappa, Pi Lambda Theta; Nat. Audubon Soc. Author publ. in field. Home: 105 Poshard St Pleasant Hill CA 94523 Office: Vallejo City Unified Sch Dist 840 Nebraska St Vallejo CA 94591

MCCARTHY, KAREN RITCHIE, arts administrator, publicist; b. Söest, Fed. Republic Germany, Aug. 2, 1957; came to Can., 1957; d. George Fraser Burk and Margaret Dodd (Coghlin) Ritchie; m. Thomas James McCarthy, Aug. 16, 1986. BA, Queen's U., 1978. Traffic mgr. Mertens & Assocs. Advt., Toronto, Ont., Can., 1979; media asst. Burson-Marsteller Inc., Toronto, 1979; advt. and promotion coordinator The Banff Ctr., Alta., Can., 1980-82, audience devel. officer, 1982-85; publicist Calgary (Alta.) Philharmonic Soc., 1985-87, mgr. mktg., pub. relations, 1987—; workshop instr. Assn. Can. Orchs., Toronto, 1986-87. Editor Prelude mag., 1986-87. Mem. Performing Arts Publicists Assn. (steering com. 1987). Mem. Anglican Ch. Office: Calgary Philharmonic Soc, 205 8th Ave SE, Calgary, AB Canada T2G 0K9

MC CARTHY, MARY, author; b. Seattle, June 21, 1912; d. Roy Winfield and Therese (Preston) McC.; 1 son, Reuel K. Wilson; m. James Raymond West, Apr. 15, 1961. A.B., Vassar Coll., 1933; A.B. (hon.), Syracuse U., 1973, U. Hull, Eng., 1974, Bard Coll., 1976, U. Aberdeen, Scotland, 1979. Editor Covici Friede, 1936-37; editor Partisan Rev., 1937-38, drama critic, 1937-48; instr. lit. Bard Coll., 1945-46, Charles Stevenson chair of lit., 1986—; instr. English Sarah Lawrence Coll., 1948; Northcliffe lectr. Univ. Coll., London, 1980. Author: The Company She Keeps, 1942, The Oasis, 1949, Cast a Cold Eye, 1950, The Groves of Academe, 1952, A Charmed

Life, 1955, Sights and Spectacles, 1956, Venice Observed, 1956, Memories of a Catholic Girlhood, 1957, The Stones of Florence, 1959, On the Contrary, 1961, The Group, 1963, Mary McCarthy's Theatre Chronicles, 1963, Vietnam, 1967, Hanoi, 1968, The Writing on the Wall, 1970, Birds of America, 1971, Medina, 1972, The Seventeenth Degree, 1974, The Mask of State, 1974, Cannibals and Missionaries, 1979, Ideas and the Novel, 1980, Occasional Prose: Essays, 1985, How I Grew, 1987; contbr. articles to nat. mags. Guggenheim fellow, 1949-50; recipient Horizon prize, 1949; Nat. Inst. grantee, 1957; Guggenheim fellow, 1959-60. Mem. Nat. Inst. Arts and Letters, Phi Beta Kappa. Office: care Harcourt Brace & Jovanovich 1250 6th Ave San Diego CA 92101

MCCARTHY, PAMELA MAFFEI, magazine editor; b. N.Y.C., May 28, 1952; d. Rudolph Paul Maffei and Mary Frances Maresca; m. Joseph Matthews McCarthy, Sept. 16, 1978; 1 child, Joseph Winston. Student, Trinity Coll., Dublin, Ireland, 1972-73; B.A., Mt. Holyoke Coll., 1974. Mem. editorial staff Esquire mag., N.Y.C., 1974-76, copy editor, 1976-79, exec. editor, 1978-84; mng. editor Vanity Fair mag., N.Y.C., 1984—. Mem. Am. Soc. Mag. Editors. Office: Vanity Fair 350 Madison Ave New York NY 10017

MCCARTHY, PATRICIA SUSAN, chemical company executive; b. Flushing, N.Y., Apr. 22, 1955; d. Joseph William and Patricia Marion (Beacom) McC.; m. Karl W. Kaltenbach, Aug. 19, 1978; 1 child, Christopher Joseph. BS in Chemical Engring., Rensselaer Poly. Inst., 1976; SM, MIT, 1981. Project mgr. Procter & Gamble Co. Inc., Cin., 1976-80; bus. unit mgr. Orion Research Inc., Cambridge, Mass., 1981-84; v.p., co-founder Medica Corp., Bedford, Mass., 1984-86; pres. Kaltenbach, McCarthy & Assoc., Newton, Mass., 1986—; bd. dirs. Cybermation Inc., Cambridge. Author: Basic Telephones, 1987. Mem. Am. Chem. Soc. Roman Catholic. Home: 183 Walnut St Newtonville MA 02160

MCCARTHY, SHERRI NEVADA, educator of gifted and talented; b. Topeka, June 2, 1958; d. Wallace Gene and Lois Elaine (McDyson) McC.; m. Scott Newlin Tucker, Feb. 14, 1983; children: Colin Apollo, Chrysallis Altair. AA, Phoenix Coll., 1981; BA in Psychology, BEd in English, Ariz. State U., 1984, MA in Spl. Edn., 1987. Mng. editor Scottsdale (Ariz.) Free Press, 1977-78; instr. English Skills Ctr. Phoenix Community Coll., 1978-80; spl. instr. Title I Creighton Sch. Dist., Phoenix, 1980-81; gifted specialist Fountain Hills (Ariz.) Schs., 1985-87, curriculum adv. council, textbook adoption com., 1986-87; tchr. of gifted Chandler (Ariz.) Unified Schs., 1987—; free-lance writer, 1974—. Author: Metamorphosis-A Collection of Poems, 1975, Speed Communication, 1979, A Matter of Time, 1980; staff writer Ariz. Hwy. Patrolman mag., Phoenix, 1979-82; newsletter editor Ednl. Opportunity Ctr., Tempe, Ariz., 1982-83, A Death in the Family, 1988; contbr. articles to profl. jours. Dep. registrar Dems. of Phoenix, 1978—; bd. dirs. Young Astronauts, Fountain Hills, 1985-87. Recipient newswriting awards Ariz. Press Assn., 1974, 75. Mem. NEA, Ariz. Edn. Assn., Ariz. Coalition for Learning Disabilities, Ariz. Assn. for Gifted and Talented, Odyssey of the Mind (bd. govs. 1987—, creativity awards 1986, 87). Home: 201 E Fordham Tempe AZ 85283

MCCARTNEY, DONNA CONQUERGOOD, personnel manager; b. Antioch, Calif., Feb. 25, 1950; d. Thomas Herbert and Leila Fern (Clark) Conquergood; m. Michael Fannin McCartney, June 10, 1972; children: Kenneth Ward, Kristin Leanne, Catherine Loree. AA, Sacramento City Coll., 1971; BS, U. San Francisco, 1984, MS, 1986. Mgr. personnel Aromat Corp. (subs. Matsushita Electric Works of Japan), Cupertino, CA. Campaign vol. Assemblyman Jerry Lewis, San Bernardino, Calif., 1973-76, Congresswoman Shirley Pettis, San Bernardino, 1974. Mem. Internat. Personnel Mgmt. Assn. (scholarship award 1984), No. Calif. Human Resources Council, Bay Area Organizational Devel. Network. Republican. Club: Summit Orgn. (San Jose, Calif.). Home: 5323 Shelby Ct Fremont CA 94536 Office: Aromat Corp 10400 N Tantau Ave Cupertino CA 95014

MCCARTY, BARBARA SMITH, county official; b. Andalusia, Ala., Sept. 7, 1940; d. Egbert L. and Gladys (Hartin) S.; m. Lucius Edard McCarty, Apr. 21, 1961; children—Debra McCarty Slaughter, Lucius Edward, Donna McCarty Swilley. Student South Ga. Tech. Coll., 1958-60, U. Ga.-Athens, 1964—. Office mgr. to county tax commr., Americus, Ga., 1966-76; clk.-treas. Sumter County Bd. Commrs., Americus, 1976-85, chief adminstrv. officer, treas., 1985—; v.p. Assoc. Industries of Americus. Named Woman of Achievement, 1987-88. Mem. County Adminstrs. Assn. Ga., Ga. County Clks. Assn., Inst. Mcpl. Clks. Ga. Democrat. Baptist. Club: Bus. and Profl. Women's (Americus) (treas.). Lodge: Order Eastern Star (worthy matron 1979-80). Avocations: reading; walking; music. Home: PO Box 1664 Americus GA 31709 Office: County Courthouse Americus GA 31709

MCCARTY, DEBORAH HUSCH, insurance company executive; b. Washington, Aug 4, 1960; d. Jakob and Ingrid (Fischer) Husch; m. Gregory D. McCarty, Aug. 15, 1987. B.S. in Mktg., U. Md., 1982. Food and beverage mgr. Washington Boat Lines, 1982-84; dist. rep. Aid Assn. for Lutherans, Appleton, Wis., 1984—. Mem. Nat. Assn. Life Underwriters, Women's Life Underwriters Conf., D.C. Life Underwriters Assn., Nat. Assn. Fraternal Ins. Counselors (Pres.'s award 1987), Nat. Assn. Female Execs., Million Dollar Round Table. Republican. Lutheran. Avocations: aerobics; running; reading; hiking; camping. Home: 6301 Sandy St Laurel MD 20707 Office: Aid Assn for Luths 6301 Sandy St Laurel MD 20707

MCCARTY, NANCY JACKOBS, information specialist; b. Hibbing, Minn., Aug. 8, 1940; d. John Casper and Eleanor Louise (Rexeisen) Jackobs; m. Walter Birks Mc Carty, May 17, 1975. BA in Chemistry and Math., Wis. State Coll., 1962; PhD in Analytical Chemistry, Purdue U., 1967. Supr. Eastman Kodak Co., Rochester, N.Y., 1967-77; owner A&L Lab., Inc., Auburn, Maine, 1977-85, W.B. McCarty Assocs., Auburn, 1985—. Organizer Danville (Maine) Community Citizens Group, 1982—. Mem. LWV, Am. Chem. Soc. (sgt. at arms 1973), Lewiston-Auburn Career Women (organizer 1986-87), Assn. Maine Environ. Labs. Roman Catholic. Club: Golf (Auburn) (pres. 1986-87). Home: PO Box 163 Danville ME 04223 Office: WB McCarty Assocs PO Box 1537 Auburn ME 04210

MCCARTY, SHIRLEY CAROLYN, aerospace executive; b. Minot, N.D., May 2, 1934; d. Harry and Cecelia Marie (Engene) Wolhowe; m. John Myron McCarty, Apr. 3, 1958. BS in Bus. Adminstrn., U. N.D., 1958. Mem. tech. staff Douglas Aircraft, El Segundo, Calif., 1960-62; mem. tech. staff The Aerospace Corp., El Segundo, 1962-72, mgr., 1972-73, dir., 1973-79, prin. dir., 1979—; mem. adv. council Calif. State U., Northridge, 1979—, chmn., 1984-86; mem. indsl. adv. bd. Purdue U., West Lafayette, Ind., 1979-82, 1985—. Named Woman of Yr. The Aerospace Corp., 1976, Pres.'s award, 1987; recipient Spl. Judges Award for Leadership, Los Angeles YWCA, 1977, Sioux Alumni Award, U. N.D. 1982, Achievement award Los Angeles County Commn. for Women, 1987. Mem. IEEE, Purdue U. Soc. Women Engrs., Assn. for Computing Machinery, Soc. Women Engrs., Bus. and Profl. Women (Woman of Achievement 1984, Golden Nike award 1985), Women in Bus.(corp. achievement award, 1987), Women in Computing (founding mem., bd. dirs.). Home: 357 Valley St El Segundo CA 90245 Office: The Aerospace Corp 2350 E El Segundo Blvd El Segundo CA 90245

MCCARTY-WRIGHT, KAREN ANN, photographer, small business owner; b. St. Louis, July 7, 1959; d. Charles Patrick and Evelyn Lorette (Aloisio) McCarty; m. Kevin Arthur Wright, June 5, 1981; children: Jesse Charles, Glen Francis. AA, East Cen. Coll., 1978; BA, Lindenwood Coll., 1980. Typesetter, pasteup artist Tribune Newspaper, Union, Mo., 1976-77; lab. technician Plank's Color Lab, Union, 1980-81; sec. to dean edn. East Cen. Coll., Union, 1981-82; tchr. St. Clare Cath. Elem. Sch., St. Clair, Mo., 1982-84; owner, photographer Wright Photography, Union, 1984—. Home and Office: Hwy V Rt 4 Box 381 Union MO 63084

MCCARVER, BETTY LOUISE, nurse, educator; b. Hurley, N.Mex., Oct. 12, 1932; d. Carl Thomas and Stella Alberta (Kreamer) McLendon; m. Robert Roy McCarver Jr., Sept. 3, 1954 (div. Jan. 1975); children—Robert Roy III, Deborah Lynn McCarver Stenberg. Diploma in nursing U. Okla., 1954; B.S., Ariz. State U., 1972; MEd, No. Ariz. U., 1986. R.N. Supr. U. Okla. Childrens Hosp., Oklahoma City, 1954; instr. Research Hosp., Kansas City, Mo., 1954-55; charge nurse U.S. Army Dispensaries, Sendai, Japan, 1956-57; owner, mgr. Hallmac Foods and Camping Supplies, Scottsdale, Ariz., 1965-68; asst. exec. dir. Ariz. Nurses Assn., Phoenix, 1976-82; tng. dir. Ariz. Family Planning Council, Phoenix, 1983—. Author: Once Upon A Time: A Complete Guide to Baby Sitting, 1965, 86; Dear Gussie: The 1-2-3 of G.E.M.S., 1968. Editor Caduceus Crier, 1972-73. Chmn. various coms. Maricopa County Med. Aux., 1963-73, Ariz. Med. Aux., 1970-73; wilderness survival counselor Theodore Roosevelt council Boy Scouts Am., Scottsdale, 1971. Recipient award of honor Nat. Safety Council, 1965, 66. Mem. Maricopa County Med. Aux. (hon. life), Council Continuing Edn. (sec. of council on continuing edn.), Am. Nurses Assn. (dist. 18 nominating com. 1986), Ariz. Nurses Assn., Ariz. Vocat. Edn. Assn., Am. Soc. Tng. and Devel., Ariz. Pub. Health Assn., Nat. Family Planning and Reproductive Health Assn. Republican. Mem. Ch. of Jesus Christ of Latter-day Saints. Avocations: hiking; backpacking; painting; sewing; travel. Home: 7124 N Via De Amigos Scottsdale AZ 85258 Office: Ariz Family Planning Council 2920 N 24th Ave Suite 26 Phoenix AZ 85015

MCCASKILL, ANNETTTE ALYCE, sales professional; b. Peckville, Pa., Dec. 4, 1958; d. Dante Ernesto and Alyce Helen (Newcott) Cancelli; m. John J. McCaskill, Mar. 15, 1986. BS in Bus., Pa. State U., 1980. Tech. salesperson Rohm and Haas, Los Angeles, 1980-84; field mktg. rep. Mobay Chem. Corp., Raritan, N.J., 1985-86; tech. sales profl. Amoco Performance Products, Concord, Calif., 1986—. Mem. Soc. for the Advancement Material and Process Engring. (sec. 1987—). Office: Amoco Performance Products 1320 Willow Pass Rd Suite 401 Concord CA 94520

MCCASLIN, F. CATHERINE, foundation executive; b. Chattanooga, Feb. 21, 1947; d. John Jacob and Elizabeth Dorothy (Johnson) McC. AB, Hollins Coll., Roanoke, Va., 1969; MA, Ga. State U., 1972; PhD, UCLA, 1979. Assoc. dir. Ga. Narcotics Treatment Program, Atlanta, 1972-73; research assoc., dir. research Health Care Delivery Services, Inc., Los Angeles, 1974-76; sr. survey analyst Kaiser Found. Health Plan, Los Angeles, 1978-80; program officer The Robert Wood Johnson Found., Princeton, 1980-84; faculty U. Pa. Sch. Medicine, Phila., 1984-86; ptnr. Schuhmacher & McCaslin, Pottstown, Pa., 1986—; exec. dir. The H.F. Lenfest Found., Pottstown, 1988—; mem. adv. bd. Nat. Childhood Asthma Project, NHBLI, Washington, 1982-84, adv. com. Statewide Adolescent Pregnancy, New Brunswick, 1981-84; trainee NIH, 1973-79; cons. in field. Mem. editorial bd. Jour. Health & Social Behavior, 1988—; editor Med. Sociology newsletter, 1984—; contbr. articles to profl. jours. Fellow NIMH, 1975; grantee Action Office for Drug Abuse Prevention, 1972, Johnson Found., 1984. Mem. Am. Sociol. Assn. (nat. council med. sociology sect. 1984—). Am. Pub. Health Assn., Sociologists for Women in Soc. Democrat. Presbyterian. Home: 482 N Charlotte St Pottstown PA 19464 Office: The H F Lenfest Found 202 Shoemaker Rd Pottstown PA 19464

MCCAUGHRIN, WENDY BORDOFF, educator; b. Windsor, Ont., Can., Nov. 23, 1944; d. Jack and Tillie (Starker) Bordoff; B.A., Wayne State U., 1967; B.A. with honors, U. Windsor, 1974; M.A., Merrill Palmer Inst., 1977; M.S., U. Ill., 1981, PhD, 1988; m. Scott James McCaughrin, July 1, 1972. Guidance counselor, instr. high sch., Chatham, Ont., 1967-70; reading therapist, instr., Windsor, Ont., 1971-77; reading and lang. therapist The Reading Group Program, Urbana, Ill., 1980-81; researcher computer-assisted instrn. for head-injured patients, Mercy Hosp., Urbana, 1984-85; ednl. cons. Learning Abilities Program, Mercy Hosp., Urbana, 1981-87, Christie Clinic, Champaign, 1987—; researcher transition of handicapped youth from tng. programs to competitive employment, U. Ill., 1986-87; ednl. researcher, Transition Inst. U. Ill., Urbana, 1987—. Mem. Cousteau Soc., Am. Speech-Lang.-Hearing Assn., Orton Soc., Internat. Reading Assn., Kappa Delta Pi. Jewish. Author reading and writing tests. Home: 36 Hillside Ln Briar Cliff Mahomet IL 61853 Office: U Ill 110 Edu Bldg Urbana IL 61801

MCCAULEY, JENNIFER KNAPP, art director; b. Buffalo, July 22, 1958; d. Lewis Durham and Harriet (Knapp) McC. Student, Hollins Coll., 1980, Calif. Coll. of Arts, 1981-83. Asst. buyer Henger's, Buffalo, 1980-81; clothing designer K.K. Kreations, Marin County, Calif., 1981-83; art dir. McGard, Inc., Buffalo, 1983—, head McCauley Agy. Inc. affiliate, 1988—. Mem. Art Dirs. Communicators of Buffalo. Office: McGard Inc 852 Kensington Ave Buffalo NY 14215

MCCAUSLAND, ELIZABETH ANN, social worker; b. Bronxville, N.Y., May 3, 1947; d. Gary Atwell and Ann (VonOsinski) Painter; m. Richard Kibbey McCausland, Aug. 23, 1969 (div. 1982); 1 child, Michael Atwell. AA, Cazenovia Coll., 1967; BA, Ramapo Coll., 1980; MSW, Hunter Coll., 1983. Cert. social worker, N.Y. Dir. social work Social Service Fedn., Englewood, N.J., 1983-84; family therapist Bergen County Div. Family Guidance, Hackensack, N.J., 1984-87, adminstr., 1987—; pvt. practice Prospect Ctr. for Psychotherapy, Ridgewood, N.J., 1988—. Coauthor: The Bergen County Youth Substance Abuse Resource Directory, 1986. Mem. Bergen County Com. on Youth Substance Abuse, 1985—. Mem. Nat. Assn. Social Workers, Acad. Cert. Social Workers. Office: Bergen County Div Family Guidance Exptl Unit E296 Ridgewood Ave Paramus NJ 07652

MCCAUSLAND, LINDA SHOFF, financial company executive; b. Los Angeles; d. Leonard Wayne Shoff and Mary Ellen (Reiter) Carey; m. Thomas William McCausland, Aug. 22, 1954 (div.). BS, UCLA, 1955. Master tchr. UCLA, Los Angeles city schs., 1955-62; investment counselor Washington, 1962—. Chmn. Aspen (Colo.) Wildflower Beautification Com., 1987; founder Nat. Mus. Women Arts, Washington, 1986—; active Nat. Rep. Senatorial Trust, Washington, 1983—, Nat. Rep. Leadership Council, Washington, 1984—; nat. trustee Washington Opera, 1983—; trustee Corcoran Gallery Art, Washington, 1986—; apptd. by. Pres. Reagan White House Conf. for a Drug-Free Am., 1987, Nat. Parks Found., 1986. Episcopalian. Office: 4200 Massachusetts Ave NW Washington DC 20016

MCCLAIN, ELSIE TALLEY, diversified co. exec.; b. Bascom, Fla., Oct. 6, 1927; d. William Russell and Hattie Mae (Benton) Talley; student Jacksonville U., Harvard Bus. Coll., 1975-76, U. N. Fla., 1978-79; children—Elizabeth McClain Jenkins, Leslie Wayne. Sec., USDA, 1945-47; sec., bookkeeper Duval County Sch. Bd., 1959-60; with Patterson Enterprises, Jacksonville, Fla., 1960-87, exec. sec., adminstrv. asst., 1971-73, controller, 1973-82, v.p., gen. mgr., 1982-87, pres. Seaboard Cold Storage Jacksonville, v.p., gen. mgr., dir. sales Seaboard Cold Storage Orlando, Winter Haven, Tampa, 1987—. Mem. Jacksonville Equal Opportunity Council; bd. dirs. USO Internat., Internat. Assn. Refrigerated Warehouses (sec., treas. 1985, vice chmn. 1986, chmn. 1987); auctioneer Public TV, 1973-79; tchr. Sunday sch. Presbyterian Ch., ruling elder, 1980-83. Mem. Exec. Women Internat., Women in Constrn., NCR Computer Users Group, Nat. Users Constrn. Group, Adminstrv. Mgmt. Soc., Am. Soc. Personnel Adminstrn. Winner 1st place cooking contest Jacksonville Jour., 1979, 80, 81, 82, 83, 84, 85. Office: Seaboard Cold Storage of Jacksonville Inc 2481 Dennis St Jacksonville FL 32204

MC CLANAHAN, RUE (EDDI-RUE MC CLANAHAN), actress; b. Healdton, Okla.; d. William Edwin and Dreda Rheua-Nell (Medaris) McC.; 1 child, Mark Thomas Bish. B.A. cum laude, U. Tulsa, 1956. Actress: Erie (Pa.) Playhouse, 1957-58; theatrical, film and TV appearances, Los Angeles, 1959-64, N.Y.C., 1964-73; mem. cast: (TV series) Maude, 1973-78, Apple Pie, 1978, Mama's Family, 1982-84, Golden Girls, 1985— (Emmy award for best actress in a comedy show 1987); appeared on Broadway: Jimmy Shine, 1968-69, Sticks and Bones, 1972, California Suite, 1977. Recipient Obie award for leading off-Broadway role in Who's Happy Now, 1970; Emmy award Best Actress in a comedy, 1987; named Woman of Yr., Pasadena Playhouse, 1986; Spl. scholar Pasadena (Calif.) Playhouse, 1959, Phi Beta Gamma scholar, 1955. Mem. Actors Studio, Actors Equity Assn., AFTRA, Screen Actors Guild. Office: Internat Creative Mgmt 8899 Beverly Blvd Los Angeles CA 90048

MCCLAY, MERI JANE, medical technologist; b. Colorado Springs, Colo., May 9, 1944; d. Charles David and Alice (Livengood) McC.; B.A., U. Oreg., 1966. Med. technologist Sacred Heart Hosp., Eugene, Oreg., 1966-67, Highland Alameda County Hosp., Oakland, Calif., 1967-68; chief technologist Arlington (Tex.) Community Hosp., 1968-72, chief technologist N.E. Med. Ctr., Bonham, Tex., 1972—. Mem. Am. Soc. Clin. Pathologists (registered, affiliate). Presbyterian. Home: PO Box 273 Bonham TX 75418 Office: 504 Lipscomb St Bonham TX 75418

MCCLEAN, CELEITA A., aerospace marketing executive; b. Huntington, W.Va., Dec. 14, 1956; d. Raymond Ray and Sylvia May (Kinser) Breakiron. BS in Art and Edn. cum laude, W.Va. State Coll., 1980; MS in Aviation Mgmt. cum laude, Embry-Riddle Aero. U., 1985; grad. numerous aviation and mgmt. courses, U.S. Army. Lic. comml. pilot. Counselor, tutor W.Va. State Coll., Institute, 1975-80; mgr. army program GE Aerospace, Washington, 1984—. Serving as co. comdr. USAR, 1987—. Recipient Sikorsky Aircraft Rescue award U.S. Army; numerous other ribbons and badges. Mem. Assn. U.S. Army, Assn. U.S. Res., Marine Corp. Aviation Assn., Army Aviation Assn. Am., Am. Defense Preparedness Assn., Naval Helicopter Soc., Am. Helicopter Soc., Nat. Assn. Female Execs., Whirly Girls, Alpha Kappa Mu. Home: 1300 Crystal Dr Apt 608 Arlington VA 22202 Office: GE Aerospace 1331 Pennsylvania Ave NW Washington DC 20004

MCCLEAN, LENORA JAMES, nursing educator, dean; b. Jesup, Ga., Apr. 22, 1937; d. Ealey and Mary (Howard) Hayes; diploma St. Vincent's Hosp. Sch. Nursing, Jacksonville, Fla., 1958; B.S., Fla. State U., 1961; M.A., Tchrs. Coll., Columbia U., 1963, Ed.D., 1972; m. Robert William McClean, July 13, 1963; children—Anne-Marie St. John, Sharman Danielle, Tara Lauren, Marshall Hayes. Asst. prof. nursing Fla. State U., Tallahassee, 1963, Tchrs. Coll., Columbia U., N.Y.C., 1964-73; clinician Bronx Psychiat. Center, 1966-73; prof. SUNY, Stony Brook, 1973-81, dean Sch. Nursing, 1981—; cons. intervention in self-destructive behavior. Vis. fellow Sturt Coll. Advanced Edn., Bedford Park, South Australia, 1981-82; grantee. Mem. N.Y. State Nurses Assn. (v.p. 1980-82), Am. Nurses Assn. Democrat. Episcopalian. Author: (with Dorothy Anderson) Indentifying Suicide Potential, 1976; contbg. author: Comprehensive Psychiatric Nursing, 1979, 2d edit., 1982; also articles. Office: SUNY Stony Brook NY 11794 *

MCCLEARY, BERYL NOWLIN, civic worker, travel agency executive; b. Ft. Worth, Feb. 22, 1929; d. Henry Bryant and Phyllis (Tenney) Nowlin; m. Henry Glenn McCleary, May 29, 1950; children: Laura Gail, Glenn Nowlin, Neil Ray, Paul Tenney. BS in Zoology, Tex. Tech U., 1950. Owner, mgr. Beryl McCleary Travels, Chicago, 1975-81, Denver, 1981-84. Treas. Kappa Alpha Theta Ednl. Found., Tex. Christian U., Ft. Worth, 1958-61; pres. study club Jr. Woman's Club, Ft. Worth, 1959-60; pres. Symphony League, Ft. Worth, 1961-62; v.p., dir. Ft. Worth Symphony Orch. Assn. Inc., 1961; treas. Jr. Pro-Am Tarrant County, 1961-62; corr. sec. Ft. Worth Children's Mus. Guild, 1961; sec. Tarrant County (Tex.) Democratic Exec. Com., 1956-62; pres. guild, bd. dirs. Maadi Community Ch., Cairo, 1964-66; mem. women's bd. Lincoln Park Zool. Soc., Chgo, 1976-81; mem. Episcopal Ch. Women's Diocesan Bd., Chgo., 1976-79; pres., charter mem. Rainbow Investment Club, London, 1970-71, travel dir. Over the Hill Gang Ski Team Internat., Denver, 1982-84. Mem. AAAS, DAR, Geol. Geophys. Aux., Service Club Chgo., Jr. League Denver, Denver Symphony Guild, Central City Opera Guild, Houston Symphony League, Alpha Epsilon Delta, Kappa Alpha Theta (charter mem. Gamma Phi chpt. 1953). Home: 232 Warrenton Houston TX 77024

MCCLEARY, MONICA JACKELS, nurse; b. St. Paul, Aug. 21, 1952; d. Robert Thomas and Lois Elizabeth (Tiling) Jackels; m. Mark Edward McCleary, Mar. 3, 1978. BA, Coll. of St. Catherine, St. Paul, 1974, MS, U. Minn., 1978. Registered Am. Coll. Nurse-Midwives. Registered nurse Divine Redeemer Hosp., South St. Paul, Minn., 1974-75, St. Joseph's Hosp., St. Paul, 1975; cert. nurse-midwife Group Health, Inc., St. Paul, 1976—; assoc. staff mem. Fairview Hosp., Mpls.; adj. clin. faculty U. Minn., Mpls., 1978—. Mem. Am. Coll. Nurse-Midwives (assoc. chairperson Region IV chpt. 6 1986—, treas. 1983-85), Minn. Mgmt. Register, Council of Cath. Women, Alumni Assn. Coll. of St. Catherine (chairperson alumni fund 1984-85). Democrat. Roman Catholic. Office: Group Health Inc 205 S Wabasha Saint Paul MN 55107

MCCLELLAND, PAMELA STEPHENS, home economics educator; b. Russell, Ky., July 26, 1956; d. Henry and Wilma (Walton) Stephens; m. Donald Lee McClelland Jr., May 9, 1975 (div. Mar. 1986); 1 child, Donald Lee McClelland III. Student, Ashland Community Coll., 1974-76, Paducah Community Coll., 1977; BS in Home Econ., Murray State U., 1980. Sales clk. Jo-Ann Fabrics, Ashland, Ky., 1974; co-owner D III Constrn., Gilbertsville, Ky., 1976-81, kitchen designer Ward Elkins, Paducah, Ky., 1978; sales clk. Hallmark Cards and Gifts, Benton, Ky., 1979; assoc. realtor Johnson Real Estate, Gilbertsville, Ky., 1979-81; home economics agt. Coop. Extension Service, Salyersville, Ky., 1981-83; 4-H agt. Coop. Extension Service, Louisa, Ky., 1983—; mem. com. extension photography, Lexington, Ky., 1985-87, extension forestry, Lexington, 1986-87. Dir. Louisa-Ft. Gay (Ky.) Women's Softball League, 1985, Salyersville Health Fair Com., 1983; mem. home adv. com. So. States Farm, Louisa, 1985-87. Mem. Nat. Assn. of Extension 4-H Agts., Ky. Assn. of Extension 4-H Agts. (area dir. 1984-87, Communication award, 1st Place Photography award 1987, 1st Place Slide Set award 1986, 1st place News Column award 1986, 2d Place Nat. Photography award 1987). Republican. Baptist. Club: Interstate Exchange. Office: Coop Extension Service PO Box 686 Louisa KY 41230

MCCLELLAND, SHARON ELIZABETH, nurse; b. Milw., May 2, 1945; d. Henry William and Caroline Elizabeth (Kuehn) Luedtke; m. Donald Arthur McClelland, Oct. 14, 1967; children: Kristina, Matthew, Mark, Kimberly, Kari Lynn. BS, U. Wis., 1967; MS in Nursing, U. Calif.-San Francisco, 1970. RN Nursing instr. Mt. Sinai Hosp. Sch. Nursing, Chgo., 1967-68; staff nurse Mills Meml. Hosp., San Mateo, Calif., 1969-70; instr. clin. nursing DeAnza Coll., Cupertino, Calif., 1972-73, coordinator, nursing asst. program, 1973-77, 80-83. Author: Manual for Implementing a Nursing Assistant Program, 1975, Basic Patient Care, 1977, 3rd edit., 1984, A Clinical Manual for Nursing Assistants, 1986. Leader Santa Clara County council Girl Scouts U.S.A., Los Gatos, Calif., 1977, 79. Mem. Health Services Edn. Council (dir. 1977-78), Mortar Bd., Sigma Theta Tau. Republican. Mormon.

MCCLENDON, MAXINE, artist; b. Leesville, La., Oct. 21, 1931; d. Alfred Harry and Clara (Jackson) McMillan; student Tex. U., 1948-50, Tex. Woman's U., 1950-51, Pan Am. U., 1963-64; m. Edward Edson Nichols, Mar. 28, 1967; children—Patricia Ann, Joan Terri, Christopher, Jennifer. One-man shows include: Art Mus. S. Tex., Corpus Christi, 1971, McAllen (Tex.) Internat. Mus., 1976, Amarillo (Tex.) Art Center, 1982 group shows in Wichita, Kans., 1972, Marietta, Ohio, 1975, Dallas, 1977; represented in permanent collections: Mus. Internat. Folk Art, Santa Fe, Ark. Mus. Fine Art, Little Rock, McAllen Internat. Mus., Lauren Rogers Mus., Laurel, Miss.; commns. include: Caterpillar Corp., Peoria, Ill., Union Bank Switzerland, N.Y.C., Crocker Bank, Los Angeles, Tarleton U., Tex., Hyatt Regency, Ft. Worth Forbes Inc., San Francisco, First Savs. & Loan, Shreveport, La., Continental Plaza, Ft. Worth. curator Mexican folk art McAllen Internat. s., 1974-80. Recipient judges award 4th Nat. Marietta, 1975, numerous others. Mem. World Crafts Council, Am. Crafts Council (Tex. rep. 1976-80), Tex. Designer/Craftsmen (pres. 1973-74). Christian Scientist. Home and Studio: 2018 Sharyland St Mission TX 78572

MCCLINTOCK, BARBARA, geneticist, educator; b. June 16, 1902. Ph.D. in Botany, Cornell U., 1927; D.Sc. (hon.), U. Rochester, U. Mo., Smith Coll., Williams Coll., Western Coll. for Women. Instr. botany Cornell U., Ithaca, N.Y., 1927-31, research assoc., 1934-36, Andrew D. White prof.-at-large, 1965—; asst. prof. U. Mo., 1936-41; mem. staff Carnegie Instn. of Washington, Cold Spring Harbor, N.Y., 1941-47, Disting. Service mem., 1967—; cons. agrl. sci. program Rockefeller Found., 1962-69. NRC fellow, 1931-33; Guggenheim Found. fellow, 1933-34; recipient Achievement award AAUW, 1947; Nat. medal of Sci., 1970; MacArthur Found. prize; Rosentiel award, 1978; Nobel prize, 1983. Mem. Nat. Acad. Scis. (Kimber genetics award 1967), Am. Philos. Soc., Am. Acad. Arts and Scis., Genetics Soc. Am. (pres. 1945), Bot. Soc. Am. (award of merit 1957), AAAS, Am. Inst. Biol. Sci., Am. Soc. Naturalists. Office: Carnegie Instn of Washington Cold Spring Harbor Lab Cold Spring Harbor NY 11724

MCCLINTOCK, JANET MARIE, interior designer, consultant; b. Dearborn, Mich., Dec. 7, 1947; d. Gailard and Julie (Skorina) McCarty; m. Douglas Cove McClintock, Aug. 2, 1969; children: Coleen, William, Margaret. BS in Design, U. Mich., 1969. Cert. interior designer, Mich. Asst. designer interior design services U. Mich., Ann Arbor, 1968-69; interior designer KMM Assocs., Ann Arbor, 1969-70, Sperry Rand/Library Bur., Inc., Plymouth, Mich., 1971-76; dir. design Library Design Assocs., Inc., Plymouth, 1976; cons. various library projects, Mich., Ohio and Ky., 1971—. Mem. Am. Soc. Interior Designers (profl. mem., Presdl. Citation, 1983, Mich. Designer of Distinction award Mich. Chpt., 1983), Inst. Bus. Designers (profl. mem.). Roman Catholic. Office: Library Design Assocs Inc 859 S Main St Plymouth MI 48170

MCCLINTOCK, SHIRLEY SPRAGUE, govt. ofcl.; b. Flushing, N.Y., Jan. 3, 1928; d. George Wilkie and Mary Dorothea (O'Rourke) Sprague; student Cornell U., 1949-51; m. John William McClintock, Sept. 22, 1951; children—Barton, Charles, Scott. Personnel adminstr. Gen. Motors Co., 1952-54, analyst, overseas ops., N.Y.C., 1965-68; mem. U.S. Govt. Transition Com., 1968-69; housing adminstr. HUD, N.Y.C., 1969-79, 82—, Buffalo, 1979-82. . Bd. dirs. Soc. Prevention Cruelty to Children Mass., 1962-64; sec. LWV, N.Y.C., 1960-62. Recipient Cert. Superior Service, HUD, 1975. Mem. Cornell Club Greater Buffalo (pres. 1981—), Cornell U. Alumni Assn. Club: Cornell (N.Y.C.). Home: 541 E 20th St New York NY 10010 Office: 26 Federal Plaza New York NY 10278

MCCLISH, C. POLLY, finance executive; b. Lubbock, Tex., May 30, 1933; d. Hershell Lee and Carrie Maude (Johnson) Ward; four children by previous marriage. AA in Bus. Psychology, Amarillo Jr. Coll., Tex., 1966; BS in Acctg., West Tex. State U., 1968, BBA, 1970. Asst. credit mgr., collection mgr. Woolco Inc., Amarillo, Tex., 1968-74; credit mgr. Sakowitz Inc., Amarillo, 1974-79; sales mgr. Med. and Profl. Mgmt. Service, Galveston, Tex., 1979-82, v.p., gen. mgr., 1982-83; pres., bd. dirs. Colelli & Assocs., Galveston, 1983-87; founder, owner MasterCheck of Galveston-Bay Area, 1988—; cons. and lectr. in field. Mem. adv. bd. Tex. Edn. Commn.; mem. aux. U. Tex. Med. Br.; mem., div. chmn. United Fund. Named Outstanding Credit Exec. of Yr., Tex., 1976, to Galveston Women's Hall of Fame for bus. and fin. category. Mem. Internat. Consumer Credit Assn. (legis. adv. council), Am. Collectors Assn. (legis. adv. com., condr. numerous seminars), Asso. Credit Bur., Retail Mchts. Assn. Tex. (pres.), Nat. Assn. Female Execs., Soc. Cert. Consumer Credit Execs., Exec. Career Women, Bus. and Profl. Women (past pres.), C. of C. (pres.'s club, honor guard, Galveston chpt.), Credit Mgmt. Assn. Tex. (past pres.), Credit Women Internat. (past pres. Lone Star council), Am. Collectors Assn. Tex. (pres.), Forgery Investigation Assn. Tex. Club: Propeller (Galveston). Address: 4601 Ave R Galveston TX 77551

MCCLUNG, CHRISTINA JUNE, training company executive; b. Newark, N.J., Jan. 19, 1948; d. Frederick and Maria (Dallinger) Palensar; m. Kenneth Austin McClung, Mar. 21, 1975. B.A., Kean Coll., 1970; M.A. in Edn., Seton Hall U., 1973; Ed.D. in Instructional Tech., U. So. Calif., 1976. Tchr. Chatham Twp. (N.J.) pub. schs., 1970-74; instructional designer Tratec Co., Los Angeles, 1976-79; asst. prof. Lehman Coll., Bronx, N.Y., 1977-79; ind. cons., 1978-80; v.p., bd. dirs. Instructional Design Group, Morristown N.J., 1980—; gen. ptnr. MGM Investments, 1985—. Mem. Nat. Soc. Performance Instrn. (v.p. programs N.J. chpt.), Phi Delta Kappa. Author 5 book series Computers for Professionals, 1983. Office: Instructional Design Group 144 Speedwell Ave Morristown NJ 07930

MCCLURE, ANGELINE KITCHENS, human resource management executive, consultant; b. Macon, Ga., Dec. 26, 1945; d. Benjamin Grady and Reba (Atkins) Kitchens; m. Donald Wayne McClure, Nov. 2, 1974; children by a previous marriage—Leanna Kay Oliver Linnekohl, Gregory Alan Oliver. B.A. in Social Sci., Hollins Coll. (Va.), 1971; postgrad. U. Va., 1972, Commonwealth U. of Va., 1972. Tchr., Ronaoke City Pub. Schs. (Va.), 1971-73, Twiggs County Pub. Schs., Jeffersonville, Ga., 1973-75; human resource specialist Charter Med. Corp., Macon, 1975-79; personnel cons. Mut. Personnel Service, Macon, 1980-81; human resource mgr. So. Trust Ins. Co., Macon, 1981-84; mgmt. cons., owner Motivational Mgmt. Resources, Macon, 1984—; mem. employer's relation com. Ga. Dept. Labor, 1983. Mem. Gov.'s Leadership Forum for Post-Seconday Edn., State of Ga., 1983; co-chmn. employers' relations com. Am. Cancer Soc., Macon, 1984, 85; Mem. Middle Ga. Personnel Assn. (pub. relations dir. 1982, v.p. 1983, pres. 1984, bd. dirs. 1985), Am. Soc. Personnel Adminstrs., Nat. Assn. Female Execs., Career Women's Network (bd. dirs. 1986-88), Middle Ga. Employers Assn., Bus. and Industry Relations Com., Macon C. of C., Greater Macon Women Bus. Owners (charter mem., bd. dirs. 1988). Baptist. Home: 3076 Tiffin Circle Macon GA 31204 Office: Motivational Mgmt Resources PO Box 6735 Macon GA 31208

MCCLURE, ANN L., lawyer; b. Mt. Vernon, Ohio, Dec. 26, 1946; d. W. Roger and Marian E. (McBurney) Levering; married; children—Andrew Daniel, James Stephen, Mark Ian. B.A., Hanover Coll., 1968; M.L.S., Ind. U., 1970, M.B.A., 1973; J.D., South Tex. Coll. Law, 1976. Bar: Tex. 1976; librarian Southwestern Consol. Sch. Dist. Ind., Hanover, 1968-69; reference librarian Ind. State Library, Indpls., 1970-71; sole practice of law, Wichita Falls, Tex., 1976-88 ; instr. Midwestern State U., 1982-87; asst. prof. Ft. Hays State U.; city atty., Holliday, Tex., 1984-86. Bd. dirs. Northside Girls Club, 1983-86, KIDZ-Channel 13, 1983—, Library Bd., Wichita Falls, 1986—. Mem. ABA, Tex. Bar Assn., Wichita Falls Bars Assn., AAUW (pres. 1981-83), Bus. and Profl. Womens Club (pres. 1978-80), LWV. Democrat. Presbyterian.

MCCLURE, FLORENCE HELEN, management consultant; b. Chgo., July 21, 1930; d. George and Minnie (LaBarbara) Torre; m. Richard D. McClure, Feb. 16, 1952; children: Kimbert, Brian, Douglas, Ronald. Student Ind. U., 1948-50, Kent State U., 1967-68, Lake Erie Coll., Ohio, 1969-70. Elem. sch. tchr., Geneva, Ohio, 1966-71; coordinator traffic dept. True Temper Corp., Saybrook, Ohio, 1971-72; mktg. dir. Peoples Savs. & Loan, Ashtabula, Ohio, 1973-82; pres. Chem. Seal, Inc., Grand Junction, Colo., 1982-85; mktg./personnel dir. Valley Fed. Savs. & Loan, Grand Junction, 1982-87; cons. Access Profl. Search Inc., Columbus, 1988—; human resource cons., 1985—. Commr., Colo. Housing Authority, Grand Junction, 1985-87; bd. dirs. Alternative Housing Assocs., Grand Junction, 1982-87. Mem. Am. Soc. Personnel Adminstrn., Western Slope Personnel Assocs., Grand Junction C. of C. (pub. relations com. 1985-87, coll. edn. com. 1983-85). Republican. Roman Catholic. Avocations: walking, reading, traveling. Home: 6100 McNaughton Woods Dr Columbus OH 43232

MCCLURE, LESLIE ANNE LIGON, real estate company executive; b. Fort Worth, Apr. 11, 1922; d. Joseph Moses and Willie H. (Glasgow) Ligon; divorced; children—Ralston Hugh, Michele Ligon (Mrs. Everett W. Beelman), Anne Melissa (Mrs. John H. Bill). Student Brantley-Draughn, Fort Worth, 1960-61, Real Estate Inst., San Antonio, 1961-62. Salesperson Margie Burch Co., 1960, Beth Carter Realty, Fort Worth, 1962-63, Glen-Walker, Collett & Rigg (name changed to Wm. Rigg Co.), Fort Worth, 1964-65; owner, mgr. Leslie Ligon McClure Realtor, Fort Worth, 1965—. V.P. Ft. Worth Prayer Fellowship; mem. Women's Aglow Fellowship; student Bible Study Fellowship; active Tarrant County Hist. Soc. Mem. Greater Fort Worth Bd. Realtors, Tex. Assn. Realtors, Nat. Assn. Realtors, Fort Worth Jr. League, Ft. Worth Lecture Found. Clubs: Bon Soir, (treas. 1985-86), Met. Women's Republican, Ft. Worth Woman's. Home: 3716 Hamilton Fort Worth TX 76107

MCCLURE, MARGARET ANN, insurance company executive; b. Charleston, W.Va., Jan. 20, 1950; d. Jess Kowden and Betty Jeane (Campbell) McC. BA, Marshall U., Huntington, W.Va., 1971, MA, 1976. Tchr. Bedford (Va.) County Schs., 1971-74, Lynchburg (Va.) Pub. Schs., 1974-75; substitute Lincoln County Schs., Hamlin, W.Va., 1975-77; writer Progress Pub., Lynchburg, 1974-75; counselor W.Va. State Women's Prison, Pence Springs, 1976; tchr. Lincoln County Schs., Hamlin, W.Va., 1977-83; agt. State Farm Ins., Hamlin, 1983—. Contbr. articles to The Lynchburg Mag., 1974-75. Chmn. bd. dirs. New Employment for Women, Hamlin, 1983-88; bd. dirs. Lincoln Primary Care, Hamlin, 1984-88. Mem. Nat. Life Underwriters Assn., Nat. Assn. Female Execs., Marshall U. Alumni Assn. Republican. Baptist. Club: Jr. Woman's (pres. 1980-82, S.E. dist. dir. 1986-88, various offices, Dist. Jr. Mem. of Yr. 1984). Office: State Farm Ins 221 Mayor's Ln PO Box 596 Hamlin WV 25523

MCCLURE, MARY ANNE, state legislator; b. Milbank, S.D., Apr. 21, 1939; d. Charles Cornelius and Mary Lucille (Whittom) Burges; m. D.J. McClure, Nov. 17, 1963; 1 child, Kelly Joanne. BA magna cum laude, U. S.D., 1961; postgrad., U. Manchester, Eng., 1961-62; M of Pub. Adminstrn., Syracuse (N.Y.) U., 1980. Staff asst. U.S. Senator Francis Case, Washington, 1959-61; sec. to lt. gov. State of S.D., Pierre, 1963, with budget office, 1964; exec. sec. to pres. Frontier Airlines, Denver, 1963-64; tchr. Pub. High Schs., Pierre and Redfield, S.D., 1965-66, 68-70,; mem. S.D. State Senate, Pierre, 1975—, pres. pro tem, 1979-88, vice chmn. council of state govts., 1987, chmn. council of state govts., 1988. Vice chmn. sch. bd. Redfield Ind. Sch. Dist., 1970-74. Fulbright scholar, 1961-62, Bush Leadership fellow, 1977-80. Mem. Phi Beta Kappa. Republican. Congregationalist. Home: 910 E 2nd St Redfield SD 57469

MCCLURG, PATRICIA A., minister; b. Bay City, Tex., Mar. 14, 1939; d. T.H. and Margaret (Smith) McC. BA, Austin Coll., 1961; M in Christian Edn., Presbyn. Sch. of Christian Edn., 1963; BD, Austin Presbyn. Theol. Sem., 1967; postgrad., So. Meth. U., 1971-73; DD (hon.), Austin Coll., 1978. Dir. Christian edn. 2d Presbyn. Ch., Newport News, Va., 1963-65; asst. pastor Westminster Presbyn. Ch., Beaumont, Tex., 1967-71; assoc. pastor 1st Presbyn. Ch., Pasadena, Tex., 1969-71; assoc. exec. Synod of Red River, Denton, Tex., 1973-75; dir. gen. assembly mission bd. Presbyn. Ch., Atlanta, 1975-86; assoc. exec. for mission The Presbytery of Elizabeth, Plainfield, N.J., 1986—; pres. Nat. Council Chs. of Christ in the U.S.A., N.Y.C., 1988—, v.p., 1985-87; del., budget com. chmn. World Council Chs. Assembly, Vancouver, Can., 1985; sect. leader World Council Chs. Mission and Evang. Confs., Melbourne, Australia, 1980. Contbr. articles to prof. jours. Mem. chs. spl. commn. on South Africa, N.Y.C., 1985—, Anti-Pollution Campaign, Pasadena, 1970. Recipient Disting. Alumni award Austin Coll., 1979. Democrat. Presbyterian. Lodge: Rotary. Office: Presbytery of Elizabeth 525 E Front St Plainfield NJ 07060

MCCOLLUM, ADRIENNE MARIE, consulting company executive; b. Los Angeles, Sept. 14, 1937; d. Luther Slayton and Joe Ann Marie (Goodson) Slayton Hale; m. Rubin Dale McCollum, June 14, 1959; children—Cheryl Kimberly, Kristin Elise, Kacie Charmion. A.A., Los Angeles City Coll., 1957; B.S., Calif. State U., 1972; Ed.D., U. Mass., 1975. Grad. asst. U. Mass., Amherst, 1972, assoc. to dir. urban edn., 1972-74; exec. dir. Springfield Day Nursery (Mass.), 1974-75; sr. assoc. Roy Littlejohn and Assocs., Washington, 1975-77; v.p. Thomas Buffington & Assocs., Washington, 1977-79; pres. Research Assessment Mgmt., Inc., Silver Spring, Md., 1980—; cons. Dept. Edn., Washington, 1978-82, Child Devel. Assn., Washington, 1973-74, D.C. Sch. System, 1980. Contbr. articles to profl. jours. Active Tots 'n Teens, Howard County, Md., 1981—. Mem. exec. bd. trustees Benedict Coll. Recipient Appreciation award Bur. Edn. Handicapped, Washington, 1978. Mem. Am. Assn. Black Women Entrepreneurs, Nat. Council Negro Women (service award 1981), Zeta Phi Beta (meritorious award 1981, 85, Superior Leadership award 1987, nat. dir. economic devel.). Presbyterian. Office: Research Assessment Mgmt Inc 1320 Fenwick Ln Silver Spring MD 20910

MCCOLLUM, ALMEDIA, real estate executive; b. Jamesville, N.C., May 11, 1940; d. Earley and Olivia (James) Whitehurst; m. Leslie McCollum, Dec. 24, 1960; children: Karen, Leslie Jr., Lawrence. Student, Fayetteville State Coll., 1957-60. V.p. Colmedia Corp., N.Y.C., 1978—. Mem. Nat. Assn. Female Execs. Home: 435 E 57th St Brooklyn NY 11203

MCCOMBS, SUSAN GENE WALKER, trade association field representative; b. Rainelle, W.Va., Apr. 11, 1948; d. Eugene Wilson and Sue (Vickers) Walker; m. Robert Marvin McCombs, 1973; 1 child, Lucas Fyn. Student in interior design, LaSalle Extension U., Chgo., 1973. Field rep. U.S. C. of C., Washington, 1985—. Democrat. Baptist. Home: PO Box 211 Quinwood WV 25981

MCCONNELL, ANN ELIZABETH, interior design warehouse manager; b. Coshocton, Ohio, Feb. 3, 1947; d. Russell Earl and Helen Mary McC. BS in Edn., Kent (Ohio) State U., 1969; MS in Phys. Edn., U. N.C., Greensboro, 1971. Instr., coach Hiram (Ohio) Coll., 1969-70; tchr., coach Paulding County Bd. Edn., Dallas, 1971-72, Fulton County Bd. Edn., Atlanta, 1972-74; instr., coach Agnes Scott Coll., Decatur, Ga., 1974-79; dir. health club Marriott Hotel Downtown, Atlanta, 1979-80; pro-tour massage therapist Women's Tennis Assn., San Francisco, 1980-82; furniture refinisher Columbus (Ohio) Home Furnishings, 1984-86; warehouse mgr. Richard R. Sherman Interior Design, Columbus, 1986—; message therapist U.S. Men's Olympic Weightlifting Team, Colorado Springs, Colo., 1981, U.S. Wrightman Cup Team, London, 1980, Chgo., 1981. Mem. Lamplighters' League (capt. Columbus chpt. 1986—), Riverview Golf League (capt. Columbus chpt. 1983—). Republican. Roman Catholic. Home: 125 B W 1st Ave Columbus OH 43201 Office: Richard R Sherman Interior Design 240 N 5th St Suite 100 Columbus OH 43215

MCCONNELL, JANICE DIANE, art gallery director; b. Chgo., Oct. 29, 1942; d. Raymond Louis and Eleanor Elizabeth (Witt) Recknagel. BFA in Art Edn., U. Denver, 1967; MA in Anthropology, U. No. Colo., 1979. Instr. art Denver Pub. Schs., 1967-87; owner, dir. Artistic Visual Products, Denver, 1986—, The Artwell Gallery, Denver, 1987—; cons. Jefferson County Pub. Schs., Golden, Colo., 1983. Illustrator: (book) Ancient Celtic America, 1986; (newspaper cartoon series) Life on Capitol Hill, 1985—; producer video prodns., 1983—. Vol. Denver Mus. Natural History, 1979-83, local TV stations, 1985—. Recipient vol. award Denver Mus. Natural History, 1982. Mem. Internat. TV Assn., Nat. Press Photographer's Assn., Colo. Art Edn. Assn. (bd. dirs. 1984-85), Colo. Lawyers for Arts, Colo. Fedn. of Arts (adv. bd. 1984-85), Profl. Picture Framers Assn., Talarian. Office: The Artwell Gallery 1915 Clarkson St Denver CO 80218

MCCONNELL, MARGARET LEE, foundation administrator; b. Hazard, Ky., Mar. 31, 1937; d. Wallace Mason and Levisa Mae (Goff) Combs; m. John Joel Watson, Oct. 5, 1968 (div. 1970); children: Kevin, Alissa, Michelle, Patrick; m. Kenton Rawls McConnell, Apr. 23, 1970 (div. 1977); 1 child, Fiona Siobhan. BA, summa cum laude, U. Ky., 1961; postgrad., U. Mass., 1967-68, Oxford (Eng.) U., 1968. Sci. editor, researcher Vanderbilt U. Med. Ctr., Nashville, 1976-85; spl. rep. George S. May Internat. Co., Park Ridge, Ill., 1986-87; pres. Am. Youth Exchange Found., 1987—; regional dir. Aspect Internat., San Francisco, 1988—; dir. student affairs S.E.E. Am. Author research papers. Sec. Charity League of Ashland, 1967; exec. sec. Nashville Arts and Edn. 1971; active Nashville Symphony Guild, 1972; vol. counselor Ednl. Found. Fgn. Study, 1986; pres. Am. Youth Exchange Fedn. NDEA fellow, 1967. Mem. Nat. Assn. Exec. Females, AAUW, Phi Beta Kappa. Democrat. Presbyterian. Avocations: travel, needlework, writing, reading, skin-diving. Home: 10 Shady Ln Covington LA 70433 Office: Aspect Internat 1940 Fillmore St San Francisco CA 94115

MC CONNELL, MARGARET MAHLER (MRS. J.H. TYLER MCCONNELL), civic worker; b. Wilmington, Del., July 3, 1944; d. John Anthony and Maggie Naomi (Davis) Mahler; m. James Hoge Tyler McConnell, Apr. 25, 1973. AA, Marjorie Webster Coll., 1964. Sec. CIA, Washington, 1964-65, Hercules, Inc., Wilmington, 1965-66; with Delaware Trust Co., Wilmington, 1966-73, asst. corp. sec., 1969-72, asst. v.p., 1972-73. Bd. dirs., corp. sec. Del. Mus. Natural History, Wilmington, 1969-79; asst. sec., treas. Cecil County (Md.) Breeders' Fair, 1969-75; sec., mem. exec. com. Fair Hill (Md.) Races, 1969-75; bd. dirs. Wilmington Vis. Nurse Assn., 1974—, sec., 1982-86; bd. dirs. Brandywine YMCA, Wilmington, 1977-82, Del. Art Mus., 1983—, Soc. Four Arts, 1985—. Mem. Nat. Assn. Bank Women, Del. Assn. Bank Women, Nat. Steeplechase & Hunt Assn., Del. Soc. Fine Arts. Democrat. Episcopalian. Clubs: Farmington (Va.) Country; River (N.Y.C.); Everglades (Palm Beach, Fla.); Bath and Tennis, Wilmington Country, Rehoboth Beach. Home: 179 Via Del Lago Palm Beach FL 33480 also: 805 Snuff Mill Rd Wilmington DE 19807

MCCONNER, ORA B., school superintendent; b. Augusta, Ga., Jan. 2, 1929; d. Landirs and Mamie (Elderidge) Williams; m. Walter R. McConner, June 27, 1953; 1 child, Susan L. BA, Paine Coll., Augusta, 1949; MA, Boston U., 1951; EdD, Nova U., Ft. Lauderdale, Fla., 1982. Instr. Paine Coll., Augusta, 1951-55; tchr. Chgo. Pub. Schs., 1956-66, adminstr., 1966-79, asst. supt., 1979—. Danforth study grantee, 1955; recipient Image award League of Black Women, 1974, Silver Beaver award Boy Scouts Am., 1985; named Educator of Yr. Chgo. Black Sch. Educators, 1984. Mem. Am. Assn. Sch. Adminstrs., Nat. Alliance of Black Sch. Educators, Council for Exceptional Children, Profl. Women's Aux. of Provident Hosp., Alpha Gamma Psi. Episcopalian. Club: Zonta (v.p., sec.). Home: 9137 S Constance Ave Chicago IL 60617 Office: Dept Pupil Personnel Services & Spl Edn 1819 W Pershing Rd Chicago IL 60609

MCCORD, JULIA ANN, internal auditing consultant; b. Waurika, Okla., May 22, 1924; d. William Solon and Eurah Pearl (Watson) Osteen; B.S., Okla. Coll. Liberal Arts, 1968; M.B.A., U. Tampa, 1980; cert. internal auditor; m. Elmer C. McCord, Jr., June 10, 1943 (div. 1974); children—Perry Houston, Linda Ann. Bookkeeper, Dyer & Watkins Ins. Agy., Durant, Okla., 1947-50, Thornton Ins. Agy., Oklahoma City, 1950-51, Gene Strauss Ins. Agy., Kansas City, Mo., 1951-52; controller Fla. Div., Am. Cancer Soc., Tampa, 1968-71; supr. auditing Sch. Bd. Hillsborough County, Tampa, 1973-87; cons. in field, 1987—; tchr. acctg., adult edn. Recipient Disting. Mem. of Yr. award Pres. Round Table of Orgns. of Greater Tampa, 1985. Mem. Inst. Internal Auditors (chpt. bd. govs. 1978-86), Nat. Assn. Accts. (chpt. sec. 1977), Fla. Assn. Sch. Bus. Adminstrs. (pres. 1984-85), LWV, AAUW (ednl. founds. chmn. 1981-82, corr. sec. 1983-86, pres. Tampa br. 1986-88), Limetree Beach Resort Homeowners Assn. (treas., bd. dirs. 1984-86). Methodist. Home: 4209 W Sevilla St Tampa FL 33629 Office: PO Box 320453 Tampa FL 33679

MCCORDUCK, PAMELA ANN, writer, educator; b. Liverpool, Eng., Oct. 27, 1940; came to U.S., 1946; d. William John and Hilda May (Bond) McC.; m. Joseph T. Traub, Dec. 6, 1969. lectr. Columbia U., 1980—. Author: Familiar Relations, 1971, Working to the End, 1972, Machines Who Think, 1979, The Fifth Generation, 1983, The Universal Machine, 1985, The Rise of the Expert Company, 1988. Mem. Am. PEN (bd. dirs. N.Y.C. chpt., 1986—. Home: 96 Battle Rd Princeton NJ 08540

MCCORMACK, CREEL C, soft drink company executive; b. N.Y.C., June 29, 1949; d. Benjamin Crawford and Flora (Campbell) Cutler; m. Robert Emmett III, May 24, 1975; children: Jessica, Kelly. BA, Marietta Coll., 1971. Various staff positions Coca-Cola Co., Atlanta, 1978-83; mgr. Coca-Cola, Atlanta, 1983—. Chair bus. and profl. women's div. Atlanta Symphony Orchestra, 1986—; bd. dirs. Ctr. for Puppetry Arts. Mem. Internat. Food Info. Council (chair pub. relations 1985—), Leadership Atlanta, Pub. Relations Soc. Am. Office: The Coca Cola Co PO Drawer 1734 Atlanta GA 30301

MCCORMACK, JUDITH GAIL, medical technologist; b. Chgo., Oct. 4, 1939; d. Milton and Marie Hedwig (Schroeder) Srail; B.S., Roosevelt U., Chgo., 1960; Med. technologist Mt. Sinai Hosp., Chgo., 1960; m. Robert George McCormack, Sept. 17, 1960. Med. technologist Mt. Sinai Hosp., 1962-65; serology supr. Meml. Hosp. DuPage County, Elmhurst, Ill., 1965-69; immunovirology supr. Lutheran Gen. Hosp., Park Ridge, Ill., 1969-82, immunology supr. Elmhurst Meml. Hosp., 1982-84; lab. info. systems mgr. Health Techs., Inc., 1984-85; exec. v.p. mktg. and edn. Bion Enterprises, Ltd., 1985—. Mem. Am. Soc. Clin. Pathologists, Am. Soc. Microbiology, South Central Assn. Clin. Microbiology, Ill. Soc. Microbiology. Mem. Ind. Fundamental Chs. Am. Home: 5 Oak Brook Club Dr Oak Brook IL 60521 Office: 656 Busse Hwy Park Ridge IL 60068

MCCORMACK, LOWELL RAY, oil producer, document examiner, graphoanalyst, lecturer; b. Ladonia, Tex., Oct. 26, 1925; d. Lowell and Orianna (McDonnold) Coney; m. Paul Ha. McCormack, June 4, 1948; children: Sharron Ann, Lowell Henry. Student Rutherford Met. Coll., Dallas, 1962, U. Tex., Arlington and Dallas, Eastfield Coll., Dallas; M. Graphoanalyst, Internat. Graphoanalysis Soc. Bookkeeper, Jot-Em-Down Gin Corp., Pecan Gap, Tex., 1947, Shedd-Bartush Foods, Dallas, 1948-52; acct., credit mgr. J. P. Ashcraft Co., Inc., Dallas, 1956-65; v.p., sec.-treas. Safari Oil Corp., Dallas, 1954—; pres. Scorpio Oil Corp., 1987—; chief fin. officer, v.p., sec.-treas. Dallas Title Co., 1965-83; instr. graphoanalysis Cooke County Coll., 1988; acctg. cons. to atty.; bd. dirs. First Nat. Bank, Cooper, Tex., Butterfield Stage, Gainesville, Tex.; lectr. in field. Leader troop Girl Scouts U.S.A., 1955-65; founder Yarn Spinners, Gainesville, 1988. Columnist Cooke County Leader, 1988—. Mem. North Tex. Oil and Gas Assn., Internat. Graphoanalysis Soc. (life, v.p. Tex. chpt. 1978, pres. 1979, named Graphoanalyst of Yr. 1987, keynote address speaker, 1987, author weekly column Cooke County Leader, 1988—), Internat. Platform Assn. Baptist. Clubs: Zonta (co-chmn. fin. com. 1982, dir., 2d v.p. 1983-84), Soroptimist, Toastmistress (pres. 1981, com. chmn. for internat. conv. 1984) (Dallas). Home: 631 S Lindsay Gainesville TX 76240

MCCORMACK, MARY BEATRICE (BEE), food manufacturing executive; b. Albany, Ga., Aug. 21, 1925; d. Robert Emmet and Anna Louise (Keller) McC. BA, Ga. Coll., 1946. Dir. personnel Bobs Candies, Inc., Albany, 1946-61; v.p. Bob's Candies, Inc., Albany, 1961—. Pres. Albany Symphony, 1972-74; co-chmn. capital funds campaign Albany Mus., 1981-82; chmn. devel. drive Albany Arts Council, 1984; dir. Albany Humane Soc., 1987—; mem. Albany Local Devel. Commn., 1986—, Albany Clean Community Commn., 1988—. Recipient Pro Deum et Juventatum medal Roman Cath. Diocese of Savannah, Ga., 1970, Alumni Achievement award Ga. Coll., Milledgeville, 1983; co-recipient Albany Woman of Yr. award, 1978. Mem. Nat. Confectioners Assn. (dir., v.p. 1979-84, Candy Mfgr. Yr. 1981), Profit-sharing Council Am. (dir. 1975-81), Profit Sharing Research Fedn (dir. 1978-81), Albany C. of C. (dir. 1982-85). Roman Catholic. Office: Bobs Candies Inc PO Box 3170 1505 Oakridge Dr Albany GA 31708

MCCORMICK, CATHERINE, school counselor; b. Pitts., Oct. 17, 1937; d. Frank John and Mary (Mullen) McC. BS in Edn., Carlow Coll., 1960; MA in Edn., Duquesne U., 1967; postgrad., Gannon coll., 1972. Cert. elem. tchr., Pa., guidance counselor. Elem. tchr. Pitts. Publ Schs., 1960-68, elem. counselor, 1968-69; elem. counselor Keystone Oaks Sch. Dist., Pitts., 1969-76, mid. sch. counselor, 1976—, mem. various coms., 1984—; tax preparer H&R Block, Inc., Pitts., 1981—; evaluator Assembly of Elem. Sch. Mid. States, 1987—. Recipient Extra Mile award Keystone Oaks Sch. Dist., 1986. Mem. Allegheny County Counselor's Assn., Keystone Oaks Edn. Assn. (sec. 1980-84), Pa. State Edn. Assn. (del. 1983), Nat. Edn. Assn., Delta Kappa Gamma Soc., Alpha Pi. Republican. Roman Catholic. Home: 662 Crystal Dr Mount Lebanon PA 15228 Office: Keystone Oaks Middle Sch 3200 Annapolis Ave Pittsburgh PA 15216

MCCORMICK, ELAINE ALICE, public relations executive; b. Jersey City, Nov. 19, 1943; d. Johannes and Anni (Gantenberg) Kratz; m. Thomas A. McCormick, Oct. 1, 1966; 1 child, Thomas John. Diploma in nursing, Mt. Sinai Sch. Nursing, 1964; BA summa cum laude, Georgian Ct. Coll., 1982. RN, N.Y., N.J. Staff nurse Holy Name Hosp., Teaneck, N.J., 1964-65, 69-70; office nurse Drs. Higdon, Beaugard and Fox, Teaneck, 1965-67; indsl. nurse Dun & Bradstreet, Inc., N.Y.C., 1967-69; camp nurse, ski area dir. Camp Arrowhead, Community YMCA, Marlboro, N.J., 1974-78; adminstrv. asst. DeJesse Advt., Woodbrige, N.J., 1982-83; staff writer Georgian Ct. Coll., Lakewood, N.J., 1983-84, dir. pub. relations, 1984—; cons. in field. Mem. adv. bd. Retired Sr. Vol. Program Ocean County, Toms River, N.J., 1987—; mem. Red Bank Cath. High Sch. PTA. Mem. Jersey Shore Pub. Relations Assn. (2d Place award 1987), Pub. Relations Soc. Am., Mercy Higher Edn. Colloquium, Sigma Tau Delta. Republican. Roman Catholic. Home: 9 Pamela St Marlboro NJ 07746 Office: Georgian Ct Coll Lakewood Ave Lakewood NJ 08701

MCCORMICK, LINDA KAY, real estate broker; b. Garden City, Kans. Sept. 6, 1947; d. Kenneth Dean and Clora Anita (Norris) Ray; m. Larry Patrick McCormick, May 2, 1970; children—Shawn Patrick, Kelli Rae. A.A. in Psychology, Dodge City Community Coll., 1967; B.S. in Elem. Edn., Ft. Hays Kans. State U., 1970. Grad. Realtors Inst. Realtor assoc. Brady Stevens Co., Joplin, Mo., 1978-80; broker, owner PRO 100, Inc., Realtors, Joplin, 1980—. Mem. adv. com. Franklin Tech. Sch. Vocat. Edn., Joplin, Mo., 1981-86; mem. adv. bd. Oakhill Hosp. Home Health Agy, 1984-86. Named Realtor of Yr., Joplin Bd. Realtors, 1983. Mem. Mo. Assn. Realtors (bd. dirs. 1982-87, mem. com. 1982-87, mem. edn. council 1984, vice chmn. edn. council 1988), Joplin Bd. Realtors (edn. chmn. 1982-85, pres. 1987), Joplin C. of C. (bd. dirs. 1982-84; mem. exec. com. 1983-84; div. chmn. 1983-84). Republican. Presbyterian. Office: PRO 100 Inc Realtors 2727 E 32nd St Joplin MO 64804

MCCORMICK, PAMELA JOY, fashion designer; b. Toronto, Can., Aug. 3, 1959; d. William Glenn and Nancy Alice McC. Degree, Pa. State U., 1981. degree ERA Real Estate, Hawaii, 1982. Prin. Pamela J. Designs, Wailuku, Hawaii, 1985; cons. Women in Bus./Womens Conf., Wailuku, 1985, Bus. Brokers of Hawaii, Wailea, hawaii, 1985. Vol. designer Theatre Arts, Pa. State U., University Park, 1985-86; producer, designer benefit luncheon Spl. Olympics, 1987. Mem. Maui Ctr. Ind. Living (designer), Hale Makua Home Health Care (designer), Maui C. of C. Republican. Episcopalian. Club: Kihei Country. Home: 215 Paka Pl Kihei HI 96753 Office: Pamela J Designs 771 Alua St Wailuku HI 96793

MC CORMICK, WILLIE MAE WARD (MRS. WALTER WITTEN MCCORMICK), city ofcl., ret. tech. specialist; b. Centerville, Tex. Oct. 17, 1908; d. William Sylvester and Lucy (Marshall) Ward; B.A., Mary Hardin Baylor Coll., 1929; M.A., Hardin Simmons U., 1931; postgrad. So. Methodist U., Tex. Woman's U.; m. Walter Witten McCormick, May 29, 1929; 1 dau., Elizabeth Ward McCormick Wilcox. Tchr. chemistry and algebra Big Spring (Tex.) High Sch., 1941-44, 45-48; weather observer for Dept. Commerce, Big Spring, 1943-44; analytical chemist Dow Chem. Co., Freeport, 1944-45; calculator Chance Vought (now Ling-Temco-Vought), Dallas, 1951-55, structural engr., 1955-63, sci. programmer, 1963-67, tech. specialist, 1967-69; sr. program analyst Univ. Computing Co., Arlington, Tex., 1970-73; adv. council 1st City Savs. of Euless (Tex.); dir. Mbank of Euless, 1985—. Mem. Euless City Council, 1973-85, mayor pro tem, 1975-85; chmn. Trinity River Authority Central Wastewater System; mem. Water Resources Council N. Central Tex.; bd. dirs. Euless Pub. Library. Mem. AAAS, Am. Chem. Soc., Math. Assn. Am., Fedn. Am. Scientists, AAUW, Trainmen's Aux. (pres. 1940-41), Internat. Platform Assn., LWV (publicity chmn.), Metro Bus. Profl. Womens Club, Acad. Scis., Inst. Am. Chemists, Soroptimist (hon.). C. of C. (dir.). Democrat. Baptist (tchr. adult dept. Sunday sch.). Clubs: Order Eastern Star (past worthy matron), Oakcrest Woman's, Altrusa. Home: 2300 N Main Euless TX 76039

MCCOWN, JUDITH KAPLAN, advertising executive; b. Memphis, Dec. 2, 1943; d. Solomon and Marianne (Uditsky) Kaplan; m. Murray Harwood McCown,Aug. 7, 1964; children: Murray Harwood Jr., Melissa Hope. BS, Memphis State U., 1967. With Tenn. Dept. Human Services, Memphis, 1967-73; sec. Country Day Sch., Memphis, 1974-80; ptnr., account exec. Tri-Mark of Greater Memphis, 1980-81; account exec. Rodney Baber & Co., Memphis, 1981—; v.p. Mid-South Direct Mktg., Memphis, 1985—. Mem. Memphis Exchange Club, 1987—; bd. dirs. Arthritis Found. Memphis Chpt., 1986—. Mem. Memphis Advt. Fedn. (bd. dirs., chmn. advt. review com.), Am Advt. Fedn. (mem. nat. advt. standards com.), Nat. Assn. Female Execs., Nat. Council Jewish Women. Jewish. Lodges: B'Nai Brith Women, Temple Israel Sisterhood.

MCCOY, CAROL, training executive, psychologist; b. Bronxville, N.Y., June 14, 1948; d. Rawley Deering and Jane (Wiske) McC.; m. Lanny Gordon Foster, Nov. 29, 1975 (div. 1985). BA, Conn. Coll., 1970; MS in Psychology, Rutgers U., 1974, PhD in Psychology, 1980. Adj. instr. psychology Rutgers U., New Brunswick, N.J., 1974-75; faculty chair dept. social sci. Misericordia Hosp. Sch. Nursing, Bronx, N.Y., 1976-79; tng. and devel. cons. Chase Manhattan Bank N.A., N.Y.C., 1980-85, tng. mgr. internat. consumer banking div., 1985—. Mem. Nat. Assn. Female Execs., Am. Soc. Tng. and Devel., Am. Psychol. Assn. Home: 771 West End Ave New York NY 10025 Office: Chase Manhattan Bank NA 195 Broadway New York NY 10081

MCCOY, CHARLOTTE ANN, school administrator; b. Knoxville, Tenn.; d. Homer L. and Nettie (Fleming) Caughron; children: Melinda Ann, Melissa Lea. BS in Bus. Adminstrn., U. Tenn.; postgrad., Pa. State U.; MS, U. Houston, 1981. With State Area Vocat. Tech. Coll., Knoxville; coordinator Vocat. Office Edn., Huffman, Tex., 1977-83; adminstr. occupational and tech. edn. Huffman Ind. Sch. Dist., 1983—; mem. adv. com. Edn. Office Curriculum Devel., 1981-82. Bd. dirs. U. Houston, Montgomery County. Mem. Am. Vocat. Assn., Tex. Vocat. Edn. Assn., Office Edn. Assn., Gulf State Ancillary Assn., Huffman Edn. Assn. (faculty rep. to exec. com.), Tex. State Tchrs. Assn., Assn. Profl. Educators, Alumni Assn. U. Tenn., Alumni Assn. U. Houston, Crosby-Huffman C. of C. (bd. dirs.). Office: Huffman Ind Sch Dist 24403 Lake Houston Pkwy Huffman TX 77336

MCCOY, FRIEDA ANN, mgmt. cons.; b. Casper, Wyo., July 15, 1945; d. William B. and Helen C. (Brattis) Noell; A.A., Casper Coll., 1965; B.S., U. Wyo., 1967; M.L.S., U. Denver, 1968; M.B.A., U. Utah, 1975; m. Gerald E. McCoy, Oct. 12, 1968. Social sci. librarian U. Utah Marriott Library, Salt Lake City, 1968-71, govt. documents dept. head, 1971-75; document control supr. Alyeska Pipeline Co., Fairbanks, 1975-77; document control supr. N.W. Alaskan Pipeline Co., Salt Lake City, 1977-78, records and data mgmt. mgr., 1978-80, records and methods dir., 1980-82; owner, pres. CRM, cons., Salt Lake City, 1982—; instr. mgmt. U. Utah Coll. Bus., 1973-75; mgmt. cons., 1972-75. Mem. Am. Mgmt. Assn., Alaska Pipeline Builders Assn. (v.p. 1982—), Assn. M.B.A. Execs., Assn. Records Mgrs. and Adminstrs., Nat. Micrographics Assn., Project Mgmt. Inst. Contbr. articles to profl. jours. Home and Office: 835 18th Ave Salt Lake City UT 84103

MCCOY, HELEN LEE, warehouse corporation executive; b. Dallas, July 8, 1939; d. Bird Pierce and Eletha Thelma (Guynes) Thomas; m. James Kent McCoy, Dec. 11, 1979; children by previous marriage: Gregory Scott Odell, Mark Aaron Odell. Student schs. Redondo Beach, Calif. Sales mgr. Stretch & Sew Fabrics, Santa Rosa, Calif., 1972-73; teller Bank of Am., Napa, Calif., 1984; bd. dirs. Stor-it Mini Warehouse, Napa, 1981—, sec., treas. Stor-it Mini Warehouse Corp., Napa, 1981—, supr., 1981—. Active Home Owners Assn., Napa. Mem. Self Service Storage Assn., Nat. Assn. Female Execs., Assn. for Bus. and Profl. Women, Napa C. of C. Republican. Avocations: reading, bicycling, crocheting. Office: Stor-in Mini Warehouse Corp 1775 Industrial Way Napa CA 94558

MCCOY, JOENNE RAE, psychiatric clinic adminstrator; b. Detroit, Jan. 26, 1941; d. Harlan and Dorothy (Simpson) Heinmiller; children: Harlan Craig, Cathi-Jo. BA, Mich. State U., 1966; MSW, U. Mich., 1983. Tchr. Owosso and Garden City pub. schs., Mich., 1962-73; psychotherapist, group leader Wayne County Hosp., Mich., 1981-82; psychotherapist East Point, Westland, Mich., 1982-83, Midwest, Dearborn, Mich., 1982-83; owner, dir. Personal Devel. Ctrs., Inc., Plymouth, Mich., 1981—; bd. dirs. Hospice Suport Services, Inc., Livonia, Mich., 1981—; cons. Westland Convalescent Ctr., Mich., 1983—; supr. grad. students U. Mich., 1986—; cons., facilitator Women-the Emerging Entrepreneurs, Wayne State U. and Small Bus. Assn., 1985—; chmn. Substance Abuse Com., Plymouth Schs., 1982; cons. Salvation Army, Plymouth. Mem. bd. advisors (newsletter) Personal Performance, Balt., 1986—. Mem. steering com. for neighborhood programs YWCA. Soroptimist scholar, 1982. Mem. Internat. Assn. Pediatric Social Workers, Internat. Platform Assn., Mich. Assn. Bereavement Counselors, Families in Crisis: Domestic Violence Inc., Nat. Assn. Social Workers (cert.), Nat. Assn. Female Execs., Am. Entrepreneurs Assn., Women's Network (pres.), Acad. Cert. Soc. Workers. Club: Agora. Avocation: flying. Home: 37644 N Laurel Park Dr Livonia MI 48152 Office: Personal Devel Ctrs Inc PC 37677 Profl Ctr Dr Suite 130C Livonia MI 48154-1114

MCCOY, KATHLEEN LYNNE, writer; b. Dayton, Ohio, Apr. 25, 1945; d. James Lyons and Ethel Elizabeth (Curtis) McC.; B.S. in Journalism, Northwestern U., 1967, M.S. in Mag. Journalism, 1968; m. Robert Miles Stover, May 28, 1977. Free lance writer, 1965—; contbr. to Glamour, Mademoiselle, Ladies Home Jour., Woman's Day, Redbook, Family Circle, Cosmopolitan, TV Guide, Readers Digest, Families, Bride's, Seventeen; feature editor 'TEEN Mag., Los Angeles, 1968-77; columnist Sex and Your Body, Seventeen mag., 1983—; frequent guest various TV, radio talk shows. Mem. Screen Actors Guild, AGVA, AFTRA, NOW, Women in Communications, Soc. Profl. Journalists. Author: Discover Yourself, 1976; Discover Yourself II, 1978; The Teenage Body Book, 1979; Your Guide to Planning Your Future, 1979; The Teenage Survival Guide, 1982, Coping with Teenage Depression: A Parents Guide, 1982; The Teenage Body Book Guide to Sexuality, 1983; The Teenage Body Book Guide to Dating, 1983; The New Teenage Body Book, 1987; Growing and Changing: A Handbook for Pre-Teens, 1987; Solo Parenting: Your Essential Guide, 1987. Home: 4629 Daleridge Rd PO Box 189 La Canada CA 91011

MCCOY, LADELLE DELPHINE, federal official; b. Detroit, Feb. 26, 1935; d. Vellpore Charlie and Mattie Lee (Smith) Newby; m. Herman Howard, Feb. 1957 (div. 1958); 1 child, Allegra Elaine; m. Beryl Lorenzo McCoy, Mar. 25, 1960; children: Valerie Jean McCoy Miller, Pamela Alyce (dec.). BS, Wayne State U., 1969; postgrad., U. Mich., Detroit and Dearborn, 1970-79. Computer programmer IRS Data Ctr., Detroit, 1969-74, computer specialist, 1974-79, systems programmer, 1982-83, security specialist, 1983-85, chief field support sect., 1985-87, chief office automation br., 1987—; sr. systems analyst Wayne State U., Detroit, 1979-82; pres. Fed. Womens' Adv. Com. IRS, Detroit, 1977-78, mem. Assn. for Improvement of Minorities, 1982-85; mem. Pres.' Commn. on Status of Women at Wayne State U., 1980-82; instr. Wayne County Community Coll., Detroit, 1975; sunday sch. tchr. Word of Faith Christian Ctr., Detroit, 1988—. Active Detroit Urban League, 1986—; mem. Founders Soc. Detroit Inst. Arts, 1981—. Recipient Spl. Achievement award IRS, 1972, Mgmt. Recognition award, 1986. Mem. Assn. Computing Machinery, Black Data Processing Assn., NAACP, Iota Phi Lambda (fin. sec. Gamma Rho chpt. 1975-77). Office: IRS Data Ctr 1300 John C Lodge Dr Detroit MI 48226

MC COY, LEE BERARD, paint company executive; b. Ipswich, Mass., July 27, 1925; d. Damase Joseph and Robena Myrtle (Bruce) B.; student U. Ala., Mobile, 1958-60; m. Walter Vincent de Paul McCoy, Sept. 27, 1943; children—Bernadette, Raymond, Joan, Richard. Owner, Lee's Letter Shop, Hicksville, L.I., N.Y., 1950-56; mgr. sales adminstrn. Basila Mfg. Co., Mobile, Ala., 1957-61; promotion mgr., buyer Mobile Paint Co., Inc., Theodore, Ala., 1961—. Curator, Shepard Meml. Library, 1972—; bd. dirs. Monterey Tour House, Mobile, 1972-78, Old Dauphin Way Assn., 1977-79, Friends of Mus., Mobile, 1978—, Miss Wheelchair Ala., 1980—; del. Civic Roundtable, 1977-78, bd. dirs., 1980-81, 1st v.p., 1980-81, pres., 1981-82; Pres.'s Com. Employment of Handicapped, 1981—; chmn. Mobile, Nat. Yr. Disabled Persons, 1982; chmn. Mobile, Internat. Decade Disabled Persons, 1983—; mem. Nat. Project Adv. Bd., 1983— Nat. Community Adv. Bd., 1983—, World Com. for Decade of Disabled Persons, 1983—; v.p. Bristol Sister City Soc.; active Mobile Area Retarded Citizens, Am. Heart Assn.; mem. City of Mobile Cultural Enrichment Task Force, 1985—. Recipient Honor award Civic Roundtable, 1979, 80; Service award Women's Com. of Spain Rehab. Center, State of Ala., 1980; award Nat. Orgn. on Disability, 1983. Mem. Spectromatic Assos., Nat. Paint Distbrs., Hist. Preservation Soc. (color mktg. group), English Speaking Union (v.p.). Republican. Methodist. Clubs: Quota (charter mem. Mobile chpt., dir. 1977—, pres. 1978-80, chmn. numerous coms., recipient Service award Dist. 8, 1979, Internat. award for serving club objectives, 1980, editor Care-Gram, Weekly newsletter for nursing homes 1980—), Bienville. Home: 1553 Monterey Pl Mobile AL 36604 Office: 4775 Hamilton Blvd Theodore AL 36582

MC COY, LOIS CLARK, county official, magazine editor; b. New Haven, Oct. 1, 1920; d. William Patrick and Lois Rosilla (Dailey) Clark; m. Herbert Irving McCoy, Oct. 17, 1943; children—Whitney, Kevin, Marianne, Tori, Debra, Sally, Daniel. B.S., Skidmore Coll., 1942; student Nat. Search and Rescue Sch., 1974. Asst. buyer R.H. Macy & Co., N.Y.C., 1942-44, assoc. buyer, 1944-48; instr. Mountain Medicine & Survival, U. Calif. at San Diego, 1973-74; cons. editor Search & Rescue Mag., 1975, Rescue mag., 1988—; coordinator San Diego Mountain Rescue Team, La Jolla, Calif., 1973-75; exec. sec. Nat. Assn. for Search and Rescue, Inc., Nashville and La Jolla, 1975-80, comptroller, 1980-82; disaster officer San Diego County, 1980-86, Santa Barbara County, 1986—; editor-in-chief Response! mag., 1982-86; cons. law enforcement div.; Calif. Office Emergency Services, 1976-77; pres. San Diego Com. for Los Angeles Philharmonic Orch., 1957-58. Bd. dirs. Search and Rescue of the Californias, 1976-77, Nat. Assn. for Search and Rescue, Inc., 1980-87, pres., 1985-87, bd. trustees, 1987—; mem. Gov.'s Task Force on Earthquakes, 1981-82; chmn. Earthquake Preparedness Task Force, Seismic Safety Commn., 1982-86. Recipient Hal Foss award for outstanding service to search and rescue, 1982, Nasar Service award, 1985. Mem. Am. Astronautical Soc., AIAA, IEEE, Am. Soc. Indsl. Security, Nat. Assn. for Search and Rescue (Service award 1985), Council for Survival Edn., Mountain Rescue Assn., Nat. Jeep Search and Rescue Assn., San Diego Mountain Rescue Team, San Diego Amateur Radio Club, Sierra Club. Episcopalian. Author: Search and Rescue Glossary, 1974; contbr. to profl. jours. Office: PO Box 91648 Santa Barbara CA 93190

MCCOY, MEREDITH, lawyer; b. Little Rock, Jan. 21, 1949; d. Travis Walton and Evelyn Lois (Greene) McC.; m. Scott Enos Slaughter, Sept. 9, 1972; children: Garrett Crawford, Evelyn McMath. BA, U. Ark., 1971; BS, Simmons Sch. Library Sci., Boston, 1972; JD, George Washington U., 1976. Bar: Va. 1977, D.C. 1978. Counsel Mergers and Acquisitions, Inc., McClean, Va., 1977; atty. Congl. Research Service, Washington, 1977-86; resident ptnr. Washington office Arnold Grobmyer & Haley, Little Rock, 1985—; cons. ABA Project on Attys.' Fees, 1978-79. Editor: Clayton Act and Mergers (ABA), 1976, Mergers and Acquisitions Jour., 1977, Fed. Bar News & Jour., 1980—. Sec. Capitol Hill Women's Polit. Caucus, Washington, 1981. Mem. Fed. Bar Assn. (sec. Younger Lawyers div. 1980, Dist. Service award 1982), Women's Bar Assn., Bar Assn. D.C. (com. on emerging bus.), Va. Bar Assn., Women's Legal Def. Fund., Women in Housing and Finance. Democrat. Methodist. Home: 3916 Aspen St Chevy Chase MD 20815 Office: Arnold Grobmyer & Haley 1629 K St NW Washington DC 20006

MCCOY, PHYLLISTINE, educational association administrator; b. Benton Harbor, Mich., Feb. 12, 1943; d. Phillip Jr. and Daisy Mae (Shaw) McC. BA, Western Mich. U., 1967, MA, 1974. Cert. tchr., Mich. High sch. reading tchr. Kalamazoo, 1967-71; reading specialist Battle Creek (Mich.) Pub. Schs., 1971-78; exec. dir. United Tchrs. of Flint, Mich., 1978-80; negotiation specialist Mich. Edn. Assn., East Lansing, 1980-83; Uniserv exec. Mich. Edn. Assn., Flint, 1983—; fin. planner A.L. Williams Assocs., Flint, 1984—; tng. specialist Conflict Mgmt. Assocs., Flint, 1987—; cons. NEA, Washington, 1983—. Trainer United Way, Flint, 1983-84, mem. edn. and planning com., 1982-85, chair mktg. task force, 1984-85. Named to Western Mich. U. Minority Alumni Wall of Distinction, 1980-87. Mem. Mich. Profl. Staff Assn. (sec. 1979-80, v.p. 1981-83), Nat. Staff Orgn., Profl. Staff Orgn., Nat. Assn. Female Execs., Indsl. Relations Research Assn., Research Services Assn. Democrat. Mem. Church of God in Christ. Home: 1153 River Hill Dr Flint MI 48532 Office: Mich Edn Assn 5095 Exchange Dr Flint MI 48507

MCCOY LAIRD, DIANE LOUISE, broadcasting company executive; b. San Louis Obispo, Calif., Oct. 13, 1950; d. Frank William and Betty Louise (Holder) Bradley; m. Daniel William McCoy, Nov. 16, 1968 (div. 1971); 1 child, Jason William; m. Andrew K. Laird, Nov. 7, 1981. Student, La. City Coll., 1976, Calif. State U., 1978. With KGRB-KBOB AM-FM, City of Industry, Calif., 1970-74; sole practice traffic-acctg. cons. City of Industry, Calif., 1976—; traffic mgr. systems mgr. Greater Media KATZ-FM, Los Angeles, 1981-84; bus. mgr. Rollins KDAY-AM, Los Angeles, 1984-86, Infinity Broadcasting KROQ-FM, Los Angeles, 1986—. Foster parent Foster Home Parent Soc., Los Angeles, 1984; program coordinator Intrax Fgn. Exchange Student Placement, Saugus, Calif., 1986. Mem. Acad. Country Music Assn. Club: KROW Snow Ski Team. Lodge: Soroptomist. Office: KROQ Radio 3500 W Olive Ave #900 Burbank CA 91505

MC CRACKEN, ALICE IRENE, psychotherapist; b. Indpls., May 4, 1942; d. Neal and Falma Dorothy (Rice) McC.; B.A. with honors, Mills Coll., 1963; M.A., U. Calif.-Davis, 1965; Ph.D., Tulane U., 1968; M.Counseling, Ariz. State U., 1975; 1 child, Tammy Maru. Library asst., head current periodicals service Ariz. State U. Library, 1968-70; community program specialist City of Scottsdale, Ariz., 1971-72; women's editor Scottsdale Daily Progress, 1972-74; activities therapist Camelback Hosp., Phoenix, 1972-74, dir. public relations, psychotherapist, 1975-78; psychotherapist Family Service Agy., Tempe, Ariz., 1978-81; pvt. practice psychotherapy, Scottsdale, Ariz., 1981—. Served with USAR, 1976-78. Recipient Ariz. Press Women editing and writing awards, 1972-75; Ariz. Bus. Communicators editing award, 1975. Mem. Am. Group Psychotherapy Assn., Phoenix Psychoanalytic Study Group, Ariz. Group Psychotherapy Soc., Am. Assn. for Counseling and Devel., Am. Mental Health Counselors Assn. Office: Dynamic Counseling Assocs 6730 E McDowell Rd #115 Scottsdale AZ 85257

MCCRACKEN, CARON FRANCIS, accounting consultant; b. Detroit, Jan. 12, 1951; d. William Joseph and Constance Irene (Kramer) McC. AS, Mott Community Coll., 1971; BS, Cen. Mich U., 1973; MA, U. Mich., 1978. Tchr. Elkton, Pigeon, Bayport (Mich.) High Sch., 1973-74, Davison (Mich.) Jr. High Sch., 1974-75; instr. Mott Community Coll., Flint, Mich., 1974-78; planning and research specialist Flint Police Dept., 1977-79; campus coordinator, programmer Systems & Computer Tech., Inc., Detroit, 1981-82, acad. specialist, 1982-83, mgr. acad. computing systems, 1983-84; mgr. adminstrv. systems Fruehauf Corp., Detroit, 1984-85, sr. communications analyst, 1985-86, 1986-87; account cons. US Sprint Communications Corp., Detroit, 1987—; adv. bd. CONTEL Bus. Networks, Atlanta, 1987. Mem. Internat. Communications Assn., Assn. for Computing Machinery, Detroit Inst. Arts. Club: Bikecentennial (Missoula, Mont.). Home: 13977 Piedmont Detroit MI 48223

MCCRACKEN, LINDA, librarian, commercial artist; b. Rochester, N.Y., Apr. 13, 1948; d. Frederick Hugh Craig and Shirley Betty (Shacter) Bickford; m. Alan Cheah, June 13, 1972 (div. 1978); m. Bruce E. McCracken, Sept. 23, 1978 (div. 1985); 1 child, Karen Elizabeth. BA in History, SUNY-Geneseo, 1970, MLS, 1970. Reference librarian Northeastern U., Boston, 1971-72; asst. librarian Burlington Pub. Library, Mass., 1972-74; research asst. Data Resources, Inc., Lexington, Mass., 1974-76; comml. artist McCracken's, Wolfeboro, N.H., 1973-87; asst. librarian N.H. Vocat.-Tech. Coll., Manchester, 1985-87; librarian N.H. Hosp., Concord, 1987—. Participant paintings Horseheads Mall Art Show (3rd place award 1968); graphic artist Rare Coin Rev. mag., 1983; layout artist quar. book: Market Media Guide, 1979; author Burlington Times-Union, 1973, Pleasant News, 1987—. Treas. Village Players, Wolfeboro, 1982-83; pub. relations com. Gov.'s Arts Council, Wolfeboro, 1982; mem. Clearlakes Chorale, Jefferson Chorus. Mem. Health Scis. Librarians, Nat. Assn. Female Execs., N.H. Library Assn., State Employees Assn. N.H. Unitarian. Avocations: skiing, gardening, singing, acting, hiking, reading, computers. Home: Box 628 Pine Hill Rd Wolfeboro Falls NH 03896 Office: NH Hosp Profl Library Annex I 105 Pleasant St Concord NH 03301

MCCRACKEN, SANDRA JAYNE, educational administrator; b. Chamblee, Ga., Nov. 9, 1942; d. James Britt and Geneva Jane (Brown) McC. BS in Bus., Western Carolina U., 1965; MEd in Adminstrn. and Supervision, U. North Fla., 1974; postgrad., U. Fla., 1981-83. Tchr. Orange Park (Fla.) Jr.-Sr. High Sch., 1965-69, dean of students, 1969-73; asst. prin. Orange Park Mid. Sch., 1973-77; dir. elem. edn. Clay County Sch. System, Green Cove Springs, Fla., 1977-79, asst. supt. bus. and fin., 1979—; bd. dirs. Ednl. Community Credit Union, Jacksonville, Fla. Mem. Clay County Dem. Exec. Com., Green Cove Springs, 1983—. Named an Outstanding Young Educator, Clay County Jaycees, 1966. Mem. Am. Assn. Sch. Bus. Officials, Southeastern Assn. Sch. Bus. Officials, Fla. Assn. Sch. Bus. Officials (pres. 1988), Fla. Assn. Sch. Fin. Officers, Jacksonville Panhellenic, Delta Kappa Gamma (pres. Beta Mu chpt. 1976-78, Outstanding Educator award 1987), Delta Zeta Alumnae (pres. Jacksonville chpt. 1972-73), Phi Delta Kappa. Methodist. Home: 2708 Lexington Dr Orange Park FL 32073 Office: Clay County Sch System 900 Walnut St Green Cove Springs FL 32043

MCCRANIE, JOANN CLAXTON, manufacturing professional; b. Jacksonville, Fla., May 17, 1941; d. Ellie Lee Jr. and Vivian (Bishop) Claxton; m. Karl Emden McCranie Sr., Oct. 14, 1961; children: Tracy McCranie Hunt, Karl E. Jr., Kirk Lee. Grad. high sch., Avondale Estates, Ga. Clk./typist Plastics Packaging Inc., Norcross, Ga., 1976-77, sec., 1977-78, mgr. customer service, 1978-84; gen. mgr. Poly/Product div. Plastics Packaging Inc., Norcross, Ga., 1984—. Dep. registrar Hall County Voter Registration, 1987. Mem. Am. Bus. Women's Assn. (pres. 1984-85, v.p. 1983-84, chmn. several coms., Woman of Yr. 1986), Nat. Assn. Female Execs. Republican. Methodist. Home: 6254 Jones Rd Flowery Branch GA 30542 Office: Poly/Products 4385 International Blvd Norcross GA 30093

MCCRARY, EUGENIA LESTER (EUGENIA CAMPBELL LESTER), civic worker, writer; b. Annapolis, Md., Mar. 23, 1929; d. John Campbell and Eugenia (Potts) Lester; A.B. cum laude, Radcliffe Coll., 1950; M.A., Johns Hopkins U., 1952; postgrad. Harvard U., spring 1953, Pa. State U., 1953-54, Drew U., 1957-58, Inst. Study of USSR, Munich, W.Ger., 1964; m. John Campbell Howard, July 15, 1955 (dec. Sept. 1965); m. 2d, Dennis Daughtry McCrary, June 28, 1969; 1 son, Dennis Campbell. Grad. asst. dept. Romance langs. Pa. State U., 1953-54; tchr. dept. math. The Brearley Sch., N.Y.C., 1954-57; dir. Sch. Langs., Inc., Summit, N.J., 1958-69, trustee, 1960-69. Dist. dir. Eastern Pa. and N.J. auditions Met. Opera Nat. Council, N.Y.C., 1960-66, dist. dir. publicity, 1966-67, nat. vice chmn. publicity, 1967-71, nat. chmn. public relations, 1972-75, hon. nat. chmn. public relations, 1976—; bd. govs., chmn. Van Cortlandt Mansion Mus., 1985—. Co-author: (with Allegra Branson) Frontiers Aflame, 1987. Mem. Nat. Soc. Colonial Dames Am. (bd. mgrs. N.Y.), Met. Opera Nat. Council, Soc. Mayflower Desc. (bd. dirs. N.Y. soc., chmn. house com.), Soc. Daus. of Holland Dames (bd. dirs., 3d directress gen.), Vestry L'Eglise Saint-Esprit, Huguenot Soc. Am. (governing council). Republican. Episcopalian. Club: Colony. Home: 24 Central Park S New York NY 10019

MCCRAY, DOLORES ROSELYN, banker; b. Youngstown, Ohio, Jan. 14, 1940; d. Cleo W. and Ada (Polnett) LaCalleaux; m. Charles Earle McCray, Jan. 18, 1957 (div.); children—Charles Earle Jr., Dolores Roselyn. A.A., B.B.A., Pace U. From teller to ops. officer Chem. Bank, N.Y.C., 1967-78; acct. Combustion Equipment Inc., N.Y.C., 1979-80; asst. treas. br. mgr. Anchor Savs. Bank, N.Y.C., 1980—. Recipient Black Achievers in Industry award, 1982, Profl. Achievement award, 1986; selected to lead banking del. to Rep. of China, 1986. Mentor, Pace U. Mem. East Midtown C. of C. (bd. dirs.), Urban Bankers Coalition (bd. dirs.), Coalition of 100 Black Women (bd. dirs.), Soc. Profl. and Exec. Women, Nat. Assn. Female Execs., Nat. Assn. Rev. Appraisers and Mortgage Underwriters, Am. Film Inst., Smithsonian Assocs. Democrat. Lutheran. Home: 345 E 93d St New York NY 10128 Office: Anchor Savs Bank 404 Fifth Ave New York NY 10018

MC CRAY, EVELINA WILLIAMS, librarian, researcher; b. Plaquemine, La., Sept. 1, 1932; d. Turner and Beatrice (Gordon) Williams II; m. John Samuel McCray, Apr. 7, 1955; 1 dau., Johnetta McCray Russ. BA, So. U., Baton Rouge, 1954; MS in Library Sci., La. State U., 1962. Librarian, Iberville High Sch., Plaquemine, 1954-70, Plaquemine Jr. High, 1970-75; proofreader short stories, poems Associated Writers Guild, Atlanta, 1982-86; library cons. Evaluation Capitol High Sch., 1964, Iberville Parish Educators Workshop, 1980, Tchrs. Core/Iberville Parish, 1980-81. Contbr. poetry New Am. Poetry Anthology, 1988, The Golden Treasury of Great Poems, 1988. Vol. service Allen J. Nadler Library, Plaquemine, 1980-82; librarian Local Day Care Ctr., Plaquemine, 1978-79. Mem. ALA, La. Library Assn., Nat. Ret. Tchrs. Assn., La Ret. Tchrs. Assn. (cons. ann. workshops 1986—, state appointee to informative and protective services com. 1988—), Iberville Ret. Tchrs. Assn. (info. and protective services dir. 1981—). Democrat. Baptist. Home: PO Box Q Plaquemine LA 70765

MCCRAY, NOELLA MARGARIET, nurse; b. Markegem, Belgium, Nov. 20, 1944; came to U.S., 1948; d. Achiel Maurice and Josephine Marie (DeWindt) DeVolder; m. Stephen Joseph McCray, Aug. 5, 1972; children: Colleen Anne, Laura Noel. BS in Nursing, Avila Coll., 1970; M in Nursing, U. Kans., 1979. RN, Kans., Mo. Clin. nurse specialist U. Kans. Med. Ctr., Kansas City, 1979-82, St. Mary's Hosp., Kansas City, Mo., 1982-85; oncology program coordinator Kansas City (Mo.) Regional Cancer Ctr., 1985—. Mem. Leukemia Soc. (bd. dirs. mid-Am. chpt. 1982—), Am. Cancer Soc. (bd. dirs. Kansas City unit 1986—), Oncology Nursing Soc. (mem. legis. com. 1983-86), Soc. Nursing Profls., Sigma Theta Tau. Roman Catholic. Home: 2919 W 50th St Westwood KS 66205 Office: Kansas City Regional Cancer Ctr 2940 Baltimore St Kansas City MO 64108

MCCREA, PATRICIA ANNE, noncommissioned army officer; b. Riverside, Calif., Oct. 7, 1945; d. Clarence Edwin and Mathilda Anne (Pfarr) McC.; m. William Louis Pagels, Oct. 7, 1963 (div. June 1982); children—Susan, Theresa, Kathryn, William Patrick. Student U. Md., Evreux, France, 1962-63; B.S., SUNY-Buffalo, 1983; postgrad. Genesee Community Coll., 1982-83. Served as enlisted person U.S. Army, USAR, 1974—, personnel mgmt. supr. for intelligence, security, ops. and tng. 390th Personnel and Adminstrn. Bn., Richmond, Va., 1985—; program asst. Coop. Extension, Batavia, N.Y., 1980-82; unit adminstr. U.S. Army Res., Richmond, Va., 1984-85; substitute tchr. Alexander Central Sch., N.Y., 1982-84; adj. faculty Genesee Community Coll., Batavia, 1982-84. Tutor, officer Literacy Vols. of Am., Batavia,

1982-84. Decorated Army Commendation medal, others. Mem. Assn. U.S. Army, Nat. Assn. Female Execs., Am. Soc. Profl. and Exec. Women, DAV (life), Mensa. Republican. Roman Catholic. Avocations: needlework; fencing; reading; quilting. Home: 1910 Repp St Highland Springs VA 23075 Home: 11269 E Bennett Rd Grass Valley CA 95945 Office: 390th Personnel and Adminstrn Bn 1305 Sherwood Ave Richmond VA 23220

MCCREARY, SALLY M., nursing administrator; b. Harrisburg, Pa., July 5, 1932; d. Clyde H. and Beulah (Kautz) McCreary. BS in Nursing, Lebanon Valley Coll., Annville, Pa., 1965; MS in Edn., Temple U., 1972. RN, 1953. Staff nurse Embudo (N.Mex.) Presbyn. Hosp., 1953-56; surg. supr., dir. nurses Harrisburg (Pa.) Osteo. Hosp., 1957-61; staff nurse Vis. Nurse Assn., Harrisburg, 1961-64; instr. Polyclinic Hosp. Sch. Nursing, Harrisburg, 1965-72; assoc. dir. edn. Indian Health Sq. Hosp., Crownpoint, N.H., 1972-74; instr. VA Med. Ctr., Sheridan, Wyo., 1974-75; assoc. chief nursing edn. VA Med. Ctr., Temple, Tex., 1975-77; asst. chief nursing VA Med. Ctr., Houston, 1977-80; chief nursing service VA Med. Ctr., Cheyenne, Wyo., 1980-82, Cin., 1982-85, St. Cloud, Minn., 1985—. Contbr. articles to profl. jours. Elder Presbyn. Ch. Avocations: needlework, animals, reading, hiking, photography. Mem. Am. Bus. and Profl. Women (sec. 1987—) AAUW (edn. found. chmn. 1986-88), Am. Orgn. Nurse Execs., Minn. Orgn. Nurse Execs. (edn. com., sec./treas. dist. D), Am. Assn. Mil. Surgeons of U.S. Republican. Lodge: Zonta. Office: VA Med Ctr Saint Cloud MN 56301

MCCREE, CYNTHIA BLANDFORD, alumni association administrator; b. Elmira, N.Y., May 4, 1956; d. William Blandford and Ardella E. Blandford Wilson; m. Wilbert A. McCree, Sept. 1977 (div. 1984); 1 child, Omari Lateef. Student, Cornell U., 1975-77, U. Liberia, West Africa, spring 1975, Ga. State U., 1986—. Paralegal Smolar & Pelletier, Atlanta, 1982-83; personnel asst. Ga. Tech. Research Inst., Atlanta, 1983-84, adminstrv. sec., tng. and devel. div., 1984-85, sec. to exec. dir., 1985; mgr., sec. to v.p. alumni affairs Ga. Tech. Alumni Assn., Atlanta, 1985—; cons. Atlanta Urban League, 1985—, Essence mag., Atlanta, 1985—, State of Ga. Women's Dept. of Health, Atlanta. Past pres., v.p., Beecher Hills Elem. Sch. PTA, Atlanta, 1986-87; mem. faculty/staff Ga. Tech Centennial Campaign com., 1987. Recipient Women of Achievement award YWCA, 1988; Bus. Men's award/scholar Men's Club of Ithaca, 1973, Am. Legion Aux. award/scholar, 1973, Rotary Internat. Exchange scholar, 1974, Advanced Study scholar Cornell U., 1975. Mem. Womens C. of C., S.W. Atlanta Youth Bus. Orgn. Democrat. Methodist. Home: 924 Cascade Ave Atlanta GA 30311 Office: Ga Tech Alumni Assn 190 North Ave Atlanta GA 30332

MCCRICKARD, RUBY ASHWELL, field representative; b. Huddleston, Va., Apr. 19, 1931; d. Harry Odell and Nellie (Cundiff) Ashwell; diploma Riverside Hosp. Sch. Nursing, 1953; cert. health care adminstrn. U. So. Calif., 1976; B.A., Goddard Coll., 1975; M.S., Med. Coll. Ga., 1977; Ph.D., Walden U., 1985; m. George T. McCrickard, Aug. 9, 1952; 1 son, George T. Operating room staff nurse, head nurse med. unit Riverside Hosp., Newport News, Va., 1953-55; asst. operating room supr., operating room staff nurse, acting operating room supr., Kecoughtan Vets. Hosp., Hampton, Va., 1955-60; intensive care and central supply supr. Lynchburg (Va.) Gen.-Marshall Lodge Hosps., 1962-66, asst. dir. nursing services, 1966-69, dir. nursing services, 1969-78, dir. nursing service, asst. adminstr., 1978-84, v.p. hosp. adminstrn., 1984-85, sr. v.p. hosp. adminstrn., 1985—; mem. Va. Bd. Health, 1981-85, chmn., 1984-85; mem. Lynchburg Coll. Nursing Edn. Adv. Council, 1979-80; mem. adv. com. respiratory therapy Central Va. Community Coll., 1978—; mem. Central Va. Health Planning Emergency Med. Adv. Council, 1975-77; mem. primary care com. S.W. Va. Health Systems Agy., Inc.; hosp. coordinator United Way, 1983. Recipient Ella T. Whitten award Registered Nurses Associated Alumnae Assn. Lynchburg, Va., 1966; Phoebe Kandel Rohrer Founders award Med. Coll. Ga., 1986. Mem. Am. Nurses Assn. (past mem. membership and by-laws coms.), Nat. League Nursing, Nat. Forum Adminstrn. Nursing Services, Am. Soc. Hosp. Nursing Service Adminstrn. (pres. Va. chpt. 1981, dir. Va. chpt. 1982, candidate, program for excellence in nursing adminstrn. 1980), Nat. Soc. Lit. and Arts, AAUW, Va. Nurses Assn. (chmn. profl. nursing practice com.), Va. League Nursing com., pres.-elect 1986—, chmn. membership com. 1984-85), Va. Hosp. Assn. (com. on nursing, com. emergency med. services), Piedmont Heart Assn. (past dir., chmn. nursing com.), Riverside Hosp. Sch. Nursing Alumnae (pres. 1959-60), Sigma Theta Tau. Baptist. Clubs: Order Eastern Star, Scottish Rite Women's Nobletts. Home: Rt 1 Box 483 Rustburg VA 24588 Office: Joint Commn on Accrediation of Health Care Orgns 875 N Michigan Ave Chicago IL 60611-9945

MCCRIMMON, BARBARA SMITH, writer, librarian; b. Anoka, Minn., May 3, 1918; d. Webster Roy and Jessie (Sargeant) Smith; m. James McNab McCrimmon, June 10, 1939; children—Kevin Mor, John Marshall. B.A., U. Minn., 1939; M.S.L.S., U. Ill., 1961; Ph.D., Fla. State U., 1973. Asst. librarian Ill. State Nat. Hist. Survey, Champaign, Ill., 1961-62; research assoc. Bur. Community Planning, U. Ill., Champaign, 1962-63; librarian Ill. Water Survey, Champaign, 1964-65; librarian Am. Meteorol. Soc., Boston, 1965-67; editorial asst. Jour. Library History, Tallahassee, 1967-69, 73-74; adj. asst. prof. Sch. Library Sci., Fla. State U., Tallahassee, 1976-77. Author: Power, Politics and Print, 1981; editor: American Library Philosophy, 1975; contbr. articles to profl. jours. Mem. ALA, Bibliog. Soc. Am., Pvt. Libraries Assn., Beta Phi Mu, Manuscript Soc. Democrat.

MC CRORY, ELLANN, radiologist; b. Butler Springs, Ala., Mar. 22, 1936; d. William Bryant and Eva Estelle (Stabler) McCrory. BS, U. Ala., 1956; MD, Med. Coll. Ala., 1960. Rotating intern Univ. Hosp., Birmingham, Ala., 1960-61; resident Bapt. Meml. Hosp., Memphis, 1961-64; instr. radiology U. Fla., 1964-65; pvt. practice radiology, Fort Payne, Ala., 1965—; chief of med. staff DeKalb County Hosp., 1977; speaker in field. Trustee, pres. Landmarks Inc., 1978-79. Recipient Bausch and Lomb Sci. award, 1953. Mem. Am. Coll. Radiology, Radiol. Soc. N.A., AMA, Am. Med. Women's Assn., So. Radiol. Assn., Am. Roentgen Ray Soc., Am. Assn. Women Radiologists (treas. 1987—), Mid-South Med. Assn., Med. Assn. Ala. (v.p. 1986-87, bd. census 1988—), DeKalb County Med. Soc. (pres. 1977), So. Med. Assn., Ala. Radiol. Soc., Fort Payne C. of C. (bd. dirs., pres. 1979-80) Ala. Hist. Soc., U. Ala. Alumni Assn. (pres. elect DeKalb County chpt. 1977, nat. dist. v.p.), Phi Beta Kappa, Alpha Lambda Delta. Methodist. Home: 1408 Alabama Ave SW Fort Payne AL 35967 Office: 309 Medical Center Dr PO Box 1298 Fort Payne AL 35967

MCCUBBIN, ANDREA MARJORIE, data processing executive; b. Geneseo, Ill., Mar. 28, 1959; d. Howard Welby and Naida Claire (Milner) Moburg; m. Jeffrey Dean McCubbin, May 10, 1986. BBa, U. Iowa, 1982. Programmer analyst Lowenberg Bakery, Inc., Ottumwa, Iowa, 1982-84; info. systems analyst Norand Corp., Cedar Rapids, Iowa, 1984-86; team leader Pioneer Data Systems, Cedar Rapids, 1986-88; project leader Norand Corp., Cedar Rapids, 1988—. Vol. programmer United Way of Wapello County, Ottumwa, 1984. Recipient Gold award Wapello County United Way, 1984. Mem. Nat. Mgmt. Assn. of Norand (sec. 1986, v.p. 1987—), Eastern Iowa Data Processing Assn. (awards chmn. 1985—), Nat. Assn. for Female Execs., Nat. Humane Soc. U.S., Iowa Alumni Assn. (life), Alpha Kappa Psi (life). Presbyterian. Home: 14861 19 Mile Rd Marshall MI 49068 Office: Norand Corp 550 Second St SE Cedar Rapids IA 52407

MCCUBBIN, SUSAN BRUBECK, real estate executive; b. Decatur, Ill., Mar. 16, 1948; d. Rodney Earl Brubeck and Marilyn Jean (McMahon) Hopkins; m. Martin Charles Resnik, May 18, 1967 (div. 1974); 1 child, Martin Charles Jr.; m. William James McCubbin, May 30, 1987. LLB, Western State U., Fullerton, Calif., 1977. Bar: Calif. 1977; lic. real estate broker, Calif. Ptnr. Blue Chip Constrn. Co., Santa Ana, Calif., 1969-73; pres. Brubeck Co., San Francisco and Newport Beach, Calif., 1973-78; sole practice San Francisco, 1978-79; sr. mktg. cons., broker Grubb & Ellis Co., San Francisco, 1979-87; pres. Greenwich Corp., San Rafael, Calif., 1987—. Columnist Automotive Age Mag., 1974-75. Chmn. U.S. Senate Primary Campaign, Orange County, Calif., 1976. Republican.

MCCUE, DONNA CAPRARI, advertising and public relations executive; b. Scranton, Pa.; d. Samuel R. and Teresa M. Caprari; m. Timothy P. McCue; 1 child, Mallorie. BA, Rosemont Coll., 1974. Program dir. hypertension screening Am. Heart Assn., Binghamton, N.Y., 1974-75; owner, pres. McCue Advt. & Pub. Relations, Inc., Binghamton, 1975—; lectr. Broome Community Coll., SUNY-Binghamton. Bd. dirs. Am. Heart Assn., Binghamton, 1982—, Broome County Child Devel. Council; active Broome Tioga Pvt. Industry Council, 1984-87, communications com. local chpt. United Way, 1985—. Mem. Pub. Relations Soc. Am. (accredited), Pub. Relations Soc. So. Tier (v.p. and sec.), Broome County C. of C. Office: 91 Riverside Dr Binghamton NY 13905

MCCULLOCH, RACHEL, economics educator; b. Bklyn., June 26, 1942; d. Henry and Rose (Offen) Preiss; m. Gary Edward Chamberlain; children: Laura Meressa, Neil Dudley. BA, U. Pa., 1962; MA in Teaching, U. Chgo., 1965, MA, 1971, PhD, 1973; student, MIT, 1966-67. Economist Cabinet Task Force on Oil Import Control, Washington, 1969; instr., asst prof. Grad. Sch. Bus., U. Chgo., 1971-73; asst. prof. then assoc. prof. econs. Harvard U., Cambridge, Mass., 1973-79; assoc. prof. U. Wis., Madison, 1979-83, prof., 1983-87; prof. Brandeis U., Waltham, Mass., 1987—; mem. Pres.' Commn. on Indsl. Competitiveness, 1983-84; mem. adv. council Office of Tech. Assessment U.S. Congress, 1979-88; cons. World Bank, Washington, 1984-86; mem. com. on internat. relations studies with People's Rep. China, 1984—; research assoc. Nat. Bur. Econ. Research, Cambridge, 1985—; mem. adv. com. Inst. for Internat. Econs., Washington, 1987—. Author: Research and Development as a Determinant of U.S. International Competitiveness, 1978; contbr. articles to profl. jours. Grantee NSF, 1975, Hoover Inst., 1984-85, German Marshall Fund of U.S., 1985. Mem. Am. Econ. Assn. (dir. summer program for minority students Madison 1983-84). Home: 10 Frost Rd Lexington MA 02173 Office: Brandeis Univ Dept of Economics Waltham MA 02254

MCCULLOH, JUDITH MARIE, editor; b. Spring Valley, Ill., Aug. 16, 1935; d. Henry A. and Edna Mae (Traub) Binkele; m. Leon Royce McCulloh, Aug. 26, 1961. BA, Ohio Wesleyan U., 1956; MA, Ohio State U., 1957; PhD, Ind. U., 1970. Asst. to dir. Archives of Traditional Music, Bloomington, Ind., 1964-65; asst. editor U. Ill. Press, Champaign, 1972-77, assoc. editor, 1977-82, sr. editor, 1982-85, exec. editor, 1985—; advisor John Edwards Meml. Forum, Los Angeles, 1973—; mem. adv. bd. Urban Traditions, Chgo., 1986—; bd. dirs. Singlejack Books, San Pedro, Calif., 1987—. Mem. Editorial Bd. Jour. Am. Folklore, Washington, 1986—; co-editor Stars of Country Music, 1975; editor (LP) Green Fields of Ill., 1963, Ethnic Recordings in America, 1982. Trustee Am. Folklife Ctr., Library of Congress, Washington, 1986—. Fulbright grantee, 1958-59; NDEA grantee, 1961, 62-63; grantee Nat. Endowment for the Humanities, 1978. Mem. Am. Folklore Soc. (pres. 1986-87), Soc. for Ethnomusicology (treas. 1982-86), Sonneck Soc., Women in Scholarly Pub., Am. Anthropological Assn. Democrat. Office: U Ill Press 54 E Gregory Dr Champaign IL 61820

MCCULLOUGH, KATHRYN SPRINGS, university adminstrator; b. Phila., Apr. 21, 1941; d. L. David and Kathryn E. (Eisele) Springs; m. Charles V. McCullough, Sept. 12, 1964 (div. Apr. 1984); children: Cristin Lee, Elizabeth Anne. BS in Fashion Merchandising, Pa. State U., 1964. Exec. sec. Coll. of Bus. Pa. State U., University Park, 1964-65; owner, operator Roost Sewing Ctr., State College, Pa., 1971-81; exec. sec. Locus, Inc., State College, 1981-84; adminstrv. asst. Coll. Engring. Pa. State U., University Park, 1984—. Author: (textbook) Sewing Knit Fabrics, 1977. Mem. Boalsburg (Pa.) Heritage Mus., 1987. Mem. Nat. Assn. for Female Execs., Sierra Club. Club: Penn State Figure Skating (University Park) (test chmn. 1983—, pres. 1986—). Office: Pa State Univ 101 Hammond Bldg University Park PA 16802

MCCULLOUGH, MARY LOUISE, communications executive; b. Columbus, Ohio, Dec. 11, 1951; d. John Lawrence and Louise (Bishop) McC.; m. Frank Coakley, June 5, 1976; 1 child, Evan Lawrence. BA, Denison U., 1973; postgrad., Northwestern U., 1977-78. Reporter Winchester (Va.) Evening Star, 1973, Pioneer Press Inc., Wilmette, Ill., 1974-76; editor Northwestern U., Evanston, Ill., 1976-78; account exec. Carl Byoir and Assocs.Chgo., Chgo., 1978-81; cons., writer MLM Communications, Chgo., 1981-83; mgr. communications Sara Lee Inc., Chgo., 1983-84; sr. communications cons., practice leader William M. Mercer-Mcidinger Hansen Inc., Richmond, Va., 1985-88; ptnr. Coakley and Assocs., Richmond, Va., 1988—. Co-author: A Taste of the West from Coors, 1982. Asst. to campaign mgr. Bakalis for Gov., Chgo., 1978; reader Blind Services Assn., Chgo., 1982; tutor 4th Presbyn. Ch., Chgo., 1981-83. Mem. Internat. Assn. Bus. Communicators (Gold Quill award 1983). Democrat. Presbyterian.

MCCULLOUGH-WIGGINS, LYDIA STATORIA, pharmacist, consultant; b. Chgo., May 14, 1948; d. George Robert and Isabell (King) Boulware; m. Robert Dale McCullough, Aug. 1, 1970 (div. Oct. 1977); m. 2d, James Calvin Wiggins, Nov. 3, 1979. Student Wis. State U.-Whitewater, 1966-69; B.S. in Pharmacy, U. Ill.-Chgo., 1972; cert. UCLA, 1976-78. Registered pharmacist, Ill. Registered pharmacy apprentice Lefel Drugs, Chgo., 1971-72; pharmacy mgr. Fernwood Pharmacy, Chgo., 1972-73, Sapstein Bros. Pharmacy, Chgo., 1973-74; dir. pharmacy Martin Luther King Neighborhood Health Ctr., Chgo., 1974-80; pharmacist in charge Walgreens, Chgo., 1980—. Bd. dirs. Nia Comprehensive Ctr. Developmental Disabilities, Inc. Author: M.L.K. Drug Formulary, 1978. Recipient Cert. of Leadership, YMCA Met. Chgo., 1979; Kizzy award 1980 Black Women Hall of Fame Found., Chgo., 1981; Ann. Med. Achievement award Greater Chgo. Met. Community, 1981. Mem. Chgo. Pharmacists Assn., Am. Pharm. Assn., Ill. Pharm. Assn., Nat. Pharmacists Assn. (exec. bd.), Nat. Assn. Female Execs., U. Ill. Alumni Assn. Democrat. Baptist. Club: Christian Novice (pres. 1977-78) (Chgo.). Home: 618 S Marshall St Bellwood IL 60104

MCCULLY, RUTH ALIDA, educator; b. Port Huron, Mich., Feb. 13, 1933; d. Leon Eugene Lounsberry and Rachel Elizabeth (DeSerano) Lounsberry-Maser; m. Donald Cecil McCully, Feb. 8, 1952; children: Stephen Donald, Robert Leon, Julie Ann. BS, Ea. Mich. U., 1976, MA, 1980. Asst. children's librarian Monroe County Library, Mich., 1962-64; dir. Weekday Nursery Sch., Youngstown, Ohio, 1964-71; dir. children's programs Lake-in-the-Woods, Ypsilanti, Mich., 1974-76; tchr. 1st grade Dundee Community Schs., Mich., 1976—. Lay speaker Ann Arbor Dist., United Meth. Ch., 1979—; chmn. Dundee Community Caring and Sharing, 1982—; active Monroe County Food Bank, 1983—, Dundee Interfaith Council, 1984—, Dundee Area Against Substance Abuse, 1984—. Named Woman of Yr., United Meth. Women, Dundee United Meth. Ch., 1983. Mem. NEA, Mich. Edn. Assn., Mich. Sch. Vols. Assn., Monroe County Edn. Assn., Mich. Reading Assn. Club: Dundee School Employees (sec. 1985-86). Avocations: playing piano/guitar, needlework, sketching/painting, gardening, reading. Home: 510 E Monroe St Dundee MI 48131

MCCURDY, SUSAN REPLOGLE, tax and accounting practitioner; b. Marshalltown, Iowa, Feb. 12, 1949; d. Paul Gilmore and Doris Mae (Schulz) Replogle; m. John William McCurdy, Dec. 21, 1968; children—William (dec.), Kathryn, Elizabeth. A.A., Marshalltown Community Coll., 1969, B.A., U. No. Iowa, Cedar Falls, 1970; postgrad. Iowa State U., Ames, 1980—, M.A., U. No. Iowa, 1983. With McCall Monument Co., Oskaloosa, Iowa, 1968-72; sr. sec. Grace United Meth. Ch., Marshalltown, 1971-72; exec. sec. Elim Luth. Ch., Marshalltown, 1977-80; founder, ptnr. Su McCurdy Bus. Alternatives, Marshalltown 1978—; faculty Marshalltown Community Coll., 1983—. Recipient Fisher Gov. Found. scholarship, 1968-69, Lloyd V. Douglas award U. No.Iowa, 1984. Mem. Nat. Assn. Tax Practitioners; Nat. and Iowa Bus. Edn. Assns., Accts. Assn. Iowa, Marshalltown C. of C., Nat. Assn. Female Execs., Assn. Bus. Communication, Iowa Jr. Coll. Honor Soc. (permanent mem.), Honor Soc. Bus. Majors, Kappa Delta Pi, Delta Pi Epsilon (Excellence in Research award 1984). Baptist. Home and Office: 405 E South St Marshalltown IA 50158

MCCURRY, VIRGINIA MARIE, funeral home executive; b. Brunswick, Mo., Aug. 13, 1928; d. Otto John and Bertha S. (Reigelsberger) Reichert; m. Laurance Elmo McCurry, Jan. 10, 1949; (dec. Dec. 1971); children—Gregory, Kenneth, Carolyn, Debra, Laurance, Richard, Kelly, Mark. Student pub. schs., Brunswick. Funeral dir. McCurry-Berry Funeral Home, Brunswick, 1965—. Active St. Mary's Alter Soc., Brunswick. Mem. Mo. Funeral Dirs. Assn., Nat. Funeral Dirs. Assn., TTT Soc. Democrat. Roman Catholic. Home: 309 Vine Brunswick MO 65236 Office: McCurry-Berry Funeral Home 511 W Broadway Brunswick MO 65236

MCCUTCHAN, JEAN ANNALEE, family counselor; b. Cleve., Aug. 20, 1952; d. H. Robert and Myrna Jean (Flory) Gemmer; BA, Manchester Coll., North Manchester, Ind., 1974; MA, Ball State U., Muncie, Ind., 1975; postgrad. Ind. U., South Bend, Andrews U., Berrien Springs, Mich.; cert. Human Devel. Tng. Inst., 1979, Effectiveness Tng. Inst., 1979; m. Larry J. McCutchan, Dec. 24, 1973; 1 child, Eric Daniel. Sch. psychologist Baugo-Concord-Wa-Nee Spl. Edn. Coop., Wakarusa, Ind., 1975-80, dir. spl. edn., 1980-85; family counselor Family Learning Ctr., Elkhart, Ind., 1985—; lectr. Andrews U., Berrien Springs, Mich., 1977, 80; vis. instr. Ind. U., South Bend, 1979; coordinator Elkhart (Ind.) County Pediatric/Ednl. Survey, 1978-79; mem. Elkhart County Presch. Screening Com., 1982—, coordinator, 1982-85; mem. Elkhart County Schs. Comprehensive System of Personnel Devel., 1980-85, chair., 1982-85; frequent community speaker, 1985—. Bd. dirs. H.C. Gemmer Family Christian Found., 1977—, Family Counseling Service, Elkhart County, 1980-85; mem. Elkhart County Adv. Council Children and Youth, 1979—. United Christian Missionary Soc. scholar 1970; Gt. Books scholar, 1965. Fellow Am. Orthopsychiat. Assn.; mem. Am. Assn. Counseling and Devel., Nat. Assn. Sch. Psychologists. Home: 22660 Remington Ct Elkhart IN 46514 Office: Family Learning Ctr 301 W Franklin Elkhart IN 46516

MCCUTCHEN, AUDREY JEAN, educator, counselor; b. Chgo., Mar. 23, 1942; d. Charles John and Theresa Mary (Sudlik) Walters; 1 child, Joel D. BA in Elem. Edn., Colo. State Coll., 1962; MA in Guidance and Counseling, U. Denver, 1968; MA in Mgmt., Human Relations and Orgnl. Behavior, U. Phoenix, Denver, 1984. Cert. profl. elem. edn. tchr., Colo. Tchr. Mapleton Pub. Schs., Denver, 1962-68, ednl. counselor, 1968—, counselor, adminstrv. asst., 1976-77, counselor, spl. edn. case mgr., 1979—, counselor added dist. drop out research, 1983—; assoc. Carlson Corp.-Performax System Internat., Denver, 1985—. Contbr. articles to profl. jours. Sch. liaison sch., hosp. and agy. com. Children's Hosp., Denver, 1986—; parenting instr. Mapleton Pub. Schs., 1987; counselor, parenting coordinator Unity Ch. of Denver, 1986—; bd. dirs. Northglenn City Bd. of Adjustments, 1985—; instr. Parks Jr. Coll., Denver, 1988. Mem. NEA, Colo. Edn. Assn., Mapleton Edn. Assn., Am. Assn. for Counseling and Devel., Assn. for Humastic Ednl. Devel., Colo. Counseling Inst. (counselor, bd. dirs. 1985—), Kappa Delta Pi. Republican. Roman Catholic. Home: 1283 W 103d Pl Denver CO 80221

MCCUTCHEON, LINDA ELLORIENT, publishing executive; b. Middletown, N.Y., Apr. 18, 1955; d. Edward Jay and Elorient Jane (Everett) McC.; m. Thomas J. Conneally, Mar. 22, 1986. BA, Boston U., 1977. Dir. market research Ms. Mag., N.Y.C., 1980-82; research mgr. Bus. Week, N.Y.C., 1982-84, mgr., new product devel., 1984-86; dir., N. Am. The Economist, N.Y.C., 1986—. Mem. Mag. Publisher's Assn. (mem. research com. 1980-84, 86—). Presbyterian.

MCDANIEL, AUDREY MAY, author, radio personality, nonprofit foundation executive; b. Washington, Feb. 24, 1908; d. Dwight David and Jenette Marie (Nolan) Stansell; m. Valrie Shields McDaniel, 1941; 1 child, Val. Pres. Audrey McDaniel Faith and Hope Found., Arlington, Va., 1974—; featured personality Sta.-WFAX, Falls Church, Va., and other stas., 1963—, Abiding Love, 1974—. Featured in series Faith and Life, Sta.-WRC-TV, NBC, Washington, 1973, A Christmas Rose spl., Sta.-WTKK-TV, Manassas, Va., 1982, in series Capital Life, Sta.-WTKK-TV, 1973. Author books, including: (inspirational) The Greatest of These is Love, 1962, Forget-Me-Nots of Love, 1964, Garden of Hope, 1966, God is There, 1969, A Christmas Rose, 1971, Abiding Love, 1973, Only Believe in Him, 1977, Love's Promise, 1980, Hope for Every Heart, 1986; (autobiography) Touched by the Master, 1975; author words: Hymn Gems From Sacred Memory Time, 1967. Author, narrator audiocassette: Faith, Hope and Love, 1986. Mem. Nat. League Am. Pen Women (D.C. br.) (past nat. chaplain, Disting. Pen Woman award 1979), ASCAP. Methodist. Home and Office: 5800 N 11th St Arlington VA 22205

MC DANIEL, JEANNE ADELE, school administrator; b. Battle Creek, Mich., Aug. 26, 1914; d. Arnold Herman and Viola May (Rice) Kambly; R.N., Michael Reese Hosp. Sch. Nursing, Chgo., 1935; m. Lloyd G. McDaniel, Feb. 6, 1937 (dec. 1980); children—Lloyd Kambly, Stephanie McDaniel Wirt, Patricia McDaniel Paddock. Asst. to dir. Lanham Fund Day Care Centers, Battle Creek Pub. Schs., 1945-46; dir., pres. bd. dirs. Kambly Sch. Retarded Children, Battle Creek, 1959—. Bd. dirs. Woodlawn Nursery; sponsor troop Boy Scouts Am. Mem. Michael Reese Nurses Alumnae Assn., D.A.R., Council Exceptional Children, Calhoun County Assn. Retarded Children, Beta Sigma Phi. Republican. Presbyn. Home: 115 Irving Park Dr Battle Creek MI 49017 Office: 1003 North Ave Battle Creek MI 49017

MCDANIEL, MYRA ATWELL, former state official, lawyer; b. Phila., Dec. 13, 1932; d. Toronto Canada, Jr. and Eva Lucinda (Yores) Atwell; m. Reuben Roosevelt McDaniel Jr., Feb. 20, 1955; children—Diane Lorraine, Reuben Roosevelt III. BA, U. Pa., 1954; JD, U. Tex., 1975; LLD, Huston-Tillotson Coll., 1984, Jarvis Christian Coll., 1986. Bar: Tex. 1975, U.S. Dist. Ct. (we. dist.) Tex. 1977, U.S. Dist. Ct. (so. and no. dists.) Tex. 1978, U.S. Ct. Appeals (5th cir.) 1978, U.S. Supreme Ct. 1978, U.S. Dist. Ct. (ea. dist.) Tex. 1979. Asst atty. gen. State of Tex., Austin, 1975-81, chief taxation div., 1979-81, gen. counsel to gov., 1983-84, sec. of state, 1984-87; asst. gen. counsel Tex. R.R. Commn., Austin, 1981-82; gen. counsel Wilson Cos., San Antonio and Midland, Tex., 1982; assoc. Bickerstaff, Heath & Smiley, Austin, 1984, ptnr., 1987—; mem. asset mgmt. adv. com. State Treasury, Austin, 1984-86; mem. legal affairs com. Criminal Justice Policy Council, Austin, 1984-86; mem. legal affairs com. Inter-State Oil Compact, Oklahoma City, 1984-86; bd. dirs. Austin Cons. Group, 1983-86; lectr. in field. Contbr. articles to profl. jours., chpts. to books. Del. Tex. Conf. on Libraries and Info. Scis., Austin, 1978, White House Conf. on Libraries and Info. Scis., Washington, 1979; mem. Library Services and Constrn. Act Adv. Council, 1980-84, chmn., 1983-84; mem. long range plan task force Brackenridge Hosp., Austin, 1981; clk. vestry bd. St. James Episcopal Ch., Austin, 1981-83; bd. visitors U. Tex. Law Sch., 1983—, vice chmn., 1983-85; bd. dirs. Friends of Ronald McDonald House of Cen. Tex., Women's Advocacy, Inc., Capital Area Rehab. Ctr.; trustee Episcopal Found. Tex., 1986—, St. Edward's U., Austin, 1986—; chmn. div. United Way/Capital area campaign, 1986. Recipient Tribute to 28 Black Women award Concepts Unltd., 1983; Focus on women honoree Serwa Yetu chpt. Mt. Olive grand chpt. Order of Eastern Star, 1979, Woman of Yr. Longview Metro C. of C., 1985, Woman of Yr. Austin chpt. Internat. Tng. in Communication, 1985, Citizen of Yr. Epsilon Iona chpt. Omega Psi Phi. Mem. ABA, Am. Bar Found., Tex. Bar Found. (trustee 1986—), Travis County Bar Assn., Travis County Women Lawyers' Assn., Austin Black Lawyers Assn., State Bar Tex. (chmn. Profl. Efficiency and Econ. Research subcom. 1978-84), Golden Key Nat. Honor Soc., Omicron Delta Kappa, Delta Phi Alpha, Order Coif (hon. mem.). Democrat. Home: 3910 Knollwood Dr Austin TX 78731 Office: San Jacinto Ctr Suite 1800 98 San Jacinto Blvd Austin TX 78701

MCDANIEL, SANDRA MARLENE, mental health consultant; b. Terre Haute, Ind., Feb. 20, 1939; d. Paul Allen Ellis and Clarabell (Stoneking) Reynolds; m. Theodore J. McDaniel, Feb. 20, 1960. Student, St. Mary-of-the-Woods, Ind., 1988—. Staff. advt. dept. Terre Haute (Ind.) Tribune-Star, 1956-63, J.C. Penney, Terre Haute, Ind., 1963-65; bookeeper, salesman, display Steiger's Furs, Inc., Terre Haute, Ind., 1965-73; buyer, salesman, display Wiandt's Jewelers, Inc., Terre Haute, Ind., 1973-82; salesman, display, customer relations Meis Illiana, Terre Haute, Ind., 1983; epilepsy cons. Ind. Epilepsy Service, Hamilton Ctr., Terre Haute, Ind., 1983-87. Publicity Mayoral candidate, Terre Haute, 1983, Sheriff's candidate, 1986. Mem. Chamber Health Council, Epilepsy Found. of Am., Epilepsy Awareness Groups, Am. Bass Fisherman of Ind. (pub. sec., treas. 1977-79). Democrat. Methodist. Office: Ind Epilepsy Services 500 8th Ave Terre Haute IN 47804

MCDAVID, JANET LOUISE, lawyer; b. Mpls., Jan. 24, 1950; d. Robert Matthew and Lois May (Bratt) Kurzeka; m. John Gary McDavid, June 9, 1973; 1 child, Matthew Collins McDavid. B.A., Northwestern U., 1971; J.D., Georgetown U., 1974. Bar: D.C. 1975, U.S. Supreme Ct., 1980, U.S. Ct. Appeals D.C. 1976, U.S. Ct. Appeals (5th cir.) 1983, U.S. Ct. Appeals (9th cir.), 1986. Assoc. Hogan & Hartson, Washington, 1974-83, ptnr., 1984—; gen. counsel ERAmerica, 1977-83. Contbr. articles to profl. jours. Mem. ABA (vice chmn. civil practice com. antitrust sect.), Washington Council Lawyers, D.C. Bar Assn., Fed. Bar Assn., Womens Legal Def. Fund, ACLU. Democrat. Office: Hogan & Hartson 555 13th St NW Washington DC 20004

MC DERMID, ALICE MARGUERITE CONNELL (MRS. RALPH MANEWAL MCDERMID), civic and political worker, lectr.; b. Sterling, Ill., May 25, 1910; d. William Hayes and Margaret (Durr) Connell; A.B., U. Ill., 1931; m. Ralph Manewal McDermid, Nov. 28, 1931; children—Ralph Manewal, Jane Dillon (Mrs. Anders Wiberg), Michael Metcalf, John Fairbanks. Bd. dirs. Scarsdale (N.Y.) Woman's Exchange, 1953-60; mem. social service bd. N.Y. Infirmary, 1960-76, vice chmn., 1964-76; trustees team United Hosp. Fund, 1965-75; case policy bd. Spence-Chapin Adoption Service, 1960—; fund raising Greer Sch., 1958-73, Vis. Nurse Assn., 1960-64; co-chmn. UN Program, Westchester County; founder Jane Todd Meml. Scholarship, 1966; mem. adv. council Morse Gallery of Art, Winter Park, Fla., 1974—; sec. exec. com. Morse Gallery Art Assocs., 1977-78, v.p., 1978-80, pres., 1980-82; bd. dirs. Council Arts and Scis. Central Fla., 1975-86 , v.p., 1976-78; bd. dirs. Charles Hosmer Morse Found., 1980-82. Sec., Young Republicans Ill., 1930-31; bd. dirs. Scarsdale (N.Y.) Women's Rep. Club, 1961-67, pres., 1965-67, legis. chmn., 1981—; del. Washington Conf. Nat. Fed. Rep. Women, 1965-72; mem. council Fedn. Women's Rep. Clubs N.Y. State, 1967-76; Rep. dist. leader, 1967-75; del. Rep. Jud. Conv., 1969-71; vice chmn. Rep. Town Com., 1969-75, mem. Rep. Presidents Club, Scarsdale; mem. N.Y. State Rep. Com., 1970-72; N.Y. Rep. committee woman 90th Assembly Dist., 1970-72. Recipient Rep. Woman of Yr. award, Scarsdale, 1974, other awards. Mem. Women's Rep. Federated Club of Winter Park (pres. 1978-80), Lock Haven Art Center, Friends of Winter Park Library, Winter Park Hist. Soc., English Speaking Union U.S., Town Club Winter Park, Morse Mus. Am. Art., Morse Mus. Art Assocs., Friends of Cornell Fine Arts, Loch Haven Arts Soc., Alpha Xi Delta. Episcopalian. Clubs: Scarsdale Women's, Ladies Harvard, Women's Nat. Rep. (N.Y.C.); Women's of Winter Park (dir. 1977-79), Racquet (Winter Park). Home: 1445 Granville Dr Winter Park FL 32789

MCDERMOTT, CHERYL LYNN, entertainment company executive, lawyer; b. Glendale, Calif., Dec. 28, 1953; d. Henry Lawrence McDermott and Phyllis (Markel) Grisso. Student, U. Colo., 1977-78; BA, Immaculate Heart Coll., Los Angeles, 1980; JD, Loyola U., Los Angeles, 1983. Bar: Calif., 1983. Paralegal antitrust div. Colo. Atty. Gen. Office, Denver, 1978; legal researcher MGM/UA Entertainment Co., Culver City, Calif., 1983-85, sr. contract adminstr., 1985-86; dir. internat. TV distbn. Turner Entertainment Co., Culver City, 1986—. Participant Names Project, Los Angeles, 1988. Mem. Acad. TV Arts and Scis. (blue ribbon panel for Emmy awards 1987-88), Lawyers for Human Rights. Office: Turner Entertainment Co 10100 Venice Blvd Culver City CA 92032

MCDERMOTT, ELYSA JEAN, naval officer; b. Danvers, Mass., Feb. 9, 1960; d. Harold James and Barbara (Teel) McD.; m. Thomas Ray Drillette, Sept. 1, 1985. BSE in Indsl. Engrng. cum laude, U. Mich., 1982. Designated naval aviator tactical jets. Commd. ensign USN, 1982, advanced through grades to lt., lt. tactical electronic warfare squadron, 1986—, comdr.naval air forces, hdqrs. staff, 1988—. Recipient numerous awards. Mem. U. Mich. Alumni Assn., Tail Hook Assn. Roman Catholic. Office: CNAP Code 33 NASNI San Diego CA 92135-5100

MCDERMOTT, LYNDA CARYL, managment consultant, investor; b. Columbus, Ohio, Sept. 23, 1950; d. Ned Roland and Marian Carlotta (Johnson) Green; m. William W. Waite, May 30, 1975. B.A. in Psychology, Miami U., Oxford, Ohio, 1972; M. Orgn. Devel., Bowling Green State U., 1983. Mgr. data processing Ohio Bell Telephone, Columbus and Cleve., 1972-78; cons. AT&T, Denver and N.Y.C., 1976; mgmt. cons. Ernst & Whinney, Cleve. and N.Y.C., 1978-82; dir. human resources cons. KMG Main Hurdman, N.Y.C., 1982-86; exec. v.p., prin. Corp. Resources, Inc., N.Y.C., 1986-87; chmn., chief exec. officer EquiPro Devel., Inc., 1985—; owner Sparks Tune-Up of Autopro, Inc., 1986—. Contbr. articles to profl. jours. Mem. resource com. Girls Clubs Am.; bd. dirs. Friends of the Joffrey Ballet. Mem. Am. Soc. Personnel Adminstrs., Am. Compensation Assn. (bd. dirs.), N.Y. Human Resources Planners, Am. Soc. Tng. and Devel. (dir. orgn. devel. and bd. dirs. 1977-87, treas. 1986-87, Torch award 1986), Orgn. Devel. Network. Republican. Clubs: Atrium, Saugatuck Yacht. Office: EquiPro Devel Inc 331 Madison Ave Suite 701 New York NY 10017

MCDERMOTT, PATRICIA ANN, nurse; b. Bklyn., July 10, 1943; d. John J. and Lillian E. (Sweeney) Skelly; m. Joseph Kevin McDermott, Oct. 5, 1963; children—Colleen Mary, John Joseph. Diploma, Kings County Hosp. Ctr. Sch. Nursing, Bklyn., 1963; B.S. in Health Care Adminstrn., St. Francis Coll., Bklyn., 1979. Staff nurse Kings County Hosp., Bklyn., 1963-66, head nurse outpatient dept., 1966-74; evening supr. Park Nursing Home, Rockaway Park, N.Y., 1974-83; day supr. Hyde Park Nursing Home, Staatsburg, N.Y., 1984-85, dir. nursing, 1985—; propr. retail liquor bus. Active local Girl Scouts U.S.A., 1971-78, Boy Scouts Am., 1978-82, Stella Maris Parents Club, 1978-82, St. Francis de Sales Altar and Rosary Soc., 1970-83, St. Francis de Sales Little League, 1978-80, also softball coach, 1974-77. Republican. Roman Catholic. Avocations: knitting; crocheting; roller skating; bowling; oil painting. Home: 286A Shadblow Ln Clinton Corners NY 12514 Office: Hyde Park Nursing Home Rt 9 Staatsburg NY 12580

MCDERMOTT, PATRICIA LOUISE, lawyer. d. Peter A. and Emily W. McDermott;. Student, Creighton U., 1955-56; BA in Polit. Sci., Idaho State U., 1958; JD, George Washington U., 1961, LLM in Labor Law, 1964. Bar: U.S. Dist. Ct. D.C. 1961, U.S. Ct. Appeals (D.C. cir.) 1961, U.S. Supreme Ct. 1965, Idaho 1966, U.S. Dist. Ct. (ea. dist.) Idaho 1966, U.S. Ct. Appeals (9th cir.) 1966. Mem. staff U.S. senator Frank Church, 1958-61; house counsel United Planning Orgn., Washington, 1964-65; cons. office of manpower U.S. Labor Dept., 1966; sr. ptnr. McDermott, Zollinger, Box & Olley, Pocatello, Idaho, 1966—; instr. communications law Idaho State U., 1974-77, Rocky Mountain Labor Sch., 1975, 79; speaker various schs. and orgns. Regional v.p. Idaho Young Dems., 1966-68; mem. legis. council Idaho State Legislature, 1973—, Ho. of Reps., 1968—, house minority leader, 1975-80; mem. Idaho Bicentennial Commn., 1969-77, Idaho State Commn. on Women, 1969-72, Employment Security Adv. Council, 1983—; mem. adv. bd. Idaho Alcohol Safety Commn., 1968-76; bd. dirs. State Legislature Leaders Found., 1978-80; bd. dirs. Idaho Spl. Olympics Inc., 1985-87; mem. Idaho Commn. on the Bicentennial of U.S. Constitution, 1985—. Recipient Cert. of Appreciation Assn. of Idaho Cities, 1974, Cert. of Appreciation Associated Students Idaho State U., 1975. Mem. ABA, Idaho Bar Assn. (criminal law seminar, 1971, corrections com., grading team 1975, 76, 78, 80, 82, 87), 6th Jud. Dist. Bar Assn. (sec., treas. 1968), Assn. Trial Lawyers Am., Idaho Trial Lawyers Assn., Eagleton Inst. of Politics, Idaho State U. Alumni Assn. (bd. dirs. 1972—, pres. 1976), NAACP (Martin Luther King award 1970), Pocatello Am. Legion, Idaho Fedn. Bus. and Profl. Women (Woman of Yr. 1976), Pocatello C. of C. (govtl. affairs com.), Pi Sigma Alpha, Alpha Omicron Pi. Office: McDermott Zollinger Box & Olley Box 3 Pocatello ID 83204 Other Address: 218 N 10th Pocatello ID 82301

MC DEVITT, ELLEN, physician; b. Shubuta, Miss., Sept. 3, 1907; d. James Andrew and Alma (McManus) McDevitt; A.B., Miss. State Coll. for Women, 1930; M.D., U. Utah, 1949. Chief technician vascular clinic N.Y. Post Grad. Hosp., 1934-46; intern Meadowbrook Hosp., Hempstead, N.Y., 1949-50; asst. resident Hackensack (N.J.) Hosp., 1950-51, Bellevue Hosp., N.Y.C., 1953-54; research asso. medicine N.Y. Hosp.-Cornell U. Med. Coll., 1951-52; provisional asst. physician out patient dept. N.Y. Hosp., 1951-52; mem. staff, chief 2d med. div. vascular clinic Bellevue Hosp.; instr. medicine Cornell U., 1954-56, asst. prof., 1957-63, asso. prof., 1963-72; former asso. attending N.Y. Hosp., dir. vascular sect., 1968-72, now hon. mem. med. staff. Recipient award for excellence Miss. U. for Women, 1984. Fellow Am. Soc. Geriatics; mem. AMA, Miss., East Miss. med. socs., Am. (fellow council on circulation, fellow council on stroke), N.Y., Miss. heart assns., Sigma Xi. Contbr. articles to profl. jours. Home: 1520 Olive St Gulfport MS 39501

MCDEVITT, SHEILA MARIE, energy company executive; b. St. Petersburg, Fla., Jan. 15, 1947; d. Frank Davis and Pauline (Binns) McD. AA, St. Petersburg Jr. Coll., 1966; BA in Govt., Fla. State U., 1968, JD, 1978. Bar: Fla. 1978. Research asst. Fla. Legis. Reference Bur., Tallahassee, 1968-69; adminstr., research assoc. Constitution Revision Commn. Ga. Gen. Assembly, Atlanta, 1969-70; adminstrv. asst., analyst Fla. State Sen., Tallahassee, Tampa, 1970-79; assoc. McClain, Walkley & Stuart, P.A., Tampa, Seminole, Fla., 1979-81; govtl. affairs counsel Tampa Electric Co., 1981-82, corp. counsel, 1982-86; sr. corp. counsel Teco Energy, Inc., Tampa, 1986—; mem. Worker's Compensation Adv. Council Fla. Dept. Labor, Tallahassee, 1984-86. Bd. dirs. Vol. Ctr. Hillsborough County, Tampa, 1984-85, trustee Tampa Lowry Park Zoo Soc., 1986—, also legal advisor; mem. Fla. State Rep. Exec. Com., Tallahassee, 1974-75, Hillsborough County Reps., 1974-75, transition team Fla. Gov. Bob Martinez, 1986-87. Mem. ABA, Fla. Bar (vice-chmn. then chmn. energy law com. 1984-87, jud. nominating procedures com. 1986—), Hillsborough County Bar Assn. (chmn. corp. counsel com. 1986-87), Am. Corp. Counsel Assn. (bd. dirs. Cen. Fla. chpt. 1986-87). Republican. Roman Catholic. Clubs: Centre, Tiger Bay (Tampa). Home: 105A S Lauber Way Tampa FL 33609 Office: Teco Energy Inc 702 N Franklin St Box 111 Tampa FL 33601

MCDILL, VICKI, office manager; b. Petaluma, Calif., Jan. 5, 1942; d. Victor and Dorothy (Tomasini) Bottari; m. William Cameron McDill, Mar. 30, 1963; children: Kathleen Maria, Michael Cameron, Kevin Cameron. BS, U. Calif., Davis, 1964. Sales, asst. mgr. Beverly Fabrics, Calif., 1976-79; gen. mgr. T.J. Importers, Ltd., Calif., 1979-84; office mgr. Novato Phys. Therapy Ctr., Calif., 1984—. Sec., treas. v.p. Novato (Calif.) Boys Club Aux., 1972-79; sec. bd. dirs. Novato Boys Club, 1980-85; bd. dirs. Marin Athletic Found.; pres. sec. San Marin High Sch. Athletic Booster Club, Novato, 1982—; pres., v.p., sec. San Marin High Sch. Parent Faculty Club, Novato, 1982-85. Republican. Roman Catholic. Home: 18 San Luis Ct Novato CA 95945 Office: Novato Phys Therapy Ctr 1555 Grant Ave Novato CA 94945

MCDOLE, JULIE ANN WERNER, engineering librarian; b. Massillon, Ohio, Oct. 27, 1957; d. Jerome Thomas and Suetta Aline (Miller) W. BS in polit. sci. cum laude, Vanderbilt U., 1980, MLS, 1981. Head librarian AVCO Aerostructures div. Textron, Nashville, 1982—; lectr. Vanderbilt U.; rep. Govt. Industry Data Exchange Program, Corona, Calif. Local campaign worker for Sen. Hubert Humphrey, Pres. Jimmy Carter, Sen. J. William Fulbright, Sen. George McGovern, Pres. Lyndon Johnson, 1965—; asst. to Sen. Jim Sasser, 1982. Wall scholar Vanderbilt U., 1977-80. Mem. ALA, Tenn. Library Assn., Nat. Mgmt. Assn., Beta Phi Mu. Democrat. Roman Catholic. Office: AVCO Aerostructures Div PO Box 210 Nashville TN 37202

MCDONALD, ALICE COIG, state education official; b. Chalmette, La., Sept. 26, 1940; d. Olas Casimere and Genevieve Louise (Heck) Coig; m. Glenn McDonald, July 16, 1967; 1 child, Michel. B.S., Loyola U., New Orleans, 1962; M.Ed., Loyola U., 1966; cert. rank I sch. adminstrn., Spalding Coll., 1975. Tchr. St. Bernard Pub. Schs., Chalmette, La., 1962-67; counselor, instructional coordinator Jefferson County Schs., Louisville, 1967-77; ednl. adviser Jefferson County Govt., Louisville, 1977-78; chief exec. asst. Office of Mayor, Louisville, 1978-80; dep. supt. pub. instrn. Ky. Dept. Edn., Frankfort, 1980-83, supt. pub. instrn., 1984—; bd. dirs., com. mem. Ky. Council on Higher Edn., 1984—, Ky. Juvenile Justice Com., 1984—, Ky. Ednl. TV Authority, 1984—, So. Regional Council Ednl. Improvement, 1984—. Mem. Pres.'s Adv. Com. on Women, 1978-80; active Democratic Nat. Convs., 1972, 76, 80, 84; pres. Dem. Woman's Club Ky., 1974-76 Ky. mem. Nat. Dem. Com., 1976-79, mem. exec. com. 1977—. Mem. Council Chief State Sch. Officers, Women in Sch. Adminstrn., NEA, Ky. Edn. Assn., River City Bus. and Profl. Women. Home: 6501 Gunpowder Ln Prospect KY 40059 Office: Ky Dept Edn Capital Plaza Tower 1st Floor Frankfort KY 40601

MC DONALD, BARBARA ANN, psychotherapist; b. Mpls., July 15, 1932; d. John and Georgia Elizabeth (Baker) Rubenzer; B.A., U. Minn., 1954; M.S.W., U. Denver, 1977; m. Lawrence R. McDonald, July 27, 1957; adopted children—John, Mary Elizabeth. Day care cons. Minn. Dept. Public Welfare, St. Paul, 1954-59; social worker Community Info. Center, Mpls., 1959-60; exec. dir. Social Synergistics Co., Littleton, Colo., 1970—; cons. to community orgns., Indian tribes. Family therapist , 1979—. Named 1 of 8 Women of Yr. and featured on TV spl. Ladies Home Jour., 1974; Clairol scholar, 1974; Am. Bus. Women's Assn. scholar, 1974; Alpha Gamma Delta scholar, 1974; lic. psychotherapist, Colo. Mem. Minn. Pre-Sch. Edn. Assn. (hon. life), Nat. Assn. Social Workers, Am. Bus. Women's Assn., Alpha Gamma Delta (Disting. Citizen award 1975). Club: Altrusa (hon.). Author: Selected References on the Group Day Care of Pre-School Children, 1956; Helping Families Grow: Specialized Psychotherapy with Hearing Impaired Children and Their Families, 1984. Office: 13720 Franciscan Dr Sun City West AZ 85375

MCDONALD, BARBARA BLACK ROBERTSON, packaging and product design consultant; b. N.Y.C., Mar. 7, 1951; d. Donald Black Robertson and Elizabeth Morton (Stout) McD. Student Western New Eng. Coll., 1969-70, Fashion Inst. Tech., N.Y.C., 1970-71, Sch. Visual Arts, N.Y.C., 1971-72. Designer, Unique Studios, N.Y.C., 1972-74; assoc. art dir. CBS, N.Y.C., 1974-77; creative dir. Remco Toys, N.Y.C., 1977-80; sr. design mgr. Lever Bros., N.Y.C., 1980-81; pres., owner B. McDonald, N.Y.C., 1981—. Recipient Excellence award Nat. Paperbox and Packaging Assn., 1987. Mem. Graphic Artists Guild, Package Designers Council (award of excellence 1979, 80), Internat. Platform Assn., N.Y.C. C. of C., Nat. Assn. Female Execs. Democrat. Avocations: wind surfing; racquetball; canoeing; writing; reading. Office: 1123 Broadway Suite 817 New York NY 10010

MC DONALD, COLLEEN, social work administrator; b. Duluth, Minn., Mar. 17, 1950; d. Thomas Joseph and Lillian Clara (Hedlund) Mc Donald. B.F.A., U. Wis., 1973; MS in Urban Affairs, Hunter Coll., 1987. Adminstrv. asst. British Steel Corp., London, 1973-75, CBS News, N.Y.C., 1976-77; coordinator CBS, Inc. Sch. of Mgmt., N.Y.C., 1977-81; social worker, supr. Westside Cluster, N.Y.C., 1981-83, project dir. Ctr. for Homeless Women, 1983—; mem. Coalition for Homeless, N.Y.C., 1981—, speaker, 1984—. Founding mem. Com. for Women in Crisis, N.Y.C., 1986; mem. Ansonia Dems., N.Y.C., 1985, West 71st St. Assn., N.Y.C., 1986. Democrat. Office: Westside Cluster 257 W 30th St New York NY 10001

MCDONALD, COLLEEN ANNE, infosystems specialist; b. Ogden, Utah, Oct. 16, 1957; d. Robert Louis McDonald and Loyce Joyce (Froberg) Deely; m. Timothy Howard Gegax, Mar. 18, 1978 (div. Sept. 1982); m. John R. Koven. Student, Ind. Cen. U., 1977-83. Mgr. computer dept. Cord, Frick, Wilson & Assocs. CPA, Indpls., 1980-81, Stephen R. Frick, CPA, Indpls., 1981-83; data processing coordinator Komputrol, Cicero, Ind., 1983—. Office: Komputrol 126 W Jackson St Cicero IN 46034

MCDONALD, GABRIELLE ANNE KIRK, judge; b. St. Paul, Apr. 12, 1942; d. James G. and Frances R. Kirk; m. Mark T. McDonald; children: Michael, Stacy. LLB, Howard U., 1966. Bar: Tex. 1966. Staff atty. NAACP Legal Def. and Ednl. Fund, N.Y.C., 1966-69; ptnr. McDonald & McDonald, Houston, 1969-79; judge U.S. Dist. Ct., Houston, 1979—; asst. prof. Tex. So. U., Houston, 1970, adj. prof., 1975-77; lectr. U. Tex., Houston, 1977-78. Bd. dirs. Community Service Option Program; bd. dirs. Alley Theatre, Houston, Nat. Coalition of 100 Black Women, ARC; trustee Howard U., from 1983; bd. vistors Thurgood Marshall Sch. Law, Houston. Mem. ABA, Nat. Bar Assn., Houston Bar Assn., Houston Lawyers Assn., Black Women Lawyers Assn. Democrat. Congregationalist. Office: US Dist Ct 9535 US Courthouse 515 Rusk Ave Houston TX 77002 *

MCDONALD, JACKIE LANELL, adminstrative assistant; b. Plainview, Tex., Aug. 16, 1961; d. Harlan Ulysses and Laverne Nell (Howard) Wallingsford; m. Donny Wayne McDonald, Nov. 16, 1979. Grad. high sch., Plainview, Tex. Sec. Wicks & Lee Law Firm, Ralls, Tex., 1979-82; adminstrv. asst. Triumph Seed Co., Ralls, Tex., 1983—. Sec. Ralls Sesquicentennial com., 1984-86. Fellow Nat. Notary Assn.; mem. Ralls Young Homemakers of Tex. (pres. 1983-84, 85-86), Region I Young Homemakers of Tex. (pres. 1985-86). Democrat. Baptist. Home: 1705 North Ave I Box 1048 Ralls TX 79357 Office: Triumph Seed Co Inc Hwy 62 Bypass Box 1050 Ralls TX 79357

MCDONALD, JANE FRANCES, insurance company executive; b. Winthrop, Mass., Dec. 19, 1940; d. William Francis and Isabelle Frances (Mythen) Moran; m. James Joseph McDonald, Aug. 21, 1965 (div. 1976); children—Maureen Lynn, Susan Jill, Kevin James. B.S. in Edn., Salem State Coll., Mass., 1962; Assoc. in Underwriting, Ins. Inst., Malvern, Pa., 1983. Tchr., East Hartford Sch. System, Conn., 1962-66; acct. Watkin Bros. Piano & Organ, Hartford, 1975-76; policy analyst Hartford Steam Boiler Insp. & Ins., 1976-80, supervising underwriter Am. Nuclear Insurers, Farmington, 1981—. Mem. Nat. Assn. Ins. Women (cert.), Am. Nuclear Soc., Nat. Assn. Female Execs., N.Y. Acad. Scis., Hartford Assn. Ins. Women (by-laws chmn. 1984-85), Hartford Women's Network. Democrat. Roman Catholic. Avocations: reading, handwriting analysis, travel, crewel embroidery. Home: 675 Graham Rd South Windsor CT 06074 Office: Am Nuclear Insurers 270 Farmington Ave Farmington CT 06032

MCDONALD, JEWEL, cosmetics distributing company executive; b. Jackson, Miss., Jan. 15, 1946; d. Ambrogers and Florence (Ward) McD. BS, U. Hawaii, 1981. Mgr. Whitmore Restaurant, Honolulu, 1977-79; security officer Pearlbridge Shopping Ctr., Aiea, Hawaii, 1979-81; tchr. social studies Waianai (Hawaii) High Sch., 1981-83, owner Jewel's Hair and Beauty Aids Distbrs., Honolulu, 1983—. Mem. Afro-Am. Assn. (corr. sec. Honolulu chpt. 1985—). Lodge: Eastern Star. Home: 2215 Aloha Dr Apt 6K Honolulu HI 96815 Office: Jewel's Hair and Beauty Aids Distbr 1088 Bishop St Suite 1005 Honolulu HI 96813

MCDONALD, JOANNE, high technology company executive; b. San Diego, June 10, 1947; d. Paul and Dolores (Paganucci) McD. B.A., U. Md., 1970. High tech. exec. ENSCO Inc., Springfield, Va., 1981—. Bd. dirs. Yorktowne Sq., Falls Church, Va., 1981. Mem. Am. Soc. Tng. and Devel., Internat. Assn. Personnel Women, Am. Soc. Personnel Adminstrs., Internat. Assn. Bus. Communicators. Office: ENSCO Inc 5400 Port Royal Rd Springfield VA 22151

MCDONALD, KAY, controller; b. Mpls., May 7, 1952; d. John Clark and Inez Joan (Weber) McD.; 1 child, Marcus John. BS, St. Lawrence U., 1974; MEd, Boston U., 1975; MBA, Rivier Coll, 1984. Dir. Alcohol Rehab. Ctr., Framingham, Mass., 1975-78; personnel mgr. Prestolite Wire and Cable, Hudson, Mass., 1978-79; EEO mgr. Sanders Assocs., Nashua, N.H., 1979-81, coordinator, coll. recuriter, 1981-83, program adminstr., 1983-85; controller, ops. mgr. The Mumps Collaborative, Inc., Newton, Mass., 1985—; prof. MBA program Rivier Coll., Nashua, 1984-85. Mem. Small Bus. Assn., Newton C. of C. Greater Boston Track, New Eng. Bike (Boston). Home: 57 Kennedy Dr North Chelmsford MA 01863 Office: The Mumps Collaborative Inc 246 Walnut St Newton MA 02160

MCDONALD, LYNN, Canadian legislator; b. New Westminster, B.C., July 15, 1940; d. Robert Stevenson and Mary Alice (Eakins) McD. Ed. U. B.C., London Sch. Econs. Mem. Can. House of Commons 1982—; pres. Can. Nat. Action Com. on the Status of Women, 1979-81. Mem. Can. Sociology and Anthropology Assn. Mem. New Dem. Party. Office: House of Commons, Centre Block Room 653D, Ottawa, ON Canada K1A 0A6 *

MCDONALD, MARIANNE, classicist; b. Chgo., Jan. 2, 1937; d. Eugene Francis and Inez (Riddle) McD.; children: Eugene, Conrad, Bryan, Bridget, Kirstie, Hiroshi. BA magna cum laude, Bryn Mawr Coll., 1958; M.A., U. Chgo., 1960; Ph.D., U. Calif., Irvine, 1975. Teaching asst. classics U. Calif., Irvine, 1972-74, instr. Greek, Latin and English, mythology, modern cinema, 1975-79, researcher Thesaurus Linguae Graecae Project, 1979—; dir. Centrum. Bd. dirs. Am. Coll. of Greece, 1981—, Scripps Hosp., 1981; Am. Sch. Classical Studies, 1986— ; ; mem. bd. overseers U. Calif. San Diego, 1985—; nat. bd. advisors Am. Biog. Inst., 1982—. Recipient Ellen Browning Scripps Humanitarian award, 1975; Disting. Service award U. Calif.-Irvine, 1982, Medal, 1987; named Philanthropist of Yr. Honorary Nat. Conf. Christians and Jews, 1986. Mem. Am. Philol. Assn., Am. Classical League, Philol. Assn. Pacific Coast, MLA, Am. Comparative Lit. Assn., Modern and Classical Lang. Assn. So. Calif., AAUP, Hellenic Soc., Calif. Fgn. Lang. Tchrs. Assn., Internat. Platform Assn. Republican. Greek Orthodox. Clubs: KPBS Producers, Hellenic Univ. (dir.). Author: Terms for Happiness in Euripides, 1978; Semilemmatized Concordances to Euripides' Alcestis, 1977; Cyclops, Andromache, Medea, 1978; Heraclidae, Hippolytus, 1979; Hecuba, 1982; Euripides in Cinema: The Heart Made Visible, 1983; Hercules Furens, 1984, Electra, 1985, Ion, 1985; translator: The Cost of Kindness and Other Fabulous Tales (Shinichi Hoshi), 1986; contbr. numerous articles to profl. jours. Home: Box 929 Rancho Santa Fe CA 92067 Office: U Calif Thesaurus Linguae Gracae Project Irvine CA 92717

MCDONALD, PEGGY ANN STIMMEL, automobile company official; b. Darbyville, Ohio, Aug. 25, 1931; d. Wilbur Smith and Bernice Edna (Hott) Stimmel; missionary diploma with honor Moody Bible Inst., 1952; B.A. cum laude in Econs. (scholar), Ohio Wesleyan U., 1965; M.B.A. with distinction, Xavier U., 1977; m. George R. Stich, Mar. 7, 1953 (dec.); 1 son, Mark Stephen (dec.); m. Joseph F. McDonald, Jr., Feb. 1, 1986. . Missionary in S. Am., Evang. Alliance Mission, 1956-61; cost acct. Western Electric Co., 1965-66; acctg. mgr. Ohio Wesleyan U., 1966-73; fin. specialist NCR Corp., 1973-74, systems analyst, 1974-75, supr. inventory planning, 1975, mgr. material planning and purchasing control, 1976-78; materials mgr. U.S. Elec. Motors Co., 1978, with Gen. Motors Corp., 1978—, shift supt. materials, Lakewood, Ga., 1979-80, gen. ops. supr. material data base mgmt. Central Office, Warren, Mich., 1980, dir. material mgmt. Gen. Motors Truck and Bus. div., Balt., 1980-87; vis. lectr. Inst. Internat. Trade, Jiao Tong U., Shanghai, China, 1985, Inst. Econs. and Fgn. Trade, Tianjin, China, 1986-87; part time instr. Towson (Md.) State U., 1986-87. Mem. Am. Prodn. and Inventory Control Soc., Am. Soc. Women Accts., AAUW, Balt. Exec. Women's Network, Balt. Council on Fgn. Relations, Baptist. Home: 125 Arbutus Ave Baltimore MD 21228 Office: Gen Motors Truck and Bus 2122 Broening Hwy PO Box 148 Baltimore MD 21203

MCDONALD, PENNY S(UE), educational administrator; b. Portland, Oreg., May 1, 1946; d. Norman James and Edna (Kaufmann) McD. BA, Oreg. State U., 1968, MEd, 1974; EdD, Portland State U./U. Oreg., 1981, Harvard U., summer 1987. Tchr. English, Fleming Jr. High Sch., Los Angeles, 1968-69; tchr. lang. arts and social studies Highland View Jr. High Sch., Corvalis, Oreg., 1970-72; tchr. English, dir. student activities Crescent Valley High Sch., Corvallis, 1973-78; grad. asst. Portland State U., Oreg., 1978-80; evaluation intern N.W. Regional Edn. Lab., Portland, 1980; Nat. Inst. Edn. assoc., edn. policy fellow Nat. Commn. on Excellence in Edn., Washington, 1981-83; prin. Inza R. Wood Middle Sch., West Linn Sch. Dist., Wilsonville, Oreg., 1983-88; adminstr. in residence for ednl. adminstrn. Lewis & Clark Coll., Portland, 1988—; cons. Oreg. Dept. Edn., 1980-81; sr. counselor Oreg. Assn. Student Councils Camps, 1976-78, 80; adj. prof. ednl. adminstrn. Lewis & Clark Coll., 1987-88. Named to Outstanding Young Woman Am., U.S. Jaycees; AFL-CIO scholar Oreg. State U., Corvallis, 1964; Univ. scholar Oreg. State U., 1965-68; nat. Alpha Delta Pi scholar Oreg. State U., 1967-68; Delta Kappa Gamma scholar Portland State U./U. Oreg. 1979-81. Mem. Nat. Assn. Student Councils, Oreg. Assn. Activities Advisors (chmn. 1976-77, bd. dirs. 1977-78), Oreg. Assn. Student Councils, Confedn. Oreg. Sch. Adminstrs. (curriculum commn. 1985-86, asst. chmn., sec. 1986-87, chmn. 1987-88, ex-officio mem. exec. bd. 1987-88), Nat. Assn. Secondary Sch. Prins., N.W. Women in Ednl. Adminstrn., Am. Ednl. Research Assn., Nat. Sch. Pub. Relations Assn., Assn. Supervision and Curriculum Devel., Edn. Policy Fellowship Alumnae, Oregon Assn. Secondary Sch. Admintrs., Delta Kappa Gamma (chpt. rec. sec.), Phi Delta Kappa. Democrat. Office: Lewis & Clark Coll Grad Sch Profl Studies Ednl Adminstrn Program Portland OR 97219

MCDONALD, PRISCILLA ANN, nurse, educator; b. New Brunswick, N.J., Sept. 15, 1953; d. John Sherlock and Louise Bertha (Marcks) Hilman; m. Francis Leo McDonald, June 24, 1978; children—Elizabeth Louise, Colleen Ann. B.S., Salve Regina Coll., 1975; M.A., Central Mich. U., 1980; M of Nursing in Gerontology U. Mass.-Amherst, 1988. Staff nurse Med. Coll. Va., Richmond, 1975-76; staff nurse Queens Med. Ctr., Honolulu, 1978; pub. health nurse Upjohn Home Health Agy., Honolulu, 1979-80; staff nurse Hardin Meml. Hosp., Kenton, Ohio, 1981; charge nurse Hardin County Home, Kenton, 1982, Poet Seat Nursing Home, Greenfield, Mass., 1983; instr. clin. nursing Greenfield Community Coll., 1983-87; clin. nurse specialist gerontology VA Med. Ctr., Northampton, Mass. Vol. sch. nurse Holy Trinity Nursery Sch., Greenfield, 1983-84; vol. nurse YMCA Health Clinic, Greenfield, 1983; sec.-treas. New Eng. Fedn. Coll. Republicans, Boston, 1973-75; sec. Ohio No. U. Law Wives and Assocs., Ada, 1982-83; vol. mgr. Girl Scouts U.S.A., Hardin County, Ada, 1981-82; bd. dirs. Franklin County Home Care Corp., 1984—. Served to lt. (j.g.) USN, 1976-78; elected to sch. com. Town of Greenfield, 1987—. Mem. Am. Nurses

Assn. (mem. com. on gerontol. nursing 1986), Mass. Nurses Assn. (nominations com. 1987-88), Res. Officers Assn. Democrat. Roman Catholic. Home: PO Box 295 62 Peabody Ln Greenfield MA 01302 Office: Greenfield Community Coll Dept Nursing College Dr Greenfield MA 01302

MCDONALD, REBECCA ANN, natural gas company executive; b. Phoenix, June 14, 1952; d. William Robert and Regenia Lucille (Hall) Kennedy; m. James Phillip Hurst, Jan. 19, 1974 (div. Oct. 1975); m. John Edward McDonald Sr., May 26, 1977; 1 child, John Edward Jr. BS, Stephen F. Austin State U., 1973. Project procurement mgr., buyer Fluor Engrs. and Constructors, Houston, 1974-79; pvt. practice cons. Houston, 1979-81; devel. mgr. Panhandle Ea. Pipeline, Houston, 1981-82, mgr. customer relations, 1982-84, mgr. sales, 1984-85; mgr. gas sales Panhandle Trading Co., Houston, 1985-88, v.p., gen. mgr., 1988—; cert. power trainer Situation Mgmt. Systems, Plymouth, Mass., 1981—. Bd. trustees The Chinquapin Sch., Highlands, Tex., 1986—; mem. Houston Jr. Forumm, 1986—. Mem. Natural Gas Men of Houston, Am. Soc. of Tng. and Devel. (membership chair 1975-76, most valuable mem. award 1976). Episcopalian. Clubs: River Oaks Luncheon, Profl. Women's Breakfast. Office: Panhandle Trading Co 24 Greenway Plaza Houston TX 77005

MCDONALD, ROSA NELL, federal research and indirect budgets manager; b. Boley, Okla., Feb. 12, 1953; d. James and Beatrice Irene (Hayes) McD. BS., Calif. State U.-Long Beach, 1975; M.B.A., Calif. State U.-Dominquez Hills, 1980, also postgrad. Acct., The Aerospace Corp., El Segundo, Calif., 1976-77; analytical accountant, 1977-79, budget analyst, 1979-81, sr. budget analyst, 1981-84, budget adminstr., 1984-86, mgr. indirect budgets, 1986—. Vol., Youth Motivation Task Force, El Segundo, 1980—, Holiday Project, El Segundo, 1984, 85. Recipient Adminstrn. Group Achievement award The Aerospace Corp., 1985, Robert Herndon Image award, 1988; named Woman of Yr, Aerospace Corp., 1987. Mem. Am. Bus. Woman's Assn., Nat. Assn. Female Execs., Beta Gamma Sigma. Democrat. Avocations: dancing; aerobics; reading; contests. Office: 2350 E El Segundo Blvd M3 364 El Segundo CA 90245

MCDONALD, RUTH DUNCAN, pianist, educator; b. St. Joseph, Mo., May 26, 1921; d. Harry E. and Muriel G. (Hockett) Duncan; B.Mus., Kansas City (Mo.) Conservatory Music, 1942; grad. diploma Juilliard Sch. Music, 1946; m. Patrick Sandys, Aug. 11, 1948; children—Patricia, Karen, Michael; m. 2d, Charles McDonald, Feb. 19, 1966. Concert tours, 1950-55; jazz pianist, Montgomery, Ala., 1956-57, Roosevelt Hotel, Jacksonville, Fla., 1957-60, DeSoto Hotel, Savannah, Ga., 1960-64, Dinkler Hotel, Atlanta, 1964, Hilton Inn, Atlanta, 1965; mem. faculty Ga. State U., Atlanta, 1966—, asst. prof. piano, 1971-77, assoc. prof. piano, 1977-86, prof., 1986—, coordinator Internat. Congress on Women in Music, 1986; performed at Keele U., U. Sussex (Eng.), 1978, Internat. Piano Workshop, Honolulu, 1981, Innsbruck, Austria, 1982. Mem. Nat. Fedn. Music Clubs (state student adviser, audition chmn.), AAUP (Internat. Women's Year award in performing arts 1975), Music Educators Nat. Conf., Mu Phi Epsilon. Author articles; pianist tapes for blind students; performed N.Y. premier of Meyer Kupferman Sonata, 1976, Am. Women Composers in Mexico City, 1984; also rec. performed Am. music Wigmore Hall, London, 1977. Home: 751 Briar Park Ct Atlanta GA 30306 Office: Ga State Univ University Plaza Atlanta GA 30302

MCDONALD, SAMMANTHA LYNNE MARIE HAYWARD, customer service official; b. Pasadena, Calif., Nov. 18, 1949; d. Louis George and Ethelyn Georgia (Hale) Nichols; A.S., San Diego Mesa Coll., 1976; B.B.A., Nat. U., 1980, M.B.A., 1983; m. Jerry Boone McDonald, July 31, 1983; 1 dau., Nicole Charise. Customer info. rep. San Diego Gas and Electric, 1970-72, 1974-80, customer info. analyst, 1980-81, customer service supr. Beach Cities Dist. Office, 1981-85, regional customer tng. supr. No. Region, 1985-86, applications analyst consumer database design project, 1986—. Seminar leader, trainer Energy Speakers Corps, 1980—; mem. adv. bd. Women's Opportunity Week, publicity chmn., 1985, chair, 1986-87. Mem. citizens adv. com. Sandburg Elem. Sch., San Diego, 1974-75, v.p., 1974, pres., 1975; area coordinator San Diego Sch. Bond Election, 1974. Recipient Sch. Citizens Adv. Com. Service award San Diego City Schs., 1975, Woman of Achievement award, 1985-87, Spl. Commendation San Diego City Council, 1986-87. Mem. Mira Mesa Scripps Ranch C. of C. (bd. dirs., membership chmn., pres. 1985), Rancho Penasquitos C. of C., Am. Mgmt. Assn. Democrat. Mem. editorial bd. Women's Basic Tng. Manual, 1981-82. Home: 13530 Longfellow Ln San Diego CA 92129 Office: San Diego Gas & Electric PO Box 1831 San Diego CA 92112

MCDONNELL, KATHLEEN MARIE, sales executive; b. London, Eng., May 16, 1947; d. John Joseph and Mary Bridget (Lunney) McDonnell; A.S. in mktg., Westchester Community Coll., 1967. With W.T. Grant Co., various locations, 1963-70, asst. buyer N.Y. Office, 1970-71, buyer, 1971-76; v.p. Mothercare Stores Inc., 1976-81; dir. Merchandising Borg Textile, 1981-82; v.p. sales and mktg. First Phillips Mfg. Co., Sunbury, Pa., 1983—, mgr. nat. sales Playskool Baby, Northvale, N.J. 1984—. Home: 6 Westward Pl Elmsford NY 10523 Office: Playskool Baby Northvale NJ 07647

MC DONNELL, LORETTA WADE, educator; b. San Francisco, May 31, 1940; d. John H. and Helen M. (Tinney) Wade; B.A., San Francisco Coll. for Women, 1962; M.A., Stanford U., 1963; grad. Coro Pub. Affairs Tng. Program for Women, 1976; m. John L. McDonnell, Jr., Apr. 27, 1963 (div.); children—Elizabeth, John L. III, Thomas. High sch. tchr. East Side Union High Sch. Dist., San Jose, Calif., 1962-63; project coordinator Inter Agency Collaboration Effort, Oakland, Calif., 1977—; legal asst. Pacific Gas and Electric Co., 1980—. Bd. dirs. Carden Redwood Sch., 1975-77, St. Paul's Sch., 1974-75; budget panelist United Way of Bay Area, 1975-77; community v.p. Jr. League, 1976-77, nat. conv. del., 1976; bd. dirs. Alameda County Vol. Bur., 1973-74; chmn. speakers panel Focus on Am. Women, 1973-74. Mem. Jr. League of Oakland-East Bay, Inc., Stanford Alumni. Democrat. Roman Catholic. Clubs: Stanford San Francisco Luncheon, Commonwealth. Assoc. editor The Antiphon, 1971-74.

MCDONNELL, MARY THERESA, travel service executive; b. N.Y.C., Nov. 9, 1949; d. John J. and Mary B. (Lunney) McD. Mgr. Kramer Travel Agy., WHite Plains, N.Y., 1967-79; owner, mgr. New Trends Travel, Rye, N.Y., 1979—. Office: New Trends Travel Ltd 55 Purchase St Rye NY 10580

MCDONOUGH, MAMIE, public relations executive; b. Plainfield, N.J., Mar. 24, 1952; d. Peter J. and Elizabeth (Driscoll) McD. BA, Elmira Coll., 1974. Protocol asst. U.S. Dept. State, Washington, 1974-75; staff asst. Office of U.S. V.P., Washington, 1975-77; dir. info. service Rep. Nat. Com., Washington, 1977-79; pres. Festive Occasions, Inc., Washington, 1979-81; staff asst. Office of Dep. Chief of Staff The White House, Washington, 1981-82; sr. ptnr. Britt-McDonough Assocs., Washington, 1982-86; owner The McDonough Group, Washington, 1986—; Co-author, developer Student/Corp. Jr. Bd. Dirs. Program, 1984. Admissions rep. Washington area Elmira Coll., 1975-76; bd. dirs. Jr. League Washington, 1977—, Camp Fire Boys and Girls, Washington area, 1985—; mem. fin. com. various Rep. congl. campaigns, 1979—; corp. bd. Vanderbilt Mus., 1985—. Recipient Outstanding Service award Camp Fire Council, 1986. Roman Catholic. Office: 2555 M St NW Washington DC 20037

MCDONOUGH, STACY JEAN, graphics designer, broadcast executive; b. Bklyn., Sept. 3, 1955; d. Eugene Hanson and Helen Porter (Bell) McD. Cert., Katharine Gibbs Sch., 1977; AA, Suffolk County Community Coll., Selden, N.Y., 1977; BFA, N.Y. Inst. Tech., Old Westbury, N.Y., 1978. Assoc. producer High Bar Prodns., N.Y.C., 1979-80; freelance electronic graphics designer N.Y.C., 1979-83; electric graphics designer, computer graphics designer Nat. Broadcasting Co., Inc., N.Y.C., 1980-86, mgr. prodn. services for Olympics, 1987—. Mem. Nat. Acad. Arts and Scis. Office: Nat Broadcasting Co Inc TV 30 Rockerfeller Plaza Room 501 W New York NY 10112

MCDONOUGH, SUSAN EDITH, private school administrator, consultant; b. Quincy, Mass., July 22, 1944; d. James Edward and Edith Elizabeth (Fekkes) Egan; m. William J. McDonough, Oct. 8, 1977; children: James Edward Dickman, Peter Martin Dickman. Diploma in Nursing, Quincy Hosp. Sch. Nursing, 1965; cert. in teaching, Montessori Tchr.'s Edn. Inst. New Eng., 1983; MEd, Antioch New Eng. Grad. Sch., 1984. RN, cert. tchr., Mass. Nurse operating room Quincy City Hosp., 1965-66, Hale Hosp., Haverhill, Mass., 1966-68; head nurse Brackbill Assocs., Georgetown, Mass., 1968-71; Montessori tchr. North Shore Children's House, Danvers, Mass., 1971-73; founder, head of sch. Harborlight Montessori Sch., Beverly, Mass., 1973—; cons., lectr. Sch. Mgmt. Services, Beverly, 1980—; treas. North Shore Gifted and Talented Edn., Beverly, 1984-85. First pres. North Shore Mid. Sch., Beverly, 1977-78; fin. chairperson Sinfonie by the Sea, Beverly, 1984-85, pres., 1985—. Mem. Assn. Montessori Internationale, Am. Montessori Soc., Montessori Schs. Mass. (pres. 1985—), Nat. Assn. Edn. Young Children, North Am. Montessori Tchr.'s Assn., Educators Soc. Responsibility. Mem. Unitarian Ch. Club: Bass River Tennis (Beverly). Home: 55 Abbott St Beverly MA 01915 Office: Harborlight Montessori Sch 243 Essex St Beverly MA 01915

MCDOUGALL, BARBARA JEAN, Canadian government official; b. Toronto, Ont., Can., Nov. 12, 1937; d. Robert James and Margaret Jean (Dryden) Leamen; m. Peter McDougall, Sept. 6, 1963 (dec.). B.A., U. Toronto. V.p. A.E. Ames and Co. Ltd.; mgr. Portfolio Investment N.W. Trust Co.; v.p. Dominion Securities Ames Ltd.; mem. Can. Ho. of Commons, Ottawa, Ont., 1984—, minister of state for fin., 1984-86, minister of state for privatization, 1986—; minister responsible for status of women, minister responsible for regulatory affairs 1986—, minister of employment and immigration, 1988—; investment analyst Odlum Brown Ltd.; market research analyst Toronto Star Ltd.; econ. analyst Can. Imperial Bank of Commerce. Fin. columnist Chatelaine mag.; fin. commentator CBC Take 30; bus. columnist City Woman mag.; bus. journalist CITV Edmonton, Vancouver Sun. Chmn. City of Toronto Salvation Army 1984 Red Shield Appeal; bd. dirs. Community Occupational Therapy Assocs., chmn., 1982-84; bd. dirs. Enoch Turner Schoolhouse; counsellor Oakhalla Province Prison for Women; vice chmn. Elizabeth Fry Soc.; past pres. Rosedale Progressive Conservative Assn. Office: House of Commons, Ottawa, ON Canada K1A 0A6

MCDOW, HOLLY ANNE, field engineer; b. Portsmouth, Va., Oct. 28, 1953; d. Louis Anthony and Joanne Marie (Fox) Socorso; A.A., Seminole Jr. Coll., 1973; student Fla. Tech. U., 1974, Hinds Jr. Coll., 1976; B.S., Middle Tenn. State U., 1979; m. B. David McDow, Dec. 28, 1977. Chief chemist Tenn. Oil & Refining, Portland, 1979-80; tech. rep. Recra Environ. & Health Scis., Nashville, 1980-81, ind. cons. oil re-refining, Nashville, 1981; mgr. mktg. Gulf Coast ops., Canonie Environ. Services, Houston, 1981-82; prin., oil recycling cons. H.A. Assocs., Houston, 1982-84; field engr. Hewlett Packard Analytical Instruments, Tulsa, 1984—. Mem. ASTM (vice chmn. P-VI and P III of subcom. P 1979-84, sec. subcom. P 1983-84), Nat. Assn. Female Execs., ACS (sec. Tulsa sect. 1987—), Internat. Platform Assn., Beta Beta Beta. Republican. Contbr. articles to profl. jours. Office: 6655 S Lewis Suite 105 Tulsa OK 74136

MCDOWELL, CECELIA MARIE, human resources administrator; b. Jacksonville, Fla., Aug. 8, 1952; d. Henry Welburn and Joyce Annette (Remion) McD. Cert., U. Ga., 1969; BS in Psychology and Spl. Edn., Armstrong State Coll., Savannah, Ga., 1972. Cert. in employee relations law. Asst. to v.p. Hilton Head (S.C) Co., 1972; land clk. Sea Pines Plantation Co., Hilton Head Island, 1972; asst. to account supr. Palmetto Elec. Co-op., Ridgeland, S.C., 1972-75; employment interviewer dept. labor State of Ga., Savannah, 1975-79; supr. employment adminstrn. Gulfstream Aerospace Corp., Savannah, 1979-87, supr. human resources, 1987—; Co-owner Easy-Does-It Mobile Home Service, Savannah, 1984-86, Rayce Enterprises, Savannah, 1984-86. Mem. adv. council Savannah Area Vo-Tech. Sch., 1981-87, Beaufort Jasper Career Ctr., Ridgeland, 1982—, Savannah Displaced Homemakers Program, 1981—; sec. Chatham Savannah Humane Soc., 1982—; instr. Ga. State Dept. Edn., 1983, Savannah Women in Mgmt. program, 1984; presenter Hodge Found., Savannah, 1894-85; trustee Savannah Tech. Found., 1987—. Mem. Am. Soc. Personnel Adminstrs., Internat. Mgmt. Council, Gulfstream Mgmt. Assn. Republican. Lutheran. Home: 608 E 49th St Savannah GA 31405 Office: Gulfstream Aerospace Corp Box 2206 D-03 Savannah GA 31402-2206

MCDOWELL, DONNA SCHULTZ, lawyer; b. Cin., Apr. 23, 1946; d. Robert Joseph and Harriet (Parronchi) Schultz; m. Dennis Lon McDowell, June 20, 1970; children—Dawn Megan, Donnelly Lon. B.A. with honors in English, Brandeis U., 1968; M.Ed., Am. U., 1972; C.A.S.E. with honors, Johns Hopkins U., 1979; J.D. with honors, U. Md., 1982. Bar: Md. 1982. Instr., Anne Arundel & Prince George's Community Coll., Severna Park and Largo, Md., 1977-78; coll. adminstr. Bowie State Coll. (Md.), 1978-79; assoc. Miller & Bortner, Lanham, Md., 1982-83; sole practice, Lanham, 1983-87; ednl. cons. Chmn. Housing Hearing Com., Bowie, 1981-83; trustee Unitarian-Universalist Ch., Silver Spring, Md., 1979-83; bd. dirs. New Ventures, Bowie, 1983, Second Mile (Runaway House), Hyattsville, Md., 1983. Recipient Am. Jurisprudence award U. Md., 1981. Mem. ABA, Assn. Trial Lawyers Am., Md. Trial Lawyers Assn., Prince George's Bar Assn. Democrat. Club: Soroptimist. Home and Office: 24308 Hipsley Mill Rd Gaithersburg MD 20879

MCDOWELL, DOTTIE ALICE, personnel director; b. Phila., Sept. 4, 1934; d. William E. and Helen (Maire) Delk; m. Jerry Luciano, Sept. 5, 1950 (dec. 1964); children: Terry Anne, Shelly Anne, Gerald Joseph; m. Donald B. McDowell, Dec. 31, 1966. BA, Orange Coast Coll., Costa Mesa, Calif., 1966; grad. in bus., Westminster Coll., Orange, Calif., 1968. Mgr. Tempo Temporary Help, Irvine, Calif., 1967-74; personnel mgr. Thiokol Corp., Logan, Utah, 1977-79, Herff-Jones Yearbook, Logan, 1979-81; personnel mgr., buyer Logan Mfg. Co., 1981—; cons. Bus. Dept. Utah State U., Logan, 1982-84, Logan Bd. Edn., 1982-85; speaker Utah Bus. Women's Assn., Logan, 1983-85. Campaigner Logan Rep. Women, 1985. Recipient letter and plaque, Am. March of Dimes, Logan, 1985. Mem. Am. Soc. Personnel Adminstrs. (v.p. 1983-84, pres. 1982-83, plaque 1982-84). Mormon. Home: 1126 Thrushwood Logan UT 84321

MCDOWELL, JENNIFER, sociologist, composer, playwright; b. Albuquerque, May 19, 1936; d. Willard A. and Margaret Frances (Garrison) McD.; m. Milton Loventhal, July 2, 1973. BA, U. Calif., 1957, MLS, 1963; MA, San Diego State U., 1958; PhD, U. Oreg., 1973. Tchr. English Abraham Lincoln High Sch., San Jose, Calif., 1960-61; freelance editor Soviet field, Berkeley, Calif., 1961-63; research asst. sociology U. Oreg., Eugene, 1964-66; editor, pub. Merlin Papers, San Jose, 1969—, Merlin Press, San Jose, 1973—; research cons. sociology San Jose, 1973—; music pub. Lipstick and Toy Balloons Pub. Co., San Jose, 1978—; composer Paramount Pictures, 1982—; tchr. writing workshops; poetry readings, 1969-73; co-producer radio show lit. and culture Sta. KALX, Berkeley, 1971-72. Author: Black Politics: A Study and Annotated Bibliography of the Mississippi Freedom Democratic Party, 1971, Contemporary Women Poets: An Anthology of California Poets, 1977, Ronnie Goose Rhymes for Grown-ups, 1984; co-author (plays off-off Broadway) Betsy and Phyllis, 1986, Mack The Knife Your Friendly Dentist, 1986, The Estrogen Party To End War, 1986, The Oatmeal Party Comes to Order, 1986; contbr. poems, plays, essays, short stories, book revs. to lit. mags. and anthologies; researcher women's autobiog. writings, contemporary writings in poetry, Soviet studies, civil rights movement and George Orwell, 1962—; writer: (songs) Money Makes A Woman Free, 1976, 3 songs featured in Parade of Am. Music; co-creator: musical comedy Russia's Secret Plot to Take Back Alaska, 1988. Recipient 8 awards Am. Song Festival, 1976-79, Bill Casey award in Letters, 1980; AAUW doctoral fellow, 1971-73; grantee Calif. Arts Council, 1976-77. Mem. Am. Sociol. Assn., Soc. Sci. Study of Religion, Soc. Study of Religion under Communism, Poetry Orgn. for Women, Dramatists Guild, Phi Beta Kappa, Sigma Alpha Iota, Beta Phi Mu, Kappa Kappa Gamma. Democrat. Office: care Merlin Press PO Box 5602 San Jose CA 95150

MCDOWELL, KAREN ANN, lawyer; b. Ruston, La., Oct. 4, 1945; d. Paul and Opal Elizabeth (Davis) Bauer; m. Norman MacKay MacDonald, Aug. 10, 1970 (div. Dec. 1977); m. Gary Lee McDowell, Dec. 22, 1979. BA, N.E. La. U., 1967; JD, U. Mich., 1971. Bar: Ill. 1973, U.S. Dist. Ct. (so. dist.) Ill. 1973, Colo. 1977, U.S. Dist. Ct. Colo. 1977. Reference library assoc. Ill. State Library, Springfield, 1972-73; asst. atty. gen. State of Ill., Springfield, 1973-75; sole practice Boulder, Colo., 1978-79, Denver, 1979—. Facilitator Denver Wings, Inc., 1987. Mem. ABA, Colo. Bar Assn., Denver Bar Assn., Colo. Womens Bar Assn. (editor newsletter 1982-84), Phi Alpha Theta, Sigma Tau Delta, Alpha Lambda Delta, Mensa (sec. Ann Arbor, Mich. 1968). Republican. Club: Toastmasters (Aurora, Colo.) (pres. 1981). Office: 1614 Gaylord St Denver CO 80206

MCDUFFIE, DEBORAH JEANNE, composer; b. N.Y.C., Aug. 8, 1950; d. Thomas Elliott and Nan Ruth (Woods) McD.; B.A., Western Coll. Women; children—Kijana Babatu, Kemal. Music producer, composer McCann-Erickson Advt., Inc., N.Y.C., 1971-81; music dir. Mingo Group, 1981—; pres. Jana Prodns, Inc., Janée Music Co., Great Music Mgmt. Co., N.Y.C., 1977—; profl. singer, composer, arranger, producer. Recipient numerous advt. awards. Mem. ASCAP, Screen Actors Guild, AFTRA, Am. Fedn. Musicians, Nat. Acad. Rec. Arts and Scis., Nat. Assn. Female Execs. Vocal arranger: I'd Like to Teach the World to Sing, 1972; composer, producer Miller High Life campaigns, 1980—; album: I Am an Illusion, 1981, Damaris, 1984; composer Hooray for Love; producer We Shall Overcome by Roberta Flack, 1986, Simon Estes, Cindy Valentine, Al Green.

MCDUNN, KATHLEEN EVELYN, nurse, nursing educator; b. Chgo., Apr. 29, 1954; d. William Dorcey and Evelyn Sylvia (Drabik) McDunn. B.S., DePaul U., 1976; M.S., No. Ill. U., 1985. Staff nurse U. Ill. Hosp., Chgo., 1976-78, asst. head nurse, 1978-80, acting head nurse, 1980; instr. nursing Little Co. of Mary Hosp. Sch. Nursing, Evergreen Park, Ill., 1980-84, acad. advisor, 1980-84; hosp.-home care coordinator Health Care at Home, Hinsdale, Ill., 1985-86; maternal child health nurse cons. Ill. Infant Mortality Reduction Initiative, Cook County Dept. Pub. Health, 1986-88, pub. health nursing supr., 1988—; instr. cardiopulmonary resuscitation Chgo. Heart Assn., 1982—. Mem. Am. Nurses' Assn., Am. Pub. Health Assn., Am. Nurses Found., Assn. for Care of Children's Health, Ill. Nurses Assn., DePaul U. Dept. Nursing Alumni Assn., Sigma Theta Tau. Roman Catholic. Home: 10343 S 74th Ave Palos Hills IL 60465 Office: Cook County Dept Pub Health 16501 S Kedzie Pkwy Markham IL 60426

MCELROY, EMILIE LIN, mental health professional; b. San Francisco, Jan. 10, 1954; d. Earl Edwin and Carolyn Ardell (Brickley) McE.; m. Robert Louis Hitsman Jr., Feb. 25, 1984; 1 child, Lynda Nicole. Student, U. Calif., Davis, U. Louisville, 1986—. Artistic dir., gen. mgr. Sunshine Children's Theatre, Davis, 1977-83; counselor Progress Ranch, Inc., Davis, 1981-83; youth worker shelter house YMCA, Louisville, 1983-84, house coordinator, 1984-85; house dir. Schizophrenia Found. Ky., Louisville, 1985—; dir. Creative Cons., Lyndon, Ky., 1985—; advocate, counselor Louisville Rape Relief Ctr., 1984—. Organizer Calif. Dem. State Conv., 1982; apptd. spl. advocate Jefferson County (Ky.) Juvenile Ct. Dependency Docket. Mem. Nat. Assn. Female Execs. Roman Catholic. Home: 9110 Farham Rd Lyndon KY 40222 Office: Schizophrenia Found 1382 S 3d St Louisville KY 40208

MCELROY, JUNE PATRICIA, sales consultant; b. Atlantic City, Sept. 26, 1929; d. Edmund N. and Dorothy R. (McDowell) Ricchezza; m. David Waycott Carson, Apr. 8, 1947 (div. 1954); m. Ottavio Gelmi, Dec. 16, 1954 (div. 1964); 1 child, Alessandra; m. Robert Joseph McElroy, Oct. 16, 1970 (dec. May 1974). Student Temple U., 1947-48, Inst. linguistics, Georgetown U., 1951-53. Mem. staff Am. consulate gen., Milan, Italy, 1954; legis. asst. U.S. Senate, Washington, 1956; social sec. to ambassador of Finland, Washington, 1958; legis. asst. to congressman, Washington, 1960-65; sr. assoc. Gillmore M. Perry Co., Washington, 1965-76; sales exec./cons. furniture industry, Hilton Head, S.C., 1985-87; ptnr. Mfrs. Representative Internat., 1987—. Mem. Georgetown U. Alumni Assn. Republican. Roman Catholic. Club: Army Navy (Washington). Home: 4101 Cathedral Ave NW Washington DC 20016

MCELWAIN, JUANITA MURIEL, music therapy educator; b. Geneva, Ohio, Jan. 17, 1928; d. George Myron and Muriel Maude (Randolph) Stilwell; B.M.E., Fla. State U., 1958, M.M.E., 1959, M.Mus., 1974, Ph.D., 1978; m. O.D. McElwain, Aug. 21, 1948; 1 son, Thomas George. Tchr., Jennings (Fla.) Public Sch., 1961-62; tchr. piano, organ Monterey Bay Acad., Watsonville, Calif., 1962-67; tchr. organ, piano Antillian Union Coll., Mayàguez, P.R., 1967-69; music therapist Sunland Tng. Center, Marianna, Fla., 1978-80; asst. prof., dir. music therapy Sch. Music, Eastern N.Mex. U., Portales, 1980-85; assoc. prof., dir. music therapy Phillips U., Enid, Okla., 1985—; condr. workshops on music in spl. edn. Mem. profl. adv. com. Community Services Portales, 1981-85; bd. dirs. Campfire Girls, Portales, 1982-85. Mem. Nat. Assn. Music Therapy, Pi Kappa Lambda. Adventist. Home: 418 W Oak Ave Enid OK 73701 Office: Phillips U Enid OK 73702

MCELWAIN, LOUISA REDFIELD, artist; b. Nashua, N.H., May 3, 1953; d. William Home and Mary (Redfield) McE.; m. Daniel Kellogg McCoubrey, May 27, 1978 (div. Sept. 1985); m. Peter R. Houghton, May 16, 1987. BFA, U. Pa., 1977. Designer, muralist Venturi, Rauch and Scott-Brown, Phila., 1981-85; represented by C.C. Rein Galleries, Mpls., Houston, Denver, Santa Fe, Scottsdale, Ariz., 1985—; designer landscape Fairmount Park, Phila., 1983. Executed mural "Cretaceous Swamp" in Treehouse, Phila. Zool. Gardens, 1985. Home: PO Box 8146 Santa Fe NM 87504

MCELWREATH, SALLY CHIN, public relations executive; b. N.Y.C., Oct. 15, 1940; d. Toon Guey and Jean B. (Wong) Chin; m. Joseph F. Callo, Mar. 17, 1979; 1 child, R.J. McElwreath III. BA, Pace Coll., 1963; MBA, Pace U., 1969. Copywriter O.E. McIntyre, N.Y.C., 1963-65; editorial asst. Sinclair Oil Corp., N.Y.C., 1966-70; account exec. Muller, Jordan & Herrick, N.Y.C., 1970-71; regional mgr. pub. relations United Airlines, N.Y.C., 1971-79; dir. corp. communications Trans World Airlines, N.Y.C., 1979-86; v.p. pub. relations TWA Mktg. Services, Inc., N.Y.C., 1987—. Serves as commdr. USNR, 1973—. Named Woman of Yr., YWCA, 1980, Alumnus of Yr., Pace U., 1976. Mem. N.Y. Airline Pub. Relations Assn. (chmn. 1978-79), Aviation and Space Writers Assn., USN Mktg. Review Bd. Clubs: Wings (N.Y.C.), Naval and Mil. (London), Ski Club Great Britain. Office: TWA Mktg Services 605 Third Ave New York NY 10158

MCELYEA, LOUANN, automated systems and artificial intelligence consultant; b. Poplar Bluff, Mo., Sept. 10, 1946; d. Arthur Eugene and Hazel Irene (Trosper) McE.; BS, Washington U., St. Louis, 1975; MBA, Lindenwood Coll., 1982. Dir. adminstrv. services Washington U., 1972-77; account exec. Bache, Halsey-Stuart Shields, Inc., St. Louis, 1977-78; project mgr. office systems dept. Mallinckrodt, Inc., St. Louis, 1978-80; pres., founder Info. Systems, Inc., St. Louis, 1980—. Mem. Alpha Sigma Lambda. Baptist. Home: 806 Bailey St Campbell MO 63933 Office: Info Systems Inc Campbell MO 63933

MCENEANEY, MARGARET EILEEN, corporate executive; b. Jersey City, Jan. 26, 1945; d. Michael George and Marie Agnes (Henehen) McE. BEd, Jersey City State U., 1968; postgrad., New Sch., N.Y.C. Lic. tchr., N.J. Sales asst. Internat. Flavor St. Fragrances, N.Y.C., 1968-69; mktg. analyst Ziff-Davis Pub. Co., N.Y.C., 1968-72; asst. pub. Stereo Rev. Mag., N.Y.C., 1972-79; asst. promotion dir. Ziff-Davis Pub. Co., 1979-81; adminstrv. dir. N.H. Bettigole Co., Paramus, N.J., 1982-84; v.p. adminstrn. N.H. Bettigole Co., Paramys, N.J., 1985—; owner The Poorhouse restaurant, Lyndhurst, N.J., 1976-77, The Peasant Rose restaurant, Passaic, N.J., 1985-87. Editor: Vietnam Investigations of a Winter Soldier, 1972; author poetry. Mem. Nat. Assn. Female Execs., N.J. Soc. Profl. Women, Nat. Orgn. Women. Democrat. Home: 70 Ridgeview Ave New Providence NJ 07974 Office: NH Bettigole Co 601 Bergen Mall Paramus NJ 07653

MCENTIRE, REBA N., entertainer; b. McAlester, Okla., Mar. 28, 1955; d. Clark Vincent and Jacqueline (Smith) McE. Student elem. edn., music, Southeastern State U., Durant, Okla., 1976. Rec. artist Mercury Records, 1978-83, MCA Records, 1984—. Albums include Whoever's in New England (Gold award), 1986, What Am I Gonna Do About You (Gold award), 1987, Greatest Hits (Gold award), 1987, The Last One To Know (Gold award), 1988, Reba (Gold award 1988). Spokesperson Middle Tenn. United Way, 1988, Nat. 4-H orgn., Bob Hope's Hope for a Drug Free Am. Recipient numerous awards in Country music including Disting. Alumni award Southeastern State U., Female vocalist award Country Music Assn., 1984, 85, 86, 87, Grammy award for Best Country Vocal Performance, 1987; named Entertainer of Yr., Country Music Assn., 1986. Mem. Country Music Assn., Acad. County Music, Nat. Acad. Rec. Arts and Scis., Gran Ol' Opry, AFTRA.

MCEVOY-JOHNSTON, PAMELA, clinical psychologist; b. Forest Hills, N.Y., Mar. 8, 1937; d. Renny T. and Pamela Shipley (Sweeny) McE.; B.A., U. La Verne, 1978, M.S., 1980; Ph.D., U.S. Internat. U., 1982; children—Michael B. Anderson, Jeffery A. Thomas, Candy L. Anderson-Smith, Kenneth L. Anderson. Data processing coordinator Ernest Righetti High Sch., Santa Maria, Calif., 1974-78; instr. psychology-sociology Allan Hancock Coll., Santa Maria, 1977-78; mental health asst. Santa Barbara City Alcoholism Dept., 1977-78; gen. mgr. Profl. Suites, San Diego, 1978-81; therapist Chula Vista (Calif.) Community Counseling Ctr., San Diego, 1978-85; research asst. U.S. Internat. U., 1979-82; research coordinator Mil. Family research Ctr., San Diego, 1981-82; assoc. dir. Acad. Assoc. Psychotherapists, 1982-86; pvt. practice, San Diego, 1982—, pres. Rancho Bernardo Psychology Ctr., 1987—; bd. dirs. Women's Internat. Ctr., 1984-86. Bd. dirs. San Diego County Mental Health Assn., 1978-80; pres. Chula Vista Counseling Ctr., 1978; mem. Delinquency Prevention Commn., 1978. State fellow, 1979, 80, 81, 82, Calif. State scholar, 1976-77. Mem. Am. Psychol. Assn., Am. Assn. Marriage and Family Therapists, Calif. Assn. Marriage and Family Therapists. Republican. Roman Catholic. Home: PO Box 8946 Rancho Sante Fe CA 92067

MCFADDEN, ELLEN ANN, nursing educator; b. Jersey City, N.J., Nov. 4, 1941; d. Joseph John and Frances Regina (Burns) McF. Diploma in nursing, Christ Hosp., 1963; BS in Nursing, U. Va., 1973; MS in Child Psychiat. Nursing, U. Md., Balt., 1975; PhD in Edn. Adminstrn., U. Md., 1986. Asst. prof. U. Md., Balt., 1975-87, U. Del., Newark, 1987—. Contbr. articles to profl. jours. Mem. Sigma Theta Tau (1st v.p. 1985-87). Office: U Del Coll Nursing McDowell Hall Newark DE 19716

MC FADDEN, MARY JOSEPHINE, fashion industry executive; b. N.Y.C., Oct. 1, 1938; d. Alexander Bloomfield and Mary Josephine (Cutting) McF.; 1 dau., Justine. Ed., Sorbonne, Paris, France, Traphagen Sch. Design, 1957, Columbia, 1959-62; DFA, Internat. Fine Arts Coll., 1984. Pub. relations dir. Christian Dior, N.Y.C., 1962-64; merchandising editor Vogue South Africa, 1964-65; polit. and travel columnist Rand (South Africa) Daily Mail, 1965-68; founder sculptural workshop Vukutu, Rhodesia, 1968-70; spl. projects editor Vogue U.S.A., 1970; pres. Mary McFadden, Inc., N.Y.C., 1976—; bd. dirs., advisor Sch. Design and Merchandising Kent State U., New Mus. Contemporary Art, Sundance Inst., Eugene O'Neill Meml. Theatre Ctr., Nat. Am. Mus., Am. Indian Coll. Fund.; profl. com. Cooper-Hewitt Mus., Smithsonian Inst., Nat. Mus. of Design. Fashion and jewelry designer, 1973—; recipient Am. Fashion Critics award-Coty award 1976, 78, Audemars Piguet Fashion award 1976, Rex award 1977, More Coll. Art award 1977, Pa. Gov.'s award 1977, Roscoe award 1978, Pres.'s Fellows award R.I. Sch. Design 1979, Neiman Marcus award of excellence 1979, named to Fashion Hall of Fame 1979. Mem. Fashion Group, Council of Fashion Designers of Am. (v.p., dir., bd. dirs., advisor), Nat. Endowment for the Arts (bd. dirs., advisor). Office: 240 W 35th St New York NY 10001

MCFADDEN, ROSEMARY THERESA, mercantile exchange executive; b. Scotland, Oct. 1, 1948; came to U.S. 1951, naturalized 1967; s. John and Winifred (Quinn) McFadden.; m. Brian Doherty, May 26, 1973. B.A., Rutgers U., 1970, M.B.A., 1974; J.D., Seton Hall U., 1978; hon. doctorate St. Elizabeth's Coll.-Convent Station, N.J., 1985. Spl. Asst. office of the Mayor, Jersey City, 1973-76; exec. dir. Hudson Health System, Jersey City, 1976-81; assoc. legal counsel N.Y. Merc. Exchange, N.Y.C., 1981-82, exec. v.p., 1982-84, pres., 1984—; mem. deans adv. council Rutgers U. Grad. Sch. Mgmt., Newark, 1985. Bd. dirs. Jersey City Med. Ctr., 1985—. Named Alumna of Yr., Rutgers U., 1985. Mem. N.J. Bar Assn., ABA, Am. Petroleum Inst., Soc. Ind. Gas Mktg., Rutgers U. Alumni Assn. Roman Catholic. Avocations: travel; antique collecting. Office: New York Mercantile Exchange 4 World Trade Center New York NY 10048

MCFADDEN, SUSAN MEADE, occupational therapist; b. Washington, Nov. 13, 1941; d. Seibert Dwight and Josephine (Blacklock) Meade; m. John J. McFadden Jr., June 19, 1971. BS in Occupational Therapy, Va. Commonwealth U., 1963; MEd, Pa. State U., 1973. Staff occupational therapist Richmond (Va.) Cerebral Palsy Ctr., 1964-65, James Ryder Randall Elem. Sch., Clinton, Md., 1965-67; resource occupational therapist Prince George's County Pub. Schs., Upper Marlboro, Md., 1967-71; ednl. cons. State Coll. (Pa.) Presbyn. Ch., 1972-73; chief occupational therapy dept. Child Devel. Ctr., U. Tenn., Memphis, 1973-78, head occupational therapy dept., 1980—; sr. lectr. in occupational therapy Western Australian Inst. of Technology, Perth, 1978-80; occupational therapy cons. Memphis, 1980—. Co-author Feeding Management of a Child with a Handicap, 1982; contbr. articles to profl. jours. Fellow Am. Occupational Therapy Assn.; mem. Tenn. Occupational Therapy Assn. (Outstanding Occupational Therapist of the Yr. 1978, cert. Appreciation, 1984, 86), World Fedn. of Occupational Therapists. Home and Office: 1100 Perkins Terr Memphis TN 38117

MC FADDEN, SYBILL MARTIN, museum curator; b. Pitts., Mar. 22, 1918; d. Alfred Nicholas and Rachel (Church) Martin; B.A. in Journalism, Pa. State U., 1941; m. William Patrick McFadden, Aug. 19, 1942; children—Suzanne Sybill, William Patrick, Gary J. Public relations dir. advt. ARC, Eastern Area Hdqrs., Alexandria, Va., 1941-46; owner, curator Mus. Antique Dolls and Toys, Lakewood, N.Y., 1960—; artist, one-woman shows, N.Y. and Fla.; writer, photographer nat. doll and toy mags., antiques mag.; writer, columnist Hobbies Mag. Mem. United Fedn. Doll Clubs, Inc., Western N.Y. Doll Club, Fla. West Coast Doll Collectors, Doll Study Club Jamestown (founder), Doll Collectors of America. Author: Portraits in Porcelain. Home and Office: 96 W Summit Ave Lakewood NY 14750

MCFARLAND, DONNA REYNE, illustrator, educator, consultant; b. Charleston, W.Va., Oct. 24, 1948; d. Clyde Freeman and Ruby June (Summerfield) Armstrong; m. Elmer Reace McFarland, Oct. 28, 1966; children—Kelli Reyne, Jay Reace, B.A. in Art cum laude, W.Va. State Coll., 1985, postgrad. Marshall Univ., 1986—. Art dir. Calvary Bapt. acad., Hurricane, W.Va., 1980-84; art judge State Accelerated Christian Edn. High Sch. Competition, Jacksons Mill, W.Va., 1981— (Internat. Competition judge, 1987); owner, tchr. art Donna McFarland Studio, Scott Depot, W.Va., 1983—; art cons. Brandywine, Hurricane, W.Va., 1985—. Illustrator Kanawha's Black Gold and the Miner's Rebellions (book by V.B Harris, 1987). Wonderful W.Va. Mag., 1983. Pres. Teays Village Homeowners Assn., Scott Depot, 1986. Fellow Allied Artists W.Va.; mem. W.Va. Artists and Craftsmen's Guild. Republican. Baptist. Avocations: reading; classical music; walking; cooking. Home and Studio: 2642 Putnam Ave Hurricane WV 25526

MCFARLAND, JANE ELIZABETH, librarian; b. Athens, Tenn., June 22, 1937; d. John Homer and Martha Virginia (Large) M. AB, Smith Coll., 1959; M in Divinity, Yale U., 1963; MS in LS, U. N.C., 1971. Tchr. hist. and religion Northfield Schs., Mass., 1961-62; head librarian reference and circulation Yale Divinity Library, New Haven, Conn., 1963-71; head librarian Bradford (Mass.) Coll., 1972-77; reference librarian U. Tenn., Chattanooga, Tenn., 1977-80; head librarian reference dept Chattanooga-Hamilton County Bicentennial Library, Tenn., 1980-86, acting dir., 1986, dir., 1986—. Mem. Chattanooga Library Assn., Tenn. Library Assn., Southeastern Library Assn., Am. Library Assn., Phi Beta Kappa (treas. 1987). Democrat. Roman Catholic. Home: 1701 Estrellita Circle Chattanooga TN 37421 Office: Chattanooga-Hamilton County Bicentennial Library 1001 Broad St Chattanooga TN 37402

MCFARLAND, KAY ELEANOR, state justice; b. Coffeyville, Kans., July 20, 1935; d. Kenneth W. and Margaret E. (Thrall) McF. BA magna cum laude, Washburn U., Topeka, 1957, JD, 1964. Bar: Kans. 1964. Sole practice Topeka, 1964-71; probate and juvenile judge Shawnee County, Topeka, 1971-73; dist. judge Topeka, 1973-77; justice Kans. Supreme Ct., 1977—. Mem. Kans. Bar Assn. Office: Kans Supreme Ct Kansas Judicial Ctr 301 W 10th St Topeka KS 66612

MCFARLAND, MARY ANN, nursing educator, academic administrator; b. Boston, July 19, 1939; d. Mario and Eva Mary (Luciano) Brambilla; m. Joseph Roy McFarland, Apr. 26, 1970; 1 child, Stephen Roy. Diploma, Mass. Gen. Hosp. Sch. Nursing, Boston, 1960; BS, Boston Coll., 1965; MS in Nursing, U. Pa., 1967; postgrad., Portland (Oreg.) State U., 1984—. Staff nurse, asst. head nurse Mass. Gen. Hosp., 1960-67; clin. nurse specialist U. Minn. Hosps., Mpls., 1967-70; asst. prof. nursing Columbus (Ga.) Coll., 1970-71, 74-75; from instr. to asst. prof. U. Hawaii, Honolulu, 1971-74; asst. prof. Oreg. Health Scis. U., Portland, 1975-77, assoc. prof., 1977—, assoc dean undergrad. studies, sch. nursing,, 1983—. Author: Interpreting Cardiac Arrythmias, 1975, Nursing Implications of Laboratory Tests, 1982, 87; contbr. articles to profl. jours. Recipient Disting. Service award Hawaii Heart Assn., Honolulu, 1974; grantee USPHS, 1964-65, 65-67. Mem. Am. Nurses Assn., Oreg. Nurses Assn., Nat. League for Nursing, Sigma Theta Tau, Phi Kappa Phi, Kappa Delta Pi. Roman Catholic. Home: 507 Palo Alto Dr Vancouver WA 98661 Office: Oreg Health Scis U 3181 SW Sam Jackson Park Rd Portland OR 97201

MCFARLAND, VIOLET VIVIAN, author; b. Seattle, Feb. 26, 1908; d. Judson Loring and Annie (Conners) Sweet; M. J. Lamar Butler, 1944 (div. 1953); m. Glen W. McFarland, 1958 (div. 1965). B.A., Wash. State U., 1928, M.A., Columbia U., 1933. Tchr., Konawaena High Sch., Kealakekua, Hawaii, 1928-30, Am. Sch. in Japan, Tokyo, 1930-31; soc. editor Japan Times, Tokyo, 1930-31, Hong Kong Telegraph, 1940; edit. asst. U.S. Dept. Justice, Washington, 1934-43; real estate assoc. Long Beach Bd., Calif., 1961—. Author (as Violet Sweet Haven): Hong Kong for Weekend, 1939; Many Ports of Call, 1940; Gentlemen of Japan, 1944. Contbr. articles to profl. jours. Recipient numerous internat. lit. awards. Fellow Internat. Inst. Arts and Letters (life); mem. Nat. Press Club (life), Calif. Bd. Realtors, Delta Zeta. Avocations: travel; curator Oriental art and lit. Address: PO Box 872 Lake Elsinore CA 92330

MCFARLANE, BETH LUCETTA TROESTER, mayor; b. Osterdock, Iowa, Mar. 9, 1918; d. Francis Charles and Ella Carrie (Moser) Troester; M. George Evert McFarlane, June 20, 1943 (dec. May 1972); children: Douglas, Steven (dec.), Susan, George. BA in Edn., U. No. Iowa, 1962, MA in Edn., 1971. Cert. tchr. Tchr. rural and elem. schs., Iowa, 1936-50, 55-56; elem. tchr. Oelwein Community Schs., Iowa, 1956-64, jr. high reading tchr., 1964-71, reading specialist, 1971-83; mayor of Oelwein, 1982—; evaluator North Cen. Accreditation Assn. for Ednl. Programs; mem. planning team for confs. for Iowa Cities, N.E. Iowa, 1985; v.p. N.E. Iowa Regional Council for Econ. Devel., 1986—; mem. Area Econ. Devel. Com. N.E. Iowa, 1985, Legis. Interim Study Com. on Rural Econ. Devel., 1987-88; mem. policy com. Iowa League Municipalities, 1987—; bd. dirs. Celwein Indsl. Devel. Corp., 1982—, Oelwein Betterment Corp., 1982—. V.p. Fayette County Tourism Council, 1987—. Named Iowa Reading Tchr. of Yr., Internat. Reading Assn. Iowa, 1978; recipient Outstanding Contbrn. to Reading Council Activities award Internat. Reading Assn. N.E. Iowa, 1978. Mem. N.E. Iowa Reading Council (pres. 1975-77), MacDowell Music and Arts Orgn. (pres. 1978-80), Oelwein Bus. and Profl. Women (Woman of Yr. 1983), Oelwein Area C. of C. (bd. dirs. 1986—, Humanitarian award 1987), Delta Kappa Gamma (pres. 1980-82). Republican. Mem. Reorganized Ch. of Jesus Christ of Latter Day Saints. Avocations: bicycling, refinishing antiques, gardening. Home: 512 7th Ave NE Oelwein IA 50662 Office: City of Oelwein 20 2d Ave SW Oelwein IA 50662

MCFARREN, GRACE WERNER, artist; b. Phila., Feb. 6, 1914; d. George Frederick and Amelia Louise (Brauninger) Werner; m. Gerald Werner McFarren, Jan. 17, 1942; children: Dorna Louise McFarren Toone, Gerald Werner. Student, Sch. of Design for Women, Phila., 1933; studies with various instrs. including, Clayton Bachtel, Peter Dubaniewicz, Joseph McMCullough, Marion Bryson, Doris Peters, Edgar Whitney. Owner, operator Wilmington (Del.) Circulating Gallery of Paintings, 1960-86. Mem. Del. Art Mus. Mem. Del. Mus. Art, Rehoboth Art League, Chester County Art Assn., Am. Watercolor Soc. Home: 3 Winterbury Circle Wilmington DE 19808

MC FATE, PATRICIA ANN, educator, foundation executive; b. Detroit, Mar. 19, 1936; d. John Earle and Mary Louise (Bliss) McF. B.A. (Alumni scholar), Mich. State U., 1954; M.A., Northwestern U., 1956, Ph.D., 1965; M.A. (hon.), U. Pa., 1977. Assoc. prof. English, asst. dean liberal arts and scis. U. Ill., Chgo., 1967-74; assoc. prof. English, assoc. vice chancellor acad. affairs U. Ill., 1974-75; assoc. prof. folklore Faculty Arts and Scis., U. Pa., Phila., 1975-81; prof. tech. and soc. Coll. Engring. and Applied Sci., 1975-81, vice provost, 1975-78; dep. chmn. Nat. Endowment for Humanities, Washington, 1978-81; exec. v.p. Am.-Scandinavian Found., N.Y.C., 1981-82, pres., 1982—; vis. assoc. prof. dept. medicine Rush U., Chgo., 1970-85; dir. Carson Pirie Scott Co., Phila. Nat. Bank, CoreStates Fin. Corp., Celebrations International, Inc. Raoul Wallenberg com. of U.S.. Author: The Writings of James Stephens, 1979, Uncollected Prose of James Stephens, 1983; contbr. articles in fields of sci. policy and lit. to various jours. Bd. dirs. Inst. Cancer Research, Bishop Anderson House Found. Decorated officer Order of Leopold II Belgium, comdr. Order Icelandic Falcon, comdr. Royal Order of Polar Star (Sweden), comdr. Order of Lion (Finland), comdr. Royal Norwegian Order Merit, Knight 1st class Royal Order Dannebrog (Denmark); U. Ill. Grad. Coll. faculty fellow, 1968; Swedish Bicentennial Fund grantee, 1981. Fellow N.Y. Acad. Scis.; mem. Acad. Scis. Phila. (founding mem., corr. sec. 1977-79), AAAS (chmn. com. on sci., engring. and pub. policy 1984-87), Am. Com. Irish Studies, N.Y. Sci. Policy Assn., Am. Women for Internat. Understanding, Internat. Assn. Anglo-Irish Studies, MLA, Theta Alpha Phi, Omega Beta Pi, Delta Delta Delta. Club: Cosmopolitan (Phila.). Office: The Am-Scandinavian Found 127 E 73rd St New York NY 10021

MCFAUL, PATRICIA LOUISE, editor; b. Jersey City, June 28, 1947; d. James Leo and Ethel Louise (Shea) McF.; 1 child, Jennifer Jeanne. Student Nassau Community Coll., 1969-70. Pub. info. officer L.I. Cath. Newspaper, Hempstead, N.Y., 1967-68, researcher, 1968-70, staff writer, 1970-73, copy editor, 1973-78, layout and copy editor, 1978—, readership surveyor, Rockville Centre, N.Y., 1971, 75; mem., com. chmn. Diocesan Family Life Bd., Rockville Centre, 1978-82. Researcher: Mission to Latin America, 1976. Pres. Florence A. Smith Sch. PTA, Oceanside, N.Y., 1982-84, Oceanside High Sch. Marching Band Parents Assn., 1987-88; chmn. talented and gifted com. Oceanside Council P.T.A.s, 1984-85; elem. tchr. aide, 1985—; mem., sec.-treas. L.I. Interfaith Council, Rockville Centre, 1977-80. Recipient Citation, Diocese of Rockville Centre, 1984, 88. Mem. Cath. Press Assn. (U.S. and Can. citations 1985; mem. research com. 1975-80, mem., chmn. credentials and inspectors of elections com. 1976—, 1st place award design 1978, 86, citations 1980-85). Democrat. Roman Catholic. Avocations: flying, classical music. Home: 37 Rodney Pl Rockville Centre NY 11570 Office: The LI Catholic 115 Greenwich St Hempstead NY 11550

MCFAUL, SARAH RUTH, business owner, researcher.; b. Cin., Mar. 17, 1919; d. Van W. and Ruth N. (Conner) Hayes; m. Edmund C. McFaul (dec. Feb. 1966); 1 child, Eileen Claire. Grad. high school, Cin. Owner Cincinnati Store, 1966—. Mem. Am. Chem. Soc. Home and Office: 8990 Lyneris Dr Cincinnati OH 45242

MCGAFFIGAN, PEGGY WEEKS, former legislative assistant; b. Houlton, Maine, June 27, 1952; d. Francis P. and Ruth Conrad (Steeves) Weeks; B.A., U. Maine, Orono, 1974; M.A., Tufts U., 1975; m. Edward McGaffigan, Jr., July 3, 1982; children: Edward Francis, Margaret Ruth. Analyst div. nat. security and internat. affairs Congl. Budget Office, Washington, 1975-79; legis. asst. to Senator William S. Cohen, Washington, 1979-84. Mem. Phi Beta Kappa. Home: 4818 N 37th St Arlington VA 22207

MCGAHA, BARBARA JOYCE, municipal administrator; b. Fairmount, Ind., Dec. 2, 1936; d. Gerald Oscar and Ruby Juanita (Ice) Earlywine; m. C.D. Merchant, Sept. 12, 1960 (div. 1974); children: Robin Lee, Steven Bradley, Kimberly Jo; m. H. Eugene McGaha, Oct. 8, 1983; stepchildren: Allison Lea, Teresa Lynn, Terra Kay and Tina Mae (twins). Student, Long Beach (Calif.) State Coll., 1961-62, Ivy Tech., 1974-75. Sec. Howard County Sheriff's Dept., Kokomo, Ind., 1975-76, IDACS coordinator, 1975-82, jail officer, 1976-82; tax assessor Ctr. Twp., City of Kokomo, 1983—; mem. Howard land com. Ctr. Twp. of Howard County, Kokomo, 1987. Vice co-chairperson Howard County Dem. Cen. Com., Kokomo, 1982, co-chairperson, 1982-85. Mem. Ind. Assessors Assn., Howard County Womens Golf Assn. (pres. 1980-81). Office: Ctr Twp Assessor of Howard Howard County Ct House Room 204 Kokomo IN 46902

MC GANN, GERALDINE, government official; b. Bklyn., Dec. 21, 1937; d. Daniel and Geraldine (LeGrande) Essex; B.A. with honors, Hofstra U., 1974; M.Profl. Studies in Health Care Adminstrn. with honors, C.W. Post Coll., L.I. U., 1978; m. Edward J. McGann, Apr. 7, 1956; children—Daniel, Kevin, Kellie, Jacqueline. Tchr. Hempstead and East Rockaway Schs.; coordinator sr. citizen services Town of Hempstead, N.Y., 1974-78, dep. commr. dept. services for aging, 1978-81; spl. asst. to regional adminstr. HUD, N.Y.C., 1981-83, exec. asst. to regional adminstr., 1983-87; regional dir housing, U.S. Dept. HUD Region II, 1987—. Chairperson Island Park (N.Y.) Housing Authority, 1975-81; village trustee, Island Park, N.Y., 1982—; bd. trustees, St. Christopher Ch., Ottilie; mem. Republican Nat. Com. Mem. Am. Soc. Public Adminstrn., Assn. Pub. Adminstrn. and Health Care Profls., Women in Housing and Fin., Pi Alpha Alpha. Republican. Home: 42 Roosevelt Pl Island Park NY 11558 Office: 26 Federal Plaza New York NY 10278

MCGAREY, DIANNE WEST, entertainment executive; b. Murray, Ky., July 24, 1947; d. Joseph Denzel and Jeanne Lazelle (Tucker) West; m. Thomas Francis McGarey, Oct. 27, 1979. BS in Bus. and Radio/TV Communications cum laude, Murray State U., 1973. Legal sec. Sutherland Asbill & Brennan, Atlanta, 1973-74; free-lance singer Atlanta, 1974-78; sec. Axtell Entertainment Inc., Atlanta, 1978-79, account exec., 1979-83, v.p., 1983-85, pres., 1985—; guest lectr. Ga. State U. event planner Zoo Atlanta, 1987. Mem. Meeting Planners Internat., Nat. Assn. Catering Execs., Ga. Soc. Account Execs., Country Music Awards, Women's Commerce Club. Mem. Ch. of God. Club: Atlanta Ski. Office: Axtell Prodns Internat 1645-F Tullie Circle NE Atlanta GA 30329

MCGARRY, MARCIA LANGSTON, probation and parole officer; b. Washington, Dec. 9, 1941; d. Emil Sylvester and Bernice B. (Bland) Busey. B.S., Morgan State U., 1964. Cert. tchr., law enforecment officer, Fla. Payroll clk., jr. acct. U.S. Dept. Labor, Washington, 1964-65; English tchr., Taiwan, 1968-70; tchr. Monroe County Sch. Bd., Key West, Fla., 1971-81; exec. dir. Monroe Assn. Retarded Citizens, Key West, 1977-79; dep. sheriff Monroe County Sheriff's Dept., Key West, 1979-83, 1986—; probation/parole officer Fla. State Dept. Corrections, Key West, 1983—; instr. Fla. Keys Community Coll., 1983—. Active local polit. campaigns; co-founder day schs. for under-privileged children; active Big Bros/Big Sisters Am. (mem. com. 1985-86), Spouse Abuse. Recipient cert. of appreciation Lions Club, 1978, 79; Career Week award Harris Elem. Sch., 1981. Mem. Nat. Assn. Female Execs., Fla. Police Benevolent Assn., Key West Profls., Lutheran Ch. Women, Delta Sigma Theta. Home: 3 Villa Patricia 2nd St SI PO Box 2648 Key West FL 33040 Office: 1111 12th St Key West FL 33040

MC GAW, JESSIE BREWER, author, educator; b. Clarksville, Tenn., Oct. 17, 1913; d. Lewis Vernon and Birdie (Basford) Brewer; A.B., Duke U., 1935; M.A., Peabody Coll., 1940; postgrad. Columbia U., 1948-50, (Fulbright scholar) Am. Acad. Rome, 1959; m. Howard Franklin McGaw, Dec. 28, 1939 (div. 1958); children—Miriam Katherine, Vernon Howard; m. Harold L. Geis, Aug. 1964 (div. 1972); m. George P. Bickford, May 24, 1986. Tchr. Latin, Ward Belmont Sch., Nashville, 1938-40; tchr. Lausanne Sch., Memphis, 1940-42; asso. prof. English and Latin, U. Houston, 1952—. Bd. dirs. YWCA, 1957-59, Day Care Assn., 1956-61, Houston Civic Music Assn., 1958-60, Houston Council Human Relations. Recipient Cokesburg Juvenile award; Theta Sigma Phi lit. award. Fulbright grantee Am. Acad. in Rome, 1959; research grantee, 1964, 72; Delta Kappa Gamma ednl. grantee, China, 1981. Mem. Tex. Folklore Soc., South Central Modern Lang. Assn., Houston Council, Tchrs. Fgn. Lang. (treas.), League Women Voters, AAUW, Tex. Inst. Letters, U. Houston Women's Assn. (pres. 1967-68), Mus. Fine Arts (asso.), Delta Kappa Gamma, Kappa Kappa Gamma. Democrat. Methodist. Club: University Houston Woman's (pres. 1954-55, 67-68). Author: How Medicine Man Cured Paleface Woman, 1956, History of Houston YWCA, 1957, Painted Pony Runs Away, 1958, Little Elk Hunts Buffalo, 1961, Chief Red Horse Tells About Custer, 1981, The Aztec Downfall, 1987. Translator: Heptaplus (Pico delia Mirandola), 1977. Home: 2411 Reba Houston TX 77019

MCGEE, DOROTHY HORTON, author, historian; b. West Point, N.Y., Nov. 30, 1913; d. Hugh Henry and Dorothy (Brown) McG.; ed. Sch. of St. Mary, 1920-21, Green Vale Sch., 1921-28, Brearley Sch., 1928-29, Fermata Sch., 1929-31. Asst. historian Inc. Village of Roslyn (N.Y.), 1950-58; historian Inc. Village of Matinecock, 1966—. Author: Skipper Sandra, 1950; Sally Townsend, Patriot, 1952; The Boarding School Mystery, 1953; Famous Signers of the Declaration, 1955; Alexander Hamilton—New Yorker, 1957; Herbert Hoover: Engineer, Humanitarian, Statesman, 1959, rev. edit., 1965; The Pearl Pendant Mystery, 1960; Framers of the Constitution, 1968; author booklets, articles hist. and sailing subjects. Chmn., Oyster Bay Am. Bicentennial Revolution Commn., 1971—; historian Town of Oyster Bay, 1982—; mem. Nassau County Am. Revolution Bicentennial Commn.; hon. dir. The Friends of Raynham Hall, Inc.; treas. Family Welfare Assn. Nassau County, Inc., 1956-58; dir. Family Service Assn. Nassau County, 1958-69. Recipient Cert. of award for outstanding contbn. children's lit. N.Y. State Assn. Elem. Sch. Prins., 1959; award Nat. Soc. Children of Am. Revolution, 1960; award N.Y. Assn. Supervision and Curriculum Devel., 1961; hist. award Town of Oyster Bay, 1963; Cert. Theodore Roosevelt Assn., 1976. Fellow Soc. Am. Historians; mem. Soc. Preservation L.I. Antiquities (hon. dir.), Nat. Trust Hist. Preservation, N.Y. Geneal. and Biol. Soc. (dir., trustee), Oyster Bay Hist. Soc. (pres. 1971-75, chmn. 1975-79, trustee), Theodore Roosevelt Assn. (trustee), Townsend Soc. Am. (trustee). Republican. Address: Box 142 Locust Valley NY 11560

MCGEE, JOYCE FANTINO, government official, accountant; b. Chgo., July 31, 1947; d. John and Yolande Paule (MacDuff) Fantino; m. David Lee McGee, May 29, 1976; children: Erin Lillian, Richard Cody. BS, Fla. State U., 1979. CPA, Fla. Staff acct. Williams, Cox, Weidner, Cox, Tallahassee, 1979-83; tax audit specialist III Fla. Dept. Revenue, Tallahassee, 1983-85, bur. chief returns accountability, 1985-87, bur. chief of fin. and acctg., 1987-88; dir. internal audit Fla. Dept. Health and Rehabilitative Services, Tallahassee, 1988—. Fla. Inst. CPAs ednl. found. scholar., 1979; recipient Top Student award, Ernst & Ernst, 1976; Nat. Key award, Phi Chi Theta, 1978-79; Fashion Design award, 1978-79, Mildred Pepper scholar, 1968. Mem. Am. Inst. CPAs, Fla. Soc. CPAs, Phi Kappa Phi, Beta Gamma Sigma, Beta Alpha Psi. Democrat. Office: Fla Dept Health & Rehab Services 1317 Winewood Blvd Rm 412 Bldg 1 Tallahassee FL 32399-0700

MCGEE, LINDA MACE, lawyer; b. Marion, N.C., Sept. 20, 1949; d. Cecil Adam and Norma Jean (Hogan) Mace; m. B. Gary McGee, Dec. 19, 1970; children: Scott Adam, Jeffrey Sean. BA, U. N.C., 1971, JD, 1973. Bar: N.C. 1973. Exec. dir. N.C. Acad. Trial Lawyers, Raleigh, 1973-78; assoc. Finger, Watson & di Santi, Boone, N.C., 1978-80; ptnr. Finger, Watson, di Santi & McGee, Boone, 1980—; mem. trustee panel U.S. Bankruptcy Ct., Greensboro, N.C., 1980—; bd. dirs. Legal Services of N.C., Raleigh, 1980-84. Vice-chairperson Watauga County Council on Status of Women, Boone, 1979-82; trustee Caldwell Community Coll. and Tech. Inst., Hudson, N.C., 1980—; mem. exec. bd. N.C. Assn. Community Coll. Trustees, 1983-85. Mem. N.C. Assn. Women Attys. (charter, treas. 1980-84), N.C. Bar Assn. (bd. govs. 1983-86), ABA, N.C. Acad. Trial Lawyers (editor legal mag. 1973-78), N.C. State Bar, Assn. Trial Lawyers Am., Boone C. of C. (bd. dirs. 1982—), N.C. Bus. and Profl. Womens Clubs (chair polit. action com. 1982-83; named Young Career Woman 1980), N.C. Bd. Law Examiners, Boone Bus. and Profl. Women's Club (Woman of Yr. 1980), N.C. Women's Forum, AAUW, LWV. Democrat. Presbyterian. Home: 1041 16th Ave Pl NW Hickory NC 28603 Office: Finger Watson di Santi & McGee PO Box 193 Boone NC 28607

MCGEE, MARY ALICE, health science research administrator; b. Winston-Salem, N.C., Oct. 14, 1950; d. C.L. Jr. and Mary Hilda (Shelton) McG. AB, Meredith Coll., 1972. Tchr. Augusta (Ga.) Schs., 1972-73; specialist grants Med. Sch. Brown U., Providence, R.I., 1974-76; dir. research adminstn. Med. Sch. Brown U., Providence, 1976—, bd. dirs., 1983—. Mem. Sojourner House, Providence. Mem. Soc. Research Administrs., Nat. Council U. Research Administrs. Club: Golden Retriever Am. Home: 121 Plain St Rehoboth MA 02769 Office: Brown U Med Sch Box G Providence RI 02912

MCGEE, PATRICIA ANN, computer management consultant; b. N.Y.C., July 22, 1939; d. Patrick James and Bridget Mary (O'Leary) Brennan; B.A., CCNY, 1961; 1 dau., Ayn Maureen. Sr. cons., analyst Western Ops., Inc., San Francisco, 1968-71; data processing mgr. R. H. Lapin & Co., San Francisco, 1971-73; project leader, systems analyst Transmaerica Corp., San

Francisco, 1973-74; systems analyst United Vintners, Inc., San Francisco, 1974-75; systems planner Fiberboard Corp., 1975-76; customer rep. Computer Scis. Corp., 1976-78; project mgr. Crocker Nat. Bank, 1978-80; cons. Bechtel Co., 1980, Mason-McDuffie & Co., 1980, Pacific Telephone Co., 1980-81; partner The Profls., San Francisco, 1981-83; computer cons. Risk Mgmt. Applications, San Francisco, 1983-84; cons. Bank of Am., Wells Fargo Realty Fin., 1985, Pacific Gas & Elec., 1986—. Mem. Am. Mgmt. Assn., Republican Women San Francisco, Women Entrepreneurs, World Affairs Trade Council, Profl. Women's Network, Assn. System Mgrs. Republican. Roman Catholic. Clubs: Commonwealth of California; San Francisco Bay. Home and Office: 430-10th Ave San Francisco CA 94118

MCGEHEE, KATHE A., newspaper administrator; b. Helena, Mont., June 12, 1946; d. Lorry M. and Helen T. (Schatz) McG.; m. Paul S. Willis, Oct. 1, 1981 (div. 1984). BA in Sociology, Journalism, U. Mont., 1969. Info. specialist State of Mont., Helena, 1971-78; editor, v.p. Art West Mag., Kalispell, Mont., 1978-81; owner Vixen Enterprises, Kalispell, 1982-86; mgr. advt. services Great Falls (Mont.) Tribune, 1987—; instr. Flathead Valley Community Coll., 1980-83; cons. Media Ranking Service, 1978-84; dir. investigative authors' league, Big Fork, Mont., 1980-84. Contbr. interviews to various mags., 1980—. Role cons. Big Brothers-Big Sisters, 1971-75; founder Handicap Aquatics Program, 1981; tchr. Gifted Talented Program, 1982-83; bd. dirs. United Way, Kalispell, 1981-83. Roman Catholic. Home: PO Box 3374 Great Falls MT 59403

MCGERITY, MARGARET ANN, lawyer; b. Boston, Aug. 23, 1949; d. Francis Charles and Margaret Mary (Ford) McG.; m. Max Folkenflik, Apr. 3, 1971; 1 child, Alexander. BA, Columbia U., 1978; JD, Benjamin N. Cardozo Sch. Law, 1981. Artist, 1970-75; asst. U.S. atty. U.S. Atty.'s Office for So. Dist. N.Y., N.Y.C., summer 1980; asst. dist. atty. Bronx Dist. Atty.'s Office, 1981-84; assoc. Wistendahl & Folkenflik, N.Y.C., 1984—. Mem. ABA, N.Y. County Bar Assn., N.Y. Woman's Bar Assn., Assn. Bar City of N.Y. Democrat. Roman Catholic. Home: 320 Riverside Dr New York NY 10025

MCGHEE, PATRICIA LOUISE, technical editor, communications consultant; b. Cin., Apr. 27, 1949; d. Patrick James Bates and Lois Ethelda (Walker) Cameron; m. Maxie Bennett McGhee, Jan. 21, 1977; children: Sarah, Kerri, Kelli. BA in Journalism, French, Edn., U. Wis., 1972; postgrad. in Communications, Pub. Relations, U. Fla., 1987-88. Cert. in French lang. and culture. Tech. writer, editor Environ. Sci. & Engring., Inc., Gainesville, Fla., 1977-78, sr. tech. writer, editor, 1978-80, mgr. project coordination, 1980—; cons., editor, writer, Ill., Minn., Gainesville, 1972—; adj. instr. U. Fla., Gainesville, 1983—. Contbr. articles to profl. and health mags., 1971—. Mem. Gateway Council Girl Scouts U.S., Gainesville, 1977—; ticket mgr. Gainesville Chamber Orch., 1987-88; bd. dirs. Gainesville Suzuki Players, 1987-88. Mem. Soc. Tech. Communication, Women in Communications, Inc., Assn. Edn. in Journalism and Mass Communications, Pi Rho Sigma. Republican. Methodist. Home: 715-203 SW 75th St Gainesville FL 32607 Office: Environ Sci & Engring Inc PO Box ESE Gainesville FL 32602

MC GHEE, PATRICIA LOUISE OHLSEN, educator; b. Monticello, Wis., Sept. 14, 1934; d. Michael Peter and Alicia Alma (Ellefson) Ohlsen; B.A., U. Ariz., 1956; M.A., Marquette U., 1958; postgrad. U. Wis-Madison, 1972-74; m. John Ferdinand; 2 children. Tchr. social studies pub. schs., Milw., 1960-62, Fox Point-Bayside (Wis.), 1963-67, Shorewood, Wis., 1971-72, Waukesha, Wis., 1974—; tchr. social studies Milw. Area Tech. Coll., 1968-74; participant NEH-Carnegie-Mellon project on social history, summer 1981; prescreening chairperson Am. Film and Video Fest., 1987. Sec. Ozaukee County Democratic party, 1973; participant Wis. Conf. on Arms Control, Wingspread, 1978; mem. adv. com. Wis. Pub. TV Network, 1985-86. Author: Gambling with Students' Minds, Lives, and Futures? Time for New Techniques. Taft fellow, 1975; Newspaper in Edn. scholar, 1980. Mem. Historians Film Com., Internat. Assn. for Audio-Visual Media in Hist. Research and Edn., Am. Ednl. Research Assn., Assn. for Ednl. Communications and Tech., Smithsonian Assocs., Ednl. Film Library Assn., Gamma Phi Beta, Pi Gamma Mu. Home: 2615 N University Dr#4 Waukesha WI 53188 Office: 401 E Roberta Ave Waukesha WI 53186

MCGILL, DONNA JEAN, hotel executive; b. Kansas City, Kans., Dec. 7, 1953; d. Donald Eugene and Helen Irene (Morgan) Hamilton; m. Larry C. McGill, Apr. 12, 1979 (div. Aug. 1986); children: James G. O'Connor, S. Patrick O'Connor, Cori Beth, Larry C. Jr. Student, Brown Machie Bus. Sch., 1973. Adminstrv. asst. Cencor Services, Kansas City, Mo., 1975-77; legal sec. various law firms, Kansas City, 1977-80; adminstrv. asst. Grand American Hotel Corp, Overland Park, Kans., 1980-85, project coordinator, purchasing agent, 1986—; Owner the Perfectionist Cleaning Services, Shawnee, Kans., 1985-86. Mem. Nat. Assn. Female Execs., Johnson County Businesswomen (sec. 1986-87, pres. elect 1987-88, pres. 1988—), Women's Resource Ctr. (charter 1986—), Jaycees (pres. 1973-74), Beta Sigma Phi. Office: Grand Am Mgmt Inc 8801 Ballentine Suite 5 Overland Park KS 66214

MCGILL, LORI BETH, educator; b. Orange, N.J., Dec. 20, 1957; d. William Joseph and Patricia Frances (Blatt) Smith; m. John Edward McGill. BA in Elem. Edn., U. R.I., 1979; MA in Elem. Edn., Hofstra U., 1987. Cert. aerobics instr. Tchr. I.S. 155 Pub. Sch., Bronx, N.Y., 1981, Deauville Gardens Sch., Copiague, N.Y., 1981-82; computer teaching specialist Summit Lane Sch., Levittown, N.Y., 1982-85, 3d grade tchr., 1985—; dist. tutor Copiague Pub. Schs., 1982-85, pvt. tutor, 1984—; tchr. summer program Levittown Pub. Schs., 1985—. Contbr. articles to profl. jours. Hofstra U. scholar, 1986, 87. Mem. Kappa Delta Pi. Clubs: Summit Lane, Aerobics (pres. 1985—), Grumman Scuba (sec. 1984-86). Home: 7 Patricia Ct Smithtown NY 11787

MCGILLEY, SISTER MARY JANET, college president; b. Kansas City, Mo., Dec. 4, 1924; d. James P. and Peg (Ryan) McG. B.A., St. Mary Coll., 1945; M.A., Boston Coll., 1951; Ph.D., Fordham U., 1956; postgrad., U. Notre Dame, 1960, Columbia U., 1964. Social worker Kansas City, 1945-46; joined Sisters of Charity of Leavenworth, 1946; tchr. English Hayden High Sch., Topeka, 1948-50, Billings (Mont.) Central High Sch., 1951-53; faculty dept. English St. Mary Coll., Leavenworth, Kans., 1956-64; pres. St. Mary Coll., 1964—. Contbr. articles, fiction and poetry to various jours. Chmn. United Way of Leavenworth, 1966-85; mem. Mayor's Adv. Council, 1967-72, Leavenworth Planning Council, 1977-78; bd. dirs. Kans. Ind. Coll. Fund, 1964—, exec. com., 1985-86, vice-chmn., 1984-85, chmn., 1985-86. Recipient Alumnae award St. Mary Coll., 1969; Disting. Service award Baker U., 1981, Leavenworth Bus. Woman of Yr. Athena award, 1986. Mem. Nat. Council Tchrs. English, Nat. Assn. Ind. Colls. and Univs. (bd. dirs. 1982-85), Kans. Ind. Coll. Assn. (bd. dirs. 1964—, treas. 1982-84, v.p. 1984-85, chmn. exec. com. 1985-86), Am. Council Edn. (com. on women in higher edn. 1980—), Am. Assn. Higher Edn., Kans. City Regional Council for Higher Edn. (bd. dirs. 1965—, treas. 1984-85, v.p. 1986-88), Ind. Coll. Funds Am. (exec. com. 1974-77, trustee-at-large 1975-76), North Cen. Assn. Colls. and Schs. (exec. commr. Com. on Insts. Higher Edn. 1980—, vice chair 1985-86, chair 1987-88), Leavenworth C. of C. (bd. dirs. 1964—), Assn. Am. Colls. (commn. liberal learning 1970-73, com. on curriculum and faculty devel. 1979-82), St. Mary Alumni Assn. (hon. pres. 1964—), Delta Epsilon Sigma. Democrat. Office: St Mary Coll Leavenworth KS 66048

MCGILVRAY, JOAN BAILEY, stockbroker; b. Monrovia, Calif., Nov. 4, 1926; d. William James and Helen Jane (Davis) Bailey; student Stanford U., 1944-47; divorced; children: Alexander Crane, Jr., Mark Rankin, Lynn. Assoc. v.p. Dean Witter & Co., Pasadena, Calif., 1966-76; 1st v.p. Bateman Eichler Hill Richards, Los Angeles, 1976-84; pres. McGilvray & Assocs., Carlsbad, Calif., 1984—. Mem. Nat. Options Soc. (founding dir.), So. Calif. Options Soc. (pres. 1978). Republican. Club: Live Oak Tennis. Home: 76 St Malo Beach Oceanside CA 92054 Office: 2777 Jefferson St Carlsbad CA 92008

MCGILVRAY-RIVET, SUSAN JEAN, school administrator; b. Newark, May 14, 1955; d. James Craig Ferguson and Joan Ruth (Sears) McGilvray; m. Michael Leo Rivet, June 26, 1982; 1 child, Caitlin Suzanne. BA, Wittenberg U., 1977; EdM, Boston U., 1982, postgrad. in edn., 1985—. Bilingual elem. tchr. Lawrence (Mass.) Pub. Schs., 1977-82, coordinator transitional bilingual edn., 1982—. Session mem. Burlington (Mass.) Presbyt. Ch., 1979-82; bd. dirs. YWCA, Lawrence, 1984-86. Mem. Nat. Assn. for Bilingual Edn., Assn. Supervision and Curriculum Devel., Mass. Assn. Bilingual Edn., Mass. Assn. Tchrs. of Speakers of Other Langs. Home: 25 Leeds Terr Lawrence MA 01843 Office: Lawrence Pub Schs 58 Lawrence St Lawrence MA 01840

MCGILVREY, SAKURA LEE, telecommunications executive; b. South Haven, Mich., Feb. 10, 1949; d. Joseph and Mieko (Takeichi) Bowers; m. Arthur W. WIlliams, July 1, 1966 (div. July 1974); children: Teresa E., Bruce K.; m. Richard L. Johnson, Apr. 3, 1976 (dec. Mar. 1986); 1 child, Erin N.; m. Frank B. McGilvrey III, Aug. 21, 1987. Student, Cameron State Coll., Lawton, Okla., 1967-69, No. Va. Community Coll., Annandale, 1975-80, 87, George Washington U., 1978-80. Supr. engring. records C&P Telephone Co. of Va., Fairfax, 1973-76, staff asst. budgeting, 1976-77; engring. clk. C&P Telephone Co. of Va., Arlington, 1969-73, supr. network adminstrn., 1977-83, supr. switching control, 1983-86; staff supr. planning new tech. C&P Telephone Co. of Md., Silver Springs, 1986-87; mgr. switching control ctr. C&P Telephone Co. of Washington, 1987—. Mem. Telephone Pioneers Am., Nat. Assn. Female Execs., Am. Philatelic So., Assn. Research & Enlightenment.

MCGINLEY, NANCY ELIZABETH, lawyer; b. Columbia, Mo., Feb. 29, 1952; d. Robert Joseph and Ruth Evangeline (Garnett) McG. BA with high honors, U. Tex., 1974, JD, 1977. Bar: Tex. 1977, U.S. Dist. Ct. (no. dist.) Tex. 1979. Law clk. U.S. Dist. Ct. (no. dist.) Tex., Fort Worth, 1977-79; assoc. Crumley, Murphy and Shrull, Fort Worth, 1979-81; staff atty. SEC, Fort Worth, 1981-87; br. chief SEC Los Angeles Regional Office, 1987—. Mem. editorial staff Urban Law Rev. Mem. Tarrant County Young Lawyers Assn., Women Lawyers of Tarrant County, Fort Worth Bus. and Profl. Women's Assn., Mortar Bd., Phi Beta Kappa, Phi Kappa Phi, Alpha Lambda Delta. Methodist. Home: 3121 Sondra Dr Apt 203E Fort Worth TX 76107 Office: SEC 411 W 7th St 8th Floor Fort Worth TX 90036-3648

MCGINNIS, CYNTHIA WOLF, microbiologist; b. Lancaster, Pa., Jan. 17, 1949; d. H. LeMar and Rosemary A. (Snyder) Wolf; student Millersville Coll., 1979—. Staff technician St. Joseph Hosp., Lancaster, 1966-67; staff technician Lancaster Osteo. Hosp., 1968-72, microbiology supr., 1972—, mem. infection control com., 1973—; mem. adv. panel Med. Lab. Observer, 1979-81, 85-86; lab. systems mgr., 1986— . Mem. Am. Med. Technologists, Am. Soc. Microbiology, Central Pa. Microbiology Assn., Pa. Soc. Med. Technologists, N.Y. Acad. Scis., Nat. Cert. Agy. Med. Lab. Personnel. Roman Catholic. Office: 1100 E Orange St Lancaster PA 17604

MCGINNIS, JANE, real estate executive; b. North Adams, Mass., Sept. 9, 1940; d. Guido L. and Ellen D. (Curran) Cimonetti; m. Gordon S. McGinnis, Sept. 15, 1962. BA in English, Cardinal Cushing Coll., 1962. English tchr. Arkanne Sch., Tehran, Iran, 1976-77; broker Century 21, Robert Stone Inc., Braintree, Mass., 1979-85; owner Brava Real Estate, Inc., Weymouth, Mass., 1985—; yoga tchr. Braintree Adult Edn. and Parks Dept., 1979-85. Troop leader Girls Scouts U.S.A., Braintree; den mother Boy Scouts Am., Braintree; tchr. St. Clares Ch., Braintree. Mem. Nat. Assn. Realtors, Quincy Bd. Realtors (trainer success series for brokers 1985-88), Grad. Realtors Inst. (cert.). Roman Catholic. Home: 19 Summit Ridge Dr Braintree MA 02184 Office: Brava Real Estate Inc 59-61 Washington St Weymouth MA 02188

MCGIVERN, MARY ELIZABETH, chemical engineer; b. Parkersburg, W.Va., Jan. 28, 1954; d. William Edward and Glenda Louise (Bowers) McG.; m. James R. McKinley, Feb. 29, 1980. B in Chem. Engring., W. Va. U., 1975; MBA, U. Houston, 1982. Process engr. Gulf Oil Chem. Co., Baytown, Tex., 1975-76, ops. specialist, 1976-79, zone supr., 1979-80, bus. analyst, Houston, 1980-85, asst. product mgr., 1985—. Vol. adviser Jr. Achievement, 1975-78. Recipient Woman of the Yr. award YWCA, Houston, 1980. Mem. Houston Bus. Forum (bd. dirs.), Am. Inst. Chem. Engrs. Republican. Roman Catholic. Address: 20202 Atascocita Shores Dr Humble TX 77346

MCGLAMERY, BARBARA COGGINS, homebuilder; b. Atlanta, Aug. 19, 1939; d. Robert Allen and Minnie (Reed) Coggins; m. Gerald G. McGlamery, Nov. 26, 1960; children—Gerald G. Jr., George L. B.A., Auburn U., 1961. Sales assoc. Ronald Warren Real Estate, Florence, Ala., 1978-83, property mgr., 1984-86; v.p. So. Heritage Homes, Florence, 1985—. Mem. adv. bd. Kennedy-Douglass Ctr. for Arts, Florence, 1976-83; bd. dirs. Kennedy-Douglass Vols., 1976-83; mem. Salvation Army Aux. Mem. Nat. Assn. Homebuilders, Nat. Assn. Realtors, Ala. Assn. Realtors, Grad. Realtors Inst. Alpha Omicron Pi (adv. bd. Alpha Kappa chpt. 1970-82). Presbyterian. Home: 214 Robin Hood Dr Florence AL 35630 Office: So Heritage Homes PO Box 674 Florence AL 35630

MC GLASSON, CHRISTINE LOUISE, advertising director, consultant; b. Glendale, Calif., Nov. 13, 1944; d. Howard Allen and Christine (Fee) Mc G. Student, Am. Acad. of Dramatic Arts, 1964; BA in Radio and TV, Fla. State U., 1966; MA in Communications, Calif. State U., 1980. Asst. dir. of news program Sta. WFSU-TV, Fla. State U., Tallahassee, 1965-66, radio announcer Sta. WFSU-FM, 1964-66; copywriter and programming asst. Sta. WSB-AM-FM, Atlanta, Ga., 1966; continuity dir., announcer and promotion dir. Sta. KCTC, Sacramento, Calif., 1968-72; copy supr. and account exec. Brown, Clark & Elkus Co., Sacramento, 1972-73; writer and comml. producer for Sta. KCRA-TV, Sacramento, 1974-75; propr., creative dir. Chris McGlasson & Assos., Communications Cons., Sacramento, 1976—; mktg. dir. Rancho Murieta Properties, Inc., near Sacramento, 1976-80, also gen. mgr. Rancho Murieta Country Club, 1977-78; Western region media mgr. Seven-Up U.S.A., 1982-85; dir. advt. and sales promotion Blue Diamond Almonds, Sacramento, 1985—; contbr. feature articles to local publs.; guest lectr. on communications and broadcasting to local secondary schs. and jr. colls., 1972—; dir. Sacramento Better Bus. Bur., 1975-76. Broadcast chmn. Sacramento Red Cross, 1970-73; publicity chmn. Soc. for the Prevention of Cruelty to Animals, 1976-77; music festival chmn. Sacramento Symphony Assn., 1977-80, bd. dirs., 1979-82; mem. publicity com. Sacramento Opera Guild, 1977-79. Served to capt. USAF, 1966-70; lt. col. with Calif. State Info. Office Air NG, 1972—. Recipient Sacramento C. of C. award, 1970, Nat. Retail Advt. award, 1972, Am. Radio/TV Commls. awards (Clios), 1972-73, Am. Advt. Fedn. award, 1973, Calif. Assn. Realtors award (3), 1978, Superior Calif. Builders Assn. awards (4), 1978, 79, Cable Car awards San Francisco Ad Club, 1979, mktg. Dir. of Yr. award Superior Calif. Bldg. Industries, 1979, Appreciation awards for public service by various community and civic orgns., 1973-77; named Sacramento Advt. Person of Yr., 1975; High Achievement award Seven-Up, 1985. Mem. Am. Acad. of Advt., Sacramento Advt. Club (past pres.; 80 awards for creativity 1971-87), Sacramento Women in Advt., Internat. Communications Assn., Sacramento Mktg. Assn. (pres.), Nat. Guard Assn., Capitol City Chpt. Episcopalian.

MCGLYNN, JACQUELYN MARGARET, radiological technician; b. Houston, May 2, 1949; d. John Francis and Margaret Sultana (Smirl) McG. Cert. radiology technician, Meml. Hosp., Houston, 1971; AA, Tyler Jr. Coll., 1985; student, Midwestern State U. Radiology technician Ledbetter Clinic, Houston, 1971-79, Meml. Hosp. Southeast, Houston, 1979-83, Mother Frances Hosp., Tyler, Tex., 1983—. Mem. Am. Soc. Radiologic Technologists, East Tex. Soc. Radiologic Technologists. Home: PO Box 131363 Tyler TX 75713 Office: Mother Francis Hosp 800 E Dawson Tyler TX 75701

MCGOLDRICK, RUTH FRANCES, religious organization administator; b. Quincy, Mass., Oct. 13, 1934; d. Orrin Francis and Florence Elizabeth (Taylor) McG. BS in Bus. Edn., Boston Coll., 1959; M in Religious Edn., St. Mary's Sch. Theology, 1965. Instr. theology and spirituality New England area, 1959-73; formation coordinator Sisters of Providence, Holyoke, Mass., 1969-73; exec. dir. Religious Formation Conf., Washington, 1973-76; program dir. Genesis Spiritual Life Ctr., Westfield, Mass., 1976—; workshop and retreat dir. Genesis Spiritual Life Ctr., U.S.A., Can., Eng. and Ireland; mem. exec. council Sisters of Providence, 1977-85; writer, speaker Women of Providence in Collaboration, 1980-86; active numerous religious orgns. Coeditor, author: Facets of Future: Religious Life, 1976; editor (newsletter) In-Formation, 1974-76; founding editor (newsletter) In-Formation; contbr. numerous articles to profl. jours. and private pubs. Mem. nat. adv. com. Internat. Women's Yr., Washington, 1976; liaison, participant nat. bicentennial projects, Washington, 1976, mem. bd. sponsors Nat. Intensive Jour. Program, N.Y.C., 1977—; founding mem. Diocesan support groups for separated and divorced people, 1981-83; exec. adv. bd. The Neurofibromatosis Assn. Inc., Granby, Mass., 1986—. Recipient Women's award Springfield (Mass.) Dailey News, 1967, Inst. Women Today award, 1976, White House invitation Gerald Ford, 1976. Mem. Inst. for Research in Spirituality (v.p. 1976—), Retreats Internat. Democrat. Roman Catholic. Home and Office: Manna House 53 Mill St Westfield MA 01085

MCGONIGAL, PEARL, lieutenant governor; b. Melville, Sask., Can., June 10, 1929; d. Fred and Kathryne Kuhlman; m. Marvin A. McGonigal, Nov. 3, 1948; 1 dau., Kimberly Jane. Ed. in, Melville, Sask.; LL.D. (hon.), U. Man. Formerly engaged in banking; then mdse. rep.; mem. St. James-Assiniboia (Man.) City Council, 1969-71; mem. Greater Winnipeg (Man.) City Council, 1971-81, chmn. com. on recreation and social services, 1977-79, dep. mayor and chmn. exec. policy com., 1979-81; lt. gov. Man., 1981—; mem. adv. bd. Royal Trust Co., 1987—; trustee First Can. Mortgage Fund; bd. dirs. Mediacom. Inc., Can. Inperial Bank of Commerce. Author: Frankly Feminine Cookbook, 1975; weekly columnist: Reliance Press Ltd. Newspapers, 1970-81. Bd. dirs. Winnipeg Conv. Centre, 1975-77, Red River Exhbn., 1975-81, Rainbow Stage, 1976-81, Man. Blue Cross; ex-officio mem. Man. Theatre Centre, 1977-81; mem. Winnipeg Conv. and Visitors Bur., 1973-75, Man. Environ. Concil, 1974-76, Man. Aviation Council, 1974-77; mem. selection com. Faculty Dental Hygiene, U. Man., 197-80; bd. mgmt. Winnipeg Home Improvement Program, 1979-81; chmn. adv. com. Sch. Nursing, Grace Gen. Hosp., 1972—; past chmn. St. James-Assiniboia Interfaith Immigration Council; former mem. vestry St. Andrew's Anglican Ch.; former vol. Lions Manor, Sherbrook Day Centre; chmn. bd. mgmt. Grace Gen. Hosp., 1987—; chmn. bd. reference Catherine Booth Bible Coll., 1987. Recipient award Dist. 64 Toastmasters, 1974, award Winnipeg lodge Elks, 1975, nat. B'nai Brith Humanitarian award, 1984, Citizen of Yr. award Knights of Columbus, 1987; decorated dame Order of St. John; named hon. col. 735 Communications Regt. Mem. Beta Sigma Phi (1st Lady of Yr. 1986). Liberal. Club: Winnipeg Winter. Lodge: KC (Citizen of Yr. 1987). Home: 51-361 Westwood Dr, Winnipeg, MB Canada R3K 1G4 Office: Rm 235 Legis Bldg, Winnipeg, MB Canada R3C 0V8

MCGOUGH, ALICE MARIE, chem. co. purchasing agt.; b. Tarentum, Pa., June 25, 1937; d. Edward Albert and Frances Amelia (Gross) Gase; BA magna cum laude, Carlow Coll., 1957; postgrad. U. Pitts., 1958-59; children: Mary Gase, Paul Aidan, Daniel John. Research asst. in biophysics U. Pitts., 1957-59; lab. technician GAF Corp., Wayne, N.J., 1973, chems. buyer, 1973-76; buyer organic chems. div. Am. Cyanamid Co., Bound Brook, N.J., 1976-78, purchasing agt. materials planning and procurement div., 1978-81, purchasing agt. chems. group, 1981—. mem. exec. bd. LWV of Wayne Twp., N.J., 1969-72; vol. Paterson (N.J.) Task Force, Day Care Ctr., 1972, phone worker Teleministries, Morris, Passaic Counties, N.J., 1987—, Contact Teleministries, Morris and Passaic Counties, 1987—. Mem. Smithsonian Instn. Democrat. Roman Catholic. Club: Sierra. Office: One Cyanamid Plaza Wayne NJ 07470

MCGOVERN, ANN, writer, publisher; b. N.Y.C., May 25, 1930; d. Arthur and Kate (Malatsky) Weinberger; m. Martin L. Scheiner, June 6, 1970; children: Peter, Charles, Annie, James. BA, U. N.Mex., 1952. Freelance writer 1953—; editor Scholastic Books, N.Y.C., 1960-67; pub., editor The Privileged Traveler Mag., Pleaseantville, N.Y., 1985-87; lectr. to ednl. and conservation groups. Author 40 books for young people; contbr. articles to mags. Fellow Explorers Club; mem. PEN, Soc. Women Geographers, Circumnavigators Club, Internat. Food, Wine and Travel Writers, Am. Soc. Journalists and Authors. Home and Office: 42 Usonia Rd Pleasantville NY 10570

MCGOVERN, CONSTANCE MADELINE, historian, educator. BA cum laude, Coll. Our Lady Elms, Chicopee, Mass., 1960; MA in History, U. Mass., 1971, PhD in History, 1976. Instr. history, vis. lectr. continuing edn. U. Mass., Amherst, 1976-77; vis. lectr. Bridgewater (Mass.) State Coll., 1976-77; asst. prof. Kalamazoo (Mich.) Coll., 1977-78, U. Ariz., Tucson, 1978-80; asst. prof. U. Vt., Burlington, 1980-86, assoc. prof., 1986—; Mem. gov.'s commn. Women, Women's History Task Force, faculty standards com. Coll. Arts Sci. U. Vt., 1987-89, acad. standards com., 1983-86, del. Nat. Acad. Advising Assn. Conf., 1984, pre-law adv. com., 1981-86, asst. marshall commencement, 1982—; manuscript reviewer Columbia U. Press, U. Press New Eng., Johns Hopkins U. Press, Vt. History; cons. Pa. Hosp., Vt. Hist. Soc. Author: Masters of Madness: Social Origins of the American Psychiatric Profession, 1985; contbr. numerous articles and revs. to profl. jours.; speaker various confs. Speaker, commentator, cons. New Eng. Constn. Series (NEH), various locations, 1986-87, Vt. Council Humanities and Pub. Issues, Am. Biography Series, 1984-85, numerous other hist. awareness projects. Grantee Am. Council Learned Socs., 1984, U. Ariz. Found., 1979, Am. Philos. Soc., 1979, NEH, 1981; fellow U. Vt. Summer Research, 1982, 85, NEH/Rockefeller, Newberry Library Inst. Quantitative History, 1978. Mem. Orgn. Am. Historians, New Eng. Hist. Assn., Vt. Hist. Soc., Vt. Acad. Arts Scis. Home: 132 Iroquois Ave Essex Junction VT 05452 Office: Univ Vt Dept History Burlington VT 05401

MCGOVERN, DONNA MARIE, assistant controller; b. Chgo., Nov. 1, 1956; d. Theodore and Marie B. (Sadilek) Machatka; m. James Charles McGovern, Aug. 2, 1942; children: James Eugene, Matthew Nicholas. AA in Gen. Bus., Coll. DuPage, 1978; BS in Acctg., York Coll. Pa., 1983. Sec. Chemetron, Chgo., 1974-78; jr. fin. analyst Alloy Rods, Hanover, Pa., 1978-81, fin. analyst, 1981-83, fin. planning coordinator, 1983-84; sr. fin. analyst Coopervision, Irvine, Calif., 1984-85, mgr. fin. reporting, 1985-86; asst. controller Monogram Sanitation, Redondo Beach, Calif., 1987—. Republican. Office: Monogram Sanitation 4030 Freeman Blvd Redondo Beach CA 90278-1180

MCGOVERN, LORETTA ELISABETH, advertising executive; b. Brookline, Mass., Nov. 3, 1949; d. Robert Frederick and Ines (Steigmann) F.; m. James McGovern, Oct. 13, 1984; 1 child, Caitlin Marie. BFA, U. Mass., Boston, 1973. Model Fashions First WCNB-TV, Boston, 1960-61; copyright asst. Machat & Kronfeld, N.Y.C., 1969-70; model, Boston, 1970-73; legal asst. Hertzberg, Childs & Shiotani, Beverly Hills, Calif., 1974-76; dir. pub. relations Parsons, Friedmann & Central, Boston, 1978—; pres. Projects, Boston, 1982—. Creator The Original Baby Trench, 1987. Democrat. Jewish. Mem. Nat. Assn. Female Execs., Advt. Club Greater Boston.

MC GOVERN, MAUREEN THERESE, entertainer; b. Youngstown, Ohio, July 27, 1949; d. James Terrence and Mary Rita (Welsh) McG. Student pub. schs., Youngstown. Exec. sec. Youngstown Cartage Co., 1968-69; sec. Assocs. in Anesthesiology, Youngstown, 1970-71. Entertainer, 1972—; stage appearances include: The Sound of Music, 1981, The Pirates of Penzance, 1981, South Pacific, 1982, Nine, 1984, Brownstone, 1984, Guys and Dolls, 1984; cameo appearance in movie The Towering Inferno, 1975; appeared in film Ky. Fried Theater's Airplane, 1979; albums recorded include: The Morning After, 1973 (Gold Record award), Nice To Be Around, 1974, Academy Award Performance, 1975, Maureen McGovern, 1979, Another Woman In Love, 1987; composer: Midnight Storm, 1973, If I Wrote You a Song, 1973, All I Want, 1974, Memory, 1974, Little Boys and Men, 1974, Love Knots, 1974, You Love Me Too Late, 1979, Thief in the Night, 1979, Don't Stop Now, 1979, Hello Again, 1979, Halfway Home, 1980, others. Recipient Gold Record for single The Morning After, Record Industry Assn. Am., 1973; Can. RPM Gold Leaf award, 1973; Australian gold award, 1975; resolution for bringing fame and recognition to Ohio, Ohio Senate, 1974; Grand prize Tokyo Music Festival, 1975. Mem. ASCAP, Am. Fedn. Musicians, AFTRA, Screen Actors Guild. Office: care Warner Bros Records 3300 Warner Blvd Burbank CA 91510 *

MCGOVERN, MICHELLE, sales representative; b. Birmingham, Mich., Mar. 15, 1962; d. Philip Joseph II and Dolores Rita (Dugal) McGovern. Course study fashion mdse., Parson's Sch. Design, Paris, 1983; BS, Western Mich. U., 1984. Asst. buyer, asst. mgr. J.L. Hudson, Detroit, 1983-84; mdse. mgr. Hattie's, Inc., Birmingham, Mich., 1984; asst. buyer, asst. mgr. Bloomingdale's, N.Y.C., 1984-86; sales rep. Advanced Word Processing, N.Y.C., 1986-87, I.B. Diffusion, N.Y.C., 1987—. Mem. Nat.

Assn. Female Execs., Alpha Phi. Republican. Roman Catholic. Home: 190 Columbus Ave Apt 4-C New York NY 10023 Office: I B Diffusion 1410 Broadway New York NY 10018

MCGOWAN, KATHLEEN JOAN, social worker; b. Berwyn, Ill., July 24, 1946; d. Robert Emmet and Joan P. (Rakas) McG.; m. Terrance P. McGuire, May 10, 1985. BA, Loyola U., Chgo., 1969; MSW, U. Ill., Chgo., 1975. Cert. social worker, Ill. Caseworker Cath. Charities, Chgo., 1969-75, supr. foster care, 1975-79, program dir. child protective services, 1979-84, dir. staff devel. and edn., 1984—; cons., lectr. Alexian Bros. Hosp., St. Louis, 1985, Alexian Bros. Med. Ctr. and Health System, Elk Grove Village, Ill., 1986 ; cons. Sisters of St. Joseph 3d Order of St. Francis, Bartlett, Ill., 1986; lectr. Loyola U. Grad. Sch. of Social Work, Chgo., 1987—. Editor: (with others) Divorce and Beyond, 1983. Mem. devel. bd. Sisters of St. Joseph, LaGrange, Ill., 1983-86, adv. bd., 1985—. Mem. Cath. Charities U.S.A. (chair membership com. 1984—), Nat. Assn. Social Workers, Acad. Cert. Social Workers, Ill. Tng. and Devel. Assn. Home: 21780 W Washington Grayslake IL 60030 Office: Cath Charities 126 N Desplaines Chicago IL 60606

MCGOWAN, MARYANNE ELIZABETH, accountant, consultant; b. Cin., Dec. 5, 1948; d. Elmer Peter and Mary Rose (Lisi) McG.; m. David Marcus Fiala, Jan. 4, 1969 (div. 1986); 1 child, Michael. BA, BS, U. Cin., 1970; MBA, Xavier U., Cin., 1986. Social worker Health and Human Service Dept., Cin., 1969-72, supr. med. unit, 1972-74, chief certification div., 1974-81; tax acct. Hengehold, Hengehold and Co., Cin., 1981-86; coordinator system devel. U. Cin., 1986-88; chief fin. officer Dames & Moore Ltd., Cin., 1988—; cons. Hengehold Group, 1984-86, Schenz Theatrical Supply Co., 1984-85, Copin Inc., Cin., 1986—, Williams Subaru Inc., 1987—. Chmn. Jr. League Cin., 1978—; mem. com. Nat. Commn. Pub. Broadcasting, Washington, 1976, exec. com. Children's Hosp. Med. Ctr., Cin., 1985; adv. bd. Arthritis Found., 1977, WCET-TV, Cin., 1969—, Pub. Broadcasting Service award, 1979; treas., bd. dirs. Internat. Folk Festival, Cin., 1987-90. Nat. Dorothy Shaw Leadership award Alpha Delta Pi, Macon, Ga., 1970. Mem. Nat. Assn. Female Execs., Am. Bus. Women's Assn. (nat. grantee 1985), Univ. and Coll. Mid Univ. Level Adminstrs., Phi Beta (Pi Alpha Mu Scroll award 1972). Club: Seven Hills Garden (Cin.) (chmn. com. 1986-87). Home: 5913 Quailhill Dr Cincinnati OH 45233 Office: Dames & Moore Ltd 644 Linn St Suite 501 Cincinnati OH 45203

MCGOWEN, SANDRA GRANT, interior designer; b. Shreveport, La., Dec. 4, 1942; d. Ellis Elva and Mary Lou (McMahen) Grant; m. Norman Douglas McGowen, Mar. 14, 1964 (dec. 1972); children: Amanda Laine, Norman Douglas Jr. BS in Home Econs., La. Tech. U., 1965; BVA in Interior Design, Ga. State U., 1978. Interior designer Rich's, Atlanta, 1978-85; dir. design Comml. Interior Designs, Atlanta, 1985; pres. McGowen Interiors Inc., Atlanta, 1985—. Elder, treas. East Point (Ga.) Presbyn. Ch., 1986; bd. dirs. Niskey Lake, Atlanta, 1986; design judge March of Dimes, Birmingham, Ala., 1987. Mem. Am. Soc. Interior Designers (Presdl. citation, 1981, 87, newsletter editor 1986, 87, treas. 1987, 88), Nat. Trust for Hist. Preservation, Ga. Trust for Hist. Preservation, High Mus. Art, Atlanta Decorative Arts, Ga. Citizens for Arts, Atlanta Preservation Soc., Mercedes Benz Club Am. (sec. Peachtree sect.). Gamma Phi Beta (pres. Mother's Club, U. Ga., 1987-88). Republican. Presbyterian. Home and Office: 2244 DeFoors Ferry Rd Atlanta GA 30318

MCGRADY, CORINNE YOUNG, design company executive; b. N.Y.C., May 6, 1938; d. Albert I. and Reda (Bromberg) Young; m. Michael Robinson McGrady; children—Sean, Siobhan, Liam. Student, Bard Coll., Annandale-on-Hudson, N.Y., 1960, Harvard U., 1968-69. Founder, pres. McGrady Corp., East Northport, N.Y., 1970—. Acrylic works exhibited in group shows at Mus. Contemporary Crafts, N.Y.C., 1969-70, Smithsonian Instn., 1970-71, Pompidou Ctr., Paris, 1971, Mus. Sci. and Industry, 1970; sculpture exhibited at Guild Hall Show, Southampton, N.Y., 1968, Hecksher Mus., 1968. Vice pres. Woman's Internat. League for Peace and Freedom, Huntington, N.Y., 1971. Recipient Design Rev. award Indsl. Design, 1969, 70; Instant Supergraphic Indsl. Design Rev. award, 1971. Patentee cookbook stand. Home: 95 Eatons Neck Rd Northport NY 11768 Office: Corinne McGrady Designs The McGrady Corp 29 Brightside East Northport NY 11731

MCGRAIL, JEAN KATHRYN, artist, educator, poet; b. Mpls., May 1, 1947; d. Robert Vern and Mary Virginia (Kees) McGrail; m. Theodore Esser III, Sept. 28, 1985. B.S., U. Wis.-River Falls, 1970; M.F.A., Cranbrook Acad. Art, 1972; postgrad. Sch. of Art Inst. of Chgo., 1985. One woman shows include Gallery at the Commons, Chgo., 1982; group exhbns. include Saginaw Art Mus., Mich., 1972, Met. Mus. Art, Miami, Fla., 1974, Lowe Mus. Art, Coral Gables, Fla., 1974, 76, Miller Galleries, Coconut Grove, Fla., 1978, 80, Cicchinelli Gallery, N.Y.C., 1980-82, Harper Coll., 1984; represented in permanent collections at Miami-Dade Pub. Library, U. Wis.-River Falls, MacGregor Found., others. Cranbrook Acad. Art scholar, 1971; recipient Poster Competition award Vizcaya Mus., 1974; Print award Auction WPBT, 1979. Mem. Coll. Art Assn., Women's Caucus for Art, Chgo. Artists Coalition. Democrat. Home: 607 Columbia Ave Elgin IL 60120

MCGRAIL, SUSAN KING, travel agency executive, accountant; b. Richmond, Va., Mar. 7, 1952; d. William Jr. and Anne Winn (Gibson) King; m. John Patrick McGrail, Jr., June 2, 1979; children: Katharine Anne, Patricia Lynn. BBA, Coll. William and Mary, 1974. CPA, Va. Employment counselor Avante Gard of Richmond, Inc., 1970-73; staff acct. Touche Ross & Co., Washington, 1974-75, Richmond, 1975-78; controller Continental Cablevision, Richmond, 1978-81; v.p. fin. Warner Amex Cable Communications, Cin., 1981-85; prin. Travel Agts. Internat., Cin., 1985—; sec., treas. Warner Amex Minority Loan Fund, Cin., 1981-85. Alumni career advisor Coll. William and Mary, Williamsburg, Va., 1982—, fund raiser, 1984—. Fellow Am. Inst. CPA's, Va. Soc. CPA's; mem. Am. Soc. Travel Agts., Greater Cin. C. of C. (pres.'s roundtable), Pi Beta Phi. Republican. Episcopalian. Avocations: scuba diving, snorkeling, reading. Home: 2207 Spinningwheel Ln Cincinnati OH 45244 Office: Travel Agts Internat Montgomery 10778 Montgomery Rd Cincinnati OH 45242

MCGRATH, CAROL ELIZABETH, controller; b. Pitts., Sept. 11, 1939; d. William Conrad Egerter and Helen Marie (Gates) Cloherty; m. James L. McGrath Sr., May 2, 1959 (div. Oct. 1986); 1 child, James L. Jr. Student, Reynolds Sch., 1986. Adminstrv. asst. North Hills Passavant Hosp., Pitts., 1961-64; office mgr. Stone Buick, Clearwater, Fla., 1981-85; sec., treas. St. Petersburg (Fla.) Jeep/Renault, 1985-86; comptroller Thunder Marine, Clearwater, 1986—, Smith Leasing, Clearwater, 1986—, Clearwater Nissan, 1986—; sec./treas. Sherwood Coal Corp., Pitts., 1974-78, J. L. McMgrath Corp., Clearwater, 1978—. Mem. Nat. Assn. Female Execs. Office: Clearwater Nissan 2123 U S 19 S Clearwater FL 33546

MCGRATH, ELEANOR BURNS, magazine editor, journalist; b. Gloucester, Mass., July 28, 1952; d. Edward James and Julie Ann (Holloran) McGrath, m. Paul A. Witteman, May 5, 1984. A.B. magna cum laude, Mt. Holyoke Coll., 1974. Researcher Time-Life Books, N.Y.C., 1974-76; reporter-researcher Time Mag., N.Y.C., 1976-78, staff writer, 1978-81, edn. writer-editor, 1981-86; sr. editor Women's Sports & Fitness mag., 1986-88. Trustee, Mt. Holyoke Coll., 1976-79; pres. Greater N.Y. Athletic Assn., N.Y.C., 1980-83. Time fellow Duke U., 1981; recipient Journalist-in-Residence award Nat. Endowment Humanities, U. Mich., 1984-85. Home: 199 Caselli Ave San Francisco CA 94114

MCGRATH, PAMELA LYNN, sales executive; b. Akron, Ohio, Oct. 5, 1955; d. James Tiernan and Naomi Ruth (Long) McG. BA in Communications, U. Akron, 1980. Account exec. Sta. WFTP Radio, Ft. Pierce, Fla., 1980; asst. to v.p. mktg. Sun Bank, Ft. Pierce, Fla., 1980-83; regional account salesperson Sta. WOAC-TV, Canton, Ohio, 1983-84; regional account exec., mgr. office Wells, Rich, Greene, Cleve., 1984-87; mgr. account western region Lois Pitts Gershon Pon/GGK, Los Angeles, 1987; v.p., field mgr. Lois Pitts Gershon Pon/GGK, Valencia, 1987—. Co-producer (film) The Treasure Coast-St. Lucie County, 1983 (2 Addy awards); co-producer, writer (TV comml.) Remlinger Christmas Message, 1984 (Silver Mona award). Mem. Nat. Assn. Female Execs., Mortar Bd. Republican. Roman Catholic. Office: Lois Pitts Gershon Pon GGK Valencia Exec Plaza Suite 201 27201 Tourney Rd Valencia CA 91355

MCGRAW, JANET GOLLER, executive secretary; b. Tulsa, Sept. 23, 1930; d. Walter Henry and Caroline Wilhelmina (Pedersen) Goller; m. Russell McGraw, Oct. 11, 1958; children: Theresa A. McGraw-French, Jeanne M. McGraw Garalis, Mary K. McGraw Tidwell, Alice Elizabeth. Cert. in acctg., DeKalb Community Coll., 1983, cert. profl. sec., 1986; cert. of mgmt., U. Ga., 1988. Sec. to mgr. Merrill, Lynch, Pierce, Fenner & Smith, Miami Beach, Fla., 1954-59; sec. to v.p. Am. Bonded Mortgage Co., Miami, Fla., 1960-62; sec. John Nicholas, Miami, 1962-72; exec. sec. to fire chief DeKalb County Fire Services, Decatur, Ga., 1973—. Mem. Profl. Sec. Internat. (membership coms. 1985-86, ways and means com. 1985-86, publicity 1986-87), CPS Service Commn. (chmn. 1988), Nat. Assn. Female Execs., Am. Soc. Profl. and Exec. Women, Ga. Council of Notaries Public, Beta Sigma Phi (life). Office: DeKalb County Dept Pub Safety 4400 Meml Dr Complex Decatur GA 30032

MCGRAW, LAURA KAY, special education supervisor; b. Peoria, Ill., June 17, 1960; d. James Michael and Marilyn Joyce (Kelley) McG. BS in Spl. Edn., Ohio U., 1982; MS in Edn. Adminstrn., U. Dayton, 1985. Cert. supr., prin., spl. edn. tchr., elem. edn. tchr. Severe behavior handicap tchr. Montgomery County Pub. Schs., Dayton, 1982-85, severe behavior handicap supr., 1985—. Coach United Cerebral Palsy, Dayton, 1980—, summer camp dir., 1982-86, tng. program coordinator, 1986—. Mem. Internat. Council for Exceptional Children (liaison 1986—), Ohio Council for Exceptional Children (liaison 1986—, editor newsletter 1985—), Council for Children with Behavioral Disabilities, Nat. Assn. Female Execs., Phi Delta Kappa. Democrat. Roman Catholic. Home: 292 Silver Bugle Ln West Carrollton OH 45449 Office: 650 St Paul Ave Dayton OH 45410

MCGRAW, LAVINIA MORGAN, retail company executive; b. Detroit, Feb. 26, 1924; d. Will Curtis and Margaret Coulter (Oliphant) McG. AB, Radcliffe Coll., 1945. Sales assoc. The May Corp., Washington, 1977—. Mem. Phi Beta Kappa. Avocation: hiking. Home: 2501 Calvert St NW Washington DC 20008

MCGUFFIE, GINGER ALLAN, lawyer, accountant; b. Ft. Worth, Sept. 9, 1944; m. Allan L. Wulff, Oct. 1, 1977. BBA, Georgetown U., 1966, JD, 1973. Bar: Md., D.C., Va.; CPA, D.C., Tex. Acct. Raymond Lang & Co., Washington, 1966-68; tax specialist Coopers & Lybrand, Dallas, 1968-70; tax law specialist Internal Revenue Service, Washington, 1970-74; mng. ptnr. Ginger McGuffie & Assoc., Washington, 1974-83, McGuffie & Wiese, Washington, 1983-87, McGuffie, Handal & Wiese, Washington, 1987—; corp. counsel Assn. Devel. Council of Washington, 1987—. Author: BNATax Portfolio - 1244 Stock, 1983. Mem. Va. Bar Assn., Md. Bar Assn., D.C. Bar Assn., Va. Trial Lawyers Assn., Am. Arbitration Assn., N.Y. Stock Exchange. Office: McGuffie Handal & Wiese 1211 Connecticut Ave NW Washington DC 20036

MCGUIGAN, CORRINE ANN, education educator, consultant; b. Spokane, Wash., Feb. 2, 1950; d. R. Patirck and Betty (Teddy) McG. AB, Seattle U., 1972; MEd, U. Wash., 1975; PhD, U. Idaho, 1979. Tchr., researcher U. Wash., Seattle, 1973-75; researcher, technical advisor U.S. Dept. Edn., varied, 1975-79; asst. prof. St. John's U., N.Y.C., 1975-79; assoc. prof., dept. chair St. Mary's Coll., Notre Dame, Ind., 1980-86; sr. cons. Designs for Human Devel., Notre Dame, 1976—. Author: Time Management, 1984, Teachers' Resource Guide, 1979; mem. editorial bd.: Jour. Ednl. and Psychological Research; contbr. articles to profl. jours. Recipient Title VI-G, VI-D research awards U.S. Dept. Edn., 1975-86, disting. service award Nat. Cath. Assn., 1985. Mem. Council Exceptional Children, Assn. Severely Handicapped. Democrat. Catholic. Office: St Mary's Coll Notre Dame IN 46545

MCGUINN, JACQUELINE E., communications company executive; b. Oak Park, Ill., Mar. 10, 1951; d. Herbert Eugene and Margaret (Martin) Parks; children: Charles William, Tamra Ann. Sec. RJR Foods, Rolling Meadows, Ill., 1974-77; asst. to pub. Ednl. Communications, Inc., Lake Forest, Ill., 1977—. Mem. Nat. Bus. Adv. Council, Office Edn. Assn., Dist. Edn. Clubs Am. (nat. adv. bd. 1980—). Office: Ednl Communications Inc 721 N McKinley Lake Forest IL 60045

MCGUINNESS, DEBORAH LOUISE, research scientist; b. Drexel Hill, Pa., Mar. 28, 1958; d. Richard Charles and Eleanor Louise (Rothermel) McG. BS in Computer Sci., Duke U., 1980; MS in Computer Sci., U. Calif., Berkely, 1981. Research scientist devel. AT&T Bell Labs., Indpls., 1980-84; research scientist Artificial Intelligence and Computing Environments AT&T Bell Labs., Murray Hill, N.J., 1984-86, research scientist Artificial Intelligence Principles Research, 1986—. Mem. Am. Assn. Artificial Intelligence, Assn. Computational Linguistics, IEEE, Phi Eta Sigma, Phi Beta Kappa. Office: AT&T Bell Labs 600 Mountain Ave Murray Hill NJ 07974

MCGUINNESS-MUKERJEE, JOANNE HELENE, nursing administrator, consultant; b. Providence, Aug. 22, 1942; d. John William and Helen Louise (McCormack) McGuinness; m. Dilip K. Mukerjee, Feb. 6, 1975 (div. 1979). BS in Nursing, Simmons Coll., 1979; MEd, Cambridge Coll., 1982. Clin. specialist Lawrence (Mass.) Gen. Hosp., 1980-81; asst. dir. nursing Essex Hall, Beverly, Mass., 1981-82, Greenery Rehab. Ctr., Brighton, Mass., 1982-83; dir. nursing Elder Care Services, Tewksbury, Mass., 1983-84; asst. adminstr. Webster Manor, Mass., 1984-85, adminstr., exec. dir., 1985—; lectr. in field. Author: An Understanding of Policy Analysis, 1982. Mem. Am. Coll. Health Care Execs., Mass. Nurses Assn. (mem. nominating com. dist. IV 1987-88, mem. long term care task force, convenor for nurse practice act legis.), Mass. Fedn. Nursing Homes (program chair 1984-85), Am. Nurses Found., Am. Nurses Assn. (cert. adminstr., mem. gerontol. council). Roman Catholic. Avocations: private and comml. pilot multiengine rating, golf, collecting 17th and 18th century French antiques. Home: 97 Larch Row Wenham MA 01984 Office: Webster Manor 745 School St Webster MA 01570

MCGUIRE, DEBORAH, banker. Pres. First Women's Bank, Rockville, Md. Office: First Women's Bank Office of the Pres 1800 Rockville Pike Rockville MD 20852 *

MCGUIRE, JOAN FRANCES SNUGGS, data processing executive, consultant; b. Washington, July 8, 1934; d. John Louis and Ethel Mary (Troutman) Snuggs; m. William Henry McGuire, Feb. 3, 1956 (div. May 1966); 1 child, Alan David. AA in Psychology and Edn., Daytona Beach (Fla.) Community Coll., 1973; BS in Clin. Psychology and Spl. Edn. magna cum laude, Bethune-Cookman Coll., Daytona Beach, 1976; MPA, Atlanta U., 1978; postgrad. in philosophy, Ariz. State U. Pvt. tutor, homebound instr. Newport News (Va.) Ind. Sch. Dist., 1962-66; chem. research technologist Dow-Badische Corp., Williamsburg, Va., 1962-68; proofreader Daytona Beach News Jour., 1971-76; recreation specialist bur. parks, recreation, libraries and culture City of Atlanta, 1976-78; Presdl. mgmt. intern Social Security Adminstrn., Balt., 1978-79, spl. asst. to dir. Office Assessment, 1979-81, computer specialist Office Systems Ops., 1981-87; claims rep. Office Field Ops. Social Security Adminstrn., Mesa, Ariz., 1987—; project mgr., designer office automation Social Security Adminstrn., 1982-87. Exec. bd. mem. Atlanta Regional Commn., 1976-78; active Ga. Conservancy, Atlanta, 1976-78, Ga. Commn. on Women, Atlanta, 1977, Polio Echo, 1988—, Ariz. Bridge to Living; Ga. rep. Nat. Parks and Recreation Adminstrn., Washington and Atlanta, 1976-78; bd. dirs. Waterways Unltd., Hampton Roads, Va., 1968-70. Dept. Health and Human Service Pub. Service fellow, 1976-78; United Negro Coll. Fund Freedman scholar, 1975. Mem. Internat. Ethernet Decision Makers Users Group (local host 1985), Govt. Ethernet Decision Makers Users Groups (chairperson 1984-87), Ethernet Decision Makers Users Group, Mid-Atlantic Xerox Users Group (chairperson 1985-86), Social Security Adminstrn. Xerox Users Group (chairperson 1985-86), Md. Assn. for Pub. Adminstrs., Assn. Fed. Info. Resources Mgrs., Am. Assn. Univ. Women, Federally Employed Women Assn., Women's Equity Action League, Feminine Action Alliance (coordinator 1976-77), Presdl. Mgmt. Intern Assn. (pres.), LWV, Alpha Kappa Mu, Phi Theta Kappa. Democrat. Episcopalian. Home: 717 W University Rd Mesa AZ 85201 Office: Social Security Adminstrn 1050 W Main St Mesa AZ 85201

MCGUIRE, KAREN LEE, educator; b. Washington, Dec. 21, 1946; d. Reane DeCavreal and Myra Elaine (Neitzey) Chilson; m. Thomas Francis McGuire, Feb. 7, 1946 (div. 1978); 1 child, Thomas Lee. BS, Palm Beach Atlantic Coll., 1985; MEd, Fla. Atlantic U., 1987. Editorial asst. Library of Congress, Washington, 1964-67; sec. Temple Hills (Md.) Bapt. Ch., 1970-73; legal sec. Giordano, Alexander, Hass, et al, Oxon Hill, Md., 1973-78; sec. Dept. of the Air Force, Washington, 1978-79; protocol asst. Dept. of Def., Washington, 1979-80; confidential asst. Dept. of Energy, Washington, 1980-81; adminstrv. asst. Bapt. Joint Com. Pub. Affairs, Washington, 1981-82; assoc. dean of students Palm Beach Atlantic Coll., West Palm Beach, Fla., 1982-87; staff asst. HUD, Washington, 1987. Edn. asst. Columbia Bapt. Ch., Falls Ch., Va., 1987—. Named one of Outstanding Young Women, 1983. Mem. Nat. Assn. Female Execs. Baptist. Home: 500 N Roosevelt Blvd Apt 601 Falls Church VA 22044

MCGUIRE, PATRICIA A., health advocate, lobbyist; b. Park Falls, Wis., Sept. 4, 1936; d. William Paul and Rose Marie (Szymik) Bautch. Diploma in Nursing, Sacred Heart Sch. Nursing, Spokane, 1957. Gen. duty Sacred Heart Hosp., Spokane, 1957-58; staff nurse So. Pacific R.R. Hosp., San Francisco, 1958-61, Andrews AFB Hosp., Washington, 1961-63; supr. claims processing Blue Cross-Blue Shield of Nat. Capital Area, Washington, 1963-72; dir. govt. relations Nat. Assn. Blue Shield Plans, 1972-77; asst. dir. fed. affairs (lobbyist) AMA, Washington, 1977—; Lobbyist, founder Health on Wednesday Assn., Washington, 1978—, Women in Govt. Relations, Washington, 1978—; keynote spkr. 29th congress Am. Operating Rm. Nurses Assn., 1982; mem. mayoral task force on infant mortality and cardiac services. Active Nat. Women's Rep. Forum, Washington, 1978—; mem. statewide health coordinating com. on health planning, Washington, 1977-82; cons. Pres. Ronald Reagan Health Platform, Washington, 1981. Served to capt. USAF, 1961-63. Recipient Personal Recognition award Sec. Otis Bowen, Dept. HHS, 1986, Personal Recognition awards Mayor Barry, Washington, 1977, 82. Mem. Sacred Heart Sch. Nursing Alumni Assn. Republican. Roman Catholic. Office: AMA 1101 Vermont Ave NW Washington DC 20005

MCGUIRE, SANDRA LYNN, nursing educator; b. Flint, Mich., Jan. 28, 1947; d. Donald Armstrong and Mary Lue (Harvey) Johnson; BS in Nursing, U. Mich., 1969, MPH, 1973; m. Joseph L. McGuire, Mar. 6, 1976; children—Matthew, Kelly, Kerry. Staff nurse Univ. Hosp., Ann Arbor, Mich., 1969; pub. health nurse Wayne County Health Dept., Eloise, Mich., 1969-72; instr. Madonna Coll., Livonia, Mich., 1973; pub. health coordinator Plymouth Ctr. for Human Devel., Northville, Mich., 1974-75; asst. prof. community health nursing U. Mich., Ann Arbor, 1975-83; asst. prof. U. Tenn., Knoxville, 1983—; resource person Gov.'s Com. Unification of Mental Health Services in Mich.; speaker profl. assns. and workshops; dir. Kids Are Tomorrow's Srs. Program; bd. dirs. Ctr. Understanding Aging, 1987—. Bd. dirs. Mich. chpt. ARC, 1980-83, Knoxville chpt., 1984-85 . USPHS fellow, 1972-73. Mem. Nat., Mich. leagues nursing, Am., Mich. (chmn. mental health sect. 1976) pub. health assns., Nat., Mich. (dir., co-chmn. residential services com. 1976-79, chmn. health services 1979-82), Plymouth (chmn. residential services com. 1975-77) assns. retarded citizens, Sigma Theta Tau, Pi Lambda Theta, Phi Kappa Phi. Author: (with S. Clemen. and D. Eigsti) Comprehensive Family and Community Health Nursing, 1981, 2d edit., 1987. Home: 11008 Crosswind Dr Knoxville TN 37922 Office: 1200 Volunteer Blvd Knoxville TN 37916

MCGUIRE, SONDRA LEE, automotive executive; b. Columbus, Ohio, Nov. 9, 1941; d. Charles Richard Whitehurst and LaVerne Adele (Harlow) Battelle; m. Brandt B. Shumate, June 2, 1958 (div. Dec. 1978); children: Raymond Murl, Russell James; m. Clyde Leon McGuire, May 29, 1982. Student, U. Ariz., 1975-76, Pima Coll., 1977-81. Sales audit, payroll Levy's Dept. Store, Tucson, 1960-61; office mgr. Shumate's Custom Interiors, Tucson, 1962-78; chief exec. officer Auto Trimmer's Supply, Tucson, 1978—; cons. curriculum Sunnyside High Sch., Tucson, 1983. Contbr. articles to profl. jours. Mem. Exec. Women's Council, So. Ariz., 1980. Recipient Cert. of Appreciation award Beacon Found., 1984. Mem. Auto Service Industry Assn. (program chmn. 1985, exec. bd. dirs. Auto Trim div.1981-88, chairperson 1987, 88, cert. of appreciation award 1985, 87, Hall of Fame plaque 1987), Tucson C. of C. Republican. Baptist. Home: 8900 Bears Path Tucson AZ 85749 Office: Auto Trimmers Supply Inc 2958 E 22d St Tucson AZ 85713

MCGUIRE, SUSANNE GIROUX, marketing professional; b. Burlington, Vt., Mar. 10, 1952; d. Bernard A. and June (Tabor) G.; m. Edward B. McGuire, Apr. 4, 1987. MS, U. Vt., 1974, MBA, 1983. Mktg. adminstr. Gen. Electric, Burlington, Vt., 1974-79; mktg. rep. Gen. Electric, Nashville, Tenn., 1979-80; purchasing agt. IBM, Essex Junction, Vt., 1980-85, mktg. rep. internal accts., 1985—. Instr. Decisions Program, Burlington, 1985—; mem. Gov.'s Comm. on Children and Youth, Montpelier, Vt., 1968-76. Libertarian. Roman Catholic. Home: Rd 2 Box 354 Pine Shore Rd Hinesburg VT 05461

MCGUIRI, MARLENE DANA, lawyer, educator, librarian; b. Hammond, Ind., Mar. 22, 1938; d. Daniel David and Helen Elizabeth (Baludis) Callis; A.B., Ind. U., 1956; J.D., DePaul U., 1963; M.A. in L.S., Rosary Coll., 1965; LL.M., George Washington U., 1978; postgrad. Harvard U., 1985; m. James Franklin McGuirl, Apr. 24, 1965. Law library asst. DePaul Coll. Law Library, 1961-62, asst. law librarian, 1962-65; admitted to Ill. bar, 1963, Ind. bar, 1964, D.C. bar, 1972; reference law librarian Boston Coll. Sch. Law Library, 1965-66; law librarian D.C. Bar Library, 1966-70; library cons. Nat. Clearinghouse on Poverty Law, OEO, 1967-69, Northwestern U. Nat. Inst. for Edn. in Law and Poverty, 1969, D.C. Office Corp. Counsel, 1969-70; instr. legal librarianship Grad. Sch., Dept. Agr., 1968; lectr. legal lit., law for librarians, advanced legal lit. grad. dept. library sci., Cath. U., 1972-73, adj. asst. prof., 1973—; asst. chief Am.-Brit. law div. Library Congress Law Library, Washington, 1970, div. chief, 1970—; instr. Ph.D. program in Am. civilization George Washington U., 1976, 79, lectr. environ. law, 1979—; pres. Hamburger Heaven, Inc., Palm Beach, Fla., 1981—; pres. L'Image de Marlene, Ltd., Washington, Heads and Hands, Inc., Washington, Clinique de Beauté, Inc., Washington, Horizon Design & Mfg. Co., Easton, Md. Mem. Georgetown Citizens Assn.; del. Ind. Democratic Conv., 1964; trustee D.C. Law Students in Ct. Recipient Meritorious Service cash award Library Congress, 1974. Mem. Am. (facilities of Law Library of Congress com. 1976-85), Fed. (mem. council Capitol Hill chpt. 1972-76), Ill., D.C. (inter-Am. bar relations com. 1968-70, memls. com. 1969-70), Women's (treas. 1970-72, pres. 1972-73, exec. bd. 73-77, parliamentarian 1975, chmn. constn. and by-laws com. 1975-76) bar assns., D.C. Bar (election bd. 1973-75, specialization com. 1975-76), Am. Bar Found. (library service com. 1969-72), Nat. Assn. Women Lawyers (co-chmn. legis. com. 1976-77), Internat. (program chmn. 1974), Am. (co-chmn. stats. com. 1970-72, chmn. legis. and legal devels. 1972-73, exec. bd. 1973-77, chmn. indexing periodical lit. com. 1979-82, chmn. copyright com.) assns. law libraries, Law Librarians Soc. Washington (pres. 1971-73), Brit. and Irish Assn. Law Librarians, Assn. Am. Library Schs. (prison libraries com. 1975-76), Exec. Women in Govt. Clubs: Nat. Lawyers, Zonta. Contbr. articles to profl. jours. Home: 3416 P St NW Washington DC 20007 Office: Library of Congress Am-Brit Law Div Law Library Washington DC 20540

MCGUNIGLE, DOROTHY GREENE, interior designer, artist; b. Providence, Jan. 24, 1914; d. Dutee Thomas and Carrie May (Stewart) Greene; m. Douglas Campbell McGunigle, June 14, 1941 (dec. 1958); children—Jane Douglas (dec.), Bruce Campbell. Grad. R.I. Sch. Design, 1935. Interior designer Healy & Helgeson, Providence, 1935-36, Merriam Co., Providence, 1936-43; mgr. interior decorating dept. Shepard Co., Providence, 1960-69; owner Dorothy McGunigle Interiors, East Greenwich, R.I., 1970—; tchr. adult edn. Providence YMCA, 1958-59, Cranston High Sch., 1962, Warwick High Sch., 1964, East Greenwich High Sch., 1970-71; art shows include: Providence Art Club, 1972, 74, 76, 78, 80, 82; Indsl. Nat. Bank, Providence, 1974, 76; Warwick Pub. Library, 1980; cons. hist. restoration Varnum House Mus., 1963—. Bd. dirs. East Greenwich Preservation Soc., 1972-77, chmn. consultation com. hist. restoration; active East Greenwich Civic Club. Recipient Hon. Mem. award Continental Ladies, Varnum House Mus., 1970. Mem. AID, ASID, R.I. Hist. Soc. Clubs: Providence Art (picture custodian 1976—, chmn. ladies bd. 1978-79), Providence Pottery and Porcelain (pres. 1981-83), Colonial Dames, Mayflower Descendants, DAR.

MCHENRY, CHARLOTTE SWALES, nurse, educator; b. Orange, N.J., July 14, 1946; d. William Grant and Mamie E. (Speights) Swales, m. James Douglas McHenry, Apr. 3, 1969; 1 child, Angela Nicole. BS in Nursing, U. Miss., 1968; MS, U. Md., 1970; PhD, Fla. State U., 1985. Asst. prof. nursing U. So. Miss., Hattiesburg, 1970-71, assoc. prof., 1973-81; acting dean, assoc. prof. Delta State U., Cleveland, Miss., 1981-85; assoc. prof. U. Miss., Jackson, 1985—; cons. Delta State U., Cleveland, 1985; project dir. Nat. Inst. Mental Health, Hattiesburg, 1973-78. Contbr. articles to profl. jours. Chmn. youth pub. edn. Miss. div. Am. Cancer Soc., Jackson, 1985, chmn. profl. edn., Bolivar County, 1983-85, chair state pub. edn., bd. dirs., exec. com. 1987-88. Recipient Appreciation award Am. Cancer Soc., 1985. Mem. Am. Nurses Assn., Soc. Gen. Systems Research, AAUW, Assn. for Instl. Research., Women's Missionary Union, Phi Delta Kappa, Sigma Theta Tau. Office: U Miss Med Ctr 2500 N State St Jackson MS 39216-4505

MCHENRY, NANCY CASSIDY, infosystems specialist, consultant; b. Parkesburg, Pa., May 25, 1957; d. Francis Vincent and Lois Fay (Juhl) Cassidy; m. John Steven McHenry. BBA, Indiana U. of Pa., 1978. Mgmt. info. systems analyst Aluminum Co. Am., Pitts., 1978-80; sr. sytems analyst Rockwell Internat., Reading, Pa., 1980-82; with info. systems dept. AT&T, Reading, Pa., 1982-87; pvt. practice info. systems Reading, Pa., 1987—; cons. data processing Rockwell Internat., 1982—, Info. Sytems Dept. AT&T, 1987—. Auditor Newry (Pa.) Borough, 1978. Fellow Am. Prodn. and Inventory Control Soc. (cert. 1978). Roman Catholic. Home: Rt 3 Kames Hill Rd Columbia PA 17512

MCHUGH, BETSY BALDWIN, sociologist, educator, small business owner; b. Concord, N.H., Jan. 2, 1928; d. Walter Killenbeck and Elizabeth Alice (Hunt) Slater; m. Michael Joseph McHugh, Dec. 19, 1954; children: Betsy Slater, Michael Brooks. MusB in Vocal Music, Syracuse (N.Y.) U., 1954; postgrad., U. South Fla., 1985—. Tchr. pub. schs. Juneau, Alaska, 1966-85; owner, founder Cashé Pub. Co., Tampa, Fla., 1985—. Named one of Outstanding Educators Gov. Alaska Woman's Comm., 1985. Home: 5932 Montgomery St Juneau AK 99801 Office: 13101 18th St Apt N Apt #110 Tampa FL 33612

MCHUGH, JEANNE O'LEARY, lawyer; b. Brighton, Mass., Mar. 14, 1956; d. James Robert and Anne Louise (Kelleher) O'Leary; m. John Gerald McHugh, Sept. 3, 1984. BA, Suffolk U., 1978, JD, 1981. Bar: Mass., U.S. Dist. Ct., U.S. Ct. Appeals (1st dist.), U.S. Supreme Ct. Assoc. Law Offices of Vincent P. Cahalane, Brockton, Mass., 1982-84, Kendrick & Gormley, Cohasset, Mass., 1984-87; in-house counsel Kemper Ins., Quincy, Mass., 1987-88, Long, McTaggart, Anderson & Kohler, Boston, 1988—. Mem. ABA, Mass. Bar Assn., Mass. Acad. Trial Attys. Democrat. Roman Catholic. Home: 100 Mediterranean Dr A39 Weymouth MA 02189 Office: Long McTaggart Anderson & Kohler 200 State St Boston MA 02109

MCHUGH, JOSEPHINE FLAHERTY, medical facility administrator; b. Pontiac, Mich., May 13, 1947; d. Joseph Francis and Mary Burns Flaherty; m. Richard Alan McHugh, Aug. 31, 1974; children: Sean Joseph, Bridget Kathleen. Grad. summa cum laude, Romana Sch., Rome, 1967; grad., Chandler Secretarial Sch., 1969. Sr. sec. Mass. Eye and Ear Infirmary, Boston, 1969-73; exec. sec. Dean's Office Preventative Medicine U. Colo. Health Scis. Ctr., Denver, 1973-80; clin. coordinator U. Hosp., Denver, 1980—; Mem. task force U. Hosp., 1986—, communications focus group leader, 1986—. Mem. Bldg. Adv. com. and Communications subcom. Douglas County (Colo.) Sch. Dist., 1987, 88. Mem. Am. soc. Profl. and Exec. Women, Nat. Assn. Female Execs. Republican. Roman Catholic. Clubs: Parker (Colo.) Breakfast Club (pres. 1987, 88), Kiwann. Home: 11464 Bonanza Circle Franktown CO 80116 Office: U Hosp Denver CO 80262

MC HUGH, MARGARET ANN GLOE, psychologist; b. Salt Lake City, Nov. 8, 1920; d. Harold Henry and Olive (Warenski) Gloe; B.A., U. Utah, 1942; M.A. in Counseling and Guidance, Idaho State U., 1964; Ph.D. in Counseling Psychology, U. Oreg., 1970; lic. psychologist; nat. cert. counselor; m. William T. McHugh, Oct. 1, 1943; children—Mary Margaret McHugh-Shuford, William Michael, Michelle. Tchr. kindergarten, Idaho Falls, Idaho, 1951-62, tchr. high sch. English, 1962-63; counselor Counseling Center, Idaho State U., Pocatello, 1964-67; instr. U. Oreg., Eugene, 1967-70; asst. prof. U. Victoria, B.C., Can., 1970-76; therapist Peninsula Counseling Center, Port Angeles and Sequim, Wash., 1976-81, McHugh & Assocs. Counseling Center, 1981—. Served with WAVES, 1943-44. Mem. Am. Psychol. Assn., Am. Assn. for Counseling and Devel., Am. Assn. Marriage and Family Therapy, Wash. Psychol. Assn. Research on women in relationships, also depression and women, sexual abuse. Home: 249 F Cameron Rd Sequim WA 98382

MCHUGH, TONI WALTER, sales executive; b. Milw., Nov. 25, 1946; d. Harland Anton Walter and Elizabeth (Abel) Walter Adamson; m. Harry Miller McHugh, Aug. 31, 1968; children: Meagan Elizabeth, Hilary Barbree. BBA, U. Wis., 1968; MBA, Fairleigh Dickinson U., 1985. Exec. trainee, asst. buyer B. Altman & Co., N.Y.C., 1968-69; spot TV buyer J. Walter Thompson, N.Y.C., 1969-72; founder, mgr., owner The Cheese Shop, Ridgefield, Conn., 1972-75; account rep., Sta. WSYX, Columbus, Ohio, 1986—; chair membership com. LWV, Chester, N.J., 1976; chair March of Dimes Mothers March, Vernon, N.J., 1978, Adoption Fair, N.J., 1982-83, Family Services Ball, Morristown, N.J., 1985; pres. Edna Gladney N.Y. Area Aux., N.Y.C., 1980; founder, chair N.J. Com. for Adoption, 1980-83; bd. dirs. Nat. Com. for Adoption, Washington, 1980-86, chair, 1983-85; fundraiser New Vernon (N.J.) Vol. Fire Dept., 1982; fundraiser Peck Sch., Morristown, 1982-85. Named Friend of Adoption, Nat. Com. for Adoption, 1985. Mem. Jr. League of Columbus (Ohio). Republican. Avocations: tennis, golf, reading, cooking. Home: 1261 Clubview Blvd N Worthington OH 43235

MCINERNEY, JANET MARIE, financial editor; b. Boston, Jan. 22, 1944; d. Timothy Joseph and Marguerite Patricia (Kirby) McI; m. Bruce D. Sargent, 1 child, Matthew D. BA, Newton Coll. Sacred Heart, 1965; MBA, Fordham U., 1981. Social worker N.Y. Foundling Hosp., N.Y.C., 1965-68; research asst. A. G. Becker, N.Y.C., 1968-69; researcher Boyden Assocs., N.Y.C., 1969-71; research asst. Middendorf Colgate, N.Y.C., 1971-72, Estabrook, N.Y.C., 1972-73; mng. editor, v.p. Morgan Stanley, N.Y.C., 1973—. Mem. Money Marketeers. Republican. Roman Catholic. Home: 424 E 52nd St New York NY 10022 Office: Morgan Stanley 1251 Ave of the Americas New York NY 10020

MCINTEE-LARENAS, TERRI LEE, human resource information systems analyst; b. Cleve., Nov. 9, 1955; d. Edward Franklin and Janet Rae (Porter) McIntee; m. Romulo David Larenas, Jan. 3, 1980. B.A., Ohio State U., 1978; postgrad. Hunter Coll., 1983, Baruch Coll., 1985-86, NYU, 1985-86, New Sch. for Research, 1986—. Benefit approver Equitable Life Assurance Co., Cleve., 1978-79, mem. flying squad team, Equitable Life, N.Y.C., 1979-80, coverage coordinator, system specialist, 1970-82; clin. adminstr. Lenox Hill Hosp., N.Y.C., 1982-84; compensation specialist Securities Industry Automation Corp., N.Y.C., 1984-87, human resource info. systems analyst, 1987—. Mem. AAUW, Internat. Assn. Personnel Women, Human Resource Info. Systems Profls., Nat. Assn. Executive and Profl. Women, Wall St. Compensation Assn., Nat. Assn. Female Execs. Avocations: swimming, horseback riding, reading. Home: 810 Hudson on Harbour Dr Poughkeepsie NY 12601 Office: Securities Industry Automation Corp 55 Water St New York NY 10041

MCINTIRE, LEANNE, script supervisor; b. Shirley, Mass., Jan. 27, 1957; d. Larry Richmond and Lydia Maria (Lourenco) McI. BS in Photography with high honors, Rochester Inst. Tech., 1980; MA in Communications, U. Md., 1982. Instr.'s aid, photographer Rochester (N.Y.) Inst. Tech., 1979-80; instr. film, TV U. Md., College Park, 1980-82; instr. TV, radio Tex. Christian U., Ft. Worth, 1982-83; freelance script supr. Ft. Worth Prodns., 1983-84; asst. unit mgr. ABC News, Dallas, 1984; script supr. Earl Owens Corp., Shelby, N.C., 1984-87; freelance script supr. Hollywood, Calif., 1987—. Scipps-Howard scholar, 1980-82. Mem. Nat. Assn. Female Execs., Am. Film Inst., Phi Eta Sigma, Alpha Lamda Delta. Democrat. Episcopalian. Home and Office: 4912 Tujunga Ave #1 N North Hollywood CA 91601

MCINTOSH, CYNTHIA JEAN, health science facility administrator; b. Detroit, Aug. 28, 1942; d. Frank Edward and Lillian Barbara (Herbster) Ott; m. Paul Archie McIntosh, Oct. 3, 1959; children: Scott Peter, Kathleen Sue McIntosh Hansen, David Paul. BS, Edgewood Coll., 1973; MA, Cen. Mich. U., 1981. Lab. mgr. Meth. Hosp., Madison, Wis., 1975-87; mktg. mgr. Shared Lab. Services, Madison, 1985-87; dir. Gen. Med. Labs., Madison, 1988—. Mem. Clin. Lab. Mgmt. Assn., Am. Soc. for Med. Tech., Madison Area Doll Club (pres. 1987—). Democrat. Home: 4535 Winnequah Rd Monona WI 53716 Office: Gen Med Labs 36 S Brooks St Madison WI 53715

MCINTOSH, EDITH MARIE, psychologist; b. Beaumont, Tex., Aug. 3, 1938; d. Edith Malone (Hill) Brown; m. Jesse Charles McIntosh, Mar. 19, 1953; children: Jonathon, Joseph, Madeline. BS, Stephen F. Austin U., 1951; MEd, U. Tex., El Paso, 1964, MA, 1977; PhD, Fla. Inst. Tech., 1981. Lic. clin. psychologist, Tex. Tchr. Beaumont Schs., 1951-54, Camp Lejeune (N.C.) Schs., 1955-57, Dade County Schs., Miami, Fla., 1958-60; tchr., therapist El Paso Schs., 1960-77; assoc. psychologist Ysleta Schs., El Paso, 1978-82; pvt. practice clin. psychologist El Paso, 1980—; clin. psychologist El Paso Neuropsychiatric Clinic, 1984-86, El Paso Pain and Stress Clinic, 1986—; mem. staff Providence Hosp., Sun Valley Hosp., Sun Towers Hosp., El Paso, 1983—; cons. Clint and Fabens Sch. Dists., El Paso, 1986—. Dir. Immanuel Bapt. Ch. Sch., El Paso, 1970-83, bd. dirs., 1982-84; mem. pilot program West Tex. Council on Aging, El Paso, 1983-85; mem. Tex. Task Force on Parenting, Austin, 1983. Mem. Am. Psychol. Assn., Tex. Psychol. Assn., El Paso Psychol. Assn., Am. Assn. Marriage and Family Therapists (cert.), Am. Bd. Med. Psychotherapists, Mental Health Assn. Tex. (chair edn. div. 1982-86, Outstanding Citizen award El Paso 1984). Republican. Home: 413 Stewart Dr El Paso TX 79915 Office: Schuster Heights Med Park 1201 Schuster El Paso TX 79902

MCINTOSH, LOUISA AICHEL, interior design firm and art gallery executive; b. Atlanta, June 1, 1925; d. Siegfried Louis and Margaret Katura (Rosser) Aichel; m. Alexander Preston McIntosh, Sept. 2, 1947 (dec. Jan. 1966); children: Alexa Louis McIntosh Selph, Preston Stuckey, Peter Aichel, Patricia Amelia. BA, Agnes Scott Coll. Owner Louisa McIntosh Interiors, Atlanta, 1967—; owner, dir. McIntosh Gallery, Atlanta, 1982—; design cons. Fed. Res. Bank, Atlanta, 1975-78, Sci. Atlanta, 1976-80, English Lang. Sch., Atlanta, 1980-82, Nat. Bank of Ga., 1984-85, Lantel Co., 1985. Treas., life mem. Midtown Bus. Assn., Atlanta, 1978, pres., 1979; trustee Atlanta Pub. Library, vice chmn. bd., 1981-82; trustee Atlanta Fulton Pub. Library, chmn. bd., 1983-85. Mem. Inst. Bus. Design, Women Bus. Owners. Episcopalian. Home: 75 Inman Circle NE Atlanta GA 30309 Office: Louisa McIntosh Interiors 1421 Peachtree St NE Atlanta GA 30309

MCINTOSH, MICHAELE D., group controller; b. Warsaw, Ind., Mar. 12, 1946; d. Paul E. and Dorothy E. (Seiffert) Hodges; B.B.A., U. Miami (Fla.), 1968; cert. in acctg. UCLA, 1976; m. J.W. McIntosh, Apr. 8, 1972 (div. Mar. 1988); 1 son, James Kyle. Asst. dist. credit mgr. W.T. Grant Co., Los Angeles, 1969-70; v.p., treas. R & B Enterprises, Los Angeles, 1970-80; pres., exec. dir. L.I.F.E. Inc., Warsaw, Ind., 1981; recreational vehicles group controller Coachmen Industries, Middlebury, Ind., 1981—; mgmt. cons. City of Warsaw; real estate broker, Ind. Trustee, Kosciusko Leadership Acad.; mem. Madison Sch. Parent-Tchr. Orgn. Mem. Nat. Bd. Realtors, Ind. Bd. Realtors, Kosciusko County Bd. Realtors, Chi Omega. Club: Women of Moose. Home: 718 Front St Syracuse IN 46567

MCINTOSH, RHODINA COVINGTON, lawyer, international development analyst; b. Chicago Heghts, Ill., May 26, 1947; d. William George and Cora Jean (Cain) Covington; m. Gerald Alfred McIntosh, Dec. 14, 1970; children: Gary Allen, Garvey Anthony, Ayana Kai. BA cum laude, Mich. State U., 1969; JD, U. Detroit, 1978. Asst. to dir. equal opportunity program Mich. State U., East Lansing, 1969-70; law clk. Bell & Hudson, P.C., Detroit, 1977-79; main rapporteur 1st All-Africa Law Conf., U. Swaziland and Botswana, 1981, lectr., 1981-83; chief info. and tech. assistance Office Pvt. and Vol. Cooperation, U.S. AID, Washington, 1983-87, chief info. and program support, 1987-88; corp. counsel Automated Research Systems Ltd., Alexandria, Va., 1988—; founding bd. mem. Women's Justice Ctr., Detroit, 1975-77; coordinator women's leadership conf. Wayne State U., Detroit, 1979, participant confs. and workshops. Contbr. articles and documents to profl. publs. Rep. coordinator urban program, Lansing, Mich., 1979-81; chair fgn. relations subcom. Nat. Black Women's Polit. Caucus, Washington, 1984; bd. dirs. Mayor's Com. to Keep Detroit Beautiful, 1980, Detroit Urban League, 1981, Am. Opportunity Found., Washington, 1984—. Nat. Achievement scholar Ednl. Testing Service, Princeton, N.J., 1965, Martin Luther King Jr. Ctr. for Social Change scholar, Atlanta, 1976; recipient Detroit Edison award, 1980, New Repubs. award, Mich., 1981, Disting. Leadership award ABI, 1987. Mem. Nat. Assn. Female Execs., GOP Women's Network, Delta Sigma Theta. Roman Catholic. Office: Automated Research Systems Ltd 4480 King St Suite 500 Alexandria VA 22302

MCINTYRE, JOAN CAROL, computer software company executive, author; b. Portchester, N.Y., Mar. 1, 1939; d. John Henry and Molly Elizabeth (Gates) Daugherty; m. Stanley Donald McIntyre, Aug. 24, 1957 (div. Jan. 1986); children—Michael Stanley, David John, Sharon Lynne. Student Northwestern U., 1956-57, U. Ill., 1957-58. Assoc. editor Writer's Digest, Cin., 1966-68; instr. creative writing U. Ala.-Huntsville, 1975; editor Strode Pubs., Huntsville, 1974-75; paralegal Smith, Huckaby & Graves (now Bradley, Arant, Rose & White), Huntsville, 1976-82; exec. v.p. Micro Craft, Inc., Huntsville, 1982-85, pres., 1985—; also dir. and co-owner. Author 8 computer-operating mans. for law office software, 1978-85; co-author: Alabama and Federal Complaint Forms, 1979; Alabama and Federal Motion and Order Forms, 1980; also numerous articles, short stories, poems, 1955-84. Editor: Alabama Law for the Layman, 1975. Bd. dirs. Huntsville Lit. Soc., 1976-77. Hon. scholar Medill Sch. Journalism, Northwestern U., 1956. Republican. Methodist. Office: Micro Craft Inc 688 Discovery Dr Huntsville AL 35806

MCINTYRE, JOY ADELE, public relations executive, journalist; b. Mt. Holly, N.J., Aug. 4, 1952; d. Arthur Francis and Mary Adele (Zuczek) McI.; m. William Harris Tobolsky, Oct. 14, 1978. A.B. in English, Princeton U., 1974; student Mansfield Coll., Oxford, Eng., summer 1972; postgrad. Seton Hall Law Sch., 1977-78. Reporter, intern Home News, New Brunswick, N.J., summer 1973; reporter Bergen Record, Hackensack, N.J., 1974-76, N.Y. Daily News, West Orange, N.J. and N.Y.C., 1976-79, Phila. Bull., 1979; reporter Phila. Daily News, 1979-82; dir. info. services div. Ednl. Testing Service, Princeton, N.J., 1982—. Mem. Women in Communications, Sigma Delta Chi (1st prize award 1973). Office: Ednl Testing Service Rosedale Rd Princeton NJ 08541

MCINTYRE, KATHY ANN, special education administrator; b. River Vale, N.J., May 15, 1956; d. Henry McIntyre and Lorraine (Klein) Kelly. BA, William Paterson Coll., 1978, MEd, 1983. Cert. elem. tchr., prin., sch. bus. adminstr., N.J. Respite care worker Bergen County Spl. Services, Paramus, N.J., 1975-77; human services asst. North Jersey Devel. Ctr., Totowa, N.J., 1978, teaching asst., 1978-79, tchr. handicapped, 1979-84, family life rep., 1980—, vol. People Who Need People, 1981-83, supr. ednl. programs, 1984—, human rights rep., 1985—, affirmative action trainer, 1986—, gastrostomy ad hoc rep., 1986—; instr. William Paterson Coll., 1986—. Mem. Council for Exceptional Children, Assn. for Severely Handicapped, Assn. for Supr. and Curriculum Devel. Roman Catholic. Home: 21 Parks Rd Denville NJ 07834 Office: North Jersey Devel Ctr Minnisink Rd Totowa NJ 07512

MCINTYRE, KAYE MARIE, nonprofit organization executive; consultant; b. Hartford, Conn., Oct. 13, 1950; d. Richard Arthur and Helen Marie (von Richter) Tillotson; m. Daniel Brian McIntyre, Feb. 21, 1969; (div. Dec. 1979). A.S. in Human Services, Northwest Conn. Community Coll., Winsted, 1983; B.S. in Bus. Adminstrn., Charter Oak Coll., Hartford, 1985; postgrad. Wesleyan U., Middletown, Conn., 1987—. Counselor, McCall House, Torrington, Conn., 1979-80; freelance photographer, Torrington, 1980—; exec. dir. Warner Theatre, Torrington, 1982-84; exec. dir. Elderly Health Screening Service, Inc., Waterbury, Conn., 1982—; cons. in field. Asst. coordinator Conn. Earth Action Group, Litchfield, 1971; regional coordinator Conn. Citizens Action Group, Litchfield County, Conn., 1971-72; pres. Northwest Conn. Assn. for the Arts, Inc., Torrington, 1981-84; bd. dirs. Torrington Trust for Historic Preservation, Inc., 1981—; 6th dist. coordinator Office of Protection and Advocacy for the Handicapped and Developmentally Disabled, Litchfield County, 1982; chairperson adult programming com. YWCA of Waterbury, 1985—; v.p. Thomaston Opera House Found., 1985—. Recipient citation Conn. Soc. Prevention of Blindness, 1984; citation Conn. Gen. Assembly, 1984, 86; Project Health award, U.S. Dept. HHS Adminstrn aging, 1986; Secs. Excellence award U.S. Dept. HHS Community Health Promotion Program, 1986. Mem. Nat. Assn. Female Execs., Am. League Hist. Theatres, Conn. Assn. Hist. Theatres (pres. 1984—), Internat. Platform Assn., Nat. Trust for Hist. Preservation. Republican. Taoist. Club: Mensa (Litchfield County coordinator). Avocations: photography; writing; hiking. Office: Elderly Health Screening Service Inc 24 Central Ave Waterbury CT 06702

MCINTYRE, LORETTA MILLER, sporting goods manufacturing company executive; b. Lancaster, Pa., Nov. 18, 1944; d. Benedictand Edna (Smoker) Miller; m. Earl E. Louer, Jan. 13,1967 (div. Mar. 1971); m. Ray G. McIntyre, Sept. 15, 1977. Student pub. schs., Umatilla, Fla. Cert. tchr.; cert. dental asst. Sec. W.T. Grant Co., Mt. Dora, Fla., 1962-64; cashier Winn Dixie, Winter Park and Eustis, Fla., 1964-65; dental asst. Dr. Ray G. McIntyre, Eustis, 1966-76, Dr. Leonard Kaplan, Eustis, 1977-79; v.p., sec. Warren and Sweat Mfg. Co., Eustis, 1983—; dental assistance instr. Lake County Vocational Sch., 1970-79. Republican. Baptist. Home: Box 446 Grand Island FL 32735 Office: Warren and Sweat Mfg Co Hwy 19 N Dona Vista FL 32784

MCINVALE, SHIRLEY B., controller; b. Plainwell, Mich., Apr. 22, 1939; d. Robert O. Button and Beatrice May (Myers) Peet; m. George T. McInvale, June 21, 1958; children: Cindy, Debby. Clk. Ludman Industries, Miami, 1957-58, Eli Witt Cigars, Ft. Lauderdale, Fla., 1958-60, Union (S.C.) County Supr., 1977; traffic dir. WBCU, Union, 1977-82, adminstrv. asst., 1982-84; bookkeeper WYAK, Myrtle Beach, S.C., 1984-87, office mgr., 1985-87; cons. Resont Broadcasting Inc., Richmond, Va., 1985-87; asst. controller Jones-Eastern Radio Inc., Charleston, S.C., 1987—; pres. Bus. and Profl. Women, Union, 1983-84. Pres. Stephen Foster PTA, Ft. Lauderdale, 1971, Buffalo PTA, 1973. Republican. Baptist.

MCIVER, SUSAN BERTHA, zoology educator; b. Hutchinson, Kans., Nov. 6, 1940; d. Ernest Dale and Thelma Faye (McCrory) McIver; B.A., U. Calif., Riverside, 1962; M.S., Wash. State U., 1964, Ph.D., 1967. Asst. prof. dept. parasitology U. Toronto (Ont.), 1967-72, assoc. prof., 1972-81, prof. dept. zoology, 1981-84; prof., chmn. dept. environ. biology U. Guelph (Ont., Can.), 1984—; cons., surgeon gen., U.S. Army, 1977-82; cons. tropical med. parasitology NIH; mem. exec. Biol. Council Can. Recipient C. Gordon Hewitt award Entomol. Soc. Can., 1978; Vis. Scientist award Med. Research Council Can., 1978; InterAm. Fellow in tropical medicine NIH, 1973. Mem. Entomol. Soc. Ont. (pres. 1981), Entomol. Soc. Can. (dir. 1975-78, pres. 1984), Entomol. Soc. Am. (chmn. sect. 1982), Canadian Soc. Zoologists, Am. Soc. Parasitologists, Micros. Soc. Can. Contbr. articles to various publs. Office: U Guelph Dept Environ Biology, Guelph, ON Canada N1G 2W1

MCKAIG, DIANNE L., lawyer, former soft drink company executive; b. Massillon, Ohio, Nov. 17, 1930; d. Sherman J. and Kathryn (Shaidnagle) McK. B.A., U. Ky., 1952, J.D., 1954; LL.M., Harvard U., 1955. Bar: Ky. 1954, Mass. 1956, D.C. 1984. Law clk. Ky. Ct. Appeals, Frankfort, 1954; mem. firm Palmer, Dodge, Gardner & Bradford, Boston, 1955-56; individual practice law Boston, 1956-58; atty. adviser Dept. Labor, Washington, 1958-62; regional dir. Office of Solicitor, Dept. Labor (Women's Bur.), Atlanta, 1963-66; chief div. legis. and standards Office of Solicitor, Dept. Labor (Women's Bur.), Washington, 1966-68; dir. Office Consumer Services, 1968-69; spl. asst. for consumer interests to sec. HEW, Washington, 1968; exec. dir. Mich. Consumers Council, 1969-72; asst. v.p. consumer affairs Coca-Cola Co., Atlanta, 1972-74; v.p. Coca-Cola Co., 1976-83; with Jones and McKaig, Washington; v.p. Coca-Cola U.S.A., 1974-76; dir. Fleet Fin. Group; mem. Maj. Appliance Consumer Action Panel, 1970-72; spl. lectr. Coll. Indsl. Mgmt., Ga. Inst. Tech., 1974; vis. com. U. Ky. Law Sch., 1981-84. Assoc. editor: Ky. Law Jour, 1953. Bd. dirs. Nat. Council Family Fin. Edn., 1970-72, Nat. Council Better Bus. Burs., 1971-72, Girl Scouts U.S., 1982-87, Met. Atlanta chpt. ARC, 1982-83; chmn. pub. affairs com. Food Safety Council, 1977; trustee Pace Acad., Atlanta, 1981-83; bd. govs. ARC, 1985—. Mem. Ky. Fed., Mass., D.C. bar assns., Soc. Consumer Affairs Profls. (dir. 1973-77, pres. 1975-76), Soc. Consumer Affairs Profls. Found. (chmn. 1984-85), U.S. C. of C. (consumer affairs com.), U. Ky. Alumni Assn. (pres. Washington 1962), Bus. and Profl. Women's Clubs, Order of Coif, Mortar Bd., Alpha Delta Pi (chpt. outstanding alumna 1965), Eta Sigma Phi, Phi Beta. Home: 3256 Jones Ct NW Washington DC 20007 Office: Jones and McKaig 1819 H St NW Suite 800 Washington DC 20006

MCKAY, ALICE VITALICH, school system administrator; b. Seattle, Sept. 6, 1947; d. Jack S. and Phyllis (Bourne) Vitalich; m. Larry W. McKay, Aug. 14, 1973 (div. Jan. 1983). BA, Wash. State U., 1969; MEd, U. Nev., Las Vegas, 1975; EdD, U. Nev., Reno, 1986. High sch. tchr. Clark County Sch. Dist., Las Vegas, 1972-77, specialist women's sports, 1977-80, high sch. counselor, 1980-84, high sch. asst. prin., 1984—; pres. Lotus Profit, Inc., Las Vegas, 1985-86. Mem. Am. Assn. Counseling and Devel. (committee on women 1985—), Nev. State Counseling and Devel. (pres. 1985-86), Nat. Assn. Female Execs., AAUW, Phi Delta Kappa (exec. bd. 1980-82). Office: Clark County Sch Dist 2832 E Flamingo Rd Las Vegas NV 89121

MCKAY, CONSTANCE GADOW, hotel executive; b. Aurora, Ill., Mar. 7, 1928; d. William H. and Esther E. (Olson) Gadow; student U. Ill., U. Wis.-Madison, U. Wis.-Milw.; widow; children—Richard A., Scott A., Mark G. Dir. catering Arlington Park (Ill.) Race Track, 1966-68, Arlington Park Hilton Hotel, Arlington Heights, Ill., 1969-85, O'Hare Kennedy Holiday Inn, 1985—. Commr., Arlington Heights Bd. Local Improvements, 1979—, Arlington Heights Relocation of Post Office Com., 1958-59, Arlington Heights Zoning Bd., 1959-60; commr. Youth Commn., 1981—. Named Outstanding Bus. Woman, Paddock Publs., Arlington Heights, 1977. Mem. Catering Execs. Club Am. Republican. Home: 604 S Waterman Ave Arlington Heights IL 60004 Office: O'Hare Kennedy Holiday Inn Hotel 5440 N River Rd Rosemont IL 60018

MCKAY, CONSTANCE MARIE FARMER, dietitian; b. Ft. Belvoir, Va., Sept. 19, 1955; d. Nathaniel Jr. and Lora Lee (Cobb) Farmer; m. Montgomery Bernard McKay, Sept. 4, 1983. BS with honors, U. Southern Miss., 1976, MS with honors, 1978; AS with honors, South Cen. Career Coll., 1984. Registered dietitian. Dietitian Valley Food Service, Jackson, Miss., 1976-78; asst. mgr. Valley Food Service, Jackson, 1978-80, mgr.and dir., 1980-85; nutrition cons. Div. Aging and Adult Services, Little Rock, 1987—. Author: Mother Goose Recycled, 1977, Food Service Supervisors Training Manual, 1979. Employer, coordinator coed program Hall High Sch., Little Rock, 1983; workshop coordinator Ark. Enterprises for the Blind, Little Rock, 1982; fund-raiser Spl. Olympics, Little Rock, 1986. Mem. Am. Dietetic Assn. (preceptor for tng. HIEFFS course), Nat. Assn. Female Execs., AMBA Mgrs. Assn., Am. Council of the Blind (Ark. council membership chmn. 1986—, Pres.'s award 1985), Alumni Assn. of U. of Southern Miss. Democrat. Baptist. Office: Div Aging & Adult Services 1428 Donaghey Bldg 7th & Main Sts Little Rock AR 72203

MCKAY, LOLA MERLE, marketing executive, consultant; b. Jacksonville, Tex., Jan. 6, 1930; d. Clarence Malcomb and Joe Dee (Rountree) Reagan; m. Lawrence Brian McKay, Mar. 10, 1950 (dec. Oct. 1982). A.A., Jacksonville Jr. Coll., 1948; B.A., So. Meth. U., 1950. Pub. relations asst. to pres. city council and acting mayor, N.Y.C., 1950-54; corp. sec., dir. Exec. Search and Tech. Recruiting Co., N.Y.C., 1954-59; adminstrv. asst. internat. relations Nat. Acad. Sci.-NRC, Washington, 1959-62; ptnr., mgmt. cons. Mktg. Innovations Co., Washington and Arlington, Va., 1962-70, Houston, 1977-83, owner, mgmt. cons., Alexandria, Va., 1983—; gen. services adminstr. Ferris & Co., Inc., Washington, 1970-77. Sustaining mem. Republican Nat. Com., 1976—; mem. Rep. Senatorial Com., 1980—; mem. Commonwealth Rep. Women's Club, Alexandria, Va., 1984—. Mem. Am. Mktg. Assn., Alexandria C. of C. Methodist. Home and Office: 375 S Reynolds Apt 502 Alexandria VA 22304

MCKAY, RENEE, artist; b. Montreal, Que., Can.; came to U.S., 1946, naturalized, 1954; d. Frederick Garvin and Mildred Gladys (Higgins) Smith;

B.A., McGill U., 1941; m. Kenneth Gardiner McKay, July 25, 1941; children—Margaret Craig, Kenneth Gardiner. Tchr. art Peck Sch., Morristown, N.J., 1955-56; one woman shows: Pen and Brush Club, N.Y.C., 1957, Cosmopolitan Club, N.Y.C., 1958; group shows include: Weyhe Gallery, N.Y.C., 1978, Newark Mus., 1955, 59, Montclair (N.J.) Mus., 1955-58, Nat. Assn. Women Artists, Nat. Acad. Galleries, 1954-78, N.Y. World's Fair, 1964-65, Audubon Artists, N.Y.C., 1955-62, 74-79, N.Y. Soc. Women Artists, 1979-80, Provincetown (Mass.) Art Assn. and Mus., 1975-79; traveling shows in France, Belgium, Italy, Scotland, Can., Japan; represented in permanent collections: Slater Meml. Mus., Norwich, Conn., Norfolk (Va.) Mus., Butler Inst. Am. Art, Youngstown, Ohio, Lydia Drake Library, Pembroke, Mass., many pvt. collections. Recipient Jane Peterson prize in oils Nat. Assn. Women Artists, 1954, Famous Artists Sch. prize in watercolor, 1959, Grumbacher Artists Watercolor award, 1970; Solo award Pen and Brush, 1957; Sadie-Max Tesser award in watercolor Audubon Artists, 1975, Peterson prize in oils, 1980; Michael Engel prize Nat. Soc. Painters in Casein and Acrylic, 1983. Mem. Nat. Assn. Women Artists (2d v.p. 1969-70, adv. bd. 1974-76), Audubon Artists (pres. 1979, dir. oils 1986-88), Artist Equity (dir. 1977-79, v.p. 1979-81), N.Y. Soc. Women Artists, Pen and Brush, Nat. Soc. Painters in Casein and Acrylic M.J. Kaplan prize 1984, Nat. Arts Club, Provincetown Art Assn. and Mus. Club: Cosmopolitan. Address: 200 E 66 St New York NY 10021

MCKEE, CHERYL ANN EAVES, day camp director; b. Compton, Calif., July 22, 1945; d. Elmer Norris and Wilma (Mitchell) Eaves; m. Allan Witney, May 21, 1966; children: Erinn Amber, Shannah, Carrie. AA, Pierce Coll., 1971; BA, U. Cin., 1987; postgrad., U. Ky., 1988. Mgr. credit Sherwin-Williams, Honolulu, 1968-70; pres. Calif. State Property Mgmt., Van Nuys, 1979-82; dir. Forrest Hills Day Camp, Cookeville, Tenn., 1985—. Sec. Gideon's Auxilary, Cookeville, 1984-86; organizer peer group Fairfield Sch.Dist., 1987—. Mem. Psi Chi (career advisor 1986—). Republican. Baptist. Home: 4 Pebble Beach Ct Fairfield OH 45014

MCKEE, DYANA CARLYNE, home health company executive, consultant, educator; b. Springfield, Ohio, June 26, 1941; d. Carl Golden and Betty Mae (Kunkle) McK.; m. James C. Shepherd, Nov. 17, 1958 (div. Mar. 1980); children—Carlton Shepherd, James Shepherd, Roy-J. Shepherd. Adminstrv. asst. cert. MATA, Dayton, Ohio, 1961; secretarial cert. Inst. Tech., Dayton, 1963; cert. in acctg. Met. Coll., Knoxville, Tenn., 1965; student Jefferson State Jr. Coll., Center Point, Ala., 1981-83. Co-owner, co-operator Rex-James Assocs., Trussville, Ala., 1962-71; owner, operator Dreamway Inc., Trussville, 1973-80; control coordinator St. Vincent Hosp., Birmingham, Ala., 1980-81; v.p. Medicare Convalescent Aids, Birmingham, 1981-86; br. mgr. Foster Med. div. Avon Home Care; cons. in field. Author: I Was Abused, 1979. Vol. cons. Cerebral Palsy, Birmingham, 1969-78, St. Jude Children's Research, Memphis, 1970-80; chmn. Toys for Tots, 1970-78; instr. Am. Cancer Soc. of Ala., 1971-76; lectr. Medaids, Birmingham, 1984—. Named to Outstanding Young Women Am., 1977, Outstanding Young Woman of Yr. in State of Ala., 1976; recipient Birmingham Woman of Yr. award Profl. Women, 1978; Fund Raiser of Yr. award St. Jude Children's Research, 1978. Mem. Med. Social Services Orgn. (charter mem., audio visual chairperson 1986—), Epsilon Sigma Alpha (chpt. pres. 1978-79, state Girl of Yr. award 1976). Republican. Lutheran. Home: 29 M Pinewood Dr Trussville AL 35173 other: 703 Memorial Dr Bassemer AL 35023

MCKEE, EDITH MERRITT, geologist; b. Oak Park, Ill., Oct. 9, 1918; d. Eustis Ewart and Edith (Frame) McK.; B.S., Northwestern U., 1946. Geologist, U.S. Geol. Survey, 1943-45, Shell Oil Co., 1947-49, Arabian Am. Oil Co., 1949-54, Underground Gas Storage Co. Ill., 1956-58; ind. cons. geologist, Winnetka, Ill., 1958—; mem. environ. adv. com. Fed. Energy Adminstrn., 1974; mem. Nat. Adv. Com. Oceans and Atmosphere, 1975; speaker, cons. in field. Commr., Winnetka Park Bd., 1976-79. Fellow Marine Tech. Soc., Geol. Soc. Am.; mem. Am. Geol. Inst., Am. Inst. Profl. Geologists (cert., charter), Assn. Engring. Geologists, Ill. Geol. Soc., Am. Oceanic Orgn. Research on shore erosion, mapping of Gt. Lakes basins and deep ocean basins, global econ. devel. programs and mineral exploration. Address: PO Box 3 Good Hart MI 49737

MCKEE, KATHRYN DIAN GRANT, bank executive; b. Los Angeles, Sept. 12, 1937; d. Clifford William and Amelia Rosalia (Shacher) Grant; m. Paul Eugene McKee, June 17, 1961; children: Scott Alexander, Grant Christopher. BA, U. Calif., Santa Barbara, 1959; grad. Sch. Mgmt. Exec. Program, UCLA, 1979. Accredited compensation and benefits. Mgr., Mattel, Inc., Hawthorne, Calif., 1963-74; dir. Twentieth Century Fox Film Corp., Los Angeles, 1975-80; sr. v.p. 1st Interstate Bank, Ltd., Los Angeles, 1980—; treas. Personnel Accreditation Inst., 1983-86, pres., 1986. Contbr. articles to profl. jours. Pres. GEM Theatre Guild, Garden Grove, Calif., 1984-86; bd. dirs. Vis. Nurses Assn., Los Angeles, 1984—, ASPA, 1986—, trustee Garden Grove Assn. for Arts, 1985—, pres., 1988. Recipient Sr. Honor Key, U. Calif., Santa Barbara, 1959; named Outstanding Sr. Woman 1959. Mem. Internat. Assn. Personnel Women (various offices, past nat. pres., Mem. of Yr. 1986), Orgn. Women Execs., Women in Bus., Am. Compensation Assn. (William Winter award 1986). Club: Los Angeles Athletic. Office: 1st Interstate Bank Ltd 707 Wilshire Blvd Los Angeles CA 90017

MC KEE, MARGARET JEAN, federal agency executive; b. New Haven, June 20, 1929; d. Waldo McCutcheon and Elizabeth (Thayer) McKee; A.B., Vassar Coll., 1951. Staff asst. United Republican Fin. Com., N.Y.C., 1952; staff asst. N.Y. Rep. State Com., N.Y.C., 1953-55; staff asst. Crusade for Freedom (name later changed to Radio Free Europe Fund), N.Y.C., 1955-57; researcher Stricker & Henning Research Assocs., Inc., N.Y.C., 1957-59; exec. sec. New Yorkers for Nixon (name later changed to N.Y. State Ind. Citizens for Nixon Lodge), N.Y.C., 1959-60; asst. to Raymond Moley, polit. columnist, N.Y.C., 1961; asst. campaign com. Louis J. Lefkowitz for Mayor, N.Y.C., 1961; research programmer, treas. Consensus, Inc., N.Y.C., 1962-67; spl. asst. to U.S. Senator Jacob K. Javits, N.Y., 1967-73, adminstrv. asst., 1973-75; dep. adminstr. Am. Revolution Bicentennial Adminstrn., 1976, acting adminstr., 1976-77; chief of staff Perry B. Duryea (minority leader) N.Y. State Assembly, 1978; public affairs cons., 1979-80; dir. govt. relations Gen. Mills Restaurant Group, Inc., 1980-83; exec. dir. Fed. Mediation and Conciliation Service, 1983-86; dir. Interam. Life Ins. Co. Mem. N.Y. State Bingo Control Commn., 1965-72 . U.S. Adv. Commn. on Public Diplomacy, 1979-82; pres. Bklyn. Heights Slope Young Republican Club, 1955-56; co-chmn. Bklyn. Citizens for Eisenhower-Nixon, 1956; chmn. 2d Jud. Dist. Assn. N.Y. State Young Rep. Clubs, Inc., 1957-58, vice-chmn., mem. bd. govs., 1958-60, v.p., 1960-62; pres., 1962-64; mem. exec. com. Fedn. Women's Rep. Clubs N.Y. State, Inc., 1960-64, mem. council, 1964-70; mem. exec. com. N.Y. Rep. State Com. 1962-64; bd. mem. Fedl. Labor Relations Authority, 1986—; co-chmn. spl. assts. Rockefeller for Pres. Nat. Campaign com., N.Y.C., 1964; co-dir. N.Y. Rep. State Campaign Com., 1964; asst. campaign mgr. Kenneth B. Keating for Judge Ct. Appeals, N.Y., 1965; dir. scheduling Gov. Rockefeller campaign, 1966, Sen. Charles E. Goodell campaign, 1970; dir. scheduling and speakers' bur. N.Y. Com. to Re-elect the Pres., 1972; dir. planning, strategy and women's programs Reagan-Bush campaign. Mem. bd. govs. Women's Nat. Rep. Club, N.Y.C., 1963-66. Mem. Jr. League of Bklyn. (past (dir.), Exec. Women in Govt. (chmn. 1986), Nat. Women's Edn. Fund (mem. bd.), Am. Newspaper Women's Club, Nat. Soc. Colonial Dames Am. Episcopalian. Club: Vassar (past dir.) (Bklyn.). Home: 3001 Veazey Terr NW Washington DC 20008

MCKEE, MARTHA ELLEN, financial consultant; b. Des Moines, Apr. 2, 1960; d. William Edward and Alice (Anderson) McK. BA in Econs., Northwestern U., 1982; MBA, U. Mich., 1984. Cons. Peterson & Co., Chgo., 1984—. Mem. AAUW. Office: 3110 N Sheridan Rd Apt 1704 Chicago IL 60657

MCKEE, SANDRA LEE, art administrator, artist; b. Cleve., May 18, 1946; d. Donald Keith and Norma May (Boeff) McK.; m. James Vincent Moisan, Nov. 28, 1968 (div. 1983); m. Ivan Lewis Taub, Dec. 2, 1983. Student, Parsons Sch. Design, 1964-66, U. Oreg., 1970-72. Instr. Lane Community Coll., Eugene, Oreg., 1972-74, U. Oreg., Eugene, 1973-76; art adminstr. Home Mag., N.Y.C., 1983-84, Am. Health Mag. and Mother Earth News, N.Y.C., 1984—; curator Mudd Club, N.Y.C., 1981, Pan Arts, N.Y.C., 1985. Exhibited in one woman shows including U. Mont. Mus. Art, Missoula, 1972, U. Oreg. Mus. Art, 1974, Anne Hughes Gallery, Portland, 1975, Aarun Gallery, Los Angeles, 1978, A's, N.Y.C., 1980, L.I. U., N.Y.C., 1981, Gwendolyn Moon Gallery, N.Y.C., 1987, Inst. Guatemala Am. in Guatamala City and Q; group shows include Institutionen for Konstvetanskap, Fack, Sweden, 1978, Haags Gemeentemuseum, The Netherlands, 1981, Interart Ctr., N.Y.C., 1981, Hunter Coll., N.Y.C., 1981, Metronom, Barcelona, Spain, 1981, Gracie Mansion Gallery, N.Y.C., 1982, U. Ill., 1982, Altos de Chavon, Dominican Republic, 1983, Seoul Fine Arts Ctr., Korea, 1983, Royal Swedish Embassy, Stockholm, 1984, Yokohama City Art Hall, Japan, 1984, Civico Instituto, Genoa, Italy, 1984, N.Y. Art Dir.'s Club, 1987; contbr. articles to profl. jours.. Mem. Found. for the Community of Artists. Home: 106 Ridge St New York NY 10002

MCKEEGAN, SHARON KATHLEEN, hospital quality assurance professional; b. Albany, Calif., Nov. 6, 1942; d. Bernard Rolland and Helen Mary (McCullough) McK.; 1 child, Meghan Marie. BA in Psychology, Calif. State U., Northridge, 1970. Eligibility worker Calif. Dept. Welfare, Panorama City, 1970-71; coordinator pvt. and govt. health projects Calif., 1972-75; cons. healthcare industry Alameda, Calif., 1975-77; supr. Wells Fargo Bank, San Francisco, 1978-79; quality assurance/audit coordinator Ralph K. Davies Med. Ctr., San Francisco, 1979-80; quality assurance coordinator Eden Hosp., Castro Valley, Calif., 1980-84; quality assurance, utilization/diagnostic related groups coordinator Wheeler Hosp., Gilroy, Calif., 1984-85; quality assurance coordinator Kaiser Santa Teresa Hosp., San Jose, Calif., 1986—; entrepreneur. Holder patents. Mem. Patient Care Assessment Council (advisor 1979-82, pres. 1981-82, Appreciation award 1982). Home: 500 West 10th St #43 Gilroy CA 95020

MCKEEL, RACHEL VIOLA, telephone company executive; b. Roseau, Minn., July 23, 1941; d. J. Martin and Ruth Elsa (Skoglund) Svensson; m. Jon Stewart McKeel, June 8, 1962; children: John, Kristin, Ruth. Student, Ball State U., 1960-61, 62-63; BS in German and English, Moorhead State Coll., 1966. Tchr. German and English Pub. Schs., 1966-76; mgmt. trainee in mktg./sales promotion State Bank of Freeport (Ill.), 1977-78; mgr. mktg./pub. relations Northwestern Telephone Co., Freeport, 1979-80; residential mktg. coordinator Contel of Ill., Sycamore, 1980-87, pub. affairs specialist, 1987—. Mem. publicity com. Community Chest, Freeport, 1977, sect. leader, 1979, publicity chmn. centennial com. Hillcrest Covenant Ch., 1982, bd. trustees, 1984-86. U.S. Dept. Edn. grantee, 1967. Mem. Am. Mgmt. Assn., Internat. Assn. Bus. Communicators, Nat. Assn. Female Execs., No. Ill. Communicators, Ill. Telephone Assn. Office: Contel of Ill Inc 112 W Elm St Sycamore IL 60178

MCKEEMAN, CHRISTINE ELAINE, lawyer; b. Austin, Tex., Apr. 25, 1953; d. Bruce Bingham and Wanda Lee (Dunlap) Batchelor; m. Leland Paul McKeeman, May 25, 1985; children—John Edward Potter, Ryan Keith McKeeman. B.A. with highest honors, U. Tex., 1975; J.D., 1982. Bar: Tex. 1982. Planner, City of Austin (Tex.), 1977-79; briefing atty. Tex. Supreme Ct., Austin, 1982-83; assoc. Rinehart & Nugent, Austin, 1983-85; with McKeeman, Tuttle & Hein, Austin, 1985—. Mem. State Bar Tex., Travis County Bar Assn., Austin Young Lawyers Assn., Phi Beta Kappa, Phi Kappa Phi. Office: McKeeman Tuttle & Hein 5407 N Interregional Hwy Suite 300 Austin TX 78723

MCKEEN, LYNN MARIE, insurance company executive; b. Mars Hill, Maine, June 26, 1951; d. Theodore Frank and Lois Marie (Hubbard) Durost; m. James Elwood McKeen, Apr. 18, 1970 (div. Aug. 1980). Cert. profl. ins. woman. Legal sec. Stewart, Griffiths & Quigley, Presque Isle, Maine, 1969-71; sec., file clk. Maine Mut. Group, Presque Isle, 1971-75, policy typist, 1975-76, rating clk., 1976-77, asst. underwriter, 1977-82, staff underwriter, 1982-83, underwriting supr., 1983-85, underwriting mgr., 1986—; v.p. Maine Mut. Fire Ins. Co. Mem. Maine Community Vol. Fire Prevention Program. Mem. Nat. Assn. Ins. Women (pres. Aroostook 1981-82, 87-88, state dir. 1983-85, Ins. Woman of Yr. 1982, state Speak-off winner 1983, regional Speak-off winner 1984). Home: 22d Strawberry Bank Presque Isle ME 04769 Office: Maine Mutual Group Ins Cos 551 Main St Presque Isle ME 04769

MC KELVEY, JEAN TREPP, industrial relations educator; b. St. Louis, Feb. 9, 1908; d. Samuel and Blanche (Goodman) Trepp; m. Blake McKelvey, June 29, 1934. A.B., Wellesley Coll., 1929; M.A., Radcliffe Coll., 1931, Ph.D., 1933. Faculty Sarah Lawrence Coll., 1932-45; faculty N.Y. State Sch. Indsl. and Labor Relations, Cornell U., Ithaca, N.Y., 1946—; asst. prof., asso. prof., prof. indsl. relations N.Y. State Sch. Indsl. and Labor Relations, Cornell U., 1946—; vis. prof. Cornell U. Law Sch., 1977-78; pub. panel mem., hearing officer and arbitrator Nat. War Labor Bd., 1944-45; mem. N.Y. State Bd. Inquiry into Rochester Transit Dispute, 1952; pub. mem. adv. com. to sec. labor, 1953; mem. N.Y. State Bd. Mediation, 1956- 66; mem. pub. rev. bd. U.A.W., 1960—; presdl. Emergency Bd., Ry. Shopcrafts Dispute, 1964, Ry. Signalmen Dispute, 1971; mem. Fed. Service Impasses Panel, 1970—. Author: The Uses of Field Work in Teaching Economics, 1939, AFL Attitudes Toward Production, 1952, Dock Labor Disputes in Great Britain, 1953, Fact Finding in Public Employment Disputes, 1969, Sex and the Single Arbitrator, 1971. Editor: The Duty of Fair Representation, 1977; The Changing Law of Fair Representation, 1985, Cleared For Takeoff: Airline Labor Relations Under Deregulation, 1988; also several vols. on arbitration. Mem. Nat. Acad. Arbitrators (past pres.), Am. Fedn. Tchrs. (pub. rev. bd. 1969-73), Am. Arbitration Assn. (nat. panel), Indsl. Relations Research Assn., Phi Beta Kappa. Home: 53 Aberthaw Rd Rochester NY 14610 Office: Cornell U 277 Alexander St Rochester NY 14607

MCKELVEY, JUDITH GRANT, lawyer, educator, university dean; b. Milw., July 19, 1935; d. Lionel Alexander and Bernadine R. (Verdun) Grant. B.S. in Philosophy, U. Wis., 1957, J.D., 1959. Bar: Wis. 1959, Calif. 1968. Atty. adv. FCC, Washington, 1959-62; adj. prof. U. Md., Europe, 1965; prof. law Golden Gate U. Sch. Law, San Francisco, 1968—; dean Golden Gate U. Sch. Law (Sch. Law), 1974-81. Contbr. to: Damages Book, 1975, 76. Bd. dirs. San Francisco Neighborhood Legal Assistance Found. Fellow Am. Bar Found.; mem. ABA, Wis. Bar Assn., Calif. Bar Assn., San Francisco Bar Assn. (dir. 1975-77, chmn. legis. com., sec.-treas., pres.-elect 1980-83, pres. 1984), Calif. Women Lawyers (1st pres.), Law in a Free Soc. (exec. com.), Continuing Edn. of Bar (chmn. real estate subcom., mem. joint adv. com.), legal services to children, Inc. (pres. 1987-88), San Francisco Neighborhood Legal Assistance Found. (dir. and exec. com. 1985-87), lawyers com. for Urban Affairs (dir. and exec. com. 1985-87). Office: Golden Gate U Sch Law 536 Mission St San Francisco CA 94105

MCKENNA, FAY ANN, electrical manufacturing company executive; b. Bennington, Vt., Jan. 7, 1944; d. George Francis and Barbara Mae (Youngangel) Hoag; m. James Dennis McKenna, Sept. 3, 1963 (div. 1983); children: Russell (dec.), Laura, James, Sean, Michael. Student, Mercy Coll. Key punch operator N.Y. State Taxation and Fin. Dept., Albany, 1960-61; receptionist Trine Mfg./Square D Co., Bronx, 1972-76; clk. Square D Co., Bronx, 1976-78, exec. sec., 1978-79, personnel mgr., 1979-86; mgr. mktg. adminstrn. Trine Products Corp., 1986—. Mfg. Fund raiser YMCA, Bronx, 1979—; mem. Community Bd. #9, Bronx, 1984—; Recipient Service to Youth award YMCA, 1985. Mem. Adminstrv. Mgmt. Soc. Republican. Roman Catholic. Avocations: physical fitness, reading, interior decorating. Home: 4100-20 Hutchinson River Pkwy E Bronx NY 10475 Office: Trine Products Corp 1430 Ferris Pl Bronx NY 10461

MCKENNA, MARY CATHERINE, nutritional biochemist, educator; b. Bethesda, Md., Dec. 17, 1945; d. John Reilly and Mary Cusack (McManus) McK.; m. Alan Mink, Dec. 18, 1974; 1 child, John Morris McKenna Mink. BA, U. Md., 1968, PhD, 1979. Stewardess, Overseas Nat. Airways, N.Y.C., 1969-72; grad. teaching and research asst., dept. chemistry U. Md., College Park, 1973-78, affiliate asst. prof. dept. food, nutrition and inst. adminstrn., U. Md., College Park, 1983—; research asst. prof. dept. pediatrics U. Md. Sch. Medicine, Balt., 1982—; staff fellow, nutritional biochemistry sect. Lab. of Nutrition and Endocrinology, Nat. Inst. Arthritis, Diabetes, Digestive and Kidney Disease, NIH, Bethesda, Md., 1979-82. Recipient Sigma Xi research excellence award and research grant, 1977. Mem. Am. Inst. Nutrition (tellers com. 1986-88, chmn. 1988), Am. Chem. Soc., Am. Oil Chemists Soc., N.Y. Acad. Scis., AAAS, Am. Forestry Assn., Sierra Club, Cousteau Soc., Sigma Xi. Home: 13088 Williamfield Dr Ellicott City MD 21043 Office: U Md Sch Medicine Dept Pediatrics Div Pediatric Research Baltimore MD 21201

MCKENNA, SHIRLEY LEE, tile company executive; b. Chgo., Apr. 4, 1935; d. Joseph M. and Estelle N. (Blasch) Warnell; m. Robert McKenna, June 18, 1955; children: Susan, Judi, Michael. Student, U. Chgo., 1954, Art Inst. Chgo., 1955. Sec. Lisle (Ill.) High Sch., 1967-69; mgr. I.B.C. Bookstore, Lisle, 1970-78, v.p., designer McKenna Tile, Naperville, Ill., 1978—; cons. CTDI, Chgo., 1985—. Mem. NFIB, Springfield, Ill., 1987. Mem. Nat Fedn. Ind. Bus., U.S. C. of C., Naperville Area C. of C. Roman Catholic. Office: McKenna Tile Co Inc 2385 S Washington Naperville IL 60540

MCKENNEY, AUDREY CAROL, telecommunications company executive; b. Denver, May 29, 1959; d. William James and Muriel Anita (Donchain) McK. BS, U. Colo., Denver, 1981. Teller Omni Bank, Aurora, Colo., 1980-81; controller Wilderness Taxidermy, Aurora, 1980-87; mgr. corp. books Mountain Bell West, Denver, 1981-84; mgr. fin. reports US West, Englewood, Colo., 1984-86, dir. investor relations, 1986—. Cons. Jr. Achievement, Denver, 1987; mem. Colo. Humane Soc., Denver, 1987. Mem. Nat. Investors Relations Inst., 50 for Colo., Nat. Assn. Female Execs. Lutheran. Home: 1873 S Sedalia Circle Aurora CO 80017 Office: US West 7800 E Orchard Rd Englewood CO 80111

MCKENZIE, ANTONIA (TONI) LYNN HATCHER, pet school director; b. Louisville, Oct. 15, 1954; d. Charles L. and Nancy L. (Sanders) Hatcher; m. Dale H. McKenzie, Sept 10, 1972 (div. Apr. 1978); 1 child, Jessica Marie. Grad. high sch., Ashland, Ky. Store mgr. Unicorn Pet Shop, Ashland, Ky., 1971-73, groomer, 1973-83; grooming instr. Merryfield Acad. Animal Technicians, Ft. Lauderdale, Fla., 1984, staff supr., 1984-86, dir. edn., 1986—; lectr. in field; certifier Internat. Profl. Groomers, Inc., Dallas, 1986—. Author: Knowing the AKC Dog Book, 1987. Mem. Briard Club Am., Nat. Dog Groomers Assn. Am., Ft. Lauderdale Dog Club, South Fla. Poodle Club. Office: Merryfield Acad Animal Technicians 5040 NE 13 Ave Fort Lauderdale FL 33334

MCKENZIE, ELAINE MARY, real estate broker; b. Detroit, June 23, 1941; d. Spencer Milton and Leona Josephine (Gelgota) Clark; m. Thomas Joseph McKenzie Sr., Oct. 6, 1962; children: Thomas J. Jr., Craig A.; adopted children: David A., Jeffrey R. Student, Detroit Bus. Sch., 1959-61. Clk. Nat. Wholesale Drug Co., Detroit, 1961-62; teller Detroit Bank and Trust Co., 1962-63; accounting clk. Budd Co., Detroit, 1963-64, 65-66; assoc. realtor Bachler Realty, Marine City, Mich., 1980-81, Real Estate One-Westrick Assn., Marine City, 1981-82; assoc. broker Schweitzer Real Estate, St. Clair, 1982-88, O'Connor Realty, Marysville, Mich., 1988—. Chmn. Cystic Fibrosis, Marine City, 1980-87. Mem. St. Clair County Bd. Realtors (Port Huron Realtor Polit. Action Com. chmn. 1987, 88), Women's Council Realtors (pres. 1984, Cystic Fibrosis chmn. 1987, award of Excellence 1986). Roman Catholic. Lodge: Women of the Moose. Home: 156 S Elizabeth St Marine City MI 48039 Office: O'Connor Realty 2801 Gratiot Blvd Marysville MI 48040

MCKENZIE, MARY ELIZABETH, chemical engineer; b. Port Hueneme, Calif., Apr. 1, 1955; d. Robert William and Nell (Cowart) McK.; m. Ralph Eugene Vincent, May 28, 1977 (div. Nov. 1985); children: William Joseph (dec.), Emily Rose; m. John W. Hebert, Jan. 3, 1987; 1 child, Rachel Leigh. BSCE, La. State U., 1977. Design engr. PPG Industries, Inc., Lake Charles, La., 1977-79; environ. engr. Walk, Haydel & Assocs., Inc., New Orleans, 1984-87; environ. control engr. Ashland (Ky.) Petroleum Co., 1987—. Mem. Nat. Assn. Female Execs., Soc. Women Engrs. Republican. Episcopalian. Office: Ashland Petroleum Co PO Box 391 Ashland KY 41114

MCKENZIE, PAMELA JEAN, physician; b. Denver, Apr. 24, 1940; d. John and Vashti Keefe (Muxlow) McK.; divorced; 1 child, Duncan. MD, U. Colo., Denver, 1965. Intern, then resident Yale New Haven (Conn.) Hosp., 1965-67; fellow in child devel. Yale Child Study Ctr., New Haven, 1967-69, from instr. to asst. prof., 1969-71; asst. prof. JFK Child Devel. Ctr., Denver, 1971-76, Kempe Child Abuse Ctr., Denver, 1976-78; dir. child devel. ctr. The Children's Hosp., Denver, 1978—. Editor: (book) The Fragile X Syndrome, 1984; contbr. articles to profl. jours. Fellow Am. Acad. Pediatrics. Democrat. Office: The Childrens Hosp 1056 E 19th Ave Denver CO 80218

MCKENZIE, SARAH DARLENE, sales executive; b. Middletown, Ohio, Sept. 20, 1947; d. Clinton and Gladys Marie (Thomas) Rogers; m. Gary C. Lilly, Aug. 17, 1968 (div. Feb. 1981). AA, South Ea. Coll., 1968; student, Fla. So. Coll., 1969-70; BA, Ohio State U., 1973. Cert. tchr., Ohio, Pa., Calif. Social worker Allegheney County Welfare Agy., Pitts., 1973-74; computer technician Reynolds & Reynolds Co., Pitts., 1974-77; with computer sales, specialist mktg. Los Angeles, 1977-81; with computer software sales O.S. Systems, Los Angeles, 1981-84; with office automation product sales Alexanders Stationers Corp., Los Angeles, 1984—; founder Edn. Plus Orgn., Pitts., 1974-76, SHOW-BIZ Network Ltd., Teleprodns. Co., Northridge, Calif., 1986—; instr. Barbizon Modeling Sch., Sherman Oaks, Calif., 1983-85, Learning Tree Inst., Los Angeles, 1984-87. Mem. End Hunger Network/Hands Across Am., Los Angeles, 1985—; recording sec. Thalians Charity/Thalians Mental Health Ctr. at Cedars Sinai Med. Ctr., Los Angeles, 1988—. Mem. So. Calif. Motion Picture Council, Mensa. Democrat. Home: PO Box 902 Reseda CA 91335

MCKEON, SHIRLEY, human services administrator; b. Pittson, Pa., Feb 11, 1931; d. Sandy and Grace (DeTato) Mazzeo; children: David, Elaine. BA, Glassboro (N.J.) State, 1974, MA, 1976. RN, Pa., N.J. Career counselor Burlington County Coll., Pemberton, N.J., 1976; unit mgr. Turning Point Drug Program, Blackwood, N.J., 1977; employment counselor N.J. Dept. Labor and Industry, Mt. Holly, N.J., 1978-82; social worker Mental Retardation div. N.J. Dept. Human Services, Bordentown, N.J., 1982-84; plan coordinator Devel. Disabilities div. N.J. Dept. Human Services, Pemberton, 1984—. Served to capt. USAF, 1953-57. Office: NJ Dept Human Services 222 S Warren St Trenton NJ 08625

MCKEOWN, KATHLEEN MARY, business consultant; b. New Haven, Dec. 11, 1941; d. Edward J. and Elizabeth Grace (Sullivan) McK. B.A., Notre Dame of Md., 1963; postgrad. San Francisco Art Inst., 1967, Acad. Art, 1968. Art supr. pub. schs., Wolcott, Conn., 1963-66; interior decorator, San Francisco, 1966-69; office mgr. Multiple Line Engring. Service, San Francisco, 1970-73; bus. mgr. Uniplan Corp., San Francisco, 1973-74, dir. prodn. control, 1974-75, dir. client services, 1976-77, v.p., 1977-78; dir. franchise resales Swensens, Inc., San Francisco, 1979; mgmt. cons. China Books & Periodicals, San Francisco, 1980—, also dir.; cons. Chinese papercuts exhibit Berkshire Mus. Art, Lenox, Mass., 1982—; graphics cons. Fgn. Lang. Press, Beijing, 1983—, New World Press, Beijing, 1983—; photographer Terwiliger Found., Tiburon, Calif., 1981—. Bus. affiliate Citizens Adv. Com. to San Francisco Police Dept., 1976-77. Mem. Embarcadero Ctr. Forum (pres. 1978), Book Publicists No. Calif., Grey Panthers. Democrat. Roman Catholic. Home: 35 Iris Ave San Francisco CA 94108

MCKEOWN, MARY ELIZABETH, educational administrator; d. Raymond Edmund and Alice (Fitzgerald) McNamara; B.S., U. Chgo., 1946; M.S., DePaul U., 1953; m. James Edward McKeown, Aug. 6, 1955. Supr. high sch. dept. Am. Sch., 1948-68, prin., 1968—, trustee, 1975—, v.p., 1979—. Mem. Nat. Assn. Secondary Sch. Prins., Central States Assn. Sci. and Math Tchrs. Nat. Council Tchrs. Math., Assn. for Supervision and Curriculum Devel., Adult Edn. Assn., LWV. Author study guides for algebra, geometry and calculus. Home: 1469 N Sheridan Rd Kenosha WI 53140 Office: 850 E 58th Chicago IL 60637

MCKERNAN-MARKOFF, JANIS LEIGH, nurse, union official, investigator; b. New London, Conn., June 17, 1949; d. Joseph Bernard and Joyce Louise (Davis) (dec.) McK.; Shirley Mae (Kenyon) (stepmother) McK.; m. Henry E. Markoff, Sept. 27, 1983. R.N., Hartford (Conn.) Hosp. Sch. Nursing, 1972; BS in Mgmt., Salva Regina Coll., 1984, postgrad. 1987—. Charge nurse R.I. Hosp., 1972-73, Butler Hosp. 1973-74, Day Kimball Hosp. 1983; supr. Inst. Mental Health, 1974-82; nat. v.p. Nat. Assn. of Govt. Employees, 1980-82; staff nurse St. Joseph Hosp., 1983-86; investigator Medicaid Fraud Control Unit, Dept. R.I. Atty. Gen., 1986-87; staff nurse intensive care unit, R.I. Hosp., 1987—; lobbyist for Alliance for Better Nursing Home Care, 1987—. Served with Nurse Corps, US Army, 1975, to maj. USAR, 1975—. Author, researcher Alzheimer's Disease Victim's Long-Term Health Care Facilities project, 1985. Fellow Internat. Biographical Assn.; mem. Am. Nurses Assn., R.I. Nurses Assn., Res. Officers Assn.,

Assn. U.S. Army, Nat. Fedn. Rep. Women, R.I. Lung Assn., Hartford Hosp. Sch. Nursing Alumni Assn., Salve Regina Coll. Alumni Assn. Home: 28 Mozart St Cranston RI 02920

MCKIERNAN, SUSAN PAOLANO, university director, art educator; b. Barberton, Ohio, June 30, 1947; d. Aldo Roosevelt and Mary Josephine (Platner) Paolano; m. Brian D. McKiernan, July 29, 1967 (div. Apr. 1980); children: Sean Mathias, Kara Meaghan. BFA, U. Akron, Ohio, 1977, MS in Edn., 1987, postgrad., 1987—. Lab. asst. metals dept. U. Akron, 1977-79, instr. metals, 1979—, asst. head art dept., 1980-87, asst. dir. Sch. Art, 1987—; instr. field trip course to manor houses, Eng., summers 1986—. Author: Walking Tour of Downtown Akron, History of Peninsula, Ohio, History of Weymouth, Ohio. Charter mem. Progress Through Preservation, Summit County, Ohio, 1983, Mus. Contemporaries, 1984; mem. Akron Art Mus., Medina County Hist. Soc.; pres. Hower House Victorians, Akron, 1984. Named one of Outstanding Young Women Am., 1982. Mem. Nat. Council Arts Adminstrs., Ohio Assn. Women Deans and Adminstrs., Ohio Assn. for Counseling and Devel., Kappa Kappa Gamma. Democrat. Episcopalian. Office: U Akron Sch of Art Akron OH 44256

MCKILLOP, LUCILLE, college president; b. Chgo., Sept. 28, 1924; d. Daniel and Catherine (Hamill) McK. B.A., St. Xavier Coll., 1951; M.S., U. Notre Dame, 1959; Ph.D., U. Wis., 1965. Vis. prof. Ill. Inst. Tech., Chgo., 1969; faculty St. Xavier Coll., Chgo., 1958-59, 63-73; pres. Salve Regina Coll., Newport, R.I., 1973—; dir. Old Colony Coop. Bank, Providence, 1976-81; mem. Gov.'s Adv. Commn. Ednl. TV, 1977-82, R.I. Postsecondary Edn. Commn., 1979—, Gov.'s Commn. on Taxation, 1981-83, Gov.'s Commn. on R.I. Legis. Compensation, 1980. Trustee Newport Hosp., 1976-80; mem. corp. R.I. Blue Cross/Blue Shield, 1980—; bd. dirs. Council for Advancement Small Colls., 1978-82, Newport Music Festival, 1978—; chmn. Washington Office on Haiti, 1984—; bd. dirs. NCCJ of R.I. Inc., 1983—. Mem. Nat. Assn. Ind. Colls. and Univs. (dir. 1977-82), R.I. Ind. Higher Edn. Assn. (exec. com.), Associated Cath. Colls. and Univs. (exec. com. coll. and univ. dept. 1977-80). Office: Newport Coll Salve Regina Ochre Point Ave Newport RI 02840

MCKINLEY, CANDACE EILEEN, advertising executive; b. Tillamook, Oreg., July 15, 1946; d. Loren Dhue and Mary Eileen (Sessions) McK. Student, Portland State U., 1964-67, Oreg. State U., 1964-67. V.p., creative dir. Marx, Knoll & Mangels Advt., Portland, Oreg., 1970-82; v.p., copy dir. Coates Advt., Portland, 1982-88; free-lance copywriter, producer Cleve., 1988—. Bd. dirs. Lukemia Assn. of Oreg., Portland, Hoyt Square Homeowners Assn., Portland; vol. copywriter for numerous civic events. Recipient of numerous awards including CLIO, IBA, LULU, ADDY, Best in West, Telly and Chgo. Film Festival.

MCKINLEY, ELLEN BACON, priest; b. Milw., June 9, 1929; d. Edward Alsted and Lorraine Goodrich (Graham) Bacon; m. Richard Smallbrook McKinley, III, June 16, 1951 (div. Oct. 1977); children—Richard IV, Ellen Graham, David Todd, Edward Bacon. BA cum laude, Bryn Mawr Coll., 1951; MDiv Yale U., 1976; STM, Gen. Theol. Sem., N.Y.C., 1979; M in Philosophy, Union Theol. Sem., N.Y.C., 1986, PhD, 1988. Ordained deacon Episcopal Ch. 1980, priest, 1981. Intern St. Francis Ch., Stamford, Conn., 1976-77; pastoral asst. St. Paul's Ch., Riverside, Conn., 1979-80, curate, 1980-81; priest assoc. St. Saviour's Ch., Old Greenwich, Conn., 1982—; asst. St. Christopher's Ch., Chatham, Mass., 1987-88. Mem. Episcipal Election Com., Diocese of Conn., 1986-87, Com. on Human Sexuality, 1987—; Com. on Donations and Bequests Diocese of Conn., 1987—; sec., Greewich Com. on Drugs, 1970-71; bd. dirs. Greenwich YWCA, 1971-72. Mem. Conn. Clergy Assn. (Episcopal), Episcopal Women's Caucus, New Eng. Women Ministers Assn., Greenwich Fellowship of Clergy, Colonial Dames Am., Jr. League. Clubs: Sulgrave, Rocky Point. Avocations: theatre, concerts, swimming, sailing, reading, architecture, building and remodeling houses. Office: St Saviour's Ch 350 Sound Beach Ave Old Greenwich CT 06870

MCKINLEY, RUTH JOANN, hospice administrator, psychotherapist; b. Los Angeles, Sept. 24, 1933; d. Ward Ivan and Lilah May (Conger) Hallin; B.A., Calif. State U.-Northridge, 1966; M.S.W., U. So. Calif., 1972; Ph.D. cum laude, Am. Western U., 1981; m. John Clyde McKinley, Nov. 19, 1954 (dec. 1972); children—Terance Phillip Green, Mark Stuart. Diplomate Am. Bd. Clin. Social Work. Adminstr., Pacoima (Calif.) br. San Fernando Valley Child Guidance Clinic, 1965-68; dependency supr. placement services Los Angeles County Juvenile Ct., Van Nuys, Calif., 1968-72; psychotherapist Simi Valley and Conejo Mental Health, Ventura County Mental Health Services, Thousand Oaks, Calif., 1972-83; exec. dir. Hospice of the Conejo, 1984-86, pvt. practice psychotherapy Capper Psychiat. Med. Group, Camarillo, Calif., after 1979; exec. dir. Hospice of Conejo, 1984-86; pvt. practice Mc Kinley Assocs., 1983—; cons., tng. cons. Conejo Community Hotline. Dir., Lifeline, Westlake Village, Calif., 1972-75; mem. White Ho. Conf. on Children and Youth, 1970; mem. Ventura County Coalition Against Household Violence, 1980. Children's Bur. Fed. grantee, 1970-72. Mem. Acad. Cert. Social Workers, Soc. Clin. Social Work. Office: 199 E Thousand Oaks Blvd Thousand Oaks CA 91361

MCKINNEY, BETTY COOPER, banker; b. Lynchburg, Va., Apr. 24, 1940; d. Norman Henry and Virginia Campbell (Thomas) Cooper; m. James Elliott McKinney, May 6, 1972; 1 child, Virginia Elizabeth. BA in English, Lynchburg Coll., 1962. English tchr. Amherst (Va.) County High Sch., 1962-63; asst. woman's editor Lynchburg News, 1963-65; city desk asst. Charlotte (N.C.) News, 1965-66; asst. woman's editor Fayetteville (N.C.) Observer, 1966-68; reporter Amherst New Era Progress, 1969-70; adminstrv. asst. Cen. Fidelity Bank, Lynchburg, 1970-72, advt. officer, 1972-74, employment officer, 1974-79, asst. v.p., mktg. officer, 1979-83, v.p. mktg., 1983—; instr. English and mktg. Am. Inst. Banking, Lynchburg, 1978—. Author Lynchburg travel guide. Publicity chair James River Day Sch., Lynchburg, 1978-82; bd. dirs. Friends of Jones Meml. Library, 1979, Lynchburg YWCA, 1978, Broadway Theater League, Lynchburg, 1978; mem. steering com. Festival by the James, 1987-88. Mem. United Daus. of the Confederacy. Republican. Baptist. Home: 305 Buckingham Dr Lynchburg VA 24502

MCKINNEY, JENNY HSUN NI, manufacturing executive; b. Taichung, Taiwan, Republic of China, Jan. 29, 1952; d. Cher-shing Tao and Shin-ching Chang; m. Bruce Evan McKinney, Apr. 23, 1977; children, Thomas Craig, Adelaide Kathryn. BA, Fu Jen U., Taipei, Republic of China, 1973. Gen. mgr. Imex Source, Inc., Taipei, 1976-81; gen. mgr. Tradex Orient, Ltd., Taipei, 1977-82, pres., 1982—; v.p. Consol. Dutchwest, Inc., Plymouth, Mass., 1983—. Office: Consol Dutchwest Inc 40 Industrial Park Rd Plymouth MA 02360

MCKINNEY, PHYLLIS LOUISE KELLOGG HENRY, school administrator, management consultant; b. Mason City, Iowa, May 3, 1932; d. Wilbur Rhode and Dorothy Margaret (Bauer) K.; children—Curtis Dean Henry, Catherine Rose Henry Jones, David Russell Henry. A.A. in Elem. Teaching, U. No. Iowa, 1953; B.A. Calif. State U.-Los Angeles, 1963, M.A., 1968. Cert. elem. tchr., cert. reading specialist, sch. adminstrn. credential. Tchr., Arlington pub. schs., Iowa, 1951-52, St. Louis Park pub. schs., Minn., 1953-55; tchr., supr. ABC Sch. Dist., Cerritos, Calif., 1963-69; cons. in reading State Dept. of Calif., Sacramento, 1969-70; cons. in edn. Orange County Dept. Edn., Santa Ana, Calif., 1970-75; sch. adminstr. Oakwood Sch., Long Beach, Calif., 1975—; chmn. bd. dirs. New City Bank, Orange, Calif.; cons. in field. Author: Song of Sounds, 1969; (with others) Beginnings for Christian Schools, 1976. Conf. coordinator State Dept. Edn., Calif., Sacramento, Santa Barbara, 1970 (Outstanding Leadership award 1974-75). Mem. Nat. Ind. Pvt. Sch. (v.p. 1982-83, dir. seminars 1983), Pre-Sch. Assn. Calif. (legis. chair 1978-84), Reading Specialists Calif. (pres. 1970-73). Republican. Avocations: skiing; scuba diving; painting; photography; travel. Home: 4438 Heather Rd Long Beach CA 90808 Office: Oakwood Sch 2650 Pacific Ave Long Beach CA 90806

MCKINNEY, RITA ESTELLE, needlework designer, instructor; b. Los Angeles, Oct. 25, 1946; d. Virgil William and Herticina (Russell) McCue; m. Edward Derrell McKinney, Mar. 20, 1969; 1 child, Jason Bowden. Student Cerritos Coll., Calif., 1970-71, El Camino Coll., Torrance, Calif., 1966-68; cert. of completion Acad. of Arts, San Francisco, 1965. Asst. art dir. Kierulff Electronics, Los Angeles, 1970-76; prodn. mgr. EPI Advt., Los Angeles, 1972-76; artist, designer The Garden, Downey, Calif., 1976-79; owner, artist, designer Etcetera Designs, Los Angeles, Hanford, Visalia, Calif., 1979-82, Rita Designs, Tulare, Calif., 1982—; pub. relations dir. SDA Orgn., Kings County, Calif., 1980-83. Contbr. articles to Sun Newspapers. Mem. Embroiderers Guild Am., Am. Needlepoint Guild. Home and office: Rita Designs 448 W Allstar Ave Tulare CA 93274

MCKINNIES, DEBORAH ANN, sales executive; b. Marrero, La., Nov. 12, 1962; d. Johnny Melvin Sr. and Jessie (Wilson) McK. BS, Tex. So. U., 1985. Salesperson Sakowitz, Houston, 1984; intern Wiseman/Hogrobrooks, Houston, 1985; area mgr. Mervyn's, Gretna, La., 1985—. Co-leader Girl Scouts Harvey La. chpt. Mem. Nat. Assn. for Female Execs., Delta Sigma Theta (pres. 1984-85), Iota Phi Lambda. Baptist. Office: Mervyn'n 197 Oakwood Shopping Ctr Harvey LA 70053

MCKINNISS, PATRICIA PERKINS, bank executive; b. Glendale, Calif., Jan. 15, 1955; d. Edwin Ray and Dolores (Vogelsang) Perkins; m. Steven Wayne Mount, July 26, 1975 (div. July 1977); m. Michael Jones McKinniss, Nov. 30, 1979; 1 child, Caroline Greenleaf. Student Mt. San Antonio Coll., 1973-78, Calif. State U.-Los Angeles, 1978-80. Part-time salesperson Sears Roebuck, Covina, Calif., 1973-75; personnel interviewer United Calif. Bank, Los Angeles, 1975-79; recruiter, personnel officer Coast Fed. Savs. & Loan Assn., Los Angeles, 1979-80; personnel officer Crocker Nat. Bank, Los Angeles, 1980-82; asst. v.p., personnel officer Security Pacific Bank, Glendale, Calif., 1983, v.p., employment mgr., 1983-85; human resources mgr. Security Pacific Brokers, Inc., 1985-87; v.p. Employee Benefits Security Pacific Bank, 1987; mgr. Country Gourmet, 1988—; freelance human resources cons. Vol., SecuriTeam, Glendale, 1984; elder Moorpark Presbyn. Ch., 1988—. Mem. Assn. Personnel Adminstrn., Human Resource Planning Soc. Republican.

MCKINNON, BARBARA JEANE, personnel executive; b. North Baltimore, Ohio, July 30, 1939; d. Charles Wayne Miller and Francis Olive (Leathers) Rector; m. James Raymond Austin, May 11, 1957 (div. 1963); 1 child, David Arnold; m. Angus Stuart McKinnon, Nov. 30, 1963; 1 child, MaryEllen. Student, Jackson (Mich.) Community Coll., 1977-78. Sec. U.S. Govt., Anchorage, 1957-61, Quality Aluminum Prod., Coldwater, Mich., 1961-62; personnel sec. Hayes-Albion Corp., Jackson, Mich., 1964-72; personnel coordinator Hayes-Albion Corp., Jackson, 1972-74, personnel supr., 1974-80, personnel mgr., 1980-85, corp. benefits mgr., 1985—. Adv. bd., mgmt./mktg., Jackson Community Coll., 1980-85. Mem. Jackson Mfrs. Assn., Am. Bus. Women (pres. 1978; Woman of the Year 1979), Jackson Indsl. Relation Assn. Republican. Episcopalian. Office: Hayes-Albion div Harvard Industries 2701 N Dettman Rd Jackson MI 49203

MCKINNON, LUANNE, curator, art dealer; b. Sikeston, Mo., Aug. 11, 1955; d. Ronald Jack and Geraldine Weltha (Badgley) McK.; m. Peter Dawson Standish, Dec. 17, 1977 (div. 1983). BA, U. Dallas, 1977; MFA, Tex. Christian U., 1983. Dir. Shaindy Fenton, Inc., Ft. Worth, 1983-85; pres. Luanne McKinnon, Inc., Dallas and N.Y.C., 1985-87; curator for The Crescent Gallery, Dallas, 1986, 87; research asst. Rauschenberg Overseas Cultural Exchange, 1985; dir. ACA Contemporary. Author exhibition catalogue Narrative Images, 1987. Mem. exec. com. Cystic Fibrosis Found., Dallas, 1986-87. Named Outstanding Young Woman Tex., 1984; recipient Ann Heller Maberry award U. Dallas, 1977, Anne Giles Kimbrough award Dallas Mus. Art, 1984.

MCKINSTRY, BONNIE MARIE, banker; b. Kenmore, N.Y., Mar. 30, 1956; d. Robert James and Joanne Mary (Harrington) McK. Student U. Houston. Asst. loan adminstr. Wells Fargo Realty Advisors, Inc., Houston, 1981-85; asst. v.p. 1st City Nat. Bank of Austin, Tex., 1985—; assoc. Renaissance Bus. Assocs., Loveland, Colo., 1985—; founder, co-owner Quality Assessments Mystery Shoppers, Austin, 1986—. Mem. Austin Restaurant Assn. (bd. dirs.). Office: First City Nat Bank 9th and Congress Austin TX 78767

MCKINSTRY, GRENETTA, microbial geneticist; b. Birmingham, Ala., Oct. 10, 1947; d. Willie D. and Willie Gertrude McKinstry; A.B. cum laude, Biology, Stillman Coll., 1968; M.A. (NDEA fellow) in Microbiology, Ind. U., 1970; Ph.D., Ohio State U., 1979; 1 son, Robert L. Harris. Researcher, Eli Lilly Pharm. Co., Indpls., 1970-72; tech. asst. dept. microbiology Ohio State U., 1972-76, teaching asst., 1976-79; tutor European Molecular Biology Orgn., U. Erlangen-Nurnberg (W. Ger.), 1979; postdoctoral asso. Max Planck Inst. for Molecular Genetics, West Berlin, 1979, Ohio State U., 1979; microbial geneticist Abbott Labs., North Chicago, Ill., 1980-85; sr. microbial geneticist Oak Ridge Research Inst., 1985-87; sr. microbiologist PEER cons., 1987—. Recipient Presdl. award, 1982. Mem. Am. Soc. for Microbiology, Assn. for Women in Sci., AAAS, N.Y. Acad. Scis., Am. Phytopath. Soc., Sigma Xi. Baptist. Contbr. articles on microbial genetics to sci. publs. Office: 575 Oak Ridge Turnpike Oak Ridge TN 37830

MCKINSTRY, KATHERINE ANN, retail executive; b. Mpls., Feb. 26, 1956; d. William Boyd and Joyce Barbara (Diehl) McK. BA, Reed Coll., Portland, Oreg., 1978; postgrad., Wash. State U., 1979. Pres. Opal, Inc., St. Simons Island, 1979-86, P.D.L., Inc., St. Simons Island, Ga., 1979—; pres., chmn. bd. dirs. Okefenokee Caps, Inc., St. Simons Island, 1980-86, Custom Imprints, Inc., St. Simons Island, 1982-86; pres. Dreamcastles, Inc., St. Simons Island, 1984-86. Trustee Reed Coll., 1986—. Office: PDL Inc 3600 Frederica Rd Saint Simons Island GA 31522

MCKNIGHT, BARBARA ANN FERRELL, land development company executive; b. Austin, Tex., June 28, 1938; d. Floyd E. Ferrell and Virginia Louise (Casparis) Ferrell Edwards; divorced; children—William Keith, Wendy Kay, Wesleye Karen. Student Baylor U., 1956-57, Durham Bus. Coll., 1967, Houston Community Coll., 1979-80. Lic. real estate assoc., Tex. Adminstrv. asst. Ryland Group, Houston, 1973-80; project mgr. Gibraltar Savs. Assn. of Tex., Houston, 1980-84; v.p. Rheinhold Corp., Houston, 1984-85, Tex. Investment and Devel. Corp., Houston, 1985—; owner, mgr. Barbara McKnight Cons., Houston, 1985—. Alternate, Tex. Rep. Conv., Houston, 1976, del., Austin, 1980. Mem. Nat. Assn. Female Execs. Baptist. Office: First Southwestern Title Agy Inc 7322 Southwest Freeway Suite 300 Houston TX 77074

MCKNIGHT, SUSAN KAREN, water filtration equipment executive; b. Detroit, Aug. 30, 1954; d. William Ross and Jean Marie Lyda (Thompson) McK. BA cum laude, Eastern Mich. U., 1975, MA in Sociology, 1977. Instr. sociology Henry Ford Community Coll., Dearborn, Mich., 1976-78; adminstr. Lake County, Waukegan, Ill., 1978-81; reseacher, project mgr. No. Ill. U., DeKalb, Ill., 1981-83; prin. Quality Flow, Waukegan, 1983—; prin., v.p. On Tap Premium Quality Water, Wheeling, Ill., 1985-87, Quality Flow Inc., Buffalo Grove, Ill., 1987—. Bd. dirs. Waukegan Crime Stoppers, 1981-82, Lake County Council Against Sexual Assault, 1988—; mem. Lake County Literacy Vols., 1986—; Dem. Committeeman, Lake County, 1986. Recipient NaCo award, Nat. Assn. Counties. Mem. Water Quality Assn., Women in Mgmt. (chair program com.), Achievement Seminars/Franz Bador, Greenpeace, Chgo. Anti-Cruelty Soc. Lutheran.

MCKNIGHT, TANDY CAROL, systems analyst; b. Huntsville, Ala., Nov. 28, 1956; d. William Baldwin and Helen (Bowling) McK. Student, U. of the South, 1974-76; BS in Math., U. Ala., 1978. Proctor electrical engring. U. Ala., Tuscaloosa, 1977-78; data processing analyst Shell Oil Co., Houston, 1979; programmer/analyst Shell Oil Co., New Orleans, 1979-82; systems analyst Shell Oil Co., Houston, 1982-88; group leader Shell Oil Co., New Orleans, 1988—; mem. various coms. Shell Oil Co., Houston, 1982-87. Republican. Methodist. Club: Cercle Francais (sec. Sewanee, Tenn., 1975-76). Home: 2100 Sawmill Rd Bldg 10-C Apt 203 Harahan LA 70123 Office: Shell Oil Co 701 Poydras New Orleans LA 70160

MCKOWEN, DOROTHY KEETON, librarian; b. Bonne Terre, Mo., Oct. 5, 1948; d. John Richard and Dorothy (Spoonhour) Keeton; m. Paul Edwin McKowen, Dec. 19, 1970; children: Richard James, Mark David. BS, Pacific Christian Coll., 1970; MS in Library Sci., U. So. Calif., 1973; MA in English, Purdue U., 1985. Librarian-specialist Doheny Library, U. So. Calif., Los Angeles, 1973-74; asst. librarian Pacific Christian Coll., 1974-78; serials cataloger Purdue Univ. Libraries, 1978-88; head children's and young adult services Kokomo-Howard County Pub. Library (Ind.), 1988—; librarian Brady Ln. Ch. of Christ, 1986—; vice chairperson Christian Edn. Com., 1986-87, chairperson, 1987—, pianist, 1978—; bd. dirs. Purdue Christian Campus House, 1985—, vice chairperson, 1986-88. Mem. ALA (resources and tech. services div., bd. dirs. 1986—, vice chairperson, chairperson-elect council of regional groups 1986-88, chairperson 1988—, conf. program com. 1986-88, internat. relations com. 1986-88, micropub. com., 1986-87, subject analysis com., subcom. to rev. Dewey 621.38, 1987, membership com. 1988—, Library Resources and Tech. Services editorial bd. 1988—), Ind. Library Assn. (vice chmn. tech. services div. 1983-84, chmn. 1984-85), Ohio Valley Group Tech. Services Librarians (vice chmn. 1984-85, chmn. 1985-86). Republican. Home: 7625 Summit Ln Lafayette IN 47905 Office: Kokomo-Howard County Pub Library 220 N Union Kokomo IN 46901

MCKOWN, PAMELA ANN, infosystems specialist, educator; b. Fullerton, Calif., Oct. 5, 1962; d. William Ralph and Billie Mae (Pope) McK. AA, Cerritos (Calif.) Jr. Coll., 1982; BA, U. Calif., Irvine, 1983; M in Communication, Calif State U. Los Angeles, 1985. Assoc. prof. Calif. State U. Los Angeles, 1983—, asst. dir. forensics, 1983-84; asst. appraiser Los Angeles County Appraiser's Office, 1984-85; systems analyst Northrop Advanced Systems Div., Pico Rivera, Calif., 1985—; cons. communication enhancement, Mayor Bradley's Youth Council, Los Angeles, 1985, The Gas Co., Los Angeles, 1986. Active Red Cross, Redondo Beach, Calif., 1986—, Rape Crisis Ctr., Torrance, Calif., 1987. Mem. Nat. Exec. Women's Council, Calif. Faculty Assn. Democrat. Baptist. Home: 613 1/2 S Esplanade Ave Redondo Beach CA 90277 Office: Calif State U Los Angeles Dept Communication Studies 5151 State University Dr Los Angeles CA 90023

MCKUSICK, ANN STARK, nonprofit association executive; b. Coral Gables, Fla., Sept. 27, 1950; d. Marwood Wellington and Nora (Levin) Stark; m. Richard Alan McKusick, Dec. 10, 1983. B.A. in English magna cum laude, Spring Hill Coll., 1972; M.A. in Human Devel., Pacific Oaks Coll., 1977—; postgrad. in theology Fuller Theol. Sem., 1980-81. Resident dir. Regency Park Retirement Home, Pasadena, Calif., 1978-80; dir. festival devel. Pasadena Arts Council, 1980-81; dir. donor communication World Vision, Pasadena, 1981-84, dir. pub. relations, 1984-85, dir. resource devel., 1985—; advisor Diakonos, Pasadena, 1985—; mem. adv. bd. for devel. edn. Overseas Devel. Council/Interaction, Washington, 1985—; co-chmn., founder Africa Crisis Employee Response, Monrovia, Calif., 1984-85. Recipient Best Media Materials award Pub. Relations Soc. Los Angeles, 1985. Mem. Nat. Assn. Exec. Females, Publicity Club. Republican. Mem. Swedish Evangelical Covenant Ch. Office: World Vision 919 W Huntington Dr Monrovia CA 91016

MCLAIN, AMBER LAURIE, telecommunications executive; b. Jacksonville, Fla., June 13, 1962; d. Nicholas Edward and Maureen (O'Leary) McL. BA, Wells Coll., 1984. Fin. advisor John Hancock, Amsterdam, N.Y., 1984-85; sucessively sales rep., account exec., sales mgr., account mgr. RCI Corp., Albany, N.Y., 1985-88; account exec. Computer Telephone Co., Albany, 1988—. Recipient Gold medals at Empire State Games, N.Y., 1984, 85. Mem. Nat. Assn. Female Execs., Capital Area Telecommunications Assn. Republican. Club: Schenectady Winter Sports. Home: 13 Valley View Ave Latham NY 12110 Office: Computer Telephone Corp 21 Lodge ST Albany NY 12207

MCLAINE, ALICE JEANETTE, athletic trainer, educator; b. Caribou, Maine, July 17, 1958; d. Robert Eugene and Melba Fern (Davis) McN.; m. Lawrence West McLaine, Nov. 24, 1985. B.Edn., Ohio U., 1980; M.S., W.Va. U., 1981. Grad. asst. athletic trainer W.Va. U., 1980-81; head women's athletic trainer Iowa State U., Ames, 1981—. Recipient Al Hart Scholarship award, 1979-80. Mem. Nat. Athletic Trainers Assn., Iowa Athletic Trainers Assn. Methodist. Home: 505 25th St Ames IA 50010 Office: Iowa State U 111 Phys Edn Bldg Ames IA 50011

MCLAINE, CAROL JUNE, social worker; b. Waycross, Ga., Jan. 11, 1949; d. Robert Ray and Maxie Laverne (Willis) Brown; m. Kenton Eisenhower McLaine, July 28, 1967; 1 child, Jennifer Carol. Student, Waycross-Ware Tech., 1968, Waycross Jr. Coll., 1981. Sec. to purchasing agt. Standard Container Co., Homerville, Ga., 1968-70; clk. Clinch County (Ga.) Dept. Family and Children's Services, Homerville, 1970-72, casework aide, 1972-74, caseworker, 1974-82, head, 1982-87, social services specialist, 1987—. Contbr.: (poem) Great Poems of the Western World, 1980. Youth Leader Homerville Congl. Meth. Ch., 1968-70, stewardess, 1980-82, Sunday Sch. tchr., 1984-86; mem. Head Start Bd., 1979—; alderman City of Homerville, 1987-88. Club: Athletic Boosters. Home: 308 Rose St Homerville GA 31634

MCLANE, SUSAN NEIDLINGER, state legislator; b. Boston, Mass., Sept. 28, 1929; d. Lloyd Kellock and Marion (Walker) Neidlinger; m. Malcolm McLane, 1948; children: Susan B., Donald W., Deborah, Alan, Ann Lloyd. Ed. Mt. Holyoke Coll; LLD (hon.), New England Coll., 1983. Mem. N.H. Ho. of Reps., 1969-80, chmn. Ways & Means Com., 1976-80; mem. N.H. Senate, 1980—; del., Rep. Nat. Conv., 1976; pres., N.H. Council For. Affairs, 1976-80. Republican. Office: NH Senate State Capitol Concord NH 03301 also: 205 Mountain Rd Concord NH 03301 •

MCLAREN, MARILYN PATRICIA, corporate human resources administrator, aviator; b. Jamaica, N.Y., July 5, 1942; d. Raymond Lionel and Katherine Marie (Doepp) Cowan; student various aviation schs., St. Joseph's Coll., N.Y., cert. in leadership and human resources mgmt.; m. Richard Edward McLaren, July 17, 1976; 1 son, Paul William Hibner. Exec. sec. to chief design Wiedersum Assocs., architects and engrs., Valley Stream, N.Y., 1960-61; officer mgr., interior designer Keith I. Hibner, architect, Hicksville and Garden City, N.Y., 1961-73; owner, pres. Hibner Atelier, Ltd., interior design and gen. constrn., Garden City, 1968-75; office mgr. Ward Assocs./Planning Assocs., architects and engrs., Bohemia, N.Y., 1975-76; flight/ground aviation instr. Islip Aviation, Ltd. (N.Y.), 1974-77; exec. asst. to pres. Arkay Packaging Corp., Hauppauge, N.Y., 1977-86, in-house constrn. mgr., 1980-82, adminstrn. and human resources mgr., 1986—; ind. aviation flight/ground instr. airplane and instrument, 1977—; safety counselor FAA, 1974—, Eastern Region Counselor Coordinator, 1985-86; past bd. dirs., officer Aviation Council L.I.; founder Seminar on Air Travel for Everyone (S.A.F.E.), 1975, Fly-C-Cure/We Air Condition People, 1979. Mem. nat. panel Consumer arbitrators Nat. Consumer Arbitration Program, Better Bus. Bur. Lic. comml. pilot, flight and ground instr. Mem. Ninety-Nines (past chmn. L.I. chpt., founding internat. chmn. safety edn., Amelia Earhart Bronze medal 1975), Aircraft Owners and Pilots Assn., Nat. Assn. Flight Instrs., Am. Soc. Personnel Adminstrn., Nat. Assn. Female Execs., Adminstrv. Mgmt. Soc. Specialist on fear of flying; author articles, seminar syllabus. Home: 3 Park St Lake Grove NY 11755 Office: 22 Arkay Dr Hauppauge NY 11787

MCLARNAN, MARTHELLA GLOVER, municipal health agent; b. N.Y.C., Aug. 30, 1922; d. John Murray and Gertrude (Carter) Glover; m. James Conard McLarnan, June 2, 1972; children: Patrick McLarnan, David Corbly Andrews, Joan Andrews O'Brien. BSNE, U. Oreg., 1944; MSN, Ohio State, 1971. Registered nurse. Program planner Bur. Crippled Children, Columbus, Ohio, 1971; dir. nursing Marion (Ohio) Tech. Coll., 1971-74, cons. nursing, 1974-81; health commr. Knox County Health Dept., Mt. Vernon, Ohio, 1981-87; lectr. Ohio State U., Columbus, 1948-52, 71-80. Bd. dirs. Mid Ohio Health Planning Fedn., Columbus, 1972-82. Mem. Am. Nurses Assn., Assn. of Ohio Health Commrs., Sigma Theta Tau. Republican. Congregationalist. Office: County Health Commr 117 E High St Mount Vernon OH 43050

MCLARNON, ALICE THERESA, insurance company executive; b. Darby, Pa., Oct. 20, 1945; d. John Morrison and Alice Theresa (Browne) McL.; m. John David Roggie, Dec. 6, 1973; stepchildren: Deborah, Elizabeth. BS in Secondary Edn., St. Joseph's U., Phila., 1968. Tchr. Camden (N.J.) Sch. System, 1967-72; tng. analyst JC Penney Co., N.Y.C., 1972-76, tng. specialist, 1974-76, mgr. tng. ctrs., 1976-79; mgr. personnel JCPenney Fin. Services, N.Y.C., 1979-82, mgr. personnel and adminstrn., 1982-85; asst. to exec. v.p. JC Penney Co., N.Y.C., 1985; sr. v.p. spl. projects JC Penney Casualty Ins. Co., Westerville, Ohio, 1985-87, pres., 1987—. Office: JC Penney Casualty Ins Co 800 Brookside Blvd Westerville OH 43081

MC LAUGHLIN, ANN DORE, federal official; b. Newark, Nov. 16, 1941; d. Edward Joseph and Marie (Koellhoffer) Lauenstein; m. John Joseph McLaughlin, Aug. 23, 1975. B.A., Marymount Coll. Supr. network comml. schedule ABC, N.Y.C., 1963-66; dir. alumnae relations Marymount Coll., Tarrytown, N.Y., 1966-69; account exec. Myers-Infoplan Internat. Inc., N.Y.C., 1969-71; dir. communications Presdl. Election Com., Washington, 1971-72; asst. to chmn. and press sec. Presdl. Inaugural Com., Washington, 1972-73; dir. Office of Pub. Affairs, EPA, Washington, 1973-74; govt. relations and communications exec. Union Carbide Corp., N.Y.C. and Washington, 1974-77; pub. affairs, issues mgmt. counseling McLaughlin & Co., 1977-81; asst. sec. for pub. affairs Treasury Dept., Washington, 1981-84; under sec. Dept. of Interior, Washington, 1984-87; cons. Ctr. Strategic and Internat. Studies, Washington, 1987; Sec. of Labor Dept. of Labor, Washington, 1987—; mem. Am. Council on Capital Formation, 1976-78; mem. environ. edn. task force HEW, 1976-77; mem. Def. Adv. Com. of Women in the Services, 1973-74. Mem. Washington Woman's Forum. Republican. Roman Catholic. Clubs: City. Office: 200 Constitution Ave NW Room S-2018 Washington DC 20210

MCLAUGHLIN, CLARA JACKSON, television station executive; b. Brunswick, Ga., Oct. 22, 1946; d. Dave and Arnetta (Lundy) Jackson; m. Richard A. McLaughlin, Oct. 1968; children—Rinetta A., Ricky A. B.A., Howard U., 1972. Founder, chmn., chief exec. officer Sta. KLMG-TV, Longview, Tex., 1980—. Author: Black Parents' Handbook—A Guide to Healthy Pregnancy, Birth and Child Care, 1976. Bd. dirs. United Cerebral Palsy, Houston, 1976-80, chmn. bd., 1978-80; trustee Tex. So. U., Houston, 1978—; mem. Aux. to AMA, 1974—. Mem. Leadership Tex. Office: 10303 Northwest Freeway KLMG-TV East Texas Television Network Suite 430 Houston TX 77092 *

MCLAUGHLIN, DEBORAH ANN, public relations executive; b. Hoisington, Kans., Nov. 12, 1952; d. Kenneth Theodore and Mildred Marie (Steiner) Siebert; m. Donald Raymond McLaughlin, July 17, 1976; 1 child, Kalla Dawn. AS, Barton County Coll., Great Bend, Kans., 1972; BS, Kans. State U., 1975. News editor Great Bend Tribune, 1975-76; deposition indexer Turner & Boisseau, Great Bend, 1976-77; feature editor Mid-Kans. Ruralist, Hoisington, 1977-78; copywriter, audio-editor Advt. Assocs., Great Bend, 1978-79; photographer, sales mgr. Clay Ward Color Portraits, Great Bend, 1979-80; news editor, photographer St. John (Kans.) News, 1980-83; freelance writer, photographer Great Bend, 1984-85; pres., owner McLaughlin Pub. Relations Agy., Great Bend, 1985-87; with Creative Mktg. Services, Great Bend, 1988—; pub., owner Cen. Kans. Sunrise mag., Great Bend, 1987—. Contbr. articles and photographs to various publs. Mem. Coalition for Prevention Child Abuse, Great Bend, 1986-87; mem. 75th anniversary com. Kansas State U. Coll. Journalism and Mass Communications, Manhattan, 1976. Mem. Kans. Press Women, Nat. Assn. Female Execs., Kansas State U. Alumni Assn., Great Bend C. of C. (mktg. cons.). Roman Catholic. Home: 1427 21st St Great Bend KS 67530 Office: 1012 Washington Great Bend KS 67530

MCLAUGHLIN, DOROTHY CLAIRE, sociologist, consultant; b. Kansas City, Mo.; d. Earl H. and Hazel Loucille (Allen) Klopfenstine; m. Patrick M. McLaughlin, Feb. 20, 1968; children by previous marriage: Michael L. Gant (dec.), Margaret C. Gant. BA in Sociology, Calif. State U., Los Angeles, 1976; MBA Columbia Pacific U., 1987; postgrad. Eastern Mont. Coll., 1977—. Student governance coordinator Calif. State U., Los Angeles, 1974-76; dir. Am. Assn. Ret. Persons Sr. Community Service Employment Program, Billings, Mont. 1977-81, Dallas, 1981-87; sociologist, Dallas, 1987-88, Billings, 1988—; cons., lectr., speaker in field. Co-founder Gray Panthers Dallas, 1985; rep. pub. sector Employment Security Council, Helena, Mont., 1979-81; mem. aging com. Mental Health Aging Program, Dallas, 1981-82. Recipient Superior Achievement honors Pasadena City Coll., 1974, Pres.'s Club award Avon Products, Inc., 1973, Rosalyn Carter Community Service award Assn. Women Entrepreneurs Dallas Speaker's Bur., 1987. Mem. AAUW (chmn. women's issues 1979), Assn. Bus. Profl. Women, Am. Sociol. Assn., Nat. Assn. Accts., Am. Personnel Guidance Assn., Mont. Assn. for Female Execs. (co-founder 1980). Home: PO Box 1314 Billings MT 59103 Office: 2423 Pine St Billings MT 59101

MCLAUGHLIN, MARGUERITE P., third-term state senator, logging company executive; m. Bruce McLaughlin; 3 children. Owner, operator contract logging firm, Orofino, Idaho; former mem. Idaho Ho. of Reps.; now mem. Idaho Senate. Trustee Joint Sch. Dist. 171; pres. Orofino Celebration, Inc. Democrat. Offfice: Idaho State Senate Boise ID 83720

MCLAUGHLIN, MARY RITTLING, magazine editor; b. Buffalo; d. Joseph and Irene (Meyer) Rittling; m. Charles Edward McLaughlin, June 21, 1962 (div. June 1981) children—Daniel, Maud Rosie. B.A., Manhattanville Coll., Purchase, N.Y. Previously reporter Buffalo Evening News; then copywriter Harper's Bazaar, N.Y.C.; editor McCall's Mag., N.Y.C., 1973-79; mng. editor Working Mother Mag., N.Y.C., 1979-85; exec. editor Working Mother Mag., 1985—. Mem. Am. Soc. Mag. Editors. Office: Working Mother Mag 230 Park Ave New York NY 10169

MCLAUGHLIN, NANCY ESTHER, stockbroker, realtor; b. Yauco, P.R., May 26, 1947; d. Eli Caraballo and Catalina Antonia (Quiros) Cintron; m. Edward Charles McLaughlin, Mar. 6, 1971 (div. June 1979); children: Elisa, Eric, Matthew. Student, Old Dominion U., 1965-67; BA, U. Md., 1970; postgrad., Hartford County Community Coll., Bel Air, Md., 1974-76, 79-80. Mgr. sales Am. Foresight, Inc., Balt., 1969-70; exec. trainee Sears, Roebuck & Co., Norristown, Pa., 1970-71; asst. mgr. Lerner Shops, S. Portland, Md., 1971-74; legal sec. Lester V. Jones, Inc., Bel Air, 1980-82; realtor Russell T. Baker & Co., Bel Air, 1979-82; fin. planner Conn. Mut. Ins. Co., Norfolk, Va., 1982-83; realtor Century 21, Virginia Beach, Va., 1982—; stockbroker Dean Witter Reynolds, Inc., Virginia Beach, 1983—; lectr. in field, Va., Md., N.C., 1969—. Contbr. articles to profl. jours. Chmn. community service Hartford County Welcome Wagon, Bel Air, 1974-76, March of Dimes Walk-A-Thon, Bel Air, 1979-80, sch. adv. com. Forest Hill (Md.) Elem. Sch., 1980-81, food and clothes dr. St. Luke's Cath. Ch., Virginia Beach, 1986—; mgr. Joseph Tydings Senatorial campaign, College Park, Md., 1969-70; pres. PTA, 1979-80; sus. mem. Repub. Nat. Com. Named Outstanding Community Citizen, City of Balt., 1981; recipient Outstanding Performance award, March of Dimes, 1979, 80. Mem. N.Y. Stock Exchange, Nat. Assn. Securities Dealers, Tidewater and Virginia Beach Bd. Realtors, Nat. Assn. Realtors, Women's Stockbrokers Nat. Assn. Roman Catholic. Home: 884 Stacey Pl Virginia Beach VA 23464 Office: Dean Witter Reynolds Inc 4460 Corporation Ln Virginia Beach VA 23462

MCLAUGHLIN-HATCH, AMY ELIZABETH, interior design consultant; b. Framingham, Mass., June 14, 1961; d. Charles Marion and Virginia Lee (Kindler) McLaughlin; m. Dennis Charles Hatch, June 9, 1985. BA, Boston Coll., 1983. Sales rep. Wang Labs., N.Y.C., 1984-86; asst. mgr. Laura Ashley, Freeport, Maine, 1986-87; interior design cons. Maine Paint Service, Portland, 1987. Mem. Nat. Assn. Female Execs. Democrat. Roman Catholic. Club: Boston Coll. of Maine (v.p. 1986—). Home and Office: 410 S Washington St North Attleboro ME 02760

MCLAURIN, MARTHA REGINA, parking service company executive; b. Raleigh, N.C., Feb. 17, 1948; d. William Lentis and Martha Catherine (Hester) McL. BA, Meth. Coll., 1970. V.p., chief fin. officer McLaurin Parking Co., Inc., Raleigh, 1970—; dir. So. Nat. Bank, Cary, N.C., 1980—. V.p., bd. dirs. Raleigh Mchts. Bur., 1988—; mem. Cary Town Council, 1987—; chmn. Wake County Planning Bd., 1983-86. Named Outstanding Bus. Alumnus Meth. Coll., 1985, Cary's Outstanding Woman Cary Jaycettes, 1984. Mem. Nat. Parking Assn. (dir. 1979—), Parking Ind. Inst. (vice chmn., dir. 1987—). Lodge: Zonta (dir. 1987—). Office: McLaurin Parking Co Inc PO Box 781 Raleigh NC 27602

MCLAURY, PATRICIA OWEN, nurse; b. Oklahoma City, Mar. 7, 1945; d. Edgar Eugene and Zulma Gertrude (White) Owen; m. Ralph Leon McLaury, Jan. 21, 1967; children: Ralph Leon, Clara Courtney, Molly Reagan (dec.). BS in Nursing, Okla. U., 1968. Pediatric clinic nurse Children's Meml. Hosp., Oklahoma City, 1971-72; staff devel. instr. Hillcrest Osteo. Hosp., Oklahoma City, 1972-73; head nurse Variety Health Ctr., Oklahoma City, 1973-74; county health nurse Washington County, Bartlesville, Okla., 1974-85; dir. nursing service Heritage Villa Nursing Ctr., Bartlesville, 1985-86; interim dir. Washington County Elder Care, Bartlesville, 1986-87; health nurse Caney Valley Pub. Schs., Ramona, Okla., 1987—; cons. Copan (Okla.) Pub. Schs., 1987—, Specilialized Rehabliltaion Services, Inc., Irving, Tex., 1987—. Mem. homemaker adv. council of Washington County Elder Care, 1984—, Disaster Services Com. Red Cross (Washington chpt.). Mem. Washington County Mental Health Assn., Washington County Child Guidance Assn. (v.p. 1983-84, pres. 1984-85), Council of Social Agys. Republican. Home: 1637 Johnstone Bartlesville OK 74003

MCLEAN, B(ONNIE) HEATHER, manufacturing company executive, photographer, ski instructor; b. Nyack, N.Y., Mar. 28, 1958; d. C. Clifford and Carol (Hunsicker) McL. AAS, Rochester Inst. Tech., 1978, BFA, 1980. Photog. sales person Blumenthals, Olean, N.Y., 1976-78; night mgr. clothing sales The Silo, Mt. Kisco, N.Y., part-time 1980-83; tech. sales rep. Majestech, Somers, N.Y., 1981-84, Schaumburg, Ill., 1984-87; spl. projects mgr. for mktg. and sales Precision Screen Machines, Inc., Hawthorne, N.J., 1987—; ski instr. Catamount, Hillsdale, N.Y., part-time 1981-84; regional mgr. Autotype USA, Elk Grove, Ill., 1984—; condr. screenmaking seminar Rochester Inst. Tech., 1986. Recipient Internat. Sales award Stretch Devices, Phila., 1983. Mem. Screen Printing Assn. Internat., Conn. Screen Printers Assn. (chpt. bd. dirs. 1982-83, sec. 1983-84), Profl. Ski Instrs. Am., Exec. Female. Episcopalian. Avocations: skiing, golf, music, aerobics, racquetball, sewing, photography. Office: 44 Ulter Ave Hawthorne NJ 07506

MCLEAN-WAINWRIGHT, PAMELA LYNNE, psychology educator; b. Rockville Centre, N.Y., Oct. 25, 1948; d. George Clifford Sr. and Violet Maude (Jones) McLean; m. Joseph Charles Everest Wainwright Jr., Jan. 20, 1982; children: Joseph Charles Everest III, Evan Clifford Jerome. BE, NYU, 1973; MEd, Fordham U., 1974; MSW, Adelphi U., 1986. Tchr. Martin Deporres Day Care Ctr., Bklyn., 1973-77; dir. student personnel services Ujamaa Acad., Hempstead, N.Y., 1977-78; coordinator Youth Employment and Tng. Program Hempstead, 1978; Ednl. Opportunity Counselor SUNY, Farmingdale, 1978-79; asst. prof. psychology Nassau Community Coll., Garden City, N.Y., 1979—; program dir. Adult Individual Multi-Service Program, Garden City, 1985—. Mem. L.I. Coalition for Full Employment, community adv. council for Nassau Tech. Ctr., Women-on-the-Job Task Force, Port Washington, N.Y.; advisor Region 2 Displaced Homemakers Network; bd. dirs. Children's Greenhouse Inc., 1987—, mem. founding com., 1980-81; Civil Rights advocate, 1963, 81; mem. adv. bd. Long Island Cares, Hempstead, 1986-87. Recipient Women's History Month Citation County of Nassau, 1988. Mem. Assn. Black Women in Higher Edn. (bd. dirs.), Nat. Assn. Black Coll. Alumni, Nat. Assn. Female Execs., Women's Faculty Assn. Nassau Community Coll. (pres. 1987—), L.I. Women's Council for Equal Edn. Tng. and Employment, Assn. of Black Psychologists. Office: Nassau Community Coll Stewart Ave Garden City NY 11530

MCLELLAN, MARY THERESA, assistant state librarian, legislative researcher; b. Quincy, Mass., Feb. 25, 1927; d. John Patrick and Theresa Mary (O'Reilly) Johnson; m. George Bernard Savage, Nov. 2, 1947 (div. 1969); 1 dau., Kathleen Mary; m. 2d, Vincent Bernard McLellan, May 13, 1971; children—Vincent, Elaine, Mary Joy, Mark, Anne, Christopher. Student Commonwealth Mass. Univ. Extension, Boston, 1944-46, 63-65, Boston U., 1946-47, Inst. Govtl. Services, Boston, 1983-84, Suffolk U., Boston, 1976-78. Cert. librarian, Mass.; lic. real estate broker, Mass. Jr. asst. Thomas Crane Pub. Library, Quincy, 1944-46, sr. asst., 1947, 1962-69; asst. librarian Bethlehem Steel Co., Quincy, 1946; pvt. practice as real estate broker, 1953-62; reference librarian Mass. State Library, Boston, 1969-73, legis. reference librarian, 1973-82, asst. state librarian, 1982—. Author: Interns Guide to Legislative Research, 1973; Guide to Massachusetts Legislative and Government Research, 1981. Contbr. chpt. to Handbook of Legal Research in Massachusetts. Mem. Assn. Boston Law Libraries. Democrat. Roman Catholic. Office: Mass State Library 341 State House Boston MA 02133

MCLENDON-MCCULLOUGH, BEVERLY J., city official; b. Daytona Beach, Fla., July 28, 1949; d. George McLendon Jr. and Bernice Lillian (Wiley-McLendon) Thompson; m. Tyrone L. McCullough, June 28, 1980; 1 dau., Kendle Joi. B.Sc., Ky. State U., 1971; M.Sc., Howard U., 1973. Adult edn. tchr. Washington Sch. Dist., 1972-73; curriculum specialist Howard U., Washington, 1971-73; price stabilization analyst Cost of Living Council, Washington, 1973-75; housing mgr. Community Devel. Div., City of Houston, 1975-79, housing adminstr., 1979-82; community liaison aide Police Dept., Houston, 1982—; cons. Social Systems Intervention, Washington, 1972-74. Co-author: (tng. manual), Training of Community Personnel in Health Maintenance Organizations, 1972. Mem. Am. Assn. Pub. Adminstrs., Omicron Nu. Democrat. Office: Office of Police Chief 61 Riesner Houston TX 77002

MCLENNAN, JEAN GLINN, virologist; b. Feb. 8, 1934; d. John Manning and Irene Mae (Pool) Glinn; m. William Eldon McLennan, Sept. 17, 1961. BA, U. Penn., 1955; postgrad., Hunter Coll., 1960-61; BSBA, U. Nebr., Omaha, 1983. Chief technician infectious disease lab. Emory U. Dept. Medicine, Atlanta, 1955-57; microbiologist virology labs. Sch. Medicine Emory U., Atlanta, 1963-66; chief technician infectious disease lab. Sch. Medicine Cornell U., N.Y.C., 1957-61; microbiologist Ga. State Dept. Pub. Health, Atlanta, 1961-62; microbiologist, virologist Cutter Labs., Berkeley, Calif., 1967-75; virologist Burns Biotech Labs., Elkhorn, Neb., 1975-86, Schering Animal Health, Elkhorn, 1986—. Mem. Am. Soc. Microbiology, N.Y. Acad. Sci., Am. Bus. Women's Assn., Pacific Height Improvement Assn. (treas. 1980-84, pres. 1986-88). Democrat. Lutheran. Home: 1442 S 163rd St Omaha NE 68130

MCLEOD, KATHLEEN COX, marketing professional; b. Pulaski, N.Y., Nov. 28, 1947; d. Cameron Clyde and Edith Marie (Switzer) Cox; m. Thomas H. McLeod, Aug. 29, 1970; children: Jonathon R., Cameron S. BA in Econs, Syracuse U., 1969; MLS, Simmons Coll., 1976; MBA, Babson Coll., 1984. Children's librarian Patten Pub. Library, Tewksbury, Mass., 1977-79; sales adminstr. dataCon, Inc., Burlington, Mass., 1980-84; sales adminstrv. mgr. dataCon Inc, Burlington, Mass., 1984-86, nat. sales adminstrv. mgr., 1986—. Chair Personnel Bd., Tewksbury, 1981—; mem. Friends of Pub. Library. Mem. Am. Mgmt. Assn. Home: 31 Babicz Rd Tewksbury MA 01876

MCLEOD, MARILYNN HAYES, educational administrator, farmer; b. Lake View, S.C., Jan. 2, 1924; d. Cary Victor and Benna (Price) Hayes; B.A., Furman U.; M.Ed., U. S.C., 1952, EdD, 1986; m. Charles Edward McLeod, Aug. 24, 1947; children—Cary Franklin, Mary Marilynn. Tchr., Hamer-Kentyre Sch., Hamer, S.C., 1944-45, Bennettsville (S.C.) City Schs., 1946-59, Clio (S.C.) Elem. Sch., 1960-63; asst. prof. elem. edn. St. Andrews Presbyn. Coll., Laurinburg, N.C., 1964-67; instr. U. S.C., Florence, 1971; reading supr. Marlboro County Sch. Dist., Bennettsville, S.C. 1967-86; prin. Marlboro County Child Devel. Ctr., 1986-87; asst. prin. Bennettsville High Sch., 1987—; farmer, 1960—. Author: The History of Education in Marlboro County, South Carolina, 1737-1895, 1988. Chmn. adminstrv. bd. Trinity United Meth. Ch., 1982—, chmn. pastor-parish relations com., 1979—, trustee Permanent Com. Meml. Fund; trustee Epworth Children's Home, chmn. personnel com., Columbia, S.C. Mem. NEA (life), Internat. Reading Assn., S.C. Edn. Assn., S.C. Reading Assn., Assn. Secondary Prins., S.C. Internat. Reading Assn., Marlboro County Edn. Assn., Pee Dee Internat. Reading Assn., Delta Kappa Gamma. Democrat. Methodist. Home: PO Box 38 127 S Main St Clio SC 29525 Office: 127 S Main St Bennettsville SC 29512

MCLEOD, NANCY JANE, city official; b. St. Louis, June 19, 1946; d. Kenneth Leroy and Velma Jane (Muchmore) McL.; B.A., U. Ariz., 1967, M.B.A., 1970; postgrad. Ariz. State U., 1981—. Adminstrv. aide LEAP dept. City of Phoenix, 1972-73, planning asst., 1973-74, chief program planner, 1974-75, planning coordinator dept. human resources, 1975-83, asst. dir. dept., 1983—. Mem. Bus. and Profl. Women of Phoenix (1st v.p. 1978-80, pres. 1980-82), Soc. Advancement of Mgmt. (dir. 1977-81), Am. Mgmt. Assn., Am. Soc. Pub. Adminstrn., Am. Planning Assn., Acad. Polit. Sci., Internat. City Mgmt. Assn. Club: Toastmasters. Home: 3753 E Bloomfield Rd Phoenix AZ 85032 Office: 302 W Washington St Phoenix AZ 85003

MCLIN, RHINE LANA, funeral director, educator; b. Dayton, Ohio, Oct. 2, 1948; d. C. Josef, Jr., and Bernice (Cottman) McL. B.A. in Sociology, Parsons Coll., 1969; M.Ed., Xavier U., Cin., 1972; postgrad. in law U. Dayton, 1974-76. Lic. funeral dir. and notary pub.; cert. tchr., Ohio. Tchr. Dayton Bd. Edn., 1970-72; divorce counselor Domestic Relations Ct., Dayton, 1972-73; law clk. Montgomery Common Pleas Ct., Dayton, 1973-74; v.p., mgr. McLin Funeral Homes, Dayton, 1972—; instr. Central State U., Wilberforce, Ohio, 1982—; speaker Dayton Pub. Schs., 1980—. Author 6-series article: Death and Dying, 1980. Adv. bd. Dayton Contemporary Dance Co., 1977, Montgomery County Welfare and Social Services, Dayton, 1983, Nat. Council on Women's Edn. Programs, 1980; mem. Democratic Voters League, Dayton, 1969; mem. Ohio Lottery Commn., 1983—; trustee Greater Dayton Sr. Citizens, 1984. Recipient Friendship award St. Mark's Masonic Lodge 165, 1980, Brotherhood award Upshaw African Meth. Episcopal Ch., 1983, Recognition award Fed. Women's Program, Dayton, 1981; One in a Million award Columbus 10-City Rally of Nat. Council Negro Women, 1984. Mem. Nat. Funeral Dirs. Assn., Ohio Funeral Dirs. Assn., Montgomery County Funeral Dirs. Assn., Women Bus. Owners Assn., NAACP (life), Nat. Council Negro Women (life), Delta Sigma Theta (recognition award 1981). Home and Office: 1130 Germantown St Dayton OH 45408

MCLOONE, JEANNE HOWE, interior designer, realtor; b. Newark, Aug. 18, 1950; d. William Benjamin and Gloria Mae (Vela) Howe; m. Mark Edward McLoone, July 8, 1975 (div. July 1982); 1 child, Angus Howe. BA, Mary Baldwin Coll., Staunton, Va., 1972. Asst. office mgr. Baker & Botts, Washington, 1973-74; asst. interior designer Jane Zivney Interiors, Phoenix, 1975-78; pres. Jeanne McLoone Designs, Inc., 1979—; interior designer, salesperson Barrow's Furniture, Phoenix, 1983—; realtor Merrill Lynch Realty, 1987—; interior designer Rosson House. Mem. Phoenix Art Mus., 1978—, league bd., 1982, co-chmn. Festival of Trees, 1982, chmn. Benefactor's Trees Com., 1986; active Hospice of Valley Ann. Fall Fundraiser. Recipient cert. Assuiduité Institut de Touraine, Tours, France, 1967. Mem. Inst. Bus. Designers (affiliate). Republican. Episcopalian. Avocations: tennis, skiing, sailing, gourmet cooking, travel. Home: 6134 N 13th St Phoenix AZ 85014 Office: Barrow's Exec Furniture 2301 E Camelback Phoenix AZ 85016 also: Merrill Lynch Realty 3165 E Lincoln Dr Phoenix AZ 85016

MC LOUGHLIN, ELLEN VERONICA, editor; b. Utica, N.Y.; d. James Henry and Mary Frances (Riley) McL. Student, Utica Free Acad.; A.B., Smith Coll., 1915; postgrad., Radcliffe Coll., 1921-22; L.H.D. (hon.), Lincoln Coll., 1949. Asst. editor woman's page Country Gentleman, 1915-17; circulation promoter Crowell Pub. Co., 1922-24; asst. advt. mgr. Grolier Soc., 1924-34, advt. mgr., 1934-41, editorial dir., 1947-59, v.p., 1956- 64; mng. editor Book of Knowledge, Children's Ency., 1936-42; editor Book of Knowledge Annuals, 1940-53, Book of Knowledge, 1942-60, Story of Our Time, 1947-53, L'Encyclopédie de la Jeunesse, 1948-60, Le Livre de l'Année, 1950-61, La Science Pour Tous, 1960-64; pres. Cragsmoor Free Library Assn., 1965-69. Author: (with Lucile Rathbun, Anetia McLoughlin) The Murder of Doctor Casenova, 1934; contbr. verse to mags. Roman Catholic. Home: 118 Genesee St New Hartford NY 13413

MCMAHAN, ALISON JILL, writer, filmmaker; b. Los Angeles, July 27, 1960; d. David Bruce and Jill Lauren (Harvick) McM.; m. Steven Bluestone, June 11, 1988. BFA in Drama, Cath. U., 1982; MFA in Film Prodn., NYU, 1987. System mgr. Manhattan Day Sch., N.Y.C., 1984-85; prodn. coordinator Interactive Med. Communications, N.Y.C., 1986-87; freelance writer N.Y.C., 1986—; film producer Guadalupe Prodns., N.Y.C., 1987—. Writer, dir., producer various films and documentaries, 1985-87; screenwriter various screenplays; contbr. articles to profl. jours. Active NOW, Fla., 1982; vol. N.Y. Circus, 1987; mem. Williamsburg Around the Bridge Block Assn., N.Y.C., 1987. Mem. Assn. for Ind. Film and Video Makers, Film Video Arts, Internat. Women's Writing Guild. Democrat. Roman Catholic. Club: Appalachian Mountain. Office: Guadalupe Prodns PO Box 366 Prince St Sta New York NY 10012

MCMAHAN, CELESTE TINA, development and construction administrator; b. Denver, Jan. 4, 1948; d. Frank McMahan and Jean Dolores (Graves) Kauno; m. George Cardinal Richards, Dec. 2, 1977. BS in Urban Studies, U. Colo., 1976, MS in Urban and Regional Planning, 1977, postgrad. in architecture, 1977. Lic. real estate sales rep. Colo. Housing sales coordinator Gt. Western United, Colorado City, Colo., 1970-74; dir. parks and recreation City of Edgewater, Colo., 1975-76; intern WICHE, 1976; intern planner City of Aurora, Colo., 1976-77; project mgr./architect Stanford U., Calif., 1977-79; designer, facilities planner Sacramento Savs., 1979-80; project mgr. Crocker Bank, San Francisco, 1980-81, Bank of Am., San Francisco, 1981-85, team mgr. No. Calif. project devel., 1985—; owner McMahan Assocs., Vallejo, Calif., 1979—. Author: A Market Analysis of Downtown, 1976; Housing Market and Population Projections, 1976; Tales From the Old Country, 1984. Photographer. Mem. archtl. com. San Francisco Traditional Jazz Found., 1985; commr. Archtl. Rev. Bd., Menlo Park, Calif., 1978; mem. com. Gov.'s Housing Policy Com., Rural Subcom. on Housing Legis., Social Concerns Legis. Com., Denver, liason com. to form Aurora Community Devel. Corp., 1976; bd. dirs. Bay Area Lawyers for the Arts; mem., trustee, mem. congl. council Grace Cathedral, 1987-88, devel. com., 1986-87; bd. dirs. San Francisco Friends of Arts, 1984-88, Inst. for Study of Natural Systems, 1987-88. Recipient 1st place award Music Educators Assn. Ensemble Festival, 1965; ednl. grantee U. Colo., 1974-77. Mem. Orgn. Women Architects, AIA, Nat. Assn. Women in Constrn., Women Evening Orgn. (v.p.), Grace Cathedral Devel. Com., Bay Area Lawyers for the Arts (bd. dirs.), Nat. Assn. Corp. Real Estate Execs., Downtown Aurora Mchts. Assn. (hon.), Internat. Acad. Lymphology (Cert.), Internat. Platform Assn., Stanford U. Alumni Assn. Episcopalian. Club: Commonwealth (San Francisco). Home: 464 Moonraker Dr Seaview-Vallejo CA 94590 Office: Bank of Am Corporate Real Estate Dept 560 Davis San Francisco CA 94111

MCMAHON, CATHERINE DRISCOLL, lawyer; b. Mineola, N.Y., Apr. 28, 1950; d. Matthew Joseph and Elizabeth (Driscoll) McM.; m. Gregory Arthur McGrath, Sept. 10, 1977; children—Elizabeth Driscoll, Kerry Margaret, Michael Riley. B.A., Simmons Coll., 1972; J.D., Boston Coll., 1975; postgrad. Suffolk U., 1972-73; LL.M., NYU, 1980. Bar: N.Y. 1976, D.C. 1979, U.S. Supreme Ct. 1980. Tax atty. asst. Exxon Corp., N.Y.C., 1975-76, asst. tax atty., 1976-77, sr. tax atty., 1979-81; tax atty. Exxon Internat. Co., N.Y.C., 1977-79; tax mgr. Exxon Research & Engring. Co., Florham Park, N.J., 1981—. Bd. dirs. Southeast Morris chpt. ARC, Madison, N.J., 1983. Recipient TWIN award YMCA, Plainfield/Westfield, N.J., 1983. Mem. ABA, N.Y. State Bar Assn., D.C. Bar Assn. Roman Catholic. Office: Exxon Research & Engring Co PO Box 101 Florham Park NJ 07932

MCMAHON, MARY ALICE, corporation executive; b. Pittsfield, Mass., June 3, 1945; d. George Joseph and Alice (Griffin) McM.; m. Ronald Francis Krysiek, Dec. 29, 1982. BBA and BA in Spanish, Siena Coll., 1967; MA in Ednl. Adminstrn., Mich. State U., 1975. Dir. program Christian Bros. Coll., Memphis, 1968; tchr. Immaculate Conception High Sch., Memphis, 1968-70, Am. Sch. Found., Mex., 1970-73; bd. dirs. Mich. Task Force on Woman Alcoholics, Lansing, 1973-75; assoc. exec. v.p. Health Care Assn. Mich., Lansing, 1975-79; dir. govt. affairs Mich. Dental Assn., Lansing, 1979-80; cons. health care Scottsdale, Ariz., 1980-82; exec. dir. Ariz. Optometric Assn., 1982-84; exec. v.p. Queen of Diamonds Enterprises Inc., Scottsdale, 1985—; also bd. dirs. Queen of Diamonds Enterprises Inc.; co-founder, pres. Links: Your Contact Connection Inc., 1986—, sec./treas. Wis. br., 1986—, also bd. dirs.; pres. MBA/McMahon Bus. Arrangers, 1987—; co-owner Credit Resources, 1987—; v.p., sec. Credit Matters Inc., 1988—. Author: Best Happy Hours in Valley of the Sun, 1983; contbr. articles to profl. jours.; editor: Jour. Ariz. Optometric Assn., 1982-84. Mem. Phoenix and Valley of Sun Conv. Bur., Scottsdale YWCA, Scottsdale C. of C., Nat. Assn. Female Execs., Ariz. Networking Council, Ariz. Soc. Assn. Execs., Am. Bus. Women's Assn. (named Woman Yr. 1985). Republican. Roman Catholic. Office: 7311 E Thomas Rd Scottsdale AZ 85251

MCMAHON, MARY FRANCES, state legislator, lawyer; b. Providence, Apr. 2, 1955; d. Paul Bernard and Mary Patrice (Schuette) McM.; B.A., St. Mary's Coll., 1977; J.D., Suffolk U., Boston, 1980. Bar: R.I. 1980, Mass. 1980. Assoc. McMahon, Hendel & Mc Mahon, Pawtucket, R.I., 1980—;

mem. R.I. Ho. of Reps., 1981—; lectr. R.I. Coll., Community Coll. R.I., 1986, R.I. Sch. Real Estate, 1987. Co-author: Welcome to Our House: An Introductory Guide to the Legislative Process, 1985. Chmn. Adv. Bd. Library Commrs., 1981—; mem. Nat. Conf. State Legislatures, 1981—; mem. rules com. Democratic Nat. Com., 1984—; del. Dem. Nat. Conv., 1988, alternate del., 1984. Named Legislator of Yr. R.I. Library Assn., 1984, 85, Outstanding Young Alumna, St. Mary's Coll., 1985. Mem. R.I. Bar Assn., Mass. Bar Assn. Roman Catholic. Office: 200 Main St Suite 350 Pawtucket RI 02860

MCMAHON, ROBERTA CLABEAUX, health facility administrator; b. Buffalo, Sept. 25, 1952; d. Donald and Rosemary (Zwick) Clabeaux; m. Robert F. McMahon (div. May 1986). AS, Trocaire Coll., 1972; BS in Radiology, Alderson-Broaddus Coll., 1974. Cert. Am. Bd. Abdominal Medicine, Am. Bd. Ob-Gyn, Am. Bd. Radiology, Am. Bd. Cardiology. Chief radiological tech. Southwestern Health Ctr., Pitts., 1976-81; dir. diagnostic lab. M.D. Cardiology Assocs., Ltd., Pitts., 1981-83; adminstr. Shared Health Systems, Pitts., 1983—; also bd. dirs. Shared Health Systems; assoc. prof. diagnostic ultrasound program Community Coll. of Allegheny, Pitts., 1983-86, bd. advs. med. sonographer program; lectr. Community Coll. Nat. Bd. Review, Pitts., 1983-85. Chmn. edn. com. Monessen (Pa.) Valley Progress Council, 1985. Mem. Am. Inst. Ultrasound in Medicine, Nat. Assn Female Execs., Am. Register Radiol. Tech. Republican. Roman Catholic. Home: Park Place 1750 Patrick Pl Library PA 15129 Office: Shared Health Systems 5850 Centre Ave Pittsburgh PA 15206

MCMAHON, YVONNE WADDELL, educational consultant; b. East Bernard, Tex., Nov. 23, 1940; d. William Robert and Ruth (Bernard) Waddell; m. Thomas Carter McMahon, Jan. 17, 1970 (div. Oct. 1978); children—Simone, Nicole. B.S., Lamar U., 1963; postgrad. St. Thomas U., 1968-69; M.Ednl. Psychology, U. Houston, 1972. Tchr., Houston Ind. Sch. Dist., 1963-70; ednl. diagnostician, 1972—; cons. spl. edn., ednl. diagnostics and evaluation specialist, Houston, 1977—; cons. Harris County Dept. Edn., Houston, 1977. Teller, Nat. Women's Conf., Houston, 1977. Mem. Tex. Assn. Ednl. Diagnosticians (pres. 1978-79), Houston Met. Assn. Ednl. Diagnosticians (pres. 1976-77), Council Exceptional Children. Republican. Episcopalian. Clubs: Les Trés Gaies Women's. Home: 5123 Forest Haven Houston TX 77066

MCMANAMA, TRUDY E., psychologist; b. Pitts., Mar. 30, 1945; d. Francis J. and Mary Margaret (McDonough) Figura; m. Patick J. McManama, Nov. 25, 1967 (div. 1977); 1 child, Steven Patrick. B.S., Mansfield U., 1967; M.S., So. Conn. U., 1973, 6th yr. degree, 1974. Tchr. New Milford Schs., Conn., 1967-69; tchr. Shepaug Valley High Sch., Washington Depot, Conn., 1969-72; tng. cons. Danbury Area Unified Social Services, Conn., 1971-72; psychologist Bd. Coop. Services, Poughkeepsie, N.Y., 1974-75; psychologist Berrien County Ind. Sch. Dist., Berrien Springs, Mich., 1975—; cons. Stanley Clark Sch., South Bend, Ind., 1981-88; adj. prof. Ind. U., South Bend, 1979—; instr. St. Joseph Hosp., South Bend, 1985—; elected trustee South Bend Sch. Corp., 1987, pres. 1988. Vol. Internat. Spl. Olympics, 1987; pres., Neighborhood Watch Program, South Bend, 1982-83; hospice vol., South Bend; bd. dirs. Child Abuse and Neglect Coordination Orgn., South Bend, 1986—; mem. Handicapped Camping Bd., 1986—; mem. Democratic Precinct Com., South Bend, 1980-82; del. Ind. Dem. State Conv., 1984. Berrien County Task Force grantee, 1979. Mem. Assn. Supervision and Curriculum Devel., Nat. Assn. Female Execs., Nat. Assn. Sch. Psychologists. Democrat. Roman Catholic. Avocations: Jogging; reading; cross country skiing. Home: 2725 Erskine Blvd South Bend IN 46614 Office: Berrien County Intermediate Sch Dist 711 St Joseph Ave Berrien Springs MI 49103

MCMANNIS, CYNTHIA ANN, dietitian; b. Canton, Ohio, Mar. 3, 1942; d. Georgia Alberta McM.; B.S. in Home Econs., Ohio U., 1964, M.B.A., 1984; dietitian cert. Drexel U., 1965. Therapeutic dietitian Lankenau Hosp., Phila., 1965-68; chief therapeutic dietitian Whelan Food Service at St. Mary Hosp., Phila., 1969-72; patient service dietitian Inst. Pa., Phila., 1972-75; adminstrv. dietitian St. Vincent Hosp. and Med. Center, Toledo, 1975-87; cafeteria mgr., U. Cin. Hosp., 1987—; adv. Northwest Ohio Hosp., Institutional, Ednl. Food Service Soc. Committee woman Republican Party, Phila., 1972-74. Cert. food service mgr., vocat. tchr., Ohio. Mem. Am. Dietetic Assn. (registered dietitian), Ohio Dietetic Assn., Am. Mgmt. Assn. Republican. Methodist. Home: 740-H Northland Rd Cincinnati OH 45240 Office: 234 Goodman St Cincinnati OH 45270

MCMANUS, SISTER MARGARET MARY, hospital executive; b. N.Y.C., Nov. 28, 1932; d. Thomas J. and Bridget F. (McGoey) McM. BBA, St. Bonaventure U., 1968; MHA, U. Minn., 1970. Joined Franciscan Sisters, Roman Cath. Ch., 1950. Bus. mgr., controller St. Joseph's Hosp., Providence, 1951-61, adminstr., 1961-66; asst. adminstr. St. Joseph's Hosp., Tampa, Fla., 1970-72; adminstr. St. Francis Hosp., Miami Beach, Fla., 1972-83, chief exec. officer, 1983—; bd. dirs. Cath. Hospice Miami, Fla. Mem. Miami Beach Health Adv. Com. Fellow Am. Coll. Healthcare Execs. Roman Catholic. Office: St Francis Hosp 250 W 63d St Miami Beach FL 33141

MCMASTER, GLORIA MAE BUGNI, mezzo soprano, educator; b. Montreal, Wis., Oct. 22, 1926; d. Anton George and Rose (Gatto) Bugni; m. Chester L. McMaster (dec. 1972); children—Chester Anthony, Raymond Dale, Brian Monroe, Maureen Anne, Heather Lynn; m. Martin Juhn, July 30, 1977. Student U. Minn.; B.S., Juilliard Sch. Music, N.Y.C.; postgrad. Columbia U., U. Detroit, SUNY-Brockport; Mus.M., Eastman Sch. Music, U. Rochester. Lic. real estate broker, Fla. Prin., voice instr. McMaster Music Studios, Rochester and Dansville, N.Y., 1987—. Performed in concert, oratorio, opera throughout U.S., including solo appearances with Juilliard Opera Theater, Chautauqua Opera Assn., Rochester Opera Theater; appeared as soloist with Mpls. Symphony, Rochester (N.Y.) Philharm. Buffalo Philharm. Music Theater of Rochester, Eastman Rochester Symphony, Rochester, Hornell (N.Y.) Symphony; recitals at Youngstown, Ohio, Ironwood, Mich., Hornell, Alfred and Rochester, N.Y.; concerts Nazareth Art Ctr., Nat. Opera Assn., New Orleans, Sarasota, Fla.; dir. Dansville Music Theater; asst. prof. Youngstown State U., State U. Coll., Geneseo, N.Y.; assoc. prof. Houghton (N.Y.) Coll.; prof. music Alfred (N.Y.) U.; owner, broker Sarasun Properties, Sarasota, Fla. Soloist Republican Nat. Convention, Miami; appeared in title role Nat. Edn. Television prodn. The Medium; appeared in plays by Phil Gelb, Sarasota, 1986-87. Mem. pres.'s leadership council U. Rochester. Mem. AAUW (past pres. Dansville area br.), AAUP (past chpt. exec. bd.), Nat. Opera Assn., Nat. Assn. Tchrs. Singing, Juilliard Alumni Assn., Eastman Alumni Assn., N.Y. Music Tchrs. Assn. Home: 8470 Mt Morris Rd Dansville NY 14437

MCMASTER, JULIET SYLVIA, English language educator; b. Kisumu, Kenya, Aug. 2, 1937; emigrated to Can., 1961, naturalized, 1976; d. Sydney Herbert and Sylvia (Hook) Fazan; m. Rowland McMaster, May 10, 1968; children: Rawdon, Lindsey. B.A. with honors, Oxford U., 1959; M.A., U. Alta., 1963, Ph.D., 1965. Asst. prof. English U. Alta., Edmonton, Can., 1965-70; assoc. prof. U. Alta., 1970-76, prof. English, 1976-86, Univ. prof., 1986—. Author: Thackeray: The Major Novels, 1971, (ed.) Jane Austen's Achievement, 1976, Jane Austen on Love, 1978, Trollope's Palliser Novels, 1978, (with R.D. McMaster) The Novel from Sterne to James, 1981, Dickens the Designer, 1987; contbr. articles to profl. jours. Can. Council fellow, 1969-70; Guggenheim fellow, 1976-77; Killam fellow, 1987-89. Fellow Royal Soc. Can.; mem. Victorian Studies Assn. Western Can. (founding pres. 1972), Assn. Can. Univ. Tchrs. English (pres. 1976-78), MLA, Jane Austen Soc. N.Am. (dir. 1980—). Office: Dept English Univ Alta, Edmonton, AB Canada T6G 2E5

MCMATH, DORIS JEANNETTE BACCUS, educator, consultant; b. Dallas, Aug. 12, 1927; d. Jasper and Edna (Nixon) Baccus; m. LeRoy McMath, Dec. 18, 1954; 1 dau., Linda. B.S., Tuskegee Inst., 1948; M.A., So. Meth. U., 1971; Dr. Metaphysics (hon.), Am. Bible Inst., 1981. Tchr. 3d grade Dallas Ind. Schs., 1948-51; instr. sci. Southwestern Christian Coll., Terrell, Tex., 1952-54; tchr. 5th grade Waco (Tex.) Pub. Schs., 1954-56; dir. early childhood Am. Sch., Phalsbourg, France, 1957-60; tchr. 2d grade Dallas Sch. Dist., 1965-71, instructional resource tchr., 1972—; curriculum writer Dallas Ind. Schs., 1975-76. Vol. dep. registrar Dallas County Tax Office, Dallas, 1979-81; membership chmn. YWCA, United Way, Dallas, 1983. Recipient Meritorious award Dallas Ind. Sch. Dist., 1977; Merit award Southwestern Christain Coll., 1978; Dedicated Service award Tex. State Tchrs. Assn., 1982; Goodwill People Travel Program award People to People Internat., 1983. Mem. NEA (del. conv. 1978-79), Internat. Reading Assn. (sec. 1978-79, mem. com. Tex. council 1984), Tex. Assn. Childhood Edn. (v.p. 1983-84), Dallas Assn. Childhood Edn. (pres. 1981-82), Classroom Tchrs. Dallas (faculty rep. 1979-82, service award 1979), Dallas Hist. Soc., Dallas Mus. Art, Internat. Platform Assn., Epsilon Delta Chi. Republican. Mem. Ch. of Christ. Club: Tuskegee (v.p. 1980-81) (Dallas). Home: 1817 Goldwood Dr Dallas TX 75232

MCMILLAN, CHARLA SUE, airline administrator; b. Stillwater, Okla., Oct. 3, 1949; d. Jack Ikard and Betty Jean (Bowling) Fryrear; m. Victor K. McMillan, Sept. 2, 1981. BS in French, Okla. State U., 1970, MS in Personnel and Guidance, 1974. Cert. tchr., Okla. Job counselor Payne/Noble Community Action Found., Stillwater, 1974-75; inventory clerk Okla. State Dept. Vocat.-Tech. Edn., Stillwater, 1975-76; high sch. French and English tchr. Perkins-Tryon (Okla.) Pub. Schs., 1976-77; lead inventory clerk Dale Carter Lumber Co., Tulsa, 1977, adminstrv. asst., 1978; data support clerk Am. Airlines, Tulsa, 1979-80, engine records clerk, 1980-85, prodn. control floor planner, 1985, master data record planner, 1986—. Photographer Three Windows at Oxford, 1982, Grand prize, 1983. Crisis counselor Stillwater Personal Contact Ctr., 1975-77. Mem. Nat. Assn. Female Execs., Okla. Forestry Assn. Democrat. Home: 7806 N 121st East Ave Owasso OK 74055

MCMILLAN, LYNN CAROL, manufacturing executive; b. Washburn, Wis., Feb. 24, 1940; d. Edwin Robert Phillips and Ina Sylvia (Anderson) Miller; m. Richard Alvin McMillan, Aug. 1964 (div. 1975); children: Jeffrey Wayne, Steven Lloyd; m. William Yates, May 22, 1987. Student, Citrus Coll., 1963-65, Mt. San Antonio Coll., 1964-67, Calif. State Polytechnical U., 1972. Cert. in personnel mgmt., Calif. Office mgr., med. asst. Drs. J. & M. Provonsha, Azusa, Calif., 1961-67, Yucaipa, Calif., 1967-69; ins. mgr. Butka Med. Group, Pomona, Calif., 1969-71; conf. coordinator Kellogg West, Pomona, Calif., 1971-80; exec. sec. Calif. Soc. Radiologic Techs., Anaheim, Calif., 1980-82; dir. personnel Tandberg Data Inc., Orange, Calif., 1982-85; mgr. ins., personnel and security Shepherd Mgmt. Services, Industry, Calif., 1985; v.p. fin., adminstrn. Poly Products Corp., Orange, 1985—; chief fin. officer TCG Inc., Orange, 1985-87, Poly Products Corp., Orange, 1987—. Mem. Nat. Assn. Female Execs., Am. Mgmt. Assn., Nat. Assn. Ind. Bus., Nat. Assn. Self Employed. Republican. Club: Friendship (sec. 1980, 81). Office: Poly Products Corp 625 W Katella Ave #17 Orange CA 92667

MCMILLAN, MARGARET LANGSTAFF, librarian; b. Eaglegroove, Iowa; d. Harry C. and Elizabeth Louise (Tryon) McM.. BS, Cen. Mo. State U., 1921; MS, U. Mo., 1923; postgrad., U. Neuchatel, Switzerland, 1947. Dir. ibrary Columbia (Mo.) Coll., 1926-59; librarian Mo. State Hist. Soc., Columbia, 1959-60; ref. librarian Mid Continent Library Service, Independence, Mo., 1961-76; dir. library Kingswood Manor, Kansas City, Mo., 1982—; mem. faculty summer sessions Cen. Mo. State U., Warrensburg, Northwest Mo. State Coll., Maryville, U. Mo., Columbia; speaker various local groups. Recipient Pioneer Sprit award, 1985. Mem. State Hist. Soc., Pi Lambda Theta, Delta Kappa Gamma. Republican. Methodist. Club: Women's City (Kansas City). Home: 2605 Lee's Summit Rd Independence MO 64055

MC MILLAN, MARIE ELIZABETH (MRS. JAMES BATES MCMILLAN), airport public information official; b. Exeter, Calif., Aug. 1, 1926; d. James Martin and Eva Marie (Cash) Stever; student Calif. Sch. Fine Arts, 1943, U. Calif., 1944-45, San Jose State U., 1956; U. Nev., 1966, 75-76; m. James Bates McMillan, June 20, 1964; children—Michelle (dec.), John, Jeffrey. Sec., U. Calif. Radiation Lab., 1956-60; adminstrv. sec. AEC, Las Vegas, Nev., 1960-65; employment interviewer State of Nev. Employment Security, Las Vegas, 1965-67; mgr. McMillan Ranches, Reedley, Calif., also aviation lectr. and ferry pilot, 1974-80; v.p., aviation dir. Presdl. Casino, Port Harcourt, Nigeria, 1980-85; pub. info. rep. McCarran Internat. Airport, 1985—. Recipient Amelia Earhart medals, 1974, 76; named Woman Pilot of Yr., 1976-77, S.W. sect. 99's, Las Vegas chpt., 1973-76. Mem. The Ninety-Nines, Nat. Aero. Assn., All Woman Transcontinental Air Race Assn., Soaring Soc. Am., Aircraft Owners and Pilots Assn., CAP, Nev. Safety Council (aviation com.). Democrat. Holder world and U.S. nat. records for speed over recognized course between Fresno and Las Vegas, 1978, for time to climb 3,000 meters, 1979, holder 656 world and U.S. nat. aviation speed records from Las Vegas to Hermosillo, Mazatlán, Puerto Vallarta, Guadalajara, Mexico City, Acapulco, all Caribbean islands and return to Las Vegas, 1985, others. Home: 705 Twin Lakes Dr Las Vegas NV 89107-2158 Office: McCarran Internat Airport Postal Box 11005 Las Vegas NV 89111-1005

MCMILLAN, MARY IRENE, pilot; b. Boulder, Colo., June 17, 1952; d. James Thomas and Mary Irene (Hall) McM. Grad. high sch., Lyons, Colo. Sheepherder, camp tender Manning and Allemand Livestock Co., Hanna, Wyo., 1971-75; owner, operator C.J. Bar Ranch Inc., Douglas, Wyo., 1975-81; real estate broker Johnston Realty, Douglas, 1981-85; pilot aircraft sales dept. Casper (Wyo.) Air Service, 1985-86; pilot, capt. States West Airlines, Phoenix, 1986-87, chief pilot, 1987—. Mem. Bd. Adjustments Town of Douglas, 1983-84. Mem. Aircraft Owners and Pilots Assn. Office: States-west Airlines 2871 Sky Harbor Blvd Phoenix AZ 85034

MCMILLAN, PATRICIA ANNE, marketing professional; b. Camden, N.J., Mar. 2, 1948; d. James Henry and Charlotte Ernst (Tilton) McCullough; m. Earl Daniel McMillan, Jan. 26, 1986; 1 child, Thomas Francis Clayton. BS in Mgmt., Maryville Coll., 1988. Telemktg. rep. Southwestern Bell Yellow Pages, Dallas, 1973-74, supr. prodn., 1974-76, telemktg. supr., 1976-77, mgr. distbn., 1977-79, mgr. tng., 1979-82; dist. mgr. sales, tng. Southwestern Bell Yellow Pages, St. Louis, 1983-84, dir. corp. labor relations, 1984-87, dir. telemktg. support, 1987-88, div. sales mgr., 1988—; dist. mgr. sales reviews AT&T, Parsippany, N.J., 1982-83; mem. Women in Leadership-Coro Found., St. Louis, 1985-87. Mem. Jr. League, St. Louis; counselor Jr. Achievement, Dallas. Mem. Nat. Assn. Female Execs.

MCMILLAN-BLAKE, DENISE, sales and marketing executive; b. Ann Arbor, Mich., Oct. 27, 1960; d. Harold Foster and Josephine Elaine (Kauffman) McM.; m. Philip George Blake, Dec. 30, 1983. BS, No. Mich. U., 1982; postgrad., Contractors Sch. Ariz., U. Phoenix. Lic. real estate and securities broker, Ariz. Mgr. sales and mktg. Modulaire Industries, Phoenix, 1982—. Founder, sec. Covey 8 Homeowners, Phoenix, 1986-87. Mem. Phoenix C. of C., No. Mich. U. Alumni (Phoenix chpt.). Club: Lacamarilla (Scottsdale, Ariz.). Home: 4315 E Highlands Dr Paradise Valley AZ 85253 Office: Modulaire Industries 2902 S 44th St Phoenix AZ 85040

MCMILLEN, LINDA LOUISE, lawyer; b. Ft. Worth, Dec. 20, 1947; d. James M. and Helen Dorrace (Taylor) McM.; m. Burke William Biow, Dec. 1968 (div. 1973); 1 child, Heather Lyn McMillen. BS with high honors, Tex. Wesleyan Coll., 1977; JD, Baylor U., 1980. Bar: Tex. 1980, U.S. Dist. Ct. (no. dist.) Tex. 1980. With Ryan Mortgage Co., Arlington, Tex., 1973-75; law clk. Wash, Hodges & Segrest, Waco, Tex., 1978-79; assoc. Kinkead Law Offices, Amarillo, 1980-81; lectr. bus. law, U. Tex., Arlington, 1984-86; sole practice, Arlington, 1981—. Vol. legal counselor Arlington Womens' Ctr., 1987—, advisor, 1988—; bd. dirs. Mother's Day Out/Day Care Ctr., 1st Christian Ch., Arlington, 1987—, TV com., crew 1st Christian Ch., 1987—, deacon, 1987—; sub. judge Teen Ct. of Arlington, 1988—; sec., bd. dirs. Am. Thai Found. Edn., Arlington, 1982—; mem. Am.-Thai Christian Found., Arlington, 1982-85. Author: The Shadow of Man, 1983, Eiphaun, 1986. Mem. State Bar Tex., ABA, Tarrant County Family Bar Assn., Tarrant County Women Lawyers, Tarrant County Bar Assn., Arlington Bar Assn., others. Home: 2904 Friendswood Arlington TX 76013 Office: PO Box 14246 Arlington TX 76094

MCMILLER, ANITA WILLIAMS, army officer, educator; b. Chgo., Dec. 23, 1946; d. Chester Leon and Marion Claudette (Martin) Williams; m. Robert Melvin McMiller, July 29, 1967 (div. 1980). BS in Edn., No. Ill. U., 1968; MBA, Fla. Inst. Tech., 1979. Social worker Cook County, Chgo., 1968-69; recruiter, dir. personnel, analyst State of Ill., Chgo., 1969-75; commd. 1st lt. U.S. Army, 1975, advanced through grades to maj., 1984; served U.S. Army, U.S. and Fed. Republic Germany, 1986—; instr. Cen. Tex. Coll., Hanau, Fed. Republic Germany, 1981-83, Phillips Bus. Coll., Alexandria, Va., 1983-84. Author articles in field. Child advocate, foster mother Army Community Service, Hanau, 1980-83; tutor Parent-Tchr. Club Hanau Schs., 1981-83; vol. Vis. Nurses Assn. No. Va., 1983-85; coordinator, English tutor Adopt-a-Sch. Project, Washington, 1983-85. Mem. Nat. Def. Transp. Assn., Assn. U.S. Army, Fedn. Bus. Profl. Women, Alpha Kappa Alpha (treas. 1982-83). Home: care M C Williams 803 E 87th Pl Chicago IL 60619 Office: MTMC Bremerhaven TML APO New York NY 09069

MCMILLIN, CAROLYN HEARD, public relations executive; b. Baton Rouge, July 15, 1960; d. William Lee ad Carolyn (Greer) Heard; m. David Lee McMillin, Dec. 29, 1984. BBA, U. Miss., 1982, MA in Journalism, 1985. Pub. relations dir. Sr. Bowl, Mobile, Ala., 1985—; communications dir. Christ United Meth. Ch., Mobile, 1987. Mem. Pub. Relations Council of Ala., Nat. Assn. Female Execs., Ole Miss Alumni Assn. (sec., treas. 1986—), Jr. League of Mobile. Democrat. Club: Southridge Garden, Press of Mobile (Mobile). Home: 6240 Southridge Rd N Mobile AL 36609 Office: Senior Bowl 63 S Royal St Suite 107 Mobile AL 36602

MCMILLIN, JEANIE BYRD, biochemist, medical educator; b. Spartanburg, S.C., Sept. 26, 1939; d. Walter Louis and Frances Elizabeth (Austell) McM.; m. Wallace Barry VanWinkle, 1987; children: Elizabeth, David Emerson. BA, Converse Coll., 1961; Ph.D. in Biochemistry, U. N.C., 1967; Research assoc., instr. U. N.C., Chapel Hill, N.C., 1967-68; research assoc. Cornell Med. Coll., N.Y.C., 1968-69; instr. Baylor Coll. Medicine, Houston, 1969-72, asst. prof., 1972-80, assoc. prof. medicine, biochemistry and pediatrics, 1980-85, prof., 1985-86; prof. medicine and cell biology, dir. cardiac biochemistry U. Ala.-Birmingham, 1986—; cons. NIH, 1979—, mem. cardiovascular pulmonary study sect., 1982-86; ad hoc cons. bd. sci. counselors Nat. Inst. on Aging, 1987; mem. cen. research rev. com. Am. Heart Assn., 1981-86, Ala. affiliate, 1986—, mem. exec. bd. Basic Sci. Council; cardiol. adv. com. Nat. Heart, Lung and Blood Inst., 1987—. Fulbright fellow in chemistry, 1961-62; NASA fellow, 1962-66; USPHS fellow, 1966-67; grantee Am. Heart Assn., 1978-81, Muscular Dystrophy Assn., 1980—, NIH, 1977—. Mem. Internat. Study Group for Research in Cardiac Metabolism, Biophys. Soc., Cardiac Muscle Soc., Am. Soc. Biol. Chemists, Am. Physiol. Soc., Sigma Xi (fellow cardiovascular sect., treas. U. Ala-Birmingham chpt.). Democrat. Editorial bd. Am. Jour. Physiology, 1980—, Circulation, 1986—, Jour. Molecular Cell Cardiology, 1986—; contbr. articles to various publs. Office: U Ala Birmingham Sta Dept Medicine Div Cardiovascular Disease Birmingham AL 35294

MCMILLIN, SUE LYNN, reporter; b. Jackson, Mich., Apr. 5, 1954; d. William Irwin and Jean Louise (Lake) McM.; m. Rodney Russell Fink, Apr. 12, 1981. BA in Journalism, Mich. State U., 1976. Staff reporter Spinal Column and Lakeland Tribune, Union Lake, Mich., 1976-77, Plymouth (Wis.) Rev., 1977-78; free-lance writer Lansing mag., Flint mag., other newspapers, cen. Mich., 1978-79; staff writer Lansing (Mich.) mag., 1979-80; police beat reporter Gazette Telegraph, Colorado Springs, Colo., 1981, mil. affairs reporter, 1981-85, 86—, asst. city editor, 1985-86. Mem. Soc. Profl. Journalists, Colorado Springs Press Assn. (treas. 1983-84, pres. 1985). Office: Gazette Telegraph 30 S Prospect St Colorado Springs CO 80901

MCMINN, TAMZIN MACDONALD, lawyer; b. N.Y.C.; m. Robert William McMinn; children—Virginia, Donald R. BA., Swarthmore Coll., 1958; MA, Drew U., 1978; JD, Rutgers U., 1981. Bar: N.J. 1981, U.S. Dist. Ct. N.J. 1981, U.S. Ct. Appeals (3d cir.) 1982. Fellow Drew U., Madison, N.J., 1980-82; assoc. Pitney, Hardin, Kipp & Szuch, Newark, also Morristown, N.J., 1981-84; chief of staff Congressman Dean A. Gallo, 11th Dist. N.J. Chmn. 25th Reunion fund drive Swarthmore Coll (Pa.), 1983; v.p. Chatham Twp. Bd. Edn. (N.J.), 1972-75; mem. Chatham Twp. Bd. Adjustment, 1975-77; bd. dirs. SE Morris unit ARC, Madison, 1984; bd. govs. Union Coll., Cranford, N.J., 1986—. Named Vol. of Yr., Jr. League Morristown, 1976. Mem. ABA, Md. D.C. Bar Assn. Republican. Episcopalian. Clubs: Morris County Golf (Morristown); Kenwood Country (Bethesda). Office: 1318 Longworth House Office Bldg Washington DC 20515

MCMORRIS, GRACE ELIZABETH, banker; b. Malden, Mass., Feb. 6, 1922; d. John Edward and Selma Florence (Swanson) O'Brien; B.A., Boston U., 1944; postgrad. Ariz. State U., 1962; m. William Michael McMorris, May 14, 1944 (dec.); children—Sheila Elizabeth McMorris Christenson, Michael, James, John. Clk., Parlin Meml. Library, Everett, Mass., part-time, 1938-40; clk. student post office Boston U., 1941-42; supr. classified advt. desk The Boston Post, 1942-44; substitute tchr. public schs., Randolph, Mass., 1956-57; with Valley Nat. Bank Ariz., Phoenix, 1960-87, trust adminstr., 1969-73, trust officer, 1973-75, asst. v.p., 1975-78, v.p., 1978-87, corporate trust mgr., 1977-87, ret., 1988. Mem. Nat. Assn. Bank Women (sec. 1974-75, dir. 1973-75), Am. Soc. Corp. Secs. (treas. Phoenix chpt., v.p.), Pi Lambda Sigma (nat. treas. 1947-48). Roman Catholic. Office: Valley Nat Bank Ariz 241 N Central Ave Phoenix AZ 85004

MCMORROW, MARGARET MARY, elementary school educator; b. N.Y.C., Dec. 18, 1924; d. Patrick Joseph and Ellen Veronica (Quinn) McIntyre; m. Joseph Patrick McMorrow, Oct. 12, 1948; children: Linda Karen, Robert Michael, Patrice Ann, Jane Ellen. BS, Queens Coll., 1946; MS in Edn., Hofstra U., 1959. Space controller Am. Airlines Co., N.Y.C., 1946-48; bus. rep. N.Y. Telephone Co., N.Y.C., 1948-52; tchr. Elwood Sch. Dist, Huntington, N.Y., 1965—. Fellow Elwood Tchrs. Assn., L.I. Scribes, N.Y. State United Tchrs., Mensa; mem. Alpha Lambda Omicron. Roman Catholic. Office: Elwood Sch Dist 286 Cuba Hill Rd Huntington NY 11801

MCMORROW, THERESA MARIE, graphic artist; b. Omaha, Sept. 14, 1956; d. Thomas Leo McCoy and Rita Jean (Volcek) Gannett; m. James Leslie Anzalone, May 3, 1980 (div. Jan. 1985); 1 child, Warren Spencer Anzalone; m. Edward James McMorrow Jr., Sept. 6, 1986. Student, Parsons Sch. Design, N.Y.C., 1975-76, Kansas City (Mo.) Art Inst., 1976-77, Am. U. in Aix-en-Provence, France, 1978-79. Comml. artist Orent Express, Omaha, 1979-82; free-lance artist Omaha, 1982-85; owner Studio 24, Omaha, 1985—. Contbr. (newsletter) Greater Resources of Omaha Women, 1985—. Mem. Omaha Fedn. Advertisers. Republican. Roman Catholic. Office: Studio 24 4034 S 24th St Omaha NE 68107

MCMULLEN, BARBARA ELIZABETH, data processing company executive, writer; b. Phila., Aug. 2, 1942; d. Walter Woodrow and Nellie Elizabeth (Rojewski) Ludman; m. John F. McMullen, May 12, 1978; stepchildren: Claire Ann, Luke John. BS in Math., Pa. State U., 1963; postgrad. Pratt Inst., 1971, N.Y. Sch. Interior Design, 1973; MPA in Pub. Fin., NYU, 1976. Supr. AT&T, Mt. Kisco, N.Y., 1963-65; sr. programmer Pan Am. World Airways, N.Y.C., 1965-67; analyst N.Y. Stock Exchange, N.Y.C., 1967-69; project leader Bache Halsey Stuart, N.Y.C., 1974-76; mgr. Morgan Stanley & Co., N.Y.C., 1976-78; pres. McMullen & McMullen, Inc., Jefferson Valley, N.Y., 1978—; mem. faculty NYU, 1980-82, New Sch. for Social Research, N.Y.C., 1981—. Author: (with John F. McMullen) Microcomputer Communications, 1982; contbg. editor Computers & Electronics, 1984-85, Computer Living, 1985—, Computer Shopper, 1985—; contbg. editor PC Clones mag., 1988—; contbr. chpt. to book, articles to profl. jours. Recipient Lepesqueur award N.Y.U., 1976. Bd. dirs. Osceola Heights Assn., Jefferson Valley, 1984. Mem. Big Apple Users Group (sec. and bd. dirs. 1981-84), Boston Computer Soc., Assn. for Computing Machinery, N.Y. Personal Computer Club (sec., bd. dirs. 1982—), N.Y. Amateur Computer Club, Westchester IBM Users Group, Pa. State U. Club of N.Y. Roman Catholic. Clubs: Downtown Athletic (N.Y.C.); Jefferson Valley Racquet (N.Y.). Avocations: pvt. pilot, painting, needlework, tropical fish breeding, amateur radio. Home: Perry St Jefferson Valley NY 10535 Office: McMullen & McMullen Inc McM Plaza Jefferson Valley NY 10535

MCMULLEN, CAROL BUECHNER, manufacturing company human resource executive; b. Jersey City, Sept. 3, 1929; d. Clarence A. and Elsie (Erdman) Buechner; m. Randolph B. McMullen, June 16, 1951; children—Gail, Carolyn, Randolph. B.A., Moravian Coll., 1951. System service supr. Info. Sci., Montvale, N.J., 1970-76, systems analyst, 1976-79; human resource systems supr. Grand Met. U.S.A., Montvale, 1979-84; personnel systems mgr. Lehn & Fink Products Group, Sterling Drug Inc., Montvale, 1984—. Mem. Assn. for Women in Computing (v.p. program 1983-84), Human Resource Systems Profession, NOW, AAUW, LWV. Republican. Home: 55 Montebello Rd Suffern NY 10201 Office: Lehn & Fink Products 225 Summit Ave Montvale NJ 07645

MCMULLEN, MELINDA KAE, public relations executive; b. Japan, July 20, 1957; d. Paul K. and Valerie C. McMullen. BA in Communications, U. Pacific, 1979. Account exec. Ketchum Communications, San Francisco, 1979-80, Burson-Marsteller, N.Y.C., 1980-81; mgr. pub. relations Am. Express, N.Y.C., 1981-86; dir. pub. relations Firemans Fund Ins., Novato, Calif., 1986-87; sr. v.p. Edelman Pub. Relations, San Francisco, 1987—. Recipient Silver Anvil Pub. Relations Soc. Am., 1979. Mem. Nat. Investor Relations Inst. Office: Edelman Pub Relations 550 California St San Francisco CA 94104

MCMULLIN, JOYCE ANNE, general contractor; b. Tulsa, Jan. 6, 1952; d. Junior Lawrence Patrick and Carol Anne (Morris) McM.; m. David Lawrence Tupper, Jan. 1, 1980 (div. May 1982). BFA, Calif. Coll. Arts and Crafts, 1973. Interior designer Design Assocs., Oakland, Calif., 1974; interior designer, sales rep. Sullivan's Interiors, Berkeley, Calif., 1975; supr. bldg. maintenance Clausen House, Inc., Oakland, 1975-82; owner New Life Renovation, Lafayette, Calif., 1981—. Contbr. articles to mags., newspapers. Mem. AAUW, Bus. and Profl. Women, Contra Costa County Women's Network, Nat. Assn. Female Execs., Self-Employed Tradeswomen (sec. 1984).

MCMULLIN, MARY JO, nurse; b. Sedalia, Mo., July 8, 1933; d. Robert Henry and Rose Mary (Alt) Welliver; R.N., St. Mary's Hosp., Kansas City, Mo., 1954; m. Jesse Francis McMullin, Nov. 26, 1955; children—James, Tom, Rose, Jane. Staff nurse St. Mary's Hosp., 1954-55; mem. nursing staff Bothwell Hosp., Sedalia, Mo., 1955-58, head nurse, 1958-70, asst. dir. nursing, 1970-83, dir. patient care services, 1983-85, dir. nursing, 1985—, tchr. stoma care, 1976—. 4-H Club leader, 1975—; pres. Pettis County Extension Council, 1983-84. Mem. Am. Nursing Assn., Mo. Nursing Assn., 10th Dist. Nursing Assn. (v.p. 1987), Profl. Nurses Assn. Bothwell Hosp. Roman Catholic. Home: Route 2 La Monte MO 65337 Office: PO Box 1706 Sedalia MO 65301

MCMULLIN, RUTH R., publishing company executive; b. N.Y.C., Feb. 9, 1942; d. Richard Thomas and Virginia (Goodwin) R.; m. Thomas Ryan McMullin, Apr. 27, 1968; 1 child, David Patrick. BA, Conn. Coll., 1963; student, Yale U. Sch. Orgn. and Mgmt., 1979. Market researcher Aviation Week mag., 1962-64; assoc. editor Doubleday & Co., 1964-67; mgr. Natural History Press, 1967-70; mgr., later v.p., treas. Weston (Conn.) Woods, Inc., from 1970; sr. v.p. Gen. Electric Capital Markets Group, until 1987; exec. v.p., chief operating officer John Wiley & Sons, Inc., N.Y.C., 1987—; also bd. dirs. John Wiley & Sons, Inc. Office: John Wiley & Sons Inc 605 3rd Ave New York NY 10158 *

MCMURRIN, TRUDY ANN, publishing consultant, editor; b. Los Angeles, May 28, 1944; d. Sterling Moss and Natalie (Cotterel) McM.; m. William M. Howard, Mar. 9, 1963 (div. 1967); 1 child, Natalie Roberta Howard; m. Robert Bruce Evans, Sept. 24, 1969 (div. 1971); m. Mick McAllister, June 16, 1982. BA in History and Philosophy, U. Utah, 1981. Editor U. Utah Press, Salt Lake City, 1967-74, asst. dir., 1974-80, editor-in-chief, 1980-83; dir. So. Meth. U. Press, Dallas, 1983-86; adj. prof. dept. communication Weber State Coll., Ogden, Utah, 1986—; mem. bus. adv. council Westminster Coll. of Salt Lake City, 1986—; cons. and lectr. in field. Dir. art, codesigner award-winning books, 1972—. Mem. adv. bd. Children's Mus. Utah, 1979-81; bd. dirs. Howe Bros. Pub. Co., 1979—; mem. symposium on quality in pre-coll. edn. Rowland Hall-St. Mark's Sch., 1980-81; mem. Coalition to Save Our Sch. Libraries, 1981—, Salt Lake City Ballet Guild, Utah Symphony Guild, Utah Opera Guild, Friends of Salt Lake City Library. Fellow Am. Assn. State and Local History Nat. Endowment for Humanities, 1977, Inst. Am. West, 1981-82; recipient Maud Powell Found. award, 1988. Mem. Assn. Utah Pubs. (pres. 1978-83, bd. dirs. 1987—), Western Lit. Assn. (mem. exec. council 1987—), Soc. for Scholarly Pub., Women in Scholarly Pub., Western Writers Am., Medieval Acad. Am., Tex. Folklore Soc., Rocky Mountain Book Pubs. Assn., Com. Small Mag. Editors and Pubs. Office: Editorial and Pub Services 1260 E Stratford Ave Salt Lake City UT 84106-2727

MCNAIR, LOIS I. D., speech therapist; b. New Brunswick, Can.; d. George W. and Mary (McColl) McN.; B.Sc., Emerson Coll., 1967; M.Ed., Boston State Coll., 1969, postgrad., 1969-70; postgrad. Boston U., 1975-76; Ph.D., Heed U., Fla., 1982. Radiologic technician Can. Dept. Vets. Affairs, 1947-62, 67-68; tchr. speech and hearing Boston Sch. System, 1969; radiographer Radiologic Group Greater Boston, 1970-71; counselor, tchr. speech and hearing Manchester (N.H.) Sch. System, 1970-71; tchr. speech therapy Houlton (Maine) Sch. System, 1972—; mem. Nat. Stuttering Project. Cert. tchr., Maine, Mass., N.H. Mem. Can. Med. Radiation Technologists, Royal Soc. Health, Nat. Council Family Relations, NEA, Am. Personnel and Guidance Assn., Maine Personnel and Guidance Assn., Maine Speech and Hearing Assn., Am. Public Health Assn., AAAS, Speech Communication Assn. Home: PO Box 393 Houlton ME 04730

MCNAIR, RUTH DAVIS, chemist, consultant; b. Flint, Mich., Mar. 18, 1921; d. Harry S. and Mary Katharine (Hogan) Davis; m. Donald Robert McNair, Oct. 14, 1950; children: Catherine Ruth, James D. BA, U. Mich., 1941; BS in Edn., U. Cin., 1942; PhD in Biochemistry, Wayne State U., 1948. Diplomate Am. Bd. Clin. Chemistry. Tchr. St. Clair (Mich.) Pub. Schs., 1942-44; clin. chemist Providence Hosp., Southfield, Mich., 1948-83; cons. clin. chemist Garden City (Mich.) Hosp., 1972—; cons. clin. chemist Northland Oakland Med. Lab., Southfield, Mich., 1973-76, Oakland Med. Ctr., Pontiac, Mich., 1970-77. Contbr. articles to profl. jours. Fellow Am. Assn. for Clin. Chemistry (chmn. Mich. sect., various coms.), AAAS, Am. Inst. Chemists; mem. Am. Bd. Clin. Chemistry (bd. dirs. 1976-84, v.p. 1981-83, pres. 1983-84), Am. Chem. Soc., Sigma Xi.

MCNALLY, REBECCA ANN, management consultant; b. Detroit, Feb. 24, 1946; d. Myron Allen and Eleanor Kathaleen (Renfroe) Wilson; m. John R. McNally, Mar. 19, 1973; 1 child, Amy Yvonne. Student, Sinclair Coll., 1975-77. With media accounts payable Marsteller, Inc., Chgo., 1967-70; office adminstr. Fairlane Assocs., Dearborn, Mich., 1970-73; real estate salesperson J.M. Kingston Realty, Dayton, Ohio, 1975-79; media coordinator Rushmore Sch., Dayton, 1979-84; comptroller Dyna-Graphics Corp., Eden Prairie, Minn., 1984-87; cons. to mgmt. Stenberg-Gruetzmacher, Mpls., 1987—; women's image cons., Mpls., 1984—; bus. systems cons., Mpls., 1985—. Writer, producer ednl. TV programs, 1981-83. Advisor 4-H Clubs of Am., Ohio and Minn., 1974—; county sec. 4-H Clubs of Am., Greene County, Ohio, 1976-79; troop leader Girl Scouts Am., Dayton, 1979-80; bd. dirs. Wright-Patterson Officers' Wives Clubs, Dayton, 1975-76. Recipient Award of Recognition 4-H Clubs of Am., 1980, Cert. of Appreciation Rushmore Sch., 1983, Community Service award Eden Prairie High Sch., 1985. Mem. Am. Mgmt. Assn.

MCNAMARA, ANN DOWD, medical technologist; b. Detroit, Oct. 17, 1924; d. Frank Raymond and Frances Mae (Ayling) Sullivan; BS, Wayne State U., 1947; m. Thomas Stephen Dowd, Apr. 23, 1949 (dec. 1980); children—Cynthia Dowd Restuccia, Kevin Thomas Dowd; m. Robert Abbott McNamara, June 15, 1985. Med. technologist Woman's Hosp. (now Hutzel Hosp.), Detroit, 1946-52, St. James Clin. Lab., Detroit, 1960-62; supr. histopathology lab. Hutzel Hosp., Detroit, 1962-72, Mt. Carmel Mercy Hosp., 1972-87. Mem. Am. Soc. Clin. Pathologists, Am. Soc. Med. Technology, Mich. Soc. Med. Technology, Nat. Soc. Histotechnology, Mich. Soc. Histotechnologists, Wayne State U. Alumni Assn., Smithsonian Assos., Detroit Inst. Arts Founders Soc. Home: 29231 Oak Point Dr Farmington Hills MI 48331

MCNAMARA, ELSA MAE BROESAMLE, sales executive; b. Pitts., June 7, 1958; d. Herman R. and Eva P. (Province) Broesamle; married May 28, 1988. Sales rep. Dardenell Publs., Pitts., 1978-80; sales rep. Advo System, Inc., Houston, 1980-82, sales mgr., 1982-83; dist. mgr. Cleve., 1983-84; regional mgr. Pitts., 1984-85; v.p. Fla. region 1985—. Mem. Am. Mgmt. Assn., Nat. Assn. Female Execs. Office: Advo System Inc 2203 N Lois Ave #418 Tampa FL 33607

MCNAMARA, JO ANNE, nurse; b. Emmetsburg, Iowa, July 23, 1932; d. Joseph Michael and Mary Victoria (Roper) McN. BSN, Briar Cliff Coll., 1956; MA, U. Redlands, Calif., 1979. Registered nurse. Pediatric supr. St. Joseph Mercy Hosp., Sioux City, Iowa, 1955-57; staff nurse Good Samaritan Hosp., West Palm Beach, Fla., 1957-58; psychiat. supr. Glenwood Hills Hosp., Mpls., 1958-61; surg. staff nurse VA Hosp., Mpls., 1961-62; pediatric nurse Mt. Sinai Hosp., Los Angeles, 1963-64, instr. inservice, 1964-69; instr. nursing Los Angeles Unified Sch., 1970-74; edn. coordinator Century City Hosp., Los Angeles, 1975-85; coordinator quality assurance Temple Community Hosp., Los Angeles, 1986—, dir. edn., 1986—. Vol. Crisis Intervention Ctr., Los Angeles, 1984. Mem. Quality Assurance Profls., Health Edn. Council, Patient Care Assessment Council, Spina Bifida Assn., B'nai B'rith Women. Democrat. Roman Catholic. Club: Toastmasters (sec.). Home: 20130 Lorne St Canoga Park CA 91306 Office: Temple Community Hosp 235 N Hoover St Los Angeles CA 90004

MCNAMARA, JULIA M(ARY), academic administrator, foreign language educator; b. N.Y.C., Dec. 13, 1941; d. John P. and Julia (Dowd) McN. BA in History and French, Ohio Dominican Coll., 1965; MA in French, Middlebury Coll., Paris, 1972; PhD in French Language and Lit., Yale U., 1980; DHL (hon.), Sacred Heart U., Hamden, Conn., 1984. Mem. faculty St. William Sch., Pitts., 1963-64, Holy Spirit Sch., Columbus, Ohio, 1964-65, Newark (Ohio) Cath. High Sch., 1965-66, Northwest Cath. High Sch., West Hartford, Conn., 1966-69, St. Vincent Ferrer High Sch., N.Y.C., 1969-70, St. Mary's High Sch., New Haven, 1971-74; lectr. french Albertus Magnus Coll., New Haven, 1976-80, dean of students, 1980-82, acting pres., 1982-83, pres., 1983—; adj. prof. french Albertus Magnus Coll., 1981—; mem. Conn. Health and Edn. Facilities Authority, Hartford, 1983—; mem. exec. com. Conn. Conf. Ind. Colls., Hartford, 1982—, sec.-treas. 1986—; lectr. in field; assoc. fellow Yale U., Morse Coll. Chairperson United Way Greater New Haven, 1987; bd. dirs. St. Mary's High Sch., New Haven, 1982—, ARC; trustee Yale/New Haven Hosp., 1984—, mem. bioethics com., mem. investment com., chmn. investor responsibility com.; adv. bd. Bank of Boston-Conn., 1983-87; adv. com. Jr. League Greater New Haven, 1985; trustee Hartford Sem., 1985—. Fulbright fellow, Paris, 1977-78; Yale U. fellow, 1974-78, Am. Council on Edn. fellow, 1981; recipient Disting. Woman in Leadership award New Haven YWCA, 1984, Veritas award Providence Coll., 1987. Mem. Fulbright Alumni Assn., New Haven C. of C. (bd. dirs. 1984—), New England Assn. Schs. and Colls. Appeals Bd. Roman Catholic. Office: Albertus Magnus Coll Office of Pres 700 Prospect St New Haven CT 06511

MC NAMARA, MARY ELLEN, marketing executive; b. Long Branch, N.J., May 26, 1942; d. Edward Ward and Alice Marie (Reynolds) McN.; B.A., Glassboro State U., 1965; M.B.A., N.Y.U., 1975, Advanced Profl. Cert., 1980. Tech. asst. Bell Labs., Holmdel, N.J., 1965-66, sr. tech. asst., 1966-68; programming analyst, IBM, N.Y.C., 1968-71, systems programmer, 1971-72, bus. planner, 1972-74, industry planning adminstr., Princeton, N.J., 1974-77, industry mktg. adminstr., 1977-81, product mktg. adminstr., White Plains, N.Y., 1981-83, mgr. engring. sci. programming, Boca Raton, Fla., 1983-84, mem. market research staff, White Plains, N.Y., 1984-85, mgr. market devel., Valhalla, N.Y., 1986—. Mem. Computer Soc. (chmn. 1981, v. chmn. N.J. sect. 1979-81), IEEE (sr. mem., vice chmn. Palm Beach sect. 1984), AAAS, Assn. Computing Machinery, AAUW, Assn. Women in Computing, Nat. Council Women U.S.A., Women's Econ. Roundtable, Exec. Women of Palm Beaches, N.Y. Acad. Sci., N.Y. U. Alumni Assn., Glassboro State U. Alumni Assn., Beta Gamma Sigma. Republican. Roman Catholic. Home: PO Box 21 Allenhurst NJ 07711 Office: 400 Columbus Ave Valhalla NY 10595

MCNAMARA, SUSAN LOUISE, data processing executive; b. Boston, May 26, 1952; d. Thomas Joseph and Louise (Downey) McN.; divorced, 1983; 1 child, Michael Peter Walsh. BS, Simmons Coll., 1973; MEd, Harvard U., 1986. Tchr. Walpole (Mass.) Sch., 1973-74; programmer Savs. Mgmt. Computer Corp., Boston, 1974-76; project mgr. William Filenes & Sons, Boston, 1976-82; instr. mgmt. info. systems Massasoit Community Coll., Brockton, Mass., 1982-84; team leader Peter R. Johnson & Assocs. Inc., Westwood, Mass., 1986-88; v.p. McNamara & Assocs., Inc., Quincy, Mass., 1988—; lectr. mgmt. info. systems Northeastern U., Boston, 1978—; instr. New Eng. Banking Inst., Boston, 1982—, chmn. acad. area for mgmt. info. systems, 1986—, mem. edn. com., 1986—. Treas. Simmons Class of '73, 1978-83, v.p., 1988—. Roman Catholic.

MCNAMEE, CATHERINE, educational association executive; b. Troy, N.Y., Nov. 13, 1931; d. Thomas Ignatius McNamee and Kathryn McNamee Marois. B.A., Coll. of St. Rose, 1953, D.H.L. (hon.), 1975, M.Ed., Boston Coll., 1955, M.A., 1958; Ph.D., U. Madrid, 1967. Grad. asst. Boston Coll., 1954-55; asst. registrar Boston Coll. (Grad. Sch.), 1955-57; acad. v.p. Coll. St. Rose, Albany, N.Y., 1968-75; dir. liberal arts Thomas Edison Coll., Trenton, 1975-76; pres. Trinity Coll., Burlington, Vt., 1976-79, Coll. St. Catherine, St. Paul, 1979-84; dean Dexter Hanley Coll., U. Scranton, Pa., 1984-86; pres. Nat. Cath. Ednl. Assn., Washington, 1986—. Bd. dirs. Am. Forum, Edn. Systems, Kotz Grad. Sch. Mgmt., Minn., UN Assn. Greater Scranton. Spanish Govt. grantee, 1965-67; OAS grantee, 1967-68; Fulbright grantee, 1972-73. Mem. Am. Assn. Execs., Assn. Cath. Colls. and Univs., Internat. Fedn. Cath. Univs. (v.p. 1980—), Delta Epsilon Sigma, Delta Kappa Gamma. Roman Catholic. Club: Zonta. Office: Nat Cath Ednl Assn Suite 100 1077 30th St NW Washington DC 20007

MCNAUGHT, JUDITH, author; b. San Luis Obispo, Calif., May 10, 1944; d. Clifford Harris and Rosetta (Prince) Spath; m. J. Michael McNaught, June 1, 1974 (dec. 1983); children—Whitney, Clayton. B.S., Northwestern U., 1966. Pres. Pro-Temps, Inc., St. Louis, 1983-84, Eagle Syndication, Inc., Dallas, 1987—. Author Tender Triumph, 1983 (Critics Choice award 1983); Double Standards, 1984; Whitney, My Love (Best Hist. Novelist 1985), Once and Always, 1987 (Best Hist. Novel 1987), Something Wonderful, 1988. Mem. Romance Writers Assn. Roman Catholic. Club: Gleneagles Country (Plano, Tex.). Avocations: racquetball, skiing.

MCNEAL, BARBARA LOUISE, contract administrator; b. Cleve., Oct. 6, 1953; d. John Wesley Jones and Ruth Mae (Fields) Johnson; m. Ronald William McNeal, Apr. 12, 1979; 1 child, Rian David. BA in Psychology, Case Western Res. U., 1975; MA in Bus., Cen. Mich. U., 1979. CPA, Va. Mgr. data configuration Tex. Instruments, Inc., Dallas, 1979; counselor Arlington (Va.) County Pub. Schs., 1979-80; sr. staff, contract adminstr. JWK Internat. Corp., Annandale, Va., 1980-83; contract adminstr. Tech. Applications, Inc., Alexandria, Va., 1983-84, mgr. contracts, 1984-85, dir. contracts, 1985-86, bus. mgr., program mgr., 1987—; pvt. practice acctg., Dumfries, Va., 1985—. Ct. rep. Williamstown H.D. Assn., Dumfries, 1985—. Served with U.S. Army, 1976-79. Mem. Nat. Assn. Accts. (team capt. 1986—), Nat. Contract Mgmt. Assn., Nat. Assn. Black Accts. Methodist. Office: Tech Applications Inc 6101 Stevenson Ave Alexandria VA 22304

MCNEAL, GRACE HOOPER, military officer; b. Columbus, Ind., Mar. 5, 1943; d. Thomas Fluharty and Grace Hooper (Smith) McN. AA, St. Mary's Jr. Coll., 1963; BS, The Johns Hopkins U., 1969, MEd, 1972. RN. Commd. 2d lt. USAF, 1972, advanced through grades to lt. col., 1987; staff nurse Greater Balt. Med. Ctr., 1966-68; instr. sch. of nursing Ch. Home and Hosp., Balt., 1968-71; ednl. coordinator USAF Hosp., Sheppard AFB, Tex., 1972-74, Elmendorf AFB, Ark., 1974-77; med. systems analyst Office of the Air Force Surgeon Gen., Washington, 1977-80, med. readiness tng. mgr., 1983-85; med. readiness tng. mgr. Office of Commd. Surgeon, Ramstein AFB, Fed. Republic Germany, 1980-83; ednl. coordinator USAF Hosp., Pease AFB, N.H., 1985—; instr. N.H. Vocat. Tech. Inst., 1985—. Instr. ARC, 1958—, Am. Heart Assn., 1985—. Mem. Aviation Space and Environ. Medicine, Air Force Assn., The Jr. League. Republican. Presbyterian. Home: PSC #3 Box 16308 APO San Francisco CA 96432-0006 Office: USAF Regional Med Ctr Clark/SGHNE APO San Francisco CA 96274-5300

MCNEAL, NANCY LYNN, educational superintendent; b. Marshall, Tex., June 14, 1947; d. Noel Carneal and Billie Maxine (Kinser) Brackman; m. Paul Leman McNeal Jr., June 5, 1965; children: Jeff, Devona. BS, East Tex. Bapt. Coll., 1973; MEd, Stephen F. Austin State U., 1977; EdD, East Tex. State U., 1983. Tchr. St. Joseph's Cath. Sch., Marshall, 1973-74, Karnack (Tex.) Ind. Sch. Dist., 1974-76, Carthage (Tex.) Ind. Sch. Dist., 1976-80; curriculum dir. Jefferson (Tex.) Ind. Sch. Dist., 1980-82, high sch. prin., 1982-86; dep. supt. Fairfield (Tex.) Ind. Sch. Dist., 1986—. Mem. Tex. Assn. Sch. Adminstrs., Tex. Council Women Sch. Execs. (pres. 1988—), Delta Kappa Gamma, Kappa Delta Pi, Phi Delta Kappa. Democrat. Baptist. Home: 563 E Main Fairfield TX 75840 Office: Fairfield Ind Sch Dist 615 Post Oak Rd Fairfield TX 75840

MCNEAR, BARBARA BAXTER, communications executive, consultant; b. Chgo., Oct. 9, 1939; d. Carl Henden and Alice Gertrude (Parrish) Baxter; m. Robert Erskine McNear, Apr. 13, 1968 (div. 1981); 1 child, Amanda Baxter; m. Glenn Philip Eisen, June 7, 1987. B.S. in Journalism, Northwestern U., 1961. Editorial asst. Scott Foresman & Co., Chgo., 1961; pub. relations dir. Market Facts Inc., Chgo., 1961-63; acct. supr. Philip Lesly Co., Chgo., 1963-68, 69; acct. exec. Burson-Marsteller, Chgo., 1968; dir. communications CNA Fin. Corp., Chgo., 1969-74; dir. pub. relations Gould Inc., Chgo., 1974; v.p. Harris Bank., Chgo., 1974-80, Fireman's Fund Ins. Co., San Francisco, 1980-83; sr. v.p. First Chgo. Corp., 1983-86; v.p. communications Xerox Fin. Services, Inc., Norwalk, Conn., 1987—. Bd. visitors Medill Sch. Journalism Northwestern U., Evanston, Ill.; bd. dirs. Pace Inst. Mem. Pub. Relations Soc. Am., Nat. Investor Relations Inst. (pres. Chgo. chpt. 1974-75, bd. dirs. Chgo. chpt.). Episcopalian. Club: Cliffdwellers. Home: 23 Telva Rd Wilton CT 06897 Office: Xerox Fin Services Inc 401 Merritt 7 Norwalk CT 06856

MCNEELY, JERRY J., health care administrator; b. Dallas, June 3, 1943; d. Delbert C. and Nina (Orr) McN. m. Jerry D. Elrod, Aug. 4, 1962 (div. 1970); 1 child, Joel D.; m. David W. Tees, July 26, 1985. BS, U. Nebr., 1976; MS, North Tex. State U., 1984. Project dir. Planned Parenthood of Am., Kansas City, Mo., 1970-71; exec. dir. Nova Health Systems, Dallas, 1972-80; med. office adminstr. Kaiser Found. Health Plan, Dallas, 1980-83; v.p. ops. Sheppard Dental Ctrs., Dallas, 1983—; cons. Fountainhead, Arlington, Tex., Hollis H. Bond Corp., Arlington, 1st Commonwealth, Chgo. Co-founder, v.p. Clergy Counseling Ctr., Omaha, 1969-70; v.p. Dallas Women Against Rape, 1977-78. Mem. Dental Group Mgmt. Assn. Democrat. Home: 218 Westview Terr Arlington TX 76103

MC NEESE, WILMA WALLACE, social worker; b. Chgo., Apr. 30, 1946; d. Nettie Fletcher Wallace; student Wilson City Coll., 1964-66; B.A., So. Ill. U., 1969; M.S.W., Loyola U., Chgo., 1976; m. Mose D. McNeese, Dec. 27, 1969; children—Derrick, Christina. Program coordinator Intensive Tng. and Employment Program, East St. Louis, Ill., 1970-71; methods and procedures adviser Ill. Dept. Pub. Aid, Chgo., 1972-73; social work intern Robbins (Ill.) Presch. Center, 1974; with U.S. Probation Office, Chgo., 1975; officer U.S. Pretrial Services Agy., Chgo., 1976-87; chief U.S. pretrial services officer for western dist. Pa., 1987—; fieldwork instr. Aurora Coll., 1981, Chgo. State U., 1981-82; grad. fieldwork instr. U. Ill. Social Work Dept., 1986. Recipient Community Service award Village of Robbins, 1975; advanced tng. cert. Fed. Jud. Center.; cert. social worker, Ill. Mem. Nat. Assn. Social Workers, Acad. Cert. Social Workers, Fedn. Probation Officers Assn. Baptist. Home: 833 Chalmers Pl Pittsburgh PA 15243 Office: 1000 Liberty Ave Room 315 Pittsburgh PA 15222

MCNEIL, BARBARA JOYCE, radiologist; b. Cambridge, Mass., Feb. 11, 1941; d. Archibald Pius and Katherine (Joyce) McN. A.B., Emmanuel Coll., 1962; M.D., Harvard U., 1966, Ph.D., 1972. Diplomate: Am. Bd. Nuclear Medicine. Intern Mass. Gen. Hosp., Boston, 1966-67, resident in nuclear medicine, 1971-73; prof. radiology and clin. epidemiology Harvard Med. Sch. and Brigham & Women's Hosp., Boston, 1983—, dir. ctr. for cost effective, 1980—; chmn. dept. health care policy Harvard Med. Sch., 1988—; chmn. Blue Cross-Mass. Hosp. Assn. Fund for coop. Innovation, 1981—; mem. Prospective Payment Assessment Commn. Editor: Critical Issues in Medical Technology, 1982; contbr. articles to profl. jours. Fellow AAAS; mem. Inst. Medicine, Fleischner Soc., Nat. Council on Radiation Protection, Am. Coll. Radiology, Soc. Nuclear Medicine. Office: Brigham and Women's Hosp Dept Radiology 75 Francis St Boston MA 02115

MCNEIL, GLENOLA CHRISTINE, real estate professional; b. Hillsdale, Mich., June 21, 1931; d. Harold Reynolds and S. Joyce (Caywood) Brown; divorced; children: David Lawrence McNeil, Matthew Wayne McNeil. Lic. real estate agt., Mich. With The Real Estate Ctr., Hillsdale, Mich., 1977-83, assoc. broker, 1983-86; state pres.p. Realtor's Land Inst., Hillsdale, 1986—; regional v.p. "Big 10", 1988—. Named Realtor of Yr. Lenawee County Bd. Realtors. Address: 917 1/2 E Butler St Adrian MI 49221

MCNEIL, JEAN ANNE, lawyer; b. Boone, Iowa, June 23, 1954; d. Ronald Dean and Marjorie Ruth (Minson) McNeil; m. David W. Dunn. BS in Microbiology, U. Iowa, 1976; JD, U. Ill., 1981. Bar: Iowa 1981. Ptnr., Davis, Hockenberg, Wine, Brown, Koehn & Shors, Des Moines, 1981—; part-time instr. Des Moines Area Community Coll., Ankeny campus, 1983. Mem. instnl. rev. com. Mercy Hosp. Med. Ctr., Des Moines, 1983—; active YMCA. Recipient Freshman Chemistry award Des Moines Area Community Coll., 1973. Mem. ABA, Iowa State Bar Assn., Polk County Bar Assn., Polk County Women's Bar Assn., Phi Delta Phi. Democrat. Methodist. Office: Davis Hockenberg Wine et al 2300 Financial Ctr Des Moines IA 50309

MCNEILL, VICKI S., mayor. m. James P. McNeill; 2 children. BS, Simmons Coll., 1947. Appointed mem. Spokane (Wash.) City Council, 1982, elected mem., 1983-85; mayor City of Spokane, 1985—. Pres. Wash. State Pavilion Fund; trustee Spokane Symphony Soc., Spokane C. of C., Spokane Centennial Commn. Recipient Golden Deeds award Exchange Club, 1975, Distinction award Women in Communications, 1979, Outstanding Achievement Leadership award YWCA, 1983. Office: Office of Mayor W 808 Spokane Falls Blvd Spokane WA 99201 *

MCNENY, MARGARET RYCE, occupational therapist; b. Richmond, Va., July 3, 1954; d. Robert and Anna Margaret (Bell) Ryce; m. Samuel Thomas McNeny II; 1 child, Samuel Thomas McNeny III. BS in occupational therapy, Va. Commonwealth U., 1976. Cert. Am. Occupational Therapy Bd. Staff occupational therapist rehab. unit Med. Coll. Va. Hosps., Richmond, 1977-85, occupational therapist head injury rehab. unit, 1985—. Contbr. articles to profl. jours. Mem. Am. Occupational Therapy Assn., Va. Occupational Therapy Assn. (legis. chmn. 1984), Am. Congress Rehab. Medicine, Nat. Head Injury Found., Va. Head Injury Found., Internat. Assn. Cognitive Retraining (steering com.). Baptist. Club: Women's of Walton Park. Home: 13201 Groveton Terr Midlothian VA 23113 Office: Med Coll Va Hosps Box 428 MCV Station Richmond VA 23298

MCNITT, MIRIAM ELIZABETH, craft artist; b. Syracuse, Kans., Feb. 13, 1916; d. Frank Dunham and Nina (Kirkpatrick) Davis; student Coll. of Sequoias, 1952—; m. William O'Neal McNitt, June 30, 1934; children: Nela (Mrs. David J. Dunaway), Nancy (Mrs. Bernard K. Knoll). Accountant, office mgr. Delta Mosquito Abatement Dist., Visalia, Calif., 1951-56; office mgr. Hathaway Nursery, Visalia, 1956-58; office mgr. Anchor of Calif., Fresno, 1958-62; personal studio craft artist, Fresno, 1962-68, 75—; adminstrv. asst. Yosemite Nat. Park, Calif., 1968-72, Merced Coll., 1972-75. One-man show McHenry Mus., Modesto, Calif., 1985, Carnegie Ctr. for Arts, Turlock, Calif., 1986, U. Pacific, 1984; exhibited Elders Gallery, Fresno, 1980, Ansel Adams Studio, Yosemite Nat. Park, 1976, 81, Le Entrepreneur Gallery, Fresno, Bank of Calif., Modesto, 1982, Farmers & Mchts Bank, Modesto, 1982; exhibited juried shows ACC S.W. Crafts Fair, San Francisco, Presdl. Mus., Odessa, Tex., The Art Place, Pen Women's Art Show, Modesto, Gallo Winery, Modesto, Yosemite Nat. Park, Fresno Arts Center, mural for McHenry Mus., Modesto, Calif., Profl. Artists Show, Fresno, Needlework Show, Woodlawn Plantation, Mt. Vernon, Va., No. Calif. Artists Show, Crocker Mus., Sacramento, State Women's Club (blue, red ribbon awards), San Francisco, U. Pacific Gallery, Stockton, Calif.; miscellaneous programs on stitchery techniques; exhibitor Manteca Quilt Show (Calif.); exhibitor, acquisition chmn. Luncheon and Quilt Show, McHenry Found.; commd. work Yosemite Nat. Park, McHenry Mus., Modesto, Calif. Vol. mem. Area 4 Neighborhood Council, Fresno, 1979—; Christmas Seal sale chmn. Tulare Kings Counties Tb Assn., 1956-57, sec.-treas., 1954-58; v.p. Fresno County Epilepsy Soc., 1965-68; mem. docent council McHenry Mansion Found., 1983-86; active Camp Fire Girls, Reseda, Calif., Van Nuys and North Hollywood (Calif.) Girl Scouts, Visalia and El Portal (Calif.) 4-H Clubs. Mem. Calif. Congress Parents and Tchrs. (life), Visalia Bus. and Profl. Women (radio TV chmn. 1956-58), Am. Craftsmans Council N.Y., Central Calif. Art League, Modesto Symphony Assn., Turlock (Calif.) Regional Arts Council, Benicia (Calif.) Community Arts. San Joaquin Valley Town Hall,

Yosemite Natural History Assn., Nat. Mus. Women in the Arts (charter). Republican. Club: Calif. Fedn. Women's Clubs (art chmn. 1965-67), Modesto Woman's, Progressive Woman's. Address: 1141 Cambridge Ct Modesto CA 95350

MCNULTY, NANCY GILLESPIE, business writer, consultant; b. Greenville, Pa., May 1, 1919; d. Stanley A. and Bess (Anthony) Gillespie; m. Arthur P. McNulty, July 16, 1942 (dec. 1961); 1 son, Terence. BA, Thiel Coll., 1940; MA, NYU, 1948. Industry analyst Equity Corp., 1940-42; writer spl. devel. project Time Inc., N.Y.C., 1942-45; freelance bus. writer/researcher, 1957-67; ind. bus. cons., N.Y.C., 1967—; founder, dir. Internat. Survey of Mgmt. Edn., N.Y.C., 1968—; cons. Chase (Bank) World Info. Service, Japan Soc., N.Y. State Commn. on Edn., Walker & Co., Time Inc., Reader's Digest, Doubleday, Time/Life Co., Fortune, Am. Heritage. Author: Management Education to Meet the Challenge of Tomorrow, 1968; Training Managers: The International Guide, 1969; Markets of the Seventies, 1970; Newspaper Publishing, 1972; Kamaz, the Billion Dollar Beginning, 1974; European Management Education Comes of Age, 1975; Business Education and Training of Americans for Business Relations with Japan, 1977; Management Development by Action Learning, 1979; Management Development Programs: The World's Best, 1980; Action Learning's International Adaptation, 1983; The International Directory of Executive Education, 1985. Ford Found. scholar, 1968, 78. Fellow Acad. Mgmt.; mem. N.Am. Mgmt. Council (bd. dirs.), Internat. Cons. Found., European Found. Mgmt. Devel., Internat. Found. Action Learning. Episcopalian. Club: Yale of N.Y.C. Home and Office: 55 W 89th St New York NY 10024

MCNULTY, SHARON LEE, lawyer; b. Tulsa, Sept. 28, 1950. BS, Cornell U., 1972; JD, Union U., 1977; MPA, Maxwell Sch. Citizenship and Pub. Affairs, 1983. Bar: N.Y. 1978, U.S. Dist. Ct. (we. dist.) N.Y. 1978. Asst. pub. defender Monroe Co. Pub. Defenders Office, 1977-80; lectr., clin. staff atty. Syracuse (N.Y.) U. Coll. Law, 1980-82; assoc. counsel Gov's. Office: Dir. of Criminal Justice, Albany, 1983-84; asst. counsel N.Y. State Police, Albany, 1984-87; staff counsel N.Y. State Commn. on Govt. Integrity, 1987—; Mem. adv. bd. exec. tng. program Victim Services Agy., N.Y.C., 1987—; speaker on police liability, condr. seminars in field. Spl. contbns. editor Law Review, 1976-77; contbr. articles to profl. jours. Fellow Rockefeller Inst., 1982. Mem. Am. Acad. Forensic Scis., N.Y. State Bar Assn., N.Y. State Dist. Attys. Assn., N.Y. State Assn. Chiefs of Police. Democrat. Roman Catholic. Home: 111 Knollwood Terr Albany NY 12203 Office: NY State Commn on Govt Integrity 330 Broadway Albany NY 12207

MCNUTT, KRISTEN WALLWORK, consumer affairs executive; b. Nashville, Nov. 17, 1941; d. Gerald M. and Lee Wallwork; m. David McNutt, Sept. 13, 1969. BA in Chemistry, Duke U., 1963; MS in Nutrition, Columbia U., 1965; PhD in Biochemistry, Vanderbilt U., 1970; JD, DePaul U., 1984. Bar: N.Y. 1984, D.C. 1984. Exec. dir. Nat. Nutrition Consortium, Washington, 1979-81; asst. prof. pub. health U. Ill., Chgo., 1981-83; assoc. dir. Good Housekeeping Inst., N.Y.C., 1982-85; v.p. consumer affairs Kraft Inc., Glenview, Ill., 1985—. Author: Nutrition and Food Choices, 1979; editor: Sugars in Nutrition, 1975. Bd. dirs. Better Bus. Bur., Chgo. and No. Ill., 1986—. Mem. Fedn. Am. Socs. Experimental Biology (Congl. Sci. fellow), N.Y. Bar Assn., D.C. Bar Assn., Soc. for Nutrition Edn. (pres. 1983-84), Am. Inst. Nutrition, Soc. Consumer Affairs Profls. Home: 1742 Asbury Ave Evanston IL 60201 Office: Kraft Inc Kraft Court 2-N Glenview IL 60025

MCPHEE, PENELOPE L. ORTNER, television producer, writer; b. Louisville, Nov. 24, 1947; d. Alvin B. and Loyce (Levenson) Ortner; m. Raymond Hunter McPhee, Aug. 25, 1973; 1 child, Cameron Brook. BA with honors, Wellesley Coll., 1969; MS in Journalism, Columbia U., 1970. Dir. pub. relations Am. Sch. in Switzerland, Lugano, 1970-71; writer, researcher Sta. WTVJ-TV, Miami, Fla., 1972-73; prof. journalism and film Fleming Coll., Florence, Italy, 1972-73; free-lance writer, producer, Miami, 1973-80; writer, cons. Burger King Corp., Miami, 1979; exec. producer for cultural programming Sta. WPBT-TV, Miami, 1980—; instr. documentary filmmaking Fla. Internat. U., 1987-88. Author: Martin Luther King, Jr.: A Documentary, Montgomery to Memphis, 1976 (Best of Best Books award ALA 1983), Beauty Ency., 1978, King Remembered, 1986, Your Future in Space, 1986; contbg. author: Underwater Photography for Everyone, 1978. Recipient Iris award Nat. Assn. TV Program Execs., 1983, Children's Programming award Corp. for Pub. Broadcasting, 1982, local program award Corp. Pub. Broadcasting, 1984, Emmy award, 1984, N.Y. State Martin Luther King, Jr. medal of freedom, 1986; Sackett scholar Columbia U., 1970. Trustee Dade County Art in Pub. Places Trust, 1985. Mem. Women in Communications. Club: Miami Wellesley (v.p. 1976-80, admissions rep. 1980-85). Office: 7221 SW 166th St Miami FL 33157

MCPHERSON, BRENDA GAYLE, psychologist; b. Higgins, Tex., Dec. 1, 1952; d. Leo Ray and Winifred Georgia (Ruf) Schwab; m. Hollace Keller McPherson, Jan. 28, 1973. AS, St. Peter Jr. Coll., Clearwater, Fla., 1972; BA, U. Cen. Fla., 1982, MS, 1985. Counselor Orlando (Fla.) Regional Med. Ctr., 1983—, sch. psychologist, 1985—, developmentalist, 1986—; clin. supr. U. Cen. Fla., Orlando, 1984—. Co-producer (video) From Womb to NICU: A Stressful Transition, 1986. Mem. Nat. Assn. Sch. Psychology, Fla. Assn. Sch. Psychology, Fla. Consortium Newborn Intervention Programs, Parents of Premature and High-Risk Infants Internat., Bereaved Parents Resource Network.

MCPHERSON, CHERRY, organization development administrator; b. Dallas, Sept. 23, 1947; d. James C. Jr. and Billie (Cherry) McP.; m. John S. Turner, July 5, 1976 (div. 1980); m. V. Wayne Widdis, June, 11, 1982. BA, Augusta (Ga.) Coll., 1970, MEd, 1975, EdD, 1978. Tchr. Augusta County Bd. of Edn., 1970-73, head media ctr., 1973-74; research asst. U. Ga., Athens, 1974-76, research coordinator, 1976-78; asst. prof. Ohio State U., Columbus, 1978-82; dir. orgns. and edn. effectiveness Women's Coll. Hosp., Toronto, 1982-85, adminstrv. dir., 1985-87; orgn. devel. adminstr. San Diego Gas & Electric, 1988—; cons. edn and health related orgns., U.S., Can., 1975—; spkr. in field. Mem. adv. bd. Centre Stage Forum, Toronto, 1985-86. Mem. Nat. Conf. for Generalists in Med. Edn. (co-founder, chmn. 1980-81), Am. Ednl. Research Assn., Am. Soc. of Tng. and Devel., Phi Kappa Phi, Kappa Delta Phi. Presbyterian. Office: San Diego Gas & Electric San Diego CA 92112

MCPHERSON, GAIL, advertising and real estate executive; b. Fort Worth; d. Garland and Daphne McP. Student U. Tex.-Austin; B.A., M.S., CUNY. Advt. sales exec. Harper's Bazaar mag., N.Y.C., 1974-76; sr. v.p., fashion mktg. dir. L'Officiel/USA mag., N.Y.C., 1976-80; fashion mgr. Town and Country mag., N.Y.C., 1980-82; v.p. advt. and mktg. Ultra mag., Tex. and N.Y.C., 1982-84; fragrance, jewelry and automotive mgr. M. Mag., N.Y.C., 1984-85; sr. real estate sales exec. Fredric M. Reed & Co., Inc., N.Y.C., 1985—. Sponsor Southampton Hosp. Benefit Com., N.Y.; mem. jr. com. Mannes Sch. Music, N.Y.C., Henry St. Settlement, N.Y.C. Mem. Fashion Group N.Y., Advt. Women N.Y., Real Estate Bd. N.Y. Tex. Alumni Assn. of N.Y. (v.p.). Republican. Presbyterian. Clubs: Corviglia (St. Moritz, Switzerland), Doubles, El Morocco (mem. jr. com. 1976-77), Le Club (N.Y.C.). Home: 429 E 52d St New York NY 10022 Office: 405 Park Ave New York NY 10022

MCPHERSON, MARY PATTERSON, college president; b. Abington, Pa., May 14, 1935; d. John B. and Marjorie Hoffman (Higgins) McP. A.B., Smith Coll., 1957, LL.D., 1981; M.A., U. Del., 1960; Ph.D., Bryn Mawr Coll., 1969; LL.D. (hon.), Juniata Coll., 1975, Princeton U., 1984, U. Rochester, 1984; Litt.D. (hon.), Haverford Coll., 1980; L.H.D. (hon.), Lafayette Coll., 1982, U. Pa., 1985; LHD (hon.), Med. Coll. Pa., 1985. Instr. philosophy U. Del., 1959-61; asst., fellow and lectr. dept. philosophy Bryn Mawr Coll., 1961-63, asst. dean, 1964-69, assoc. dean, 1969-70; dean Bryn Mawr Coll. (Undergrad. Coll.), 1970-78, assoc. prof., from 1970; acting pres. Bryn Mawr Coll., 1976-77, pres., 1978—; dir. Provident Nat. Bank of Phila., Provident Nat. Corp., 1979-83, Bell Telephone Co. Pa.; mem. commn. on women in higher edn. Am. Council on Edn., bd. dirs., 1979-82. Bd. dirs. Agnes Irwin Sch., 1971—; bd. dirs. Shipley Sch., 1972—, Phillips Exeter Acad., 1973-76, Wilson Coll., 1976-79, Greater Phila. Movement, 1973-77, Internat. House of Phila., 1974-76, Josiah Macy, Jr. Found., 1977—, Carnegie Found. for Advancement Teaching, 1978-86, Univ. Mus., Phila., 1977-79, University City Sci. Center, 1979-85, Brookings Inst., 1984—, Phila. Contributionship, 1985—, Carnegie Corp. N.Y., 1985—, Nat. Humanities Ctr., 1986—, Amherst Coll., 1986—. Mem. Soc. for Ancient Greek Philosophy, Am. Philos. Soc. Clubs: Fullerton, Cosmopolitan. Office: Bryn Mawr Coll Office of Pres Merion Ave Bryn Mawr PA 19010

MCPHETRIDGE, EMMIE RICHESON, insurance company representative; b. Kobe, Japan, Nov. 5, 1951; came to U.S., 1953; d. James Edward Lloyd and Kazue (Tanaka) Fuller; m. Ronald Wayne McPhetridge, Apr. 27, 1985; children: David Keith, Midori Blake. Student Middle Tenn. State U., 1967-71, U. South Fla., 1972, U. Tenn., Chattanooga, 1982. Adminstrv. asst. ARC, Tampa, Fla., 1972-75; office services rep. Manpower Inc., Chattanooga, 1975-81; supr. records and retention Blue Cross Blue Shield, Chattanooga, 1981-84, supr. claims control, 1984-86; provider service rep. Blue Cross Care Choice, Knoxville, 1986—. Vol. tchr. Chattanooga Area Literacy Movement, 1981-85, Outstanding Contbn. award, 1983. Mem. Nat. Assn. Female Execs., Am. Records Mgrs. Assn., Chattanooga C. of C. (vice chmn. diplomat corps, program chmn.), Adminstrv. Mgmt. Soc. (past pres., chmn. bd.), Acad. Cert. Adminstrv. Mgrs. Republican. Baptist. Avocations: writing; dancing; reading. Home: 6822 Cochise Dr Knoxville TN 37918 Office: Blue Cross Blue Shield CareChoise 1611 Magnolia Ave NE Knoxville TN 37917

MCQOUWN, JUDITH HERSHKOWITZ, publishing consultant; b. N.Y.C., Apr. 8, 1941; d. Frederick Ephraim and Pearl (Rosenberg) Hershkowitz; m. Harrison Roth, Dec. 8, 1985. BA, Hunter Coll., 1963; postgrad., N.Y. Inst. Fin., 1965-67. Analyst Walston; chief underwriting Div. Mcpl. Securities City of N.Y., 1972-73; pres. Judith H. McQuown and Co., N.Y.C., 1973—. Author: Inc. Yourself: How to Profit by Setting Up Your Own Corporation, 1977, 79,, 81, 84, 86, 87, The Fashion Survival Manual, 1981, Playing the Takeover Market, 1982, How to Profit After You Incorporate Yourself, 1985, the Passionate Shopper's Guide to the British Isles, 1987, The Passionate Shopper's Guide to the Continent, 1988; contbg. editor Boardroom Reports Mag., 1978-87, Fin. World Mag., 1985-87. Mem. Am. Soc. Journalists and Authors. Office: 444 E 86th St New York City NY 10028

MCQUAID, PHYLLIS W., state legislator; b. Mar. 26, 1928; m. Joseph McQuaid; 8 children. Ind. Rep. mem. Minn. State Senate 1983—. Office: 4130 Yosemite Ave S Saint Louis Park MN 55416 *

MCQUEEN, KATHRYN LYNN, special education and English language educator; b. Kansas City, Mo., Dec. 4, 1952; d. Hurtle Grover and Ruby Janet (Henderson) McQ. AA, Muskegon (Mich.) Community Coll., 1972; BA in Social Work, Mich. State U., 1974; postgrad. in counseling and guidance, U. of Consortium, 1974; cert. in elem. teaching, U. Tenn., 1978; postgrad., U. Madrid, U. Spain, 1980; MS in Edn., U. Tenn., 1981. Cert. spl. edn. and elem. tchr., Mich. Senate aide Mich. State Senate, Lansing, 1975; assistance payments worker Oceana County Dept. of Social Services, Hart, Mich., 1975-76; counselor Tenn. State Dept. of Corrections, Jackson, 1977; instr. lang. arts, reading Obion County Migrant Edn. Program, Union City, 1979; tchr. spl. edn. Black Oak Elem. Sch., Obion County, Tenn., 1979-86; tchr. English Colego Hamilton Elem. Sch., Mexico City, 1986-87; tchr. pre-first The Am. Sch. Found., Mexico City, 1987—; substitute tchr. Cen. Elem. Sch., 1978; instr. gen. ednl. devel. Obion County Sch. Participant Chimes for Charity, seven yrs.; vol. Spl. Olympics, seven yrs.; sponsor Easter Seals. Mem. Nat. Ednl. Assn., Tenn. Ednl. Assn. (spl. tutor), Council for Exceptional Children. Democrat. Home: Rt 2 Box 168 Garrett-Williams Union City TN 38261

MCQUEEN, SANDRA MARILYN, educator; b. Greenville, S.C., Nov. 30, 1948; d. Clement Edgar and Sara Elizabeth (Gentry) McQ.; BA, Presbyn. Coll., Clinton, S.C., 1970; MA, Presbyn. Sch. Christian Edn., Richmond, Va., 1972; PhD, Ga. State U., 1987. Dir. Christian edn. Rock Spring Presbyn. Ch., Atlanta, 1972-74; tchr. Thomasville Heights Elem. Sch., Atlanta, 1974-80; tchr. gifted students Sutton Middle Sch., Atlanta, 1980 , chmn. dept. gifted students, 1982—; ex-officio div. Christian Concern Atlanta Presbytery, 1985-86; cons. in field. Mem. chancel choir Rock Spring Presbyn. Ch., chmn. Mission Com., 1987—; mem. camps and confs. Presbyn. Synod S.E.; mem. Women's Advocacy Task Force, Atlanta Presbytery, 1980—, co-pres., 1985-86; mem. Young Careers of High Mus., 1985—; chmn. Missions Rock Spring Presbyn. Ch., 1987-88; elder Rock Spring Presbyn. Ch., 1986-88; sec. Calvin Task Force, 1974-79. Named Sutton Tchr. of Yr., 1985. Mem. Assn. Supervision and Curriculum Devel., NEA, Ga. Edn. Assn., Atlanta Assn. Educators, Ch. Sch. Tchrs., Presbyn. Coll. Alumni Assn. (pres. Atlanta club 1982-83), Ga. State U. Doctoral Fellows, Sigma Kappa, Kappa Delta Pi. Office: 4360 Powers Ferry Rd NW Atlanta GA 30327

MCQUERN, MARCIA ALICE, newspaper editor; b. Riverside, Calif., Sept. 3, 1942; d. Arthur Carlyle and Dorothy Louise (Krupke) Knopf; m. Lynn Morris McQuern, June 7, 1969. BA in Polit. Sci., U. Calif., Santa Barbara, 1964; MS in Journalism, Norhtwestern U., 1966. Reporter The Press-Enterprise, Riverside, 1966-72, city editor, 1972-74, capitol corrs., 1975-78, dep. mng. editor news, 1984-85, mng. editor news, 1985-87, exec. mng. editor, 1987—; asst. metro editor The Sacramento Bee, 1974-75; editor state and polit. news The San Diego Union, 1978-79, city editor, 1979-84; juror Pulitzer Prize in Journalism, 1982, 83. Mem. editorial bd. Calif. Lawyer mag., San Francisco, 1983—. Recipient Journalism award Calif. State Bar Assn., 1967, Sweepstakes award Twin Counties Press Club, Riverside and San Bernardino, 1972. Mem. Am. Soc. Newspaper Editors, Calif. Soc. Newspaper Editors, AP Mng. Editors, Soc. Profl. Journalists, U. Calif. Alumni Assn. (bd. dirs. 1983—). Home: 5717 Bedford Dr Riverside CA 92506 Office: The Press-Enterprise 3512 14th St Riverside CA 92501 *

MCQUIDE, PAMELA ANN, nurse; b. Racine, Wis., Oct. 7, 1951; d. Arthur C. and Carol Jean (Frudenwald) Massmann; m. Lawrence J. Drexler, Apr., 1972 (div. May, 1980); m. Scott Little McQuide, Sept. 4, 1982. Diploma in nursing, Columbia Hosp. Sch. of Nursing, Milw., 1977; BA in French, U. Wis., 1979; BSN, Alverno Coll., 1986. Staff nurse Columbia Hosp., Milw., 1978-80, unit tchr., staff nurse, 1980-83, asst. head nurse, 1980-83, nurse mgr., 1985-87, patient services coordinator, 1986-87, nurse mgr., 1987—. Columnist Nursing Dimension, 1986-87, Synapse, 1987; interviewer TV show Milwaukee Observer, 1987. CPR instr., trainer Am. Heart Assn., Milw., 1978—; mem. steering com. Coalition for Recruitment and Retention of Nurses, Milw., 1987—, Sane Nuclear Energy, Washington, 1986-87. Mem. Am. Assn. Neurosci. Nurses (legis. chair 1987—, rep. 1988—), Am. Nurses Assn., Wis. Nurses Assn. (chmn. Milw. Dist. legis. com. 1987—, pres.-elect 1988—), Nat. League of Nursing, Nat. Orgn. Female Execs., Alliance Francaise. Democrat. Episcopalian. Home: 4474 N Murray Shorewood WI 53211 Office: Columbia Hosp 2025 E Newport Shorewood WI 53211

MCQUILLA, KATHLEEN ROSE, law enforcement official; b. Jersey City, July 4, 1957; d. Richard and Mary (Glover) McQ. B.A., St. Peter's Coll., Jersey City, 1979; M.A., Seton Hall U., 1983. Asst. sociol. researcher St. Peter's Coll., Jersey City, 1978-79; youth counselor Hudson County C.E.T.A., Bayonne, N.J., 1978-82; tchr. Bayonne Bd. Edn., 1979-80; mgr. Smitty's Auto Repair, Bayonne, 1979—; alcohol counselor Womanpower Projects, Newark, 1982; probation/hearing officer Hudson County Probation Dept., Jersey City, 1983-86; child support hearing officer, Supreme Ct. N.J., 1986—. Co-coordinator NAACP Youth Group, Bayonne, 1980—; big sister Hudson County Big Bros./Sisters, Jersey City, 1978-80. Mem. Hudson County Reading Council, Nat. Black Alcohol Council, Nat. Soc. Notaries. Methodist. Office: Adminstrv Office of the Cts Richard J Hughes Complex Trenton NJ 00625

MCQUILLAN, FRANCES CARROLL, artist; b. Chgo.; d. Thomas William and Jane Ellen (Connors) Carroll; B.A., Caldwell Coll., 1975; postgrad. Parsons Sch. Design, 1932; m. Edward J. McQuillan, Apr. 23, 1941; children—Thomas, Kathleen. Fashion artist, N.Y. and Chgo. papers, 1933-35; freelance window display, N.Y. and N.J., 1936-38; instr. art Yard Art Sch., 1967-69, 83-84, Montclair Art Mus. Sch. Art (N.J.), 1950—; one person shows Argent Galleries, N.Y.C., Seton Hall U., Newark, Caldwell (N.J.) Coll.; exhibited in group shows Nat. Arts Club, N.Y.C., Dayton Art Inst., Conn. Acad. Fine Arts, Seton Hall U., Paris, Exposition Continental, Monaco and Dieppe, France, Mus. Fine Arts, Springfield, Mass. Mem. Am. Artists Profl. League, N.J. Watercolor Soc., Montclair Art Mus., Art Centre N.J. Home: 3 Godfrey Rd Upper Montclair NJ 07043 Office: South Mountain Ave Montclair Mus Montclair NJ 07042

MC QUILLAN, MARGARET MARY, publishing company executive; b. N.Y.C.; d. John A. and Margaret (Higgins) McQ.; A.B., Coll. New Rochelle, 1945; M.A. Columbia U., 1948. With Harcourt Brace Jovanovich, Inc. (formerly Harcourt, Brace & World), N.Y.C., 1949—; asst. sec., 1960-70, sec., 1971—, v.p. 1975-78, adminstrv. v.p., 1978-80, sr. v.p., 1980—. Home: 125 Crestwood Ave Tuckahoe NY 10707 Office: Harcourt Brace Jovanovich Inc Orlando FL 32887

MCQUOWN, JUDITH HERSHKOWITZ, author, consultant; b. N.Y.C., Apr. 8, 1941; d. Frederick Ephraim and Pearl (Rosenberg) H.; m. Michael L. McQuown, Jan. 13, 1969 (div. 1980); m. Harrison Roth, Dec. 8, 1985. AB, Hunter Coll., 1963; postgrad., N.Y. Inst. Fin., N.Y.C., 1965-67. Chief underwriting div. mcpl. securities City of N.Y., 1972-73; prin. Judith H. McQuown & Co., Inc., N.Y.C., 1973—. Author: Inc. Yourself: How to Profit by Setting Up Your Own Corporation, 6th edit., 1988, Tax Shelters That Work for Everyone, 1979, The Fashion Survival Manual, 1981, Playing the Takeover Market, 1982, How to Profit After You Inc. Yourself, 1985, Keep One Suitcase Empty: The Bargain Shopper's Guide to the Finest Factory Outlets in the British Isles, 1987, Keep One Suitcase Empty: The Bargain Shopper's Guide to the Finest Factory Outlets in Europe, 1988; contbg. editor Boardroom Reports, Physician's Fin. World, Physician's Guide to Money Mgmt. Mem. Am. Soc. Journalists and Authors. Home and Office: 444 E 86th St New York NY 10028-6480

MCRAE, DEE (DOROTHY SUE), writer, editor; b. Huntsville, Ala., May 29, 1939; d. Alan and Dorothy Adel (Heffernan) McR., Jr.; student Florence (Ala.) State Coll., 1957-59; B.J., U. Mo., Columbia, 1961; m. Paul W. Chesser, May 29, 1973; 1 son, Timothy Paul. With Florence Herald, 1962-63; newsroom writer, editor USIA, Washington, 1963-64, editor, writer Am. Illustrated mag., 1964-67, picture editor Topic mag., 1967-69, mem. pamphlets staff, editor, writer, 1969-72; freelance writer, editor, picture editor, 1972-74; asst. editor Smithsonian Mag., Washington, 1974-77, asso. editor, 1977-81; freelance writer/editor, 1981—; assoc. for revs. Smithsonian mag., 1985—. Home: Dragonlair Saint George Island MD 20674

MCRAE, HELENE WILLIAMS, education educator; b. N.Y.C.; d. John Henry and Gertrude E. (Chevers) Williams; m. Lemuel C. McRae. BS, Trenton State Coll., 1945; EdD, Lehigh U., 1974; MA, Columbia U., 1948, Profl. Diploma, 1965. Tchr., chmn. dept. math. Bates High Sch., Annapolis, Md., 1945-52; tchr., acting dir. child study team Lawrence Twp. (N.J.) Bd. Edn., 1952-68; prof. spl. edn. Trenton (N.J.) State Coll., 1968—; cons. Trenton Bd. Edn., 1973—. Contbr. articles to profl. jours. Dir. fed. grant, Tchrs. of Presch. Handicapped, 1983-86; co-dir. state grant Reading in the Content Area Urban Sec. Schs., 1977-78; trustee Friends Trenton Pub. Library, 1981—; bd. dirs. Carolyn Stokes Day Nursery, Trenton, 1983—. Mem. AAUP (chpt. pres. 1977-79), CEC, Internat. Reading Assn., Alpha Kappa Alpha. Episcopalian. Clubs: Links, Inc. (chpt. treas. 1980-85), Girlfriends, Inc. (treas. 1987—) (Trenton). Office: Trenton State Coll Dept Spl Edn Trenton NJ 08618

MCRAE, NORA FRANCES STONE, lawyer; b. Columbus, Miss., Nov. 2, 1955; d. Douglas Clyde and Betty Ruth (Boyls) Stone; m. Vaughan Watkins McRae, Apr. 17, 1982. B.A., U. of South, 1977; J.D., U. Miss., 1980. Bar: Miss. 1980. Law clk. Miss. Supreme Ct., Jackson, 1980-81; assoc. firm Barnett, Alagia & Pyle, Jackson, 1981-82; in house counsel Miss. Power & Light Co., Jackson, 1983-85. Mem. Galloway Players; v.p. Miss. Opera Guild, 1984-86, pres., 1987-88; bd. dirs. Young Jacksonians for Symphony, Jackson, 1984; mem. Jr. League Jackson, 1984—, bd. dirs., 1987-88, co-chmn. for pub. affairs, 1988-89; project chmn. Impressions Gallery, 1987-88; mem. Jackson Symphony League, 1983-84, Jackson Ballet Guild, 1983-84, Symphony League, Ballet Guild, Mus. Aux.; mem. exec. com., bd. dirs. Miss. Opera Assn.; instr. Bethel Bible Series at Galloway Meml. United Meth. Ch. Mem. ABA, Miss. Bar Assn., Miss. Women Laywers Assn., Hinds County Bar Assn., Miss. Mus. Art Aux., Jackson Young Lawyers Assn. Methodist. Home: 1515 N State St Jackson MS 39202

MCREYNOLDS, MARY ARMILDA, lawyer; b. Carthage, Mo., Sept. 2, 1946; d. Allen and Virginia Madeliene (Hensley) McR. BA, Mt. Holyoke Coll., 1968; JD, Georgetown U., 1971; LL.M., Harvard U., 1973. Bar: D.C. 1971, U.S. Ct. Appeals (D.C. cir.) 1971, U.S. Ct. Appeals (2d cir.) 1975, U.S. Ct. Appeals. (4th cir.) 1979, U.S. Ct. Appeals. (1st, 5th, 6th, 9th, 10th cirs.) 1980, U.S. Supreme Ct. 1980, U.S. Ct. Appeals. (11th cir.) 1981, U.S. Ct. Appeals (3d, 7th, 8th cirs.) 1983, U.S. Ct. Appeals (Fed. cir.) 1988. Law clk. U.S. Ct. Appeals for D.C. circuit, 1971-72; assoc. Wilmer, Cutler & Pickering, Washington, 1973-77; sr. trial atty. civil div. fed. program br. U.S. Dept. Justice, 1977-79, mem. appellate staff, 1979-81; ptnr. McReynolds & Mutterperl, Washington, 1981-83; ptnr. Wilner & Scheiner, 1983—. Mem. bd. dirs., gen. counsel Washington Bach Consort, 1985—. Mem. ABA, Bar Assn. D.C., Fed. Bar Assn., Am. Soc. Legal History. Episcopalian. Clubs: Racquet (Washington); Kenwood (Bethesda, Md.). Contbr. articles to profl. jours. Home: 2101 Connecticut Ave Apt 26 Washington DC 20008

MCREYNOLDS, MARY MAUREEN, municipal environmental administrator, consultant; b. Tacoma, July 15, 1940; d. Andrew Harley and Mary Leone (McGuire) Sims; m. Gerald Aaron McReynolds, Dec. 10, 1964. Student Coll. Puget Sound, 1957-59; BA, U. Oreg., 1961; PhD, U. Chgo., 1966; postgrad. San Diego State U., 1973-75. NIH postdoctoral fellow U. Tex., Austin, 1966-68, mem. adj. faculty, 1980-82, mem. biohazards com., 1981—; research assoc. Stanford U., Calif., 1968-71; chemist assoc. Syva Co., Palo Alto, Calif., 1972; environ. specialist County of San Diego, Calif., 1973-75; dept. head City of Austin, 1976-84, chief environ. officer, 1984-85, utility environ. mgr., 1985—; cons. enologist Mirassou Vineyards, San Jose, Calif., 1969-72; lectr. Wright Inst., Berkeley, Calif., 1971-72; instr. San Diego State U., 1974-75. Contbr. articles to profl. pubs. U.S.-Mexico Sister Cities del., 1983-85; sponsor, chaperone Tex.-South Australia Youth Exchange, 1986; active Leadership Austin, 1987-88. USPHS tng. grantee U. Chgo., 1961-64; univ. fellow U. Chgo., 1961-66. Mem. Water Pollution Control Fedn. (v.p. 1988—), Am. Planning Assn., Am. Inst. Cert. Planners (cert.), Assn. Environ. Profls., AAAS, Am. Water Resources Assn., Austin Soc. Pub. Adminstrn., Nat. Assn. Female Execs., Zeta Tau Alpha. Lodges: Soroptimists (dir. Soroptimist Manor 1978-80, 83-85, v.p. chpt. 1983-85, pres. chpt. 1985-87, chpt. dir. 1987-88), Toastmasters (club pres. 1981, 88, area gov. 1981-82, div. lt. gov. 1983-84, Able Toastmaster award 1983, Dist. 56 Table Topics award 1986, Disting. Toastmaster award dist. 56 no. div. 1987). Avocations: gourmet food and wine. Office: City of Austin PO Box 1088 Austin TX 78767

MCROBERTS, JUNE HATTIE, interior designer; b. Grosse Pointe, Mich., Mar. 26, 1931; d. Willard Winfield and Cleo Velma (Holloway) Bishop; m. Nelson Leon McRoberts, June 6, 1953; children: Ann McRoberts Johnson, Eric, Sara McRoberts Mascetti. AA, Coll. DuPage, 1972; postgrad., Chgo. Acad. Fine Arts, 1974-75; BA, No. Ill. U., 1981. Owner, designer June McRoberts Interiors, Batavia, Ill., 1971—; pres. Flutes & Swags Ltd., Batavia, 1988—. Contbr. pub. newsletter The Designing Eye, 1980-82. Mem. adv. com. interior design program Coll. DuPage, Glen Ellyn, Ill., 1973-80. Mem. Interior Design Soc. (copywriter newsletter 1983-85, pres. Chgo. chpt. 1985-87). Baptist. Home: 1255 Woodland Ave Batavia IL 60510

MCROY, RUTH GAIL, social worker, educator; b. Vicksburg, Miss., Oct. 6, 1947; d. Horace David and Lucille A. (McKinney) Murdock; B.A. in Sociology and Psychology, U. Kans., 1968; M.S.W., 1970; Ph.D. in Social Work (Danforth Found. fellow 1980-81, Black Analysis, Inc. fellow 1980-81), U. Tex.- Austin, 1981; m. June 5, 1968 (div.); children—Myra Louise, Melissa Lynn. Marriage counselor Family Consultation Service, Wichita, Kans., 1970-71; adoption specialist Kans. Children's Service League, Wichita, 1971-73; asst. prof. social work U. Kans., Lawrence, 1973-77; asst. prof. sociology and social work Prairie View A&M U., 1977-78; tech. asst. specialist Region VI Adoption Resource Center, Austin, 1979-81; assoc. prof. social work U. Tex., Austin, 1981—; guest speaker in field; cons. adoptions; instr. in continuing edn.; pres. bd. dirs. Black Adoption Program and Services, Kansas City, Kans., 1976-77; pres. bd. dirs. George Washington Carver History Mus., 1983-86. Mem. Nat. Assn. Social Workers, Council Social Work Edn., Phi Delta Kappa, Phi Kappa Phi. Episcopalian. Author: Black Homes for Black Children, 1974; Instructor's Guide to Accompany Human Responses to Social Problems, 1981; Transracial and Inracial Adoptees: The Adolescent Years, 1983. Contbr. articles to profl. jours. Office: 2609 University Ave Austin TX 78712

MCSHEA, BETTY JANE, purchasing executive; b. Baldwin Park, Calif., Mar. 23, 1948; d. George Henry and Amelia Gloria (Pappacena) Cagle; m. Michael P. McShea, Aug. 17, 1965 (div. 1971); children: Michael Patrick Jr., Traci E. BA, U. Houston, 1985; postgrad., Western State U., 1986-87, U. Calif., Irvine, 1987—, Northrop U., 1988—. Jr. buyer Reuland Electric, Industry, Calif., 1971-74; sr. buyer W.P.M. Systems, Inc., Claremont, Calif., 1974-76; buyer Aramco, Houston, 1976-78; purchasing agt. Vector Cable, Houston, 1978-79; purchasing mgr. NL Shaffer, Houston, 1979-83; pvt. practice paralegal cons. Houston, 1983-85; purchasing agt. NL Shaffer, Brea, Calif., 1985-86; purchasing supr. Pheion Corp., Santa Ana, Calif., 1986—. Mem. Purchasing Mgmt. Assn., Women in Purchasing, Nat. Contract Mfg. Assn. Republican. Roman Catholic. Home: 32831 Samuel Circle Dana Point CA 92629

MCSHERRY, KATHLEEN ANN, advertising agency executive; b. Bklyn., May 12, 1951; d. Joseph Francis and Mary Maguire (Lemmon) McS. Student, Sch. Visual Arts, N.Y.C., 1969-72. From asst. art dir. to art dir. Young & Rubicam Inc., N.Y.C., 1972-77; art dir. Grey Advt. Inc., N.Y.C., 1977-79; sr. dir. Benton & Bowles, N.Y.C., 1979-80, creative supr., v.p., 1980-86; creative group head, sr. v.p. D'Arcy Masius Benton & Bowles, N.Y.C., 1986—; instr. Pratt Inst., Bklyn., 1978-81, Sch. Visual Arts, 1986—; guest lectr. Cooper Union, N.Y.C., 1977, U. Vt., Burlington, 1978. Recipient cert. The One Show, 1977, cert. Art Dirs. Club, 1977, Bronze medal Internat. Film and TV Festival N.Y., 1981, 82, Addy, 1982, Clio cert., 1983, Silver medal Internat. Film and TV Festival N.Y., 1983, Bronze medal Internat. Advt. Festival N.Y., 1984.

MCSHIRLEY, SUSAN RUTH, gift industry company executive, consultant; b. Glendale, Calif., July 31, 1945; d. Robert Claude and Lillian Dora (Mable) McS. B.S., U. Calif.-Berkeley, 1967. Nat. sales dir. McShirley Products, Glendale, Calif., 1967-71, Viade Products, Camarillo, Calif., 1972-80; pres. SRM Press, Inc., Los Angeles, 1980—; nat. sales cons. Warner Bros. Records, Burbank, Calif., 1985. Author: Racquetball: Where to Play, USA, 1978. Patentee picture pen. Creator novelty trademarks including Collectable Critters, Preppy Pen, Dependable Heart. Mem. Calif. Alumni Assn., Alpha Omicron Pi. Avocations: travel; photography; tennis; foreign languages. Home: 15947 Temecula St Pacific Palisades CA 90272 Office: SRM Press Inc 4216 1/2 Glencoe Ave Marina del Rey CA 90292

MCSWEENEY, JUNE ELIZABETH, printing company executive; b. Boston, June 18, 1932; d. William Earnest and Mabel Evelyn (Ricker) Mortimer; m. Charles Edward McSweeney, June 21, 1952; children: David Charles, Donna Marie, Diane June. Student Boston U., 1948-52; A.S., Northeastern U., 1970, B.S., 1974. Policywriter, T.C. Curran Ins., Hyde Park, Mass., 1948-56; office mgr. Slattery Ins., Abington, Mass., 1954-70; v.p., treas. Fairmount Press, Inc., Rockland, Mass., 1967—. Chmn. edn./bus. community Alliance Rockland pub. schs., 1982—; bd. dirs. White Island Pond Conservation Alliance, East Wareham, Mass., 1986—. Editor: Federation Topics, 1988—. Mem. Printing Industries Am., Sigma Epsilon Rho. Club: Mass. State Fedn. Women's Clubs (trustee endowment fund 1982-84, dir. evening div. 1986-88) (Quincy). Home: 250 Barker Rd East Wareham MA 02538 Office: Fairmount Press Inc 496 Union St Rockland MA 02370

MCTAGGART, DEBRA JO, insurance company executive; b. Pratt, Kans., Nov. 10, 1953; d. Raymond Earl and Maxine Emith (McClauskey) McT.; m. Galen Leroy Trinkle, July 1, 1972; 1 child, Keri McTaggart Trinkle. Grad. high sch., Pratt, 1971; student, Wichita Bus. Coll., 1971-72. Sec. Mass. Mut. Life Ins. Co., Wichita, Kans., 1974-76; adminstrv. asst. Mass. Mut. Life Ins. Co., San Francisco, 1976-77; group service rep. Mass. Mut. Life Ins. Co., Indpls., 1977-80, Greensboro, N.C., 1980-83; group sales rep. Mass. Mut. Life Ins. Co., Kansas City, Mo., 1983-86; mgrn group rep. Met. Life Ins. Co., Overland Park, Kans., 1986—. Active Girl Scouts U.S. Mem. Nat. Assn. Life Underwriters, Kansas City Employee Benefits Profls. Assn., Nat. Assn. Female Execs. Office: Met Life Ins Co 9200 Indian Creek Pkwy Suite 100 Overland Park KS 66210-2008

MCTEAGUE, LINDA BRAGDON, preservation planner, consultant; b. Rahway, N.J.; d. Lyle M. and Garnet (Gowdy) Cooper; m. John W. Bragdon; children: David A., Lucinda J. AB, Rutgers U., 1966, M of City and Regional Planning, 1984. Tchr. secondary history and Eng. Rahway High Sch. and The Vail Deane Sch., Elizabeth, N.J., 1966-84; preservation planner Union County, N.J., 1984—; adj. prof. Rutgers U., New Brunswick, 1986-87; advisor N.J. State Hist. Preservation Plan, 1987—; mem. Resource Recovery Aesthetics Rev. Com. of Union County Utilities Authority; cons. in field. Editor, Author: Preserving New Jersey, 1986, rev. edit., 1987; editor, designer: Rediscovery of Rahway, 1976; contbr. articles to profl. jours. State coordinator Washington Inaugural Bicentennial Project, 1988—; trustee Proprietary House Assn., Perth Amboy, N.J., 1988—. Mem. Am. Planning Assn., Nat. Trust for Hist. Preservation. Home and Office: 1208 Pierpont St Rahway NJ 07065

MCTEER, MAUREEN ANNE, lawyer; b. Cumberland, Ont., Can., Feb. 27, 1952; d. John J. and Beatrice E. (Griffith) McT.; B.A., U. Ottawa (Ont.), 1973, LL.B., 1977; m. Charles Joseph Clark, June 30, 1973; 1 dau., Catherine Jane. Called to Ont. bar, 1980. Bd. govs. U. Ottawa, 1980—. Named Woman of Future, Ladies Home Jour., 1979, Chatelaine Woman of yr., 1984. Mem. Nat. Council Women of Can. (hon. pres.), Nat. Assn. Women and Law, Nat. Action Com. on Status of Women. Progressive Conservative. Author: Residences: Homes of Canada's Leaders, 1980, Parliament: Canada's Democracy and How it Works, 1987. Roman Catholic.

MCTIERNAN, MIRIAM, government executive; b. Limerick, Ireland, May 2, 1952; arrived in Can., 1973; d. Michael and Marjorie (Woulfe) Lynch; m. Timothy Patrick McTiernan, Oct. 31, 1972; 1 child, Leah Rhiannon. BA with honors, Nat. U. Ireland, U. Coll. Dublin, 1972, diploma in archival studies, 1973; diploma in pub. sector mgmt. U. Victoria, 1985. Coll. archivist Douglas Coll., New Westminster, B.C., 1973-76; univ. archivist U. B.C., Vancouver, 1975; credit union archivist B.C. Cen. Credit Union, Vancouver, 1976-79; govt. records archivist Govt. of Yukon, Whitehorse, Yukon Ter., 1979-80, territorial archivist, 1980-84, dir. libraries and archives, 1984—. Contbr. articles to profl. jours. Mem. Assn. Can. Archivists (bus. archives com. 1976-79, treas. 1981-83, v.p. 1983-84, pres. 1984-85, chmn. nominations and elections com. 1985-87), Bur. Can. Archivists, Assn. B.C. Archivists (sec.-treas. 1976-78, pres. 1978-80), Can. Council of Archives (Yukon rep. 1985—, bd. dirs. 1987—, chair planning and priorities com. 1987), Yukon Geog. Names Bd., Yukon Hist. and Mus. Assn. (treas. 1981), Soc. Am. Archivists, Assn. Records Mgr. and Adminstrs., Inst. Pub. Adminstrn. Can.

MCVAY, VIVINA HELEN, publishing executive; b. Holton, Kans., Mar. 25, 1953; d. Stephen Eugene and Vivina Helen (Hrenchir) Freel; m. Barry Lee McVay, Mar. 14, 1981; 1 child, William Randall. AA, Highland (Kans.) Community Jr. Coll., 1973; BA, Emporia (Kans.) State U., 1975; postgrad., Cen. Mich. U., 1980. Contract specialist Tank Command, U.S. Army, Detroit, 1975-77; contract specialist Missile Command Huntsville, Ala., 1977-78; specialist small bus. Materiel Command, Alexandria, Va., 1981-84; chief contract adminstrn. Mil. Traffic Mgmt. Command, New Orleans, 1978-79; analyst procurement Nat. Park Service, Washington, 1979-81; pres. Panoptic Enterprises, Woodbridge, Va., 1982—. Mem. Internat. Assn. Ind. Pubs., Pubs. Mktg. Assn., Network Entrepreneurial Women, Nat. Assn. for Female Execs., Handgun Control, Women's Action for Nuclear Disarmament, Prince William County C. of C. Democrat. Roman Catholic. Home: 3911 Findley Rd Woodbridge VA 22193 Office: Panoptic Enterprises PO Box 1099 Woodbridge VA 22193

MCVEY, MARCIA ALICE, educational administrator; b. San Jose, Calif., Aug. 31, 1934; d. Charles Thurston and Thelma (Hackett) McV.; B.A., Pomona Coll., 1955; M.A., Claremont Grad. Sch., 1959; Ed.D. (Delta Kappa Gamma Scholar), U. So. Calif., 1978. Tchr., Glendora Sch. Dist., 1955-59; tchr. Covina Valley Unified Sch. Dist., 1959-65, counselor, jr. high sch., 1965-67, asst. prin. jr. high, 1967-68, prin., 1968-72, 73-79; dir. curriculum and instruction Norwalk (Calif.) LaMirada Unified Sch. Dist., 1979-83; asst. supt. Centralia Sch. Dist., Buena Park (Calif.), 1983-86; deputy supt. Duarte Unified Sch. Dist., Calif., 1986—; ednl. cons.; mem. Calif. Dept. Edn. task force on conflict resolution in secondary schs., 1972-73. Bd. dirs. HEAR Center, Pasadena, 1976—; community vol. Pomona Coll. Assocs.; mem. Calif. Curriculum Devel. and Supplemental Materials Commn., 1984—. Kettering IDEA fellow, 1981. Mem. Assn. Calif. Sch. Adminstrs., Calif. Assn. Gifted, Profl. Advocates for Gifted Edn., Assn. Supervision and Curriculum Devel., AAUW, Phi Delta Kappa, Delta Kappa Gamma. Contbr. articles to profl. jours. Office: 1427 Buena Vista Ave Duarte CA 91010

MCVICAR, ANN LAMONT, librarian; b. Seattle, Sept. 1, 1935; d. Ralph Howell and Vivian Hazel (Effinger) Lamont; m. Forrest B. McVicar, Mar. 21, 1959; children—Mary, Helen, Bruce Lamont. B.A. in Am. Lit., U. Wash., 1957, M.L.S., 1960; Cert. Advanced Study North Tex. State U., 1985. Profl. Librarian's cert., N.J.; State Bd. Cert. for Librarian, Wash. Br. librarian and reference librarian Library Assn. Portland, 1971-74; head reference dept. Old Bridge Pub. Library, N.J., 1975-79; dir. library Nat. Office Boy Scouts Am., Irving, Tex., 1979-85; mgr. corp. library Mobil Products div. Motorola, Inc., Ft. Worth, Tex., 1985—; adminstrv. asst. to pres. Tex. Library Assn., Dallas, 1984—. Precinct committeeperson Republican Party, Portland, 1972; pres. P-TSA George Smith Elem. Sch., Portland, 1972-73. Mem. Am. Library Assn., Tex. Library Assn., Special Libraries Assn. Club: Church Women United (vice pres. 1975-76). Office: Motorola Inc Fossil Creek Library PO Box 2931 Fort Worth TX 76113

MCVICKER, MARY ELLEN HARSHBARGER, museum director, art history educator; b. Mexico, Mo., May 5, 1951; d. Don Milton and Harriet Pauline (Mossholder) Harshbarger; m. Wiley Ray McVicker, June 2, 1973; children: Laura Elizabeth, Todd Michael. BA with honors, U. Mo., 1973, MA, 1975, postgrad. Adminstrv. Sec. Engring. Surveys, Columbia, Mo., 1976-77. Instr. Columbia U., Mo., 1977-78, Cen. Meth. Coll., Fayette, Mo., 1978-85, mus. dir., 1980-85; project dir. Mo. Com. for Humanities, Fayette, 1981-85, Mo. Dept. Natural Resources Office Hist. Preservation, 1978-85; owner, Memories of Mo., Inc., 1986—. Author: History Book, 1984. V.p. Friends Hist. Boonville, Mo., 1982-87; bd. dirs. Mus. Assocs. Mo. U., Columbia, 1981-83, Mo. Meth. Hist. Soc., Fayette, 1981-84; chmn. Bicentennial Celebration Methodism, Boonville, Mo., 1984. Mem. Mo. Heritage Trust (charter), AAUW (treas. 1977-79), Am. Assn. Museums, Centralia Hist. Soc. (project dir. 1978), Mus. Assocs. United Meth. Ch. (charter, bd. dir. 1981-83), Phi Beta Kappa, Mortar Bd. Democrat. Clubs: Women's (treas. 1977-79), United Meth. Women's Group (charter mem.). Avocations: collecting antiques, gardening, family farming, singing, travelling. Home: 813 Christus Dr Boonville MO 65233 Office: Memories of Mo Inc PO Box 228 Boonville MO 65233

MCWHINNEY, MADELINE H. (MRS. JOHN DENNY DALE), economist; b. Denver, Mar. 11, 1922; d. Leroy and Alice (Houston) McW.; B.A., Smith Coll., 1943; M.B.A., N.Y.U., 1947; m. John D. Dale, June 23, 1961; 1 child, Thomas Denny. Economist, Fed. Res. Bank N.Y., 1943-73, chief fin. and trade statis. div., 1955-59, mgr. market stats. dept., 1960-65, asst. v.p., 1965-73; pres. First Women's Bank, N.Y.C., 1974-76; trustee Retirement System Fed. Res. Bank, 1955-58; vis. lectr. N.Y.U. Grad. Sch. Bus., 1976-77; pres. Dale, Elliott & Co., Inc., Red Bank, N.J., 1977—; mem. N.J. Casino Control Commn., 1980-82, Women's Econ. Round Table, 1978—, chmn. 1987—; bd. govs. Am. Stock Exchange, 1977-81. Trustee, Carnegie Corp. N.Y., 1974-82, Central Savs. Bank of N.Y., 1980-82, Charles F. Kettering Found., 1975—, chmn. 1987—, Inst. Internat. Edn., 1975—, Investor Responsibility Research Center, Inc., 1974-81; asst. dir. Whitney Mus. Am. Art, 1983-86; dir. Atlantic Energy Co., 1983—; trustee Mgr. of Mgr. Funds, 1983—; adv. bd. Grad. Sch. Bus., Denver U.; mem. adv. com. prof. ethics N.J. Supreme Ct., 1983—. Recipient Smith Coll. medal, 1971, Alumni Achievement award N.Y.U. Grad. Sch. Bus. Adminstrn. Alumni Assn., 1971; N.Y.U. Crystal award, 1982. Mem. Am. Fin. Assn. (past dir.), Money Marketeers (v.p. 1960, pres. 1961-62), Nat. Assn. Bank Women, Alumni Assn. Grad. Sch. Bus. Admin. N.Y.U. (dir. 1951-63, pres. 1957-59), Am. Econ. Assn., Soc. Meml. Center, Women's Econ. Roundtable (chmn. 1986—), N.J. Com. for Humanities, Phi Beta Kappa Assocs. (v.p. 1979-87). Home: 24 Blossom Cove Rd Red Bank NJ 07701 Office: PO Box 458 Red Bank NJ 07701

MCWHIRTER, DIANE BALTZELLE, lawyer; b. Miami Beach, Fla., Sept. 12, 1958; d. Conner and Mary Athria (Marney) Baltzelle; m. John McWhirter. BA in Philosophy, Duke U., 1979; JD, U. Fla., 1982; postgrad. in comparative law Magdalen Coll., Oxford, Eng., summer 1980. Bar: Fla. 1983, U.S. Dist. Ct. (mid. dist.) Fla. 1983, U.S. Ct. Appeals (11th cir.) 1984. Asst. pub. defender, Pub. Defender's Office, Lake City, Fla., 1983-84, Orlando, Fla., 1984-86; sole practice, Orlando, 1987-88, gen. counsel Fla. United Meth. Children's Home, Inc., Enterprise, Fla., 1988—, trustee, 1985-88; teaching fellow Holland Law Ctr., Gainesville, Fla., 1982; lectr. Pub. Defender Spring Conf., 1985. Editor family law, Legal Aid Handbook, 1981-82. Mem. Fla. Symphony League, Orlando, 1983-84, Columbia Assn. for Retarded Children, Lake City, 1984; mem. choir 1st United Presbyn. Ch., Lake City, 1984; Sunday sch. tchr. 1st United Meth. Ch., Orlando, 1983, 85, mem. choir, 1986—; trustee Fla. United Meth. Children's Home, 1985-87. Mem. ABA, Fla. Bar Assn. (evidence com. 1985-86), Orange County Bar Assn. (vice chmn. law and edn. com. 1986-87), Phi Delta Phi (clk. 1981-82, historian 1982, cert. of merit 1981, 82). Democrat. Home: 180 N Clark St Enterprise FL 32725 Office: 51 Main St Enterprise FL 32725

MCWHORTER, SHARON LOUISE, business executive, inventor, consultant; b. Detroit, Feb. 22, 1951; d. Leroy Byron Harris Jr. and Josiebell (Richards) Harris Aaron; m. Abner McWhorter II, Mar. 15, 1969 (div. Aug. 1974); 1 child, Abner III. BA, Wayne State U., 1988; cert., SBA, Detroit, 1978; cert. in sound engring. Detroit Rec. Inst., Warren, Mich., 1982. Directory asst. Mich. Bell Telephone Co., Detroit, 1969; quality control clk. Chevrolet Gear & Axle, Detroit, 1971-74; circulation clk. Wayne County Community Coll., Detroit, 1977-85, mem. library standing com. and open house com., 1983-84; pres. Galactic Concepts & Designs, Detroit, 1977-88, cons., 1983—; gen. ptnr., mgr. S.M.J. Corridor Devel., Detroit, 1982—, hist. researcher, 1982; del. Small Bus. Conf., 1981; ad-hoc mem. Minority Tech. Council, 1981-82; elected alt. Mich. del. White House Conf. on Small Bus., Washington, 1985-86. Author, editor Creative Dilemma newsletter, 1985—. Co-patentee cup holding apparatus. Vol. counselor Barat House/March of Dimes, Detroit, 1977; active Concerned Citizens Cass Corridor, Detroit, 1982-87, Cass Corridor Citizen's Patrol, Detroit, 1983-84; pres. Wayne County chpt. Mothers Against Drunk Driving, Mich., 1987-88. Recipient Hist. Landmark award Dept. Interior, 1983, cert. appreciation Tri-County Substance Abuse Awareness Com., 1984. Mem. Inventors Council Mich. (bd. dirs. 1985—), Black Women in Bus. (sec. 1984-85), Greater Detroit C. of C., South Cass Bus. Assn. (v.p. 1987-88, pres. 1988—), Detroit Econ. Club. Democrat. Methodist. Avocations: inventing; writing, re-adaptive furniture design, photography, video production. Office: SMJ Corridor Devel Co 453 Myrtle Suite 102 Detroit MI 48201

MCWILLIAMS, CONNIE OPAL, insurance company executive; b. Magnolia, Iowa, June 28, 1947; d. Thomas E. and Ila M. (Vore) Chatburn; m. Dale Roy McWilliams, Sept. 29, 1973. Sec. Kovar Agy., Inc., Missouri Valley, Iowa, 1965-76; owner McWilliams Enterprises, Missouri Valley, 1976—. Chairperson, Harrison County (Iowa) March of Dimes, 1970-73; commr. Iowa Jud. Qualifications Commn., 1981-85. Mem. Assn. Life Underwriters, (past pres. chpt.), Christian Legal Soc., Toppers Club of Farmers Ins. Group, Iowa C. of C. (bd. dirs. Missouri Valley 1987—), Lifemasters Club, Comml. Masters Club. Democrat. Mem. Reorganized Ch. of Jesus Christ of Latter-day Saints. Club: Community Band and Chorus (dir. 1981). Home: Rural Rt 2 Box 172 Logan IA 51546 Office: 301 E Erie St Missouri Valley IA 51555

MEAD, ANN MARIE, personnel agency executive; b. Charleston, W.Va., Jan. 10, 1943; d. Lester G. and Eleanor Segerman. BBA, U. Cin., 1966. Pres. A. Job Bank Ltd., Alexandria, Va., 1974-84, Alexander, Mead & Assocs. Inc., Old Town Alexandria, Va., 1984—; pres. J.B. Temps Inc., 1978-82. Mem. corp. bd. Alexandria Hosp., 1967—. Mem. Alexandria C. of C., Va. Assn. Personnel Services, Nat. Assn. Female Execs., Am. Bus. Women's Assn. Home: 6003 Liberty Bell Ct Burke VA 22015 also: Casa D'Marchesa Hedgesville WV 25427 Office: 1408 King St Alexandria VA 22314

MEAD, CATHERINE SMITH, librarian; b. Sharon Springs, N.Y., July 11, 1924; d. Elmer Charles and Marguerite (Brady) Smith; B.A. in English, N.Y. State Coll. Tchrs., Albany, 1944, B.S. in L.S., 1947; m. John Mead, Feb. 6, 1947; 1 son, Gregory. Post librarian Camp Drake, Japan, 1953-55; cataloger post library Fort Hood, Tex., 1955-63, Pa. State Library, Harrisburg, 1964-65; asst. state librarian info. resources State Library Ohio, Columbus, 1971-83, head reference and info services. Mem. ALA, Ohio Library Assn., Ohio Assn. Archivists. Office: 65 S Front St Columbus OH 43215

MEAD, DENISE JOY, medical facility administrator; b. Endicott, N.Y., Feb. 19, 1965; d. Eldon Raymond and Judith Marie (Riek) M. BS, Mercer U., 1987. Ops. mgr. North Atlanta Ob-Gyn, P.A., 1987—. Judge Phi Beta Lambda, Atlanta, 1988. Mem. Nat. Assn. for Female Execs. Republican. Office: North Atlanta Ob-Gyn PA 980 Johnson Ferry Rd Suite 410 Atlanta GA 30342

MEAD, HARRIET COUNCIL, librarian, author; b. Franklin, Va., Jan. 11; d. Hutson and Ollie (Whitley) Council; m. Berne Matthews Mead, Jr., Dec. 2, 1940; children—William Whitley, Charles Council. B.A., Coll. William and Mary, 1935; postgrad. Rollins Coll., 1966, 70, 84; student Fla. State U., 1958-62. County librarian Carroll County, Hillsville, Va., 1935-36; city librarian Suffolk City Schs., Va., 1936-41; librarian, media specialist Orange County Schs., Orlando, Fla., 1961-80. Author: The Irrepressible Saint, 1983, A Family Legacy, 1987. Contbr. article to mag., 1983. Sustaining mem. Jr. League Orlando, Winter Park, 1985, Soc. Colonial Dames in State of Fla., Orlando, 1987, Orange County Hist. Soc., 1987, LWV, Orlando, 1987. Mem. Friends of Library, Fla. Council Libraries, Orange County Media Specialists (pres. 1968-69), Nat. Soc. Colonial Dames, DAR, Orange County Ret. Educators. Democrat. Episcopalian. Avocation: watercolor painting. Home: 500 E Marks St Orlando FL 32803

MEADE, DONNA LYNN, fundraising executive; b. Salem, N.J., June 19, 1949; d. C. Lewis and Elizabeth Ann (Griscom) M.; m. Donald L. Pendley, Oct. 14, 1984; 1 chil, Katelyn. BA in History, Montclair State Coll., 1971. Dir. devel. Women's Action Alliance, N.Y.C., 1974-76; assoc. dir. devel. Polytech. Inst., Bklyn., 1976-77; ptnr. Meade-Pendley, Inc., Montclair, 1977-83; dir. devel. N.J. Hist. Soc., Newark, 1983-86; dir. capital campaign Coll. of St. Elizabeth, Convent, N.J., 1986—; instr. Cheyney (Pa.) Acad. for Exec. Mgmt., 1980-81. Trustee Montclair State Coll. Found., Upper Montclair, 1985—, alumni rep. 1984-86. Noyes Found. scholar, 1967-71. Mem. Conf. of Pres. of State Colls. Alumni Assns. (co-founder 1985), Montclair State Coll. Alumni Assn. (pres. 1984—), Pi Delta Epsilon. Republican. Mem. Soc. Friends. Home: 32 Hamilton Rd Glen Ridge NJ 07028 Office: Coll of St Elizabeth Convent Rd Convent Station NJ 07961

MEADE, PATRICIA SUE, hospital executive; b. Columbus, Ohio, Mar. 14, 1960; d. Harold Eugene and Glenna Rhae (Croaff) M. BS in Communications, Ohio U., 1982, M in Sports Adminstrn., 1984, MS in Communications, 1986. Dir. advt. The Pensacola (Fla.) Civic Ctr., 1984-85; asst. dir. mktg. Ohio Ctr. Co., Columbus, 1985-86; asst. v.p. mktg. Doctors Hosp., Columbus, 1986—; cons. in field, 1987—. Mem. Am. Mgmt. Assn., Ohio Hosp. Assn., Internat. Assn. Bus. Communicators, Am. Mktg. Assn., Nat. Assn. Female Execs. Club: Scandanavian Health Spa. Office: Doctors Hosp 1087 Dennison Ave Columbus OH 43201

MEADLOCK, NANCY B., computer graphics company executive; b. 1938; married. BSMA, Athens Coll., 1969. With Intergraph Corp., 1969—, v.p. for adminstrn., now exec. v.p. Office: Intergraph Corp 1 Madison Industrial Park Huntsville AL 35807 *

MEADOR, WILMA JEAN, broadcast company executive; b. Gravelly, Ark., June 15, 1932; d. Ernest Cecil and Sue Frances (Poindexter) Wilson; m. John M. Meador III, Aug. 31, 1951; children: John M. IV, Matthew Warren. Student, Okla. Bapt. U., 1949-51, Okla. U., 1974-76. Exec. sec. various attys., Okla., 1953-68; adminstrv. asst. First. Am. Bank, Purcell, Okla., 1968-78; mktg. dir. Telum, Inc., Provo, Utah, 1979-86; v.p. media services Am. Telemedia Network, Provo, 1986-87, v.p. pub. relations, investor relations, 1987—; sr. v.p., vice chmn. bd. Mall Mktg., Inc., Ariz., 1988—; lectr. communication seminars various cos., Utah, 1985—. Mem. Pub. Relations Soc. Am., Nat. Assn. Female Execs., Am. Mgmt. Assn. Republican. Baptist. Office: Am Telemedia Network 890 Quail Valley Dr Provo UT 84604

MEADORS, GAYLE MARLEEN, lawyer; b. Chgo., Sept. 13, 1946; d. Howard C. and Eileen M. (Baker) M.; m. William Frank Fortuna II, June 11, 1983. AB in English Lit. with honors, U. Ill., 1969; MA in Library Sci., U. Chgo., 1973; JD magna cum laude, DePaul U., 1977. Bar: Ill. 1977. Cons. Hewitt Assocs., Lincolnshire, Ill., 1976-83; sr. counsel Am. Hosp. Supply Corp., Evanston, Ill. 1983-84; assoc. Katten, Muchin, Zavis, Pearl, Greenberger & Galler, Chgo., 1984-87; assoc. Pope, Ballard, Shepard & Fowle, Ltd., Chgo., 1987—; adj. mem. faculty Inst. for Fin. Services Training Roosevelt U., Chgo. Mem. ABA, Chgo. Heart Assn. (vol. mgmt. services), Ill. State Bar Assn., Chgo. Bar Assn., Chgo. Council Lawyers, Women in Employee Benefits, Phi Beta Kappa. Home: 530 E Prospect Lake Bluff IL 60044 Office: Pope Ballard Shepard & Fowle Ltd 69 W Washington Chicago IL 60602

MEADOWS, EDITH ELIZABETH (LISA), transportation company professional; b. Jacksonville, Fla., Dec. 22, 1957; d. Malvern Dean and Mary Elizabeth Wallace (Royle) Laudenslayer; m. Richard Dell Meadows, June 25, 1983. Student, Valdosta (Ga.) State Coll., 1975-77; AA in Mktg., Fla. Jr. Coll., 1978; BBA in Mktg., U. North Fla., 1981. Asst. dept. mgr. May Cohens, Jacksonville, 1982; adminstr. asst. Kee Transp. Co., Jacksonville, 1982-85; adminstr. asst. Unit Distbn. Fla., Jacksonville, 1985-87, coordinator corp. values com., 1986-87; adminstrv. asst. Seminole Kraft Corp., Jacksonville, 1987—. Sec. K & C Pet Rescue, Jacksonville, 1987—, pres., 1988. Mem. Women's Traffic Assn. Jacksonville, Inc. (publicity com. 1984-85, treas. 1985-86, corr. sec. 1986-87, bd. dirs., Dir.'s award 1985, Officer's award 1986, 87, 1st v.p. 1988), Delta Nu Alpha (auditing com. 1986, sec. 1988-89). Democrat. Episcopalian. Home: 11318 Rustic Wheel Ct Jacksonville FL 32223 Office: Seminole Kraft Corp 9469 Eastport Rd Jacksonville FL 32218

MEADOWS, JERRILEE "SKIP", small business owner; b. Akron, Ohio, Jan. 16, 1942; d. Hulbert Harold and Geraldine F. (Lehnert) Hickman; m. Robert T. Meadows, June 23, 1962; children: Michael, Andrew, David. BS in Edn., Akron U., 1978. Lic. real estate broker; cert. tchr. bus. Tchr. Akron Pub. Schs., 1978-79; sales exec. Macinnis Realty, Akron, 1978-80, Eriksen Bus. Machines, Canton, Ohio, 1980-81, Jeter Systems Corp., Akron, 1981-85; owner Meadows Bus. Systems, Inc., Clearwater, Fla., 1985—. Mem. Women's Polit. Caucus, Akron, 1982-84, Witan Civic Orgn., Akron, 1982-85, Espiritu Santo Cath. Ch. Women's Guild; mgr. Robert Meadows City Council Campaign, Akron, 1983; bd. dirs. Pinellas Office Devel. Council, Clearwater, 1986-87. Mem. Nat. Assn. Female Execs., Assn. Records Mgrs. and Adminstrs. (1st v.p. Tampa, Fla. chpt. 1986-87), Network Exec. Women (historian Tampa chpt. 1986-87). Democrat. Office: 2535 Landmark Dr Suite 117 Clearwater FL 34621

MEADS, PATRICIA JEAN, marketing specialist; b. Fargo, N.D., Apr. 10, 1950; d. Raymond Byron and Isabel Edith (Barrett) Whiting; student So. Meth. U., 1968-69; B.A., U. Minn., 1971. Advt. coordinator Sun Newspapers, also mng. editor Zenith Express, 1973-74; dir. consumer communications A.S. Industries, Mpls., 1974-76; sales promotion coordinator Carlson Mktg. Group div. Carlson Cos., Mpls., 1976-79, dir. mktg. services, 1979-86, dir. creative services Carlson Promotion Group div. Carlson Cos., Mpls., 1986—. Mem. Women in Communications (past pres. Twin Cities chpt.), Minnetonka Chorale. Contbr. to Pro-Con Mag. Home: 18900 Shady Ln S Minnetonka MN 55345 Office: 12755 Hwy 55 Minneapolis MN 55441

MEAGHER, CYNTHIA NASH, journalist; b. Detroit, Dec. 24, 1947; d. Frederick Copp and Carolyn (Coffin) Nash; 1 child, Lydia Anne. BA, U.

Mich., 1969. Reporter, Detroit News, 1970-75, sports columnist, 1975-77, Life Style columnist, 1977-79, Life Style editor, 1979-82; news features editor Seattle Times, 1983, asst. mng. editor Sunday Seattle Times, 1983-86, assoc. mng. editor, 1986—. Club: City. Office: Seattle Times PO Box 70 Seattle WA 98111

MEALIA, JOANNE SCHRAM, marketing professional; b. Dearborn, Mich., Mar. 9, 1957; d. Joseph Herman and Joan Frances (Mulkeen) Schram; m. John Joseph Mealia, Oct. 23, 1982; 1 child, Alexandra Marie. BA in Bus., Mich. State U., 1979. Teaching asst. Mich. State U., East Lansing, 1977-78; computer science mktg. intern Quaker Oats Co., Chgo., 1978; mktg. rep. IBM, Indpls., 1979-81; regional specialist IBM, Toronto, Ont., Can., 1982, mktg. rep., 1983-85, advt. mktg. rep., 1986-87; adv.instr., entry level tng. —, Toronto, Ont., 1988—. Contbr. short story, Detroit News, (award 1968). Bd. dirs. St. Aidan Parish, Livonia, Mich., 1975; facilitator St. Gabriel Passionist Parish, Willowdale, Ont. 1983—; fellow Jr. League, Toronto, 1986—; organizer Lunches with Leaders program, Toronto, 1974. Recipient Mich. competitive scholarships; named one of Outstanding Teenagers of Am. Fellow Women's Roundtable (sec. 1984-85); mem. Phi Beta Kappa, Kappa Delta. Republican. Roman Catholic. Club: Bayview Golf and Country (Toronto). Home: 307 Ontario St, Toronto Can M5A 2V8 Office: IBM Canada Ltd, 243 Consumers Rd, Suite 900, North York Can M2J 4W8

MEANS, MARIANNE, political columnist; b. Sioux City, Iowa, June 13, 1934; d. Ernest Maynard and Else Marie Johanne (Andersen) Hansen; m. Warren Weaver, Jr. B.A., U. Nebr., 1956; J.D., George Washington U., 1977. Copy editor Lincoln (Nebr.) Jour., 1955-57; woman's editor No. Va. Sun, Arlington, 1957-59; Washington bur. corr. Hearst Newspapers, 1959-61, White House corr., 1961-65; polit. columnist King Features Syndicate, 1965—; commentator Spectrum CBS radio, Mut. Broadcasting Network, Voice of Am. Author: The Woman in the White House, 1963. Recipient Front Page award N.Y. Newspaper Women, 1962; Tex. Headliners award, 1976. Mem. White House Corrs. Assn., Women in Communications, Nat. Press Found. (bd. dirs.), Phi Beta Kappa, Delta Delta Delta, Sigma Delta Chi (Hall of Fame). Clubs: Fed. City, Gridiron, City Tavern. Home: 1521 31st St NW Washington DC 20007 Office: 1701 Pennsylvania Ave Washington DC 20006

MEANY, SARAH ANN, occupational therapist; b. Warren, Ohio, Feb. 20, 1928; d. Edward Anthony and Ida May (Van Cleef) M. BA, Lake Erie Coll., 1950; cert. in Occupational Therapy, Wash. U. Sch. Medicine, St. Louis, 1962. Occupational therapist Canton (Ohio) Rehab. Clinic, 1962-64, Children's Rehab. Ctr., Warren, 1964-66; dir. occupational therapy dept. Hillside Rehab. Hosp., Warren, 1966-75; owner, operator Pirate Sam, Ltd., San Salvador, The Bahamas, 1975-78; occupational therapist Wingate Oaks Ctr., Ft. Lauderdale, Fla., 1980—; owner Expertise Co., Broward County, Fla., 1987—. Author: Begin with Success - A Logical Approach to the Dressing Training of Children, 1988. Recipient Cert. Appreciation Fla. Lang. Speech and Hearing Assn., 1985. Mem. Am. Occupational Therapy Assn., Fla. Occupational Therapy Assn., Fla. Alliance of Occupational and Phys. Sch. Therapists, Council for Exceptional Children. Republican. Presbyterian. Home: 1281 NW 46th St Pompano Beach FL 33064 Office: Wingate Oaks Ctr 1211 NW 33d Terr Fort Lauderdale FL 33311

MEARA, ANNE, actress, writer; b. Bklyn., Sept. 20; d. Edward Joseph and Mary (Dempsey) M.; m. Gerald Stiller, Sept. 14, 1954; children: Amy, Benjamin. Student, Herbert Berghoff Studio, 1953-54. Apprentice in summer stock, Southold, L.I. and Woodstock, N.Y., 1950-53; off-Broadway appearances include A Month in the Country, 1954, Maedchen in Uniform, Ulysses in Uniform, 1955 (Show Bus. off-Broadway award), Ulysses in Nightown, 1958, The House of Blue Leaves, 1970, Spookhouse, 1983, Bosoms and Neglect, 1986, also with Shakespeare Co., Central Park, N.Y.C., 1957, Romeo and Juliet, 1988; film appearances include The Out-of-Towners, 1968, Lovers and Other Strangers, 1969, The Boys From Brazil, 1978, Fame, 1979, Nasty Habits (with husband Jerry Stiller), 1976; comedy act, 1963—; appearances Happy Medium and Medium Rare, Chgo., 1960-61, Village Gate, Phase Two and Blue Angel, N.Y.C., 1963, The Establishment, London, 1963; syndicated TV series Take Five With Stiller and Meara, 1977-78; numerous appearances on TV game and talk shows, also spls. and variety shows; rec. numerous comml s. for TV and radio; star TV series Kate McShane, 1975; other TV appearances Archie Bunker's Place, 1979 (Co-recipient Voice of Imagery award Radio Advt. Bur. 1975), series The Odd Couple; actress TV series Alf, 1986, writer, 1987. Office: 200 W 57th St #603 New York NY 10019

MEBANE, BARBARA MARGOT, service company executive; b. Sylacauga, Ala., July 21, 1947; d. Audrey Dixon and Mary Ellen (Yaikow) Baxley; m. James Lewis Mebane, Dec. 31, 1971; 1 child, Cieson Brooke. Grad. high sch., Albany, Ga. Line performer J. Taylor Dance Co., Miami, Fla., 1964-65; sales mgr. Dixie Readers Service, Jackson, Miss., 1965-67; regional sales mgr. Robertson Products Co., Texarkana, Tex., 1967-75; owner, pres. Telco Sales, Service and Supply, Dallas, 1976—; mem. Dance Masters, Miami, 1975—; cons. Lewisville Ballet, Gallerie Dance Ensemble, 1982; choreographer music videos for pay/cable TV, 1985. Author: Paper on Positive Thinking, 1983. Sponsor, St. Jude's Research Hosp., Memphis, Cancer Research Ctr., Dallas. Mem. Nat. Fedn. Ind. Businesses, Female and Minority Owned Bus. League, Assoc. Gen. Contractors (assoc.), Female Exec. Club N.Y.C. Avocations: working with children; teaching dance; writing. Home: 3701 Twin Oak Ct Flower Mound TX 75028 Office: Telco Sales Service and Supply PO Box 29763 Dallas TX 75229

MECHLER, BARBARA ADAMS ELLIOTT, real estate trainer, educator; b. Hartford, Conn., Apr. 13, 1952; d. Welles Vorce and Grace Dorothy (Webster) A.; m. Peter Starr Elliott (div.); 1 child, Kevin Scott; m. David Harold Mechler. Tchr. pub. schs. Fairfax County, Va., 1974-75, Meriden, Conn., 1975-82; coordinator Christian Edn. 1st Ch. Christ, New Britain, Conn., 1983-86; sales assoc. Westledge Assocs., Realtors, Middletown, Conn., 1984-85; dir. relocation Westledge Assocs., Realtors, Avon, Conn., 1985-86, dir. tng., 1987—; br. sales mgr. Westledge Assocs., Realtors, Wallingford, Conn., 1986-87; instr. real estate U. New Haven, 1987—, Grad. Realtors Inst., 1987—. Mem. Nat. Assn. Realtors, Cen. Conn. Bd. Realtors (chair edn. com. 1982—). Republican. Congregationalist. Home: 34 Quaker Farms Rd Oxford CT 06483 Office: Westledge Assocs Realtors 300 W Main St Avon CT 06001

MEDARIS, FLORENCE ISABEL, osteopathic physician and surgeon; b. Kirksville, Mo.; d. Charles Edward and Nellie (Finley) Medaris; B.A., Coll. Wooster, 1932; D.O., Kirksville Coll. Osteopathy and Surgery, 1939; postgrad. U. Wis., Marquette U. Pvt. practice osteo. medicine and surgery, Milw., 1940—. Active Milwaukee County Mental Assn., Milw. Art Center, Friends of Art; mem. med. bd. dirs. Milw. Soc. Multiple Sclerosis Soc., 1973—; mem. Mayor's Beautification Com., 1968—. Dir. Zonta Manor, 1957-67, Brace Fund Bd. of Advt. Women of Milw., 1958-64, pres. bd., 1962-63, 77—; bd. mem. Bookfellows Milw.; finance com. Coll. Womens Club Found., 1971-78. Mem. Am. Osteo. Assn. (com. mental health 1964), Wis. Assn. Osteo. Physicians and Surgeons, Milw. Dist. Soc., Osteo. Physicians and Surgeons, Am. Coll. Gen. Practitioners, Applied Acad. Osteopathy, Am. Assn. U. Women, Inter-Group Council Women (pres. 1947-49, dir.), Wis. Pub. Health Assn., Council for Wis. Writers, Photog. Soc. Am., Wis. Acad. Scis., Arts and Letters, Delta Omega (nat. pres. 1952-53). Presbyn. Club: Zonta (bd. mem. Milw. 1968-69). Home: 1121 N Waverly Pl Milwaukee WI 53202 Office: 161 W Wisconsin Ave Milwaukee WI 53203

MEDDAUGH, LAURA JENEAN, accounting director; b. Santa Monica, Calif., Oct. 31, 1956; d. Rogers Arthur and Al Mae (Tryon) Hornsby; m. Robert Howard Meddaugh, Dec. 26, 1976; 1 child, Tiffany Beth. BS in Indsl. Psychology, Calif. State U., Hayward, 1981. From mgmt. trainee to dir. merchandise acctg. I. Magnin, San Francisco, 1982-84, 85—; mgr. sales audit Ross Stores, Inc., Newark, Calif., 1985. Commr. Hayward Environ. Quality Comm., 1986—. Mem. Golden Gate Retail Fin. Execs. Assn. (assoc.). Democrat. Office: I Magnin 185 Berry St San Francisco CA 94107

MEDEIROS, BARBARA DENIS JEAN, accountant; b. Honolulu, Feb. 7, 1934; d. Anthony Sebastian and Rose (Furtado) Denis; m. Carlos Louis Medeiros, Mar. 28, 1953; children: Carlos Louis Jr., Matthew Mark, Joel Carter, Timothy Francis. Sec. The Med. Group, Kailua, Hawaii, 1956-62; preparer vital stats. Castle Med. Ctr., Kailua, 1962-77; tax preparer H&R Block Exec. Tax Service, Honolulu, 1979—, instr. income tax preparation, 1981—. Author: Eight Lines of Family Geneology, 1986. Mem. Beta Sigma Phi (pres. Honolulu chpt.). Democrat. Roman Catholic. Home: 619 Kaha St Kailua HI 96734 Office: Holland Mgmt and Tax Service 629-A Kailua Rd Suite 3 Kailua HI 96734

MEDEROS, CAROLINA LUISA, federal executive; b. Rochester, Minn., July 1, 1947; d. Luis O. and Carolina (del Valle) M. BA, Vanderbilt U., 1969; MA, U. Chgo., 1971. Adminstrv. asst. Lt. Gov. of Ill., Chgo., 1972; sr. research assoc. U. Chgo., 1972; project mgr., cons. Urban Dynamics, Inner City Fund and Community Programs Inc., Chgo., 1972-73; legis. asst. to Senate pres. Ill. State Senate, Chgo. and Springfield, 1973-76; program analyst Dept Transp., Washington, 1976-79, chief, trans. assistance programs div., 1979-81, dir. programs and evaluation, 1981-88, chairwoman, sec.'s safety rev. task force, 1985-88; deputy asst. sec. for safety Dept Transp., 1988—. Recipient award for Meritorious Achievement, Sec. Transp. 1980, Superior Achievement award U.S. Dept. Transp., 1981, Sec.'s Gold Medal Award for Outstanding Achievement, 1986, Presdl. Rank award, 1987. Mem. Am. Assn. Budget and Program Analysis, Exec. Women in Govt., Womens Trans. Seminar, World Affairs Council of Washington, D.C. Home: 2723 O St NW Washington DC 20007 Office: US Dept Transp 400 Seventh St SW Washington DC 20590

MEDLENKA, CONNIE LEE, furrier; b. Kansas City, Mo., Jan. 1, 1936; d. Glenn Wilson Griggs and Therresia Juanita (Holland) Booher; m. Ramon Joseph Medlenka; children: Becky Pursley, Paula Meharg. Grad. high sch., Ft. Worth. Furrier Sanger Harris Dept. Store, Dallas, 1967-81, R.E. Cox & Co. (name changed to Stripling and Cox), Ft. Worth, 1981—. Roman Catholic. Office: Stripling & Cox 6370 Camp Bowie Fort Worth TX 76116

MEDLEY, SHERRILYN, auditor; b. Oneida, Ky., Sept. 7, 1946; d. Ora E. and Rheba (Allen) Rice; m. James F. Laughlin, Sept. 20, 1966 (div. Apr. 1969); m. James Silas Medley, Jan. 25, 1980. B.S. in Acctg., U. Ky., 1975; M.B.A., Xavier U., 1986. Cert. internal auditor. Tchr., Ky. Bus. Coll., Lexington, 1976-78; claims approver Met. Life Ins. Co., Lexington, 1967-73; staff acct. Jerrico, Inc., Lexington, 1976-77, acctg. supr., 1977-80, sr. auditor, 1980-82, internal audit supr., 1982-86; internal audit mgr., 1986-87; sr. internal. audit mgr., 1988—. Vol., Cen. Bapt. Aux., Lexington, 1984. Mem. Inst. Internal Auditors (chpt. pres. 1985-86), Nat. Assn. Accts., Bluegrass Soc. MBA's, Am. Assn. Female Execs. Beta Alpha Psi. Republican. Home: 118 Dundee Dr Lexington KY 40503

MEDLIN, DOROTHY ANN, retail executive; b. Chattanooga, July 1, 1935; d. Garry S. and Ida (Schmidt) M. Exec. asst. Dillard Smith Constrn. Co., Chattanooga, 1956-87; v.p. WOAGO, Inc., Chattanooga, 1986—; pres. Mistletoe and Memories, Chattanooga, 1987—. Named to Hon. Order of Ky. Cols. Gov. Commonwealth of Ky. Mem. Assn. Am. Bus. Women (Woman of Yr. 1972, 79), Chattanooga Bus. and Profl. Women (numerous offices), Freedoms Found. (corr. sec. Chattanooga chpt. 1986—), Tenn. Assn. Parliamentarians (treas.), Tenn. Assn. Parliamentarians (v.p.). Home: 104 Parkdale Ave Chattanooga TN 37411

MEDWAY, MARCIA LUTZ, internal auditor; b. Phila., Dec. 28, 1955; d. Arnold David and Elaine (Entliss) L.; m. Frederic Jeffrey Medway; Aug. 13, 1977; children: Lauren Jessica, Scott Jonathan. BSBA, Phila. Coll. of Textiles and Sci., 1977. Acct. II S.C. Dept. of Youth Services, Columbia, 1978-81, audit supr., 1981-87; dir. internal audits Midlands Tech. Coll., Columbia, 1987—. Mem. Orgn. for Rehab. Tng., Columbia, 1986—; fund raiser chmn. Girl Scouts of Am., Columbia, 1987—. Mem. Inst. Internal Auditors (gov. 1983, sec. 1988), S.C. State Internal Auditors Assn. (exec. com. 1982—, Achievement award 1985), Assn. Coll. and Univ. Auditors, Am. Assn. of Women in Jr. and Community Colls., S.C. Tech. Edn. Assn., Cen. State Adv. Fin. Com. (chtr.). Home: 101 Larkspur Rd Columbia SC 29212 Office: Midlands Tech Coll PO Box 29202 Columbia SC 29202

MEDWIN, MICHELE BRAND, optometrist; b. Queens, N.Y., Aug. 24, 1954; d. David and Marilyn Brand; m. Steven J. Medwin, June 6, 1976; children: Daniel, Rachel. BS with honors, Cornell U., 1976; OD, Pa. Coll. Optometry, 1980. Optometrist Dr. Allen Levine, Wilmington, Del., 1980-83; pvt. practice optometry Wilmington, Del., 1982—; staff optometrist Nemours Health Clinic, Wilmington, Del., Wilmington Hosp. Bd. dirs. Albert Einstein Acad., Wilmington, 1985-86. Mem. Am. Optometric Assn. (licensure and regulation com.), Del. Optometric Assn. (pres. 1986-88). Office: 2004 Foulk Rd Wilmington DE 19810

MEEDER, JEANNE ELIZABETH, food technologist; b. Erie, Pa., Mar. 5, 1950; d. Theodore Roosevelt and Linnie Loretta (Drury) M. BA, Houghton Coll., 1972; postgrad. Kent State U., 1978-81. Product devel. technician Welch Foods Inc., Westfield, N.Y., 1972-73, tech. asst., 1973, assoc. tech. asst., 1973-76, sr. tech. asst., 1976; research and devel. technologist Stouffer Foods Corp., Solon, Ohio, 1976-77, entree team leader, 1977-82; sr. food technologist Del Monte Corp., Walnut Creek, Calif., 1982-84, prin. food technologist, 1984-85, mgr. product devel., 1985-86, mgr. exploratory research, 1986-88; dir. new product devel. Kibun Products Internat., Inc., Raleigh, N.C., 1988—. Mem. Home Economists in Business (treas. San Francisco sect. 1986-88), Nat. Food Processors Inst., Am. Home Econs. Assn., Inst. Food Technologists, Am. Culinary Fedn., Internat. Microwave Power Inst., San Francisco Profl. Food Soc., East Bay Culinary Assn., Nat. Assn. Female Execs., Women's Network of Contra Costa County, D.A.R., West County Hist. Soc. Republican. Presbyterian. Lodge: Order of Eastern Star. Avocations: antiques, refinishing furniture, gardening, literature, travel. Home: 5031-C Wallingford Dr RaleighCreek NC 27604 Office: Kibun Products Internat Inc 5609 Departure Dr Raleigh NC 27604

MEEHAN, DENISE DUFFY, journalist; b. Huntington, N.Y., Oct. 14, 1954; d. Francis Xavier and Myrtle (Dionne) Duffy; m. John Faulkner Meehan, Jan. 3, 1981; 1 child, Sean. BA in Am. Studies, SUNY, Old Westbury, 1977; cert. in Pub. Relations, NYU, 1980; cert. in antique appraisal, Hofstra U., 1985. Vocat. counselor Nassau County Neighborhood Youth Corps., Hempstead, N.Y., 1976-79; pub. relations asst. Internat. Air Transport Assn., Montreal, 1979-81; publicity dir. Chris Lockwood & Assocs., N.Y.C., 1981; v.p. communications Chris Lockwood Communications, N.Y.C., 1981-82; assoc. editor Travel-Holiday Mag., Floral Park, N.Y., 1982-85; restaurant editor Goodliving Mag., Jericho, N.Y., 1985—. freelance editor various mags., Huntington, N.Y., 1977. counselor Coalition for Abused Women, East Meadow, N.Y., 1977-78, Divorce Info. Ctr., Garden City, N.Y., 1977-78; Nassau consumer rep., plan devel. com. Nassau-Suffolk Health Systems Agy., Melville, N.Y., 1978-79; bd. dirs., editor newsletter Parent Resource Ctr., Port Washington, 1986-87. Home: 8 Stuyvesant St Huntington NY 11743

MEEHAN, KANDY LEE, real estate executive; b. Alva, Okla., Mar. 17, 1951; d. Robert Leonard and Jeanette A. (Wade) Sams; m. J. Kevin Meehan, May 5, 1984; 1 child, Caitlin Elizabeth. BS, Kans. State U., 1973, MS cum laude, 1974. Lic. broker Kans., Mo. Prof., head dept. Benedictine Coll., Atchison, Kans., 1974-76; sub. tchr. various sch. dists., Buffalo, 1977-78; prof. SUNY, Buffalo, 1978-79; sales exec., mgr. Louis R. Trigg & Assocs., Overland Park, Kans., 1979-82; mgr., broker Coldwell Banker, Overland Park, 1983-87, Kansas City, Mo., 1987—. Mem. Nat. Assn. Realtors, Kansas City Bd. Realtors, Johnson Bd. Realtors, Nat. Assn. Female Execs., Bus. and Profl. Women, Omicron Nu. Office: Coldwell Banker 4137 Pennsylvania Kansas City MO 64111

MEEHAN, MARY JANE, state agency administrator; b. Elizabeth, N.J., June 11, 1945; d. Michael and Louise Ann (Balboa) Miglorie; divorced; children: Kelly, Frank, Michael, Jennifer. BS in Nursing, Seton Hall U., 1971, MS in Nursing, 1983. Med./surg., intensive care staff nurse St. Elizabeth Hosp., Elizabeth, N.J., 1971-76; intensive care staff nurse Rahway (N.J.) Hosp., 1976, intensive care/coronary head nurse, 1976-78, edn. adminstr., 1978-83; spl. agt. for the commr. N.J. Dept. of Labor, Trenton, 1983-84, dir. div. of employment, tng., 1984-86, asst. commr. of labor, human resources, 1986—; departmental design cons. Elizabeth Gen. Med. Ctr., 1984-86; expert witness consultation, testimony including ct. appearances for law firms, 1980-86. Mem. Gov's. Employment Policy Task Force, Trenton, Gov's. Commn. for Bus. & Job Retention, Trenton, PTA Arthur L. Johnson Regional High Sch., 1980—; chairwoman N.J. Judiciary Dept., Youth Services Commn., Trenton. Mem. Am. Assn. of Critical Care Nurses (cert.), N.J. State Nursing Assn., Exec. Women of N.J., Seton Hall Alumni Assn., Sigma Theta Tau. Republican. Roman Catholic. Home: 86 Broadway Clark NJ 07066

MEEHAN, MARY JO, hospital administrator; b. Orange, N.J., Dec. 29, 1949; d. Eugene Joseph and Mary Fitzgerald (Lee) M. BA, Seton Hall U., 1972, MA, 1974. Rehab. counselor Mt. Carmel Guild, Union City, N.J., 1974-75; rehab. counselor Passaic-Clifton (N.J.) Community Mental Health Ctr., 1975-78, dir. transitional services, 1978-80; dir. Marian Ctr., 1980-83; dir. mental health St. Mary's Hosp., Passaic, 1983-88; asst. adminstr. St. Vincent's Hosp., Harrison, N.Y., 1988—; cons. in field. Trustee Passaic Mental Health Clinic, 1987—. Mem. Am. Rehab. Counseling Assn. (pres. Passaic County 1980-81), Nat. Rehab. Assn. (v.p. Passaic County 1986—), N.J. Psychosocial Rehab. Assn. (v.p. 1987—). Democrat. Roman Catholic. Home: 47 N Fullerton Ave Montclair NJ 07042 Office: St Mary's Hosp 211 Pennington Ave Passaic NJ 07055

MEEK, MARTHA ANNE, editor; b. Martin, Tenn., Aug. 20, 1936; d. Paul and Martha Washington (Campbell) M.; m. Robert Kelly Roney III, June 14, 1957, (div. Feb. 1985); children: Robert Kelly IV, Lisa Claire. BS, U. Tenn., Martin, 1959; MS, U. Tenn, Knoxville, 1969; EdD, U. Tenn., Knoxville, 1976. Cert. elem. tchr., Tenn. Tchr. city and county schs., Tenn., 1965-75; prin. Knox County Schs., Tenn., 1976-79, supr., 1979-87; mng. editor Ednl. Leadership Assn. for Supervision and Curriculum Devel., Alexandria, Va., 1987—; cons. State of Tenn. Dept. Edn., Maryville City Schs., Memphis City Schs., Shelby County Schs., Scott County Schs., Oak Ridge Mental Health Ctr., Maine Assn. for Supervision and Curriculum Devel.; reviewer Internat. Reading Assn., Allyn and Bacon. Contbr. and editor articles for profl. jours. V.p. Greater Knoxville Beautification Bd., 1981-84, pres. 1984-85; mem. Devel. Com., U. Tenn., Martin, 1984-87. Mem. Tenn. Edn. Assn. (bd. dirs. local assn. 1986-87), NEA, Tenn. Assn. Supervision and Curriculum Devel. (jour. com. chmn. and editor, 1981-87, recipient Outstanding Service award 1986), Phi Delta Kappa. Democrat. Methodist. Office: Assn Supervision Curriculum Devel 125 N West St Alexandria VA 22314

MEEKER, ARLENE DOROTHY HALLIN (MRS. WILLIAM MAURICE MEEKER), manufacturing company executive; b. Glendale, Calif., June 13, 1935; d. Haddon Eric and Martha (Randow) Hallin; grad. John Muir Jr. Coll., 1953; student Los Angeles Valley Coll., 1956-58, B.A., Whittier Coll., 1973, M.B.A., 1980; m. William Maurice Meeker, Aug. 19, 66; 1 son, William Michael. Statewide sec. pub. relations United Reps. Calif., Los Angeles, 1964; personnel specialist Sanford Mgmt. Services, Inc., Los Angeles, 1964-66; v.p. personnel Grover Mfg. Corp., Montebello, Calif., 1966-75, pres., 1975—, dir., 1969—, chmn. of bd. 1975—; dir. Brit. Marine Industries, Montebello, 1969-86, chmn. bd. 1986—. Grover Ltd., Bandon, County Cork, Ireland, 1986—, Grover Internat., 1969—. Mem. City of Whittier Transp. and Parking Commn., 1976-84, chmn. commn., 1977-79, vice chmn., 1982-84; council mem. Los Angeles County Art Mus., 1969-80; chmn. fine arts bd. Hillcrest Congl. Ch., mem. Ch. council, 1977-79; trustee Oxford Prep. Sch., Whittier, Calif., 1981-86. Patron KCET Ednl. TV, Action for Children's TV, Whittier Guild, Children's Hosp.; visitors bd. Whittier Coll., 1983—; press chmn. Whittier Rep. Women Federated, 1977-78, 1st v.p., 1981-83; Rep. precinct capt., 1964; pres. Whittier Lincoln Club, 1982-84. Mem. Docian Soc. (pub. relations chmn. 1967-68), Los Angeles World Affairs Council, AAUW, Friendly Hills Property Owners Assn. (pres. 1982-84). Conglist. Clubs: Newport Harbor Yacht (Newport Beach, Calif.); Friendly Hills Country (Whittier, Calif.). Author: Stress Differences Between Male and Female Executives, 1982. Home: 9710 Portada Dr Whittier CA 90603 Office: 620 S Vail St Montebello CA 90640

MEEKS, CAROLLE JEAN, data processing executive; b. St. Louis, May 22, 1943; d. Hubert H. and Bernice (Apel) Hoog. BS, Tex. Christian U., 1972, Masters in Mgmt. Sci., 1973; postgrad., U. Tex., Arlington, 1973-74, 78-81; MS in Indsl. Engring., U. Pitts., 1978. Cert. in data processing. Systems analyst Kimbell, Inc., Ft. Worth, 1972-75; mgr. systems and program devel. Fox Grocery Co., Belle Vernon, Pa., 1975-77; project leader Giant Eagle Corp., Pitts., 1977-78; sr. systems analyst The Drawing Bd., Dallas, 1978-79, Zale Corp., Dallas, 1979-81; system planner Sperry Flight Systems, Phoenix, 1981-83; dir. computer services Cen. Ariz. Coll., Coolidge, 1983—. Mem. Cause, Nat. Assn. Female Execs., Alpha Sigma Lambda. Republican. Roman Catholic. Home: Rt 3 Box 335-A Casa Grande AZ 85222 Office: Cen Ariz Coll Woodruff and Overfield Rd Coolidge AZ 85228

MEEKS, TERRI LYNN, social services administrator; b. Bessemer, Ala., May 30, 1962; d. Bobby Harris Meeks and Jo Ann (Winslett) McGee. BS, Auburn U., 1985. Lab. technician Gordon County Farm Co., Calhoun, Ga., 1985-86; adminstr. Crisis Ctr. of E. Ala., Auburn, 1986—. Mem. Dept. of Vol. Services, Lee County, Ala., 1986—; vocat. evaluator Lee County Youth Devel. Ctr., Opelika, 1986—. Recipient Linly Heflin Scholarship, 1980-85. Mem. Nat. Assn. Female Execs. Club: Rehab (Auburn U.) (v.p. 1986-87). Home: 1218 Wrights Mill Rd Auburn AL 36830 Office: Crisis Ctr of E Ala Inc PO Box 1949 Auburn AL 36831

MEELHEIM, HELEN DIANE, nurse, nursing administrator; b. Charleston, W.Va., Mar. 25, 1952; d. Richard Young and Dolores (Frick) M. BS in Nursing, U. N.C., 1974; MS in Nursing, East Carolina U., 1982. Charge nurse Pitt County Health Dept., Greenville, N.C., 1974-77; nursing adminstr. East Carolina U. Sch. of Med., Greenville, N.C., 1978—, clin. instr., 1986—; cons. Eastern Area Health Edn. Ctr., Greenville. Served to capt. Army Nurse Corps, U.S. Army Res. Mem. Oncology Nurses Soc., Am. Nurses Assn. (cert. family nurse practitioner), N.C. State Nurses Assn., Hospice of E. Carolina. Democrat. Episcopalian. Avocation: painting. Home: 32 Flemington Rd Chapel Hill NC 27514 Office: East Carolina U Sch Medicine Dept Surgery Greenville NC 27834

MEESE, CELIA EDWARDS, pharmaceutical and nutritional supplement company executive; b. San Diego, May 10, 1938; d. Roy Clifford Edwards and Bessie Lucille (Lang) Hill; m. Jed D. Meese, July 6, 1963; 1 son, Scott Edwards. Student U. Calif.-Sacramento, 1958-60; B.A., U. Wis., 1964; B.A. (hon.), U. Taiwan, 1965. Office mgr. Pacific Telephone, San Jose, Calif., 1965-72; pres. Vitaline Corp., Incline Village, Nev., 1972—; v.p. RenalChem, Inc., San Jose, Calif., 1982—, Formulations Tech., Inc., Oakdale, Calif., 1982—; dir. Spectra Diagnostics, San Jose. Bd. dirs. Sierra Council on Alcoholism, Kings Beach, Calif., 1980—. English-Chinese Exchange Council, Taipei, 1964-65; vol. Brandon House, San Jose, 1965—, Children's Home Soc., San Jose, 1965—; mem. steering com. U.S. Rep. Mineta, Calif., 1974. Mem. Pharm. Mfrs. Assn., Am. Soc. Bariatric Physicians, Mensa (proctor 1985). Home: PO Box 4772 Incline Village NV 89450 Office: Vitaline Corp PO Box 6757 Incline Village NV 89450

MEGAL, CAROLYN ANN, chemical company executive; b. Stevens Point, Wis., Apr. 12, 1952; d. Ambrose A. and Ester (Iwanski) M. BS in Chemistry, U. Wis., Stevens Point, 1974. Devel. engr. Velsicol Chem., Ann Arbor, Mich., 1974-79; chemist Tech. Service, Pontiac, Mich., 1980-81; acctg. mgr. Ciba-Geigy Corp., Madison Heights, Mich., 1981—. Mem. Am. Soc. Body Engrs., Soc. Automotive Engrs., Soc. for Advancement of Material and Process Engring., Soc. Plastics Engrs., LWV, NOW. Home: 3490 Oak Knoll Brighton MI 48116

MEGDAL, SHARON BERNSTEIN, economics educator, consultant; b. Newark, Apr. 4, 1952; d. William B. and Ann (Kopatonsky) Bernstein; m. Ronald G. Megdal, Aug. 18, 1974. A.B. in Econs., Rutgers U., 1974; M.A. in Econs., Princeton U., 1977, Ph.D. in Econs., 1981. Asst. prof. econs. U. Ariz., Tucson, 1979-87, pres., owner MegEcon Cons. Group, 1987— ; vis. assoc. prof. No. Ariz. U., 1987-88; commr. Ariz. Corp. Commn., 1985-87. Bd. dirs. Tucson Issues Forum, Tucson Tomorrow; mem. First Leadership Am. Class. Contbr. articles on econs. to profl. jours. Vol. United Way of Greater Tucson, 1982-85, 87-88. Richard D. Irwin fellow, 1977-78; fellow Princeton U., 1974-78. Mem. Am. Econs. Assn. (com. on status of women 1983—), Women Execs. in State Govt., Nat. Assn. Regulatory Utility Commrs. (com. on electricity), Phi Beta Kappa, Beta Gamma Sigma.

MEGOFNA, C(HRISTINE) GAIL, administrator, medical corporation manager, nurse; b. New Britain, Conn., Aug. 12, 1949; d. Edward Lucian and Mary Dorothy (Cappello) Jacynowicz; 1 child, William John, Jr. A in Bus. Adminstrn./Med. Scis., Briarwood Coll., Southington, Conn., 1969; R.N., Tunxis Sch. Nursing, Farmington, 1981; postgrad., 1981-86; A in Mktg., Tunxis Community Coll., 1984. Cert. in counseling and human services. Kinetic therapist Kinetic Concepts, San Antonio, Tex., 1981-83; mktg. cons. JM Mktg., Rocky Hill, Conn., 1983-87; area mgr. PCS div. EMPI, Fridley, Minn., 1984-85; mktg. mgr. H.L. Moore Med. Corp., New Britain, 1985-87; adminstr. Nursefinders of Hartford, Inc., 1987—; cons., owner, pres. correctional health care. Pres. Briarwood Coll., Southington, 1967-69. Mem. Nat. Assn. Female Execs., Sales and Mktg. Execs., Conn. Bus. and Industry Assn., Am. Correctional Assn., Am. Correctional Health Services Assn. (bd. dirs.), Am. Jail Assn. (chmn. profl. adv. com.). Democrat. Roman Catholic. Club: New Britain Jr. Woman Club (health chmn. 1977, treas. 1977, sec. 1978). Avocations: golf, reading music, coaching little league. Home: 422 Clinton St New Britain CT 06053

MEGRATH, ROSANNE, company sales executive; b. Mt. Vernon, N.Y., Oct. 7, 1947; d. Vincent James and Antonina (LaRocca) Costantino; 1 dau., Catherine Anne. B.A., U. Bridgeport, 1969. Sec. John Carey, Architect, Pleasantville, N.Y. 1973-75; instr. Manatee Jr. Coll., Bradenton, Fla., 1978-80; sec. Tropicana Products, Bradenton, 1975-79; adminstrv. asst. to v.p., sales and mktg. Tropicana Products Sales, Inc., Bradenton, 1979-83, mgr. mil. sales, 1983—. Mem. PTA, Bradenton, 1977-84. Mem. Am. Logistics Assn. Am. Mgmt. Assn. Republican. Roman Catholic. Home: 3212 21st Ave Dr West Bradenton FL 34205 Office: Tropicana Products Sales Inc PO Box 338 Bradenton FL 34206

MEHERIN, MARGARET WILSON, accountant; b. Mobile, Ala., Jan. 5, 1955; d. Joseph Henry Jr. and Rose Patricia (McNamara) W.; m. Dennis Peter Meherin, May 31, 1975; children: Bridget Claire, Molly Margaret. BS in Commerce, Spring Hill Coll., 1975. CPA, Ala. Staff acct. L.E. Nicholas & Co., Mobile, Ala., 1975, Morrison and Smith, CPA's, Mobile, Ala., 1975-77; pvt. practice acctg. Mobile, Ala., 1977-88; sec., treas. Gulf Coast Electronics, Inc., Mobile, Ala., 1980-81, Wilson Electric Co., Inc., Mobile, Ala., 1980—. Sec., treas. Med. Clinic Bd. Second City of Mobile, 1980-82; bd. dirs. St. Dominic's Sch., Mobile, 1985-86. Mem. Am. Inst. CPA's, Am. Women's Soc. CPA's, Ala. Soc. CPA's, Am. Soc. Women Accts. Roman Catholic. Home and Office: 1283 Skywood Dr Mobile AL 36693

MEHLING, DAPHNE KAY, computer professional; b. Newark, Ohio, Feb. 17, 1960; d. Wilfred Louis and Mary Jane (Ridenour) M. B, Bowling Green (Ohio) State U., 1983. Programmer, analyst ALLTEL, Twinsburg, Ohio, 1984—. Mem. Nat. Assn. for Female Execs. Roman Catholic. Home: 38365 N Lane G204 Willoughby OH 44094 Office: ALLTEL 2000 Highland Dr Twinsburg OH 44087

MEHTA, EILEEN ROSE, lawyer, real estate development executive; b. Colver, Pa., Apr. 1, 1953; d. Richard Glenn and Helen (Wahna) Ball; m. Abdul Rashid Mehta, Aug. 31, 1973. Student Miami U., Oxford, Ohio, 1971-73; B.A. with high distinction, Fla. Internat. U., 1974; J.D. cum laude U. Miami (Fla.), 1977. Bar: Fla. 1977. Law clk. U.S. Dist. Ct. (so. dist.) Fla., Miami, 1977-79; asst. county atty. Dade County Atty.'s Office, Miami, 1979—; v.p., dir. Shalimar Trucking, Inc., 1984—, Coral Reef Cruises, Inc., 1984—, Mehtatron Enterprises, Inc., 1985—; guest lectr. U. Miami Law Sch., Coral Gables, Fla., 1982, 83. Alumni scholar Miami U., Oxford, 1971-73. Mem. ABA, Fla. Bar Assn. Office: 111 NW 1st St Dade County Atty's Office Met-Dade Ctr Suite 2810 Miami FL 33128

MEIDL, KATHLEEN JOAN, marketing professional; b. Watsonville, Calif., Apr. 18, 1945; d. Joseph Herbert Meidl and Norma Marie (Sears) Vucinich; 1 child, Jason Blaine. BA, U. Ariz., 1967. Sales clk., mgr. night Budget Rent-A-Car, San Francisco, 1967-68; sec., bookkeeper Kling Oil Co., Redwood City, Calif., 1968-69; adminstrv. asst. Renault and Handley, Palo Alto, Calif., 1969-73; office mgr. Barnett-Winston, Menlo Park, Calif., 1973-74; mgr. office adminstrn. Louis Allen Assocs., Palo Alto, Calif., 1974-78; mgr. mktg. adminstrn. Dysan Corp., Santa Clara, Calif., 1978-84; mgr. product Dysan Corp., Santa Clara, 1984-86; analyst mktg. Santa Cruz Ops., Calif., 1986—. Mem. Santa Clara Word Processing Assn. (dir. 1978-80). Republican. Episcopalian. Office: Santa Cruz Operation 400 Encinal St Santa Cruz CA 95060

MEIER, ENGE, university administrator; b. N.Y.C., Jan. 17, 1929; d. Rudolf and Kate (Furstenow) Pietschyck; m. Alfred August Meier, Sept. 11, 1948; children: Kenneth Randolph, Philip Alan. Student, Mercy Coll., 1980-84; BBA, Western States U. Tchr. nursery sch. Neu Ulm, Fed. Republic Germany, 1963-64; sec. Brewster (N.Y.) Mid. Sch., 1969-72; teaching asst. Brewster Elem. Sch., 1972-73; office asst. Bd. Coop. Edn., Yorktown Heights, N.Y., 1973-76; sec. Am. Can. Co., Greenwich, Conn., 1976-77, adminstrv. sec., 1977-79, exec. sec., 1979-84; adminstrv. asst. U. Tex., Austin, 1984-85, adminstrv. assoc., 1985-86, sr. adminstrv. assoc., 1986—. Vol. Laguna Gloria, Austin, 1984; docent LBJ Library & Mus., Austin, 1984—; usher Performing Arts Ctr., Austin, 1986—. Mem. Profl. Sec. Internat. (bd. dirs. Austin chpt. 1985-86), Women in Mgmt., Bus. & Profl. Women (bd. dirs. Austin chpt. 1987—), Nat. Assn. for Female Execs., Am. Payroll Assn. Presbyterian. Office: U Tex 6th and Colorado Sts Austin TX 78701

MEIER, KAREN LORENE, educator; b. Davenport, Iowa, Aug. 17, 1942; d. Charles Frank and Minnie Louise (Arp) Meier; BA, U. Iowa, 1963, MA, 1974. Tchr., librarian Plano (Ill.) High Sch., 1963-67; tchr. social studies Moline (Ill.) High Sch., 1967—, also secondary social studies coordinator; registered rep. 1st Investors Corp., 1987-88. Bd. dirs. Quad-City World Affairs Council; active LWV. Recipient regional award Ill. State Hist. Soc. Mem. Nat. Council Social Studies, Ill. Council Social Studies (sec. 1973-74, v.p. 1974-75, 86-87, pres.-elect 1987—, bd. dirs. 1982-83, treas. 1984-86), Iowa Council Social Studies, NEA, Ill. Edn. Assn. (sec.-treas. regional council 1975-79, legis. chairperson 1980-81), Moline Edn. Assn. (pres. 1977-78), Am. Soc. Profl. and Exec. Women, Social Studies Suprs. Assn., Assn. Supervision and Curriculum Devel., AAUW, Women in Ednl. Adminstrn., (dir. 1985, pres. 1985-86, past pres. 1986-87, asst. pres. 1986-87, bd. dirs. 1987-88, bd. dirs. at large 1987-88), Iowa Women in Ednl. Leadership, Alpha Delta Kappa. Home: 1855 14th St Bettendorf IA 52722 Office: 3850 Blackhawk Rd Rock Island IL 61201

MEIER, NANCY JO, nursing consultant; b. Sidney, Nebr., Dec. 15, 1951; d. Donald William and Clara Jo (Miller) M. BA, Midland Luth. Coll., 1974; diploma in Nursing, Immanual Hosp. Sch. Nursing, Omaha, 1974; MS in Nursing Edn., Tex. Women's U., 1978. RN, Tex. Staff nurse St. Lukes Episcopal Hosp./Tex. Heart Inst., Houston, 1974-75, Park Plaza Hosp., Houston, 1976; clin. nursing specialist Houston Thoracic and Cardiovascular Assn., 1977-78; instr. clin. nursing Cedar Sinai Med. Ctr., Los Angeles, 1978-79; dir. dept. nursing edn. Los Angeles New Hosp., 1979-80; ind. cons. nursing edn. Los Angeles, 1980-81; systems support specialist IVAC Corp., San Diego, 1981-83; med. specialist, advt. account exec. Kenneth C. Smith & Assocs., La Jolla, Calif., 1983-87; ind. nursing cons. San Diego, 1987—; cons. nursing edn. Nat. Med. Enterprises, Saudi Arabia, 1980-81, Nursing Services Internat., Los Angeles, 1980, Grossmont Hosp., San Diego, 1985; instr. cardiac life support Los Angeles chpt. Am. Heart Assn., 1978-84; lectr. in field. Organist United Meth. Ch., Sidney, 1967-69, Immanual Sch. Nursing, 1971-74, Meml. Luth. Ch., Houston, 1977-78; bd. dirs. Bluffs of Fox Run Homeowners Assn., San Diego, 1984-85, pres., 1985-86. Mem. Am. Nurses Assn., Am. Assn. Operating Room Nurses, Med. Mktg. Assn., Sigma Theta Tau. Republican. Lutheran. Home and Office: 2963 Old Bridgeport Way San Diego CA 92111

MEIER-VOTIK, BARBARA ELLEN, electronics company executive; b. Clearwater, Fla., Apr. 10, 1944; d. James O. and Ethel Constance White; m. J. Carl Votik Jr., Sept. 21, 1985; children: Harvey J., MaryEllen. BS in Bus Edn., James Madison U., 1965; student, U. Va., 1978-79. Cert. bus. tchr. Tchr. Prince William (Va.) county sch. dist., Manassas, 1966-67, bus. tchr., 1975-80; bus. tchr. Temple Bus. Sch., Alexandria, Va., 1967-69, Greenville County (Va) Sch. Dist., Emporia, 1981-82; account rep. Weaver's Bus. Machines, Charlotte, N.C., 1983-84; market support rep. Brother Internat. Corp., Atlanta, 1984-85; sales devel. mgr. Brother Internat. Corp., Piscataway, N.J., 1985-86; dist. sales mgr. Brother Internat. Corp., Miami, Fla., 1986—. Author: (book) Brother Dealer Guide, 1986, (tng. guides) Self Paced Training, 1984, 85; editor: (book) Brother Training Guide, 1986. Club: Toastmasters. Home: 882 N Fig Tree Ln Plantation FL 33317

MEIKLEJOHN, (LORRAINE) MINDY JUNE, political organizer; b. Staunton, Colo., June 9, 1929; d. Edward H. and Erna E. (Schwabe) Mindrup; student Ill. Bus. Coll., 1948, Red Rocks Community Coll., 1980-81; m. Alvin J. Meiklejohn, Apr. 25, 1953; children—Pamela, Shelley, Bruce, Scott. Pvt. sec. Ill. Liquor Commn., 1948-51, David M. Wilson, Ill. Sec. of State's Office, 1951-52; flight attendant Continental Airlines, 1952-53, pvt. sec. to mgr. flight services office, 1953-54; organizational dir. Colo. Republican Party, Denver, 1981-85, mem. Cen. Com., 1987—; campaign coordinator Hank Brown's Exploratory Campaign for Gov., 1985; mgr. Hank Brown for Congress, 1985-86; dep. campaign dir. Steve Schuck for Gov., 1985-86; vice chmn. 2d Congl. Cen. Com. Colo.; active campaigns; del., alt. to various, county, state, dist. and nat. assemblies and convs.; Colo. chmn. Citizens for Am., 1987—. Mem. Jefferson County Hist. Commn., Colo., 1974-82, pres., 1979; vol. Jefferson County Legal Aid Soc., 1970-74; vice chmn. Jefferson County Rep. Party, 1977-81, exec. com., 1987; vice chmn. Colo. State Rep. Party, 1981-85; chmn. Rep. Nat. Pilot Project on Volunteerism, 1981; mem. adv. council U.S. Peace Corps, 1982-84; sect. chmn. Jefferson County United Way Fund Drive; mem. exec. bd. Colo. Fedn. Rep. Women; pres. Operation Shelter, Inc., 1983—; bd. dirs. Jefferson County chpt. Am. Cancer Soc., 1987—. Lutheran. Club: Jefferson County Women's Rep. (edn. chmn. 1987—). Home: 7540 Kline Dr Arvada CO 80005

MEIL, KATE, accountant; b. N.Y.C., June 15, 1925; d. Jacob and Becky (Lichtman) Meil; 1 child, Maria Rebecca Black. B.B.A. in Acctg., CCNY, 1949. Acct. chem., printing, garment, machine and tool, film industries, 1943-73; office mgr., acct. Barrie Imports, Inc., Upper Saddle River, N.J., 1973—. Sculptor: Mein Kind, 1976, Determined to Be, 1977, Inner Mirror, 1979, Zeyda, 1980, Meydele, 1985. Leader Hudson Ave Area Residents Assn., Edgewater, 1973. Recipient Red and Blue Ribbons 3d Ann. N.J. Woodcarving and Wildlife Art Show, 1987. Mem. Salute to Women in Arts, Whittle Ones, Ethical Culture Soc. Clubs: Dumont Chessmates (N.J.); Palisades Nature Assn. (Alpine, N.J.). Avocations: chess; theater; folk dancing. Office: Barrie Imports Inc 145 Route 17 Upper Saddle River NJ 07458

MEILACH, DONA ZWEIGORON, author, lecturer, consultant; b. Chgo.; d. Julius and Rose (Don) Zweigoron; m. Melvin M. Meilach, Feb. 15, 1948; children: Susan Meilach Seligman, Allen. Student, Art Inst. Chgo. and Chgo. Jr. Colls., 1958-64, Palomar Jr. Coll., 1979-81; PhB, U. Chgo., 1946; MA in Art History, Northwestern U., 1969. Tchr. Evergreen Park (Ill.) High Sch., 1958-65; tchr. fundamentals of art Moraine Valley Jr. Coll., Palos Park, Ill., 1970-71; instr. art history and crafts Purdue U., Hammond, Ind., 1969-71; lectr. arts and crafts at various colls. and workshops in U.S. and Can. 1970—; pres. CompuWrite, Carlsbad, Calif., 1984—; appeared in various radio and TV programs including: Arlene Francis Show, 1972, Good Morning Show, 1973, Not For Women Only, 1975, Sun-Up San Diego, 1979. Author books on art-crafts, 1964—, including Creating Modern Furniture, 1975, Decorative and Sculptural Ironwork, 1977, Exotic Needlework, 1978, Basketry Today, 1979, Ethnic Jewelry, 1981; books on other subjects include: Art of Belly Dancing, 1975, Jazzercise 1978, How to Relieve Your Aching Back, 1979, Homemade Liqueurs, 1979, Homemade Cream Liqueurs, 1986; books on computers include Before You Buy a Computer, 1983, Before You Buy Word Processing Software, 1984, Before You Buy a Used Computer, 1985, Dynamics of Computer Graphics, 1986, Better Business Presentations, 1988; contbr. numerous articles to various newspapers and mags. including: Chgo. Sun-Times, N.Y. Times, Redbook, Cosmopolitan mag., Today's Health mag., PC mag., Bus. Software and others; contbr. articles to World Book Ency.; syndicated columnist Creative Crafts, 1974-77; editor Sphere mag., 1973; contbg. editor Computer Graphics Today, 1986—; contbr. numerous photographs to various newspapers and mags. Judge Oreg. State Fair, 1976, So. Calif. Expn. State Fair, 1977, Crocker Art Gallery, 1979; colleague San Diego County Dept. Edn., 1986, 87; arts commr. City of Carlsbad, Calif., 1986—. Mem. Author's Guild Am., Nat. Assn. Sci. Writers, Am. Craft Council, Artist-Blacksmith Assn. of N.Am., Nat. Computer Graphics Assn., SIGGRAPH, Sigma Delta Chi. Address: 2018 Saliente Way Carlsbad CA 92009

MEINERSMANN, KAREN LEE, service company executive; b. Waukegan, Ill., June 4, 1948; d. Herman Theodore and Rosalie Vera (Bronenkart) M. BSBA, U. Phoenix, 1987. Applications engr. Fairchild Test Systems, San Jose, 1979-81, mfg. project mgr., 1981-82; applications supr. GenRad Semiconductor Test, Milpitas, Calif., 1982-85; area sales mgr. NW and MW Aehr Test Systems, Menlo Park, Calif., 1985-87; owner Hanlee Services, Wichita, Kans., 1987—; cons. engring. Effective Search Inc., Wichita, 1987—. Mem. Nat. Assn. Female Execs., Nat. Assn. Women Bus. Owners. Presbyterian.

MEIS, JEANETTE KAY, elementary educator; b. Greeley, Colo., July 16, 1959; d. Gerald Martin and Kathryn Ella Jean (Chessmore) M. BA, U. No. Colo., 1980, MA, 1986. Cert. elem. tchr., Colo. Tchr. kindergarten Hugo (Colo.) Pub. Sch., 1981, tchr. 4th grade, 1981-82; tchr. Greeley Pub. Schs., 1982-83, tchr. 2d grade, 1983—; activity coordinator Colo. Camp Cherith, Woodland Park, 1978—, dir., 1988—. Mem. Alpha Delta Kappa. Baptist. Home: 1622 14th Ave Greeley CO 80631

MEIS, NANCY RUTH, marketing and fundraising executive; b. Iowa City, Aug. 6, 1952; d. Donald J. and Theresa (Dee) M.; m. Paul L. Wenske, Oct. 14, 1978; children—Alexis Meis Wenske, Christopher Meis Wenske. B.A., Clarke Coll., 1974; M.B.A., U. Okla., 1981. Cultural program supr. City of Dubuque, Iowa., 1974-76; community services dir. State Arts Council of Okla., Oklahoma City, 1976-78, program dir., 1978-79; mgr. Cimarron Circuit Opera Co., Norman, Okla., 1979-82, bd. dirs., 1982—; account exec. Bell System, Kansas City, Mo., 1982; mgr. special services Holy Land Christian Mission/Children Internat., Kansas City, 1983-86; dir. mktg. and fund raising, 1986—, dir. devel., 1987—; speaker in field. Named Outstanding Young Woman in Am., 1977, 78. Mem. Nat. Soc. Fund Raising Exec. (Kansas City chpt. program com. 1985), Nat. Network Bus. Sch. Women (rep. 1980), Nat. Assn. Female Execs., Greater Kansas City Council on Philanthropy. Roman Catholic.

MEISEL, CINDY LEE, retail executive; b. Detroit, Sept. 24, 1961; d. Paul Edgar and Colleen Anne (Leavy) M. BA, Heidelberg Coll., Tiffin, Ohio, 1983; MBA, Baldwin-Wallace Coll., Berea, Ohio, 1985. Mgr. The Candy Shop, Vermilion, Ohio, 1978-85; co-mgr. Youthland, Parma, Ohio, 1985-86; mgr. Warren, Ohio, 1986, Youngstown, Ohio, 1987, Beachwood, Ohio, 1987-88, Charlotte, N.C., 1988—. Named one of Outstanding Young Women in Am., 1986. Mem. Assn. Bus. and Profl. Women (treas. 1984-85, individual devel. rep. 1985, Young Careerist 1984), VFW. Democrat. Roman Catholic. Home: 2500 Eastway Dr 29C Charlotte NC 28205 Office: Youthland Inc 5639A Central Ave Charlotte NC 28212

MEISELMAN, MARIAN RUTH FLUM, training and hazard communications executive, industrial hygiene consultant; b. East Orange, N.J., Aug. 26, 1945; d. Louis and Florence (Gluck) Flum; m. Michael Fanwick Meiselman, Nov. 21, 1970; 1 child, Deborah Elaine. BA, U. Fla., 1968. Biochem. research asst. U. Miami (Fla.) Med. Sch., 1968-71, Johns Hopkins U., Balt., 1971-81; program adminstr. Md. Com. Occupational Safety & Health, Balt., 1981-82; asbestos tng. coordinator Md. Dept. Health & Mental Hygiene, Balt., 1982-84; mgr. tng. and hazard communications Biopherics, Inc., Rockville, Md., 1984-88; asst. dir. Biopherics, Inc., Beltsville, Md., 1988—. Contbr. articles to profl. jours. Newsletter editor Howard County Friends Cen. Am., 1986—. Mem. Am. Indsl. Hygiene Assn., Am. Pub. Health Assn., Nat. Environ. Tng. Assn., NOW. Office: Biopherics Inc 12051 Indian Creek Ct Beltsville MD 20705

MEISLER, BARBARA ALTMAN, speech pathologist; b. Wilkes-Barre, Pa., Oct. 5, 1943; d. Julius and Ann (Garber) Altman; B.A. in Speech Correction, George Washington U., 1965, M.A., 1967; m. Jules Murray Meisler, July 4, 1965; children—Marc Alan, Jan David. Speech clinician and lectr. George Washington U., Washington, 1967-68; tchr. Silver Spring (Md.) Nursery Learning Center, 1973-75, speech-lang. pathologist, 1972-79; speech pathologist Silver Spring Speech and Lang. Center, 1974-77; pvt. practice speech pathology, 1977—; cons. Learning Diagnostics, Inc., Silver Spring, 1976-79; guest lectr. Montgomery County public schs., 1979; v.p. Speech and Hearing Discussion Group, 1971-73. Liaison to bd. dirs. Silver Spring Jewish Center, 1973-79, sisterhood pres. 1975-79; bd. dirs., v.p. Hebrew Day Inst., Rockville, Md., 1979-82, pres., 1982-84, exec. dir., 1985—, pres. day sch., 1982-84, trustee, 1986—; bd. dirs. Sisterhood Young Israel Shomrei Emunah, Silver Spring, 1982—; mem. women's div. United Jewish Appeal Fedn., recipient award of merit, 1980, 81; co-chmn. Marge Freedman Mus. Endowment Talented Children, 1984-86. Recipient Service award Silver Spring Jewish Center, 1978; award Hebrew Day Inst., 1984; Md. Council Bus. Service award Montgomery County, 1987; award of merit Hebrew Day Inst., 1985. Mem. Am. Speech and Hearing Assn., Md. Speech and Hearing Assn., D.C. Speech and Hearing Assn., Sigma Alpha Eta (pres. 1964-65, hon. mem. award 1965). Democrat. Jewish. Home: 11411 Monticello Ave Silver Spring MD 20902 Office: care Hebrew Day Inst 11710 Hunters Ln Rockville MD 20852

MEISLER, MERYL ANN, artist; b. Bronx, N.Y., Oct. 24, 1951; d. Jack Meisler and Sylvia Frances (Schulman) Donenfeld. Student, Cornell U., 1972; BS, SUNY, Buffalo, 1973; MA, U. Wis., 1975. CETA photographer Am. Jewish Congress, N.Y.C., 1976-78; tchr. photography Learning to Read Through the Arts, N.Y.C., 1978-80; tchr. art of photography intermediate sch. #291 N.Y.C. Bd. Edn., Bklyn., 1975—, chair art dept., 1986—; illustrator (book) Wild Things, 1975, Sea Otters-Little Clowns of the Sea, 1985, State History of Ga., 1986, also various bookjackets, newspapers, mag. articles. Am. Jewish Congress grantee 1976. Mem. Graphic Artists Guild, Park Slope Artists Council, N.Y.C. Art Tchrs. Assn., Profl. Women Photographers (bd. dirs., sec. 1985—, newsletter editor 1985—), Women's Caucus of the Arts, Graphic Artists Guild. Democrat. Jewish. Home: 553 8th St Apt 1L Brooklyn NY 11215

MEISTAS, MARY THERESE, endocrinologist, diabetes researcher; b. Grand Rapids, Mich., July 22, 1949; d. Frank Peter and Anne Therese (Karsokas) M. MD, U. Mich., 1975. Diplomate Am. Bd. Internal Medicine, Am. Bd. Endocrinology. Intern, then resident in internal medicine Cleve. Clinic Hosp., 1975-78, endocrinology fellow, 1978-79; fellow in pediatric endocrinology Johns Hopkins Hosp., Balt., 1979-81; diabetes researcher Joslin Diabetes Ctr., Boston, 1981-86; assoc. in medicine Brigham and Women's Hosp., Boston, 1981-86; asst. in medicine, diabetes researcher Mass. Gen. Hosp., Boston, 1986—. Contbr. articles to profl. jours. Mem. ACP, Am. Diabetes Assn., Am. Fedn. Clin. Research, Endocrine Soc. Office: Mass Gen Hosp Fruit St ACC-508 Boston MA 02114

MEIXNER, BECKI, cosmetic company executive, make-up artist; b. Cookville, Tenn., May 15, 1956; d. Epi Stephan and Reba (Denny) Bilak; m. Timothy Mark Meixner, July 10, 1976; children: Jeffrey Paul, Nicole Marie. Student Abilene Christian U., 1973-76. Field exec. Aloette Cosmetics, Niagra Falls, Ont., Can., 1981-85; pres. Aloette Cosmetics Southeastern Mich., Inc., Ann Arbor, Mich., 1985—. Mem. Nat. Assn. Female Execs. (network dir. 1985-86), Women's Assn. Vital Ednl. Services, Ladies Assocs. Mich. Christian Coll., Greater Detroit C. of C., Ann Arbor C. of C. Office: 912 N Main Ann Arbor MI 48104

MEJIA, BARBARA OVIEDO, chemistry educator; b. San Francisco, Apr. 14, 1946; d. Louis Jerome and Alice May (Beall) O.; m. Michael Scot Ellison, June 7, 1969 (div. Jan. 1977); m. Richard S. Mejia, Sept. 15, 1982. AA, Sierra Coll., 1967; BS, U. Calif., Davis, 1969, PhD, 1973. Cert. community coll. tchr., Calif. Lectr. U. Calif., Davis, summer 1977; lectr. Calif. State U., Chico, 1973-76, asst. prof., 1976-80, assoc. prof., 1980-85, prof., 1985—. Contbr. articles to profl. jours. Judge Calif. Cen. Valley Sci./Engring. Fair, Chico, 1977, 80, 81, 82, 88, bd. dirs. 1978-79; judge Butte County Sci. Fair, Chico, 1985, 86, 87, 88. Mem. AAAS, Am. Chem. Soc., Congress of Faculty Assns., Cal Aggie Alumni Assn., Assn. Calif. State Univ. Profs., Sigma Xi. Home: 4 Jasper Dr Chico CA 95928 Office: Calif State U Dept Chemistry Chico CA 95929-0210

MELAMED, CAROL DRESCHER, lawyer; b. N.Y.C., July 12, 1946; d. Raymond A. and Ruth W. (Schwartz) Drescher; children—Stephanie Weisman, Deborah Weisman; m. Arthur Douglas Melamed, May 26, 1983; children: Kathryn, Elizabeth. A.B. magna cum laude with high honors in English Lit., Brown U., 1967; M.A.T., Harvard U., 1969; J.D., Catholic U. Am., 1974. Bar: Md. 1974, D.C. 1975, U.S. Ct. Appeals, (D.C. cir.) 1975, U.S. Dist. Ct. D.C. 1981, U.S. Supreme Ct. 1982. Tchr. English, Wellesley High Sch., Mass., 1968-69; law clk. U.S. Ct. Appeals, (D.C. cir.), Washington, 1974-75; assoc. Wilmer, Cutler & Pickering, Washington, 1975-79; assoc. counsel The Washington Post, 1979—. Mem. Phi Beta Kappa. Office: The Washington Post 1150 15th St NW Washington DC 20071

MELANI, BETTY LOU, academic administrator; b. Pitts., Oct. 1, 1932; d. Cesare and Rosemary (Valdiserri) M. BS, U. Pitts., 1980. Exec. asst. Ionics Inc., Bridgeville, Pa., 1963-73; adminstrv. asst. Western Psychiat. Inst. and Clinics U. Pitts., 1973-82, asst. adminstr., 1983—, exec. adminstr. sch. medicine, 1984—; bd. dir. Renaissance Ctr., Pitts., 1984—. Sec., bd. dirs. Foster Parents, 1968—. Mem. Exec. Women's Council. Democrat. Roman Catholic. Office: U Pitts Sch Medicine M246 Scaife Hall Pittsburgh PA 15261

MELARA, ANA LAURA MARTINEZ, insurance company professional; b. San Salvador, El Salvador, July 4, 1936; came to U.S., 1964; d. Miguel de Jesus and Maria Juana (Uribe) Martinez; m. Carlos Alberto Melara, Apr. 2, 1960; children: Ana Sylvia, Carolina, Carlos Eduardo. BS and Letters, Colegio La Sagrada Familia, San Salvador, 1953. Actuary Amex Life Assurance Co., San Rafael, Calif., 1983-85, reserve analyst, 1985-86, sr. reserve analyst, 1986—. Pres. Club Hispanoa Americano Sonoma County, Petaluma, Calif., 1983-85, v.p. 1985-86. Fellow Life Mgmt. Inst. Democrat. Roman Catholic. Home: 743 Rancho Way Petaluma CA 94952 Office: Amex Life Assurance Co 1650 Los Gamos Dr San Rafael CA 94903-1899

MELCHIONNE, LAURA ANNE, graphics engineer, illustrator; b. Belleville, N.J., Aug. 19, 1958; d. Anthony Joseph and Yvette Marie (Santos) M. B.F.A., Rochester Inst. Tech., 1980, M.S., 1986. Supr. art dept. Rochester Inst. Tech. Print Shop, N.Y., 1978-81; graphics engr. Xerox Corp., Fremont, Calif., 1981—; free-lance illustrator, San Francisco. Mem. Nat. Assn. Female Execs., Graphics Arts Guild, U.S. Ski Assn. Club: Far West Masters (Incline Village, Nev.). Avocations: running; skiing. Office: Xerox Corp Electronic Typewriter Printer Div 901 Page Ave Fremont CA 94537

MELICK, KATHERINE, publishing company manager; b. Carteret, N.J., Feb. 4, 1924; d. Stephen and Mary (Ginda) M.; m. Stanley R. Niemiec, Apr. 24, 1948 (dec. 1973). B.L., Rutgers U., 1944. Manual writer G.M. Corp., Linden, N.J., 1944-46; news asst., sec. Wall Street Jour., N.Y.C., 1946-55; exec. sec. Dow Jones & Co., Inc., N.Y.C., 1955-72, asst. to promotion mgr., 1972-74, adminstrv. mgr. mktg. services, 1975—. pres., N.J. Fedn. Women's Clubs, Carteret, 1953-55. Mem. Advt. Women N.Y., Japan Soc., AAUW, Am. Mgmt. Assn. Clubs: Rutgers (N.Y.C.), Douglass Coll. Alumnae Assn. (New Brunswick, N.J.). Office: Dow Jones & Co Inc 420 Lexington Ave New York NY 10170

MELKIN, AUDREY DALE, sales executive; b. Washington, May 4, 1947; d. Gilbert and Jean Ann (Thur) M. BA in Sociology and Anthropology with honors, Swarthmore Coll., 1969. Research asst. Ednl. Testing Service, Princeton, N.J., 1969-70; resident counselor SHAC, Burlington, Vt., 1972-73; counselor Sr. Health and Counseling Service, Glen Cove, N.Y., 1975-76; examiner Nassau County Food Stamp Program, Mineola, N.Y., 1976-78; copywriter Oxford Univ. Press, N.Y.C., 1978-80, mgr. exhibits, 1980-83, trade sales rep., 1981-83; mgr. sales promotion John Wiley & Sons, Inc., N.Y.C., 1983-85, mgr. library sales, 1985—. Mem. C.G. Jung Found., N.Y.C., 1984—. Mem. Assn. Am. Pubs. (mem. library com. gen. pub. div. 1986—), Soc. for Scholarly Pub., ALA (mem. pub. vendor library relations com. 1988). Home: 243 E 33d St Apt 2A New York NY 10016 Office: John Wiley & Sons Inc 605 Third Ave New York NY 10158

MELL, GLENDINE FRANCES, health administrator, psychologist; b. Madison, Ill., Jan. 30, 1951; d. Glenwood Frances and Zetta Lucille (Eaton)

M.; m. David Robert Jordan, Sept. 18, 1982. BS, So. Ill. U., Edwardsville, 1973, MS, 1975. Lic. psychologist, Mich. Counselor job placement CDI Temps, St. Louis, 1976-82; cons. St. Louis County Spl. Sch. Dist., 1977-78, sch. psychologist, 1978-83; pvt. practice psychology Kalamazoo, 1983-86; adminstr., psychologist Blue Care Network, Kalamazoo, 1985—; with Kellogg Community Coll., Battle Creek, Mich., 1988—. Mem. Am. Assn. Counseling and Devel., Am. Psychol. Assn. (assoc.). Home: 7344 YZ Ave E Vicksburg MI 49097

MELLEN, NANCY E., manufacturing company executive; b. Waterbury, Conn., Aug. 28, 1953; d. Robert W. and Sara E. (Emery) Brown; m. Howard B. Mellen, Aug. 6, 1977 (div. Mar. 1985). AB in Math, Physics with honors, Mount Holyoke Coll., 1975; MBA in Operation Mgmt., U. Rochester, 1979. Assoc. physicist Johns Hopkins Applied Physics Lab., Laurel, Md., 1975-78; inventory strategy analyst Xerox Corp., Rochester, N.Y., 1979-83, supr. material control, 1983-85, mgr. direct mktg. sales support, 1985-87, mgr. asset planning, 1987—. Mem. Am. Mgmt. Assn., Nat. Assn. Female Execs., Sigma Xi. Home: 33 Keswick Way Fairport NY 14450

MELLEN, SUZANNE ROBERTA, real estate appraiser, consultant; b. N.Y.C., Mar. 19, 1953. Student, Carnegie-Mellon U., 1971-73; BS, Cornell U., 1976. Jr. cons. Harley, Little Assocs., Toronto, Ontario, Can., 1976; mgmt. trainee Westin Hotel, N.Y.C., 1976-78; appraiser, cons. Helmsley-Spear, N.Y.C., 1978-80; real estate analyst Morgan Guaranty Trust Co., N.Y.C., 1980-81; dir. cons. valuation Hospitality Valuation Services, Mineola, N.Y., 1981-85; ptnr. in charge Hospitality Valuation Services, San Francisco, 1986—. Mem. Am. Inst. Real Estate Appraisers (edn. com. 1985, chairperson workshop 1987), Am. Hotel/Motel Assn., Calif. Hotel/Motel Assn., Calif. Assn. Realtors, Cornell Soc. Hotelmen. Club: Commonwealth (San Francisco). Home: 1980 Sutter St #304 San Francisco CA 94115 Office: Hospitality Valuation Services 116 New Montgomery St San Francisco CA 94105

MELLEY, MAURA LINEEN, lawyer, insurance company executive; b. Hartford, Conn., Apr. 29, 1951; d. William Joseph Melley and Rita (Murphy) Melley-Coyne. BA, St. Joseph Coll., Hartford, 1973; JD, Western New England Coll., 1978. Bar: Conn. 1979. Mgr. corps. div. Office of Sec. of State of Conn., Hartford, 1978-81; dep. sec. of state State of Conn., Hartford, 1981-82, sec. of state, 1982-83; v.p. Ins. Assocs. Conn., Hartford, 1983-85; asst. v.p. Hartford Ins. Group, 1985—; v.p., bd. dirs. Camp Horizons, Inc., Hartford. Vol. Big Bros./Big Sisters, Hartford; mem. Wethersfield (Conn.) Charter Rev. Com., 1984-85, Dem. Town Com., Wethersfield, 1985-86. Named Outstanding Young Alumna, St. Joseph Coll., 1985. Mem. Conn. Bar Assn., Hartford Assn. Women Attys. Hartford County Bar Assn., NOW. Roman Catholic. Home: 456 Main St Wethersfield CT 06109 Office: Hartford Ins Group Hartford Plaza Hartford CT 06115

MELLON, JACKIE SUE, geological engineer; b. Plainview, Nebr., July 5, 1956; d. Henry and Norma Ann (Barnes) Ruterbories; m. Steven Allen Mellon, Oct. 18, 1953. BS in Geol. Engring., S.D. Sch. Mines and Tech., 1978; postgrad., So. Meth. U., 1986—. Geologist Carbon Coal Co., Mentmore, N.Mex., 1978; geologist AMAX, Inc.-Mt. Tolman Project, Grand Coulee, Wash., 1979-80, mining engr., 1980-82; geologist N.Am. Cons., Inc., Dallas, 1982; geologist Trinity Project N.Am. Coal Corp., Dallas, 1982-83, geol. engr., 1983-84, sr. geol. engr., project mgr., 1984—. Mem. Am. Mgmt. Assn., NSPE, Soc. Mining Engrs. of AIME, Soc. Econ. Geologists, Tex. Soc. Profl. Engrs. Roman Catholic. Home: 401 Kentucky Ln Fairview TX 75069 Office: The NAm Coal Corp 13140 Coit Rd Suite 400 Dallas TX 75240

MELLON, JOAN ANN, educator; b. Massena, N.Y., Nov. 29, 1932; d. Leo Herbert and Irene (Tyo) French; m. Donald Emmett Mellon, Aug. 24, 1963. B.A., Coll. St. Rose, 1954; M.Ed., St. Lawrence U., 1956; M.Ed., Tchrs. Coll. Columbia U. 1972, Ed.D., 1985. Tchr. math. Copenhagen Sch. Dist., N.Y., 1954-57, Massena Sch. Dist., N.Y., 1957-62; supr. student tchrs. SUNY-Albany, 1962-63; asst. prof. math SUNY-Potsdam, 1963-67; tchr. math. Long Beach Sch. Dist. (N.Y.), 1967-70; chmn. math. dept. Edgemont Sch. Dist., Scarsdale, N.Y., 1971—; instr. inservice course for elem. tchrs. SUNY-Potsdam, 1965; instr. Inst. for Jr. High Sch. Tchrs., 1966; vis. com. Middle States Assn., 1973, 76, 79. Vice grand regent Cath. Daus. Am., Norwood, N.Y., 1959, grand regent, 1960; treas. St. Lawrence Deanery of Council Cath. Women, Ogdensburg, N.Y., 1958; chmn. Jr. Cath. Daus., Norwood, 1964. Mem. Assn. Math. Tchrs. N.Y. State (exec. council 1977-78), N.Y. Assn. Math. suprs. (v.p. 1978-79), Nat. Council Tchrs. Math., Math. Assn. Am., Edgemont Tchrs. Assn. (pres.), Delta Kappa Gamma. Republican. Roman Catholic. Home: 8 Woodhaven Dr New City NY 10956 Office: Edgemont High Sch White Oak Ln Scarsdale NY 10583

MELNIKOFF, SARAH ANN, gem importer, jewelry designer; b. Chgo., Feb. 12, 1936; d. Harry E. and Marie Louise (Straub) Caylor; m. Casimir Adam Jestadt, Feb. 27, 1959 (div. Sept. 1972); 1 child, Christina Marie Jestadt-Russo; m. Sol Melnikoff, July 31, 1981. Student Gemol. Inst. Am., 1968-69, Am. Acad. Art, Chgo., 1952-56, Art Inst. Chgo., 1953, Mundelein Coll., Chgo., 1953-54. Pres., Casmira Gem, Inc., Chgo., 1963—; comml. artist, Chgo., 1957-78; U.S. del. Internat. Colored Gemstone Dealers Assn., W.Ger., 1985; lectr., cons. in field. Mem. Chgo. Salesman's Alliance, MINK Inc., Am. Gem Trade Assn. (nat. sec. 1982-86), Am. Horse Show Assn., Am. Saddlebred Horse Show Assn., Mid-Am. Horse Show Assn. (dir. 1980-83). Republican. Roman Catholic. Avocation: horses.

MELTON, JOAN SPINKS, musician, educator; b. Albemarle, N.C., Feb. 19, 1938; d. John Spinks and Helen Louise (McMillan) M.; children from previous marriages: Joan Catherine Lynch Noble, Christopher Todd Smith. MusB, U. Miss., 1961, MusM, 1962; PhD, U. N.C., 1977; postgrad., Am. Acad. Dramatic Arts, 1987—, Nat. Theatre Conservatory, 1988. Instr. Hinds Jr. Coll., Raymond, Miss., 1962-63, U. N.C., Chapel Hill, 1964-66, N.Y. Cen. U., Durham, 1966-67; chair dept. music Peace Coll., Raleigh, N.C., 1974-78; instr. Manhattan Sch. of Music, N.Y.C., 1983-85; free lance musician Claremont, Calif.; dir. New Music Assocs., N.Y.C., 1983-86; dir. music and commn. sch. of music Lexington United Meth. Ch., N.Y.C., 1980-86; research assoc. Nat. Council of Chs., N.Y.C., 1978-81; guest clinician Ea. Dist. Choral Festival, 1977; guest conductor All-City Choral Festival, Raleigh, 1976. Composer numerous works for piano, orch., and chamber ensembles; author music course combining phys. exercise with vocal technique, 1986; model/actress various daytime dramas CBS, ABC, 1981-82; contbr. articles to music jours. Mem. arts edn. panel N.C. Cultural Adv. Council, 1978. Recipient Nat. Guild scholarship and Paderewski Gold medal Nat. Guild Piano Tchrs., 1951, 55; Miss N.C. scholar, 1956; Ford Found. fellow, 1966-68. Mem. AFTRA, Choral Conductors Guild, Am. Fedn. Musicians, N.C. Music Educators Assn. (sec. higher edn. sect. 1975-78). Democrat. Mem. Ch. of Religious Sci.

MELTON, LAURIE ALISON, service company administrator; b. Santa Ana, Calif., Feb. 25, 1964; d. Thomas Albert and Kathleen Mary (Thompson) Cox; m. David Fiester; children: Robert Daniel, Alicia Michelle. Grad. high sch., Oakland Park, Fla., 1982. Horse trainer, mgr. various show horse stables, U.S. and Europe, 1975-80; office mgr. Land Title Ins. Co., Ft. Lauderdale, Fla., 1979-82; gen. mgr. Boca Travel Trailer Resort, Boca Raton, Fla., 1982-85; asst. mgr. credit Boca Raton Hotel and Country Club, 1985—. Mem. U.S. Dressage Assn.

MELTON, PATRICIA J., money broker; b. Kankakee, Ill., Mar. 11, 1932; d. Aime A. and Armella R. (Holler) Guimond; m. William J. Melton, oct. 30, 1970; children: Pamela, Frank, Dawn, Danielle. Real estate broker Peoria, Ill., 1971-74; v.p. First Fin. Savs. and Loan, Arlington Heights, Ill., 1976-82; underwriter Camper Mortgage Assn., Ft. Lauderdale, Fla., 1983-86; broker Melton Diversified, Inc., Ft. Lauderdale, 1987—, Melton Mortgage Corp., Ft. Lauderdale, 1986—; bd. dirs. Plato Investments, Inc., Miami, Fla.; v.p. Samor Corp., Ft. Lauderdale, 1984—; lectr. Pub. Mortgage Seminars, Ft. Lauderdale, 1986—, lectr. Conventional Lending Seminars. Author conventional mortgage manual. Mem. Fla. Assn. Mortgage Brokers. Office: Melton Mortgage Corp 2701-B E Oakland Park Blvd Fort Lauderdale FL 33306

MELTON-SCOTT, MARY MEULI, hospital administrator, consultant; b. Dec. 4, 1943; d. August Martin and Vada Irene (Matthews) Meuli; m. James Lynn Bell, May 23, 1961 (div. 1964); 1 child, James Lynn; m. Charles David Scott, Jr., Sept. 18, 1964 (div. 1969); 1 child, Charles David III; m. Charles Tabb, Jr., June 23, 1970 (div. 1973); 1 child, Erika Elizabeth; m. Johnny Wayne Scott, 1983. BA, McMurry Coll., 1971; MS, Wright State U., 1978; PhD, Columbia Pacific U., 1983; MBA, Xavier U., Cin., 1986. Cert. alcoholism counselor, 23 states, including Ohio. High sch. tchr. Dayton pub. schs., Ohio, 1972-74; therapist Greene Hall, Greene Meml. Hosp., Xenia, Ohio, 1975-77; clin. dir. Bur. Alcoholism Services, Dayton, 1978-83; v.p. Dettmer Hosp./Upper Valley Med. Ctr., Troy, Ohio, 1983-86; adminstr. Valley View Hosp., Las Cruces, N.Mex., 1986—; owner, pres. Melton-Scott Enterprises, Tipp City, Ohio, 1983—, So. N.Mex. D.W.I. Programs, 1988—; cons. WORAC, Dayton, 1978-83; exec. dir. Miami County Mental Health, Ohio, 1984—. Mem. Nat. Assn. Female Execs., Assn. Mental Health Adminstrs., Nat. Assn. Alcoholism Counselors, Nat. Council on Alcoholism (Ohio chpt.), Am. Coll. Health Care Adminstrs., Sigma Delta Tau. Avocations: writing, gardening, needlework, sports. Home: 4248 Mission Bell Ave Las Cruces NM 88001 Office: 1029 E Spruce Ave Las Cruces NM 88001

MELTZER, MIRIAM SCHLESINGER, social worker, administrator; b. Pitts., Oct. 3, 1938; d. Hymen and Ida Rose (Mirowitz) Schlesinger; m. Donald Meltzer, Apr. 15, 1961; children—Deborah, Alan. B.A., U. Mich., 1960; M.S.W., U. Md., 1966. Counselor, Counseling and Testing, So. Ill. U., Carbondale, 1966-67, dir. social service Meml. Hosp., 1973-75; social worker Sch. Dist. No. 95, Carbondale, 1975-76; field ops. asst. U.S. Census Bur., Belleville, Ill., 1980; dir. truancy alternate program Regional Supt. Schs., Murphysboro, Ill., 1983—; mem. panel specialists Ill. Dept. Rehab., 1985-87. Advisor Welfare Rights Orgn., Carbondale, 1973; pres. Beth Jacob Sisterhood, Carbondale, 1979, 80, 81, Lincoln Jr. High Sch. PTA, Carbondale, 1981-82; bd. dirs. Temple Beth Jacob, 1979, 80, 81; area chmn. United Jewish Appeal Women's Drive, 1987-89. Home: 3007 W Kent Dr Carbondale IL 62901 Office: Regional Supt Schs Courthouse Murphysboro IL 62966

MELUSKEY, VALERIE, therapist; b. N.Y.C., July 21, 1939; d. John J. and Willys (Morieau-Jones) McCarthy; m. Benjamin L. Meluskey (div. Oct. 1975); children: Michael, Julianne, Alexander. BA, Bucknell U., 1961; MA, Goddard Coll., 1978. Pvt. practice therapist, tchr., writer 1970—. Contbr. articles to profl. jours. and mags. Mem. Am. Dance Therapy Assn. (N.J. chpt. pres. 1981), Assn. Study Dreams, Assn. Research and Enlightment, Aikido Koki Kai Internat., Reiki Soc.

MELVIN, MARGARET, nurse, consultant; b. Thomasville, Ga., July 13, 1927; d. Robert and Lorene Elizabeth (Barrett) M. BS in Nursing, Duke U., 1953. Cert. Occupational Health Cons. Head nurse Duke U. Med. Ctr., Durham, N.C., 1947-54; charge nurse med. clinic U. Mich. Med. Ctr., Ann Arbor, 1955-59; occupational health nurse State Farm Ins. Co., Jacksonville, Fl., 1960-65; dir. ins. edn. Baptist Hosp. Med. Ctr., Jacksonville, 1965-68; various positions Wausau Ins. Co., Orlando, Fla., 1968-80; sr. cert. occupational health cons. Wausau Ins. Co., Orlando, 1980—; lectr. various hosps. and orgns. Developed, created nat. teaching program for back problems, 1976, program for emergency care industry, 1974. Am. Cancer Soc. grantee, 1968. Mem. Am. Nurses Assn., Am. Assn. Occupational Health Nurses, Fla. State Assn. Occupational Health Nruses (chmn. 1982, conf. sec. 1980-84), Am. Bd Occupational Health Nurses. Republican. Home: 244 Windmeadows Dr Altamonte Springs FL 32701

MEMMER, MARY MARGARET, nursing educator; b. St. Paul, Apr. 23, 1936; d. Philip Loren and Georgia Mildred (Rose) Kelly; m. David Jay Memmer, June 24, 1972. B.S. in Nursing, U. Nebr., 1958; M. in Nursing Edn., U. Minn., 1960; postgrad. U. Wash., 1966-67. R.N., Calif., Nebr.; cert. pub. health nurse, Calif. Staff nurse U. Nebr. Hosp., Omaha, 1958-59, U. Minn. Hosp., Mpls., 1959; instr. U. Nebr., Omaha, 1961-62; instr., then asst. prof. U. Mich., Ann Arbor, 1962-66; instr. U. Wash., Seattle, 1967-68; from asst. prof. to prof. nursing Calif. State U.-Chico, 1968—. Author of learning modules (5) Intercampus Nursing Project. Contbr. articles to profl. jours, chpts. to Nursing Textbook, 1987. Mem. Chico Symphony Orch., 1975—. Grantee U. Mich., 1965, Calif. U. and Coll. System, 1974-75, 73-74, Calif. State U.-Chico, 1977-78, 81. Mem. Nat. League Nursing Calif., Calif. Faculty Assn., U. Nebr. Sch. Nursing Alumnae Assn., Sierra Club, Sigma Theta Tau. Democrat. Methodist. Office: Calif State U Chico CA 95926

MEMORY, CATHERINE ANN, psychologist; b. Boston, Sept. 8, 1939; d. Roger and Mary (Loftus) Keane; A.B. magna cum laude, Regis Coll., 1960; Ed.M., Harvard U., 1961; postgrad. Boston U., 1964-69; m. Robert Edward Memory, Oct. 12, 1969; 1 son, Robert James. Tchr. public schs., Stoneham, Mass., 1961-63, sch. counselor, 1963-68; sch. counselor, Brookline, Mass., 1968-70; psychologist, public schs., Attleboro, Mass., 1970-83; adminstr. spl. edn., 1983—; cons. Bridgewater State Coll. spl. edn. workshop, 1974; instr. Bristol Community Coll., Fall River, Mass., 1972-73; guest panelist Boston Catholic Family Life program, 1970-80 ; lectr. Project Interserv Tchr. and Parent Tng. Program, 1975—; presenter Project IMPACT Parent Edn. Program, 1978-79. Mem. City of Attleboro Social Services Com., 1970-74; South Attleboro residential chmn. Attleboro United Fund, 1973; mem. pack com. Cub Scouts Am., 1981-85. NDEA grantee, San Diego State Coll., 1965; recipient Stoneham Jaycees Outstanding Young Educator award, 1967. Mem. Am. Psychol. Assn., Attleboro PUb. Sch. Adminstrs. Assn. (sec. 1984-86, v.p. 1986—), Regis Coll. Alumnae Assn., Delta Epsilon Sigma. Researcher with hyperkinetic children; contbr. paper on subject to profl. confs. Home: 145 Park Circle South Attleboro MA 02703

MENAKER, SHIRLEY ANN LASCH, psychology educator, academic administrator; b. Jersey City, July 22, 1935; d. Frederick Carl and Mary Elizabeth (Thrall) Lasch; m. Michael Menaker, June 4, 1955; children: Ellen Margaret, Nicholas. BA, Swarthmore Coll., 1956; MA, Boston U., 1961, PhD, 1965. Adminstrv. asst. N.J. State Fedn. Dist. Bds. Edn., Trenton, 1956-59; trainee clin. psychology Mass. Mental Health Ctr., Boston, 1960-61; intern clin. psychology Thom Guidance Clinic for Children, Boston, 1961-62; research assoc. ednl. psychology U. Tex.-Austin, 1964-67, asst. prof. edn. psychology, 1967-70. assoc. prof. ednl. psychology, 1970-79, assoc. dean grad. sch., 1975-77, psychology cons. Research and Devel. Ctr. for Tchr. Edn., 1965-67, faculty investigator, 1967-74; assoc. prof. counseling psychology U. Oreg., Eugene, 1979-85, prof., 1985-87 , assoc. dean grad. sch., 1979-84, acting dean grad. sch., 1980-81, 82-83, dean grad sch., 1984-87; assoc. provost for acad. support, prof. gen. faculty, U. Va., Charlottesville, 1987—. Bd. dirs. Nat. Grad. Record Exam. Bd. and Policy Council-Test of English as Fgn. Lang., Ednl. Testing Services, 1984-87. Contbr. articles to profl. jours. NIMH fellow, 1963-64. Home: 1640 Owensville Rd Charlottesville VA 22901 Office: U Va Madison Hall Charlottesville VA 22903

MENCHACA, SANDRA, accountant; b. Port Neches, Tex., June 28, 1953; d. Travis Rex Corley and Fannie-Bell (Porter) Chancellor; m. Ruben Paul Menchaca, Sept. 25, 1970; 1 child, Veronica Ann. BBA, Lamar U., 1978. CPA, Tex. Acct. Dixilyn-Field Drilling Co., Houston, 1978-80, sr. acct., 1980-81, acctg. supr., 1981-84, acctg. mgr., 1984-87; controller Gyrodata, Inc., 1987—. Mem. Am. Inst. CPA's, Tex. Soc. CPA's, Internat. Assn. Drilling Contractors. Roman Catholic. Home: 4122 Summit Valley Houston TX 77082 Office: Gyrodata Inc 1682 N West Belt Houston TX 77046

MENDELSOHN, NAOMI, pharmaceutical company executive. BA, NYU; MA, Boston U.; PhD, CUNY, 1975. Fellow Meml. Sloan-Kettering Cancer Ctr., N.Y.C., 1975-78; asst. prof. Mt. Sinai Med. Ctr., N.Y.C., 1978-82; assoc. sci. dir. Sterling Drug, Inc. Internat., N.Y.C., 1982—; adjunct asst. prof. Mt. Sinai Med. Ctr., 1982—. NSF fellow, 1969, NIH fellow 1975-78. Mem. Am. Assn. Advancement Sci., Am. Chem. Soc., Am. Soc. Hematology, Fedn. Am. Socs. Exptl. Biology, Am. Heart Assn., N.Y. Acad. Scis. (Women Sci. com., Planning com. 1983-85). Office: Sterling Drug Inc 90 Park Ave New York NY 10016

MENDEZ, JANA LYNN, senator; b. Moscow, Idaho, Jan. 18, 1944; d. Earl Dean and Alverta (Dalberg) Hall; m. Richard Albert Mendez, Sept. 16, 1965; children: Amy, Jennifer, Christopher. BS in Journalism, U. Colo., 1981. Community and issue activist Boulder County Housing Authority and Citizens for the Right To Vote, Longmont, Colo., 1975-83; legis. asst. Senate Minority Leader, Denver, 1982-84; Colo. state senator, 1985—; asst. whip minority leader, 1986. Author: (with others) Chile From The Ground Up, 1982. Dem. precinct leader, area coordinator, senate dist. chmn. Boulder County, Colo., 1975-84; chair, commr. Boulder County Housing Authority, 1974-83. Regents scholar, 1963, Cervi scholar, 1980; U. Colo. Women's Ctr. grantee, 1980; named Outstanding Freshman Senator Colo. Social Legis. Com., 1985. Mem. Kappa Tau Alpha. Avocations: gardening, reading, photography, cooking. Office: State Capitol Room 274 Denver CO 80203

MENDEZ, OLGA A., state legislator; b. Mayaguez, P.R.. BA, U. P.R.; MEd, Columbia U., 1960; PhD in Ednl. Psychology, Yeshiva U., N.Y.C., 1975. Previously assoc. prof. SUNY-Stony Brook, research psychologist Albert Einstein Coll. Med., N.Y.C., dep. commr. N.Y.C. Agy. for Child Devel, N.Y. state senator, 1978—; del. Dem. Nat. Conv., 1980. Address: 1215 Fifth Ave Apt #15-D New York NY 10029 *

MENDREY, KATHLEEN LOUISE, management consultant; b. Trenton, N.J., Aug. 22, 1946; d. Francis Stephen Gregory and Kathryn May (Church-Rothermel) M.; m. Robin A. Magowan Jr., Nov. 4, 1973 (div. 1976). BFA summa cum laude, Calif. Coll. Arts and Crafts, 1970; MA (hon.), U. Pa., 1976; MBA, Harvard U., PhD. Photog. operator 3M Color Separations Packaging Fortune 500, 1963—; asst. to pres. Spring Mill Co., Phila., 1963; with Lambertville (N.J.) Nuclear Power Condenser, 1963; tchr. Valley Day Sch., Edgewood, Pa., 1965; colorist Contilla Fabrics Madison Ave., N.Y.C., 1966-67; pres., prof. Centering Sch. Arts, San Francisco and Oakland, Calif., 1970-73; dir. Restoration/French Project, Vitteaux, France, 1973-76; v.p. Island Fragrance Co., St. Thomas, V.I., 1976; pres. Presdl. Cons. Co., Boston, San Francisco, N.Y.C., and Europe, 1976—; cons. dir. Heinz Corp., Safeway Corp., Columbia Pictures, Trump Corp., U.S. Congress, Pres. of U.S., Fiat, Doubleday Co., Van Heusen Corp., Met. Mus., Baccarat, Boston Opera Co., Atomic Energy Commn., NBC, CBS, Harvard U., Dept. of Def., Boston Ballet Co., Boston Symphony, U.S. Treasury Dept., Ralph Lauren and others. Art works exhibited in group shows in Oakland and San Francisco, 1968-73. Mem. Nat. Trust for Hist. Preservation, 1985, NatTrust for a Nuclear Freeze, 1967, Mus. Fine Arts, 1987, Artists Found., 1980-87; pres. Internat. Arts Fraternity, 1964. Mem. Women's Ednl. Bur., Jr. League, Union for Concerned Scientists, Bucks County Geneal. Soc., Colonial Williamsburg Found., Phi Beta Kappa. Mem. Soc. Friends. Club: Trenton Country. Home and Office: Presdl Cons Co 791 Tremont St W 403 Boston MA 02118

MENDRY, KATHLEEN LOUISE, public relations consultant. Student, Keuka Coll. Women, 1964-66; BFA summa cum laude, Calif. Coll. Arts Crafts, 1970; MA (hon. commemorative), U. Pa., 1978. Asst. to dir. N.J. State Mus., Trenton, 1964; head colorist Continella Fabrics, N.Y.C., 1967; head photographic ops. Hucks Press Service, Oakland, Calif., 1968-70; founder, dir. Centering Sch. Arts, Oakland, 1970-73; dir. restoration project French Project, Vitteaux, Cote D'Or, Burgundy, France, 1973-76; ind. cons. Boston, 1976—; cons., liaison numerous projects including Preservation Nature Series, Radcliffe Women's Art Slide Library fundraiser, An Wang request for Sarah Caldwell, House the Homeless, Pulitzer Prize choices, Nuclear Waste Sites, Calif. lottery, gifted students program, research Parkinson disease, Boston Pub. Library, Mary Ball Washington Mus. and Library, Andy Warhol sale of lithographs, Colonial Williamsburg Found. Mem. Internat. Solar Energy Soc., Nat. Trust Hist. Preservation, Nat. Council Nuclear Freeze, NOW, Nat. Audubon Soc., Friends of Earth, Womens Edn. Bur., Soc. Preservation New Eng. Antiquities, Com. Debutante Assembly. Home and Office: West 403 791 Tremont St Boston MA 02119

MENES, PAULINE H., state legislator; b. N.Y.C., July 16, 1924; d. Arthur B. and Hannah H. Herskowitz; m. Melvin Menes, Sept. 1, 1946; children: Sandra Jill, Robin Joy Menes Elvord, Bambi Lynn. BA in Bus. Econs. and Geography, Hunter Coll., N.Y.C., 1945. Economist Quartermaster Gen. Office, Washington, 1945-47; geographer Army Map Service, Washington, 1949-50; chief clk. Prince George's County Election Bd., Upper Marlboro, Md., 1963; substitute tchr. Prince George's County High Schs., Md., 1965-66; elected mem. Md. Ho. of Reps., Annapolis, 1966—; mem. Md. Ho. Judiciary com., Annapolis, 1979—, Ho. Com. on Rules and Exec. Nominations, 1979—; chair Spl. Com. on Drug and Alcohol Abuse, Annapolis, 1986—. Active Md. State Arts Council, Balt., 1968—, Md. State Commn. on Aging, Balt., 1975—; parlimentarian Nat. Found. for Women Legislators, Washington, 1986-87; 2d v.p. Prisoner's Aid Assn., Balt., 1971—. Recipient Internat. Task Force award Women's Yr., 1977; named to Hall of Fame Hunter Coll. Alumni Assn., 1986. Mem. Nat. Conf. State Legislators (com. on drugs and alcohol 1987), Md. NOW (Ann London Scott Meml. award for Legis. Excellence 1976), Md. Assn. Elected Women (bd. dirs. 1979—), Nat. Order Women Legislators (pres. 1979-80), Women's Polit. Caucus, LWV. Clubs: Women's Nat. Dem. (Washington); BPW Women's Club (College Park, Md.). Lodge: B'nai B'rith Women. Address: 3517 Marlbrough Way College Park MD 20740 Office: Md House Dels 3210 Lowe State Office Bldg Annapolis MD 20740

MENESES-IMBER, SARA NATALIA, diplomat; b. Caracas, Venezuela, Dec. 28, 1944; came to U.S., 1975; d. Guillermo Meneses and Sofia (Imber) de Rangel; m. Jose R. Serritiello, Sept. 18, 1964 (div. 1973); 1 child, Guillermo J. Serritiello. BA in Sociology, U. Cen. Venezuela, 1966; MA in Internat. Devel. Edn., Stanford U., 1979, MA in Sociology, 1981, PhD in Internat. Devel. Edn., 1983. Sociologist, advisor ednl. com. Caracas City Council, 1969-75; head Venezuelan Scholarship Program, San Francisco, 1981-82; ofcl. Venezuelan Consulate, San Francisco, 1983-84; attaché Venezuelan Consulate, Washington, 1984, 2d sec., 1984-85; 1st sec. Mission to OAS Venezuelan Office Fgn. Affairs, Washington, 1985-87; counselor Venezuelan Mission OAS, Washington, 1987—; cons. Stanford Research Inst., Menlo Park, Calif., 1982, Stanford Program Internat. in Culture and Edn., 1982-84, Calif. Bd. Edn., 1983-84. Postdoctoral fellow Stanford U., 1983-84; grantee Procter & Gamble, 1981, Venezuela Ministry Edn., 1975-77, Venezuela Govt. Found., 1977-81. Mem. Latin Am. Student Assn., Stanford Alumni Assn., Colegio Sociologos y Antropologos, Sociedad Venezolana Criminologia, Phi Delta Kappa. Roman Catholic. Office: Mission of Venezuela to OAS 4201 Connecticutt Ave NW #609 Washington DC 20008

MENGE, DANNETTE MARIE, petroleum engineer; b. New Orleans, Feb. 26, 1958; d. Laurence Hewitt and Gloria (Louviere) Menge. B.S. in Mech. Engring., U. New Orleans, 1981; M.S. in Petroleum Engring., Tulane U., 1987. Registerd engr.-in-tng., La. Petroleum engr. Chevron USA, Inc., New Orleans, 1981—. Mem. ASME (treas. 1980-81), La. Engring. Soc. (assoc.), Soc. Petroleum Engrs., Am. Welding Soc. (charter mem.). Democrat. Roman Catholic. Avocations: scuba diving and swimming, running, snow skiing, camping, fishing. Home: 801 Sena Dr Metairie LA 70005 Office: Chevron USA Inc 935 Gravier St New Orleans LA 70112

MENNELLA, CHARLOTTE AGNES, accountant, tax consultant; b. Burlington, Vt., Jan. 16, 1951; d. Robert Russell Brothers and Constance Ella (Couture) Callahan; stepdaughter of David C. Callahan; m. Steven M. Farnsworth, Oct. 3, 1970 (div. Jan. 1979); children: Bill Joseph Farnsworth, David M. Farnsworth; m. Anthony C. Mennella, Mar. 8, 1987; stepchildren: Anthony S., C. Mark, Barbara J., Wendy A., Scott A., David A., Tricia M. A in Acctg., Lowell U., 1981, BS in Acctg. cum laude, 1984. Stenographer U.S. Army, Ft. McNair, Ind. and Washington, 1969-70; sr. tech. typist Lincoln Lab., MIT, Lexington, Mass., 1972-79; tax cons. C&D Bus. Services, Dracut, Mass., 1980-81, Cafco Tax Service, Dracut, 1981-83; acct. A&C Video, Inc., Dracut, 1982-87; pvt. practice acctg. and tax cons. Oklawaha, Fla., 1988—; owner, operator Johnson's Beach and Cottages, Oklawaha, Fla.; acctg. cons. Racal-Redac Corp., 1987. Mem. Nat. Assn. Female Execs. Home and Office: PO Box 457 Oklawaha FL 32679

MENNEN, DOROTHY RUNK (MRS. HAROLD E. MENNEN), retired performing arts educator; b. Marshfield, Wis., July 17, 1915; d. Jon Cleveland and Minnie Pearle (Walker) Runk; B.S. in Edn., Kent State U., 1938; M.A., Purdue U., 1964; m. Harold E. Mennen, Jan. 5, 1943; children: Ferol, Laurel (Mrs. Bruce Miller Robb). Tchr., choral dir. Twinsburg (Ohio) pub. sch., 1938-41; tchr. speech, English Aurora (Ohio) High Sch., 1941-42; tchr. Cuyahoga Falls (Ohio) High Sch., 1941-42; tchr. English, Wea High Sch.,

Tippecanoe County, Ind., 1951 53; tchr vocal music West Lafayette (Ind.) pub. schs., 1957-60; assoc. prof. theatre Purdue U., West Lafayette, Ind., also vocal coach, from 1964, chmn. senate, 1979-80; now prof. emeritus; contralto soloist, 1946—. Editor: Directory of Voice and Speech Specialists in Actor Training Programs in U.S. and Canada, 1981. Bd. dirs. Lafayette Symphony, 1958-60, Civic Theatre, Lafayette, 1972-73, 1986—, The Bach Chorale Singers, Inc., 1980—. Mem. Am. Theatre Assn. (nat. chairperson theatre, speech and voice 1968-71, 73-75, Outstanding Leadership and Performance award Univ.-Coll. Theatre div. 1985), Nat. Assn. Tchrs. of Singing (treas. Ind. chpt.), Voice and Speech Trainers Assn., Inc., (pres. 1986—), Speech Communication Assn., AAUP (chairperson com. W on Status of Women 1972-74, pres. chpt. 1974-75, 75-77), LWV. Democrat. Methodist. Home: 1804 Ravinia Rd West Lafayette IN 47906 Office: Theater Dept Creative Arts Stewart Center Purdue U Wes t Lafayette IN 47907

MENOUSEK, LORIA FRANCES, nurse, educator; b. New Britain, Conn., May 21, 1943; d. Joseph Albert and Ruth (Patterson) M. Student, Skidmore Coll., 1966; M of Nursing, Emory U., 1968. Staff nurse, team leader Hartford (Conn.) Hosp., 1966-67; patient care coordinator Wesley Woods Health Ctr., Atlanta, 1967-68; clin. specialist rehab. nursing Grady Meml. Hosp., Atlanta, 1969-70; clin. coordinator Northside Hosp., Atlanta, 1970-71; staff nurse New Britain Meml. Hosp., 1971; instr. U. No. Colo., Greeley, 1971-73; dir. nursing U. Miami-Jackson Meml. Med. Ctr., Fla., 1973-75, instr., 1975-79; clin. specialist rehab. nursing VA Med. Ctr., Bay Pines, Fla., 1979-86, instr., 1986—; workshop planner, lectr. VA regional med. edn. programs, 1982-87. Mem. USCG Aux., 1986—. Mem. Am. Nurses Assn., Assn. Rehab. Nurses (cert.), Am. Congress Rehab. Medicine, Sigma Theta Tau. Home: 1201 Seminole Blvd #537 Largo FL 34640 Office: VA Med Ctr Dept Nursing Bay Pines FL 33504

MENSCH, LINDA SUSAN, lawyer, educator; b. N.Y.C., Mar. 12, 1951; d. Max Robert and Judith (Keller) M.; m. Michael Gerald Heyman, Aug. 28, 1977, 1 child, Jessica. Student, U. Salzburg, Austria, 1971-72, Collegium Palatinum, Heidelberg, Ger., 1972, Caius and Gonville Colls., Cambridge U. (Eng.), 1972; BA, Kirkland Coll., 1973; JD, NYU, 1976. Bar: N.Y. 1977, Ill. 1977. Law clk. Snadowsky & Fox, N.Y.C., 1974-76, Women's Rights Project, ACLU, N.Y.C., 1975; adj. prof. Columbia Coll., Chgo., 1978-85; assoc. law firm Shelton, Kalcheim & Cotnoir, Chgo., 1977-82, Katten, Muchin, Zavis, Pearl & Galler, Chgo., 1982-84, Linda S. Mensch, P.C., 1985—; v.p., gov., gen. counsel Nat. Acad. Rec. Arts and Scis., Chgo., 1979—, nat. trustee, 1985—; bd. dirs. Lawyers for Creative Arts, Chgo., 1982—; entertainment mgmt. cons. Chgo. Entertainment Network, 1983—. Exec. producer record album Back to Chicago Duke Tumatoe, 1983, Heavy Manners, 1983. Vice-pres., bd. dirs. Midwest Rec. Arts Found., Chgo., 1983—. N.Y. State Regents scholar, 1969-73. Mem. Chgo. Bar Assn. (creative arts com., patent, trademark and copyright com. 1983—), Nat. Assn. Women Bus. Owners, ABA, Ill. State Bar Assn., Nat. Acad. Rec. Arts and Scis., Women in Film (founding mem. sec. 1984). Home: 1158 S Plymouth Ct Chicago IL 60605 Office: 33 N Dearborn Suite 506 Chicago IL 60602

MENTZER, MERLEEN MAE, adult education educator; b. Kingsley, Iowa, July 25, 1920; d. John David and Maggie Marie (Simonsen) Moritz; m. Lee Arnold Mentzer, June 1, 1944. Student Westman Coll., 1939, Wayne State U., Nebr., 1942, Bemidji State U., 1950, Mankato Coll., 1978, U. Minn.-St. Paul, 1979. Tchr., Kingsley, Iowa, 1938-41; owner, mgr. Mentzer's Sundries, Hackensack, Minn., 1946-76, House of Mentzers, Pine River, Minn., 1974-77; instr. Hennepin Tech., Eden Prairie, Minn., 1978—. Mem. Mpls. C. of C., Hackensack C. of C., (v.p. 1970-76), Northern Lights Federated Woman's Club (pres. 1958-59). Republican. Lutheran. Avocations: dancing; bowling; reading; theatre; seminars. Home: 6781 Tartan Curve Eden Prairie MN 55344

MENTZER, SUSAN STERNBERG, psychologist; b. N.Y.C., Mar. 22, 1949; d. Theodore and Aida Selma (Tucker) Sternberg; m. Richard Alan Mentzer, Aug. 29, 1971; children: Kimberly Lynn, Michelle Lauren. BA, Pa. State U., 1971; MA, Ohio State U., 1972, PhD, 1975. Lic. psychologist, Ohio; cert. sch. psychologist, Ohio. Intern Springfield (Ohio) City Schs., 1973-74, psychologist, 1974-78; psychologist Columbus (Ohio) Pub. Schs., 1978—. Mem. Summerfield Civic Assn., Pickerington, Ohio, 1978—, Fairfield Elementary Sch. PTO, Pickerington, 1981—, Pickerington Middle Sch., Pickerington, 1987—. Mem. NEA, Nat. Assn. Sch. Psychologists, Ohio Edn. Assn., Columbus Edn. Assn., Phi Beta Kappa, Phi Kappa Phi, Psi Chi. Home: 13136 Summerfield Way Pickerington OH 43147 Office: Columbus Pub Schs Sch Psychology Services 2571 Neil Ave Columbus OH 43202

MENYUK, PAULA, developmental psycholinguistics educator; b. N.Y.C., Oct. 2, 1929; d. Louis and Helen (Weissman) Nichols; m. Norman Menyuk, Mar. 5, 1950; children—Curtis R., Diane F., Eric D. B.S., NYU, 1951; Ed.M., Boston U., 1955, Ed.D., 1961. Chief lang. therapist Mass. Gen. Hosp., Boston, 1952-54; teaching fellow Boston U., 1957-60; NIMH post-doctoral fellow MIT, Cambridge, 1961-64; mem. research staff MIT, 1964-72; prof. edn. Boston U., 1972, dir. div., 1981-87; cons. Children's Hosp., Boston, 1964—, Kennedy Hosp., Boston, 1981—, NIH, Bethesda, Md., 1972-80, Nat. Found. March of Dimes, White Plains, N.Y., 1977—; research assoc. MIT, 1972—. Author: Sentences Children Use, 1969, Acquisition and Development of Language, 1971, Language and Maturation, 1977, Language Development: Knowledge and Use, 1988. NIH fellow, 1958-64; Fulbright fellow, 1971. Fellow Am. Speech, Lang. and Hearing Assn. (Disting. Service award 1976); mem. Soc. Research in Child Devel., Linguistic Soc. Am., Internat. Soc. Study Behavioral Devel., AAAS, Am. Assn. Phonetic Scis. Home: 162 Mason Terr Brookline MA 02146 Office: Boston U 605 Commonwealth Ave Boston MA 02215

MENZIES, JEAN STORKE (MRS. ERNEST F. MENZIES), retired newspaperwoman; b. Santa Barbara, Calif., Dec. 30, 1904; d. Thomas More and Elsie (Smith) Storke; B.A., Vassar Coll., 1927; M.A. in Physics, Stanford, 1931; m. Ernest F. Menzies, Oct. 20, 1937; children—Jean Storke (Mrs. Dennis Wayne Vaughan), Thomas More. Teaching asst. dept. physics Stanford, 1927-29; instr. of physics Vassar Coll., 1929-30; tchr. math., chemistry, gen. sci. Sarah Dix Hamlin Sch., San Francisco, 1931-34; sec. to Dr. and Mrs. Samuel T. Orton, N.Y.C., 1935-36; press reporter, spl. writer Santa Barbara News-Press, 1954-63. Rec. sec. nat. YWCA, India, Burma and Ceylon, 1941-42; rec. sec., Calcutta YWCA, 1942-47, v.p., 1949-51; sec. Tri-County adv. council Children's Home Soc., Santa Barbara, 1952-54; founding dir., sec. corp. Santa Barbara Film Soc., Inc., 1960-66. Bd. dirs. Santa Barbara County chpt. Am. Assn. UN, 1954-59, Friends U. Calif. at Santa Barbara Library, 1970-74, Small Wilderness Area Preservation, 1971-79; sec. bd. trustees Crane Country Day Sch., 1955-57; trustee Mental Hygiene Clinic of Santa Barbara, 1956-60, U. Calif. Santa Barbara Found., 1974-80, Santa Barbara Mus. Natural History, 1977-81; adv. council Santa Barbara Citizens Adult Edn., 1958-62, v.p., 1960-62; bd. dirs. Internat. Social Sci. Inst., sec., 1963-68, mem. adv. bd., 1969; bd. dirs. Planned Parenthood Santa Barbara County, Inc., 1964-65, adv. council, 1966-67; trustee Santa Barbara Botanic Garden, 1967-81, hon. trustee, 1981—; trustee. Santa Barbara Trust for Historic Preservation, 1967-68, 72-77; mem. affiliates bd. dirs. U. Calif. at Santa Barbara, 1960-61, 67-70, 72-77; sec. Santa Barbara Mission Archive-Library, 1967—; mem. Santa Barbara Found., 1977-81. Mem. Santa Barbara Hist. Soc. (dir. 1957-62, founding mem. women's projects com. 1959-63, sec. 1961-62), Channel City Women's Forum (v.p. 1969-73, bd. dirs. 1973-87), Phi Beta Kappa, Sigma Xi. Club: Vassar of Santa Barbara and the Tri-Counties (1st v.p., founding com. 1956-57, 2d v.p. 1959-61, chmn. publicity com. 1961-73). Home: 2298 Featherhill Rd Santa Barbara CA 93108

MÉRAS, PHYLLIS LESLIE, journalist; b. Bklyn., May 10, 1931; d. Edmond Albert and Leslie Trousdale (Ross) M.; BA, Wellesley Coll., 1955; MS in Journalism, Columbia U., 1954; Swiss Govt. Exchange fellow, Inst. Higher Internat. Studies, Geneva, 1957; m. Thomas H. Cocroft, Nov. 3, 1968. Reporter, copy editor Providence Jour., 1954-57, 59-61; feature writer Ladies Home Jour. mag., 1957-58; editor Weekly Tribune, Geneva (Switzerland), 1961-62; copyeditor, travel sect. N.Y. Times, 1962-68; mng. editor Vineyard Gazette, Edgartown, Mass., 1970-74, contbg. editor, 1974—; asso. editor Rhode Islander, Providence, 1970-76; travel editor Providence Jour., 1976—; editor Wellesley Alumnae mag., 1979—; assoc. in journalism U. R.I., 1974-75; adj. instr. Columbia U. Sch. Journalism, 1975-76; Author: First Spring: A Martha's Vineyard Journal, 1972, A Yankee Way With Wood, 1975, Miniatures: How to Make Them, Use Them, Sell Them, 1976, Vacation Crafts, 1978, The Mermaids of Chenonceaux and 828 Other Tales: An Anecdotal Guide to Europe, 1982; co-author: Christmas Angels, 1979, Carry-out Cuisine, 1982, New Carry Out Cuisine, 1986, Exploring Rhode Island, 1984. Pulitzer fellow in critical writing, 1967. Mem. Soc. Am. Travel Writers. Home: Music St West Tisbury MA 02575 Office: Providence Jour Providence RI 02902

MERCADO, EVELYN, sales professional; b. N.Y.C., Sept. 8, 1959; d. Manuel Barrios and Carmen (Colon) M. Grad. high sch., Floral Park, N.Y. Customer service rep. John Barnes Inc., N.Y.C., 1980-83, office mgr., 1984-86, sales rep., 1987; sales asst. Contract Furnishings & Systems, N.Y.C., 1984; sales rep. Vertical Surfaces div. Maharam Fabric Corp., N.Y.C., 1987—. Mem. Nat. Assn. Female Execs. Home: 167 Hoffman Ave Elmont NY 11003 Office: Maharam Fabric Corp 979 Third Ave Suite 1223 New York NY 10022

MERCADO, JESSICA THERESA, marketing representative; b. Fontana, Calif., Oct. 29, 1954; d. Raul Joseph and Rose (Caballero) M. AA in Fashion Merchandising, Brooks Coll., Long Beach, Calif., 1974; BA, Calif. State U., Fullerton, 1980. Mktg.-sales support staff Pacific Bell, Los Angeles, 1982—. Mem. Nat. Assn. Female Execs., Statue of Liberty Found., Beta Sigma Phi (exec. bd., v.p., treas., pres., sec.). Avocations: cooking, aerobics, nutritional awareness. Office: Pacific Bell 1010 Wilshire Blvd Los Angeles CA 90017

MERCE, ANNE MARIE, insurance underwriter; b. Denison, Ohio, Nov. 5, 1947; d. Russel and Leona (Berry) M. Student, Alderson Broaddus Coll., 1967-68; B Mus. Edn., Westminster Choir Coll., 1972. Cons., tchr. Nat. Keyboard Arts Assocs., Princeton, N.J., 1972-73; homeowners underwriting clk. Walter B. Howe, Inc., Ins., Princeton, 1973; adminstrv. asst. E.D. Sayer, Inc., Princeton, 1974-79, asst. v.p., underwriter, 1979-84; treaty underwriter GRE-Re of Am. Corp., Princeton, 1984-85; account rep. GRE/Albany-Atlas Ins. Group, Princeton, 1985—. Mem. Nat. Assn. Female Execs., Soc. Profl. and Exec. Women, Assn. Profl. Ins. Women. Republican. Baptist. Home: 189 Princeton Arms N Cranbury NJ 08512

MERCHANT, DONNA RAE, marketing professional; b. Wichita, Kans., Aug. 29, 1948; d. Raymond Houston and Edna Brooks (Waddell) Hobbs; m. Christopher Wayne, Aug. 31, 1968 (div. Aug. 1973); 1 child, Shauna Layne. Student, Wichita State U., 1966-68. Adminstrv. asst. postgrad. edn. U. Kans. Med. Sch., Wichita, 1974-80; activity coordinator continuing med. edn. Wesley Med. Ctr., Wichita, 1980-84; mgr. support services 9th dist. Farm Credit Services, Wichita, 1984-88; mktg. coordinator Greater Oreg. Travel Inc., Eugene, 1988—; cons. Jr. Leauge Wichita, 1983, Plancon, Inc., Martinsville, N.J., 1987—. Mem. Wichita Conv. and Visitors Bur., 1987, events com. Wichita Festivals, Inc., 1987; mem. Eugene Conv. and Visitors Bur., 1988—. Mem. Am. Mktg. Assn., Admsnstrv. Mgmt. Soc., Forum for Exec. Bus. Women, Great Plains Bus. Adminstrn. Group, Eugene C. of C., Delta Gamma Alumni Assn. Republican. Mem. Ch. Nazarene. Home: 87 E 33d St Eugene OR 97405 Office: Greater Oreg Travel 205 E 14th Eugene OR 97401

MERCHANT, GAIL WORTH, sales executive; b. Bridgeport, Conn., Aug. 27, 1955; d. Donn Hamilton and Rosemary (Fettinger) Worth; m. Kenneth Allen Merchant, Mar. 21, 1987. BS in Environ. Design, Syracuse U., 1977. Asst. buyer Abraham and Straus, Bklyn., 1977-79; acct. exec. Bus. Interiors, Boston, 1979-82; sr. acct. exec. Philips Info. Systems, Boston, 1983-84; acct. exec. Autographix Inc., Waltham, Mass., 1984-87; dist. sales rep. Steelcase Inc., Boston, 1987—. Fundraiser Mass. Youth Leadership Found., Boston, 1980-84. Mem. Women in Sales, Nat. Assn. Female Execs., Am. Mktg. Assn. Home: 100 Leslie Rd Waltham MA 02154

MERCINCAVAGE, JANET ELAINE, accountant, educator; b. Wilkes-Barre, Pa., July 19, 1954; d. George Michael and Anna Margaret (Chesavage) M. BS in Bus. Adminstrn. and Spanish, Juniata Coll., 1976; MBA, Temple U., 1984. CPA, Pa. Sr. acct. Ernst & Whinney, Reading, Pa., 1976-78; asst. to treas. Reading Alloys, Inc., 1978-80; asst. prof. acctg. King's Coll., Wilkes-Barre, 1980—. Named one of Outstanding Young Women in Am., 1981, 86. Mem. Am. Inst. CPA's, Pa. Inst. CPA's (chair bus., govt. and edn. Northeast chpt. 1987). Republican. Roman Catholic. Home: 85 N Thomas Ave Kingston PA 18704

MERCOUN, DAWN DENISE, manufacturing company officer; b. Passaic, N.J., June 1, 1950; d. William S. and Irene F. (Micci) M. BS in Bus. Mgmt., Fairleigh Dickinson U., 1978. Personnel payroll coordinator Bentex Mills, Inc., East Rutherford, N.J., 1969-72; employment mgr. Inwood Knitting Mills, Clifton, N.J., 1972-75; gen. mgr. Consol. Advance, Inc., Passaic, 1975-76; v.p. human resources Gemini Industries, Inc., Clifton, 1976—. Mem. Am. Soc. for Personnel Adminstrn., Am. Compensation Assn., Internat. Found. Employee Benefits, Earthwatch Research Team. Republican. Episcopalian. Office: 215 Entin Rd Clifton NJ 07014

MERDINGER, SUSAN, marketing, sales executive; b. Boston, Oct. 5, 1943; d. J. George and Bertha (Lotten) Greenfield; m. Edward Franklin Merdinger, Dec. 21, 1963; children: Mindy Beth, Matthew Joseph. AA, Green Mountain Coll., 1963. Asst. dir. pub. relations Filene's, Boston, 1963; real estate sales, Marlboro, N.J., 1970-78; nat. dir. edn. Network of Homes, Babylon, N.Y., 1978-79; v.p. homefinding Employee Transfer Co., Chgo., 1979-81; dir. mktg. Merrill Lynch Realty, Stamford, Conn., 1981-83, asst. v.p. communications and promotional services, 1983-84, dir. mktg. services, 1984-86; founder, pub. mag. Fine Homes, 1982-87; v.p. Fine Homes Internat., 1986-87; v.p. mktg. services, 1987-88, v.p. internat. mktg., 1988—; lectr. in field. Pres., founder Hadassah, Marlboro, N.J., 1972-75, mem. nat. membership com., 1972-75. Mem. N.J. Realtors Assn., Nat Speakers Assn., Mag. Pubs. Assn., Am. Mgmt. Assn. Office: Merrill Lynch Realty Assocs 10 Stamford Forum Stamford CT 06901

MEREY, DAISY, physician; b. Tangiers, Morocco, Feb. 1, 1949, came to U.S., 1961; d. Theodore and Lilly (Roth) Breuer; m. John Howard Merey, Dec. 26, 1967; children: DeAnne, Andrew. BA, Barnard Coll., 1964; PhD, NYU, 1971; MD, St. George's U., 1979. Resident Broward Gen. Med. Ctr., Ft. Lauderdale, Fla., 1979-80; practice medicine, West Palm Beach, Fla., 1981—; med. cons. Vis. Nurse Assn., 1981-83. Recipient Founder's Day award NYU, 1970. Fellow Am. Soc. Bariatric Physicians, Interam. Physicians Assn.; mem. AMA (Physicians Recognition award 1982, 86), Am. Bariatric Assn., Internat. Bariatric Assn., Internat. Acad. Bariatric Physicians (internat. pres.), Am. Soc. Clin. Nutrition (cert.), Am. Soc. Contemporary Medicine and Surgery, Exec. Women Palm Beaches. Office: 900 N Olive Ave West Palm Beach FL 33401

MERIC, HAVVA JALE, marketing educator; b. Karsiyaka, Turkey, Sept. 9, 1948; came to U.S., 1970.; d. Mustafa Selahattin and Nevin (Esmin) M.; children: Ali, John. BS in Econs. and Fin., Ankara U., Turkey, 1969; MBA, George Washington U., 1973; PhD in Mktg., U. N.C., 1979. Fin. analyst Ministry of Fin., Ankara, 1969-70; asst. prof. East Carolina U., Greenville, N.C., 1978-84, assoc. prof. mktg., 1984—; cons. Lawrence Behr Assocs., Greenville, 1983, Torboro (N.C.) Clinic P.A., 1987. Contbr. numerous articles to profl. jours. Mem. Am. Mktg. Assn., Assn. Health Services Mktg., Assn. Consumer Research, So. Mktg. Assn. (reviewer), Inst. Decision Scis. (discussant SE chpt.), Pilot Club Internat. Office: East Carolina U Sch of Bus Dept Mktg Greenville NC 27834

MERINOFF, BARBARA LEE, advertising executive; b. Manhasset, N.Y., Mar. 26, 1962; d. Herman Irwin and Susan Leah (Kletz) M. BA in Communications, U. Mich., 1984. Asst. acct. exec. Grey Advt., N.Y.C., 1984-86, acct. exec., 1986—. Big sister Ann Arbor Community Services, 1981—. Mem. Nat. Assn. Female Execs., Kappa Kappa Gamma. Home: 360 E 72d St New York NY 10021 Office: Grey Advt 777 Third Ave New York NY 10017

MERJOS, ANNA, financial analyst, securities researcher; b. N.Y.C., Apr. 1, 1923; d. Stavros and Helen (Papavasiliou) M. B.A., Hunter Coll., N.Y.C., 1944. Vice pres. Merrill Lynch, Pierce, Fenner & Smith Inc., N.Y.C., 1951—. Contbr. articles to profl. jours. Mem. Pi Mu Epsilon, Phi Beta Kappa. Greek Orthodox. Office: Merrill Lynch & Co Merrill Lynch World Hdqrs North Tower World Fin Ctr New York NY 10281-1214

MERKEL, SANDRA IRENE, nurse, consultant; b. LeMars, Iowa, Mar. 20, 1944; d. Dale Wilfred and Dorothy Maire (Seggerman) Dorr; m. David Patrick Merkel, June 12, 1971; children: Martha, Leigh. BSN, U. Iowa, 1966; MS, U. Mich., 1977. Registered nurse, Mich. Staff nurse C. S. Hosp., Colon, Panama, 1970-71; head nurse C. S. Mott Children's Hosp., Ann Arbor, Mich., 1972-75; clinician II C. S. Mott Children's Hosp., Ann Arbor, 1975-77; adj. instr. sch. nursing U. Mich., Ann Arbor, 1982—; clin. nurse specialist C. S. Mott Children's Hosp. U. Mich. Med. Ctr., Ann Arbor, 1977—, Diabetes Research and Tng. Ctr., Ann Arbor, 1978-82. Author videotape Spinal Fusion: What You Need to Know, 1984, Children in Pain: A Special Challenge; contbr. articles to profl. jours. V.p. PTA, Chelsea, Mich., 1984. Mem. Am. Nurses Assn., Mich. Nurses Assn., Dist. 51 Nurses Assn. (v.p. 1983-87), Assn. for Care of Children in Hosps., Sigma Theta Tau. Home: 252 Shoreview Chelsea MI 48118 Office: CS Mott Children Hosp F2438/0216 Ann Arbor MI 48109

MERKER, MATHILDA SUE, nursing educator, nursing consultant; b. Richmond, Va., Oct. 23, 1942; d. Frank F. and Edith Marjorie (Greer) Merker; m. Robert C. Acuff, Feb. 7, 1970 (div. Oct. 1982). B.S. in Nursing, Med. Coll. Va., 1965; M.S., Va. Commonwealth U., 1975. Cert. clin. specialist. Asst. dir. nursing Mid-Mo. Mental Health Ctr., Columbia, 1980-81; staff devel. instr. Sheppard and Pratt Hosp., Balt., 1981-82, cons., 1981—; instr. psychiat. nursing Sch. Nursing, U. Md., Balt., 1982-87, adult admissions adminstr., 1988—; cons. A Safe Place, 1985—. Served to lt. U.S. Navy, 1967-70. Mem. Am. Nurses Assn., Md. Nurses Assn., Sigma Theta Tau Psi. Democrat. Methodist. Office: PO Box 1034 Severna Park MD 21146

MERKIN, JANE PAULA, management executive; b. Bklyn., Feb. 26, 1945; d. Allan and Mindell (Schaff) M. BA, George Washington U., 1966, MPA, 1983. Office mgr. Office Senator Joseph Tydings, Washington, 1966-68; adminstrv. asst. Tydings & Rosenberg, Balt., 1968-70; asst. press sec. Tydings for Senate Campaign, Balt., 1970; scheduling dir. Office Senator Birch Bayh, Washington, 1970-78; dir. scheduling liaison HUD, Washington, 1978-81; pres. Details, Inc., Washington, 1981-88; freelance meeting planning cons. Bethesda, Md., 1988—; instr. continuing edn. George Washington U., 1984-85; speaker Meeting World, 1985, 86, 87. Mem. exec. com. Am. Diabetes Assn. Montgomery County, Md. chpt., 1987—; mem. adv. council Sec. Md. Dept. Human Resources, 1987—; vol. dem. polit campaigns, Washington, Md., 1964—. Mem. Phi Beta Kappa. Democrat. Jewish. Office: Bethesda MD 20817

MERKLE, HELEN LOUISE, hotel executive; b. Carrington, N.D., May 23, 1950; d. Orville F. and Lillian M. (Argue) M. BS, N.D. State U., 1972. Asst. dir. food mgmt. Stouffer's Atlanta Inn, Atlanta, 1972-74; dir. food mgmt. Stouffer's Indpls. Inn, 1974-78; adminstrv. dir. food mgmt. Stouffer's Riverfront Towers, St. Louis, 1978-80; food mgmt. cons. Fraser Mgmt., Westlake, Ohio, 1980-83; exec. chef Marriott Hotel, Cleve., 1983—. Recipient First Place award for soups Taste of Indpls., 1976. Mem. Am. Culinary Fedn., Cleve. Culinary Assn., Food Service Execs. Assn., Nat. Assn. Female Execs. Democrat. Lutheran. Home: 4137 W 160th St Cleveland OH 44135 Office: Marriott Hotel Cleve 4277 150th St Cleveland OH 44135

MERKLE, JUDITH ASTRAIA, political science educator, writer; b. Brunswick, Maine, Jan. 14, 1942; d. Theodore Charles and Helene Rafaela Antonia (Suarez) M.; m. W. Parkes Riley, II, June 19, 1971; children—Elizabeth Antonia, Marlow Francis Parkes. B.A., U. Calif.-Berkeley, 1962, Ph.D., 1974; A.M., Harvard U., 1964. Mgmt. intern Dept. Def., Washington, 1964-65, research mgr., 1965-66; research and teaching asst. U. Calif., Berkeley, 1967-69, acting instr., 1969-70, lectr. pub. adminstrn., 1970-71; asst. prof., dir. Russian and East European Studies Ctr., U. Oreg., Eugene, 1971-82; assoc. prof. polit. sci. Claremont McKenna Coll., Calif., 1982—; mem. faculty Claremont Grad. Sch.; cons., guest lectr., book reviewer; books include: Management and Ideology: The Legacy of the International Scientific Management Movement, 1980, A Vision of Light, 1989; contbr. articles to profl. jours. Vice pres. Lane County Diabetes Assn., 1981; pres. Oreg. State Employees Assn., 1981. NSF grantee, 1969; Mellon grantee, 1985; Deutscher Akademischer Austauschdienst, Council European Studies, 1975. Mem. Acad. Mgmt., Am. Pollt. Sci. Assn., Am. Soc. Pub. Adminstrn., Am. Assn. Advancement Slavic Studies, Phi Beta Kappa, Alpha Mu Gamma, Pi Sigma Alpha. Democrat. Episcopalian. Office: Claremont McKenna Coll Dept of Govt Claremont CA 91711

MERKLE, LINDA L., legal administrator, corporate controller; b. Washington, Apr. 6, 1947; d. Robert Clifton, Shreeves II and Esther A. (Harrison) Cumming; lic. real estate, Prince Georges Community Coll., Largo, Md., 1972; children: Christina L., Regina L. Various secretarial positions, 1964-65, 67-72; real estate saleswoman, 1973-74; div. sec. Prince Georges Community Coll., 1974-75; real estate saleswoman Harvest Realty Inc., Clinton, Md., 1974-75; legal adminstr., property mgr., investment mgr. firm Tucker, Flyer, Sanger, Reider & Lewis P.C., Washington, 1975-84; legal adminstr. Anderson, Heibey, Nauheim & Blair, Washington, 1984-85; v.p. fin. and adminstrn. Barnes, Morris & Pardoe, Inc., Washington, 1985—; dir. Md. Corp.; pres. Lawtabs Inc. Del. Corp.; cons., speaker Mem. Assn. Legal Adminstrs. (chmn. new adminstrs. and gen. adminstrn. sect. 1984-85), ABA (assoc.). Home: 4100 N River St Arlington VA 22207 Office: 919 18th St NW Washington DC 20006

MERKLE, PEGEEN FARRELL, technical training manager; b. Stamford, Conn., Dec. 18, 1958; d. Robert Ernst and Marie Cecilia (Koch) Farrell; m. Walter John Merkle, Oct 15, 1983. Student, So. Conn. State U., 1976, Western Conn. State U., 1980—. Adminstrv. asst. Village Bank & Trust Co., Ridgefield, Conn., 1979-80; asst. dir. Grolier Internat., Inc., Danbury, Conn., 1980-81; program adminstr. Union Carbide Corp., Danbury, 1981-87; mgr. tng. Ultimate Data Systems, Inc., Wilton, Conn., 1987-88. Tchr. Spanish High Sch. Affiliation, Stamford, 1974-75, swimming Italian Ctr., Stamford, 1975-76, catechism St. Francis of Assisi, New Milford, Conn., 1982-83; instr. aerobics Nancy Strong, New Milford, 1983-84; vol. St. Joseph's Hosp., Stamford, 1975; rep. Am. Heart Assn., Stamford, 1975; donator ARC, Danbury, 1981—. Named to Spanish Honor Soc., Stamford, 1975. Mem. Am. Soc. Tng. and Devel., Nat. Assn. Female Execs. Roman Catholic. Club: Union Carbide Bowling (Brewster, N.Y.).

MERKLIN, LINDA LEE, food products executive; b. Akron, Ohio, Nov. 18, 1958; d. Raymond Lee and Barbara Jean (Robb) Vittitoe; m. Randall Douglas Merklin, Dec. 29, 1979; children: Daniel, Nicholas. BA in Dietetics, U. Akron, 1981. Supr. foodservice Akron Children's Med. Ctr., 1979-81; mgr. foodservice SAGA/Marriott Foodservice Co., Toledo, 1981-85; dir. foodservices Riverside Hosp., Toledo, 1985—; bd. dirs. Women's, Infants and Children Adv. Com., Toledo, 1985—; bd. dirs. steering com. Quality Circle, Toledo, 1986—. Mem. Am. Dietetic Assn., Toledo Dietetic Assn., Nat. Assn. Female Execs., Am. Soc. Hosp. Foodservice Adminstrs. Presbyterian. Lodge: Internal Order of Foresters. Home: 527 Richards Rd Toledo OH 43607 Office: Riverside Hosp 1600 Superior St Toledo OH 43604

MERMELSTEIN, ISABEL MAE ROSENBERG, adminstrative financial planner; b. Houston, Aug. 20, 1934; d. Joe Hyman and Sylvia (Lincove) Rosenberg; m. Robert Jay Mermelstein, Sept. 6, 1953 (div. July 1975); children: William, Linda, Jody. Student U. Ariz., 1952, Mich. State U., 1974, Lansing (Mich.) Community Coll., 1975. Exec. dir. Shiawassee County YWCA, Owosso, Mich., 1975-78; real estate developer F&S Devel. Corp., Lansing, Mich., 1978-79, Corum Devel. Corp., Houston, 1979-81; adminstrv. fin. planner Investec Asset Mgmt. Group, Inc., Houston, bd. dirs. Living Hope Care Ctr. 1981-85, Living Hope Care Paraclete Found. Author: For You! I Killed the Chicken, 1972. Mem. 1st Ecumenical Council of Lansing. Recipient State of Mich. Flag, 1972, Key to City, City of Lansing, 1972-73. Mem. Internat. Women's Pilot Orgn. (The 99's). Republican. Jewish. Lodges: Zonta, Licoma, B'nai B'rith, Hadassah, Nat. Fedn. Temple Sisterhoods. Flew All Women's Transcontinental Air Race (Powder Puff Derby), 1972, 83. Avocations: flying, gourmet cooking, needlepoint, knitting, snow skiing. Home: 4030 Newshire Houston TX 77025

MERMELSTEIN, PAULA, broadcasting executive; b. N.Y.C., Nov. 8, 1947; d. Robert and Dorothy Blanche (Asch) M.; m. Francis W. James, Fr., Nov. 23, 1975; 1 son, Robert Austin. B.A. cum laude, Bklyn. Coll., 1968. Promotion writer, producer NBC, N.Y.C., 1970-78; supervising writer, producer NBC, 1978-79, dir. on-air promotion, 1979, v.p. on-air promotion, 1979-80, v.p. on-air promotion and print copy, 1980-82, creative dir. East Coast, 1982-87, exec. dir. copy, 1985-87; freelance advt. writer and producer N.Y.C., 1987; creative group head broadcast advt. Spring, O'Brien, House, N.Y.C., 1988—; mem. editorial staff Joe Garagiola's Memory Game quiz show; prodn. asst. Macy's Thanksgiving Day Parade, 1969. Author: (Reader column) Glamour mag., 1970. Recipient First Place in News Promo U.S. TV Commls. Festival, 1977; recipient Silver award Broadcasters Promotion Assn., 1983, Gold award Chgo. Internat. Film Festival, 1986, 2 Gold awards Broadcast Promotion and Mktg. Execs., 1987. Mem. Writers Guild Am. Jewish.

MEROLA, MARY LOUISE FRANCES, physician; b. N.Y.C., Oct. 9, 1950; d. John A. and Mary T. (Guidera) M. BS in Biology, St. John's U., Jamaica, N.Y., 1972; MD, U. Bologna (Italy), 1979. Resident in family practice Community Hosp., Glen Cove, N.Y., 1979-82, asst. dir. family practice residency program, 1982—; pvt. practice specializing in family practice; Baldwin, N.Y., 1985—; attending physician South Nassau (N.Y.) Community Hosp. Glen. Mem. Am. Assn. Family Practitioners, AMA, Am. Med. Women's Assn., N.Y. Acad. Scis., Nassau Acad. Medicine.

MERRIAM, MARY-LINDA SORBER, college president; b. Jeannette, Pa., May 31, 1943; d. Everett Sylvester Calvin and Madeleine (Case) Sorber; m. E. William Merriam, Dec. 14, 1969 (div. 1975). Student, Grove City Coll., 1961-63; B.A., Pa. State U., 1963-65, M.A., 1965-67, Ph.D., 1967-70. Research assoc. Penn. State U., University Park, 1970-72; asst. prof. Emerson Coll., Boston, 1972-74, dir. continuing edn., 1974-77, spl. asst. to pres., 1977-78, v.p. adminstrn., 1978-79; asst. to pres. Boston U., Boston, 1979-81; pres. Wilson Coll., Chambersburg, Pa., 1981—; cons. Govt. E.S.E.A. Title III, Alameda County, Calif., 1968, Avon Products, Inc., N.Y.C., 1977; bd. dirs. United Telephone Systems-Ea. Group. Bd. dirs. Sta. WITF-TV, Harrisburg, Pa., 1982—, Boston Zool. Soc., 1980-81, Arts, Boston, 1979-81, Scotland Sch. for Vets.' Children, Pa., 1984—, Chambersburg Hosp., Pa., 1984—; mem. higher edn. com. Gen. Assembly Presbyn. Ch., 1987—, chmn., 1987-88; elder Falling Spring Presbyn. Ch., 1988—. Recipient Athena award Chambersburg C. of C., 1988; named Disting. Alumna The Pa. State U., 1984, Disting. Daughter of Pa., 1986; fellow Am. Council Edn., 1977-78. Mem. Speech Communication Assn., Nat. Acad. TV Arts and Scis. (bd. govs. New England chpt. 1980-81), Pa. Assn. Colls. and Univs. (exec. com. 1984—), Assn. Presbyn. Colls. and Univs. (exec. com. 1983-88, pres. 1986-87), Am. Assn. Higher Edn., Nat. Soc. Arts and Letters, Phi Kappa Phi, Rho Tau Sigma, AAUW. Presbyterian. Home: 1301 Philadelphia Ave Chambersburg PA 17201 Office: Wilson Coll Chambersburg PA 17201

MERRICK, SUE ALICE, realtor; b. Chgo., Oct. 1, 1943; d. Henry Maynard and Margaret Kathryn (McNulty) Hintz; m. Michael D. Merrick, Oct. 19, 1959 (div. 1987); children: Theresa, Kenneth, Sandy, Michael, Keith, Jennifer, Michelle. Student, Clark County Community Coll., 1978-83. Realtor Centurion Properties, Las Vegas, 1979-80; sales assoc. U.S. Home Corp., Las Vegas, 1980-81, Chism Homes, Inc., Las Vegas, 1981-83; realtor Sellwood Realty, Las Vegas, 1983-85; realtor, dept. mgr. Americana Group Realtor, Las Vegas, 1985-87; broker Heritage Homes Inc., Las Vegas, 1987—. mem. Gov.'s Conf. for Women, Las Vegas, 1987. Mem. Women's Council Realtors (chair reservations 1983-85, pres. Las Vegas chpt. 1986—, program chmn. 1986, pres.-elect Nev. state chpt. 1988), So. Nev. homebuilders, So. Nev. polit. caucus), Las Vegas Bd. Realtors (bd. dirs.), Realtors Active in Politics. Democrat. Roman Catholic. Office: Heritage Homes Inc 17255 S Rainbow #22 Las Vegas NV 89102

MERRIGAN, MARY ELLEN, sales executive; b. Maryville, Mo., July 7, 1951; d. James Robert and Coletta Marie (Seipel) M. BA in Speech, Northwest Mo. State U., 1973. Account exec. Sta. WMKC Radio, Oshkosh, Wis., 1973-74, Sta. KHAK Radio, Cedar Rapids, Iowa, 1974-77; account exec. Sta. KARN Radio, Little Rock, 1977-79, sales mgr., 1979-80; account exec. Sta. KCKN Radio, Kansas City, Kans., 1980-81; account exec. Sta. KMJQ Radio, Houston, 1981-85, sales mgr., 1985-86, gen. sales mgr., 1986—. Mem. Am. Mgmt. Assn., Mind-Body Connection Inst. Office: Sta KMJQ 24 Greenway Plaza Suite 1508 Houston TX 77046

MERRILL, DALE MARIE, sales executive; b. Melrose, Mass., Feb. 21, 1954; d. Richard Paul and Rosemarie Reine (Porelle) M. BA in English, U. of Lowell (Mass.), 1976; MA in Am. Studies, Boston Coll., 1983. Sales rep. A-Copy Inc., Natick, Mass., 1976-77; sales mgr. Jan Optical Co., Waltham, Mass., 1977-78; market researcher Decision Research Co., Lexington, Mass., 1979-81; sales rep. Henco Software Co., Waltham, 1981-82; account mgr. Univ. Computing Co., Chgo., 1982-83; regional sales mgr. CompuServe Data Techs. (formerly Software House), Cambridge, Mass., 1983—; bd. dirs. M.T. Corp., Woburn, Mass. Author, editor: Seeds mag. (Poetry award 1972), 1971-72; contbr. poetry to mags. Organizer 18x72 project, Stoneham, Mass., 1970-71; bd. dirs. Stoneham Hist. Commn., 1976-77. Recipient Top Sales award A-Copy Inc., 1976-77, Interviewer award Decision Research Co., 1981, Triple Crown Sales award, 1985, 86, 87, Million Dollar Sales Club award, 1987. Mem. Nat. Assn. Female Execs., NOW, Digital Equipment Co. User Soc. (DECUS). Democrat. Avocations: skiing, photography, painting, sculpturing, karate. Home: PO Box 2586 Woburn MA 01888 Office: CompuServe Data Techs 1000 Massachusetts Ave Cambridge MA 02138

MERRILL, JANE LAYTON, health facility administrator; b. Annapolis, Md., Oct. 21, 1951; d. Donald Merrill and Kathleen (Gingras) Layton; 1 child, Scott Haussler. BA, Calif. Poly. State U., 1973; MPH, UCLA, 1982; MS in Psychology, U. La Verne, 1983. Cert. marriage family child counselor. Adminstrv. dir. Haussler Oil Prodn., St. Maria, Calif., 1971-79, Fin. Exec. Recruiter, Westlake, Calif., 1980-82, Calif. Psychoednl., Claremont, Calif., 1982-83; exec. dir. Project S.I.S.T.E.R., Claremont, 1982-84, Community Hospice, Modesto, Calif., 1984—. Mem. Mayor's Council for Handicapped, Modesto, Oncology Planning Com., Modesto. Recipient Award of Excellence Nat. Hospice Orgn., 1987. Mem. Am. Assn. Marriage Family Therapists, Calif. Assn. Marriage Family Therapists, Am. Mgmt. Assn., Nat. Assn. Female Execs., Stepfamily Assn. Am. Home: 3612 Forest Glenn Dr Modesto CA 95355 Office: Community Hospice 601 McHenry #C Modesto CA 95350

MERRILL, LOIS JEAN, university dean, nursing educator; b. New Haven, Aug. 3, 1932; d. Robert Warner and Lydia Mabel (Crook) M.; B.S., U. Conn., 1955; M.S., U. Colo., 1960; Ph.D., U. Nebr., 1978. RN Cin. Gen. Hosp., 1955-56; asst. instr. U. Cin., 1956-58; RN Presbyn. Hosp., Denver, 1959-60; instr. nursing Syracuse U., N.Y., 1960-63; assoc. prof. U. Ky., Lexington, 1963-69; assoc. prof., assoc. dean, U. Nebr., Lincoln, 1969-76; prof., dean of nursing U. Evansville, Ind., 1978-86; prof., dean nursing U. N.D., Grand Forks, 1986—. Editor: Global Hunger, 1986; mem. editorial bd. Nurse Educator, 1975-84, Jour. Profl. Nursing, 1987—; contbr. articles to profl. jours. Mem. adv. bd. Evansville-Vanderburg County Health Occupations Programs, 1978-86; bd. dirs. Vandenburgh City Sch. Practical Nursing, Evansville, 1978-86, Greater Evansville Diabetes Assn., 1985-86. Recipient Mentor award Eta Lambda/Sigma Theta Tau, 1986. Mem. Am. Nurses Assn. (state pres. 1972-74), Nat. League for Nursing (bd. dirs. 1974-76, accreditation visitor 1984—), Am. Edn. Research Soc., Midwest Nursing Research Soc. Office: U ND Sch Nursing PO Box 8195-Univ Sta Grand Forks ND 58202

MERRILL, LYNNE BARTLETT, marketing and advertising company executive; b. Southampton, N.Y., Mar. 17, 1953; d. William Stuart and Marilyn (Bake) Bartlett; m. John Albee Merrill, June 1, 1974; 1 child, Michael Bartlett. BS, Boston U., 1975. Intern U.S. Ho. of Reps., N.H., 1974; account exec. Creative Promotions, Dover, N.H., 1974-75; pres., owner Merrill Assocs., Inc., Kingston, N.H., 1975—; real estate salesman Kingston Real Estate, 1974—. Past chmn., current judging chmn. Graniteers Awards, Inc., 1986-87; chmn. save the ch. com. Kingston Hist. Soc. Recipient numerous Laurel awards for best radio comml. Cadillac Motor Car Div., 1985, 87, best TV comml., 1987, numerous Graniteer awards, Test TV Comml. award, 1987. Mem. Pub. Relations Soc. Am. (accredited), Advt. Club N.H. (past pres.), Kingston Bus. and Profl. Womens Club, Haverhill C. of C. (bd. dirs., v.p.), Portsmouth C. of C., Seacoast Communications Network. Republican. Congregationalist. Avocations: boating, swimming, sewing, reading, gardening. Office: Merrill Assocs Inc 11 Church St PO Box 757 Kingston NH 03848

MERRIMAN, ILAH COFFEE, financial executive; b. Amarillo, Tex., Mar. 22, 1935; d. Oran and Frances Elizabeth (Rocque) Coffee; children—Pamela, Michael. B.S. in Math., Tex. Tech. U. Cert. secondary tchr., Tex. Pres., chief exec. officer H&R Block Inc., Houston ; pres. H&R Block Inc. Tex.; Trustee, bd. dirs. exec. bd. Tex. Tech U. ex students assn., pres. elect; mem. steering com. Pres.'s Council, bd. dirs. Tex. Tech. Double T Connection, Tex. Tech. Found., Southwest Athletic Conf., Women's Basketball Tournament; mem. enterprize fund Dallas Chpt., Texas Tech. U.; Mem. Dallas Mus. Fine Art, Houston Mus. Fine Art, Dallas Shakespeare Festival, Dallas Theater Ctr., Dallas Symphony Assn., Dallas Hist. Soc., Fort Worth's Kimball Mus., AAUW. Methodist. Office: 8808 Greenville Ave Suite 101 Dallas TX 75243

MERRITT, DORIS HONIG, pediatrician; b. N.Y.C., July 16, 1923; d. Aaron and Lillian (Kunstlich) Honig; children: Kenneth Arthur, Christopher Ralph. B.A., City U. N.Y., 1944; M.D., George Washington U., 1952. Diplomate: Nat. Bd. Med. Examiners, Am. Bd. Pediatrics. Pediatric intern Duke Hosp., 1952-53; teaching and research fellow pediatrics George Washington U., 1953-54; pediatric asst. resident Duke U. Hosp., 1954-55, cardiovascular fellow pediatrics, 1955-56, instr. pediatrics, dir. pediatric cardiorenal clinic, 1956-57; exec. sec. cardiovascular study sect., gen. medicine study sect. div. research grants NIH, 1957-60; dir. med. research grants and contracts Ind. U. Sch. Medicine, 1961-62, asst. prof. pediatrics, 1961-68, asst. dean med. research, 1962-65, asst. dir. med. research, aerospace research application center, 1963-65, asso. dir. med. research, 1965-68, asst. dean for research, office v.p. research and dean advanced studies, 1965-67, dir. sponsored programs, asst. to provost, 1965-68, asso. dean for research and advanced studies, office v.p. and dean for research and advanced studies, 1967-71, assoc. prof. pediatrics, 1968-73, prof., 1973-80; spl. asst. to dir. NIH, 1978-87, research tng. and research resource officer, 1980-87, acting dir. Nat. Ctr. Nursing Research, 1986-87; prof. pediatrics, assoc. dean Sch. of Medicine, Ind. U., 1988—; cons. USPHS, NIH div. research grants Div. Health Research Facilities and Resources, Nat. Heart Inst., 1963-78, Am. Heart Assn., 1963-67, Ind. Med. Assn. Commn. Vol. Health Orgns., 1964-67, Bur. Health Manpower, Health Profession's Constrn. Program, 1965-71, Nat. Library Medicine, Health Center Library Constrn. Program, 1966-72; dir. office sponsored programs Ind. U.-Purdue U. Indpls. Office Chancellor, 1968-71, dean research and sponsored programs, 1971-79; mem. Nat. Library Medicine biomed. communications rev. com., 1970-74. Contbr. articles to profl. jours. Chmn. Indpls. Consortium for Urban Edn., 1971-75; v.p. Greater Indpls. Progress Com., 1974-79; mem. Community Service Council, 1969-75; bd. dirs. Bd. for Fundamental Edn., 1973-77, Ind. Sci. Edn. Found., 1977-78, Community Addiction Services Agy., Inc., 1972-74; trustee Marian Coll., 1977-78; exec. com. Nat. Council U. Research Adminstrs., 1977-78; bd. regents Nat. Library Medicine, 1976-80; chmn. adv. screening com. for life scis. Council Internat. Exchange of Scholars, 1978-81. Served to lt. (j.g.) USNR. Fellow Am. Acad. Pediatrics; mem. AAAS, George Washington U., Duke U. med. alumni assns., Phi Beta Kappa, Alpha Omega Alpha. Office: Ind U Sch Medicine FH312 Indianapolis IN 46223

MERRITT, NANCIE LEE, insurance company adminstrator; b. New Castle, Pa., Dec. 9, 1941; d. Clarence Edgar and Ethel Mae (Wagner) McGaffic; m. Andrew Charles Merritt, Feb. 24, 1968 (div. 1984); children: Gregory Lawrence, Douglas Charles. BA in Anthropology, Drew U., 1981; MA in Human Resources, New Sch. for Social Research, 1987. Supr. of staffing Ins. Services Office, Inc., N.Y.C., 1984—. Bull. editor League of Women Voters, Indpls., 1973-74, Maplewood, N.J., 1975-76. Mem. Phi Beta Kappa. Democrat. Office: Ins Services Office Inc 160 Water St New York NY 10038

MERRITT, PATRICIA ANNE, data processing executive; b. Rochester, N.Y., Jan. 12, 1945; d. Richard Henry and Florence Elizabeth (Adams) M.; m. Steve Verderber, March 1981. Student Long Beach (Calif.) City Coll., 1972-74, Foothill Jr. Coll., 1974-77; grad. Bryman Paramed. Sch., San Jose, Calif., 1977; m. Steve Verderber. Data processing clk. Lincoln Rochester Trust Co., Rochester, N.Y., 1965-67; keypunch operator Eastman Kodak, Rochester, 1967-70; keypunch and verify operator Reliance Steel Co., Los Angeles, 1971; keypunch operator Automatic Data Processing, Long Beach, 1971, Fed. Civil Service, Los Alamitos, Calif., 1971-73, Varian Assos., Palo Alto, Calif., 1973-78; tech. typist, word processor lead-operator Watkins Johnson, Palo Alto, 1978-79, 79-81; supr. office systems Smith Kline Instruments, Sunnyvale, Calif., 1981-82; owner I.P.S. Info. Processing Systems, 1982-86; word processor sr. operator Palo Alto Unified Sch. Dist., 1979; independent personal beauty cons., Mary Kay Cosmetics, 1987—. Leader, Monroe County council Girl Scouts U.S.A., Rochester, 1969-70, Santa Clara County council, Mountain View, Calif., 1978-80; commr. City of Santa Clara Hist. Commn., 1983-85. Mem. Beta Sigma Phi.

MERROW, TONI SUE, public relations specialist; b. Springfield, Mo., Mar. 24, 1940; d. Haldene Kemp and Ruth Darlene (Jordan) Holt; m. Maesil LeGrand Merrow, May 13, 1961 (dec.); children—Dene O., Scott J., Regina L. Haney. Student pub. schs., Denver. Exec. sec. Colo. Brick Co., Denver, 1959-60; sec. Stanley Aviation, Denver, 1960-61; sec. to service specialist Ford Motor, Tractor div., Denver, 1961-77; sec. to v.p. advt. communications KWAL Paints, Inc., Denver, 1979-84; sec., asst. to v.p. Intermountain Network, Denver, 1985-88; pub. relations cons. The Osburn Band, Denver, 1977—. Vice pres. Hallet Sch. PTA, Denver, 1971-73; active various charitable orgns.; mem., pub. relations cons. Blue Knights Drum and Bugle Corps Parents Orgn., Littleton, 1983-84; historian, pub. relations cons. Highland High Sch. Booster Assn., Thornton, 1983-84. Cert. of Commendation, City of Thornton, 1975. Mem. Nat. Assn. Female Execs., Scholastic Gold Key. Club: Thornton Women's. Avocations: antiques; geneology; reading; camping. Home: 2502 E 90th Pl Thornton CO 80229

MERRY, MARILYN DIANA HOOVER, cartographer; b. St. Louis, July 28, 1946; d. Roscoe C. S. and Elnora (Monigan) H.; m. Allan Preston Merry (div. Sept. 1978); children: Jason Kimball Ward, Meana Linette Ward. Clk., typist Army Recruit and Inductions Sta., St. Louis, 1966-67; printing control clk. U.S. Mobility Equipment Command, St. Louis, 1968-70; supply clk. U.S. Troop Support Command, St. Louis, 1970-71; clk.-typist Inst. Heraldry, Alexandria, Va., 1971-72, Med. Intelligence, Washington, 1972-73; office mgr. Yodi Enterprises, E. St. Louis, Ill., 1973-74; sec. Defense Mapping Agy., Washington, 1974-79, cartographic tech., 1979-82, cartographer, 1982—. Exec. Bd. Am. Cancer Soc., sec., 1985-87, Pres.'s award, 1985; active Coalition of Black Trade Unionist; exec. bd. Washington Area Labor Com. on Cen. Am. and the Caribbean, 1986—; candidate Town Council, Capitol Heights, 1986. Recipient Pres.' award Am. Cancer Soc. Mem. NAACP, Coalition Labor Union WOmen, Federally Employed Women (sec. 1979-80, 1987-88), A. Philip Randolph Inst., Nat. Council Negro Women, Am. Fedn. Govt. Employees (women's coordinator 14th dist. 1984-88), London Woods Community Assn. (adv. com. 1984-86). Baptist. Home: 5803 Falkland Pl Capitol Heights MD 20743

MERSEREAU, BOBBI, claims manager, administrator; b. Boston, Dec. 30, 1945; d. George William and Nellie (David) M. Cert., Vesper George Sch. Art, Boston, 1972-73; Cert. Legal Prins., Am. Ednl. Inst., Basking Ridge (N.J.), 1983. With Fireman's Fund Ins. Co., Boston, 1963—, claims rep., 1972-76, claims supr., 1976-78, sr. claims supr., 1978-82, line sr. Fidelity & Surety, 1982-84; asst. claims mgr. administration, 1984—; analyst Coca-Cola, Atlanta, 1977; bus. analyst Am. Mgmt. Systems, Inc., 1978-80, pring. 1981, v.p., dir., 1982—; arbitrator Ins. Arbitration Forums, Woburn, Mass., 1982—. Account exec. United Way Mass. Bay, Boston, 1982, 83, sect. chmn., 1984; mem. com. Boston Paralympic Com., 1983; vol. Spl. Olympics, Boston, 1983; vol. Nikee Pikee Roadrace for Spl. Olympics, 1982, 83; active Beacon Hill Civic Assn., 1985-86, Charleston Preservation Soc., 1987-88. Republican. Home: 2 Lawnwood Place Suite #1 Apt 12A Charleston MA 02129

MERSKEY-ZEGER, MARIE GERTRUDE FINE, retired librarian; b. Kimberley, South Africa, Oct. 10, 1914; came to U.S., 1960, naturalized, 1965; d. Herman and Annie Myra (Wigoder) Fine; m. Clarence Merskey, Oct. 8, 1939 (dec. 1982); children: Hilary Pamela Merskey Nathe, Susan Heather Merskey Sinistore, Joan Margaret Merskey Schneiderman; m. Jack I. Zeger, July 15, 1984. Grad. Underwood Bus. Sch., Cape Town, South Africa, 1934; BA, U. Cape Town, 1958, diploma librarianship, 1960. Sec. to Chief Rabbi Israel Abrahams, South Africa, 1945-49, Jewish Sheltered Employment Council, 1954-56; reference librarian New Rochelle Pub. Library, 1960-63; research librarian Consumers Union, Mt. Vernon, 1963-66; asst. readers services, head union catalog Westchester Library System, 1966-69, mem. adult services com., 1973-74; dir. Harrison Pub. Library and West Harrison Br., 1969-84; acting dir. Mamaroneck (N.Y.) Free Library, 1987—, also trustee. Pub. edn. officer USCG Aux. Flotilla 63. Author: History of the Harrison Libraries, 1980. bd. dirs. Shore Acres Point Corp., Mamaroneck, 1985—. Recipient Brotherhood award B'nai B'rith, 1974; named Woman of Yr., Harrison, 1984. Mem. ALA, Westchester Library Assn., N.Y. Library Assn. (adult edn. com. for continuing edn. 1971-75, adult services com. 1973-75, vice chmn., 1975, exec. bd. 1981-82), Pub. Library Dirs. Assn. (tech. services com. chmn. Westchester County 1971, exec. bd. 1974-75, vice chmn. 1975), Clubs: Harrison Women's, YMCA, Harrison Hist. Soc. (bd. dirs. Charles Dawson History Ctr. (founder), Hadassah, (Harrison, N.Y.), USCG Aux. Contbr. articles to local newspapers. Home: 316 S Barry Ave Mamaroneck NY 10543

MERSMANN, CYNTHIA ANN, nurse; b. Buffalo, July 31, 1957; d. John A. and Judith F. (Detig) M. BS in Nursing, U. Rochester, 1979; MS in Nursing, Hunter Coll., 1984; doctoral candidate, NYU, 1985—. Registered nurse obstet. Staff nurse NYU Med. Ctr., 1979-80, nurse clinician, 1980, asst. head nurse, 1980-82, head nurse, 1982-84, clin. coordinator, 1984—. Vol. Jr. Achievement, 1979-83. Mem. Nurse's Assn. of Am. Coll. Obstetricians and Gynecologists, Internat. Childbirth Ednl. Assn., Sigma Theta Tau. Home: 340 E 34th #16K New York NY 10016

MERTEN, KAROL KAY, speech communication educator; b. Hays, Kans., Oct. 19, 1934; d. Albert R. and Louise (McKinley) Papes; m. Robert W. Merten, July 15, 1956. BS, U. Kans., 1956, MA, 1963; PhD, U. Denver, 1976. Speech, hearing clinician Shawnee County Schs., Topeka, 1956-57, Hoisington Pub. Schs., Kans., 1959-61; pvt. practice speech, lang. pathologist Great Bend, Kans., 1962-65; asst. prof. dept. speech pathology and audiology U. Denver, 1965-77, chmn., assoc. prof. dept. speech pathology and audiology, 1977-86, assoc. prof. dept. speech communication, 1986—; co-project dir. Listen Found., Denver, 1983-85; project dir. U.S. Dept Edn. Rehab. Services, Washington, 1977-86, U.S. Dept. Edn., Washington, 1977-86. Vol. cons. Cleft Palate Clinic Children's Hosp., Denver, 1975—, Vets. Adminstrn. Hosp., Denver, 1976—; mem. com. service rehab. Colo. Cancer Soc., 1977—; loaned exec. Mile Hi United Way, Denver, 1986. Fellow Am. Speech-Lang.-Hearing Assn. (legis. council 1973-76); mem. Colo. Speech-Lang.-Hearing Assn. (DiCarlo award 1984), Speech Communication Assn. Democrat. Home: 1751 Glen Garry Dr Lakewood CO 80215

MERWIN, JANE HURLEY, printing and data processing company executive; b. Clinton County, Ohio, Sept. 4, 1934; d. Alton Brock and Ethel Marie (Davis) Hurley; m. Roy Layton Merwin, July 24, 1954; children—Minda Jane, Maureen Jo, Brock Layton. B.A. in History, Stetson U., 1966. Sec. Brown-Brockmeyer Co., Dayton, Ohio, 1951-53, Gen. Electric Co., Dayton, Ohio, 1953-54, First Bapt. Ch., Sarasota, Fla., 1962; sales rep. Capitol Homes, Schenectady, N.Y., 1957-58; owner The Spinning Wheel, Indialantic, Fla., 1960-61; tchr. Daytona Beach (Fla.) Jr. High Sch., 1966-67, Athens (Ala.) High Sch., 1967; newscaster Sta. KTMF, New Prague, Minn., 1970-72; sales rep. Sta. KYMN, Northfield, Minn., 1972-74; profl. bldg. mgr. Apple Valley Exec. Offices, Apple Valley, Minn., 1974-75; service rep. Nat. Bus. Lists, Apple Valley, 1975-77; v.p. adminstrn. EU Services, Rockville, Md., 1977—; sec., treas. Hurley Industries, Inc., Rockville, Md., 1965—; co-owner Clockwork Computers, Rockville, 1982—. Mem. Mid-Montgomery Bus. and Profl. Women, Am. Soc. Personnel Adminstrn., Sigma Kappa. Presbyterian. Office: EU Services 649 N Horners Ln Rockville MD 20850

MESCHKE, DEBRA JOANN, polymer chemist; b. Elyria, Ohio, Oct. 22, 1952; d. Loren Willis and JoAnne Elizabeth (Meyer) M. BS, U. Cin., 1974; MS, Case Western Res. U., 1976, PhD, 1979. Sr. chemist Union Carbide Corp., South Charleston, W.Va., 1979-82, project scientist, 1982-85, chair research and devel. Exempt Women's Group, 1980-81, chair research and devel. Ctr. Safety Team, 1981-82, coordinator Polymer Methods Course, 1982-83; project scientist Union Carbide Corp., Tarrytown, N.Y., 1985-86; sr. prin. research chemist Air Products and Chems. Inc., Allentown, Pa., 1986—, chmn. waste disposal com., 1986-88. Author chpts. in textbooks; patentee in field. Bd. dirs. Overbrook Home Owners Assn., Macungie, Pa., 1987. Case Western Res. U. grad. fellow, 1974-79. Mem. AAAS, Am. Chem. Soc. (Polymer div.), Iota Sigma Pi. Home: 6401 Mulberry Ln Macungie PA 18062

MESENZEFF, DOLORES ANN, clothing store executve; b. Bath, Maine, Feb. 6, 1941; d. Charles Alvin Rossiter and Alberta Elva Ella (Bailey) Dorr; m. Walter Mesenzeff, Apr. 3, 1959 (div. Apr. 1980); children: Lorica Ann, Danita Dawn, Julie May. Grad. pvt. sch., Dresden, Maine. Mgr. new accounts Gardiner (Maine) Savs. Inst., 1963-67; regional sales mgr. for Maine Sarah Coventry Inc., Newark, N.Y., 1968-79; dir.'s asst. Kennebec Valley C. of C., Augusta, Maine, 1979-81; regional sales mgr. for Maine Contempo Fashions, Shawnee Mission, Kans., 1981-83; radio sales mgr. Tanist Broadcasting Co., Augusta, 1983-84; pvt. practice bookkeeping Augusta, 1968-88; owner, mgr. Fashion Plate, Augusta, 1988—; ptnr. Ms. Capital Investors, Treas., 1987. Sec., v.p. woman's aux. Gardiner Gen. Hosp., 1966-68, mem. hosp. bd., 1968-69; chmn. Cerebral Palsy Found., Richmond, Maine, 1966-67. Mem. Al-Anon, Nat. Honor Soc. Republican. Methodist. Office: Fashion Plate 283 State St Suite A Augusta ME 04330

MESKE, EUNICE BOARDMAN, music educator; b. Cordova, Ill., Jan. 27, 1926; d. George Hollister and Anna Bryson (Feaster) Boardman; m. Delmar Christ Meske, June 24, 1972. B. Mus. Edn., Cornell Coll., 1947; M. Mus. Edn., Columbia Tchrs. Coll., 1951; Ed.D., U. Ill., 1963. Tchr. music pub. schs., Iowa, 1947-55; prof. music edn. Wichita State U., Kans., 1955-72; vis. prof. mus. edn. Normal State U., Ill., 1972-74, Roosevelt U., Chgo., 1974-75; prof. mus. edn. U. Wis., Madison, 1975—, dir. Sch. Music, 1980—. Author: Musical Growth in Elementary School, 1963, 5th rev. edit., 1986, Exploring Music, 1966, 3d rev. edit., 1975, The Music Book, 1980, 2d rev. edit., 1984, Holt Music, 1987. Mem. Soc. Music Tchr. Edn. (chmn. 1984-86), Music Educators Nat. Conf. Office: U Wis Sch Music Madison WI 53706

MESLER, IDA MARIE, finance executive; b. Miami, Fla., June 14, 1942; d. Walter W. and Louise (Ritts) Mertens; m. Jack W. Mesler, Oct. 19, 1963 (div. Feb. 1982); 1 child, Colleen Marie; m. Stephen K. Jack, Apr. 15, 1988. Grad. high sch., Miami. Investor JIA Investments & Loans, Atlanta, 1985—; owner, operator JIA Purchase Lease & Sales, Atlanta, 1985—. Mem. Better Bus. Bur., Broadcast Music Inc., Nat. Acad. Recording Arts and Scis., Nat. Hist. Preservation Soc., U.S. C. of C. Office: JIA Inc 6075 Roswell Rd #615 Atlanta GA 30328

MESNEY, DOROTHY TAYLOR, mezzo soprano, pianist, composer, educator; b. Bklyn., Sept. 15, 1916; d. Franklin and Kathryn Munro Taylor; diploma Berkeley Inst., 1934; B.A., Sarah Lawrence Coll., 1938; postgrad. Columbia U., 1938-41, Juilliard Sch. of Music, 1963-71, Manhattan Sch. Music, 1971-73; m. Peter Michael Mesney, Oct. 15, 1942; children—Douglas, Kathryn, Barbara. Mezzo-soprano, operetta, mus. comedy, concert and oratorio; ch. soloist, N.Y.C., 1956—; debuts include: N.Y. Cultural Center, 1971, Carnegie Recital Hall, 1974; leading roles with local opera and Gilbert and Sullivan groups, (as Hedi Munro) comedienne and songwriter various nightclubs and cabarets; dir. a-capella vocal quintet The Notebles; rec. artist Folkways Records, Musicanza Records; dir. American Experience ensemble, also An Elizabethan Encounter; tchr. piano and singing, Douglaston, N.Y., 1958—, also tchr. introduction music classes; founder, dir. children's series Concerts for Children; founder Introduction to Music for Preschoolers; performer early Am. music for mus., hist. socs., schs., colls.; performer Renaissance music N.Y. State Renaissance Festival, 10 yrs.; 2c authority on Am. and Renaissance music. Com. chmn. PTA, Douglaston, 1952-55; den mother Greater N.Y. council Cub Scouts Am., 1953-56; Brownie leader Greater N.Y. council Girl Scouts U.S.A.; bd. dirs. Community Concerts Assn. of Great Neck, N.Y. Mem. Nat. Piano Tchrs. Guild, Nat. Fedn. Music

Clubs (N.Y. chpt.), Met. Opera Guild, Tuesday Morning Music Club (pres. 1979-81). Democrat. Congregationalist. Composer hymns, songs, instrumental quartets and trios, ballades also songs for children.

MESSENGER, ELLEN S. LANGER, video business owner; b. Miami Beach, Fla., June 16, 1955; d. Jerome George and Leona (Emer) Langer; m. Gary Howard Messenger, Aug. 7, 1977. BS in Criminology, Fla. State U., 1976, BA, 1977. Dept. head J. Byron Fine Jewelry, Tallahassee, 1975-77, Montgomery Wards Camera, Durham, N.C., 1977-78; mgr. big dipper Hakan and Corley, Durham, 1978-79; regl. supr. Cookie Factory, Durham, 1979-81; owner, chief exec. officer N.Am. Video Ltd., Durham, 1981—. Bd. dirs. YWCA, Durham. Mem. Video Software Dealers Assn., Chapel Hill, Durham and Raleigh C. of C., Small Bus. Forum. Democrat. Jewish. Home: 3120 Buckingham Rd Durham NC 27707 Office: N Am Video Ltd 3411 University Dr Durham NC 27707

MESSER, SONIA, collector toys designer, manufacturer and importer wholesale toys; b. Los Angeles, Nov. 23, 1932; d. George Messer and Milena Messer-Brozovich; m. Anthony Randazzo, June 21, 1970; one child, Monica Milena. Student pub. schs., Alhambra. Head bookkeeper Seaboard Fin. Co., Los Angeles, 1950-59; owner, operator Stuyvesant Travel, N.Y.C., 1959-65; owner, operator, designer Sonia Messer Imports, Los Angeles, 1965—. Designer over 400 pieces of collector dollhouse furniture, 1969—, ltd. edit. collector dolls, 1982-85. Bd. dirs. Nat. Charity League, Los Angeles, 1983—, Jr. Tennis League, Los Angeles, 1984—, Glendale Citizens Assn. Funding for Children; mem. council Marlborough Sch. Mem. Western States Toy Assn., Los Angeles Gift Assn., Hobby Assn. Am. Republican. Episcopalian. Avocations: miniature collector; tennis; skiing; classical music. Home: 2785 E Valley Rd Montecito CA 91304 also: 4811 Glencairn Rd Los Angeles CA 90027

MESSER-REHAK, DABNEY LEE, physical therapist; b. Des Moines, Iowa, June 21, 1951; d. Joseph Thomas and June (Grady) Messer; m. Thomas James Rehak, June 27, 1981. BS, Chgo. Med. Sch., 1974; MS, U. Wis., 1984. Physical therapist Loyola U. Hosp., Maywood, Ill., 1974-78; faculty U. Ill. Med. Ctr., Chgo., 1978-81; physical therapist U. Wis. Hosp., Madison, 1982-84; lectr. Baxter-Travenol Labs., Deerfield, Ill., 1984—; cons. Mercy Ctr. for Health Care Services, Aurora, Ill., 1985—, dir. physical therapy, 1986—; cons. Edward Hosp., Napervlle, 1984. Contbr. articles to profl. jours. Mem. Am. Physical Therapy Assn. (vice chair dist. 1986—), Am. Coll. Sport Medicine, Bus and Profl. Women, Nat. Assn. Female Execs. Presbyterian. Office: Mercy Ctr for Health Care Services 1325 Highland Ave Aurora IL 60506

MESSERSCHMITT, NORMA FLORINE, nurse; b. Long Beach, Calif., Jan. 3, 1928; d. John Homer and Bernice Mildred (Miller) Mauk; m. John Arthur Messerschmitt, Nov. 8, 1947; children—John, James, Jarrett. R.N., Long Beach City Coll., 1972. Nurse, Pioneer Hosp., Artesia, Calif., 1972-73; lab. nurse supr. Clin. Lab. St. Mary's Hosp., Long Beach, 1973—, instr. health technologies Long Beach City Coll., 1976—. Mem. Nat. Phlebotomy Assn., Internat. Platform Assn. Republican. Home: 8001 Ring St Long Beach CA 90808 Office: 1050 Linden Ave Long Beach CA 90813

MESSIN, MARLENE ANN, gift store executive; b. St. Paul, Oct. 6, 1935; d. Edgar Leander and Luella Johanna (Rahn) Johnson; m. Frank Messin; children—Rick, Debora, Ronald, Lori, Carlson; 5 stepchildren. Bookkeeper Jeans Implement Co., Forest Lake, Minn., 1952-53, part-time bookkeeper, 1953-57; bookkeeper Great Plains Supply, St. Paul, 1960-62; bookkeeper Plastic Products Co., Inc., Lindstrom, Minn., 1962-75, pres., major owner, 1975-81; co-owner Gustaf's Fine Gifts, Lindstrom, Minn., 1985—. Bookkeeper, Trinity Lutheran Ch., Lindstrom, 1976-81. Mem. Nat. Assn. Women Bus. Owners, Soc. Plastic Engrs. (chmn. membership com.), Swedish Inst. Home: 28940 Olinda Trail Lindstrom MN 55045 Office: 30355 Akerson St Lindstrom MN 55045

MESSING, CAROL SUE, communications educator; b. Bronx, N.Y.; d. Isidore and Esther Florence (Burtoff) Weinberg; m. Sheldon H. Messing; children: Lauren, Robyn. BA, Bklyn. Coll., 1967, MA, 1970. Tchr. N.Y.C. Bd. Edn., 1967-72; assoc. prof. Lang. arts Northwood Inst., Midland, Mich., 1973—; owner Job Marh, Midland, 1983-85; cons. Mich. Credit Union League, Saginaw, 1984-87, Nat. Hotel & Restaurant, Midland, Mich., 1985, 86, External Degree program, Continuing Edn. program, Northwood Inst., 1986-87, Dow Chem. Employees' Credit Union, 1988—. Author: (anthology) Symbiosis, 1985, rev. edit., 1987, Controlling Communication, 1987. Mem. Nat. Council Tchrs. English, LWV, Kappa Delta Pi, Delta Mu Delta. Office: Northwood Inst 3225 Cook Rd Midland MI 48640

MESSING, JANET AGNES KAPELSOHN, economist, educator; b. Bklyn., Oct. 12, 1918; d. Louis and Kate (Cohen) Kapelsohn; m. Joseph Messing, Feb. 1, 1948 (dec. July 1986); children—Robert, Alice. A.B., Hunter Coll., 1939; M.S., Columbia U., 1940; Ph.D., NYU, 1959. C.P.A., N.Y. Acct. Seidman and Seidman, C.P.A.s, N.Y.C., 1943-46; mem. faculty dept. econs. Hunter Coll., 1943-69, prof., 1969; prof. Herbert H. Lehman Coll. CUNY, Bronx, 1975—, chmn. dept. econs., 1982-85; tax cons. N.Y.C., 1960; mem. core faculty Walden U., summers 1980-82; mem. women's study council Lehman Coll., 1981—; treas. PSC/CUNY Welfare Fund, 1974-83, del., 1960-83, del. to NEA/Am. Fedn. Tchrs., 1972-75, trustee, 1966—, del. to N.Y. State United Tchrs., Am. Fedn. Tchrs.-CIO, 1976—. Author: (with Joshua Wachtel) Tax Considerations in Non-Profit Organizations-The Treatment of Exempt Organizations under the Income Tax Laws, 1978, rev. edit., 1979, 80, 81, 82, 83; contbr. articles and book revs. to profl. jours. V.p. Queensborough Library Council, 1960-68. Mem. Am. Econ. Assn., Eastern Econ. Assn., Am. Inst. C.P.A.s, Am. Soc. Women Accts., Met. Econ. Assn., Lehman Coll. Retirees Assn. Home: 35-23 171st St Flushing NY 11358 Office: CUNY HH Lehman Coll Bedford Park Blvd W Bronx NY 10468

MESSNER, KATHRYN HERTZOG, civic worker; b. Glendale, Calif., May 27, 1915; d. Walter Sylvester and Sadie (Dinger) Hertzog; B.A., UCLA, 1936, M.A., 1951; m. Ernest Lincoln, Jan. 1, 1942; children—Ernest Lincoln, Martha Allison Messner Cloran. Tchr. social studies Los Angeles schs., 1937-46; mem. Los Angeles County Grand Jury, 1961. Mem. exec. bd. Los Angeles Family Service, 1959-62; dist. atty.'s adv. com., 1965-71, dist. atty.'s adv. council, 1971-82; mem. San Marino Community Council; chmn. San Marino chpt. Am. Cancer Soc.; bd. dirs. Pasadena Rep. Women's Club, 1960-62, San Marino dist. council Girl Scouts U.S.A., 1959-68, Am. Field Service, San Marino, 1983—; pres. San Marino High Sch. PTA, 1964-65; bd. mem. Pasadena Vol. Placement Bur., 1962-68; mem. adv. bd. Univ. YWCA, 1956—; co-chmn. Dist. Atty.'s Adv. Bd. Young Citizens Council, 1968-72; mem. San Marino Red Cross Council, 1966—, chmn., 1969-71, vice chmn., 1971-74; mem. San Marino bd. Am. Field Service; mem. atty. gen.'s vol. adv. com., 1971-80; bd. dirs. Los Angeles Women's Philharm. Com., 1974—, Beverly Hills-West Los Angeles YWCA, 1974-85, Los Angeles YWCA, 1975-84, Los Angeles Lawyers Wives Club, 1974—, Pacificulture Art Mus., 1976-80, Reachout Com., Music Center, Vol. Action Center, West Los Angeles, Calif., 1980-85, Stevens House, 1980—, Pasadena Philharm. Com., 1980-85, Friends Outside, 1983—, Internat. Christian Scholarship Found., 1984—; hon. bd. dirs. Pasadena chpt. ARC, 1978-82. Recipient spl. commendation Am. Cancer Soc., 1961; Community Service award UCLA, 1981. Mem. Pasadena Philharmonic, Las Floristas, Huntington Meml. Clinic Aux., Nat. Charity League, Pasadena Dispensary Aux., Gold Shield (co-founder), Pi Lambda Theta (sec. 1983—), Pi Gamma Mu, Mortar Bd., Prytanean Soc. Home: 1786 Kelton Ave Los Angeles CA 90024

METCALF, LYNNETTE CAROL, naval officer, journalist, educator; b. Van Nuys, Calif., June 22, 1955; d. William Edward and Carol Annette (Keith) M.; m. Scott Edward Hruska, May 16, 1987. BA in Communications and Media, Our Lady of Lake, 1978; MA in Human Relations, U. Okla., 1980; MA in Mktg. Webster U., 1986. Enlisted U.S. Air Force, 1973, advanced through grades to sgt., 1975; intelligence analyst, Taiwan, Italy and Tex., 1973-76; historian, journalist, San Antonio, 1976-78; commd. officer U.S. Navy, 1978, advanced through ranks to lt. comdr., 1988; pub. relations officer, Rep. of Panama, 1979-81; mgr. system program, London, 1981-82; ops. plans/tng., McMurdo Sta., Antarctica, 1982-84; exec. officer transient personnel unit Naval Tng. Ctr., Great Lakes, Ill., 1984-86, comdg. officer transient personnel unit, 1986-87; asst. prof. naval sci. U. Notre Dame NROTC, 1987—; nat. coordinator Seapower/Maritime Affairs curriculum, 1987—; anchorwoman USN-TV CONTACT, 1986-87. Contbr. articles to profl. jours.; editor Naval Station Anchorline, 1979-81, WOPN Caryatides, 1985-86; author: Winter's Summer, 1983. Sec. San Vito Dei Normanni theatre group, Italy, 1975-76; coordinator Magic Box Theater, Zion, Ill., 1984-86; dir. "Too Bashful for Broadway" variety show, Naval Tng. Ctr., 1986-87. Decorated Antarctic Service medal, 1983, Sec. Navy Letter of Commendation, 1984, Navy Commendation, 1987, Expert Marksman medal, 1985. Mem. Nat. Assn. Female Execs., Women Officers' Prof. Network. (communications chair 1985-86, programs chair 1986-87), Patron Michiana Arts & Scis. Council, Ladies of Notre Dame. Clubs: McMurdo; Soc. of South Pole. Avocations: golf, scuba diving, travel, reading, writing, performing. Office: Notre Dame U Dept Naval Sci South Bend IN 46556

METCALF, MARGARET LOUISE FABER, infosystems specialist, small business owner, consultant; b. Washington, Jan. 1, 1943; d. Marshall Lee and Martha Noreen (Mogan) Faber; m. George Taft Metcalf, June 1, 1968. BA in Math., U. Denver, 1966; JD, South Tex. Coll. of Law, 1974. Mathematician Falcon Research and Devel., Denver, 1965-67; systems analyst Chrysler Space Div., Slidell, La., 1967-68, Philco Ford, Houston, 1968-69, Lockheed Corp., Houston, 1969-70; sr. programmer Celanese Chem. Corp., Bayport, Tex., 1970-72; ch. adminstr. Epis. Ch. of the Redeemer, Houston, 1974-85; dir. Altar Guild, Houston, 1974-84; owner Celebration Designs, Houston, 1983—; cons. GTM Tech., Houston, 1986—, assoc. systems analyst, 1987—; corp. sec. Eastwood Ltd., Inc., Houston, 1982-83. Mem. Div. of World Missions, Bd. of Missions, Episcopal Diocese of Tex., 1981—. Recipient Zonta award, 1960, Amelia Earheart award. Mem. Soc. Women Engrs. (assoc.), IEEE, Assn. of Computing Machinery (local treas. 1967-72), Assn. Women Attys., South Tex. Coll. of Law Alumni Assn., U. Denver Alumni Assn. Club: Episcopal Ch. Women. Home and Office: 4609 University Oaks Blvd Houston TX 77004

METROS, MARY TERESA, librarian; b. Denver, Nov. 10, 1951; d. James and Wilma Frances (Hanson) Metros. BA in English, Colo. Women's Coll., 1973; MA in Librarianship, U. Denver, 1974. Adult services librarian Englewood (Colo.) Pub. Library, 1975-81, adult services mgr., 1983-84; library systems cons. Dataphase Systems, Kansas City, Mo., 1981-82; circulation librarian Westminster (Colo.) Pub. Library, 1983; pub. services supr. Tempe (Ariz.) Pub. Library, 1984—. Mem. ALA, Pub. Library Assn., Ariz. Library Assn. Democrat. Home: 1001 N Pasadena 28 Mesa AZ 85201 Office: Tempe Pub Library 3500 S Rural Rd Tempe AZ 85282

METTLER, MARILYNN VIRGINIA, nurse educator; b. Topeka, Kans., Feb. 23, 1926; d. Isaac Webb and Dickey Jewell (Fish) Vernon; m. Marvin Dean Mettler, Apr. 6, 1947 (div. 1969); 1 son, Max Vernon. Diploma Hutchinson Jr. Coll., 1946, William Newton Sch. Nursing, 1959; B.S. in Nursing, U. Mo., 1962; M.S., U. Colo., 1965; postgrad. in computer sci. U. So. Colo., 1982-84; postgrad. PhD program, Tex. Woman's U., 1986-88. Cashier, acct. Barton Salt Co., Hutchinson, Kans., 1948-56; staff nurse, supr. William Newton Meml. Hosp., Winfield, Kans., 1959-60, instr. nursing, 1960-61; staff nurse U. Mo. Med. Ctr., Columbia, 1961-62; dir. nursing edn. Butler County Community Coll., El Dorado, Kans., 1965-74, St. Johns Coll., Winfield, Kans., 1974-80; mem. faculty U. So. Colo., Pueblo, 1980—, assoc. prof., interim asst. dean, 1980-81, assoc. degree nursing coordinator, 1981-86, faculty 1986— . Mem. Am. Nurses Assn., Nat. League for Nursing (assoc. degree nursing accreditation visitor 1983-88 , bd. rev. 1984-88), NEA, Sigma Theta Tau. Democrat. Methodist. Club: Soroptimist (Winfield, Kans.). Home: 1243 Ln 28 Pueblo CO 81006 Office: U So Colo 2200 Bonforte Blvd Pueblo CO 81006

METTLER, MARY A., business executive; b. Akron, Ohio, Oct. 9, 1937; d. William M. and Margaret E. (Young) M. BA in Econs., Stanford U., 1959; cert. in bus. adminstrn., Harvard U., 1960; MBA, Am. U., 1962. Dir. research Ferris & Co., Washington, 1060-63; systems engr. IBM, San Francisco, 1964-68; pres. Western Ops., Inc., San Francisco, 1968-74; dir. fin. United Vintners, San Francisco, 1975-79; sr. v.p., chief fin. officer Lawrence Systems, Inc., San Francisco, 1979-84; v.p. fin. San Francisco Newspaper Agy., 1984—; bd. dirs. Rosie's Cafe, Inc., Tahoe City, Calif. Bd. dirs. San Francisco Friends of the Urban Forest, 1985. Recipient Elijah Watt Sells award Am. Inst. CPA's, 1974. Mem. Internat. Newspaper Fin. Execs. Club: Commonwealth, World Trade (San Francisco). Home: 4462 24th St San Francisco CA 94114 Office: San Francisco Newspaper Agy 925 Mission St San Francisco CA 94103

METZ, MARY SEAWELL, college president; b. Rockhill, S.C., May 7, 1937; d. Columbus Jackson and Mary (Dunlap) Seawell; m. F. Eugene Metz, Dec. 21, 1957; 1 dau., Mary Eugena. B.A. summa cum laude in French and English, Furman U., 1958; postgrad., Institut Phonetique, Paris, 1962-63, Sorbonne, Paris, 1962-63; Ph.D. magna cum laude in French, La. State U., 1966; H.H.D. (hon.), Furman U., 1984; LL.D. (hon.), Chapman Coll., 1985. Instr. French La. State U., 1965-66, asst. prof., 1966-67, 1968-72, assoc. prof., 1972-76, dir. elem. and intermediate French programs, 1966-74, spl. asst. to chancellor, 1974-75, asst. to chancellor, 1975-76; prof. French Hood Coll., Frederick, Md., 1976-81, provost, dean acad. affairs, 1976-81; pres. Mills Coll., Oakland, Calif., 1981—; vis. asst. prof. U. Calif.-Berkeley, 1967-68; mem. commn. on leadership devel. Am. Council on Edn., 1981—; mem. adv. council SRI, 1985—; assoc. Gannett Ctr. for Media Studies, 1985—; bd. dirs. PG&E, Lucky Stores, Pacific Telesis, PacTel & PacBell, Rosenberg Found. Author: Reflets du monde francais, 1971, 78, Cahier d'exercices: Reflets du monde francais, 1972, 78, (with Helstrom) Le Francais a decouvrir, 1972, 78, Le Francais a vivre, 1972, 78, Cahier d'exercices: Le Francais a vivre, 1972, 78; standardized tests; mem. editorial bd.: Liberal Edn., 1982—. bd. dirs. Rosenberg Fedn., 1985-87. NDEA fellow, 1960-62, 1963-64; Fulbright fellow, 1962-63; Am. Council Edn. fellow, 1974-75. Mem. Western Coll. Assn. (v.p. 1982-84, pres. 1984-86), Assn. Ind. Calif. Colls. and Univs. (exec. com. 1982), Nat. Assn. Ind. Colls. and Univs. (govt. relations adv. council 1982-85), So. Conf. Lang. Teaching (chmn. 1976-77), World Affairs Council No. Calif. (dir. 1984—), Bus.-Higher Edn. Forum, Women's Forum West, Women's Coll. Coalition (exec. com. 1984—), Phi Kappa Phi, Phi Beta Kappa. Office: Mills Coll Office of Pres Oakland CA 94613

METZ, NANCY HERRON, medical technologist; b. Guthrie County, Iowa, Nov. 8, 1940; d. Raymond E. and Lillian M. Herron; B.S., Wheaton Coll., 1962; cert. in med. tech. U. Kans., 1964; m. William Mason Metz, Aug. 14, 1966; children—Steven James, Gail Leanne, Marcia Jane. Staff technologist Blood Bank Lab., U. Kans. Med. Center, Kansas City, 1964-70; staff technologist lab. and x-ray Lookout Meml. Hosp., Spearfish, S.D., 1971—. Mem. Am. Soc. Clin. Pathologists. Home: 821 10th St Spearfish SD 57783

METZEL, REBECCA ANN, city executive; b. Cardington, Ohio, Feb. 21, 1936; d. William Harrison and Violet (Glass) Casto; m. Edward Carl Metzel, June 29, 1957; children—Anne E. Metzel Linc, Linda S. Metzel Alderfer, Edward C., III. Student Malone Coll., 1954-56. Mem. secretarial pool Hydraulic Mfg. Co., Mt. Gilead, Ohio, 1956-57; sec. credit dept. Johns-Manville, Cleve., 1957-58; sec. Cleve. Heights, Ohio, 1978; asst. commr. central services, City of Cleveland Heights, 1978-80, supr. central services, 1980—. Mem. Task Force for Devel. of Minority Bus. Enterprise Plan. Mem. Nat. Assn. Govt. Purchasing. Methodist. Avocations: gardening; sewing; antique collecting; cut glass; traveling. Office: Supr Cen Services 40 Severance Circle Cleveland Heights OH 44118

METZGER, DIANE HAMILL, paralegal, poet; b. Phila., July 23, 1949; d. David Alexander Sr. and Eunice (Shelton) Hamill; m. Frank Allen Metzger, Aug. 29, 1973; 1 child, Jason Frank. AA in Bus. Adminstrn. magna cum laude, Northampton Coll., 1980; BA in Polit. Sci. magna cum laude, Bloomsburg U., 1987; paralegal cert., Pa. State U., 1988. Statistician Am. Viscose div. FMC Corp., Phila., 1967-72; research asst. Temple U., Phila., 1972-73; clk. II State Correctional Instn. at Muncy, Pa., 1977—; freelance writer and paralegal. Author: (poems) Coralline Ornaments, 1980; lyricist: Come Now, Shepherds, 1979, Sleep Now, My Baby, 1986; poetry pub. in numerous mags., publs. including Gravida, Inside/Out, Working Parents, South Coast Poetry Jour. Recipient numerous awards for poetry including 2d place award Phila. Writers Conf., 1969, 1st prize PEN Writing Awards, 1985, 2d prize Carver Prize Essay Competition, 1986; also Citation for Outstanding Achievement Pa. Ho. of Reps., 1988, Citation for Outstanding Achievement Pa. Senate, 1988. Mem. ASCAP, Poetry Soc. Am., Mensa. Democrat. Home: 313 Barker St Ridley Park PA 19078 Office: SCIM #5634-PO Box 180-Rt 405 Muncy PA 17756

METZGER, KATHLEEN ANN, computer systems specialist; b. Orchard Park, N.Y., Aug. 4, 1949; d. Charles Milton and Anna Irene (Matwijow) Wetherby; m. Robert George Metzger, Aug. 29, 1970. BS in Edn. cum laude, SUNY Coll., Buffalo, 1970; postgrad., SUNY, Fredonia, 1975. Cert. secondary tchr. Math. tchr. Crestwood High Sch., Mantua, Ohio, 1970-71; sec., bookkeeper Maple Bay Marina, Lakewood, N.Y., 1972; math., bus. tchr. Falconer (N.Y.) High Sch., 1972-76; bookkeeper Darling Jewelers, Lakewood, 1977-78; computer operator Ethan Allen Inc., Jamestown, N.Y., 1978-79, So. Tier Bldg. Trades, Jamestown, 1979; program analyst TRW Bearings Div., Inc., Jamestown, 1980-82, Fla. Power Corp., St. Petersburg, 1982—. campaign advisor United Way, St. Petersburg, 1985. Kappa Delta Pi. Republican. Roman Catholic. Home: 13799 Gull Way N Clearwater FL 34622 Office: Fla Power Corp 3201 34th St S Saint Petersburg FL 33711

METZGER, LAURA HELEN, advertising agency executive; b. N.Y.C., June 20, 1950; d. Robert Louis and Ann (Rittenberg) M. B.A., U. Pa., 1971. Research analyst Bank of Am., San Francisco, 1971-73, systems liaison officer, 1974; mktg. research Crown Zellerbach Corp., San Francisco, 1975-76; project dir. Grey Advt., Los Angeles, 1976-78, sr. project dir., 1978-81, v.p., dir. research services, 1981-82; v.p. so. ops., research dir. Ogilvy & Mather, Houston, 1982-85, v.p., dir. strategy devel., 1985-88; v.p. dir. mktg. services, 1988—; guest lectr. local univs., 1981—. Recipient EFFIE award for advt. effectiveness, 1983, 85. Mem. Am. Mktg. Assn., Bus. Vols. for the Arts, Mensa, Research Round Table. Office: Ogilvy & Mather 1415 Louisiana Houston TX 77002

METZGER, MARIAN, management consultant; b. Bklyn., Mar. 19, 1931; d. William David and Marian (Kemmet) Averell; m. Lester W. Metzger, June 17, 1951 (div. Nov. 1965); children: Edward L., Leslie I. Bowden; m. Robert L. Hirsh, June 16, 1973. Grad. high sch., Bellmore, N.Y., 1948. Administrv. asst., office mgr. Profl. Mgmt. Corp., Bayshore, N.Y., 1958-65, v.p., 1965-83; exec. v.p. R.L. Hirsh Assocs., Ltd., Bayshore, N.Y., 1972-85, R.L. Hirsh Assocs., Inc., Key Largo, Fla., 1985—. Editorial advisor Types of Medical Practice, 1982; editorial cons. Physicians Mgmt. mag., 1974—, New Practice Planning mag., 1980—, Physicians Mktg. mag., 1985—; contbr. articles to profl. jours. Mem. Med.-Dental Hosp. Burs. Am. (pres. 1986-87), Soc. Profl. Bus. Cons. (sec., treas. 1979-82), Profl. Secs. Internat. (pres. 1966-67, Sec. of Yr. award 1969). Republican. Jewish.

METZLER, JACQUELINE ANN, veterinarian, research scientist; b. Medford, Wis., Aug. 11, 1949; d. Joseph Leonard and Florence Marie (Prust) M. BA, U. Wis., 1969; PhD, Stanford U., 1973; VMD, U. Pa., 1985. Postdoctoral fellow, neurobiology Harvard U., Cambridge, Mass., 1973-75; postdoctoral fellow in neuroscience Ctr. for Systems Neuroscience, Amherst, Mass., 1975-77; asst. prof. neurosurgery lab. Yale U. Med. Sch., New Haven, 1977-81; veterinarian, research sci. U. Pa. Sch. Vet. Medicine, Phila., 1985—. Editor: Systems Neurosci., 1977; cons. editor: Can. Jour. Psychology, Cognitive Psychology, Jour. Neurosci., Trends in Neurosci.; contbr. articles to profl. jours. Scholarships Phi Kappa Phi, 1969, Stanford U., 1969-70, William Goldman Found., 1982, 83, 84, Windham County Kennel Club, 1983, U. Pa. Vet. Med. Sch., 1984, N.Y. Farmers' Fund, 1984, Second Century Fund, 1985, E & A. Roebuck Found., 1985; fellow NIMH, 1970-73, Grass Found., 1982; grantee Sigma Xi, 1972, NINCDS, 1978-81, NIH, 1983, 84, U. Pa. Research Found., 1986—. Mem. Am. Animal Hosp. Assn., AAAS, Am. Assn. Feline Practitioners, Am. Assn. Wildlife Vets., Am. Physiol. Soc., Am. Psychol. Assn., AVMA, Assn. Research in Vision and Ophthalmology, Fedn. Am. Scientists, Psychonomic Soc., Soc. Neurosci., Phi Beta Kappa, Sigma Xi, Phi Kappa Phi, Phi Zeta. Home: 2651 Lenape Rd Philadelphia PA 19131 Office: U Pa Sch Vet Medicine 3800 Spruce St Philadelphia PA 19104

MEUSE, ANN TERRELL, insurance company official; b. Massillon, Ohio, Jan. 16, 1943; d. Douglass Fuqua and Jane (Chidester) Terrell; B.A. magna cum laude, Coll. White Plains (N.Y.), 1974; diploma paralegal edn. N.Y. U., 1975; m. Lewis Andrew Meuse, Apr. 16, 1960; children—Ann W., Laura A. Corp. sec., compliance dir. Gerber Life Ins. Co., White Plains, 1974-78; dir. legis. and policy research services Colonial Penn Group, Inc., Phila., 1978-82; asst. v.p., field mktg. The Signature Group, Chgo., 1982—. Mem. Chgo. Assn. Direct Marketers, Soc. Profl. Journalists, Sigma Delta Chi, Women's Direct Response Group of Chgo. Club: Toastmasters. Office: Signature Group 200 N Martingale Rd Schaumburg IL 60194

MEUSEL, JANIS LYNN, accountant; b. St. Albans, N.Y., Feb. 2, 1956. BA, Thiel Coll., 1977; A in Applied Sci., Hudson Valley Community Coll., 1982; BBA, Siena Coll., 1985. Acctg. clk. N.Y. State United Tchrs., Albany, 1979-81, jr. acct., 1981-83, acct., 1983-85, spl. funds acct., 1985—; treas. Meusel Bus. Services, Clifton Park, N.Y., 1986—. Treas. Christ Luth. Ch., Albany, 1982-85. Mem. Am. Payroll Assn. Republican. Club: Clifton Park Keglers (treas. 1987-88); E&A Mixed Bowling (Albany) (treas. 1986-87). Office: NY State United Tchrs 159 Wolf Rd Box 15-008 Albany NY 12212 5008

MEYER, ALICE SHERMAN, fashion marketing director writer; b. N.Y.C., Mar. 22, 1936; d. Sidney and Rose (Cheiten) Sherman; m. Norman Meyer, Dec. 20, 1953 (dec. 1978). B.A., NYU, 1956; grad. Profl. Program in Bus. and Mktg., NYU, 1978. Fashion researcher Lord & Taylor, N.Y.C., 1956-66; fashion coordinator Bloomingdales store, N.Y.C., 1966-76; fashion dir. R.H. Stearns, Boston, 1976-78; v.p. Abbracci, Ltd., U.S. and Italy, 1978-80; pres. Fashion Dirs., N.Y.C., 1980—; cons. to Italian and Israeli fashion industries, 1980-86; U.S. fashion mktg. dir. Govt. of Israel, 1986—. Author: Clotheswise, 1982; Stop the Clock Dressing, 1987. Contbr. articles in field to publs. Mem. Fashion Group, Fashion's Inner Circle. Democrat. Mem. Religious Sci. Ch.

MEYER, ANNE STRINGER, association executive; b. Decatur, Ala., Nov. 20, 1930; d. William Lowe Stringer and Corinne Annabelle (Stritzinger) Stringer Stanton; m. William Andrew Meyer, Sept. 9, 1949 (div. Jan. 1977); children—William Andrew, Jr., Robert Moore, Anne Elizabeth. B.A., Tulane U., 1976. Real estate agt. Stan Weber & Assocs., Metairie, La., 1971-76; owner Chateau Florist, Kenner, La., 1978-82; pub. relations dir. Goodwill Industries, New Orleans, 1982-84; community relations coordinator East Jefferson Gen. Hosp., 1984-86; prin. Anne Meyer and Assoc., Pub. Relations Cons., 1986—; free-lance artist, writer. Chmn. bus. and profl. group Goodwill Industries Vol. Services, 1984-85; chmn. thank you com. United way, 1985; mem. mayor's adv. com. City of Kenner. Recipient awards for drawings, 1971-72. Mem. Women in Communications (local v.p. 1983—), Pub. Relations Soc. Am., Kenner Bus. Assn. (co-founder, 1st v.p. 1979), Internat. Assn. Bus. Communicators (v.p. programs 1985), Kenner Women's Profl. Assn. (Businesswoman of Month, 1986), Kenner Bus. Assn., Jefferson Pvt. Industry Council (exec. com. 1986—), Friends of Zoo, McGehee Sch. Alumnae Assn. (sch. class rep. 1950—), Newcomb Alumnae Assn. Republican. Roman Catholic. Club: Press (New Orleans). Home and Office: 3408 Connecticut Ave Kenner LA 70065

MEYER, BETTY JANE, former librarian; b. Indpls., July 20, 1918; d. Herbert and Gertrude (Sanders) M.; B.A., Ball State Tchrs. Coll., 1940; B.S. in L.S., Western Res. U., 1945. Student asst. Muncie Public Library (Ind.), 1936-40; library asst. Ohio State U. Library, Columbus, 1940-42, cataloger, 1945-46, asst. circulation librarian, 1946-51, acting circulation librarian, 1951-52, adminstrv. asst. to dir. libraries, 1952-57, acting asso. reference librarian, 1957-58, cataloger in charge serials, 1958-65, head serial div. catalog dept., 1965-68, head acquisition dept., 1968-71, asst. dir. libraries, tech. services, 1971-76, acting dir. libraries, 1976-77, asst. dir. libraries, tech. services, 1977-83, instr. library adminstrn., 1958-63, asst. prof., 1963-67, asso. prof., 1967-75, prof., 1975-83, prof. emeritus, 1983—; library asst. Grandview Heights Public Library, Columbus, 1942-44; student asst. Case Inst. Tech., Cleve., 1944-45; mem. Ohio Coll. Library Center Adv. Com. on Cataloging, 1971-76, mem. adv. com. on serials, 1971-76, mem. adv. com. on tech. processes, 1971-76; mem. Inter-Univ. Library Council, Tech. Services Group, 1971-83; mem. bd. trustees Columbus Area Library and Info. Council Ohio, 1980-83. Ohio State U. grantee, 1975-76. Mem. ALA, Assn. Coll. and Research Libraries, AAUP, Ohio Library Assn. (nominating com.

1978-81), Ohioana Library Assn., Ohio Valley Group Tech. Services Librarians, No. Ohio Tech. Services Librarians, Franklin County Library Assn., Acad. Library Assn. Ohio, PEO, Beta Phi Mu, Delta Kappa Gamma. Club: Ohio State U. Faculty Women's. Home: 970 High St Unit H2 Worthington OH 43085

MEYER, CYNTHIA KAY, nurse; b. Wichita Falls, Tex., Mar. 6, 1952; d. Harry Lewis and Nancy Jane (Daily) Harris; m. Larry Francis Meyer, Sept. 1, 1973; children: Eric Q., Bryce J. B of Health Mgmt., U. Mo., 1987. Staff nurse Meml. Community Hosp., Jefferson City, Mo., 1973-74; staff, then charge nurse St. Mary's Health Ctr., Jefferson City, 1974-77, 80-81; nurse practitioner Capitol Childrens' Clinic, Jefferson City, 1977-80; project dir., nurse practitioner Planned Parenthood Cen. Mo., Jefferson City, 1981-85; nursing cons. Mo. Dept. Health, Jefferson City, 1985—; cons. Mo. Community Health Corp., Jefferson City, 1984, Head Start Region Vii U.S. Pub. Health Service div. of material and Child Health, instr. pub. health courses Jefferson City. Contbr. chpts. to state govt. document Two Generations at Risk, 1987. Vol. Am. Cancer Soc., 1983, 87, Boy Scouts Am., 1985-86, United Way, 1987—, all Jefferson City. Mem. Mo. Perinatal Assn., Mo. Family Planning Assn., Mo. Pub. Health Assn. Home: 5013 Sharon Dr Jefferson City MO 65109 Office: Mo Dept Health 1738 E Elm Jefferson City MO 65101

MEYER, EMMA LYNNE, health care organization administrator; b. St. Petersburg, Fla., Jan. 25, 1952; d. Lewis Merle and Hazel (MacIver) Trubey; m. Ronald W. Meyer, May 18, 1980. BS in Nursing, U. Fla., 1974; MBA, Western Carolina U., 1983—. RN. Nurse St. Josephs Hosp., St. Petersburg, Fla., 1974-75; pub. health nurse Pinellas County Health Dept., St. Petersburg, 1975-77; clinic coordinator Henderson County Health Dept., Hendersonville, N.C., 1978-80; health services adminstr. Westinghouse Electric Corp., Arden, N.C., 1980-83, communucations coordinator, 1983-86; v.p., co-founder Med. Bus. Assocs., Etowah, N.C., 1986—. Campaign coordinator United Way Buncombe County, Arden, N.C., 1983-85; speaker Opportunity House, Hendersonville, 1986—. Mem. Nat. Assn. Female Execs., Brevard C. of C., Hendersonville C. of C. Republican. Presbyterian. Club: Hendersonville (pres. 1988). Lodge: Soroptimists. Office: Med Bus Assocs PO Box 1479 Hwy 64 W Etowah NC 28729

MEYER, GEORGIA ERNA, therapy assistant; b. Richland Center, Wis., Aug. 20, 1958; d. Edmund and Helen (Meyer) M. Assoc., Acad. Health Sci., San Antonio, 1978. Cert. occupational therapist asst. Bethesda Luth. Home, Watertown, Wis., 1978-84, Beaver Dam (Wis.) Hosp., 1984, Therapy Assocs., Mequon, Wis., 1984—. Mem. Ground Zero, Watertown, 1983, Rehab. Assocs., 1984 . Served with U.S. Army, 1976-82. Mem. Am. Occupational Therapy Assn., Wis. Occupational Therapy Assn. Home: 617 S 7th St Watertown WI 53094

MEYER, IVAH GENE, social worker; b. Decatur, Ill., Nov. 18, 1935; d. Anthony and Nona Alice (Gamble) Viccone; A.A. with distinction, Phoenix Coll., 1964; B.S. with distinction, Ariz. State U., 1966, M.S.W., 1969; postgrad. U.S. Internat. U.; m. Richard Anthony Meyer, Feb. 7, 1954; children—Steven Anthony, Stuart Allen, Scott Arthur. Social worker Florence Crittendon Home, Phoenix, 1969-70; social worker Family Service of Phoenix, 1970-73; faculty asso. Ariz. State U., 1973; field supr. Pitzer Coll., Claremont, Calif., 1977—; social worker Family Service of Pomona Valley, Pomona, Calif., 1975—; field supr. Grad. Sch. Social Services, U. So. Calif., 1978—; pvt. practice Chino (Calif.) Counseling Center. Lic. clin. social worker, Calif. Mem. Nat. Assn. Social Workers, Acad. Cert. Social Workers. Republican. Roman Catholic. Home: 778 Via Montevideo Claremont CA 91711 Office: 12632 Central Ave Chino CA 91710

MEYER, LINDA DOREEN, writer; b. Santa Barbara, Calif., Apr. 2, 1948; d. John Floyd and Dorothy Lucidie (Baker) Potter; m. Donald Lee Meyer, Sept. 6, 1969; Joshua Scott, Matthew Sean. BA, San Jose State U., 1971. Pres. Charles Franklin Press, Edmonds, Wash., 1979—. Mem. Nat. Writers Club, Pacific NW Writers Conf. Office: PO Box 524 Lynnwood WA 98036-0524

MEYER, LYNN NIX, lawyer; b. Vinita, Okla., Aug. 10, 1948; d. William Armour and Joan Ross Nix; m. Lee Gordon Meyer; children: Veronica, Victoria, David. BA, Baldwin Wallace Coll., 1978; JD, Case Western Res. U., 1981. Bar: Ky. 1982, Colo. 1984. Paralegal Texaco Devel., Austin, Tex., 1976-77; legal asst. Alcan Aluminum, Cleve., 1977-79; assoc. Wyatt, Tarrant & Combs, Lexington, Ky., 1982-83; ptnr. Meyer Legal Advisors, Denver, 1984—; pres. Cherokee Fuel Systems Inc.; gen. counsel Carbon Fuels Corp., Denver. Mem. ABA, Am. Trial Lawyers Assn., Colo. Bar Assn., Ky. Bar Assn., Arapahoe County Bar Assn. Republican. Home: 10487 E Ida Ave Englewood CO 80111 Office: 5105 DTC Pkwy# 317 Englewood CO 80111

MEYER, M. KATHERINE, sociologist, educator; b. Balt., Apr. 4, 1943; d. Walter Francis and Winifred Marie (Kenney) M.; A.B., Trinity Coll., Washington, 1964; M.A., U. N.C., Chapel Hill, 1971, Ph.D., 1974; m. John Seidler, June 25, 1978; children—Anne Meyer Seidler, Elizabeth Meyer Seidler. Tchr. jr. high sch., Balt., 1964-67, Hyattsville, Md., 1967-68; assoc. prof. sociology Ohio State U., 1974—. NIMH trainee, 1969-73, fellow, 1979; Johns Hopkins Deans fellow, 1979; NSF grantee, 1970-74; Ohio State U. grantee, 1977, 88. Mem. Am. Sociol. Assn., N. Central Sociol. Assn., So. Sociol. Assn. Democrat. Roman Catholic. Contbr. articles to profl. jours. Home: 1179 Middleport Dr Columbus OH 43225 Office: Ohio State U Dept Sociology Columbus OH 43210

MEYER, MARILYN CLARITA, school administrator; b. Cin., June 22, 1942; d. George William and Clarita (Hueil) Strassell; m. Edward Walter Meyer, May 14, 1966 (div. 1980). BS, Edgecliff Coll., 1964; M, Xavier U., Cin., 1976. Cert. supt., Ohio. Tchr. Our Lady of Lourdes Sch., Cin., 1964-66; tchr. Greenhills Forest Park City Sch., Cin., 1967-72, tchr. resource, 1972-77, instructional analyst, 1977-79; coordinator career edn. Great Oaks Joint Vocat. Sch., Cin., 1979-88, Ohio HiPoint Joint Vocat. Sch., Bellefontaine, Ohio, 1988—. Treas. Birthright, Cin., 1979-80, Scholarship Fund, Cin.; trustee, treas. Imperial Oaks Condominium, Cin.; chairperson Mayer for Ho. of Reps. campaign, Cin.; mem. state task force for career edn., 1984-86. Mem. Career Edn. Assn. (pres. 1985-86), Buckeye Assn. Sch. Adminstrs. (profl. growth com. 1984-86), Ohio Vocat. Assn. (del. 1985), Phi Delta Kappa. Republican. Roman Catholic. Club: Longhunters Assn. (treas. 1986-87). Office: Ohio Hi Point Joint Vocat Sch 2240 Rt 540 Bellefontaine OH 43311

MEYER, MARION M., editor; b. Sheboygan, Wis., July 14, 1923; d. Herman O. and Viola A. (Hoch) M.; B.A., Lakeland Coll., 1950; M.A., N.Y.U., 1957. Payroll clk. Am. Chair Co., Sheboygan, 1941-46; tchr. English and religion, dir. athletics Am. Sch. for Girls, Baghdad, Iraq, 1950-56; mem. edn./publ. staff United Ch. Bd. for Homeland Ministries, United Ch. Press/Pilgrim Press, 1958-64, sr. editor, 1965—; cons. to religious orgns. on editorial matters, copyrights, hymnals. Incorporating mem. Contact Phila., Inc., 1972, bd. dirs., 1972-75, v.p., chmn. com. to organize community adv. bd., chmn. auditing com., editor newsletter, 1972-74, pres., 1974-75, assoc. mem., 1977—. Mem. ofcl. bd. Old First Reformed Ch., Phila., 1984—; deacon United Ch. Christ, 1984—, mem. Mid-East Com. of Pa. SE Conf. United Ch. Christ, 1986—. Honored as role model United Ch. of Christ, 1982, 85. Mem. AAUW. Contbr. articles to various publs. Home: 1900 JF Kennedy Blvd Philadelphia PA 19103 Office: 132 W 31st St New York NY 10001

MEYER, MARY ANN IRENE, chemist; b. Glassport, Pa., Feb. 10, 1935; d. Alfred Andrew and Irene Elizabeth (Cavanaugh) Babyak; m. Frank Meyer. BS in Chemistry, DuQuesne U., 1956. Research asst. Mellon Inst. Chem. Hygiene, Pitts., 1956-59; research assoc. Indsl. Health Found., Pitts., 1959-67, research chemist, 1971-76; sr. research assoc. U. Pitts. Grad. Sch. Pub. Health, Pitts., 1959-67; chemist I Calgon Corp., Pitts., 1976-80, regulatory specialist, 1980—. Contbr. articles to profl. jours. Mem. Am. Chem. Soc., Soc. Analytical Chemists of Pitts., Pitts. Toxicology Club, Am. Water Resources Assn., Am. Indsl. Hygiene Assn. (sec., treas. Pitts. chpt. 1975-76). Democrat. Roman Catholic. Home: 5832 Steubenville Pike McKees Rocks PA 15136 Office: Calgon Corp PO Box 1346 Pittsburgh PA 15230

MEYER, MARY-LOUISE, art gallery owner; b. Boston, Feb. 21, 1922; d. Alonzo Jay and Louise (Whitledge) Shadman; m. Norman Meyer, Aug. 9, 1941; children—Wendy C., Bruce R., Harold Alton, Marilee, Laurel. B.A., Wellesley Coll., 1943; M.S., Wheelock Coll., 1965. Head tchr. Page Sch., Wellesley Coll., Mass., 1955-60; instr. early childhood edn. Pine Manor Coll., Brookline, Mass., 1960-65; chaplain/counselor Charles St. Jail, Boston, 1974-79; Christian Sci. practitioner, Wellesley, Mass., 1974—; owner Alpha Gallery, Boston, 1972-87 ; cons. Living & Learning Centers, Boston, 1966-69; 2d reader Christian Sci. Ch., 1979-82. Contbr. articles to profl. jours. Overseer Sturbridge Village, 1981—, trustee, 1986; visitor Am. Decorative Arts dept. Mus. Fine Arts, Boston, 1973—; chmn. Wellesley Voters Rights Com., 1983-84; state organizer Ednl. Channel 2 Group, Boston, 1960; co-founder Boston Assn. for Childbirth Edn., 1950; overseer Strawberry Banke Living Mus., 1987. Mem. Farnsworth Mus., Waldoboro Hist. Soc., Soc. for Pres. New Eng. Antiquities. Club: Wellesley Coll.

MEYER, NANCY J., financial executive; b. Iowa; d. Frank Jacob and Marjorie Estelle (Duhme) M.; B.A., Barnard Coll., 1969; Dipl. Supérieur, Alliance Francaise, Paris, 1980; m. Charles Linzner, Nov. 14, 1970. With Krambo Corp., N.Y.C., 1969-76, San Francisco, 1976-77, v.p. and treas., 1973-77, also dir.; 2d v.p., sr. budget officer Chase Manhattan Corp., N.Y.C., 1977, 2d v.p., project mgr. system support, 1980-81, div. exec./ops. fin. planning, 1981-83, v.p., 1982-83; sr. fin. officer Rainier Nat. Bank, Seattle, 1983-85, v.p., 1985; asst. v.p., corp. strategy/acquisitions and divestitures, CIGNA Corp., 1985—. Chartered fin. analyst, 1976; Nat. Merit scholar, 1965-69. Fellow Fin. Analysts Fedn.; mem. Inst. Chartered Fin. Analysts, N.Y. Soc. Security Analysts, The Fin. Analysts of Phila., Corp. Planning 100, The Planning Forum, Barnard Coll. Alumnae Assn. Home: PO Box 6539 Lawrenceville NJ 08648 Office: 1 Logan Square 29th Floor Philadelphia PA 19103

MEYER, NATALIE, state official; b. Henderson, N.C., May 20, 1930; d. Ranie Thomas and Mary Osborne (Johnson) Clayton; m. Harold Meyer, June 17, 1951; children—Mary, Becky, Amy. Student in bus. and edn., U. No. Iowa, 1951. Formerly tchr. pub. schs. Jefferson County; past tchr. and prin. Ascension Luth. Ch. Midweek Sch.; past leasing mgr. for office comple; sec. of state State of Colo., Denver, 1982—. Past vice chairperson Arapahoe County Republicans, Colo.; mgr. Senator Bill Armstrong's 1974 Fifth Congl. Campaign; exec. dir. Pres. Reagan's 1976 Colo. Campaign; dir. Ted Strickland's 1978 Gubernatorial Race; mgr. Phil Winn's race for Rep. state chmn., 1978; author, adminstr. Colo. program for Rep. legis. races, 1980, other statewide campaign plans; coordinator Draft Phil Winn effort. Office: Colo State Dept 1560 Broadway Suite 200 Denver CO 80202 *

MEYER, PATRICIA HANES, psychiatric social worker; b. Champaign, Ill., Feb. 10, 1947; d. Walter Ernest and Mary Kathryn (Kemp) Hanes; B.A., Carroll Coll., Waukesha, Wis., 1969; M.S.W., Cath. U. Am., 1976; m. Scott Kimbrough Meyer, June 15, 1969; children—Jennifer Suzanne, Claire Catherine, John Andrew. Dir. family therapy program Fairfax County Juvenile Ct., Fairfax, Va., 1970-77; clin. instr. Georgetown U. Med. Sch., Washington, 1976-84; pvt. practice family psychiatry, 1976—. Mem. Am. Orthopsychiat. Assn., Am. Family Therapy Assn., Nat. Assn. Social Workers. Adv. editor The Family, 1977-84. Home: 3419 Tilton Valley Dr Fairfax VA 22033 Office: 10805 Parkridge Suite 230 Reston VA 22091

MEYER, PRISCILLA ANN, Russian language and literature educator, writer, translator; b. N.Y.C., Aug. 26, 1942; d. Herbert Edward and Marjorie Rose (Wolff) M.; m. William L. Trousdale, Sept. 15, 1974; 1 dau., Rachel V. B.A., U. Calif.-Berkeley, 1964; M.A., Princeton U., 1966, Ph.D., 1971. Lectr. in Russian lang. and lit. Wesleyan U., Middletown, Conn., 1968-71, asst. prof., 1971-75, assoc. prof., 1975-88, prof., 1988—; vis. asst. prof. Yale U., 1973; tchr. John Lyman Elem. Sch., Middlefield, Conn., 1982, 83. Editor: Dostoevsky and Gogol, 1979; Life in Windy Weather (by Andrei Bitov), 1986; Collected Works of Vasily Aksenov (6 vols.), Find What The Sailor Has Hidden: Vladimir Nabokov's Pale Fire, 1988; translator stories; contbr. articles to profl. jours. Sr. scholar exchange Internat. Research and Exchange Bd., 1973; Ford Found. grantee, 1964-68, 70. Mem. Am. Council Tchrs. Russian (dir. 1983—), Am. Assn. Tchrs. Slavic and East European Langs., Am. Assn. for Advancement of Slavic Studies, Vladimir Nabokov Soc., Conn. Acad. Arts and Scis. Office: Russian Dept Wesleyan U Middletown CT 06457

MEYER, RUTH KRUEGER, museum administrator, art historian; b. Chicago Heights, Ill., Aug. 20, 1940; d. Harold Rohe and Ruth Halbert (Bateman) Krueger; m. Kenneth R. Meyer, June 15, 1963 (div. 1978); 1 child, Karl Augustus. B.F.A., U. Cin., 1963; M.A., Brown U., 1968; Ph.D., U. Minn., 1980. Lectr. Walker Art Ctr., Mpls., 1970-72; instr. U. Cin., 1973-75; curator Contemporary Arts Ctr., Cin., 1976-80; dir. Ohio Found. Arts, Columbus, 1980-83, Taft Mus., Cin., 1983—. Pub. Dialogue Mag., Columbus, 1980-83; author (exhbn. catalogue) Brad Davis: The Pines, 1984, (exhbn. catalogue) The American Weigh, 1983, (exhbn. catalogue) New Epiphanies, 1982. Recipient research award Kress Found., 1967,76. Mem. Assn. Art Mus. Dirs., Internat. Assn. Art Critics, Coll. Art Assn., Am. Assn. Mus. Democrat.

MEYER, SALLY CAVE, personnel director; b. Coulee Dam, Wash., Oct. 20, 1937; d. Verl Edwin and Etha Laree (Moore) Cave; m. Ronald Lee Meyer, July 27, 1957; children: John Lee, Deanna Meyer Brayton, Michael Ron, Geri Anne, Deborah Sue. BA, Wash. State U., 1959, postgrad., 1986. Cert. tchr., Wash. Tchr. English Colfax (Wash.) High Sch., 1959-60; tchr. Pasco (Wash.) High Sch., 1961-62, Chief Joseph Jr. High Sch., Richland, Wash., 1968-69; instr. Columbia Basin Community Coll., Pasco, 1962-70; mem. staff Wash. State U., Pullman, 1955-61, 71-77, dir. faculty, adminstrv., and profl. personnel, 1977—, acting dir. affirmative action program, 1986-87; coordinator Nat. Faculty Exchange Wash. State U., 1986—; dep. chmn. Wash. State Employees Combined Fund Drive, 1987—. Sec. Camp Fire Girls Am., Pullman, 1979-82; mem. Wash. State U. Pres.'s Commn. on of Status Women. Mem. NW Women's Studies Assn., Coll. and Univ. Personnel Assn., Nat. Assn. Female Execs., Lakewood Research Tng. Group, Wash. State U. Alumni Assn., Phi Delta Kappa. Office: Wash State U French Adminstrn 446 Pullman WA 99164-1049

MEYER, SANDRA W(ASSERSTEIN), communications, financial and consulting services company executive; b. N.J., Aug. 20, 1937; children—Jenifer Anne Schweitzer, Samantha Boughton Schweitzer. Student, U. Mich.; B.A. cum laude, Syracuse U., 1957; postgrad., London Sch. Econs., 1958. Advt. account exec. London Press Exchange, 1959-63; product mgr. Beecham Products Inc., Clifton, N.J., 1963-66; with Gen. Foods Co., White Plains, N.J., 1966-76; mktg. mgr. coffee div. Gen. Foods Co., 1973-74, dir. corp. mktg. planning, 1975-76; with Am. Express Co., N.Y.C., 1976-84; pres. communications div. Am. Express Co., 1980-84; mng. dir. Russell Reynolds Assocs., N.Y.C., 1985—; dir. Anchor-Hocking Corp., Lancaster, Ohio, Munsingwear Inc., Mpls. V.p., trustee Met. Opera Guild; bd. dirs. N.Y. Urban Coalition; mng. dir. Met. Opera Assn.

MEYER, SUSAN THERESA, personnel industry executive; b. Ames, Iowa, Mar. 29, 1950; d. Robert William Keirs and Jeanne Marion (Thomas) Kaufer; m. John Allen Meyer, Dec. 18, 1972; children: Katherine Jeanne, Robert John. BS cum laude, U. Wis., 1972; MBA, Ea. Mich. U., 1982. Cert. spl. edn. tchr. Spl. edn. tchr. Prince George (Va.) Pub. Schs., 1972-73; acct. DEMPUBCO Printing Co., Colorado Springs, Colo., 1973-74; adminstr., dir. EEO Dept. of Army, Frankfurt, Fed. Rep. of Germany, 1974-77; program coordinator Wake Up La., New Orleans, 1977-78; buyer Ford Motor Co., Dearborn, Mich., 1978-81; fgn. procurement specialist Ford Motor Co., Dearborn, 1981-85; pres., gen. mgr. Mgmt. Recruiters of No. Del., Wilmington, 1985—; pres. Profl. Images, 1987—; cons. Fed. Women's Program, Frankfurt, 1974-77. Bd. dirs. Milford (Mich.) Hist. Soc., 1983-85; bd. dirs. Milford Parks and Recreation Dept., 1983-85. Mem. Wilmington Women in Bus., Nat. Assn. Female Execs. Republican. Roman Catholic. Home: 16 N Cliffe Dr Wilmington DE 19809 Office: Mgmt Recruiters 501 Silverside Rd Suite 140 Wilmington DE 19809

MEYER, URSULA, library director; b. Free City of Danzig, Nov. 6, 1927; came to U.S., 1941; d. Herman S. and Gertrud (Rosenfeld) M. BA, UCLA, 1949; M.L.S., U. So. Calif., 1953; postgrad., U. Wis., 1969. Librarian Butte County (Calif.) Library, 1961-68; asst. div. library devel. N.Y. State Library, Albany, 1969-72; coordinator Mountain Valley Coop. System, Sacramento, 1972-73; dir. library services Stockton (Calif.)-San Joaquin County Pub. Library, 1974—; chair 49-99 Coop. Library System, 1974-84. Higher Edn. Title II fellow, 1968-69. Mem. ALA (council 1979-83, chmn. nominating com. 1982-83, legis. com. 1985-87), Calif. Library Assn. (pres. 1978, council 1974-82 Am. Assn. Pub. Adminstrs., AAUW, LWV, Common Cause. Lodges: Rotary, Soroptimists. Office: Stockton-San Joaquin County Pub Library 605 N El Dorado St Stockton CA 95202

MEYER, WILLA DEAN, former newspaper editor; b. Farmington, Mo., Oct. 10, 1932; d. Lawrence and Clara Evalina (Williams) Thurman; m. Arthur Francis Meyer, Apr. 14, 1956; children: Cynthia Ann Meyer Butterbaugh, Larry Joe, Kevin Lee. Grad. high sch., Farmington. Sec. Mo. Dept. Revenue, Farmington, 1950-59, auditor, 1959-64; sec. Presbyn. Ch., Farmington, 1968-78; soc. editor Farmington Press, 1978-80, news editor, 1980-88. Active Farmington PTA, 1976—; mem. Uptown Farmington. Mem. Mo. Press Assn., Farmington C. of C. Democrat. Roman Catholic. Home: 1 Airline Dr Farmington MO 63640

MEYERROSE, SARAH LOUISE, bank holding company executive; b. Jefferson City, Mo., Nov. 26, 1955; d. William J. and Mary L. (Fricke) Wollenburg; m. Michael J. Meyerrose, Aug. 18, 1978. BA, Vanderbilt U., 1978, MBA, 1987. Chartered fin. analyst. Corp. fin. asst. Commerce Union Corp., Nashville, 1978-80, money market sales rep., 1980-82; asst. treas. First Tenn. Nat. Corp., Memphis, 1982-84, v.p., treas., 1984—; guest lectr. Vanderbilt U., 1987; instr. Am. Inst. Banking, Memphis, 1985, Tenn. Bankers Assn., Nashville, 1987, 88. Office: First Tenn Nat Corp PO Box 84 Memphis TN 38101

MEYERS, BARBARA, marketing consultant company executive; b. Passaic, N.J., July 28, 1953; d. Eugene Richard and Matilda (Mycek) M. BA, George Washington U., 1975, MA, 1976. Editorial asst. Nat. Rehab. Assn., Washington, 1974; dir. news service Forum for the Advancement Students in Sci. and Tech., Washington, 1974-75; writer, cons. Nat. Acad. Sci., Washington, 1976; project mgr. Capital Systems Group, Rockville, Md., 1976-78; mktg. research assoc. Am. Chem. Soc., Washington, 1978-82; v.p. Reliance Graphic Arts Cons. Group, N.Y.C., 1983; pres., founder Meyers Cons. Services, Adelphi, Md., 1983—. Editor: Federal Environmental Data: Selected Information Sources, 1977; assoc. editor: Improving the Dissemination of Scientific and Technical Information: A Practitioners Guide to Innovation, 1978; contbr. articles to profl. jours.; speaker in field. Mem. Soc. Scholarly Publishing (co-founder, bd. dirs. 1978-84), Washington Women's Info. Network (co-founder, coordinator 1983—), Council Biology Editors, Women's Nat. Book Assn. (Washington chpt. bd. dirs. 1986—). Roman Catholic.

MEYERS, CHRISTINE LAINE, publishing and media executive, consultant; b. Detroit, Mar. 7, 1949; d. Ernest Robert and Eva Elizabeth (Laine) M.; 1 child, Kathryn Laine. BA, U. Mich., 1968. Editor, indsl. relations Diesel div. Gen. Motors Corp., Detroit, 1968; nat. advt. mgr. J.L. Hudson Co., Detroit, 1969-76, mgr. internal sales promotion, 1972-73, dir. pub., 1973-76; nat. advt. mgr. Pontiac Motor div., Mich., 1976-78; pres., owner Laine Meyers Assocs., Troy, Mich., 1978—; dir. Internat. Inst. Met. Detroit, Inc. Contbr. articles to profl. publs. Mem. bus. adv. council Cen. Mich. U., 1977—. Named Mich. Ad Woman of Yr., 1976, One of Top 10 Working Women, Glamour mag., 1978, One of 100 Best and Brightest, Advt. Age, 1987. Mem. Women in Communications (Vanguard award 1986), Internat. Assn. Bus. Communicators, Adcraft Club, Women's Advt. Club (1st v.p. 1975), Women's Econ. Club (pres. 1976-77), Internat. Women's Forum Mich. (pres. 1986—), Internat. Inst. of Detroit (bd. dirs. 1986—), Detroit C. of C., Mortar Board, Quill and Scroll, Pub. Relations Com. Women for United Found., Founders Soc. Detroit Inst. Arts, Fashion Group, Pub. Relations Soc. Am., First Soc. Detroit (exec. com. 1970-71), Kappa Tau Alpha. Home: 1780 Kensington Bloomfield Hills MI 48013 Office: Laine Meyers Inc 3645 Crooks Rd Troy MI 48084

MEYERS, DEBRA D., advertising executive; b. Angola, Ind., July 22, 1957; d. J. William and Ruth E. (Brooks) M. BA with honors, Mich. State U., 1981. Advt. asst. Tangier Restaurant and Cabaret, Akron, Ohio, 1981-84; media buyer Bonsib Inc. Mktg. Services, Ft. Wayne, Ind., 1984-87; sales devel. specialist Ft. Wayne Newspapers, 1987—; bd. operator Sta. WOWO-AM, Ft. Wayne, 1985—; freelance artist. Mem. theatre crew 1st Presbyn. Ch., Ft. Wayne, 1986—; sec., bd. dirs. Opus 18 Vocal Chamber Ensemble; mem. publicity com. Three Rivers Fesitval, 1988. Mem. Advt. Assn. Ft. Wayne, Mensa (editor 1987—, nat. nominating com. 1988). Republican. Home: 2205 1/2 California Ave Fort Wayne IN 46805 Office: Ft Wayne Newspapers 600 W Main St Fort Wayne IN 46802

MEYERS, DOROTHY, gerontologist, writer; b. Chgo., Jan. 9, 1927; d. Gilbert and Harriet (Levitt) King; B.A., U. Chgo., 1945, M.A., 1961, also postgrad.; postgrad. Columbia U., New Sch. Social Research, Northwestern U.; m. William J. Meyers, Oct. 9, 1947; children—Lynn, Jeanne. Instr. sr. adults, Chgo. Bd. and/City Colls. Chgo., 1961-78; coordinator pub. affairs forum and health maintenance program City Colls. Chgo.-Jewish Community Centers, Chgo., 1975-78; lectr. adult program City Colls. Chgo., 1984; tchr. Dade County Adult Edn. Program, Miami, Fla., 1983-85; discussion leader Brandeis U. Adult Edn., 1985-86; cons., lectr. in field. Chmn. legislation PTA; discussion leader Great Decisions, 1984-86; chmn. civic assembly Citizens Sch. Com.; v.p. community relations Womens Fedn. and Jewish United Fund; discussion leader LWV, Gt. Decisions, Fgn. Policy Assn.; program chmn. Jewish Community Centers, 1966-67, also mem. sr. adult com.; bd. dirs. council Jewish Elderly, Open U.; mem. art and edn. com. Chgo. Mayor's Com. for Sr. Citizens and Handicapped; mem. com. on media Met. Council on Aging. Mem. Am. Sociol. Assn., Gerontol. Assn., Nat. Council Aging, Chgo. Met. Sr. Forum (media com.), Council Women Chgo. Real Estate Bd., Women in Communications, Chgo. Real Estate Bd., Nat. Assn. Real Estate Bds., Art Inst. Chgo., Mus. Contemporary Art, Soc. Contemporary Art. Contbr. articles to profl. jours. Office: 77 Washington St W Chicago IL 60602

MEYERS, JAN, congresswoman; b. Lincoln, Nebr.; m. Louis Meyers; children—Valerie, Philip. A.A. in Fine Arts, William Woods Coll., 1948; B.A. in Communications (hon.), U. Nebr.-Lincoln, 1951; LittD, William Woods Coll., 1986. Mem. Overland Park City Council, Kans., 1967-72; also pres; mem. Kans. Senate, 1972-84, chmn. pub. health and welfare com., local govt. com.; mem. 99th, 100th Congresses from 3d Kans. Dist., mem. com. foreign affairs, small bus. com., select com. on aging, others; re-elected 100th Congress. 3d dist. co-chmn. Bob Dole for U.S. Senate, 1968; chmn. Johnson County Bob Bennett for Gov., 1974; mem. Johnson County Community Coll. Found.; bd. dirs. Johnson County Mental Health Assn. Recipient Outstanding Elected Ofcl. of Yr. award Assn. Community Mental Health Ctrs. Kans., Woman of Achievement Matrix award Women in Communications, Disting. Service award Bus. and Profl. Women Kansas City, Community Service award Jr. League Kansas City, 1st Disting. Legislator award Kans. Assn. Community Colls., Outstanding Service award Kans. Library Assn., United Community Services, Kans. Pub. Health Assn., award Gov.'s Conf. Child Abuse and Neglect, Outstanding Legislator award Kans. Action for Children, Friend award Nat. Assn. County Park and Recreation Ofcls., 1987, numerous others. Mem. LWV (past pres. Shawnee Mission). Methodist. Office: US House of Reps 315 Cannon House Bldg Washington DC 20515

MEYERS, JUDY YVONNE, wholesale executive; b. Puyallup, Wash., May 22, 1938; d. John Harry and LaVerne (LaBrash) Poolman; m. Victor A. Meyers, Nov. 12, 1978 (dec. June 1981); children: Angela, Donald Jay. Assoc. in Nursing, Bellevue Community Coll., 1970; postgrad. in Adolescent Medicine, U. Wash., 1970-74. RN. Staff RN Echo Glen Children's Ctr., Snoqualmie, Wash., 1970-75; intravenous nurse Swedish Hosp. Med. Ctr., Seattle, 1975-86; exec. v.p. Sweats Unltd. Inc., Kirkland, Wash., 1985—. Republican. Roman Catholic. Home: 935 1st St South #2 Kirkland WA 98033 Office: Sweats Unltd Inc 13513 NE 126th Pl Kirkland WA 98034

MEYERS, LYNN BETTY, architect; b. Chgo., Dec. 2, 1952; d. William J. and Dorothy (King) M.; m. Dana Terp, May 17, 1975; children: Sophia, Rachel. Student, Royal Acad. Architecture, Copenhagen, Denmark, 1971; BArch, Washington U., St. Louis, 1974, MArch, 1977. Registered architect,

Ill. Architect Holabird & Root Architects, Chgo., 1973, 76, Hist. Pullman Found., Chgo., 1975, Jay Alpert Architects, Woodbridge, Conn., 1976, City of Chgo. Bur. Architects, 1978-80; sole practice architecture Chgo., 1980-82; prin., architect Terp Meyers Architects, Chgo., 1982—. Exhbns. include: Centre George Pompidou, Paris, 1978, Fifth Internat. Congress Union Internat. Des Femmes Architects, Seattle, 1979, Frumkin Struve Gallery, Chgo., 1981, Art. Inst. Chgo., 1983, Inst. Francais d'Architecture, Paris, 1983, Mus. Sci. and Industry, Chgo., 1985; pub. in profl. jours. including Progressive Architecture, Modo Design, Los Angeles Architect; work featured in various archtl. books; exhibited 150 Yrs. of Chgo. Architecture, Mus. Sci. and Industry, Chgo., 1985. Recipient Progressive Architecture mag. award, 1980; First Place Los Angeles AIA Real Problems Competition, 1986. Mem. AIA (task force com. for 1992 World's Fair), Union Internat. Des Femmes Architects, Chgo. Women in Architecture (v.p. 1980-81, Allied Arts award 1974), Young Chgo. Architects. Office: Terp Meyers Architects 919 N Michigan Ave Chicago IL 60611

MEYERS, MARY DAVIS, social services administrator; b. Omaha, May 22, 1943; d. Donald Nelson and Harriet (Davis) M. AA, Cottey Coll. for Women, 1963; BA, U. Nebr., 1965; MA, U. Iowa, 1967. Coordinating counselor ednl. services State of Iowa Cen. Office, Des Moines, 1967-69; dir. activity therapies State of Iowa Vet.'s Home, Marshalltown, 1969-74; coordinator rehab. medicine service VA Med. Ctr., North Chicago, Ill., 1975-80; chief work restoration VA Med. Ctr., Northport, N.Y., 1980-82, coordinator rehab. medicine service, 1982-83, coordinator comprehensive rehab. ctr., 1983-87; dir. post traumatic stress disorder in-patient services VA Med. Ctr., Togus, Maine, 1987—; adj. prof. Chgo. Med. Sch., North Chicago, 1976-80; instr. Webster Grad. Coll. Human Services, St. Louis, 1976-77; mem. faculty VA Regional Med. Ednl. Seminars, 1980—, exec. bd. Suffolk Rehab., 1980-83; pres. adv. bd. Hofstra U., 1987; ctr. rep. Dist. Planning Council, 1984-87. Bd. dirs. Guide Dog Found. for Blind, Smithtown, N.Y., 1983—, v.p. 1985-87. Office: VA Med Ctr Togus ME 04841

MEYLOR, COLLEEN BETH, steelmill product specialist, educator; b. Milw., Nov. 29, 1957; d. Michael Bernard and Karole Joan (Kabbeck) M. BSCE, U. Wis., Madison, 1979; MBA, Baldwin Wallace Coll., 1987. Devel. engr. Foseco, Inc., Cleve., 1980-82, foundry product specialist, 1982-85, sr. product devel. specialist, 1985-86, steelmill product specialist, 1986—; instr. Cast Metals Inst., Am. Foundry Soc., Chgo., 1984—; bd. dirs. Foseco Employees Fed. Credit Union, 1983—, treas. 1986. Mem. Profl. Engring. Soc., Am. Foundryman's Soc., Am. Women in Metal Industries, Nat. Assn. Female Execs., Iron & Steel Soc., U. Wis. Alumni Assn. Avocations: piano, sports. Home: 32747 Willowbrook Ln North Ridgeville OH 44039 Office: Foseco Inc 20200 Sheldon Rd Cleveland OH 44142

MEYNER, HELEN STEVENSON, former congresswoman, co. dir.; b. N.Y.C., Mar. 5, 1929; d. William Edward and Eleanor (Bumstead) Stevenson; B.A. in History, Colo. Coll., 1950, LL.D. (hon.), 1973; m. Robert B. Meyner, Jan. 19, 1957. With ARC, Korea, 1950's; later with UN, N.Y.C. then consumer adv. TWA; staff Adlai E. Stevenson; columnist Newark Star Ledger, 1962-69; hostess TV interview program, 1965-68; mem. 94th and 95th Congresses from 13th N.J. Dist.; dir. Prudential Ins. Co., 1979—.Opened N.J. gov.'s mansion Morven to public; mem. N.J. Rehab. Commn., 1961-75. Bd. dirs. Newark Mus. Mem. N.J. Democratic Policy Council; congressional candidate from 13th N.J. Dist., 1972. Home: 16 Olden Ln Princeton NJ 08540

MEYNINGER, RITA, civil engineer; b. 1935 Newark; B.S. in Civil Engring., Newark Coll. Engring., 1958; MS in Civil Engring., NYU, 1973; candidate DEng, N.J. Inst. Tech. With Clinton Bogert & Assos., Ft. Lee, N.J., 1970-74; v.p., gen. mgr. Resource Planning div. Hydrosci., Inc., Emerson, N.J., 1974-78; regional dir., region II, Fed. Emergency Mgmt. Agy., N.Y.C., 1979-81; fed. coordinating officer in emergency declaration at Love Canal, N.Y. State, 1980; fed. coordinating officer in drought emergency declaration in N.J., 1980; sr. v.p. Enviresponse, Inc., subs. Foster Wheeler Corp., Livingston, N.J., 1980-88; pres. pres. Environ. Systems Mgmt. and Design, Fort Lee, N.J., 1988—. Recipient Alumni Honor Roll award N.J. Inst. Tech., 1980; named Eminent Engr. Mem., Tau Beta Pi, 1986. Mem. ASCE, Am. Water Works Assn., Water Pollution Control Fedn. Home: 300 Winston Dr Cliffside Park NJ 07010

MICELI, DOROTHY WERBER, publishing company executive, editorial associate, business administrator; b. Bklyn., Dec. 20, 1939; d. Howard Clifford and Helen Clare (Mangold) Werber; m. Frank Joseph Miceli, Sept. 24, 1960; children—Frank Albert, Carolyn Louise, Stephen Joseph, Andrew James. Student Los Angeles City Coll., 1958-59. Typist, Savoy Real Estate, South Ozone Park, N.Y., 1956-57; stenographer/typist Western Electric, N.Y.C., 1957, sec., 1958; sec. Coldwell Banker & Co., Los Angeles, 1958-61; biller, typist Microfilm Pub. Inc., Larchmont, N.Y., 1976, circulation, advt. mgr., 1976—; advt. and bus. mgr. Internat. Micrographics Source Book, Larchmont, 1976—; asst. pub.-editor Micrographics Newsletter, Larchmont, 1985—. Typist New Rochelle Little League, 1980-82; eucharistic minister Ch. of Holy Family, New Rochelle, 1984—. Democrat. Roman Catholic. Clubs: Salesian High Sch. Parents Guild (v.p. 1986—), Salesian Cooperators (v.p. 1982—) (New Rochelle). Home: 333 Mayflower Ave New Rochelle NY 10801 Office: Microfilm Pub Inc PO Box 950 Larchmont NY 10538

MICELI, MOTHER IGNATIUS, missionary sister; b. N.Y.C., Mar. 14, 1918; d. Joseph and Celelia (Torre) M. BS, Regis Coll.; MEd, Loyola U., New Orleans; M Religious Edn., Seattle U.; postgrad., U. Denver, 1968-69. Coordinator religious programs All Souls Ch., Englewood, Colo., 1968-71, dir. home instr. for adults, 1971-72, dir. adult edn., 1972—; dir. religious edn. Assumption, Welby, Colo., 1973-77, Holy Cross, Thornton, Colo., 1971-73; instr. religion various missions, 1968—. Author: (poems) Leaves Of Thought, 1980, Random Thoughts and Meditations, 1968, Colorado and St. Francis Xavier Cabrini, M.S.C. Mem. Internat. Bibl. Assn., Religious Edn. Assn. U.S., Religious Edn. Assn. Can., Kappa Delta Phi. Home: Cabrini Shrine Golden CO 80401 Office: All Souls Ch Religious Edn Office 435 Pennwood Circle Englewood CO 80110

MICHAEL, COLETTE VERGER, educator; b. Marseille, France, May 3, 1937; d. Raymond Marc and Fanny (Kindler) Verger; B.Phil., U. Wash., 1969, M.A. in Roman Langs., 1970; M.S. in History of Sci., U. Wis., 1975, Ph.D. in French, 1973; children—Barbara, Peggy, Monique, Alan, David, Gerard. Tchr. French, U. Wis., 1973-75, Shimer Coll., Mt. Carroll, Ill., 1976; prof. French, No. Ill. U., DeKalb, 1977. Fellow Ford Found., 1970-73, NEH, summer 1977. Mem. Am. Assn. Tchrs. French, Fedn. Internat. Professeurs Francais, Am. Philos. Assn., 18th Century Studies Assn., Aircraft Owners and Pilot Assn. Author: Choderlos de Laclos: The Man, His Work and His Critics, 1982; (poetry) Intemperies, 1982, Sens Dessus Dessous, 1984; Choderlos de Laclos, Les Milieux Philosophiques et le Mal, 1984; The Marquis de Sade: The Man, His Works, and His Critics, 1986; Les tracts féministes, 1986; Negritude: An Annotated Bibliography, 1988; Le Divorce en France, 1988. Home: 5 Moraine Terr DeKalb IL 60115 Office: No Ill U 315 Weston Hall DeKalb IL 60115

MICHAEL, DOROTHY ANN, nurse, naval officer; b. Lancaster, Pa., Sept. 20, 1950; d. Richard Linus and Mary Ruth (Hahn) Michael. Diploma, R.N., Montgomery Hosp. Sch. Nursing, Norristown, Pa., 1971; BS Nursing, George Mason U., 1980; MS in Nursing U. Tex. Health Sci. Ctr., 1985. Commd. lt. (j.g.) U.S. Navy, 1970, advanced through grades to lt. comdr. Nurse Corps, 1980; staff nurse Nat. Naval Med. Ctr., Bethesda, Md., 1971-73; charge nurse Naval Hosp., Guantanamo Bay, Cuba, 1973-74, Naval Regional Med. Ctr., Phila., 1974-76, Naval Hosp., Keflavik, Iceland, 1977, Naval Hosp., Bethesda, 1980-84, sr. nurse, asst. officer-in-charge Br. Med. Clinic, Naval Weapons Ctr., China Lake, Calif., 1986—; splty. advisor to dir. Navy Nurse Corps, Navy Med. Command, Washington, 1983-84. V.p. Deepwood Homeowners Assn., Reston, Va., 1978-82; advisor, com. mem. Reston Found., 1979. Mem. Am. Nurses Assn., Calif. Soc. for Nursing Service Adminstrs. (cert.), Am. Pub. Health Assn. (cert.), Vietnam Vets Am., Nat. Assn. Female Execs., Nat. Assn. Quality Assurance Profls., Sigma Theta Tau. Roman Catholic. Home: 136 N Gwen Dr Ridgecrest CA 93555

MICHAEL, MARIE BRAGAW, health care administrator; b. Washington, Oct. 3, 1947; d. Neal Dawson Jr. and Margaret Elizabeth (Sager) Bragaw; divorced; children: J., Bryan. BA in Vocat. Edn., Ottawa U., 1979; MA in Health Care Adminstrn., Cen. Mich. U., 1986. Cert. med. asst., Mo. Coordinator, instr. Penn Valley Community Coll., Kansas City, 1975-79; asst. dir. Sullivan Ednl. Ctrs., Kansas City, 1980-82; account exec. Portamedic, Kansas City, 1982-84; dir. prog. devel. Med. Systems, Inc., Kansas City, 1984-87; dir. Physician Cons. Services, Kansas City, 1987—. Mem. Life and Health Claim Assn., Heart of Am. Benefit Conf., Mo. C. of C. Republican. Episcopalian. Clubs: Quivira Yacht, Quivira Gourmet (sec./treas.). Home: 132 Terrace Trail W Lake Quivira KS 66106 Office: Met Med Soc 3036 Gillham Rd Kansas City MO 64108

MICHAEL, MARY LOUISE, health administrator; b. Rochester, N.Y., Apr. 5, 1932; d. Charles Caramel and Margaret Blanche (O'Connor) Mandia; m. William Robert Michael, Apr. 5, 1962 (div. 1975); children: R. Brendon, Robert, Christopher, Sean;m. Clifford Augustus Reynolds, July 20, 1976. BS in biology, Nazareth Coll., Rochester, 1953; degree in med. tech., Rochester Gen. Hosp., 1955. Research chemist U. Rochester AEC, 1955-56; med. technologist St. Joseph's Hosp., Ann Arbor, Mich., 1956-57; research chemist Rochester Gen. Hosp., 1957-58; med. technologist William Beaumont Hosp., Royal Oak, Mich., 1958-60; chemistry supr. Sinai Hosp. Detroit, 1961-67, chief med. technologist, 1969-73, lab. services supr., 1974-80, asst. adminstrv. technologist, 1980-86, asst. adminstrv. dir., 1986—. Mem. Am. Soc. Clin. Pathologists (cert.), Am. Soc. Med. Technologists, Hosp. Lab. Mgrs. Assn., Mich. Humane Soc., Nat. Audubon Soc., Detroit Zool. Soc. Roman Catholic. Office: Sinai Hosp Detroit 6767 W Outer Dr Detroit MI 48235

MICHAEL, MIRIAM GRACE, miltary officer, substance abuse consultant; b. Hazelton, Pa., Apr. 5, 1956; d. Thomas Fredrick and Grace Elaine (Cannon) Van Horn; m. Staton Scott Kieffer, Aug. 9, 1975 (div. Dec. 1977); m. Gregory Lee Michael, Mar. 14, 1983. AS, Community Coll. of Air Force, Maxwell, Ala., 1981; BS in Aviation Mgmt. with high honors, So. Ill. U., 1982; MS in Human Resources, Golden Gate U., 1984. Enlisted USAF, 1979, advanced through grades to capt.; air traffic control trainee Air Traffic Control Sch., Keesler, Miss., 1979; augment controller Fresno Air Terminal Control Tower USAF, Fresno, Calif., 1981; air traffic control operator 2067 Communications Squadron USAF, George AFB, Calif., 1979-82; officer trainee Officers Tng. Sch. USAF, Medina AFB, Tex., 1982-83; air traffic control officer rapcon-radar 2021 Communications Group USAF, Tyndall AFB, Fla., 1983; dep. chief air traffic control ops. 1925 Communications Squadron, Edwards AFB, Calif., 1983-85; exec. officer 6510 Test Wing/F-16 Test USAF, Edwards AFB, Calif., 1985-86; asst. air traffic control operator 33 Communications Group, March AFB, Calif., 1986-87; ground safety officer 452 AREFW/SE USAFR, March AFB, Calif., 1987—; orof. Golden Gate U., George AFB, 1984— Embry Riddle U., March AFB, 1986—; cons. High Desert Family Ctr., Victorville, Calif., 1987—. Contbr. articles to profl. jours. Mem. Victor Valley Child Abust Task, Victorville, Calif., 1987—, mem. exec. com., awards chmn. Combined Fed. Campaign, Los Angeles, 1986; vice chmn. Career Conf. Women Victor Valley Coll., 1987; fundraiser Family Violence Intervention, Victorville, 1987—. Mem. AAUW (chmn. women's issues 1987—), Fed. Women's Program (speaker 1973), Air Force Speakers Bur. (speaker Edwards AFB and March AFB 1983-87), Air Force Assn., Am. Film Inst., Soccer Referee Assn. Office: PO Box 2792 Apple Valley CA 92307

MICHAEL, PHYLLIS CALLENDER, composer; b. nr. Berwick, Pa., Dec. 24, 1908; d. Bruce Miles and Emma (Harvey) Callender; grad. Bloomsburg Coll., 1928; B. Mus., U. Extension Conservatory, Chgo., 1953; m. Arthur L. Michael, Aug. 21, 1933; children: Robert Bruce, Keith Winton. Elem. tchr. Berwick Schs., 1928-33; substitute tchr. Shickshinny and Northwest Area, Pa., 1954-66; tchr. Northwest Area High Sch., 1966-71; gen. tchr. piano, organ, theory and voice, 1943—; hymnwriter, poet, author, composer, 1943—. Recipient first place in Nat. Favorite Hymns contest for Take Thou My Hand, 1953, Cert. of Merit for disting. service to composition outstanding hymns, 1967, and others. Adv. mem. MBLS. Mem. Nat. Ret. Tchrs. Assn., Internat. Platform Assn., Nat. Soc. Lit. and the Arts, Hymn Soc. Am. Author: Poems for Mothers, 1963, Poems From My Heart, 1964, Beside Still Waters, 1970, Fun to Do Showers, 1971, Bridal Shower Ideas, 1972, Is my Head on Straight, 1976, This Is Christmas, 1985, Quotes, 1986, Surely Goodness and Mercy, 1986, Hi, Lord!, 1987; contbr. songs, articles, poems to books, hymn-books, booklets, mags. Address: Oak Haven RFD 3 Shickshinny PA 18655

MICHAELS, JOANNE, editor; b. N.Y.C., Dec. 30, 1950; d. Lawrence William and Renee M.; m. Stuart A. Ober, Sept. 20, 1981; 1 child, Erik Michaels-Ober. BA, U. Conn., 1972. Asst. editor Viking Press, N.Y.C., 1972-74; editor David McKay Co., N.Y.C., 1974-76, St. Martin's Press, N.Y.C., 1977-78; v.p. mktg. and dir. Beekman Pub., Woodstock, N.Y., 1978-82; editor-in-chief Hudson Valley mag., Woodstock, 1982-86; instr. Marist Coll., Poughkeepsie, N.Y., 1985; pub. JMB Publs., 1986—. Hostess Speak Out Show, Sta. HV-TV, Port Ewen, N.Y., 1982-83; author: Living Contradictions: The Women of the Baby Boom Come of Age, 1982, The Best of the Hudson Valley and Catskills, 1988, Famous Woodstock Cooks, 1988. Mem. Women in Communications, Authors Guild, Internat. Women Writers Guild. Home: PO Box 888 Woodstock NY 12498 Office: PO Box 425 Woodstock NY 12498

MICHAELS, SHARON LEE, lawyer; b. Chgo.; d. Robert Anthony and Marjorie (Richardson) M. B.S. in Journalism, Northwestern U., 1975; M. Pub. Adminstrn., Govs. State U., Park Forest South, Ill., 1980; J.D. magna cum laude, U. Houston, 1983. Bar: Tex. 1983. Caseworker Ill. Dept. Pub. Aid, Harvey, Ill., 1975-80; briefing atty. Tex. 1st Ct. Appeals, Houston, 1983-84. Contbr. chpt. to book. Recipient Am. Jurisprudence award, 1983. Mem. Houston Trial Lawyers Assn., Houston Bar Assn., Tex. Young Lawyers Assn., Kappa Tau Alpha. Democrat. Roman Catholic. Club: University (Houston). Office: 3050 Post Oak Blvd Suite 1700 Houston TX 77056

MICHAELSON-FISHER, BONNIE LEE, psychologist; b. N.Y.C., Aug. 7, 1948; d. Robert and Lillian (Pecker) Barber; m. Roger I. Michaelson, Dec. 21, 1969 (div. June 1985); m. H. Edward Fisher, Aug. 23, 1986. BA cum laude, NYU, 1970; MA, Temple U., 1972, PhD, 1974. Lic. psychologist, Md., Del. Dir. counseling ctr. Washington Coll., Chestertown, Md., 1973—; clin. cons. Kent County Health Dept., Chestertown, 1974-87; clin. dir. Tressler Ctr., Dover, Delaware, 1985—, Project 801 Aid-in-Dover, 1980—. Mem. Newark Symphony Orch., Del., 1976—. Mem. Am. Psychol. Assn. Home: 54 Bohemia Ln Earleville MD 21919 Office: Washington Coll Chestertown MD 21620

MICHAK, HELEN BARBARA, educator, nurse; b. Cleve., July 31; d. Andrew and Mary (Patrick) M. Diploma Cleve. City Hosp. Sch. Nursing, 1947; BA, Miami U., Oxford, Ohio, 1951; MA, Case Western Res. U., 1960. Staff nurse Cleve. City Hosp., 1947-48; pub. health nurse Cleve. Div. Health, 1951-52; instr. Cleve. City Hosp. Sch. Nursing, 1952-56; supr. nursing Cuyahoga County Hosp., Cleve., 1956-58; pub. information dir. N.E. Ohio Am. Heart Assn., Cleve., 1960-64; dir. spl. events Higbee Co., Cleve., 1964-66; exec. dir. Cleve. Area League for Nursing, 1966-72; dir. continuing edn. nurses, adj. assoc. prof. Cleve. State U., 1972-86. Trustee N.E. Ohio Regional Med. Program, 1970-73; mem. adv. com. Dept. Nursing Cuyahoga Community Coll., 1967-87; mem. long term care com. Met. Health Planning Corp., 1974-76, plan devel. com. 1977—; mem. policy bd. Ctr. Health Data N.E. Ohio, 1972-73; mem. Rep. Assembly and Health Planning and Devel. Commn., Welfare Fedn. Cleve., 1967-72; mem. Cleve. Community Health Network, 1972-73; mem. United Appeal Films and Speakers Bur., 1967-73; mem. adv. com. Ohio Fedn. Lic. Practical Nurses, 1970-73; mem. tech. adv. com. TB and Respiratory Disease Assn. Cuyahoga County, 1967-74; mem. Ohio Commn. on Nursing, 1971-74; mem. Citizens com. nursing homes Fedn. Community Planning, 1973-77; mem. com. on home health services Met. Health Planning Corp., 1973-75. Mem. Nat. League Nursing (mem. com. 1970-72), Am. Nurses Assn. (accreditation visitor 1977-78, 83-85) Ohio Nurses Assn., (com. continuing edn. 1974-79, 82-84, chmn. 1984-85), Greater Cleve. (joint practice com. 1973-74, trustee 1975-76) Nurses Assn., Cleve. Area Citizens League for Nursing (trustee 1976-79), Am. Soc. Tng. and Devel., Am. Assn. Univ. Profs., Zeta Tau Alpha. Home and Office: 4686 Oakridge Dr North Royalton OH 44133

MICHALEC, DIANE MARIE, nutritionist; b. Detroit, Mar. 29, 1941; d. Roland Elwood and Victoria (Serpetti) Trebilocock; divorced; children: Brian Keith, Jeffrey Edward, Joseph Roland. Associate degree, Columbus (Ohio) Tech., 1983; BS in Nutrition, U. Mich., 1986. Nutritionist Worthington (Ohio) Pub. Schs., 1981-84; nutritionist, dir. programs Weight Watchers, Farmington Hills, Mich., 1984-87; pvt. practice nutritionist Southgate, 1987—. Author: nutrition column, 1984. Mem. Detroit Dietetic Assn. (com. mem.), Am. Dietetic Assn., Am. Fitness Assn. Republican. Roman Catholic. Home and Office: 14615 Burns Southgate MI 48195

MICHALIK, GERALDINE ADELE VERONICA, oil company executive; b. Jersey City, Apr. 27, 1949; d. Benjamin Aloysius and Helen Rita (Dominski) M. Student, U. Stockholm, 1969-70; BA cum laude, St. Peter's Coll., 1971; MBA, NYU, 1973. Petroleum analyst Exxon Internat., N.Y.C., 1973-74, transp. analyst, 1974-75; sr. planning analyst, transp. planning, Marine Fleet Planning, and Pipeline, Ocean Terminal Planning div. Mobil Oil Corp., N.Y.C., 1975-80, sr. analyst ops. and analysis unit sales and Supply div., 1980-81, sr. economist, corp. planning and econs., 1981-87, sr. fin. advisor, corp. treasurers, 1987—. Mem. Internat. Econs. Group, N.Y. Assn. Bus. Economists (coodinator internat. econs. workshop), Nat. Assn. Bus. Economists, Japan Soc., Women's Econ. Round Table. Office: Mobil Oil Corp 150 E 42d St New York NY 10017

MICHALS, LEE MARIE, travel agency executive; b. Chgo., June 6, 1939; d. Harry Joseph and Anna Marie (Monaco) Perzan; B.A., Wright Coll., 1959; children—Debora Ann, Dana Lee, Jami. Internat. travel sec. E.F. MacDonald Travel, Palo Alto, Calif., 1963-69; pres. Travel Experience, Santa Clara, Calif., 1973—; ptnr. Cruise Connection, Mountain View, Calif., 1983-85 . Mem. Am. Soc. Travel Agts., Inst. Cert. Travel Agts., Bay Area Travel Assn., Pacific Area Travel Agts. Office: Travel Experience 3255 7F Scott Blvd Santa Clara CA 95051 also: 1622 El Camino Real Mountain View CA 94040

MICHAM, NANCY SUE, information systems executive; b. Toledo, May 15, 1956; d. Charles Edward and Dorothy Ruth (Bittner) Linker; m. Donald Thomas Kerner, June 20, 1975 (div. June 1980); m. Ray David Micham, III, May 19, 1984. AS with high honors, U. Toledo, 1980; BSM cum laude, Pepperdine U., 1983. Cert. systems profl. Programmer, Owens-Ill., Toledo, 1973-80; programmer analyst Smith Tool Co., Irvine, Calif., 1980-82; systems analyst Denny's, Inc., La Mirada, Calif., 1982-83; sr. corp. systems analyst, mgr. corp. systems group Libbey-Owens-Ford Co., Toledo, 1983-86, pres. Seagate Systems Cons., 1986—. Participant ToledoScape. Mem. Nat. Mgmt. Assn., Assn. Systems Mgmt., Inst. for Cert. of Systems Profls., Nat. Assn. Female Execs. Republican. Roman Catholic. Avocations: travel, backpacking, bicycling, aerobics teaching.

MICHAUD, ADELE DEMERISE AUDET, pharmacist; b. Salem, Mass., Jan. 19, 1955; d. Henri Joseph and Alice (Levesque) Audet; m. Brian S. Michaud, July 24, 1988. BS in Pharmacy, Mass. Coll. Pharmacy, 1978. Registered pharmacist, Mass. C.V.S. Beverly, Mass., 1984—; staff educator NUVA Inc., Gloucester, Mass., 1985—. Parent coordinator Project Charlie, Beverly sch. system PTO, 1985—; co-chair Cape Ann Council for Children, Beverly, 1988—; mem. Cape Ann/Danvers/Salem children's com. Mass. Dept. Mental Health, 1988—. Mem. Mass. Pharm. Assn. (bd. dirs. 1987—, Pharmacist of Yr. award 1987). Home: 4 Davis St Apt 2 Beverly MA 01915 Office: CVS 446-448 Rantoul St Beverly MA 01915

MICHEL, SHARON LEE, systems and programming executive; b. Waterloo, Wis., Dec. 23, 1946; d. Charles Raymond and Harriet Agatha (Sheridan) M. BS, U. Wis., Stevens Point, 1969. Systems analyst Employee Trust Funds State of Wis., Madison, 1976-79, dir. systems mgmt. bur., 1979-84; chief applications devel. Natural Resources State of Wis., Madison, 1984—. Vice chmn. orgn. Dem. Party of Dane County, Madison, 1986, co-chmn., 1987-88. Mem. Data Processing Mgmt. Assn. (v.p./sec. So. Wis. chpt. 1983, v.p. 1984, Individual Performance award 1985), Nat. Assn. Female Execs., Nat. Women's Polit. Caucus, Nat. Orgn. of Women. Democrat. Roman Catholic. Home: 4849 Sheboygan Ave #319 Madison WI 53705 Office: Natural Resources State of Wis 101 S Webster Madison WI 53707

MICHELSON, CINDY MELINDA, small business owner; b. Balt., May 25, 1957; d. Baird Isreal and Roslyn Ruth (Greenberg) M. BS in Communications, Emerson Coll., 1978. Asst. promotional dir. Sta. WBRC-TV, Birmingham, Ala., 1978-80; prodn. asst. Straight Furrow Prodns., Birmingham, 1980-81; owner, pres. Errand Express, Inc., Birmingham, 1981—. Named one of Congress of Outstanding Young Citizens, Birmingham Jaycees, 1986, Small Bus. Woman of Yr., Birmingham Bus. Jour., 1986, one of Top Ten Outstanding Alabamians, Alabama Jaycees, 1987. Mem. Entrepreneurship Roundtable, Entrepreneurship Forum (speaker 1987, 88), Forum Network, Breakfast Club Network, Chamber Womens Forum. Democrat. Jewish. Office: Errand Express 2719 S 19th St Suite 147 Birmingham AL 35209

MICHETTI, SUSAN JANE, print media specialist; b. Kenosha, Wis., Dec. 20, 1948. BA cum laude, U. Wis., 1981; Cert. A, B, C for real estate law, appraisal and mktg., Gateway Tech. Inst., Kenosha, 1979; postgrad., Carthage Coll., Kenosha, 1984. Lic. real estate appraiser. Wis. Project dir. Big Bros/Big Sisters of Kenosha Co., Wis., 1978-79; tchr. Kenosha Unified Sch. Dist., 1979-84; newspaper editor U. Wis.-Parkside, 1980-81; news reporter Milw. Sentinel, 1982-83; nes reporter, newscaster WRJN Radio, Racine, Wis., 1982-84; quar. rpt. writer, editor, designer Kenosha Unified Sch. Dist., 1983-84; book editorial and prodn. coordinator McDougal, Littel, Skokie, Ill., 1985, Scott, Foresman and Co., Glenview, Ill., 1985—; proprietor Michetti Multi-Media Assocs., Kenosha, 1971—; mng. editor Nat. News Syndicate, Washington, 1982—; cons. in field. Contbr. articles to profl. jours. Media coordinator Tony Earl Gov. campaign, Kenosha, 1982; media cons. Friends of Peter Barca for State Legis., Kenosha, 1985—; art fair asst. Friends of Kenosha Pub. Mus., 1986—; prog. devel. com. Racine Hist. Soc. and Pub. Mus., 1984-85. Scholar, Kenosha Found., 1979-81, Kenneth L. Greenquist, 1980, Vilas, 1968-71, Ida D. Altemus, 1969-70. Mem. Nat. Assn. Female Execs., Am. Soc. Profl. and Exec. Women, Nat. Writers Union, Chgo. Women in Pub., Sierra Club (conservation chmn. 1983-86).

MICHLIN, DONNA C., foundation administrator; b. Bethesda, Md., July 23, 1954; d. Walter Edward and Helen (Lingenfelter) Cushen; m. Paul Robert Michlin, Sept. 16, 1978; 1 child, Alexander Eric. BA, Western Md. Coll., 1976. Teller Washington Fed. Savs. & Loan, 1976-77, secondary loan processor, 1977; safety dir. ARC, Bridgeport, Conn., 1977; service coordinator Ansonia, Conn., 1981-82; safety services program coordinator ARC, Farmington, Conn., 1982-84, health services adminstr., 1984-87; life ins. asst. Conn. Gen. Life Ins., Greenwich, 1978; br. dir. ARC, Windsor Locks, Conn., 1987—; instr. health services, ARC, 1973—; health services instr. trainer ARC, Farmington chpt., 1983—, trainer, 1983—, disaster worker; caseworker to Service to Armed Forces and Vets. Treas. Milford (Conn.) Newcommer's Club, 1978. Recipient Loaned Exec. award Capitol Region United Way, 1985. Mem. CNCA Am. Canoe Assn. Methodist.

MICHUL, CYNTHIA LOUISE, economic development executive; b. Cleve., Oct. 6, 1949; d. Constantine J. and Irene Joan (Reinke) M.; m. James M. Musser, June 14, 1969 (div. Dec. 1984); children: Karl, Lisa. Student, Ohio State U., 1967-69; BA with high honors, Grand Valley State Coll., 1971. Coordinator Oak Park (Ill.) Housing Ctr., 1983-85, dir., 1986—; v.p. Oak Park Devel. Corp., 1985—; mem. Fair Housing Alliance, Chgo., 1984-85. Bd. dirs. Grand Rapids (Mich.) Pub. Mus., 1975-76; mem. Yesteryear 2000 Com., Oak Park, 1986—. Mem. LWV (bd. dirs. Milw. chpt. 1976-79, Oak Park chpt. 1987—). Roman Catholic. Office: Oak Park Devel Corp 104 N Oak Park Ave Oak Park IL 60301

MICKA, SALOMEA SOPHIE (SALLY), information systems executive; b. Milford, Conn., May 9, 1940; d. Stanley John and Sophie Frances (Ignatowski) Kamykowski; m. Edward John Micka, June 16, 1962; children—Edward John, Sally. B.A. in Physics, Cath. U. Am., 1962. Data base cons., various orgns., 1968-76; br. chief Energy Research and Devel. Agy., Germantown, Md., 1976-77; mgr. Internat. Atomic Energy Agy., UN, Vienna, 1977-81; asst. to dir. Dept. Energy, Germantown, 1981-83; group mgr., v.p. Technassociates, Inc., Rockville, Md., 1983—; pres. SEMCOM Assocs., Inc., Gaithersburg, Md., 1984-87; v.p. Maxima Data Systems Corp., 1986-88; regional mgr. Oracle Corp., Bethesda, Md., 1988—; Mem. AimS-2K Data Base Mgmt. Users Group (pres. 1976-770, Nat. Assn. Female Execs., Assn. Women in Computing, Nat. Assn. Women Bus. Owners, Montgomery County C. of C. Democrat. Roman Catholic. Club: Women's Golf Montgomery County. Avocations: golf, reading, hiking. Home: 8307 Warfield Rd Gaithersburg MD 20879

MICKELSEN, SUSAN KAY, computer company executive; b. Salt Lake City, Nov. 12, 1943; d. Woodrow S. and Frances (Seaton) M.; children: Lori Beth, Alan David. BA cum laude, Brigham Young U., 1966; MSW, U. Utah, 1974. Cert. secondary tchr., Utah; lic. social worker, Utah. Adminstrv. aide Gov. Utah, Salt Lake City, 1973-75; asst. to gov. State of Iowa, Des Moines, 1975-81; v.p. Evans & Sutherland, Salt Lake City, 1981—. Author: (legislation) Utah Privacy Act, 1975, Iowa Corrections Master Plan, 1976. Precinct chmn. Des Moines Reps., 1980-81, Salt Lake City Reps., 1982; bd. dirs. Utah State Bd. Juvenile Corrections, Salt Lake City, 1981-83, Children's Service Soc., Salt Lake City, 1983-86. Republican. Mormon. Office: Evans & Sutherland PO Box 8700 Salt Lake City UT 84108

MICKEY, KATHLEEN KNIGHTS, journalist; b. Buffalo, Dec. 21, 1944; d. Allen Coby and Jean Dorothy (Wolf) Knights; m. William R. Mickey, Aug. 27, 1966; children: William, Jr., Jessica Nell. BA in Govt., MacMurray Coll., 1966. Reporter Photo News, Monroe, N.Y., 1980-85, asst. editor, 1981-84, editor, 1984-85; reporter Gannett Westchester/Rockland Newspapers, Harrison, N.Y., 1986—. Vice-chmn. Dem. Town Com., Greenwich, Conn., 1978-79. Mem. Woodbury Hist. Soc. (founding mem., bd. dirs. 1983). Episcopalian.

MICKEY, LISA, magazine editor; b. Johnstown, Pa., Sept. 23, 1963; d. James Earl and Linda Lou (Kelly) M.; m. Robert Michael Sanetrik, July 26, 1986. AA in Journalism, Potomac State Coll., 1983; BS in Journalism, W.Va. U., 1985. Dir. pub. affairs Wholesale Florists and Florist Suppliers Am., Arlington, Va., 1985-86, editor Link mag., 1986—. Mem. Nat. Assn. Women in Horticulture (chmn. 1988-89), Nat. Assn. for Female Execs. Republican. Lutheran. Home: 2154 N Pollard St Arlington VA 22207 Office: Wholesale Florists and Florist Suppliers Am 5313 Lee Hwy Arlington VA 22207

MICKLUS, CAROLE LUTZ, association executive; b. Phila., Oct. 3, 1938; d. William Charles and Mildred Katrina (Holl) Lutz; m. Ceasar Samuel Micklus, June 28, 1958; children: Denise Lynn, Barton Allan, Samuel William. Grad. high sch., Merchantville, N.J., 1956. Exec. dir. OM Assn., Inc., Glassboro, N.J., 1982—; bd. dirs. Creative Competitions, Glassboro, 1979—. Author: OM Program Handbook, 1986. Mem. Mgmt. Inst. Home: 205 Lehigh Rd Glassboro NJ 08028 Office: OM Assn Inc 114 E High St Glassboro NJ 08028

MICUCCI, PATRICIA, primary educator; b. Chgo., Mar. 30, 1934; d. Charles Pasquale and Mildred (Damato) M. BEd, Nat. Coll. Edn., 1955; MEd, U. Ill., 1963. Cert. tchr., Ill. Tchr. kindergarten School Dist. #74, Lincolnwood, Ill., 1955-74, tchr. pre-kindergarten, 1974—, chmn. dept. early childhood, 1982—; mem. kindergarten curriculum com. Lincolnwood, 1986—. Author kindergarten curriculum handbooks; contbr. articles to profl. jours. Named Outstanding Tchr., Grade Tchr. mag., 1968, one of Outstanding Young Women of Am., 1970. Mem. PTA, Instr. Pre-school Book Club, Delta Kappa Gamma. Republican. Roman Catholic. Office: School Dist #74 6950 N East Prarie Rd Lincolnwood IL 60645

MIDDLEBROOK, GRACE IRENE, nurse/educator; b. Los Angeles, Mar. 5, 1927; d. Joel P. and Betty (Larson) Soderberg; dip. West Suburban Hosp., 1950; B.S. in Nursing, Wheaton Coll., 1951; M.A. in Edn., Ariz. State U., 1965, Ed.D., 1970; m. Albert William Middlebrook, July 7, 1950; children—Alberta Elizabeth, Jo Anne. Office nurse, Dr. G.A. Hemwall, Chgo., 1950-51; supr. Bates Meml. Hosp., Bentonville, Ark., 1955-58; instr. Sparks Meml. Hosp. Sch. Nursing, Ft. Smith, Ark., 1959-61; instr., coordinator med.-surg. nursing Sch. of Nursing, Good Samaritan Hosp., Phoenix, 1961-64, asst. dir. Sch. Nursing, 1964-73, dir. edn. and tng., 1968-80; corp. dir. edn. Samaritan Health Service, Phoenix, 1969—; adj. prof. Samaritan Coll. Nursing, Grand Canyon Coll. Mem. speakers bur. Sch. Career Days, 1970—. Recipient award for leadership co-op programs Phoenix Union High Sch., 1980, Sammy award Samaritan Health Service and Samaritan Med. Found., 1981. Mem. Ariz. Nurses in Mgmt. (bd. dirs. 1983-85), Am. Hosp. Assn., Nat. League Nursing, Ariz. League for Nursing, Adult Edn. Assn., Ariz. Heart Assn. (instr.), Pi Lambda Theta, Kappa Delta Pi, Sigma Theta Tau. Home: 4242 N 15th Dr Phoenix AZ 85015 Office: Samaritan Health Service Edn Ctr 1500 E Thomas Rd Phoenix AZ 85014

MIDDLETON, CAROLE FOSTER, insurance broker, consultant; b. Weymouth, Mass., Dec. 24, 1946; d. David Warren and Hazel Margaret (McRae) Foster; B.A., Coll. St. Catherine, 1968; B.S., Rutgers U., 1974; MA, Webster U., 1987; m. Finley N. Middleton, II, Mar. 23, 1974. Claims supr. Allstate Ins. Co., 1969-74; asst. account exec. Johnson & Higgins, Brazil, 1974-76; new bus. prodn. mgr. Edward Lumley & Sons, South Africa, 1976-77; asst. v.p. Johnson & Higgins, N.Y.C., 1977-81; asst. v.p. Alexander & Alexander, N.Y.C., 1981-83; pres. Lynmar Internat., Yonkers, N.Y., 1983—, Foxberry Press, Gourmet Internat., Shopping & Mailing Internat. (all subs.); adj. faculty mem. Webster U., Leiden campus; speaker on sales techniques, internat. ins., fgn. investment in the U.S., women in ins., women's networking, multinat. corps. Bd. dirs. Bklyn. YWCA, 1980-83, chmn. fin. com., treas., 1982; chair Republicans Abroad-Netherlands, 1987-88. Mem. Nat. Assn. Ins. Women, Am. Mgmt. Assn., Nat. Fedn. Bus. and Profl. Women, Assn. Profl. Ins. Women (adv. bd. 1982-83), Women's Econ. Round Table, Am. Women's Club Denmark (pres. 1986-87). Presbyterian. Clubs: Wall St. Bus. and Profl. Women's (past pres.); Women's Nat. Rep. Columnist Wall St. Woman, 1979-80; editor Chronicle mag., 1984-86; author: Managing Foreign Risks, 1988.

MIDDLETON, DIRONDA LYNN (PEMBERTON), accountant, tax consultant; b. Clovis, N.Mex., Oct. 29, 1950; d. Robert James and Ruby Joyce (Pond) Pemberton; m. Michael H. Williams, Aug. 30, 1968 (div. Apr. 1978); children: Diedra Michelle, Robert Michael, Matthew Aaron; m. David Owen Middleton, Oct. 26, 1980; 1 adopted child, Chadlee Donald Michael. Grad. high sch., Clovis. Tax cons. H & R Block, Topeka, 1973-74; saleswoman Stanley Home Products, Topeka, 1974-75, Sara Coventry, Topeka, 1977-78; owner, mgr., acct., tax cons. Facts 'n' Figures, Topeka, 1974-81, Small Bus. Bookkeeping and Tax Services, Topeka, 1981-; asst. Mize, Houser, Mehlinger, Kimes, CPA's, Topeka, 1978; acct. Hwy Oil Co., Topeka, 1978-79, Cobler and Cummings, CPA's, Topeka, 1979-1981. Baptist. Avocations: water and snow skiing, interior decorating. Office: Small Bus Bookkeeping and Tax Services PO Box 2603 Topeka KS 66601

MIDDLETON, PAULETTE BAUER, atmospheric chemist; b. Beeville, Tex., Dec. 8, 1946; d. Paul Wylie and Lillian Grace (Schoppe) Bauer; m. John William Middleton, July 12, 1970; children—Mären Katherine, Erin Ann. BA, U. Tex., 1968, MA, 1971, PhD, 1973. Research asst., then instr. chemistry U. Tex., 1968-73, research assoc. chem. engring., 1973-75; postdoctoral fellow Nat. Ctr. Atmospheric Research, Boulder, Colo., 1975-76, sci. visitor, 1977-79, spl. project scientist, 1979, staff scientist, 1979-87; research assoc. then sr. research assoc. Atmospheric Scis. Research Ctr., SUNY, Albany, 1987—; lectr., seminar leader in field. EPA grantee, 1982—. Author over 50 papers. Mem. Air Pollution Control Assn., AAAS. Home: 2385 Panorama Ave Boulder CO 80302 Office: Nat Ctr Atmospheric Research PO Box 3000 Boulder CO 80307

MIDDLETON, SUSAN ALEXIS, lawyer, accountant; b. San Fransisco, Dec. 11, 1943; d. John Squier Middleton and Barbara Jean Hover Lomma; m. Sarath C. Vidanage, Feb. 6, 1965 (div. Mar. 1983); children: Sharmaine E., Srimalie Anne, Stuart H.; m. Vincent A. Pillai, Dec. 15, 1985. BS in Bus., U. Calif., Berkeley, 1967; JD, Western State U., Fullerton, Calif., 1986. CPA, Calif. CPA, staff auditor Touche & Co., San Fransisco, 1967-69; internal auditor County of Santa Clara, San Jose, Calif., 1969-71; adminstrv. asst. City of San Jose, 1972-73; assoc. Law Offices M. T. Kenney, Santa Ana, Calif., 1987-88; with Orange County Pub. Defenders, Orange, Calif., 1988; CPA pvt. practice, Irvine, Calif., 1969—. Planning editor law rev. Western States U., 1986. Team mgr. Bobby Sox Softball, Irvine, 1982-86; dist. coordinator, den leader Boy Scouts Am., Irvine, 1983-85. Mem. ABA, Calif. Bar Assn., Orange County Bar Assn. Home: 5571 Sierra Verde Rd Irvine CA 92715

MIDLER, BETTE, singer, entertainer, actress; b. Honolulu, 1945; m. Martin von Haselberg, 1984; 1 child, Sophie. Student, U. Hawaii, 1 year. Debut as actress film Hawaii, 1965; mem. cast Fiddler on the Roof, N.Y.C., 1966-69, Salvation, N.Y.C., 1970, Tommy, Seattle Opera Co., 1971; nightclub concert performer on tour, U.S., from 1972; appearance Palace Theatre, N.Y.C., 1973; TV appearances include Tonight Show; appeared Clams on The Half-Shell Revue, N.Y.C., 1975; recs. include The Divine Miss M, 1973, Bette Midler, 1973, Broken Blossom, 1977, Live at Last, 1977, Thighs and Whispers, 1979, New Depression, 1979, Divine Madness, 1980, No Frills, 1984; motion picture appearances include The Rose, 1979, Jinxed, 1982, Down and Out in Beverly Hills, 1986, Ruthless People, 1986, Outrageous Fortune, 1987, Big Business, 1988; appeared in cable TV (HBO) prodn. Bette Midler's Mondo Beyondo, 1988; author: The Saga of Baby Divine, 1983. Recipient After Dark Ruby award, 1973; Grammy award, 1973; spl. Tony award, 1973; Emmy award for NBC Spl., Ol' Red Hair is Back, 1978. Office: care Atlantic Records 75 Rockefeller Plaza New York NY 10019 *

MIEL, VICKY ANN, municipal government executive; b. South Bend, Ind., June 20, 1951; d. Lawrence Paul Miel and Virginia Ann (Yeagley) Hernandez. BS, Ariz. State U., 1985. Word processing coordinator City of Phoenix, 1977-78, word processing adminstr., 1978-83, chief dep. city clk., 1983-88, city clk. dir., 1988—; assoc. prof. Phoenix Community Coll., 1982-83, Mesa (Ariz.) Community Coll., 1983; speaker in field, Boston, Santa Fe, Los Angeles, N.Y.C. and St. Paul, 1980—. Author: Phoenix Document Request Form, 1985, Developing Successful Systems Users, 1986. Judge Future Bus. Leaders Am. at Ariz. State U., Tempe, 1984; bd. dirs. Fire and Life Safety League, Phoenix, 1984. Recipient Gold Plaque, Word Processing Systems Mag., Mpls., 1980, Green Light Productivity award City of Phoenix, 1981, Honor Soc. Achievement award Internat. Word Processing Assn., Willow Grove, Pa., 1981. Mem. Assn. Info. Systems Profls. (internat. dir. 1982-84), Internat. Inst. Mcpl. Clks. (cert.), Am. Records Mgrs. Assn., Assn. Image Mgmt., Am. Soc. Pub. Adminstrs., Am. Mgmt. Assn. Lodge: Soroptimists. Office: City of Phoenix 251 W Washington Phoenix AZ 85003

MIER, PHYLLIS JEAN, program analyst; b. Muncie, Ind., Aug. 9, 1949; d. Philip Wilber and Helen Elizabeth (Moore) M. BA, Ball State U., 1971; postgrad., U. Md. LicensedMd., Va., D.C., Ind. Tchr. Montgomery County Pub. Schs., Rockville, 1971-74; tchr., mgr. Sears, Roebuck and Co., Arlington, Va., 1974-77; cons. Greenhorne and O'Mara, Inc., Riverdale, Md., 1977-78; program analyst Fed. Emergency Mgmt. Agy., Washington, 1978—; asst. coordinator, driver Sunderland (Md.) Vanpools, 1980—; transportation, tour cons. Calvert Transportation Systems, Sunderland, 1980—; prin. Mier Computer Services, Huntingtown, Md., 1987. Mem. Nat. Assn. Female Execs. (Who's Who in Female Execs. 1987), Beta Sigma Phi (pres. 1977, 81, 84, 85, council pres. 1977, 84). Home: 1847 Cliff Dr Huntingtown MD 20639 Office: Fed Emergency Mgmt Agy 500 C St SW Washington DC 20472

MIESSE, MARY ELIZABETH (BETH), educator; b. Amarillo, Tex.; M.Ed. in Guidance and Counseling, M.A., W. Tex. State U., Canyon, 1952, M.B.A., 1960; M.Personnel Service, U. Colo., Boulder, 1954. With various bus. firms and radio stas., 1940-47; prof. Amarillo (Tex.) Coll., 1947-63; tchr. pvt. and pub. schs., also TV work, 1963-78; spl. edn. cons., writer, 1978—. Mem. NEA, Nat Fed. State Poetry Socs., Poetry Soc. Tex., Tex. State Tchrs. Assn., Bus. Profl. Womens Assn., Toastmistress Internat., Am. Psychol. Assn., North Plains Assn. for Children with Learning Disabilities, AAUP, AAUW. Pioneered in ednl. TV in West Tex.; recipient awards in typewriting and ednl. TV; elected to Top Ten Women of Yr., Am. Bus. Women's Assn., 1962, Certified in spl. edn. supr., spl. edn. counselor, ednl. diagnostician, spl. edn. (lang. and/or learning disabled, mentally retarded) tchr., profl. counselor, profl. tchr., supt., prin., Tex. Editor, Tex. Jr. Coll. Tchrs. Assn. publ., 7 yrs. Producer radio poetry show. Home and Office: PO Box 3133 Valle de Oro Boys Ranch TX 79010

MIGALA, LUCYNA JOZEFA, broadcaster, journalist, arts administrator, singer, radio station executive; b. Krakow, Poland, May 22, 1944; d. Joseph and Estelle (Suwala) M.; came to U.S., 1947, naturalized, 1955; student Loyola U., Chgo., 1962-63, Chicago Conservatory of Music, 1963-70; B.S. in Journalism, Northwestern U., 1966. Radio announcer, producer sta. WOPA, Oak Park, Ill., 1963-66; writer, reporter, producer NBC news, Chgo., 1966-69, 1969-71, producer NBC local news, Washington, 1969; producer, coordinator NBC network news, Cleve., 1971-78, field producer, Chgo., 1978-79; v.p. Migala Communications Corp., 1979—; program dir., on-air personality Sta. WCEV, Cicero, Ill., 1979—; lectr. City Colls. Chgo., 1981, Morton Coll., 1988. Columnist Free Press, Chgo., 1984-87. Soloist, artistic dir. and gen. mgr. Lira Singers, Chgo., 1965—; mem., chmn. various cultural coms. Polish Am. Congress, 1970—; bd. dirs. Nationalities Services Center, Cleve., 1973-78; exec. com. Ill. Humanities Council, 1985-86, bd. dirs. 1983—; bd. dirs., v.p. Cicero-Berwyn Fine Arts Council, Cicero, Ill.; mem. City Arts I and II panels Chgo. Office of Fine Arts, 1986—; v.p. Chgo. chpt. Kosciuszko Found., 1983-86; bd. dirs. Polish Women's Alliance Am., 1983-87; gen. chmn. Midwest Chopin Piano Competition, 1984-86 ; mem. ethnic and folk arts panel Ill. Arts Council, 1984-87. Recipient AP Broadcasters award, 1973, Emmy award Nat. Acad. TV Arts and Scis., 1974; Washington Journalism Center fellow, spring 1969. Mem. Sigma Delta Chi. Office: Sta WCEV 5356 W Belmont Ave Chicago IL 60641

MIGUEL, SUSAN JANE, management service executive; b. New Bedford, Mass., Sept. 6, 1962; d. John and Barbara (Mello) M. BA, Boston Coll., 1984; postgrad. in tech. writing, Southeastern Mass. U., 1985—. Asst. Naval Underwater Systems Ctr., Newport, R.I., 1980-81; sci. programmer Input Output Computer Services, Waltham, Mass., 1981-83; security analyst Kyran Research Assocs., Inc., Middletown, R.I., 1984-85, Aquidneck Mgmt. Assocs., Newport, 1985-88; pres. Info. Mgmt. Services, Ltd., Portsmouth, R.I., 1986—. V.p. Jr. League Fall River, 1986-88, pres., 1988—. Republican. Roman Catholic. Home: PO Box 313 Tiverton RI 02840 Office: Info Mgmt Services Ltd 2140 E Main Rd Portsmouth RI 02871

MIHALKO, PATRICIA JOYCE, secondary physical education educator; b. Detroit, Dec. 19, 1940; d. Joseph and Helen Christine (Mohnach) M. BS, SUNY, Cortland, 1963; MS, Ind. U., 1969. Permanent cert. in phys. edn., N.Y. Tchr. Cooperstown (N.Y.) High Sch., 1963—. Founder Cooperstown Internat. Field Hockey Trips, 1975—; state chmn. Empire State Games, Field Hockey, 1978; coach "C" Camp Olympic Devel. Program, Smith Coll., Mass., 1982. Named to Hall of Fame Inductee SUNY, 1985, Amateur Sports Hall of Fame, Johnstown, Pa., 1985. Mem. N.Y. Pub. Sch. Athletic Assn. (sports chmn., Service Honor 1980), N.Y. State Coaches Assn., Nat. Fedn. Interscholastic Coaches (Outstanding Coach 1984), N.Y. State Tchrs. Assn., Nat. Edn. Assn. Democrat. Roman Catholic. Clubs: Adirondack Mountain (Lake Placid, N.Y.), Mohawk Bicycle (Utica, N.Y.). Home: Cary Park Rd Box 275 Richfield Springs NY 13439 Office: Cooperstown Cen Sch Linden Ave Cooperstown NY 13326

MIHRAM, DANIELLE, librarian, bibliographer, educator; b. Alexandria, Egypt, July 23, 1942; came to U.S., 1965; d. Albert and Aimee (Seidman) Redibaum; m. George Arthur Mihram, Dec. 22, 1965. B.A. with honors, U. Sydney (Australia), 1964; diplôme d'études supérieures, Ecole des Hautes Etudes, Paris, 1965; Ph.D., U. Pa., 1970; M.L.S., Rutgers U., 1982. Vis. lectr. Swarthmore (PA.) Coll., 1971; asst. prof. Haverford (Pa.) Coll., 1971; vis. lectr. U. Pa., 1974; bus./research assoc. G. A. Mihram, Cons., Haverford, Pa., 1974-79; library staff Princeton U., 1980-82; reference librarian NYU, N.Y.C., 1982—; adj. asst. prof. NYU, 1985—. Editorial bd. WESS Newsletter, 1986—; contbr. articles to profl. jours. British Commonwealth scholar Australian Govt., U. Sydney, 1959-65; NATO travel grantee, 1977. Mem. ALA, Assn. Internat. de Cybernétique, (Titre Scientifique), Assn. for Computers and the Humanities, Assn. Coll. and Research Libraries, Modern Lang. Assn., Assn. Computers and the Humanities. Home: 4 Washington Sq Village New York NY 10012 Office: NYU EH Bobst Library 70 Washington Square S New York NY 10012

MIKA, MARY JANE, physician; b. Chgo., Mar. 8; d. John and Mary (Milas) M.; student U. Ill., 1960-62; B.S. (scholar), Roosevelt U., 1965, M.S. 1970; Ph.D., U. Ill. Med. Center, Chgo., 1973; M.D., Universidad Autonoma de Ciudad Juarez (Mexico) Escuela de Medicina, 1978. Reviewer current gas chromatography lit. Preston Tech. Abstracts Co., Evanston, Ill., 1968-73; contbg. editor Internat. Jour. Pharm. Abstracts, Am. Soc. Hosp. Pharmacists, Washington, 1972-73; asst. in chemistry U. Ill. Coll. Pharmacy, Chgo., 1970-73; biochem. researcher VA Hosp., North Chicago, Ill., 1975-76; intern in internal medicine Cook County Hosp., Chgo., 1978-79, fellow in gastroenterology, 1981-83; resident in internal medicine St. Francis Hosp., Evanston, 1979-81; staff physician Med. Networks, Chgo., 1986—. Research in gaso-chromatography in flavor volatiles, mass spectrometric analysis of aromatic amines.

MIKEL, CHARLENE ANN, social worker, consultant, lecturer, editor; b. Oswego, Kans., Sept. 30, 1938; d. Warren Fowler and Gladys Maude (Hoke) Hardwick; m. Robert Andrew Mikel, Oct. 22, 1960 (div. July 1979); children—Cassandra, Mark. B.S. in Edn., Kans. State Coll., 1960; M.S.S.W., U. Mo., 1968. Social worker State of Kans., Topeka, 1964-66, 67-69, med. social worker 1976-82; social worker S.E. Kans. Mental Health, Humboldt, 1970-74; cons. Charlene Mikel Cons., Oswego, 1982—, editor, 1984—; lectr. Labette Community Coll., Parsons, Kans., 1983—, Barton County Community Coll., Great Bend, Kans., 1982—. Active 4-H. Mem. Nat. Assn. Social Workers, Kans. Soc. Clin. Social Workers (membership com. 1985—), Am. Legion Aux. (past pres. local chpt.). Republican. Methodist. Avocations: sewing; reading; travel. Home and Office: PO Box 204 Oswego KS 67356

MIKE-NARD, BEVERLY JEAN, nurse; b. Youngstown, Ohio, Nov. 3, 1957; d. Michael Ablen and Marion Charlotte (Saba) Mike; m. Kenneth Robert Nard Sr., May 27, 1979 (div. May 1985); children: Stacy Nicole, Kenneth Robert Jr. Nursing diploma, St. Elizabeth Hosp. Med. Ctr., 1978. Nurse asst. St. Elizabeth Hosp. Med. Ctr., 1977-78, nurse orthopaedic dept., 1978-81, RN Neonatal ICU, 1982—. Active PTA, Austintown, Ohio, 1985—. Mem. Nat. Assn. Neonatal Nurses, Nurses Assn. Am. Coll. Ob-Gyn (cert.), Nat. Apostolate of Maronites. Democrat. Roman Catholic. Home: 120 Georgetown Place Youngstown OH 44515-2219 Office: St Elizabeth Hosp Med Ctr 1040 Belmont Ave Youngstown OH 44515

MIKESELL, MARY (JANE), therapist; b. Rockledge, Fla., Oct. 29, 1943; d. John and Mary C. (Leighty) Wagner. B.A., Calif. State U.-Northridge, 1967; M.A., Pacific Oaks Coll., 1980; postgrad. Calif. Grad. Inst. Psychology, 1984—. Tchr., Los Angeles pub. schs., 1966-69; photog. lab. dir. Oceanograficos de Honduras, Roatan, 1969-70; supr. Los Angeles Life Ins. Co., 1970-72; customer service rep. Beverly Hills Fed. Savs. & Loans, Calif., 1972-73; mem. staff counseling ctr. Calif. State U.-Northridge, 1974-78; head office services Pacific Oaks Coll., Pasadena, Calif., 1978-79; prodn. supr. Frito-Lay, Inc., Los Angeles, 1979-81; circulation supr. Daily News, Van Nuys, Calif., 1981-82; ednl. therapist/MFCC intern Barr Counseling Ctr., 1982-86 and Victory-Tampa Psychol. Ctr. (now Reseda Psychol. Ctr.), San Fernando Valley, Calif., 1982—; project coordinator Carlson Rockey & Assocs., Brentwood, Calif., 1983-84; staff mem Southland Olympic News Bur., Sub-Ctr. Steward, Press Ops., Olympic Water Polo Venue, LAOOC, 1983-84; project coordinator/communications and systems specialist Student Ins. div. William F. Hooper, Inc., Brentwood, 1985-87; cons. Designer Collection by Pingy, 1985, others. Photographer. Mem. Nat. Assn. Female Execs., Planetary Soc., Calif. Scholarship Fedn., Calif. Inst. Psychology Grad. Student Assn. (v.p. 1985-88). Democrat. Club: CSUN Anthropology. Avocations: photography; writing; laser research; astronomy; sports. Office: CGI Counseling Ctr 1100 Glendon Ave 11th Floor Los Angeles CA 90049

MIKESELL, SUSAN GAIL, psychologist; b. Cleve., Nov. 21, 1946; d. Jack J. and Violette A (Czerpa) Smith; m. Richard H. Mikesell, June 5, 1970; children: Elizabeth Suzanne, Theodore Richard. BS in Nursing, Cath. U., 1973, MSW, 1975; PhD, U. Md., 1981. Lic. psychologist, Md., D.C. Psychiat. social worker Glass Mental Health Ctr., Balt., 1975-77; pvt. practice psychiat. social work Washington, 1977-81; psychology trainee North Mental Health Ctr., Washington, 1981-82; pvt. practice psychology Washington, 1982—; cons. psychologist In Vitro Fertilization Program Columbia Hosp. for Women, Washington, 1983—; mem. adv. panel Office Tech. Assesment Infertility Prevention and Treatment, Washington, 1985-88. Pres. Resolve of D.C., 1985-86; leader Brownie troop Girl Scouts of Am., Washington, 1986-88. Mem. Am. Psychol. Assn., Am. Fertility Soc., Am. Orthopsychiat. Assn. Office: 4545 42d St NW Suite 202 Washington DC 20016

MIKIEWICZ, ANNA DANIELLE, marketing representative; b. Chgo., Dec. 22, 1960; d. Zdislaw and Lucy (Magnusewska) K. B.S. in Mktg., Elmhurst Coll., 1982; postgrad. Triton Coll. Asst. to Midwestern regional mgr. Meister Pub. Co., Chgo., 1983; sales rep. First Impression, Elk Grove, Ill., 1984; mktg. and customer services rep. Airco Ind. Gases, Broadview and Carol Stream, Ill., 1985, Yamazen USA, Inc., Schaumburg, Ill., 1985—. Named Chgo. Polish Queen, Polish Am. Culture Club, 1983-84. Mem. Nat. Assn. Female Execs. Republican. Roman Catholic.

MIKKELSEN, PAULA MAE, museum curator, malacologist; b. Lewiston, Maine, Nov. 17, 1953; d. George Mitchell and Lucia Helen (Yurkston) Cowles; m. Paul Stephen Mikkelsen, Aug. 3, 1973 (div. Mar. 1988). BS, Bates Coll., 1976. Med. librarian Fla. Inst. Tech., Melbourne, 1976-78; mus. aide, technician Smithsonian Inst., Ft. Pierce, Fla., 1978-1982; asst. curator Harbor Br. Oceanographic Inst., Ft. Pierce, 1982—; cons. malacology Continental Shelf Assocs., Tequesta, Fla., 1978—, SeaPharm Inc., Ft. Pierce, 1987-88, Applied Biology Inc., Jensen Beach, Fla., 1986—; cons. computer programs Logix Inc., Vero Beach, Fla., 1986-88. Contbr. articles to profl. jours., 1981—. Mem. Am. Malacological Union (corr. sec. 1983—, editor newsletter 1984—), Am. Assn. Zool. Nomenclature, Biol. Soc. Washington, Unitas Malacologia, Paleontol. Research Instn., Sigma Xi. Club: Astronaut Trail Shell (Melbourne) (chmn. identification 1980-87). Office: Harbor Br Oceanographic Inst 5600 Old Dixie Hwy Fort Pierce FL 34946

MIKOLAIZYK, DEBORAH FRANSISCO, pharmacist; b. Detroit, Mar. 15, 1956; d. Theodore Joseph and Phyllis Irene (VanZant) F.; m. Gerald John Norris, Aug. 21, 1976 (div. May 1981); m. Michael Gene Mikolaizyk, Feb. 11, 1987. BS in Pharmacy, Ferris State Coll., 1978. Pharmacist, asst. mgr. Cunningham Drug Stores, 6 stores in met. Detroit area, 1978-81; cons. Specialized Pharmacy Services, Livonia, Mich., 1981-83; ptnr. Village Pharmacies, Harrison and Beaverton, Mich., 1983—. Mem. Cen. Mich. Pharmacists Assn. (sec. 1983-85), Nat. Assn. Retail Druggists. Republican. Avocations: cross country skiing, sailing. Home: 192 Hillcrest Harrison MI 48625 Office: Village Pharmacy 158 N 1st St Harrison MI 48625

MIKOS, KATHERINE CHARLOTTE, manufacturing executive; b. Chgo., July 8, 1953; d. Donald G. and Charlotte M. (Jethon) Lutzow; m. Gary A. Mikos, Oct. 29, 1976 (div. July 1981); children: Kimberly A., Kristen J. Student, Harper Coll., Palatine, Ill., 1971-72, 85-87. Office mgr. Arthur Treacher's Fish and Chips, Des Plaines, Ill., 1972-75, Sika Chem. Corp., Des Plaines, 1975-79; adminstrv. asst. RDN Mfg. Co., Elk Grove Village, Ill., 1981-82; mgr. distbn. ctr. Merit Abrasive Products, Wood Dale, Ill., 1982—. Sec. bd. dirs. Elk Grove Village Community Day Ctr., 1986—. Mem. Am. Prodn. and Inventory Control Soc., Inc. Lutheran. Office: Merit Abrasive Products 860 Lively Blvd Wood Dale IL 60191

MIKULSKI, BARBARA ANN, senator; b. Balt., July 20, 1936; d. William and Christina Eleanor (Kutz) M. B.A., Mt. St. Agnes Coll., 1958; M.S.W., U. Md., 1965; LL.D. (hon.), Goucher Coll., 1973, Hood Coll., 1978. Tchr. Mt. St. Agnes Coll., 1969; tchr. Community Coll. Balt., 1970-71, VISTA Tng. Ctr., 1965-70; with Balt. Dept. Social Services, 1961-63, 66-70, York Family Agy., 1964, Assoc. Catholic Charities, 1958-61; former mem. Balt. City Council; mem. 96th-99th congresses from 3d Md. Dist., 1979-87, mem. interstate and fgn. commerce com., mcht. marine com.; mem. U.S. Senate appropriations environment and pub. works, labor and human relations, small bus. coms. 100th Congress from 3d Md. Dist., 1987—; mem. Congl. Steel Caucus, Congresswomen's Caucus, Democratic Study Group, Environ. Study Conf., Mems. Congress for Peace Through Law; cons. Nat. Ctr. Urban Ethnic Affairs, others. Contbr. articles to mags. and newspapers. Bd. dirs. Valley House; nat. bd. dirs. Urban Coalition; mem. Polish Women's Alliance, Polish Am. Congress, Citizens Planning and Housing Assn., S.E. Community Orgn.; chmn. com. community devel. Archdiocesan Urban Commn.; mem. nat. com. Muskie for Pres., 1971-72; chmn. com. del. selection and party structure Dem. Nat. Com.; Dem. nominee U.S. Senate, 1974, Ho. of Reps., 1976; mem. Dem. Nat. Strategy Council. Named Woman of Yr. MS. mag., 1987. Mem. Nat. Women's Polit. Caucus, Nat. Bus. and Profl. Women's Assn., Am. Fedn. Tchrs., Nat. Assn. Social Workers, LWV. Office: US Senate 320 Hart Office Bldg Washington DC 20510-2003

MILANO, HEATHER CASEY, educator; b. St. John, N.B., Can., Mar. 2, 1934; B.A. in L.S., St. Francis Xavier U., Antigonish, N.S., Can., 1956; M.Sc. in Audiovisual Edn., Western Conn. State Coll., Danbury, 1976; married, 2 children. Librarian various schs., 1957-59; library media specialist Putnam Valley (N.Y.) Central Sch. Dist. 2, 1972—. Mem. cultural com. Putnam Valley Pub. Library, 1972-74; media council rep. to Bd. Coop. Ednl. Services, Yorktown Heights, N.Y., 1973—. Mem. N.Y. State United Tchrs., Sch. Librarians of Southeastern N.Y. Pi Lambda Theta. Certified library media specialist, N.Y. State. Home: 2730 Quaker Church Rd Yorktown Heights NY 10598 Office: Putnam Valley Jr High Sch Peekskill Hollow Rd Putnam Valley NY 10579

MILDON, MARIE ROBERTA, association executive; b. Pittsburg, Calif., Apr. 18, 1935; d. Samuel Ward and Roberta Alice (Trumpower) Wilson; m. James Lee Mildon, Sept. 17, 1958; 1 dau., Laura Marie. B.S., U. Nev.-Reno, 1983. News editor Seaside News Sentinel (Calif.), 1956-58; adminstrv. asst. for corp. devel. Crown Zellerbach, San Francisco, 1959-64; assoc. dir. Nat. Council Juvenile and Family Ct. Judges, Reno, Nev., 1969—; tng. dir. Nat. Coll. Juvenile Justice, Reno, 1971-72; apptd. cons. to task force on abused and neglected children Mo. Supreme Ct. Alt. trustee John Shaw Field Found., Reno, 1979-85. Co-author: Model Statute for Termination of Parental Rights, 1976; Model Statute on Juvenile and Family Court Records, 1981; My World To Share, 1982. Editor: Judicial Concern for Children in Trouble, 1974; Juvenile and Family Law Jour., 1985—; prodn. editor Juvenile and Family Law Digest, 1986—. Office: U Nev Campus Jud Coll Bldg Reno NV 89557

MILES, BARBARA ANN, health care facility administrator, nurse; b. Huron, S.D., July 4, 1940; d. Marvin Christian and Lucy Johanna (DeYoung) Roesch; m. Frederick Dean Miles Jr., May 6, 1967; 1 child, Frederick Dean III. R.N., Presbyn.-St. Luke's Hosp. Sch. of Nursing, Chgo., 1961; student U. Ill.-Chgo., 1965, Case Western Res. U., 1963-65. R.N., Ill., Ohio, Ariz. Asst. head nurse Tucson Med. Ctr., 1971-72; supr. Desert Samaritan Hosp., Mesa, Ariz., 1972-74; nurse mgr. McDowell facility Cigna Health Plan of Ariz., Phoenix, 1974-83, assoc. adminstr., 1983-85, adminstr., 1985—; state chairperson nursing contest Vocat. Indsl. Clubs of Am., Phoenix, 1984—, nat. chairperson nursing contest, 1985—. Mem. Am. Acad. Ambulatory Nursing Adminstrs., Chandler C. of C. Methodist. Avocations: playing piano; reading; crafts. Home: 1019 E Vinedo Ln Tempe AZ 85284 Office: Cigna Health Plan of Ariz 1349 W Chandler Blvd Chandler AZ 85224

MILES, DEBRA ANN, software trainer; b. N.Y.C., Mar. 12, 1953; d. Alexander Acey and Easter Alma (Brown) M. MusB, Boston U., 1975; MusM, North Tex. State U., 1983. Instrumental music instr. Boston Pub. Schs., 1975-78; music instr. Dallas Ind. Sch. Dist., 1978-83; systems engr. Computer Lang. Research, Carrollton, Tex., 1983-85; client support rep. Nat. FSI, Dallas, 1985-86; customer support rep. Magna Software, Inc., N.Y.C., 1987—. Vol. Girl Scouts Am., Dallas, 1980. Recipient Key and cert. Pi Kappa Lambda, 1983. Mem. Nat. Assn. Female Execs. Methodist.

MILES, JOANNA, actress; b. Nice, France, Mar. 6, 1940; came to U.S., 1941, naturalized, 1941; d. Johannes Schiefer and Jeanne Miles; m. William Burns, May 23, 1970 (div. 1977); m. Michael Brandman, Apr. 29, 1978; 1 child, Miles. Grad., Putney (Vt.) Sch., 1958. Mem. Actors Studio, N.Y.C., 1966, Los Angeles Classic Theatre, 1986. Appeared in: motion pictures The Way We Live Now, 1969, Bug, 1975, The Ultimate Warrior, 1975, Golden Girl, 1978, Cross Creek, 1983, As Is, 1986, Findings, 1987; numerous television films, including In What America, 1965, My Mothers House, 1968, Glass Menagerie, 1974 (2 Emmy awards), Born Innocent, 1974, Aloha Means Goodbye, 1974, The Trial of Chaplain Jensen, 1975, Harvest Home, 1977, Fire in the Sky, 1978, Sophisticated Gents, 1979, Promise of Love, 1980, Sound of Murder, 1983, All My Sons (PBS), 1986, 87, The Right To Die, 1987; episodes in numerous TV series including Barney Miller, Dallas, St. Elsewhere, The Hulk, Trapper John, Kaz, Cagney and Lacey; stage plays Walk-Up, 1962, Once in a Life Time, 1963, Cave Dwellers, 1964, Drums in the Night, 1968, Dracula, 1968, Home Free, 1964, One Night Stands of A Noisy Passenger, 1972, Dylan, 1973, Dancing for the Kaiser, 1976, Debutante Ball, 1985; performed in radio shows Sta. KCRW Once in a Lifetime, 1987, Babbit, 1987; playwright, v.p. Brandman Productions. Pres. Children Giving Children. Recipient Am. Women in Radio and TV award, 1974, Actors Studio Achievement award, 1980. Mem. Acad. Motion Picture Arts and Scis., Acad. TV Arts and Scis., Dramatists Guild. Also: 250 W 57th St New York NY 10019

MILES-LAGRANGE, VICKI, state legislator; b. Oklahoma City, Sept. 30, 1953; d. Charles and Mary (Greenard) Miles; m. Jacques Lagrange. BA, Vassar Coll., 1974; LLB, Howard U., 1977. Formerly trial atty. U.S. Dept. Justice; congl. aide Speaker of the Ho., Rep. Carl Albert; mem. Okla. Senate from Dist. 48, 1987—. Democrat. Baptist. Address: 4020 N Lincoln #204 Oklahoma City OK 73105 *

MILKS, SALLY ANN, food service manager, dietitian; b. Bradford, Pa., Nov. 29, 1949; d. John David and Pearl Marie (Meier) Morrison; m. Frank Elmer Milks, Aug. 18, 1973 (div. 1978); 1 child, Jason Michael. B.S. in Edn., Mansfield State Coll., 1971; student Indiana U. of Pa., 1969-71. Registered dietitian. Clin. dietitian St. Vincent Med. Ctr., Erie, Pa., 1971-72, 73-74; dietetic intern Shadyside Hosp., Pitts., 1972-73; cons. dietitian Sheridan Manor Nursing Home, Buffalo, 1975-77; nutrition instr. E.J. Meyer Sch. Nursing, Buffalo, 1975-77, chief clin. dietitian, 1977-78; asst. dir. food services ARA Services, Erie County Med. Ctr., 1978-79, dir. food services, 1979-82, dist. mgr., Phila., 1982—; mem. adv. council Buffalo State U., 1985—; guest lectr. food and nutrition dept., 1980—. Ho. of dels. United Way of Buffalo and Erie County, 1983-85. Mem. Am. Dietetic Assn., Erie County Assn. for Retarded Children (2d v.p. 1983-85, chmn. residential services com. 1981-87). Home: 17 Apollo Dr Amherst NY 14120 Office: ARA Services 11103 Pepper Rd Hunt Valley MD 21031

MILLANE, LYNN, town official; b. Buffalo, N.Y. Oct. 14, 1928; d. Robert P. Schermerhorn and Justine A. (Ross) m. J. Vaughan Millane, Jr.; Aug. 16, 1952 children—Maureen, Michele, John, Mark, Kathleen ED.B. Grad., U. Buffalo, 1949, Ed.M., in Health Education 1951. Mem. Amherst Town Bd., 1982—. Pres., E.J. Meyer Hosp. Jr. Bd., 1962-64; pres. Aux. to Erie County Bar Assn., 1966-68; pres. Women's Com. of Buffalo Philharm. Orch., 1976-78, v.p. adminstrn., 1975-76, v.p. pub. affairs, 1974-75, chmn. adv. bd., 1979-82; v.p. Buffalo Philharm. Orch. Soc., Inc., 1976-78, mem. council, trustee, 1979-87, bd. overseers, 1987—; 1st v.p. Fans for 17, 1980-82; 1st. v.p. Friends of Baird Hall, SUNY-Buffalo, 1980-82; exec. bd. mem. Longview Protestant Home for Children, 1979-85, 2d v.p., 1982-85; bd. dirs. ARC, Town of Amherst br., 1982—, by-laws com., 1981, 84, chmn. sr. concerns com., 1982—; bd. dirs. Amherst Symphony Orch. Assn., 1981-87, roster chmn., 1982-84, nominating chmn., 1985-86; nat. music com. Women's Assn. for Symphony Orchs. in Am. and Can., 1977-79; council mem. Am. Symphony Orch. League; sec. Amherst Sr. Citizen's Adv. Bd., 1980-81, liaison from Amherst Town Bd., 1982—; mem. 1st adult day services adv. bd., 1st records mgmt. adv. bd.; dir.-at-large community adv. council SUNY-Buffalo, 1981—; co-assoc. chmn. maj. gift div. capital campaign Daeman Coll., 1983-84; co-chmn. Women United Against Drugs Campaign, 1970-72; founding mem. Lunch and Issues, Amherst, 1981—; mem. edn. com. Network in Aging of Western N.Y., Inc., 1982—, bd. dirs., 1982—, housing com., 1987—; bd. dirs. Amherst Elderly Transp. Corp., 1982—; liaison to and established 1st adult day services adv. bd. in Amherst, 1988; committeeman dist. Town of Amherst Republican Com.; treas. Town and Country Rep. Club, 1980-81; mem. nominating com. Fedn. Rep. Women's Clubs Erie County, 1980; exec. bd. mem. Women's Exec. Council of Erie County Rep. Com., 1969-71; dir. Amherst Rep. Women's Club, 1960-66; Pi Lambda Theta National Honorary-1950. Named Homemaker of Yr., Family Circle Mag., 1969; Woman of Substance, 20th Century Rep. Women, 1983; Woman of Yr., Buffalo Philharm. Orch. Soc., Inc., 1982; Outstanding Woman in Community Service, SUNY-Buffalo, 1985; recipient Good Neighbor award Courier Express, 1978; Merit award Buffalo Philharm. Orch., 1978; award Fedn. Rep. Women's Clubs Erie County, 1982; Disting. Service award Town of Amherst Sr. Ctr., 1985. Mem. Amherst C. of C. (VIP dinner com. 1984), LWV, SUNY-Buffalo Alumni Assn. (life, presdl. advisor 1977-79). Lodge: Zonta (pres. Amherst chpt. 1986-88). Office: 5583 Main St Amherst NY

MILLAN-FALK, NICOLE INA, foundation executive; b. Jamaica, N.Y., Apr. 15, 1953; d. Meyer and Garie (Solomom) Millman; m. Douglas Lawrence Falk, Nov. 24, 1979; 1 child, Ruussell Aaron. BS in Journalism, Boston U., 1975; MA in Media Studies, New Sch. for Social Research, N.Y.C., 1980. Editorial asst. Exceptional Parent mag., Boston, 1974-75; asst. editor Area Devel. mag., N.Y.C., 1975-77; mgr. editor N.Y. Dental Jour., N.Y.C., 1977-80; asst. exec. dir. Dental Soc. State N.Y., N.Y.C., 1980-83; pres. Millamn-Falk & Assocs., New Millford, N.J., 1983—; exec. dir. Nurses Ednl. Funds Inc., N.Y.C., 1985—. Editor: Park/Garden Maintenance Manual, 1983; contbr. articles to profl. jours. Journalism award Internat. Coll. Dentists, 1979, 83. Mem. N.Y. Soc. Assn. Execs. (assoc. mem. adv. com. chmn.), Soc. Women Engrs. (editor, pub. relations cons.), Am. Soc. Assn. Execs., Nat. Assn. Female Execs., Nat. Alliance Homebased Businesswomen, Women in Prodn. (bd. dirs. 1978-80, editor 1980-86), Boston U. Alumni Club (bd. dirs. 1977-80). Jewish. Home: 281 Birchwood Rd New Milford NJ 07646 Office: Nurses Ednl Funds Inc 555 W 57th St New York NY 10019

MILLAR, MARGARET ELLIS, author; b. Kitchener, Ont., Can., Feb. 5, 1915; d. Henry William and Lavinia (Ferrier) Sturm; m. Kenneth Millar (pseudonym Ross Macdonald), June 2, 1938 (dec.); 1 dau., Linda Jane (dec.). Student, U. Toronto, 1933-36. Author: The Invisible Worm, 1941, The Weak-Eyed Bat, 1942, The Devil Loves Me, 1942, Wall of Eyes, 1943, Fire Will Freeze, 1944, The Iron Gates, 1945, Experiment in Springtime, 1947, It's All in the Family, 1948, The Cannibal Heart, 1949, Do Evil in Return, 1950, Vanish in an Instant, 1952, Rose's Last Summer, 1952, Wives and Lovers, 1954, Beast in View, 1955, An Air That Kills, 1957, The Listening Walls, 1959, A Stranger in My Grave, 1960, How Like an Angel, 1962, The Fiend, 1964, The Birds and the Beasts Were There, 1968, Beyond This Point Are Monsters, 1970, Ask for Me Tomorrow, 1976, The Murder of Miranda, 1980, Mermaid, 1982, Banshee, 1983, Spider Webs, 1986; also writer short stories and TV plays. Recipient Edgar award for Beast in View Mystery Writers Am., 1956, Grandmaster award Mystery Writers Am., 1983. Mem. Mystery Writers Am. (pres. 1957). Home: 87 Seaview Dr Santa Barbara CA 93108

MILLARD, LAVERGNE HARRIET, free-lance artist; b. Chgo., July 8, 1925; d. Lewis and Julia (Smolk) Bassmire; student Chgo. Art Inst., 1937-39; m. Samuel Costales, 1943 (div. 1957); m. Bailey Millard, Mar. 9, 1958 (div.); children—Bryan Lewis Costales, Julianne, Juanita Crump, Candace Lynn Millard. Cocktail waitress Verdis, Grant Street, Concord, Calif., 1955-61; mgr. used book shop Joyce Book Shop, Concord, 1964-79, seller art works, own prints; freelance artist, 1979—. Recipient ribbons local fairs, art shows. Republican. Copyright holder for pastel art work. Home and Office: 1890 Farm Bureau Rd Apt 11 Concord CA 94519

MILLARD, PATRICIA LEWIS, communications executive; b. Washington, Mar. 7, 1956; d. James Judson and Philippa Beatriz (Muse) M. BS in Criminal Justice, Old Dominion U., 1979. Assoc. editor Am. Correctional Assn., College Park, Md., 1983-84, mng. editor, 1984-86, dir. communication and publs., 1986—. Vol. Norfolk Ct. Juvenile Domestic Relations, 1977-78, Arlington Ct. Juvenile and Domestic Relations; vol., coordinator ; law related edn. project Phi Alpha Delta, Washington, 1981-835. Office: Am Correctional Assn 4321 Hartwick Rd Suite L 208 College Park MD 20740

MILLARD, REGINA ELIZABETH, personnel management specialist; b. Kane, Pa., Oct. 5, 1949; d. Evan Clifford and Ovenia Gertrude (Tims) M. BS, U. Oreg., 1971, MS, 1972. Correctional officer Fed. Bur. Prisons, San Pedro, Calif., 1973; rehab. program mgr. New Cumberland (Pa.) Army Depot, 1973-75; personnel specialist U.S. Mil. Acad., West Point, N.Y., 1975-78; personnel mgr. HHS, Laguna Niguel, Calif., 1978-81, Dallas, Tex., 1981-85; program analysis officer Social Security Adminstrn., Arlington, Va., 1985-87; personnel mgmt. specialist U.S. Naval Observatory Defense Mapping Agy., Washington, 1987—. Office: Def Mapping Agy US Naval Observatory Washington DC 20305

MILLER, ADELE ENGELBRECHT, educator; b. Jersey City, July 31, 1946; d. John Fred and Dorathea Kathryn (Kamm) Engelbrecht; m. William A. Miller, Jr., Dec. 21, 1981. BS in Bus. Edn., Fairleigh Dickinson U., 1968, MBA magna cum laude, 1974; cert. in public sch. adminstrn. and supervision, Jersey City State Coll., 1976. Bus. tchr. Jersey City Bd. Edn., 1967—, coordinator coop. office edn. programs, 1973—, acting v.p., 1985-86, prin. of summer sch., 1986; adj. instr. St. Peter's Coll., 1974-75; curriculum cons. Cittone Bus. Sch., 1981-82; mem. adv. council Dickinson High Sch., 1973—, chmn., 1978-80; organizer, bd. dirs. Frances Nadel and Cooke-Connolly-Coffey-Witt Faculty Meml. Scholarships, 1978—; trustee Dickinson High Sch. Parents Council, 1985—. Co-author: New Jersey Cooperative Office Education Coordinators Resource Manual, 1984; author coop. office edn. study course Jersey City Public Schs., 1980, 84. Mem. Citizens Adv. Council to Mayor of Jersey City, 1968-71; organizer, dir. Jersey City Youth Week, 1970-72; mem. juvenile conf. com. Hudson County Juvenile Ct., 1978—; v.p., sec., trustee, chmn. dinner-musicale Jersey City Coll.-Community Orch., 1979—; Explorer Scouting adv. bd. Hudson-Hamilton council Boy Scouts Am., 1985—; trustee Jersey City YWCA, 1988—. Recipient Dickinson High Sch. Key Club Tchr. of Yr. award, 1971; named Educator of Yr. award Dickinson High Sch. Parents Council, 1986, 88. Mem. NEA, N.J. Edn. Assn., Jersey City Edn. Assn. (bldg. dir.), N.J. Coop. Office Edn. Coordinators Assn. (sec., dir., treas., v.p.), N.J. Fedn. Women's Clubs, Jersey City Women's Club (scholarship chmn., adviser Jr. Woman's Club), AAUW N.J. Div. (edn. chmn., sec., del. to White House briefing on edn., women's issues, arms control); AAUW-Coll. Club of N.J. (pres., v.p., sec., treas.). Clubs: Jersey City (pres.), N.J. Fedn. Women's (jr. membership dept., chmn. conv. exhibits 1969, dist. drama chmn.), Jersey City Jr. Woman's (v.p., sec., treas.). Lodge: Rotary. Home: 91 Sherman Pl Jersey City NJ 07307 Office: Dickinson High School 2 Palisade Ave Jersey City NJ 07306

MILLER, AILEEN ETTA MARTHA, medical association administrator, consultant; b. Sullivan, Ind., Oct. 4, 1924; d. Arthur Henry and Alice Marie (Michael) Dettmer; m. Robert Charles Miller, Sept. 1, 1945; children: Robert Conrad, Debra Carol, Theresa Marie. D of Chiropractic, Palmer Coll. Chiropractic, 1945. Sec. Soroptimist Internat., East Detroit, Mich., 1951-52, Mich. State Chiropractic Assn. Dist. 1, East Detroit, 1957-58, Macomb County Chiropractic Assn., East Detroit, 1982-86; pres. Macomb County Chiropractic Assn., Warren, Mich., 1986-87; cons. Chiropractic Physicians, Warren, 1986—. Mem. Internat. Chiropractic Assn., Mich. State Chiropractic Assn., Nat. Upper Cervical Chiropractic Assn., Roy Sweat Research and Edn. Found., Mich. Chiropractic Council, Am. Chiropractic Assn., Found. Chiropractic Edn. and Research, Palmer Coll. Alumni, Atlas Orthogonal Assn. Republican. Office: Chiropractic Physicians 30020 Schoenherr Warren MI 48093

MILLER, ALICE LYNN, social services administrator; b. chgo., Jan. 24, 1929; d. John Henry and Alice Olive (Lynn) Bamberger; m. Wesley H. Miller, Sept. 23, 1950 (div. Feb. 1976). BSW, Fla. Internat. U., 1972; MS, Calif. Coast U., 1987. Counselor Henderson Mental Health, Ft. Lauderdale, Fla., 1972-75; diagnosis, assessment ct. cons. Broward County Alcohol & Drug Div., Ft. Lauderdale, 1975-83, supr., 1986—; mental health clin. specialist Seminole Indian Tribe of Fla., Hollywood, 1983-86; bd. dirs. Seminole Drug Bd., Hollywood, 1972-75, Women's Detention Ctr., Ft. Lauderdale, 1980-83, Cert. Addiction Profls., Tallahassee, 1985—, FAC-B, Tallahassee, 1982-85, CDC Ctrs., Ft. Lauderdale, 1987—. Mem. Nat. Assn. Alcohol and Drug Abuse Counselors, Fla. Alcohol and Drug Abuse Assn. Office: Broward County Alcohol & Drug Div 1011 SW 2d Ct Fort Lauderdale FL 33312

MILLER, BARBARA, physical therapist; b. Lakewood, N.J., Dec. 31, 1954; d. Robert and Carolyn (Seiden) M.; m. Joel Behar, Dec. 22, 1985. B.S.P.T., Washington U., 1977. Staff therapist, then sr. therapist Nassau Hosp., Mineola, N.Y., 1977-82; sr. phys. therapist Jewish Inst. Geriatric Care-Geriatric Community Health Center, New Hyde Park, N.Y., 1982-87; pvt. practice Glen Cove, N.Y., 1977—; supr. phys. therapy Jewish Inst. for Geriatric Care, Long Term Home Health Care Program, New Hyde Park, N.Y., 1986—; staff therapist Pain Alleviation Ctr., Roslyn, N.Y., 1987—; guest lectr. Current researcher in efficacy of helium neon laser stimulation on wound healing. Mem. Am. Phys. Therapy Assn. Home: 11 Clement St Glen Cove NY 11542

MILLER, BARBARA ANN, computer consulting firm executive; b. N.Y.C., July 5, 1952; d. Charles John and Catherine (Ponkrashoff) M. B.A., U. Vt., 1974. Systems analyst Honeywell Info. Systems, Billerica, Mass., 1978-80, sr. systems rep., Houston, 1980-82, Tandem Computers, Houston, 1983-84; tech. support rep. Allied Data Research, Houston, 1982-83; sr. v.p. Neu-Sound of Houston, 1984—; cons. Honeywell Info. Systems, Tallahassee, Fla., 1985-86, MidCon Mktg. Co., Houston, 1987—; bd. dirs. Neu-Sound of Houston; v.p., dir. Neu-Comp of Houston, 1987—. Recipient Pacemaker award Honeywell Info. Systems, 1981, 82. Roman Catholic. Avocations: sailing, skiing, tennis, raquetball, photography. Home: 3700 Watonga Blvd #406 Houston TX 77092 Office: Neu-Sound of Houston PO Box 271569 Houston TX 77277

MILLER, BARBARA ANN(BOBBE), educator; b. Cleve., Aug. 16, 1943; d. Julius and Marie Rose (Pekarek) Mosonics; m. David Leighton Miller, July 31, 1965. BS in Edn., Ohio State U., 1965; MS in Spl. Edn., U. Akron, 1973; postgrad., Nat. Coll. Edn., 1977, Kent State U., 1984—. Cert. elem., spl. edn. tchr. Tchr. Strongsville (Ohio) City Schs., 1965-67, tchr. spl. edn., 1967-69, cons., 1969-72; ednl. diagnostician Proviso Area Exceptional Children, Maywood, Ill., 1972-73, supr. learning disabilities, 1973-77, asst. dir. spl. edn., 1977-80; tchr. educator and dir. U. Akron (Ohio), 1980—; cons. N.W. Ohio Spl. Edn. Regional Resource Ctr., Bowling Green, 1982-85; adv. faculty Student Council for Exceptional Children, Akron, 1980—; cons., vol. Handicapped Student Services, Akron, 1981—; adv. spl. edn. Ohio Coalition/Edn. Handicapped Children, Columbus, 1986—. Author: (with others) (monograph) Preparing Teachers of Students Who are Handicapped, 1987; (index) Individualized Computerized Learning Centers, 1979, (computer program) Mainstreaming at the Secondary Level, 1982; director (with others)Improving Integrative Services, 1985. Mem. adv. bd. dirs. Summit Company Assn. for Retarded Citizens, Akron, 1982—; puppeteer Kids on the Block, Akron, 1982-85; vol. Mentor (Ohio) Police Crime Prevention, 1982-86, Am. Cancer Soc., Cleve., 1986—. Mem. Council for Exceptional Children (leadership participation award 1986, Ohio Fedn. pres. 1986-88), Tchr. Edn. Div., EdLums: Ohio State U., Phi Delta Kappa. Clubs: Lake County Ohio State U. Alumni (treas. 1983—), Mentor Jr. Women's. Home: 9940 Juniper Ct Concord Township OH 44060 Office: U Akron Carroll Hall 117 Akron OH 44325

MILLER, BARBARA ELLEN, pharmacist; b. Rochester, N.Y., June 2, 1955; d. Ivan Wilbur and Shirley Jean (Kreigh) M. BS in Pharmacy, Mass. Coll. Pharmacy, 1977; MPH, Boston U., 1983. Staff pharmacist Harvard Community Health, Boston, 1978-83; chief pharmacist Harvard Community Health, Braintree, Mass., 1983—. Mem. Am. Soc. Hosp. Pharmacists, Mass. Soc. Hosp. Pharmacists, Rho Chi Soc. Republican. Lutheran. Home: 54 Alton Pl Brookline MA 02146 Office: Harvard Community Health 111 Grossman Dr Braintree MA 02184

MILLER, BARBARA STALLCUP, medical foundation administrator; b. Montague, Calif., Sept. 4, 1919; d. Joseph Nathaniel and Maybelle (Needham) Stallcup; m. Leland F. Miller, May 16, 1946; children—Paula Kay, Susan Lee, Daniel Joseph, Alison Jean. B.A., U. Oreg., 1942. Women's editor Eugene (Oreg.) Daily News, 1941-43; law clk. to J. Everett Barr, Yreka, Calif., 1943-45; mgr. Yreka C. of C., 1945-46; Northwest supr. Louis Harris and Assocs., Portland, Oreg., 1959-62; dir. pub. relations and fund raising Columbia River council Girl Scouts U.S.A., 1962-67; pvt. practice pub. relations cons., Portland, 1967-72; adviser of student publs., asst. prof. communications U. Portland, 1967-72, dir. pub. relations and info., asst. prof. communications, 1972-78, dir. devel., 1978-79, exec. dir. devel., 1979-83; assoc. dir St. Vincent Med. Found., 1983—. Pres. bd. dirs. Vols. of Am. of Oreg., Inc., 1980-84, pres. regional adv. bd., 1982-84; chmn. bd. dirs. S.E. Mental Health Network, 1984—, Oreg. Black History Project; nat. bd. dirs. Vols. of Am., Inc., 1984—. Recipient Presdl. Citation, Oreg. Communicators Assn., 1973, Matrix award, 1976, 80, Miltner award U. Portland, 1977. Mem. Nat. Assn. Hosp. Devel., Nat. Soc. Fundraising Execs., Women in Communications (NW regional v.p. 1973-75), Nat. Fedn. Press Women, Oreg. Press Women (dist. dir.), Pub. Relations Soc. Am. (dir. local chpt.), Oreg. Fedn. Womens Clubs (communications chmn. 1978-80), Alpha Xi Delta. Unitarian. Clubs: Portland Zenith (pres. 1975-76, 81-82), City Club of Portland. Contbr. articles to profl. jours. Home: 5930 SW Meadows Rd Lake Oswego OR 97035 Office: 9205 SW Barnes Rd Portland OR 97225

MILLER, BERNICE J., college administrator, consultant; b. Chgo., Oct. 7, 1920; d. Archibald Perkins and Hattye (Jones) Johnson; m. George Benjamin Miller, Mar. 18, 1944; children: Benita Charlotte, Michael Benjamin. BA, Roosevelt U., 1947; MA, Chgo. Tchrs. Coll., 1965; CAS, Harvard U., 1970, EdD, 1972. Tch. English Chgo. Pub. High Schs., 1947-50; elem. sch. tchr. McClellan Pub. Sch., Chgo., 1950-64; mem. faculty, assoc. in edn., lectr. Harvard Grad. Sch. of Edn., Cambridge, Mass., 1967-75; assoc. dean Jackson Coll. Tufts U., Medford, Mass., 1968-70; instr. seminar on day care, adminstrn. and child care Radcliffe Inst., Cambaridge, 1970-73; assoc. dir. Ctr. Urban Studies Harvard Grad. Sch. Edn., Cambridge, 1971-75; prin. Lucy Stone Sch. Boston Pub. Schs., 1977-78; sr. officer Office Curriculum and Competency, Boston, 1978-83; dir. Harvard/Boston High Tech. Project Harvard Grad. Sch. Edn., Boston, 1983-84; pres. Loop Coll. City Coll. Chgo., 1984—; mem. Whitney Women Study on Urban Coll., Medford, 1971-73; ednl. cons. Sci. Research Assocs., Chgo., 1965-68, Urban Research Corp., Chgo., 1968-72; con. Inner-City Cons. New Eng. Bell, Medford, spring 1969. Contbr. articles to profl. jours. Mem. Women Involved, Boston, 1970-73, Women in Politics, Boston, 1968-84, Mayor's Commn. on Women, Chgo., 1986—, Ind. Precinct Orgn. Ind. Voters of Ill., Chgo., 1986—. Recipient Black Achiever's award YMCA of Greater Boston, 1980, Freedom award Roosevelt U., 1984, Outstanding Achievement award in edn. Leadership Acad. YWCA, 1986; named Educator of Yr. Boston Negro Bus. and Profl. Club, 1984, Disting. Alumni of Yr., Chgo. State U., 1984. Mem. AAUW, Am. Assn. Community and Jr. Colls. (internat. council), Chgo. Network. Democrat. Office: Loop Coll City Coll Chgo 30 E Lake St Chicago IL 60601

MILLER, BETTY BROWN, free-lance writer; b. Altus, Ark., Dec. 21, 1926; d. Carlos William and Arlie Gertrude (Sublett) Brown; B.S., Okla. State U., 1949; M.S., U. Tulsa, 1953; student Am. U., 1966-68; m. Robert Wiley Miller, Nov. 15, 1953; children—Janet Ruth, Stephen Wiley. Tchr., LeFlore (Okla.) High Sch., 1947-48, Osage Indian Reservation High Sch., Hominy, Okla., 1948-50, Jenks (Okla.) High Sch., 1950-51; instr. Sch. Bus., U. Tulsa, 1950-51; tchr. Tulsa public schs., 1951-54; instr. Burdette Coll., Boston, 1954-55; reporter Bethesda-Chevy Chase Tribune, Montgomery County, Md., 1970-73; freelance writer, contbr. newspapers and mags., 1973—. Vice-pres. Kenwood Park (Md.) Citizens Assn., 1960; mem. Ft. Sumner Citizens Assn., editor newsletter, 1969; mem. Md. State PTA, editorial coordinator leadership conf., 1973-74; chmn. Montgomery County Forum for Edn., 1970-75. Mem. Nat. Soc. Arts and Letters (past editor mag., dir. public relations, past nat. corr. sec.), Nat. League Am. Pen

Women (budget chmn., past nat. treas.) PEO, Montgomery County Press Assn., Internat. Platform Assn., Capital Speakers Club of Washington (past pres.), Adventures Unltd., U.D.C., Soc. Descs. of Washington's Army at Valley Forge (nat. bd., insp. gen.), DAR, Huguenot Soc. (Pa. bd.). Republican. Clubs: Washington; Sedgeley (pres. 1985-88) (Phila.). Address: PO Box 573 Valley Forge PA 19481

MILLER, BETTY JO, machine manufacturing company executive; b. Pitts., July 27, 1924; d. Paul Haines and Ella Irene (Berkey) Young; m. Clifford Miller, Feb. 16, 1946; 1 child, Paul David. B.S. in Bus., Burdett Coll., 1950; postgrad. MIT, 1960. With engring. dept. Armstrong Cork, Braintree, Mass., 1942-44; pvt. sec. F.S. Webster Co., Boston, 1944-46; acct., treas. Braintree Tool Co., Inc., 1952-75, pres., 1975—; acct. Blackburn Sheetmetal, Braintree, 1954-78, Micro Hydraulic Valves, Braintree, 1955-80, Mandel E. Cohen, M.D., Boston, 1964—, Howie and Cramond, Inc., Quincy, Mass., 1974—, Smith Harrison Co., Inc., 1969—; notary pub. Mass., 1970—; IRS rep. Holtsville, N.Y., 1984. Patentee electric undercutter and armature turning tools. Clk. of the polls, Braintree, 1964—; sec. Hampshire Shores Assn., 1967—; acct., tax specialist Braintree gardners guild, 1983—. Mem. Braintree Bd. Trade, Nat. Fedn. Ind. Bus., South Shore C. of C., U.S. SBA, Nat. Bus. Assn., Braintree Women's Club (pres. 1982-83) treas., auditor 1968—), Gen. Fedn. Women's Clubs, State Fedn. Womens Clubs. Republican. Avocations: golf; bowling; bridge. Office: Braintree Tool Co Inc PO Box 253 Braintree MA 02184

MILLER, BEVERLY WHITE, college president; b. Willoughby, Ohio; d. Joseph Martin and Marguerite Sarah (Storer) White; m. Lynn Martin Miller, Oct. 11, 1945 (dec. 1986); children: Michaela Ann, Craig Martin, Todd Daniel, Cass Timothy, Simone Agnes. A.B., Western Res. U., 1945; M.A., Mich. State U., 1957; Ph.D., U. Toledo, 1967; L.H.D. (hon.), Coll. St. Benedict, St. Joseph, Minn., 1979; L.L.D. (hon.), U. Toledo, 1988. Chem. and biol. researcher 1945-57; tchr. schs. in Mich., also Mercy Sch. Nursing, St. Lawrence Hosp., Lansing, Mich., 1957-58; mem. chemistry and biology faculty Mary Manse Coll., Toledo, 1958-71; dean grad. div. Mary Manse Coll., 1968-71, exec. v.p., 1968-71; acad. dean Salve Regina Coll., Newport, R.I., 1971-74; pres. Coll. St. Benedict, St. Joseph, Minn., 1974-79, Western New Eng. Coll., Springfield, Mass., 1980—; cons. U.S. Office Edn., 1980; cons. in field.; mem. Pvt. Industry Council, exec. com., 1984—, Springfield. Author papers in field. Corporator Mercy Hosp., Springfield, Mass. Recipient President's citation St. John's U., 1979; also various service awards. Mem. Am. Assn. Higher Edn., AAAS, Assn. Cath. Colls. and Univs. (exec. bd.), Internat. Assn. Sci. Edn., Nat. Assn. Ind. Colls. and Univs. (govt. relations adv. com.), Nat. Assn. Biology Tchrs., Assn. Ind. Colls. and Univs. of Mass. (exec. com. 1981—, chmn. 1986-87, vice-chmn. 1985-86), Nat. Assn. Research Sci. Teaching, Springfield C. of C. (dir.), Delta Kappa Gamma, Sigma Delta Epsilon. Office: Western New England Coll 1215 Wilbraham Rd Springfield MA 01119

MILLER, BILLIE RUTH, guidance counselor; b. Abilene, Tex., July 9, 1924; d. George Bruce and Cordelia (Chaffin) Darnell; m. Lloyd Nathaniel Hawkins, Sept. 6, 1942 (dec. June 1962); children—Billy Loyd, Garry Lynn, Bruce Russell; m. J. Robert Miller, Mar. 27, 1969. BA, McMurry Coll., 1966; M.Ed., Hardin Simmons U., 1971; postgrad. U. Tex.-Arlington, 1972, No. Ariz. U., 1973, Abilene Christian U., 1977. Cert. counselor, Tex.; nat. cert. counselor. Cons. Cogdell News Co., Abilene, 1945-47, sec., acct., 1942-45; tchr., counselor Kayenta Boarding Sch., Ariz., 1966-67; head guidance dept. Crownpoint Boarding Sch., N.Mex., 1967-71; edn. service officer 96 CSG/DPE, Dyess AFB, Tex., 1973-75, guidance counselor, 1971-73, 75—, edn. lectr., 1971—, edn. service officer, 1986—; pvt. practice counseling, Abilene, 1971—, guest appearances TV stas., Abilene. Vice pres. Abilene Art Forum, 1954; pres., historian N.A.T.I.O.N.S Club, Abilene, 1960, 61. Recipient Superior Performance award Civilian Personnel Dyess AFB, Tex., 1984, achievement award Dir. Personnel Dyess AFB, 1983, Notable Achievement, 1987, Cert. Appreciation, 1987; Ora Negra Am. Bus. Women Assn. ednl. scholar, 1967. Mem. Am. Assn. Counselor Devel. (nat. cert. 1983), Nat. Vocat. Counselor Devel., Tex. Assn. Counseling Devel. (cert. 1983), Mil. Edn. Counselor Assn. (treas. 1981-82), Western Horizon Am. Bus. Women Edn. Assn. (chmn. 1983, Woman of Yr. 1979), Mensa (sec. Abilene chpt. 1963-64), United Daus. Confederacy (sec. 1947-48). Republican. Baptist. Lodge: Order of Ea. Star (worthy matron 1957-58, dep. grand matron 1960), Dau. of Nile, 1987. Avocations: amateur archaeology; astronomy; camping and rafting; painting; knitting. Home: 1857 Sycamore Abilene TX 79602 Office: 96 CSG/DPE Dyess AFB Abilene TX 79607

MILLER, CAROLYN HANDLER, screenwriter; b. San Francisco, Nov. 30, 1941; d. Marvin and Louise (Haas) Handler; m. Jerry Miller, Apr. 25, 1971 (div. 1978); m. Daryl Francis Warner, Mar. 14, 1982. BA, Cornell U., 1963; MS in Journalism, Northwestern U., Evanston, Ill., 1965. Reporter Fairchild Publs., N.Y.C., 1965-67; staff writer The Many Worlds of Music, N.Y.C., 1967; freelance writer 1967—; scriptwriter TV series Captain Kangaroo, 1975-77. Author: The Illustrated Television Directory, 1978, (script) Mystery at Fire Island, 1981, Sometimes I Don't Love My Mother (Emmy nomination 1983), (with Daryl Warner) Jigsaw, 1987. Mem. Am. Acad. TV Arts and Scis. (Blue Ribbon panel 1984-86), Writers Guild Am. West (mem. informational films com. 1984—, co-chair women's com. 1986—), Women in Film. Democrat. Jewish.

MILLER, CATTIE LOU, state government commissioner; b. Horse Cave, Ky., Apr. 1, 1923; d. Robert Emmett and Cattie Lieu (Rowntree) M. Student, Bowling Green U., 1941, U. Louisville, part-time 1947-65. Civilian chief clk. Armored Forces Hdqrs., Ft. Knox, Ky., 1941-43; exec. sec. to works mgr. Consol. Vultee Aircraft Corp., Louisville, 1943-45; with Ky State Govt., Frankfort, 1947—; sec. to govs., sec. gov's cabinet 1947-55, clk. State Election Commn. and Ky. Bd. Registration and Purgation, 1947-56, exec. asst. to gov., 1959-60, commr. Dept. Pub. Info., 1960-67, chief adminstrv. asst. to gov., 1966-67, exec. asst. to gov., 1967-71, adminstrv. asst. to gov., 1971-72, commr. Dept. Personnel, 1972-75, chief of personnel auditing, 1976, exec. dir. Bd. Claims, 1976-79, exec. dir. Crime Victims Compensation Bd., 1976-79, dep. sec. adminstrn. Dept. Fin., 1979-81; exec. dir. Pub. Service Commn. State of Ky., 1982; commr. Dept. Adminstrn., Fin. and Adminstrn. Cabinet, 1981-82, 83—, commr. and acting dept. sec., 1982-83; adminstrv. asst. to exec. v.p. Morton Frozen Foods, Inc., 1956; advt. mgr. Louisville C. of C., 1957-59; trustee Ky. Employees Retirement System, 1966-75, 82—, past mem. investment com., mem. legis. com. 1982—; mem. Fin. Disclosure Rev. Commn., 1975-76.c. Trustee Ky. Hist. Soc., 1977-81; mem. adv. com. Sch. Pub. Affairs Ky. State U., 1980-81. Recipient Forestry Practices award Courier-Jour., 1963, Forest Service award U.S. Dept. Agr., 1980. Mem. Nat. Assn. State Gen. Service Officers (vice chair 1986—), Ky. Watercolor Soc., Lexington Art League. Democrat. Baptist.

MILLER, CHERYL MARION, academic association purchasing agent; b. Mooselake, Minn., May 27, 1947; d. Alfred Herman and Frances Beatrice (Beckman) Pofahl; m. Lloyd James Miller, Sept. 15, 1968; 1 child, Elizabeth Hope. Student, U. Colo., 1965-67. Teller First Nat. Bank Denver, 1967-68, Boulder (Colo.) Nat. Bank, 1968-69; purchasing agt. U. Colo., Boulder, 1969—. Mem. Nat. Assn. Purchasing Mgmt., Nat. Assn. Ednl. Buyers (profl. devel. com.). Republican. Lodge: Rebakahs. Home: 11682 Hillcrest Rd Golden CO 80403

MILLER, CHRISTINA JOYCE, foundation administrator; b. Hollywood, Calif., Jan. 22, 1952; d. Richard Francis and Harriet Joyce (Puffer) M. BE, U. Fla., 1976. Cert. elem. tchr., Fla. Owner, dir. Montessori Sch., Gainesville, Fla., 1977-79, millhopper, 1979—; owner, developer Dynamic Didactic Developware, Gainesville, 1985—; founder, ednl. dir. Children's Resource Ctr., Gainesville, 1988—. Benefactor Gainesville Civic Ballet; U.S. rep. London Montessori Tchr. Tng., 1987; pres. Children's Theater for the Deaf, Gainesville, 1987—. Mem. Gainesville C. of C., Apple Developer. Office: Montessori Sch 4840 NW 23d Ave Gainesville FL 32606

MILLER, CHRISTINE MARIE, communications executive, consultant; b. Williamsport, Pa., Dec. 7, 1950; d. Frederick James and Mary Elizabeth (Wurster) M.; m. Robert M. Ancell Jr., Mar 30, 1985. BA in Speech and Drama, U. Kans., 1972; MA in Radio and TV, Northwestern U., 1978, PhD in Radio, TV and Film, 1982. With pub. relations dept. Bedford (Pa.) County Commissioners, 1972-73; grad. asst. Northwestern U., Evanston, Ill., 1977-80; asst. prof. broadcasting U. Ala., Tuscaloosa, 1980-82; asst. prof. communications Loyola U., New Orleans, 1982-85; vis. prof. journalism Ind. U., Bloomington, 1985-86; cons. in communication info. Nat. Inst. Fitness and Sport, Indpls., 1986-88; dir. nat. prog. Nat. Entrepreneurship Acads., Bloomington, Ind., 1986—. Contbr. articles to profl. jours. Pres. Coll. Park Assn., Indpls., 1987, Vet. Day Assn., Indpls., 1987. Served with USN 1973-77, USNR, 1977—. Named Outstanding Woman Am., 1984, 87. Mem. Entrepeneurial Alliance (bd. dirs. 1986), Navy League (sec. 1985), Popular Culture Assn., Internat. Communications Assn., Naval Reserve Assn, Nat. Assn. Female Execs. Presbyterian. Club: Press of Indpls. Home: 9021 Clemson St N Indianapolis IN 46268 Office: Subaru-Isuzu Automotive Inc 3701 State Rd 26 East PO Box 5689 Lafayette IN 47903

MILLER, DAPHNE ELAINE, business executive; b. Wallington, Surrey, Eng., Oct. 6, 1943; d. Reginald Arthur and Leila Beatty (Cherry) Wills; m. Alan Oliver Roberts, Oct. 6, 1962 (div. Feb. 1973); children: Diane E., Paul A.; m. Peter Hugh Miller, Apr. 30, 1973; 1 child, Stuart A. Educated pub. schs., Eng., 1959, 79, 80. Jr. clk. Philips Elec. Industries, Wallington, 1960-62; typist Park Webb Foundries, Wigan, Eng., 1970-73; sec. Allied Breweries Ltd., Haydock, Eng., 1978-80; sr. sec. Barclays Bank Pub. Ltd. Co., Manchester, Eng., 1980-84; coordinator membership com. Escondido (Calif.) Bd. Realtors, 1984-86; office mgr. Vista (Calif.) Hill Nursery, 1986-87, fin. controller, 1987-88; pres. Miller Systems, Vista, 1988—; Bd. dirs. Peter H. Miller & Son, Vista. Mem. Am. Soc. Profl. Exec. Women, Bus. Women's Inst., Nat. Assn. for Female Execs. Republican. Methodist. Office: Miller Systems 1021 Torole Circle Vista CA 92084

MILLER, DARLENE, microbiologist; b. Boston, Aug. 28, 1951; d. Fred Lee and Carrie Lee (Jones) M.; 1 child, Crispin Stanley. B.S. in Med. Tech., U. Miami, 1978; M.A. in Microbiology, U. Miami, 1984. Med. technologist clin. microbiology South Miami Hosp., Fla., 1977-80, Mercy Hosp., Miami, 1981-83; supr. microbiology Bascom Palmer Eye Inst., Anne Bates Leach Eye Hosp., U. Miami, 1983—, cons., 1983—. Contbr. articles to profl. jours. Mem. Am. Soc. Microbiology, Am. Soc. Clin. Pathologists, Fla. Soc. Med. Technologists, Woodson Williams Marshall Assn., Nat. Council Negro Women, Nat. Assn. Female Execs., Assn. Research in Vision and Ophthalmology. Avocations: cycling, bowling, chess, reading, music. Home: 14780 Monroe St Miami FL 33176 Office: AR Abrams Ophthalmic Microbiology Lab Bascom Palmer Ey e Inst Anne Bates Leach Eye Hosp U Miami Dept Ophthalmology 900 NW 1 Miami FL 33176

MILLER, DEANE GUYNES, styling salon exec.; b. El Paso, Tex., Jan. 12, 1927; d. James Tillman and Margaret (Brady) Guynes; degree in bus. adminstrn. U. Tex., El Paso, 1947; m. Richard George Miller, Apr. 12, 1947; children—J. Michael, Marcia Deane. Owner four Merle Norman Cosmetic Studios, El Paso, 1967—; pres. The Velvet Door, Inc., El Paso, 1967—; dir. Mountain Bell Telephone Co. Pres. bd. dirs. YWCA, 1967; v.p. Sun Bowl Assn., 1970; bd. dirs. El Paso Symphony Assn.; bd. dirs., treas. El Paso Mus. Art; chmn. bd. El Paso Internat. Airport; bd. dirs., sec. Armed Services YMCA, 1987. Named Outstanding Woman field of civic endeavor, El Paso Herald Post. Mem. Women's C. of C. (pres. 1969, now dir.), Pan Am. Round Table (dir., pres. 1987). Home: 1 Silent Crest St El Paso TX 79902 Office: 122 Thunderbird St El Paso TX 79912

MILLER, DEBORAH LEE, laboratory manager; b. Teaneck, N.J., Sept. 1, 1953; d. Henry Thomas and Dorothy Grace (Davison) Miller. B.S. in Med. Tech., Caldwell Coll., 1975; diploma in Med. Tech. Mountainside Hosp., Montclair, N.J., 1975; M.S. in Med. Tech. and Lab. Adminstrn., St. John's U., Jamaica, N.Y., 1984. Med. technologist Bergen Pines County Hosp., Paramus, N.J., 1975; med. technologist Holy Name Hosp., Teaneck, N.J., 1975-82, mgr. out-patient lab. services, 1982-83, supr. immunochemistry, 1983; dir. mktg. Clin Path Inc., Hackensack, N.J., 1983-85; lab. mgr. St. Francis Hosp., Jersey City, 1985—. Mem. Am. Soc. Clin. Pathologists, Am. Soc. Med. Tech., N.J. Soc. Med. Tech., Md. Geneal. Soc., Md. Hist. Soc. Roman Catholic. Home: 52 Phelps Ave Bergenfield NJ 07621 Office: 25 McWilliams Pl Jersey City NJ 07302

MILLER, DEBRA ANN, nurse; b. New Castle, Pa., July 6, 1954; d. James Wilber and Ruth Marie (Miles) Chill; m. James Edward Miller, Sept. 2, 1978; children: Aaron James, Travis Adam. BS in Nursing, Slippery Rock U., 1982. With Ellwood City (Pa.) Hosp., 1975—, nursing quality assurance coordinator, 1985—. Mem. Nat. Assn. Female Execs., Slippery Rock U. Alumni, Am. Nurses Assn. Democrat. Home: 3507 Nearwood Dr New Castle PA 16101 Office: Ellwood City Hosp 724 Pershing St Ellwood City PA 16117

MILLER, DEBRA LEE, insurance agency executive; b. Tulsa, Nov. 4, 1955; d. Raymond L. and Vivian Lee Moreland; m. Greg Miller, June 5, 1982 (div. Apr. 1985); 1 child, Tishey Lee. B.S., Okla. State U., 1977. Adminstrv. asst. United Gen. Agy., Inc., Tulsa, 1977-79, exec. v.p., 1979-84, pres., 1984—; mem. ins. task force Nat. Grocers Assn., Washington, 1985; mem. leaders council Atlas Life Ins. Co. Cert. ins. counselor Soc. Cert. Ins. Counselors. Mem. Profl. Ins. Agts. of Okla., Ins. Women of Tulsa (fin. chmn. 1988—), Ind. Ins. Agts. of Tulsa, Tulsa C. of C., Okla. Retail Grocers Assn. Republican. Club: Tulsa Panhellenic Soc. Home: 10007 S Maplewood Pl Tulsa OK 74137 Office: United Gen Agy Inc 7146 S Braden Suite 100 Tulsa OK 74136

MILLER, DIANE DORIS, executive search consultant; b. Sacramento, Calif., Jan. 18, 1954; d. George Campbell and Doris Lucille (Benninger) M. B.A., U. Pacific, 1976; BA, Golden Gate U., 1985, MBA, 1987. Mgr., A.G. Spanos, Sacramento, 1977-81, Lee Sammis, Sacramento, 1981-83; v.p. Consolidated Capital, San Francisco, 1983-86; exec. McCracken, Wilcox & Bertoux, Sacramento, 1986—. Bd. dirs. Sacramento Symphony En Corps, 1982-84, Sacramento Ballet, 1983-84, 86—, Sacramento Symphony Assn., 1988—, Oakland Ballet, Calif., 1984-85. Named Vol. of Yr. Junior League, 1983. Mem. U. Pacific Alumni Assn. (bd. dirs. 1978-85). Republican. Avocations: ballet, water sports.

MILLER, DIANE DROPSEY, hospital administrator; b. Gary, Ind., Apr. 29, 1929; d. Lawrence Alton and Tirzah Catherine (Butler) Dorsey Dropsey; children—Michael, Phillip, William, David. R.N., Gary Meth. Hosp. Sch. Nursing, 1952. Staff nurse Gary Meth. Hosp., Ind., 1952-53, asst. head nurse, 1960, night supr., 1961-62; office nurse Dr. H.M. English, Gary, 1953-54; pvt. duty nursing, Gary, 1954-60; nursing services adminstr. Harrison County Hosp., Corydon, Ind., 1962-70, assoc. exec. dir., 1970—; cons. Accreditation Standards for Hosps., Ind. and Ky., 1978-85. Mem. adv. com. Ind. U. Sch. Nursing, 1981-83; mem. Fed. Relations Com., Ind., 1984; chairperson adminstrv. bd. Corydon Meth. Ch.; bd. dirs. Harrison County Hosp. Found., 1985—, vol. Hospice, 1988; mem. steering com. Village of Corydon, 1987-88, Main Street Corydon Inc., 1987-88. Mem. Am. Soc. Nursing Service Adminstrs. (membership com. 1981-82), Am. Nurses Assn., Bus. and Profl. Women's Assn. (v.p. 1976; Outstanding Woman of Yr. 1985), Nursing Adminstrn. Council, Meth. Hosp. Sch. Nursing Alumni (past pres.), Ind. Soc. Nursing Service Adminstrs. (past pres., bd. dirs. 1976-77, 79, 80, 81, 83), Ind. State Bd. Nursing (registration and edn. com.), Ind. State Nurses Assn. (commn. on practice 1983), Ind. Hosp. Assn.(council on manpower and edn., 1984—), Southeastern Ind. Soc. Hosp. Nursing Service Adminstrs. (past pres.). Democrat. Home: 425 Williar Ave Corydon IN 47112 Office: Harrison County Hosp 245 Atwood St Corydon IN 47112

MILLER, DORIS PARSONS, artist; b. Bangor, Pa., Aug. 6, 1927; d. Alfred H. and Evelyn May P.; student Baum Sch. Art, Allentown, Pa., 1955-58; pvt. studies in art; m. Lewis E. Miller, June 10, 1946; 1 son, Alex Lewis. Portrait artist, 1955-63; pvt. studio artist, Wyomissing, Pa., 1977—; works represented in pvt. and permanent collections in U.S.; one-woman shows include: Nat. Bank of Boyertown, Jacksonwald, Reading, Pa., 1981; group shows: Berks Art Alliance, 1978-80, Nat. Portrait Seminar, N.Y.C., 1979, Catherine Lorillard Wolfe Art Club, N.Y.C., 1980. Sec. women's com. Reading Symphony Orch., 1972-77. Mem. Berks Art Alliance, Berks Art Council (1st prize 1980), Portrait Club Am., Catherine Lorillard Wolfe Art Club (asso.), DAR (Nat. award of excellence 1982), Daus. Am. Colonists (chpt. librarian 1982—). Episcopalian. Home: 19 Birchwood Rd Wyomissing PA 19610

MILLER, ELIZABETH GAMBLE, language educator, translator; b. Boston, May 31, 1926; d. Fred Ridley and Leona Aileen (Crain) Gamble; m. Frederick James Miller, Jr., July 15, 1949; children: Frederick James III, Janice Elaine Miller Jones, David Earl. BA, Tex. Christian U., 1946; MA, So. Meth. U., 1965; PhD, U. Tex., Dallas, 1981. Instr. So. Meth. U., Dallas, 1947-49, 62-72, asst. prof., 1972-84, assoc. prof. Spanish lang. and lit., 1984—. Translator Sólo La Voz, 1984, Fabulas, 1985, numerous poems, short stories, essays; mem. editorial bd. Translation Review; contbr. articles to profl. jours. Named Académica Correspondiente, El Salvador, 1985. Mem. Am. Lit. Translators Assn. (charter, editor newsletter 1983—, mem. editorial bd., sec.-treas. 1983-85), South Cen. Modern Langs. Assn. Mem. Christian Ch. Office: So Meth U Hillcrest at Daniel Dallas TX 75275

MILLER, ELVA RUBY CONNES (MRS. JOHN R. MILLER), civic worker; b. Joplin, Mo.; d. Edward and Ada (Martin) Connes; student Pomona Coll., part-time, 1936-56; m. John R. Miller, Jan. 17, 1934 (dec. Nov. 1968). Entertainer various night clubs, supper clubs, also Hollywood Bowl, 1967; TV appearances; rec. artist Capitol Records, 1966—, Amaret Records, 1969—; appeared in motion pictures. Active Girl Scouts U.S.A., 1933-58; hon. mem. Mayor's Com. for Sr. Citizens, Los Angeles, 1966; mem. Disabled Am. Vets., Comdrs. Club, Music Ctr. Los Angeles County. Recipient awards including Thanks badge Girl Scouts U.S.A., 1956, Key to City, Mayor San Diego, 1967, plaque Dept. of Def. for trip to Vietnam, 1967. Mem. Gen. Alumni Assn. U. So. Calif. (life). Republican. Presbyterian. Home: 9585 Reseda Blvd Northridge CA 91324

MILLER, ENID M., real estate sales professional; b. Joplin, Mo., Sept. 25, 1932; d. Virgil G. and Isabelle C. (Higdon) Pearson; m. Bobby A. Jones, Nov. 16, 1952, (div.); children: Larry B., Kimberly K. Jones-Booker; m. Robert E. Miller, Aug. 16, 1965 (div. Sept. 1985); 1 child, Zachary K. Student, Memphis State U., 1965-67. Office mgr. De Witt Real Estate, Hickman Mills, Mo., 1957-64; with sales dept. Bateman Realtors, Pontiac, Mo., 1972-75; real estate broker Max Broock, Inc., Birmingham, Mich., 1976—. Mem. Am. Bus. Women's Assn. (treas. local chpt. 1955), Mich. Metaphysical Soc. Avocations: metaphysical studies, teaching. Home: 593 Hanna Birmingham MI 48009 Office: Max Broock Inc 411 S Woodward #610 Birmingham MI 48011

MILLER, ERICA T(ILLINGHAST), aesthetician, skincare and cosmetics company executive, writer; b. Laramie, Wyo., Oct. 17, 1950; d. Walter McNab and Martha (Brown) M. Student Sophia U., Tokyo, 1969-72, U. Md., Tokyo, 1969-72, Simultaneous Interpreting Acad. Tokyo, 1974; cert. Christian Shaw Sch. Beauty, London, 1973, Kanebo Total Beauty Acad., 1974; internat. diploma CIDESCO, 1977. Instr., Nakano Am. English Ctr., Tokyo, 1969-72; instr., researcher Kanebo Cosmetics Inc., Tokyo, 1973-76, internat. cons., 1976—; dir. edn. Aestheticians Internat., Dallas, 1976-79; pres. Correlations Inc., Dallas, 1979—; cons. Nieman Marcus Greenhouse, Arlington, Tex., 1981—. Assoc. pub., editor Aesthetics World Mag., 1980-85. Contbr. articles to various publs.; translator tech. film. Mem. Aestheticians Internat. (dir. edn. 1976-79), Am. Inst. Esthetics (lectr.), Nat. Hairdressers and Cosmetology Assn. (dir. skin care sect. aesthetics com.), Dallas C. of C., North Dallas C. of C. Republican. Episcopalian. Avocations: tennis; English riding; swimming; care and training of animals. Office: Correlations Inc 4803 W Lovers Ln Dallas TX 75209

MILLER, FRANCES HALL, lawyer, educator; b. Boston, Dec. 25, 1938; d. Addison Smith and Frances Winston (Ivey) Hall; m. Hugh Miller, June 3, 1961; children—Hugh III, Christopher Graham. A.B., Mt. Holyoke Coll., 1960; J.D. cum laude, Boston U., 1965; postgrad. London Sch. Econs. (Eng.), 1965-66. Bar: Mass. Prof. law Boston U., 1968—, prof. Med. Sch. 1983—; assoc. Powers & Hall, Boston, 1973-76; of counsel Widett, Slater and Goldman, Boston, 1976—; commr. Mass. Rate Setting Commn., 1974; mem. ethical-legal bd. Urban Med. Group, Inc., Boston, 1983-85; mem. adv. bd. Adolescent Consultation Service, Inc., Cambridge, 1980—; chmn. Mass. Health Facilities Appeals Bd., 1986—. Contbr. articles to profl. jours. Trustee Mt. Holyoke Coll., South Hadley, Mass., 1976-81; mem. human rights rev. com. Judge Baker Clinic of Children's Hosp., Boston, 1976—; bd. dirs. New Eng. Legal Found., Boston, 1982—. W.K. Kellogg Found. fellow, Battle Creek, Mich., 1983-86. Mem. ABA (spl. com. on profl. med. liability reform). Club: Longwood Cricket (sec. 1981, gov. 1980-83). Office: Boston U Sch of Law 765 Commonwealth Ave Boston MA 02215

MILLER, GAYNOR ANN, physical therapist; b. Belfast, Maine, Nov. 16, 1948; d. Stanley Malcolm and Mildred Arlene (Perkins) Whitney; m.Lauren Andrew Hebert; children: Jason, Jamie Lynn. BS in Physical Therapy, U. Conn., 1971. Chief therapist Aroostook Convalescent Ctr., Presque Isle, Maine, 1972-73, A.R. Gould Meml. Hosp., Presque Isle, 1973-76, Androscoggin Home Health Agy., Auburn, Maine, 1976-78; staff therapist Kennebec Valley Med. Ctr., Augusta, Maine, 1980-83; pres., owner Orthopedic Physical Therapy Ctr., Augusta, 1983—. Author Taking Care of Your Back, 1984. Mem. adv. bd. YMCA, Augusta, 1987—; bd. dirs. Back to Work Ctr., Augusta, 1987—. Mem. Am. Physical Therapy Assn. (chair dist. 1985—, chair membership 1984-86), Pvt. Practice Specialty Group. Lodge: Eastern Star. Office: Orthopedic Physical Therapy Ctr 12 Spruce St Augusta ME 04330 also: The Back to Work Ctr 5 Wabon St Augusta ME 04330

MILLER, GENEVIEVE, medical historian; b. Butler, Pa., Oct. 15, 1914; d. Charles Russell and Genevieve (Wolford) M. A.B., Goucher Coll., 1935; M.A., Johns Hopkins U., 1939; Ph.D., Cornell U., 1955. Asst. in history of medicine Johns Hopkins Inst. of History of Medicine, Balt., 1943-44, instr., 1945-48, research assoc., 1979—; asst. prof. history of medicine Sch. Medicine, Case Western Res. U., Cleve., 1953-67, assoc. prof., 1967-79, assoc. prof. emeritus, 1979—; research assoc. in med. history Cleve. Med. Library Assn., 1953-62, curator Howard Dittrick Mus. of Hist. Medicine, 1962-67, dir. Howard Dittrick Mus. Hist. Medicine, 1967-79. Author: William Beaumont's Formative Years: Two Early Notebooks 1811-1821, 1946; The Adoption of Inoculation for Smallpox in England and France (William H. Welch medal Am. Assn. for History of Medicine 1962), 1957; Bibliography of the History of Medicine of the U.S. and Canada, 1939-1960, 1964; Bibliography of the Writings of Henry E. Sigerist, 1966; Letters of Edward Jenner and Other Documents Concerning the Early History of Vaccination, 1983; assoc. editor Bull. of History of Medicine, 1944-48, acting editor, 1948, mem. adv. editorial bd. 1960—; mem. bd. editors Jour. of History of Medicine and Allied Scis., 1948-65; editor Bull. of Cleve. Med. Library, 1954-72; editor newsletter Am. Assn. for History of Medicine, 1986—; contbr. articles in field to profl. jours. Am. Council Learned Socs. fellow, 1948-50; Dean Van Meter fellow, 1953-54. Alumna trustee Goucher Coll., Balt., 1966-69. Hon. fellow Cleve. Med. Library Assn.; mem. Am. Assn. for History of Medicine (pres. 1978-80, mem. council 1960-63), Am. Hist. Assn., Internat. Soc. for History of Medicine, Soc. Archtl. Historians, Phi Beta Kappa; corr. mem. fgn. socs. for history of medicine. Democrat. Club: Johns Hopkins (Balt). Home and Office: Judson Manor 1890 E 107 St Apt 816 Cleveland OH 44106

MILLER, GENEVIEVE RUTH, broadcasting, cable, marketing professional; b. Watertown, N.Y., May 9, 1945; d. Clifford Arthur and Genevieve (Farmer) Damon; m. Edward Robert Miller, Nov. 23, 1963; children: Edward R., Kimberly L. Student, Jefferson Community Coll., 1981-82, 85. Sec. Jefferson County Health Assn., Watertown, 1963-64; sec., receptionist Dr. Burton Silver, Watertown, 1965-66; sec. Gen. Electric Cablevision (now United Artists Cablesystems of Watertown), Watertown, 1967-68, chief clerk, 1972-81, office mgr., mktg. supr., personnel adminstr., 1981—. Mem. Nat. Assn. Female Execs., Watertown C. of C. Roman Catholic. Lodge: KC. Office: United Artists Cablesystems of Watertown 340 Eastern Blvd Watertown NY 13601

MILLER, GERALDINE, clinical psychologist; b. Jersey City, Nov. 30, 1946; d. Gerard and Nora Miller; m. Walter Greenberg, Apr. 1984. B.A., magna cum laude, CCNY, 1971; M.Ph., CUNY, 1979, Ph.D., 1980. Clin. intern Columbia Presbyn. Med. Center, N.Y. State Psychiat. Inst., N.Y.C., 1974-75; staff psychologist Albert Einstein Med. Coll. Substance Abuse Service, Bronx, 1978-79; assoc. psychologist Pilgrim Psychiat. Center, West Brentwood, L.I., 1980—, treatment team leader, 1984—. Sec., patient relations com. Presbyn. Hosp. Community Health Council, 1979-82. Recipient numerous awards CCNY, Employee Recognition award Pilgrim Psychiat. Center, 1981, 84, 87, Lic. psychologist, N.Y. Mem. Am. Psychol. Assn. (membership chmn. clin. psychology sect. 1982-86), Eastern Psychol. Assn.,

N.Y. State Psychol. Assn. (Ph.D. dissertation award 1982), N.Y. Soc. Clin. Psychologists. Suffolk County Psychol. Assn., Phi Beta Kappa.

MILLER, HARRIET SANDERS, art center director; b. N.Y.C., Apr. 18, 1926; d. Herman and Dorothy (Silbert) S.; m. Milton H. Miller, June 27, 1948; children—Bruce, Jeffrey, Marcie. B.A., Ind. U., 1947; M.A., Columbia U., 1949; M.S., U. Wis., 1962, M.F.A., 1967. Dir. art sch. Madison Art Ctr., Wis., 1963-72; acting dir. Center for Continuing Edn., Vancouver, B.C., 1975-76; mem. fine arts faculty Douglas Coll., Vancouver, 1972-78; exec. dir. Palos Verdes Arts Center, Calif., 1978-84; dir. Junior Arts Center, Los Angeles, 1984—; one woman exhibits at Gallery 7, Vancouver, 1978, Gallery 1, Toronto, Ont., 1977, Linda Farris Gallery, Seattle, 1975, Galerie Allen, Vancouver, 1973. Mem. Calif. Art Edn. Assn., Calif. Confedn. of Arts, Museum Educators of So. Calif., Arts and Humanities Symposium. Office: Junior Arts Ctr 4814 Hollywood Blvd Los Angeles CA 90027

MILLER, HELEN MARIE DILLEN (MRS. J. CARTER MILLER), bus. exec.; b. Sedalia, Mo.; d. John Barney and Lulu (Blume) Dillen; student Central Coll., 1936-37; m. J. Carter Miller, Dec. 3, 1941; 1 son, J. Carter. Sec.-treas. Midwest Supply Co., Lansing, Ill., 1946—, Midwest Supply Co. of Can., 1946—; sec.-treas. Carter Controls, Inc., Lansing, also Livonia, Mich., 1952—, v.p., 1956—; v.p. Carter Controls Internat., Windsor, Can., Antwerp, Belgium, 1960—; sec.-treas. Carter Controls U.K. Ltd., Sheffield, Eng., Carter Controls, GmbH, Busingen, Germany, Carter Controls., A.G., Schaffhausen, Switzerland. Social worker ARC, Hammond, Ind., 1942-44. Mem. Principia Patrons No. Ind. (pres. 1963-65), Chgo. Symphony, Sarah Siddons Soc., Chgo. Art Inst. Christian Scientist. Clubs: Principia Mothers (dir. Chgo. 1962-64); Fortnightly, Woman's Athletic (Chgo.); Woodmar Country (Hammond); Everglades (Palm Beach, Fla.). Home: 1731 Wilson Ave Munster IN 46321 also: Ibis Isle Rd Palm Beach FL Office: 2800 Bernice Rd Lansing IL 60438

MILLER, JACQUELINE K. THOMSON, educational consultant; b. Flora, Inc., March 5, 1940; d. Jack O. and Betty L. (Tolen) T.; children: Elizabeth Ann Miller-Frederick, Victoria Lynne . AS, Mankato State U., 1978; BA, Metro State U., St. Paul, 1980; MA, St. Mary's Coll., 1982. Instr. adult edn. Iowa Community Colls. and YMCA, 1970-75; dir. aquatics Faribault Family YMCA and Faribault Community Services, Minn., 1975-78; tech. sales/tng. rep. Ames div. Miles Labs., Mpls., 1978-80; med. lab. instr. Normandale Community Coll., Boomington, Minn., 1978-80; staff edn. coordinator St. Joseph's Hosp., Marshfield, Wis., 1981-84; dir. ednl. services Fairview Ridges Hosp., Burnsville, Minn., 1984-85; owner, prin. J. Miller Assocs., Burnsville, 1979—; presenter various profl. confs. including Nat. Whim Humor Confs., 1986-88. Developer wellness program Life Styling, 1979, mobile fitness test ctr. Health on Wheels, 1982; author-dir. video programs Body Mechanics, 1982. Chmn. Girl Scouts, Kokomo, Ind., 1964-69; vol. swim instr. ARC, Corning, Iowa, 1970-75, Faribault, Minn., 1975-78. Recipient Traveling Art awards Ia. State Lending Library, Des Moines, Iowa, 1973-74; artist in residence Corning Community Schs., Iowa, 1972. Mem. Mpls. C. of C., Burnsville C. of C., Am. Soc. Tng. and Devel. (bd. dirs. Central Wis. 1982-83, mem. career devel. task force So. Minn. 1986, mem. program com. 1985-86, chair conf. com. 1987), Nat. Wellness Assn. (nat. membership chmn. 1983-85), Am. Soc. Health Edn. and Tng., Am. Soc. Med. Technologists, Am. Soc. Clin. Pathologists, Nat. Assn. Female Execs., Delta Kappa Gamma. Episcopalian. Avocations: art; swimming; gardening; sailing. Home: 12309 Oak Leaf Ct Burnsville MN 55337 Office: J Miller Assocs Box 1377 Burnsville MN 55337

MILLER, JACQUELINE ROSE, public speaker, consultant; b. Columbus, Ohio, Aug. 28, 1946; d. Edison Charles and Juanita Rose (Wiley) Heyder; divorced; children: P.J., Brande; m. Dale Lee Miller, June 15, 1985; stepchildren: Stephanie, Eric. Student, Ariz. State U., 1964-65, Phoenix Coll., 1965-68. Acctg. clk. Occidental Oil Shale, Grand Junction, Colo., 1976-77; with purchasing dept., buyer Barru Homes, 1977-78; dir. pub. relations Ridges Devel. Corp., 1978-79, asst. project mgr., 1981-82; owner Heyder and Assocs., Grand Junction and Denver, 1981—; sales exec. Western Slope Telephone, Grand Junction, 1982-83; cons. media Sta. KREX, 1983, Mesa Broadcasting, 1983-84; co-owner TriStar Cons., Englewood, Colo., 1986—. Author: The Lopsided Gal, 1987. Vol. trainer Denver Chamber and Tech. Assistance Corp., 1986-87; bd. dirs. The Enablers, Denver; chairperson women's golf tournament Heart Assn., 1986; trainer, cons. Va. Neal Blue Ctrs., Denver, 1986—. Mem. Denver Businesswomen's Network, Denver C. of C. (cons. 1987). Republican. Clubs: Penrose (bd. dirs. 1986—) (Denver); Sporting (Englewood). Home: 6145 S Flamingo Ct Littleton CO 80121 Office: TriStar Cons 8101 E Prentice Ave Suite M-250 Englewood CO 80111

MILLER, JACQUELINE WINSLOW, library director; b. N.Y.C., Apr. 15, 1935; d. Lynward Roosevelt and Sarah Ellen (Grevious) W.; 1 child, Percy Scott. B.A., Morgan State Coll., 1957; M.L.S., Pratt Inst., 1960; grad. profl. seminar, U. Md., 1973. Cert. profl. librarian. With Bklyn. Pub. Library, 1957-68, young teen specialist, 1960-63, br. librarian, 1963-64, dir. young teen services, 1964-68; head extension services New Rochelle (N.Y.) Pub. Library, 1969-70; dir. Yonkers Pub. Library, 1975—. Mem. commr.'s Com. Statewide Library Devel., Albany, N.Y., 1980; resource person Task Force on Fed. Depository Library Service in N.Y., Albany, 1982; bd. dirs. Community Planning Council, Yonkers, N.Y., 1987; mem. Yonkers Black Women's Polit. Caucus, 1987. Recipient Yonkers Citizen award Ch. of Our Saviour, 1980, Community Service award Women's Civic Club of Nepperhan Inc., 1982; named Outstanding Profl. Woman Nat. Assn. Negro Bus. and Profl. Women's Clubs Inc., 1981. Mem. ALA (councilor 1987—), N.Y. Library Assn., Pub. Library Dirs. Assn. (exec. bd.), N.Y. State Pub. Library Dirs. Assn., Westchester Library Assn., Coalition for Pub. Library Legis., N.Y. Library Club (council mem. 1979-82), Community Planning Council, Yonkers C. of C. Office: 7 Main St Yonkers NY 10701

MILLER, JANEL HOWELL, psychologist; b. Boone, N.C., May 18, 1947; d. John Estle and Grace Louise (Hemberger) Howell; B.A., DePauw U., 1969; postgrad. Rice U., 1969; M.A., U. Houston, 1972; Ph.D., Tex. A&M U., 1979; m. C. Rick Miller, Nov. 24, 1968; children—Kimberly, Brian, Audrey, Rachel. Asso. sch. psychologist Houston Ind. Sch. Dist., 1971-74; research psychologist VA Hosp., Houston, 1972; asso. sch. psychologist Clear Creek Ind. Sch. Dist., Tex., 1974-76; instr. psychology, counseling psychology intern Tex. A. and M. U., 1976-77; clin. psychology intern VA Hosp., Houston, 1977-78; coordinator psychol. services Clear Creek Ind. Sch. Dist., 1978-81, assoc. dir. psychol. services, 1981-82; pvt. practice, Houston, 1982—; faculty U. Houston-Clear Lake, 1984—; adolescent suicide cons., 1984—. DePauw U. Alumni scholar, 1965-69; NIMH fellow U. Houston, 1970-71; lic. clin. psychologist, sch. psychologist; lic. profl. counselor, Tex. Mem. Am. Psychol. Assn., Tex. Psychol. Assn., Houston Psychol. Assn. (media rep. 1984-85), Southeastern Psychol. Assn., Am. Assn. Marriage and Family Therapists, Tex. Assn. Marriage and Family Therapists, Houston Assn. Marriage and Family Therapists. Home: 806 Walbrook Dr Houston TX 77062 Office: Southpoint Psychol Services 11550 Fugua St Suite 450 Houston TX 77034

MILLER, JANICE, interior designer; b. Jacksonville, Fla., Oct. 5, 1925; d. Paul Jerome and Tola (Sherman) Walker; m. John Edwin Miller, June 7, 1949; children: Rebecca Ann M., Patricia Blair. BFA cum laude, Wesleyan Coll., Macon, Ga., 1947; MFA, Boston U., 1966. Pvt. art tchr. Weston, Mass., 1962-63; tchr. Brookline (Mass.) pub. schs., 1963-66; faculty mem. State Coll. Mass., Bridgeport, 1966-67; designer Ruth Batchelder, 1967-71; dir. Janice Miller Assocs., Brookline, 1971—, Art for Industry, 1972—. Mem. Am. Archives of Art New Eng., Am. Soc. Interior Designers, Boston U. Visual Arts Alumni Assn., Boston C. of C. (mem. exec. club), Brookline Arts Ctr., Friends of Boston Art, Boston Ctr. for Charity, Nat. Art Dealers Assn., Internat. Furnishing & Design Assn. (pres. 1980, nat. dir. 1982-83), New Eng. Sculptures Assn., New Eng. Women's Bus. Owners, Mus. Fine Arts. Episcopalian. Home: 19 Winchester St #907 PO Box 38 Westport Point MA 02791

MILLER, JANIS DIANE, marketing professional; b. Chgo., Oct. 6, 1946; d. James Ellis and Marjorie Marion (Sykes) Turner; m. Rock Miller, Apr. 15, 1967; children: Shari, Diane. Student, IIT, 1963-64, U. Ill., 1964-66; BSBA, Thomas A. EdisonState Coll., 1983. Cert. data processing, 1975. Acct. exec. SCM Corp., Hillside, N.J., 1967-68; sr. tech. cons. Standard Security Life, N.Y.C., 1968-76, [illegible] mgr. AT&T, Morristown, N.J., 1979-82, sales channel planner, 1983-84; product mktg. AT&T S.W., Morristown, N.J., 1985-86, product mgr., 1987—; chmn. Bus. Adminstrn. Degree Program, Trenton, N.J., 1984-86; bd. dirs. Thomas Edison Acad. Council, Trenton; mem. council Inst. Cert. Computer Profls., Chgo., 1976-81; citizen ambassador China for U.S., 1988. Author: (with others) Financial Analysis of Life Insurance Industry, 1982, Life Insurance Market Plan, 1982, Certificate in Data Processing Study Guide, 1982. Fundraiser Decade of Woman, 1985; mem. Nat. Congress Black Women, Washington, 1986—. Recipient Bus. Woman of Yr. award Boston Coll., 1978, Fast Trackers award Datamation, 1979, Role Model award Ebony Mag., 1979. Fellow Life Mgmt. Inst.; mem. Internat. Platform Assn., Am. Soc. Profl. and Exec. Women. Club: SOMAC. Home: 358 Beech Spring Rd South Orange NJ 07079 Office: AT&T 1776 On The Green Morristown NJ 07960

MILLER, (KATHRYN) JEAN, township zoning inspector; b. Canton, Ohio, Mar. 7, 1944; m. Richard W. Miller, June 29, 1963; children: Michelle, Tiffany, Stephanie. Grad. high sch., Uniontown, Ohio. Bookkeeper Hartville, Ohio, 1979-80; real estate agt. Century 21, Uniontown, 1979-83; with acctg. dept. Stark County Engrs., Canton, 1983-86; zoning inspector Lake Twp., Hartville, 1986—; clk., sec. Zoning Bd. Appeals, Hartville, 1986—, Zoning Commn., 1986—. Active Canton Bapt. Temple. Mem. Am. Planners Assn., Ohio Planners Assn. Home: 10154 Carlswood Ave Hartville OH 44632

MILLER, JEAN ANN, computer operations supervisor; b. York, Pa., Sept. 12, 1951; d. Dale Vernon and Betty Jane (Kimmons) M. BA in Math., Lebanon Valley Coll., 1973. Advt. mgr. K-Mart Store 4313, York, 1973-78; computer operator Borg-Warner Air Conditioning, York, 1978-82, software analyst, 1982-85; computer operations supr. York Internat. Corp., York, 1985—; pvt. tutor in math and computers, Red Lion, Pa., 1976—. Chmn. advt. bd. Shenberger's Chapel Ch., 1986—. Mem. Nat. Assn. Female Execs., Mensa. Democrat. United Methodist. Home: RD 1 Box 358-3 Red Lion PA 17356 Office: York Internat Corp PO Box 1592 York PA 17405

MILLER, JEANNE-MARIE ANDERSON (MRS. NATHAN J.), educator, administrator; b. Washington, Feb. 18, 1937; d. William and Agnes Catherine (Johns) Anderson; B.A., Howard U., 1959, M.A., 1963, Ph.D., 1976; m. Nathan John Miller, Oct. 2, 1960. Instr. dept. English Howard U., Washington, 1963-76, asst. prof., 1976-79, assoc. prof., 1979—, also asst. dir. Inst. Arts and Humanities, 1973-75, asst. acad. planning office v.p. for Acad. Affairs, 1976—; cons. Am. Studies Assn., 1972-75, Silver Burdett Pub. Co., Nat. Endowment for Humanities, 1978—; adv. bd. D.C. Library for Arts, 1973—, John Oliver Killens Writers Guild, 1975—, Afro-Am. Theatre, Balt., 1975—. Mem. Washington Performing Arts Soc., 1971—, Friends of Sta. WETA-TV, 1971—, Mus. African Art, 1971—, Arena Stage Assos., 1972—, Washington Opera Guild, 1982—, Wolf Trap Assocs., 1982—, Ford Found. fellow, 1970-72; So. Fellowships Fund fellow, 1972-74; Howard U. research grantee, 1975-76; Am. Council Learned Socs. grantee, 1978-79; Nat. Endowment Humanities grantee, 1981-84. Mem. Nat. Council Tchrs. of English, Coll. English Assn., Am. Studies Assn., Am. Theatre Assn., AAUP, AAUW, D.C. LWV, Common Cause, ACLU, Am. Acad. Polit. and Social Sci., Coll. Lang. Assn., MLA, Am. Assn. Higher Edn., Nat. Assn. Women Deans, Adminstrs. and Counselors, Friends Kennedy Center for Performing Arts, Pi Lambda Theta. Democrat. Episcopalian. Editor, Black Theatre Bull., 1977—; Realism to Ritual: Form and Style in Black Theatre, 1983; asso. editor Theatre Jour., 1980-81; contbr. articles to profl. jours. Home: 1100 6th St SW Washington DC 20024

MILLER, JO ANN, small business owner, public relations executive; b. Buffalo, Mar. 1, 1953; d. Walter Joseph and Norrine Opal (Lang) M. Student in consumer bus., SUNY, Buffalo, 1974; student in fashion mktg., Fashion Inst. Tech., N.Y.C., 1975. Actress TV commls. and film Ford Talent Agy., N.Y.C., 1975-80; sales and mktg. mgr. Natures Organic Plus, N.Y. and New England, 1980-82, Vidal Sassoon, New England, 1982-83; mktg. mgr. Colony Swimwear, N.Y.C., 1983; sales and mktg. mgr. J.I. Sopher and Co., N.Y.C., 1983; press coordinator The White House, Washington and N.Y.C., 1983-84; owner J.A. Miller & Assocs., Beverly Hills, Calif., 1984—; cover girl Albion Cosmetics, Tokyo, 1977; spokesperson Tourist Council of Mex., 1978, Jamaican Tourist Council, 1978; cons. in field. Hon. chair Multiple Sclerosis Soc., N.Y., 1973; exec. dir. Los Angeles Variety Club, 1985-86; pub. relations com. Beverly Hills Presbyn. Ch., 1985—. Named Miss Dance Am., 1972, Miss New York State (Miss America contestant), 1973. Mem. Nat. Assn. for Female Execs. Office: 342 N Rodeo Dr Beverly Hills CA 90210

MILLER, JO CAROLYN, family and marriage counselor, educator; b. Gorman, Tex., Sept. 16, 1942; d. Leonard Lee and Vera Vertie (Robison) Dendy; m. Douglas Terry Barnes, June 1, 1963 (div. June 1975); children—Douglas Alan, Bradley Jason; m. Walton Sansom Miller, Sept. 19, 1982. B.A., Tarleton State U., 1964; M.Ed., N. Tex. State U., 1977. Tchr., Mineral Wells (Tex.) High Sch., 1964-65, Weatherford (Tex.) Middle Sch., 1969-74; counselor, instr. psychology Tarrant County Jr. Coll., Hurst, Tex., 1977-82; pvt. practice family and marriage counseling, Dallas, 1982—. Author: (with Velma Walker, Jeannene Ward) Becoming: A Human Relations Workbook, 1981. Mem. womens' com. Dallas Ballet; vol. Am. Heart Assn. in Tex., Dallas chpt., 1983-84. Mem. Tex. State Bd. Examiners Profl. Counselors, Tex. Assn. Counseling and Devel., Am. Assn. Counseling and Devel., Am. Mental Health Counselors Assn., North Central Tex. Assn. for Counseling and Devel., Tex. Mental Health Counselors Assn. Methodist. Clubs: Highland Park Sports, So. Meth. U. Mothers (Dallas). Home: 3556 Binkley Ave Dallas TX 75205

MILLER, JOYCE LAVERTY, marketing writer; b. Coral Gables, Fla., Sept. 16, 1941; d. Clevis Owen and Marie Lucille (Gravelle) Laverty; m. Walter W. Miller Jr. (div. Nov. 1985); 1 child, Dorothy E. AB, Boston U., 1963; MA, Bryn Mawr Coll., 1965, PhD, 1970. Instr. Boston U., 1966-70; cons. Boston, 1970-72; research assoc. Harvard U., Cambridge, Mass., 1973-79; feature editor Concord (Mass.) Patriot, 1979-80; promotional writer GenRad Inc., Concord, 1980-85, mktg. communications mgr., 1985-86; lead mktg. specialist Cullinet Software Inc., Westford, Mass., 1986-87; sci. and mktg. writer BBN Labs. Inc., Cambridge, 1987—. Contbr. articles to profl. jours. Mem. adv. council Silver Bay (N.Y.) Assn. YMCA, 1975-85; mem. fin. com. Town of Concord, 1986-87; bd. dirs. Concord Family Services, 1983, Concord Mcpl. Light Plant, 1981-85, 87—. Scholar history Boston U., 1963-64; Fulbright fellow, 1966. Mem. Am. Hist. Assn., Phi Beta Kappa (bd. dirs. 1970-73), Phi Alpha Theta. Office: BBN Labs Inc 10 Moulton St Cambridge MA 02138

MILLER, JUNE FASESKY, retail department store public relations executive; b. Bethlehem, Pa., June 27, 1955; d. Walter Franklin and Frances Helene (Broczkowski) Fasesky. B.A. in Journalism, Lehigh U., 1977. Exec. trainee Bamberger's, Newark, 1977, employee communications asst. mgr., 1977-78; mdse. tng. coordinator Chas. A. Stevens, Chgo., 1978-80, fashion events coordinator, 1980, media/mktg. coordinator, 1980-81; employee communications supr. J. W. Robinson's, Los Angeles, 1981, mdse. promotions mgr., 1981-82, spl. programs mgr., 1982-84, sr. mgr. spl. events, 1984-86; div. v.p. pub. relations and spl. events The Broadway, Los Angeles, 1986-87, div. v.p. mktg. promotions, 1987—. Mem. Jr. League Los Angeles. Mem. Fashion Group (program com. Los Angeles chpt.), Lehigh U. Alumni Club (pres.). Home: 1014 Arroyo Dr #1 South Pasadena CA 91030 Office: The Broadway 3880 N Mission Rd Los Angeles CA 90031

MILLER, KAREN JEAN, occupational therapist, activity therapy administrator; b. Massillon, Ohio, Jan. 6, 1951; d. Clyde Albert and Jean Evelyn (Baker) M. B of Music Edn., Capital U., 1973; B of Music Therapy, Mich. State U., 1974; M of Occupational Therapy, Western Mich. U., 1979. Youth counselor, supr. ops. Roush Treatment and Rehab. Ctr., Lima, Ohio, 1975-79; occupational therapist Riverside Hosp., Toledo, 1979-80, St. Charles Hosp., Toledo, 1980-82; dir. dept occupational therapy Kings Daughter's Hosp., Ashland, Ky., 1982-85; supr. dept. occupational therapy Cen. State Hosp., Louisville, 1985-87; cons. KMI Med. Ctr. (name now Ten Broeck), Louisville, 1986-87, dir. therapeutic activities, 1987—; cons. Jefferson Hosp., Jeffersonville, Ind., 1986—, Louisville Luth. Home, 1987—. Author: Treatment with Music, 1979. Mem. Am. Occupational Therapy Assn., Ky. Occupational Therapy Assn. (sec. 1986—), Nat. Assn. for Music Therapy, [illegible] Female Execs., Nat. Assn. Activity Therapy and Rehab. Programs. Home: 10709 Colonial [illegible] KY 40223 Office: Ten Broeck 8521 LaGrange Rd Louisville KY 40242

MILLER, KIM ELIZABETH, educational services company executive; b. Bridgeport, Conn., July 7, 1956; d. Robert Joseph and Mary Barbara (Monahan) Loch; m. David R. Miller, Aug. 31, 1979 (div. Nov. 1988). Student, Trinity Coll., Burlingtn, Vt., 1974-75; BA in English, Regis Coll., 1978; MA in English, Goergetown U., 1984. Cert. secondary tchr., Conn. Tchr. Dept. Def. Dependent Schs., Okinawa, Japan, 1979-82; sales rep. Sta. KHFM, Albuquerque, 1982-84; asst. prof. English Strayer Coll., Washington, 1984-86; writer 1985 Armed Forces Inaugural Com., Washington, 1984-85, chief plans div. for 1989., 1986—; mgr. emergency mgmt. tng. program U.S. Army Corps of Engrs., Washington, 1985-86; pres., owner Essential Edn. Services, Annapolis, Md., 1986—; cons. Ketron, Inc., Carlisle, Pa., 1987—, Dewberry & Davis, Fairfax, Va., 1988—. Yearbook advisor Kubasaki High Sch., Okinawa, 1979-82; pres. Am.-Japanese Welcome Club, 1980-81; mem. South River Manor Civic Assn. Recipient Comdr.'s award Dept. Army, 1985, commendation, 1986. Mem. Am. Soc. for Tng. and Devel., Am. Def. Preparedness Assn., Nat. Assn. Female Execs., Soc. Am. Mil. Engrs. Republican. Office: Essential Edn Services 428 4th St Suite 4 Annapolis MD 21403

MILLER, LANORA ETOILE, real estate broker; b. Lubbock, Tex., Aug. 7, 1929; d. Robbie Roy and Wanda Lavelle (Smith) Graham; m. Harry Eugene Miller, Aug. 12, 1951; children: Robert Eugene, Thomas Allen, Gary Edward. B.A., Eastern N.Mex. U., 1950. Tchr. Coronado Elem. Sch., Hobbs, N.Mex., 1951-52, elem. sch., House, N.Mex., 1952-53; substitute tchr. Inst. Logopedics and Stanley Elem. Sch., Wichita, Kans., 1976-77; real estate agt. Carl Chuzy Co., Wichita, 1977-78; ptnr. Holleman, Price & Miller Realty, Nacogdoches, Tex., 1978—. Mem. Nacogdoches County Bd. Realtors (sec. 1983, pres. 1984, 87, bd. dirs. 1985—), Nat. Assn. Realtors, Tex. Assn. Realtors, Stephen F. Austin Univ. Women, Nacogdoches County C. of C. (Ambassadors Club), Nacogdoches County Crime Stoppers Bd. Republican. Mem. Ch. of Christ. Home: 1604 Victoria St Nacogdoches TX 75961 Office: Holleman Price & Miller Realty 920 University Dr Nacogdoches TX 75961

MILLER, LINDA CLOYD, engineering educator; b. Siloam Springs, Ark., Jan. 4, 1947; d. Ralph and Helen (Carter) Cloyd; m. John William Adams, May 30, 1970 (div. Mar. 1976); m. Steven Karl Miller, June 19, 1982. BSEE, U. Ark., 1970; postgrad., Memphis State U., 1972-73, U. Mo., Columbia, 1984—. Substa. loading engr. Memphis Light, Gas and Water Co., 1971-76; customer engr. Hewlett-Packard Corp., King of Prussia, Pa., 1976-78, logistics mgr., 1978-81; asst. prof. St. Louis Community Coll., 1983-85, chmn. dept. engring., 1985—; electronics instr. Memphis State Tech. Inst., 1974-76. Recipient Leadership award YWCA St. Louis, 1985. Mem. Am. Soc. Engring. Edn. (campus rep. 1984—, ETD sec. 1988—), Am. Vocat. Assn., Mo. Vocat. Assn., Soc. Women Engrs. (sr.), Mo. Trade and Tech. Assn. (pres. 1987—, Outstanding Tchr. 1987). Republican. Mem. Christian Church (Disciples of Christ). Office: St Louis Community Coll 3400 Pershall Rd Saint Louis MO 63135

MILLER, LINDA LAEL, writer; b. Spokane, Wash., June 10, 1949; d. Grady Eugene and Hazel Lorraine (Bleecker) Lael; m. Rick Martin Miller, Oct. 12, 1968 (div. July 1987); 1 child, Wendy Diane. Author: Fletcher's Woman, 1983, Desire and Destiny, 1983, Banner O'Brien, 1984, Willow, 1984, Snowflakes on the Sea, 1984, Part of the Bargain, 1985, State Secrets, 1985, Corbin's Fancy, 1985, Memory's Embrace, 1986, Lauralee, 1986, Ragged Rainbows, 1986, Wanton Angel, 1987, Moonfire, 1988. Recipient Most Sensual Historicals award Romantic Times mag., 1985. Mem. Romance Writers Am. Methodist. Office: c/o Pocket Books 1230 Ave of the Americas New York NY 10020

MILLER, LISA ANN, pharmaceutical company representative; b. Englewood, N.J., Mar. 23, 1959; d. Alfred and Janet (Pelton) M. BA in English, Douglass Coll., Rutgers U., 1981. Adminstrv. asst. Klemtner Advt. Inc., N.Y.C., 1982, asst. account exec., 1983, account exec., 1983-84; account exec. Botto, Roessner, Home & Messinger Inc., N.Y.C., 1984-85; account mgr. Baxter, Gurian & Mazzei Inc., Mountain View, Calif., 1985-86; pharm. rep. Hoffmann-La Roche, Nutley, N.J., 1986—. Mem. Med. Mktg. Assn., Nat. Assn. Female Execs., The Mus. Soc., Ariz. Pharm. Reps. Assn., Ariz. Bicycle Club, Ariz. Bicycling Assn., A.Y.H. Avocations: bicycling, hiking, volleyball, swimming, creative writing. Office: Hoffmann-LaRoche 240 Kingsland Rd Nutley NJ 07110

MILLER, LOIS ANN, health educator, nurse; b. Detroit, Sept. 10, 1953; d. Donald Joseph and Bernice (Zarek) Deneweth; m. Larry Duane Miller, Oct. 18, 1980; children: Lori Ann, Brett Donald. BS in Nursing cum laude, Nazareth (Mich.) Coll., 1975. Nurse. Inservice educator Fremont (Ohio) Hosp., 1975-76; sr. nursing instr., staff nurse Providence Hosp. Sch. Nursing, Sandusky, Ohio, 1976-79; inservice dir. to asst. dir. nursing to dir. edn. to educator Rockdale Hosp., Conyers, Ga., 1979—; aerobics instr. LZ Inc. Aerobics, Conyers, Ga., 1986—; basic cardiac life support instr./trainer Am Heart Assn.; diabetes educator-support group leader, CPR coordinator, Rockdale Hosp. Editor: Tennis Talk newsletter, 1986-87; contbr. article Tennis Talk; created seminar program Body Lean - Body Fat, 1986-87, Working up to a Work-Out, 1987; choreographed Kids Aerobics for middle sch., 1987. Mem. Ga. Soc. Hosp. Educators and Trainers, Nat. Dance Exercise Instrs. Tng. Assn. (cert.), Internat. Dance Exercise Assn (cert.), Diabetes Assn. Atlanta, Honey Creek Tennis Assn. (sec. 1986—). Roman Catholic. Office: Rockdale Hosp 1412 Milstead Ave Conyers GA 30207

MILLER, LOIS LEA, artist; b. Texarkana, Tex., Sept. 16, 1929; d. George Newton and Daisy Rena (Alford) Gage; m. Jack Curtis Miller, Sept. 1, 1950 (div. 1963); 1 child, Jackie Lee. B.F.A., U. Houston, 1977, M.A., 1983. Artist, NASA, Johnson Space Ctr., Houston, 1960—; judge art scholarship com. Houston Livestock Show and Rodeo, 1983—. Chmn. bd. dirs. Krishen Found. for Arts and Scis., 1981—. Mem. Am. Fedn. Govt. Employees (1st v.p. legis. coordinator, 1980—), Soc. for Tech. Communications, Am. Bus. Women's Assn., AAUW, U. Houston Alumni Assn. Democrat. Roman Catholic. Clubs: Toastmasters, Mensa. Home: 9702 Palmfield St Houston TX 77034 Office: NASA Johnson Space Ctr Mail Code JM2 Houston TX 77058

MILLER, LYNNE CATHY, parasitologist; b. Washington, Dec. 25, 1951; d. Albert and Lorraine Shirley (Snyder) M.; m. Gary Franklin Clark, July 25, 1982; 1 child, Nicole Beth. B.S. in Pharmacy, U. R.I., 1974; M.S. in Biol. Scis., U. Tex., El Paso, 1977; Ph.D. in Biology, N.Mex. State U., 1980. Registered pharmacist Meml. Gen. Hosp., Las Cruces, N.Mex., 1979; postdoctoral research asso. dept. entomology and plant pathology N.Mex. State U., Las Cruces, 1980-81; assoc. prof. biology and allied health Bloomsburg U. (Pa.), 1981—; Giardiasis cons., 1983—; parasitology and pub. health field worker, Mexico, El Paso, Tex. Sponsor, Creature-Feature program, 1981—. Recipient Disting. Faculty Teaching award Bloomsburg U., 1985; Bloomsburg U. faculty research grantee, 1981—; Commonwealth of Pa. grantee, 1981—. Mem. AAAS, Rocky Mountain Conf. Parasitologists, Entomol. Soc. Am., Helminthological Soc. Washington, Sigma Xi, Beta Beta Beta, Phi Kappa Phi. Contbr. sci. articles to profl. jours. Office: Biology and Allied Health Bloomsburg U Bloomsburg PA 17815

MILLER, MADELYN SUE, advertising executive; b. Chgo., Mar. 4, 1947; d. Seymour and Estelle (Klotwogg) Jensky; student NYU, 1966-67; B.A. in Journalism, U. Mich., 1968; m. Howard Brian Miller, May 26, 1968; children—Mallorie Ann, Gregory Scott. Copywriter, Young & Rubicam, Detroit, 1968-69, Yaffe Stone August, Huntington Woods, Mich., 1969-70, Dancer Fitzgerald Sample, N.Y.C., 1970-71, Neiman-Marcus, Dallas, 1975-76; sr. copywriter Tracy, Dallas, 1976-81; pres. Madelyn Miller, Inc., Dallas, 1982—. Adv. bd. Dallas Art Inst. Recipient Clio award, 1981; Matrix award Outstanding Dallas Woman in Advt., 1981; Effie award, 1980; Addy award (2), 1980; cert. of merit Dallas Soc. Visual Communications, 1979, Dallas Ad League, 1979; Bronze medal Dallas Soc. Visual Communications, also Bronze award, 1979; Bravo award (4) Detroit Art Dirs. Club, 1981; numerous others. Mem. Dallas Soc. Visual Communications, Women in Communications (student pres. 1968), Dallas Advt. League, Women in Communications, Internat. Assn. Bus. Communicators, Bus. and Profl.

Advt. Assn., Am. Inst. Graphic Artists, Northwood Inst. Am. Women in Radio and TV, Dallas C. of C. (pub. relations chmn., small bus. council). Jewish. Clubs: Hadassah Nat. Fedn. Jewish Women, CEO. Home: 9619 Rocky Branch Dallas TX 75243 Office: 10100 N Central Expressway Suite 430 Dallas TX 75231

MILLER, MARGARET ANN, graphoanalyst; b. Custer, Okla., June 26, 1937; d. Eddie Arthur and Pansy Opal (Harrall) Friesen; m. Marvin James Miller, May 20, 1955 (div.); children: Wayne Douglas, James Russell, Richard Don; m. Carl Vincent Ferrera, 1988. Student in social work, U. Okla., 1972-74. Legal asst. U. Okla., Norman, 1972-74; contract adminstr. Pizza Inn, Inc., Dallas, 1974-77; real estate saleswoman Joe Chitwood Real Estate, Arlington, Tex., 1977-80, Hamilton Owen Real Estate, Dallas, 1980-83; office mgr., legal asst. Brown & Shapiro, Dallas, 1983-84; dir. real estate Lone Star Lubrications, Dallas, 1985-86; cons. real estate Kentucky Fried Chicken, 1987—. Asst. chmn. Neighborhood Crime Watch, Dallas, 1983; chmn. Gov.'s com. Employment Handicapped Archtl. Barriers, 1980-82; mem. Dallas Mayor's Com. Employing Handicapped; chmn. AID/Handicapped Housing Com., 1979-82; mem. City Dallas 1981 Internat. Yr. Disabled Persons Access Com.; mem. Women's S.W. Fed. Credit Union; vol. Com. to Aid Abused Women. Recipient Lois Hair Bernays award Dallas Bd. Realtors, 1980. Mem. Women's Polit. Caucus of Reno (sec.), Reno Women's Network (sec.), Internat. Graphoanalysis Soc., Am. Handwriting Analysis Found., Gov.'s Conf. for Women Organizational Com. Democrat. Home: University Station PO Box 8876 Reno NV 89507

MILLER, MARGARET HAIGH, librarian; b. Ashton-under-Lyne, Lancashire, Eng., Feb. 26, 1915; came to U.S., 1915, naturalized, 1919; d. Errwood Augustus and Florence (Stockdale) Savage; m. Mervin Homer Miller, June 30, 1940; children—Nancy Elaine Reich, Edward Stockdale, Jame Elizabeth Miller-Dean. B.S. in Edn., Millersville U. (Pa.), 1937; M.S. in L.S., U. So. Calif., 1952; postgrad. in supervision Calif. State U.-Northridge, 1957-59. High sch. librarian Phoenixville Sch. Dist. (Pa.), 1937-40; jr. high sch. librarian Los Angeles Unified Sch. Dist., 1952-55, coordinating librarian, 1955-62, coll. head librarian, 1959-62, supr. library services, 1962-83; lectr. children's lit. U. So. Calif., Los Angeles, 1959-76, advisor Sch. Library and Info. Sci., 1980-83; resource person Nat. Council for Accreditation Tchr. Edn., Washington, 1976—; cons. Pied Piper Prodns., Glendale, Calif., 1978—, David Sonnenshein Assocs., Los Angeles, 1983-85, Baker & Taylor Co., Inc., N.Y.C., 1979-83, H.W. Wilson Co., N.Y.C., 1975—, Mook & Blanchard, La Puente, Calif., 1985—, Enslow Pub., Inc., Hillside, N.J. Editor: Book List for Elementary School Libraries, 1966; Books for Elementary School Libraries, 1969; Children's Catalog, 13th edit., 1976; Multicultural Experiences in Children's Literature, Grades K-6, 1978; Periodicals for School Libraries, Grades K-12, 1977; Multicultural Experiences in Literature for Young People, Grades 7-12, 1979; School Selection Guide, K-12, 1980, 81, 82, 83; Supplement to Multicultural Experiences in Children's Literature, 1982; Special Books for Special People: A Bibliography about the Handicapped, 1982. Bibliographer: Concepts in Science, Levels 1 through 6 students' edits. (P. Brandwein et al), 1972; Concepts in Science Teacher's Education, 1972. Columnist, book reviewer Los Angeles Times, various jours. Mem. Los Angeles Sch. Library Assn. (cons. 1952-83), Calif. Assn. Sch. Librarians (pres. So. sect. 1971-72, state pres. 1975-76, many coms. 1952-77), Calif. Media and Library Educators Assn. (various coms. 1977—), ALA (many coms. Young Adult Services Div.), Am. Assn. Sch. Librarians, Assn. Library Service to Children, Friends Children and Lit. (dir. 1979—, pres. 1987-88), So. Calif. Council on Lit. for Children and Young People (dir. 1961—, pres. 1973-74, 1st v.p. 1986, 3d v.p. 1987-88), Calif. Library Assn., Young Adult Reviewers Booklist Com., Assn. Adminstrs. Los Angeles Unified Sch. Dist., Beta Phi Mu (dir. 1977-79, 84-86, pres. 1979-80), Pi Lambda Theta (chpt. pres. 1964-66), Delta Kappa Gamma (chpt. sec. 1962-64). Republican. Home: 4321 Matilija Ave Sherman Oaks CA 91423

MILLER, MARGERY SILBERMAN, psychologist, speech and language pathologist, higher education administrator; b. Roslyn, N.Y., May 7, 1951; d. Bernard and Charlotte (Schatzberg) Silberman; m. Mark Howard Miller, Sept. 5, 1971; children—Kip Lee, Tige Justice. Lic. speech pathologist, N.Y., Md.; cert. tchr. nursery-6th grades, spl. edn., N.Y., advanced profl. tchr. speech and hearing, Md.; cert. sch. psychologist, Md. B.A., Elmira Coll., 1971; M.A., NYU, 1972; Ed.S., M.S., SUNY-Albany, 1975; postgrad. in psychology Georgetown U., 1984—. Speech and lang. pathologist Mental Retardation Inst., Flower and Fifth Ave. Hosp., N.Y.C., 1971-72; community speech/lang. pathologist N.Y. State Dept. Mental Hygiene, Troy, dir. speech and hearing services, 1972-74; instr. communication disorders dept. Coll. of St. Rose, Albany, N.Y., 1975-77; clin. supr. U. Md., College Park, 1978; speech/lang. pathologist Md. Sch. for Deaf, Frederick, 1978-84; auditory devel. specialist Montgomery County Pub. Schs., Rockville, Md., 1984-87; coordinator Family Life program Nat. Acad. Gallaudet U., Washington, 1987—; part-time assoc. prof. psychology Gallaudet U.; instr. sign lang. program Frederick Community Coll.; dance instr. for deaf adolescents; diagnostic cons. on speech pathology; mem. editorial rev. com. Gov.'s Devel. Disabilities Council of Md., 1984; presenter at confs. Author: It's O.K. To Be Angry, 1976; contbr. chpt. to Cognition, Education, and Deafness: Directions for Research and Instruction, 1985; contbr. articles to profl. jours. Former vol. Am. Cancer Assn., Heart Assn., Muscular Dystrophy Assn.; vol. Emergency Interpreting for Deaf; choreographer Miss Deaf Am. Pageant, 1984. Office of Edn. Children's Bur. fellow, 1971. Mem. Am. Speech, Lang. and Hearing Assn. (cert. clin. competence in speech/lang. pathology), Md. Speech, Lang. and Hearing Assn., D.C. Speech, Lang. and Hearing Assn., Nat. Assn. of Deaf. Jewish. Home: 12316 Triple Crown Rd Gaithersburg MD 20878 Office: Gallaudet U 800 Florida Ave NE Washington DC 20002

MILLER, MARILYN LOUSHIN, principal; b. Palo Alto, Calif., Oct. 26, 1943; d. Andrew Joseph and Anne (Duzanica) Loushin; m. Arthur Joseph Miller, Aug. 21, 1965; children: Garreth Josh, Ashleigh Jennifer, Heath Grahame. BA, U. Calif., Berkeley, 1963; postgrad., San Jose State U., 1963-65; MA, Notre Dame U., 1980. Tchr. Los Angeles City Schs., 1965-68, Beverly Hills (Calif.) Unified Sch. Dist., 1968-70, Hinsdale (Ill.) Sch. Dist., 1970-75; tchr. Hillborough (Calif.) City Sch. Dist., 1975-80, elem. prin., 1980-84, prin. mid. sch., 1984—; mem. prin.'s forum planning team Stanford U., Palo Alto, 1987—. Mem. Am. Ctr. Students and Artists, Assn. Supervision and Curriculum Devel., Phi Delta Kappa. Democrat. Roman Catholic. Home: 160 Leslie Dr San Carlos CA 94010 Office: Hillsborough City Sch 300 El Cerrito Hillsborough CA 94010

MILLER, MARJORIE CAVINS LEEPER (MIDGE), educator, former state legislator; b. Morgantown, W.Va., June 8, 1922; d. Lorimer V. and Neva (Adams) Cavins; student Spokane Jr. Coll., 1939-40, Morris Harvey Coll., 1940-41; B.A., U. Mich., 1944; M.S., U. Wis., 1962; m. Harry Dean Leeper, Nov. 5, 1944 (dec. 1954); children—Steven Lloyd, David Dean, Linda Jean, Kenneth Chandran; m. Edward Ernst Miller, May 12, 1963; stepchildren—Mark, Sterling, Jeffrey, Nancy, Randy. Teen-age program dir. Ann Arbor YWCA, 1944-45; married women's program dir. New Haven YWCA, 1945-46; teaching asst. U. Wis., Madison, 1957-60, asst. dean letters and sci., 1960-66, coordinator univ. religious activities, 1966-68; mem. Wis. Assembly, 1970-84, chmn. commerce and consumer affairs, 1977-82, state affairs com., 1975-76, higher and vocat. edn., family and econ. assistance, 1983-84; co-chmn. law revision com., 1979-84; vice chmn. Dane County Democratic Com., 1967-68; mem. Dem. Nat. Com., 1975-84; mem. nat. adv. bd. Interchange Resource Center; founder Nat. Council Alternative Work Patterns; founder, chmn. The Madison Inst. Mem. Nat. Orgn. Women Legislators (nat. adv. com.), Nat. Women's Polit. Caucus. Methodist.

MILLER, MARLENE ROBERTA, college administrator; b. Malden, Mass., Feb. 28, 1949. Grad. high sch., Ridgecrest, Calif. Office mgr. Liberty Nat. Life Ins., Inglewood, Calif., 1968-70; asst. bookkeeper Wheel Distbrs., Ontario, Calif., 1970-74; personnel mgr. Tri-Tex Industries, Ontario, 1974-81; dir. personnel and phys. plant Coll. Osteo. Medicine, Pomona, Calif., 1981—. Mem. Merchants and Mfrs. Assn., Nat. Assn. Female Execs., Coll. and Univ. Personnel Assn., David Margaret Home for Girls (bd. dirs.), Assn. Phys. Plant Adminstrs. Home: 1521 Eucalyptus Ct Ontario CA 91761 Office: Coll Osteo Medicine Coll Plaza Pomona CA 91766-1889

MILLER, MARY ANGELA, dietitian; b. Youngstown, Ohio, Jan. 15, 1956; d. John Francis and Angeline M. (Frazzini) M.; m. James M. Lucente; children: Angela, Carlin. BS, Youngstown State U., 1978; MS, Case Western Res. U., 1985. Registered dietitian, Ohio. Nutrition counselor Procare, Youngstown, 1977-78; intern Ind. U. Med. Ctr., Indpls., 1979; clin. dietitian Lakewood (Ohio) Hosp., 1979-82; cardiothoracic surgery dietitian Cleve. Clinic Found., 1982-83, critical care dietitian, 1983-85, nutrition care coordinator, 1985-87; dir. weight mgmt. Dublin (Ohio) Med. Clinic, 1987—. Contbr. articles to profl. jours. Recipient Estee Corp. award, 1984; Case Western Res. U. scholar, 1985. Mem. Am. Dietetic Assn., Ohio Dietetic Assn., Cleve. Dietetic Assn. (chair career guidance, 1986—), Dietitians in Nutritional Support (legisl. com. 1985-87), Soc. for Parenteral/Enteral Nutition, Am. Heart Assn., Nat. Assn. Research Nurses and Dietitians. Home: 171 Greenbank Rd Gahanna OH 43230 Office: Dublin Med Clinic 6350 Frantz Rd Dublin OH 43017

MILLER, MARY ELLEN, labor union administrator; b. Kansas City, Mo., Aug. 11, 1948; d. William Mansfield and Dorothy Ellen (Hassel) M.; m. Gerald Dee Powell, 1966 (div. 1973); 1 child, Paige Anjanette; m. Jerry Michael Krasovec, May 12, 1979; children: Mimi Renee, Joshua M. Flight attendant Trans World Airlines, Kansas City, 1969-77; nat. officer Transport Workers Union, Kansas City, 1974-76; founder Ind. Fedn. of Flight Attendants, Kansas City, 1977, officer, contract negotiator, 1977-83, dir. safety, health, legisl. and communication, 1984—; mem. speakers bur. United Labor Com. of Mo., 1977-78; chmn. supervisory com. TWA Credit Union, Kansas City, 1979-86; mem. supervisory com. United Labor Credit Union, Kansas City, 1986—. Editor: The 6:30 News, 1984—; dir. video IFFA, 1985. del. Dem. Conv., N.Y.C., 1980; campaign coordinator Mondale/Ferraro for Pres., Kansas City, 1984; Jackson County (Mo.) Dem. committee woman, 1984—; vice chair Com. for County Progress, Jackson County, 1985—; Jackson County commr. Office of Human Relations, 1985-87. Mem. Labor Mgmt. Council (exec. com. 1984—), Nat. Transp. Safety Assn. (adv. com. 1984—), NOW. Presbyterian. Home: Rt 1 Box 256 B Grain Valley MO 64029 Office: Ind Fedn Flight Attendants 6301 Rockhill Rd Suite 418D Kansas City MO 64131

MILLER, MARY JEANNETTE, office management specialist; b. Washington, Sept. 24, 1912; d. John William and David Evengeline (Hill) Sims; m. Cecil Miller, June 17, 1934 (dec.); children—Sylvenia Delores Doby, Ferdi A., Cecil Jr. Student Howard U., 1929-30, U. Ill., 1940-42, Dept. Agr. Grad. Sch., 1957-59, U. Md., 1975; cert. in Vocat. Photography, Prince George's Community Coll., 1986. Chief mail processing unit Bur. Reclamation, Washington, 1940-57; records supr. AID, Manila, Korea, Mali, Guyana, Dominican Republic, Indonesia, Laos, 1957-71; office engr. Bechtel Assos., Washington, 1976-79; real estate asso; tchr. English as 2d lang. Ministry of Edn., Seoul, Korea, 1960-61, Ministry of Fin., Laos, 1968-70; cons. to Ministry of Fin. Royal Lao Govt., 1971-74; cons. AID missions to Yemen, Sudan, Somalia, 1982; records mgmt. cons. AID, Monrovia, Liberia, 1980-81, Sri Lanka, 1984; docent Mus. African Art Smithsonian Inst., Washington, 1986—. Author handbooks on office mgmt. Mem. Mayor's Internat. Adv. Council. Mem. Soc. Am. Archivists, Am. Mgmt. Assn., Montgomery County Bd. Realtors, Am. Fgn. Service Assn., Nat. Trust Hist. Preservation, Zeta Phi Beta. Roman Catholic. Home and Office: 1008 Avery Pl Largo MD 20772

MILLER, MARY PATRICIA, medical technologist; b. Chgo., Nov. 5, 1953; d. Daniel Patrick and Eleanor Therese (Halford) McNeill; m. Thomas Edward Miller, Mar. 29, 1986; 1 child, Matthew. AAS in Med. Tech., Moraine Valley Community Coll., 1977; BA in Allied Health Mgmt. and Edn., Nat. Coll. Edn., 1985. Cert. med. technologist. Med. technologist BioSci. Labs., Bellwood, Ill., 1977-85; lab. supr. Damon Labs., Berwyn, Ill., 1985-86, Interstate Med. Labs., Lansing, Ill., 1986—; mem. safety com. BioSci. Labs., Chgo., 1983-85. Mem. Am. Soc. Clin. Pathologists, Am. Chem. Soc., Am. Inst. for Cancer Research. Home: 7824 W 80th St Bridgeview IL 60455

MILLER, MARYGRACE, advertising executive; b. Toledo, Dec. 3, 1946; d. George John and Leona Marie (Johnson) Chovanec; m. Jerome K. Miller (separated); 1 child, Joel J. Grad., Notre Dame Acad., Toledo, 1964. Lic. life ins. agt., Ohio. Sec. Spartan Chem. Co. Inc, Toledo, 1964-66; sec., bookkeeper ARC, Fulda, Fed. Republic of Germany, 1966-68; exec. sec. Spartan Chem. Co. Inc., Toledo, 1968-77, advt. mgr., 1977—. Republican. Roman Catholic. Home: 29644 E River Rd Perrysburg OH 43607

MILLER, MORGAN JANE LAUREN, business executive; b. Hamilton, Ont., Can., June 13, 1945; d. Beverly Montford and Vera Ellen (Wordon) Hills; m. David Allan Wright, Mar. 1967 (div. Dec. 1972); children: Christopher David, Patrick Montford Allan; m. William David Miller, Mar. 28, 1987; children: Karen Elizabeth, Debra Sharon. BFA, N.S. Coll. Art and Design, Halifax, 1973. Med. photographer Halifax Infirmary, 1972-75; filmmaker Nat. Film Bd. Can., Halifax, 1975; pvt. practice design cons. Halifax, Seattle and Vancouver, B.C., 1976-84; women and youth coordinator Ministry Industry and Small Bus., Vancouver, 1985-86; gen. mgr. Bus. Devel. Group Tiem Can. Inc., Vancouver, 1986-88; pres. Morgan Design Inc., Vancouver, 1988—; v.p. Pacific Northwest Inst. Neurolinguistics, Seattle and Vancouver, 1982-84; cons., speaker various womens' orgns. Producer and director documentary film for Nat. Film Bd. Can.: Cancer in Women, 1975. Mem. Vancouver Bd. Trade, Downtown Vancouver Assn., Western Businesswomen's Assn. Club: British Columbia. Office: Morgan Design Inc, 200 - 1534 W 2d Ave, Vancouver, BC Canada V6J 1H2

MILLER, NANCY GREENE, hospital administrator; b. Syracuse, N.Y., Aug. 29, 1934; d. Franklin Irvine and Eleanor (Grant) Greene; m. W. Porter Miller, Nov. 16, 1956; 1 child, Cynthia. BA, Wheaton Coll., Norton, Mass., 1956. Asst. to pres. Cazenovia Coll., N.Y., 1962-75; asst. mgr. Syracuse Mall, 1975-77; dir. vol. services Community Gen. Hosp., Syracuse, 1977—. Profl. adv. com. Caring Coalition/Hospice, 1984—. Mem. Am. Soc. Dirs. Vol. Services, Syracuse C. of C. (downtown com.), Adminstrs. Vol. Services of Cen. N.Y. (pres. 1979-81, exec. com. 1979—), N.Y. State Assn. Dirs. Vol. Services (dir. 1985—). Republican. Club: Jr. League. Office: Community Gen Hosp Broad Rd Syracuse NY 13215

MILLER, PAMELA GARDINER, lawyer; b. Newark, May 29, 1948; d. Herbert and Adele (Hoffman) Gardiner; m. David Edward Miller, Dec. 28, 1974. B.A., U. Wis., 1971; M.A., Columbia U., 1972; J.D., Case Western Res. U., 1975. Bar: Ohio 1975, Wis. 1982. Legal intern Pub. Defender Office, Cleve. 1973-75; asst. trust officer Cleve. Trust Co., 1975-78; asst. dean student acad. affairs Coll. of Letters and Sci., U. Wis., Madison, 1978-84; exec. dir. Madison Festival of the Lakes, Inc., Madison, 1984—. Mem. Wis. Bar Assn., ABA.

MILLER, PATRICIA ANN, educational administrator; b. Lancaster, Pa., May 15, 1939; d. Ivan Crosley and Elsie Irene (Blocher) M.; divorced; 1 child, Jonathan Thomas Bayne. BS in Secondary Edn., Kent (Ohio) State U., 1961; MS in Secondary Edn., Wilkes Coll., 1971. Cert. tchr., Pa., Ill., Ariz. Tchr. Clearview High Sch., Lorain, Ohio, 1961, Manheim Twp. High Sch., Neffsville, Pa., 1961-65; instr. Pa. State U., Wilkes-Barre, 1965-69; asst. dir. instructional TV Sta. WVIA-TV, Pittston, Pa., 1971-74; program devel. Oswego (Ill.) High Sch., 1974-77; exec. dir. program devel. Youth, E.T.C., Phoenix, 1978-85; exec. dir. Ariz. Sch. Services through Ednl. Tech. program, Sta. KAET-TV, Tempe, 1985—; bd. dirs. Youth, E.T.C., Ednl. Access Gov.'s Bd. pub. access channel 34, Phoenix; vice-chmn. DLS Council Pacific Mountain Network, Denver, 1985—. Program devel. Pathway Day Support Therapy, 1979, Youth, E.T.C. Skills Ctr., 1980, Second Start Residential Treatment Girls' Facility, 1985; bd. dirs. Ariz. Masterworks Chorale, 1983—, pres. 1982, 83. Mem. AAUW, Assn. for Edn., Communications & Tech., Ariz. Ednl. Media Assn. Republican. Home: 210 E Betty Elyse Phoenix AZ 85022 Office: Ariz State U ASSET Program/Sta KAET-TV Tempe AZ 85287

MILLER, PATRICIA LEE, nursing administrator; b. Atlanta, June 4, 1950; d. Harold Blaine and Sarah Elizabeth (Burgamy) M. BS in Nursing, Med. Coll. of Ga., 1978, MS in Nursing, 1979. Cert. Nursing Adminstrn., advanced. Emergency room staff nurse Ga. Bapt. Hosp., Atlanta, 1971; intensive care unit staff nurse Savannah (Ga.) Meml. Hosp., 1971; commd. 2d lt. USAF, 1971; Intensive care, critical care staff nurse Burnham City Hosp., Champaign, Ill., 1974-76; with nurse corps USAF, 1971-74; supr. intensive care, critical care units St. Joseph Hosp., Augusta, Ga., 1976-79; dir. ambulatory care nursing Med. Coll. of Ga., Augusta, 1979-85; dir. ambulance care nursing Tulane U., New Orleans, 1985—; temporary faculty Parkland Coll., Champaign, Ill., 1975-76; cons., adminstr., surveyor Joint Commn. Accreditation Hosps., Chgo., 1986—. Author: (books) Initial Assessment of Patient with Acute Myocardial Infarction, 1980, Complications of Patient with Acute Myocardial Infarction, 1980, Arrhythmia Recognition and Intervention, 1980, Patient Education and Rehabilitation, 1981; contbr. articles to profl. jours. Served to 1st lt. USAF, 1971-74, as maj. with USAFR. Recipient Environ. Health and Safety award Tulane U., 1987. Mem. Am. Nurses Assn., Ga. Nurses Assn. (nurse of the year 1982), Am. Acad. of Ambulatory Nursing Adminstrn. (pres. 1986-87), Sigma Theta Tau. Episcopal. Office: Tulane U Med Group 1415 Tulane Ave New Orleans LA 70112

MILLER, PATRICIA LOUISE, state senator, nurse; b. Bellefontaine, Ohio, July 4, 1936; d. Richard William and Rachel Orpha (Williams) Miller; m. Kenneth Orlan Miller, July 3, 1960; children—Tamara Sue, Matthew Ivan. R.N., Meth. Hosp. Sch. Nursing-Indpls., 1957; B.S., Ind. U., 1960. Office nurse A.D. Dennison, M.D., 1960-61; staff nurse Meth. Hosp., Indpls., 1959, Community Hosp., Indpls., 1958; representative, State of Ind., Dist. 50, Indpls., 1982-83, senator, State of Ind., Dist. 32, Indpls., 1983—, mem. edn., health welfare and aging, labor and pension, legis. apportionment and elections coms., chmn. interim study com. pub. health and mental health Ind. Gen. Assembly, 1986. Mem. Bd. Edn., Met. Sch. Dist. Warren Twp., 1974-82, pres., 1979-80, 80-81; mem. Warren Twp. Citizens Screening Com. for Sch. Bd. Candidates, 1972-74, 84, Met. Zoning Bd. Appeals, Div. I, City-County Council, 1972-76; bd. dirs. Central Ind. Council on Aging, Indpls., 1977-80; mem. State Bd. of Voc. and Tech. Edn., 1978-82, sec., 1980-82; mem. Gov.'s Select Adv. Commn. for Primary and Secondary Edn., 1983; precinct committeeman Republican Party, 1968-74, ward vice chmn., 1975-78, ward chmn., 1978-85, twp. chmn., 1985—; del. Rep. State Conv., 1968, 74, 76, 1980, sgt. at arms, 1982, mem. platform com., 1984; del. Rep. Nat. Conv., 1984; active various polit. campaigns; bd. dirs. PTA, 1967-81; pres. Grassy Creek PTA, 1971-72; state del. Ind. PTA, 1978; mem. child care adv. com. Walker Career Center, 1976-80, others; bd. dirs. Ch. Fedn. Greater Indpls., 1979-82, Christian Justice Center, Inc., 1983-85, Gideon Internat. Aux., 1977—; mem. United Meth. Bd. Missions Aux. of Indpls., 1974-80, v.p., 1974-76; bd. dirs. Lucille Raines Residence, Inc., 1977-80; exec. com. S. Ind. Conf. United Meth. Women, 1977-80, lay del. S. Ind. Conf. United Meth. Ch., 1977—, fin. and adminstrn. com., 1979—, planning and research com., 1980—; sec. Indpls. S.E. Dist. Council on Ministries, 1977-78, pres., 1982; chmn. council on ministries Cumberland United Meth. Ch., 1969-76; chmn. stewardship com. Old Bethel United Meth. Ch., 1982-85, fin. com., 1982-85, adminstrv. bd., mem. council on ministries, 1981-85. Recipient Phi Lambda Theta Honor for outstanding contbr. in field of edn., 1976; Woman of the Year, Cumberland Bus. and Profl. Women, 1979; Ind. Voc. Assn. citation award, 1984, others. Mem. Indpls. Dist. Dental Soc. Women's Aux., Ind. Dental Assn. Women's Aux., Am. Dental Assn. Women's Aux., others. Clubs: Warren Twp. Rep. Franklin Rep., Lawrence Rep., Center Twp. Rep., Fall Creek Valley Rep., Marion County Council Rep. Women, Ind. Women's Rep., Indpls. Women's Rep., Ind. Fedn. Rep. Women, Nat. Fedn. Rep. Women, Beech Grove Rep., Perry Twp. Rep. Address: 1041 S Muesing Rd Indianapolis IN 46239

MILLER, PHYLLIS JANE, nurse, educator; b. Kansas City, May 18, 1956; d. Ivan Eugene and Floris S. (Jantz) M. AA, Hesston Coll., 1976; BS, Ea. Mennonite Coll., 1978; MS, U. Md., 1985. RN, Md., Va., D.C. Nurse George Washington U. Med. Cen., Washington, 1978; dir. nursing services Mennonite Bethesda Hosp. Soc. Inc., Goessel, Kans., 1979-80; clinical preceptor Greater SE Community Hosp., Washington, 1980-81, specialist edn., 1981—. Mem. MASHET (pres. 1983-86), Am. Soc. Healthcare Edn. and Tng. (chmn. 1985-87), Am. Nurses Assn. (mem. Council Continuing Edn. recruitment com. 1985—), Sigma Theta Tau. Democrat. Home: 1117 Palmer Rd #8 Fort Washington MD 20744 Office: Greater SE Community Hosp 1310 Southern Ave SE Washington DC 20032

MILLER, ROSEMARY MARGARET, accountant; b. Jersey City, Jan. 3, 1935; d. Joseph John and Marguerite (Delatush) Corbin; m. James Noyes Orton, 1956 (div. 1977); m. Julian Allen Miller, Oct. 14, 1978; children: Alexandria Lynn Hayes, Jennifer Ann Orton Cole. Student Barnard Coll., 1953-54, Rutgers U., Newark, 1954-56, Howard U., 1962-63, No. Va. Community Coll., 1976-83; AA, Thomas A. Edison State Coll., 1981; BS in Acctg., U. Md., 1987; cert. H & R Block, 1981. Bookkeeper Gen. Electronics, Inc., Washington, 1970-73; cost acct. Radiation Systems, Inc., Sterling, Va., 1973-80; acct. Bilsom Internat., Inc., Reston, Va., 1980-83; sales mgr. Bay Country Homes, Inc., Fruitland, Md., 1984; sr. staff acct. Snow, Powell & Meade, Salisbury, Md., 1985-86; acct. Meadows Hydraulics, Inc., Fruitland, Md., 1987-88; acct. Porter & Powell CPAs, Salisbury, 1988—; owner, prin. RCOM Cons., acctg., bookkeeping, taxes, Princess Anne, Md. Mem. Accreditation Council for Accountancy (accredited 1981), Nat. Soc. Public Accts., Nat. Acct. Assn., Nat. Student Bus. League, Alpha Kappa Mu. Democrat. Lutheran. Home: Rt 2 Box 255 E 33 Princess Anne MD 21853 Office: PO Box 153 107 High St Salisbury MD 21801

MILLER, SELAINA AUNOA LEVI, employment and training executive; b. Apia, Western Samoa, May 5, 1946; came to U.S., 1962, naturalized, 1969; d. Arius and Avasa (Niu) Levi; m. Charles M. Miller, Dec. 14, 1974; 1 child, Jamila Atamai. AA, Chabot Coll., 1969; BA, Calif. State U., Hayward, 1971. Cert. tchr., Calif. Program developer/coordinator Alameda County Assn. Mentally Retarded, Oakland, Calif., 1969-71; program dir., tchr. Contra Costa Assn. Retarded/Richmond Calif. Sch. Dist., Walnut Creek, Calif., 1971-74; mgr. regional services MidWillamette Jobs Council, Pvt. Industry Council, Salem, Oreg., 1975—; mem. adv. bd. study on unemployment problems of Samoans, N.W. Regional edn. Lab., Portland, Oreg., 1982-83; participant vocation extern program for tchrs. and trainers Oreg. State U. and Oreg. Alliance for Program Improvement, Corvallis, 1985-86. Participant region 9-Oreg. Joint Action for Community Service, 1982-85; bd. dirs. Green Thumb Agy. for Older Workers, Oreg.-Wash., 1985-86, Community Action Orgn. Info. and Referral, Stayton, 1985-86; mem. community adv. bd. spl. programs for students Salem-Keizer Sch Dist., 1986-88, South Marion County Secondary Sch. Programs, 1987-88; active Metro Work Experience Coordinators Oreg., 1986-88, commn. bd. Mid-Willamette Child CAre, 1988. Mem. Soc. for Training Devel., Nat. Assn. Female Execs., Oreg. Employment and Tng. Assn. Avocations: sewing, gardening, swimming, volleyball, travel. Home: 18874 Old Mehama Rd SE Stayton OR 97383 Office: Mid Willamette Jobs Council 1495 Edgewater NW Suite 225 Salem OR 97304

MILLER, STEPHANIE LEE, federal agency administrator; b. Los Angeles, Mar. 7, 1950; d. Robert Wilson and Estella Elizabeth (Halle) Lee; m. Phillip Van Miller, June 13, 1976 (div. Oct. 1981). B.A., Calif. State U.-Dominquez Hills, 1971; M.A., Occidental Coll., 1975. Cons. Coro Found., Los Angeles, 1973-77; fundraiser Legal Def. Fund NAACP, Los Angeles, 1978-79; owner, mgr. Contact Calif., Beverly Hills, 1979-81; spl. asst. Dept. Commerce, Washington, 1981-83; asst. sec. pub. affairs HHS, Washington, 1983—; mem. U.S. del. to Internat. Women's Conf., Nairobi, Kenya, 1985, UN Commn. on Status of Women, 1987. Vice chmn. community and govt. affairs council United Way, Los Angeles. Mem. Los Angeles C. of C. (bd. dirs. women's div.), Nat. Council Negro Women, Delta Sigma Theta. Republican. Home: 116 G St SW Washington DC 20024 Office: Dept Health and Human Services 200 Independence Ave SW Washington DC 20201

MILLER, SUSAN GILLETT, teacher; b. Bklyn., Aug. 9, 1936; d. Samuel Lawrence and Charlotte (Merkin) Gillett; m. Richard James Miller, Oct. 7, 1956; children: Jody Ann, Lawrence Samuel. AA with highest honor, Broward Community Coll., Ft. Lauderdale, Fla., 1970; BA in Edn. with honors, Fla. Atlantic U., 1975; MS, Nova U., 1984. Cert. tchr. Fla., reading specialist, early childhood edn. Substitute tchr. Broward County Schs., Ft. Lauderdale, 1975, assoc. mem. curriculum council, 1983-84, com. mem. reading cadre, 1984-85, inservice facilitator, 1981, inservice instr., 1984-85, devel. examiner Gesell tng. early childhood, 1985-87; reading resource Sunshine Elem. Sch., Miramar, Fla., 1976, second grade tchr., 1976-77, co-chairperson career edn., 1977-78, 79-80, com. chairperson rep. accreditation study, 1982-83, grade chairperson, 1983-84, first grade tchr., 1977—; spl. edn. program tutor mailman ctr. Nova U., Ft. Lauderdale, 1983-84. Contbr. articles to profl. jours. Unit chairperson League of Women Voters, Hollywood Fla. chpt., 1963-64, v.p., Broward County, 1964-65; v.p. Orgn. for Rehab. Through Tng., Hollywood, 1966-68; vol. Nova-Blanche Forman Elem., Ft. Lauderdale, 1968-69. Mem. AAUW, Broward County Reading Council, Phi Kappa Phi. Home: 4200 Taylor St Hollywood FL 33021

MILLER, SUSAN HEILMANN, newspaper publishing executive; b. Yuba City, Calif., Jan. 13, 1945; d. Paul Clay and Helen Christine (Sterud) Heilmann; m. Allen Clinton Miller III, June 24, 1967. BA, Stanford U., 1966; MS, Columbia U., 1969; PhD, Stanford U., 1976. Info. officer Montgomery County Schs., Rockville, Md., 1970-71, Palo Alto Schs., Calif., 1969-70, 71-73; news-features editor Bremerton Sun, Wash., 1976-80; night city editor Peninsula Times Tribune, Palo Alto, 1980-81; exec. editor News-Gazette, Champaign, Ill., 1981-85; dir. editorial devel. Scripps Howard Newspapers, Cin., 1985—. Contbr. articles to profl. jours. Bd. dirs. Vol. Illini Projects, U. Ill., 1983-85, Washington Journalism Ctr., 1985; mem. Pulitzer Prize Nominating Jury, 1986-87, accrediting com. Accrediting Council on Journalism and Mass Communication. Mem. Am. Soc. Newspaper Editors (bd. dirs. 1985—), Assoc. Press Mng. Editors (bd. dirs.1984—), Ill. AP Mng. Editors (bd. dirs. 1984-85). Clubs: Executive (Champaign, Ill.) (bd.dirs. 1984-85); Bankers (Cin.). Office: Scripps Howard Newspapers 1100 Central Trust Tower Cincinnati OH 45202

MILLER, SYDELL LOIS, cosmetics executive, marketing professional; b. Cleve., Aug. 10, 1937; d. Jack Harvey Lubin and Evelyne (Saltzman) Brower; m. Arnold Max Miller, Oct. 19, 1958; children: Lauren Beth, Stacie Lynn. Student, U. Miami, 1955-56. Mgr. Hair Salon, Cleve., 1958-60; pres., owner Women's Retail Store, Cleve., 1960-72; exec. v.p. Ardell, Inc., Solon, Ohio, 1972-84; exec. v.p. and owner Matrix Essentials, Inc., Solon, 1980—; pres. Lauren Stacy Mktg., Inc., Solon, 1972—. Editor ednl. books and newsletter, Salons, 1981—. Mem. Mt. Sinai Hosp. Aux., Cleve., 1972—, Beachwood (Ohio) Mus., 1981—, Cleve. Fashion Group. Mem. Am. Beauty Assns. (bd. dirs. 1988—, named Woman of Yr. 1985), Beauty and Barber Supply Inst., Inc., Cosmetic, Toiletry and Fragrance Assn., Inc. Office: Matrix Essentials Inc 30601 Carter St Solon OH 44139

MILLER, THERESA MARY HEALY, health facility administrator; b. Phila., Pa., Sept. 18, 1950; d. John Thomas and Margaret Mary (Lavelle) H. A in Nursing, Bucks County Community Coll., 1974; B in Nursing Sci., Gwynedd Mercy Coll., 1976; M in Health Adminstrn., St. Joseph U., Phila., 1983. Staff nurse Thomas Jefferson U. Hosp., Phila., 1974-78, dir. home care, 1984—; staff nurse Home Health Services Greater Phila., Elms Park, 1978-80, supr., 1980-83; dir. home care Roxborough Meml. Hosp., Phila., 1983-84. Mem. Hosp. Home Care Dirs. (chairperson 1985-87), Am. Nurses Assn. (cert. nursing adminstr.), Southeastern Pa. Home Health Assn. (chairperson 1987—), Pa. Nurses Assn., Montgomery County Nurses Assn. (bd. dirs. 1986), Phila. County Nurses Assn., Iota Kappa, Sigma Theta Tau. Democrat. Roman Catholic. Office: Jefferson Home Health Services 127 S 10th St Philadelphia PA 19107

MILLER, TRUDY JOYCE, retail executive, publisher; b. Chgo.; d. Leonard John and Evelyn Grace (Winter) Clarke; m. William Robert Miller, Oct. 8, 1960; children: William, James, Brian, Catherine. Student, Marycrest Coll., 1959; student in Interior Design, Art, Prairie State Coll., 1975; student in Publishing, Northwestern U., 1983. Reporter, feature writer Hammond (Ind.) Times, 1967-73, Village Press, South Holland, Ill., 1973-75; owner The Emporium, Glenwood, Ill., 1975-76, Second Thoughts, Chicago Heights, Ill., 1976—; pres. retail outlet Second Thoughts Inc., Chicago Heights, 1984—; editor Second Thoughts Publishing, Chicago Heights, 1982—; bd. dir. Fashion Consortium, Chgo., 1984-86; speaker in field. Author: 1983 Guide to Suburban Resale and Thrift Shops, Where to Find Everything For Practically Nothing in Chicagoland, 1984, 86. Bd. dirs. econ. devel. Thornton Coll., South Holland, 1983-85; mem. small bus. adv. bd. Prairie State Coll., Chicago Heights, 1984-85; fashion show coordinator Operation ABLE Past 50 Job Fair, Chicago Heights, 1985. Mem. Nat. Assn. Resale and Thrift Shops (founder, bd. dirs., sec. 1984-86, pres. 1986—, editor newsletter 1987—, coordinator 1st ann. conf. 1988), Internat. Assn. Independant Pubs., Chgo. Women in Pub., Nat. Assn. Women Bus. Owners, South Suburban Assn. Commerce and Industry, Women in Mgmt. S. Suburban Network (bd. dirs., editor newsletter 1984-85). Roman Catholic. Club: Toastmasters (v.p. 1984-85). Office: Second Thoughts Inc 153 Halsted Chicago Heights IL 60411

MILLER, ZOYA DICKINS (MRS. HILLIARD EVE MILLER, JR.), civic worker; b. Washington, July 15, 1923; d. Randolph and Zoya Pavlovna (Klementinovska) Dickins; grad. Stuart Sch. Costume Design, Washington, 1942; student Sophie Newcomb Coll., 1944, New Eng. Conservatory Music, 1946; grad. Internat. Sch. Reading, 1969; m. Hilliard Eve Miller, Jr., Dec. 6, 1943; children: Jeffrey Arnot, Hilliard Eve III. Fashion coordinator, cons. Mademoiselle mag., 1942-44; instr. Stuart Summer Sch. Costume Design, Washington, 1942; fashion coordinator Julius Garfinckel, Washington, 1942-43; star TV show Cowbelle Kitchen, 1957-58, Flair for Living, 1958-59; model mags. and comml. films, also nat. comml. recs., 1956—; dir. program devel. Webb-Waring Lung Inst., Denver, 1973—. Mem. exec. com., bd. dirs. El Paso County chpt. Am. Lung Assn., 1954-63; mem. exec. com. Am. Lung Assn. Colo., 1965-84, bd. dris. 1965-87, chmn. radio and TV council, 1963-70, mem. med. affairs com., 1965-70, pres., 1961-68, procurer found. funds, 1965-70; developer nat. radio ednl. prodns. for internat. use Nat. Tb and Respiratory Disease Assn., Am. Lung Assn., 1963-70, coordinator statewide screening programs Colo., other states, 1965-72, chmn. benefit fund raising El Paso County Cancer Soc., 1963; founder, coordinator Colorado Springs Debutante Ball, 1967—; coordinator Nat. Gov.'s Conf. Ball, 1969; mem. exec. com. Colo. Gov.'s Comprehensive Health Planning Council, 1967-74, chmn., 1972-73; chmn. Colo. Chronic Care Com., 1969-73, chmn. fund raising, 1970-72, chmn. spl. com. congressional studies on nat. health bills, 1971-73; mem. Colo.-Wyo. Regional Med. Program Adv. Council, 1969-73; mem. Colo. Med. Found. Consumers Adv. Council, 1972-78; mem. decorative arts com. Colorado Springs Fine Arts Ctr., 1972-75; founder, state coordinator Nov. Noel Pediatrics Benefit Am. Lung Assn., 1973-87; founder, state chmn. Newborn Hope, 1987. Recipient James J. Waring award Colo. Conf. on Respiratory Disease Workers, 1963; Zoya Dickins Miller Vol. of Yr. award established Am. Lung Assn. of Colo., 1979; Nat. Pub. Relations award Am. Lung Assn., 1979, Gold Double Bar Cross award, 1980, 83; named Humanitarian of Yr., Am. Lung Assn. of Colo., 1987. Lic. pvt. pilot. Mem. Nat. (chmn. nat. father of year contest 1956-57), Colo., El Paso County (pres. 1954, TV chmn. 1954-59) cowbelle assns., Colo. Assn. Fund Raisers. Club: Broadmoor Garden (ways and means chmn. 1967-69, civic chmn. 1970-71, publicity chmn. 1972)(Colorado Springs, Colo.). Contbr. articles, lectures on health care systems and fund raising. Home: 74 W Cheyenne Mountain Blvd Colorado Springs CO 80906

MILLER-MCMILLEN, KAREN JO, personnel director, consultant; b. Allentown, Pa., June 10, 1956; d. Paul Henry and Ruth Ann (Bartholomew) M.; m. Robert Glenn McMillen, Oct. 14, 1978; 1 child, Kelsey Jordan. BS with distinction, Pa. State U., University Park, 1978; MA, Ind. U. of Pa., 1982. Caseworker Indiana (Pa.) County Child Welfare Services, 1978-83; caseworker supr. Ind. (Pa.) County Child Welfare Services, 1983-84; human services coordinator Indiana County Planning Commn., 1984; testing and assessment specialist Susquehanna Employment and Tng. Corp., Lebanon, Pa., 1984-85; personnel dir. Cedar Haven, Lebanon, 1985-87, dir. human resources, 1987—; cons. personnel various orgns., Indiana, 1979-84, Lebanon, 1987—; bd. dirs. Ind. County Head Start, Inc., 1979-82; correspondent Lebanon (Pa.) Daily News, 1986-87; co-chmn. Employer Adv. Com., Lebanon, 1987—. Mem. Lebanon Area Personnel Assn., Appalachian Hosp. Personnel Soc., Am. Soc. for Personnel Adminstrn. (article reviewer 1987—), Am. Bus. Women's Assn. (Woman of Yr. 1987), Pa. State U. Alumni Assn. (alumni rep. 1985—), Nat. Assn. for Female Execs., Cen. Pa. Assn. Female Execs., Phi Kappa Phi. Republican. Presbyterian. Home: 1425 E Walnut St Annville PA 17003 Office: Cedar Haven 590 S 5th Ave Lebanon PA 17042

MILLER-PATTERSON, BARBARA ANNE, dance instructor; b. Harrisburg, Pa., May 13, 1953; d. Warren Eugene Miller and Mary Martha (Laudenslayer) Sanderson; m. Earl F. Burnett, May 15, 1976 (div. May 1979); m. Bruce Reed Patterson Jr., May 31, 1980 (separated). AA in Comml. Art, Harrisburg Area Community Coll., 1980. Trust clk. Cumberland Co. Nat. Bank, Camphill, Pa., 1972-74; contract expediter Naval Ships Parts Control Ctr., Mechanicsburg, Pa., 1974-75; receptionist/clk. Black, Davis & Shue Ins. Agy., Harrisburg, 1977-81; sales support United Republic Life Ins. Co., Harrisburg, 1977-81; owner Proficient Printing, York, Pa., 1981-82; mgr. office services Educators Mut. Life Ins. Co., Lancaster, Pa., 1982-87; dance instr. Arthur Murray Studio, Lancaster, Pa., 1986—. Instr. graphic arts YWCA, Lancaster, 1985, Jr. Achievement, 1986; mem. spl. events com. United Way, 1984—; alternate Goodwill Ins. Bus. Adv. Council; chmn. spl. events. Democrat. Methodist. Office: Arthur Murray Dance Studio 1357 Fruitville Pike Lancaster PA 17601

MILLETT, KATHERINE MURRAY (KATE MILLETT), political activist, sculptor, artist, writer; b. St. Paul, Sept. 14, 1934; m. Fumio Yoshimura, 1965. B.A. magna cum laude, U. Minn., 1956; postgrad. with 1st class honors, St. Hilda's Coll. Oxford, Eng., 1956-58; Ph.D., Columbia U., 1970. Instr. English U. N.C. at Greensboro, 1958; file clk. N.Y.C., kindergarten tchr., 1960-61; tchr. Barnard Coll., 1964-68; formerly tchr. English Bryn Mawr (Pa.) Coll.; disting. vis. prof. Sacramento (Calif.) State Coll., from 1973. Sculptor, Tokyo, 1961-63; co-producer, co-dir. film Three Lives, 1970; one-woman shows Minami Gallery, Tokyo, Judson Gallery, Greenwich Village, 1967, Noho Gallery, N.Y.C., 1976, 78, 80, 82, 84, 86, Women's Bldg., Los Angeles, 1977, one-woman shows drawings, Andre Wanters Gallery, N.Y.C., 1977, Chuck Levitan Gallery, N.Y.C, deVille Galerie, New Orleans, Emma Gallery, Berlin, 1980; author: Sexual Politics, 1970, The Prostitution Papers, 1973, Flying, 1974, Sita, 1977, The Basement, 1979, Going to Iran, 1982. Mem. Congress of Racial Equality, from 1965; chmn. edn. com. NOW, 1966, active supporter women's liberation groups. Mem. Phi Beta Kappa. Office: care Georges Borchardt Inc 136 E 57th St New York NY 10022

MILLEY, JANE ELIZABETH, academic administrator; b. Everett, Mass., May 20, 1940; d. Walter R. and Florence (Leach) M. MusB, Boston U., 1961; MA in Music, Columbia U., 1966; PhD in Higher/Post Sec. Edn.-Adminstrn., Syracuse (N.Y.) U., 1977; piano study with Claude Frank, Martin Canin and Maria Clodes, 1963-75. Coordinator, founder, pianist Elmira (N.Y.) Coll. Fine Arts Trio, 1967-75; instr. music Elmira Coll., 1967-70, asst. prof. music, 1970-75, dir. arts and scis. program, 1974-75; research assoc. Syracuse U., 1975-76; adminstrv. asst. to dean Coll. Arts and Scis., Syracuse U., 1976-77; div. dean humanities and fine arts Sacramento City Coll., 1977-80; assoc. dean sch. fine arts, prof. music Calif. State U., Long Beach, 1980-81, interim dean, sch. fine arts, prof. music, 1981-82, dean, sch. fine arts, prof. music, 1982-84; arts advisor to chancellor Calif. State Univ. System, 1983-84; chancellor N.C. Sch. Arts (a constituent instn. of U. N.C.), 1984—; speaker, cons. in field. Contbr. articles to profl. jours. Ex officio bd. dirs. Regional Arts Found., 1982-84, N.C. Scenic Studios, 1984—, N.C. Dance Theatre, 1984—, N.C. Shakespeare Festival, 1984—; bd. dirs. Sacramento Film Festival, 1979-80, Long Beach Grand Opera, 1980; charter mem., founder Sacramento Exptl. Theatre, 1978-84. Commendation for outstanding service Los Rios Community Coll. Bd. Trustees, 1980, Sacramento City Coll., 1980. Mem. Am. Assn. State Colls. and Univs. (chmn. arts com. 1986—), Nat. Assn. State Univs. and Land Grant Colls. (U. N.C. rep. commn. on arts 1986—), AAUW (found. adv. com. 1987—), Internat. Council Fine Arts Deans, N.C. Women's Forum, N.C. Assn. Women Deans Adminstrs. Counselors, Winston-Salem Leadership Group, Kappa Delta Pi, Pi Kappa Lambda.

MILLICAN, MARIE CLAIRE, laboratory administrator; b. Wilmington, N.C., July 21, 1942; d. H.W. and Patty (Craig) M. BS, U. N.C., 1964; attended, Va. Commonwealth U., 1975. Staff technologist James Walker Meml. Hosp., Wilmington, 1964-65; hematology supr. Wake County Med. Ctr., Raleigh, N.C., 1965-66; hematology supr. St. Mary's Hosp., Richmond, Va., 1966-68, asst. dir. lab. services, 1968-71, dir. lab. services, 1971—; cons. Bon Secours Health Care System, Balt., 1983—, mgmt. devel. task force, lab. computer task force; adj. faculty mem. J. Sargent Reynolds Community Coll., Richmond, 1974—, adv. bd. Med. Lab. Program. Active Richmond YMCA. Recipient Zenith award St. Mary's Hosp., 1975, Marion award, 1985. Mem. Am. Soc. Med. Tech., Va. Soc. Med. Tech. (frequent speaker), Clin. Lab. Mgmt. Assn. Club: Piankatank Shores (Hartfield, Va.). Office: St Mary's Hosp Lab 5801 Bremo Rd Richmond VA 23226

MILLIGAN, CHRISTINE, documentation research manager; b. Troy, N.Y., Jan. 3, 1962; d. Rex Vincent and Carol (LeFevre) M. BA in English cum laude, Brigham Young U., 1984. Tech. writer, mgr. documentation Novell, Inc., Provo, Utah, 1985—; cons. Netline, Provo, 1985. Mem. Nat. Assn. for Exec. Women. Office: Novell Inc 122E 1700 S Provo UT 84601

MILLIGAN, JANET LOUISE, organization executive; b. Seattle, June 21, 1954; d. Gilbert Anton and Lillian Lahja (Niemi) Matson; m. Douglas Scott Milligan. BS, Wash. State U., 1978. Dir. camping services Camp Fire Inc., Claremont, Calif., 1978-83; exec. dir. Vols. for Outdoor Wash., Seattle, 1985; exec. dir. Pacific NW region Leads Club/Contacts, Carlsbad, Calif., 1985—; pres., bd. dirs. Vols. Outdoor Washington, 1987-88. Mem. Am. Camping Assn. (bd. dirs. 1980-84, cert. appreciation 1984). Home and Office: 10421 NE 143d Pl Bothell WA 98011

MILLIGAN, SHIRLEY ANN, educator; b. Bklyn., Sept. 27, 1957; d. Eddie and Louise (Everett) M.; 1 child, Bryan. BA, Bklyn. Coll., 1982, MS, 1986. Tchr. Bd. Edn., Bklyn., 1982-84, 1984—; dir. Kiddie Christian Nursery, Bklyn., 1986—. Mem. Nat. Assn. Female Execs. Democrat. Baptist. Home: 724 E 27th St Brooklyn NY 11210 Office: Clara Barton High Sch 901 Classon Ave Brooklyn NY 11225

MILLIKEN, SUSAN JOHNSTONE, mathematician, educator, government official; b. Woodstock, Conn., 1922; d. Francis U. and Violet Floyd (Ward) Johnstone; m. Peter H. Milliken, Dec. 15, 1950; children: Peter H. III, Frances U. Johnstone Balsam. AB, Vassar Coll.; MA, Columbia U. Chief statistician, research analyst E. W. Axe & Co., investment counsel, N.Y.C., 1940-42, 48-52; economist War Prodn. Bd., Washington, 1943-44; chief economist for sugar and allied products OPA, Washington, 1945-46; head sugar price control USDA, 1947-52; profl. genealogist Washington, 1953—; tutor in stats., math., French, econs. Columbia U., 1962-66, N.Y. Bd. Edn., 1966-83. Author articles in field. Life mem. Gov. William Bradford Compact, editor bull., 1963-69. Mem. Colonial Dames Am. (docent, co-chmn., house com. mus., hospitality com.), Soc. Daus. Holland Dames, N.Y. Geneal. and Biog. Soc. Episcopalian. Club: Barnard. Home: 423 W 120th St New York NY 10027

MILLNER, LYNDA DAYLE, museum director; b. Refugio, Tex., Oct. 2, 1942; d. Jesse C. and A. Fay (LeBleu) Millican; m. Richard A. Millner, June 15, 1962; children: R. Adam, Jill, David. Grad. high sch., Corpus Christi, Tex. Mus. dir. Dickinson County Hist. Soc., Abilene, Kans., 1982—; trustee Dickinson County Hist. Soc., 1980-82. Mem. 1st United Meth. Ch., Abilene; mem. Kans. Downtown Devel. Assn. Mem. Nat. Trust for Hist. Preservation, Kans. State Hist. Soc., Kans. Mus. Assn., Mountain Plains Mus. Assn., Am. Assn. State and Local History, Abilene Area C. of C. (pres. 1985, v.p. 1984). Republican. Clubs: Abilene Country (bd. dirs. 1980-81), PEO (GY chpt.) (recording sec.). Home: 902 N Buckeye Abilene KS 67410 Office: Dickinson County Hist Soc PO Box 506 Abilene KS 67410

MILLS, CAROL MARGARET, trucking company executive; b. Salt Lake City, Aug. 31, 1943; d. Samuel Lawrence and Beth (Neilson) M.; B.S. magna cum laude, U. Utah, 1965. With W.S. Hatch Co., Woods Cross, Utah, 1965—, corp. sec., 1970—, traffic mgr., 1969—, dir. publicity, 1974—; dir. Hatch Service Corp., Nat. Tank Truck Carriers, Inc., Washington; bd. dirs. Intermountain Tariff Bur. Inc., 1978—, chmn., 1981-82, 1986-87. Fund raiser March of Dimes, Am. Cancer Soc., Am. Heart Assn.; active senatorial campaign, 1976, gubernatorial campaign, 1984, 88, vice chair voting dist., 1988—; witness transp. com. Utah State Legislature, 1984, 85; mem. Pioneer Theater Guild, 1985—. Recipient service awards W. S. Hatch Co., 1971, 80; appointed gov. Utah to bd. trustees Utah Tech. Fin. Corp., 1986, exec. com., 1988—; mem. Pioneer Theatre Guild, 1985—. Mem. Nat. Tank Truck Carriers, Transp. Club Salt Lake City, Am. Trucking Assn. (public relations council), Utah Motor Transport Assn. (dir. 1982—), Internat. Platform Assn., Beta Gamma Sigma, Phi Kappa Phi, Phi Chi Theta. Home: 77 Edgecombe Dr Salt Lake City UT 84103 Office: W S Hatch Co 643 S 800 W Woods Cross UT 84087

MILLS, DANIELLE COLE, social services administrator; b. Ft. Eustis, Va., Dec. 17, 1953; d. Daniel McCoy and Isabella Aileen (Jeffreys) Cole; m. Melvin Levester Mills, Oct. 29, 1983. BS in Mental Health Counseling, Gannon U., 1975, M in Counseling, 1977. Program field exec. Girl Scouts U.S., Washington, 1978-82, unit mgr. Camp Potomac Woods, 1982; document info. specialist Informatics Gen. Corp., Rockville, Md., 1983-84; dir. summer youth employment program So. Md. Tri-County Community Action Com., Hughsville, 1985—, dir. employment support program, 1984—; mem. So. Md. SDA Coordination com., career and employability devel. br. Md. State Dept. Edn., Tri-County Coordination com. for Youth Services. Active Nat. Kidney Found., Lupus Found. Office: So Md Tri-County Community Action Com PO Box 280 Hughesville MD 20637

MILLS, DENISE YVONNE, librarian; b. Compton, Calif., July 19, 1946; d. Clifford Clinton and Lois Catherine (Eaton) Mills; children—Randall, Marisa, Nicholas. B.A. in Sociology, Calif. State U.-Long Beach, 1968; profl. diploma in elem. edn. U. Hawaii, 1976, M.L.S., 1980. Sch. librarian Stevenson Intermediate Sch., Honolulu, 1981-82, Bloomington (Calif.) High Sch., 1983—; librarian San Bernardino County Library, Fontana br., 1985—; instr. San Bernardino Valley Coll., 1987-88; research sec. Johns Hopkins U., Balt., UCLA, U. Calif.-Irvine, 1972-74. Mem. steering com. ednl. media task force San Bernardino County Supt. Schs., Calif., 1983-84; mem. Young Adult Services Media Library Educators Network. Mem. ALA, Calif. Media Library Educators Assn., Am. Assn. Sch. Librarians. Republican. Presbyterian. Home: 6615 Churchill St San Bernardino CA 92407 Office: Bloomington High Sch 10750 Laurel St Bloomington CA 92316

MILLS, ELIZABETH ANN, librarian; b. Cambridge, Mass., Apr. 1, 1934; d. Ralph Edwin and Sylvia Elizabeth (Meehan) McCurdy; m. Albert Ernest Mills, July 6, 1957; 1 dau., Karen Elizabeth. B.A., Duke U., 1956; M.S., Simmons Coll., 1973; postgrad. Boston Coll., Framingham State U., Bridgewater State U. Sec. Lowell House, Harvard U., Cambridge, 1956-57; substitute librarian, tchr. Wellesley High Sch. (Mass.), 1972-73, Needham High Sch. (Mass.), 1972-73; librarian Tucker Sch. Media Ctr., Milton Pub. Schs. (Mass.), 1973—, chmn. computer com., bldg. coordinator gifted program, 1981—. Contbr. articles to profl. jours. Active Girl Scouts U.S.A., U.S. Power Squadron, Gt. Blue Hill, Mass., 1974—. Mem. ALA, Am. Assn. Sch. Librarians, Assn. Library Service Children, Mass. Assn. Ednl. Media, Beta Phi Mu, Kappa Delta, Delta Kappa Gamma. Republican. Episcopalian. Home: 177 Jarvis Circle Needham MA 02192 Office: Tucker Sch 187 Blue Hills Pkwy Milton MA 02187

MILLS, HELEN SLABY, English language educator, writing consultant; b. Cleve., Apr. 8, 1923; d. Ollie F. and Nettie J. (Hejl) Slaby; B.A. magna cum laude, Western Res. U., 1944; M.A., Calif. State U., Sacramento, 1965; m. LeRoy Kenneth Mills, June 12, 1948 (dec. Aug. 1983); children—Marilyn Antoinette, David Ellsworth. Women's editor Cleve. Citizen, 1945-48; tchr. (part-time) Western Res. U., Cleve., 1945-48; sec. to dir. Cleve. Inst. Art, 1948-50; x-ray technician and mgr. pvt. med. office, Sacramento, 1957-65; prof. English, Am. River Coll., Sacramento, 1965-84, part-time instr., 1984—; instr. U. Calif. Extension, Davis, 1972; instr. various workshops for tchrs., 1972—; writing cons. for bus. and govt., 1984—; book reviewer Harper & Row Publishers, 1972, Scott Foresman & Co., 1974—, Holt, Rinehart and Winston Co., 1975; free-lance writer, 1984—. Mem. Calif. State U. Alumni Assn., Kappa Delta Pi. Author: Commanding Communication, 1972; Commanding Sentences, 1974, 3d edit., 1983; Commanding Paragraphs, 1977, 2d edit., 1981; Commanding Essays, 1978, 2d edit., 1982; Commanding Composition, 1980; Connecting and Combining in Sentence and Paragraph Writing, 1982; contbr. articles on learning to profl. jours.; editorial bd. Jour. Personalized Instruction, 1974-81. Home: 3157 Oak Cliff Circle Carmichael CA 95608

MILLS, KAREN CELESTE, marketing professional, consultant; b. Chester, Pa., Aug. 29, 1955; d. Virgil Jess and Virginia Mae (Jagloski) M.; m. Thomas Lee Morris, Aug. 1, 1981 (div. Oct. 1987). BA in Communications and Bus., U. Pitts., 1977; AS in Electronic Tech., Am. Acad. Broadcasting, 1978. Engr., videotape editor Ctr. City Video, Phila., 1978-79; sales equipment trainee RCA Broadcast Systems, Camden, N.J., 1979-80; network sales rep. N.Y.C. Tektronics, Inc. div. Grass Valley (Calif.) Group, 1980-81; product mgr. EECO, Inc., Santa Ana, Calif., 1981-83; dir., vendor distbn. EasyLink for Western Union, Upper Saddle River, N.J., 1984; product mgr. Boeing Computer Services, San Francisco, 1985-86, Ampex Corp., San Francisco, 1986-87; dir. worldwide mktg. Visulux, Sunnyvale, Calif., 1988—. Mem. Soc. of Motion Pictures and TV Engrs., Internat. TV Assn., San Francisco Commonwealth Club, Soc. of Broadcast Engrs., Nat. Assn. of Female Execs., Aircraft Owners and Pilots Assn. Home: 796 Dartshire Ct Sunnyvale CA 94087 Office: Visulux 404 Tasman Dr Sunnyvale CA 94089

MILLS, LINDA S., public relations executive; b. San Antonio, June 26, 1951; d. Frank M. and Betty A. (Young) M. BA, St. Mary's U., 1971. Asst. dir. Paseo Del Rio Assn., San Antonio, 1971-74; mktg. officer Frost Nat. Bank, San Antonio, 1974-79; account exec. Fleishman Hillard Inc., St. Louis, 1979-81, v.p., sr. ptnr., 1981-85, exec. v.p., sr. ptnr., 1985-86, dir. corp. planning, 1986—; bd. dirs. Fleishman Hillard U.K. Ltd., London, FH et Associes, Paris. Mem. Pub. Relations Soc. Am. Club: Noonday (St. Louis) (bd. dirs.). Office: Fleishman Hillard Inc 200 N Broadway Saint Louis MO 63102

MILLS, MARCIA JOAN, lawyer; b. Evanston, Ill., Dec. 14, 1948; d. Fred Edward and Faye K. (Kohn) Ryherd; m. Gerald Edward Mills; children: Michael Edward, Amanda Susan. BA in English, U. Ill., 1970; JD cum laude, Fla. State U., 1975. Bar: Fla. 1975, Wis. 1977, U.S. Dist. Ct. (we. dist.) Wis. 1977, Tex. 1986. Research asst. Fla. State Ct. Appeals 1st Dist., Tallahassee, 1975-76; ptnr. Glinski, Haferman, Ilten, Mills, Dreier, SC, Stevens Point, Wis., 1976-85; asst. gen. counsel Res. Life Ins. Co., Dallas, 1985—. Bd. dirs. Womens Resource Ctr., Stevens Point, 1978-85; Cen. Wis. Alcohol and Drug Abuse Ctr., Stevens Point, 1978-85; Bd. dirs. Cen. Wis. Pvt. Industry Council, Wisconsin Rapids, 1981-85. James scholar U. Ill., 1966. Mem ABA, Dallas Council Insurance Attys. Home: 1911 Espinosa Dr Carrollton TX 75007 Office: Reserve Life Ins Co 403 S Akard St Dallas TX 75202

MILLS, MARGARET, association executive; b. Levenshulme, Eng., Dec. 16, 1921; came to U.S., 1953, naturalized, 1973; d. Leonard and Katharine (Howard) M. Student, U. London, 1939-42, Colegio Superior de Vicosa, Minas Gerais, Brazil, 1943-45. Translator, writer O Observador Economico, Rio de Janeiro, 1945-47; researcher Brazilian Embassy, London, 1948-53; asst. dir. purchasing commn. Brazilian Treasury Del., N.Y.C., 1954-64; asst. Cheryl Crawford Prodns., 1965-67; asst. to dir. AAAL, N.Y.C., 1968-73, exec. dir., 1973—. Democrat. Office: Am Acad Arts & Letters 633 W 155th St New York NY 10032

MILLS, MARGARET MARIE, lawyer, consultant; b. Norfolk, Va., Dec. 6, 1946; d. David Johnathan and Sarah Louise (Jackson) M.; m. Dwight J. Williams, June 30, 1967 (div. 1969). BA, Spelman Coll., 1970; MA, Temple U., 1974; JD, Golden Gate U., 1978. Bar: S.C. 1979, U.S. Ct. Appeals (4th cir.) 1980, U.S. Dist. Ct. S.C. 1980. Teaching asst. sch. law Golden Gate U., San Francisco, 1977-78; staff atty. Greenville (S.C.) Legal Services, 1979-80; sole practice Greenville, 1981—; ind. research asst., San Francisco, 1974-78; pres. Margaret M. Mills & Assocs. Ltd., Greenville, S.C., 1979—. Past pres. counseling program Nat. Urban League; 2d v.p. Girl Scouts U.S. Old Ninety-Six council; mem. Greenville Profl. Women's Forum, 1984; moderator Legal Viewpoints. Mem. ABA, Nat. Bar Assn. (pub. relations coordinator Phila. chpt. 1973), Nat. Council Negro Women, Nat. Assn. Female Execs., Greenville Bar Assn., S.C. Bar Assn., Greenville C. of C. Home and Office: 202 Lavinia Ave Greenville SC 29603

MILLS, NANCY LOUISE, accountant; b. Coral Gables, Fla., Sept. 29, 1960; d. Alfred Preston and Josephine Elizabeth (Sullivan) M.; m. David Edward Soderholm, July 9, 1988. B.S. in Acctg., U. Fla., 1983; M.Profl. Acctg., U. Miami, Fla., 1984; grad. Dale Carnegie Inst., 1987. C.P.A., Fla. Intern, Occidental Chem. Co., White Springs, Fla., 1982; staff auditor

Touche, Ross & Co., C.P.A.s, Miami, 1985-86; internal auditor Internat. Controls Corp., Coral Gables, Fla., 1986-87; sr. acct. Dryclean-USA, Inc., Miami, 1987—. Mem. Am. Inst. CPA's, Fla. Inst. CPA's, Nat. Assn. Female Execs., Am. Bus. Women's Assn., Am. Women's Soc. CPA's, U.S. Tennis. Assn., So. Fla. Orchid Soc., Beta Gamma Sigma. Clubs: Royal Palm Tennis, Tropical Rose Soc. (Miami). Avocations: tennis, water sports, camping, roses, orchids and cactus. Home: 9133 SW 147 Ct Miami FL 33196 Office: Dryclean-USA 9100 S Dadeland Blvd Miami FL 33156

MILLS, ROBIN KATE, law librarian; b. Chgo., Jan. 10, 1947; d. Dumont Cromwell and Virginia Anne (Nordeng) M.; A.B., Ind. U., 1969, M.L.S., 1970; J.D., U. S.C., 1976. Circulation/reference librarian Ind. U. Sch. Law, Bloomington, 1970-73; asst. law librarian U. S.C. Sch. Law, Columbia, 1973-76, asst. prof. law and law librarian, 1976-81, asso. prof. law and law librarian, 1981-84; assoc. prof. law, law librarian, 1984-87, Emory U. Sch. Law, Atlanta, 1987—. Mem. Am. Assn. Law Libraries (chpt. pres. 1980-82), Am. Bar Assn., S.C. Bar Assn., S.C. Library Assn. Author: South Carolina Legal Research Handbook, 1976. Office: Emory U Law Library Gambrell Hall Atlanta GA 30322

MILLS, SUSAN LEE, insurance underwriter; b. Troy, Mo., Dec. 29, 1960; d. James Kenneth and Kathleen Marie (Fleming) Hardy; m. Ronald Graydon Mills, Sept. 8, 1984. BS in Bus. Adminstrn., Cen. Meth. Coll., 1983. Asst. mgr. Wal-Mart, Inc., Bentonville, Ark., 1983-84; asst. dir. admissions and fin. aid Cen. Meth. Coll., Fayette, Mo., 1984-86; multi-line underwriter Shelter Ins., Columbia, Mo., 1986—. Mem. Nat. Assn. Ins. Women. Roman Catholic. Club: Lawrence Talbot Study. Home: 332 Reynolds Fayette MO 65248 Office: Shelter Ins 1817 W Broadway Columbia MO 65218

MILLS, SUSEN FINCH, consulting company executive; b. Newark, Mar. 14, 1952; d. Frederick John and Mary Lou (Schwarz) Finch; m. Darrell M. Mills, May 22, 1983. BSEE, Ariz. State U., 1974, MBA, 1986. Cert. data processor. Engr. Sperry Flight Systems, Phoenix, 1974-76; computer programmer, analyst Am. Express, Phoenix, 1977-85; research asst. coll. bus. Ariz. State U., Tempe, 1985-86; pres. Human Horizons Corp., Mesa, Ariz., 1986—; sec., treas. Human Horizons Inst., 1987—. Recipient Entrepreneurial scholarship Assn. for Corp. Growth, 1985-86. Mem. Data Processing Mgmt. Assn. (sec. 1984-85), Soc. Women Engrs., Eta Kappa Nu.

MILLWARD, CELIA MCCULLOUGH, English language educator; b. Endicott, N.Y., July 27, 1935; d. Ross William and Ruth (Williams) McCullough; m. Richard Bolster Millward, Sept. 7, 1954 (dec. 1986); 1 child, James Andrew. AB, Syracuse (N.Y.) U., 1955; MA, Brown U., 1963, PhD, 1966. Editor Bur. Bus. Research, Ind. U., Bloomington, 1957-60; from instr. to prof. English Boston U., 1966—. Author: Imperative Constructions in Old English, 1971, Handbook for Writers, 1980, A Biography of the English Language, 1988. Fellow NSF, NEH. Mem. Am. Name Soc. (mem. editorial bd.), Linguistic Soc. Am., Modern Lang. Assn., Am. Dialect Soc., Medieval Acad. Am. Home: 53 Forest St Providence RI 02906 Office: Boston U 236 Bay State Rd Boston MA 02215

MILNAR, ROSA FAY, management consultant; b. New Orleans, July 16, 1947; d. Grover Cleveland and Agnes (Ehrhardt) Walk; m. Lawrence Milnar, Aug. 12, 1971 (div. Sept. 1975); 1 child, Christopher Ray. BA in English, U. New Orleans, 1969, MA in English, 1971; MS in Human Resource Mgmt., Nova U., 1981. English lang. instr. Nicholls State U., Thibodaux, La., 1971-72; real estate mgr. Bond, Inc., New Orleans, 1972-74; mgr. tng. Ochsner Hosp., New Orleans, 1978-79, Gen. Motors, George Engine Co., New Orleans, 1979-81; supr. Coopers & Lybrand, Houston, 1982-86; prin. Mercer-Meidinger, Houston, 1986; assoc. King, Chapman & Broussard, Inc., Houston, 1986—; chair learning resources div. Delgado Coll., New Orleans, 1974-76, adj. faculty, 1974-81, N. Harris County Coll., Houston, 1982—; cons. in field, New Orleans, 1976-81, Orgnl. Mgmt. Assn., New Orleans, 1981-82; adj. mgmt. Ind. U., 1978-81; author, presenter seminars in field, 1976—. Contbr. articles on mgmt. to profl. jours., horse tng. to Horse Sheet Mag. Leader Girl Scouts, New Orleans, 1971-73, Boy Scouts Am., New Orleans, Houston, 1981-85; mem. Pres. Council Basic Edn., Washington, 1977-81. Recipient Cert. Appreciation Mayor of Houston, 1985, Mayor of Austin, 1985; named Outstanding Leader Boy Scouts Am., 1983-85. Mem. Am. Bus. Women's Assn., Nat. Female Exec. Assn., Am. Soc. Tng. and Devel. (Nat. com. 1979-80, bd. dirs. New Orleans 1979-81, Outstanding Trainer 1980, bd. dirs. Houston, 1982-84), U.S. Dressage Found., Houston Dressage Soc. Democrat. Roman Catholic. Club: Appaloosa Horse. Home: #5 Cassowary Ln Woodlands TX 77380 Office: Saint Jerome Elem Sch 8825 Kempwood Houston TX 77080

MILNE, ROBIN JAYN LAUTENBACH, sales executive; b. El Paso, Tex., Nov. 2, 1955; d. William Earl and Jacqueline Renee (Whitt) Lautenbach; m. Richard William Milne, Jr., Apr. 20, 1985. BBA, Ariz. State U., 1978. Sales rep., interior designer TOTAL/Interiors, Scottsdale, Ariz., 1975-79; sales rep. Am. Hosp. Supply, San Francisco, 1979-81, sales mgr., 1981-82, sales mgr., Sacramento, 1982-83; region mgr. H.B.O. & Co., San Francisco, 1983-85, sales dir., Scottsdale, 1985-86, v.p., Los Angeles, 1986-88—; dist. dales mgr. Oracle, Phoenix, 1988—. Mem. Nat. Assn. Profl. Saleswomen (founding pres. San Francisco 1981-82, nat. pres. 1983-85, Cross Pen Outstanding Sales Woman award 1982, rep. Am. Bus. Women's Day White Ho. Luncheon 1983), Bus. and Profl. Women's Assn. (Young Careerist award 1985, Young Career Woman award 1986). Republican. Club: Soroptomists. Avocations: racquetball, public speaking. Home: 4551 N 65th St Scottsdale AZ 85251 Office: Oracle 2600 N Central 8th Floor Phoenix AZ 85004

MILNER, BRENDA ATKINSON LANGFORD, neuropsychologist; b. Manchester, Eng., July 15, 1918; emigrated to Can., 1944; d. Samuel and Leslie (Doig) Langford. B.A., Cambridge (Eng.) U., 1939, M.A., 1949, Sc.D., 1972; Ph.D., McGill U., 1952; LL.D. (hon.), Queen's U.; ScD (hon.) U. Manitoba, U. Lethbridge, Mt. Holyoke Coll., U. Laval, U. Toronto, Mt. St. Vincent U.; Hon. D. U. de Montréal. Exptl. officer U.K. Ministry of Supply, 1941-44; prof. agrégé Institut de Psychologie, Université de Montréal, 1944-52; research asso. psychology dept. McGill U., Montreal, 1952-53, lectr. dept. neurology and neurosurgery, 1953-60, asst. prof., 1960-64, asso. prof., 1964-70, prof. psychology, 1970—; head neuropsychology research unit Montreal Neurol. Inst., 1953—; Clothworkers fellow Girton Coll., Cambridge, 1972-73. Mem. editorial bd.; Neuropsychologia, 1973—, Behavioral Brain Research, 1980. Career investigator Med. Research Council Can., 1964—; recipient Disting. Sci. Contbn. award Am. Psychol. Assn., 1973; Karl Spencer Lashley award Am. Philos. Soc., 1979; Izaak Walton Killam Meml. prize Can. Council, 1983; Hermann Von Helmholtz prize Cognitive Neuroscience Inst., 1984; Officier de l'Ordre nat. du Que., 1985; Ralph W. Gerard prize Soc. for Neuroscience USA, 1987; named Officer Order of Can., 1984. Fellow Royal Soc. London, Royal Soc. Can., Am. Psychol. Assn., AAAS, Can. Psychol. Assn.; mem. Am. Epilepsy Soc., Am. Neurol. Assn., Association de Psychologie Scientifique de Langue Française, Brit. Soc. Exptl. Psychology, Psychonomic Soc., Eastern Psychol. Assn., Internat. Neuropsychology Symposium, Soc. Neurosci. (Ralph W. Gerard prize 1987), Nat. Acad. Scis. (fgn. asso.), Am. Acad. Neurology (asso.), Assn. Research in Nervous and Mental Diseases (asso.), Royal Soc. Medicine (affiliate), Sigma Xi. Office: Montreal Neurol Inst, 3801 University St, Montreal, PQ Canada H3A 2B4

MILNER, SARAH HANDLIN, economist, educator; b. N.Y.C., July 13, 1922; d. Joseph and Ida (Young) Handlin; m. Samuel Milner, July 10, 1948; children: Eve Deborah, Elizabeth Rose. BA, Bklyn. Coll., 1944; postgrad., U. Chgo., 1945; MA, Harvard U., 1947, postgrad., 1947. Economist Internat. Monetary Fund, Washington, 1947-67; prof. econ. Trinity Coll., Washington, 1960; prof. econs. Dunbarton Coll., Washington, 1968-69; economist Orgn. Am. States, Washington, 1970-87; dir. nat. office Orgn. Am. States, Barbados, 1977-84; sr. specialist Orgn. Am. States, Washington, 1984—. Mem. exec. bd. Women in Devel., Bridgetown, Barbados, 1977—. Mem. Soc. Internat. Devel. Democrat. Jewish. Home: Apt G2H-B 3900 Watson Pl NW Washington DC 20016 Office: Orgn Am States 1889 1st St NW Washington DC 20006

MILNER, ZELDA WINOGRAD, government executive; b. Cleve., Dec. 17, 1919; d. Maurice Aaron and Rae (Garber) Winograd; m. Irvin Myron Milner, Aug. 15, 1943. AB magna cum laude, Case Western Res. U., 1941. Tchr., Cleve. Pub. Schs., 1941-42; economist War Labor Bd., Cleve., 1943-46; asst. editor ency. World Pub. Co., Cleve., 1946; economist Wage Stabilization Bd., Cleve., 1946-47; with U.S. Dept. Commerce, 1947-86, dep. dir., Cleve., 1970-80, dir., 1980-86, mem. field ops. mgmt. council, 1980-81, regional mgr., 1980-81; dep. dir. U.S. Aircraft Trade Mission, Sudan, Kenya, Nigeria, 1978; writer, voice radio scripts Sta. WGAR, 1961-77. Editor: Bull. of Commerce, 1947-64, Bus. America-Ohio, 1965-86. Mem. adv. com. Cleve. State U., 1985—, Cuyahoga Community Coll., Cleve., 1965—; mem., exec. sec. Minority Bus. Opportunity Com., Cleve., 1970-80; exec. sec. No. Ohio Dist. Export Council, Cleve., 1980-86; exec. sec. Nat. Def. Exec. Res., Cleve., 1980-86; mem. vis. com. Western Res. Coll., 1979—; bd. overseers Case Western Res. U., 1982—, mem. univ. council, 1987—; Ohio rep. World Trade Info. Ctr. Inc., Estes Park, Colo., 1987-88. Recipient Silver medal Sec. of Commerce, 1957, Creative Communication award, 1965; Fed. Career Service award Greater Cleve. Growth Assn., 1968; Spl. Achievement award Bur. of Census, 1971; Outstanding Achievement award Fed. Exec. Bd., 1976-83; Case Centennial scholar Case Inst. Tech., Case Western Res. U., 1980. Mem. Cleve. Bus. Economists Club, Phi Beta Kappa (pres. Cleve. chpt. 1968-69). Club: Women's City Cleve. (bd. dirs. 1978-83, bd. dirs. found. 1984—). Office: US Dept Commerce 666 Euclid Ave Cleveland OH 44114

MILOSIC, JUDITH STEPHANIE, academic administrator; b. Detroit, Sept. 7, 1950; d. Henry Thomas and Helen Virginia (Borowicz) Ham; m. Michael J. Milosic, Aug. 7, 1971 (div. July 1983). BS in Math, Lawrence Inst. Tech., 1976; MBA, Oakland U., 1983. Student asst. Lawrence Inst. Tech., Southfield, Mich., 1968-71, sec., 1971-73, chief acct., 1973-80, asst. dir. bus. affairs, 1980—, instr., 1984—, mem. audit review and budget review bds., 1985—. Vol. St. John's Youth Group, 1985, St. Michael's Women's Club, 1986. Nat. Assn. Female Execs., Engring. Soc. Detroit, Lawrence Inst. Tech. Alumni Assn. (sec. 1986—). Roman Catholic. Home: 25650 Circle Dr Southfield MI 48075 Office: Lawrence Inst Tech 21000 W Ten Mile Rd Southfield MI 48075

MILSTEAD, JESSICA LEE, consultant; b. Bryans Road, Md., June 4, 1939; d. J. Woodrow and Margret E. (Downs) M. AB, Ea. Nazarene Coll., Quincy, Mass., 1960; MS, Columbia U., N.Y.C., 1965; DLS, Columbia U., 1969. Asst. prof. Columbia U., N.Y.C., 1969-72, Queens Coll., N.Y.C., 1972-74; assoc. prof. St. John's U., N.Y.C., 1974-79; mgr. indexing dept. Research Publs. Inc., Woodbridge, Conn., 1979-82; v.p. NewsBank, Inc., New Canaan, Conn., 1982-86; prin. The Jelem Co., Ridgefield, Conn., 1986—. Author: Subject Headings, 1969, Subject Access Systems, 1984 (Book of Yr. 1985); contbr. numerous articles to profl. jours. Mem. ALA, Am. Soc. Indexers, Am. Soc. for Info. Sci. (chair numerous coms., exec. bd., 1987-88), Conn. Cactus and Succulent Soc. Office: The Jelem Co PO Box 1126 Ridgefield CT 06877

MILSTIEN, JULIE BLOCK, chemist; b. Waynesboro, Va., Oct. 11, 1942; d. LeRoy Pelton and Carolyn Victoria (Stitely) B.; m. Sheldon Milstien, July 3, 1966 (div. 1984); children: Sarah Susan, Benjamin. AB in Chemistry, Randolph Macon Woman's Coll., 1964; PhD in Biochemistry, U. So. Calif., Los Angeles, 1968. Staff fellow NIH, Bethesda, Md., 1968-72; spl. fellow Nat. Cancer Inst., Bethesda, 1972-73; cons. Litton Bionetics, Inc., Bethesda, 1973; research chemist FDA, Rockville, Md., 1974—; cons. Pan-Am. Health Orgn., Washington, 1983—.

MILTON, MICHELLE SANDERS, hospital quality assurance administrator; b. Arlington, Va., Oct. 9, 1958; d. Hilary Herbert and Patty (Sanders) M. BS, Samford U., 1980, MBA, 1984. Jr. programmer Cen. Computer Services, Birmingham, Ala., 1978-79; system programmer Samford U., Birmingham, 1979-81; programmer, analyst Protective Corp., Birmingham, 1981-85; cons. Peat, Marwick & Main Co., Atlanta, 1985-87; quality assurance adminstr. Crawford W. Long Med. Ctr.-Emory Univ., Atlanta, 1987—. Mem. jr. women's aux. com. Ala. Symphony, Birmingham, 1982-86; vol. Girls Club Am., Atlanta, 1986. Named one of Outstanding Young Women Am., 1981, 83, 84. Presbyterian. Home: 3057 Pharr Ct North Unit #C-4 Atlanta GA 30305 Office: Crawford Long Hosp 550 Peachtree St NE Atlanta GA 30365

MINARIK, ELSE HOLMELUND (BIGART), author; b. Aarhus, Denmark, Sept. 13, 1920; d. Kaj Marius and Helga Holmelund; B.A., Queens Coll., 1940; m. Walter Minarik, July 14, 1940 (dec.); 1 dau., Brooke Ellen; m. 2d Homer Bigart, Oct. 3, 1970. Tchr. 1st grade, art, pub. schs., Commack, N.Y., 1950-54; author children's books: Little Bear, 1957; Father Bear Comes Home, 1959; Little Bear's Friend, 1960; Little Bear's Visit, 1961; No Fighting, No Biting, 1958; Cat and Dog, 1960; The Winds That Come From Far Away, 1960; The Little Giant Girl and the Elf Boy, 1963; A Kiss for Little Bear, 1968; What If, 1987; Percy and the Five Houses, 1988. Mem. PEN Club. Home: Rural Delivery Barrington NH 03825

MINDEL, ADRIENNE RAUCHWERGER, historian, educator; b. Bayonne, N.J.; d. Joseph and Blanche (Vitriol) Rauchwerger; m. Robert G. Spivack, 1940 (dec. 1970); children—Lorna Ellen Spivack, Miranda Sheila Spivack; m. 2d, Joseph Mindel, 1975. B.A., NYU, 1941; M.A., Am. U., 1966, Ph.D., 1976. Editorial assoc. Roscoe Drummond, newspaper columnist, Washington, 1960-63; teaching asst. Am. U., Washington, 1966-68, Massey fellow, 1968-69, univ. fellow, 1969-70; asst. prof. history Hood Coll., Frederick, Md., 1970-76, assoc. prof., 1976-84, prof., 1984—; commentator Duquesne U. History Forum, 1985; mem. Wye faculty seminar Aspen Inst., 1983; cons. town planning Town of Reston (Va.), 1963-64; humanities scholar and panelist Md. Com. for Humanities, 1977, 78, com. mem., 1979-86; panelist Western Soc. for French Hist. Annual Conf., 1986. Assoc. editor Contemporary Affairs, 1963-64; contbg. editor: China and U.S. Far East Policy, 1967; contbr. articles to profl. jours. Mem. Va. Gildersleeve Internat. Fund for Univ. Women, 1981—; mem. Md. br. Nat. Coordinating Com. for Promotion of History, 1982—, AAUW Coll. Faculty Program scholar, 1964. Mem. Am. Hist. Assn., French Hist. Studies Assn., AAUP, AAUW, So. Assn. Women Historians, Phi Alpha Theta. Office: Hood Coll Dept History Frederick MD 27101

MINEKA, SUSAN, psychology educator; b. Ithaca, N.Y., June 2, 1948; d. Francis Edward and Muriel Leota (McGregor) M. BA in Psychology magna cum laude, Cornell U., 1970; PhD, U. Pa., 1974. Lic. psychologist, Ill. Prof. psychology U. Wis., Madison, 1974-85, U. Tex., Austin, 1986-87; prof. Northwestern U., Evanston, Ill., 1987—. Contbr. articles to profl. jours. NSF grantee, 1977-88. Fellow Am. Psychol. Assn.; mem. Psychonomic Soc., Assn. for Advancement of Behavior Therapy, Internat. Primatological Soc., Internat. Soc. for Research on Emotion, Sigma Xi, Phi Beta Kappa. Democrat. Home: 1825 N Lincoln Plaza #1609 Chicago IL 60614 Office: Northwestern U Psychology Dept Evanston IL 60201

MINEMIER, BETTY M(ITCHELL), educational media specialist, computer consultant; b. Dansville, N.Y., July 13, 1928; d. Marshall Bradley and Joyce (Kenney) Mitchell; m. Robert Stansbury Minemier; children: Diana, Robert Stansbury, Ronald, Leah, Martin. BS in Edn. summa cum laude, SUNY-Geneseo, 1961, MLS, 1965, MS in English, 1971. Cert. library media specialist, N.Y. Library media specialist Central Sch., Arkport, N.Y., 1961-64; library media specialist Central Sch., Dansville, 1964—, dist. coordinator, 1981—; presenter computer workshops, 1979—; vis. prof. U. Buffalo, 1987; mem. Rochester Area Resource Exchange (N.Y.), 1979—; cons. microcomputers, 1979—. Reviewer for reference books Instr., 1964-80; mem. adv. council Scholastic, Inc., 1980-83. Clk. of session Presbyterian Ch., Dansville, 1979-86; jour. clk. Genesee Valley Presbytery; mem. coll. council SUNY Coll.-Alfred, 1981—; mem. alumni council SUNY-Geneseo, 1983—. Mem. ALA, N.Y. Library Assn., Greater Rochester Area Sch. Media Sect. (mem. RESOURCES), N.Y. State Tchrs. Assn., Genesee Valley Tchrs. Assn., Am. Assn. Sch. Librarians, Dansville Tchrs. Assn., Internat. Platform Assn., Assn. Council Mems. and Coll. Trustees of SUNY, Delta Kappa Gamma (pres.), Kappa Delta Pi. Home: 20 Chestnut Ave Dansville NY 14437

MINER, CAROL SPALDING, educator; b. Louisville, Jan. 6, 1950; d. Wallace H. and Martha Lee (Ratterree) S.; BA in Internat. Studies, U. Louisville, 1972; MA in Human Resource Mgmt., Pepperdine U., 1976; m. John Boyd Miner, Oct. 2, 1971. Instr., Fla. Community Coll. at Jacksonville, 1972-77, coordinator/counselor offender assistance program, 1975-77; assoc. dir. Jacksonville Community Council, 1977-81; dir. continuing edn. Fla. Jr. Colls., 1981-85, dean Open Campus, 1985—. Mem. United Way rev. com., 1977-78; pres. Spring Homeowners Assn., 1980-83; chmn. state public affairs com. Jr. League; host Politics is Your Business, LWV; bd. dirs. Leadership Jacksonville; v.p. Goodwill Industries; bd. dirs. Tree Hill, pres., 1985. Mem. Am. Soc. Pub. Adminstrn. (dir.), Jacksonville Women's Network (v.p., EVE award). Home: 1968 Largo Pl Jacksonville FL 32207 Office: Fla Community Coll 101 W State St Jacksonville FL 32202

MINER, JACQUELINE, political consultant; b. Mt. Vernon, N.Y., Dec. 10, 1936; d. Ralph E. and Agnes (McGee) Mariani; B.A., Coll. St. Rose, 1971, M.A., 1974; m. Roger J. Miner, Aug. 11, 1975; children—Laurence, Ronald Carmichael, Ralph Carmichael, Mark. Ind. polit. cons., Hudson, N.Y.; instr. history and polit. sci. SUNY, Hudson, 1974-79. Republican county committeewoman, 1958-76; vice chmn. N.Y. State Ronald Reagan campaign, 1980; candidate for Rep. nomination for U.S. Senate, 1982; co-chair N.Y. state steering com. George Bush for Pres. campaign; chmn. Coll. Consortium for Internat. Studies; mem. White House Outreach Working Group on Central Am.; co-chmn. N.Y. State Reagan Roundup Campaign, 1984—; mem. nat. steering com. Fund for Am.'s Future. Mem. U.S. Supreme Ct. Hist. Soc., P.E.O. Address: RD 2 Box 110E Hudson NY 12534

MINGHENELLI, ANTOINETTE, personnel executive; b. Orange, N.J., Sept. 21, 1946; d. John and Julia (Lepore) Verducci; 1 child, Michael C. BS in Mgmt., Fairleigh Dickinson U., 1988. Exec. asst. Breeze Corps., Union, N.Y., 1967-80; personnel adminstr. Internat. Paint, Union, 1981-83, personnel mgr. ea. div., 1983-84, corp. personnel mgr., 1984—. Mem. Am. Soc. for Personnel Adminstrs., Adminstrv. Mgmt. Soc., Am. Mgmt. Assn., Union Twp. C. of C., Phi Omega Epsilon, Phi Zeta Kappa. Office: Internat Paint 2270 Morris Ave Union NJ 07083

MINGOUS, LOUADA FRANCES, hospital supervisor; b. Indpls., Oct. 27, 1947; d. Francis Olandon Mingous and Clara Katherine (Lucas) Fuel. AS, Purdue U., 1981, BS, 1983. Various sec. positions Meth. Hosp., Indpls., 1969-82, office mgr. fiscal services, 1982-83, sec. med. technology, 1984, adminstrv. sec. quality assurance, 1984-85, supr. clin. lab. office, 1986—. Bd. dirs. Christian Youth Crusaders, Indpls., 1970-71, Young Teens Free Meth. Ch., Indpls., 1972. Mem. Profl. Secs. Internat. (bd. dirs. 1983-84, 1st v.p. 1985-86, pres. chpt. 1986-87, com. chmn. 1987—), Nat. Assn. Female Execs., Mut. Services Assn. Avocations: music, profl. cake decorating, bowling, reading. Office: Meth Hosp Inc 1701 N Senate Blvd Indianapolis IN 46202

MINICK, PHYLLIS BRIDGE, editor; b. Los Angeles, Jan. 15, 1929; d. Louis A. and Gertrude E. Bridge; m. Stanley R. Minick, Jan. 25, 1951; children—Lloyd Scott, Ricky Patrice. B.A., UCLA, 1952. Freelance editor, writer, 1967—; contbr. articles to Dive Mag., Skin Diver, Genie, San Diego Mag, Aquarius, Atlante; oceanographic statis. researcher, scuba diver Fathoms Plus, Inc., 1967-70; sci. writer Health Communications, Inc., 1973-74; sr. house editor Scripps Clinic and Research Found., La Jolla, Calif., 1974—; instr. extension div. U. Calif., San Diego; lectr. tech. English. Mem. Soc. Tech. Communications (past chmn. San Diego chpt.), Am. Med. Writers Assn. (nat. bd. dirs.), Council Biology Editors. Home: 5860 Cactus Way La Jolla CA 92037 Office: 10666 N Torrey Pines Rd La Jolla CA 92037

MINK, MAXINE MOCK, realtor; b. Lakeland, Fla., Jan. 17, 1938; d. Idus Frank and Elizabeth (Warren) Mock; student Fla. So. Coll.; children—Lance Granger, Justin Chandler. With Union Fin. Co., Lakeland, Fla., 1956-62; partner/owner S & S Ent. & Arrow Lake Mobile Home Pk., Lakeland, Fla., 1957-66; head bookkeeper Seaboard Fin., Lakeland, 1964-68; partner Custom Chem., Inc., Lakeland, 1968-75; partner Don Emilio Perfumers, Newport Beach, Calif., 1978-79; owner Maxine Mink Public Relations, Newport Beach, 1978-83; fine homes and relocation specialist Merrill Lynch Realty, Newport Beach, 1985—. Bd. dirs. Guild of Lakeland Symphony Orch., 1972-75; mem. Lakeland Gen. Hosp. Aux., 1974-76, Mus. Modern Art. Mem. Newport Beach C. of C., Hoag Hosp. Aux., Nat. Assn. Female Execs., Orange County Music Center Guild. Republican. Clubs: Lido Isle Women's, Balboa Bay, Sherman Library and Gardens, The 552. Home: 115 Via Undine Newport Beach CA 92663 Office: PO Box 1262 Newport Beach CA 92663

MINN, SHYN CHYN, restaurant owner, educator; b. Guei-Yoñg, China, Jan. 15, 1946; came to U.S., 1968; d. Yu-Wen and Chon Show (Yu) Inn; m. Wen Jiun Minn, Aug. 24, 1968; 1 child, Andy. MA, N.E. Mo. State U., Kirksville, 1982. Owner Minn's Tea House, Kirksville, Mo., 1972—, Minn's Cuisine, Kirksville, 1983—; tchr. N.E. Mo. State U., Kirksville, 1986—. Mem. Chinese Lang. Teaching Assn. Home: 2209 East St Kirksville MO 63501

MINNAUGH, VICKI ANN, real estate broker; b. Louisville, Ky., Mar. 25, 1949; d. William Robert and Norma Jean (Fehribach) Neumeister, Sr.; m. Robert Emmett Minnaugh, June 10, 1977. AA, Miami Dade Jr. Coll., 1969; BS, Fla. State U., 1971; MS, Barry U., 1973. Tchr. Highlands County Schs., Sebring, Fla., 1971-72; tchr. Archdiocese of Miami, 1972-78, asst. prin., 1978-83; broker Zinkil Realty, Inc., Cooper City, Fla., 1983—; bd. dirs. Madonna Acad., Hollywood, Fla.; tchr. Hollywood Area Bd. Realtors, 1987. Bd. dirs. Rock Creek, Inc., Cooper City, Fla., 1978—. Mem. Nat. Assn. Realtors, Fla. Assn. Realtors,. Republican. Roman Catholic. Home: 3605 Bay Way Hollywood FL 33026 Office: 5806 S Flamingo Rd Cooper City FL 33026

MINNELLI, LIZA, singer, actress; b. Los Angeles, Mar. 12, 1946; d. Vincente and Judy (Garland) M.; m. Peter Allen, 1967 (div. 1972); m. Jack Haley, Sept. 15, 1974 (div.); m. Mark Gero, Dec. 4, 1979. Appeared in Off-Broadway revival of Best Foot Forward, 1963; recorded You Are For Loving, 1963, Tropical Nights, 1977, Liza Minelli at Carnegie Hall, 1987; appeared with mother at London Palladium, 1964; appeared in Flora, the Red Menace, 1965 (Tony award), The Act, 1977 (Tony award), The Rink, 1984; nightclub debut at Shoreham Hotel, Washington, 1965; films include Charlie Bubbles, 1967, The Sterile Cuckoo, 1969, Tell Me That You Love Me, Junie Moon, 1970, Cabaret, 1972 (Oscar award), That's Entertainment, 1974, Lucky Lady, 1975, A Matter of Time, 1976, Silent Movie, 1976, New York, New York, 1977, Arthur, 1981, Rent A Cop, Arthur on the Rocks, 1988, Sam Found Out, 1988; appeared on TV in own spl. Liza With a Z, 1972 (Recipient Emmy award 1978); other TV appearances include Goldie and Liza Together, 1980, Baryshnikov on Broadway, 1980, The Princess and the Pea, Showtime, 1983, A Time to Live, 1985. Address: care Creative Mgmt Assocs 40 W 57th St New York NY 10022 *

MINNER, RUTH ANN, state senator; b. Milford, Del., Jan. 17, 1935; m. Roger Minner. Student Del. Tech. and Community Coll. Former mem. Del. Ho. of Reps.; now mem. Del. Senate. Democrat. Office: Rt 3 Box 694 Milford DE 19963 *

MINNETTE, RHONDA WILLIAMS, sales marketing representative; b. Evansville, Ind., Oct. 10, 1952; d. Raymond Howard and Bonnie (Huebner) Williams; m. Timothy Lee Minnette, July 11, 1982; 1 child, Erin Ashly. BS in Edn., Ind. State U., 1974; MA in Curriculum and Instrns., Fla. Atlantic, Boca Raton, 1978-79. Tchr. Broward County Sch. System, Ft. Lauderdale, Fla., 1974-81; sales rep. Breon Labs., Ft. Lauderdale, 1981-82, Glaxo, Inc., Ft. Lauderdale, Fla., 1982—. Co-writer Ft. Lauderdale Emergency Sch. Aid Act, 1981. Mem. Women in Sales, Classroom Tchrs. Assn.-NEA (del. 1975-76). Republican. Office: Glaxo Inc 5 Moore Dr Research Triangle Park NC 27709

MINNICK, SANDRA LEE, counselor, social worker; b. Watsonville, Calif., June 25, 1954; d. Warren Richard and Mary Grace (Miller) Ingram; m. Ronald John Minnick, June 1, 1975; 1 child, Megan Lyn. BA in Psychology magna cum laude, Chapman Coll., 1982; MA, U. No. Colo., 1984. Adminstrv. asst. Chapman Coll., Warren AFB, Wyo., 1979-81; program coordinator Safe House Program, Inc., Cheyenne, Wyo., 1981-86; pre-sch. tchr. La Petite Acad., Inc., Simi Valley, Calif., 1987-88, asst. dir., 1988—; social worker Children's Protective Services, Ventura, Calif., 1988—; psychology instr. Chapman Coll., Warren AFB, 1985. Contbd. foreword to book: It's Not Your Fault, 1985. Chairperson Laramie County Incest Task Force, Cheyenne, 1983, sec., 1982-83, 84-85; sec. Wyo. Coalition on Family Violence and Sexual Assault, 1983-85. Served to sgt. USAF, 1974-78. Democrat. Home: 300 S Moorpark Ave #408 Moorpark CA 93021 Office: Children's Protective Services 4651 Telephone Rd Suite 201 Ventura CA 93001

MINNICK, SHIRLEY BERNECE, state agency director; b. Santa Monica, Calif., May 18, 1946; d. Harry Phillip Jr. and Frances Marian (Schroder) Becher; m. Michael Wayne Minnick, Sept. 12, 1970. BA, Calif. State U., Sacramento, 1969; MPA, Golden Gate U., 1981. Mgmt. cons. Calif. Dept. Consumer Affairs, Sacramento, 1977-80, budget analyst, 1980-81, mgr. budget ops., 1981-83, dep. chief div. consumer services, 1983-85; dep. dir. Calif. State Pub. Def.'s Office, Sacramento, 1985—; coordinator Gov.'s Task Force on Proposition 13; negotiator mgmt. bargaining team Calif. State Attys., Sacramento, 1985—. Mem. Am. Mgmt. Assn., Nat. Assn. Female Execs., Am. Arbitration Assn., Am. Soc. Personnel Adminstrs., Calif. Forum on Info. Tech. (exec. com.), Alpha Chi Omega. Democrat. Episcopalian. Office: Calif State Pub Defs Office 1107 9th St Suite 650 Sacramento CA 95814

MINNIE, MARY VIRGINIA, social worker, educator; b. Eau Claire, Wis., Feb. 16, 1922; d. Herman Joseph and Virginia Martha (Strong) M. BA, U. Wis., 1944; MA, U. Chgo., 1949, Case Western Reserve U., 1956. Lic. clin. social worker, Calif. Supr. day care Wis. Children Youth, Madison, 1949-57; coordinator child study project Child Guidance Clinic, Grand Rapids, Mich., 1957-60; faculty, community services Pacific Oaks Coll., Pasadena, Calif., 1960-70; pvt. practice specializing in social work various cities, Calif., 1970-78; cons., educator So. Calif. Health Care, North Hollywood, Calif., 1978—; med. social worker Kaiser Permanente Home Health, Downey, Calif., 1985-87; assoc. Baby Sitters Guild, Inc., 1987—; cons. Home Health, 1987—; pres. Midwest Assn. Nursery Edn., Grand Rapids, 1958-60; bd. dirs., sec. So. Calif. Health Care, North Hollywood; bd. dirs., v.p. Baby Sitters Guild Inc., South Pasadena; cons. project Head Start Office Econ. Opportunity, Washington, 1965-70. Mem. Soc. Clin. Social Workers, Nat. Assn. Social Workers, Nat. Assn. Edn. Young Children (1960-62). Democrat. Club: Altrusa (Laguna Beach, Calif.) (pres. 1984-87). Home and Office: 1622 Bank St S Pasadena CA 91030

MINNINGER, SANDRA L., retail company administrator; b. Boyertown, Pa., Oct. 6, 1960; d. William Lewis and Hazel Leah (Stoudt) M. Grad. high sch., Boyertown, 1978. Store detective Jefferson Ward, Pottstown, Pa., 1981-84; mgr. loss prevention, safety Jefferson Ward, Pottstown, 1984-85; mgr. regional loss prevention Radio Shack/Tandy Corp., Phila., 1985—. Mem. Nat. Assn. Female Execs. Office: Radio Shack Loss Prevention Office 1101 Woodland Rd Wyomissing PA 19610

MINOR, ADDINE E., civic leader; b. Tupelo, Miss., June 22, 1919; d. George Bradley and Myrtle (Guyton) Jones; m. William Minor, Oct. 11, 1941; children: Ramona June Warhurst, Deborah Merle Ruff, William Bradley, Bonnie Sue Shannon. AA, So. Bapt., 1974; student, Parke Coll. Sec., bookkeeper Sinclair Refining Co., Osceola, Ark., 1948-53, Judge A.F. Barham, Osceola, 1953-59; sec., then welfare counselor State of Ark., Blytheville and Osceola, 1959-63; substitute tchr. State of Ark., Luxora and Osceola, 1983-86; sec., counselor U.S. Govt., Blytheville AFB, 1963-83; exec. sec. Calvary Bapt. Ch., Osceola, 1986—; class sec. bible study First Bapt. Ch., Osceola, 1985-86; mem. Calvary Bapt. Ch. 1971—, leader tng. union, 1986—, tng. union dir., 1988—, served baptismal com., 1986-88; ch. clk., 1988—. Recipient English award State Miss., 1936, PMIT Golden Fingers award Hdqrs. SAC Offutt AFB NE, 1978, 79, 80, Presdl. Cert. U.S. Govt., Washington, 1983. Mem. Explorer Bible First Bapt. Ch., Home Bible Study, Women's Missionary Union, Farm Bur., Nat. Assn. Female Execs., Homemaker's Extension Club (sec., treas. to 1987), Gen. Fedn. Women's Clubs, Profl. Women's Orgn., Worldwide Communications. Republican.

MINSHULL, RUTH ELLEN, publishing executive, writer; b. Battle Creek, Mich., Oct. 9, 1926; d. Vernon Bradley and Laura Minerva (Percy) Convis; m. Robert T. Minshull, June 5, 1948 (div. 1965); children: Paul Robert, Lee Steven. Student, Albion (Mich.) Coll., 1946-47. Pub., writer SAA Pub., Northport, Mich., 1968—. Author: Miracles For Breakfast, 1968, How to Choose Your People, 1972, Logic Puzzles, 1981, Free Money, 1985, numerous others. Mem. Nat. Writers Club, Mensa. Office: SAA Pub Box 117 Northport MI 49670

MINSK, JANNA, land use planner; b. Los Angeles, Aug. 16, 1955; d. Stanley Carl and Hetty Rose (Herman) M. BA in Sociology and Social Scis., U. Calif., Santa Barbara, 1977; MA City and Regional Planning, Calif. Poly. State U., 1988. Code enforcement officer planning dept. San Luis Obispo County, Calif., 1983-85; community planner City of Santa Barbara, 1985-86; regional planner Ventura (Calif.) County Resource Mgmt. Agy., 1986—; transp. cons. Area Council Govts., mktg. cons., supr., permit processor Public Works Agy., San Luis Obispo, 1982-83. Mem. Am. Planning Assn., Calif. Chpt. Am. Planning Assn., Sierra Club. Jewish. Home: 6645 Thille St #191 Ventura CA 93003 Office: Ventura County RMA Planning 800 S Victoria Ave Ventura CA 93003

MINTON, KATHRYN LYNETTE, dentist; b. Independence, Mo., Sept. 8, 1958; d. Donald Ray and Marilyn Yvonne (Smith) Thomas; m. Mark V. Minton, Aug. 8, 1981; 1 child, Elizabeth Anne. DDS, Baylor U., 1984; BS, U. Mo., Kansas City, 1987. Nursing asst. Bethany Med. Ctr., Kansas City, Kans., 1978-81; dir. off campus housing U. Mo., Kansas City, 1979-80; pvt. practice dentistry Dallas, 1984—; clin. instr. Baylor U., Dallas. Mem. ADA, Acad. Gen. Dentistry, Tex. Acad. Gen. Dentistry, Am. Assn. Dental Research, Metroplex Assn. Women Dentists, Dallas County Dental Soc. Republican. Mem. Reorganized Ch. of Jesus Christ of Latter-day Saints. Club: Young Lawyers' Wives Aux. (Dallas). Office: Kathryn L Minton DDS 7475 Skillman St #101-C Dallas TX 75231

MINTZ, GILDA YOLLES, public relations company executive; b. N.Y.C.; d. Naftali and Sarah Pearl (Langner) Yolles; B.A., Hunter Coll., 1956; children—Louis Neil, Stephen Matthew. With Ruder Finn & Rotman Inc., N.Y.C., 1960-85, account supr., 1970-85, sr. v.p., 1978-85; pres. Gilda Yolles Mintz & Assocs., Inc., pub. relations and mktg., 1986-87; sr. v.p. Dorf & Stanton Communications, Inc., 1987—. Chmn. pub. relations adv. bd. Twp. of Teaneck (N.J.). Mem. Pub. Relations Soc. Am. (Silver Anvil award), Nat. Home Fashions League (v.p., past dir.), Am. Soc. Interior Designers. Office: 111 5th Ave New York NY 10003

MINUZZO, ANTOINETTE, educator; b. Lake Forest, Ill., Nov. 20, 1938; d. Frank and Maria Minuzzo; B.A., Lake Forest Coll., 1960; M.A., Northwestern U., 1967. Tchr., Oak Terrace Sch., Highwood, Ill., 1960—; cons. Xerox Ednl. Pubs., My Weekly Reader. Local and state edn. lobbyist; chmn. Ill. Polit. Action Com. for Edn., 1974-80. Bd. dirs. Literacy Vols. of Lake County, 1983-88. Recipient Those Who Excel award, 1974. Mem. NEA, Ill. Edn. Assn. (dir. 1972-80), Highwood-Highland Park Edn. Assn. (pres. 1987-89), Nat. Assn. Female Execs., AAUW, Phi Delta Kappa, Delta Kappa Gamma (pres. chpt. 1982-84, state legis. chmn. 1981-85, state rec. sec. 1985-87, 1st v.p. 1987—). Home: 813 Jenkisson Rd Lake Bluff IL 60044

MIRABELLA, GRACE, magazine editor; b. Maplewood, N.J., June 10, 1930; d. Anthony and Florence (Bellofatto) M.; m. William G. Cahan, Nov. 24, 1974. B.A., Skidmore Coll., 1950. Mem. exec. tng. program Macy's, N.Y.C., 1950-51; mem. fashion dept. Saks Fifth Ave., N.Y.C., 1951-52; with Vogue mag., N.Y.C., 1952-54, 56-88; assoc. editor Vogue mag., 1965-71, editor-in-chief, 1971-88; mem. pub. relations staff Simonetta & Fabiani, Rome, Italy, 1954-56; hon. bd. dirs. Catalyst; lectr. New Sch. Social Research. Adv. bd. Columbia U. Sch. Journalism; hon. bd. advisers Kent State U. Sch. Fashion Merchandising. Decorated cavalier Order of Merit Republic of Italy; recipient Outstanding Grad. Achievement award Skidmore Coll., 1972; Fashion Critics award Parsons Sch. Design, 1985; Woman of Distinction award Birmingham-So. Coll., 1985, Girl Scouts Am. Leadership award, 1987, Excellence in Media award Susan G. Komen Found., 1987, Equal Opportunity award NOW, 1987. Mem. Women's Forum N.Y. Office: Vogue Condé Nast 350 Madison Ave New York NY 10017

MIRABELLA, KAREN RAE, communications executive; b. Colorado Springs, Colo., Mar. 2, 1945; d. Orville A. and Dorothy R. (Wallace) Parsons; m. Emil John Mirabella Jr., Mar. 14, 1968 (div. Mar. 1984); 1 child, Marcus John. BS in Sociology-Anthropology, Colo. State U., 1967. Trainee U.S. Army Logistics Mgmt. Systems Agy., St. Louis, 1968-70; applications programmer USAF Acctg. and Fin. Ctr., Denver, 1970-75, communications systems programmer, 1975-79, communications analyst, 1979-85, supr. data communications, 1985-87; computer communications specialist Pentagon USAF, Washington, 1987—. Mem. Am. Soc. Mil. Controllers, Air Force Assn. Democrat. Methodist. Office: AFAFC/SCCC Lowry AFB Denver CO 80279-5000 Office: USAF Hdqrs/SCCM Pentagon Rm 5E 165 Washington DC 20330

MIRAGLIO, ANGELA MARIA, dietitian; b. Chgo., Sept. 12, 1944; d. Charles A. and Rose C. (Moles) M.; m. Robert S. Schwartz, Oct. 22, 1983. BS, Mundelein Coll., 1966; MS, U. Chgo., 1975. Registered dietitian. Clin. nutrition dir. West Suburban Kidney Ctr., Oak Park, Ill., 1974-78; clin. nutritionist Pediatric Outpatient Clinics U. Chgo., 1978-83; owner AMM Nutrition Services, Hinsdale, Ill. and Chgo., 1984—; part-time instr. Chgo. City-Wide Coll., 1979-81; lectr. DePaul U. Sch. Nursing, Chgo., 1978-80. Author: Food Composition Tables for Renal Diets, 1978; contbr. articles to profl. jours. Bd. dirs. Dorridge Condominium Assn., Chgo. Mem. Am. Dietetic Assn. (bd. dirs. Chgo. chpt.), Am. Diabetes Assn., Am. Assn. Diabetes Educators, Soc. for Nutrition Edn., Chgo. Dietetic Assn. (sec. 1969-71), Chgo. Nutrition Assn. Roman Catholic. Home: 5402 S Dorchester #2 Chicago IL 60615 Office: AMM Nutrition Services 120 E Ogden Ave Suite 13 Hinsdale IL 60521

MIRKIN, MARSHA PRAVDER, psychologist; b. N.Y.C., Apr. 14, 1953; d. Sidney and Ann Toby (Goldman) P.; m. Mitchell I. Mirkin, Oct. 2, 1983; 1 child, Allison Sarah. B.A. (Regents scholar 1969-73, Sullivan award 1973), SUNY, Stony Brook, 1973; Ph.D., SUNY, Albany, 1979. Tchr. high sch. English, 1973-74; unit psychologist O.D. Heck Devel. Center, Schenectady, 1976-77; group home supr. Bosco House of St. Catherine's Center Children, Albany, 1977-78; intern Children's Psychiat. Center, Red Bank, N.J., 1978-79; adolescent clin. cons. Charles River Counseling Center, Newton, Mass., 1979-81; coordinator adolescent psychotherapy Charles River Hosp., Wellesley, Mass., 1981, dir. adolescent psychotherapy, 1981-84, dir. adolescent internship tng., 1984-85, dir. psychology tng., 1985; pvt. practice psychotherapy, consultation and tng., Newton, 1985—; supr. Am. Assn. Marriage and Family Therapy; clin. instr. psychiatry Boston U. Med. Sch., 1981-84, asst. clin. prof., 1984—; guest lectr., cons., workshop leader in field. Mem. Am. Psychol. Assn., Am. Orthopsychiat. Assn., Soc. Family Therapy and Research, Women's Action for Nuclear Disarmament, Am. Family Therapy Assn. Jewish. Editor: Social and Political Contexts of Family Therapy; co-editor: Handbook of Adolescents and Family Therapy. Author papers in field. Office: 53 Langley Rd Suite 300 Newton Center MA 02159

MIRSKY, SONYA WOHL, librarian, curator; b. N.Y.C., Nov. 12, 1925; d. Louis and Anna (Steiger) Wohl; m. Alfred Ezra Mirsky, Aug. 24, 1967 (dec. June 1974). B.S. in Edn., CCNY, 1948; M.S.L.S., Columbia U., 1950. Asst. librarian Rockefeller U., N.Y.C., 1949-60, assoc. librarian, 1960-77, univ. librarian, 1977—; v.p., trustee Med. Library Ctr. N.Y., 1980—; cons. library mgmt. Mem. Bibliog. Soc. Am., Bibliog. Soc. Can., Bibliog. Soc. Gt. Britain, Soc. Bibliography of Natural History. Home: 500 E 63rd St Apt 15C New York NY 10021 Office: Rockefeller U Library 1230 York Ave New York NY 10021

MIRSKY, SUSAN, personnel director; b. N.Y.C., Nov. 5, 1939; d. Ira Albert and Ethel Maxine (Goldstein) Schur; m. Stanley Mirsky, Jan. 24, 1963; children: Jennifer L., Jonathan S. BA, Smith Coll., 1961; postgrad., NYU, 1961-62. Employment interviewer Met. Life Ins. Co., N.Y.C., 1962-63, supr. employment, 1963-66; personnel adminstr. J. Walter Thompson Co., N.Y.C., 1981-82, personnel mgr., 1982-84, v.p., dir. U.S. personnel, 1985-86, sr. v.p., worldwide personnel dir., 1986—. Adv. mem. Boys Harbor, N.Y.C., 1963—; mem. dr.'s com. Mt. Sinai Med. Ctr., N.Y.C., 1985—. Mem. N.Y. Persnnel Mgmt. Assn., N.Y. Human Resource Planners. Office: J Walter Thompson Co 466 Lexington Ave New York NY 10017

MIRUSKI, ELIZABETH ANN, school system administrator; b. Stonega, Va., Dec. 22, 1932; d. James Malcolm and Lula Ethel (Betchman) L.; m. Michael Miruski, Jr., Oct. 29, 1955; 1 child, Michele Ann. Student, Radford U., 1951-53; BS in Edn., Cen. State U., Edmond, Okla., 1972, MEd, 1976; Cert. in Computer Edn., U. Okla., 1986. Cert. secondary edn. tchr., Okla. Sec. Forman & Parrish Law Firm, Alexandria, Va., 1953-55; court reporter Dept. Army C.E., Camp Drum, N.Y., 1956-57; sec. Topeka Savs. Assn., 1957-58; sec., compositor Gen. Electric Co., Syracuse, N.Y., 1959-62; sec. Gen. Electric Co., Oklahoma City, 1962-66; tchr. Bishop McGuinness High Sch., Oklahoma City, 1971-72, Putnam City High Sch., Oklahoma City, 1972-74; curriculum coordinator office adminstrn. Putnam City Ind. Schs., Oklahoma City, 1974—; bd. dirs. Regional Apple Computer Educators Consortium, Okla. Educators Telecommunications and Teleconferencing. Author: Introduction to Business Technology; contbr. articles to profl jours; designer various ednl. tng. programs. Dir. Jr. Achievement, Oklahoma City, 1983—. Mem. Okla. Bus. Edn. Assn. (pres. 1975-76), Okla. Council Econ. Edn., Okla. Soc. for Curriculum, Future Tchrs. Am. (advisor Oklahoma City chpt. 1972-79), Okla. Microcomputer Edn. Assn., Nat. Assn. Female Execs., Okla. Women Female Execs., Okla. Career Edn. Assn., Am. Soc. Curriculum Devel., Delta Kappa Gamma, Kappa Delta Pi. Home: 6440 N Sterling Dr Oklahoma City OK 73132 Office: Putnam City Schs 5401 NW 40th St Oklahoma City OK 73132

MIRZA, LEONA LOUSIN, educator; b. Chgo., July 1, 1944; d. Max B. and Opal Lousin; B.A. in Math., North Park Coll., Chgo., 1965; M.A. in Edn., Western Mich. U., Kalamazoo, 1967, Ed.D. in Edn., 1972; m. David B. Mirza; children—Sara Anush, Elizabeth Ann. Tchr. Kalamazoo Pub. Schs., 1965-69; asso. prof. edn. North Park Coll., 1969—. Chmn. adv. com. on edn. in Ill., 1975-77. Mem. Nat., Ill. assns. supervision and curriculum devel., Ill. Assn. Colls. of Tchr. Edn., Ill. Assn. Tchrs. Edn. in Pvt. Colls. (officer 1974-86). Contbr. articles to profl. jours. Specialist in elem. curriculum and adminstrn. Home: 795 Lincoln Ave Winnetka IL 60093 Office: 3225 W Foster Ave Chicago IL 60625

MISCHELL, PATRICIA LUCILLE, author, minister; b. Hurricane, W.Va., July 5, 1936; d. William and Gladys Lou (Tabor) Chapman; children—Rene Victoria, Cynthia Ann, Steven Joseph Zang. Student pub. schs., Blue Ash, Ohio. Founder, Hope Ministries and Positive Living Ctr.; pres. World of ESP; cons. Sci. Bur. of Investigation in N.Y.; affiliated with Tour Crafters of Cin.; lectr. in field; parapsychologist. Author: Beyond Positive Thinking, 1985. Mem. PSI Center, Positive Living Found., Assn. for Spiritual Devel. and Research, Spiritual Frontiers Fellowship, The Rosicrucian Order, Assn. for Research and Enlightenment, Internat. Entrepreneurs Assn., Nat. Fedn. Ind. Bus., Noohra Found. Office: Positive Living Center-Hope Ministry 8425 Vine St Cincinnati OH 45216

MISCIOSCIA, JOSEPHINE ELIZABETH, translator; b. N.Y.C., Mar. 19, 1939; d. Jack Joseph and Elisa (Bologna) Cecchini; m. Andrew Miscioscia (div. 1985). AAS, Latin Am. Inst., 1960; BA in Polit. Sci., U. Rome, 1962; student, Fordham U., 1962-63. Research and exec. asst. Carnegie Endowment and U.S. Mission to UN, N.Y.C., 1962-65; admissions counselor, instr. diplomatic history Latin Am. Inst., N.Y.C., 1965-68; tchr. Holy Family Sch., N.Y.C., 1968-71; Italian affairs specialist U.S. State Dept., Washington and N.Y.C., 1972—; cons. UN and U.S. State Dept., 1972—; translator U. Rome Internat. Confs., 1984. Editor: Long Road to Freedom, 1960; contbr. various profl. jours. Docente Raynham Hall, Coe Hall, Oyster Bay, N.Y., 1985—; active Am. Cancer Soc., 1981—, Am.-Italian Cultural Com., 1958—, Am. Com. for Italian Migration, 1968—, Italy-Am. Soc., 1962—. Recipient Pope Pius X award N.Y. Roman Cath. Archdiocese, 1986. Mem. Acad. Polit. Sci., U.S. Equestrian Team, L.I. Historical Soc. (merit award). Conservative. Roman Catholic. Club: Rosary Soc. (Glen Cove) (pres. 1984, 85). Home: 98 Pound Hollow Rd Old Brookville NY 11545

MISHKIN, HERMINE PENNY, occupational therapist; b. N.Y.C., Nov. 4, 1949; d. Sidney and Jeanne (Silverstein) Mishkin. BA, NYU, 1971; MS, Columbia U., 1978. Registered occupational therapist. Publicity asst. Grosset & Dunlap, N.Y.C., 1972-73; editorial asst. Random House, N.Y.C., 1973-75; supr. occupational therapy Blueberry Sch., Bklyn., 1979-81; sr. occupational therapist St. Vincent's Hosp., N.Y.C., 1981—; cons. Mt. Sinai Hosp., 1985-86, The Children's House Presch., 1986—. Mem. Am. Occupational Therapy Assn., Met. N.Y. Dist. Occupational Therapy Assn., N.Y. State Occupational Therapy Assn., Ctr. for Study of Sensory Integration Internat. (cert.). Clubs: Atrium, East River Tennis.

MISHOE, RAINELLE DIXON, small business owner; b. Burlington, N.C., Feb. 18, 1950; d. James Milo and Nellie (Rainey) Dixon; m. Harmon W. Mishoe Jr., Apr. 23, 1988; 1 child from previous marriage, Jessica Rainelle Tinsley. BA in English, N.C. State U., 1972. Cert. tchr., real estate broker. Tchr. Richard B. Harrison Jr. High Sch., Selma, N.C., 1972-73, Flat Rock (N.C.) Jr. High Sch., 1973-79; owner, designer The Finishing Touch, Carolina Beach, 1981-87; tchr. lang. arts Lake Forest Jr. High Sch., Carolina Beach, 1987-88; tchr. English Haggard High Sch., 1988—; chmn. curriculum com. Henderson County Bd. Edn., Hendersonville, N.C., 1978-79; mem. archtl. rev. bd. Old Chimney Homeowners Assn., 1985-86. Feature writer Hendersonville Times News, 1976-77. Pres. Hendersonville Jaycettes, 1975, treas., 1976, chmn. bd. dirs., 1977; mem. family life com. First United Meth. Ch., Hendersonville, N.C. Recipient Dist. Spoke award Hendersonville Jaycettes, 1977; named Outstanding Jaycette, Hendersonville Jaycettes, 1976. Mem. Nat. Home Furnishings Assn., So. Home Furnishings Assn., Cape Fear Sales and Mktg. Assn. (social chmn. 1986), Kappa Kappa Iota (historian 1977, v.p. 1978, pres. 1979, chmn. bd. dirs. 1980-81). Democrat. Methodist. Club: Jr. Woman's (Hendersonville). Home: 214 Chimney Ln Wilmington NC 28403

MISNER, KIMBERLY IRENE, chiropractor, nurse; b. Neptune, N.J., Nov. 3, 1955; d. Ray Hunting and Lelia Ruth (Ledden) M. BS in Nursing, Trenton State Coll., 1978; D of Chiropractic, Sherman Coll. of Straight Chiropractic, 1984. Registered nurse, N.J. RN Jersey Shore Med. Ctr., Neptune, 1980-81; pvt. practice chiropractic medicine Neptune, 1984—. Mem. Internat. Chiropractic Soc., Monmouth and Ocean County Women's Chiropractic Soc., Monmouth and Ocean County Chiropractic Soc., Asbury Park (N.J.) C. of C. (past bd. dirs.). Republican. Methodist. Home: 185 W Sylvania Ave Neptune City NJ 07753 Office: Misner Chiropractic Health Ctr 185 W Sylvania Ave Neptune City NJ 07753

MISNER, LORRAINE, laboratory technologist; b. Fitchburg, Mass., June 24, 1948; d. Cedric Winfield and Pearl Erma (Hallisey) M. BA in Biology, Fitchburg State Coll., 1971; MS in Med. Technology, Anna Maria Coll., 1983. Lab. technologist Leominster (Mass.) Hosp., 1971-87; research asst. U. Lowell (Mass.) Research Found., 1987—. Piccolo Townsend (Mass.) Military Band, 1964—; mem. choir United Ch. of Christ. Mem. Am. Soc. of Clin. Pathologists (assoc., registrant), Am. Soc. for Med. Technology, Mass. Soc. for Med. Technology.

MITCHAM, KAREN JO, management, sales development training company executive; b. Erie, Pa., Nov. 12, 1946; d. Chrstian Niels and Marguerite Lucille (Shaffer) Blumensaadt; B.F.A., Mercyhurst Coll., 1969; m. John B. Stoeckley, Nov. 14, 1981; 1 son, Clark Shaffer; children by previous marriage, Aaron Urie, M. Denton; 1 stepson, Reed B. Owner, The Crow's Nest, retail store, Oil City, Pa., 1973-77; pres. Karen Mitcham Assos., mfrs. rep., Monroeville, Pa., 1974-78; mktg. dir., culinary cons. Cousances div. Schiller & Asmus, Inc., Chgo., 1978-80; exec. adminstr. Ingrid At Home, direct selling, North Chicago, Ill., 1980-83; v.p. mktg. and sales Wicker World Enterprises Inc., Bensenville, Ill., 1984-85; exec. dir. Skin Care Internat. (doing bus. as Peau Soin Internat.), direct selling, Sandy, Utah, 1985-86; trainer, account exec., Nat. Tng. Programs, Inc., Clarendon Hills, 1986—; freelance pub. speaker. Vice pres. Assn. Promotion Oil City, 1976; bd. dirs. Greater Pitts. Mdse. Mart, 1977; vestrywoman Calvary Episcopal Ch., Louisiana, 1986—. Democrat. Home: Route 1 Box 193A Louisiana MO 63353

MITCHAM, PATRICIA ANN HAMILTON, educator; b. El Paso, Tex., Sept. 8, 1942; d. Leverett Chandler and Annabelle Hamilton; m. Eugene Louis Mitcham III, Apr. 20, 1968; children: Shirley Dianne, Steven Craig. BA, Tex. Western Coll., 1964; postgrad., U. Calif., Irvine, 1983-85. Educator U. Tex., El Paso, 1964-66; instr. Hardin Simmons U., Abilene, Tex., 1966-67; educator El Paso Pub. Schs., 1968-70, 74-59; English instr. Los Angeles Unified Sch. Dist., 1979-87; instr. social studies Huntsville (Ala.) City Schs., 1988—; tng. supr. of vols. Army Community Service, Ft. Bliss, Tex., 1971-73, asst. supr., 1973-74. Aerospace edn. officer CAP, dep. comdr; mem. Decatur Composite. Mem. DAR, Assn. Supervision and Curriculum Devel., Internat. Platform Assn., Nat. Council Tchrs. of English, Computer Using Educators, Huntsville Gem and Mineral. Soc. (recording sec. 1988). Republican. Episcopalian. Home: 1919 McDowling Huntsville AL 35803 Office: Stone Mid Sch 2620 Clinton Ave W Huntsville AL 35805

MITCHELL, ALICE SCHAFFER, lawyer; b. Mobile, Ala., Jan. 23, 1950; d. William James and Alice Martii (Ford) Schaffer; m. Timothy Allen Mitchell, Mar. 6, 1976; children: Meghan Ann, Kathleen Christine. B.S., U. Ala.-Tuscaloosa, 1971, J.D., 1974. Bar: Ala. 1975, Okla. 1976, U.S. Dist. Ct (we. dist.) Okla. 1980, U.S. Supreme Ct. 1981. Contractman, Texaco, Inc., Tulsa, 1974-77; landman, atty. Sabine Corp., Oklahoma City, 1977-79; trial examiner Corp. Commn., Oklahoma City, 1979, conservation atty., 1980-82; atty. Linn & Helms, Oklahoma City, 1979-80; div. atty. Inexco Oil Co., Oklahoma City, 1982-85; ptnr. Mitchell & Mitchell, Edmond, Okla., 1985—; lectr. Okla. U., Norman, 1982. Mem. Okla. Bar Assn. Interstate Oil Compact Commn., Oklahoma City Mineral Lawyers, Women's Exec. Network (v.p.), Oklahoma City Title Attys., Jefferson Bryan State Dem. Club (pres.), Dem. Women's Club, DAR. Democrat. Roman Catholic. Club: Zonta. Office: 2 East 11 Suite 7 Edmond OK 73034

MITCHELL, ANDREA LOUISE, journalist; b. N.Y.C., Oct. 30, 1946; d. Sydney and Cecile Mitchell. B.A., U. Pa., 1967. Polit. reporter KYW Newsradio, Phila., 1967-76; polit. corr. Sta. KYW-TV, Phila., 1972-76; corr. Sta. WTOP-TV, Washington, 1977-78; gen. assignment and energy corr. NBC News, Washington, 1978-81; White House corr. NBC News, 1981—; instr. Gt. Lakes Colls. Assn., 1974-76. Recipient award for public affairs reporting Am. Polit. Sci. Assn., 1969; Public Affairs Reporting award AP, 1976; AP Broadcast award, 1977; Communicator of Yr. award Phila. chpt. Women in Communications, 1976. Mem. Sigma Delta Chi (award for broadcast reporting Phila. chpt. 1975). Club: Nat. Press. Office: 4001 Nebraska Ave NW Washington DC 20016

MITCHELL, BARBARA BILLINGS, pharmacist, educator; b. Elkin, N.C., Sept. 26, 1945; d. Thomas Carmel and Eva Mae (Johnson) Billings; m. Jackson Taylor Pugh, Feb. 28, 1969 (div. 1979); children: Miriam Ashley, David Taylor; m. William Paul Mitchell, June 22, 1984. BS, U. N.C., Greensboro, 1967. Engring. asst. Beaunit Fibers, Research Triangle Park, N.C., 1967-69; instr. Pamlico County Tech. Coll., Grantsboro, N.C., 1970-71; exec. sec. N.C. State U., Raleigh, 1977-80; office mgr. George Smart Architects, Raleigh, 1981-83; pharmacy edn. adminstr. Glaxo Inc., Research Triangle Park, 1983-87, mgr. continuing edn., 1987—. Mem. Nat. Assn. Female Execs., Am. Pharm. Assn., Am. Assn. Colls. Pharmacy, Am. Soc. Hosp. Pharmacists, Nat. Assn. Retail Druggists. Democrat. Methodist. Office: Glaxo Inc Five Moore Dr Research Triangle Park NC 27709

MITCHELL, BETTY JO, writer, publisher; b. Coin, Iowa, May 2, 1931; d. Edith Darrah McWilliams; B.A., S.W. Mo. State U., Springfield; M.S.L.S., U. So. Calif. Asst. acquisitions librarian Calif. State U., Northridge, 1967-69, librarian for personnel and fin., 1969-71, acting asso. library dir., 1971-72, asso. dir. univ. libraries, 1972-81; owner Viewpoint Press, Tehachapi, Calif.; cons. Western Interstate Commn. for Higher Edn. USOE Inst. for Tng. in Staff Devel. Problem Solving; participant workshops in field. Bd. dirs. San Fernando Valley council Girl Scouts U.S.A., 1974-77, employed personnel com., 1979—; bd. dirs. Bear Valley Springs Condominium Owners Assn., 1978, Empyrean Found., 1978—. Mem. Assn. Women in Computing (bd. dirs. 1987—), ALA (mem., chmn. various coms.), Nat. Library Assn., Calif. Library Assn., Assn. Calif. State U. Profs. (sec., exec. com., 1971-72), AAUP, Pi Beta Chi, Alpha Mu Gamma. Co-author: Cost Analysis of Library Functions: A Total System Approach, 1978; author: ALMS: A Budget Based Library Management System, 1982; co-author: How to See the U.S. on $12 a Day; speaker profl. confs.; contbr. writings to profl. publs.; editor Staff Development column in Special Libraries, 1975-76. Home: Star

Route 3 Box 4600-7 Tehachapi CA 93561 Office: PO Box P Tehachapi CA 93561

MITCHELL, CAROLANN, nursing educator; b. Portsmouth, Va., Aug. 31, 1942; d. William Howell and Eleanor Bertha (Wesarg) M.; m. David Alan Friedman, June 17, 1971 (div. 1988). Diploma, NYU, 1963; BS, Columbia U., 1968, MA, 1971, EdM, 1974, EdD, 1980. Charge nurse Nassau County Med. Ctr., East Meadow, N.Y., 1963-65; staff nurse Meml. Hosp., N.Y.C., 1965-68; head nurse, supr. Community Hosp. at Glen Cove (N.Y.), 1969-71; assoc. prof. dept. nursing Queensborough Community Coll. CUNY, Bayside, 1971-80; assoc. prof. Marion A. Buckley Sch. Nursing Adelphi U., Garden City, N.Y., 1981-88; ednl. cons. Nat. League for Nursing, N.Y.C., 1980-81; prof. sch. nursing SUNY, StonyBrook, 1988—, chmn. adult nursing, 1988—; mem. faculty Regents Coll. degrees in nursing program U. State U. N.Y., Albany, 1978—, cons., 1978—. Editor Scholarly Inquiry in Nursing Practice jour., 1983—; contbr. articles to profl. jours. Robert Wood Johnson clin. nurse scholar postdoctoral fellow U. Rochester (N.Y.), 1983-85. Mem. Am. Nurses Assn., Nat. League for Nursing, Gerontol. Soc. Am., N.Am. Nursing Diagnosis Assn., Soc. for Research in Nursing Edn.

MITCHELL, CHERRY ANNE, financial planner; b. Glendale, Calif., Nov. 14, 1950; d. John R. and Mabel B. (Stevenson) M. AA in Nursing, Los Angeles Valley Coll., 1971. Cert. Fin. Planner; RN, Calif. Agt., registered rep. Prin. Fin. Group, Visalia, Calif., 1984-87; registered rep. Foothill Securities, Inc., Visalia, 1987-88, Southmark Fin. Services Inc., Fresno, Calif., 1988—. Vol. Hospice of Tulare County, Visalia, 1986-87. Mem. Internat. Assn. Fin. Planners, Inst. Cert. Fin. Planners, Networking for Women (bd. dirs. Visalia chpt. 1986—), Tulare-Kings Assn. Life Underwriters (sec./treas. 1985—), Estate Planning Council of Tulare County, Visalia C. of C. Republican. Baptist. Club: Visalia Coin Collectors. Home: 5621 W Elowin Dr Visalia CA 93291 Office: Prosperity Planning Services 350 W Caldwell Ave Visalia CA 93277

MITCHELL, CHERYL ELAINE, marketing executive; b. Oceanside, N.Y., Dec. 27, 1951; d. Harold Bertram and Doris Meredith (Hose) M. BA in History, Polit. Sci., Hartwick Coll., 1973; postgrad., Syracuse U., 1973-75. Campaign staffer Udall for Pres., N.Y., 1975-76; sr. writer Syracuse (N.Y.) Record, 1976-78; assoc. nat. dir. pub. relations Cushman & Wakefield, Inc., N.Y.C., 1978-81; sr. account exec. JP Lohman Orgn., N.Y.C., 1981-84; v.p. SPGA Group, N.Y.C., 1984-86; pres. Mitchell & Assocs., N.Y.C., 1986—; lectr. in field. Contbr. articles to profl. jours; prin. works include numerous art brochures. Recipient ANDY ward Art Dirs. N.Y., 1983. Mem. Assn. Real Estate Women, Nat. Assn. Female Execs. Democrat. Lutheran. Office: Mitchell & Assocs 30 W 21st St New York NY 10022

MITCHELL, CONSTANCE AYER, design analyst; b. Painesville, Ohio, Oct. 9, 1952; d. Russell Ayer and Jean Ann (Hanna) Poxon; m. Leslie Olan Mitchell, Feb. 5, 1972; children—Bryan, Brandon. A.A., Lakeland Coll., Ohio, 1973. Programmer, analyst Curtis Industries Inc. div. Congoleum, Eastlake, Ohio, 1973-79; asst. to sr. v.p. Lake Nat. Bank, Painesville, 1979-81; sr. programmer analyst Picker Internat., Highland Heights, Ohio, 1981-83; sr. analyst George Worthington Co., Mentor, Ohio, 1983-86; with application devel. The Lubrizol Corp., Wickliffe, Ohio, 1986—; cons. and lectr. in field. Co-author: data processing systems. Mem. Nat. Assn. Female Execs. Episcopalian. Avocations: reading; photography. Home: 91 Chatfield Dr Painesville OH 44077 Office: The Lubrizol Corp 29400 Lakeland Blvd Wickliffe OH 44092

MITCHELL, ELIZABETH IRWIN, interior designer; b. Buffalo, May 20, 1957; d. Robert James Armstrong Irwin and Barbara Butler (Baird) Palladino; m. William Avery Mitchell, May 14, 1988. BFA, Ringling Sch. of Art and Design, 1985. Interior designer Gasparilla Interiors, Boca Grande, Fla., 1985-87; co-owner Interarc Assocs., Sarasota, Fla., 1987—. Mem. Am. Soc. Interior Designers. Republican. Episcopalian. Home: 637 Corwood Dr Sarasota FL 34234 Office: Interarc Assocs 22 S Palm Ave Sarasota FL 34236

MITCHELL, GAIL ELLEN, state agency administrator; b. N.Y.C., Sept. 23, 1951; d. Howard Bernard and Veronica Thelva (LeDoux) M.; BA, Boston U., 1973; MS, NYU, 1975; postgrad. St. John's U. Transp. planner Office Upper Manhattan Planning and Devel., 1974-75; sr. planner N.J. Dept. Community Affairs, 1975-78; sales rep. Xerox Corp., N.Y.C., 1978; market adminstr. N.Y. Tel., N.Y.C., 1978-83, sales compensation specialist, fin. mgr., staff compensation mgr., tech. cons. AT&T, 1983-87; pub. adminstr. Port Authority N.Y. & N.J., N.Y.C., 1987—. Recipient various awards N.Y. Tel.; grantee Boston U., N.Y. U. Mem. NAACP, Nat. Urban League, Am. Mgmt. Assn., Nat. Assn. Female Execs., Delta Sigma Theta. Office: 1 World Trade Ctr 71S New York NY 10048

MITCHELL, JACQUELINE KEATON, English language educator; b. Jackson, Miss., Feb. 15, 1935; d. Randall Calvin and Leanna (Hayes) Anderson; m. William D. Keaton, July 27, 1958 (div. 1966); children: Leslie D., Linda D.. AB, Fisk U., 1958; MEd, Washington U., St. Louis, 1972; PhD, Iowa State U., 1984. Tchr. St. Louis Pub. Sch. System, 1963-73, head English Dept., 1972-73, asst. prin., 1972-82; research asst. Iowa State U., Ames, 1982-84; asst. prof. English Tex. Woman's U., Denton, 1984—, mem. faculty senate, 1988-90, cons. pvt. edn., Metroplex Area, Tex., 1984—, Effective Teaching, Tchr. Evaluation and Instrnl. Leasership; dir. Computer Assisted Tchr. Evaluation, Ames, 1983-84; instr. St. Louis U., 1983; guest lectr. various sch. dists., 1984—. Co-author: Computer Assisted Teacher Evaluation/Suprevision, 1986, Professinal Growth Plans for Texas Teachers: The Appraiser's Guide, 1986, A Compendium of Validated Professional Improvement Commitments, 1986, Writing Professional Growth Plans, 1987; contbr. articles to profl. jours. Washington U. fellow, 1971-72; scholar Iowa State U., 1982-84; recipient Outstanding Acad. Achievement award Minority Student Affairs, 1983, 84. Mem. Assn. for Supervision and Curriculum Devel., Tex. Profs. Ednl. Adminstrn., Assn. Black Journalists (faculty advisor), Tex. Woman's U. (faculty advisor), Phi Delta Kappa, Pi Lambda Theta (faculty advisor), Alpha Sigma. Methodist. Home: 4815 Westgrove Dr Apt 2504 Dallas TX 75248 Office: Tex Woman's Univ PO Box 23029 TWU Station Denton TX 76204

MITCHELL, JANET ALDRICH, fund raising executive, reference materials publisher; b. Providence, Jan. 12, 1928; d. Norman Ackley and Janet (Gordon) Aldrich; m. Raymond Warren Mitchell, Jan. 9, 1954 (div. 1967); children—Lydia Aldrich, Polly Burbank. A.B., Smith Coll., 1949; M.Ed., Rutgers U., 1975. Engaged in devel. various non-profit orgns., 1954-72; dir. devel. Wilson Fellowship Found., Princeton, N.J., 1972-74; dir. spl. projects N.J. Dept. Higher Edn., Trenton, 1974-76; pub., editor-in-chief Mitchell Guide, Princeton, 1976-87; pres., chmn. Mitchell Guide, 1987—; cons. to numerous non-profit orgns., 1976-86; lectr. Adult Sch., Princeton, 1983-84. Editor: Directory of Woodrow Wilson Fellows, 1968; Guide to Federal Aid to Higher Education, 1975; Higher Education Exchange, 1978; A Community of Scholars, 1980. Exec. officer Princeton Community Democratic Orgn., 1984-86; mem. Princeton Twp. Com., 1987—; mem. NAACP Legal Def. Fund, 1980—; trustee N.J. Hist. Soc., 1984-86. Episcopalian. Clubs: Smith Coll. (pres. 1968-70), Princeton Dog (bd. dirs. 1962-68). Avocation: breeding and showing standard poodles. Home: 390 Rosedale Rd Princeton NJ 08540 Office: Mitchell Guide PO Box 413 Princeton NJ 08542

MITCHELL, JANET MARIE, financial and strategic planner; b. Greenwich, Conn., June 2, 1958; d. Walter Booth James and Margaret Mary (Brennan) M. BBA, Babson Coll., 1981; MBA, U. Conn., 1986. Fin. mgr. CBS, Inc., Greenwich, 1981-84; sr. fin. analyst Internat. Playtex, Inc., Stamford, Conn., 1984-86; bus. planner The Dannon Co., Inc., White Plains, N.Y., 1986—. Mem. Beta Sigma Pi, Alpha Kappa Psi. Home: 85 Washington St Norwalk CT 06854

MITCHELL, JEANNE OLSON, mining and minerals company executive; b. Orlando, Fla., Oct. 10, 1959; d. Carl Howard and Mary Jane (Jattuso) Olson; m. Douglas Keith Mitchell, Feb. 16, 1985. AA, Lake-Sumter Community Coll., Leesburg, Fla., 1978; BS, U. Fla., 1980, MS, 1981. Grad. asst., U. Fla., Gainesville, 1981, interium dir. instr. materials, 1982; info./press relations staff mem. Future Farmers Am., Alexandria, Va., 1982-83; dir. pub. relations Fla. Sugar Cane League, Clewiston, Fla., 1983-86; pub. relations advisor Mobil Mining & Minerals Co., Nichols, Fla., 1986—. bd. dirs. Polk County Econ. Devel. Council; adv. council Associated Industries Fla., Inc.; mem. Lakeland Chamber Host Task Force. Author and editor curriculum guides. Mem. Nat. Assn. Female Execs., Pub. Relations Soc. Am., Fla. Pub. Relations Assn. (bd. dirs. 1985, 86, 87, 88, Golden Image award 1983, 84, 85, 87), Mulberry C. of C. (1st v.p., bd. dirs.), Fort Meade C. of C. (bd. dirs.), Mulberry Service Ctr. (v.p.). Baptist. Office: Mobil Mining & Minerals Co PO Box 311 Nichols FL 33863

MITCHELL, JERYL ARLENE, employee development manager; b. Newburgh, N.Y., Mar. 9, 1959; d. George James and Harriet (Kilpatrick) M. BS, Syracuse U., 1981, MS, 1982. Tng. coordinator Niagara Mohawk Power Co., Syracuse, 1982-85; founding assoc. Tng. Systems Inst., Syracuse, 1982—; sr. assoc. Orgnl. Devel. Systems, Alexandria, Va., 1986—; human resource coordinator Niagara Mohawk Power Corp., Syracuse, 1985-88; corp. mgr. employee devel. Gould Pumps Inc., Seneca Falls, N.Y., 1988—; adj. asst. prof. Syracuse U., 1987—; program developer Goddard Space Flight Ctr. NASA, Washington, 1987, cons. Cen. N.Y. Sch. Study Council, Syracuse, 1987. Editor nat. newsletter The Bottom Lines, nuclear div. newsletter Happenings, 1986-87. Mem. Am. Soc. Tng. Devel. (utilities ind. group dir. 1984-85, council ind. group rep. 1984-87, chmn. council ind. group 1987—, conf. design com. 1986-87), Nat. Assn. Female Execs. Democrat. Baptist. Office: Gould Pumps Inc 240 Fall St Seneca Falls NY 13148

MITCHELL, JO BENNETT, educator, civic worker; b. Laredo, Tex., Jan. 14, 1928; d. Hilary Joseph and Inez Bell (Drake) Bennett; B.A., N.Mex. State U., 1949; postgrad. Hartford Sem. Found., 1951-52, U. Wash., 1973; M.A., Pacific Oaks Coll., 1981; m. Robert Curtis Mitchell, Aug. 30, 1949; children—Drake Curtis, John Douglas, Mary Cecilia. Day care tchr. Seattle Day Nursery, 1949-50, University Heights Sch., 1950-51; nursery sch. and kindergarten tchr. Campus Sch., N.Mex. State U., 1961-65; child care cons. HELP, Albuquerque, 1965; early childhood edn. faculty Cent. Wash. U., 1970-82; dir. Alaska/N.W. Extension Center, San Francisco Theol. Sem., Seattle, 1982-87. Mem. policy bd. Kittitas County Head Start, 1967-70; trustee Westminster Found. United Presbyterian Ch. Synod Alaska N.W., 1979-82; bd. dirs. United Ministries in Higher Edn., Central Wash. U., 1975-82; mem. planning com. Christian Century Lectureship Northwest, 1984-87, United Ministries in Higher Edn. Pacific Northwest, 1985—; mem. Task Force on Ch. Housed Chid Care of Family Life Task Force of Ch. Council Greater Seattle; Ecumenical Child Care Network of Nat. Council Chs. Mem. NOW, Fellowship of Reconciliation, Phi Delta Kappa. Home: Route 5 Box 880 Ellensburg WA 98926

MITCHELL, JOAN, abstract expressionist painter; b. Chgo., 1926; d. James Herbert and Marion (Strobel) M. Student, Smith Coll., 1942-44; M.F.A., Art Inst., Chgo., 1947; hon. degree, Western Coll., Ohio, 1972. One-person shows, Stable Gallery, N.Y.C., 1952-64, Galerie Fournier, Paris, 1967-78, Everson Mus., Syracuse, N.Y., 1972, Whitney Mus., N.Y., 1974, Art Club, Chgo., 1974, Carnegie Mus., Pitts., 1974, Corcoran Gallery Art, Washington, 1975, Xavier Fourcade Gallery, N.Y.C., 1981, 83, 85, 86 others; group shows include Pa. Acad. Fine Arts, Phila., 1966, Mus. Modern Art, N.Y.C., U. Ill., 1967, Jewish Mus., N.Y.C., 1967, Mass. Inst. Tech., bienniale Corcoran Gallery Art, 1981, Haus der Kunst, Munich, 1981-82, Richard Gray Gallery, Chgo., 1981-82, Xavier Fourcade Gallery, N.Y.C., 1982, Hirshhorn Mus. and Scultpure Garden, 1980; biennial Whitney Mus., 1983; Mus. of Art, Ft. Lauderdale, 1986; represented in permanent collections, including Basel (Switzerland) Mus., Albright-Knox Art Gallery, Buffalo, Art Inst. Chgo., Mus. Modern Art, Phillips Collection, Washington, Whitney Mus. Am. Art, Musee National d'Art Moderne, Paris, Corcoran Gallery of Art, Washington, Solomon R. Guggenheim Mus., N.Y., Fogg Art Mus., Mass.; tour in Japan, India and Australia, 1967. Recipient Creative Arts citation Brandeis U., 1973; Art Inst. Chgo. Traveling fellow, 1947. Office: care Robert Miller Gallery 41 E 57th St New York NY 10022

MITCHELL, JONI (ROBERTA JOAN ANDERSON), singer, songwriter; b. Ft. Macleod, Alta., Can., Nov. 7, 1943; d. William A. and Myrtle M. (McKee) Anderson; m. Chuck Mitchell (div.); m. Larry Klein, Nov. 21, 1982. Student, Atla. Coll. Albums include Song to a Seagull, Clouds, Ladies of the Canyon, Blue, For the Roses, Court and Spark, 1974, Miles of Ailes, Hissing of Summer Lawns, 1975, Hejira, Don Juan's Reckless Daughter, Mingus (Jazz Album of Year and Rock-Blues Album of Year, Downbeat mag. 1979), Shadows and Light, 1980, Dog Eat Dog, 1986, Chalk Mark in a Rainstorm, 1988; compositions include Both Sides Now, Michael from Mountains, Urge for Going, Circle Game, Beat of Black Wings, The Tea Leaf Prophecy. Address: care Geffens Records Distbr Warner Bros 3300 Warner Blvd Burbank CA 91510 *

MITCHELL, JOSEPHINE GRAY, musician; b. Bonham, Tex.; d. Moses Vashti and Bertie (Hoy) Gray; B.S., Tex. Woman's U., 1926, M.A., 1971; m. T.A. Mitchell, Mar. 21, 1929; children—Richard Gray, Thomas Albert. Pianist in profl. concerts in Tex., Okla., and Colo., 1927—; tchr. music Port Arthur (Tex.) High Sch., 1928-29; lectr. on Tex. music and composers; established Southwestern Folk Music Archive in Ft. Worth Library; chmn. in establishment of Tex. Composers Manuscript Archives in Dallas Pub. Library; mem. bd. Tex. Girls' Choir Youth Orch. Greater Ft. Worth; chmn., adv. Tex. Composers Commn. Fund, 1978—, founder, chmn., 1980-82; mem. contest Van Cliburn Piano Quadrennial Contest, 1976-82; bd. dirs. Fine Arts Soc. Tex., 1980—, S.W. Ballet Assn.; presented hist. ballet with commd. composers and choreographers Tex. Women's U., 1980; established Modern Dance-Ballet Archive, Lyndon Baines Johnson Library, Austin, Tex., 1980; bd. dirs. S.W. Ballet Ctr.; chmn. Tex. Composers Commn. Fund, 1984—. Recipient various citations; named 1st Lady of Music in Ft. Worth, 1967. Mem. Am. Coll. Musicians, Ft. Worth League Composers (founder 1958, pres. 1958-76), Fine Arts Guild, Nat. Fedn. Music Clubs (folk music archivist 1963-65, research chmn. 1958-68), Tex. Fedn. Music Clubs (dist. pres. 1964-65), Tex. Composers Guild (pres. 1952-76, adv. 1978-82), Tex. Woman's U. Alumnae Assn. (past pres.), Ft. Worth Ballet Assn. (charter), Symphony League (charter), Ft. Worth Opera Guild (charter), Fine Arts Soc. Tex. (charter dir.), Tex. Hist. Assn., Tarrant County Hist. Soc., Nat. Guild Piano Tchrs. (nat. adjudicator), Sigma Alpha Iota (pres. 1961-62). Episcopalian. Clubs: Ft. Worth Piano Forum, Ft. Worth Women's, Euterpean Music (pres. 1952-54), E. Clyde Whitlock Music (charter, past pres.). Editor: Texas Composers Handbooks, 2d edit., 1974; author: Creative Music of Texas, 1836-1986. Column editor Tex. Composers News, 1978—.

MITCHELL, JUDITH MARIE, research associate, counselor; b. Los Angeles, Oct. 1, 1950; d. Glen H. and Carla Jane (Bilderback) Taylor; m. Paul Francis Mitchell, Dec. 29, 1969 (div.); 1 child, Jennifer Ann. BA, Calif. State U., Northridge, 1976, MA, 1980; PhD, UCLA, 1987. Research and data mgmt. asst. County Office Alcohol Abuse, Los Angeles, 1977-78; vocat. youth counselor, statis. reporter Seventh Step Found., Los Angeles, 1978-79; rehab. counselor San Fernando (Calif.) Valley Assn. for Retarded, 1979-80; vocat. counselor, VA Hosp., Sepulveda, Calif., 1980-81; staff research assoc. Neuropsychiat. Inst. UCLA, 1981-85; postgrad. research assoc. Sch. Pub. Health UCLA, 1986—. Contbr. articles to profl. jours. Fellow Mabel W. Richards Assn., 1974-77, Calif. State U., Northridge, 1974-76, U. Women's Club, 1978, UCLA, 1981-84, 85-86. Mem. Am. Psychol. Assn.

MITCHELL, KAYE, employee benefits consultant; b. Oklahoma City, Sept. 17, 1941; d. Leila (Easttam) Pritchett; m. Wayne Mitchell. Student, Southeastern State U., 1959-60, Eastfield Coll., 1972-74. Asst. corp. sec. Dallas Bus. Capital Corp., 1972-76; asst. v.p. Fidelity Union Life Ins. Co., Dallas, 1976-80; employee benefit specialist Jenkens & Gilchrist, Attys., Dallas, 1980-84; pres. Creative Employee Benefit Services, Inc., Bastrop, Texas, 1984—. Editor digest CEBS' SAY, 1987; contbr. poem to State Book of Poetry, 1959. Fellow Internat. Soc. Cert. Employee Benefit Specialists (bd. dirs. Dallas/Ft. Worth chpt. 1984-87); mem. Bus. Profl. Women's Assn. Office: Creative Employee Benefit Rt 2 Box 145 BA Bastrop TX 78602

MITCHELL, LAURA ANN, lawyer; b. Miles City, Mont., Oct. 21, 1952; d. Wilmer Ashford and Avis Jean (Baldwin) M.; m. John Walker Ross, Nov. 21, 1981. BA in Polit. Sci. with high honors, U. Mont., Missoula, 1975; JD with honors, George Washington U., 1978. Bar: Mont. 1978. Law clk., U.S. Dist. Ct. for Mont., Billings, 1978-79; assoc. Crowley, Haughey, Hanson, Toole & Dietrich, Billings, 1979-83; ptnr. Crowley, Haughey, Hanson, Toole & Dietrich, 1983—. Mem. adv. panel spl. projects Mont. Arts Council, 1980-82; bd. dirs. Billings Preservation Soc., 1988—, St. Labre Indian Edn. Assn., 1988—. Mem. Am. Judicature Soc., ABA, Mont. Bar Assn., Yellowstone County Bar Assn. Office: Crowley Haughey Hanson Toole & Dietrich 500 Transwestern Plaza II 490 N 31st St Billings MT 59101

MITCHELL, MADELEINE ENID, home economist, educator; b. Jamaica, W.I., Dec. 14, 1941; came to U.S., 1963, naturalized, 1974; d. William Keith and Doris Christine (Levy) M. B.Sc. in Home Econs., McGill U., Montreal, Que., Can., 1963; M.S., Cornell U., 1965, Ph.D., 1968. Asst. prof. Wash. State U., Pullman, 1969-77, assoc. prof., 1978—, acting chmn. home econs. research ctr., 1981-83, asst. dir. Agri Research Ctr., Coll. Agr. and Home Econs., 1984-86; nutrition scientist U.S. Dept. Agr., Washington, 1980-81. Mem. Am. Dietetics Assn., Assn. Faculty Women, Sigma Xi, Phi Kappa Phi, Omicron Nu. Episcopalian. Avocations: genealogy, music. Office: Wash State U Dept Food Sci/Human Nutrition Pullman WA 99164-2032

MITCHELL, MARGARET ANNE, Canadian legislator; b. Brockville, Ont., Can., July 17, 1925; d. Clarence W. and Earnestine (Dutton) Learoyd; m. Claude Frederick Mitchell, May 6, 1956. Ed., McMaster U., Hamilton, Ont., U. Toronto, Ont. Mem. Can. Ho. of Commons, 1979—; community devel. worker. Mem. B.C. Assn. Social Workers. Mem. New Democratic Party. Address: 1176 Skeena St, Vancouver, BC Canada V5K 4V5 *

MITCHELL, MARION MIRANDA MCWILLIAMS (MRS. WILLIAM HENRY MITCHELL), former social work adminstrator; b. Elgin, Ill., Nov. 14, 1914; d. Henry Edgar and Ada (Young) McWilliams; m. William Henry Mitchell, Jan. 11, 1941. BA, U. Chgo., 1936, MA, 1959. Caseworker Chgo. Relief Adminstrn., 1938-41; library asst. Chgo. Pub. Library, 1941-42; caseworker Chgo. Orphan Asylum, 1943-44, spl. day care project, 1947-50; probation officer Juvenile Ct. Cook County, Ill., 1945-47; caseworker Chgo. Child Care Soc., 1950-54, supr. child placement and adoptions, 1954-74, dir. foster care and adoption, 1974-78, ret., 1978; chmn. Chgo. chpt. Nat. Council on Illegitimacy, 1966-70; del. to Ill. Commn. on Children, 1970, mem. state cooperating orgns. com., 1970-87, mem. adoptions com., 1972-73, com. on rights of minors, 1975-77; mem. adv. com. Subsidies for Black Adoptions, 1972-74; chmn. Adoption Info. Service Assn., 1974-77; mem. Com. Youth and the Law Ill. Commn. Children, 1977—; mem. adoptions adv. com. Ill. Dept. Children and Family Services, 1979-81; mem. statewide com. Ill. White House Conf. on Children, 1979-80; bd. dirs. Midwest Adoption Facilitating Service, 1971-77, treas., 1974-77; bd. dirs. Council on Unplanned Pregnancy, 1971-73. Mem. Human Services Assn. (study course com. 1965-83, dir. 1972-87, 3d v.p. 1975-77), Nat. Assn. Social Workers, Nat. Conf. Social Welfare, Child Care Assn. Ill., Acad. Cert. Social Workers. Home: 7552 S Wabash Ave Chicago IL 60619

MITCHELL, MARY ELLEN, psychologist, educator; b. Dover, N.J., Apr. 6, 1853; d. William H. and Mary E. (Jesness) M.; m. Patrick H. Tolan, May 30, 1984. BA, Kirkland Coll., 1975; MA, Fairleigh Dickinson U., 1978; PhD, U. Tenn., 1983. Assoc. psychologist Peninsula Psychiat. Hosp., Louisville, Tenn., 1979-80; clin. assoc. Helen Ross McNabb Ctr., Knoxville, Tenn., 1980-81, psychol. examiner, 1982-84; staff developer Southlake Ctr. for Mental Health, Merrillville, Ind., 1984—, staff psychologist, coordinator gerontol. services, 1984-85, supr. outpatient dept. main ctr., 1985-87; asst. prof. Ill. Inst. Tech., Chgo., 1988—; vis. asst. prof. Ill. Inst. Tech., 1987-88; adj. mem. faculty Ill. Sch. Profl. Psychology, Chgo., 1986—. Contbr. articles to profl. jours. Mem. Am. Psychol. Assn., Soc. for the Exploration of Psychotherapy Integration, Nat. Register of Health Service Providers. Office: Ill Inst Tech Chicago IL 60061

MITCHELL, MAURA ANN, health science facility administrator; b. N.Y.C., Mar. 25, 1954; d. James Francis and Catherine Daly (Stewart) M.; m. Verne Owen Sedlacek, Oct. 10, 1981. Diploma, St. Peter's Med. Ctr. Sch. Nursing, 1975; BS in Nursing, Seton Hall U., 1980; MA, Columbia U., 1981, EdM, 1985. RN, N.J., Va., Mass. Staff nurse St. Peter's Med. Ctr., New Brunswick, N.J., 1975-77, Beth Israel Med. Ctr., Newark, 1977-80; assoc. dir. nursing St. John's Episc. Hosp. South Shore, Far Rockaway, N.Y., 1980-82, asst. adminstr., dir. nursing, 1982-83; dir. nursing Brookline (Mass.) Hosp., 1983-85, assoc. dir., 1985—. Active Beacon Hill Civic Assn., Boston, 1987. Mem. Am. Orgn. Nurse Execs., Am. Soc. Hosp. Planning and Mktg., Mass. Orgn. Nurse Execs. (co-chairperson joint legis. com. with Council of Nurse Mgrs. 1986—). Roman Catholic. Home: 1 Pinckney St Boston MA 02114 Office: Brookline Hosp 165 Chestnut St Brookline MA 02146

MITCHELL, MOZELLA GORDON, educator, minister; b. Starkville, Miss., Aug. 14, 1936; d. John Thomas and Odena Mae (Graham) Gordon; m. Edrick R. Woodson, Mar. 20, 1953 (div. 1974); children: Cynthia LaVern, Marcia Delores Woodson Miller. AB, LeMoyne Coll., 1959; MA in English, U. Mich., 1963; MA in Religious Studies, Colgate-Rochester Divinity Sch., 1973; PhD, Emory U., 1980. Instr. in English and Speech Alcorn A&M Coll., Lorman, Miss., 1960-61; instr. English, chmn. dept. Owen Jr. Coll., Memphis, 1961-65; asst. prof. English and religion Norfolk State Coll., U. Norfolk, Va., 1965-80; asst., then assoc. prof. U. South Fla., Tampa, 1981—; pastor Mount Sinai AME Zion Ch., Tampa, 1982—; co-dir. Ghent VISTA Project, Norfolk, 1969-71; vis. asst. lectr. U. Rochester, N.Y., 1972-73; vis. assoc. prof. Hood Theol. Sem., Salisbury, N.C., 1979-80; cons. Black Women and Ministry, Interdenominational Theol. Ctr. Author: Spiritual Dynamics of Howard Thurman's Theology, 1985; staff writer AMEXION Sunday sch. lit., 1981—; editor Martin Luther King Meml. Series in Religion, Culture, and Social Development, 1987—; contbr. articles to profl. jours., essays to books. Bd. dirs. Nat. Farmworkers' Ministry, Tampa, 1987—, AME Zion Ch. Connectional Council, Charlotte, N.C., 1984—; mem. Tampa-Hillsborough County Human Relations Council, 1987—; pres. Fla. Council Chs., Orlando, 1988—. Nat. Doctoral Fund fellow, 1978-80; NEH grantee, 1981; recipient King Unsung Hero award STOP Orgn., 1988. Mem. Coll. Theology Soc., Am. Acad. Religion, Soc. for the Study of Black Religion, Joint Ctr. for Polit. Studies, Black Women in Ch. and Soc., Alpha Kappa Alpha. Democrat. Methodist. Office: U South Fla 310 CPR 4202 Fowler Ave Tampa FL 33620

MITCHELL, NANCY DENICE, nurse anesthetist; b. Houston, Sept. 27, 1956; d. Carl Dewie and Marlene (Eakin) Mitchell. A.S. in Nursing, San Jacinto Coll., Pasadena, Tex., 1976; dipl. Harris County Sch. Nurse Anesthesia, Houston, 1981. R.N., cert. registered nurse anesthetist. From staff nurse to head nurse surg. intensive care, Ben Taub Hosp., Houston, 1976-79; nurse anesthetist, cardiovascular operating room Fondren-Brown Meth. Hosp. Houston, 1981—; clin. inst. Baylor Coll., 1981—. Mem. Gulf Coast Assn. Nurse Anesthetists, Am. Assn. Nurse Anesthetists, Tex. Assn. Nurse Anesthetists. Home: 8327 Sandy Glen Ln Houston TX 77071

MITCHELL, PAMELA DEE ANN, programmer; b. Canadian, Tex., Aug. 4, 1959; d. James Austin and Linda Darlene (Walker) Carnagey; m. Ricky James Hickernell, June 30, 1979 (dec. July 1981); m. Mark Robert Mitchell, May 11, 1985. AA in Computer Sci., Amarillo (Tex.) Coll., 1985. Computer operator, programmer Tom F. Marsh, Inc., Dallas, 1978—. Mem. Nat. Assn. of Female Execs. Office: Tom Marsh Inc 1999 Bryan St Dallas TX 75201

MITCHELL, PAMELA HOLSCLAW, nursing educator, researcher; b. Denver, June 27, 1940; d. Harold Leslie and Maurine Agnes (Boatman) Holsclaw; m. Donald Waldo Mitchell, Sept. 17, 1966; children: Robert Edward, Kenneth Pearce, Andrew David. BS in Nursing, U. Wash., 1962; MS, U. Calif., 1965. Diplomate Am. Bd. Neurosci. Nurses. Asst. head nurse Mass. Gen. Hosp., Boston, 1962-64; pub. health nurse II Dane County Health Dept., Madison, Wis., 1966-67; nursing instr. Emory U., Atlanta, 1967-68; asst. prof. U. Wash., Seattle, 1970-71, 72-78, assoc. prof., 1977-82, prof. physiol. nursing, 1982—; research affiliate Wash. Regional Primate Ctr., Seattle, 1978-82; specialist U. Wash. div. Neurology, 1978—; acting chmn. physiologic nursing U. Wash., 1984-85;project dir. Am. Assn. Critical Care Nurses, Newport Beach, Calif., 1986—. Co-author: Neurological Assessment for Nursing Practice, 1984 (Am. Jour. Nursing Book of Yr. award 1984); author: Concept Basic to Nursing, 1973, 77, 81, translated to Norwegian, Danish, Spanish; editor Neuroscience Nursing, 1988; contbr. articles to jours. Mem. adv. bd. local chpt. Nat. Multiple Sclerosis Soc., Seattle, 1977—, ARC, 1979—. Recipient Disting. Writing award Wash. and Am. jours. nursing, 1983, Disting. Teaching award sch. nursing U. Washington, 1986; Am. Acad. Nursing fellow, 1980. Mem. Am. Assn. Neurosci. Nurses (chmn. clin. reference 1983—), Am. Assn. Critical Care Nurses (recipient Disting. Research award 1984), Am. Nurses Assn., Am. Councils of Nurse Researchers, Internat. Platform Assn., Clin. Nurse Specialists, Med. Surg. Practice. Democrat. Congregationalist. Home: 6016 Upland Terr S Seattle WA 98118 Office: U Wash Dept Physiol Nursing SM 28 Seattle WA 98195

MITCHELL, PAULA RAE, nursing educator; b. Independence, Mo., Jan. 10, 1951; d. Millard Henry and E. Lorene (Denton) Gates; m. Ralph William Mitchell, May 24, 1975. B.S. in Nursing, Graceland Coll., 1973; M.S. in Nursing, U. Tex., 1976; postgrad. N.Mex. State U. R.N., Tex., Mo.; cert. childbirth educator. Commd. capt. U.S. Army, 1972; ob-gyn nurse practitioner U.S. Army, Seoul, Korea, 1977-78; resigned, 1978; instr. nursing El Paso Community Coll. (Tex.), 1979-85, dir. nursing, 1985—, acting div. chmn. health occupations, 1985-86, div. chmn., 1986—, curriculum facilitator, 1984-86; ob-gyn nurse practitioner Planned Parenthood, El Paso, 1981-86, mem. med. com., 1986-87. Founder, bd. dirs. Health-C.R.E.S.T., El Paso, 1981-85; mem. pub. edn. com. Am. Cancer Soc., El Paso, 1983-84. Decorated Army Commendation medal, Meritorious Service medal. Contbr. articles to profl. jours. Mem. Nat. League for Nursing (mem. resolutions com. Assocs. Degree council, 1987—), Am. Soc. for Psychoprophylaxis in Obstetrics, Nurses Assn. of Am. Coll. Obstetricians and Gynecologists (cert. in ambulatory women's health care; chpt. coordinator 1979-83, nat. program rev. com. 1984-86, correspondent 1987-88), Advanced Nurse Practitioner Group El Paso (coordinator 1980-83 legislative committee 1984), Orgn. for Advancement of Assoc. Degree in Nursing (Tex. membership chmn. 1985—), Am. Vocat. Assn., Am. Assn. Women in Community and Jr. Colls., Nat. Council Occupational Edn. (mem. articulation task force, regional rep. AD nursing), Sigma Theta Tau. Mem. Christian Ch. (Disciples of Christ). Home: 4616 Cupid Dr El Paso TX 79924 Office: El Paso Community College PO Box 20500 El Paso TX 79998

MITCHELL, PAULINE ALLEN, public information director; b. Newport News, Va., Nov. 1, 1929; d. Toliver H. and Lalie Catherine (Muffet) Allen; m. Ashton Daniel Mitchell; children: Ashton, Timothy A., Paul B., Mary C., Susan R., Anne L. ABA, Va. Intermont Coll., 1949; BS, Va. Commonwealth U., 1974. Corp. dir. community relations Cen. Va. Ednl. TV, Richmond, 1973-78; info. dir. Va. Dept. Mental Health and Mental Retardation, Richmond, 1978-83; v.p. Ashton Mitchell and Assocs. Advt., Richmond, 1983-84; dir. news and pub. info. Chesterfield County, Chesterfield, Va., 1984—. Founding chairperson pub. info. sect. Va. Mcpl. League, 1985—; mem. adv. bd. visitors Mary Baldwin Coll., Staunton, Va., 1978—; chairperson Social Services Bd., Powhatan, 1969-73, 25th anniversary ch. Huguenot Acad., Powhatan, 1984-85; vestry woman St. Luke's Episcopal Ch., Powhatan, 1982—; sec. Henricus Found., Richmond, 1985—; bd. dirs. emergency med. services adv. bd., Va., 1974-78, Va. Lung Assn., 1973-78, Richmond Area Heart Assn., 1978-84. Mem. Nat. Assn. Counties Info. Officers (dir. mid-eastern region 1986-88). Republican. Club: Fed. Hill (Powhatan).

MITCHELL, RIE ROGERS, psychologist, counseling educator; b. Tucson, Feb. 1, 1940; d. Martin Smith and Lavaun (Peterson) Rogers; student Mills Coll., 1958-59; B.S., U. Utah, 1962, M.S., 1963; postgrad. San Diego State U., 1965-66; M.A., UCLA, 1969, Ph.D., 1969; m. Rex C. Mitchell, Mar. 16, 1961; 1 child, Scott Rogers. Tchr., Coronado (Calif.) Unified Sch. Dist., 1964-65; sch. psychologist Glendale (Calif.) Unified Sch. Dist., 1968-70; psychologist Glendale Guidance Clinic, 1970-77; asst. prof. ednl. psychology Calif. State U., Northridge, 1970-74, asso. prof., 1974-78, prof., 1978—, chmn. dept. ednl. psychology, 1976-80, acting exec. asst. to pres., 1981-82; acting exec. asst. to pres. Calif. State U., Dominguez Hills, 1978-79; cons. to various Calif. sch. dists.; pvt. practice psychology, Calabasas, Calif. Recipient Outstanding Educator award Maharishi Soc., 1978; Woman of Yr. award U. Utah, 1962. Mem. Calif. Assn. Counselor Edn., Supervision and Adminstrn. (dir. 1976-77), Western Assn. Counselor Edn. and Supervision (officer 1978-82, pres. 1980-81), Assn. Counselor Edn. and Supervision (dir. 1980-81, program chmn. 1981-82, treas. 1983-86, Presdl. award 1986, Leadership award 1987), UCLA Doctoral Alumni Assn. (pres. 1974-76), Am. Psychol. Assn., Am. Ednl. Research Assn., Calif. Women in Higher Edn. (pres. chpt. 1977-78), Calif. Concerns (treas. 1984-86), Pi Lambda Theta (pres. chpt. 1970-71, chairwoman nat. resolutions 1971-73). Contbr. numerous articles on group process, juvenile delinquency, adminstrn., counselor edn. to profl. jours. Home: 22945 Paul Revere Dr Calabasas CA 91302 Office: Calif State U Northridge CA 91330

MITCHELL, RUTH ELLEN (BUNNY), advertising executive; b. Mpls., Jan 2, 1940; d. Burt and Helen (Bolnick) Horwitz; div.; children: Cathy Ann, Thomas Charles, Andrew Robert. Student UCLA, 1957, U. Minn., 1960. Substitute tchr. Holy Innocents' Sch., Atlanta, 1972-76; mem. staff Issues Dept., Carter-Mondale, Atlanta, 1976; office mgr. Atlanta Area Family Psychiatry Clinic, 1976-79; account exec. Am. Advt. Distributors, Atlanta, 1979-81, Brown's Guide Ltd., Atlanta, 1981-82; account mgr. Billian Pub., Atlanta, 1983-85; regional sales dir. Am. Hosp. Pub., Inc., Chgo., 1985—; cons. G.C.C., Inc., Atlanta, 1982-83. Bd. dirs. Nat. Council Jewish Women, Mpls., 1963-70, Temple Israel Sch., Mpls., 1964-68, Minn. Symphony Assn., Mpls., 1963-71; The Temple Sisterhood, Atlanta, 1972-77, Holy Innocents' Sch., Atlanta, 1973-77; vol. fundraiser KTCA-TV Pub. Broadcasting Service, Mpls., 1968-71, WETV-TV, Atlanta, 1976-80; vol. Northside Hosp., Atlanta, 1971-77, Arts Festival of Atlanta, 1971-80, Holy Innocents' ch. summer program, 1974-76, Buckhead Mental Health Clinic, Atlanta, 1975-77. Mem. Nat. Assn. Profl. Saleswomen, Bus./Profl. Advt. Assn., Am. Advt. Fedn., Atlanta Advt. Club, Mag. Advt. Reps. of the South (sec. 1982-83, v.p. 1983-84, 88-89), High Mus. Art., Atlanta Symphony Orch., Found. for Hosp. Art Assn. (spl. events coordinator 1987—), Atlanta Ballet, Southeastern Hosp. Conf. (mem. exhibits com. 1988). Home: 7155 Roswell Rd #57 Atlanta GA 30328 Office: 1117 Perimeter Ctr W 5th Floor E Atlanta GA 30338

MITCHELL, SHEILA MARIE, hospital administrator; b. Monticello, Minn., Nov. 24, 1959; d. Robert Linn and Mary Kathleen (Ward) M.; m. Robert Gerard Kerekes, Feb. 11, 1984 (div. July 1987). BS in Liberal Arts, Ariz. State U., 1982. Asst. mgr. Lerner Shops, Phoenix, 1982-84; supr. Cottonwood Hosp. Med. Ctr., Murray, Utah, 1984, Swedish Hosp. Med. Ctr., Seattle, 1985-88, Providence Hosp. Med. Ctr., Seattle, 1988—. Mem. Implant Mgrs. Assn., Nat. Assn. Female Execs. Democrat. Roman Catholic. Home: 3419 Wallingford Ave N #3 Seattle WA 98103 Office: Providence Hosp 500 17th St Seattle WA 98104

MITCHELL, SUSAN EVELYN, computer marketing executive; b. Patterson, Calif., Oct. 20, 1953; d. Carl William and Luanna (Scott) M.; m. Michael Stankovic, Sept. 17, 1950; children: Brandi L., Daniel R. BA, Skadron Bus. Coll., 1972. Exec. sec. Tymshare, Inc., Newport Beach, Calif., 1974-75, applications cons., 1975-77, sales rep., 1977-80; br. mgr. The Computer Co., Richmond, Va., 1980-83; v.p. sales Bankmatic Systems, Portland, Oreg., 1983-85; pres., founder Mydas Mktg., Boulder City, Nev., 1985—; cons. Palo Alto (Calif.) Research Group, 1985-87; assoc. Western Ind. Bankers, Oakland, Calif., 1985—. Editor: Micro-Computer Software, 1986. Assoc. PTA, Boulder City, 1985—, Girl Scouts U.S., Las Vegas, 1986—. Mem. Nat. Assn. Female Execs. Republican. Episcopalian. Office: Mydas Mktg 557 California St Suite 56 Boulder City NV 89005

MITCHELL, SUSAN MILLER, insurance executive; b. Appleton, Wis., Apr. 13, 1945; d. James Frederick and Bernice Eileen (Bleick) Miller; B.A. magna cum laude, Lawrence U., Appleton, 1967; M.A. in Journalism, U. Wis., 1970; m. George Allen Mitchell, Oct. 28, 1973; children—Margaret Kim, Mary Eleanor. Tchr., Wakefield (Mass.) Elem. Schs., 1967-68; reporter Wall St. Jour., Chgo., 1970-72, San Francisco Examiner, 1972-73, Riverside (Calif.) Press Enterprise, 1973; exec. asst. Wis. Dept. Regulation and Licensing, 1975-78, sec., 1978-79; commr. ins. State of Wis., 1979-82; exec. v.p. adminstrn. Milw. Ins., 1983-86, sr. v.p. ops. gen. life, 1986; pres. gen. life, 1986-88; ptnr. The George A. Mitchell Co., Inc., 1988—. Mem. Milw. Council on Alcoholism, Wis. Hosp. Rate Rev. Com. Recipient award Center Public Representation, Madison, 1981. Home: 4516 N Ardmore Ave Shorewood WI 53211 Office: George A Mitchell Co 1863 N Farwell Milwaukee WI 53202

MITCHELL, VALERIE ANNE, pharmaceutical company executive; b. Teaneck, N.J., Mar. 9, 1959; d. Joseph Paul and Beatrice Louise (Frisch) Weglarz; m. Clifford Michael Mitchell, Aug. 25, 1985. Student, Oxford (Eng.) U., 1979; BA, Susquehanna U., 1981; postgrad., Ramapo Coll., 1986. Asst. mgr. DialAmerica Mktg., Teaneck, 1981-82; supr. Suburban Assocs., Ridgewood, N.J., 1982-84; office mgr. Thomas S. Boron, Inc., Glen Rock, N.J., 1984-85, ops. mgr., 1985—. Mem. Healthcare Businesswomens Assn. (newsletter dir. 1986-87, recording sec. 1987—). Home: 3 Hilary Ct Stockholm NJ 07460 Office: Thomas S Boron Inc 139 Harristown Rd Glen Rock NJ 07452

MITCHELL, VELDA JEAN, filter manufacturing company personnel executive; b. Alton, Ill., July 27, 1937; d. Glenn Kessinger and Eunice Ruth (Jarvis) Saxton; m. Spencer L. Middlecoff, Oct. 20, 1957 (div. 1980); children—Laura A. Middlecoff Decker, Mark S. m. Robert E. Mitchell, May 31, 1986. Student in bus. mgmt. Sinclair Coll., Dayton, Ohio, 1986—. Exec. sec. Sinclair Refining, Hartford, Ill., 1955-58, Laclede Steel Co., Alton, Ill., 1958-71; personnel specialist Fram Corp., Greenville, Ohio, 1974-80, personnel adminstr., 1980-83, supr. human resources, 1983-84; supr. employee relations Fram Corp. div. Allied Aftermarket, Greenville, 1984—; mem. adv. bd. Blue Cross/Blue Shield, 1978—; audit com. Fram Credit Union. Mem. adv. bd. Ansonia Schs. Bus. Edn., 1980—;, Greenville Schs. Bus. Edn., 1982—; adv. com. individualized study, Sinclair Coll., Dayton, Ohio. Mem. Personnel Assn. SW Ohio, Nat. Assn. Female Execs., Indsl. Mgmt. Assn. Office: Fram Allied Aftermarket Martz & Jackson St Greenville OH 45331

MITCHELL, VERNICE VIRGINIA, nurse, poet, author; b. Scott, Miss., Mar. 11, 1921; d. Isaiah and Martha Magdalene (Edwards) Smith; m. Willis Mitchell, Aug. 17, 1940; children: Elaine, Kenneth, Liethia, John, Ransom, Paul. Diploma, Princeton Continuation Coll., 1955. Lic. practical nurse Cook County Sch. Nursing, Chgo., 1951-59, U. Ill. Hosp., Chgo., 1959-67, Grant Hosp., Chgo., 1967-78, Northwestern Meml. Hosp., Chgo., 1979-84; Aetna Nurse's Registry U. Ill. Hosp., Chgo., 1984—. Author: The Book Success Through Spiritual Truths, 1987, (poems) A Women, Chicago, The 12 Months; also numerous poetry and musical lyrics; guest poet on Dial-A-Poem, Chgo., 1988-89. Recipient merit cert. Am. Poetry Assn., 1982, World of Poetry, 1983, 85; Golden Poet award World of Poetry, 1985. Club: 6700 Emerald Ave. Block (pres. 1971—).

MITCHELSON, MARY SUE, lawyer; b. Joplin, Mo., Mar. 17, 1951; d. L. R. and Mildred (Mathes) M. BA, U. Kans., 1973; JD, Georgetown U., 1976. Asst. dean Georgetown U. Law Ctr., Washington, 1976-78; law clk. to Hon. Harold Greene U.S. Dist. Ct. D.C., Washington, 1978-79; trial atty. civil div. comml. litigation br. U.S. Dept. Justice, Washington, 1979-86, asst. dir. civil div. comml. litigation br., 1986—. Office: US Dept Justice 550 11St NW Washington DC 20530

MITCHEM, MARY TERESA, publishing company marketing executive; b. Atlanta, Aug. 31, 1944; d. John Reese and Sara Letitia (Marable) Mitchem. BA in History, David Lipscomb Coll., 1966. Sch. and library sales mgr. Chilton Book Co., Phila., 1972-79; dir. market devel. Baker & Taylor Co. div. W.R. Grace, N.Y.C., 1979-81; dir. mktg. R.R. Bowker Co. div. Xerox Corp., N.Y.C., 1981-83, dir. mktg. research, 1983-85; mktg. mgr. W.B. Saunders Co. div. Harcourt, Brace & Jovanovich, Phila., 1985-87; mktg. dir. Congl. Quarterly Inc., Washington, 1987—. Mem. Book Industry Study Group, Inc. (chairperson stats. com. 1984-86), Mktg. Research Assn. Home: 4625 Tilden St NW Washington DC 20016 Office: Congl Quarterly Inc 1414 22nd St NW Washington DC 20037

MITCHUM, DIANE, financial analyst; b. Toledo, Sept. 13, 1950; d. John D. and Bonnie (Gilchrist) M. AA, U. Toledo, 1976, BS, 1978, MBA, 1980. Product planner AT&T, Chgo., 1980-81, mfg. acct., 1981-83, acctg. supr., 1983-85, fin. analyst, 1985—. Served with USN, 1969-72; capt. Ill. Army NG, 1980—. Mem. Nat. Black MBA Assn. (sec. 1983-84), Ill. Police Fedn. Assn. Democrat. Baptist. Home: 401 Hyde Park Hillside IL 60162 Office: AT&T 1 S Wacker Dr 6-F Chicago IL 60606

MITELMAN, BONNIE COSSMAN, advertising executive, writer, lecturer; b. Flint, Mich., Feb. 15, 1941; d. Maurice B. and Frieda H. (Ragir) Cossman; student U. Mich., 1958-61; B.A., Northwestern U., 1969; M.A., Manhattanville Coll., 1977; m. Stanley D. Lelewer, Mar. 12, 1961 (div. 1969); children—Joanne, Stephen; m. 2d, Alan N. Mitelman, July 23, 1972; 1 son, Geoffrey. Copywriter trainee Dancer-Fitzgerald-Sample, Inc., Chgo., 1956-60; advt. copywriter Spiegel, Inc., Chgo., 1961-63; freelance advt. and public relations writer, Chgo., N.Y., 1963—; co-founder Mitelman & Assocs., Briarcliff Manor, N.Y., 1972—; adj. lectr. dept. history Mercy Coll., Dobbs Ferry, N.Y., 1979—; contbr. articles to N.Y. Times, Reform Judaism, 1977—. Mem. Am. Hist. Assn., Women in Communications, Authors Guild. Author: Mothers Who Work: Strategies for Coping; mem. editorial bd. Reform Judaism, 1977—. Home: 639 Pleasantville Rd Briarcliff Manor NY 10510

MITRANY, DEVORA LANG, software firm executive, writer; b. Oak Park, Ill., Mar. 20, 1947; d. John Joseph and Frances Elizabeth (Kirke) L.; m. Douglas Allen Braun, Sept. 16, 1967 (div. Sept. 1976); m. Stanton Mitrany, Feb. 7, 1988. BA cum laude, Beloit Coll., 1969; postgrad. Boston U., 1971-72. Tchr. First Baptist Presch., Oak Park, 1966, 67-68, St. Brigid Sch., Boston, 1969-72; regional adminstr. TRW Fin. Systems, Wellesley, Mass., 1972-76; mgr. mktg. communications Computer Sharing Services, Denver, 1976-82; dir. corp. communications Corp. Mgmt. Systems, Denver, 1982-85; sr. copywriter On-Line Software Internat., Fort Lee, N.J., 1985-86; mgr. corp. communications Health Mgmt. Systems, N.Y.C., 1986—. Warden, vestry mem. Trinity Ch., Wrentham, Mass., 1974-76; mem. vestry St. Philip and St. James Episcopal Ch., Denver, 1983; vol. Hospice of Holy Spirit, Lakewood, Colo., 1980-83; bd. dirs. Talia Hadassah, 1986—; dir. pub. relations Bus. Roundtable on Nat. Security, Colo., 1983-84. Mem. Denver Advt. Fedn. (bd. dirs. 1981-83, Alfie award 1984), Colo. Conf. Communicators (Denver Advt. Fedn. liasion 1981-84), Bus. Execs. for Nat. Security, Am. Sephardi Fedn. (edn. com. 1987—), Jewish. Democrat. Home: Box 718 Long Beach NY 11561 Office: Health Mgmt Systems 401 Park Ave S New York NY 10016

MITRE, BLIMA KIRMAYER, pathologist; b. Romania, Aug. 15, 1942; came to U.S., 1968, naturalized, 1978; d. Moses and Regina Kirmayer; m. Ricardo J. Mitre, Oct. 7, 1967; children—Edward, Sandra, Marcie, Richard James. Grad. Universidad Mayor de San Simon, 1967. Intern Viedma Hosp., Cochabamba, Bolivia, 1967-68; resident in pathology Bapt. Meml. Hosp., Jacksonville, Fla., 1968-70; with Presbyn. Hosp., Pitts., 1970-72, Children's Hosp., Pitts., 1972-73; assoc. pathologist St. Margaret Meml. Hosp., Pitts., 1974-83, Suburban Hosp., 1983—; clin. asst. prof. pathology U. Pitts. Med. Sch., 1970—. Mem. Internat. Acad. Pathology, Am. Soc. Clin. Pathologists, Coll. Am. Pathologists, Pa. Assn. Clin. Pathologists. Office: Suburban Gen Hosp S Jackson St Pittsburgh PA 15202

MITTELSTAEDT, JOAN NAOMI, educator, consultant; b. Fond du Lac, Wis., Feb. 9, 1950; d. H. Arthur and Naomi Genevieve (Maltby) Steiner; 1 child, Robert John. BS in Edn., U. Wis., Stevens Point, 1972, MS in Edn., 1978; doctoral studies, Oxford U., summer 1986, 87. Cert. English and speech tchr., Wis.; cert. Amway Gold Direct Distbr. Tchr. Menasha (Wis.) High Sch., 1972—, also owner Fox Valley Bus. Cons., Neenah, Wis., 1978—; tchr. English, facilitator Wis. Dept. Edn.; tchr. positive mental attitude classes for bus. people; leader sales tng. seminars; curriculum and sales tng. system developer; pub. speaker on free enterprise, entrepreneurship and assertiveness, 1978—. Mem. Republican Presdl. Task Force, 1982. Mem. Nat. Council Tchrs. of English, Wis. Council Tchrs. of English, Wis. Regional Writers, Worldwide Diamond Assn., Nat. Assn. Female Execs. (network dir.), Am. Mgmt. Assn., Citizens Choice, Am. Fedn. Tchrs. (local sec. 1974-76), Assn. Supervision and Curriculum Devel., Internat. Platform Assn., Am. Assn. Univ. Women, Delta Zeta, Delta Kappa Gamma. Episcopalian. Research on imagists influence on contemporary poets. Home: 304 Quarry Ln Neenah WI 54956

MITTLER, DIANA, music educator and administrator, pianist; b. N.Y.C., Oct. 19, 1941; d. Franz and Regina (Schilling) Mittler; m. Victor Battipaglia, Sept. 5, 1965 (div. 1982). B.S., Juilliard Sch., 1962, M.S., 1963; D.M.A., Eastman Sch. Music, 1974. Choral dir. William Cowper Jr. High Sch. and Springfield Gardens Jr. High Sch., Queens, N.Y., 1963-68, coordinator of music Flushing High Sch., Queens, 1968-79; asst. prin. music Bayside High Sch., Queens, 1979-86; assoc. prof. music Lehman Coll. CUNY, 1986-87, prof., 1987—, choral dir., 1986—; dir. ednl. projects New World Records, 1987—; cons. Sta. WNET; assoc. condr. Queens Borough-Wide Chorus, 1964-70; pianist, founder Con Brio Chamber Ensemble, 1978; faculty So. Vt. Music Festival, 1979-83; soloist with N.Y. Philharmonic, 1956; solo and chamber music appearances; examiner N.Y.C. Bd. Edn. Bd. Exams., 1985—. Author: 57 Lessons for the High School Music Class, 1983. Choral dir. and accompanist various charitable, religious, mil., civic holiday functions. N.Y. State Regents scholar, 1958-62; scholarships, Juilliard Sch. and Eastman Sch. Music. Contbr. articles to music publs. Mem. Music Edn. Nat. Conf., Delta Kappa Gamma. Democrat. Home: 108-57 66th Ave Forest Hills NY 11375 Office: Lehman Coll Music Dept Bedford Pk Blvd West Bronx NY 10468

MITZEN, NANCY ELIZABETH, graphic designer; b. Pitts., May 5, 1955; d. Lawrence David and Elizabeth Ann (Williamson) M. BA in Graphic Design, Columbia Coll., Chgo., 1983; MA in Communications Arts with honors, N.Y. Inst. Tech., 1987. Prodn. coordinator ASN Pub., Chgo., 1981-83; designer Tech. Advt. Service, Bryn Athyn, Pa., 1983-88; dir. art O'Brien Design, Audubon, N.J., 1988—; free-lance designer Mitzen Graphics, Huntingdon Valley, Pa., 1981—, computer artist, 1986—. Mem. Am. Inst. Graphic Arts, Soc. Typographic Arts, Women in Design Chgo., Am. Film Inst. Home: 1810 Autumn Leaf Ln Huntingdon Valley PA 19006

MITZO, KAREN LYNN, engineer; b. Lakewood, Ohio, July 16, 1962; d. Andrew Edward and Beatrice Evelyn (Skowronski) M. BS in Indsl. Engring., Purdue U., 1985. Indsl. engr. Moore Bus. Forms, Northbrook, Ill., 1985-87; project engr. Martin Brower, Des Plaines, Ill., 1987; with Sedlak Mgmt. Cons., Cleve., 1987—. Mem. Inst. Indsl. Engrs., Soc. Women Engrs., Warehouseing Edn. Research Council, Nat. Assn. Female Execs., Am. Soc. Profl. and Exec. Women. Methodist. Home: 2755A Lochraven Blvd Copley OH 44321

MIXON, VERONICA, editor; b. Phila., July 11, 1948; d. Mathew and Bertha Lee (Goodwine) Mixon. Student L.I. U., 1970-74. With Food Fair, 1966-68, Social Security Adminstrn., 1968-70; editor Starlight Romances, Doubleday & Co. Inc., N.Y.C., 1974—; reviewer VM Media Service, Carib News, 1983—. Democrat. Baptist. Co-editor (book): Freshtones: Women's Anthology, 1979, The World of Octavia Butler; (mag.) Essence, 1979. Home: PO Box 694 Grand Central Sta New York NY 10163 Office: Doubleday 666 Fifth Ave New York NY 10103

MIZWA, MARY JANE HOUSE, publishing executive, antique dealer; b. Nacogdoches, Tex., Oct. 16, 1936; d. Garnet Reed and Johnnie Rhae (Simons) House; m. Tad S. Mizwa, Mar. 12, 1965; children: John, Michael, Michelle, Stephen; m. Barnett J. Jones, Sept. 1, 1956 (div. May 1964). AA, Lon Morris Coll., 1955; BEd, U. Tex., 1958. Advt. and editorial asst. Horseman mag., Houston, 1967-70; advt. salesman, 1970-73; assoc. editor Western Outfitter mag., Houston, 1973-75, editor, 1975-80; ops. mgr. Cordovan Corp., Houston, 1980-82, mgr. circulation adminstrn., 1982-85; dir. circulation S.W. Art mag., 1985-87, v.p. circulation, 1987—; owner Past Tense Antiques, Houston, 1983-85; v.p. Antique Panache Inc., 1984—. Republican. Presbyterian. Home: 1205 Krist Dr Houston TX 77055 Office: Southwest Art Mag Ben Franklin Tower 5444 Westheimer Suite 1440 Houston TX 77056

MLAY, MARIAN, government official; b. Pitts., Sept. 11, 1935; d. John and Sonia M.; A.B., U. Pitts., 1957; postgrad. (Univ. fellow) Princeton U., 1969-70; J.D., Am. U., 1977. Mgmt. positions HEW, Washington, 1961-70, dep. dir. Chgo. region, 1971-72, dir. div. consol. funding, 1972-73, dep. dir. office policy devel. and planning USPHS, Washington, 1973-77; dir. program evaluation EPA, Washington, 1978-79, dep. dir. Office of Drinking Water, 1979-84, dir. Office of Ground Water Protection, 1984—. Bd. dirs. D.C. United Fund, 1979-80. Recipient Career Edn. award Nat. Inst. Public Affairs, 1969. Mem. ABA, D.C. Bar (steering com. energy, environment and natural resources sect.). Author articles in field. Home: 3747 1/2 Kanawha St NW Washington DC 20015 Office: 401 M St SW Washington DC 20460

MLODOCK, JEAN CAROL, publishing company executive; b. Highland Park, Ill., Apr. 27, 1961. BA in Journalism, U. Wis., 1983. Prodn. mgr. Vanides-Mlodock, Inc., Chgo., 1983-86, Alexander Communications, Inc., Chgo., 1986-88, Western Pub. Co., Inc., Racine, Wis., 1988—. Club: Okauchee Lake Yacht. Home: 1130 S Main #205 Racine WI 53403 Office: Western Pub Co Inc 1220 Mound Ave Racine WI 53404

MMAHAT, ARLENE CECILE, steel company executive, civic activist; b. New Orleans, Oct. 5, 1943; d. John Alden and Margaret Therese (Nuccio) Montgomery; m. John Anthony Mmahat, Aug. 12, 1967; children—Arlene, Amy, John Anthony, Jr. B.A., La. State U., 1965. Clk., Shell Oil Co., New Orleans, 1965; claims rep. Social Security, New Orleans, 1966-67; chmn. bd. New Era Tubulars, New Orleans, 1979-84; chief exec. officer Olympia Tubular Corp., New Orleans, 1984—. Bd. dirs. New Orleans Symphony, 1983-86 , chmn. musicians adv. com., 1984, 85, membership chmn., 1985, oil and gas chmn. devel. com., 1983, devel. chmn. pub. sector, 1984; mem. Houston Bus. Council, 1980—, Dallas Regional Bus. Council, 1987—, New Orleans Mus. Art Odyssey, 1987; Ind. Women's Orgn., 1968—steering com. Internat. Gastroenteroly Research Fellowship Fund, Tulane U. Med. Ctr.; mem. adv. bd. Kennedy Ctr. for Performing Arts, 1980, Loyola U. Sch. Music, 1982—, New Orleans Mus. Art, 1986— ; fin. advisor New Orleans Symphony Soc. Jr. Com., 1977-79, fin. chmn., 1976; bd. dirs. Young Audiences, Inc., 1985—; mem. nat. adv. bd. on tech. and the disabled U.S. Dept. HHS; bd. dirs. Leukemia Soc. Am., Inc., 1978, corp. del., 1979; founder Ladies Leukemia League, Nat. Assn. Women Bus. Owners chpt. 1980; Odyssey Weekend chmn. New Orleans Mus. Art, 1985, fellows, 1983; mem. adv. com. St. Michael's Sch. for Spl. Students, 1978—, fin. chmn., 1977, mem. fin. com., 1973-76; fin. chmn. La. Landmarks Soc., 1973-75; bd. dirs. Preservation Resource Ctr., 1980, ways and means com., 1979, Christmas Benefit advisor, 1975, 76, mem. Women in Bus./ Women in Politics, Acad. Sacred Heart Adv. Study Com. Assoc. producer Film Am., Inc. Gottschalk, A Musical Portrait, 1986. Named One of 10 Outstanding Persons, New Orleans Inst. Human Understanding, 1977; One of 83 People to Watch in 1983, New Orleans Mag.; recipient Vol. Activist award Germain Monteil and D.H. Holmes Co., Ltd., 1977. Democrat. Roman Catholic. Home: 1239 1st St New Orleans LA 70130 Office: Olympia Tubular Corp 348 Baronne St Suite 602 New Orleans LA 70112

MOATS, PAMELA HELENE, educator; b. Los Angeles, Feb. 21, 1949; d. Richard Tashne and Luba (Kaplan) Scott; divorced; 1 child, Kristy Nicole. BS, U. Nev., Las Vegas, 1971; M in Ednl. Adminstrn., U. Nev., 1976. Cert. tchr., adminstr. endorsement, Nev. Instr. Opportunity Sch., Las Vegas, Nev., 1975-78, Western High Sch., Las Vegas, 1978-84, Bonanza High Sch., Las Vegas, 1984—. Grantee Nev. Gaming Found. for Ednl. Excellence, NSEA. Mem. NEA, Nat. Acad. Child Devel., Nat. Assn. Women in Adminstrn., Clark County Classroom Tchrs. Assn. Republican. Home: 3259 Astoria Dr Las Vegas NV 89121 Office: Bonanza High Sch 6665 Del Rey Ave Las Vegas NV 90106

MOBLEY, MONA LEJEUNE, writer, lecturer, Bible educator; b. Lucedale, Miss., Aug. 29, 1933; d. Cecil and Birdie Lee (Adams) McLeod; m. Harold Dean Mobley, Dec. 19, 1952; children—Stephen, Tamara, Stephen, Timothy. Student Freed-Hardeman Coll., 1952; French lang. cert. Grenoble Inst., Florence, Italy, 1970. Legal sec. for various attys., Wichita Falls, Tex., 1975-79; missionary Ch. of Christ, Florence, Italy, 1961-71, Montreal, Can., 1971-75; lectr., writer, 1961—; tchr. Ch. of Christ, Channelview, Tex., 1979—, counselor, Tex., Italy, Can., 1961—; lectr. various religious functions, Europe and U.S., 1961—. Author: Joyful Hospitality, 1983; Because I'm a Woman ... Please Understand, 1983; From Mom With Love, 1985, also articles. Sec. Forest River Estates Civic Club, Channelview, 1980. Democrat. Avocations: painting; various crafts; homemaking; volunteer work.

MOBLEY, NORMA MASON GARLAND, real estate corporation officer; b. Rocky Mount, N.C., Sept. 6, 1923; d. Roscoe Gibbs and Elizabeth Estelle (James) Garland; m. Joseph Kinsey Murrill, Jr., Dec. 29, 1942 (div. Oct.

1983); children: Joseph K. III, James B.; m. Leon Jay Mobley. Student, Va. Intermount Jr. Coll., 1942, Mary Washington U., 1942, Edgecombe Community Coll., 1979, U. N.C., 1980. Lic. real estate broker, N.C. Assoc. broker Charter Assocs., Rocky Mount, 1980-83, Wayne Ferrell Real Estate, Rocky Mount, 1983-84, Gary Mortan and Assocs., Jacksonville, N.C., 1984-85; pres., broker-in-charge Wright Properties, Inc., Jacksonville, 1985—. Officer, bd. dirs. Rocky Mount Jr. Guild, 1953-84; bd. dirs. YWCA, 1961-65. Mem. Jacksonville Bd. Realtors, N.C. Assn. Realtors, Nat. Assn. Realtors, Nat. Assn. Real Estate Appraisers. Republican. Methodist. Home: RR 02 Box 109 Beulaville NC 28518 Office: Wright Properties Inc 405 Johnson Blvd Jacksonville NC 28540

MOCK, BETTE MARIE, computer executive; b. Pontiac, Mich., July 2, 1937; d. John Phillips and Rosalie (Custer) Coder; m. Charles Robert Mock, June 18, 1960; children: Steven, Douglas, Katherine. BS, U. Md., 1959. Instr. zoology U. MD., College Park, 1958-60; supr. tchr. Dept. Edn. U. Md., College Park, 1963; sci. tchr. Prince George's County Schs., Hyattsville, Md., 1960-63; trainer, tester Gallaudet U., Washington, 1973-81; owner Mock's Computer Services, Bowie, Md., 1983—; researcher USDA, Washington, 1958, 59, 61; ednl. specialist U.S. Weather Bur., Washington, 1962; cons. Incoming Calls Mgmt. Inst., Annapolis, Md., 1984—, v.p. 1986—; v.p., sec., treas., editor Service Level Newsletter, Inc., Bowie, 1986—. Treas. St. Matthews United Meth. Ch., Bowie, 1984—, Gloria Ringers Handbell Choir, Bowie, 1984—. Named one of Outstanding Young Women Am., 1965; recipient Vol. award Bowie Recreation Council, 1979. Mem. Internat. Customer Service Assn., Newsletter Assn., Nat. Assn. Female Execs., Washington Apple Pi. Democrat. Home and Office: Mock's Computer Services 3516 Moylan Dr Bowie MD 20715

MODEEN-WATKINSON, MARY, artist, educator; b. Madison, Wis., July 14, 1953; d. James Howard and Dorothy (Johnston) Modeen; m. James F. Modeen-Watkinson, June 21, 1983; 1 stepchild, Obadiah J. BA, Alma Coll., 1974, BFA, 1975; MA, NE Mo. State U., 1976; MFA, La. State U., 1982. Extension instr. NE Mo. State U., Kirksville, 1976-77, dir. publs., 1976-77; instr. art Ottumwa (Iowa) Heights Coll., 1977-79; asst. prof. art Darmouth Coll., Hanover, N.H., 1983—; Artist-in-residence Peacock Printmakers, Aberdeen, Scotland, 1988—. Contbr. articles to periodicals; exhibited works in various shows. Recipient research grants Dartmouth Coll., 1983-87, sabbatical in France, 1986. Mem. Coll. Art Assn. Am., Nat. Assn. Female Execs., Phila. Print Club. Home: 7 Fletcher Circle Hanover NH 03755 Office: Dartmouth Coll Visual Studies Dept Hanover NH 03755

MODELSKI, JULIA ANN, nurse; b. Bryn Mawr, Pa., July 2, 1952; d. Joseph Peter and Julia (Carr) M. AA, Wesley Coll., Dover, Del., 1976; BA, Glassboro (N.J.) State U., 1980; MS in Nursing, Gwynedd (Pa.) Mercy Coll., 1984. Cert. pediatric nurse practitioner. Pediatric nurse practitioner Osborn Family Health Ctr., Camden, N.J., 1981-84, UMD N.J.-SOM, Stratford, 1985-86, Edward B. Brown, Sewell, N.J., 1986—. Mem. Nat. Assn. Pediatric Nurse Assocs. and Practitioners, Sigma Theta Tau. Roman Catholic. Home: 106 Canterbury Cove Sicklerville NJ 08081

MOE, VIDA DELORES, civic worker; b. Ryder, N.D., Feb. 29, 1928; d. John Nelson and Inga Marie (Lewis) Ahlgran; m. Placido Ferdinand, July 28, 1950 (div.); children: Terrence Paul, Star Marie; m. Edgar Louis Moe, May 24, 1970 (dec. 1983). Student, Minot State U., 1964-66; diploma interior decorating, LaSalle Extension U., 1976. Clk.-typist Base Supply, Minot AFB, N.D., 1960-61, clk.-stenographer Base Housing, 1961-62, 74, with MIADS Direction Ctr., 1962-63, with QC Br., 1963-64, with dept. acctg. and fin., 1964-65, with USAF Regional Hosp., 1965-66, with Minuteman AFSC, 1966-67, 74-75, with 5th Bomb Wing, 1967-70, with 1st Missile Wing, 1973-74, with dept. mil. personnel, 1975-76, sec. disaster preparedness, 1987—; sec., salesperson Allen Realty, Minot, 1980-85. Pres. Carnegie Restoration and Art Ctr. Project, City Art League, 1977-79, 86-87, chair, 1980—; bd. dirs. Patrons of Library, Minot, 1978—, sec., 1979-80, v.p., 1981, pres., 1982-83; v.p. 40/50 Rep. Women Minot, 1982, chair decorations com., 1983; historian Minot Rep. Women, 1984-86. Recipient Superior Performance award 5th Bomb Wing, Minot AFB, 1968, Devotion to Vol. Duty award USAF Regional Hosp., Minot, 1983, 86. Mem. N.D. Bus. and Profl. Women's Club (rec. sec. 1978-79, 81-82), Minot Bus. and Profl. Women's Club (pres. 1981-82), Am. Legion Aux. (judge jr. art posters contest 1980-82, pres. 1982-84), Minot Shrine Hosp. Aux. (v.p. 1984, 85, pres. 1986, 87), Beta Sigma Phi (v.p. Laureate Epsilon chpt. 1981-82, pres. 1983-85, Valentine Queen 1985, Girl of Yr. 1985, preceptor Eta chpt., Girl of Yr., 1980). Lutheran. Club: MidState Porcelain Artists Guild (v.p. 1983, pres. 1984). Lodge: Order Eastern Star (North Dakota Grand chpt. dist. dep. 1982-83, chair credentials com. 1983-84, chair registration com. 1986-87, Worthy Matron Minot chpt. 1976, 87-88, Grand Martha 1984-85, Grand Electa 1985-86). Avocations: china painting, oil painting, sewing, tennis, embroidery. Home: 705 25th St NW Minot ND 58701

MOE-FISHBACK, BARBARA ANN, counselor, educator; b. Grand Forks, N.D., June 24, 1955; d. Robert Alan and Ruth Ann (Wang) Moe; m. William Martin Fishback. BS in Psychology, U. N.D., 1977, MA in Counseling and Guidance, 1979, BS in Elem. Edn., 1984. Cert. elem. counselor, Ill. Tchr. United Day Nursery, Grand Forks, 1977-78; social worker Cavalier County Social Services, Langdon, N.D., 1979-83; elem. sch. counselor Douglas Sch. System, Ellsworth AFB, S.D., 1984-87, Jacksonville (Ill.) Sch. System, 1987—. Vol. Big Sister Program, Grand Forks, 1978-84; leader Pine to Prairie Girl Scout council, Langdon, N.D., 1980-82; tchrs. asst. Head Start Program, Grand Forks, 1979. Mem. Am. Assn. Counseling and Devel., NEA, AAUW (local br. newsletter editor 1980-81, br. sec. 1981-83), Ill. Edn. Assn., Am. Sch. Counselor Assn., Kappa Alpha Theta (newsletter, magazine article editor 1976-77). Club: Jaycettes (Langdon) (dir. 1982-83). Avocations: cooking, camping, curling, ceramics, creative writing. Home: 1712 Nita Ln Jacksonville IL 62650 Office: Jacksonville Sch Dist Jacksonville IL 62650

MOELLER, BEVERLEY BOWEN, agribusiness executive; b. Long Beach, Calif., Oct. 12, 1925; d. George Walter and Agnes Ruth (Coffey) Bowen; B.A., Whittier Coll., 1956; M.A., UCLA, 1965, Ph.D., 1968; m. Roger David Moeller, Dec. 11, 1955; children: Roger Bowen Shelton, Wendell Shelton, Claire Agnes, Barbara Bowen, Thomas David. Writer, Valley News and Green Sheet, Van Nuys, Calif., 1961-64; scholar-tchr. Valley Coll., Los Angeles, 1968-69, UCLA, 1970; instr. Petróleos Brasileiros, Salvador, Bahia, Brazil, 1972-73; pres. Nova Pioneira Agroindustrial Ltda., Belém Pará, Brazil, 1982—; dir. Associacão Cultural Brasil-Estados Unidos, 1972-73. Mem. Calif. Regional Water Quality Control Commn., 1970-71; bd. dirs. Dallas Council World Affairs, 1988—. Mem. Dallas Arboretum and Bot. Soc., Dallas Zool. Soc., Internat. Soc. Tropical Foresters, Forest History Soc., Kappa Kappa Gamma. Republican. Author: Phil Swing and Boulder Dam, 1971. Home: 7802 Glenn Eagle Dallas TX 75248

MOELLER, MARY ELLA, home economist, educator, radio commentator; b. Southampton, N.Y., Mar. 11, 1938; d. Harry Eugene and Edith Leone (Reester) Parsons; m. James Myron Moeller, Aug. 5, 1961; 1 dau., Mary Beth. B.S. in Home Econs., U. Nebr., 1960; M.L.S., SUNY-Stony Brook, 1977. Tchr. home econs. Port Jefferson Schs., N.Y., 1960-70; home econs. program asst. Suffolk County Coop. Extension of Cornell U., Riverhead, N.Y., 1972-82; tchr. home econs. Eastport High Sch., N.Y., 1982-85, South County Schs., Bellport Middle Sch., N.Y., 1985—; host Ask Your Neighbor, Sta. WRIV, Riverhead, 1982-87; trainer Home Econs. Entrepreneurship N.Y. State Edn. Dept., 1986—; mem. home and career skills regional team N.Y. State Edn. Dept., 1984—. Contbr. monthly articles to consumer publs. Mem. consumer homemaking adv. bd. Bd. Coop. Edn. Mem. N.Y. State Home Econs. Assn., Suffolk County Home Econs. Assn., DAR (historian 1985). Lodge: Eastern Star (matron 1970). Home: PO Box 377 Miller Place NY 11764 Office: Bellport Middle Sch Kreamer St Bellport NY 11713

MOELLER, TAMERRA PICKFORD, psychologist; b. Fresno, Calif., Mar. 15, 1943; d. Robert Donald and Ruth (Aynesworth) Pickford; m. James Ralph Moeller, July 22, 1967; 1 child, Ethan. BA with great distinction, Stanford U., 1965; PhD, U. Mich., 1974. Lic. clin. psychologist, N.J., Pa.; cert. sch. psychologist, N.J., N.Y. Intern in psychology State of N.J., 1978-79; staff psychologist Cath. Charities, East Brunswick, N.J., 1979-81; asst. prof. U. Pa. Med. Sch., Phila., 1981-84; dir. psychology St. Laurence Rehab. Ctr., Lawrenceville, N.J., 1984—; instr. U. Mich., Ann Arbor, 1971-83; vice chairperson West Windsor Commn. Aging and Sr. Services, N.J., 1978—; mem. instl. rev. bd. N.J. Dept. Health, 1987; cons. N.J. Dept. Human Services, 1983—, N.J. Dept. Community Services, 1986—. Mem. editorial adv. bd. Advice for Adults with Aging Parents, 1986—; dir., creator (mus. exhibit and film) What About Aging: Your Changing Senses, 1981-84; cons., developer (film) The Sixth Sense, 1984-86 (Nat. Media award 1986); contbr. articles to profl. jours. Mem. Consumer Adv. Panel, N.J., 1985—, advocacy com. West Windsor Sr. Ctr., N.J., 1985—; vice chmn., mem. consumer adv. panel N.J. Pub. Service Electric and Gas Co. Disting. Teaching fellow U. Mich., 1970; recipient Tribute to Women and Indstry and Govt. award YWCA, 1986. Mem. Am. Psychol. Assn., N.J. Psychol. Assn., N.J. Gerontol. Assn., Phi Beta Kappa. Democrat. Home: 201 Varsity Ave Princeton NJ 08540

MOEN, BARBARA JEAN, newspaper executive, controller; b. St. Cloud, Minn., Oct. 8, 1941; d. Clarence Carl and Mildred Augusta (Schmelzel) Hoffman; m. Charles Edward Moen, Sept. 30, 1961; children: Wendi Bryn, Kelly Elise (dec.). Student, Vermilion Community Coll., 1972; cert. in acctg., Fresno City Coll., 1985. Personnel asst. Northwestern Nat. Bank, Mpls., 1959-61; bookkeeper Tech. Tooling Co., Mpls., 1961-62; payroll, accounts payable bookkeeper St. Lukes Hosp., Duluth, Minn., 1967-71; br. mgr. Queen City Fed., Ely, Minn., 1973-77; loan officer Queen City Fed. Savs. & Loan, Virginia, Minn., 1977-79; advt., acctg. bookkeeper Fresno (Calif.) Bee, 1979-80, asst. bus. ops. mgr., 1980-84, bus. ops. mgr., 1984—; treas. Bus. and Profl. Women's Club, Ely, 1975-77; bd. dirs. Leadership Fresno Alumni, 1986—, Sta. PBS-TV, 1987—; acctg. adv. bd. Fresno City Coll., 1986—. Mem. Fresno C. of C., Ely C. of C. (sec., treas. 1976), Mrs. Jaycee's (treas. 1968), Internat. Newspaper Fin. Execs., News Media Internal Auditors, Ltd., Nat. Assn Women Accts., Exec. Women's Internat., Nat. Assn. Female Execs., Am. Payroll Assn. Republican. Lutheran. Lodge: Rotary (COGS chmn. 1988-89). Home: 329 E Pontiac Way Fresno CA 93704 Office: The Fresno Bee 1626 E St Fresno CA 93786-0001

MOFFAT, MARYBETH, automotive company executive; b. Pitts., July 25, 1951; d. Herbert Franklin and Florence Grafe (Knerem) M.; m. Brian Francis Soulier, Nov. 30, 1974 (div.). B.A., Carroll Coll., 1973. Indsl. engring. technician Wis. Centrifugal Co., Waukesha, Wis., 1976-77; indsl. engr. Utility Products, Inc., Milw., 1977-79; indsl. engring. mgr. Bear Automotive, Bangor, Pa., 1980—. Group home house parent Headwaters Regional Achievement Ctr., Lake Tomahawk, Wis., 1974. Mem. Am. Inst. Indsl. Engrs., MTM Assn. for Standards Research, Indsl. Mgmt. Soc., Alpha Gamma Delta (standards chmn. 1971-72). Republican. Methodist. Avocations: skiing; horseback riding; swimming; reading. Home: Spring Ridge Apts #P-23 Whitehall PA 18052 Office: Bear Automotive Service Equipment Co S Main and Werner Sts Bangor PA 18013

MOFFATT, MINDY ANN, teacher, educational and researcher consultant; b. Mpls., Aug. 3, 1951; d. Ralph Theron and La Vone Muriel (Bergstrom) M. Student, U. Calif., :Los Angeles, 1972-73; BA, Calif. State U., Fullerton, 1975, postgrad. Cert. elem. tchr., Calif. Tchr. early childhood edn. program Meadows Elem. Sch., Valencia, Calif., 1977-78; tchr. United Parents Against Forced Busing, Chatsworth, Calif., 1978-80; founding tchr. Gazebo Two Sch. for Young Gifted and Creative Children, Summerville, S.C., 1980-81; tchr. Anaheim Union High Sch. Dist., Anaheim, Calif., 1981—, mentor, tchr., 1985-88; cons. writing project U. Calif., Irivne, 1982—; textbook cons. McDougal, Littell & Co., Evanston, Ill., 1984-86; mentor tchr. Anaheim Union High Sch. Dist., Calif., 1985-88; facilitator Summer Tech. Tng. Inst., Irvine, 1987. Author: The Gifted and Talented Education Way to English, 1984; co-author: Practical Ideas for Teaching Writing as a Process, 1986, 87. Mem. Friends of the River, San Francisco, Handgun Control, Inc., Washington; active The Nature Conservancy, Arlington, Va.; sponsor English Council Orange County. Mem. NEA, Calif. Assn. Tchrs. of English, Students Assn., NOW , Nat. Writing Project, Sierra Club, Friends of the River, Handgun Control Inc., English Council of Orange County, PTA. Democrat. Unity Ch. of Truth. Club: Our Ultimate Recreation (Orange County, Calif.) (social com. chairperson 1983, backpacking chairperson 1983).

MOFFATT, PAMELA JEANNE, real estate broker, marketing professional; b. Lincoln, Nebr., June 28, 1949; d. Harold William and Mary Ann (Gregory) Ohlrich; m. John Edmund Fair, May 31, 1970 (div. Oct. 1973); children: Tiffanie Nicole, Blaine Nichols; m. Brian T. Moffatt, Aug. 29, 1987. BS, Okla. State U., 1971. Lic. real estate broker, Tex. Stenographer mktg. Texaco, Inc., Houston, 1971-78; regional ops. mgr. RRS, Inc., Houston, 1978-82; broker Real Property Mgmt., Inc., Houston, 1982-84; mgr. transferee services S.W. region Merrill Lynch, 1984-86; liquidation asst. FDIC, 1986-88; mktg. officer, Fed. Savings and Loan Ins. Corp., 1988—; substitute tchr. Houston Community Coll., 1982. Active Nat. Trust for Hist. Preservation. Fellow Nat. Assn. Realtors; mem. Nat. Geographic Soc., Tex. Assn. Realtors, Houston Bd. Realtors (cert. comml. investment mem.). Republican. Episcopalian. Home: 7847 El Pastel Dallas TX 75248

MOFFETT, PAMELA AMY, hospital executive; b. Ephrata, Wash., June 4, 1954; d. George Edward and Amy Elizabeth (Bailey) M. Student, Everett (Wash.) Community Coll., 1973, USN Hosp. Corps Sch., Great Lakes, Ill., 1974. Psychiat. nursing asst. Ingleside Hosp., Rosemead, Calif., 1980-82, adminstrv. coordinator, 1982-85, dir. materials mgmt., 1985—. Vol. Nixon re-election campaign, Everett, 1972. Served with USN, 1974-76. Mem. Calif. Assn. Hosp. Purchasing and Materials Mgrs. (sec. Los Angeles, Orange, San Bernadino and Riverside Counties, 1986—), Rainbow Girls. Methodist. Office: Ingleside Hosp 7500 E Hellman Ave Rosemead CA 91770

MOFFORD, ROSE, state official; b. Globe, Ariz., June 10, 1922; m. T.R. Mofford (div.). Attended pub. schs. Sec. to Joe Hunt, Ariz. State Treas., 1941-43, Ariz. State Tax Commr., 1943-54, Wesley Bolin, Ariz. Sec. of State, 1954-55; asst. sec. of state State of Ariz., Phoenix, 1955-75; asst. dir. of revenue State of Ariz., 1975-77, sec. of state, 1977-88, governor, 1988—. Democrat. Office: Office of Gov 1700 W Washington St Phoenix AZ 85007 *

MOGFORD, SHARON MARIE, state official; b. Kerrville, Tex., Mar. 4, 1959; d. Harold Lamar, Sr., and Mary Elizabeth (Phipps) M. B.B.A., S.W. Tex. State U., 1981. CPA, Tex. With State Auditor's Office, Austin, Tex., 1981—, asst. state auditor, 1981-83, in-charge asst. state auditor, 1983-85, supervising asst. state auditor, 1985—. Mem. Am. Inst. CPA's. Republican. Baptist. Avocations: scuba diving, softball, snow skiing. Home: 2207 Hollybush 103 Dallas TX 75228

MOGGE, HARRIET MORGAN, educational association executive; b. Cleve., Jan. 2, 1928; d. Russell VanDyke and Grace (Wells) Morgan; m. Robert Arthur Mogge, Aug. 17, 1948 (div. 1977); 1 child, Linda Jean. BME, Northwestern U., 1959; postgrad., Ill. State U., 1969. Instr. piano, Evanston, Ill., 1954-58; instr. elem. music pub. schs., Evanston, 1959; editorial asst. archivist Summy-Birchard Co., Evanston, 1964-66, asst. to editor-in-chief, 1966-67, cons., 1968-69, ednl. dir., 1969-74, also historian, 1973-74; supr. vocal music jr. high sch., Watseka, Ill., 1967-68; asst. dir. profl. programs Music Educators Nat. Conf., Reston, Va., 1974-84, dir. meetings and convs., 1984—, mgr. direct mktg. service, 1981—. Mng. editor Am. Suzuki jour., 1972-74, Gen. Music Today, 1987—; mgr. diplay advt. Model T Times, 1971—. Active various community drives. Mem. Music Educators Nat. Conf., Am. Choral Dirs. Assn., In and About Chgo., Music Educators Assn. (bd. dirs.), Suzuki Assn. Ams. (exec. sec. 1972-74), Nat. Assn. Exposition Mgrs. (cert.; mem. edn. com. 1979—, chmn. edn. com. 1985-87, bd. liaison edn. com. 1987—, bd. dirs. Washington chpt. 1983-85, nat. bd. dirs. 1986—), Mu Phi Epsilon, Kappa Delta (province pres. 1960-66, 72-76, regional chpts. dir. 1976-78, nat. dir. scholarship 1981-84). Republican. Presbyterian. Clubs: Bus. and Profl. Women's (Watseka) (bd. dirs. 1968-70); Antique Automobile (registrar ann. meeting 1961-86), Model T Ford Internat. (v.p. 1971-72, 76-77, pres. 1981, treas. 1983-87, bd. dirs. 1971-87). Home: 1919A VillaRidge Dr Reston VA 22091 Office: 1902 Association Dr Reston VA 22091

MOGYORDY, LAURA JANE, religious organization director; b. Cleve., June 18, 1960; d. Steven Zoltan and Margaret (Volchko) M. BS in Mktg., Miami U., Oxford, Ohio, 1982. Credit analyst asst., credit statement processor The Standard Oil Co. Ohio, Cleve., 1980-81; agt. asst., receptionist Stone & Youngberg investment Securities, La Jolla, Calif., 1982; optometrist asst. Assocs. in Vision Care, Inc., Cleve., 1983; telemarketing rep. Ohio Bell Telephone Co., Cleve., 1983; pub. relations writer, asst. Josh McDowell Ministryof Campus Crusade for Christ, Richardson, Tex., 1983-84; advt., promotions mgr. Josh McDowell Ministry of Campus Crusade for Christ, Richardson, Tex., 1985-88; dir. mktg. Christian Leadership Ministries of Campus Crusade for Christs, Dallas, 1988—. Vol. phone counselor Richardson Crisis Ctr., Richardson, 1986. Mem. Am. Mktg. Assn. (Outstanding mem. 1981-82, copy editor, ad salesman Scope mag., nat. publ. award 1982) , Quill and Scroll, Mu Kappa Tau, Pi Sigma Epsilon. Office: Christian Leadership Ministries 14679 Midway Rd Suite 100 Dallas TX 75244

MOHLER, MARY GAIL, editor; b. Milaca, Minn., Dec. 15, 1948; d. Albert and Deane (Vedders) M.; m. Paul Rodes Trautman, June 5, 1976; children: Elizabeth Deane, David Albert Rodes, Theodore DeForest Lloyd. B.A., U. Calif.-Davis, 1974; M.A. in Lit., SUNY-Stony Brook, 1976. Asst., then editor-reporter Family Circle Mag., N.Y.C., 1979-81; editorial coordinator Ladies' Home Jour., N.Y.C., 1981; assoc. articles editor Ladies' Home Jour., 1982, mng. editor, 1982—. Medieval philosophy fellow SUNY-Binghamton, 1978. Mem. MLA, Am. Soc. Mag. Editors, Phi Beta Kappa. Club: Medieval. Office: Ladies' Home Jour 100 Park Ave New York NY 10017

MOHR, JEAN HOLLY, newspaper account executive; b. New Rochelle, N.Y., Jan. 27, 1955; d. John Henry and Ethel Jane (Zimmerman) MBA in Advt. and Pub. Relations, Tex. Tech. U., 1977; postgrad. U. Houston. Scheduling coordinator nat. advt. Houston Chronicle, 1977-78, account rep. retail advt., 1978-83, account coordinator advt. spl. event retail, 1983-85, retail advt. mktg. cons. southwest, 1985—, promotional asst. Houston Livestock Show and Rodeo, 1983; judge Mktg. Distbr. Edn. Competitions, Houston, 1978-79, 86. Vol. Ronald McDonald House, Houston, 1983. Named Salesperson of Month, 100 Club mem. Houston Chronicle, 1985, 86, 87. Mem. Nat. Assn. Female Execs., Tex. Tech. Ex-Students Assn., Delta Delta Delta (pres. Houston 1985-86). Methodist. Avocations: jazzercise; tennis. Home: 8151 Misty Ridge Ln Houston TX 77071 Office: Houston Chronicle 10635 Richmond Ave Houston TX 77042

MOHRMAN, BARBARA ANN, engineering company executive; b. N.Y.C., Dec. 27, 1950; d. Harry Laemmle and Dorothy (Fletcher) M. BS, U. N.H., 1973; M of Urban Affairs, Boston U., 1978. Vol., Mus. Fine Arts, Boston, 1985—; chmn. Amelia Earhart award com., 1987-88, membership com. Women's Ednl. & Indsl. Union, Boston, 1985—; APA rep. Joint Regional Transp. Com., 1986—. Mem. Am. Planning Assn. (sec. MA sect. 1986—), Women's Transp. Seminar, Internat. Assn. for Impact Assessment. Office: Stone & Webster Engring Corp 245 Summer St Boston MA 02107

MOITRA, PATRICIA AVRIL, architect; b. Chelmsford, Essex, Eng., Apr. 25, 1933; d. Harold Joseph and Helen May (Philpott) Berry; m. St. John Rivers Coplans, Aug. 23, 1959 (div. 1963); m. Deepak Kumar Moitra, Sept. 1, 1978. BA, Mid Essex Coll., Chelmsford, 1952; intermediate degree, Royal Inst. Architects, London, 1955; grad. degree in Architecture, London U., 1959. Architect/trainee Architects Co.-Partnership, London, 1956-60; architect Campbell and Wong, San Francisco, 1961-63, Wurster, Bernadi and Emmons, San Francisco, 1963-64; architect, ptnr. Burger and Coplans, San Francisco, 1964-78; architect, owner Moitra Designs, Phoenix, 1978—. Bd. dirs. Ariz. Opera League, 1987—. Mem. Am. Inst. Architects (Excellence Community Architecture citation 1969, Homes Better Living award 1970, 73, 79, Bay Area Honor award 1969, 74, 79, Archtl. Record award for design 1972, 73, U.S. Dept. Housing Urban Devel. award 1970, Sunset Mag. Western Home award 1972, 74, Holiday Mag. Beautiful Am. award 1970). Republican. Hindu. Club: English Speaking Union (Phoenix).

MOLEE, NANCY ANNE, educator; b. Newark, Dec. 9, 1938; d. Charles and Jennie (Fiocca) Vitale; m. Casper S. Molee, Nov. 22, 1959; children: Linda Jaye, Lenore M., Anthony. BA, Montclair State Coll., 1960, MA, 1985. Tchr. Bloomfield (N.J.) Bd. Edn., 1975—, guidance counselor, 1986-87, team leader, 1986—; participant QUEST-Skills for Adolescence, Hofstra U., Hempstead, N.Y., 1986, in-house cons. Bloomfield Schs., 1986-87. Developed social sci. curriculum for Bloomfield Schs., 1986. Sec. Bloomfield Local Assistance Bd., 1983; committeewoman Bloomfield Rep. Party, 1972-87, ward chmn., 1978-79; sec. Unico Ladies' Aux., 1970-71; active Bloomfield Boys' Club Ladies' Aux. Robert A. Taft fellow, 1985. Mem. NEA, N.J. Edn. Assn., Bloomfield Edn. Assn., Assn. Am. Geographers. Republican. Roman Catholic. Home: 56 Mountain Ave Bloomfield NJ 07003 Office: Bloomfield Middle Sch 60 Huck Rd Bloomfield NJ 07003

MOLER, ELIZABETH ANNE, lawyer; b. Salt Lake City, Jan. 24, 1949; d. Murray McClure and Eleanor Lorraine (Barry) M.; m. Thomas Blake Williams, Oct. 19, 1979; 1 child, Blake Martin Williams. BA, Am. U., 1971; postgrad., Johns Hopkins U., 1973; JD, George Wash. U., 1977. Bar: D.C. 1978. Law clk. Sharon, Pierson, Semmes, Crolius & Finley, Washington, 1975-76; chief legis. asst. Senator Floyd Haskell, Washington, 1973-75; sr. counsel com. on energy and natural resources U.S. Senate, Washington, 1976—; bd. dirs. Inst. Study of Regulation, Washington, 1985—. Mem. ABA. Democrat. Home: 1537 Forest Ln McLean VA 22101 Office: Com Energy Natural Resources US Senate Washington DC 20510

MOLES, SUSAN ANN, environmental laboratory executive, chemist; b. Hot Springs, Ark., June 29, 1956; d. James Webster and Anna Laura (Phillips) Kendall; m. James Fredrick Denton, Nov. 30, 1973; m. Danny Ray Moles, Nov. 15, 1986. Student Garland County Community Coll., 1977-79. Lab. dir. Weyerhaeuser Co., Hot Springs, Ark., 1980-86, Entek Labs., Hot Springs, 1986, Enseco Houston, 1987— . Resource vol. Nat. Park Service, Hot Springs, 1983—. Mem. Am. Chem. Soc., Assn. Ofcl. Analytical Chemists, Nat. Assn. Female Execs. Democrat. Avocations: motorcycles; cats; water sports. Home: 1351 Greens Pwy Houston TX 77067

MOLINE, MARY, publisher, author; b. Bretz, W.Va., May 30, 1932; d. John Sommavilla and Mary Joan (Sbardella) M. Purchasing agt. Fergueson Door Mfg. Co., Los Angeles, 1953-55; freelance writer nat. publs. Los Angeles, 1967-71; newspaper pub. The Condenser, Los Angeles, 1971-74; pres. Rumbleseat Press, Inc., Cayucos, Calif., 1971—, Green Valley World, Inc., Cayucos, 1981—; internat. authority of Norman Rockwell art and Henry Ford of Ford Motor Co. Author 14 books; inventor new method to produce cloth-faced dolls; creator series of collectible porcelain dolls based on Norman Rockwell's art; motivational speaker. Mem. Norman Rockwell Soc. Republican. Club: San Francisco Press. Office: 41 S Ocean Ave Cayucos CA 93430

MOLINO, PATRICIA MARY, communications executive; b. Jersey City, N.J., Nov. 20, 1946; d. Nicholas and Jean (Rocco) M.; m. Ronald J. Sullivan. BS, NYU, 1968, MA, 1987. Writer Am. Mus. Nat. History, N.Y.C., 1968-69; dir. pub. affairs N.Y. Bot. Garden, N.Y.C., 1969, Hunter Coll. CCNY, N.Y.C., 1970-74; dir. communications Deutsch, Shea & Evans, N.Y.C., 1975; mgr. pub. info. Meml. Sloan-Kettering Concern Ctr., N.Y.C., 1976-84; pres. Patricia Molino Communications, N.Y.C., 1985—; cons. Gen. Motors, N.Y.C., 1980—, Altro Health & Rehab., N.Y.C., 1984—, Am. Cancer Soc., 1987—, Health Ins. Plan N.Y., 1987—, Hebrew Home for the Aged, Riverdale, N.Y., 1988—. Bd. dirs. Family Dynamics, N.Y.C., 1986—. Mem. AAAS, Pub. Relations Soc. Am., N.Y. Acad. Scis. Democrat.

MOLITOR, SISTER MARGARET ANNE, nun, former college president; b. Milford, Ohio, Sept. 19, 1920; d. George Jacob and Mary Amelia (Lockwood) M. B.A., Our Lady of Cin. Coll., 1942; M.Ed., Xavier U., 1950; LL.D.; M.A., Catholic U. Am., 1963, Ph.D., 1967. Joined Sisters of Mercy, 1943; tchr. elementary schs. Cin., 1946-50, secondary schs., Cin. and Piqua, Ohio, 1951-60; faculty Edgecliff Coll., Cin., 1962-73; pres. Edgecliff Coll., 1973-80; provincial archivist Sisters of Merchy, Cin., 1980—; archivist Cin. Province Sisters of Mercy; research cons. various religious communities. Bd. dirs. Citizens Com. on Youth; trustee Chatfield Coll.; mem. Area Council Planning Task Force, Cin. Community Devel. Adv. Council. Recipient Woman of Year award Cin. Enquirer, 1977. Mem. Greater Cin.

Consortium Colls. and Univs. (pres. 1980). Address: 2335 Grandview Ave Cincinnati OH 45206

MOLL, KATHY LORRAINE, financial company adminstrator, market analyst; b. Kansas City, Mo., Mar. 3, 1954; d. Donald Eugene and Mary Evelyn (Seeley) M. Student, U. Mo., 1972-73; AA, Penn Valley Community Coll., 1974. Adminstrv. asst. Exec. Selection Internat., Dallas, 1980-81, corp. acctg. asst., 1981, mgr. corp. publs., 1981-82; sr. sec. MBank Dallas, 1982-84; exec. sec. MTrust Corp., Dallas, 1984-85, adminstrv. coordinator state-wide ops., 1985-88, market analyst, 1988—. Am. Bus. Women's Assn. scholar, 1972. Home: 6318 Richmond #3303 Dallas TX 75214 Office: MTrust Corp Main at Ervay Dallas TX 75201

MOLLICA, SUSAN CATHERINE, marketing executive; b. New Brunswick, N.J., Oct. 22, 1953; d. Anthony Joseph and Theresa Marie (Vella) M. BA, Rutgers U., 1978, MA, 1980; MBA, Fairleigh Dickinson U., 1983. Ops. analyst Burroughs Computer Systems, Piscataway, N.J., 1980-82; advt. sales exec. Cardinal Pub. Co., Trenton, N.J., 1983; software designer Digital Learning Systems, Inc., Parsippany, N.J., 1983-85, mgr. software devel., 1985-86, dir. mktg. and creative media, 1986—. Mem. Am. Mktg. Assn., Pub. Relations Soc. Am., Nat. Assn. Female Execs., AAUW, N.J. Music Assn., Phi Sigma Iota. Republican. Home: 213 Learnington Way Somerset NJ 08873

MOLLISON, CHAR, women's rights activist; b. Michigan City, Ind., Mar. 31, 1945; d. Isaac and Mildred Ruth (Brooklyn) Jolles; m. Andrew Ramsay Mollison, Jr., Dec. 27, 1967. B.A, Mich. State U., 1972; M.A. in Comparative Lit., CUNY, 1985. Teaching fellow dept. English, Queens Coll., N.Y.C., 1977; with Women's Equity Action League, Washington, 1977—, exec. dir., 1980—. Bd. dirs. House of Ruth, Washington, 1983—, bd. v.p., 1987, Planned Parenthood of Met. Washington, 1986—; speaker women's rights, nonprofit mgmt. and fundraising. Author articles. Sarah Lawrence Coll. and Smithsonian Instn. scholar Inst. Women's History, 1979. Office: Women's Equity Action League 1250 1st St NW Suite 305 Washington DC 20005

MOLLMAN, JENNIFER ELLEN, retail executive; b. East Alton, Ill., Oct. 20, 1954; d. Edward Lee and Jacqueline (Laney) M. A in Retail Merchandising, U. Maine, 1976. Mgr. advt. sales Greater Boston Conv. and Tourist Bur., 1976-80; mfrs. rep. Boston Gear, Quincy, Mass., 1980-82; sales rep. Classic Computers Co., Braintree, Mass., 1983-84; mgr. retail store NE Computer Stores, Stoneham, Mass., 1984-85; adminstr. retail distbn. Torrington (Conn.) Co., 1985. Mem. Nat. Assn. Female Execs., Assn. Bus. Computer Dealers, North Shore C. of C., Woburn Bus. Assn., Hartford Track Club. Home: 78 Alan Dr Weatogue CT 06089 Office: The Torrington Co 59 Field St Torrington CT 06790

MOLT, CYNTHIA MARYLEE, author, publisher; b. Sierra Madre, Calif., Nov. 1, 1957; d. Lawrence Edward and Evelyn Mary (Novak) Molt. BA in English Lit., Calif. State U., Long Beach, 1980. Mng. editor Assoc. Graphics, Arts and Letters, Monrovia, Calif., 1981-87, pub., sr. and mng. editor, 1987—, authenticator, 1981—; author McFarland and Co., Inc., Pubs., Jefferson, N.C., 1988. Author: Gone With the Wind: A Complete Reference, 1988; author, editor mag. The Wind, 1981—, Calif. Film, 1987—; spl. corr. Monrovia News-Post, 1985; corr. : G.W.T.W. Collector's Club Newsletter, 1979-82, Monrovia Rev., 1975. Vol. adminstrv. asst. student activities Monrovia High Sch., 1976. Mem. Gone with the Wind Soc. (pres. 1985—), Vivien Leigh Fan Club (pres. 1987—), Clark Gable Fan Club (pres. 1987—), Grace Kelly Fan Club (pres. 1987—). Republican. Roman Catholic. Home and Office: 364 N May Ave Monrovia CA 91016

MOLTENI, BETTY PHILLIPS, painter; b. Norfolk, Va., Dec. 15, 1913; d. William Henry and Margaret (Brownley) Phillips; A.B., Coll. William and Mary, 1938; student art U. Nev., Reno, 1966-71; m. Peter G. Molteni, Jr., July 22, 1939; children—Peter G. III, Margaret Elizabeth, Christopher Phillips, Marianne Stephanie. Founder, chmn. Armed Forces Art Show Hawaii, 1962; one woman shows Artist Co-op., Reno, 1978, 81, Mother Lode Nat. Art Exhbn., Sonora, Calif., 1977, 79, Delta Art Assn. Show, Antioch, Calif., 1978; exhibited group shows Nev. Women Art Show Las Vegas, 1976, Nat. League Am. Pen Women, Salt Lake City, 1973, Sacramento, 1978, Washington, 1984, Lodi Art Ann., Acampo, Calif., 1979, 84, Tahoe Erhman Mansion Arts Festival, 1979-80, Sierra Nev. Mus., 1983, Nev. Watercolor Soc., 1984, New Artists Gallery, Celebration Watercolor Las Vegas Art Mus., 1986, Brewery Art Ctr., Carson City, Nev., 1986, 2d nat. miniature show Furman U., S.C.; represented in pvt. collections, also Sierra Nev. Mus. Art, Reno. Bd. dirs. Nev. Art Gallery, 1975-78; del. Sierra Arts Assembly, 1977-78, 80-81. Mem. Nat. League Am. Pen Women (v.p. 1973, treas. Reno br. 1979, pres. 1980, state pres. 1982-84), Soc. Western Artists, Latimer Art Club (art scholarship chmn. 1986, pres. 1971, treas. 1978), Carson City Alliance (charter), Nev. Artists Assn., Nev. Art Gallery, Sierra Arts Assembly, Artist Co-op. (charter, v.p. 1983), Sierra Nevada Mus. Arts Aux., Reno Philharmonic League, Cath. Daus. Republican. Roman Catholic. Home: 1130 Alpine Circle Reno NV 89509

MOLTZAN, JANET ROZDIL, library administrator; b. Bridgeport, Conn., Jan. 6, 1945; d. Andrew Peter and Helen (Botsko) Rozdil; m. Herbert John Moltzan, July 30, 1976. B.S. in L.S., Tex. Woman's U., Denton, 1967, M.L.S., 1973. Spl. counselor Tex. Woman's U., 1967-68; children's librarian Dallas Pub. Library, 1968-74, asst. library mgr., 1974-76, mgr., 1976-85, asst. dir. pub. services, 1985—; cons. Lamplighter Sch., Dallas, 1971; mem. Caldecott Award Jury, 1982-84; cons. on book Reminiscences: A Glimpse of Old East Dallas, 1983; ex-officio mem. Lakewood Library Friends Bd., Dallas, 1982-85; participant NDEA Inst. Pub. and Sch. Library Work with Gifted Children, Denton, 1970. Contbr. articles to profl. jours. Friends of Dallas Pub. Library scholar, 1973. Mem. ALA (conf. chmn. 1978-79), Tex. Library Assn. (legis. coordinator 1976-78, children's roundtable v.p. 1975-76, pres. 1976-77, recognition award 1980, chmn. continuing edn. com. 1987-88) Pub. Library Assn. (chmn. services to children com. 1976-77), Assn. Library Services to Children (nominating com. 1980, publs. com. 1984, chmn. Centennial Celebration Task Force, 1987—), Lakewood C. of C. Zonta Internat. Office: Dallas Pub Library 1515 Young St Dallas TX 75201

MOMIYAMA, NANAE, artist, lecturer; b. Tokyo; came to U.S., 1954; d. Tokutaro and Kimie Momiyama; divorced; children—Haniwa, Anne-Kesa, Richard. B.F.A., Bunka Gakvin Coll., Japan; M.F.A., Tokyo Women's Coll. Free lance artist; one woman shows include: Seibu Gallery, Tokyo, 1974, 77, 79, 82, 87, Weinwright House, Rye, N.Y., 1979, Galeries Raymond, Duncan, Paris, 1975, 78, Ligoa Duncan Gallery, N.Y., 1975, Mudo Gallery, Tokyo, 1977, Bruce Mus., Greenwich, Conn., 1970, 72, Gima Gallery, Honolulu, 1962, Brata Gallery, N.Y., 1958, 59; exhibited in group shows: Museo Nazionale dell'Accademia Itaria, 1983, Met. Mus., Tokyo, City Mus., Kyoto, City Mus., Osaka, Nat. Assn. Women Artists Ann. and Group Exhbn., Nat. Acad. Fed. Bldg., N.Y., 1968-88, Lever House, Union Carbide, Equitable Bldg., N.Y. World Trade Ctr., N.Y., Weintraub Gallery, Duncan Gallery, Landmark Gallery, N.Y., many others throughout U.S., Europe and Japan. Lectr. numerous colls. and univs. Recipient Jury award Grand Prix Internat. Inst. painting, 1972, Silver medal Grand Prix Humanitaire de France, 1975, Gold medal Acad. Italy, 1979, Stature Victory World Culture prize Centro Studie Ricerche dell Nazioni, 1983. Japanese Artists Assn. N.Y. (pres. 1978-81), Nat. Assn. Women Artists (jury 1979-81, C.W. Meml. prize 1978), Modern Art Assn. (dir. N.Y. chpt. 1966—), Internat. Assn. Artists. Studio: 155 Bank St New York NY 10014

MOMMAERTS, BARBARA GLORIA, placement and career development director; b. Shawano, Wis., Jan. 19, 1939; d. August Christian and Maebelle Mary (Cleveland) Herrmann; m. Richard Davis Mommaerts, Aug. 19, 1961; children: Michele, Dirk, Paul. BS in Edn., U. Wis., Oshkosh, 1961, MS in Counseling, 1972. Tchr. Plymouth, Wis., 1961-62, Oakfield, Wis., 1962-64, Green Bay, Wis., 1966-67; counselor U. Wis., Green Bay, 1971-74; asst. dir. Placement and Career Devel., U. Wis., Green Bay, 1974-79, assoc. dir., 1979-84, dir., 1984—; affirmative action dir. U. Wis., Green Bay, 1980-84; workshop presenter, pub. speaker Women in bus., Vocat. Services to Handicapped Persons, Employee Assistance Program, Sta. WFRV-TV, Human Relations Seminar, and other profl., edni., and civic orgns. Mem. Bay Area of Wis. Epilepsy Assn., Green Bay, 1972-75; mem. steering com. Community Affirmative Action Task Force, Green Bay, 1981. Mem. Wis. Career Planning and Placement Assn. (past chmn. membership com., bd. dirs., sec., now pres.), Midwest College Placement Assn. (affirmative action com.), Assn. for Sch., Coll., and Univ. Staffing, Wis. Assn. Sch. Personnel Adminstrs (audit com.), Nat. Assn. Female Execs. Lodge: Zonta Internat. Club: Mgmt. Women. Office: U Wis 2420 Nicolet Dr Green Bay WI 54301-7001

MON, LOURDES GAGUI, school principal; b. Bangar, Philippines, Mar. 6, 1944; came to U.S., 1967; d. Crispin Yabut and Josefa Vergara (Agas) Gagui; m. Francis Lopez Mon, July 17, 1968; children: Catherine, Joey. BS in Elem. Edn., U. of East, Manila, 1963; MEd, Loyola U., Chgo., 1976. Tchr. San Sebastian Coll., 1963-64, St. Joseph's Coll., Philippines, 1964-67, Beloit (Wis.) Pub. Schs., 1967-69, Immaculate Conception Sch., Chgo., 1969-83; prin. St. Josaphat Sch., Chgo., 1983—; ex-officio mem. St. Josaphat Sch. Bd., 1983—; coordinator U.S. State Dept. Confs. for Minorities and Women. Contbg. editor: Maynila mag., 1983-85; contbg. writer: I M Herald, 1983-85; assoc. editor: VIA Times mag., 1984-86, columnist, 1984—, sr. editor, 1986—. Pres. Asian Human Services, Chgo., 1986-88; active Am. Profls. Civic Alliance; vol. Immigration and Naturalization Program, 1985—; exec, dir. immigration program Am. Filipino Profls. Civic Alliance; mem. Filipino Am. Council Bd., 1983-85; co-founder, bd. dirs. Sining Kayumanggi Theatre Group. Named Outstanding Asian of Yr., Asian Am. Coalition Chgo., 1986. Mem. Assn. for Supervision and Curriculum Devel., Archdiocesan Prins. Assn., Nat. Cath. Edn. Assn., Filipino Am. Women's Network (chmn. Ill. chpt. 1987—). Republican. Roman Catholic. Lodge: Lions (v.p. Chgo. chpt. 1984—). Office: St Josaphat Sch 2245 N Southport Ave Chicago IL 60614

MONACO, KATHLEEN M., district manager marketing; b. Danbury, Conn., Oct. 24, 1950; d. Marvin Victor and Mary Veronica Crowley; m. Joseph E. Monaco Jr., June 12, 1971 (div. July 1977). BA, U. Conn., 1972; MBA, U. New Haven, 1986. Various positions, then dist. mgr. mktg. So. New Eng. Telephone, New Haven, 1973—. Mem. Am. Mktg. Assn. Republican. Roman Catholic. Home: Oronoque Forest 552 Muirfield Rd New Haven CT 06515

MONAGAN, MARILEE, state agency administrator; b. Stockton, Calif., Sept. 9, 1947; d. Robert Timothy JR. AND Margaret Ione (Angwin) M. AA, Am. River Coll., Sacramento, 1981; BA, Nat. U., Sacramento, 1986. Legis. sec. Calif. State Senate, Sacramento, 1968-73; info. service dir. Calif. Research, Sacramento, 1973-74; cons. Calif. State Assembly, Sacramento, 1974-81; spl. asst. U.S. Dept. Health and Human Services, Washington, 1981-83; exec. officer Calif. Dept. Social Services, Sacramento, 1983—; mem. State Maternal, Child and Adolescent Health Bd., Sacramento, 1985—, Child Devel. Programs adv. com., Sacramento, 1986—. Mem. Sacramento Pub. TV, 1975—, Sacramento Pub. Radio, 1986—, Sacramento Symphony Support Group, 1983—, Citizens for a Better Sacramento, 1988—; co-founder Gov.'s Women Appointees Council State of Calif., 1984—; chair Rep. task force Nat. Women's Polit. Caucus of Calif., 1980-81; bd. dirs. Calif. Rep. League, 1975—. Mem. Child Welfare League of Am., Sacramento Women's Network, Friends of 6. Club: Comstock (Sacramento). Home: 2912 Pasatiempo Pl Sacramento CA 95833

MONAGHAN, NANCY C., journalist; b. Olean, N.Y., May 13, 1945; d. Stephen Francis Cipot and June (Butler) Cipot Duffey; m. G. Patrick Monaghan Jr., June 24, 1967 (div. 1973). Student U. Rochester, 1974-75. Mng. editor City Newspapers, Rochester, N.Y., 1973-75; pres. Mill Sq. Communications, Rochester, 1975-77; reporter, day metro editor Democrat and Chronicle, Rochester, 1977-82, metro editor, 1982; nat. editor, day nat. editor USA Today, Washington, 1982-84, mng. editor, news, 1984—. Chmn. Nat. Communications Council, Va. Tech., Blacksburg, 1986—. Recipient Matrix award Women in Communications, 1982, Spot News Reporting award N.Y. State AP, 1979, 82, Legal Reporting award N.Y. State Bar Assn., 1981, Govt. Reporting, award N.Y. State Pubs. Assn., 1973, 74, Polit. Reporting award N.Y. State Pubs. Assn., 1975. Mem. AP Mng. Editors (gen. news com.), Nat. Soc. Profl. Journalists (nat. membership chmn. 1984-85, Rochester chpt. pres. 1980-81, Washington chpt. treas. 1988—). Office: USA Today PO Box Washington DC 20044

MONAHAN, DOROTHY IRENE, manufacturing executive; b. Paterson, N.J., Jan. 13, 1950; d. Peter Thomas and Dorothy Adele (Gehring) M.; m. Edward Guratosky, Aug. 24, 1975 (div. 1983). Grad. high sch., Paterson. Head cashier Food Fair Stores, Paterson, 1967-68; with Medallion Industries, Paterson, 1968—; v.p. mfg. Medallion Industries subs. C.N. Burman Lamp Co., Paterson, 1986—; real estate saleswoman Molke Real Estate, Bloomingdale, N.J., 1984—. Mem. Nat. Assn. Female Execs., Am. Prodn. and Inventory Control Assn., Am. Mgmt. Assn., Am. Legion. Club: E.P. Rifle & Gun (treas. 1974-75). Office: Medallion Industries T/A CN Burman Lamp Co 781 River ST Paterson NJ 07524

MONAHAN, FRANCES DONOVAN, nurse, educator; b. Lawrence, Mass., Aug. 29, 1943; d. Francis Jeremiah and Isabel Rita (Torpey) Donovan; m. William Thomas Monahan; children: Michael McCain, Kerryane Torpey. AB in Psychology, Emmanuel Coll., 1964; BS in Nursing, Columbia U., 1966, MS in Med. Surg. Nursing, Boston U., 1968; PhD in Nursing, NYU, 1980. RN, N.Y. Staff nurse Lawrence Gen. Hosp., 1967, Columbia Presbyn. Hosp., N.Y.C., 1969; instr. Beth Israel Hosp. Sch. Nursing, N.Y.C., 1969-71; asst. assoc. professor Dept. Nursing Rockland Community Coll., Suffern, N.Y., 1971-82, prof., chmn., 1983—; staff nurse Columbia Prebyn. Hosp., N.Y., 1969; camp nurse Model Cities Program, Highland Falls, N.Y., summer 1972-73, Ladycliff Coll., 1971-74; adj. faculty State U. Coll. at New Paltz, N.Y., 185-86, fall 87; site visitor accreditation Nat. League for Nursing, N.Y., 1987; manuscript reviewer Little Brown & Co., Boston, 1984; program chmn. State U. N.Y. Conf. on Nursing Edn., Albany, N.Y., 1985; item writer Regents Coll. Examination, 1980-87. Author: Medical-Surgical Nursing, 1984; co-author: Writing Across the Curriculum Handbook of Strategies, 1983; contbr. articles to profl. jours. Mem. adv. com. Dept. Nursing Dominican Coll., Blauvelt, N.Y., 1982—, Dept. Nursing Coll. New Paltz, 1984—, parents adv. council Willow Ave. Sch., Cornwall, 1983-84. Mem. North Am. Nursing Diagnosis Assn. (charter), Am. Nurses Assn., Mid Atlantic Regional Nursing Assn., N.Y. State Assoc. Degree Nursing Council, N.Y. State Assn. of Two Yr. and Jr. Colls., NYU Alumni Assn, Sigma Theta Tau (Alpha Zeta chpt.). Office: Rockland Community Coll 145 College Rd Suffern NY 10901

MONAHAN, JEANNETTE, hospital management development specialist; b. Dallas, May 9, 1949; d. John I. and Julia M. (Galloway) Welsh; m. Terence F. Meany, Mar. 17, 1977; 1 dau., Theresa K. Monahan. B.A. in English, U. Tex.-Austin, 1971; M.P.A., U. Colo., 1975; diploma of competency in systems renewal consultation Internat. Inst. for Study of Systems Renewal, Seattle, 1981. Intern, City of Boulder (Colo.), summer 1975, Dept. Regulatory Agys., State of Colo., Denver, summer 1976; tng. specialist Municipality of Met. Seattle, 1977-78; mgr. employee tng. and devel. U. Wash. Hosps., Seattle, 1978-82; dir. mgmt. devel. Virginia Mason Med. Ctr., Seattle, 1982—; supervisory cons. U. Ky. Teaching Improvement Project, 1986—. Mem. parish council St. Patrick's Cath. Ch., Seattle, 1984-88, pres., 1988—. Recipient Suggestion award Municipality of Met. Seattle, 1978. Mem. Am. Soc. for Tng. and Devel. (recipient outstanding contbn. award 1977, 78, mem. region VIII conf. planning com. 1983), Am. Soc. Healthcare Edn. and Tng. (nat. program planning com. 1982, 83). Democrat. Roman Catholic. Club: Toastmasters Internat. Contbr. articles on organizational devel. to profl. jours. Office: Virginia Mason Med Ctr 925 Seneca St PO Box 1930 Seattle WA 98111

MONAHAN, MARIE TERRY, lawyer; b. Milford, Mass., June 26, 1927; d. Francis V. and Marie I. (Casey) Terry; m. John Henry Monahan, Aug. 25, 1951; children: Thomas F., Kathleen J., Patricia M., John Terry, Moira M., Deirdre M. AB, Radcliffe Coll., 1949; JD, New Eng. Sch. Law, 1975. Bar: Mass. 1977, U.S. Dist. Ct. Mass. 1978, U.S. Supreme Ct. 1982. Tchr. French and Spanish Holliston (Mass.) High Sch., 1949-52; sole practice Newton, Mass., 1977—. Fellow Mass. Bar Found.; mem. ABA, Mass. Bar Assn., Nat. Assn. Women Lawyers, Assn. Trial Lawyers Am., Mass. Assn. Women Lawyers (pres. 1986), Mass. Acad. Trial Attys., Mass. Assn. Women Lawyers Scholarship Fund. (exec. bd. 1986-87), Boston Bar Assn. Home and Office: 34 Foster St Newtonville MA 02160

MONAHAN, MARILYN GRACE, educational administrator; b. Holyoke, Mass., Feb. 11, 1948; d. Michael and Grace (Ramondetta) M. BEd, Westfield State Coll., 1970; MEd, U. N.H., 1975. Tchr. Elem. Sch., Alton, N.H., 1970-72, Goffstown, N.H., 1972-83; pres. Nat. Edn. Assn., N.H., 1983—. Mem. Gov.'s Adv. Com. Educational Block Grants 1981, N.H. Constitutional convention, 1984. Mem. Nat. Edn. Assn. (st. exec. bd. 1977—, v.p. 1981-83), Nat. Council St. Edn. Assns., N.H. Educators Polit. Action Com., St. Council Tchr. Edn. Roman Catholic. Home: 962 Goffstown Rd Manchester NH 03102 Office: NEA 103 N State St Concord NH 03301

MONCARZ, ELISA SHAFRAN, accounting educator; b. Havana, Cuba, Oct. 10, 1949; came to U.S., 1960; d. Benjamin and Felicia (Steinberg) Shafran; m. Raul Moncarz, May 31, 1973; children: Felippe, Roger, Benjamin. BBA, CUNY, 1966. CPA, Fla., N.Y. Asst. acct. Ernst & Whinney, N.Y.C., 1966-69, supr., 1969-72; rev. mgr. Spear, Sheldon and Safer, CPA., Miami, Fla., 1972-74, asst. prof. acctg. Fla. Internat. U., Miami, 1974-79, assoc. prof., 1979—; cons. various hospitality orgns., 1974—. Author: Financial Accounting for Hospitality Management, 1986; contbr. articles to profl. jours. Mem. Am. Inst. CPA's, Fla. Inst. CPA's, Cuban-Am. CPA Assn. (bd. dirs. 1986—, treas.). Office: Fla Internat U Dept Acctg Tamiami Trail Miami FL 33199

MONCHEK, LANA TERI, university administrator; b. Bronx, N.Y., Sept. 17; d. Sydney and Pearl (Ungar) M. BE, SUNY, Buffalo, 1968; MEd, U. Miami, 1969; EdS, U. Fla., 1974; JD, U. Miami, 1981; PhD, U. Fla., 1982. Bar: Fla., 1981. Tchr. Broward County Pub. Schs., Hollywood, Fla., 1969-81, Dade County Pub. Schs., Miami, Fla., 1982-83; asst. dir. devel. research U. Miami, Coral Gables, Fla., 1983-85, dir. devel. research, 1985—. Bd. dirs. Goldstein Hebrew Acad., Miami, 1985-87; vol. Miami Youth Mus., 1985-86; mem. Ctr. for Fine Arts, Miami, Dade County Planned Giving Council, 1985—, Council Advancement and Support of Edn., 1983—; mem. bench and bar unit B'nai B'rith, Dade County, Fla.; vol. guide Vizcaya, Dade County, 1986. Office: U Miami Dept Devel Research 5807 Ponce de-Leon Blvd Miami FL 33124 also: PO Box 248073 Miami FL 33124

MONCURE, JANE BELK, educator, author, consultant; b. Orlando, Fla., Dec. 16, 1926; d. John Blanton and Jennie Bruce (Wannamaker) B; m. James Ashby Moncure; 1 child, James Ashby II. BS in Elem. Edn., Va. Commonwealth U., 1952; MA in Early Childhood Edn., Columbia U., 1954. Tchr., and various directorships schs. and chs., N.Y., Va., 1952-66; instr. early childhood edn. Va. Commonwealth U., Richmond, 1966-72; instr. children's lit. U. Richmond, 1973-74; tchr. early childhood edn. Burlington, N.C., 1974-78; author, cons. early childhood edn. 1979-87; lectr. seminars and workshops, Va., N.C., Ill., Ind. Author: Word Bird Series for Young Readers, Wise Owl Series for Young Readers, Sound Box Books, Alphabet Books, various language arts books including All By Myself, I Never Say I'm Thankful, But I Am, Where Things Belong, Magic Monsters series, Child Development, Creative Dramatics series, Creative Expression series, Special Day Arts and Crafts, Science and Social Science series, Values series, Religious Education series, First Steps to Reading series, First Steps to Math series, Magic Castle Readers series. Recipient C.S. Lewis Gold medal, 1984. Mem. Va. Assn. for Early Childhood Edn. (Outstanding Service to Young Children in Va.), So. Assn. for Children Under Six, Nat. Assn. for the Edn. Young Children, Early Learning Resouce Co., Delta Kappa Gamma. Home and Office: Seven Lakes Box 750 West End NC 27376

MONDOU, MARIE ANNE, infosystems specialist; b. Iowa City, Sept. 21, 1961; d. Eugene Raymond and Irene Lucienne (Arguin) M. BA, SUNY, Potsdam, 1983; postgrad., Va. Poly. Inst. & State U. Software engr. MCI/Satellite Bus. Systems, McLean, Va., 1983—. Mem. Nat. Assn. Female Execs. Roman Catholic. Home: 2303 Freetown Ct #2B Reston VA 22091

MONFERRATO, ANGELA MARIA, entrepreneur; b. Wissembourg, Alsace-Loraine, France, July 19, 1948; came to U.S., 1950; d. Albert Carmen and Anna Maria (Vieri) Monferrato; m. Perry S. Itkin, Nov. 9, 1978. Diplomate, Pensionnat Florissant, Lausanne, Switzerland, 1966-67; BS in Consumer Related Studies, Pa. State U., 1971. Simultaneous translator Inst. for Achievement of Human Potential, Phila., 1976-78; art dir. The Artworks, Sumneytown, Pa., 1975-76; asst. productionist Film Space, State College, Pa., 1976; real property mgr. Plaza 15 Condominium, Ft. Lauderdale, Fla., 1979-80; legal asst. Perry S. Itkin, P.A., Ft. Lauderdale, Fla., 1981—; real estate salesperson Rising Sun The Real Estate Corp. S. Fla., Ft. Lauderdale, 1986—. Filmmaker, Red Cross Canoe and Kayak Safety Film, 1976; patentee reflective vest. Mem. Ft. Lauderdale Bd. Realtors. Home: 2524 Barcelona Dr Fort Lauderdale FL 33301 Office: Night Life Inc 106 SE 9th St Fort Lauderdale FL 33316

MONFORT, MYRA HARRIET, lawyer; b. Newark, July 4, 1938; d. Benjamin Victor and Alice Cohen; m. Kenneth Warren Monfort, Sept. 23, 1982; children from previous marriage: Bradley Ben Ellins, Rachel Starr Ellins. B.A. cum laude, Barnard Coll., Columbia U., 1960; J.D., U. Colo., 1975. Bar: Colo. 1975. Clk. to judge Colo. Ct. Appeals, 1975-76; staff atty., assoc. gen. counsel then gen. counsel Monfort of Colo., Inc., Greeley, 1976—; v.p., sec. Monfort of Colo., Inc., 1980—; group v.p. adminstrv. services Monfort of Colo. Inc., Swift Independent Corp. and Swift Independent Packing Co., 1988—; grad. asst. Ctr. Labor Edn. and Research, U. Colo., 1975. Republican committeewoman, 1979-80; mem. lawyer's com. Am. Meat Inst.; bd. dirs., trustee, mem. house com. North Colo. Med. Ctr., 1985—; appointed mem. Colo. State Bd. for Community Colls. and Occupational Edn., 1986—; bd. dirs. Greeley Philharmonic Orch., 1986—. Mem. ABA, Colo. Bar Assn., Weld County Bar Assn., Colo. Assn. Corp. Counsels. Jewish. Office: Monfort of Colo Inc PO Box G Greeley CO 80632

MONGOLD, SANDRA K., corporate executive; b. Springfield, Ohio, Aug. 14, 1947; d. Robert Harold and Norma Jean (Fennessy) Rine; m. Alan Darrell Mabry, Aug. 18, 1968 (div. 1977); m. Danny Willard Mongold, Nov. 16, 1979; children: Brian Alan Mabry, Krista Marie Mabry. Student, Wright State U., Urbana Coll., So. State Coll., Ohio. Acctg. clk. Irwin Co., Wilmington, Ohio, 1968-80, asst. treas., 1980-85, treas., 1985—, new product com., 1985—. Mem. adv. bd. So. State Coll. Mem. Nat. Assn. Accts., Nat. Assn. Female Execs., Am. Mgmt. Assn., Nat. Corp. Cash Mgmt. Assn., Wilmington C. of C. (dir., bd. dirs.). Republican. Presbyterian. Avocations: golf, bowling. Home: 330 Washington Ave Wilmington OH 45177 Office: Irwin Co 92 Grant Wilmington OH 45177

MONICAL, MARY CHRISTINE, biotechnology marketing executive; b. Cin., Apr. 6, 1950; d. Robert Duane and Carol Arnetha (Dean) M. B.S., U. Miami, 1972, postgrad., 1973; postgrad. Butler U., 1980. Tech. specialist Am. Dade div. Am. Hosp. Supply Corp., Miami, Fla., 1976-79; sales rep. Gen. Diagnostics Co., Morris Plains, N.J., 1980-81, microbiology specialist, 1981-83; sales rep. Coulter Immunology, Hialeah, Fla., 1983-85, regional sales mgr., 1985-86, mktg. dir. FAST Systems, Inc., Rockville Md., 1986—. Recipient best sales tng. performance award Gen. Diagnostics, 1980; named to Pres.'s Club, Outstanding Sales Rep., Coulter Electronics, 1984-85, 85-86. Home: 20415 Sunbright Lane Germantown MD 20874

MONIHAN, MARY ELIZABETH, lawyer; b. Cleve., Mar. 22, 1957; d. Michael Reilley and Donna Mae (Warner) M. BS in Econ., John Carroll U., 1979; JD, Cleve.-Marshall Coll. of Law, 1984. Trust analyst AmeriTrust Co., Cleve., 1979-81, legal asst., 1981-84, assoc., 1984-85; assoc. Jones, Day, Reavis & Pogue, Cleve., 1985—. Mem. Citizens League, Cleve., Jr. com. Cleve. Orchestra. Mem. ABA, Ohio State Bar Assn., Cleve. Bar Assn., Estate Planning Council of Cleve. Home: 990 Som Ctr Rd Mayfield Village OH 44143 Office: Jones Day Reavis & Pogue 901 Lakeside Ave Cleveland OH 44114

MONIZ, SARA JANE, public relations director; b. Norwalk, Conn., May 7, 1946; d. Harry Wilson and Freda Julia (Hylen) Bouton; m. Robert Henry Mahler Jr. (div. 1980); children: Melissa Victoria, Robert Henry; m. Bryan Joseph Moniz. Grad. high sch., Norwalk, Conn., 1964. Exec. sec. H&J Electronic Seal, Norwalk, 1964-70; mgr. pub. relations Atlantic Environ., Norwalk, 1970-75, Strategic Innovations, Westport, Conn., 1975-79; exec. adminstrv. asst. Vitam Ctr., Norwalk, 1979-83; mgr. pub. relations El Conquistador Country Club, Bradenton, Fla., 1983—. Mem. Nat. Assn. Female Execs., Manatee County C. of C. Republican. Methodist. Home: 5427 4th

St Ct E Bradenton FL 34203 Office: El Conquistador Country Club 4350 El Conquistador Pkwy Bradenton FL 33507

MONIZE, COLETTE RUTH, correctional education administrator; b. Chicopee, Mass., Apr. 8, 1933; d. Frederic Joseph and Lillian A. (Quenneville) Demers; m. Walter Carl Monize, Aug. 13, 1960. BA, U. New Orleans, 1973; MA, U. Ariz., 1975, PhD, 1988. Assoc. faculty Pima Community Coll., Tucson, 1975-85; career counselor Ariz. State Prison Complex, Tucson, 1981-86, supr. correctional edn., 1986—; mem. long range planning com. Ariz. Dept. Corrections, 1985-87. Writer, editor women's newspaper Source, 1977-80; adv. inmate newspaper Inside the Wire (first class award, 1982). Mem. Ariz. Vocat. Assn., Correctional Edn. Assn. (developer constn. and by-laws state chpt., 1st pres. Ariz. chpt. 1988), Nat. Assn. Female Execs. Home: 308 Hazzard St Bisbee AZ 85603 Office: ASPC-Douglas PO Drawer 3867 Douglas AZ 85608

MONK, JANICE WALLS, special education coordinator; b. Detroit, Oct. 29, 1954; d. George Oscar and June Pauline (Strohm) Walls; m. Charles Stanton Monk, Aug. 28, 1981; 1 child, Jessica Lauren. BS in Edn., U. Ga., 1974, MEd, 1975, PhD in Mental Retardation, Ga. State U., 1987. Speech pathologist DeKalb County Schs., Decatur, Ga., 1975-77, 80, Health Authority, Gateshead, Eng., 1977-79, Cobb County Schs., Marietta, Ga., 1980-82; research asst. Ga. State U., Atlanta, 1982-83; coordinator spl. edn. Atlanta pub. schs., 1983—; adv. Ga. State U. Speech Pathology Program, Atlanta, 1984—; guest lectr., 1982—. Mem. Young Republicans, Ga., 1976, 80-81. Fellow Ga. State U., 1982-83, U. Ga., 1975. Mem. Am. Speech and Hearing Assn., Council for Exceptional Children, Ga. Council for Exceptional Children, (membership chmn. div. on career devel. 1983—), Phi Kappa Phi, Phi Delta Kappa. Presbyterian. Avocations: Duplicate bridge; gourmet cooking; wine tasting. Home: 1708 Hickory Grove Trail Acworth GA 30101 Office: Atlanta Pub Schs 2930 Forrest Hill Dr SW Atlanta GA 30315

MONK, JULIA FLORENCE, architect; b. Chgo., Nov. 2, 1954; d. Clarence Burleigh and Lorene (Bullard) M. BArch, Ball State U., 1978, B in Environ. Sci., 1978. Project designer Welton Becket, Chgo., 1978-82; project architect Welton Becket, N.Y.C., 1982-84; assoc. Brennan, Beer, Gorman, N.Y.C., 1984—. Mem. Mus. Modern Art, N.Y.C. Mem. AIA, Am. Soc. Interior Designers, ADPSR. Office: Brennan Beer Gorman Monk 515 Madison Ave New York NY 10022

MONK, TRACIE ELIZABETH, science policy analyst; b. Pecos, Tex., Sept. 17, 1958; d. Sherman Wayne and Anity May (Phillips) M.; m. Daniel Todd Westrick, May 27, 1984. BA in Polit. Sci., U. Tex., 1980; MA in Sci. Policy, George Washington U., 1983, postgrad., 1984—. Adminstrv. asst. NSF, Washington, 1980-82; research analyst J.F. Coates, Inc., Washington, 1983; mgr. The BDM Corp., McLean, Va., 1983-88; ind. mgmt. cons. Jakarta, Indonesia, 1988—; cons. George Washington U., Washington, 1980-83, Carnegie Inst. of Washington, 1982-83. Publicity chmn. Young Democrats of Tex., Austin, 1979; state youth coordinator Krueger U.S. Senate campaign, Austin, 1978. Recipient Sustained Superior Performance award NSF, 1982. Mem. Assn. for Sch., Tech. and Innovation (pres. 1985-86), Soc. for Internat. Devel., AAAS. Democrat. Home: 1917 S Randolph St Arlington VA 22204 Office: Jalan Gumuk 24/26 #2, Kemang, Jakarta Indonesia

MONKS, KAREN ELIZABETH, nursing educator; b. Grand Rapids, Mich., Nov. 3, 1936; d. Louis Francis and Evelyn Anne (Hammerschmidt) McGough; m. Patrick Joseph Monks, Nov. 26, 1966; children—Laura Anne, Joseph Patrick. Diploma in nursing Mercy Central Sch. Nursing, Grand Rapids, 1956; B.S. in Nursing, Marquette U., 1965; M.S. in Nursing, U. Tex. Med. Br., Galveston, 1984. R.N., Mich., Wis., Ariz. Staff nurse St. Mary's Hosp., Grand Rapids, 1957-58; staff nurse, then head nurse Kent County Hosp., Grand Rapids, 1958-62; staff nurse part-time St. Joseph's Hosp., Milw., 1962-65, head nurse, 1965-66; staff nurse, then house supr. Yuma Regional Med. Ctr. (Ariz.), 1966-72; nursing instr. Ariz. Western Coll., Yuma, 1972—, div. chmn. human services, 1984—; bd. dirs. Yuma Regional Med. Ctr., 1980—, sec./treas., 1987vice-chmn., 1988, chmn. personnel/nominations, 1981-84; chmn. Ariz. Council Assoc. Drgree Nursing Programs, 1985-86; co-chmn. Ariz. Council on Nursing Edn., 1985-86. Mem. Nat. League Nursing (legis. network, accreditation visitor, 1985—). Democrat. Roman Catholic. Home: 1946 London Dr Yuma AZ 85364 Office: Ariz Western Coll Box 929 Yuma AZ 85364

MONO, MADELEINE, cosmetics company executive; b. London, Aug. 7, 1935; d. Arthur and Elizabeth Lillian (Emanuel) M.; m. Joseph Berry (div.); children—Gail Lynne, Louise Ann, Craig Justin, Grant Lloyd; m. 2d, Arthur Levene, Nov. 25, 1972. Stage actress, London, 1947; antique dealer, London, 1968-72; founder, pres., creative dir. Madeleine Mono Cosmetics Ltd., Great Neck, N.Y., 1972—; cons. on make-up to mags. Author: Make eyes With Madeleine Mono, 1980. Bd. dirs. Nassau Reperatory Theatre, L.I. Mem. Fragrance Found., Cosmetic/Toiletry Fragrance Assn., Am. Women's Devel. Corp., Foragers. Lodge: Daus Brit. Empire. Office: Madeleine Mono Cosmetics Ltd 925-2 Lincoln Ave Holbrook NY 11741

MONROE, KATHLEEN JEANNE, laboratory administrator; b. Somerville, Mass., Aug. 25, 1954; d. Gerald Michael and Eugenia Ethel (Bernier) Creedon; divorced; children: Megan Guinevere, Briana Moya. BS in Animal Sci., U. Calif., Davis, 1981; MBA, Golden Gate U., 1986. Technician animal health Animal Hosps. Inc., Vallejo, Calif., 1976-77, research asst. GenenTech Inc., South San Francisco, 1981-83; mgr. lab. Genen Tech Inc., South San Francisco, 1983—. Mem. Am. Soc. Microbiologists, Nat. Assn. Female Execs., Tissue Culture Assn. Home: 1660 Sweetwood Dr Daly City CA 94105 Office: Genentech Inc 460 Pt San Bruno Blvd South San Francisco CA 94080

MONROE, YVONNE LIS, marketing executive; b. Amsterdam, N.Y., June 14, 1957; d. Charles John and Rose Emily Lis; B.S. cum laude, SUNY, Albany, 1978; M.B.A., San Francisco State U., 1979. Adminstrv. asst. Office Lt. Gov. N.Y. State, Albany, 1975-78; price adminstrn. supr. Intel Corp., Santa Clara, Calif., 1979-80, corp. planner, 1980-81, customer mktg. engr., 1981-82; product mktg. mgr. Shugart Corp., Sunnyvale, Calif., 1982-84; product line mgr. Ampex Corp., Cupertino, Calif., 1984-85; product mgr. Fujitsu Am. Inc., San Jose, Calif., 1985-86, acct. rep., 1986-87, sales devel. mgr., 1987—. Mem. Am. Mktg. Assn., Assn. M.B.A. Execs. Roman Catholic. Office: Fujitsu Am Inc 3055 Orchard Dr San Jose CA 95134

MONSEN, ELAINE RANKER, educator, nutritionist, editor; b. Oakland, Calif., June 6, 1935; d. Emery R. and Irene Stewart (Thorley) Ranker; m. Raymond Joseph Monsen, Jr., Jan. 21, 1959; 1 dau., Maren Ranker. B.A., U. Utah, 1956; M.S. (Mead Johnson grad. scholar), U. Calif., Berkeley, 1959, Ph.D. (NSF fellow), 1961; postgrad. NSF sci. faculty fellow, Harvard U., 1968-69. Dietetic intern Mass. Gen. Hosp., Boston, 1956-57; asst. prof. nutrition, lectr. biochemistry Brigham Young U., Provo, Utah, 1960-63; mem. faculty U. Wash., Seattle, 1963—; prof. nutrition and medicine U. Wash., 1984—, prof. nutrition, adj. prof. medicine, 1976-84, chmn. div. human nutrition, dietetics and foods, 1977-82; chmn. Nutrition Studies Commn., 1969-83; vis. scholar Stanford U., 1971-72; mem. sci. adv. com. food fortification Pan-Am. Health Orgn., São Paulo, Brazil, 1972; tng. grant coordinator NIH, 1976—. Editor Jour. Am. Dietetic Assn., 1983—; author research papers on lipid metabolism, iron absorption. Bd. dirs. A Contemporary Theatre, Seattle, 1969-72; trustee, bd. dirs. Seattle Found., 1978—, vice chmn., 1987—; pres. Seattle bd. Santa Fe Chamber Music Festival, 1984-85. Grantee Nutrition Found., 1965-68, Agrl. Research Service, 1969—, Center Research Oral Biology, 1970-72. Mem. Am. Inst. Nutrition, Am. Soc. Clin. Nutrition (sec. 1987—), Am. Dietetic Assn., Soc. Nutrition Edn., Am. Soc. Parenteral and Enteral Nutrition, Wash. Heart Assn. (nutrition council 1973-76), Phi Beta Kappa, Phi Kappa Phi. Office: Human Nutrition Univ Wash DL-10 Seattle WA 98195

MONSON, CAROL LYNN, osteopathic physician, psychotherapist; b. Blue Island, Ill., Nov. 3, 1946; d. Marcus Edward and Margaret Bertha (Andres) M.; m. Frank E. Warden, Feb. 28, 1981. B.S., No. Ill. U., 1968, M.S., 1969; D.O., Mich State Coll. Osteo. Medicine, 1979. Lic. physician, Mich., diplomate Am. Bd. Osteo. Gen. Practitioners, Am. Bd. Osteo. Gen. Practice. Expeditor-psychotherapist H. Douglas Singer Zone Ctr., Rockford, Ill., 1969-71; psychotherapist Tri-County Mental Health, St. Johns, Mich., 1971-76; pvt. practice psychotherapy, East Lansing, Mich., 1976-80; intern Lansing Gen. Hosp., Mich., 1979-80; pvt. practice osteo. medicine, Lansing, 1980—; mem. staff Ingham Med. Hosp., Lansing Gen. Hosp., chmn. gen practice, 1987—; field instr. Sch. Social Work, U. Mich., 1973-76; clin. instr. Central Mich. Dept. Psychology, 1974-75; clin. prof. Mich. State U., 1980—; mem. adv. bd. Substance Abuse Clearinghouse, Lansing, 1983-85, Kelly Health Care, Lansing, 1983-85, Americor Health Services, Lansing, 1984—; chairperson dept. gen. practice Lansing Gen. Hosp. Mem. Am. Osteo Assn., Internat. Transactional Analysis Assn., Mich. Assn. Physicians and Surgeons, Ingham County Osteo. Assn., Nat. Assn. Career Women (conv. com. 1984—), Lansing Assn. Career Women. Lodge: Zonta (chmn. service com. Mid Mich. Capital Area chpt.). Avocations: gardening; orchid growing; antique collecting. Office: 3320 W Saginaw St Lansing MI 48917

MONTALBANO, ANGELA (BROGNA), advertising agency executive; b. Bklyn., Nov. 4, 1942; d. Salvatore and Ann (Taibi) Brogna. Student New Sch. for Social Research, 1970-71, Warren Robertson Sch. Drama, 1968-70. Casting dir. Norman Craig & Kummel Advt. Co., N.Y.C., 1968-73; v.p., talent rep. Lester Lewis Agy., N.Y.C., 1973-78, Bob Waters Agy., N.Y.C., 1978-80; ptnr., v.p., casting dir. City Limits Casting, N.Y.C., 1980-81; talent mgr. Curtis-Brown Mgmt., N.Y.C., 1981-82; v.p., dir. casting/celebrity negotiator William Esty Co., N.Y.C., 1982—; bd. dirs., cons. Assoc. Casting Group, Miami, Fla.; new bus. cons. Show People, Inc., N.Y.C., 1982, Westside Arts, N.Y.C., 1984; comml. acting instr. seminars, schs.; acting coach theatre, film and comml. technique; image impact cons. Mem. Nat. Assn. Talent Reps., Nat. Acad. TV Arts and Scis.

MONTANT, JANE, editor. With Gourmet Mag., N.Y.C., 1958—, formerly editorial asst., travel editor, sr. editor, exec. editor, now editor-in-chief. Office: Gourmet Magazine 560 Lexington Ave New York NY 10022 *

MONTEE-CHAREST, KAREN ANN, legal historian; b. Montclair, N.J., May 15, 1957; d. Bobby Dean and Barbara Joyce (Thatcher) Montee; m. Stephen Glenn Charest, Aug. 14, 1982. BA, U. Nebr., 1979, JD, 1982. Bar: Nebr. 1982, U.S. Dist. Ct. Nebr. 1982, Ariz. 1984. Assoc. Elsken Law Offices, Lincoln, Nebr., 1984; ptnr. Elsken & Montee-Charest, Lincoln, 1985-86; grad. asst. dept. history U. Nebr., 1986-87; ind. researcher, cons. Fed. Republic Germany, 1988—; adj. faculty Chapman Coll., Tucson, 1983-84; adj. prof. history and bus. law Park Coll., Tucson, 1983-84. Omaha Lawyers Wives' grantee, 1981; Mildred F. Thompson fellow, 1985-86. Mem. ABA, Nebr. Bar Assn., Ariz. Bar Assn., Am. Judicature Soc. Democrat. Roman Catholic.

MONTELLA, SUSAN CALLAGHAN, nursing administrator and educator; b. Bklyn., Nov. 29, 1949; d. Francis Joseph and Katherine (Nugent) Callaghan; m. Chris Montella, May 29, 1977; children: Kristin Lauran, Kerrin. BS in Nursing, Hunter Coll., 1971; MA, NYU, 1975. RN. From staff nurse to head nurse Bellevue Hosp. Ctr., N.Y.C., 1971-78, clin. supr., 1978-82, asst. dir. nursing emergency services, 1982-85, edn. coordinator, cons. emergency care inst., 1985—. Bd. dirs. A Very Spl. Place Day Treatment and Community Ctrs., Staten Island, N.Y., 1981—, pres., 1981-86, v.p. 1986-87; bd. dirs. Educare: Early Childhood Ctr., N.Y.C., 1983—, v.p., 1986—. Mem. Emergency Nurses Assn., N.Y.C. Emergency Med. Services Assn. (911 nurse adv. com. 1985-87), N.Y. Heart Assn. (testing/tng. com. emergency cardiac care 1987—). Office: Bellevue Hosp Ctr 27 St and 1st Ave New York NY 10016

MONTGOMERY, DENISE KAREN, nurse, N.Y.C., Dec. 23, 1951; d. Thomas Cornell and Dorothy Marie (Castine) Simons; m. Timothy Bruce Montgomery, July 19, 1974 (div. Feb. 1981); m. Joseph Samuel Montgomery, Aug. 20, 1983. A.D.N., San Jacinto Coll., 1971. R.N., Tex. Charge nurse Aaron's Women's Clinic, Houston, 1977; research asst. dept. ob-gyn Baylor Coll. Medicine, Houston, 1977-81, nursing supr., 1979-81, program coordinator population control program, 1979-81; nurse Dr. Eric J. Haufrect, Houston, 1982-83; office mgr., supr. Dr. J.S. Montgomery III, 1987—; Dr. Samuel Law, Houston, part-time, 1983-84. Contbr. articles to med. jours. Recipient Disting. Pub. Service award Am. Heart Assn., 1976; grantee in field. Mem. Nat. Assn. Coll. Ob-Gyn. Democrat. Roman Catholic. Home: 8014 Argentina Houston TX 77040

MONTGOMERY, EVANGELINE JULIET, exhibits and museum specialist, artist; b. N.Y.C., May 2, 1933; d. Oliver Paul and Carmelite Thompson. Student Calif. State U-Los Angeles, 1958-62, U-Calif., Berkeley, 1969-70; A.A., Los Angeles City Coll., 1958; B.F.A., Calif. Coll. Arts and Crafts, 1969. Ethnic art cons. Oakland (Calif.) Mus., 1968-74; freelance art and hist. exhibits and mus. specialist, Calif. and Washington, 1968—; exhibits and workshops coordinator Am. Assn. for State and Local History, Nashville, 1979; dir. community affairs WHMM-TV, Washington, 1980; v.p. bd. dirs. Ark Urban Systems Inc., 1973-77. Exhibited in one man shows including: Bowie State Coll., 1973, Hampton Inst. Mus., 1974, Taylor Gallery, 1974, De Paul U. Gallery, 1974, Seattle World Expo Black Pavilion, 1974; group shows include: travelling exhibit Mills Coll. Art Gallery, 1971-73; Oakland (Calif.) Mus., 1974; Berkeley Arts Center, 1975; Brook Meml. Gallery, Memphis, 1979; represented in permanent collections including: Los Angeles Bd. Edn., Oakland Mus., So. Ill. U., Normal, Mus. Afro-Am. Artists, Roxbury, Mass.; mem. San Francisco Art Commn., 1976-79, chmn. visual arts com., 1976-79. Smithsonian fellow, 1973; Nat. Endowment for Arts grantee, 1973; Third World Fund grantee, 1974. Mem. Am. Assn. Mus., Nat. Conf. Artists (nat. coordinator regions 1973-79), Am. Assn. for State and Local History, Am. Craftsmen Council, Nat. Assn. for Negro Bus. and Profl. Women (nat. fine arts dir. 1976-79), Metal Arts Guild Calif. (pres. 1972-74). Baptist. Home: 1237 S Masselin Ave Los Angeles CA 90019

MONTGOMERY, GINGER KELLAR, social services professional; b. Conway, Ark., May 28, 1945; d. Herman Robert and Una D. (Ethridge) Kellar; m. James Smith Montgomery, May 10, 1985; children: Laura Gebhardt, Michael Gebhardt, Mark Doyle. BA in Criminal Justice, Sociology with honors, U. Ark., Little Rock, 1980. Claims processor State of Ark., Little Rock, 1975-76; rep. social service I Morrilton, Ark., 1986—; adminstrv. asst. Wilson Drywall Constrn., Little Rock, 1983-85, Mac's Wholesale, Little Rock, 1985-86; adminstrv. asst. Neighborhood Adv., Little Rock, 1976-78; tchr. Conway Sch. Dist., 1980-85; ind. sales agt., 1982-85. Lay therapist SCAN, Conway, 1979-80. Recipient cert. City of Little Rock, 1978, cert. Ark. State Police, 1979. Democrat. Mem. Ch. of Christ. Office: Ark Dept Human Services PO Box 228 Morrilton AR 72110

MONTGOMERY, JEAN OLIVE, antique dealer; b. Springerville, Ariz., June 1, 1919; d. Henry T. and Cordelia Carol (Shideler) Miller; B.A. with honors, U. Pacific, Stockton, Calif., 1939; M.S. with honors, Simmons Coll., Boston, 1940; m. George W. Montgomery, Jr., Feb. 21, 1942. Owner, mgr. Montgomery Antiques, Los Gatos, Calif., 1948—; treas. Los Gatos Heritage Preservation Soc. Mem. Calif. Republican Central Com., 1962-64; officer, mem. bd. Los Gatos-Saratoga Rep. Assembly, 1950-68; founding mem. bd. Calif. Rep. League, 1960-73; bd. dirs. Bellringer Preservation Project. Mem. Antique Dealers Assn. Calif., Antique Dealers Orgn. No. Calif., U. Pacific Alumni Assn., Pi Kappa Delta, Pi Gamma Mu. Club: Wiscasset Yacht. Home: 262 E Main St Los Gatos CA 95032 Other: Middle St Wiscasset ME 04578 Office: 262 E Main St Los Gatos CA 95032

MONTGOMERY, JOYCE POLLACK, financial services executive, consultant; b. N.Y.C., Dec. 8, 1949; d. Sidney Joshua and Dorothy Belle (Muskat) Pollack; m. Robert M. Montgomery, July 20, 1979 (div. Dec. 1982). B.A. in Math. with honors cum laude, Barnard Coll., 1970; M.B.A. in Acctg., NYU, 1978. C.P.A., N.Y., N.J. Br. mgr. Allen-Babcock Computing, N.Y.C., 1970-71; sr. project mgr. Arlen Realty & Devel., N.Y.C., 1971-73; sr. mgmt. cons. Touche Ross & Co., N.Y.C., 1974-78; v.p. Chase Manhattan Bank, N.Y.C., 1978—. V.p. Friends of the Joffrey Ballet, 1984-87, pres., 1987—; bd. dirs. the Joffrey Ballet, 1987—. Named Young Career Woman of 1972, Bus. and Profl. Women's Fedn., N.J.; named to Outstanding Young Women Am., U.S. Jaycees, 1980. Mem. Am. Inst. C.P.A.s, Fin. Women's Assn. (corp. bd. com. 1982-84), Barnard Bus. and Profl. Women (pres. 1979-80, bd. dirs. 1979-82), Barnard Alumnae Assn. (bd. dirs. and chmn. budget and fin. com. N.Y.C. chpt. 1984-87). Republican. Home: 49 Sherwood Dr Morris Township NJ 07960 Office: Chase Manhattan Bank 80 Pine St 22d Floor New York NY 10081

MONTGOMERY, JUDY G(LASS), child care center executive; b. Jacksonville, Fla., July 19, 1945; d. Paul H. and Pearle V. (Greene) Glass; m. Jack T. Montgomery, Jan. 4, 1970; 1 child, Sean Christopher. BS in Math., La. State U., 1967. Group chief operator South Central Bell Telephone Co., Baton Rouge, 1967-69; systems analyst Sperry Univac, Baton Rouge, 1969-70; pres. M & M Playland Inc., Baton Rouge, 1973-87, L'Ecole, Inc., Baton Rouge, 1976-87, Child Care Info., Baton Rouge, 1984—; cons. in field. Author: Door To Learning, 1983; contbg. author and mem. adv. bd. for tng. manuals Day Care Directions, 1984. Chairperson La. Women's Conf. on Day Care, Baton Rouge, 1977; day care rep. Senator Thomas Hudson, Baton Rouge, 1977; mem. Gov.'s Council on Children, La., 1980; lobbyist children's services Baton Rouge, 1976—; bd. dirs. Baton Rouge Vocat. Tech. Sch., 1980—. Mem. Nat. Alliance Child Devel. Assns., La. Fedn. Child Devel. Ctrs. (lobbyist 1976-81, pres. 1978-81), Baton Rouge C. of C. (edn. com. 1980). Avocations: reading, sewing. Office: Child Care Info Inc PO Box 45212 Dept 223 Baton Rouge LA 70895

MONTGOMERY, MARTHA BARBER, academic administrator, philosophy educator; b. Palo Alto, Calif.; d. Willard Foster and Gladys Rebecca (Dorris) B.; children: DeWitt Hall, Mary W. Montgomery Sickles, Owen C., Ruth Montgomery Platoff. BA, Bryn Mawr Coll.; MA, U. Pa., 1971, PhD, 1972. Asst. prof. philosophy Drexel U., Phila., 1972-76; assoc. prof. Drexel U., 1976-81, prof., 1981—; head dept. humanities and communication Drexel U., Phila., 1976-85, dir. research devel., 1985-87, asst. v.p. for program evaluation, 1987—; evaluator commn. on edn. Middle States Assn. Colls. and Schs.; resource person Aspen Inst. for Humanistic Studies, Ctr. for Internat. Leadership; referee grant proposals NEH, NSF, Am. Assn. Colls.; educator, pub. mem. Nat. Architecture Accrediting Bd., 1984—, also head task force on liberal studies and student devel.; speaker and advisor Am. Psychoanalytic Assn., Am. Orthopsychiat. Assn., ASCE, ASME, Nat. Council Engring. Examiners, Del. Assn. Profl. Engrs., AAAS. Contbr. articles to profl. jours. Mem. exec. com. Pa. Humanities Council, 1983, chmn., 1986—; chair rev. panel in humanities Gov.'s Task Force on Cultural Affairs, 1987—; nominating com. for Corps., Haverford Coll.; pub. mem. Pa. Bd. Landscape Architects, 1983-86. Recipient awards NEH, 1976, Nat. Project on Philosophy and Engring. Ethics, 1978, 81, Dascher award Am. Soc. Engring. Edn., 1981. Mem. Soc. of Friends. Home: 2320 Perot St Philadelphia PA 19130

MONTGOMERY, ROSEANNE RULTENBERG, librarian; b. Phila., May 27, 1950; d. Max and Mildred Gert (Rabinowitz) R.; m. Michael Wylie Montgomery, Oct. 10, 1987; 1 child, Daniel. B.A. in Fine Arts cum laude, Hofstra U., 1971; M.S. in Info. Sci., Drexel U., 1975; studied painting with John Laub, 1980-83. Cataloger, Free Library of Phila., 1975-77, reference librarian for young adults, 1977-78, children's librarian, 1978-88, head br. library, 1984, storyteller, performer, 1978-88, chmn. printed book lists, 1980, 84, asst. mgr. Library Info. Systems, 1988—; cons. programs for gifted students Sch. Dist. of Phila., 1983-84. Exhibited paintings and photographs Bushrod Library, Phila., 1982, Frankford Women's Clubs, Phila., 1983, Cheltenham Art Ctr. (Pa.), 1983; illustrator: The Work, 1970, 71. Judge photography show Northeast Regional Library, Phila., 1979. Mem. ALA, Women's Caucus on the Arts. Office: Free Library of Phila 19th St and Benjamin Franklin Pkwy Philadelphia PA 19103

MONTGOMERY, VELMANETTE, state senator; b. Tex. M.Ed., NYU; student U. Ghana. Mem. N.Y.C. Dist. 13 Sch. Bd., 1977-80, pres., from 1977; former co-dir. advocacy group Child Care Inc.; mem. N.Y. Senate, 1984—, mem. child care, consumer protection, health, social services, commerce and mental hygiene coms. Fellow Inst. Ednl. Leadership, 1981, Revson Found., 1984. Democrat. also: 70 Lafayette Ave Brooklyn NY 11217

MONTGOMERY-CLIFFORD, MARY, managing editor; b. Chgo., Dec. 21, 1948; d. Neil Simeon and Irene Mary (Mitchell) M.; Winslow Williams Clifford, May 19, 1984. BA, U. Ill., Chgo., 1971. Clk. U.S. Postal Service, Chgo., 1971-74; tchr. Chgo. Pub. Sch. System, 1974-80; mng. editor EXTRA Publs., Chgo., 1980—, ptnr., 1987—. Pres. Hispano Alcoholic Services Bd., Chgo., 1980—; chmn. Operation Graduation/Network for Youth Services, Chgo., 1986—; fundraising com. Easter Seals, Chgo., 1988; bd. dirs. Safer Found.-Humboldt Park, Chgo., 1981—, Logan Square YMCA, Chgo., 1987—. Recipient Quill & Scroll award Clemente Community Acad., Chgo., 1987. Mem. Nat. Assn. Hispanic Publs. Office: EXTRA Publs 3918 W North Ave Chicago IL 60647

MONTONI, ANDREA MANGINO, publishing executive; b. Portland, Maine, Feb. 22, 1956; d. Samuel Albert and Pauline (Beem) Mangino; m. Richard Alphonse Montoni, June 25, 1983. BS, Emerson Coll., 1978. Retail promotion dir. for New Eng. A&M Records, Inc., Boston, 1978-79; regional promotion and publicity mgr. Columbia Pictures, N.Y.C., 1980-82; pub. relations and spl. events dir. May D&F, Denver, 1982-83; promotion dir. KPKE-FM Radio, Denver, 1983-84; pub. relations mgr. The Denver Post, 1984—. Pub. relations vol. Rocky Mountain Adoption Exchange, Denver, 1983-84; bd. dirs. Child Abuse Prevention Vols., Inc., Denver, 1986—. Recipient Outstanding Promotion Efforts award A&M Records, Inc., Los Angeles, 1978. Mem. Denver Advt. Fedn., Denver Internat. Film Soc. (bd. dirs. 1986—), Internat. Assn. Bus. Communicators (Silver Quill award of merit 1986, award of excellence 1986, Gold Quill award of excellence 1987), Pub. Relations Soc. Am., Internat. Alliance Theatrical Stage Employees, Publicists Guild Am. Roman Catholic. Office: The Denver Post Inc 650 15th St Denver CO 80202

MONTOYA, FRIEDA M., government official; b. Albuquerque, Oct. 14, 1923; d. Max Emiliano and Emilia (Gurule) Montoya; m. Frank Wolfel Montoya, June 20, 1945; children—Maxine Berea, Frank Wolfel. Student La. Junta Jr. Coll. (Colo.), 1943-45. Clk., interviewer U.S. Army and Air Force Recruiting Sta., Albuquerque, 1949-53; sales unit mgr. Stanley Home Products, Albuquerque, 1953-56; sec. ACF Industries, Inc., Albuquerque, 1956-57; sec. U.S. Dept. Energy, Albuquerque, 1967-80, mgr. fed. women's program, 1980; sec. to dir. VA Med. Ctr., Albuquerque, 1980-82; exec. dir. Fed. Exec. Bd., Albuquerque, 1982-84; with command sect. field command Def. Nuclear Agy., Kirtland AFB, N.Mex., 1984—; chmn. Fed. Women's Program, Albuquerque, 1974-75. Author: Upward Mobility for Women, 1974. Coordinator, U.S. Savs. Bonds, Albuquerque, 1983-84, Combined Fed. Campaign, Albuquerque, 1983-84, United Blood Service, Albuquerque, 1983-84, ARC, Albuquerque, 1983-84; commentator, lector, eucharistic minister St. Charle's Ch., Albuquerque. Mem. Am. Soc. Pub. Adminstrn. Roman Catholic. Club: Toastmistress Am. (sec./treas. 1960, v.p. 1961, pres. 1962, mem. council 1963, pres. cert. competetant toastmaster, 1986). Office: Field Command Def Nuclear Agy Kirtland AFB NM 87106

MONTY, GLORIA, television producer; b. Union City, N.J.; d. Joseph and Concetta M. (Mango) Montemuro; m. Robert Thomas O'Byrne, Jan. 8, 1952. B.A., NYU; M.A., Columbia U. Dir. New Sch. of Research, N.Y.C., 1952-53; dir. Old Towne Theatres, Smithtown, N.Y., 1952-56, Abbey Theatre Workshop, N.Y.C., 1952-56; cons. ABC. Dir. numerous TV shows including Secret Storm, 1956-72, Bright Promise, numerous episodes ABC Wide World Entertainment; exec. producer General Hospital, 1977-86, The Hamptons, 1983-85, made-for-TV movies including Confessions of a Married Man, 1982, The Imposter, 1984; exec. producer in devel. for primetime TV 20th Century Fox, 1987—. Recipient Emmy awards, 1982, 84, award Am. Soc. Lighting Dirs., 1979, Most Successful TV Show in History of TV award ABC, 1982, Spl. Editors award Soap Opera Digest, numerous others; named Woman Yr., Paulist Choristers So. Calif., 1986. Mem. Women in Film, Dirs. Guild Am. (exec. com.), Stuntman's Assn. (hon.). Clubs: Thunderbird Country (Rancho Mirage, Calif.); Bel Air Country (Calif.).

MONYEK, MARCIA E., public relations executive; b. Chgo., Oct. 30, 1959; d. Robert H. and Harice (Kinsler) M. BA, DePaul U., 1980; JD, Wake Forest U., 1983. Bar: Ill. Staff mktg. promotions Crain Communications, Chgo., 1980-81; acct. exec. Hill and Knowlton, Inc., Chgo., 1981-83, acct. supr., 1983-84, v.p., 1984-86, pub. relations staff, 1986—; asst. adj. prof. Ill. Inst. Tech. Sch. Bus., Chgo., 1984-86. Mem. Alumni in Admissions, Wake Forest U., Chg., 1985-87; bd. dirs., Gilbert and Sullivan, Chgo., 1985-86; mem. Jr. League of Chgo., 1984-86. Mem. Nat. Investor Relations Inst. (sec.

1985-86, v.p. programs 1986-87), Young Execs. Club (v.p. communications 1986-87). Clubs: Standard (limited members com. 1986-87), Internat. Home: 2800 Lake Shore Dr Chicago IL 60657 Office: Hill and Knowlton Inc 111 E Wacker Suite 1700 Chicago IL 60601

MOODY, BARBARA GAREY, real estate executive; b. Medford, Mass., June 23, 1931; d. DeMelle and Mildred (Holman) Garey; B.A., William Jewell Coll., Liberty, Mo., 1953; M.Ed., Northeastern U., Boston, 1964; M.B.M., Leslie Coll., Boston, 1983; m. Richard H. Moody, May 15, 1954; children—Meredith, Heather, Richard B., Janice. Dir. personnel P.W. Moody Co., Andover, Mass., 1954-70, guidance counselor Lawrence (Mass.) Gen. Hosp. Sch. Nursing, 1971-77, asst. dir. nursing, 1980-81; adminstrv. asst. in nursing New Eng. Deaconess Hosp., Boston, 1977-80, adminstrv. asst., 1981-87, mgr. budget and fin., 1987—; with Howe Real Estate Agy., Andover, 1987—; asso. dir. Lawrence Coop. Bank, 1976-80. Dir., sec. Gale Systems, 1972-74; dir. Coulter Fibers, Inc., 1968-77. Pres. Andover Vis. Nurse Assn., 1964-74. Mem. Andover Sch. Com., 1963-66. Bd. dirs. Andover council Girl Scouts, 1956-60, Andover YMCA, 1968-73; bd. dirs. Greater Lawrence Family Service, 1972-77, v.p., 1971-78. Mem. Nat. Assn. Women Deans, Adminstrs. and Counselors, LWV, Mass. Assn. Hosp. Fin. Mgrs., Nat. League Nursing, Am. Personnel and Guidance Assn., Pi Kappa Delta. Mem. United Ch. Christ (clk., past mem. bd. Christian edn.). Club: Andover Tennis, Andover Garden. Home: 95 Sunset Rock Andover MA 01810 Office: Howe Real Estate Agy Andover MA 01810

MOODY, EVELYN WILIE, consulting geologist; b. Waco, Tex.; d. William Braden and Enid Eva (Holt) Wilie; student Baylor U., 1934-35; B.A. with honors in geology and edn. U. Tex., 1938, M.A. with honors in geology, 1940; children—John D., Melissa L., Jennifer A. Geologist, Ark. Fuel Oil Co., Shreveport, La., New Orleans and Houston, 1942-45; teaching asst. Colo. Sch. Mines, Golden, 1946-47; exploration cons. geologist Gen. Crude Oil Co., Houston, 1975-77; ind. cons. geologist, Houston, 1977—; exploration cons. geologist Shell Oil Co., Houston, 1979-81; faculty dept. continuing edn. Rice U., Houston, 1978. Cert. profl. geologist. Treas., Sipes Found., 1984, pres., 1985, treas., 1984, editor Sipes Bulletin, 1983-1985 . Recipient Sipes Found. Nat. award for Outstanding Service, 1988, Sipes Houston Chpt. Chmn. award for Outstanding Service to Sipes, 1986. Mem. Am. Assn. Petroleum Geologists, Soc. Ind. Profl. Earth Scientists (sec. 1978-79, vice chmn. 1979-80, chpt. chmn. 1980-81, nat. dir. 1982-85), Geol. Soc. Am., Watercolor Soc. Houston, Art Students League N.Y.C., Art Assn., Am. Inst. Profl. Geologists, Houston Geol. Soc., Pi Beta Phi (nat. officer 1958-60, 66-68), Pi Lambda Theta. Republican. Presbyterian. Contbr. articles to profl. jours.; editor: The Manual for Independence, 1983, The Business of Being a Petroleum Independent (A Road Map for the Self Employed), 1987. author: How (To Try) To Find An Oil Field, 1981. Office: 956 The Main Bldg 1212 Main St Houston TX 77002

MOODY, MARILYN DALLAS, librarian; b. Little Rock, Aug. 28; d. Corbin Luther and Marian (Ricks) Dallas; m. W. I Moody Jr., June 1, 1970 (div. 1987). Student, Hendrix Coll, Conway, Ark., 1959, U. Ark., 1960, Drexel U., 1964. Librarian Free Library of Phila., 1964-70, cons. librarian, 1971-76, coordinator dist. library ctr. services, 1976-82, chief extension services div., 1982—. Recipient Cert. of Merit, 1981. Mem. ALA (councilor 1983-86), Pa. Library Assn. Office: Free Library of Phila Logan Sq Philadelphia PA 19103

MOODY, VIRGINIA LAREECE (GOODIN), commercial realtor, small business owner; b. Oakland, Calif., Dec. 22, 1942; d. True Pete and Essie Mae (Lemons) Goodin; m. Robert Dean Walker, Sept. 15, 1962 (div. Sept. 1970); children: Kimberly, Kelly; m. William Francis Moody, Aug. 23, 1980 (div. 1988); stepchildren: Eric, Brandon. Student Orange County Jr. Coll., 1963-65, Midwestern U., 1961-62, Tarrant County Jr. Coll., 1975-83. Clk., agt., dispatcher Chgo. Rock Island R.R., Fort Worth, 1967-80; v.p., mgr. farms ops. Moody Farms, Inc., North Richland Hills, Tex., 1980—; comml. realtor Roseberry Comml. Real Estate Co., North Richland Hills, 1985—; owner Moody's Tex. Gifts. Mem. council City of North Richland Hills, 1984—; mem. women in Govt., Nat. League of Cities, 1984; bd. dirs. Indsl. Devel. Council, NE Tarrant County, 1984—, North East Fin Arts League, 1986—. Mem. Nat. Assn. Female Execs., Fort Worth Bd. Realtors, Comml. Real Estate Women, Haltom-Richland C. of C. Democrat. Episcopalian. Avocations: hist. areas, fine arts, video games. Home: 7722 Jennifer Ln North Richland Hills TX 76180 Office: Moody's Tex Gifts 902 North Hills Mall North Richland Hills TX 76180

MOOK, BARBARA HEER HELD, civic worker; b. Akron, June 9, 1919; d. Harold Edward and Helen Wilhelm (Heer) Held; student Coll. Wooster, 1937-39; diploma Actual Business Coll., 1941; m. Conrad Payne Mook, Sept. 6, 1941; children—Patricia Ann Mook Harris, Mary Ann Mook Barnum. Tchr., lectr. DAR Museum, Washington, 1973-79; sr. nat. asst. organizing sec. Children of the Am. Revolution, Washington, 1974-76, hon. sr. nat. v.p., 1977-83. Troop leader Girl Scouts U.S.A., Arlington, Va., 1951-53, neighborhood chmn., 1953-55, mem. program com. Arlington County council, 1955-56; rec. sec. Thomas Nelson chpt. DAR, Arlington, 1963-65, 73-75, librarian, 1967-69, regent, 1965-67. Recipient medal of appreciation SAR, 1981, Martha Washington medal, 1984. Mem. Va. Hist. Soc., Ohio Geneal. Soc., First Families Ohio, Soc. Descs. of Washington's Army at Valley Forge (charter v.p. 1976-78), Daus. of Union Vets. of Civil War 1861-65 (sr. v.p. 1978-80, pres. 1981-82), Children of Am. Revolution (sr. nat. officers club), Potomac Regents Club DAR (treas. 1974-75, librarian historian 1983-84), Aux. Sons Union Vets. of Civil War (patriotic instr. 1981-84, pres. 1984-85). Home: 5222 26th Rd N Arlington VA 22207

MOON, KAY KAREN, nurse; b. Grove City, Pa., July 1, 1945; d. Kenneth Harvey and Marian Elizabeth (Burns) M. Diploma in Nursing, Trumbull Meml. Hosp. Sch. Nursing, 1967. Staff nurse Trumbull Meml. Hosp., Warren, Ohio, 1967-68, Bashline Hosp., Grove City, Pa., 1968-69, Warren Gen. Hosp., Warren, Ohio, 1969-70, Packard Electric div. Gen. Motors, Warren, 1970—. Republican. Home: 15 Arms Blvd Apt 5 Niles OH 44446 Office: Packard Electric Box 431 Warren OH 44486

MOON, LINDA ELLEN, medical center researcher; b. Corpus Christi, June 10, 1946; d. Troy William and Beatrice Claire (Cryer) Moon; m. Jerry Preston Reid, Oct. 29, 1965 (div. 1971); 1 son, James Troy; m. Jack James Flagg, Feb. 6, 1986. BA, U. Tex., 1969. Research asst. Tex. A&M U. Research and Extension, Overton, 1969; lab. technician East Tex. Chest Hosp., Tyler, 1970-73; med. tech. James M. Gray & Assocs., Houston, 1974, Motley Clin. Labs., Inc., Houston, 1974-75; med. technician III, U. Tex. Cancer Ctr., M.D. Anderson Hosp., Houston, 1976-84; sr. research asst. dept. surgery/organ transplant U. Tex. Health Sci. Ctr., 1984-87; gen. supr. flow cytometry labs. Cytology Tech., Inc., Houston, 1987-88; tech. dir. Diagnostic Genetics, Inc., Houston, 1988—. Republican. Methodist. Home: 3215 Elmridge Houston TX 77025 Office: Diagnostic Genetics Inc 2600 S Loop W Suite 600 Houston TX 77054

MOON, MARJORIE RUTH, former state treasurer; b. Pocatello, Idaho, June 16, 1926; d. Clark Blakeley and Ruth Eleanor (Gerhart) M. Student, Pacific U., 1944-46; A.B. in Journalism cum laude, U. Wash., 1948. Reporter, Pocatello Tribune, 1944; Reporter Caldwell (Idaho) News-Tribune, 1948-50; Salt Lake City bur. chief Deseret News, Boise, Idaho, 1950-52; owner, operator Idaho Pioneer Statewide (weekly newspaper), Boise, 1952-55; founder, pub. Garden City (Idaho) Gazette, 1954-68; partner Sawtooth Lodge, Grandjean, Idaho, 1958-60, Modern Press, Boise, 1958-61; treas. State of Idaho, Boise, 1963-86; owner, pub. Kuna-Melba News, 1987—. Chmn. Idaho Commn. on Women's Programs, 1971-74; del. Dem. Nat. Nominating Conv., 1972, 76, 80, 84; Dem. candidate Lt. Gov., Idaho, 1986; mem. Idaho Comn. for the Blind, 1987—. Mem. Nat. Assn. State Treas. (sec.-treas. 1976-78, regional v.p. 1978-79, 84-85), Nat. Fedn. Press Women, Idaho Press Women (past pres.). Congregationalist. Clubs: Soroptimists (Boise) (pres. club 1971-73), Women's Ltd. (Boise) (pres. 1984, dir. 1983-84). dir.). Office: 2227 Heights Dr Boise ID 83702

MOONAN, GLORIA JEAN, retail products executive; b. Bowling Green, Ky., Nov. 3, 1950; d. Albert M. and Lenora (Hayes)Paschal; m. Michael C. Moonan (div.); 1 child, Shelly. Mgr. Alexander Wallcovering, Falls Church, Va., 1976-81; decorator Duron Paints and Wallcovering, Beltsville, Md., 1982-84, sales rep., 1984-85, archtl. rep., 1985-86, dir., 1986—. Mem. Constrn. Specification Inst., Interior Design Soc., Nat. Assn. Female Execs., Washington Sales and Mktg. Council Republican. Episcopalian. Home: 7488 Tangier Way Manassas VA 22110 Office: Duron Paints and Wallcoverings 10406 Tucker St Beltsville MD 20705

MOONEY, LORI, county official; b. Atlantic City, Aug. 22, 1929; d. Joseph Aloysius and Alice Marie Inemer; m. Charles H. Calvi (div.); children: Joseph P., Stephen C., Christina L.; m. Thomas Christopher Mooney; children: Thomas C., Timothy C. Service rep. Bell Telephone Co., Atlantic City, 1950-58; sr. evaluator U.S. Census Bur., N.J., 1960-63; coordinator Nat. Small Bus. Com. for Johnson and Humphrey, Washington, 1964; owner, mgr. Lori Mooney & Co., Realtors, Atlantic County, N.J., 1965-77; commr. Atlantic County Bd. Elections, from 1970, also chmn. 5 yrs.; county clk. County of Atlantic, Mays Landing, 1978—; mem. Active Corps Execs., Nat. SBA; chmn. county clk. liaison com. N.J. Supreme Ct., 1984-86. Del. Democratic Nat. Conv., 1972, 76, 84, 88; mem. study team N.J. Div. Youth and Family Services, 1982; mem. U.S. Senator Bill Bradley's Citizen Adv. Com. Recipient Woman of Achievement award N.J. Fedn. Bus. and Profl. Women, 1985. Mem. Internat. Platform Assn., Internat. Assn. Clks., Recorders, Election Ofcls. and Treas., Atlantic County Realtors Assn., Bus. and Profl. Women Atlantic County (scholarship chmn. 1982-85), County Officers Assn. N.J. (bd. dirs. 1978—), N.J. Assn. County Clks. (chmn. 1984-86), N.J. Assn. Realtors, Nat. Assn. Realtors, N.J. League Municipalities, Assn. Records Mgrs. and Administrs., Atlantic City Women's C. of C., Nat. Assn. Female Execs. Home: 62 E Wright St Pleasantville NJ 08232 Office: Atlantic County Clerks Office Main St Mays Landing NJ 08330

MOONEY, PATRICIA MAY, physicist; b. Bryn Mawr, Pa., July 12, 1945; d. William Henry and May (Howson) M. AB, Wilson Coll., 1967; MA, Bryn Mawr Coll., 1969, PhD, 1972. Asst. prof. physics Hiram (Ohio) Coll., 1972-74; research assoc. physics dept. SUNY, Albany, 1977-78; asst. prof. physics Vassar Coll., Poughkeepsie, N.Y., 1974-80; mem. research staff IBM T.J. Watson Research Ctr., Yorktown Heights, N.Y., 1980—; vis. scientist U. Paris VII, 1979-80, Fraunhofer IAF, Freiberg, Fed. Republic of Germany, 1987-88. Contbr. articles to profl. jours. Mem. Am. Phys. Soc., Materials Research Soc. Office: IBM Thomas J Watson Research PO Box 218 Yorktown Heights NY 10598

MOONIE, LIANA MARIA, artist; b. Trieste, Italy, Mar. 22, 1922; came to U.S., 1947, naturalized, 1950; d. Angelo and Maria (Canciani) Gabrielli. B.A., U. Trieste, 1940; student Robert Brachman, Art Students League, Edgar Whitney. One-woman shows and numerous juried and invitationals in galleries and mus. throughout U.S. and Europe; works exhibited in pvt. and corp. collections; contbg. editor Beaux Arts mag., 1974-77; lectr. and juror in field. Chmn. Beaux Arts Project, Westchester, N.Y. Recipient numerous art awards. Mem. Am. Soc. Contemporary Artists (N.Y.C. watercolor award 1983, dir.), Nat. Assn. Women Artists (pres., N.Y.C. oil award 1984, watercolor award 1983, 85, dir.), Allied Artists Am. (oil award 1985), Scarsdale Art Assn. N.Y., Silvermine Artists Guild, Hudson River Contemporary Artists (past pres.), Mamaroneck Artists Guild (past pres.). Club: Salmagundi (N.Y.C.). Address: 10 Baldwin Farms S Greenwich CT 06831

MOOR, DINA MAVIS, advertising agency executive; b. Phoenix, Aug. 23, 1943; d. Isaac Lowery and Anna Mavis (Stinson) M.; student State U. Iowa, 1961-62; B.A., So. Meth. U., 1967; M.B.A., U. Dallas, 1976; 1 child, Aaron Michael. Freelance model, 1965-71; sec. to academic dean U. Dallas, 1971-72, asst. to dean, 1972-74, dir. affiliated programs, 1974-76; dir. Mgmt. Labs. Am., Exec. Edn. Inst., Center for Publishing, 1974-76; owner Moor and Assocs., Inc., Dallas, 1976—; bd. dirs. Peninsula MarCom Exchange; owner Standby Club, Highlands Trading Co.; dir. Lynn Weiss & Assos.; bd. dirs. Screen Actors Guild and AFTRA, 1967-70. Recipient Wall St. Jour. award, 1976. Mem. Savs. Instns. Mktg. Soc. Am., Sales and Mktg. Execs. Dallas, Women in Communications, Inc., Peninsula Mktg. Assn., North Dallas C. of C., Grad. Sch. Mgmt. Alumni Assn. (past pres.), The Mktg. Corp., Inc. (pres.), Peninsula Mktg. Communications Exchange (bd. dirs.), IABC, PRSA, Sigma Iota Epsilon. Episcopalian. Clubs: Slipper, 500 Inc. (past dir.). Office: 1249 Hoover Menlo Park CA 94025

MOORE, ALDERINE BERNICE JENNINGS (MRS. JAMES F. MOORE), club woman; b. Sacramento, Apr. 17, 1915; d. James Joseph and Elise (Thomas) Jennings; A.B., U. Wash., 1941; m. James Francis Moore, Aug. 14, 1945. Sec. to div. Plant supr. Pacific Tel. & Tel. Co., Sacramento, 1937-39; exec. sec. Sacramento Community Chest Fund Raising Dr., 1941; sec. USAAF, Mather Field, Sacramento, 1942; statistician Calif. Western States Life Ins. Co., 1943; treas. Women's Aux. Stranger's Hosp., Rio de Janeiro, Brazil, 1964-65. Vice pres. Douglaston (N.Y.) Women's Club, 1955; mem. Douglaston Garden Club, 1951-55; pres. Nina Opland chpt. Women's Cancer Assn. U. Miami, 1960-61; corr. sec. Coral Gables (Fla.) Garden Club, 1960-62; pres. Miami Alumnae Club of Pi Beta Phi, 1961-62; mem. Putnam Hill chpt. D.A.R., Greenwich Conn., 1967-75, Palm Beach chpt., 1978—; mem. Woman's Club, Greenwich, Conn., 1967-75; mem. Women's Panhellenic Assn., Miami, 1961-62; internat. treas. Ikebana Internat., Tokyo, Japan, 1966-67, parliamentarian Tokyo chpt., 1966-67, N.Y. chpt., 1968-69; mem. Coll. Women Assn. Japan, 1965-66; mem. Tchrs. Assn. Sogetsu Sch. Japanese Flower Arranging, 1966—. Served to lt. USNR, 1943-45. Mem. Internat. Platform Assn., AAUW, Pi Beta Phi (local v.p. alumnae club 1969-71). Baptist. Club: Steamboat Investment (pres. 1972-73). Home: 316 Fairway Ct Atlantis FL 33462

MOORE, AMANDA LEE, lawyer; b. Phila., June 27, 1949; d. Maurice Lee and Charlotte (Holg) M. BA cum laude, Northwestern U., 1971; JD cum laude, George Washington U., 1974; PhD, Cambridge (Eng.) U., 1983; cert., Nat. Inst. for Trial Advocacy, 1987. Law clk. Office Telecommunications Policy, Exec. Office of the Pres., Washington, 1973-74; atty., policy cons. Moore Assocs., Bronxville, N.Y., 1974—; rapporteur U.S. Space WARC Adv. Com., Washington, 1981—; vice chmn. NGOS Unispace, Vienna, 1980-82; UN rep. L5 Soc., Nat. Space Soc., Rensselaerville, N.Y. Inst., 1980—; mem. U.S. del. World Adminstrv. Radio Conf., 1985. Author: Astrobusiness-A Guide to the Law and Commerce of Outer Space, 1984, ORB'85-Is There Enough Space in Space?, 1985; contbr. articles to profl. jours. Chmn. ch. com. Bronxville League for Service, 1984-86, chmn. programs com., 1986-88; mem. Jr. League Bronxville; treas., bd. dirs. Eastchester Meals on Wheels, 1984-88. Grantee George Bidder Fund, Cambridge, 1974-75, Hattie M. Strong Found., 1975, Psi Psi Psi Internat., 1976. Mem. ABA (vice chmn. aerospace law com. 1977-79), Assn. Bar City of N.Y., Am. Soc. Internat. Law (moot ct. Judge 1980), U.S. Assn. Internat. Inst. Space Law (treas. 1984-86), LWV, Phi Delta Phi, Delta Delta Delta. Home and Office: 7 Brookside Circle Bronxville NY 10708

MOORE, BETH COOK, public relations executive; b. Atlanta, Oct. 18, 1954; d. Albert Womack and Betty Anne (Clontz) Cook; divorced; 1 child, Albert Hunter; m. Harry Galt Moore, Jr., Aug. 23, 1986. BA, Brenau Coll., 1975. Asst. dir pub. relations ARC, Atlanta, 1976-77, Erlanger Med. Ctr., Chattanooga, 1977-80; dir. pub. relations Daniels & Assocs., Chattanooga, 1980-81; dir. communications United Way, Chattanooga, 1981-82; dir. mktg. Humana Hosp., Chattanooga, 1982-87; employment cons. Provident Life and Accident Ins. Co., Chattanooga, Tenn., 1987—. Active Leadership Chattanooga, 1985-86; bd. dirs. Jr. League, 1978-85. Named Outstanding Young Citizen Chattanooga Jaycees, 1987, One of Outstanding Young Women of Am. Mem. Internat. Assn. Bus. Communicators (pres. Chattanooga chpt. 1980-82). Home: 1009 Scenic Hwy Lookout Mountain TN 37350 Office: Provident Life and Accident Co One Fountain Sq Chattanooga TN 37402

MOORE, BETTIE JO, designer, artist, consultant; b. Shawnee, Okla., July 4, 1928; d. Cedric and Verna H. (Avery) M. Student Ringling Art Sch., Sarasota, Fla., 1945; B.F.A., U. Colo., 1969; M. Vocat. Edn., Colo. State U., 1973. Cert. vocat. edn., Colo. Dir./designer Moore Display & Design Studio, Aurora, Colo., 1955—; sch. dir. Visual Merchandising Inst., Aurora, 1979-81; cons. sales dir. Goodwill Industries Denver, 1981-83; exhibited in one-woman shows: Okla. Bapt. U., Shawnee, 1945; group shows include: U. Colo., 1969, Salito (Mex.) Gallery, 1972; represented in permanent collections: Okla. Bapt. U., Ringling Mus., Sarasota, Fla.; cons. visual merchandising; lectr., seminar instr. Denver Merchandising Mart, 1980-83; instr. visual merchandising Colo. State U., Ft. Collins, 1973. Author: Basic Display And Advertising, 1970. Nat. rep. to Goodwill Conf. for Goodwill Aux. Denver, 1983. Recipient First place award for store design Visual Merchandising and Store Design Internat. Competition, 1951, 75, also 3 hon. mention awards, 1960-82; recipient numerous first, second and third place awards from various art shows, 1969-80. Mem. Bus. Women's Club Am. (chairperson speakers 1979), Aurora Art Guild, Rocky Mountain Graphologists, Kappa Pi. Office: Goodwill Industries 6850 N Fed Blvd Denver CO 80205

MOORE, BETTY ANN, nursing consultant; b. Florence, S.C., Oct. 7, 1955; d. Robin Eugene Moore and Juanita (Powell) Lee; m. Lawton W. Evans, Nov. 18, 1973 (div. 1976). AS in Nursing, Florence-Darlington Tech. Coll., 1976. Cert. nurse, S.C. Staff nurse Florence Gen. Hosp., 1976-77; charge nurse emergency McLeod Meml. Hosp., Florence, 1977-78; supr. Grand Strand Gen. Hosp., Myrtle Beach, S.C., 1978-79; charge nurse emergency Charleston (S.C.) County Hosp., 1979-80; nurse recruiter, staff nurse Cedars of Miami, Fla., 1980-83; staff nurse Med Cen., Florence, 1983-85; health profl. recruiter Snelling & Snelling Columbia, S.C., 1985-86; nurse cons. Cynmco, Columbia, 1986-87; v.p. St. Charles Group, Columbia, 1987—. Mem. Am. Nurses Assn., S.C. Nurses Assn. (CERC com. 1986—), Self-Insurer's Assn., S.C. Assn. Rehab. Profls., Literacy Council, LWV (bd. dirs. S.C. 1987), Soil Conservation Soc. Democrat. Home: Rt 1 Box 233 Jenkinsville SC 29065 Office: St Charles Group PO Box 11994 Columbia SC 29211

MOORE, BEVERLY BARRETT, library director; b. Evanston, Ill., Mar. 17, 1934; d. James Henry and Louise (Miller) Barrett; m. James O. Moore, Oct. 6, 1957 (div. Sept. 1967); children: Louis Barrett, Ann Louise Cushman. AA, Hutchinson Jr. Coll., 1954; BA, U. No. Colo., 1957; MLS, Denver U., 1970. Br. librarian Pueblo (Colo.) Library Dist., 1966-70; documents librarian U. So. Colo., Pueblo, 1970-74, head catalog librarian, 1974-76, library dir., 1970—; co-chair Colo. Acad. Library com., 1982—; treas. Arkansas Valley Regional Library Services System, 1984—. Coauthor: Colorado Academic Master Plan, 1985. Mem. Colo. Library Assn. (pres. 1985), ALA, LWV, AAUW, Beta Phi Mu. Democrat. Congregationalist. Home: 1719 Jerry Murphy Rd Pueblo CO 81001 Office: Univ So Colo Pueblo CO 81001-4901

MOORE, CECELIA MORRIS, health care administrator; b. Memphis, Tenn., Aug. 3, 1950; d. Bessie Louise (Morris) Cathey; divorced; 1 child, Tracie L. Moore. BA, Rhodes Coll., 1972; M of Pub. Adminstrn., Memphis State U., 1978. Operator computer 1st Tenn. Bank, Memphis, 1969-72; rep. service Social Security Adminstrn. Dept. HHS, Memphis, 1972-73; demographer Regional Med. Program, Memphis, 1973-76; dir. data collection-analysis Mid-South Med. Ctr. Council, Memphis, 1976-80; dir. adminstrn. Midtown Mental Health Ctr., Memphis, 1980-84; dir. patient fin. services Regional Med. Ctr. Memphis, 1984—; bd. dirs. Memphis Health Ctr., treas. 1984—. Active United Way, 1986; bd. dirs. YWCA, Habitat Humanity, Memphis, 1986. Mem. West Tenn. Chpt. Admitting Mgmt. Assn. (sec.), Am. Guild Patient Account Mgmt., Hosp. Fin. Mgmt. Assn., Coalition 100 Black Women (bd. dirs. 1984—). Democrat. Baptist. Home: 2169 Vollintine Memphis TN 38108

MOORE, CLEAH TONYA, geologist, small business owner; b. Norman, Okla., Apr. 27, 1959; d. James Bartel and Jimmie Pauline (Goodman) Urban; m. Halton Joe Moore, Jan. 23, 1982. BS in Geology, U. Okla., 1981. Registered profl. sanatarian. Geologist Camplin Petroleum, Oklahoma City, 1981-84; geologist-cons. Van Helsdingen Exploration, Oklahoma City, 1985-86; geologist Moore Petroleum Investment Corp., Oklahoma City, 1984-87; bus. co-owner Moore Petroleum Investment Corp., Norman, Okal., 1987—. Author: Hungry Hound Cookbook, 1987. Mem. Am. Assn. Petroleum Geologists, Delta Gamma (rec. sec. 1979-80). Republican. Episcopalian. Club: Oklahoma City Obedience Tng. (trophy chmn. 1987, 88, 98, pres. 1988-89). Home: 710 Heatherhill Dr Norman OK 73072

MOORE, CYNTHIA RICH, marketing professional; b. Painesville, Ohio, Apr. 26, 1964; d. Howard Lynn and Evie Shepard (Gibbs) Rich; m. Eric K. Moore, Nov. 28, 1987. BSBA, U. So. Calif., 1985. Area sales mgr. Baxter Health Care, Chgo., 1985—. Republican. Episcopalian. Home: 11305 Foster Overland Park KS 66210

MOORE, DIANE ELAINE, marketing professional, researcher; b. Albany, N.Y., Feb. 5, 1957; d. Willis Eugene and Sarah (Davidson) M.s. BS in Chemistry and Math., Western Mich. U., 1978; MS in Chem. Engrin., Wayne State U., 1980. Staff scientist Energy Conversion Devices, Troy, Mich., 1980-82; dir. plating material devel. Ovonic ThermoElectric, Troy, 1982-84, sales engr., 1984-86; internat. sales mgr. Glasstech Solar, Inc., Denver, 1986-87; sales engr. UMI, Inc., 1987—. Inventor thermoelectric material, solders for thermoelectric material. Mem. Am. Inst. Chem. Engrs. (chmn. membership com. 1985-86), Am. Chem. Soc., Nat. Assn. Female Execs., Tau Beta Pi. Home: 42419 Old Bridge Canton MI 48188 Office: Solaronics Inc 704 Woodward Ave Rochester MI 48063

MOORE, EDWINA VESTA, educator, violinist; b. Detroit, Feb. 2; d. Edwin Allen and Vesta Rae (Ellison) Pierse; m. H. Chester Moore, June 23, 1973 (div. 1982). BMus, U. So. Calif., 1950, postgrad., 1960. Cert. elem. and secondary tchr., Calif. Tchr. instrumental music Long Beach (Calif.) Unified Schs., 1950—; concertmaster Long Beach Symphony, 1965-73, 1st violinist, 1973—; violinist Pacific Symphony, Orange, Calif., 1982-84, Southcoast Symphony, Costa Mesa, Calif., 1986—, Irvine (Calif.) Symphony, 1986—; 1st violinist Heritage String Quartet, Long Beach, 1987—. U. So. Calif. scholar, 1948-50. Mem. Music Educators Nat. Conf., Musicians Union (life mem. Long Beach local). Republican. Home: 3933 Virginia Rd Apt 204 Long Beach CA 90807

MOORE, (MARGARET) ELEANOR MARCHMAN, ret. librarian; b. Pinckard, Ala., Nov. 6, 1913; d. Robert Lee and Eleanor Rowena (Paris) Marchman; A.B., Fla. State Coll. for Women, 1936; B.S. in L.S., George Peabody Coll. for Tchrs., 1947, M.A. in Library Sci., 1962; m. James William Moore, Feb. 22, 1934 (div. 1940); 1 son, John Robert. Tchr. Alva (Fla.) High Sch., 1938-40, Wacissa (Fla.) Jr. High Sch., 1940-43; librarian Bartow (Fla.) Sr. High Sch., 1943-45, 48-67, Bartow Pub. Library, 1945-48; cataloger Roux Library, Fla. So. Coll., Lakeland, 1967-70, reference librarian, 1970-75; co-sponsor Polk County Student Library Assn., 1957-59; intern tchr. Fla. State U.; former mem. evaluating team So. Assn. Secondary Schs. and Colls. Recipient Polk County Career Increment award, 1961. Mem. NEA, Beta Phi Mu, Delta Kappa Gamma. Democrat. Baptist. Address: 251 Marilyn Dr Lafayette LA 70503

MOORE, ELIZABETH DAVIS, home fashion products specialist; b. Charleston, S.C., June 15, 1961; d. Victor M. and Ina Elizabeth (Anderson) Davis; m. William Scott Moore, June 21, 1986. BS in Mktg. summa cum laude, U. Ala., 1983. Dept. mgr. Parisian, Inc., Birmingham, Ala., 1983-84, Tuscaloosa, Ala., 1984-85; interior products specialist Phifer Wire Products, Inc., Tuscaloosa, 1985—. Mem. Color Assn. of U.S. Methodist. Home: PO Box 152 Berry AL 35546

MOORE, ELIZABETH GRAY, cultural organization administrator; b. Virginia Beach, Va., May 28, 1957; d. Wynn Victor and Melissa Gorham (Hillard) Whidden; m. Winston Fredrick Moore, Feb. 27, 1982. BBA, Longwood Coll., Farmville, Va., 1979. Processor ticket sales Wolf Trap Found., Vienna, Va., 1976-79, clk. acctg., 1979-80, asst. mgr. fin., 1980-82, asst. to mng. dir., 1982-84, dir. fin., 1984-85, dir. adminstrn., 1985—. Republican. Episcopalian. Home: 3834 Inverness Rd Fairfax VA 22033 Office: Wolf Trap Found 1624 Trap Rd Vienna VA 22180

MOORE, FAY LINDA, computer programmer; b. Houston, Apr. 7, 1942; d. Charlie Louis and Esther Mable (Banks) Moore; m. Noel Patrick Walker, Jan. 5, 1963 (div. 1967); 1 child, Trina Nicole Moore. Student, Prairie View Agrl. and Mech. Coll., 1960-61, Tex. So. U., 1961. Instr. Internat. Bus. Coll., Houston, 1965; keypunch operator IBM Corp., Houston, 1965-67, sr. keypunch operator, 1967-70, programmer technician, 1970-72, asst. programmer, 1972-73, assoc. programmer, 1973-84; sr. assoc. programmer, 1984-87, staff programmer, 1987—. Mem. Internat. Platform Assn., Booker T. Washington Alumni Assn., Ms. Found. for Women, Inc., Data Processing Mgmt. Assn., Nat. Assn. Female Execs. Inc. Democrat. Roman Catholic. Club: First Osborne Group. Avocations: personal computing, board games. Office: IBM Corp 3700 Bay Area Blvd MC 6402A Houston TX 77058-1199

MOORE, GLORIA SPEARS, health science facility administrator; b. New Orleans, Nov. 4, 1948; d. William Alexander and Alma (Gills) Spears; m. Gilbert Moore, June 23, 1968; children: Vanessa Danielle, Gilbert Jr. BA, Lesley Coll., 1974, MEd in Psychology, 1977, postgrad., 1977-79. Lic. clin. social worker; cert. counselor. Aux. instr. Lesley Coll., Cambridge, Mass., 1980-81; sr. area supr. protective and preventive services Dept. Social Services, Boston, 1981-82; counselor, instr. writing DeKalb Schs. Writing Ctr., Decatur, Ga., 1984-85; dir. personnel and employee assistance West End Med. Ctrs., Atlanta, 1985—; psychotherapist, supr. Putnam Children and Family Clinic, Boston and Roxbury, Mass., 1978-80; regional coordinator child abuse hotline and adolescent programs Dept. Social Services, Middleton, Mass., 1981-82; counselor, tchr. Univ. NOW Princeton (N.J.) Lab., 1971-74; counselor outreach program U.S. Dept. Labor, Oakland, Calif.; cons. Cameroon & Assocs., Atlanta, 1987—; lectr. in field. Mem. Morehouse Women's Aux., Atlanta, 1984—, Ga. Women's Polit. Caucus, Atlanta, 1985—. Mellen Found. grantee, 1973. Mem. Assn. Black Psychologists, Ga. Assn. Black Psychologists, Nat. Assn. for Female Execs., Employee Assts. Assn., Minority Assn. for Ind. Schs. (exec. bd. mem., co-chairperson upper sch.), Atlanta Profl. Womens Network. Democrat. Home: 4585 Runnemede Rd NW Atlanta GA 30327 Office: West End Med Ctrs 319 Westlake Ave NW Atlanta GA 30318

MOORE, HAZEL BROWNING, health planning analyst; b. Greenville, N.C., May 29, 1950; d. Daniel Robert and Helen Nelson (Shelton) Gay; 1 child from previous marriage, Lauran Shelton; m. Frank Douglas Moore, Oct. 16, 1987. BS in Nursing, East Carolina U., 1972, MS in Rehab. Counseling, 1976, MS in Nursing, 1979. Staff nurse Pitt Meml. Hosp., Greenville, N.C., 1972-73; office nurse Dr. David Pearsall, Greenville, N.C., 1973; nursing instr. East Carolina U., Greenville, 1973-77, asst. prof. nursing, 1977-80; asst. prof. nursing Duke U., Durham, N.C., 1980-82; assoc. exec. dir. N.C. Nurses Assn., Raleigh, N.C., 1982-87; project analyst div. Facility Services, Dept. Human Resources, Raleigh, 1987—. Mem. Am. Nurses Assn., Nurses Assn. of Am. Coll. Obstetricians and Gynecologists, N.C. Nurses Assn., N.C. Nurses Assn. of Am. Coll. Obstetricians and Gynecologists (mem. adv. council), Rho Lambda, Sigma Theta Tau. Democrat. Presbyterian. Home: 4305 Sunbelt Dr Raleigh NC 27612 Office: Cert of Need Sect 701 Barbour Dr Raleigh NC 27603

MOORE, HELEN ELIZABETH, free-lance reporter; b. Rush County, Ind., Dec. 19, 1920; d. John Brackenridge and Mary Amelia (Custer) Johnson; m. John William Sheridan, July 6, 1942 (dec. Jan. 1944); m. Harry Evan Moore, May 15, 1954; 1 child, William Randolph. BS, Ind. U., 1972, MS, 1973. Ofcl. ct. reporter 37th Jud. Cir., Brookville, Ind., 1950-60; freelance reporter Rushvile, Ind., 1960—; conv. reporter various assns. Served with USMC, 1943. Recipient Sagamore of the Wabash award Gov. Ind., 1984. Mem. Women Marines Assn. (charter, nat. pres. 1966-68), Am. Legion Aux. (various offices 1950—, pres. Ind. dept. 1966-67, conv. reporter), Bus. and Profl. Women (dist. dir., various offices 1967—), Nat. Shorthand Reporters Assn., (registered profl. reporter), Ind. Shorthand Reporters Assn. (state treas., edit. Hoosier Reporter, chmn. Legal directory), Ind. German Heritage Soc. (state bd. dirs. 1984-86, recording sec.). Democrat. Methodist. Home and Office: PO Box 206 Rushville IN 46173

MOORE, HERBERTA GRISSOM, small food business executive; b. Knoxville, Tenn., Aug. 30, 1944; d. Herbert Gist and Grace (Gass) Grissom; m. Farris F. Moore Jr., Sept. 17, 1976. Grad. high sch., Nashville. Office mgr., v.p. Mrs. Grissom's Salads, Inc., Nashville, 1964—. Mem. Beta Sigma Phi. Methodist. Office: Mrs Grissoms Salads Inc 2500 Bransford Ave PO Box 40231 Nashville TN 37204

MOORE, JANET MARIE, state official; b. Butler, Pa., Mar. 13, 1947; d. Jesse Robert and Katherine Mae (Pisor) Moore; Asso. in Specialized Bus., New Castle Bus. Coll., 1972. Cost accountant Package Products Inc., Pitts., 1967-68; audit clk. Liberty Mut. Ins. Co., New Castle, Pa., 1968-71; acct. S.R. Snodgrass & Co., C.P.A.s, New Castle, 1971-74; clerical supr. Pa. vital records Pa. Dept. Health, New Castle, 1974—; pvt. practice acctg., Volant, Pa., 1974—. Mem. Owner Handler Assn., Nat. Rifle Assn. (life). Democrat. Presbyterian. Club: New Castle Kennel (sec. 1978, dir. 1977-81, v.p. 1979-81). Home: RD 3 Box 101 Volant PA 16156 Office: PO Box 1528 New Castle PA 16103

MOORE, JANET RUTH, nurse, educator; b. Bridgeport, Conn., Sept. 19, 1949; d. Robert Harland and Florence (Merritt) Bessom; m. William James Moore, Sept. 5, 1971; children: Jeffrey, Gregory. AA, Green Mountain Coll., 1969; diploma, Mass. Gen. Hosp., 1974; BS in Nursing, Am. Internat. Coll., 1980. RN, Mass. Nurse's aide Lynn (Mass.) Hosp., 1967-69, staff nurse, 1972-73; nursing asst. U.S. Army Hosp., Ft. Polk, La., 1971-72; staff nurse Ludlow (Mass.) Hosp., 1980-85; staff edn. instr. Springfield (Mass.) Mcpl. Hosp., 1985—; nurse Camp Wilder, Springfield, 1981-84. Mem. Jr. League of Springfield, 1981—, Community Health Edn. Council for Children and Adolescents; bd. dirs. Mass. Soc. for Prevention of Cruelty to Children, Springfield, 1985—. Mem. Mass. Nursing Assn., Mass. Gen. Alumni Assn., Wilbraham (Mass.) Jr. Women's Club, Alpha Chi. Home: 104 Burleigh Rd Wilbraham MA 01095 Office: Springfield Mcpl Hosp 1400 State St Springfield MA 01109

MOORE, JEANETTE EVELYN, cosmetics company executive; b. Terre Haute, Ind., Apr. 19, 1946; d. Earl Brown and Nola Helen (Griffen) McCarty; m. Frederick Steven Moore, Dec. 27, 1971; children—Carter Alan, Todd Jason. Student Brigham Young U., 1964-65; grad. Roper Sch. Real Estate, 1970, Dublin Beauty Coll., 1982. Coordinator, Charted Services Calif., Hayward, 1974-76; v.p. Ins. Rev. Agy., Hayward, 1975-76; loan officer Sierra Home Loans, Grass Valley, Calif., 1978-82; ins. broker Moore Ins. Agy., San Ramon, Calif., 1976-82; pres. Boughatti Internat., Pleasanton, Calif., 1983—, mktg. dir., 1983-85. Author: Boughatti Sales/Training Manual, 1983; 10 Steps of Basic Nail Care, 1983; My Nails-Sculptured Nail Manual, 1983. Den mother Boy Scouts Am., San Ramon, Calif., 1978. Mem. Nat. Assn. Female Execs., Nat. Write Your Congressman Orgn., Nat. Assn. Nail Artists. Republican. Avocations: waterskiing; snow skiing; dancing; bowling. Home: 9425 Alcosta Blvd San Ramon CA 94583

MOORE, JEANNE MADELINE, writer; b. Marysville, Calif., June 28, 1943; d. Frederick William and Madeline Rose (Cassidy) Weimann; m. Charles T. Moore, May 22, 1982; 1 child, Charles Thomas. BA in English, Skidmore Coll., 1965; MS in Journalism, Northwestern U., 1968; MA in Ednl. Media, Fairfield U., 1988. Catalog copywriter Montgomery Ward & Co., N.Y.C., 1966-67; dictionary lexicographer R.R. Donnelley & Sons, Evanston, Ill., 1967-68; retail copywriter Carson Pirie Scott & Co., Chgo., 1968-70; corp. copywriter Continental Assurance Co., Chgo., 1970-71; agy. copywriter Foote, Cone & Belding, Chgo., 1971-78; author Academy Press, Chgo., 1978-81; dir. TJM Creative Services, Monroe, Conn., 1982—. Author: The Fair Women, 1982; co-author: Equality in Print, 1978; editor HERS Healthy Kit, 1977; co-editor: Chicago Women's Directory, 1974; contbr. editor World's Fair Journal, 1982—, Antique Almanac, 1984—, Victorian Homes, 1985—; contbr. articles to profl. jours. and pop. mags. including Americana, MS, Newsday, 1982—. Mem. Lockwood-Mathews mansion, Norwalk, Conn., 1985—. Mem. Women in Communications, Am. Numismatic Assn. (speaker, Wayte-Raymond Literary award 1982). Roman Catholic. Home: 15 Cheryl Dr Monroe CT 06468

MOORE, JOYCE KRISTINA, controller; b. Phila., June 19, 1955; d. Oscar Herbert Hariu and Virginia Wilson (Guss) Leas; m. Timothy Meanor BuBon, Oct. 4, 1975 (div. 1977); m. William Burns Moore, June 20, 1980; children: William Patrick, Kristofer Sean. Student, Beloit Coll., 1973-74, U. Pa., 1974-75, Lafayette Coll., 1984-88. With photographic sales staff MacCallum Stores, Ardmore, Pa., 1974-77; photographer Clair Pruett Studios, Drexel Hill, Pa., 1977-80; photographic cons. Dan's Camera City, Allentown, Pa., 1980-81; controller BioService, Inc., Bethlehem, Pa., 1986—. Former mem. Warren County Dem. Com., Phillipsburg, N.J., 1981-83; overseer Religious Soc. Friends, 1986—; bd. dirs. Spring Garden Children's Sch., Easton, Pa. Mem. LWV (bd. dirs. Easton area 1987—), Lower Nazareth C. of C. Office: BioService Inc 4383 Hecktown Rd Suite E Bethlehem PA 18017

MOORE, JULIA MARTIN, restaurant industry executive; b. Dec. 27, 1955; d. Carol Walton and Ruth (Hines) Martin; m. Gregory Allen Moore, Nov. 10, 1979; children—Junius Gregory, Margaret Burlie. Student St. Mary's Coll., Raleigh, N.C., 1974-76; B.A. in Psychology, U. N.C., 1978. Social worker John Umstead Hosp., Butner, N.C., 1978-79; adminstrv. asst. C & S Bank, Charleston, S.C., 1979-81; corp. sec. SCNB, Inc., Jacksonville, N.C., 1981—; owner, developer Smithfield's Chicken-n-Bar BQ, N.C., 1981-85; sec.-treas. Smithfield Mgmt. Corp., Jacksonville, 1985—. Mem. Nat. Rep. Com. Mem. Nat. Restaurant Assn., N.C. Restaurant Assn. (bd. dirs., restaurateur of yr. 1988), N.C. C. of C. Republican. Episcopalian. Club: Jacksonville Christian Women's. Avocations: tennis, reading. Home: 2226 Warrenton Way Jacksonville NC 28540 Office: Smithfield Mgmt Corp 825 Gun Branch Rd Suite 130 Jacksonville NC 28541

MOORE, LINDA MARIE, travel company owner; b. Binghamton, N.Y., Feb. 2, 1943; d. Louis Paul and Mary (Opryshka) Fearns; m. Charles Edward Moore, Feb. 2, 1963; children: Kimberly Anne, Robert Charles. AS in Bus. Adminstrn., Bryant Coll., 1963; postgrad., Eastern Coll., St. Davids, Pa., 1970. Sales mgr. Avon Products, Inc., Newark, Del., 1973-78; account exec. Encore Travel, Naperville, Ill., 1984-86; owner The Traveler's Connection, Naperville, 1986-87; owner, pres. Travel Mktg. Assocs., Wilmington, N.C., 1987—. Author leisure travel guide books. Leader Girl Scouts U.S., Wayne, Pa., 1960-72; asst. leader Boy Scouts Am., 1987-88; sec. Rowland PTA, 1973-74; previously vol. Am. Heart Assn., Wayne; v.p. Naperville Welcome Wagon, 1983-84; funding com. Mill Street Sch., Naperville, 1983-84; tchr. St. Timothy's Luth. Ch., Naperville. Named Woman of Achievement Town of Wilmington, N.C., 1988. Mem. Nat. Network Women in Sales (membership sales 1985, Leadership Award 1986, nat. pres. 1987), Women in Mgmt., Nat. Assn. Female Execs., Travel Council N.C., Chgo. Travel Women's Club, Execs. Breakfast Club Oakbrook, Upper Main Line Women's Investment Assn., Bus. and Profl. Women Assn. (conv. del. 1975), Am. Soc. Assn. Execs., Wilmington C. of C. Club: Naperville Jr. Women's.

MOORE, LINDA MAYE, computer programmer; b. Petersburg, Va., July 14, 1963; d. Harold and Ella Elizabeth (Peele) M. BS in Computer Sci., Tenn. Tech. U., 1985. Programmer analyst Milliken & Co., Spartenburg, S.C., 1985—. Mem. Nat. Assn. Female Execs. Home: 2479 Country Club Rd 950M Spartanburg SC 29302 Office: Milliken & Co PO Box 1926 M-335 Spartanburg SC 29304

MOORE, LINDA PERIGO, writer; b. Evansville, Ind., Nov. 25, 1946; d. John Myrl and Loraine Jeannette (Hudson) Perigo; m. Stephen Howard Moore, Aug. 12, 1967; 1 child, Jackson Staurt Moore. B.S., Miami U., Oxford, Ohio, 1968; M.S., M.Ed., U. Louisville, 1973. Instr., St. Joseph Infirmary, Louisville, 1969-71; tng. dir. Park-DuValle Neighborhood Health Ctr., Louisville, 1971-74; counselor Charlestown High Sch. (Ind.), 1974-75; tng. dir. Midtown Mental Health Ctr., Indpls., 1977-79; freelance writer, 1980—; cons. Kelly & Assocs., Indpls., 1977-81; instr. Ind. U., Indpls., 1979-81, instr., U. So. Ind., 1986. Bd. dirs. Jr. League Evansville, 1982-84, Mothers Assn. Evansville Day Sch., 1985-87. Author: Does This Mean My Kid's a Genius?, 1981; (with Mary Kay Ash) On People Management, 1984, 2nd. ed., 1986; You're Smarter Than You Think, 1985; (with Bart Conner) Winning the Gold, 1985; (with Richard Simmons) Reach for Fitness, 1986; also articles in mags. and trade jours; tv appearences include: Oprah Winfrey Show, Today, Sonya Live, Larry King. Bd. dirs. Planned Parenthood Southwestern Ind., Evansville, 1983, Evansville Mus. Arts and Scis. Guild, 1983-87.

MOORE, LINDA PICARELLI, insurance executive; b. Bklyn., Jan. 13, 1943; d. Anthony Joseph and Alma Patricia (D'Angio) Picarelli; m. William H. Moore, Nov. 11, 1962 (div. 1974); 1 child, David A.; m. Spiro D. Demetriou, Dec. 9, 1977. Student, Wagner Coll., 1976, Coll. Ins., 1977-80. Licensed ins. broker. Ins. clk. Tchrs. Ins. and Annuity Assn., N.Y.C., 1959-61; claim examiner Aetna Life and Casualty Co., N.Y.C., 1961-63; claim supr. Northeastern Life Ins. Co., N.Y.C., 1963-66; correspondent collector Dun and Bradstreet, Staten Island, N.Y., 1972-73; asst. underwriter Duncanson and Holt, Inc., N.Y.C., 1973-76; underwriting mgr. CNA Ins. Cos., N.Y.C., 1976-85; account mgr. Marsh and McLennan Group Assn., N.Y.C., 1985-87; asst. mgr. Home Ins. Co., N.Y.C., 1987—; v.p. Naxos Inc., d/b/a Dr. Nick's Transmissions. Mem. Am. Spl. Risk Assn., Amnesty Internat. Democrat. Roman Catholic.

MOORE, LOIS JEAN, health science facility administrator. married; 1 child. Grad., Prairie View (Tex.) Sch. Nursing, 1957; BS in Nursing, Tex. Woman's U., 1970; MS in Edn., Tex. So. U., 1974. Nurse Harris County (Tex.) Hosp. Dist., 1960-77; adminstr. Jefferson Davis Hosp., Houston, 1977-88, exec. v.p., chief ops. officer, 1988—; Mem. adv. bd. Tex. Pub. Hosp. Assn. Contbr. articles to profl. jours. Mem. Mental Health Needs Council Houston and Harris County, Congressman Mickey Leland's Infant Mortality Task Force; bd. dirs. Greater Houston Hosp. Council. Named Nurse of Yr. Houston Area League Nursing, 1976-77, Outstanding Black Achiever YMCA Century Club, 1974. Mem. Am. Coll. Hosp. Adminstrs., Tex. Hosp. Assn. (chmn. pub. hosp. com.), Young Hosp. Adminstrs., Nat. Assn. Pub. Hosps. (bd. dirs., mem. exec. com. Tex. assn.), License Vocat. Nurses Assn. Home: 3837 Wichita St Houston TX 77004

MOORE, LOIS LAVERNE, comptroller; b. Sulphur Springs, Tex., Apr. 7, 1936; d. Lowell Lee and Lillie Dee (Smith) Patterson; children: Eric Dwight, Rhonda Darlene. Student, Mountain View Coll., 1975-77. Gen. office clk. Am. Gen. Ins. Co., Dallas, 1954-56, Voice of Healing Pub. Co., Dallas, 1956-59; bookkeeping clk. Tex. Am. Bank, Dallas, 1959-63, acct. Delta Comml., Dallas, 1963-71, Cathey Office Designs, Dallas, 1973-77; auditor/comptroller Brook Hollow Golf Club, Dallas, 1977—. Active United Way Dallas; v.p. Dallas/Ft. Worth Hospitality Assn. Mem. Internat. Assn. Hospitality Accounts Inc., Tex. Hospitality Accts. Assn., Club Controllers North Tex., Am. Soc. Notaries. Republican. Baptist. Home: 2046 Robin Hill Ln Carrolton TX 75007-1611 Office: Brook Hollow Golf Club 8301 Harry Hines Dallas TX 75235

MOORE, LOIS MARIE, oil and gas company personnel trainer; b. Clarendon, Tex., Mar. 14, 1933; d. Frank Johnson and Gladys Irene (Johnson) Hommel; m. James Andrew Moore ; children—Danny Lynn, Jacquelynn McDuffee, James Hayden, Mark Tremaine. B.S. in Bus. Mgmt., Wayland Baptist U., 1985 and Owens Grad. Sch. Mgmt., Vanderbilt U. Cert. instr. Interaction Mgmt.; cert. program dir. Devel. Dimensions Internat. asst. personnel dir. City of Amarillo, Tex., 1961-70; employment interviewer and DOE program coordinator Mason & Hanger, Amarillo, 1970-78; staffing and tng. mgr. Diamond Shamrock Corp. Exploration Co., Amarillo, 1978-86; pres., owner LM Consulting, Amarillo, 1986; human resources devel. cons. Procorp Group, Inc., San Antonio, 1987—. Bd. dirs. Music Festival, Amarillo, 1979-83, Guidance and Counseling Ctr., Amarillo, 1980-83, United Way Employee Assistance, Amarillo, 1979-82; adv. Amarillo Coll. and West Tex. State U., Amarillo, Canyon, Tex., 1976—; mem. personnel com. Young Women's Christian Organ., Amarillo, 1981-82. Mem. Am. Soc. Tng. and Devel. (pres.-elect 1982-84, pres. 1984, bd. dirs. 1985—, outstanding pres. award 1984), Panhandle Personnel Assn. (nominating com. 1982, tng. and devel. adv. com. 1985). Republican. Baptist. Avocations: reading, music, listening to motivational and inspirational tapes, Sunday sch. tchr., pianist. Office: Procorp Mgmt Group 4211 Gardendale Suite A-102 San Antonio TX 78229

MOORE, MARTHA BECK, financial consultant; b. Jackson, Miss.; d. Earl Crafton and Lorraine (Harrington) Beck; B.A., Duke U.; cert. bus. adminstrn., Harvard U.-Radcliffe Coll. Grad. Bus. Sch.; cert. N.Y. Sch. Interior Design; m. Edward S. Moore, III (dec.); children—Diana, John Donelson. Investment research analyst Tri-Continental Corp., also Union Service Funds, N.Y.C.; fin. asso. corp. fin. Smith, Barney & Co., Inc., investment bankers; interior designer Village Residential Design, Lost Tree Village, Fla.; designer, prin. Martha Smith, Inc., Palm Beach, Fla.; now with Citicorp Trust, Palm Beach; vol. restoration worker. Mem. Am. Soc. Interior Designers (asso.), Phi Beta Kappa. Republican. Episcopalian. Office: Royal Palm Way Palm 140 Royal Palm Way Beach FL 33480

MOORE, MARY FRENCH (MUFFY), potter, community activist; b. N.Y.C., Feb. 25, 1938; d. John and Rhoda (Teagle) Walker French; B.A. cum laude, Colo. U., 1964; m. Alan Baird Minier, Oct. 9, 1982; children—Jonathan Corbet, Jennifer Corbet, Michael Corbet. Ceramics mfr., Wilson, Wyo., 1969-82, Cheyenne, Wyo., 1982—; commr. County of Teton (Wyo.), 1976-83, chmn. bd. commrs., 1981, 83, mem. dept. public assistance and social service, 1976-82, mem. recreation bd., 1978-81, water quality adv. bd., 1976-82. Bd. dirs. Teton Sci. Sch., 1968-83, vice chmn., 1979-81, chmn., 1982; bd. dirs. Teton Energy Council, 1978-83; mem. water quality adv. bd. Wyo. Dept. Environ. Quality, 1979-83; Democratic precinct committeewoman, 1978-81; mem. Wyo. Dem. Central Com., 1981-83; vice chmn. Laramie County Dem. Central Com., 1983-84, Wyo. Dem. nat. committewoman, 1984-87; chmn. Wyo. Dem. Party, 1987—; del. Dem. Nat. Conv., 1984, mem. fairness commn. Dem. Nat. Com., 1985, vice-chairwoman western caucus, 1986—; chmn. platform com. Wyo. Dem. Conv., 1982; mem. Wyo. Dept. Environ. Quality Land Quality Adv. Bd., 1983-86; mem. Gov.'s Steering Com. on Troubled Youth, 1982, dem. nat. com. Compliance Assistance Commn., 1986-87; legis. aide for Gov. Wyo., 1985, 86; project coordinator Gov.'s Com. on Childrens' Services, 1985-86; bd. dirs. Wyo. Outdoor Council, 1984-85. Recipient Woman of Yr. award Jackson Hole Bus. and Profl. Women, 1981. Mem. Jackson Hole Art Assn. (bd. dirs., vice chmn. 1981, chmn. 1982), Pi Sigma Alpha. Home: 8907 Cowpoke Rd Cheyenne WY 82009

MOORE, MARY JUNE, transportation executive; b. Belvidere, Ill., July 7, 1950; d. Richard Carl Waterstraat and Dardnell Leone Rambow Guell; m. Gregory F. McCormick, Aug. 31, 1968 (div. Mar. 1973); 1 child, Robbie C.; m. John W. Moore, Sep. 9, 1978; 1 child, Daniel W. Grad. high sch., Belvidere, Ill. Ops. mgr. Van Lines Co., Phoenix, 1974-79, acct. mgr., 1979-81; ops. mgr. Comml. Transp. Co., Phoenix, 1981-84, v.p., adminstr., 1984—; bd. dirs. Express Pack and Crating, Inc., Phoenix; mem. Womens's Transp. Seminar; corp. sec. U.S. Express, Inc., Phoenix, 1984—. Mem. Phoenix Traffic Club. Republican. Baptist. Office: US Express Inc 50 S 43d Ave Phoenix AZ 85009

MOORE, MARY TYLER, actress; b. Bklyn., Dec. 29, 1936; d. George and Marjorie Moore; m. Richard Meeker; 1 child, Richard (dec.); m. Grant Tinker, 1963 (div. 1981); m. Robert Levine, 1983. Chmn. bd. MTM Enterprises, Inc., Studio City, Calif. Appeared in TV series Richard Diamond, Private Eye, 1957-59, Dick Van Dyke Show, 1961-66, Mary Tyler Moore Show, 1970-77, Mary, 1978, Mary Tyler Moore Hour, 1979, Mary, 1985, miniseries Gore Vidal's Lincoln, 1988; in TV movies Love American Style, 1969, Run a Crooked Mile, 1969, First You Cry, 1978, Heartsounds, 1984, Finnegan Begin Again, 1984, numerous others; in films X-15, 1961, Thoroughly Modern Millie, 1967, Don't Just Stand There, 1968, What's So Bad About Feeling Good?, 1968, Change of Habit, 1969, Ordinary People, 1980 (Acad. Award nominee for best actress 1981), Six Weeks, 1982, Just Between Friends, 1986; appeared on Broadway in Whose Life Is It Anyway?, 1980, Sweet Sue, 1987; in TV spl. How to Survive the Seventies, 1978. Recipient Emmy award Nat. Acad. TV Arts and Scis. 1964-65, 73-74, 76, Golden Globe award 1965, 81; named to TV Hall of Fame, 1985. Office: care Agy Performing Arts Inc 9000 Sunset Blvd Suite 1200 Los Angeles CA 90069

MOORE, MARYLOU AGNES, nurse; b. Jersey City, N.J., May 27, 1957; d. Frank Anton and MaryAnn Patricia (Reehill) Prekop; m. Clifford Pederson Moore, May 17, 1954; 1 child, Meghan Elizabeth. BSN, Seton Hall U., 1979, postgrad., 1984—. Charge nurse Univ. Hosp., Newark, 1979-82; nurse preceptor intensive care Mountainside Hosp., Montclair, N.J., 1982-84; clin. research scientist Pharmacia Inc., Piscataway, N.J., 1984-86, mgr. clin. research, 1986—. Screener Eyewitness News, N.Y.C., 1981-82; study coordinator N.Y. ARA, N.Y.C., 1985—; mem. curriculum team Transplant Found., New Jersey, 1987. Mem. N.J. State Nurses Assn., Sigma Theta Tau. Roman Catholic. Home: 637 Reba Rd Landing NJ 07850 Office: Pharmacia Inc 800 Centennial Ave Piscataway NJ 08854

MOORE, MELANIE ETHEL, sales executive; b. Swainsboro, Ga., Mar. 19, 1952; d. William Walker and Elizabeth (DuPree) M. Student, Ga. State U., 1975, 78 80; BA, Agnes Scott Coll., 1974. Research assoc. Emory U., Atlanta, 1974-77; customer service rep. VWR Sci., Atlanta, 1978-80, interactive purchasing, 1980-81, sales rep., 1981-83; regional mgr. Precision Sci., Chgo., 1983-84; regional sales mgr. Ohaus Scale Corp., Florham Park, N.J., 1984—. Contbr. articles to profl. jours. Grantee NSF, 1973. Mem. AAUW, Nat. Assn. Female Execs., DAR. Methodist. Home: 2977 Villa Esta Dr Chamblee GA 30341

MOORE, MILDRED ELIZABETH, farm market and greenhouse owner; b. Burlington, N.J., May 20, 1921; d. Scott Moore; m. George Francis Moore; children: Frances, George, Scott. Owner, mgr. Moores Farm Market, Bayville, N.J., 1952—. Mem. Better Bus. Bur., Toms River, N.J., 1979—. Named to Better Bus. Women of Ocean County 1st Nat. Bank Toms River, 1979. Mem. Toms River C. of C. Home: 35 Locker St Bayville NJ 08721 Office: Moores Farm Market 66 Atlantic City Blvd Bayville NJ 08721

MOORE, PAMELA DIANE, optometrist; b. Great Bend, Kans., Dec. 28, 1954; d. Samuel J. and Jean (Murphy) M. BS, U. Nev., Las Vegas, 1977, So. Calif. Coll. Optometry, Fullerton, 1979; OD, So. Calif. Coll. Optometry, Fullerton, 1981. Pvt. practice optometry Las Vegas, 1981-86; assoc. optometrist Nev. Eye Care Assocs., Las Vegas, 1986—; cons. Sexequity Awareness Program of So. Nev., 1985-87, preprofl. adv. bd. of U. Nev., Los Vegas, 1982-85. V.P., bd. dirs. Planned Parenthood So. Nev., 1984-85, pres. bd. dirs., 1986-87. Mem. Am. Optometric Assn., Nev. Optometric Assn., So. Nev. Optometric Assn., U. Nev. at Las Vegas Alumni Assn. (bd. dirs. 1986-87), Greater Las Vegas C. of C. (women's council 1984-85). Democrat. Club: Irish-Am. Lodge: Soroptimist. Office: Nev Eye Care Assocs 3507 Maryland Pkwy Las Vegas NV 89121

MOORE, PATRICIA KAY, market research administrator; b. Peoria, Ill., Jan. 20, 1947; d. David Harold and Mary Jane (Gregoryk) Jenkins; m. James Christopher Moore, Jan. 11, 1980. BS in Bus. Adminstrn., U. Mo., 1978, MBA, 1981. Planning analyst Emerson Electric Corp., St. Louis, 1972-79; mgr. mktg. adminstrn. Emerson Electric WED, Houston, 1979; dir. mktg. adminstrn. HBE Corp., St. Louis, 1979-82; mgr. market research Emerson Electric ESD, St. Louis, 1982—; instr. U. Mo.; cons. project bus. Recipient Woman Leader award YWCA. Mem. Am. Mktg. Assn., U. Mo. Alumni Assn., Beta Gamma Sigma. Roman Catholic. Home: 1940 N Geyer Rd Frontenac MO 63131 Office: Emerson Electric ESD 8100 W Florissant St MS 3216 Saint Louis MO 63136

MOORE, PEARL B., nurse; b. Pitts., Aug. 25, 1936; d. Hyman and Ethel (Antis) Friedman; diploma Liliane S. Kaufmann Sch. Nursing, 1956; B.S. in Nursing, U. Pitts., 1968, M. Nursing, 1974; 1 dau., Cheryl. Staff nurse Allegheny Gen. Hosp., Pitts., 1957-60; instr. Liliane S. Kaufman Sch. Nursing, Pitts., 1960-70, asst. dir., 1970, dir., 1970-72; cancer nurse specialist Montefiore Hosp., Pitts., 1974-75; coordinator Brain Tumor Study Group, Pitts., 1975-83; exec. dir. Oncology Nursing Soc., 1983—; adj. asst. prof. U. Pitts., 1983—. Mem. Am. Nurses Assn., Oncology Nurses Soc., Am. Soc. Clin. Oncology, Am. Soc. Assn. Execs., Nurses Alumnae U. Pitts., Sigma Theta Tau. Contbr. articles in field to profl. publs. Home: 4221 Winterburn Ave Pittsburgh PA 15207 Office: 1016 Greentree Rd Pittsburgh PA 15220

MOORE, PEGGY SUE, corporation financial executive; b. Wichita, Kans., June 16, 1942; d. George Alvin and Marie Aileene (Hoskinson) M. Student, Wichita State U., 1961-63, Wichita Bus. Coll., 1963-64. Controller Mears Electric Co., Wichita, 1965-69; exec. v.p., sec., treas., chief fin. officer CPI Corp., Wichita, 1969—, also bd. dirs.; Trustee Fringe Benefits Co., Kansas City, Mo., 1984-85. Mem. Rep. Nat. Com., Washington, 1985-86, task force 1986—; bd. dirs. Good Shepherd Luth. Ch., Wichita, 1980-85. Mem. Nat. Assn. Female Execs. Inc, Wichita C. of C., Women's Nat. Bowling Assn. (bd. dirs., pub. com. 1969-76), Internat. Platform Assn., DAR. Office: CPI Corp 816 E Funston Wichita KS 67211

MOORE, RUTH, author; b. St. Louis; d. William Dunn and Ethel (Sledd) M.; m. Raymond W. Garbe. AB, MA, Washington U., St. Louis; DLitt., McMurray Coll., 1955. Staff writer Chgo. Sun-Times newspaper, 1943-70, Washington corr., 1943-50. Author: Man, Time, and Fossils, 1953, Charles Darwin-A Great Life in Brief, 1955, The Earth We Live On, 1956, The Coil of Life, 1961, Evolution, 1962, Niels Bohr: His LIfe, His Science and the World They Changed, 1966, (with Sherwood L. Washburn) Ape Into Man,

1973, rev. edit, Ape Into Human, 1980, Man in the Environment, 1975. Chmn. Prarie Ave. Historic Dist., 1974-82; mem. Commn. on Chgo. Hist. and Archtl. Landmarks, 1974-86; pres. women's bd. U. Chgo., 1973-77; pres. Chgo. Architecture Found., 1978-80; trustee Washington U. Recipient ann. award Friends of Lit., 1955, Alumni citation, Washington U., 1963, Champion Fighter for a Better Chgo. award Met. Housing and Planning Council, $1 million endowment Ruth and Norman Moore Professorship in Architecture and Urban Design Washington U., St. Louis, 1986; $1 million endowment Ruth (Moore) and Raymond Garbe Professorship in Urban Design, Harvard U., 1987; named Chgo. Preservationist of Yr., 1981. Mem. AIA (hon.), AAAS (standing com. on pub. understanding sci.), Phi Beta Kappa. Clubs: Women's Nat. Press (Washington); Fortnightly (Chgo.). Home: 2190 Washington St San Francisco CA 94109

MOORE, RUTH JOHNSTON, health education administrator; b. Washington, Pa., Mar. 25, 1939; d. Warren and Wilma Bell (McDaid) Johnston; divorced; 1 child, Dean Jason. BS in Nursing, Fla. Internat. U., 1978; MEd, Fla. Atlantic U., 1980, EdS, 1986, EdD, 1987. Adj. faculty nursing Broward Community Coll., Ft. Lauderdale, Fla., 1978-80, div. chmn. continuing edn. and health-related professions, 1980-83, 1983—; cons., instr. local hosps., Ft. Lauderdale, 1979—; mem. adv. council Area Health Ednl. Ctr., Palm Beach, Fla., 1986—, Hot Coalition, Ft. Lauderdale, 1986—, Health Edn. and Research Founds., Ft. Lauderdale, 1986. Mem. com. Coordinating Council Broward County, Ft. Lauderdale, 1984—, Broward County Sch. Bd., 1985—. Mem. Am. Nurses Assn. (edn. com., council on continuing edn.), Am. Soc. Health Care Edn., Fla. Assn. Nurse Educators (council), South Fla. Nurse Educators (bd. dirs. 1985—), Phi Kappa Phi. Mem. Unity Ch. Office: Broward Community Coll 3501 SW Davie Rd Bldg 8 Fort Lauderdale FL 33314

MOORE, SARA JO, financial planner; b. Moline, Ill., July 30, 1954; d. Joseph K. and Anne Marie (Spaeth) Hanson; m. Robert Dean Moore, Aug. 25, 1985. BA, U. Ill., 1976. Dealer mgmt. rep. John Deere Co., Kansas City, Mo., 1976-82, territory mgr., 1982-84; sr. analyst Deere & Co., Moline, Ill., 1985; account exec. Sta. KSYZ, Grand Island, Nebr., 1985-86; registered rep. Waddell & Reed, Inc., Lincoln, Nebr., Moline, 1986—. Vol. United Way, Grand Island, 1986. Mem. Bus. and Profl. Womens Club, Jaycee Women. Republican. Roman Catholic. Club: Newcomer's, Poker Flats Investment (fin. ptnr., 1986—) (Grand Island). Home: 2920 16th Ave Moline IL 61265 Office: Waddell & Reed Inc 3450 38th Ave Moline IL 61265

MOORE, SHEILA JOYCE, federal agency administrator; b. Rugby, N.D., Apr. 17, 1954; d. Michael J. and Tekla H. (Tuchscherer) Hoffart. BA in Human Resources Adminstrn., St. Leo Coll., 1982. Office adminstr. U.S. Dept. Agrl., Savannah, Ga., 1979-82; city carrier U.S. Postal Service, Hinesville, Ga., 1982-85, supr. mails and delivery, 1985-86, supt. postal ops., 1986-87; officer in charge U.S. Postal Service, Hazlehurst, Ga., 1987; supt. postal ops. U.S. Postal Service, Waycross, Ga., 1987—. Served with U.S. Army, 1973-79. Mem. Am. Bus. Womens Assn., Nat. Assn. Female Execs. Roman Catholic. Home: PO Box 93 Waycross GA 31502-0093 Office: US Postal Service 601 Tabeau St Waycross GA 31501-9998

MOORE, SHIRLEY BEAHAM, real estate broker, civic worker; b. Tucson, July 28, 1934; d. Thomas Graham and Virginia (Ruthrauff) Beaham; m. Jack K. Moore, Jr., June 30, 1956 (div. June 1969); children: Catherine Lee Puccetti, Alan Graham. BA, Scripps Coll., 1956. Exec. dir. Pima chpt. Ariz. Kidney Found., Tucson, 1977-81; realtor assoc. Roy H. Long Realty, Tucson, 1982—; organizer, participant Southwestern Sch. Behavioral Health Studies, Tucson, 1977-78. Civic worker, Tucson, 1958—; bd. dirs. Planned Parenthood So. Ariz., 1959-65, v.p., 1962, pres., 1963-64; bd. dirs. Jr. League Tucson, 1962-73, Alsoholism Council Tucson, 1977-87; bd. dirs. St. Luke's in Desert, Inc., 1975-86; mem. planning com., 1984—; area chmn. ARC, 1964; bd. dirs. St. Luke's Bd. Visitors, 1968-78, v.p., 1974, pres., 1975; co-chmn. U.S. Senatorial Campaign, Pima County, 1972; invitations and gen. arrangements chmn. Tucson Symphony Cotillion, 1973, 74; participant Ariz. Town Hall, Grand Canyon, 1975; mem. Ariz. Acad., 1975-84; rep. alumnae admissions Scripps Coll., 1979-84. Mem. Tucson Bd. Realtors. Republican. Episcopalian. Club: President's. Lodge: Elks. Home: 7000 E Calle Arandas Tucson AZ 85715 Office: Roy H. Long Realty 6424 E Tanque Verde Tucson AZ 85715

MOORE, SHIRLEY THROCKMORTON (MRS. ELMER LEE MOORE), accountant; b. Des Moines, July 4, 1918; d. John Carder and Jessie (Wright) Throckmorton; student Iowa State Tchrs. Coll., summers 1937-38, Madison Coll., 1939-41; M.C.S., Benjamin Franklin U., 1944; m. Elmer Lee Moore, Dec. 19, 1946; children—Fay, Lynn Dallas. Asst. bookkeeper Sibley Hosp., Washington, 1941-42, Alvord & Alvord, 1942-46, bookkeeper, 1946-49, chief accountant, 1950-64, fin. adviser to sr. partner, 1957-64; dir. Allen Oil Co., 1958-74; pvt. practice acctg., 1964—. Mem. sch. bd. Takoma Acad., Takoma Park, Md., 1970—. Recipient Disting. Grad. award Benjamin Franklin U., 1961. C.P.A., Md. Mem. Am., D.C. (pub. relations com. 1976—) insts. C.P.A.s, Am. Women's Soc. C.P.A.s, Am. Soc. Women Accts. (legislation chmn. 1960-62, nat. dir. 1952-53, nat. treas. 1953-54), Bus. and Profl. Women's Club (treas. D.C. 1967-68), Benjamin Franklin U. Alumni Assn. (Disting. Alumni award 1964, charter, past dir.), D.A.R., Md. Assn. C.P.A.s (charter chmn. membership com. Montgomery Prince George County 1963-64, chmn. student relations com. 1964-67, pres. 1968-69, mem. fed. tax com. 1971-73). Mem. Seventh Day Adventist Ch. Contbr. articles to profl. jours. Home and Office: 1007 Elm Ave Takoma Park MD 20912

MOORE, SUSAN EVELYN, chemist, biologist; b. Mobile, Ala., July 20, 1954; d. Thurston Theodore and Evelyn (Patty) M. BS magna cum laude, Mobile Coll., 1976; postgrad. U. South Ala. Tech. dir. Ala. Lions Eye Bank, Birmingham, 1979-81; chem. cons. Merck & Co., Inc., Birmingham, 1981-84; indsl. chemist Ashland Co., Huntsville, Ala., 1984-85; electron microscopist U. Ala., Birmingham, 1986—. Mem. choir Shades Mountain Baptist Ch., 1980—. U. South Ala. research grantee, 1977-79. Mem. Nat. Assn. Female Execs. (charter), Electron Microscopy Soc. Am., Ala. Soc. Electron Microscopists, Nat. Assn. Sports Ofcls. (charter), Nat. Fedn. Interscholastic Ofcls. Assn. (charter), Ala. High Sch. Athletic Assn. (basketball and football approved), Amateur Softball Assn. (umpire). Republican. Baptist. Avocations: tennis, antique refinishing, softball, basketball. Home: 1219-I Beacon Pkwy E Birmingham AL 35209 Office: U Ala Comprehensive Cancer Ctr 1824 6th Ave S WTI 262 Birmingham AL 35294

MOORE, SUSAN LYNN, association executive; b. Freeport, N.Y., Mar. 21, 1949; d. Robert Emmett Moore and Margaret Ann (Moline) Reich; m. Frank Badalucco (div. Dec. 1974); 1 child, Lisa; m. Gary Wayne Sitton, May 22, 1981. A. in Gen. Studies, Pima Community Coll.; postgrad. U. Ariz. Lic. real estate salesperson, Ariz.; commd. peace officer, Ariz. Pvt. investigator, L.I., N.Y., 1969-73; investigator Office of Spl. Investigations, N.Y. Dept. Social Services, Bayshore, 1973-74; sgt. USAF, Davis Monthan AFB, Tucson, Ariz., 1974-77; sr. investigator criminal div., Pima County Atty.'s Office, Tucson, 1977-80, 88-crime program dir. (CrimeStoppers), 1980-87; exec. v.p. Southern Ariz. Home Builders Assn., 1988—; founding mem., dir. CrimeStoppers USA, 1980-82; hon. dir. La Hacienda Foster Care Resource Ctr., Tucson, 1985—. Mem. Republican Women's Club, Tucson, 1984—, U.S. Congressman Kolbe's Women's Issues Com., Tucson, 1985—, Gov. Bruce Babbitt's Crime Commn., Phoenix, 1984; dir. Tucson Community Found., 1985—; founder, chmn. Missing Children's Task Force, Tucson, 1985—. Named to Teaching Individuals Positive Solutions/Protective Strategies Adv. Council Ariz. Supreme Ct., 1985—. Mem. Am. Soc. Indsl. Security (Tucson chpt.), Tucson Met. C. of C. (Outstanding Community Service award 1984, prevention com. 1983—). Club: Soroptimist Internat. of Desert (Tucson). Lodge: Fraternal Order of Police. Avocations: aerobics; free weights; running. Home: 1871 S Skyview Pl Tucson AZ 85748 Office: Southern Ariz Homebuilders Assn 2840 N Country Club Tucson AZ 85716

MOORE, VIRGINIA BRADLEY, librarian, educator; b. Laurens, S.C., May 13, 1932; d. Robert Otis Brown and Queen Esther (Smith) Bradley; m. David Lee Moore, Dec. 27, 1957 (div. 1973). B.S., Winston-Salem State U., 1954; M.L.S., U. Md., 1970. Cert. in library sci. edn. Tchr., John R. Hawkins High Sch., Warrenton, N.C., 1954-55, Happy Plains High Sch., Taylorsville, N.C., 1955-58, Young and Carver elem. schs., Washington, 1958-65; librarian Davis and Minor elem. schs., Washington, 1965-72, Ballou Sr. High Sch., Kramer Jr. High Sch., Washington, 1972-75, 78-80, Anacostia Sr. High Sch., Washington, 1975-77, 80—; class, club sponsor, 1975—; chmn. competency-based curriculum D.C. Pub. Schs., 1978—; speaker, presenter Ch. and Synagogue Library Assn., 1975, 80, 83; dir. ch. library workshops Asbury United Methodist Ch., Washington, 1972-74, 76; mem. 1st library and info. sci. del. to People's Republic China, 1985. Author: (bibliography) The Negro in American History, 1619-1968, 1968; TV script for vacation reading program, 1971, sound/slide presentation D.C. Church Libraries' Bicentennial Celebration, 1976; video script and tchr.'s guide for Nat. Library Week Balloon Launch Day, 1983; bibliography Black Literature/Materials, 1987. Rec. sec. Washington Pan-Hellenic Council, 1975; librarian Mt. Carmel Baptist Ch., Washington, 1984. Recipient certs. of award D.C. Pub. Library, 1980, D.C. Pub. Schs., 1983; NDEA scholar Central State Coll., Edmond, Okla., 1969, U. Ky., 1969; scholar Ball State U., 1969; grad. fellow U. Md., 1969. Mem. NEA (life), LWV, Internat. Assn. Sch. Librarians, Am. Assn. Sch. Librarians (coms. 1973-83), D.C. Assn. Sch. Librarians (pres. 1971-73, citation 1973, newsletter editor 1971-75, 83, Soc. Sch. Librarians, Freedom to Read Found., ALA (councilor-at-large 1983-91), D.C. Library Assn., Md. Ednl. Media Orgn., Internat. Platform Assn., Prince Georges County LWV, Zeta Phi Beta (v.p. chpt. 1972-74), Delta Kappa Gamma. Democrat. Club: S.E. Neighbors. Home: 2100 Brooks Dr Apt 721 Forestville MD 20747 Office: Anacostia Sr High Sch 16th and R Sts SE Washington DC 20020

MOORE-CARROLL, PATRICIA SUSAN, hairdresser, make-up artist; b. Toledo, Ohio, June 14, 1957; d. Wilford Henderson and Beatrice Ann (Otting) Moore; married, Oct. 10., 1986. Lic. cosmetologist. Hairdesigner Country Charm Beauty Salon, Swanton, Ohio, 1975; mgr. Tory's Services, Inc., Swanton, 1975-80; owner Patty and Co. Hairdesigners, Swanton, 1980—; owner Jhirmack Lyceum, Redding, Calif., 1979; advisor Penta County Cosmetology Dept; adv. com., Penta County Vocat. High Sch., 1979—. Mem. Nat. Hairdresser and Cosmetology Assn. Democrat. Roman Catholic. Office: Patty and Co 137 Airport Hwy Swanton OH 43558

MOORE-DAY, BONNIE LOU, corporate professional; b. East Orange, N.J., July 10, 1956; d. Clinton Hoyt and Hannabel (Borst) Moore; m. Garrison Glenn Day, Dec. 12, 1987. AA, East Los Angeles Jr. Coll., 1977; BA in Early Childhood Edn., Calif. State U., Los Angeles, 1985. Tchr. Gerber's Child Ctr., Los Angeles, 1977-78; options prin. Bateman Eichler, Los Angeles, 1978-84; compliance dir. Cantor Fitzgerald & Co., Inc., Los Angeles, 1984—. Mem. Nat. Assn. Securities Dealers (bd. arbitrators), Nat. Soc. Compliance Profls. Republican. Presbyterian. Lodge: Order Ea. Star (matron 1986-87). Home: 4633 Ocean View Blvd La Canada CA 91011 Office: Cantor Fitzgerald & Co Inc 1840 Century Park East 9th Floor Los Angeles CA 90067

MOOREHEAD, VICTORIA ROSE, marketing and sales executive; b. Cleve., Aug. 24, 1951; d. Walter George and Stella (Petrella) Tuleta; m. Richard Manford Moorehead, Sept. 11, 1971 (div. 1982). BA, Cleve. State U., 1974. Cert. secondary edn. tchr., Ohio, W.Va., Pa. Dist. mgr. Revco Drug Stores, Inc., Cleve., 1969-78; sales mgr. Revlon Beauty Care div., N.Y.C., 1978-79; sales mgr. spl. commodity div. Carolina Freight Carriers Corp., Weirton, W.Va., 1979-82; sales rep. gen. commodity div. Carolina Freight Carriers Corp., Cherryville, N.C., 1982; mgr. nat. accts. Tenn. Ohio Express div. Service Transport, Inc., Nashville, 1982—. Mem. Future Bus. Leaders Am. (pres. 1968-69), Traffic Club Cleve., Akron, Delta Nu Alpha. Democrat. Roman Catholic. Home: 12520 Edgewater dr #910 Lakewood OH 44107 Office: Service Transport Inc PO Box 171066 Nashville TN 37217

MOORE-RUSSELL, MARTHA ELIZABETH, psychologist, substance abuse counselor. m. James Witham Moore-Russell, June 15, 1968; 1 child, Donald. AB, Skidmore Coll., 1968; MEd, Auburn U., 1971; PhD, Rutgers U., 1978. Lic. psychologist, N.Y. Chief psychologist Mt. Loretto, Staten Island, N.Y., 1980-84; clin. cons. YMCA Counseling Service, Staten Island, 1982—; clin. dir. Woodbridge Child Diagnostic, Avenel, N.J., 1984—; tng. assoc. Narcotics and Drug Research, N.Y.C., 1985—; instr. Hunterdon Council on Alcoholism, Flemington, N.J., 1986—; pres. Div. Youth and Family Services, Clin. Staff Orgn., 1986—. Recipient Bevier Grad. Fellowship, Rutgers U., 1977; research NIMH, 1978-80. Mem. Am. Psychol. Assn. Home: 63 Lillie St Princeton Junction NJ 08550 Office: Woodbridge Child Diagnostic 15 Paddock St Avenel NJ 07001

MOORHEAD, ROLANDE ANNETTE REVERDY, artist, educator; b. Périgueux, France, Sept. 24, 1937; d. RémyJean and Andrée Marcelle (Lavollée) Reverdy; liberal arts degree Coll. Technique, Nice, France, 1954; m. Elliott Swift Moorhead, III, Sept. 30, 1960; children—Edward Marc, Roland Elliott, Rémy Bruce. Bi-lingual sec., France, 1957-58, French Embassy, 1959-60, 1968-70; chmn. exhibit com. Lauderdale-By-The-Sea Art Guild, Ft. Lauderdale, Fla., 1972-75, v.p., 1972-74; charter mem. Gold Coast Water Color Soc., Ft. Lauderdale, 1976; mem. exhibit com. Broward Art Guild, Ft. Lauderdale, 1976; treas., dir. Alliance Française, Miami, Fla., 1973-75; one-man shows include: numerous banks Ft. Lauderdale area, 1971—, Ocean Club Art Gallery, Ft. Lauderdale, 1971-74, Pier 66 Gallery, Ft. Lauderdale, 1973, 75, 76, Ft. Lauderdale City Hall, 1974, 77, 78, 81, 82, 83, 84, 85, St. Basil Orthodox Ch., North Miami Beach, 1977, Galerie Vallombreuse, Biarritz, France, 1977, Galerie du Palais des Fêtes, Périgueux, 1978, Le Club Internationale, Ft. Lauderdale, 1979; exhibited in group shows: Broward Art Guild, Ft. Lauderdale, 1971, 73, 74, Point of Am. Gallery, Ft. Lauderdale, 1971, 73, Internat. Festival, Miami, 1976, Internat. Salon, Biarritz, 1977, Internat. Summer Salon, Paris, 1977, Fine Art Gallery Show and Competition, Long Galleries, Ft. Lauderdale, 1979, Pembroke Pines (Fla.) City Hall, 1982, Hollywood (Fla.) City Library, 1982, also area banks, chs. and libraries, numerous local art festivals; represented in permanent collections: Ft. Lauderdale City Hall, DAV Hdqrs., Washington, Associated Aircraft Co., March of Dimes Bldg. (both Ft. Lauderdale), U.S. Air Force Mus., Ohio, Main Line Fleets, Inc., Palm Beach, Fla., Creditre form, Dusseldorf, W.Ger., St. Front Cathedral, Périgueux, St. Sacerdoce Cathedral, Sarlat, France, also numerous pvt. collections, U.S. and Europe. Recipient Best in Show award Internat. Salon, Biarritz, 1977. Mem. Fla. Watercolor Soc., Miami Watercolor Soc., Palm Beach Watercolor Soc., Wo/Man's Showcase (dir. visual arts div. 1982—, chmn. edn. com. 1983), Am. Bus. Women's Assn., Nat. League Am. Penwomen, Lauderdale-By-The Sea Art Guild, Broward Art Guild, Boca Raton Center for Arts, Gold Coast Water Color Soc. (pres. 1984-86), Del Ray Beach Art Guild, Fla. League of Arts, Artists Equity, Everglades Artists, Çercle Français of Ft. Lauderdale, Alliance Française of Dade County, Internat. Platform Assn., Union des Français de l'Etranger. Office: PO Box 8692 Fort Lauderdale FL 33310

MOORHOUSE, LINDA VIRGINIA, symphony orchestra administrator; b. Lancaster, Pa., June 26, 1945; d. William James and Mary Virginia (Wild) Moorhouse. BA, Pa. State U., 1967. Sec., San Antonio Symphony, Tex., 1970-71, adminstrv. asst., 1971-75, asst. mgr., 1975-76; gen. mgr. Canton Symphony, Ohio, 1977—. Mem. Ohio Arts Council Music Panel, 1980-82, 86-88. Mem. Met. Orch. Mgrs. Assn. (pres. 1983-85), Orgn. Ohio Orchestras (pres. 1985, 86), Am. Symphony Orch. League (bd. dirs. 1983-85). Office: Canton Symphony Orch 1001 Market Ave N North Canton OH 44702

MOOSBRUGGER, MARY COULTRIP, marketing research consultant; b. Urbana, Ill., Sept. 1, 1947; d. Donald Lyle and Charlotte Carol (Barber) Coultrip; m. John R. Moosbrugger, Apr. 24, 1971; children—Peter John, Kathryn Rose. B.A., U. Ill., 1969; M.B.A., U. Chgo., 1982. Research analyst Leo Burnett Co., Chgo., 1969-71; study dir. Booz Allen & Hamilton, Chgo., 1972-73; research supr. Quaker Oats Co., Chgo., 1974-75; mgr. mktg. research Kitchens of Sara Lee, Deerfield, Ill., 1975-77; pres., owner Moosbrugger Mktg. Research, LaGrange, Ill., 1977—; speaker profl. assn. confs. Mem. Am. Mktg. Assn. Roman Catholic. Home: 934 N Brainard Ave LaGrange Park IL 60525 Office: Moosbrugger Mktg Research 901 W Hillgrove LaGrange IL 60525

MOOSE, SANDRA OHRN, management consultant; b. Boston, Feb. 17, 1942; d. Fritz Andrew and Esther Helen (Bastey) Ohrn. Student U. Vienna, Austria, 1962; BA summa cum laude, Wheaton Coll., 1963; MA, Harvard U., 1965, PhD, 1968. Tutor, Harvard U., Cambridge, Mass., 1964-65, cons. FDIC, Washington, 1966-68; pres. Sandra O. Moose, Inc., Chestnut Hill, Mass., 1981—; v.p., dir. The Boston Cons. Group, Boston, 1968-81, 84—; dir. GTE Corp., Rohm & Haas, New Eng. Life Mut. Funds. Contbr. articles to profl. jours. Trustee, Wheaton Coll., Norton, Mass., 1981—; bd. dirs., treas. Arts Boston, 1976—; mem. Dana Farber Cancer Inst.; corporator New England Deaconess Hosp., Boston, 1981—; trustee Hampshire Coll., 1976-83. Woodrow Wilson fellow, 1963-64; recipient 100th Anniversary award, Wheaton Coll. Alumnae Assn., 1970. Mem. Am. Econs. Assn., Com. of 200. Club: Union. Home: 53 Beverly Rd Chestnut Hill MA 02167 Office: The Boston Cons Group Exchange Pl Boston MA 02109

MOOSSY, YVONNE REESE, medical journal editor; b. McComb, Miss., Oct. 11, 1927; d. James Ottsray and Jewette Marie (Mulkey) Reese; m. John Moossy, March 15, 1951; children: John Jefferson, Joan Marie. BS, La. State U., 1950; MLS, U. Pitts., 1967. Nurse Charity Hosp., New Orleans, 1950; instr. nursing Touro Infirmary, New Orleans, 1951; nurse New Orleans Pvt. Duty Assn., 1951-53; asst. librarian Salem Coll., Winston-Salem, N.C., 1968-69; librarian Sch. Med. Bowman Gray Sch., Winston-Salem, 1969-72; mng. editor Journal Neuropathology and Experimental Neurology, Pitts., 1981—. Mem. Council Biology Editors, Nat. Standards Council Embroiderers (sec. 1974-80, chmn. traveling show 1974, 76, 78, 80). Home: 1600 Powers Run Rd Pittsburgh PA 15238 Office: Jour Neuropathology and Exptl Neurology Div Neuropathology Sch Med U Pitts Pittsburgh PA 15261

MORA, JUDITH STEVENS, financial institution consultant; b. Oakland, Calif., Dec. 5, 1946; d. Russell Norman and Lorraine C. Stevens; m. Gilbert Mora, Feb. 26, 1977. BA, U. Hawaii, 1969; MA in Mgmt., U. Redlands, 1980. Acting editor ofcl. publ. Navy C.E.C. and Seabees, Pearl Harbor, Hawaii, 1967-70; mgr. pub. relations and advt. Bishop Trust Co., Ltd., Honolulu, 1970-73; mgr. mktg. and promotions Ala Moana Ctr. Dillingham Corp., Honolulu, 1973-75; mus. cons., Hilo, Hawaii, 1975-76; cons. Edward Carpenter & Assocs., Los Angeles, 1976-79; pres., cons. J. Mora & Assocs., Inc., Orange, Calif. and Stafford, Va., 1979—. Contbr. to Hawaii Ency., 1977. Mem. spl. gifts and pub. relations coms. Am. Cancer Soc., 1973-76. Mem. Women in Communications (past chpt. pres.), Bank Adminstrn. Inst. (assoc.), Am. Heart Assn. Office: 2230 W Chapman Ave Orange CA 92668 Office: 1116 Richmond Dr Stafford VA 22554

MORADIANS-GOSS, TANYA JOY, clinical social worker; b. Chgo.; B.A., U. Calif., Berkeley, 1958; M.S.W., U. So. Calif., 1971; Ph.D., Inst. Clin. Social Work, 1981. Clin. social worker Olive View Children's Psychiat. Service, Sylmar, Calif., 1974-77, Olive View Psychiat. Emergency Service, 1970-75, Olive View Adult Psychiat. Outpatient Clinic, 1970-81; pvt. practice psychotherapy, Sherman Oaks, Calif., 1971—; asst. clin. prof. Neuropsychiat. Inst., UCLA. Cert. group psychotherapist. Mem. Social Work Treatment Service (dir.; outstanding service award), Acad. Cert. Social Workers, Soc. Clin. Social Work (dir.), Los Angeles Group Psychotherapy Soc. (dir.), Nat. Assn. Social Workers, Am. Group Psychotherapy Assn. Office: 15422 Ventura Blvd Suite 204 Sherman Oaks CA 91403

MORAITIS, KAREN KARL, real estate broker; b. Orange, Tex., Sept. 28, 1943; d. Richard Louis and Betty (Crandall) Karl; m. George Reynold Moraitis, Aug. 14, 1965; children: George Reynold Jr., Alexandra. BS in Advt., U. Fla., 1965; MEd, Fla. Atlantic U., 1968, EdS, 1974. Cert. real estate broker. Welfare worker State of Fla., Ft. Lauderdale, 1967; guidance counselor Broward County Pub. Schs., Ft. Lauderdale, 1968-70; adj. faculty Fla. Atlantic U., Boca Raton, 1971-74; real estate assoc. Blackwell Realty, Ft. Lauderdale, 1976-77; real estate broker Karen Moraitis Realty, Inc., Ft. Lauderdale, 1978—. Editor: Official Florida Publications, 1966. Mem. Pres.'s Council U. Fla., 1980—, scholarship ptnr. Gator Boosters, 1983—; pres. Harborside at Hillsboro Beach (Fla.) Condominium Assn., 1982, Parent Tchr. Student Orgn. Ft. Lauderdale High Sch., 1985—, Parent Tchr. Student Assn. Sunrise Middle Sch., Ft. Lauderdale, 1986; v.p. PTA Bayview Elem. Sch., Ft. Lauderdale, 1980; chmn. Winter Cotillion, Ft. Lauderdale, 1986—; bd. dirs. Sunrise Intracoastal Homeowners Assn., 1977, Broward County Zoning Bd., 1980-81, Imperial Village Condominium Assn., Ft. Lauderdale, 1983; ambassador edn. City of Ft. Lauderdale, 1986—. Served with USN, 1965. Mem. Ft. Lauderdale Bd. Realtors, Nat. Assn. Realtors, Fla. Assn. Realtors. Democrat. Club: Ft. Lauderdale High Sch. Boosters (pres. 1984-85, 87—). Office: Karen Moraitis Realty Inc 915 Middle River Dr Suite 502 Fort Lauderdale FL 33304

MORALES-SIMON, KATHLEEN ELIZABETH, artist, nutrition consultant; b. Milw., Oct. 25, 1958; d. Jorge Alarcon and Margaret Agnes (Vaughn) Morales; m. Michael Lester Simon, Sept. 10, 1978; 1 child, Lauren Elizabeth. Student, Milw. Inst. of Art and Design, 1976-82. Nutritional cons. Nutrition World, Inc., Milw., 1982-86; freelance artist KMS Art & Design, Milw., 1986—. Artist: sculpture Series on Women, 1987. Mem. Nat. Assn. of Female Execs., Milw. Inst. of Art and Design Alumni Assn., Milw. Inst. of Art and Design Alumni Assn. Figure Drawing Group. Democrat. Home: 3801 W Good Hope Rd Milwaukee WI 53209 Office: KMS Art and Design 3801 W Good Hope Rd Milwaukee WI 53209

MORAN, JULIETTE M., management consultant; b. N.Y.C., June 12, 1917; d. James Joseph and Louise M. B.S., Columbia U., 1938; M.S., NYU, 1948. Research asst. Columbia U., 1941; jr. engr. Signal Corps Lab., U.S. Army, 1942-43; with GAF Corp. (formerly Gen. Aniline & Film Corp.), 1943-82; successively jr. chemist process devel. dept., tech. asst. to N.Y. process devel. dept., tech. asst. to dir. Central Research Lab., tech. asst. to dir GAF Corp., 1953-55, supr. tech. service comml. devel. dept., 1955-59, sr. devel. specialist, 1959-60, mgr. planning, 1961, asst. to the pres., 1962-67, v.p., 1967-71, sr. v.p., 1971-74, exec. v.p., 1974-80, dir., 1974-83, vice chmn., 1980-82, cons., 1984—; dir. Am. Savs. Bank. Bd. dirs. N.Y. State Sci. and Tech. Found. Recipient Greater N.Y. Advt. award for excellence in communications N.Y. chpt. Assn. Indsl. Advertisers, 1972, Alumni Achievement award N.Y. U. Grad. Sch. Arts and Scis., 1977. Fellow AAAS, Am. Inst. Chemists; mem. Am. Chem. Soc., Comml. Devel. Assn. Home: 10 W 66th St New York NY 10023

MORAN, LORI ELLEN, oil company manager, small business owner; b. Albion, N.Y., Oct. 20, 1955; d. Ralph Joseph Babcock and Barbara Ellen (Lancto) Reynolds; m. John Gordon Moran, Apr. 30, 1983; 1 child, Jonathan MacKenzie. Student Plattsburgh State Coll., N.Y., 1973-74. Cert. applicator Structural Pest Control Bd. Tex. Office mgr. ABC Truck Rental and Leasing, Houston, 1979-80; with dept. accounts payable Forney Oil Co., Houston, 1980-81, accounts payable supr. with dept. accounts receivable, 1981-82, mgr. acctg. dept., 1982-87. Mem. Nat. Assn. Female Execs. Democrat. Roman Catholic. Avocations: bicycling; gardening; reading; boating. Home: 11214 Crayford Ct Houston TX 77065 Office: Lone Star Pest Control Service PO Box 650245 Houston TX 77065

MORAN, PATRICIA KIELTY, government official; b. Wilkes-Barre, Pa., Dec. 11, 1927; d. Patrick Francis and Mary Flanagan Kielty; children—Patrick, Francis, Edward, Mary. B.A., Marymount Coll., Tarrytown, N.Y., 1949; M.A., Catholic U. Am., Washington, 1953. Reporter, Broadcasting mag., Washington, 1952-54, feature editor, N.Y.C., 1954-55; spl. projects editor Nat. Assn. Broadcasters, Washington, 1955-57; dir. info. Nat. Assn. Ednl. Broadcasters, Washington, 1966-71; dir. info. and editorial services Council of Better Bus. Burs., Inc., Washington, 1971-73; dir. corp. communications DATRAN, Washington, 1973-76; communications cons., Washington, 1976-80; dir. Office of Pub. Info., GAO, Washington, 1980—. Mem. Nat. Assn. Govt. Communicators, Washington Women's Network. Club: Nat. Press. Office: US Gen Acctg Office 441 G St NW Washington DC 20548

MORAN, PEG, writer; b. Hartford, Conn., Feb. 28, 1940; d. James Thomas and Margaret (Lynch) M.; m. William J. Ziegler Jr., June 26, 1965 (div. 1971); 1 child, John William. BA, Coll. of New Rochelle, 1962; MA, Trinity Coll., 1966. Tchr. high sch. Conn., 1962-67; owner, operator Treillage Shop, Petaluma, Calif., 1971-76; free-lance writer Petaluma, Calif., 1976-78, 80; pub. info. officer Sonoma County CETA Program, Santa Rosa, Calif., 1978-79, program planner, 1979; small bus. cons. 1981—; instr. U. Calif., Berkeley, 1985-86, Santa Cruz, 1986; rep. White House Conf. on Small Bus., 1979, Econ. Devel. Program, 1979. Author: Invest in Yourself, 1981, Running Your Business Successfully, 1983; contbr. articles to mags. Pres. Spl. Olympics, Santa Rosa, 1986-87.

MORANDA, NANCY LEIGH, retail executive; b. Canandaigua, N.Y., Sept. 17, 1957; d. Wilfred Thurston and Mary Elizabeth (Cotton) M.; m. Leslie Edward Sacani, Sept. 20, 1986. BS, Rochester (N.Y.) Inst. Tech., 1979. Asst. buyer Sibley, Lindsay & Curr, Co., Rochester, 1979; from asst. market rep. to market rep. Assoc. Dry Goods Corp., N.Y.C., 1979-83; market rep. May Merchandising Corp., N.Y.C., 1983—. Republican. Methodist. Office: May Merchandising Corp 1120 Ave of Americas New York NY 10036

MORATH, INGE, photographer; b. Graz, Austria, May 27, 1923; d. Edgar Eugen and Mathilde (Wiesler) M.; m. Arthur Miller, Feb. 1962; 1 child, Rebecca Augusta. B.A., U. Berlin; D.H.C. in Fine Arts, U. Hartford, 1984. Formerly translator and editor ISB Feature Sect., Salzburg and Vienna, Austria; later editor lit. monthly Der Optmist, Vienna and Austrian editor Heute Mag.; former free-lance writer for mags. and Red White Red Radio Network; with Magnum Photos, Paris and N.Y.C., 1952—; mem. Magnum Photos, 1953—; tchr. photography course Cooper Union, 2 years; lectr. at various univs. including U. Miami, U. Mich. Exhibited photographs one-woman shows, Wuehrle Gallery, Vienna, 1956, Leitz Gallery, N.Y.C., 1958, N.Y. Overseas Press Club, 1959, Chgo. Art Inst., 1964, Oliver Woolcott Meml. Library, Litchfield, Conn., 1969, Art Mus., Andover, Mass., 1971, U. Miami, 1972, U. Mich., 1973, Carlton Gallery, N.Y.C., 1976, Neikrug Galleries, N.Y.C., 1976, 79, Grand Rapids (Mich.) Art Mus., 1979, Mus. Modern Art, Vienna, 1980, Kunsthaus, Zurich, Switzerland, 1980, Burden Gallery Aperture Inc., N.Y.C., 1987; numerous group shows include, Photokina, Cologne, Ger. and, World's Fair, Montreal, Que., Can.; represented in permanent collections, Met. Mus. Art, Boston Mus. Art, Art Inst. Chgo., Bibliothèque Nationale, Paris, Kunsthaus, Zurich, Prague (Czechoslovakia) Art Mus.; photographer for: books Guerreà la Tristesse (Dominique Aubier), 1956, Venice Observed (Mary McCarthy), 1956, (with Yul Brynner) Bring Forth the Children (Yul Brynner), 1960, From Persia to Iran (Edouard Sablier), 1961, Tunisia (Claude Roy, Paul Sebag), 1961, Le Masque (drawings by Saul Steinberg), 1967, In Russia (Arthur Miller), 1969, East West Exercises (Ruth Bluestone Simon), 1973, Boris Pasternak: My Sister Life (O. Carlisle, translator), 1976, In The Country (Arthur Miller), 1977, Chinese Encounters (Arthur Miller), 1979, Salesman in Beijing (Arthur Miller), 1984; Images of Vienna (Barbara Frischmuth, Pavel Kohout, Andre Heller, Arthur Miller), 1981, Inge Morath: Portraits, 1987; editor, co-photographer: books Paris/Magnum, Aperture Inc.; biography: Grosse Photographen unserer Zeit, 1975; contbr. numerous photographs to European, U.S., S. Am., Japanese mags., and to numerous anthologies including Life series on photography and photographic yearbooks. Recipient various citations for shows. Mem. Am. Soc. Mag. Photographers. Home: Tophet Rd Box 320 Roxbury CT 06783 Office: Magnum Photos 72 Spring St New York NY 10012

MOREAU, PATRICIA ANN, legal administrator; b. Beaumont, Tex., Dec. 16, 1944; d. Woodrow Wilson and Virginia Lorraine (Turner) Leone; m. Kenneth D. Moreau, Dec. 28, 1969 (div. 1986); children: Blake Allen, Jessie Lorraine. AS cum laude in Acad. Studies, Lamar U., Beaumont, 1985. Legal sec. Lefler, Walker & Lefler, Beaumont, 1963-71, Benckenstein, Norvell, Beaumont, 1971-83; adminstr. Benckenstein, Norvell, Bernsen & Nathan, Beaumont, 1983—. Exec. sec. Sesquicentennial Com., Beaumont, 1987. Mem. State Bar of Tex. Legal Adminstrs. Div. (charter mem., dir., sec. 1987-88), Nat. Assn. Legal Adminstrs., Beaumont C. of C. (ambassador 1988). Democrat. Roman Catholic. Club: Tower (social com.). Lodge: Soroptimist (v.p. 1988—). Home: 2812 Nashville St Nederland TX 77627 Office: Benckenstein Norvell et al 2615 Calder Suite 600 Beaumont TX 77702

MOREHEAD, LOIS KATHRYN, educator; b. Columbus, Ohio, Jan. 4, 1944; d. Elwood and Kathryn ed. Chico State U.; m. Jon Franklin Morehead, June 28, 1963; chidren—Michael, Michele, Mindy, Matt. Sec., Track & Field News, Los Altos, Calif., 1959-60; sec. Sch. Planning Lab., Stanford U., 1961-62; tchr., Rosedale Elem. Sch., 1965-66, Chico Unified Sch. Dist., 1966-67; tchr. Citrus Sch., Chico, 1967—; Amway Corp. voting mem. Recipient Outstanding Service award PTA, 1986, Outstanding Edn. award Masons, 1987. Mem. NEA, Chico Unified Tchrs. Assn., Omega Nu. Clubs: Chico Racquet, Sports Medicine. Home: 2200 Oak Park Ave Chico CA 95928 Office: Citrus Sch 1350 Citrus Chico CA 95926

MOREHEAD, PATRICIA S., state senator; b. Falls City, Nebr., July 21, 1936; d. Leo L. and Luella (Dowell) Stalder; m. Kenneth Edwin Morehead, 1967; Student MacMurray Coll., 1954-55; B.S., U. Nebr., 1958. Mem. Nebr. State Senate, 1983—. Mem. Gage County Democratic Women. Mem. PEO, Blue Valley Home Economists, Am. Trap Shooting Assn., Phi Upsilon Omicron, Chi Omega. Democrat. Office: 2317 Elk St PO Box 369 Beatrice NE 68310 *

MOREHOUSE, BARBARA ROGERS, educator; b. Norwich, Conn., Mar. 4, 1936; d. Samuel Eugene and Louise E. (Hollenback) Rogers; m. Robert Noble Morehouse, July 18, 1959; children: Ellen Morehouse Langsner, Robert Eugene, Gail Elizabeth. BS in Edn., U. Vt., 1958. Tchr. Essex Junction (Vt.) Elem. Sch., 1954-55, Manhattan (Kans.) Northview Elem. Sch., 1955-56, Penn Brook Sch., Georgetown, Mass., 1968—. Named Conservation Tchr. Essex Conservation Dist., 1985, Outstanding Elem. Tchr. nom. Outstanding Elem. Tchrs. of Am., 1973; recipient Golden Apple award Mass. Agrl. in Classrm., U. Amherst, 1986; grantee Horace Mann, 1986-87. Mem. Mass. Assn. Sci. Tchrs., Nat. Edn. Assn., Mass. Tchrs. Assn., Georgetown Tchrs. Assn., Oceanographic Research and Edn. Soc., Nat. Marine Edn. Assn., Country Garden Club. Mem. United Ch. of Christ. Home: 57 Jewett St Georgetown MA 01833 Office: Penn Brook Sch Elm St Georgetown MA 01833

MOREL, DONNA JEAN, controller; b. Berwyn, Ill., Apr. 14, 1961; d. Thomas C. and Antoinette Genevieve (Trumpick) M. AA in Acctg. honors, Coll. DuPage, 1981; BS in Acctg., U. Ill., 1982. Mgr., bookeeper Regency Gift Shop, Naperville, Ill., 1980-82; analyst contract cost Gas Research Inst., Chgo., 1982-83; asst. controller Owens-Corning Fiberglas, Summit, Ill., 1983—. Lector, reader Ascension Cath. Ch., Oakbrook Terr., Ill. 1983—. Mem. Nat. Assn. Accts., Nat. Assn. Female Execs., Alpha Lambda Epsilon. Office: Owens-Corning Fiberglas 5824 S Archer Rd Summit IL 60501

MORELAN, PAULA KAY, ballet company director; b. Lafayette, Ind., Nov. 24, 1949; d. Dickie Booth and Marian Maxine (Fetterhoff) M.; m. Kerim Sayan, Aug. 10, 1974. Student U. Utah, 1968-69; B.F.A., Tex. Christian U., 1972; student El Centro Coll., 1969-70. Tchr., Rosello Sch. Ballet, Dallas, 1972-74; mgr., tchr. Ballet Arts Ctr., Dallas, 1974-76; owner, tchr. Ballet Classique, Garland, Tex., 1976—, Garland Ballet Acad., 1977-87; asst. to Mythra Rosello, Tex. Civic Ballet, Dallas, 1972-74; assoc. artistic dir. Dance Repertory Theatre Dallas, 1974-75; artistic dir. Dance Repertory Theatre Dallas, 1975-76, Garland (Tex.) Ballet Assn., 1977—, Classical Ballet Acad., Performing Arts Sch., 1987—; resident choreographer Garland Civic Theater, 1988—. Office: Garland Ballet Assn 3112 N Jupiter Suite 410 Garland TX 75042

MORELLA, CONSTANCE ALBANESE, congresswoman; b. Somerville, Mass., Feb. 12, 1931; d. Salvatore and Mary Christine (Fallette) Albanese; m. Anthony C. Morella, Aug. 21, 1954; children: Paul, Mark, Laura; guardians of: Christine, Catherine, Louise, Rachel, Paul, Ursula. AA, Boston U., 1950, AB, 1954; MA, Am. U., Washington, 1967. Tchr. Montgomery County (Md.) Pub. Schs., 1956-60; instr. Am. U., 1968-70; prof. Montgomery Coll., Rockville, Md., 1970—; mem. Md. Ho. Dels., Annapolis, 1979-86, 100th congress from 8th Md. dist., 1987—. Trustee Capitol Coll., Laurel, Md., 1977—, Trinity Coll., Washington, 1984—; mem. found. bd. Shady Grove Hosp., Rockville, 1986—; pres. Montgomery County Commn. for Women, Rockville, 1973-74; vice chair adv. com. C & O Canal Nat. Hist. Park, 1976-78. Recipient Disting. Alumna award Am. U., 1980, 82, Disting. Legislator award Md. Victims Advocacy Network, Annapolis, 1985; named to Collegium of Disting. Alumni, Boston U., 1987; named Woman of Commitment, ADL, 1987, Woman of Yr. Nat. Assn. Women Judges Dist. 4, 1987. Mem. AAUW, Women's Inst., League of Women Voters, Bus. and Profl. Women at Large, Montgomery County Hospice Soc. Republican. Roman Catholic. Lodge: Zonta (hon., Woman of Yr. 1984). Office: US House of Reps 1024 Longworth House Office Bldg Washington DC 20515

MOREN, SALLY ANN, graphic design company owner; b. Providence, Aug. 15, 1953; d. John August and Arlene A. (Tait) M.; m. Harold Houston Woollard III, Oct. 4, 1987. BA, Coll. William and Mary, 1975; MA, Mills Coll., 1977. Graphic designer Murphy Advt., Williamsburg, Va., 1977-78, The Va. Gazette, Williamsburg, 1978-80; art dir. Spectrum Tng. Corp., Salem, Mass., 1980-82; creative supr. Woollard Advt., Boston, 1982-84; traffic mgr. Ingalls Assocs., Boston, 1984-85; mktg. dir. The Lodge at Harvard Sq., Newton, Mass., 1985-86; owner Moreno Design, Inc., Boston, 1986—; tchr. art Santa Catalina Sch., Monterey, Calif., 1977-78; tchr. ballet Williamsburg Recreation Dept., 1978; founder, prin. Freelance Dance Co., 1977-78. Mem. Nat. Assn. Female Execs., Delta Delta Delta. Republican. Home: 1 Chickatabot Rd Quincy MA 02169

MORENO, BARBARA R., accountant; b. Kingston, Pa.; d. Theodore G. and Arline (Rhodes) Rodgers; m. James H. Moreno, Mar. 1, 1957; children: James H., Arline M. BA magna cum laude, Newark State Coll., 1961; MA, Rutgers U., 1965, MBA, 1979. CPA, N.J. Asst. prof. Newark State Coll., Union, N.J., 1963-69, adj. prof., 1970-80; acct. J.H. Cohn and Co., Roseland, N.J., 1980-82; pvt. practice South Plainfield, N.J., 1982—; adj. instr. Rutgers U., 1982. Nat. Sci. Found. grantee, 1965. Fellow N.J. Soc. CPA's; mem. Am. Inst. CPA's, Kappa Delta Pi, Beta Gamma Sigma. Avocations: reading, swimming, biking. Home and Office: 109 Whispering Hills Rd South Plainfield NJ 07080

MORENO, ROSEMARIE TRAINA, brokerage house executive; b. N.Y.C., Aug. 7, 1957; d. Anthony Nicholas and Mary Caroline (Brand) Traina; m. George Moreno Sr., Oct. 21, 1984. B, CUNY, 1980; M, Fordham U., 1981. Adminstrn. coordinator Nesbitt Thompson Securities, Inc., N.Y.C., 1981-83; registered rep. Shearson Lehman Bros., Inc., N.Y.C., 1983-88, R.L. Renck Holdings, Inc., N.Y.C., 1988—; cons. Townhill Cons., Inc., N.Y.C., 1985—. Mem. Met. Opera Guild, N.Y.C., 1986; vol. presdl. re-election campaign, 1980. Recipient Italian/Am. award Italian Tchrs. Assn., 1973. Mem. Publicity Club N.Y., Pub. Relations Soc. Am.

MORESKY, LANA, organization executive; b. Youngstown, Ohio, Feb. 23, 1946; d. Edward S. and Rose (Gelfand) Zatell; B.S., Pa. State U., 1967; m. Marc Moresky, July 30, 1967; children—Rachel, Joanna. Mem. NOW, 1970—, pres. Ohio chpt., 1974-75, mem. nat. bd. dirs., 1976-77, pres. Cleve. East chpt., 1980-81, cons., 1981—; mem. Ohio Atty. Gen. ERA Implementation Task Force Sexism in Edn., 1975, Ohio Internat. Women's Year Coordinating Com., 1977; mem. Cuyahoga County steering com. White House Conf. Families, 1979. Mem. platform com., del. Democratic Nat. Conv., 1980; mem. Cuyahoga County Dem. Exec. Com., 1978; chmn. 22d Congl. Dist. Caucus, 1980; bd. dirs. Cleve. chpt. Ams. for Democratic Action, 1982, pres., 1985, nat. bd. dirs., 1984—. Recipient Susan B. Anthony award NOW, 1975, Ohio and Cuyahoga local Women in Bus. Advocate award SBA, 1984, 85; named Woman of Yr., Coalition Labor Union Women, 1980; honored by Ohio Women's Hall of Fame, 1983. Jewish. Address: 3918 Washington Blvd Cleveland OH 44118

MORETTI, ARDEN WELLS, freelance writer; b. Orillia, Ont., Can., Jan. 18, 1932, came to U.S., 1973; d. Kenneth McNeill and Audrie (Sinkins) Wells; m. Frank Joseph Moretti, Sept. 10, 1955; children—John, Lauren, Lisa. B.A., U. Western Ont., 1955; postgrad. U. Houston, 1978-82. Freelance writer, Houston, 1978-84: contbr. articles to Ultra Mag., Houston City Mag., Houston Home and Garden mag.; editor, writer Houston Working Woman's Jour., 1980-81; contbr. Houston Downtown, 1978-82; columnist, feature writer Southwestern Argus, 1978-79; editor, writer, layout and photography Univ. Village Assn. News, 1979-83; reviewer Tex. Episc. Churchman, 1984-86; research asst. Mus. Fine Arts, Houston, 1985-86; freelance writer, Houston. Mem. Women in Communications (Matrix award 1982), Golden Key Honor Soc. Home: 2125 Goldsmith St Houston TX 77030

MORETTO, JANE ANN, nurse; b. Belgium, Ill., Apr. 9, 1934; d. Bernard James and Mildred Bertha (Sutton) Moretto; R.N., Mercy Hosp. Sch. Nursing, Urbana, Ill., 1955; B.S. in Nursing, St. Joseph Coll., Emmitsburg, Md., 1969. Relief head nurse, staff nurse Mercy Hosp., Urbana, Ill., 1955-57; staff nurse in psychiatry VA Hosp., Danville, Ill., 1957-59; staff nurse pulmonary disease VA Hosp., Long Beach, Calif., 1959-60, staff nurse surg. unit, Los Angeles, 1960-61, staff nurse operating room, 1961-64; staff nurse USPHS Hosp., Galveston, Tex., 1964-66, staff nurse tumor ICU, Balt., 1967, asst. operating room supr., New Orleans, 1969-71, operating room supr., Brighton, Mass., 1971-78, dep. dir. nursing, dir. inservice edn. Carville, La., 1978-80, dir. nurses Nat. Hansen's Disease Center, 1980—; cons. in field; lectr. in field. Commd. lt. comdr., USPHS, 1969, advanced through grades to capt., 1975—. Recipient Superior Performance award, USPHS Hosp., Galveston, 1966, Outstanding Service medal for exemplary performance of duty Dept. Health Human Services-Pub. Health Service, 1986. Mem. Am. Nurses Assn., La. Nurses Assn., La. Hosp. Assn., La. Soc. Nursing Service Adminstrs., Nat. Assn. for Uniformed Services, Assn. Mil. Surgeons of U.S., Assn. Operating Room Nurses, Alumnae Assn. of Schlarman High Sch., Alumnae Assn. of St. Joseph Coll., Commd. Officers Assn. USPHS. Roman Catholic. Home: 303 Bridgett St Westville IL 61883 Office: Nat Hansen's Disease Ctr Carville LA 70721

MOREY, MARTHA ANN, geneticist, educator; b. Sanford, Fla., Aug. 8, 1923; d. Marvin Conley and Myrtle Manora (Cummings) Ballew; m. Donald Franklin Morey; children: Ann Janine, Noralane, Darcy. AA, Chesbrough Sem., 1941; AB, Greenville Coll., 1943; MS, U. Rochester, 1949; RN, BS, Graceland Coll., 1980. Tchr. sci. Los Angeles Pacific Coll., 1948-50; physical edn. tchr. Hart High Sch., Newhall, Calif., 1950-51; founder, dir. day care ctr. Liberty (Mo.) Christian Ch., 1972-79; genetic counselor Children's Mercy Hosp., Kansas City, Mo., 1976—; genetics instr. Clin. Pediatric Genetics, U. Mo. Med. Sch., Kansas City, 1985—. Author numerous poems; contbr. articles to profl. jours. Med. chair 10th Habitat for Humanity, Kansas City, 1986; contbr. So. Poverty Law Ctr., Ala.; charter mem. Nat. Mus. Women in Arts. Mem. AAUW, Am. Soc. Human Genetics. Mem. Christian ch.

MORFESIS, ANASTASIA, chemist, researcher; b. Lancaster, Pa., Dec. 31, 1957; d. Andreas and Tsidonis Morfesis; m. Robert Gregory Swisher, Aug. 31, 1985. BS in Chemistry, Math., Chatham Coll., 1979; MS in Chemistry, U. Mass., 1983, PhD in Chemistry, 1986. Chemist Gulf Research and Devel., Pitts., 1980-81; teaching asst. chemistry U. Mass., Amherst, 1981-83, research asst. chemistry, 1983-86; teaching asst. Smith Coll., Northampton, Mass., 1984; research assoc. U. Pitts., 1986—; computer programmer, cons. Pitts., 1980-81. Mem. Am. Chem. Soc. (div. of Colloid and Surface Sci.), Soc. Analytical Chemists of Pitts., Soc. Plastics Engrs. Office: U Pitts Chemistry Dept Pittsburgh PA 15260

MORGAN, AUDREY, architect; b. Neenah, Wis., Oct. 19, 1931; d. Andrew John Charles Hopfensperger and Melda Lily (Radtke) Anderson; m. Earl Adrian Morgan (div); children: Michael A., Susan Lynn Heiner, Nancy Lee, Diana Morgan Lucio. B.A., U. Wash., 1955. Registered architect, Wash.; cert. NCARB. Project mgr. The Austin Co., Renton, Wash., 1972-75; med. facilities architect The NBBJ Group, Seattle, 1975-79; architect constrn. rev. unit Wash. State Dept. Social and Health Services, Olympia, 1979-81; project dir., med. planner John Graham & Co., Seattle, 1981-83; pvt. practice architecture, Seattle, 1983—, also health care facility cons., code analyst. Contbr. articles to profl. jours. and govt. papers; prin. works include quality assurance coordinator for design phase Madigan Army Med. Ctr., Ft. Lewis, Wash.; med. planner and code analyst Rockwood Clinic, Spokane, Wash. Cons. on property mgmt. Totem council Girl Scouts U.S.A., Seattle, 1969-84, troop leader, cons., trainer, 1961-74. Mem. AIA (subcoms. codes and standards, health planning and mental health of nat. com. on architecture for health 1980—, and numerous other coms., founding mem. Wash. council AIA architecture for health panel 1981—,recorder 1981-84, vice chmn., 1987, chmn. 1988, bd. dirs. S.W. Wash. chpt. 1983-84), Nat. Forest Products Assn., Soc. Am. Value Engrs., Am. Hosp. Assn., Assn. Western Hosps., Wash. State Hosp. Assn., Seattle Womens Sailing Assn., Audubon Soc., Alpha Omicron Pi. Lutheran. Clubs: Coronado 25 Fleet 13 (Seattle) (past sec., bull. editor); GSA 25 Plus. Home and Office: 4216 Greenwood Ave N Seattle WA 98103

MORGAN, BARBARA JOAN, real estate broker; b. Mattoon, Ill., July 5, 1940; d. Wendel Lewis and Helen Irene (Adkins) Huddlestun; m. David A. Morgan, Aug. 22, 1958; children—Wendy A., Eric W., D. Gregory. B.S. in Edn., Ea. Ill. U., 1962. Tchr. Lincoln Sch., Mattoon, Ill., 1962-66; real estate broker, Paris, Ill. 1974—; real estate broker, owner Paris Realty, 1978—; real estate tchr. Lakeland Jr. Coll., Mattoon, 1980—; appointed to Region 23 Pvt. Industry Council, 1987. Pres. Paris Newcomers club, 1974-75; chair United Way of Edgar County, 1988. Named Paris Woman of Yr., 1985-86. Mem. Ill. Assn. Realtors (inst. grad. 1977, cert. residential specialist 1979), East Central Ill. Bd. Realtors (pres. 1978-79), Bus. and Profl. Women Paris (pres. 1983-84), Paris C. of C. (v.p. 1984-86). Republican. Clubs: Altrusa, Prairies Edge Toastmaster's (charter mem.). Lodge: Order Eastern Star. Office: Paris Realty 207 N Central St Paris IL 61944

MORGAN, EVELYN BUCK, nursing educator; b. Phila., Nov. 3, 1931; d. Kenneth Edward and Evelyn Louise (Rhineberg) Buck; m. John Allen McGeary, Aug. 15, 1958 (div. 1964); children—John Andrew, Jacquelyn Ann McGeary Keplinger; m. Kenneth Dean Morgan, June 26, 1965 (dec. 1975). R.N., Muhlenberg Hosp. Sch. Nursing, 1955; B.S. in Nursing summa cum laude, Ohio State U., 1972, M.S., 1973; Ed.D., Nova. U., 1978. R.N., N.J., Ohio, Fla., Calif.; cert. specialist Am. Nurses Assn. Psychiat.-Mental Health Clin. Specialists; advanced R.N. practitioner Fla. Bd. Nursing. Staff nurse Muhlenberg Hosp., Plainfield, N.J., 1955-57; indsl. nurse Western Electric Co., Columbus, Ohio, 1957-59; supr. Mt. Carmel Hosp., Columbus, 1960-65; instr. Grant Hosp. Sch. Nursing, 1965-72; cons. Ohio Dept. Health, 1972-74; prof. nursing Miami (Fla.)-Dade Community Coll., 1974—; family therapist Hollywood Pavilion Hosp., 1977-82; pvt. practice family therapy, Ft. Lauderdale, Fla., 1982—. Sustaining mem. Democratic Nat. Com., 1975—. Mem. Am. Nurses Assn., Fla. Council Psychiat.-Mental Health Clin. Specialists, Am. Nurses Found., Am. Holistic Nurses Assn., Sigma Theta Tau. Democrat. Roman Catholic.

MORGAN, GAIL MARLYS, personnel and rental management executive; b. Turtle Lake, N.D., Nov. 15, 1954; d. Sam Darwin and Delores Ann (Stoering) Eng; m. Kenneth Stuart Morgan, May 10, 1975 (div. Sept. 1984); children: KarLee Kay, Leah Christina, Patrick McDonald. Student, U. Minn., 1973-74, Patricia Stevens Fashion and Modeling Schs., Mpls., 1973-74. Dept. mgr. Herberger's, Bismarck, N.D., 1974; asst. mgr. Holly, Inc., White Bear Lake, Minn., 1974-76; exec. sec. Beulah (N.D.) Secretarial Services, 1983-84; sec.-treas. Brandy Corp., Beulah, 1984-85, pres., 1985-86; owner, mgr. Brandy Contract Personnel Service, Beulah, 1986—, Bodies by Brandy, Beulah, 1987—, Brandy Rental Mgmt., Beulah, 1987—; devel. mgr. Delta (Utah) Temporary Services, 1984-85; asst. Fields Photography, Beulah, 1985—; fin. advisor RAZ, Inc., Beulah, 1987—. Mem. Adminstrv. Mgmt. Soc., Nat. Assn. Female Execs., N.D. Lignite Council, Beulah C. of C. Lutheran. Club: Women of Today (Beulah). Office: Brandy Personnel Service Hwy 49 N PO Box 479 Beulah ND 58523

MORGAN, GALE LYNN, marketing executive; b. Balt., Aug. 20, 1959; d. Gerald David and Ruth Pearl (Bryant) M. BBA in Mktg., U. Phoenix, 1985. Mktg. cons. Leffler Agy., Balt., 1978-79; account rep. Ciani Jewelry Co., N.Y.C., 1979-81; adminstrv. sec. Century 21 of the South, Mobile, Ala., 1982, Century 21 of the SW, Phoenix, 1982; inquiry, community relations Kachina Health Care Services, Scottsdale, Ariz., 1983; dir. mktg. The Regent Health Care COrp., Scottsdale, 1984-85; v.p. mktg. Retirement Living Afiliates, Scottsdale, 1986—. mem. planning com. Sr. Ctr., Scottsdale, 1985-86. Republican. Roman Catholic. Office: Retirement Living Afiliates 6991 E Camelback Rd Suite C-250 Scottsdale AZ 85251

MORGAN, GLENDA ANDERSON, municipal government official, educator; b. Liberty, Tex., July 19, 1944; d. Edgar Lloyd and Verley Lanell (Barnes) Anderson; m. Howard Lamont Morgan. AA, Copiah-Lincoln Jr. Coll., 1964; BA, Miss. State Coll. for Women, 1966; MRE, New Orleans Bapt. Theol. Sem., 1968; postgrad., U. South Ala., 1971—. Cert. mcpl. personnel adminstr., Ala. Youth dir. Woodmont Bapt. Ch., Mobile, Ala., 1968; sec. Daupin Way Bapt. Ch., Mobile, 1968-70; tchr., guidance counselor 1st Ind. Meth. Ch. Sch., Mobile, 1970-76; personnel officer Mobile Pub. Library, 1976-85; tchr. 20th Century Coll., Mobile, 1980-85, U. South Ala., Mobile, 1984—; asst. city clk. City of Mobile, 1985—; owner, operator Frames & Things, Mobile, 1969—; tchr. Ala. Christian Coll., Mobile, 1975-76, Bishop State Jr. Coll., Mobile, 1984-85. Sec. Daupin Way Bapt. Ch., Mobile, 1968-70; v.p. Mobile County Merit System Employee Assn., 1979-80, pres., 1980-84. Mem. Ala. Assn. Personnel Adminstrs., Ala. Assn. Mcpl. Clks. and Adminstrs., Ala. City Mgmt. Assn., Mobile Personnel Assn., Internat. Inst. Mcpl. Clks., Phi Theta Kappa. Baptist. Home: 1906 Navco Rd Mobile AL 36605 Office: City of Mobile 111 S Royal Mobile AL 36601

MORGAN, INGA BORGSTROM, educator, pianist; b. Amarillo, Tex.; d. August and Charlotte (Jonsson) Borgstrom; grad. Amarillo Jr. Coll., 1938; Mus.B., Eastman Sch. Music, 1940, Mus.M., 1944, performer cert., 1942; postgrad. Sommer Akademie, Mozarteum, Salzburg, Austria, 1969, 71; student Friederich Wuhrer, Max Landow, Lilly Larsen, Esther Jonsson, Radie Britain; m. Edwin Phillip Morgan, Aug. 23, 1942; 1 child, Kent August. Mem. faculty, dept. music Coll. Fine Arts, U. Tex., Austin, 1942-43, N. Tex. State U., Denton, 1944-45; prof. music and piano Sch. Music, U. N.C., Greensboro, 1946—; cons.; concert pianist, harpsichordist, lecture-recitalist, accompanist. Mem. Am. Liszt Soc., Coll. Music Soc., Music Tchrs. Nat. Assn., N.C. Music Tchrs. Assn., Greensboro Music Tchrs. Assn., Am.-Scandanavian Found., Vasa Order (officer), Pi Kappa Lambda, (past officer), Mu Phi Epsilon. Presbyterian. Club: Euterpe Music. Home: 1005 Guilford Ave Greensboro NC 27401 Office: 209 Music Bldg U NC Greensboro NC 27412

MORGAN, JULIE FAY, personnel administrator; b. Plaquemine, La., Mar. 7, 1959; d. Arthur and Ida Mae (Brooks) Ganaway. BS Psychology, Calif. State U., Los Angeles, 1983, MS in Devel. Psychology, 1985. Human resources adminstrv. aide Los Angeles Times, 1983-85, employee benefits asst., 1985-87, sr. employee benefits analyst, 1987—. counselor The Phone, Baton Rouge, La., 1978-79, U. So. Calif. Psychiat. Hosp., Los Angeles, 1982, Angelus Plaza retirement Housing Facility, Los Angeles, 1984-85. Mem. Calif. Assn. of Counseling and Devel., Nat. Counsel on Aging, Nat. Assn. of Older Worker Employment Services, Internat. Soc. of Pre-Retirement Planners (v.p. So. Calif chpt. 1987—), Nat. Notary Assn., Los Angeles C. of C., Psi Chi, Phi Kappa Phi. Office: Los Angeles Times Times Mirror Sq Los Angeles CA 90053

MORGAN, KAREN R., advertising sales executive; b. Washington, Dec. 7, 1957; d. Nelson and Sara (Raudenbush) Richards; m. David Gerald Morgan, Sept. 17, 1983; 1 child, Peter. BA, Mary Washington Coll., Fredericksburg, Va., 1981. Store mgr., dist. mgr. Cargo Furniture, Richmond, Va., 1981-84; br. mgr. BSA Advt., Landover, Md., 1984-88; sales mgr. Ea. region Personal Selling Power, Fredericksburg, Va., 1988—. Mem. Nat. Assn. Female Execs., Nat. Mus. of Women in the Arts. Episcopalian. Home and Office: 9206 Tunemaker Terr Columbia MD 21045

MORGAN, KATHY G., sales executive; b. Cin., Nov. 2, 1957; d. Jack Robert and Mae S. (Sams) Morgenroth. B.S. in Econs., No. Ky. U., 1983. Sales rep. Dodge, Datsun, and Chevrolet dealers, Cin., 1979-84; mfg. sales rep. State Chem., Cin., 1984-86; dist. sales mgr. Chevrolet Zone, Cin., 1986—; staff analyst operations Chevrolet Zone, Cin., 1987—. Advisor Jr. Achievement, 1984-85. Recipient 1st Timers award Ohio Jaycees, 1985. Republican. Methodist. Clubs: Cin. Ski, Hyde Park Methodist (Cin.). Avocations: water skiing; snow skiing; volleyball; softball. Home: 4902 Chalet Dr # 703 Cincinnati OH 45217 Office: Chevrolet Zone Office 155 Tri County Pkwy Cincinnati OH 45246

MORGAN, KERRY DARLENE, automotive executive; b. Sparta, Mich., Feb. 23, 1953; d. William Cecil and Karla Marie (Hunter) Newton; children: Tanya Beth Shinew, Hilary Eve Shinew. Grad. high sch., Grant, Mich. Enlisted U.S. Army, Ft. Hood, Tex., 1980, with clerical/med. depts., 1980-83; with clerical/med. depts. USAR, Mich., 1983-86; with BSR Components, Newaygo, Mich., 1983-85; producer CPC Group div. Gen. Motors Corp., Grand Rapids, Mich., 1985—. Recipient cert. of merit White Cloud (Mich.) Social Services Dept., 1986. Mem. Nat. Assn. Female Execs. Democrat. Home: 2295 120th St Grant MI 49327-9803 Home: Production Dept 300 36th St Grand Rapids MI 49508

MORGAN, LUCY W., journalist; b. Memphis, Oct. 11, 1940; d. Thomas Allin and Lucile (Sanders) Keen; m. Alton F. Ware, June 26, 1958 (div. Sept. 1967); children—Mary Kathleen, Andrew Allin; m. Richard Alan Morgan, Aug. 9, 1968; children—Lynn Elwell, Kent Morgan. A.A., Pasco Hernando Community Coll., New Port Richey, Fla., 1975; student, U. South Fla., 1976-80. Reporter Ocala Star Banner, Fla., 1965-68; reporter St. Petersburg Times, Fla., 1967-86, capitol bur. chief, 1986—. Recipient Paul Hansel award Fla. Soc. Newspaper Editors, 1981, First in Pub. Service award Fla. Soc. Newspaper Editors, 1982, First Place award in pub. service Fla. Press Club, 1982, Pulitzer award for investigative reporting Columbia U., 1985, First Place award in investigative reporting Sigma Delta Chi, 1985. Home: 1727 Brookside Blvd Tallahassee FL 32301 Office: St Petersburg Times 336 E College Ave Tallahassee FL 32301

MORGAN, LYNN KASNER, librarian, educator, lecturer; b. N.Y.C., Oct. 13, 1950; d. Edward Paul and Michaela (Lipton) Kasner; m. Nicky N. Morgan, June 25, 1978. B.A., SUNY-Binghamton, 1972; M.L.S., SUNY-Albany, 1972. Coordinator N.Y. and N.J. Regional Med. Library, N.Y.C., 1976-78; dir. N.Y. and N.J. Regional Med. Library, 1978-80; assoc. librarian N.Y. Acad. Medicine, N.Y.C., 1981-83; dir. Levy Library, Mt. Sinai Sch. Medicine, N.Y.C., 1983—; instr. med. edn. Mt. Sinai Sch. Medicine, %; cons. Albany Sch. Library and Info. Service, SUNY-Albany, 1975, Mt. Sinai Sch. Continuing Edn. in Nursing, 1976-77, N.Y. State Nurses Assn., Albany, 1978-79; adj. lectr. Queens Coll., N.Y.C., 1984-86, Sch. Library Sci., Columbia U., N.Y.C., 1985—; trustee Med. Library Ctr. of N.Y., 1985—, N.Y. Met. Reference and Research Library Agy., 1985—, treas., 1987—; regional adv. council Greater Northeastern Regional Med. Library Program, 1985—. Editor N.Y. and N.J. Regional Med. Library News, 1976-80; asst. editor N.Y. State Nurses Assn. Jour., 1975-76; contbr. articles to profl. jours. Grantee, Nat. Library of Medicine Contract, Regional Med. Library Services, 1980-82. Mem. AAAS, ALA, Assn. Coll. and Research Libraries, Med. Library Assn. (cert.), Beta Phi Mu. Home: 20 Marquette Rd Upper Montclair NJ 07043 Office: Mt Sinai Med Ctr Levy Library One Gustave L Levy Pl New York NY 10029

MORGAN, M. JANE, computer systems consultant; b. Washington, July 21, 1945; d. Edmond John and Roberta (Livingstone) Dolphin; 1 child, Sheena Anne. Student U. Md., 1963-66, Montgomery Coll., 1966-70; BA in Applied Behavioral Sci. with honors, Nat. Coll. Edn., 1987. With HUD, Washington, 1965-84, computer specialist, 1978-84; pres., chief exec. officer Systems and Mgmt. Assocs., 1983-87; dir. systems engring. Advanced Technology Systems, Inc., Vienna, Va., 1984-86; chief tech. staff Tech. and Mgmt. Services, Inc., 1986—. Mem. Am. Mgmt. Assns. Episcopalian. Club: Order Eastern Star. Office: Care Systems and Mgmt Assocs 10252 Cherry Walk Ct Oakton VA 22124

MORGAN, MARITZA LESKOVAR, painter; b. Zagreb, Yugoslavia, Nov. 20, 1920; came to U.S., 1929, naturalized, 1930; d. Josef and Paula Mihailovic (Yunkovic) Leskovar; M.A., Cornell U., 1944; m. Norman Charles Morgan, May 10, 1941; children—Vincent, Penelope, Jonathan, Christopher, Catherine. Music editor Chautauguan Dailey, Chautaugua, N.Y., 1969—; one woman shows: Central Cathedral, N.Y.C., 1982, Downtown Cathedral, Rochester, N.Y., 1982, Bryn Mawr (Pa.) Presbyn. Ch., 1982, 86, Univ. Christian Ch., Austin, Tex., 1986, Old Scots' and Pine St. Ch., 1987 (pres.), Princeton Theol. Sem. (in conjunction with 175th anniversary of its founding), N.J., 1988, represented in permanent collections Hurlbut Ch., Chautaugua, All Souls Unitarian Ch., Tulsa, Downtown Presbyn. Ch., Rochester, Presbyn. Ch., Warren, Pa., St. Joseph Ch., Erie, Pa.; ofcl. artist Presbyn. Ch.'s 200 Anniversary of First Synod, St. Louis and Phila., 1988—; executed mural Mellon Cathedral, Pitts. Transl.: The Cunning Little Vixen (Rudolf Tesnohildek), 1984. Home: 10 Forest Ave Chautaugua NY 14722

MORGAN, MARTHA LOUISE, nurse; b. Ripley, Tenn., June 7, 1955; d. Columbus and Martha Mae (Taylor) M. Diploma in Nursing, St. Joseph Hosp. Sch. of Nursing, Memphis, 1976; student, Coll. of St. Francis, Joliet, Ill., 1987—. RN, Tenn., Ind. cert. in cardiac life support Am. Heart Assn. Nurse in charge med. surg. unit St. Joseph Hosp., Memphis, 1973-78; nurse intensive CCU Meth. Hosp. Memp, Memphis, 1978-79; nurse intensive CCU Meth. Hosp. Memp, Gary, Ind., 1979-87, asst. projects coordinator, 1987, dir. ICU and CCU, 1987—; owner, designer Silk Flower Creations, Gary. Recipient INd. Nurses Week Ideal Nurse award Meth. Hosp., Gary, 1985, 86. Mem. Am. Assn. Critical Care Nurses, Midtown RN Orgn. (publicity com. 1986—), NAACP (bd. dirs., community coordinator Gary br. 1988), Ind. Coalition for Black Jud. Officials, Smithsonian Assocs. Democrat. Baptist. Home: 578 S Vermillion Pl Apt 311 Gary IN 46403 Office: Meth Hosp of Gary 600 Grant St Gary IN 46402

MORGAN, RUTH ANN, publishing computers company executive, b. Chgo., June 4, 1958; d. Jimmy Louis and Esther Nancy (Sorensen) Sorensen; m. Bradford Rex Morgan, Aug. 11, 1979. Student Dana Coll., 1976-77, U. No. Iowa, 1977-79. With Deer Valley Dude Ranch, Nathrop, Colo., 1978, Am. Entertainment Prodns., Columbus, Ohio, 1979; typesetter, designer K&J Typographers, Streamwood, Ill., 1980-81; applications engr. Atex, Chgo., 1982-84; cons. Morgan & Assocs., Roselle, Ill. and King of Prussia, Pa., 1984—. Vol., Spl. Olympics, Phila., 1986. Nebr. Bd. Regents scholar, 1976. Mem. Nat. Assn. Female Execs., Printing Industries of Am., Multiple Computer Bull. Bds. Republican. Avocation: horses. Office: 1504 Canbury Ct Wheeling IL 60090

MORGAN, RUTH MILDRED, medical technologist; b. Indpls., Mar. 8, 1917; d. James Franklin and Lula Floy (Heiny) M.; B.S. in Allied Health Edn., Ind. U.-Purdue U., Indpls., 1976; student Ind. U., 1954-57, 76-77, Butler U., 1958. Dental asst., med. asst. and med. technologist, Indpls., 1953—; tchr. hematology Med. Lab., 1970-79, supr. hematology, 1960-79, gen. supr., 1980—. Fin. chmn. 8th precinct 20th Ward of Indpls., 1977-79. Recipient citation Mayor Richard Lugar, 1976; registered med. technologist, lic. health facility adminstr. Mem. Am. Soc. Clin. Pathologists (affiliate), Am. Soc. Profl. and Exec. Women, Marion County Council Republican Women, Nat. Fedn. Republican Women, Am. Coll. Health Care Adminstrs. (assoc. Ind. chpt.), Brown County Art Gallery Assn., Ind. Soc. Med. Technologists. Club: Eastern Star (matron 1950). Inventor, patentee cabinets for indsl. use. Home: 2625 N Meridian St Apt 921 Indianapolis IN 46208 Office: 8801 N Meridian St Indianapolis IN 46250

MORGAN, THERESA BEASLEY, nurse; b. Pontotoc, Miss., Sept. 17, 1925; d. William C. and Mary V. (Lyon) Beasley; children—Mary Wise, Marguerite Chapman, John D. Morgan, Sherrie Farley, Barbara Halberg. B.S., Calif. Bapt. Coll., 1972; student Miss. State Coll. for Women, 1943-44, George Peabody Coll., 1948; R.N., Bapt. Meml. Hosp. Sch. Nursing, Memphis, 1947. Cert. nurse practitioner, 1975. Staff nurse Riverside Community Hosp., Calif., 1955-57; head nurse Riverside Gen. Hosp., 1957-59; dir. student health service Calif. Bapt. Coll., 1961-76; dir. nurses Beverly Enterprises, Riverside, 1976-79; adult nurse practitioner Parkview Indsl. Sports Clinic, Riverside, 1979-84; R.N. charge nurse Warner Brown Hosp., El Dorado, Ark., 1984-87, Union Med. Ctr., 1987—. Charter mem. Presdl. Task Force, 1984; sustaining mem. Republican Nat. Com., 1984-86; tchr. Bible study East Main Bapt. Ch., El Dorado, 1985—, dir. women's missionary union, 1985—. Recipient awards Easter Seal Soc., Am. Heart Assn., Am. Lung Assn. Mem. Ark. Nurses Assn., Diploma Nurses Ark., Nat. Assn. Female Execs. Club: Altrusa. Avocations: reading; golf; civic work. Home: PO Box 1833 El Dorado AR 71731

MORGAN, TIMI SUE, lawyer; b. Parsons, Kans., June 16, 1953; d. James Daniel and Iris Mae (Wilson) Baumgardner; m. Rex Michael Morgan, Oct. 28, 1983; 1 child, Tessa Anne. BS, U. Kans., 1974; JD, So. Meth. U., 1977. Bar: Tex. 1977, U.S. Dist. Ct. (no. dist.) Tex. 1978, U.S. Ct. Appeals (5th cir.) 1979, U.S. Tax Ct. 1980. Assoc. Gardere & Wynne, Dallas, 1977-79; assoc. Akin, Gump, Strauss, Hauer & Feld, Dallas, 1979-83, ptnr., 1984-86; of counsel Stinson, Mag & Fizzell, Dallas, 1986—. Mem. Dallas Symphony Orchestra League Innovators; bd. dirs. Dallas Urban League Inc. Mem. State Bar Tex., Dallas Bar Assn., Tex. Young Lawyers Assn., Dallas Assn. Young Lawyers, So. Meth. U. Law Alumni Council (sec. 1985-86), Order of Coif, Beta Gamma Sigma. Republican. Episcopalian. Home: 3416 Amherst Dallas TX 75225 Office: Stinson Mag & Fizzell 4000 Lincoln Plaza 500 N Akard Dallas TX 75201

MORGAN, WANDA BERNICE BUSBY, health science facility administrator; b. Cromwell, Okla., Aug. 27, 1930; d. Charles C. and Gladys J. (Beaty) Busby; m. James O. Morgan, Oct. 23, 1954; children: Terri, Kathleen, Martha. BA, Lincoln (Ill.) Christian Coll., 1954; MA, Kans. State U., 1973; postgrad., Cen. State U., Edmond, Okla., 1976-78, U. Okla., 1980-84; posrgrad., Purdue U., 1983. Prof. Manhattan (Kans.) Christian Coll., Lincoln, 1970-74, Bethany (Okla.) Nazarene Coll., 1981-84; instr. Moravian Coll., Bethlehem, Pa., 1984-85, Allentown Coll., Center Valley, Pa., 1985—; edn. coordinator Sacred Heart Health Care System, Allentown, Pa., 1985-87, v.p., 1987—; cons. Communication Arts, Ltd., Allentown, 1978—; advisor Okla. Dept. Edn., Oklahoma City, 1981; tchr., cons. U. Okla. Dept. Edn., Norman, 1980—, Okla. Writing Project, 1980—. Author: Bridging the English Gap, 1983; co-author: Grammar, Ltd., 1983. Mem. adv. bd. Lehigh County (Pa.) Human Services Dept., 1986—. Fellow U. Okla., 1980. Mem. Am. Soc. for Healthcare Edn. and Tng., Okla Council Tchrs. of English (v.p. coll. sect. 1983-84). Democrat. Episcopalian. Home: 3547 Pleasant Ave Allentown PA 18103 Office: Sacred Heart Hosp 421 Chew St Allentown PA 18102

MORGAN-JOHNSTON, CHERYL DIANNA, data processing specialist; b. St. Louis, Apr. 27, 1959; d. Joseph and Evelyn (Hardy) Morgan; m. Charles Anthony Johnston, June 12, 1982. BA in Maths., U. Mo., St. Louis, 1981; cert. in Artifical Intelligence, Washington U., St. Louis, 1988. Asst. staff mgr. Southwestern Bell Telephone Co., St. Louis, 1982-85; tech. specialist McDonnell Aircraft Co., St. Louis, 1985—. Contbr. articles profl. mags., 1986-87. Asst. musician Jerusalem Missionary Bapt. Ch., St. Louis, 1973—; vol. Frair Communications Ctrs. Mem. Nat. Assn. Female Execs., Cen. Computer Communications Monitor (v.p. 1987), St. Louis IBM Personal Computer User's Group, Profl. Spl. Interest Group. Democrat. Home: 804 N Hills Dr Saint Louis MO 63121-2451

MORGENTHAL, BECKY HOLZ, computer service company owner; b. Altadena, Calif., Aug. 5, 1947; d. E. William and Elizabeth (DeLong) Holz; m. Roger Mark Morgenthal, Aug. 12, 1972. AA, Goldey Beacom Coll., 1967; student, Wilson Coll., 1986—. Clk. Hercules, Inc., Wilmington, Del., 1969-71; acct. Beth Products, Lebanon, Pa., 1971-72; adminstrv. asst. Legal Services, Inc., Carlisle, Pa., 1973-76; office mgr. CEMI Corp., Carlisle, 1976-77; acct. Tressler Luth. Services, Camp Hill, Pa., 1978-79, Benatec Assocs., Inc., Camp Hill, 1979-82; fin. analyst Electronic Data Systems, Camp Hill, 1983-87; owner B.H. Morgenthal Computer Services, Carlisle, 1982—. Pres. Carlisle Jr. Civic Club, 1979-80, v.p., 1978-79; active Diocese of Harrisburg, Pa., 1985—, chmn. pro-life com., 1988—; mem. Council of Cath. Women, Carlisle, 1986—. Republican. Home: 1311 Windsor Ct Carlisle PA 17013-3562

MORGENTHAU, JOAN ELIZABETH, physician; b. N.Y.C., Oct. 9, 1923; d. Henry and Elinor M.; A.B., Vassar Coll., 1945; M.D., Columbia U., 1949; m. Fred Hirschhorn, Jr., Oct. 6, 1957; children—Elizabeth, Joan, Elinor. Intern, Maimonides Hosp., Bklyn., 1949-50; resident N.Y. Hosp., 1950-54; instr., then asst. prof. pediatrics Cornell U. Med. Sch., 1954-67; dir. adolescent health center Mt. Sinai Hosp., N.Y.C., 1968-81, prof. clin. pediatrics, 1975-81; assoc. dean Mt. Sinai Sch. Medicine, 1976-81; professional lectr. pediatrics and community medicine, 1982—; dir. health service Smith Coll., Northampton, Mass., 1981—, adj. prof. psychology, 1981—. Trustee, Henry J. Kaiser Family Found., Vassar Coll. Mem. Am. Acad. Pediatrics, Am. Public Health Assn., Soc. Adolescent Medicine, Ambulatory Pediatrics Assn. Club: Cosmopolitan (N.Y.C.). Contbr. articles to profl. jours. Home: 55 Binney Ln Old Greenwich CT 06870 Office: 69 Paradise Rd Northampton MA 01060

MORIE, MARY ANN, non-profit administrator; b. Lee's Summit, Mo., Apr. 10, 1939; d. Philip Edson and Erma Lee (Gibson) Whiting; m. Gerald Prescott Morie, June 3, 1961; children: Christopher Scott, Gregory Vaughn, Bradley Ryan. BS in Edn., Cen. Mo. State U., 1961; postgrad., Ohio State U., 1961-65, Presbyn. Sch. of Christian Edn., 1981-82. Cert. dir. of Christian edn., elementary sch. tchr. Tchr. elem. Columbus Ohio Sch. System, 1961-65; dir. Christian edn. First Presbyn. Ch., Kingsport, Tenn., 1981-85; exec. dir. Vol. Kingsport, 1987—. Program dir. Dirs. of Vols. in Agys., Tenn., 1987—, Kingsport Social Services, 1987—, Vol.: The Nat. Ctr., Arlington, Va., 1987—; elder Waverly Rd. Presbyn. Ch., Kingsport, 1986—; pres. Kingsport PTA, 1980-87; cons. Serving People in Need, Church Hill, Tenn., 1987; bd. dirs. Waverly Rd. Day Care Ctr., adv. bd. Link House, 1987—; treas. Families and Community Together, 1985-87. Mem. Kingsport Jr. League. Democrat. Home: 4522 Mitchell Rd Kingsport TN 37664 Office: Vol Kingsport 1501 McCoy St Kingsport TN 37664

MORIMOTO, AKIKO CHARLENE, educator; b. Los Angeles, May 2, 1948; d. Satosu Don and Midori Jean (Ohira) M. B, Calif. State U., Los Angeles, 1971. Cert. secondary tchr., Calif., adult edn. tchr., Calif. Tchr. Los Angeles City Schs., 1972-77; instr. U. Calif., San Diego, summers 1983-85; tchr. Vista (Calif.) Unified Sch. Dist., 1977—; cons. San Diego Area Writing Project, La Jolla, Calif., 1981—; bd. dirs. Greater San Diego Council Tchrs. of English; table leader Calif. Assessment Program-Writing, San Diego, 1987—. Co-author: (with others) Foundations of Art Education, 1973; editor (dist. lit. mag.) Visions of Our Youth, 1986, 87. Mem. Old Globe Theatre, San Diego, 1985—. Named Vista Mentor Tchr. U. San Diego, 1985-88. Mem. Calif. Assn. Tchrs. of English, Assn. San Diego Educators of Gifted, Calif. Assn. of Gifted, Nat. Council Tchrs. of English, Nat. Writing Project, Greater San Diego Council Tchrs. English (Excellence in Classroom award 1988). Democrat. Home: 704 C-6 Regal Rd Encinitas CA 92024 Office: 740 Olive Ave Vista CA 92083

MORIN, CLAUDETTE, financial executive; b. Lewiston, Maine, Jan. 21, 1946; d. Albert Donat and Diane Clarice (Veilleux) M.; children: Malik Nevels, Baraka Nevels. Pre-med. student, Roosevelt U., 1970-71. Floor mgr. Brandt & Assocs., Chgo., 1978-86; v.p. First Options of Chgo., 1986—. Mem. Nat. Assn. Female Execs. Roman Catholic. Office: First Options of Chgo 440 S LaSalle Suite 1400 Chicago IL 60605

MORIN, NANCY RUTH, botanist; b. Albuquerque, N.Mex., Feb. 16, 1948; d. Seale E. Fuller and Nan (Dunford) Rearick; m. Jerome Morin, 1969 (div. 1971). AA, City Coll. of San Francisco, 1973; AB, U. Calif., Berkeley, 1975; PhD, U. Calif., 1980. Research/teaching asst. U. Calif., Berkeley, 1975-80; postdoctoral fellow Smithsonian Instn., Washington, 1980-81; editor Annals of the Mo. Bot. Garden, St. Louis, 1981-86; curator of herbarium Mo. Bot. Garden, St. Louis, 1981—, head dept. botany, 1981—, co-editor Herbarium News, 1981—; convening editor Flora of North Am. Project, St. Louis, 1983—; adj. prof. U. Mo., St. Louis, 1983—. NSF grantee, 1977-79. Mem. AAAS, Am. Inst. Biol. Scis., Am. Soc. Plant Taxonomists, Bot. Soc. Am., Internat. Assn. Plant Taxonomy, Mo. Native Plant Soc. (editor Missouriensis 1983-86), Phi Beta Kappa. Democrat. Home: 6035 Eitman Saint Louis MO 63139 Office: Mo Botanical Garden 2344 Shaw Blvd Saint Louis MO 63110

MORISATO, SUSAN CAY, actuary; b. Chgo., Feb. 11, 1955; d. George and Jessie (Fujita) M.; m. Thomas Michael Remec, Mar. 6, 1981. BS, U. Ill., 1975, MS, 1977. Actuarial student Aetna Life & Casualty, Hartford, Conn., 1977-79; actuarial asst. Bankers Life & Casualty, Chgo., 1979-80, asst. actuary, 1980-83, assoc. actuary, 1983-85, health product actuary, 1985-86, v.p., 1986—; participant individual forum Health Ins. Assn. Am., 1983. Fellow Soc. Actuaries; mem. Am. Acad. Actuaries, Health Ins. Assn. Am. Long Term Care Task Force, Chgo. Actuarial Assn. (sec. 1983-85, program com. 1987—), Phi Beta Kappa, Kappa Delta Pi, Phi Kappa Phi. Office: Bankers Life & Casualty Co 4444 W Lawrence Ave Chicago IL 60630

MORISSEAU, DOLORES SCHANNÉ, psychologist, government agency official; b. N.Y.C., Dec. 1, 1936; d. Lawrence Charles and Anne Lucy (Jelincic) Schanné; B.A. summa cum laude, George Mason U., 1978, M.A. in Psychology, 1980; m. Kenneth Clay Morisseau, May 3, 1958; children—Anne Lavita, Kenneth Clay. Stewardship editor Luth. Woman's Quarterly, St. Louis, 1969-75; mng. editor patient newsletter Georgetown U. Center for Continuing Health Edn., Washington, 1975, faculty moderator, 1974-75; instr. activated patient skills Nat. Public Broadcasting, 1975; fed. intern, personnel psychologist, U.S. Office Personnel Mgmt., Washington, 1979; lectr. psychology No. Va. Community Coll., Loudoun, 1981—; tng. and assessment specialist U.S. Nuclear Regulatory Commn., Washington, 1981—. Mem. Fairfax (Va.) Hosp., Aux., 1969-78, coordinator library service for patients, publicity chr., 1971-76. Mem. Am. Psychol. Assn., Human Factors Soc., AAUW, Alpha Chi, Psi Chi. Contbr. articles in field to profl. jours. Home: 11800 Breton Ct 32B Reston VA 22091

MORLEY, FAITH NOLLNER, realtor; b. Carthage, Tenn., Feb. 4, 1934; d. James and Carrie (Browning) Nollner; m. Ronald Britton Morley, May 23, 1957; children: Lisa, Regina Marie, Andrea Catherine. AB cum laude, Maryville Coll., 1956; MA in Teaching, Vanderbilt U., 1957; postgrad., Midwestern U., 1968; grad., Tex. Realtors Inst. Cert. residential specialist. Instr. Ricker Coll., Houlton, Maine, 1962-63, U. Md., Coll. Park, 1963-66, 74-77; pub. info. dir. Tex. Dept. Human Resources, Abilene, 1978-80; regional adminstr. Concepts of Care, Abilene, 1981-82; realtor Senter Realtors, Abilene, 1983-85, Re/Max Abilene, 1985—. Dir. U.S. Bicentennial Celebration San Vito dei Normanni Ari Sta., Brindisi, Italy, 1976; organizer, 1st chmn. Noah Project Women's Shelter, Abilene, 1980—; chmn. Abilene Centennial Parade Com., 1983. Mem. North Tex. Cert. Realtors, Abilene Bd. Realtors, Abilene Women's Club. Republican. Presbyterian. Office: Re/Max of Abilene 2481 S Danville Abilene TX 79605

MORONEY, LINDA LELIA SUSAN (MUFFIE), lawyer, educator; b. Washington, May 27, 1943; d. Robert Emmet and Jessie (Robinson) M.; m. Clarence Renshaw II, Mar. 28, 1967 (div. 1977); children: Robert Milnor, Justin W.R. BA, Randolph-Macon Woman's Coll., 1965; JD cum laude, U. Houston, 1982. Bar: Tex. 1982, U.S. Ct. Appeals (5th cir.) 1982, U.S. Dist. Ct. (so. dist.) Tex. 1982, U.S. Supreme Ct. 1988. Law clk. to assoc. justice 14th Ct. Appeals, Houston, 1982-83; assoc. Pannill and Reynolds, Houston, 1983-85, Gilpin, Pohl & Bennett, Houston, 1985—; adj. prof. law U. Houston, 1986—. Mem. ABA, State Bar of Tex., Houston Bar Assn., Order of the Barons, Phi Delta Phi. Episcopalian. Home: 3730 Overbrook Lane Houston TX 77027 Office: Gilpin Pohl & Bennett 1300 Post Oak Blvd Suite 2300 Houston TX 77056

MOROZE, LINDA GALVANI, insurance company executive; b. Stockton, Calif., Sept. 24, 1955; d. Benjamin Robert and Isabel Constance (Lopez) Galvani; m. Chester Moroze, Feb. 2, 1985. B.A. cum laude, U. Pacific, 1977; postgrad. Columbia U. Law Sch., 1986—. Broker's asst. Stockton Ins. Exchange, 1978-80; program coordinator I, West Ins. Mgrs., Stockton, 1980-81; corp. ins./employee benefits mgr. Am. Savs., Stockton, 1981-84; asst. risk mgr. Fin. Corp. Am., Los Angeles, 1984; asst. to risk mgr. N.Y. Times, 1984-85. Contbr. articles to profl. jours. Mem. Risk and Ins. Mgmt. Soc., Ins. Women of San Joaquin County (rec. sec. 1978, bull. chmn. 1980). Democrat. Buddhist.

MORPHEW, DOROTHY RICHARDS-BASSETT, artist, real estate broker; b. Cambridge, Mass., Aug. 4, 1918; d. George and Evangeline Booth (Richards) Richards; grad. Boston Art Inst., 1949; children—Jon Eric, Marc Alan, Dana Kimball. Draftsman, United Shoe Machinery Co., 1937-42; blueprinter, advt. artist A.C. Lawrence Leather Co., Peabody, Mass., 1949-51; propr. Studio Shop and Studio Potters, Beverly, Mass., 1951-53; tchr. ceramics and art, Kingston, N.H., 1953—; real estate broker, pres. 1965-81; two-man exhbn. Topsfield (Mass.) Library, 1960; owner, operator Ceramic Shop, West Stewartstown, N.H. Served with USNR, 1942-44. Recipient Profl. award New Eng. Ceramic Show, 1975; also numerous certificates in ceramics. Home: 557 Palomino Trail Englewood FL 34223 Studio: Intervale Rd York Cliffs ME 03910

MORPHOS, DIANE BELOGIANIS (MRS. PANOS PAUL MORPHOS), civic worker; b. Chgo.; d. Demetrios and Alice (Rousseas) Belogianis; B.S., U. Chgo., 1937, M.A., 1938; m. Panos Paul Morphos, Dec. 11, 1948; children—Evangeline, Paul. Mem. faculty U. Chgo. Orthogenic Sch., 1938-45, U. Chgo. Remedial Reading Clinics, 1945-48; vis. lectr. Tulane U., 1947. Bd. dirs. S.E. La. council Girl Scouts U.S.A., New Orleans, 1959-65, v.p., 1965-68, pres., 1968—; bd. dirs. AAUW, New Orleans, 1969, v.p., 1970-75, pres., 1975-80; Republican candidate for La. 2d Congl. Dist., 1974. Mem. Athenee Louisianais, France-Amerique. Mem. Greek Orthodox Ch. Home: 1404 Audubon St New Orleans LA 70118

MORR, HELEN YVONNE, small business owner; b. Middletown, Ohio, Sept. 4, 1938; d. Volnia Alexander and Dora Katherine (Gilbert) Gentry; m. Jack L. Phillips, Sept. 8, 1961 (div. Sept. 1972); 1 child, Karla Renae Spitzlel; m. Fred E. Morr, Nov. 20, 1973. Student, Middletown Bus. Coll., 1965-67, Mt. St. Joseph Coll., 1979. Office mgr. Congl. Office 24th Dist., Middletown, 1967-71, Ohio River Basin Commn., Cin., 1971-78; sec., treas. Continental Farm and Land Mgmt. Co., Cin., 1974—; co-owner F.E. & H.Y. Morr Ins. Co., Cin., 1978-85; dir. Molitor Loan and Bldg. Co., Cin., 1978-85; pres., record producer MoPro Records, Inc., Cin., 1981—; talent booker MoPro Midwest Booking Agy., Cin., 1987—. Producer numerous jazz albums. Field coordinator Lukens for Gov. campaign State of Ohio, 1970; hosp. vol. Womens Aux. St. Francis Hosp., Cin., 1980-81; campaign coordinator Morr for Congress, 1st Congl. Dist., 1986. Mem. Nat. Acad. Recording Arts and Sci., Internat. Assn. Jazz Record Collectors, Nat. Assn. Jazz Educators, Cin. Jazz Forum, Cin. Jazz Soc. Republican. Episcopalian. Clubs: Bankers, Western Hills Country (Cin.); Capital Hill (Washington). Home: 375 Compton Rd Cincinnati OH 45215 Office: MoPro Records Inc 2959 Kling Ave Cincinnati OH 45211

MORREALE, JANE M., foundation administrator; b. N.Y.C., Nov. 29, 1949; d. Anthony Vito and Jane Margaret (Mauro) Ruggiero; m. Charles Morreale, Nov. 21, 1976 (dec. June 1985); 1 child, Jena. AAS, Manhattan Community Coll., 1970; BBA, CUNY, 1976. Systems analyst/programmer Dept. Budget, City of N.Y., 1970-73; mgr. systems and programming Nat. Bd. YMCA's, N.Y.C., 1973-80; dir. info. systems Am. Cancer Soc., N.Y.C., 1980-88; asst. v.p. adminstrn. N.Y.C. and Atlanta, 1988—; lectr. in field. Mem. AMA. Office: Am Cancer Soc 90 Park Ave New York NY 10016

MORRELL, JAYNE ELLEN, municipal official; b. Milw., June 4, 1948; d. David Arthur and Lenore Lillian (Dretzka) M. BA in Sociology, U. Tex., Arlington, 1970, MA in Urban Studies, 1973. Research assoc. Ptnrs. in Career Edn., Arlington, 1972-77; adminstrv. asst. mgmt. services City of Dallas, 1977-78, adminstrv. asst. city mgr.'s office, 1978-81, mgr. spl. collections, 1981-82, mgr. tax collections, 1982-85, asst. dir., tax assessor/collector, 1985—; legislative lobby Tex. Mcpl. Leauge, Austin, 1987—. Mem. Internat. Assn. Assessing Officers, Tex. Assn. Assessing Officers (trustee State Bd., sec.-treas.North Tex. chpt. 1988), Tex. Assn. Mcpl. Tax Adminstrs., Nat. Assn. Female Execs., Assn. Women Execs. (v.p. 1985-86, 88-89). Democrat. Roman Catholic. Home: 3756 Kiest Valley Pkwy Dallas TX 75233 Office: City Dallas Dept Fin 1500 Marilla 2BS Dallas TX 75201

MORRELLI, RITA LORENE, sales executive; b. El Paso, Tex., July 30, 1960; d. George Wesley and Carol Antoinette (Bachechi) M.; m. David Paulsen, May 1, 1980 (Sept. 1984). Student, Va. Poly. U., 1986. Telemktg. agt. Coordinated Programming Ins., Costa Mesa, Calif., 1976-79; leasing agt. Airport Exec. Suites Inc., Newport Beach, Calif., 1979-81; food service broker C. Noblett & Assocs. Inc., Santa Ana, Calif., 1981-85; v.p. sales and mktg. Climax Insulated Bag Co., Plano, Tex., 1985—. Mem. Nat. Frozen Food Assn. (Golden Penguin award, 1987), Nat. Roundtable for Women in Foodservice (sec. Los Angeles chpt. 1985-86, v.p. Dallas chpt. 1986—), So. Calif. Deli Council, Dallas C. of C., Plano C. of C., Tex. Restaurant Assn. Republican. Roman Catholic. Clubs: Holiday Health, Balboa Ski. Office: Climax Insulated Bag 740 Ave F #301 Plano TX 75074

MORRICE, EILEEN, service executive; b. N.Y.C., Mar. 13, 1961. AS, Johnson and Wales Coll., Providence, R.I., 1981, cert. of mixology, 1982. Front desk agt., hotel internship instr. R.I. Inn/Johnson and Wales Coll., 1981-83; reservations mgr., food and beverage asst., personnel mgr. Hilton Inn, St. Petersburg Beach, Fla., 1983-85; front office mgr., catering service mgr. Comfort Inn, Dedham, Mass., 1985-87; asst. to gen. mgr. Crowne Plaza Holiday Inn, Natick, Mass., 1987—. Roman Catholic. Home: 138 Wilson St Norwood MA 02062 Office: Crowne Plaza Holiday Inn 1360 Worcester St Natick MA 01760

MORRIN, VIRGINIA WHITE, educator; b. Escondido, Calif., May 16, 1913; d. Harry Parmalee and Ethel Norine (Nutting) Rising; B.S., Oreg. State Coll., 1952; M.Ed., Oreg. State U., 1957; m. Raymond Bennett White,

1933 (dec. 1953); children: Katherine Anne, Marjorie Virginia, William Raymond; m. 2d, Laurence Morrin, 1959 (dec. 1972). Social caseworker Los Angeles County, Los Angeles, 1934-40, 61-64; acctg. clk. War Dept., Ft. MacArthur, Calif., 1940-42; prin. clk. USAAF, Las Vegas, Nev., 1942-44; high sch. tchr., North Bend-Coos Bay, Oreg., 1952-56, Mojave, Calif., 1957-60; instr. Antelope Valley Coll., Lancaster, Calif., 1961-73; ret., 1974. Treas., Humane Soc. Antelope Valley, Inc., 1968—. Mem. Nat. Aero. Assn., Calif. State Sheriffs' Assn. (charter assoc.), Oreg. State U. Alumni Assn. (life). Mailing: 3153 Milton Dr Mojave CA 93501

MORRIS, AURELIA LOUISE, auditor; b. Cin., Dec. 25, 1956; d. Fredward and Louisa Marjorie (Bonner) M.; m. Johnny E. Roberts, May 21, 1988; children: Dion Dici Thornton, Desire Louise. BS, Ohio State U., 1979. Br. auditor BancOne Corp., Columbus, Ohio, 1979-81; statis. clk. Warner Cable Community, Inc., Cin., 1983-84; sr. auditor Soc. Bank Corp., Dayton, Ohio, 1984-86; auditor Union Fed Savs. Bank (name formerly Community Fed. Savs. Assn.), Hamilton, Ohio, 1986—. Democrat. Baptist. Home: 802 Burns Ave Wyoming OH 45215 Office: Union Fed Savs Bank 445 Main St Hamilton OH 45013

MORRIS, BERNADETTE REGINA, personnel director; b. Bklyn., Dec. 16, 1952; d. James Francis and Agnes (Morell) M. BA in English, U. Colo., Denver, 1976. Adminstr. employee relations Cen. Bank Denver, 1976-79; mgr. corp. personnel Beverage Distbn. Corp., Denver, 1979-83; adminstr. human resources grocery products div. Beatrice Food Co., Nashville, 1984-85; dir. human resources Beatrice Cos. doing bus. as Frozen Spltys. Inc., Archbold, Ohio, 1985—, Beatrice Cos. doing bus. as Pet Spltys. Inc., Nashville, 1985—; cons. Command Fin. Services, Nashville, 1986. Mem. Nashville YMCA; hon. mem. King Bees Pvt. Businessmen's Fund Raising for Charity, Denver, 1980-82; chmn. Colo. State-Employers Job Service council, 1979. Recipient Gov.'s award Employers-CETA Program Colo. Dept. Labor, 1978. Mem. Am. Soc. Tng. and Devel., Am. Soc. Personnel Adminstrs., Nashville Assn. Personnel Adminstrs. Roman Catholic.

MORRIS, CAROLINE JANE MCMASTERS STEWART (MRS. FRANCIS J. MORRIS), librarian; b. Ridley Park, Pa., Sept. 14, 1923; d. James Sterrett and Mildred M. (McCloskey) Stewart; BS in Commerce, Drexel U., 1950, MLS, 1964; m. Francis Joseph Morris, Feb. 3, 1951; 1 son, Edward James. Adminstrv. trainee John Wanamaker, Phila., 1946-50; serials librarian Penn Morton Colls., Chester, Pa., 1964-65; dir. libraries and archives Pa. Hosp., Phila., 1965—; cons., 1970—; instr., leader several library workshops Am. Hosp. Assn., Cath. Hosp. Assn., Med. Library Assn. Mem. Emergency Aid Pa., 1960—. Served with WAVES, 1943-45. Mem. ALA, AAUP, AAUW, Nat. Med. Library Assn. (sect. chmn. 1970 pres. local chpt. 1978—), Spl. Libraries Assn., Med. (local chpt. pres. 1969-70), Prospect Park library assns., D. of R. (pres. Pa. 1947—), Victorian Soc. Am., Soc. Am. Archivists, Manuscript Soc., Delaware County Hist. Soc., Hist. Delaware County, Soc. Preservation Landmarks, Hist. Soc. Pa., Oral Hist. Soc., Geneol. Soc. Pa., Hort. Soc. Pa., Dames Loyal Legion (state pres. 1966-68), Phila. Mus. Art, Am. Assn. Records Mgrs., Am. Soc. Profl. and Exec. Women, Drexel U. Alumni Assn. (pres. 1969-71). Club: Art Alliance (Phila). Home: 1553 Schiavello Dr Swarthmore PA 19081 Office: Pa Hosp 8th and Spruce Sts Philadelphia PA 19107

MORRIS, CHRISTINA MARIA LINDBERG, law firm executive; b. Vansbro, Sweden, Jan. 10, 1950; came to U.S., 1975; d. Charles George and Britt Maria (Larsson) Lindberg; m. Jack W. Morris, Nov. 23, 1975; children: Jason, Charlie. Bachelors in econs., Norrkoping U., 1970; MBA in Civil Econs., Uppsala (Sweden) U., 1974. Mgr. fin. services Mills, Shirley, Eckel & Bassett, Galveston, Tex., 1977—. Mem. Assn. Legal Adminstrs., State Bar Tex. (charter mem. #59 legal adminstrn. div.), Nat. Assn. Female Execs., Bus. and Profl. Women Orgn., Swedish Women's Ednl. Assn. Lutheran. Clubs: Gulf Coast Scandinavian, Swedish (Houston). Home: 815 13th St Galveston TX 77550 Office: Mills Shirley Eckel & Bassett 2228 Mechanic Galveston TX 77550

MORRIS, CHRISTINE COALSON, financial services executive; b. Orange, Calif., Dec. 24, 1952; d. Coalson Clyde and Jessie Jean (Crawford) M. BS, U. Utah, 1975; postgrad., Loma Linda (Calif.) U., 1975-77. Corp. sec. Jefcol, Laguna Beach, Calif., 1977-79, N. Laguna Fin., Laguna Beach, 1979-81, Perry Morris Corp., Newport Beach, Calif., 1981-82; v.p. Perry Morris Corp., Newport Beach, 1982-83, exec. v.p., 1983-88; with U. So. Calif. Assocs., Los Angeles, 1988—. Mem. Found. Christian Living, Pauling, N.Y., 1984-88; corp. sponsor Fine Arts Mus. of San Francisco, 1988; sponsor Spl. Olympics, Orange County, Calif., 1988. Mem. San Francisco C. of C., San Jose C. of C., Western Assn. Equipment Lessors, Am. Assn. Equipment Lessors, Delta Gamma. Republican. Presbyterian. Club: Primetime Athletic (Burlingame, Calif.). Office: Perry Morris Corp 2929 Campus Dr Suite 350 San Mateo CA 94403

MORRIS, CRYSTAL LEFTWICH, accountant; b. Bedford, Va., Sept. 27, 1954; d. Paul W. and Lorraine (Holdren) Leftwich; m. Steve A. Morris, July 15, 1977; 1 child, Charlie P. II. AAS magna cum laude, Cen. Va. Community Coll., 1974; BS cum laude, Lynchburg Coll., 1982. Dir. acctg. Lynchburg (Va.) Coll., 1982-85; staff acct. Dalton, Pennell & Co. CPAs, Lynchburg, 1986; dir. acctg. Westminster-Canterbury, Lynchburg, 1986—. Treas. Altrusa Club Lynchburg, 1984. Mem. Gold Key Honor Soc. Methodist. Home: Route 4 Box 272 Forest VA 24551 Office: Westminster-Canterbury 501 VES Rd Lynchburg VA 24503

MORRIS, ELIZABETH TREAT, physical therapist; b. Hartford, Conn., Feb. 20, 1936; d. Charles Wells and Marion Louise (Case) Treat; B.S. in Phys. Therapy, U. Conn., 1960; m. David Breck Morris, July 10, 1961; children—Russell Charles, Jeffrey David. Phys. therapist Crippled Children's Clinic No. Va., Arlington, 1960-62, Shriners Hosp. Crippled Children, Salt Lake City, 1967-69, Holy Cross Hosp., Salt Lake City, 1970-74; pvt. practice phys. therapy, Salt Lake City, 1975—. Mem. Am. Phys. Therapy Assn., Am. Congress Rehab. Medicine, Salt Lake Area C. of C., Friendship Force Utah, U.S. Figure Skating Assn. Home: 4177 Mathews Way Salt Lake City UT 84124 Office: 2178 So 900 East Suite 3 Salt Lake City UT 84106

MORRIS, EMMA WARD, marketing executive; b. Lafayette, Ind., Sept. 6, 1952; d. Curtis Howard and Charlotte Berkley (Reed) Ward; m. John Harry Morris, Jr., Sept. 12, 1975. Student Sorbonne, Paris, 1972-73; BA in French cum laude, Emory U., 1974; MBA in Mktg., U. S.C., 1976. Tchr. math. and French, Ashley Hall Sch., Charleston, S.C., 1975-76; systems engr. IBM Corp. Columbia, S.C., 1976-79, mktg. rep., Charleston, 1979-81; v.p. mktg. Cambar Bus. Systems, Charleston, 1981-83; sr. mgr. mgmt. cons. Ernst & Whinney, Atlanta, 1983-85; dir. industry mktg. Mgmt. Sci. Am., Inc., Atlanta, 1985-87, v.p. mktg., 1987—; co-owner, pres. Computer Catch Up, Charleston, 1982-83. Mem. industry adv. bd. U. Ga., 1983—; adv. bd. Charleston County Vocat. Edn., 1981-83. Named Young Career Woman of Yr., Bus. and Profl. Women Charleston, 1981. Mem. Assn. Systems Mgrs., Assn. Small Computer Users (com. chmn.), Bus. and Profl. Women (pres. 1982-83), Atlanta C. of C., Nat. Assn. Elec. Distbrs. (chmn. nat. EDP fair com. 1982-83). Republican. Baptist. Avocations: sailing, traveling, handcrafts, camping, singing. Home: 3791 Ridge Rd Smyrna GA 30080 Office: 3445 Peachtree Rd NE Atlanta GA 30326

MORRIS, JACQUELYN MCCOY, university library administrator; b. Columbus, Ohio, June 14, 1942; d. Donald Richard and Jeanne (Clark) McCoy; m. Richard David Morris, Mar. 19, 1960; children: Patricia A., Michelle A. BA cum laude, Syracuse U., 1971, MS in Library Sci., 1972. Asst. librarian SUNY, Syracuse, 1972-79; head reference div. Albert Mann Library, Cornell U., Ithaca, N.Y., 1979-82; assoc. dean of library U. Pacific, Stockton, Calif., 1982-86; library dir. Occidental Coll., Los Angeles, 1986—; dir. N.Y. Libraries Instructional Clearinghouse, SUNY, Syracuse, 1974-79; cons. U.S. Presdl. Council Environ. Quality, 1980. Author: Library Searching—Research and Strategies, 1978, Teaching Library Skills for Academic Credit, 1985, ACRL College Library Standards, 1986. Bd. dirs Tierra del Oro council Girl Scouts N.Am., cen. Calif., 1985-86. Recipient Chancellors award, SUNY, 1978. Mem. Am. Library Assn. (chmn. com.), Calif. Library Assn., AAAS, 49/99 (mem. exec. council, bd. dirs. 1984-86), Phi Alpha Theta, Beta Phi Mu. Office: Occidental Coll MN Clapp Library 1600 Campus Rd Los Angeles CA 90041

MORRIS, JANINE INEZ, marketing executive; b. Hampton, Va., June 1, 1956; d. Owen Glenn and Moree (Glover) M.; m. Kerry James Comeaux; 1 child, Kyle Jarrett. BS, Tex. A&M U., 1978. Programmer, analyst St. Luke's Episcopal Hosp., Houston, 1978-79; systems analyst Exxon Chemical, Houston, 1979-81; advanced systems specialist United Gas Pipeline, Houston, 1981-84, supr. human resource info., 1984-86, supr. compensation and human resource info., 1986-87, supr. benefits, 1987-88; supr. contract adminstrn. LASER Mktg. Co., Houston, 1988—. Capt. United Way campaign, Houston, 1985, 86; com. mem. St. Giles Presbyn. Ch., Houston, 1987; sec. Oaks of Inwood Civic Assn., Houston, 1987. Named Outstanding Woman of Yr. Houston YWCA's, 1986. Mem. Am. Mgmt. Assn., Am. Compensation Assn., Human Resource Systems Profls. Office: United Gas Pipeline PO Box 1478 Houston TX 77001

MORRIS, JULIA ANN, banker; b. Chgo., Sept. 11, 1956; d. John and Emily (Coffee) M. AA, Oliver-Harvey Coll., Chgo., 1976. Sr. investigator Continental Ill. Nat. Bank of Chgo., 1974—. Home: 901 E 104th St Apt C227 Chicago IL 60628 Office: Continental Ill Nat Bank Chgo 231 S LaSalle Chicago IL 60693

MORRIS, KRISTINE ANNE, executive recruiter; b. Lynn, Mass., Apr. 26, 1954; d. Edward Austin and Vivian Muriel (Fuhrer) M. AB in German summa cum laude, Occidental Coll., 1981. Owner, operator Comml. Fisherperson, San Francisco, 1974-75; assoc. dir. Occidental Coll., Los Angeles, 1981-83; dir. Search Assocs., Inc., Sherman Oaks, Calif., 1983-84; v.p., ptnr. Paul Cowen Assocs., Pasadena, Calif., 1984—. Mem. Tounament of Roses Assn., Pasadena, Pasadena Heritage, Pasadena Hist. Soc., Town Hall of Calif., Los Angeles, Occidental Coll. Pres.'s Circle. Mem. Calif. Exec. Recruiter's Assn., Pasadena C. of C., Phi Beta Kappa. Office: Paul Cowen Assocs 100 S Los Robles Ave #420 Pasadena CA 91101

MORRIS, LOIS LAWSON, educator; b. Antoine, Ark., Nov. 27, 1914; d. Oscar Moran and Dona Alice (Ward) Lawson; m. William D. Morris, July 2, 1932 (dec.); 1 child, Lavonne Morris Howell. B.A., Henderson U., 1948; M.S., U. Ark., 1951, M.A., 1966; postgrad. U. Colo., 1954, Am. U., 1958, U. N.C., 1968. History tchr. Delight High Sch., Ark., 1942-47; counselor Huntsville Vocat. Sch., 1947-48; guidance dir. Russellville Pub. Sch. System, Ark., 1948-55; asst. prof. edn. U. Ark., Fayetteville, 1955-82, prof. emeritus, 1982—; ednl. cons. Ark. Pub. Schs., 1965-78. Mem. Commn. on Needs for Women, 1976-78; pres. Washington County Hist. Soc., 1983-84. Named Ark. Coll. Tchr. of Year, 1972; recipient Plaque for outstanding services to Washington County Hist. Soc., 1984. Mem. Ark. Council Social Studies (sec.-treas.), Washington County Hist. Soc. (exec. bd. 1977-80), NEA, Nat. Council Social Studies, Ark. Edn. Assn., Ark. Hist. Assn., AAUW, U. Ark. Alumni Assn., LWV, Phi Delta Kappa, Kappa Delta Pi, Phi Alpha Theta. Democrat. Episcopalian. Address: 1601 W 3d St Russellville AR 72801

MORRIS, LUMMIE DENE, business manager; b. Elbert, Tex., Sept. 4, 1931; d. Conley Clarence and Lora Alma (Fulton) Smith; student St. Marys U., 1968-70; m. Edwin J. Morris, Sept. 15, 1955 (dec.); children—Robin Dee, Atiyeh, Tracy Lee Morris Hair. Instr. interior design St. Marys U., San Antonio, evenings, 1970-71; asst. dir. Faye Neri Modeling Studio, San Antonio, 1970-72; interior designer, San Antonio, 1972-77; v.p. Communications Services, Inc., San Antonio, 1977-79, pres., 1984—; gen. mgr. Nat. Electric Corp., San Antonio, 1979-80; mgr. trucking div. Agribusiness Services, Inc., San Antonio, 1981-83; v.p. Morton & Assocs., Inc., 1984—; lectr. San Antonio high schs. Coordinator family services program USAF, Zweibruecken, W. Ger., 1968. Mem. Internat. Guild Accredited Interior Designers, Beta Sigma Phi. Republican. Mem. Ch. of Christ. Home: 1983 Oakwell Farms Pkwy #1807 San Antonio TX 78218 Office: 4850 Whirlwind San Antonio TX 78217

MORRIS, LYNNE LOUISE, psychotherapist; b. Youngstown, Ohio, Nov. 5, 1946; d. Richard Davies and Elsie Margaret Raymond) B.A., Westminster Coll., Pa., 1969; MSW, NYU, 1971. Cert. clin. social worker. Social worker Community Service Soc., N.Y.C., 1971-74, Altro Health and Rehab. Services, Inc., N.Y.C., 1974-79; field instr. Hunter Coll. Sch. Social Work, NYU Grad Sch. Social Work, 1974-79; clin. coordinator Montefiore Hosp. and Med. Center, Bronx, N.Y., 1979-81; asst. dir. II, social service dept. Montefiore Hosp., Bronx, 1981-83; pvt. practice psychotherapy, N.Y.C., 1976—; sr. staff therapist Counseling and Human Devel. Center, N.Y.C., 1979—. Contbr. articles of profl. jours. including Jour. Geriatric Psychiatry, 1975; abstractor Abstracts for Social Workers, 1975. Fellow N.Y. State Soc. Clin. Social Work Psychotherapists; mem. Nat. Assn. Social Workers (clin. diplomate), Acad. Cert. Social Workers, Am. Assn. Pastoral Counselors (profl. affiliate). Mem. profl. adv. com. Cary Addis Meml. Found. Home and office: 161 W 75th St 2C New York NY 10023

MORRIS, MARGARET ELIZABETH, marketing professional; b. N.Y.C., Nov. 1, 1962; d. John Daniel and Jean Bingham (MacCollom) M. BA in English, Georgetown U., 1984. Mem. staff mktg. programs AT&T Nat. Fed. Mktg., Arlington, Va., 1985; mktg. tech. cons. AT&T Fed. Systems, Washington, 1985-87; technical cons. computer mktg. Cin. Bell Telephone Co., Ohio, 1987—. Editor: (newsletter) District Action Project RAP, 1981-82. Intern Citizen's Complaint Ctr., Washington, 1981-82. Mem. Nat. Network of Women in Sales (Cin. chpt. hotel liaison), Data Processing Mgmt. Assn. (student chpt. liaison), Nat. Assn. Female Execs., Healthcare Fin. Mgmt. Assn. Club: Women's City (Cin.). Lodge: Soroptimist Internat. Office: Cincinnati Bell Telephone Co 201 E 4th St Room 102-1115 Cincinnati OH 45202

MORRIS, MARNA JAY, public relations executive; b. Amityville, N.Y., Sept. 14, 1949; d. Theodore Sylvan and Bernice Rose (Plotnick) Berusch; m. Joel Rosenstock, Aug. 28, 1971 (div. Sept. 1978); children: Scott Adam, Todd Stuart; m. James L. Morris III, Aug. 9, 1985. BA in Edn., SUNY, Cortland, 1970; postgrad., U. Louisville, 1979-81. Tchr. Mid. Country Pub. Schs., Centereach, N.Y., 1970-71, St. John's English Sch., Brussels, 1971-76, Luhr Elementary Sch., Louisville, 1978-80, Seneca High Sch., Louisville, 1980-83; pres. Star Drive Inc., Louisville, 1983—; free-lance writer Louisville, 1983—; v.p. M.J. Morris Inc., Louisville, 1985—; mng. ptnr. Sports Ventures, Inc., 1987—, Sportsfare, Inc., 1987—; cons. Remmers & Victor Inc., Louisville, 1985—. Contbr. articles to profl. jours. Bd. dirs. Cain Ctr. for Disabled, Louisville, 1986—; spl. dep. Jefferson County Police Dept., Louisville, 1984-86; vol. sta. WHAS Crusade for Children, Louisville, 1980—. Mem. Nat. Assn. Female Execs., Nat. Writers Club, Country Music Assn., Entrepreneur Soc. Democrat. Jewish. Office: MJ Morris Inc Box 22413 Louisville KY 40224

MORRIS, MARSHA RENEE, real estate owner; b. Cordell, Okla., Aug. 1, 1951; d. Leslie and Frankie Mae (Flaming) Hinds; m. Gary Thomas Morris, May 28, 1971; children: Justin Lance, Kyle Derek. Student, Southwestern State U., Weatherford, Okla., 1969-71, Okla. State U., 1986—. Agent/assoc. Red Carpet Realtors, Stillwater, Okla., 1976-77; personnel asst. Equitable Life Ins. Co., Stillwater, 1977-80; spl. agt. Northwestern Mut. Life Ins., Stillwater, 1980-84; co-owner G.M. Mgmt., Stillwater, 1984—. Previously fund raiser for Am. Heart Assn., Am. Cancer Soc. Stillwater; treas. Stillwater Apt. Assn., 1985-86, v.p., 1986-87, pres., 1988—. Mem. Nat. Apt. Assn. (pres.'s council 1988), Okla. Real Estate Bd., Nat. Life Underwriters Assn., Stillwater Life Underwriters Assn. Republican. Mem. Ch. of Christ. Club: Stillwater Gymnastics. Home: 1615 Celia Ln Stillwater OK 74074 Office: GM Mgmt Inc 2222 W 12th Stillwater OK 74074

MORRIS, MARY SUE, real estate investor, developer; b. Wichita Falls, Tex., Oct. 5, 1938; d. William Willard and Ruth (Maxey) Gibson; m. Bill Morris, 1972 (div. 1985). Student, Okla. U., 1956-57; BBA, So. Methodist U., Dallas, 1960; student, NYU, 1981-84. V.p. mktg. Paragon Industries, Inc., Dallas, 1960-64; dir. pub. relations and advt. Haggar Slacks, Dallas, 1964-67; dir. women's sales Am. Airlines, N.Y.C., 1968-72; cons. mgmt. constrn. and mktg. Unit, Inc., Columbus, Ohio, Lexington, Ky., 1972-74; developer The Left Bank, Cin., 1974-81; owner, mgr. Tennis Is My Racket, Cin., 1974-81; owner, developer Amanda, Cin., 1977-81; head of real estate devel. Cumberland, Inc., N.Y.C., 1981-84; pres. founder The Sheridan Group, N.Y.C., 1984—. Bd. dirs. Contemporary Art Council, Cin., 1974; mem. Mayor's Council, Cin., 1981. Mem. Pi Beta Phi. Methodist. Clubs: Town Tennis, City, West Side Tennis, University. Home: 1 Sheridan Sq PH-N New York NY 10014 Office: The Sheridan Group In 444 Madison Ave New York NY 10022

MORRIS, MIRANDA JANE, outdoor advertising company executive; b. Hinesville, Ga., Sept. 17, 1957; d. Stanley Lewis and Juanita (Brockman) Sexton; divorced; 1 child, Nathaniel Ryan. BA, U. Ky., 1979. Cert. elem. tchr., Ky. Spa technician, asst. mgr. 21st Century Health Spa, Louisville, 1981; staff counselor Physician's Weight Loss Ctr., Middletown, Ohio, 1981; sales rep. Louisville Automobile Club of AAA, 1982; asst. mgr. Lerner Shops, Inc., Louisville, 1982; asst. dir. Fun Skool and Gagel Elem. Sch., Louisville, 1983—; kindergarten tchr. Louisville, 1984; sales rep. Columbia Sussex Corp., Louisville, 1984-86; account exec. Naegele Outdoor Advt., Louisville, 1986—. Active Jullian Carroll for Gov. Campaign, 1987; publicity chmn. Wheeler Sch. PTA, Louisville, 1986-87, 2d v.p., 1987. Named hon. capt. Mayor of Louisville, 1986; named to Hon. Order Ky. Cols. Mem. Nat. Assn. Female Execs. Democrat. Mem. Christian Church (Disciples of Christ). Home: 10801 Cherry Grove Ct Louisville KY 40299 Office: Naegele Outdoor Advt 1501 Lexington Rd Louisville KY 40207

MORRIS, NANCY MITCHELL, research chemist; b. Griffin, Ga., Jan. 9, 1940; d. Roy Eugene and Winifred Florence (Puckett) Mitchell; m. Cletus Eugene Morris, June 5, 1962; 1 child, Kendall Eugene. AB in Chemistry, LaGrange Coll., Ga., 1960; MS, Auburn U., Ala., 1964. Chemist, West Point-Pepperell, Shawmut, Ala., 1964-65; chemist So. Regional Research Ctr., USDA, New Orleans, 1966-72, research chemist plant products analysis research, 1972-76, indsl. environ. health research, 1982-85, composition and properties research, 1985—. Contbr. articles to profl. publs, chpt. to book. Mem. Am. Chem. Soc. (treas. La. sect. 1987, 88), Am. Assn. Textile Chemist and Colorists (sec. gulf coast sect. 1978-79), Soc. Applied Spectroscopy (sec. La. sect. 1984-86, sec.-treas. 1986-87, chmn.-elect 1987-88, chmn. 1988—), Orgn. Profl. Employees of Dept. Agrl. (v.p. 1983, pres. 1984), Sigma Xi (treas. New Orleans chpt. 1981-82, sec. 1986-87, pres.-elect 1987-88, pres. 1988—). Methodist. Office: So Regional Research Ct PO Box 19687 1100 Robert E Lee Blvd New Orleans LA 70179

MORRIS, SANDRA RHEA, elementary educator; b. Blue Ridge, Tex., July 2, 1949; d. William Marshel and Lena Marie (Braswell) M.; m. Jack Watson Dana, July 15, 1972 (div. Aug. 1975). BS, Tex. Wesleyan Coll., 1971; M in Early Childhood Edn., E. Tex. State U., 1977. Cert. elem. sch. tchr., Tex. Elem. tchr. St. Rita's Cath. Sch., Ft. Worth, 1970-71; kindergarten tchr. La Petite Acad., Arlington, Tex., 1971-72, Community I.S.D., Nevada, Tex., 1973—; dir. All God's Children Learning, Farmersville, Tex., 1986, Little Brave Day Care, Nevada, 1987. Mem. NEA, Tex. State Tchrs. Assn., Kindergarten Tchrs. Tex., Tex. Elem., Kindergarten, and Nursery Educators, Gamma Sigma Sigma. Republican. Baptist. Office: Community ISD Box 400 Nevada TX 75073

MORRIS, SUSAN ELIZABETH, computer company administrator; b. Louisville, Jan. 10, 1952; d. Adam and Agnes Bertha (Huber) M.; B.S. in Commerce, U. Louisville, 1978. Paralegal law firm Wyatt, Grafton & Sloss, Louisville, 1973-79; systems installer HBO & Co., Inc., San Mateo, Calif., 1979-81; systems specialist Whittaker Medicus, Evanston, Ill., 1981-83; product installation mgr. Computer Synergy, Inc., Oakland, Calif., 1983; adv. analyst, mgr. Shared Med. Systems, Oakland, 1983-88, mgr. mktg. support, 1988—. Active Third Century, Louisville, 1978-79. Mem. Bus. and Profl. Women's Assn., NOW, Ky. Hist. Soc., U. Louisville Alumni Assn., U.S. Capital Hist. Soc., Greenpeace, Internat. Platform Assn., Calif. Hist. Soc., Sierra Club; Louisville Preservation Alliance. Democrat. Roman Catholic. Club: Filson. Home: 325 Kitty Hawk Rd #201 Alameda CA 94501

MORRIS, SUSAN MCDONALD, financial institution executive; b. Orange, Calif., Mar. 1, 1946; d. Coalson Clyde and Jesse Jean (Crawford) Morris; B.A., U. So. Calif., 1968. Press sec. Orozco for Congress, 1968; coordinator field services U. So. Calif., Los Angeles, 1969; dir. donor relations U. So. Calif., 1971, dir. event planning from 1976; pres., owner McDonald Morris & Assocs., Inc., Los Angeles, 1981-85; v.p. Perry Morris Corp., Newport Beach, Calif., 1985—. Mem. Los Angeles World Affairs Council, Town Hall Calif. Republican. Presbyterian. Club: Los Angeles Athletic. Home: 438 Goldenrod Corona Del Mar CA 92625 also: 438 Goldenrod Corona Del Mar CA 92625 also: PO Box 54123 Los Angeles CA 90054

MORRIS, SUSAN STEERS, service executive; b. Detroit, Dec. 24, 1929; d. Philip John and Lucille (Garvie) Steers; divorced; children: Steven C., Sandra L., Scott W., Bradley A., Vivian G. BS, Tex. Christian U., 1950. Pres. The Idea House, Inc., Baton Rouge, 1966-76; sales rep. Bekins Van Lines, Baton Rouge, 1977-80; pres. Career Cons., Inc., Baton Rouge, 1980-83, So. Comfort Bed and Breakfast Reservation Service, Baton Rouge, 1983—; exec. dir. Bed and Breakfast Reservation Services Worldwide, Inc. Trade Assn., Baton Rouge, 1985—; pres. Person to Person Travel Prodns., Inc., Baton Rouge, 1985—; organized first Mardi Gras Krewe of Phoenix, Ariz., 1987. Recipient Order of the Pelican, La. Dept. Tourism, 1987. Republican. Methodist.

MORRIS, SYLVIA MARIE, administrative manager; b. Laurel, Miss., May 6, 1952; d. Earlene Virginia (Cameron) Stewart; m. James D. Morris, Jan. 29, 1972; children: Cedric James, Taedra Janae. Student, U. Utah, 1970-71. From adminstrv. sec. to adminstrv. mgr. mech. and indsl. engring. U. Utah, Salt Lake City, 1972—. Mem. Community Devel. Adv. Bd., Salt Lake City, Utah, 1984—; nom. chmn. and del. to Dem. Mass Meeting, 1988. Mem. NAACP, Nat. Assn. Female Execs., Consortium Utah Women in Higher Edn. Baptist. Home: 964 No 1500 W Salt Lake City UT 84116 Office: Univ Utah Mech and Indsl Engr Dept Salt Lake City UT 84112

MORRIS, THERESA CELESTINE, military officer; b. Ocala, Fla., Dec. 17, 1949; d. Louis Mack Sr. and Lillie Mae (Steele) M.; 1 child, Terri Snowden. BA in Psychology, Temple U., 1974; M in Health Services, Lincoln U., Oxford, Pa., 1979. Commd. 2d lt. USAF, 1979, advanced through grades to capt., 1983; mental health worker Hahnneman Hosp. Med. Ctr., Phila., 1974-77, Einstein Med. Coll. and Hosp., Phila., 1977-79; adminstrn. officer 366 Tactical Fighter Wing, Mountain Home AFB, Idaho, 1979-81; squadron commander 3d Aircraft Generation Squadron, Clark AFB, Philippines, 1981-83; hdqrs. squadron commander 3d Combat Support Group, Clark AFB, Philippines, 1983-85; chief site support, emergency actions officer 750Z Munitions Support Squadron, Norvenich AB, Fed. Republic Germany, 1985—. Decorated Achievement medal, Meritorious Service medal, Commendation medal with oak leaf cluster USAF. Home: Box 15 750Z MunSS APO NY 09072-5360

MORRIS, UNA LORRAINE, physician; b. Kingston, Jamaica, W.I., Jan. 17, 1949; came to U.S., 1965; d. Arthur Samuel and Lydia (Reid) Morris; m. Charles Cecil Chong, Mar. 27, 1981; children—Keone Tremaine, Cheynne Jehon, Wei-Lin Lorraine Chong. M.D., U. Calif.-San Francisco, 1974. Diplomate Am. Bd. Radiology. Intern, Kaiser Permanente Hosp., Oakland, Calif., 1974; resident in radiology Martin Luther King Jr. Gen. Hosp, Los Angeles, 1975-79; fellow U. Calif.-Irvine; practice medicine specializing in radiology, Los Angeles, 1980—; asst. prof. radiology U. So. Calif., Los Angeles, 1984—; program coordinator San Gabriel Women Physicians Assn., 1982—; organizer, liaison Jamaican Med. Airlift, Los Angeles, 1982—. Contbr. articles to profl. jours. Named Sportswoman of Yr. for Jamaica, Jamaica Amateur Athletic Assn., 1964, 65, 66; mem. Olympic team 1964, 68, 72. Mem. Radiol. Soc. N.Am. Baptist. Address: 1617 Homewood Dr Altadena CA 91001

MORRIS, VICKY WATSON, educator; b. Powhatan Point, Ohio, Sept. 26, 1944; d. Viola Viktoria (Toniola) Watson; m. David Clinton Morris, Sept. 21, 1963; children: Scott David, Matthew Clinton. BS summa cum laude, Ball State U., 1984, MA in Edn., 1987. Cert. elem. tchr., Ind. Sec. U.S. Govt. Agys., Washington and Columbus (Ohio), 1962-68; bookkeeper, sales rep. Postal Instant Press, Muncie, Ind., 1975-79; research tech. Ball State U., Muncie, 1980-81, instr., 1986—. Vol. Well Baby Clinic, Muncie, 1981-86, WIPB Pub. TV Telesale, Muncie, 1982-86. Scholar Ball State U., 1981-84. Mem. Gold Key Nat. Honor Soc. (lif). Democrat. Home: 1415 W Sheffield Dr Muncie IN 47304 Office: Ball State U Burris Lab Sch 2000 University Ave Muncie IN 47306

MORRISON, ALEXIA, lawyer; b. Los Angeles, Apr. 9, 1948; d. Alexander and Sarah Edith (Blayney) M.; m. Robert A. Shuker, Feb. 11, 1978; 1 child, Amanda Meighan. BA, Douglass Coll., 1969; JD, George Washington U., 1972. Bar: D.C. 1973, U.S. Dist. Ct. (D.C. dist.) 1975, U.S. Ct. Appeals (D.C. cir.) 1975, U.S. Supreme Ct. 1980. Legal asst. U.S. Dept. Justice, Washington, 1972-73; asst. U.S. Atty. Washington, 1973-81, chief grand jury sect., 1978-79; chief felony trial div. U.S. Dist. Ct. D.C., Washington, 1979-81; chief litigation counsel SEC, 1981-85; ptnr. Swidler & Berlin, Washington, 1985—; mem. adv. bd. Racketeer Influenced and Corrupt Orgns. Act Bur. Nat. Affairs, Washington, 1986—. Recipient U.S. Dept. Justice Dir.'s award, 1980, Sr. Exec. Service Performance bonus, 1983, Presdl. Rank award, 1985. Mem. ABA (litigation sect.), D.C. Bar (v.p. long range planning com. 1985—, chmn. steering com. litigation div. 1985-86), Asst. U.S. Atty.'s Assn. (pres. 1986-87). Republican. Office: Swidler & Berlin 3000 K St NW Suite 300 Washington DC 20007

MORRISON, BARBARA LANE, vocational educator; b. Houston, June 24, 1939; d. Nathan and Dorothy (Chasnoff) Blum; m. Richard A. Lane, Jan. 3, 1960 (div. Feb. 1972); children: David A., Lori A.; m. Richard L. Morrison, Jan. 23, 1974. BS, Drake U., 1964; postgrad., So. Meth. U., 1973. Tchr. Saydell Ind. Sch. Dist., Des Moines, 1961-64, Carrollton (Tex.) Framers Br. Ind. Sch. Dist., 1964-65; real estate salesperson Guion Gregg Realtors, Dallas, 1969-71, Meyers & Meryers Realtors, Dallas, 1971-72, Dal Capri Realtors, Dallas, 1972-74; founder, owner, instr. Real Estate Career Coll., Dallas, 1976—. Named Affiliate of Yr. Greater Dallas Bd. Realtors, 1984. Mem. Greater Dallas Bd. Realtors (com. mem., Affiliate of Yr. 1984), Ft. Worth Bd. Realtors (com. mem.), North East Tarrant County Bd. Realtors (com. mem.), Women's Council Realtors, Real Estate Ecducators Assn., Tex. Real Estate Tchrs. Assn. (bd. dirs. 1981-82, treas. 1982, 83), Tex. Assn. Realtors, Nat. Assn. Realtors. Office: 107 Dal-Rich Village Richardson TX 75080

MORRISON, BETTY LEE YARBOROUGH, corporate executive; b. Pinehurst, N.C., Mar. 12, 1946; d. Charlie D. and Jessie Lee (Wallace) Yarborough; m. Arthur Dale Morrison, Feb. 1, 1964; children: Lindale Maire, Melanie Anne. Student, Sandhills Community Coll., 1977. Office mgr. Pinehurst (N.C.), Inc., 1973-77; controller Morrison, Inc., West End, N.C., 1977-79; controller, sec., treas. Stuart-Fitchett, So. Pines, N.C., 1979—. Chmn. Miss Noel Pageant, Pinehurst, 1985-87; mem. campaign com. United Way, So. Pines, 1986. Mem. Bus. and Profl. Women's Club (Woman of Yr. 1986, v.p. local chpt.), League Women Voters, So. Pines Jaycees. Democrat. Baptist. Lodge: Does. Home: Rt 1 Box 333 West End NC 27376 Office: Stuart-Fitchett PA Architects 180 E Connecticut Ave Southern Pines NC 28387

MORRISON, DELCY SCHRAM, psychodramatist; b. Chgo., Apr. 15, 1935; d. Harry Samuel and Gertrude (Hackman) Schram; married, June 29, 1958 (div. Sept. 1968); children: John, Christopher. BA, Columbia Pacific U., 1982, MA, 1984. Asst. to dir. psychodrama dept. Camelback Hosp., Phoenix, 1974-78; co-dir. Western Inst. for Psychodrama, Phoenix, 1978—; supr. psychodrama dept. Scottsdale (Ariz.) Camelback Hosp., 1980—; cons. Northern Ariz. Univ. Counseling Dept., Flagstaff, 1978—, Holocaust Remembrance Conf., West Lafayette, Ind., 1984, United Hosp., Grand Forks, N.D., 1985, St. Joseph Hosp., Wichita, 1986. Author: (with Elaine Eller Goldman) Psychodrama: Experience and Process, 1984; contbr. articles to psychol. jours. Fellow Am. Soc. Group Psychotherapy and Psychodrama; mem. Am. Group Psychotherapy Assn., Ariz. Group Psychotherapy Soc., Fedn. Trainers and Tng. Programs in Psychodrama.

MORRISON, (GRACE) DORIS, painter, lecturer; b. Alameda, Calif., Apr. 21, 1906; d. Edward Alexander and Emma Doris (Harris) Cochran; m. Robert Rixford Morrison, Feb. 19, 1927 (dec. May 1982). Grad., Cleve. Inst. Art, 1948, BFA, 1949; student, Coll. Marin, 1961-62, Santa Barbara Coll., 1982-83. Various works exhibited Cabrillo Art Ctr., Santa Barbara, 1980-85; one-woman show Astra Gallery El Paseo Santa Barbara, 1988. Mem. Mayor's Bicentennial Cultural Arts Com. fund raising for library, Santa Barbara 1976; co-dir. gallery Santa Barbara Arts Council, 1987—. Mem. Marin Soc. Artists (life pres. 1965-66), Santa Barbara Art Assn. (pres. 1977-78) Artists Equity, (bd. dirs. Santa Barbara chpt. 1986-87). Home: 333 Old Mill Rd Santa Barbara CA 93110

MORRISON, EILEEN ELIZABETH, educator; b. Bridgeport, Conn., Nov. 4, 1948; d. Edward J. and Edna J. (Nuttall) M.; 1 child, Grant Edward Ellis. A in Applied Sci., Broome Community Coll., 1969; BS, U. Tenn., 1972, M in Pub. Health, 1973; EdD, Vanderbilt U., 1982. Dental hygienist Matthew Walker Health Ctr., Nashville, 1969-70; state tng. officer Head Start, Knoxville, Tenn., 1973-74; asst. prof. East Tenn. State U., Johnson City, 1974-76; health edn. coordinator Cumberland County Health Dept., Fayetteville, N.C., 1976-77; instr. Tenn. State U., Nashville, 1979-82; prof. Tex. Woman's U., Denton, 1982—; Cons. USPHS, Washington, 1980-82, ADA, Chgo., 1980-85, Tex. Health Studies, Arlington, Tex., 1986—. Mem. Sigma Phi Alpha. Democrat. Roman Catholic. Office: Tex Woman's U PO Box 23716 Denton TX 76204

MORRISON, GRACE BLANCH SIMPSON, auditor, accountant, government official; b. Waterloo, Iowa, Dec. 18, 1933; d. Lyle Meredith and Grace Luella Blanch Simpson; B.S., So. Meth. U., 1956; M.Ed., U. Houston, 1973; C.P.A., Tex.; m. Glenn Harry Murphree, July 2, 1955 (dec.); children—Gregory Alan, Gina Grace; m. 2d, Henry Joseph Morrison, Jr., July 23, 1974. Tchr. math., Mesquite (Tex.) Ind. Sch. Dist., 1957-58, Clear Creek Ind. Sch. Dist., Seabrook, Tex., 1967-73, Richardson (Tex.) Ind. Sch. Dist., 1973-74; equal opportunity asst. Office for Civil Rights, HEW, Dallas, 1974-75; govt. relations specialist, consumer affairs officer Region VI, Dept. Energy, Dallas, 1975-81; audit acctg. aide IRS, Dallas, 1981-82, revenue agt., 1982-85. Mem. Mensa, White Rock Bus. and Profl. Women's Club, Nat. Assn. Parliamentarians, Puppeteers Am., Assn. Govt. Accts., Am. Soc. Women Accts. Unitarian. Home: 4116 Amy Dr Mesquite TX 75150 Office: 1100 Commerce St 3B17 Dallas TX 75242

MORRISON, GWENDOLYNN SUE SLOVER, bank executive; b. Armstrong, Mo., Feb. 21, 1945; d. Leon A. and Dorothy R. (Robinson) Slover; m. Donald Joe Morrison, Sept. 13, 1963; children: Tracy, Kent. Program dir. Econ. Devel. Program, Georgetown, Tex., 1982-84; bus. devel. officer First Nat. Bank, Georgetown, 1984—, also bd. dirs.; bd. dirs. Economic Devel. Program, Georgetown. Mem. Women's Polit. Caucus; bd. dirs. Goergetown Pub. Library, 1985—, Handcrafts Unltd., Georgetown, 1987—, Downtown Georgetown Assn.; chmn. Tourism Devl. Bd., Georgetown. Mem. Am. Bus. Women, Nat. Assn. Bank Women, Nat. Assn. Female Execs., So. Indsl. Devel. Council, Tex. Indsl. Devel. Council, Georgetown C. of C. (exec. dir. 1988—). Home: 219 Serenada Dr Georgetown TX 78628 Office: First Nat Bank 624 Austin Ave Georgetown TX 78627

MORRISON, JANE ANN, dental health administrator; b. Fargo, N.D., Apr. 17, 1956; d. Dale Frederick Rasmusson and Gladys Mildred (Sebring) Lucha; m. David Alexander Morrison, Jan. 3, 1987. AA, Orange Coast Coll., 1977; BA, U. Calif., Irvine, 1982. Nurse aid Park Superior Health Care Coll., Costa Mesa, Calif., 1977-79; customer relations Nat. Health Care System, Irvine, 1979-83; dir. Dental Assn. N.Am. Calif., Irvine, 1979-83; state dir., adminstr. Nat. Health Care Systems, Bismarck, N.D., 1983-84; st. project dir. Nat. Health Care Systems, Albuquerque, 1984-86; adminstr., mktg. dir. Nat. Health Care Systems, Salt Lake City, 1986—; mktg. cons. Dental Assn. N.Am., N.Mex., Oreg., Calif., N.D., Ariz., 1979—. Acitve Rep. Youth Assocs., Orange County, Calif., 1979-83; bd. dirs. Dwight Eisenhower Bd. Trustees, Orange County, 1980—. Newport Women's League Scholar, Costa Mesa, 1979. Office: Nat Dental Health Assn 3761 S 700 East #200 Salt Lake City UT 84106

MORRISON, JUDITH PARKER, management consultant; b. Boston, Aug. 8, 1946; d. Arnold and Gertrude (Caro) Parker; m. Malcolm H. Morrison, Aug. 20, 1967; children: Andrew, Seth. Student, U. Mich., 1968; BA, Boston U., 1968; MS, The Johns Hopkins U., 1978, postgrad. Curriculum developer Griggs Assocs., Bethesda, Md., 1978-81; pres., sr. lectr. ACT II Mgmt. Cons. Co., Columbia, Md., 1985—; sr. trainer Office Personnel Mgmt., Washington, 1986—, Soil Conservation Dept. USDA, Washington, 1987, U.S.C.O.E., Huntsville, Ala., 1984, U.S. Dept. Navy, Rosslyn, Va., 1987; instr. The Johns Hopkins U., Balt., 1986—; lectr., cons. Fed. Bur. Prisons, Devel. Career Devel. Model, Washington, 1987—; cons. U. Balt., 1986—. Mem. Am. Soc. Tng. and Devel., Chi Sigma Iota. Home and Office: 5053 Castlemoor Dr Columbia MD 21044

MORRISON, LINDA, music educator; b. Fort Deposit, Ala., June 19, 1939; d. Clarence Alexander and Buena Ethyl (Murray) Morrison; Mus.B., Samford U., 1961; Mus.M., So. Bapt. Theol. Sem., 1965; D.M.A., North Tex. State U., 1984; children—Eric, Allen. Pvt. piano and organ tchr., 1963—; minister of music Crescent Hill Baptist Ch., Louisville, 1973-76; faculty La. Coll., Pineville, 1976-83, asst. prof. music, 1979-83; choral dir. Louisville Collegiate Sch, 1983-85; faculty Jefferson Community Coll. Mem. Am. Guild Organists, Baptist. Home: 3003 Lexington Rd Louisville KY 40206

MORRISON, PAULETTE HARKELROAD, accountant; b. Kingsport, Tenn., Dec. 22, 1944; d. George Kelly and B. Jane (Harris) Harkelroad; m. F. Wayne Morrison, Juner 21, 1966 (div. Sept. 1982); 1 child, Cynthia. Cert., Whitney Bus. Coll., Kingsport, 1963. Staff acct. Hoover Harrison Assocs., Kingsport, Tenn., 1963—. Mem. Kingsport VFW. Republican. Baptist. Lodges: Moose. Home: 1356 Garden Dr Kingsport TN 37664 Office: Hoover Harrison Asscs 440 E Sullivan St Kingsport TN 37662

MORRISON, TONI (CHLOE ANTHONY MORRISON), novelist; b. Lorain, Ohio, Feb. 18, 1931; d. George and Ella Ramah (Willis) Wofford; children—Harold Ford, Slade Kevin. B.A., Howard U., 1953; M.A., Cornell U., 1955. Tchr. English and humanities Tex. So. U., 1955-57, Howard U., 1957-64; editor Random House, N.Y.C., 1965—. Author: The Bluest Eye, 1970, Sula, 1974, Song of Solomon, 1977, Tar Baby, 1983, Beloved, 1987 (Pulitzer prize and Robert F. Kennedy Book award, 1988). Mem. Author's Guild (council). Office: care Random House 201 E 50th St New York NY 10022 *

MORRISON, WINIFRED ELAINE HAAS, rehabilitation agency executive, educator; b. Buffalo, Aug. 31; d. Edward Albert and Elaine Magdalene (McNamara) Haas; m. Robert Charles Morrison; children: Robert Edward, James Richard. BS in Edn., SUNY, Buffalo, MS in Edn. magna cum laude, 1964, PhD, 1984, postgrad.; MLS, SUNY, Geneseo, 1969; postgrad., Harvard U., UCLA. Instr., Genesee Community Coll., 1972-78, 80, also asst. prof. State U. Coll., Buffalo, 1973-77; instr. corr. course Empire State Coll., Saratoga Springs, N.Y., 1975-78; dir. early edn. div. Park Sch., Buffalo, 1960-74, dir. lower sch., 1974-78; mem. faculty ednl. studies, lectr., SUNY, Buffalo, also coordinator child care adv. service Early Childhood Research Ctr., Amherst campus, 1978-80; dir. children's services Erie County Assn. for Retarded Children, 1980-83, exec. dir., 1983—; chmn. early childhood com. Nat. Office Gifted and Talented, HEW, 1976; panelist symposium Chautauqua Inst., 1974. Author: This Book is About Your School, Early Education Unit, 1976, Primary Unit, 1977, You Are Your Child's First Teacher, 1974, (with Carol Woodard) You Can Help Your Baby Learn, 1979, (with Betty Jenkins) (screening materials) Kiddy Kards, 1982. Pres. bd. dirs. Day Care Council Western N.Y., 1971-72; adv. com. parenthood edn. project Buffalo and Erie County council Girl Scouts U.S., 1972-76; child adv. com. child/adult edn. project Western N.Y. div. Salvation Army, 1977-82; TV and reading com. WNED-TV Public Broadcasting, 1977-79; chmn. community com. Erie Community Coll., 1971-72; hon. chmn. Week of the Young Child; pres. Erie County Adv. Council on Disabled, 1986-88. Recipient Outstanding Service award Villa Maria Coll. Child Devel. Adv. Council, 1979, 84, Outstanding Achievement award YWCA of Buffalo and Erie County, 1985. Mem. AAUW, Nat. Assn. Edn. of Young Children, Council Exceptional Children, World Orgn. Presch. Edn., Ctr. Women in Mgmt. (bd. dirs. 1983-88, Mgr. of Yr. award 1987), Am. Mgmt. Assn., ALA, Nat. Assn. Supervision and Curriculum Devel., N.Y. State Council for Children, Pi Lambda Theta (pres. Alpha Nu chpt. 1985-87, sec. N.E. region 1988—, Outstanding Pi Lambda Thetan award 1987), Phi Delta Kappa (v.p. Alpha Psi chpt.). Lodges: Zonta (v.p.), Rotary. Home: 13 Karen Dr Tonawanda NY 14150 Office: 101 Oak St Buffalo NY 14203

MORRISS, MARY RACHEL, art educator, painter; b. Memphis; d. William Dale and Lizzie Hennie (Woodward) M. B.S., Memphis State U., 1927; postgrad. U. Colo., 1931, 34, 37, 40; various art workshops Maxine Masterfield, 1983, 84. Cert. high sch. tchr., Tenn. Tchr., Bellevue Sch., Memphis, 1936-66; ret.; pvt. art classes, Memphis, 1966—; represented by Art Gallery East, Memphis. Exhibited in group juried shows Central South Parthenon, Nashville, Hunter Annual Show, Delta Annual, Little Rock, Mid-Am., Owensboro, Ky., 1979, Mid-South Memphis Brooks Gallery, So. Watercolor Soc., 1983, Patrons' Watercolor Gala, Oklahoma City, 1983, 84, Tenn. Watercolor Soc. Annual Traveling Show, Ga. Watercolor Soc., 1986, and many others; represented in numerous pub. and pvt. collections. Recipient Best Cotton Design award Brooks Art Gallery; Purchase prize Mid-South Fair, 1971, Best in Show and 1st in watercolors, 1985, 86; Md. prize J.J. White 1988 Meml. Watercolor juried exhbn.; Doochin of Madison award Central South, 1984, and many other awards. Mem. Tenn. Watercolor Soc. (David Wade Meml. award 1988), So. Watercolor Soc., Friends of Dixon Gallery, Memphis Watercolor Soc., Ga. Watercolor Soc. Presbyterian. Home: 4819 Parkside Ave Memphis TN 38117

MORRONE, ANNA L., theatrical artistic director, publicist; b. Hackensack, N.J., Dec. 8, 1956; d. Fred James and Antoinette (Pesce) M. BA, Ramapo Coll., 1978. News corr. United Artists Columbia Cable TV, Oakland, N.J., 1977-78; dir. publicity Ctr. Stage, Inc., Englewood, N.J., 1979-81; assoc. producer N.J. Actors Repertory Co., Paramus, N.J., 1981-82; mng. dir. Playhouse on the Mall, Paramus, 1982-85; artistic dir. Miana Prodns., Paramus, Hackensack, 1985—; cons. Yates Musical Theatre, East Orange, N.J., 1981—, Papermill Playhouse, Milburn, N.J., 1982; instr. drama The Theatre Sch., Inc., Teaneck, N.J., 1983-85; drama coach, dir. Hackensack High Sch., 1986. Dir. numerous theatrical prodns. Roman Catholic. Office: Miana Prodns PO Box 1035 Maywood NJ 07607

MORROW, CHERYLLE A., accountant, consultant; b. Sydney, Australia, July 3, 1950; came to U.S., 1973; d. Norman H. and Esther A. E. (Jarrett) Wilson. Student U. Hawaii, 1975; diploma Granville Tech. Coll., Sydney, 1967. Acct., asst. treas. Bus. Investment, Ltd., Honolulu, 1975-77; owner Lanikai Musical Instruments, Honolulu, 1980-86, Cherylle A. Morrow Profl. Services, Honolulu, 1981—; fin. managerial cons. E.A. Buck Co., Inc., Honolulu, 1981-84; controller, asst. trustee THC Fin. Corp., Honolulu, 1977-84, bankruptcy trustee, 1984—. Mem. Small Bus. Hawaii PAC, Lanikai Community Assn., Arts Council Hawaii, vol., mem. Therapeutic Horsemanship for Handicapped, Small Bus. Adminstrn. (women in bus. com. 1987—). Mem. Australian-Am. C. of C. (dir. 1985—, corp. sec. 1986—, v.p. 1988—), Nat. Assn. Female Execs. Avocations: reading, music, dancing, sailing, gardening, computers. Office: PO Box 1621 Honolulu HI 96806

MORROW, MARGERY SACHS, educator; b. Ft. Leavenworth, Kans., Sept. 19, 1948; d. Edward Irving and Marguerite F. (Ott) Sachs; m. Julian Philip Morrow, May 15, 1971. BA, Vassar Coll., 1969; MS, Bank St. Coll., 1975. Cert. elem. tchr., N.Y. Tchr's. asst. Lower West Side Childrens Ctr., N.Y.C., 1970; child care worker St. Christopher's Sch., Dobbs Ferry, N.Y., 1970-71; tchr's. aide Grants Pass (Oreg.) High Sch., 1971-72; student tchr. Bank St. Coll., N.Y.C., 1973-74; tchr. Village Community Sch., N.Y.C., 1974-81, Churchill Sch., N.Y.C., 1981-84, Byram Hills Sch. Dist., Armonk, N.Y., 1984—; free-lance writer Dobbs Ferry, 1986-87; tutor pvt. practice for learning disabled children, Dobbs Ferry, 1984-85. Mem. Am. Fedn. Tchrs., N.Y. State United Tchrs. Democrat. Home: 102 Southlawn Ave Dobbs Ferry NY 10522

MORROW, SHARON M., university official; b. Pierce County, Wash., Aug. 26, 1953; d. Kenneth L. and Patsy R. (Cepicky) M. B.S., Ball State U., 1975, postgrad., 1975-77; postgrad. Miami U., 1977-79. Teaching grad. asst. English Ball State U., Muncie, Ind., 1975-76, publs. grad. asst., 1976-77; editorial asst. Old N.W. Miami U., Oxford, Ohio, 1977-79; admissions counselor Kans. Wesleyan U., Salina, 1979-80; publs. editor Western Mich. U., Kalamazoo, 1980-83; dir. publs. Bradley U., Peoria, Ill., 1983-86, mem. publs. council, 1983-86; publs. dir. Kans. State U., Manhattan, 1986—; mem. commencement com. Open House Coordinating Council. Treas. Commn. Status of Women, Western Mich. U., 1981-82; conf. com. mem. Council Advancement and Support Edn., Dist. 5, 1984. Recipient Adams award Peoria Advt. and Selling Club, 1985. Mem. Women in Communications, Nat. Assn. Female Execs.; Faculty Women's Caucus. Democrat. Office: Kans State U Univ Publs 5 Anderson Hall Manhattan KS 66506

MORROW, SUSAN DAGMAR, psychic, educator, writer, consultant; b. Harrisburg, Pa., July 10, 1932; d. William Lime and Margaret Louise (Deckard) Brubaker; m. Henry Taylor Morrow, June 9, 1952 (div. Mar. 1984); children—Quenby Anne Morrow Smith, Christopher Brian. Student Carnegie Inst. Tech., 1950-52, U. Ariz., 1952-54, U. Calif.-Berkeley Ext., 1960-72, Foothill Coll., 1980-81. Self-employed psychic, psychic tchr., Palo Alto, Calif., 1976-80, Mountain View, Calif., 1980—; psychic, tchr. Seekers Quest Profl. Ctr., San Jose, Calif., 1983—; tchr. San Andreas Health Council, Palo Alto, 1981-83; lectr. U. Calif.-Berkeley, 1979, Foothill Coll., Los Altos, Calif., 1980; lectr. in field; cons. in cases of mental disorientation to psychologists, Palo Alto and Mountain View, 1978-84. Contbr. articles on psychic awareness to various publs. Mem. Assn. Psychic Practitioners (co-founder, v.p. 1982-83, editor and writer newsletter 1982-83), Assn. Research and Enlightenment, Friends of the Animals. Democrat. Methodist. Avocations: mediumship; painting; swimming; sailing; skiing.

MORROW, SUSAN H., interior designer; b. Bklyn., Aug. 27, 1943; d. Murray and Roslyn (Benjamin-Polsky) Chalkin; m. Robert Morrow (div.); children: Christopher, Andrew. BFA, Syracuse U., 1964; MA, NYU, 1965; cert. Post Coll. With Bagatelle Assocs., Roslyn, N.Y., 1972-74, The Wallpaper Place, Roslyn, 1974-75, Trio Designs, Huntington, N.Y., 1975-80, SHS Designs, Inc., North Hills, N.Y., 1980—; designer Designs For ..., Manhasset, N.Y., 1981—, ptnr., 1982—; pres. Wallpapers and ..., 1985—; designer Cinderella Project, Bklyn. Union Gas Urban Renewal, 1979, Human Resources, Ind. Living Project, 1982—; designer and converter Class Reunion, 1987. Designer Showcase Mansions; contbr. articles to mags. Co-chairperson budget adv. com. Roslyn Schs.; v.p. Norgate Civic Assn., Roslyn. Named Woman of Yr., Hadassah, 1974. Mem. Am. Soc. Interior Designers, 110 Assn. Profl. Women, Assn. Environ. Designers, Mensa, Internat. Platform Assn., LWV (v.p.). Home: PO Box H Sea Cliff NY 11579 Office: Designs For... 24 Skillman St Roslyn NY 11576

MORSE, CLAIRE KREBS, psychology educator; b. Cleve., Nov. 12, 1943; d. Gerhard and Ellen (Quinn) Krebs; m. Lawrence Bowen Morse; children: Jennifer Quinn, Jessica Elizabeth. BA, Oberlin (Ohio) Coll., 1965; PhD, Yale U., 1968. From asst. to assoc. prof. psychology Tougaloo (Miss.) Coll., 1968-72, assoc. prof., 1975-76; prof. Universidad Centroamericana Jose Simeon Canas, San Salvador, El Salvador, 1973-75; assoc. prof. Guilford Coll., Greensboro, N.C., 1976—. Contbr. articles to profl. jours. Bd. dirs. headstart program Community Edn. Extension, Jackson, Miss., 1971-72; mem. Hazardous Waste Task Force, Greensboro. Recipient Excellence in Teaching award Guilford Coll., 1980; NSF grantee, 1969-70. Mem. Am. Psychol. Assn. Home: 224 Kensington Greensboro NC 27403 Office: Guilford Coll 5800 W Friendly Ave Greensboro NC 27410

MORSE, DEBRA SUE, fashion designer; b. Gaylord, Mich., Aug. 20, 1952; d. Robert Buford Abbott and Mary Esther (Skingley) Lokken; m. Bleecker Morse Jr., Mar. 8, 1975 (div. Apr. 1981). AA in Fashion Merchandising, Fashion Inst. Am., Atlanta, 1972. Asst. fashion coordinator Rich's Dept. Store, Atlanta, 1972-74, asst. fabric fashion coordinator, 1974; workshop coordinator, admissions rep. Art Inst. Atlanta, 1974-80, dir. continuing edn., 1980; pvt. clothier Atlanta, 1980—; head designer Morse Designs, Atlanta, 1980—; pvt. wardrobe cons. Atlanta, 1986—. Contbr. articles to profl. jours. Mem. Fashion Group of Atlanta, Assn. for Wardrobe Consultants of Kennesaw Coll. Home and Office: PO Box 12388 Atlanta GA 30355

MORSE, ELEANOR MEREDITH, art dealer; b. Bklyn., June 2, 1926; d. Daniel and Salley Beatrice Hershey; B.B.A., CCNY, 1947; m. Mitchell Ian Morse, Dec. 24, 1947; children—Jeffrey Aslan, Andrea Urdang. Vice pres. Art Gallery on Wheels, Floral Park, N.Y., 1953-54; product designer, v.p. Wall Decor, Inc., Cedarhurst, and Lawrence, N.Y., 1954-70; free-lance window designer, 1955-61; interior designer, 1961-68; sec./treas. Mann-Morse Graphics, N.Y.C., 1968-69, Morse-Sun Art Assocs., Inc., N.Y.C., 1972-75; v.p., Mitch Morse Gallery, Inc., N.Y.C., 1966-85, pres., 1985—; v.p. Yogre Bldg. Assocs., Lawrence, 1964—, Art Spectrum, 1979—, Whitney Morse Art Group, Inc., 1988—; sec. China Spectrum, Inc., N.Y.C., 1981-86; watercolorist; one-person show jewelry design, Annapolis, Md., 1983. Office: 334 E 59th St New York NY 10022

MORSE, HAZEL RED, investment services specialist; b. Bar Harbor, Maine, June 19, 1937; d. Forrest L. and Beulah (Ramsdell) Hamblen; divorced; children: Raymond Lee, Cheryl Barg, Lowell Lee. Student, Broward Community Coll., 1969; cert. in real estate, U. Conn., 1979; BS, Nova U., 1986. Cert. real estate assoc.; registered rep. in mut. funds. Office mgr. Ramada Inn, Ft. Lauderdale, Fla., 1969-70; receptionist Le Club Internat., Ft. Lauderdale, 1970-71; acct. City of Ft. Lauderdale, 1971-75; supr. admissions Nova U., Ft. Lauderdale, 1975-79; billing registrar North Cen. Conn. Health Maintenance Orgn., East Hartford, 1979-80; auditor Beach Club Hotel, Ft. Lauderdale, 1980-82; payroll coordinator North Broward Med. Ctr., Pompano Beach, Fla., 1982-87; rep. 1st Investors, Ft. Lauderdale, 1987—; chairperson edn. com. North Broward Med. Ctr., 1986-87, bd. dirs. credit union, 1985-87. Mem. fin. com. Rep. party, Ft. Lauderdale, 1985; re. United Way, Ft. Lauderdale, 1982-86. Mem. Nova Univ. Alumni Assn., Notary Pub. Assn., Nat. Assn. Female Execs., Fla. Govtl. Secs. Assn. (bd. dirs. 1972-75), Mensa. Home: 1111 NE 30th Dr Fort Lauderdale FL 33334

MORSE, TAMARA ELEANOR, financial services consultant; b. Portland, Oreg., Feb. 4, 1945; d. Frederick Baker and Eleanor (Arkell) M. B.A. with highest distinction Purdue U., 1965, M.S. with distinction, 1968, M.B.A., 1978. Registered rep. Integrated Resources Equity Corp. Instr. Moraga Sch. Dist., Calif., 1968-75, Fluor Internat., Ahwaz, Iran, 1976-77; sales tng. program Chevron, U.S.A., Anchorage, Seattle, and Portland, 1978-79, orgn. cons., San Francisco, 1979-80, staff supr., Seattle, 1980-81, div. analyst, 1981-86; pres. Morse Mgmt. Services, Bellevue, Wash., 1983-86; assoc. Fin. Resources Group, Bellevue, 1986—. Contbr. articles to profl. jours. Account exec. United Way of King County, Seattle, 1981. Mem. Am. Mgmt. Assn., ASTD, Internat. Assn. Fin. Planners, Delta Gamma, Delta Rho Kappa. Office: Fin Resources Group 10800 NE 8th St Suite 512 Bellevue WA 98004

MORSON, EVA INGEBORG, publishing executive; b. Nuernberg, Bavaria, Fed. Republic of Germany, Apr. 29, 1940; came to U.S., 1961; d. Gustave and Anna (Kratzer) Fuchs; m. Walter Gerald Morson, June 23, 1963; children: Peter Gregory, Vanessa Christina. Cert. in bus. adminstrn., Kaufmännische Berufsschule, Nuernberg, 1960; Diploma in French, Alliance Française and Sorbonne, Paris, 1964; Diploma in Italian, Am. Italy Soc., 1985. Bus. adminstr. Metrawatt A.-G., Nuernberg, 1960-61; bilingual sec. Badische Annilin & Soda Fabric Co., N.Y.C., 1962-63; bus. adminstr. Edits. Mayer, Paris, 1965-66; bus. exec., owner Edits. Pub., N.Y.C., 1966—; cons., bd. dirs. Elisa Monte Dance Co., N.Y.C., 1986—. Office: Edits Pub PO Box 339 New York NY 10028

MORTENSEN, SUSAN MARIE, manufacturing company executive; b. Portland, Oreg., Jan. 24, 1950; d. Leslie Dean Mortensen and Kathryn Merdell Huff; m. José Garcia Ruiz, Oct. 25, 1986. BA, U. Portland, 1972. Advt. dir. B.A.C. Inc., Portland, 1972-76, v.p., 1976-81; exec. dir. Econ. Devel. Assn. Skagit County, Inc., Mt. Vernon, Wash., 1982-86; mgr. Sugiyo U.S.A., Inc., Anacortes, Wash., 1986-87, exec. dir., 1987—. Active Skagit County Tourism Task Force., Washington, 1984; rep. Team Wash. Asian Mission, Japan, 1986; ambassador Wash. Partnership for Econ. Devel., 1984—. Mem. Japan-Am. Soc., Econ. Devel. Execs. Wash. (bd. dirs. 1985—), Anacortes C. of C. Jansen Found. grantee, 1985, Team Wash. Dept. Trade, 1985, Local Devel. Fund Matching Dept. Com. Devel., Washington, 1986.

MORTHAM, SANDRA BARRINGER, state legislator; b. Erie, Pa., Jan. 4, 1951; d. Norman Lyell and Ruth (Harer) Barringer; m. Allen Mortham, Aug. 21, 1950; children: Allen Jr., Jeffrey. AS, St. Petersburg Jr. Coll., 1971; postgrad., Eckerd Coll., 1986—. Personnel dir. Capital Formation Counselors, Inc., Bellair Bluffs, Fla., 1972—; commr. City of Largo, Fla., 1982-86, vice mayor, 1985-86; mem. Fla. Ho. of Reps., 1986—. Bd. dirs. Performing Arts Ctr. & Theatre, Clearwater, Fla.; exec. com. Pinellas County Rep. Com., Rep. Nat. Com. Recipient Women Honoring Women award

Soroptomists Pinellas County, 1980. Mem. Am. Legis. Exchange Council, Nat. Rep. Legislators Assn., Largo C. of C. (bd. dirs. 1987—). Presbyterian. Clubs: Largo Jr. Woman's (pres., Woman of Yr. award 1979), Suncoast Community Woman's (pres., Ouststanding Service award 1981, Woman of Yr. award 1986), Suncoast Tiger Bay, Greater Largo Rep., Belleair Rep. Woamn's, Clearwater Rep. Woman's. Home: 2860 Vernon Terr Largo FL 33540 Office: 152 8th Ave SW Largo FL 34640

MORTHLAND, CONSTANCE AMELIA GRANT (MRS. ANDREW MORTHLAND), civic worker; b. Eng., Mar. 31, 1915 (came to U.S. 1919, naturalized 1940); d. Douglas Gordon and Maud (Smith) Grant; ; A.B. summa cum laude, Stanford, 1936; m. Andrew Morthland, Aug. 8, 1937; children—Joan (Mrs. Warren C. Hutchins), Patricia (Mrs. James F. Draper). Research asst. RKO Studios, 1936-39; story dept. analyst Paramount Studios, 1941-46; free lance writer, 1955-60; cons. overseas program Stanford U. Pres. Friends of Claremont Colls., 1976-78; mem. Friends of Radcliffe Coll., 1962-70; chmn. fin. com. Episcopal Ch. Women, 1959-60; mem. exec. bd. Assistance League, 1968-69; staff mem. Laguna-Moulton Community Playhouse, 1961-69, editor Callboard, 1955—; community adviser Jr. League, 1973-75. Trustee Pitzer Coll., Claremont, Calif.; bd. overseers Claremont Coll., 1965-73; bd. dirs. Lyric Opera Assn. Orange County, 1973-84, Continuing Edn. at Claremont Coll., 1973-77; trustee South Coast Med. Center, 1978-84; exec. bd. Assocs. of House Ear Inst., 1982-84; bd. dirs. Research Assocs. U. Calif.-Irvine Coll. Medicine, 1983—. Recipient Journalism award Sigma Delta Chi, 1936, Calif. Internat. Woman award 1971. Mem. Soc. Preservation Rural Eng. (hon.), Daus. Brit. Empire (regent 1972-73, 80—), Aircraft Owners and Pilots Assn., Ninety-Nines. Clubs: Stanford (Orange County sec.); Stanford Profl. Women's; Women's University (London); Newport Harbor Yacht; El Miguel Country; N.Y. Yacht. Home: 165 Moss Point Laguna Beach CA 92651

MORTMAN-FRIEDMAN, BETH-LYNN, graphic designer; b. Jersey City, Dec. 17, 1950; d. Abraham and Martha (Yochel) Mortman; 1 child, Alexis Paige. AAS, Queensborough Community Coll., 1972; BS, Buffalo State U., 1975; MS, Pratt Inst., 1988. Cert. art tchr., N.Y. Asst. art dir. Transhigh Corp., N.Y.C., 1976-78; graphic art designer, tchr. Lowell Sch., Queens, N.Y., 1978-82; art dir., owner Visual Persuasion Studio, Jericho, N.Y., 1982—; cons. and lectr. in field. Art dir. numerous print ads, brochures, flyers. Recipient numerous nat. design award. Fellow Buffalo State Alumni Assn., Am. Inst. Graphic Artists, Graphic Artist Assn. Office: Visual Persuasion Studio 2 Deer Ln Jericho NY 11753

MORTON, ANN MAYO TILDEN, civic worker, genealogist; b. Concord, N.H., Dec. 3, 1931; d. Sidney Edward and Wanda Louise (Tapp) Tilden; m. Robert Basil Brazil, Jan. 29, 1953 (div. 1956); m. 2d Donald John Morton, Aug. 16, 1958; children—Saundra Kay Morton Hannaford, Donald John, Mary Ann Morton Kasperson. B.S. in Biology, N.Mex. State U., 1953. Cert. Am. Lineage Research Specialist. Organizing chpt. regent Capt. Samuel Wood chpt. Nat. Soc. DAR, Northborough, Mass., 1972, state recording sec., Mass., 1974-77, state vice regent, 1977-80, state regent, 1980-83, v.p. gen. Nat. Soc. DAR, 1983-86; nat. chmn. geneal. com. Nat. DAR, 1986—; registrar gen. Soc. Descs. Colonial Clergy, 1986—; Nat. Soc. Old Plymouth Colony Descs., 1984—; state recording sec. Daus. of Colonial Wars in Commonwealth of Mass., Ind., 1980-83, state registrar, 1983—; state pres. Mass. Soc., Nat. Soc. Colonial Dames XVII Century, 1985-87. Mem. Nat. Soc. of Dames of Ct. of Honor, Hereditary Order of Descendants of Colonial Govs., Nat. Soc. Daus. of Founders and Patriots of Am., Gen. Soc. Mayflower Descendants, Nat. Soc. New Eng. Women, Piscataqua Pioneers (asst. registrar 1985—), Nat. Geneal. Soc., Mass. Soc. Genealogists (state corr. sec. 1985—), Conn. Soc. Genealogists, New Eng. Hist. Geneal. Soc., Essex Soc. Genealogists, Knox County (Ill.) Geneal. Soc., Maine Old Cemetery Assn., Geneal. Soc. Vt. Episcopalian. Home: 12 Westchester Dr Auburn MA 01501

MORTON, AUDREY FARRAR, public administrator; b. Washington, June 24, 1937; d. John Ollie and Massie (Hollard) Farrar; divorced; children: Michelle Bernadette, Michael Nathaniel, Brian Anthony, Brenda Anne. BA, Regis Coll., Denver, 1971; MPA, U. Colo., 1973, postgrad. Tchr. Cure D'ars Cath. Sch., Denver, 1968-71; alcoholism counselor Denver Opportunity, Inc., Denver, 1971-72; asst. to city mgr. Aurora (Colo.) City Govt., 1973-79; doctoral program coordinator U. Colo., Denver, 1980-82; instr. Met. State Coll., Denver, 1980-83; dep. regional dir., intergovtl. affairs Office of Sec. HHS, Denver, 1983-86; spl. asst. to dir. Office Minority Health HHS, Washington, 1986-87, dir. Office of Civil Rights, 1987—; lobbyist Denver Pub. Sch. System, Denver, 1983; affirmative action officer Longmont City (Colo.) Govt., 1983; keynote speaker various confs., meetings on role of women, family issues, legislation, and minorities throughout midwest U.S., 1975-86. Mem. Black Edn. Adv. Council, Denver, 1982-86, Women's Health Care Com., Denver, 1984-86, Colo. Healthy Mothers-Healthy Babies Coalition, Denver, 1986, Dist. 8 Jobs Task Force, Denver, 1984; precinct committee woman Rep. Party, Denver, 1981-82, capt. dist. 7, 1983; vice chairperson Colo. Black Rep. Council, Denver, 1981-82; Rep. candidate Colo. Ho. of Reps., Denver, 1982; mem. Colo. Black Caucus; bd. dirs. Ecumenical Housing, Denver, 1984. MPA fellow HUD, 1972-73; recipient Service award Denver Pub. Schs. Bd. Edn., 1986. Mem. Colo. City Mgmt. Assts. Assn. (v.p. 1975-76, pres. 1976-77) Disting. Service 1977), Colo. City Mgmt. Assn. (sec.-treas. 1978-79), Alpha Kappa Alpha. Roman Catholic. Office: Dept Health & Human Services Civil Rights 330 Independence Ave SW Washington DC 20201

MORTON, BERNICE FINLEY, nurse; b. Detroit, Aug. 29, 1923; d. Virgil and Minnie Alice (Batchelor) Finley; B.S.N., Wayne State U., 1954, M.S.N., 1961; Ph.D., U. Mich., 1980; m. Donald Allen Morton, Oct. 1, 1949; children—Donna Jean, Mildred Ellen. Staff nurse Grace Hosp., Detroit, 1948; public health nurse Detroit Dept. Health, 1948-58; instr. Deaconess Sch. Nurses, Detroit, 1960-62; instr. med. terminology Highland Park (Mich.) Community Coll., 1962; asst. dir. Met. Hosp., Detroit, 1962-63; mem. faculty Wayne State U., 1963—, assoc. prof. nursing, chmn. community health nursing, 1973—, minority affairs officer, 1977—, also mem. speakers' bur. vis. prof. Howard U., 1983-84; dir. nursing service Model Neighborhood Comprehensive Health Care Center, 1969-72; mem. Mayor Detroit Adv. Com. Health, 1970-72; cons., reviewer in field. Horace Rachkam fellow, 1975; grantee USPHS, 1959; Martin L. King/Rosa Parks scholar, Oakland U., Rochester, MI, 1988. Mem. AAUP, Am. Nurses Assn., Nat. League Nursing, Am. Pub. Health Assn., Detroit Dist. Nurses Assn., Am. Assn. for History of Nursing, Mus. African-Am. History, Wayne State U. Wayne State U. Alumni Assn., Smithsonian Assocs., Sigma Theta Tau, Delta Sigma Theta, Chi Eta Phi. Author papers in field. Address: 3790 Sturtevant Ave Detroit MI 48206

MORTON, CAROLINE JULIA, devel. co. exec.; b. N.Y.C.; B.S. in Edn., U. Pa.; M.B.A., N.Y. U.; grad. cert. in profl. writing and effective communication, CCNY. Vice pres. mktg. mgmt. V-TEC Corp., Hopewell, Va.; pres. CMR Co., Hopewell; past cons. Advt. Women of N.Y. Mem. Am. Mktg. Assn. (past dir.), Advt. Women of N.Y., Fedn. Profl. Bus. Women, Am. Mgmt. Assn., AAUW. Contbr. articles to profl. jours. Address: PO Box 841 Hopewell VA 23860

MORTON, HELEN K., utilities executive; b. Jacksonville, Fla., June 29, 1950; d. Hoke Smith and Ellen Emily (McCall) Harden; m. Christopher Lynn Morton, June 24, 1978; 1 child, Elizabeth Ann. Student, Purdue U., 1986-87. With service dept. Praetorian Mut., Dallas, 1968-71; mgr. Prudential Water Co., Jacksonville, 1971-74; service supr. Jacksonville Suburban, 1974-82, asst. mgr., 1982-86; mgr. West Lafayette (Ind.) Water Co., 1986-88, Gen. Water Works, Baton Rouge, 1988—. Mem. Am. Water Works Assn., Nat. Assn. Water Cos., Home Builders Assn. Democrat. Episcopal. Office: Werik Office Bldg 651 Laurel St Baton Rouge LA 70802

MORTON, JOANNE MCKEAN, computer educator, consultant; b. New London, Conn., Dec. 3, 1953; d. Newton Hubbard and Lucille (Paganetti) McK.; m. Michael McNally Morton, Sept. 16, 1978. BA, Conn. Coll., 1976; MBA, Rensselaer Poly. Inst., 1985. Dept. mgr. Great Atlantic & Pacific Tea Co., Inc., Springfield, Mass., 1976-84; research asst. Hartford Grad. Ctr., Conn., 1985, adj. lectr. Sch. Mgmt., 1986—; lectr. courses in mktg. and mgmt; owner, operator, Personal Income Tax Preparation and Counseling Service, 1986—; ind. small bus. computer cons. and trainer, 1986—. Avocations: personal investing, basketry, collecting watercolors, Conn. wine industry. Office: The Hartford Grad Ctr 275 Windsor St Hartford CT 06120-2991

MORTON, MARGARET E., state legislator; b. Pocahontas, Va., June 23, 1924; m. James F. Morton. Formerly mem. Conn. Ho. of Reps.; now mem. Conn. Senate; vice-chair Conn. Legis. Black and Hispanic Caucus. Del. Dem. Nat. Conv., 1980, 84. Mem. Nat. Council Negro Women (life), NAACP, NOW, Nat. Black Caucus State Legislators. Home: 25 Currier St Bridgeport CT 06607 Office: Office of the State Senate State Capitol Bldg Hartford CT 06106 *

MORVAY, RUTH GANEK, advertising agency executive; b. Newark, Aug. 10, 1922; d. Benjamin and Sarah (Wexelman) Ganek; m. Leonard Samuel Morvay, Dec. 17, 1944; d. Roslyn Barbara, Judith Morvay Bridges, Steven Elliott. B.A., N.J. State Tchrs. Coll., 1943; M.A., Kean Coll., 1962, Ph.D., 1974. Tchr., Irvington Bd. Edn. (N.J.), 1946-47, Orange Bd. Edn. (N.J.), 1947-50; master tchr. So. Mountain Sch., Millburn, N.J., 1958-81, pres. Morvay Advt. Agy. Inc., South Orange, N.J., 1982—; therapist learning disability children, 1984—. Mem. Essex County Republican Com., 1982—; bd. dirs. Family Counseling, Child Guidance, 1983—. Mem. Alpha Delta Kappa (past pres.). Republican. Jewish (sec. sisterhood 1970). Club: Maplewood (N.J.) Country (pres. ladies aux. 1985—). Home: 31 S Mountain Rd Millburn NJ 07041 Office: Morvay Advt Agy Inc 177 Valley St South Orange NJ 07079

MORWOOD, BETTY JO, psychiatrist, physician; b. Burlington, Vt., Nov. 8, 1948; d. Nicholas Abraham and Alice (Thamer) M.; 1 child, Sophia Ruth. BA, U. Vt., 1970, MD, 1974, fellow, 1978-80. Diplomate Am. Bd. Psychiatry and Neurology. Resident Stanford (Calif.) U., 1976-77; fellow U. Vt., Burl, 1978-80; med. dir. Cath. Social Services, San Jose, Calif., 1977-78; sr. staff psychiatrist Santa Clara County, San Jose, 1977-78; practice medicine specializing in psychiatry Burlington, 1980—; staff physician Med. Ctr. Vt. Mem. Am. Psychiatry Assn., Vt. Psychiatry Assn. Office: Champlain Valley Psychiatry Services 1 Kenneky Dr South Burl VT 05403

MORYADAS, VIRGINIA HILL, real estate executive; b. N.Y.C., Nov. 28, 1937; d. Egon and Therese (Fantin) Hill; m. Subramaniam Moryadas; children: Yashvant, George, Anita. BA, U. Md., 1959; M in Urban and Regional Planning, George Washington U., 1973. Lic. in real estate. Planner Prince George's County, Upper Marlboro, Md., 1969-76, So. Md. Health Systems Agy., Clinton, 1976-77, Med. Service Cons., Inc., Arlington, Va., 1978-79; realtor PGP Realtors, Roper Real Estate, Shannon and Luchs Realtors, Prince George County, 1977—; corp. sec. Health Plus, Riverdale, Md., 1980-84. Bd. dirs. Am. Heart Assn. of So. Md., Riverdale, 1977-84; mem. citizen adv. com. on master plan City of Langley Park, Md., College Park, Greenbelt, Md., 1984—. Mem. Md. Assn. Realtors (bd. dirs. 1985-86), Prince George's County Bd. Realtors (bd. dirs. 1984-86). Home: 11-J Ridge Rd Greenbelt MD 20770 Office: Shannon and Luchs Realtors 6000 Greenbelt Rd Greenbelt MD 20770

MOSBY, CAROLYN BROWN, state legislator; b. Nashville, May 10, 1932; d. Alvin Thomas and Mary Elizabeth (Snelling) Brown; m. William Edward Jordan, Jr., 1950; 1 son, William Edward; m. 2d, John Oliver Mosby, Feb. 5, 1966 (dec. Apr. 1, 1988); 1 dau., Carolyn Elizabeth. Adminstrv. asst. dept. econs. U. Chgo., 1961-80; mem. Ind. Ho. of Reps., 1979-82, Ind. Senate, 1982—; pres., owner Gary Image Ctr., 1980—. Mem. com. on platform accountability Democratic Nat. Com. Recipient Women's Agenda for Action award, 1981, Omega Psi Phi Outstanding Citizen award, 1981, INFO Newspaper awards as Outstanding Citizen in Politics, 1983, in Govt., 1983, Outstanding Citizen award City of Gary, 1983, Ovington award NAACP, 1987; Harvard U. fellow, 1986. Mem. LWV, N.W. Ind. Forum (bd. dirs. 1985-88), Gary C. of C. (dir. 1981-83). Baptist. Clubs: Toastmistress, Jack and Jill Am. Mem. editorial bd. AIM mag., 1980-82. Office: 530 Broadway Gary IN 46402

MOSE, SHERRY LEE, social services administrator; b. Mamou, La., Feb. 26, 1960; d. Hurley Sr. and Levia Janice M. BA, U. Southwestern La., 1982. Social worker neighborhood ctr. Ctr. of Lafayette, La., 1981-82; dir. child care food program La. Dept. Edn., Baton Rouge, 1983—; sec. La. State Child Care Com., Baton Rouge, 1984-85, chairperson, 1985. Hdqrs. coordinator La. senatorial campaign, New Orleans, 1985. Mem. Nat. Assn. Female Execs. Home: Rt 6 Box 210 Ville Platte LA 70586 Office: La Assn Community Action Agy 7360 Tom Dr Suite D Baton Rouge LA 70806

MOSELEY-NERO, ROBERTA, lawyer; b. Hudson, N.Y., Dec. 7, 1957; d. Robert Joseph and Patricia (Montague) M. B.A. in Econs., Russell Sage Coll., 1978; J.D., Syracuse U., 1979. Bar: N.Y. 1980, U.S. Supreme Ct. 1984. Legal asst. to county atty. Columbia County, Hudson, N.Y., 1980-82; asst. dep. counsel N.Y. State Dept. Taxation and Fin., Albany, 1982—. Com. mem. Columbia County Democratic Com., Hudson, 1981—. Recipient Evans award Hudson Housing Services Corp. (bd. dirs.), Russell Sage Coll., 1976. Mem. N.Y. State Bar Assn., Columbia County Bar Assn., State Women's Bar Assn. (bd. dirs. Capital Dist. chpt., sec.), Zonta (charter mem., 1st pres. Columbia-Greene area), Omicron Delta Epsilon. Roman Catholic. Home: 736 Union St Hudson NY 12534 Office: NY State Dept Taxation and Fin State Campus Office Bldg Albany NY 12227

MOSELLA, NANCY LEE, health science facility administrator; b. Railroad, Pa., Sept. 24, 1939; d. Lloyd Wilson and Ruth Alma (Holloway) Schuman; m. Anthony Paul Mosella, June 15, 1962. BS, York (Pa.) U., 1983. RN, Pa. Asst. charge nurse York Hosp., 1961-66; charge nurse Dr. L.G. Cooper's Office, York, 1966-72; staff nurse Community Health Ctr., York, 1972-74; charge nurse Drs. Mulligan & Woerthwein, York, 1974-79; asst. dir. nursing Leader Nursing and Rehab. Ctr., Dallastown, Pa., 1979-81, dir. nursing, 1981-83, asst. adminstr., 1983-85, adminstr., 1985—; sec. adv. council York County Area Agy. on Aging, 1985—. Pres. Aux. to Paid Firefighters, York, 1975-76. Recipient Vol. Services award York County Human Services Agys., 1986. Mem. Pa. Health Care Assn., Sigma Theta Tau. Republican. Lutheran. Club: Quota (York) (2d v.p. 1986-87, 1st v.p. 1987-88). Home: 159 Kirch Rd York PA 17402 Office: Leader Nursing and Rehab Ctr 100 W Queen St Dallastown PA 17313

MOSER, ELIZABETH KOHN, state agency administrator; b. Balt., Jan. 23, 1930; d. Martin Benno and Rosa (Rosenthal) Kohn; m. Martin Peter Moser, June 14, 1949; children: Martin Peter Jr., Deborah Moriah, Jeremy Richard. Student, Smith Coll., 1947-49, Simmons Coll., 1949-50; MA in Economic Geography, Johns Hopkins U., 1966. Research analyst, project dir. Morton Hoffman and Co., Balt., 1966-76; planner, adminstr. Office of the Sec. Md. Dept. Transpn., Balt.-Washington Internat. Airport, 1976-87, dep. dir. Office of Policy and Program Analysis, 1984—. Bd. dirs. Md. Jewish Hist. Soc., 1985—; chmn. bd. dirs. Balt. chpt. Am. Jewish Com., 1962-63. Mem. Women's Transpn. Seminar. Democrat. Home: 119 W Lee St Baltimore MD 21201

MOSER, MARTHA ANN, healthcare consultant, nurse; b. Lubbock, Tex., Dec. 7, 1941; d. John Cecil and Etta Mae (McDonald) Elam; m. Dennis Robert Moser, Mar. 3, 1962; children: Mitch Elam, Shanna Kaye. Student, West Tex. State U., 1960-62; BS in Nursing with distinction, U. Minn., 1972; postgrad., U. Houston, 1987—. RN. Staff nurse U. Minn. Hosps., Mpls., 1972-73, Combined Nursing Service, Mpls., 1973-74; team leader Vis. Nursing Assn., Portland, Oreg., 1974-76; educator patients St. Louis Park (Minn.) Med. Ctr., 1976-77; dir. nursing Med. Personnel Pool, Mpls., 1977-79; dir. home services Fairview Community Hosps., Mpls., 1980-84; mgr. nursing systems The Meth. Hosp., Houston, 1984-85; v.p., prin., cons. Dennis R. Moser and Assocs. Inc., Kingwood, Tex., 1985—. Mem. Altar Guild Episcopal Ch., Kingwood, 1986-87. Mem. Nat. Assn. Home Care Agys. (mem. panel annual meeting 1986), Nat. Hospice Orgn., AAUW (chmn. women's issues com. Kingwood chpt. 1984-85), Minn. League Nursing (chmn. legis. com. 1983-84), Tex. Assn. Home Care Agys. (legis. com. 1986-87), Tex. Assn. Home Health Agys., Tex. Hosp. Assn. (speaker annual meeting 1987), Alpha Delta Pi. Republican. Office: Dennis R Moser & Assocs 1975 Kingwood Dr Suite 204 Kingwood TX 77339

MOSER, ROSEMARIE SCOLARO, psychologist; b. Hackensack, N.J., June 16, 1954; d. Giovanni Natale and Mary (Bellaera) Scolaro; m. Robert Lawrence Moser, June 4, 1978; children: Rachel Ann, Alexander Robert. Student, Lafayette Coll., 1972-74; BA, U. Pa., 1976, MS, 1977, PhD, 1981. Lic. psychologist, N.J., Pa., Md.; cert. sch. psychologist, N.J., Pa., Del., Md. Doctoral intern Towson (Md.) State U. Counseling Ctr., 1979-80; counseling psychologist U. Md., Balt., 1980-84; sch. psychologist Lawrence Pub. Schs., Lawrenceville, N.J., 1984-85, Mercer County Non-Pub. Schs., Hamilton Square, N.J., 1985; pvt. practice psychology Morrisville, Pa. and Lawrenceville, N.J., 1985—; lectr. U. Pa., Phila., 1985-87; staff psychologist Helene Fuld Med. Ctr., Trenton, N.J., 1986—. Contbr. articles on psychology in profl. jours. Mem. Mercer County Med. Soc. Aux., N.J., 1987. Named one of Outstanding Young Women Am., 1980, Act-Discover grantee, 1986-87, Am. Assn. Counseling & Devel. Profl. Enhancement research grantee, 1986-87. Fellow Pa. Psychology Assn.; mem. Am. Psychology Assn. Div. 17, Am. Mental Health Counselors, N.J. Psychology Assn., N.J. Acad. Psychology (Psychologist Recognition award 1987), Ea. Psychol. Assn., Am. Assn. for Counseling and Devel. (proj. dir., grant recipient 1987-88). Office: 3131 Princeton Pike Bldg 6 Suite 101 Lawrenceville NJ 08648

MOSER, SARAH GUNNING, manufacturing engineer, small business owner; b. Seattle, Sept. 17, 1953; d. Harvey Dade and Grace Wills (Bell) Gunning; m. Lawrence Herman Moser, May 18, 1985; 1 child, Grace Elizabeth. BA in Archtl. Planning, The Evergreen State Coll., Olympia, Wash., 1975; mfg. engrng. cert., Boeing Mfg. Engrng. Sch., Everett, Wash., 1980. Asst. variety dept. mgr. The Safeway Corp., Seattle, 1977-79; mfg. engr. Boeing Co., 747/767 div., Everett, 1980-82; sr. mfg. engr. McDonnell Douglas Helicopter Co., Mesa, Ariz., 1982-87; engrng. trainer McDonnell Douglas Helicopter Co., Mesa, 1986-87, procedure writer, 1986-87; procedure writer The Boeing Co., Everett, 1981. Community outreach spkr. Alcohol Pub. Info. Com., Wash., 1976-80, 88, Evergreen State Coll.; coordinator Women's Ctr., Olympia, 1973-74; trainer, bd. dirs. Sta. KAOS-FM, Olympia, 1972-74; soloist Unity Ch. of Truth, Seattle, Everett, 1978-82; guest soloist various churches. Recipient Cost Savs. awards Boeing Co., 1980-82. Assoc. fellow. Am. Inst. Aeronautics and Astronautics; mem. Soc. Mfg. Engrs., Nat. Assn. Female Execs., Internat. Exec. Devel. Inc. Mem. Unity Ch. of Truth. Home and Office: Rt 5 Box 365C Vashon WA 98070 Office: Moser Design Assocs Rt 5 Box 365C Vashon WA 98070

MOSES, GLORIA ANN, investment management consultant; b. Berkeley, Calif., Nov. 7, 1938; d. Benjamin and Gertrude (Key) Golberger; m. Richard L. Hayden, July 18, 1958 (div. May 1972); children: Pamela, Jeffrey Hayden; m. David L. Moses, May 29, 1976. AA, U. Calif., 1958, student, 1958-60; student, Marin Community Coll., 1972-73. Field supr. S.R. Ctr. U. Calif., Berkeley, 1963-71; real estate broker Beacock & Maxson, Marin County, Calif., 1971-74; comml. broker, pres. Gloria Moses & Assoc., Newport Beach, Calif., 1974-79; comml. real estate broker J. McIntosh & Assoc., Bellevue, Wash., 1979-82; account exec. Drexel Burnham Lambert, Seattle, 1982-85; v.p. Oppenheimer & Co., Inc., Seattle, 1985-87, Shearson Lehman Hutton, Bellevue, Wash., 1987—; v.p., bd. dirs. DGM Corp., Seattle, 1985—; bd. dirs. Chautauqua, 1988—. Contbr. articles to profl. jours. Mem., contbr. Brandeis U.-Yeshiva, Jewish Fedn., Seattle, 1986. Mem. Nat. Assn. Securities Dealers, Am. Stock Exchange, N.Y. Stock Exchange, Investment Mgmt. Cons. Assn., Alaska State C. of C. Jewish. Club: Bellevue Athletic. Office: Shearson Lehman Hutton 10900 NE 8th St Suite 1500 Bellevue WA 98004

MOSHER, SALLY EKENBERG, lawyer; b. N.Y.C., July 26, 1934; d. Leslie Joseph and Frances Josephine (McArdle) Ekenberg; m. James Kimberly Mosher, Aug. 13, 1960 (dec. Aug. 1982). MusB, Manhattanville Coll., 1956; postgrad., Hofstra U., 1958-60, U. So. Calif., 1971-73; JD, U. So. Calif., 1981. Bar: Calif., 1982. Musician, pianist, tchr. 1957-74; music critic Pasadena Star-News, 1967-72; mgr. Contrasts Concerts, Pasadena Art Mus., N.Y., Los Angeles, 1971-72; rep. Occidental Life Ins. Co., Pasadena, 1975-78; v.p. James K. Mosher Co., Pasadena, 1961-82, pres., 1982—; pres. Oakhill Enterprises, Pasadena, 1984—; assoc. White-Howell, Inc., Pasadena, 1984—. Contbr. articles to various publs. Bd. dirs. Pasadena Arts Council, 1966-68, 86—, Jr. League Pasadena, 1966-67, Encounters Concerts, Pasadena, 1966-72, U. So. Calif. Friends of Music, Los Angeles, 1973-76, Pasadena Arts Council, 1986—, I Cantori, 1988—; mem. Citizen's Com. on Pub. Fin., Pasadena, 1985—, v.p. Pasadena Chamber Orchestra, 1986—; v.p., bd. dirs. Pasadena Chamber Orch., 1986—, pres., 1987—; mem. Calif. 200 Council for Bicentennial of U.S. Constn., 1987—. Manhattanville Coll. hon. scholar, 1952-56. Fellow Aspen Inst. for Humanistic Studies, Fellows of Contemporary Art (Los Angeles); mem. ABA, Calif. Bar Assn., Los Angeles Bar Assn., Pasadena Bar Assn., Nat. Assn. Realtors, Am. Assn. Realtors, Calif. Assn. Realtors, Pasadena Bd. Realtors, Assocs. of Calif. Inst. Tech., Kappa Gamma Pi, Mu Phi Epsilon, Phi Alpha Delta. Republican. Club: Athenaeum. Home: 1260 Rancheros Rd Pasadena CA 91103 Office: 711 E Walnut St Suite 407 Pasadena CA 91101

MOSHER STUMP, JOLENE (JO), journalist, publishing executive. d. Alfred Clinton and Geraldine Iva Mae (Sheldon) Hodges; m. Al J. Stump; children: Robyn Jean, Sharyn Lee. Student, Los Angeles City Coll., 1940, Glendale (Calif.) Coll., 1941, UCLA, 1941, 43, U. So. Calif., 1945-47. Journalist S.E. News, Downey, Calif., 1950-55, Palos Verdes (Calif.) Newspapers, 1965-67, Press Telegram, Long Beach, Calif., 1967-78, Los Angeles Herald Examiner, 1968-84; owner, pres. Celebrity Press, Los Angeles, 1984—. Columnist Wish You Were Here, 1969-84 (10 awards), Ala Carte; editor spl. sect. House and Garden, 1967 (1st pl. 1967). Bd. dirs. sch. extension in journalism UCLA, 1983-85; sec. Am. Nat. Theater Aux.; mem. Meml. Med. Found., Long Beach, 1986—. Recipient Miss Today Flying award Pvt. Pilots Assn., 1967, Flying Orchard award Delta Air Lines, 1975. Mem. Soc. Profl. Journalists, Nat. Press Women, Am. Women in Radio and TV. Club: Greater Los Angeles Press (bd. dirs. 1970-86, sec. edn. found. 1980-86, pres. 1984, hon. life mem.).

MOSKAL, JANINA, high technology manufacturing executive; b. Czerna, Poland, June 6, 1944; came to U.S., 1963; d. Stanislaw and Agata (Kleczek) Kot; m. Tadeusz J. Moskal, Dec. 29, 1960 (div. 1981); children: Robert R., Thomas L. Student, L.I. U., 1976-78; AAS, Nassau Community Coll., 1980. Machine operator Photocircuits Corp., Glen Cove, N.Y., 1966-70, programmer, 1970-72, supr., 1972-81, engr. process support, 1981-83, systems mgr. laser graphics, 1984-86; gen. mgr., ptnr. NC Design Corp., Williston Park, N.Y., 1983-84; systems mgr. Parlex Corp., Methuen, Mass., 1984-87; mfg. specialist Rothtec Engraving Corp., New Bedford, Mass., 1987—; owner, prin. JM Cons., Glen Cove, 1987—; organizer, instr. tech. courses and seminars, 1980-81, 1986-87. Officer Polish Nat. Home, Glen Cove, 1975-79, Polonia, Glen Cove, 1978. Republican. Roman Catholic. Office: JM Cons Co 109 Shore Rd Glen Cove NY 11542

MOSKOWITZ, RANDI ZUCKER, nurse; b. N.Y.C., Oct. 19, 1948; d. Seymour and Gertrude (Levy) Zucker; R.N., Jewish Hosp. & Med. Center Sch. Nursing, 1969; B.A., Marymount Manhattan Coll., 1975; M.S., Hunter Coll., 1979; postgrad. in bus. Baruch Coll.; m. Marc N. Moskowitz, July 11, 1976. Gen. staff nurse neurosurgery unit, N.Y. Hosp., N.Y.C., 1969-71, sr. staff nurse Recovery Room, 1971-76, nurse coordinator utilization rev., 1976-79; health educator Office of Cancer Communications, Meml. Sloan-Kettering Cancer Center, 1979-81; adminstrv. nurse oncologist Bklyn. Community Hosp. Oncology Program, Meth. Hosp., 1981-83, grants coordinator radiotherapy dept., 1983-86; adminstr. Ambulatory Oncology Ctr., Columbia-Presbyn. Med. Ctr., N.Y.C., 1986—. instr. Div. Gen. Studies, Community Health and Health Adminstrn., St. Joseph's Coll., 1979-86. Mem. Am. Public Health Assn., Oncology Nursing Soc. (sec. N.Y.C. chpt. 1983-87), Soc. for Pub. Health Edn. (sec. tri-state chpt. 1982-84, membership chmn. 1984-87), Nat. Hospice Orgn., City-Wide Adv. Council on Sch. Health (sec. 1983-87), Patient Edn. Consortium, Am. Cancer Soc. Contbr. articles to profl. jours. Home: 222 E 80th St New York NY 10021 Office: 161 Ft Washington Ave New York NY 10032

MOSS, BARBARA WONG, public relations executive; b. Berkeley, Calif., Apr. 14, 1934; d. Wing and Ruth (Lee) W.; m. Arthur H. Moss, Aug. 20, 1960 (div. June 1980); 1 child, John A. BA, U. Calif., Berkeley, 1955; MBA, Drexel U., 1980. Cert. tchr., Calif., Pa. Tchr. Calif. Schs., 1955-58, Japan, Germany, 1958-60; mgr. planning Bell of Pa., Phila., 1980-83, mgr. mktg., 1983-86, mgr. pub. relations, 1986—; cons. computers, Phila., 1985—. Pres. LWV, Radnor, Pa., 1974-76; planner Radnor Twp., 1985—; trustee Delaware County Community Coll., Pa. 1980—, chmn. bd. 1986—. Mem. Phi Beta Kappa. Republican. Unitarian. Home: 121 Poplar Ave Wayne PA 19087 Office: Bell of Pa One Pkwy Philadelphia PA 19102

MOSS, DORIS LANETTE, engineer; b. Miami, Fla., Dec. 13, 1954; d. Ollie E. and Clara Parker; m. Joseph I. Moss, Dec. 5, 1977; children: Angela Christine, Terri Nicole. BS, Fla. Internat. U., 1977; postgrad., Barry U., 1985—. Cert. tchr., Fla. Tchr. math. Dade County Pub. Schs., Miami, 1977-78; rep. service So. Bell Telephone Co., Miami, 1978-80, engr. outside plant facilities, 1981—. Leader Girl Scout U.S.A., Miami, 1980—. Mem. Nat. Orgn. Profl. Women. Democrat. Home: 10814 SW 141st Ln Miami FL 33176 Office: So Bell Telephone Co 9500 SE 180 St Miami FL 33157

MOSS, ELIZABETH LUCILLE (BETTY), transportation company executive; b. Ironton, Mo., Feb. 13, 1939; d. James Leon and Dorothy Lucille (Russell) Rollen; m. Elliott Theodore Moss, Nov. 10, 1963 (div. Jan. 1984); children: Robert Belmont, Wendy Rollen. BA in Econs. and Bus. Adminstrn., Drury Coll., 1960. Registrar, transp. mgr. Cheley Colo. Camps, Inc., Denver and Estes Park, 1960-61; office mgr. Washington Nat. Ins. Co., Denver, 1960-61; sec. White House Decorating, Denver, 1961-62; adminstrv. asst. Ringsby Truck Lines, Denver, Oakland, Calif., and Los Angeles, 1962-67, System 99 Freight Lines, Los Angeles, 1967-69; terminal mgr. System 99 Freight Lines, Stockton, Calif., 1981-84; adminstrv. asst. Yellow Freight System, Los Angeles, 1969-74, Hayward, Calif., 1974-77; ops. mgr. Yellow Freight System, Urbana, Ill., 1977-80; sales rep. Calif. Motor Express, San Jose, 1981; regional sales mgr. Schneider Nat. Carriers, Inc., No. Calif., 1984-86; account exec. TNT-Can., Nev. and Cen. Calif., 1986-88; mgr. Interstate-Intermodal Divs. HVH Transp., Denver, 1988—; chmn. operation council for San Joaquin and Stanislaus Counties Calif. Trucking Assn., 1983-84; planning adv. com. Truck Accident Reduction Projects, San Joaquin County, 1987—. Mem. Econ. Devel. Council Stockton C. of C., 1985-86; active Edison High Sch. Boosters, 1982-88. Mem. Nat. Def. Transp. Assn. (bd. dirs. 1986-87), Stockton Traffic Club (bd. dirs. 1982-84), Delta Nu Alpha (bd. dirs. Region 1 1982-84, v.p. Chpt. 103 1984-85, pres. 1985-86, chmn. bd. 1985-87, regional sec. 1987—, Outstanding Achievement award 1986). Methodist. Stockton Traff (Trucker of Yr. 1983). Home: 8735 W Cornell #6 Lakewood CO 80227

MOSS, JEANINE LAURA, publisher, consultant; b. Frederick, Md., Jan. 16, 1955; d. Leonard James and Gertrude (Honegger) Spielberger; m. Stanley Lewis Moss, Nov. 3, 1948. Student, Santa Barbara (Calif.) City Coll., 1972-73, Forest Park Coll., St. Louis, 1973-74, San Francisco State U., 1974-76, U. So. Calif., 1978. V.p. Slade, Gross & Assocs., Santa Barbara, 1976-78; asst. dir. Davies Advt. Inc., Santa Barbara, 1978-79; exec. asst. Corp. Property Investors, N.Y.C., 1980-81; exec. Gerald Schoenfeld Inc., N.Y.C., 1981-83; pub. Woman's Travel Connections, N.Y.C., 1983-86; pres. Travel Trends Pub. Inc., N.Y.C., 1984—; cons. Northwest Airlines Inc., Mpls., 1987—. Contbr. articles to profl. jours. Founding dir. Katastromsa Soc. , N.Y.C., 1980—; bd. dirs. U.S. Art from Planet Earth, N.Y.C., 1987—; mem. Nat. Mus. Women's Art, Washington, 1986. Recipient Monty McKinney award Am. Assn. Advt. Agys., Los Angeles, 1978. Mem. Women Execs. in Travel and Tourism, Profl. and Exec. Women, Newsletter Assn. Club: Santa Barbara Garden. Office: Travel Trends Pub Inc PO Box 6117 New York NY 10150

MOSS, KAREN MANDLEBAUM, law librarian; b. Boston, Mar. 11, 1938; d. Daniel and Naomi (Kranson) Mandlebaum; children: Lauren Rachel, Jonathan David. BA in Edn., Wayne State U., 1959, MS of Library Sci., 1971. Cert. law librarian. Tchr. elem. sch. Southfield, Mich., 1959-61; staff tech. services Oakland County Law Library, Pontiac, Mich., 1972-75; tech. services librarian Adams-Pratt Oakland County Law Library, Pontiac, 1975-76; librarian U.S. Dist. Ct. (ea. dist.) Mich., Detroit, 1977-79; cir. librarian U.S. Ct. Appeals (1st cir.), Boston, 1979—; dir. Law Library Microform Consortium, Honolulu, 1985—. Contbr. articles to profl. jours. Mem. Friends of the Library, Lincoln, Mass., 1986—. Mem. Am. Assn. Law Libraries, Law Librarians of New Eng. (pres. 1983), Assn. Boston Law Librarians, Fed. Ct. Librarians User Group (chairperson 1981). Democrat. Jewish. Clubs: The Boston. Office: US Ct Appeals Library 1208 McCormack Courthouse and Post Office Boston MA 02109

MOSS, PATRICIA ARLENE, union official; b. Cleve., May 6, 1947; d. Shirley Leon and Pauline (Frelich) Moss. B.A., Ohio U., 1969; J.D., Cleve. Marshall Coll. Law, 1981. Bar: Ohio 1981. Adminstrv. specialist Cuyahoga County Welfare Dept., Cleve., 1969-72; gen. rep. Ohio Council 8, Am. Fedn. State, County and Mcpl. Employees, AFL-CIO, Cleve., 1972-87, regional dir., 1987—; bd. dirs. Council Econ. Opportunities Greater Cleve., 1986-87; trustee Ohio Council 8 Health and Welfare Fund, Cleve., 1983—. Mem. Columbus (Ohio) Democratic Exec. Com., 1983—; trustee, sec. bd. Council for Econ. Opportunities Greater Cleve., 1980—. Mem. ABA, Ohio Bar Assn., Audubon Soc., Smithsonian Assoc., Cousteau Soc. Roman Catholic. Home: 1289 W 103d St Cleveland OH 44102 Office: 2975 Superior Ave Ohio Council 8 AFSCME AFL-CIO Cleveland OH 44114

MOSS, PATRICIA DIANE, bank examiner; b. Richwood, W.Va., Aug. 22, 1960; d. James Russell and Sandra June (Hamric) M. BBA, Fairmont State Coll., 1982. Nat. bank examiner Office of the Comptroller of the Currency, Washington, 1981—. Mem. Moral Majority. Mem. Nat. Assn. Female Execs. Republican. Baptist. Office: Comptroller of the Currency 6100 Fairview Rd Charlotte NC 28210

MOSS, ROSE, management consultant; b. Johannesburg, Republic of South Africa, Jan. 2, 1937; d. David Hirsch and Yetta (Eides) Rappaport; m. Stanley Felix, Apr. 30, 1964 (div. 1981); 1 child, Duncan John. BA, U. Witwatersand, Johannesburg, 1957; Degree in English, U. Natal, 1959; MBA, Boston U., 1983. Lectr. Wellesly (Mass.) Coll., 1972-82; pres. Rose Moss Assocs., Newton, Mass., 1984—; assoc. Synectics, Cambridge, Mass., 1984. Author: The Family Reunion, 1974, The Terrorist, 1979 (New Fiction Soc. award 1979); published several articles, stories, poems. Fellow Yaddo Found, 1977, MacDowell Colony, 1976, 79, Mellon Found, 1980. Mem. Poets Essayists Novelists. Home and Office: 580 Walnut St Newtonville MA 02160

MOSS, SANDRA HUGHES, law firm administrator; b. Atlanta, Dec. 24, 1945; d. Harold Melvin and Velma Aileen (Norton) H.; m. Marshall L. Moss, May 1, 1965; children—Tara Celise, Justin Hughes. Student W. Ga. Coll., 1964-65. Legal sec. Smith, Cohen, Ringel, Kohler & Martin, Atlanta, 1965-78; real estate salesman Century 21-Phoenix, College Park, Ga., 1978-80; office mgr./personnel dir. Smith, Cohen, Ringel, Kohler & Martin, Atlanta, 1980-85; dir. adminstrn. Smith, Gambrell & Russell, Atlanta, 1985—. Bd. dirs., sec. North Clayton Athletic Assn., Riverdale, Ga., 1981-83; sec. E.W. Oliver PTA, Riverdale, 1981; exec. com. E.W. Oliver and N. Clayton Jr. PTA, Riverdale, 1980, 81, 82; den leader Cub Scouts, Pack 959, Riverdale, 1984. Mem. Am. Soc. Personnel Adminstrs, Assn. Legal Adminstrs. (sec. Atlanta chpt. 1988). Home: 1627 Laurancea Way Riverdale GA 30296 Office: Smith Gambrell & Russell 2400 First Atlanta Tower 2 Peachtree St Atlanta GA 30383

MOSS, SUSAN LINDA, nurse; b. Charlotte, N.C., Sept. 29, 1948; d. Edward and Rose (Goldstein) M. BS in Nursing, U. Fla., 1971; MS in Health Care Adminstrn., U. South Fla., 1977. RN. Fla. Nurse Shands Teaching Hosp., Gainesville, Fla., 1971; head nurse Walston Army Hosp., Ft. Dix, N.J., 1971-72; nurse Bay Pines (Fla.) VA Med. Ctr., 1973-74, 75-77, Gainesville VA Med. Ctr., 1974-75; instr. Bay Pines VA Med. Ctr., 1977-78, supr., 1978-81; asst. chief nursing service Shreveport (La.) VA Med. Ctr., 1981-83, Jerry L. Pettis Meml. VA Hosp., Loma Linda, Calif., 1983-85, Durham (N.C.) VA Med. Ctr., 1985-87; chief nursing service Jerry L. Pettis Meml. VA Hosp., Loma Linda, Calif., 1987—; bd. dirs. Desert Area Wellness Network, Palm Springs, Calif. 1984-85; pres. Triangle chpt. Mission Air, Durham 1987—; chmn. task force Identify Health Care Needs Female Vets., 1985; instr., organizer Regional Edn. Program 1982. Organizer Spl. Olympics, St. Petersburg, Fla., 1979-80. Named Citizen Yr., Kiwanis Club St. Petersburg, 1979. Mem. Sigma Theta Tau (mem. selection com. 1986-87). Home: 355 Highlander Dr Riverside CA 92507 Office: Jerry L Pettis Meml VA Hosp Benton St Loma Linda CA 92357

MOSS, VICKI, journalist; b. N.Y.C., Sept. 8, 1936, d. Max and Minnie (Weissman) Dresher; m. Lawrence Moss, Mar. 18, 1956 (div. Nov. 1972); children: Ronald Scott, Andrew Lewis. B in Philosophy, CCNY, 1969; M in English, Colo. State U., 1984; M in Philosophy, CUNY, 1987. Lectr. philosophy CCNY, N.Y.C., 1970-73; dir. women's dept. Cen. State Bank, N.Y.C., 1974-77; founder, pres. Personomics, N.J. and N.Y., 1975-79; reporter The Record, Hackensack, N.J., 1979-82; lectr. English Colo. State U., Ft. Collins, 1982-84; reporter The Coloradoan (Gannett), Ft. Collins, 1984-85; free-lance journalist consumer and trade press, N.Y.C., 1985—; lectr. English Queens Coll., N.Y.C., 1985—; speaker Fin. Problems of Women, 1977. Author: Leaving Home, 1980 (CCNY award 1981); author Masks, 1984; contbr. articles to profl. jours. Counselor domestic violence shelters, Hackensack, N.J., 1977, Paterson, N.J., 1978-82. Recipient award Investigative Reporting Gannett, 1984, The Coloradoan, 1984. Mem. Women in Communications Inc., N.Y. Assn. Women Bus. Owners (founder 1976), New Amsterdam Writers Collective, Salute to Women in the Arts. Home: 394 Clinton St Brooklyn NY 11231

MOSSE, SHARON BETH, advertising executive; b. Pitts., May 26, 1950; d. Daniel T. and Cecelia (Mason) M. BA, Williams Coll.; MBA, U. Pa. Account exec. Ogilvy & Mather, N.Y.C., 1976-80; v.p., account supr. Ted Bates Advt., N.Y.C., 1980-84, sr. v.p., mgmt. rep., 1984-86; exec. v.p. Backer-Spievogel Bates, N.Y.C., 1987—; bd. dirs., cons. Starlight Found., N.Y.C., 1986-87. Office: Backer-Spielvogel Bates 1515 Broadway New York NY 10036

MOSSER, MARLA BIANCO, management consultant; b. Easton, Pa., July 20, 1953; d. Thomas S. and Alvera (Tomaino) Bianco; m. Bart H. Mosser, Feb. 23, 1979. BS in Edn. cum laude, West Chester U., 1975, MA in Psychology, 1977; M in Mgmt., Northwestern U., 1986. Teaching asst. psychology dept. West Chester (Pa.) U., 1975-76, psychology intern Counseling Ctr., 1976-77; counselor-therapist Devereux Found., Exton, Pa., 1976-77, psychotherapist, 1977-78; cons. Crawford Rehab. Services, Phila., 1978-79, Boston, 1979-80; v.p. J.M. Boros and Assoc., Ltd., Chgo., 1980-86; cons. Marla B. Mosser Assocs., 1987—; lectr. in field. Bd. dirs. Ctr. for Grieving Children, 1988—; mem. planning com. Maine State Council for Vols., 1988. Mem. Women in Mgmt. (career devel. com. Chgo. chpt. 1983-84), Am. Soc. Personnel Adminstrs., Northwestern U. Profl. Women's Assn., Kappa Delta Pi, Psi Chi.

MOTHERSHEAD, ALICE BONZI (MRS. MORRIS WARNER MOTHERSHEAD), retired college administrator, civic worker; b. Milan, Italy, Dec. 25, 1914; came to U.S. 1920, naturalized 1925; d. Ercole and Alice (Spalding) Bonzi; pvt. pupil music and art; student Pasadena City Coll., 1958-60; m. Morris Warner Mothershead, Sept. 15, 1935; children: Warner Bonzi, Maria (Mrs. Andrei Rogers). Partner Float Toy Co., Pasadena, Calif., 1942-44; community adv. Fgn. Student Program, Pasadena City Coll., from 1952, past dir. Community Liaison Center. Chmn., Am. Field Service Internat. Scholarships, Pasadena, 1953-55; mem. West Coast adv. com. Inst. Internat. Edn., San Francisco, 1957-70. Vice pres. San Rafael Sch. PTA, Pasadena, 1945-46; active Community Chest, ARC, Pasadena; chmn. Greater Los Angeles Com. Internat. Student and Visitor Services, 1962; mem. Woman's Civic League Pasadena, chmn. city affairs com., 1985, pres., 1986-87; bd. dirs. Fine Arts Club of Pasadena, 1983-85, Friends of Caltech Y, 1984—, Pasadena City Coll. Found., 1983-85; commr. City of Pasadena Cultural Heritage Commn., 1984—. Decorated knight Govt. of Italy, 1975. Mem. Nat. Assn. Fgn. Student Affairs (life, chmn. community sect. and v.p. 1964-65, chmn. U.S. study abroad com. 1969-70), Am. Assn. UN (chpt. 2d v.p. 1964), Soc. Women Geographers, Am. Friends Middle East, Zonta Internat., Omicron Mu Delta. Club: International (Pasadena). Author: Social Customs and Manners in the United States, 1957; Dining Customs Around the World, 1982; co-author: 15 Years of the Foreign Student Program at Pasadena City College, 1965. Editor: Students to People to Future, 1971. Lodge: Lions. Home: 675 Burleigh Dr Pasadena CA 91105

MOTLEY, CONSTANCE BAKER (MRS. JOEL WILSON MOTLEY), judge, former city official; b. New Haven, Sept. 14, 1921; d. Willoughby Alva and Rachel (Huggins) Baker; m. Joel Wilson Motley, Aug. 18, 1946; 1 son, Joel Wilson, III. A.B., N.Y. U., 1943; LL.B., Columbia U., 1946. Bar: N.Y. bar 1948. Mem. Legal Def. and Ednl. Fund, NAACP, 1945-65; mem. N.Y. State Senate, 1964-65; pres. Manhattan Borough, 1965-66; U.S. dist. judge So. Dist. N.Y., 1966-82, chief judge, 1982-86, sr. judge, 1986—. Mem. N.Y. State Adv. Council Employment and Unemployment Ins., 1958-64. Mem. Assn. Bar City N.Y. Office: US Dist Ct US Courthouse Foley Sq New York NY 10007

MOTT, KAREN RENÉ, geophysicist; b. Sulpher, La., Mar. 23, 1959; d. Edgar Dewey and Eunice Pauline (Pond) M. A in Bus. Adminstrn., Alvin Community Coll., 1979; BS in Geophysics, Tex. A&M U., 1980. Exploration geophysicist Gulf Oil, Houston, 1981, Unocal, Houston, 1982—. Active S.E. Tex. chpt. M.S. Soc., Houston, 1986—; mem. Alley Theatre Guild, Houston, 1986—; chair com. Brazoria Kennel Assn., Angleton, Tex., 1985-87. Mem. Soc. Exploration Geophysics, Geophys. Soc. Houston, Nat. Assn. Female Execs. Roman Catholic. Office: Unocal 4635 SW Freeway Suite 275 Houston TX 77027

MOTT, MARY ELIZABETH, educator; b. West Hartford, Conn., July 10, 1931; d. Marshall Amos and Mary Salome (Herman) M. B.A., Conn. Coll. Women, 1953; M.A., Western Res. U., 1963. Cert. tchr., Ohio; cert. computer tchr., Ohio. Mgr. sales promotion Cleve. Electric Illuminating Co., 1953-60; tchr. Newbury Bd. Edn., Ohio, 1960-67, West Geauga Bd. Edn., Chesterland, Ohio, 1967—; chmn. state certification com. in computers ECCO, Mayfield, Ohio, 1983—, exec. bd., 1980—. Asst. dir. West Geauga Day Camp, Chesterland, 1968. Mem. Ednl. Computer Consortium Ohio, Delta Kappa Gamma. Republican. Clubs: MAC Users Group, NEO Apple Corps, Nat. Assn. Playing Card Collectors. Avocations: golf, travel, reading, gardening, computers. Office: Westwood Sch 13738 Caves Rd Chesterland OH 44026

MOTTOLO, DEBORAH, interior designer; b. Cambridge, Mass., Oct. 23, 1965; d. Gerald Joseph and Carol Ann (Vitagliano) M. A in Interior Design, Endicott Coll., Beverly Mass., 1985. Kitchen designer, sales Internat. Design Assocs., Boston, 1984-85, Andover (Mass.) Kitchen and Bath Ctr., 1985—. Mem. Nat. Kitchen and Bath Assn. Home: 1 Morse Ave Wilmington MA 01887 Office: Andover Kitchen & Bath Ctr 2 Stevens St Andover MA 01810

MOTZKIN, EVELYN HERSZKORN, psychiatrist; b. Warsaw, Poland, Jan. 12, 1933; d. Joseph and Eda (Itzkowitz) Herszkorn; m. Donald Motzkin, 1955; children: Patricia, Linda, Neil, Nancy, Richard, Lisa. M.D., SUNY, 1958; Ph.D. in Psychoanalysis, So. Calif. Inst. Psychoanalysis, 1978. Intern, Vassar Bros. Hosp., 1958-59; fellow in endocrinology Baylor U., Houston, 1960-62, resident in psychiatry, 1962-64; resident in psychiatry VA Hosp., Sepulveda, Calif., 1965-67; practice psychiatry and psychoanalysis, Encino, Calif., 1967—; cons. Sepulveda VA Hosp., 1967-68, Jewish Home for Aged, 1968-71; clin. instr. UCLA Neuropsychiat. Inst., 1969-71; instr. So. Calif. Psychoanalytic Inst., 1980—; coordinator U. Judaism Extension Div. and So. Calif. Psychoanalytic Inst., 1983; mem. staff Woodview Calabasas Hosp., Med. Ctr. Tarzana, Calif., Encino Hosp., Calif., Rancho Encino Hosp. Initiator, chmn. psychiat. div. San Fernando Valley United Jewish Welfare Fund, 1977, 78; major gifts co-chmn. United Jewish Appeal, San Fernando, 1979; mem. community relations council United Jewish Fedn., 1982-86, bd. dirs. 1986-88; bd. dirs. Assn. Mental Health Affiliation with Israel; pres. Women's pro-Israel Nat. Polit. Action Com., 1986-88. Recipient Ben Gurion award San Fernando Valley State of Israel Bonds Med. Div., 1977. Mem. So. Calif. Psychoanalytic Soc. (exec. com. 1980-81, sec. treas. 1981-83, chmn. membership com. 1983), Am. Psychiat. Assn., So. Calif. Psychiat. Assn., Internat. Psychoanalytic Assn., Am. Psychoanalytic Assn., Israeli Med. Assn., Physicians for Israel. Office: Motzkin Med Corp 5353 Balboa Blvd Encino CA 91316

MOUBAYED, MARIA NABIH, insurance sales professional; b. Lebanon, May 8, 1962; d. Nabih Jamil and Rima Hana (Khayat) Z. B of Organizational Behavior, U. Houston, 1984. Asst. at circulations desk M.D. Anderson Library at U. Houston, 1980-84; asst. mgr. K-Mart Apparel Corp. K-Mart Corp., Houston, 1984, ins. agt. K-Mart Ins. Co., 1985; ins. agt. Mem.'s Life Ins. div. Tex. League Credit Union, Houston, 1985—. Mem. Arabic choir and festival St. George Orthodox Ch., Houston. Mem. Nat. Assn. Female Execs. Greek Orthodox. Home: 14811 Scotter Houston TX 77015 Office: Mem's Ins Co 3303 Main St Houston TX 77226

MOULTON, KATHERINE KLAUBER, hotel executive; b. Buffalo, Nov. 28, 1956; d. Murray Joseph and Joanna (Brown) Klauber; m. Michael Arthur Moulton, July, 10, 1982. BS, Cornell U., 1978. Hotel and restaurant designer Cini-Grissom Assoc., Potomac, Md., 1978-82; gen. mgr. Colony Beach Resort, Longboat Key, Fla., 1982—; owner Le Tennique, Longboat Key, 1982—; exec. v.p., cons., designer Total Environments, Longboat Key, 1982—; exec. v.p. The Reserve Devel., Longboat Key, 1985—. Contbr. articles to restaurant and hotel design mags. Mem. Coquille, Sarasota, Fla., 1982—; organizer, fund raiser St. Jude's Children's Research Hosp., 1982—. Mem. Cornell Soc. of Hotelmen. Office: Colony Beach Resort 1620 Gulf of Mexico Dr Longboat Key FL 34228

MOUNDS, LEONA MAE REED, educator; b. Crosby, Tex., Sept. 9, 1945; d. Elton Phillip and Ora Lee (Jones) Reed; m. Aaron B. Mounds Jr., Aug. 21, 1965 (div.); 1 dau., Lisa Nichelle. B.S. in Elem. Edn., Bridgewater State Coll., 1973; M.A. in Mental Retardation, U. Alaska, 1980. Cert. tchr. Alaska, Colo., Tex., Mass., cert. adminstrv. prin. 1985. Tchr., Sch. Dist. 11, Colorado Springs, Colo., 1973-75; tchr. Anchorage Sch. Dist., 1976-78, 80—, mem. math. curriculum com., reading contact tchr., mem. talent bank. Tchr. Del Valle (Tex.) Sch. Dist., 1979-80. Bd. dirs. Urban League, 1974; 1st v.p. PTA, Crosby, Tex.; del. Tex. Democratic Conv., 1980, dist. 13 chair Dem. party, Anchorage; tchr. religious edn., lay Eucharist minister St. Martin De Pores Roman Cath. Ch., St. Patrick's Ch. Served with USAF, 1964-66. Alaska State Tchr. Incentive grantee, 1981; Ivy Lutz scholar, 1972. Mem. NEA (human relations coordinator Alaska chpt., region 6 bd. dirs., Alaska chpt. bd. dirs., vice chmn. women's caucus), Anchorage Edn. Assn. (minority chmn. 1982—, mem. Black Caucus polit. action com., v.p. programs 1986-88), Black Educators of Pikes Peak Region (pres. 1974), Anchorage Edn. Assn. (v.p. programs com. 1986-87, women's caucus), Assn. Supervision and Curriculum Devel., Alaska Women in Adminstrn., Council for Exception Children, NAACP.

MOUNT, WARD (PAULINE WARD), painter, sculptor; b. Batavia, N.Y., Jan. 8, 1898; d. Fred Kendall and Nellie L. (Dowsey) Ward; m. Elmer M. Mount, M.D.; 1 son, Marshall. Grad., Flushing High Sch.; student, New York Univ., Art Students League; pupil of, Gertrude Gardner, Kenneth Hayes Miller, Albert P. Lucas, Joseph P. Pollia. Former head of dept., oil painting and sculpture N.J. State Tchrs. Coll.; founder, former dir. of art classes at the Jersey City Med. Center, N.J.; dir., instr. Ward Mount Art Classes. Represented by paintings and sculptures in permanent collections pvt. colls., art museums, U.S. and fgn., including, N.A.D., Library of Congress, Nat. Sculpture Soc., Archtl. League N.Y., Allied Artists Am., Allied Arts Mus., N.Y.C., Acad. Allied Arts, N.Y.C., Am. Brit. Art Center, Kearny Mus., Mont Clair Art Mus., Audubon Artists, Pa. Acad., Westchester Art Assn., Mus. Modern Art, N.Y.C., Macy Galleries, Smithsonian Inst., The Carlebach Galleries, N.Y.C., Worlds Fair N.Y., Medallic Art, Lever House, N.Y. Hist. Soc., Columbia U. Library, Marquis Biog. Library, Chgo., Riverside Mus., Nat. Arts Club, Am. Heart Assn., Trenton State Mus., Audubon Artists, Hudson River Mus., Delgado Mus., Jersey City Mus., Provincetown Art Gallery, Bergen County (N.J.) Mus.; Designed: bronze Medal of Honor for, Painters and Sculptors Soc. N.J., 1947; Christmas card for, Am. Heart Assn., 1971. Hon. fellow J.F. Kennedy Found. Recipient numerous awards and prizes for sculpture and painting, including Gold medal Woman of Achievement, Jersey Jour., 1971; Plaque of Honor, Jersey City Mus., 1980, citation Jersey City Hist. Assn., 1987; named Artist of Yr., Hudson Artists, 1984; honoree at Statue of Liberty Gala, 1986. Fellow Royal Soc. of Arts (Eng.), Internat. Inst. Arts and Letters; mem. Painters and Sculptors Soc. N.J., Inc. (founder, hon. pres.), Artists Equity, Internat. Platform Assn., DAR, Women of the Arts Mus. (charter), Acad. of Italy (gold medal mem.), several other artists and sculptors assns. Studio: 74 Sherman Pl Jersey City NJ 07307

MOUNTZ, LOUISE CARSON SMITH, media consultant; b. Fond Du Lac, Wis., Oct. 20, 1911; d. Roy Carson and Charlotte Louise (Scheurs) Smith; m. George Edward Mountz, May 4, 1935 (dec. Oct. 1951); children: Peter, Pamela. Student, Western Coll., 1929-31; AB, The Ohio State U., 1933; MA, Ball State U., 1962; postgrad., Manchester Coll., 1954, Ind. U., 1960-61. Cert. tchr. (life), Ind. Tchr. Monroeville (Ind.) High Sch., 1953-54, Riverdale High Sch., St. Joe, Ind., 1954-55; librarian High Sch., Avilla, Ind., 1955-58; head librarian Penn High Sch., Mishawaka, Ind., 1958-67, Northwood Jr. High Sch., Ft. Wayne, Ind., 1967-69, McIntosh Jr. High Sch., Auburn, Ind., 1969-74; dir. Media Ctr. DeKalb Jr. High Sch., Auburn, Ind., 1974-78; ret. 1978; cons. media ctr. planning Penn-Harris-Madison Sch. Corp., Mishawaka, 1966-67. Author: Biographies of Junior High Schools; contbr. articles to profl. jours. Bd. dirs. DeKalb County chpt. ARC, 1938-42, 51-53, DeKalb County Heart Assn., 1946-52, DeKalb County Community Concert Assn., 1946-58, Am. Field Service Mishawaka chpt., 1960-67. Mem. AAUW, ALA, World Confedn. Orgns. Teaching Professions, Nat. Council Tchrs. English, NEA, Ind. Sch. Librarians Assn. (dir. 1963-67), Internat. Assn. Sch. Librarianship, Ft. Wayne Art Mus., Ind. Assn. Ednl. Communication and Tech., Assn. Ind. Media Educators, Ind. Tchrs. Assn., Ind. Garrett, DeKalb County, Allen County, Ft. Wayne Hist. Socs., DeKalb County Ind., Nat. Ret. Tchrs. Assns., Ft. Wayne YWCA, Nat. Trust Hist. Preservation, Delta Kappa Gamma (charter mem., v.p. Beta Beta chpt. 1960-62), Kappa Kappa Kappa (st. officer 1941-45, pres. Alpha Chi chpt. 1938-40, Garrett Assoc. chpt. 1971-73), Delta Delta Delta (house pres.), Epsilon Sigma Omicron, DeKalb Meml. Hosp. Women's Guild (life). Methodist. Lodge: Order Ea. Star. Clubs: Greenhurst Counrty, Ft. Wayne Women's, Athena Lit. (hon. mem.), Auburn Ladies Lit.

MOUSSATOS, MARTHA ANN TYREE, librarian; b. Parris Island, S.C., Sept. 18, 1936; d. Frank La Prade and Vireen Florrie (Varn) Tyree; m. Apostolos Harilaos Moussatos, June 27, 1959; children—Vasiliana Vireen, Harilaos Apostolos. B.A., Columbia Coll., 1958; M.L.S., U. Ariz., 1974. Asst. reference librarian U. S.C., Columbia, 1958-59; librarian Fulton High Sch., Atlanta, 1962; substitute tchr. pub. schs., Sierra Vista, Ariz., 1967-68; librarian Naco Elem. Sch. (Ariz.), 1968-70, Benson High Sch. (Ariz.), 1970-75; head librarian Depot Library, Parris Island, S.C., 1975—. Author: Hagar (play), 1980; Young Eliza (play), 1958; Marshgrass and Muscadines (poetry), 1980; Scuppernong Wine at Room Temperature (poetry), 1984; contbr. articles to profl. jours. and popular mags. Mem. Historic Port Royal Found. (S.C.), 1976—, bd. dirs., 1981—. Recipient award as head of outstanding single parent family Beaufort County Homebuilders Assn. (S.C.), 1980. Mem. ALA, Library Assn. Beaufort County, S.C. Library Assn. (editorial com. 1979—), Poetry Soc. S.C. (bd. dirs. 1980-83). Methodist. Home: 3011 Hickory St Burton SC 29902 Office: Depot Library PO Drawer 5-055 Parris Island SC 29905

MOUSSEAU, DORIS NAOMI BARTON, elementary school principal; b. Alpena, Mich., May 6, 1934; d. Merritt Benjamin and Naomi Dora Josephine (Pieper) Barton; m. Bernard Joseph Mousseau, July 31, 1954. AA, Alpena Community Coll., 1954; BS, Wayne State U., 1959; MA, U. Mich., 1961, postgrad., 1972-75. Profl. cert. ednl. adminstr., tchr. Elem. tchr. Clarkston (Mich.) Community Schs., 1954-66; elem. sch. prin. Andersonville Sch., Clarkston, 1966—, Bailey Lake Sch., Clarkston, 1979—. Cons., research com. Youth Assistance Oakland County Ct. Services, 1968—; leader Clarkston PTA, 1967—; chairperson Clarkston Sch. Dist. United Way Campaign, 1985, 86; mem. allocation com. Oakland County United Way, 1987-88. Recipient Outstanding Service award Davisburg Jaycees, Springfield Twp., 1977, Vol. Recognition award Oakland County (Mich.) Cts., 1984. Fellow Assn. Supervision and Curriculum Devel., MACUL (State Assn. Ednl. Computer Users); mem. NEA (del. 1964), Mich. Assn. Elem. and Middle Sch. Prins. (treas., regional del. 1982—, pres.-elect region 7 1988, pres. 1988—), Mich. Edn. Assn. (pres. 1960-66, del. 1966), Clarkston Edn. Assn. (author, editor 1st directory 1963), Women's Bowling Assn., Phi Delta Kappa, Delta Kappa Gamma (pres. 1972-74, past state and nat. chmn., Woman of Distinction 1982). Republican. Club: Spring Meadows Golf. Lodge: Elks. Home: 6825 Rattalee Lake Rd Clarkston MI 48016 Office: Clarkston Community Schs Bailey Lake Sch 8051 Pine Knob Rd Clarkston MI 48016

MOUSTOUKAS, VIKI PAPPAS, personnel director; b. Houston, Sept. 29, 1956; d. John Dan and Despina (Kleoudis) Pappas; m. Nick M. Moustoukas, Mar. 25, 1978; children: Diana Nicole, John Nicholas. BBA in Mktg., U. Houston, 1978. Profl. in human resources designation. Purchasing agt. N.L. Baroid, Houston, 1974-78; personnel mgr., asst. v.p. Johnson & Higgins of La., Inc., New Orleans, 1978—. Active New Orleans United Way, 1987; organist, pianist, local ch. Mem. Am. Soc. Personnel Adminstrn., Ins. Personnel Mgmt. Assn., New Orleans C. of C. (team capt. corp. challenge 1987). Greek Orthodox. Home: 1413 Papworth Metairie LA 70005 Office: Johnson & Higgins of La Inc PO Box 60183 New Orleans LA 70160

MOXLEY, ANN WEIMER, psychologist; b. N.Y.C., Mar. 14, 1946; d. Rae Otis and Ruth (Meister) Weimer; m. James E. Moxley, Mar. 16, 1968 (div. 1981). BA with honors, U. Fla., 1967, MS, 1968, PhD, 1970; postgrad. in neuropsychology, VA Hosp., San Francisco, 1988. Lic. clin. psychologist, Calif.; diplomate Am. Bd. Psychology. Intern U. Rochester, N.Y., 1970; assoc. psychologist Monroe Devel. Ctr., Rochester, 1971-73, prin. psychologist, 1973-78; psychologist Calif. Sch. Deaf, Fremont, 1978-79; supr. No. Calif. Assessment Ctr. Hearing Impaired, Fremont, 1979—; clin. instr. psychiatry U. Rochester, 1973-78; cons. N.Y. State Vocat. Rehab., 1977-78, Community Support Services, 1976-77. Contbr. articles to profl. jours. Mem. Am. Psychol. Assn., Phi Beta Kappa, Phi Kappa Phi. Home: 130 Sea Bridge Alameda CA 94501 Office: Calif Sch Deaf 39350 Gallaudet Dr Fremont CA 94538

MOY, AUDREY, retail buyer; b. Bronx, N.Y., May 6, 1942; d. Ferdinand Walter Melkert and Stella (Factorow) Schroff; m. Edward Moy, Aug. 16, 1974. B.A. in Biology, Hunter Coll., 1964, M.A. in Biology, 1966. Asst. buyer Bonwit Teller, N.Y.C., 1961-68; dept. mgr. Franklin Simon, N.Y.C., 1968; asst. buyer Saks Fifth Ave., N.Y.C., 1968-73; buyer Martins, Bklyn., 1973, Belk Store Services, N.Y.C., 1974—. Mem. Nat. Assn. Female Execs. Democrat. Avocations: cooking; bird watching; fishing.

MOYER, KERRI SALLS, marketing executive; b. Framingham, Mass., May 3, 1954; d. Frederick Hedderman and Therese Jane (Healy) S.; m. Alan James Moyer, Feb. 11, 1984; 2 children. BA, Bates Coll., 1976; MBA, Boston U., 1984. Tchr. Peace Corps., Dassa-Zoumé, Benin, West. Africa, 1976-78; tech. aide Mitre Corp., Bedford, Mass., 1979-80; tech. writer Data Gen., Westboro, Mass., 1980-81; sr. tech. writer Atex Inc. (subs. Kodak), Bedford, 1982-83, supr. tech. documentation, 1984, mgr. tech. documentation, 1985, sr. mgr. product comml. mktg., 1986-88; pres. DocTech, Westford, Mass., 1988—. Mem. Natural Resource Council Maine, Augusta, 1976—, Westford Conservation Commn., Mass. 1985—, coordinator Bahá'í area Mass. Mem. Soc. Tech. Communicators, Nat. Assn. Female Execs., Mgmt. Women's Assn., Am. Mgmt. Assn., Phi Sigma Iota (chpt. pres. 1975-76), Boston Computer Soc. Home: 51 Forrest Rd Westford MA 01886 Office: 51 Forrest Rd Westford MA 01886

MOYER, NANCY KAY, management consultant; b. Omaha, Aug. 3, 1942; d. Stewart Harlan and Dorothy Irene (Evans) M. BA in Sociology, Psychology, Northwestern Coll., Mpls., 1964; MA in Mgmt., Claremont Grad. Sch., 1983. Asst. to pres World Vision, Monrovia, Calif., 1969-82; pres. Nancy Moyer & Assocs., Monrovia, 1983-86; exec. asst., sr. pastor Hollywood (Calif.) Presbyn. Ch., 1986-87; assoc. cons. Visionary Mgmt. Group, 1987—. Office: Visionary Mgmt Group 150 N Santa Anita Arcadia CA 91006

MOYLAN, LEIGH ANN, communications executive; b. Peoria, Ill., Nov. 22, 1957; d. William Richard and Patricia Ann (Jacquin) M. BA in History, Calif. Poly. State U., San Luis Obispo, 1975-79. Traffic coordinator Sta. KSON-AM/FM Radio, San Diego, 1980-81; customer support rep. Automated Bus. Concepts, San Diego, 1981-83; media broker The Holt Corp., 1983—; bus. mgr. Sta. WGCM-AM-FM, Gulfport, Miss., 1983—; exec. v.p., chairperson Sta. WBNE-FM Div. Holt Assoc. Group, Gulfport, Miss., 1986—; pres. L.A.M. Assocs., Inc., Bethlehem, 1984—. Mem. Am. Women in Radio and TV, Jr. League Lehigh Valley, Pa., Gamma Phi Beta. Republican. Roman Catholic. Home: 797 Elva St Bay Saint Louis MS 39520

MOYNAHAN, KAREN PEELER, arts administrator; b. Balt., May 12, 1957; d. Richard N. and Frances A. (Signorelli) P.; m. J. Patrick Moynahan, Aug. 11, 1979. MusB, St. Mary's Coll., Notre Dame, Ind., 1979; MBA, Loyola Coll., Balt., 1987. Asst. dir. various assns., Reston, Va., 1981—. Orchestral mgr. Prince William Symphony Orch., Woodbridge, Va., 1981-84. Mem. Percussive Arts Soc. Republican. Roman Catholic. Office: Nat Assn Schs Music 11250 Roger Bacon Dr #21 Reston VA 22090

MOYNIHAN-BRADT, CAROLYN JEAN, family therapist, consultant; b. San Diego, Aug. 17, 1943; d. Donald Eugene and Katherine Elaine (Wright) Johnson; m. Robert Moynihan, Aug. 6, 1966 (div. 1972); m. Jack O. Bradt, Aug. 17, 1974; children: Mitchell, Ann Elise, Marca. BA, Immaculate Heart Coll., 1965; MSW, Cath. U. of Am., 1967. Family therapist dept. child psychiatry Georgetown U. Med. Ctr., Washington, 1965-67, clin. instr. dept. psychiatry, Family Ctr., 1966-76; lectr. dept. sociology Georgetown U., 1978-80; family therapist Overbrook Children's Ctr., Arlington, Va., 1967-70; co-founder, dir. clin. services Groome Ctr. for Families, Washington, 1969-78, clin. lectr., supr. tng. program family systems, psychotherapy, 1978-85, dir. tng., 1977-78; pvt. practice family therapy Washington, 1977—; guest lectr. U. Pa., Phila., 1980-87, U. Man., Can., 1981, U. Tenn., Nashville, 1978, Carnegie-Mellon U., Columbia U., Cath. U. Editor: Systems Therapy, 1972; author (with husband) Family Resources, 1987. Mem. Am. Family Therapy Assn., Am. Assn. Marriage and Family Therapists (clin.), Nat. Assn. Social Workers (cert.), Women's Colloquium. Democrat. Roman Catholic. Home: 8283 N Riley Rd Verona WI 53593

MOZER, DORIS ANN, writer; b. July 10, 1929; d. Charles Ross and Mary Margaret (Redmiles) Werner; B.A., N.Mex. State U., 1963, M.A. in English, 1970; postgrad. in English, U. Md., 1982; div.; children—Stephen, Judith, Mary Catherine, Laura, John. Grad. asst. N.Mex. State U., 1963-65, instr., 1969-75; free-lance editor, 1969—; editor Sibyl-Child, women's arts and cultural jour., 1976—; grad. asst. U. Md., College Park, 1976-78, dir. Writing Center, 1978-80, acad. adviser, internship coordinator, 1980-82; tech. writer Environ. Satellite Data, Inc., Suitland, Md., 1982-84, RCA, Moorestown, N.J., 1984—. Vice pres., publicity chmn. Las Cruces (N.Mex.) Children's Theatre, 1968; pres., publicity chmn. Las Cruces Theater Guild, 1969. Folger Shakespearean Inst. fellow, 1979. Mem. Phi Kappa Phi. Democrat. Unitarian. Author: (poetry) The Quickest Promise Home. Home: 102 Fourth Ave 2R Mount Ephraim NJ 08059 Office: RCA Advanced Tech Labs Moorestown NJ 08057

MRKONICH, DOROTHY EVANSON, nursing educator; b. Echo, Minn., July 10, 1938; d. August Alfred and Tilda (Sollom) Evanson; B.S.N., St. Olaf Coll., 1960; M.Ed., U. Minn., 1961, Ph.D., 1982; m. Thomas Mrkonich, Aug. 15, 1959; children—Jana Kaye, Kirsten DeAnn, Jon Thomas. Mem. faculty dept. nursing Coll. of St. Catherine, St. Paul, 1961-62; mem. faculty dept. nursing St. Olaf Coll., Northfield, Minn., 1970—, prof., 1986—, chmn. dept. nursing, 1979-86; mem. Minn. Bd. Nursing, 1981—, pres., 1984; dir. Minn. Intercollegiate Nursing Consortium. Mem. Am. Nurses Assn., Minn. Nurses Assn., Sigma Theta Tau, Pi Lambda Theta. Office: St Olaf Coll Northfield MN 55057

MUCCIANO, STEPHANIE LYONS, hospitality, travel, and tourism executive; b. Pitts., Jan. 8; d. Ross Cooper and Catherine Dorothy (Perrone) Lyons; m. Richard Francis Mucciano, Apr. 17, 1963 (dec. 1972); 1 child, Stephanie Lynn. Student St. Petersburg Jr. Coll., 1963-64, Alamogordo Bus. Coll., 1970-71. Sales mgr. Bahama Cruise Line, Tampa, Fla., 1978-82; dir. mktg./sales AAA Holidays/St. Petersburg Motor Club, Fla., 1982-84; dir. mktg./sales Travel and Tourism Resources, Inc., St. Petersburg, 1986, prin., pres., 1986—; dir. mktg./sales Island Harbor Resort, Cape Haze, Fla., 1984-86; mgr. Hotel Radisson-Pan-Am. Ocean Hotel, Miami Beach, Fla., 1987—; mktg. cons., bd. dirs., adv. bd. Travel Marketplace, Royal Fiesta Cruises, Clearwater; seminar leader, internat. industry speaker. Mem. Fla. Gulf Coast Symphony Guild, St. Petersburg, 1975—, All Childrens Hosp. Guild, 1975—, Infinity League to Aid Abused Children, 1981—, Pinellas Assn. for Retarded Adults, 1975—, St. Petersburg Internat. Folk Fair Soc.; pres. Travel and Tourism Resources, Inc. Recipient Cert. of Recognition, George Greer County Commr., Pinellas, 1986. Mem. Pacific Area Travel Assn. (dir.), Sun Coast Travel Industry Assn., Sales & Mktg. Execs. Internat., Travel & Tourism Research Assn., C. of C., Women Execs. in Travel, Travel and Tourism Research Assn., Fla. Assn. Sales Execs., Hotel Sales and Mktg. Assn., Nat. Assn. Female Execs., Fla. Women's Network, Am. Soc. Travel Agts., Am. Mktg. Assn. Republican. Clubs: Italian-Am.; St. Petersburg Internat. Folk Fair Soc.; S.K.A.L. Avocations: reading, volunteer work. Office: Radisson Pan Am Ocean Hotel 17875 Collins Ave Miami Beach FL 33160

MUCH, KATHLEEN, editor; b. Houston, Apr. 30, 1942; d. C. Frederick and Ortrud V. (Lefevre) M.; m. W. Robert Murfin, Aug. 17, 1963 (div. 1981); children—Brian C., Glen M.; m. Paul Stanley Peters Jr., Jan. 1, 1988. B.A., Rice U., 1963, M.A., 1971, postgrad., 1978. Clk., Tex. State Library, Austin, 1963-64; tchr. Kinkaid High Sch., Houston, 1964-66; editorial asst. Rice U., 1969-71, assoc. editor, 1972-81; freelance writer Houston and Palo Alto, Calif., 1971—; dir. info. Meth. Hosp., Houston, 1981-84; sr. editor Addison-Wesley Pub. Co., Menlo Park, Calif., 1984-86; editor Ctr. for Advanced Study in Behavioral Scis., Stanford, Calif., 1986—. dir. Tex. Wordworks, Inc. Active Houston Ballet Guild, Rice U. Fund Council, Friends of Stanford String Quartet, Stanford Music Guild, Bus. Vols. for Arts, Houston Grand Opera, Tex. Chamber Orchestra. Internat. Assn. Bus. Communicators, Soc. Tech. Communication, Phi Beta Kappa. Editor, contbr. profl. jours. Office: Ctr for Advanced Study 202 Junipero Serra Blvd Stanford CA 94305

MUCHISKY, LINDA LEE, health care consultant; b. Redwood City, Calif., Nov. 6, 1962; d. Thomas Peter Muchisky and Jean Marie (Montgomery) Cross. BSBA, Washington U., St. Louis, 1983, MHA, 1985. Acct. Washington U., 1980-82, health care cons., 1988—; sales and service rep. Goodyear Tire and Rubber Co., Lincoln, Nebr., 1983; adminstrv. intern S.W. Community Health Services, Albuquerque, 1984; adminstrv. resident St. Anthony's Med. Ctr., St. Louis, 1985-86, ops. mgr. ambulatory services, 1986-87. Mem. St. Louis Squires and Ladies Charitable Found., St. Louis, 1986. Mem. Women in Health Adminstrn., Med. Group Mgmt. Assn., Soc. Ambulatory Care Profls., Healthcare Fin. Mgmt. Assn. Home: 2007 Green Glen Apt 301 Kirkwood MO 63122 Office: 701 Market St Suite 1400 Saint Louis MO 63101

MUCHMORE, PATSY WILLINE, author, photographer; b. Holdenville, Okla., June 28, 1937; d. Mennis Miller and Olive Faye (Ballard) Noblett; m. Gareth Bruce Muchmore, Oct. 16, 1977 (dec. Sept. 22, 1983); children by previous marriage: Kerry James Redmond, Kathryn Joy Pruitt, Darla Sue Duncan. Student, Okla. State U., 1968, 74. Soc. editor Holdenville Daily News, 1960-62; news editor Wewoka (Okla.) Daily Times, 1962-63; reporter Kingfisher (Okla.) Free Press, 1964; aux. staffer Enid (Okla.) Morning News, 1965; news wire editor Ponca City (Okla.) Daily News, 1965-74; freelance writer Africa and Cen. Am., 1974-75, asst. and assoc. editor, 1974-75; asst. and assoc. editor Dental Econs., Tulsa, 1975-77, editor, 1977-82, contbg. editor, 1983—; cons. dental firms, newspapers; speaker in field. Author: Guide to Collections, 1979; (with others) As Your Practice Grows, 1977, How to Hire an Associate, 1982; contbr. numerous articles to newspapers, periodicals and jours. Bd. dirs. Ponca City Art Assn., 1984, Tulsa County Hist. Soc., 1986-89. Recipient hon. mention Golden Pen award, 1977, hon. mention Golden Pencil award, 1980; 1st runner-up AP Creative Writing award, 1969. Mem. Author's Guild, Am. League Authors, Okla. Writers Fedn., Sigma Delta Chi. Republican. Presbyterian. Office: 4405 S Columbia Ave Tulsa OK 74105

MUCHNIC, SUZANNE, art critic, educator, lecturer; b. Kearney, Nebr., May 16, 1940; d. Walter Marian Ely and Erva Nell Liston; m. Paul D. Muchnic, 1963; B.A., Scripps Coll., 1962; M.A., Claremont Grad. Sch., 1963. Art instr. Weber State Coll., Ogden, Utah, 1972-73; art history instr. Los Angeles City Coll., 1974-82; editor for So. Calif., Artweek, 1976-78; art critic Los Angeles Times, 1978—; art criticism instr. Claremont Grad. Sch., 1984. Author: Tim Nordin retrospective catalogue, 1982, Martha Alf retrospective catalogue, 1984, Mark Lere Catalogue, 1986. Recipient Disting. Alumna award Claremont Grad. Sch., 1982, Disting. Alumna award Scripps Coll., 1987. Mem. Coll. Art Assn., Internat. Assn. Art Critics. Office: Los Angeles Times Times-Mirror Sq Los Angeles CA 90053

MUCKLER, JULIE ROBINSON, communications executive; b. Mpls., Jan. 4, 1951; d. William Joseph and Martha (Snider) Robinson; B.S., Iowa State U., 1973, M.S., 1978; m. Richard D. Muckler, June 1, 1974. Personnel rep. John Deere, Des Moines, 1975-77; dir. recruitment and selection Social Services, Des Moines, 1978-79, asst. dir. field ops., 1979-80; co-owner, prin. Applied Mgmt. Assocs., 1980—; compensation and devel. mgr. Pioneer Hi-Bred, Internat., Inc., Des Moines, 1983-86, dir. communications, 1986—. Mem. Pub. Relations Soc. Am., Am. Soc. Tng. and Devel., Am. Soc. Personnel Adminstrn., Midwest Coll. Placement Assn., Agrl. Relations Council, Nat. Assn. Mfrs., Internat. Assn Bus. Communicators. Republican. Methodist. Office: Pioneer Hi-Bred Internat Inc 6800 Pioneer Pkwy Johnston IA 50131

MUDD, ANNE CHESTNEY, mathematics educator; b. Macon, Ga., June 30, 1944; d. Bard Sherman Chestney and Betty (Bartow) Houston; m. Charles Lee Mudd, Dec. 28, 1963; children: Charles Jr., Richard, Robert Jason. BA, U. Louisville, 1966, MA, 1976. Math statistician U.S. Bur. Census, Jeffersonville, Ind., 1966-70; instr. math. U. Louisville, 1975-77, Coll. DuPage, Glen Ellyn, Ill., 1978-85; tchr. math., substitute tchr. Lyons Twp. High Sch., La Grange, Ill., 1986—; math tutor Louisville 1969-77, Western Springs, Ill. 1977—. Mem. steering com. Village Western Springs, 1986-87. Mem. Children's Theater Western Springs (bd. dirs. 1987—), LWV (pres. 1983-85, bd. dirs. 1981-86), Lyons Twp. High Sch. Com. Student Discipline, Western Springs Hist. Soc., Nat. Council Tchrs. Math. Club: Met. Math. of Chgo. Home: 3958 Hampton Ave Western Springs IL 60558

MUDGE, JEAN MCCLURE, writer, filmmaker; b. Fort Benning, Ga., Dec. 4, 1933; d. Robert Battey and Eva Eugenia (Colby) McClure; m. Lewis Seymour Mudge, June 15, 1957; children—Robert Seymour, William McClure, Anne Evelyn. B.A., Stanford U., 1955; M.A., U. Del., 1957; Ph.D., Yale U., 1973. Reader, Smith Coll., Northampton, Mass., 1963-65, lectr., 1972-73; curator Amherst (Mass.) Coll., 1965-76; filmmaker, Amherst, 1971—; vis. scholar China Trade Mus., Milton, Mass., 1977—; cons. Peabody Mus., Salem, Mass., 1980—, Essex Inst., Salem, 1980—; lectr. Field Mus., Chgo., 1982—. Author: Chinese Export Porcelain for the American Trade, 1785-1835, 1962, rev. edit., 1987; Emily Dickinson and the Image of Home, 1975; Chinese Export Porcelain in North America, 1986; author films: Emily Dickinson, 1978; Herman Melville, 1982; Sanctuary in Chicago, 1985, Mary Lyon: Precious Time, 1987. Winterthur fellow H. F. duPont Mus., Wilmington, Del., 1955-57; Danforth Found. fellow, 1969-71; recipient Red Ribbon, N.Y. Film Festival, 1978, finalist, 1982; Chris Plaque, Columbus Film Festival, 1978, 82. Mem. NOW, MLA, Oriental Ceramic Soc., Winterthur Grads. Assn. Democrat. Home: 130 Bolinas Ave San Anselmo CA 94960

MUDRON, MAUREEN DOLORES, lawyer; b. Joliet, Ill., June 7, 1948; d. Francis Raymond and Veronica Marie (McGuire) M. BA, U. Ill., 1970; JD, John Marshall Law Sch., Chgo., 1974. Bar: Ill. 1974. Staff atty. Ill. Dept. Mental Health and Devel. Disabilities, Chgo., 1974-78, asst. to chief counsel, 1978-80, chief legal counsel, 1980-84, counsel spl. projects., 1984-85; staff atty. Am. Hosp. Assn., 1985-87, sr. counsel, 1987—; speaker in field. Mem. Nat. Abortion Rights Action League. Mem. ABA, NOW, Ill. Bar Assn., Chgo. Council Lawyers, Lawyer's Alliance for Nuclear Arms Control. Office: Am Hosp Assn 840 N Lake Shore Dr Suite 8 E Chicago IL 60611

MUEHLBAUER, RENICE ANN, public relations administrator, consultant; b. Milw.; d. Fredrick and Lucia (Stewart) Fregin; m. Thomas George Muehlbauer; children: Jennifer Jean, Whitney Susan. Student, U. San Diego, 1986—. Pres. Chubby Bumpkins Inc., Houston, 1980-82; contracts adminstr. Gulf States Computer Service, Houston, 1980-82; pres. RAM Prodns., Houston, 1981-82, Pizza Internat. Inc., Houston, 1982-84; contracts adminstr. 1st Alliance Corp., Houston, 1982-85; free-lance pub. relations cons. San Diego, 1985—. Tutor U. San Diego writing ctr., 1987—; founder, dir. pub. relations-tng. Montgomery County Crisis Action Line, Houston, 1979-84; founder, v.p., bd. dirs. Montgomery County Rape Crisis Coalition, 1982-84; speaker Trauma Rape Coalition, 1982-84; mem. prodn. com. Community Women Together, 1980-82; YWCA Woman Yr., 1981, 82; pres. Living Arts Council, Houston, 1980-81. Mem. Am. Assn. Bus. Women (dir. activities Houston chpt. 1983-84), Bus. Women's Forum (dir. community awareness Houston chpt. 1982-83), Assn. Women Bus. Owners, Montgomery County C. of C. (spl. events com. 1983-84), Phi Alpha Delta. Club: Ladies (Houston) (com. chair 1981-82). Lodge: Lions (hon. dir. pub relations).

MUEHLENTHAL, CLARICE KELMAN, travel consultant; b. Cleve., Nov. 16, 1924; d. William and Ann (Teitel) Kelman; m. Arnold G. Muehlenthal, Dec. 17, 1950 (dec. Sept. 1980); children—Shelley Muehlenthal Mitchell, David M. Cert., Draughons Bus. Coll., 1945; cert. travel counselor, Inst. Cert. Travel Agts., 1980. Owner, Cee-Jay Bus. Service, Riverhead, N.Y., 1952-55; travel cons. Journey House Travel, Dallas, 1967-73; ptnr. Alpha Travel, Dallas, 1973-76; owner World Wide Travel Service, Dallas, 1976—. Round Table chmn. Dallas North dist. Boy Scouts Am., 1971-73; charter mem. Tex. Cultural Alliance, 1975—; courier Hands Around the World, Tex., 1975—. Recipient Dist. Award of Merit, Boy Scouts Am., Circle Ten, Dallas, 1973; Internat. Fellowship, Tex. Cultural Alliance, Dallas, 1982; named Ambassador of Goodwill, State Tex., 1975. Mem. Am. Soc. Travel Agts., The 3020 Soc. (sec.-treas. 1982—), Inst. Cert. Travel Agts (study group leader 1983, life 1982), Assn. Retail Travel Agts., Travel Agy. Council N. Tex. (sec. 1981-83), Phi Sigma Alpha. Address: PO Box 59327 Dallas TX 75229 Office: PO Box 52327 World Wide Travel Service 2860 Walnut Hill Ln Suite 106 Dallas TX 75229

MUEHLNER, SUANNE WILSON, library director; b. Rochester, Minn., June 29, 1943; d. George T. and Rhoda (Westin) Wilson. Student Smith Coll., 1961-63; A.B., U. Calif.-Berkeley, 1965; M.L.S., Simmons Coll., 1968; M.B.A., Northeastern U., Boston, 1979. Librarian, Technische Univ. Berlin, Germany, 1970-71; earth and planetary scis. librarian MIT Libraries, Cambridge, 1968-70, 1971-73; personnel librarian, 1973-74, asst. dir. personnel services, 1974-76, asst. dir. pub. services, 1976-81; dir. libraries Colby Coll., Waterville, Maine, 1981—. Mem. New Eng. Assn. Coll. and Research Librarians (v.p., pres. elect 1985—, sec.-treas. 1983-85), Maine Library Assn. (chmn. intellectual freedom com. 1984—), Nelinet (bd. dirs. 1985—), ALA. Office: Colby Coll Miller Library Waterville ME 04901

MUELLER, AUDREY EDNA, public relations specialist, psychic counselor; b. Nazeing, Essex, Eng., Oct. 2, 1932; came to U.S., 1954; d. William and Lilian Gertrude (Schirn) Hale; m. Robert Estes Hegwood, Sept. 22, 1952 (div. Jan. 1967); children—Robert, Beverly, Irene, Virginia, David; m. Larry Emerson Mueller, May 3, 1969 (div. July 1985). Ed. English schs. Copywriter, advt. sales rep. Springfield (Ohio) Advertiser, 1966-1967; copywriter, mng. editor New Carlisle (Ohio) Sun, 1967-79; advt. specialist Dayton Tire & Rubber Co. (Ohio), 1979-80; pub. relations and fund devel. dir. Am. Lung Assn., Dayton, 1980—; speaker; dir., coordinator Miami Valley Coalition Smoking Or Health, 1982—; pub. relations cons. Am. Lung Assn.; coordinator, promoter Stop Smoking Clinics, Dayton, 1983—; tchr. psychic devel. groups Greater Dayton area. Recipient Optimists Creed award New Carlisle Rotary Club, 1973; Voice of Democracy award VFW, Medway, Ohio, 1978; Recognition award Tire Rev. Mag., 1980, Nat. VFW, 1979. Mem. Pub. Relations for Health (pres. 1984), Ohio Congress Lung Assn. Staff (sec.-treas. 1982-84), Assn. Research and Enlightenment, Internat. Assn. Bus. Communicators (sec. 1984), Women in Communications, Inc. Democrat. Unitarian. Clubs: English Accents of New Carlisle (sec., founder, past pres.), Rotary (hon.) (New Carlisle). Home: 433 E Carpenter Dr New Carlisle OH 45344 Office: American Lung Assn Miami Valley 226 Belmonte Park E Dayton OH 45405

MUELLER, BETTY JEANNE, social work educator; b. Wichita, Kans., July 7, 1925; d. Bert C. and Clara A. (Pelton) Judkins; children—Michael J., Madelynn J. M.S.S.W., U. Wis., Madison, 1964, Ph.D. (E.B. Fred fellow, Nat. Inst. Child Health and Human Devel. fellow), 1969. Asst. prof. U. Wis., Madison, 1969-71; vis. asso. prof. Bryn Mawr (Pa.) Coll., 1971-72; asso. prof., dir. social work Cornell U., Ithaca, N.Y., 1972-78, prof. human services studies, 1978—; nat. cons. Head Start, Follow Through, Appalachian Regional Commn., N.Y. State Office Planning Services, N.Y. State Dept. Social Services, N.Y. State Div. Mental Hygiene, Nat. Congress PTA. Author: (with H. Morgan) Social Services in Early Education, 1974; contbr. articles to profl. jours. Grantee HEW, 1974-76, 79-80, State of N.Y., 1975—, Israeli Jewish Agy., 1985-87, Israeli Nat. Council for Research, 1986-87. Mem. Am. Sociol. Assn., Nat. Conf. Social Welfare, Nat. Assn. Social Workers, Council Social Work Edn., Groves Family Conf., Chi Omega. Democrat. Unitarian. Home: 11 Forest Ln Ithaca NY 14850 Office: Cornell U Human Services Studies N139MVR Hall Ithaca NY 14853

MUELLER, DOROTHY ANN, academic administrator; b. Feb. 10, 1938; d. George Henry and Caroline (Schoettlin) M. AB, Birmingham So. Coll., 1959; MA, George Peabody Coll., 1961. Intern med. librarian UCLA, 1961-62; reference librarian Duke U. Med. Ctr. Library, Durham, N.C., 1962-65; circulation librarian U. Ala. Med. Ctr. Library, Birmingham, 1965-66; trainee Nat. Library Medicine, Bethesda, Md., 1966-67; chief searcher Ala. MEDLARS Ctr., Birmingham, 1967-70; assoc. dir. Lister Hill Library, Birmingham, 1970-76; assoc. dir. instnl. study program U. Ala., Birmingham, 1972-73, asst. dean adminstrn., 1976-77, asst. to v.p. research and grad. studies, 1977-83, asst. v.p. research and instnl. advancement, 1983-88, asst. v.p. for research devel., 1988—; speaker at profl. meetings. Contbr. articles to profl. publs. Loaned exec. United Way, 1987; trustee St. John's Evangel. Ch., Birmingham, 1983-85. Mem. AAUW (honoree 1986), Ala. Assn. Univ. Administrs., Ala. Assn. Women Deans, Adminstr. and Counselors (pres. 1984-86), Am. Assn. Affirmative Action, Med. Library Assn. (chmn. So. regional group 1973-74), Birmingham Library Club. Lodge: Zonta. (pres. Birmingham chpt. 1986-88). Home: 3236 Georgetown Pl Birmingham AL 35216 Office: U Ala Birmingham AL 35294

MUELLER, HENRIETTA WATERS, psychologist, artist; b. Pitts., Apr. 13, 1915; d. William Sydney and Helen Losey (Kirkwood) Waters; m. Werner A. Mueller, June 15, 1940; children: Christopher Bradford, Richard Kirkwood. BFA with honors, Art Inst. of Chgo., 1938; MA, U. Wyo., 1948, MEd, 1960. Tchr. art Boulder (Colo.) Valley Sch., 1969-75; sch. clin. psychologist Jefferson County Sch. Dist., Lakewood, Colo., 1973-75; dir. speech and lang. clinic U. Wyo., Laramie, 1976; ednl. cons. Natrona County Sch. Dist., Casper, Wyo., 1976-85; prof. printmaking, art edn. U. of the Pacific, Stockton, Calif., summers 1970-71. Marshall grantee Cummington (Mass.) Found., 1953; recipient purchase awards U. N.C., 1958, U. Wyo. Mus. Art, 1975. Fellow Handworks Gallery, Art Emporium; mem. Alpha Chi Omega. Democrat. Presbyterian. Lodge: Zonta. Home: 520 Mapleton Ave Boulder CO 80302 Studio: 1309 Steele St Laramie WY 82070

MUELLER, KATHLEEN ANN, small business owner, consultant; b. St. Louis, Apr. 7, 1950; d. Gerald J. and Constance L. (Courtney) Reiser; m. Roy L. Mueller, Dec. 10, 1977; children: Christopher L., Jennifer M., Nicholas A. AA, Florissant Valley, 1982; student, Washington U., St. Louis, 1982—. Asst. v.p. fin. CMC Corp., St. Louis, 1977-79; asst. cash mgr. Consol Aluminum Corp., St. Louis, 1979-81; spl. document coordinator McCarthy Bros., St. Louis, 1981-83; ops. mgr. MIS Am. Soybean Assn., St. Louis, 1983-86; owner la Debug, St. Louis, 1985—; vocat. instr. part-time various community colls., St. Louis, 1986—; instr. Personal Computer Inst., St. Louis, 1986—; course designer Word Processing Inst, St. Louis, 1986—. Editor newsletter Communique, 1986-87; Contbr. articles to numerous publs. Mem. Nat. Assn. Female Execs., 5520 Users Group (bd. dirs. 1984-86), IBM Personal Computer Users Group (chariperson, bd. dirs. 1986—). Office: la Debug PO Box 140164 Saint Louis MO 63114

MUELLER, LOIS M., psychologist; b. Milw., Nov. 30, 1943; d. Herman Gregor and Ora Emma (Dettmann) M.; B.S., U. Wis.-Milw., 1965; M.A., U. Tex., 1966, Ph.D., 1969. Postdoctoral intern VA Hosp., Wood, Wis., 1969-71; counselor, asst. prof. So. Ill. U. Counseling Center and dept. psychology, Carbondale, 1971-72, coordinator personal counseling, asst. prof., 1972-74, counselor, asst. prof., 1974-76; individual practice clin. psychology, Carbondale, 1972-76, Clearwater, Fla., 1977—; owner, dir. Adult and Child Psychology Clinic, Clearwater, 1978—; staff mem. Med. Center Hosp., Largo, Fla., 1979—; mem. profl. adv. com. Mental Health Assn. Pinellas County, 1978, Alt. Human Services, 1979-80; cons. Face Learning Center, Hotline Crisis Phone Service, 1977—; advice columnist Clearwater Sun newspaper, 1983—; public speaker local TV and radio stas., 1978, 79; talk show host WPLP Radio Sta., Clearwater, 1980-83, WTKN Radio Sta., Clearwater, 1988—. Campaign worker for Sen. George McGovern presdl. race, 1972. Lic. psychologist, Ill., Fla. Mem. Am., Fla., Ill., Pinellas (founder, pres. 1978) psychol. assns., Assn. Advancement Psychology, Am. Soc. Clin. Hypnosis, Fla. Soc. Clin. Hypnosis, Acad. Family Psychology, Bus. and Profl. Women of Clearwater, Assn. Women in Psychology. Contbr. articles to profl. jours. Office: 2901 US 19 N Suite 202 Clearwater FL 34621

MUELLER, MARGARET REID, social worker; b. Cleve., Aug. 20, 1929; d. James Sims and Felice (Crowl) Reid; B.A., Smith Coll., 1951; M.A., Case Western Res. U., 1969, M.S.W., 1973; m. Werner D. Mueller, Sept. 6, 1952; children—Fred, John, Lydia, Felice, Omar. Social worker Cleve. Soc. for the Blind, 1969-71; social worker Childrens Services, Cleve., 1973-75; social worker Cuyahoga County Juvenile Ct., Cleve., 1975—, supr. probation dept., 1975—. Candidate for U.S. Ho. of Reps. Mem. Acad. Certified Social Workers, Nat. Assn. Social Workers. Republican. Presbyterian. Clubs: Kirtland Country, Womenspace, Jr. League. Home: 8848 Music St Novelty OH 44072

MUELLER, MARY BETH, automotive executive; b. Cleve., June 3, 1944; d. Charles Frederick and Sarah (McDonald) Kocher; m. William Leo Mueller, Oct. 8, 1966 (div. Nov. 1976); children: Eric Lee, Mark Andrew. BA in Math., Wayne State U., 1965; MBA, Oakland U., Rochester, Mich., 1987. Systems engr. IBM Corp., Detroit, 1965-68; systems analyst Automated Mktg. Services, Detroit, 1976-78; systems cons. Allen Services, Detroit, 1978-79; systems mgr. Citation Computing Co., Southfield, Mich., 1979-82; leader purchasing project Chrysler Motors Corp., Highland Park, Mich., 1982-84, supr. fin. mgmt. program, 1984-86, specialist fin. and systems, 1986—. Mem. Data Processing Mgrs. Assn., Nat. Assn. Female Execs., Mensa. Lutheran. Home: 918 Durham Troy MI 48084 Office: Chrysler Motors Corp 2800 Oakland Blvd Highland Park MI 48203

MUELLER, MARY ELSIE, medical technologist; b. Buffalo, Nov. 10, 1939; d. Thomas Michael and Elsie Mary (Kienke) Rusch; B.A., diploma med. tech., U. Buffalo and Buffalo Gen. Hosp. Sch. Med. Tech., 1961; m. Peter M. Mueller, Mar. 21, 1964; 1 son, Thomas P. Microbiology technologist, then microbiology supr. Buffalo Gen. Hosp., 1961-71, microbiology teaching supr., 1971—; temporary supr. lab, West Seneca, 1983; computer writer Spirit Graphics, 1985—; clin. instr. area colls. and univs. Sunday Sch. supt. Resurrection Luth. Ch., Buffalo, 1983—. Mem. Am. Soc. Clin. Pathologists, Nat. Cert. Agy. Med. Lab. Personnel. Lutheran. Home: 75 Chesterfield Dr Buffalo NY 14215 Office: 100 High St Buffalo NY 14215

MUELLER, NINA RHODES, insurance company executive; b. Muncie, Ind., Dec. 22, 1944; d. John Waddington and Nina Mapleton (Cricks) Rhodes; m. James Thomas Moon, Nov. 14, 1964 (div. May 1973); 1 child, Scot Aaron; m. Franz Mueller, Aug. 3, 1974; 1 child, Tamara Lynne. AAS in Supervision, Purdue U., 1981, BS in Psychology, 1981. CLU, ChFC. Asst. coordinator Midwest Hydro Corp., Ft. Wayne, Ind., 1981-83; mgr. life sales Mut. Sec. Life, Ft. Wayne, 1983-86; dir. advanced underwriting Midwestern United Life, Ft. Wayne, 1986—. Mem. steering com. Ft. Wayne Women's Bur., 1986-87. Mem. Nat. Assn. Life Underwriters, Ft. Wayne Assn. Life Underwriters, Am. Soc. CLU's and ChfC's, Ft. Wyane CLU's and ChFC's (Huebner chair 1987—), Ft. Wayne Estate Planning Council. Home: 10813 Oak Wind Ct Fort Wayne IN 46845 Office: Midwestern United Life 7551 W Jefferson Fort Wayne IN 46804

MUELLER, PATTY PUIG, oil company executive; b. Laredo, Tex., Oct. 12, 1931; d. Valentine L. and Louise (Payne) Puig; m. Joseph P. Mueller, Sept. 4, 1954; children: Michelle, Martha, Mary Pat, Paul, Julianna. Student, Ward-Belmont Coll. for Women; BS in Edn., U. Tex., 1954. Tchr. Corpus Christi (Tex.) ISD, 1954-56; bookkeeper J.P. Mueller Cons., Corpus Christi, 1957-70, acct., 1970-76; controller Mueller Engrng. Corp., Corpus Christi, 1976-84, v.p. fin./controller, 1984—; v.p. treas. Mueller Exploration Inc., Corpus Christi, 1977—. Chmn., bd. dirs. City Pub. Libraries, Corpus Christi, 1975-86; treas. Bond Drive Support Group, Corpus Christi, 1981; vice chmn. adv. council South Texas Library Systems, 1980-81; pres. Friends of Corpus Christi Pub. Libraries, 1964-79; trustee The Hearth, 1973-79; pres., chmn. fin. Amigos de las Americas, 1984-85, Bond Drive Support Group, Corpus Christi, treas. 1981; mem. Gov.'s Conf. on Libraries, 1974. Named Sustaining Mem. of Yr. Jr. League of Corpus Christi, 1981, disting. citizen Corpus Christi city council, 1987. Mem. Am. Mgmt. Assn., Human Resources Mgmt. Assn., State of Tex. Pan-Am. Round Table (treas. 1983-85, dir. 1987—), Chi Omega. Republican. Roman Catholic. Clubs: Corpus Christi Town, Nueces. Home: 206 Indiana Corpus Christi TX 78404

MUELLER, PEGGY JEAN, dance educator, choreographer, rancher; b. Austin, Tex., June 14, 1952; d. Rudolph George Jr. and Margaret Jean (Locke) M.; m. John Yerby Tarlton, June 24, 1972 (div. June 1983). BS in Home Econs., Child Devel., U. Tex., 1974. Dance tchr. Shirley McPhail Sch. Dance, Austin, 1972-75; dance tchr. Jean Tarlton Sch. Dance, Alpine, Tex., 1975-77, College Station, Tex., 1977-80; dance tchr. Sul Ross State U., Alpine, 1975-77; dance tchr. Tex. A&M U., Coll. Station, 1977-80, dance tchr. consol. community edn. dept., 1977-78; dance tchr. Jean Mueller Sch. Dance, Austin, 1980—, U. Tex., Austin, 1980—; dancer, contest judge Great Tex. Dance-Off, Austin, 1985-86; equestrian com. mem. Austin-Travis County Livestock Show and Rodeo, 1980—, trail ride chmn., 1986—; trail boss, pres. Austin Founders Trail Ride, 1986—; choreographer, head cheerleader Austin Texans Pro Football Team, 1981. Dancer Oklahoma, Austin, 1969, Kiss Me Kate, Austin, 1970; choreographer, lead role Cabaret, Alpine, 1976. Active Women's Symphony League Austin, 1972—, Settlement Club, Austin, 1987—; mem., recreation chmn. St. Martin's Evang. Luth. Ch., Austin, 1972—. Recipient Outstanding Trail Rider of Yr. award Wild Horse Trail Ride, Okla., 1984; named Tex. First Lady Trail Boss Gov. Mark White, Mayor Frank Cooksey, Austin City Council, 1986, Outstanding Intramural Sports Team Mgr./Player Tex. A&M U., 1978-79. Mem. Tex Assn. Tchrs. of Dancing, Inc., U.S. Twirling and Gymnastics Assn., Univ. Tex. Ex-Students Assn., Tex. Execs. in Home Econs., Am. Vet. Med. Assn. Aux. (v.p. 1978-79, pres. 1979-80), Am. Horse Shows Assn., Internat. Arabian Horse Assn., Austin Women's Tennis Assn. (v.p. 1985-86, pres. 1986—), Houston Salt Grass Trail Ride Assn., San Antonio Alamo Trail Ride Assn., Ft. Worth Chisholm Trail Ride Assn., U. Tex. Longhorn Alumni Band, Austin C. of C., Zeta Tau Alpha (alumnae photographer, social advisor, 1982-87, treas. 1987—), Omicron Nu Nat. Honor Soc. (v.p. 1973-74). Republican. Clubs: Cen. Tex. Arabian Horse, Capitol Area Quarter Horse Assn., Jr. Austin Woman's. Home: 1506 Hardouin Ave Austin TX 78703 Office: Jean Mueller Sch Dance PO Box 14762 Austin TX 78761

MUELLER, VICKI LYNNE BONEBRIGHT, health sciences executive; b. St. Paul, Apr. 21, 1962; d. Max Eugene Bonebright and Elizabeth (Fanning) Veskrna. Student, U. Oreg., 1980-81, San Diego State U., 1982-84. Employer coordinator Greater San Diego Health Plan, 1981-85; account exec. Group Health Plan, St. Louis, 1985-86, Physicians Health Plan, St. Louis, 1986-88, Corroon and Black of Mo., 1988—. Mem. Profl. Sales Women St. Louis, Nat. Assn. Female Execs. Republican. Roman Catholic. Home: 6207 Coronado Ave Saint Louis MO 63116

MUENSTER, KAREN, state legislator. m. Ted Muenster, 1965; children: Ted, Mary, Thomas. Ed. U. Nevada. Councilperson City of Vermillion, S.D., 1975-77; mem. S.D. State Senate 1985—; mem. Dem. Forum, Nat. Dem. Policy Commn. Mem. LWV, Questers, Alpha Xi Delta. Office: 117 N Duluth Ave Sioux Falls SD 57104 *

MUENSTER, MARGARET ANN, health care administrator, educator; b. Jersey City, July 4, 1953; d. Walter P. and Mary Eileen (Rafter) M. BA, Caldwell (N.J.) Coll., 1975; MPA, Temple U., 1977. Evaluator Middlesex County Govt., New Brunswick, N.J., 1977-78, fiscal assessment coordinator, 1978-80, mgmt. info., 1980-82; instr. polit. sci. and pub. adminstrn. Trenton (N.J.) State Coll., 1980; product devel. coordinator N.J. Blue Shield, Newark, 1982-86; project mgr. PPO Alliance, Cypress, Calif., 1986-87; freelance health care cons. Calif., 1987—. Elks scholar, 1971; named one of Outstanding Young Women in Am., 1984. Mem. Am. Mktg. Assn., Am. Soc. for Pub. Adminstrn. (membership, budgeting, fin. mgmt. sect.), CAldwell Local C. of C. (guest speaker 1974-75). Roman Catholic. Home and Office: 2016 A Nelson Ave Redondo Beach CA 90228

MUETH, JANE ELLEN, educator; b. Bellville, Ill., Feb. 19, 1946; d. Charles John and Marjorie Jane (Hempen) M. BA, So. Ill. U., Edwardsville, 1969, MA, 1976. Cert. secondary tchr. in speech and theater. Tchr. speech, drama, film Dist. 201 West Pub. Schs., Belleville, 1970—; facilitator Transformational Fantasy, Belleville, 1987—. Reader for blind Our Lady of Snows Ch., Belleville, 1980-84; founder Comet Prodns., Belleville, 1982, sec.-treas., 1982-84. Mem. Internat. Listening Assn., Nat. Council on Self Esteem. Home: 8 Dale Allen Dr Belleville IL 62223 Office: Dist 201 BTHS West 2600 W Main St Belleville IL 62223

MUGGLI, CLARA BARBARA, civic worker; b. Hebron, N.D., Nov. 10, 1927; d. Matt and Mary (Schneider) Maershbecker; student Dickinson State Coll.; m. Ewald Muggli, Sept. 27, 1948; children—Allen, Linda, Joyce, Carol, Gary, Holly. Tchr. rural schs., 1945-48; county chmn. establishment Bookmobile, 1960, bd. dirs., 1960—, bd. dirs., librarian Glen Ullin (N.D.) Public Library, 1956—; social services home health aide, 1972-76; co-owner, mgr. Rock Mus., Glen Ullin, 1970—, also instr. rocks and minerals, 1970—; sec. Glen Ullin Hist. Soc., 1978—; tchr. Sacred Heart Ch., 1969—, dir. religious edn., 1982—; weekly columnist Glen Ullin Times, 1977-84. Recipient State Homemakers award for Cultural Arts, 1975; K. C. Religious Edn. award, 1979; Best of Show award Dakota Gem and Mineral Show, 1979, 84. Mem. Morton County Hist. Soc., Central Dakota Gem and Mineral Assn., Badlands and Knife River Rock Clubs, Art Assn., Am. Legion Aux. Club: Homemakers. Co-author: Glen Ullin Yesteryears, 1983, A Century of Catholicism, 1984. Home: 701 Oak Ave E Glen Ullin ND 58631 Office: Sacred Heart Ch Glen Ullin ND 58631

MUHAMMAD, ALBERTA, nurse; b. Norristown, Pa., Apr. 20, 1937; m. Jace and Mattie Anna (Culbreath) Henley; m. Ellsworth Hadley, Sept. 3, 1962 (div. Oct. 1965). Diploma in nursing, Temple U., Phila., 1960; BS in Nursing, Moravian Coll., Bethlehem, Pa., 1961. Cert. mental health and psychiat. nurse. Psychiat. head nurse Norristown State Hosp., 1960-63, 78-87, Commonwealth of Pa., Phila. and Embreeville, 1963-67; pvt. duty nurse to Hon. Elijah Muhammad, leader of Nation of Islam Chgo., 1967-75; staff nurse Chgo. Osteo. Med. Ctr., 1975-78; nursing instr. sick com. Nation of Islam, 1970-78; psychiatric nurse instr. Norristown State Hosp. and Embreeville State Hosp., 1965-67. Mem. Pa. Nurses Assn., Prog. Women's League, Inc. (pres. 1986-87). Democrat. Muslim. Home: 21 E Freedley St Norristown PA 19401

MUHAMMAD, KHALEEDAH, entrepreneur, sales and marketing consultant; b. Berkeley, Calif., Nov. 2, 1943; d. Samuel Taylor Odom and Robbie Lee (Taylor) Gordon; m. O.B. Britt, Jan. 2, 1963 (div. 1972); children: Raymie, Jamal; m. Ansar El Muhammad, June 12, 1974; children: Tamishi, Ansar El II. BA, Los Angeles State Coll., 1965; postgrad., Calif. State, Hayward, 1971-72. Caseworker Pacoima (Calif.) Child Guidance Clinic, 1965-68; probation officer Los Angeles Probation Dept., 1968-72; ednl. opportunity program counselor U. Calif., Berkeley, 1974-79; community cons. YWCA, Richmond, Calif., 1979-81; owner, sales mgr. Touch of Class Boutique, Richmond, 1981-84; owner, mktg. cons. Nature's Co., Richmond, 1982-84, Unique Home Services, Richmond, 1984—; part-owner, mktg. cons. Cora's Kitchen, Oakland, Calif., 1987—, Halal Mktg. Services, Oakland, 1987—; sales, mktg. cons. The Fox Factory, Richmond, 1985-87. Author: (pamphlet) It's Not Easy Being a Parent, 1979. Vice chairperson Unity Orgn., Richmond, 1979-83; founder People United For Coops., Richmond, 1983; bd. dirs. Richmond chpt. Reading Is Fundamental, 1979-83, Minority Arts Network, Contra Costa, Calif., 1987. Mem. Nat. Assn. Female Execs. Democrat. Islam.

MUHLERT, JAN KEENE, art museum director; b. Oak Park, Ill., Oct. 4, 1942; d. William Henry and Isabel Janette (Cole) Keene; m. Christopher Layton Muhlert, Jan. 1, 1966; 1 son, Michael Keene. B.A. in Art and French, Albion (Mich.) Coll., 1964; M.A. in Art History, Oberlin (Ohio) Coll., 1967; student, Neuchatel (Switzerland) U., Inst. European Studies, Paris, Inst. de Phonetique, Acad. Grande Chaumiere. Asst. curator Allen Meml. Art Mus., Oberlin, 1967-68; asst. curator 20th Century painting and sculpture Nat. Collection Fine Arts, Smithsonian Instn., Washington, 1968-73; assoc. curator Nat. Collection Fine Arts, Smithsonian Instn., 1974-75; dir. U. Iowa Mus. Art, 1975-79, Amon Carter Mus., Ft. Worth, 1980—. Author museum brochures, catalogues. Mem. Nat. Mus. Act Adv. Council, 1980-83, vis. com. Allen Meml. Art Mus. of Oberlin (Ohio) Coll., 1987—. Grantee Nat. Endowment Arts-Donner Found., 1979. Mem. Assn. Art Mus. Dirs. (trustee 1981-82, 84-86, chmn. govt. and art com. 1982-84), Western Assn. Art Mus. (regional rep. 1978-79), Am. Assn. Mus. (commn. for new century 1981-84), Am. Arts Alliance (dir. 1980-86, vice-chmn. 1982-84). Office: 3501 Camp Bowie Blvd PO Box 2365 Fort Worth TX 76113

MUHLNICKEL, ISABELLE, mental health counselor; b. Strong, Colo., May 11, 1931; d. Albert and Frances (Martinez) Quintana; m. Ludwig Albert Muhlnickel, Jan. 13, 1952; children: Ludwig Albert, Elizabeth, Mary Karolyn. BA in Sociology, Met. State Coll.-Denver, 1980. Lic. psychiat. technician, Colo. Ednl. loan officer Lowry Fed. Credit Union, Denver, 1972-76; mgr., dir. Teamsters Credit Union, Denver, 1980-81; psychiat. technician State of Colo., Wheatridge, 1981—; del. to China Research Soc. Modernization of Mgmt., The China Assn. Sci. and Tech., People to People Internat., People's Republic China, 1988.; founder, exec. dir. Fathers Crisis Center, Denver, 1984—. Met. State Coll. Colo. Scholars award, 1977, 78, 79. Mem. Nat. Assn. Female Execs., Inst. Internat. Edn. Democrat. Roman Catholic. Avocations: travel, photography, skiing, hiking, painting.

MUIR, HELEN, journalist, author; b. Yonkers, N.Y., Feb. 9, 1911; d. Emmet A. and Helen T. (Flaherty) Lennehan; student public schs.; m. William Whalley Muir, Jan. 23, 1936; children—Mary Muir Burrell, William Torbert. With Yonkers Herald Statesman, 1929-30, 31-33, N.Y. Evening Post, 1930-31, N.Y. Evening Jour., 1933-34, Carl Byoir & Assos., N.Y.C., and Miami, Fla., 1934-35; syndicated columnist Universal Service, Miami, 1935-38; columnist Miami Herald, 1941-42; children's book editor, 1949-56; woman's editor Miami Daily News, 1943-44; freelance mag. writer, numerous nat. mags., 1944—; drama critic Miami News, 1960-65. Trustee, Coconut Grove Library Assn., Friends U. Miami Library, Friends Miami-Dade Public Library; vis. com. U. Miami Libraries; bd. dirs. Miami-Dade County Public Library System; mem. State Library Adv. Council, 1979—, past chmn. Recipient award Delta Kappa Gamma, 1960; Fla. Library Assn. Trustees and Friends award, 1973; trustee citation ALA, 1984; named to Fla. Women's Hall of Fame, 1984. Mem. Women in Communications (Community Headliner award 1973), Soc. Women Geographers. Clubs: Florida Women's Press (award 1963); Cosmopolitan (N.Y.C.); Biscayne Bay Yacht. Author: Miami, U.S.A., 1953, Biltmore: Beacon for Miami, 1987. Home: 3855 Stewart Ave Miami FL 33133

MUIR, JEANNE ELIZABETH, computer information professional; b. Huntingdon, Pa., Feb. 2, 1961; d. Jay Robert and Judith Leigh (Knox) M. BS, Pa. State U., 1982. Staff distbn. systems Eastman Kodak Co., Rochester, N.Y., 1982-85; staff mil. and data systems ops. Gen. Electric Co., Valley Forge, Pa., 1985-87; software test mgr. govt. electronic systems div. Gen. Electric Co., Syracuse, N.Y., 1987—. Rape crisis counselor Crime and Victims Assn. of Chester County, West Chester, Pa., 1986-87, Planned Parenthood Assn. of Monroe County, Rochester, N.Y., 1985-86. Nat. Assn. of Female Execs. Republican. Home: 985 Westmoreland Ave Syracuse NY 13210

MUJAHED, MARY ELIZABETH, small business owner; b. Cheyenne, Calif., Mar. 16, 1929; d. Frank Ralph and Elsie Fern (Patterson) Yager; m. Saleh Ramadan Mujahed, July 24, 1952; children: Susan Elizabeth, David Saleh. BA in Liberal Arts, Scripps Coll., 1951. Library asst. Contra Costa (Calif.) County Library System, 1965-69; publisher Orion Pub. Co., Walnut Creek, Calif., 1982—. Editor: How To Stop Smoking, 1982. Mem. Nat. Congl. Rep. Com., Washington, 1977—; sustaining mem. Rep. Nat. Com., 1977—. Recipient Medal Merit Rep. Presdl. Task Force, 1981. Mem. Fine Arts Mus's. San Francisco. Methodist. Club: Commonwealth (San Francisco).

MUKA, BETTY LORAINE OAKES, lawyer; b. McAlester, Okla., Jan. 30, 1929; d. Herbert La Fern and Loraine Lillian (Coppedge) Oakes; m. Arthur Allen Muka, Sept. 6, 1952; children: Diane Loraine, Stephen Arthur, Christopher Herbert, Martha Ann, Deborah Susan. Student Monticello Coll., 1946-47; BS, Okla. U., 1950; MS, Cornell U., 1953, MBA, 1970; JD, Syracuse U. 1980. Bar: R.I. 1983, U.S. Dist. Ct. R.I. 1984. Mgr. dining room Anna Maude's Cafeteria, Oklahoma City, 1950-51; faculty dining room mgr. V.P.I., Blacksburg, Va., 1955-56; owner, mgr. The Cottage Restaurant, 1959-60; lectr., lab. instr. foods and organic chemistry Cornell U., 1961; owner, mgr. student housing, 1965-68; jr. acct. Maxfield, Randolph & Carpenter, CPA's, Ithaca, N.Y., 1970-71; income tax cons. H & R Block, Ithaca, 1971-73; atty. pro se, 1972—; hostess-bookkeeper Holiday Inn, Ithaca, 1972-73; salesperson Investors Diversified Services, Ithaca, 1972-73, NASD, 1973; agt. Inventory Control Co., 1975-78; law clk. 1978-79; sole practice, Providence, 1983-85; lectr. in fin. Tompkins Cortland Community Coll. Leader various youth groups, Ithaca, 1964-71. Mem. ABA, N.Y. State Bar Assn., R.I. Bar Assn., R.I. Trial Lawyer's Assn., Assn. Trial Lawyers Am., Mortar Bd., Delta Delta Delta Alumnae (pres. 1974), Phi Delta Phi (bd. dirs. 1980, J. Mark McCarthy award 1980), Sigma Delta Epsilon. Club: Toastmasters. Home and Office: 113 Kay St Ithaca NY 14050

MUKALLA, CLAUDETTE JOAN, publisher; b. Detroit, June 14, 1946; d. Michael A. and Lily (Sayegh) M.; Grad. high sch., Detroit. Asst. dir. Librarie du Liban, Beirut, 1972-73; owner, operator Internat. Book Ctr., Troy, Mich., 1973—. Vol., Beaumont Hosp., Oak Park, Mich., 1975. Mem. Nat. Women's Book Assn., Mich. Assn. Ednl. Reps., Founders Soc. Detroit Inst. Art, Troy C. of C. Republican. Roman Catholic. Avocations: green belt karate, oil painting, yoga. Office: Internat Book Ctr PO Box 295 Troy MI 48099

MUKOYAMA, HELEN KIYOKO, social worker; b. Paia, Maui, Hawaii, Nov. 13, 1914; d. Ginichi and Shio (Takahashi) Takehara; m. Teruo Mukoyama, June 11, 1936 (div. 1956); children: Marshall H., Howard T., Wesley K. BA, Simpson Coll., 1937; postgrad., U. Denver, 1936; MA, U. Chgo., 1943. Caseworker Chgo. Welfare Adminstrn., 1938-41; Caseworker Cook County Dept. Welfare, Chgo., 1945-46, cons. to Japanese Ams. relocating to Chgo., 1945-46; cons. to Japanese Ams. relocating to Chgo. Ill. Public Aid Commn., Chgo., 1945-46, welfare adminstrv. aide supr., 1949-69; caseworker Travelers Aid Soc.-Immigrants Service, Chgo., 1951-65; intake worker Homemaker Service, Chgo., 1951-65, Salvation Army Family Service, Chgo., 1957-65; social work supr. intake Ill. Dept. Children and Family Services, Chgo., 1965-67; caseworker III Salvation Army Family Service, Chgo., 1967-72; casework supr. Jewish Family and Community Services, Chgo., 1972-73; supr. intake Council for Jewish Elderly, Chgo., 1973-77, supr. community aides and welfare adminstrv. coordinator, 1977-79; coordinator elderly housing Japanese Am. Service Com., Chgo., 1977-79; mgr. Heiwa Ter. Japanese Am. Elderly Housing, Chgo, 1980—; mem. Japanese Am. Housing Bd. Contbr. articles to profl. jours. Mem. Council of Ministries, Welfare Div. United Meth. Ch., 1963-69. Recipient Cert. Merit award Japanese Am. Service Com., 1963, 82, Plaque Japanese Housing Corp. Heiwa Terr., 1984, Spl. award Japanese Am. Redress Com., 1983. Mem. Acad. Cert. Social Workers, Nat. Assn. Social Workers, Ill. Cert. Social Workers, Chgo. Human Relations Commn., Japanese-Am. Citizens League, Japanese-Am. Soc., Art Inst. Chgo., Epsilon Sigma, Pi Gamma Mu. Methodist. Home: 912 S Mason Ave Chicago IL 60644 Office: 920 W Lawrence St Chicago IL 60640

MULARSKI, VICTORIA A., consultant flavor analyses; b. Adams, Mass.; d. Walter F. Sr. and Frances (Meczywor) M. BA, Syracuse U., postgrad. Research asst. N.Y. Hosp., Cornell Med. Ctr., N.Y.C.; biochemist Lahey Clinic, Boston; mem. staff Arthur D. Little, Inc., Cambridge, Mass., 1954-70, asst. dir. flavor profile panel tng., 1956-67, dir. flavor profile panel tng., 1967-70; cons. flavor profile Adams, Mass., 1970—. Profl. mem. Inst. Food Technologists. Roman Catholic. Home and Office: 68 Orchard St Adams MA 01220

MULDAUR, DIANA CHARLTON, actress; b. N.Y.C., Aug. 19, 1938; d. Charles Edward Arrowsmith and Alice Patricia (Jones) M.; m. James Mitchell Vickery, July 26, 1969 (dec. 1979); m. Robert J. Dozier, Oct. 11, 1981. B.A., Sweet Briar Coll., 1960. Actress appearing in: Off-Broadway theatrical prodns., summer stock, Broadway plays including A Very Rich Woman, 1963-68; guest appearances on TV in maj. dramatic shows; appeared on: TV series Survivors, 1970-71, McCloud, 1971-73, Tony Randall Show, 1976, Black Beauty, 1978; star: TV series Born Free, 1974, Hizzoner, 1979, Fitz & Bones, 1980, NBC miniseries A Year in the Life, 1986, TV movie Murder in Three Acts; motion picture credits include McQ. Bd. dirs. Los Angeles chpt. Asthma and Allergy Found. Am.; bd. advisors Nat. Ctr. Film and Video Preservation, John F. Kennedy Ctr. Performing Arts, 1986. Mem. Acad. Motion Picture Arts and Scis., Screen Actors Guild (dir. 1978), Acad. TV Arts and Scis. (exec. bd., dir., pres. 1983-85), Conservation Soc. Martha's Vineyard Island. Office: care Clarke Lilly 333 Apolina Ave Balboa Island CA 92662

MULDER, SUSAN LEWIS, paralegal; b. Houston, Aug. 5, 1957; d. Richard Victor Lewis and Margery Marie (Bryan) Gentry; m. Orous Alan Mulder, Nov. 22, 1986. AA in Gen. Studies, Austin (Tex.) Community Coll., 1988, AS in Psychology, 1988. Legal sec. Clint Parsley, Atty., Austin, 1984-86; legal sec., legal asst. Mauro, Wendler, Sheets, Austin, 1986; litigation paralegal Earl H. Staelin Atty., Austin, 1987—. Mem. ABA (legal asst. div.), State Bar Tex. (legal asst. div.), Nat. Assn. Female Execs., Alpha Gamma Delta, Phi Theta Kappa. Republican. Methodist. Club: P.E.O. Sisterhood (Austin) (recording sec. 1984-85, treas. 1985-87). Home: 3206 Bryker Dr Austin TX 78703 Office: Earl H Staelin Atty 812 San Antonio #525 Austin TX 78701

MULDOON, BETTY P., restaurant company executive; b. Chgo., Mar. 13, 1953; d. John Edmund and Alice Therese (McCormick) M. BA in Modern Langs., Knox Coll., 1971-75; cert. French studies, Universite De Besanqon, France, 1974-75; postgrad., Colo. State U., 1974, 1975-76; cert., Nat. Cooking Inst., Denver, Colo., 1979; postgrad., Goldenwest Coll. and Coastline Coll., Huntington Beach, Calif., 1984-87. Cert. performax systems trainer. Mgr. Shakey's Inc., Denver, 1976-80, area supr., 1980-82; franchise field cons. Shakey's Inc., Santa Ana, Calif., 1982-84; v.p. Clausen Enterprises, Anaheim, Calif., 1984—; cons. Golden Triangle, Longmont, Colo., 1980-82. Author Delivery Manual, 1982, Training Manual, 1985. Mem. Nat. Restaurant Assn., Nat. Assn., Female Execs. Club: Toastmasters (sec. ednl. v.p., Best Club Speaker of Yr. 1986, 87, pres. 1988). Home: 6600 Warner Ave #102 Huntington Beach CA 92647 Office: Clausen Enterprises 2795 W Lincoln Suite F Anaheim CA 92801

MULDROW, TRESSIE WRIGHT, psychologist; b. Marietta, Ga., Feb. 1, 1941; d. Festus Blanton and Louise Williams Wright Summers; BA, Bennett Coll., 1962; MS, Howard U., 1965, PhD, 1976; 1 child, DeJuan Denise. Research asst. W.C. Allen Corp., Washington, 1966-68; personnel research psychologist Dept. Navy, Washington, 1968-73, Office Personnel Mgmt., CSC, 1973-79; chief, adv. council on alternative selection procedures Office Personnel Mgmt., Washington, 1979-86, chief consultative services, 1986—; lectr. Howard U., 1979. Mem. Washington Inter-Alumni council United Negro Coll. Fund, 1970—, pres., 1988—; trustee Bennett Coll., vice chmn., 1985—; v.p. Family Life Ctr. Br., Boys and Girls Clubs of Washington, 1984—. Named Alumnae of Yr., United Negro Coll. Fund, 1971, recipient Individual Achievement award, 1985; Outstanding Alumnae Morehouse Coll., 1978. Mem. Bennett Coll. Alumnae Assn. (nat. pres. 1978-85, Alumnae of Yr. award 1987), Am. Psychol. Assn., Nat. Assn. Black Psychologists Delta Sigma Theta. Presbyterian. Contbr. articles to profl. publs. Office: 1900 E St NW Washington DC 20415

MULHAUSEN, HEDY ANN, biochemist; b. Cleve., Dec. 5, 1940; d. William Michael and Hedy (Koechle) M. BA, Ursuline Coll., 1962; MS, Ohio State U., 1965, PhD, 1967, postdoctoral studies, Winter, Spring 1968; postdoctoral studies, U. Ga., 1969. Editorial analyst Chem. Abstracts Service, Columbus, Ohio, 1970-80, customer service, 1980-81, tech. services rep., 1981—. Co-Author:(with others) Methods In Enzymology, 1975; contbr. articles to profl. jours. Mem. Big Brothers/ Big Sisters, 1981—. Mem. Am. Chem. Soc. Roman Catholic. Clubs: Buckeye Wanderfreunde, Heart of Ohio Hikers. Office: Chem Abstracts Service PO Box 3012 Columbus OH 43210

MULHAUSER, KAREN, organization executive; b. Burlington, Vt., Nov. 5, 1942; d. Harold H. and Leta H. Webber; B.A. in Biology, Antioch Coll.,

1965; m., Aug. 18, 1968; 1 child, Christopher. Research asso. Albert Einstein Coll. of Medicine, Bronx, N.Y., 1965-67; sci. tchr. Cambridge Sch., Weston, Mass., 1967-70; family planning trainer/educator HEW Region X, Seattle, 1970-73; lobbyist Nat. Abortion Rights Action League, Washington, 1973-75, exec. dir., 1975-81; polit. cons., 1988; exec. dir. Citizens Against Nuclear War, Washington, 1982-87; exec. dir. Ctr. for Edn. on Nuclear War, Washington, 1982—; mem. Scoville Peace Fellowship Bd., adv. bd. Peace Media Project; bd. dirs. Ind. Action, Scoville Fellow; chmn. Women for a Meaningful Summit, 1985—; mem. exec. com. Nuclear Weapons Freeze Campaign. Mem. Planned Parenthood Met. Washington, past pres., bd. dirs.; bd. dirs. Center for Population Options; sec., mem. exec. com. Voters for Choice; mem. exec. com. Friends of Family Planning; pres. Antioch U. Alumni Assn. Democrat. Office: 1201 16th St NW Washington DC 20036

MULHOLLAND, SHEILA LEE, lawyer, educator; b. Glens Falls, N.Y., Aug. 7, 1951; d. Leo Daniel Dennis and Florence Elta (Wilson) M. BA, Alfred U., 1974; JD, Western New Eng. U., 1978; LLM, Boston U., 1986; postgrad., U. Houston, 1987. Bar: Mass. 1978, U.S. Fed. Ct. (1st cir.). Assoc. atty. Guy R. Peznola, Springfield, Mass., 1978; asst. dist. atty. Hampden County, Springfield, 1978—; adj. prof. Holyoke (Mass.) Community Coll., 1987—; lect. Project Drug Awareness, Prevention Abuse of Elderly, Springfield, 1986-88. Mem. Nat. Coll. Dist. Attys., Greater Springfield Mental Health Assn. (trustee 1981-83), Western New Eng. U. Alumni Assn. (trustee 1979-81). Democrat. Roman Catholic. Home: 15 Park St Springfield MA 01103 Office: Hampden County DA's Office 50 State St Springfield MA 01103

MULLEEDY, JOYCE ELAINE, nursing service administrator, educator; b. Paterson, N.J., Aug. 30, 1948; d. Edward and Jane (Van De Weert) Schuurman; m. Philip Anthony Mulleedy, May 14, 1982. BS, Paterson State Coll., 1970. RN, cert. emergency nurse, emergency med. technician, paramedic. Pub. health nurse Vis. Nurse Assn. of No. Bergen County, Ramsey, N.J., 1970-72; health dir. Camp Fowler Assn., Speculator, N.Y., 1973-76; exec. dir. Am. Cancer Soc., Speculator, 1976-77; pub. health nurse Hamilton County Nursing Service, Lake Pleasant, N.Y., 1977-80, supervising pub. health nurse, 1980-82, dir. patient services, 1982-86; quality assurance specialist Susquehanna-Adirondack Regional Emergency Med. Services Program, 1986—; cons. dir. Home Health Care of Hamilton County, Inc., Indian Lake, N.Y., 1979-84. Author instructional booklet: Assessing Your Patients, 1983, (pamphlet) A Note to Parents, 1985. Bd. dirs. Am. Cancer Soc.-Hamilton County Unit, Speculator, 1972-76, Speculator Vol. Ambulance Corps, Inc., 1974-81, ARC-Hamilton County chpt., Lake Pleasant, N.Y., 1981—; mem. adminstrv. bd. dirs. Grace United Meth. Ch., Speculator, 1982—. Martha Hazen Scholar Am. Legion, 1966; recipient Service award Am. Legion, 1977. Mem. N.Y. State Assn. County Health Ofcls., Adirondack-Appalachian Regional Emergency Med. Services Council (chmn. 1982—), Emergency Nurses Assn., Hamilton County Emergency Med. Services Council (sec.-treas. 1974—, instr. 1974—), Dirs. of Northeastern N.Y. Home Health Agys. Republican. Home: PO Box 203 Elm Lake Rd Speculator NY 12164 Office: Susquehanna Adirondack Regional Emergency Med Services Program PO Box 212 Speculator NY 12164

MULLEN, ANDREA, corporation executive, television personality; b. Evanston, Ill., Mar. 6, 1959; d. Edwin and Geraldine Anna (Rejsek) Shapiro; m. Carter Kane Mullen, Sept. 25, 1982 (div. Nov. 1985). Student, Ariz. State U., 1977-78. Ad, pub. relations coordinator Plaza 3, Phoenix, 1980-81; merchandise publicity coordinator JC Penny Co. Inc., Phoenix, 1981-84; dir. spl. events Diamond's, Phoenix, 1984; dir. pub. relations Ramada Inc., Phoenix, 1984-87; pres. Plaza 3 Models, Talents, Phoenix, 1987—; anchorwoman Sta-KTSP-TV, Phoenix, 1986—. Editor Ariz. Bus. Gazette Corporate Style, 1984, East Valley Mag. Lifestyle, 1983-84; reporter PM Magazine Consumer Reports, 1984. Mem. Rio Salado Support Group, 1987. Mem. Women In Communications, Ad 2, Pub. Relations Soc. Am. Roman Catholic. Office: Plaza 3 Models Talents 4343 N 16th St Phoenix AZ 85016

MULLEN, FRANCES ANDREWS, educational consultant, psychologist, educator; b. Chgo., Nov. 27, 1902; d. Edmund Lathrop and Ethel (Baker) Andrews; m. Urban Joseph Mullen, Oct. 11, 1929 (div. 1947); 1 child, Urban Edmund; adopted children: Ann Mullen Cramer, William J., Katherine Mullen Dane. Ph.B., U. Chgo., 1923, M.A., 1927, Ph.D., 1939, postdoctoral student, 1943-44; postdoctoral student clin. psychology Michael Reese Hosp., 1943-44, Western Res. U., 1942, Inst. Juvenile Research Chgo., 1942-43. Diplomate in clin. psychology Am. Bd. Examiners in Profl. Psychology. High sch. tchr., Chgo. pub. schs., 1925-39, sch. psychologist, 1939-47, elem. sch. prin., 1947-49, dir. Bur. Mentally Handicapped Children, 1949-53, asst. supt. schs. for spl. edn., 1953-66; cons. sch. adminstrs. and parents, 1966-75; editor Internat. Psychologist, 1968-73, World Go Round, 1972-74; co-editor Sch. Psychology at Mid Century, 1955; pres. Internat. Council Psychologists (award 1987), Sherman Oaks, Calif., 1976-77, sec. gen., 1977-79; chmn. SHARE, Internat. Hospitality, Sherman Oaks, 1953-84; pres. Council Adminstrs. Spl. Edn. Local Sch. Dists., Chgo., 1961-62; vis. prof. or instr. summer and evening courses in field Northwestern U., U. S.C., U. Ariz., Calif. State U., Northridge, Chgo. Tchrs. Coll., Roosevelt U.; part time faculty dept. psychology Calif. State U., Northridge, 1977-78; cons. Ariz. Dept. Mental Health, 1959, Waukesha Pub. Schs. Wis., 1960, Univs. Lahore and Indiana, Pakistan, 1966, N.Z. Dept. Edn., 1967, Worcester Pub. Schs., Mass., 1968, U.S. Office Edn., 1968, Interprofl. Research Commn. on Pupil Personnel Services, 1967-69, Washington Pub. Schs., 1970, Bangalore, India, 1971, Jinnah Postgrad. Med. Ctr. Karachi, Pakistan, 1971; mem. psychology adv. panel Office Vocat. Rehab., HEW, 1961-63; mem. various panels U.S. Office Edn., 1953-66; co-chmn. Thayer Conf. on Sch. Psychology, N.Y., 1954; co-chmn., organizer 1st Internat. Colloquium Sch. Psychology, Munich, W.Ger., 1975. Author: Educating Handicapped Children, 1969; Achievement and Adjustment of Educable Mentally Handicapped Children, 1961. Contbr. chpts. to books, articles to profl. pubs. Past mem. bds. and adv. coms. Inst. Juvenile Research, Chgo., Ill. Soc. Crippled Children and Adults, United Cerebral Palsy, Chgo., Retarded Children's Aid, Girl Scouts Chgo. Recipient awards Ill. Council for Exceptional Children, 1967, Chgo. Council for Exceptional Children, 1966, State St. Salute award, Nat. Bus. and Profl. Women, 1966. Fellow Am. Psychol. Assn. (pres. div. sch. psychologists 1951-53, award 1971), Am. Assn. Mental Deficiency; mem. Internat. Council Exceptional Children (pres. div. Council Adminstrs. Spl. Edn. in Local Sch. Systems 1955-56). Democrat. Presbyterian. Clubs: Am. Alpine (N.Y.); Can. Alpine (Banff); Sierra (San Francisco); Chgo. Mountaineering (pres.). Home: 4014 Cody Rd Sherman Oaks CA 91403

MULLEN, MAUREEN ANN, interior designer; b. Chgo., Mar. 22, 1949; d. Robert Vincent and Mary Geraldine (Woelfel) M. BA, U. Ill., 1971; MEd, Coll. of William and Mary, 1974; postgrad., U. Chgo., 1985—. Programmer Computer Task Group, N.Y.C., 1980-81; analyst, programmer Guy Carpenter, N.Y.C., 1981-82; analyst C.N.A. Ins., Chgo., 1982-84; analyst, programmer Lakeshore Nat. Bank, Chgo., 1984-85; customer service rep. Sterling Software, Chgo., 1986; owner Mullen Designs, Chgo., 1987—. Worker crisis hotline, Chgo., 1986; mem. adv. bd. Lakeview Mental Health Ctr., Chgo., 1986; mem. Chgo. Council on Fgn. Relations, 1986-87; vol. Thomas Hynes Campaign, Chgo., 1987. Mem. Nat. Assn. Female Execs., Mensa.

MULLEN, PAMELA ANN, school principal; b. Biddeford, Maine, Mar. 12, 1949; d. Rudolph Arthur and Lois Ailene (Cameron) Martin; children: Matthew, Tamara. BA in Music, Wheaton Coll., Mass., 1971; MA in Edn. Adminstrn., U. So. Maine, 1981. Tchr. Old Orchard Beach (Maine) Schs., 1972-86; tchr., vice prin. Jameson Primary, Old Orchard Beach, 1982-86, prin., 1986. Recipient grant Maine Dept. Edn. and Cultural Services, 1979, 86. Mem. Maine Elem. Prins. Assn. Methodist. Home: 8 W Old Orchard Ave PO Box 309 Old Orchard Beach ME 04064 Office: Jameson Primary Sch Jameson Hill Rd Old Orchard Beach ME 04064

MULLEN, PATRICIA ANN, chemical executive; b. Flushing, N.Y., July 10, 1935; d. Peter Charles and Julie (Plzak) M. BA, Seton Hill Coll., Greensburg, Pa., 1957; MA, Mt. Holyoke (Mass.) Coll., 1961. Research chemist Am. Cyanamid Co., Stamford, Conn., 1961-71; group leader Am. Cyanamid Co., Clifton, N.J., 1971-77; dir. fragance application Naarden Internat., N.Y.C., 1977-85; gen. mgr. Exotherm, Inc., Beverly, Mass., 1985-87; pres., chief exec. officer Inatex, Ltd., Babylon, N.Y., 1987—. Mem. Am. Chem. Soc., Soc. Cosmetic Chemists.

MULLENAX, JEAN STAYTON, municipal services administrator; b. Glenwood Springs, Colo., Nov. 15, 1932; d. Ruel Wesley and Elsie May (Yandell) Stayton; m. Mervil Jay Mullenax, Dec. 25, 1950; children: Elizabeth Sandra, Gregory Kim. Student, U. Colo., 1962-63, Loretto Heights Coll., 1978-81. Cost acct. Colo. Office Supply, Denver, 1959-61; tax cons., office mgr. Loren Penny Tax Service, Arvada, Colo., 1961-68; exec. sec. Aspen (Colo.) Constrn. Corp., 1968-71; controller RJ Mullenax, Inc., Rifle, Colo., 1979—; dist. mgr. Town of Snowmass (Colo.) Water and Sanitation Dist., 1972—. Mem. Water Pollution Control Fedn., Am. Water Works Assn., New Castle Hist. Soc. Lodge: Order of Eastern Star. Home: 128 West Ave Rifle CO 81650

MULLENIX, LINDA SUSAN, lawyer, educator; b. N.Y.C., Oct. 16, 1950; d. Andrew Michael and Roslyn (Rosenthal) Marasco; m. James William Mullenix, Sept. 26, 1981; children—Robert Bartholomew, John Theodore, William Joseph. B.A., CCNY, 1971; M. Philosophy, Columbia U., 1974, Ph.D. (Pres.'s fellow), 1977; J.D., Georgetown U., 1980. Bar: D.C. 1981, U.S. Dist Ct. D.C. 1981, U.S. Supreme Ct. 1986. U.S. Ct. Appeals (D.C. cir.) 1981. Assoc. prof., lectr. George Washington U., Washington, 1977-80; asst. prof. Am. U., Washington, 1979; clin. prof. Loyola U. Law Sch., Los Angeles, 1981-82, vis. asst. prof., 1982-83; vis. asst. prof. Catholic U. Law Sch., Washington, 1983-84, asst. prof., 1984-86, assoc. prof., 1986—; assoc. Pierson, Ball & Dowd, Washington, 1980-81; adj. instr. Fordham U., N.Y.C., 1975-76, adj. asst. prof. 1977; adj. asst. prof. CCNY, 1977; adj. instr., adj. asst. prof. Cooper Union Advancement Sci., Art, N.Y.C., 1977; instr. N.Y. Inst. Tech., N.Y.C., 1976, U. Md. European div., Ramstein, Germany, 1974. Editor bibliographies Political Theory, A Jour. Polit. Philosophy, 1972-74; The Tax Lawyer Jour., 1978-80; contbr. articles to profl. publs. Alt. del. Va. Democratic State Conv., 1980. Fellow NDEA, 1971-74, Georgetown U. Law Sch., 1978; N.Y. State Regents scholar, 1967-71. Mem. D.C. Bar Assn., Women's Bar Assn. D.C., ABA, Phi Beta Kappa, Phi Alpha Delta. Home: 6221 Redwing Rd Bethesda MD 20817 Office: Cath U Am Columbus Sch Law Washington DC 20064

MULLER, ADELYN CAMERON, retired educator; b. Greenville, Tex., Mar. 5, 1913; d. Frank Clifton and Hortense (White) Cameron; B.A., B.A. in English and Math., E. Tex. State U., Commerce, 1934; M.A. in Math. Edn., U. Mo., Kansas City, 1968; Ph.D. in Math. Edn., Kans. State U., Manhattan, 1975; m. John G. Muller; children—Ken Cameron, Jon Tackaberry. Tchr., Greenville (Tex.) Pub. Schs., 1936-40; aero. liasion engr. Ft. Worth Consol.-Vultee, 1943-46; coordinator math. Valley View Sch. Dist., Overland Park, Kans., 1960-69, Shawnee Mission (Kans.) Pub. Schs., 1969-70, adj. prof. Kans. State U., U. Mo., Kansas City. Mem. AAUW, Shawnee Mission Pub. Sch. Adminstrs. Assn., Nat. Council Tchrs. Math., Phi Delta Kappa, Delta Kappa Gamma. Recipient Nat. Edn. Assn. Pacemaker award, 1969. Participant in HEW 3-month tour of India; Nat. Sch. Assn. people-to-people tour Russia, Switzerland, France, Eng. Contbr. articles in field to profl. jours. Home: 370 Terrace Trail W Lake Quivira KS 66106

MULLER, CHARLOTTE FELDMAN, economist, educator; b. N.Y.C., Feb. 19, 1921; d. Louis and Lillian (Drogin) Feldman; m. Jonas N. Muller, 1942 (dec.); m. Carl Schoenberg; children: Jeremy Lewis Muller, Sara Linda Muller. A.B., Vassar Coll., 1941; A.M., Columbia U., 1942, Ph.D. in Econs., 1946. Instr. econs. Bklyn. Coll., 1943; lectr. Barnard Coll., 1943-46; asst. prof. Occidental Coll., 1947; asst. study dir. Survey Research Center, U. Mich., 1948; research assoc. U. Calif., Berkeley, 1948-50; lectr. Yale U. Sch. Public Health, 1952-53; asst. prof. Columbia U. Sch. Public Health, 1957-67; assoc. dir. Center for Social Research CUNY, 1967-86, prof. econs., 1978—, prof. sociology, 1982—, prof. urban studies Center for Social Research, 1967-78; v.p. CUNY Acad. for Humanities and Scis., 1985-88; prof. health econs. Mt. Sinai Sch. Medicine, 1986—, dir. div. health econs., 1988—; cons. U.S. VA Health Care Financing Adminstrn.; disting. Alumna speaker Vassar Centennial, 1971. Mem. editorial bd. Research on Aging, Am. Jour. Pub. Health, 1980-84, Women and Health; contbr. numerous articles on health econs. to profl. pubs. Mem. N.Y.C. Mayor's Com. on Prescription Drug Abuse, 1970-73; bd. dirs. Alan Guttmacher Inst., 1972-81, CUNY Research Found., 1985- ; vice chmn. Med. and Health Research Assn., N.Y.C.; mem. health care tech. study sect. Nat. Center Health Services Research, 1976-79; mem. commn. on nat. policy Am. Jewish Congress. Ford/Rockefeller Founds. grantee, 1972-73, 75-76; Russell Sage Found. grantee, 1985—. Mem. Am. Econs. Assn., Am. Public Health Assn., NOW. Jewish. Office: Mt Sinai Sch Medicine 1 Gustave L Levy Plaza New York NY 10029

MULLER, CLAUDYA BARBARA, librarian; b. Furth, Germany, Sept. 14, 1946; came to U.S., 1952; d. Ralph Leon and Elfriede Katherine (Hilpert) Burkett; m. William Albert Muller III, Dec. 12, 1965 (div. 1986); 1 child, Martha Genevieve. B.A., Ga. So. Coll., 1967; M.L.S., Emory U., 1968. Asst. to head circulation Ga. State U., 1968-69; asst. dir. War Woman Regional Library, 1970-72; assoc. dir. Ottumwa Heights Coll. Library, Iowa, 1973; bookmobile librarian Gallia County Dist. Library, Ohio, 1976; dir. Jackson County Pub. Library, W.Va., 1976-78, Worcester County Library, Md., 1978-83; state librarian State of Iowa, Des Moines, 1983-86; dir. Suffolk Coop. Library System, 1986—. Editor: University Press Books for Public Libraries, 1979, 80. Timmie Dora Barker fellow Emory U., 1967; recipient Good Citizenship award Rotary, Snow Hill, Md., 1983. Mem. ALA (editor procs. small and medium sized libraries sect. 1981, mem. standards com., 1986—, mem. architecture for pub. libraries com., 1987—), Library Adminstrn. and Mgmt. Assn., Pub. Library Assn. (chmn. orgn. com. 1983-84, mem. publs. com. 1984-85, chair publs. com. 1985-87, new standards task force), Iowa Library Assn., Biblio. Ctr. for Research (trustee, budget and fin. com., by-laws com.). Office: Suffolk Coop Library System 627 N Sunrise Service Rd Bellport NY 11713

MULLER, ELSIE FERRAR, psychotherapist, psychiatric social worker; b. Worcester, Mass., Apr. 7, 1913; d. Frederic and Anne (Binns) Bonnet; B.S., Alfred U., 1934; M.S.W., U. Mo., Columbia, 1969; postgrad. U. Mo., Kansas City, 1962-63; m. Frederick Wentworth Muller, Oct. 10, 1936 (div. 1961); 1 dau., Jean Ferrar Muller Mackimmie. Lic. clin. social worker. Art. instr. Alfred U., 1935-36; art therapist Gillis Home, Kansas City, Mo., 1958-70; psychotherapist Ozanam Home, Kansas City, Mo., 1970—; art therapy cons. Jackson County, Kansas City, Mo., 1975-78, Wyandotte County Sch. Social Workers, Kansas City, Kans., 1978—. Mem. Nat. Assn. Social Workers, Acad. Social Workers, Am. Art Therapy Assn. (hon. life), Am. Soc. Psychopath. Expression (editorial adv.), Nat. Register Clin. Social Workers. Episcopalian. Home: 1420 Upper Dr NE Pullman WA 99163-4305

MULLER, ESTHER UNTERMAN, retail executive, consultant; b. Haifa, Israel, Jan. 12, 1947; d. Mike and Frieda (Halpert) M.; m. Jerrold Unterman (div. July 1982); m. Peter Muller, Jan. 4, 1987; 1 child, Richard. BA cum laude, Bklyn Coll., 1975. Pres. On-Site Realty, N.Y.C., 1979-83, Aca Joe Ea., N.Y.C., 1983-86; chmn. bd. Aca Joe Retail, San Francisco, 1986—; sec., treas. Real Estate N.Y., 1983-86. Vol. Fairfield (Conn.) Hosp. Mental Health, 1976-79. Mem. Young Men's Real Estate Assn., B'nai B'rith Real Estate Assn. Home: 21 E 66th St New York NY 10021 Office: 475 Park Ave South New York NY 10016

MULLETTE, JULIENNE PATRICIA, research astrologer, author, lecturer, television personality and producer, editor, holistic health center administrator; b. Sydney, Australia, Nov. 19, 1940; came to U.S., 1953; d. Ronald Stanley Lewis and Sheila Rosalind Blunden (Phillips) M.; m. Fred Gillette Sturm, Nov. 24, 1964 (div. Dec. 1969); m. Kenneth Walter Gillman, Dec. 27, 1971 (div. Dec. 1978); children—Noah Khristoff Mullette-Gillman, O'Dhaniel Alexander Mullette-Gillman. B.A., Western Coll. for Women, Oxford, Ohio, 1961; postgrad. Harvard U., 1964, U. Sao Paulo, Brazil, 1965, Inst. do Filosofia, Sao Paulo, 1965, Miami U., Oxford, 1967-69. Tchr. English, High Mowing Sch., Wilton, N.H., 1962-64, Stoneleigh-Prospect Hill Sch., Greenfield, Mass., 1964; seminar dir. Western Coll., Oxford, Ohio, 1967-69; pres. Family Tree, The Home Univ., Montclair, N.J., 1978-80; dir. Pleroma Holistic Health Ctr., Montclair, 1980—; dir. Astrological Research Ctr., Sydney, Australia, 1983; hostess You and the Cosmos talk show WFMU, East Orange, N.J., 1985, The Juliette Mullette Show, Connections TV, Newark, 1985—, The Juliette Mullette Show WFDU-FM, Fairleigh Dickinson U., N.J., 1986—; founder Spiritual Devel. Research Group 1986—, Spvt. astrology counselor, 1962—; lectr., speaker worldwide, 1968—; guest on radio and TV shows, U.S. and Can., 1962—; host syndicated radio talk show The Juliette Mullette Show, N.Y., N.J., 1987—; owner, pres. Moonlight Pond, Woodbourne, N.Y., 1988—; founder The Spiritual Devel. Ctr., 1986—. Author: The Moon— Understanding the Subconscious, 1973; also articles, 1968—. Founding editor KÓSMOS mag., 1968-78, The Jour. of Astrological Studies, 1970, The Signs of the Times, 1986—. Founder local chpt. La Leche League, Montclair, 1974. Mem. AAUW (chair cultural affairs Montclair chpt.), Spiritual Devel. Group (founder 1987), Internat. Soc. Astrological Research (founding pres. 1968-78), Am. Fedn. Astrologers (cert.), Societé Belge d'Astrologie, Am. Assn. Humanistic Psychology, AAUW (dir. cultural affairs 1987—), Nat. Assn. Female Execs., Internat. Llamas Assn. Avocations: competitive tennis, local theatre, singing, breeding and training of Llamas. Home: 89 A Star Rt Woodbourne NY 12788

MULLIKIN, LOLETA ROSE HATFIELD, educator; b. Princeton, Ind., Nov. 4, 1931; d. Commodore Worthington and Cleda Marie (Ashby) Hatfield; m. James Harold Mullikin, Dec. 22, 1956. BS in Elem. Edn., Ind. State U., 1957, MA in Elem. Edn., 1967. Tchr. Vigo County Sch. Corp., Terre Haute, Ind., 1957-87; classroom student tchr. supr. Ind. State U., 1970-87; Vigo County Sch. Corp. Ednl. Specifications Com., 1977-78, 86. Mem. NEA, Ind. State Tchrs. Assn., Vigo County Tchrs. Assn., Ind. Reading Assn., Kappa Kappa. Republican. Club: Terre Haute Country. Home: 170 Gardendale Rd Terre Haute IN 47803

MULLINS, ELIZABETH IONE, sociology educator; b. Colemaine, Minn., Sept. 6, 1928; d. Edgar R. and Bess (Redhed) M. B.A., Miami U., Oxford, Ohio, 1950; M.A., U. Ill., 1954; Ph.D., Ind. U., 1975. Tchr., Blue Ash High Sch., Ohio, 1950-53; student personnel rep. Ind. U., Bloomington, 1954-57; coordinator activities devel. ctr. So. Ill. U., Carbondale, 1957-65; vis. lectr. Ind. U., 1972-73; asst. prof. sociology Kent State U., Ohio, 1973—. Co-editor Sociol. Focus, 1980—. Mem. ACLU, Common Cause, North Central Sociol. Assn. (exec. council 1980—), Am. Sociol. Assn. (com. 1972-75), NOW, Women Studies Assn., AAUP, Alpha Kappa Delta (v.p. 1974-78). Office: Kent State U Lowery Hall Kent OH 44242

MULLINS, NANCY RUTH, firefighter-paramedic; b. Rockledge, Fla., June 8, 1959; d. Alfred Emanuel and Jacqueline Ruth (Combs) Rubins; m. George Ray Mullins, June 2, 1984; children: Gregory Raymond, Lorraina Irene. Cert. paramedic, Miami (Fla.) Dade Coll., 1976-78, cert. firefighter, 1980; student in sci., Valencia Community Coll., Orlando, Fla., 1984—. Emergency med. technician South Miami Hosp., 1977-78; emergency room technician Jackson Meml. Hosp., Miami, 1978-79; paramedic Brevard County Emergency Med. Services, Merritt Island, Fla., 1979-80; firefighter/paramedic Kissimmee (Fla.) Fire Dept., 1980-81; firefighter, paramedic Rescue Squad Orange County Fire Dept., Orlando, Fla., 1981—; auxilliary dep. sheriff Orange County Sheriff's Office, Orlando, 1985-88, sgt., 1988—; vol. firefighter Brevard County, 1979-81; vocat. tchr. Orange County Sch. Bd., Orlando, 1987—; flight medic Orange County Fire Rescue, Orlando, 1982—, dive team, 1982-86. CPR instr. Am. Heart Assn., Orlando, 1986—; first aid instr. ARC, Orlando, 1986—; trainer citrus council Girl Scouts U.S., Fla., 1986—, leader, 1983-87; mem. PTA, Orange County, 1984—; mem. Orange County Fire/Rescue Rappelling Team, 1981-84; mem. emergency response team coordinator ARC, 1986; post adviser emergency med. services Boy Scouts Am., 1988—. Named Firefighter/Paramedic of Yr. Fla. VFW, 1987-88; recipient Spl. Commendation Orange County Rescue Squad, 1988. Mem. Internat. Assn. Firefighters, Women in Fire Suppression, Nat. Assn. Emergency Med. Technicians, Greenpeace, Sierra Club. Democrat. Methodist. Home: 1304 Angeline Ave Orlando FL 32807-1313 Office: Orange County Fire/Rescue div 4700 Lake Underhill Rd Orlando FL 32807

MULLINS, OBERA, microbiologist; b. Egypt, Miss., Feb. 15, 1927; d. Willie Ree and Maggie Sue (Orr) Gunn; B.S., Chgo. State U., 1974; M.S. in Health Sci. Edn., Governors State U., 1981; m. Charles Leroy Mullins, Nov. 2, 1952; children—Mary Artavia, Arthur Curtis, Charles Leroy, Charlester Teresa, William Hellman. Med. technician, microbiologist Chgo. Health Dept., Chgo., 1976—. Mem. AAUW, Am. Soc. Clin. Pathologists (cert. med. lab. technician). Roman Catholic. Home: 9325 S Marquette St Chicago IL 60617 Office: 3026 S California Ave Chicago IL 60623

MULRONEY, MILA PIVNICKI, wife of Canadian prime minister; b. Sarajevo, Yugoslavia, 1953; d. Dmitrije and Bogdanka Pivnicki; m. (Martin) Brian Mulroney, May 6, 1973; children—Caroline Anne, Benedict Martin, Robert Mark, Daniel Nicolas Dimitri. Student Sir George Williams U. (now Concordia U.), Montreal, Que., Can. Office: care Office of Prime Minister, Langevin Block Parliament Bldgs, Ottawa, ON Canada K1A 0A2 *

MULVANEY, MARY JEAN, educator; b. Omaha, Jan. 6, 1927; d. Marion Fowler and Blanche Gibons (McKee) M. B.S., U. Nebr., 1948; M.S., Wellesley Coll., 1951; LHD (hon.), U. Nebr., 1986. Instr. Kans. State U., Manhattan, 1948-50; instr. U. Nebr., Lincoln, 1951-57, asst. prof., 1957-62; asst. prof. U. Kans., Lawrence, 1962-66; assoc. prof. phys. edn. U. Chgo., 1966-76, prof., 1976—, chmn. women's div., 1966-76, chmn. dept. phys. edn. and athletics, 1976—; mem. vis. com. on athletics MIT, 1978-81, Wellesley Coll., 1978-79. Recipient honor award Nebr. Assn. Health, Phys. Edn. and Recreation, 1962. Mem. Nat. Collegiate Athletic Assn. (council 1983-87), Collegiate Council of Women Athletic Adminstrs., Midwest Assn. Intercollegiate Athletics for Women (chmn. 1979-81), Nat. Assn. Collegiate Dirs. Athletics (exec. com. 1976-80), Ill. Assn. Intercollegiate Athletics for Women (chmn. 1978-80), AAHPERD, Mortar Bd., Univ. Athetic Assn. (sec. 1986—, exec. com. 1986—, dels. com., chmn. atheletic adminstr.'s com. 1986-88), Alpha Chi Omega. Office: U Chgo Dept Phys Edn & Athletics 5640 S University Ave Chicago IL 60637

MULVANEY, MAUREEN GAIL, lecturer, counselor, educator; b. Norfolk, Va., Oct. 2, 1950; d. Paul Leo and Mary Patricia (Landry) M.; m. James Matthew Keith, July 10, 1976 (div. Nov. 1985). B.A., Troy State U., 1972; Ed.M., Boston U., 1980. Social services asst. U.S. Govt., Augsburg, W.Ger., 1980; clin. psychologist William Beaumont Army Med. Ctr., El Paso, Tex., 1984; counselor Adlerian Family Counseling Ctr., Litchfield Park, Ariz., 1984—; instr. Grand Canyon Coll., Phoenix, 1984—; profl. speaker, Phoenix, 1985—; cons. stress mgmt. corp. orgns., Phoenix, 1985-86; cons. Carl Hayden High Sch., Phoenix, 1986, Maryvale High Sch., Phoenix, 1986. Author: The Stress Strategists, 1986. Active Mothers Against Drunk Drivers, El Paso, 1985. Recipient Certs. of Achievement, Dept. of Army, 1981. Mem. Am. Personnel and Guidance Assn., Nat. Speakers Assn., Am. Assn. Female Execs., NOW, Phoenix C. of C. Democrat. Roman Catholic. Avocation: cons. to women's athletic teams. Home: 8118 N 38th Ave Phoenix AZ 85051

MULVEY, HELEN FRANCES, emeritus history educator; b. Providence, Feb. 22, 1913; d. William James and Anna (Nelson) M. A.B., Pembroke Coll., 1933; A.M., Columbia U., 1934; A.M., Radcliffe Coll., 1942; Ph.D., Harvard U., 1949. Instr. history Russell Sage Coll., Troy, N.Y., 1944-46; asst. prof. to prof. history, Conn. Coll., New London, 1946-83, prof. emeritus, 1983—, Brigida Pacchiana Ardenghi chair, 1975-78; vis. prof. Brit. history, U. Wis., Madison, 1971-72; vis. lectr. Yale U., 1974-83; lectr. Irish history, Pfizer Adult Edn., Groton, Conn., 1983-84; vis. scholar Phi Beta Kappa, Washington, 1982-83. Author articles, essays Irish and Brit. history; co-editor bibliog. vol. in A New History of Ireland, 9 vols. Anne Crosby Emery fellow, Brown U., 1933. Mem. Am. Hist. Assn., Am. Com. for Irish Studies, Conf. on Brit. Studies, AAUP (chpt. pres. 1962-64), Phi Beta Kappa. Club: Providence Art. Office: Conn Coll Box 1508 Mohegan Ave New London CT 06320

MULVEY-WRIGHT, MAUREEN ELIZABETH, telecommunications executive; b. Chgo., Nov. 7, 1954; d. John James and Mary Maxine (Steinberg) M. BA, So. Ill. U., 1978, MBA, 1983. Pres. Solution Mktg., Carbondale, Ill., 1978-85; lectr. mktg. Coll. of Bus. So. Ill. U., Carbondale, 1983-85; research analyst new bus. devel. GTE Airfone, Inc., Oak Brook, Ill., 1985-87; product mgr. Airfone Internat. div. GTE Airfone Inc., Oak Brook, Ill., 1987-88; sr. mgr. mktg. and bus. planning Metro Fiber Systems Inc., Chgo., 1988—; cons. in field. Mem. Am. Mktg. Assn., Direct Mktg. Inst. (cert.), Alpha Mu Alpha. Roman Catholic. Home: 2421 Grape St Joliet IL 60435 Office: Metro Fiber Systems Inc 35 E Wacker Dr Suite 670 Chicago IL 60601

MULVIHILL-RUSSO, LINDA JOYCE, real estate executive; b. Houston, June 9, 1951; d. John William and Joyce Laverne (Bryant) M. Student Gulf Coast Sch. Real Estate, Houston, 1978. Lic. real estate salesman, Tex. Exec. sec. Musemeche/Assocs., Architect, Houston, 1969-70; personnel sec. A.B. Chance Co., Houston, 1970-72; property mgmt. sec. Gerald D. Hines Interests, Houston, 1972-76; property mgr. Kilburn G. Moore Co., Houston, 1976-78; project mgr. Mel Powers Investment, Houston, 1978-83; comml. leasing agt. Horne Co., Houston, 1983—. Mem. Young People in Real Estate, Houston Bd. Realtors. Republican. Roman Catholic.

MULZET, JANE, sales executive; b. Bethlehem, Pa., June 9, 1952; d. Joseph John and Elizabeth Agnes (Wilk) M. BS in Nursing, Pa. State U., 1974; M in Nursing, UCLA, 1981. Staff nurse coronary div. Allentown (Pa.) Sacred Heart Med. Ctr., 1974-75; charge nurse neurosurgery Wilford Hall Med. Ctr., San Antonio, 1975-77; charge nurse of clinic Ramstein, Fed. Republic of Germany, 1977-79; surg. instr. Los Angeles County Med. Ctr., U. So. Calif., 1981-83; sales rep. UHI Corp., Los Angeles, 1983-85; sales trainer Kinetic Concepts, Inc., Los Angeles, 1985-87, regional sales mgr., 1987—; Served to capt. USAFR, 1975—. Served to maj. USAF, 1975—. Mem. Air Force Assn., Res. Officers Assn. Office: Kinetic Concepts 2437 Lillyvale Ave Los Angeles CA 90032

MUMM, BETTY JANE CASTILLO, educator; b. Lihue, Hawaii, Feb. 15, 1951; d. Philip N. and Irmgard (Ebner) Castillo. BA, Chapman Coll., Orange, Calif., 1973; MA, U. Hawaii, 1976. Cert. tchr., Hawaii, Tex. Ednl. research assoc. Curriculum Research & Devel. Group U. Hawaii, Honolulu, 1976-82; tchr., state child devel. assoc., tech. specialist head start tng. program State of Hawaii, Honolulu, 1982-84; research tchr. Kamehameha Schs., Honolulu, 1984-85; tchr. San Antonio Ind. Sch. Dist., 1986—; mem. Alliance for Drama Edn., Honolulu, 1980-85. Author: Exploring the Island, 1980, Parent Assistant Program, 1981; editor: Hawaii Assn. for Edn. of Young Children, Honolulu, 1982-84. Bd. dirs., chair vol. com. Hawaiian Islands chpt. Multiple Sclerosis Soc., 1977-79, sec. bd. dirs., 1979-80. Mem. Assn. Tex. Profl. Educators, Kindergarten Tchrs. Tex. Home: 2306 Quail Hollow San Antonio TX 78232

MUNCY, MARTHA ELIZABETH, newspaper publisher; b. Dodge City, Kans., Nov. 5, 1919; d. Jess C. and Juliet Mildred (Pettijohn) Denious.; m. Howard E. Muncy, June 5, 1943 (div. 1969); children: Martha Juliet, Suzanne Gilbert, Howard E. Jr. Student, Lindenwood Coll. for Women, 1937-38; BA, U. Kans., 1941. Advt. mgr. Dodge City Broadcasting Co., 1942-43, copywriter, 1944-46, pres., 1973—; saleswoman Boot Hill Mus., Inc., Dodge City, 1963; pub., pres. Dodge City Daily Globe, 1973—. Mem. Kans. Cavalry, Topeka, 1976—; bd. dirs. Arrowhead West, Inc., Dodge City, 1976—, Dodge City Roundup, Inc., 1976—, Dodge City Crimestoppers, 1985—; bd. dirs., sec. Ford county Hist. R.R. Preservation and Found., Dodge City, 1984—; trustee William Allen White Found., Lawrence, Kans., 1984—. Recipient Outstanding Service award Dodge City Lions, 1981; named Kans. Outstanding Rehab. vol. Kans. Rehab. Assn., 1985. Mem. Kans. Press Women (Woman of Achievement award 1984), S.W. Kans. Press Women, S.W. Kans. Edit. Assn. (Outstanding Journalism award 1982), Dodge City Media Pros, Kans. Press. Assn., Kans. Assn. Broadcasters, Am. Assn. Univ. Women, Dodge City Women's C. of C., Dodge City C. of C., The Philomaths, DAR, Sigma Delta Chi. Republican. Presbyterian. Home: 511 Annette Dodge City KS 67801 Office: Dodge City Daily Globe 705 Second Ave Dodge City KS 67801

MUNGER, SHARON, marketing research firm executive. Pres., chief operating officer M/A/R/C, Inc., Irving, Tex. Office: M/A/R/C Inc 7850 N Belt Line Rd Irving TX 75063 *

MUNHALL, RUTH BEATRICE, business and financial consultant; b. Mendon, Mass., Feb. 8, 1929; d. Lawrence B. and Elsie B. (Gaskill) M. Grad. Salvation Army Officers Coll., Bronx, N.Y., 1951; M.B.A., Calif. Coast U., 1980, Ph.D., D.B.A., 1981. Civilian supr. U.S. Army and VA Hosp., Framingham, Mass., 1946-50; ordained clergywoman; officer Salvation Army centers in Mass., N.Y. and N.J., 1951-64; owner, operator acctg. and real estate firm, N.Y.C., 1964-68; supr. fiduciary and individual taxation Bank of N.Y., N.Y.C., 1968-79; cons. non profit orgns. founder R.M. Scholarship Info. Services, Ark., N.Y., Mass. and Israel, 1981—; pres., chief exec. officer Munhall, Monahan, Chapman Fiduciary Animal Charities, Inc., 1984—; pres. Munhall Research Sci. Corp., 1985—; cons. in field. Recipient 5 Yr. Civil Def. award Gov. N.Y. State. Mem. Am. Mgmt. Assn., DAR, Alumni Assn. Calif. Coast U. Republican.

MUNNELL, ALICIA HAYDOCK, economist; b. N.Y.C., Dec. 6, 1942; d. Walter Howe Haydock and Alicia (Wildman) Haydock Roux; m. Thomas Clark Munnell (div.); children—Thomas Clark Jr., Hamilton Haydock; m. Henry Scanlon Healy, Feb. 2, 1980. B.A. in Econs., Wellesley, 1964; M.A. in Econs., Boston U., 1966; Ph.D. in Econs., Harvard U., 1973. Staff asst. bus. research div. New Eng. Telephone Co., Boston, 1964-65; teaching fellow econs. dept. Boston U., 1965-66; research asst. for dir. econ. studies program Brookings Instn., Washington, 1966-68; teaching fellow Harvard U., Cambridge, Mass., 1971-73; asst. prof. econs. Wellesley Coll., Mass., 1974; economist Fed. Res. Bank Boston, 1973-76, asst. v.p., economist, 1976-78, v.p., economist, 1979-84, sr. v.p., dir. research, 1984—; mem. Gov.'s Task Force on Unemployment Compensation, Mass., 1975; associated staff Brookings Instn., 1975—; mem. spl. funding adv. com. for Mass. pensions, 1976; mem. Mass. Retirement Law Commn., 1976-82; staff dir. joint com. on pub. pensions Nat. Planning Assn., 1978; mem. adv. com. for urban inst. HUD grant on state-local pensions, 1978-81; mem. pension research council Wharton Sch. Fin. and Commerce, U. Pa., 1979—; mem. adv. group Nat. Commn. for Employment Policy, 1980-81; mem. adv. bd. Nat. Aging Policy Ctr. in Income Maintenance, Brandeis U., 1980-84; participant pvt. sector retirement security and U.S. tax policy roundtable discussions Govt. Research Corp., 1984; mem. supervisory panel Forum Inst. of Villers Found., 1984; mem. Medicare working group, div. of health policy research and edn. Harvard U., 1984-87; mem. Commn. on Coll. Retirement, 1984-86; mem. com. to plan major study of nat. long term care policies Inst. Medicine, Nat. Acad. Scis., 1984—; mem. steering com. Am. Assn. Ret. Persons, 1987—; mem. adv. council Am. Enterprise Inst., 1987—; com. mem. Inst. Medicine, Nat. Acad. Scis. Human Rights Com., 1987—; cofounder, pres. Nat. Acad. Social Ins., 1986—; bd. dirs. Pension Rights Ctr.; mem. program rev. com. Brigham and Women's Hosp., 1988—; mem. Commn. to Rev. Mass. Anti-Takeover Laws, 1988—. Author: The Impact of Social Security on Personal Saving, 1974, Future of Social Security (various awards), 1977, Pensions for Public Employees, 1979, The Economics of Private Pensions, 1982; editor: Lessons from the Income Maintenance Experiments, 1987; (with others) Options for Fiscal Reform in Massachusetts, 1975; contbr. chpts. and articles to profl. jours. Mem. Inst. Med. Nat. Acad. Scis., Nat. Acad. Pub. Adminstrn. Office: Fed Res Bank Boston 600 Atlantic Ave Boston MA 02106

MUNRO, ALICE, author; b. Wingham, Ont., Can., July 10, 1931; d. Robert Eric and Anne Clarke (Chamney) Laidlaw; m. James Armstrong Munro, 1951 (div. 1976); children: Sheila, Jenny, Andrea; m. Gerald Fremlin, 1976. Student, U. Western Ont., 1949-51. Author: (short stories) Dance of the Happy Shades (Gov.-Gen.'s Lit. award 1969), 1968, Lives of Girls and Women (Can. Booksellers award), 1971, (short stories) Something I've Been Meaning To Tell You, 1974, Who Do You Think You Are?, 1978, Stories of Flo and Rose (Gov.-Gen.'s Lit. award 1979), 1979, The Moons of Jupiter, 1982, (short stories) The Progress of Love (Gov.-Gen.'s Lit. award 1987), 1987. Recipient Can.-Australia Lit. Prize. Office: care Alfred A Knopf Inc 201 E 50th St New York NY 10022 *

MUNRO, JUNE EDITH, librarian; b. Echo Bay, Ont., Can., June 20, 1921; d. Neil and Agnes (MacLeod) M.; B.J., Carleton U., 1961; B.L.S., U. Toronto, 1962, M.L.S., 1972. Head children's library services Sault Ste. Marie (Ont., Can.) Public Library, 1941-51; children's librarian London (Ont.) Public Library, 1951-53; head children's library services Leaside Public Library, 1953-56; asst. to exec. dir., publs. prodn. editor Canadian Library Assn., 1956-61; supr. extension service, editor Ont. Library Rev., Ont. Provincial Library Service, 1961-70; book acquisition adv. Coll. Bibliocentre, Toronto, Ont., 1970-72; chief public relations div. Nat. Library Can., Ottawa, Ont., 1972-73; dir. library services St. Catharines (Ont., Can.) Public Library, 1973-82; sessional lectr. Sch. Librarianship, U. B.C., 1983; mem. exec. Shaw Theatre Guild, past chmn. bd. dirs. Carousel Players, St. Catharines, Ont.; bd. dirs. YWCA, St. Catharines. Recipient St. Catharines YWCA award to Woman, 1986; named Librarian of Year, Ont. Library Trustees Assn., 1971. Mem. ALA, Can. Library Assn., Ont. Library Assn. Clubs: Golf and Country, Univ. Women's (St. Catharines). Editor Ont. Library Rev., 1961-70.

MUNROE, DONNA SCOTT, data processing management consultant, statistician; b. Cleve., Nov. 28, 1945; d. Glenn Everett and Louise Lenox (Parkhill) S.; m. Melvin James Ricketts, Dec. 23, 1968 (div. Aug. 1979); 1 child, Suzanne Michelle; m. Peter Carlton Munroe, Feb. 14, 1981. BS in Sociology, Portland (Oreg.) State U., 1976, BS in Philosophy, 1978, MS in Sociology, 1983. Lectr. Portland State U., 1977-79; writing, editorial cons. Worth Pubs., N.Y.C., 1978-79; statis. cons. Oreg. U. Sch. Health Sci. and Morrison Ctr. for Youth and Family Services, Portland, 1979-82; tech. writer Equitable Savs & Loan, Portland, 1981-82; account ops. mgr. Electronic Data Systems, Portland, 1982-87; sr. mgmt. cons. to govt. div. Computer Mgmt. Systems, Inc., Portland, 1987—. Mem. Am. Mgmt. Assn., Sigma Xi. Democrat. Episcopalian. Club: City of Portland. Home: 1435 SW Harrison Portland OR 97201 Office: Computer Mgmt Systems Inc 0234 SW Bancroft Portland OR 97201

MUNROE, MARY LOU SCHWARZ (MRS. ROBERT E. MUNROE), educational administrator; b. Denver, Nov. 18, 1927; d. John Anthony and Lutie A. (Benefiel) Schwarz; m. Robert E. Munroe; children: Robert M., Carol E., John E. Dir. Jr. and Collegiate Great Books Program, Archdiocese of Denver, 1961-71, leader tng. staff, 1963-71, archdiocesan dir. grade and high sch., 1966-71; undergrad. counselor Sch. Edn. U. Denver, 1971-74; adminstrv. dir., ednl. coordinator adolescent unit Mt. Airy Psychiat. Ctr., Denver, 1975—; feature writer Register, Denver, 1963-71; lectr., workshop dir. Loretto Heights Coll., 1966, regional tng. ctrs. for religion tchrs., 1967—. Author: Counseling the Parishoner, 1967. Mem. steering com. Cinema Critique Series of Denver, 1967; mem.-at-large Bd. Cath. Edn. of Denver Met. Area, 1969—, pres., 1974-75; mem. Denver Met. Adv. Com. Cath. Edn., 1968-69, Juvenile Ct. Task Force, 1969. Named Woman of Yr., Archdiocese of Denver Edn. Assn., 1971; named to Denver Post Gallery of Fame, 1975; recipient papal medal Pro Ecclesia et Pontifice, 1975. Mem Cath. Edn. Guild, Mortar Bd., Ednl. Forum Colo. (charter), Phi Beta Kappa, Kappa Delta Pi, Delta Kappa Gamma, Phi Delta Kappa, Delta Gamma. Home: 3131 E Alameda Ave Apt 802 Denver CO 80209

MUNSELL, ELSIE LOUISE, lawyer; b. N.Y.C., Feb. 15, 1939; d. Elmer Stanley and Eleanor Harriet (Dickinson) M.; m. George P. Williams, July 14, 1979. A.B., Marietta Coll., 1960; J.D., Marshall-Wythe Coll. William and Mary, 1972. Bar: Va. 1972. Tchr. Norview High Sch., Norfolk, Va., 1964-69; asst. Commonwealth atty. Commonwealth Atty.'s Office, Alexandria, Va., 1972-73; asst. U.S. atty. Alexandria, Va., 1974-79; U.S. magistrate U.S. Dist. Ct. (ea. dist.)Va., Alexandria, 1979-81; U.S. atty. Dept. Justice, Alexandria, Va., 1981-86; sr. trial atty. Office Gen. Counsel Dept. Navy, 1986—. Mem. Va. Commn. on Status of Women, 1966-74; bd. vistors Coll. William and Mary, 1972-76; mem. Atty. Gen.'s Adv. Com. U.S. Attys., 1981-83. Mem. ABA, Fed. Bar Assn., Va. Women Attys. Assn. Republican. Episcopalian. Office: Office Gen Counsel Office Litigation Dept Navy Washington DC 20360-5110

MUNSON, JANIS ELIZABETH TREMBLAY, engineering company executive; b. Beverly, Mass., Dec. 17, 1948; d. Louis Story Tremblay and Doroth Ellen (Burnham) Tonkin; divorced. BS in Geology summa cum laude, Boston U., 1976, M in Urban Planning, 1982. Librarian United Engrs. and Constrn., Boston, 1971-73, land use planner, 1973-76, lead land use planner, 1976-80, supervising lic. engr., 1980-87, head mktg. analysis services group power div., 1987—. Bd. dirs. Ctr. City Residents Assn., Phila., 1986; mem. Multiple Sclerosis Soc.; vol. for disabled. Mem. Am. Planning Assn., Am. Inst. Cert. Planners (assoc.), World Affairs Council. Republican. Congregationalist. Home: 2401 Pennsylvania Ave 3C-50 Philadelphia PA 19130 Office: United Engrs and Constructors 300 S 17th St Philadelphia PA 19101

MUNSON, LINDA FREYTAG, environmental and radiation protection consultant; b. Hayward, Calif., Apr. 6, 1948; d. John J. and Mildred (Huff), F.; m. Leo H. Munson, Apr. 23, 1976. BA in Chemistry, U.S. Internat. U., 1968; MS Chemistry, Iowa State U., 1971. Scientist U. Minn., St. Paul, 1971-73; environ. engr. UNC Nuclear Industries, Richard, Wash., 1973-77, mgr. indsl. safety, 1977-80; assoc. sect. mgr. Battelle N.W., Richland, 1980-88; pres. Evergreen Innovations, Richland, 1988—; cons., health and safety appraiser Oak Ridge Associated Us., 1988—; project mgr. Tech. Assistance to U. S. Nuclear Regulatory Commn., Richland, 1983-87. Active Benton County Annexation Review Bd., Wash., 1973-76. Mem. Columbia Chpt. Health Physics Soc. Republican. Episcopalian. Club: Atomic Ducks Dive. Office: Evergreen Innovations Inc 2323 Snohomish Richland WA 99352

MUNSON, LUCILLE MARGUERITE (MRS. ARTHUR E. MUNSON), real estate broker; b. Norwood, Ohio, Mar. 26, 1914; d. Frank and Fairy (Wicks) Wirick; R.N., Lafayette (Ind.) Home Hosp., 1937, A.B., San Diego State U., 1963, student Purdue U., Kans. Wesleyan U.; m. Arthur E. Munson, Dec. 24, 1937; children—Barbara Munson Papke, Judith Munson Andrews, Edmund Arthur. Staff and pvt. nurse Lafayette Home Hosp., 1937-41; indsl. nurse Lakey Foundry & Machine Co., Muskegon, Mich., 1950-51, Continental Motors Corp., Muskegon, 1951-52; nurse Girl Scout Camp, Grand Haven, Mich., 1948-49; owner Munson Realty, San Diego, 1964—. Mem. San Diego County Grand Jury, 1975-76, 80-81; charter mem. Calif. Grand Jurors Assn. Mem. San Diego Bd. Realtors. Presbyterian. Home: 5765 Friars Rd Apt 200 San Diego CA 92108 Office: 2999 Mission Blvd # 102 San Diego CA 92109

MUNSON, MARY KATHLEEN, education educator; b. Junction City, Kans., Jan. 7, 1943; d. Gaylord Russel and Josephine May (Grammer) M. BS in Secondary Edn., Kans. State U., 1965, PhD in Adult Edn., 1978; MS in Social Scis., Emporia (Kans.) State U., 1968. Cert. secondary sch. tchr., Kans. Grad. teaching asst. Emporia State U., 1966-67; tchr. Atchison (Kans.) Pub. Schs., 1967-68, Topeka Pub. Schs., 1968-69; 4-H youth leader Iowa State U. Extension, Ames, 1969-76; grad. teaching asst. Kans. State U., Manhattan, 1976-78; extension specialist 4-H/youth, assoc. prof. U. Ill. Coop. Extension Service, Urbana, 1978—; cons. USDA, Washington, 1987—, Conn. Coop. Extension, Storrs, 1987—, Mo. Coop. Extenison, Columbia, 1987—. Author, editor (series) Leadership: Skills You Never Outgrow, 1986-87, ednl. package. Elder worship and music com., chmn. asst. treas. Westminster Presbyn. Ch. Mem. Internat. 4-H Youth Assn. U.S.A. (treas. 1969-70, bd. dirs. 1968-70), Nat. Assn. Adult and Continuing Edn., Nat. Assn. Extension 4-H Agts., Disting. Service award 1981), Ill. Assn. Extension Advisers (youth programs com. 1979—, Disting. Service award 1981), AAUW, IFYE (orientation com. Ill. region 1979—), Epsilon Sigma Phi (banquet com. 1982, outstanding program award 1976, Shuman award 1986). Republican. Presbyterian. Office: Ill State 4-H Office 1901 University Inn 302 E John Champaign IL 61820

MUNSON, NANCY KAY, lawyer; b. Huntington, N.Y., June 22, 1936; d. Howard H. and Edna M. (Keenan) Munson. Student, Hofstra U., 1959-62; JD, Bklyn. Law Sch., 1965. Bar: N.Y. 1966, U.S. Supreme Ct. 1970, U.S. Ct. Appeals (2d cir.) 1971, U.S. Dist. Ct. (ea. and so. dists.) N.Y. 1968. Law clk. to E. Merritt Weidner Huntington, 1959-66, sole practice, 1966—; mem. legal adv. bd. Chgo. Title Ins. Co., Riverhead, N.Y., 1981—. Trustee Huntington Fire Dept. Death Benefit Fund; pres., trustee, chmn. bd. Bklyn. Home for Aged Men Found. Mem. ABA, Suffolk County Bar Assn., Bklyn. Bar Assn., N.Y. State Bar Assn., Nat. Rifle Assn. Republican. Christian Scientist. Club: Soroptimist (past pres.). Office: 197 New York Ave Huntington NY 11743

MUNSON, NORMA FRANCES, biologist, ecologist, nutritionist, educator; b. Stockport, Iowa, Sept. 22, 1923; d. Glenn Edwards and Frances Emma (Wilson) M.; B.A., Concordia Coll., 1946; M.A., U. Mo., 1955; Ph.D. (NSF fellow 1957-58, Chgo. Heart Assn. fellow 1959), Pa. State U., 1962; postgrad. Ind. U., 1957, Western Mich. U., 1967, Lake Forest Coll., 1971, 72, 78; student various fgn. univs., 1964-71. Tchr., Aitkin (Minn.) High Sch., 1946-48, Detroit Lakes (Minn.) High Sch., 1948-54, Libertyville (Ill.) High Sch., 1955-79; researcher in nutrition, Libertyville, 1965—; lectr. in counseling and nutrition. Ruling elder First Presbyn. Ch., Libertyville, 1971-77; pres. Lake County Audubon Soc., 1975—, Libertyville Edn. Assn., 1964-67; active Rep. Party of Ill., Citizens to Save Butler Lake, Citizens Choice, The Defenders; mem. U.S. Congl. Adv. Bd., 1985—; bd. dirs. Holy Land Christian Mission Internat. Recipient Hilda Mahling award, 1967, C. of C. award, 1971, Ill. Best Teacher's award, 1974; Best Biology of Yr. award, 1971; NSF fellow, 1957, 58, 60-62, 70-71. Mem. Nat. Biology Tchrs. Assn. (award 1971), AAAS, Am. Inst. Biol. Sci., Am. Biog. Inst., Ill. Environ. Council, Ill. Audubon Council, Nat. Health Fedn., Internat. Platform Assn., Nat. Wildlife Fedn., N.Y. Acad. Scis., Parks and Conservation Assn., Delta Kappa Gamma. Contbr. research articles to publs. Home and Office: 206 W Maple Ave Libertyville IL 60048

MUNTS, MARY LOU, lawyer, economist, state commissioner; b. Chgo., Aug. 21, 1924; d. Thomas Hunton and Elizabeth (Vinsonhaler) Rogers; m. Raymond Munts, July 19, 1947; children—Lisa Munts Redburn, Polly, Andy. Student Swarthmore Coll., 1941-44; M.A. in Econs., U. Chgo., 1947; J.D., U. Wis., 1976. Bar: Wis. 1976. Research asst. U.S. Treasury Dept., Paris, France, 1947-48; instr. Sch. Bus., Wilkes Coll., Wilkes-Barre, Pa., 1949-50; asst. to Congressman Robert Kastenmeier, Washington, 1960; econ. research asst. Robert Nathan Assocs., Washington, 1964-66; admissions sec. Ctr. for Devel., U. Wis., Madison, 1967-72; state rep. Wis. Legislature, Madison, 1972-84; mem. Wis. Pub. Service Commn., 1985—, chair 1986-87; mem. conservation com. Nat. Assn. Regulatory Commrs., 1985—. Co-editor: The Future of Small Bus., 1967. Recipient Recognition award Dane County Assn. for Retarded Children Ann. 1973, 74, 81; Layperson of Year award Wis. Psychol. Assn., 1975; EPA Environ. Quality award, 1975; Citizen of Yr. Wis. Assn. Mental Health, 1975; Pub. Service award. Ctr. of Pub. Representation Inc., 1976; Disting. Service award Wis. Assn. for Retarded Citizens, 1977; Wis. Women's Polit. Caucus award 1979, 86; Legislator of Yr., Wis. Wildlife Fedn. 1981; Wis. NOW Woman of the Year, 1982, Wis. Assn. Marriage and Family Therapy ann. award 1982, Human Services Adv. award 1985, Weatherization Operators Wos. award 1986, Wis. Women's Network Stateswomen of Yr award 1986, others. Democrat.

MUNZER, MARTHA EISEMAN, writer; b. N.Y.C., Sept. 22, 1899; d. Samuel and Stella (Stettheimer) Eiseman; m. Edward M. Munzer, June 15, 1922 (dec. 1960); children: Edward Munzer Jr. (dec.), Martha Amato, Stella Loeb; m. Isaac Corkland, Apr. 30, 1980 (dec. 1986). BS in Electrochem. Engring., MIT, 1922. Tchr. chemistry, chairperson community services Fieldston Sch., N.Y.C., 1930-54; writer Conservation Found., N.Y.C., 1954-68, Wave Hill Ctr. for Environ. Studies, Riverdale, N.Y., 1968-73; freelance writer Ft. Lauderdale, Fla., 1978—. Author: Teaching Science Through Conservations, 1960, Unusual Careers, 1962, Planning Our Town, 1964, Pockets of Hope, 1966, Valley of Vision, 1969, Block by Block, 1973, New Towns, 1974, Full Circle, 1978, The Three R's of Ecology: A Personal Collection, 1986; contbr. articles to profl. jours. Mem. conservation adv. commn. Town of Larchmont, N.Y., 1964-78, planning and zoning bd. Lauderdale by the Sea, Fla., 1985—. Recipient Oscar R. Foster award Chemistry Tchrs. Club, 1947. Fellow Soc. Women Engrs.; mem. AAUW (chairperson lit. group 1985—), Fla. Engring. Soc. (award for engring. journalism 1985), LWV (mem. natural resources com.). Democrat. Home and Office: 4411 Tradewinds Ave E Lauderdale by the Sea FL 33308

MURALI, LAKSHMI, physician; b. Madras, India, Aug. 4, 1943; d. Rangaswami and Jeya Krisna Swami; m. Raj Murali, Apr. 7, 1972; children—Sujatha, Ram. M.B.B.S., U. Madras, 1967. Diploma child health Royal Coll. Physicians and Surgeons, Glasgow, 1974; diplomate Am. Bd. Phys. Medicine and Rehab. Intern, Govt. Gen. Hosp., Madras, 1967-68; sr. house officer internal medicine Bensham Gen. Hosp., Gateshead, Eng., 1968-69, 70-72; sr. house officer pediatrics Queen Elizabeth Hosp., Gateshead, 1971-72; sr. house officer, registrar phys. medicine and rehab. Astley Ainslie Hosp., Edinburgh, Scotland, 1972-75; resident in phys. medicine and rehab. Inst. Rehab. Medicine, NYU Med. Ctr., N.Y.C., 1975-77; clin. instr. rehab. medicine NYU Med. Ctr., 1977-82; assoc. attending rehab. medicine Bellevue Hosp Med. Ctr., N.Y.C., 1977—; cons. rehab. medicine Astoria Gen. Hosp. (N.Y.), 1982—; attending physician St. Vincent's Hosp. and Med. Ctr., N.Y.C., 1982—, dir. Amputee and Prosthetic Clinic, 1983—; asst. prof. rehab. medicine N.Y. Med. Coll., Valhalla. Mem. Am. Spinal Injury Assn., Gen. Med. Council Gt. Britain, Am. Acad. Phys. Medicine, Internat. Soc. Prosthetics and Orthotics, Am. Congress Phys. Medicine and Rehab., Internat. Rehab. Medicine Assn., Am. Spinal Injury Assn., N.Y. Acad. Medicine, N.Y. Soc. Phys. Medicine. Hindu. Office: 130 W 12th St Suite 2G New York NY 10011

MURASKIN, ROSLYN, criminal justice educator; b. N.Y.C., Mar. 5, 1941; d. Sydney and Alice (Kroll) Cashman; m. Matthew Muraskin; children: Seth, Craig, Tracy. BA, Queens Coll., 1961; MA, NYU, 1963; postgrad., CUNY, 1987—. Asst. supr. Vera Inst. Justice, N.Y.C., 1962-65; supr. release on recognizance project Dept. Probation, City N.Y., 1965-68; instr. to chmn. dept. criminal justice L.I. U., Brookville, N.Y., 1980—; cons. Legal Aid Soc. Nassau county, N.Y., 1978—. Author: Outline Series in Criminal Justice, 1987; editor: Victims of Crime, 1985, Women, Victims of Rape, 1986, The Future of Criminal Justice Education, 1987; reviewer: The Annals. Vol. Women's Am. Organ. Rehab. through Tng., 1967—, mem. communications com., L.I., N.Y., 1987—. Recipient Outstanding Service awards Alpha Phi Sigma, 1985-86, Criminal Justice Assn., Brookville, 1985, 86, 87; L.I. U. grantee, 1986, N.Y. Council for Humanities grantee, 1985. Mem. Acad. Criminal Justice Scis., Am. Soc. Criminology, Correctional Edn. Assn., Acad. Security Educators. Home: 3060 Riverside Dr Wantagh NY 11793 Office: LI Univ CW Post Dept Criminal Justice Brookville NY 11548

MURDOCK, MONI (MARY MARGARET), marriage and family therapist; b. Mishawaka, Ind., Jan. 19, 1938; d. Joseph Weldon and Evelyn Mary (Diroll) Hennessy; m. Charles William Murdock, May 25, 1963; children: Kathleen Tracy, Michael Hennessy, Kevin Charles, Sean Joseph. BS cum laude, Marquette U., 1959; MSW, Loyola U., Chgo., 1961; postgrad., The Family Inst., Ill., 1977-79. Caseworker Ill. Children's Home and Aid Soc., Chgo., 1961-64; clin. social worker Logan Ctr., South Bend, Ind., 1973, St. Joseph County Mental Health Ctr., South Bend, 1974-75; clin. social worker Doyle Ctr. Loyola U., Chgo., 1975-77, clin. supr., 1977—; pvt. practice psychotherapy The Family Ctr., Evanston, 1979—; mem. adv. bd. Ctr. for Family Studies inst. psychiatry Northwestern Meml. Hosp., 1978—, pres. alumni bd., 1980-83, part time faculty mem., 1983—; chair gov. bd. Family Inst. Chgo., 1987—; mem. adj. faculty Loyola U. Sch. Social Work, 1984—; chmn. Chgo. family therapy conf. Ctr. for Family Studies, 1980. Co-author: Getting to Know Us., 1983. Bd. dirs., co-founder Little Flower Montessori Sch., South Bend, 1969-74; chmn. adult edn. Little Flower Parish, South Bend, 1971-73, St. Athanasius Parish, Evanston, 1976-79; del. Nat. Assembly Cath. Laity, Notre Dame, Ind., 1981. Grantee HEW, 1959-60; stipentee VA, 1960-61. Mem. Am. Family Therapy Assn. (charter), Am. Assn. Marriage and Family Therapy (clin., approved supr.), Nat. Assn. Social Workers (cert., clin.), Register Clin. Social Workers (clin. diplomat). Democrat. Home: 2527 Marcy Ave Evanston IL 60201 Office: The Family Ctr 1830 Sherman Ave Evanston IL 60201

MURDOCK, PAMELA ERVILLA, wholesale travel company executive, retail travel company executive; b. Los Angeles, Dec. 3, 1940; d. John James and Chloe Conger (Keefe) M.; children—Cheryl, Kim. BS, U. Colo., 1962. Pres., Dolphin Travel, Denver, 1972-87, Mile Hi Tours, Denver, 1974—, MH Internat., 1987—. Named Wholesaler of Yr., Las Vegas Conv. and Visitors Authority, 1984. Mem. Am. Soc. Travel Agts., Colo. Assn. Commerce and Industry, Nat. Fedn. Independant Businessmen. Republican. Office: Mile Hi Tours Inc 2120 S Birch Denver CO 80222

MURFIN, TWILA DEARBORN, production engineer; b. Fairhope, Ala., Mar. 19, 1958; d. William Harold and Emily Rose (Heidelberg) Dearborn; m. Martin Joseph Murfin, June 20, 1981; children: Joseph Riley, Kristina Alayne. BS in Indsl. Engring., Auburn U., 1981. Indsl. engr. Scott Paper Co., Mobile, Ala., 1981-83, project indsl. engr., 1983-84; prodn. engr. Rohr So. Industries, Foley, Ala., 1984-86, sr. prodn. engr., 1986—. Hon. mem. Ala. Sheriff's Assn. Boy's & Girl's Ranches, Inc., Boys Ranch, Ala., 1987; treas. Rohr Recreation Com., 1987. Mem. Nat. Assn. Female Execs., Bus and Profl. Women's Club (v.p. 1987, pres. 1988), AAUW. Baptist. Home: 9797 Pleasant Rd Daphne AL 36526 Office: Rohr So Industries Corner of Fern & Airport Foley AL 36535

MURLAS, MARY KAY, data processing executive; b. Turlock, Calif., Dec. 30, 1949; d. D. Keith and Mary Gertrude (Farmer) Winton; m. Christopher George Murlas, Nov. 25, 1978; 1 child, Brittany Kirsten Quinn. BS, U. Calif., Berkeley, 1973; MBA, San Francisco State U., 1980. Adminstrv. asst. Assn. Bay Area Govts., Oakland, Calif., 1976-78; adminstrv. asst. Systems Applications, Inc., San Rafael, Calif., 1978-79, project adminstr., 1979-80, contract adminstr., 1980-81, asst. controller, 1981-82; mgr. acctg. Times Mirror Videotex Services, Santa Ana, Calif., 1982-83, controller, 1983-84; exec. v.p. Info. Tech. Devel. Corp., Cin., 1985—, also bd. dirs.; bd. dirs. Columbia Research Group, Cin. V.p. Alzheimer's Disease Assn., Newport Beach, Calif., 1982-84, Cin., 1986, program chair, Cin., 1985-86. Democrat. Club: Garden (Cin.). Office: Info Tech Devel Corp 4000 Executive Park Ln Suite 310 Cincinnati OH 45241

MURNIN, BETTE F., retired government executive; b. Omaha, Mar. 10, 1918; m. Joseph Albert Murnin, Mar. 9, 1971; children—Robert Manning, Christopher Hill Maxwell. BS, Baker U. 1940; MS in Edn., Ind. U.-Bloomington, 1960; postgrad. various schs. 1961-85. Field supr. Ind. Dept. Pub. Instruction; dir. guidance Merrillville, Ind.; tchr. Jr. high sch., Elkhart, Ind.; program officer Office Edn. Dept. Edn., 1968-84; pres. U.S. Dept. Edn. Region VIII Am. Fed. Govt. Employees Local Union #3898, 1977-82; nat. exec. bd. Am. Fed. Govt. Employees Nat. Council #252 U.S. Dept. Edn., 1982-84; mem. Sixth Congl. Dist. Edn. Com., 1984—. Bd. dirs. Gary Players, 1961-64, Lake County chpt. Am. Cancer Soc., 1960-72, sec. 1962, 64, state bd. dirs. 1965, 72; pres. PTA, Merrillville, 1965; program chmn. 1964; nat. committeewoman Colo. Young Democrats, 1950; capt. Jefferson County Democrats, 1949-52; program chmn. Jefferson County Jane Jeffersons; bd. dirs. Jefferson County Community Chest 1949-55; chmn. Roosevelt Jr. High Sch. faculty. Baker U. scholar; U.S. Govt. grantee. Mem. Ind. Personnel and Guidance Assn. (founder), Alpha Chi Omega.

MURO-GARCIA, LINDA CHRISTINE, organization and behavior consultant; b. San Bernadino, Calif., Dec. 29, 1951; d. Paul and Mary Esther (Garcia) Muro; children: Gina Marie, Steven Michael. AA, San Bernadino Valley Coll., 1978; BS, U. San Francisco, 1987. Supr. San Bernadino County Health Dept., San Bernadino, 1972-77; program coordinator Human Studies Ctr., Santa Ana, Calif., 1978-86; dir. seminars and consultation services London Assocs. Internat., Santa Ana, 1986—. Mng. editor ABCD Reports, 1988; assoc. editor Internat. Bull. Medicine and Psychology. Honorary Fellow, Milton H. Erickson Advanced Inst., Sydney, Australia, 1984. Mem. Soc. Clin. and Experimental Hypnosis (conf. co-chmn., 1987), Nat. Assn. Social Workers, Soc. Clin. Social Work. Office: London Assocs Internat 1125 E 17th St Suite E-209 Santa Ana CA 92701

MURPHY, ANNE MARIE, library system director; b. N.Y.C., July 24, 1926; d. Timothy D. and Mary A. Murphy. AB, Coll. Mt. St. Vincent, 1948; BLS, Pratt Inst., 1950. Profl. asst. N.Y. Pub. Library, N.Y.C., 1950-51, asst. br. librarian, 1951-54; asst. dir. for pub. services Fordham U., Bronx, 1954-56, assoc. librarian, 1956-70, dir. libraries, 1970—; trustee N.Y. Met. Reference and Research Library Agy., 1983—. Mem. ALA, Cath. Library Assn. Office: Fordham Univ Duane Library Bronx NY 10458-5151

MURPHY, ARLENE MARIE, hotel coordinator; b. Madison, Wis., Nov. 23, 1960; d. Keith Lawson and Ruth Lillian (Lackey) M. Grad. high sch., Milton, Ont., Can. Front office mgr., then catering rep. Delta Meadowvale Inn, Missisauga, Ont., 1980-84; front office mgr. Hyatt Regency Vancouver, B.C., 1984-85; account exec. Sheraton Hamilton, Ont., 1985-86; events coordinator Hamilton Conv. Ctr., 1986-88; conf. ctr. mgr. Sheraton Ctr. Toronto, 1988—. Mem. Meeting Planners Internat. Home: 705 King St W, Apt 509, Toronto, ON Canada M5V 2W8 Office: Sheraton Ctr Toronto, 123 Queen St W, Toronto, ON Canada M5H 2M9

MURPHY, BERNADETTE BARTELS, stock market analyst; b. N.Y.C.; d. Joseph Francis and Julia (Flynn) Bartels; m. Eugene F. Murphy. BA, Our Lady of Good Counsel, White Plains, N.Y. Sr. v.p. Shaw & Co., N.Y.C., 1965-86; exec. dir. strategies and selections div. M. Kimelman & Co., N.Y.C., 1986—; panelist TV program Wall St. Week, Md. Ctr. for Pub. Broadcasting, 1979—; Lubin lectr. Pace U.; trustee Stovall/21 Century Consistent Return Fund, 1986—; bd. dirs. Mtrs. Life Ins. Co. Advisors Corp. Contbr. articles to profl. jours. Trustee Pace U., 1978-82. Mem. N.Y. Soc. Security Analysts (pres. 1984-85, dir. 1974-86), Fin. Analysts Fedn. (bd. dirs. 1982—, chmn., 1988—, sec.-treas. 1986—, vice chmn. investment analysis standards bd. 1985—, exec. com. 1985—, mem. admissions com.), Market Technicians Assn. (pres. 1977-78), Internat. Soc. Fin. Analysts (bd. dirs. 1985—, pres. 1986-88),Fin. Womens Assn. (pres. 1973-74, dir. 1972-78). Home: Bronxville Office: M Kimelman & Co 100 Park Ave New York NY 10017

MURPHY, BETTY JANE SOUTHARD (MRS. CORNELIUS F. MURPHY), lawyer; b. East Orange, N.J.; d. Floyd Theodore and Thelma (Casto) Southard; m. Cornelius F. Murphy, May 1, 1965; children: Ann Southard, Cornelius Francis Jr. AB, Ohio State U.; postgrad., Alliance Française and U. Sorbonne, Paris; JD, Am. U., 1958; LLD (hon.), Eastern Mich. U., 1975, Capital U., 1976, U. Puget Sound, 1986; LHD, Tusculum coll., 1987. Bar: D.C. 1958. Corr., free lance journalist Europe and Asia, UPI, Washington; pub. relations counsellor Capital Properties, Inc. of Columbus (Ohio), Washington; atty. Appellate Cts. br. NLRB, Washington, 1958-59; practiced in Washington, 1959-74; mem. firm McInnis, Wilson, Munson & Woods (and predecessor firm), 1959-70; gen. partner firm Wilson, Woods & Villalon, 1970-74; dep. asst. sec., adminstr. Wage and Hour div. Dept. Labor, 1974-75; chmn. and mem. NLRB, 1975-79; ptnr. firm Baker & Hostetler, 1980—; adj. prof. law Am. U., 1972—; mem. adv. com. on rights and responsibilities of women to sec. HEW; mem. panel conciliators Internat. Center Settlement Investment Disputes, 1974-85 ; mem. Adminstrv. Conf. U.S., 1976-80, Public Service Adv. Bd., 1976-79; mem. human resources com. Nat. Center for Productivity and Quality of Working Life, 1976-80; mem. Presdl. Commn. on Exec. Exchange, 1981-85. Trustee Am. U., Mary Baldwin Coll.; nat. bd. dirs. Med. Coll. Pa., bd. corporators, 1976-85; bd. dirs. Center for Women in Medicine; bd. govs. St. Agnes Sch., 1981-87; mem. exec. com. Commn. on Bicentennial of U.S. Constn., chmn. instnl. adv. com. Recipient Ohio Gov.'s award, 1980, fellow award, 1981, Outstanding Pub. Service award U.S. Info. Service, 1987; named Disting. Fellow John Sherman Myers Soc., 1986. Mem. Am. Bar Assn. (adminstrv. law sect., chmn. labor law com. 1980-83, chmn. internat. and comparative law adminstrv. law sect. 1983—), Fed. Bar Assn., Inter-Am. Bar Assn. (editor Newsletter 1960-69, Silver medal 1967, co-chmn. labor law com. 1975-83), Bar Assn. D.C., World Peace Through Law Center, Internat. Soc. for Labor Law and Social Security, Am. Arbitration Assn. (dir.), Am. U. Alumni Assn. (dir. 1964-65, sec. law sch. 1965-66, pres. 1966-69, chmn. bd. govs. law sch. alumni 1969-73), Mortar Board, Kappa Beta Pi, Order Eastern Star. Republican. Episcopalian. Office: Baker & Hostetler 1050 Connecticut Ave NW Suite 1300 Washington DC 20036

MURPHY, BETTY PERRY, refuse service executive; b. Milton, W.Va., June 11, 1947; d. William Clinton and Dorothy Elizabeth (Wise) Perry; divorced; children: Amber Clagg, Gerald Clagg; m. Jarrell Sargent. Sec., payroll clk. Pinkerton's, Inc., Huntington, W.Va., 1971-76; mgr. Gen. Refuse Service, Inc., Milton, 1976-82, owner, pres., 1982—; devel. commercial mall, Milton. Pres. W.Va. Pumpkin Festival, Milton, 1987. Mem. Nat. Solid Waste Assn. (steering com. 1983—), W.Va. Solid Waste Assn. (pres.), Milton Bus. and Improvement Assn. Lodge: Order Eastern Star (sec. 1984, 87). Office: Gen Refuse Service Inc 1511 W Main St PO Box 219 Milton WV 25541

MURPHY, CAROL C(ATHERINE), judge; b. Chgo., June 17, 1933; d. James I. and Catherine F. (Glasgow) Gibbons; m. Frank P. Murphy, Sept. 13, 1952; children: Eileen, Catherine Cox, Frank Jr., Stephen, Daniel, Christine, Robert, E. Patricia, John. BA summa cum laude, Fla. So. Coll., 1975; JD with honors, Stetson U., 1978. Bar: Fla. 1979, U.S. Dist. Ct. (mid. and so. dists.) Fla. 1979, U.S. Dist. Ct. (no. dist.) Fla. 1981, U.S. Ct. Appeals (5th and 11th cirs.) 1981, U.S. Supreme Ct. 1984. Staff atty. Fla. Rural Legal Services, Bartow, Fla., 1979-82; sole practice Lakeland, Fla., 1982-84; judge Polk County Ct., Bartow, 1985—. Bd. dirs. Mental Health Assn., Polk County, 1984—, Cath. Social Services, Polk County, 1983—; mem. adv. bd. United Way Cen. Fla., 1984—; mem. Fla. Ctr. Children and Youth, Fla. Council Crime and Delinquency. Mem. ABA (nat. conf. spl. ct. judges), Am. Judges Assn., Fla. Bar Assn. (chmn. consumer protection law com. 1983-84), Lakeland Bar Assn., Nat. Assn. Women Lawyers, Nat. Assn. Women Judges, Fla. Assn. Women Lawyers (past. pres. 10th cir. chpt.), Conf. County Ct. Judges Fla. (bd. dirs. 1986-87), Pionette Bus. and Profl. Women, Polk County LWV, AAUW. Club: Toastmasters (Lakeland). Office: PO Box 928 Bartow FL 33830

MURPHY, CAROLE JOYCE, insurance sales executive, consultant; b. Chgo., Nov. 26, 1942; d. Adolph Orger and Frances Rose (Villa) Amundsen; m. Michael Brendan Murphy, Sept. 10, 1969; children—Angela Catherine, Martin Ignatius. Lic. life, accident, health, property and casualty ins. agt.; registered investment rep. Exec. sec. New Am. Library, N.Y.C., 1964-66; registrar M.B.A. program Northwestern U., Chgo., 1966-68; exec. sec. Mktg. Inst., Dublin, Ireland, 1968-70; analyst, supr. Motorola, Schaumburg, Ill., 1978-80; sales rep. Met. Ins. Co., Elgin, Ill., 1980-81; agt. Prudential Ins. Co., Schaumburg, 1981-84, sales mgr., 1984-86; dir. agys. Met. Life Ins., 1986—; br. mgr. Council mem. St. Margaret Mary Roman Catholic Ch., Algonquin, Ill., 1980-83, religious edn. tchr., 1982-83; mem. adv. com. Medic Alert Found. Internat., 1983-87. Mem. Nat. Assn. Life Underwriters, Am. Mgmt. Assn., Ill. Life Underwriters Assn., Chgo. Area Life Underwriters, Women Life Underwriters Council, Nat. Assn. Female Execs. (network dir. 1983-88), Crystal Lake C. of C. (editor Legis. Briefing 1983-88). Republican. Home: 310 Crestwood Ct Algonquin IL 60102 Office: Metropolitan Life Ins Co 1827 Walden Office Sq Suite 308 Schaumburg IL 60173

MURPHY, CAROLYN LOUISE, insurance company executive; b. Chgo., Dec. 12, 1944; d. Frank Joseph and Louise Mary Tomecek; student U. Chgo., 1965-67; B.S. in Math., Coll. of St. Francis, Joliet, Ill., 1965; M in Math., U. Chgo., 1967. Mktg. mgr. IBM, Chgo., 1976-77; exec. asst. to chief exec. officer CNA Ins., Chgo., 1977-78, v.p. personnel, 1978-80, v.p. adminstrn., 1980-83, v.p. field ops., 1984—. Office: CNA Ins CNA Plaza Chicago IL 60685

MURPHY, CHRISTINA ALINE, service executive; b. Jacksonville, Fla., Dec. 13, 1947; d. Charlie and Anna (Payden) M. BS, Edward Waters Coll., 1974; AS, Fla. Community Coll., 1988. Community resource councilor N.E. Fla. Community Action Inc., Jacksonville, 1971-74, child advocacy worker, 1974-76, consumer edn. coordinator, 1976-79, county services program asst., 1979-80, dir. human services, 1980-82, dir. community services, 1982—; instr. adult devel. services Fla. Community Coll., Jacksonville, 1981—; vice-chmn. Fla. State Weatherization Adv. Council, Tallahassee, 1984-86; resource person Feminization of Women Council, Jacksonville, 1986—; community facilitor black on black crimes com. Jacksonville Sheriff Community Relations, 1987—; bus. mgr. High Chapparal Sch. of Dance, Jacksonville, 1984—; mem. adv. com. housing and urban devel. City of Jacksonville, 1988—; mem. need assessment task force Jacksonville Human Service Coalition, 1987—; mem. community crime prevention program Jacksonville Sheriff's Office, 1988—. Vol. block chmn. Am. Cancer Soc., Jacksonville, 1985, U.S. Commodity Distbn. Program, Jacksonville, 1984-85; bd. dirs. Jacksonville Sickle Cell Found., 1986—; vita vol. IRS, Jacksonville, 1975—; United Way Emergency Service Council, Jacksonville, 1985—; mem. Jacksonville Human Service Coalition Task Force, 1987—, HUD Community Devel. Adv. Com., 1988—; active Jacksonville Sheriff's Office Neighborhood Crime Prevention program, 1987—. Recipient award of Appreciation Brotherhood of Police Officers, 1987, award of appreciation Neighborhood Resource Ctr., 1985, award of appreciation Fla. Dept of Correction-JCCC, 1986. Mem. Fla. Assn. Community Action (planning com. 1986—), Fla. Weatherization Assn., Creative Cons. Service (sec. 1984—), Edward Water Coll. Alumni Assn. (correspondent 1987—). Baptist. Club: Federate Garden Circle (program chmn. 1986—). Lodge: Elks (chmn. 1979-80). Home: 429 Linwood Ave Jacksonville FL 32206

MURPHY, COLLEEN FRANCES, public relations executive; b. Litchfield, Ill., Mar. 17, 1960; d. Carl Maurice and Margaret Evelyn (McAnarney) M.; m. James Arnold Buck, Jan. 10, 1987. BS, So. Ill. U., 1982. Pub. relations rep. Ill. Consol., Mattoon, 1982-84; mktg. mgr. Mercy Hosp., Urbana, Ill., 1984-86; account exec. Cohn & Wolfe/Burson-Marstellar, Atlanta, 1987; sr. account exec. DKB Pub. Relations, Atlanta, 1988; ind. pub. relations cons. Decatur, Ill., 1988—; cons. pub. relations Families First, Atlanta, 1987—. Mem. Pub. Relations Soc. Am. (bd. dirs. Cen. Ill. chpt. 1986, v.p. 1987). Home and Office: 9 Powers Lane Pl Decatur IL 62522

MURPHY, DEBORAH JUNE, lawyer; b. Clinton, Tenn., Dec. 19, 1955; d. Robert Carlton and Mary Ruth (Melton) M.; m. Charles L. Beach, Dec. 9, 1987. BS, U. Tenn., 1977; postgrad. Vanderbilt U., 1983; JD, Nashville YMCA Law Sch., 1987. Bar: Tenn. 1987. Bank officer C&C Bank, Oak Ridge, 1975-76; tax auditor State of Tenn., Knoxville, 1977-82, Nashville, 1983-85, legal advisor, 1985-86; with office legal services Tenn. Gen. Assembly, Nashville, 1986-87; atty. U.S. Dept. Treasury, 1987—; instr. Draughons Coll., Knoxville, 1978-81. Mem. Tenn. Homecoming 1986 Com. Mem. ABA, Tenn. Bar Assn., Assn. Trial Lawyers Am., Tenn. Trial Lawyers Assn., Anderson County Bar Assn., Lawyers Assn. for Women, The Young Lawyers Conf., Sigma Delta Kappa. Democrat. Methodist. Avocation: travel. Home: Rt 6 Oakwood Ave Clinton TN 37716 Office: IRS 710 Locust St Knoxville TN 37902

MURPHY, DIANA E., federal judge; b. Faribault, Minn., Jan. 4, 1934; d. Albert W. and Adleyne (Heiker) Kuske; m. Joseph E. Murphy, Jr., July 24, 1958; children: Michael, John E. B.A. magna cum laude, U. Minn., 1954, J.D. magna cum laude, 1974; postgrad., Johannes Gutenberg U., Mainz, Germany, 1954-55, U. Minn., 1955-58. Bar: Minn. 1974. Mem. firm Lindquist & Vennum, 1974-76; mcpl. judge Hennepin County, 1976-78; Minn. dist. judge 1978-80; U.S. dist. judge Minn. Mpls., 1980—; instr. Law Sch. U. Minn., Atty. Gen.'s Advocacy Inst.;. Bd. editors: Minn. Law Rev. Bd. dirs. Spring Hill Conf. Ctr., 1978-84, Mpls. United Way, 1985—; bd. dirs. Bush Found., 1982—, chmn. bd., 1986—; bd. dirs. Amicus, 1976-80, also organizer, 1st chmn. adv. council; mem. Mpls. Charter Commn., 1973-76, chmn., 1974-76; bd. dirs. Ops. De Novo, 1971-76, chmn., 1974-75; mem. Minn. Constl. Study Commn., chmn. bill of rights com., 1971-73; regent St. Johns U., 1978-87, vice chmn. bd., 1985-87; trustee Twin Cities Pub. TV, 1985—. Fulbright scholar; recipient U. Minn. Outstanding Achievement award; Amicus Founders' award; YWCA Outstanding Achievement award. Fellow Am. Bar Found.; mem. Am. Bar Assn. (Ethics and Profl. Responsibility Judges Adv. Com. 1981—), Minn. Bar Assn. (bd. govs. 1977-81), Hennepin County Bar Assn. (gov. council 1976-81), Am. Law Inst., Am. Judicature Soc. (bd. dirs. 1982—, v.p. 1985—), Nat. Assn. Women Judges, Minn. Women Lawyers, U. Minn. Alumni Assn. (bd. dirs. 1975-83, pres. 1981-82), Fed. Judges Assn. (bd. dirs. 1982—, v.p. 1984—), Order of Coif, Phi Beta Kappa. Office: US Dist Ct 670 US Courthouse 110 S 4th St Minneapolis MN 55401

MURPHY, E. ANNE, business services and consulting company executive; b. Charleston, S.C., Feb. 26, 1936; d. Barnwell H. and Miriam Elizabeth (Hilton) Limehouse. Pres., Finders Internat. Ltd. Inc., 1968; v.p., dir. Comprehensive Acctg. Corp., Aurora, Ill., 1979-84; pres., chief operating officer Pop-In, Inc., Columbiana, Ohio, 1984-85; pres., chief exec. officer, chmn. bd. PMA Ent., Inc., Aurora, Ill., 1984—, PMA, Inc., Aurora, 1984—; pres., chief exec. officer Gen. Mgmt. Services, Elmhurst, Ill., 1986, pres. chief operating officer Jobstores Inc, 1987. Contbr. articles to profl. jours. Author: Recruiting, Hiring and Training, 1983, Prairie State 2000 Authority, 1986. Served with USN, 1955-59. Mem. Women in Mgmt., Nat. Alliance of Female Execs., Womens Ednl. Services Assn. (Ill. Businesswoman of Yr. 1984). Mem. Pentecostal Assemblies of God. Avocations: music; theater.

MURPHY, EDRIE LEE, hospital laboratory administrator; b. Redwood Falls, Minn., Dec. 4, 1953; d. Melvin Arthur and Betty Lou (Wenholz) Timm; m. David Joseph Murphy, July 30, 1984. B.S. in Med. Tech. summa cum laude, Mankato State U., 1976; M.B.A., Coll. of St. Thomas, 1984. Registered med. technologist. Med. technologist Children's Hosp., St. Paul, 1976-81, chemistry supr., 1981-85, lab. mgr., 1985—. Contbr. articles to profl. jours. Charles H. Cooper scholar, 1975. Mem. Am. Soc. Med. Tech., Minn. Soc. Med. Tech., Am. Assn. Clin. Chemists, Clin. Lab. Mgmt. Assn., Phi Kappa Phi. Club: Elan Vital Ski (v.p. membership 1981-82) (Mpls.). Avocations: photography, sailing, skiing, tennis, travel. Office: Children's Hosp 345 N Smith Saint Paul MN 55102

MURPHY, ELIZABETH ANNE, nurse manager; b. Windsor, Ont., Can., Nov. 24, 1954; came to U.S., 1985; d. Edward William and Maxine Annie (Percy) M; m. Dennis J. Piper, June 28, 1975 (div. 1984). BA, BS in Nursing, U. Windsor, 1976; postgrad., Madonna Coll., Livonia, Mich., 1984—. Cert. critical care nurses, nursing adminstrn., advanced cardiac life support. Profl. nurse Met. Hosp., Windsor, 1976-79; nurse mgr. Sinai Hosp. of Detroit, 1979—; instr. St. Clair Coll., Windsor, 1982. advisor Detroit Met. Youth Found., 1987. Mem. Assn. Critical Care Nurses, Nat. Assn. Exec. Females, Women's Econ. Club, Sigma Theta Tau (nat. honor soc. 1988). Home: 23656 Rowe Pl Dearborn MI 48124 Office: Sinai Hosp of Detroit 6767 W Outer Dr Detroit MI 48235

MURPHY, EVELYN F., state official; b. Mass., 1940. AB, Duke U., PhD; MS, Columbia U. Lt. gov. Commonwealth of Mass., 1987—. Office: Lieutenant Governors Office Room 259 State House Boston MA 02133 *

MURPHY, IRENE HELEN, publishing executive; b. Boston; d. Charles Leo and Irene Muriel (Finney) M. BA, Regis Coll., 1958; MA, Boston Coll., 1963, Northeastern U., Boston, 1968, Manhattanville Coll., 1969. Tchr. elem. sch. Boston, high sch. dir. guidance, ednl. adminstr., prof. master tchr. program; prof. N.Y.C.; cons; dir. sch. services Glencoe Pub. Co., Mission Hills, Calif., v.p.; vis. lectr. univs., Australia, Can. Author series ednl. games for children. Recipient Gold Seal Recognition award Today's Cath. Tchr., 1987. Mem. Nat. Cath. Edn. Assn., Nat. Assn. Female Execs., AAUW. Democrat. Roman Catholic. Clubs: Woman's (Plymouth, Mass.); Adminstrs., Passport. Home: 59 Summer St Plymouth MA 02360 also: 2677 SW Thunderbird Trail Stuart FL 33497 Office: Glencoe Pub Co 15319 Chatsworth St Mission Hills CA 91345

MURPHY, JANET GORMAN, college president; b. Holyoke, Mass., Jan. 10, 1937; d. Edwin Daniel and Catherine Gertrude (Hennessey) Gorman. B.A., U. Mass., 1958, postgrad. 1960-61, Ed.D., 1974, LL.D. (hon.) 1984; M.Ed., Boston U., 1961. Tchr. English and history John J. Lynch Jr. High Sch., Holyoke, 1958-60; tchr. English, Chestnut Jr. High Sch., Springfield, Mass., 1961-63; instr. English and journalism Our Lady of Elms Coll., Chicopee, 1963-64; mem. staff Mass. State Coll., Lyndonville, Vt., 1977-83; pres. Mo. Western State Coll., St. Joseph, 1983—. Mem. campaign staff Robert F Kennedy Presdl. Campaign, 1967. Recipient John Gunther Tchr. award NEA, 1961, award Women's Opportunity Com., Boston Fed. Exec. Bd., 1963; named one of 10 Outstanding Young Leaders of Greater Boston Area, Boston Jr. C. of C., 1973. Office: Mo Western State Coll Office of Pres Saint Joseph MO 64507

MURPHY, JOANNE MARIE, health care equipment company sales executive; b. Chgo., Jan. 17, 1938; d. Charles John and Catherine Elizabeth (Nallon) M. Student, Clarke Coll., 1955-57, St. Francis Hosp. Sch. Med. Tech., Evanston, Ill., 1957-58. Registered med. technologist. Med. technologist J.B. Hartney, M.D., Oak Park, Ill., 1959-61; chem. lab. supr. St. Anne's Hosp., Chgo., 1961-67; tech. sales rep. Hycel, Inc., Chgo., 1967-72; adminstr. Gen. Med. Lab., Chgo., 1972-76; sales rep. Instrumentation Lab., Chgo., 1976-79, S.W. area sales mgr., Houston, 1979-84; central regional sales mgr. Radiometer Am., Inc., Dallas, 1985—. Bd. dirs. Bayou Woods Condo Assn., 1982-84. Recipient Pres.'s Club awards Instrumentation Lab., Lexington, Mass., 1978, 79. Mem. Am. Soc. for Med. Tech., Am. Assn. for Clin. Chemistry, Clin. Lab. Mgmt. Assn., Nat. Assn. Female Execs. Roman Catholic. Office: 2750 Northaven #305 Dallas TX 75229

MURPHY, JOANNE MILLER, marketing executive; b. Holyoke, Mass., Dec. 31, 1957; d. LeRoy Paul and Rose Marie (Danehey) Miller; m. Dennis Francis Murphy III, June 2, 1979; 1 child, Dennis Francis IV. AS in Bus. Studies, Holyoke Community Coll., 1979; BA in Mktg., U. Mass., 1980. Account rep. Xerox Corp., Hartford, Conn., 1980-82; sr. account exec. Exxon Office Systems, Stamford, Conn., 1983-85; area sales cons. ShareTech, Hartford, 1985-86; sr. mktg. rep. Honeywell Info. Systems, Glastonbury, Conn., 1986-87; account mgr. CompTech, Inc., 1987—. Editor shared tenant newsletter, 1985. Mem. Data Processing Mgmt. Assn., Orgn. for Profls. in Telecommunication. Republican. Roman Catholic. Avocations: skiing, tennis, golf, personal computers. Home: 20 Partridge Ct Simsbury CT 06070 Office: CompTech Inc 500 Winding Brook Dr Glastonbury CT 06033

MURPHY, JOY WALDRON, journalist, communications executive; b. Boston, Nov. 4, 1942; d. Albert Leo Jr. and Agnes Josephine (Cuddy) Waldron; m. Logan H. Roots, Oct. 6, 1962 (div. 1975); children: April E. Roots, Logan M. Roots, Ellen H. Roots; m. Larry E. Murphy, Mar. 20, 1982. Student, Northeastern U., 1960-62; BA in English, Coll. Santa Fe, 1977; postgrad., U. N.Mex., 1978-79. Editor Harvard U., Cambridge, Mass., 1963-66, U. Wash., Seattle, 1966-67; writer, editor smallpox eradication program WHO, Niamey, Niger, 1968-70; tchr. Berlitz Sch. Languages, Seattle, 1971-73; pvt. practice cons. Santa Fe, 1977-78; pub. info. officer Sec. of State N.Mex., Santa Fe, 1978-79, State of N.Mex. Health and Environment Dept., Santa Fe, 1979-80; pres. Joy Murphy & Assocs., Santa Fe, 1980—; cons. pub. relations, Santa Fe, 1980—; cons. writing State of N.Mex. Dept. Econ. Devel. and Tourism, Santa Fe, 1982—. Contbr. more than 200 articles to profl. jours. Home: PO Box 5815 Santa Fe NM 87502

MURPHY, KATHRYN MARGUERITE, archivist; b. Brockton, Mass.; d. Thomas Francis and Helena (Fortier) M. A.B. in History, George Washington U., 1935, M.A., 1939; M.L.S., Cath. U., 1950; postgrad. Am. U., 1961. With Nat. Archives and Records Service, Washington, 1940—, supervisory archivist Central Research br., 1958-62, archivist, 1962—, mem. fed. women's com. Nat. Archives, 1974, rep. to fed. women's com. GSA, 1975; lectr. colls., socs. in U.S., 1950—; lectr. Am. ethnic history, 1978-79. Founder, pres. Nat. Archives lodge Am. Fedn. Govt. Employees, 1965—, del. conv., 1976, 78, 80, recipient award for outstanding achievement in archives, 1980. Recipient commendation Okla. Civil War Centennial Commn., 1965; named hon. citizen Oklahoma City, Mayor, 1963. Mem. ALA, Soc. Am. Archivists (joint com. hosp. libraries 1965-70), Nat. League Am. Pen Women (corr. sec. Washington 1975-78, pres. chpt. 1978-80), Bus. and Profl. Women's Club Washington, Phi Alpha Theta (hon.). Contbr. articles on Am. ethnic history to profl. publs. Home: 1500 Massachusetts Ave NW Washington DC 20005 Office: Nat Archives and Records Service 7th and Pennsylvania Aves NW Washington DC 20408

MURPHY, LINDA SUE, city official; b. Lynchburg, Va., June 7, 1948; d. Carter P. and Dorothy L. (Clark) Tucker; m. Daniel K. Murphy, Mar. 25, 1972; 1 child, Krystal Grace. Student, Longwood Coll., 1966-68. Exec. sec. First Nat. Bank of Anchorage, Seward, Alaska, 1976-80; clk. of ct., asst. magistrate Alaska Ct. System, Seward, 1980-81; city clk., personnel officer City of Seward, 1981—. Sec., Seward Concert Assn., 1982; chmn. Seward Sch. Adv. Bd., 1983; v.p. bd. dirs. Seward Life Action Council, 1983-84, pres. bd. dirs., 1984-86; chmn. Seward-Obihiro Sister City Com., 1984. Mem. Internat. Inst. Mcpl. Clks., Alaska Assn. Mcpl. Clerks (sec. 1984-85, v.p. 1985-86, pres. 1986-87), Alaska Women in Govt. (v.p. 1985-87). Democrat. Club: Bus. and Profl. (Seward) (v.p. 1988—). Lodge: Rotary. Home: NHN Salmon Creek Rd Seward AK 99664 Office: Seward City Hall PO Box 167 Seward AK 99664

MURPHY, MARCIA GAUGHAN, lawyer, educator; b. Cleve., Nov. 23, 1949; d. John James and Alma Marie (Friedman) Gaughan; m. James Paul Murphy, Sept. 5, 1975; 1 child, Meghan Gaughan. AB with honors in English, Smith Coll., Northampton, Mass., 1972; JD summa cum laude, U. Notre Dame, 1975. Bar: Ohio 1975. Assoc. Jones, Day, Reavis & Pogue, Cleve., 1975-77; asst. prof. law Case Western Res. U., 1977-81, assoc. prof., 1981-83, prof., 1983; vis. prof. law Am. U., Washington Coll. Law, 1983, prof., 1984—, acting dep. dean, 1985-86; referee Ct. Common Pleas, Cleve., 1980; participant Law & Econs. Conf. for Lawyers, Hanover, N.H., 1983. Assoc. editor: Couse's Ohio Form Book, 1985; contbr. articles to law jours. Div. chmn. Campaign for Notre Dame U., 1979; mem. Women's Com. Nat. Symphony Orch., Washington. Mem. ABA, Women's Bar Assn. D.C. Roman Catholic. Office: Am U Washington Coll Law 4400 Massachusetts Ave NW Washington DC 20016

MURPHY, MARGARETTE CELESTINE EVANS, educator, writer; b. Chgo., June 25, 1926; d. Crawford and Ethel Hazel (Cartman) Evans; Ph.B., U. Chgo., 1945, M.A., 1949, postgrad., 1950-79, Ph.D., Colo. Christian

Coll., 1972; m. Robert H. Murphy, Sept. 25, 1949; children: Linda, Michelle. Tchr., English, Spanish and French, Willard Elem. Sch., 1950-52, McKinley High Sch., 1952-60, chmn. fgn. langs. dept. Crane High Sch., 1960-64, Harlan High Sch., Chgo., 1967—; tchr. TESL, Chgo. City Jr. Colls., 1976—. Mem. Women's Share in Pub. Service, Brazilian Soc. Chgo., Am. Security Council (nat. adv. bd.), U. Chgo. Alumni Assn., AAUW, Esperanto Soc. Chgo., Alpha Kappa Alpha. Republican. Roman Catholic. Club: 1200 of Chgo. Author: Note on Martinez Zuviría, Argentinian Novelist, 1949. Home: 8214 S Evans Ave Chicago IL 60619 Office: care Mrs Eva C Martin and Linda M Murphy 907 Polk Ave Memphis TN 38104

MURPHY, MARIE CLARE, business educator. BS, Boston U., 1967, MA, Columbia U., 1970. Cert. tchr., N.Y., Mass. Instr. SUNY, Bklyn., 1973-75; prof. of bus., CUNY, 1975—. Mem. AAUW (mem. ednl. task force N.Y. State Div. 1985-86, pres. 1979-81, Marie C. Murphy named Gift award presented 1987), Virginia Gildersleeve Internat. Found. U. Women, Nat. Bus. Edn. Assn., Jr. League, Bklyn Mus. (council mem. 1988), Bklyn Hist. Soc., Delta Pi Epsilon (pres. 1973-75 Tau chpt.). Club: Point O Woods (L.I.). Home: 101 West 12th St New York NY 10011

MURPHY, MARION Z., media director; b. N.Y.C., Aug. 12, 1954; d. James Leo Jr. and Sylvia (Zakim) M. BA in Acting and Directing, Montclair State Coll., 1976; Lic. in Real Estate, NYU, 1982. Stage mgr. Westchester-Rockland Regional Theatre, Harrison, N.Y., 1976-78; asst. dir. corp. devel. World Wildlife Fund-U.S., N.Y.C., 1977-80; prodn. stage mgr. Non Son Gallery Prodns., N.Y.C., 1978-83; direct mail mgr. Sotheby's Internat. Real Estate, N.Y.C., 1980-83; prodn. stage mgr. Greek Theatre N.Y., N.Y.C., 1981; assoc. dir. devel. Wunderman Ricotta & Kline, N.Y.C., 1984-86; producer MZM Prodns. Inc., N.Y.C., 1983—; media dir. NW Ayer Direct, N.Y.C., 1986—; mem. exec. com. NW Ayer Direct, 1986—. Author (plays): Holy Suit, 1986, The Party, 1987, The Renaissance, 1988. sec. Manhattan Plaza Tenants Assn., N.Y.C., 1981-83. Mem. AFTRA, Actors Equity Assn., Direct Mktg. Assn. Democrat. Jewish. Club: Players Alumni. Home: 400 W 43d St 37K New York NY 10036

MURPHY, MARY C., state legislator. B.A., Coll. St. Scholastica; postgrad. U. Minn., Macalester Coll., U. Wis.-Superior, Am. U. High sch. tchr.; mem. Minn. Ho. of Reps., 1976—, mem. appropriations, commerce, econ. devel./housing, labor-mgmt. relations coms. Trustee St. Mary's Hosp., Duluth, Minn.; bd. dirs. Minn. Alliance for Sci. and Tech.; mem. adv. com. Home Econs. Vocat. program Hermantown Community Schs.; active del. Duluth Central Labor Body AFL-CIO; mem., lector St. Raphael's Parish; dir. State Democratic Farmer-Labor Party, 1972-74, chmn. 8th Dist. credentials com., 1974—, chmn. St. Louis County Legis. Delegation, 1985-86. Mem. Duluth Fedn. Tchrs. (1st v.p. 1976-77, various coms.), Minn. Fedn. Tchrs. (legis. com. 1972-75), Am. Fedn. Tchrs. (del. nat. convs.), Coalition Labor Union Women, Minn. Hist. Soc., Alpha Delta Kappa. Office: State Office Bldg Saint Paul MN 55155

MURPHY, MARY KATHLEEN CONNORS, college administrator, writer; b. Pueblo, Colo.; d. Joseph Charles and Eileen E. (McDermott) Connors; m. Michael C. Murphy, June 6, 1959; children—Holly Ann, Emily Louise, Patricia Marie. AB, Loretto Heights Coll., 1960; MEd, Emory U., 1968; PhD, Ga. State U., 1980. Tchr. English pub. schs., Moultrie, Ga., 1959, Sacramento, 1960, Marietta, Ga., 1960-65, DeKalb County, Ga., 1966; tech. writer Ga. Dept. Edn., 1966-69; editorial asst. So. Regional Edn. Bd., Atlanta, 1969-71; dir. alumni affairs The Lovett Sch., Atlanta, 1972-75, dir. publs. and info. services, 1975-77; coordinator summer series in aging Ga. State U., 1979; dir. devel. found. relations Ga. Inst. Tech., 1980-87; dir. devel., 1988—; state coordinator for Ga., Am. Council on Edn. nat. identification program for women in higher edn. adminstrn., 1983-85; presenter profl. confs.; freelance edn. writer, 1968—; contbr. and contbg. editor numerous articles on teaching, secondary edn., higher edn., and fund raising to profl. publs.; columnist Daily Jour., Marietta, 1963-67, The Atlanta Constn., 1963-68. Bd. advisors Bridge Family Counseling Center, 1981-86, Northside Sch. Arts, 1981-83; bd. dirs. Atlanta Women's Network, 1982-84, v.p., 1983-84; bd. dirs. Sch. Religion, Cathedral of Christ the King, 1979-84; publicity chmn. Phoenix Soc. Atlanta, 1981—; mem. allocations com., exec. com United Way Met. Atlanta, 1983; bd. counseling Fulton Service Ctr., Met. Atlanta chpt. ARC, 1982-83; mem. Leadership Atlanta, class of 1983-84; group facilitator, 1984-85, co-chmn. edn. program, 1987. NDEA fellow, 1965-66; Adminstrn. of Aging fellow, 1977-79; recipient Image Maker award Atlanta Profl. Women's Directory, Inc. 1984. Mem. Council for Advancement and Support of Edn. (publs. com., alumni adv. com., dist. III bd. 1981—, chmn. corp. and found. support conf. 1985, maj. donor research conf. N.Y.C. 1985, dist. III conf. chmn. 1986) Nat. Assn. Ind. Schs. (publs. com.), Edn. Writers Assn., Am. Vocat. Assn., Nat. Soc. Fund Raising Execs. (v.p. chpt. 1985, pres. 1986-87, mem.-at-large nat. bd. 1985—, chmn. pub. relations com. 1985-87, asst. treas., mem. exec. com. 1988—), Phi Delta Kappa, Kappa Delta Pi (pres. 1980-81). Co-author: Fitting in as a New Service Wife, 1966; editor handbook on found. fund raising, 1988. Home: 2903 Rivermeade Dr NW Atlanta GA 30327

MURPHY, MARY KATHRYN, industrial hygienist; b. Kansas City, Mo., Apr. 16, 1941; d. Arthur Charles and Mary Agnes (Fitzgerald) Wahlstedt; m. Thomas E. Murphy Jr., Aug. 26, 1963; children: Thomas E. III, David W. BA, Avila Coll., Kansas City, 1962; MS, Cen. Mo. State U., 1975. Cert. in comprehensive practice of indsl. hygiene. Indsl. hygienist Kansas City area office Occupational Safety and Health Adminstrn., 1975-78, regional indsl. hygienist, 1979-86; dir. indsl. hygiene Chart Services, Shawnee, Kans., 1986-87; dir. indsl. hygiene activities Hall-Kimbrell Environ. Services, Lawrence, Kans., 1987—; asst. dir. safety office U. Kans. Med. Ctr., 1978-79. Summer talent fellow Kaw Valley Heart Assn., 1961. Mem. Am. Indsl. Hygiene Assn. (sec.-treas. Mid-Am. sect. 1978-79, bd. dirs. 1981, mem. auditcom.), Am. Chem. Soc., Am. Conf. Govt. Indsl. Hygienists (mem. chem. agts. threshold limit value com.), Am. Acad. Indsl. Hygiene, N.Y. Acad. Scis., AAAS, Internat. Soc. Environ. Toxicology and Cancer, Am. Coll. Toxicology, Am. Conf. on Chem. Labeling. Home: 10616 W 123rd Street Overland Park KS 66213 Office: Hall-Kimbrell Envirn Services 4840 W 15th St Lawrence KS 66044

MURPHY, MARYNELL, business owner; b. Waco, Tex., Apr. 21, 1954; d. James Austin and Betty (Thaxton) M. BS, So. Meth. U., 1976, MBA, 1977. Owner Four Leaf Clover, Dallas, 1978-85, In the Pub. Eye, Dallas, 1985—. Mem. Jr. League Dallas, Wadley Guild, Dallas, Susan Komen Found., Dallas, Art Reach Aux., Dallas. Recipient So. Meth. U. scholarship, 1975. Mem. So. Meth. U. Alumni Assn., So. Meth. U. MBA Assn. Democrat. Episcopalian. Clubs: Cotillion (pres. 1982-83), Slipper (Dallas) (treas. 1983-84). Home: 4333 Druid Ln Dallas TX 75205 Office: In the Pub Eye 5526 Dyer Suite 1113 Dallas TX 75206-5021

MURPHY, MELISSA SUZANNE, company executive; b. Teaneck, N.J., Sept. 13, 1958; d. Loyola Harry and Rita Floria (Forment) M. Diploma, Roman Acad., Hawthorne, N.J., 1983. Pres., chief exec. officer Glory B, Inc., Montclair, N.J., 1986—; owner Melissa Hair Fixer-Upper, Montclair. Mem. Paramus Animal Welfare Soc., Glen Rock, N.J., 1977—; mem. Irish-Am. Unity Conf., Clifton, N.J., 1987, People for Ethical Treatment of Animals, Washington, 1987, Celtic League, Am. br., N.Y.C., 1988. Democrat. Home: 142 Ellsworth Terr Glen Rock NJ 07452 Office: Glory B Inc 412 Bloomfield Ave Montclair NJ 07042

MURPHY, NANCY ANN, code enforcement officer; b. Columbus, Nebr., May 15, 1936; d. Chester Thomas and Louise Frances (Byrnes) Isgrig; m. James Gordon Reisner, Aug. 22, 1957 (div. Aug. 1971); children: Christopher A., Frances L., Thomas W., Andrew P.; m. John Michael Murphy, July 8, 1978; stepchildren: Linda K., Timothy C. Student, U. Nebr., 1954-57, Lower Columbia Coll., 1969-79. Pvt. practice residential design Omaha, 1958-66; engring. technician Trojan nuclear project Wismer & Becker, Rainier, Oreg., 1975-76; engring. technician Weyerhauser Co., Longview, Wash., 1976-80; field engr. Weyerhauser Co., Columbus, Miss., 1980-82; zoning and housing officer bldg. dept. City of Columbus, 1983—. Mem. exec. bd. Cowlitz County Health Systems Agy., Longview, 1978-79; chmn. citizens rev. com. United Way of Lowndes County, Columbus, 1985—. Mem. Nat. Assn. Women in Constrn. (charter, bd. dirs. 1978-79), Miss. Women in Mcpl. Govt., Bus. and Profl. Women's Club (treas. 1986—, pres. 1988—), DAR. Republican. Episcopalian. Clubs: Mustang, Scuba (Columbus). Home: 207 Jones Circle Columbus MS 39701 Office: City of Columbus Bldg Dept 513 Main St PO Box 1408 Columbus MS 39703

MURPHY, PATRICIA, speech and language pathologist, learning specialist; d. Michael and Nora (Dennehy) M. B.A. in Speech Pathology and Audiology, Hunter Coll., 1968, M.A. in Communication Scis., 1970; M.A. in Learning Disabilities and Reading, NYU, 1977; postgrad. in Ednl. Psychology, Columbia U., NYU Grad. Sch. of Social Work, 1986—. Speech-lang. pathologist Goldwater Meml. Hosp. NYU Med. Ctr., 1970-78; lang. learning specialist in child and adolescent psychiatry N.Y. Med. Coll.; instr. psychiatry Met. Hosp., N.Y.C., 1980-85, 86—; cons. speech-lang. pathologist Mary Manning Walsh Nursing Home, N.Y.C., 1974—. Mem. Am. Speech Lang. and Hearing Assn., Orton-Dyslexia Soc., Internat. Reading Assn., NYU Alumni Assn., Hunter Coll. Alumni Assn. Club: Appalachian Mountain.

MURPHY, R(OSALINA) LEE M(ARY), educator; b. Worcester, Mass., July 16, 1930; d. Pantaleo and Teresa (Patruno) DiPilato; m. William A. Murphy; children: Leo, Janice, Donna, William B. BSBA cum laude, Clark U., 1981; MEd, Worcester State Coll., 1983; cert. advanced grad. study, U. Mass., 1987. Cert. bus., social studies tchr., principal, supt. Sec. Crompton & Knowles Loom Works, Worcester, Mass., 1948-52; sr. stenographer Coll. of the Holy Cross, Worcester, Mass., 1968-73; adminstrv. asst. to pres. Assumption Coll., Worcester, Mass., 1973-78; managerial sec. Clark U., Worcester, Mass., 1979-81; bus. instr. Leicester (Mass.) High Sch., 1981-82, Salter Sch., Worchester, Mass., 1983—, David Prouty High Sch., Spencer, Mass., 1984—. Den mother Worcester council, Cub Scouts Am.; mem. Ecumenical com of Interreligious Affairs, Worcester, 1974-76, Leicester Supt. of Schs. Adv. com., 1981—; vol. Assumption Coll., 1973—; sec. Worcester Parent-Teachers Council, 1962-65. Mem. New Eng. Bus. Assn., R.I. Bus. Edn. Assn., Mass. Bus. Edn. Assn. Home: 17 Massasoit Dr Leicester MA 01524 Office: David Prouty High Sch 302 Main St Spencer MA 01562

MURPHY, SANDRA, human resources director; b. Pitts., Sept. 20, 1957; d. Adelmino Domenic and Patricia Ann (Davidson) DiLucente; m. Kevin C. Murphy, July 12, 1980. BA in Liberal Arts, Pa. State U., 1979. Asst. planner Community Action Com. of Lehigh Valley, Bethlehem, Pa., 1980-81, planner, 1981-82, exec. dir., 1982—. Speaker sex equity program Northampton County Community Coll., Bethlehem, 1985—; mem. consumer adv. panel Met. Edison, Easton, Pa., 1986—; mem. higher edn. adv. bd. Lehigh County Community Coll., Schnecksville, Pa., 1987. Mem. Pa. Dirs. Assn. for Community Action (exec. bd. 1986-88, pres. 1988—), Coalition Women Execs., Allentown-Lehigh County C. of C. Home: 237 Franklin St Quakertown PA 18951 Office: Community Action Com of Lehigh Valley 520 E Broad St Bethlehem PA 18018

MURPHY, SUSAN JANE, small business owner; b. Williamsport, Pa., Dec. 26, 1950; d. Jack W. and Edythe J. (Grier) M.; m. Michael J. Sanchez, Dec. 30, 1979. BBA, Pa. State U., 1978. Gen. mgr. Murphy Swift Homes, Hummelstown, Pa., 1970-75; owner, operator Murphy's Home Ctr., Hummelstown, 1975-79, 1985—; mgr. Builder's Emporium, San Diego, 1979-80; entrepreneur Castle in the Sand, San Diego, 1980-83; adminstr. Murphy's Home Ctr., Hummelstown, Alaska, 1983-85; cons. in field; dealer Servistar Home Ctrs. Photographs displayed at San Diego Art Inst. Vol. Hershey (Pa.) Free Ch. Donald MacIntyre scholar, 1979, Class of 1920 scholar, 1979, Congressman Kunkel scholar, 1979. Mem. Pa. Hardware Assn., Hummelstown C. of C., Better Bus. Bur. Evangelical Christian.

MURPHY-SCHEUMANN, DEBRA LYNN, magistrate; b. Newton, Iowa, July 27, 1954; d. Kenneth Earl and Beverly Louise (Shaffer) murphy; m. Max Leroy Morrow (div.); children: Charity Ann, Shannon Brent, Joshua Kent; m. Brent Alan Scheumann; children: Austin Kenneth, Allison Kim, Alex Kim. BSWi, U. No. Iowa, 1984, MEd, 1987; cert. practical nurse, Hawkeye Tech., 1985. Nurse Dr. W.H. Verduyn, Reinbeck, Iowa, 1979-85; edn. coordinator Allen Clinic, Waterloo, Iowa, 1985—; judicial magistrate State of Iowa, 1981—. Mem. Reinbeck Theater Guild, 1976—, Internat. Families, Black Hawk County, 1986—; foster parent Dept. HUman Services, Grundy County, 1982—. Mem. Iowa Assn. of Judges of Ltd. Jurisdiction (sec. 1983-85, v.p. 1985—, legisl. com., pres.). Democrat. Lutheran. Office: State Of Iowa Courthouse Grundy Center IA 50638

MURR, DEIRDRE ANN, data processing documentation consultant, b. Tulsa, Feb. 4, 1948; d. Hugh Orville and Pamela Hilda (Comley) Steavenson. BA in History, U. S.C., 1971. Mgr. data control Sterling Computers Co., Houston, 1977-78; supr. ops. Weingartens Co., Houston, 1978-80; cons. data processing The Leslie Corp., Houston, 1981; documentarian, trainer Barbour Computer Service, Houston, 1981-83; prin., owner Docutext Co., Houston, 1983—, mgr. internat. tech. publs. competition, 1988—. Mem. Soc. Tech. Communication, Tex Hist. Soc., Women in Data Processing, Houston Assembly Delphian Chpts. Episcopalian. Club: Quitters Guild Houston. Office: Docutext PO Box 29089 Houston TX 77227

MURRAY, ANGIE ANNA ALICE, government official; b. Thibodaux, La., July 6, 1949; d. Edward Justin Paul and Anna Angelina (Himmler) Hebert; m. Walter Thomas Murray, Mar. 21, 1970; children: Thomas Joseph, Anthony Michael. Speedwriting Cert., Sawyer Secretarial Sch., 1974. Mem. customer service staff European Exchange System, Ramstein, Ger., 1967-68; buyer, expeditor Thurow Electronics, Tampa, Fla., 1968-70; quotation clk. Thomas & Betts Co., Elizabeth, N.J., 1970-75; cost acct., girl Friday, Fulton Shirt Co., Elizabeth, 1975-76; office sec. Rapides Parish Police Jury, Alexandria, La., 1977-81, parish sec., 1981—; sec. Rapides Parish Stormwater Mgmt. and Drainage Dist., 1983—. Recipient Journalism award Noncommd. Officers Wives Club, 1967. Mem. Am. Soc. Notaries, Sec.-Treas. Orgn. of La. (region 8 exec. bd.), VFW Aux. Democrat. Roman Catholic. Avocations: reading; handicrafts. Home: PO Box 187 Elmer LA 71424 Office: Rapides Parish Police Jury PO Box 1150 Alexandria LA 71309

MURRAY, ANITA JEAN, data processing executive, consultant; b. Pitts., May 22, 1943; d. Julius and Nancy (Betza) Czujko; m. Christopher H. Murray, Apr. 6, 1968 (div. 1976). BS in Psychology, U. Pitts., 1964; MS in Stats., Stanford U., 1967. Cert. data processor. Systems analyst Pan Am. World Airways, N.Y.C., 1967-69; asst. controller Bunge Corp., N.Y.C., 1969-79; prin. nat. office Arthur Young & Co., N.Y.C., 1979-82; v.p. mgmt. info. systems Murjani Internat. Ltd., Saddle Brook, N.J., 1982-85; pres. Amston Mgmt., Inc., N.Y.C., 1985—; seminar leader Am. Mgmt. Assn., N.Y.C., 1979-82. Author: Minicomputer Bus. Solutions, 1981. Pres. Married Ams. for Tax Equality, N.Y.C., 1973-76; chmn. office mgmt. com. Community Bd. 1, N.Y.C., 1983. Mem. Data Processing Mgmt. Assn. (speaker 1981-82), Internat. Platform Assn., Am. Women Entrepreneurs. Club: Skating of N.Y. Avocations: photography, design. Office: Amston Mgmt Inc 52 Laight St New York NY 10013

MURRAY, ANNE, singer; b. Springhill, N.S., Can., June 20, 1945; d. Carson and Marion (Burke) M.; m. William M. Langstroth, June 20, 1975; children: William Stewart, Dawn Joanne. B.Phys. Edn., U. N.B., 1966, D.Litt. (hon.), 1978; D.Litt. (hon.), St. Mary's U., 1982. Rec. artist for, Arc Records, Can., 1968, Capitol Records, 1969; appeared on series of TV spls., CBC, 1970-81; star CBS spls., 1981-85; toured, N. Am., Japan, England, Germany, Holland, Ireland, Sweden, Australia and New Zealand, 1977-82. Hon. chmn. Can. Save the Children Fund, 1978-80. Recipient Juno awards as Can.'s top female vocalist, 1970-81; Can.'s Top Country Female Vocalist, 1970-86; Grammy award as top female vocalist-country, 1974; Grammy award as top female vocalist-pop, 1978; Grammy award as top female vocalist-country, 1980, 83; Country Music Assn. awards, 1983-84; named Female Rec. Artist of Decade, Can. Rec. Industry Assn., 1980, Top Female Vocalist 1970-86; star inserted in Hollywood Walkway of Stars, 1980; Country Music Hall of Fame Nashville; Decorated companion Order of Can. Mem. AFTRA, Assn. Canadian TV and Radio Artists, Am. Fedn. Musicians. Office: Balmur Ltd, 4881 Yonge St, Suite 412, Toronto, ON Canada M2N 5X3

MURRAY, BARBARA BATEMAN, economics educator; b. Detroit, Aug. 31, 1933; d. Ralph Charles and Mabel Evelyn (Gracey) B; m. John McLay Murray, Nov. 1955; children: Kevin B., Sharron D. BS, Mich. State U., 1955; MBA, U. Detroit, 1961; MA, Wayne State U., 1964, PhD, 1967. Asst. prof. U. Detroit, 1971-75, assoc. prof., 1975-77; economist Ford Motor Co., Dearborn, Mich., 1977-78; assoc. prof. Sch. of Mgmt. U. Mich., Dearborn, 1978—; pres. Barbara B. Murray Assocs. contbr. articles to profl. jours. Trustee Bus. Edn. Alliance. Resources for the Future fellow, 1967. Mem. Midwest Bus. Assn., Economic Club of Detroit. Club: Detroit. Home: 33742 York Ridge Dr Farmington Hills MI 48331 Office: U Mich at Dearborn Sch Mgmt 4823 Evergreen Dearborn MI 48223

MURRAY, CAROLINE FISH, psychologist; b. Buenos Aires, Argentina, Mar. 28, 1920; came to U.S., 1924; d. Alfred Dupont and Caroline Johnston (Ramsay) Chandler; m. Henry A. Murray, May 17, 1969; children by previous marriage: Caroline D. Janover, Alexander M. Davis, Ann Kelso D. MacLaughlin, Quita D. Palmer, Maude I. Fish. AB magna cum laude, Smith Coll., 1942; MEd, U. N.H., 1962; EdD, Boston U., 1967. Exec. sec. to dir. Alfred I. duPont Inst., Wilmington, Del., 1953-55; tchr. Kingston (N.H.) Pub. Schs., 1962-63; instr. Boston U., 1966-67, asst. prof. psychology, 1967-71, co-dir. psycho-educational clinic, 1966-70, coordinator headstart evaluation and research ctr., 1966-69, cons., 1969-83; mem. clin. staff Mass. Mental Health Ctr., Boston, 1983—; lectr. psychology dept. psychiatry Harvard Med. Sch., 1983—; mem. profl. adv. com. Mass. Dept. Mental Health, 1983-85. Bd. dirs. Wediko Children's Services, 1975-85; bd. dirs. Shaker Village, Hancock, Mass.; bd. dirs. Douglas A. Thom Clinic, Boston, 1974-77, pres., 1977; chmn. bd. Ariel Chamber Music, Cambridge, 1979; bd. dirs. Mass. Children's Lobby, 1978-82, pres., 1979-81; chmn. statewide adv. council Office for Children, 1980-82. Mem. Am. Psychol. Assn., Am. Assn. Advancement Psychology, Mass. Psychol. Assn., Eastern Psychol. Assn., N.Y. Acad. Scis., Assn. for Advancement Psychology, Fedn. Am. Scientists, Jean Piaget Soc., Pi Lambda Theta. Democrat. Home: 22 Francis Ave Cambridge MA 02138

MURRAY, CHERRY ROBERTS, artist, fine arts educator; b. Colfax, La., Jan. 3, 1921; d. John Bunyon and Mary (Procter) Roberts; student U. N.Mex., 1940-41; B.F.A., U. Tex., 1942; student Nagayama Studio, Tokyo, 1955; studied under numerous profl. artists, including Ward Lockwood, Best-Mougourd, Maynard Dixon, Millard Sheets, Peter Hurd, Georgia O'Keefe, Vincent Farrell; m. John Lewis Murray, May 2, 1942; children—John Roberts, James Procter (dec.), Cherry Ann, Nancy Lee. Tchr. painting, U.S., 1939-54, 70—, Japan, 1954-56, 60-64, Pakistan, 1957-60, Korea, 1965-68, Indonesia, 1968-70; instr. fine arts Pima Coll. East, Tucson, 1979—; exhbns. include: Baluche Regiment, Cherat, West Pakistan, 1965-68, Am. Embassy Residence, Seoul, Korea, 1965-68, Djarkarta, Indonesia, 1968-70, Abba Gallery, 1978-80, Kay Bonfoey Gallery, 1980, Rentschler Gallery, 1980, Casa Grande Art Gallery, Tucson, 1980; represented in permanent and pvt. collections: U. Tex., U. N.Mex., Nagayama Studio, Tokyo, Ayub Kahn, Baluche Regiment, West Pakistan, Mitha Collection, Lahore, Pakistan, Sir Ian McKensie, Brit. Isles, H. Allen Loomes, Australia, Ambassador Yehuda Horam, Israel, Chote-Kholgvista, Thailand, Kopper, Indonesia, Galbraith, Washington, USIS, Indonesia, Am. Embassy, Djarkarta, Am. Embassy, Seoul, Lathrum, Hicks, Woods, Elliott collections (all Washington), Valley Nat. Bank, City of Douglas, Old Adobe Patio Gallery, others. Recipient 56 awards, 1975-86, including: Creative Artist of Yr. award, 1976; 1st pl. award So. Ariz. Watercolor Guild, 1978; Merit award Watercolor Southwest III, Houston, 1978; Best of Show award Nat. League Am. Pen Women, 1978; Tchr. of Yr. award Pima Coll. East, 1983. Mem. U. Tex. Art Assn. (1st pres.), So. Ariz. Watercolor Guild, Tubac Center of the Arts, Santa Cruz Valley Art Assn., Sierra Vista Art Assn., Ariz. Watercolor Soc., Archeol. and Hist. Soc., Nat. Soc. Arts and Letters, Southwestern League Fine Arts, Gem and Mineral Soc., Nat. League Am. Pen Women, AAUW, Pilot Internat. Democrat. Presbyterian. Home: 12420 Calle del Gorrion Tucson AZ 85748 Office: Pima Community College 8202 E Poinciana Dr Tucson AZ 85730 Office: Pima Coll E Tucson AZ 85710

MURRAY, CLAIRE F., nurse administrator, educator; b. Troy, N.Y., Nov. 22, 1942; d. William F. and Clara (Bowen) M. Grad. in nursing, St. Mary's Hosp., Troy, 1963; BS in Nursing, Russell Sage Coll., 1973, MS in Nursing, 1984. Staff nurse St. Mary's Hosp., Troy, 1963-66, head nurse, 1966-69, inservice edn. coordinator, 1968-70, patient care coordinator, 1970-72, 73-77, assoc. dir. nursing, 1977-78, dir. nursing, 1978-82, v.p. nursing servicesthen v.p. patient services, 1982—; adj. prof. grad. program Russell Sage Coll., Troy, 1985—; cons. VA Med. Ctr., Albany, 1986-87; lectr. in field. Contbr. articles to profl. jours. Active Rensselaer County Health Dept.; founding mem. Task Force on Substance Abuse in Nursing, 1985—. Mem. Am. Nurses Assn. (bd. dirs. 1987—, cert. nursing adminstrn.), N.Y. State Nurses Assn. (bd. dirs. 1984-86), Capital Dist. Nurses Assn. (pres. 1980-81, sec. 1978-79, bd. dirs. 1975-78, 81-83), Am. Orgn. Nurse Execs., Northeastern N.Y. Orgn. Nurse Execs. (exec. com. 1984—), Sigma Theta Tau, LWV. Democrat. Home: 1501 Twelfth Ave Watervliet NY 12189 Office: St Mary's Hosp Patient Services 1300 Massachusetts Ave Troy NY 12180

MURRAY, CYNTHIA ANN, lumber executive, real estate agent; b. Marlin, Tex., Dec. 27, 1956; d. Johnny Hilton Sr. and Wilta June (Johnson) Stewart; m. Lawrence James Murray, May 22, 1976; 1 child, Jason Ray. Cert. in real estate, Temple (Tex.) Jr. Coll., 1979. Lic. real estate broker, Tex. Exec. asst. Oasis Water Co., Waco, Tex., 1975-76, Air Systems, Inc., Temple, 1976-77; exec. asst., property mgr. Reagan Investments, Temple, 1977-79; sales and adminstrn. mgr. Tumac Lumber Co., Inc., Irving, Tex., 1979—; cons. Reagan Investments, Temple, 1979-82. Recipient Sales award Willamette Industries Surelam Div., 1985. Mem. Nat. Assn. for Female Execs. Republican. Baptist. Club: Los Colinas Sports (Irving). Home: 414 Santa Fe Trail #95 Irving TX 75063 Office: Tumac Lumber Co Inc 9901 E Valley Ranch Pkwy #2080 Irving TX 75063

MURRAY, ELIZABETH ANN, therapist; b. Phila., Oct. 21, 1947; d. Donald Shipley and Elizabeth Burton (Friedenwald) M. BS in Edn., U. Pa., 1969; MEd, U. Del., 1974; ScD, Boston U., 1987. Tchr. Sch. Dist. of Phila., 1969-72, 73-74; asst. dir. occupational therapy, research asst. Div. for Disorders in Deve. Learning U. N.C., Chapel Hill, 1976-78; asst. dir. occupational therapy Shriver Ctr., Waltham, Mass., 1978—; adj. asst. prof. Boston U., 1980—; mem. faculty Sensory Integration Internat., Los Angeles, 1976—. Fellow Boston U., 1985-86. Mem. Am. Occupational Therapy Assn., Mass. Assn. Occupational Therapy, Nat. Council Tchrs. of Maths., Boston Computer Soc. Home: 26 Lake Rd Wayland MA 01778 Office: Shriver Ctr 200 Trapelo Rd Waltham MA 02254

MURRAY, FLORENCE KERINS, state supreme court justice; b. Newport, R.I., Oct. 21, 1916; d. John X. and Florence (MacDonald) Kerins; m. Paul F. Murray, Oct. 21, 1943; 1 child, Paul F. A.B., Syracuse U., 1938; LL.B., Boston U., 1942; student, R.I. Coll. Edn., 1942, Ed.D. (hon.), 1956; grad., Nat. Coll. State Trial Judges, 1966; LL.D. (hon.), Bryant Coll., 1956; LL.D., R.I. U., 1963, Mt. St. Joseph Coll., 1972, Providence Coll., 1974, Roger Williams Coll., 1976, Salve Regina Coll., 1977, Johnson and Wales Coll., 1977. Bar: Mass., R.I., U.S. Supreme Ct. Sole practice Newport, 1947-52; mem. firm Murray & Murray, Newport, 1952-56; assoc. judge R.I. Superior Ct., 1956-78; presiding justice Superior Ct. R.I., 1978-79; assoc. justice R.I. Supreme Ct., 1979—; staff, faculty adv. Nat. Jud. Coll., Reno, Nev., 1971-72, dir., 1975-80, chmn., 1979-87; legal adv. R.I. Girl Scouts; sec. Commn. Jud. Tenure and Discipline, 1975-79. Mem. R.I. Senate, 1948-56; chmn. spl. legis. com.; mem. Newport Sch. Com., 1948-57, chmn., 1951-57; mem. Gov.'s Jud. Council, 1950-60, White House Conf. Youth and Children, 1950, Ann. Essay Commn., 1952, Nat. Def. Adv. Com. on Women in Service, 1952-58, Gov.'s Adv. Com. Mental Health, 1954, R.I. Alcoholic Adv. Com., 1955-58, R.I. Com. Youth and Children, Gov.'s Adv. Com. on Revision Election Laws, Gov.'s Adv. Com. Social Welfare, Army Adv. Com. for 1st Army Area; mem. civil and polit. rights com. Pres.'s Commn. on Status of Women, 1960-63; mem. R.I. Com. Humanities, 1972—, chmn., 1972-77; mem. Family Ct. Study Com., R.I. com. Nat. Endowment Humanities; bd. dirs. Newport YMCA; sec. Bd. Physicians Service; bd. visitors Law Sch., Boston U.; bd. dirs. NCCJ; mem. edn. policy and devel. com. Roger Williams Jr. Coll.; trustee Syracuse U.; pres. Newport Girls Club, 1974-75. Served to lt. col. WAC, World War II. Decorated Legion of Merit, Army Commendation ribbon; recipient Arents Alumni award Syracuse U., 1956; Carroll award R.I. Inst. Instn., 1956; Outstanding Woman award Bus. and Profl. Women, 1972; Brotherhood award NCCJ, 1983. Mem. Am. Arbitration Assn., Nat. Trial Judges Conf. (state chmn. membership com., sec. exec. com.), New Eng. Trial Judges Conf. (com. chmn. 1967), ABA (chmn. credentials com. nat. conf. state trail judges 1971-73), Am. Judicature Soc.

(dir.), Boston U. Alumni Council, Am. Legion (judge adv. post 7, mem. nat. exec. com.), AAUW (chmn. state edn. com. 1954-56), Bus. and Profl. Women's Club (past state v.p., past pres. Newport chpt., past pres. nat. legis. com.), Alpha Chi Omega, Kappa Beta Pi. Club: Auota (past gov. internat., past pres. Newport chpt.). Home: 2 Kay St Newport RI 02840 Office: RI Supreme Ct 250 Benefit St Providence RI 02903

MURRAY, GERI D., real estate salesperson; b. Chgo., Oct. 7, 1927; d. Frances Edward and Geraldine (Luce) Dunlap; m. Donald James Murray, Oct. 9, 1948; children: Cheryl, Lynda, Donald D., Patrick, Michael, Joyce, Janyce. Student, DePaul U., 1948, Triton Coll.; BS, U. Mo., 1975. Asst. supr. bidding and contract div. Hauserman Co., Hillside, Chgo., 1967-72; asst. to pres. First Fed. Savs. and Loan Proviso Twp., Hillside, Ill., 1972-74; asst. mgr. product sales R.W. Mitchell & Co., Bellwood, Ill., 1974-75; agt. purchasing Reynolds Electric, Maywood, Ill., 1975-77; exec. dir. West Suburban Neighborhood Preservation Agy., Bellwood, 1978-83; salesman real estate Remax, Elmhurst, Ill., 1983—; cons., tchr. Network Rehab.-Cook County, Bellwood, 1976-83, pres. 1984. Pres. PTA West Suburbs, 1954-75; dir. Hillside Planning Commn., 1972-84; mem. adv. council Suburban Cook County Area Agy. Aging, 1984. Mem. Nat. Assn. Housing Rehab. Ofcls., Am. Planning Assn. (past state Ill. membership chmn.), Met. Planning Assn., Bellwood C. of C. (dir. 1984). Republican. Roman Catholic. Lodge: Women Moose. Home: 1 S 278th Stratofrd Ln Villa Park IL 60181 Office: Tri-Plex Mgmt Corp 1127 S Manheim Rd Westchester IL 60153

MURRAY, IRENE JUANITA, dental hygienist; b. Newark, July 17, 1940; d. Thomas Oliver Miles and Irene Vivian (Thibaudeau) M.; divorced; children: Robert, Rachel Marie. AA, No. Va. Community Coll., 1982. Lic. dental hygienist, Va. Dental hygienist Dr. John A. Marino, Annandale, Va., 1982—. Den leader/coach Cub Scouts Am., Alexandria, Va., 1972-73; mem. Fairfax County Rep. Com., 1974—; pres. Booster Club, Congl. Sch., Falls Church, Va., 1975-76, Columbia Elem. Sch. Parents Assn., Annandale, Va., 1976-77, Monticello Council Rep. Women, 1977-78; del. Rep. State Convs., 1978, 79, 82, 85, 88. Mem. Am. Dental Hygienists Assn., Va. Dental Hygienists Assn. (state sec. 1982-88), No. Va. Dental Hygienists Assn., Concerned Women for Am., Phi Theta Kappa. Home: 6800 Algonquin Ct Annandale VA 22003

MURRAY, JANE ELLEN, advertising executive; b. Chgo., Aug. 21, 1927; d. Thomas F. and Mildred (Spacek) M.; m. Edwin R. Wentz. B.A., Vassar Coll., 1948; postgrad. Northwestern U.-Ill. With J. Walter Thompson, Chgo., 1948—, assoc. creative dir., 1968-70, v.p., 1970—, creative dir., 1976—; initiated advt. campaigns for Libby, Swift, Alberto-Culver, Quaker, Kraft, Better Homes and Gardens and others. Contbr. articles to profl. jours. Mem. adv. bd. MacCormac Jr. Coll.; bd. dirs. Vassar Club, Chgo., 1978. Recipient Spl. citation Blue Ribbon award Chgo. Daily News Writing Contest, 1958; Am. TV Comml. Festival award, 1964; Bur. Advt. Am. Newspaper Pubs. Assn. award, 1968; Hermes award, 1969, Cleo award, 1985; cert. of appreciation for profl. services Sch. of Journalism, No. Ill. U., 1975; YWCA Leadership award, 1977; Advt. Woman of Yr. award, 1978; Chgo. Addy award, 1980. Mem. Jr. Women's Advt. Club (pres., founder), Women's Advt. Club of Chgo. (rec. sec., corr. sec., bd. dirs. 1978-79, pres. 1979-80, 80-81), Chgo. Copywriter's Club (sec.), Chgo. Soc. Communicating Arts (membership chmn. 1969, 2d v.p. 1970, 1st v.p. 1972, pres. 1973); faculty AM. Acad. of Art, 1987. Author: (book, lyrics of musical prodn.) Fear of Filing, 1987. Republican. Roman Catholic. Home: 1120 N Lake Shore Dr Chicago IL 60611 Office: J Walter Thompson Co 875 N Michigan Ave Chicago IL 60611

MURRAY, JULIA KAORU (MRS. JOSEPH EDWARD MURRAY), occupational therapist; b. Wahiawa, Oahu, Hawaii, 1934; d. Gijun and Edna Tsuruko (Taba) Funakoshi; m. Joseph Edward Murray, 1961; children—Michael, Susan, Leslie. BA, U. Hawaii, 1956; cert. occupational therapy U. Puget Sound, 1958. Therapist, Inst. Logopedics, Wichita, Kans., 1958; sr. therapist Hawaii State Hosp., Kaneohe, 1959; part-time therapist Centre County Ctr. for Crippled Children and Adults, State College, Pa., 1963; vice chmn. adv. bd. Hosp. Improvement Program, East Oreg. State Hosp., Pendleton, 1974; v.p. Ind. Living, Inc., 1976-79; job search instr.; mem. adv. com. Oreg. Ednl. Coordinating Commn., 1979-82; mem. Oreg. Bd. Engring. Examiners, 1979-87; occupational therapist Fairview Tng. Ctr., Salem, Oreg. Rep. from Umatilla County Commrs. to Blue Mountain Econ. Devel. Council, 1976-78; mem. Ashland Park and Recreation Bd., 1972-73; vice chmn. adv. bd. LINC, 1978; mem. exec. bd. Liberty-Boone Neighborhood Assn., 1979-83. Mem. Am., Oreg., Hawaii (sec. 1960) occupational therapy assns., LWV (bd. dirs. Pendleton 1974, 77-78, pres. 1975-77; bd. dirs. Oreg. 1979-81, Ashland 1967-71, v.p. 1970). Office: Fairview Tng Ctr 2250 Strong Rd SE Salem OR 97310

MURRAY, KAREN ROSSINI, accountant; b. Framingham, Mass., Mar. 8, 1954; d. Albeno A. and Marguerite M. (Kiely) Rossini; m. Patrick F. Murray Sr., Aug. 25, 1979; children: Patrick F. Jr., Kiely Marguerite. BBA, Boston Coll., 1976; MBA, Northeastern U., 1977. Sales rep. Met. Life Ins. Co., Brookline, Mass., 1977-79; sales mgr. Met. Life Ins. Co., Peobody, Mass., 1979-80; advanced acct. John Hancock, Boston, 1980-84, adminstr., 1984-85, sr. acct., 1985—. Mem. Pre-Cannan Team, St. Mary's Catholic Ch., Hollingston, Mass., 1980-82, religious education tchr. , 1987; treas. John Hancock United Way, Boston, 1982, 83. Named one of Outstanding Young Woman Am., 1986. Home: 212 Marked Tree Rd Holliston MA 01746 Office: John Hancock 200 Clarendon St Boston MA 02111

MURRAY, KATHLEEN ANNE, lawyer; b. Los Angeles, Feb. 14, 1946; d. Francis Albert and Dorothy (Thompson) M.; 1 child, Anne Murray Ladd. BA, U. Mich., 1967; JD, Hastings Coll. of Law, 1973. Bar: Calif. 1973, U.S. Dist. Ct. (no. dist.) Calif. 1973, U.S. Ct. Appeals (9th cir.) 1973. Sr. staff atty Child Care Law Ctr., San Francisco, 1979-84, cons. child day care law and regulation, 1984-86; atty Epstein & Harris, San Francisco, 1985-86; gen. counsel Fisher Friedman Assocs., San Francisco, 1986—; exec. dir., mem. editorial adv. bd. Parenting Mag., 1985—. Editor: Child Care Center Legal Handbook; Tax Guide for California Child Care Providers; contbr. articles to profl. jours. Mem. adv. council Humanities West Inc., 1986—, North of Market Child Devel. Ctr., San Francisco, 1987—. Democrat. Episcopalian.

MURRAY, KATHLEEN VIRGINIA, editor; b. Charleroi, Pa., Nov. 7, 1939; d. William Albert Carney and Virginia (Behanna Carney) Clark; B.A. cum laude in Communications, Mundelein Coll., 1980; m. David Lee Murray, Dec. 29, 1961 (div. June 1987); children—Clark David, Timothy Lee. Div. sales mgr. Port-A-Bookstore, Palatine, Ill., 1973-74; editor Murray Communications, Evanston, Ill., 1975-81; assoc. editor The Guarantor, Chgo. Title & Trust Co., 1981-83, editor, 1983, editor, communications officer, 1984-85; tng. and communications cons. Career Exchange Network, Carlsbad, Calif., 1985-87; Murray Communications, San Diego, 1987—. Mem. Internat. Assn. Bus. Communicators, Women in Communications, North Shore Choral Soc. (dir.), Kappa Gamma Pi. Editor: You, Your Children and Divorce, New Decision, 1981; mng. editor PACE, 1980. Office: Murray Communications PO Box 82991 San Diego CA 92138

MURRAY, KIMBERLY LOUISE, structural engineer; b. Akron, Ohio, June 9, 1955; d. George Wendell and Shirley Ann (Tibbens) M. Student, Miami U., Oxford, Ohio, 1973-76; BSCE, Ohio State U., 1979; postgrad., Manhattan Coll., 1986—. Registered profl. engr., Ohio, N.Y. Engr. Howard, Needles, Tammen and Gronquist, Cleve., 1979-81; bridge engr. Adache-Ciuni-Lynn, Cleve., 1982-84; project engr. Steinman, Boynton, gronquist and Birdsall, Hoboken, N.J., 1984-86, Lichtenstein Engring. Assocs., N.Y.C., 1986—. Mem. ASCE, Ohio State U. Alumni Assn. Home: 288 7th St Jersey City NJ 07302 Office: Lichtenstein Engring Assocs 21 W 38th St New York NY 10018

MURRAY, LOIS A. HEIL, lawyer; b. Marshfield, Wis., June 3, 1953; d. Frank N. and Bertha J. (Hafenbreadl) Heil; B.A., B.S. in Acctg., U. Wis., River Falls, 1974; J.D. cum laude, U. Minn., 1978; m. Alan E. Murray, Aug. 18, 1973. Tax examiner Minn. Dept. Revenue, 1974-75; admitted to Wis. bar, 1978, Minn. bar, 1978, U.S. Dist. Ct. bar, 1978; law clk. firm Ralph Senn, River Falls, 1976; research asst. to prof. law and asso. dean Sch. Law, U. Minn., Mpls., 1976-78; law clk. Honeywell, Inc., Mpls., 1977; assoc. firm Heywood, Cari & Murray and predecessor, Hudson, Wis., 1978-80, partner, 1980—; mem. faculty Wis. Indianhead Tech. Inst., Hudson Community Edn. Bd. dirs. West Central Wis. Action Agy., 1984-85. Mem. State Bar Assn. Wis., State Bar Assn. Minn., Am. Bar Assn., St. Croix Valley Bar Assn., AAUW, LWV, Hudson Area C. of C. Roman Catholic. Home: 600 7th St Hudson WI 54016 Office: Micklesen Bldg 204 Locust St Hudson WI 54016

MURRAY, LYNN, lawyer; b. Paterson, N.J., Mar. 2, 1956; d. James Lindsay and Joan (Van Winkle) M. B.A., Purdue U., 1978; J.D., Rutgers U., 1981. Bar: Ind. 1981. Assoc. firm Sandy, Deets & Kennedy, Lafayette, Ind., 1981-82; staff atty. UAW legal services plan Gen. Motors Corp., Kokomo, Ind., 1983-86, supervising atty., 1986—. Contbr. articles to legal publs. Active Democrats of Howard County, Ind. Hist. Soc. Mem. ABA, Ind. Bar Assn., Howard County Bar Assn., Purdue U. Alumni Assn., Phi Alpha Delta, Pi Sigma Delta, Phi Alpha Theta. Methodist. Home: 323 N Berkley Ave Kokomo IN 46901 Office: UAW Legal Services Plan 1817 Dogwood Ct Kokomo IN 46902

MURRAY, MARY MCFARLANE, genealogist; b. Tulsa, Dec. 28, 1947; d. John Robert Kincaid and Letha Nadine (Robertson) Hansen; m. Richard Walter Berge, Feb. 21, 1965 (div. 1972); children: Renae Marie Gehardstein, Rachelle Ann Dunne; m. Timothy Winslow Murray, Feb. 14, 1987. Student, Grossmont Coll., 1977, U. Md., Berlin, 1983. Various positions Dept. Motor Vehicles, Sacramento, Calif., 1971-74; various positions acctg. Calif. Bd. Equalization, Sacramento, 1975-79; asst. tax collector, treas. County of Madera, Calif., 1986—. Served as sgt. U.S. Army, 1980-86. Mem. Madera County Geneology Soc. Democrat. Unitarian. Lodge: Soroptimists. Home: 19420 Panoramic Dr Madera CA 93638 Office: Madera County Govt Ctr 209 W Yosemite Madera CA 93637

MURRAY, MARY RAYMOND, public relations executive; b. Gardner, Mass., Sept. 22, 1947; d. Paul Henry and Mary Raymond (Proctor) M. BA in English with honors, LeMoyne Coll., 1969. Asst. pub. info. Bus. Sch. Harvard U., Boston, 1969-71; mng. editor Bus. Atlanta Mag., 1972-75, editor, 1975-77; market analyst Land Data Corp., Atlanta, 1974-77; account exec. Daniel J. Edelman Inc., Chgo., 1977-79, account supr., 1979-81, v.p., 1982-83, sr. v.p., 1983-84; exec. v.p., gen. mgr. Daniel J. Edelman Inc., St. Louis, 1984—. Contbr. articles to Bus. Atlanta Mag. Mem. V.P. Fair Found. Pub. Relations Com., St. Louis, 1985—; chmn. recruitment/devel. com. vol. action ctr. United Way, St. Louis, 1986—, vice chmn., 1988—; bd. dirs. St. Louis Charitable Found., St. Louis, 1986—; instr. Jr. Achievement Project Bus., St. Louis, 1987—. Recipient Golden Trumpet-Mktg. award Publicity Club Chgo., 1981, Merit Mktg. award Publicity Club Chgo., 1983, Merit Communications award Internat. Assn. Bus. Communicators, 1986, Silver Quill award Internat. Assn. Bus. Communicators, 1987. Mem. Pub. Relations soc. Am. (Silver Anvil Mktg. award 1984). Office: Daniel J Edelman Inc 515 Olive St Saint Louis MO 63101

MURRAY, MELITA FRANCES, sales executive; b. Mt. Vernon, Tex., Sept. 9, 1931; d. Luther Henry J. and Nora Ethel (King) Johnson; 1 child, Lanora Reneé Rivers. Grad., Mt. Pleasant High Sch. With Stanley Home Products, Mt. Pleasant, Houston, Springfield, Mo., 1960—, div. mgr., 1960-67, area mgr., 1967-74, regional mgr., 1975-84; v.p. sales Stanley Home Products, Westfield, Mass., 1985—. Mem. Ch. of Christ. Home: 608 Raton Pass Irving TX 75063 Office: Stanley Home Products 333 Western Ave Westfield MA 01085

MURRAY, META RUTH, lawyer; b. Glens Falls, N.Y., Apr. 12, 1951; d. Russell Bernard and Marguerite Ruth (Merkel) M.; m. George B. Pfeiffer, Oct. 12, 1980; 1 dau., Meghan Ruth. B.A., St. Lawrence U., 1973; J.D., Albany Law Sch., 1977. Bar: N.Y., U.S. Dist. Ct. (no. dist.) N.Y. Adminstrv. asst. Ways and Means Com. N.Y. State Senate Assembly, Albany, 1973-75; legal intern N.Y. State Senate, Albany, 1976, N.Y. State Office of Ct. Adminstrn., Albany, 1977; sr. atty. N.Y. State Dept. Law, Albany, 1977-85, N.Y. State Dept. Environ. Conservation, Albany, 1986—. Mem. ABA, N.Y. State Bar Assn., Phi Alpha Theta. Republican. Jewish. Home: 25 Owen Ave Glens Falls NY 12801 Office: Environ Conservation 50 Wolf Rd Albany NY 12233-1500

MURRAY, MURIEL JOHNSON, state government official; b. Istanbul, Turkey, May 20, 1950; came to U.S., 1951; AB, Brown U., 1971; JD, George Washington U., 1976; MBA, U. Richmond, 1986. Bar: Va. 1976, U.S. Supreme Ct. 1980. Sole practice Falls Church, Va., 1978-81; lawyer, lobbyist Thomas & Sewell, Richmond, Va., 1978-79; legis. aide Ho. of Dels. Majority Leader Thomas W. Moss, Richmond, 1982; exec. dir. Va. State Edn. Assistance Authority, Richmond, 1982—; bd. dirs. Madison Research Assocs., Inc., Syria, Va., Electronic Cottage Industries, Inc., Richmond. Contbr. articles to profl. jours. Coordinator Northern Va. Chuck Robb for Lt. Gov., Falls Church, 1976-78; asst. legal counsel, counsel to compliance rev. commn., counsel to credentials com. Dem. Nat. Com., Washington, 1979-80. Named Va. Woman of Achievement in Govt. Va. Commn. on Status of Women, 1985. Mem. Va. Assn. Student Fin. Aid Adminstrs., Nat. Council Higher Edn. Loan Programs (chmn. lender relations 1983-84, sec. 1984-85), Beta Gamma Sigma. Office: State Edn Assistance Authority 6 N 6th St #300 Richmond VA 23219

MURRAY, PATRICIA ANN, periodontist; b. Cambridge, Mass., Oct. 6, 1949; d. William John Jr. and Edna Lucille (Maguire) M.; m. Joseph David Thornton, Aug. 29, 1970 (div. July 1974). BA magna cum laude, Boston Coll., 1971; DMD, U. Conn., 1979; PhD, SUNY, Buffalo, 1984. Tchr. Scarborough (Maine) High Sch., 1971-74; postdoctoral fellow SUNY, 1979-83, asst. prof. U. Calif., San Francisco, 1983—; dental cons. Letterman Hosp., San Francisco, 1983—; grad. program dir. U. Calif., San Francisco, 1984—; continuing edn. dir. U. Calif., San Francisco, 1986. Co-author: Anaerobic Bacteria, 1983; contbr. articles to sci. jours. NIH postdoctoral fellow, 1979-83; grantee 1985—; recipient Young Scientist award 1983-86, Research Career Devel. award, 1988-92. Fellow Am. Acad. Periodontology; mem. ADA, Internat. Assn. Dental Research, Am. Soc. Microbiologists. Roman Catholic. Home: 372 24th Ave San Francisco CA 94121 Office: U Calif HSW 661 Box 0650 San Francisco CA 94143

MURRAY, PATTI ANN, educator, microbiologist; b. Syracuse, N.Y., Nov. 5, 1956; d. Robert Dennis and Bette Ann (Symonds) M.; m. Mark Steinberger, July 20, 1985; 1 child, David Michael Steinberger. BS cum laude, LeMoyne Coll., 1978; PhD, Cornell U., 1985. Grad. teaching asst. Cornell U., Ithaca, N.Y., 1978-82, grad. research asst., 1982-84; postdoctoral research fellow Mich. State U., East Lansing, 1985-86; visiting asst. prof., biochemistry Rutgers U., Piscataway, N.J., 1986-87; microbiology research affiliate N.Y. State Dept. Health, Albany, 1987—. Contbr. articles to profl. jours. Recipient summer research fellow Cornell U., 1983, tuition and fees scholarship, 1978. Mem. AAAS, Am. Soc. for Microbiology. Democrat. Roman Catholic. Home: 29 Woodstead Rd Ballston Lake NY 12019 Office: Dept Environ Scis Wadsworth Ctr Labs Research Empire State Plaza Albany NY 12201

MURRAY, SUSAN CAROL, military services administrator; b. Washington, Dec. 20, 1957; d. Porter Dale and Mary Louise (Brown) M. Student, U. Md., 1976, 87—. Enlisted USAF, 1977, advanced through grades to tech. sgt., 1986; mgr. restaurant Seymour Johnson AFB, Goldsboro, N.C., 1978-80; mgr. Hickam AFB, Honolulu, 1980; dir. food and beverage Andrews AFB, Camp Springs, Md., 1980-81, personnel specialist, 1981-82, specialist air passengers, 1982-84, mgr. in-flight services, 1984—; exec. mgr. 101 Enterprises/Ponderosa Steaks, Reston, Va., 1982; cons. N.G. Bur., Washington, 1984—, Air N.G. Support Ctr. Andrews AFB, Camp Springs, 1985—, Colo. Air N.G., Denver, 1986. Inventor aircraft engine cover, 1978. Coach Andrews Little League Soccer, Camp Springs, 1983; active Combined Fed. Campaign, Camp Springs, 1984-86. Mem. Nat. Assn. Female Execs. Democrat. Office: USAF Detachment One Hdqrs DCAir NG Bldg 1233 Andrews AFB MD 20331-6519

MURREL, KATHLEEN RICE, computer services company executive; b. Ann Arbor, Mich., Mar. 4, 1953; d. Thomas Russell and Thelma Joyce (Mullreed) Rice; m. Richard Lee Murrel, Sept. 18, 1982. A.B.A., Cleary Coll., Ypsilanti, Mich., 1973, A.B.A. in Data Processing, 1983; B.B.A. in Data Processing, 1986. Sec., Midwest Microwave, Ann Arbor, 1973-75; office asst. Kurkjian-Samborn, Ann Arbor, 1975-76; legal asst. Dever Profl., Ann Arbor, 1977-78; computer installation expeditor Mfg. Data Systems, Ann Arbor, 1979-83; mgr. office adminstrn. Anvil Corp., Ann Arbor, 1984—; owner, pres. Murrel's Word Processing Services, Ann Arbor, 1976—. Mem. Nat. Assn. Female Execs. Avocations: reading; sports, gardening. Home: PO Box 220 Dexter MI 48130-0220 Office: Anvil Corp PO Box 1088 Ann Arbor MI 48106

MURRILLO, KATHLEEN MARIE, construction company official; b. Elizabeth, N.J., Mar. 21, 1956; d. Gerald Anthony and Beverly Ann (Dearstyne) M. Grad. high sch., Middlesex, N.J. Helper Dumar, Inc., Bound Brook, N.J., 1979-80; journeyman roofer Dumar, Inc., Bound Brook, 1980-81, formeman, 1981-83, supr., 1983-84, project coordinator, 1984-87; project coordinator Dumar Constrn. Service, Middlesex, 1987—. Home: 1511-B W Camplain Rd Manville NJ 08835 Office: Dumar Constrn Services 5 Ivanhoe St Bridgewater NJ 08807

MURRY, DONNA ELAINE, educational therapist; b. San Angelo, Tex., Jan. 22, 1939; d. Kenneth Van and Frances Elizabeth (Reed) Ausmus; m. Rudolph Henry Zacharias, July 4, 1965 (div. 1968); 1 child, Rudolph Kenneth; m. Peter Randle Murry, May 30, 1970; 1 child, Peter Eric. BS, East Tex. U., 1961; cert. spl. edn., Baylor U., 1965; MS in Rehabilitation Services, Am. Tech. U., Killeen, Tex., 1980. Tchr. Waco (Tex.) Ind. Sch. Dist., 1961-64; ednl. specialist Mexia (Tex.) State Sch., 1981-82; ednl. therapist Waco Ctr. for Youth, 1982—; exec. dir. Transition House, Inc., 1988—. Mem. LWV, Tex. State Tchrs. Assn., Alpha Lambda. Democrat. Roman Catholic. Home: 1810 A Azalea Dr Temple TX 76502

MURTHA, GERILYNN QUATAMA, environmental specialist; b. New York, Aug. 25, 1956; d. James E. and Eileen V. (Riess) M. BS in Biology/Geology, SUNY, Purchase, 1978. Cert. safety executive. Mgr. quality assurance United Abrasives, Mt. Vernon, N.Y., 1977-78; environ. specialist Dames & Moore, Cranford, N.J., 1978-82; environ. specialist Storch Engrs., Florham Park, N.J., 1982-84, assoc., 1984-87, ptnr., 1987—, dir. environtl., 1986—. tchr., counselor Spl. Children Assn., N.Y., 1978. Mem. Nat. Water Well Assn., Hazardous Waste Control Research Inst., World Safety Execs. (cert.), N.J. Engring. Assn. (cons. 1986). Office: Storch Engrs 220 Ridgedale Ave Florham Park NJ 07932

MURTHA, JO ANN PATRICE, magazine account executive, sales representative; b. Bronx, N.Y., Sept. 6, 1963; d. Richard Joseph and Joan Ann (Looney) M. BS in Mktg., SUNY, Plattsburgh, 1985; student, Careers for Women Sch., 1986. Governess, household mgr. Coppotelli's Residence, Southampton, N.Y., 1983-84; resident asst. SUNY, Plattsburgh, 1984-85; jr. account exec. Ultra Mag., N.Y.C., 1985-86; sales rep. Citicorp, N.Y.C., Rockland, 1986-87; account exec. Am. Office Dealer, N.Y.C., 1987—. Counselor Crisis Ctr., Plattsburgh, 1983. Mem. Am. Mktg. Assn., Nat. Assn. Exec. Females, Omicron Delta Kappa. Democrat. Roman Catholic. Home: 12 Slater Dr Stony Point NY 10980 Office: Am Office Dealer 49 E 21st St New York NY 10010

MUSA, CONNIE JOY, insurance company executive; b. Greenville, S.C., Aug. 22, 1952; d. Ben Hill and Marjorie (Gwinn) Davis; m. Thomas John Musa, Aug. 24, 1974; 1 child, Michael Davis. Student in bus., Greenville Tech. Coll., 1971-72. Agent, mgr. Root Ins. Agy., East Haddam, Conn., 1977—. Mem. East Haddam Dem. Com., 1982—, bd. fin. Town of East Haddam, 1983—. Mem. Profl. Ins. Agents Assn. (mem. edn. com. Wethersfield, Conn. chpt. 1985—), East Haddam C. of C. (pres. 1983-84). Democrat. Baptist. Home: 276 Petticoat Ln East Haddam CT 06423 Office: Root Ins Agy Inc 30 Main St East Haddam CT 06423

MUSANTE, BARBARA CLAIRE, infosystems specialist; b. Des Moines, Oct. 4, 1945; d. John Winslow and Elizabeth Muldrow (McCool) Corrigan; m. Dennis John Musante, Oct. 24, 1970. BA, U. Calif., Santa Barbara, 1967; MBA, Golden Gate U., 1985. Programmer, analyst Lockheed Missles and Space Corp., Sunnyvale, Calif., 1967-70, United Vintners, San Francisco, 1970-71, Bank of Calif., San Francisco, 1971; sr. programmer, analyst Pacific Intermountain Express, Oakland, Calif., 1971-73; project mgr. Fairchild Camera and Instrument, Mountain View, Calif., 1973-74; dir. Mgmt. Info. Systems Pacific Stereo, Emeryville, Calif., 1974-86; dir. MIS Calny, Inc., San Mateo, Calif., 1986-87; pres. Infocus Solutions, Alamo, Calif., 1986—; v.p. systems engring. Comml. Solutions, San Francisco, 1987—; bd. dirs. Comml. Solutions, San Francisco, 1986—. Democrat. Episcopalian. Office: Comml Solutions 8 Coso Ave San Francisco CA 94110

MUSE, MARTHA TWITCHELL, foundation executive; b. Dallas, Sept. 1, 1926; d. John Blackburn Muse and Kathryn (Poole) Muse Burbank. B.A., Barnard Coll., 1948; M.A., Columbia U., 1955; D.H.L., Georgetown U., 1981. Exec. dir. Tinker Found., N.Y.C., 1965-68, pres., 1968—, chmn., 1975—; bd. dirs. Irving Bank Corp., Irving Trust Co., May Dept. Stores Co., N.Y. Stock Exchange. Bd. dirs. Am. Council Germany, Americas Found., Americas Soc. Inc., Internat. Univ. Found.; trustee emeritus Columbia U., N.Y.C.; vice chmn., bd. dirs. Spanish Inst.; bd. visitors Edmund A. Walsh Sch. Fgn. Service, Georgetown U., 1973—; adv. com. Center for Strategic and Internat. Studies, 1974—; bd. dirs. Am. Portuguese Soc.; mem. Wilson Council Woodrow Wilson Internat. Center for Scholars; mem. council Internat. Exec. Service Corps; mem. public policy com. Advt. Council. Decorated Assoc. Dame Order St. John of Jerusalem, Great Britain, Lazo de Dama de la Orden del Merito Civil (Spain), Comdr. Orden del Sol del Peru; recipient Alumni award for excellence Columbia U. Grad. Faculties, 1987. Mem. N.Y.C. Council Fgn. Relations, Huguenot Soc., Nat. Soc. Colonial Dames., N.Y. Sci. Policy Assn. Episcopalian. Clubs: Colony (N.Y.C.), Met (N.Y.C.), Internat. (Washington), Rockefeller Ctr. Luncheon. Home: 267 Westport Rd Wilton CT 06897 Office: Tinker Found Inc 55 E 59th St New York NY 10022

MUSE, PATRICIA ALICE, writer, educator; b. South Bend, Ind., Nov. 27, 1923; d. Walter L. and Enid (Cockerham) Ashdown; student Columbia U., 1946; B.A., Principia Coll., 1947; postgrad. Seminole Community Coll., 1977, U. Central Fla., 1978, 79, 80, 81, 82; m. Kenneth F. Muse, Dec. 2, 1950; children—Patience Eleanor, Walter Scott. Substitute tchr. public schs., Key West, Fla., also Brunswick, Ga., 1962-68; free lance writer, Casselberry, Fla., 1968—; novels: Sound of Rain, 1971, The Belle Claudine, 1971, paperback, 1973, Eight Candles Glowing, 1976; creative writing instr., Valencia Community Coll., 1974-75; instr. various writers confs. Community resource vol. Orange County (Fla.) Sch. Bd. (cert. of appreciation 1975, 76, 77); tutor Adult Literacy League, 1983—.

MUSE, VONCEIL FOWLER(MRS. BERT C. MUSE), school librarian, educator; b. Tyler, Tex., July 12, 1915; d. Dennis Cleveland and Elva Mary (Wallace) Fowler; m. Bert Cromwell Muse, Dec. 28, 1938 (dec. Jan. 1983). B.A., Tex. Coll., 1936; M.S.L.S., U. So. Calif., 1953; postgrad. NDEA seminars (grantee) Tex. Women's U., 1965. Cert. profl. all levels, Tex. Elem. tchr. Jasper (Tex.) Schs., 1936-37, Trinidad (Tex.) Schs., 1937-39; tchr.-librarian Stanton Rural High Sch., Whitehouse, Tex., 1940-46; co-owner, Tyler (Tex.) Tribune, 1946-49; tchr.-librarian Tyler Schs., 1949-52; sch. librarian Dallas Pub. Schs., 1952-78; past dir. Women's Southwest Fed. Credit Union, Dallas, 1975-80; yearbook chmn. Dallas Sch. Librarians, 1976; mem. social com. Dallas Ret. Tchrs., 1979. Founder, Glenview Neighbors Assn., Dallas, 1980; mem. Mental Health Assn. Dallas County, 1978, Community Connection, Dallas, 1983, South Central Dallas Civic Group, 1984; mem. Maria Morgan br. YWCA, Friends Vis. Nurses Assn. (charter Dallas chpt.), Mus. African Am. Life and Culture, Women's Ctr. of Dallas, Dallas Classroom Tchrs. (bldg. rep. 1969-78), Dallas Ret. Tchrs. Assn., Am. Assn. Ret. Persons (Red Bird chpt. bd. dirs. 1984-85), United Tchrs. Tex. State Tchrs. Assn. (life), NEA (life), Tex. Ret. Tchrs. Assn. (life), Tex. Library Assn., ALA, Tex. and Southwestern Cattle Raisers Assn., Mitchell County Hist. Commn., Tex. Coll. Nat. Alumni, (life), Tex. Coll. Alumni Assn. of Dallas, Alpha Kappa Alpha life). Democrat. Mem. Christian Methodist Episcopal Ch. Lodge: Court of Calanthe.

MUSGRAVE, CHERYL LYNN, insurance agent; b. Titusville, Pa., Nov. 26, 1963; d. Eleanor (Hall) M. A Bus. Adminstrn., Pa. State U., Erie, 1984. Sub agent Pfeffer Ins. Agy., Erie, Pa., 1984—; sales assoc. Kaufmann's, Erie, Pa., 1983—; gymnastic instr. Erie Gymnastic Ctr., Erie, Pa., 1985-87. Mem. Nat. Assoc. Ins. Women. Republican. Lodge: Order of the Eastern Star, ch.21. Home: 7790 East Lake Rd Erie PA 16511 Office: Pfeffer Ins Agy 518 Holland St Erie PA 16507

MUSGRAVE, THEA, composer, conductor; b. Edinburgh, Scotland; m. Peter Mark, 1971. Ed., Edinburgh U., Paris Conservatory; Mus.D. (hon.). Composer: opera A Christmas Carol (first performed Va. Opera Assn., 1979), Harriet, the Woman Called Moses (1st performed Va. Opera 1985); ballet Beauty and the Beast, 1969; The Phoenix and the Turtle and The Five Ages of Man for choir and orch, Triptych for tenor and orch; opera Mary Queen of Scots; clarinet, horn and viola concertos Night Music for chamber orch; chamber concertos 1, 2 and 3, other vocal, chamber and orchestral works. Address: care Theodore Presser Co Presser Pl Bryn Mawr PA 19010

MUSICK, MILDRED BERNICE, association executive; b. Harrison, Ark., Sept. 2, 1922; d. Wiley Homer and Eva Francis (Murphy) Slavens; m. John Melvin Musick, July 20, 1940; children: John Melvin Jr., Janet Bernice Watkins, Jack L. Student, Coll. Commerce, 1943-44. Nat. organizer, treas. Nat. Fedn. Grandmother Clubs Am. Inc., Chgo., 1978-80, sec., 1980-82, 2d v.p., 1982-84, 1st v.p., 1984-86, pres., 1986-88; treas. sixth dist. Gen. Fedn. Women's Club Am., Springfield, 1983-85; pres. Mo. Fedn. Women's Clubs, Springfield, 1986-88. Bd. dirs. Mo. Against Drugs; Dem. election judge City of Springfield, 1983-88. Baptist. Home: 2316 N Franklin Springfield MO 65803 Office: Nat Fedn Grandmothers Club Am 203 N Wabash Ave Suite 702 Chicago IL 60601

MUSOLINO-ALBER, ELLA MARIE, professional tennis executive; b. N.Y.C., Apr. 22, 1942; d. Frank and Eva Patricia (Yarusevich) Grassi; m. Ronald J. Musolino, Oct. 14, 1962 (div. 1978); 1 child, Dennis Alexander; m. Robert E. Alber, Jan. 31, 1988. Sec. U.S. AEC, N.Y.C., 1959-61; sales asst. De La Rue Banknote Co., N.Y.C., 1961-66; sales and service rep. U.S. Banknote Corp., N.Y.C., 1966-67; gen. mgr. N.Y. Apples Team Tennis, N.Y.C., 1976-78; pres., founder Sports Etcetera, Inc., N.Y.C., 1978—; tournament mgr. U.S. Open Tennis Championships, 1969-75; tournament dir. Avon Championships, Madison Sq. Garden, 1979-82, Va. Slims Championships, 1983—. Mem. Women's Profl. Tennis Assn. Republican. Roman Catholic. Office: Sports Etcetera Inc 4 Penn Plaza New York NY 10001

MUSSELMAN, KAREN WALKER, savings bank executive. d. Joseph L. and Betty J. (Riley) Walker; m. Roddy Wix Musselman, Sept. 5, 1981; 1 child, Hillary Elisabeth. AS in Bus., Palm Beach Jr. Coll., 1982; student, Barry U., 1986—. Lic. stock broker, life and health ins. agt. Retirement dept. mgr. Cateret Savs. Bank, Delray Beach, Fla., 1982-84; asst. v.p. fin. services Cateret Savs. Bank, Delray Beach, 1984—. Named one of Outstanding Young Women Am., 1983. Mem. Inst. Fin. Edn. (bd. dirs., v.p. 1986—), Soc. Savs. Officer (pres. 1986), Delray Beach C. of C. Republican. Lutheran. Office: Cateret Savs Bank 645 E Atlantic Ave Delray Beach FL 33444

MUSSER, DONNA JEAN, educator; b. Bell, Calif., July 8, 1938; d. Houston Howard and Mary Irene (Burkleo) Bailey; m. William Adolph Musser (dec. Jan. 8, 1987); children: Tamra Annette, Kimra Irene. BA, San Diego State U., 1961; postgrad., San Diego State U., Lansing Sch. for Blind and U. San Diego. Physical edn. tchr. Roosevelt Jr. High Sch., San Diego, 1961-64, spl. edn. tchr., 1964-69; physical edn. tchr. Pacific Beach Jr. High Sch., San Diego, 1972-77, ESL tchr., 1978-84; social studies tchr. Pacific Beach Jr. High Sch., Ray A. Kroc Mid. Sch., San Diego, 1984—. Mem. NEA, Calif. Tchrs. Assn., San Diego Tchrs. Assn. Democrat. Episcopalian. Office: Ray A Kroc Mid Sch 5050 Conrad San Diego CA 92109

MUSSER, ELLYN ZUNKER, physician; b. Chgo., July 25, 1937; d. Albert August and Fern Grace (Wiesbach) Zunker; m. Eugene H. Musser, June 1972 (div. Dec. 1978); 1 child, Kathy Ann. BS with honors, Loyola U., Chgo., 1958; student Med. Sch., U. Ill., Chgo., 1958-60; MD, U. Miami, 1962. Intern Grady Meml. Hosp., Atlanta, 1962-63, resident in pediatrics, 1963-65; practice medicine specializing in pediatrics Marietta, Ga., 1965—. Fellow Am. Acad. Pediatrics; mem. Med. Assn. Ga., Am. Med. Women's Assn. Home: 441 The North Chace Atlanta GA 30328 Office: Suite 303 2480 Windy Hill Rd Marietta GA 30067

MUSSMAN, CAROL LYNNE, lawyer; b. Salt Lake City, Oct. 6, 1957; d. S. Mark and Barbara (Rampton) Johnson; m. William E. Mussman III. AB, Bryn Mawr Coll., 1979; JD, Duke U., 1982. Bar: Tex. 1982, Calif. 1987. Assoc., Strasburger & Price, Dallas, 1982-86; assoc. Pettit & Martin, San Francisco, 1986—. Mem. ABA, State Bar Tex., State Bar Calif., Phi Delta Phi. Republican. Mormon. Author: Preparation of a Financing Statement to Perfect a Security Interest Under the U.C.C., 1986, The Secured Lender. Office: Pettit & Martin 101 California St San Francisco CA 94111

MUSSO, ANGELA, pharmacist; b. Elizabeth, N.J., Aug. 20, 1957; d. Giuseppe and Lucia (Corsentino) M. BS, Rutgers U., 1981; postgrad., Kean Coll., 1987. Registered pharmacist, N.J. Pharmacy technician Holmdel (N.J.) Village Pharmacy, 1977-78, Elmora Pharmacy, Elizabeth, 1978; pharmacy extern Clark (N.J.) Drugs, 1980, Schering Corp., Kenilworth, N.J., 1980, Alexian Bros. Hosp., Elizabeth, 1980; pharmacist Rahway (N.J.) Hosp., 1981—, speaker edn. dept., 1981—, mem. speakers bur. community relations dept., nutritional support com., 1985-87, asst. pharmacy adminstr., 1987—; relief pharmacist Horowitz Pharmacy, Elizabeth, 1981. Performer and asst. dir. various local plays, 1982-86. Mem. N.J. Assn. Hosp. Pharmacists, Am. Pharm. Assn. (political action com. 1981—), Pharmacists Against Drug Abuse (lectr. 1986—), Pi Alpha Alpha. Democrat. Roman Catholic. Club: Cranford Dramatic (set painting chmn. 1985-87). Home: 513 Maple Ave Linden NJ 07036 Office: Rahway Hosp 865 Stone St Rahway NJ 07065

MUSTO, MICHELE LYNN, medical personnel agency executive; b. Jamaica, N.Y., Dec. 24, 1954; d. Jack Davis and Charlene Mildred (Sparks) M. BS in Nursing, Keuka Coll., 1976; MS in Nursing, SUNY, Binghamton, 1981. Charge nurse Binghamton Gen. Hosp., 1976-81; asst. clin. supr. Dr.'s Hosp. of Prince George's County, Lanham, Md., 1981-84; mgr. Hosp. Temporaries, Inc., Washington, 1984-86; prin., pres. Med. Personnel Assocs., Hyattsville, Md., 1986—; med. equipment cons. Bradford Communications, Greenbelt, Md., 1984; mgmt. cons. Personal Touch Home Care, Towson, Md., 1986. Mem. Sigma Theta Tau. Republican. Office: Med Personnel Assocs Inc 7515 Annapolis Rd Suite 307 Hyattsville MD 20784

MUSTONE, AMELIA P., state legislator; b. Salem, Mass., July 16, 1928; d. Udo A. and Alberta (Durand) Poppey; m. John J. Mustone, 1950; children—John, Lisa, Mary Ellen, Anastasia, Jessica. B.A., Goddard Coll., Vt. Pres., Meriden Bd. Edn., Conn., 1974-78; mem. Conn. State Senate from 13th Dist., 1979—, dep. majority leader, 1987. Mem. Nat. Conf. State Legislators, Council on State Govts., Caucus New Eng. State Legislators, Conn. Women's Polit. Caucus, Conn. Student Loan Found.; mem. Martin Luther King Jr. Commn.; active YMCA. Recipient Citizen of Yr. award Civitan Club, 1978. Mem. AAUW, Meridan LWV, Latin Am. Soc. (hon.), NAACP. Roman Catholic. Lodge: Soroptimist Internat. Home: 34 Tunxis Circle Meriden CT 06450

MUTCHLER, JANE FRANCES, acct.; b. Janesville, Wis., Feb. 26, 1941; d. Frederick Gerald and Anne Marie (Healy) M.; B.A. in Edn., U. S. Fla., 1973, B.A. in Acctg., 1976, M.Acctg., 1977; Ph.D., U. Ill., 1983; children—Tami Jeanne, Susan Marie (Parr). Tchr., United Day Care Center, Tampa, Fla., 1971-73; instr. U. South Fla., Tampa, 1976-78; adminstrv. asst. intermediate acctg. program Arthur Andersen & Co., Champaign, Ill., summers 1979-81; grad. research asst., grad. teaching asst. U. Ill., Champaign, 1978-82; asst. prof. acctg. Ohio State U., fall 1983; mgmt. cons., 1977-82. Contbr. articles to Jours. Expert Systems and Acctg. Research and Auditing, Jour. Practice and Theory; mem. editorial bd. Auditing: a Jour. Practice and Theory, The Acctg. Review. Am. Soc. Women Accts. Margaret Keldie scholar, 1979-80; Am. Inst. C.P.A.s fellow, 1982; recipient Research Opportunities in Auditing award Peat Marwick, 1983, research fellow, 1986. C.P.A., Fla. Mem. Am. Acctg. Assn., Fla. Inst. C.P.A.s. Office: Ohio State U Faculty Acctg 1775 College Rd 408 Hagerty Hall Columbus OH 43210

MUTISYA, BRENDA [illegible], [illegible] adminstrator; b. Durham, N.C., Nov. 17, 1958; d. Gene Berkley and Frances Mac ([illegible]) [illegible] Commonwealth U., 1976-78; B.S., Hampton Inst., 1982; MS in Nursing, 1987. R.N., N.C., Va. nurse asst. VA, Hampton, 1978-79; profl. nurses asst. Duke U. Hosp., Durham, N.C., 1980-81; ICU nurse Whittaker Meml. Hosp., Newport News, Va., 1982; adminstrv. supr. Hillcrest Convalescent, Durham, 1983; nursing supr. Hillhaven LaSalle, Durham, 1984; nurse Duke U. Hosp., Durham, 1982—; assoc. dir. nursing HH Corp., 1987. Hampton U. scholar, 1985-86. Mem. Nat. League Nursing. (com. chmn.), Am. Nurses Assn. (del. conv. 1984), Nat. Black Nurses Assn., Am. Heart Assn., N.C. Nurses Assn., Chi Eta Phi. Democrat. Baptist.

MUTO, SUSAN ANNETTE, religious educator, academic administrator; b. Pitts., Dec. 11, 1942; d. Frank and Helen (Scardamulia) M. BA in Journalism and English, Duquesne U., 1964; MA, U. Pitts., 1967, PhD in English Lit., 1970. Asst. dir. Inst. of Formative Spirituality, Duquesne U., Pitts., 1965-80, dir., 1980—, faculty coordinator grad. programs in foundational formation, 1979—, prof., 1981—; guest lectr. formative reading various colls. and community orgns., 1970—. Author: (with Adrian van Kaam) The Emergent Self, 1968, (with Adrian van Kaam) The Participant Self, 1969, Approaching the Sacred: An Introduction to Spiritual Reading, 1973, Steps Along the Way, 1975, A Practical Guide to Spiritual Reading, 1976, The Journey Homeward: On the Road of Spiritual Reading, 1977, Tell Me Who I Am, 1977, Celebrating the Single Life, 1982, Blessings That Make Us Be, 1982, Pathways of Spiritual Living, 1984, Mediation in Motion, 1986; contbr. articles to religious and secular publs. Mem. Edith Stein Guild, Epiphany Assn., Phi Kappa Phi. Home: 2223 Wenzell Ave Pittsburgh PA 15216 Office: Duquesne Univ Inst of Formative Spirituality Pittsburgh PA 15282

MUZZY, DIANA LEE, bicycle clothing manufacturing company executive; b. Hanover, Pa., Oct. 28, 1949; d. Leo Esiah and Alice Wilkinson (Rudolph) M. B.S., U. Calif.-Berkeley, 1972. Lic. animal health technician, Calif. Asst., Orinda Vet. Clinic, Calif., 1971-74; animal health technician Wilson Animal Hosp., Concord, Calif., 1974-78; co-owner, co-operator Vigorelli, Oakland, 1979—. Cons. Battered Women's Alternatives, Concord, Calif., 1981-84. Mem. Women's Sports Found. Democrat. Avocation: running. Office: Vigorelli 2200 Adeline St Suite 250 Oakland CA 94607

MYATT, SUE HENSHAW, gerontological activity therapy consultant; b. Little Rock, Aug. 16, 1956; d. Bobby Eugene and Janett Lanell (Ahart) Henshaw; m. Tommy Wayne Myatt. BS in Psychology, Old Dominion U., 1978, MS in Ednl. Counseling, 1982. Cert. activity dir., cons. Nat. Cert. Council of Activity Dirs. and Cons. Dir. activity Manning Convalescent, Portsmouth, Va., 1983-84, Camelot Hall, Norfolk, Va., 1984-86; coordinator activity Beverly Manor, Portsmouth, 1986—. Mem. Nat. Assn. Activity Profl. (cert., legis. com.), Va. Assn Activity Profl. (v.p. 1986-87, creator logo), Va. Recreation and Park Soc. (sr. sect.), Hampton Roads Activity Profls. Assn. (sec. 1985-86, pres. 1986-87, v.p. 1987—). Home: 705 Gladesdale Dr Chesapeake VA 23322

MYERS, CAROLE ANN, health transportation service executive; b. Henderson, Ky., June 14, 1938; d. James Newton and Rosalene Alberta (Eakins) Wade; m. Lawrence William Myers, Dec. 28, 1957 (dec. Feb. 1980); children: Patti Myers Crisler, Nancy Myers Allen, Sandra Myers Kowalski, Mark William. Cert., St. Francis Hosp., 1971; student, Butler U., 1979. Cert. emergency med. tech., paramedic. Pres., chief exec. officer Myers Ambulance Service, Greenwood, Ind., 1966—. Bd. dirs. Greenwood Sr. Citizens Ctr.; mem. Rep. Sen. Inner Circle, Washington, 1984. Named Disting. Hoosier by Gov. of Ind., 1984. Mem. Ind. Ambulance Assn. (pres. 1983-85, treas. 1986—), Ind. Emergency Med. Services Commn., Am. Ambulance Assn. (sec. 1983-84, treas. 1985-86, v.p. 1987—, pres.-elect, woman of yr. 1983), Greater Greenwood C. of C. (sec. exec. bd.). Home: 150 N Madison Ave Greenwood IN 46142 Office: Myers Ambulance Service Inc 325 W Wiley St Greenwood IN 46142

MYERS, CONNIE LYCANS, laboratory administrator, educator; b. Huntington, W.Va., May 18, 1950; d. Billy and Loretta Bea (Bentley) Lycans; B.S., Marshall U., 1972; MS, Coll. of St. Francis, 1988; cert. Cabell Huntington Hosp. Sch. Med. Tech., 1972; m. Terry Lee Myers, June 15, 1971; 1 dau., Leigh Lycans. Med. technologist St. Mary's Hosp., Huntington, 1972, supr. microbiology, 1974-79; dept. supr. Halifax Med. Center, Daytona Beach, Fla., 1973-74; clin. instr. Marshall U., Huntington, 1975-79; clin. lab. supr./edn. coordinator Sch. Med. Tech., Decatur (Ill.) Meml. Hosp., 1979-81, lab. mgr., program dir., 1981—; clin. instr. Western Ill. U., Macomb, 1980—, Eastern Ill. U., Charleston, 1980—, Millikin U., Decatur, 1980—, Ill. State U., Normal, 1980—. Chmn., Decatur Meml. Hosp. Red Cross Blood Drive, 1979-80; solicitor United Way, 1979-87, Am. Cancer Soc., 1982-83; v.p., bd. dirs. March Dimes, 1987-88. Mem. Am. Soc. Clin. Pathologists, Accreditation and Inspection Team, Vol. Hosp. Am., Inc. (chmn. Ill. Lab. com. 1987-88), Midwest Assn. Edn. Resource Sharing in Clin. Med. Tech., Clin. Lab. Mgmt. Assn. Home: 1375 W Sunset St Decatur IL 62522 Office: 2300 N Edward St Decatur IL 62526

MYERS, DORIS JORDAN, nurse; b. Hunstville, Ala., Sept. 7, 1931; d. Alex and Ola (Milliner) Jordan; m. Arvine H. Myers Jr.; children: Arvine III, Russell, Eric, Michael, Amy. BS in Health Care Adminstrn., St. Joseph's Coll., 1984; diploma, Birmingham Bapt. Hosp. Sch. Nursing, 1952. Staff nurse Birmingham (Ala.) Bapt. Hosp., 1952; staff nurse Massillon Community Hosp., 1954-56, pvt. duty nurse, 1959-63, charge nurse, 1963-78, mem. procedure com. sch. nursing, 1973-83, head nurse mgr., 1978-83; dir. nursing service Joel Pomerene Meml. Hosp., Millersburg, Ohio, 1983-85; asst. instr. Massillon (Ohio) State Hosp., 1953-54, staff and charge nurse, 1957-59, staff nurse, 1985—. Den mother Boy Scouts Am., Massillon, 1967; mem. gymnastics com. YMCA, Massillon, 1970-76, Choir Parents Washington High Sch., Massillon, 1974-79; pres. Faith Lutheran Ch. Women, Massillon, 1971-77. Mem. Am. Hosp. Assn., Am. Nurses Assn. Democrat. Lutheran. Home: 1041 Bennington Ave NE Massillon OH 44646 Office: Massillon State Hosp PO Box 540 Massillon OH 44046-0048

MYERS, GERRY LYNN, public relations, marketing and advertising consulting firm executive; b. Dallas, July 23, 1943; d. Saul H. and Helen Frances (Hafter) Golden; children: Richard Scott, Deborah Ruth, Kenneth Andrew. BS cum laude, U. Tex., 1964; MBA, North Tex. State U., 1980. Account supr. Dykeman & Assocs., Dallas, 1978-81; account exec. Teich Communications Co., Dallas, 1981; exec. v.p., ptnr. Shiroma & Myers, Inc., Dallas, 1981-87, pres., owner, The Myers Group, 1987—. Mem. Pub. Relations Soc. Am., Addison Bus. Assn., Metrocrest C. of C. Republican. Jewish. Lodge: B'nai Brith Women (past pres. Starlight chpt., Best Communications award 1972). Home: 6812 St Anne St Dallas TX 75248 Office: The Myers Group 16950 Dallas Pkwy Suite 100 Dallas TX 75248

MYERS, HELEN DEE, small business owner; b. Denver. Student in med. tech., U. Colo., 1953-55. Cert. meeting profl. Owner Preferred Sales, Inc., Las Vegas, Nev., 1962-81, Creative Convs., Las Vegas, Nev., 1978—. Author, publisher: (book) The Business of Seminars, 1982. Coordinator Mary Gojack for Congress, Nev., 1982, Elect Bob Miller, Las Vegas, 1986; chmn. Women Bus. Owners Polit. Action Com., 1987-88. Mem. Nat. Assn. Women Bus. Owners (sec. 1985-86, bd. dirs. 1983-85), Nat. Speakers Assn., Meeting Planners Internat. Democrat. Home: 2304 Windjammer Way Las Vegas NV 89107 Office: Creative Conventions 218 W Wyoming Las Vegas NV 89102

MYERS, HELEN LORETTA, property manager; b. Hammond, Ind., Sept. 22, 1934; d. Leslie Gilbert and Bessie Vickers (Pollard) Coapstick; m. Ivan Oteen Myers, Dec. 2, 1961 (dec. 1978). Student, St. Joseph's Coll., East Chicago, Ind., 1957-59. Sec., State Farm Ins., Griffith, Ind., 1969; owner, operator Myers' Restaurant, Hartford, Ky., 1969-77, Highland Body Shop, Ind., 1977-84; supr. Kelly Services, Merrillville, Ind., 1984-86, resident br. mgr., Chgo., 1985-87; property mgr. Cypress Trace Shipping Ctr., Ft. Myers, Fla., 1987—; mem. adv. com. Daley Coll., Chgo.; mem. Hyde Park C. of C., Automotive Service Councils (sec.-treas. 1977-86). Republican. Club: Scherwood Golf (Schererville, Ind.). Lodge: Eastern Star (matron 1967-68, state appts., Grand rep. to Ala. 1974-78). Avocations: golf, reading, hand crafts, walking, bicycling. also: 14662 Triple Eagle Ct Fort Myers FL 33912 Office: Kelly Services 7601 S Kostner Chicago IL 60652

MYERS, KATHERINE BELL, health facility administrator; b. Tampa, Fla., Sept. 25, 1952; d. Lewis Albert and Elizabeth Virginia (Richards) Bell; m. John Karl Myers, [illegible] 1981. Cert. records technician, Am. Med. Record Assn., Chgo., 1974. Med. transcriptionist [illegible] Gen. Hosp., 1972-75, specialist quality assurance, 1975-82; supr. med. records Lakeland Regional Med. Ctr., 1982-85, asst. dir. med. records, 1985-87, dir. med. records, 1987—. Mem. Am. Med. Record Assn., Gulf Coast Med. Record Assn., Fla. Med. Record Assn. (by-laws com. 1981, alt. del. 1988, editor jour. 1985, del. adv. 1988). Home: 4607 N Strauss Rd Plant City FL 33566 Office: Lakeland Regional Med Ctr Med Record Dept PO Box 95448 Lakeland FL 33804

MYERS, KATHY J., accountant; b. Anderson, Ind., Nov. 28, 1958; d. Jack K. and Edna B. Myers. BS, Butler U., 1980; MBA, Ball State U., 1984, BS in Acctng., 1987. Acct. St. John's Med. Ctr., Anderson, 1980-86, cost acct., 1986-88, mgr. cost and reimbursement, 1988—. Home: [illegible] E 8th St Anderson IN 46012

MYERS, LAVONA MAY, social services administator; b. Huntington, Ind., Apr. 3, 1925; d. Von Everett and Ethel L. (Trout) Jackson; m. Clarence F. Myers, Apr. 19, 1947; children: Coleen J., Mavis B., Eric K., Lloyd G. Grad. high sch., Huntington County, Ind. Exec. asst. ARC, Huntington, 1973-75; exec. dir. Huntington County Council on Aging, 1975—. Bd. dirs. Roanoke Bible Sch., Jackson Twp., Ind., 1956-66, Roanoke Red Cross Bloodmobile, Jackson Twp., 1965-75; leader Limberlost Girl Scouts U.S., Jackson Twp., 1954-65, Jackson Twp. 4-H Club, Huntington County, 1965-75. Mem. Ind. Sr. Cits. Drs. (bd. dirs.), Assn. for Homes (sec. 1976—). Methodist. Club: Altrusa (leader). Home: 3048 E 900 North Roanoke IN 46783 Office: Huntington County Council on Aging 208 W State PO Box 86 Huntington IN 46750

MYERS, LINDA BERNICE JAMES, psychologist, educator; b. Hugoton, Kans., Nov. 4, 1948; d. Harold Franklin and Fay Elnora (Brown) James; m. Roger Weldon Myers, Aug. 4, 1950; children: Ikenna, Ptah. BS in Edn. in Psychology and Spl. Edn., Emporia State U., 1970, MS in Sch. Psychology, 1971; PhD in Clin. Psychology, Ohio State U., 1975. Licensed psychology. Asst. prof. dept. Black studies Ohio State U., Columbus, 1974-80, assoc. prof. dept. Black studies, psychology, psychiatry., 1980—. Author: Understanding an Afrocentric World View: Introduction to an Optimal Psychology, 1988; contbr. articles to jours. Bd. dirs. Choices for Victims of Domestic Violence, Columbus, Ohio, 1985—, CompDrug, 1986. Recipient Outstanding Service award Ohio State U. Black Graduate Student Orgn., 1986. Mem. Cen. Ohio Assn. Black Psychologists (pres., founder 1976—), Nat. Assn. Black Psychologists (sec. 1985-86), Am. Psychol. Assn., Am. Assn. U. Profs. Office: Ohio State Univ 486 UH 230 N Oval Mall Columbus OH 43210

MYERS, MARGARET SHAFFER, insurance broker; b. McAllen, Tex., Sept. 10, 1936; d. Leigh Wesley and Adah Martha (Moss) S.; m. James Wareham, June 8, 1957; children: Melonye Elaine, Jamie Sue. Student, U. Tex., 1954-57; BS, West Tex. State U., 1976. Owner, prin. Adventure Land Sch., Amarillo, Tex., 1964-78; owner, mgr. The Red Caboose Toy Store, Amarillo, 1978-80; ins. agt. Fidelity Union Life, Austin, Tex., 1981-84; ins. broker Tex. Assoc. Agy., Austin, 1985—. Pres. Austin Edn. Young Children, Amarillo, 1974-75, Wellington Sq. Mchts. Assn., Amarillo, 1979-80; docent U. Tex. Art Mus., Austin, 1981-83. Mem. Women Life Underwriters Assn. (pres. 1983-84), Austin Assn. Life Underwriters, Austin Assn. Health Underwriters, Nat. Assn. Female Execs. (chairperson 1988), Nat. Assn. Profl. Saleswomen (sec. 1987-88). Episcopalian. Home: 7402 Chelsea Moor Austin TX 78759 Office: Tex Assoc Agy Ins Inc 901 Mopac Expressway S Barton Oaks Plaza Two Suite 400 Austin TX 78746

MYERS, MARIAN KATHRYN, pediatrician, educator; b. Fulton, N.Y., July 30, 1940; d. Michael and Mary (Frank) Solowy; m. Terry Lewis Myers, June 26, 1971; children: Wesley, Terry. BS, U. Fla., 1962, MD, 1966. Intern, then resident in pediatrics Upstate Med. Ctr., Syracuse, N.Y., 1966-68; resident in pediatrics U. Va., Charlottesville, 1968-69, fellow, 1969-71; instr. pediatrics U. Va., Charlottesville, Va., 1969-71, asst prof. pediatrics, 1971-73; assoc. prof. pediatrics Creighton U., Omaha, 1973-78; assoc. prof. pediatrics, Ob-Gyn East Tenn. State U., Johnson City, 1978-87, prof. pediatrics, 1987—; dir. div. of Neonatology East Tenn. State U., Johnson City, 1978—. Mem. Phi Beta Kappa. Office: East Tenn State U Coll Medicine Pediatrics Dept Johnson City TN 37614

MYERS, MYRA SUE, scientist; b. Oberlin, Ohio, May 1, 1947; d. Ralph Leroy and Betty Jean (Garrett) M. AA, Lorain (Ohio) County Community Coll., 1967; BS in Med. Tech., Ohio State U., 1969; MS in Mgmt. and Supervision, Cen. Mich. U., 1981. Sr. technician chemistry lab. Ohio State Univ. Hosps., Columbus, 1970-75; evening supr. lab. Mansfield (Ohio) Gen. Hosp., 1975-82; from lab. coordinator to lab. computer coordinator Our Lady of the Lake Regional Med. Ctr., Baton Rouge, 1982—. Mem. Christian personhood com. United Meth. Women, 1984-86; bd. dirs. Jefferon United Meth. Ch., mem. adminstrv. bd., 1988. Mem. Am. Soc. for Med. Tech. (Omicron Sigma award 1987), La. State Soc. for Med. Tech. (student advisor 1984-85, chair student bowl com. 1985-86, 87, 88, bd. dirs. 1985—), LWV (bd. dirs. Baton Rouge chpt. 1983-86, sec. 1986—, state sec. 1987—), Common Cause (state sec. 1983—), Nat. Assn. Parliamentarians (registered). Home: 7344 Meadowview Baton Rouge LA 70810 Office: Our Lady of the Lake Regional Med Ctr 5000 Hennessy Blvd Baton Rouge LA 70809

MYERS, PATRICIA LYNN, accountant; b. Oklahoma City, Nov. 21, 1950; d. George and Julia Dorothy (Thompson) Morgan; m. Larry Wayne Myers, July 17, 1981. BBA in Acctg., Tex. Tech. U., 1972. CPA, Tex. Sr. staff tax analyst Tenneco, Inc., Houston, 1973—. Mem. Am. Inst. CPA, Tex. Soc. CPA, Houston Payroll Tax Assn. (chmn. 1985-86). Republican. Presbyterian. Home: 9555 Pagewood Houston TX 77063 Office: Tenneco Inc 1010 Milan Houston TX 77252

MYERSON, ELEANOR, state representative; b. Winthrop, Mass., May 9, 1922; d. Jacob B. and Rebecca Lillian (Cohen) Applebaum; m. Morton Myerson, Dec. 3, 1942; children—Joseph, Ann. B.A. magna cum laude, Smith Coll., 1943. Selectman Town of Brookline, Mass., 1970-82; mem. Mass. Ho. of Reps., 1983—. State sec. Americans for Democratic Action, Boston, 1969; bd. dirs. Mass. Assn. for Blind, Brookline, 1984—, Brookline Com. on the Arts, 1984—. Democrat. Office: State House Boston MA 02133

MYHRE, JANET KLIPPEN, mathematician; b. Tacoma, Sept. 24, 1932; d. Leif Christian Klippen and Thelma (Fenney) Dickenson; 1 child, Karin. BA, Pacific Luth. U., 1954; MA, U. Wash., 1956; PhD, Inst. Math. Stats. U. Stockholm, Sweden, 1968. Research engr. Boeing Math. Services Unit and Sci. Research Labs., 1956-58; stats. cons. U. Stockholm, 1958-60; instr. math. Harvey Mudd Coll., Claremont, Calif., 1961-62; prof. math. Claremont (Calif.) McKenna Coll., 1962—; mem. math. grad. faculty Claremont Grad. Sch., 1968—; assoc. editor Technometrics, Claremont, 1969-75; vis. prof. U. Stockholm, Eidgenossiche Technische, Zurich, Switzerland, 1971-72; pres. Math. Analysis Research Corp., 1973—; bd. dirs. Inst. Decision Sci. Claremont McKenna Coll., 1975—; editorial bd. Quality Mag., 1981—. Contbr. numerous articles to profl. jours. Recipient Austin Bonis award Am. Soc. for Quality Control, 1984. Me. Inst. Math. Stats., Statis. Assn. of Am., Am. Assn. Quality Control, Phi Beta Kappa, Sigma Xi. Office: Math Analysis Research Corp 4239 Via Padova Claremont CA 91711

MYLES, ANN ETHEL, agricultural credit company executive; b. Pennsauken, N.J., July 30, 1927; d. William Joseph and Ethel (Schaffer) M. Student St. Elizabeth's Coll., Convent Station, N.J., Acad. Advanced Traffic, Phila., St. Joseph's Coll. Indsl. Relations, Phila. Asst. mgr. Farm Credit Service of Moorestown (N.J.), 1963-72, mgr., aquatic loan officer, 1972-76, gen. mgr., 1976-81; pres., chief exec. officer Fed. Land Bank Assn. Moorestown, 1981—, Farmers Prodn. Credit Assn. Moorestown, 1981—, T/A Farm Credit Service Moorestown, 1981—. mem. Food Industry Adv. Com.; bd. dirs. Pineland Devel. Credit Bank. Bd. dirs. United Way of Burlington County. Mem. N.J. Agrl. Soc. Club: Moorestown Field. Office: Farm Credit Service Main St PO Box 226 Rancocas NJ 08073

MYRDAL, ROSEMARIE CARYLE, legislator; b. Minot, N.D., May 20, 1929; d. Harry Dirk and Olga Jean (Dragge) Lohse; m. B. John Myrdal, June 21, 1952; children: Jan, Mark, Harold, Paul, Amy. BS, N.D. State U., 1951. Registered profl. first grade tchr., N.D. Tchr. various sch. dists., Park River, Gardar and Edinburg, N.D., 1951-71; bus. mgr. Edinburg Sch. Dist., 1974-81; mem. N.D. Legislature, 1985—; sch. evaluator Walsh County Sch. Bds. Assn., Grafton, N.D., 1983-84; evaluator, work presenter N.D. Sch. Bds. Assn., Bismarck, N.D., 1983-84; sch. bd. dirs. Edinburg Sch. Dist., 1981-87. Co-editor: Heritage '76, 1976. Precint committee Rep. Party, Gardar Twp, 1980-86; leader Hummingbirds 4-H Club, Edinburg, 1980-83; bd. dirs. Camp Souix Diabetic Children, Grand Forks, N.D., 1980-86. Mem. AAUW (pres. 1982-84 Pembina County area), Pembina County Hist. Soc. (historian 1976-84), Northeastern N.D. Heritage Assn. (pres. 1986-87), Red River Valley Heritage Assn. (bd. dirs. 1985—). Lutheran. Club: Agassiz Garden (Park River) (pres. 1968-69). Home: Rt 1 Box 151 Edinburg ND 58227

MYRICK, DEBORAH DIANE, telecommunications systems engineer; b. Ogdensburg, N.Y., Jan. 4, 1951; d. Harold LeRoy Myrick and Alecia Ethel (Chase) Hartt. BA, U. Conn., 1973; cert., Paralegal Inst., 1973; postgrad., Northeastern U. Communications rep. ITT Communications Systems, Boston, 1976-80; sales engr. GTE Bus. Communications Systems, Needham, Mass., 1980-81; product mgr. Wang Labs, Inc., Lowell, Mass., 1981-84; sr. sales engr. SONECOR Systems, Burlington, Mass., 1984-86; mgr. installation and deployment Project Athena, MIT, Cambridge, 1986—. Chmn. Dem. Election Primary Com., Pelham, N.H., 1984; mem. Town Cable Com., Pelham, 1983. Mem. Inst. Celtic Studies. Democrat. Roman Catholic. Club: Irish Unity Conf. (Boston). Avocations: reading, needlecrafts, gardening. Home: 4 Woodlawn Dr Pelham NH 03076 Office: MIT 77 Massachusetts Ave Cambridge MA 02139

MYRICK, SANDRA DEPRIEST, data processing executive; b. Eden, N.C., Sept. 27, 1957; d. Jerry Todd and Helen May (Tapp) DePriest; m. Larry Keith Myrick, Aug. 2, 1975; children: Melody Anne, Bradley Keith. AS in Computer Sci. with honors, Bluefield (W.Va.) State Coll., 1978. Programmer S.W. Va. Nat. Bank, Bluefield, 1979-81, Princeton (W.Va.) Bank and Trust, 1981-82, Sutphin & Son Oil Co., Bluefield, 1982-83; programmer 1st Community BancShares, Inc., Princeton, 1983-86, sr. programmer, 1987—; programmer, developer Jack Henry & Assocs., Monett, Mo., 1986. Democrat. Baptist. Lodge: Order of Eastern Star (conductress Bluefield chpt. 1985). Home: PO Box 70 Bland VA 24315-0070 Office: 1st Community BancShares Inc 1001 Mercer St Princeton WV 24740

MYRICK, SUELLEN, advertising agency executive; b. Tiffin, Ohio, Aug. 1, 1941; d. William Henry and Margaret Ellen (Roby) Wilkins; m. Wilbur Edward Myrick Jr., Sept. 11, 1977; children: Mia, Greg, Miesa, Alex, Dan. Student, Heidelberg Coll., 1959-60. Exec. sec. to mayor and city mgr. City of Alliance, Ohio, 1962-63; dir. br. office Stark County Ct. of Juvenile and Domestic Relations, Alliance, 1963-65; pres. Myrick Agy., Charlotte, N.C., 1971—; v.p. Saxby's of Va., Inc., Charlotte, 1981—; mayor of Charlotte, 1987—. advt. and pub. relations account exec. Charlotte Transit System; mem. adv. bd. U.S. Small Bus. Adminstrn. Active Heart Fund, Multiple Sclerosis, March of Dimes, PTA, Sch. Boosters Clubs, Arts and Scis. Council Fund Dr.; mem. adv. bd. Children's Theatre, Charlotte, 1981-84, Substance Abuse Council of Mental Health Authority, Charlotte, Uptown Shelter, Share a Home, Hezekiah Alexander House; mem. Friendship Force of Charlotte, Vocat. Edn. Adv. Council, Charlotte/Mecklenburg Citizen's Forum, Transit Mall Citizen's Adv. Com., Uptown Homeless Task Force, Safe Drive Com.; bd. dirs. N.C. Inst. Politics; founder, coordinator Charlotte vol. tornado relief effort; bd. dirs. Handicapped Organized Women; mem.-at-large Charlotte City Council, 1983-85; mayor City of Charlotte, 1987—; pub. relations chairperson Mecklenburg Rep. Exec. Task Force; trustee, Sunday sch. tchr. 1st United Meth. Ch.; treas. Mecklenburg Ministries; mayor City of Charlotte, 1987—. Recipient Woman of Yr. award Harrisonburg, Va., 1968; named one of Outstanding Young Woman of Am., 1968. Mem. LWV, Women's Polit. Caucus, Nat. Assn. Women Execs., Charlotte C. of C. (chair small bus. action council), Jaycettes, Beta Sigma Phi. Republican. Club: Tower. Lodge: Elks Aux. Home: 310 W 8th St Charlotte NC 28202 Office: 505 N Poplar St Charlotte NC 28202

NACHMAN, FRAN GAIL, industrial cleaning company executive; b. Phila., Feb. 17, 1951; d. Harold and Rose (Gold) N. BA in Theater, Pa. State U., 1972; MBA, Temple U., 1982. Gen. mgr. Film Makers Phila. Inc., 1972-79; v.p. AAA Indsl. Cleaning Services, Inc., Abington, 1979—, T/A Airways Cleaning and Fireproofing, Abington, 1979—. Mem. NOW, Soc. Am. Baseball Research, Nat. Assn. Female Execs. Home: 773 N 27th St Philadelphia PA 19130 Office: Airways Cleaning & Fireproofing 1646 Old York Rd Abington PA 19001

NACOL, MAE, lawyer; b. Port Arthur, Tex., June 15, 1944; d. William Samuel and Ethel (Bowman) N.; children—Shawn Alexander Nacol, Catherine Regina Nacol. B.S., Rice U., 1965; student, So. Tex. Coll. Law. Bar: Tex. 1969, U.S. Dist. Ct. (so. dist.) Tex. 1969. Diamond buyer/appraiser Nacol's Jewelry, Houston, 1961—; sole practice, Houston, 1969—. Chmn. bd., nat. dir. A.R.M.S. of Am. Ltd., Houston, 1984-85. Recipient Mayor's Recognition award City of Houston, 1972; Ford Found. fellow So. Tex. Coll. Law, Houston, 1965. Mem. Houston Bar Assn. (chmn. candidate com. 1970, chmn. membership com. 1971, chmn. lawyers referral com. 1972), Tex. Trial Lawyers Assn., Nat. Assn. Women Lawyers, Am. Judicature Soc. Presbyterian. Office: Nacol & Assoc 500 Jefferson #1915 Houston TX 77002-7334

NADEL, BARBARA ANNE, architect; b. N.Y.C., June 13, 1953; d. George and Ruth Lillian (Friedman) N. Student, Cornell U., 1973, Hofstra U., 1974; BA in Pre-Architecture, SUNY, Binghamton, 1975; BFA, R.I. Sch. Design, 1977, BArch, 1978; Cert. in Mgmt., U. R.I., 1979. Lic. architect, N.Y. Architect VA Med. Ctr., Providence, 1978, Keyes Assocs., Architects and Engrs., Providence, 1978-80, Haines, Lundberg, Waehler, N.Y.C., 1980-82; assoc. Perkins and Will, Architects and Engrs., N.Y.C., 1982-84; project mgr. Norman Rosenfeld AIA Architects, N.Y.C., 1984-86, Cannon, N.Y.C. and Boston, 1986-88; dir. health care facilities design Hellmuth, Bata & Kassabaum, Architects and Engrs., N.Y.C., 1988—. Mem. AIA (mem. com. on architecture for health), Forum for Health Care Planning. Democrat. Jewish.

NADER, JULIANNA CHAPMAN, computer company administrative assistant; b. Pitts., Sept. 14, 1935; d. Robert James and Hazel Taylor (Snyder) Chapman; m. Philip Robert Nader, June 29, 1959 (div. Dec. 1982); children: Richard Harrison, Stephanie Taylor. B Music Edn., Coll. of Wooster, Ohio, 1957. Cert. elem., secondary and jr. coll. tchr. Music tchr. Pitts.-Crescent Pub. Sch., 1957-59; vocal music tchr. elem. and jr. high West Irondequoit (N.Y.) Pub. Schs., 1959-61; tutor and substitute tchr. Rochester (N.Y.) Pub. Schs., 1961-63; voice instr. Galveston Coll. and La Marque High Sch., Tex., 1974-84; administr. ASK Computer Systems, Inc., Los Altos, Calif., 1984—; vocal music judge Atlanta and Tex., 1965-80. Contbr. 6 articles to Galveston Daily News; alto soloist Pitts., Rochester, San Francisco Lyric Theater, 1959-84. Com. mem. Citizens for Quality, Integrated Edn., Rochester, 1959-63; com. chairperson Rochester Area Women for Peace, 1966-69; weekly vol. ednl. TV sta., Rochester, 1966-73; edn. com. Ch. Women United, Rochester, 1968-72; founder Galveston Chamber Music Soc., 1976, Galveston County Lupus Support Group, 1978; co-founder Mid-Peninsula Lupus Support Group, 1980; founding mem. Clean Galveston Com., 1981, Kick Illegal Drugs, Galveston, 1982; organizer Health Project Olympics, U. Tex. Med. Sch., 1982; bd. dirs. Youth Shelter of Galveston, 1976-79. Recipient Citizenship award Am. Legion, 1949. Mem. Calif. Assn. Profl. Music Tchrs., Music Tchrs. Nat. Assn., Inc., Nat. Assn. Tchrs. of Singing, Inc., LWV (bd. dirs. Galveston chpt. 1974-78, co-moderator radio program 1982-83), Scola Cantorum. Democrat. Methodist. Club: Stanford Singles (Calif.) (membership com.). Home: 457 Sierra Vista Apt 8 Mountain View CA 94043-2981 Office: ASK Computer Systems Inc 2440 El Camino Real W PO Box 7640 Mountain View CA 94039-7640

NADERI, JAMIE BENEDICT, owner hazardous waste services brokerage firm; b. New Castle, Pa., June 6, 1951; d. Harold James and June Marilyn (Sipe) Benedict; m. David Lynn Martin, June 25, 1970 (div.); children: Robert Brian, Eric James; m. David James Fanning, Feb. 16, 1980 (div.); m. Bijhan A. Naderi, Sept. 16, 1985. Student, New Castle Bus. Coll., 1967-69, Truckee Meadows Community Coll., 1979-82. Lic. practical nurse, Pa. Nurse Dr. William Stechschulte, Pitts., 1973-76, Dr.'s S & R Ramos, Reno, 1977-81, St. Mary Hosp., Reno, 1979-81; restaurant critic PM Mag., Reno, 1979-81; v.p. BioNova Industries, Irvine, Calif., 1981-83; mgr. Hyatt Regency, Nashville, 1983-84; pres. Moheat, Inc., Houston, 1984—. Treas. Reno Little Theatre, 1979-80, 80-81. Mem. Women in Constrn., Nat. Assn. Female Execs., Physicians Nurses Assn., Nat. Found. of Lic. Practical Nurses. Presbyterian. Office: Moheat Inc 430 Hwy 6 Suite 202 Houston TX 77079

NADZICK, JUDITH ANN, accountant; b. Paterson, N.J., Mar. 6, 1948; d. John and Ethel (McDonald) N.; B.B.A. in Acctg., U. Miami (Fla.), 1971. Staff accountant, mgr. Ernst & Whinney, C.P.A.s, N.Y.C., 1971-78; asst. treas. Gulf & Western Industries, Inc., N.Y.C., 1979-83, asst. v.p., 1980-82, v.p., 1982-83; v.p., corp. controller United Mchts. and Mfrs. Inc., N.Y.C., 1983-85, sr. v.p., 1985-86, exec. v.p., chief fin. officer, 1986—, also bd. dirs. 1987—. C.P.A., N.J. Mem. Am. Inst. C.P.A.s, Nat. Assn. Accts., N.Y. State Soc. C.P.A.s, U. Miami Alumni Assn., Delta Delta Delta. Roman Catholic. Home: 2 Lincoln Sq Apt 15G New York NY 10023

NAFTULIN, ROSE IRENE, artist; b. Phila., Aug. 31, 1925; d. Morris and Sara (Goldman) Freedman; m. Morton Naftulin, Mar. 17, 1945 (dec. 1977); children—Louis, Elise, Nancy. Student Phila. Coll. Art, 1944-45, Barnes Found., 1962-64. Tchr. Cheltenham Art Ctr., Pa., 1961-79, Woodmere Art Mus., Phila., 1977-81; free-lance painter, Wyndmoor, Pa., 1961—; represented by Gross McCleaf Gallery, Phila. Represented in permanent collections Burlington Industries, Johnson and Johnson Co., Provident Bank, Phila., Zeitlin Corp., Phila., Shnader, Harrison, Segal and Lewis, Phila., E.I. DuPont de Nemours and Co., Fed. Nat. Mortgage Assn., Woodmere Art Mus., Prescott Forbes; numerous pvt. collections U.S. and Can. Recipient Cert. Merit Nat. Acad. design, Purchase prize Woodmere art Mus., David Humphreys prize Allied Artists Am. Publications: American Artists, 1984; with Elizabeth Leonard, Painting Flowers, 1986. Office: Gross-McCleaf Gallery 127 S 16th St Philadelphia PA 19102

NAGEL, EVELYN, symphony association executive; b. Portland, Oreg., Apr. 8, 1928; d. Aaron and Rose (Freedbaum) Davis; m. Stanley Blair Nagel, Aug. 21, 1949; children—Scott, Robert. Student U. Oreg., 1946-48. Comptroller Fountain Gallery of Art, Portland, 1966—; dir. devel. Oreg. Symphony Assn., Portland, 1973—; bd. dirs., v.p., sec. Oreg. Symphony Assn., 1970-74; mem. founding com. Oreg. Advocates for the Arts, Portland, 1980-81; mem. selection jury for architects Performing Arts Ctr., Portland, 1981-82; advisor to bd. dirs. Pacific Ballet Theatre, Portland, 1984—. Trustee, Congregation Beth Israel, Portland, 1972-84, sec. bd. trustees, 1975-80. Recipient 1st ann. spl. award Past Presidents of Women's Assn. of Oreg. Symphony, 1985. Mem. Am. Symphony Orch. League, Willamette Valley Devel. Officers (co-founder 1977-78). Republican. Jewish. Avocation: music. Office: Oreg Symphony Assn 813 SW Alder St Portland OR 97205

NAGEL, GAYLE KATHLEEN, telecommunications specialist; b. Chgo., Feb. 17, 1947; d. George Karl and Violet Margaret (Salaba) Rohner; m. James Donald Nagel, July 21, 1973; 1 child, Zackary. BS in Acctg., So. Ill. U., 1969. Acct. U.S. Gypsum Co., Chgo., 1969-72, mktg. research analyst, 1972-75, systems analyst, 1975-78; cons. Lindenhurst, Ill., 1979-80; sr. communications coordinator USG Corp., Libertyville, Ill., 1980—. Office: 1913 Woodlane Dr Lindenhurst IL 60046

NAGEL-SMILEY, CHERYL, educator; b. Englewood, N.J., Dec. 1, 1947; s. John Francis and Mary (Gozdenovich) Nagel; m. Roger John Gottlieb, June 22, 1969 (div. 1976); m. Calvin Smiley Jr., Dec. 21, 1985; 1 child, Calvin John. BA, Jersey City State Coll., 1969; MEd, Trenton State Coll., 1977; postgrad., Kean Coll. of N.J., 1978. Tchr. spl. edn. Hubbard Mid. Sch., Plainfield, N.J., 1969—, also mem. various curriculum and report card coms. Named Tchr. of Yr., State of N.J., 1985-86. Mem. NEA (rep. assembly 1980-84), N.J. Edn. Assn. (del. assembly 1981-86), Plainfield Edn. Assn. (chair grievance com. 1979-86, rep.), Union County Edn. Assn. (2d v.p. 1982-84). Lutheran. Office: Hubbard Mid Sch 661 W 8th St Plainfield NJ 07060

NAGEL-VIOLAND, MARYANN MELISSA, actress; b. Bay Village, Ohio, Nov. 27, 1952; d. Clarence Thomas and Melissa Elizabeth (Smith) Nagel; m. George Michael Violand, Aug. 17, 1985. BA, Webster Coll., 1975. Actress A Contemporary Theatre, Seattle, 1975-76, Bann & Plantation Theaters, St. Louis, 1976-78, Globe Theatre, Los Angeles, 1978, Gt. Lakes Theatre festival, Cleve., 1979; freelance actress Cleve., 1983—. Mem. Actors Equity Assn., Actors Guild., AFTRA (bd. dirs. Cleve. chpt.).

NAGLE, JUSTINE TERESA, advertising executive; b. N.Y.C., Feb. 3, 1940; d. Nicholas J. and Marguerite P. (Battle) N.; m. Edward Dillon, Sept. 14, 1957 j(div. May 1964); children: Justine, Stacy. Student, Pace Coll., 1955-59, Cornell Labor Coll., 1972—, New Sch. Social Research, 1981—. Asst. producer Geyer Advt., 1957-58; coordinator Rose Marie Reid Bathing Suits, 1958-59; dir. advt. Temas Mag., N.Y.C., 1959-63; with Commerce Advt., N.Y.C., 1963—; v.p., account exec. 1969—; owner, pres. Elgan Communications, N.Y.C.; owner J. Nagle Assocs., 1980—, Kibbe Cab Co., 1979—; owner, pres. Commerce Advt., Inc., 1985—. Vol. The Shelter. Mem. Advt. Womens Club, Conservative Club, Met. Opera Guild, Mus. Natural History, Mus. Art. Republican. Clubs: Belle Harbor Yacht, N.Y. Athlete (assoc.), Gaslight, Atrium. Home: 301 E 47th St New York NY 10017 also: 537 Beach 130 St Belle Harbor NY 11694 Office: 220 E 23d St 8th Floor New York NY 10018

NAGLE, NANCY ELIZABETH, automotive manufacturing executive; b. Houston, Mar. 27, 1951; d. John Ware and Elizabeth Geraldine (Dawkins) Nagle; m. William Edward Zinsmeister, Oct. 22, 1983. B.F.A., So. Meth. U., 1973; M.B.A., U. Tex., 1977. Creative asst. Clinton Frank Advt., Dallas, 1974-75; teaching asst. U. Tex., Austin, 1976-77; trainee Ford Motor Co., Houston, 1978, zone mgr., 1979-81, dealer leasing and rental mgr., 1982, bus. mgr., 1983-84, car merchandising mgr., 1984; sales devel. mgr., 1985, coordinator light truck tng., 1986, mgr. light truck mechandising, 1986; coordinator contemporary markets, Detroit, 1987— ; adj. prof. Coll. of Mainland, 1985. Author: Role Models of Educated Women Regarding Marriage and Career, 1977. Mem. Detroit Inst. of the Arts, Daus. Am. Republic, Daus. Republic Tex., Magna Carta Dames, Tex. Ex-Students Assn., So. Meth. U. Alumni Assn. Episcopalian. Home: 780 Greenwood Birmingham MI 48009 Office: Ford Motor Co PO Box 43320 300 Renaissance Ctr Detroit MI 48243

NAGY, ISABEL GEORGETTE YVONNE, writer, television producer; b. Parry Sound, Ont., Can., July 2, 1955; came to U.S., 1961; d. Louis and Denise (Ktorza) N. Diploma in French lang. and lit., Inst. Etrangers, Aix-en-Provence, France, 1976; BA, Calif. State U., Northridge, 1979. Editor Burbank (Calif.) Scene, 1979; reporter Burbank Daily Rev., 1979; mng. editor San Fernando Valley Mag., Studio City, Calif., 1980; writer, producer Sta. KTLA News, Los Angeles, 1980-82, Sta. KCBS News, Los Angeles, 1982-87, Lifetime Med. TV, Los Angeles, 1987—. Recipient Best Local TV Feature award Odyssey Inst., cert. appreciation Ctr. Improvement Child Caring, 1982. Mem. Writers Guild Am. (outstanding script award 1987), Acad. TV Arts Scis. (Emmy 1982), Internat. Documentary Assn. Home: 2112 Pearl St Santa Monica CA 90405 Office: Lifetime Med TV 3575 Cahuenga Blvd Suite 500 Los Angeles CA 90068

NAH, CAROLYN BROWN, federal agency professional; b. Rochelle, Ga., Sept. 26, 1945; d. Frances Brown; m. Anthony W. Nah, Feb. 1, 1975; children: Leroy, Robert Mathis, Harold. BS in Human Service, N.H. Coll., 1980; MS in Edn., U. Bridgeport, 1987. Asst. contract mgmt., Contract Adminstrn. U.S. Dept. Def., Stratford, Conn., 1971—; prin. Nah & Brown Assocs., Bridgeport, Conn., 1986—. Dir. edn. NAACP, Bridgeport, 1984-85, exec. sec., 1986-87. Mem. Black Women Corp. Am. (sec. 1985—), Nat. Assn. Female Execs. Club: Jack and Jill Am. (Bridgeport) (assoc.). Home: 44 Lewis St Bridgeport CT 06605

NAHIGIAN, ALMA LOUISE, technical writer, editor; b. Peabody, Mass., Sept. 17, 1936; d. Walter Daniel and Alma Edith (Knowles) Higgens; m. Franklin Roosevelt Nahigian, April 30, 1961; children: Ellen Elise, Dana Leigh, Catherine Elizabeth. AA, Boston U., 1956, BS, 1958, MS in Communcications, 1963. Nat. and spl. projects editor Boston U. News Bur., 1959-61; writer, editor Nutrition Found., N.Y.C., 1961-63; writer, editor, cons. Cambridge (Mass.) Communicators, Tech. Edn. Research Ctr., Harvard U., Cambridge, Smart Software, Inc., Belmont, Mass., 1970-82; tech. editor Digital Equipment Corp., Bedford, Mass., 1979-84; prin. tech. writer, editor Wang Labs, Inc., Lowell, Mass., 1984—; instr. Harvard U., Cambridge, 1988; guest lectr. Northeastern U., Boston, 1979, 88, Radcliffe Coll., Cambridge, 1979. Contbr. numerous articles to profl. pubs. Active, LWV, Arlington, Mass., 1963-73. Mem. Soc. for Tech. Communication. Democrat. Roman Catholic. Home: 30 Venner Rd Arlington MA 02174 Office: Wang Labs Inc One Industrial Ave Lowell MA 01851

NAIDA, JOANN ORNOSKY, hospital education administrator; b. Monroe, Mich., Sept. 23, 1936; d. Joseph Paul and Phyllis Barbara (Theisen) Ornosky; m. David Daniel Naida, Sept. 8, 1956; children: Jean Ann, Linda Kay, John David, Paul David. BS in Nursing, Eastern Mich. U., 1981, MA, 1982, MA in Counseling, 1987. Staff nurse Mercy Meml. Hosp., Monroe, 1957-62, 67-69, nursing supr., 1969-74, head nurse, 1974-77, utilization coordinator, 1978-81, staff devel. instr., 1982-83, edn. dir., 1983—; instr. Monroe County Community Coll., 1978-79, 84-87; v.p. Detroit-Dearborn (Mich.) area br. Continuing Health Edn. Soc., 1984-87. Pres. Community Staff Devel., Ann Arbor, Mich., 1984-87; chmn. profl. edn. Am. Cancer Soc., Monroe, 1985-87; asst. clk. London Twp., Maybee, Mich., 1956-64. Named Disting. Alumni Eastern Mich. U., 1986. Mem. Am. Nurses Assn., Mich. Nursing Diagnosis Assn., Nat. Assn. Female Execs., St. Vincent Sch. Nursing Alumni Assn., Sigma Theta Tau, Eta Rho. Democrat. Roman Catholic. Office: Mercy Meml Hosp 718 N Macomb St Monroe MI 48161

NAISMITH, LAURIE, state executive; b. Norfolk, Va., Apr. 21, 1952; d. George and Mary Helen (Campbell) N. BS in Polit. Sci., Old Dominion U., Norfolk, 1975; postgrad., Va. Exec. Inst., 1983, Inst. Policy Scis. and Pub. Affairs Exec. Edn. Program, Duke U., 1984, London Sch. Econs. and Polit. Scis. Mem. legis. staff Nat. Student Lobby, Washington, 1973; legis. asst. to Robert E. Washington Norfolk, 1974-76; cons. Va. Internship Program, Richmond, 1975; field dir. Elmo Zumwalt's U.S. Senate Campaign, Richmond, 1976; dir. pub. affairs program office Lt. Gov. of Va., Richmond, 1978-81; scheduler Robb for Gov., Richmond, 1981; mem. transition team gov.-elect Robb, Richmond, 1981-82; sec. of state Commonwealth of Va., Richmond, 1982-85; mem. Official U.S. Elections Observation Del. to El Salvador, 1984, gov.'s exec. com., Va.-Israel Commn., 1986. Hon. sec. Va. Young Democrats, 1983; del. Dem. Convs., 1972, 76, 77, 78, 80, 81; bd. dirs. Central Va. Council Girl Scouts U.S.A., 1984-85; mem. adv. bd. Internat. Inst. Plastic, Reconstructive and Specialized Surgery, 1985; mem. Commn. on Intergovt. Cooperation, 1982; Va. rep. nat. adv. com. Eleanor Roosevelt Centennial Commn., 1984; participant Women in Leadership Conf. to USSR, 1986; del. Am. Council Young Polit. Leaders Study Tour of India, 1986; bd. dirs. Richmond Symphony Orch., Va. Cultural Laureate Soc., Va. Stage Co., Richmond Metro. Blood Service. Named One of Outstanding Young Women Am., 1980; recipient Exec. Dir.'s award Nat. Black Assn. for Speech, Lang. and Hearing, 1983; Fast Track Favorite award Commonwealth Mag., 1983. Mem. Council State Govts., Women Execs. in State Govt. (conf. program chmn. 1984), Nat. Assn. Secs. State (chmn. fin. com. 1982), Nat. Assn. Extradition Ofcls., Pi Sigma Alpha. Democrat. Presbyterian. Home: 16 Mecklenburgh Sq, London WCIN 2AD, England Office: Va Alcoholic Beverage Control Bd 2401 Hermitage Rd Richmond VA 23261

NAKAI, TERESA, mine inspector; b. Shiprock, N.Mex., Dec. 17, 1960; d. Gabriel and Virginia (Joe) N. BS in Crop and Soil Sci., N.Mex. State U., 1983. Environ. technician Utah Internat., Fruitland, N.Mex., 1982; water resource technician engrs. office State of N.Mex., Roswell, 1984-86; reclamation specialist mining and minerals div. State of N.Mex., Santa Fe, 1986—. Mem. Soil Conservation Soc. Am. Office: State of NMex Mining & Minerals Div 525 Camino de los Marquez Santa Fe NM 87501

NAKASHIMA, SUSAN ELLEN, data processing executive; b. Summit, N.J., Nov. 6, 1957; d. John Russell and Miriam (Giordano) Clayton; m. Junji Harry Nakashima, Oct. 4, 1980. BSBA, U. Redlands, Calif., 1986. From jr. to sr. word processing operator So. Calif. Edison, Rosemead, 1977-79; supr. word processing services TransAm. Fin. Services, Los Angeles, 1979-80, supr. documentation services, 1980-81, mgr. documentation services, 1982-84, mgr. systems support, 1984-86, systems cons., 1986; dir. data processing TransAm. Real Estate Tax Services, Los Angeles, 1986—; office systems analyst 1st Interstate Bank, Los Angeles, 1981-82; sr. advisor Trans-Western Inst., 1980—. Mem. Assn. Info. Specialists, United Info. Processors (v.p. 1977-79). Republican. Roman Catholic. Office: TransAm Real Estate Tax Service 1150 S Olive St Suite #1733 Los Angeles CA 90015

NALEPKA, JOYCE DEE, association executive; b. Friendsville, Md., Mar. 24, 1936; d. Randall Wayne and Yvonne Wilma (Hoye) Friend; m. Raymond John Nalepka, Jan. 19, 1963; children: Kevin Jay, Keith Eric. Student, W.Va. U., 1954-57, Waynesburg Coll., 1957. Founder Interstate Movement Moms Against Drugs (I'M MAD), Silver Spring, Md., 1977, vol. lobbyist, 1977-80; founding mem. bd. dirs. Nat. Fedn. Parents for Drug-Free Youth, Silver Spring, 1980, pres., 1984—; cons. Nat. Inst. Drug Abuse, Nat. Inst. Alcohol, Alcoholism and Alcohol Abuse, Nat. Assn. Broadcasters, USIA, Office Juvenile Justice and Deliquency Prevention, U.S. Attys., Drug Enforcement Adminstrn., McDonalds Corp., Chem. Specialties Mfrs. Assn., Nat. Assn. Life Underwriters, DuPont Pharms.; testified before U.S. Senate, U.S Ho. of Reps., Md. House Judiciary Com., Md. Senate Judiciary Com., U.S. Dept. State, U.S. Dept. Edn.; co-sponsor bill to close Md. paraphenalia shops. Contbr. articles to met. and nat. newspapers; author drug abuse prevention materials. Founder Congl. Families for Drug-Free Youth, 1984. Recipient numerous nat. and internat. awards for service and activism. Mem. Nat. Assn. Female Execs., Nat. Assn. Broadcasters, Am. Soc. Assn. Execs. Home: 1805 Tilton Dr Silver Spring MD 20902 Office: Nat Fedn Parents Drug-Free Youth 1805 Tilton Dr Silver Spring MD 20902

NALLEY, BLANCHE ALMEDIA (MEDA), real estate development executive, property management director; b. Rocky Mount, N.C., June 26, 1939; d. Walter McDonald, Jr., and Ella Blanche (Phelps) Peacock; m. Richard Kingsman Nalley, Jr., Jan. 16, 1960 (div. 1967); children—Michelle, Karen, Natalie. A.A., U. Fla., 1960. Controller, sta. WPGC, Washington, 1965-68, Trans Continental Industries, Washington, 1968-71, Atlantic Elec. and Bldrs. Hardware, Washington, 1971-74, LBG Distrbrs., Washington, 1974-79; dir. property mgmt., devel. and constrn. Ingersoll & Bloch Chartered, Washington, 1979—; renovation cons. Nunnery Assocs., Washington, 1983-85, J.C. Assocs., Washington, 1984—; constrn. cons. P St Assn., Washington, 1985-86; owners rep. 801 Pa. Ave. Assn., Washington, 1985-86; ptnr. Bldg. Services and Maintenance, Inc., Washington, 1986—. Active design and constrn. hist. structures into office space, 1985-86, renovation hist. landmark bldg., 1985-86. Vol. Alexandria Hosp., Va., 1984; v.p. Elem. Sch. PTA, Hyattsville, Md., 1975, sec. Middle Sch. PTA, 1975. Mem. Property Mgmt. Assn., Apt. Office Bldg. Assn., Multi Housing Assn. Republican. Avocations: running, aerobics, swimming, crocheting, cooking. Home: 4540 Garbo Ct Annandale VA 22003 Office: J C Assocs 1401 16th St NW Washington DC 20036

NANCE, BETTY LOVE, librarian; b. Nashville, Oct. 29, 1923; d. Granville Scott and Clara (Mills) Nance. BA in English magna cum laude, Trinity U., 1957; AM in Library Sci., U. Mich., 1958. Head dept. acquisitions Stephen F. Austin U. Library, Nacogdoches, Tex., 1958-59; librarian 1st Nat. Bank, Fort Worth, 1959-61; head catalog dept. Trinity U., San Antonio, 1961-63; head tech. processes U. Tex. Law Library, Austin, 1963-66; head catalog dept. Tex. A&M U. Library, College Station, 1966-69; chief bibliographic services Washington U. Library, St. Louis, 1970; head dept. acquisitions Va. Commonwealth U. Library, Richmond, 1971-73; head tech. processes Howard Payne U. Library, Brownwood, Tex., 1974-79; library dir. Edinburg (Tex.) Pub. Library, 1980—; pres. Edinburg Com. for Salvation Army. Mem. ALA, Pub. Library Assn., Tex. Library Assn., Hidalgo County Library Assn. (v.p. 1980-81, pres. 1981-82), Pan Am. Round Table of Edinburg (corr. sec. 1986-88), Edinburg Bus. and Profl. Womens Club (founding bd. dirs., pres. 1986-87, bd. dirs. 1987-88), Alpha Lambda Delta, Alpha Chi. Methodist. Club: Zonta (bd. dirs. West Hidalgo club 1986-88). Home: 1602 John St Apt 4 Edinburg TX 78539 Office: Edinburg Pub Library 401 E Cano St Edinburg TX 78539

NANCE, MARY JOE, educator; b. Carthage, Tex., Aug. 7, 1921; d. F. F. and Mary Elizabeth (Knight) Born; B.B.A., North Tex. State U., 1953; postgrad. Northwestern State U. La., 1974; M.E., Antioch U., 1978; m. Earl C. Nance, July 12, 1946; 1 child, David Earl. Tchr., Port Isabel (Tex.) Integrated Sch. Dist., to 1979; tchr. English, Splendora (Tex.) High Sch., 1979-80, McLeod, Tex., 1980-81, Bremond, Tex., 1981-84. Served with WAAC, 1942-43, WAC 1945. Recipient Image Maker award Carthage C. of C., 1984; cert. bus. educator. Mem. Nat. Bus. Edn. Assn., NEA, Tex. Tchrs. Assn., Tex. Bus. Tchrs. Assn. (cert. of appreciation 1978), Nat. Women's Army Corps Vets. Assn., Air Force Assn. (life), Assn. Supervision and Curriculum Devel., Council for Basic Edn., Nat. Hist. Soc., Tex. Council English Tchrs. Baptist.

NANTAIS, DIANE EMILIE, mortgage servicing manager; b. Worcester, Mass., June 11, 1956; d. Louis J. and Mary Catherine (O'Connor) Boucher; m. Kenneth H. Nantais, Apr. 14, 1978; children: Amanda C., Julie-Beth, Erin Holly. BS in Elementary Edn. and Spl. Edn., Bridgewater State Coll., 1978. Teller Plymouth Savs. Bank, Wareham, Mass., 1978-83, sr. teller, 1983-84, head teller, 1984-85, rep. tax escrow, 1985, sr. rep. mortgage, 1985-86, mgr. mortgage servicing, 1986—. Mem. Mass. Young Mortgage Bankers Assn. Home: Main St PO Box 15 Carver MA 02330

NARAD, JOAN STERN, psychiatrist; b. N.Y.C., June 21, 1943; d. Victor and Grete (Metzger) S.; m. Richard M. Narad; children: Christine, Laurie, Michael. BA, N.Y.U., 1964; MD, woman's Med. Coll., Pa., 1968. Diplomate Am. Bd. Psychiatry, Am. Bd Child Psychiatry. Intern pediatrics Stanford (Calif.) U. Hosp., 1968-69; resident adult psychiat. Med. Coll., Phila., 1969-71, fellow child psyciat., 1971-73; resident in psychoanalysis, child psychoanalysis Phila. Psychoanalytic Inst., 1970; practicing medicine specializing in psychiatry Westport, Conn., 1987—; cons. Cath. Home Girls, Phila., Germantown Friends Sch. 1973-79; asst. prof. Child Psychiat. Med. Coll. Pa. 1975-79; chief Adolescent and Young Adult Service, Silver Hill Found, New Canaan, Conn. 1980-84, asst. clin. prof. Yale Child Study Ctr. 1979—. Fellow NIH, 1968. Mem. Am. Psychiat. Assn., AMA, Am. Med. Women's Assn., Pa. Psychiat. Soc., Pa. Med. Soc., Alumnae Assn. Med. Coll. Pa. (chpt. sec./treas. 1970-72), Am. Acad. Child and Adolescent Psychiat., Am. Psychoanalytic Assn., Western New Eng. Psychoanalytic Soc., Conn. Council Child Psychiatrist. Office: Med Coll Pa Dept of Psychiatry 3300 Henry Ave Philadelphia PA 19129

NAREL, DOROTHY ALMA, bank executive; b. Newark, June 25, 1924; m. Aleksander Narel (dec.); children: Amy, Barbara. Asst. v.p. mktg. and communications Ulster Savs., Kingston, N.Y., 1976—. Editor Woman's Page The Daily Freeman. Bd. dirs. YWCA, Hudson Valley Philharmonic Concert Assn.; minister of music, St. John's Parish, Woodstock and West Hurley, N.Y., 1964—; past minister of music St. Mary's of the Snow, Saugerties, N.Y.; mem. commn. Ch. Music for the Archdiocese of N.Y.; music dir. Kingston Maennerchor and Damenchor; Ulster County Democratic Committeewoman, 1955-66; dir. woman's program Sta. WKNY/WKNY-TV, Kingston, N.Y. Mem. (charter) Ulster County Bus. and Profl. Women's Club, Kingston Uptown Bus. Assn. (bd. dirs.), Fin. Instits. Mktg. Assn., Bank Mktg. Assn. Democrat. Roman Catholic. Home: Box 307 Mosher Place West Hurley NY 12401

NARIN, SANDRA CAROLE GOLDBERG, lawyer; b. Phila., Apr. 2, 1941; d. Woolf and Ida (Moliver) Goldberg; m. Stephen B. Narin, Sept. 29, 1963; children—Howard Glen, Brenda Teri. B.A., Bryn Mawr Coll., 1962; M.A., U. Pa., 1963, Ph.D., 1973; J.D., Villanova U., 1983. Bar: Pa. 1983. Instr. Russian, Haverford (Pa.) Coll., 1965-66; tchr. Russian Central High Sch., Phila., 1965-66; instr. Russian, Ursinus Coll., Collegeville, Pa., 1967-68; assoc. Narin & Chait, Phila., 1983—. Mem. Lower Merion Twp. Intersch. Council, Lower Merion, Pa., 1972—, sec., pres., 1974-76, 76-78; mem. citizen adv. com. Lower Merion (Pa.) Sch. Bd., 1977-79. Mem. ABA, Pa. Bar Assn., Phila. Bar Assn. Democrat. Clubs: Green Valley Country (Lafayette Hill, Pa.); Bryn Mawr Coll. (Phila.). Home: 331 Mallwyd Rd Merion PA 19066 Office: Narin and Chait 1521 Locust St 10th Floor Philadelphia PA 19102

NARISI, STELLA MARIA, equipment manufacturing executive; b. Fort Smith, Ark., Oct. 24, 1950; d. Vincent J. and Norma J. Narisi; B.B.A., U. Tex., 1972, J.D., 1975. Admitted to Tex. bar, 1975; staff atty. enforcement div. Tex. State Securities Bd., Houston, 1975-79; corp. sec., gen. counsel Marathon Le Tourneau Co. and subs., Houston, 1979—. Mem. Am. Bar Assn., Tex. Bar Assn., Houston Bar Assn. Club: Houston. Office: Marathon Mfg Co 600 Jefferson Suite 1900 Houston TX 77002

NARNEY, JANICE WORTHINGTON, controller; b. Nowata, Okla., Jan. 25, 1957; d. James Mark Worthington and Frances Katherine (Deen) Fairless; m. Dennis Walter Narney, Apr. 20, 1984. BS in Acctg., Okla. State U., 1978, MS in Acctg., 1979. CPA, Okla. Staff mem. Deloitte, Haskins & Sells, Oklahoma City, 1980-81; mgr. spl. projects, asst. controller Texoma Resources, Inc., Oklahoma City, 1981; acctg. mgr. Sabre Oil & Gas Co., Oklahoma City, 1981-83; controller Hill Resources, Inc., Oklahoma City, 1983-88, Cox Cable, Oklahoma City, 1988—; lectr. in field. Vol. Odyssey, fundraiser Oklahoma City Symphony, 1985; mem. advance gifts team Children's Miracle Network Telethon, Oklahoma City, 1986; chair advance gifts team Children's Miracle Network Telethon, 1987; mem. allocation com. United Way, 1988—. Mem. The Forum (membership chair 1986-87, officer 1987-88, treas., chmn. 1988—), Am. Inst. CPA's, Oklahoma Soc. CPA's, Pi Beta Phi.

NARON, CONNIE COX, food company executive; b. Vicksburg, Miss., Oct. 22, 1950; d. Melvin O'Neal and Grace Belinda (Brouilette) Cox Benner; m. James Randolph Naron, June 2, 1966; children—Cyndi, Sonya, Andrew, Jon. Student, U. Ark. Sales rep. Cox's Relish Co. Inc., Dermott, Ark., 1977-83, sec.-treas., Daingerfield, Tex., 1983-84, v.p. adminstrn., 1984-87; v.p. sales/adminstrn., bd. dirs., Wisconsin Potato Chip Co., Antigo, 1987—. Mem. Nat. Assn. Female Execs., U.S. C. of C., Nat. Food Processors Assn., Snack Food Assn., Antigo C. of C., Tex. Dept. Agr. Avocations: art; poetry; photography; travel. Office: Wis Potato Chip Co Inc 309 Superior Antigo WI 54409

NAROV, FRUMA, structural engineer; b. Germany, Oct. 25, 1947; d. Abraham and Paula Arieli; B.S., Technion, Israel Inst. Tech., 1968; m. David Narov, Jan. 25, 1970; children—Hilla, Yoav. Structural engr. Lev Zetlin Assocs., Inc., N.Y.C., 1970-72, sr. structural engr., 1972-76, assoc., 1978-84, v.p., 1984—; project engr. Cannon Design Inc., Buffalo, 1977-78. Served to lt. Israeli Def. Forces, 1968-70. Registered profl. engr., N.Y. Mem. ASCE. Jewish. Office: Lev Zetlin Assocs Inc 641 Ave of Americas New York NY 10001

NARRIN, JANE ANNE, corporate recruiting executive, career management cons.; b. Detroit, Aug. 12, 1945; BA, Fla. Atlantic U., 1966, MA, 1970. Cert. social worker. Counselor, Broward County Schs., Fort Lauderdale, Fla., 1970-74; pres. J.A. Narrin and Assocs., Inc., Computer Search Firm, Bloomfield Hills, Mich., 1975—; mgmt. cons. hitech. industries, 1986—; cons. resource mgmt., mktg., communications, Detroit, 1984—. Pub. Options Newsletter, 1984—. Recipient Leadership award Bus. Assn. Mem. Nat. Wildlife Fedn., Save the Whale Found., Project Hope. Avocations: writing, photography, creative arts, video prodn. Office: J A Narrin and Assocs Inc 1000 S Woodward Suite 105 Birmingham MI 48009

NARRIN, ROBERTA PETRONELLA, financial consultant; b. Providence, Oct. 11, 1939; d. Anthony and Maria G. (Barra) Petronella; m. Sidney Narrin, April 22, 1961 (div. Nov. 1971); children: Christine E. De Pari, Anthony F. Student, Bryant Coll., 1959; cert., Nat. Assn. Securities Dealers, 1978. CLU, Pa. Exec. sec., adminstrv. asst. Allied Adjustment Services, Providence, 1967-71; account exec. Advertisers Workshop, East Providence, R.I., 1971-75; pres. Roberta Narrin Assocs., Providence, 1975-77, A Chris Corp., Providence, 1980—; fin. cons. Phoenix Mut. Life Ins., One-120 Assocs. MBF, Inc., Providence, 1977—. Pres. PTA, No. Providence, 1969; v.p. R.I. Assn. Brain Injured, No. Providence, 1968; sec. The Learning Ctr., Providence, 1977-79, R.I. Assn. Retarded Children, 1970—. Mem. Nat. Assn. Female Execs., R.I. Assn. Life Underwriters (Nat. Quality award 1981—), R.I. Chpt. CLU's, R.I. Estate Planning Council, Million Dollar Round Table. Home: 300 Smithfield Rd North Providence RI 02904 Office: 2 Richmond Sq Providence RI 02906

NARUSIS, REGINA GYTÉ FIRANT, lawyer; b. Kaunas, Lithuania, Oct. 12, 1936; came to U.S., 1949, naturalized, 1955; d. Victor and Eugenia S. (Cesnavicius) Firant; m. Bernard V. Narusis, June 19, 1959; children: Victor John, Ellen Marie, Susan Marie. BA, U. Ill., 1957, JD, 1959. Bar: Ill. 1960. Ptnr. Narusis & Narusis, Cary, Ill., 1961—; atty. City of McHenry (Ill.), 1973—; village atty. Fox River Grove, Ill., 1967-73; asst. state's atty., McHenry County, Ill., 1968-75, head juvenile div., 1968-75. Mem. McHenry County Bd. Health, Woodstock, Ill., 1964-75, McHenry County Welfare Services Com., 1968-75; mem., pres. Dist. 46 Sch. Bd., McHenry County, 1964-79, mem. adminstrv. council, mem. exec. bd. Marian Cen. Cath. High Sch., 1981—; bd. dirs. Cath. Found. for People of Diocese of Rockford, Ill., 1988—. Mem. Ill. Bar Assn., McHenry County Bar Assn., Women's Bar Assn., Am. Judicature Soc., Nat. Dist. Attys. Assn., Kappa Beta Pi. Address: 213 W Lake Shore Dr Cary IL 60013

NASALROAD, KENNIETH JEAN, import executive; b. Oak Harbor, Wash., Dec. 10, 1950; d. Edward Clifton and Norma Jean (Kent) Bickmore; m. Ralph Floyd Nasalroad, June 15, 1974; children: Raymond Douglas, Ralph Eric. AA in Math., Reedley (Calif) Jr. Coll., 1972. Adminstrv. asst. Kings Canyon Unified Sch. Dist., Reedley, 1970-72; computer operator Sequoia Forest Industries div. Wickes Co., Dinuba, Calif., 1972-74; office mgr. Therm'x Corp. div. Buchmin Glass Corp., Reedley, 1974-78, gen. mgr., 1978—. Treas. Monday Mixed 4-Some Bowling league, Dinuba, 1973-76, Noah's Ark Child-Care Ctr., Reedley, 1981-83; sec. Reedley-Kings Canyon Youth Soccer, 1983-84, pres. 1986-87. Mem. Warehouse Distbrs. Assn., Nat. Assn. Female Execs., Orange Cove Women's Club (mem. chmn. 1984-85). Republican. Home: 110 Sixth St Orange Cove CA 93646 Office: Therm'x Corp 835 S Frankwood Ave Reedley CA 93654

NASH, HELEN ELIZABETH, pediatrician; b. Atlanta, Aug. 8, 1921; d. Homer Erwin and Marie (Graves) N.; B.A., Spelman Coll., 1942; M.D., Meharry Med. Coll., 1945; m. James B. Abernathy, Aug. 1, 1964. Intern, resident Homer Phillips Hosp., St. Louis, 1945-49; asso. prof. clin. pediatrics Washington U., St. Louis, 1949—; practice medicine specializing in pediatrics, St. Louis, 1949—; pediatric supr. H.G. Phillips Hosp., 1949-64; mem. staff St. Louis Children's Hosp., St. Luke's Hosp., Jewish Hosp. of St. Louis, St. Louis Maternity Hosp.; mem. Mo. Welfare Commn., 1969-73. Diplomate Am. Bd. Pediatrics. Mem. St. Louis Med. Soc. (Hon. life), Mo. Med. Soc., AMA, Am. Acad. Pediatrics, St. Louis Pediatric Soc. Home: 5783 Lindell Blvd St Louis MO 63112 Office: 1441 N Grand St Saint Louis MO 63106

NASH, MARILYN JEAN, editor, author; b. Houston, Oct. 17, 1950; d. Alfred Leroy and Doris Jean (Anderson) Lewis; B.B.A., U. Houston, 1975; m. Shannon T. Nash, Apr. 11, 1980; 1 dau. by previous marriage, Angela Christine Rittel. Acctg. clk. Fin. Services, Gulf Oil Corp., Houston, 1971-75; mktg. rep. AM Internat., Houston, 1976-80; self-employed copywriter, 1980-86, cons. communications Hewitt Assocs., 1987—. Mem. Phi Gamma Nu Alumni. Office: 25231 Grogans Mill Rd The Woodlands TX 77380

NASH, NANCY JEAN, banker; b. New Haven, June 21, 1956; d. Joseph Edward and Jean Ninita (Crowell) Byrnes; m. Paul Anthony Nash, Sept. 29, 1984. BA, U. Conn., Storrs, 1978; MBA, U. Conn., Stamford, 1980. Asst. br. mgr. Peoples Bank, Bridgeport, Conn., 1980-83, br. mgr., 1983-84, asst. v.p., br. ops. mgr., 1984-86, v.p. electronic funds transfer and delivery ops., 1986—. Sec. Bd. Christian Concerns Ch., Bridgeport, 1983-84; deacon United Congl. Ch., Bridgeport, 1985—. Named one of Outstanding Young Women in Am., 1982. Mem. Nat. Assn. Bank Women, Nat. Honor Soc. Secondary Schs., AAUW. Republican. Office: Peoples Bank 899 Main St Bridgeport CT 06604

NASH, NANCY LYNNE, Spanish educator; b. Detroit, June 21, 1949; d. Willard James and Bessie Louise (Terry) Towers; children: Gregory Thomas, Cristina Lynne. Student, U. Madrid, 1969-70; BA in Spanish, Vocal Music, We. Mich. U., 1971; MA in Spanish, Mich. State U., 1977; MA in Bus. Edn., Wayne State U., 1984. Spanish tchr. Rochester (Mich.) Community Schs., 1971—, dept. rep., 1985-87. Software reviewer Modern Language Jour., 1985—. Mem. Am. Assn. Tchrs. of Spanish and Portugese, Oakland Fgn. Language Assn. (pres. 1987—). Home: 397 Nakomis Dr Lake Orion MI 48035 Office: Adams High Sch 3200 W Tienken Rd Rochester MI 48063

NASH, RUTH COWAN (MRS. BRADLEY D. NASH), journalist; b. Salt Lake City, Utah; d. William Henry and Ida (Baldwin) Cowan; A.B., U. Tex., 1923; m. Bradley D. Nash, June 30, 1956. Tchr. pub. high sch., San Antonio, 1924-27; reporter San Antonio Evening News, 1928, United Press, 1929; corr. AP, Chgo., 1929-40, Washington, 1940-43, 45-56, war corr., North Africa, Gt. Britain, Europe, 1943-45, retired, 1956; free lance journalist, 1956—; asst. to undersec. of health edn. and welfare, 1958-61; pres. Travelers Service, Inc., Charles Town, W.Va. Cons., pub. relations dir. women's div., Republican Nat. Com., Washington; mem. Def. Adv. Com. on Women in the Services, 1958-61. Clubs: Nat. Press, Washington Press (pres. 1947-48), Overseas Press, Am. Newswomen's; Writer and Press (London). Home: High Acres Farm Box 122 Route 3 Harpers Ferry WV 25425

NASH, SYLVIA D., religious organization executive, consultant; b. Montevedio, Minn., Apr. 25, 1945; d. Owen Donald and Selma A. (Tollefson) Dotseth; 1 child from previous marriage, Elizabeth Louise; m. Thomas L. Nash, Dec. 20, 1986. Student, Calif. Luth. Bible Sch., 1965. Office mgr. First Congl. Ch., Pasadena, Calif., 1968-75; adminstrv. asst. Pasadena Presbyn. Ch., 1975-78; dir. adminstrv. services Fuller Theol. Sem., Pasadena, 1978-81; chief exec. officer Christian Ministries Mgmt. Assn., Diamond Bar, Calif., 1981—; bd. dirs. Evang. Council Fin. Accountability, Washington, Gospel Lit. Internat., Rosemead, Calif.; mem. adv. com. Christian Mgmt. Rev., Chgo., 1986—; cons. various orgns., 1985—. Editor: The Clarion, 1975-78, The Christian Mgmt. Report, 1981-86; contbr. articles to profl. jours. Chmn. bd. Lamb's Players, National City, Calif., 1985—. Mem. Nat. Assn. Ch. Adminstrs. (sec. 1979-81), Nat. Assn. Female Execs., Am. Soc. Assn. Execs. Office: Christian Ministries Mgmt Assn PO Box 4638 Diamond Bar CA 19765

NASH, THERESE MARY, marketing professional; b. Neenah, Wis., July 14, 1959; d. Edward Frederick and Lucille (Mottl) N. BS in Psychology magna cum laude, U. Wis., Oshkosh, 1982; degree, U. of Mex., Cuernavaca, 1983. Counselor Tamarack Home, Oshkosh, 1980-82; sr. sales rep. The Computer Store, Rochester, N.Y., 1983-84; dist. sales mgr. Computer Depot, Rochester, 1984; mktg. support Apple Computer, Inc., Chgo., 1984-86; with product devel. and sales dept. Apple Computer, Inc., Cupertino, Calif., 1986-87, with edn. mktg. dept., 1987—; bd. dirs. Furry Friends, Morgan Hill, Calif., 1986—; mentor Electronics Acad., San Jose, Calif., 1986-87. Curriculum adv. bd. com., sci. dir. Independence High Sch., San Jose, 1987. Recipient Spl. Optimist award City of Neenah, 1977. Mem. Nat. Assn. Female Execs., Psi Chi (pres. Wis. chpt.). Clubs: Macintosh User's Group, Macintosh Developers. Office: Apple Computer Inc 20525 Mariani Ave Cupertino CA 95014

NASHER, PATSY RABINOWITZ, art collector; b. Dallas, Sept. 15, 1928; d. Myer Alexander and Ivy (Topletz) Rabinowitz; m. Raymond Donald Nasher, July 25, 1949; children: Andrea Dani, Joan Dru, Nancy Arnole. Student, Hockaday Jr. Coll., Dallas, 1944-46, So. Meth. U., 1946-47; BA, Smith Coll., Northampton, Mass., 1947-49; PhD (hon.), Northwood Inst., 1988. Pvt. art collector, Dallas; art cons. NorthPark Nat. Bank, Dallas, 1974—; mem. com. Art in Pub. Places, Dallas, 1982—; assoc. organizer various exhbns. NorthPark Ctr., Dallas, 1974—, Dallas Mus. Art, 1987, Nat. Gallery of Art, Washington, 1987-88, The Centro de Art Reina Sofia, Madrid, 1988, Forte di Belvedere, Florence, Italy, 1988. Mem. bd. Dallas Mus. Acquisition Com., 1982—, Am. Craft Council, N.Y.C., 1986—, Smith Coll. Mus. of Art, Northampton, 1985—; mem. adv. bd. Ft. Worth Art Mus. Acquisition Com., 1980—; founder, bd. dirs. Maureen Connolly Brinker Found., Dallas, 1974—. Recipient Obelisk award Dallas C. of C., 1982, 87, Exhbn.-Textile Collection award Dallas Mus. of Art, 1980, Exhbn.-Master Art Collection award So. Meth. U., 1978. Democrat. Jewish. Office: 8950 N Central Expwy Suite 202 Dallas TX 75231

NASH-HOFF, MICHELLE MARIE, manufacturers representative; b. Chgo., July 16, 1942; d. Ancil John and Lois Mae (Anderson) Bernard; m. Robert Charles Nash, Feb. 24, 1962 (div. 1983); children: Melanie Marie, Jeffrey Eric; m. Michael Lorin Hoff, Sept. 1, 1984. BA in French, San Diego State U., 1962. Sec. Mektron div. Calif. Gen., San Diego, 1960-62, sec. Cubic Corp., San Diego, 1962-67, adminstrv. asst., dept. mgr., 1965-67; pre-sch. tchr. Goose & Gander Nursery, San Diego, 1973; instr. Spanish Marvin Elem. Sch., San Diego, 1974-75; cosmetic sales Beauty Counselor, San Diego, 1976-78; tchr. Carden Sch., Del Mar, Calif., 1979-82; office mgr., v.p. Cambridge Assocs., San Diego, 1982-85; owner, pres. Electrofab Sales, San Diego, 19856. Mem. Nat. Assn. Female Execs., San Diego Electronics Network (programs com. 1983—), Electronic Reps. Assn. (edn. chmn. 1985—), Soc. Mfg. Engrs., Torrey Pines Ski Club, Don Diego Ski Club.

NASH-MORGAN, LEONORA ELIZABETH, surgeon; b. Holyoke, Mass., Aug. 13, 1910; d. George Harlan and Edna Doris (Snell) Nash; B.A., Mt. Holyoke Coll., 1932, M.A., 1933; fellow Harvard U., 1933-34; M.D. (W.K. Kellogg grantee), U. Mich., 1939; m. John Dickinson Morgan, Aug. 27, 1940; children—John Dickinson, Leonora Elizabeth, Harlan Kellogg, Elizabeth Emily. Intern, resident U. Mich., 1938-39; physician Iowa State Coll., Cedar Falls, 1939-40; practice medicine and surgery, Erie, Ill., 1941-54, Moline, Ill., 1954—; chmn. utilization rev. com. Oak Glen Nursing Home, Coal Valley, Ill.; lectr. medicine, childhood, adolescence, marriage; mem. staff Lutheran, Moline Public hosps. Mem. Moline Youth Commn., 1964-68; physician Rock Island County Free Venereal Disease Clinic, 1975-77; mem. Center Study of the Presidency, 1976—, nat. adv. council, N.Y.C., 1979—. Recipient article of recognition Moline Dispatch, 1982. Fellow Am. Acad. Family Physicians; mem. Ill. Acad. Family Physicians (past pres., past dir., past del. Rock Island chpt.), Rock Island County Med. Soc., Ill. Med. Soc., Am. Assn. Physicians and Surgeons, AMA, Internat. Soc. Advanced Edn., Photog. Soc. Am., Alpha Epsilon Iota. Republican. Episcopalian. Clubs: Harvard (Chgo.); Sanderling (Sarasota, Fla.). Research on permeability of capillaries, lymphatic system, tetanus; inventor specialized humidifier, 1975.

NASON, THELMA STEIN (TEMA NASON), writer, teacher; b. N.Y.C.; d. Gerson and Bella (Czernitzski) Stein; m. Alvin Nason, Oct. 18, 1944 (dec. Jan., 1978); children—Deborah R., Steffi R., Jean L., Gerson S., Benjamin M. B.A., Bklyn Coll., 1941; postgrad. U. Chgo., 1941-42; M.A., Johns Hopkins U., 1968. Instr. econs. Williams Coll., Williamstown, Mass., 1942-43; wage and disputes analyst War Labor Bd., Chgo., N.Y.C., 1943-44; labor rep. CIO, N.Y.C., Washington, San Francisco, 1944-47; cons. Md. Planning Commn., 1952-53; instr. writing Johns Hopkins U., Balt., 1969-78; freelance writer, Balt., 1958—; sr. research assoc. sociology Brandeis U., Waltham, Mass., 1980—. Author: A Stranger Here, Myself, 1977, short stories. Contbr. articles to jours., newspapers. Vice pres. PTA, Mt. Washington, Balt., 1956-58; vis. scholar Bunting Inst., Radcliffe Coll., Cambridge, Mass., 1979-80. Fellow MacDowell Colony, Peterborough, N.H., 1973, 74, 76, Va. Ctr. for Creative Arts, Sweetbriar, 1984, 85, 86, 88. Mem. PEN, Poets and Writers Assn., Nat. Writers Union. Avocations: theatre; reading; music; swimming; walking.

NAST, CAROL ANN, laboratory executive; b. Champaign, Ill., Nov. 8, 1945; d. Christian Ulrich and Lelia Mae (Glover) Nast; B.S., M.S., Tex. Christian U. Med. technologist Harris Hosp., Ft. Worth, 1967-72; chief med. technologist Presbyn. Hosp., Dallas, 1972-73; mfg. dir. Nuclear Med. Labs., Dallas, 1973-85; ops. mgr. Bio Rad Labs., Hercules, Calif., 1985—; adv. bd. Women in Sci. Program U. Tex., Arlington. Mem. Am. Prodn. and Inventory Control Soc., Am. Soc. Clin. Pathologists (asso. mem., cert. med. technologist), Nat. Purchasing Mgmt. Assn., Sierra Club, Tamalpa Runners, Mensa, Macs of Marin. Home: 2305 Las Gallinas San Rafael CA 94903 Office: 1000 Alfred Nobel Hercules CA 94547

NAST, DIANNE MARTHA, lawyer; b. Moorestown, N.J., Jan. 30, 1946; d. Henry Daniel and Anastasia (Lovenduski) Nast; m. Joseph Francis Roda, Aug. 23, 1980; children: Michael, Daniel, Joseph, Joshua. BA, Pa. State U., 1965; JD, Rutgers U., 1976. Bar: Pa. 1976, N.J. 1976, U.S. Dist. Ct. N.J. 1976, U.S. Dist. Ct. Ariz. 1985, U.S. Ct. Appeals (3d and 7th cirs.) 1976, U.S. Supreme Ct. 1982. Dir., v.p. Kohn, Savett, Klein & Graf, P.C., Phila., 1976—; mem. lawyers adv. com. U.S. Ct. Appeals (3d cir.), 1982-84, chmn., 1983-84, mem. com. on revision jud. conf. conduct rules, 1982-84; mem. U.S. Ct. Appeals for the 3d Dist. Jud. Conf. Permanent Planning Com., 1983—; bd. dirs. Phila. Pub. Def., chmn. lawyers adv. com. U.S. Dist. Ct. (ea. dist.) Pa., 1982—, bd. dirs. hist. soc. Active various charitable and fund raising orgns. Mem. Phila. Bar Assn. (bd. govs. 1985-87, chmn. bicentennial com. 1986-87, chmn. bench bar conf. 1988—) Pa. Bar Assn. (ho. of dels. 1983—, co-chmn. anti-trust com. litigation sect., chmn. bicentennial com. 1986-87, mem. bd. govs. 1985-87), ABA (com. litigation sect. 1984-86, co-chmn. anti-trust com. litigation sect. 1984-86), Am. Law Inst., Am. Judicature Soc., Pa. Bar Assn. (ho. dels. 1983), N.J. Bar Assn., Pa. Trial Lawyers Assn., Pa State U. Alumni Assn., Rutgers Law Sch. Alumni Assn., Pa. Acad. Fine Arts, Pa. Farm Mus. of Landis Valley Assocs., Community Gallery of Lancaster County, Lancaster County Hist. Soc., Rockford Found., Phila. Zool. Soc., Nat. Acquatic Soc., Smithsonian Instn., Met. Mus. Art N.Y. Clubs: Union League Phila., Peale (Phila.). Home: 1059 Sylvan Rd Lancaster PA 17601 Office: Kohn Savett Klein & Graf PC 1100 Market St Suite 2400 Philadelphia PA 19107

NATHAN, NANCY BUTTON, producer, lawyer; b. Wilmington, Del., Mar. 22, 1946; d. Daniel E. and Rebecca (Pool) Button; m. David A. Nathan, Aug. 29, 1969; children: Susannah Day, Elizabeth Bronne Root. AB, Mt. Holyoke Coll., 1968; JD, St. Louis U., 1977; MA, Am. U., 1984. Bar: D.C. 1977. Atty. Fed. Election Commn., Washington, 1980-84; reporter MacNeil-Lehrer News Hour, Washington, 1984-86; producer NBC News, Washington, 1986—. Reporter: (TV coverage) Space Shuttle Challenger Explosion, 1986 (emmy nomination 1987); contbr. article to mag. Recipient Sesquicentennial award Mt. Holyoke Coll. Alumnae Assn., 1987, Mary Lyon award Mt. Holyoke Coll. Alumnae Assn., 1988, Nat. Mag. award, 1985. Mem. Bar Assn. of D.C. Home: 5615 Midwood Rd Bethesda MD 20814 Office: NBC News 4001 Nebraska Ave NW Washington DC 20016

NATHAN, WINIFRED ANTONETTE, lawyer; b. Racine, Wis., Oct. 10, 1936; d. Joseph William and Harriet Marie (James) M.; m. Arthur Bennet Nathan, Sept. 14, 1983; children: Peter J., Angela M., Raissa V. BA, Alverno Coll., 1958; MSW, U. Wis., Milw., 1976; JD, Marquette U., 1983. Police woman Racine Police Dept., 1959-61; social worker Racine County Dept. Social Services, 1969-75, Racine County Human Services Dept., 1976-78; pvt. practice psychotherapy Milw., 1978-80; prin. Nathan Law Office, S.C., Racine, 1984—. Mem. publicity com. The Clearing, Ellison Bay, Wis., 1985-87; bd. dirs. Health and Nutritious Service, Inc., Racine, 1986-87, The Rushes Condominium Assn., Ltd., Door County, Wis., 1987—; Zoning Bd. Village of Wind Point, 1985—. Mem. ABA, State Bar Wis., Racine County Bar Assn., AAUW (bd. dirs. 1984-87), Racine Area Alumnae Campaign Alverno Coll. (chmn. 1987). Home: 5103 Park Place Racine WI 53402 Office: Nathan Law Office SC 524 Monument Square Suite 302 Racine WI 53402

NATHANSON, A. LYNN, broadcasting executive; b. Sydney, N.S., Can., Dec. 4, 1955; came to U.S., 1970, permanent resident, 1978; d. Norris Lionel and Reva (Brook) N.; m. Mark Joseph Pandiscio, Oct. 8, 1978; 1 child, Jennifer Cara. AB in Music and French, Brown U., 1977. Program mgr., announcer Sta. CJCB-FM, Sydney, 1978; floor dir., asst. dir. Sta. WJAR-TV, Providence, R.I., 1979-80; devel. officer Boston Biomed. Research Inst., 1980-81; concert mgr. Mus. Fine Arts, Boston, 1980-81, mgr. Remis Auditorium, 1981-82; sr. v.p. Sta. WCRB, Charles River Broadcasting, Waltham, Mass., 1982-87; sr. v.p., gen. mgr., 1987—; cons. Stas. CJCB-AM, CKPE-FM, Sydney. Chmn. Flights of Fancy Gala fundraiser Dana Farber Cancer Inst., Boston, 1986; bd. dirs. Friends of Dana Farber Cancer Inst., 1985—; mem. benefit com. Pro Arte Chamber Orch., 1986. Mem. Classic Music Broadcasters Assn., Concert Music Broadcasters Assn. (bd. dirs. 1987—, v.p. 1988—), Assn. for Classical Music, Advt. Club of Boston, Boston Symphony Assn. Vols. Jewish. Avocations: piano, singing, swimming, skiing. Home: 241 Perkins St J-202 Boston MA 02130 Office: Sta WCRB Charles River Broadcasting 750 South St Waltham MA 02254

NATHANSON, LINDA SUE, software training consultant, technical writer; b. Washington, Aug. 11, 1946; d. Nat and Edith (Weinstein) N.; m. James F.

Barrett. BS, U. Md., 1969; MA, UCLA, 1970, PhD, 1975. Tng. dir. Rockland Research Inst., Orangeburg, N.Y., 1975-77; asst. prof. psychology SUNY, 1978-79; pres. Cabri Prodns., Inc., Ft. Lee, N.J., 1979-81; research supr. Darcy, McManus & Masius, St. Louis, 1981-83; mgr. software tng., documentation On-Line Software Internat., Ft. Lee, 1983-85; pvt. practice cons. Ft. Lee, 1985-87; founder, exec. dir. The Edin. Group, Inc., Gillette, N.J., 1987—. Author: (with others) Psychological Testing: An Introduction to Tests and Measurement, 1988; contbr. articles to mags. and profl. jours. Recipient Research Service award 1978; Albert Einstein Coll. Medicine Research fellow, 1978-79. Mem. Am. Psychol. Assn., Ind. Computing Cons.'s Assn. (editor Interface newsletter of N.Y./N.J. chpt.). Jewish. Home and Office: 102 Sunrise Dr Gillette NJ 07933

NATHANSON, MAUREEN REILLY, manufacturing company executive; b. Lynn, Mass., Aug. 20, 1942; d. Matthew Louis and Kathleen (Coyne) Reilly; children—Robin, Neal, Matthew. Student pub. schs., Lynn. Demonstrator, Polaroid Corp., Cambridge, Mass., 1967-77, mdse. rep., 1977-79. mktg. rep., 1979-82, area mgr., 1982-84, mktg. rep., 1984-85, dist. sales mgr. N.E., 1985-88; dealer., mgr., U.S. Ops., 1988—. Mem. Women in Sales. Roman Catholic. Avocations: tennis, reading; nautilus; travel. Home: 25 Nickerson Rd Lexington MA 02173 Office: Polaroid Corp 575 Tech Sq Cambridge MA 02138

NATHANSON, NANCY ELLEN, systems consultant; b. Framingham, Mass., July 15, 1958; d. Arnold Norman and Gloria Ruth (Beroff) N. BS in Indsl. and Labor Relations, Cornell U., 1980; MBA., Boston U., 1988. Office automation specialist Word Systems, Inc., Burlington, Mass., 1981-82; customer support analyst Wang Labs., Inc., N.Y.C., 1982-84, dist. systems cons., 1984-85; systems cons. Wang Labs., Inc., Boston, 1985-87, sr. systems cons., 1987—. Mem. Combined Jewish Philanthropies. Home: 33 Pond Ave #1017 Brookline MA 02146 Office: Wang Labs Inc 185 Kneeland St Boston MA 02111

NATHANSON, REBECCA BELLE, psychologist; b. Detroit, Sept. 15; d. Maurice and Sally Stockman; m. Leonard M. Nathanson, Aug. 6, 1960; children: Keith, Shelley, Wendy. BA, Wayne State U., 1955, MA, 1957. Psychologist Henry Ford Hosp., Detroit, 1956-66, Bloomfield Hills (Mich.) Bd. Edn., 1967-68, Ten-Southfield (Mich.) Clinic, 1968-84, William Beaumont Hosp. Neurol. Edn. Ctr., Royal Oak, Mich., 1976-82, Cons. Clinic, Southfield, 1984-86, Mich. Comprehensive Health Services, Oak Park, Mich., 1984-85, Mich. Counseling Ctrs., Ctr. Line, Mich., 1985-86, Rehab. and Placement Assn., Troy, Mich., 1986—. Mem. Am. Psychol. Assn., Am. Radio Relay League. Home: 29203 Lake Park Dr Farmington Hills MI 48018 Office: 3250 W Big Beaver Suite 245 Troy MI 48084

NATIONS-FAULKENBERRY, CYNTHIA ANNE, educator; b. El Paso, Tex., July 5, 1945; d. Jack F. Chew and Doise Louise (Walker) Farrington; m. Edward H. Nations, Nov. 20, 1968 (div. Feb. 1979); children: Kimberly Nations, Kristin Nations; m. Murrel Brooks, July 20, 1985. BS in Edn., U. Tex., 1967. Cert. elem. tchr., Tex. Tchr. elem. schs. Houston, 1967-73, El Paso, Tex., 1979-87. Contbr. articles to profl. jours. Mem. Nat. Tchrs. Assn. (sch. rep. 1986-87, bldg. rep. 1986-87), Tex. State Tchrs. Assn. (sch. rep. 1986-87, bldg. rep. 1986-87), Socorro Tchrs. Assn. (bldg. rep. 1986-87), U.S. Tennis Assn., Greater El Paso Tennis Assn. Republican. Episcopalian. Home: 11223 Les Peterson El Paso TX 79936

NATORI, JOSIE CRUZ, apparel executive; b. Manila, May 9, 1947; came to U.S., 1964; d. Felipe F. and Angelita A. (Almeda) Cruz; m. Kenneth R. Natori, May 20, 1972; 1 child, Kenneth E.F. BA in Econs., Manhattanville Coll., 1968. V.p. Merrill-Lynch Co., N.Y.C., 1971-77; pres. The Natori Co., N.Y.C., 1977—; bd. dirs. Fashion Group, N.Y.C. Recipient Human Relations award Am. Jewish Com., N.Y.C., 1986, Harriet Alger award Working Woman, N.Y., 1987, Castle award Manhattanville Coll., Purchase, 1988. Mem. Com. of 200. Home: 45 E 62d St New York NY 10021 Office: The Natori Co 40 E 34th St 18th Floor New York NY 10016

NATURALE, JOAN MARIE, instructional specialist; b. Abington, Pa., Apr. 11, 1955; d. Anthony Daniel and Ailene (Schutz) N. BA in English, Gallaudet Coll., 1980; MEd, Western Md. Coll., 1983. Student tchr. sign lang. George Mason Elem. Sch., Alexandria, Va., 1981; substitute tchr. Lake Dr. Sch. Hearing Impaired, Mountain Lakes, N.J., 1983; instr. reading, writing Ala. State Sch. Deaf, Talladega, 1984-85; instructional specialist English Northwestern Conn. Community Coll., Winsted, Conn., 1985—; English tutor Gallaudet Coll., 1978-81. Contbr. articles to profl. jours. Mem. Council Edn. Deaf (cert. Ala., N.J.), Conn. Assn. Deaf (coordinator Deaf Awareness Week 1986, founder Conn. assn. deaf blind), Council Tchrs. Deaf, Teaching English Speakers Other Langs., Conn. Educators Hearing Impaired (sec. 1987—), Nat. Assn. Deaf (self help for hard of hearing com.). Roman Catholic. Home: 12 B E Farms Rd Torrington CT 06790 Office: Northwestern Conn Community Coll Park Pl E Winsted CT 06798

NATYSON, FRANCES, psychologist, health educator; b. New Haven, Nov. 20, 1923; d. John Harry and Rozalia N.; grad. Yale New Haven Hosp. Sch. Nursing, 1946; B.A., Hunter Coll., 1969; M.A., New Sch. Social Research, 1972; Ed.D., Columbia U., 1982. Nurse, Bellevue Hosp., N.Y.C., Presbyn. Hosp., N.Y.C., Meml. Hosp. for Cancer and Allied Disease, Roosevelt Hosp., N.Y.C.; team leader, alcoholism counselor Cabrini Med. Center, N.Y.C., 1972—; pvt. practice as psychotherapist; asst. to dir. SEEK program Hunter Coll., 1969-70; tchr. biology Haarem High Sch., N.Y.C., 1971. Mem. Mayors Com., 1973. Mem. N.Y. State Nurses Assn., Am. Psychol. Assn., Soc. Behavioral Medicine, Am. Nurses Assn., Soc. Public Health Edn., Inst. Society, Ethics and Life Scis., Union Concerned Scientists, Kappa Delta Pi. Contbr. articles to profl. jours. Home: 562 West End Ave New York NY 10024

NATZKE, PAULETTE ANN, manufacturing executive; b. Wausau, Wis., Oct. 23, 1943; d. Milton L. and Geraldine J. (Henrichs) Marth; m. Kenneth A. Natzke, June 29, 1963; children: Jerome E., Julie J. Sec. Marth Wood Shavings Supply, Marathon, Wis., 1973-85; pres. Marth Wood Shavings Supply, Marathon, 1985—; v.p. Marth Transp. Inc., Marathon, 1984—; bd. dirs. Marth Found., Marathon. Mem. Cen. Wis. Ceramic Assn. (cert. tchr., Best Show award 1981, Best Booth Show award 1982). Republican. Lutheran. Home: Rt 2 Box 139 Marathon WI 54448 Office: Marth Wood Shavings Supply Inc Rt 2 Marathon WI 54448

NAUGHTON, ANN ELSIE, educator; b. N.Y.C., Apr. 27, 1942; d. George and Wilma (Lubitz) Bruning; m. Gerald Richard Naughton, Dec. 26, 1965 (dec. Apr. 1983); 1 child, Jonathan. BA, CUNY, 1963; MA, Columbia U., 1965; postgrad., Greenburgh Inst. Tchrs. Social worker div. child and family welfare Westchester County, Yonkers, N.Y., 1963-64; tchr. Hastings-on-Hudson (N.Y.) Pub. Schs., 1965—; tchr. Lincoln Ctr. Inst., N.Y.C., 1986—. Mem. Hastings Tchrs. Union (mem.-at-large exec. com. 1982—, state facilitator and trainer N.Y. parent tchr. confs. 1988—). Republican. Home: 31 Walbrook Rd Scarsdale NY 01058-0003 Office: Hastings-on-Hudson Pub Schs Hastings-on-Hudson NY 10706

NAUGHTON, ELIZABETH MAY, museum director; b. Washington, Dec. 16, 1933; d. A. Nelson and May H. (Laudenslager) Sayre; m. Frank H. Naughton III, Sept. 13, 1958; children: Stephen, Elizabeth. BA, Wellesley Coll., 1956. Museum dir. Hartshorn Arboretum, Short Hills, N.J., 1977—; chmn. Environ. Commn. (planning bd. mem.), Millburn, N.J., 1981-87. Mem. Jr. League. Office: Hartshorn Arboretum 324 Forest Dr S Short Hills NJ 07078

NAUGHTON, JODIE-KAY MARIE, telecommunications company executive; b. Chgo., Sept. 9, 1951; d. Joseph Martin and Evelyn Marie (Milne) N.; A.B.A., Wright City Coll., 1979; B.A., Lakeland Coll., 1984; m. Robert Anthony Memmel, Jr., Nov. 17, 1979 (div. July 1984). With Western Electric Co., various locations, 1969—, customer service rep., 1979-80, payroll and acctg. specialist, Milw., 1980; now with Ameritech Services, Inc., Arlington Heights, Ill. Bd. dirs. Future Pioneers, 1979, Concerner Consumers League Inc., Milw.; adviser Jr. Achievement, 1974, 75; v.p. Wright Newman Ctr., 1977; creator Weco Wackos, clown troupe, 1978; asst. adminstr. Midwest Region Hunger Project, 1980; info. chmn. Telephone Pioneers, 1986-87. Served with USNR. Home: 433 N Maple Ln Hillside IL 60162 Office: 3040 W Salt Creek LN Arlington Heights IL 60005

NAUGHTON, MARIE ANN, corporate manager; b. Boston, Feb. 19, 1954; d. Robert J. and Beatrice T. (McDonald) N.; B.S. in Speech magna cum laude, Emerson Coll., 1976; M.A., Ind. U., 1977. Speech-lang. pathologist Dedham (Mass.) public schs., 1977-79; speech-lang. pathologist Mass. Gen. Hosp., Boston, 1979-81; speech pathologist Mt. Auburn Hosp., Cambridge, Mass., 1982-84; mgr. Curtis-Newton Corp., Spltys. Div., 1984—. Fellow Soc. for Ear, Nose and Throat Advances in Children; mem. Am. Speech, Lang. and Hearing Assn. (cert. clin. competence), Mass. Speech and Hearing Assn., Zeta Phi Eta. Club: Northeastern Young Lumber Execs. Author: A Coarticulation Manuel for the Remediation of /S/, 1979. Home: 77 Circuit Rd Dedham MA 02026 Office: 963 Watertown St West Newton MA 02165

NAUMANN, MARY LYNN, insurance company executive; b. Houston, July 19, 1940; d. James Reuben and Sarah Gladys (Foster) Spaulding; m. Halmude Naumann, Jr., Aug. 29, 1958; children—Dana Lynn, Halmude III. Student St. Louis Inst. Music, 1958, U. Houston, 1959. C.P.C.U., Tex. Real estate broker, Houston, 1962-65; underwriting asst. Royal Globe Ins., Houston, 1965-67; sr. underwriter Indsl. Indemity, Houston, 1967-75; casualty supr. Aetna Ins. Co., Houston, 1975-80; asst. v.p. Emett & Chandler Tex., Houston, 1980-81; S.W. regional mgr. AIG Risk Mgmt., Houston, 1981-86; pres. RM Ins. Agy., Inc., Houston, 1986-87; field underwriting adminstr. Am. Gen. Fire & Casualty Co., 1988—; adj. prof. U. Houston, 1975-79, 88—, Houston Bapt. U., 1979-82; instr. Houston Sch. Ins., 1975-78. Mem. Houston C.P.C.U. Assn. (pres. 1981-82, dir. 1978—), Nat. Soc. C.P.C.U.s (com. mem.), Houston Casualty Roundtable (v.p. 1975-76). Home: 7343 Birchtree Forest Houston TX 77088 Office: Am Gen Fire & Casualty Co PO Box 1502 Houston TX 77251

NAUTS, HELEN LANCASTER COLEY, health science association administrator; b. Sharon, Conn., Sept. 2, 1907; d. William Bradley and Alice (Lancaster) Coley; m. william Boone Nauts, Sept. 22, 1928; children: Nancy Coley, Phyllis Lancaster. Student sch. landscape architecture, Columbia U., 1927-28; D Sci. (hon.), Hartwick Coll., 1986. Pvt. practice landscape architecture N.Y. and Conn.; founder, exec. dir. Cancer Research Inst., N.Y.C., 1953-82, dir. Sci. Med. Communications, 1982—; exec. dir. Brearley Alumnae Assn., N.Y.C., 1940-48, mng. editor Brearley Bulletin, 1946-48; trustee Cancer Research Inst., 1953-66; lectr. cancer confs. France, Germany, Eng., Japan, China, U.S. Author, editor scientific papers in cancer research, 1953-87, monographs on cancer immunology, 1946-87. Recipient William B. Coley Meml. award, 1985, Commandeur de l'Ordre Nat. de Merite Pres. Valery Giscard d'Estaing, 1981; named Francis Riker Davis alumnae Brearley Sch., 1980. Democrat. Presbyterian. Club: Cosmopolitan (N.Y.C.). Home and Office: Cancer Research Inst 1225 Park Ave New York NY 10128-1707

NAVARRO, KARYL KAY, educator; b. Detroit, Dec. 6, 1956; d. Richard Charles and Vera Clair (Gemeinhardt) Carlson; m. Andrew J. Navarro, June 24, 1986. MusB, U. Mich., 1979; MS in Music Edn., U. Ill., 1982. Cert. tchr., Fla. Tchr. elem. music Community Sch. Dist. 5, Franklin Sch., Sterling, Ill., 1979-81; tchr. Hialeah-Miami Lakes High Sch. Dade County Pub. Schs., Hialeah, 1982—, supervising tchr., 1984-88; tchr. Miami Lakes Jr. High Sch. Dade County Pub. Schs., 1984—; pvt. instr. piano and voice, 1979—; adjudicator solo-ensemble Dist. 5, Moline, 1980; choreographer HML Singers, Hialeah, 1982—; condr. Honors Music Festival Dade County Pub. Schs., Miami, Fla., 1985; accompanist Civic Chorale U. Miami, 1985; tchr. summer choral camp U. Miami, Coral Gables, Fla., 1987; clinician U. Miami Honor Choir Festival. Arranger marching band and choral music, 1979—; dir., producer: (musicals) L'il Abner, 1982, Aria da Capo, 1982. Mem. Miami Zool. Soc., 1985, gallon donor club ARC, Miami, 1986; dir. HML Singers, Young Ams. Nat. Invitational Performance Choir Festival, Hollywood, Calif., Festival Internat. de Musique, Quebec, Can.; peer tchr., Dade County Pub. Schs. Recipient Fla. Master Tchr. award State of Fla., 1986. Mem. Am. Choral Dirs. Assn., Music Educators Nat. Conf., Fla. Music Educators Assn., Dade County Music Educators Assn. (treas. 1986-87), Fla. Vocal Assn. (dist. chair 1987—), United Tchrs. Dade, U. Mich. Alumni Assn. Republican. Home: 2200 Charleston Fort Lauderdale FL 33326 Office: Hialeah-Miami Lakes High Sch 7977 W 12th Ave Hialeah FL 33014

NAVE, JEAN RUSSELL, marketing and management training company executive; b. Burbank, Calif., Jan. 18, 1949; d. Gale Paul and Carolyn Margaret (Ludwig) Bartlett; m. Thomas R. Russell, June 18, 1968 (div. 1973); 1 child, Robert Gale; m. 2d, Claude Felix Nave, Aug. 6, 1983. Student Antelope Valley Coll., 1967, also numerous pvt. sales tng. courses. Mktg. rep. Bank of Am., Los Angeles, 1968-73; maj. account rep. Xerox Corp., Los Angeles, 1974-75; advisor, mktg. rep. Service Bur. Co., Los Angeles, 1975-79; field sales rep. Hewlett Packard Co., Santa Ana, Calif., 1979-80; mktg. mgr. Automatic Data Processing, Portland, Oreg., 1980-82; pres. Motivational Dynamics, Inc., Portland, 1981—, also dir.; mktg. cons. J.T. Warren Computer Service, Portland, 1983—; host TV show Bus. Upbeat; dir. Author: (book, tapes) Women ... The World's Greatest Salesmen, 1984, Traveling the Road of Success, Sales in a Nutshell, 1986, The Quest for Real Success-A Search for American Business Values, 1987. Active Republican polit. campaigns, Calif. and Oreg., 1970—. Mem. Am. Mktg. Assn., Project Mgmt. Inst. (v.p. 1981), Inst. Profl. and Managerial Women. Baptist. Club: Portland City. Home: 360 SW Breeze Ct Portland OR 97225 Office: Motivational Dynamics Inc PO Box 25104 Portland OR 97225

NAVIAUX, LAREE DEVEE, psychologist; b. Lewellen, Nebr., Aug. 18, 1937; d. Prosper Leo and Dorothy DeVee (Walters) N.; m. Frank Anthony D'Abreo, June 16, 1973. B.S., U. Nebr., 1959; M.S., Iowa State U., 1963; Ph.D., Duquesne U., 1973. Instr. Iowa State U., Ames, 1963-65; asst. prof. Kans. State U., Manhattan, 1965-66; grad. faculty Carnegie-Mellon U., Pitts., 1966-69; asst. prof. West Ga. Coll., Carrollton, 1969-72; regional dir. Children's Mental Health, Charleston, W.Va., 1973-80; therapist, educator Community Mental Health Center, Charleston, 1980-82; pvt. practice, 1982—; asst. clin. prof. W.Va. U., 1977—. Active Family and Children Together Speaker's Bur., 1980-83; bd. dirs. Creative Arts Clinic, 1981-83, Parents Anonymous of W.Va., 1979-82. Humanities Found. W.Va. grantee, 1978, 79, 81, 82. Fellow Menninger Found.; mem. U. Nebr. Alumni (life), Iowa State U. Alumni (life), Am. Psychol. Assn., Assn. for Humanistic Psychology, Mental Health Assn. (life), Inst. Noetic Scis. Democrat. Roman Catholic. Clubs: Kanawha Players, Gourmet, Friendship Force, Indian Assn. Contbr. articles to profl. jours. and books. Office: 3500 Staunton Ave Charleston WV 25304

NAVRATIL, JEAN, librarian, missionary; b. Houston, Aug. 17, 1950; d. Louis Anton and Annie Kamila (Slansky) Navratil; m. Colin Cumming, July 1, 1982 (div. June 1987). A.A., Wharton County Jr. Coll., 1970; B.A., Tex. Woman's U., 1972; postgrad. Unification Theol. Sem., 1980—. Library technician Project Job, U.S. Civil Service Commn., Dallas, 1972; clk.-typist Menasco, Fort Worth, 1972-73; fin. mgr. Internat. Exchange Press, San Francisco, 1974-75; library clk., adminstrv. clk. Bechtel Power Corp., San Francisco, 1974-75; exec. sec. Internat. Cultural Found., N.Y.C., 1975-80; cataloguer Unification Theol. Sem., Barrytown, N.Y., 1981-83, dir. tech. services, 1984-87, dir. tech. and pub. services, 1987-88, assoc. dir., 1988—. Vol. community work Unification Ch. Home Ch. Program Harlem, N.Y., 1976-80. Mem. ALA, Internat. Cultural Found. Confs. (exec. sec.). Home: 17 South St #9 Rhinebeck NY 12572 Office: Unification Theol Sem Library 10 Dock Rd Barrytown NY 12507

NAVRATILOVA, MARTINA, professional tennis player; b. Prague, Czechoslovakia, Oct. 18, 1956; came to U.S., 1975, naturalized, 1981; d. Miroslav Navratil and Jana Navratilova. Student, schs. in Czechoslovakia. Profl. tennis player 1975—. Author: (with George Vecsey) Martina, 1985. Winner Czechoslovak Nat. singles, 1972-74, U.S. Open singles, 1983, 84, 87 U.S. Open doubles, 1977, 78, 80, 83, 84, 87, U.S. Open mixed doubles, 1987, Va. Slims Tournament, 1978, 83, 84, 85, 86, Wimbledon singles, 1978, 79, 82, 83, 84, 85, 86, 87, Wimbledon women's doubles, 1976, 79, 81, 82, 83, 84, 86, Wimbledon mixed doubles, 1985, French Open singles, 1982, 84, Australian Open singles, 1981, 83, 85, Grand Slam of Women's Tennis, 1984; named Hon. Citizen of Dallas, AP Female Athlete of Yr., 1983. Mem. Women's Tennis Assn. (dir., exec. com.). Office: care Sargent Hill 525 Bailey Fort Worth TX 76107

NAYAR, SHAMILA BEHAL, auditor; b. Nairobi, Kenya, June 29, 1956; came to U.S., 1984; d. Ved Parkash and Savitri (Bassi) Behal. B.S. with Honors, London Sch. of Econs., 1978; M.B.A., McGill U., 1984. Economist, Ministry of Fin., Nairobi, 1978-79; auditor Touche Ross & Co., London, 1979-82; sr. auditor, N.Y.C., 1984-86; mgr. policies and procedures Am. Express Travel-Related Services, N.Y.C., 1987—. Treas. UN Youth Orgn., London, 1977. Mem. Nat. Assn. of Accts., Nat. Assn. Female Execs., Inst. of Chartered Accts. Students Soc. Club: U. London Bridge (sec. 1975-76). Avocations: horseback riding; tennis; international affairs; reading. Office: Am Express World Fin Ctr New York NY 10285

NAYLE, PATRICIA LYNN, state personnel officer; b. Columbus, Ind., Sept. 26, 1951; d. Ray Herman and Mary Lucille (Buckles) N. B.S. in Home Econs., Merchandising, So. La. U., 1974; postgrad. U. Houston, 1976-81. Personnel clk. Tex. Dept. Human Services, Houston, 1975-76, personnel asst., 1976-80, personnel officer, 1980—. Mem. Nat. Assn. Female Execs., Houston Personnel Assn., AAUW, Phi Kappa Phi, Alpha Sigma Tau (alumnae chpt. pres. 1977-79, dist. pres. 1980-82, dir. expansion nat. council 1982-86, nat. historian 1976-80, nat. pres. 1986—). Office: Tex Dept Human Services PO Box 16017 Houston TX 77022

NAZARIO, LUCY, real estate company vice president; b. Rio Piedras, P.R., Oct. 8, 1941; came to U.S., 1960; d. Rafael Montañez and Providencia Sanchez; m. Carmelo Nazario, Feb. 23, 1963; children: Wilbert, Jimmy. Sales rep. Coopercraft Guild, Jersey City, 1972-74; tax preparation specialist H & R Block, Jersey City, 1974-76; real estate sales rep. Robert DeRuggiero, Inc., Union City, N.J., 1976-84; sales rep. R.E. Bulin Assocs., North Bergen, N.J., 1984-85, office mgr., 1985-86, v.p., 1987—. Chairperson St. Joseph Sch. for Blind Christmas Party. Named Assoc. of Yr. N.J. Assn. of Realtors, 1983, 84. Mem. North Hudson Bd. Realtors (1st v.p., 1988, 2d v.p. 1987, treas. 1986, assoc. of yr. 1984). Democrat. Roman Catholic. Office: R E Bulin Assocs 2241 Kennedy Blvd North Bergen NJ 07047

NAZARUK, PAMELA ANNE, publishing executive; b. Rockville Centre, N.Y., Feb. 21, 1954; d. Fred Ehnatey and Luella Henderson (Muir) N. BS, U. Fla., 1976. Dir. pub. relations Fla. Mcpl. Utilities Assn., Tallahassee, 1977-79; asst. editor pubs. Am. Pub. Power Assn., Washington, 1979-81; dir. communications Valve Mfrs. Assn. Am., Washington, 1981-87; mng. editor CPI Purchasing mag. Cahners Pub. Co., Newton, Mass., 1987—. Editor and compiler various trade pubs. Mem. Pub. Relations Soc. Am. (accredited), Am. Soc. Assn. Execs. (mgmt. achievement award Washington chpt. 1985, gold circle award 1983, 86), Ski Club of Washington (ski trip leader 1979-87), Alpha Chi Omega (alumni mem. 1976—). Democrat. Presbyterian. Office: CPI Purchasing Mag Cahners Pub Co 275 Washington St Newton MA 02158

NEAL, ANNE DEHAYDEN, lawyer; b. Indpls., Mar. 22, 1955; d. James Thomas and Georgianne (Davis) N.; m. Thomas Evert Petri, Mar. 26, 1983. A.B. in Am. History and Lit., Harvard U., 1977, J.D., 1980. Bar: N.Y. 1981, U.S. Dist. Ct. (so. dist.) N.Y. 1981, U.S. Dist. Ct. (ea. dist.) N.Y. 1981, U.S. Ct. Claims 1982, U.S. Ct. Appeals (fed. cir.) 1982, D.C. 1984, Wis. 1986. Assoc., Rogers & Wells, N.Y.C., 1980-82; gen. counsel Office of Adminstrn., Exec. Office Pres., Washington, 1982-84; assoc. Wiley, Rein & Fielding, Washington, 1984-87; dep. gen counsel Recording Industry Assn. Am. Inc., 1987—. founding mem. Nat. Mus. of Women in Arts, 1984—, bd. dirs., 1987—, chmn. nominating com., 1987—; chmn., bd. dirs., v.p., ho. of reps. Child Care Ctr. Inc., 1986—; chmn. New Leadership Fund, 1985—. Pulliam journalism fellow Indpls. News, 1977. Mem. Fed. Communications Bar Assn., ABA, Communications Law Forum, Colonial Dames Am., Phi Beta Kappa. Republican. Methodist. Club: Dramatic (Indpls.). Office: Rec Industry Assn of Am Inc 1020 19th St NW Suite 200 Washington DC 20006

NEAL, BONNIE JEAN, real estate sales associate; b. Kansas City, Mo., Apr. 24, 1930; d. David Ira and Juanita Mae (Duncan) Johnson; m. Howard Stranton Neal, July 24, 1948 (div. Oct. 1972); children: Randall Stranton, William Scott, Douglas Kelly. Student, U. Omaha, 1980-86, Londay Sch. Real Estate, Omaha, 1987. Data processing supr. Enron Corp., Omaha, 1980-85, adminstrv. support analyst, 1985-86; real estate sales agt. Allen, Young Assocs., Omaha, 1987-88, Coldwell Banker Action Real Estate, Bellevue, Neb., 1988—; Active PTA, Council Bluffs, Iowa, 1957-59; vol. March of Dimes, Council Bluffs, 1963—; mem. com. Realtors Polit. Action. Fellow Omaha Bd. Realtors; mem. Women's Bowling Assn. Democrat. Baptist. Lodge: Order Eastern Star (25-yr. award 1980). Home: 3303 6th Ave Council Bluffs IA 51501 Office: Coldwell Banker Action Real Estate 1313 Harlan Dr Bellevue NE 68005

NEAL, CHARLOTTE ANNE, education specialist; b. Hampton, Iowa, May 8, 1937; d. Sebo and Marion Bradford (Boutin-Clock) Reysack; B.A., U. No. Iowa, 1958; M.Ed., DePaul U. (Chgo.), 1966; postgrad. No. Ill. U.; m. Paul Gordon Neal, Mar. 29, 1969; children—Rachel Elizabeth, Kory Bradford. Tchr., 4th grade, Des Moines Ind. Sch. Dist., 1958-59; tchr., 3d grade Glenview (Ill.) Pub. Schs., 1959-61, tchr. 3d grade, psychol. ednl. diagnostic Schaumburg Dist. Schs., Hoffman Estates, Ill., 1961-69; supr. learning disabilities and behavior disorders Springfield (Ill.) Pub. Schs., 1969-73; psycho-ednl. diagnostician Barrington (Ill.) Sch. Dist. 220, 1973-77; ednl. strategist Area Edn. Agy. 7, Cedar Falls, Iowa, 1978—; ednl. cons. Spl. Edn. Dist. Lake County, Gurnee, Ill., summer, 1968. Certified K-14 teaching and supervising in guidance, counseling, elementary supervisory K-9, elementary K-9 teaching, spl. K-12 learning disabilities. Mem. NEA, Ill. Edn. Assn. Author: Handbook for Learning Disabilities Tchrs., 1971. Home: 1102 Sunset Dr Parkersburg IA 50665 Office: 3712 Cedar Hts Dr Cedar Falls IA 50613

NEAL, CONSTANCE ANN TRILLICH, lawyer, librarian, minister; b. Chgo., Apr. 16, 1949; d. Lee and Ruth (Goodhue) Trillich; m. Robert Dale Neal, Dec. 25, 1972 (div. 1988); 1 son, Adam Danforth. BA in French, U. Tenn., 1971, cert. Sorbonne, 1970; MLn, Emory U., 1979; JD, Mercer Law Sch., 1982. Bar: Ga. 1982; cert. Reiki therapist level II. Reservationist AAA, Tampa, Fla., 1971-72; library tech. asst. I, Mercer U., Macon, Ga., 1973-74, library tech. asst. II, 1974-78; teaching asst. Mercer Law Sch., Macon, 1981; asst. prof. Mercer Med. Sch., Macon, 1980-82; sole practice, Macon, 1982-86; minister Ch. Tzaddi, 1986—; minister Alliance of Divine Love, 1988—; research asst. Ctr. Constl. Studies, Macon, 1983; instr. bus. Wesleyan Coll., Macon, 1982. Bd. dirs. Unity Ch., Middle, Ga., 1987, Sec., 1987. Bd. dirs. Macon Council World Affairs, 1981-82; mem. Friends Emory Libraries, Atlanta, 1980—; mem. Friends Eckerd Coll. Library, St. Petersburg, Fla., 1980—. Mem. ABA, Am. Soc. Law and Medicine, Am. Judicature Soc., DAR (Kaskaskia chpt.), Mercer U. Women's Club (treas. 1974, pres. 1986, bd. dirs. 1987), Am. Assn. U. Women, Friends of the Library, Mid. Ga. Gem and Mineral Soc., Macon Mus. Arts and Scis., La Leche League (sec. 1985), Phi Alpha Delta. Republican.

NEAL, KATHY, civic worker, former city official; b. Los Angeles, Aug. 9, 1949; d. Elvin Vernon and Doris Eva (Golden) N.; m. Elihu M. Harris. student U. So. Calif., 1974-75; B.A., Calif. State U., Los Angeles, 1975; M.P.A., U. San Francisco, 1983; cert. in Spanish, U. Salamanca, 1967. Dir., Little Playmates Childrens Center, Los Angeles, 1971-74; legis. analyst Los Angeles City Council, 1975-84; mng. ptnr. 24K, 1984; fund raising cons.; dir. Builders Mut. Surety Co. Vice pres. bd. govs. Calif. Community Colls., also chmn. legis. and adminstrv. com., 1981-86; mem. bd. govs. Calif. State Bar, 1987—, Calif. Democratic Central Com., 1979—; sponsor, adv. Black Womens Forum, 1979-84; bd. dirs. Miss Watts Summer Pageant, 1976—, Westside Women's Clinic, 1985—; chmn. politics com. Coordinating com. Internat. Womens Yr. State Conf., 1977; asst. coordinator telethon United High Blood Pressure Found., 1978; co-founder, chmn. Black Edn. Network, 1985—; chmn. Speaker's Bur., Crenshaw-West Adams-Leimert Consortium, 1985—, Oakland Zoo Devel. com. Mem. Alpha Kappa Alpha.

NEAL, LEORA LOUISE HASKETT, social services administrator; b. N.Y.C., Feb. 23, 1943; d. Melvin Elias and Miriam Emily (Johnson) Haskett; m. Robert A. Neal, Apr. 23, 1966; children: Marla Patrice, Johnathan Robert. BA in Psychology and Sociology, City Coll. N.Y., 1965; MS in

Social Work, Columbia U., 1970, asst. adoption specialist, 1977; IBM cert. community exec. tng. program, N.Y., 1982. Cert. social worker N.Y. State. Caseworker N.Y.C. Dept. Social Service, 1965-67, Windham Child Care, N.Y.C., 1967-73; exec. dir. Assn. Black Social Workers Child Adoption Counseling and Referral Service, N.Y.C., 1975—; Cons. adoption, adoption tng. N.Y. State Dept. Social Service, Columbia U. Sch. Social Work, N.Y.C. Human Resources Adminstn., U. La. New Orleans. Mem. Nat. Assoc. Female Execs., Columbia U. Alumni Assn., City Coll. N.Y. Alumni Assn. Democrat. Club: Missionary Com. Revival Team (outreach chairperson 1982—). Office: Assn Black Social Workers Adoption Service 271 W 125th St Room 414 New York NY 10027

NEAL, MARGARET SHERRILL, intelligence research specialist; b. Memphis, Apr. 13, 1950; d. Wilburn Franklin and Merle Aileen (Willis) N. BA, Memphis State U., 1972, postgrad., 1973; MS, Columbia Pacific U., 1984. Air traffic controller FAA, Memphis, 1974-76, New Bern, N.C., 1976-81, Vero Beach, Fla., 1981-83; detection systems specialist U.S. Customs Service, Miami, 1983-87, intelligence research specialist, 1987—. Mem. NOW, Smithsonian Inst., Mensa, Nat. Trust for Hist. Preservation, Assn. for Research and Enlightenment. Republican. Baptist.

NEAL, MARY, home economics educator; b. Green Bay, Va.; d. Emmitt P. and Viola (Warren) N. BS, St. Paul's Coll., Lawrenceville, Va., 1953; MA, Columbia U., 1955, diploma, 1963. Dietitian various hosps., Welfare Island, N.Y.C., 1953-54; instr. food and nutrition Alcorn Coll., Lorman, Miss., 1955-56; instr. home econ. and phys. sci. Benedict Coll., Columbia, S.C., 1956-58; asst. prof. home econs. Morris Brown Coll., Atlanta, 1959-62; tchr. home econs. and consumer math. Wyandanch (N.Y.) High Sch., 1963-66; tchr. home arts Hicksville (N.Y.) High Sch., 1966—; lyceum chmn. Morris Brown Coll., Atlanta, 1959-62; mem. mid. states evaluation team Mid. States Assn. Schs., Hicksville, N.Y., 1978; mem. curriculum devel. com. various colls. Lorman and Atlanta, 1955-62. Sunday sch. tchr., hostess Benedict Coll., Columbia, 1956-58; sec. McAlister summer camp, Huguenot, N.Y., 1966; hostess Episcopal Students Canterbury House, Atlanta, 1960-62; chaperone St. John's Episcopal Ch., Hempstead, N.Y., 1975-82. Mem. Nat. Home Econs. Assn., L.I. Home Econs. Assn. (legis. chmn. 1966), Hicksville Tchrs. Assn., Alpha Kappa. Democrat. Club: Crafts (L.I.).

NEAL, SUSAN CAROL, security officer; b. Cinn., Nov. 3, 1951; d. Donald Stanley and Marilyn (Huber) Sammons; m. Frederick E. Neal, July 5, 1979; 1 child, Charles D. BS in Criminology, U. Md., 1978, BS in Paralegal Studies, 1985; postgrad., Cen. Mich. U., 1982—. Counter intelligence agt. U.S. Army, worldwide, 1975-80; counter intelligence technician U.S. Army, Ft. Meade, Md., 1980-85; supr. security ops. Bendix Field Engring. Corp., Columbia, Md., 1985—. Pres. Parents Orgn. Post Pre-Sch., Ft. Meade, 1986-87, mem. 1985-86. Mem. Nat. Class Mgmt. Soc., Am. Soc. for Indsl. Security, Nat. Paralegal Assn., Nat. Assn. Female Execs. Office: Bendix Field Engring Corp One Bendix Rd Columbia MD 21045

NEAL-DANIELS, SHERRY ANN, accountant; b. Helena, Ark., Oct. 1, 1959; d. Jerry and Melvina (Williams) N. BBA, Memphis State U., 1981. Acctg. asst. Gen. Telephone of the Southwest, San Angelo, Tex., 1981-83, acct., 1983-85, sr. acct., 1985-87; budget statistician Gen. Telephone of the Southwest, Irving, Tex., 1987—. Mem. Nat. Assn. Accts., Nat. Assn. Female Execs. Office: Gen Telephone Co SW 290 E Carpenter Freeway Irving TX 75015

NEALE, DEBORAH LORETTO, chemical company executive; b. Rocky River, Ohio, June 29, 1947; d. James Anthony and Loretto Murray (Seedhouse) N. BA, U. Dayton, 1969, MA, 1970. Asst. buyer Higbee's Dept. Store, Cleve., 1970-71; tchr. Rocky River (Ohio) Sch. System, 1971-73; group coordinator Med. Mut. of Cleve., 1973-78, dir. govt. relations, 1978-81; mgr. state govt. relations BF Goodrich, Akron, Ohio, 1981-83; dir. state govt. relations BF Goodrich, Akron, 1983-85, exec. dir. govt. relations, 1985-87; dir. external affairs BF Goodrich, Cleve., 1987-88; exec. dir. state govt. relations BF Goodrich, Akron, Ohio, 1988—. Mem. Pub. Affairs Com., Cleve., 1978—, Women in Govt. Relations, Washington, 1979—; com. mem. Gov.'s Ohio Adv. Com. on Energy, Columbus, 1984; chmn. govt. relations com. Hwy. Users Fedn., Washington, 1985—; chmn. exec. com. NE Ohio March of Dimes, Cleve., 1987; chmn. Calif. Plastics Polit. Action Com., Sacramento, 1987; com. mem. Summity City United Way, Akron, Ohio, 1987; mem. planning fedn., Cleve. Mem. Soc. of the Plastics Industry Inc. (com. chmn. 1986—), Chem. Mfrs. Assn., Ohio Chpt. of Plastics Industry (chmn. 1986—), CA Aerospace Alliance (state govt. affairs council 1983—), Ohio Press Club, Operation Life Safety (vice chmn. Washington chpt.). Club: Women's City. Office: BF Goodrich 3925 Embassy Pkwy Akron OH 44313 Office: BF Goodrich 6100 Oak Tree Blvd Cleveland OH 44131

NEAL-RICKER, NORMA CANDACE, engineer, construction company executive; b. Berkeley, Calif., Aug. 19, 1947; d. Charles Edward and Norma Alice (Davidson) Neal; m. Frederick Augustin Ricker; children: Candace Victoria, Chelsea Elizabeth. BS, Oreg. State U., 1969; MBA, Golden Gate U., 1977. Rep. employee relations Bechtel, Inc., San Francisco, 1969-73, coordinator contracts, 1973-75, mgr. contracts, 1975-78, exec. rep. ETSI pipeline project, 1981-84; mgr. ETSI pipeline project Bechtel Power Corp., San Francisco, 1984—, rep. bus. devel., 1978-81. Bd. trustees Sausalito (Calif.) Found., 1975-84; bd. govs. San Francisco YMCA, 1976-83; chmn. San Rafael (Calif.) YMCA, 1979-80; bd. dirs. Marin County (Calif.) YMCA, 1976—. Mem. Comml. Club of San Francisco, Commonwealth Club. Republican. Episcopalian. Club: Sausalito Women's. Home: 88 Monte Vista Rd Fairfax CA 94930 Office: Bechtel Inc PO Box 3965 San Francisco CA 94119

NEARING, HELEN KNOTHE, writer, farmer; b. N.Y.C., Feb. 23, 1904; d. Frank Frederick and Maria (Obreen) Knothe; widowed. Studied violin, Amsterdam, Holland, Vienna. Author: Our Home Made of Stone, Simple Food for the Good Life, Wise Words on the Good Life, The Good Life Picture Album; author (with Scott Nearing): Living the Good Life, Continuing the Good life, The Maple Sugar Book, USA Today. Home: Forest Farm Harborside ME 04642 Office: Social Sci Inst Harborside ME 04642

NEASE, JUDITH ALLGOOD, marriage and family therapist; b. Arlington, Mass., Nov. 15, 1930; d. Dwight Maurice Allgood and Sophie (Wolf) Allgood Morris; student Rockford Coll., 1949-50; B.A., N.Y.U., 1953, M.A., 1954; M.S., Columbia U. Sch. Social Work, 1956; m. Theron Stanford Nease, Sept. 1, 1962; children—Susan Elizabeth, Alison Allgood. Social worker Bellevue Psychiat. Hosp., N.Y.C., 1956-59; psychiat. social worker St. Luke's Hosp., N.Y.C., 1959-62; asst. psychiat. social worker supr. N.J. Neuropsychiat. Inst., Princeton, 1962-64; marriage and family therapist Druid Hills Pastoral Counseling Service, Atlanta, 1973-76, asst. dir. social work supr., co-leader group, 1973-84 ; asst. dir., co-leader Pastoral Counseling Service, Columbia Theol. Sem., 1973-82 ; marriage and family therapist Catholic Social Services, Atlanta, 1978-87; chief Community Mental Health Clinic, Atlanta, Ga., 1987—; pvt. practice marriage and family therapy. Mem. Nat. Assn. Social Workers, Acad. Cert. Social Workers, Am. Assn. Marriage and Family Therapy, Atlanta Group Psychotherapy Assn. Republican. Episcopalian. Home: 4678 Cedar Park Way Stone Mountain GA 30083

NEASE, VIRGINIA LEE, social worker; b. Toronto, Ont., Can., May 5, 1939; d. Norman Miller and Willie Belle (Terry) Dunn; m. Corley Harrell Nease, Dec. 30, 1967; children—Michael Lovett, Paul Robert. B.A., Fla. State U., 1962; M.S.W., Tulane U., 1966. Social work aide ARC, Charleston, S.C., 1962-64; social work supr., Columbus, Ga., 1966-68; social work supr. Child Guidance Clinic, Savannah, Ga., 1968-71; social work supr. Community Mental Health Center, Savannah, 1971-74; service coordinator Tidelands Community Mental Health Center, Savannah, 1974—; family therapist pvt. practice Savannah, 1979—. Bd. dirs. Hospice, Savannah, 1980-84, sec., 1983-84; employee assistance counselor for human affairs Internat. and Personal Performance Con. Scholarship in her name awarded by Nat. Assn. Social Workers, 1973—. Mem. Aux. Ga. Optometric Assn. (pres. 1972-73), Nat. Assn. Social Workers (pres. S.E. chpt. 1971), Nat. Assn. Social Workers, Acad. Cert. Social Workers (lic. clin. social worker, marriage and family therapist). Episcopalian. Home: 4 Margrave Ln Savannah GA 31411 Office: 7203 Hodgson Meml Dr Savannah GA 31406

NEAVEILL, DARLA PETERS, lawyer; b. Peoria, Ill., Aug. 2, 1956; d. Ralph and Wilma Francis (Neaveill) P. BS in Chemistry, U. South Fla., 1977; postgrad., Stetson U., St. Petersburg, Fla., 1981-82; JD, Ind. U., 1984. Bar: Ohio 1984, U.S. Patent Office 1985, Minn. 1987. Patent atty. Procter & Gamble Co., Cin., 1984-86, Minn. Mining and Mfg. Co. div. 3M, St. Paul, 1986—. Com. mem. Ramsey Hill Hist. Soc., St. Paul, 1987. Mem. ABA, Minn. Bar Assn., Minn. Patent Law Assn., Am. Intellectual Property Law Assn. (mem. com.), Nat. Assn. Female Execs., Phi Delta Phi. Home: 79 Western Ave N Apt 608 Saint Paul MN 55102 Office: 3M 3M Ctr PO Box 33427 Saint Paul MN 55133-3427

NEBEKER, TERESA SKURA, communications company executive; b. Washington, Aug. 28, 1959; d. Joseph Eugene and Lois (George) Skura; m. William Mark Nebeker, Sept. 15, 1984. BA in English Lit. and French Lang., U. Va., 1981; postgrad. in film and video, Am. U., 1986—. Editorial asst. Assn. for Ednl. Communications and Tech., Washington, 1981-82, program asst. basic edn. skills through tech., 1982-83; info. coordinator Mainstream, Inc., Washington, 1982; assoc. producer Fay Communications, Inc., Washington, 1983-84, producer, 1984-86, v.p. prodn., 1986—. Co-producer videoconference The New Resource Conservation and Recovery Act, 1984 (Gold award Assn. Visual Communicators). Mem. Internat. TV Assn., Am. Women in Radio and TV., Women in Film and Video, Nat. Assn. Female Execs. Roman Catholic. Office: Fay Communications Inc 2111 Wilson Blvd Suite 421 Arlington VA 22201

NECSULESCU, CRISTINA, engineer; b. Bucharest, Romania, Feb. 10, 1946; came to Can., 1980; d. Silviu and Elena-Rodica (Vrabie) Bogdan; m. Dan-Sorin Necsulescu, Apr. 27, 1974; 1 child, Philip-Ioan. B of Engring., Poly. Inst., Bucharest, 1968, M of Engring., 1968. Profl. engr., Province of Ont. Research engr. Poly. Inst., Bucharest, 1969-72; sr. system engr. Power System Studies and Design Inst., Bucharest, 1972-80; analytical planning engr. Nat. Energy Bd., Ottawa, Ont., 1981—. Author papers in field. Mem. Assn. Profl. Engrs. Ont., IEEE. Home: 1505 Forest Valley Dr, Gloucester, ON Canada K1C 5R5 Office: Nat Energy Bd, 473 Albert St, Ottawa, ON Canada K1A 0E5

NEDERVELD, RUTH ELIZABETH, real estate executive; b. Hudsonville, Mich., Oct. 29, 1933; d. Ralph and Hattie (Ploeg) Schut; m. Terrill Lee Nederveld, June 6, 1952; children: Courtland Lee, Valerie Lynn Nederveld Heisey, Darwin Frederic. Degree in real estate, U. Mich., 1979; grad., Pa. State U., Centre Hall, 1973, Aquinas Coll., Grand Rapids, Mich., 1974; degree, Grad. Realtors Inst., 1979. Cert. residential specialist; registered securities agt. With sales dept. Field Enterprises, Lancaster, Pa., 1962-72; sales assoc. E. James Hogan, Lancaster, 1972-74, C-21 Packard, Grand Rapids, Mich., 1974-80; assoc. broker comml. div. Markland Devel., Inc., Grand Rapids, 1980-86, Am. Acquest Realty, Inc., Grand Rapids, 1986—. Pres. Civic Nucomers of Grand Rapids, 1978; trustee, elder Forest Hills Presbyn. Ch., Cascade, Mich., 1983-86. Mem. Nat. Assn. Realtors (mem. comml. dept. 1973—), Mich. Assn. Realtors, Grand Rapids Real Estate Bd., Woman's Council Realtors (corr. sec. 1986-87), Nat. Assn. Female Execs., Assn. Sales and Mktg. Execs. (exec. dir. internat. chpt. 1977-84, pres. Grand Rapids chpt. 1986-87). Republican. Lodge: Order of Eastern Star. Office: Am Acquest Inc 5958 Tahoe SE Grand Rapids MI 49506

NEDROW, FAY MARCELLE, optical dispensary professional, model; b. Breckenridge, Tex., July 30, 1946; d. Woodrow Benton and Georgia Fay (Huffman) Mason; m. James L. Nedrow, Sept. 23, 1967; children: Brooke T., Blake J. Student, Tex. Tech U., 1965-67. Artist, copywriter Dunlaps, Lubbock, Tex., 1967, Lipman-Wolfe, Portland, Oreg., 1968-69; sec. to pres. Pershing Coll., Beatrice, Nebr., 1970-73; copywriter Sta. KWBE Radio, Beatrice, 1973-74; owner, mgr. Reflections, Beatrice, 1977-80; buyer, mgr. The Optical Dispensary, Beatrice, 1980—, dress designer, 1986—; exec. dir. Miss S.E. Nebr./Am., Beatrice, 1986; model Miller and Paine, Lincoln, Nebr., 1985-86; model, actress, instr. Nancy Bounds Agy., Lincoln and Omaha, 1986; model, actress Jackie Beavers Agy., Lincoln, 1986; instr. Nancy Bounds Studio, 1986—. Actress Lubbock Community Theatre, 1966 (Best Supporting actress award 1966); designer, creator Community players costumes, 1975-86. Pres., bd. dirs. YWCA, Beatrice, 1986, chmn. ann. fund raiser, 1985, chmn. teen programs, 1985; vol. United Way Campaign, Beatrice, 1985-86, Teen Pregnancy Program, 1985-86, March of Dimes Jail and Bail Fund Raiser, Beatrice, 1985, Reagan for Pres., Nebr., 1978, 85, Bob Kerry for Gov., Nebr., 1982, Charly Thone for Gov., Nebr., 1978; artist, vol. Gage County Reps., Beatrice, 1986; chmn. Community Players Ann. Fund Raiser, Beatrice, 1980-82; pres. Parent Tchr. League St. Paul's Sch., Beatrice, 1984-85; mem. exec. bd. Children's Library Guild, Beatrice, 1975-77, Beatrice Community Hosp. Guild, 1984-85; chmn., organizer Seymour Safely Program, Nebr., 1977; mem. Am. Charter Adv. Bd., 1986-87; state coordinator Mrs. Nebr. America Pageant, 1987; adv. bd. Salvation Army, 1987—; vol. United Way, 1985-88, Am. Cancer Soc., 1988—; host mother Am. Field Service Internat., 1987-88; bd. dirs. Blue Valley Found.; state coordinator Mrs. Nebr. Peageant, 1987-88. Named Mrs. Nebr., 1985, Bus. Profl. Women, 1987, Am. Cancer Vol., 1988. Mem. Nebr. Optometric Auxiliary (pres 1978-79, sec., treas. 1977-78, Outstanding Mr. O.D. 1980), Bus. and Profl. Women, Beatrice C. of C., Beta Sigma Phi. Lutheran. Lodge: Rotary.

NEDZA, SANDRA LOUISE, manufacturing executive; b. Chgo., Aug. 20, 1951; d. Thomas and Ina Louise (Wilson) Ingle; m. James Owen Earnest, May 5, 1973 (div. Nov. 1984); m. Ronald Edward Nedza, Nov. 22, 1986; 1 child, Thomas Edward. Student acctg., Met. Sch. Bus., Chgo., 1970. Accounting clk. Gane Bros. & Lane, Inc., Chgo., 1967-72; advanced from expeditor to buyer Hammond Organ Co., Chgo., 1972-84; buyer Indsl. Research Products, Inc., Elk Grove Village, Ill., 1984—. Mem. Jobs Daughters, 1967—. Mem. Alpha Iota. Lutheran. Clubs: Juke Box Sno-Riders (sec. 1986-87) (Fox Lake, Ill.) Lodge: Lioness (v.p. 1985-88, pres. 1988—) (Chgo.). Home: 1418 S Robert Dr Mount Prospect IL 60056 Office: Indsl Research Products Inc 409-415 Busse Rd Elk Grove Village IL 60007

NEE, SISTER MARY COLEMAN, college president emeritus; b. Taylor, Pa., Nov. 14, 1917; d. Coleman James and Nora Ann (Hopkins) N. A.B., Marywood Coll., 1939, M.A., 1943; M.S., Notre Dame U., 1959. Joined Order of Sisters, Servants of Immaculate Heart of Mary, 1941; asso. prof. math. Marywood Coll., Scranton, Pa., 1959-68; pres. Marywood Coll., 1970-88, advisor, 1988—; apostolic coordinator Sisters, Servants Immaculate Heart of Mary, Scranton, Pa., 1968-70. Office: Marywood College 2300 Adams Ave Scranton PA 18509

NEEDHAM, MARTHA ELAINE, city manager; b. Memphis, Feb. 23, 1947; d. Charles D. Riley and Lorraine M. (Bennett) Yulich; m. Peter L. Needham, Nov. 30, 1969 (div. 1979); children: John Michael, Kelly Lyn. BA in Polit. Sci., U. Mo., 1979; M in Pub. Adminstrn., U. Kans., 1982. Adminstrv. asst. City Mgr., Bonner Springs, Kans., 1980; city mgr. Osage City, Kans., 1980-81; cons. mcpl. and county govts., bus. 1981-82; city mgr. New Carlisle, Ohio, 1982-84; cons. bus. Mo., 1984-86; asst. city mgr. Mankato, Minn., 1986-87; account exec. Blinder Robinson, Investment Bankers, Overland Park, Kans., 1988—. Office: Blinder Robinson 6600 College Blvd Suite 300 Overland Park KS 66211

NEEDLE, SUSAN JUDITH, business executive, paramedical makeup specialist, consultant; b. Newark, June 18, 1941; d. Joseph J. and Betty (Levinson) N.; m. Robert J. Henderson. BEd, U. Miami (Fla.), 1962; MA in Human Resources and Psychology, U. Houston, 1979. Tchr. pub. schs., Fla., 1963-72, Houston, 1973-77; part-time profl. model, 1974-79; sales mgr. ADF Services, Houston, 1975-80; event mgr. Summit Arena, Houston, 1980-83; pres. Colorific, Inc., Houston, 1976-87, Can. Am. Energy Corp., 1983-87; assoc. prof. Coll. of Mainland, Dickinson, Tex., 1984-87; v.p., sec. Total H.E.L.P., Inc., Houston, 1984-87; behavior edn. counselor Nutri System, Ft. Myers. Fla., 1987; owner, pres. R.J.H. Cosmetic and Skin Care Ctr., Cape Coral, Fla., 1987—, pres. R.J.H. & Assocs., 1987—; makeup artist, instr. Naples Internat. Studio, 1988— assoc. prof. Edison Community Coll. Ft. Myers, Fla., 1987—; distbr. RCMA Profl. Makeup, Fla., 1988. Fashion and beauty editor Clear Lake Voice. Author: Fashion Impact, 1986. Named Outstanding Educator in Fla., 1968. Mem. Nat. Assn. Female Execs. (dir.), Exec. Link, Am. Inst. Esthetics, Hotel Sales Mgmt. Assn., Performax, Am. Bus. Women's Assn. (ways and means, hospitality chmn., pres. 1984-85, v.p. 1985-86, Woman of Yr. Bay Area chpt. 1987), Fla. Motion Picture and TV Assn., Profl. Image Cons. Assn. Internat., Nat. Fashion and Image Cons. Assn. (pres. Bay Area chpt.), Profl. Speakers Internat., Internat. Platform Assn., Assn. Bus. and Profl. Women, Phoenix Soc., Alpha Epsilon Phi, Alpha Kappa Alpha. Democrat. Jewish. Lodge: Zonta Internat. Home: 3315 SW 8th St Cape Coral FL 33991 Office: RJH Cosmetic and Skin Care Ctr 1417 Del Prado Blvd Suite 480 Cape Coral FL 33990

NEEDLEMAN, ELLEN SUE, television producer; b. N.Y.C., May 30, 1955; d. Sheldon and Rita (Fagen) N. BA, Duke U., 1976; MA, R.I. Sch. of Design, 1981. Free-lance line producer N.Y.C., 1981-82; sr. cost analyst Darcy Masius Benton and Bowles, N.Y.C., 1982-86; free-lance exec. producer Boston, 1986—. Producer TV commls. (Clios award 1981-86, Hatch award 1987-88). Mem. Advt. Club of New England. Democrat. Jewish. Home: 18 Upton St Boston MA 02118

NEEL, JUDY MURPHY, association executive; b. Rhome, Tex., Sept. 16, 1926; d. James W. and Linna B. (Vess) Neel; m. George E. Tashjian, Dec. 15, 1946 (div.); children—Mary B. Tashjian Schmidt, Janet E. Tashjian Wescott, Susan E. Tasjian Salinas; m. Ellis F. Murphy, Jr., Dec. 30, 1975. B.S., Northwestern U., 1976; M.B.A., Roosevelt U., 1983. Cert. assn. exec. Vice pres. Murphy, Tashjian & Assocs., Chgo., 1960-73; exec. dir. Automotive Affiliated Rep. Assn., Chgo., 1973-78; mgr. Automotive Service Ind. Assn., Chgo., 1978-80; exec. dir. Am. Soc. Safety Engrs., Park Ridge, Ill., 1980—. Mem. Chgo. Soc. Assn. Execs. (bd. dirs. 1979—, pres. 1985—), Am. Soc. Assn. Execs. (found. dir. 1986—, Key award 1986), Council Engring. and Sci. Socs., AAAS. Republican. Office: Am Soc Safety Engrs 1800 Oakton St Des Plaines IL 60018

NEELY, K. ELAINE, nursing home adminstrator; b. Dorchester, Mass., July 21, 1943; d. James Walter and Dorothy May (Billings) Hickey; m. Thomas W. Neely Jr., Oct. 14, 1967; children: Matthew, Brevard. BA, Skidmore Coll., 1965; postgrad., NYU, 1966-67. Research analyst Dun & Bradstreet Inc., N.Y.C., 1965-66; mktg. research analyst Westvaco, N.Y.C., 1966-68; adminstr. Sweet Brook Nursing Home Inc., Williamstown, Mass., 1968—, treas., 1985—; v.p. Crescent Manor Nursing Home Inc., Bennington, Vt., 1979—, treas., 1985—; exec. dir. Sweetwood, Williamstown, 1985—; chair Mass. Bd. Registration Nursing Home Adminstrs., Boston, 1981; bd. dirs. adv. bd. 1st Agrl. Bank, Williamstown, 1982—. Chmn. Williamstown Fin. Com., 1982—. Episcopalian. Office: Sweet Brook Nursing Home Inc 1561 Cold Spring Rd Williamstown MA 01267

NEES, SUSAN LYNN, automobile company administrator; b. Cadillac, Mich., Feb. 20, 1949; d. H. Iver and H. Lila (Hancock) Walenjus; m. William O. Nees, Aug. 5, 1979; children: Brian W., Kristen L., Stephanie L. B in Social Sci. with highest honors, Mich. State U., 1976; M in Mgmt., Aquinas Coll., 1985. Adminstrv. asst. Bank of Lansing, Mich., 1972-75; vol. U.S. Peace Corps., 1976-77; interviewer Gen. Motors of Lansing, 1977-81, benefit rep., 1981-82, personnel adminstrv. rep., 1982-85, supr. personnel adminstrn., 1985—. Mem. council Bus. Edn. Adv. Bd., Lansing, 1982-85; acctg. vol. Capital Area United Way, Lansing, 1984-85; bd. dirs. Human Relations Council, Lansing, 1985—, Office for Young Children Planning, Ingham County, Mich., 1987. Mem. Nat. Assn. Female Execs., Personnel Assn. Mid-Mich.

NEESE, GERTRUDE ELIZABETH FLESH LOCKHART KENNEDY, real estate executive; b. N.Y.C., Mar. 9, 1925; d. Bernard William and Dorothy Katherine (Reimund) Flesh; B.A., U. Havana (Cuba), 1944; m. Alonzo Aldrich Neese, Nov. 10, 1978 (dec. Aug. 1981); children—Christopher H. Bohner, Stephen Edward Bohner, Karen Bohner Hyden. Stewardess-purser Pan Am. World Airways, 1945-47; pvt. investments, Rio de Janeiro, Brazil, Coral Gables, Fla. and N.Y.C., 1947-57; pres. Lockhart Realty, Inc., Sewall's Point, Stuart, Fla., 1957—, also dir.; pres., dir. Sewall's Point Estates, Inc., Stuart, Lockhart Sales, Inc., Stuart, Lockhart Devel., Inc., Sewall's Point, Neese Land Co.; v.p., dir. Dunes Club, Hutchinson Island, Stuart, Fla.; chmn. Sewall's Point Code Enforcement Bd. Pres. United Fund of Sewall's Point, 1958-70, bd. dirs., 1958—; pres. patrons of Ctr. for Liver Disease, U. Miami, 1986; trustee Martin County (Fla.) Library, Martin County Hist. Soc.; bd. dirs. Am. Cancer Soc. Mem. Nat. Inst. Real Estate Brokers, Am. Inst. Real Estate Appraisers, NAREB, World Wings Internat., Fla. Assn. Realtors. Clubs: Sailfish Point, Yacht and Country (dir.) (Stuart); Sakonnet Golf (Little Compton, R.I.). Home: 87 S River Rd Stuart FL 34996 Office: 2 N Sewall's Point Rd Stuart FL 33494

NEFF, FRANCINE IRVING (MRS. EDWARD JOHN NEFF), former federal treasurer; b. Albuquerque, Dec. 6, 1925; d. Edward Hackett and Georgia (Henderson) Irving; m. Edward John Neff, June 7, 1948; children: Sindle, Edward Vann. A.A., Cottey Coll., 1946; B.A., U. N.Mex., 1948. Div. and precinct chmn. Republican Party, Albuquerque, 1966-71; mem. central com. Bernalillo County (N.Mex.) Republican Party, 1967-74, mem. exec. bd., 1968-70; mem. N.Mex. State central com. Republican Party, 1968-74, 77-82, mem. exec. bd., 1970-74, 81-83; Rep. nat. committeewoman State of N.Mex., 1970-74, also mem. exec. com.; Treas. of U.S. U.S. Dept. Treasury, Washington, 1974-77; nat. dir. U.S. Savs. Bonds, 1974-77; mktg. v.p. Rio Grande Valley Bank, Albuquerque, 1977-81; dir. Hershey Foods Corp., Pa., E-Systems Inc., Dallas, La.-Pacific Corp., Portland, Oreg. N.Mex. state adviser Teenage Reps., 1967-68; del. Rep. Nat. Conv., Miami, 1968, 72; campaign coordinator Congressman Lujan of N.Mex., 1970; pres. Albuquerque Federated Rep. Women's Club, 1977; Leader Camp Fire Girls, Albuquerque, 1957-64; pres. Inez (N.Mex.) PTA, 1961; den mother Cub Scouts Am., Albuquerque, 1964-65; exec. bd. United Way of Albuquerque; mem. adv. council Mgmt. Devel. Center, Robert O. Anderson Grad. Sch. Bus. and Adminstrv. Scis., U. N.Mex.; mem. Def. Adv. Com. on Women in the Services, 1980-83; trustee Cottey Coll., Nevada, Mo., 1982—. Recipient Exceptional Service award Dept. Treasury, 1976, Horatio Alger award, 1976. Mem. P.E.O. (pres. Albuquerque chpt. 1958-59, 63-64), Albuquerque City Panhellenic Assn. (pres. 1959-60), Greater Albuquerque C. of C. (bd. dirs. 1978-81), Alpha Delta Pi, Sigma Alpha Iota, Phi Kappa Phi, Pi Lambda Theta, Phi Theta Kappa. Episcopalian.

NEFF, JEANNETTE (BUNNY), insurance agent, real estate broker; b. Spartanburg, S.C., Nov. 16, 1934; d. William and Cecilia (Huseman) Bobo; m. Raymond Michael Neff, May 27, 1956; children: Susan Neff Letzig, David M., Patrick L., John R. Grad., Travelers Sch. Ins., 1964. Legal sec. Lyles & Lyles Law Firm, Spartanburg, 1953-54; sec. Chevrolet Motor Div., Charlotte, N.C., 1954-56, Gen. Motors Parts Div., Oklahoma City, 1956-57; owner Jeannette B. Neff, Tax Service, Sayre, Okla., 1962—; v.p., sec. The Mike Neff Co., Sayre, 1962—; dean, asst. dean, moderator Sch. Ins., U. Okla., Norman, 1974-75. Deacon First Presbyn. Ch., Sayre, elder, 1985—; dist. com. mem., instr., counselor Boy Scouts Am., Sayre; organizer Crimestoppers Hotline; safety coordinator State of Okla. Mem. Nat. Assn. Master Appraiser, Profl. Ins. Agts., Nat. Assn. Female Execs., Okla. Assn. Ind. Ins. Agts., Okla Leader Users Group (dir. 1986-88), Sayre C. of C., P.E.O. Sisterhood (past pres. local chpt.). Republican. Club: En Avant Fed. Women's (Sayre) (past pres.). Office: The Mike Neff Co 119 E Main St PO Box 338 Sayre OK 73662

NEGIN, JENNIE LEE, infosystems specialist; b. Tampa, Fla., Sept. 25, 1939; d. Mottie and Frances Nettie (Prince) N.; m. Harold Lindsey Folley, Mar. 11, 1987; children: Rachel Claire Boring, Neil Edward Boring. BS in Edn., U. Fla., 1960, MA in Math, 1962. Tchr. Alachua County Pub. Schs., Gainesville, Fla., 1962-63; research asst., computing supr. U. Fla. Computing Ctr., Gainesville, 1963-68; mem. staff Los Alamos (N.Mex.) Nat. Lab., 1968-74; cons. U. N.Mex. Law Sch. and Anthropology Mus., Albuquerque, 1974-75; mem. staff Sandia Nat. Labs., Albuquerque, 1975-86, supr. mgmt. info. systems, 1986-88, mgr. tech. library, 1988—. Contbr. articles to profl. jours. Pres. Women's Am. Orgn. Rehab. through Tng., Albuquerque, 1981-83; loaned exec. United Way of Greater Albuquerque, 1982-83, speakers bur., 1983-84, div. chair, 1987; active Leadership Albuquerque, 1986-87. Recipient Women on the Move award YWCA, Albuquerque, 1987, Gov.'s award, 1988. Mem. Assn. for Computing Machinery (state pres. 1974-76), N.Mex. Network for Women in Sci. and Engring. (program 1986-87). Democrat. Jewish. Office: Sandia Nat Labs PO Box 5800 Albuquerque NM 87185

NEHRING, SUSAN BUSCH, public relations executive; b. St. Paul, Nov. 28, 1955; d. Richard Robert and Betty (Fogel) Busch; m. Gary Kenneth

Nehring, Feb. 14, 1987. BA, U. Minn., 1977. Copywriter PBA, Inc., Mpls., 1977-78, creative promotions adminstr., 1978-80; advt. mgr. ITT Life Ins., Mpls., 1980-81; communications cons. Control Data Corp., Mpls., 1981-83, corp. pub. relations mgr., 1983-86; account mgr. Colle and McVoy Pub. Relations, Mpls., 1986—. Mktg. com. mem. U. Minn. Found., Mpls., 1986-87; mem. Minn. Meeting, St. Paul, 1986-87. Mem. Pub. Relations Soc. Am., Nat. Investor Relations Inst., Minn. Press Club. Home: 5537 Bartlett Blvd Mound MN 55364 Office: Colle and McVoy Pub Relations 7900 International Dr Bloomington MN 55420

NEIDHART, CAROL LYNN, medical representative; b. Mt. Vernon, OH, Sept. 18, 1953; d. Clair Edwin and Merry Evelyn (Burke) Neidhart. BA, Miami U., Oxford, Ohio, 1975. Sr. med. rep. CIBA-Geigy Co., Summit, N.J., 1976—; clin. conf. moderator 1980—. Mem. Nat. Assn. Female Execs. Republican. Methodist. Home: 90 Blenheim Rd Columbus OH 43214

NEIHART, CARLENE ROSE, organist, choral director; b. Girard, Kans., Nov. 11, 1929; s. William Earl and Florene Ella (Morrison) Schifferdecker; m. James Leroy Neihart, 1950; children—Robert Earl, David James, Carl William. B.A. in Music, Pittsburg State U., 1950; M.A. in Music, Kans. U., 1955, postgrad., 1955-65. Mem. faculty Park Coll., Parkville, Mo., U. Mo., Kansas City; organist St. Paul's Episcopal Ch., Kansas City, Kans., 1955-59, St. Andrew's Episcopal Ch., Kansas City, Mo., 1959-76; artist in residence Mid America Nazarene Coll., Olathe, Kans., 1978—; organist, dir. music New Reform Temple, Kansas City, Mo., 1980—, Central Presbyterian Ch., Kansas City, 1976—; presenter of approximately 20 concerts each year on the pipe organ for universities, Am. Guild of Organists chapters, and for dedication of new church organs; presenter of workshops on playing and teaching the pipe organ. NEA grantee 1984. Represented the U.S. in 1982 by appearing in 9 concerts throughout Netherlands in celebration and recognition of 200 years of Dutch-U.S. Relationships; selected by NEA to give organ recitals in the Arts Am. program overseas, 1982. Mem. Am. Guild Organists (Mo. chmn. 1976-84, performer nat. and regional convs.).

NEIL, SUE, truck company official; b. Columbus, Ohio, Jan. 13, 1941; d. Edgar Gordon and Marian Ida (Scheuffler) Beckemeyer; m. James G. Neil, June 28, 1968; children—James G. II, Chadwick G. B.S., Ohio State U., 1962, postgrad., Antioch U., 1986—. Personnel supr. Bloomingdale's Dept. Store, N.Y.C., 1962-64; tng. supr. United Mchts. & Mfrs., N.Y.C., 1964-66; tng. dir. Accuray Corp., Columbus, 1966-71; asst. v.p., mgr. First Interstate Bank of Wash., Seattle, 1974-79; with Kenworth Truck Co., Seattle, 1979—, mgr. employee relations Seattle factory, 1981-87; corp. dir. tng. Paccar, Inc., Bellevue, Wash., 1987—; instr. City U., Seattle; cons. to bus. and govt.; lectrs. Mem. Am. Soc. Tng. Devel. (pres. Wash. State chpt. 1979, regional v.p. for West Coast, 1981-82, nat. dir. 1981-82, Nat. Torch award 1981), Futurist Soc. Am., Am. Soc. Personnel Adminstrn., Mortar Bd. Home: 21711 SE 259th St Maple Valley WA 98038 Office: Paccar Inc 777 106 NE Bellevue WA 98004

NEILL, LAQUITA JOYCE BELL, educator, home economist, librarian; b. Humphreys County, Miss., Aug. 10, 1930; d. Clarence Marvin and Dorothy (Parker) Bell; m. Robert Wood Neill, Apr. 29, 1956; 1 child, Robert Wood, Jr. BS in Home Econs., Delta State U., Cleve., 1952, MLS, 1977; grad. Miss. Ednl. Adminstrn. Leadership Inst. for Women U. So. Miss., 1987. Asst. home economist Panola County, Miss. Cooperative Extension Service, Batesville, 1952-54, home economist Carroll County, Carrollton, Miss., 1954-57; bookkeeper, teller Peoples Bank & Trust Co., North Carrollton, 1959-61; instr. home econs. Leflore County, Greenwood, Miss., 1961-62, Carroll County, Carrollton, 1962-77; media dir. Leflore County High Sch., Itta Bena, Miss., 1977-78, Winona Elem. Sch., Miss., 1978-79, J.Z. George Sch., North Carrollton, 1979—; ptnr. Bell Farms, Tchula and Belzoni, Miss.; dir. Neill Forest Products, Inc., Carrollton, Neill Realty, Inc., Carrollton. Trustee, mem. adminstrv. bd. Carrollton United Methodist Ch. Named Regional Star Tchr. Miss. Econ. Council, 1973. Mem. Miss. Library Assn., Miss. Assn. Media Educators, ALA, Miss. Archeol. Assn. (Cottanlandia chpt.), Miss. Assn. Educators, NEA, Delta State Univ. Alumni Assn., UDC (The H. D. Money chpt.), Carroll Soc. for Preservation of Antiquites, Internat. Bell Soc. (bd. govs.), Bell Family Assn. of U.S. (charter mem.), Clan Bell Descendants, Council of Scottish Clan Assns., Zeta State (Alpha Phi chpt.), Delta Kappa Gamma. Club: Cherokee Rose Garden. Home: 204 Washington St Carrollton MS 38917 Office: PO Box 264 Carrollton MS 38917

NEIMAN, TANYA MARIE, lawyer; b. Pitts., June 28, 1949; d. Max and Helen (Lamaga) N. AB, Mills Coll., 1970; JD, U. Calif., San Francisco, 1974. Bar: Calif. 1975. Law assoc. Boalt Hall U. Calif., Berkeley, 1974-76; pub. defender State of Calif., San Francisco, 1976-81; assoc. gen. counsel, dir. vol. legal services Bar Assn. San Francisco, 1982—. Mem. ABA (speaker 1985—, Harrison Tweed award 1985), Calif. Bar Assn. (exec. com. 1984—, legal services sect.), Golden Gate Bus. Assn. Found. (v.p. grant making 1985—), Nat. Conf. Women and Law (speaker 1975—)Nat. Lawyers Guild. Office: Bar Assn San Francisco 685 Market St San Francisco CA 94105

NELIPOVICH, SANDRA GRASSI, artist; b. Oak Park, Ill., Nov. 22, 1939; d. Alessandro and Lena Mary (Ascareggi) Grassi; m. John Nelipovich Jr., Aug. 19, 1973. BFA in Art Edn., U. Ill., 1961; postgrad., Northwestern U., 1963, Gonzaga U., Florence, Italy, 1966, Art Inst. Chgo., 1968; diploma, Accademia Universale Alessandro Magno, Prato, Italy, 1983. Tchr. art Edgewood Jr. High Sch., Highland Park, Ill., 1961-62, Emerson Sch. Jr. High Sch., Oak Park, 1962-77; batik artist Calif., 1977—; illustrator Jolly Robin Publ. Co., 1988—; supr. student tchrs., Oak Park, 1970-75; adult edn. tchr. ESL, ceramics, Medinah, Ill., 1974; mem. curriculum action group on Human Dignity, EEO workshop demonstrator, Oak Park, 1975-76, guest lectr. Muckenthaler Ctr., Fullerton, Calif., 1980; fabric designer for fashion designer Barbara Jax, 1987. One-woman shows include Lawry's Calif. Ctr., Los Angeles, 1981-83, 1982, Whittier (Calif.) Mus., 1985-86, Anaheim (Calif.) Cultural Ctr., 1986-88; also gallery exhibits in Oak Brook, Ill., 1982, La Habra, Calif., 1983; represented in permanent collections McDonald Corp., Oak Brook, Ill., Glenkirk Sch., Deerfield, Ill., and in galleries in Laguna Beach, Calif., Maui, Hawaii; fashion designer for Barbara Jax, 1987; illustrator for Jolly Robin Pub. Co., 1988—. Recipient numerous awards, purchase prizes, 1979—. Mem. AAUW (hospitality chmn. 1984-85), Oak Park Art League, Orange Art Assn. (jury chairperson 1980), Anaheim Art Assn., Muckenthaler Ctr. Circle. Roman Catholic. Club: Anaheim Hills Women's. Home and Office: 5922 Calle Cedro Anaheim CA 92807

NELKIN, DOROTHY, sociology and science policy educator, researcher; b. Boston, July 30, 1933; d. Henry and Helen (Fine) Wolfers; m. Mark Nelkin, Aug. 31, 1952; children: Lisa Nelkin Epstein, Laurie. B.A., Cornell U., 1954. Research assoc. Cornell U., Ithaca, N.Y., 1963-69, sr. research assoc., 1970-72, assoc. prof., 1972-76, prof. sci. tech. soc. program, 1976—, prof. dept. sociology, 1977—; Clare Boothe Luce Vis. Prof. NYU, 1988-90; cons. OECD, Paris, 1975-76, Inst. Environ., Berlin, 1978-79; maitre de conference U. Paris, 1975-76; maitre de recherche Ecole Polytechnique, Paris, 1980-81. Author: The Creation Controversy, 1982, Workers at Risk, 1984, The Atom Besieged, 1981, Controversy: Politics of Technical Decision, 1979, Science as Intellectual Property, 1983, Selling Science: How the Press Covers Science and Technology, 1987. Adviser Office Tech. Assessment, 1977-79, 82-83; expert witness ACLU, Ark., 1982. Vis. scholar Resources for the Futures, 1980-81; vis. scholar Russell Sage Found., N.Y.C., 1983; Guggenheim fellow, 1983-84. Fellow Hastings Inst. Soc. Ethics and Life Scis., AAAS (bd. dirs.); mem. Council for Advancement Sci. Writing (bd. dirs.), Medicine in the Pub. Interest (bd. dirs.), Soc. for Social Studies Sci. (pres. 1978-79). Home: 119 Heights Ct Ithaca NY 14850 Office: Cornell U Clark Hall Ithaca NY 14853

NELL, PATRICIA ANN, allergist; b. Marshfield, Wis., Aug. 10, 1935; d. Harry William and Sarah Alice (Ingraham) m. Lewis Edwards Gibson, Dec. 27, 1986. BA, State U. of Iowa, 1957, MD, 1960. Rotating intern Phila. Gen. Hosp., 1960-61; resident in pediatrics Cin. Children's Hosp., 1961-62, St. Christopher's Hosp., Phila., 1964-65; resident in allergy and immunolgy U. Wis., Madison, 1969-71; practice medicine specializing in pediatrics, allergies West Side Clinic, Green Bay, Wis., 1971-73; tng. program faculty, chief allergy St. Christopher Hosp., Temple U., Phila., 1973-78; chief pediatric allergy dept., asst. prof. pediatrics U. Ill., Chgo., 1978-86; clin. dir. pediatrics, allergy Anchor HMO, Oak Park, Ill., 1986—; asst. prof. Rush-Presbyn. St. Luke Med. Ctr., Chgo., 1986—. Contbr. articles to profl. jours. Served to maj. USAF, 1962-68, res. 1981—, served to col. USAFR. Fellow Am. Acad. Pediatrics, Am. Thoracic Soc., Am. Acad. Allergy-Immunology; mem. Am. Med. Women Assn., Phila. Allergy Soc. (sec. 1975-78), Chgo. Immunology Soc., Pediatric and Allergy Immunology Soc. Methodist. Club: St. Christopher (Phila.) (treas. 1974-78). Office: Anchor HMO 1049 Lake St Oak Park IL 60301

NELLI, ELIZABETH ROLFE, university dean; b. Toronto, Ont., Can., Feb. 14, 1935; came to U.S., 1956, naturalized; d. George Millar and Anne Noela (Scaborne) Thomson; BA, U. Chgo., 1959; MA, U. Ky., 1974, EdD, 1980; m. Bert S. Nelli, Dec. 28, 1961; children: Steven, Christopher, William. Elem. sch. tchr., Toronto, 1955-56, Chgo., 1956-59, Vancouver, B.C., Can., 1959-61; nursery sch. tchr. U. Chgo., 1964-65; kindergarten tchr. Inner City Vol. Programs, Lexington, Ky., 1969-72; research asst./asso. U. Ky., Lexington, 1974-79, asst. to dean, 1979-80, asst. dean Coll. Edn., 1980-84; asst. dir. tchr. edn. and Cert. Ky. Dept. Edn., 1984—; mem. nat. accreditation teams Nat. Council for Accreditation Tchr. Edn., 1980—. Contbr. articles to profl. and acad. jours. Mem. Assn. Tchr. Educators, Landscape Architecture accreditation Bd., Nat. Assn. Edn. Young Children, Bluegrass Assn. Children under Six, Ky. Citizens for Child Devel., Phi Delta Kappa. Office: Ky Dept Edn Div Tchr Edn and Cert Frankfort KY 40601

NELLOR, REGINA ANGELA, management and advertising executive; b. Yonkers, N.Y., May 11, 1943; d. Edward Kenneth and Regina Helena (Dziuban) N. AB in English Lit., Wheeling Coll., 1965; postgrad., U. Chgo., 1965-66. Western regional mgr. SmokEnders, Inc., Woodland Hills, Calif., 1978-79; spl. asst. to pres. SmokEnders, Inc., Phillipsburg, N.J., 1979; sr. v.p. SmokEnders, Inc., Reseda, Calif., 1979-80, chmn. nat. div., 1980-81; ptnr., owner Wo Is Me, Northridge, Calif., 1981-83, Ready to Show, Northridge, 1983-84, Chellor Mktg. Coop., Northridge, 1984—; pres., chief exec. officer Chellor Assocs., Inc. & DMMC, Inc., Sherman Oaks, Calif., 1985—; sec., also bd. dirs. DMMC, Inc., Sherman Oaks, Calif. Contbr. articles to profl. jours. Mem. Nat. Assn. Female Execs., Direct Mktg. Assn., Gamma Pi Epsilon. Republican. Roman Catholic. Office: DMMC Inc 15301 Ventura Blvd Suite 300 Sherman Oaks CA 91403

NELSON, ARLENE B., state legislator; b. Doniphan, Nebr., July 15, 1925; m. Milford R. Nelson, 1946; children: Donna, Dennis. Student, U. Nebr. Program asst. Agrl. Stabilization Conservation Service, 1983-84; mem. Nebr. State Legislature, 1984—. Mem. LWV. Methodist. Office: 3127 Woodridge Blvd Grand Island NE 68801 •

NELSON, AUDREY ELAINE, nurse educator; b. York, Nebr., Jan. 7, 1949; d. Milton Lars and Audrey Elizabeth (Watson) Nelson. Student U. Nebr., 1967-69; B.S. in Nursing, U. Nebr. Med. Center-Omaha, 1972; M.S. in Nursing, U. Wis., 1974. Registered nurse; CPR cert. Staff nurse York Gen. Hosp., 1972-73; asst. prof. nursing U. Nebr. Coll. Nursing, Omaha, 1974-78, second yr. coordinator, 1978-80, asst. prof., 1980—; part time staff nurse U. Nebr. Hosp., Omaha, 1979—; cons. Community Coll., Wichita, Kans., 1979, others; speaker in field. Mem. ARC, 1972; active York County (Nebr.) 4-H Clubs, 1955-67. March of Dimes Scholar, 1970-72; partipant Maternal-Child Health Service Project U. Wis., 1972-74; named one of Outstanding Young Women in Am., 1980. Mem. Am. Nurses Assn., Nebr. Nurses Assn. (cabinet mem. nursing practice 1980-84 , spl. recognition awards 1980, 84, other awards), Nebr. Nurses Assn. Dist. II (pres. 1982-84, profl. achievement award 1981, excellence in nursing practice award 1986), U. Wis. Sch. Nursing Alumni Assn., U. Nebr. Coll. Nursing Alumni Assn. (life), Sigma Theta Tau (charter mem. chpt.), Phi Delta Gamma (pres. chpt. 1984; nat. conv. chmn. 1982, nat. dir. fin. 1984-88), Oncology Nursing Soc., N.Am. Nursing Diagnosis Assn., Midwest Nursing Research Soc., Phi Delta Kappa. Democrat. Lutheran. Club: U. Nebr. Faculty Women's. Office: U Nebr Coll Nursing 4111 Dewey Ave Omaha NE 68105

NELSON, BARBARA ANNE, lawyer; b. Mineola, N.Y., Jan. 16, 1951; d. Richard William and Dorothee Helen (Thorne) N. BA, Inter Am. U. P.R., 1972; JD, New Eng. Sch. Law, 1975. Legal editor Prentice Hall Pub. Co., Englewood Cliffs, N.J., 1976-77; assoc. Antonio C. Martinez Law Firm, N.Y.C., 1977-79, Pollack & Kramer, N.Y.C., 1979-83; sole practice N.Y.C., 1983—. Authro, speaker tng. film. Mem. Am. Immigration Lawyers Assn., Legal Aid Soc. N.Y., Amnesty Internat., Asia Soc. Home: 324 W 14th St Apt 5-A New York NY 10014 Office: 132 Nassau St Suite 219 New York NY 10038

NELSON, BARBARA KAY, insurance agent, financial services consultant; b. Dayton, Ohio, May 20, 1947; d. Orville James and Catherine Ann (Pentenburg) Weber; m. Theodore Joseph Nelson II, Nov. 8, 1969; children—Theodore Joseph III, Jason Michael. B.A., U. Dayton, 1969; M.A., Webster U., 1985. TV co-host Sta. WHIO-TV, Dayton, 1969; dept. mgr. Elder-Beerman, Dayton, 1969-70; customer service rep. Ohio Bell Telephone, Dayton, 1970; adminstrv. coordinator AmeriSource, San Antonio, 1984-86; agt. N.Y. Life Ins., 1986—. sec. bd. dirs. Network Power Tex., 1987—. Mem. exec. bd. Oak Grove Elementary Sch. PTA, San Antonio, 1981-83; mem. San Antonio Assn. Life Underwriters, San Antonio C. of C., religious edn. com. St. Mark's Ch., San Antonio, 1983-84; mem. North San Antonio Chamber/Pub. Art, 1984-85. Mem. Nat. Assn. Female Execs. Club: FLW Officers Wives (pres. 1980-81). Avocations: art; jogging; bicycling; racquetball; reading.

NELSON, BONNIE KAY, educator; b. Paso Robles, Calif., Aug. 3, 1950; d. Vernon Carroll and Hilda Marie (Engelke) N. Degree in standard elem. edn., Calif. Poly. State U., San Luis Obispo, 1973, cert. early childhood edn., 1976. Tchr. kindergarten Paso Robles Union Elem. Sch. Dist., 1973—; sch. improvement project coordinator Paso Robles Union Elem. Sch. Dist., 1980-83, sch. site council chmn., 1981-82. Recipient service award, Paso Robles PTA, 1983; named Outstanding Young Educator for Paso Robles, Paso Robles Jaycees, 1985, Outstanding Young Educator for State Calif., Jaycees, 1986. Mem. Paso Robles Tchrs. Assn. (pres. 1980-82), Computer Using Educators, Cen. Coast Math Council, North County Athletic Assn., San Luis Obispo Antique Bottle Soc. (communications officer 1980—) Phi Delta Kappa, Delta Kappa Gamma (communications officer 1982-84). Republican. Baptist. Home: 124 21st St Paso Robles CA 93446

NELSON, CAROL LEE SYVERTSEN, personal computer specialist; b. Plainfield, N.J., Nov. 30, 1960; d. Harry and Doris (Butler) Syvertsen; m. David Thomas Nelson, July 16, 1983. BA magna cum laude, Gettysburg (Pa.) Coll., 1982. Support analyst BPI System, Austin, Tex., 1984-85; mgr. tech. support Computer Support Corp., Carrollton, Tex., 1985-87; salesperson STB System, Richardson, Tex., 1987; product mktg. mgr. Conductor Software, Irving, Tex., 1987—. Home: 118 Meadow Run Coppell TX 75019

NELSON, CHARLOTTE ANN, accountant, supervisor; b. Albertville, Ala., Nov. 12, 1950; d. Clarence Gerald and Flonell (Berry) N. BS summa cum laude, U. Ala., Tuscaloosa, 1985. Accounts payable clk. Dixie Poultry Supply, Albertville, 1968; sec., invoice clk. Continental Grain Co., Albertville, 1968-80, computer terminal operator, 1980-82, acct., 1982-87, accounting supr., 1987—. Sec. to chmn. United Givers Fund, Albertville, 1976, 81; active Friends of Library, Albertville, 1982. Named one of Outstanding Young Women of Am., 1982. Jehovah's Witness.

NELSON, CHRISTINE A., occupational therapist; b. Hartford, Conn., Apr. 30, 1937. BS in Occupational Therapy, Va. Commonwealth U., 1959; MS in Child Devel., U. Wis., 1963; cert. in Neurodevelopmental Treatment, Dr. Karel and Mrs. Berta Bobath, Madison, Wis., 1963; PhD in Human Devel., U. Md., 1973. Evaluator of blind and physically handicapped children Sunland Tng. Ctr., Gainesville, Fla., 1960-62; creator occupational therapy program, in-service staff instr. Cen. Wis. Colony, Madison, 1962-65; dept. dir. Easter Seal Community Agy., Balt., 1965-67; cons. Children's Guild, Balt., 1967-76; pvt. practice specializing in therapy for neurologically impaired children, Richmond, Va., 1967-77; devel. cons. Maternal-Infant Health Care Project div. Balt. City Health Dept., 1969-74; coordinator cert. courses in Neurodevel. Treatment 1975—; clin. practitioner, clin. coordinator Centro de Aprendizaje de Cuernavaca, Mexico, 1977—. Contbr. articles to profl jours. Office: Cuernavaca Rio Balsas 14, Col Vista Hermos, 62 Morelos Mexico

NELSON, CLARA SINGLETON, aerospace company executive; b. Union Ridge, Tenn., Apr. 10, 1935; d. Ernest Caldwell and Willie Emma (Hord) Singleton; m. Joe Edward Nelson, July 26, 1953; children—Drexel Edward, Dorissia Lynett. Student Tenn. State U., 1961-62, Middle Tenn. State U., 1984; AS, Motlow Coll., 1978. Cert. personnel specialist. Sec., adminstrv. asst. Bedford County Sch., Shelbyville, Tenn., 1957-64; sec., personnel asst. Aro, Inc., Arnold Air Force Sta., Tenn., 1964-71; mem. pub. relations staff, job interviewer Employment Security, Shelbyville, 1971-81; personnel rep. Calspan Corp., Arnold Air Force Sta., 1981—; mem. adv. bd. Tenn. Area Vocat. Sch., Shelbyville, 1979—, Bedford Moore Vocat. Ctr., Shelbyville, 1979—; cons., dir. Career Devel. Workshops, Shelbyville. Chmn. adv. commn. Equal Employment Opportunity, 1983—, improvement com. Tullahoma Job Service, Tenn., 1985—; mem. Tenn. Gov.'s Better Schs. Com., 1985—; mem. Patrons Council Argie Cooper Library, Shelbyville; Bus. Adv. Group Motlow State Coll., Tullahoma; trustee Motlow Coll. Found. Recipient cert. of appreciation ARC, 1985. Mem. Highland Rim Personnel Assn. (treas. 1983-84, 87, sec. 1988), Nat. Assn. Female Execs. (network dir. 1985), Tenn. State U. Cluster (chmn. com. 1984—), Tenn. Placement Assn. Club: Better Homes and Gardens (v.p. Shelbyville). Methodist. Avocations: reading, gardening. Home: 118 Scotland Heights Shelbyville TN 37160 Office: Calspan Corp Mail Stop 430 Arnold Air Force Station TN 37389

NELSON, CYNTHIA HILTON, data processing consultant; b. Tulsa, Aug. 21, 1950; d. Thomas Leonard and Lois (Warf) Hilton; m. Kenneth S. Nelson, May 31, 1980. Student, Okla. State U., 1968-69; BS in Edn., U. Tulsa 1972, postgrad., 1973. Programmer trainee Williams Cos., Tulsa, 1973-75; programmer Am. Airlines, Tulsa, 1975-78; computer systems designer Martin Marietta Corp., Denver, Bethesda, Md., 1978-81; sr. programmer analyst Planning Resource Corp., McLean, Va., 1981-84; sr. systems engr. Nat. Cash Register, Washington, 1984-85; cons., sec.-treas., bd. dirs. Corp. Tech., Inc., Washington, 1985—. Area coordinator Neighborhood Watch Crime Prevention Program, Seabrook, Md., 1982—; mem. Citizens' Adv. Com., Bowie, Md., 1982—, Citizens' Adv. Bd. to Chief of Police, Forestville, Md., 1984—; vol. Spl. Olympics, Tulsa, 1970-74. Mem. Tulsa Backgammon Soc., Okla. State Soc., Convergent Tech. User's Group (bd. dirs., v.p. membership com. 1986-87). Avocations: bridge, jogging, backgammon. Home: 6709 Woodstream Dr Seabrook MD 20706

NELSON, CYNTHIA LEE, medical facility administrator; b. Kansas City, Mo., Oct. 4, 1955; d. John Angelo and Helen Deane (Gelsinger) Drago; m. Gregory Lee Nelson; children: Jennifer Lee, Mary Louisa. BS in Pub. Adminstrn., Emporia State U., 1977, postgrad., 1977-78; postgrad., U. Kans., 1978. Unit mgr. med. intensive and coronary care units VA Med. Ctr., Houston, 1979, adminstrv. asst. medicine, 1980—; adminstrv. coordinator medicine Baylor Coll. of Medicine, Houston, 1980-84, adminstrv. asst. medicine, 1984-85, sr. adminstrv. asst. medicine, 1985—, adminstr. program on aging, 1987-88; adminstr. Roy M. and Phyllis Gough Huffington Ctr. on Aging, Houston, 1988—. Presenter Family Life Services, Houston, 1986—. Mem. Tex. Hosp. Assn., Nat. Council on the Aging, Young Hosp. Adminstrs. of Houston, Adminstrs. Internal Medicine. Democrat. Roman Catholic. Office: Baylor Coll of Medicine One Baylor Plaza Houston TX 77030

NELSON, DEBORAH JEAN, chemical company executive; b. Somers Point, N.J., Feb. 9, 1953; d. Harmon Frederich and Helen Marie (Ryan) Lindner; m. Rodney Francis Nelson, Oct. 1, 1977. Cert. respiratory technician, Atlantic Community Coll., 1972, student, 1974-75; student, Miami Dade Community Coll., 1985-86. Respiratory technician, supr. Shore Meml. Hosp., Somers Point, 1971-74, coordinator med. records, 1974-77; supr. outpatient lab. Diagnostic Med. Services, St. Petersburg, Fla., 1978-79; supr. customer service, import/export B&B Chem. Co., Inc., Hialeah, Fla., 1979-87; adminstrv. asst. to pres. Cyclo Corp., Miami, 1987-88; sales rep. SunPetals, Miami, 1988—. Author: The Sand, 1986; contbg. poet: Beggers Velvet. Active March of Dimes Walkathon, Coconut Grove, Fla., 1986-87, Harley Owners Group collection for charity, Miami, 1986-87; civilian attache Starfleet/USS Encounter, Dade and Broward County. Mem. Nat. Assn. Female Execs. Republican. Club: Blue Blaze Irregulars. Home: 4810 NW 79th Ave #207 Miami FL 33166 Office: SunPetals 3330 NW 60th St Miami FL 33142

NELSON, DEBORAH LYDIA, mortician; b. Winona, Minn., Dec. 30, 1960; d. Lloyd Eldridge and Bernice Helen Hertha (Rumsch) N. Student U. Wis.-LaCrosse, 1979-80, summer 1982, Winona State U., summers 1979-82; B.S. in Mortuary Sci., U. Minn.-Mpls. with high distinction, 1982; cert. in eye enucleation, U. Iowa, 1984. Lic. mortician, Minn., Iowa, Tex.; registered Conf. Funeral Service Exam. Bds. Practicum student Bradshaw-Hauge Funeral Homes, St. Paul, 1982; mortician Dykeman-Huisman-SchumacherFuneral Home, Denver and Waterloo, Iowa, 1982-84, Greenwood/Mt. Olivet Funeral Homes, Ft. Worth, 1984—; sub-registrar State of Minn.; organist 1st Baptist Ch., Winona, 1978-80, Community United Methodist Ch., Columbia Heights, Minn., 1980-82. Named one of Outstanding Young Women of Am. Mem. Nat. Assn. for Female Execs., Internat. Platform Assn., Minn. Alumni Assn., Phi Kappa Phi. Democrat. Lutheran. Avocations: flying, skiing, bicycling, music, swimming. Office: Greenwood Funeral Home PO Box 9450 3100 White Settlement Rd Fort Worth TX 76107

NELSON, DIANA, former state legislator, association executive; b. Berlin, Wis., Oct. 15, 1941; d. Llewellyn James and Virginia Laurel (Shaver) Walker; B.S., U. Wis., 1963; m. Thomas David Nelson, Aug. 22, 1964; children—Stephanie, Brian. Mem. Ill. Ho. of Reps., 1981-85; exec. dir. Mental Health Assn. Ill., 1986—. Congl. candidate Ill. 13th Dist., 1984; candidate Cook County Clk., 1986; Dole dele., primary election, 1988. Republican. Congregationalist. Home: 5025 Woodland Ave Western Springs IL 60558

NELSON, DIANNE ELLEN, sales executive; b. Decorah, Iowa, Oct. 27, 1947; d. Vincent A. and Norma P. (Gjetley) Lerdall; m. F. Walter Nelson, July 31, 1967 (div. Feb. 1983); children: Tanya, Nicole. Student, U. Iowa, 1965-67. Dance instr. Decorah, 1967-72; head designer fasion dept. May D&F Dept. Store, Denver, 1973-74; head customer service Harts Drug, Littleton, Colo., 1974-75; dietitian Jefferson County Sch. System, Littleton, 1978-79; traffic and sales staff Harmon/Ft. Howard Paper Co., Westbury, N.Y., 1980-83; v.p. sales and purchasing N&V Internat., Inc. and Atlantic Coast Fibers Inc., Teterboro, N.J., 1983—. Mem. Nat. Assn. Recyclers Inc. (del. nat. conv. 1987), N.J. Assn. Waste Dealers and Mill Suppliers, Nat. Assn. U.S. C. of C. Republican. Episcopalian. Home: 227 Valley Blvd. Woodridge NJ 07075 Office: N&V Internat ACF Inc 200 North St Teterboro NJ 07608

NELSON, DONIE ALBERTA, television production executive; b. Los Angeles, June 13, 1942; d. Raymond Oscar and Corinne (Valdez) N.; A.A., Santa Monica City Coll., 1972; student U. Calif., Berkeley, 1960-61, UCLA, 1971; m. Foster George Phelps, May 30, 1981; 1 child, Molly Corinne. Asst. story editor MGM Films, Culver City, Calif., 1972-75, story editor, 1975-77; dir. creative affairs Christiana Prodns., Los Angeles, 1977-79; freelance creative cons., story editor, ind. producer for TV, 1979-82; freelance mag. writer, pub. cons., book editor, Los Angeles, 1979-82; feature writer, asst. to editor Showcase mag., Encino, Calif., 1981-82; dir. devel. feature film, TV and cable Solofilm Co., Los Angeles, 1982; dir. devel. TV and cable Sherwood Prodns. Inc., Culver City, 1982-83; interviewer Natural History of AIDS Research Project, Sch. Pub. Health, UCLA, 1984-85; dir. network devel. Procter & Gamble Prodns., Los Angeles, 1985—; guest speaker Los Angeles Career Planning Center, 1979, U. So. Calif. Film Sch., 1980. Vol., Hollygrove Home for Children, 1975-77; sec. Culver City Employees Assn., 1970, Culver City Parks and Recreation Commn., 1969-70, sec. Farragut Sch. PTA, Culver City Edn. Com., Parent Edn. Com., Farragut Sch. Site Council. Recipient Service award Los Angeles chpt. Women in Communications, Inc., 1978; Outstanding Journalism Student of Year award Warren High Sch., Downey, Calif., 1960. Mem. Acad. TV Arts and Scis., Women in Communications (past Los Angeles chpt. pres., Woman of Achievement award Far West region 1983), Women in Film (co-chmn. election com.), NOW, Am. Film Inst. Asso. producer Like Normal People, 1979.

NELSON, DOROTHY WRIGHT (MRS. JAMES F. NELSON), judge; b. San Pedro, Calif., Sept. 30, 1928; d. Harry Earl and Lorna Amy Wright; m. James Frank Nelson, Dec. 27, 1950; children: Franklin Wright, Lorna Jean. B.A., UCLA, 1950, J.D., 1955, LL.M., U. So. Calif., 1956. Bar: Calif. 1954. Research assoc. fellow U. So. Calif., 1953-56; instr. 1957, asst. prof. 1958-61, assoc. prof., 1961-67, prof., 1967, assoc. dean., 1965-67, dean., 1967-80; judge U.S. Ct. Appeals for 9th Circuit, 1980—; cons. Project STAR, Law Enforcement Assistance Adminstrn.; mem. select com. on internal procedures of Calif. Supreme Ct., 1987—. Author: Judicial Administration and The Administration of Justice, 1973; Contbr. articles to profl. jours. Co-chmn. Confronting Myths in Edn. for Pres. Nixon's White House Conf. on Children, Pres. Carter's Commn. for Pension Policy, 1974-80; bd. visitors U.S. Air Force Acad., 1978; bd. dirs. Council on Legal Edn. for Profl. Responsibility, 1971-80, Constnl. Right Found., Am. Nat. Inst. for Social Advancement; adv. bd. Nat. Center for State Cts., 1971-73. Named Law Alumnus of Yr. UCLA, 1967; recipient Profl. Achievement award, 1969; named Times Woman of Yr., 1968; recipient U. Judaism Humanitarian award, 1973; AWARE Internat. award, 1970; Ernestine Stalhut Outstanding Woman Lawyer award, 1972; Coro award for edn., 1978. Fellow Am. Bar Found., Davenport Coll., Yale U.; mem. Bar Calif. (bd. dirs. continuing edn. bar commn. 1967-74), Am. Judicature Soc. (dir.), Assn. Am. Law Schs. (chmn. com. edn. in jud. adminstrn.), Am. Bar Assn. (sect. on jud. adminstrn., chmn. com. on edn. in jud. adminstrn. 1973—), Phi Beta Kappa, Order of Coif (nat. v.p. 1974-76), Jud. Conf. U.S. (com. to consider standards for admission to practice in fed. cts. 1976-79). Office: US Ct of Appeals 312 N Spring St Los Angeles CA 90012

NELSON, ETHELYN BARNETT, civic worker; b. Bessemer, Ala., Jan. 16, 1925; d. Laurence McBride and Ethel Victoria Fortesque (King) Barnett; student Huntingdon Coll., 1943, U. Ala., 1948, George Washington U., 1948-49, 74; m. Stuart David Nelson, May 6, 1949; children—Terryl Lynn, Cynthia Dianne, Jacqueline Margo. Sec., U.S. Air Force, Montgomery, Ala. and Panama Canal Zone, 1944-49; sec. to dep. undersec. U.S. Dept. State, Washington, 1951-53, U.S. Ho. of Reps. and U.S. Senate, 1959-60; adminstrv. asst. editorial div. Nat. Geog. Soc., Washington, 1962-65; rec. sec. Dist. IV, Nat. Capital Area Fedn. Garden Clubs, Inc., Washington, 1981-83. Mem. Women's Com. Nat. Symphony Orch., The English-Speaking Union, Vols. for Washington Ballet, Washington Opera Guild. Mem. Salvation Army Aux., Suburban Hosp. Assn. Republican. Clubs: Landon Woods Garden (pres. 1978-80), Congressional Country; Capital Speakers (Washington). Patentee. Home: 6410 Maiden Ln Bethesda MD 20817

NELSON, GAIL F., transportation company executive; b. Dumont, N.J., Oct. 28, 1960; d. Clifton Bernard and Rita Margaret (McNamara) N. Grad., Montclair (N.J.) State Coll., 1982. Ride-sharing coordinator People Ridesharing Systems, Newark, 1982-83; spl. projects mgr. People Ridesharing Systems, 1983-84, dir. program devel., 1984-86, v.p. program devel., 1986—. Mem. Assn. Commuter Transp., Nat. Assn. Female Execs., ACLU, Greenpeace, N.J. Bicycle Touring Club. Office: People Ridesharing Systems 844 McCarter Hwy Newark NJ 07102

NELSON, HEDWIG POTOK, financial and investment advisor, small business consultant; b. Detroit, Oct. 6, 1954; m. Richard Alan Nelson. BA with honors, U. Mich., 1976; MBA, Am. U., 1980. Fin. asst. antitrust div. U.S. Dept. Justice, Washington, 1979-80; fin. analyst corp. treasury Martin Marietta Corp., Bethesda, Md., 1980-81, fin. adminstr. aggregates div., 1981-83, sr. fin. adminstr. bus. devel. data systems div., 1983, mgr. fin. planning and analysis, 1983-85; mgr. mergers and acquistions M/A-COM Devel. Corp., Rockville, Md., 1985-87; fin. and investment advisor, small bus. cons. Fulton, Lauroesch and Assocs., Bethesda, 1987—. Mem. Internat. Assn. Fin. Planners, Nat. Assn. Female Execs. (treas. Montgomery County chpt. 1987—), Nat. Women's Econ. Alliance, Bethesda/Chevy Chase C. of C. Home: 4601 N Park Ave #319 Chevy Chase MD 20815 Office: Fulton Lauroesch & Assocs 7201 Wisconsin Ave Suite 310 Bethesda MD 20814

NELSON, JANET KATHRYN, broadcast engineer; b. Indpls., Jan. 15, 1954; d. Robert Eddinger and Carol Jean (Nelson) N.; m. Phillip Edward Callighan, Sept. 6, 1975; 1 child, Elliot Nelson. BA, North Cen. Coll., Naperville, Ill., 1975; tech. cert. DeVry Inst. Broadcast personality Sta. WGSB, Geneva, Ill., 1975-79, Sta. WYEN-FM, Des Plaines, Ill., 1977-79; sales rep. MCI Telecommunications, Chgo., 1979-80; asst. engr.-charge WGN-TV, Chgo., 1981—; v.p. Ctr. Communications, Inc., Lombard, Ill., 1985—. Mem. Nat. Acad. TV Arts and Scis., Alumni Bd. North Cen. Coll. Avocations: music, sports. Home: 6340 Americana Dr Unit 618-A Willowbrook IL 60514 Office: Ctr for Communications Inc 945 Springer Dr Lombard IL 60148

NELSON, JANIE RISH, hospital executive; b. Gloster, Miss., Mar. 1, 1941; d. William Hubert and Essie Dell (Davis) Rish; m. John Preston Nelson, Jr., Aug. 19, 1984. Student S.W. Miss. Jr. Coll., 1959-61, Stephens Coll., 1981. Accredited record technician. Admissions clk. Field Hosp., Centreville, Miss., 1963-68, asst. dir. med. records, 1968-73; dir. med. records West Feliciana Parish Hosp., St. Francisville, La., 1976—. Med. records cons. Beverly Enterprises & Centreville Health Care, 1983-84. Mem. nat. adv. bd. Am. Security Council, 1984-85, mem. U.S. Congl. Adv. Bd. for La., 1985; fund raiser Republican Com., 1984. Mem. Am. Med. Records Assn., La. Med. Records Assn., Nat. Assn. Female Execs., Tumor Registration Assn. La., Miss. Sheriffs Assn. (hon.). Republican. Presbyterian. Club: Civic. Avocations: Reading; public speaking; gardening. Home: PO Box 374 Centreville MS 39631

NELSON, JULIE D., lawyer; b. N.Y.C., Sept. 8, 1954; d. John D. and Eileen M. (Canning) Krohn; m. James L. Nelson, Dec. 29, 1973; children—Morgan, Max. B.S., U. Iowa, 1975, J.D., 1978. Bar: D.C., Colo., Tex. Law clk. to presiding justice Iowa Supreme Ct., Des Moines, 1978-79; assoc. Sidley & Austin, Washington, 1979-84; atty. AT&T Info. Systems, Denver, 1984-87, AT&T Communications, Austin, Tex., 1987—; instr. U. Iowa Sch. Law, summer 1983, U. Phoenix, 1986-87. Mem. Order of Coif, Phi Beta Kappa. Democrat. Office: AT&T Communications 4412 Spicewood Springs Rd Suite 600 Austin TX 78759

NELSON, KATHY ANN, foundation administrator; b. Williamsport, Pa., Sept. 21, 1954; d. Dan LeRoy and Shirley Joann (Klein) Hoover; m. James Michael Nelson, Oct. 23, 1976 (div. 1983). BS in German Edn., Ind. U. of Pa., 1976; postgrad., Pa. State U., 1978-83. Tchr. German Hollidaysburg (Pa.) Area Sch. Dist., 1977-85; adminstr. Carlisle (Pa.) Project, 1985; dir. fin. devel. and pub. relations Am. Lung Assn., York, Pa., 1986; exec. dir. Adams County United Way, Gettysburg, Pa., 1987—; dir. Adams Community TV, Gettysburg, 1987—, Adams Area Postal Customer Council, Gettysburg, 1988—. Press sec. Nancy Kulp's campaign for 9th Congl. Dist., Pa., 1984; mem. Downtown Gettysburg, 1987—, 125th Battle of Gettysburg Anniversary Commn., 1988. Fulbright/Goethe Haus scholar, Stuttgart, Fed. Republic of Germany, 1982. Mem. Bus. and Profl. Women, Am. Bus. Women's Assn., Nat. Assn. Female Execs., Cen. Pa. Assn. Women Execs. (charter), Alpha Omicron Pi. Democrat. Lutheran. Home: 2566 Old Route 30 Orrtanna PA 17353 Office: Adams County United Way PO Box 3545 Gettysburg PA 17325-3545

NELSON, LAURA KAY, editor; b. Larned, Kans., May 12, 1962; d. Keith Charles and Thelma Wandalee (Wright) N. A.A., Dodge City Community Coll., 1982; B.S., U. Kans., 1984. Reporter Tiller & Toiler, Larned, Kans., 1984; area reporter Tribune, Great Bend, Kans., 1984-85; assoc. editor High Plains Jour., Dodge City, Kans., 1985—. Mem. U. Kans. Alumni Assn. and Journalism Soc., Kans. Authors Club, Kans. Anthrop. Soc. Democrat. Avocations: archeology; frontier history. Home: 100 Plains Apt 15 Dodge City KS 67801 Office: High Plains Jour 1500 E Wyatt Earp Blvd Dodge City KS 67801

NELSON, LAURIE CAROLYN, lawyer; b. N.Y.C., Oct. 13, 1955; d. Daniel Jack and Norma Augusta (Ranard) Nelson. B.A. with distinction, Swarthmore Coll., 1977; J.D., Bklyn. Law Sch., 1982. Bar: N.Y. 1983. Generalist paralegal Mcpl. Employees Legal Services, N.Y.C., 1977-79; assoc. Lewis & Clarkson, N.Y.C., 1982-86; assoc. Proskauer Rose Goetz & Mendelsohn, N.Y., 1986—. Contbr. articles to profl. jours.; editor Bklyn. Law Rev., 1981-82. Recipient Am. Jurisprudence award, 1980, 81. Mem. ABA, N.Y. County Bar Assn., N.Y.C. Bar Assn. Democrat. Unitarian. Club: Swarthmore of N.Y. Home: 101 Perry St Apt 2E New York NY 10014 Office: Proskauer Rose Goetz & Mendelsohn 300 Park Ave New York NY 10022

NELSON, LINDA HERMINA EHRLICH FLETCHER, educator; b. Honolulu, Oct. 4, 1938; d. Alexander Eugene and Myrle Louise (Mossholder) Ehrlich; m. Richard John Nelson, Mar. 14, 1959; children: Alex Jon, Lisa Katherine. BA in Home Econs., Calif. State U., Sacramento, 1965, MA in Health Edn., 1976. Lic. real estate agt., Calif. Instr., dept. chmn. Roseville (Calif.) High Sch. Dist., 1965-68; program dir. nutrition Dairy Council Calif., Sacramento, 1968-72; instr. nutrition Calif. State U., Sacramento, 1972; instr. Sierra Coll., Rocklin, Calif., 1972-73; instr., dept. chmn. Elk Grove (Calif.) High Sch., 1973-81; salesman J. F. Lazar & Assocs., Roseville, 1981-84; instr. Cosumnes River Coll., Sacramento, 1987—; cons. Excalibur Corp., Sacramento, 1982. Author (with others) teaching curricula. NDEA grantee, 1967, U.S. Govt. tng. grantee, 1979-80. Democrat. Home: 8400 King Rd Loomis CA 95650 Office: Cosumnes River Coll 8401 Center Pkwy Sacramento CA 95823

NELSON, MARTHA JANE, magazine editor; b. Pierre, S.D., Aug. 13, 1952; d. Bernard Anton and Pauline Isabel (Noren) N. BA, Columbia U., 1976. Mng. editor Signs: Jour. of Women in Culture, N.Y.C., 1976-80; sr. editor Ms. Mag., N.Y.C., 1980-85; editor-in-chief Women's Sports and Fitness Mag., Palo Alto, Calif., 1985—. Editor: Women in the American City, 1980; contbr. articles to profl. jours. Bd. dirs. Painting Space 122, N.Y.C., 1982-85, Urban Athletic Assn. Mem. Am. Soc. Mag. Editors, Western Pubs. Assn. Office: Women's Sports Mag 501 2d St San Francisco CA 94115

NELSON, MARY, state legislator; b. Boston, May 3, 1943; children: John, Michael, Jamie. Tchr. Perkins Sch. Blind, 1967-77; lectr. River Coll., 1977-78; selectman Nashua, N.H., 1983-85; mem. N.H. Ho. of Reps., 1983-85, N.H. State Senate, 1986—; del. Dem. State Conv., 1982, 84; cons. on employment and tng. of handicapped, 1977—. Mem. N.H. Order of Women Legislators (pres. 1986—), Phi Delta Kappa. Democrat. Roman Catholic. Address: 18 Stanley Ln Nashua NH 03062 *

NELSON, MARY CARROLL, artist, author; b. Bryan, Tex., Apr. 24, 1929; d. James Vincent and Mary Elizabeth (Langton) Carroll; m. Edwin Blakely Nelson, June 27, 1950; children: Patricia Ann, Edwin Blakely. BA in Fine Arts, Barnard Coll., 1950; MA, U. N.Mex., 1963. Juror Am. Artist Golden Anniversary Nat. Art Competition, 1987; moderator Harwood Found. Art History Conf., 1987; curator Shrines, 1988. Group shows include: Southwestern Watercolor Soc., Dallas, N.Mex. Watercolor Soc., Nat. League Am. Pen Women, N.Mex. State Fair, N.Mex. Mus. Fine Arts Biennial, 1987; represented in pvt. collections in: U.S., Fed. Republic of Germany, Eng. and Australia; author: American Indian Biography Series, 1971-76, (with Robert E. Wood) Watercolor Workshop, 1974, (with Ramon Kelley) Ramon Kelley Paints Portraits and Figures, 1977, The Legendary Artists of Taos, 1980, (catalog) American Art in Peking, 1981, Masters of Western Art, 1982, Connecting, The Art of Beth Ames Swartz, 1984, (catalog) Layering, An Art of Time and Space, 1985, (catalog) Layering/Connecting, 1987; contbg. editor Am. Artist, 1976—. Mem. Soc. Layerists in Multi-Media (founder 1982), Albuquerque Mus. Found., Nat. Fedn. Press Women, N.Mex. Press Women, Albuquerque Arts Bd. Home: 1408 Georgia St NE Albuquerque NM 87110

NELSON, MERLE CHANDLER, real estate executive; b. Nicholson, Ga., June 30, 1908; d. Berry G. and Addie Lavina (Harris) Chandler; m. Ealton Louis Nelson, Dec. 2, 1938; children: Joan Harris Nelson Mulholland, Jean Nelson Amann. Student, Am. U., 1938-41, George Washington U., 1937-38. Exec. sec. Civil Aeros. Bd., Washington, 1938-41; real estate broker No. Va. Bd. Realtors, Fairfax, 1957-87; pres. Nelson Realty, Inc., Arlington, Va., 1957-87, also chmn. bd. dirs. Mem. Arlington County Dem. com., Arlington, 1955-56. Mem. Lake Barcroft Civic Assn. Democrat. Home: 3816 Lakeview Terr Falls Church VA 22041 Office: Nelson Realty Inc 5537 Lee Highway Arlington VA 22207

NELSON, NANCY ELEANOR, pediatrician, educator; b. El Paso, Apr. 4, 1933; d. Harry Hamilton and Helen Maude (Murphy) N. B.A. magna cum laude, U. Colo., 1955, M.D., 1959. Intern, Case Western Res. U. Hosp., 1959-60, resident, 1960-63; practice medicine specializing in pediatrics, Denver, 1963—; assoc. clin. prof. U. Colo. Sch. Medicine, Denver, 1977—, asst. dean Sch. Medicine, 1982—. Mem. Am. Acad. Pediatrics, AMA, Denver Med. Soc. (pres. 1983-84), Colo. Med. Soc. (bd. dirs. 1985—). Home: 1265 Elizabeth Denver CO 80206 Office: 4200 E 9th Ave Denver CO 80262

NELSON, NANCY JANE, savings and loan company executive, mortgage broker, account executive; b. Greenwood, S.C., Apr. 11, 1956; d. George Dewey and Mary Helen (Capps) N.; m. Terry Alan Evans, Aug. 23, 1975 (div. 1979); 1 child, Brandon Gregory. Grad., Nova U., Ft. Lauderdale, Fla., 1983. Cert. tchr.; lic. mortgage broker. Emergency room clk. Self Meml. Hosp., Greenwood, 1974-78; gen. mgr. First Fla. Sanitation, Ft. Lauderdale, Fla., 1979-82; export mgr. Carvel Corp., Ft. Lauderdale, Fla., 1983-86; account exec. Guardian Savs. and Loan, Ft. Lauderdale, Fla., 1987—. Contbr. short stories, poems to mags. Mem. Ft. Lauderdale C. of C. Republican. Baptist. Office: Guardian Savs and Loan 6520 N Andrews Ave Fort Lauderdale FL 33310

NELSON, NANCY MELIN, editor, consultant; b. Cleve., Feb. 15, 1941; d. Myron Alexander and Irma (Sell) M.; m. Milo Gabriel Nelson, Feb. 15, 1980. BA, Mt. Union Coll., Alliance, Ohio, 1962; MA, Wayne State U., 1972; MLS, Simmons Coll., 1972. Serials librarian U. Vt., Burlington, 1972-75, Central Mich. U., Mt. Pleasant, 1975-78; library systems analyst Research Library Group, Stanford, Calif., 1979, Online Computer Library Ctr., Columbus, Ohio, 1980; serials librarian CUNY Grad. Ctr., N.Y.C., 1981-82; editor-in-chief Library Hi Tech, 1982-83, Library Hi Tech News and Library Software Rev., 1982—, Serials Rev., 1978-83, Ref. Services Rev., 1980-83, Small Computers in Libraries, 1984—, CD-Rom Librarian, 1987—, prin. Nelson Assocs., 1982—. Editor: Serials Collection, 1982; Serials Management in an Automated Age, 1982; International Subscription Agents, 1978; Serials and Microforms, 1983; Library Standards 1984; CD-Roms in Print, 1987; author: Essential Guide to the Library IBM PC, 1985, vols. 1, 8, 1987; contbr. articles to profl. jours. Mem. ALA. Democrat.

NELSON, NEVIN MARY, interior designer; b. Cleve., Nov. 5, 1941; d. Arthur George Reinker and Barbara Phyllis (Gunn) Parks; m. Wayne Nelson (div. 1969); children: Doug, Brian. BA in Interior Design, U. Colo., 1964. Prin. Nevin Nelson Design, Boulder, Colo., 1966-70, Vail, Colo., 1970—; program chmn. Questers Antique Study Group, Boulder, 1969. coordinator Bob Kirscht for Gov. campaign, Eagle County, Colo., 1986; state del. Denver Repub. Conv., 1986, 88; county coordinator George Bush for Pres. campaign, 1988. Mem. Am. Soc. Interior Designers. Episcopalian. Club: Pro Denver. Home: Box 1212 Vail CO 81658 Office: 108 S Frontage Rd Vail CO 81657

NELSON, PAMELA LEIGH, publishing company executive; b. Des Moines, Oct. 18, 1947; d. Clare S. and Eleanor (Greef) Orth; B.S., U. N.Mex., 1969; M.S., U. Kans., 1975. Tchr., Albuquerque Public Schs., 1969-72, Shawnee Mission (Kans.) Public Schs., 1972-76; cons. Macmillan Pub. Co., Kansas City, 1976-79; dir. mktg. services Am. Book Co., N.Y.C., 1979-81; product mgr. D. C. Heath & Co., Lexington, Mass., 1981-82; sr. product mgr. Allyn and Bacon Inc., Newton, Mass., 1982-85; product line mgr., dir. market research Silver Burdett and Ginn and Co., 1985-88; dir. reading Open Ct. Pub., Chgo., 1988—. Mem. Assn. Am. Pubs., Internat. Reading Assn., Nat. Council Social Studies, Nat. Council Tchrs. English, Phi Mu Alumni Assn., Kans. U. Alumni Assn., U. N.Mex. Alumni Assn. AAUW, Jr. League, Women in Communications. Republican. Presbyterian. Club: PEO. Office: Open Ct Pub Co 315 5th St Peru IL 61354

NELSON, PATRICIA LEE, real estate broker, commercial artist; b. El Paso, Tex., Dec. 3, 1949; d. Edward Adam and Carol Ann (Conlee) Walsh; m. Ben Scott Nelson, June 5, 1971; children: E. Carl, C. Katharine. BFA, N.Mex. State U., 1971. Head artist Trend Binder, Bryan, Tex., 1971-72; artist Tex. A&M U. Printing Ctr., College Station, 1972-74; free lance comml. artist, Las Vegas, N.Mex., 1974-83; real estate agt. Realty of Las Vegas, 1980-81; real estate broker Olafson Agy., Las Vegas, 1981-85; assoc. broker, 1985-87, Ochterbeck Agy., Las Vegas, 1987—; also photographer. Project leader San Miguel County 4-H, Las Vegas, 1975-83; sec. San Miguel County Fair Assn., 1981-83, pres. 1985; bd. dirs. Northeastern Regional Hosp., 1988. Recipient cert. of appreciation as outstanding project leader N.Mex. State U., 1975-82, Outstanding Leader award for 4-H Photography Project, Eastman Kodak, 1981, photography awards, 1982-83. Mem. Nat. Bd. Realtors, N.Mex. Bd. Realtors, Las Vegas Bd. Realtors (sec. 1981-82), Las Vegas-San Miguel C. of C. (pres. 1988, bd. dirs. 1986), Santa Fe Bd. Realtors, PEO (pres. 1984-85), Zeta Tau Alpha Alumnae. Republican. Methodist. Home: 1201 8th St Las Vegas NM 87701 Office: Ochterbeck Agy 524 6th St Las Vegas NM 87701

NELSON, PATRICIA SWEAZEY, international management consultant, exec. coach, psychotherapist; b. Seattle, Mar. 5, 1927; d. Manley Earl and F. Pauline (Pickard) S.; m. Russell Paul Nelson; children—Cynthia, Andrea, Barry. B.A. magna cum laude, U. Wash., 1971; postgrad. Whitworth Coll., 1985. Interpreter Italian prisoners of war U.S. Army, Seattle, 1944-45; interpreter, adminstr. trouble-shooter Pomona Valley Community Hosp., 1951-53; head tchr. of Kindergarten, program developer, co-dir. Alpental Kinderschule, Seattle Day Nursery, 1956-69, export/import mgr. Warn Internat., Seattle, 1971-72; trainer computer transition and corp. hdqrs. mgmt. devel team Unigard Ins., Seattle, 1972-74; dir. Nelson Internat. Assocs., Seattle, 1974—; researcher/cons. Swissair Transport, 1982—, expatriate families abroad. Author: Guide to Girl Scout Backpacking, 1965. Council cons. in Alpine travel Girl Scouts U.S.A., Seattle, 1960-67, also trainer, leader, explorer advisor; designer, dir. commissary program, bd. dirs. King County Search and Rescue Assn., 1967-74; dir. sites, program developer, Lichtenfeld Backpacking Encampment, 1964-67; adj. faculty City Univ. Seattle, 1975-79, Cen. Washington Univ., 1978—. Mem. Assn. for Tng. and Devel., Soc. for Internat. Edn., Tng. and Research.

NELSON, PAULA MORRISON, educator; b. Memphis, Mar. 26, 1944; d. Fred Ford and Julia (Morrison) Bronson: m. Jack Marvin Nelson, July 13, 1968; children: Eric Allen, Kelly Susan. BS, U. N. Mex., 1967; MA, U. Colo., Denver, 1985. Physical edn. tchr. Grant Union Sch. Dist., Sacramento, Calif., 1967-68; physical edn. tchr. Denver Pub. Schs., 1968-74, with program for pupil assistance, 1974-80, chpt. 1 reading specialist, 1983—; tchr. English as a second lang. Douglas County Pub. Schs., Parker, Colo., 1982-83; demonstration tchr. Colo. Edn. Assn., 1970-72; curriculum com. mem. Denver Pub. Schs., 1970-72, Douglas County Accountability Com., Castle Rock, Colo., 1986-88. Co-author: Gymnastics Teacher's Guide Elementary Physical Education, 1973; producer: slide shows Brotherhood, 1986, We the People...Our Dream Lives On, 1987. Pub. Edn. Coalitoin grantee, Denver, 1987, Rocky Mountain Global Edn. Project grantee, Denver, 1987, Wake Forest Law Sch. grantee, Winston-Salem, N.C., 1988. Mem. Denver Classroom Tchr.'s Assn., Colo. Edn. Assn., Nat. Edn. Assn., Colo. Council Internat. Reading, Internat. Reading Assn., Nat. Soc. for the Study of Edn. Republican. Methodist. Home: 10488 E Meadow Run Parker CO 80134

NELSON, PRISCILLA SPOERER, principal, consultant; b. Providence, Feb. 9, 1952; d. Henry George and Florence May (Mennie) Spoerer; m. Eric Charles B. Nelson, Oct. 11, 1986. BS, Gordon Coll., 1974; MEd, Boston U., 1980. Cert. elem. tchr., prin., Mass. Classroom tchr. Bessie Buker Sch., Wenham, Mass., 1974-79; prin., chief exec. officer North Shore Christian Sch., Lynn, Mass., 1979—; vis. lectr. Gordon Coll., Wenham, 1981-85, 1987—. Mem. Nat. Educators Fellowship (pres. New Eng. North Shore chpt. 1975-77), New Eng. Assn. Christian Edn. (bd. dirs. 1985—), Assn. Christian Schs. Internat. (adminstrs. fellowship 1985—), Evangelistic Assn. New Eng. (bd. dirs. 1986—), Gordon Coll. Alumni Assn. (bd. dirs. 1985—), Wash. Street Bapt. Womens Assn. (bd. dirs. 1987—). Home: 22 Linwood Rd Lynn MA 01905

NELSON, ROBIN JACOBS, business supply company professional; b. Boston, Nov. 19, 1959; d. Joel Robert and Betty Patricia (Spero) Jacobs; m. Michael Ellis Nelson, Sept. 13, 1986. AA, Stephens Coll., 1980, BA in Advt., 1981. Sales service Bowers Record Sleeve, Indpls., 1981-83, sales rep., 1983-86; key account mgr. Bower Envelope Co., Indpls., 1986—. Vol. Dance Kaleidescope, Indpls., 1985-86; vol., hostess Hoosier Dome, Indpls., 1986. Mem. Nat. Assn. Female Execs., Chgo. Assn. Direct Mktg., Direct Mktg. Assn. Office: Bowers Envelope Co 5331 N Tacoma Ave Indianapolis IN 46205

NELSON, SALLY IRENE, insurance agency executive; b. Rockland, Maine, Mar. 15, 1941; d. Edward Michael and Anne Laura (Taylor) Gluse; divorced; children: Erik O., Gayle Anne. Grad. high sch., S. Portland, Maine. Sales rep. Blue Cross/Blue Shield, Portland, Maine, 1975-80, Turner Barker, Portland, Maine, 1980-85; pres. Nelson, Desmond and Payne, Inc., Falmouth, Maine, 1984—. Legis. chairperson State of Maine, 1987—; mem. fin. com. Martin's Point Health Care Ctr., 1987—; bd. dirs. United Way, 1984—. Mem. Maine Assn. Life Underwriters (bd. dirs. 1983—, legis. chair 1983—), Nat. Assn. Life Underwriters (mem. sub-com. 1986—, Recognition of Quality and Achievement Com. 1988—), Am. Bus. Women's Assn. (named Woman of Yr., 1984), Nat. Assn. Female Execs. Democrat. Home: 113 Granby Rd South Portland ME 04106 Office: Nelson Desmond and Payne Inc 366 US Rt 1 Falmouth ME 04105

NELSON, SANDRA, educator; b. N.Y.C., Oct. 3, 1936; d. Harry Mitchell and Ann Frances (Mellin) Hochman; m. Bernard Nelson, Nov. 20, 1955; children: Michael Jay, Pamela Susan. AA in Fashion Design, Fashion Inst. Tech., 1955; BS in Art magna cum laude, Hofstra U., 1975; MS in Art, L.I. U., 1978, MS In Spl. Edn., 1982. Cert. remedial reading and diagnosis educator, N.Y. Pvt. practice sportswear design N.Y.C., 1954-63, pvt. practice custom dressmaking and designing, 1964—; tchr., asst. coordinator Consumer Home Econs. Ctr., Roosevelt, N.Y., 1975-81; instr. ceramics Baldwin (N.Y.) Sch. System, 1976-78, Roosevelt Jr. and Sr. High Sch., 1977-81; tchr. spl. edn. N.Y.C. Pub. Schs., Ozone Park, N.Y., 1981—. Mem. Internat. Reading Assn., L.I. Art Tchrs. Assn., Kappa Pi, Alpha Sigma Lambda.

NELSON, SARAH MILLEDGE, archaeology educator; b. Miami, Fla., Nov. 29, 1931; d. Stanley and Sarah Woodman (Franklin) M.; m. Harold Stanley Nelson, July 25, 1953; children: Erik Harold, Mark Milledge, Stanley Franklin. BA, Wellesley Coll., 1953; MA, U. Mich., 1969, PhD, 1973. Instr. archaeology U. Md. extension, Seoul, Republic Korea, 1970-71; asst. prof. U. Denver, 1974-79, assoc. prof., 1979-85, prof. archaeology, 1985—, chair dept. anthropology, dir. women's studies program, 1985—; vis. asst. prof. U. Colo., Boulder, 1974. Grantee Southwestern Inst. Research on Women, 1981, Acad. Korean Studies, Seoul, 1983, Internat. Cultural Soc. Korea, Seoul, 1986. Fellow Am. Anthrop. Assn.; mem. Soc. Am. Archaeology, Assn. Asian Studies, Royal Asiatic Soc., Sigma Xi (sec.-treas. 1978-79). Democrat. Home: 4970 S Fulton St Englewood CO 80111 Office: U Denver Dept Anthropology Denver CO 80208

NELSON, SHERRY LUCILLE WILLIAMS, infosystems specialist, consultant; b. Ripley, Tenn., Mar. 10, 1956; d. John Walter and Lucille (Sanders) Williams. BBA, U. Miss., 1978. Software specialist Burroughs Corp., Memphis, 1978-80; mgr. accounts payable Carlson Co., Mpls., 1981-83; acct. Memphis State U., 1983; cons. Touche Ross, Memphis, 1984-86, Ernst and Whinney, Memphis, 1986—. Vol. Ramesses the Great Exhibition, Memphis 1987, Memphis May Activites 1987. Republican. Methodist. Home: 3722 Charleston Sq Memphis TN 38122 Office: Ernst and Whinney 1400 One Commerce Sq Memphis TN 38103

NELSON, TONI COOKE, real estate broker; b. Houston, Sept. 9, 1949; s. Alan Theodore Jr. and Lydia (Parker) Cooke; m. William Crayton Nelson Jr., Nov. 27, 1970; children: Tricia Leigh, William Crayton III. Student, Tex. Tech U., 1967-70; BBA in Mktg., U. Houston, 1971; grad., Realtors Inst., 1984. Field supr. market research Higginbotham Assocs., Houston, 1971-76; agt. Laguardia, Gavrel and Kirk Real Estate, Houston, 1982-83; mgr., broker Gary Greene Realtors/Better Homes and Gardens, Missouri City, Tex., 1983—, also bd. dirs.; instr. Mktg. Specialist Sch., 1987; pres. Ft. Bend County Bd. Realtors, 1988—. Author Real Estate Data Market Report, 1985. Chmn. Community Revitalization Com., auction Ft. Bend chpt. Texans War on Drugs, 1988; sponsor Tex. War on Drugs, Sugar Land, 1987, auction chmn., 1988, Women's Refuge Ctr./Ft. Bend, Sugar Land, 1987; sequincentennial life mem. Tex. Real Estate Polit. Action Com., Sugarland, 1984—. Mem. Tex. Assn. Realtors (bd. dirs.), Ft. Bend County Bd. Realtors (bd. dirs. 1984-86, pres. 1988), Ft. Bend C. of C. (leadership 2000, pres.' council), Women's Council Realtors (liaison 1987), Realtors Nat.

Mktg. Inst. (cert. residential specialist 1985, cert. residential broker 1986). Republican. Episcopalian. Home: 1418 Sugar Creek Blvd Sugar Land TX 77478 Office: Gary Greene Realtors 3536 Hwy 6 Sugar Land TX 77479

NELSON, VITA JOY, editor, publisher; b. N.Y.C., Dec. 9, 1937; d. Leon Abraham and Bertha (Sher) Reiner; m. Lester Nelson, Aug. 27, 1961; children: Lee Reiner, Clifford Samuel, Cara Ritchie. BA, Boston U., 1959. Promotion copywriter Street & Smith, N.Y.C., 1958-59; asst. to mng. editor Mademoiselle Mag., N.Y.C., 1959-60; mcpl. bond trader Granger & Co., N.Y.C., 1960-63; founder, editor, publisher Westchester Mag., Mamaroneck, N.Y., 1968-80, L.I. Mag., 1973-78, Moneypaper, Larchmont, N.Y., 1981—. Bd. dirs. Westchester Tourism Council, Westchester County, N.Y., 1974-75, Sackerpath council Girl Scouts U.S.A., White Plains, N.Y., 1976-79; bd. govs. v.p. Am. Jewish Com., Westchester, N.Y., 1979—. Recipient citation Council Arts, 1972; Media award Pub. Relations Soc. Am., 1974. Mem. Women in Communications (Outstanding Communicator award 1983), Sigma Delta Chi. Democrat. Home: Pleasant Ridge Rd Harrison NY 10528 Office: Temper of the Times Communications 930 Mamaroneck Ave Mamaroneck NY 10543

NELSON, WANDA LOUISE KOESTER, controller, consultant; b. Cin., Oct. 8, 1949; d. Louis Charles and Bertha O'Delle (St. Clair) Chretien; m. John Wesley Nelson Jr., Jan. 23, 1971 (div. Apr. 1979). AA in Acctg., Coll. of DuPage, Glen Ellyn, Ill., 1976; BA in Acctg., Aurora (Ill.) U., 1980, MS in Bus. Mgmt., 1983. Statis. clk. David J. Joseph Co., Cinn., 1968-71; acctg. clk. Vulcan Materials, Countryside, Ill., 1971-72; supr. accounts payable C.G. Conn, Ltd., Oak Brook, Ill., 1972-77; mgr. acctg. office Authentic Furniture Products, Aurora, Ill., 1977; acct. Wil-Fred's, Inc., Naperville, Ill., 1977-78, supr. acctg., 1978-80; cost acct. Alcan Ingot & Powders, Joliet, Ill., 1981-83; controller Ingersoll-Rand, Naperville, 1983-87, Carol Stream, Ill., 1987—; computer cons. Kupco Constrn. Co., Houston, Miami, Fla., 1983—. Treas. Pebblewood Home Owners Assn., Naperville, 1974-75, bd. dirs., 1973-74. Named one of Outstanding Young Women of Am., 1982. Mem. Nat. Assn. Female Execs., NOW. Democrat. Methodist. Home: 9 Pebblewood Tr Naperville IL 60540 Office: Ingersoll-Rand Co 125 Tubeway Dr Carol Stream IL 60188

NELSON-HUMPHRIES, TESSA (UNTHANK), English language educator, writer, lecturer; b. Yorkshire, Eng.; came to U.S., 1955; m. Kenneth Nelson Brown, June 1, 1957 (dec. 1962); m. Cecil H. Unthank, Sept. 26, 1963 (dec. 1979). BA, U. London, 1953; MA, U. N.C., 1965; PhD in English, U. Liverpool (Eng.), 1973. Head English dept. Richard Thomas Girls Sch., Elmore Green Sch., Walsall, Eng., 1956-58; dir. English studies Windsor Coll., Buenos Aires, Argentina, 1958-59; prof. English, Cumberland Coll., Williamsburg, Ky., 1964—. Best Actress award Carlsbad (N.Mex.) Little Theatre, 1962, Cumberland Coll., 1979; Fulbright fellow, 1955-56, Danforth fellow, 1971, James Still fellow, 1983; Mellon travel/study grantee, China, 1981, 87; recipient awards for fiction Eng., 1986, 87, 88. Fellow AAUW; mem. Soc. Women Writers and Journalists (Short Story prize 1975, 87, Julia Cairns Silver trophy for Poetry, 1978, article prize, London, 1986), Nat. Council Tchrs. English, Soc. Children's Book Writers, Vegetarian Soc. (life), Mensa. Episcopalian. Contbr. articles to Cats Mag., Let's Live, The Lookout, Child Life, Vegetarian Times, Alive!, The Dalesman, Mich. Quar. Rev., Bull. of Soc. Children's Book Writers, Bull. Soc. Women Writers and Journalists, others; columnist, British Vegetarian mag., 1987; contbr. poetry to various mags. including Joycean Lit. Arts Guild, Z-Miscellaneous.

NELSON-SHULMAN, YONA, psychology consultant; b. Norwich, Conn., Jan. 14, 1946; d. Zev K. and Florence (Strum) Nelson; m. Herbert B. Shulman, June 16, 1973; children: Serena Florence, Larissa Anne. BA, Brandeis U., Waltham, Mass., 1967; MS, London Sch. Econs., 1970; PhD, CUNY, 1981. Vis. fellow Yale U., New Haven, 1972-73; lectr. in psychology CUNY, N.Y.C., 1973-80; cons. Drexel Burnham Lambert, N.Y.C., 1981—; cons. AT&T, Bellevue Hosp., J. Robinson Devel. Corp. N.Y. Housing Authority, Port Authority, Securities Ind. Assocs., UN, N.Y.C. area, 1980-85; sec. Orgn. for Women in Psychology, N.Y., 1971-73. H. Greenberg scholar, 1964-65; CUNY fellow, 1974-75. Mem. Am. Psychol. Assn., Assn. Applied Psychologists, Am. Soc. for Tng. and Devel. (chairperson sales and mktg. com. 1985—). Jewish. Home and Office: 521 Marl Rd Colts Neck NJ 07722

NEMCHEK, LEE RACHEL, law librarian; b. Phila., Oct. 27, 1954; d. Philip H. Nemchek and Elaine Harriet (Shapiro) Harrison. B.A. magna cum laude, Loyola U., Chgo., 1976; M.F.A. in Theater, UCLA, 1978; M.S. in Library Sci., U. So. Calif., Los Angeles, 1981. Library asst. II, U. So. Calif. Dental Library, 1979-80; library technician I, Pasadena (Calif.) Pub. Library, 1979-81; asst. law librarian Irell & Manella, Los Angeles, 1981-83; library asst. Cedars-Sinai Med. Ctr., Los Angeles, 1983-84; law librarian Pepper, Hamilton & Scheetz, Los Angeles, 1983-84, Manatt, Phelps, Rothenberg & Tunney, Los Angeles, 1984-85, Morrison & Foerster, Los Angeles, 1985—; cons. Nat. Health Law Program, Los Angeles, 1983, Library Mgmt. Systems, Los Angeles, 1984-85, Hanna & Morton, Los Angeles, 1986. Contbr. articles to profl. jours. Named outstanding grad. in Theatre, Loyola U. Theater dept., 1976; Schmidt Found. scholar Loyola U., 1976, Wilson Found., U. So. Calif., 1980, Libraria Sodalitas, U. So. Calif., 1981. Mem. Am. Assn. Law Libraries, ALA, Theatre Library Assn., So. Calif. Assn. Law Libraries, LRMA. Democrat. Home: 1523 S Wooster St Apt #2 Los Angeles CA 90035 Office: Morrison & Foerster 333 S Grand Ave Los Angeles CA 90071

NEMETH, PATTI MARIE, biomedical research scientist, educator; b. Tulsa, Nov. 8, 1946; d. Eugene M. and Juanita V. Cox; m. Michael Hatlelid; children: Tessa Elisabeth, Ryan Mason, Rebecca Lane. B.S., U. Ariz., 1969; Ph.D. (USPHS fellow 1972-77), UCLA, 1977. Alexander von Humboldt fellow in biomed. research U. Konstanz (W.Ger.), 1977-80, postdoctoral fellow in biomed. research Univ. Coll., London, 1978; asst. prof. neurology, neurosurgery, anatomy, and neurobiology Washington U., St. Louis, 1980-86, assoc. prof., 1986—. NIH, Muscular Dystrophy Assn. grantee. Mem. Biophys. Soc. Am., Nat. Inst. Neurol. and Communicative Disorders of Stroke, Soc. Neurosci., Am. Assn. Anatomists, Fedn. European Biochem. Socs. Mem. editorial bd. Experimental Neurology Jour.; contbr. articles in field to profl. jours. Office: Washington U Sch Medicine Dept Neurology Saint Louis MO 63110

NEMETH, VALERIE ANN, lawyer; b. Sutton Surrey, Eng., Mar. 23, 1954; d. Gerald Arnold and Louise Marian (Ross) N.; m. Larry Nagelberg, Dec. 28, 1978 (div. Nov. 1979); m. Hyman Joseph Zacks, Oct. 28, 1984. BA, UCLA, 1976; JD, Whittier Coll., 1979. Assoc. Grayson, Gross, Friedman, Los Angeles, 1979-80; gen. counsel Red Wind Prodns., Los Angeles, 1979-80; sole practice Los Angeles, San Diego, 1980—; gen. counsel, ptnr. MarValUs Entertainment Co., Los Angeles, 1984—; arbitrator Los Angeles County Superior Ct., 1985—, San Diego Superior Ct., 1985—; legal con. Centre Devel., San Diego, 1985—. Mem. legal com. Fairbanks Ranch Assn., Rancho Santa Fe, Calif., 1987—; adminstrv. dir. community services dist. Fairbanks Ranch. Mem. Am. Film Inst., State Bar Calif. (mem. intellectual property sect.), Variety Clubs Internat., Hadassah (life), Zool. Soc. San Diego. Democrat. Jewish. Office: 500 S Sepulveda Blvd #400 Los Angeles CA 90049 also: 619 S Vulcan Ave Suite 208 Encinitas CA 92024

NEMETZ, ANNETTE MARIE, materials engineer; b. Whitehall, Pa., May 13, 1954; d. Stephen Andrew and Anna Julia (Schadl) N. AA, Lehigh County Community Coll., 1975; BS, Rensselaer Poly. Inst., 1980; postgrad. Stanford U., 1988—. Devel. engr. Combustion Engring., Inc., Windsor, Conn., 1980-82, prin. startup engr., Palo Verde, Ariz., 1982—; co-owner, mgr. The Happy Llama Co., Telluride, Colo., 1985—. Co-founder, mem. C-E Women's Network; mem. Com. on East-West Econ. Relations. Mem. AAUW, Stanford Bus. Sch. Student Assn., Alpha Sigma Mu, Mensa. Roman Catholic. Club: Palo Verde Ski (founder, pres. 1984-86). Avocations: skiing, outdoor activities, tennis, art, travel-investments. Home: 638 College Ave Palo Alto CA 94306 Office: Stanford U Grad Sch Bus Stanford CA 94305

NEMIRO, BEVERLY MIRIUM ANDERSON, writer, educator; b. St. Paul, May 29, 1925; d. Martin and Anna Mae (Oshanyk) Anderson; m. Jerome Morton Nemiro, Feb. 10, 1951 (div. May 1975); children: Guy Samuel, Lee Anna, Dee Martin. Student Reed Coll., 1943-44; B.A., U. Colo., 1947; postgrad., U. Denver. Tchr., Seattle Pub. Schs., 1945-46; fashion coordinator, dir. Denver Dry Goods Co., 1948-51; fashion model, Denver, 1951-58, 78—; fashion dir. Denver Market Week Assn., 1952-53; free-lance writer, Denver, 1958—; moderator TV program Your Preschool Child, Denver, 1955-56; instr. writing and communications U. Colo. Denver Ctr., 1970—, U. Calif., San Diego, 1976-78; dir. pub. relations Fairmont Hotel, Denver, 1979-80; free lance fashion and TV model; author: The Complete Book of High Altitude Baking, 1961, Colorado a la Carte, 1963, Colorado a la Carte, Series II, 1966, (with Donna Hamilton) The High Altitude Cookbook, 1969, The Busy People's Cookbook, 1971 (Better Homes and Gardens Book Club selection 1971), Where to Eat in Colorado, 1967, Lunch Box Cookbook, 1965, Complete Book of High Altitude Baking, 1961, (under name Beverly Anderson) Single After 50, 1978, The New High Altitude Cookbook, 1980. Co-founder, pres. Jr. Symphony Guild, Denver, 1959-60; active Denver Art Mus., Denver Symphony Group. Recipient Achievement Rewards for Coll. Scientists, Sante Fe Opera, Denver Ear Inst., Top Hand award Colo. Authors' League, 1969, 72, 79-82, 100 Best Best Books of Yr. award N.Y. Times, 1969, 71; named one of Colo.'s Women of Yr., Denver Post, 1964. Mem. Pub. Relations Soc. Am., Am. Soc. Journalists and Authors, Nat. Writers Club, Colo. Authors League (dir. 1969—), Authors Guild, Authors League Am., Friends Denver Library, Sigma Delta Chi, Kappa Alpha Theta. Address: 420 S Marion Pkwy Apt 1003 Denver CO 80209

NEMITZ, JOY ANN, sales and marketing professional; b. Erie, Pa., Feb. 9, 1959; d. Angelo Anthony and Winifred Marie (Reese) Mezzacapo; m. Timothy J. Nemitz, June 20, 1981. BA, Villa Maria Coll., 1981; MS, Nova U., 1983. Cert. elem. and secondary level tchr. Educator Cathedral Ctr., Erie, 1979-81, Linvoln Ave Elem. Sch., Lakeland, Fla., 1981-83, St. Cecelia Sch., Clearwater, Fla., 1983-84; performance specialist Jack Eckerd Corp., Clearwater, 1984-86; mgmt. developer Citicorp, Tampa, Fla., 1986; sales tng. mgr. NCNB Nat. Bank, Tampa, 1986-88, mktg. product mgr., 1988—. Mem. Am. Soc. Tng. and Devel. (conf. registrar 1985, treas. 1986), Nat. Soc. Performance and Instrn. Democrat. Roman Catholic. Office: NCNB Nat Bank 400 Ashley Tampa FL 33602

NEMKO, BARBARA GAIL, academic coordinator, educational planner; b. Bronx, N.Y., Jan. 24, 1945; d. Herbert and Leona (Beder) Padrid; m. Martin Nathan Nemko, Dec. 26, 1976; 1 child, Amy Helene. B.A., Queens Coll., 1964, M.S., 1972; Ph.D., U. Calif.-Berkeley, 1981. Dir. of evaluation (partnership) U. Calif.-Berkeley, 1978-80; project dir. Calif. State Dept. Edn., U. Calif.-Davis, 1979—; cons. Berkeley Unified Sch. Dist., 1974-75, Sonoma State U., Rohnert Park, Calif., 1983—, Calif. State U.-Sacramento, 1983—, Calif. State U.-Los Angeles, 1985—; mem. regional action team State Dept. Edn., Sacramento, 1984—. Author: Resources, Strategies, and Directions to Better Serve Disadvantaged Students in Career-Vocational Programs, 1983; (with M. Nemko) How to Get Your Child a Private School Education in a Public School. Mem. Calif. Assn. Vocat. Educators, Am. Vocat. Assn. Jewish. Avocations: tennis, theatre, music, reading. Home: 5936 Chabolyn Terr Oakland CA 94618 Office: U Calif Dept Applied Behavioral Scis AOB 4 Davis CA 95616

NEMMERS, SHERRY J., advertising company executive; b. Blue Mountain Lake, N.Y., Aug. 11, 1954; d. Michael John and M. Jane (Santoro) Jacobs; m. Barry H. Nemmers, May 6, 1978. Student, Dartmouth Coll., 1974-75, U. Strasbourg, France, 1975; AB, Vassar Coll., 1976. Writer Grey Advt., N.Y.C., 1976-77; writer Dancer Fitzgerald Sample, Inc., N.Y.C., 1977-82, v.p., head creative group, 1982-83, sr. v.p., assoc. creative dir., 1983-84; sr. v.p., creative dir. DFS/Dorland Worldwide, N.Y.C., 1984-87, Saatchi & Saatchi DFS Compton, N.Y.C., 1987—; judge CLIO Awards, N.Y.C., 1980-82, The Hatch Awards, Boston, 1982; cons. Chandelle Farms, Holcomb, N.Y., 1986-87; cons., bd. dirs. Profl. Media Services, Boston, 1985-87. Creator: (animated character) McGruff, the Crime Dog (Pub. Service award 1987); founder, editor Out of the Blue, 1975, The Vassar Quar., 1979; contbr. articles to Dan's Papers, 1974-77. Writer Ad Council, Nat. Crime Coalition, N.Y.C., 1977-87, Fresh Air Fund, N.Y.C., 1980-87, Breast Exam. Ctr. Harlem, N.Y., 1982-85; mem. Blue Mountain Lake Performing Art Ctr., 1980-87. Recipient CLIO awards, N.Y.C., 1980-84, Effie awards, N.Y.C., 1983-85, The One Show award, N.Y.C., 1984, 85, 86, Internat. Radio and TV award Cannes (France) Film Festival, 1985. Mem. Advt. Women of Am. Roman Catholic. Club: Yale. Home: 1326 Madison Ave New York NY 10128 Office: Saatchi and Saatchi DFS Compton 405 Lexington Ave New York NY 10174

NENNER, VICTORIA CORICH, nurse; b. Marshall, Tex., Jan. 17, 1945; d. Bernard Paul and Mary DeLayne (Bowen) Corich; B.S. in Nursing (Regents scholar, Krost-Freeman scholar, Mary Gobbs Jones Nursing scholar), Tex. Women's U., 1966; cert. U. Paris, summer 1966; M.S. in Nursing, U. San Diego, 1984; m. Paul Edwin Nenner, Aug. 12, 1970. Mem. nursing staff St. Thomas Hosp., London, 1966-67, Parkland Meml. Hosp., Dallas, 1967-68; coordinator nursing continuing edn. Scripps Meml. Hosp., La Jolla, Calif., 1974-85; pres. Marvik Ednl. Services, Inc.; mem. part-time faculty U. Calif., San Diego; mem. vis. faculty U. B.C.; mem. Inservice Council San Diego and Imperial Counties, 1974—, pres., 1976-77; mem. San Diego Community Colls. Health Edn. Adv. Bd., 1976—. Served to capt. Nurse Corps, USAF, 1968-73. Named Tex. Student Nurse of Year, 1966. Mem. Am. Soc. Health Edn. and Tng., Nat. League Nursing, Am. Nurses Assn., Nat. Assn. Female Execs., Sigma Theta Tau. Author articles in field; producer oncology nursing ednl. videotapes. Home: 3937 Southview Dr San Diego CA 92117

NENSTIEL, SUSAN KISTHART, social services administrator; b. Hazleton, Pa., Aug. 21, 1951; d. Frank W. and Mary A. (Price) Kisthart; m. David W Nenstiel, June 4, 1977. BS, Pa. State U., 1973; MBA, Wilkes (Pa.) Coll., 1982. Control mgr. Barrett, Haentjens & Co., Hazleton, 1973-79, export mgr., 1979-86; exec. dir. Leadership Hazleton, 1986-87; devel. officer Planned Parenthood of NE Pa., Wilkes-Barre, 1986-87. Pres. YWCA, Hazleton, 1983-85, Womens Coalition of Greater Hazleton, 1987—; sec. Govt. Study Commn., Hazleton, 1984-85; bd. dirs. United Way Greater Hazleton, 1986; trustee, sec. Hazleton Area Pub. Library, 1987—; chair Luzerne County Commn. for Women, 1988—. Named one of Outstanding Women Penns Woods Council Girl Scouts U.S.A., 1977, Outstanding Young Women in Am., 1985, Woman of Yr. Soroptomist Internat., 1984. Mem. AAUW (pres. 1977-79, sec. 1981-83, treas. 1983-85, Br. Outstanding Woman 1980). Republican. Home: 537 W Diamond Ave Hazleton PA 18201

NESBITT, LENORE CARRERO, federal judge; m. Joseph Nesbitt; 2 children: Sarah, Thomas. A.A., Stephens Coll., 1952; B.S., Northwestern U., 1954; student U. Fla. Law Sch., 1954-55; LL.B., U. Miami, 1957. Private practice, Nesbitt & Nesbitt, 1960-63; spl. asst. attorney gen., 1961-63; research asst., Dade County Circuit Ct., 1963-65; with Law Offices of John Robert Terry, 1969-73; counsel, Fla. State Bd. Med. Examiners, 1970-71; with Petersen, McGowan & Feder, 1973-75; judge, Fla. state courts, 1975-82; judge, U.S. Dist. Ct. (so. dist.) Fla., Miami, 1983—. Mem. Am., Fla. bar assns. Office: US Dist Ct 301 N Miami Ave Miami FL 33128-7784 *

NESBITT, MARA LINDSEY, therapist; b. N.Y.C., Sept. 18, 1952; d. Saul M. and Esta (Feuerman) N. AA, Kirkwood Community Coll., 1973; student, U. Iowa, 1973-74, East-West Coll., 1983-84. Exec. dir. NOW, Portland, Oreg., 1975-76; adminstrv. asst. Harry's Mother Counseling Agy., Portland, 1976-78; events and info. coordinator N.W. Artists Workshop, Portland, 1980-83; telemktg. supr. Willamette Week Newspaper, Portland, 1981-84; owner The Nesbitt Massage, Portland, 1984—; Mem. adv. bd. Ample Opportunity, Portland, 1985-86. Organizer Portland Performing Arts Marathon, 1975. Mem. Oreg. Massage Technicians Assn. (sec. 1985-86). Democrat. Taoist. Office: The Nesbitt Massage 1509 SW Sunset Blvd Portland OR 97201

NESBITT, MARGOT LORD (MRS. CHARLES R. NESBITT), fine arts appraiser; b. Tonbridge, Kent, Eng., Feb. 13, 1927; d. Douglas G.R. and Octave (Waghorne) Lord; came to U.S., 1930, naturalized, 1937; BA in English Lit., U. Okla., 1950, BFA in Art History, 1970, MA, 1975, PhD, 1988; m. Charles R. Nesbitt, June 6, 1948; children—Nancy Margot, Douglas Charles, Carolyn Jane. Ordained deacon Episcopal Ch., 1988. Appraiser fine arts, Oklahoma City, 1968—; treas. Apollo Oil Corp., 1974—. Mem. Okla. Arts and Humanities Council, 1971-76; mem. women's com. Oklahoma City Symphony, 1964—; life mem. Okla. Art Center, women's bd., 1962-63; chmn. art collection State of Okla., 1975-76; bd. dirs. Okla. Found. for Disabled, 1972-75; bd. advisers Nat. Trust Historic Preservation, 1976-81. Mem. English Speaking Union, Okla. Hist. Soc. (dir. 1975-85), Hist. Preservation Oklahoma City (treas. 1977-80), Am. Soc. Appraisers (sr. mem.; pres. Okla. chpt. 1978-79), Appraisers' Assn. Am., Kappa Alpha Theta (pres. alumni chpt. 1962-64, Okla. chmn. Theta Link 1965-66, treas. corp. bd. 1976-77). Democrat. Episcopalian (treas. assemblies 1971-72, mem. women's bd. 1971-72, treas. altar guild 1972-73, treas. St. Paul's Cathedral 1976-78, mem. vestry 1978-85, jr. warden 1978-82, 84-85). Clubs: Connoisseur (pres. 1956-57); Early American Glass (treas. 1973-75). Address: 1703 N Hudson St Oklahoma City OK 73103

NESIUS, MARY ELLEN, telecommunications executive, consultant; b. Milw., Jan. 27, 1947; d. Paul and Mary Josephine (Kamps) Noelke; m. Robert Charles Nesius, Aug. 29, 1970; children: Elizabeth, Catherine. Editor advt. Detroit News, 1970-71; tchr. English and humanities Crestwood High Sch., Dearborn Heights, Mich., 1971-72; chmn. English dept. St. Mary's High Sch., Perth Amboy, N.J., 1972-74; tchr. humanities Randolph (N.J.) High Sch., 1976-81; cons. bus. Bell Labs., Murray Hill, N.J., 1980-82; cons. tng. AT&T, Bell Labs., Parsippany and Plainfield, N.J., 1982-84; cons. documentation AT&T Technology, Parsippany, 1984-85; PBX product mgr. AT&T Info. Systems, Parsippany, 1985—; writing cons. Animal Brands, Pottersville, N.J., 1980-85. Contbr. articles to profl. jours. Vice chmn., bd. trustees Family Leisure Times, Inc., Lake Hopatcong, N.J., 1986—. Mem. Am. Mgmt. Assn., Am. Assn. Univ. Women (bd. dirs. Flemington chpt. 1978). Office: AT&T 5 Woodhollow Rd Parsippany NJ 07054

NESSMITH, KITTY BURKE, accounting educator, accountant, consultant; b. Millen, Ga., Jan. 14, 1948; d. Charles Edward and Hazel (Cloy) Burke; m. Randy Nessmith, June 3, 1968 (div. Nov. 1982); 1 child, Jodi Allyson. BBA, Ga. So. Coll., 1971, MBA, 1981. CPA, Ga.; cert. info. systems auditor, 1987. Acct. Smith Supply Co., Statesboro, Ga., 1971-72; staff acct. Fuller & DeLoach, CPA's, Statesboro, 1972-75; instr. acctg. Ga. So. Coll., Statesboro, 1978-82, asst. prof., 1982—; systems analyst Computer Knowledge, Atlanta, 1983; ptnr. Bethel and Nessmith, Sylvania, Ga., 1985—. Named one of Outstanding Young Women of Am., 1981. Mem. Am. Inst. CPA's,. Ga. Soc. CPA's, Am. Acctg. Assn., Nat. Assn. Accts., Ga. Assn. Acctg. Instrs., Assn. Govtl. Accts., Beta Sigma Phi, Pi Sigma Epsilon, Beta Gamma Sigma, Beta Alpha Psi. Republican. Baptist. Home: 101 Greenbriar Trail Statesboro GA 30458 Office: Ga So Coll LB 8141 Statesboro GA 30460

NESTOR, BRENDA DIANA, real estate executive; b. Palm Beach, Fla., Nov. 10, 1955; d. John Joseph and Marion O'Connor N. Student, U. Miami, Fla., 1978. Lic. real estate agent, Fla. Salesman Oscar E Dooley, Inc., Miami, Fla., 1978-80; prin. Brenda Nestor Assocs, Inc., Miami Beach, Fla., 1980—. Named Ms. Charity City of Miami, 1985. Mem. Miami Beach Bd. of Realtors (bd. dirs. 1984—), Real Estate Securities and Exchange Com.. Roman Catholic. Clubs: Le Club (N.Y.C.); La Gorce Country (Miami Beach), Surf (Miami Beach). Home and Office: 6917 Collins Ave Miami Beach FL 33141

NETHERLAND, PATRICIA JANE, counselor; b. Texarkana, Ark., July 26, 1937; d. James Edward and Leota Christina (Fleming) Cunningham; m. David Austin Metts, July 21, 1957 (div. Dec. 1979); children: Alison Elizabeth, Leslie Christine; m. Robert Neil Netherland, Nov. 17, 1981. AA, Texarkana Coll., 1957; BA in Art, U. Tex., Odessa, 1974, MA in Edn., 1977. Cert. substance abuse counselor, social work assoc. Sec. J.B. Beaird Co., Shreveport, La., 1957-60, U. Ark., Fayetteville, 1960, Texaco, Midland, Tex. and Roswell, N.Mex., 1961-63; co-owner, counselor Talk It Over Consulting Service, Midland, 1983—; cons. High Sky Girls' Ranch, Midland, 1983-86; cons., counselor Culver Youth Home, Midland, 1983—; artist Netherland Art Gallery, Midland, 1983-86; adj. instr. counseling Odessa Coll., 1984— . Mem. Tex. Assn. of Drug and Alcoholism Counselors (v.p. 1985-86), Bus. and Profl. Women (local v.p. 1987), Nat. Assn. Female Execs. (network dir. 1983—). Club: Pilot charter mem.). Home: 2819 Maxwell Midland TX 79705 Office: Talk It Over PO Box 8162 Midland TX 79708

NETHERY, ANN ETTA, business broker executive, realtor; b. Vernon, Tex., Mar. 2, 1950; d. Paul Fuston and Helen Louise (Mayes) Nethery; children—Jeffrey Paul, Kristen Nicole. Realtor, owner Garland Assocs., Inc., Tex., 1976-86; broker, owner Metroplex Bus. Brokerage, Garland, 1982—. Mem. Garland Bd. Realtors (bd. dirs. 1982-86, Realtor of Yr. 1985), Counseling Inst. Tex. (bd. dirs. 1988), Garland C. of C. (bd. dirs. 1983-86). Baptist.

NETSCH, DAWN CLARK, state senator; b. Cin., Sept. 16, 1926; B.A. with distinction, Northwestern U., 1948, J.D. magna cum laude, 1952; m. Walter A. Netsch. Admitted to Ill. bar; individual practice law, Washington, Chgo.; law clk. U.S. Dist. Ct. Chgo.; adminstrv. and legal aide Ill. Gov. Otto Kerner, 1961-65; prof. law Northwestern U., 1965—; mem. Ill. Senate. Del. Ill. Constl. Conv.; adv. bd. Nat. Program Ednl Leadership, LWV, Mus. Contemporary Art, Ill. Welfare Assn. Democrat. Author: (with Daniel Mandelker) State and Local Government in a Federal System; contbr. articles to legal jours. Office: State Capitol Room 121C Springfield IL 62706 also: 715 W Armitage Chicago IL 60614

NETTER, CORNELIA ANN, real estate broker; b. N.Y.C., July 11, 1933; d. Frank H. and Mary (MacFadyen) N.; divorced: 1 child, Cornelio Jr. Student, U. Denver, 1951-53, C.W. Post Coll., 1958-60; BS, N.Y. State Regents, 1972. Sec. Newsday Bus. Office, Garden City, N.Y., 1959-61; adminstrv. asst. to U.S. Senator J. K. Javits N.Y., 1961-66; spl. asst. to Gov. Nelson A. Rockefeller Office of Gov., N.Y.C., 1966-69; pub. affairs dir. N.Y. State Health Planning Commn., 1969-72; dir. Office of Planning Services N.Y. State Human Resources Planning Commn., Albany and N.Y.C., 1972-76; pres. Netter Communications, N.Y.C., 1976-83, Netter Real Estate, N.Y.C., 1982-88, Independent Brokers Network, 1988—. Founding mem. N.Y. State Women's Polit. Caucus, Albany, 1971; mem. N.Y. State Del. Appilachian Regional Commn., 1973-75, Rep. Family Com., N.Y.C., 1986—; mem. steering com. Breakthru Found., N.Y.C., 1983-85; bd. dirs. N.Y. Citiworks, 1987—; dept. campaign mgr. Rockefeller Gubernatorial, N.Y.C., 1966, dir. spl. groups, 1970; co-campaign mgr. N.Y. Nixon Presdl., 1968, dir. ethnic and spl. groups, 1972; candidate N.Y. State Assembly, 1974. Mem. Nat. Assn. Realtors, Nat. Assn. Real Estate Appraisers (CREA designation 1986), Ind. Brokers Network (pres. 1988—), Real Estate Bd. of N.Y., Greenwich Village C. of C. (bd. dirs. 1988—). Republican. Office: Netter Real Estate 853 Broadway #1007 New York NY 10003

NETTESHEIM, CHRISTINE COOK, judge; b. Oakland, Calif., Aug. 25, 1944; d. Leo Marshall and Carolyn Grant (Odell) Cook; m. Paul Henry Nettesheim, Feb. 18, 1978. BA, Stanford U., 1966; JD, U. Utah, 1969. Bar: Utah 1969, D.C. 1972, Calif. 1982. Clk. to chief judge U.S. Ct. Appeals (10th cir.), 1969-70; trial atty. U.S. Dept. Justice, Washington, 1970-72, Fed. Trade Commn., Washington, 1972-74; litigation Hogan & Hartson, Washington, 1974-76; spl. counsel Pension Benefit Guaranty Corp., Washington, 1976-78; asst. gen. counsel U.S. Ry. Assn., Washington, 1978-80; litigation Shack & Kimball P.C., Washington, 1980-83; judge U.S. Claims Ct., Washington, 1983—. Mem. State Bar Assn. Calif., D.C. Bar Assn., Utah State Bar Assn., ABA (mem. tax, pub. contract and jud. adminstrv. div.), Order of Coif. Republican. Presbyterian. Club: City Tavern (Washington). Office: US Claims Ct 717 Madison Pl NW Washington DC 20005

NEU, IRENE DOROTHY, historian, educator; b. Cin.; d. Frederick Francis and Mary Clara (Holterman) N.; B.A., Marietta Coll., 1944; M.A., Cornell U., 1945, Ph.D., 1950; m. Robert Leslie Jones, Nov. 25, 1976. Fellow, Research Center Entrepreneurial History, Harvard U., 1950-51; instr. Rockford (Ill.) Coll., 1951-52, Conn. Coll., New London, 1953-54; asso. prof. S.E. Mo. State Coll., Cape Girardeau, Mo., 1956-62, prof., 1962-64; asso. prof. Ind. U., Bloomington, 1964-70, prof. history, 1970-86, prof. emeritus history, 1986—. Fulbright fellow Italy, 1954-55; Social Sci. Research Council faculty fellow, 1960-61; Eleutherian Mills Hist. Library sr. fellow, 1970. Mem. Am. Hist. Assn., Orgn. Am. Historians, Econ. History Assn., Bus. History Conf., Ind. Hist. Soc., Phi Beta Kappa. Author: Erastus Corning, Merchant and Financier, 1794-1872, 1960; co-author: The American Railroad Network, 1861-1890, 1956; contbr. articles in field to profl. jours. Home: 206 Brentwood St Marietta OH 45750

NEUBELT, MELANIE MARY, real estate investor, electrical engineer; b. Red Bank, N.J., Aug. 5, 1961; d. James Arthur and Lorraine (Lechleiter) O'Keefe; m. Michael James Neubelt, Nov. 1, 1986. BS in Engring. Physics, Stevens Inst. Tech., Hoboken, N.J., 1983; MS in Elec. Engring., Columbia U., 1987. Engr., sci. McDonnell Douglas Astronautics, Huntington Beach, Calif., 1983-85; mem. tech. staff Bell Communications Research, Red Bank, N.J., 1985-87; pvt. practice real estate investor Asbury Park, N.J., 1987—. Treas., bd. dirs. Wyndmoor at the Highlands (N.J.), 1986—. Roman Catholic. Home: 11 Ivy Pl Asbury Park NJ 07712 Office: Bell Communications Research 331 Newman Springs Rd NVC 3C-109 Red Bank NJ 07701-7020

NEUFELD, ELIZABETH FONDAL, biochemist, educator; b. Paris, Sept. 27, 1928; U.S. citizen; m. 1951; Ph.D., U. Calif., 1956; D.H.C. (hon.), U. Rene Descartes, Paris, 1978; D.Sc. (hon.), Russell Sage Coll., Troy, N.Y., 1981, Hahnemann U. Sch. Medicine, 1984. Asst. research biochemist U. Calif.-Berkeley, 1957-63, Nat. Inst. Arthritis, Metabolism and Digestive Diseases, Bethesda, Md., 1963-84, research biochemist, 1963-73, chief sect. human biochem. genetics, 1973-79, chief genetics and biochem. br., 1979-84; prof. chmn. dept. biol. chemistry UCLA Sch. Medicine, 1984—. USPHS fellow U. Calif., Berkeley, 1956-57. Recipient Dickson prize U. Pitts., 1974, Hillebrand award, 1975, Gairdner Found. award 1982; Albert Lasker Clin. Med. Research award, 1982; Elliott Cresson Medal, 1984; Wolf Found. prize, 1988. Mem. Nat. Acad. Sci., Am. Acad. Arts and Sci., Am. Soc. Human Genetics, Am. Chem. Soc., Am. Soc. Biol. Chemists, Am. Soc. Cell Biology, Am. Soc. Clin. Investigation. Office: UCLA Sch Medicine Dept of Biological Chemistry Los Angeles CA 90024

NEUFELD, JUDITH B., librarian; b. Bklyn., Nov. 7, 1935; d. Jesse and Miriam (Horowitz) Ginsberg; m. Meyer P. Neufeld, Dec. 18, 1966; children: Sandra, Deborah, Laura. BA, Queens Coll., Flushing, N.Y., 1956; B Hebrew Lit., Jewish Theol. Sem., N.Y.C., 1956; MLS, Columbia U., 1958, cert. in advanced librarianship, 1966. Librarian Ramaz Sch., N.Y.C., 1956-57; adminstrv. librarian Jewish Theol. Sem., N.Y.C., 1957-68; asst. dir. L.I. Library Resources Council, Stony Brook, 1974—; free-lance indexer. Mem. ALA, N.Y. Library Assn., Suffolk County Library Assn. (pres. 1984), Assn. Jewish Librarians. Home: 87 Roe Blvd W Patchogue NY 11772 Office: LI Library Resources Council Melville Library Bldg Suite E5310 Stony Brook NY 11794-3399

NEUFELD, NAOMI DAS, pediatric endocrinologist; b. Butte, Mont., June 13, 1947; d. Dilip Kumar and Maya (Chaliha) Das; m. Timothy Lee Neufeld, Nov. 27, 1971; children: Pamela Anne, Katherine Louise. AB, Pembroke Coll., 1969; M. in Med. Sci., Brown U., 1971; MD, Tufts U., 1973. Diplomate Am. Bd. Pediatrics, Am. Bd. Endocrinology. Intern R.I. Hosp., Providence, 1973-74, resident in pediatrics, 1974-75; fellow in pediatric endocrinology UCLA, 1975-78; staff endocrinologist Cedars-Sinai Med. Ctr., Los Angeles, 1978-79, chief pediatric endocrinology sect., 1979-85, dir. pediatric endocrinology, 1985—; asst. research pediatrician UCLA, 1978-79, asst. prof.-in-residence pediatrics, 1979-85, assoc. prof.-in-residence, 1985—. Contbr. articles to profl. jours. Mem. bd. deacons Pacific Palisades Presbyn. ch. 1988—. Named Clin. Investigator, NIH, 1978; grantee United Cerebral Palsy Soc., 1979, March of Dimes, 1981, NIH, 1983-88. Mem. Am. Diabetes Assn., Soc. Pediatric Research, Endocrine Soc., Juvenile Diabetes Found. (research grantee 1980). Presbyterian. Home: 16821 Charmel Ln Pacific Palisades CA 90272 Office: Cedars Sinai Med Ctr 8700 Beverly Blvd Los Angeles CA 90048

NEUGARTEN, BERNICE LEVIN, social scientist; b. Norfolk, Nebr., Feb. 11, 1916; d. David L. and Sadie (Segall) Levin; m. Fritz Neugarten, July 1, 1940; children: Dail Ann, Jerrold. B.A., U. Chgo., 1936, Ph.D., 1943; D.Sc. (hon.), U. So. Calif., 1980. Research asst. dept. edn. U. Chgo., 1937-39; fellow Am. Council on Edn., 1939-41; instr. psychology Englewood Coll., Chgo., 1941-43; research assoc. Com. on Human Devel., U. Chgo., 1948-50, asst. prof., 1951-60, assoc. prof., 1960-64, prof., 1964-80, chmn., 1969-73; prof. social service adminstrn. U. Chgo., 1978-80, mem. com. on policy studies, 1979-80; prof. edn. and sociology Northwestern U., 1980—; mem. council U. Chgo. Senate, 1968-71, 72-75, 78-80, chmn. council com. on univ. women, 1969-70, mem. tech. com. research and demonstration White House Conf. on Aging, 1971; tech. adv. com. on aging research HEW, 1972-73; nat. adv. council Nat. Inst. on Aging, 1975-76, 78-81, Fed. Council on Aging, 1978-81; dep. chmn. White House Conf. on Aging, 1980-81; mem. various adv. bodies. Author: (with R.J. Havighurst) American Indian and White Children: A Social-Psychological Investigation, 1955, reprint, 1969, Society and Education, 1957, rev., 1962, 67, 75, (with Assocs.) Personality in Middle and Late Life, 1964, reprint, 1980, (with J.M.A. Munnichs et al) Adjustment to Retirement, 1969, (with R.P. Coleman) Social Status in the City, 1971; editor: Middle Age and Aging, 1968; co-editor: (with H. Eglit) Age Discrimination, 1981, Age or Need? Public Policies for Older People, 1982; assoc. editor Jour. Gerontology, 1958-61, Human Devel., 1962-68; adv. or cons. editor other profl. jours., 1959—; author monographs, research papers and reports. Bd. dirs. Internat. Ctr. Social Gerontology. Recipient Am. Psychol. Found. Disting. Teaching award, 1975, Disting. Psychologist award Ill. Psychol. Assn., 1979; named to Chgo. Sr. Citizens Hall of Fame, 1983. Fellow AAAS, Am. Psychol. Assn. (council rep. 1967-69, 73-76, Disting. Sci. Contbn. award for div. 20, 1980), Am. Sociol. Assn., Gerontol. Soc. Am. (pres. 1968-69, Kleemeier award for research in aging 1971, Brookdale award for disting. contbn. 1982, Sandoz Internat. Prize for Gerontol. Research, 1987), Am. Acad. Arts and Scis., Internat. Assn. Gerontology (governing council 1975-78, chmn. N. Am. exec. com. 1983-85); mem. Inst. Medicine of Nat. Acad. Scis (sr., com. on aging soc. 1982-87), Am. Assn. for Internat. Aging (bd. dirs.), Sigma Xi, Phi Delta Kappa, Pi Lambda Theta. Home: 5801 Dorchester Ave Chicago IL 60637

NEUHAUS, RUBY HART, health services administration educator; b. Dec. 23, 1932; s. Coy Elkin and Pauline (Thorn) Hart; m. Sept. 3, 1955; children—Leah, Paul, Rachel. B.A., Bklyn. Coll., 1955; M.S.W., Fordham U., 1957; Ph.D., NYU, 1973. Cert. social worker, N.Y. State. Adminstrv. asst. dir. Lutheran Med. Ctr., 1953-55; unit dir. U. Minn. Hosp. Psychiat. Div., 1957-59; supr. Lutheran Social Services, Mpls., 1959-64; field work preceptor adminstrn. U. Minn., 1960-62; adminstrv. dir. N.Y. Counseling and Consultation Service, 1964-72; dir. fieldwork program Adelphi U., 1972-74, adj. lectr. dept. sociology, 1972; regional dir. Nassau County Mental Health Clinic, 1975-77, St. Anthony's Guidance Clinic; asst. prof. pub. adminstrn. SUNY Empire State Coll., 1974-75; assoc. prof. dept. health services Lehman Coll. CUNY, 1977—, chmn. dept., 1980—; adj. lectr. sociology L.I. U., 1972; adj. asst. prof. urban studies SUNY, Old Westbury, 1976. Author: (with other) Family Crises, 1980, Successful Aging, 1983, Interdisciplinary health Team Development, 1983, others. Bd. dirs. Consumer Council, Health Ins. Plan of N.Y. Hicksville Ctr., East Nassau, 1981-82. Recipient Bklyn. Coll. CUNY All Coll. award, 1955; Founders Day award NYU, 1974; fellow Wheatridge Found., 1955-57, NYU, 1970-71, Inst. on Man and Sci., 1983; grantee Robert Wood Johnson Found., 1988. Mem. Contemporary Authors, Nat. Assn. Social Workers, Am. Sociol. Assn., Am. Soc. Pub. Adminstrn., Am. Acad. Health Adminstrn., Assn. Univ. Programs in Health Adminstrn., Beta Mu (award 1955). Office: Herbert H Lehman Coll CUNY Bedford Park Blvd W Bronx NY 10468

NEUMAN, DEANNE ELAINE, editor; b. Webster City, Iowa, June 20, 1945; d. Bernard John and Palma Merle (Lande) Neuman; m. Peyton R. Neal Jr., June 25, 1985. BA in Journalism and Polit. Sci. with honors, U. Iowa, 1967. Mng. editor internat. trade report Bur. Nat. Affairs, Inc., Washington, 1967—; editorial cons. Steven K. Herlitz, Inc., N.Y.C., 1968-73. Club: Internat. (Washington). Home: 1738 Irving St NW Washington DC 20010 Office: Bur Nat Affairs Inc 1231 25th St NW Washington DC 20037

NEUMEISTER, SUSAN MARY, librarian; b. Buffalo, May 23, 1958; d. Edward John and Regina Mary (Winnicki) N. BA in Geography, SUNY, Buffalo, 1980, MLS, 1982. Clk. Health Scis. Library SUNY, Buffalo, 1978-81, grad. asst., 1981-82, library aide, 1982, cataloger cen. tech. services, 1982—. Librarian Buffalo chpt. ARC, 1983—. Grantee, 1987-88. Mem. ALA, N.Y. Library Assn., SUNY Librarians Assn., Online Audiovisual Catalogers, Western N.Y./Ont. ACRL. Democrat. Roman Catholic. Home: 16 Block St Buffalo NY 14211 Office: SUNY Cen Tech Services Lockwood Library Bldg Buffalo NY 14260

NEUTZE, LOUISE ELIZABETH, leasing company executive; b. Phila., Feb. 9, 1948; d. Lee Lange and Marion Margaret (Trautman) Zell; m. William C. Neutze, July 16, 1967 (div. 1978); children—Marlee F., Roxanne L. Student U. Balt., 1966-67. Small fleet rep. Comml. Credit, Balt., 1976-79; controller L-J Leasing, Balt., 1979-84; v.p. 1st Eastern Leasing, Balt., 1984-86; mgr. controller L-J Leasing, Balt., 1986—. Pres. Lutherville Timonium Recreation Council, Timonium, Md., 1983-86, 87-88; Republican candidate Balt. County Council. Mem. Eastern Assn. Equipment Lessors, Engring. Soc. Episcopalian. Clubs: Soroptimist Internat. (treas. 1985-86, pres. 1986-88), Friendshp (1st v.p. 1985-86) (Balt.). Avocations: bowling; coaching softball and basketball. Home: 31 Pickburn Ct Cockeysville MD 21030 Office: L-J Leasing Co 600 Reisterstown Rd Baltimore MD 21208

NEUWIRTH, BEBE, dancer, actress; b. Newark, Dec. 31; d. Lee Paul and Sydney Anne Neuwirth; m. Paul Dorman. Student, Juilliard Sch., 1976-77. Appeared on Broadway and internationally as Sheila in A Chorus Line, 1978-81; other Broadway appearances include West Side Story, 1981, Little Me, 1981, Sweet Charity, 1985-87 (Tony award for Best Supporting Actress in a Musical, 1985-86); prin. dancer Dancin', 1982; appeared with Pa. Stage Co. in Just So, 1984; choregrapher, leading dance role Kicks, 1984; appeared with N.Y.C. Comedy Cabaret in Upstairs at O'Neal's, 1982-83. Vol. performances for March of Dimes Telethon, 1986, Cystic Fibrosis Benefit Children's Ball, 1986, Ensemble Studio Theater Benefit, 1986, Circle Repertory Co. Benefit, 1986, all in N.Y.C. Democrat.

NEUWIRTH, GLORIA S., lawyer; b. N.Y.C., Aug. 16, 1934; d. Nathan and Jennie (Leff) Salob; m. Robert S. Neuwirth, June 9, 1957; children: Susan Madeleine, Jessica Anne, Laura Helaine, Michael Jonathan. BA, Hunter Coll., 1955; JD, Yale U., 1958. Bar: N.Y. 1959, Fla. 1979, U.S. Supreme Ct. 1976, U.S. Dist. Ct. (so. and ea. dists.) N.Y. 1976. Assoc. dir. Joint Research Project on Ct. Calendar Congestion, Columbia U., N.Y.C., 1958-61; assoc. Kridel and Friou, N.Y.C., 1974-76; ptnr. Kridel, Slater and Neuwirth, N.Y.C., 1976-82; assoc. Kaye, Scholer, Fierman, Hays and Handler, N.Y.C., 1982-84; assoc. Graubard Moskovitz McGoldrick Dannett & Horowitz, N.Y.C., 1984-86; ptnr. Kridel & Neuwirth, N.Y.C., 1986—; vol. arbitrator Better Bus. Bur. Author: (with R.B. Hunting) Who Sues in New York City: A Study of Automobile Accident Claims, 1962; contbr. articles to law jours. Trustee Blueberry Inc., 1962-70, Riverdale Country Sch., 1981—; trustee, v.p., sec. Nat. Kidney Found. Inc., N.Y./N.J., 1980—, trustee nat. office, 1980—. Recipient C. LaRue Munson prize Yale Law Sch., 1958. Fellow Am. Coll. Probate Counsel; mem. ABA, N.Y. State Bar Assn. (vice chmn. com. on persons under disability), Assn. Bar City N.Y., Estate Planning Council of N.Y., Nat. Health Lawyers Assn., Fed. Bar Council, Sierra Club. Club: Appalachian Mountain. Office: Kridel & Neuwirth 360 Lexington Ave New York NY 10017

NEVES, CAROL PATTERSON, security analyst; b. Montclair, N.J.; d. Charles and Agnes (Patterson) Neves. B.A., Trinity Coll., 1954; M.B.A., Harvard U., 1955. Research trainee Merrill Lynch, N.Y.C., 1955-60, security analyst, 1960-68, sr. security analyst, comglomerates, 1968—, v.p., 1974-88, first v.p., 1988—; mem. All-Am. Research Team Instnl. Investors, 1978-87. Contbr. articles to profl. jours. Trustee Trinity Coll., Washington, 1986—. Mem. Diversified Cos. Analyst Group (founder, pres. 1979-80, treas. 1980-82), N.Y. Soc. Security Analysts; Women's Bond Club N.Y. Clubs: Spring Lake Bath and Tennis, Spring Lake Golf, Harvard.

NEVILLE, JANICE NELSON, dietitian; b. Schenectady, Dec. 1, 1930; d. William Anthony and Margaret (Adams) Nelson; B.S., Carnegie Inst. Tech., 1952; M.S. (research fellow 1953), U. Ala., 1953, M.P.H., 1962; D.Sc., U. Pitts., 1964; divorced; children—James Gleeson, Lynn Marie. Clinic dietitian, instr. Univ. Hosps., Birmingham, Ala., 1954, research dietitian alcoholism, obesity, serum lipids and diet Grad. Sch. Public Health, 1956-64, asst. research prof. nutrition, 1965; mem. faculty Case Western Res. U., 1965—, prof. nutrition, 1977—, chmn. dept., 1974-82; trustee, chmn. various coms. N.E. Ohio affiliate Am. Heart Assn., 1975-87, v.p., 1985-86, pres.-elect, 1986-87, trustee, 1975-88; adv. com. FDA, 1977-78; mem. grant and contract rev. com. USPHS, NIH. Recipient Meritorious Service medal N.E. Ohio affiliate Am. Heart Assn. Mem. Am. Dietetic Assn. (chmn. nat. adv. com. Dial-a-Dietitian 1975-78, area coordinator 1978-81, speaker House of Dels., 1983-84, dir. 1982-86, pres.-elect 1986-87, pres. and chmn. bd. 1987-88), AAAS, Am. Pub. Health Assn., Soc. Nutrition Edn., Am. Home Econs. Assn., Am. Coll. Nutrition (cons. editor), Dietetic Practice Groups, N.Y. Acad. Scis., Ohio Dietetic Assn. (pres. 1973-75; Pres.'s award 1981), Cleve. Dietetic Assn. (Disting. Service award), Sigma Xi. Author articles in field, chpts. in books. Office: Dept Nutrition Case Western Res U Cleveland OH 44106

NEVINS, SHEILA, television director and producer; b. N.Y.C.; d. Benjamin and Stella N.; B.A., Barnard Coll., 1960; M.F.A. (Three Arts fellow), Yale U., 1963; m. Sidney Koch; 1 son, David Andrew. TV producer Great Am. Dream Machine, NET, 1970-72, The Reasoner Report, ABC, 1973, Feeling Good, Children's TV Workshop, 1975-76, Who's Who, CBS, 1977-78; dir. documentary programming Home Box Office, N.Y.C., 1978-86, v.p. family programming and documentaries, 1986—; pres. Spinning Reels, Inc., 1982-86. Bd. dirs. Women's Action Alliance. Recipient Peabody award, 1986. Mem. Writers Guild Am., Women in Film.

NEVIUS, DISA KIRSTEN, marketing professional; b. New Haven, Aug. 29, 1962; d. Stuart Clark and Ester Evelyn (Gustavsson) Pratt; m. Martin Kenneth Nevius, Sept. 20, 1986. BA in Internat. Mgmt. and Spanish, Simmons Coll., 1984. Lic. realtor assoc. Sales rep. Packing Soap div. Procter and Gamble, Hartford, Conn., 1984-85; mktg. rep. Vantage Computer Systems, Wethersfield, Conn., 1985-86; franchise mktg. cons. Realty World Corp., San Diego, 1986-87; v.p. mktg. Homestate Team, San Diego, 1987—. Vol. ARC, Cohasset, Mass., 1976-84; student advisor, counselor Simmons Coll., Boston, 1982-84; vol. translator Mass. Gen. Hosp., Boston, 1983. Twice named All-State actor/actress Boston Globe. Mem. Women in Sales Assn., Nat. Assn. Female Execs. Home: 4353-64 Nobel Dr San Diego CA 92122

NEW, SUSAN CUBBEDGE, chemical company process engineer; b. Aiken, S.C., Dec. 5, 1956; d. Ira Bengamin and Janet (Epting) N. BS in Chem. Engring., Clemson U., 1979. Chem. engr. Dow Chem. Co., Plaquemine, La., 1979-81, Amoco Chem. Co., Mt. Pleasant, S.C., 1981—. Fund drive worker, Jr. Achievement; Charleston, S.C., 1985-86, United Way, 1985. Named Young Career Woman Fort Sumter Bus. and Profl. Woman's Club Inc., 1986. Mem. Internat. Mgmt. Council (Charleston chpt. pub. relations 1987—, publicity 1988—), Am. Inst. Chem. Engrs., Nat. Assn. Female Execs. Republican. Office: Amoco Chem Co Cooper River Plant PO Box 987 Mount Pleasant SC 29464

NEWBERG, DOROTHY BECK (MRS. WILLIAM C. NEWBERG), portrait artist; b. Detroit, May 30, 1919; d. Charles William and Mary (Labedz) Beck; student Detroit Conservatory Music, 1938; m. William C. Newberg, Nov. 3, 1939; children: Judith N. Bookwalter, Robert Charles, James William, William Charles. Trustee Detroit Adventure, 1967-71, originator A Drop in Bucket Program for talented inner-city children. Bd. dirs. Bloomfield Art Assn., 1960-62, trustee 1965-67; bd. dirs. Your Heritage House, 1972-75, Franklin Wright Settlement, 1972-75, Meadowbrook Art Gallery, Oakland U., 1973-75; bd. dirs. Sierra Nevada Mus. Art, 1978-80; deacon St. John's Presbyn. Ch., Reno. Recipient Heart of Gold award, 1969; Mich. vol. leadership award, 1969. Mem. Sierra Art Found., Birmingham Soc. Women Painters. Home: 2000 Dant Blvd Reno NV 89509

NEWBERG, ELLEN JOYCE, library administrator; b. Wellman, Iowa, Sept. 29, 1941; d. Carl Clarence and Elda Grace (White) Herr; m. Alan Keith Newberg, June 11, 1965. B.A., Sioux Falls Coll., 1962; M.L.S., U. Ill., 1963. Asst. dir. library Sioux Falls Coll., S.D., 1963-66; library cataloger U. Wyo., Laramie, 1966-67, U. Oreg., Eugene, 1967-69; asst. library dir. Rocky Mountain Coll., Billings, Mont., 1969-73; head tech. services library Parmly Billings Library, 1973-82, dir., 1982—; Western Library Network retrospective conversion trainer Mont. State Library, 1981-82; OCLC installation trainer Dowling Coll. Library, Oakdale, N.Y., 1978-79. Contbr. articles to profl. jours. Recipient Great Performance in the Library award Exxon, 1985. Mem. Mont. Assn. Female Execs., ALA, Mont. Library Assn. (various offices), Pacific Northwest Library Assn. (Mont. rep. 1980-82, joint planning team 1981-82). Avocations: gourmet cooking; gardening; hiking. Office: Parmly Billings Library 510 N Broadway Billings MT 59101

NEWBERRY, ELIZABETH CARTER, owner greenhouse and floral company; b. Blackwell, Tex., Nov. 25, 1921; m. Weldon Omar Newberry, Sept. 24, 1950 (dec. Nov. 1984); 1 child. Student Hardin Simmons U., 1938-39. Office mgr. F. W. Woolworth, Abilene, Tex., 1939-50; acct. Western Devel. & Investment Corp., Englewood, Colo., 1968-72; owner, operator Newberry Bros. Greenhouse and Florist, Denver, 1972—; bd. dirs. Western Devel. and Investment Corp. Englewood, Colo., 1979-87. Pres. Ellsworth Elem. Sch. PTA, Denver, 1961-62; v.p. Hill Jr. High Sch. PTA, Denver. Home: 201 Monroe Denver CO 80206 Office: Newberry Bros Greenhouse 201 Garfield Denver CO 80206

NEWBERRY, JUDITH MARY, hospital consortium executive, nurse; b. Columbus, Ohio, June 11, 1940; d. Franklin J. and Dolores E. (Theado) Eyerman; m. David A. Strickland Jr., Sept. 24, 1961 (div. July 1975); children: Deborah, Barbara, David A. III; m. James S. Newberry, Sept. 30, 1983. Diploma, Mt. Carmel Sch. Nursing, 1961; BS in Bus. Adminstrn. and Acctg., Franklin U., 1980; postgrad., U. Mo., 1983-84. RN, Ohio; cert. profl. in healthcare mgmt. material. Nurse Mt. Carmel Med. Ctr., 1961-63, Venice (Fla.) Hosp., 1963-65; nurse Sarasota (Fla.) Hosp., 1965-67, emergency room nurse, 1969-71; day and operating room surp. Doctor's Hosp., Sarasota, 1967-68; dir. nursing East Manor Extended Care Facility, Sarasota, 1968-69; coordinator continuing edn. Mt. Carmel East Hosp., Columbus, Ohio, 1971-74, supr. operating room, 1974-78, material mgr., 1978-82; asst. adminstr. hosp. and clinics U. Mo., Columbia, 1982-87, cons., 1982-83; corp. dir. material and supplies purchasing program U. Hosp. Consortium, Inc., Oakbrook Terrace, Ill., 1987—; speaker in field. Author: Operating Room Technician Training, 1976; contbr. articles to profl. jours; producer patient teaching video, 1977. Pres. Little League Football Team Mothers Assn., Gahanna, Ohio, 1980. Mem. Health Care Material Mgmt. Soc. (internat. pres. 1985-87), Am. Prodn. and Inventory Control Soc., Assn. Operating Room Nurses (del. 1973-78). Democrat. Roman Catholic. Club: Fortnightly (Columbia). Office: U Hosp Consortium Inc 1 Mid America Plaza Suite 700 Oakbrook Terrace IL 60181

NEWBERRY, TRUDELL MCCLELLAND, educator; b. Junction City, Ark., Jan. 30, 1939; d. Roosevelt and Margaret (Knighten) McClelland; div.; children: FeLesia Michelle, Thomas W. III. BA, U. Ark., 1962; MA, Roosevelt U., 1980; postgrad., Gov.'s State U., Arlington Heights, Ill., 1982-84. Cert. tchr., Ark., Ill. Tchr. Almyra (Ark.) Pub. Schs., 1962-65; social worker Franklin-Wright Settlement, Detroit, 1965-69; tchr. North Chicago (Ill.) Sch. Dist. #64, 1970—. Recreational supr. Foss Park Dist., North Chicago, 1982-83; mem. North Chicago Library Bd., 1982-86; North Chicago Alderperson, 1983-87; mem. North Chicago High Sch. PTO, Booster Club, 1984—. Mem. North Chicago Tchrs. Assn. (bldg. rep. 1986-87, rep. to Lake County Fedn. Tchrs. Local #504 1987—), Am. Fedn. Tchrs. (adv.), Lake County Fedn. Tchrs. Exec. Bd., Ill. Fedn. Tchrs., AFL-CIO. Democrat. Baptist. Lodge: Eureka Temple. Home: 2111 S Lewis Ave North Chicago IL 60064

NEWBILL, SALLIE PULLER, state senator; b. Roanoke Rapids, N.C., June 23, 1940; d. Timberlake Meredith and Mary Gillam (Williams) Puller; m. Thomas Carroll Newbill, July 2, 1966; children: Sallie Gillam, Thomas Carroll III. MA, U. Va., 1961; MEd, Ga. State U., 1972. Tchr. San Diego Unified Sch. System, 1961-63, Tauranga Girls Coll., New Zealand, 1963-64, Bangkok Internat. Sch., Thailand, 1964-65; journalist Richmond (Va.) Times Dispatch, 1965-66; tchr. Fulton County, Atlanta, 1966-68; research writer Ga. State Dept. Edn., Atlanta, 1968-70; state senator Ga. Gen. Assembly, 1986—; v.p. S&N Enterprises, Atlanta, 1984-86; state news dir. Rep. House Caucus, Atlanta, 1983-86. V.p. Rep. Women, Atlanta, 1985-86, Fulton County Reps., Atlanta, 1985-86. Mem. Sandy Springs C. of C. Methodist. Clubs: Greater Marietta Rep. Womens; Rep. Women of Northside. Office: State Capitol Atlanta GA 30334

NEWBOLD, SUSAN KAY, nurse, computer analyst; b. Chicago Heights, Ill., Oct. 23, 1953; d. Barbara Fay (Gast) Ward; m. Henry Cree Newbold, April 7, 1973. BS in Nursing, Ball State U., 1975; MS in Nursing, U. Md., 1983. Nurse Hosp. Commn. Prince Georges County, Laurel and Cheverly, Md., 1976-77, asst. head nurse, 1977-78, head nurse, 1978-81; nursing supr. St. Agnes Hosp., Balt., 1981-82, patient care system coordinator, 1982-84; clin. application specialist Travenol Labs., Inc., Reston, Va., 1984-85, mgr. health care applications, 1985-87; field support rep. IBM Corp., Rockville, Md., 1987—. Instr. CPR Am. Heart Assn., Md., 1978—, breast self-examination Am. Cancer Soc., Md., 1978—. Mem. Am. Nurses Assn. Council on Computer Applications in Nursing (liaison), Nursing /Computer Roundtable (co-chmn.), Sigma Theta Tau. Office: IBM Corp 11300 Rockville Pike Suite 501 Rockville MD 20852

NEWBORN, ELLEN MARIE, municipal official; b. Columbus, Ohio, Nov. 24, 1948; d. Kenneth Melvin and Mary Jane (McCluggage) Spear; m. David Reeves Newborn, Nov. 26, 1966 (dec. Dec. 1977); children: Cynthia Denise Newborn Kinter, Brett Michael. Student, Polk Community Coll., Winter Haven, Fla., 1967; grad., Fla. State U., 1985. Cert. mcpl. clk. Dep. city clk. City of Lake Alfred, Fla., 1969-71, city clk., 1971—. Mem. Internat. Inst. Mcpl. Clks. (cert.), Fla. Assn. City Clks., Polk County City Clks. Assn. (coordinator 1985). Democrat. Home: 245 S Rochelle Ave Lake Alfred FL 33850 Office: City of Lake Alfred 120 E Pomelo St Lake Alfred FL 33850

NEWCOMBE, JOANNE PAULINE, educational administrator; b. Chicopee, Mass., July 10, 1947; d. Eugene L. and Veronica Rita Maciolek Galuska; m. Randall William Helweg, Aug. 29, 1970 (div.); m. Edward Jeffrey Newcombe, Oct. 9, 1982. B.A., U. Mass., 1969; M.Ed., U. Lowell, 1975, Ed.D., Northeastern U., 1985. Cert. tchr., adminstr., Mass., Mich., Conn., N.H. Tchr. Ellsworth Sch., Windsor, Conn., 1969-70, Muraco Sch., Winchester, Mass., 1970-75; asst. prin. Londonderry Jr. High Sch., (N.H.), 1975-78; prin. South Sch., Londonderry, 1978-80, Birch Hill Sch., Nashua, N.H., 1980-84; dir. instructional services Ludington Area Schs. (Mich.), 1984-86; supt. schs., Auburn, Mass., 1986—; mem. faculty Lesley Coll., Cambridge, Mass., 1971-74, Worcester (Mass.) State Coll., 1987—. Speaker nat. convs. on ednl. adminstrn. Mem. Nashua Assn. Sch. Prins. (pres. 1983-84), N.H. Coalition Ednl. Leaders (pres. 1980-82), N.H. Assn. Sch. Prins. (exec. bd. 1982-84, regional v.p. 1978-80, regional pres. 1980-82), Am. Assn. Sch. Admins., Mass. Assn. Sch. Supts., Assn. Supervision and Curriculum Devel., Mass. Assn. Supervision and Curriculum Devel., NE Coalition Ednl. Leaders, Nat. Supts. Acad. (cert. of excellence 1986), Phi Delta Kappa, Kappa Delta Pi, Delta Kappa Gamma. Democrat. Roman Catholic. Home: 25 Old Meeting House Rd Auburn MA 01501 Office: Auburn Pub Schs 5 West St Auburn MA 01501

NEWCOMER, MARCIA LIND, management information systems analyst; b. Omaha, Aug. 7, 1961; d. Stephen Kaysing and Elisabeth Anne (Richards) Newcomer. Student. U. Kans., 1979-80, U. No. Iowa, 1980-81; BS, Bentley Coll., 1984. Programmer, analyst Delphi Assocs. Inc., Lowell, Mass., 1984-86; mgmt. information systems analyst KHP Services Inc., Camp Hill, Pa., 1986-87; cons. Hickory Brewster Internat., Inc., Phila., 1987—. Republican. Congregationalist. Clubs: Slim Time Health Spa, Livingwell Lady.

NEWCORN, CLAUDIA DANA, consumer products company executive, helicopter pilot; b. N.Y.C., Aug. 9, 1958; d. Andrew Robert and Ruth Ann (Duplain) N. BA, Wellesley Coll., 1981; MBA, Northeastern U., 1986. Research asst. Harvard Bus. Sch., Boston, 1981-82; dir. mktg. research Gen. Computer Co., Cambridge, Mass., 1982-84; asst. mgr. internat. mktg. services Polaroid Corp., Cambridge, 1985; asst. editor Nolan, Norton & Co., Lexington, Mass., 1985-86; asst. product mgr. Silkience Brand, Gillette Corp., Boston, 1986-87, assoc. product mgr. Toni Homewaves Brand, 1987—. Author (poems): Tent: Napkin Poems, 1988; co-author: Tentatively: Bit Parts, 1986; author numerous pub. poems (named golden Poet 1985-87). Wellesley Coll. scholar, 1981. Mem. Am. Mktg. Assn., Nat. Assn. Female Execs., Smithsonian Instn., Cousteau Soc., Sigma Xi (assoc.), Beta Gamma Sigma, Phi Kappa Phi. Avocations: scuba diving, helicopter flying, mountain climbing, chess, costume design. Home: 503 Beacon St #7 Boston MA 02115

NEWELL, ELIZABETH JEANIE BROOME, brokerage company executive; b. Washington, Dec. 8, 1956; d. Eugene Macon Broome Sr. and Margie Elizabeth (Hodge) Goodyear; m. Clifford Anthony Newell, Aug. 16, 1975; 1 child, Lauren Elizabeth. BA, U. S.C., 1976, BS, 1979, MBA, 1981; real estate diploma, Columbia (S.C.) Real Estate, 1980. Lic. real estate broker, S.C. First v.p. Gene Broome Systems, Columbia, S.C., 1976-81; fin. cons. Merrill Lynch, Columbia, 1981-87; resident v.p., mgr. Prudential-Bache Securities, Columbia, 1987—; bd. dirs. Gene Broome Systems, Inc., Columbia, 1979—, BT's Sportswear, Columbia, 1986—; cons. Electronic Realty Inc., Columbia, 1982—; instr. Dale Carnegie, Columbia, 1984. Author: Policies and Procedures, 1981; editor: Super Stocks, 1986. Speaker United Way of Midlands, Columbia, 1983, 84; liaison Adopt a Sch. Program, Columbia, 1983-85; mem. Ednl. TV Endowment, Columbia, 1987—; project bus.coordinator Jr. Achievement, 1988—. Mem. Columbia C. of C. (charter mem.), Columbia Zool. Assn., Mensa (dir. memberships 1986—), Carolina Bus. and Profl. Women (1st v.p. 1983-84, 87—, pres. 1984-85), Columbia Sales and Mktg. Execs. (dir. memberships 1984), McKissick Mus., Gibbes Planetarium, Columbia Mus. Art. Club: Landmark Sertoma. Home: 141 Kerryton Rd Columbia SC 29223 Office: Prudential Bache Securities 1330 Lady St Suite 205 Columbia SC 29201

NEWELL, GLADYS ELIZABETH, former educator, civic worker; b. Ticonderoga, N.Y., Aug. 31, 1908; d. Charles R. and Elizabeth (Ives) N.; A.B., SUNY, Albany, 1930, M.A., 1935. Tchr., Corinth (N.Y.) High Sch., 1930-33, Bethlehem Central High Sch., Delmar, N.Y., 1933-45; supr. social studies Bethlehem Central Schs., Delmar, 1946-71; mem. N.Y. State Regents Com. on Exams., 1950-53, N.Y. Social Studies Council Curriculum Com., 1961-63, N.Y. State Mental Health Planning Commn., 1963-64. Bd. dirs., v.p. SUNY, Albany Benevolent Assn.; adv. com. N.Y. delegation White House Conf., 1955. Recipient Bus. and Profl. Women Outstanding Citizen award Tri-Village area, 1953; State Coll. Alumni Bertha E. Brimmer award for outstanding teaching, 1955; Citizenship Conf. Outstanding Tchr. award Syracuse U., 1962; Distinguished Alumnus award State U. at Albany, 1969. Mem. N.Y. State Tchrs. Assn. (dir. 1950-69, pres. 1966-67), Eastern Zone Bethlehem Central (a founder, past pres.), Albany Supervisory Dist. (past pres.) tchrs. assns., NEA (life mem., rep. of N.Y. State Tchrs. Assn. at tchr. edn. and profl. standards meetings), N.Y. State (past pres.), Capital Dist. (past pres.), Nat. councils social studies, LWV (past pres. Albany County), UN Assn. U.S.A. (past chpt. dir.), World Affairs Council (past dir. Albany), AAUW (1st v.p. Essex County br.), Fort Carillon Bus. and Profl. Women's Club, N.Y. State Ret. Tchrs. Assn. (del. to Gov.'s Conf. Libraries 1978), N.Y. Ret. Tchrs. Assn., Delta Kappa Gamma, Pi Gamma Mu. Methodist. Club: New Horizons. Contbr. articles to profl. jours. Home: 17 John St Ticonderoga NY 12883

NEWELL, KATHERINE ANN, lawyer; b. Phila., May 5, 1947; m. Francis P. Newell, Aug. 16, 1975. AB magna cum laude, Temple U., 1969; JD cum laude, Villanova U., 1975; LLM, Georgetown U., 1979. Bar: Pa. 1975, D.C. 1980. Atty.-advisor Office of Chief Counsel, Dept. Treasury, Washington, 1975-78; assoc. firm Schnader, Harrison, Segal & Lewis, Phila., 1978-86; ptnr. Baskin, Flaherty, Elliott & Mannino, P.C., Phila., 1986—; mem. adj. faculty grad. tax program Villanova U. Law Sch., 1983—. Mem. ABA (tax-exempt fin. com. sect. taxation 1982—), Pa. Bar Assn., D.C. Bar Assn., Phila. Bar Assn. Office: Baskin Flaherty Elliott & Mannino P C 3 Mellon Bank Ctr Suite 1800 Philadelphia PA 19102

NEWELL, REBECCA G., psychiatric nurse; b. Savannah, Ga., July 4, 1953; d. Henry Morgan and Julia (Rogers) Grimes; AA, Armstrong State Coll., 1973, BS in Nursing, 1980; postgrad. Sch. Grad. Nursing, Med. Coll. Ga., 1980-81; m. E. Andrew Newell, June 14, 1980. With Charter Hosp.of Savannah (Ga.), 1973—, coordinator utilization rev. and staff devel., 1975-80, asst. dir. nursing, 1980-82, nursing adminstr., 1982—; adj. faculty Armstrong Coll. Sch. Nursing. cons. Council Recruitment and Retention of Nurses, 1978—; profl. staff exchange cons. Recipient Leadership award Vocat. Indsl. Clubs Am., 1971. Mem. Am. Nurses Assn., Ga. Nurses Assn., Ga. Hosp. Assn. Soc. Nursing Service Adminstrs., Ga. Orgn. Nurse Execs., Ga. Hosp. Assn., Armstrong State Coll. Hon. Soc. for Nursing, Ga. So. Coll. Hon. Soc. for Nursing. Baptist. Home: 11 Ramsgate Rd Savannah GA 31419 Office: 1150 Cornell Ave Savannah GA 31406

NEWELL, SALLY OTTAWAY, veterinarian; b. Ypsilanti, Mich., July 2, 1936; d. Henry Jackson and Ruth Marie (Montgomery) Ottaway; B.S., E. Carolina U., 1958; D.V.M., U. Ga., 1970; m. John Richard Newell, June 28, 1958 (div. 1985); children—Deonne Marie, Mary Jo, Penni Sue. Research asst. N.C. State U., Raleigh, 1958-60; research asso. U. Ga., 1970-73; gen. practice vet. medicine, Elberton, Hartwell, and Athens, Ga., 1973-74; coordinator U. Ga. Lab. Animal Care, Athens, 1974—. Mem. Am. Assn. Lab. Animal Sci. (pres. 1982), AVMA, Am. Soc. Primatologists, Am. Soc. Lab. Animal Practitioners, Sigma Xi. Episcopalian. Author articles in field. Home: 187 Highland Park Dr Athens GA 30605 Office: U Ga Office of the vp for research Athens GA 30602

NEWFIELD, LAUREL NANCY, county government official; b. N.Y.C., Oct. 13, 1960; d. Howard Burton and Bernice (Rosenblatt); m. Geoffrey William Pollak, May 31, 1981 (div. 1986). AS, Camden County Coll., 1980; BA, Rutgers U., 1982. Cert. compute programmer, data processor. Bookkeeper Pathmark, Corp., Jencho, N.Y., 1976-78; crt operator Burlington County Trust Co., Moorestown, N.J., 1979-80; student safety officer Rutgers U. Police, Camden, N.J., 1980-82; office technician Sherwin-Williams Co., Reno, 1983-84; inventory control mgr. Sherwin-Williams Co., Dayton, Ohio, 1984-87; real estate assessment mgr. Montgomery County Auditors Office, Dayton, Ohio, 1987-88, personal property tax compliance coordinator, 1988—. Mem.Temple Beth Or Sisterhood, Kettering, Ohio, dir. temple youth group. Named one of Outstanding Vols. Dana Stamps-Montgomery County Auditors, 1986-87. Mem. Am. Mgmt. Assn., LWV, Nat. Assn. Female Execs., Assn. Female Execs. Jewish. Club: Miami Valley Rep. (chmn. pub. relations 1986-87, treas. 1987—). Home: 2270 Bonnie Birch Ct Centerville OH 45459 Office: Montgomery County Auditor 451 W 3d St Dayton OH 45422

NEWITT, RENÉE, designer; b. Tooele, Utah, June 28, 1936; d. George and Carol (Millward) Buzianis; m. Kenneth L. Hatch, May 19, 1961 (div. 1972); children: Sean Michael, Ryan Lee. Student, U. Utah. Supr. placement Snelling & Snelling, Seattle, 1972; sec. mgr. Rainier Bank, Mercer Island, Wash., 1973-88; designer, sales rep., ptnr. Floorcraft, inc., Redmond, Wash., 1974-87; designer, cons. Renée Newitt Design, Bellevue, Wash., 1987—; cons., v.p. Newitt Constrn., Redmond, 1974-84; pres. C.F.S., Inc., Hardwood Distbrs., 1988; Reweenewitt Des., 1973-88. Designer Street of Dreams, Bellevue, 1985; contbr. articles to profl. jours. Mem. Master Builders. Democrat. Mem Ch. Latter Day Saints. Office: Floorcraft Inc 7842 159th Pl NE Redmond WA 98004

NEWLANDS, SHEILA ANN, financial director; b. Worcester, Mass., Mar. 8, 1953; d. Joseph and Doris Edna (Bachand) N; m. Domenic Victor Testa Jr., Oct. 2, 1976 (div. 1983). BA summa cum laude, Worcester State Coll., 1975; cert. interior design, Bunkerhill Community Coll., 1976; MS, Simmons Coll., 1976; MBA, Suffolk U., 1983. Cert. real estate broker, Mass. Dir. health scis. library Lynn Hosp., Mass., 1976-78, Mt. Auburn Hosp., Cambridge, 1978-81; assoc. fin. analyst Data Gen., Westboro, Mass., 1981-82, fin. analyst, 1982-84, sr. fin. analyst, 1984; fin. analyst Chateau Sainte Michelle Winery, Woodinville, Wash., 1985-86, dir. fin., 1986—; guest lectr. Simmons Coll. Sch. Library Sci., Boston, 1980-81. Mem. Burlington (Mass.) Conservation Commn., 1978-84. Mem. Fin. Mgmt. Honor Soc., Phi Alpha Theta. Club: Mountaineers (Seattle). Home: PO Box 514 Issaquah WA 98027 Office: Chateau Sainte Michelle Winery One Stimson Ln Woodinville WA 98072

NEWMAN, AMY SUZANNE, psychologist, educator; b. Pitts., Oct. 10, 1954; d. William Reece Elton and Margie Ruth (Pollard) N.; m. Eric James Van Denburg, Oct. 11, 1986. BA in Psychology with honors, U. Utah, 1977; MA in Psychology, Washington U., St. Louis, 1980, PhD in Psychology, 1984. Intern U. Tex. Health Sci. Ctr., Dallas, 1979-80; research asst. Washington U., St. Louis, 1981-82; staff psychologist Cardinal Glennon Meml. Hosp. for Children, St. Louis, 1982-84; postdoctoral fellow Orange (Calif.) County Juvenile Ct. Evaluation and Guidance Unit, 1984-85; clin. psychologist Clin. Psychology Assocs., Bloomingdale, Ill., 1985-86; clin. psychologist, coordinator tng. Michael Reese Hosp. and Med. Ctr., Chgo., 1986—; instr. George Warren Brown Sch. Social Work Washington U., St. Louis, 1982, 83; assoc. faculty Ill. Sch. Profl. Psychology, Chgo., 1986—; pvt. practice specializing in clin. psychology, Chgo., 1987—; peer reviewer Jour. Behavioral Medicine, Lynchburg, Va., 1987—. Author: (with others on book chpt.) Adherence, Generalization, and Maintenance in Behavioral Medicine, 1982; contbr. articles to profl. jours. Mem. Am. Psychol. Assn., Soc. Behavioral Medicine, Phi Beta Kappa, Mortar Bd., Phi Kappa Phi, Phi Eta Sigma. Democrat. Baptist. Office: Michael Reese Hosp and Med Ctr 3033 S Cottage Grove Chicago IL 60616

NEWMAN, ANITA NADINE, physician; b. Honolulu, June 13, 1949; d. William Reece Elton and Margie Ruth (Pollard) Newman; m. Frank Ellis Burkett, Dec. 30, 1978; children—Justin Ellis, Chelsea Newman, Andrew Frank. AB, Stanford U., 1971; MD, Dartmouth Coll., 1975. Diplomate Am. Bd. Otolaryngology. Intern, resident in gen. surgery Northwestern Meml. Hosp., Chgo., 1975-77, resident in otolaryngology, 1977-78; resident UCLA Hosp. and Clinics, 1979-82, asst. prof., 1982—; staff surgeon Wadsworth VA Hosp., Los Angeles, 1982-84; research fellow in neurotology UCLA, 1984—. Contbr. articles to med. jours. Mem. alumni admissions support com. Darmouth Med. Sch. Alumni Council, 1983—. Mem. Am. Acad. Otolaryngology, Am. Med. Women's Assn., Los Angeles County Med. Women's Assn., Assn. Research in Otolaryngology, Stanford Women's Honor Soc. Democrat. Office: UCLA Hosp and Clinics Div Head and Neck Surgery Westwood CA 90024

NEWMAN, ANNETTE GOERLICH, shopping center manager; b. Fresno, Calif., Jan. 19, 1940; d. David August and Mary Eloise (Simpson) Goerlich; Pharm.D., U. Calif., San Francisco, 1963; children—Anne Kristen, Mark David, Gregory Hartley. Pharmacist, Village Drug, 1963-69; relief pharmacist, 1969-72; store mgr. The Drug Store of Fig Garden Village, 1972-77; mgr. Fig Garden Village Shopping Center, Fresno, 1977—; dir. Fig Garden Mcht. Assn.; sec. bd. dirs. Fig Garden Village, Inc. Active Fresno Community Analysis Citizens Com., Littlest Angel chpt. Children's Home Soc., Ladies Aid to Retarded Children, Women's Symphony League; bd. dirs. St. Agnes Med. Found., St. Agnes Endowment Com.; mem. women's adv. com. Senator Ken Maddy 14th Dist., 1988—; mem. adv. bd. Sch. Arts and Humanities Adv. Bd. Calif. State U., Fresno, 1988—; mem. council of 100, Fresno Art Ctr. Women's Yr. Nominee, Rosalie M. Stern award, 1971, 72; registered pharmacist, Calif. Mem. Fresno-Madera Pharm. Assn., Pharm. Alumni Assn. U. Calif., Nat. Assn. Female Execs., Jr. League of Fresno, AAUW, Alpha Phi. Club: Soroptimists. Home: 3909 W Fir Ave Fresno CA 93711 Office: 5082 N Palm Ave Suite A Fresno CA 93704

NEWMAN, BARBARA MILLER, psychologist, educator; b. Chgo., Sept. 6, 1944; d. Irving George and Florence (Levy) Miller; student Bryn Mawr Coll.; A.B. with honors in Psychology, U. Mich., 1966, Ph.D. in Devel. Psychology, 1971; m. Philip R. Newman, June 12, 1966; children—Samuel Asher, Abraham Levy, Rachel Florence. Undergrad. research asst. in psychology U. Mich., 1963-64, research asst. in psychology, 1964-69, teaching fellow, 1965-71, asst. project dir. Inst. for Social Research, 1971-72, univ. lectr. in psychology and research assoc., 1971-72; asst. prof. psychology Russell Sage Coll., 1972-76, assoc. prof., 1977-78; assoc. prof. dept. family relations and human devel., chmn. dept. family relations and human devel. Ohio State U., 1978-83, prof., 1983-86, assoc. provost for faculty recruitment and devel., 1987—. Mem. Eastern Psychol. Assn., Soc. Research in Child Devel., AAAS, Am. Psychol. Assn., Nat. Council Family Relations, Groves Conf. on Marriage and Family, N.Y. Acad. Scis., Midwestern Psychol. Assn., Western Psychol. Assn., Am. Home Econs. Assn. Author books including: (with P. Newman) Living: The Process of Adjustment, 1981; Development Through Life, 1987; Understanding Adulthood, 1983; Adolescent Development, 1986; contbr. chpts., articles to profl. publs. Office: Ohio State U Office Acad Affairs 203 Bricker Columbus OH 43210

NEWMAN, CLAIRE POE, corporate executive; b. Jacksonville, Fla., Dec. 12, 1926; d. Leslie Ralph and Gertrude (Criswell) Poe; student Fla. State Coll. for Women, 1944-45, Tulane U., 1971-73; m. Robert Jacob Newman, July 3, 1948; children—Leslie Claire, Robert, Christopher David. Co-owner Vineyards in Burgundy, France; v.p., dir. Carrollton Realty Co. of New Orleans, 1956—. Mem. various coms. New Orleans Mus. Art. Mem. Women's com. New Orleans Philharmonic Symphony Assn., 1961—, chmn. orch. relations com., 1961-63; chmn. New Orleans Easter Seal Drive, 1963; La. trustee Nat. Soc. Crippled Children and Adults, 1963-65. Mem. Women's Aux. C. of C., New Orleans Soc. Archeol. Inst. Am. (v.p. 1972-74), Confrérie des Chevaliers du Tastevin, Sigma Kappa. Club: Metairie Country, Kitzbuehel (Austria) Golf, Golden Skibook (Kitzbuehel), Pass Christian (Miss.) Yacht; Ski (Arlberg). Home: 1111 Falcon Rd Metairie LA 70005 : Tiemberg Kitzbuehel, Austria

NEWMAN, DONNA MARIE, communications specialist, consultant; b. Balt., Dec. 26, 1948; d. Edward Arthur and Elsie Muriel (Erdman) N. BA in Math., Hood Coll., 1970. Programmer USN, Jacksonville, Fla., 1970-73, Oxford Chem., Atlanta, 1973-75; programmer, analyst Emory U., Atlanta, 1976-78; analyst First Atlanta, Atlanta, 1978-81; data communications cons. So. Bell/AT&T, Atlanta, 1981-84; satellite and internat. communication systems cons. AT&T, Atlanta, 1985—. Mem. Council on Battered Women, Atlanta, 1978—; exec. dir. Feminine Action Alliance Edn. Found., Atlanta, 1978-79; bd. dirs. Women's Coalition of Ga., Atlanta, 1982-83; pres. Feminist Action Alliance, Atlanta, 1983-85. Recipient Woman of Achievement award Bus. and Profl. Womens Club, 1985. Mem. Nat. Assn. of Female Execs.

NEWMAN, DORA JEAN, financial manager, real estate developer; b. Maysville, Ky., July 1, 1958; d. Laton Mitchell and Teresa Irene (Kirby) N. BA in Econs., Xavier U., 1980. Analyst Congl. Budget Office, Washington, 1980; cost acct. mgr. Folger Coffee Co., San Francisco, 1980-81; fin. mgr. Folger Coffee Co., Cin., 1981-85; group mgr. cost forecast Procter & Gamble Mfg. Co., Cin., 1985-86; fin. analyst dept. mgr. Crush Internat., Cin., 1986—; cons. Jr. Achievement, Cin., 1984. Trip leader Cin. Ski Club, 1983—. Mem. Nat. Assn. Female Execs. Republican. Office: Procter & Gamble One Procter & Gamble Plaza Cincinnati OH 45201

NEWMAN, DOROTHY ANNE, educator; b. Minden, La., Jan. 25, 1947; d. George Malcolm and Neva Estelle (Reeder) Temple. AA, Kilgore Coll., 1967; BA summa cum laude, East Tex. Bapt. Coll., 1972; MA, Stephen F. Austin State U., 1979. Cert. tchr., Tex. Tchr. social studies Marshall (Tex.) Ind. Sch. Dist., 1974—, sponsor student council, 1975—; bd. dirs. Tex. Energy Edn. Day Project, Austim, 1982—. Mem. regional planning com. Youth Alcohol and Treatment Conf., Austin, 1983, Tex. PTA (life). Recipient awards for energy edn. day project, nat. student safety program, alcohol edn. project, Excellence award for outstanding high sch. tchrs. U. Tex., Austin, 1988; named Outstanding High Sch. Tchr. So. Meth. U., 1988. Mem. Tex. Classroom Tchrs. Assn. (membership chmn. 1981-82), Nat. Council for Social Studies, Tex. Council for Social Studies, East Tex. Council on Social Studies, Nat. Assn. Workshop Dirs., Tex. Assn. Student Councils (state sec. 1981-82, 88—, parliamentarian 1983-84), Phi Alpha Theta, Alpha Chi. Republican. Methodist. Office: Marshall High Sch 1900 Maverick Dr Marshall TX 75670

NEWMAN, EILEEN MERYL, computer executive; b. Queens, N.Y., June 6, 1961; d. Lorraine (Siegel) N. BS in Engring., U. Pa., 1982, MS in Engring., 1983; MBA, Hofstra U., 1985. Assoc. engr. Sperry Corp., Great Neck, N.Y., 1983-85, computer instr., 1984-85; product mgr., sr. engr. Gen. Instrument, Hicksville, N.Y., 1985—. Mem. IEEE, Assn. of Old Crows, U. Pa. Alumni Club. Home: 6 Holiday Park Dr Williston Park NY 11596 Office: Gen Instrument Corp 600 W John St Hicksville NY 11802-0709

NEWMAN, ELLEN MAGNIN, consultant; b. San Francisco, Apr. 19, 1928; d. Cyril Isaac and Anna Smithline Magnin; student Stanford U., 1945-48; m. Walter Simon Newman, Sr., Oct. 15, 1950; children—Walter Simon, Robert Magnin (dec.), John Donald. With Joseph Magnin Co., San Francisco, 1948-69, women's apparel buyer, 1948-54, developer sales tng., 1954-60, dir. product devel., 1960-64, dir. new products and new brs., 1964-69; spl. asst. to pres. Joseph Magnin, San Francisco, 1969-72; in house cons. consumer affairs Amfac, Honolulu, 1972-74; pres. Ellen Newman Assos., San Francisco, 1974—; dir. Wells Fargo & Co., Wells Fargo Bank, San Francisco. Mem. Mayor's Fiscal Adv. Com. City San Francisco; v.p. bd. govs. San Francisco Symphony; council mem. SRI Internat.; mem. adv. council Grad. Sch. Bus., Stanford U.; chair U. Calif. San Francisco Found. Mem. Com. 200, Women's Forum West, San Francisco C. of C. (v.p., bd. dirs.). Clubs: Metropolitan, City (bd. govs.). Office: 323 Geary St Suite 507 San Francisco CA 94102

NEWMAN, ESTELLE RUTH, rehabilitation counselor, occupational therapist; b. N.Y.C., Apr. 25, 1935; d. Nathan and Clara (Wattman) Glotzer; m. Malcolm Newman, June 11, 1955; children: Roberta, Leonard, Alisa. BS in Occupational Therapy, Columbia U., 1956; MEd in Rehab. Counseling, Hofstra U., 1978. Occupational therapist L.I. Devel. Ctr., Melville, N.Y., 1969-71; sr. occupational therapist L.I. Devel. Ctr., Melville, 1979; vocat. rehab. counselor Office Vocat. Rehab. N.Y. Edn. Dept., Hauppauge, 1979-82, sr. vocat. rehab. counselor, 1982—; cons. in home modifications and adapted equipment Office Vocational Rehab. N.Y. Edn. Dept., 1979—. Bd. dirs. Kehillath Shalom Synagogue, Cold Spring Harbor, N.Y., 1986—, Huntington (N.Y.) NOW, 1986—; mem. Witness for Peace, Washington, D.C., N.C., 1986—. Mem. Nat. Rehab. Assn., Am. Occupational Therapy Assn., L.I. Rehab. Assn., L.I. Dist. Occupational Therapy Assn., Rehab. Engring. Soc. N. Am., Mensa. Democrat. Jewish. Home: 12 Beal Ct Huntington NY 11743 Office: OVR NYSED NYSOB Veteran's Hwy Hauppauge NY 11788

NEWMAN, FRANCES MAE, real estate management executive; b. Elm Grove, Ohio, Dec. 15, 1938; d. Earl E. and Phena (Dunn) Whitworth; student Ohio U., 1960—; A in Acctg. Internat. Accts. Soc., 1969; m. Carson Newman, July 13, 1958; children: Brad, Carmen. Office mgr., credit mgr. Clarence Valley Sons, Inc., Waverly, Ohio, 1956-74; v.p. RMS Mgmt. Corp., Chillicothe, Ohio, 1974-85; sec. to bd. RMS Properties (merged with RMS Mgmt. Corp. 1985), 1980—, v.p., 1985—; owner, operator Clothes Corral, men and women's apparel, Waverly, 1981-83, Carmen's, 1983—. Instr. cert. apt. mgr. tng. courses. Mem. Waverly Jaycettes (pres. 1970), Bus. and Profl. Womens Club (dist. dir. 1985-86), Nat. Assn. Female Execs. Home: 90 Prosperity Rd Waverly OH 45690 Office: 126 W 2d St Waverly OH 45690

NEWMAN, JANICE MARIE, lawyer, business owner; b. N.Y.C., Aug. 11, 1951; d. Robert (dec.) and Clara (White) Swindler; m. Roger Kevin Newman, Jan. 20, 1972 (div. July 1980); 1 child, Germaine M. Swindler-Newman (dec.). BA, Smith Coll., 1973; JD, Rutgers U., 1980. Bar: N.J. 1983, U.S. Supreme Ct. 1987. Adminstrv. asst. Corp. Ann. Reports, N.Y.C., 1972-73; pub. relations asst. Lippincott & Margulies, N.Y.C., 1973; journalist Essex Forum Newspaper, East Orange, N.J., 1973; pub. info. officer City of Newark, 1974-82; asst. communications dir. Mayor's Office, Newark, 1982-86; producer, host Newark and Reality, 1974-84, Newark Report, 1974—; pres., owner J.M. Newman & Assocs.; producer, host Newark and Reality TV show, 1974-84, Newark radio Report, 1974—. Mem. editorial bd. N.J. Lawyer mag., 1987—; contbr. articles to mags. Trustee Interest on Lawyers Trust Accounts, 1988—; bd. dirs. Instructions, Exposures, Experiences, 1983-87. Recipient Pub. Service award N.J. Voice Newspaper, 1977, Achievement award Minority Contractors and Craftsmen Trade Assn., 1982, award Nat. Council Negro Bus. and Profl. Women Legal Achievement, 1987, award N.J. Unit Nat. Assn. Negro Bus. and Profl. Women's Clubs, 1987; named to Outstanding Young Women Am. U.S. Jaycees, 1984. Mem. Nat. Assn. Media Women (rec. sec. 1985-87, Media Woman of Yr. award 1985, pres. N.J. chpt. 1986—), N.J. Women Lawyers Assn. (pres. 1986-88, chair pub. relations com., mem. women's rights sect.), Nat. Council Negro Women, Garden State Bar Assn. (bd. dirs. 1986-87), N.J. State Bar Assn. (chair pub. relations com. 1987—, asst. sec. women's rights sect.). Republican. Episcopalian. Home: 115 Sunset Ave PO Box 6070 Newark NJ 07106

NEWMAN, JEANNE LOUISE, association executive; b. Boston, June 29, 1946; d. William Collyer and Barbara (Bailey) Smith; m. Harry Stephen Newman, June 9, 1968 (div. 1977); children: Michael Stephen, Catherine Louise. BSBA, Am. U., 1968. Bookkeeper Am. Pharm. Assn., Washington, 1968-69; bus. mgr. Soc. Photog. Scientists and Engrs., Washington, 1969-73; controller Nat. Ctr. for Vol. Action, Washington, 1973-75; fin. officer Bur. Rehab., Washington, 1975-79; acting dir. bus. affairs Assn. Am. Med. Colls., Washington, 1979-88, dir. fin. services, 1988—. Treas. Potomac Valley Civic Assn., 1975-77; pres. Franconia Commons Homeowners Assn., Alexandria, Va., 1982—. Mem. Nat. Assn. Female Execs., Am. Soc. of Assn. Execs. Office: Assn Am Med Colls 1 DuPont Circle NW Washington DC 20036

NEWMAN, LIBBY, painter, printmaker, curator; b. Rockland Del., Nov. 17, 1925; d. Hyman and Dora (Horowitz) Goldberg; children—Don, Andrea Newman Orsher. B.F.A., Phila. Coll. Art; postgrad. U. Pa., Villanova U. Mem. visual arts panel Pa. Council on Arts, 1971-76; artist-in-residence/curator exhbns. University City Sci. Ctr., Phila., 1975—; co-curator sculpture Gov.'s Mansion, Harrisburg, Pa., 1979—; one-man shows Phila. Art Alliance, 1971, 81, Mangel Gallery, Phila., 1972, 75, 78, 84, University City Sci. Ctr. Gallery, Phila.; group shows include Mangel Gallery, 1972-86, Pa. Acad. Fine Arts, Phila., Peale Galleries of Pa. Acad. Fine Arts, Woodmere Art Gallery, Chestnut Hill, Pa., Moore Coll. Art, Phila., Fritz Miller Gallery, N.Y.C., William Penn State Mus., Harrisburg, Pa., Fountain Gallery, Portland, Oreg., Del. Art Mus., Wilmington, Phila. Mus. Art, Circle Gallery, N.Y.C., Chgo., So. Alleghenies Mus. Art, Loretto, Pa., Mus. Phila. Civic Ctr., Moore Coll. Art, Phila., 1982, Sichuan Fine Arts Inst., Changging, People's Republic China, 1985, Tianjin Fine Arts Coll., People's Republic China, 1986, Art in City Hall, Phila., 1986; represented in permanent collections Phila. Mus. Art, Nat. Mus. Belgrade (Yugoslavia), Mus. Modern Art, Buenos Aires, Argentina, U. Pa. Law Sch., Mus. Phila. Civic Ctr., Temple U. Law Sch., Phila., Glassboro State Coll. (N.J.), Free Library Phila., University City Sci. Ctr., Phila., St. Joseph's Coll., Phila., St. Charles Borromeo Sem., Overbrook, Pa., Temple U. Health and Sci. Ctr., Phila., Nationalities Service Ctr., Phila., Phila. Assn. Clin. Trials. Editor: R. Buckminster Fuller Sketchbook, 1981; A City Sketched: A Guide to the Art and History of Philadelphia, 1976. Mem. Mayor's Com. for Sci. and Tech., 1979-82. Recipient Fleischer Art Meml. award; Cheltenham Nat. Graphic award; Best Pictures of the Yr. award Phila. Art Alliance; Carl Zigrosser Nat. Meml. award Am. Color Print Exhbn.; chosen for vis. artist project Brandywine Graphics, 1984; Nat. Endowment grantee, 1973. Mem. Artists Equity Assn. (pres. Phila. chpt. 1969-71), Am. Color Print Assn., Phila. Art Alliance, Phila. Watercolor Club. Home: 327 Meeting House Ln Merion PA 19066 Office: University City Sci Ctr 3624 Market St Philadelphia PA 19104

NEWMAN, LINDA, construction executive; b. Bklyn., July 10, 1937; d. Max and Mae (Goldlust) Lukin; m. Morton Newman, Dec. 29, 1956; children: Jeffrey H., Karen M., Susan L. Student, Hunter Coll., 1955-56. Adminstrv. asst. Princeton Park, Shoreham, N.Y., 1971-73; ops. mgr. Imperial Gardens, Woodmere, N.Y., 1973-80, v.p. ops., 1980-83; dir. sales, mktg. and advt. DiCanio, Smithtown, N.Y., 1983—. Recipient Best Newspaper Advertisement award Profl. Builder Mag., 1987. Mem. Nat. Assn. Home Builders, Women's Am. Orgn. for Rehab. and Tng. (charter, Imperial Woods chpt. pres. 1981-82), L.I. Builders Inst. (cert.). Office: DiCanio Orgn 712 Smithtown Blvd Smithtown NY 11787

NEWMAN, LINDA JOYCE, magazine advertising executive; b. Newark, May 2, 1945; d. Daniel and Beatrice (Birnbaum) N. m. Neil Goldstein, 1986. BA, U. Pitts., 1966. Pub. relations dir. N.Y.C. Dept. Cultural Affairs, N.Y., 1968-70; N.Y. State Council Arts, 1970-74; communication dir. N.Y.C. Bicentennial, 1974-76; v.p., advt. dir. OMNI Mag., N.Y.C., 1978—; cons. in field. Fund raising coordinator, Mayor Ed Koch, N.Y., 1976; mem. young leadership council United Jewish Appeal, N.Y., 1983-84; career conf. chmn. Advt. Women of N.Y., 1984; fund raiser N. Am. Conf. Ethiopian Jewry, N.Y., 1985. Avocations: snow skiing, tennis.

NEWMAN, LOIS EDA, editor, writer, animal welfare activitist; b. Los Angeles, May 14, 1934; d. Aaron Senderman and Lois G. (Jaffe) Newman. AB, Marymount Coll., 1956; AM, Smith Coll., 1958; MA in Library Sci., Immaculate Heart Coll., Los Angeles, 1965. Tchr. high sch. various schs., Los Angeles, 1958-62; instr. Edgemont Coll., Madison, Wis., 1962-63; librarian Rand Corp., Santa Monica, Calif., 1965-74; owner, operator Lois Newman Books, Boulder, Colo., 1974-77; abstracts editor Sage Publs., Beverly Hills, Calif., 1978-79; freelance editor, writer Los Angeles,

1979—. Author: (newspaper column) Your Cat, 1987—. Pres., founder Have A Heart Found., Los Angeles, 1986—. Mem. Freelance Network, Animal Protection Inst., Humane Soc. U.S., Nat. Wildlife Fedn., Fund for Animals. Republican. Office: 6546 Hollywood Blvd Suite 201 Los Angeles CA 90028

NEWMAN, MARGARET ANN, nurse; b. Memphis, Oct. 10, 1933; d. Ivo Mathias and Mamie Love (Donald) N.; B.S.H.E., Baylor U., 1954; B.S.N., U. Tenn., Memphis, 1962; M.S., U. Calif., San Francisco, 1964; Ph.D., N.Y.U., 1971. Dir. nursing, asst. prof. nursing Clin. Research Center, U. Tenn., 1964-67; asst. prof. N.Y.U., 1971-75, asso. prof., 1975-77; prof. in charge grad. program and research dept. nursing Pa. State U., 1977-80, prof. nursing, 1977-84; prof. nursing U. Minn., 1984—. Recipient Outstanding Alumnus award U. Tenn. Coll. Nursing, 1975; Disting. Alumnus award NYU Div. Nursing, 1984; Am. Jour. Nursing Scholar, 1979-80. Fellow Am. Acad. Nursing. Author: Theory Development in Nursing, 1979; Health as Expanding Consiousness, 1986; editor: (with others) Source Book of Nursing Research, 1973, 2d edit., 1977. Research on movement, time perception and consciousness as indices of health. Home: 289 E 5th St Saint Paul MN 55101 Office: 6-101 Health Scis Unit F 308 Harvard St Minneapolis MN 55455

NEWMAN, MAXINE PLACKER, insurance consultant; b. Haslem, Tex., Nov. 21, 1922; d. L. H. and Beatrice Rosetta (Stuart) Placker: B.S., Stephen F. Austin State U., 1943; m. Robert Wayne Newman, May 23, 1975; 1 son, Stephen Randall Hillin (by previous marriage). Acct., Lamar U., Beaumont, Tex., 1956-58; office mgr. Williamson Ins. Agy., Beaumont, 1958-72; v.p. Alexander & Alexander, Dallas, 1972-79; cons. Bellefonte Ins. Co., Cin., 1979—; v.p. Ralph K. Kemp & Assocs., Inc. office mgr., treas. Ralph K. Kemp & Assocs., Inc., Dallas, 1979—. . Mem. Am. Bus. Women Assn. (Woman of Yr. 1979), Nat. Assn. Ins. Women, Dallas Assn. Ins. Women, Beta Sigma Phi (Woman of Yr. 1966). Republican. Baptist. Clubs: Trophy, Women's, Trophy Ladies Golf Assn. Address: 114 Carnoustie Dr Trophy Club TX 76262

NEWMAN, MELVA JEWELL, social worker; b. Shreveport, La., Mar. 3, 1932; d. William and Minnie Lee (Burton) Collins; m. Joseph Newman, June 27, 1957; children: Sheri, Toni, Colette. BA in Psychology, UCLA, 1953, MSW, 1957. Asst. prof. Calif. State U., Northridge, 1969-70, Los Angeles, 1970-78; lectr. Calif. Poly. Inst., Pomona, 1978-79; prin. Family Actualization, Altadena, Calif., 1980—; cons. Frederick Douglas Child Devel. Ctr., Los Angeles, 1982—; vis. faculty Pacific Oaks Coll., Pasadena, Calif., 1982—. Mem. Adv. Council Child Abuse Prevention, Calif., 1978, Adv. Bd. Office Creative Connections, Pasadena, 1985-86. Named Woman of Yr. Zeta Phi Beta, 1983, one of Women of Distinction Soroptimists Internat., 1985; recipient 2d Century award Pasadena YWCA, 1985. Mem. Nat. Assn. Social Workers, Assn. Black Social Workers of Greater Los Angeles (life), Assn. Black Social Workers in Family Service, So. Calif. Group Psychotherapy Assn. Home and Office: 524 E Loma Alta Dr Altadena CA 91001

NEWMAN, PAULINE, federal judge; b. N.Y.C., June 20, 1927; d. Maxwell Henry and Rosella N. B.A., Vassar Coll., 1947; M.A., Columbia U., 1948; Ph.D., Yale U., 1952; LL.B., NYU, 1958. Bar: N.Y. 1958, U.S. Supreme Ct. 1972, U.S. Ct. Customs and Patent Appeals 1978, Pa. 1979, U.S. Ct. Appeals (3d cir.) 1981, U.S. Ct. Appeals (fed. cir.) 1982. Research chemist Am. Cyanamid Co., Bound Brook, N.J., 1951-54; mem. patent staff FMC Corp., N.Y.C., 1954-75; mem. patent staff FMC Corp., Phila., 1975-84, dir. dept. patent and licensing, 1969-84; judge U.S. Ct. Appeals (fed. cir.), Washington, 1984—; bd. dir. Research Corp., 1982-84; program specialist Dept. Natural Scis. UNESCO, Paris, 1961-62; mem. State Dept. Adv. Com. on Internat. Indsl. Property, 1974-84; lectr. in field. Contbr. articles to profl. jours. Bd. dirs. Med. Coll. Pa., 1975-84, Midgard Found., 1973-84; trustee Phila. Coll. Pharmacy and Sci., 1983-84. Mem. ABA (council sect. patent trademark and copyright 1983-84), Am. Patent Law Assn. (bd. dirs. 1981-84), U.S. Trademark Assn. (bd. dirs. 1975-79, v.p. 1978-79), Am. Chem. Soc. (bd. dirs. 1972-81), Am. Inst. Chemists (bd. dirs. 1960-66, 70-76), Pacific Indsl. Property Assn. (pres. 1979-80). Clubs: Vassar, Yale. Office: US Ct Appeals 717 Madison Pl NW Washington DC 20439

NEWMAN, PHYLLIS, counselor, therapist, hypnotist; b. N.Y.C., Aug. 20, 1933; d. Max and Frieda Yetta (Pechter) Hershkowitz; B.S., Mercy Coll., 1977; M.S., L.I.U., 1979; m. Milton Newman, Dec. 28, 1952; children—Renee Holly, Eileen Sharon, Jeffrey Mark. Pvt. practice hypnosis and therapy, Peekskill, N.Y., 1977—; lectr. in field; lectr. Pepsico Fitness Ctr., Purchase, N.Y., 1984, Purdue U., 1986, 88; dir. counseling Hypnosis Group, 1979—. Mem. parents exec. bd. Purdue U., 1978-83, mem. pres.' council, 1983—; mem. Hand to Mouth Players, Garrison, N.Y. Mem. Am. Assn. Counseling and Devel., Am. Mental Health Counselors Assn., N.Y. Soc. Ericksonian Hypnosis, Am. Assn. Profl. Hypnotherapists. Contbr. articles to profl. jours. Club. Deans. Address: 2 Gallows Hill Rd RFD Box 2 Peekskill NY 10566

NEWMAN, RACHEL, magazine editor; b. Malden, Mass., May 1, 1938; d. Maurice and Edythe Brenda (Tichell) N.; m. Herbert Bleiweiss, Apr. 6, 1973. B.A., Pa. State U., 1960; cert., N.Y. Sch. Interior Design, 1963. Accessories editor Women's Wear Daily, N.Y.C., 1964-65; designer, publicist Grandoe Glove Corp., N.Y.C., 1965-67; asso. editor McCall's Sportswear and Dress Merchandiser mag., N.Y.C., 1967; mng. editor McCall's You-Do-It Home Decorating, 1968-70, Ladies Home Jour. Needle and Craft mag., N.Y.C., 1970-72; editor-in-chief Am. Home Crafts mag., N.Y.C., 1972-77; fashion dir. Good Housekeeping mag., N.Y.C., 1977-78; home bldg. and decorating dir. Good Housekeeping mag., 1978-82; editor Country Living mag., 1978—; founding editor Country Cooking mag., 1985—. Pa. State U. Alumni fellow, 1986; named Disting. Alumni Pa. State U., 1988. Mem. N.Y. Fashion Group, Nat. Home Fashions League, Am. Soc. Interior Designers, Am. Soc. Mag. Editors. Office: Country Living 224 W 57th St New York NY 10019

NEWMARK, ANDREA, nutrition consultant and researcher, financial adviser; b. Freeport, N.Y., Dec. 8, 1960; d. Barry Oscar and Phyllis Helena (Schiffer) N. B.S. in Biochemistry, SUNY-Binghamton, 1982. Regional distbr. Munch-A-Bunch, Hicksville, N.Y., 1983-84; pres. ACN Analysis, Levittown, N.Y., 1984—; educator Yours, Ours, Mine Ctr., Levittown, 1983-84; cons. Fantasy Gifts, Levittown, 1985—, Floating Expressions, Garden City, N.Y., 1985—; owner, operator Purveyor of Smiles; lectr., leader workshops in field, N.Y.C. area, 1986—. Author pamphlets in field. Editor A Healthy Outlook, 1986—. Canvasser, N.Y. Pub. Interest Research Group, 1982-83. Mem. Nat. Assn. Female Execs. Avocations: travel, kite flying. Home: 273 N Newbridge Rd Levittown NY 11756 Office: Floating Expressions 621 Chestnut St Garden City NY 11530

NEWSOM, BARBARA JOAN, association controller, golf club owner; b. Indpls., June 10, 1936; d. Floyd Herbert and Cora Eleanor (Gabel) Dreyer; m. Drextle Lee Newsom, Oct. 15, 1954; children—Diana Lee, Cynthia Lou, John Adam, Patricia Kay. Student pub. schs., Indpls. Clk. typist Allison div. Gen. Motors Co., 1954, 56; bookkeeper Greenfield Country Club Pro Shop (Ind.), 1956-59; mgr., bookkeeper Hazelden Country Club, Brook, Ind., 1959-60; bookkeeper Harrison Lake Country Club Pro Shop, Columbus, Ind., 1960-73; co-owner, Golf Club of Ind., Zionsville, 1973-86; bookkeeper nat. hdqrs. Amateur Athletic Union, Indpls., 1974-76, bus. mgr., 1976-81, comptroller, 1981—. Leader 4H Club, 1971-73, 79-86; sec. PTA, 1967-69; treas. PTO, 1974-75; deacon, elder Christian Ch. (Disciples of Christ). Home: 8585 N 925 E Brownsburg IN 46112 Office: 3400 86th St W Indianapolis IN 46268

NEWSON, VICKY LYNN, municipal official; b. Chgo., Mar. 15, 1946; d. Vernon Bruce and Velda Elizabeth (Wright) N. AA, Morton Coll., 1966; BS in Edn., Cen. Mo. State U., 1974, MS, 1975. Cert. tchr., Mo., Ga. Instr. Sure Driving Sch., Inc., La Grange, Ill., 1967-71, owner, pres., 1971-72; tchr. Cen. State Hosp., Milledgeville, Ga., 1975-76, Carver High Sch., Columbus, Ga., 1976-77; dist. grants mgmt. specialist State of Fla. Dept. Health and Rehab. Services, Ft. Lauderdale, 1977-80; projects planner, coordinator City Mgr.'s Office City of Boca Raton, Fla., 1980—. Bd. dirs. United Way of Greater Boca Raton, 1987. Mem. Nat. Assn. Telecommunication Officers and Advisers, Fla. Assn. Telecommunication Officers and Advisers (charter). Republican. Methodist. Clubs: Underseas Adventurers (Ft. Lauderdale), Boca Raton Road Runners, Pack and Paddle. Home: 4901 NW 77th Ct Pompano Beach FL 33073 Office: City of Boca Raton 201 W Palmetto Park Rd Boca Raton FL 33432

NEWTON, BRENDA LEE, lighting company executive; b. Warren, Ohio, Aug. 9, 1960; d. Donald Robert and Carol Lee (DeHoff) Parker; m. Michael Macardel Newton, Oct. 19, 1985. BBA in Graphics, Youngstown State U., 1982; AA in Interior Design, John Hopkins U., 1985. Buyer cosmetic, cons. May Co., Youngstown, Ohio, 1979-82; mgr., cons. comml. Excello Lighting, Balt., 1982-84; mgr. project, cons. comml. Dorman & Assoc., Balt., 1984-85; designer Kesco Lighting, Virginia Beach, Va., 1985-86; br. mgr. showroom, designer lighting Noland Co., Chesapeake, Va., 1986—. Author editorial Wall Street Jour., 1985, poems. Inventor light fixtures. Mem. advt. com. Am. Cancer Soc., 1981-82. Served to Sgt. U.S. Air Force, 1982-86. Mem. Illuminating Engr. Soc., Tidewater Builders Assn., Tidewater Women's Aux., Am. Lighting Inst., Nat. Assn. Female Execs., Am. Home Lighting Inst., TBA Remodeling Council, TBA Comml. Com., C. of C. Republican. Presbyterian. Home: 116A Budding Ave Virginai Beach VA 23452 Office: Noland Co 663 Wood Lake Dr PO Box 1426 Chesapeake VA 23320

NEWTON, DEIDRA ELLEN, communications executive; b. Miami, Fla., Sept. 23, 1959; d. Peter Bradshaw and Lovda (Williams) N. AA, Palm Beach Jr. Coll., 1980; BS, Fla. Atlantic U., 1983. Cons. Easy Writer Communications, West Palm Beach, Fla., 1983-86; v.p. Sun Communications, West Palm Beach, 1986-88, pres., 1988—. Vol. ARC, Palm Beach County, Fla., 1977—, Sunfest, Palm Beach County, 1985—; vol., coordinator community parks cleanup and improvement project City of Riviera Beach, Palm Beach County, 1986; shelter mgr. Red Cross Internat., Palm Beach County, 1985-86. Recipient Most Dependable Writer award Beachcomber Newspaper, Palm Beach County, 1984. Mem. Fla. Pub. Relations Assn., Women in Communications. Office: Sun Communications 1616 N Florida Mango Rd West Palm Beach FL 33409

NEWTON, GALE JOANN, investment account executive, financial consultant; b. Mich., Nov. 23, 1954; d. Gilbert Allen Sr. and Marjorie J. (Lockard) N. Student, Grand Valley State U., Allendale, Mich., 1978; cert., Life Underwriter Tng. Council, 1983, 85, 87. Registered rep. Investors Diversified Services, Grand Rapids, Mich., 1980-83; acct. exec. Primus Fin. Services Inc., Grand Rapids, 1983-87, cons., 1987—. Grant Taggart scholar Am. Coll., 1985. Mem. Nat. Assn. Profl. Sales Women, Mich. Profl. Sales Women, Nat. Assn. Female Execs., Nat. Assn. Life Underwriters, Mich. and Grand Rapids Life Underwriters. Office: Primus Fin Services Inc 4450 Cascade Rd SE Grand Rapids MI 49506

NEWTON, LISA HAENLEIN, philosophy educator; b. Orange, N.J., Sept. 17, 1939; d. Wallen Joseph and Carol Bigelow (Cypiot) Haenlein; m. Victor Joseph Newton, June 3, 1972; children: Tracey, Kit, Cynthia Perkins, Daniel Perkins, Laura Perkins. Student, Swarthmore Coll., 1957-59; B.S. with honors in Philosophy, Columbia U., 1962, Ph.D., 1967. Asst. prof. philosophy Hofstra U., Hempstead, N.Y., 1967-69; asst. prof. philosophy Fairfield U., Conn., 1969-73, assoc. prof., 1973-78, prof., 1978—, dir. program in applied ethics, 1983—, dir. program in environ. studies, 1986—; lectr. in medicine Yale U., 1984—; lectr., cons. in field. Contbr. articles to profl. jours. Mem. exec. bd. Conn. Humanities Council, 1979-83. Mem. Am. Soc. Value Inquiry (pres.), Am. Philos. Assn., Am. Soc. Polit. and Legal Philosophy, Acad. Mgmt., Am. Soc. Law and Medicine, Phi Beta Kappa. Home: 4042 Congress St Fairfield CT 06430 Office: Fairfield U Dept Philosophy Fairfield CT 06430

NGO, TERESITA WY, economics educator; b. Manila, Sept. 18, 1949; came to U.S., 1972; d. In Ngo and Rosita Uy. BA cum laude, U. Santo Thomas, Manila, 1970; MA, U. Colo., 1976, U. So. Calif., 1979; PhD in Econs., U. So. Calif., 1982. Fin. economist Western Alarm Supply Co., Denver, 1982-84; asst. prof. econs. Regis Coll., Denver, 1983-84; assoc. prof. Pepperdine U., Malibu, Calif., 1984—. Mem. Inst. Mgmt. Sci., Nat. Assn. Female Execs. Office: Pepperdine U Sch Bus Mgmt 400 Corporate Pointe Culver City CA 90230

NGUYEN, ANN CAC KHUE, pharmaceutical and bioorganic chemist; b. Sontay, Vietnam; came to U.S., 1975; naturalized citizen; d. Nguyen Van Soan and Luu Thi Hieu. BS, U. Saigon, 1973; MS, San Francisco State U., 1978; PhD, U. Calif., San Francisco, 1983. Teaching and research asst. U. Calif., San Francisco, 1978-83, postdoctoral fellow, 1983-86; research scientist U. Calif., 1987—. Contbr. articles to profl. jours. Recipient Nat. Research Service award, NIH, 1981-83; Regents fellow U. Calif., San Francisco, 1978-81. Mem. Am. Chem. Soc., AAAS, Bay Area Enzyme Mechanism Group, Nat. Coop. Drug Discovery Group. Roman Catholic. Home: 1488 Portola Dr San Francisco CA 94127 Office: U Calif Dept Pharmaceutical Chemistry San Francisco CA 94143

NIARCHOS, MARY ANNE, geologist; b. N.Y.C., Nov. 5, 1953; d. Demetri and Sylvia (Ellis) N. BSc, U. Queensland, Brisbane, Australia, 1975; MSc, Queen's U., Kingston, Ont., Can., 1982. Research asst. Geology dept. U. Queensland, 1972-74; editorial asst. Plenum Press, N.Y.C., 1976-77, Engring. and Mining Jour. McGraw-Hill Corp., N.Y.C., 1977-79; geologist U.S. Borax, Los Angeles, 1980; strategic planner explorations Utah Internat., San Francisco, 1982-87; mng. ptnr. Ubiqore Mineral Explorers, Toronto, Ont., 1987—. Fellow Geol. Assn. Can.; mem. Soc. Mining Engrs., N.W. Mining Assn., Can. Inst. Mining and Metallurgy. Greek Orthodox. Home: 870 UN Plaza New York NY 10017 Office: 72 Howland Ave, Toronto, ON Canada M5R 3B3

NICCOLINI, DIANORA, photographer; b. Florence, Italy, Oct. 3, 1936; d. George and Elaine (Augsbury) Niccolini; came to U.S., 1945, naturalized, 1960; student Hunter Coll., 1955-62, Art Students League, 1960, Germain Sch. Photography, 1962. Med. photographer Manhattan Eye, Ear and Throat Hosp., 1963-65; organizer med. photography dept., 1st chief med. photographer Lenox Hill Hosp., 1965-67; organizer, head dept. med. and audio visual edn. St. Clare's Hosp., N.Y.C., 1967-76; mem. Third Eye Gallery, N.Y.C., 1974-76; owner Dianora Niccolini Creations, 1976—; instr. photography Camera Club N.Y., 1978-79, Germaine Sch. Photography, 1978-79, N.Y. Inst. Photography, 1981—; one woman shows 209 Photo Gallery, Top of the Stairs Gallery, Third Eye Gallery, 1974, 75, 77, West Broadway Gallery, N.Y.C., 1981, Camera Club N.Y., 1982, Photographics Unltd. Gallery, N.Y.C., 1981; project dir. Photography over 65, N.Y.C., 1978; pub. portfolios. Mem. Women Photographers N.Y. (founder 1974), Biol. Photog. Assn., Assn. Ind. Video and Filmmakers, Internat. Center Photography, Am. Soc. Mag. Photographers, Am. Soc. Picture Profls., Profl. Women Photographers (coordinator 1980-84), Unity Center Practical Christianity. Author: Women of Vision, 1982; Men in Focus, 1983; editor: P.W.P. Times, 1981-82; contbr. to photog. books, 1979, 80; contbg. editor Functional Photography, 1979-80, N.Y. Photo Dist. News, 1980. Home: 356 E 78th St New York NY 10021 Office: Dianora Niccolini 2 W 32d St Suite 200 New York NY 10001

NICHOLAS, CAROL LYNN, lawyer; b. Berkeley, Calif., July 28, 1938; d. Frederick Mortimer and Carolyn (Wright) Nicholas; m. Donald Herrick Maffly, Aug. 24, 1958 (div. 1973); children: Donald Herrick, Brian A. E., Elizabeth Lynn. Student, Conn. Coll., 1956-58; AB, U. Calif., Berkeley, 1971; JD, U. San Francisco, 1975; LLM, Georgetown U., 1982. Bar: Calif. 1976. Staff atty. SEC, San Francisco, 1976-79, Crocker Nat. Bank, San Francisco, 1979-81, Fed. Home Loan Bank, San Francisco, 1983-84; assoc. Rosen, Wachtell & Gilbert, San Francisco and Los Angeles, 1984-86, Lewis, D'Amato, Brisbois & Bisgaard, Los Angeles, 1986—. Contbr. book revs. and articles to profl. jours. Mem. ABA (fed. regulation of securities com.). Democrat. Episcopalian. Home: 2738 Webster St Berkeley CA 94705 Office: Lewis D'Amato Brisbois & Bisgaard 261 Figueroa St Suite 300 Los Angeles CA 90012

NICHOLAS, COLOMBE MARGARET, fashion licensing executive; b. Larchmont, N.Y., Nov. 6, 1944; d. Dimitri Paul and Colombe Irene Nicholas; student Coll. de Montreaux (Switzerland), 1960; B.A., U. Dayton, 1964; J.D., U. Cin., 1968; m. Leonard Rosenberg. Buyer Macy's 1970-75; buyer, divisional mdse. mgr. Bloomingdale's, 1975-78; v.p., mdse. mgr. Bonwit Teller, 1978-80; pres. Christian Dior N.Y., Inc., N.Y.C., 1980—. Mem. Young Pres.'s Orgn. Office: Christian Dior 1372 Broadway New York NY 10018 *

NICHOLAS, MAY THERESA, string instrument company executive; b. Phila., Aug. 8, 1944; d. Charles B. and Irene L. Nicholas. BS in Applied Music, Temple U., 1966; cert., Internazionale Sommerakademie des Mozarteums, Salzburg, Austria, 1965; diploma, Orff-Institut, Salzburg, 1965, M.W. Funk Real Estate Inst., 1984. With House of Primavera, Phila., 1964-79, sec.-treas., 1968-79; sec.-treas. Phila. Sales Co. Inc., 1971-79; gen. mgr. RW Service and Supplies div. Italo-Am. String Instrument Co., Inc., Cherry Hill, N.J., 1979-82; gen. mgr., chief fin. officer Triad Mus. Supplies, Inc., 1986—; prin., cons. small bus. mgmt. Nicholas Services; violin maker. Recipient Vira I. Heinz award, 1965; N.J. State scholar, 1962-65. Mem. Violin Soc. Am. (charter), Nat. Assn. Music Mchts., Phila. Direct Mktg. Democrat. Presbyterian. Home: 6338 Irving Ave Pennsauken NJ 08109 Office: PO Box 1002 Merchantville NJ 08109

NICHOLAS, NICKIE LEE, industrial hygienist; b. Lake Charles, La., Jan. 19, 1938; d. Clyde Lee and Jessie Mae (Lyons) N.; B.S., U. Houston, 1960, M.S., 1966. Tchr. sci. Pasadena (Tex.) Ind. Sch. Dist., 1960-61; chemist FDA, Dallas, 1961-62, VA Hosp., Houston, 1962-66; chief biochemist Baylor U. Coll. Medicine, 1966-68; chemist NASA, Johnson Spacecraft Center, 1968-73; analytical chemist TVA, Muscle Shoals, Ala., 1973-75; indsl. hygienist, compliance officer Occupational Safety and Health Adminstrn., Dept. Labor, Houston, 1975-79, area dir., Tulsa, 1979-82, mgr., Austin, 1982—; mem. faculty VA Sch. Med. Tech., Houston, 1963-66. Recipient award for outstanding achievement German embassy, 1958, Suggestion award VA, 1963, Group Achievement award Skylab Med. Team, NASA, 1974; Personal Achievement award Dept. Labor Fed. Women's Program, 1984. Mem. Am. Chem. Soc. (dir. analytical group Southeastern Tex. and Brazosport sects. 1971, chmn. elect 1973), Am. Assn. Clin. Chemists, Am. Harp Soc., Fed. Exec. Assn. (pres. 1984-85), Kappa Epsilon. Home: 1305 Shannon Oaks Austin TX 78746 Office: 611 E 6th St Suite 303 Austin TX 78701

NICHOLS, ALLIE JO, telecommunications executive; b. Wickes, Ark., Nov. 5, 1932; d. Luther Sebrin Nichols and Ruth May (Ross) Ford; m. Clarence Lee Cook, Jan. 29, 1960 (div. 1965). Student, Coll. of the Ozarks, 1951-52; A in Bus., St. Joseph Coll., 1957; AS, North Am. Inst., 1959; student, Ariz. State U., 1963-65. Mgr. communications exec. offices Ramada Inns, Phoenix, 1965-67; mgr. traffic Mountain Bell, Phoenix, 1967-73; facilities planner Mountain Bell, Denver, 1973-78, intra-lata planner, 1980-83, product specialist, 1983-85; toll switch planner AT&T, Denver, 1973-80; mgr. product selection, evaluation U.S. West, Denver, 1983—. Mem. N. Mex. Grassroot Dems., Santa Fe, 1955—; officer Sloan's Lake Citizen Group, Denver, 1977—; mem. NW Denver Dems., 1980—; adv. bd. Denver Ch. Assn., 1981—; mem. Our Lady of the Bell, Denver. Mem. Soc. of Women Engrs., U.S. West Women, Alliance of Profl. Women, Pioneers of Am. Roman Catholic. Home: 2764 Yates St Denver CO 80212 Office: US West 1801 California Denver CO 80211

NICHOLS, ALLISON SUE, engineer; b. New Haven, Mar. 15, 1957; d. Philip Paul and Arlene Janice (Lieberman) Donenfeld; m. Malcolm Swift Nichols, Dec. 30, 1979. B.S.C.E., Union Coll., Schenectady, 1977; M.B.A., Golden Gate U., 1981. Intern N.Y. State Energy Office, Albany, N.Y., 1976-77, editor bull., 1976; assoc. resident mgr. Gen. Electric Co., Louisville, 1977-78, resident mgr., Schenectady, 1978-79; project engr. Swinerton & Walberg Co., San Francisco, 1980-81, asst. project mgr., 1981-83, project mgr., 1983-85; project mgr. George Hyman Constrn. Co., Boston, 1985-86; sr. project mgr., 1986—. Contbr. articles to Seventeen mag., Empire State Energy News. Actress various theatres, including for Danville Old Towne Theater (Calif.), 1982, Eugene O'Neill Soc., Lafayette, Calif., 1983. Mem. ASCE (assoc.; v.p. student chpt. 1976-77), Nat. Assn. Female Execs. Republican. Jewish. Lodge: B'nai B'rith (Danville). Home: 10 Wescott Circle Tewksbury MA 01876 Office: George Hyman Constrn Co 410 Boylston St Boston MA 02116

NICHOLS, CAROL JEAN, management consultant; b. Kansas City, Kans., Nov. 13, 1954; d. Ernest Alfred and Lila Jean Rousselot; m. Dennis Dean Nichols, Dec. 22, 1979. Student, San Diego State U., 1975-77; BS, U. Mo., 1979; postgrad., W. Conn. State U., 1982. Tchr. Blue Springs (Mo.) Sch. Dist., 1979-82; group move coordinator Merrill Lynch Relocation Mgmt., St. Paul, 1983; project cons. Merrill Lynch Relocation Mgmt., White Plains, N.Y., 1984-86, mng. cons., 1986-87; sr. mng. cons. Premier Decision Mgmt., Overland Park, Kans., 1987—. Leader Girl Scouts of Am., Mo., 1972-82. Mem. Employee Relocation Counsel, Am. Assn. Personnel Adminstrs., Am. Mgmt. Assn. Democrat. Home: 3541 W 129th Terr Leawood KS 66209 Office: Premier Decision Mgmt 4500 College Blvd Suite 210 Overland Park KS 66211

NICHOLS, CYNTHIA LEIGH, lawyer; b. Gainesville, Fla., Aug. 3, 1957; d. Donald Gilbert and Betty Catherine (Bullard) Nichols. B.S., Fla. State U., 1978; J.D., Stetson U., 1980. Bar: Fla. 1981. Law clk. Fla. Supreme Ct., Tallahassee, 1981; asst. state atty. State of Fla., Jacksonville, 1981-82; sole practice, Jacksonville, 1982-83; ptnr. Nichols & Nichols, Jacksonville, 1983—. Bd. dirs. P.A.C.E. Ctr. for Girls. Mem. ABA, Fla. Bar Assn., Jacksonville Bar Assn., Assn. Trial Lawyers Am. Democrat. Baptist. Office: Nichols & Nichols 340-1 E Adams St Jacksonville FL 32202

NICHOLS, EDIE DIANE, real estate executive; b. Grahamstown, Eastern Cape Province, Republic of South Africa, Mar. 28, 1939; came to U.S., 1963; d. Cyril Doughtry and Dorothy Ethel (Nottingham) Tyson; m. John F. Nichols, Dec. 16, 1962; 1 child, Ian Tyson. Adminstrv. asst. Am. Acad. Medicine, N.Y.C., 1963-64, Jack Lenor Larsen, Inc., N.Y.C., 1964-70; v.p. John Scott Fones, Inc., N.Y.C., 1971-76, Howard J. Rubenstein Assocs. Inc., N.Y.C., 1976-80; dir. communications Carl Byoir & Assocs., N.Y.C., 1981-83; account supr. Hill and Knowlton, N.Y.C., 1983-85; with Cross & Brown Co., N.Y.C. Trustee Cen. Park Hist. Soc., N.Y.C., 1978-80. Mem. NOW, N.Y. Women in Communications (pub. relations chair 1980-81, v.p., programs bd. dirs 1985-87). Republican. Episcopalian. Club: City of N.Y. (trustee, v.p., fin. and devel. 1987—). Home: 16 Stuyvesant Oval New York NY 10009 Office: Cross & Brown Co 63 Wall St New York NY 10005

NICHOLS, ELIZABETH EMBRY, travel agency owner, president; b. Gresston, Ga., Mar. 31, 1927; d. Walter Colquitt and Frances Commella (Pierce) Embry; m. William A. Denson; m. Nelvie Edward Nichols, Oct. 12, 1963; children: Commella, William. Student, Pan Am Bus. Sch., Miami, 1952. Certified travel cons. Acctg. clk. Ea. Air Lines, Inc., Miami, Fla., 1954-63; office mgr. Ga. Motor Club, AAA, Albany, Ga., 1965-72; travel agt. Albany Travel, Inc., Albany, 1973-76; owner, pres. Trinity Travel, Inc., Albany, 1977—; Active Citizens' Adv. Council, Albany, 1981—; bd. dirs. United Way Dougherty County, Albany, 1985—; bd. dirs. Girl's Club Albany, 1986—. Mem. Albany C. of C. (bd. dirs.), Am. Soc. Travel Agts., Ga. Hospitality and Tourism Assn. (v.p. Albany chpt. 1987). Democrat. Presbyterian. Office: Trinity Travel Inc 501 Pine Ave Albany GA 31701

NICHOLS, IRENE DELORES, real estate professional, paralegal; b. Kansas City, Mo., Mar. 7, 1938; d. Verne Keith Covell and Louise Lena (Janeski) Covell Jackson; children: Todd Martin Hesher, Tedd Matthew Hesher. BS, U. Fla., 1980; AA in Tech. Arts, Johnson County Coll., 1986. Cert. paralegal, Mo.; lic. securities, ins. dealer, Mo. Legal sec. Lathrop, Koontz, Righter, Clagett, Parker and Norquist, Kansas City, 1972-75; fashion model Patricia Stevens Agy., Kansas City, 1975-76; with legal dept. U.S. Dept. Treasury, Kansas City, 1981-84; fin. planner, rep. IDS Am. Express, Overland Park, Kans., 1984-85; with real estate dept. Gage and Tucker, Kansas City, 1985—. Mem. Kansas City Ballet Guild, 1970, Clay County Task Force for Juvenile Detention, Liberty, Mo., 1970; life mem. Nat. PTA, 1970—; sch. dist. lobbyist to Mo. Ho. Reps., Senate, Jefferson City, 1971; v.p. North Kansas City Dem. Club, 1976. Mem. Kansas City Assn. Legal Assts., Kansas City Chpt. Internat. Assn. Fin. Planners. Club: Brookridge Country (Overland Park). Office: Gage and Tucker 2345 Grand Ave Kansas City MO 64108

NICHOLS, JACQUELINE BRUCE, archeologist; b. Harlan, Ky., Oct. 14, 1941; d. Jack Corum and Martha Jayne (Miracle) Bruce; B.A., Wellesley

Coll., 1963; M.A., SUNY, Albany, 1977; m. David Edward Nichols, Mar. 4, 1963; children—Corinna Elizabeth, David Andrew, Patrick Edward. Tchr., Bedford (Eng.) Schs., 1963-64; dir. Archeol. Field Labs., SUNY, Albany, 1976-77, Cath. U., 1978; v.p. Gt. Basin Found. for Archeol. Research, 1979; pres. Atechiston, Inc., Albuquerque, 1980—; co-founder, editor Flintknappers Exchange, 1977; founder, pub. Contract Abstracts & CRM Archeology, 1980—; pub. Am. Archeology. Wallace Stegner fellow, 1963-64. Mem. AAAS, Soc. Am. Archaeology, Nat. Assn. Women Bus. Owners, Soc. Archeol. Sci., Found. for Desert Archaeology (dir. 1980—). Republican. Office: 4426 Constitution NE Albuquerque NM 87110

NICHOLS, JANET ELLEN, educator; b. Rockville Centre, N.Y., Apr. 7, 1950; d. John B. and Virginia Florence (Raupp) Greenhouse; m. John G. Nichols, June 9, 1973; 1 dau., Virginia Anne. B.A., Adelphi U., 1971; M.S., Lehigh U., 1973; postgrad., Colo. State U., 1973-76. Teaching asst. Lehigh U., Bethlehem, Pa., 1971-73, Colo. State U., Ft. Collins, 1973-76; instr. math. U. So. Colo., Pueblo, 1977-79, asst. prof., 1979—. NDEA Title IV fellow, 1971-73. Mem. Am. Math. Soc., Math. Assn. Am., Sigma Xi, Pi Mu Epsilon, Delta Tau Alpha, Delta Phi Alpha. Home: PO Box 214 Canon City CO 81212 Office: U So Colo Dept Math Pueblo CO 81001

NICHOLS, JUDITH ELLEN, academic administrator; b. N.Y.C., Aug. 20, 1947; d. Harold and Rosalyn (Yanover) Nadler; m. Michael Earl Eisenkraft, Oct. 6, 1966; Divorced; children: Brian David, Stacey Lynne; m. Jonathan David Nichols, Sept. 19, 1981; 1 child, Cassandra Beth. BA in English, CCNY, 1969; MBA, N.Y. Inst. Tech., 1983. mem. fin. and devel com. Detroit Area Pre Coll. Engring. Program,1986-87. Pvt. cons. mktg. N.Y. and N.J., 1970-76; dir. mktg. YMCA's Greater N.Y.C., 1976-79; dir. devel. N.Y.C. Coll. Podiatric Medicine, 1979-81; exec. dir. alumni relation N.J. Inst. Tech., Newark, 1981-85; exec. dir. univ. devel. Wayne State U., 1985-87; v.p. for devel. Portland (Oreg.) State U., 1987—. Mem. mktg. com. YMCA Greater Detroit, 1986-87. Mem. Nat. Assn. Fund Raising Execs. (cert., active long-range plan com. 1986—, bd. dirs. Oreg. chpt., chair philanthropy day 1988), Council Support and Advancement Edn. Office: Portland State U PO Box 751 Portland OR 97207

NICHOLS, MARGARET ROWELL, social worker; b. Malden, Mass., Aug. 1, 1920; d. John Munn and Edith (Temple) Rowell; m. Paul R. Nichols, June 22, 1941; children—David R., Barbara Nichols Pierimarchi, Carol Nichols Friesen. A.B., Denison U., Granville, Ohio, 1943; M.S.W., Boston U., 1950. Admitting officer, social worker Carney Hosp., Boston, 1948-52; mem. Disability Rev. Team, Boston, 1952-53; social worker Mass. Gen. Hosp., Boston, 1953-55; clin. social worker West Roxbury VA Med. Ctr., Boston, 1955-57; clin. social worker, fieldwork supr. VA, Boston, 1957-64, clin. social worker, student supr. Psychiatry Clinic, 1964—. Recipient Hands and Heart award VA, 1981. Mem. Nat. Assn. Social Workers, Acad. Cert. Social Workers, Boston Gerontologic Psychiatry, Mass. Acad. Psychiat. Social Workers, Nat. Registry Health Care Providers., Baptist Womens Soc. (past pres., deaconess, past chairperson missionary bd. Needham, Mass.). Baptist. Office: VA Boston Psychiatry Clinic 17 Court St Boston MA 02108

NICHOLS, MARY PEROT, communications executive; b. York, Pa., Oct. 11, 1926; d. Charles Poultney and Dorothy (Leonard) Perot; BA in Polit. Sci., Swarthmore Coll., 1948; m. Robert Brayton Nichols, Oct. 11, 1953 (div. 1967); children: Kerstin, Duncan, Eliza. Reporter, polit. columnist Village Voice, N.Y.C., 1958-66, city editor, columnist, 1968-75; dir. public relations N.Y.C. Parks, Recreation and Cultural Affairs Adminstrn., 1966-68; freelance journalist, investigative columnist Boston Herald Am., 1975-76; dir. communicatios Office of Mayor, Boston, 1977-78; pres. sta. WNYC Radio/TV Communications Group, public broadcasting stas. assoc. with Nat. Public Radio and Public Broadcasting System, 1978-80; dir. communications U. Pa., Phila., 1980-83; dir. WNYC Radio/TV, N.Y.C. Mcpl. Broadcasting System, 1984—; dir. Eastern Public Radio Network, 1979-80. Trustee Broadcasting Found. Am., 1978-80, Com. for Arts in Pa., Parks Council N.Y.C., 1969-75; bd. dirs. Public Interest Law Center Phila. Recipient Rosebuds award for investigation of organized crime, journalism rev. More, 1973. Mem. Forum Exec. Women (exec. bd.), Phila. Art Alliance, Am. Women in Radio and TV, Phila. Athenaeum (bd. dirs.), Nat. Acad. Radio and TV (N.Y. chpt.), Nat. Constn. Ctr. Democrat. Clubs: Coffee House, City N.Y., Women's City (dir. 1972-74), Cosmopolitan (Phila.). Contbr. articles to various publs., including Barron's, New Republic. Address: 505 La Guardia Pl New York NY 10012 Office: Mcpl Bldg One Centre St New York NY 10007

NICHOLS, NANCY, financial consultant; b. Monroe, Mich., Dec. 1, 1939; d. Joseph William and Eva Arlene (Smith) Smith; m. Raymond Arlyn Nichols, Jan. 17, 1959; children—Anita Marie Nichols Baran, Amy Beth Nichols Forrest. Student U. Mich., 1972, Siena Heights Coll., 1983. Sales staff Glover Real Estate, Adrian, Mich., 1972-75; mgr. Bennett Ambulance, Tecumseh, Mich., 1972-75; acting dir. Lenawee Health Dept., Adrian, 1975-78; owner, capt. Anywhere Sports Fishing, Monroe, 1978—; assoc., cons. Stauder, Barch & Assoc., Ann Arbor, Mich., 1985—; speaker in seminars concerning pub. health laws and regulations, unification of health systems, county govt., women in decision making roles. Bd. dirs. U. Mich. Sch. Pub. Health, 1980-85, Community Mental Health Bd. Lenawee County, 1975-84; vice-chmn. exec. bd. Tecumseh Housing Commn., 1975—; chmn. exec. com. South Central Substance Abuse Commn., 1976-84; chairperson Human Service Bd., 1976-78, Lenawee County Democratic Party, Adrian, 1972—, chmn. 1985—, Lenawee County Health Bd., 1976-78, Lenawee County Energy Task Force, 1980-81; candidate for state rep. Lenawee County, 1984; county commnr. Lenawee County, 1974-84; mem. Industry/Edn. Coordinating Council (3 counties), 1983-85, State Health Coordinating Council, 1980-84, Selection com. for State Dir. Pub. Health, 1981, State Mich. com. for Unification of Pub. Mental Health System, 1979, State Mich. Substance Abuse Consolidation Task Force, 1975-76, Mich. Assn. Bds. Health, 1976-84, pres. 1983; bd. dirs. Mich. Mid-South Health Systems Agy., 1976-83, pres. 1981; mem. adv. com. Great Lakes Fishery, 1986—. Named Democrat of Yr. Lenawee Democratic Party, 1985; recipient Mich. Legis. Cert. Tribute for Outstanding Service in Health field, 1983, 85, Mich. Minuteman Citation Honor for Promoting Mich. and community, 1979; Namesake of the Nancy Nichols Award for Outstanding contribution to the Substance Abuse field by the Substance Abuse Program Directors in Calhouns, Hillsdale, Jackson and Lenawee Counties, 1983. Mem. Bus. and Profl. Women. Democrat. Methodist. Clubs: Safari (sec. 1984—) (Tecumseh). Lodge: Order Eastern Star (past matron). Home: 216 North Oneida St Tecumseh MI 49286 Office: Stauder Barch & Assoc 3989 Research Park Ann Arbor MI 48108

NICHOLS, ROBERTA JEAN, automotive executive; b. Venice, Calif., Nov. 29, 1931; d. Robert Fulton and Winifred Elaine (Vos) Hilts; m. William A. McDonald; children: Kathleen, Robert; m. Alfred Lynn Yakel, Nov. 2, 1974. BS in Physics, UCLA, 1968; MS in Environ. Engring., U. So. Calif., Los Angeles, 1975, PhD in Engring., 1979. Mathematician Douglas Aircraft Co., Santa Monica, Calif., 1957-58; computer tech. Space Tech. Lab, Inc., Redondo Beach, Calif., 1958-60; tech. staff The Aerospace Corp., El Segundo, Calif., 1960-79; prin. research engr. Ford Motor Co., Dearborn, Mich., 1979—; cons. State of Calif. Synthetic Fuels Programs, Sacramento, Calif. 1978-79, Office Tech. Assessment, U.S. Congress, Washington, 1982-83. Contbr. articles to profl. jours.; patentee in field. Precinct worker Rep. Party, Calif., 1972. Recipient Pursuit of Excellence award Auto Warehouse Dealers Assn., 1982; named Outstanding Engr. Inst. for Advancement of Engrs., 1974. Mem. Soc. Automotive Engrs., Am. Soc. Mechanical Engrs., The Combustion Inst., Soc. Women Engrs. (sr. mem., pres. Los Angeles sect. 1972-73, Achievement award 1988), Nat. Drag Boat Assn. (chmn. 1964-72, nat. bd. dirs. 1964-72), Sigma Xi. Republican. Clubs: Nat. Drag Boat Assn (pres.), Internat. Gull Wing Group, Inc. (pres. 1977-78). Office: Ford Motor Co 20000 Rotunda Dr PO Box 2053 Dearborn MI 48121-2053

NICHOLS, VICKI ANNE, financial consultant, librarian; b. Denver, June 10, 1949; d. Glenn Warner and Loretta Irene (Chalender) Adams; B.A., Colo. Coll., 1972; postgrad. U. Denver, 1976-77; m. Robert H. Nichols, Oct. 28, 1972 (div.); children—Christopher Travis, Lindsay Meredith. Treas., controller, dir. Polaris Resources, Inc., Denver, 1972-86; controller InterCap Devel. Corp, 1986-87; treas., controller, dir. Transnat. Cons., Ltd., 1986—; librarian Jefferson County (Colo.) Pub. Library, 1986—; dir., owner Nichols Bus. Services. Home: 4305 Brentwood St Wheat Ridge CO 80033 Office: 1825 Lawrence St Suite 333 Denver CO 80202

NICHOLS, VICKI LYNN, business official; b. Cin., July 4, 1955; d. Dale Peter Nichols and Janet Josephine (Nagele) Nichols Mortimer. File clk. Dayco Corp., Cin., 1974-75, order entry processor, 1975-76, br. mgr., sec., 1976-77, sec., regional sales mgr., 1977-78, inside sales coordinator, West Chester, Ohio, 1978-80, sr. inside sales coordinator, 1980-87, office mgr., 1982-87, adminstrv. asst. indsl. hose mktg., 1987—. Author: Branch Training Manuals, 1980 (cert. of accomplishment 1982). Roman Catholic. Avocations: travel; bowling; reading; collecting Star Trek memorabilia. Home: 402 Old St Unit #7 Monroe OH 45069 Office: Dayco Products Inc Corp Hdqtrs Ct 33 W First St Dayton OH 45402

NICHOLS, VIRGINIA V., insurance agent, accountant; b. Monroe County, Mo., Oct. 26, 1928; d. Elmer W. and Frances L. (McKinney) N.; student Belleville (Ill.) Jr. Coll., 1959-60, Rockhurst Coll., 1964-65, Avila Coll., Kansas City, Mo., 1981-84. Sec., Panhandle Eastern Pipeline Co., Kansas City, Mo., 1964-65, St. Louis County Dept. Revenue, 1965-69, Forest Park Community Coll., 1969-71, Nooney Co., St. Louis, 1971-77, J. A. Baer Enterprises, St. Louis, 1979; acct. Panhandle Eastern Pipe Line Co., Kansas City, Mo., 1979-85. Vol., ARC, 1965—. Mem. Am. Soc. Women Accts., Profl. Secs. Internat. (Sec. of Year 1969, sec. Mo. div. 1975-76), Jr. Women's C. of C. (Girl of Year 1975, pres. 1974-75). Republican. Episcopalian. Home: PO Box 5832 Kansas City MO 64111

NICHOLSON, AIDEEN, state legislator; b. Dublin, Ireland, Apr. 29, 1927. Student, Trinity Coll., Dublin, U. London, London Sch. Econs. Former social worker Ont. Dept. Correctional Services, Can., from 1965; exec. dir. Cradleship Creche of Met. Toronto, Can., 1969-74; mem. Can. Ho. of Commons; Founding mem. Ont. Commn. on the Status of Women. Recipient Centennial medal, 1967. Mem. Liberal Party. Address: 723 Ossington Ave, Toronto, ON Canada M6G 3T6 *

NICHOLSON, EDNA ELIZABETH, retired public health official; b. Redwood Falls, Minn., Dec. 23, 1907; d. Ernest Crawford and Alma (Bordeaux) N.; A.B., U. Mich., 1930, M.S. in Pub. Health, 1931, cert. social work, 1931. Nat. Tb Assn. fellow in social research, 1930-31; med. social work ARC, U.S. Naval Hosp., Great Lakes, Ill., 1931-33; asst. dir. med. relief service Cook County Bur. Public Welfare, Chgo., 1933-35; instr. social aspects of nursing Cook County Sch. Nursing and asst. dir. social service Cook County Hosp., Chgo., 1935-37; dir. med. relief service Chgo. Relief Adminstrn., 1938-42; vis. lectr. Sch. Hygiene and Pub. Health, U. Mich., 1939; cons. on med. assistance, bur. pub. assistance Fed. Security Agency, 1942-44; dir. Central Service for Chronically Ill, Inst. Medicine, Chgo., 1944-54; exec. dir. Inst. Medicine of Chgo., 1955-64; sr. specialist program ops. and standards Med. Services Adminstrn., HEW, 1964-71; spl. lectr. program in hosp. adminstrn. Northwestern U., 1945-60; tech. adviser Commn. on Chronic Illness, 1949-56. Recipient Cancer Care award Nat. Cancer Found., 1955. Mem. Am. Public Health Assn., Phi Beta Kappa, Delta Omega, Sigma Kappa. Author: Terminal Care for Cancer Patients, 1950; Surveying Community Needs and Resources for Care of the Chronically Ill, 1950; The Nurse and Chronic Illness: Planning New Institutional Facilities for Longterm Care, 1956; A Comprehensive Community Plan for Meeting the Problems of Chronic Illness, 1959. Contbr. to profl. jours. Home: 315 N LaGrange Rd LaGrange Park IL 60525

NICHOLSON, JEAN HAGEWOOD, school adminstrator; b. Tullahoma, Tenn., Jan. 14, 1935; d. Leroy Irving and Mildren Angeline (Prince) Hagewood; m. Stuart Edwin Nicholson, June 9, 1962; 1 child, Brian Edwin. BS, Peabody Coll., 1956; MS, U. Colo., 1959; PhD, Peabody of Vanderbilt U., 1980. Tchr. Cleve. Bd. EDn., 1956-60; tech. writer Gen. Electric Co., Cleve., 1960-62; research asst. Vanderbilt Hosp., Nashville, 1965-67; adj. prof. Trevecca Nazarene Coll., Nashville, 1987—; tchr., adminstr. Nashville Bd. Edn., 1967—; cons. U.S. Office Edn., Miami, Fla., 1986-87, Metro Bd. Edn., Nashville, 1976-78. Bd. dirs. Chem. Awareness Nashville, 1986—, Alcohol/Drug Abuse Council, Nashville, 1988—; vol. Bob Clement Congl. Campaign, Nashville, 1987—. Peabody Coll. scholar, 1953-56. Mem. Metro Edn. Roundtable (pres. 1981-82), Nat. Edn. Assn., Tenn. Edn. Assn., Met. Nashville Edn. Assn., Mid. Tenn. Edn. Assn., Phi Delta Kapp (v.p. 1982-84). Office: McGavock High Sch 3150 McGavock Pike Nashville TN 37214

NICHOLSON, MYREEN MOORE, researcher, artist; b. Norfolk, Va., June 2, 1940; d. William Chester and Illeen (Fox) Moore; m. Roland Quarles Nicholson, Jan. 9, 1964 (div. 1978); children: Andrea Joy, Ross; m. Harold Wellington McKinney II, Jan. 18, 1981; 1 child, Cara Isadora. BA, William and Mary Coll., 1962; MLS, U. N.C., 1971; postgrad. Dominion U. 1964-67, 75-87, The Citadel, 1968-69, Hastie Sch. Art, 1968, Chrysler Mus. Art Sch., 1964-64. English tchr., Chesapeake, Va., 1962-63; dept. head, Portsmouth (Va.) Bus. Coll., 1963-64; tech. writer City Planning/Art Commn., Norfolk, 1964-65; art tchr. Norfolk pub. schs., 1965-67; prof. lit., art Palmer Jr. Coll., Charleston, S.C., 1968; librarian Charleston Schs., 1968-69; asst. to asst. dir. and dir. City Library Norfolk, 1970-72, art librarian, 1972-75, research librarian, 1975-83, asst. head fiction, 1983—; dir. W. Ghent Arts Alliance, Norfolk, 1978—. Poet-in-schs., Virginia Beach, Va., 1987. Book reviewer Art Book Revs., Library Jour., 1973-76; editor, illustrator Acquisitions Bibliographies, 1970—; contbr. art and poetry to various publs. Mem. Virginia Beach Arts Ctr., 1978—, Peninsula Art Ctr., 1983—; bd. dirs. W. Ghent Art/Lit. Festival, 1979. Recipient various art and poetry contests; Coll. William and Mary art scholar, 1958; Nat. Endowment Arts grantee, 1975. Mem. ALA (poster sessions rev. com. 1985-87, pub. relations judge, subcom. communications 1988-90), Pub. Library Assn. (com. bylaws and orgns 1988-90), Va. Library Assn. (pub. relations com. 1984-86, grievance and pay equity com. 1986-88, Logo award 1985), Southeastern Library Assn. (Rothrock award com. 1986-88), Poetry Soc. Va. (eastern pres. 1986—) Art Libraries Soc. N.Am., Tidewater Artists Assn., Southeastern Coll. Art Assn., Acad. Am. Poets, Internat. Platform Assn. (artists assn., selected judge speaking ladder 1988—), Old Dominion U. Alumni Assn. (artistic dir.), Southeastern Soc. Archtl. Historians, Ikara (pres. 1986—). Home: 1404 Gates Ave Norfolk VA 23507 Office: Norfolk Pub Library 301 E City Hall Ave Norfolk VA 23510

NICHOLSON, RUBY NELL PEAKE, education educator; b. Phil Campbell, Ala., May 13, 1940; d. Freeman A. and Ruby E. (Wood) Peake; m. Lawrence Cummings Jr., May 18, 1955 (div. June 1967); children: Sharon L. Wells, Reneé Cummings, Julie Cummings; m. Hugh P. Nicholson, Feb. 13, 1975 (div. June 1982). BS in Edn., U. North Ala., 1962, MA, 1967; EdD, U. Ala., 1970. Classroom tchr. Tuscumbia (Ala.) Bd. Edn., 1962-67; assoc. prof. Ala. Agrl. and Mech. U., Huntsville, 1970-75, prof., 1975—, chair dept. elem. early childhood edn., 1981—; cons., instr. U.S. Army Corps Engrs., Huntsville, 1978-86. Author: Reading and Self-Concept, 1970. Apptd. mem. Ala. Women's Commn., Montgomery, 1983—, sec., 1986-88. Mem. Phi Delta Kappa (pres. 1985—), Kappa Delta Pi (counselor, nat. com. 1986-88). Home: 3714 Oakdale Ct Huntsville AL 35810 Office: Ala Agrl and Mech U Meridian St Box 281 Normal AL 35762

NICHOLSON BOLLING, CAROL, personnel director; b. Jamaica, N.Y., Jan. 28, 1952; d. Paris Oliver Jr. and Miriam (Riley) N.; m. Bruce Bolling, Dec. 27, 1980. BA, SUNY, 1976. Group leader collections Gillette Co., Boston, 1977-78, group leader adjustments, 1978, asst. supr. sales order, 1978-80, supr. records and files, 1980-81, administr. affirmative action, 1983-84, recruiter personnel, 1981-83, sr. rep. personnel, 1984-86, corp. mgr. employee relations, 1986-87; mgr. human resources Sta. WCVB-TV, Needham, Mass., 1987—; bd. dirs. Roxbury Comprehensive Health Ctr., 1988. Bd. dirs. Big Sisters Assn., 1985—, Robert F. Kennedy Action Corp., 1987—. Named one of 10 Outstanding Young Woman of Boston, Jaycees, 1986, one of Outstanding Young Women of Am, Outstanding Young Women of A. Assn., 1984. Mem. Black Enterprise Mag. Forum (mem. com. 1987), Boston Black Profl. Media Dialogue (mem. com. 1987), YMCA (bd. dirs. 1988), Mus. Afro Am. History (bd. dirs. 1986—), Personnel Mgmt. Council, Assn. Affirmative Action Profls. Democrat. Methodist. Club: New England Circle. Home: 64 Harold St Boston MA 02119 Office: Sta WCVB-TV 5 TV Place Needham MA 02192

NICKEL, CATHERINE ANN, Spanish language educator; b. Urbana, Ill., June 2, 1946; d. Curtis Gerald Chapman and Dorothy (Stahle) Chapman Ealy; m. Robert K. Nickel, Dec. 18, 1971. Student, El Colegio de Mex., Mexico City, 1966-67; BA, U. Calif., Berkely, 1968; MA, U. Nebr., 1974, PhD, 1984. Mng. editor Jour. Spanish Studies: Twentieth Century, 1979-80, Soc. of Spanish and Spanish-Am. Studies, 1980-86; asst. editor Anales de la Literatura española contemporánea, 1985—; asst. prof. Spanish U. Nebr., Lincoln, 1985—; bd. dirs. Mid-Am. Conf. on Hispanic Lit., 1987. Mem. editorial bd. Studies in Twentieth Century Lit., 1979-80; contbr. articles on Spanish lit. to profl. jours. George Rogers fellow U. Nebr., 1979-84, Fling fellow, summer 1987. Mem. MLA, Am. Assn. Tchrs. of Spanish and Portuguese, Twentieth Century Spanish Assn. of Am. Office: U Nebr Dept Modern Langs and Lit 1110 Oldfather Hall Lincoln NE 68588-0315

NICKEL, ROSALIE JEAN, reading specialist; b. Hooker, Okla., Oct. 10, 1939; d. Edwin Charles and Esther Elizabeth (Wiens) Ollenburger; m. Ted W. Nickel, June 3, 1960; 1 child, Sandra Jean. BA, Tabor Coll., 1961; MA, Calif. State U., Fresno, 1970. Cert. tchr., Calif. Elem. tchr. Visalia (Calif.) Pub. Schs., 1961-62; overseas tchr. Kodaikanal Internat. Sch., Madras State, India, 1963-65; tchr. Mendota (Calif.) Jr. High Sch., 1966; elem. tchr. Fresno Pub. Schs., 1966-68, reading specialist, 1987—; elem. tchr. Inglewood (Calif.) Pub. Schs., 1976-78; spl. reading tchr. Tulsa Pub. Schs., 1974-81; salesperson, mgr. Compaq, Marion, Kans., 1981-85; gifted student tchr. Wichita (Kans.) Pub. Schs., 1986; evaluator State Textbook Com., Tulsa, 1976, 78. Newsletter editor Marion County Arts Council, 1981-82. Co-dir. Am. Field Service, Tulsa, 1980-81; v.p. Women's Federated Clubs Am., Marion, 1985-86. Mem. Internat. Reading Assn., Tulsa Reading Assn., Fresno Area Reading Council. Home: 6600 N Marls #59 Fresno CA 93711 Office: Fresno United Sch Dist Tulare and M Sts Fresno CA 93701

NICKEL, SUSAN EARLENE, physical education educator, financial analyst; b. Fort Madison, Iowa, June 27, 1951; d. Earl Dean and Irma Ellen (Ivins) N. BE, Northeast Mo. State U., 1973. Phys. edn. tchr. Ft. Madison (Iowa) Sr. High. Sch., 1974-79; phys. edn. specialist Los Angeles Unified Schs., 1979—; fin. planner, then mgr. Martin Fin. Services, Marina Del Rey, Calif., 1986—. Bd. dirs. Connexxus Womens' Ctr., Los Angeles, 1985-87, profl. women's facilitator, 1984—; vol. facilitator Los Angeles Womens' Ctr., 1981-84; vol. Spl. Olympics, U.S. Assn. for Blind Athletes, Exceptional Games, Women's Wheelchair Basketball Assn., all Los Angeles. Mem. Los Angeles Adapted Phys. Edn. Assn. (bd. dirs.), Calif. Assn. Health, Phys. Edn., Recreation and Dance, Bus. and Profl. Alliance, Nat. Assn. Female Execs. Office: Martin Fin Services 13160 Mindanao Way Marina del Rey CA 90292

NICKELL, SHERI MARIE, gift company owner; b. Kalispell, Mont., Oct. 11, 1945; d. Reuben F. and Mildred M. (Frye) Hoiland; m. Delmer A. Nickell, Oct. 18, 1963 (div. 1987); children: Lynn Marie, Jay D. Grad., Ellensburg (Wash.) High Sch., 1963. Homemaker, dressmaker, sales rep. Montgomery Wards, Ellensburg, 1967-71, Sears, Ellensburg, 1967-71; founder, owner Agapesound Prodns., Ellensburg, 1970-79; freelance comml. artist Ellensburg, 1963-83; founder, owner Am. Heartwarmer, Ellensburg, 1983—. Republican. Roman Catholic. Office: Am Heartwarmer Rt 1 Box 318 Ellensburg WA 98926

NICKERSON, RUTH, sculptor; b. Appleton, Wis., Nov. 23, 1905; d. Robert Wellington and Kate Mary (Ellis) N.; m. Edmund Greacen, Jr., Dec. 30, 1935; children: Elizabeth Ruth, Barbara Eleanor. Ed., Simcoe Collegiate Inst., 1921-23, Nat. Acad. Schs., 1928-32. Works represented in permanent collections, Newark Mus., Cedar Rapids, Iowa, Art Assn., New Brunswick, N.J., Post Office, Eden, N.C., children's br. Bklyn. Pub. Library, New Rochelle City Hall, Grasslands Hosp., Valhalla, N.Y., Montclair (N.J.) Mus. Art, Interchurch Center, N.Y.C. Mem. White Plains Civic Arts Commn., 1948-60. Recipient Nat. Arts Club medal, 1933, Saltus Gold medal N.A.D., 1933, Montclair Mus. medal, 1936, Am. Artists Profl. League medal, 1947, Allied Artists Religious award, 1981, Therese Wright Richard award Nat. Sculpture Soc., 1982; Guggenheim fellow, 1946-47. Fellow Nat. Sculpture Soc. (council 1981-83); mem. N.A.D. (diplomate, council mem. 1978-81), Audubon Artists. Address: 106 Woodcrest Ave White Plains NY 10604

NICKERSON, SANDRA L., personnel services company executive; b. Denver, Oct. 26, 1943; d. Edward Kell and Bettye Aileen (Murphy) Brinsa; m. Stanley R. Nickerson, Sept. 2, 1961; children: David Wayne, Robert Edward. Grad. high sch., Englewood, Colo. Sales rep. Russell Stover Candies, Kansas City, Mo., 1977-80, Perma Temps, Denver, 1980-82; personnel asst. Swedish Med. Ctr., Denver, 1982-83; sales rep. Stivers Temp. Personnel, Denver, 1983-84, asst. br. mgr., 1984-85, br. mgr., 1985-87, dist. mgr., 1987—; speaker in field. Mem. Nat. Mgmt. Assn. (bd. dirs. 1985—), Colo. Assn. Temp. Services (bd. dirs. 1986—). Lutheran.

NICKLAS, DEBORAH SIMON, hospital planning and marketing administrator; b. Washington, Dec. 30, 1955; d. Martin Stanley and Rita Edith (Scheinhorn) S. B.A., Ithaca Coll., 1978; M.P.A. (scholar), U. So. Calif., 1981. Asst. dir. admissions Ithaca Coll. (N.Y.), 1978-79; research analyst Nat. Med. Enterprises, Los Angeles, 1979-80, adminstrv. resident Inter-Community Med. Ctr., Covina, Calif., 1980-81, dir. planning and mktg., 1981-85, v.p. planning and mktg., 1985—; instr. U. So. Calif., 1982, 84, U. La Verne, 1985-87; mem. Hosp. Council Planning Com., 1983-87; editor Exchanges, So. Calif. Soc. Hosp. Planners, 1983. Mem. community adv. bd. Charter Oak Hosp., Covina, 1981-84; residency adv. com. U. So. Calif., 1981-87; mem. United Way Task Force on Aging. Mem. Women in Health Adminstrn. (area rep. 1982), Am. Mktg. Assn., Soc. Hosp. Planning, Am. Coll. Health Care Execs., Health Care Execs. So. Calif., U. So. Calif. Health Services Adminstrn. Alumni Assn. pres. 1984-85), Soc. Health Care Planning and Mktg. (pres. 1987). Office: Inter Community Med Ctr 303 N Third Ave Covina CA 91723

NICKLES-MURRAY, ELIZABETH ANNE, advertising executive, writer; b. Miami Beach, Fla., May 29, 1947; d. Arnold C. and Audrey (Reid) Nelson. B.S., Northwestern U., 1968; M.A., DePaul U., 1970. Creative supr. Esquire Inc., Chgo., 1975-76; copy supr. Marsteller Inc., Chgo., 1976-77; assoc. creative dir. J. Walter Thompson, Chgo., 1977-80; sr. v.p. D'Arcy MacManus Masius, Chgo., from 1980; now exec. v.p., creative dir., Warwick Advertising, N.Y.C.; cons. ptnr. Nickles & Ashcraft, Chgo., 1978—; founder & dir. Update: Women, research survey, 1980—. Author: The Coming Matriarchy, 1982, Girls in High Places, 1986. Contbr. articles to popular mags. Named Outstanding Young Woman Achiever Nat. Council Women U.S., 1982, All Time Top 10 Working Women Glamour Mag., 1984. Mem. Women's Advt. Club Chgo. (named Advt. Woman of Yr., 1982.). Office: Warwick Advt Inc 875 Third Ave New York NY 10022 *

NICKOLS, JO ANN MARY, health service administrator; b. Chgo., Aug. 21, 1949; d. Joseph Paul and Patricia (Tancredi) Ballerine; m. Joseph S. DePergola, May 15, 1971 (div. Nov. 1981); children: Stacy, B.J., Joseph; m. Albert L. Nickols, Mar. 30, 1987. Cert. in nursing, St. Mary of Nazareth Hosp. Ctr., Chgo., 1970. Staff nurse St. Mary of Nazareth Hosp. Ctr., Chgo., 1970-73; supr. Oxford Ln. Nursing Ctr., Naperville, Ill., 1979-81, dir. nursing, 1981-84; adminstr. Countryside Plaza Nursing Ctr., Dolton, Ill., 1984—. Bd. dirs. Critical Care Consultants, Woodridge, Ill., 1984. Mem. Ill. Council Long-Term Care. Democrat. Roman Catholic. Office: Countryside Plaza 1635 E 154th Dolton IL 60149

NICOL, MARJORIE CARMICHAEL, research psychologist; b. Orange, N.J., Jan. 6, 1926; d. Norman Carmichael and Ethel Sarah (Siviter) N.; BA, Upsala Coll., MS, 1978; MPh, PhD, CUNY, 1988. Art dir. Finneran Advt. Co., N.Y.C., 1944-47; mgr. advt. prodn. RCA, Harrison, N.J., 1948-58; advt. mgr., writer NPS Advt., East Orange, N.J., 1960-67; pres. measurement and eval., chief exec. officer, psychol. evaluator F.L. Merritt, Inc., Montclair, N.J., 1967—, chief exec. officer., dir. Rafiki, Essex County, N.J., 1965—; officer Montclair Rehab. Orgn., 1981-86; founder Met. Opera at Lincoln Center. Republican. Presbyterian. Author: Nicol Index. Home: 89 Linden St Millburn NJ 07041 Office: PO Box 111 Millburn NJ 07041

NICOLAÏ, JUDITHE, import-export company executive; b. Lawrence, Mass., Dec. 15, 1945; d. Victor and Evelyn (Otash) Abisalih; m. Charles M.J. Nicolaï (div. 1979); children: Michelle Marie, Monique Therese. Student in photography, Los Angeles City Coll., 1967, UCLA, 1971; AA in Fgn. Langs., Coll. of Marin, 1983; hon. degree, Culinary Inst., San Francisco, 1981. Photographer Scott Paper Co., N.Y.C., 1975; owner, operator restaurant The Raincheck Room, West Hollywood, Calif., 1976; photographer fashion Photographie, Nice, France, 1977; instr. catering and cooking Back to Basics, San Francisco, 1980; photographer exhbn. Agri-Bus. U.S.A., Moscow and Washington, 1983; head transp. U.S. Summer Olympics, Los Angeles, 1984; interpreter, prin. Intertrans div. NIS, San Francisco; founder, pres. Nicolaï Internat. Services, San Francisco, 1985; pres., chief exec. officer Photographie and Back-to-Basics divs. NIS, San Francisco, 1985—. Contbr. column on food and nutrition to jour., 1983-84. Episcopalian. Office: Nicolaï Internat Services and Intertrans-Photographie BTB 2269 Chestnut St Suite 237 San Francisco CA 94117

NICOLL, EMILY MARGARET WEBER, optometrist; b. Bklyn., Jan. 17, 1943; d. Peter Gerard and Emily (Schuerger) Weber; m. John Andrew Nicoll, May 20, 1967; children: Kathleen Ann, Michelle Marie. Student, Manhattanville Coll. Sacred Heart, 1961-63; BS, Pa. Coll. Optometry, 1965, OD, 1967. Pvt. practice optometry Wilmington, Del., 1967—; mem. State Bd. Examiners, Dover, Del., 1980-87, sec., 1982-85. Leader Girl Scouts U.S., Wilmington, 1978—. Recipient Appreciation award Capitol Trail Lions Club, 1974, Appreciation award Hockessin Yorklyn Lions Club, 1976. Mem. Am. Optometric Assn., Del. Optometric Assn. (sec. 1969-75), Better Bus. Bur. Roman Catholic. Home and Office: 2501 Limestone Rd Wilmington DE 19808

NICOLL, MARGARET GIBSON, marketing executive; b. Cape Girardeau, Mo., Apr. 23, 1950; d. Alexander Blair and Ruth Iva (Craig) Gibson; m. Phillip Grant Nicoll, Mar. 31, 1977; children: Meaghan Blair. BA, Duke U., 1973. Asst. editor Alumni Affairs, Duke U., Durham, N.C., 1973-76; reporter, editor Gazette Telegraph, Colorado Springs, Colo., 1977-83; asst. mktg. mgr. The Citadel/Rouse Co., Colorado Springs, 1983-84, mktg. mgr., 1984-85; group mktg. mgr. Salem Mall/Rouse Co., Dayton, Ohio, 1986-88, Westlake Ctr./Rouse Co., Seattle, 1988—. Mem. nominating com. Jr. League of Colorado Springs, 1979-84; bd. dirs. Colorado Springs Dance Theatre, 1979-82. Mem. Internat. Council of Shopping Ctrs., Colorado Springs Press Club (bd. dirs. 1980, Honorable Mention award 1979, 80). Lutheran. Office: Westlake Ctr Assoc 414 Olive Way Suite 500 Seattle WA 98101

NICOLOSI, DOROTHY EMILY, non-profit organization executive; b. N.Y.C., July 15, 1931; d. Thomas and Aurora (Scoppa) Nicolosi; B.S. in Edn., Fordham U., 1963, cert. Introductory Mgmt. Devel., 1967, cert. Advanced Mgmt. Devel., 1968; M. Public Adminstrn., N.Y. U., 1979. Exec. sec. Arabol Mfg. Co., N.Y.C., 1950-55; research asst. Smith Richardson Found., N.Y.C., 1955-60; cons. Robert A. Taft Meml. Found., Washington, 1960-61; asst. sec., office mgr. United Student Aid Fund, Inc., N.Y.C., 1961-63; sec., treas., exec. adminstr. Nat. Strategy Info. Center, Inc., N.Y.C., 1963-84, v.p., treas., 1984—, dir., 1978—. Mem. Am. Acad. Polit. and Social Sci., Am. Soc. Public Adminstrn., Acad. Polit. Sci. Republican. Roman Catholic. Home: 3103 Fairfield Ave Riverdale NY 10463

NIDETCH, JEAN, health service executive; b. Bklyn., Oct. 12, 1923; d. David and May (Rodin) Slutsky; children—David, Richard. Founder, pres. Weight Watchers Internat., Inc., Manhasset, L.I., until 1973, now cons.; cons. N.Y. State Assembly Mental Hygiene Com., 1968; adviser Joint Legis. Com. on Child Care Needs, Legislature N.Y.; pres. Weight Watchers Found. Author: Jean Nidetch: Weight Watchers Cookbook, 1966, The Story of Weight Watchers, 1970, Weight Watchers Party & Holiday Cookbook, 1984. Named Marketing Woman of Yr., Hon. Adm. Gt. Navy Nebr.; Woman of Year, Forest Hills Youth Assn.; recipient Woman of Achievement award, Speakers award Sales Promotion Execs. Assn. Mem. Washington Sq. Bus. and Profl. Womens Club, AFTRA. *

NIEBRUGGE, VICTORIA VIRGINIA, human resources executive; b. Detroit, Nov. 1, 1952; d. Frederick Gilbert and Dorothy Helen (McClary) N. BA, Ea. Mich. U., 1974, MA, 1976; grad. with highest hons., Am. Inst. Paralegal Studies, N.J., 1987. Cert. in employee relations law, Nat. Bd. Cert. Counselors. Mgr. corp. human resources Gelman Scis., Inc., Ann Arbor, Mich., 1975—; dir. Nova Group, Ann Arbor, 1986—, cons. Turning Point, Ann Arbor, 1984-86. Pres. SOS Community Crisis Ctr., Ypsilanti, Mich., 1983—; loaned exec. Washtenaw United Way, Ann Arbor, 1986-88; bd. dirs. Huron Residential Services For Youth, Ann Arbor, 1986—. Named one of Outstanding Young Women Am., 1987. Mem. Am. Bus. Woman's Assn. (pres. 1986-87, Woman of Yr. 1987), High Technol. Personnel Assn. (pres. 1987—), Profl. Speakers Assn. Mich. (bd. dirs. 1987—), Tau Beta Sigma. Home: PO Box 3236 Ann Arbor MI 48106

NIED, HARRIET THERESE, landscaping company executive; b. Elyria, Ohio, Apr. 3, 1923; d. Henry Andrew and Kataryn Patricia (Siekierska) Zaremba; m. Michael Ernest Nied, Aug. 22, 1942; children: Kathryn Marie, Judith Boynton, Michaeline Wideman, Ellan Murphy, Gregory Michael. With Censorship Office, El Paso, 1942-43; promotional salesperson Aluminum Co. Am., 1945-51; store mgr. Nied Garden Ctr. Co., Northfield, Ohio, 1960-78, sec., treas., 1978—. Consumer advocate. Recipient Commendation plaque Nordonia Hills C. of C., 1986. Mem. Women in Bus. (mem. scholarship com.), Nordonia PTA. Democrat. Roman Catholic.

NIEDERMEIER, CHRISTINE MARIE, lawyer, former state legislator; b. Bridgeport, Conn., Oct. 21, 1951; d. Jerome J. and Marie Perkins N.; A.B. in Govt., Georgetown U., 1973, J.D., 1977. Legis. analyst in housing and urban affairs Library of Congress, Washington, 1973-74; staff asst. to Gov. of Conn., Hartford, 1975; legis. asst. Congressman Christopher J. Dodd of Conn., Washington, 1975-77; assoc. Day, Berry and Howard, Hartford, Conn., summer 1976; schedule and advance aide Nat. Presdl. Campaign of Gov. Edmund G. Brown, Jr., 1976; admitted to Conn. bar, 1977, U.S. Dist. Ct. bar, 1977, D.C. bar, 1979; assoc. firm Trager and Trager, Fairfield, Conn., 1977-81, Winthrop, Stimson, Putnam and Roberts, Stamford, Conn., 1982-87; ptnr. Pullman, Comley, Bradley & Reeves, 1987—; mem. Conn. Ho. of Reps., 1979-87, former mem. appropriations com., govt. adminstrn. and elections com., energy and pub. utilities com., ad hoc legis. com. on arts, past chmn., ranking mem. transp. com., past chmn., mem. transp. and communications com. Nat. Conf. State Legislators. Lawyers com. rep. United Way Campaign, 1977-79; mem. Fairfield Rep. Town Meeting, 1977-79; mem. Democratic Town Com., Fairfield; bd. dirs. Conn. Audubon Soc.; mem. U. Bridgeport Law Sch. Fund Com., also bd. assocs.; former mem. Fairfield Parking Authority Adv. Com.; mem. Parents and Friends of Retarded Citizens, Inc.; former vice chmn. president's council Sacred Heart U.; mem. Fairfield County Heart Assn.; bd. dirs. Urban League Greater Bridgeport, Family Services, Woodfield, Music Found. for Handicapped; former mem. pub. affairs com., YWCA Greater Bridgeport Inc.; trustee Mus. Art, Sci. and Industry. Recipient Disting. Service award Georgetown U., 1973. Mem. ABA, Conn. Bar Assn., D.C. Bar Assn., Greater Bridgeport Bar Assn., Fairfield C. of C., Fairfield LWV.

NIEDLING, HOPE HOTCHKISS, dietitian; b. Meriden, Ill.; d. Bert and Myrle Glenn (Vaughn) Hotchkiss; student North Central Coll., 1939-40; B.S., U. Ill., 1943; M.S. in Food Sci. and Nutrition, U. Wis. 1974; m. Ivan Martin Niedling, June 26, 1948. Teaching dietitian Univ. Hosp., Balt., 1944; dietitian public sch. cafeterias, Balt., 1944-48; dir. admissions Thomas Sch. Retailing, Phila., 1954-55; instr. foods U. Wis., Stevens Point, 1967-68; food service supr., instr. Mid-State, N.Central and Fox Valley Tech. Insts., Wis., 1973-75; cons. dietitian nursing homes in Wis., 1973—. Chmn. Village of Plover Cancer Fund Drive, 1977-78; bd. dirs. Stout Found., U. Wis., 1977-87; sec.-treas. Joint Com. Edn. State of Wis., 1978—. Recipient Loyalty award U. Ill., 1978, award of merit U. Ill. Home Econs. Assn., 1979. Mem. Am. Dietetic Assn. (ho. of dels. 1974-77), Wis. Dietetic Assn., No. Wis. Dietetic Assn. (pres. 1971-73), Soc. Nutrition Edn., Nutrition Today Soc., Nutritionists in Bus., Wis. Assn. Registered Parliamentarians (state corr. sec. 1978-80), Wis. Fedn. Women's Clubs (1st v.p. 1978-80), U. Ill. Home Econs. Alumni Assn. (bd. dirs. 1972-78), Daus. Am. Colonists, Nat. Assn. Registered Parliamentarians, Wis. Public Health Assn. (mem. aging com. 1974-78), Portage County Humane Soc. (sec. 1973-84), Wis. Fedn. Women's Clubs (pres. 1980-82), Gen. Fedn. Women's Clubs (sec.-treas. region 1982-84, chmn. internat. aid div. 1982-84, pres. Gt. Lakes region 1984-86, fundraiser chmn. Gt. Lakes Regional 1986-88), Colonial Dames XVII Century (chpt. 1st v.p. 1981-83, chpt. pres. 1983—), DAR (sec. 1977-80, 1st vice regent 1980-83, state regent 1983-86, chpt. regent 1972-77, chpt. registrar 1977—, pres. Wis. state officers club 1976-77, nat. bd. mgmt. 1983—, v.p. gen. 1987-90, pres. v.p. gens. club, 1988—, nat. chmn. lineage research com. 1986-89, nat. social mem. commn. 1986—), AAUW (pres. br. 1968-72, state corr. sec. 1970-72), U. Ill. Alumni Assn. (dir. 1973), NCCJ (disting. merit citation 1976; vice chmn. Wis. region 1975—; Portage County chmn. Nat. Brotherhood Week 1972—), Portage County Bicentennial of Const. of U.S., Wis. Soc. Children Am. Revolution (sr. state corr. sec. 1984-86, sr. state 1st v.p. 1986—), Wis. Soc. Am. Revolution (state organizing sec.), Children of the Am. Revolution, Nat. Soc. Women Descendants Ancient and Honorable Artillery Co., Nat. Soc. Daughters Founders and Patriots of Am., Soc. Descendants Washington's Army at Valley Forge, Hereditary Order of First Families of Mass., Wis. Fedn. Republican Women (dist. chmn. 1969-74), Gamma Sigma Delta, Epsilon Sigma Omicron. Methodist. Clubs: Stevens Point Area Woman's (pres. 1972-74, 76-78). Lodge: Order Eastern Star, Order of Amaranth, Order White Shrine of Jerusalem. Address: 1008 3rd St Stevens Point WI 54481

NIEDOJADLO, LINDA FRANCES, manufacturing executive, small business owner; b. Norwich, Conn., July 5, 1943; d. Charles Lord Webster and Josephine A. Murawski; m. Robert J. Niedojadlo, Dec. 20, 1963 (div.). Grad. high sch., Colchester, Conn., 1959. Lic. greyhound breeder, Conn., Mass., N.H., Vt. From field acct. to acctg. mgr. F. H. McGraw & Co., Hartford, Conn., 1959-69; from controller to v.p. ACME Enterprises Corp., Hartford, 1969-82; acctg. mgr. Savage Engring., Inc., Bloomfield, Conn., 1982-84; with Nutmeg Piping Services, Inc., Colchester, 1984—; from acct mgr. to pres. Nutmeg Pipe Supply, Inc., Colchester, 1985—; owner Linwood Greyhounds Trg. and Breeding Facilities, Oneco, Conn., 1987—. Mem. Nat. Greyhound Assn., Conn. Soc. Genealogists. Home: Mac Donald Rd Colchester CT 06415 Office: Nutmeg Pipe Supply Homonick Rd Colchester CT 06415 also: Linwood Greyhounds PO 216 Rt 14A Oneco CT 06373

NIELSEN, LISA TAGE, marketing consulting company executive; b. Glen Ridge, N.J., June 8, 1946; d. Axel Tage and Winifred Phyllis (Eisenhart) N.; divorced; children: Abby, Molly. Student Skidmore Coll., 1964-65; BA, U. Miami, 1968, MBA, 1973. Circulation trainee Miami Herald Pub. Co. (Fla.), 1972-74, research mgr., 1974-76; research mgr. Gannett Rochester Newspapers (N.Y.), 1976-77; sr. media analyst Market Opinion Research, Detroit, 1977-78, mgr. media div., 1978-81, v.p. media research, 1981-84; owner, pres. Market Link Co., 1984-88; v.p. Market Opinion Research, Detroit, 1988—. Mem. Women in Communications (v.p. Detroit chpt. 1981-82), Internat. Newspaper Promotion Assn. Episcopalian. Clubs: Econ. of Detroit, Women's Econ. Home: 19961 Norton Ct Grosse Pointe Woods MI 48236 Office: 19830 Mack Ave Grosse Pointe Woods MI 48236

NIELSEN, NANCY ANNE, data processing specialist; b. Salem, Mass., Sept. 12, 1934; d. Frank Ellwood and Myrtle Annie (Peterson) Root; B.A. in Math., U. N.H., 1957; m. Glenn Foster Nielsen, Nov. 27, 1959; children—Peder Root, Edward Stapleford. Programmer Rand Corp., Hanscom Field, Lexington, Mass., Topsham AFS, Maine, 1957-58; sr. programmer analyst System Devel. Corp., Santa Monica, Calif., 1958-60, 1960-62; engring. programmer Litton, Canoga Park, Calif., 1964; programming cons. Am. Inst. for Research, West Los Angeles, 1963-64; sr. programmer analyst System Devel. Corp., Santa Monica, 1965-69, sect. head, 1969-79, computer systems specialist, 1979-84, sr. systems specialist, staff systems specialist Systems Devel. Corp. (now part of Unisys Corp.), 1984—; tech. cons. U.S. Air Force. Den leader, troop com. sec. Boy Scouts Am., 1971-75; vestry mem. St. Martin-in-the Fields Episcopal Ch., 1972-74, clk. of the vestry, 1984. Mem. System Devel. Corp. Mgmt. Assn. Club: Canoga Park Jr. Women's. (safety chmn., treas. 1963-65). Home: 5774 Willow View Dr Camarillo CA 93010

NIELUBOWICZ, MARY JOAN, retired naval officer, nurse; b. Shenandoah, Pa., Feb. 5, 1929; d. Joseph John and Ursula Elizabeth (Czepukaitis) N. Diploma in Nursing, Misericordia Hosp., Phila., 1950; B.S. in Nursing, U. Colo., 1961; M.S. in Nursing, U. Pa., 1965. R.N., Pa. Commd. ensign U.S. Navy, 1951, advanced through grades to rear admiral 1983, retired, 1987; dir. nursing service, Portsmouth, Va., 1979-83, dep. comdr. health care ops. Naval Med. Command, Washington, from 1983, dir. Navy Nurse Corps, from 1983-87. Decorated Navy Commendation medal, Meritorious Service award, Legion of Merit. Mem. Am. Nurses Assn., Nat. League Nursing, Assn. Nurse Execs., Assn. Mil. Surgeons of U.S. (chmn. nursing sect. 1984), Sigma Theta Tau. Republican. Roman Catholic.

NIEMANN, CHRISTI CAY, paralegal; b. Valparaiso, Ind., Oct. 5, 1956; d. Harold Wilson Jr. and Alice Eileen (Wild) Williams; m. Richard Roy Niemann, Nov. 1, 1980; 1 child, Jeffrey Patrick. BA, Bethany Bible Coll., 1978. Lic. ins. adjuster, Alaska; cert. tchr. Calif. Tchr. Foothill Christian Sch., Milpitas, Calif., 1978-79; account exec. Murray, Bradley & Peterson Pub. Relations, Anchorage, Alaska, 1979-81; claims adjuster Providence Washington Ins., Anchorage, 1981-82; workers compensation claims supr. Am. Internat. Adjustment Co., Anchorage, 1982-83; paralegal Staley, DeLisio, Code & Sherry, Anchorage, 1983-84, Mason & Griffin, Anchorage, 1985—. Co-editor: Lighter Than Air Cookbook, 1980. Bd. dirs. Abbott Loop Community Council, Anchorage, 1982-84. Mem. Alaska Pub. Interest Research Group, Alaska Assn. Legal Assts., Pub. Relations Soc. Am., Advt. Fedn. Alaska, Alaska Adjusters Assn. Republican. Office: Mason & Griffin 1600 A St Suite 101 Anchorage AK 99501

NIEMEYER, MAXINE BREWER, ins. exec.; b. Detroit, Jan. 14, 1920; d. Daniel Frederick and Ella (Case) Niemeyer; student Detroit Coll. Bus., 1938-39, Exec. Sec. Asso. (hon.), 1960; grad. Dale Carnegie course, 1946; student Wayne U., 1958, Wayne State and U. Mich. Extension Schs., 1961-64, 65—. Gen. office clk. Hart Sewing Machine Supplies Co., Detroit, 1938-39; cashier, sec. N.Am. Life Assurance Co., Detroit, 1939-41, office mgr., 1942-43; office mgr. L.A. Walden & Co., Detroit, 1943-46; asst. office mgr. Dr. Ralph H. Pino, Ophthalmologist, Detroit, 1946-48; registrar Leadership Tng., Inc., Detroit, 1948-50; sec. to mgr. market analysis and dealer orgn dept. Sales div. Chevrolet Motor Co., Detroit, 1950-56; office mgr., sec. to Walter R. Cavanaugh, C.L.U., 1956—, corp. sec. 1958—, mgr. policyholders service and sales promotion, 1966; agy. mgr. Phoenix Mut. Life, also owner and pres. M.B. Niemeyer CLU & Assos., 1966—; pres. Bus. and Estate Fin. Coordinators Inc.; advanced underwriting cons., agt., surplus lines mgr. Phoenix Cos.; registered rep. Phoenix Equity Planning Corp. Named Detroit Sec. of Yr. Detroit chpt. Nat. Secs. Assn. Internat., 1960, One of Top Ten Working Women Central Bus. Dist. Assn., Detroit, 1965; C.L.U.; chartered fin. counselor; lic. life ins. counselor. Mem. Nat. Secs. Assn. (pres. Detroit chpt. 1962-64), Detroit Assn. Life Underwriters (pres. 1974-75), Am. Soc. C.L.U.s (past regional dir.; pres. Detroit chpt. 1973-74), Am. Coll. C.L.U.s (trustee), Million Dollar Round Table, Fin. and Estate Planning Council Detroit (dir.), Life Ins. Leaders Mich., Mich. Assn. Life Ins. Counselors (dir.), Internat. Assn. Fin. Planners, Alpha Iota Internat. (chpt. pres. 1944). Presbyterian. Club: Soroptimist (pres. 1972—) (Grosse Pointe, Mich.). Home: 1792 Vernier Rd Grosse Pointe Woods MI 48236 Office: 3000 Town Ctr Suite 202 Southfield MI 48075

NIEMI, JANICE, state legislator, lawyer; b. Flint, Mich., Sept. 18, 1928; d. Richard Jesse and Norma (Bell) Bailey; m. Preston Niemi, Feb. 4, 1953; children—Ries, Patricia. B.A., U. Wash., 1950, LL.B., 1967; postgrad. U. Mich., 1950-52; cert. Hague Acad. Internat. Law, Netherlands, 1954. Bar: Wash. 1968. Assoc. firm Powell, Livengood, Dunlap & Silverdale, Kirkland, Wash., 1968; staff atty. Legal Service Ctr., Seattle, 1968-70; judge Seattle Dist. Ct., 1971-72, King County Superior Ct., Seattle, 1973-78; acting gen. counsel, dep. gen. counsel SBA, Washington, 1979-81; mem. Wash. State Ho. of Reps., Olympia, 1983-87, chmn. com. on state govt., 1984; mem. Wash. State Senate, 1987—; sole practice, Seattle, 1981—; mem. White House Fellows Regional Selection Panel, Seattle, 1974-77, chmn., 1976, 77; incorporator Sound Savs. & Loan, Seattle, 1975. Bd. dirs. Allied Arts, Seattle, 1971—, Ctr. Contemporary Art, Seattle, 1981-83, Women's Network, Seattle, 1981-84, Pub. Defender Assn., Seattle, 1982-84; bd. visitors dept. psychology U. Wash., Seattle, 1983-87; bd. visitors dept sociology, 1987— . Named Woman of Yr. in Law, Past Pres.'s Assn., Seattle, 1971; Woman of Yr., Matrix Table, Seattle, 1973, Capitol Hill Bus. and Profl. Women, 1975. Mem. Wash. State Bar Assn., Wash. Women Lawyers. Democrat. Office: 226 Summit Ave E Seattle WA 98102

NIEMI, KAROL TONI, interior designer; b. Longview, Wash., Feb. 16, 1949; d. Albert Howard and Toini Kathryn (Vahala) N.; m. Dennis Eugene Datke, Oct. 19, 1973. B in Interior Architecture, U. Oreg., 1971. Sr. designer Zimmer, Gunsul, Frasca Architects, Portland, Oreg., 1971-76, Yakeley Assocs., Architects, Cambridge, Eng., 1977-78; owner, prin. Karol Niemi Assoc. Interior Planning and Design, Portland, 1978—. Prin. works include Providence Med. Ctr., Pacific NW Bell Lincoln Bldg., VNA Corp. Hdqrs., Wanke Cascade Hdqrs., St. Vincent's Med. Ctr., Emanuel Hosp and Health Ctr., Crabbe-Huson Corp. Hdqrs.; works represented in profl. jours.; contbr. articles to profl. jours. Bd. dirs. Pacific Ballet Theatre, Portland, Oreg., 1984-85; bd. dirs. Oreg. Sch. Design, Portland, 1984-87; mem. bd. visitors U. Oreg. Recipient Am. Cermaic Tile Inst. award, 1982. Mem. Inst. Bus. Designers (corp. mem.), Found. for Interior Design Edn. Research (mem. nat. bd. vis. 1985-88). Office: Karol Niemi Assocs 1020 SW Taylor Suite 880 Portland OR 97205

NIES, HELEN WILSON, federal judge; b. Birmingham, Ala., Aug. 7, 1925; d. George Earl and Lida Blanche (Erckert) Wilson; m. John Dirk Nies, July 10, 1948; children: Dirk, Nancy, Eric. B.A., U. Mich., 1946, J.D., 1948. Bar: Mich. 1948, D.C. 1961, U.S. Supreme Ct. 1962. Atty. Dept. Justice, Washington, 1948-51, Office Price Stblzn., Washington, 1951-52; assoc. Pattishall, McAuliffe and Hofstetter, Washington, 1960-66; resident ptnr. Pattishall, McAuliffe and Hofstetter, 1966-77; ptnr. Howrey & Simon, Washington, 1978-80; judge U.S. Ct. Customs and Patent Appeals, 1980-82, U.S. Ct. Appeals Fed. Circuit, 1982—; mem. jud. conf. U.S. Com. on Bicentennial of Constitution; mem. public adv. com. trademark affairs Dept. Commerce, 1976-80; mem. adv. bd. BNA's Patent Trademark and Copyright Jour., 1976-78; bd. visitors U. Mich. Law Sch., 1975-78; adv. for restatement of law of unfair competition Am. Law Isnt., 1986; speaker World Intellectual Property Orgn., Forum of Judges, Calcutta, 1987; lectr. in field. Contbr. articles to legal jours. Anne E. Shipman Stevens scholar, 1945-47; recipient Athena Outstanding Alumna award U. Mich., 1987. Mem. ABA (chmn. com. 203, 1972-74, com. 504, 1975-76), Bar Assn. D.C. (chmn. patent trademark copyright sect. 1975-76, dir. 1976-78), U.S. Trademark Assn. (chmn. lawyers adv. com. 1974-76, dir. 1976-78), Am. Patent Law Assn., Fed. Bar Assn., Nat. Assn. Women Lawyers (Woman Lawyer of Year 1980), Order of Coif, Phi Beta Kappa, Phi Kappa Phi. Office: US Court of Appeals 717 Madison Pl NW Washington DC 20439

NIETFELDT, CHERYL M., real estate executive; b. Central City, Nebr., May 20, 1952; d. Joe A. and Helen M. (Janky) Ruzicka; m. Norman L. Nietfeldt, June 30, 1973; children: Ryan N., Bradley J. Student, Spencer Sch. Bus., 1971, Dale Carnegie, 1985. Office sec. Hornady Mfg., Grand Island, Nebr., 1971-72; receptionist Da-ly Realty, Grand Island, Nebr., 1972-74; real estate salesperson Winkler Realty, Grand Island, Nebr., 1974-75; receptionist, sec. Alvin Alms, CPA, Grand Island, Nebr., 1975-76; with admissions St. Francis Med. Ctr., Grand Island, Nebr., 1976-79; bookkeeper Nietfeldt Plumbing Co., Grand Island, Nebr., 1978—; real estate salesperson Realty World-F.J. Pollard & Assocs., Grand Island, Nebr., 1983—. Mem. Grand Island Bd. Realtors (mem. com. 1985-86, sec., treas. 1986-87, v.p. 1987-88, bd. dirs. 1986-88), Nebr. Realtors Assn. (hon. soc. 1986-87), Million Dollar Club. Democrat. Lutheran. Club: Grand Island Saddle. Lodge: Eagles. Office: Realty World-F J Pollard & Assocs 2504 N Webb Rd Grand Island NE 68803

NIEVES, PRISCILLA, commodities trading co. exec.,; b. San Juan, P.R., Dec. 14, 1950; d. Benito and Benita (Nieves-Jimenez) Nieves-Baez; B.A. (Alice Baldwin scholar), Duke U., 1972; M.B.A., U. N.C., 1977; m. Andrew E. Cardwell, July 2, 1981. Part-owner Waste Paper & Equipment, Durham, N.C., 1976-79; asst. brand mgr. Legg's Products div. Hanes Hosiery, Winston-Salem, N.C., 1977-79; asst. brand mgr. Miller Brewing Co., Milw., 1979; brand mgr. Wine Spectrum, Coca-Cola, Atlanta, 1979-82; partner Cardwell Nieves Inc., Atlanta, 1982—. Mem. High Mus. Art, Found. of Truth. Roman Catholic. Address: 15 Parkgate Dr Atlanta GA 30328

NIEWEGLOWSKI, CONNIE SUE, business program analyst; b. Red Bud; d. John Eugene and Lona Frances (Miller) N. BS in Computer Sci., Quincy Coll., 1984. Assoc. bus. programmer McDonnell Douglas Corp., Hazelwood, Mo., 1985-86; bus. programmer, analyst McDonnell Douglas Corp., Hazelwood, 1986-88; program analyst Southwestern Bell Telephone, St. Louis, 1988—. Roman Catholic.

NIGHORN, SHARON KAY, nurse educator, psychotherapist; b. Chgo., Mar. 21, 1956; d. Richard Louis and Catherine Nighorn. AA, AAS, Harper Coll., 1975; BS in Nursing, No. Ill. U., 1977; MS, U. Ill. Med. Ctr., 1980. Cert. clin. specialist adult psychol. mental health, substance abuse counselor. Staff nurse N.W. Community Hosp., Arlington Heights, Ill., Ill. State Psychiat. Inst., Chgo.; supervising nurse Barclay Hosp., Chgo.; staff nurse Northwestern Meml. Hosp., Chgo., asst. head nurse; clin. mgr. Weiss Hosp. Lifeline Program, Chgo., 1985; instr. Rush Presbyn. St. Luke's, Chgo., 1986—, practitioner, tchr., 1986—; psychotherapist, group and independent practice, Chgo., 1987—; treas. Hypoglycemia Info. & Support Services, Chgo., 1985-88; v.p., bd. dirs. Peer Assistance Network for Nurses, Chgo., 1987, v.p., 1988. Mem. Nat. Assn. Female Execs., Nat. Nurses Soc. on Addiction, Nat. Assn. Neuro Linguistic Programmers (assoc.), Ill. Nurses Assn., ANA Council Clin. Specialists. Office: Rush Presbyn Sheridan Rd Hosp 6130 N Sheridan Chicago IL 60660

NIGHTINGALE, ELENA OTTOLENGHI, physician, geneticist, administrator; b. Livorno, Italy, Nov. 1, 1932; came to U.S., 1939; d. Mario Lazzaro and Elisa Vittoria (Levi) Ottolenghi; m. Stuart L. Nightingale, July 1, 1965; children—Elizabeth, Marisa. A.B. summa cum laude, Barnard Coll., 1954; Ph.D., Rockefeller U., 1961; M.D., NYU, 1964. Asst. prof. Cornell U. Med. Coll., N.Y.C., 1965-70; asst. prof. Johns Hopkins U., Balt., 1970-73; fellow in clin. genetics and pediatrics Georgetown U. Hosp., Washington, 1973-74; sr. staff officer Nat. Acad. Scis., Washington, 1975-79; sr. program officer Inst. Medicine, Nat. Acad. Sci., Washington, 1979-82, sr. scholar in residence, 1982-83; spl. advisor to pres. Carnegie Corp. of N.Y., N.Y.C., 1983—; vis. assoc. prof. Harvard U. Med. Sch., Boston, 1980-84, vis. lectr., 1984—; mem. recombinant DNA adv. com. NIH, Bethesda, Md., 1979-83. Editor: The Breaking of Bodies and Minds: Torture, Psychiatric Abuse and the Health Professions, 1985, Prenatal Screening, Policies and Values: The Example of Neural Tube Defects, 1987; contbr. numerous sci. articles to profl. publs. Bd. dirs. Ctr. for Youth Services, Washington, 1980-84, Sci. Service Inc., Washington, 1985—. Sloan Found. fellow, 1974-75. Fellow N.Y. Acad Scis., AAAS (chmn. com. on sci. freedom and responsibility 1985-88); mem. Harvey Soc., Am. Soc. for Microbiology, Am. Soc. for Human Genetics (social issues com. 1982-85), Genetics Soc. Am., Inst. of Medicine (chmn. com. on health and human rights), Nat. Acad. Scis., Phi Beta Kappa, Sigma Xi. Office: Carnegie Corp of NY 437 Madison Ave New York NY 10022

NIGOGHOSIAN, ALICE MARIE, university press executive, publishing consultant, editor; b. Detroit, Apr. 9, 1939; d. Sam and Agnes O. (Vartanian) N. B.A. in Mass Communications, Wayne State U., Detroit, 1969. Editorial and prodn. sec. Wayne State U. Press., Detroit, 1961-68, asst. prodn. mgr., 1968-69, 70-77, publishing prodn. coordinator, 1977-79, prodn. and design mgr., 1979—, assoc. dir., 1986—; on air promotion supr., writer Sta. WKBD-TV, Southfield, Mich., 1969-70. Editor: On the Urban Scene, 1972; The Professor & the Public, 1972; To Enforce Education, 1974; Detroit and Its Banks, 1974; Forty Years On: A History of Cranbrook School, 1976; Smith, Hinchman & Grylls, 1978, others; publishing cons. various books. Mem. Soc. Scholarly Pub., Founders Soc., Detroit Inst. Arts. Club: Book of Detroit. Office: Wayne State Univ Press 5959 Woodward AVe Detroit MI 48202

NIKLAUSKI, MARIANNE NANCY, cytotechnologist; b. Phila., Aug. 19, 1942; d. Edward S. and Pauline S. (Polner) Bay; student Pa. State U., 1960-63; degree in cytotech. U. Pa., 1964; m. Leonard Niklauski, Oct. 27, 1977. Cytotechnologist, Lower Bucks County Hosp., Bristol, Pa., 1964-65; supr. cytology, clin. lab. Walter G. Sawchak, Trenton, N.J., 1965-80; cytotechnologist MDS Labs., Cherry Hill, N.J., 1980-81; supr. cytology Torresdale div. Frankford Hosp., Phila., 1981—. Am. Cancer Soc. grantee, 1963. Mem. Am. Soc. Clin. Pathologists, Del. Valley Soc. Cytotechnologists. Home: 211 Cleveland Ave Edgewater Park NJ 08010 Office: Frankford Hosp Red Liom and Knights Rd Philadelphia PA 19114

NILES, BARBARA ELLIOTT, psychotherapist; b. Boston, Jan. 31, 1930; d. Byron Kauffman and Helen Alice (Heissler) Elliott; m. John Denison, June 25, 1960 (div. 1981); children: Catherine, Andrew. AA, Briarcliff Coll., 1958; BA, SUNT, 1984; MSW, Hunter Coll., 1986. Cert. social worker. Exec. com. Legal Aid Soc. Women's Aux., 1965-67; sec. Water Quality Task Force Scientists' Com. for Pub. Info., 1973-74; founding dir., sec. Consumer Action Now Inc., 1970-77; dir. devel. Consumer Action Now's Council Environ., 1976-77; dir. 170 Tenants Corp., 1979-81; mem. pub. interest com. Cosmopolitan Club, 1979-82; dir. INFORM Inc., 1978-84; pvt. practice psychotherapy and psychoanalysis 1986—. Editor: biography: Off the Beaten Track, 1984. Mem. Nat. Assn. Social Workers. Clubs: Cosmopolitan (N.Y.C.), The Vincent (Boston). Home: 170 E 79th New York NY 10021 Office: 903 Park Ave New York NY 10021

NILSEN, BARBARA YVONNE, lawyer, water utility executive; b. Glendale, Calif., Oct. 23, 1941; d. Allen Blair and Ina Lee (Stewart) Scott; A.A., San Jose City Coll., 1972; B.S. in Bus., San Jose State U., 1974; J.D. Lincoln U., 1983; m. William Nilsen, May 15, 1976; children—Tina, Valerie, Jamie Ng, Michael Ng. Dir. personnel, sec. San Jose Water Co., Calif., 1964—. Chmn. allocations panel Santa Clara County United Way, 1983, vice chmn. bd. trustees, 1986; bd. dirs. Central chpt., 1983-88; pres. League of Friends on Commn. Status of Women, 1984; pres. Seven Trees Village Homeowners Assn., 1974. Named Disting. Citizen of Yr., City of San Jose, 1981. Mem. Am. Water Works Assn. (sec. Calif./Nev. chpt. 1980, dir. 1982, conf. dir. 1986). Democrat. Roman Catholic. Clubs: Fairway Glen Women's Golf, San Jose Quota (pres. 1978-79). Office: 374 W Santa Clara St San Jose CA 95196

NINO, DIANNE DENISE, employment and training executive; b. Trinidad, Colo., Mar. 13, 1949; d. Vincent and Margaret (Romero) Abeyta; m. George Leonard Trancoso, Oct. 11, 1969 (div. Nov. 1976); 1 son, Brian; m. 2d, Daniel P. Nino, Dec. 10, 1983. Student Colo. Women's Coll.; A.A., Trinidad State Jr. Coll., 1969. Clk. U. Colo., 1967-68; loan clk. Mattel Credit Union, City of Industry, Calif., 1970-71; asst. office mgr. Power Equipment Co., Baldwin Park, Calif., 1972-73; office mgr. M.R. Schwarts, M.D., El Monte, Calif., 1973-74; personnel counselor SER-Jobs for Progress, Denver, 1974-77; tech. assistance specialist Nat. SER Office, Denver, 1977-80; exec. dir. SER-Jobs for Progress, 1980—; sec.-treas. El Dorado Denver Industries, 1983-85, chmn. bd., 1985—; treas. Denver Central Corp., 1982—. Chmn. bd. Denver Community Devel. Corp., 1981-84; vol. counselor Resource Ctr. for Battered Women, 1979; com. chmn. Hispanic Ann. Salute, Denver, 1980—; vol. campaigns Councilman Sandos and Mayor Pena, 1982-83, 87; mem. Denver Voter Registration and Edn. Project, 1983-87. Recipient Good Citizen award DAR, Trinidad, 1967; named Nat. SER Dir. of Yr., 1984; selected one of 20 nationally to participate in Leadership Initiative for Hispanic Women, Rutgers U., Harvard U., 1988. Mem. Nat. Assn. Female Execs., Am. G.I. Forum (Mile Hi chpt. chmn. 1979—), Nat. Assn SER Programs (2d v.p. 1987—). Democrat. Roman Catholic. Office: Denver SER-Jobs for Progress 2915 W 7th Ave Denver CO 80204

NISH, CATHY SONTAG, magazine publishing executive; b. N.Y.C., Dec. 21, 1959; d. Rollin Henry and Joan (Seltzerman) Sontag; m. James B. Nish, June 8, 1985. BBA, George Washington U., 1981. Home furnishings asst. Bloomingdale's, N.Y.C., 1981-82; research asst. Warner Pub. Services, N.Y.C., 1982-84; circulation analyst Hearst Corp., N.Y.C., 1984-85, bus. mgr. Motor Boating and Sailing mag., 1985-87, bus. mgr. Redbook mag., 1985—. Mem. Nat. Assn. Female Execs. Jewish. Office: The Hearst Corp 224 W 57 St New York NY 10019

NISHIO, DENYSE ANN, physician; b. Detroit, Feb. 19, 1951; d. John James and Pauline Marie (Mercier) Fox; m. James Neal Nishio, Dec. 30, 1976. B.S., U. Mich., 1972, M.D., 1976. Intern in ob-gyn U. Mich., 1976-77, intern in internal medicine, 1977-78, resident in internal medicine, 1978-80; practice medicine specializing in internal medicine; dir. acute care clinic U. Calif.-Davis, Sacramento, 1980—. Mem. Am. Med. Women's Assn. Home: 5050 Keane Dr Carmichael CA 95608

NIX, BARBARA LOIS, real estate broker; b. Yakima, Wash., Sept. 25, 1929; d. Martin Clayton and Norma (Gunter) Westfield; A.A., Sierra Coll., 1978; m. B.H. Nix, July 12, 1968; children—William Martin Dahl, Theresa Irene Dahl; step-children—Dennis Leon, Denise Lynn. Bookkeeper, office mgr. Lakeport (Calif.) Tire Service, 1966-69, Dr. K.J. Absher, Grass Valley, Calif., 1972-75; real estate sales and office mgr. Rough and Ready Land Co., Penn Valley, Calif., 1976-77, co-owner, v.p., sec., 1978—, also of Wildwood West Real Estate and Lake of the Pines Sales. Youth and welfare chmn. Yakima Federated Jr. Women's Club, 1957; den mother Cub Scouts, 1959-60; leader Girl Scouts, 1961-62; bd. dirs. Friends Hospice Sierra, Nev. Meml. Hosp. Found. Recipient Pres.'s award Sierra Coll., 1973; others. Mem. Penn Valley C. of C., Nat. Assn. Female Execs., Antique Soc. Penn Valley (founder, pres. 1978), St. Mary's Coll. Aux., Sierra Nevada Meml. Hosp. Aux., Nevada County Arts Council. Democrat. Roman Catholic. Clubs: Job's Daus. (life), Lady Elks. Home: 19365 Wildflower Dr Penn Valley CA 95946 Office: PO Box 191 Rough and Ready CA 95975

NIX, TISH ANDERSON, management consultant; b. Atlanta, May 7, 1950; d. Joe Terrell and Ellen (Brooks) Anderson; m. Paul Warren Nix, May 19, 1984; stepchildren: Warren, Brandee. BS in Criminology, West Ga. Coll., 1972. Mgr. Rich's, Atlanta, 1972-78; v.p. Garr Cons. Group, Marietta, Ga., 1978-85; prin. The Phoenix Ptnrship., Atlanta, 1985-86; sr. cons. Kurt Salmon Assocs., Atlanta, 1986—. Mem. Nat. Assn. Female Execs. Republican. Baptist.

NIX, YVONNE MARIA, corporate administrator; b. De Bilt, The Netherlands, Aug. 27, 1952; came to U.S., 1960; d. Leo and Tonia (Reiche) Nix. BSBA, Calif. State U., Los Angeles, 1975. Coordinator pub. relations Davis, Johnson, Mogul & Columbatto Advt., Los Angeles, 1975-77; rep. govt. relations ARCO, Los Angeles, 1977-79, adminstr. polit. action com., 1979-81, field coordinator civic action program, 1981-84, assoc. dir. polit. affairs, 1984-86, dir. polit. affairs and edns., 1986—, vice chair programs com. ARCO Forum, 1986-87, mem. programs com. ARCO Forum, 1987—. v.p. downtown Los Angeles chpt. Calif. Rep. League, 1984—, bd. dirs., 1984—, v.p. state, 1985—; assoc. mem. Calif. Rep. State Cen. Com., 1984-86, mem., 1986—. Named to Hon. Order Ky. Cols., 1981. Mem. Young Execs. Am. (chmn. communications Los Angeles county chpt.), Women in Pub. Affairs, Theta Gamma Chi. Republican. Roman Catholic. Office: ARCO 515 S Flower St Room 4079 Los Angeles CA 90071

NIXON, AGNES ECKHARDT, television writer, producer. m. Robert Nixon; 4 children. Student, Sch. Speech, Northwestern U. Writer for radio and TV; freelance writer for: TV programs Hallmark Hall of Fame, Robert Montgomery Presents, Studio One; creator, packager, head writer: daytime TV series All My Children; creator nighttime mini-series The Manions of America; creator, packager daytime TV series One Life to Live; creator, packager: daytime TV series Loving; co-creator: daytime TV series As The World Turns; formerly head writer, The Guiding Light, daytime TV series Another World. Recipient Trustees award Nat. Acad. TV Arts and Scis., 1981; Super Achiever award Jr. Diabetes Found.; Wilmer Eye Inst. award. Mem. Internat. Radio and TV Soc., Nat. Acad. TV Arts and Scis. Address: 774 Conestoga Rd Rosemont PA 19010

NIXON, JOYCE ELAINE, chiropractor, educator, consultant; b. Corning, N.Y., Feb. 17, 1925; d. Douglas Lewis and Mina Phiolana (Barnes) Williams; m. Lewis Earl Nixon, June 21, 1946 (div. Nov. 1958); 1 child, Deborah Joy. BA, Webster U., 1945; postgrad., SUNY, Geneseo, 1952-53; student, PBTS Bible Inst., 1946. Adminstr., chiropractic technician Dr. DeLue, Nunda, N.Y., 1958-85, cons., 1986—; instr. Sacro Occipital Research Soc. Internat., Inc., Omaha, 1966-79. Active Genessee Valley Council on Arts, Geneseo, 1967—; pres., bd. dirs. Nunda Community Home, Inc., 1983—. Mem. Internat. Platform Assn., N.Y. State Chiropractic Women's Aux., Nat. Assn. for Female Execs. (N.Y. State chpt.), Sacro Occipital Research Soc. (internat. sec. 1965-70, officer 1976, Disting. Profl. Service Founder's award 1976, Pres.' award 1980), N.Y. State Bus. and Profl. Women's Assn. (bd. dirs. 1963-71), Internat. Fedn. Bus. and Profl. Women, Geneva Bus. and Profl. Womens Clubs Inc. Republican. Home: 3 Meadowbrook Terr Dansville NY 14437

NIXON, (THELMA CATHERINE) PATRICIA RYAN, wife of former President of U.S.; b. Ely, Nev., Mar. 16, 1912; m. Richard Milhous Nixon, June 21, 1940; children: Patricia (Mrs. Edward Finch Cox), Julie (Mrs. Dwight David Eisenhower II). Grad. cum laude, U. So. Calif., 1937, L.H.D., 1961. X-ray technician N.Y.C., 1931-33; tchr. high schs. Cal., 1937-41; govt. economist 1942-45. Promoter of world wide humanitarian service, volunteerism in U.S. Decorated grand cross Order of Sun for relief work at time of massive earthquake, 1971; Peru; grand cordon Most Venerable Order Knighthood Pioneers Liberia, 1972; named among most admired women George Gallup polls, 1957, 68, 69, 70, 71. •

NIXON, TAMARA FRIEDMAN, economist; b. Cleve., June 3, 1938; d. Victor and Eva J. (Osteryoung) Friedman; B.A. with honors in econs. (Wellesley scholar), Wellesley Coll., 1959; M.B.A. (fellow), U. Pitts., 1961; m. Daniel D. Nixon, June 14, 1959; children—Asa Joel, Naomi Devorah, Victoria Eve. Asst. economist Fed. Res. Bank, N.Y.C., 1959-60, 61-62; economist R.P. Wolff Econ. Research, Miami, Fla., 1972-75; econ. cons., Miami, 1975-79; sr. v.p. Washington Savs. & Loan Assn., Miami Beach, Fla., 1979-81; pres. T.F. Nixon Econ. Cons. Inc., 1982—; sr. v.p. CenTrust Savs. Bank, 1984—; real estate feasibility cons.; investment adminstr. Land use chmn. Dade County chpt. LWV, 1975-76. Mem. Econ. Soc. S. Fla. (v.p. programs, dir.), Am. Econ. Assn. Office: CenTrust Savs Bank One CenTrust Fin Ctr Miami FL 33131

NJUGUNA, BEVERLY WOHNER, lawyer; b. Milw., Aug. 18, 1940; d. Joseph C. and Bernice (McCoy) Thomas; m. George M. Njuguna, Apr. 18, 1971 (div. Sept. 1982); 1 child, Mbugua. B.S. in Bus. Adminstrn., Roosevelt U., 1964; M.S.W., U. Wis.-Milw., 1968; J.D., U. Wis., 1979. Bar: Wis. 1980. Tng. coordinator Jane Addams Tng. Center for VISTA, Chgo., 1968-69; sch. social worker Chgo. Bd. Edn., Chgo., 1969-73; dir. social services Martin Center, Inc., Milw., 1974-77; assoc. Miller Law Offices, Milw., 1980-85, dir. YWCA Phillips Ctr., 1985-86, assoc. exec. dir. YWCA Greater Milw., 1987—. Mem. Task Force on Regulations and Restrictions, Gov.'s Conf. on Small Bus.; pres. Black Women's Network, Inc., 1980-82, 85—; regional coordinator Networking Together, Inc., 1984-86. Mem. ABA, State Bar Wis., Nat. Assn. Black Women Attys., Delta Sigma Theta. Baptist. Home: 1618 N 24th Pl Milwaukee WI 53205 Office: YWCA Greater Milw 3112 W Highland Blvd Milwaukee WI 53208

NOAH, HOPE ELLEN, editor, speech educator, broadcaster, writer; b. N.Y.C., Sept. 17, 1943; d. Mortimer and Anne (Forscher) Shaff; m. Lester Noah, Oct. 30, 1969 (div. July, 1985); children: Meredith Ayn, Allison Jane. BS in Speech, Emerson Coll., 1965. Cert. tchr. speech, English, drama, N.Y., N.J. Film producer Rossmore Prodns. and Selling Methods, Inc., N.Y.C., 1965-66; high sch. English tchr. New City, and Mt. Vernon, N.Y., Fair Lawn, N.J., 1966-73; pvt. teaching practice, profl. speech writer and cons. various locations, 1972—; sales rep. Wordex Corp., Fair Lawn, 1978-80; spl. assignment, summer sch. tchr. Fair Lawn Bd. Edn., 1980-81; writer weekly column A Single Look and spl. feature articles Bergen News, Palisades Pk., N.J., 1982—; producer, programmer, host weekly program "Hope with Singles" Sta. WMCA-Radio, N.Y.C., 1983-84; columnist, cons. Single Times, N.Y.C., 1984—; editor-in-chief N.J. Singles Mag., Totowa, 1985—, Single People mag., Dynasty Media Pubs., Englewood Cliff, N.J., 1985-86, Pizzazz, N.Y.C. tri-state entertainment mag., U.S. Pub. Inc., Rutherford, N.J., 1986—; pvt. practice advt. and pub. relations, small bus. cons., 1982—; dir. creative advt., creator of "Hope" columns, TODAY newspapers, Wayne, N.J., 1982-84; pub. speaker, guest radio and TV shows including The David Letterman program; cons. to industry, hosps.; performer comml. voice-overs; lectr. in field. Author: The Conversation Cookbook, 1988; columnist News Pub. Co., 1986—, Spotlight mag. 1987—. V.p., then pres. Ridgewood, N.J. B'Nai B'rith Women, 1976-78. Named one of Eighty-Five N.J. Residents to Watch N.J. Monthly Mag., 1985. Mem. AFTRA, Emerson Coll. Alumni Assn. Jewish. Home: 26 Leone Ct Geln Rock NJ 07452 Office: US Pub Inc 17 Sylvan St Rutherford NJ 07070

NOAKES, BILLIE SUSAN, cable television production manager; b. Aurora, Ill., Feb. 3, 1955; d. Richard Orville and Joan Susan (Melling) N.; m. Thomas Jeffrey Hart, July 26, 1975 (div. Nov. 1978). Editor Pinellas Park (Fla.) Beacon, 1979-81; pub. affairs dir. Vision Cable of Pinellas, Clearwater, Fla., 1981-85, pub. access dir., 1984-87, prodn. mgr., 1987—; free lance script writer, 1984—; cons., media specialist MediaMuses, Pinellas Park, 1986—. Author, editor: (with Tim Caddell) Selected Works of Incomplete Poets, 1986; contbr. articles to newspapers. Mem. Pinellas Park Library Bd., 1984—, Pinella Park Art Soc.; pres. Girls Club of Pinellas Park, 1985-87. Named one of Outstanding Young Women Am., 1982; recipient Broadcaster of Yr. award Pub. Relations Network, Pinellas County, 1986, Women Helping Women award Soroptomists Pinellas Park, 1987. Mem. Nat. Fedn. Local Cable Programmers, Pinellas C. of C. (bd. dirs. 1982-86, Outstanding Citizenship Service award 1982), Mensa (exec. com. Tampa Bay, Fla. 1985-87), Tampa Bay Objectivists. Republican. Club: Bay Area Rennies (Clearwater) (bd. dirs. 1987). Office: Vision Cable of Pinellas 2530 Drew St Clearwater FL 34625

NOBEL, JEAN ANNE, cytotechnologist, histologist; b. N.Y.C., Feb. 28, 1934; d. Robert and Irene May (McCullough) Ritchie; Cert. lab. tech., St. Francis Hosp., Jersey City, 1956; cert. histology East Orange Gen. Hosp., 1960; cert. cytology Presbyterian Hosp., Newark, 1971; m. James L. Nobel, Oct. 30, 1954 (div. Aug. 1986); 1 dau., Donna Jean Nobel Marsula. Supr. histology Kimball Med. Ctr., Lakewood, N.J., 1965-73, supr. histology and cytology, 1982—; supr. cytology Walson Army Hosp., Ft. Dix., N.J., 1973-75; cytotechnologist Obstet. Assocs., Bricktown, N.J., 1975-82. Leader Monmouth County and Ocean County councils Girl Scouts U.S.A., 1964-70; instr. Spl. Olympics Swimming, Ft. Dix, 1973-75. Mem. Greater N.Y. Assn. Cytotechnologists, N.J. Assn. Cytotechnologists, N.J. Histology Soc. Home: 22 Field St Toms River NJ 08753 Office: Kimball Med Ctr Lakewood NJ 08701

NOBLE, BARBARA RUTH, small business owner; b. Washington, Oct. 2, 1952; d. Franklin Eugene and Mary Ellen (Nash) Smith; m. Clay Alan Noble, Sept. 20, 1975; children: Beverly Ruth, Carol Anne, Craig Alan. BS in Nursing, Baylor U., 1975; cert., Southwestern Paralegal Inst., 1978. RN. Dir. nurses Permian Lodge, Inc., Midland, Tex., 1975-76; charge nurse Meml. Hosp., Seminole, Tex., 1977-78; head nurse, relief supr. Citizens Gen. Hosp., Houston, 1978—; legal asst. ed. malpractice Andrews & Kurth, Houston, 1978-80; legal asst. personal injury Butler & Binion, Houston, 1980-83; owner Noble Services, Houston, 1983—; lectr. in field. Contbg. author: State Bar of Tex. Seminar publ., 1983. Mem. Houston Legal Assts. Assn. (1st v.p. 1981-82, corr. sec. 1985-87, treas. 1980-81), Legal Assts. State Bar Tex. Republican. Episcopalian. Office: Noble Services 18303 Oakhampton Dr Houston TX 77084

NOBLES, LAURA EDWARDS, retail executive; b. Hartford, Ala., Nov. 13, 1954; d. Beverly Eugene and Laura (Ward) Edwards; m. Carl Wesley Nobles II, June 26, 1976 (div. Feb. 1982). Cert. in fashion merchandise, Bauber Fashion Coll., 1974. Asst. mgr. Leon's, Montgomery, Ala., 1974-75; mgr. dept. Pizitz, Montgomery, 1975-76; mgr. store, tng. Brooks, Montgomery, 1976-79; owner, mgr. Rag House, Wetompka, Ala., 1979-81; mgr. store Added Dimensions, Montgomery, Ala., 1981-82; mgr. area Added Dimensions, Jacksonville, Fla., 1982-83; mgr. dist. Added Dimensions, Ala., Miss., Fla., 1983—. Mem. Nat. Assn. Female Execs. Methodist. Home: 409 Green St Wetumpka AL 36092 Office: Added Dimensions 2981 E S Blvd Montgomery AL 36116

NOBLITT, MARTHA JANE, principal, educator; b. Shelby, N.C., Sept. 5, 1936; d. Perry Gold and Annie Mae (Grigg) N. BS, Appalachian State U., 1958, MS, 1963. Cert. tchr., N.C., S.C. Tchr. Gaston County Schs., Lowell, N.C., 1958-62; tchr., coach Lancaster (S.C.) High Sch., 1963-71, asst. prin., 1971-77; prin. McDonald Green Elem. Sch., Lancaster, 1977—. Mem. Palmetto State Tchrs. Assn. Democrat. Methodist. Home: PO Box 273 Lancaster SC 29720 Office: McDonald Green Elem Sch Rt 8 Jones Crossroads Lancaster SC 29720

NOBLITT, NANCY ANNE, aerospace engineer; b. Roanoke, Va., Aug. 14, 1959; d. Jerry Spencer and Mary Louise (Jerrell) N. B.A., Mills Coll., Oakland, Calif., 1982. Data red specialist, Universal Energy Systems, Beaver Creek, Ohio, 1981; aerospace engr. turbine engine div. components br. turbine group aero-propulsion lab. Wright-Patterson AFB, Ohio, 1982-84, engine assessment br. spl. engines group, 1984-87; lead analyst cycle methods computer aided engr. Gen. Electric Co., Lynn Mass., 1987—. Math and sci. tutor Centerville Sch. Bd., Ohio, 1982-86, math. and physics tutor Marblehead Sch. Bd., Mass., 1988—. Recipient Notable Achievement award U.S. Air Force, 1984; receipient Special award Fed. Lab. Consortium, 1987 . Avocation: book collecting. Home: 35 State St Marblehead MA 01945 Office: Gen Electric Co AEBG Lynn MA 01910

NOBOA-STANTON, PATRICIA LYNN, printing company executive; b. Cin., Sept. 6, 1947; d. William Emile and Marie Virginia (Ballbach) Hakes; m. Donald R. Stanton, Nov. 10, 1987; children from previous marriage: Aric Israel, Rene Carlos. Diploma Presbyn.-St. Luke's Sch. Nursing, Chgo., 1967. Supr. patient care Alexandria Hosp., Va., 1976-78; pres. Renaissance Reprographics, Inc., Reston, Va., 1985—; pres. Va. Leasing & Copying Inc., Reston, 1978—. Pres. Reston Bd. Commerce, 1985, founding bd. dirs. 1982-85, v.p. 1984, sec. 1983; v.p. Planned Community Archives, Inc., 1985-88; mem. regional com. United Way, 1985-87; Dulles Area Regional Council steering com., 1985-88; bd. dirs. N. Va. Local Devel. Corp., 1987—; bd. dirs. Fairfax Symphony. Named Reston Citizen of Yr., 1985; named Small Bus. Person of Yr. Fairfax County Commn. for Women, 1985-87. Mem. Nat. Assn. Quick Printers (bd. dirs. Capital chpt. 1984—, vice chair 1987—), Internat. Platform Assn., Fairfax County C. of C. (bd. dirs. 1985-86, 87—), Herndon C. of C., Washington-Dulles Task Force. Episcopalian. Lodge: Rotary. Avocations: computers, music, flying. Office: Reston Copy Ctr 11800 Sunrise Valley Dr Reston VA 22091 also: Renaissance Reprographics 13873 Park Center Rd Suite 137 Herndon VA 22071

NOCHMAN, LOIS WOOD KIVI (MRS. MARVIN NOCHMAN), educator; b. Detroit, Nov. 5, 1924; d. Peter K. and Annetta Lois (Wood) Kivi; A.B., U. Mich., 1946, A.M., 1949; m. Harold I. Pitchford, Sept. 6, 1944 (div. May 1949); children: Jean Pitchford Horiszny, Joyce Lynn Pitchford McGinnis; m. 2d, Marvin A. Nochman, Aug. 15, 1953; 1 son, Joseph Asa. Tchr. adult edn., Honolulu, 1947, Ypsilanti (Mich.) High Sch., 1951-52; spl. instr. English, Wayne State U., Detroit, 1953, 54; tchr. Highland Park (Mich.) Coll., 1950-51, instr. English, 1954-83. Mem. exec. bd. Highland Park Fedn. Tchrs., 1963, 64, 65, 66, 71, 72, mem. 1st bargaining team, 1965-66, 73, del. to Nat. Conv., 1964, 71, 72, 73, 74, rep. higher edn. to Mich. Fedn. Tchrs. Exec. Com., 1972, 73, 74, 75, 76; mem. faculty adv. com. Gov.'s Commn. on Higher Edn., 1973—. Tchr. Baha'i schs., Davison, Mich., 1954, 55, 58, 59, 63, 64, 65, 66, Beaulac, Que., Can., 1960, Greenacre, Maine, 1965; sec. local spiritual assembly Baha'is, Ann Arbor, 1953, sec., Detroit, 1954, chmn., 1955; mem. nat. com. Baha'is U.S., 1955-68; sec. Davison Bahai Sch. Com. and Council, 1956, 58, 63, 64, 65, 66, 67, 68; Baha'i lectr. Mem. Modern Lang. Assn., Nat. Council Tchrs. English, Mich. Coll. English Assn., Am. Fedn. Tchrs., Nat. Soc. Lit. and Arts, Women's Equity and Action League (sec. Mich. chpt. 1975-79), Alpha Lambda Delta, Alpha Gamma Delta. Contbr. poems to mags. Home: 25227 Parkwood Huntington Woods MI 48070

NODINE, BARBARA FRACASSI, psychologist, educator; b. N.Y.C., July 19, 1937; d. Renator D. and Charlotte (Dallmer) Fracassi; m. Calvin F. Nodine, Sept. 6, 1958; children: Renee, Linda, Richard. BA, Bucknell U., 1959; PhD, U. Mass., 1962. Asst. prof. psychology Chatham Coll., Pitts., 1967-68; prof. Beaver Coll., Glenside, Pa., 1969—; cons. faculty devel. various colls., 1981—; chair Com. on Undergraduate Edn., Washington, 1982-84. Author: Study Guide for Introductory Psychology; co-author Writing in the Arts and Sciences, 1981, Readings in the Arts and Sciences. Recipient Lindbach Disting. Teaching Lindbach Found., 1975. Fellow Am. Psychol. Assn.; mem. Am. Ednl. Research Assn., Council for Exceptional Children, Nat. Council Tchrs. of English. Office: Beaver Coll Glenside PA 19038

NOE, ELNORA (ELLIE), chemical company executive; b. Evansville, Ind., Aug. 23, 1928; d. Thomas Noe and Evelyn (West) Dieter; student Ind. U.-Purdue U., Indpls. Sec., Pitman Moore Co., Indpls., 1946; with Dow Chem. Co., Indpls., 1960—, public relations asst. then mgr. employee communications, 1970-87, mgr. community relations, 1987—, Dow Consumer Products Inc., 1986—; mem. steering com. Learn About Bus. Recipient 2d place award as Businesswoman of Yr., Indpls. Bus. and Profl. Women's Assn., 1980, Indpls. Profl. Woman of Yr. award Zonta, Altrusa, Sorptomist & Pilot Service Clubs, 1985. Mem. Am. Bus. Women Assn. (Woman of Yr. award 1965; past pres.), Ind. Assn. Bus. Communicators (communicator of yr. 1977), Women in Communications (Louise Eleanor Kleinhenz award 1984), Nat. Fedn. Press Women, Women's Press Club Ind. (past v.p.). Lodge: Zonta (dist. public relations chmn. 1978-80, area dir. 1980-82, pres. Indpls. 1977-79). Office: PO Box 68511 Indianapolis IN 46268

NOEL, TALLULAH ANN, nurses' employment agency executive; b. Detroit, Oct. 21, 1945; d. Harry Carababas and Ruby Dimple (Gentry) Caruso; m. Vernon E. Noel (div. 1965); children: Cynthia L. Robbins, Kimberly J. Wise. AA in Nursing, Morton Coll., Cicero, Ill., 1976; BS, Coll. St. Francis, Joliet, Ill., 1983; postgrad., Rosary Coll., River Forest, Ill., 1984—. RN. Staff nurse Mt. Sinai Hosp., Chgo., 1976-78, head nurse, 1978-79, critical care nurse, 1979-80, oncology clinician, 1980-82; head nurse McNeal Hosp., Berwyn, Ill., 1982-84; dir. nursing Nursefinders of Elmwood Park (Ill.), 1984-86; dir. profl. services Nursefinders of Chgo., Elmwood Park, 1986-87, v.p. profl. services, 1987—. Bd. dirs. Morton Coll. Found., 1987—, Chgo. Heart Assn., 1985—, Grant Works Children's Ctr., Cicero, 1982-85. Mem. Women's Health Exec. Network, Nat. League Nursing, Oncology Nursing Soc., Am. Fedn. Home Health Agys., Assn. Critical Care Nurses, others. Democrat. Roman Catholic. Office: Nursefinders 593 N York Rd Elmhurst IL 60126

NOETH, CAROLYN FRANCES, speech and language pathologist; b. Cleve., July 21, 1924; d. Sam Falco and Barbara Serafina (Loparo) Armaro; m. Lawrence Andrew Noeth Sr., June 29, 1946; children: Lawrence Andrew Jr. (dec.), Barbara Marie Heaney. AB magna cum laude, Case Western Res. U., 1963; MEd, U. Ill., 1972; postgrad., Nat. Coll. Edn., 1975—. Speech therapist Chgo. Pub. Schs., 1965; speech, lang. and hearing clinician J. Sterling Morton High Schs., Cicero and Berwyn, Ill., 1965-82, tchr. learning disabilities/behavior disorders, 1982, dist. ednl. diagnostician, 1982-84; Title I Project tchr., summers 1966-67, lang. disabilities cons., summers 1968-69, in-service tng. cons., summer 1970, dir. Title I Project, summers 1973-74, learning disabilities tchr. W. Campus of Morton, 1971-75, chmn. Educable-Mentally Handicapped-Opportunities Tchrs. Com., 1967-68, spl. edn. area and in-sch. tchrs. workshops, 1967—. Precinct elections judge, 1953-55; block capt. Mothers March of Dimes and Heart Fund, 1949-60; St. Agatha's rep. Nat. Catholic Women's League, 1952-53; collector for charities, 1967; mem. exec. bd. Morton Scholarship League, 1981-84, corr. sec., 1981-83; vol. Am. Cancer Soc., 1985—; vol. judge Ill. Acad. Decathlon, 1988—. First recipient Virda L. Stewart award for Speech, Western Res. U., 1963, recipient Outstanding Sr. award, 1963. Mem. Am. (certified), Ill. speech and hearing assns., Council Exceptional Children (div. for learning disabilities, chpt. spl. projects chmn., exec. bd. 1976-81, chpt. pres. 1979-80), Assn. Children with Learning Disabilities, Council for Learning Disabilities, Profls. in Learning Disabilities, Internat. Platform Assn., Kappa Delta Pi, Delta Kappa Gamma (chmn., co-chmn. chpt. music com. 1979—, mem. state program com. 1981-83, chpt. music rep. to state 1982—). Roman Catholic. Clubs: St. Norbert's Women's (Northbrook, Ill.), Case-Western Res. U., U. Ill. Alumni Assns., Lions (vol. Northbrook, 1966—). Chmn. in compiling and publishing Student Handbook, Cleve. Coll., 1962; contbr. lyric parodies and musical programs J. Sterling Morton High Sch. West Retirement Teas, 1972-83. Home and Office: 1849 Walnut Circle Northbrook IL 60062

NOETH, PATRICIA ANN, computer engineer; b. Stamford, Conn., Mar. 4, 1960; d. Gerard Joseph and Frances Loretta (Karp) N. BS, Boston Coll., 1982; postgrad., Iona Coll. Computer engr. Xerox Co., Rochester, N.Y., 1981; programmer analyst AT&T Co., White Plains, N.Y., 1982—; cons. in field. Tchr., workshop leader, asst. co-ordinator Literacy Vols. Am., NW and So. Bergen County, N.J., 1987. Mem. Nat. Assn. Female Execs., IEEE. Democrat. Roman Catholic. Office: AT&T Co 600 Lanidex Plaza Parsippany NJ 07054

NOGRADY, SUSAN, lawyer, financial services and real estate investor; b. Lancaster, Calif., Feb. 23, 1953; d. Leslie John Nogrady and Martha (Sipos)

Feher; 1 child, Nicole Suzanne. A.A., Los Angeles Valley Coll., 1974; B.A., Pepperdine U., 1976; J.D., Western State U., 1982; M.A. (hon.) U. Rome, 1976. Exec. asst. Congressman R.K. Dornan, Washington, 1976-77; dir. adv. councils Republican Nat. Com., Washington, 1977-78; campaign mgr. Goedeke for Congress, Santa Ana, Calif., 1978; v.p. Meridian Land, Malibu, Calif., 1980-82, pres. Meridian Land Devel., Inc., 1982—; pres. Lenders Processing Services, Inc.; sr. ptnr. Golden Earth Investment Co., Granada Hills, Calif.; ptnr. Golden Vale Properties, Malibu; legal cons. Network & Telephone Systems, Inc., Laguna Niguel, Calif., 1983—. Fundraiser Com. to Reelect Pres. Ford, Los Angeles, 1976, Citizens for Republic, Santa Monica, Calif., 1978, Reagan for Pres., Santa Monica 1980. Recipient Am. Jurisprudence award West Pub. Co., 1981. Roman Catholic. Home: 21771 Regal Way Lake Forest CA 92630

NOGUEIRAS, MARY, travel agent; b. Havana, July 18, 1929; d. Jose Antonio and Carmen (Carrasco) Gonzalez; m. Humberto Mario Nogueiras, June 28, 1952; children—Diane Michelle, Eileen Lillian, Denise Susan, Brenda Lynn. A.S., Havana Bus. U., 1948; student Sch. Bus. Edn., U. Miami, 1948-52. Bilingual sec. U. Miami fgn. student dept., Coral Gables, 1949-52; bilingual sec., asst. to mgr. Brown & Bigelow, Mpls., 1952-54; salesperson, various cos., Miami, 1960-75; owner, mgr. Directions in Design, Miami, 1980-83; pres. Bermar Travel Inc., Coral Gables, Fla., 1983—. Bd. dirs. Doctors Hosp. Aux. Coral Gables, 1960-75, Dade County Med. Aux., 1960-66, pres., 1966-67. Mem. Am. Soc. Travel Agts., Meeting Planners Assn., Riviera Country Club Womens Golf Assn. (past pres.). Republican. Roman Catholic. Office: Bermar Travel Inc 6851 Yumuri St Miami FL 33146

NOLAN, ELIZABETH ANNE, military officer, pharmacist; b. Pitts., Oct. 4, 1954; d. John Edward and Dorothea Josephine (Scheuermann) N. Student, St. Mary's Coll., Notre Dame, Ind., 1972-74; BS in Pharmacy, Duquesne U., 1977. Lic. pharmacist, Pa., Calif. From intern to pharmacist Magee Womens Hosp., Pitts., 1975-79; pharmacist St. Claire Hosp., Pitts., 1979, Duvall's Drug Store, Pitts., 1979; commd. ensign USN, 1979, advanced through grades to lt., 1981, promoted lt. commdr., 1988, pharmacy officer Naval Hosp. Phila., 1979-82, Naval Hosp. Br. Clinic Treasure Island, San Francisco, 1982-85; asst. head pharmacy Naval Hosp. Pensacola (Fla.), 1985-88, head pharmacy, 1988—. Mem. Am. Soc. Cons. Pharmacists, Am. Soc. Hosp. Pharmacists, Assn. Mil. Surgeons U.S., Aircraft Owners and Pilot's Assn., Multiple Sclerosis Soc., Nat. Assn. for Female Execs., Mortar Bd. Republican. Roman Catholic. Club: Navy Aero (Alameda, Calif., Pensacola), (treas. Alameda chpt. 1984-86). Home: 4458 Bellview Ave Pensacola FL 32506 Office: Naval Hosp Pensacola Pensacola FL 32512

NOLAN, KAREN LORI, advertising and public relations executive; b. Paterson, N.J., Nov. 18, 1958; d. Martin Alek and Florence (Miller) Rosenthal; m. Timothy Reynolds Nolan, June 24, 1984. B.S., Montclair State Coll., Upper Montclair, N.J., 1981; postgrad. Fairleigh Dickinson U., 1982—. Mktg. asst. Kem Mfg. Co., Inc., Fairlawn, N.J., 1975-80; graphics mgr. The Montclarion Inc., Upper Montclair, N.J., 1978-80; advt. mgr. Meadox Med., Inc., Oakland, N.J., 1980-82; account exec. McGovern Advt., Inc., Red Bank, N.J., 1984-85; sr. account exec. Allen Cons., Inc., Holmdel, N.J., 1986-87; mgr. advt. and pub. relations, Tarkett Inc., Parsippany, N.J., 1987—. Mem. Bus./Profl. Advt. Assn. (mem. exec. bd. 1982—), Am. Mktg. Assn., Montclair Athletic Comm. (dir. 1979-80). Democrat. Jewish. Home: 3 Lyons Pl Morristown NJ 07960 Office: 800 Lanidex Plaza Parsippany NJ 07054

NOLAN, KATHERINE ANN, automotive services executive; b. Kansas City, Kans., Dec. 1, 1959; d. Matthew William and Dorothy Helen (Kulhanek) Hogan; m. Francis Joseph Nolan, Jan. 31, 1988. BS in Fin., Kans. State U., 1982; MBA in Fin. and Mktg., Rockhurst Coll., 1986. Successively asst. customer rep., wholesale rep., customer rep., sr. customer rep. Ford Motor Credit Co., Kansas City, 1982-85; internal auditor Ford Motor Credit Co., Kansas City and Detroit, 1985-86; supr. dealer services Ford Motor Credit Co., San Francisco, 1986—; student adv. Jr. Achievement, Plymouth, Mich., 1985-86. Mem. Nat. Assn. Female Execs., Am. Mgmt. Assn., Am. Soc. Profl. Exec. Women. Republican. Roman Catholic.

NOLAN, LONE KIRSTEN, real estate investment counselor and executive; b. Copenhagen, Oct. 9, 1938; d. Johannes and Elizabeth (Zachariassen) Jansen; came to U.S., 1957, naturalized, 1964; m. Gene Nolan, Mar. 19, 1973; children—Glenn Muller, Erik Muller. Lic. securities broker; adminstrv. asst. Am. Nat. Bank and Trust, Morristown, N.J., 1967-72; asst. cashier First Nat. Iron Bank, 1972; comptroller and ops. officer Panama City Nat. Bank, 1973-74; asst. v.p. Lee County Bank, Ft. Myers, Fla., 1974-76; Priscilla Murphy Realty, Sanibel, Fla., 1976-77; pres. Century 21 Nolan Realty, Ft. Myers, 1977-80; pres. AAIM Realty Group, Ft. Myers, 1980-81; real estate investment counselor Merrill Lynch, Boca Raton, Fla., 1982-85; mgr. Merrill Lynch Realty, Palm Beach, Fla., 1984-85; mgr. J.W. Charles Realty, Inc., Boca Raton, 1985—; mem. A.L. Williams Agy. Mem. Internat. Real Estate Fedn., Nat. Assn. Realtors, Realtors Nat. Mktg. Inst., Fla. Real Estate Exchangors, Nat. Assn. Securities Dealers. Home: 21380 Placida Terr Boca Raton FL 33433 Office: JW Charles Realty Inc 21301 Powerline Rd Suite 210 Boca Raton FL 33433

NOLAN, LOUISE MARY, school system administrator, author; b. Boston, Sept. 28, 1947; d. John Joseph and Helen (Spiers) Nolan; B.A., Regis Coll., 1969; M.Ed., Boston U., 1971 postgrad., 1981-82; postgrad Fitchburg State Coll., 1972-74, Salem State Coll., 1977-79; Ph.D., Boston Coll., 1986. Counselor, Camp Thoreau, Inc., Concord, Mass., 1964-68; tchr., chmn. sci. dept. John F. Kennedy Meml. Jr. High Sch., Woburn, Mass., 1969-86; asst. supt. schs. for curriculum and instrn. Woburn Pub. Schs., 1986—; co-owner Ruth and Louise Silkscreening, Lexington, Mass., Fancypants, Carlisle, Mass.; dir. ecology program Curry Coll., Milton, Mass., summer 1977. Active New Eng. League Mid. Schs., Nat. League Mid. Schs. Vice chmn. Mass. Sci. Fair Com. NSF grantee, 1972-73, 77-79, 81-82; chemistry fellow Boston U., 1983-84; For a Cleaner Environment grantee, 1984-86. Mem. Mass. Tchrs. Assn., NEA, AAAS, Nat. Assn. Sci. Tchrs., Mass. Assn. Sci. Tchrs., Nat. Assn. Biology Tchrs., Nat. Assn. Research in Sci. Teaching, Middlesex County Tchrs. Assn., Biology Roundtable, Woburn Tchrs. Assn., Mass. Supts. Assn., Beta Beta Beta, Pi Lambda Theta. Democrat. Roman Catholic. Clubs: Museum Fine Arts, Lit. Guild, Concord Art Assn., Mus. of Sci., Theatre Guild. Author: Y.E.S.-A Comprehensive Guide to Students Educating Youth in Environmental Sciences; Bioluminescence—An Experimental Guide; Marine Plankton; Heath Physical Science, 1983, 87; also papers. Home: 9 Stevens Rd Lexington MA 02173 Office: Joyce Jr High Sch Adminstrn Offices Locust St Woburn MA 01801

NOLAN, MARY CATHERINE, architectural analyst, construction company executive; b. Ft. Meade, Md.; d. John Joseph and Emma Mae (Sheaffer) N.; m. Daniel Patrick Ensor, Sept. 4, 1981. BA, Montclair State Coll., Upper Montclair , N.J., 1976; MS, Rutgers U., 1980, PhD, 1984. Teaching asst. Rutgers U., New Brunswick, N.J., 1978-83, lab asst., 1982-83; software programmer Estate Systems, Costa Mesa, Calif., 1984; adminstrv. dir. Hill Pinckert Architects, Inc., Irvine, Calif., 1984-87, research analyst, 1987; v.p. Ensor Constrn., Laguna Niguel, Calif., 1985-87; cons. in field. Grantee Rutgers U., 1983. Mem. AAAS, Am. Assn. Female Execs., Am. Mgmt. Assn., Bot. Soc. Am. Republican. Roman Catholic. Office: Hill Pinckert Architects 16969 Von Karman Suite 105 Irvine CA 92714

NOLAN, PATRICIA ANN, computer consultant; b. New London, Wis., Feb. 13, 1961; d. Cliff Francis and Elizabeth Jane (Groholski) N. BBA, U.Wis., Eau Claire, 1983. Programmer M&I Data Services, Milw., 1984-85, info. ctr. cons., 1985-86; solution ctr. cons. S.C. Johnson & Son., Racine, Wis., 1986—; prof. Milw. Area Tech. Sch., 1985—. Advisor Jr. Achievement, Milw., 1986. Mem. SE Wis. Info Ctr. Users Group. Office: SC Johnson & Son 1525 Howe MS80 Racine WI 53403

NOLAND, ANNGINETTE ROBERTS, national sorority executive; b. Stillwater, Okla., Sept. 30, 1930; d. Cecil Andrew and Gladys Leah (Woods) Roberts; m. Thomas Vaughan Noland, June 11, 1949; children: Nanette Noland Crocker, Thomas Vaughan Noland, Bruce Andrew Noland. Student, Okla. State U., 1948-49; cert. in planning, U. Wis. Chpt. advisor Kappa Delta Sorority, Stillwater, 1953-54, Baton Rouge, 1956-59; province pres. Kappa Delta Sorority, Miss., 1970-77; regional dir. Kappa Delta Sorority, cen. U.S., 1977-84, nat. dir. scholarship program, 1984-87, past mem. evaluation com., chmn. conv. scholarship banquet com., 1985, chmn. fellowships evaluation com., 1984-87. Recipient Outstanding Service award WLOX-TV, 1977. Mem. Nat. Assn. Female Execs., DAR (treas. Biloxi chpt. 1983—), Colonial Dames XVII Century (corr. sec. local chpt. 1985-87, pres. 1987—), United Daus. of the Confederacy, Gulf Coast Community Concert Assn., Hibernia Soc. Republican. Episcopalian. Club: Biloxi Yacht (aux. corr. sec. 1986-88). Home: 2441 Old Bay Rd Biloxi MS 39531 Office: Sta WLOX-TV PO Box 4596 Biloxi MS 39535-4596

NOLAND, PATRICIA HAMPTON, editor, writer, poet; b. New Orleans, Dec. 24, 1924; d. Leon Maxwell and Clara Hampton (Whittle) Noland. BA, U. Houston, 1981; Dr. Leadership in Poetry (hon.), Internat. Acad. Leadership, Philippines, 1969; DLH (hon.) Free U. Asia, 1973; diploma of merit in lit., U. Arts, Salsomaggiore Terme, Italy, 1982; postgrad., Rice U., 1987. Vol. Mental Health Ctr., St. Joseph's Hosp., Houston, 1970-71; founder, pres., editor monthly newsletter Internat. Poetry Inst., Houston, 1969—. Author: Poems, 1960; editor: Whoever Heard a Birdie Cry?, 1970. Chmn. music com. 1st Ch. of Christian Scientist, Houston. Named Hon. Internat. Poet Laureate, United Poets Laureate Internat., Manila, 1969. Mem. Am. Hort. Soc., Mus. Fin Arts Houston, Met. Opera Guild, Smithsonian Instn., Colonial Williamsburg Found., Nat. Trust Hist. Preservation, Cousteau Soc., Met. Mus. Art, Boston Mus. Fine Arts, Isabella Stewart Gardner Mus., Norton Gallery and Sch. Art, New Orleans Mus. Art, Mus. for Women in Art, Internat. Platform Assn., English-Speaking Union, Mus. of Art of Am. West, Chgo. Art Inst., L'Alliance Française. Democrat. Club: Jr. League Luncheon. Home: 2400 Westheimer Rd Apt 215W Houston TX 77098 Office: PO Box 53087 Houston TX 77052

NOLD, CONNIE JO, writer; b. Flint, Mich., Sept. 20, 1954; d. Richard George and Shirley Ann (Willey) N. BA in Communications, Mich. State U., 1976; MA in Personnel Mgmt., Cen. Mich. U., 1986. Supr. Gen. Motors Corp., Flint, Mich., 1976-78, statistician, 1979-83; staff writer Detroit, 1984—. Mem. Am. Bus. Women's Assn, Nat. Assn. for Female Execs., Sigma Iota Epsilon.

NOLEN, BARBARA JEAN, social worker; b. Chgo., Jan. 8, 1955; d. Willie and Maudine (Cochran) N. BA, DePaul U., 1979, MA, 1981. Supr. Oak Community Ctr., Oak Park, Ill., 1979-80; social worker Dept. Mental Health, Chgo., 1980—, Ill. Dept. Children and Family Services, Chgo., 1980—. Home: 1919 S 3d Ave Maywood IL 60153

NOLIN, MARTA VICTORIA, psychotherapist; b. Eastchester, N.Y., May 23, 1952; d. Joseph H. and Victoria B. (Toteff) N.; B.A. magna cum laude, Boston U., 1974; M.A., Assumption Coll., 1977. Residence hall dir. Boston U., 1974-75; head of residence U. Mass., Amherst, 1977-78, sr. head of residence, 1978-79; asst. dean for student life Ohio Wesleyan U., Delaware, 1979-83; counselor Project Self Discovery U. Mo.-Columbia, 1983-84, counselor intern Women's Ctr., 1984-85, intern psychologist Univ. Counseling Services, 1985-87, asst. to dir. Univ. Counseling Services, 1987—. Mem. Am. Coll. Personnel Assn., Am. Assn. Counseling and Devel., Am. Psychol. Assn. Democrat. Office: U Mo Counseling Services 204 Parker Hall Columbia MO 65211

NOLL, LINDA SUE, insurance company executive; b. Hastings-on-Hudson, N.Y., July 20, 1955; d. Donald Richard and Ronda Frances (Moore) N. AS, Fisher Jr. Coll., 1975; BS in Bus. Mgmt., Roger Williams Coll., 1982. Life group asst. Liberty Mut. Ins. Co., Boston, 1979-81, underwriter, 1981-82, underwriter spl. risks, 1982-84, coordinator fin. plans, 1984-86, asst. mgr. fin. disbursements, 1986—. Mem. Mus. of Fine Arts, Boston, 1987—; active United Way, Spl. Olympics. Republican. Methodist. Office: Liberty Mut Ins Co 175 Berkeley St Boston MA 02117

NOLTE, JOAN HENDERSON, personnel and risk management manager; b. Atlanta, Mar. 18, 1955; d. Thomas Roy and Mary Theron (Roberts) Henderson; m. Brian Charles Nolte, Jan. 29, 1955. BA in Journalism/Advt., U. Ga., 1977. Mgmt. trainee Six Flags Over Ga., Atlanta, 1977, promotions coordinator, 1977-79, personnel staff asst., 1979-81; sales account exec. L.S. Brown Co., Atlanta, 1981-83; personnel mgr. Six Flags Atlantis, Ft. Lauderdale, Fla., 1983—; personnel and risk mgmt. mgr. Six Flags Corp., Chgo., 1984—. vol. Leukemia Soc., Ft. Lauderdale, 1986-87. Mem. Am. Soc. for Personnel Adminstrn. (cert. profl. human resources), Am. Mgmt. Assn., Personnel Assn. of Broward County, Am. Soc. of Tng. and Devel. Republican. Presbyterian. Home: 3731 NW 114th Ave Coral Springs FL 30365 Office: Six Flags Atlantis 2700 Stirling Rd Hollywood FL 33021

NOLTE, JUDITH ANN, magazine editor; b. Hampton, Iowa, Sept. 17, 1938; d. Clifford P. and Sigrid M. (Johnson) N.; m. Randers H. Heimer, May 7, 1971. B.S., U. Minn., 1960; M.A. in English, N.Y. U., 1965. Tchr. English Middletown (N.Y.) High Sch., 1960-62, High Sch. of Commerce, N.Y.C., 1962-64; merchandising editor Conde Nast Publs., N.Y.C., 1964-69; editor-in-chief Am. Baby mag., N.Y.C., 1969—, Weight Watchers mag., 1980-83; hostess Am. Baby Cable TV Show. Chmn. media adv. bd. N.Y. chpt. March of Dimes. Mem. Am. Soc. Mag. Editors (pres. 1986-88), Mortar Bd., Delta Gamma. Office: American Baby Magazine 475 Park Ave S New York NY 10016

NOONAN, MELINDA DUNHAM, nurse, educator; b. Peoria, Ill., Feb. 19, 1954; d. Emmett Maxwell Dunham and Dixie Maurine (DeCounter) Widner; m. Robert Joseph Noonan; children: Alissa, Meris. Diploma, Ravenswood Hosp. Sch. Nursing, 1977. Med. asst. James J. Hines, M.D., S.C., Chgo., 1973-76; staff nurse Northwestern Mem. Hosp., Chgo., 1978-79, asst. head nurse, 1979-80, staff nurse, 1980-83, parent educator, 1983—; founder, bd. dirs. Mothers Organized for Mutual Support, Chgo, 1981—; creator, coordinator Beyond The Birth Experience Program, Chgo., 1983—. Mem. Family Resource Coalition, Nurses Assn. of Am. Coll. Ob-Gyn, Internat. Childbirth Edn. Assn. Democrat. Roman Catholic. Lodge: Rebekah (v. grand 1981-82, noble grand 1982-83). Home: 3414 W Glenlake Chicago IL 60659 Office: Northwestern Mem Hosp 333 E Superior Room 1085 Chicago IL 60611

NOONER, MARIANNA REBECCA, fashion executive; b. Corpus Christi, Tex., Sept. 9, 1951; d. R.C. and Evelyn Helen (Habeeb) Nooner. BSE, U. Ark., 1973; MA, U. Tex., 1979. Sales rep. Am. Can. Corp., Dallas, 1973-77, Mobil Chem. Co. div. Mobil Oil Co., Dallas, 1977-80; acct. exec. Calvin Klein Menswear, Dallas, 1980-86, Giorgio Armani Menswear, 1986—. Mem. Women's Com. Dallas Ballet; active Dallas Mus. Art. Named Salesman of Yr. Calvin Klein Sportswear, 1982. Mem. Delta Gamma. Republican. Episcopalian. Home: 9612 Glenacre Circle Dallas TX 75243

NORBACK, DIANE HAGEMAN, pathologist; b. Comfrey, Minn., Mar. 22, 1946; d. Evan Herman and Emma Alvina (Meier) Hageman; B.A., Luther Coll., 1966; M.A.T., Northwestern U., 1967; Ph.D., U. Wis., 1973, M.D., 1974; m. John Palmer Norback, Aug. 20, 1966; children—Christopher James, Nathaniel Charles. Asst. prof. dept. pathology U. Wis., Madison, 1975-81, assoc. prof., 1981—, dir. hematology lab. Clin. Sci. Center, 1982—; chief electron microscopy VA Hosp., Madison, 1977-82. Am. Cancer Soc. Jr. Faculty fellow, 1977-80. Mem. Am. Assn. Pathologists, Soc. Toxicology, Internat. Acad. Pathology, Electron Microscopic Soc. Am., Wis. Soc. Pathologists, Soc. Analytical Cytology. Home: 2551 Arboretum Dr Madison WI 53713 Office: Dept of Pathology Univ Wis Madison WI 53706

NORCEL, JACQUELINE JOYCE CASALE, educational administrator; b. Bklyn., Nov. 19, 1940; d. Frederick and Josephine Jeanette (Bestafka) Casale; m. Edward John Norcel, Feb. 24, 1962. BS, Fordham U., 1961; MS, Bklyn. Coll., 1966; 6th yr. cert. So. Conn. State U., 1980; postgrad. Bridgeport U. Elem. tchr., pub. schs., N.Y.C., 1961-80; prin. Coventry Schs., Conn., 1980-84, Trumbull Schs., Conn., 1984—; guest lectr. So. Conn. State U., 1980—; cons. Monson Schs., Mass., 1984; mem. adj. faculty Sacred Heart U., Fairfield, Conn., 1985—. Editor: Best of the Decade, 1980. Contbr. articles to profl. jours. Chmn. bldg. com. Trumbull Bd. Edn., 1978-80; chmn. Sch. Benefit Com., Trumbull, 1985-86; catechist Bridgeport Diocese, Roman Cath. Ch., Conn., 1975-85, youth minister, 1979—, coordinator, evaluator leadership tng. workshops for teens and adults, 1979-84. Recipient Town of Trumbull Service award, 1982, Nat. Disting. Prin. award, 1988. Mem. N.E. Regional Elem. Prins. Assn. (rep. 1984-86, sec. 1986-87), Elem. Middle Sch. Prins. Assn. (pres. 1985-86, Pres.'s award 1981-85), Adminstrn. and Supervision Assn. (sec. 1980-81, pres. 1981-82, exec. bd. 1982-83), Hartford Area Prins. and Suprs. Assn. (local pres. 1981-82), Nat. Assn. Elem. Sch. Prins. (zone I dir. 1987-90, Conn. State Prin. Acad. Adv. Bd. 1986-88, del. to gen. assemblies 1984-88, bd. dirs. 1987—), Assn. Supervision and Curriculum Devel., Conn. Assn. Supervision and Curriculum Devel., Eastern Conn. Council of Internat. Reading Assn., New Eng. Coalition Ednl. Leaders, Associated Tchrs. of Math. in Conn., Phi Delta Kappa, Pi Lambda Theta (Beta Sigma chpt.), Delta Kappa Gamma. Republican. Home: 5240 Madison Ave Trumbull CT 06611 Office: Tashua Sch 401 Stonehouse Rd Trumbull CT 06611

NORCROSS, LOIS MANLEY, communications professional; b. Orange, Conn.; d. Roy Ellis and Viola Agnes (Ericson) N.; A.A., Centenary Coll. for Women; B.S., Quinnipiac Coll.; M.A., Fairfield U. Dir. public relations Greater New Haven C. of C., 1966-68; acting dir. Better Bus. Bur. Greater New Haven, 1968-69; communications specialist Olin Corp., New Haven, 1969-74; editor employee newsletters, cons. editor employee communications Olin chem. plants in U.S., 1974-78; info. services coordinator Communications Office, Dept. Adminstrv. Services, State of Conn., 1978-81, editor State Scene, 1979-85, info. services officer Personnel Devel. Ctr., 1985—. Cons. publicity adv. bd. Conn. Public TV, 1981-82. Recipient Outstanding Service award Conn. chpt. Internat. Assn. Bus. Communicators, 1980. Mem. Women in Communications, Internat. Assn. Bus. Communicators (chpt. pres.), Conn. State Women in Mgmt. (pres. 1984). Congregationalist. Club: Appalachian Mountain. Office: Personnel Devel Ctr 61 Woodland St Hartford CT 06105

NORD, DEANNA LYNN, marketing company executive, consultant; b. Detroit Lakes, Minn., Apr. 20, 1956; d. Donald Harris Steen and Ellen Marie (Bratlien) N. BA, Macalester Coll., St. Paul, 1980; postgrad., U. Minn., 1981-82, St. Catherine's Coll., St. Paul, 1985. Research asst. Minn. Energy Agy., St. Paul, 1977-79; mgr. product devel. Control Data, Mpls., 1980-83, mgr. mktg., 1983-85, account mgr., edn., 1985-86; pvt. practice bus. devel, mktg. cons. Mpls., 1986—; pres., bd. dirs. Self Reliance Ctr., Mpls., 1980-87; mem. U. Minn. Inst. Agrl. Adv. Council, Mpls., 1984-88; sr. cons. Internat. Bus. Cons., St. Paul, 1985-87. Contbr. articles to profl. jours. Founder, mem. Mpls. Food Policy Task Force, 1985-87, Minn. Solar Sustenance Team, Mpls., 1978-80; participant Nat. Gov.'s Task Force Image of Agrl. Project, Mpls, 1985. Mem. Minn. Women's Network, Minn. Women for Agrl. (pres. 1982-84), Minn. Food Assn. (research, community involvement coms.), Nat. Assn. Female Execs., Upper Midwest Flute Assn. Home: 721 Kenwood Pkwy Minneapolis MN 55403

NORDEEN, PEGGY ANN, advertising executive; b. Muscatine, Iowa, July 27, 1946; d. Gene E. and Marylou Nordeen; B.A. in Journalism and English, U. Iowa, 1968. Gen. assignment news reporter Davenport (Iowa) Times-Democrat, 1966-69; with Sperry-Boom Inc., Chgo., 1970-78, v.p., dir. 1976-78; pres. Starmark, Inc., Chgo., 1978—. Mem. Viking Ship Restoration Com., Chgo., 1979; Iowa Realtors Assn. scholar, 1964. Mem. Am. Mktg. Assn. (v.p. communications Chgo. chpt. 1974), Publicity Club Chgo. (sec., dir. 1973-74), Gamma Phi Beta. Mem. Christian Ch. (Disciples of Christ). Home: Elm St Chicago IL 60611 Office: Starmark Bldg 240 E Ontario Chicago IL 60611

NORDHAGEN, HALLIE HUERTH, nursing home administrator; b. Sarona, Wis., Apr. 2, 1914; d. Mathias James and Ethel Elizabeth (Fann) Huerth; B.Ed., U. Wis., Superior, 1938, M.A., 1949; m. Carl E. Nordhagen, May 24, 1947; children—Bruce Carl, Brian Keith. Prin., tchr. Wis. Public Schs., 1932-46; supervising tchr. Wis. Community Coll., 1946-48; psychiat. adminstr. Trempealeau County Health Care Center, psychiat. nursing home, Whitehall, Wis., 1959—; mem. Wis. Nursing Home Adminstrs. Examining Bd.; fellow Menninger Clinic, Topeka, 1979-81. Recipient Disting. Service award in edn. and hosp. adminstrn., London, 1967, award for services to human services programs Wis. Assn. Human Services, 1972, award for outstanding services to exceptional children Assn. Retarded Children, 1978, award for accomplishments in human resources Trempealeau County Conservation Service, 1981; Wis. State Senate citation, 1983; citatioin Wis. Gov., 1984. Mem. Wis. Assn. County Homes, Wis. Edn. Assn., Wis. Assn. Human Services Programs, Internat. Platform Assn., Am. Lutheran Ch. Women. Clubs: Whitehall Country, Women's. Author: Wisconsin Indians, 1966. Home: 2220 Claire St Whitehall WI 54773

NORDIN, PHYLLIS ECK, sculptor, designer, consultant; b. Chgo. Student Beloit Coll., Wayne State U.; B.S., U. Toledo, 1963, B.A. cum laude, 1972; postgrad. Sch. Design, Toledo Mus. Art. Design and art cons. various builders, chs., businesses and individuals, 1972—; instr. Lourdes Coll. Sylvania, Ohio, 1972—, U. Toledo, 1986—. Prin. works include large bronze sculptures Lucas County Main Library, Toledo, Christ figure St. Joan of Arc Ch., Maumee, Ohio, Ronald McDonald House, Toledo, First English Evangel. Luth. Ch., Grosse Pointe Woods, Mich., Christ Presbyn. Ch., Covenant Presbyn. Ch., Toledo, Toledo Hosp., Reynolds Br. Library, Toledo, stone wall mural Epworth United Methodist Ch., Toledo, Beloit Coll., Wis., bronze fountain U. Toledo, bronze life-size children T.C. Mall, Stuart, Fla., Treasure Coast Mall, Stuart, Fort Defiance Park, Defiance, Ohio, welded steel sculptures Town Ctr. Mall, Port Charlotte, Fla., Carey (Ohio) Bank, Toledo Bank, Centennial Park, Toledo, wood wall carvings 1st Meth. Ch., LaGrange, Ill., numerous others; exhibited Allied Artists Am., Salmagundi Club, numerous others. Represented by Collectors Corner Toledo Mus. Art, 1970—. Recipient Alpha award Foothills Art Ctr., 1983, 1st prize Ann. Nat. Art Exhbn., 1978, also numerous others. Mem. Arts Commn. Greater Toledo, Toledo Design Rev. Bd., Nat. Assn. Women Artists, Interfaith Forum Religion Art Architecture, Ohio Designer Craftsmen, Toledo Modern Art Group (trustee 1982-87), Phi Kappa Phi. Home and Studio: 4035 Tantara Rd Toledo OH 43623

NORDMANN, NANCY OLIVIA, educational services administrator; b. Atlanta, June 5, 1945; d. Robert Foster Jr. and Leila (Howard) House; m. Gary Arnold Nordmann, June 9, 1966 (div. 1982); 1 child Leila Olivia. BS in Edn. cum laude, U. Ga., 1966; MA, U. Chgo., 1974. Instr. U. Chgo., 1974-75, Roosevelt U., Chgo., 1975; extraordinary services provider children psychiat. unit Michael Reese Hosp., Chgo., 1978-80; therapeutic interventional specialist Children's Day Hosp., Rush-Presbyn. St. Luke's Med. Ctr., Chgo., 1980-81; ednl. dir. Children and Family Services Shelter, Chgo., 1981-83; diagnostic resource specialist Chgo. Bd. Edn., 1983—; rec. sec. Bur. Spl. Needs, Chgo., 1985-86; bd. dirs. Spl. Needs Adv. Council, 1985-86, sec. 1986-87. Active local arrangements com. Council for Exceptional Children, Spl. Arts Festival com., Jr. League Chgo.; vice-chmn. mgmt. assistance to nonprofit orgns. Support Ctr., 1985-86; sec. bd. dirs. Lincoln Park Plaza Assn., 1985—. USPHS fellow, 1972-73, 1973-74, U. Chgo. fellow, 1981-82; Ill. Dept. Mental Health and Devel. Disabilities grantee, 1981. Mem. Nat. Assn. Women Execs., PEN. Clubs: Women's Athletic, Mill Creek Hunt (Lake Forest, Ill.). Home: 1926 N Mohawk St Chicago IL 60614

NORDMEYER, MARY BETSY, vocational specialist educator; b. New Haven, May 19, 1939; d. George and Barbara Stedman (Thompson) N. ABPhil, Wheaton Coll., Norton, Mass., 1960; MA, San Jose State U., 1968; AS in Computer Sci., West Valley Coll., 1985. Cert. tchr. spl. edn., Calif.; cert. secondary tchr., Calif. Instr. English Santa Clara (Calif.) Unified Sch. Dist., 1965-77, vocat. specialist, 1977—, dir. project work ability, 1984—. Author poetry, 1960, Career and Vocat. Edn. for Students With Spl. Needs, 1986; author/designer Career English, 1974, Career Information, 1975. Facilitator Project Work-Ability Region 5, 1985—; mem. community adv. com. Santa Clara Unified Sch. Dist. Recipient Outstanding Secondary Educator award, 1975, Award of Excellence, Nat. Assn. Vocat. Edn., 1984; named Tchr. of Yr. in Spl. Edn., Santa Clara Unified Sch. Dist., 1984-85. Mem. Calif. Assn. Work Experience Educators, Sierra Club, Epsilon Eta Sigma. Democrat. Home: 14920 Sobey Rd Saratoga CA 95070 Office: Santa Clara Unified Sch Dist 1889 Lawrence Rd Santa Clara CA 95052

NORDYKE, ELEANOR COLE, population researcher, public health nurse; b. Los Angeles, June 15, 1927; d. Ralph G. and Louise Noble (Carter) Cole; m. Robert Allan Nordyke, June 18, 1950; children: Mary Ellen Nordyke-Grace, Carolyn Nordyke Cozzette, Thomas A., Susan E., Gretchen C. BS, Stanford U., 1950; P.H.N. accreditation, U. Calif.-Berkeley, 1952; MPH, U.

Hawaii, 1969. RN. Pub. health nurse San Francisco Dept. Health, 1950-52; nurse-tchr. Punahou Sch., Honolulu, 1966-67; clinic coordinator East-West Population Inst., East-West Ctr., Honolulu, 1969-75, population researcher, 1975-82, research fellow, 1982—; cons. Hawaii Commn. on Population, Honolulu, 1970-83; mem. Hawaii Policy Action Group for Family Planning, Honolulu, 1971—, chmn., 1976-77. Author: The Peopling of Hawaii, 1977, rev. edit., 1989, A Profile of Hawaii's Elderly Population, 1984; (with Robert Gardner) The Demographic Situation in Hawaii, 1974; mem. editorial bd. Hawaiian Jour. History, 1980—; contbr. articles to profl. jours. Bd. dirs. YMCA Central, Honolulu, 1970—, vice chmn. bd., 1978-79; bd. dirs. Hawaii Planned Parenthood, Honolulu, 1974-78, Friends of Library of Hawaii, 1985—, Camp Erdman YMCA of Honolulu, Mokuleia, Hawaii, 1985—; trustee Hawaiian Hist. Soc., 1978-82; trustee Arcadia Retirement Residence, Honolulu, 1978-87. Mem. Population Assn. Am., Population Reference Bur., Hawaii Pub. Health Assn., Am. Statis. Assn., Hawaii Econ. Assn., Hawaiian Hist. Soc., Stanford Nurses Alumni Assn., Phi Beta Kappa. Democrat. Congregationalist. Clubs: Gen. Fed. Women's, History (Honolulu). Home: 2013 Kakela Dr Honolulu HI 96822 Office: Population Inst East-West Ctr 1777 East-West Rd Honolulu HI 96848

NOREIKA, SOFIA, real estate corporation officer; b. Naples, Italy, Aug. 20, 1945; d. Antonio and Anna (Gambardella) DeFelice; m. Peter Charles Noreika, Apr. 29, 1972; children: Timothy J., Steven P. Student, Greater Hartford Community Coll., 1970-71; real estate sales lic., U. Conn., 1980, diploma in real estate appraisal, 1985. Hostess Holiday Season Restaurant, Waterbury, Conn., 1974-79; owner Sofia Tops Plus, Woodbury, Conn., 1979-84; realtor RE/MAX Properties Unltd., Southbury, Conn., 1984—; land developer Middlebury, Conn. Den mother Boy Scouts of Am., Bethlehem, Conn., 1980-83; vol. Bethlehem Elem. Sch., 1980-85; fund raiser Little League Baseball, Bethlehem, 1983-85. Mem. Waterbury Bd. Realtors, Nat. Assn. Realtors, Conn. Assn. Realtors, Multiple Listing Service, RE/MAX Hundred Percent Club, RE/MAX Internat. Referral Network. Republican. Roman Catholic. Club: 100% of RE/MAX Internat. Home: 132 Carriage Dr Middlebury CT 06762 Office: RE/MAX Properties Unltd 800 Main St S Southbury CT 06488

NOREK, FRANCES THERESE, lawyer; b. Chgo., Mar. 9, 1947; d. Michael S. and Viola C. (Harbecke) N.; m. John E. Flavin, Aug. 31, 1968 (div.); 1 child, John Michael. B.A., Loyola U., Chgo., 1969, J.D., 1973. Bar: Ill. 1973, U.S. Dist. Ct. (no. dist.) Ill. 1973, U.S. Ct. Appeals (7th cir.) 1974. Assoc. Alter, Weiss, Whitesel & Laff, Chgo., 1973-74; asst. states atty. Cook County, Chgo., 1974-86; assoc. Clausen, Miller, Gorman, Caffrey & Witous P.C., 1986—; mem. trial practice faculty Loyola U. Sch. Law, Chgo., 1980—; judge, evaluator mock trial competitions, Chgo., 1978—; lectr. in field. Recipient Emil Gumpert award Am. Coll. Trial Lawyers, 1982. Mem. Womens Bar Assn. Ill., Chgo. Bar Assn. (instr. fed. trial bar adv. program young lawyer's sect. 1983-84). Office: Clausen Miller Gorman et al 10 S La Salle St Chicago IL 60603

NORELLI, PATRICIA ANN, educator; b. McKeesport, Pa., July 13, 1941; d. Patrick and Lillian (Colaizzi) N. B.A., Clark U., 1963, M.A., 1964. Tchr. English, Stoneham High Sch., Mass., 1966—. Named Horace Mann Tchr. of the Yr., 1986-88. Mem. Stoneham Tchrs. Assn., Mass. Tchrs. Assn., NEA, Nat. Council Tchrs. English. Roman Catholic. Avocations: Gardening; running. Home: 3 Harrison St Stoneham MA 02180

NOREM, BONNIE LOU, electronics executive; b. Columbus, Ohio, July 4, 1936; d. William Paul Atwood and Lena Bell (Coey) Wolford; m. David Marlowe Norem, Mar. 20, 1965; children: Kimberlie, Mark, Chris, Jon. Student, Capital U., 1954-55, Ohio State U., 1955-58, Am. U., 1963-64; BS in Psychology, George Mason U., 1978. Sr. systems programmer Gen. Electric, Bethesda, Md., 1961-65, Arlington, Va., 1975-79; project leader Inco., Inc., McLean, Va., 1979-81; prin. engr. H.R.B. Singer Inc., Lanham, Md., 1981-83; sr. systems analyst Ultra Systems, Inc., Hanover, Md., 1983-86; pres. MAI Enterprises, Inc., Annandale, Va., 1986—. Pres. Bethlehem Women's Orgn., Fairfax, Va.; treas. Bethlehem Luth. Ch., Fairfax; mem., capt. FISH; mem. FOCUS. Mem. IEEE, Assn. Study of Dreams (mem. chmn. 1986—). Republican. Club: Washington Dream Group (co-chmn. 1986). Home: 6612 Spring Valley Dr Alexandria VA 22312

NORFLEET, BARBARA PUGH, photographer, lecturer; b. Lakewood, N.J., Feb. 18, 1926; d. Joseph Pugh and Henriette (Plangère) N.; m. Alfred B. Cohn; children: Stephen, Frederic, Timothy. BA, Swarthmore (Pa.) Coll., 1947; MA, Radcliffe Coll., 1950, PhD, 1951. Staff research ctr. group MIT, Cambridge, 1947-48; teaching fellow Harvard U., Cambridge, 1948-51, resident asst. advanced stats., 1951-52, dir. photography collection, 1975—, photography curator, 1972—, lectr., 1960-81, sr. lectr., 1981—; resident asst. Harvard U. Med. Sch., Boston, 1949; cons. Ednl. Devel. Corp., Cambridge, 1968-69. Author: Wedding, 1979, The Champion Pig, 1979, Killing Time, 1982, All The Right People, 1986; exhibited in shows at Inst. Contemporary Art, Boston, 1983, Friends of Photography, Carmel, Calif., 1984, George Eastman House, Rochester, N.Y., 1986, Internat. Ctr. Photography, N.Y.C., 1987, Mus. Modern Art, N.Y.C., 1987. Nat. Endowment for the Humanities fellow, 1975-77, Mass. Artists fellow, 1982, 87, Guggenheim fellow, 1984, Nat. Endowment for the Arts fellow, 1985. Democrat. Episcopalian. Home: 79 Raymond St Cambridge MA 02140 Office: Harvard U VES Dept 24 Quincy St Cambridge MA 02138

NORKIN, CYNTHIA CLAIR, physical therapist; b. Boston, May 6, 1932; d. Miles Nelson and Carolyn (Green) Clair; BS in Edn., Tufts U., 1954; cert. phys. therapy Bouve Boston Coll., 1954; MS, Boston U., 1973, EdD, 1984; m. Stanislav A. Norkin, Feb. 19, 1955 (dec. 1970); 1 child, Alexandra. Instr., Bouve-Boston Coll., 1954-55; staff phys. therapist New Eng. Med. Center, Boston, 1954-55; staff phys. therapist Abington Meml. Hosp., Abington, Pa., 1965-70, Eastern Montgomery County Vis. Nurse Assn., 1970-72; asst. prof. phys. therapy Sargent Coll., Boston U., 1973-84; assoc. prof. phys. therapy, dir. Sch. Phys. Therapy, Ohio U., Athens, 1984—; cons. Boston Center Ind. Living, Cambridge Vis. Nurse Assn., Mass. Medicaid Cost Effectiveness Project, 1978; sec. Health Planning Council Greater Boston, 1976-78. Trustee Brimmer and May Sch., 1980. Mem. Am. Phys. Therapy Assn., Mass. Phys. Therapy Assn. (chmn. Mass. quality assurance com. 1980-85), Am. Public Health Assn., AAAS, Mass. Assn. Mental Health, Athens County Vi. Nurse Assn. (sec. adv. council 1984—). Episcopalian. Author: (with others) Joint Structure and Function: A Comprehensive Analysis, 1983; (with D.J. White) Joint Measurement: A Guide to Goniometry, 1985. Home: 42 Stroud's Run Athens OH 45701 Office: Ohio U Convocation Ctr Athens OH 45701

NORMAN, CHERIE SHELTON, lawyer; b. Ft. Collins, Colo., Sept. 25, 1950; d. Willie L. and Doris E. (Hoopes) Shelton; m. J. Thomas Norman, May 27, 1972; children—Elizabeth Ella, Robert Thomas, Victoria Cherie, Virginia Elaine. B.S., U. Wyo., 1973, M.S., 1974, J.D., 1979. Bar: Wyo. 1979, U.S. Dist. Ct. Wyo. Assoc. John Burk, P.C., Casper, Wyo., 1979-82; sole practice law, Casper, 1982-85; prin. Monroe & Norman, Casper, 1985—; trustee chpt. 7 in bankruptcy, Casper, 1982—. Co-author Bankruptcy Update in Wyoming, 1986, Basic Bankruptcy in Wyoming, 1987. Pres. Ross Law Forum, Laramie, 1978-79. Dir. Community Recreation, Inc., Casper, 1980-84; Casper Rep. Women, 1st.v.p. 1984, pres. 1985-87; parliamentarian Wyo. Rep. Women, Casper, 1983—. Mem. ABA, Wyo. Bar Assn., Assn. Trial Lawyers Am., Wyo. Trial Lawyers, Assn. Bankruptcy Trustees, Bus. and Profl. Women., Am. Bankruptcy Inst., Sigma Alpha Eta (v.p. Laramie 1972). Episcopalian. Home: 4361 S Ash Casper WY 82601 Office: 232 E 2nd Suite 200 Casper WY 82601-2544

NORMAN, CORA ELLEN GARNER, state official, b. Columbia County, Ark., Nov. 7, 1926; d. Robert Everett and Jewel Melissa (Beasley) Garner; m. William Harvey Norman, May 28, 1946; children—Robert Henry, Judith Ellen Norman Bratton. B.A., U. Tex.-El Paso, 1949; M.S., U. Miss., 1964, Ph.D., 1975; postgrad. Inst. of Edn. Mgmt. and Inst. Lifelong Mgmt., Harvard U., 1978, 79, U. London, 1985. Tchr., Holly Springs High Sch. (Miss.), 1964-65; sci. tchr. Lafayette County High Sch., Oxford, Miss., 1965-66; adminstrv. asst. to dir. continuing edn. U. Miss., 1966-69; exec. dir. Miss. Humanities Council, Jackson, 1972—. Chmn. Miss. Polit. Women's Caucus, 1978; pres. Miss. Women's Cabinet Pub. Affairs; active Virginia Gildersleeve Internat. Fund for Univ. Women, Miss. State Adv. Com. to U.S. Commn. on Civil Rights. Recipient citation for leadership community and social devel. Rust Coll., 1974, Woman of Achievement award Oxford, 1982; Distinguished Alumni award So. Ark. U., 1986; One of 14 Ole Miss Alumnae cited for success Ole Miss Alumni Rev., 1982. Mem. LWV (chpt. pres. 1971), AAUW (state pres. 1974-76; Coll. Faculty award 1963, v.p. Ednl. Found. 1985—, Woman of Achievement award, Miss. div., 1987). Democrat. Methodist. Office: Miss Com for Humanities 3825 Ridgewood Rd Room 111 Jackson MS 39211

NORMAN, MARILYN FAY, construction company executive; b. Ord, Nebr., July 19, 1958; d. Clayton Leo and Dorothy Maxine (Anderson) Montanye; m. Michael Lee Norman, June 2, 1979; children—Cody Christina, Ciara Cain. A.A.S., Lincoln Sch. Commerce, 1978. Cert., Nat. Secs. Assn. Office mgr. Vance D. Rogers, Republican candidate for Gov., Lincoln, 1977-78; sec.-treas. Peterson Constrn. Co., Lincoln, 1978-86; sec.-treas. Lincoln Home Builders, Inc., 1986—. Republican. Roman Catholic. Avocations: Reading; fishing. Home: 2400 N 63d St Lincoln NE 68507 Office: Lincoln Home Builders Inc 3225 S 13th St Lincoln NE 68502

NORMAN, MARSHA, playwright; b. Louisville, Sept. 21, 1947; d. Billie Lee and Bertha Mae (Conley) Williams. B.A., Agnes Scott Coll., 1969; M.A.T., U. Louisville, 1971. Tchr. in Ky.; work with disturbed children Ky. Central State Hosp.; book editor, reviewer for Louisville Times; author (plays) Getting Out (John Gassner New Playwrights Medallion, Outer Critics Circle) 1977; other plays include Third and Oak, 1978, Circus Valentine, 1979, The Holdup, 1980, 'Night, Mother, 1982, Traveler in the Dark, 1984; author (novel) The Fortune Teller, 1987. Recipient Susan Smith Blackburn prize for 'Night, Mother, 1982; Pulitzer prize for drama for 'Night, Mother, 1983; Nat. Endowment for Arts grantee, 1978-79; Rockefeller playwright-in-residence grantee, 1979-80. Office: care Pat Galloway/Wm Morris Agy 1350 Ave of the Americas New York NY 10019

NORMAN, MARY MARSHALL, college president; b. Auburn, N.Y., Jan. 10, 1937; d. Anthony John and Zita Norman; B.S. cum laude, LeMoyne Coll., 1958; M.A., Marquette, U., 1960; Ed.D., Pa. State U., 1971. Tchr., St. Cecilia's Elem. Sch., Theinsville, Wis., 1959-60; vocat. counselor Marquette U., Milw., 1959-60; dir. testing and counseling U. Rochester (N.Y.), 1960-62; dir. testing and counseling, dean women, asso. dean coll., asst. dean students, dir. student activities, asst. prof. psychology Corning (N.Y.) Community Coll., 1962-68; research asst. Center for Study Higher Edn., Pa. State U., University Park, 1969-71; dean faculty South Campus, Community Coll. Allegheny County, West Mifflin, Pa., 1971-72, exec. dean, coll. v.p., 1972-82; pres. Orange County Community Coll., 1982—; cons. Boricua Coll., N.Y.C., 1976-77; reader NSF, 1977-78; mem. govtl. commn. com. Am. Assn. Community and Jr. Colls., 1976-79, bd. dirs., 1982—; mem. and chmn. various middle state accreditation teams. Bd. dirs. Orange County United Way. Mem. Am. Assn. Higher Edn., Nat. Assn. Women Deans Counselors, Am. Assn. Women in Community and Jr. Colls. (charter, Woman of Yr. 1981), Pa. Assn. Two-Yr. Colls., Pa. Assn. Acad. Deans, Pitts. Council Women Execs. (charter), Am. Council on Edn. (Pa. rep. identification women for adminstrn. 1978—), Pa. Council on Higher Edn., Orange County C. of C., Gamma Pi Epsilon. Contbr. articles to profl. jours. Home: 8 Crabapple Ln Middletown NY 10940 Office: 115 South St Middletown NY 10940

NORMAN, MARYANNE, financial analyst; b. Passaic, N.J., Aug. 21, 1949; d. John Clifford and Arlene (Redling) Anema; m. Wayne Jonathan Norman. AS cum laude, Ocean County Coll., 1977; BS, Salisbury State Coll., 1979; MBA, Fairleigh Dickinson U., 1985. Clk. typist elec. command U.S. Army, Ft. Monmouth, N.J., 1968-73, budget asst. elec. command, 1973-77, budget analyst proj. mgr. optads, 1981-84; budget analyst system command U.S. Army, Ft. Lee, Va., 1984-85; budget analyst, research and devel. dir. CECOM U.S. Army, Monmouth, 1985-86, supervisory budget analyst, prodn. and system mgmt. dir. CECOM, 1986—. Mem. Nat. Assn. Female Execs., Army Comptrollership. Lodge: Moose. Home: 597 Vision Ave Toms River NJ 08753

NORMAN, SYLVIA REAVES, engineer; b. Rock Hill, S.C., Sept. 22, 1956; d. Titus and Mary Ruth (Jennings) Reaves; m. Jacob Aubrey Norman, Aug. 30, 1980; 1 child Nicholas Alexander. BCE, N.C. State U., 1978. Engr. Raleigh (N.C.) Dept. Transp., 1975-76, So. Bell Telephone Co., Charlotte, N.C., 1977; sr. engr. E. I. DuPont de Nemours, Brevard, N.C., 1978—. Chmn. Nat. Bus. and Profl. Women, Western, N.C., 1983; records officer Transylvania County core com., Brevard, N.C., 1986; active Big Bros./Big Sisters. Named Young Careerist of Western N.C. Nat. Bus. & Profl. Women, 1983. Mem. Nat. Bus. and Profl. Women (chmn. young careerist selection com.). Home: 120 Hawthorne Dr Brevard NC 28712 Office: E I Dupont de Nemours Station Rd Cedar Mountain NC 28718

NORMANDIN, MARY ANNE, educational administrator, consultant; b. Portland, Oreg., Feb. 4, 1928; d. Thomas Eben and Anne Marie (Schmit) Shea; m. Talbot Herbert Normandin, Sept. 24, 1949 (dec.); children—John Louis, Sue Marie, Paul Herbert, Frederick Lyle, Frank Talbot. B.A., Marylhurst Coll., 1949; postgrad. U. Oreg., Oreg. State U., 1965-70, Journalism and pub. relations faculty, dir. pub. info. and publs. Marylhurst Coll., Lake Oswego, Oreg., 1963-70; asst. to dean Northwestern Sch. Law of Lewis and Clark Coll., Portland, Oreg., 1970-71, asst. to pres., 1971—; dir. AMFAC, Inc., Honolulu, 1979—, chmn. audit com., 1983—. Bd. dirs. Roger Bounds Found., Hermiston, Oreg., 1981—; bd. dirs. Oreg. Arts Found., Portland, 1975-87, pres. 1977-82; bd. dirs. Oreg. Bus. Com. for Arts, 1987—, City Club Found., Portland, 1980-83, St. Andrews Legal Clinic, Portland, 1983—, Contemporary Crafts Assn., Portland, 1978-85; active Oreg. Community Found., Oreg. Hist. Soc., Portland Art Assn., Met. Mus. Art. Mem. Nat. Council Univ. Research Adminstrs. (exec. com. 1977-80), Am. Council on Edn. State of Oreg. Nat. Identification Program (chmn. 1983-86); mem. City of Portland Cable Regulatory Commn., 1984—, Met. Arts Commn., 1985—; mem. adv. com. Portland Performing Arts Ctr., 1984-87. Republican. Roman Catholic. Office: Lewis and Clark Coll 0615 SW Palatine Hill Rd Portland OR 97219

NORMILE, BARBARA, systems manager, consultant; b. Trenton, N.J., Jan. 4, 1951; d. William Donald and Beatrice Marie (Noon) N. BS in Edn., St. Francis Coll., Loretto, Pa., 1972; postgrad., Pa. State U., State College, Pa., 1976; student, Mercer County Community Coll., Trenton, N.J., 1983, 85-86. Cert. elem. and secondary math. tchr. Tchr. math. and sci. St. Anthony Sch., Trenton, 1972-77; tchr. math Cumberland Regional High Sch., Seabrook, N.J., 1977-82; programmer N.J. Dept. Human Services, Trenton, 1982-84; programmer/analyst Computer Services Group, Trenton, 1984; sr. computer systems designer Martin Marietta Data Systems, Princeton, N.J., 1984-86; sr. systems mgr. Storey/Ross/Barker, Inc., Lambertville, N.J., 1987—; union rep. Cumberland Regional Edn. Assn., Seabrook, mem. negotiating team, 1980-81; computer tchr. West Windsor/Plainsboro (N.J.) Adult Edn., 1983-86. Dem. committeewoman, Bridgeton, N.J., 1980. Mem. N.J. Novell Users Group, Nat. Assn. Female Execs., Gamma Sigma Sigma (v.p. 1971-72). Home: 249 Hobart Ave Trenton NJ 08629 Office: Storey/Ross/Barker Inc 9B Church St Lambertville NJ 08530

NORNIELLA, IRMA, import and wholesale distributer; b. Havana, Cuba, Feb. 4, 1939; came to U.S., 1969; d. Joaquin and Josephine (Nodal) N.; m. Richard Valdes, Nov. 25, 1962 (div. Nov. 1985); children: Maggie Alonso, Richard Jr.; m. Francis Richardson, May 5, 1987. BS, Villanova U., Havana, 1960; BS in Econs., St. Peters Coll., 1978. Gen. mgr. prodn. Unisa Am., Inc., Miami, Fla., 1978-86, head accessory div., 1987—; gen. mgr. prodn. Terra Island, Inc., Miami, 1986-87. Republican. Roman Catholic. Home: 9115 SW 123d Ave Ct Miami FL 33186 Office: Unisa Am Inc 6900 NW 52d Ave Miami FL 33166

NORRGARD, KRISTIN ANN, publisher; b. London, June 19, 1957; d. John Thomas and Barbara Ann (Erikson) N. BA, William Smith Coll., Geneva, N.Y., 1979. Account mgr. Media Book, Inc., N.Y.C., 1979-80; dir. advt. Ad Forum mag., N.Y.C., 1980-83; nat. account mgr. Ladies' Home Jour., N.Y.C., 1983-85; dir. advt. Savvy mag., N.Y.C., 1985-86, pub., 1986—. Active Jr. League of N.Y.C., 1979—, Fountain House, N.Y.C., The Manhattan Soc., N.Y.C. Mem. Advt. Women of N.Y. Republican. Club: N.Y. Health and Racquetball (N.Y.C.). Office: Savvy Mag Family Media Inc 3 Park Ave New York NY 10016

NORRIS, BARBARA THERESA, financial manager, stockbroker, insurance broker; b. Bklyn., Nov. 20, 1948; d. William Valentine and Stella (Laskowski) N.; diploma, L.I. Coll. Hosp. Sch. Nursing, 1968; B.S. magna cum laude, City U. N.Y., 1982. Charge nurse medicine/surgery L.I. Coll. Hosp., Bklyn., 1968-69, asst. head nurse labor/delivery unit, 1969-72, asst. dir. nursing, 1972-74, staff devel. instr., 1974-79, staff cons. materials mgmt. and nursing recruitment, 1979-80, staff cons. materials mgmt., 1980-83; mktg. cons., 1982-83; pres. Barbara Norris, Inc. Recipient N.Y. State Regents Incentive award, 1966; Nursing Sch. scholar Women's Floral Assn., 1968; lic. nurse, N.Y. Mem. L.I. Coll. Hosp. Sch. Nursing Alumnae Assn., Am. Assn. Critical Care Nurses, N.Y. Heart Assn., Smithsonian Assocs., Nat. Mus. Women in the Arts (charter), Arline Shahmanesh Hodgkins Research Orgn. Editor Nursing Communications, 1976-79. Contbr. poetry to anthologies. Home: 51-A Douglass St Brooklyn NY 11231 Office: Allied Capital Group Inc 11 Broadway New York NY 10004

NORRIS, DOROTHY MARIE, interior designer, consultant; b. Chgo., Aug. 19; children: William, Rebecca. Cert., Harrington Inst. Interior Design, 1965; B of Gen. Studies, Roosevelt U., 1972. Interior design coordinator Sears, Roebuck and Co., Chgo., 1965-69; display coordinator Laura Ashley, Inc., Chgo., 1981-84, regional interior design consultant, 1984—. Mem. Nat. Assn. Female Execs., Inc. Office: Laura Ashley 835 N Michigan Ave Chicago IL 60611

NORRIS, ELIZABETH DOWNE, librarian; b. White Plains, N.Y., Apr. 25, 1914; d. Albro Farwell and Alice Elizabeth (Morse) Downe; B.A., Smith Coll., 1936; M.Div., Yale U., 1939; M.L.S., Columbia U., 1955; 1 son, Donald E. Norris. Asst. residence dir. New Haven YWCA, 1940-42; religious edn. librarian Union Theol. Sem., N.Y.C., 1953-57; librarian NCCJ, N.Y.C., 1957-63; head librarian Nat. Bd. YWCA, N.Y.C., 1963—, dir. Nat. Bd. Archives Project, 1976—, YWCA historian, 1980—. Recipient Henry Foote Lewis prize in religion, 1934. Mem. Spl. Libraries Assn., Soc. Am. Archivists. Mem. United Ch. Christ. Editor: Feminine Figures: Selected Facts about American Women and Girls, 1968-72; Subject Headings on Women, 1973; Recent Trends in Professionalism, 1973; The YWCA Advances Women's Rights, 1855-1983, 1983; Dairy of a Volunteer, 1983; Women and Children First; a Century of YWCA Services to Children, 1984; contbg. librarian Mental Health Book Rev. Index, 1961-72; editor, mem. adv. com. Books for Brotherhood, ann. 1957-76; contbr. articles to jours. Home: 505 La Guardia Pl New York City NY 10012 Office: 726 Broadway New York NY 10003

NORRIS, FRANCES MCMURTRAY, government official; b. Jackson, Miss., Mar. 27, 1946; d. William and Helen Frances (Dutton) McMurtray; m. Stephen Leslie Norris, Oct. 8, 1981. B.S., U. Miss., 1968, postgrad. in law, 1973; M.S.L.S., U. Ky., 1970; postgrad. program for med. librarians, U. Tenn., 1970-71. Legis. asst. to G. V. Montgomery, U.S. Ho. of Reps., Washington, 1974-78; staff asst. to Trent Lott rules com. U.S. Ho. of Reps., Washington, 1979-80; asst. to Republican whip U.S. Ho. of Reps., Washington, 1981-82; dir. legis. liaison Dept. Edn., Washington, 1983; dep. asst. sec. for legis. Dept. Edn., 1984-85, asst. sec. for legislation, 1986—. Pres. Miss. Soc. of Washington, 1983-84. U.S. Govt. fellow U. Ky., Lexington, 1969-70. Republican. Presbyterian. Home: 1000 Heather Hill Ct McLean VA 22101 Office: Dept of Edn Office of Sec 400 Maryland Ave SW Washington DC 20202

NORRIS, MARUJA MIRANDA, giftware retailer; b. Havana, Cuba, Mar. 19, 1933; came to U.S., 1957; d. José and María (García) González; m. Robert M. Norris, Nov. 18, 1951; children—Robert, Josephine. Grad. Sacred Heart Sch., Havana, 1951, BA Sacred Heart Coll., Havana, 1955; diploma Chgo. Sch. Interior Decoration, 1965. Owner Miranda's, Rockford, Ill., 1984—. Bd. dirs. Spanish Services, Keith County Day Sch., Rockford; vol. County Med. Aux., Rockford, 1961-84. Mem. (lifetime) St. Anthony Med. Ctr. Aux. Republican. Roman Catholic. Clubs: Rockford Country, City, Woman's (Rockford). Home and Office: 3510 Val Mark Terr Rockford IL 61107

NORRIS, PATRICIA KILMER, public relations executive; b. New Rochelle, N.Y., Feb. 7, 1933; d. Hugh and Patricia (Polk) Kilmer; student Sweet Briar Coll., 1951-52, Westchester Comml. Sch., 1953-54; m. James Alexander Norris, Feb. 16, 1957; children—Melissa Polk, Benjamin White II. Asst. beauty editor Glamour mag., N.Y.C., 1954-55; sr. exec. sec. McCann-Erickson Inc., N.Y.C., 1955-59; sec. to pres., office mgr. Thomson-Leeds Co., Inc., N.Y.C., 1959-62; dir. pub. relations Glenview (Ill.) Park Dist., 1975-78; freelance writer/pub. relations, Glenview, 1978—. Rec. sec. Glenview Aux., 1968-70, pres., 1970-72, v.p. pres.'s council of all auxs. Skokie Valley Hosp., 1972-73, pres., 1973-74; active Glenview Bi-Centennial Commn., 1976; active Northfield Twp. Republican Women's Club, 1974—, publicity chmn., 1977-79, active 10th Dist. Rep. Women's Club, 1974—; publicity chmn. Glenbrook So. High Sch. Instrumental League, 1978-79, Glenview Area Hist. Soc. Coach House/Library, 1978-79; pres. Grove Heritage Assn., Glenview, 1979-83, pres.' adviser, 1983-84; founder, rec. sec. Save the Grove Com., 1973-75; mem. Citizens' Adv. Com. for the Grove, 1975-76; active Glenview Independence Day Commn., 1986—; mem. Glenbrook Chpt. Valparaiso (Ind.) U. Guild; women's bd. dirs. Youth Services Boys div. Lawrence Hall, Chgo., 1982—, 1st v.p., 1986-88; publicity chmn., bd. dirs. Episcopal Ch. Women, 1983-85; guild mem. and bd. dirs. Holy Trinity Episcopal Ch., Glenview, sec., 1983-85, 1st v.p., 1986—, ch. acolyte, 1987—. Recipient Cert. of Merit, Village of Glenview. Mem. LWV (chmn. local environ. study com. 1983—, bd. dirs. 1987—, observors chmn. 1984-86, sec. 1986-87, pres. 1987—). Episcopalian. Club: North Shore Public Relations. Home: 4121 Kennicott Ln Glenview IL 60025

NORRIS, THOMASINE PARKER, educator, academic administrator; b. Quitman, Tex., May 19, 1940; d. Clyde and Bennie (Taylor) Parker; m. James Earl Norris, Sept. 10, 1960; children: Victor Devereaux, James Tyrone. BS, Bishop Coll., 1963; MA, Azuza Pacific U., 1982. Tchr. Overseas Dependent Schs., Naha, Okinawa, Japan, 1966-68; counselor Community Action Prog., Jacksonville, N.C., 1968-69; tchr. Del Norte Elem. Sch., Roswell, N.M., 1969-70; bank teller Santa Monica (Calif.) Bank, 1970-71; tchr. Loren Miller Elem. Sch., Los Angeles, 1971-77, Mt. Washington Elem. Sch., Los Angeles, 1977-79; resource specialist Grandview Jr. High Sch., Valinda, Calif., 1979-82, El Monte Union (Calif.) High Sch., 1983-85; asst. prin. Chapel Hill Mid. Sch., Tyler, Tex., 1985—; cons. Los Angeles Tchrs'. Aides, 1971-77. Mem. Am. Assn. Educators, Profl. Bus. Women Am., Tex. Adminstrs. Assn., Delta Sigma Theta. Baptist. Home: 4805 Commanche Trail Tyler TX 75707 Office: Chapel Hill Mid Sch Rt 7 Box 34 Tyler TX 75707

NORSMAN, ANNETTE SONJA, health association administrator, educator; b. Council Bluffs, Iowa, May 5, 1941; d. George Waldemar and Martha Desideria (Olson) Wahlin; m. Jerry Lynn Norsman, June 15, 1963 (div. 1988); children: Brian Jerome, Brent Andrew, Caroline Louise. AA, Riverside Coll., 1961; BA, Augustana Coll., 1963; MS, U. Wis., 1987. Cert. tchr., Ill., Conn., Calif., Wis. Tchr. Hartford (Conn.) Pub. Schs., 1963-64, Berkeley (Calif.) Pub. Schs., 1964-65, Milw. Pub. Schs., 1965-66, Madison (Wis.) Pub. Schs., 1966-68; coordinator grants project Assn. Retarded Citizens, Madison, 1975-77, dir. tng. outreach, 1977-80; exec. dir. Wis. Assn. Devel. Disabilities, Madison, 1980-87, Wis. Ret. Tchrs. Assn., Madison, 1987—; Mem. nat. adu. bd. Accreditation Standards Commn. on Accreditation Rehab. Facilities, Tucson, 1985; mem. nat. consortium community health service Adminstrn. Devel. Disabilities, Washington, 1987. Co-producer (video tape) Commit to the Community 1986, Are We Ready to Listen? 1985; author/editor: (instructional series) Patterns for Participation, 1984. Chmn., pres. Wis. Coalition Arts and Human Needs, Milw., 1984-86; bd. dirs. Madison Art Ctr., 1976-78; v.p., pres. Madison Art Ctr. League, 1974-78; mem. Symphony League, Madison. Mem. Assn. Retarded Citizens (nat. adv. self advocacy 1984-86, nat. conv.program com. 1984-86) Am. Assn. Mental Deficiency, Council Advancement Citizenship, Independent Sector. Democrat. Lutheran. Home: 4213 Manitou Way Madison WI 53711 Office: Wis Ret Tchrs Assn 2564 Branch St Middleton WI 53562

NORTH, KATHRYN E. KEESEY (MRS. EUGENE C. NORTH), retired educator; b. Columbia, Pa., Jan. 25, 1916; d. Issac and Elizabeth (French) Keesey; B.S., Ithaca Coll., 1938; M.A., N.Y. U., 1950; m. Eugene C. North, Aug. 18, 1938. Dir. music Cairo (N.Y.) Central Sch. Dist., 1938; music edn.

cons. Argyle (N.Y.) Central Sch. Dist., 1939; dir. gen. music curriculum Hartford (N.Y.) Central Sch. Dist., 1939; mem. staff Del. Dept. Pub. Instrn., Dover, 1943; dir. music edn. Herricks (N.Y.) Pub. Schs., 1944-71; ret., 1971. Vis. lectr. Ithaca Coll., summers 1959, 60, 62-65, Fairleigh-Dickinson U., Rutherford, N.J., summer 1966, Albertus Magnus Coll., New Haven, summer 1968; instr. Adelphi Coll., 1954-55, Sch.. Edn., N.Y.U., 1964-65. Mem. Music Educators Nat. Conf., N.E.A., N.Y. State Sch. Music Assn., N.Y. State Tchrs. Assn., Nassau Music Educators Assn. (exec. bd. 1947-58), N.Y. State Council Adminstrs. Music Edn. (chpt. v.p. 1967-68), Herricks Tchrs. Assn. (pres. 1948), Sigma Alpha Iota. Mem. Order Eastern Star. Home: 1616 Calle Camille La Jolla CA 92037

NORTHCROSS, LYDIA ANN, probation officer, social worker; b. Detroit, Oct. 15, 1955. BS in Social Work, Eastern Mich. U., 1978; MSW, Wayne State U., 1984. Cert. social worker, Mich. Youth counselor Comprehensive Youth Services, Detroit, 1979-80; case mgr. Wayne Ctr. for Retarded, Detroit, 1980-82; social work therapist Devel. Ctrs., Inc., Detroit, 1982-83; juvenile probation officer Wayne County Probate Ct., Detroit, 1984—; prin. Met. Residential Care Systems, Detroit, 1987—; prodn. asst. Mental Health Performing Arts Assn., Detroit, 1983. Mem. Nat. Assn. Social Workers, Mich. Residential Care Assn., Nat. Assn. Female Execs., Nat. Assn. Residential Care Facilities, Mich. Soc. Clin. Social Work, NAACP, Ea. Mich. U. Alumni Assn., Wayne State U. Alumni Assn., Fraternal Order of Police. Democrat. Office: Wayne County Juvenile Ct 1025 E Forest Ave Detroit MI 48207

NORTHCUTT, MARIE ROSE, learning disabilities specialist; b. White Plains, N.Y., Feb. 2, 1950; d. Carlo and Marcelline Marie Rose (Benoit) DeMarco; m. Kenneth Walter Northcutt, Mar. 17, 1984; 1 child, James Lee. BA, Lynchburg Coll., 1972; MA, Columbia U., 1977. Cert. elem. and secondary tchr., N.Y. Tchr. Petersburg (Va.) Pub. Schs., 1972-74; asst. relocation mgr. Ticor Co., White Plains, 1974-75; 3d grade tchr. Resurrection Sch., Rye, N.Y., 1975-76; 6th grade tchr. Harrison (N.Y.) Cen. Sch. Dist., 1976-78, learning disabilities specialist, 1981—; tchr. of emotionally handicapped N.Y.C. Schs., 1978-80; learning evaluator Empire State Coll., White Plains, 1981-82; ind. evaluation cons., White Plains, 1981—. Mem. Harrison High Sch. PTA, 1980—. Mem. Assn. for Children with Learning Disabilities, Westchester County Assn. for Children with Learning Disabilities, Orton Soc., Phi Delta Kappa. Roman Catholic. Home: 81 Griffin Pl White Plains NY 10603 Office: Harrison Cen Sch Dist Union Ave Harrison NY 10528

NORTHRUP, CHRISTIANE LOUISE, gynecologist-obstetrician; b. Buffalo, Oct. 4, 1949; d. George Wilbur and Edna (Zwilling) N,; m. Kenneth Moller III, May 3, 1975; children: Ann Christiane, Kate Northrup. BA, Case Western Res., 1971; MD, Dartmouth Coll., 1975. Diplomate Am. Bd. Ob-Gyn. Intern Tufts New Eng. Med. Ctr. Affiliated Hosps., Boston, 1975; intern then resident Tufts New Eng. Med. Ctr., Boston, 1976-79; assoc. clin. prof. ob-gyn Tufts U. Sch. Medicine, Boston, 1979-80; clin. instr. ob-gyn U. Vt. Coll. Med., Portland, Maine, 1980-85, asst. clin. prof. ob-gyn, 1985—; practice medicine specializing in ob-gyn Gynecol. Assocs., South Portland, 1979-85, Women's Health Care Orgn. Women to Women, Yarmouth, Maine, 1986—; Mem. high risk perinatal group Maine Med. Ctr., Portland, 1981-83; bd. trustees Proprioceptive Writing Ctr., 1987—. Contbr. various articles on women's health to profl. jours. Fellow Am. Coll. Ob-Gyn; mem. Am. Holistic Med. Assn. (sec. 1986-88, pres.-elect 1988—), Am. Holistic Med. Found. (pres. 1986—). Office: Women to Women 1 Pleasant St Yarmouth ME 40496

NORTHWAY, WANDA L., realty company executive; b. Columbia, Mo., July 11, 1942; d. Herman W. and Goldie M. (Wood) Proctor; m. Donald H. Northway, June 12, 1965; 1 child, Michelle D. Student U. Mo., 1966. Lic. real estate agt., Mo.; grad. Realtors Inst. Realtor, assoc. Gentry Real Estate Co., Columbia, 1969-80; realtor Griffin Real Estate Co., 1980-81; pres., realtor, ptnr. House of Brokers Realty, Inc., Columbia, 1981—; pres., organizer Realtor-Assoc. Sales Club, Columbia, 1975; pres. Columbia Bd. Realtors, 1982. Contbr. articles to realty mags. Sunday sch. tchr., girls' aux. leader Baptist Ch.; vol. ARS, local hosp; campaign worker for Columbia legislators; mem. allocation com. United Way; active vol. Am. Cancer Soc. and Heart Assn. Named Realtor Assoc. of Yr., Columbia Bd. Realtors, 1974, Realtor of Yr., 1980. Mem. Mo. Assn. Realtors (state dir. 1974-77, Realtor Assoc. of Yr. award 1977), Realtors Nat. Mktg. Inst. (cert. residential specialist 1978), Nat. Assn. Realtors, (nat. dir. 1977), Epsilon Sigma Alpha (state corr. sec., local pres.). Republican. Baptist. Clubs: Million Dollar; Federation of Women's (pres. Mo. 1980). Office: House of Brokers Realty Inc 1316 Parkade Blvd Columbia MO 65203

NORTON, ANDRE ALICE, author; b. Cleve.; d. Adalbert and Bertha Stemm N. Librarian Cleve. Public Library, until 1951. Author 109 books. Mem. Authors League, Penwomen, Sci. Fiction Writers Am.

NORTON, ANITA, taxidermist; b. Delta, Colo., July 18, 1941, d. Arthur Boyd and Avalon Mae (Payne) Wilhelm; m. Lawrence Alford Norton, July 10, 1970; stepchildren: Rick Norton, Linda Norton Christiansen, Brenda Norton. Cert. in keypunching, Mesa Coll., 1964. Bus driver Mesa County Sch. Dist., grand Junction, Colo., 1964-68; data entry op. First Security Bank-Computer, Salt Lake City, 1968-72, quality supr., 1972-79; prin. Norton's Minor Home Repair, Bountiful, Utah, 1979-80; apprentice taxidermist Wildlife West Taxidermy, West Jordan, Utah, 1980-82; prin. Norton Taxidermy, Inc., Bountiful, Utah, 1982—; also bd. dirs. Norton Taxidermy, Inc., Bountiful; instr. Norton Taxidermy, Inc., Bountiful, Utah, 1982-87, Utah Taxidermist Assn., Provo, Utah, 1983-87; lectr. Utah Wood Carvers Assn., Bountiful, 1985-86; judge taxidermy Utah State Fair, Salt Lake City, 1984-87. Recipient various awards for works; named distinguished taxidermist Taxidermy Review mag., 1986. Mem. Nat. Taxidermists Assn. (Henry Wichers Inchumuk award 1987), Utah Taxidermist Assn. (area dir. 1983—, master taxidermist, 1986), Internat. Guild of Taxidermy, Nat. Wildlife Fedn. Home and Office: 177 W 3000 South Bountiful UT 84010

NORTON, BILLIE FOSTINA, social services administrator; b. Topeka, Sept. 10, 1927; d. Verlette Floyd Williams and Ann Leona (Foster) Card; m. Ralph G. Norton (div.); children: Michael, Audré Marie, Anthony. BA in Behavioral Sci., Ursuline Coll., 1976; MSW, Smith Coll., 1983. Cert. alcoholism counselor. Lab. technician Blood Bank of ARC, Cleve., 1951-70; alcoholism social worker Hough-Norwood Health Ctr., Cleve., 1972-77; treatment specialist Alcoholism Services of Cleve., 1977-79; staff counselor employee assistance program Cuyahoga County Commrs., Cleve., 1980-81; alcoholism and chem. dependency treatment coordinator Ctr. for Human Services, Cleve., 1981—; mem. exec. com. Regional Council on Alcoholism, Cleve., 1981—; pvt. practice, 1979—. Mem. Nat. Assn. Female Execs., Nat. Black Alcoholism Assn., Cleve. Chpt. Alcoholism Counselors Ohio. Club: Toastmistress. Office: West Ctr for Human Services 3929 Rocky River Dr Cleveland OH 44111

NORTON, CYNTHIA LOUISE, publishing executive, art director; b. Milton, Mass., Apr. 14, 1955; d. Ralph Arnold and Mary Elizabeth (McDonald) N. BFA in Archtl. and Graphic Design, U. Mass., 1977. Graphic designer Garber Travel, Inc., Brookline, Mass., 1977-78; graphic and exhibit designer Rust Craft, Inc., Dedham, Mass., 1978-80; corp. advt. artist Morse, Inc., Canton, Mass., 1980-83; pvt. practice designer Boston, 1983-84; asst. art dir. Cahners Pub. Co., Newton, Mass., 1984-86, art dir., 1986-87; art dir. Knapp, Inc., Brockton, Mass., 1987—; guest speaker Mt. Ida Jr. Coll., Newton, 1980. Designer graphs and charts for Vols. I and II State Budget Commonwealth of Mass., 1982; art dir. Mini Micro Systems, 1984-87. Mem. Art Dirs. Club Boston, Kappa Kappa Gamma (alumni, pres. 1975-76). Roman Catholic. Home: 13 Connell St Quincy MA 02169 Office: Knapp Inc One Knapp Centre Brockton MA 02401

NORTON, KAREN ANN, accounting executive; b. Paynesville, Minn., Nov. 1, 1950; d. Dale Francis and Ruby Grace (Gehlhar) N. B.A., U. Minn., 1972; postgrad. U. Md., 1978; cert. acctg. U.S. Dept. Agr. Grad. Sch., 1978; postgrad. Calif. State Poly. U.-Pomona, 1984—. C.P.A., Md. Securities transactions analyst Bur. of Pub. Debt., Washington, 1972-79, internal auditor, 1979-81; internal auditor IRS, Washington, 1981; sr. acct. World Vision Internat., Monrovia, Calif., 1981-83, acctg. supr., 1983-87; sr. systems liaison specialist, Home Savs. Am., 1987—; cons. (vol.) info. systems John M. Perkins Found., Pasadena, Calif., 1985-86. Author (poetry): Ode to Joyce, 1985 (Golden Poet award 1985). Second v.p. chpt. Nat. Treasury Employees Union, Washington, 1978, editor chpt. newsletter; mem. M-2 Prisoners Sponsorship Program, Chino, Calif., 1984-86. Recipient Spl. Achievement award Dept. Treasury, 1976, Superior Performance award, 1977-78; Charles and Ellora Alliss scholar, 1968. Mem. Christian Ministries Mgmt. Assn., Nat. Assn. Accts. Mem. Covenant Ch. Avocations: chess; racquetball; mountain climbing; whitewater rafting.

NORTON, VIRGINIA SKEEN (MRS. JOHN H. NORTON, JR.), civic worker; b. Atlanta, June 1, 1907; d. Lola Percy and Rebecca (Baldwin) Skeen. A.B., Agnes Scott Coll., 1928; student Columbia U., 1934-35; m. John Hughes Norton, Jr., Dec. 16, 1938; children—Virginia Skeen Norton Kraft, John Hughes III. With personnel dept. Retail Credit Co., Atlanta, 1929-31, sec. to v.p., gen. mgr. Davison-Paxon, Co., Atlanta, 1931-34; with Aluminium Ltd., N.Y.C., 1935-41, sec. to pres., 1937-41; sec. to pres. Colonial Williamsburg, Inc., N.Y.C., 1943-44. Bd. dirs. North Shore Assos. Chgo. Commons, 1951-54, Infant Welfare Soc. Chgo., 1953-54, Catherine Morrill Day Nursery, Portland, Maine, 1956-59. Mem. Central Fla. Civic Theater Guild, Loch Haven Arts Soc., Winter Park Meml. Hosp. Aux., Morse Art Gallery Assocs. (dir. 1982-84), Nat. Soc. Colonial Dames Am. Episcopalian. Address: 111 S Lakemont Ave Winter Park FL 32792

NORWOOD, CONNIS MARIE, clinical nurse specialist; b. Pickens, S.C., Feb. 14, 1955; d. William Wright and Connis Virginia (Durham) N. AA, Clemson U., 1975; BS in Nursing, Med. Coll. Ga., 1984, MS in Nursing, 1986. cert. critical-care RN, Ga. Staff nurse Univ. Hosp., Augusta, Ga., 1975-79, 83-85, shift supr., 1979-82, critical-care clin. nurse specialist, 1985—. Mem. Am. Assn. Critical Care Nurses (pres. local chpt. 1983-84, sec. 1986-87), Sigma Theta Tau (nominating com. Beta Omicron chpt. 1987—, award Beta Omicron chpt. 1985). Methodist. Home: 8 Foxhil Dr North Augusta SC 29841 Office: Univ Hosp 1350 Walton Way Augusta GA 30910

NORWOOD, JANET LIPPE, government official; b. Newark, Dec. 11, 1923; d. M. Turner and Thelma (Levinson) Lippe; m. Bernard Norwood, June 25, 1943; children—Stephen Harlan, Peter Carlton. B.A., Douglass Coll., 1945; M.A., Fletcher Sch. Law and Diplomacy, 1946, Ph.D., 1949; LL.D., Fla. Internat. U., 1979, Carnegie Mellon U., 1984. Instr. Wellesley Coll., 1948-49; economist William L. Clayton Center, Fletcher Sch. Law and Diplomacy, 1953-58; with Bur. Labor Statistics, Dept. Labor, Washington, 1963—; dep. commr., then acting commr. Bur. Labor Statistics, Dept. Labor, 1975-79, commr. labor stats., 1979—. Author papers, reports in field. Recipient Disting. Achievement award Dept. Labor, 1972, Spl. Commendation award, 1977, Philip Arnow award, 1979, Elmer Staats award, 1982, Pub. Service award, 1984; named to Alumni Hall of Fame, Rutgers U., 1987/. Fellow Am. Statis. Assn. (pres.-elect), AAAS, Royal Statis. Soc., Nat. Assn. Bus. Economists; mem. Am. Econ. Assn., Indsl. Relations Research Assn., Royal Statis. Soc., Women's Caucus in Stats., Com. Status Women Econs. Profession, Internat. Statis. Inst., Internat. Assn. Official Statistics, Nat. Acad. Pub. Adminstrn., Soc. Disting. Achievement. Home: 6409 Marjory Ln Bethesda MD 20817 Office: Dept of Labor Bureau of Labor Stats 441 G St NW Washington DC 20212

NORWOOD, JOY JANELL, corporate real estate executive; b. Barnes, Kans., Aug. 25, 1936; d. Howard Clayton and Gladys Melveno (Wells) Cook; divorced; 1 child, Rebecca. Student, U. Colo., 1958-63; grad., Realtors Inst. Ohio State U., 1977. Lic. real estate agt., Ohio. Registered rep. First Investors Corp., Boston, 1966-68; area supr. Wohl Shoe Co., Boston, 1968-70; residential real estate broker Coldwell Banker, Cin., 1970-78, comml. real estate broker, 1978-80; comml. real estate broker Rubloff, Cin., 1980-82; sr. real estate rep. Ky. Fried Chicken, Louisville, 1982-86; v.p. Otto Realty Corp., Cin., 1987—. Jr. high sch. tchr. Mason (Ohio) Ch. Christ, 1986—, mem. choir., 1986—. Served with U.S. Army, 1955-58. Mem. Nat. Assn. Corp. Real Estate Execs., Internat. Council Shopping Ctrs., Cin. Bd. Realtors (polit. affairs com. 1974, Million Dollar Club award, 1972-79), Cin. Hist. Soc. Republican. Club: Flying Neutrons (Cin.). Home: 8547 Ashwood Dr Westchester OH 45069 Office: Otto Realty Corp 2311 Grandin Rd Cincinnati OH 45208

NORWOOD, JUANITA HILL, medical center administrator; b. Washington, Oct. 22, 1935; d. Leroy and Sarah (Wilcher) Hill; widowed; children: Shelton, Clarence. Student, Morgan State U., 1953-55; M. Lincoln U., Lincoln University, Pa., 1984. Personnel mgmt. specialist VA Med. Ctr., Phila., 1975—, equal employment specialist, 1978-80; cons. dept. personnel City Phila., 1985-87, Pa. Coalition Against Domestic Violence, Harrisburg, Pa., 1986; EEO investigator Office VA, Washington, 1977-82; founder Norwood's Sporting Goods Inc., Phila., 1984, J.H. Norwood Inc., Phila., 1987. Pres. Strawberry Sq. Mchts. Assn., Phila., 1987-88; bd. dirs. Phila. Council Community Advancement, 1984—, Girls Coalition of S.E. Pa., Phila., 1985-87. Recipient of Bus. and Econ. Devel. award Com. for a Better N. Phila., 1988. Mem. Fed. Mgrs. Assn. (chpt. convenor 1987, pres. 1988), United Black Bus. Assn. (fin. sec. 1986—), NOW (pres. SW Phila. chpt. 1980—), Utilities Emergency Services Fund (bd. dirs.). Office: Norwoods Sporting Goods/Leisure 2827 N 22d St Philadelphia PA 19132

NORWOOD, REGINA ANN, insurance company executive; b. Richmond, Calif., June 13, 1956; d. Raymond L. and Bernieta F. (Heyer) Terrill; m. Wynton C. Norwood, Feb. 6, 1982. Student, Old Dominion U., 1974-75; BS in Medicine, U. Md., 1979. Ins. agt. Southwestern Life Ins. Co., Washington, 1979-82, Little Rock, 1982; co-owner, v.p. Atwood-Norwood Agy., Inc., Little Rock, 1983—. Chair Am. Lung Assn., Pulaski County, 1984-85. Mem. Women Life Underwriters Assn., Little Life Underwriters Assn., Nat. Assn. Female Execs., Little Rock C. of C. (com. mem.), Chi Omega Alumni Assn. Republican. Baptist. Club: Maumelle (Ark.) Country (com. chair). Home: #12 Fairway Woods Maumelle AR 72118 Office: Atwood-Norwood Agy Inc 2024 Arkansas Valley Dr Apt 306 Little Rock AR 72212

NOTARIUS, BARBARA ANN, association executive; b. New Rochelle, N.Y., Sept. 22, 1946; d. Seymour and Florence (Schulman) N.; m. George Klein, Oct. 28, 1972, divorced; 1 child, Cydney. BS, Elmira Coll., 1968; MS, CCNY, 1972, cert. in advt., 1975; postgrad., Fla. Inst. Tech., 1979. Lic. pediatric psychologist. Tchr. N.Y.C., 1968-72; psychologist Harlem Hosp., N.Y.C., 1974-79; pres. Bed and Breakfast U.S.A., Ltd., Croten, N.Y., 1981—; charter pres. Bed and Breakfast Reservation Services Worldwide, 1985-87, chmn. bd. 1987—. Author: Open Your Own Bed and Breakfast, 1987; editor: The Bed and Breakfast Directory. Mem. Croten Beautification Com., 1985-86. Mem. County C. of C. (Westchester winner), Albany C. of C., N.Y.C. C. of C., Croton C. of C. Jewish. Office: Bed and Breakfast USA 129 Grand St Croton-on-Hudson NY 10520

NOTHHELFER, NANCY EVANS, human relations educator, psychotherapist; b. Reading, Pa., Oct. 23, 1934; d. Olin Law and Dorothy Bishop (Ermentrout) Evans; m. John Odell Nothhelfer, Sept. 20, 1958 (dec. July 1976); children: Anne Louise, John Evans. BS, Ursinus Coll., 1957; M of Profl. Studies, N.Y. Theol. Seminary, 1977. Biochemistry technician Jefferson Hosp., Phila., 1955; research asst. in chemotherapy Meml. Sloan Kettering Cancer Ctr., N.Y.C., 1957-59, 62; pvt. practice trainer, facilitator, cons. in human relations Greenwich, Conn., 1971—; pvt. practice psychotherapist Greenwich, 1974—; adj. instr. human relations, Princeton (N.J.) Theol. Sem., 1971-84, Syracuse (N.Y.) U. Sch. Mgmt., 1972-74; guest instr. Pace U., Pleasantville, N.Y., 1974-77; counselor, cons. Pathways, Greenwich, 1983-86, asst. dir. 1986-87, dir. residential services, 1988—. Dir. client services Shelter for the Homeless, Stamford, Conn., 1985-86; facilitator, edn. com. mem. Alternatives to Violence Project, N.Y.C., 1981—; past clk., past mem. ministry and counsel Soc. of Friends. Mem. Assn. for Creative Change (profl., steering com. 1979-82), Lab. Trainers and Cons. Network (bd. dirs. 1982-85). Office: Pathways 175 Milbank Ave Greenwich CT 06830

NOTO, JOANNE MARIE, publisher, dental hygiene educator; b. Mesa, Ariz., June 24, 1950; d. Joseph and Pauline Ann (Mazzone) N.; m. Jimmie Wayne Wylie, May 7, 1983. BS in Dental Hygiene, U. Calif., 1972; MA in Edn., San Francisco State U., 1983. Dental hygienist various pvt. offices, Mountain View, Calif., 1972-86; pub. Apogee, Carmel, Calif., 1985—; instr. Apogee, Los Altos Hills, Calif., 1982-87, U. Calif., San Francisco, 1984-87; educator Chabot Coll., Hayward, Calif., 1984-86, Foothill Coll., Los Altos Hills, 1983-88. Author: Use of the Ultrasonic Scaler, 1984; editor: Coronal Publishing for the Registered Dental Assistant, 1987, Study Guide for the Registered Dental Assistant, 1987, Radiology, 1987; presentor in field. Examiner Calif. State Bd. Dental Examiners, Sacramento, 1979. Calif. Community Colls. grantee, 1986. Mem. Am. Denatl Hygienisit's Assn., Calif. Dental Hygienist's Assn., No. Calif Dental Hygienist's Assn. (exec. officer 1975-80, editorialist 1978-79), Monterey Bay Dental Hygiene Soc. Republican. Home: 27959 Berwick Dr Carmel CA 93923 Office: Apogee Press PO Box 223191 Carmel CA 93922

NOUVELLE, CAMEO, investment advisor; b. Salem, Oreg., May 14, 1959; d. Ram S. and Jean Marie (Hewitt) Gursahani. Producer, dir. Cameo Prodns., Honolulu, 1979-81; asst. pub. Middle East Media Orgn., Mclean, Va., 1981-83; real estate broker Luke n' Luke Realty, Honolulu, 1983-85; registered investment adv. Ferris n Co., Washington, 1985—; pres. Unique Gift Baskets, Unltd., Va., 1987—; bd. dirs., v.p. membership com. Nat. Economists Club, Washington. Contbr. articles to profl. jours. Vol. Nat. Assn. Arab Ams., Washington, 1986. Mem. Am. Soc. Assn. Execs. Club: AMEX. Home: 3101 S Manchester St #522 Falls Church VA 22044 Office: Ferris n Co 1720 Eye St NW Washington DC 20006

NOVAK, ANN-NADINE, data processing manager; b. Cleve., Sept. 14, 1951; d. Joseph Paul and Evelyn Johanna (Suchina) N. BS in Math., Cleve. State U., 1972, BS in Computer Info. Scis., 1974, MS in Indsl. Engring., 1978. Programmer/analyst Standard Oil Co., Cleve., 1973-75, systems analyst/programmer, 1975-78, systems analyst, 1978-81; sr. systems analyst Ernst & Whinney, Cleve., 1981-84, supr., 1985, mgr., 1985—. Mem. Cleve. Chpt. Am. Inst. Indsl. Engrs. (numerous com. positions, acting treas. 1985-86, immediate past pres. 1986-87, bd. dirs. 1987—, Excellence award 1982, 85), Data Processing Mgmt. Assn., Am. Mgmt. Assn., Am. Assn Individual Investors.

NOVAK, CAROL ANN, multi-company executive; b. Plankington, S.D., Nov. 8, 1925; d. Frederick Laurence and Vera Marie (Lindekugel) Lindekugel; m. Kenneth R. Novak, Feb. 14, 1953 (dec. May 1982); children—Charles Arnold, Tanna Ann Novak Scriven, Nancy Ann. Student, Yankton Coll., 1943-44. Sec., State Auditor, Pierre, S.D., after 1944, U.S. Geol. Survey, Pierre, 1947; cutter, folder Boeing Airplane Co., Seattle, 1949-51; sec. Western Airlines, Seattle, 1951-55; sec.-treas., Novak Homes, Seattle, 1953—; sec. SEA-KOTA, Inc., Seattle, 1955-82, pres., 1983—; sec. Cascade Door Co., Seattle, 1957-83, pres., 1983—; owner, operator Agate & Crescent Beach Park, Port Angeles, Wash., 1962-77, Carols Crescent Beach, 1985—; sec. Agate & Crescent Beach Tree Farm., Port Angeles, 1965—. Home: 3440 Crescent Beach Rd Port Angeles WA 98362 Office: Agate & Crescent Beach 3454 Crescent Beach Rd Port Angeles WA 98362

NOVAK, DIANE MARIE, nurse; b. Chgo., June 7, 1951; d. William Charles and Bertha Marie (Rich) N.; R.N., Augustana Hosp., Chgo., 1971; postgrad. Loop Coll., Chgo., Northeastern Ill. U. Mem. nursing staff Augustana Hosp. (now Luth. Gen. Hosp.), Lincoln Park, Ill., 1971-73, 74-86, asst. coordinator med.-surg. unit, 1976-80, staff nurse dept. pediatrics, 1980-86, asst. unit coordinator pediatrics and stroke unit, 1982-83, staff nurse obstetrics, 1983-86; labor and delivery nurse Luth. Gen. Hosp., Park Ridge, Ill., 1986-87, asst. head nurse for labor and delivery, 1987—; staff nurse surg. and burn unit Evanston (Ill.) Hosp., 1973-74; in-service instr., CPR tchr. Mem. Transcultural Nursing Soc., Nurses Assn. of the Am. Coll. of Obstetricians and Gynecologists. Office: Luth Gen Hosp 1775 Dempster St Park Ridge IL 60068

NOVAK, ELIZABETH ANN, personnel executive; b. Detroit, Dec. 22, 1935; d. Ralph Bernard and Ida Margaret (Burgess) N. AAS, Westchester Community Coll., 1956; BA, Wayne State U., 1974, MBA, 1979. Sec. Dykema, Wheat, Spencer, Goodnow, Trigg, Detroit, 1966-68, Chrysler Corp., Highland, Mich., 1968-76; personnel recruiter Chrysler Def., 1976-78; instrl. devel. Gen. Dynamics Land Systems, Warren, Mich., 1978-83; supr., tech. trnr. Chrysler Def., Gen. Dynamics Land Systems, Warren, 1983—. Mem. Soc. Logistics Engrs. (chpt. officer 1979-88), Logistics Edn. Found. (sec. 1981-85), Am. Soc. Tng. and Devel. Democrat. Roman Catholic. Office: Gen Dynamics Land Systems 6700 E 14 Mile Rd Warren MI 48090

NOVAK, JO-ANN STOUT, chemical engineer; b. Glen Ridge, N.J., June 25, 1956; d. Herbert Austin and Anna (Messina) Stout; m. John Robert Novak Jr., Oct. 30, 1976; B.Chem. Engring., Ga. Inst. Tech., 1977; M.B.A., Oakland U., 1984. Cert. engr.-in-tng., Ga.; registered profl. engr., Mich. Trainee AC Spark Plug div. Gen. Motors Corp., Flint, Mich., 1977-78, chemist, 1978-79, exptl. chemist, 1979-81, mfg. engr., 1981-84, sr. mfg. engr., 1984-87; sr. mfg. project engr., 1987—. Mem. Am. Electroplaters Soc. (dir. Saginaw Valley br. 1981-83, ednl. chmn. 1984-85, sec.-treas. 1985-86, 2d v.p. 1986-87, 1st v.p. 1987-88, pres. 1988-89), Am. Inst. Chem. Engrs., Soc. Mfg. Engrs. Office: AC Spark Plug Div Gen Motors Corp 1300 N Dort Hwy Flint MI 48556

NOVAK, NINA, lawyer; b. Basking Ridge, N.J., Oct. 2, 1952; d. Edward Lawrence and Rita Virginia (Myers) N. B.A., Roanoke Coll., 1974; J.D., U. Richmond, 1976. Bar: Va. 1977, D.C. 1987. Assoc. Taylor, Walker & Adams, Norfolk, Va., 1977-80; asst. resident counsel Va. Hosp. Assn., Richmond, Va., 1980-82; assoc. Miles & Stockbridge, Washington, 1982-85, health law cons., 1986-88; v.p. Dudley & Co., Inc., Washington, 1987—; ptnr. Novak & Dudley, Washington, 1988—. Mem. ABA (governing com., forum com. on health law), Va. Bar Assn., Am. Acad. Hosp. Attys., Nat. Health Lawyers Assn., Roanoke Coll. Alumni Assn. (pres. 1981—). Republican. Office: 1620 Eye St NW Suite 501 Washington DC 20006

NOVAK, RENA ANN, travel and restaurant executive; b. Torrance, Calif., Nov. 12, 1951; d. John B. and Mary E. (Olufsen) Depue; m. Robert Paul Novak, Apr. 18, 1970; 1 child, Brenda Suzanne. A.A. in Computer Sci., Control Data Corp., 1971. Travel counselor Flying Tiger Line, Los Angeles, 1973-77, Am. Express, Torrance, Calif., 1977-78; mgr. comml. Thomas Cook Travel, Newport Beach, Calif., 1978-79; pres. Oui Travel, Inc., Medford, Oreg., 1979—; owner, pres. Bear Creek Travel, Medford, 1984—, Baccala's Pizza, Medford, 1982—. Vice-pres. pub. relations Medford chpt. Muscular Dystrophy Assn., 1980-81; sec. Medford-Alba Sister City Com.; bd. dirs. Visitors and Conv. Bur.; assoc. bd. dirs. Peter Britt Festival. Mem. Inst. Cert. Travel Agts. (study group leader 1980—), Am. Bus. Women's Assn. (chair coms.). Republican. Roman Catholic. Club: Soroptimists (chair coms.). Avocation: travel. Home: 2533 Southport Way Medford OR 97504 Office: Bear Creek Travel 820 Crater Lake Ave Suite 111 Medford OR 97504

NOVAK, SHIRLEY A., librarian; b. Rochelle, Ill., May 29, 1936; d. Don and Irma (Olson) Archer; B.S. in Elementary Edn., No. Ill. U., Dekalb, 1970. M.S. in Instructional Tech., 1975; cert. media instrn. and supervision; m. Leonard S. Novak; children—Lance Kendall, Pamela Kay. Tchr., Durand (Ill.) Elementary Sch., 1955-56, Pecatonica (Ill.) Elementary Sch., 1957-58, Windsor Sch., Loves Park, Ill., 1959-70, learning center dir., 1970-74, head librarian Harlem High Sch., 1974-84, learning ctr. dir. Harlem Jr. High Sch., 1984—. Vice pres. Rockford area TI Users Group, 1983-85; pres. Friends of the North Suburban Dist. Library, 1984-85. Mem. ALA, Am. Assn. Sch. Librarians, NEA, Ill. Edn. Assn., Harlem Educators Assn. (treas. 1980-81), Ill. Audio-Visual Assn. (Woman Yr. 1985, v.p. 1985, corr. sec. 1983), No. Ill. Media Assn., Am. Bus. Women's Assn. (corr. sec. Blackhawk chpt., 1983, v.p. 1986, Woman of Yr. 1985) Lutheran. Certified in teaching, media instructiion. Home: 5412 Garden Plain Ave Loves Park IL 61111 Office: 735 Windsor Rd Loves Park IL 61111

NOVECK, CAROLYN SCHNURER, fashion consultant, chef; b. N.Y.C., Jan. 5, 1907; d. Henry Goldsand and Rebecca Bronner; m. Lawrence Noveck, Aug. 27, 1967; 1 child, Anthony T. Schnurer. Student, N.Y. Tchrs. Tng. Sch., 1927, Acad. Design, 1929; BA, NYU, 1931. Tchr. art, music Queens (N.Y.) Pub. Schs., 1927-31; instr. fashion, retailing NYU, 1934-38; designer Bert Schnurer Cabana, N.Y.C., 1938-41; designer, mfr., dir. pub. relations, co-owner Carolyn Schnurer Inc., N.Y.C., 1941-57; advisor fashion merchandising J.P. Stevens and Co., N.Y.C., 1957-1964; v.p. Bus. Careers, N.Y.C., 1964-70; v.p., v.p. catering, cons. Lawrence Noveck Inc., N.Y.C., 1970—; critic, advisor R.I. Sch. Design; advisor students Parsons Sch.

Design; lectr. Fashion Inst. Tech., 1969-70; v.p., bd. dirs. Fashion Group Inc. Author: Culinary Fashions in Food and Table Presentations; contbr. articles to fashion pubs.; designed clothes represented in permanent collections at Costume Inst. Met. Mus. Art, Fashion Inst. Tech., Bklyn. Mus. Art. Recipient Coty, Sports Illustrated, Cotton Council, Internat. Sportswear, Am. Women Achievers Fashion Group, New Orleans, Boston Fashion Group awards. Mem. Fashion Group Inc. Home and Office: 44 Cocoanut Row Palm Beach FL 33480

NOVELLO, ANTONIA COELLO, pediatric nephrologist, research administrator; b. Fajardo, P.R., Aug. 23, 1944; d. Antonio and Ana D. (Flores) Coello; m. Joseph R. Novello, May 30, 1970. BS, U. P.R., Rio Piedras, 1965; MD, U. P.R., San Juan, 1970; MPH, Johns Hopkins Sch. Hygiene, 1982. Diplomate Am. Bd. Pediatrics. Intern in pediatrics U. Mich. Med. Ctr., Ann Arbor, 1970-71, resident in pediatrics, 1971-73, pediatric nephrology fellow, 1973-74; pediatric nephrology fellow Georgetown U. Hosp., Washington, 1974-75; project officer Nat. Inst. Arthritis, Metabolism and Digestive Diseases NIH, Bethesda, Md., 1978-79, staff physician, 1979-80; exec. sec. gen. medicine B study sect., div. of research grants NIH, Bethesda, 1981-86; dep. dir. Nat. Inst. Child Health & Human Devel., NIH, Bethesda, 1986—; clin. prof. pediatrics Georgetown U. Hosp., Washington, 1986—; mem. Georgetown Med. Ctr. Interdepartmental Research Group, 1984—; legis. fellow U.S. Senate Com. on Labor and Human Resources, Washington, 1982-83; mem. Com. on Research in Pediatric Nephrology, Washington, 1981—; participant grants assoc. program seminars Nat. Inst. Arthritis, Diabetes and Digestive and Kidney Diseases, NIH, Bethesda, 1980-81; pediatric cons. Adolescent Medicine Service, Psychiat. Inst., Washington, 1979-83; nephrology cons. Met. Washington Renal Dialysis Ctr. affiliate Georgetown U. Hosp., Washington, 1975-78; phys. diagnosis class instr. U. Mich. Med. Ctr., Ann Arbor, 1973-74. Contbr. numerous articles to profl. jours. and chpts. to books in field; mem. editorial bd. Internat. Jour Artificial Organs, Jour. Mexican Nephrology. Served to capt. USPHS, 1978—. Recipient Intern of Yr. award U. Mich. Dept. Pediatrics, 1971, Woman of Yr. award Disting. Grads. Pub. Sch. Systems, San Juan, 1980, PHS Commendation medal HHS, 1983, PHS Citation award HHS, 1984, Cert. of Recognition, Div. Research Grants NIH, 1985. Fellow Am. Acad. Pediatrics; mem. AMA, Internat. Soc. Nephrology, Am. Soc. Nephrology, Latin Am. Soc. Nephrology, Soc. Pediatric Research, Am. Soc. Artificial Internal Organs, Assn. Mil Surgeons U.S., Am. Soc. Pediatric Nephrology, Pan Am. Med. and Dental Soc. (pres. elect, sec. 1984), Va. State Med. Soc., D.C. Med. Soc. (assoc.). Home: 1315 31st St NW Washington DC 20007 Office: Nat Inst Child Health & Human Dev Dept Health & Human Services Bldg 31 Room 2A03 9000 Rockville Pike Bethesda MD 20892

NOVEMBRINI, ROSEMARIE T., library media specialist; b. Beverly, Mass., Sept. 16, 1953; d. James W. and Rose Marie (Valletta) Tarolli; m. Joseph August Novembrini, May 10, 1986. AA, Onondaga Community Coll., 1973; BS, Evang. Coll., 1975; MLS, Syracuse (N.Y.) U., 1978. Dir. Solvay (N.Y.) Pub. Library, 1977-79; library media specialist Solvay Sch. Dist., 1978—; co-coordinator gifted and talented program Hazard St. Sch., Solvay, 1985—. Editor: newsletter The Hotline, 1979—. tchr. Sunday sch. Solvay Assembly of God, 1975—, co-leader youth dept., 1985—. Mem. Librarians Unltd., Cen. N.Y. Media Specialists, Solvay Tchrs. Assn. (exec. com. 1979—). Home: 320 Higgins Dr Baldwinsville NY 13027 Office: Hazard St Sch Hazard St Solvay NY 13209

NOVEY, LINDA SIMMONS, management consultant; b. Dyersburg, Tenn., Oct. 18, 1940; d. L. Doyle and Mary Jane (Alsup) Moore; m. George Thomas Novey, Apr. 1, 1981; children: Lori, Jane, Paula; stepchildren: George, Clifford. BA, U. Calif., Berkeley, 1962; postgrad., U. Tenn., U. So. Calif. Pres. Simmons Conventions Inc., Columbia, S.C., 1975-79; mng. ptnr. Abbott Simmons Mktg. Assocs., Memphis, 1979-81; exec. v.p. Cohen & Henry, Virginia Beach, 1981-84, Hospitality Standards Ltd., Skokie, Ill., 1981—; pres. Novey Enterprises, Atlanta, 1984—; mem. adv. bd. Discovery Learning Inc., Atlanta, Atlanta Concierge Assocs.; vis. asst. prof. Ga. State U., Atlanta; cons. Ga. Hospitality and Tourism div., Atlanta; guest lectr. Ohio State U., U. Ark., internationally; graduation speaker Brighton (Eng.) Poly. Coll. Author: The Smile Parade, 1980. Mem. adv. com. Max Clelland Sec. State Ga. Recipient Spl. Person of Yr. award S.C. C. of C., 1972; named Woman of Yr. Fla. Jr. Woman's Club, 1975. Mem. Ga. Hospitality and Tourism Assn., Nat. Assn. Female Execs., Ga. Exec. Women's Network, Nat. Assn. Profl. and Bus. Women, Atlanta Consultants Soc. (founding bd.). Republican. Office: Novey Enterprises Box 97 Norcross GA 30091

NOVICK, BEVERLY, jewelry designer, consultant; b. N.Y.C., Sept. 27, 1942; d. Samuel and Dorothy (Gross) Drezin; m. Lawrence Novick (div.); 1 child, Paige Rachel. BA in Edn., Queens Coll., 1965, MS in Edn., 1970. Tchr. P.S. 140, N.Y.C., 1965-66, Flushing Country Day Sch., Queens, N.Y., 1970-73; dir. Sky Line Towers, Flushing, N.Y., 1974-75; owner Beverly Novick Jewelry Design, Briarwood, N.Y., 1978-83, N.Y.C., 1984—. Author: Stop Wasting Money on Jewelry, 1987; contbr. articles to N.Y. Times, others, 1986—; TV appearnces include The Morning Show, ABC, 1987, others. Mem. Assn. Fashion Image Cons., The Fashion Group, Am. Women's Econ. Devel., Women Bus. Owners N.Y. (chairperson round tables 1983-86), N.Y. C. of C. and Industry (leader task force 1987), Nat. Assn. Female Execs. Club: President's (N.Y.C.).

NOVICK, REBECCA FRIEDMAN, financial consultant, stockbroker; b. Jackson, Tenn., Feb. 3, 1955; d. Fred Martin and Jeanette (Platt) Friedman; m. Mark Douglas Novick, Dec. 23, 1978 (div. Nov. 1981). BS in Nursing, U. Tenn., 1979. RN, Tenn. Registered nurse emergency room Le Bonheur Children's Hosp., Memphis, 1979-80; registered nurse Clin. Research Ctr. U. Tenn. Coll. Medicine, Memphis, 1980-82; fin. cons. Merrill Lynch Corp., Memphis, 1982—. Mem. Nat. Assn. Securities Dealers, Network, Internat. Assn. Fin. Planners. Republican. Unitarian. Office: Merrill Lynch 6750 Poplar Suite 800 Memphis TN 38138

NOVIE, MARY KELTZ, manufacturing company executive; b. Lawrence, Kans., Mar. 23, 1949; d. Harold L. and Dorothy C. (Cohen) Keltz; m. Jan Novie, July 7, 1972 (div. Feb. 1983). BA, Colo. Coll., 1971. Sales rep. Livingston's, San Francisco, 1971, buyer, 1972-80, mdse. mgr., 1981-84; v.p. Circa Corp., San Francisco, 1985—. Grantee Ford Found., 1971. Mem. Fashion Group (past treas., past program chmn.), Friends of Ethnic Art, Women's Profl. Network. Democrat. Club: Commonwealth (San Francisco). Office: Circa Corp 2300 Harrison St San Francisco CA 94110

NOVINA, TRUDI (MRS. CHARLES E. COAKLEY), fibers company official; b. Bklyn., Dec. 8; d. Isidor and Lilian (Greenberg) Novina; B.A., Bklyn. Coll., 1950; M.B.A., Fordham U., 1981; m. Leo H. Papazian, June 24, 1956 (dec. 1964); children—Lyssa D., Gregory M.; m. Charles E. Coakley, Apr. 27, 1968. Reporter, N.Y. World Telegram & Sun, N.Y.C., 1950-54, asst. woman's editor, 1954-57, home furnishings editor, 1957-60; free-lance writer, 1960-64; account exec., dir. home fashions publicity Donald Degnan Assos., N.Y.C., 1964-69; mgr. publicity Allied Fibers, Allied-Signal Corp., N.Y.C., 1969—. Mem. Am. Inst. Interior Designers, Nat. Home Fashions League (chpt. v.p. 1972-73), Fashion Group. Club: Overseas Press (N.Y.C.). Editor: House and Garden Decorating Book, 1965. Contbr. articles to various mags. Home: 34 W 89th St New York NY 10024 Office: 1411 Broadway New York NY 10018

NOVOTNY, DEBORAH ANN, microcomputer consultant; b. Oak Lawn, Ill., Sept. 23, 1964; d. Russell Anthony and Barbara J. (Doran) N. BA in Econs., Northwestern U., 1986. Mgr. lab., cons. Northwestern U., Evanston, Ill., 1983-86; asst. mgr. microcomputer services Sara Lee Corp., Chgo., 1986; sr. cons. Lante Corp., Chgo., 1987—. Active teen retreat team St. Michael's Ch., Orland Park, Ill., 1982—. Ill. State scholar. Mem. Macintosh Users Group, Chi Omega Rho (charter, chmn. housing assn. 1986—). Home: 14424 West Ave Orland Park IL 60462 Office: Office Corp 100 S Wacker Dr Suite 1110 Chicago IL 60606

NOWAK, CAROL A., city official; b. Buffalo, Mar. 5, 1950; d. Walter S. and Stella M. (Gurowski) N. AAS in Bus. Adminstrn., Erie Community Coll., Buffalo, 1986; student, SUNY, Buffalo, 1986—. With Liberty Nat. Bank/Norstar, Buffalo, 1968-70; with City of Buffalo, 1970-74, asst. adminstrn. and fin., 1974-82, pension clk., adminstr. city police and fire pension fund, city clk., 1982—. Artist, designer holiday greeting cards, 1984—. Mem. Nat. Assn. Female Execs. Home: 422 Dingens St Buffalo NY 14206 Office: City of Buffalo City Clerk's Office 1308 City Hall Buffalo NY 14202

NOWAK, JACQUELYN LOUISE, state official; b. Harrisburg, Pa., Sept. 2, 1937; d. John Henry and Irene Louise (Clark) Snyder; children—Andrew Alfred, IV, Deirdre Anne. Student Pa. State U., 1973-74; B.A., Lycoming Coll., 1975. Editorial writer Patriot News Co., Harrisburg, Pa., 1957-58; dir. West Shore Sr. Citizens Ctr., New Cumberland, Pa., 1969-72; exec. dir. Cumberland County Office Aging, Carlisle, Pa., 1972-80; dir. Bur. Advocacy, Pa. Dept. Aging, Harrisburg, 1980-88, owner D&J Productions, Art and Handcrafted Teddy Bears. Recorder, Pa. Gov's. Council Aging, Central Region, 1972-74; chmn. pub. relations, 1973-74; mem. state planning com. Pa. State Conf. Aging, 1974, panelist, 1975-78; mem. state bd. Pa. Council Homemakers-Home Health Aide Services, 1972-80, v.p., 1975, chmn. ann. meeting, 1973-75; sr. citizens subcom. chmn. Pa. Atty. Gens. Commn. to Prevent Shoplifting, 1983; mem. adv. com. Tri-County Ret. Sr. Vol. Program, 1972-74; bd. dirs. Council Human Services Cumberland, Dauphin, and Perry Counties, 1973-74; mem. service com. Family and Children's Service Harrisburg, 1970-74, mem. policy com., 1973-74, bd. dirs. Cumberland County unit Am. Cancer Soc., 1964-76, state del., 1964-66, chmn. county pub. relations, 1965-66, cancer crusade chmn., 1964. Recipient Herman Melitzer award, Pa. Conf. Aging, 1978; named Woman of the Year WIOO Radio, Carlisle, Pa., 1979. Mem. Nat. Assn. Area Ags. on Aging (dir. 1975-80, pres. 1976-77; sec. 1978-79), Pa. Watercolor Soc., Harrisburg Art Assn., Mechanicsburg Art Ctr. (pres. 1987-88, bd. dirs. 1984—), Gerontol Soc. Am., Am. Trauma Soc. (Pa. div. state bd. 1985—), Older Women's League (founder chpt.), Lycoming Coll. Alumni Assn.. Clubs: Federation of Women's (div. chmn. 1972-76), Torch (pres. 1987-88, 2d v.p. 1985-86). Lodge: Zonta Internat. (sec. 1986-88). Home: 505 Geary Ave New Cumberland PA 17070 Office: Pa Dept Aging Bur of Advocacy 231 State St Harrisburg PA 17101

NOWAK, PATRICIA ANN, insurance executive; b. Lynn, Mass., Feb. 17, 1946; d. Richard H. and Gertrude M. (Barry) Kiely; m. Robert D. McCarthy, Apr. 16, 1966 (div. June 1982); children: Christine, Robert, Alison; m. Robert C. Nowak, July 24, 1982; children: Richard, Peter. BS in Edn., Salem State Coll., 1967; postgrad., U. Vt., 1974-76. CLU. Owner, tchr. pvt. school Colchester, Vt., 1971-80; agt., rep. N.Y. Life Ins. Co., South Burlington, Vt., 1979-87; owner Nowak Fin. Group, Williston, Vt., 1983—. Assoc. trustee St. Michael's Coll., Winooski, Vt., 1987—. Fellow Life Underwriter Tng. Council, mem. Nat. Fedn. Bus. and Profl. Women (past state pres. 1984, Nat. Speak-off winner 1979), Vt. Fedn. Bus. and Profl. Women Assn. (local pres. 1978, Vt. Speak-off winner 1979), Nat. Life Underwriters Assn., Vt. Life Underwriters Assn. (local pres.-elect), Nat. Assn. Female Execs. Democrat. Roman Catholic. Home: 98 Logwood St South Burlington VT 05403 Office: Nowak Fin Group 8 Blair Pk Suite 103 Williston VT 05495

NOWELL, ELIZABETH CAMERON CLEMONS, author; b. Berkeley, Calif.; d. Alfred George and Edith (Catton) Cameron; A.B. San Jose State Coll., 1928; M.A., Stanford U., 1937; m. Wood Clemons, Dec. 22, 1946 (div. Dec. 1958); m. Arthur G. Robinson, May 27, 1961 (dec. Jan. 1967); m. Nelson T. Nowell, Feb. 15, 1969 (dec. Sept. 1973). With edn. dept. San Jose State Coll., 1928-39, in service tng. U. Calif. Extension Div., 1939-42; elem. editor The John C. Winston Co., 1942-43, Silver Burdett Co., 1943-44, D.C. Heath, 1944-46; instr. English dept. U. Minn., 1947; writing, editing publs. services Gen. Mills, 1947-50; freelance writer, 1950—; mem. faculty Monterey Peninsula Coll., Monterey, Calif., 1978-83; reading cons. Monterey City Sch., 1959-62, asso. editor Calif. edit. Am. Home Mag., 1965-70; mem. seminar faculty Embroiderers Guild, 1980, Monterey Peninsula Coll., 1978-82; judge needle-work Good Samaritan Hosp., Los Angeles, 1977, 79, 83, 87, Montalvo Center for Arts, Saratoga, Calif., 1980, 82, Status Needle Art Show, Burlingame, Calif., 1982, Altrusa Needlework Exhbn., Santa Maria, Calif., 1982, Scripps Meml. Hosp., La Jolla, Calif., 1980, 86, others. Bd. dirs. Community Hosp. Aux.; bd. dirs. Harrison Meml. Library, 1971-76, Monterey Symphony Assn., 1974-75; vestryman St. Dunstan's Episcopal Ch., 1974-77. Mem. Nat. League Am. Pen Women, Authors Guild, LWV, Nat. Embroidery Tchrs. Assn. (nat. dir. 1978-81), Embroiderers Guild Am. (nat. dir. 1978-81, nat. fin. com. 1984-87; nat. fin. guidelines chmn. 1986-87; nat. judges cert. com. 1984—, chmn. 1986; pres. chpt. 1977-78; judge needlework exhbns. 1977—), Kappa Alpha Theta, Pi Lambda Theta, Delta Phi Upsilon, Kappa Delta Pi, Delta Kappa Gamma. Republican. Clubs: Casa Abrego (historian 1979-83), Monterey Peninsula Country, Soroptimist. Author: The Pixie Dictionary, 1953; the Catholic Child's First Dictionary, 1954; The Winston Dictionary for Canadian School Children, 1955; Away I Go, 1956; All About Baby, 1956; I Live on A Farm, 1956; A Wish for Billy, 1956; Wings, Wheels, and Motors, 1957; The Big Book of Real Fire Engines, 1958; The Big Book of Real Trains, 1958; The Big Book of Real Trucks, 1958; Rodeo Days, 1960; Shells Are Where You Find Them, 1960; Rocks and The World Around You, 1960; Big and Little, 1961; Tide Pools and Beaches, 1964; Tides, Waves, and Currents, 1967; Here and There Stories; Now and Then Stories; Near and Far Stories; A Source Book for the Teaching of Literature for Children (all 1967); The Seven Seas, 1971; The Friendly Frog, 1971; What I Like, 1971; Guidelines for Treasurers, 1987; also feature articles in nat. mags. Address: PO Box 686 Carmel CA 93921

NOWIK, DOROTHY ADAM, medical equipment company executive; b. Chgo., July 25, 1944; d. Adam Harry and Helen (Kichkaylo) Wanaski; m. Eugene Nicholas Nowik, Aug. 9, 1978; children—George Eugene, Helen Eugene. A.A., Columbia Coll., 1980. Sec., adminstrv. asst. to pres. Zenco Engring Corp., Chgo., 1970-71; sales rep. Medizenco USA Ltd., Chgo., 1971-73; ptnr. Pacific Med. Systems, Inc., Bellevue, Wash., 1973-76, pres., 1976—. Mem. Nat. Assn. Female Execs. Mem. Orthodox Ch. Am. Home: 10249 SE 7th St Bellevue WA 98004 Office: 15055 NE Bel-Red Rd Bellevue WA 98007

NOWLIN, JANET, utilities executive, data processing executive; b. Buffalo, July 16, 1953; d. Sam Angelo and Josephine (Sciolino) Conti; m. Harry Wayne Nowlin, Nov. 30, 1973; 1 child, Wesley Wayne. Student, Phoenix Coll., 1972-73; cert., IBM Tech., 1986. Cert. data processor and programmer. Supr. data processing Levitz Furniture, Phoenix, 1970-74; mgr. data processing dept. Ariz. Water Co., Phoenix, 1974—, cons., 1984. Mem. Data Processing Mgmt. Assn., Postal Customer Council, Beta Sigma Phi (sec. 1985-86). Republican. Roman Catholic. Home: 4008 W Danbury Glendale AZ 85308 Office: Ariz Water Co 2612 N 16th St Phoenix AZ 85006

NOXON, MARGARET WALTERS, community volunteer; b. Detroit, Dec. 16, 1903; d. George Alexander and Ethelwyn (Taylor) Walters; grad., Liggett Sch. for Girls, Det., 1922; life teaching certificate Wayne State U., 1925; student Columbia Tchrs. Coll., 1939-40; m. Herbert Richards Noxon, July 15, 1926 (dec. Aug. 4, 1971). Bd. dirs. Coll. Club, Detroit, 1925-30; mem. Salvation Army Aux., Detroit, 1926—; mem. Coll. Club, Summit N.J., 1941—; historian D.A.R., N.Y.C., 1943-46, vice regent, 1946-49; dir. New Eng., Women, 1961-64; dir. Woodycrest-Five Points Child Care, 1961-77; bd. dirs. ARC, Summit, N.J., service com. chmn. uniforms and insignias, 1943-45; v.p. N.Y. Infirmary Aux., N.Y.C., 1948-58, bd. dirs., 1959-80. Recipient award for meritorious personal service ARC, 1945. Mem. Nat. Inst. Social Scis., Grand Jury Assn. N.Y. County, D.A.R. (dir. 1950-70), St. David's Soc. State N.Y., English-Speaking Union, Daus. Am. Colonists, AAUW, Southampton Colonial Soc., Nat. Woman's Farm and Garden Assn. (dir. met. br. 1975—, dir. N.Y. State div. 1978-80, mem. nat. council 1978-80), Ch. Women's League for Patriotic Service, Women's Bible Soc. N.Y., Alpha Sigma Tau. Republican. Presbyterian. Clubs: Southampton (N.Y.) Bath and Tennis, City Gardens (dir. 1963-68, mem. adv. com. 1968-74, dir. 1974-80, adv. bd. 1980-83), York (bd. govs. 1965-66, 73-77), Barnard (trustee 1979-81), Sorosis (v.p. 1979-81), Regency (N.Y.C.). Home: 1100 Madison Ave Apt 10C Box 86 New York NY 10028

NOYES, ELISABETH JOYCE, university system administrator; b. Hilversum, The Netherlands, Oct. 15, 1940; came to U.S., 1951, naturalized, 1966; d. Louis Jan and Wilhelmina Louise (Bollee) van Epen; m. Arnold Eugene Noyes, Sept. 2, 1961; children: James Louis, Edwin Willard. Postgrad., Middlebury Coll., 1961; MA, U. Mass., 1962; MEd, Salem (Mass.) State Coll., 1966; EdD, Nova U., 1976. Instr. German and English North Shore Community Coll., Beverly, Mass., 1965-68, assoc. prof., 1970-76, div. chairperson, 1972-74; dept. chairperson White Pines Coll., Chester, N.H., 1968-70; prof. Mt. Wachusett Community Coll., Gardner, Mass., 1974-75; div. chairperson Bunker Hill Community Coll., Boston, 1976-78, asst. dean, 1978-83; acad. program officer Mass. Bd. Regents of Higher Edn., Boston, 1983-87; dir. planning and program devel. Univ. System N.H., Durham, 1987—; mem. N.H. Post Secondary Edn. COmmn., 1987—; cons., evaluator N.J. Dept. Higher Edn., Trenton, 1986-87. Trustee White Pines Coll., Chester, 1974-85, Notre Dame Prep. Sch., Fitchburg, Mass., 1980-85, Nashoba Community Hosp., Ayer, Mass., 1983—, chmn. nursing home com. 1985—, 1985—; chairperson Shirley (Mass.) Sch. Com., 1974-80; moderator Town of Shirley, 1983—. Grantee Internat. Edn. Consortium, 1978 Am. Assn. Community & Jr. Colls., 1981—. Mem. Nat. Council Tchrs. English, Conf. on Coll. Composition and Communication, Mass. Women in Pub. Higher Edn. (exec. com. 1982-86, treas. 1983-86), N.E. Regional Conf. on English in two-yr. colls. (exec. com. 1981-84, treas. 1982-84), Greater Boston Regional Edn. Council (vice chmn., chair 1978-86), Nat. Council State Dirs. Community and Jr. Colls., Modern Language Assn., NE Regional Conf. on Teaching Fgn. Languages, Chi Omega. Unitarian. Lodge: Altrurian. Home: Lancaster Rd Shirley MA 01464 also: Harvey Lake Northwood NH 03261 Office: Univ System New Hampshire Dunlap Ctr Durham NH 03824

NOZIGLIA, CARLA MILLER, director forensics, forensic scientist; b. Erie, Pa., Oct. 11, 1941; d. Earnest Carl and Eileen (Murphy) Miller; m. Keith William Noziglia, Nov. 21, 1969; children: Pama, Kathryn. BS, Villa Maria Coll., 1963; MS, Lindenwood Coll., 1984. Pathologist's assoc. Galion (Ohio) Comm. Hosp., 1969-75; dir. crime lab. Mansfield (Ohio) Police Dept., Richland County Crime Lab., 1978-81; crime lab. supr. St. Louis County Police, Clayton, Mo., 1981-84; dir. lab. services Las Vegas (Nev.) Met. Police, 1984-88, dir. forensic services, 1988—. Tech. abstracts editor Jour. Police Sci. and Adminstrn., 1983—. Recipient Ohio award Ohio House of Reps., 1971, Alumni of Yr. award Villa Maria Coll., 1981; named Woman of Yr., Am. Bus. Women's Assn., 1988, Outstanding Cath., Erie Diocese N.W. Pa., 1988. Fellow Am. Acad. Forensic Sci. and Criminalistics (sect. sec. 1986—, sect. chmn. 1987, bd. dirs. 1988—); mem. Am. Soc. Crime Lab. Dirs. (bd. dirs. 1980-87, treas. 1981-82, pres. 1986-87), Am. Soc. Pub. Adminstrn., Am. Acad. Forensic Services (bd. dirs. 1988—). Home: 1025 Pagosa Way Las Vegas NV 89128 Office: Las Vegas Met Police Forensic Services 6765 W Charleston Blvd Las Vegas NV 89102-9003

NUCCI, ANNAMARIA, psychiatrist; b. Nicastro, Catanzaro, Italy, June 4, 1945; d. Thomas and Tina (Pagnotta) N. BA, Montclair (N.J.) State Coll., 1961; MusM, Rosary Coll., 1962; MD, Universita Cattolica, Rome, 1971; PhD, NYU, 1976. Practice medicine specializing in psychiatry N.Y.C. and Cedar Grove, N.J, 1976—; asst. clin. prof. N.Y. Med. Coll., N.Y.C., 1980—; adj. prof. music NYU, 1976-79; attending psychiatrist Gracie Sq. Hosp., N.Y.C., 1977-79, Mountainside Hosp., Montclair, 1978—, N.Y. Hosp., N.Y.C., 1978—; instr. child psychology Cornell U. Med. Sch., N.Y.C., 1978—; cons. Kateri Residence, N.Y.C., 1985—. Author: Music and Medicine, 1976; (booklet) Layman's Guide to Psychiatry, 1975; poetry. Dir. Italian-Am. Concert Artists Auditions, N.Y.C., 1980-84; bd. dirs. Symphony for the UN, N.Y.C., 1980-84, N.Y.C. Yr. 2000 Com., 1985—. Recipient Anabel Mack Taylor award Pius XII Inst., 1972, Schmidt award J. Schmidt Found., 1979; Named Doctor of Yr., Columbia Found., 1978. Mem. Am. Med. Women's Assn. (dir. pub. relations 1981-83), Arts Medicine Assn., N.Y. County Med. Soc., Morgagni Med. Soc., Congress Italian-Am. Orgns. (bd. dirs. 1984—), Ctr. Italian Culture (pres. 1964-68). Republican. Roman Catholic. Home: 5 Westview Ct Cedar Grove NJ 07009 Office: 80 Central Park W New York NY 10023

NUGENT, CHRISTINE MURPHY, educator; b. Suffern, N.Y., Nov. 30, 1951; d. Thomas William and Kathleen Christina (Connors) Murphy; A.A., Edward Williams Coll., 1975; B.S., Fairleigh Dickinson U., 1978, M.B.A., 1982; m. William R. Nugent, Jan. 30, 1971; 1 dau., Maura Kathleen. Adminstrv. asst. to dir. product mgmt. Thomas J. Lipton, Inc., Englewood Cliffs, N.J., 1972-75, adminstrv. asst. to exec. v.p. mktg., 1975-78, consumer promotions adminstr., 1979, sales promotion analyst, 1979-83; prof. Edward William Coll., Fairleigh Dickinson U., 1983—. Republican. Roman Catholic. Office: Edward Williams Coll 150 Kotte Pl Hackensack NJ 07601

NUGENT, MAXINE E., bank executive; b. Canton, Tex., Sept. 26, 1931; d. John C. and Ora Frances (Pettit) Gamel; m. Chester L. Nugent, Aug. 4, 1953; children: LeAnne Nugent McClure, Karen F. Student, Longview Comml. Coll., 1951. With Peoples Loan Service, Longview, Tex., 1950-53, 1954-55; with Federated Dept. Store, Longview, 1953, AAA Automobile Service, Longview, 1953-54, San Francisco Tex. Consumer Fin. Corp., 1958-65; v.p. Union Modern Mortgage Corp., Longview, 1973—. Tchr. Valley View Bapt. Ch., Longview, 1977—. Mem. Longview Bd. Realtors. Republican. Home: 1211 Columbia Dr Longview TX 75601 Office: Union Modern Mortgage Corp 2169 Gilmer Rd Longview TX 75604

NUGENT, NELLE, theatrical producer; b. Jersey City, May 24, 1939; d. John Patrick and Evelyn Adelaide (Stern) N.; m. Donald G. Baker, June 6, 1960 (div. 1962); m. Benjamin Janney, June 22, 1969 (div. Apr., 1980); m. Jolyon Fox Stern, Apr. 7, 1982; 1 child, Alexandra Fox Stern. B.S., Skidmore Coll., 1960, D.H.L. (hon.), 1981. Chmn. bd. McCann & Nugent, Prodns. Inc. (mgmt. and prodn. co.), N.Y.C., 1976-86; pres. Foxboro Prodns., Inc., 1985—. Stage mgr. various off-Broadway shows, 1960-64; prodn. asst.: Broadways plays Any Wednesday, 1963-64, Dylan, 1964, Ben Franklin in Paris, 1964-65; stage mgr. Broadway shows, 1964-68; prodn. supr., then gen. mgr., 1969-70, asso. mng. dir. Nederlander Corp., operating theaters and producing plays in, N.Y.C. and on tour, 1970-76; producer: Dracula, 1977 (Tony award), The Elephant Man, 1978 (Tony award, Drama Critics award), Morning's at Seven, 1980 (Tony award), Home, 1980 (Tony nomination), Amadeus, 1981 (Tony award); also produced: Rose and Piaf, 1980, The Life and Adventures of Nicholas Nickleby, 1981 (Tony award, Drama Critics award), The Dresser (Tony award nominee), 1981, Mass Appeal, 1981; The Lady & The Clarinet, 1982; The Glass Menagerie (revival), 1983; Painting Churches (Obie award), 1983; Total Abandon, 1983; All's Well That End's Well, 1983; Pilobolus Dance Company, 1983; Pacific Overtures (revival), 1984; Much Ado about Nothing/Cyrano de Bergerac (repertory) (Tony award nominees), 1984; Leader of the Pack (Tony award nominee), 1985, The Life and Adventures of Nicholas Nickleby (revival) (Tony award nominee), 1986; producer: TV spls.; Morning's At Seven, Piaf; Pilobolus; producer A Fighting Choice, Walt Disney Prodns., 1986, Phoenix Entertainment Group, 1986—, A Conspiracy of Love, New World TV, 1987; exec. producer CBS TV pilot Morning Maggie, 1987. Bd. dirs. Los Angeles Theatre Co., A.W.E.D. Office: Foxboro Prodns 311 W 43rd St Suite 702 New York NY 10036

NUNES, PEPSI, marine biologist; b. Makati, Philippines, Aug. 9, 1952; came to U.S., 1969.; d. Carlos Maria da Luz and Pureza (d'Eca) N. BS, U. Miami, 1973; PhD, U. Alaska, 1984. Lab. supr. dept. med. chemistry Northeastern U., Boston, 1973-74; research technician Biochem. div. Arthur D. Little, Inc., Cambridge, Mass., 1974-75; physiologist Nat. Marine Fisheries Service, Tiburon, Calif., 1975-76; staff research assoc. Bodega Marine Lab., U. Calif., Berkeley, 1976-78; research asst. Inst. Marine Science, U. Alaska, Fairbanks, 1978-82; fisheries biologist Nat. Marine Fisheries Service, Kodiac, Alaska, 1982-83; aquatic biologist Harza Engring., Anchorage, 1983-84; oceanographer U.S. Fish and Wildlife Service, Slidell, La., 1984-85; sr. fisheries biologist Kinnetic Labs., Inc., Anchorage, 1985-87; pres., owner BIOSPHERE, Anchorage, 1987—; adj. prof. marine science U. Alaska, 1987—; v.p. Alaska Internat. Devel., Inc., Anchorage, 1987—; mktg. rep. New Horizons Telecommunications Contrn. Co., Anchorage, 1987—; mem. Alaska World Affairs Council, 1982—. Mem. Alaska Assn. Environ. Profls., Nat. Shellfisheries Assn., Am. Soc. Limnology and Oceanography, Am. Fisheries Soc., Sigma Xi. Roman Catholic.

NUNN, BARBARA ELAINE, educator; b. Washington, Mar. 14, 1947; d. Charles Edward Nunn and Elsie Eunice (Smith) Press. B.A., U. Fla., 1969; M.Ed., U. Miami, 1975. Tchr. math. Miami Sr. High Sch., 1969-76, Coral Springs High Sch., Fla., 1976-82, Taravella High Sch., Coral Springs, 1982-83, Coral Springs High Sch., 1983—; coordinator high sch. summer math inst. Broward County Schs., Ft. Lauderdale, 1984, 85; speaker in field. Named Broward County High Sch. Math. Tchr. of Yr., Broward County Council Tchrs. Math., 1985; state finalist Presdl. award for excellence in math. teaching, 1984, 85. Mem. Fla. Council Tchrs. Math. (pres. 1981), Broward County Council Tchrs. Math. (pres. 1977-78), Nat. Council Tchrs.

Math., Delta Kappa Gamma (chpt. pres. 1984-86), Phi Delta Kappa. Democrat. Presbyterian. Home: 8821 Hampshire Dr #204 Coral Springs FL 33065 Office: Coral Springs High Sch 7201 W Sample Rd Coral Springs FL 33065

NUNNALLY, NANCY KATHLEEN, human resource executive, journalist; b. Oklahoma City, June 9, 1950; d. Robert Milton and Winifred Julia (Allen) N.; m. David Craig Hood, Feb. 22, 1977 (dec. Dec. 1981). BS, Okla. State U., 1972; M in Criminal Justice Adminstrn., Okla. State U., Oklahoma City, 1976. Reporter Sta. KTOK, Oklahoma City, 1973-76; capitol reporter Sta. KWTV-TV, Oklahoma City, 1976-77; pub. info. officer dept. corrections State of Okla., 1977-82, employee relations and mgmt. tng. office personnel mgmt., 1982—; editorial columnist Okla. Gazette, 1986—. columnist weekly editorial On Point, 1986—; co-author mgmt. research employees legal rights, 1986, employee motivation, 1987. Mem. Am. Soc. Tng. Devel., Nat. Assn. State Tng. Devel. Dirs., Nat. Cert. Pub. Mgr. Consortium. Democrat. Office: State Okla Office Personnel Mgmt 2101 N Lincoln Blvd Oklahoma City OK 73105

NURMELA, CATHERINE ANN, nurse; b. Marquette, Mich., July 15, 1953; d. Peter Marcus and Gladys Geraldine (Nopola)N. AA, Suomi Coll., Hancock, Mich., 1973; BA, St. Olaf Coll., 1975; BSN, Idaho State U., 1980; MS in Exercise Physiology/Cardiac Rehab., Northeastern Ill. U., 1988. RN; cert. various nursing specializations. Charge nurse Bannock Meml. Hosp., Pocatello, Idaho, 1980-81; nurse St. Joseph Hosp., Chgo., 1981-84, nursing quality assurance nurse, 1984—, diabetic instr., 1984-86, cardiac rehab. nurse educator. Mem. Am. Nurses Assn., Ill. Nurses Assn., Ill. Assn. Quality Assurance Profls., Sigma Theta Tau. Democrat. Lutheran. Home: 3621 N Pine Grove Chicago IL 60613 Office: St Joseph Hosp 2900 N Lake Shore Dr Chicago IL 60657

NUSBAUM, ADELE HELEN, government official; b. Toronto, Ont., Can.; d. Louis J. and Edith Nusbaum. BA magna cum laude, U. Rochester, 1940; MA, Columbia U., 1942; postgrad., Am. U., 1971. Info. specialist War Food Adminstrn., N.Y.C., 1942-45; staff assoc. C.M. Bayer Pub. Relations, N.Y.C, 1945-47, Sally Dickson Assocs., N.Y.C., 1947-49, United Jewish Appeal Fedn., N.Y.C., 1950-55; dir. pub. relations United Jewish Fedn., Pitts., 1955-64; dir. pub. relations B'nai B'rith Women, Washington, 1964-68, communications cons. for urban affairs, 1968-69; sr. writer bur. health manpower NIH, Bethesda, Md., 1969-71; dir. fed. women's program NIH, Bethesda, 1971-74; program dir. communications devel. Nat. Cancer Inst., Bethesda, 1974-82, spl. asst., 1982—. Mem. Pub. Relations Soc. Am., Nat. Press Club, Nat. Assn. Govt. Communicators, Am. Pub. Health Assn., Am. Soc. Pub. Adminstrn., Am. News Women's Club, Phi Beta Kappa. Home: 2829 Connecticut Ave NW Washington DC 20008 Office: 9000 Rockville Pike Bethesda MD 20892-4200

NUSCHLER, LISA MONICA, insurance professional; b. New Orleans, May 23, 1952; d. Christian Jr. and Clara Louise (Ledet) N.; m. Des Roger Mothe, Dec. 27, 1974 (div. Oct. 1983). Student, Am. River Coll., 1970-72; BA in Communications, U. New Orleans, 1975. Sec. Radio for the Blind & Print Handicapped, New Orleans, 1976-77; exec. sec. Johnson & Higgins of La., New Orleans, 1977-80; asst. ins. property Gulf States Theatres, New Orleans, 1981-83; rep. customer service J. Everett Eaves, Inc., New Orleans, 1984—; solicitor La. Ins. Commn., Baton Rouge, 1979—. Mem. Animal Protection Inst. (Gold mem.), People for Ethical Treatment of Animals, Greenpeace.

NUSIM, ROBERTA, publisher; b. N.Y.C., Dec. 1, 1943; d. Seymour and Ranna (Weiner) Nusim; m. Stephen Jablonsky, Aug. 29, 1965. B.A. in English, CCNY, 1964; M.A., CUNY, 1966. Tchr. N.Y.C. Bd. Edn., 1964-73; v.p. program devel. Mind, Inc., Westport, Conn., 1973-76; pres. Mind Media, 1976-78; founder, pres. Lifetime Learning Systems, Fairfield, Conn., 1978—; founder dir. The Film Study Guild, 1979—. Editor: Let's Talk About Health, 1980. Mem. Am. Film Inst., Women in Communications, Home Economists in Bus. Avocations: reading; painting. Office: Lifetime Learning Systems Inc 79 Sanford St Fairfield CT 06430

NUSSDORF, GERRIE E., psychologist; b. Bklyn., Feb. 2, 1944; d. Edith Posner and Oscar Nussdorf. Ph.D. in Psychology, Fordham U., 1975. Cert. psychoanalyst and psychotherapist. Computer programmer, 1966-69; psychology intern Fairfield Hills Hosp., Newtown, Conn., 1972-73; staff psychologist Nyack (N.Y.) Cons. Ctr., 1975-78; assoc. psychologist Rockland Psychiat. Ctr., Orangeburg, N.Y., 1978-80; therapist, tng. candidate adult program Postgrad. Ctr. Mental Health, N.Y.C., 1977-81; prin. psychologist Manhattan Psychiat. Ctr., N.Y.C., 1980—; pvt. practice psychology, N.Y.C., 1981—; adj. instr. psychology Marymount Manhattan Coll., 1974; tri-state coordinator Assn. Women in Psychology, 1975-76. NDEA Title IV teaching fellow, 1969-72; Regents scholar, 1961-65. Mem. Am. Psychol. Assn., Assn. Women in Psychology, Ea. Psychol. Assn., Postgrad. Ctr. Mental Health Psychoanalytic Soc., Austin Healey Club Am., Sports Car Club Am. Home: 305 W 13th St New York NY 10014 Office: Manhattan Psychiat Ctr Dept Psychology Wards Island New York NY 10035

NUTT, ANNE BAILEY, aerospace company community relations executive; b. Los Angeles, Oct. 16, 1940; d. Wilbur and Margaret (Robinson) Bailey; m. Stephen Douglas Nutt, Sept. 1, 1962 (div. Nov. 1982); children—Elizabeth Anne, Kathleen Margaret. B.A. in Polit. Sci., Stanford U., 1962; M.S. in Library Sci., U. So. Calif., 1968. Asst. to office mgr. Forster Gemmill & Farmer, Los Angeles, summers 1959, 60, 65; elem. asst. Agnes Irwin Sch., Rosemont, Pa., 1963-64; research asst. to law librarian Stanford U. Law Sch., Palo Alto, Calif., 1966-67; jr. museum librarian Met. Mus. Art, N.Y.C., 1971-74; intern in pub. affairs Coro Found., Orange County, Calif., 1979; mgr. community relations Northrop Corp., Anaheim, Calif., 1982—. Bd. dirs. Jr. League, N.Y.C., 1974-76, chairperson provisional tng., 1974-76, bd. dirs., Newport Harbor, Calif., 1976-82, rec. sec., 1978-79, pres., 1981-82; mem. Area VI council Assn. Jr. Leagues, 1980-81, editor child advocacy programs, 1980-81; v.p. devel. Orange County Arts Alliance, 1982-84, v.p. planning and bus. affairs, 1984-86; mem. agy. relations com. United Way Orange County, 1982—, chairperson info. and referral task force, 1983-87, bd. dirs., 1987—, chairperson community problem-solving com., 1988—; v.p. bd. dirs. New Directions for Women, Inc., Costa Mesa, Calif., 1982-85; mem. women's exec. cabinet Orange County chpt. March of Dimes, 1982—; chairperson adv. council for furniture and equipment for non-profits Vol. Ctrs. Orange County, 1983-86; bd. dirs. Performing Arts Assn. Orange County, 1983—, now chmn. bd. dirs.; mem. adv. com. Tech. Exchange Ctr., 1984-87; mem. adv. bd. North Orange County YWCA, 1984—; mem. Orange County Needs Assessment Adv. Com., 1984-86; mem. mktg. com. Exploratory Learning Ctr., Santa Ana, Calif., 1983-86, mem. adv. com., 1986—; pres. Red Ribbon 100 chpt. ARC, 1985-86; chair silver medallion recognition YWCA, 1985-86. Recipient cert. appreciation and recognition N.Y. State Dept. Correction, 1975, cert. merit Orange County Bd. Suprs., 1982, Outstanding Service award Orange County Arts Alliance, 1983. Mem. Orange County C. of C. (exec. com., bd. dirs. 1985—, chmn. membership com. 1988), Orange County Community Relations Council (pres. 1985-86), Corp. Vol. Council Los Angeles/Orange County, ALA. Republican. Presbyterian. Office: Northrop Corp ElectroMech Div 500 E Orangethorpe Anaheim CA 92801

NUTT, NAN, church administrator; b. Pasadena, Calif., Dec. 25, 1925; d. Paul Geltmacher and Estelle Boggs (Love) White; m. David Ballard Norris, Jan. 8, 1944 (div. 1967); children: Teresa, Anita, Carol, Steven; m. Evan Burchell Nutt, July 14, 1967. AA, Chaffee Jr. Coll., Calif., 1967; BA, Pomona Coll., 1969. Adminstrv. asst to dept. head sch. elec. engring. U. Tenn., Knoxville, 1952-53; adminstrv. asst. to minister of ch. edn. United Congl. Ch., Claremont, 1955-62; adminstrv. asst. to personnel dir. Pomona Coll., Claremont, 1962-63; bus. mgr. 1st Congl. Ch., Long Beach, Calif., 1982-86, ch. adminstr., 1986—. Chmn. Nat. Women's Polit. Caucus, Tucson, 1972, nat. rep., Ariz., 1973-79, chmn. greater Long Beach, 1981, vice chmn., Calif.; pres. Coalition for ERA, Ariz., 1973-79; commr. Cultural Heritage Commn., Long Beach, 1985-87, chair 1987—. Democrat.

NYCUM, SUSAN HUBBELL, lawyer. B.A., Ohio Wesleyan U., 1956; J.D., Duquesne U., 1960; postgrad., Stanford U. Bar: Pa. 1962, U.S. Supreme Ct. 1967, Calif. 1974. Sole practice law Pitts., 1962-65; designer, adminstr. legal research system U. Pitts., Aspen Systems Corp., Pitts., 1965-68; mgr. ops. Computer Ctr., Carnegie Mellon U., Pitts., 1968-69; dir. computer facility Computer Ctr., Stanford U., Calif., 1969-72, Stanford Law and Computer fellow, 1972-73; cons. in computers and law 1973-74; sr. assoc. MacLeod, Fuller, Muir & Godwin, Los Altos, Los Angeles and London, 1974-75; ptnr. Chickering & Gregory, San Francisco, 1975-80; ptnr.-in-charge high tech. group Gaston Snow & Ely Bartlett, Boston, NYC, Phoenix, San Francisco, Calif., 1980-86; ptnr. Palo Alto office Kadison, Pfaelzer, Woodard, Quinn & Rossi, Los Angeles, Washington, Newport Beach, Palo Alto, Calif., 1986-87; ptnr. Baker & McKenzie, Palo Alto, 1987—; trustee EDUCOM, 1978-81; mem. adv. com. for high tech. Ariz. State U. Law Sch., Santa Clara U. Law Sch., Stanford Law Sch., U. So. Calif. Law Ctr., law sch. Harvard U. U. Calif.; U.S. State Dept. del. OECD Conf. on Nat. Vulnerabilities, Spain, 1981; invited speaker Telecom, Geneva, 1983; lectr. N.Y. Law Jour., 1975—, Law & Bus., 1975—, Practicing Law Inst., 1975—; chmn. Office of Tech. Assessment Task Force on Nat. Info. Systems, 1979-80. Author:(with Bigelow) Your Computer and the Law, 1975, (with Bosworth) Legal Protection for Software, 1985, (with Collins and Gilbert) Women Leading, 1987; contbr. monographs, articles to profl. pubs. Mem. Town of Portola Valley Open Space Acquisition Com., Calif., 1977; mem. Jr. League of Palo Alto, chmn. evening div., 1975-76. NSF and Dept. Justice grantee for studies on computer abuse, 1972—. Mem. ABA (sect. on sci. and tech. chmn. 1979-80, chmn. elect 1978-79), Internat. Bar Assn. (U.S. mem. computer com. of corps. sect.), Assn. Computing Machinery (mem. at large of council 1976-80, nat. lectr. 1977—, chmn. standing com. on legal issues 1975—), Computer Law Assn. (v.p. 1983-85, pres. 1986—, bd. dirs. 1975—), Calif. State Bar Assn. (founder first chmn. econs. of law sect., vice chmn. law and computers com.), Nat. Conf. Lawyers and Scientists (rep. ABA). Address: 35 Granada Ct Portola Valley CA 94025

NYE, MIRIAM MAURINE BAKER, writer; b. Castana, Iowa, June 14, 1918; d. Horace Boies and Hazel Dean (Waples) Hawthorn; B.A., Morningside Coll., 1939, postgrad., 1957-58; postgrad. U. Ariz., 1973, U. S.D., 1975-77, New Coll., U. Edinburgh (Scotland), 1974; m. Carl E. Baker, June 21, 1941 (dec. 1970); children—Kent Alfred, Dale Hawthorn; m. 2d, John Arthur Nye, Dec. 25, 1973. Tchr. jr. high sch., Rock Falls, Ill., 1939-41, Moville (Iowa) Community Sch., 1957-62, Woodbury Central Community Sch., Climbing Hill, Iowa, 1962-64; homemaking columnist Sioux City (Iowa) Jour.'s Farm Weekly, 1953-81; author: Recipes and Ideas From the Kitchen Window, 1973; But I Never Thought He'd Die: Practical Help for Widows, 1978; speaker, Iowa, Nebr., Minn., S.D. Counselor, Iowa State U., 1972—; county adv. Iowa Children's and Family Services, 1980-84; mem. public relations com. Farm Bur., Woodbury County, 1980-82; advisor nat. orgn. for help to widows THEOS, Sioux City chpt., 1981—; lay del. Iowa United Meth. Conf., 1981-83. Recipient Alumni award Morningside Coll., 1969, Service award Woodbury County Fair, 1969, Friend of Extension award Iowa State U., 1981. Mem. AAUW, Iowa Fedn. Women's Clubs (dist. creative writing chmn. 1978-80), Common Cause, Alpha Kappa Delta, Sigma Tau Delta. Methodist. Home and Office: Box 193 Route 2 Moville IA 51039

NYHOLM, CAROL JOYCE, training consultant, association executive, social worker; b. Wenatchee, Wash., Mar. 12, 1932; d. Edward and Flora Agnes (Bray) Nyholm. B.A. in Sociology, Wash. State U., 1954; M.S.W., U. Mich., 1967. Cert. social worker. Program dir. YWCA, Long Beach, Calif., 1954-60; teenage dir. YWCA, San Diego, 1960-61; youth program YWCA Mid-Peninsula, Palo Alto, Calif., 1961-65; city wide youth program YWCA, Pitts., 1967-69, assoc. exec., 1969-72, exec. dir., 1972-77; exec. dir. YWCA, Long Beach, Calif., 1977-84; tng. cons. YWCA of USA Leadership Devel. Ctr., Phoenix, 1984-85; exec. dir. YWCA of Maricopa County, Phoenix, 1985—. Bd. dirs. South Coast Ecumenical Council, 1980-82, chmn. community action com., 1980-82; bd. dirs. Bouggess-White Scholarship Found., 1979-80; steering com. Shalom Ctr., 1979-81; mem. United Way Campaign Cabinet, 1980, council of execs., 1977-84; mem. equitable salaries com. Pacific S.W. Conf. United Meth. Chs., 1981-84. Grace H. Dodge Merit fellow YWCA, 1965-66, Florence Allen Roblee scholar YWCA 1966-67. Named Boss of Yr. Jubilee chpt. Am. Bus. Women's Assn., 1978, Susan B. Anthony Woman of Yr., Long Beach chpt. NOW. Mem. Nat. Assn. Social Workers, Nat. Assn. Female Execs., Nat. Conf. Social Welfare. Methodist. Home: 5043 W Sweetwater Ave Glendale AZ 85304 Office: 755 E Willetta St Phoenix AZ 85006

NYQUIST, CORINNE ELAINE, librarian; b. Minnesota Falls, Minn., Nov. 1, 1935; d. Clair Francis and Ebba Ingeborg (Lindgren) Johnson; m. Thomas Eugene Nyquist, Dec. 22, 1956; children: Jonathan Eugene, Lynn Marie. BA, Macalester Coll., 1956; MALS, U. Minn., 1960. Asst. librarian U. Minn., Mpls., 1959-60, Evanston (Ill.) Pub. Library, 1962-64, Skokie (Ill.) Pub. Library, 1965-66; asst. librarian, research asst. Rhodes U., Grahamstown, Republic of South Africa, 1967; asst. librarian to librarian SUNY, New Paltz, 1968—, ombudsman, 1983-85; co-project dir. Ford Found. Human Rights Bibliographic Project, 1986-87; cons. N.Y. State Edn. Dept., Albany, 1980-82; chmn. SUNY Internat. Librarians Com., 1984—. Contbr. articles to profl. jours. Chmn. Town Dem. Com., New Paltz, 1984-86. Recipient Chancellor's award, 1986; grantee SUNY Research Found., 1975, 84-86, Ford Found., 1986. Mem. ALA (chmn. human rights task force 1986—), N.Y. African Studies Assn. (co-editor newsletter 1974—), Ulster Co. Librarians Assn. (exec. com. 1984-86), African Studies Assn., Dutchess County Library Assn., Mid. East Librarians Assn., SUNY Librarians Assn. Home: 62 S Chestnut St New Paltz NY 12561 Office: SUNY Sojourner Truth Library G14 New Paltz NY 12561

NYREN, DOROTHY ELIZABETH, librarian; b. Portland, Maine, Sept. 29, 1929; d. Johann and Ethelreda (Mullaney) Schmidt; divorced; children: Neil Sebastian Nyren, Eve Nyren Okawa. BA, Boston U., 1952, MA, 1954; MLS, Simmons Coll., 1960; cert., U. Md., 1978. Lic. librarian N.Y., Ill., Mass. Head spl. services Ginn and Co., Boston, 1953; dir. Young Library, Daytona Beach, Fla., 1955-57; librarian Free Library, Concord, Mass., 1959-64; asst. head pub. ALA, Chgo., 1964-65; chief librarian Pub. Library, Northbrook, Ill., 1965-69; coordinator adult services Pub. Library, Bklyn., 1969-71, chief cent. library, 1971-77, chief pub. services, 1977-80, chief cen. library and spl. services, 1981—. Author: Modern American Literature, 1976, Modern Romance Literature, 1968; editor: Voices of Brooklyn, 1973, Community Service, 1970. Mem. ALA (mem. library outreach com. 1988—, publs. com. Reference and Adult Services div. 1987—, bd. dirs. 1976-79, Notable Books Council 1983-87), Phi Beta Kappa. Democrat. Office: Bklyn Pub Library Grand Army Plaza Brooklyn NY 11238

OAKAR, MARY ROSE, congresswoman; b. Cleve., Mar. 5, 1940; d. Joseph M. and Margaret Mary (Ellison) O. BA in English, Speech and Drama, Ursuline Coll., Cleve., 1962, LHD (hon.); MA in Fine Arts, John Carroll U., Cleve., 1966; LLD (hon.), Ashland (Ohio) Coll. Instr. English and drama Lourdes Acad., Cleve., 1963-70; asst. prof. English, speech and drama Cuyahoga Community Coll., Cleve., 1968-75; mem. Cleve. City Council from 8th Ward, 1973-76, 95th-100th Congresses from 20th Dist. Ohio; mem. banking, fin. and urban affairs com., select com. on aging, post office and civil service com., com. on house adminstrn., also numerous subcoms. Founder, vol.-dir. Near West Side Civic Arts Center, Cleve., 1970; ward leader Cuyahoga County Democratic Party, 1972-76; mem. Ohio Dem. Central Com. from 20th Dist., 1974; trustee Fedn. Community Planning, Cleve., Health and Planning Commn. Cleve., Community Info. Service Cleve., Cleve. Soc. Crippled Children, Public Services Occupational Group Adv. Com., Cuyahoga Community Coll., Cleve. Ballet, Cleve. YWCA. Recipient Outstanding Service awards OEO, 1973-78, Community Service award Am. Indian Center, Cleve., 1973, Community Service award Nationalities Service Center, 1974, Community Service award Club San Lorenzo, Cleve., 1976, Cuyahoga County Dem. Woman of Yr., 1977, Ursuline Coll. Alumna of Yr. award, 1977, awards Irish Nat. Caucus, awards West Side Community Mental Health Center, awards Am. Lebanese League, awards Spanish Christian Orgn., awards Cleve. Fedn. Am.-Syrian Lebanese Clubs; cert. appreciation City of Cleve.; Woman of Yr. award Cuyahoga County Women's Polit. Caucus, 1983; decorated Knight of Order of St. Ladislaus of Hungary. Office: US House of Reps 2231 Rayburn Washington DC 20515 also: 523 Federal Courthouse 215 Superior St Cleveland OH 44114 *

OAKES, DEBORAH GILLIAM, quality engineer; b. Kingsport, Tenn., Mar. 15, 1954; d. George W. and Stella Mae (Garber) Gilliam; m. James Gilbert Oakes, Nov. 12, 1983; 1 child, James Gilliam. BS in Engring. Tech., Memphis State U., 1977; postgrad., U. Tenn., 1981-82. Quality assurance engr. TVA, Knoxville, 1977-84; quality engr. Watts Bar Nuclear Plant TVA, Spring City, Tenn., 1985—. Adv. Knoxville, Tenn. chpt. Jr. Achievement, 1983-84. Mem. Am. Bus. Women Assn. (mem. communication com.). Democrat. Baptist. Office: TVA-Quality Assurance Dept Quality Engring PO Box 2000 Spring City TN 37381

OAKES, ELLEN RUTH, psychotherapist, health institute administrator; b. Bartlesville, Okla., Aug. 19, 1919; d. John Isaac and Eva Ruth (Engle) Harboldt; m. Paul Otis Oakes Sr., June 12, 1937 (div. April 1974); children: Paul Otis Jr., Deborah Ellen Wallain, Nancy Elaine Masters; m. Siegmar Johann Knopp, Nov. 24, 1975. BA in Sociology, Psychology summa cum laude, Oklahoma City U., 1961; MS in Clin. Psychology, U. Okla., 1963, PhD, 1967. Lic. clin. psychologist, Okla. Chief psychometrist Okla. U. Guidance Service, Oklahoma City, 1962; psychology trainee VA Hosp., Oklahoma City, 1962-64, Cerebral Palsy Ctr., Norman, Okla., 1964-65; psychology intern Guidance Service, Norman, 1965-66, staff psychologist, 1966-67; asst. prof. psychology Okla. U. Med. Sch., Oklahoma City, 1967-70; supr. psychology interns Okla. Univ. Health Scis. Ctr., 1967-80; founder, dir. Timberridge Inst., Oklahoma City, 1970—, pres., 1980—; pvt. practice clin. psychologist Oklahoma City, 1970—; instr. Okla. U. extension course, Tinker AFB, Oklahoma City, 1963, U. Okla., 1965-66; discussion leader Inst. for Tchrs. of Disadvantaged Child Oklahoma City Sch. System, 1966; leader group therapy sessions Asbury Meth. and Westminster Presbyn. Chs., Oklahoma City, 1966; mem. psychology team confs. for hearing disorders, Okla. U. Med. Sch., 1967-70; cons. Oklahoma City Pub. Schs., 1970-72; cons., group leader halfway house, 1972; lectr. chs., PTAs, hosps.; reviewer Am. Psyhol. Assn. Civilian Health and Med. Program of the Uniformed Services, 1978—. Contbr. articles to profl. jours. Speaker Okla. County Mental Health Assn. Ann. Worry Clinic, St. Luke's Ch., Oklahoma City, 1968—; speaker psychology dept. Sorosis Club, St. Luke's Ch. Mem. Am. Psychol. Assn., Okla. Psychol. Assn. (pres. 1975-76), Okla. State Psychologist Licensing Bd. Office: Timberridge Inst 6001 N Classen Blvd Oklahoma City OK 73118

OAKLAND, VELMA LEANE, educator; b. Moorhead, Minn., Dec. 29, 1939; d. Alfred J. and Annie (Klusman) Kuvaas; m. Aug. 17, 1959 (div. 1986); 1 child, Terry Lee. BS in Edn., Mayville State U., 1966; MS in Edn., N.D. State U., 1969. Cert. elem. tchr., Minn. Tchr. Granville (N.D.) Pub. Schs., 1960-62, Tappen (N.D.) Pub. Schs., 1962-64, Hughes Elem. Sch., 1964—. Head start dir. Inter County Community council, Red Lake Falls, Minn., 1970-73; comr. HUD, 1988; mem. Red Lake County Fair Bd., 1988—; mem. exec. com. 7th Congrl. Dist., 1988. Mem. Minn. Edn. Assn. (sec. 1979—, treas. 1983—, exec. com. 1983—), Pine to Prairie Coop. Ctr. (adv. com.), Delta Kappa Gama. Home: 118 Main Ave Red Lake Falls MN 56750 Office: Hughes Elem Sch Red Lake Falls MN 56750

OAKLEY, DEBORAH JANE, researcher, educator; b. Detroit, Jan. 31, 1937; d. George F. and Kathryn (Willson) Hacker; B.A., Swarthmore Coll., 1958; M.A., Brown U., 1960; M.P.H., U. Mich., 1969, Ph.D., 1977; m. Bruce Oakley, June 16, 1958; children—Ingrid Andrea, Brian Benjamin. Dir. teenage and adult programs YWCA, Providence, 1959-63; editorial asst. Stockholm U., 1963-64; research investigator, lectr. dept. population planning U. Mich., 1971-77; asst. prof. community health programs U. Mich., Ann Arbor, 1977-79, asst. prof. nursing research, 1979-81, asso. prof., 1981—. Trustee, Womens Health Research Inst., 1981—. Recipient Margaret Sanger award Washtenaw County Planned Parenthood, 1975; Outstanding Young Woman of Ann Arbor award Jaycees, 1970. Mem. Am. Public Health Assn. (chmn. population sect. council), Internat. Union Sci. Study Population, Midwest Nursing Research Soc., Population Assn. Am., Delta Omega. Democrat. Author: (with Leslie Corsa) Population Planning, 1979; contbr. articles to profl. jours. Home: 5200 S Lake Rd Chelsea MI 48118 Office: U Mich Sch Nursing Ann Arbor MI 48109

OAKLEY, MARY ANN BRYANT, lawyer; b. Buckhannon, W.Va., June 22, 1940; d. Hubert Herndon and Mary F. (Deeds) Bryant; m. Godfrey P. Oakley, Jr., Sept. 2, 1961; children—Martha, Susan, Robert. A.B., Duke U., 1962; M.A., Emory U., 1970, J.D., 1974. Tchr., Winston-Salem/Forsyth County Schs., N.C., 1961-65; assoc. Margie Pitts Hames, Atlanta, 1974-80; ptnr. Stagg Hoy & Oakley, Atlanta, 1980-83, Oakley & Bonner, Atlanta, 1984—. Contbr. articles to law jours. Notes and Comments editor Emory Law Jour., 1973-74. Author: Elizabeth Cady Stanton, 1972; Bd. dirs. Atlanta Met. YWCA, 1975-79, lst v.p., 1978-79; mem. Leadership Atlanta, 1979; bd. dirs. Ga. chpt. ACLU, 1981-83; trustee Unitarian Universalist Congregation Atlanta, 1977-80, pres., 1979-80, mem. Unitarian Universalist Commn. Appraisal, 1980-85; bd. dirs. Unitarian Universalist Service Com., 1984—, v.p., 1986-88, pres. 1988—. Nat. Merit scholar, 1958. Mem. ABA, Am. Judicature Soc., State Bar Ga. (chmn. individual rights sect. 1979-81, chmn. bench and bar com. 1984-87), Atlanta Bar Assn., Lawyers Club Atlanta, No. Dist. Bar Council, 1982-86, Ga. Assn. Women Lawyers, Ga. State Bar Disciplinary Bd., 1985-88, chmn., 1987-88, Assn. Trial Lawyers of Am., Ga. Women's Polit. Caucus, LWV, Phi Beta Kappa, Order of Coif. Home: 897 Barton Woods Rd NE Atlanta GA 30307 Office: 133 Carnegie Way Suite 508 Atlanta GA 30303

OAKS, M. MARLENE, minister; b. Grove City, Pa., Mar. 30, 1940; d. Allen Roy and Alberta Bell (Pinner) Eakin; m. Lowell B. Chaney, July 30, 1963 (dec. Jan. 1977); children: Christopher, Linda; m. Harold G. Younger, Aug. 1978 (div. 1986); Gilbert E. Oaks, Aug. 3, 1987. BA, Calif. State U., Los Angeles, 1972. Ordained Ch. of Religious Sci. minister, 1978. Educator Whittier (Calif.) Sch. Dists., 1972-74, Fullerton (Calif.) Coll., 1974-75, Garden Grove (Calif.) Sch. Dist., 1974-78; minister, founder Community Ch. of the Islands now Ch. of Religious Sci., Honolulu, 1978-80; minister Ch. of Divine Sci., Pueblo, Colo., 1980-83; minister, founder Ch. Religious Sci., Palo Alto, Calif., 1983-86; minister Ch. Religious Sci., Fullerton, 1986—; workshop leader Religious Sci. Dist. Conv., San Jose, Calif., 1985, Internat. New Thought Alliance Conference, Las Vegas, 1984, Calgary, Alta., Can., 1985, Washington, 1988, Golden Valley Unity Women's Advance, Mpls., 1986, 87, Qume Corp., San Jose, 1985. Author: (books) Old Time Religion is a Cult, 1985, Beyond Forgiveness, 1985, Stretch Marks On My Aura, 1987; contbr. booklets and articles for profl. jours. Mem. Fullerton Interfaith Ministerial Assn. (sec., treas. 1987—), United Clergy of Religious Sci., Internat. New Thought Alliance (pres. Orange County chpt.), Kappa Delta Pi. Republican. Lodge: Soroptimist Internat. (chmn. com. for internat. coop. and goodwill, 1987—). Office: First Ch Religious Sci 117 N Pomona Fullerton CA 92632

OATES, JOYCE CAROL, author; b. Lockport, N.Y., 1938; d. Frederic James and Caroline (Bush) O.; m. Raymond Joseph Smith, Jan. 23, 1961. BA, Syracuse U., 1960; MA, U. Wis., 1961. Prof. English U. Detroit, 1961-67, U. Windsor, Ont., Can., 1967-87; writer-in-residence Princeton (N.J.) U., 1978-81, prof., 1987—. Author: (short story collections) By the North Gate, 1963, Upon the Sweeping Flood, 1966, The Wheel of Love, 1970, Marriages and Infidelities, 1972, The Hungry Ghosts, 1974, The Goddess and Other Women, 1974, Where Have You Been, 1974, The Poisoned Kiss and Other Portuguese Stories, 1975, The Seduction and Other Stories, 1975, Crossing the Border, 1976, Night-Side, 1977, (novels) With Shuddering Fall, 1965, A Garden of Earthly Delights, 1967, Wonderland, 1971, Do With Me What You Will, 1973, The Assassins, 1975, Childwold, 1976, The Triumph of the Spider Monkey, 1977, Son of the Morning, 1978, Unholy Loves, 1979, Cybele, 1979, Bellefleur, 1980, A Sentimental Education, 1981, Angel of Light, 1981, A Bloodsmoor Romance, 1982, Mysteries of Winterthorn, 1984, Solstice, 1985, Wild Nights, 1985, Marya, 1986, You Must Remember This, 1987, On Boxing, 1987, The Lives of the Twins, 1987, (essays) On Boxing, 1987, (poetry collections) Women in Love, 1968, Expensive People, 1968, Them, 1969 (Nat. Book award 1970), Anonymous Sins, 1969, Love and Its Derangements, 1970, Angel Fire, 1973, Dreaming America, 1973, Men Whose Lives Are Money, 1978, (plays) The Sweet Enemy, 1965, Sunday Dinner (produced at Am. Place Theatre), 1970, Miracle Play, 1974, Daisy (produced at Cubioulo Theatre), N.Y.C., 1980, (essays) The Edge of Impossibility, 1971, The Poetry of D.H. Lawrence, 1973, New Heaven, New Earth, 1974; editor: Ont. Rev., The Best American Short Stories, 1979, also fiction in nat. mags. Recipient O. Henry Prize Story award, 1967-68; Guggenheim fellow, 1967-68. Mem. Am. Acad. and Inst. Arts and Letters. Office: Princeton U Dept English Princeton NJ 08544 *

OATNEY, CECILIA KAY, military officer; b. McCall, Idaho, May 18, 1956; d. Cecil Edward and Ruby Ilene (Wine) O. BBA in Acctg., Idaho State U., 1978; MS in Econs. and Ops. Research, Colo. Sch. Mines, 1987. Commd. 2d lt. U.S. Army, 1978, advanced through grades to capt., 1982; platoon leader A, B & C Cos. 8th signal bn. U.S. Army, Bad Kreuznach, Fed. Republic of Germany, 1978-81, bn. logistics officer 8th signal bn., 1981; div. radio officer 142d signal bn. U.S. Army, Ft. Hood, Tex., 1982-83, co. comdr. C Co. 142d signal bn., 1983-85, asst. ops. officer 142d signal bn., 1985; chief market analysis 6th recruiting brigade U.S. Army, Ft. Baker, Calif., 1987—. Pres. 4-H Club, Valley County, Idaho, 1973-74. Mem. Armed Forces Communication-Electronics Assn., Assn. U.S. Army. Home: PO Box 92 Donnelly ID 83615 Office: 6th Recruiting Brigade USARCW-RMS Fort Baker CA 94129

O'BANNION, MINDY MARTHA MARTIN, registered nurse; b. Cushing, Okla., Aug. 19, 1953; d. John William and Martha Florence (Vineyard) Martin; student Okla. State U., 1971-73, Oscar Rose Jr. Coll., 1973; grad. St. Anthony Sch. Nursing, 1975; m. William Neal O'Bannion, Oct. 9, 1976; children—Mindi Martha Mae, William Neale Aaron. Nursing asst. Cushing Mcpl. Hosp., 1973-75, head nurse surg. floor, 1975-76, charge nurse med. unit, 1978-79, 82-83; staff nurse Met. Hosp., Dallas, 1985; staff nurse med. unit Mesquite Community Hosp., Tex., 1985-87; nurse post partum unit Trinity Med. Ctr., Carrollton, Tex., 1987—. Mem. social com. Royal Haven Bapt. Ch. Women's Missionary Union, Dallas, 1977-78; mem. extension dept. nursery First Bapt. Ch., Cushing, 1979-82, extension dept. presch., 1982-84; mem. extension dept preschool Royal Haven Bapt. Ch., Dallas, 1986-87; treas., mem. nominating com. Joyce Harms group Women's Missionary Union. Mem. Am., Tex., Okla. State nurses assns., St. Anthony Hosp. Sch. Nursing Alumnae, Alpha Xi Delta (corr. sec. 1973), Tau Beta Sigma. Baptist. Home: 2939 Oxfordshire Ln Farmers Branch TX 75234

OBARA, PATRICIA EVELYN, banker, lawyer; b. Springfield, Mass., Sept. 26, 1952; d. Adam John and Evelyn Victoria (Pazik) O.; m. Walter W. Wronka, Jr., Oct. 8, 1977; children—Matthew Obara, Marissa Obara. B.A., Colgate U., 1974; J.D., Rutgers U., 1977. Bar: N.J. 1977. Vice-pres., asst. counsel, asst. sec. United Jersey Banks, Princeton, N.J., 1979—. Mem. ABA, N.J. Bar Assn., Somerset County Bar Assn., Princeton Bar Assn., Corp. Counsel Assn., Bank Counsel Group N.J., N.J. Bankers Assn. Roman Catholic. Office: United Jersey Banks 301 Carnegie Ctr Princeton NJ 08540

OBBINK, KRISTINE GARNERO, dietitian; b. Monterey, Calif., Oct. 6, 1952; d. Frank Peter and Gloria Jane (Fassio) Garnero; m. Rick Garrett Obbink, July 25, 1951; 1 child, Alex. BS, Calif. Poly. State U., 1975. Registered dietician, Calif., Oreg. Food service asst. Cal Poly Food Found., San Luis Obispo, Calif., 1970-75; food service supr. Cabrillo Convalescent Hosp., San Luis Obispo, 1975-77; staff dietician Woodland Park Hosp., Portland, Oreg., 1978-79; asst. dir. nutrition services Portland Sch. Dist., 1979—; cons. Take Off Pounds Sensibly, Portland, 1986-87; instr. Portland Community Coll., 1986—; guest lectr. Oreg. Council for Health, Fitness and Sports, Inc., Portland, 1987. Author: Get a Healthy Emotional Attitude Towards Dieting, 1985; co-author: Training Table: A Complete Sports Nutrition Program, 1987. Campaign chair United Way, Portland, 1984-85; vol. Children's Learnign Fair, Portland, 1985. Mem. Am. Sch. Food Service Assn. (guest lectr. 1987, Nutrition Standards com.)0, Oreg. Sch. Food Service Assn. (sec. 1983-85, chair exhibit, 1983-85, lectr. 1986), Assn. Central Adminstrn. Personnel (chair membership com. 1986, sec., treas. 1987-88, Outstanding Dept. award 1983), Am. Dietetic Assn., Oreg. Nutrition Council. Club: Toastmaster. Home: 2737 NE 48th Ave Portland OR 97213

OBERHAUSEN, JOYCE ANN, aircraft company executive, artist; b. Plain Dealing, La., Nov. 12, 1941; d. George Dewey and Jettie Cleo (Farrington) Wynn; m. James J. Oberhausen, Oct. 15, 1966; 1 dau., Georgann; m. Dale Estein, Sept. 15, 1958 (div. 1960); children—Darla Renee Estein Oberhausen Minor, Dale Henry Estein Oberhausen. Student Ayers Bus. Sch., Shreveport, 1962-63, U. Ala., 1964-65. Stenographer, sec. Lincoln Nat. Life Co., Shreveport, 1965-66; sec. Baifield Industries, Shreveport, 1975-86; internat. art tchr., Huntsville, Ala., 1974—; v.p. Precision Splty. Co., Huntsville, 1966—, Mil. Aircraft, Huntsville, 1979—; pres. Wynnson Enterprises, Huntsville, 1983—; owner Wynnson Galleries Pvt. Collections, Florist, Meridianville, 1987. Mgr. basketball team Meridianville, 1985-86; founder Nat. Mus. Women in Arts. Mem. Internat. Porcelain Guild, Nat. Assn. Female Execs., People to People, porcelain Portrait Soc., United Artists Assn., Am. Soc. of Profl. and Executive Women Hist. Soc. Avocations: oil painting, antiques, handcrafts, gourmet cooking, horseback riding. Home: 156 Spencer Dr Meridianville AL 35759 Office: Precision Splty Corp 150 Wells Rd Meridianville AL 35759

OBERLY, KATHRYN ANNE, lawyer; b. Chgo., May 22, 1950; d. James Richard and Lucille Mary (Kraus) O.; m. Daniel Lee Goelzer, July 13, 1974 (div. Aug. 1987); 1 child, Michael W. Student, Vassar Coll., 1967-69; BA, U. Wis., 1971, JD, 1973. Bar: Wis. 1974, D.C. 1981. Law clk. U.S. Ct. Appeals, Omaha, 1973-74; trial atty. U.S. Dept. Justice, Washington, 1974-77, spl. asst., 1977-81, spl. litigation counsel, 1981-82, asst. to Solicitor Gen., 1982-86; ptnr. Mayer, Brown & Platt, Washington, 1986—. Mem. ABA (environ. quality com. sect. on natural resources law), Wis. State Bar Assn., D.C. Bar Assn. Democrat. Office: Mayer Brown & Platt 2000 Pennsylvania Ave NW Washington DC 20006

OBERNDORFER, JANET, home economist; b. Flushing, N.Y., Jan. 6, 1941; d. Colonel Abbott and Molly Boone (Spencer) O. B.S. in Home Econs., U. R.I., 1963; grad. (with honors) advt. and mktg. edn. program Advt. Club of N.Y. Tchr. home econs. Central Islip Sr. High Sch. (N.Y.), 1963-65; home economist Borden, Inc., N.Y.C., 1966-69, Wheat Flour Inst., Chgo., 1970-72; mgr. home econs. Sharp Electronics, Paramus, N.J., 1973; asst. to circulation dir. market letter Merrill Lynch, N.Y.C., 1974-80; pres. Lady Resourceful, Inc., Garden City, N.Y., 1980—. Contbr. articles to mags. Mem. adv. council Coll. Human Sci. Services, U. R.I., Kingston, 1982, founder Home Econs. Endowment for Study of Bus., 1982. Mem. Home Economists in Bus., Am. Home Econs. Assn., N.Y. State Home Econs. Assn., L.I. Dist. Home Econs. Assn. (pres. 1986-87), Culinary Historians of N.Y., L.I. Communicators' Assn., Soc. Nutrition Edn., Women in Communications (v.p. fin. N.Y. chpt.), Garden City Hist. Soc., Nat. Trust for Historic Preservation, Met. Mus. Art, North Shore Preservation Soc. Club: Appalachian Mountain (N.Y.-N.J. chpt.). Office: Lady Resourceful Inc Box 7241 Garden City NY 11530

OBLINGER, JOSEPHINE KNEIDL HARRINGTON (MRS. WALTER L. OBLINGER), state legislator; b. Chgo., Feb. 14, 1913; d. Thomas William and Margaret (Kneidl) Harrington; B.S., U. Ill., 1933; J.D., U. Detroit, 1968; L.H.D., Sioux Empire Coll., 1966; m. Walter L. Oblinger, Apr. 27, 1940; 1 son, Carl D. Tchr. Lanphier High Sch., Springfield, Ill., 1951-62; clk. Sangamon County, assessor Capital Twp., Springfield, 1962-69; asst. dir. Ill. Dept. Registration and Edn., Springfield, from 1970; exec. dir. Gov.'s Com. on Voluntary Action, 1970-73; asst. to pres. Lincoln Land Community Coll., 1973-77; dir. Ill. Dept. on Aging, 1977-78; mem. Ill. Ho. Reps., 1978-85; dir. Gov.'s Office Sr. Involvement, 1985—. Sec. Springfield and Sangamon County Community Action, 1965-70 pres., 1970-74; mem. finance com. Child and Family Service, Springfield, 1965-70; mem. Nat. Com. for Day Care of Children, from 1960; mem. I-SEARCH Task Force on Alzheimer's Disease of So. Ill. U.; pres. Springfield Fedn. Tchrs. AFL-CIO, 1957-59, Ill. Fedn. Tchrs. AFL-CIO, 1959-63; mem. adv. com. to Gov.'s ACTION Office; mem. Planning Consortium for Services to Children in Ill., pres., 1978-79; chmn. mothers' march Sangamon County March of Dimes, 1980; bd. dirs., sec. Villa Vianney Retirement Ctr., Ill. Humanities Council, YWCA, Fed. Council on Aging, officer, Republican Women's Luncheon Club, 1959, pres., 1963-67; chmn. Sangamon County Rep. com., from 1965; past pres. Ill. Fedn. Rep. Women. Del. to White House Conf. on Children, 1960; chairperson Com. Women's Affairs White House Conf. Aging, 1981. Bd. dirs., pres. Sangamon-Menard County Council on Alcoholism and Drugs, Nat. Center Vol. Action; mem. bd. Sangamon County Salvation Army, Ret. Sr. Vol. Program, Edn. Alumnae Assn., Sangamon County Lit. Council. Recipient Golden Anniversary Salute to Older Illinoisans award Blue Cross/Blue Shield, 1987. Mem. Ill. Assn. County Clks. and Recorders (past pres.), Am. Bus. Women's Assn., Am., Ill., Sangamon County bar assns., Am. Assn. Vol. Services Coordinators (dir., chmn. pub. policy com.), NAACP (exec. bd.), Urban League, Am. Arbitration Assn., U. Ill. Alumni Assn., Nat. Assn. Recorders and Clks., Sangamon County Hist. Soc., Ill. Council Continuing Edn. (exec. com.), P.E.O., Kappa Delta Pi, Sigma Delta Pi, Delta Delta Delta. Clubs: Springfield Women's; Altrusa (pres. 1968-70) (Springfield). Home: RR 1 Williamsville IL 62693 Office: Gov's Office Sr Involvement Stratton Bldg Room 107 Springfield IL 62706

OBLINGER, NANCY L(EE), communications executive; b. Fort Sill, Okla., May 18, 1945; d. Richard Lee and Jane Catherine (Fleig) O.; student U. Calif., Santa Barbara, 1963-64, Kent State U., 1964-65. Adminstrv. asst. VanBarneveld & Ellis Public Relations, Los Angeles, 1965-67, Md. Casualty Co., Los Angeles, 1968-72, prin. corp. and mktg. coms., Los Angeles, 1984, account exec. Ruder Finn & Rotman, Los Angeles, 1984-85, sr. v.p. Swett & Crawford Group, Los Angeles, 1985—, asst. v.p., mgr. corp. communications, 1976-82. Recipient awards Am. Inst. Graphic Arts Show, 1978, Communication Arts Soc. Show, 1979. Mem. Internat. Assn. Bus. Communicators, Ins. Mktg. Communication Assn. (award of excellence 1980, 86), Insurers Public Relations Council, So. Calif. Bus. Communicators (awards of excellence 1978, 86). Republican. Episcopalian. Club: Toastmasters. Office: Swett & Crawford Group 3699 Wilshire Blvd Los Angeles CA 90010

O'BOYLE, SHEILA MARY, lawyer, accountant; b. San Francisco, Aug. 28, 1956; d. Frank Vincent and Eleanor Kathryn (Rodenhausen) O'B.; m. Moshe Litman, Sept. 9, 1978; 1 child, Marissa Michelle. B.S. in Bus. Adminstrn., Calif. State U.-Northridge, 1978; J.D., U. West Los Angeles, 1982. Bar: Calif. 1982. Auditor, corp. examiner Calif. Dept. Corps., Los Angeles, 1978; acct. Transam. Ins. Services, Los Angeles, 1979; sole practice, Simi Valley, Calif., 1982—. Vice pres. Simi Republican Women; mem. Ventura County Rep. Central Com. Recipient John Gorfinkel award U. West Los Angeles, 1980; Am. Jurisprudence award Bancroft Whitney Pub. Co., San Francisco, 1981. Mem. State Bar Calif., ABA, Ventura County Bar Assn., U. West Los Angeles Alumni Assn., AAUW, Simi Valley C. of C. Home: 2779 Baywater Pl Thousand Oaks CA 91362 Office: 2333 E. Birchfield St. Simi Valley CA 93065

OBREMSKI, ARLENE JOYCE, special education educator; b. Bklyn., Mar. 13, 1944; d. Richard Edgar and Antonia Agnes (Bonsignore) Bennett; m. Robert John Obremski, Aug. 29, 1964; children: Christine Michelle, Robin Joyce. BS in History, Calif. State U., Fullerton, 1974, MS in Reading, 1977, cert. spl. edn., 1987, MS in Counseling, 1985. Gen. teaching credential; reading specialist credential, learning disabilities credential, severely handicapped credential. Tchr. Holy Redeemer Sch., College Park, Md., 1964-66, Sch. of Our Lady, Santa Ana, Calif., 1974-75; 2d grade tchr., vice prin. St. Angela's Sch., Brea, Calif., 1975-79; spl. edn. tchr. Commonwealth Sch., Fullerton, 1979-83, Orangethorpe Sch., Fullerton, 1983—; Speaker in field. Author: ABC of Ocean, 1984, Special Education in Hong Kong, Storytelling Orange Thorpe Style, Storytelling and the Arts for the Handicapped Child. Named Tchr. of Yr. Fullerton Dist., Orange County, 1987. Mem. Internat. Reading Assn., Reading Educators Guild (sec. 1983, v.p. 1984), Calif. Reading Assn., Orange County Reading Assn., Calif. Assn. Handicapped Children and Adults, Spl. Arts Orange County (adv. bd.), Storytellers Assn. Home: 19792 La Tierra Ln Yorba Linda CA 92686

O'BRIEN, ANNA BELLE CLEMENT, state senator; b. Scottsville, Ky.; m. Charles H. O'Brien; 3 stepchildren. Student McMurray Coll. Former mem. Tenn. Ho. of Reps.; mem. Tenn. State Senate, 1976—. Active Am. Legion Aux., Cumberland County Mental Health Assn., DAR, Cumberland County Beautiful Assn., Hosp. Aux.; adv. council Maccasin Bend Psychiat. Hosp., Chattanooga; bd. dirs. Plateau Mental Health Ctr., Cookeville, Tenn.; bd. dirs. Wharton Nursing Home, Cumberland County, Crossville C. of C. Mem. Bus. and Profl. Women's Club, Democratic Women's Club. Clubs: Top Town Garden, Marie Ervin Home Demonstration, Lake Tansi Village Women's. Baptist. Office: Tenn Senate State Capitol Nashville TN 37219 *

O'BRIEN, ANNE PACE, medical center administrator, real estate salesperson; b. Pittston, Pa., Feb. 2, 1930; d. Leo Aloyious Pace and Catherine (Ceceal) O'Rourke; m. Vincent Anderson O'Brien, Nov. 15, 1952; children: Lou Anne, Catherine, Vincent, Sean, Jeremy. Student, St. Joseph's Coll., 1969-70; RN, St. Mary's Hosp. Sch. Nursing, Hoboken, N.J., 1952. Pres., adminstr., owner Community Med. Ctr., Northport, N.Y., 1961—; assoc. Olita Real Estate, Kings Park, N.Y., 1966—; owner, pres., mgr. Mallow Marsh Farm Stables, Northport, N.Y., 1979—. Dir., pres. St. Charles Aux. (Northport chpt.), 1964-65; dir. St. Charles Aux. Coordinating Council, Port Jefferson, N.Y., 1966-78; Womens Aux. to Med. Soc., L.I., N.Y., 1972-82; pres. Cystic Fibrosis Found., 1974-75, dir., 1968-70. Roman Catholic. Home: 115 Sunken Meadow Rd Northport NY 11768 Office: Community Med Ctr 1014 Fort Salonga Rd Northport NY 11768-2525

O'BRIEN, BARBARA LYNN, food technologist; b. St. Louis, July 23, 1955; d. Daniel and Yetta (Derfeld) Berk; m. Timothy Patrick O'Brien, May 25, 1976. B, U. Mo., 1976, M in Food Sci., 1978; postgrad., Washington U., St. Louis, 1984—. Food technologist II Anheuser-Busch, Inc., St. Louis, 1979-84, food technologist I, 1984-87, research group leader, 1987—. Mem. Inst. Food Technologists, ASMT, Am. Soc. Brewing Chemists. Republican. Jewish. Office: Anheuser-Busch Inc 1101 Wyoming Saint Louis MO 63118

O'BRIEN, CATHERINE LOUISE, museum administrator; b. N.Y.C., July 21; d. Edward Denmark and Catherine Louise (Browne) O'B.; m. Philip R. James (div.); m. Sterling Noel (div.). B.A., Finch Coll., N.Y.C.; postgrad. Williams Coll., Williamstown, Mass., Sarah Lawrence Coll. Reprodn. mgr. Met. Mus. Art, N.Y.C., 1975—. Exhibited in group shows at Parrish Art Mus., Southampton, N.Y., 1965-70, Met. Mus. Art, N.Y.C., 1975-85, Guild Hall Exhibit, East Hampton, N.Y., 1965-85. Mem. aux. Southampton Hosp., 1970-85; founder East Hampton Horse Show, Ladies Village Improvement Soc., East Hampton, 1970—; mem. fair coms. St. James Ch., N.Y.C., St. Luke's Ch., East Hampton, 1970-85; mem. alumnae adv. bd. Marymount Coll., N.Y.C., 1984-86, Women's Nat. Rep. Club, N.Y.C. Mem. DAR (vice regent East Hampton chpt. 1974-85), Colonial Dames Am. (archives com. 1980-85), Daus. Brit. Empire (historian 1978-85), United Daus. Confederacy (state historian 1970-85), Daus. Colonial Wars (corr. sec. 1983-85), Sons and Daus. of the Pilgrims (corr. sec. 1983-85), Victorian Soc., Soc. Mayflower Descs. (life), English Speaking Union, New Eng. Soc. (mem. ball com. 1983-86), Daus. of Cin. (historian 1979-85), Squadron "A". Republican. Episcopalian. Clubs: Devon Yacht, Maidstone (East Hampton, N.Y.); Southampton Yacht (N.Y.); Metropolitan (N.Y.C.) (women's com., chmn. debutante ball 1980-84); Reciprocal/India House, St. Anthony Union League (N.Y.C.). Avocations: show horses; dogs. Home: 605 Park Ave New York NY 10021 Office: Met Mus Art Fifth Ave New York NY 10028

O'BRIEN, ELIZABETH ELLEN, sales professional; b. South Weymouth, Mass., Sept. 19, 1961; d. Robert Lincoln and Marjorie (Knapp) O'B. BA, Simmons Coll., 1983. Dept. mgr. sales Jordan Marsh Co., Boston, 1983-86, asst. buyer, 1986-87, div. sales mgr., 1987—. Home: 41 Deacon Ct Barnstable MA 02630

O'BRIEN, ELIZABETH MARESCA, marketing executive; b. Red Bank, N.J., Jan. 4, 1958; d. Paul William Michael and Roberta Gertrude (Abbes) Maresca. Student, Brookdale Community Coll., 1976-77; A Bus. Adminstrn., Tidewater Community Coll., 1988. Systems analyst Methods Research Corp., Farmingdale, N.J., 1977-79; div. mgr. Abacus Services, Inc., Virginia Beach, Va., 1979—. V.p. Charlestowne Civic League, Virginia Beach, 1983-84; bd. dirs. Arthritus Found., Norfolk, Va., 1986—; advisor Commonwealth Coll., Norfolk, 1984—. Mem. Women's Network of Hampton Rds., Hampton Roads C. of C. (com. chair 1985, 88), Williamsburg Area C. of C. (exhibit chair 1987). Republican. Roman Catholic. Office: Abacus Services Inc 860 Greenbrier Circle Suite 302 Chesapeake VA 23320

O'BRIEN, JACQUELYN KIRTLEY, state legislator; b. Cin., July 23, 1931; d. Baxter Thomas Kirtley and Paulyne (Walker) Kirtley Cronimus; m. John O'Brien, Aug. 13, 1955 (dec. Mar. 30, 1985); children: John Todd, Holly Temple, Heather Kirtley. Student, U. Cin., 1950-53. With AT&T, Cin., 1953-57; mem. Ohio Ho. Reps., Cin., 1985—, mem. Aging and Housing com., Econ. Devel. and Small Bus. com., Elections and Townships com., mem. Joint Select Com. on State House Beautification, Transpn. and Urban Affairs com., sec. Human Resources com. V.p. Anderson Mid. Sch. PTA, Turpin Mid. Sch. PTA, Forest Hills Instrumental Music Assn.; pres. St. Timothy's Episc. Ch. Women; head of vols. Salem Sr. Ctr., also bd. dirs.; area chmn. United Fine Arts Fund; trustee Anderson Twp. Library, co-founder library com.; active area polit. campaigns, school bond and levy drives, Salvation Army, Cin. Ballet Com.; bd. dirs. Anderson Hills Loan Found. Mem. Psi Psi Psi (past pres.). Republican. Club: Anderson Hills Women's (past pres.). Home: 7651 Burline Hills Ct Cincinnati OH 45244 Office: Ohio Ho Reps State House Columbus OH 43215

O'BRIEN, LORETTA SULLIVAN, lawyer; b. Boston, June 13, 1930; d. Franklin James and Frances (Sullivan) O;B.; m. William P. Shields, Aug. 27, 1949 (div. May 6, 1971); children—Candice P., Leslie A. A.B., U. Mass., 1969; cert. Simmons Sch. Social Work, 1973; J.D., New Eng. Sch. Law, Boston, 1977. Bar: Mass. 1977. Sr. social worker Mass. Dept. Pub. Welfare, Norwood, 1972-78; founder, owner, Norwood Legal Ctr., 1978—. Mem. ABA, Western Norfolk County Bar Assn. (pres. 1985—), NOW, LWV (pres.). Club: Appalachian Mountain (chmn. com. 1981—). Home: 150 S Walpole St Sharon MA 02067 Office: Norwood Legal Ctr 648 Washington St Suite 12 Norwood MA 02062

O'BRIEN, LUCREZIA FLORENCE, cosmetics company executive; b. Albany, N.Y., Jan. 28, 1940; d. Joseph John and Christina E. (Pustorino) Toste; children: Thomas, Jr., Stephanie. Lic. cosmetologist, Ill. Mgr. Face & Figure Salon, Hinsdale, Ill., 1960-70; founder, pres. LaFinesse, Inc., Lisle, Ill., 1970—. Chmn. benefit dance local Am. Cancer Soc., Riverwalk Naperville; co-developer Child Protection Program; active YMCA, Naperville Heritage Soc., Naperville Humane Soc.; vol. Good Samaritan Hosp. Mem. Nat. Cosmetologist Assn., Ill. Cosmetologist Assn., Chgo. Cosmetologist Assn. (chmn. various coms. 1984—, co-chmn. edn. com. 1986—, bd. dirs., treas. 1984—), Women in Mgmt. (program com. 1985—, spl. events com., speakers arrangement com. 1986—, Woman of Achievement award, Charlotte Danstrom award 1987), Naperville C. of C. (relations com. 1984—, chmn. ann. golf tournament, bd. dirs. 1985—, v.p. 1988—). Office: LaFinesse Inc 501 Ogden Ave Lisle IL 60532

O'BRIEN, MAREE ARLEEN, real estate company executive; b. Providence, Sept. 15, 1947; d. Alphonse Robert and Dahlia Lydia (Fiore) Testa; m. William Washburn O'Brien Jr., Apr. 27, 1967 (div. Oct. 1974); children: Dawne Alisa, Jennifer Lynn. Student, R.I. Jr. Coll., 1967-68, R.I. Coll., 1978-80, U. R.I., 1980-81. Owner, trainer, breeder Bryanook Kennels, Warwick, R.I., 1968-83; owner, saleswoman, designer Kountry Shoppe, Greenville, R.I., 1982-83; adminstr., saleswoman Orchard View Assocs., Greenville, R.I., 1983-85; gen. ptnr. RPM Assocs., Greenville, 1985-87; prin. Century 21 RPM Assocs., Inc., Greenville, 1987—; tchr. Century 21 of NE, Warwick, 1987—; mem. Century 21 Investment Soc. R.I. Mem. Nat. Assn. Realtors, R.I. Assn. Realtors, Greater Providence Bd. Realtors, Nat. Assn. Female Execs. Lodge: Rotary (sgt. at arms Smithfield, R.I. club). Office: Century 21 RPM Assocs Inc One Garnett Ln Greenville RI 02828

O'BRIEN, MARY DEVON, communications company executive, strategic planning-consultant; b. Buenos Aires, Argentina, Feb. 13, 1944; came to U.S., 1949, naturalized, 1962; d. George Earle and Margaret Frances (Richards) Owen; m. Gordon Covert O'Brien, Feb. 16, 1962 (div. Aug. 1982); children—Christopher Covert, Devon Elizabeth; m. Christopher Gerard Smith, May 28, 1983. BS, Rutgers U., 1975, MBA, 1976. Controller manpower Def. Communications div. ITT, Nutley, N.J., 1977-80, adminstr. program, 1977-78, mgr. cost, schedule control, 1978-79, voice processing project, 1979-80; mgr. project Avionics div. ITT, Nutley, 1980-81, sr. mgr. projects, 1981—; cons. strategic planning, N.J., 1983—; lectr. in field, 1977—. Author: Pace: System Manual, 1979, Voices, 1982. Chmn. Citizens Budget Adv. Com., Maplewood, N.J., 1984-87, chmn. recreation, library, pub. services, 1982-83, chmn. pub. safety, emergency services, 1983-84, chmn. schs. and edn., 1984-85; bd. dirs., officer Civic Assn., Maplewood, 1984—; first v.p. MCA, 1987—; chmn. Maple Leaf Service award Com., 1987—, nat. chmn. Project Mgmt. Jour. Survey; mem. Maplewood Zoning Bd., 1983—; officer, mem. exec. bd. N.J. Project Mgmt. Inst., 1985—, pres., 1987—, v.p., 1986; chmn. Project Mgmt. Assn. Charter Com.; chmn. Internat. Project Mgmt. Inst. Jour. and Membership survey, 1986-87, mktg. com., 1986-, long range planning and steering com., 1987—; adv. bd. Project Mgmt. Jour., 1987—, N.J. PMI Ednl., 1987—; mem. MCA/N.J.Blood Bank Drive. Recipient Anti-Shoplifting Program award Distributive Edn. Club Am., 1981, N.J. Fedn. of Women's Clubs, 1981, 82, Retail Mchts. Assn., 1981, 82; Commendation and Merit awards Air Force Inst. Tech., 1981; Pres.'s Safety award ITT, 1983; State award N.J. Fedn. of Women's Clubs Garden Show, 1982; Cert. Spl. Merit award N.J. Fedn. of Women's Clubs, 1982. Mem. Internat. Platform Speakers Assn., Grand Jury Assn., Telecommunications Group and Aerospace Industries Assn., Performance Mgmt. Assn. (bd. dirs.), Nat. Security Indsl. Assn., Assn. for Info. and Image Mgmt., ITT Mgmt. Assn., LWV. Club: Maplewood Women's (pres. 1980-82). Home: 594 Valley St Maplewood NJ 07040 Office: ITT Avionics 417 River Rd Nutley NJ 07110

O'BRIEN, MAURA ANN, bioethicist; b. Bronx, N.Y., Aug. 3, 1959; BA, Duke U., 1981; MA, Georgetown U., 1985, PhD, 1988. Congl. aide, Washington, 1982; research assoc. Masi Research Cons., Inc., Washington, 1983-85; fellow Kennedy Inst. Ethics, Georgetown U., Washington, 1983-85, 88; assoc. for ethics N.Y. State Task Force on Life and Law, N.Y.C., 1985-86; intern WHO, 1988. Video producer AIDS and Edn.: An Australian Reponse, 1988; NEH Writing Ctr. fellow, 1984-85; Inst. for Humane Studies fellow, 1985; Fulbright scholar Ctr. for Human Bioethics Australia, 1987; Fulbright scholar, 1987-88. Mem. AAUW, Hastings Ctr., Philos. Soc. Washington, Am. Soc. Law and Medicine, Am. Philos. Assn. Clubs: Washington Philosophy, Duke of Washington. Office: Georgetown U Dept Philosophy Washington DC 20057

O'BRIEN, PATRICIA NEVIN, computer scientist; b. Hanover, Pa., June 13, 1957; d. Malcolm Hugh and Lida Mae (Smith) Nevin; m. Thomas Gerard O'Brien, May 2, 1981. BS in Psychology, Towson State U., 1978, MA, 1980. Research asst. Johns Hopkins U., Balt., 1980-82; programmer-analyst Johns Hopkins U., Towson, Md., 1982; ops. research analyst U.S. Army, Aberdeen, Md., 1983-84, 86-87; officer BDM Corp., Albuquerque, 1984-85; pres. Maverick, Inc., Albuquerque, 1985-86; chief analysis div. Defense Test and Evaluation Support Agy., Albuquerque, 1987—. Mem. Am. Assn. Artificial Intelligence, Soc. for Computer Simulation, Armed Forces Communications and Electronics Assn. Home: 45 Meikle Rd Tijeras NM 87059 Office: Def Test and Evaluation Support Agy DTESA/RQA Albuquerque NM 87106

O'BRIEN, SUE, journalist; b. Waukon, Iowa, Mar. 6, 1939; d. John Gordon and Jean (Schadel) O'B.; children—Peter, Sarah, Andrew. B.A., Grinnell Coll., 1959; M.P.A., JFK Sch. Govt., Harvard U., 1985. Reporter, KTLN/KTLK Radio, Denver, 1968-70; anchor, reporter KBTR-AM, Denver, 1970-73; anchor, reporter, commentator KOA-AM/TV, Denver, 1973-75; corr. NBC Radio, N.Y.C., 1975-76; news dir., exec. editor KOA AM/FM/TV, Denver, 1976-80; press sec. Gov. Colo., Denver, 1980-85; campaign mgr. Roy Romer 1985-86; asst. city editor The Denver Post, 1987-88; assoc. prof. journalism U. Colo., Boulder, 1988—; adj. assoc. prof. U. Colo. Grad. Sch. Pub. Adminstrn., 1986—. Chmn., Christian Social Relations div. Episcopal Diocese Colo., 1964-68; chmn., editor Colo. Journalism Rev., 1974-75; press sec. Coloradans for Lamm/Dick, 1982. Recipient Headliner award Women in Communications Colo., 1972, Big Hat award U. Colo. Soc. Profl. Journalists, 1973, Alumni award Grinnell Coll., 1974. Mem. Soc. Profl. Journalists (v.p. 1977-78), Radio and TV News Dirs. Assn., Mortar Bd., Phi Beta Kappa. Democrat. Episcopalian. Club: Denver Press. Home: 17 Ogden St Denver CO 80218

O'BRIEN, SUSAN MARY, banker; b. N.Y.C., Feb. 5, 1947; d. Charles George and Francis Lucille (O'Dea) Hemberger; m. Richard Thomas O'Brien Jr., May 31, 1980. BBA, Fordham U., 1979; MBA, St. John's U., 1983. Programmer Bklyn. Union Gas Co., 1968-71, Woods, Struthers & Winthrop Co., N.Y.C., 1971; programmer analyst Storer Broadcasting Co., N.Y.C., 1971-72, Am. Electric Power Co., N.Y.C., 1972-74; programmer analyst Mfrs. Hanover Trust, N.Y.C., 1974-78, project mgr., 1978-80, sr. tech. officer, 1981, group mgr., asst. v.p., 1982-83, area mgr., v.p., 1984-85, v.p., devel. mgr., 1985—. Republican. Roman Catholic. Office: Mfr Hanover Trust 40 Wall St New York NY 10005

O'BRIEN-PENNISI, MARY EVELYN, color consultant; b. Long Beach, N.Y., Aug. 12, 1946; d. William Maddox and Agnes Elizabeth (Sweeney) O'Brien; m. Peter Pennisi, Feb. 3, 1968 (div. Nov. 1987); 1 child, Mark Edward. Student Fashion Inst. Tech., N.Y.C., 1964-65, student Brown's Bus. Sch., Rockville Center, N.Y., 1965-66, Parsons Sch. Design, White Plains, N.Y., 1975. Rep., Color Me Beautiful, Tex., 1979-83; owner, operator The Color Studio, Richardson, Tex., 1983—; prin. Communicative Seminars, Inc., Richardson, 1984—, The Color Studio Eyewear, Richardson, 1983—; realtor assoc. Henry S. Miller Residential Real Estate Services Corp., Richardson, 1987—. Author tng. manual. Mem. Am. Bus. Women's Assn., Richardson C. of C., Dallas C. of C., Dallas Better Bus. Bur. Avocations: skiing, walking, designing clothing. Home: 1202 Eton Dr Richardson TX 75080 Office: Henry S Miller Residential Real Estate Service Corp 1535 Promenade Ctr Richardson TX 75080

O'BRYON, LINDA ELIZABETH, television executive, anchor; b. Washington, Sept. 1, 1949; d. Walter Mason Ormes and Iva Genevieve (Batrus) Ranney; m. Dennis Michael O'Bryon, Sept. 8, 1973; 1 child, Jennifer Elizabeth. BA in Journalism cum laude, U. Miami, Coral Gables, Fla. News reporter Sta. KTVX, Salt Lake City, 1971-73; documentary and pub. affairs producer Sta. WPLG-TV, Miami, Fla., 1974-76; producer, reporter, news dir. then v.p. for news and pub. affairs, exec. editor and co-anchor The Nightly Business Report Sta. WPBT-TV (PBS), Miami, 1976—. Recipient award Fla. Bar, Tallahasse, 1977, 2 awards Ohio State U., 1976, 79, local Emmy award So. Fla. chpt. Nat. Acad. TV Arts and Scis., 1978, award Corp. for Pub. Broadcasting, 1978, Econ. Understanding award Amos Tuck Sch. Bus. Dartmouth Coll., Hanover, N.H., 1980, award Fla. AP, 1981, 1st prize Nat. Assn. Rea Hors, 1986. Mem. Nat. Acad. TV Arts and Scis. (former bd. dirs.), Radio-TV News Dirs. Assn., Sigma Delta Chi. Republican. Roman Catholic. Office: Sta WPBT-Channel 2 14901 NE 20th Ave Miami FL 33181

O'BYRNE, NATALIE KWASNESKI, psychiatrist; b. Bklyn., Nov. 29, 1933; d. Julian Leon and Jeannette Pauline (Kowalski) Kwasneski; BS in Chemistry cum laude, St. John's U., 1955; MD, State U. N.Y., Bklyn., 1959; m. William O'Byrne, June 13, 1959; children: Cecily, Matthew, Stephanie, Gabrielle, Luke. Intern, Kings County Hosp., N.Y.C., 1960-61; resident in pediatrics Children's Hosp., San Francisco, 1962-63, adolescent medicine fellow, 1963-64; resident in adult psychiatry St. Mary's Hosp., San Francisco, 1964-66, in child psychiatry, 1966-68; practice medicine specializing in adult, child and adolescent psychiatry, Corte Madera, Calif., 1968—; assoc. clin. prof. U. Calif. (San Francisco); sr. supervising psychiatrist Langley-Porter Children's Service; bd. dirs. Threshold, Inc. Diplomate Am. Bd. Psychiatry and Neurology, Am. Bd. Adult and Child Psychiatry. Fellow Am. Psychiat. Assn., Am. Acad. Child Psychiatry; mem. AMA, Calif. Med. Assn., Marin, San Francisco med. socs., No. Calif. Psychiat. Assn., Regional Orgn. Child-Adolescent Psychiatry. Roman Catholic. Home: 715 Butterfield Rd San Anselmo CA 94960 Office: 1556 Redwood Hwy Corte Madera CA 94925

O'CARROLL, ANITA LOUISE, legal editor, lawyer; b. Jersey City, Nov. 19, 1953; d. Henry Patrick and Anita (Babikian) O'C. B.A., Rutgers U., 1975; J.D., N.Y. Law Sch., 1978. Bar: N.J. 1983, Pa. 1983, U.S. Dist. Ct. N.J. 1983. Legal asst. to Manhattan Dist. Atty., N.Y.C., 1977, to Bergen County Counsel, Hackensack, N.J., 1977; jud. clk. City of Hackensack, 1978-79; legal editor West Pub. Co., Mineola, N.Y., 1980-85; staff atty. Social Security Adminstrn. Office of Hearings and Appeals, Newark, 1985-86; staff atty. Aetna Life and Casualty Co., Parsippany, N.J., 1986—. Author: (with others) The Guide to American Law, 1981; A Synthesis of N.Y. Case Law on the Bill of Particulars and Pretrial Discovery, 1977. Mem. ABA, Assn. Trial Lawyers Am., N.J. State Bar Assn., Pa. Bar Assn. Republican. Home: 373 Penns Way Basking Ridge NJ 07920

OCCHIUZZO, LUCIA RAJSZEL, restaurant executive; b. Casablanca, Morocco, Nov. 5, 1951; came to U.S., 1958, naturalized, 1973; d. Tadeusz Joseph and Irmina Elizabeth (Wacholska) Rajszel; m. Joel Occhiuzzo, Dec. 9, 1976. BA, Montclair U., 1974. Owner, pres. Mr. O's, Dallas, 1977-83, L n J's Restaurant & Club, Richardson, Tex., 1984—. Guest star Sta. Telecable TV, 1985; L n J's Restaurant subject of TV program, 1986; contbr. articles to newspapers. Recipient Restaurant of Month award Dallas Times Herald, 1978. Mem. Richardson C. of C., ASCAP. Republican. Roman Catholic. Avocations: music, photography, writing. Home: 156 Hidden Circle Richardson TX 75080 Office: L 'n J's Restaurant & Club 2475 Promenade Ctr Richardson TX 75080

OCHAL, BETHANY JACQUITA, law library administrator; b. Flint, Mich., Dec. 2, 1917; d. Llewellyn Lane and Idah B. (Stewart) Ziegler; m. Edward Louis Ochal, July 1, 1944 (div.); children—Myrna Irene, Edward Llewellyn. B.A., Wayne State U., 1944, J.D., 1945. Bar: Mich. sup. ct. 1945, U.S. Dist. Ct. (ea. dist.) Mich. 1945, U.S. Ct. Aplo. (6th cir.) 1960, U.S. Sup. Ct. 1964. Sole practice, Detroit, 1945-51; reference librarian Detroit Bar Assn., 1951-60, librarian, 1960-61; law librarian Wayne State U., 1961-72, dir. Legal Research program, 1962-67; dir. Orange County (Calif.) Law Library, Santa Ana, 1972—. Mem. State Bar Mich. (chmn. legal pubs. com. 1968-70), Women Lawyers Assn. Mich. (pres. 1966-67), Am. Assn. Law Libraries (chmn. com. membership 1965-67, chmn. com. chapters 1968-70, chmn. com. audio visual 1970-71, 82-83), Ohio Regional Assn. Law Libraries (pres. 1969-70), Internat. Assn. Law Libraries, AAUW. Democrat. Club: Soroptimists Internat. Contbr. in field to profl. jour. Office: Orange County Law Library 515 N Flower St Santa Ana CA 92703

OCHIPINTI, LAURA ANN, editor; b. Washington, Sept. 12, 1961; d. Samuel Joseph and Rose Marie (LaTorre) O. BS in Journalism, U. Md., 1984. Editorial asst. Law & Bus., Inc., Washington, 1984-85; assoc. editor Am. Correctional Assn., College Park, Md., 1985-86; mng. editor Am. Correctional Assn., College Park, 1986—. Author: (mag.) Corrections Today, 1985-86, (newsletters) One the Line, 1985-86, Legal Times, 1984-85. Home: 200 Fort Meade Rd #305 Laurel MD 20707 Office: Am Correctional Assn 4321 Hartwick Rd #L-208 College Park MD 20740

OCHMAN, B. L., public relations executive, writer; b. N.Y.C., Mar. 13, 1949; d. Reuben and Dorothy (Bussel) Friedman. B.A. in Journalism, U. Bridgeport (Conn.), 1968. Account exec. Leo Miller Assocs., Westport, Conn., 1968-74; pub. relations dir. M. Hohner Inc., L.I., N.Y., 1974-76; editorial dir. Ruder & Finn Pub. Relations, N.Y.C., 1976-78; account supr. Ben Kubasik Pub. Relations, N.Y.C., 1978-79; pres. Rent-A-Kvetch, Inc., N.Y.C., 1979—; pres. B.L. Ochman Pub. Relations, N.Y.C., 1979—. Mem. N.Y. C. of C., Pub. Relations Soc. Am., N.Y. Assn. Women Bus. Owners. Democrat. Jewish. Office: BL Ochman Pub Relations 109 W 27 St Suite 9-D New York NY 10001

O'CHUK, GRAYCE XENIA, school nurse; b. Zion, Ill., Oct. 21, 1919; d. Vasily Titus and Xenia (Solunanchuk) Omelianchuk; m. Jacob Stipanuk, Dec. 2, 1944 (div. Dec. 1980); children: James Jacob, Jane Paula, Jeane Grayce, Timothy Peter. RN, St. Luke's Hosp., Racine, Wis., 1944; BA, Ariz. State U., 1970; MA, U. LaVerne, 1980. Indsl. nurse Am. Motors, Kenosha, Wis., 1945-46, 53-54, gen. nurse and night supr., 1945-57; charge nurse Kenosha (Wis.) Meml. Hosp., 1952-53, 55-57; charge nurse obs. Good Samaritan Hosp., Phoenix, 1957-58; indsl. nurse Internat. Metals, Phoenix, 1958-59; inservice dir., nursing arts instr. Tempe (Ariz.) Community Hosp., 1959-62; sch. nurse Scottsdale (Ariz.) Schs., 1962-70; spl. edn. sch. nurse for severely handicapped children Los Angeles County Office of Edn., Downey, Calif., 1970-87; founder, owner House of Spl. Books, 1986; pres. Wheelchair Lab, Inc.; sub-chmn. health edn. com. Scottsdale Schs., 1967-69; instigated 1st orthopedically handicapped sch., Scottsdale, Ariz., 1965; ret., 1987. Author: Nursing Procedures-Tempe Community Hospital, 1961, High School Health Assistant Procedures, 1964, Multi-Handicapped Students, 1984-85, Special Education: Student Vision Screening, 1985, Vision Problems: Look and See, 1988; author tape/slides: A Box ZPC Memories, 1983; founder pub. co. House of Spl. Books, 1987—. Bd. dirs. San Gabriel Valley Regional Ctr., State Calif., 1978-82; ad hoc chmn. Med. Delivery System, San Francisco State U. grad. fellow, 1970; Calif. del. White House Conf. Physically Handicapped, 1977. Mem. Am. Sch. Health Assn., Council Exceptional Children, Nat. Assn. Autistic Children, Calif. Assn. Physically Handicapped, Calif. Sch. Nurses Assn., Los Angeles County Sch. Nurses Assn., Am. Heart Assn. Democrat. Home: 4348 Toyon Circle LaVerne CA 91750 Office: E San Gabriel Valley Sch 4400 N Roxburgh St Covina CA 91722

O'CONNELL, ANN, state legislator; b. Albuquerque, Aug. 3, 1934; m. Robert E. O'Connell; children: Gray, Jeff. Student, U. N.Mex. Mem. from dist. 5 Nev. State Senate. Former pres. Citizens for Pvt. Enterprise; mem. State Mental Hygiene and Mental Retardation Adv. Bd. Recipient Outstanding Citizen award City of Las Vegas, Silver Beaver award Boy Scouts Am. Republican. Home: 7225 Montecito Circle Las Vegas NV 89120 *

O'CONNELL, ANNA PORRECA, biologist; b. Phila., Apr. 26, 1937; d. Francis Paul and Anna Agnes (Donatucci) Porreca; A.B., Temple U., 1959. Mem. staff Inst. Cancer Research, Phila., 1959—, research asso., 1972-81, sr. research assoc., 1981—. Mem. Am. Soc. Microbiology, Pa. Soc. Microbiology, N.Y. Acad. Scis. Author papers in field. Office: 7701 Burholme Ave Philadelphia PA 19111

O'CONNELL, BONNIE DIKMAN, retailer, editor; b. N.Y.C., Sept. 9, 1942; d. George Henry and Ruth (Hymes) Dikman; BA in English Edn., U. South Fla., 1968; m. Jonah Henry, Aug. 11, 1963 (div. 1986); children: Shera Lyn, Scott Harris; m. Maurice Patrick O'Connell, Apr. 23, 1988.. Feature and fashion writer St. Petersburg Times, Fla., 1956-64; writer Congl. Quar., Washington, 1961-62; fashion writer Tampa Tribune, Fla., 1977-84; fashion editor On Design mag., 1983—; pres. What's New, retail sportswear store; instr. journalism U. Tampa, 1979. Contbr. articles to profl. jours. Pres. Tampa Hadassah Group, 1974-76; founder Hillel Sch., Jewish Day Sch., Tampa. Recipient Men's Fashion Assn. Am. award 1980, 81, 83, award J.C. Penney, Mo., 1980. Mem. The Fashion Group, Sigma Delta Chi. Club: Palma Ceia Jr. Women's Westcoast editor Fla. Designer's Quar. mag., 1980—. Home: 2 Adalia Ave Tampa FL 33606 Office: 1536 S Dale Mabry Tampa Fl 33629

O'CONNELL, CAROLYN ANN HOWINGTON, manufacturer's representative; b. Wasco, Calif., Aug. 13, 1949; d. Calvin Verble and Pearline (Stutts) Worley; 1 child, Todd Eugene Howington; m. Howard James O'Connell; 4 stepchildren: Bridget E., Vicki M., Tracey A., Sean P.; B.S. in Bus., N.E. La. State U., 1971. Owner, pres. R & R Sales, Inc., Tulsa, 1978-83; mktg. rep. large scale computer systems Honeywell Info. Systems, 1985-87; mktg. small scale computers Digital and Wang, 1987—. Mem. Nat. Assn. Female Execs., Am. Bus. Women's Assn., Nat. Assn. Women Bus. Owners, Okla. Minority Purchasing Council, NOW, Tulsa Theatre Drive, Blues Soc. Republican. Presbyterian. Club: So. Hills Fitness Center. Home: 11830 Mardy Dr Overland Park KS 66210

O'CONNELL, SISTER COLMAN, nun, college administrator, consultant. BA in English, Speech, Coll. St. Benedict, St. Joseph, Minn., 1950; MFA in Theater, English, Cath. U., 1954; PhD in Higher Edn. Adminstrn., U. Mich., 1979; student, Northwestern U., Birmingham U., Stratford, Eng., Denver U., Stanford U., Sophia U., Tokyo. Tchr. English Pierz (Minn.) Meml. High Sch., 1950-53, Cathedral High Sch., St. Cloud, Minn., 1950-53; chairperson theater and dance dept. then prof. theater Coll. of St. Benedict, St. Joseph, 1954-74, dir. alumnae, parent relations, ann. fund, 1974-77, dir. planning, 1979-84, exec. v.p., 1984-86, pres., 1986—; cons. Augsburg Coll., Mpls., 1983-85, Assn. Cath. Coll. and Univs., 1982, Minn. Pvt. Coll. Council, 1982, SW (Minn.) State U., Marshall, 1980-82, Wilmar (Minn.) Community Coll., 1980-82, Worthington (Minn.) Community Coll., 1980-82, U. Minn., Morris, 1980-82; bd. dirs. Security Fed. Savs. and Loan, St. Cloud, 1987—. Mem. St. Cloud Area C. of C. (bd. dirs. 1987—). Office: Coll of St Benedict Office of the Pres 37 College Ave Saint Joseph MN 56374

O'CONNELL, JEANNE, financial planner, insurance broker; b. Stoneham, Mass., Dec. 9, 1951; d. Kenneth Edward and Frances Evelyn (Matulewicz) O'C. Student U. Oreg., 1971-72; B.F.A. cum laude, U. Mass.-Amherst, 1974; U. Calif.-Sacramento, summer 1973; postgrad. Northeastern U., 1975; Exec. M.B.A., Suffolk U., M.B.A., 1984. CPCU, CLU, Chartered fin. cons.; assoc. in underwriting; cert. profl. ins. woman. Ins. clk. S.B. Swaim & Co., Boston, part time 1969-72, Hollis Perrin & Co., Boston, 1972; underwriting asst. Pub. Service Mut. Ins. Co., Newton, Mass., 1974-77; personal lines analyst Comml. Union Ins. Co., Boston, 1977-80, sr. personal lines analyst, 1980-83, tech. specialist, 1983-88; pvt. practice fin. cons., brokerage Boston, 1988—; lic. ins. agt. Mut. of N.Y.; registered rep. Mony Securities; ind. tax preparer; founder, dir. Red Dragon Arts Coop., Boston, 1983; potter, artist Radcliffe Pottery Studio, Boston, 1980-851. Mem. exec. student adv. bd. Suffolk U., 1982-83, student liaison mem. between Exec. M.B.A. Program and regular M.B.A. Program and dean's adv. bd., coordinator Exec. M.B.A. Program Policy Seminar Weekend, 1983. Mem. Internat. Assn. Fin. Planners, Nat. Assn. Life Underwriters, Nat. Assn. Female Execs., Soc. CPCU's (bd. dirs. Boston chpt., joint adv. bd. Mass. Ins. Commr.), Soc. Chartered Fin. Cons., Delta Mu Delta. Home and Office: 41 Atkins St Boston MA 02135

O'CONNELL, KATHLEEN MARIE, communications company manager; b. Cleve., Nov. 19, 1949; d. Francis Raymond and Lillian (Smigelski) O'C.; children: Hal Kirkwood, Camden Kirkwood. BS in Bus. Mgmt., Dyke Bus. Coll., Cleve., 1984; postgrad. in law, U. Akron, 1983—. Account exec. Am. Internat., Cleve., 1980-82; electronic product specialist Simplex Corp., Cleve., 1982-84; account mgr. bldg. systems constrn. Honeywell Corp., Cleve., 1984-87; account mgr. Datatel Data Communications, Cleve., 1987—; cons. in field, Cleve., 1986—. Fin. mgr. mayoral campaign, Cleve., 1984. Named one of 84 Most Interesting Clevelanders, Cleve. Mag., 1984. Mem. Am. Soc. for Heating, Air Conditioning and Refrigeration Engrs., Cleve. C. of C., Cleve. Growth Assn., Nat. Assn. Female Execs. Democrat. Roman Catholic. Home: 18924 Chagrin Blvd Shaker Heights OH 44122

O'CONNELL, MARY ANN, state senator; b. Albuquerque, Aug. 3, 1934; d. James Aubrey and Dorothy Nell (Batsel) Gray; m. Robert Emmett O'Connell, Feb. 21, 1977; children: Ervin Jeffery, Aubrey Gray. Grad. high sch. Albuquerque. Exec. dir. Blvd. Shopping Ctr., Las Vegas, Nev., 1968-76, Citizen Pvt. Enterprise, Las Vegas, 1976; media supr. Southwest Advt., Las Vegas, 1977—; owner, operator Comfort Inn, Las Vegas, 1985—; mem. Nev. Senate, 1984—; chmn. govt. affairs vice chmn. commerce and labor, mem. taxation com. Rep. Nat. Conf. State Legislators. Pres. explorer div. Boulder Dam Area council Boy Scouts Am., Las Vegas 1979-80; pres. Citizen Pvt. Enterprise, Las Vegas, 1982-84, Secret Witness, Las Vegas, 1981-82; vice chmn. Gov.'s Mental Health-Mental Retardation, Nev., 1983—; mem. community adv. bd Care Unit Hosp., Las Vegas, Kidney Found. Recipient Silver Beaver award Boy Scouts Am., 1980, Outstanding Citizenship award Bd. Realtors, 1975, Commendation award Mayor O. Grayson, Las Vegas, 1975. Republican. Mem. Christian Ch. Home: 7225 Montecito Circle Las Vegas NV 89101 Office: 525 Bonanza Rd Las Vegas NV 89120

O'CONNELL, MARY ELLEN, consulting firm executive; b. Plainfield, N.J., Nov. 3, 1956; d. John Forster and Regina Anne (McCarthy) O'Connell. B.S. in Early Childhoold Edn., Trenton State Coll., 1978. Pub. sch. tchr. Head Start, Somerville, N.J., 1978-79; account exec. Mgmt. Recruiters, Union, N.J., 1979-82; owner, search cons. Priority Search, Inc., Sewaren, N.J., 1982—. Recipient Top 10 Account Execs. East Coast award Mgmt. Recruiters, 1981. Mem. N.J. Assn. Personnel Cons. Office: Priority Search Inc 645 Fifth Ave New York NY 10022

O'CONNELL, MARY ITA, psychotherapist; b. Balt., July 3, 1929; d. Richard Charles and Ona (Buchness) O.; m. Leon Jack Greenbaum, Dec. 28, 1962 (div. Jan. 1986); children: Jessie A., Elizabeth K. BA, U. Md., 1956; postgrad., Am. U., 1960—; M in Creative Arts and Therapy, Hahnemann Med. Coll., 1978. Registered Acad. Dance Therapists. Tchr. Robert Cohan Sch. Dance, Boston, 1958-61; instr., choreographer Wheaton Coll., Norton, Mass., 1959-60, Harvard/Radcliffe Colls., Boston, 1960-62; tchr., performer, choreographer Profl. Studios, Washington, 1962-69; asst. prof., adminstr. Fed. City Coll., Washington, 1969-74; movement psychotherapist Woodburn Ctr. for Community Mental Health, Fairfax, Va., 1975-76, Gundry Hosp., Balt., 1976-77, Prince Georges' Community Mental Health Dept., Captiol Heights, Md., 1978-80; lectr. George Washington U., D.C., 1981-85; pvt. practice psychotherapy Silver Spring, Md., 1977—; sr. movement psychotherapy Regional Inst. for Children and Adults, Balt., 1983—; movement cons. Ctr. for Youth Services, Washington, 1981-83; movement psychotherapist Wickersty and Assocs., Washington, 1985—, Community for Creative Non-Violence Women's Shelter, Washington, 1986. Choreographer, soloist (dance performance) The Artist: A Theatre Happening, 1963; choreographer, co-dir. (outdoor dance event) Tree Sculpting, 1974; choreographer (dance performance) Excitations, 1967, A Dance Event, 1974; soloist, New England Opera, 1961; performer, choreographer WGBM TV/Laboratory Concert Series, 1961; performer, CBS-TV/Erika Thimey Dance Theatre, 1965; guest artist, Harford Coll. Art Festival, 1967. U. Md. scholar, 1955-56. Mem. Dance Circle of Boston (life, pres. 1959-61), Modern Dance Council of Washington (exec. bd dirs., editor 1965-69), Am. Dance Therapy Assn. (treas. metro chpt. 1977-81), Assn. Humanistic Psychology, Family Therapy Network, Am. Dance Guild, NIH (movement specialist 1978-79). Democrat. Home and Office: 16 Sussex Rd Silver Spring MD 20910

O'CONNELL, MARY JANETTE, state agency administrator; b. Durant, Okla., June 19, 1947; d. Curtis Lee and Willie Mae (Lynn) Boone; children: James Andrew, Angela Lee Ann, Amber Jo. BS, Southeastern State U., 1973; MEd, Ctl. State U., 1982. Cert. tchr., Okla. Career specialist Guthrie (Okla.) Job Corps, 1974-76; tchr. Draughon Sch. Bus., Oklahoma City, 1976, dir. edn., 1976-79; wrold work instr. Okla Dept. Vocat. Edn., Del City, 1979-81; career specialist Okla Dept. Vocat. Edn., Oklahoma City, 1981-85; state coordinator Okla Dept. Vocat. Edn., Stillwater, 1985—. Active Boy Scouts Am., Midwest City, Okla., 1977; block coordinator Yukon March of Dimes, 1979-81. Mem. Nat. Assn. Female Execs., Am. Vocat. Assn., Okla. Vocat. Assn., Okla. Career Assn., AAUW, Kappa Delta Pi. Republican. Home: 11608 Delphi Circle Yukon OK 73099 Office: State Dept Vocat Edn 1500 W 7th Ave Stillwater OK 74074

O'CONNOR, BETTY LOU, service executive; b. Phoenix, Oct. 29, 1927; d. Georg Eliot and Tillie Edith (Miller) Miller; m. William Spoeri O'Connor, Oct. 10, 1948; children: Thomas W., William K., Kelli Anne. Student, U. So. Calif., 1946-48, Calif. State U., Los Angeles, 1949-50. V.p., treas. O'Connor Food Services, Inc., Jack in the Box Restaurants, Granada Hills, Calif., 1983—; pres. Western Restaurant Mgmt. Co., Granada Hills, 1986—. Recipient Frannie award Foodmaker, Inc., Northridge, Calif., 1984. Mem. Jack in the Box Franchisee Assn., Spurs Hon. (sec. U. So. Calif. 1947-48), Associated Women Students (sec. U. So. Calif. 1946-47), Gamma Alpha Chi (v.p. 1947-48), Chi Omega. Republican. Roman Catholic. Office: Western Restaurant Mgmt Co 10727 White Oak Ave Suite 204 Granada Hills CA 91344

O'CONNOR, C. KELLY, advertising executive; b. Aurora, Ill., July 20, 1944; d. Frank William and Emily (Kish) Vargo; m. John J. O'Connor, Mar. 13, 1981 (div. July 1985). BA, St. Francis Coll., 1966. Tchr. various schs., N.Y., N.J., 1966-72; asst. dir. sales service Metromedia, Inc., N.Y.C., 1972-76; dir. divisional mktg. Paramount Pictures Corp., N.Y., 1976-86; dir. media Richard Heim Advt., N.Y.C., 1987-88; supr. media McFarland & Drier, Inc., Miami, Fla., 1988—; mktg. cons. Internor Trade Inc., N.Y.C., 1987, Chakkar Internat., London, 1987. Mem. Global Bus. Assn. (v.p. membership 1987), Nat. Assn. Female Execs.

O'CONNOR, DORIS JULIA, oil company foundation executive; b. N.Y.C. Apr. 30, 1930; d. Joseph D. and Mary (Longinotti) Bisagni; m. Gerard T. O'Connor, Oct. 8, 1950 (div. Dec. 1972); 1 dau., Kim C. B.A. cum laude in Econs., U. Houston, 1975. Adminstrv. asst. Shell Cos. Found., Inc., N.Y.C., 1966-71, asst. sec., Houston, 1971-73, sec., 1973-76, sr. v.p., dir., mem. exec. com., 1976—. Corp. assoc. United Way of Am., Washington, 1976—; corp. advisor Bus. Com. of Arts, N.Y.C., 1976—; del. Bus. Com. of Arts, Houston, 1982-87; dir. Ind. Sector, Washington, 1981—, vice chmn., 1983-87; mem. contbns. council Conf. Bd., N.Y.C., 1976—; advisor Council of Better Bus. Burs., Washington, 1975—, 1983-87. Mem. Omicron Delta Epsilon. Club: Plaza (bd. govs. 1987—).

O'CONNOR, FRANCINE MARIE, magazine editor; b. Springfield, Mass., Apr. 8, 1930; d. Wallace Harold and Celestine Margaret (Morrison) Provost; m. John Francis O'Connor, Dec. 27, 1951; children—Margaret Anne McGlynn, Kathryn Mary Boswell, Timothy John. Grad. high sch., Springfield. Editorial asst. Liguori Publs., Mo., 1975-76, assoc. editor, 1976-79, mng. editor, 1979—, also author children's bulls. and books. Author ABC's of Faith series including The Seven Sacraments, 1981, The Stories of Jesus, 1982, Stories of God and His People, 1984, The ABC's of the Rosary, 1984, Special Friends of Jesus, 1986, The ABC's of the Mass, 1988. Den mother Boy Scouts Am., Webster Groves, Mo., 1963; religious edn. tchr. Our Lady Queen of Peace Roman Catholic Ch., House Springs, Mo., 1976-77. Mem. Cath. Press Assn. Club: Focolare (Chgo.). Home: 158 Crest Manor Park House Springs MO 63051 Office: Liguorian 1 Liguori Dr Liguori MO 63057

O'CONNOR, JUNE ELIZABETH, religious studies educator; b. Chgo., June 3, 1941; d. Philip Kevin and Eva Marie (Ennis) O'C.; m. Harry Hood, Aug. 11, 1973; 1 child, Meagan Hood. BA in English Lit., Mundelein Coll., 1964; MA, Marquette U., 1966, Temple U., 1972; PhD, Temple U., 1973. Instr. theology Mundelein Coll., Chgo., 1965-69, Temple U., Phila., 1970-73; asst. prof. religion U. Calif., Riverside, 1973-79, assoc. prof., 1979—, chmn. program in religious studies, 1985—; instr. theology Rosary Coll., River Forest, Ill., 1971, cons. William H. Sadlier Pubs., N.Y., 1971-81. Author: The Quest for Political and Spiritual Liberation: A Study in the Thought of Sri Aurobindo Ghose, 1977; assoc. editor Jour. Religious Ethics, 1978-82, mem. editorial bd. 1982-85; contbr. articles to profl. jours. Grantee U. Calif., Riverside, 1975—. Mem. Am. Acad. Religion (pres. Western region 1984-85, v.p., program chmn. 1983-84, mem. nat. com. on edn. study of religion), Soc. Christian Ethics (bd. dir. 1979-83, chmn. Pacific sect. 1977-78, vice chmn., program chmn. 1976-77), Coll. Theology Soc., Danforth Found. (assoc.), Pacific Coast Theol. Soc., Soc. Values in Higher Edn. Office: U Calif Program Religious Studies Riverside CA 92521 *

O'CONNOR, KAREN ANNE, cosmetic company executive; b. N.Y.C., May 2, 1950; d. Edward Patrick and Patricia Bernadette (Hayes) O'C. BA in Eng. Lit., CUNY, 1982; postgrad., Fordham U., 1983-84, CUNY, 1984-85; student, Internat. Ctr. Photography, N.Y.C., 1984-86. Asst. Newsweek mag., N.Y.C., 1969-75; photo editor Harcourt Brace Jovanovich, N.Y.C., 1975-76; prodn. assoc. Scientific Am. mag., N.Y.C., 1976-85; dir. prodn., pub. relations Estee Lauder, Inc., N.Y.C., 1985—. Mem. Women in Prodn. (staff writer 1983—). Roman Catholic. Office: Estee Lauder 767 Fifth Ave New York NY 10153

O'CONNOR, KATHLEEN ANN, German language educator; b. Boston, Oct. 17, 1956; d. Francis Patrick and Ann Elizabeth (O'Brien) O'C. BA, Dartmouth Coll., 1978; MA, U. Va., 1980, PhD, 1987. Instr. German lang. U. Va., Charlottesville, 1983-87, lang. coordinator, 1986-87; asst. prof. Bowdoin Coll., Brunswick, Me., 1987—. Mem. Am. Assn. Tchrs. German, MLA. Office: Bowdoin Coll German Dept Brunswick ME 04011

O'CONNOR, KRISTIN KOEHLER, infosystems executive; b. Greenfield, Mass., Oct. 24, 1953; d. Paul B. and Lorraine Mary (Mahan) K.; m. Patrick J. O'Connor, May 21, 1977; children: Kathleen Lorraine, Elizabeth Mary. BS, U. Hartford, 1975; MPH, Yale U., 1977. Statistician Boehringer Ingelheim, Ridgefield, Conn., 1977-83, sr. statistician, 1983-84, mgr. clin. trial info., 1984—. Mem. Am. Statis. Assn., Biometric Assn., Soc. for Clin. Trials, Drug Info. Assn. Home: 20 Little Boston Ln West Redding CT 06896 Office: Boehringer Ingelheim 90 E Ridge Ridgefield CT 06877

O'CONNOR, MAUREEN, mayor; b. San Diego, July 14, 1946; d. Jerome and Frances O'Connor; m. Robert O. Peterson, 1977. B in Psychology and Sociology, San Diego State U., 1970. Tchr., counselor Rosary High Sch., 1970-71; council mem. City of San Diego, 1971-79, dep. mayor, 1976, mayor, 1986—; with Calif. Housing Fin. Agy., 1977-79; mem. Met. Transit Devel. Bd., 1976-81; port commr. San Diego, 1980-85; mem. Rules, Legis., and Intergovtl. Relations com.; chmn. pub. services and safety com. 1974-75; mem. League Calif. Cities' Com. on Human Resources Devel., Natl League Cities' Manpower and Income Support com.; chmn. mayor's crime commn. Roman Catholic. Office: Office of the Mayor 202 C St San Diego CA 92129 *

O'CONNOR, MICHOL, lawyer; b. Houston, Nov. 30, 1942; d. Charles Cary O'Connor and Ida Mae (Mueller) Baird; BA, U. Tex., Austin, 1966;

JD, U. Houston, 1973; 1 child, Baird James Craft. Admitted to Tex. bar, 1973; bd. cert. appellate law, Tex. Bd. Legal Specialization, 1986. law clk. 1st Ct. Civil Appeals, Houston, 1974-75; asst. dist. atty. Harris County Dist. Attys. Office, Houston, 1975-76; assoc. firm Kronzer, Abraham & Watkins, Houston, 1976-78; asst. U.S. atty. U.S. Atty.'s Office, So. Dist. Tex., Houston, 1978-81; corp. counsel Century Devel. Corp., 1981-82. Democratic nominee 1st Ct. Appeals of Tex., 1984, 88; of counsel Haight, Gardner, Poor & Havens, 1985-86; sole practice, Houston, 1986—. Recipient award for jour. article Tex. Bar Found., 1978. Mem. ABA, Tex. Bar Assn. (chmn. adminstrn. justice com.), Houston Bar Assn. (dir. 1977-79), Houston Young Lawyers (dir. 1975-76, Outstanding Contbn. award 1975), Order of Barons. Contbr. articles to profl. and polit. jours.; lectr. State Bar of Tex., advanced appellate sems., 1985, 87, 88. Office: PO Box 25337 Houston TX 77265

O'CONNOR, NANCY ANN, retail store owner; b. San Diego, Calif., Oct. 25, 1952; d. William Paul and Jean Ann (Cullenane) Connor. Grad., San Diego Coll. of Bus., 1972; student, Mesa Coll., San Diego, 1973. With Wiles and Circuit, La Jolla, Calif., 1973-74; asst. mgr. Something Mad Store, La Jolla and San Diego, 1974-75; mgr. Ziba Clothing Store, La Jolla, 1975-76; owner, operator Whistle Clothing Store, La Jolla, 1980—; designer Whistle and others, La Jolla and Los Angeles, 1982—. Contbr. articles to profl. jours. Office: Whistle 7553 Girard Ave La Jolla CA 92037

O'CONNOR, PEGGY LEE, computer company manager; b. Chgo., Apr. 20, 1953; d. William Stanley and Eleanor Sopie (Levandowski) Czaska; m. Charles B. O'Connor, III, Feb. 14, 1978. BS in Biology, Northeastern Ill. U., 1982; MBA, No. Ill. U., 1985. Emergency med. technologist, 1976-82; instr. Chgo. City Wide Colls., 1976-81; program dir. U. Ill. Hosp. 1979-81; program dir. Fermilab, Roselle, 1978-82; dist. adminstrv. mgr. Decision Data Service, Schaumburg, Ill., 1981—. Recipient Phoenix award Decision Data Service, 1983, award Summit Club, 1987. Mem. Nat. Assn. Female Execs., Women in Info. Processing, Women in Bus. Avocation: computers. Office: Decision Data Services Inc One Pierce Pl Itasca IL 60143

O'CONNOR, RUTH ELKINTON, real estate executive, consultant; b. Oakland, Calif., May 19, 1927; d. Alfred Cope and Anna (Lydia) Elkinton; m. Roger Edward O'Connor; children: Bruce E., Colleen, Lynn, Michael, John E. AA, U. Calif., 1949. Salesman Ruth Hendrickson, Realtor, Honolulu, 1966-68; salesman, broker John D. McCurry, Realtor, Honolulu, 1968-76; prin. broker O'Connor Realty, Honolulu, 1976-80; owner, pres. R.E.O. Inc., Honolulu, 1980—; pres. Farm and Land Brokers, Honolulu, 1972; mem. profl. standards com. Grievance Honor Bd., Honolulu, 1983-85. Editor: Friends of Samoa, 1979. Recipient Exchangor of the Yr. award The Investment Group, Realtors, 1968, Councelor of the Yr. award The Investment Group, Realtors, 1969, Arts Council award Govt. of Am. Samoa, 1980. Mem. Honolulu Bd. Realtors (dir. 1970-72), Hawaii Bd. Realtors, Nat. Assn. of Realtors (real estate aviation chpt.), Internat. Real Estate Fedn., Nat. Assn. Female Execs., Pan Pacific S.E. Asian Women (life), Arts Council (dir. 1976-79), The Ninety-Nines (Hawaii del. 1985), Profl. Assn. Diving Instrs., Alpha Omicron Pi. Mem. Soc. of Friends. Club: Outrigger Canoe. Office: REO Inc 417 Kanekapolei St Ste 103 Honolulu HI 96815

O'CONNOR, SANDRA DAY, justice U.S. Supreme Court; b. El Paso, Tex., Mar. 26, 1930; d. Harry A. and Ada Mae (Wilkey) Day; m. John Jay O'Connor, III, Dec. 1952; children: Scott, Brian, Jay. AB in Econs. with great distinction, Stanford U., 1950, LLB, 1952. Bar: Calif. Dep. county atty. San Mateo, Calif., 1952-53; civil atty. Q.M. Market Ctr., Frankfurt and Main, Fed. Republic of Germany, 1954-57; sole practice Phoenix, 1959-65; asst. atty. gen. State of Ariz., 1965-69; Ariz. state senator 1969-75, chmn. com. on state, county and mcpl. affairs, 1972-73, majority leader, 1973-74; judge Maricopa County Superior Ct., 1975-79, Ariz. Ct. Appeals, 1979-81; assoc. justice Supreme Ct. U.S., 1981—; referee juvenile ct., 1962-64; chmn. vis. bd. Maricopa County Juvenile Detention Home, 1963-64; mem. Maricopa County Bd. Adjustments and Appeals, 1963-64, Anglo-Am. Legal Exchange, 1980, Maricopa County Superior Ct. Judges Tng. and Edn. Com., Maricopa Ct. Study Com.; chmn. com. to reorganize lower cts. Ariz. Supreme Ct., 1974-75; faculty Robert A. Taft Inst. Govt.; vice chmn. Select Law Enforcement Rev. Commn., 1979-80. Mem. bd. editors Stanford (Calif.) U. Law Rev. Mem. Ariz. Personnel Commn., 1968-69, Nat. Def. Adv. Com. on Women in Services, 1974-76; trustee Heard Mus., Phoenix, 1968-74, 76-81, pres., 1980-81; mem. adv. bd. Phoenix Salvation Army, 1975-81; trustee Stanford U., 1976-80, Phoenix County Day Sch.; mem. citizens adv. bd. Blood Services, 1975-77; nat. bd. dirs. Smithsonian Assocs., 1981—; past Rep. dist. chmn.; bd. dirs. Phoenix Community Council, Ariz. Acad., 1970-75, Jr. Achievement Ariz., 1975-79, Blue Cross/Blue Shield Ariz., 1975-79, Channel 8, 1975-79, Phoenix Hist. Soc., 1974-77, Maricopa County YMCA, 1978-81, Golden Gate Settlement. Recipient Ann. award NCCJ, 1975, Disting. Achievement award Ariz. State U., 1980; named Woman of Yr., Phoenix Advt. Club, 1972. Lodge: Soroptimists. Address: Supreme Ct of the US 1 First St NE Washington DC 20543 *

O'CONNOR, SUZANNE MARIE, marketing professional, educator; b. Mobile, Ala., Sept. 17, 1947; d. Thomas Sidney and Sarah Mary (Pauché) O'C. BS, U. Ala., Tuscaloosa, 1969, MA in Edn., 1974. Buyer Pizitz, Inc., Birmingham, Ala., 1969-72; grad. asst. U. Ala., Tuscaloosa, 1973; mktg. edn. coordinator Huntsville (Ala.) City Schs., 1973—. Vol. Chmn. Historic Hunstville Found, 1984—; chmn. face painting Arts Council of Hunstville for Panoply, 1986, 87; active Mus. Art, Huntsville, Friends of the Symphony. Mem. Ala. Mktg. Assn. (treas. 1983—), Ala. Voc. Assn., Ala. Edn. Assn., NEA, Am. Vocat. Assn., Ala. Mktg. Edn. Assn., Distributive Edn. Clubs Am., Ala. Distributive Edn. Clubs Am., Alpha Delta Kappa (treas. 1986—). Roman Catholic. Office: Grissom High Sch 7901 Bailey Cove Rd Huntsville AL 35803

ODA, MARGARET YURIKO, educational administrator; b. Hakalau, Hawaii, Mar. 26, 1925; d. Satoru and Satoyo Kurisu; m. Glenn K. Oda (dec.); 1 child, Marjorie. B.Ed., U. Hawaii, 1947; M.A., Mich. State U., 1950; Ed.D., U. Hawaii, 1977. Tchr. Hilo Intermediate Sch., Hawaii, 1951, counselor, 1951-52, 53-56, vice prin., 1956-63; prin. Hakalau-Honomu-Pepeekeo, Hilo, 1963-64; dir. gen. edn. State Dept. Edn., Honolulu, 1965-76; prin. Kaiser High Sch., Honolulu, 1978-82; supt. Honolulu Sch. Dist., Honolulu, 1982-84; state dep. supt. Hawaii State Dept. Edn., Honolulu, 1984-87, dist. supt., 1987—; mem. Western Regional Adv. Panel Coll. Bd., 1984-86, Northwest Regional Ednl. Lab. Adv. Bd., Portland, Oreg., 1984-85, exec. bd. Chief State Sch. Officers Study Commn., 1985-86; coordinator State Edn. Policy Seminars, 1984-86. Bd. dirs. Hawaii Heart Assn., Honolulu, 1979-84, Honolulu Community Theatre, 1972-75, Honpa Hongwanji Buddhist Orgn., 1984—, Pan Pacific Found., 1982—, Jr. Achievement 1986-88, Kuakini Med. Devel.; bd. trustees Honolulu Acad. of Arts, Hawaii Pub. Sch. Found. Fellow Ctr. for Study Edn. Yale U., 1973. Mem. Am. Assn. Sch. Adminstrs., Nat. Assn. Secondary Sch. Prins., Pi Lambda Theta. Club: Japanese Women's Soc. (pres. 1983-85). Office: Honolulu Dist Supr Office 4967 Kilauea Ave Honolulu HI 96816

O'DANIEL, JEAN ELIZABETH, lawyer; b. Louisville, Aug. 16, 1955; d. Philip Benedict and Clara Elizabeth (Scott) O'D.; m. Donald Gene Keach, II, Apr. 16, 1977. BA in Social Work, U. Ky., 1975; MSW, JD, Washington U., St. Louis, 1981. Bar: Ky. 1982, U.S. Dist. Ct. (we. dist.) Ky. 1982. Intern, atty. Fayette County Legal Aid, Inc., Lexington, Ky., 1981-82; atty. Adminstrv. Office Cts., Frankfort, Ky., 1982-84; staff atty. Ky. Ct. of Appeals, Frankfort, 1984-85, Lexington, 1985—. Author: (with others) Interstate Child Custody Disputes, 1982. Big sister to Big Bros./Big Sisters, Lexington, Ky., 1985-86; mem. Ky. Foster Care External Rev. Bd., 1986—; chairperson Fayette County Bd., 1986—, State Exec. Bd., 1986-87. Mem. ABA, Ky. Bar Assn., NOW. Democrat. Home: 3900 Sundart Dr Lexington KY 40502 Office: Ky Ct of Appeals 177 N Upper St Lexington KY 40507

O'DAY, SHARON, marketing professional; b. Morristown, N.J., May 23, 1948; d. William Raymond and Jean Scott (Donaldson) O'D. Student, U. So. Calif., 1967-69, Fairfield (Conn.) U., 1977-79; MBA, U. Pa., 1981. Asst. mgr. pub. relations Carajás Iron Project Amazon, Rio de Janeiro, 1974-76; asst. to pres. Polycast Tech. Corp., Stamford, Conn., 1977-79; dir. mktg. Godiva Chocolatier S.A., Brussels, 1981-83; dir. internat. sales and mktg. Godiva Chocolatier Inc., N.Y.C., 1983; dir. mktg. Cognac Louis Royer, Jarnac, France, 1984-86; pres. Images de Marque, Inc., Miami, Fla., 1986—; cons. internat. mktg. various European corps. in Belgium, France and Italy, 1986—. Republican. Home and Office: Images de Marque Inc 14730 SW 63d Ct Miami FL 33158

O'DEA, CONSTANCE LOUISE, public finance credit analyst, former state official, educator; d. John W. J. and Valerie C. O'Dea; B.A. (Durant scholar), Wellesley Coll.; M.A. (Grad. Prize fellow), Harvard U. Asst. coordinator systems analysis group Inst. Space Research, Nat. Research Council of Brazil, Sao Paulo, 1973-74; vis. prof. Tech. Inst. Aeros., Sao Paulo, 1974; instr. Am. Sch., Rio de Janeiro, Brazil, 1975-77, coordinator research and planning N.J. Dept. Edn., Trenton, 1978-83, project mgr., 1983-85; senior analyst Moody's Investors Service, 1985—. Rep. for Rio de Janeiro-Belo Horizonte to Wellesley (Mass.) Coll., 1976-77. Ford Found. fellow Harvard U., 1969-73; Fanny Bullock Workman fellow Wellesley Coll., 1969-70. Mem. Phi Beta Kappa. Clubs: N.Y. Wellesley, St. Bartholomew Community. Editor, collaborator: The Social Economy of the Future, 1979. Home: 63 W 85th St New York NY 10024 Office: 99 Church St New York NY 10007

O'DELL, JOAN ELIZABETH, business executive, lawyer; b. East Dubuque, Ill., May 3, 1932; d. Peter Emerson and Olive (Bonnet) O'dell; children: Dominique R., Nicole L. BA cum laude, U. Miami, 1956, JD, 1958. Bar: Fla. 1958, D.C. 1974, Ill. 1978, Va. 1987; lic. real estate broker. Trial atty. U.S. SEC, Washington, 1959-60; asst. state atty. Office State Atty., Miami, Fla., 1960-64; asst. county atty. Dade County Atty.'s Office, Miami, 1964-70; county atty. Palm Beach County Atty.'s Office, West Palm Beach, Fla., 1970-71; regional gen. counsel. U.S. EPA, Region IV, Atlanta, 1971-73, assoc. gen. counsel, Washington, 1973-77; sr. counsel Nalco Chem. Co., Oakbrook, Ill., 1977-78; v.p. Angel Mining, Tenn., 1979—; pres. South West Land Investments, Miami, Fla., 1979—. Bd. dirs. Tucson Women's Found., 1982-84, U. Ariz. Bus. and Profl. Women's Club, Tucson, 1981-85; bd. dirs. LWV Tucson, 1981-85, pres., 1984-86; bd. dirs. LWV Ariz., 1985-86, chmn. nat. security study; mem. AAUW; mem. Exec. Women's Council, Tucson, 1982-85. Mem. ABA, Fed. Bar Assn., Fla. Bar Assn., D.C. Bar Assn., Va. State Bar Assn. Home: 703 S Lake Dr Lantaua FL 33462

O'DELL, KAROL JOANNE, experimental prototype company executive; b. Lafayette, Colo., Jan. 4, 1936; d. Clarence Willis and Thelma (Stoner) O'D. Student Wayne State U., 1953-56, U. Detroit, 1956-57. Sec. IBM, Detroit, 1957-59; from bookkeeper to office mgr. Jo-Ad Industries, Inc., 1959-84, v.p., 1984—. Treas. Detroit Puppeteers Guild, 1983—; active Salvation Army. Mem. Nat. Assn. Female Execs., Fellowship Christian Magicians, Puppeteers Am., Fellowship Christian Puppeteers, Unima U.S.A., Commerce Alumni Assn. Avocations: puppetry; religious education; reading.

O'DELL, LYNN MARIE LUEGGE (MRS. NORMAN D. O'DELL), librarian; b. Berwyn, Ill., Feb. 24, 1938; d. George Emil and Helen Marie (Pesek) Luegge; student Lyons Twp. Jr. Coll., La Grange, Ill., 1957; student No. Ill. U., Elgin Community Coll., U. Ill., Coll. of DuPage; m. Norman D. O'Dell, Dec. 14, 1957; children—Jeffrey, Jerry. Sec., Martin Co., Chgo., 1957-59; dir. Carol Stream (Ill.) Pub. Library, 1964—; chmn. automation governing com. DuPage Library System, v.p., 1982-85, pres. exec. com. adminstrv. librarians, 1985-86. Named Woman of Year, Wheaton Bus. and Profl. Woman's Club, 1968. Mem. ALA, Ill. Library Assn., Library Adminstrs. Conf. No. Ill. Lutheran. Home: 182 Yuma Ln Carol Stream IL 60188 Office: 616 Hiawatha Dr Carol Stream IL 60188

ODELL, MARY JANE, state official; b. Algona, Iowa, July 28, 1923; d. Eugene and Madge (Lewis) Neville; m. John Odell, Mar. 3, 1967 (dec.); children: Brad Chinn, Chris Odell; m. Ralph Sigler, Nov. 22, 1987. B.A., U. Iowa, 1945; hon. doctorate, Simpson Coll., 1982. Host public affairs TV programs Des Moines and Chgo., 1953-79; with Iowa Public Broadcasting Network, 1975-79, host Assignment Iowa, 1975-78, host Mary Jane Odell Program, 1975-79; sec. of state State of Iowa, 1980—; tchr. grad. classes in communications Roosevelt U., Chgo., Drake U., Des Moines. Chmn. Iowa Easter Seals campaign, 1979-83; mem. Midwest Com. Future Options; bd. dirs. Iowa Shares. Recipient Emmy award, 1972, 75; George Washington Carver award, 1978; named to Iowa Women's Hall of Fame, 1979. Republican. Mailing Address: 725 Hickman Rd Des Moines IA 50314 Office: Office Sec State State House Des Moines IA 50319

O'DELL, SUSAN LINDA, psychotherapist, fundraiser; b. Mpls., July 23, 1948; d. Harold Everett and Marguerite Emma (Jones) O'D. BS in Social Work-Corrections, Mankato State U., 1971; MSW, U. Minn., 1973. Psychotherapist Cambridge (Mass.) Women's Ctr., 1973-75; social worker Needham (Mass.) Youth Commn., 1973-75; housing adminstr. Youth Network Council Chgo., Inc., 1975-77; exec. dir. Winnetka Youth Orgn. and Glencoe Youth Services, Ill., 1978-81; pvt. practice psychotherapy Chgo., 1984—; fundraiser Am. Friends Service Com. Chgo., 1981—, ACLU, 1987—, United Way Chgo., 1984-86, Cambodian Assn. Ill., 1985-87, Latino Inst. Chgo., 1985. Walker fellow, 1972. Mem. Nat. Soc. Fundraising Execs., Nat. Assn. Social Workers, Acad. Cert. Social Workers (cert.). Home and Office: 3220 N Sheffield Ave Chicago IL 60657

ODEM, LAURA JUANITA BURTON, personnel executive; b. Newark, Jan. 21, 1947; d. Herman L. and Iola (Brantley) Burton; BA, Spelman Coll., 1968; postgrad. Control Data Inst., 1970; m. Jerry Odem, Sept. 4, 1970; 1 child, Veronica Michelle. Social worker Los Angeles County Public Social Services, 1968-70; chief personnel tng., 1970-72, personnel analyst with personnel dept., 1972-74, team leader, 1974-77, community devel. analyst, 1974-77, now personnel mgmt. specialist. Pres., Black Women's Network; exec. bd. dirs. Los Angeles chpt. Jack & Jill of Am., Inc.; mem. Inter-Alumni Council United Negro Coll. Fund. Mem. Calif. Personnel Mgmt. Assn., Am. Soc. Personnel Mgmt., Am. Soc. Public Adminstrn. Presbyterian. Home: 1222 Alvira St Los Angeles CA 90035 Office: 222 N Grand Ave Los Angeles CA 90012

ODOARDI, ANTOINETTE MARIE, pharmacology company project manager; b. Pietranico, Italy, Apr. 19, 1952; d. Vincent and Lucy (Colucci) O.; came to U.S., 1955, naturalized, 1961; B.S. (Scholar 1970-74), Coll. White Plains, 1974; M.S. (teaching asst. 1975-76), Fordham U., 1977, postgrad N.Y. Med. Coll., 1978-81; M.B.A. candidate U. Conn., 1984—. Clin. data analyst Revlon Health Care Group, Tuckahoe, N.Y., 1976-83; quality assurance assoc. Ayerst Labs., N.Y.C., 1983-85; project mgr. Miles Pharms., West Haven, Conn., 1985—. Mem. Project Mgmt. Assn., Pharm. Mfrs. Assn., N.Y. Acad. Sci., Sigma Xi, Beta Gamma Sigma. Home: 91 Strawberry Hill Ave Unit 230 Stamford CT 06902 Office: 400 Morgan Ln West Haven CT 06516

ODOM, CAROLYN, publishing company executive; b. Augusta, Ga.; d. Plannie C. and Marjorie (Waldo) Odom. B.A., Spelman Coll., 1966; M.A., Am. U., 1970. Dep. dir. N.Y.C. Health and Hosp. Adminstrn., 1972-76; communications coordinator Nat. Health Council, N.Y.C., 1976-77; dir. pub. affairs Earl G. Graves Ltd., N.Y.C., 1977-83, v.p. corp. communications, 1983-87, sr. v.p. 1987—. Contbr. articles to profl. jours. Named to YWCA Acad. Women Achievers. Mem. Women in Communications, The EDGES Group. Office: Earl G Graves Ltd 130 Fifth Ave New York NY 10011

ODOMIROK, MARY HELEN, educator; b. Bklyn., June 2, 1954; d. Andrew and Helen (Demko) O. BA, Queens Coll., 1976, MS, 1980; MS magna cum laude, Pace U., 1986. Cert. tchr., N.Y. State. Feature writer, editorial asst. Star Newsmag., N.Y.C., 1976-78; tchr. Ft. Hamilton High Sch., Bklyn., 1978, John Ericsson Jr. High Sch., Bklyn., 1978—; intern edn. com. N.Y.C. Council, 1985, aide to councilman, 1983—; sales assoc. Tiffancy and Co., N.Y.C., summer 1987. Campaign mgr. for N.Y. State Assemblyman, 1982; me. exec. bd. Northside Community Devel. Council, Bklyn., 1982-88. Recipient award N.Y.C. Assn. Tchrs. English, 1972. Mem. Queens Coll. Alumni Soc., Pace U. Alumni Soc. Home: 110 N 7th St Brooklyn NY 11211 Office: John Ericsson Jr High Sch 434 Leondard St Brooklyn NY 11222

O'DONNELL, ALICE LOUISE, government official, lawyer; b. Stanwood, Wash., Oct. 7, 1914; d. John James and Jeannette May (Anderson) O'D. Student, U. Wash., 1932, U. So. Calif., 1943-44, George Washington U, 1940-42; J.D., 1954. Bar: U.S. Dist. Ct. D.C., U.S. Supreme Ct., U.S. Ct. Appeals (D.C. Cir.). With staff Atty. Gen. U.S., 1945-49; mem. staff Justice Clark, Supreme Ct. of U.S., Washington, 1949-67; lawyer Fed. Jud. Center, Washington, 1968—; dir. div. inter-jud. affairs and info. services Fed. Jud. Center, 1971—; sec.-treas. Nat. Center for State Cts., 1971-81. Vice-chmn. bd. dirs. Potomac Law Sch., Washington, 1975-79. Fellow Inst. Jud. Adminstrn. (pres. elect); Mem. Am. Judicature Soc.; mem. ABA (mem. div. jud. adminstrn., chmn. 1973-74), Fed. Bar Assn., Nat. Lawyers Club, Washington (bd. govs.), Thomas More Soc. Am., Supreme Ct. Hist. Soc. (trustee, v.p.), Phi Alpha Delta. Roman Catholic. Home: The Towers 4201 Cathedral Ave NW Washington DC 20016 Office: Dolley Madison House 1520 H St NW Washington DC 20005

O'DONNELL, EILEEN ANNE, travel agency executive; b. Attleboro, Mass., Aug. 5, 1961; d. John and Elizabeth (Brennan) O'D. Diploma, Boyd Career Sch., Pitts., 1981. Cert. travel counselor, Mass., 1987. Reservationist Avis Rent a Car, Tulsa, 1981; travel agt. Walpole (Mass.) Travel Service Inc., 1982-84, mgr., 1984—. Recipient travel excellence award Am. Express Co., 1987. Mem. Inst. Cert. Travel Agts., Mansfield Jaycees. Roman Catholic. Home: 150 Gilbert St Mansfield MA 02048 Office: 942 Main St Walpole MA 02081

O'DOWD-JANA, PATRICIA MARGARET, educator, author; b. Easkey, Ireland, Mar. 23, 1949; came to U.S., 1968; d. James and Margaret Theresa (Keogh) O'Dowd; m. Denis I. Jana, June 2, 1978; 1 child, Jennifer Erin. BA, U. San Diego, 1975; MS, Pepperdine U., 1977. Cert. tchr., reading specialist, community coll. instr., Calif. Tchr., reading specialist pub. and pvt. schs. Calif., 1968-74, curriculum writer, 1974—; prof. Calif. Community Colls., 1976-83; adj. prof. Nat. U., San Diego, 1978-83; lectr. U. Calif., San Diego, 1978—, U. Hawaii, Honolulu, 1983—; prin. Pat O'Dowd Test Preparation Seminars, Del Mar, Calif, 1979—; cons. San Diego City Schs., 1982—, Hawaii and Maui City Schs., 1986—, Calif. Council for Humanities, 1986; cons. test-taking skills, 1979—. Author: Preparation for the CLEP, 1982, How to Prepare for the GRE, 1984, How to Prepare for the GMAT, 1984, Preparation for the RN Test, 1985; contbr. articles to ednl. jours. Bd. dirs. San Diego chpt. Multiple Sclerosis Soc., 1983—. Mem. Nat. Assn. Female Execs. Republican. Roman Catholic. Home: 13261 Denara Rd San Diego CA 92130 Office: Pat O'Dowd Test Prep Seminars PO Box 2074 Del Mar CA 92014

OEHLER, TEMPE ANNE (TE ANNE), clinical social worker; b. Raleigh, N.C., June 22, 1954; d. Henry Frederick Jr. and Tempe Anne (Hughes) O.; m. Thomas Peter Russo, May 31, 1986. BS in Social Work, U. N.C., Greensboro, 1976; clin. tng. degree, St. Joseph's Hospice, London, 1978; MS in Social Work, U. N.C., Chapel Hill, 1981; cert. clin. tng., Duke U., 1981. Dir. Helping Hand Crisis Ctr., Myrtle Beach, S.C., 1976; dir. social work Knollwood Hall Hillhaven, Inc., Winston-Salem, N.C., 1976-80; oncology social worker Duke U. Med. Ctr., Durham, N.C., 1980-81; acting dir., clin. social worker Meml. Med. Ctr. Hosp. Corp. Am., Savannah, Ga., 1981-84; clin. social worker S.C. Dept. Health and Environ. Control, Myrtle Beach, 1984-86; pvt. practice clin. social work Myrtle Beach, 1986—; cons. Cancer Control Com. Nat. Cancer Inst., Bethesda, Md., 1981-84, Forsyth County Hospice Inc., Winston-Salem, 1976-80, GrandStrand Pastoral Counseling, Myrtle Beach, 1986—, Holiday Inn Inc., Burlington, N.C., 1977-80, Sports Medicine Savannah, 1982-84. Author: How To Live With Kidney Failure, For You and Your Family, An Introduction to Dialysis, 1983; contbr. articles to various mags. Pres. Family Support Services of Horry Co., Conway, S.C., 1986—; chmn. pub. relations Peedee Chpt. Colonial Dames of XVII Century, 1984—; mem. Am. Cancer Soc., Myrtle Beach, 1984—. Recipient Pub. Relations award Ga. Hosp. Assn., 1983. Mem. Nat. Assn. Social Workers (diplomate 1986, presider Chgo. symposium 1985, pub. relations chrmn. bd. dirs. 1985-87), U. N.C. Alumni Assn. (admissions rep. 1986—), U. N.C. Greensboro Alumni Assn., Golden Chain Soc., Coastal Women's Network (sec. 1987-88), Myrtle Beach C. of C. (alumni rep. Leadership GrandStrand). Democrat. Presbyterian. Club: Pilot (Myrtle Beach). Home: Retreat at Glenn's Bay 316 Glenns Bay Rd 206G Myrtle Beach SC 29577 Office: PO Box 3303 4567 BackGate Properties Myrtle Beach SC 29577

OEHRLEIN, MARY LOU, architect; b. Clinton, Iowa, Dec. 7, 1950; d. Gilbert Joseph and Virginia Marie (Thrun) O.; m. David Evans Heacock, Jan. 16, 1979. BArch, Iowa State U., 1973. Registered architect, D.C., Md., Va. Staff architect Hist. Am. Bldgs. Survey U.S. Nat. Parks Service, Washington, 1972-74; archtl. conservator Universal Restoration, Inc., Washington, 1975; v.p. Bldg. Conservation Tech., Washington, 1975-83; sr. assoc., dir. Washington office The Ehrenkrantz Group, 1978-83; prin. Oehrlein & Assocs., Washington, 1984—; reviewer State of Va. Div. Hist. Landmarks, Richmond, 1985—; bd. dirs. Cosmos Club Hist. Preservation Found., Washington, 1987—. Author handbooks on hist. property and maintenance. Bd. dirs. D.C. Preservation League, 1987—, Cosmos Club Hist. Preservation Found., Washington, 1987—. Recipient Cert. Appreciation Town of Leesburg, Va., 1987. Mem. AIA (v.p. Washington chpt. 1987, pres. 1988—, numerous awards 1983-86), Assn. Preservation Tech., Constrn. Specifications Inst. (bd. dirs. Washington chpt. 1983-85), Soc. Archtl. Historians (sec. Latrobe Chpt. 1983-84), Preservation Round Table. Club: Washington. Home: 4354 Westover Pl NW Washington DC 20016 Office: Oehrlein & Assocs 1702 Connecticut Ave NW Washington DC 20009

OESTER, CAROL LEE, civic worker; b. Staten Island, N.Y., June 3, 1947; d. Stanley T. and Florence D. (Campbell) Ogrodowski; m. Alan Edward Oester; children: John, James, Chip. AS in Med. Assistance, Jr. Coll. Broward County, 1968; BS, Fla. Atlantic U., 1976. Office mgr. Kiester, Frei, Jordan, Brohamer P.A., Ft. Lauderdale, Fla., 1968-72, Drs. Tunn and Adair, Ft. Lauderdale, 1972-74; adminstrv. asst. Oester Mgmt. Cons. Services, Carmel, Ind., 1982-85. Mem. ways and means com., newcomers club Lancaster YWCA, Pa., 1979-80; v.p. St. Joseph Hosp. Aux., 1979-80; mem. com. Boy Scouts Am., Carmel, 1983-85, den mother, Carmel, 1985-86, treas. Pack 7 Old Trail Dist., Richmond, Ind., 1987; sec. Carmel Symphony Orch., 1985-86, chmn. cookbook benefit, 1986; v.p. Richmond Symphony Orch., 1987-88, bd. dirs., 1986-87; computer coordinator Charles Elem. Sch., Richmond, 1986-87; bd. dirs. PTA, v.p., 1987; organizer referendum Richmond Community Schs., 1987. Home: 944 Breckenridge Dr Richmond IN 47374

OESTREICH, LINDA LOUISE GARLAND, technical writer; b. Bklyn., June 23, 1948; d. Thomas Tennant and Muriel Jessie (Campbell) Garland; m. Patrick Kenneth Oestreich, Mar. 31, 1967 (div. 1979); 1 child, Connie Lynn. BA in English, Am. Lit., U. Calif, San Diego, 1979. Sec. Naval Ocean Systems Ctr., San Diego, 1968-76, tech. writer, 1976-86, supr. tech. writer, 1986—; instr. San Diego Mesa Coll., 1982-87; cons. in field; chairperson adv. com. San Diego Community Colls. Dept., 1985—. Mem. Am. Soc. for Tng. and Devel. (v.p. communication 1986, mem. editorial staff 1985—), Soc. for Tech. Communications (sec. 1985-86, v.p. programs 1987, pres. 1988). Home: 2938-A 39th St San Diego CA 92104-4920 Office: Naval Ocean Systems Ctr Reports Section Code 9611 San Diego CA 92152-5000

OESTREICHER, ANNETTE MURIEL, publishing company and healthcare public relations executive; b. N.Y.C., Nov. 14, 1943; d. William and Ruth (Blanshaft) O.; m. John Diamante, Sept. 5, 1969 (div. Dec. 1977). BS in Biology, City Coll. N.Y., 1965; MS in Biology, NYU, 1969. Bur. chief Internat. Med. News Group, Rockville, Md., 1973-79; asst. mng. editor Med. Tribune, N.Y.C., 1979-81; mng. dir. Ctr. for Med. Communications (div. J. Walter Thompson Healthcare), N.Y.C., 1981-83; editor, publisher Med. World News HEI Publishing, Houston, 1983-87; exec. v.p., dir. healthcare communications Cohn & Wolfe, Houston, 1987—; bd. dirs., editorial adv. bd. Hippocrates mag. Fellow NIH, 1968-69. Mem. N.Y. Acad. Scis., Nat. Assn. Sci. Writers, Am. Med. Writers Assn. Office: Cohn & Wolfe One Madison Ave New York NY 10010

OFFENHAUSER, MARTHA ANN, appraiser; b. Los Angeles, Nov. 12, 1929; d. Charles and Edna Marie (Rhine) O. BS, Immaculate Heart Coll., Los Angeles, 1964; MEd, LaVerne (Calif.) U., 1972. Tchr. Los Angeles Cath. Archdiocese, 1953-67, Sawyer Bus. Coll., Pomona, Calif., 1967-68, Bonita Unified Sch. Dist., San Dimas, 1969-76; real estate sales person Century 21-Smith, Upland, Calif., 1976-77; real property appraiser San Bernardino County Assessor, Ontario, Calif., 1977-88; tchr. Mt. San Antonio Coll., Walnut, Calif., 1986—. Author: (textbook) Introduction to Real Property Appraisal, 1986. Mem. Am. Soc. Appraisers (sr., chair seminar 1986—). Republican. Roman Catholic. Home: 208 W Wagonhorse Ave

LaVerne CA 91750 Office: San Bernardino County Assessor 320 E D St Ontario CA 91750

OFFERMAN, CHRISTIANE TOENNE, marketing consultant; b. Hannover, Germany, Apr. 30, 1947; came to U.S., 1977; d. Adolf and Eva (Kretzschmar) Toenne; m. Louis Offerman, May 15, 1983; children: Anna, Elena. MBA, U. Hamburg, Fed. Republic Germany, 1972; postgrad. Clark U., 1977-78. Project dir. GFM, Hamburg, 1973-74, Makrotest, Dusseldorf, Fed. Republic Germany, 1974-75, Delphi Marktforschung, Dusseldorf, 1975-80; ptnr. Delphi Sales Cons., Inc., Lexington, Mass. and Chatham, N.J., 1980-84, Oasis Consulting, Inc., N.Y.C., 1984—. Pub. relations coordinator Amnesty Internat., Dusseldorf, 1975-77, group leader, Worcester, Mass., 1977-78. Mem. Smaller Bus. Assn., Nat. Assn. Female Execs. Lutheran. Office: Oasis Consulting Inc 32 Broadway Penthouse New York NY 10004

OFTEDAHL, LAURA RUTH, public relations executive; b. Libertyville, Ill., June 28, 1952; d. Everett John and Elaine Doris (Van Horn) O. B.S., U. Ill., 1974. Air personality Sta. WGMW, Riviera Beach, Fla., 1974-75, Sta. WRKR, Racine, Wis., 1975; pub. service dir. Sta. WGEZ, Beloit, Wis., 1975-77; sales mgr. Frostee Foam Co., Antioch, Ill., 1977-79; field services rep. Lions of Ill. Found., Oak Park, 1979-81; dir. pub. affairs Am. Council of Blind, Washington, 1981-87; dir. pub. affairs Columbia Lighthouse for the Blind, 1987; advisor Endependence Ctr., Arlington, Va., 1982—. Editor Old Dominion Council of Blind newsletter, 1981-85, Blind Student Advocate, 1982-87; contbr. articles on recreation for blind persons for profl. jours. Bd. dirs., v.p. Old Dominion Council of Blind, 1981-85; bd. dirs., v.p. Nat. Capital Citizens with Low Vision, Washington, 1982-85, pres., 1985-87; bd. dirs. Ski for Light, Inc., Mpls., 1983—. Recipient gold medal silver medal Nat. Championships-Skiing-U.S. Assn. Blind Athletes, 1982, gold medals, 1983, gold medals, 1985, silver medals, 1986, gold medals, 1987; silver medal World Olympics for Disabled, Innsbruck, Austria, 1984; Media award for radio presentation Pres.'s Com. on Employment of Handicapped, 1985, Healthy Am. Fitness Leaders award, 1987. Mem. U.S. Assn. Blind Athletes, Women in Communications, Pub. Relations Soc. Am. Lutheran. Clubs: Ski, Potomac Pedalers Touring, Potomac Appalachian Trail (Washington); Am. Blind Bowling Assn. (Louisville), RunHers. Lodge: Sons of Norway (Washington). Home: 115 E Glendale Alexandria VA 22301 Office: Columbia Lighthouse for the Blind 1421 P St NW Washington DC 20005

OGAN, ANNE PETERSON, stockbroker; b. Balt., Apr. 28, 1947; d. Harold Leon Peterson and Grace Legate (Olmsted) Potts; m. Nicholas Ogan, Aug. 26, 1967; 1 son, Alexander Peterson. B.A., Radcliffe Coll., 1969. Security analyst Union Commerce Bank, Cleve., 1969-71, Ball Burge & Kraus, Cleve., 1971-73; asst. to pres. Technicare Corp., Cleve., 1973-74; security analyst McDonald & Co., Cleve., 1974-77; equity salesman Salomon Bros., Cleve., 1977—, First Boston Corp., Cleve. Mem. Cleve. Soc. Security Analysts (sec. 1981-82, pres. 1987-88). Club: Harvard U. (treas. 1982-84) (Cleve.). Office: First Boston Corp 100 Erieview Plaza Cleveland OH 44114

O'GARA, BARBARA ANN, soap company executive; b. Newark, Aug. 8, 1953; d. Frank Percy and Rose (Giordano) Stevens; m. Michael Larry O'Gara, Mar. 21, 1981; 1 stepchild, Jennifer Kelly. AA, Keystone Jr. Coll., 1973; BA, U. Ariz., 1976. Media buyer Wells, Rich, Green/Townsend, Irvine, Calif., 1977-80; dist. sales mgr. Armour-Dial, Phoenix, 1980-82; regional sales mgr. Guest Supply, Inc., North Brunswick, N.J., 1982-85; dir. hotel sales Neutrogena Corp., Los Angeles, 1985—. Keystone Jr. Coll. scholar, 1972, Morris County scholar, 1971; recipient Outstanding Sales Accomplishment award Armour-Dial, 1981. Mem. Am. Mgmt. Assn., Am. Hotel & Motel Assn., Nat. Assn. Female Execs. Republican. Roman Catholic. Avocations: tennis, jogging, golf. Home: 41 Carriage Hill Ln Laguna Hills CA 92653 Office: Neutrogena Corp 5755 W 96th St Los Angeles CA 90045

OGDEN, JOANNE, real estate executive; b. Cumming, Ga., Apr. 9, 1941; d. Crafton Kemp Sr. and Mary Evelyn (Willis) Brooks; m. William Rush Williams, Oct. 21, 1940 (div. 1966); 1 child, Paul Rush Williams; m. Cecil Leavern Ogden, Sr.; stepchildren: Cecil Laverne Jr., Michael Vann. Grad. high sch., Cumming. Prin. Ogden & Ogden, Milledgeville, Ga., 1966—. Candidate Baldwin County Commnr., Milledgeville, 1984. Republican. Methodist. Club: 700 (Virginia Beach). Home: 402 Allen Memorial Dr SW Milledgeville GA 31061 Office: Ogden and Ogden 2600 Irwinton Rd Milledgeville GA 31061

OGDEN, VICKI LYNN, nurse, consultant; b. San Antonio, July 11, 1962; d. Willard LeRoi and Frances Avalon (Allman) O. Cert. in nurses aide, Tex. State Tech. Inst., 1978; cert. in emergency med. tech., Clarendon Coll., 1979; AA in Nursing Sci., Amarillo (Tex.) Coll., 1983. RN.; cert. nurse specialist emergency medicine and trauma Maricopa Med. Ctr. Emergency med. tech. Met. Ambulance, Pampa, Tex., 1978-83; nurse Palo Duro Hosp., Canyon, Tex., 1983-84, Meth. Hosp., Lubbock, Tex., 1984-85, St. Mary Plains Hosp., Lubbock, 1985-87, Vanderbilt Med. Ctr., Nashville, 1987—; dir. Nurse Refresher Course, Nashville, 1987—; guest lectr. paramedic instrn. State of Tex., Amarillo, 1984-86; instr. ARC Classes, Amarillo, 1985-87. Mem. ARC Nurses, Emergency Med. Technicians (v.p. 1980-84), Cert. Emergency Nurse Assn., Emergency Nurses Assn., Top of Tex. Emergency Med. Techs. Assn. (instr. 1980). Republican. Presbyterian. Home: 1404 Brentwood Terr Nashville TN 37211

OGDEN-REID, VICTORIA ANN, accountant; b. Oakland, Calif., Dec. 7, 1957; d. John Paul and Barbara J. (Woodd) DeMoss; m. Gary Lincoln Ogden, June, 1974 (div. Feb. 1978); 1 child, David Gary; m. Travis E. Reid, Sept. 11, 1982; 1 child, Sarah Ashley. Student, Diablo Valley Coll., Pleasant Hill, Calif., 1984-86, Golden Gate U., 1986-87. Asst. mgr. Robert L. Lippert Theatres, San Francisco, 1974-78; acct. Maestri Mgmt. Corp., San Francisco, 1978-82; staff acct. Robert O. Folkoff, CPA's, San Francisco, 1982—. Mem. Women of the Motion Picture Industry (treas. San Francisco chpt. 1986-87), Variety Club of No. Calif. Office: Robert O Folkoff Inc 995 Market St 15th Fl San Francisco CA 94103

OGI, IRENE AYAKO, lawyer; b. San Jose, Calif., May 10, 1948; d. Irving Toshiro and Gladys Yukiko (Nakashima) Ogi. Student, U. Calif.-Davis, 1966-68, Internat. Christian U., Tokyo, 1968-69; B.A., U. Calif.-Berkeley, 1970; J.D., U. Calif.-Davis, 1975. Bar: Calif. 1981. Discovery coordinator Homestake Mining Co., San Francisco, 1977-81; assoc. Skjerven, Morrill, San Francisco, 1981-83; sole practice, Oakland, Calif., 1983—; judge protem Santa Clara County Superior Ct., San Jose, 1984-85; adj. prof., litigation Calif. State Univ., Hayward, 1986—, adj. instr. litigations, Santa Clara (Calif.) Univ. 1987—; guest lectr. labor law J.F.K. U., Orinda, Calif., 1984—; adj. prof. litigation U. Santa Clara, 1987-88. Mem. Japanese Am. Citizens League, Oakland, 1984—; pres. adv. bd. R.S.V.P. (Ret. Srs. Vol. Program, East Bay Peralta Colls. Dist. 1987—), Oakland, 1984—. Mem. San Francisco Trial Lawyers Assn., San Francisco Bar Assn., Alameda County Bar Assn. Republican. Buddhist. Club: Barracuda (pres. Oakland-San Francisco 1984). Office: 848 Cleveland St Oakland CA 94606

OGILVIE, MARGARET PRUETT, counselor; b. McKinney, Tex., Jan. 8, 1922; d. William Walter and Ida Mae (Houk) Pruett; B.A., Baylor U., 1943; M.Ed., Hardin Simmons U., 1968; m. Frederick Henry Ogilvie, May 13, 1943; children—Ida Margaret, James William. Tchr. pub. and pvt. schs., Tex., Calif., Alaska, W.Ger., 1944, 53-65; guidance counselor Dentsville High Sch., Columbia, S.C., 1968-69, Northwest H.S., Clarksville, Tenn., 1970-72; personal and marital counselor, Fairfield Glade, Tenn., 1972—; co-owner F & M Gems & Jewelry. Treas. Officers' Wives Club, Ft. Irwin, Calif.; chmn. vols. ARC, Ft. Irwin, 1965; pres. Women's Golf Assn., Ft. Irwin, 1965-66; v.p. Ch. Women United, Crossville, Tenn., 1972-74; bd. dirs. Cumberland County Mental Health Assn., 1975-87; mem. legis. com. and pub. affairs com. Tenn. Mental Health Assn., 1976-81, mem. exec. bd., 1977-86; vol. Christian Service Corps, 1985—, Home Mission Bd. of So. Bapt. Conv., 1985-87; mem. Middle Tenn. com. Internat. Women's Yr., 1975; bd. dirs. Battered Women, Inc., Crossville, 1984-85. Mem. Am. Personnel and Guidance Assn., Nat. Ret. Tchrs. Assn., Bus. and Profl. Women's Club (chmn. 1973-75), DAR (parliamentarian Crab Orchard chpt. 1981), Pi Gamma Mu. Democrat. Baptist (choir dir., organist 1972—). Clubs: Fairfield Glade Women's (parliamentarian 1974-77), Fairfield Glade Women's Golf Assn. (pres. 1973, 2d v.p. 1986), Fairfield Glade Sq. Dance; Order Eastern Star (Amanda chpt. IV). Home: 240 Snead Dr PO Box 1522 Fairfield Glade TN 38555

OGLE, PEGGY ANN, human services consultant; b. Washington, Feb. 3, 1950; d. William Paul and Lurlene (Lazenby) Ogle. A.A., Miami Dade Coll., 1969; B.S., Fla. State U., 1972, M.S., 1976. Cert. tchr., Fla. Spl. educator Jackson County Schs., Marianna, Fla., 1972-73; edn. dir. Sunland-Tallahassee, Fla., 1974-76; program supr. BARA, Tallahassee, 1976-77; program examiner Dept. of H.R.S., Tallahassee, 1977-79; program adminstr. Dept. of H.R.S.-V., St. Petersburg, Fla., 1979; dir. client services PARC Ctr., St. Petersburg, 1979-82; pres. Program Design Inc., St. Petersburg, 1982—, Personal Fitenss by Program Design Inc.; strategic planning cons. Ann Storck Ctr., Ft. Lauderdale, Fla., 1982-86; cons. State of Fla., Tallahassee, 1982-86; staff trainer, cons. ARA DevCon, Tallahassee, 1984-86; researcher, cons. L.R. O'Neall & Assocs., Tallahassee, 1984-86; mgr. quality assurance contract Healthcare and Retirement Corp. Am. Author: Being Human, 1983, Mirador: An Assessment Guide for Persons with Profound Functional Defecits and Complex Health Care Needs; editor: Developmental Nursing, 1985; contbr. articles to profl. jours. Chmn. Pinellas County Housing Coalition, St. Petersburg, 1982-83. State of Fla. grad. fellow, 1975; recipient Citizenship award, DAR, 1972. Mem. Am. Assn. Mental Deficiencies (gen. div. chmn. S.E. affiliate), Assn. for Severly Handicapped, Life Concepts, Inc. Avocations: tennis; swimming; skiing. Office: Program Design Inc 224 Cordova Blvd NE Saint Petersburg FL 33704

OGLETREE-BOLDEN, YVONNE THERESA, graphic designer; b. Chgo., Feb. 1, 1955; d. Lewis W. and Betty Lucille (Brown) Ogletree; m. Nathaniel Bolden, June 1986; 1 child, GaBrielle Nicole. A.A. in Graphic Design, Kennedy-King Coll., 1975; B.F.A., Ind. State U., 1979. Asst. art dir. Proctor & Gardner Advt., Inc., Chgo., 1979-82; prodn. artist Sharp Hartwig Advt., Inc., Seattle, 1982-87; freelance designer, Seattle, 1987—; prodn. artist, designer Manus Corp., Seattle, 1987—. Mem. Soc. Typographic Artists.

O'GORMAN, PATRICIA ALICE, psychologist; b. N.Y.C., May 27, 1946; d. Patrick M. and Mary L. (Kohut) O'G.; B.A., CCNY, 1968, M.S., 1970; Ph.D., Fordham U., 1975; m. Robert Allen Ross, Aug. 12, 1979. Clin. Asst. dept. sch. psychology Bklyn. Coll., 1973-74, adj. lectr., 1974; dir. dept. prevention and edn. Nat. Council on Alcoholism, N.Y.C., 1974-79; clin. instr. dept. psychiatry N.Y.U., N.Y.C., 1976-79; dir. div. prevention Nat. Inst. Alcohol Abuse, Rockville, Md., 1979-81; chief psychologist Berkshire Farm Ctr. and Services for Youth, Canaan, N.Y., 1981-84; pvt. practice psychology East Greenbush, N.Y., 1981—; nat. and internat. lectr. on alcoholism prevention; also spokesperson on radio, TV and press; cons. VA Hosp., Albany, N.Y., 1978-79, SUNY, Albany, 1979, 81, N.Y. Council on Children and Families, Albany, 1979, Ministry Labour and Social Affairs, Israel, 1981, 84; mem. grad. edn. nat. adv. com. project Physician Requirements for 1990's, 1982. Mem. Pres. Carter's Transition Task Force on Health, 1976; mem. N.Y. Gov.'s Transition Task Force on Alcohol and Substance Abuse, also chmn. com. on prevention, 1976; mem. adv. bd. Info. Exchange on the Young Adult Chronics; mem. adv. subcom. on alcoholism N.Y. State Senate, 1977-79; mem. alcohol and drug work group for promoting health and preventing disease Objectives for Nation, 1979; nat. adv. bd. Women in Crisis Conf., 1981-82. Mem. Am. Psychol. Assn., Am. Pub. Health Assn., Research Soc. on Alcoholism, Nat. Assn. Children of Alcoholics (founding exec. com.), Psychol. Assn. N.E. N.Y. (past treas.). Democrat. Author: (with P. Finn) Teaching About Alcohol, 1981; (with Phil Oliver-Diaz) Breaking the Cycle of Addiction: A Parent's Guide to Healthy Kids, 1987; (with Phil Oliver-Diaz) The Twelve Steps to Self-Parenting, 1988; also articles. Editorial bd. Focus on Women: Jour. of Addiction and Health, 1981-82. Home: Rural Delivery Box 300 East Chatham NY 12060 Office: 568 Columbia Turnpike East Greenbush NY 12061

O'GRADY, ELINOR M., secretarial service owner; b. Chgo.; d. Arthur O. and Anna L. (Miller) Atkins; m. Norman Hohnstock, Oct. 12, 1940 (div. 1945); 1 child, Judith A.; m. Michael A. O'Grady, Jr., Dec. 16, 1950; 1 child, Michael A. Office mgr. N. Soifer, M.D. & Assocs., Dayton, Ohio, 1950-79; pres. Park Ave. Secretarial Service, Dayton, 1980—. Mem. Tri-City Bus. and Profl. Women (sec. 1983-84, pres. 1987—), Profl. Secs. Internat., Am. Bus. Women Assn. (pres. 1986-88, Woman of Yr. 1987), Assn. Female Execs., Nat. Assn. Secretarial Services. Club: Pilot (pres. 1984-85) (Kettering, Ohio). Avocations: golf, landscape gardening, boating, sailing, crocheting. Home: 2513 Hackney Dr Kettering OH 45420 Office: Park Ave Secretarial Service 53 Park Ave Dayton OH 45419

O'HALLORAN, (LAVERNE M.) KATHLEEN (MRS. JOHN R. O'HALLORAN, JR.), real estate broker; b. Laurium, Mich., Nov. 15, 1921; d. Joseph Wilfred and Della K. (Gervais) Shaffer; student Fond Du Lac Comml. Coll., 1938-40, Fresno City Coll., 1965-66; m. John Richard O'Halloran, Jr., July 15, 1942; children: Sheila Ann O'Halloran Stoll, Gregory, Michael, Maureen O'Halloran Benelli, Sean, Margaret. Co-owner Hamlin Hotel, San Francisco, 1946-48, Lazy F Guest Ranch, Ellensburg, Wash., 1948-50; owner, broker Kathy O'Halloran Realty, Fresno, 1980—; pres. C & R Investments, 1974-75; broker Settlers Real Estate, Inc., Fresno, 1975-80. Charter mem. Infant of Prague Adoption Agy. Aux., 1954—, sec., 1955; mem. Mayor's Com. for Community Devel., 1963-64; charter mem. Nat. Mus. of Women in the Arts; pres. Sacred Heart Mothers Club, 1959; pres. Calif. Citizens for Decent Lit., 1961-63, Central Calif. Citizens for Decent Lit., 1959-64; precinct chmn. Goldwater campaign, 1964; chmn. Fresno County United Republicans Calif., 1962; area coordinator Clean Campaign Ballot Initiative, 1966; candidate Fresno City Council, 1961; mem. Women's League of Fresno Arts Center, 1976—, St. Agnes Service Guild, 1983—, Fresno Fiber Guild, 1985—. Mem. Fresno Bd. Realtors, Nat. Assn. Real Estate Bds. Roman Catholic. Home: 3503 N Bond St Fresno CA 93726 Office: 3503 N Bond St Fresno CA 93726

OHANESIAN, SUSAN MARIE, social service administrator; b. Bridgeport, Conn., Nov. 18, 1949; d. Nicholas Anthony and Jeanette Mary (Aniolowski) Yanosy; m. George Vaughn Ohanesian, Apr. 28, 1973. BA, U. Conn., 1971; MSSW, Columbia U., 1979; Cert. in Social Work Adminstrv., Hunter Coll., 1985. Employment interviewer State Conn. Unemployment, Bridgeport, 1971-73; legal asst. Mendes & Mount, N.Y.C., 1973-74; milieu therapist The Bridge, N.Y.C., 1976-77; asst. editor Matthew Bender & Co., N.Y.C., 1974-77; asst dir. mental health Palisades Gen. Hosp., North Bergen, N.J., 1981-85; clinic dir. C.S.S. BRC Human Services Corp., N.Y.C., 1985-86; dir. Social Service Project Return Found., Inc., N.Y.C., 1986-88, Artemis/Women's Spl. Services Project Return Found., Inc., N.Y.C., 1988—; pres. HPAE, AFT/AFL-CIO, North Bergen, N.J., 1980-81; regional coordinator E.M.H.S.P. Assn. N.J., North Bergen, 1985. Panlist N.Y. State Conf. on Substance Abuse-Relapse Prevention, 1987-88. Mem. Acad. Cert. Social Workers, Nat. Assn. Social Workers, N.Y. Assn. Social Workers, N.Y. Assn. Substance Abuse Program, N.Y. State Council on Alcoholism.

O'HARA, KATHY MARLEEN, physician; b. Bridgeport, Conn., Feb. 22, 1951; d. Walter Edgar and Grace Dorothy (Potter) Magill; B.S. cum laude in Biology, Oral Roberts U., Tulsa, 1973; D.O., Coll. Osteo. Medicine and Surgery, Des Moines, 1977. Intern, Des Moines Gen. Hosp., 1977-78; emergency room physician Salem County Meml. Hosp., Salem, N.J., 1981-87; asst. dir. emergency dept. Bridgeton and Millville Hosps., 1987—; guest speaker. Served with USN, 1978-80. Mem. Am. Osteo. Assn., Am. Med. Women's Assn., Christian Med. Soc., Assn. Mil. Osteo. Physicians and Surgeons, AAUW, Sigma Sigma Phi. Republican. Mem. Assembly of God. Home: 170 W Park Dr Bridgeton NJ 08302 Office: Bridgeton Hosp Bridgeton NJ 08302

O'HARA, SUSAN J., educator; b. Creston, Iowa, July 10, 1946; d. Ervin Adolph and Thelda Irene (Mangels) Queck; m. Dennis Michael O'Hara, Nov. 26, 1971 (div. July 1980). BA in English, Wartburg Coll., 1968; MA in Elem. Edn., Pacific Luth. U., 1970. Cert. tchr. with reading endorsement. Tchr. corps. intern Sumpter (S.C.) Pub. Schs., 1968-69, Tacoma Pub. Schs., 1969-70; tchr. 4th grade South Umpqua Sch Dist., Myrtle Creek, Oreg., 1970-79, tchr. chpt. I, 1979—; treas. edn. 1st com. Myrtle Creek, 1984—; bd. dirs. People for Improvement in Edn. OEA, Tigard, Oreg., 1984-86,; negotiators cadre Riddle (Oreg.) Edn. Assn., 1985—, Glide Edn. Assn. Contbr. articles to profl. jours. Mem. commn. Douglas County Cen. Com., Roseburg, Oreg., 1984—; del. 4th dist. Dem. Conv., Eugene, Oreg., 1985, Platform Conv., Beaverton, Oreg., 1986. Mem. NEA, Oreg. Edn. Assn. (bd. dirs. 1986—), Internat. Reading. Assn., Umpqua-Rogue UniServe Council, South Umpqua Edn. Assn. (pres. 1981-82, 85-87), Beta Sigma Phi. Democrat. Lutheran. Home: PO Box 613 Myrtle Creek OR 97457 Office: Tri-City Elem Sch 546 SW Chadwick Myrtle Creek OR 97457

OHARENKO, MARIA T., public relations official; b. Louvain, Belgium, Dec. 25, 1950; came to U.S., 1951; d. Vladimir and Lubomyra (Kotz) O. BS, Northwestern U., 1972, MS, 1973. Pub. info. officer U.S. AEC, ERDA, Dept. Energy, Argonne and Chgo., Ill., 1973-79; pub. info. and news media advance officer U.S. Dept. Energy, Washington, 1980-81; corp. press. relations mgr. Northrop Corp., Los Angeles, 1981—. Mem. Aviation/Space Writers Assn., Women in Communications, Sigma Delta Chi. Ukrainian Catholic. Office: Northrop Corp 1840 Century Park E Los Angeles CA 90067

OHLENFORST, CYNTHIA MORGAN, lawyer; b. Dallas, May 17, 1949; d. Robert Ernest and Alice Helen (Ingels) Morgan; m. Patrick Michael Ohlenforst, June 12, 1971; children—Kristen Michelle, Lauren Jennifer, Megan Kathryn. B.A., Loyola U.-New Orleans, 1970; M.A., U. Dallas, 1974; J.D. magna cum laude, So. Meth. U., 1980. Bar: Tex. 1980. Tchr., Bishop Lynch High Sch., Dallas, 1971-74, Mt. Carmel High Sch., Houston, 1974-76, Jesuit Coll. Preparatory, Dallas, 1976-77; ptnr. Hughes & Luce, Dallas, 1980—. Active Leadership Tex., 1984; Dean Search Com. So. Meth. U. Sch. Law, 1978-80; bd. dirs. Lone Star Council Camp Fire; corp. council Shakespeare Festival of Dallas. Recipient Outstanding Secondary Tchr. Am. award, 1975-76. Mem. Dallas Bar Assn., ABA, State Bar Tex. (com. legis. devel.), Tex. Young Lawyers Assn. Republican. Roman Catholic. Office: Hughes & Luce 2800 Momentum Pl Dallas TX 75201

OHLER, DENISE L., university administrator; b. Erie, Pa., Nov. 8, 1955; d. David Carpenter and Martha B. (Pencinger) O.; m. Gordon J. Herbst, May 23, 1986. BA in Sociology, Edinboro (Pa.) U., 1977, MEd, 1980, cert. sch. psychology, 1983. Cert. in secondary and guidance counseling, Pa. Social worker Family Planning Clinic of Western Pa., Erie, 1977-79; grad. asst. Edinboro U., 1979-80, exec. asst. to provost and v.p. acad. affairs, 1986—; assessment counselor Career Assessment Ctr., Erie, 1980-86. Mem. NW Pa. Guidance Assn. Lutheran. Office: Edinboro U Pa Reeder Hall Edinboro PA 16444

OHLHAUSEN, ANITA APPRILL, sales professional; b. St. Louis, Feb. 6, 1941; d. Herbert A. and Crescentia (Venverloh) Apprill; m. William George Ohlhausen, Sept. 8, 1962; children: Peter Edmund, Eric Wendel. BA, Fontbonne Coll., St. Louis, 1962; MS, U. Md., 1977. Consumer liaison FDA, Washington, 1972-77; nutrition specialist Office Asst. Sec. Health HHS, Washington, 1974-75; instr. U. Mo., St. Louis, 1977-78; cons. nutritionist Nutirition Counseling Services, St. Louis, 1980-82; sr. sales specialist Boehringer Mannheim Diagnostics Inc., St. Louis, 1982-87; sales rep. Nichols Inst. Reference Labs., Washington, 1987—. Contbr. articles to profl. jours. Speaker in field. Mem. St. Louis Forum (founding, sec. 1981-82).

OHLRICH, ELIZABETH SCHOWALTER, physician, health science administrator, educator; b. Beloit, Wis., Nov. 7, 1943; d. Clarence H. and Ruth Mildred (Knoble) Schowalter; m. Warren H. Ohlrich, Aug. 28, 1965 (div. Jan. 1976); children: Wayne Hargen, Miles Arthur. BS with honors, U. Wis., 1965, MS, 1967, PhD, 1968, MD with honors, 1980. Research assoc. Childrens Hosp. Nat. Med. Ctr., Washington, 1968-71, 72-76; intern, then resident in pediatrics U. Wis. Hosp. and Clinics, Madison, 1980-83; med. dir. eating disorders program U. Wis. Hosp., Madison, 1983—; research assoc. Walter Reed Army Inst. of Research, Washington, 1968-71; adj. asst. prof. Antioch Coll., Balt., 1970-71; asst. prof. dept. child health and Human devel. George Washington U., Washington, 1975-77; asst. prof. dept. pediatrics U. Wis. Med. Sch., Madison, 1983-87, assoc. prof., 1987—. Contbr. articles to profl. jours. NIH fellow, 1965-68. Mem. Soc. Adolescent Medicine. Democrat. Office: U Wis Hosp 600 Highland Ave Madison WI 53792

OJAKLI, SUMYA, marketing professional; b. Oklahoma City, May 10, 1961; d. Sadeddin Said and Mary Josephine (King) O. BA in Communications cum laude, L.I. U., 1984. Orientation coordinator, leadership trainer C.W. Post, Greenvale, N.Y., 1982-83, TV prodn. teaching asst., 1983-84; account exec., art dir. Nat. Imagemakers, N.Y.C., 1984-85; producer, designer Sumai Prodns., Bklyn., 1984-87; mktg. mgr. corp. communications Graphic Media Inc., N.Y.C., 1985-88; ptnr., designer Melted Ice Prodns., N.Y.C., 1988—. Published in 24 mags. Arts career adviser to coll. students, N.Y.C., 1986—. Recipient 2 DESI awards, 1986. Mem. Am. Film Inst., N.Y. Acad. TV Arts and Scis., Nat. Assn. Female Execs. Republican. Home: 351 Marine Ave Brooklyn NY 11209 Office: Billboard Mag 1515 Broadway New York NY 10036

OJANLATVA, ANSA TERTTU TELLERVO, educator; b. Piippola, Finland, Mar. 19, 1948; came to U.S., 1973; d. Leevi Johannes and Kerttu (Helmi) O.; MS, U. Ill., 1975; PhD (teaching asst.), So. Ill. U., 1977; grad. U. Jyvaskyla (Finland), 1971. Lectr. San Francisco State U., 1977-78; asst. prof. U. Houston, 1978-81; lectr. Calif. State Coll., San Bernardino, 1981-84, asst. prof., coordinator health sci. program La. State U., 1984-87; assoc. prof., chairperson Dept. Allied Health, Ind. U. of Pa., 1987—; cons. family life edn. San Diego State U., 1981; chairperson health edn. profl. edn. sect. Tex. Assn. Health, Phys. Edn. and Recreation, 1981; mem. Houston steering com. Internat. Yr. of Disabled Persons, 1981. Am.-Scandinavian Found. grantee, 1976-77; cert. sex educator. Mem. Am. Assn. Sex Educators, Counselors and Therapists (continuing edn. com. 1982-83), Internat. Union Health Edn. (publs. com.), Nat. Assn. Female Execs., Eta Sigma Gamma, Phi Delta Kappa. Editor audiovisual revs. column Hygie, 1986—; reviewer manuscripts for Health Edn., 1986—; contbr. articles to profl. jours. Office: Indiana U of Pa Dept Allied Health Profls Indiana PA 15705

OKA, HIRONO, classical musician; b. Tokyo, June 9, 1957; came to U.S., 1977; d. Kōsaku and Machiko (Tanaka) O. Student, San Francisco Conservatory Music, 1977-78; diploma, cert., Curtis Inst. Music, 1982. Violinist The Phila. Orch., 1981-83, The New Phila. Quartet, 1981-82, 87, Concerto Soloists Chamber Orch., 1983—, The Lehigh Quartet, 1988—. Home: 4 Lantern Ln Cherry Hill NJ 08002 Office: Concerto Soloists Chamber Orchestra 2136 Locust St Philadelphia PA 19103

OKA, YASU, physician; b. Japan, June 6, 1930; came to U.S., 1956; d. Kozo and Yoshi Shimada; m. Masamichi Oka, Mar. 17, 1956; children—Marie, Lisa. Intern St. Joseph Hosp., Denver, 1956; intern Bronx Mcpl. Hosp. Ctr., N.Y.C., 1957; resident in anesthesiology Albert Einstein Coll. Medicine, N.Y.C., 1959, prof., 1981—. Mem. Am. Assn. Anesthesiologists, Internat. Anesthesiologist Research Soc., N.Y. State Assn. Anesthesiologists, N.Y. Acad. Medicine, Soc. Cardiovascular Anesthesiology, N.Y. Soc. Thoracic Surgery, Am. Heart Assn. Home: 5 Crossway Scarsdale NY 10583 Office: Albert Einstein Coll Medicine Bronx NY 10461

OKEEFE, BARBARA ANN, manufacturing executive; b. St. Louis, Sept. 4, 1940; d. Henry Charles and Thelma Elizabeth (Forsythe) Warner; m. Bobby Gene Watson, Sept. 10, 1960 (div. Dec. 1980); children: Glenn Charles, Laura Ann, Vicky Lynn, Lisa Beth; m. Richard L. OKeefe, Nov. 17, 1984. Student, St. Louis Community Coll. at Meramac, 1981—. Purchasing agt. Affinitec Corp., St. Louis, 1978-85; buyer Engineered Air System, St. Louis, 1985-86, McDonnell Douglas Electronics, St. Charles, Mo., 1986—. Mem. Nat. Assn. Purchasing Mgmt. (mem. membership com. 1981—), St. Louis Women's Commerce Assn. Democrat. Presbyterian.

O'KEEFE, KATHLEEN MARY, state government official; b. Butte, Mont., Mar. 25, 1933; d. Hugh I. and Kathleen Mary (Harris) O'Keefe; B.A. in Communications, St. Mary Coll., Xavier, Kans., 1954; m. Nick B. Baker, Sept. 18, 1954 (div. 1970); children—Patrick, Susan, Michael, Cynthia, Hugh, Mardeen. Profl. singer, mem. Kathie Baker Quartet, 1962-72; research cons. Wash. Ho. of Reps., Olympia, 1972-73; info. officer Wash. Employment Security Commn., Seattle, 1973-81, dir. public affairs, 1981—; freelance writer, composer, producer, 1973—. Founder, pres. bd. Eden, Inc., visual and performing arts, 1975—; public relations chmn. Nat. Women's Democratic Conv., Seattle, 1979, Wash. Dem. Women, 1976—; bd. dirs., public relations chmn. Eastside Mental Health Center, Bellevue, Wash.,

1979-81; Dem. candidate Wash. State Senate, 1968. Recipient Black Community award for composition The Beaufort County Jail, Seattle, 1975, Silver medal Seattle Creative Awards Show for composing, directing and producing Rent A Kid, TV public service spot, 1979. Mem. Wash. Press Women. Democrat. Roman Catholic. Author handbook on TV prodn., guide to coping with unemployment; composer numerous songs, also producer Job Service spots. Home: 4426 147th Pl NE A-12 Bellevue WA 98007 Office: 212 Maple Park Olympia WA 98504

OKELL, JOBYNA LOUISE, public health administrator, accountant; b. Miami, Fla., Nov. 21, 1937; d. George Shaffer and Evelyn Maude (Pottmyer) O. B.B.A., U. Miami-Fla., 1961; postgrad. U. Miami, 1962, Nova U., 1976—. Acct. Crippled Children's Soc., Miami, Fla., 1964-65, Am. Coll. Found., Miami, 1965-66; owner Jobyna's Miniatures, Coral Gables, Fla., 1978—; exec. dir./adminstr., corp. dir. Fla. Health Profl. Services, Inc., Coral Gables, 1967—. Dist. chmn. Young Democrats Dade County and Fla., 1956-68; vice regent DAR, Coral Gables chpt., 1968-87, active Irish Georgian Soc., English Speaking Union; treas., dir. Merrick Manor Found., 1974-75; active Friends of Library, U. Miami, 1974-87; adv. bd. channeling project Miami Jewish Home and Hosp. for Aged, 1982-87. Recipient Outstanding County Young Democrat award Young Dems. Fla., 1964; Truman award Outstanding Young Dem. Young Dems. Dade County, 1965; Outstanding Jr. DAR, 1972. Mem. Am. Pub. Health Assn., Nat. League Nursing, Am. Soc. Pub. Adminstrn., Dade/Monroe Assn. Home Health Agys. (pres./dir. 1974-76), Health Planning Council South Fla., Health Systems Agy. South Fla., Fla. Assn. Home Health Agys., South Fla. In-Home Services (pres. 1985-88), Red-Sunset Merchants Assn., Nat. Assn. Miniature Enthusiasts, Internat. Guild Miniature Artisans, Ocean Waves Guild, Am. Philatelic Soc., Hawaiian Philatelic Soc., Nat. Quilting Assn., Am. Quilter's Soc., Geneal. Soc. Greater Miami (treas. 1987-88), Gamma Alpha Chi, Alpha Delta Pi. Republican. Episcopalian. Home: 715 Palermo Ave Coral Gables FL 33134 Office: Fla Health Profl Services Inc 1510 Venera Ave Coral Gables FL 33146

OKERCHIRI, CAROLYN ANN, program administrator; b. Cin., Nov. 5, 1945; d. George Washington and Daisy Marybell (Johnson) Crocheron; m. Emmanuel Okoe Okerchiri; children: Damon Albert, Ronda Marie. Student, U. Cin., 1963-64; BA, St. Mary's Coll., 1985. Task force coordinator Women's Conf., Detroit, 1978-79; pub. relations and promotions adminstr. Ren Unltd. Prodns., Fontana, Calif., 1979-81; producer, programmer Sta. WAIF-FM, Cin., 1982-83; assoc. program dir. Concerned Citizens Council, Detroit, 1985-86; founder, chief exec. officer Proving Grounds Internat., Inc., Jackson, Mich., 1986—; founder Peace of the World project, Jackson, Mich., 1986—. Author: Just Between Us Two, 1987, Talking to Myself, 1988. Bd. dirs. Assembly of Youth for Polit. Office, Jackson, 1986-87. Mem. A. Phillip Randolph Inst., St. Mary's Coll. Alumni Assn., Internat. Peace Research Assn., St. Mary's Coll. Alumni Assn., Soc. Internat. Devel., Internat. Congress Female Clergy (assoc. dir.). Lodges: Zonta, Ea. Star (assoc. conductress).

OKESON, DOROTHY JEANNE, educational association administrator; b. Garden City, Kans., Aug. 31, 1931; d. Arthur E. and Thelma Lucille (McGraw) Clements Newman; m. Arnold Leroy Okeson, Dec. 20, 1953; 1 child, Michael Leroy. BA, U. No. Colo., 1961. Cert. jr. high and secondary tchr. Tchr. Weskan (Kans.) Consolidated Sch., Weskan Unified Sch. Dist., 1962-70; corr. sec. Sherman-Wallace Assn. Retarded Children, Goodland, Kans., 1968—; mem. Gov.'s Adv. Planning Council, Topeka, 1976-80, Kans. Planning Council Devel. Disabilities, Topeka, 1980—, chmn., 1985—. Contbr. articles to Western Times newspaper. Bd. dirs. Assn. Retarded Citizens, Merriam, Kans., 1969-79; asst. campaign mgr. county gubernatorial candidates, Sharon Springs, Kans., 1986. Mem. NEA (life), AAUW (past pres., legis. chmn. 1980—), Nat. Assn. Devel. Disabilities (chmn. subcom. child devel. 1976-87, mem. council, by-laws and pub. policy com. 1987—). Republican. Lutheran. Home: Box 136 Weskan KS 67762 Office: Kans Planning Council Devel Disabilities Services Docking Bldg 5th Floor N Topeka KS 66612

OKOYE, RENEE LOLA, therapist; b. N.Y.C., Jan. 8, 1945; d. Rocklyn and Eleanor (Jordan) Clarke; m. Emmanuel Ogbunnaya Okoye, Sept. 27, 1966; children: Amaogechukwu, Nkeiruka. BS, NYU, 1966; M in Health Sci., SUNY, Stony Brook, 1978. Cert. occupational therapist. Occupational therapist St. Vincent's Hosp., N.Y.C., 1966-68; supr. clin. edn. NYU Med. Ctr., Roosevelt Island, 1969-74; asst. prof. NYU, N.Y.C., 1974-79; pvt. practice occupational therapist Wantagh, N.Y., 1978—; cons. dean's com. on grad. programs, Howard U., 1977, med. missionary cons. Children's Bible Fellowship, Carmel, N.Y., 1979—; active Scis.' Inst. for Pub. Info. Book: An Eclectic Approach, 1975, Functional Evaluation, 1976. Mem. program com. Amityville (N.Y.) Bd. Edn., 1985-86; adminstrv. asst. Highland Ave. Ch., Jamaica, 1986—. Mem. Am. Occupational Therapy Assn. (resource person 1984—, Appreciation cert. 1987), N.Y. State Occupational Therapy Assn. (Excellence in Practice award 1979). Office: Associated Therapies 1228 Wantagh Ave Wantagh NY 11793

OKUN, GAIL SHEILA, academic administrator; b. Bklyn., Apr. 6, 1943; d. Edward and Anne (Stenzler) Jasowitz; m. Clark N. Okun, Nov. 9, 1963; children: Scott Andrew, Peter Heath. BS, LIU, 1966; MEd, William Paterson Coll., 1985. Instr. high sch. N.Y.C. Pub. Schs., 1966-67, Pompton Lakes (N.J.) High Sch., 1967-69; adminstr., dir. Ft. Lee (N.J.) Montessori Sch., 1976-79; instr. The Berkeley Sch., Little Falls, N.J., 1980—, chairperson secretarial sci. and info. processing dept., 1986-87; cons. N.Y., N.J., Conn., 1981—. Dem. com. person, Wayne, N.J., 1985—. Mem. Am. Soc. Tng. and Devel., Internat. Reading Assn., Assn. Info. System Profls., Ea. Bus. Edn. Assn., N.J. Bus. Edn. Assn., N.J. Edn. Assn., Delta Pi Epsilon. Jewish. Home: 45 Princeton Pl Wayne NJ 07470 Office: The Berkeley Sch 44 Rifle Camp Rd West Paterson NJ 07424

OLAH, ELSA CRUZ, state government specialist; b. Guaynabo, P.R., Jan. 29, 1942; d. Felix Cruz and Justina (Lopez) Rivera; children: Gizella, Paul. EdM, Rutgers U., 1972. cert. tchr., Mass. Mgr. Almela Corp., Bklyn., 1958-63, Mt. Ephraim, N.Y.C., 1965-70; research asst. Rutgers U., Camden, N.J., 1976-82, teaching asst., 1980-82; trainer counsel Temple U., Phila., 1982-85; program specialist N.J. Dept. Health, Trenton, 1985—. Author Spanish poetry, plays; contbr. articles to profl. jours. Mem. Assn. Female Execs., Rutgers U. Alumni Assn., Sociedad Nacional Hispanica, Museo Del Pueblo, Kappa Delta Pi. Home: 118 N 3d St Camden NJ 08102 Office: NY Dept Health 129 E Hanover St Trenton NJ 08625-0362

OLAH, SUSAN ROSE, artist; b. Budapest, Hungary, June 14, 1947; d. Joseph and Emma (Hupcsak) Olah; came to Can., 1957, naturalized, 1962; student Art Instrn. Sch. Mpls., 1966-69, grad. 1969. One woman shows Gallery of Roof, Regina, Sask., 1973, Galerie Mouffe, Paris, 1977, Galerie Vallombreuse, Biarritz, France, 1977; exhibited in group shows Gallery of Roof, Galerie Mouffe; tchr. art Wascana Hosp., Regina, 1969-72, art cons., 1970-72. Recipient award for painting, Mpls., 1967, Gold medal Accademia Italia delle Arti e del Lavoro, 1979, Golden Centour award Accademia Italia, 1982, Gold medal Internat. Parliament for Peace and Safety, U.S.A., 1982, European Banner of Arts, Gold medal Accademia Europea, 1985, Oscar d' Italia, 1985, Fiamma d'Oro World Parliament award Accademia Italia, U.S.A., 1986, Golden Palm of Europe award Com. for the European Zrize for artist Undisputed Validity Accademia Europe, 1987. Mem. Internat. Order of Vols. for Peace. Deceased. Home: 37 Haultain Crescent, Regina, SK Canada S4S 4B4

O'LAUGHLIN, SISTER JEANNE, university administrator. Pres., Barry U., Miami Shores, Fla. Office: Barry U 11300 NE 2nd Ave Miami Shores FL 33161

OLDFATHER, PAULA MARIE, computer company executive; b. Rosenberg, Tex., Aug. 3, 1940; d. Theron Andrew and Pansy Blossom (Carpenter) O.; B.S. with honors in Math., UCLA, 1966. Mem. tech. staff RAND Corp., Santa Monica, Calif., 1964-67; analyst, programmer Auerbach Assos., Phila., 1967-69; mgr. systems and programming CARA Corp., Phila., 1969-71, v.p., 1975-82; pres. Belmont & Oldfather, Inc., Glen Mills, Pa., 1982—; tchr. SIMSCRIPT programming USAF, 1965-67. Mem. Assn. Computing Machinery, Data Entry Mgmt. Assn., Soc. Ambulatory Med. Systems, Nat. Assn. Female Execs. Author computer materials. Home: 21 Winding Way RD 5 Glen Mills PA 19342 Office: Riddle Valley 2 New Rd Aston PA 19014

OLDHAM, ELAINE DOROTHEA, educator; b. Coalinga, Calif., June 29, 1931; d. Claude Smith Oldham and Dorothy Elaine (Hill) Wilkins. AB in History, U. Calif.-Berkeley, 1953; MS in Sch. Adminstrn., Calif. State U.-Hayward, 1976; postgrad. U. Calif.-Berkeley, Harvard U., Mills Coll. Tchr. Piedmont Unified Sch. Dist., Calif., 1956—. Pres., bd. dirs. Camron-Stanford House Preservation Assn., 1979-86, adminstrv. v.p., bd. dirs., 1976-79; mem. various civic and community support groups; bd. dirs. Anne Martin Children's Ctr. Mem. Am. Assn. Museums, Am. Assn. Mus. Trustees, Internat. Council Museums, Inst. Internat. Edn., Am. Assn. State and Local History, DAR (Outstanding Tchr. Am. History award), Colonial Dames Am., Magna Charta Dames, Daus. of Confederacy, Hugeunot Soc., Plantagenent Soc., Order of Washington, Order St. George and Descs. of Knights of Garter, U. Calif. Alumni Assn. (co-chmn. and chmn. of 10th and 25th yr. class reunions), Prytanean Alumnae Assn. (bd. dirs.), Phi Delta Kappa, Delta Kappa Gamma. Republican. Episcopalian. Club: Harvard (San Francisco); Women's Athletic of Alameda County. Office: Magnolia Ave Piedmont CA 94611

OLDHAM, MAXINE JERNIGAN, real estate broker; b. Whittier, Calif., Oct. 13, 1923; d. John K. and Lela Hessie (Mears) Jernigan; m. Laurance Montgomery Oldham, Oct. 28, 1941; 1 child, John Laurence. AA, San Diego City Coll., 1973; student Western State U. Law, San Diego, 1976-77, LaSalle U., 1977-78; grad. Realtors Inst., Sacramento, 1978. Mgr. Edin Harig Realty, LaMesa, Calif., 1966-70; tchr. Bd. Edn., San Diego, 1959-66; mgr. Julia Cave Real Estate, San Diego, 1970-73; salesman Computer Realty, San Diego, 1973-74; owner Shelter Island Realty, San Diego, 1974—. Author: Jernigan History, 1982, Mears Geneology, 1985. Mem. Civil Service Commn., San Diego, 1957-58. Mem. Nat. Assn. Realtors, Calif. Assn. Realtors, San Diego Bd. Realtors, San Diego Apt. Assn., Internationale des Professions Immobilieres (internat. platform speaker), DAR, Colonial Dames 17th Century, Internat. Fedn. Univ. Women. Republican. Roman Catholic. Avocations: music, theater, painting, geneology, continuing edn. Home: 3348 Lowell St San Diego CA 92106 Office: Shelter Island Realty 2810 Lytton St San Diego CA 92110

OLDHAM, PHYLLIS VIRGINIA KIDD, librarian; b. Lafayette, Ind., Mar. 19, 1926; d. Hulbert Haven and Grace Ellene (Doup) Kidd; B.S., Purdue U., 1948, M.S., Butler U., 1966; 1 child, Stephen Kidd. Tchr. English, Jefferson High Sch., Lafayette, 1950; tchr., librarian Tudor Hall Sch., Indpls., 1954-70; librarian Park Tudor Sch., 1970—; mem. exec. bd. Central Ind. Area Library Services Authority, sec., 1983-85. Mem. People-to-People Internat., dist. dir. Student Ambassador Program, 1970-80; chmn. bd. Central Christian Ch., Indpls., 1979-81; mem. vol. council Indpls. Zool. Soc. Mem. ALA, Marion County Librarians Assn. (pres. 1969-72), Ind. Media Educators, Kappa Delta Pi, Delta Kappa Gamma (treas. Alpha Eta chpt. 1974-80), Pi Beta Phi. Lodge: Sertoma (dist. gov. 1969-70) (Indpls.). Home: 7015 Warwick Rd Indianapolis IN 46220 Office: Park Tudor Sch Library 7200 N College St Indianapolis IN 46240

OLDING, DOROTHY (MCKEOWN), literary agent; b. N.Y.C., Apr. 12, 1910; d. Addington Eric and Seraphine (Theodor) O.; student Columbia U., 1927-29; m. Edward V. McKeown, Aug. 14, 1946 (dec. 1951). Asst. fiction editor Am. mag., N.Y.C., 1929-38; with Harold Ober Assocs. Inc., lit. agy., N.Y.C., 1938—, partner, then exec. v.p., 1949-72, pres., 1972—. Home: 447 E 57th St New York NY 10022 Office: 40 E 49th St New York NY 10017

OLDS, SHARRON LEE, leasing company executive; b. Highland Park, Mich., Nov. 3, 1939; d. Emil and Sally (DiBlasi) O. Departmental sec. Wayne State U. Libraries, Detroit, 1958-76; mng. coordinator Jack Barnes Dance Ctrs., West Bloomfield, Mich., 1976-80; br. office mgr. Corp. Funding, Inc., Birmingham, Mich., 1980-84; v.p. Corp. Resources, Inc., Birmingham, 1984—. Mem. Am. Assn. Individual Investors, Nat. Assn. Female Execs. Republican. Avocations: dancing, flying, table tennis. Office: Corp Resources Inc 16231 W 14 Mile Rd Birmingham MI 48009

O'LEARY, PATRICIA ANN, nurse, educator; b. Steubenville, Ohio, May 15, 1949; d. John Paul and Rita Catherine (Andrews) O'L. L.P.N., Bellaire Sch. Practical Nursing (Ohio), 1969; R.N., Mercy Hosp. Sch. Nursing, Pitts., 1973; B.S.N., West Liberty State Coll., 1978; M.S.N., Vanderbilt U. 1980; postgrad. W.Va. U., 1981-83, U. Ala., 1987—. L.P.N., Ohio Valley Hosp., Steubenville, Ohio, 1969-73; staff nurse Cleve. Clinic, 1973-75, Ohio Valley Hosp., 1975-79; nursing supr. Royal Pavilion Extended Care Facility, Steubenville, 1979; instr. nursing West Liberty State Coll. (W.Va.), 1980-84; asst. prof. East Carolina U. Sch. Nursing, Greenville, N.C., 1984-87; U. Ala., Birmingham, 1987—. Bueleh Boyd scholar AAUW, 1979, Florence Hixson scholar, 1987-88. Contbg. author: Clinical Pharmacology and Nursing Textbook, 1988. Mem. Am. Nurses Assn., Ala. Nurses Assn., N.Am. Nursing Diagnosis Assn., West Liberty State Coll. Alumni Assn., Vanderbilt U. Alumni Assn., Vanderbilt U. Nurses Alumni Assn. Democrat. Roman Catholic. Clubs: Brenda Lee Fan. Contbr.: Adult Health Nursing Examination Review Book, 1984. Home: 518 Chalet Dr Birmingham AL 35209

O'LEARY MOORE, DONNA MARIE, radiation therapy technologist; b. Buffalo, Sept. 15, 1964; d. John Joseph and Ruth Marie (Mackey) O'L.; m. William Paul Moore, Sept. 26, 1987. AAS in Radiotherapy Option, Erie Community Coll., 1986. Radiation therapy technologist Finger Lakes Radiation Oncology, Clifton Springs, N.Y., 1986-87, Four County Radiation Oncology, Utica, N.Y., 1987—; assoc. Century 21 Advantage Real Estate Co., West Seneca, N.Y., 1988—. Author pamphlet: Radiation Therapy for Benign Bone Disorder, 1988.

OLEEN, MERRIKAY ADELLE, research epidemiologist, educator, pharmacist; b. Princeton, Minn., Oct. 30, 1949; d. Walter Burdette and Virginia Emelia (Carlson) O. BS in Pharmacy, N.D. State U., 1972, MS in Pharmacy, 1975; PhD in Social and Adminstrv. Pharmacy, U. Minn., 1985. Registered pharmacist, N.D., Minn. Pharmacist intern Mora (Minn.) Drug Co., 1972-73; pharmacy resident VA Med. Ctr., Fargo, N.D., 1973-75; asst. dir. clin.pharmacy services Brokaw Hosp., Normal, Ill., 1976-79; dir. drug info. Wash. State U., Pullman, 1979-81; Kellogg pharm. clin. scientist U. Minn., Mpls., 1981-84; research epidemiologist Upjohn Co., Kalamazoo, 1985—; adj. prof. epidemiology Coll. Health and Human Services, Western Mich. U., Kalamazoo, 1988—. Contbr. articles to profl. jours. Vol. CROP Walk, 1987-88, Planned Parenthood, 1986-87; recorder/bookkeeper organ fundraising com Prince of Peace Luth. Ch., Portage, Mich., 1987-88. Named Hosp. Pharmacist of Yr., Ill. Council Hosp. Pharmacists, 1979; Kellogg Found. fellow U. Minn., 1981-84. Mem. Am. Pub. Health Assn., Soc. Epidemiologic Research, Am. Pharm. Assn., Am. Soc. Hosp. Pharmacists, Drug Info. Assn., Indsl. Epidemiologists Forum (working group on reproductive outcomes 1987-88), LWV (sch. bd. observer Portage chpt. 1986-88). Lodge: Vasa. Home: 3762 Tartan Circle Portage MI 49081 Office: Upjohn Co 7000 Portage Rd Kalamazoo MI 49001

OLEN, BETTY ELIZABETH ANN, real estate broker; b. Pawtucket, R.I., Dec. 13, 1932; d. Albert Murray and Loretta (Pouliot) Goodrich; m. Milton William Olen, July 24, 1930 (div. May 1971); children: Milton William Jr., Floyd Stuart (dec.). Cert. in real estate, Realtors Inst., 1968. Salesperson Crowell & Co. Realtors, McLean, Va., 1964-71, Town & Country Properties, McLean, 1971-75; relocation dir. Town & Country Properties, Fairfax, Va., 1975-81; relocation and mktg. specialist Mount Vernon Realty, Alexandria, Va., 1981; salesperson Merrill Lynch Realty, Sarasota, Fla., 1982-85; owner, principal broker Mount Vernon Realty, Co. Inc., Sarasota, 1986—. Bd. dirs. Key Towers Condominium, Sarasota, 1985-87. Named Disting. Salesman, Sales and Mktg. Exec. Club, 1968, 69, 70, Salesman of Yr., No. Va. Bd. Realtors, 1974. Mem. Am. Womens Assn. (pres. Accra, Ghana, West Africa 1963), Women's Council Realtors, Sarasota Bd. Realtors, Million Dollas Assn., Sarasota C. of C. Republican. Roman Catholic. Office: Mount Vernon Realty Co Inc 3701 S Osprey Sarasota FL 34239

OLESEN, KAREN MARGRETHE, human services planner; b. Askov, Minn., Apr. 28, 1953; d. Wilford Clement and Ruth (Sorensen) O. BA in Psychology, U. Minn., 1979, MSW, 1985. Cert. work adjustment specialist. Work supr. Good Will Industries, Duluth, Minn., 1975-78, case mgr., 1978-84; grants administr. Arrowhead Regional Devel. Commn., Duluth, 1984-86, long term care project dir., 1986-87, sr. Options North project dir., 1986—; mem. Interagency Planning Council, Duluth, 1982—; bd. dirs. Assn. Retarded Citizens, Duluth, 1985—. Bd. dirs. CHUM Ch., Duluth, 1980-86; mem. Community Living Project, Duluth, 1982—; vol. docent Glensheen Mansion, Duluth, 1983—. Mem. Am. Soc. Aging, Nat. Assn. Social Workers, Phi Kappa Phi. Democrat. Lutheran. Clubs: Campaign for Real Ale; Northern Ale Stars. Home: 613 N 9th Ave E Duluth MN 55805 Office: Arrowhead Regional Devel Commn 330 Canal Park Dr Duluth MN 55802

OLIGNY, IRENE CECILIA FADER, telephone company executive; b. Roswell, N.Mex., Apr. 12, 1950; d. Justin Lindsey Fader and Alice Renee (Jacoby) Devlynd; m. Carl Joseph Olighy, Jan. 12, 1971 (div. Sept. 1984); children: Jason John, Eric Justin. AA, Hillsborough Community Coll., 1980. Buyer sports J.C. Penny Co., Tampa, Fla., 1968-69; fashion model Vantage Talent, Lakeland, Fla., 1968-73; operator Gen. Telephone Fla., Tampa, 1970, rep. customer service, 1971-74, service rep., 1974-76, service observer, 1976-77, supr. bus. office, 1977-78, mgr. phone mart, 1978-79, supr. spl. services, 1979-82, supr. bus. services, maintenance, 1982-85, sr. analyst service, 1985—; v.p., bd. dirs. Practical Applications, Tampa, 1980—; bd. dirs. MEGGA, Tampa. Bd. dirs. Spl. Olympics, Tampa, 1984—. Mem. Artists Alliance, Hyde Park Preservation Assn., Tampa Mus. Republican. Presbyterian. Clubs: Metro Action Civitan, Hyde Park Garden, Tampa Cycling. Home: 114 Targa Ct Tampa FL 33606 Office: Gen Telephone Fla Box 110 Tampa FL 33601

OLIN, LINDA FRAN, human resources executive; b. New Brunswick, N.J., Oct. 24, 1956; d. David Irwin and Nina (Segal) O. BA in Psychology, U. Md., 1978; MS in Indsl. Mgmt., Ga. Inst. Tech., 1980; JD, Ga. State U., 1987. Personnel rep. Lockheed-Aeronautical Systems Co.-Ga., Marietta, Ga., 1980-84, labor relations rep., 1984-86, labor relations arbitration coordinator, 1986-87, asst. to dir. human resources, 1987—. Mem. Indsl. Relations Research Assn., Phi Delta Phi, Phi Kappa Phi. Office: Lockheed Aeronautical Systems-Ga 86 S Cobbb Dr Dept 90-01 Marietta GA 30063

OLIPHANT, ERNIE L., safety educator, public relations executive, consultant; b. Richmond, Ind., Oct. 25, 1934; d. Ernest E. and Beulah A. (Jones) Reid; m. George B. Oliphant, Sept. 25, 1955; children—David, Wendell, Rebecca. Student, Earlham Coll., 1953-55, Ariz. State U., 1974, Phoenix Coll., 1974-78. Planner, organizer, moderator confs., programs for various women's clubs, safety assns., 1971-86; nat. field coordinator Operation Lifesaver, Inc., 1986—; assoc. dir. Operation Lifesaver Nat. Safety Council, Phoenix, 1978-86; cons. Fed. R.R. Adminstrn.; lectr. in field.; adviser Am. Ry. Engring. Assn., Calif. Assn. Women Hwy. Safety Leaders, numerous others. Mem. R.R./Hwy. grade crossing com. Ariz. Corp. Commn.; mem. transp. and system com. Ariz. Gov.'s Commn. on Environment; mem. Ariz. Gov.'s Council Women for Hwy. Safety; mem. motor vehicle traffic safety at hwy.-r.r. grade crossings com., roadway environment com., women's div. com. Nat. Safety Council; mem. Phoenix Traffic Accident Reduction Program; task force mem. U.S. Dept. Transp. on Grade Crossing Safety. Recipient Safety award SW Safety Congress, 1973; citation of Merit Adv. Commn. on Ariz. Environment, 1974; Gov.'s award for hwy. safety, 1978; Gov.'s Merit of Recognition Outstanding Service in Hwy. Safety, 1980. Mem. Assn. R.R. Editors, Nat. Assn. Female Execs., Inc., Pub. Relations Soc. Am., R.R. Pub. Relations Assn., committees Nat. Acad. Scis. (dir. transp. research, planning, adminstrn. of transp. safety com., r.r.-hwy. grade crossing safety com.), Women's Transp. Seminar, Ariz. Fedn. Women's Clubs (named pres. of yr. 1968), Ariz. Safety Assn. (safety recognition award 1975), Gen. Fedn. Women's Clubs (internat. bd. dirs.), Nat. Assn. Women Hwy. Safety Leaders, Phi Theta Kappa. Republican. Quaker. Author of tech. publs.

OLIVA, MARTHA ELOISA, health facility administrator; b. Havana, Cuba, Apr. 25, 1931; came to U.S., 1971, naturalized, 1977; d. Rafael E. and Serafina J. (Arguelles) O.; m. Ofelio P. Gutierrez, May 4, 1958 (div. Dec. 1964); 1 child, Ricardo (dec.). BS, Marianao Inst., Havana, 1950; CPA, Havana U., 1960. Accredited record technician, Fla.; cert. tumor registrar, 1983. Gen. mgr. hosp. div. Nat. Health & Welfare Ministry, Havana, 1960-62; dir. med. records U. Havana Teaching Hosp., 1962-65, assoc. prof. Sch. Nurses, 1963-65; supr. acctg. dept. Chem. Lab. Corp./Lederle Labs., Miami, Fla., 1972-74; supr. profl. activities system-mgmt. assistance program Jackson Meml. Hosp., Miami, Fla., 1974-76, supr. tumor registry, 1976-77, sr. tumor registrar, 1977-86; coordinator cancer program League Against Cancer, Inc., Miami, 1983—, adminstr., 1984—; cons. cancer program ACS, Chgo., 1981—. Author: (biography) Carlos J. Finlay, M.D., 1949 (Bronze medal 1949). Recipient diploma Instituto de Raices Cubanas, 1986. Mem. Nat. Tumor Registrars Assn. (treas. 1988—), Fla. Tumor Registrars Assn. (treas. 1980-82, chair membership com. 1982-84, pres. 1985-86, diploma 1980, 84, 85), Nat. Assn. for Female Execs., Nat. Com. to Preserve Social Security, Coalition Hispanic Am. Women. Republican. Roman Catholic. Office: League Against Cancer Inc 1895 SW 3d Ave Miami FL 33129

OLIVARIUS-IMLAH, MARY PAT, sales/advertising/marketing executive; b. Bklyn., Oct. 25, 1957; d. Kenneth William Joseph and Ann Marie (Beckley) Olivarius; m. Craig Alexander Olivarius-Imlah, Sept. 18, 1982; 1 child, Christopher Edward. BS in Mktg. and Communications, Ramapo State Coll. N.J., 1979; MBA in Mktg. and Mgmt., Fairleigh Dickinson U., 1985. Researcher, pub. relations MacNeil/Lehrer Report, WNET TV, N.Y.C., 1977; salesperson Terrace Realty, Montvale, N.J., 1977-79; direct mail advt. copywriter Prentice-Hall, Inc., Englewood Cliffs, N.J., 1979-81; editor, promotional designer Beauty & Barber Supply Inst., Englewood, N.J., 1981-83; nat. dir. advt. and pub. relations Emerson Radio Corp., North Bergen, N.J., 1983-85; founder, pres. Imagery Advt., Print Brokerage, Hinesburg, Vt., 1985—; bd. dirs. Chittenden County Ct. Diversion Program. Mem. Nat. Assn. Female Execs. Democrat. Roman Catholic. Office: Beecher Hill Rd Hinesburg VT 05461

OLIVARRI, LEAH PAGAN, management consultant; b. Houston, June 13, 1951; d. John Shaw and Shirley (Andrew) Pagan; m. George Placido Olivarri, Nov. 28, 1975. BA magna cum laude, Mt. Holyoke Coll., 1973; MA, U. Tex., 1976, postgrad., 1977-79. Project mgr., research asst. RPC, Inc., Austin, Tex., 1976-79; analyst City of Corpus Christi, Tex., 1980-81, asst. to city mgr., 1981-84, dir. adminstrv. services, 1984-86; prin. Wolfe and Assocs., Albuquerque, 1986; owner, operator Olivarri and Assocs., Corpus Christi, 1987—; v.p. Money Mgmt., Inc., Corpus Christi, 1983-86. Contbr. articles to profl. jours. Pres. Nueces County Child Welfare Bd., Corpus Christi, 1981-85; co-chair City of Corpus Christi United Way Campaign, 1982; mem. Leadership Corpus Christi, 1983, Tex. Productivity Com., Austin, 1984-86. Mem. Mt. Holyoke Alumni (rep. Tex. alumni 1982-87). Club: Am. Contract Bridge League. Home: 4934 High Meadow Corpus Christi TX 78413 Office: Olivarri and Assocs PO Box 271096 Corpus Christi TX 78427

OLIVE, AGNES W., director city literacy council; b. Havana, Ark., Mar. 22, 1919; d. George Washington and Ada Frances (Wasson) Weatherhall; m. Wiley Robert Olive (dec. Dec. 1977); children: Wiley Robert Olive Jr., Beverly Olive Payne. Student, Oklahoma City U., 1965-68. Asst. banking supr. Kerr-McGee Corp., Oklahoma City, 1953-74; literacy cons., coordinator Okla. Dept. Libraries, Dept. Edn., Oklahoma City, 1985-87; dir. Oklahoma City Literacy Council, 1987—; chmn. tng. program Oklahoma City Literacy Council, 1981-84; state rep., chmn. laubach tng. S. Cen. Literacy Action, Fayette, Ark., 1985—; dir. Okla. Literacy Coalition. Chmn. 5th dist. pres. Reagan's re-election campaign, Okla., 1984; founder Okla. Opera and Mus. Comedy Found. Soc., 1983. Recipient Award of Honor Sta. KOCO-TV, 1984, Legis. Citation award State of Okla., 1986, Assoc. Literacy award Am. Library Trustee Assn., 1987, Citizen Recognition award Okla. Library Assn., 1987. Mem. Laubach Literacy Action (named Nat. Trainer of Yr.). Republican. Baptist. Club: Zonta. Home: #10 Lytle Dr Oklahoma City OK 73127 Office: Oklahoma City Literacy Council 131 Dean A McGee Ave Oklahoma City OK 73102

OLIVE, SUSAN FREYA, lawyer; b. Durham, N.C., June 26, 1952; d. B.B. and Denyse L.A. (Edwards) O.; m. Richard Anthony Rall, June 28, 1980; children: Erin Alyssa, Park Anthony, Ashley Erica. A.B. in Med.-Legal Interface, Brown U., 1974; J.D. with distinction, Duke U., 1977. Bar: N.C.

1976, U.S. Ct. Mil. Appeals 1976, U.S. Dist. Ct. (ea. and mid. dists.) N.C. 1977, U.S. Dist. Ct. (we. dist.) N.C. 1984. Sole practice Durham, N.C., 1976-77; spl. counsel 9th Jud. Dist., Butner, N.C., 1977-79; ptnr. Olive, Faust & Olive, Durham, 1979-80; ptnr. Olive & Olive, P.A., Durham, 1980-86, v.p., 1986—; regional chmn. Brown U. Nat. Alumni Schs. Program, Central N.C., 1977—; guest lectr. Duke U. Sch. Law, Durham, 1982—, supervising atty. trial advocacy clinic outplacement, 1982-83, participant supervising atty., 1982—; guest lectr. N.C. Sch. Sci. and Math., Durham, 1983—; lectr. continuing legal edn. program N.C. Bar Found., Raleigh, 1983, 85-87; mem. N.C. Fed. Bar Adv. Council, 1984—, sec., 1984-87; mem. merit selection panel U.S. Dist. Ct. (mid. dist.) N.C., 1984, mem. atty. qualifications rev. com., 1984—; mem. research com. for ct. annexed arbitration U.S. Dist. Ct. (mid. dist.) N.C., 1985-87; presenter various workshops. Author: Brief Introduction to Trademarks and Copyrights, Copyright Basics for the General Practitioner; editor: The Durham Docket newsletter, 1977-83, Reference Guide for Area Mental Health, Mental Retardation and Substance Abuse Board Members in North Carolina, 1980. Bd. dirs. Mental Health Assn. Durham County, 1979-83, chmn. legis. com., 1980-82; bd. dirs. N.C. Prisoners' Legal Services, Inc., Raleigh, 1980—; fin. dir. Knox 1984 Gubernatorial Campaign, Durham County, 1984. Mem. N.C. Coll. Advocacy, N.C. Bar Found., Durham County Bar Assn. (sec. 1981-82, pres. 1983-84), 14th Jud. Dist. Bar (pres. 1983-84), N.C. Bar Assn. (patent, trademark and copyright law sect. 1983—, sect. sci. and tech. 1983—, anti-trust sect. 1984—, econs. of law practice 1985—, rep. to Dorothea Dix Hosp. med.-legal adv. com. 1980-84, chmn. com. on mental health law 1982-84, nominations com. 1983-84, intellectual property law com. 1984—, bar ctr. steering com. 1987, forum com. on franchising 1987—), Carolina Patent, Trademark and Copyright Law Assn., N.C. Acad. Trial Lawyers (lectr. continuing legal edn. program 1983), N.C. Assn. Women Attys., ABA (patent, trademark and copyright law sect., sect. of sci. and tech., forum com. on franchising 1984—, anti-trust sect., econs. of law practice), Am. Soc. Law and Medicine, Assn. Trial Lawyers Am., Fed. Cir. Bar Assn. Democrat. Episcopalian. Home: PO Box 2049 Durham NC 27702 Office: Olive & Olive PA 500 Memorial St PO Box 2049 Durham NC 27702

OLIVER, BETH MARIE, insurance specialist; b. Ottawa, Ill., Apr. 6, 1957; d. James Edward Oliver and Mary Lorraine (McNamara) Panter. AA in Liberal Arts, Ill. Valley Community Coll., 1977; BA in Creative Arts, Coll. St. Francis, 1981. With Profl. Med. Supply Co., Joliet, Ill., 1981-82; processor ins. claims St. Margaret's Hosp., Spring Valley, Ill., 1982—; asst. dir. Joliet Drama Guild, 1981-82. Producer Halloweenfest, Joliet, 1981. Vol. Rialto Sq. Theatre, Joliet, 1981-82; bd. dirs. Theatre Ctr. for Arts Coll. St. Francis, Joliet, 1982; mem. precinct com. Rep. Bur. County Cen. Com., Spring Valley, 1986-87. Named Outstanding Local Dir. Ill. Jaycees. Mem. Nat. Assn. Female Execs., Spring Valley Jaycees (bd. dirs. 1987—, Jaycees of Month 1987, merit award 1987), Mensa, Phi Rho Pi. Roman Catholic. Home: 403 E First Apt B Spring Valley IL 61362

OLIVER, BONNIE BONDURANT, educational telecommunications company executive, consultant; b. St. Louis, Jan. 25, 1933; d. Benjamin Burns and Florence Mary (Spencer) Bondurant; m. Donald Edgar Wiese, June 19, 1954 (div. 1972); children: Kurt Rowland, Martha Jill Wiese Reid; m. Raymond Elliott Oliver, Dec. 8, 1972. BA, Monmouth Coll., Ill., 1954; MA, U. Mo., 1957; postgrad. U. Calif., Irvine, 1963-65. Lic. tchr., Calif.; lic. in ednl. adminstrn. Sci. TV tchr. Santa Ana Schs., Calif., 1966-70; dir. dist. media Santa Ana Unified Schs., 1970-72; adminstr. Regional Ednl. TV, Downey, Calif., 1973-78; mgr. edn. tech. unit Calif. Dept. Edn., Sacramento, 1978-81; dep. dir. Calif. Pub. Broadcasting Commn., Sacramento, 1981-83; pres. Oliver and Co., Los Angeles, 1983—; project dir. Sta. KCET-TV, Los Angeles; dir. Pub. Service Satellite Consort, Washington; cons. Calif. Dept. Edn., Sacramento, Ky. Ednl. TV, Lexington; mem. Los Angeles County, Los Angeles Pub. Library Adult Reading Project Coucnil. Recipient Achievement Commendation City of Los Angeles, 1987. Contbr. articles to popular mags. Mem. friends com. Orange Commn. on Status of Women, Santa Ana, 1976, Los Angeles Southwest Coll. Literacy Council, Friends com. Coro Found.; chmn. adv. com. Internat. Childrens TV, Washington, 1979; trustee Stanford Home for Children, Sacramento, 1980-84. C-Span Cable Network fellow, Washington, 1980; recipient Susan B. Anthony Communications award Hollywood chpt. Bus. and Profl. Women, 1987. Mem. Acad. TV Arts and Sci., Calif. Media Library Edn. Assn., Am. Mgmt. Assn., Kappa Kappa Gamma Alunae Assn. Republican. Avocation: running. Home: 1309 W Bay Ave Newport Beach CA 92661 Office: Oliver and Co 1005 Dodson San Pedro CA 90732

OLIVER, BONNIE KLISCZ, mortgage company executive; b. West Bend, Wis., June 24, 1944; d. Edwin Leslie and Helen Louise (Schuppel) Ahlers; m. Anthony W. Kliscz, July 17, 1962 (div. Dec. 1982); children: Todd Anthony, Terry John; m. Wayne Darrell, Feb. 28, 1985. Grad., Realtors Inst. Cert. realtor, Wis., Minn. Reporter, writer Fremont (Nebr.) Tribune, 1970; real estate salesperson Gerrard Realty, La Crosse, Wis., 1971-74; loan officer No. Fed. Savs. & Loan, St. Paul, 1974-75; real estate salesperson Gerrard Realty & The Wheeler Co., La Crosse, 1975-82; regional loan originator Norwest Mortgage Corp., Madison, Wis., 1983; mortgage loan specialist Mortgage Options, La Crosse, 1983-85, pres., 1985—; company rep. Greater La Crosse C. of C., 1983-87. Mem. Greater La Crosse Bd. Realtors, Nat. Assn. Realtors, Wis. Realtors, Assn., La Crosse Area Home Builders Assn. Democrat. Lutheran. Home: 522 S 23d St La Crosse WI 54601 Office: Mortgage Options La Crosse 505 King St La Crosse WI 54601

OLIVER, FLORENCE DURHAM, educator; b. Balt., June 8, 1934; d. Watt Thomas and Emmer Serena (Hooker) Durham; m. John Currie Oliver; children: John Currie II, Joel Cedric, Jonica Cheryl, Javon Cory, Jeffrey C. BS, Coppin State Coll., Balt., 1961. Cert. tchr., Ill. Elem. tchr. Balt. City Pub. Schs., 1961-65; English tchr. United Christian Coll., Balt., 1962-65; elem. tchr. Alton (Ill.) Dist. 11, 1966-78; ednl. coordinator Madison County Head Start Program, Alton, 1980-81; tchr. Venice (Ill.) Head Start, 1985—. Mem. Ill. Head Start and Day Care Assn. Democrat. Baptist. Home: 607 St Peter Dr Godfrey IL 62035

OLIVER, JIMANN SMITH, educator; b. Ardmore, Okla., Feb. 12, 1934; d. Jim W. and Isabel (Foster) Smith; m. Estil H. Oliver, Dec. 20, 1953; children: Angela, Kelton, Retha, Lisa, Lanette. BA, Ill. State U., 1954; MEd, Okla. U., 1961. Tchr. mentally handicapped and learning disabled Okla. and Tex. pub. schs., 1954-75; child guidance specialist Okla. State Dept. Health, Norman, 1976-82; tchr. of gifted Washington (Okla.) Pub. Schs., 1982-85, Moore (Okla.) Pub. Schs., 1985—; instr. Hillsdale Freewill Bapt. Coll., Moore, 1974, 75; coordinator Moore Olympics of the Mind, 1985—; instr., coach winners of speech and essay contests, 1984. Mem. NEA, Okla. Edn. Assn. (past local pres., sec., other offices), Moore Classroom Tchrs. Assn., Okla. Assn. for Gifted and Talented., AAUW, Mensa. Unitarian. Home: Rt 2 Box 138 Purcell OK 73080 Office: Moore Search 2016 Regency Blvd Moore OK 73160

OLIVER, JOYCE ANNE, journalist, editorial consultant; b. Coral Gables, Fla., Sept. 19, 1958; d. John Joseph and Rosalie Cecile (Mack) O. BA in Communications, Calif. State U., Fullerton, 1980, postgrad. sch. mgmt., 1988. Corp. editor Norris Industries Inc., Huntington Beach, Calif., 1979-82; pres. J.A. Oliver Assocs., La Habra Heights, Calif., 1982—; corp. editorial cons. ALS Corp., Anaheim, Calif., 1985, Gen. Power Systems, Anaheim, 1985, MacroMarketing, Costa Mesa, Calif., 1985-86, PM Software, Huntington Beach, Calif., 1985-86, CompuQuote, Canoga Park, Calif., 1985-86, Nat. Semicondr. Can. Ltd., Mississauga, Ont., Can., 1986, Frame Inc., Fullerton, Calif., 1987-88, The Johnson-Layton Co., Los Angeles, 1988; mem. Research Council of Scripps Clinic and Research Found., 1987-88. Contbr. to Cleve. Inst. Electronics publ. The Electron, 1986-88; contbg. editor Computer Dealer mag., 1987-88; also contbr. to Can. Electronics Engrng. Mag., PC Week, The NOMDA Spokesman, Entrepreneur, Adminstrv. Mgmt., High-Tech Selling, Video Systems, Tech. Photography, Computing Canada, and Stores. Mem. Internat. Platform Assn., IEEE, Soc. Photo-Optical Instrumentation Engrs., Inst. Mgmt. Scis., Nat. Writers Club (profl.), Sigma Delta Chi/Soc. Profl. Journalists. Republican. Roman Catholic. Office: 2045 Fullerton Rd La Habra Heights CA 90631

OLIVER, MARGUERITE BERTONI, food service executive; b. Ann Arbor, Mich., June 5, 1929; d. Ralph Angelo and Margaret Amelia (Rovegno) Bertoni; m. William John Oliver, May 28, 1949; children: R. Scott, Catherine Oliver Allen, Susan M. Mgr. complaint dept. Sears Roebuck Co., Ann Arbor, 1949-50; dir. meals-on-wheels program U. Mich. Hosp., Ann Arbor, 1974-76; fund raiser U. Mich. Art Sch., Ann Arbor, 1976-80; founder Pastabilities, Ann Arbor, 1980—; participant, speaker Midwest Assn. State Depts. Agr., 1987; mem. adv. com. Gov.'s Conf. on Future of Mich. Agr., 1988. Mem. com. on aging Ann Arbor Council, 1970-74; bd. dirs. Hands-On-Mus., Ann Arbor, 1980-82; mem. mkt. commn. Ann Arbor, 1982—; founded Internat. Neighbors. Recipient Washtenaw Community Service award Washtenaw Community Coll., 1985. Democrat. Roman Catholic. Club: Women's City. Home: 2892 Bay Ridge Dr Ann Arbor MI 48103 Office: Pastabilities 212 E Kingsley St Ann Arbor MI 48104

OLIVER, MARLYS MAE, editor, writer; b. St. Paul, Mar. 23, 1930; d. Earle R. and Margaret A. (Parrott) Benner; m. Alfred Leo Oliver, Apr. 28, 1951; children—Stephanie Margaret, David Earle. A.A., Lakewood Community Coll., 1970; student Metro State U., 1976-77. Graphic artist Lakewood Community Coll., White Bear Lake, Minn., 1968-70; corr. Women Sports mag., N.Y.C., 1973-77; editor Press Publs., White Bear Lake, 1972-76; mng. editor Frogtown Forum, St. Paul, 1976-77; mayor City of Birchwood, Minn., 1977-83; editor Press Publs., White Bear Lake, 1982—; pres., dir. Cable Access Corp. Mem. White Bear Lake Arts Council, dir., 1975; bd. dirs. Lakeshore Players, 1984-85; chmn Ramsey Washington Counties Cable TV Commn. Recipient numerous awards in journalism. Mem. Minn. Newspaper Assn., Nat. Newspaper Assn., Minn. Press Women (past treas.), Suburban Newspaper Assn., Midwest Writers Conf (com.) Mem. Democratic Farm Labor Party. Lodge: Job's Daus. (Queen 1949). Contbr. numerous articles and poems to popular mags. Home: 139 Birchwood Ave Birchwood Village MN 55110 Office: Press Publs 4779 Bloom Ave White Bear Lake MN 55110

OLIVER, MARY, poet; b. Maple Heights, Ohio, Sept. 10, 1935; d. Edward William and Helen Mary (Vlasak) O. Student, Ohio State U., 1955-56, Vassar Coll., 1956-57. Chmn. writing dept. Fine Arts Work Ctr., Provincetown, 1972-73, mem. writing com., 1984; Mather vis. prof. Case-Western Res. U., Cleve., 1980, 82; vis. poet-in-residence Bucknell U., 1986; Elliston poet-in residence U. Cin., 1986. Author: No Voyage and Other Poems, 1963, enlarged edit., 1965, The River Styx, Ohio, 1972, The Night Traveler, 1978, Twelve Moons, 1979, American Primitive, 1983, Dream Work, 1986; contbr. to Yale Rev., Kenyon Rev., Poetry, Atlantic, Harvard Mag., others. Recipient Shelley Meml. award, 1970, Alice Fay di Castagnola award, 1973; Cleve. Arts prize for lit., 1979; Achievement award Am. Acad. and Inst. Arts and Letters, 1983; Pulitzer prize for poetry, 1984; Nat. Endowment fellow, 1972-73; Guggenheim fellow, 1980-81. Mem. Poetry Soc. Am., PEN. Home: care Molly Malone Cook Lit Agy Box 338 Provincetown MA 02657

OLIVER, MARY ANN URSO, lawyer; b. Tampa, Fla., Aug. 25, 1948; d. Philip and Mary (Frisco) Urso; B.A. magna cum laude, U. Mass., 1970; J.D., Boston Coll., 1973; m. Richard Allen Oliver, May 23, 1972; children—Edward Raymond, Robert Philip. Admitted to D.C. bar, 1973, Va. bar, 1975, U.S. Supreme Ct. bar, 1980; atty. electric and telephone div. U.S. Dept. Agr., Washington, 1973-77; atty. SEC, Washington, 1977-80, dep. asst. dir. div. corp. regulation, 1980-84; ptnr. Oliver & Oliver, P.C., Washington, 1984—. Mem. Am. Bar Assn., D.C. Bar Assn., Boston Coll. Alumni Assn., Phi Beta Kappa, Phi Kappa Phi. Office: 1300 New York Ave NW Suite 200 E Washington DC 20005

OLIVER, MARY WILHELMINA, law librarian, educator; b. Cumberland, Md., May 4, 1919; d. John Arlington and Sophia (Lear) O. A.B., Western Md. Coll., 1940; B.S. in Library Sci, Drexel Inst. Tech., 1943; J.D., U. N.C., 1951. Bar: N.C. 1951. Asst. circulation librarian N.J. Coll. Women, 1943-45; asst. in law library U. Va., 1945-47; asst. reference, social sci. librarian Drake U., 1947-49; research asst. Inst. Govt., U. N.C., 1951-52, asst. law librarian, 1952-55, asst. prof. law, law librarian, 1955-59, asso. prof. law, law librarian, 1959-69, prof. law, law librarian, 1969-84, prof. law and law librarian emeritus, 1984—. Mem. ABA, N.C. Bar Assn., Assn. Am. Law Schs. (exec. com. 1979-81), Law Alumni Assn. U. N.C., Order of Coif. Home: Box 733 Chapel Hill NC 27514 Office: U NC Law Library PO Box 733 Chapel Hill NC 27514

OLIVER, RENATE MENCK, management consultant; b. Luebz, German Democratic Republic, Sept. 4, 1938; came to U.S., 1958; d. Werner Johann Menck and Freifrau Margret (Huffelmann) von Dunern; m. H. Edward Oliver, Aug. 12, 1959 (div. 1963); m. Stanley E. Polchlopek, May 4, 1964 (div.); children: Robina Oliver, Walter M., Lester J.; m. William T. Olmstead, June 1, 1984. AA in Early Childhood Edn. with highest honors, Norwalk (Conn.) Community Coll., 1973; BA in Psychology magna cum laude, Western Conn. State Coll., 1975; MEd in Community Devel., Springfield (Mass.) Coll., 1976. Tchr. Wilton (Conn.) Woods Nursery Sch., 1972-74; camp dir. Wilton Family YMCA, 1973-75; asst. dir. YWCA, Springfield, 1976; program dir. ARC, Springfield, 1976-77, field rep. blood services, 1977-80; dir. non-credit div. Western New Eng. Coll., Springfield, 1980-85; free-lance mgmt. tng. specialist Springfield, 1985—. 2d v.p. Child & Family Service, Springfield, 1984; bd. dirs. VNA Div., Springfield, 1985; corporator, chair new initiatives com. United Way Pioneer Valley, Springfield, 1986; cert. vol. mediator Springfield Dispute Resolution Project, 1984—. Recipient Leadership award NOW, 1985. Mem. Am. Soc. for Tng. and Devel. (pres. Pioneer Valley chpt. 1986—, Oustanding Service award 1984, 85, 86), Women Bus. Owners Alliance of Pioneer Valley (pres. 1986—). Democrat. Lodge: Zonta (chair leadership devel. Springfield chpt. 1985—, bd. dirs. 1986—). Home and Office: 59 Chapin Rd Hampden MA 01036

OLIVERIO, MARY ELLEN, accounting educator; b. Fairmont, W.Va., Jan. 17, 1926; d. Luigi and Elizabeth C. (LaCova) O.; m. Bernard H. Newman, Dec. 26, 1964. AB, BS, Fairmont State Coll., 1947; MA, Columbia U., 1949, PhD, 1954. CPA, N.Y. Instr. Marshall U. (formerly Marshall Coll.), Huntington, W.Va., 1949-51; from asst. prof. to prof. bus. tchr. edn. and econs. Tchr.'s Coll. of Columbia U., N.Y.C., 1954-73; acct. Deloitte, Haskins & Sells, N.Y.C., 1979-80; prof. acctg. Pace U., N.Y.C., 1980—; lectr. bus. and edn. groups. Author: The Office: Technology and Procedures, 1987, numerous other high sch. edn. books; contbr. articles to profl. jours. Mem. Am. Acctg., Nat. Assn. Accts., Am. Inst. CPA's, N.Y. State Soc. CPA's, Nat. Bus. Edn. Assn. Office: Pace U Grad Sch Pace Plaza New York NY 10038

OLIVETI, SUSAN GAIL, sales promotion and public relations executive; b. Bklyn., Nov. 1, 1938; d. Peter and Nancy Jane (Wolk) Randolph; m. Fosco Anthony Oliveti, Sept. 18, 1970; children by previous marriage—Lois, Peter, Elizabeth Ruben. Student CCNY, 1956-58, NYU, 1965-69; R.N., Jewish Hosp. Sch. Nursing, 1958. Estimator, media research Ogilvy & Mather, N.Y.C., 1966-68; TV rep. Adam Young, Inc., N.Y.C., 1968-69; exec. asst. Paramount Pictures, N.Y.C., 1969-80; mgr. conv. and media events Warner Amex Satellite Enterprise Co., N.Y.C., 1980-83; exhibits specialist Siemens Med. Systems, Iselin, N.J., 1984-86; meetings mgr. U.S. Trademark Assn., N.Y.C., 1985-87; v.p. corp. communications J.R. Heimbaugh, Inc., 1986-87; mgr. sales promotions, pub. relations meetings, convs. Lightolier, Inc., Secaucus, N.J., 1988— . Recipient spl. honors United Airlines, 1978. Mem. Meeting Planners Internat. (reception com., edn. com.), Women in Cable, Nat. Cable TV Assn. (meeting planner 1980-88), N.J. Travel and Conf. Mgrs. Assn. Office: Lightolier Inc 100 Lighting Way Secaucus NJ 07094

OLMAN, MARYELLEN, human resources administrator; b. Grand Rapids, Mich., Dec. 24, 1946; d. Norman Adolph and Mary Irene (McCarthy) Olman; m. Richard Isaac Fine, Nov. 25, 1982; 1 child, Victoria Elizabeth. B.A. in Community Service, Mich. State U., 1968. Legis. researcher Hon. Gerald R. Ford, U.S. Ho. of Reps., 1969-71; spl. asst. Hon. Jack F. Kemp, U.S. Ho. of Reps., 1971-74; personnel analyst Los Angeles City Housing Authority, 1975-78; profl. placement rep. Gen. Telephone of Calif., Santa Monica, 1978-81, mgmt. staffing adminstr., 1981-84. Mem. Los Angeles Internat. Visitors Assn., 1982—; mem. founders circle Los Angeles Music Ctr. Mem. Am. Soc. Personnel Adminstrs., Coll. Placement Council, Western Coll. Placement Assn., Personnel and Indsl. Relations Assn. Republican. Home: 5331 Horizon Dr Malibu CA 90265

OLMEDO-BORECKY, STEPHANIE KATHRYN, air force officer; b. Denver, Jan. 16, 1950; d. Juanita (Morales) Putnam; m. Steven John Borecky, Sept. 23, 1978; children: Kittrick John, Kyle Stephen. M.A., U. No. Colo., 1979. Tchr. of deaf Amoskeege Sc. Dist., Claremont, N.H., 1973, Gov. Baxter Sch. for Deaf, Falmouth, Maine, 1973-75, Pueblo Sch. Dist., Colo., 1975-77; commd. 2d lt. U.S. Air Force, 1981, advanced through grades to capt., 1985; exec. support officer Ellsworth AFB, S.D., 1981-85, Dyess AFB, Tex., 1985—. Mem. Air Force Assn., Nat. Assn. Female Execs. Roman Catholic. Home: 2957 Stonecrest Dr Abilene TX 79606 Office: 96 Combat Support Group Dyess AFB TX 79607

OLMSTEAD, DIANE DULUDE, nurse, child birth educator; b. St. Albans, Vt., Aug. 31, 1956; d. Philip Charles and Beatrice J. (Desranleau) Dulude; m. Michael John Olmstead, Aug. 20, 1977; children: Michael J. II, Nicholas Charles. Student, Fanny Allen Sch. of Practiced Nursing, 1975; AS in Nursing, U. Vt., 1978, postgrad. in health edn., Johnson State Coll., 1984—. RN, Vt. Lic. practical nurse Kerbs Meml. Hosp., St. Albans, 1975-76; staff registered nurse obstetrics Northwestern Med. Ctr., St. Albans, 1978-81, relief charge nurse obstetrics, 1981-87, charge nurse ambulatory care unit, 1987—; educator child birth Franklin County Home Health, St. Albans, 1979—. Democrat. Roman Catholic. Home: 114 High St Saint Albans VT 05478 Office: Northwestern Med Ctr Fairfield St Saint Albans VT 05478

OLMSTEAD, KAREN JO, nurse; b. Port Angeles, Wash., Jan. 4, 1951; d. George Herman Jr. and Joanna (Jordan) Schoenfeldt; b. Cecil Wayne Olmstead, Dec. 20, 1967; children—Wayne Thomas, Justina Jo. A.A., 1981, A.A.S., 1982, BA in Psychology, 1988, R.N., 1982. Cert. psychiat. nurse, 1986. Group counselor Family Resource Ctr., Port Angeles, 1975-80; nurse aide Olympic Meml. Hosp., Port Angeles, 1980-81, L.P.N., 1981-82, R.N., 1982—, charge nurse psychiat. detox unit, 1984—. Parent aide Exchange Club Ctr. for Prevention of Child Abuse, Port Angeles; active Wash. Assn. County Child Abuse Councils, Seattle; founder, pres. Clallam County Parent Adv. Council for Learning Disabilities, 1984—. Recipient Most Improved Family in Entire Western Region award Exchange Club Ctr. Prevention Child Abuse, 1985. Mem. Wash. Nurses Assn., Am. Nurses Assn. Avocations: raising and riding horses; reading; crocheting; aerobics. Home: 915 Scrivner Rd Port Angeles WA 98362 Office: Olympic Meml Hosp 939 Caroline St Port Angeles WA 98362

OLMSTEAD, MARJORIE ANN, physics educator; b. Glen Ridge, N.J., Aug. 18, 1958; d. Blair E. and Elizabeth (Dempwolf) O. BA in Physics, Swarthmore Coll., 1979; MA in Physics, U. Calif., 1982, PhD, 1985. With research staff Palo Alto (Calif.) Research Ctr. Xerox Corp., 1985-86; asst. prof. Physics Dept. Physics U. Calif., Berkeley, 1986—; mem. exec. com. SSRL User's Orgn., Stanford, Calif., 1986—, chair-elect exec. com. 1987—. Contbr. articles to profl. jours. Named Presdl. Young Investigator, Nat. Sci. Found., 1987; recipient Devel. awards IBM, 1986, 87. Mem. Am. Phys. Soc., Am. Vacuum Soc., Materials Research Soc., Assn. Women in Sci., Phi Beta Kappa, Sigma Xi. Office: U Calif Dept Physics Berkeley CA 94720

OLMSTEAD, SUSAN ANN, real estate development company executive; b. Caribou, Maine, Nov. 2, 1950; d. Lawrence R. and Fern (Bushey) Guerrette; m. Dale C. Olmstead, Jr., June 22, 1968; 1 child, Craig A. ABS in Acctg., No. Maine Vocat. Tech. Inst., 1975; BS in Acctg., Husson Coll., 1977. CPA. Sr. acct. Brooks and Carter CPA's, Caribou, 1977-82; acctg. mgr. Fox and Bowden CPA's, Freeport, Maine, 1982-83; retail acctg. mgr. Emery Waterhouse, Portland, Maine, 1983-84; treas. The Dartmouth Co., Portland, Maine, 1984—. Vol. United Way Am., Presque Isle, Maine, 1977-82, Caribou Youth Orgn., 1970-73; treas. Cubscouts Am., Holden, Maine, 1975-77. Named Outstanding Vol. United Way Aroostook, Maine, 1980-81. Mem. Maine Soc. CPA's, Am. Inst. CPA's, Acctg. Soc. (v.p. 1975-77). Club: Presdl. Guide. Home: PO Box 29 Freeport ME 04032

OLMSTED, MARY SEYMOUR, foreign service officer; b. Duluth, Minn., Sept. 28, 1919; d. George Chauncey and Zadia Sarah (McDonald) O.; A.B., Mt. Holyoke Coll., South Hadley, Mass., 1941; M.A., Columbia U., 1945; postgrad. Fletcher Sch. Law and Diplomacy, Medford, Mass., 1955-56. Fgn. service officer U.S. Dept. State, 1945-79, dep. dir. personnel, Washington, 1971-74, ambassador, Port Moresby, Papua New Guinea, 1975-79. Co-author: (research pamphlet) Women At State, 1984. Recipient Herter award U.S. Dept. State, 1972, Superior Honor award, 1973. Mem. Soc. Women Geographers, Sr. Seminar Alumni Assn. (treas. 1983-84, pres. 1987—), UN Assn. (dir. capitol area div.). Democrat. Episcopalian.

OLNESS, DOLORES URQUIZA, physicist; b. Kingsport, Tenn., Mar. 20, 1935; d. Manuel Alvarez and Josephine (Wyrick) Urquiza; m. Robert J. Olness, June 17, 1957; children: James M., Gwen E., Michael F. AB, Duke U., 1957, PhD, 1961. Research assoc. Duke U., Durham, N.C., 1961, U. N.C., Chapel Hill, 1961-63; physicist U. Calif. Lawrence Livermore (Calif.) Nat. Lab., 1963-67, 74—, cons., 1967-68. Contbr. articles to profl. jours. Mem. various coms. Livermore Unified Sch. Dist., 1970—. Mem. AAUW, LWV, Am. Phys. Soc. Lutheran. Home: 4345 Guilford Ave Livermore CA 94550 Office: U Calif Lawrence Livermore Nat Lab PO Box 808 Livermore CA 94550

OLSEN, BARBARA ELLEN, medical clinic administrator; b. Paterson, N.J., July 24, 1936; d. Paul Bernhard and Helen Louise (WEmlinger) Eiden; m. Robert Stephen Walz, May 28, 1955 (div. Nov. 1963); children: Robert Stephen Jr., Paul Edward; m. Dwight Harold Olsen, Feb. 20, 1965; 1 child, Eric Dwight. Student, Bismarck Jr. Coll., 1954-55. Exec. sec. Consol. Oil and Gas Inc., Denver, 1962-66; advt. mgr. Allmand Bros. Inc., Holdrege, Nebr., 1978-81; sales dir. Mary Kay Cosmetics, Dallas, 1981-84; office mgr. H. Dale Sostad and Assocs., Holdrege, 1984-85; bus. mgr. Kearney Orthopedic and Fracture Clinic, Kearney, Nebr., 1985—. Mem. Med. Group Mgmt. Assn., Nat. Assn. Female Execs., Bus. and Profl. Women. Republican. Mem. Evang. Free Ch. Am. Club: Christian Women's (advisor 1982-84). Home: 4203 Pony Express Rd Kearney NE 68847 Office: Kearney Orthopedic and Fracture Clinic 123 W 31st St Box 2168 Kearney NE 68848

OLSEN, INGER ANNA, psychologist; b. Copper Mountain, B.C, Can., Dec. 25, 1926; d. Dagmar O.; B.S., Wash. State U., 1954, M.S., 1956, Ph.D., 1962. Psychiat. nurse Provincial Mental Health Services B.C., 1947-51, psychologist, 1956-58; psychologist Vancouver (B.C.) City Met. Health Services, 1958-60, Wash. State U. Student Counseling Center, Pullman, 1960-62; sr. psychologist Met. Health Services, Vancouver, 1962-66; instr. psychology Vancouver Community Coll., 1966-87; docent Vancouver Aquarium Assn. Bd. dirs. Second Mile Soc., 1975—. Mem. Assn. Childhood Edn. Internat., Am. Psychol. Assn., B.C. Psychol. Assn., Gerontol. Soc., Can. Assn. Gerontology, B.C. Assn. Gerontology, Phi Beta Kappa, Sigma Xi, Alpha Kappa Delta. Contbr. articles to profl. jours. Home: 1255 Bidwell St, Apt 1910, Vancouver, BC Canada V6G 2K8

OLSEN, THEODORA EGBERT PECK (MRS. SEVERT ANDREW OLSEN), artist; b. Union, N.J., Sept. 6, 1909; d. Edward Egbert and Theodorea G. (Tucker) Peck; student N.Y. Sch. Design, 1928-29, Pratt-Phoenix Sch. Design, N.Y.C., 1929-32, Coll. City N.Y., 1955, Wagner Coll., summer 1965; m. Ray Sheldon Wilbur, Sept. 8, 1933 (dec. 1966); 1 dau., Margaret Anne (Mrs. Prudhomme); m. 2d, Severt Andrew Olsen, July 17, 1967 (dec. Feb. 1975); stepchildren Arlene Christine, Severt Eugene (dec.). Exhibited at Contemporary Gallery, Newark, 1932, S.I. Mus., 1947-65, N.Y.C. Fedn. Women's Clubs exhibit, 1961, Island Art Center Gallery, New Dorp, S.I., 1961, 33d N.J. Exhbn., Montclair Art Mus., 1964, Summit (N.J.) Art Center, 1965; outdoor shows at Sailors Snug Harbour, S.I., 1956-63, Greenwich Village, N.Y.C., 1961-64, Southhampton and Westhampton (L.I.) Beach, 1964, Summit Art Center, N.J., 1967, Spring Festival Arts, Staten Island, 1968; represented in permanent collection at Wagner Coll., S.I., S.I. Mus.; prin. works include View From Guild Hall, Show Case, Variation on Theme VIII, Long Island Expressway, Seed Pods, Emergence from Chrysalis. Cons., lectr., pvt. tchr., 1934—; tchr. painting YWCA, S.I., 1968-72. Active fund-raising Richmond Mem. Hosp., 1946-54, com. to beautify halls Tottenville (S.I.) High Sch., 1958-60. Recipient S.I. Mus.-Wagner Coll. Purchase award, 1958—; Julius Weisglass award S.I. Mus., 2d prize, 1960, 1st prize, 1965; 1st prize and Honorable mention N.Y.C. Fedn. Women's Clubs competition, 1961. Founder, hon. life mem. South Shore Artists Group (pres. 1946-47, 49-61, 2d v.p. 1965-66); mem. Nat. Assn. Mil. Widows, Pratt-Phoenix Sch. Design Alumni (jury awards 1949), Epsilon Nu Sigma. Clubs:

Prince Bay Women's (pres. 1969-71); Coast Guard Officer's Wives. Home: 72 Bayview Ave Prince Bay Staten Island NY 10309 Also: 584 Main St Rt 2 Hammond NY 13646

OLSON, BECKY VEITH, marketing professional; b. Lakewood, Ohio, July 4, 1959; m. Alan J. Olson, Apr. 25, 1986. BSBA, Miami U., Ohio, 1981. Corp. salesperson Computerland, Cleve., 1983-84; mktg. sales rep. Apple Computer Inc., Cleve., 1984-85; mktg. dir. World Book Discovery Software Inc., Cleve., 1985-86; mktg. mgr. Arthur Andersen & Co., Cleve., 1986—; instr. Cuyahoga Community Coll., Cleve., 1984. Mem. allocations panel United Way, Cleve., 1987—. Mem. Pub. Relations Soc. Am., Press Club. Republican. Unitarian. Clubs: West Shore Volleyball (Lakewood); Erie Shore Ski (Cleve.). Home: 24624 Lake Rd Bay Village OH 44140 Office: Arthur Andersen & Co 1717 E 9th St Cleveland OH 44114

OLSON, BONNIE BRETERNITZ-WAGGONER (MRS. O. DONALD OLSON), civic worker; b. North Platte, Nebr., May 30, 1916; d. Floyd Emil and Edith (Waggoner) Breternitz; A.B., U. Chgo., 1947; m. O. Donald Olson, May 17, 1944; children—Pamela Lynne, Douglas Donald. Dep. clk. Dist. Ct., Lincoln County, Nebr., 1940-42; advt. researcher Burke & Assos., Chgo., 1942; contbg. newspaper columnist Chgo. Herald-Am., 1943; social worker A.R.C., Chgo., 1942-44, Sacramento, Calif., 1944, Amarillo, Tex., 1945; exec. sec. Econometrica, Cowles Commn. for Research in Econs., Chgo., 1945-47; interior designer, antique dealer. Col.; participant Chgo. Maternity Ctr. Fund Drive, 1953, Chgo. Council on Fgn. Relations, 1948-54; mem. Colo. Springs Community Council, 1956-58, chmn. children's div., 1956-58, mem. exec. bd., 1956-58, mem. budget com., 1957-58; mem. Colorado Springs Charter Assn., 1956-60, mem. exec. bd., 1957-59, sec., 1958; chmn. El Paso County PTA, Protective Services for Children, 1959-61; chmn. women's div. fund drive ARC, 1961; mem. League Women Voters, 1957—, mem. state children's law com., 1961-63; chmn. ad hoc com. El Paso County Citizens' Com. for Nat. Probation and Parole Survey, Juvenile Ct. Procedures and Detention, 1957-61; mem. children's adv. com. Colo. Child Welfare Dept., 1959-63, chmn., 1961; del. White House Conf. on Children and Youth, 1960, 70; sec. Citizens Ad Hoc Com. for Comprehensive Mental Health Clinic for Pikes Peak Region, 1966—; mem. Colorado Springs Human Relations Commn., 1968-71; sustaining mem. Symphony Guild, 1970-72, Fine Arts Ctr., 1957—; mem. Pikes Peak Mental Health Ctr., 1964-67 (bd. dirs.); Colo. observer White House Conf. on Aging, Colo. Gov.'s Conf. on Aging, 1981, Dist. Atty.'s Child Abuse Task Force, 1986. Recipient Lane Bryant Ann. Nat. Awards citation, 1971; alumni citation for pub. service U. Chgo., 1961. Mem. Am. Acad. Polit. and Social Sci., Nat. Trust Historic Preservation, Women's Ednl. Soc. Colo. Coll. (life), Council on Religion and Internat. Affairs. Episcopalian. Clubs: Quadranglar, University (Chgo.); Broadmoor Golf, Garden of the Gods (Colorado Springs). Home: 2110 Hercules Dr Colorado Springs CO 80906

OLSON, CONNIE MARLENE, medical center manager; b. Artesia, Calif., Nov. 9, 1950; d. Ross Carl and Elvera Constance (Fernandes) Zaptiff; m. Robert Earl DeBolt, Aug. 9, 1969 (div. 1971); 1 child, Leah Marlene; m. John William Olson, Aug. 4, 1979; 1 child, Erin Michele. AA, Cerritos Coll., 1970; BS in Mgmt., Cal State U., Long Beach, 1985. Supr. ins. dept. Pioneer Hosp., Artesia, 1967-78; claims processor Aetna Life and Casualty, Long Beach, Calif., 1978; mgr. Southcoast Mgmt. Sucs., La Palma, Calif., 1978-81, Meml. Med. Ctr., Long Beach, 1986—. Recipient achievement award Bank of Am., 1968. Mem. Radiologists Bus. Mgmt. Assn. Democrat. Club: CAP (pres. 1976-78). Lodge: Soroptomist (scholarship 1968). Home: 19428 Ellen Way Cerritos CA 90701 Office: Meml Med Ctr of Long Beach 2880 Atlantic Ave #260 Long Beach CA 90806

OLSON, DIANE FAYNE, psychologist; b. Mpls.; d. Douglas Donald and Mabel Dorothey (Hagen) Christensen; m. Timothy M. Olson, Sept. 21, 1968 (div. 1978); 1 child, Emily S. L. B.A. in Psychology magna cum laude, U. Minn., 1968, Ph.D., 1972. Lic. consulting psychologist. Sr. clin. psychologist Hennepin County Gen. Hosp., Mpls., 1971-73; dir. partial hospitalization unit U. Minn., 1977—; sr. clin. psychologist Pilot City Mental Health Ctr., Mpls., 1975-78; ptnr., exec. v.p. dor and associates, inc., Mpls., 1978-83; pres. Affiliated Psychol. Services, Inc., Mpls., 1983—. Bd. dirs. United Neighborhood Ctrs. Am., 1977—; pres. bd. dirs. Northside Settlement Services, Inc., 1980-82, 1st v.p. 1978-80, v.p. program and planning, 1977-78; treas., bd. dirs. Pillsbury United Neighborhood Ctr., 1983—; chmn. allocation panel United Way of Mpls., 1979—; bd. dirs. Jr. Achievement of Twin Cities, Mchts. of Old St. Anthony, Harriet Tubman Womens' Shelter; pres. Assn. Labor-Mgmt., Cons. on Alcoholism, Inc., Minn. 1980-83. Contbr. articles to profl. jours. Recipient Bronze leadership award Jr. Achievement, 1983, Gold medal award Legal Aid Soc., 1980, Disting. Service award Northside Neighborhood Services, 1979. Mem. Am. Psychol. Assn., Assn. Labor, Mgmt., Cons. on Alcoholism Inc., Mental Health Assn., Minn. Psychol. Assn., Am. Mgmt. Assn., Mchts. of Old St. Anthony, Minn. Women's Econ. Roundtable, Horizon 100. Democrat. Lutheran. Home: 169 Seymour Ave SE Minneapolis MN 55414 Office: Affiliated Psychol Services Jeffrey Bldg 1985 Piper Minneapolis MN 55402

OLSON, DONNA RAE, medical technologist; b. St. Louis, Oct. 20, 1947; d. Roy William and Ann Elizabeth (O'Donnell) O. B.A. in Biology, Cath. U. Am., 1964, B.S. in Med. Tech., 1966, M.A. in Ednl. Tech., 1973, Ed.D. in Ednl. Tech., 1985; M.A. in Health Care Mgmt. and Supervision, Central Mich. U., 1981. Cert. Clin. Lab. Scientist, Nat. Cert. Agy. for Med. Lab. Personnel, 1988. Clin. chemistry supr. Washington Hosp. Center, 1965-69, teaching coordinator Sch. Med. Tech., 1969-72; clin. chemistry technologist NIH, Bethesda, Md., 1972—. Recipient various govt. awards. Mem. Am. Soc. Clin. Pathologists (affiliate), Am. Soc. Med. Technologists, Am. Mgmt. Assn., Clin. Lab. Mgmt. Assn., D.C. Soc. Med. Tech. (ednl. coordinator 1979-81), Md. Soc. Med. Tech. Home: 6001 Landon Ln Bethesda MD 20817 Office: Clin Chem Service NIH Bethesda MD 20814

OLSON, DORISE EVELYN (MRS. RAUL J. MINA-MORA), artist; b. N.Y.C., June 8, 1932; d. Athur C. and Anna (Carlson) Olson; student Art Student's League, L.I. Art League, Woodstock, N.Y., Traphagen Sch. Design, N.Y.; m. Raul J. Mina-Mora, Oct. 27, 1967. One-man shows at Caravan House Galleries, Lord & Taylor's Galleries, Different Drummer Gallery, 1976, Nat. Art League, Wickford Art Gallery, W. Ris Galleries, N.J., Rosequist Gallery, Ariz.; exhibited in group shows at Bklyn. Mus., Nat. Arts Club, Nat. Acad., Nat. Acad. Fine Arts, Met. Mus. Arts, Community Gallery with Burr Artists, 1977, Goldsboro (N.C.) Art Mus., 1977, Parrish Art Mus., 1970, 72, Springfield (Mass.) Art Mus., Stony Brook U., Cork Gallery, Avery Fisher Hall, Lincoln Center, 1980, others; represented in pvt. collections; tchr. painting Islip Art Mus. Demonstrator watercolor for various schs. and pvt. clubs. Recipient award Bus. and Profl. Women's Club, N.Y.C., 1967; gold medal Knickerbocker Artists, 1968; Hydenryk award Catherine Lorillard Wolfe Art Club, 1969; 1st place award in watercolor Bklyn. Mus. competition, 1966, 67, 69, Windsor and Newton award, Nat. Arts League Gold medal, 70, Grumbacher award 1971, 1st prize for watercolor Malverne Artists, 1973, best watercolor award Burr Artists, 1974, Forbes award, 1981, Newman award Nat. Soc. Painters in Casein and Acrylic, 1981, others. Mem. Am. Artists Profl. League (award 1979), Allied Artists Am., Catherine Lorillard Wolfe Art Club, Nat. Soc. Painters in Casein and Acrylic, Knickerbocker Artists (award 1979), Nat. Arts Club, Audubon Artists. Address: 87 Central Blvd Box 256 Oakdale NY 11769

OLSON, GEN, state legislator. BS, U. Minn. Mayor Minnetrista, Minn., 1981-82; mem. Minn. State Senate, 1983—. Former mem. Park and Recreation Commn., Planning and Zoning Commn., Police Commn., City Council. Office: 6750 Country Rd 110 W Mound MN 55364 *

OLSON, GLORIA ELLAINE, retail executive; b. Luck, Wis., Jan. 21, 1935; d. Lewis John and Stella (Larson) Jensen; m. Dale LeRoy Olson, Mar. 5, 1953; children—William, Debra, Scott, Kari, Beth. Women's editor ABC Newspapers, Anoka, Minn., 1968-76, editor, 1976-84, asst. mng. editor, 1976-84; owner, operator GloriAnne's, Inc., Ham Lake, Minn., 1984—. With pub. info. dept. Am. Cancer Soc., Anoka County; pub. info. chmn. Star Cities Com., Ham Lake, 1983-84; mem. adv. council Assn. Retarded Citizens, Anoka County, 1983-84. Recipient Woman of Achievement award North Metro Bus. and Profl. Women, 1980-81. Mem. Press Women of Minn., Minn. Press Women (pres. 1979-81), Nat. Press Women. Democrat. Lutheran. Home: 3527 InterLachen Dr Ham Lake MN 55304 Office: 320 Crosstown Mall 17565 Central Ave NE Ham Lake MN 55304

OLSON, IRENE MALLET, human resources executive; b. Bklyn., Jan. 3, 1943; d. David and Dinah Mallet; m. Ronald I Olson. BA in Psychology, Bklyn. Coll., 1972. Supr. compensation and personnel adminstrn. U.S Plywood div. Champion Internat., Stamford, Conn., 1972-75; mgr. employee benefits Sunshine Biscuits, Inc., 1975-78; mgr. corp. personnel 1978-83; bd. dirs. Bell Brand Foods, Inc., Santa Fe Springs, Calif., 1982-85; asst. sec., mgr. corp. personnel Sunshine Biscuits, Inc. div. Am. Brands, Inc., Woodbridge, N.J., 1982-86; mgr. human resources Cluett Peabody & Co. Inc., N.Y.C., 1987—. Clubs: Miramar Yacht (bd. of govs. 1968-70, pres. Women's League 1968-70).

OLSON, JULIE ANN, systems consultant, educator; b. Oklahoma City, May 14, 1957; d. Willard Alton and Ruth Harriet (Ehlers) O.; m. Kevin Peter McAuliffe, Oct. 12, 1985. B.A. in History, Augustana Coll., 1979; postgrad. Keller Grad. Sch. Mgmt., Chgo. Systems analyst Continental Bank, Chgo., 1979-82; systems cons. Computer Ptnrs., Oakbrook, Ill., 1982—; instr. data processing Oakton Community Coll., Des Plaines, 1983—. Exec. dir., chmn. scholarship Miss Northwest Communities Inc., Des Plaines, 1984—. Mem. Data Processing Mgmt. Assn. (asst. faculty coordinator Student chpt. 1985—), Nat. Assn. Female Execs. Lutheran. Avocations: classical pianist; reading; flamenco dancing; snow skiing; cross stitch. Home: 401 S Pine Mount Prospect IL 60056-3723 Office: Computer Ptnrs 122 W 22d St Oak Brook IL 60521

OLSON, KATHY RAE, educator; b. Bismarck, N.D., Oct. 24, 1950; d. Raymond Charles and Virginia Ann (Mason) Lynch; m. Barth Eugene Olson, Aug. 11, 1973; 1 son, William Raymond. B.S., U. N.D., 1972; MS in Spl. Edn., U. N.D., 1987. Cert. elem. tchr. with spl. edn. credential, N.D. Instr., Grafton State Sch., N.D., 1972-74; tchr. spl. edn. Grand Forks Sch. Dist., N.D., 1974—; dir. Agassiz Enterprises. Bd. dirs. Assn. Retarded Citizens; dir. spl. needs recreation program Grand Forks Park Bd., 1973-76; mem. Spl. Olympics Area Mgmt. Team, 1984—. Named N.D. Tchr. of Yr., Council of Chief State Sch. Officers, 1981. Mem. AAUW, Delta Kappa Gamma (sec. 1984-86), Alpha Phi (alumni pres. 1984-86), Pi Lambda Theta. Republican. Roman Catholic. Avocations: sporting events; civic work; cross stitch; outdoor activity. Home: 3208 Walnut St Grand Forks ND 58201

OLSON, LISA MARLENE, public relations executive; b. Flint, Mich., Dec. 9, 1950; d. Julius Caesar and Leona Henrietta (Genske) Gaspar; m. Joel Aaron Ahearne, June 14, 1969 (div. 1971); 1 child, Listte; m. David Robert Olson, Aug. 18, 1972; 1 child, Elisa. Student, U. Mich, Flint, 1969-72. Polit. cons. Midwest Polit. Action Com., Flint and Lansing, Mich., 1975-79; producer, talk show host Sta. WTRX-AM, Flint, 1979; morning drive disk jockey, media cons. Sta. WWCK-FM, Flint, 1980; free-lance writer Flint, 1981-82, Buick Open Tournament, Flint, 1982-83; writer Prismatic Images Prodn., Flint, 1983; cons. Stewart-Jackson Agy., Flint, 1983-84; chmn. bd. dirs. J.T. Lions and Assocs., Inc., Flint, 1984—. Author, producer golf highlight films, 1981, 82. Pub. relations chair Handicappers Assn., Flint, 1986-87, Mayors Task Force on Handicapped Parking, Flint, 1986, cons., 1986-87; cons. Genesee Coalition for Handicappers, Flint, 1986-87; del. White House Conf. on Small Bus., Washington, 1986, Gov.'s Conf. on Small Bus., 1988; bd. dirs. Flint Twp. Econ. Devel. Council, Flint Area Planned Parenthood. Recipient certs. of appreciation, White House Conf. on Small Bus., 1986, Genesee Coalition of Handicapped, 1986, Flint NOW, 1986, Mayors Task Force Handicapped Parking, 1986. Mem. Nat. Fedn. Ind. Bus. (guardian com. 1987), Nat. Assn. Female Execs., Flint C. of C. (mem. com. women's div. 1986-87, Athena award 1987), Pvt. Industry Council, Nat. Assn. Women Bus. Owners. Democrat. Clubs: The Hundred (Flint), Economic (Detroit). Lodge: Kiwanis. Office: JT Lions and Assocs Inc G 4212 Lennon Rd Flint MI 48507

OLSON, LYNNETTE GAIL, personnel executive; b. Omaha, Oct. 9, 1945; d. Norman Lester and Harriet Grace (Carlson) Skillman; m. Gary Allen Olson, Aug. 1, 1964 (div. Oct. 1972); 1 child, Michael John. BA, Augustana Coll., 1980. Legal sec. May, Johnson, Doyle & Becker PC, Sioux Falls, S.D., 1963-76; benefits mgr. Raven Industries, Inc., Sioux Falls, 1980-87, Midcontinent Corp., Sioux Falls, 1987—. Mem. Sioux Falls Personnel Assn. Republican. Home: 4316 E 26th St #47 Sioux Falls SD 57103 Office: Midcontinent Corp 501 S Phillips Ave Sioux Falls SD 57102

OLSON, MARIAN EDNA, nurse, social psychologist; b. Newman Grove, Nebr., July 20, 1923; d. Edwrd and Ethel Thelma (Hougland) Olson; diploma U. Nebr., 1944, B.S.N., 1953; M.A., State U. Iowa, 1961, M.A. in Psychology, 1962; Ph.D. in Psychology, UCLA, 1966. Staff nurse, supr. U. Tex. Med. Br., Galveston, 1944-49; with U. Iowa, Iowa City, 1949-59, supr. 1953-55, asst. dir. 1955-59; asst. prof. nursing UCLA, 1965-67; prof. nursing U. Hawaii, 1967-70, 78-82; dir. nursing Wilcox Hosp. and Health Center, Lihue, 1970-77; chmn. Hawaii Bd. Nursing, 1974-80; prof. nursing No. Mich. U., 1984—. Mem. Am. Nurses Assn. (mem. nat. accreditation bd. continuing edn. 1975-78), Nat. League Nursing, Am. Hosp. Assn., Am. Public Health Assn., LWV. Democrat. Roman Catholic. Home and Office: 6223 County 513T Rd Rapid River MI 49878

OLSON, MARIAN KATHERINE, federal agency administrator, publisher, information broker; b. Tulsa, Oct. 15, 1933; d. Sherwood Joseph and Katherine M (Miller) Lahman, BA in Polit. Sci., U. Colo., 1954, MA in Elem. Edn., 1962; EdD in Ednl. Adminstrn., U. Tulsa, 1969; m. Ronald Keith Olson, Oct. 27, 1956. Tchr. public schs., Wyo., Colo., Mont., 1958-67; teaching fellow, adj. instr. edn. U. Tulsa, 1968-69; asst. prof. edn. Eastern Mont. State Coll., 1970; program assoc. research adminstrn. Mont. State U., 1970-75; on leave with Energy Policy Office of White House, then with Fed. Energy Adminstrn., 1973-74; with Dept. Energy, and predecessor, 1975—, program analyst, 1975-79, chief planning and environ. compliance br., 1979-83; regional dir. Region VIII Fed. Emergency Mgmt. Agy., 1987—; pres. Solar Sense of Colo., Bannack Pub. Co. Contbr. articles in field. Grantee Okla. Consortium Higher Edn., 1969, NIMH, 1974. Mem. Am. Soc. for Info. Sci., Am. Assn. Budget and Program Analysis, Women in Energy, Internat. Assn. Ind. Pubs., Kappa Delta Pi, Phi Alpha Theta, Kappa Alpha Theta. Republican. Home: 707 Poppy Dr Brighton CO 80601 Office: FEMA Denver Fed Ctr Bldg 710 PO Box 25267 Denver CO 80225-0267

OLSON, MELODIE ANN, nursing educator; b. Chicago Heights, Ill., Dec. 5, 1941; d. Melvin Richard and Gwenyth (Hills) Olson. Diploma in nursing, Ill. Masonic Hosp., 1963; B.S.N., U. Ill.-Chgo., 1966; M.S. N., DePaul U., 1970; Ph.D., U. Tex., 1982. R.N., Ill. Staff nurse Ill. Masonic Hosp., Chgo., 1963-65, instr., 1965-69; staff nurse VA Research Hosp., Chgo., 1965-66; nursing educator Luth. Sch. Nursing, Madang, Papua-New Guinea, 1969-75; assoc. prof. nursing San Antonio Coll., 1975-83; assoc. prof. nursing Med. U. S.C., Charleston, 1983—. Contbr. chpts. to books. Coordinator inservice edn. for home health Aides Sr. Citizens Ctr., 1984—. Mem. Am. Nurses Assn. (del. Nat. Conv. Ho. of Dels., 1988), S. C. Nurses Assn. (chmn. cabinet on nursing edn. 1987—, chmn. council continuing edn. 1986), Sigma Theta Tau Gamma Omicron (research com. 1987). Lutheran. Office: Med U of SC Grad Program Coll Nursing Charleston SC 29425

OLSON, RUE EILEEN, librarian; b. Chgo., Nov. 1, 1928; d. Paul H. and Martha M. (Fick) Meyers; student Herzl Coll., 1946-48, Northwestern U., 1948-50, Ill. State U., 1960-64, Middle Mgmt. Inst. Spl. Libraries Assn., 1985-87; m. Richard L. Olson, July 18, 1964; children—Catherine, Karen. Accountant Ill. Farm Supply Co., Chgo., 1948-59; asst. librarian Ill. Agrl. Assn., Bloomington, 1960-66, librarian, 1966-86, dir. library services, 1986—. Mem. area Com. Nat. Library Week, 1971, area steering com., 1972; mem. steering com. Illinet/OCLC, 1985-87; mem. adv. council of librarians Grad. Sch. Library Sci. U. Ill., 1976-79; mem. Ill. State Library Adv. Com. for Interlibrary Cooperation, 1979-80; del. Ill. White House Conf. on Library and Info. Services, 1978; coordinator Vita Income Tax Assistance, Bloomington, Ill., 1986—. Mem. Am., Ill., McLean County (pres. 1970-71) library assns., Spl. Libraries Assn. (pres. Ill. 1977-78), Internat. Assn. Agrl. Librarians and Documentalists, Am. Soc. Info. Sci., Am. Mgmt. Assn. Lodge: Zonta (pres. 1987-89). Club: Bloomington. Office: Ill Agrl Assn 1701 Towanda Ave Bloomington IL 61701

OLSON, TERESA JOYCE, brokerage house agent; b. Reed City, Mich., Apr. 19, 1958; d. William Charles and Celestine Joyce (Swem) O. Student, L'Institut des Etudes Americains, Avignon, France, 1980; BS in Bus. Adminstrn., Cen. Mich. U., 1980. Reservations mgr. Marriott Corp./Marriott Hotels, Lincolnshire, Ill., 1981, Stamford, Conn., 1981-84; telecommunications supr. Lillian Vernon Corp., New Rochelle, N.Y., 1984-85; sales asst. Robustelli Corp. Services, Stamford, 1985-86; adminstrv. asst. Drexel Burnham Lambert Inc., N.Y.C., 1986—. Mem. Nat. Assn. Female Execs., Fgn. Lang. Council, Sigma Iota Epsilon. Club: Skydiving. Office: Drexel Burnham Lambert Inc 60 Broad St New York NY 10004

OLSZEWSKI, TEENA LOUISE, education administrator; b. Hamilton, Ohio, Mar. 30, 1956; d. Leonard and Norma Lee (Pizzino) Stokley; m. Peter John Olszewski. BA, Ind. U., 1979; postgrad., No. Ariz. U., 1979, 81. Adult probation officer Monroe County Probation Dept., Bloomington, Ind., 1975-77; adj. instr. Navajo Community Coll., Tsaile, Ariz., 1979; counselor No. Ariz. U., Flagstaff, 1979; coordinator career devel. Coconino County Manpower Programs, Flagstaff, 1979-81; jud. adminstr. Ariz. Supreme Ct., Phoenix, 1981-86; dir. Ctr. Law-Related Edn. Ariz. Bar Found., Phoenix, 1987—; moderator, panelist Nat. Employment Policy Conf., San Antonio, Tex., 1980; faculty presenter Nat. Council Juvenile and Family Ct. Judges, Reno, 1984. Vol. St. Thomas the Apostle Parish, Phoenix, 1985. Arthur R. Metz scholar, 1978, Disting. Alumni scholar Ind. U., 1978. Mem. Am. Judicature Soc., Ariz. Assn. Ct. Mgmt., Nat. Assn. Female Execs. Democrat. Roman Catholic. Office: Ariz Ctr Law-Related Edn 363 N First Ave Phoenix AZ 85003

OLTERS, SANDRA CAROL, lawyer; b. Elizabeth, N.J., Jan. 18, 1955; d. Stanley Charles and Miriam Helena (Ives) O. BA, Rutgers U., 1977; paralegal cert., Inst. Paralegal Tng., 1978; JD, Georgetown U., 1984. Bar: Va. 1984; cert. tchr., N.J. Substitute tchr. Rahway and Somerville (N.J.) Pub. Schs., 1975-78; paralegal Thomas & Fiske, P.C., Alexandria, Va., 1978-84; assoc. Hyatt & Rhoads, P.C., Washington, 1984—. Author: (with others) Condominium and Homeowner Association Litigation, 1987. Mem. ABA, Va. Bar Assn., Community Assns. Inst. (speaker 1984—, author case summaries Law Reporter 1985-87, cert. Appreciation 1985, 87), Phi Beta Kappa, Kappa Delta Pi. Democrat. Presbyterian. Office: Hyatt & Rhoads 1275 K St NW Suite 1100 Washington DC 20005

OLTORIK, DIANE ELIZABETH, insurance executive; b. Washington, July 24, 1937; d. Eugene A. and Hazel Mary (Dumm) Ross; m. Thomas Francis Oltorik Sr., Apr. 23, 1960; children: Thomas F. Jr., Dennis R., Stephen M., David E., Janelle E. BA, Catholic U. Am., 1959. Cabaret performer The Ross Sisters, Washington, 1957-61; owner, operator London Antiques, Inc., Rochester, N.Y., 1975-79; sr. account exec. The Copeland Cos., Rochester, N.Y., 1979—. Choreographer, performer Rochester area community theatres, 1978—. Pres. Griffiss AFB Nursery Sch., Rome, N.Y., 1966-67; fund raising capt. Rochester United Way, 1976-78; campaign mgr. for Monroe County Legislator, Irondequoit, N.Y., 1970-78, Irondequoit Twp. Justice, 1983; pres. St. Margaret Mary Soc., Rochester, 1971-72, lector, tchr. for parish, 1969—; foster mother Cath. Charities, Rochester, 1967-71. Named Top Sales Producer The Copeland Cos., 1979-82. Mem. Catholic U. Alumni Assn. (admissions liaison 1969-70, bd. govs. 1985—). Democrat. Roman Catholic. Club: Griffiss AFB Officers (hon. life membership). Home: 350 Simpson Rd Rochester NY 14617 Office: The Copeland Cos 625 Panorama Trail Rochester NY 14625

OLZENDAM, HARRIETT STEELE, retired lawyer; b. Dover, N.H., Aug. 5, 1914; d. Enoch Ned and Lena Marion (Steele) O.; B.A., Wellesley Coll., 1936; M.A., Trinity Coll., 1942; J.D. with distinction, U. Conn., 1946. Admitted to Conn. bar, 1946, Fed. Dist. bar, 1948; with The Travelers Ins. Co., Hartford, Conn., 1937-79, chief contract underwriter, 1951-61, asst. sec., 1961-69, sec., 1969-79. Mem. residence com. YWCA, Hartford, Conn., 1964-79, dir., 1971-77, sec., 1972-74, v.p., 1974-75, pres., 1975-77, mem. fin. com., 1975-79, personnel com., 1979-82. Mem. ABA, Conn. Bar Assn., Hartford County Bar Assn., Am. Judicature Soc., Mental Health Assn. Conn. (nominating com. 1976-78, trustee 1979-81), Conn. Ins. Assn. (group com.), Conn. Health Reins. Assn. (chmn. forms com.), Soc. Group Contract Analysts, Wellesley Coll. Alumnae Assn., U. Conn. Sch. Law, Trinity Coll. alumni assns., Mark Twain Meml., Wadsworth Atheneum, Antiquarian and Landmarks Soc. Conn., Conn. Hist. Soc., Hartford Architecture Conservancy, Nat. Audubon Soc., Nat. Wildlife Fedn., Smithsonian Assos., Hartford Easter Seal Rehab. Ctr. Republican. Congregationalist. Clubs: Wellesley (fin. chmn. 1975-77, 1st v.p. 1977-79), Quota (corr. sec. Hartford 1970-78, 1st v.p. 1978-81, 2d v.p. 1981-87), Town and County (gov. 1978-82, rec. sec. 1979-80, 83-85, personnel com. 1978-82, chmn. personnel com. 1980-82, fin. com. 1979-82, 85—, exec. com. 1979-84). Address: 2012 Blvd West Hartford CT 06107

O'MALLEY, MARY PATRICIA, foundation executive; b. St. Louis, Sept. 28, 1956; d. Joseph Michael Jr. and Kathleen Gertrude (Montrey) O'Malley. BA, U. Mass., 1977. Exec. trainee The Prudential, Newark, 1978-80; found. officer The Prudential Found., Newark, 1980—; cons. various non profit orgns., N.Y., N.J., D.C. Author: Administrative Procedures, 1980. Treas. South Orange-Maplewood (N.J.) Adult Sch.; v.p. Family Service & Child Guidance Ctr., Orange, N.J.; bd. dirs. Family Enrichment Council, Port Monmouth, N.J. Recipient cert. merit Assn. for Community-Based Edn., 1987. Mem. Nat. Assn. Female Execs., Women and Founds./Corp. Philanthropy, Grantmakers in Health. Democrat. Home: 1623 May St Union NJ 07083

O'MALLEY, PATRICIA ELLEN, industrial chemicals company executive; b. Scranton, Pa., May 10, 1935; d. Stanley Francis and Clare Helen (Fadden) Coar; m. Frank Jerome O'Malley, Oct. 6, 1953; children—F. Jerome, Brian, Ellen, Kevin, Karen, Timothy, Sean, Christopher, Kathleen. B.A., Rosemont Coll., Pa., 1954. Model, Pa. and Ct., 1960-67; office mgr. pvt. med. office, Westport, Conn., 1965-67; bus. mgr. Norwalk Periodontics, 1967-75; adminstrv. dir. New Eng. Found. Allergic Diseases, Norwalk, 1975-81; asst. to pres., dir. resources Berol Chems. Inc., Westport, Conn., 1981—. Mem. Nat. Assn. Female Execs., Smithsonian Instn. Roman Catholic. Clubs: U.S. Figure Skating Assn.; Weston Racquet, Women's Guild-St. Francis Assissi. Avocations: figure skating; windsurfing; modern dance; singing. Home: 38 Tobacco Rd Weston CT 06883

OMAN, DEBORAH SUE, health science facility administrator; b. North Platte, Nebr., Aug. 26, 1948; d. Rex Ardell and Opale Louise (Smith) O. BS, Kearney State Coll., 1970. Med. technologist Physicians Pathology Labs., Lincoln, Nebr., 1970-71; med. technologist student health Colo. State U., Ft. Collins, 1971-72; supr. hematology lab. Bryan Meml. Hosp., Lincoln, 1972-76; sect. supr. hematology/coagulation Clin. Labs. of Lincoln and Pathology Med. Services, 1976—; adj. prof. sch. of med. technology Nebr. Weslyan U., Lincoln, 1979-85. Contbr. articles to profl. jours. Mem. Am. Soc. Clin. Pathologists (cert., affiliate, recognition award 1986), Lancaster Soc. Med. Technologists. Republican. Mem. Christian Ch. Club: Cornhusker Ski (pres. 1982-83). Office: Clin Labs of Lincoln Plaza Mall South 1919 S 40th St Suite 333 Lincoln NE 68506

O'MARA MCMAHON, PEGGY NOREEN, editor, publisher; b. Kenosha, Wis., May 14, 1947; d. Oliver Edward and Ruth Helen (Slater) O'Mara; m. John William McMahon, May 27, 1973; children—Lally, Finnie, Bram, Nora. B.S., U. Wis.-Milw., 1970. Tchr. high sch. Alamogordo High Sch., N.Mex., 1971-72; tchr. spl. edn. Zia Sch., Alamogordo, 1972-73; M.B.A. coordinator U. Utah, Holloman AFB, N.Mex., 1973; freelance writer, 1973-77; assoc. editor Mothering Mag., Albuquerque, 1978-80, editor, pub., Santa Fe, 1980—; leader La Leche League, Franklin Park, Ill., 1975—. Editor: Mother Poet, 1983. Bd. dirs. Midwifery Tng. Inst., Albuquerque, 1983-86, N.Mex. State Midwifery Adv. Bd., Santa Fe, 1984—. Mem. Midwives Alliance N.Am., Internat. Childbirth Edn. Assn., Nat. Fedn. Press Women (1st place award 1984), Nat. Assn. Safe Alternatives in Birth, N.Mex. Press Women (1st place awards 1984), N.Mex. Press Assn. Avocations: herb gardening; ornithology; alternative health. Home: Route 7 Box 124K Santa Fe NM 87505 Office: Mothering Publs PO Box 1690 Santa Fe NM 87504

O'MEALLIE, KITTY, artist; b. Bennettsville, S.C., Oct. 24, 1916; d. Earle and Rosa Estelle (Bethea) Chamness; m. John Ryan O'Meallie, June 27, 1939 (dec. Apr. 26, 1974); children—Sue Ryan, Kathryn Bethea; Lee Harnie

Johnson, Aug. 21, 1976. BFA Tulane U., 1937; postgrad., 1954-59. One-woman shows include Masur Mus., Monroe, La., 1979, Marlboro County Mus. of S.C., 1975, Meridian Mus. Art, Miss., 1981, 85; exhibited in group shows at New Orleans Mus. Art, Contemporary Art Ctr., Meadows Mus., Cushing Gallery, SE Ctr. of Contemporary Art, Art 80, Art Expo West, Art Expo 81. Represented in permanent collections New Orleans Mus. Art, Tulane U. Pan-Am. Life Ctr., Masur Mus. Art, Meridian Mus. Art. Nat. officer Newcomb Coll. Alumnae Assn., 1964-66; lectr. exhibitor for many charitable orgns. Recipient award WYES-TV, 1979, Hon. Invitational New Orleans Women's Caucus, 1986, numerous awards and prizes in competitive exhibitions. Mem. Artists Equity Assn., Womens Caucus for Art, New Orleans Womens Caucus for Art, Chi Omega Mothers Club (pres. 1964), Town and Country Garden Guild (pres. 1970, 1986). Avocations: bird-watching; bridge; ballroom dancing. Home and Office: 211 Fairway Dr New Orleans LA 70124

O'MEARA, ANN MARIE, sales manager; b. Bay City, Mich., May 17, 1957; d. Robert Frank and Jo Ann (Neitzel) Davis; m. Scott E. O'Meara, June 1, 1979. BSBA, U. Mo., 1979; postgrad., Rockhurst Coll., 1979-80. Sales rep. The Drackett Products Co., Kansas City, Mo., 1979-81; key account mgr. Playtex, Inc., Kansas City, 1981-84; territory mgr. Chattem, Inc., Kansas City, 1984—; fin. advisor SOK Investments, Kansas City, 1984—. Mem. Friends of Art, Kansas City; chmn. ball Bacchus Found., Kansas City, 1986-87; founding mem. Ozanam Boys Home Guild, Kansas City, 1987; bd. dirs. Muscular Dystrophy Assn., Kansas City, 1987. Mem. Kansas City Jaycees (bd. dirs. 1983-84, Outstanding Chmn. 1984-85), U. Mo. Alumni, Winnebago Yachtsmen Assn. (pres. 1986-87), Kappa Kappa Gamma Alumni. Republican. Roman Catholic. Club: The Kansas City. Home: 5519 Rockhill Rd Kansas City MO 64110

ONA-SARINO, MILAGROS FELIX, pathologist; b. Manila, May 8, 1940; came to U.S., 1965, naturalized, 1983; d. Venancio Vale Ona and Fidela Torres Felix; m. Edgardo Formantes Sarino, June 11, 1966; children—Edith Melanie, Edgar Michael, Edenn Michele. A.A., U. Santo Tomas, Manila, 1959, M.D. cum laude 1964. Diplomate Am. Bd. Pathology. Rotating intern N.Y. Infirmary, 1965-66; resident in anatomic and clin. pathology Lenox Hill Hosp., N.Y.C., 1966-71; asst. adj. pathologist, 1972-74; assoc. pathologist St. Francis Med. Ctr., Trenton, N.J., 1974-84, Hamilton Hosp., N.J., 1974-84; pathologist, chief lab. service Louis A. Johnson VA Med. Ctr., Clarksburg, W.Va., 1984—; clin. instr. pathology Columbia U. Coll. Physicians and Surgeons, N.Y.C., 1973-85; clin. asst. prof. pathology, W. Va. U. Sch. Medicine. Fellow Am. Soc. Clin. Pathologists; mem. AAAS, Internat. Acad. Pathology, N.Y. Acad. Scis. Office: Louis A Johnson VA Med Ctr Clarksburg WV 26301

ONASSIS, JACQUELINE BOUVIER KENNEDY, editor, widow of 35th president of U.S.; b. Southampton, N.Y., 1929; d. John Vernou III and Janet (Lee) Bouvier; m. John Fitzgerald Kennedy, 35th pres. of U.S., Sept. 12, 1953 (dec. Nov. 22, 1963); children: Caroline Bouvier, John Fitzgerald, Patrick Bouvier (dec.); m. Aristotle Onassis, Oct. 20, 1968 (dec. Mar. 1975). Grad., Miss Porter's Sch., Farmington, Conn., 1947; student, Vassar Coll., 1947-48, The Sorbonne, Paris, 1949; BA, George Washington U., 1951. Inquiring photographer Washington Times-Herald (now Washington Post and Times Herald), 1952; planned and conducted restoration of decor The White House, 1961-63; cons. editor Viking Press, 1975-77; assoc. editor Doubleday & Co., N.Y.C., 1978-82, editor, 1982—. Trustee Whitney Mus. Am. Art. Recipient Prix de Paris Vogue mag., 1951, Emmy award for pub. service, 1962. Address: 1041 Fifth Ave New York NY 10028 Office: Doubleday & Co 245 Park Ave New York NY 10017 *

O'NEAL, BARBARA LYNNE, corporate executive; b. Washington, May 4, 1939; d. Orton Thomas and Edna Earle (Ryals) Campbell; B.A., Baylor U., 1973; children—Kai Lynne, Carlton Clay, John F. (dec.). Legal sec. Carlton Smith, Waco, Tex., 1960-62, John F. O'Neal, Hamilton, Tex., 1962-66; tchr. Waco Ind. Sch. Dist., 1973-83; dir. field ops. Bob Krueger U.S. Senate Campaign, 1983-84; dir. personnel Tex. Comptroller of Pub. Accounts, Austin, 1984-87; v.p. Lomas & Nettleton Co., Dallas, 1988—. Sec. McLennan County Dem. Conv., 1978; del. Dem. Nat. Conv., 1980. Named outstanding tchr. of Tex., 1975. Mem. NEA, Tex. State Tchrs. Assn. (pres. 1982-83), Waco Classroom Tchrs. Assn. (pres. 1977-78), Alpha Delta Kappa. Baptist. Home: 4343 W Northwest Hwy Suite 1043 Dallas TX 75220 Office: Lomas & Nettleton Co 1600 Viceroy Dr PO Box 660723 Dallas TX 75266-0723

O'NEAL, CAROLE KELLEY, health sciences administrator; b. Lawrenceville, Ga., June 20, 1933; d. Daniel Claude Jr. and Connie Fay (Moore) Kelley; m. Donald E. O'Neal, Jan. 24, 1953; children: Sharon Lee O'Neal Altenbach, Terrence P. Student, U. Ba., 1950-52, Massey Bus. Coll., 1952-54, Oglethorpe U., 1981-82. Office mgr. Photostat Corp., Atlanta; from sec. to office mgr. pvt. physician Atlanta; pres., owner Profl. Practice Services Inc., Atlanta; cons. plastic surgery office mgmt.; mng. dir. Found. for Edn. Aesthetic Plastic Surgery, Atlanta. Contbr. articles to profl. jours. Mem. Alliance Theater Guild. Mem. Plastic Surgery Adminstrv. Assn. (pres. 1983-84), Pi Beta Phi Alumnae. Republican. Office: Profl Practice Services Inc 3312 Piedmont Rd NE Suite 322 Atlanta GA 30305

O'NEAL, DOROTHY DECKER, fabric sales company executive; b. Akron, Ohio, Dec. 8, 1923; d. Clyde Earl and Mary Iva (King) Decker; m. Robert Frank O'Neal, Dec. 4, 1943; 1 child, Aileen Adele. Purchasing agt. Firestone Tire and Rubber Co., Akron, 1941-43; free lance fashion model, Little Rock, 1944-46; freelance fashion cons., Akron, 1947-52; owner, mgr. Canal Shop, Peninsula, Ohio, 1953-60, Fashion With Fabrics, Sierra Vista, Ariz., 1979—. Editor: Bi-Centennial Cook Book, 1976; Yule in the Mules Cook Book, 1977. Chmn. Goldwater for Pres. Com., Battle Creek, Mich., 1963-64. Mem. Greater Fedn. Women's Clubs, Am. Assn. Hosp. Auxs., Internat. Platform Assn. Republican. Unitarian. Club: Fashion Group (N.Y.C.). Avocations: sewing; cooking; fashion shows; travel; career seminars. Home: 4391 Plaza Oro Loma Sierra Vista AZ 85635 Office: Fashion with Fabrics 1502 E Fry Blvd Sierra Vista AZ 85635

O'NEAL, HARRIET ROBERTS, psychologist, psycholegal consultant; b. Covington, Ky., Dec. 28, 1952; d. Nelson E. and Georgia H. (Roberts) O'N.; m. Michael Coy Acree, Oct. 5, 1985 (div. Dec. 1986). BA in Psychology, Hollins Coll., 1974; JD, U. Nebr., 1978, MA in Psychology, 1980, PhD in Psychology, 1982. Program dir., therapist Richmond Maxi Ctr., San Francisco, 1979-81; clin. coordinator, therapist Pacifica (Calif.) Youth Service Bur., 1981-83; staff psychologist Kaiser-Permanente Med. Ctr., Walnut Creek, Calif., 1983—; psycholegal cons., Nebr., Calif., 1987—; oral exam commr. Calif. Bd. Behavioral Sci. Examiners, Sacramento, 1982—; pvt. practice psychotherapy, Pleasant Hill, Calif., 1985—, Lafayette, Calif., 1987—; psycholegal cons., presenter San Francisco State U., 1980, U. Calif., San Francisco, 1980, VA Med. Ctr., San Francisco, 1983. Cons. Nebr. Gov.'s Commn. on Status of Women, 1975, 78. NIMH fellow, 1974-79. Mem. Am. Psychol. Assn., Calif. Psychol. Assn., Phi Beta Kappa, Psi Chi. Club: Commonwealth (San Francisco). Home: 286 Park Lake Circle Walnut Creek CA 94598 Office: Kaiser-Permanente Med Ctr Mental Health Dept 1425 S Main St Walnut Creek CA 94596

O'NEAL, MARGARET FUNDERBURK, consulting and purchasing firm owner; b. LaGrange, Ga., Jan. 12, 1949; d. George William and Margaret Cleaveland (Dodd) Funderburk; m. William Ennis O'Neal, Aug. 30, 1969. B.A., Agnes Scott Coll., 1971. Mgr. The Frog Pond, Inc., Atlanta, 1976-79; project mgr. ADM Assocs. Inc., Atlanta, 1979-82; pres., owner Focus Interior Contracting, Inc., Atlanta, 1982—. Methodist. Club: Women Bus. Owners (Atlanta). Avocation: reading. Office: Focus Interior Contracting 1900 Emery St Suite 450 Atlanta GA 30318

O'NEAL-SMITH, MELBA MARGO, health care executive; b. Marietta, Ohio, Mar. 29, 1951; d. Vaughn Everett and Velma May (Prine) O'Neal; m. Jay Pierce Smith, June 21, 1976 (div. Aug. 1983). BS in Nutrition, Ohio State U., 1978; postgrad., U. Phoenix, Orange County, Calif., 1984, 85. With Riverside Meth. Hosp., Columbus, Ohio, 1970-78; clinic adminstr. Ohio State U., Columbus, 1978-81; cons., mktg. rep. Control Data Corp., Cleve., 1981-83; mktg. mgr. Nat. Med. Computers, San Diego, 1983-84; ind. cons. Orange County, 1984-86; dir. mgmt. info. systems FHP, Inc., Fountain Valley, Calif., 1986-87, assoc. v.p. mgmt. info. systems, 1987—; cons., speaker in field, 1985—. Author several poetry books. Counselor Big Bros./Big Sisters Am., Cleve., 1981; counselor, sponsor Post Adoption Ctr. Research, San Francisco, 1983. Mem. Med. Group Mgmt. Assn., Nat. Assn. Female Execs., Group Health Assn. Am., Am. Hosp. Assn. Home: 31434 Flying Cloud Dr Laguna Niguel CA 92677

O'NEIL, JEAN F., policy analyst; b. Washington, Apr. 6, 1947; d. Ralph Emerson and Vivian Jean (Elliott) O'N. BS in Fgn. Service, Georgetown U., 1968; postgrad., Montgomery Coll., 1978—; M of Pub. Adminstrn., Harvard U., 1983. Caseworker U.S. House Reps., Washington, 1969-72; press asst. U.S. Ho. Reps., Washington, 1972-77, dir. spl. projects, 1977-82; cons. Washington, 1983—; dir. computer ops. Nat. Crime Prevention Council, Washington, 1984-85, dir. research and policy, mng. editor, 1986—; cons. Nat. Inst. Justice, 1987—, Benchmarks Inc., Washington, 1983—; lectr. Montgomery Coll., Rockville, Md., 1984—. Author: Making A Difference: Young People in Community Crime Prevention, 1985, Crime Prevention: Status and Trends, 1986, Ink Plus Antime, 1987; editor: What, Me Evaluate?, 1986, Preventing Crime in Urban Communities, 1986. Mem. Montgomery County (Md.) Liquor Control Task Force, 1980-81; sec./pres., bd. dirs. Plymouth Woods Condo, Rockville, Md., 1976-82; bd. dirs. LWV, 1985-87. Mem. Nat. Criminal Justice Assn., Am. Inst. Parliamentarians, Pi Sigma Alpha, Phi Alpha Theta, Gamma Pi Epsilon. Democrat. Anglican Catholic. Office: Nat Crime Prevention Council 733 15th St NW Suite 540 Washington DC 20005

O'NEILL, BARBARA MARY, home economics educator; b. Amityville, N.Y., Nov. 23, 1952; d. Francis X. and Mary (Carney) O'Neill; m. Gene M. Bronson, Aug. 20, 1977. BS, SUNY, Oneonta, 1974; MS, Cornell U., 1978. Cert. fin. planner. Home econs. tchr. Hammondsport (N.Y.) Cen. Sch., 1974-76; grad. asst. Cornell U., Ithaca, N.Y., 1976-78; assoc. prof., extension home economist Rutgers Cooperative Extension, New Brunswick, N.J., 1978—; adj. faculty College for Fin. Planning, Denver, 1985—. Contbr. articles to profl. jours. Recipient Fin. Mgmt. award Nat. Assn. Extension Home Economists, 1987. Mem. NW Jersey Home Econs. Assn. (pres. 1985-86), N.J. Home Econs. (treas. 1986—), N.J. Assn. Extension Home Economists (pres. 1988—), Inst. Cert. Fin. Planners, Assn. for Fin. Planning and Counseling Edn. Lodge: Soroptimist (Sussex county pres. 1984—). Home: 617 Limecrest Rd Newton NJ 07860 Office: Rutgers Coop Extension 330 Rt 206 S Newton NJ 07860

O'NEILL, JEANNE MARIE, legal assistant; b. Ft. Ogden, Fla., Mar. 27, 1926; d. William Andrew and Ila Mae (Waterson) O'N.; m. Adam J. Thielen, June 28, 1947 (div. 1969); children: Adam Joseph, Mary Denise, John Patrick, William Andrew, Carol Anne, Peter Stephen, Timothy Adrian, Robert Michael, Terence O'Neill, Paul Eugene, James Francis. AA, Edison Community Coll., 1978; student, Nova U.; cert., Fla. Internat. U., 1983. Exec. sec. purchasing agt., Clewiston, Fla., 1943-47; legal sec. Jules R. Israel, Miami, Fla., 1969-71, David A. Rhodes, Bradenton, Fla., 1971-72, Alonzo Shields, Dickinson, O'Riorden et al, Sarasota, Fla., 1972-76; jud. asst. Hon. Thomas S. Reese, Ft. Myers, 1976-81; supervisory legal asst. Ruden, Barnett, McClosky et al, Ft. Lauderdale, Fla., 1982-84; sr. legal asst. Robert N. Reynolds, Miami, 1984—; guest lectr. cert. legal asst. rev. courses, Fla. Internat. U., Broward Community Coll. Mem. Nat. Assn. Legal Assts. (charter, bd. dirs. 1984—), Fla. Legal Assts. (chairperson 1986—, pres. 1981-83, v.p. 1980-81, dir. region IV), Fla. Bar Exec. Council (legal asst. rep.). Democrat. Roman Catholic. Home: 3311 Meadows Circle W Miramar FL 33025 Office: Robert N Reynolds 9100 S Dadeland Blvd Miami FL 33156

O'NEILL, KATHERINE ANNE, psychologist, pharmacologist; b. Hartford, Conn., June 28, 1954; d. Robert Michael and Anne K. (Hanley) O'N.; m. Richard Eric Chipkin, Sept. 8, 1985. BS in Psychology, Emmanuel Coll., 1976; MA in Exptl. Psychology, U. R.I., 1981, PhD in Physiol. Psychology, 1983. Asst. scientist Pfizer, Inc., Groton, Conn., 1982-83; postdoctoral trainee NYU Med. Ctr., N.Y.C., 1983-84; postdoctoral fellow N.J. Med. Sch., Newark, 1984-85; cons. Ciba-Giegy Pharms., Summit, N.J., 1985-87, market research analyst, 1987—. Contbr. articles to profl. jours. Mem. AAAS, N.Y. Acad. Scis., Soc. for Neuroscience, Internat. Narcotics Research Group. Office: Ciba-Giegy Inc 556 Morris Ave Summit NJ 07901

O'NEILL, KATHERINE TEMPLETON, university administrator; b. Moline, Ill., Jan. 13, 1949; d. Morris John and Patricia (Collins) Templeton; 1 child by previous marriage, Carolyn Patricia Coquillette; m. William James O'Neill Jr., July 18, 1987; children: Alec, Sara, Jessie, Laura O'Neill. BSN, U. Mich., 1971; postgrad., St. Clare's Hall, 1971-72; MSN, Boston U., 1974. RN, Ohio, Mass. Instr. Mass. Gen. Hosp., Boston, 1974-76; assoc. prof. Ursuline Coll., Cleve., 1976-81; dir. devel. Ohio Coll. Podiatric Medicine, Cleve., 1985-86, dir. devel., pub. relations, 1986-87; project dir. Chisolm Halle Costume Wing We. Reserve Hist. Soc., Cleve., 1988—; v.p., bd. dirs. Cleve. Health Edn. Mus., 1983—; v.p., bd. dirs. Cleve. Music Sch. Settlement, Cleve., 1983—; adj. instr. Ursuline Coll., Cleve., 1976-78. Bd. dirs. Cleve. Ballet, 1987—. Mem. Nat. Assn. Female Execs., Council Advancement Support of Edn., Hathaway Brown Sch. Alumnae Assn. (pres., bd. dirs. 1984-86). Roman Catholic. Clubs: Intown, Cleve. Playhouse. Home: Glengarah South Woodland Rd Hunting Valley OH 44022 Office: Western Reserve Hist Soc 10825 East Blvd Cleveland OH 44106

O'NEILL, SISTER MARGARELLA, college administrator; b. Phila.. BS in Nursing, Georgetown U. and Cath. U. Am., 1948; MS in Nursing Edn., Cath. U. Am., 1950-52, PhD in Sociology, 1966; D of Social Sci. (hon.), Villanova U., 1983. Tchr. St. Mary Magdalen Sch., Lost Creek, Pa., 1943-44; instr. nursing edn. St. Joseph Hosp., Balt., 1948-52; co-founder, asst. prof., assoc. dir. Sch. Nursing Villanova (Pa.) U., 1952-56; dir. nursing services St. Francis Med. Ctr., Trenton, N.J., 1956-59; dir. Sch. Nursing St. Joseph Hosp. and Health Ctr., Lancaster, Pa., 1959-62; assoc. prof. sociology, acad. dean Neumann Coll.-Our Lady of Angels, Aston, Pa., 1966-74; pres. Neumann Coll.-Our Lady of Angels, Aston, 1983—; gen. councilperson Sisters of St. Francis, Phila., 1974-82. Recipient Alumnae Excellence in Service award Cath. U. Am., 1981. Mem. AAUW, Am. Sociol. Assn., Soc. for the Advancement of Religion, Sigma Theta Tau. Office: Neumann Coll Office of the Pres Aston PA 19014

O'NEILL, MARGARET, psychological counselor; b. Youngstown, Ohio, Jan. 23, 1935; d. Julius and Anna (Zakel) Huegel; m. Thomas B. O'Neill, Oct. 21, 1971 (div. 1979); children by previous marriage—Paul McCann, Kathleen McCann, Kevin McCann. B.S. in Nursing, UCLA, 1961, M.S. in Nursing, 1963; M.A. in Counseling, Calif. Luth. Coll., Thousand Oaks, 1974; Ph.D. in Psychology, U.S. Internat. U., San Diego, 1986. Cert. hypnotherapist, Calif. Instr. Ventura Coll., Calif., 1965-69, dept. chair, 1969-74, coordinator Women's Ctr., 1974-79, counselor, 1979—; marriage, family and child therapist, cons., Ventura, 1981—; trainer, cons. County of Ventura, 1984—. Bd. dirs. Ventura County chpt. ARC. Mem. Am. Assn. Holistic Health, Nat. Assn. Female Execs., Ventura County Psychol. Assn., Calif. Assn. Marriage Family Therapists. Republican. Unitarian Universalist. Avocations: reading; dancing; hiking; walking. Office: 2590 E Main St Suite 202 Ventura CA 93003

O'NEILL, MARY JANE, health agency executive; b. Detroit, Feb. 24, 1923; d. Frank Roger and Kathryn (Rice) Kilcoyne; Ph.B. summa cum laude, U. Detroit, 1944; postgrad. U. Wis., 1949-50; m. Michael James O'Neill, May 31, 1948; children—Michael, Maureen, Kevin, John, Kathryn. Editor, East Side Shopper, Detroit, 1939-45; club editor Detroit Free Press, 1945-48; reporter UP, Milw. and Madison, Wis., 1949; dir. public relations Fairfax-Falls Church (Va.) Community Chest, 1955-60; copy editor Falls Ch. Sun-Echo, 1958-60; free-lance writer, Washington, 1960-63; asso. editor Med. World News, Washington, 1963-66; dir. public relations Westchester Lighthouse, N.Y. Assn. for Blind, 1967-71; dir. public edn. The Lighthouse, N.Y.C., 1971-73, dir. public relations, 1973-80; exec. dir. Eye-Bank for Sight Restoration, Inc., 1980—. Bd. dirs. N.Y. Regional Transplant Program, 1987—. Mem. Women in Communications (pres. N.Y. chpt. 1980-81), Eye-Bank Assn. Am. (lay adv. bd. 1981-83, dir. 1983-86), Public Relations Soc. Am., Publicity Club, Women Execs. in Pub. Relations (dir. 1982—, pres. 1986-87). Club: Cosmopolitan. Office: 210 E 64 St New York NY 10021

O'NEILL, MAUREEN ANNE, arts adminstrator, city administrator; b. Seattle, Nov. 11, 1948; d. Robert P. and Barbara F. (Pettinger) O. B.A. in Sociology cum laude, Wash. State U., 1971; M.A., Bowling Green U., 1972. Grad. asst. dept. coll. student personnel Bowling Green (Ohio) U., 1971-72, asst. coordinator coll. activities SUNY-Geneseo, 1972-75, acting coordinator coll. activities, 1975-76; regional mgr. northeast Kazuko Hillyer Internat. Agy., N.Y.C., 1976-77; mgr. pub. performing arts U. Wash., Seattle, 1977-81; mgr. performing and visual arts Parks and Recreation, City of Seattle, 1981-83, recreation dist. mgr., 1983—; cons. Nat. Endowment for Arts Multi-Music Panel, 1980, 81, 88; mem. edn. com. Seattle Art Mus., 1981—; workshop presenter Nat. Recreation and Parks Assn. Regional Confs., 1985-86; mem. conf. com. Internat. NW Parks and Recreation Assn. Conf., 1986. Bd. dirs. Bumbershoot-Seattle Arts Festival, 1979, 80; bd. dirs. Northwest Folklife Festival, 1982—, treas., 1985, 86, pres. 1986—; cantor Sacred Heart Ch., Seattle, 1982—. Mem. Nat. Entertainment and Campus Activities Assn. (dir. 1969-72, Cert. of Appreciation 1975), Western Alliance Arts Adminstrs. (v.p. 1978-80), Wash. State Folklife Council, Allied Arts Seattle, Seattle Folklore Soc., Wash. Recreation and Parks Assn., Internat. NW Parks and Recreation Assn. (conf. com. 1986), Nat. Recreation and Parks Assn. (presenter workshops at regional conf. 1985-86), Phi Beta Kappa, Mu Phi Epsilon, Alpha Delta Pi. Roman Catholic. Home: PO Box 19278 Seattle WA 98109 Office: 100 Dexter Ave N Seattle WA 98109

O'NEILL, NORAH ELLEN, airline pilot; b. Seattle, Aug. 23, 1949; d. John Wilson and Bertha Ellen (Moore) O'N.; m. Scott Reynolds, Jan. 31, 1970 (div. Apr. 1973); m. Scott Edward Byerley, Jan. 29, 1983; children: Cameron, Bren Maxey. Student, U. Calif., Santa Barbara, 1967-68, San Diego State U., 1868-70; BS in Profl. Aeros., Embry-Riddle Aero. U. Lic. airline transport pilot (comml., instrument instr.). Flight instr. Reynolds Aviation, Anchorage, 1973; flight instr. Alaska Cen. Air, Fairbanks, 1973-74, mail, commuter, medivac pilot, 1974-76; DC-8 pilot Flying Tigers, Los Angeles, Seattle, N.Y.C., 1976-80; 747 pilot Flying Tigers, Los Angeles, 1980—. Mem. Airline Pilots Assn., Women Airline Pilots Soc. (co-founder 1978, v.p. 1979-80), The 99's (hon.). Home: PO Box 1504 Walla Walla WA 99362 Office: Flying Tigers 7401 World Way West Los Angeles CA 90009

O'NEILL, SUSAN FAVANT, retailing company staff member; b. Bronxville, N.Y., Jan. 16, 1951; d. Eugene Frederic and Jacqueline Marie (Terreson) F; m. William J. O'Neill, Nov. 16, 1986. Student Russell Sage Coll., 1969-70; A.A. cum laude, Green Mountain Coll., 1972; B.S., N.Y. U., 1973. Asst. buyer merchandise trainee B. Altman & Co., N.Y.C., 1973-74, sr. asst. buyer, 1974-76, sr. group mgr. ready to wear, St. David's, Pa., 1976-82, asst. store mgr., Short Hills, N.J., 1982-86; operating store mgr. B. Altman's, Paramus, N.J., 1986-87. Vol., United Way of Bronxville, 1973, Planned Parenthood of Mt. Vernon, N.Y., 1973, Lawrence Hosp., Bronxville, 1974-75. Mem. Green Mountain Coll. Alumni Assn., Edn. Alumni Assn. N.Y. U., Omicron Nu. Republican. Club: 7 Arts Soc. (Bronxville treas. 1976). Home: 838 N 27th St Allentown PA 18104 Office: B Altman's The Fashion Ctr Paramus NJ 07652

ONG, WENDY SENG, educator; b. Phoenix, Aug. 19, 1950; d. Tong and Jessie (Yee) Wong; m. Timothy Laurence Ong, Apr. 14, 1974; 1 child, Amber Nicole. B in Elem. Edn., Grand Canyon Coll., 1972; M in Spl. Edn., Ariz. State U., 1978, M in Elem. Edn., 1980. Cert. sch. prin., superintendent, supr., spl. edn. supr., tchr. emotionally handicapped and learning disabilities. Tchr. Bay City Pub. Schs., Auburn, Mich., 1972-73; tchr. Washington Sch. Dist., Phoenix, 1973-76, tchr. spl. edn., 1976-79, dir. community edn., 1979-80, tchr., 1980-82; adminstrv. instructional asst. Washington Dist., 1983-84; instrnl. leader Washington Sch. Dist., Phoenix, 1982-84, adminstrv. instructional asst., 1983-84; faculty Grand Canyon Coll., Phoenix, 1980-81, 84; prin. Osborn Sch. Dist., Phoenix, 1984—; faculty McPhearson Coll., 1984. Bd. dirs., newsletter editor Ariz. Assisting Women to Advance through Resource and Encouragement, Phoenix, 1985-87; mem. Ariz. Women's Town Hall, 1987; Sunday sch. instr. Mem. AAUW, Nat. Elem. Sch. Prins. Assn., Am. Assn. Sch. Adminstrs., Am. Evaluation Assn., Assn. of Supervision and Curriculum Devel. (bd. dirs.), Nat. Assn. Female Execs., Bus. and Profl. Women's Clubs Inc., Am. Evaluation Assn., Phi Delta Kappa, Delta Kappa Gamma. Baptist. Home: 8608 N 45th Ave Glendale AZ 85302 Office: Longview Primary Sch 1209 E Indian Sch Rd Phoenix AZ 85014

ONLEY, SISTER FRANCESCA, college president; b. Phila., Mar. 4, 1933; d. Edward Patrick and Marie (Rice) O. B.A., Holy Family Coll., 1959; M.S., Marywood Coll., 1966; Ph.D., So. Ill. U., 1985. Cert. secondary counselor, Penn. Tchr. Nazareth Acad. Grade Sch., Phila., 1952-64; tchr. Nazareth Acad., Phila., 1964-67, vice prin., counselor, 1967-72, prin., 1972-80; spl. asst. to pres. Holy Family Coll., Phila., 1980-81, pres., 1981—; bd. dirs. Comcast, Phila., 1983—. Bd. officer, sec. N.E. br. ARC, Phila., 1984—, bd. dirs., 1983—. Recipient Alumni award Holy Family Coll. Alumni 1982. Mem. Middle State Assn. Schs. and Colls., Assn. Governing Bds., Council Ind. Colls., Northeast C. of C. (bd. dirs. 1983—). Democrat. Roman Catholic. Office: Holy Family Coll Grant and Frankford Aves Philadelphia PA 19114

ONN, SHIRLEY ANN, librarian, editor; b. Montreal, Can., Nov. 4, 1940; d. Kenneth Charles and Ann Campbell (Scott) Chappell; m. G. Hewson Hickie, Feb. 20, 1959 (div. 1973); children: Kent H., Colin S., Craig H., Keith C.; m. William DeForest Onn, Oct. 28, 1977. BA in English with hon., Concordia U., Montreal, 1976; MA in Can. Lit., U. Calgary, Alberta, 1983. Librarian King's Hall Sch. for Girls, Compton, Quebec, 1971-72, C.D. Howe Research Inst., Montreal, 1976-77; edit. asst. Abstracts of English Studies, Calgary, 1980-84; manuscript editor Calgary, 1983—; asst. U. Calgary Libraries, 1984—; instr. communications U. Calgary, 1987—. Mem. Can. Library Assn. (H.W. Wilson scholar 1987), Alberta Library Assn., Foothills Library Assn., Can. Assn. Spl. Libraries and Info. Services, Freelance Editors Assn. of Can., Bibliographical Soc. Can. Office: Univ Calgary Libraries, 2500 University Dr NW, Calgary CAN T2N 1N4

ONO, YOKO, conceptual artist, singer, recording artist; b. Tokyo, Feb. 18, 1933; U.S. citizen; m. John Ono Lennon, Mar. 20, 1969 (dec. 1980); children: Kyoko, Sean; Student Peers' Sch., Gakushuin U., Tokyo, Sarah Lawrence Coll., Harvard U. One-woman shows include Alchemical Wedding, Albert Hall, London, 1967, Evening with Yoko Ono, Birmingham, 1968, Event, U. Wales, 1969, Everson Mus., Syracuse, N.Y., 1971, others; exhibited Fluxshoe, Sch. Art, Falmouth, Cornwall, Eng., 1972; recorded albums: (with John Ono Lennon) Two Virgins, 1968, Life With Lions, 1969, Wedding Album, 1970, Live Peace In Toronto (1969), 1970, Some Time in New York City, 1972, Double Fantasy, 1980 (Grammy award Album of Yr. 1981), Milk and Honey, 1984; solo albums include Yoko Ono/Plastic Ono Band, Fly, Approximately Infinite Universe, Feeling the Space, Season of Glass, Starpeace, 1985; composer numerous songs including Don't Worry Kyoko, Mummy's Only Looking For Her Hand in the Snow, Walking on Thin Ice (Grammy award nomination Best Female Rock Performance on Single 1981), Don't Be Sad. Author six film scripts, Tokyo, 1964, thirteen film score scores, London, 1967, John & Yoko Calendar, 1970, (book) Grapefruit, 1964, London, 1970, A Hole to See the Sky Through, N.Y., 1971. Office: Studio One 1 W 72nd St New York NY 10023

ONOFREY, DEBRA ANNE CATHERINE, accounting administrator; b. Lakewood, Ohio, Jan. 18, 1956; d. John Martin and Dolores Marlene (Sefcovic) O. Student, Tex. Luth. Coll., 1974-76, John Cabot Internat. Coll., Rome, 1977. Bookkeeper, clk. Ress Realty Co., Cleve., 1978-80; acctg. clk. U. Tex. SW Med. Ctr., Dallas, 1981-83, sect. coordinator, 1983-86, mgr., 1986—. Co-editor Med. Service Research and Devel. plan Monarch newsletter, 1984. Mem. Nat. Assn. Female Execs., Smithsonian Inst.. Roman Catholic. Home: 4005 N Beltline #526 Irving TX 75038 Office: U Tex SW Med Ctr 6011 Harry Hines Blvd Dallas TX 75235

OOSTERWIJK, LINDA JEAN, insurance executive; b. Cambridge, Mass., June 7, 1947; m. Gary Brian Garner, Jan. 12, 1969 (div. June 1972); children: Jeanette M., Brett A.; m. Frederik Dirk Oosterwijk, Nov. 25, 1983; 1 stepson, Jason . BS in Elem. Edn., U. Mass., 1969; postgrad., North Lake Coll., 1979-81, Quinsigamond Coll., 1985. Tchr. Pinellas County Elem. Sch., Clearwater, Fla., 1971-73; bookkeeper Dean Air Conditioning Co., Clearwater, 1973-74; claims examiner Insurnational, Inc., Dallas, 1976-77; asst. supr. Lone Star Life Ins. Co., Dallas, 1977-79, acctg. supr., 1979-81; clk., typist Consol. Group Trust, Framingham, Mass., 1974-75, supr. billing, 1975-76, 81-82, asst. mgr., 1982-85; mgr. Transport Life Ins. Co., Ft. Worth, Tex., 1985-86, sr. adminstr., 1986—. Arbitrator Better Bus. Bur., Worcester,

Mass., 1983-85; mem. Parent Adv. Bd., Worcester, 1984-85. Mem. Nat. Assn. Female Execs. Roman Catholic. Home: 6604 Constitution St Watauga TX 76148

OPAR, PATRICIA ANN, guidance counselor; b. Troy, N.Y., June 3, 1938; d. Paul and Martha Theresa (Kawola) Opar; B.A., Coll. St. Rose, 1960, M.A., 1963; M.S. in Edn., Siena Coll., 1965; postgrad. (NDEA grantee) Western Mich. U., 1965, N. Adams State Coll., SUNY, Albany, Russell Sage Coll. Nat. cert. counselor and career counselor; cert. guidance counselor, sch. dist. adminstr., elem. and secondary tchr., N.Y. State. Tchr., S. Colonie Central Sch. Dist., Albany, N.Y., 1960-65, guidance counselor, 1965—, mem. curriculum rev. bd., 1979-82, coordinator continuing edn., 1980-81; summer youth counselor div. employment N.Y. State Dept. of Labor, 1969. Bd. dirs. Colonie Youth Centers, Albany, 1979-81. Mem. Am. Assn. Counseling and Devel., (dir. Senate), Am. Sch. Counselor Assn., Nat. Career Devel. Assn., N.Y. State Assn. Counseling Devel. (sec., chmn. by-laws rev. com., exec. council, senate), Capital Dist. Counseling Assn. (pres., sec., chmn. program and in-service edn. com., trustee), N.Y. State United Tchrs., Delta Epsilon Sigma. Ukrainian Catholic. Home: 3 Kerry Ln Albany NY 12211 Office: Sand Creek Mid Sch 329 Sand Creek Rd Albany NY 12205

OPHEIM, ROBERTA CLAIRE, consulting company executive; b. Virginia, Minn., Sept. 20, 1948; d. Harden Robert and Romelle Claire (Sandberg) Bloomquist; m. Gary Warren Opheim, July 26, 1969; children: Justin Robert, Scott Warren. BA, Gustavus Adolphus Coll., 1970; cert. in small bus. mgmt., 916 Voc-Tech, 1983. Customer service rep. Northwestern Bell Telephone, St. Paul, 1971-75; owner Hickory Dickory Dock, Stillwater, Minn., 1977-86; pres. Objectives Inc., Stillwater, 1986—. Advisor Small Bus. Adv. Council, Congressman Arlan Erdahl, 1980; bd. dirs. Small Bus. Adv. Bd. 916 Voc-Tech, White Bear, 1981-83; del. Minn. Conference on Small Bus., 1981, 87; pres. Downtown Council, Stillwater, 1984; mem. Stillwater City Council, 1986—, Stillwater Parks and Recreation Commn., 1986—, Stillwater Downtown Planning Com., 1987—; mem. Mpls.-St. Paul Airport Adequacy Study Task Force Met. Council of Twin Cities. Named Outstanding Community Bus. Leader Jaycees, 1984. Mem. Nat. Assn. Female Execs., Jaycee Women (v.p. 1979, treas. 1980), Stillwater C. of C. (pres. 1986, 87). Office: Objectives Inc 324 S Main St PO Box 518 Stillwater MN 55082

OPPEDISANO, SUZANNE MARIE, marketing professional, dentist; b. Boston; d. Rocco Louis and Ruth Margaret (Webb) O. BS, Tufts U., 1976, MBA, 1986; DMD, U. Pa., 1980, MBA, 1986. Adj. faculty U. Pa. Sch. Dental Medicine, Phila., 1984-86; nat. sales analyst E.R. Squibb & Sons, Princeton, N.J., 1986-87; asst. product dir. Johnson & Johnson Dental Care Co., New Brunswick, N.J., 1988—; Intern prodn. mgmt. Pharm. div. CIBA-Geigy, Summit, N.J., 1985; student cons. Albert Einstein Hosp., Phila., 1985. Contbr. articles to profl. jours. Served to capt. U.S. Army, 1980-84. Armed Forces Health Professions scholar U.S. Army Dental Corps. Mem. ADA, Wharton Alumni Assn.

OPPENHEIM, BETH N., data processing company executive; b. Balt., July 9, 1963; d. Samuel and Rosalind (Lewis) O. BS in Computer Sci., Syracuse U., 1985; MBA in Engring. Mgmt., U. Dallas, Irving, 1987. Software design engr. Tex. Instruments, Plano, Tex., 1985—. Dem. precinct chmn., Dallas, 1986; mem. com. Jewish Fedn., Dallas, 1985—; mem. Am. Jewish Com., Jewish Community Ctr. Mem. Nat. Assn. Female Execs., Syracuse Alumni Assn. (pres. Dallas chpt.), Delta Phi Epsilon, Rho Lambda. Club: Syracuse Alumni.

OPPENHEIM, ELLEN, municipal official; b. N.Y.C., Mar. 18, 1951; d. Don Bruce and Irene (Gartner) O.; m. Steven William Davidson, June 8, 1974; 1 child, Anne Oppenheim Davidson. BA, U. Wis., 1972, MBA, 1977. Dir. mini-course U. Wis., Madison, 1974-75, mgr. ops., 1975-77; asst. dir. Tresidder Union Stanford (Calif.) U., 1977-80, dir. Tresidder Union, 1980-83, assoc. dean students, 1983-87; asst. dir. City of San Jose (Calif.) Parks and Recreation Dept., 1987—; bd. dirs. Stanford U. Fed. Credit Union, 1984-87. Mem. Am. Mgmt. Assn., Wis. Meml. Union Bldg. Assn. (voting mem. 1985—), Assn. Coll. Unions (chairperson internat. conf. com. 1983-85). Home: 304 Tioga Ct Palo Alto CA 94306 Office: City of San Jose Parks and Recreation Dept 151 West Mission St San Jose CA 95110

OPPENHEIM, IRENE GARTNER, writer; b. N.Y.C., July 26, 1928; d. Samuel and Bessie (Gersten) Gartner; m. Don Bruce Oppenheim, June 22, 1947; children: Ellen, Wendy, Barbara. BS, Pratt Inst., Bklyn., 1947; MA, NYU, 1957, PhD, 1961. Tchr. N.Y.C. Pub. Schs., 1949-50; dir. Schley St. Coop. Nursery Sch., Newark, 1954-57; tchr. Irvington (N.J.) Pub. Schs., 1957-59; asst. prof. Montclair State Coll., Upper Montclair, N.J., 1959-63; from assoc. to asst. prof. NYU, N.Y.C., 1963-68; freelance ednl. writer Princeton, N.J., 1968—; mem. pub. service adv. com. FDA, Washington, 1964-65; dir. Interdisciplinary Project for Tchrs. and Adminstrs. Wash. State U., Pullman, 1971; trustee, cons. Princeton U. League Nursery Sch., 1987; cons. in field. Author: The Family as Consumers, 1965, Management of the Modern Home, 1972, 2d edit., 1976, Consumer Skills, 1972, 2d edit., 1976, Living Today, 1981, 2d edit., 1988. Consumer rep. Senate Bank and Currency Commn., U.S. Congress, Washington, 1964. Pratt Inst. scholar, 1946-48. Mem. Am. Home Econs. Assn., Am. Council on Consumer Interests (pres. 1964-65).

OPPENHEIM, MARTHA KUNKEL, pianist, educator; b. Port Arthur, Tex., June 25, 1935; d. Samuel Adam and Grace (Moncure) Kunkel; m. Russell Edward Oppenheim, June 18, 1960; children—Lauren Susan, Kristin Lee Oppenheim Mortenson. MusB with honors, U. Tex., 1957, MusM, U. Tex., 1959; diploma in piano Juilliard Sch. Music, 1960; student Am. Conservatory, Fontainebleau, France, 1956, 58. soloist, Amarillo (Tex.) Symphony, Austin (Tex.) Symphony, U. Tex. Orch., San Antonio Symphony, Dallas Symphony, Heilbronner Kammer Orch., Heilbronn, Germany; solo and chamber music recitals in Tex., N.Y., France; mem. Halcyon Trio, 1974-77; teaching asst. U. Tex., 1957-59, 68-69; pvt. piano tchr., San Antonio, 1962—. Recipient 1st Place award Internat. Piano Recording Festival, Nat. Guild Piano Tchrs., 1956, 57, 1st Place award Tuesday Mus. Club Young Artist Competition, 1956, 1st Place award Young Artist Competition, Amarillo Symphony, 1959; 1st Place award G. B. Dealey Competition, Dallas Symphony and Dallas Morning News, 1959; Scholar U. Tex., Juilliard Sch. Music. Mem. Music Tchrs. Nat. Assn., Tex. Music Tchrs. Assn., San Antonio Music Tchrs. Assn., Sigma Alpha Iota, Pi Kappa Lambda. Presbyterian. Club: Tuesday Musical (San Antonio) (bd. dirs.). Home and Office: 9118 E Valley View Ln San Antonio TX 78217

OPPENHEIMER, JANE MARION, biologist, historian, educator; b. Phila., Sept. 19, 1911; d. James Harry and Sylvia (Stern) O. B.A., Bryn Mawr Coll., 1932; Ph.D., Yale U., 1935, postgrad. (Sterling fellow), 1935-36, Am. Assn. U. Women fellow, 1936-37; Sc.D. (hon.), Brown U., 1976. Research fellow embryology U. Rochester, 1937-38; faculty Bryn Mawr (Pa.) Coll., 1938—, prof., 1953-80, prof. emeritus, 1980—, acting dean grad. sch., 2d semester, 1946-47; Vis. prof. biology Johns Hopkins, 1966-67; exchange prof. U. Paris, 1969. Author: New Aspects of John and William Hunter, 1946, Essays in History of Embryology and Biology, 1967; editor: Autobiography of Dt. Karl Ernst von Baer, 1986; co-editor: Founds. Exptl. Embryology, 1964, editor 2d edit., 1974; assoc. editor: Jour. Morphology, 1956-58, Quar. Rev. Biol, 1963-64; mem. editorial bd.: Am. Zoologist, 1965-70, Jour. History Biology, 1967-75, Quar. Rev. Biology, 1968-75; sect. editor developmental biology: Biol. Abstracts, 1970-73. Mem. history life scis. study sect. NIH, 1966-70. Recipient Lucius Wilbur Cross medal Yale Grad. Alumni Assn., 1971; Guggenheim Meml. Found. fellow, 1942-43, 52-53; Rockefeller Found. fellow, 1950-51; NSF postdoctoral fellow, 1959-60. Fellow AAAS (sec. sect. L 1955-58, council del. sect. G 1980-83, com. on council affairs 1981-82), Phila. Coll. Physicians (hon.); mem. Am. Soc. Zoologists (treas. 1957-59, chmn. div. devel. biology 1967, pres. 1973), Am. Assn. Anatomists, History of Sci. Soc. (mem. council 1975-77), Am. Assn. History Medicine (mem. council 1971-74), Am. Soc. Naturalists, Soc. for Developmental Biology, Internat. Soc. for Developmental Biology, Am. Inst. Biol. Scis. (mem. at large governing bd. 1974-77), Internat. Soc. History Medicine, Internat. Acad. History of Sci. (Paris) (corr.), Internat. Acad. History Medicine (Paris), Am. Philos. Soc. (council 1982—, exec. com. 1984—, sec. 1987—). Office: Biology Bldg Bryn Mawr Coll Bryn Mawr PA 19010

OPPENHEIMER, SELMA LEVY (MRS. REUBEN OPPENHEIMER), artist; b. Balt.; d. William and Beatrice (Stern) Levy; A.B., Goucher Coll., 1919; student Md. Inst., 1920-22; m. Reuben Oppenheimer, June 26, 1922; children—Martin J., Joan (Mrs. Stanley Weiss). One-man show Har Sinai Synagogue, 1977, McDonough Sch., Balt., 1978; exhibited in group shows at Balt. Mus. Art, 1935-61, also invitational exhbn., 1968, Peale Mus., 1938-66, Phila. Art Alliance, 1940, So. State, 1947, Hagerstown Mus. Fine Arts, Pa. Acad., 1938, Chgo. Art Inst., 1952, Phillips Meml. Gallery, 1938, Corcoran Gallery, 1941-47, 51, 56, 57, 60, Va. Mus. Fine Arts, 1938, Ringling Mus. Art, 1960, Calif. Palace Legion Honor, San Francisco, 1938, Mus. Modern Art, N.Y.C., 1933, Smithsonian Instn., 1956, N.A.D., N.Y.C., 1938-66, Royal Acad. Galleries, Edinburgh, Scotland, 1963, Royal Birmingham (Eng.) Soc. Artists Galleries, 1963, Johns Hopkins Med. Residence Hall, 1961, Goucher Coll., 1965, 76, Jewish Community Center Retrospective Exhibit, 1967; with traveling exhbn. U.S., 1963-65, Scotland (Edinburg), 1964, France, 1965; represented in permanent collection Balt. Pub. Schs., U. Md., Loyola Coll. Chmn. art com. Jewish Community Center, Balt., 1958-65, bd. dirs., 1958-64; corr. sec. Balt. br. Council Jewish Women; publicity chmn. Md. Fedn. Women's Clubs; sec.-treas. Balt. Art Festival; vice chmn. artists com. Balt. Mus. Art, 1950, artists com., trustee, 1961-72, chmn. classical arts accessions com., 1969—. Recipient medal Md. Inst., 1933, Balt. Mus. Art, 1935, 38, Balt. Water Color Club, 1959, award oil painting Nat. Assn. Women Artists, 1952, 60, 65, purchase award Loyola Coll., 1967. Mem. Nat. Assn. Women Artists, Artists Equity Assn. (past pres. Md. chpt.), Am. Fedn. Arts, Balt. Watercolor Club. Clubs: Hamilton Street (Balt.); Suburban (Pikesville, Md.). Address: 7121 Park Heights Ave Baltimore MD 21215

OPPENHEIMER, SUZI, state senator; m. Martin J. Oppenheimer; children: Marcy, Evan, Josh, Alexandra. BA in Econs., Conn. Coll. for Women; MBA, Columbia U. Former security analyst L.F. Rothschild Co., N.Y.C.; mayor Village of Mamaroneck, N.Y., 1977-84; mem. N.Y. State Senate, 1984—, mem. edn., commerce, econ. devel. and small bus., child care, consumer protection, transp. coms., chmn. Senate Minority Task Force on Women's Issues. Former pres. Mamaroneck LWV, Westchester County Village Ofcls. Assn., Westchester Mcpl. Planning Fedn. Democrat. Office: Legis Office Bldg Albany NY 12224

OPPENHEIMER-FEINSTEIN, JOAN AMY, psychologist, educator; b. Phila., Aug. 9, 1952; d. Simon and Claire (Pogach) F. BA cum laude, Temple U., 1974, cert. grad. study, 1979, PhD, 1984; MEd, Pa. State U., 1975. Lic. psychologist, Pa.; cert. sch. psychologist. Program dir. People Acting to Help, Inc., Phila., 1976-80; pvt. practice psychology Phila., 1982—; adj. asst. prof. grad. div. Temple U., 1981—, Chestnut Hill Coll., 1988—. Mem. Am. Psychol. Assn., Am. Assn. Marriage and Family Therapy (clin.), Am. Orthopsychiat. Assn., Nat. Assn. Cert. Rehab. Counselors. Jewish. Office: Marriage & Family Resource Ctr 82 Buck Rd Holland PA 18966

ORAN, GERALDINE ANN, teacher; b. Burleson, Tex., June 27, 1938; s. Clyde Lloyd and Ruth (Baxley) Renfro; m. Francis Larry Oran, Dec. 18, 1960, children: Angelique Michelle, Jeremy Lloyd. AS summa cum laude, Roane State Community Coll., Harriman, Tenn., 1976; BS summa cum laude, U. Tenn., 1978. IBM instr., office mgr. Kelsey-Jenney Bus. Coll., San Diego, 1958-61; exec. sec. Bendix Corp., San Diego, 1961-62; ednl. adminstr. South Harriman Bapt. Ch., 1964-74; tchr. Midtown Elem., Harriman, 1979—. Mem., sec., treas., pres. PTA and PTO, Harriman, 1967-81; active Cancer, Heart Fund and March of Dimes, Harriman, 1979—; dir. vacation bible sch. South Harriman Bapt. Ch., 1983-86, tchr. women's bible sch., 1965-87; club sponsor Tenn. Just Say No to Drugs Team, Roane County, 1985-87. Named Tchr. of Yr. Roane County, 1987. Mem. Nat. Edn. Assn. (del. rep. 1985-86), Tenn. Edn. Assn. (del. rep. 1984-86, Outstanding Service award 1985-86), Roane County Edn. Assn. (membership chairperson 1984-85, pres. 1985-86), Gamma Phi Beta, Kappa Delta Pi, Phi Kappa Phi. Baptist. Home: PO Box 917 Harriman TN 37748-0917 Office: Midtown Elem Sch Rt 8 Box 188 Harriman TN 37748

ORAV, HELLE REISSAR, retired dentist; b. Tartu, Estonia, July 10, 1925; came to U.S., 1949, naturalized, 1954; d. Johan and Adele Johanna (Minski) Reissar; m. Arnold Orav, May 30, 1952; children: Ilmar Erik, Hillar Thomas. Student Friedrich Alexander U., Erlangen, West Germany, 1946-49; DDS, NYU, 1952. Practice dentistry, N.Y.C., 1952, 60, 62, 68, Valencia, Venezuela, 1953-68. Counselor, Red Cross, Valencia, 1954-55; past mem. Rotary Ladies Republican. Lutheran. Clubs: Country of Maracaibo (Venezuela); Palm Beach Polo and Country (Fla.); Korp Filiae Patriae (N.Y.C.). Avocations: Pre-Colombian art, bridge, travel, swimming, reading. Home: 860 Fifth Ave New York NY 10021

ORCHARD, DONNA LEE, box company executive; b. Kansas City, Mo., Dec. 27, 1931; d. Max Edward and Ruth Louise (Kerst) Arenson; m. Edgar L. Orchard, Feb. 5, 1957; children—Laura Ellen Orchard Massie, Barri Louise Orchard Sapp, Caroline Courtney. Student Washington U., St. Louis, 1950, U. Mo.-Kansas City, 1952. Office mgr. Gentry & Voskamp Architects, Kansas City, 1953-57; sec., synopsis editor for publ. release Sovereign TV Prodn. (Gen. Electric, Dupont Theaters), Hollywood, Calif., 1951-52; pres., owner Orchard Box Co., St. Louis, 1979—; v.p. Orco Sales Co. Patentee in field. Pres., Washington U. Women's Soc., St. Louis, 1982-84; bd. mem. Temple Israel, St. Louis, 1982-87; sec. Gateway Theater, St. Louis; life mem., v.p. Primitive Arts Soc., St. Louis Art Mus., 1980-81; bd. dirs. St. Louis Opera Guild, founder womens com. 1960-63; bd. dirs., life mem. Jewish Hosp. Aux., Brandeis U.; bd. dirs. St. Louis Symphony Womens Soc., St. Louis Zoo Assn., League of Women Voters, 1958-59; life mem. Hilton Theater, Webster Coll. Mem. Nat. Assn. Women Bus. Owners, Kansas City C. of C. (wage and hour com. 1955-57). Republican. Jewish. Club: Whitemore House. Avocations: collector of art, gardening, raising of Koi, research of art and oriental porcelains. Home: One Robindale Dr Saint Louis MO 63124 Office: Orchard Box Co 1326 Baur Blvd Saint Louis MO 63132

ORCHARD, JAYE MERRILL, courier service executive; b. West Palm Beach, Fla., May 26, 1949; d. Samuel Miller and Marcia Lee (Wooden) Turn; m. Jeffrey Campbell Orchard, Aug. 7, 1970 (div. 1980); 1 child, Zachary Campbell. AA, Stephens Coll., 1969; BS, So. Meth. U., 1971. Recreation therapist Central Island Nursing Home, Plainview, N.Y., 1976-81; parent counselor Tara Hall Home for Boys, Georgetown, S.C., 1981-82; dist. mgr. A. L. Williams Co., Wilmington, N.C., 1983—; owner, mgr. Leisurely Dash Courier Service, Wilmington, 1986—; freelance writer, photographer; editor, pub. Focus newsletter, 1986, Jobhunters newsletter, 1987. Mem. Women Helping Women (dir. pub. relations 1987—), Wilmington Bus. Women's Assn., Entrepreneurs Assn. N.C. Democrat. Presbyterian. Clubs: Wilmington Jr. Women's, Wilmington Newcomers. Home: 526 Sierra Dr Wilmington NC 28403 Office: Leisurely Dash PO Box 1062 Wilmington NC 28402

ORCUTT, BEN AVIS, social work educator; b. Falco, Ala., Oct. 17, 1914; d. Benjamin A. and Emily Olive Adams; A.B., U. Ala., 1936; M.A., Tulane U., 1939, M.S.W., 1942; D.S.W., Columbia U., 1962. Social worker, acting field dir. ARC, LaGarde Gen. Hosp., New Orleans, Fort Benning (Ga.) Regional Hosp., 1942-46; chief social work service VA regional office, Phoenix, 1946-51, chief social work service unit outpatient office, Birmingham, Ala., 1954-57, 58; research asst. Research Center Sch. Social Work, Columbia U., N.Y.C., 1960-62, field adv. social work, 1962, asso. prof. social work, 1965-76; asso. prof. social work La. State U., Baton Rouge, 1962-65; prof. social work, dir. doctoral program U. Ala., University, 1976-84; research cons. Tavistock Centre, London, 1972. Mem. alumni bd. Sch. Social Work, Columbia U., 1985—. NIMH fellow, 1957-60. Mem. Council Social Work Edn., Nat. Assn. Social Workers, Am. Assn. Orthopsychiatry, Found. Thanatology, N.Y. Acad. Scis., Ala. Conf. Social Welfare, Group for Advancement Doctoral Edn. (steering com., editor newsletter 1980-83). Episcopalian. Club: Zonta. Author: (with Harry P. Orcutt) America's Riding Horses, 1958; (with Elizabeth R. Prichard, Jean Collard, Austin H. Kutscher, Irene Seeland, Nathan Lefkowitz) Social Work with the Dying Patient and the Family, 1977; (with others) Social Work and Thanatology, 1980; editor: Poverty and Social Casework Services, 1974; editorial bd. Jour. Social Work, 1982-84; contbr. articles to profl. books and jours. Home: 222 Fox Run Tuscaloosa AL 35406 Office: PO Box 1935 University AL 35486

ORDILLE, CAROL MARIA, infosystems specialist, analyst; b. Hammonton, N.J., Aug. 4, 1943. BS in Econs., Temple U., 1965; MS in Applied Stats., Villanova (Pa.) U., 1967; PhD in Biostats., Ohio State U., 1975. Statistician Merck Sharp & Dohme, West Point, Pa., 1967-68; research statistician Schering-Plough Corp., Kenilworth, N.J., 1972-75; dir. stats. and data systems Miles Pharms., West Haven, Conn., 1975-80; mgr. biostats. DuPont Pharms., Wilmington, Del., 1980-84; database adminstr. Dept. Eviron. Protection State of N.J., Trenton, 1985-86; sr. staff analyst G.P.U. Service Corp., Parsippany, N.J., 1986—; program co-chmn. biostats. ann. mtg. Pharm. Mfrs. Assn., 1983, chmn. roundtable discussion on med. stats., 1983; cons. in field, 1984—. Mem. Am. Statis. Assn., Biometric Soc., Pi Mu Epsilon, Omicron Delta Epsilon. Office: GPU Service Corp 100 Interpace Pkwy Parsippany NJ 07054

ORDOWER, MYRNA E., insurance broker; b. Chgo., Oct. 8; d. Abe Herman and Gussie (Rubinsky) Berliner; m. Sidney L. Ordower, Mar. 4, 1961; children—Cheryl, Karyn, Steven. Student, U. Ill., Northwestern U. Underwriter, Bergman & Lefkow Ins., Chgo., 1952-61; unit mgr. Near North Ins., Chgo., 1974-82; owner, pres. Myrna Ordower Enterprises, Chgo., 1982—; v.p., stockholder Rockwood Co., 1982—, also bd. dirs. Founder, Women's Exec. Network, Chgo., 1983—; co-founder Corp. Connections, Chgo., 1985. Bd. dirs. Little City Found. for Mentally Retarded Children, Women's bd. Chgo. Urban League; fund raiser Muscular Dystrophy, Chgo.; del. White House Conf. Small Bus., 1986. Mem. Nat. Assn. Women Bus. Owners (bd. dirs.), Nat. Assn. Ins. Women. Home: 5502 S Harper Ave Chicago IL 60637 Office: Myrna Ordower Enterprises 20 N Wacker Dr Chicago IL 60606

ORDUNA-MUSLIMANI, MARIA, insurance sales executive; b. La Paz, Colombia, Feb. 11, 1959; came to U.S., 1967; d. Segismundo Orduna and Ana Lucrecia Traslavina; m. Nazeir Muslimani, July 27, 1985. BS in Lang. Arts, Georgetown U., 1982. Supr. Deak-Perera, Washington, 1983-84; ins. agt. Mut. of Omaha Cos., Washington, 1984-87, sales mgr., 1987—. Chairperson Sacred Heart Trilingual Parish Council, Washington, 1987—. Mem. Nat. Assn. Female execs., Nat. Assn. Health Underwriters (health ins. quality award 1985, 86), Nat. Council Hispanic Women. Roman Catholic. Office: Mut of Omaha 1666 Connecticut Ave NE 2d Floor Washington DC 20009

O'REGAN, PATRICE, retail executive; b. Staten Island, N.Y., Aug. 14, 1956; d. Cornelius James and Margaret Anne (Larkin) O'R. BS in Secondary Edn., Villanova (Pa.) U., 1978. Sales mgr. Macy's N.Y., Staten Island, 1978-79; asst. buyer Macy's N.Y., N.Y.C., 1979-81, assoc. merchandising adminstr., 1981, buyer gift housewares, 1981-83; sr. sales rep. Corning Glass Works, Fairfax, Va., 1983; mgr. retail sales devel. Corning Glass Works, Corning, N.Y., 1983-84; mgr. nat. accounts Crown Corning div. Corning Glass Works, Los Angeles, 1984-86, mgr. ea. regional sales Crown Corning div., 1986-87; mgr. divisional merchandising Federated Merchandising Services, N.Y.C., 1987—. Democrat. Roman Catholic. Office: Federated Merchandising Services 1440 Broadway 6th Floor New York NY 10018

O'REILLY, LOUISE, electric company executive; b. Melrose, Mass., Sept. 11, 1948; d. Whitney and Shirley (Moore) Gerrish; m. Richard Wayne Halle, May 10, 1969 (div. 1985); m. William R. O'Reilley, May 20, 1988. Student, U. Mich., 1966-69; BS in Chem. Edn., U. Mass., 1971, MEd, 1974; MS in Indsl. Adminstrn., Union Coll., 1984. Tchr. chemistry R.C. Mahar Regional Sch., Orange, Mass., 1971-74, Portland (Conn.) High Sch., 1974-76; self employed 1976-78; fuel chemist Encotech Inc., Schenectady, N.Y., 1978-80; tng. specialist Gen. Electric Co., Schenectady, 1980-84, mgr. entry level tng., 1984-86, mgr. power gen. tch. tng., 1986—. Mem. Elfun Soc., Schenectady, 1987. Mem. Am. Soc. Tng. and Devel. Office: Gen Electric Co 1 River Rd Bldg 600-129 Schenectady NY 12345

ORELLANA, SANDRA LEE, anthropology educator; b. Fredericksburg, Va., Mar. 6, 1941; d. Melvin H. and Margaret J. (Alexander) Davey; m. Carlos L. Orellana (div. 1973). BA in Internat. Relations, UCLA, 1963, MA in Polit. Sci., 1965, MA in Latin Am. Studies, 1969, PhD in Anthropology, 1976. Tchr. Instituto Brasil-Estados Undiso, Fortaleza, Brazil, 1965-66; asst. prof. anthropology Calif. State U., Dominguez Hills, 1973-78, assoc. prof., 1979-82, prof., 1982—; cons. for Latin Am. Sect. RAND Corp., Santa Monica, 1970-71, Los Angeles Bd. Edn., 1973; instr. UCLA extension, 1974—. Fellow NSF, 1969-70, Del Amo Found., 1977; recipient Affirmative Action Faculty Devel. award, 1981; Pacific Basin grantee. Mem. Acad. Internat. Bus., Am. Inst. Archaeology, Am. Soc. for Ethnohistory, World Future Soc., Robotics Internat., Southwestern Anthrop., Beverly Hills C. of C. (membership com. 1985—), U.S. Space Found., Space Studies Inst. Republican. Home: 3853 Coolidge Ave Los Angeles CA 90066 Office: Calif State U Dept Anthropology 1000 E Victoria St Carson CA 90747

OREM, SANDRA ELIZABETH, nursing administrator; b. Balt., Sept. 26, 1940; d. Ira Julius and Mabel Ruth (Peeples) O. Diploma, Ch. Home and Hosp. Sch. Nursing, 1962; BS with honors, The Johns Hopkins U., 1968; MS, U. Md., 1972. Staff, charge nurse Ch. Home and Hosp., Balt., 1962-63; asst. instr. Ch. Home and Hosp. Sch. Nursing, Balt., 1963-64, instr., 1964-70; clin. nurse specialist Johns Hopkins Hosp., Balt., 1972-77, asst. dir. nursing, 1977-79, dir. nursing, 1979—; clin. assoc. faculty The Johns Hopkins U. Sch. of Nursing, 1984—; pres. Nursing Edn. and Cons. Service, Inc., Balt., 1976-78, Oasis Health Systems, Inc., Balt., 1987—. Contbr. articles to profl. publs. Vol. Office on Aging, Balt., 1982-83, Boy Scouts Am., Balt., 1984-85. Mem. Am. Orgn. Nurse Execs., Am. Hosp. Assn., Am. Holistic Nurses Assn., Ch. Home and Hosp. Sch. Nursing Alumni Assn. (treas. 1970-72, pres.-elect 1975-76), Sigma Theta Tau. Democrat. Episcopalian.

ORIANS, MONICA ANN, sales executive, medical technologist, microbiologist; b. San Diego, Mar. 18, 1956; d. Michael Aloysius and Martha Ann (Green) Chamberlain; m. July 9, 1988. BS in Microbiology, San Diego State U., 1979. Lab. asst. San Diego State U., 1977-79, San Diego Health Dept., 1976-78; med. technologist intern El Centro Community Hosp., Calif., 1979-80; med. technologist Pioneer Meml. Hosp., Brauley, Calif., 1980-81, Sharp Meml. Hosp., San Diego, 1981-84; sales and service rep. 3M Diagnostic Systems, Mountain View, Calif., 1984-87, assoc. product mgr., Santa Clara, Calif., 1987-88; product mgr., 3M Diagnostic Systems, Santa Clara, 1988—. cons. Nutri-Fact, Encinitas, Calif., 1984-85. Vol. research fellow San Diego Zoo, 1983; vol. Old Globe Theater, San Diego, 1982. Named Tech. Service Rep. of Yr., 3M Diagnostic Systems, 1985. Mem. Am. Soc. Clin. Pathologists, Nat. Assn. Female Execs., Am. Soc. Microbiology (pres. San Diego State U. chpt. 1978-79), Calif. Assn. Med. Lab. Technologists (treas. Desert chpt. 1980-81), San Diego State U. Microbiology Alumni Assn. (chmn. fundraiser 1984). Republican. Roman Catholic. Avocations: bicycling; racquetball; skiing; gourmet cuisine. Office: 3M Diagnostic Systems 3380 Central Expressway Santa Clara CA 95051

ORKIN, RITA LOUISE, data processing executive; b. N.Y.C., Aug. 18, 1944; d. Louis Richard and Florence (Fine) O. BA in Math., Alfred (N.Y.) U., 1965. Programmer AT&T, N.Y.C., 1965-70; systems programmer S&H Promotional Services, N.Y.C., 1970-81, Penn Cen. Corp., N.Y.C., 1981-85, Comml. On-Line Systems Inc., N.Y.C., 1985—. Mem. Assn. of Women in Computing, OSERG (bd. dirs. 1982—), GUIDE Internat. (div. sec. 1981—; Pres.'s award 1986).

ORKOW, BONNIE MARIE, state social services administrator; b. Natrona Heights, Pa., June 11, 1945; d. Ralph William and Helen Frances (Rakowski) Bole; m. Alex Frank Orkow, Jan. 24, 1970. BA, Coll. of Wooster, Ohio, 1967; MSW, Washington U., 1970. Cert. social worker; lic. social worker. Med. social worker City Hosp. #1, St. Louis, 1970-71; office social worker Tri-County Dist. Health Dept., Denver, 1971-77, dir. social services, 1977-81; dir. office of evaluation Colo. State Dept. Social Services, Denver, 1981-84; div. dir. Medicaid Programs Colo. State Dept. Social Services, 1984-87, div. dir. research, evaluation, and quality control, 1987—; cons. to pvt. and civic health care orgns.; panel chmn. U.S. del. to U.S.-Soviet Conf. on Youth and Soc., Moscow, 1981. Contbr. articles to profl. jours., chpts. to textbooks. Campaign organizer Democratic Party, Denver, 1987; mem. fed. tech. adv. com. Nat. Aid to Families with Dependent Children. Mem. Nat. Assn. Social Workers. Jewish. Club: Denver City. Lodge: Temple Emanuel

Sisterhood. Home: 1625 Larimer #1907 Denver CO 80202 Office: Colo State U Dept Social Services 1575 Sherman Denver CO 80203-1714

ORLANDO, ANDREA LEE, financial planner; b. N.Y.C., Sept. 19, 1953; d. Julius Jean and Margaret Jane (Leichter) Matto; m. Dino Fontana, Aug. 4, 1974 (div. 1980); m. Gary William Orlando, June 19, 1983. BS in Acctg., Fairleigh Dickinson U., 1975, MBA in Fin., 1982. Cert. fin. planner. Owner, mgr. Dean Andre Inc., Englewood, N.J., 1974-79; asst. mgr. sales T.J. Lipton Inc., Moonachi, N.J., 1978-80; mgr. sales audit Petrie Corp., Secaucus, N.J., 1980-82; controller Data Mgmt. Services, N.Y.C., 1982-85; planner fin. Madison Fin. Group, Green Village, N.J., 1985-87; fin. planner Summit Fin. Resources, Livingston, N.J., 1987—; adviser fin. Am. Stage Corp., Teaneck, N.J., 1985—, Summit Fin. Resources, Livingston, N.J. Bd. Concerned Citizens Assn., Denville, N.J., 1985; fund raiser Am. Lung Assn., Elizabeth, N.J., 1982;. Mem. Nat. Assn. Accts., Nat. Assn. Female Execs., Internat. Assn. Fin. Planners, Internat. Conf. Fin. Planners, N.J. Assn. Women Bus. Owners, Morris County C. of C., Denville Rockaway Jr. Woman's Club. Republican. Presbyterian. Club: Rockaway River Country (Denville). Home: 8 Canterbury Ln Annandale NJ 08801

ORLANDO, JOYCE RYAN, public relations director; b. Steubenville, Ohio, Aug. 9, 1942; d. Orel B. and Alice (Mountford) Ryan; m. Joseph M. Orlando, Sept. 1, 1962 (div. Feb. 1976); children—Suzanne Elizabeth, Melissa Ann. BS in Bus. Mgmt., U. Steubenville, 1981-84. Mktg. dir. Ft. Steuben Mall, Steubenville, 1974-81; asst. dir. pub. relations U. Steubenville, 1981-83, dir. pub. relations, 1983—. Bd. dirs. Jeffco Workshop, Steubenville, 1982-87; chmn. Jefferson County Leukemia Soc., 1980-87; edn. chmn. Jefferson County United Way, 1986-87; chmn. Jefferson County Muscular Dystrophy Campaign, 1981-86; mem. Steubenville Fiesta Com., 1984-86; mem. bldg. fund com. Franciscan U. Steubenville, 1984—; past bd. dirs. Nat. Found. Birth Defects, United Way, Jefferson County Mental Retardation. Author/editor: A Guide to Steubenville for the Handicapped, 1974. Mem. Pub. Relations Soc. Am., Women in Communications Inc., Steubenville Area C. of C., Wintersville Area C. of C. Democrat. Episcopalian. Avocations: skiing, racquetball. Home: 136 Meadow Rd Wintersville OH 43952 Office: U Steubenville Franciscan Way Steubenville OH 43952

ORLING, ANNE, art consultant, appraiser; b. N.Y.C.; d. Joseph and Bertha (Elsner) Acks; B.S., in Art Adminstrn., SUNY, Old Westbury, 1977; art student Art Students League, also studied art with pvt. tchrs.; m. Michael Orling; children—Merry, Jeffrey, Alan. One-woman shows include: Silvermine Guild, Lafayette (Ind.) Art Center, U. Ariz., Tucson, Pa. State U., Hazleton, Baldwin Wallace Coll., Berea, Ohio, U. Idaho, Moscow, U. Fla., Gainesville; group shows include: Hofstra U., Hempstead, N.Y., L.I.U., Bklyn., N.Y. World's Fair Fine Arts Pavilion, Silvermine Guild, New Canaan, Conn., N.Y.C. Center, Provincetown Art Assn., NAD, Hofstra U., Heckscher Mus., Adelphi U., Fordham U., Bklyn. Coll., UN Plaza, Royal Acad., Stockholm; represented in permanent collections UN, C.W. Post Coll., many pvt. collections; former mem. staff North Shore Community Arts Center. Founder, v.p. bd. trustees Fine Arts Mus. L.I., Hempstead, N.Y. Recipient 1st prize Hofstra U., 1960, Heckscher Mus., 1960; award Silvermine Guild, 1960, East Hampton Guild, 1960, Winners Show at Hofstra U., 1964, 65; 2d prize Lincoln House, 1965. Mem. Appraisers Assn. Am., Profl. Artists Guild (pres.). Home: 166-25 Powells Cove Blvd Beechhurst NY 11357

ORMAN, BETTY, social worker, administrator; b. Detroit, Nov. 24, 1928; d. Robert Israel and Lillian (Aberson) Fleiss; B.A., Wayne State U., 1950; M.S.W. Ariz. State U., 1973; m. Bernie Orman, Oct. 22, 1950; children—Rodger, Marc. Diplomate Nat. REgistry Clin. Social Workers. With State of Mich., 1952-56; caseworker Jewish Family Service, Tucson, 1961-71, social worker, 1973-79, asst. exec. dir., 1979-83, dir. counseling services, 1983—; asso. prof. Pima Community Coll., 1979—; mem. field faculty Ariz. State U., 1977-79, 83—. Mem. Family and Social Service Task Force, City of Tucson, 1975-77. Mem. Nat. Assn. Social Workers (chairperson div. II 1982-84), Acad. Cert. Social Workers, Am. Acad. Family Mediators. Home: 7358 E Kenyon Dr Tucson AZ 85710 Office: 2424 E Broadway Suite 100 Tucson AZ 85719

ORMSBY, MARGARET ANCHORETTA, historian; b. Quesnel, B.C., Can., June 7, 1909; d. George Lewis and Margaret Turner (McArthur) O. B.A., U. B.C., 1929, M.A., 1931, D.Lit., 1974; Ph.D., Bryn Mawr Coll., 1937; LL.D. (hon.), U. Man., 1964, U. Notre Dame, Nelson, B.C., 1968, Simon Fraser U., 1971, U. Victoria, 1976. Head of history Sarah Dix Hamlin Sch., San Francisco, 1937-40; spl. lectr. in history McMaster U., 1940-43; lectr. in history U. B.C., Vancouver, 1943, asst. prof., 1946, assoc. prof., 1949, prof., 1955, head history dept., 1965-74, vis. prof. history, 1974-75; vis. prof. U. Western Ont., 1977, U. Toronto, 1978. Author: British Columbia: A History, 1958, rev. edit., 1971; A Pioneer Gentlewoman in British Columbia: The Recollections of Susan Allison, 1976. Contbr. intro. Fort Victoria Letters 1946-51, 1979; contbr. Dictionary Can. Biography, vols. IX, X, XI, XII. Mem. B.C. Heritage Adv. Bd., 1971-83; mem. Hist. Sites and Monuments Bd. Can., 1960-68, Sir John A. Macdonald Prize Com. in Can. History, 1977-79. Recipient Merit award Am. State and Local History Soc., 1959, 75, Regional History award Can. Hist. Assn., 1983; Centennial medal, 1967. Mem. Can. Hist. Assn. (pres. 1965-66), Okanagan Hist. Soc. Fellow Royal Soc. Can. Anglican. Avocation: fruit growing. Office: 12407 Coldstream Creek Rd, Vernon, BC Canada V1B 1G2

ORMSBY, MARION M. (MARTIE), marketing executive; b. Hamlet, N.C., Dec. 19, 1953; d. Adrian S. and Marion H. O. AA, Peace Coll., 1974; BA, U. N.C., 1976; MA, West Chester State U., 1978. Cert. of Clin. Competence. Speech pathologist Caswell Ctr., Kinston, N.C., 1978-79; regional sales mgr. Telex Communications, Inc., Mpls., 1978-85; account exec. N.Y. Life Ins., Atlanta, 1985; mktg. mgr. Hearing Tech., Inc., Mpls., 1985-86, nat. sales, mktg. mgr., 1986-87; v.p. sales, mktg. Hearing Tech., Inc., Eden Prairie, Minn., 1987—; speaker in field, state convs., 1986. Author: Mktg. Mag., 1986. Mem. Acad. Dispensing Audiologists, Hearing Industries Assn. (mktg. com. 1975—), Am. Speech and Hearing Assn., Nat. Hearing Aid Soc., Nat. Assn. Female Execs., Sales/Mktg. Execs. Baptist. Club: Excelsior Bay (Minn.) Yacht. Home: 5070 Arrowood Ln N Plymouth MN 55442 Office: Hearing Tech Inc 6269 Bury Dr Eden Prairie MN 55346

ORNBURN, KRISTEE JEAN, accountant; b. Moberly, Mo., Feb. 24, 1956; d. Lloyd Edward and Ruth Maxine (Major) O. AA, Moberly Jr. Coll., 1976; BSBA magna cum laude, U. Mo., Columbia, 1978. CPA, Mo. Teller City Bank & Trust, Moberly, 1974-78; supr. gen. ledger Orscheln Farm & Home Supply, Moberly, 1978-80, supr. accounts payable, 1980, supr. sr. acctg., 1981-82, mgr. acctg., 1982-86; controller Orscheln Consumer Products Div., Moberly, 1986—. Youth worker Carpenter St. Bapt. Ch., Moberly. Recipient Youth Leadership award Moberly C. of C., 1974. Mem. Am. Inst. CPA's, Mo. Soc. CPA's, AAUW (v.p.), U. Mo. Alumni Assn. Democrat. Club: Bapt. Young Women (Moberly). Office: Orscheln Farm & Home Supply 339 N Williams Moberly MO 65270

ORNELLAS, LORRAINE (LORI) B., small business owner; b. Honokaa, Hawaii, Apr. 19; d. Joseph R. and Maria (Sampaia) Bugado; m. Herbert P. Ornellas, July 1, 1928; children: Kenneth Herbert, Brenda Jane. Degree, U. Hawaii, 1976; cert., Vitousek Real Estate Sch., 1986. Owner 50th St. Bar, Hilo, Hawaii, 1956-83; real estate sales rep. Hicks Homes, Hilo, 1972-73; owner, mgr. Gift-Wrap Hawaii, Hilo, 1982—; realty assoc. Big Island Land Co., Ltd., Hilo, 1986—. Vol. Frank Fasi for Mayor Campaign, Honolulu, 1977, Dante Carpenter for Mayor Campaign, Hilo, 1985. Mem. Am. Bus. Women's Assn., Hawaii Bus. Women's Network, Hawaii Island Bd. Realtors, Hawaii Island Portuguese C. of C., Hawaii Island C. of C. Democrat. Roman Catholic. Club: Hilo Women's. Home: 64 Hale Manu Dr Hilo HI 96720 Office: Big Island Land Co Ltd 688 Kinoole St Suite 120 Hilo HI 96720

OROPILLA, TERESITA BACANI, psychiatrist; b. Naga City, Philippines, Mar. 17, 1929; came to U.S., 1973, naturalized, 1979; d. Gerardo Bacani and Policarpia Ruivivar; A.A., U. Santo Tomas, Manila, 1950, M.D. cum laude, 1956; m. Ricardo Oropilla, Oct. 29, 1960; children—Joseph Marius, Teresa Ann. Intern, U. Santo Tomas, 1955-56, rotating intern U. Louisville, 1956-57, resident in pediatrics, 1957-58, resident in psychiatry, 1976-79, asst. prof., 1980—; practice medicine specializing in pediatrics, Philippines, 1959-73; staff physician Children's Treatment Service, Louisville, 1973-78; mem. psychiat. staff, charge mental hygiene clinic VA Med. Center, 1980—; vol. med. missions, Guatemala, 1976. Diplomate Am. Bd. Psychiatry and Neurology. Mem. Jefferson County Med. Soc., Ky. Med. Assn., Filipino-Am. Soc., Philippine Med. Assn. Ky. (sec.). Roman Catholic. Home: 2517 Stonehurst Dr Louisville KY 40222 Office: 800 Zorn Ave Louisville KY 40202

OROSZ, JUDY INEZ, pediatrician; b. Woodbury, Ga., July 16, 1945; d. Joseph Michael and Ruby Inez (Brown) Orosz; student U. Ga., 1963-64; B.S. in Biology, Ga. State U., 1967; M.D., Med. Coll. Ga., 1971. Intern, Baroness Erlanger Hosp., Chattanooga, Tenn., 1971-72; resident T.C. Thompson Children's Hosp., Chattanooga, 1972-74, chief resident, 1973-74; pvt. practice medicine specializing in pediatrics, Cartersville, Ga., 1974-79; mem. staff Gracewood (Ga.) State Sch. and Hosp., 1979-81; asst. prof. pediatrics Med. Coll. Ga., Augusta, 1980-87, dir. ambulatory pediatrics, 1980-87; pres. med. staff Sam Howell Meml. Hosp., 1977,78; with med. staff Eku (Nigeria) Bapt. Hosp., 1987—. Mem. adv. bd. Bartow County Tng. Center, 1974-76; active Nat. Found. March of Dimes, 1976-77; v.p. bd. dirs. Augusta Child Advocacy Ctr., 1986. Named Dept. Pediatrics Tchr. of Yr., Med. Coll. Ga., 1981; Ann. Social Work award Univ. Hosp., 1985. Mem. Richmond County Med. Soc., Med. Assn. Ga., AMA, Am. Acad. Pediatrics, Bapt. Med.-Dental Fellowship (fin. chmn. 1983-85, v.p. Ga. chpt. 1985-86, pres. 1986-87), Nat. Perinatal Assn., Med. Coll. Ga. Alumni Assn. (treas. women physician's council 1983-84). Baptist. Contbr. articles to profl. jours. Home: 4451 Forrest Dr Martinez GA 30907 Office: 1350 Walton Way Augusta GA 30910

OROSZ, JULIA ELIZABETH, nurse, educator, consultant; b. Alliance, Ohio, Nov. 5, 1948; d. William and Rachel (Dosa) O.; m. Gerald Coker, July 3, 1976 (div. 1980). Nursing diploma Lutheran Hosp. Sch. Nursing, Cleve., 1970; BS in Nursing, U. Cin., 1973; MS in Nursing, U. Ala.-Birmingham, 1975. RN, Ohio, Tex. Staff nurse Children's Hosp. Akron, Ohio, 1970-71, 75-77; health clinic nurse U. Cin., 1972-73; asst. prof. Maryville Coll. St. Louis, 1977-80, U. Tex. Health Sci. Ctr., San Antonio, 1980-84; clin. specialist Barberton Citizen's Hosp., Ohio, 1984-85; regional perinatal edn. coordinator Children's Med. Ctr., Akron, 1985—; health care assoc. Sch. Medicine, Washington U., St. Louis, 1978-79; mem. adolescent pregnancy task force on community awareness Summit County Adolescent Services Network, 1985—; grad. asst. prof. Kent State U. Sch. Nursing, 1987; chmn. health care services Luth. Ch. Mo. Synod: Internat. Youth Gathering, 1983. Editor NeoGram, 1985—; mng. editor Northeast Ohio Perinatal Newsletter, 1985—. Vol. ARC, San Antonio, Akron, 1970—; speaker San Antonio Coalition for Children, Youth and Families, 1980-84, Children's Med. Ctr., Akron, 1985—; vol. Carter Presdl. Campaign, Akron, 1976; mem. child find subcom. Ohio Dept. Health, 1987. Named to Outstanding Young Women Am., U.S. Jaycees, 1981, 83; Klaus Meml. scholar Luth. Hosp. Sch. Nursing, 1970; grad. fellow U. Ala.-Birmingham, 1973. Mem. LWV, Am. Nurses Assn. (council perinatal nurses 1985), Tex. Nurses Assn. (chmn. dist. social com. 1982-84), Nurses Assn. of the Am. Coll. of Ob-gyn. (ednl. coordinator Ohio sect. 1987), Nat. Assn. Neonatal Nurses (charter), Nat. Perinatal Assn. (Ohio rep. to council 1986, 87), Ohio Perinatal Assn. (bd. dirs. 1986), U. Cin. Alumni Assn. (life), Nat. Mus. Women in the Arts (charter), Sigma Theta Tau. Avocations: counted cross stitch; piano; pipe organ; cooking; painting. Home: 2436 Chatham Rd Akron OH 44313 Office: Children's Med Ctr of Akron Div Neonatology 281 Locust St Akron OH 44308

O'ROURKE, MARGARET MARY, government official; b. East Chicago, Ind., Nov. 2, 1945; d. Edward J. and Helen M. (Saprony) Savage; B.A., Marygrove Coll., Detroit, 1967; M.P.A., George Washington U., Washington, 1980; grad. Nat. War Coll., 1986; m. John E. O'Rourke, May 16, 1969. Import specialist U.S. Customs Service, Detroit, 1967-71, systems analyst, Washington, 1971-76, chief mgmt. info. br., 1976-77, spl. asst. to commr. data processing, 1977-79, dir. office mgmt. insp., 1979-82, dir. office trade ops., 1982-87; dir. office design IRS, Washington, 1987—. Recipient Outstanding Performance award U.S. Customs Service, 1977, Sr. Exec. Bonus award, 1985. Mem. Sr. Exec. Assn., Am. Soc. Public Adminstrn. Home: 1211 Tulane Dr Alexandria VA 22307 Office: 1111 Constitution Ave NW Washington DC 20224

O'ROURKE, MARGUERITE PATRICIA, insurance company official; b. N.Y.C., May 10, 1950; d. William Lawrence and Olive Rose (Ponte) O'R.; B.A. in Polit. Sci. (Ednl. Opportunity grantee, N.J. State scholar), Am. U., 1972. Adminstrn. asst. Asso. Merchandising Corp., Washington, 1972-73; various positions Savage/Fogarty Co., Inc., Alexandria, Va., 1973-79; property mgr. Community Mgmt. Corp., Reston, Va., 1979-80; property mgr. Braedon Cos., Washington, 1980-81, dir. property mgmt., 1981-82; v.p. bldgs. adminstrn. Smithy Braedon Property Co., Washington, 1982-83; sr. real estate officer-asset mgmt. Northwestern Mut. Life Real Estate Div., 1983—; corp. sec. Savage/Fogarty Co., Inc., 1978-79. Intern Senator Claiborne Pell, R.I., 1971. Mem. Inst. Real Estate Mgrs., Internat. Council Shopping Ctrs., Nat. Assn. Female Execs., Washington Bd. Realtors, Save The Bay, Environ. Def. Fund, Union Concerned Scientists, Cousteau Soc., Nat. Trust for Historic Preservation, Smithsonian Instn., Am. Film Inst. Office: 1133 20th St Washington DC 20036

O'ROURKE, MARSHA CAROLYN, surgeon; b. Jacksonville, Fla., Mar. 10, 1949; d. Gerald G. and Willie O. (Martin) O'R.; m. Vincent J. Schafmeister, III, 1970 (div. 1978). B.A., Wheaton Coll., 1970; M.D., Free U. Brussels, 1977. Diplomate Am. Bd. Surgery, 1983; lic., N.Y. 1978, Calif. 1983. Intern, Albany (N.Y.) Med. Ctr. Hosp., 1977-78, resident, 1977-81, chief resident, 1981-82; gen. surgeon Community Health Plan, Latham, N.Y., 1982-85; practice gen. surgery, Augusta, Maine, 1985—; acting supt. Tintswalo Hosp., Acornhoek, South Africa, 1983. Active Women Overseas for Equality, Physicians for Social Responsibility, Physicians for Abortion Rights. Fellow ACS; mem. AMA, Sierra Club. Home: Route 1 Box 3405 Wayne ME 04284 Office: 89 Hospital St Augusta ME 04350

ORPHANOS, MARY JOAN, communications executive; b. Chgo., Apr. 23, 1960; d. George James and Mary Elizabeth (Quinn) O. AAS, Coll. Dupage, Ill., 1980. Tester Rockwell Communications, Downers Grove, Ill., 1977-81, electronic technician, 1981-85, tech. support engr., 1985—. Recipient Voice of Democracy award VFW, 1976. Democrat. Roman Catholic. Home: 214 Porter Ln Bolingbrook IL 60439 Office: Rockwell Communications 2626 Warrenville Rd Downers Grove IL 60515

ORR, ELAINE LOUISE, public policy writer; b. Washington, Aug. 14, 1951; d. Miles D. and H. Rita (Rooney) O. BA, U. Dayton, 1972; MA, Am. U., 1974. Evaluator, GAO, Washington, 1974-78, spl. asst. to asst. comptroller gen., 1979-80, dir. internat. liaison, 1979-86. Editor, Internat. Jour. Govt. Auditing, 1983-86, Nat. Young Profls. Forum News, 1982-83; assoc. editor The Bureaucrat: Jour. for PUb. Mgrs., 1987—. Elected gov. D.C. Girls State, DAR, 1968. Mem. Am. Consortium Internat. Pub. Adminstrn. (v.p., 1984-86, past bd. dirs.), Am. Soc. Pub. Adminstrn. (life, bd. dirs. women in public adminstrn. sect. 1984-85), Washington Ind. Writers, Nat Press Club. Democrat. Avocations: gardening, music, reading, theatre. Office: PO Box 5840 Takoma Park MD 20912

ORR, HELEN LOUISE, educator, consultant; b. Denver, Apr. 13, 1927; d. Fred Holcomb and Della Marie (Graff) Horr. BA, Hastings Coll., 1951; MA, San Francisco Theol. Sem., San Anselmo, Calif., 1954. Cert. elem. and secondary tchr., reading specialist. Owner Quality Photos, Denver, 1945-54; dir. Christian edn. St. Andrew's Presbyn. Ch., Newport Beach, Calif., 1954-58, First Presbyn. Ch., Colton, Calif., 1958-59; community youth dir. YWCA, Riverside, Calif., 1959-64; tchr. Chino (Calif.) Unified Sch. Dist., 1964-76; owner, prin. cons. Orrtech/Orrtronics, Inc., Chino, 1978—. Mem. Baldy View Regional Occupational Program Commn., Claremont, Calif., 1979-83, v.p. 1981-83, mem. electronics adv. com., 1983—; mem. vocat. edn. task force Chino Unified Sch. Dist., 1985—, Chino Bd. Edn., 1979-83, clk.1981-82; mem., photographer Chino Centennial Com., 1987. Mem. Chino Bus. and Profl. Women (corr. sec. 1980-81, pres. 1986-88, treas. 1988—). Club: Chino Valley Woman's (auditor 1981-83, chairperson sch. issues com. 1987). Home and Office: 12594 16th St Chino CA 91710

ORR, JAXCINE LEE, accountant, consultant; b. Beaver, Okla., Dec. 18, 1938; d. Harry Leslie Potter and Wilda Bethene (Girk) Weaver; m. Bob F. Orr (dec.); children: William Scott, Susan Orr Talley, Steven, Lonnie Frank. Student bus. adminstrn. and acctg., Wichita U., 1958-61. Acct. Orr's Acctg., Cromwell, Okla., 1965-86; plant mgr. Glass-Tex Industries, Electra, Tex., 1980-82; city clk., treas. City of Wewoka, Okla., 1984-85; officer mgr., activities dir., councellor Tri-Cities Helping Hand, Wewoka, 1986; acct., job placement councellor Acc-Temps, Electra, 1986-88, activities, social services coordinator Electra Nursing Ctr., 1988—. Bd. dirs., grant facilitator Grand Playhouse of Electra, 1987—. Mem. Nat. Assn. Female Execs., Nat. Notary Assn., Electra C. of C., Assn. of Women for Commerce and Industry (pres. Electra 1987—), Tex. Assn. Pub. Accts. Democrat. Methodist. Club: Electra Riding. Office: Electra Nursing Ctr 608 W Summit Electra TX 76360

ORR, KARIN KATHLEEN, columnist, food stylist; b. Grand Rapids, Mich., Sept. 27, 1942; d. Ray Wilson and Joan (Bosworth) McClow; BA, Albion Coll., 1964; MA, Wayne State U., 1966, PhD, 1976; m. Vance Womack Orr, Mar. 29, 1965; children: Deirdre Ellen, Caitlin Elizabeth, Maurya Kathleen, Vance W. III. Legal sec. James Knopper, atty., Grandville, Mich., 1961; artists' model Albion (Mich.) Coll., 1963-64; asst. Wayne State U., Detroit, 1964-68; instr. English, Grand Rapids (Mich.) Jr. Coll., 1968-81; dir. drama, 1969-81, sec. faculty council, 1978-81; instr. drama Aquinas Coll., 1979-81; acting instr. Grand Rapids Civic Theatre; columnist Grand Rapids Press, Wonderland mag., Cooking with Karin. Mem. Arts Council Greater Grand Rapids, 1970-80; chmn. Festival '75, Jr. Arts Council, 1975-79; co-chmn. Springfest benefit auction for art mus., 1978; bd. dirs. Opera Assn. Western Mich., 1972-81, Grand Rapids Civic Theatre, 1976-80, West Mich. Telecommunications Found., Butterworth Hosp., Women's and Children's Ctr., Very Spl. Arts/Mich.; mem. exec. bd., chmn. public affairs, 1st v.p. Jr. League of Grand Rapids, pres., 1981-82; mem. Area IV nominating com. Assn. Jr. Leagues, 1982-84 co-chmn. auction Channel 35, Public TV, 1981; mem. adv. bd. Performing Arts Center, Grand Valley State Colls., 1976-79; trustee Grand Valley State Colls.; membership chmn., exec. com. Grand Rapids Art Mus., 1983-85, Nat. Juvenile Diabetes Found.; mem. 5th dist. Women's adv. com. U.S. Senator Paul Henry. Recipient certificate merit for service Grand Rapids Art Council, 1975, Vol. of Yr. award YWCA, 1984, Tribute award YWCA, 1984, 1st Lady award Mich. Sequicentennial, 1987, Dist. Service award Arts Council Greater Grand Rapids. Mem. Alpha Xi Delta. Home and Office: 1841 Buttrick St Ada MI 49301

ORR, KAY A., governor of Nebraska; b. Burlington, Iowa, Jan. 2, 1939; d. Ralph Robert and Sadie Lucille (Skoglund) Stark; m. William Dayton Orr, Sept. 26, 1957; children: John William, Suzanne. Student, U. Iowa, 1956-57. Exec. asst. to Gov. Charles Thone, Lincoln, Nebr., 1979-81; treas. State of Nebr., Lincoln, 1981-86; gov. elect. 1986; governor State of Nebr., Lincoln, 1987—. Co-chmn. Thone for Gov. Com., 1977-78; del., mem. platform com. Rep. Nat. Conv., 1976, 80, 84, co-chmn. 1984; trustee Hastings (Nebr.) Coll., 1985—; appointed to USDA Users Adv. Bd. 1985, Pres.'s Adv. Com. for Arts John F. Kennedy Performing Arts Ctr., 1985; chmn. Nat. Rep. Platform Commn., 1988—; appointed Nat. Adv. Council on Rural Devel., 1988. Named Outstanding Young Rep. Woman in Nebr., 1969.

ORR, LILLIAN JENELL BROWN, publishing executive; b. Atlanta, Feb. 17, 1952; d. Sanford O'Neal and Clara Lillian (Simmons) Brown; m. David Paul Orr, Apr. 28, 1972; children: Deborah Cheryl, Stephanie Michelle. Grad. high sch., Conyers, Ga. Bus. mgr. Citizen Pub. Co., Inc., Conyers, 1969—. Sec., treas. Gwinnett Pentecostal Ch. Mem. Am. Bus. Women's Assn. (chair publicity com., treas. New Rochelle charter chpt., Woman of Yr. 1988), Nat. Assn. Female Execs. Office: Citizen Pub Co Inc 969 S Main St Conyers GA 30207

ORR, LINDA, educator, writer; b. Atlanta, Apr. 20, 1943; d. Henry Hammett and Marianna (de Noyelles) O. BA, Duke U., 1965; cert., lic., U. Montpellier, France, 1966; PhD, Yale U., 1971. Instr. U. Iowa, Iowa City, 1971-73; asst. prof. Swarthmore (Pa.) Coll., 1974-75; asst. prof. Yale U., New Haven, 1975-78, assoc. prof., 1978-80; vis. prof. U. Calif., Berkeley, 1980; assoc. prof. Duke U., Durham, N.C., 1980—. Author: Jules Michelet, 1976, A Certain X, 1980, critical edition Michelet's The Mountain, 1987; contbr. articles to scholarly jours.; translator French lit. Am. Council Learned Societies fellow, 1973-74, Morse fellow, 1977-78, Guggenheim fellow, 1977-78, Howard Found. fellow, 1987-88. Mem. Modern Langs. Assn., Soc. Romantic Studies. Office: Duke U Dept Romance Langs Durham NC 27706

ORR, MARLENE B., editor, consultant; b. Wichita, June 28, 1939; d. Bediah Esper and Victoria N. (Farha) Samra; m. Kenneth Thomas Orr, Dec. 28, 1963; children—Kathryn Elisabeth, Paige Marlene. B.A. cum laude, U. Wichita, 1961; postgrad. in English (grad. assistantship) U. Nebr., 1961. Copy editor Jour. Am. Med. Assn., Chgo., 1961-63; textbook editor Henry Regnery Co., Chgo., 1963-64; manuscript editor U. Chgo. Press, 1964-68; editorial dir. Langston, Kitch & Assoc., Topeka, 1977-80; cons., asst. treas., dir. mktg. com. Ken Orr & Assocs., Inc., Topeka, 1980—; editorial cons., Topeka, 1971-77. Editor: The Kansas Legislature, 1974; Recollections of an Herpetologist, 1975; Structured Systems Design, 1978; Structured Requirements Definition, 1979. Vice-pres. Dance Arts of Topeka, 1982-83; sec. PTA, Topeka, 1975-76; newsletter author Topeka Assn. Gifted, 1973. Mem. Women in Communications, Inc. (membership rev. com. 1982), Gamma Phi Beta. Democrat. Home: 104 Woodlawn Topeka KS 66606 Office: Ken Orr & Assocs Inc 1725 Gage Topeka KS 66604

ORR, N'OMI, computer graphics consulting executive; b. Atlantic City, Feb. 13, 1938; d. Walter Corson and Mary Ethel (Strockbine) Smith; m. Joel Nathanael Orr; children—David, Anne, John, Thomas, Stephen, Sharon. Pres., Orr Assocs., Inc., Washington and Danbury, Conn., 1979—, Naomi Orr Agy., 1980—; dir. The CADD/CAM Inst., Washington, 1982—; asst. dir Computer Graphics Inst. Am., Washington, Knoxville, Tenn.; pub. Honeycomb Library, 1982—. Author: A Cure for Cancer, 1984; The Common Cold: Cause and Cure, 1983; editor: The Computer Graphics Newsletter, 1976-78; The Computer Graphics Extravaganza, 1977; How to Implement CADD, 1981; The Top Ten Multistation CADD Systems, 1982; The Low Cost CADD Systems, 1983. Mem. Nat. Computer Graphics Assn. Home and Office: Orr Assocs Inc 431 River Bend Rd Great Falls VA 22066

ORR, PEARL LEE, emergency management city-county executive; b. Henderson, N.C., Oct. 27, 1931; d. William Edgar Woodlief and Reba Colon (Lee) Marshall; m. Elmer Roscoe Orr, Aug. 24, 1949; children—Susan Lee Orr Rexrode, William Roscoe. Diploma, Henderson Bus. Coll., 1950. Bookkeeper, Roth-Stewart Co., Henderson, 1961-62; legal sec. Gholson & Gholson, Henderson, 1962-66; sec. Henderson-Vance Co. CD, Henderson, 1966-78, coordinator Henderson-Vance Co., emergency mgmt., 1978—. Officer, chmn. Jr. Woman's Club, Henderson, 1957-66; ex-officio mem. adv. council Region K, Emergency Med. Services, 1985—. Named Woman of Yr., Henderson Jr. Woman's Club, 1960. Mem. Superfund Amendments and Reauthorization Act of 1986 (local emergency planning com., 1987—), N.C. Emergency Mgmt. Assn. (Gen. Edward Foster Griffin award 1984; pres. 1983-84, state rep. 1984-85), Nat. Coordinating Council on Emergency Mgmt. Democrat. Baptist. Avocations; travel; reading. Home: 115 Zollicoffer Ave Henderson NC 27536 Office: Henderson-Vance Co Emergency Mgmt PO Box 1094 Henderson NC 27536

ORRIS, MICHELE MARIE, public relations, marketing and advertising consultant; b. Norwalk, Conn., Feb. 23, 1958; d. Stephen Joseph and Arcenia (Rodriguez) O. Student, U. N.Mex., 1976-78; BA with honors, U. Bridgeport, 1980, postgrad., 1981-83. Tchr. Norwalk Pub. Schs., 1981-83; head tchr. presch. Norwalk YMCA, 1983-84; exec. dir. Norwalk Seaport Assn., 1984-86; cons. 1986-87, Barnum Festival, Bridgeport, Conn., 1987-88, P.T. Barnum Found., Bridgeport, 1987; mgr. communications Human Resources Inc., Stamford, Conn., 1987; owner, mgr. Michele Orris, East Norwalk, Conn., 1988—. Past sec., pres. Marvin Beach Assn., East Norwalk; asst. dir. pub. relations Conn. Women's Celebration, 1986; chmn. subcom. auditorium com. New City Hall, Norwalk; active numerous other civic orgns.; bd. dirs. Southwestern Conn. council Girl Scouts U.S.A., 1987—. Recipient award City of Norwalk, 1987. Mem. Greens Farms Acad. Alumni Assn. (pres., class sec.), Phi Sigma Iota (life). Democrat. Roman Catholic. Home and Office: 108 Gregory Blvd East Norwalk CT 06855

ORSINI, BETTE SWENSON, reporter; Reporter, St. Petersburg Times, Fla. Co-recipient Pulitzer Prize for nat. reporting, 1980. Office: Times Pub Co St Petersburg Times PO Box 1121 Saint Petersburg FL 33731 *

ORTBERG, NATALIE ANN JARAMILLO, aerospace engineer; b. Albuquerque, June 29, 1957; d. John Gilbert and Anita (Blackwood) Jaramillo; m. Kenneth Lynn Ortberg, Dec. 18, 1976; children: Adam Jaramillo, Katherine Lynn. BS in Bus. Mgmt., U. LaVerne, Calif., 1980. Assoc. planning analyst ITT Fed. Electric, Vandenberg AFB, Calif., 1977-80; info. systems mgr. Mountain Bell, Mesa, Ariz., 1980-82; field engr. Martin Marietta Aerospace, Vandenberg AFB, 1982-85; sr. test engr. Martin Marietta Aerospace, Denver, 1985-86, staff engr., 1986—; speaker in field. Active Sand Creek PTO, Highlands Ranch, Colo., 1986—. Mem. Nat. Mgmt. Assn., Am. Mgmt. Assn., Martin Marietta Mgmt. Assn., Career Women's Assn. Roman Catholic. Home: 2266 Thistle Ridge Circle Highlands Ranch CO 80126 Office: Martin Marietta Aerospace PO Box 179 Denver CO 80201

ORTEGA, BEVERLEY, accountant; b. London, Feb. 6, 1956; came to U.S., 1975; d. Ernest Charles and Barbara (Wiseman) Patterson; m. Alfred Ortega, Nov. 25, 1982; children: Tamara, Russell, Stuart. AAS with honors, Tacoma Community Coll., 1978; BBA with honors, U. Puget Sound, 1980. CPA, Wash. Accounts payable clk. Hillhaven Corp., Tacoma, 1975-76, staff acct., 1980-83, acquisition analyst, 1983-86; controller, chief fin. officer Tacoma Luth. Home and Retirement Community, 1987—; cons. in field, 1984—. Mem. Nat. Assn. Accts., Wash. Soc. CPA's, Am. Soc. Women Accts. Home: 4007 31st Ave NW Gig Harbor WA 98335 Office: Tacoma Luth Home and Retirement Community 1301 Highland Pkwy Tacoma WA 98406

ORTEGA, KATHERINE D., treasurer of U.S.; b. July 16, 1934. B.A., Eastern N.Mex. U., 1957. Tax supr. Peat, Marwick, Mitchell & Co., 1969-72; v.p., cashier Pan Am. Nat. Bank, 1972-75; pres. Santa Ana (Calif.) State Bank, 1975-77, Copyright Royalty Tribunal, 1982-83; Treas. U.S. Washington, 1983—. Office: Dept of Treasury Treas of the US 15th & Pennsylvania Ave NW Washington DC 20220 *

ORTEGA, LENETTE MARY HERTZ, banker; b. Joliet, Ill., Jan. 6, 1947; d. Leonard Marlyn and Julia (Zeimis) Hertz; m. Zarinelo R. Ortega, Feb. 12, 1982; children: Maximilian, Elizabeth. BS, No. Ill. U., 1969; MEd, Nat. Coll. Edn., 1978. Loan officer Fin. Resources, Chgo., 1980-81, Percy Wilson, Chgo., 1981-82, Margaretten & Co., Chgo., 1982—. Presbyterian. Office: Margaretten & Co 5519 N Cumberland #1009 Chicago IL 60656

ORTH, ARDEAN SYLVIA, nurse; b. Racine, Wis., Oct. 5, 1947; d. Alfons and Evelyn Florence (Hahnefeld) O.; R.N., Deaconess Hosp., Milw., 1968; B.S., Evangel Coll., Springfield, Mo., 1973; M.S., U. Wis., Milw., 1980. Staff nurse, then head nurse Milw. County Mental Health Center, 1968-72, 76-77; head nurse Lutheran Hosp., Milw., 1973-75; dir. Community Mental Health Nursing, Waukesha, Wis., 1977—; ednl. cons., lectr. Waukesha County Tech. Inst., 1985, 86; workshop leader, 1979—; adv. com. Mental Health Assn. Waukesha County, 1979-86. Honored by YWCA Women of Distinction, 1987. Mem. Nat. League Nursing, Evangel Coll. Alumni Assn. Republican. Baptist. Home: 8510-8 W Waterford Ave Greenfield WI 53228 Office: 25042 W Northview Rd Waukesha WI 53188

ORTIZ, IRMA, retired university administrator, interpreter; b. Calexico, Calif., May 28, 1922; d. Camilo Enrique and Emelina (Trujillo) O.; 1 adopted child, Kumari Mary Ruth Danda. AA, Imperial Valley Coll., 1942; BBA, Academia Coss y Leon, 1942. Cert. profl. sec., 1966. Stenographer U. Calif. Agrl. Extension, El Centro, 1942, sec., 1943-64; adminstrv. sec. U. Calif. Coop. Extension, El Centro, 1965-79, adminstrv. asst., 1980-86, ret.; speaker various high schs. and colls. Dir. Salvation Army, El Centro, 1968-79; chmn. Imperial Valley Coll. Community review com., Calif., 1977-78; pres. Imperial Valley Community Concert Assn., 1983-86; editor Imperial Arts Council, 1987-88; docent Imperial Valley Pioneers Mus., 1987; sec. Imperial County Retired Employees Assn., 1988. Recipient Red Feather award Community Chest, El Centro, 1953; named Employee of Yr. Imperial County, 1969. Mem. Pilot Club (sec. western region 1968-69, 1st v.p. El Centro chpt. 1969-70), Beta Sigma Phi. Republican. Roman Catholic. Club: Euterpe (Mex.) (pres. 1945). Avocations: travel, reading, music, silvercraft, painting. Home: 918 Rockwood Calexico CA 92231

ORTLUND, (ELIZABETH) ANNE, writer, musician; b. Wichita, Kans., Dec. 3, 1923; d. Joseph Burton and Mary Elizabeth (Weible) Sweet; m. Raymond Carl Ortlund, Apr. 27, 1946; children—Sherrill Anne, Margot Jeanne, Raymond Carl, Nels Robert. Student Am. U., 1941-43; B.Music, U. Redlands, Calif., 1945; Assoc. Degree, Am. Guild of Organists, 1944. Organist, Old-Fashioned Revival Hour and Joyful Sound, Radio World-Wide, 1960-75; composer hymns, anthems, N.Y.C., 1963-77; worldwide speaker to pastors, missionaries, chs. Orgn. Renewal Ministries, Newport Beach, Calif., 1980—; composer 250 anthems for hymnals including Macedonia (theme hymn Billy Graham and Christianity Today's Congress on Evangelism, Berlin, 1966); books include: Up with Worship, 1975; Disciplines of the Beautiful Woman, 1977; (with Raymond Carl Ortlund) The Best Half of Life, 1976; Discipling One Another, 1979; Children Are Wet Cement (Christie award Christian Booksellers Assn. 1982), 1981; Joanna: A Story of Renewal, 1982; Building a Great Marriage, 1984; (with Raymond C. Ortlund) Staying Power, 1986, Disciplines of the Heart, 1987. Named Profl. Woman of Yr., Pasadena Bus. and Profl. Women, 1975; recipient SESAC award Gospel Musicians, 1978. Home: 32 Whitewater Dr Corona Del Mar CA 92625 Office: Renewal Ministries 4500 Campus Dr Suite 662 Newport Beach CA 92660

ORTOLEVA, LAURA LYNN, marketing communications executive; b. Chgo., Apr. 27, 1956; d. Salvatore Henry and Loretta Elvira (Kosiba) Ortoleva. A.A., Harper Jr. Coll., 1975; B.A., U. Ill., 1977, M.S. in Advt., 1979. Instr. bus. writing U. Ill., Champaign, 1979-80; asst. promotion dept. The News-Gazette, Champaign, 1979-80; copywriter Abelson-Frankel, Chgo., 1980-82; mktg. cons. Flair Communications, Chgo., 1982-83; copy dir. Lee Hill, Inc., Chgo., 1983-84; assoc. creative dir. Storandt, Kay & Pann, Chgo., 1984-85, account mgr., 1985-86; sr. advt. specialist Computer Products div. NEC Home Electronics, 1986-87, asst. mgr., 1987—, advt. mgr., 1987—. Youth leader St. Francis Borgia Teen Club, Chgo., 1982. Campaign winner Ill. Dept. Transp., 1979, Champaign Advt. Club, 1980. Office: NEC Home Electronics 1255 Michael Dr Wood Dale IL 60191

ORULLIAN, B. LARAE, banker; b. Salt Lake City, May 15, 1933; d. Alma and Bessie (Bacon) O.; cert. Am. Inst. Banking, 1961, 63, 67; grad. Nat. Real Estate Banking Sch., Ohio State U., 1969-71. With Tracy Collins Trust Co., Salt Lake City, 1951-54; sec. to exec. sec. Union Nat. Bank, Denver, 1954-57; exec. sec. Guaranty Bank, Denver, 1957-64, asst. cashier, 1964-67, asst. v.p., 1967-70, v.p., 1970-75, exec. v.p., 1975-77, also bd. dirs.; pres., chief exec. officer, dir. The Women's Bank N.A., Denver, 1977—, Equitable Bankshares of Colo., 1980—; vice chmn. Equitable Bank Littleton; vice chmn. bd., dir. Colo. and N.Mex. Blue Cross/Blue Shield, lectr. Nat. treas. Girl Scouts U.S.A., 1981, nat. 1st v.p., chair exec. com., 1987—; bd. dirs., chair fin. Rural Ky. Mental Health Care Corp; mem. adv. bd. ABA Community Bankers Council. Mem. Bus. and Profl. Women Colo. (3d Century award 1977), Inst. for Better Govt. (bd. dirs.), Colo. State Ethics Bd., Denver C. of C. (bd. dirs., chair state and local affairs), Am. Inst. Banking, Am. Bankers Assn., Nat. Assn. Bank Women, Nat. Women's Forum, Com. of 200, Denver Partnership. Republican. Mormon. Home: 10 S Ammons St Lakewood CO 80226

OSBORN, JANET LYNN, information systems executive; b. Berea, Ohio, Dec. 25, 1952; d. Walter Martin and Mary Alice O. BS in Systems Analysis, Miami U., Ohio, 1975; MBA, U. Mich., 1984; postgrad., Universidad de las Americas, Puebla, Mex., 1974. Cons. mgmt. info. systems Arthur Andersen and Co., Cinn., 1975-77; systems analyst Consumers Power Co., Jackson, Mich., 1977-79; sr. systems analyst Consumers Power Co., Jackson, 1979-81; supr. analyst Consumer Power Co., Jackson, 1982, mgr. corp. systems, 1983-85, mgr. litigation systems, 1985-87, mgr. quality assurance, 1988—. Solicitor United Way, Jackson, 1983-84. Mem. Women's Info. Network, Nat. Assn. Female Execs., Pi Mu Epsilon, Phi Kappa Phi, Delta Delta Delta. Office: Consumers Power Co 1945 W Parnall Rd Jackson MI 49201

OSBORN, JUNE ELAINE, pediatrician, microbiologist, university dean; b. Endicott, N.Y., May 28, 1937; d. Leslie A. and Dora W. (Wright) O.; divorced; children: Philip I. Levy, Ellen D. and Laura A. Levy (twins). B.A., Oberlin (Ohio) Coll., 1957; M.D., Western Res. U., 1961. Intern, then resident in pediatrics Harvard U. Hosp., 1961-64; postdoctoral fellow Johns Hopkins Hosp., 1964-65, U. Pitts. Hosp., 1965-66; practice medicine specializing in pediatrics Madison, Wis., 1966-84; dean Sch. Pub. Health U. Mich., 1984—, prof. epidemiology, pediatrics and communicable diseases, 1984—; mem. faculty U. Wis. Med. Sch., 1966-84, prof. pediatrics and microbiology, 1975-84, asso. dean Grad. Sch., 1975-84; mem. rev. panel viral vaccine efficacy FDA, 1973-79, mem. vaccines and related biol. products adv. com., 1981-85; mem. exptl. virology study sect. Div. Research Grants, NIH, 1975-79; bd. dirs. Stetler Research Fund Women Physicians, 1971-75; mem. med. affairs com. Yale U. Council, 1981-86; chmn. life scis. associateships rev. panel NRC, 1981-84; mem. U.S. Army Med. Research and Devel. Adv. Com., 1983-85; chmn. working group on AIDS and the Nation's Blood Supply, NHLBI, 1984—; chmn. WHO Planning Group on AIDS and the Internat. Blood Supply, 1985-86. Contbr. articles to med. jours. Mem. task force on AIDS, Inst. of Medicine, 1986; mem. adv. com. Robert Wood Johnson Found. Health Services Program, 1986—; mem. nat. adv. com. on the health of the pub. program pew and Rockefeller Founds.; mem. health promotion and disease prevention. bd. IOM. Grantee NIH, 1969, 72, 74, 75; Grantee Nat. Multiple Sclerosis Soc., 1971. Fellow Am. Acad. Pediatrics, Am. Acad. Microbiology, Infectious Diseases Soc. Am.; mem. Soc. Pediatric Research, Am. Assn. Immunologists, Inst. Medicine. Office: Univ of Michigan Sch of Public Health Ann Arbor MI 48109

OSBORN, MARY JANE MERTEN, biochemist; b. Colorado Springs, Colo., Sept. 24, 1927; d. Arthur John and Vivien Naomi (Morgan) Merten; m. Ralph Kenneth Osborn, Oct. 26, 1950. B.A., U. Calif., Berkeley, 1948; Ph.D., U. Wash., 1958. Postdoctoral fellow, dept. microbiology N.Y. U. Sch. Medicine, N.Y.C., 1959-61; instr. N.Y. U. Sch. Medicine, 1961-62, asst. prof., 1962-63; asst. prof. dept. molecular biology Albert Einstein Coll. Medicine, Bronx, N.Y., 1963-66; asso. prof. Albert Einstein Coll. Medicine, 1966-68; prof. dept. microbiology U. Conn. Health Center, Farmington, 1968—; dept. head U. Conn. Health Center, 1980—; mem. bd. sci. counselors Nat. Heart, Lung and Blood Inst., 1975-79; mem. Nat. Sci. Bd., 1980-86; mem. adv. council Nat. Inst. Gen. Med. Sci., 1983-86. Asso. editor: Jour. Biol. Chemistry, 1978-80; contbr. articles in field of biochemistry and molecular biology to profl. jours. NIH fellow, 1959-61; NIH grantee, 1962—; NSF grantee, 1965-68; Am. Heart Assn. grantee, 1968-71. Fellow Am. Acad. Arts and Scis., Nat. Acad. Scis.; mem. Am. Chem. Soc. (chmn. div. biol. chemistry 1975-76), Am. Fedn. Soc. Exptl. Biology (pres. 1982-83), Am. Soc. Biol. Chemists (pres. 1981-82), Am. Soc. Microbiology. Democrat. Office: U Conn Health Ctr Dept Microbiology Farmington CT 06032

OSBORN, MICHELLE PYNCHON, journalist; b. N.Y.C., July 13, 1927; d. George Mallory Pynchon and Alice (Bennett) Dunnington; m. O'Neill Osborn, Aug. 16, 1949; children: Victoria Alice, Hugh O'Neil Pynchon, Ann Sayre, Julie Alexandra. AB, Smith Coll., 1948. Columnist Phila. Bull., 1965-69, editorial writer, 1969-70; cons. U.S. Commn. on Civil Rights, Washington, 1970-71; dir. pub. info. Bryn Mawr (Pa.) Coll., 1971-77; Bagehot fellow Columbia U., N.Y.C., 1977-78; reporter Wilmington (Del.) News-Jour., 1978-82; reporter USA Today, Arlington, Va., 1982-83, assignment editor Money sect., 1983—. Home: 2127 California St NW Washington DC 20008

OSBORNE, CAROL ANN, lawyer; b. Erie, Pa., Aug. 26, 1938; d. Clarence Henry and Grace Louise (McLaughlin) Bronson; LL.B., Western State U., 1977, J.D., 1978; m. Dwight E. Osborne, Jr., Jan. 1, 1965 (div. July 1986); children—Dwight E., Joy Louise. Bar: Calif. 1978. Legal sec., Orange County, Calif., 1967-78; individual practice, Orange, Calif., 1978-83; assoc. with Maxine L. Zazzara, Downey, Calif., 1983-85; sole practice, Downey, Calif., 1985—; instr. Probate Paralegal Course, Cerritos Coll. Active PTA Kraemer Jr. High Sch. and Van Buren Elem. Sch.; treas. Kraemer Parent Booster Club, 1979-80; mem. Valencia High Sch. PTA, others. Mem. ABA, Calif. Bar Assn., Los angeles County Bar Assn., Orange County Bar Assn., Calif. Trial Lawyers Assn., Orange County Trial Lawyers Assn., Southeast Bar Assn., Am. Bus. Women's Assn. (chpt. officer), Western State U. Alumni Assn., Nu Beta Epsilon. Club: Pico Rivera (sec. 1988-89). Lodge: Rotary. Republican. Office: 8221 3d St #307 Downey CA 90241

OSBORNE, GAYLA MARLENE, sales executive; b. Owenton, Ky., Aug. 9, 1956; d. Frederick Clay and Helen Beatrice (Mason) O. AAS, No. Ky. U., 1982, BS, 1986; certificate in Chinese Mandarin, Defense Language Inst., 1975. Personnel clk. Dept. Edn. State Ky., Frankfort, 1974; sec. Dept. Health, Edn., Welfare Nat. Inst. Occupational Safety Health, Cin., 1977-79; specialist sales promotion U.S. Postal Service, Cin., 1980, Coordinator customer liaison, task force pub. image, account rep., 1986-87. Councilmember Florence City Council, Ky. 1984-87; vol. Children's Home, Covington, 1982, 87. Served in USAF, 1974-76. Named to hon. order Ky. Cols. Mem. Disabled Am. Veterans, No. Ky. U. Alumni Assn., Nat. Assn. Postmasters U.S., Boone County Fraternal Order Police, Ky. Assn. Realtors, Nat. Bd. Realtors. Democrat. Baptist. Club: Fraternal Order Police. Home: 8395 Juniper Ln Florence KY 41042

OSBORNE, JANA YOUNG, accountant; b. Memphis, Mar. 26, 1964; d. Isaac and Martha Jane (Craine) Young; m. Anthony Osborne, Jr., Aug. 9, 1980; children: Anthony, Jr, Ashley. BS in Acctg. cum laude, Jackson State U., 1986. Computer operator Tenn. Valley Authority, Knoxville, 1984-85; computer operator C.E. Standard Enterprises, Jackson, Miss., 1985-86, controller, 1986—. Mem. Nat. Assn. Female Execs., Nat. Acctg. Soc., Delta Mu Delta, Phi Beta Lambda. Democrat. Home: 128 Wacaster Jackson MS 39209 Office: CE Standard Enterprises 1350 Livingston Rd Suite D Jackson MS 39213

OSBORNE, MAGGIE (MARGARET ELLEN), novelist; b. Hollywood, Calif., June 10, 1941; d. William Edward and Zelma Lucille (King) Prather; m. Charles Ralph Carter, Dec. 26, 1966; 1 child, Zane Earl; m. 2d, George Muncy Osborne II, Apr. 22, 1972. Flight attendant United Air Lines, Denver, 1963-67; owner Hospitality House, Denver, 1968-72; freelance writer, 1979—. Author: Alexa, 1980; Salem's Daughter, 1981; Portrait in Passion, 1981; Yankee Princess, 1982; Rage to Love, 1983; Flight to Fancy, 1984; Winter Magic, 1986; Castles and Fairy Tales, 1986, Chase The Heart, 1987, Heart Club, 1987, Where There's Smoke..., 1988. Mem. Romance Writers Am. (sec. 1983-84, nat. dir. 1983-84, pres. 1984-85, 85-86, named Denver chpt. Writer of Yr. 1984), Rocky Mountain Writers Guild (resident writer 1982-84, named Writer of Yr. 1981), Colo. Authors League, Mensa. Methodist. Club: Denver Women's Press. Home: PO Box E Dillon CO 80435

OSBORNE, MARTHA LEE, facilities manager; b. Fayetteville, N.C., May 15, 1938; d. T. Emmett and Mary Omie (Cook) Thomas; m. Stancil Ray Osborne, Feb. 9, 1961 (div. Jan. 1985); children: Sandra Lee Lewis, Sharon Lynn, Steven Ray. BA, U. Maryland, 1959. Tchr. Calvert County Bd. of Edn., Prince Frederick, Md., 1959-60, Fairfax County Bd. of Edn., Springfield, Va., 1960-62; sec. Safeway Stores, Inc., Washington, 1963-65; tchr. Prince Georges County Bd. Edn., Cheverly, Md., 1965-68, Cheverly, 1973-75; tchr. Cobb County Bd. Edn., Powder Springs, Ga., 1975-83; mgr. facilities Digital Communications Assocs., Alpharetta, Ga., 1983—; cons. Community Christmas Tree Com., Cumming, Ga., 1987—. Soloist, choir mem. 1st UMC Marietta, Ga., 1975-87; dir. music Children's Community Theater, Marietta, 1983-85; mem. Atlanta Symphony Orch. Chorus, 1975-81; dir., pres. Cumming Chorale, Ga., 1986—; pres. Cobb County Autry PTA, AcWorth, Ga., 1978. Mem. Internat. Facilities Mgmt. Assn. (sec. Atlanta chpt.), Women In Construction, Nat. Assn. Female Execs., Airline Owners and Pilots Assn., Panhellenic Assn. (Diamond Honorary 1958), Sigma Alpha Iota. Republican. Methodist. Lodge: Order Eastern Star. Home: Rural Rt 16 Box 546 Magnolia Pl Cumming GA 30130 Office: DCA 1000 Alderman Dr Alpharetta GA 30201

OSBORNE, THERESA JO, investment administrator; b. Seattle, Aug. 22, 1945; d. Stanley and Jean (Strazdas) Pospichal; m. Herbert L. Osborne Jr., June 3, 1967 (div. Feb. 1987); children: Amanda Jennifer, Maxwell Joseph. BFA in Art Printmaking, U. Nebr., Omaha, 1967; MFA in Arts Mgmt., Bklyn. Coll., 1982. Supr. art Burlington (N.J.) Twp., 1967-68, Harpswell Schs., Topsham, Maine, 1968-70; dir. spl. projects Borough of Queens City of N.Y.C., 1979-81, project coordinator Bklyn. Bridge Centennial, 1981-82, dir. cultural affairs Borough of Queens, 1982-85; community coordinator Bklyn. Acad. Music, 1980; exec. mgr., corp. sec. Live Oak Realty Corp., N.Y.C., 1985—. Trustee Old Stone House Gowanus, Bklyn., 1978, Flushing Meadows-Corona Park Corp., Queens, 1987—. Mem. N.Y.C. Jr. League (bd. mgrs. 1984-85), N.Y. Drama League, Chi Omega. Democrat. Roman Catholic. Club: Women's City (N.Y.C.). Home: 19 Ingram St Forest Hills Gardens NY 11375 Office: Live Oak Realty Corp 40 E 75th St Suite 1-A New York NY 10021

OSBURN, DEE CAMPBELL, steel supply company executive; b. Dallas, Jan. 26, 1941; d. Cipranno Granado and Santa Prisca (Sanches) Cluké; m. John Roy Osburn, July 2, 1982; children: Michael A., Joanna Mentensana. Grad. high sch., Dallas. Collections supr. J.C. Penney Credit Office, Dallas, 1963-75; cons. in fin. and credit ops. Dallas, 1975-81; v.p. Intercontinental Pipe and Steel, Dallas, 1980-86; pres. Deeferro Corp., Inc., Dallas, 1986—; mem. panel women and work, research and resource conf. of U. of Arlington, Tex., 1987. Mem. Assn. Gen. Contractors, Assn. Women Entrepreneurs, Nat. Assn. Female Execs., Dallas C. of C., Hispanic C. of C. Republican. Baptist. Office: Deeferro Corp 18601 LBJ Freeway Suite 725 Mesquite TX 75150

OSCAR, JOYCE ANNETTE, newscaster; b. Chgo., July 3, 1956; d. Edward Ambrose and Gertrude (Andrews) O. BA, Western Ill. U., Macomb, 1978. Copy writer advt. Sta. WFYR/RKO, Chgo., 1978-79; video journalist Cable News Network, Atlanta, 1980; reporter, anchor Sta. WJBF-TV ABC Affiliate, Augusta, Ga., 1980-83; news anchor Sta. WDEF-TV CBS Affiliate, Chattanooga, 1983-85; news reporter Sta. WSB-TV ABC Affiliate, Atlanta, 1985—. Talent, writer, producer Spot News Report, 1983, TV reporting, rotary, 1983. Vol. March of Dimes, Atlanta, 1986-87, pub. speaker United Way Agy., Atlanta, 1986-87; com. mem. Ga. Spl. Olympics. Unicom Ednl. TV grantee, 1975-78; recipient Spot News Reporting award, UP Internat. and W. Augusta Rotary, 1983. Mem. Ga. Assn. Newscasters, Soc. Profl. Journalists, Sigma Delta Chi, Sigma, Sigma, Sigma. Roman Catholic. Office: Sta WSB-TV 1601 W Peachtree St Atlanta GA 30309

OSCHIN, FRANCINE, journalist; b. Bklyn., Mar. 20, 1943; d. Albert and Goldie (Miller) Strauss; m. Michael Harvey Oschin, Nov. 11, 1961; children: Sheryl, Danny, Karen, Kathy. AA, Los Angeles Valley Coll., 1965; BA, Calif. State U., Northridge, 1984, MA, 1986. Condr. slide show Friends of Hawaii Pub. TV, Honolulu, 1978-81, 1st v.p., 1978-80; corr. Leader Newspapers, Glendale, Calif., 1985—. asst., writer Office Pub. Affairs, Calif. State U., Northridge, 1985—; corr. sec. Birmingham High Sch. PTSA, Van Nuys, Calif., 1987-88. Mem. Soc. Profl. Journalists/Sigma Delta Chi, Calif. State U.-Northridge Alumni Assn., Calif. State U.-Northridge Journalism Alumni Assn., Greenpeace, Sierra Club, Cousteau Soc., Consumers Union, Kappa Tau Alpha, Tau Alpha Epsilon. Home: 16027 Royal Oak Rd Encino CA 91436 Office: Glendale News Press 111 N Isabel St Glendale CA 91206

OSGOOD, LLOYD GUNTER, banker; b. Big Springs, Tex., Sept. 20, 1960; d. James Poteat and Twyla Layton (Willey) G. BA in Speech Communications, U. Va., 1982, MA in communications, 1984. Plannng specialist Bank Va., Richmond, 1984-86; sales training officer Signet Bank, Richmond, 1986-87, br. officer, 1987—; freelance cons., 1986—. Bd. mem. Va. Home for Boys, Richmond, 1986—. Mem. Am. Soc. for Training and Devel. (v.p. 1984-86). Methodist. Club: UVA (Richmond) (dir. 1985—).

OSKEY, D. BETH, banker; b. Red Wing, Minn., Dec. 23, 1921; d. Alvin E. and Effie D. (Thompson) Feldman; student U. Wis., River Falls, 1939-41; B.A., Met. State U., Minn., 1975; grad. degree in banking, U. Wis., 1973, postgrad. in banking, 1977; student in interior decorating LaSalle Extension U., Chgo., 1970; m. Warren B. Oskey, Sept. 27, 1941; children—Jo Cheryl, Warren A., Peter (dec.), Jeffrey L. Officer, Hiawatha Nat. Bank, Hager City, Wis., 1959—, cashier, 1978-79, pres., 1979, chmn. bd., 1984—, exec. v.p., dir., sec. bd. dirs., 1959—, sec., mem. discount com.; with First Nat. Bank of Glenwood, Glenwood City, Wis., 1965— pres., exec. v.p., 1979—, dir., sec. bd., 1965—, chmn. bd., 1984—, sec., mem. discount com.; speaker on women in banking. Banking com. Vo-Tech Sch., Red Wing, Minn.; former officer civic orgns. Mem. Ind. Bankers Am., Wis. Bankers Assn., Am. Bankers Assn. Republican. Lutheran. Club: Minn. Fedn. Women's Clubs (v.p. 1983—, pres. dist. III 1978—, pres. elect 1986-88, pres. 1988—). Home: 1022 Hallstrom Dr Red Wing MN 55066 also: 1561 Leisure World Mesa AZ 85206 Office: Hiawatha Nat Bank Hager City WI 54014

OSLER, DOROTHY K., state legislator; b. Dayton, Ohio, Aug. 19, 1923; d. Carl M. and Pearl A. (Tobias) Karstaedt; B.S. cum laude in Bus. Adminstrn., Miami U., Oxford, Ohio, 1945; m. David K. Osler, Oct. 26, 1946; children—Scott C., David D. Mem. Conn. Ho. of Reps., 1973—. Mem. Greenwich (Conn.) Rep. Town Meeting, 1968—, Eastern Greenwich Women's Rep. Club, 1970—; sec. Conn. Student Loan Found., 1973-83, v.p., 1983-84; mem. Spl. Edn. Cost Commn., 1976-77, Sch. Fin. Adv. Panel, 1977-78, Edn. Equity Study Com., 1980-81, Commn. on Goals for U. Conn. Health Center, 1975-76; bd. dirs. ARC, 1975. Mem. Nat. Order Women Legislators (sec. 1987-88), Conn. Order of Women Legislators (sec. 1983-84, pres. 1985-86), LWV (pres. Greenwich chpt. 1965-67, sec. Conn. chpt. 1967-72), AAUW (dir. 1971-73), Mortar Board, Phi Beta Kappa, Alpha Omicron Pi. Republican. Christian Scientist. Bi-weekly columnist local newspaper, 1973—.

OSLER, JULIE, public relations executive; b. N.Y.C., Feb. 11, 1947; d. David Saul Osler and Grace Rose (Brown) Osler Sonenblick; m. Arnold Mark Huberman, Apr. 27, 1985. BA, George Washington U., 1968; MA, Columbia U., 1969. Tchr. Lexington Sch. for Deaf, N.Y.C., 1969-73; editorial coordinator New Ingenue Mag., 1973-75; assoc. dir. pub. relations PBS, 1975-80; dir. pub. relations Showtime, 1980-81; v.p. pub. relations The Entertainment Channel, 1981-83; pres. Julie Osler Pub. Relations, 1983—; dir. pub. affairs Cablevision Systems Corp.; vis. lectr. New Sch. for Social Research, N.Y.C., 1982-83, L.I. Univ., Southhampton, N.Y., 1985-86. U.S. Office Edn. fellow 1968-69. Mem. Am. Women in Radio and TV, Internat. Radio and TV Soc., Women in Communication, Women in Cable, Pub. Relations Soc. Am., Women Execs. in Pub. Relations, Women's Media Group.

OSMINER, LINDA LEE, oil company executive; b. Chgo., Jan. 12, 1943; d. Joe William and Evelyn Marie (Lense) O'Dowd; m. Emmett Franklin Osminer, Aug. 4, 1962; children: Matthew, Erin, Allison. BBA, U. Phoenix, Denver, 1986. Numerous clerical positions Houston, Denver, 1962-81; landman Oxy Petroleum, Inc., Denver, 1982-83; lease records mgr. IREX Corp., Denver, 1983-86; div. order mgr. Apache, Denver, 1986-87; land adminstrn. mgr. NICOR Exploration, Denver, 1987—; cons., lease conversion NICOR Exploration, Denver, 1986-87. Mem. Denver Assn. of Petroleum Landmen, Denver Assn. of Div. Order Analysts (sec. 1986-87, pres. 1988), Nat. Assn. of Div. Order Analysts, Denver Assn. of Lease and Title Analysts. Presbyterian. Lodge: Order of the Easter Star. Office: NICOR Exploration 1050 17th St Suite 1100 Denver CO 80265

OSMOND, LYNN JOYCE, symphony orchestra manager; b. St. Catharines, Ont., Can., Mar. 31, 1957; d. George and Joyce Edith (Stanton) O. MusB with honors, Queens U., 1980; numerous courses and seminars in field. Adminstrv. asst. Assn. of Can. Orchs., Ont. Fedn. of Symphony Orchs., Toronto, 1980-81; exec. dir. Mississauga Symphony, Ont., 1981-83; youth orch. coordinator for Ont., Ont. Fedn. Symphony Orchs., Toronto, 1981-84; festival coordinator Ont. Youth Orch. Festival, 1983-85; gen. mgr. Thunder Bay Symphony Orch., Ont., 1983-85, Orch. London Ont., Can., 1985—; dir. Can. Assn. Youth Orchs., Banff, Alta.; mem. adv. bd. Performing Arts Mgmt. Confedn. Coll., Thunder Bay, 1984-86; bd. dirs. Performing Arts Ctr. for Tomorrow (PACT), London West Progressive Conservative Assn., London & Area Progressive Conservative Bus. Assn. Arts Mgmt. Tng. grantee Can. Council, 1984. Mem. Thunder Bay Regional Arts Council (pres.), Thunder Bay Press Club, Assn. Cultural Execs., Ont. Fedn. Symphony Orchs. (bd. dirs.), London C. of C., Dirs. Club of London, Am. Symphony Orch. League (bd. dirs. youth orch.), London West Progressive Conservative Small Bus. Assn. (exec. com., bd. dirs.), Queen's U. Alumni Assn. (class agt.). Conservative. Anglican. Avocations: music, sports. Home: 2-234 Central Ave, London, ON Canada N6A 1M8

OSMOND, MARIE, singer; b. Ogden, Utah, Oct. 13, 1959; d. George and Olive O.; m. Brian Blosil, 1986; 1 child, Stephen James. Ed. pub. schs., pvt. tutors. Appeared with The Osmond family singing group from age 7, solo act, 1973—; co-star: Donny & Marie TV show, 1976-79, Donny & Marie Christmas Spl, 1979, Osmond Family Show, 1979, Osmond Family Christmas Show, 1980; star TV spl. Marie, 1981; record albums include (with Donny Osmond): Make the World Go Away, I'm Leaving It All Up To You; songs from their TV Show Goin Coconuts; solo albums include: Paper Roses, In My Little Corner of the World, Who's Sorry Now?, This Is The Way That I Feel, There's No Stopping Your Heart, 1985, All In Love, 1988; #1 singles include Meet Me in Montana (Best Country Duo of Yr. award with Dan Seals), 1986, Read My Lips, 1986, There's No Stoppin' Your Heart, 1986, I Only Wanted You, 1987; singles include You're Still New to Me; co-author: Fun, Fame, and Family, 1973; Marie Osmond's Guide to Beauty, Health, and Style, 1980. Recipient (with Donny Osmond) Georgie award for best vocal team Am. Guild Variety Artists, 1978. Mormon.

OSORA, ANN MARCHESE, social worker; b. Middletown, Conn., Nov. 15, 1928; d. Vincenzo and Santa (Garofalo) Marchese; m. Stanley Leonard Osora, May 10, 1952; children: Grace Ann Osora Erhart, Margaret Marie. BA with high honors, U. Hartford, 1956; MS, Cet. Conn. State U., 1964. Cert. tchr., Conn. Library aide Wesleyan U. Olin Library, Middletown, 1952-56; tchr. elem. schs. Portland (Conn.) Bd. Edn., 1956-61; social worker Conn. Dept. Human Resources, Middletown, 1978—. Republican. Roman Catholic. Home: 218 College St Middletown CT 06457 Office: Conn Dept Human Resources Middletown CT 06457

OSSENBERG, HELLA SVETLANA, psychoanalyst; b. Kiev, Russia, June 10, 1930; came to U.S., 1957, naturalized, 1964; d. Anatole E. and Tatiana N. (Dombrovski) Donath; diploma langs. and psychology, U. Heidelberg (W. Ger.), 1953; M.S., Columbia U., 1968; cert. Nat. Psychol. Assn. Psychoanalysis, 1977; m. Carl H. Ossenberg, June 7, 1958. Sr. psychiat. social worker VA Mental Hygiene Clinic, N.Y.C., 1968-80, pvt. practice psychoanalysis, N.Y.C., 1975—; mem. Theodor Reik Cons. Center, 1978—; field instr. Columbia U., Fordham U. schs. social work. Mem. Nat. Assn. Social Workers, Acad. Cert. Social Workers (diplomate clin. social work), Nat. Psychol. Assn. Psychoanalysis, Nat. Assn. Advancement Phychoanalysis (Am. Bds. Accreditation and Certification), Council Psychoanalytic Psychotherapists. Home: 820 West End Ave New York NY 10025 Office: 345 W 58th St New York NY 10019

OSSOFSKY, HELEN JOHNS (MRS. ELI OSSOFSKY), physician; b. Phila., Dec. 7, 1921; d. William Calloway and Gertrude (Schindele) Johns; A.B., Mt. Holyoke Coll., 1943; student Women's Med. Coll. Pa., 1950-52; M.D., Johns Hopkins U., 1954; m. Eli Ossofsky, Aug. 8, 1950, (dec. Oct. 1950); m. Charles E. Illiff, 1987. Intern Oslev Med. Service, Johns Hopkins, 1954-55, resident Pediatrics Cornell U., N.Y. Hosp., 1955-56, Pediatrics Johns Hopkins, 1956-57; research assoc. Johns Hopkins Sch. Hygiene and Pub. Health, 1957-59; asst. prof. Georgetown U. Sch. Medicine, 1959-66, assoc. prof. pediatrics, 1966-79; supervisory med. officer D.C. Dept. Pub. Health, 1959-62, med. cons. div. mental retardation, 1967-69; child psychiatry consultation practice, McLean, Va., 1966—. Cons., Inst. Child Health and Human Devel., NIH, Bethesda, Md., 1962-63; cons. in med. tng. div. chronic diseases USPHS, 1964-65; cons. Va. Assn. Children with Learning Disabilities, Psychiatric Inst. Washington, 1972—; fellow Am. Acad. Pediatrics, 1975; lectr. Cath. U. Sch. Cardiovascular Nursing, 1959-79; mem. advisory council Cybernetic Research Inst. Mem. Fairfax County Med. Soc., AMA, Washington Psychiat. Soc., Am. Psychiat. Assn., Johns Hopkins Med. and Surg. Assn., Phi Beta Kappa. Author: Tumors of the Eye and Adnexa in Infancy and Childhood, 1962; also articles in profl. jours. Address: 1333 Merrie Ridge Rd McLean VA 22101

OSTAP, MARTINE ELIZABETH, educator; b. New Brunswick, N.J., Mar. 31, 1959; d. Helen M. O.; BA with honors, in English, with honors in Am. Studies, U. Wyo., 1981, MA in Am. Studies, 1984; MA in English, U. Tex., El Paso, 1983; postgrad. U. N.Mex., Fla State U., 1988—. Instr. English U. Tex., El Paso, 1981-83, research asst. English composition, 1982; teaching assoc. English, U. N.Mex., 1984-86; lectr. in English. U. Wyo., 1986-88. Contbr. to Jack London Newsletter. William Robertson Coe fellow, 1984. Mem. Omicron Delta Kappa. Home: 1271 N 17th St Laramie WY 82070

OSTENDORF, CAROLE GLORINE, health care facility executive; b. Little Falls, Minn., Sept. 6, 1948; d. Gilbert Frank and Monica Therese (Lange) O. BS, St. Cloud (Minn.) State U., 1973; M of Med. Sci., Emory U., 1980; MBA, U. Wis., Milw., 1987. Cert. phys. therapist. Staff phys. therapist McDowell (Ky.) Appalachia Regional Hosp., 1973-75; supr. Ebenezer Soc., Mpls., 1975-78; research asst. Emory U. Dept. Rehab., Atlanta, 1978-80; dir. phys. therapy Curative Rehab. Ctr., Milw., 1980-85, v.p., 1985—; mem. profl. adv. com. Kimberly Home Health, Milw., 1983-87. Active women's group Counseling Ctr., Milw., 1986-87. Mem. Am. Phys. Therapy Assn., Wis. Phys. Therapy Assn. (treas. 1984-85, v.p. 1985-87). Democrat. Office: Curative Rehab Ctr 1000 N 92d St Wauwatosa WI 53000

OSTER, NANCY ELIZABETH, lawyer; b. Toronto, Ont., Can., June 5, 1958; d. Walter Stuart and Lorraine Jean (Uffelman) Brown; m. Jan Christian Oster, Sept. 12, 1987. B of Aerospace Engring., U. Toronto, 1981; LLB, McGill U., 1984. Bar: B.C. 1985. Barrister, solicitor Fed. Dept. Justice, Vancouver, Can., 1985-86, 87—; aviation enforcement officer Fed. Dept. Transport, Vancouver, 1986-87. Mem. Law Soc. B.C. Mem. Anglican Church. Office: Dept Justice, 2800-1055 W Georgia St, Vancouver, BC Canada V6E 3P9

OSTER, ROSE MARIE GUNHILD, university administrator; b. Stockholm, Feb. 26, 1934; came to U.S., 1958; d. Herbert Jonas and Emma Wilhelmina (Johnson) Hagetorn; m. Ludwig F. Oster, May 17, 1956; children: Ulrika, Mattias. Fil. mag., U. Stockholm, 1956; D. Phil., Kiel (Germany) U., 1958. Postdoctoral research fellow linguistics Yale U., 1958-60, research fellow Germanic langs., 1960-64, lectr. Swedish, 1964-66; mem. faculty U. Colo., Boulder, 1966-80; assoc. prof. Germanic langs. and lits. U. Colo., 1970-77, prof., 1977-80, chmn. dept., 1972-75; assoc. dean U. Colo. (Grad. Sch.), 1975-79, assoc. vice chancellor for grad. affairs, 1979-80; dean for grad. studies and research U. Md., College Park, 1980-83; prof. Germanic langs. and lits. U. Md., 1980—; Mem. Fulbright Nat. Screening Com. Scandinavia, 1973, 83-86; mem. selection com., Scandinavia Internat. Exchange of Scholars, 1983; cons. panelist Nat. Endowment for Humanities, 1975—, mem. bd. consultants, 1980—; state coordinator Am. Council on Edn., Colo., 1978-80, Md., 1981-83; mem. exec. com. Assn. Grad. Schs., 1980-83; mem. dean's exec. com. African-Am. Inst., 1981-85; bd. dirs. dept. leadership program Am. Council on Edn.; cons. in field. Contbr. articles and revs. to profl. publs. Carnegie fellow, 1974; grantee Swedish Govt., Am. Scandinavian Found.; grantee German Acad. Exchange Service. Mem. Soc. Advancement Scandinavian Studies (pres. 1979-80), Am. Scandinavian Assn. of Nat. Capital Area (pres. 1983-86), MLA, Am.-Scandinavian Found., Am. Assn. Higher Edn., AAUP, NOW. Home: 4977 Battery Ln Bethesda MD 20814 Office: U Md Jimenez Hall College Park MD 20742

OSTERBERG, BECKY WALKER, communications executive; b. Fargo, N.D., Sept. 11, 1946; d. Robert and Edna Mae (Smith) Huxtable; m. Robert C. Osterberg Jr., Jan. 20, 1979. BA in Journalism, Ind. U., 1969. Mgr. mdse. J.C. Penney & Co., Newport Beach, Calif., 1974-77; stockbroker Merrill Lynch, Fullerton, Calif., 1977-79; cons. communications Fin. Relations Bd., Chgo., 1979-81; v.p. fin. relations Burson-Marsteller, Chgo., 1981-83; dir. investor relations Ameritech, Chgo., 1983-86; v.p. communications Premark Internat., Chgo., 1986—. Mem. Nat. Investor Relations Inst. (dir.). Republican. Office: Premark Internat Inc 1717 Deerfield Rd Deerfield IL 60015

OSTERMAN, CONSTANTINE E., Canadian provincial government minister; b. Acme, Alta., Can., June 23, 1936; m. Joe Osterman, Oct. 30, 1954; children: Theo, Kurt, Kim, Kelly, Joe Jr. MLA representing Three Hills constituency Alta. Legis. Assembly, 1979-82, 82-85, 86—, party whip, mem. edn. caucus and agr. caucus coms., 1979-82, Minister of Consumer and Corp. Affairs, mem. social planning com. of cabinet, cabinet/caucus com. on legis. rev., agr. caucus com., 1982-85, Minister of Social Services and Community Health, 1986, Minister Social Services, mem. social planning, energy, met. affairs and mgmt. policy coms. of cabinet, 1986—; served select legis. com. to rev. surface rights issue, lead role in passing of Surface Rights Act, 1983. Active exec. bds. local ch., home and sch. assns., Carstairs, Alta., 1958—, surface rights area; commr., charter mem. Alta. Human Rights Commn., 1973-78; pres. Can. Assn. Statutory Human Rights Agys. Office: Office Minister Social Services, 424 Legislature Bldg, Edmonton, AB Canada T5K 2B6

OSTERMAN, FRANCES MARGARET, nurse; b. L'Anse, Mich., Sept. 25, 1946; d. Francis Joseph and Margaret Rose (Zelinski) Whitman; m. George Patrick Osterman. Diploma in nursing, Henry Ford Hosp. Sch. Nursing, Detroit, 1967; BSN, No. Mich. U., 1987. Registered Nurse. Staff nurse Barago County Meml. Hosp., L'Anse, Mich., 1967-69, William Beaumont Hosp., Royal Oak, Mich., 1969, Henry Ford Hosp., 1970, St. Luke's Hosp., Marquette, Mich., 1971; critical care nurse St. Mary's Hosp., Marquette, 1971-72, Presbyn. Intercommunity Hosp., Klamath Falls, Oreg., 1972-77; sch. nurse Baraga (Mich.) Area Schs., 1979-85; home health nurse Western Upper Peninsula Health Dept., L'Anse, 1985; community health nurse Keweenaw Bay Indian Community, Baraga, 1985—. Bd. dirs. Bay Ambulance, Baraga, 1981—, Baraga County Meml. Hosp., 1987—, Baraga County Shelter Home (treas.), L'Anse, 1983—, Upper Peninsula Emergency Med. Services, Marquette, 1983—. Recipient of Achievement award AAUW (Mich. chpt.), 1987. Mem. NOW (pres. Copper County, Mich. chpt.), 1985—. Home: PO Box 492 Baraga MI 49908 Office: Keweenaw Bay Tribal Health Service Rt 1 Baraga MI 49908

OSTROW, GAIL ROBERTA, management consultant; b. Bklyn., Mar. 29, 1944; d. Bernard R. Ostrow and Miriam F. (Greene) Travaini; m. Fred T. Pielert (div. Dec. 1977); children: Richard Jonathan, Beth Rachel; m. Robert F. Sauerhoff. BA in Psychology, U. Minn., 1975, MA in English, 1977. Teaching asst. Dept. English U. Minn., Mpls., 1976-79; dir. publs. CPT Corp., Edina, Minn., 1979-83, Datacomm Mgmt. Scis., East Norwalk, Conn., 1983-84; dir. mgmt. info. systems Micrognosis, Inc., Danbury, Conn., 1984-86; prin., pres. Write Type, Inc., Bethel, Conn., 1986—; adj. instr. SE Community Edn. dist., Mpls., 1975-80. Editor med. textbook, 1982. Crisis intervention counselor Yes/Neon programs, Mpls., 1978-83; mem. Amnesty Internat., 1983—. Mem. Soc. for Tech. Communication, Nat. Assn. Female Execs., U.S. Power Squadron (nat. lt.), NOW, Phi Kappa Phi. Jewish. Home and Office: 3 Marvin Pl Bethel CT 06801

O'SULLIVAN, DONNA LEE, public relations executive; b. Woodbury, N.J., June 7, 1957; d. Albert Franklin and Jeanne Agnes (Rainier) Lounsbury; m. Timothy Joseph O'Sullivan, Aug. 17, 1985. BA, Kent State U., 1979. Prodn. asst. Sta. WCAU-TV, Phila., 1979-81; assignment editor Sta. WPVI-TV, Phila., 1983-85, Sta. WRBV-TV, Vineland, N.J., 1981, N.J. Network, Trenton, 1981-83; mgr. pub. relations Six Flags Great Adventure, Jackson, N.J., 1985-87; sr. account exec. Mgmt. Systems Assocs., Toms River, N.J., 1987—. Sec. Shore Region Tourism Council, Wall Twp., N.J., 1985-87; bd. dirs. Monmouth-Ocean Devel. Council, Wall Twp., 1986—. Mem. N.Y. Press Club, N.J. Press Assn., N.J. Broadcasters Assn. Presbyterian.

O'SULLIVAN-SMITH, BITTY, motion picture sound editor; b. Munich, Fed. Republic Germany, Nov. 2, 1952; d. Robert William and Lorraine Mary (Saltus) O'Sullivan; m. Mike Simpson, Feb. 4, 1976 (div. 1978); m. Philip Raymond Smith, Nov. 24, 1978; 1 child, Tristan Laine. BS in Communications, U. Tex., Austin, 1975. Sound editor Nurse, CBS-TV Series, 1983, film Places in the Heart, 1984, Three Sovereigns for Sarah, PBS miniseries, 1985, Equalizer, CBS-TV series, 1985, films Manhattan Project, 1985-86, Peggy Sue Got Married, 1986, Dead of Winter, 1986, Ishtar, 1987. Recipient Golden Reel award Motion Picture Sound Editors Assn., 1984. Mem. Internat. Assn. State and Theatrical Employees. Democrat. Home and Office: 111 3rd Ave Apt 12C New York NY 10003

OSVATH, SUSAN MARGARET, school librarian, educator; b. Holyoke, Mass., July 11, 1944; d. John Herbert Friedhaber and Anne Mary (Pruzinsky) Friedhaber Hard; m. Robert Osvath, Feb. 17, 1973; 1 dau., Rebecca Jeanne. B.A., Daemen Coll., 1967; M.L.S., State U. Coll.-Geneseo, 1974. Tchr. English, French, DeSales High Sch., Columbus, Ohio, 1967-68; housemother St. Vincent's Orphanage, Columbus, 1968; tchr. English, French, Mater Dei High Sch., New Monmouth, N.J., 1968-69; records librarian Children's Aid Soc., Buffalo, 1970; tchr. English, French, religion, library Archbishop Carroll High Sch., Buffalo, 1970-74; librarian asst. Arcade Free Library (N.Y.), 1975-81; sch. librarian Pioneer High Sch., Yorkshire, N.Y., 1981—; council mem. Cattaraugus-Allegany Sch. Library System, 1986—; lector, mem. liturgy com. St. Joseph's Ch., Bliss, N.Y., 1987—. Mem. Citizens' Activist Group to fight zoning change, Arcade, N.Y., 1982-83; tchr. St. Mary's Ch., East Arcade, N.Y., 1977-84, lector, 1980-84. Mem. ALA, N.Y. Library Assn., Sch. Library Assn. Western N.Y. Roman Catholic. Home: 2269 Sullivan Rd East Arcade NY 14009 Office: Pioneer High Sch Library PO Box 579 Yorkshire NY 14173

OSWALD, GRETCHEN, lighting manufacturing company executive, industrial motor repairs and sales company executive; b. Pitts., Oct. 23, 1945; d. V.E. and Eleanor (Hook) O. BA, DePauw U., 1967. Pres. Shop Materials, Inc., Pitts., 1981—, Electric M&R Inc., Pitts., 1983—. Mem. World Affairs Council Pitts. Republican. Presbyterian. Clubs: Duquesne, Grow and Invest Now Investment (Pitts.). Lodge: Zonta. Office: Electric M&R Inc 2025 Milford Dr Pittsburgh PA 15102

OSWALT, GENE GUNN, financial analyst; b. Pascagoula, Miss., Apr. 2, 1961; d. Clyde Hubert Jr. and Pattie Beth (Corban) Gunn; m. Ronald J. Oswalt, May 12, 1984. BA in Econs. and German, Emory U., 1983; M in Internat. Bus., U. S.C., 1985. Teaching asst. Emory U. German Div., Atlanta, 1982-83; intern Robert Bosch LTDA., Brazil, 1984-85; fin. analyst Robert Bosch Corp., Charleston, S.C., 1985—. Office: Robert Bosch Corp 8001 Dorchester Rd North Charleston SC 29418

OTERO, ANITA, accountant; b. San Antonio, Aug. 16, 1959; d. Arturo G. and Guadalupe (Rivera) O. BBA, St. Mary's U., San Antonio, 1981. Asst. controller Gunter Hotel, San Antonio, 1981-86; bookkeeper Hilton Inn West, Houston, 1986-87; controller Nassau Bay Hilton & Marina, Houston, 1987; acct. Utility Fuels, Inc., Houston, 1987—. Mem. Nat. Assn. for Female Execs. Office: Utility Fuels Inc PO Box 539 Houston TX 77001

OTHMER, MARY LINDA, accountant; b. Ames, Iowa, May 16, 1954; d. Richard Thomas and Betty Margaret (Will) O. BBA in Acctg., Tex. Tech U., 1976. CPA, N.Mex., Tex. Staff acct. Seidman and Seidman, CPA's, Houston, 1976-79; supr. then audit mgr. Washington, 1979-83; acct. adminstr. Roqoff, Diamond and Walker, Albuquerque, 1983—. Bd. dirs., treas. Artspace mag., Albuquerque, 1986. Mem. Jr. League of Albuquerque 1986—. Mem. Am. Inst. CPA's, N.Mex. Soc. CPA's. Republican. Roman Catholic. Office: Roqoff Diamond and Walker 1001 Medical Arts Ave NE Albuquerque NM 87125

OTIS, DIANE C., realtor, writer; b. Wilmington, Del., Jan. 21, 1946; d. Victor Manual and Minerva C. (Jones) Rolli; m. Fitz-Edward Otis II, Apr. 8, 1967 (div. Feb. 1984); children: Fitz-Edward III, Michelle K. BJ, Bowling Green (Ohio) State U., 1968. Lic. real estate broker, Fla. Realtor Sungate Real Estate, Sarasota, Fla., 1971-75, Merrill Lynch Realty, Sarasota, 1975-83, Michael Saunders & Co., Sarasota, 1983—. Co-editor (book) Fare by the Sea, 1985, also company newsletter. Sec.-treas. Sarasota Pack 90 Boy Scouts Am., 1985-87, Beneva Woods Homeowners Assn., Sarasota, 1976-80; vol. art instr. Girls' Club Sarasota, 1985-87; vol. Citizens for Congressman Connie Mack campaign, Sarasota, 1983—; active Sarasota Jr. League, 1985—, Power Squadron, Sarasota, 1985—, Sarasota Arts Council, 1986—. Recipient Excellence in Real Estate award Ameritrust Mortgage Corp., Sarasota, 1985-87, Million Dollar Sales Club Crossroads Fed. Savs. and Loan, Sarasota, 1976—. Mem. Nat. Assn. Realtors, Sarasota Bd. Realtors (multi-million dollar club 1971—), Power Squadron, Gulf Coast Heritage Assn. Republican. Episcopalian. Office: Michael Saunders & Co 61 S Blvd of Presidents Sarasota FL 33577

OTSTOTT, GRETA VIRGINIA, interior designer, artist; b. Dallas, July 22, 1933; d. Ramon E. and Virginia H. (Anderson) Espinosa; m. Daniel Dushane Otstott, Jan. 7, 1955; children—Dana D. Otstott Shear, Cheryl Lynn. A.A., El Centro Coll., 1975; B.A., So. Meth. U., 1954. Artist, Fenne-Vaughn Co., Dallas, 1954-55, Dallas Times Herald, 1955-57, Edward Fields Inc., Dallas, 1973-74; head design ctr. Standard Fixture Co., Dallas, 1976-81; art dir. Hancock Ltd., Dallas, 1981-82; owner, mgr. GO Enterprises, Dallas, 1982—. Pres. Richardson Unitarian Ch., Dallas, 1976-77; leader troop Girl Scouts U.S.A.; facilitator of Explore, Dallas, 1968-74. Mem. Am. Soc. Interior Designers (cert. 1980), Am. Inst. Bus. Designers, Dallas Needlework and Textile Guild, Fiber Artist Fedn. (pres. 1988-89). Author: Bride of the 50's, Woman of the 80's, 1985.

OTT, LISA MARIE, sales executive; b. Phila., June 20, 1963; d. Michael Joseph and Sheila Teresa (Mullarkey) O. BSBA, Meredith Coll., Raleigh, N.C., 1985. Sales trainee Reynolds Metals Co., Shaumburg, Ill., 1985-86, regional sales rep. consumer div., 1986-88; midwest sales mgr. primary metals div. Reynolds Metals Co., Chgo., 1988—. Republican. Roman Catholic. Office: Primary Metals div Reynolds Metals Co 1338 N LaSalle #3 Chicago IL 60610

OTTAVIANI, REGINA, psychologist; b. Towanda, Pa., Oct. 1, 1957; d. Julius James and Helen (Shanowski) O. BA, Bloomsburg State Coll., Pa., 1979; MA, The Am. U., Washington, 1983, PhD, 1985. Lic. psychologist, Md. Intern Crownsville Md. Hosp. Ctr., 1984-85; post-doctoral fellow U. Pa. Ctr. Cognitive Therapy, Phila., 1985-86; co-dir. Cognitive Therapy Ctr., Chevy Chase, Md., 1986—. Office: Cognitive Therapy Ctr 4701 Willard Ave #222 Chevy Chase MD 20815

OTTE, LAURA JEAN, county health department adminstrator; b. Concordia, Kans., July 4, 1949; d. Irwin Edgar Johnson and Carol Lee (Stanton) Williams; m. Melvin Alfred Otte, Dec. 17, 1971; children—Brenda Sue, Matthew Lee, Jason Andrew. Grad. Asbury Hosp. Sch. Nursing, Salina, Kans., 1970; part-time student Kans. State U., 1975-82. Charge nurse Morton County Hosp., Elkhart, Kans., 1970-71; ICU, emergency rm., Med. charge nurse Mitchell County Hosp., Beloit, Kans., 1971-76; adminstr. Mitchell County Health Dept., North Central Kans. Home Health, Beloit, 1977—; sch. nurse St. John Grad Sch., Beloit, St. John High Sch., Beloit, St. Boniface High Sch., Tipton, Kans., 1977—; bd. dirs., nurse, sec. Solomon Valley Hospice, Inc., Beloit, 1982—; Bloodmobile vol. nurse ARC, Beloit, 1975—; vol. nurse Am. Heart Assn., Beloit, 1978-83; publicity dir., cons. Beloit Cancer Soc. State and fed. health grantee; mem. com. Mitchell County Food Bank, 1986—; position #4 Beloit/Mitchell County Salvation Army, 1987—; pres. North Cen. Kans. Chpt. of Compassionate Friends, 1987—; sponser Luth. Youth Together 1986—, Fifth Quarter, 1986—. Mem. Mitchell County Local Emergency Planning Com. Mem. Am. Nurses Assn., Kans. Assn. Local Health Depts., Kans. State Nurses Assn. (dist. bd. dirs. 1979-80), Kans. Assn. Home Health Agys., Kans. Pub. Health Assn. Republican. Clubs: Andromeda, Willow Springs Players (Beloit) (sec. 1985-86). Home: 414 E Court St Beloit KS 67420 Office: Box 217 400 W 8th St Beloit KS 67420

OTTERSON, CECILEE ANN, accountant; b. Camp LeJeune, N.C., Dec. 19, 1955; d. Edward Alva and Cordelia Rose (Sahlberg) Raymond; widowed; children: Jessica Rose, Justin Gregory. Student, N.D. State U., 1974-75; student in acctg., Moorhead State U., 1975-76; student psychology, U. Oreg., 1976-77. Bookkeeper Tiffany Davis Drug Co., Eugene, Oreg., 1976-77; adminstrv. asst. Adams, Inc., Fargo, N.D., 1979-81; bookkeeper Bridgeman Creameries, Moorhead, Minn., 1981—. Mem. Fargo Bus. and Profl. Women (treas. 1986—), N.D. Fedn. of Bus. and Profl. Women (officer 1987—). Home: 1627 30th Ave S Fargo ND 58103 Office: Bridgeman Creameries 2103 5th Ave N Moorhead MN 56560

OTTINGER, MARY LOUISE, podiatrist; b. Valley City, N.D., July 8, 1956; d. Roy Albert and Harriet Annabelle (Noltimier) O. BS, N.D. State U., 1978; D of Podiatric Medicine, Chgo. Sch. Podiatric Medicine, 1983. Resident in podiatry J.A. Haley VA Hosp., Tampa, Fla., 1983-84; podiatrist Med. Ctr. Podiatry Group, Augusta, Ga., 1984—. Author: (with others) Podiatric Dermatology, 1985. Mem. Am. Podiatric Med. Assn., Ga. Podiatric Med. Assn., Am. Diabetes Assn., Am. Coll. Foot Surgeons (assoc.), 1987, AAUW. Methodist. Clubs: Network Augusta, Toastmasters (Augusta) (treas. 1987, pres. 1988). Office: Med Ctr Podiatry Group 1515 Laney Walker Blvd Augusta GA 30904

OTTO, CATHERINE NAN, clinical laboratory scientist; b. Stockton, Calif., Dec. 17, 1953; d. Edward Joseph Otto and Arlene Maud (Holmes) Naylor. BS in Microbiology, Oreg. State U., 1976; BS in Med. Tech., Oreg. Health Scis. U., 1981; BA in French, Portland (Oreg.) State U., 1986. Cert. clin. lab. scientist, clin. lab. supr., clin. lab. specialist in hematology, med. technologist. Med. technologist night shift Ore. Health Scis. U., Portland, 1981-85; med. technologist night shift Bess Kaiser Med. Ctr., Portland, 1985, med. technologist hematology, 1985-86; lab. supr. div. med. office Kaiser Permanente, Portland, 1986-87, lab. supr. Vancouver Med. Officer, 1987—. Bd. dirs. Friends of Ore. Pub. Broadcasting, Portland, 1985-88; mem. allied health subcom. Am. Cancer Soc., Portland, 1985-87. Assn. for Oreg. Med. Tech. (pres. 1986-87, bd. dirs. 1984-85), Portland Dist. Soc. of the Assn. for Oreg. Med. Tech. (pres. 1983-84), Am. Soc. for Med. Tech. (chair region IX immunology/immunohematology scientific assembly, 1984-87, vice chmn. 1987-88, bd. trustees 1987—), Am. Assn. Blood Banks, Am. Assn. Clin. Chemists, Nat. Assn. for Female Execs., Clin. Lab. Mgmt. Assn., AAUW. Club: Beaverton Internat. Tng. in Communication (sec. 1985-86).

OTTO, MARGARET AMELIA, librarian; b. Boston, Oct. 22, 1937; d. Henry Earlen and Mary (McLennan) O.; children—Christopher, Peter. A.B., Boston U., 1960; M.S., Simmons Coll., 1963, M.A., 1970; M.A. (hon.), Dartmouth Coll., 1981. Asst. sci. librarian M.I.T., Cambridge, 1963; Lindgren librarian M.I.T., 1964-67, acting sci. librarian, 1967-69, asst. dir., 1969-75, asso. dir., 1976-79; librarian of coll. Dartmouth Coll., Hanover, N.H., 1979—; pres., chmn. bd. Universal Serials and Book Exchange, Inc., 1980-81; bd. govs. Research Library Group, 1979—, trustee Howe Library, Hanover, 1988—. Council on Library Resources fellow, 1974; elected to Collegium of Disting. Alumnus Boston U., 1980. Mem. ALA, Assn. Research Libraries (chmn. preservation com. 1983-85, bd. dirs. 1985-87). Home: 16 Dresden Rd Hanover NH 03755 Office: Dartmouth Coll 115 Baker Library Hanover NH 03755

OTTO, ROBERTA, musician, educator, orchestra manager; b. Lebanon, Pa., Aug. 20, 1943; d. Robert March and Catherine Lucille (Mills) Johns; m. Roland Louis Otto Jr., June 24, 1967. BS in Music Edn., Lebanon Valley Coll., 1965; MA in Teaching in Music Edn., Manhattanville Coll., 1979. Tchr. music Anne Arundel Co. Schs., Annapolis, Md., 1965-67, Westport (Conn.) Pub. Schs., 1967-68, Holbrook (Mass.) Pub. Schs., 1968-69, Stamford (Conn.) Pub. Schs., 1969-79; mng. dir. Plymouth (Mass.) Philharm. Orch., 1981—; prin. flutist Annapolis Symphony Orch., 1965-67, Troupers Light Opera Co., Stamford, 1972-79; flutist Stamford Symphony Orch., 1971-74, Plymouth Philharmonic Orch., 1980—; co-curator Pilgrim Rock, Clark's Island, Plymouth; panelist Mass. Council on Arts and Humanities, Boston, 1985-86. Composer score performer TV comml., 1974. Mem. Friends of Philharm., Plymouth, 1980-83. Mem. Am. Symphony Orch. League, Duxbury (Mass.) Arts Lottery Council (sec. 1986-87), Duxbury Art Assn., Duxbury Rural and Hist. Soc. Baptist. Club: Duxbury Garden (sec. 1980-82), Duxbury Yacht. Office: Plymouth Philharm Orch 130 Court St Plymouth MA 02361

OTTO, ROSEMARY LYNNE, management consultant; b. Aitkin, Minn., Oct. 6, 1946; d. Joseph Henry Chale and Betty Anne (Murray) Greenbush; m. John Bartles Otto, July 9, 1964 (div. 1974); children: Debra Lynne, Justin Lee. Grad. high sch., Aitkin, Minn. Tax cons. H & R Block, Aurora, Minn., 1969-73; bus. mgr. Lake Mayfield Restaurant & Motel, Silver Creek, Wash., 1973-78; mgr. Maurices, Inc., Chehalis, Wash., 1978-83; mktg. dir. Lewis County Mall, Chehalis, 1983-84; pvt. practice cons. Centralia, Wash.,

1985—; chmn. Food Service com. Centralia, Wash., 1984-87, By-Laws com., Twin Cities Chamber, Chehalis, 1987; adv. mem. Suprs. Workshops, Centralia Coll., 1984-85; sec. Miracle Mile Assn. Bd. Dirs., Chehalis/Centralia, 1986-87. Mem. Am. Assn. of Profl. Cons., Twin Cities C. of C. (bd. dirs., treas. exec. com.), Nat. Assn. of Female Execs. Roman Catholic. Lodge: Moose.

OUELLETTE, ELAINE BRENDA, nurse, physician's assistant; b. Hamlin Plantation, Maine, June 20, 1955; d. Gerald Reginald and Constance B. (Duperry) Lapierre; m. Vernon Rodney Ouellette, June 1, 1977; children: Jennifer Lee, Kerri Lynne. B.S.N. with honors, U. So. Maine, 1977; cert. physician's asst., Van Buren Hosp. (Maine), 1981. R.N., Maine. Staff nurse Van Buren Hosp., 1977-78, emergency and operating supr., 1978-85; instr. adult edn., 1980—, staff edn. instr., 1981-85 ; instr. No. Maine Vocat. Tech. Inst., Presque Isle, Maine, 1983—; physician's asst. Dr. William Chan, Van Buren, 1982—; inservice coordinator Borderview Manor Nursing Home, 1984-87; instr. pharmacology Residential Care Assn., 1986—; instr. CPR, Advanced Cardiac Life Support; diabetes cons., educator; v.p. Elem. PTA; Brownie leader Van Buren Abnaki council Girl Scouts USA, town chairperson. Mem. Centennial Com., Van Buren, 1982; sec. Reunion Com. Class of '73, Van Buren, 1983; v.p. Van Buren Elem. PTA, 1986-87. Recipient Recognition award Van Buren Ambulance Service, 1982. Mem. Assn. Operating Room Nurses, Down East Assn. Physicians Assts., Am. Diabetes Assn., Diabetes Support Group, No. Maine Gymnastics Judges Assn. Democrat. Roman Catholic. Clubs: Van Buren Fire Dept. Women's Aux. (pres. 1982-83, v.p. 1983-84, sec. 1986-87, treas. 1987-88), Van Buren Hosp. Aux. Home: 21 Lynne St Van Buren ME 04785 Office: Van Buren Hosp 121 Main St Van Buren ME 04785

OUELLETTE, JANE LEE YOUNG, biology educator; b. Charlotte, N.C., Dec. 29, 1929; d. James Thomas and Nancy Isabel (Yarbrough) Young; m. Armand Roland Ouellette, Aug. 3, 1951 (dec. Oct. 1984); children—Elizabeth Anne, James Young, Emily Jane, Frances Lee. B.A., Winthrop Coll., 1950; M.A., Oberlin Coll., 1952; postgrad. Coll. Medicine, Baylor U., 1974, U. Tex.-Houston, 1976-83, Tex. Woman's U., 1980-82. Lic. tchr., Tex. Tchr. Maria Regina High Sch., Hartsdale, N.Y., 1969-70, Spring Ind. Sch. System, Tex., 1972-78; coordinator biology program, instr., North Harris County Coll., Houston, 1979—. Mem. Internat. Assn. for Study of Pain, Internat. Pain Found., N.Y. Acad. Sci., AAAS, Internat. Chronobiol. Soc., People to People Internat. Democrat. Home: 1619 Big Horn St Houston TX 77090 Office: North Harris County Coll 2700 W Thorne Dr Houston TX 77073

OUNJIAN, MARILYN J., career counseling executive; b. Harrisburg, Pa., Oct. 24, 1947; d. Stanley Wolf and Rebecca (Darrow) Freeman; m. Irving Henry Schwartz, Aug. 24, 1974 (dec. May 1975); 1 child, Jennifer; m. George Edward Ounjian, July 31, 1982; children: Jonathan, Kori. Student, U. Md. Pres. Today's People, Phila., 1973-81; chmn., founder, chief exec. officer The Career Inst., Phila., 1981—; pres., chief exec. officer Careers USA, Phila., 1981—. Mem. Rep. Senatorial Inner Circle. Mem. Cen. City Proprietors Assn., Nat. Assn. Female Execs. Inc., Nat. Assn. Women Bus. Owners, Greater Phila. C. of C., Pa. C. of C., Assn. Venture Founders. Club: Gov.'s Del. Office: Careers USA 1825 JFK Blvd Philadelphia PA 19103

OURS, TINA CHARLENE, marketing professional; b. Tipton, Ind., Sept. 26, 1966; d. Charles W. and Evelyn D. (Stanholtz) O. Cert., Midwest Travel Acad., Indpls., 1985. Travel agt. Fifth Season Travel, Indpls., 1985-86; account exec. Total Travel Mgmt., Anderson, Ind., 1986—. Home: Rural Rt 2 Elwood IN 46036

OUTHWAITE, LUCILLE CONRAD, ballerina, educator; b. Peoria, Ill., Feb. 26, 1909; d. Frederick Albert and Della (Cornett) Conrad; m. Leonard Outhwaite, Mar. 1, 1936 (dec. 1978); children—Ann Outhwaite Maurer, Lynn Outhwaite Pulsifer. Student, U. Nebr., 1929-30, Mills Coll., 1931-32; student piano, Paris, 1933-35, Legat Sch., London, 1934, N.Y.C. Ballet, N.Y.C., 1936-41, Royal Ballet Sch., London, 1957-59. Tchr. ballet Perry Mansfield, Steamboat Springs, Colo., 1932, Cape Playhouse, Dennis, Mass., 1937-41, Jr. League, N.Y.C., 1937-41, King Coit Sch., N.Y.C., 1937-41; toured with Am. Ambassador Ballet, Europe and S. Am., 1933-35; owner, tchr. dance sch., Oyster Bay, N.Y., 1949-57. Producer, choreographer ballets Alice in Wonderland, 1951, Pied Piper of Hamlin, 1952. Author: Birds in Flight, 1984. Mem. English Speaking Union, Preservation Soc., Alliance Française, Delta Gamma. Republican. Episcopalian. Clubs: Mills Coll., Spouting Rock Beach, Clambake (Newport, R.I.). Office: Beachmound Bellevue Ave Newport RI 02840

OUTTZ, JANICE HAMILTON, demographic researcher; b. Monroe, La., June 18, 1951; d. O'sha James and Virgie Mae (Richmond) Hamilton; m. James Lawrence Outtz, June 3, 1972; children—Jabari Hamilton, Hasina Hamilton. B.A., Howard U., 1972, M.A., 1976; postgrad. U. Md. Counselor, D.C. Juvenile Ct., 1970; research asst. Washington Ctr. Metro. Studies, 1971-76; instr. Montgomery Coll., Takoma Park, Md., 1975; program analyst Nat. Adv. Council, Washington, 1976; ednl. researcher Howard U., Washington, 1976-79; research assoc. Greater Washington Research Ctr., Washington, 1979-85; research cons. Lanham, Md., 1985—; survey researcher cons. Howard U., 1978, Hutchinson Family Service (Kans.), 1979, Community Found., Washington, 1980; analyst poverty data United Planning Orgn., Washington, 1981. Contbr. research articles to profl. jours. 1st v.p. Nat. Council Negro Women, Washington, 1984-86; mem. Prince George County LWV (Md.); newsletter editor Nat. Council Negro Women, 1980, 83-84; bd. dirs. Nat. Capital Area LWV, 1985-87. Howard U. fellow, 1973; named to Dean's Honor Roll, Howard U., 1971; recipient Mary McLeod Bethune award Nat. Council Negro Women, 1981. Mem. Assn. Pub. Policy Analysis, Govt. Research Assn., Am. Statis. Assn., Leadership Washington Alumni. Democrat. Roman Catholic. Home and Office: 7208 Martins Ct Lanham MD 20706

OUZOUNIAN, ARMENUHI, dentist; b. Mosul, Iraq, Feb. 17, 1942; came to U.S., 1974; d. Yervant and Warda (Efram) O. DDS, U. Baghdad, Iraq, 1962, degree in anesthesiology, 1966. Cert. U.S. Bd. Dentistry; lic. dentist, Ill. Resident Fed. Teaching Hosp., Baghdad, 1963-66; anesthesiologist Maternity Hosp., Baghdad, 1966-73; gen. practice dentistry Baghdad, 1967-73; asst. various offices, Chgo., 1975-83; gen. practice dentistry Chgo., 1984—. Active Smithsonian Inst., Washington. Mem. Internat. Platform Assn., ADA, Am. Women Dentists Assn., Ill. Dental Soc., Chgo. Dental Soc. Home: 2253 N Kildare Chicago IL 60639 Office: 3503 W 26th St Chicago IL 60623

OVERCASH-ANTHONY, CHERYL ANN, investment analyst; b. Abington, Pa., Feb. 12, 1955; d. Clifton Odel and Christine Ruth (von Brauchitsch) Overcash; m. David Banks Anthony, Jr., Aug. 29, 1981. B.A., Hollins Coll., 1977; M.B.A. Tex. Christian U., 1979. Chartered fin. analyst, 1987. Acctg. mgr. Sanger Harris Co., Dallas, 1979-81; bus./market analyst Xerox Corp., Dallas, 1981-83; investment analyst Inter First Investment Mgmt., Dallas, 1983-85; investment analyst, portfolio mgr. Boulder Asset Mgmt., Denver, 1985—; chmn. women's fitness com. YMCA; part-time prof. continuing edn. Tex. Christian U., mem. Dallas Opera Guild. Office: 5331 Mercedes Ave Dallas TX 75206

OVERFIELD, THERESA, nursing educator, researcher; b. Buffalo, July 22, 1935; d. Norbert J. and Mary (Waver) O.; m. David B. Morris. Diploma in Nursing, Sisters of Charity Sch. Nursing, 1956; BS in Nursing, D'Youville Coll., 1958; MPH, Columbia U., 1962; PhD in Phys. Anthropology, U. Colo., 1975. Registered nurse. Instr. nursing Canisius Coll., Buffalo, 1957-58; itinerant pub. health nurse Alaska Dept. Health, Bethel, 1959-61; nurse epidemiologist Arctic Health Research Ctr., USPHS, Anchorage, 1962-65; cons. nursing Colo. Dept. Pub. Health, Denver, 1966-69; research asst. prof. U. Utah, Salt Lake City, 1975-76, asst. prof. nursing, 1976-78; assoc. prof. nursing Brigham Young U., Salt Lake City, 1978-84, dir. research Coll. Nursing, 1979-86, prof. nursing, 1984—; clin. instr. U. Colo., Denver, 1967-68; adj. prof. anthropology U. Utah, 1976-85, research prof. 1985—; cons. in field; mem. adv. bd. Western Jour. Nursing Research, 1978-82; mem. research steering com. Western Commn. Higher Edn. in Nursing, 1978-82; mem. peer rev. group Div. Nursing USPHS, 1979. Contbr. articles, revs. on nursing, phys. anthropology, plant toxicology, and genetics to profl. jours. Bd. dirs. Salt Lake Indian Health Ctr., 1981-82, also mem. adv. com.; mem. nursing research com. VA Med. Ctr., Salt Lake City, 1982—, sci. rev. com. Recipient Excellence in Writing award Am. Jour. Nursing, 1981; grantee USPHS, NSF, Am. Nurses Found., U. Utah. Mem. Am. Nurses Assn., Utah Nurses Assn. (chairperson transcultural nursing conf. group 1978-80, mem. newsletter research com. 1985—), Am. Assn. of Phys. Anthropologists, Soc. Med. Anthropologists, Human Biology Council, AAAS, Western Soc. Research in Nursing, Council Nursing and Anthropology, Soc. Study Human Biology, Utah Pub. Health Assn. (bd. dirs. 1983-86), Am. Pub. Health Assn.

OVERGAARD, MARY ANN, lawyer; b. Mason City, Iowa, May 29, 1951; d. Gunnar S.M. and Claudia May (Michalek) O.; m. David Earl Cook, Aug. 19, 1972; 1 child, Nels David Overgaard-Cook. BS, U. Nebr., 1972, JD, 1975. Bar: Nebr. 1975, U.S. Dist. Ct. Nebr. 1975, Oreg. 1983, U.S. Dist. Ct. Oreg. 1984, U.S. Supreme Ct. 1985. Counsel Nebr. Regional Med. Program, Lincoln, 1975-76, Nebr. Dept. of Revenue, Lincoln, 1977-78; legal counsel Nebr. Dept. of Edn., Lincoln, 1978-81; legal policy advisor Oreg. Bur. of Labor, Portland, 1981-84; legal advisor Portland Police Bur., 1984—. V.p. Planned Parenthood, Lincoln, 1979; commr. Lincoln/Lancaster Planning Commn., 1980-81; legis. chairperson Oreg. Womens Polit. Caucas, 1986—; v.p., bd. dirs. Portland YWCA, 1985—. Mem. ABA, Multnomah County Bar Assn. Democrat. Unitarian. Clubs: Portland City, Oreg. Road Runners. Home: 2772 NE Wiberg Ln Portland OR 97213 Office: Portland Police Bur 1111 SW 2d Ave Room 1526 Portland OR 97204

OVERHOLT, BETTYE O'DELL, educator; b. Newport, Tenn., Feb. 4, 1930; d. Aaron L. O'Dell and N. Belle Clark; m. Dale Hawkins Overholt, Mar. 3, 1924; children: Carl Edward, Jill Overholt Fishburn. AS, Walters State Community Coll., 1978; BS, Carson-Newman Coll., 1979; MS, U. Tenn., 1982. Bookkeeper, sec. Mohawk Roller Mills, Newport, Tenn., 1950-62; operator switchboard Hamilton Bank, Morristown, Tenn., 1969-70; sec. G. H. Hatfield Enterprises, Morristown, Tenn., 1970-76; tchr.'s aide Morristown City Schs., 1976-79, tchr., 1979-85; tchr. Hamblen County Sch. System, Morristown, 1985—. Parent-tchr. coordinating rep. ARC, Morristown, 1982—; mem. hospitality com. Lakeway Reading Council, Morristown, 1984-85, sec., 1985-86, mem. spl. project com., 1986—; library-aide Manley Bapt. Ch., Morristown, 1986—; mem. Morristown PTA, 1986—. Mem. Internat. Reading Assn., NEA, Tenn. Edn. Assn., Hamblen County Edn. Assn., Am. Bus. Women's Assn. (sec. Davy Crockett chpt. 1984-85), Alpha Delta Kappa. Republican. Lodge: Lioness (pres. Morristown chpt. 1974-75, sec. 1976-77). Home: 1710 Joe Stephens Rd Morristown TN 37814

OVERLAND, WANDA IDELLE, university administrator; b. Harvey, N.D., Sept. 15, 1953; d. Ingwald T. and Edna M. Overland; BS, N.D. State U., 1975, MS, 1982. Tchr. home econs. N.H. high schs., 1975-78; head resident residential life/housing N.D. State U., 1978-81, adminstrv. asst. Coll. Home Econs., 1978-81; exec. dir. YMCA at N.D. State U., 1981-84, student affairs officer, 1984—; tchr. adult edn. courses; speaker, cons., workshop leader in field. Chmn. N.D. State U. Campus Equity, 1982. Christine Finlayson scholar, 1978-80; Elsie Stark Martin scholar, 1974; named Hillsboro Outstanding Young Educator, 1978, Outstanding Faculty Mem., Alpha Tau Omega, 1986, Disting. Educator Blue Key Nat. Hon. Fraternity, 1988; recipient citation of Honor Theta Chi, 1985. Mem. Am. Personnel and Guidance Assn., Assn. Coll. Unions (internat. mem., steering com.), N.D. Coll. Personnel Assn. (pres.-elect 1988), Kappa Delta Pi, Phi Upsilon Omicron (treas. alumni chpt.), Assn. Fraternity Advisors, Phi Mu (chpt. fin. advisor). Republican. Lutheran. Lodge: Zonta Internat. (sec. Fargo-Moorhead chpt. 1985-87). Office: ND State U Memorial Union Fargo ND 58105

OVERMYER, ELIZABETH CLARK, television executive; b. Toledo, Ohio, July 1, 1957; d. Daniel Harrison and Shirley Ann (Clark) O. B.A., U. Denver, 1979. Assoc. producer ABC Sports Inc., N.Y.C., 1980-82; prodn. mgr. ABC Sports 1984 Olympic Unit, N.Y.C., 1983-84; prodn. mgr. Ohlmeyer Communications Cos., N.Y.C., 1985-86; sr. prodn. mgr. ABC Sports 1988 Olympic Games, Calgary, 1986-88; free-lance prodn. TV and films, 1988—. Recipient Emmy award for TV series American Sportsman, 1981. Mem. Women in Communications, Inc. Republican. Episcopalian.

OVERTON, HELEN PARKER (MRS. SAMUEL WATKINS OVERTON), Realtor; b. Memphis, Dec. 30, 1920; d. William and Pearl (Pinkston) Parker; m. Samuel Watkins Overton, Sept. 3, 1952; children—Helen Parker (Mrs. William Barron Brown), Napoleon Hill. Exec. sec. Memphis State U., 1941-43, Chgo. and So. Air Lines, 1943-46, Memphis Bd. Edn., 1948-50; dir. women's programs Sta. WHBQ-TV, Memphis, 1950-52. Pres., Beethoven Club, 1960-66, 72-78, 1988—, Mid-South Opera Guild, 1967-85; dir. auditions Mid-South region Met. Opera, 1960-71, mem. nat. council, 1960-71; chmn. Tenn. Arts Commn., 1968-70; bd. dirs. Opera Memphis, 1956—, Arts Appreciation, 1960-87, Tenn. Arts Commn., 1967-74. Mem. Sigma Alpha Iota, Alpha Gamma Delta. Clubs: Memphis Country (Memphis). Home: 5476 Collingwood Cove Memphis TN 38119

OVERTON, MEREDITH ANN, management executive; b. Kansas City, Mo., Jan. 4, 1947; d. James Howard and Viola May (Moats) Holloway. BS in Home Econs., Kans. State U., 1969; MS, U. Kans., 1973; postgrad., U. Mo., 1974-75. Dietetic intern Houston VA Hosp., 1969-70; admistrv./clin. dietitian Mpls. VA Hosp., 1970-71; dietitian coordinator for nutrition edn. med. students U. Kans. Med. Ctr., 1972-74, clin. dietitian, instr., 1973-74; clin. dietitian/trainee counselor Good Samaritan Hosp. and Med. Center, Portland, Oreg., 1975-76; sales rep. nutritional div. Mead Johnson, Portland, 1976-78; asst. prof., dir. dietetic internship Oreg. Health Scis. U., Portland, 1978-84; mem. faculty Clackamas Community Coll., 1976-78, Portland State U., 1978-81; sr. territory mgr. Am. Continue Care/Travacare, 1984-87; gen. mgr. Care Plus, 1987—; mem. dietetic adv. council Oreg. State U. Author: (with B.P. Lukert) Clinical Nutrition-A Physiologic Approach, 1977, (with A.L. Fortuna) 1981 Dietetic Internship Funding Survey, 1982; contbr.: The Taste of Success: Dysphagia Intervention for the Adult, 1983. Active March of Dimes, Multiple Sclerosis. AAUW scholar, 1966-67, Midwest Fish and Frozen Seafood scholar, 1967-68, Martha S. Pittman scholar, 1968-69, Bessie Brooks West scholar, 1968-69. Mem. Am. Dietetic Assn., Wash. Dietetic Assn., Greater Seattle Dietetic Assn., Am. Council Sci. and Health, Western Region Coll. and Univ. Tchrs. of Foods and Nutrition, Soc. Nutrition Edn., Oreg. Nutrition Council, Am. Diabetes Assn., Am. Home Econs. Assn., Phi Kappa Phi, Omicron Nu, Phi Upsilon Omicron, Alpha Lambda Delta. Methodist. Home and Office: 15204 NE 8th St B-3 Bellevue WA 98007

OVERTON, ROSILYN GAY HOFFMAN, financial services executive; b. Corsicana, Tex., July 10, 1942; d. Billy Clarence and Ima Elise (Gay) Hoffman; B.S. in Math., Wright State U., Dayton, Ohio, 1972, M.S. in Applied Econs. (fellow), 1973; postgrad. N.Y. U. Grad. Sch. Bus., 1974-76; m. Aaron Lewis Overton, Jr., July 2, 1960 (div. Mar. 1975); children—Aaron Lewis III, Adam Jerome. Cert. fin. planner. Research analyst Nat. Security Agy., Dept. Def., 1962-67; bus. reporter Dayton Jour.-Herald, 1973-74; economist First Nat. City Bank, N.Y.C., 1974, A.T. & T. Co., 1974-75; broker Merrill Lynch, N.Y.C., 1975-80; asst. v.p. E.F. Hutton & Co., N.Y.C., 1980-84; v.p., nat. mktg. dir. investment products Manhattan Nat. Corp., 1984-86; pres. R.H. Overton Co., N.Y.C., 1986—. Friend N.Y.C. Mayor's Commn. on Status of Women. Named Businesswoman of Yr., N.Y.C., 1976. Mem. Nat., N.Y. Assns. Bus. Economists, Nat. Fedn. Bus. and Profl. Women, Internat. Assn. Fin. Planners, Women's Econ. Roundtable, Gotham Bus. and Profl. Womens Club, Wright State U. Alumni Assn. (dir.), Mensa. Methodist. Lodge: Zonta (area dir.). Office: 56 Pine St New York NY 10005

OVIATT, PATRICIA ANN, human resources executive; b. Cleve., Mar. 29, 1949; d. John and Mary (Herzak) Sivulka; m. Roger Oviatt, May 1, 1971 (div. May 1980); m. Donald O. Wheeler, Aug. 22, 1982; 1 child, Nicholas Brett Sivulka Wheeler. Cert., Inst. Am. Univs., Aix-en-Provence, France, 1970; BS in Internat. Studies, Miami U., Oxford, Ohio, 1971; MBA, John Carroll U., Cleve., 1980. Personnel asst. Stouffer Corp., Cleve., 1971-73; labor relations adminstr. Kaiser Permanente Co., Cleve., 1973-80; dir. human resources Kaiser Permanente Co., White Plains, N.Y., 1985—; mgr. compensation and benefits Dictaphone Corp., Rye, N.Y., 1980-85; Newsweek, Inc., Manhattan, N.Y., 1982-85. Mem. Am. Compensation Assn. (v.p. 1982-85, pres. Ea. region 1985-86, bd. dirs. 1986—), N.Y. Compensation Assn., No. Met. Hosp. Assn. of N.Y. Republican. Office: Kaiser Permanente 7-11 S Broadway White Plains NY 10601

OVITT, BETSY JEAN, nurse; b. Nashvillw, Oct. 30, 1946; d. David Wilkie and Elizabeth Louella (Wright) O. BS in Nursing, U. Wis., 1968; MS in Nursing, Marquette U., 1985. Staff nurse U. Wis. Hosp., Madison, 1968-69, Fairview Southdale Hosp., Edina, Minn., 1969-70, Anchorage Community Hosp., 1971-73; biomed. instr. Geophys. Inst. U. Alaska, Fairbanks, 1973-74; unit dir. burn ctr. St. Mary's Hosp., Milw., 1976-87; nurse mgr. burn ctr. Tampa Gen. Hosp., Fla., 1987—; instr. Advanced Cardiac Life Support, 1978-86. Contbr. articles to profl. jours. Mem. Am. Burn Assn., Am. Assn. Critical Care Nurses, U. Wis. Alumni Assn. Home: 2608 Crestfield Dr Valrico FL 33594

OWCZARZAK, RUTH IRENE, finance executive; b. Saginaw, Mich., June 17, 1929; d. Henry W. and Elsie E. (Eich) Voight; m. Leonard F. Owczarzak, Apr. 23, 1949; children: Steven L., Rick M., David P. A in Acctg., Delta Coll., 1977; B in Mgmt., Saginaw Valley State Coll., 1988. Head bookkeepr Saginaw Twp. Community Schs., 1968-74; office mgr. Saginaw Floor Covering, 1974-75, Artnoey, Inc., Saginaw, 1975-76; dep. clk. Saginaw Twp. Office, 1976-77; fin. and credit mgr. Fruehauf Corp., Saginaw, 1977-87; credit mgr. Fruehauf Corp., Detroit, 1987—. catechism instr. St. Thomas Aquinas Sch., 1973-74; sec., bookkepper Can America Games, Saginaw, 1977-79; vol. Saginaw County Social Service. Mem. Nat. Assn. Female Execs., LWV, Am. Soc. Women Accts. (sec. 1980-82). Republican. Roman Catholic. Home: 3580 Midland Rd Saginaw MI 48603

OWEN, BARBARA LOOP, clinical social worker, consultant; b. Toledo, Mar. 9, 1937; d. Alan Bevingten and Eleanor (Wilcox) Loop; children: Timothy Allyn, Corinna Ruess. BA in Philosophy magna cum laude, Mt. Holyoke Coll., 1959; MSW, U. Ill., Chgo., 1970. Dir. religious edn. St. Paul's Ch., Natick, Mass., 1959-60, St. John's Ch., Beverly Farms, Mass., 1960-62; dir. family counseling Gad Hill Settlement House, Chgo., 1964-68; social worker Youth Guidance, Chgo., 1970-75, coordinator of research and statistics, 1972-75, clinic dir., 1973-75; also bd. dirs. Youth Guidance; student supr. MSW div. U. Ill, Chgo., 1974-75; staff supr. North River Youth Commn., Chgo., 1973-74; pvt. practice Northbrook, Ill., 1974-77, Poughkeepsie, N.Y. and Litchfield, Conn., 1977-81, Natick and Cambridge, Mass., 1977—; cons. in field; dir. numerous workshops and tng. programs. Bd. dirs. Chgo. Internat. Programs for Youth Leaders and Social Workers, 1963-74, Episcopal Family Resource Ctr., New Haven, 1978-80, Divorce Ctr., 1983—. Mem. Nat. Assn Social Workers, Assn. for Humanistic Psychology, Assn. for Transpersonal Psychology, Acad. Cert. Social Workers, Am. Psychol. Assn., Mass Psychol. Assn. Home: 50 Fresh Pond Place Cambridge MA 02138 Office: 16 E Central St Natick MA 01760

OWEN, CAROL ELAINE, academic administrator; b. Kingsport, Tenn., July 11, 1957; d. Carroll Cortland and Joy Elaine (Campbell) O. Student, Union U., Jackson, Tenn., 1975-78, U. Tenn., Martin, 1979; BS, Mid. Tenn. State U., 1980; MEd, Vanderbilt U., 1985. Asst. pub. relations Bates, Campbell & Co., Union City, Tenn., 1980-81; with dept. communications Bapt. Sunday Sch. Bd., Nashville, 1981-84; mgr. campaign services Belmont Coll., Nashville, 1984-85, specialist corp. and found. relations, 1985-88, dir. annual giving, 1988—; adj. faculty, vol. State Community Coll.; cons. mktg. research J. Robert Clark & Assocs., Memphis. Contbr. articles to profl. publs. Program leader Am. Cancer Soc., Nashville, 1987; leader conf. Tenn. Bapt. Conv., Nashville; Case 1989 Dist III Planning Com. Mem. Nat. Soc. Fundraising Execs. (bd. dirs. Nashville chpt.), Council for Advancement and Support Edn. (scholar 1986), Nat. Assn. YMCA Devel. Officers. (conf. leader), Nashville Area C. of C. (mem. pres's com. 1987, 88), Zeta Tau Alpha, Sigma Alpha Iota, Alpha Psi Omega. Republican. Home: 675 Harding Pl Nashville TN 37211 Office: Belmont Coll Nashville TN 37212

OWEN, DEBORAH MYRA, library director; b. Evanston, Ill., Nov. 21, 1953; d. Richard Harding and Belle Florence (Kallet) Willens; m. Thomas Edward Owen III, Aug. 3, 1974; 1 child, Joseph Benthomas. BA, U. Ill., 1975, MS, 1976. Bibliographer, cataloger Wash. U., St. Louis, 1976-77; head pub. services Belleville (Ill.) Pub. Library, 1977-79; dir. Fairview Heights (Ill.) Pub. Library, 1979—. chmn. adminstrv. com. library fundraiser, Fairview Heights, 1988—; mem. Library Bldg. Com., Fairview Heights, 1984—. Mem. ALA, Ill. Library Assn.

OWEN, GINA KAY, marketing executive; b. Ft. Worth, Tex., Aug. 25, 1958; d. Dewey DeWayne and Barbara Ann (Green) Martin; m. William Edward Owen, Mar. 25, 1952; children, Tyson Edward, James Andrew. BS in Criminal Justice, MSSC, 1978. Teller World Savs., Kansas City, 1978-79; receptionist Cessna Aircraft, Kansas City, Mo., 1979-81; sec. KC Biol., Lenexa, Kans., 1981-82, internat. coordinator, 1982-83; mktg. asst. Tallgrass Technologies, Overland Park, Kans., 1983-85; mktg. mgr. Adacom Corp., Overland Park, 1985—. Mem. Silicon Prairie Assn. (v.p., founder 1986-87). Republican. Home: 8432 W 113th St Overland Park KS 66210 Office: Adacom 8871 Bond St Overland Park KS 66214

OWEN, IRIS ANNE, petroleum executive; b. Texarkana, Aug. 4, 1938; d. Gilford Holt Nash and Bertha (Miller) Payne; m. O.M. Owen (div. 1971); 1 child, Kelly Lynn. Student, Southwestern Coll. Bus., 1958; ins. cert., Ins. Inst. Am., 1976. Underwriter Offenhauser & Co., Texarkana, 1967-72, Marsh & Mclennan, Dallas, 1972-74; account mgr. Alexander & Alexander, Dallas, 1974-79; account exec. Fred S. James & Co., Dallas, 1979-81; gen. mgr. Innkeepers Internat. Ins., Garland, Tex., 1981-86; risk mgr. Star Service & Petroleum Co., Corsicana, Tex., 1986—. Mem. Nat. Assn. Ins. Women (cert. profl.), Risk Ins. Mgrs. Soc. Republican. Episcopalian. Home: 1556 W 5th Ave Corsicana TX 75110 Office: Star Service & Petroleum 101 N Beaton Suite 700 Corsicana TX 75110

OWEN, LAURA ELLEN, electrical engineer; b. Tucumcari, N.Mex., Nov. 26, 1939; d. Luther Moody and Ida Floy (Hutchens) O. BS in Geophysics, N.Mex. Inst. Mining and Tech., 1961; BEE, U. Tex., 1969. Registered profl. engr., Tex. Engr. Schlumberger, Houston, 1961-66, TOC, Houston, 1968-73; project engr. Zapata Corp., Houston, 1973-74; salesperson Ocean Research Engring., Falmouth, Mass., 1974; mgr. power, controls TOC, Houston, 1974-76; engr. Mobil Oil Corp., Beaumont, Tex., 1976—; ptnr. Copa de Leche, Beaumont, 1979-81. Campaign mgr. Alice Edwards for Commr., Beaumont, 1978; asst. chmn. Tex. Women's Polit. Caucus, Austin, 1979; county coordinator Bob Krueger for U.S. Senate, Beaumont, 1980; bd. dirs. Rape Crisis Ctr. for Southeast Tex., Beaumont, 1980-82. Mem. AAAS. Democrat.

OWEN, PATRICIA ROSE, investment company executive; b. Chattanooga, Feb. 13, 1955; d. David G. and Elsie E. (Newman) Owen; m. Joseph Edward Thompson, May 2, 1987. AA, Broward CommunityColl., 1974; BA, U. S. Fla., 1976; MBA, Nova U., 1985. Cert. USCG ocean operator, 1983. Tchr. Dade County Sch. System, Miami, 1976-78; v.p. Securities Research and Mgmt., Inc., Ft. Lauderdale, Fla., 1977-82, exec. v.p., 1982-84, dir., 1984—, pres., chief exec. officer, 1986—. Contbr. various poetry publs. Episcopalian. Clubs: Coconut Grove Sailing (Miami, Fla.); Seven Seas Cruising Assn. (Ft. Lauderdale, Fla.), Cruising Assn. (London). Office: Securities Research & Mgmt Inc 800 Corporate Dr Suite 602 Fort Lauderdale FL 33334

OWEN, SUE ANN, poet; b. Clarinda, Iowa, Sept. 5, 1942; d. Theodore Reynold and Elizabeth (Roderick) Matthews; m. Thomas Charles Owen, Aug. 29, 1964; B.A. in English, U. Wis., 1964; M.F.A. in Writing, Goddard Coll., 1978. Poet in schs. Arts and Humanities Council, Baton Rouge, 1980-81, vis. artist, 1982—; participant writing confs. Author: Nursery Rhymes for the Dead, 1980, The Book of Winter, 1988 (Ohio State Univ. Press/The Jour. award 1988); contbr. poems to mags., anthologies, including Harvard Mag., Iowa Rev., The Nation, Poetry, Ploughshares, So. Rev., The Best of Intro., others; readings in Boston, N.Y.C., Washington, San Francisco, New Orleans. Mem. Poetry Soc. Am., Associated Writing Programs, Poets and Writers, Arts and Humanities Council (Baton Rouge). Home: 2015 General Cleburne Baton Rouge LA 70810

OWEN, SUZANNE, savings and loan executive; b. Lincoln, Nebr., Oct. 6, 1926; d. Arthur C. and Hazel E. (Edwards) O.; B.S. in Bus. Adminstrn., U. Nebr., Lincoln, 1948. With G.F. Lessenhop & Sons, Inc., Lincoln, 1948-57; with First Fed. Lincoln, 1963—; v.p., dir. personnel, 1975-81, 1st v.p., 1981—, sr. v.p., 1987— . Mem. Adminstrv. Mgmt. Soc. (past bd. dirs. local chpt.), Lincoln Personnel Mgmt. Assn., Phi Chi Theta. Republican. Christian Scientist. Clubs: Altrusa, Wooden Spoon, Twig Daniels Network (bd. dirs. 1987-88), Exec. Women's Breakfast Group, Pi Beta Phi Alumnae, Order of Eastern Star (Lincoln). Office: First Fed Lincoln 13th and N Sts Lincoln NE 68508

OWEN, TAMARA TEAGUE, real estate appraiser; b. Canton, Ga., Sept. 20, 1953; d. Charles Robert and Doris (Haley) Teague; m. Kenneth Warren Owen, Sept. 25, 1971; children: Kyle Previs, Kendra Glynn. Grad. high sch., Canton. Lic. real estate broker, Fla. Contract supr. Diamondhead Corp., Waleska, Ga., 1974-75; office mgr. sales and rentals Cousins Properties, Big Canoe, Ga., 1975-80; office mgr. Allgood's, Ft. Walton Beach, Fla., 1981-84; v.p. Shores Mgmt. Services, Inc., Seagrove Beach, Fla., 1984—; cons. Zenith Group, Destin, Fla., 1985-86, Pointe Mgmt. Okaloosa, Destin, 1985—. Mem. Destin PTO, 1986-87. Mem. Nat. Assn. Realtors, Fla. Assn. Realtors, Ft. Walton Beach Bd. Realtors, Community Assn. Inst. Democrat. Baptist. Home: Rt 10 Box 143 Scott Rd Canton GA 30114 Office: Shores Mgmt Services Inc PO Box 4611 Seaside FL 32459

OWENS, ALICE GERTRUDE, director of communications; b. Elmer, N.J., Aug. 10, 1955; d. William Robert and Alice Ethel (Shipley) Owens. AS in Aviation Bus. Adminstrn., Embry-Riddle Aeronautical U., 1987. Pvt. br. exchange operator Embry-Riddle Aeronautical U., Daytona Beach, Fla., 1976-78, supr. communications, 1978-80, dir. communications, 1980—; instr. communications counselor course Bell System, Jacksonville, Fla., 1980; customer adminstrn. panel operator tng., Southern Bell Telephone Co., Jacksonville, 1981; participant Southern Bell Large User Confs. Mem. Assn. Coll. and Telecommunications Adminstrs., Embry-Riddle Vet's Club (sec. 1987), Embry-Riddle Bowling League (v.p., treas., staff advisor 1976—). Home: 1301 Freedom Ln Daytona Beach FL 32019 Office: Embry-Riddle Aeronaut U Daytona Beach FL 32014

OWENS, BARBARA ANN, telecommunications company manager; b. Memphis, Sept. 1., 1948; d. Harwood Casey and Anna Lou (Webb) Owens; m. Carroll Lynn Hughes, Feb. 24, 1978; 1 child, Kimberlyn Casey. B.S.Ed. summa cum laude, U. Tenn.-Knoxville, 1970; M.S. in Social Work, U. Tenn., 1975. Caseworker, supr. Tenn. Dept. Human Services, Knoxville, 1970-75; dir. social services ARC, Knoxville, 1975-77; bus. office supr. South Central Bell Tel. Co., Knoxville and Maryville, 1977-80; phone ctr. supr. South Central Bell, Maryville, Tenn., 1980-82; asst. staff mgr. BellSouth Services, Birmingham, Ala., 1983-87, Nashville, 1987—. Mem. Nat. Assn. Female Execs., Future Telephone Pioneers. Methodist. Clubs: Birmingham Big Orange. Avocations: personal computers; basketball; spectator sports. Home: 300 Ridgetop Ct Franklin TN 37064 Office: Bell South Services Rm 3-840 MSC Brentwood Data Ctr 402 Franklin Rd Brentwood TN 37027

OWENS, BRENDA OWEN, data processing professional; b. Marianna, Fla., May 14, 1951; d. Carl Junior and Thelma Grace (Kirkland) Owen; m. Robert John Owens, June 27, 1981. BS in Mgmt. Info. Systems, Fla. State U., 1984. Acctg. clk. Southwestern Corp., Nashville, 1971-72, gen. acctg. supr., 1972-74; computer operator Fla. Dept. Law Enforcement, Tallahassee, 1974-76, supr. computer ops., 1976-82, communications specialist, 1982-84, mgr. computer ops., 1984-86, mgr. data processing, 1986—; hardware, communications expert AFIS Tech. Com., Fla. Dept. Law Enforcement, 1986—, mgr. statewide project, 1988; info. security mgr. Info. Resource Com., Tallahassee, 1986—. Mem. Phi Chi Theta (past sec., treas.), Phi Theta Kappa (past v.p., treas.). Democrat. Baptist. Home: 5660 Nature Ln Tallahassee FL 32303-6727 Office: Fla Dept Law Enforcement 100 W Virginia St Tallahassee FL 32302

OWENS, CAROLE EHRLICH, therapist; b. Mpls., Dec. 7, 1942; d. Jerome D. and Amy Ann (Scott) Schein; B.A., U. Md., 1970; M.A., Cath. U. Am., 1977; D of Social Work Yeshiva U., 1987; m. Robert O. Owens, Oct. 5, 1975; children: Todd Frederick, Joseph Eric. Cert. Mental Health Clinician, Mass. Youth advocate, leader Montgomery (Md.) County Recreation Dept., 1970-72, counselor, supr. preadjudication diversion program, Crisis Home Program, Family Service, 1972-74, adminstr. Karma House (residential drug treatment), 1974-75; program devel. dir. Jewish Social Service Agy., Montgomery County, 1975-77, United Jewish Appeal Fedn. of Montgomery County, 1977-79; therapist, educator, writer, cons. in field, Englewood, N.J., 1979—; instr. Cath. U. Cons. to Montgomery County Exec. candidate, 1974; appointee Governor's Task Force, Md., 1978; bd. dirs. Jewish Community Center, 1981—, Temple Sinai Sisterhood, Bergen County, N.J., 1981—; pres. chpt. LWV, 1983. Mem. Internat. Platform Assn., AAUW, Am. Assn. Marriage and Family Therapy (clin.), Am. Assn. Jewish Communal Workers, Nat. Assn. Social Workers, LWV (pres. 1983-84), N.Y. Acad. Scis. Author: The Berkshire Cottages: A Vanishing Era, 1984, Clinical Vs. Psychometric Judgement of Alcohol Use; editor: Fund-Raising (Elton J. Kernes); reviewer Kirkus Revs.; contbr. articles in field to profl. jours. Home and Office: 100 Dwight Pl Englewood NJ 07631 Home: Box 1207 Stockbridge MA 01262

OWENS, DONNA, mayor; b. Aug. 24, 1936. Student, Stautzenberger Bus Coll. Past v.p. Lucas County Bd. Edn., Ohio; mem. Toledo City Council, 1980-84; mayor City of Toledo, 1984—. Mem. Toledo-Lucas County Council for Human Services, Internat. Inst. Greater Toledo, Lucas County Improvement Corp., Toledo Area Employment and Tng. Consortium, St. Vincent Hosp. and Med. Guild, Ohio Sch. Bd. Assn., Assn. of Two Toledos, Toledo Econ. Planning Council, Criminal Justice Coordinating Council, Toledo Mus. of Art; mem. exec. com. Toledo Met. Area Council of Govts.; bd. dirs. pub. broadcasting WGTE-TV; bd. mgrs. West Toledo YMCA; bd. dirs. YMCA, Substance Abuse Service, Inc.; adv. bd. U.S. Conf. of Mayors. Recipient Legion of Leaders award YMCA, 1976; Community Service award Post 606 VFW. Office: Office of the Mayor City of Toledo One Government Center Toledo OH 43604 *

OWENS, DONNA LEE, small business owner, consultant; b. Buffalo, Aug. 19, 1939; d. Millard Douglas and Arlene Josephine (Schalk) Shriver; m. Perry B. Owens, Dec. 31, 1960 (div.); children: Brandon Joseph, Kimberly Ann, Devney, Megan. Student, Mundelein Coll., Chgo., 1957-59, 66-67, Harper Coll., Rolling Meadows, Ill., 1972-73. Cost acct. Signode Steel Strapping, Glenview, Ill., 1960-63; travel cons. Ask Mr. Foster, Barrington, Ill., 1978-83; pres. C-Chgo., Barrington, 1978-83; dir. corp. sales Ill. Corp. Travel, Schaumburg, 1983—; pres. Sprotours, Inc., Barrington Hills, Ill., 1983—. Benefit chmn. The Cradle Soc., Evanston, Ill., 1965-67; vol. Chgo. Mental Health Assn., 1970-72. Republican. Roman Catholic. Club: The Meadow (Rolling Meadows). Home and Office: 90 Meadowhill Rd Barrington Hills IL 60010

OWENS, JOAN D., writer, producer; b. Los Angeles, June 2, 1942; d. Albert Lazar and Esther (Lipson) Kaplan; BA in History, U. Calif., Berkeley, 1964, postgrad., 1965; postgrad. Sorbonne, Cours de Civilisation Français, 1964. Assoc. producer pub. affairs KHJ-TV, Los Angeles, 1965-66; assoc. producer, producer, writer David L. Wolper Prodns., Metromedia Producers Corp., Alan Landsburg Prodns., Alan Sloan Prodns. and CRM Prodns., Los Angeles, 1967-75; writer CBS and ABC network children's programming, Hollywood, Calif., 1976-77; exec. producer KOCE-TV, 1982-85. Recipient Gold medal Internat. Film and TV Festival N.Y., 1975; Chris Bronze plaque Columbus Film Festival, 1975; Silver medal V.I. Internat. Film Festival, 1975; award for creative excellence U.S. Internat. Film Festival, 1975, Blue Ribbon Am. Film and Video Festival, 1975, 88, Golden Apple award Nat. Edn. Film and Video Festival, 1988. Mem. Women in Film (bd. dirs. 1976-78), Writers Guild Am. West. Writer, producer numerous TV documentaries and ednl. films including Say Goodbye (assoc. producer), 1971, It Takes a Lot of Love, 1972, The Explorers, 1973, French nat. TV spls., 1979-80, 87-88, Disney Telecommunications, 1981, 86-88, Painting with Elke Sommer, 1984, Filmation Studios, 1985, Children of Japan, 1987.

OWENS, JUDITH ANNE, social services agency director; b. Freeport, N.Y., Nov. 6, 1941; d. Arthur Ernest and Jayne Elizabeth (Killian) Williamson; m. David C. Owens, June 8, 1973 (div. 1980). BS, Western Mich. U., 1965; MSW, Ariz. State U., 1972. Dir. occupational therapy Creighton Meml. Hosp., Omaha, 1965-67; sr. occupational therapist Ft. Logan Mental Health Ctr., Denver, 1967-70; psychiat. social worker U. Ariz. Med. Ctr., Tucson, 1972-74; social work supr. Natrona County, State of Wyo., Casper, 1974-76; clin. social worker Cen. Wyo. Counseling Ctr., Casper, 1976-78; child protection supr. Natrona County, State of Wyo., Casper, 1979-81, children services supr., 1981-85; div. dir. The Casey Family Program, Cheyenne, Wyo., 1985—, lectr. psychology U. Ariz., 1972-74; field instr. Ariz. State U., Tempe, 1973-74, U. Wyo., Laramie, 1980-81. V.p. Residential Intervention Ctr., Tucson, 1972-74; vice chair Women's Self-Help Ctr., Casper, 1978-80; trainer women's conscientious groups NOW, Casper, 1980-82. Mem. Nat. Assn. Social Workers, Acad. Cert. Social Workers. Democrat. Office: The Casey Family Program 3116 Old Faithful Rd Cheyenne WY 82001

OWENS, KAREN RUTH, accountant; b. Decatur, Ala., Apr. 16, 1960; d. John Franklin and Betty Ruth (Fuller) O. BS, Jacksonville State U., 1982. Acct. Valley Home Constrn., Inc., Decatur, 1985—. Mem. Ch. of Christ. Home: 107 Bob White Dr SE Decatur AL 35603 Office: Valley Home Constrn Inc Rt 2 Box 33 Decatur AL 35603

OWENS, LINDA HARRIMAN, educator; b. Alexandria, Va., Nov. 10, 1952; d. Edward Eugene and Jean Carolyn (Buescher) Harriman; m. Steven Mark Owens, Aug. 6, 1977; 1 child, Mark Edward. BS, Va. Poly. and State U., 1974, MA, 1976; PhD, Fla. State U., 1981. Adminstrv. services asst., Office Sec. USAF, Washington, 1974-75; asst. to v.p. student affairs Va. Poly. and State U., Blacksburg, 1975-79; account exec. Mgmt. Recruiters Internat., Tallahassee, 1981-82; planning specialist Dept. Edn. State of Fla., Tallahassee, 1982-83; research specialist Dept. Edn., Tallahassee, Fla., 1983-86; fiscal analyst State of Fla., Tallahassee, 1986, policy analyst office commr. of edn., 1986—; guest lectr. Fla. State U., Tallahassee, 1980-83; program presenter Nat. Assn. Student Personnel Adminstrs. Conf., N.Y.C., 1981, S.E. Regional Conf. Women in Higher Edn., Williamsburg, Va., 1982, Leadership Vitality Conf., Tallahassee, 1982. Contbr. numerous articles to profl. jours., 1982—. Active Tallahassee Jr. Mus., 1985—, Family YMCA, 1979—; bd. dirs. Arbor Hill Neighborhood Assn., chmn. improvement-beautification com., 1982-86; bd. dirs. Creative Employment Found., 1982-83. Marjorie Rice fellow, 1979-80. Mem. Am. Assn. Higher Edn., Assn. Study Higher Edn., Delta Gamma Alumni Assn. (pres. 1978-79), Phi Upsilon Omicron, Phi Delta Kappa. Home: 2625 Vassar Rd Tallahassee FL 32308 Office: Fla Dept Edn Rm 1701 The Capitol Tallahassee FL 32399

OWENS, LORRAINE LUCILLE, handwriting analyst, cons.; b. Pettus, Tex., Sept. 19, 1927; d. Bernard Phillip and Lucille Lillian (Newman) Hopkins; B.A. in Psychology, Ottawa (Kans.) U., 1977; m. George Erwin Owens, Feb. 5, 1947; children—Janet Lucille, George Erwin, David M., Lynn L. Partner, Allen and Owens, Kansas City, Mo., 1970-80; pres. Kaleidoscope Corp., Kansas City, Mo., 1980—; lectr., seminar speaker; psychology instr. Graphoanalysis Congress, Chgo., 1978-81; cons. with psychologist Lansing State Prison, Marillac Sch. Bd. dirs. Marillac Sch., Kansas City, Mo., 1977-82; troop, troop organizer Mid Continent council Girl Scouts U.S.A., 1962-72. Mem. Internat. Graphoanalysis Soc. (certificate of merit, 1979). Republican. Unity Ch. Author: Different Ways to Describe Traits, 1976; Handwriting Analysis Dictionary, 1981, rev. edit. 1987, Dual Aspects of Traits, 1987. Home: 6300 Verona Shawnee Mission KS 66208 Office: 1524 Crystal Kansas City MO 64126

OWENS, MARGARET ALMA, educational administrator; b. Houston, Mar. 10, 1938; d. Leon Edgar and Velma Rotha (Miller) Owen; m. Robert Harvey Owens, May 28, 1958 (div. 1975); children—Robert Stephen, Keith Randall. BS, Mary-Hardin Baylor U., 1960; MEd, Tex. Woman's U., 1972; supervision cert., 1975; postgrad., 1979-82. Cert. mid-mgmt. adminstr. Tex. Vocat. home economist Tex. A&M U., Bryan, Tex., 1960-64; substitute tchr. Dallas Ind. Sch. Dist., 1965-67, permanent substitute tchr. in home econs. and sci., 1968-69, tchr. spl. edn., 1969-71; jr. acct. Burgess Manning Co., Dallas, 1967-68; asst. dir. Camp Nerby, Oak Cliff YMCA, Dallas, 1968; tchr. spl. edn. Austin Ind. Sch. Dist., Tex., 1972-74, supr. secondary spl. edn., 1974—; adminstrv. intern SW Tex. State U., San Marcos, 1973; cons. San Marcos Bapt. Acad., Tex., 1976; mem. student tchr. adv. com. U. Tex., Austin, 1984—; citizen ambassador of edn. to China, 1986. Author, editor, advisor various profl. tng. materials. Active various Tex. councils Boy Scouts Am., 1968—. Recipient The Golden Measure Achievement award Grand Prairie YMCA, 1968; Outstanding Leadership award Boy Scouts Am., 1971; Fed. edn. grantee, 1971-72. Mem. Council for Exceptional Children (v.p. 1971), Austin Assn. Pub. Sch. Adminstrs. (chmn. task force), Alpha Delta Kappa (former officer), Phi Delta Kappa (sec. Austin 1987-89), Pi Lambda Theta. Baptist. Clubs: Paramount Theatre, World-Wide Vacation, Hyde Park Singles. Lodge: Demolay (pres. Mother's Aux. 1977-78). Avocations: reading, travel, art collecting, theatre, gourmet cooking. Home: 1777 Cricket Hollow Dr Austin TX 78758 Office: Austin Ind Sch Dist 6016 Dillard Circle Austin TX 78752

OWENS, PAMELA RAE, small business executive; b. Portsmouth, Va, Aug. 27, 1949; d. Charles Ray and Virginia Adele (Lowe) O. Cert., Reporting Acad. of Virginia Beach, Ltd. Registered profl. reporter, La. Exec. sec. Norfolk Naval Shipyard, Portsmouth, 1967-79; official court reporter 19th Jud. Dist. Ct., Baton Rouge, 1979—; pres. Profl. Typing Services, Baton Rouge, 1980—; transcriber to confidential informants, narcotics div. Dept. Pub. Safety, Baton Rouge, 1980—. Mem. Am. Bus. Women's Assn. (exec. bd. Portsmouth chpt. 1971-79, Cypress chpt. 1980-81, Pelican chpt. 1982—, various local chpt. offices, Woman of Yr., 1972, newsletter editor, 1972), Nat. Shorthand Reporters Assn., La. Shorthand Reporter Assn. (newsletter editor 1985—), Capital Area Shorthand Reporters Assn. Presbyterian. Office: 19th Jud Dist Ct 222 St Louis St Room 752 Baton Rouge LA 70801

OWENS, PATTI-REBA, dance educator, actress, model; b. Houston, Feb. 3, 1953; d. Jessye Goode Owens. Student, Southwestern Acad., Houston, 1969-70, Columbia Sch. Broadcasting, 1971-72, U. Houston, 1973-75. Model Montgomery Ward, Seventeen mag., Bobby Brooks, and others, Houston, N.Y.C., 1968-69; model, dancer vaious locations, 1969-74; dancer, choreographer Buddy Brock Talent Agy., Houston, 1974-76; model mags., commls. 1968-76; owner, tchr. Patti Owens Dance Acad., Houston, 1976—; owner, choreographer Patti Owens Dancers, Houston, 1977—, Patti Owens Jazz Co., Houston, 1979—. Author: Year of the Texas Sesquicentennial, 1986; designer dance wear; choreographer ballet "Love Songs," 1986. Active various charitable orgns. Recipient various community/civic awards. Mem. Tex. Press Assn., Better Bus. Bur., Dance Educators of Am., Nat. Assn. Dancers, Nat. Assn. Female Execs. Office: Patti Owens Dance Acad 8225 Broadway Houston TX 77061

OWENS, RHONELLA C., counseling, career training administrator; b. Detroit, Mar. 11, 1950; d. Harley W. and Violette C. (Smith) Owens. BS, Western Mich. U., 1971; MEd, Antioch Grad. Sch., Phila., 1976; postgrad., Calif. Inst. Integral Studies, 1984—. Coordinator time counseling Lincoln U., Pa., 1976-78; counselor, instr. U. San Francisco, 1978-79; administrv. asst. Programming Resources, San Francisco, 1979-80; logistical coordinator Urban Inst. Human Services, San Francisco, 1980-81, project mgr., 1981-82; career counselor Career Devel. Inst., San Francisco, 1982-84; counselor, trainer Organize for Success, San Francisco, 1984—; counselor City Coll. San Francisco, 1985—, coordinator women's re-entry program, 1987—; workshop facilitator Options for Women, San Francisco, 1973-76, chair edn. com. Minority Women's Career Workshop, 1984; trainer Oakland (Calif.) Youth Corp., 1976—; field services coordinator Calif. Head Start Tng. Program, San Francisco, 1982-84. Mem. Pi Omega Pi.

OWENS, SHELBY JEAN, electrologist; b. Flintville, Tenn., Dec. 18, 1936; d. Harvey Chrethton and Emma Lucille (McDonald) Langford; m. David Randall Owens, Mar. 12, 1953 (div. Feb. 1970); children—Karen, Kristie, Kaylon; m. Richard Allen Brewer, May 26, 1977. Diploma Hoffman Electrolysis Inst., N.Y.C., 1968, postgrad. cert., 1970; cert. clin. electrologist. Tech. typist Thiokol Chem. Corp., Huntsville, Ala., 1957-60; exec. sec. CFW Constrn. Co., Fayetteville, Tenn., 1961-65; pvt. practice electrolysis, Winchester, Tenn., 1968-70, Huntsville, 1970-77, Pensacola, Fla., 1975—. Founder, Hirsutes Anonymous Initiating Removal Reform, Inc., 1986—; mem. Pensacola chpt. Freedoms Found. Recipient Pres.'s award Am. Electrolysis Assn., 1984. Mem. Internat. Platform Assn., Soc. Clin. and Med. Electrologists, Electrolysis Soc. Fla. (lobbyist 1979-86, pres. 1982-86), Am. Bus. Women's Assn. (Pensacola charter chpt.) (past pres., Woman of Yr. award 1984). Democrat. Avocations: sewing, writing. Home: 3801 N 12th Ave Pensacola FL 32503 Office: 5113 N Davis Suite 8 Pensacola FL 32503

OWENS, TERESA F(AY), marketing/sales executive; b. Cheoah, N.C., May 18, 1954; d. Clarence Edward and Doris Pauline (Quilliams) O. BA, Mars Hill Coll., 1975; postgrad. U. Louisville, 1975-76. Social worker Sheltered Workshop, Louisville, 1976-77, River Region Mental Health Bd., Louisville, 1977-78; dist. sales rep. Chromalloy Photographics, Louisville, 1978; mktg. rep. McDonnell Douglas Automation, St. Louis, 1978-81, account mgr., Altanta, 1981-84; account mgr. Info. Sci., 1984-85; mktg. mgr. Mgmt. Sci. Am., 1985; mktg. mgr. HBO & Co., 1986—; sr. mktg. mgr. McDonnell Douglas Health Systems, 1986—. Active Ga. Council on Battered Women, Atlanta Children's Shelter; mem. Peachtree Presbyn. Ch. Mars Hill Coll. Pres.'s scholar, 1972. Mem. Nat. Assn. Female Execs., Atlanta Women's Network, Ga. Women's Polit. Caucus, LWV, High Mus. Art. Home: 7120 Stonington Dr NE Atlanta GA 30328

OWENS-POTE, KAREN ASKEY, nutrition consultant; b. Indiana, Pa., Dec. 3, 1945; d. William Anthony and Cleo Margaret (Lyons) Askey; B.S. in Home Econs., Indiana U. of Pa., 1967; M.S. in Food and Nutrition, Va. Poly. Inst. and State U., 1970; postgrad. in bus. mgmt. Pepperdine U., 1979-80; m. Wilfred D. Pote, Feb. 14, 1981. Dir. dietetics and food service Somerset (Pa.) Community Hosp., 1970; food mgr. supr. Restaurant-Hotel div. Stouffer Food Corp., Cleve., 1967-68; allied health nutritionist, sr. dietitian City of Hope Nat. Med. Center, Duarte, Calif., 1970-71; chief nutritionist U. Calif. Med. Center-Irvine, Orange, Calif., 1971-74; prin. K.A. Owens Assos., Sierra Madre, Calif., 1972-80; pres. K.A. Owens & Assos., Inc., St. Paul and San Diego, 1981—; health editor Copley Radio Network, 1986—; mgr. nutritional affairs Gen. Foods Corp., White Plains, N.Y., 1980-81; instr. public health nutrition U. Minn., Mpls., 1981—; chmn., asst. prof. home econs. and dietetics Pepperdine U., Malibu, Calif., 1974-80; adj. prof. social ecology U. Calif., Irvine, 1972-74; lectr., researcher in human nutrition Va. Poly. Inst. and State U., Blacksburg, 1968-70; syndicated broadcast journalist Health Note; condr. ednl. seminars in field, Calif., Idaho, Minn.; health editor Copley Radio Network, 1986—; cons. Henkel U.S.A., Bozell & Jacobs, Manning Selvage & Lee, Schwan's Sales Enterprises, Kane-Miller Corp., Anderson-Hendrickson & Co., Van de Kamp Frozen Foods, Pillsbury Co., Robert Marston and Assocs., Inc., Hunt-Wesson Foods, Inc., Dinah's Place, NBC-TV, Longevity Centers, Inc., Glass Packaging Inst., Home Savs. and Loan Assn., Squirt and Co., Daniel J. Edelman, Inc.; Office: 4416 Topa Topa Dr Suite 300 La Mesa CA 92041

OWINGS, MARGARET WENTWORTH, conservationist, artist; b. Berkeley, Calif., Apr. 29, 1913; d. Frank W. and Jean (Pond) Wentworth; m. Malcolm Millard, 1937; 1 child, Wendy Millard Benjamin; m. Nathaniel Alexander Owings, Dec. 30, 1953. A.B., Mills Coll., 1934; postgrad., Radcliffe Coll., 1935. One-woman shows include Santa Barbara (Calif.) Mus. Art, 1940, Stanford Art Gallery, 1951, stitchery exhbns. at M.H. De Young Mus., San Francisco, 1963, Internat. Folk Art Mus., Santa Fe, 1965. Commr. Calif. Parks, 1963-69, mem., Nat. Parks Found. Bd, 1968-69; bd. dirs. African Wildlife Leadership Found., 1968-80, Defenders of Wildlife, 1969-74; founder, pres. Friends of the Sea Otter, 1969—; pres. Calif. Mountain Lion Preservation Found., 1987; trustee Environmental Def. Fund, 1972-83; Regional trustee Mills Coll., 1962-68. Recipient gold medal, Conservation Service award Dept. Interior, 1975, Conservation award Calif. Acad. Scis., 1979, Am. Motors Conservation award, 1980, Joseph Wood Krutch medal Humane Soc. U.S., 1980, Nat. Audubon Soc. medal, 1983, A. Starker Leopold award Calif. Nature Conservancy, 1986. Home: Grimes Point Big Sur CA 93920

OWNBEY, VIRGINIA KAY, architect; b. Miami, June 2, 1946; d. Hal Norwood and Mary Virginia (Williams) Buchanan; B.Arch., Okla. State U., 1970; m. Charles Lewis Ownbey, Aug. 11, 1974; children—Christine Vanessa, Wade Preston. Archtl. draftsperson Frank L. Hope & Assos., Santa Ana, Calif., 1970-73, Am. Devel., Torrance, Calif., 1973-74, J. Ward Dawson, Architect, Tustin, Calif., 1975-76; architect Archi & Tekton, Newport Beach, Calif., 1977-79; individual practice, Tustin, 1979-83, Manitou Springs, Colo., 1983—. Nat. Endowment Arts grantee, 1969. Mem. Women's Archtl. League. Methodist. Address: 810 Crystal Park Rd Manitou Springs CO 80829

OWSLEY, MICHELE MALEK, aerospace engineer; b. Hackensack, N.J., Oct. 11, 1950; d. Leo Edward and Virginia (Brown) Malek; m. Robert Lamar Owsley, Sept. 20, 1974; 1 child, James Edward. BS in Aeronautical Engring., Rensselaer Poly. Inst., 1972; MS Aerospace Engring., Tex. A&M U., 1974. Aerospace engr. Boeing Comml. Airplane Co., Renton, Wash., 1974-77; aerospace engr. FAA, Ft. Worth, 1977-85, project mgr., 1985—. Mem. Experimental Aircraft Assn., Aircraft Owners and Pilots Assn. Club: Toastmasters (editor newsletter 1979-80). Home: 979 Trophy Club Dr Roanoke TX 76193-0150 Office: FAA 4400 Blue Mound Rd Fort Worth TX 76106

OWSNITZKI, GABRIELE ANNA J., marketing professional; b. Osnabrück, Fed. Republic of Germany, Mar. 5, 1957; came to U.S., 1960; d. Johannes Franz Karl and Theresia Paula (Richter) O. Student, Fairleigh Dickinson U., 1978—. Office, showroom mgr. Dynasty and Eterna, Mido Watches, N.Y.C., 1975-77; adminstrv. asst. Leber Katz Ptnrs., N.Y.C., 1977-78, Art Carved and Rosenthal Jewelry, N.Y.C., 1978-80; asst. product mgr. Art Carved Inc., N.Y.C., 1980-83, product mgr., 1983; dir. of merchandising Hirsch U.S.A., Inc., River Edge, N.J., 1983-87; brand mgr. Pulsar Time Inc., Mahwah, N.J., 1987—. Mem. Delta Mu Delta, Phi Zeta Kappa, Nat. Assn. Female Execs. Office: Pulsar Time Inc 1111 Macarthur Blvd Mahwah NJ 07430

OXLEY, ANN, television executive; b. Canton, Ohio, Aug. 3, 1924; d. Edward and Dorothy (Duffy) Adang; B.A. with distinction, Ind. U., 1974, M.P.A., 1982; m. Jack Raymond Oxley, Aug. 10, 1946; children—Kathleen Oxley Wiggins, Maureen Oxley Gaff, Joseph, Jeffrey, Christeen Oxley Rhodes, Daniel, Julie Marie, Jamie, Kevin, Valerie, Amy. Advt. account salesperson Ft. Wayne (Ind.) Jour. Gazette, 1945-47; office mgr. Ind. Equestrian Assn., Ft. Wayne, 1971-73; research dir. Taxpayers Research Assn., Ft. Wayne, 1974-76; exec. dir. Ft. Wayne Pub. TV Inc., 1976-86; founder, owner Akin Assocs., 1987—. Active Bicentennial Com., 1976; adviser Media Arts Panel Ind. Arts Commn. Mem. AAUW, Service Corp Retired Execs., publicity chair., 1986, Mensa Internat., C. of C. (cultural com.), Phi Alpha Alpha. Roman Catholic. Home: 4305 Arlington St Fort Wayne IN 46807 Office: PO Box 11303 Fort Wayne IN 46866

OXLEY, GERALDINE MOTTA, insurance company executive; b. N.J., June 25, 1930; d. Edward J. and Mary (Green) E.; m. John E. Oxley, Sept. 19, 1953. B.S., Coll. Mt. St. Vincent, 1951. With N.Y. Life Ins. Co., N.Y.C., 1951—; 2d v.p. N.Y. Life Ins. Co., 1975-78, v.p. info. systems and services, 1978—. Trustee Manhattan Coll. Mem. Assn. Computer Machinery. Home: 169 E 69th St New York NY 10021 Office: NY Life Ins Co 51 Madison Ave New York NY 10010

OYLER, SUSAN DEBORAH, microbiologist; b. Roanoke, Va., Apr. 21, 1950; d. Dalton Oliver and Margaret Clay (Waldron) O.; B.A. in Biology, U. Va., 1972; Med. Technologist, Duke U., 1973; M.S. in Microbiology (A.D. Williams fellow 1973-74, NIH grantee 1974-76), Med. Coll. Va., 1976. Mgr. lab. Family Med. Center, Richmond, Va., 1975-76; gen. lab. supr. Physicians Clin. Labs., Richmond, 1976-78; supr. biol. formulation Technicon Corp., Middletown, Va., 1978-80; specialist fermentation tech. support Abbott Labs., N. Chicago, Ill., 1980-87; prodn. mgr. Sybron Chemicals, Inc., Salem, Va., 1987—; mem. faculty J. Sargeant Reynolds Community Coll., Richmond, 1976-77. Regional rep. Va. Democratic Conv., 1976. Mem. Am. Soc. Clin. Pathologists, Soc. Ind. Microbiologists, Am. Soc. Microbiologists, Am. Mgmt. Assn., Nat. Assn. Female Execs. Home: 243 Plymouth Dr Roanoke VA 24019

OZAN, MARILYN FRANCES RALEY, mailing service executive; b. Memphis, Jan. 31, 1946; d. Claude Mason and Mary Reba (Pruett) Raley; m. Richard Vance Ozan, June 29, 1968; 1 child, Melynda Ellen. BA, Baylor U., 1968. Cert. secondary tchr. Advtg. dir. Baylor Bookstore, Waco, Tex., 1965-68; substitute tchr. Orange County Ind. Sch. Dist., Orlando, Fla., 1969; tchr. San Antonio Ind. Sch. Dist., 1971-77; owner, pres. The Mailing Service, Greensboro, N.C., 1978—; sec. Ozan Communications, Greensboro, 1983—; prof. music, choral dir. Lehman Coll., CUNY, 1986—; pianist Lehman Trio, 1987—; dir. ednl. activities New World Records, 1986—. Stage mgr. City

Stage, United Arts Council, Greensboro, 1984-86; active local Girl Scouts U.S., 1982. Author: 57 Lessons for the High School Music Class, 1983. Recipient cert. appreciation Lowell Jr. High Sch. PTA, San Antonio, 1975. Mem. World Interest Group (cert. of appreciation Greensboro chpt. 1987), Piedmont Triad Advt. Fedn. (mailing coordinator, Cert. Appreciation), Postal Customer Council Greater Greensboro (vice chmn. 1987—), Greensboro Area C. of C. Republican. Avocations: spiritual exploration, metaphysical awareness, photography, reading, automobile racing. Home: 106 E Brentwood St Greensboro NC 27403 Office: Lehman Coll Music Dept Bedford Park Blvd W Bronx NY 10468

OZER, LISA GOLDBERG, lawyer; b. Kileen, Tex., Feb. 14, 1954; d. Nathaniel and Renee (Slutzky) Goldberg; m. Robert H. Ozer, May 13, 1979. BA summa cum laude, Tufts U., 1976; JD, U. Pa., 1979. Bar: U.S. Dist. Ct. (so. and ea. dists.) N.Y. 1980, U.S. Dist. Ct. N.J. 1985. Assoc. Kronish, Lieb, Weiner & Hellman, N.Y.C., 1979-86; acting legal advocate Jersey Battered Women's Services, Morristown, N.J., 1987—. Mem. Phi Beta Kappa. Home: 187 Great Hills Dr South Orange NJ 07079

OZICK, CYNTHIA, author; b. N.Y.C., Apr. 17, 1928; d. William and Celia (Regelson) O.; m. Bernard Hallote, Sept. 7, 1952; 1 dau., Rachel Sarah. BA cum laude with honors in English, NYU, 1949; MA, Ohio State U., 1950; LHD (hon.), Yeshiva U., 1984, Hebrew Union Coll., 1985, Williams Coll., 1986, Hunter Coll., 1987, Jewish Theol. Sem. Am., 1988, Adelphi U., 1988. Author: Trust, 1966, The Pagan Rabbi and Other Stories, 1971, Bloodshed and Three Novellas, 1976, Levitation: Five Fictions, 1982, Art and Ardor: Essays, 1983, The Cannibal Galaxy, 1983, The Messiah of Stockholm, 1987, Metaphor and Memory: Essays, 1988; also poetry, criticism, revs., translations, essays and fiction in numerous periodicals and anthologies. Phi Beta Kappa orator, Harvard U., 1985. Recipient Mildred and Harold Strauss Living award Am. Acad. Arts and Letters, 1983, Rea award for short story, 1986; Guggenheim fellow, 1982. Mem. PEN, Am. Inst. Arts and Letters, Authors League, Am. Acad. of Arts and Scis., Phi Beta Kappa. Office: care Alfred A Knopf Co 201 E 50th St New York NY 10022

OZOLS, LIA, medical technologist; b. Riga, Latvia, Jan. 4, 1929; came to U.S., 1950, naturalized, 1959; d. Karlis and Olga Rozenfelds; B.S., U. Minn., 1957; postgrad. Metro State U., Minn., 1980; m. Laimons Ozols, Mar. 19, 1956; children—Ingemars, Arnis. Med. technologist U. Minn. Hosps., 1957-61; chief adminstrv. technologist Abbott Hosp., Mpls., 1957-77; administrv. lab. dir. Abbott-Northwestern Hosp., 1977-79; dir. Les Soeurs Orgn., Mpls., 1979—. Chair adv. bd. City of Richfield (Minn.) Dept. Health; bd. dirs. South Hennepin Human Services Council, Minn., 1986. Recipient Key to City, Richfield, 1985. Mem. Am. Soc. Clin. Pathologists, Am. Soc. Med. Technology, Minn. Microbiologists, Minn. Soc. Med. Technology, Minn. LWV, Women's Equity Action League (v.p. 1981-82), Women's Consortium, Minn. Women's Network, Exec. Females. Club: Selga (pres. 1981-82). Home: 2012 W 68th St Minneapolis MN 55423

OZOLS, SANDRA LEE, lawyer; b. Casper, Wyo., June 24, 1957; d. Virgil Carr and Doris Louise (Conklin) McC.; m. Ojars Herberts Ozols, Sept. 2, 1978 (div.); children: Michael Ojars, Sara Ann, Brian Christopher. BA with distinction, U. Colo., 1978; JD magna cum laude, Boston U., 1982. Bar: Colo. 1982, U.S. Dist. Ct. Colo. 1985. Assoc. Cohen, Brame and Smith, Denver, 1983-84, Parcel, Meyer, Schwartz, Ruttum and Mauro, Denver, 1984-85, Mayer, Brown and Platt, Denver, 1985-87; region counsel Gen. Electric Capital Corp., Englewood, Colo., 1987—. Mem. Denver Bar Assn., Colo. Bar Assn., Phi Beta Kappa, Phi Delta Phi. Republican. Mem. Ch. of Christ. Home: 8086 S Willow Ct Englewood CO 80112 Office: Gen Electric Capital Corp 7409 S Alton Court #208 Englewood CO 80112

OZZARD, JANET LUCILLE, publisher; b. Phila., Dec. 17, 1927; d. Frederic Twining and Elizabeth (Evans) Harris; m. Norbert E. Turek, May, 1948 (dec. 1965); children: Leslie Turek Deluccia, Allison Turek Isherwood, Peter Alan, Ginger Turek-Brown, Norbert E. Jr., Janet E. Ozzard; m. William E. Ozzard, June 10, 1967. Student, Vail Deane Sch., Elizabeth, N.J., 1946, Barmore Sch., N.Y.C., 1947, Raritan Valley Community Coll., 1986. Artist Embree Printing, Elizabeth, N.J., 1947-48; asst. records clk. N.J. Gen. Assembly, 1948-49; reporter Legis. Index of N.J., Inc., Elizabeth, N.J., 1953-66; pub., pres. Legis. Index of N.J., Inc., Somerville, N.J., 1966—. Pres. Westfield Council of PTAs, 1959; active United Way of Somerset County, 1980. Mem. Soc. Mayflower Descendents in State of N.J. (sec. 1985-88), N.J. Trail Conf., Appalachian Trail Conf. Republican. Episcopalian. Home: 1908 Mountain Top Rd Bridgewater NJ 08807 Office: Legis Index of NJ Inc 27 N Bridge St Somerville NJ 08876

PAARDECAMP, SUSAN LYNN, marketing professional; b. Short Hills, N.J., Feb. 17, 1962; d. James Brian and Phyliss Patricia (Tiger) P. BA, Franklin & Marshall Coll., 1984. Ednl. services rep. Christian Sci. Monitor, Boston, 1984-85, lists project coordinator, 1985-86, dir. mail supr., 1987-88, circulation dir., 1988—. Vol. probation officer Vols. in Probation/Parole, Lancaster, Pa., 1982-84; vol. Mass. Adoption Resource Exchange, Boston, 1985, YWCA Big Sister Program, Lancaster, 1981. Mem. Ch. Christ Scientist. Home: 26 Cumberland St Boston MA 02115 Office: Christian Sci Monitor Ednl Service P701 1 Norway St Boston MA 02115

PACANIA, ADORACION BUENSUCESO, therapist; b. Samal Bataan, Philippines, Jan. 29, 1946; came to U.S., 1969; d. Pedro Magpoc and Francisca (Buensuceso) Albelda; m. Eleno Sadian Pacania, Aug. 17, 1971; children: Lener, Adora, Peter, Darrell, Elena. BE, Far Eastern U., Manila, 1966; MEd, Wayne State U., 1986. Cert. spl. edn., elem. tchr. Tchr. Philippine Pub. Sch. System, Bataan, 1966-69; instr. for adult edn. Social Resources, Inc., Utica, Mich., 1982-84; supr., Warren Activity Ctr. Social Resources, Inc., Utica, 1984-86; mental health program coordinator ARC Services of Macomb, Mt. Clemens, Mich., 1986-87; cognitive therapist Genesis Group, Southfield, Mich., 1987-88; spl. educator Havenwyck Hosp., Auburn Hills, Mich., 1988—. Roman Catholic. Home: 39164 Hyland Dr Sterling Heights MI 48310 Office: Genesis Group 20755 Greenfield Rd Southfield MI 48705

PACE, CAROLINA JOLLIFF, communications executive, commercial real estate investor; b. Dallas, Apr. 12, 1938; d. Lindsay Gafford and Carolina (Juden) Jolliff; student Holton-Arms Jr. Coll., 1956-57; B.A. in Comparative Lit., So. Meth. U., 1960; m. John McIver Pace, Oct. 7, 1961. Promotional advisor, dir. season ticket sales Dallas Theatre Center, 1960-61; exec. sec. Dallas Book and Author Luncheon, 1959-63; promotional and instl. cons. Henry Regnery-Reilly & Lee Pub. Co., Chgo., 1962-65; pub. trade rep. various cos., instl. rep. Don R. Phillips Co., Southeastern area, 1965-67; Southwestern rep. Ednl. Reading Service, Inc.-Troll Assocs., Mahwah, N.J., 1967-72; v.p., dir. multimedia div. Melton Book Co., Dallas, 1972-79; v.p. mktg. Webster's Internat., Inc., Nashville, 1980-82; pres. Carolina Pace, Inc., 1982—; mem. adv. bd. Nat. Info. Center of Spl. Edn. Materials; mem. materials rev. panel Nat. Media Center for Materials of Severely-Profoundly Handicapped, 1981; mem. mktg. product rev. bd. LINC Resources, 1982, 83, 84, mktg. task force, 1983, adv. bd., 1987; reviewer spl. edn. U.S. Dept. Edn., 1975-79, 85; rev. cons. HHS, 1982, 83, 84, 86; product rev. taskforce CEC, 1984, 85, 86; cons. Ednl. Cable Consortium, Summit, N.J. Mem. adv. council Grad. Sch. Library and Info. Sci. Found., U. Tex. Mem. Women's Nat. Book Assn., Nat. Audio Visual Assn. (conf. speaker), Internat. Communications Industries Assn., Assn. Ednl. and Communications Tech., Assn. Spl. Edn. Tech. (nat. dir., v.p. publicity 1980-82), Women in Communications, Dallas Founders, Friends of the West End (pres. 1988—), West End Assn. Dallas (chmn. subcom. on traffic and parking 1986-87, com. demographic study 1987—), Pub. Relations Soc. Am., Council Exceptional Children (dir. exhibitors com., chmn. publ. com. 1979 conf., conf. speaker 1981), DAR, Dallas Mus. of Art, ALA, Sothern Meml. Dallas Art Assn., Press Club of Dallas, Alpha Delta Pi. Presbyterian. Producer ednl. videos; contbr. articles to profl. jours. Home: 4524 Lorraine Ave Dallas TX 75205

PACE, CHERYL FIDA, banker; b. St. Paul, Aug. 27, 1953; d. Frank J. and Roselyn M. (Donofri) Fida; m. G. Allen Pace, Jr., Sept. 25, 1976; 1 child, Jonathan Derek. BA in Fin., Wichita (Kans.) State U., 1980. Comml. banking officer Tex. Commerce Bank-Reagan, Houston, 1981-83; asst. v.p. Tex. Commerce Bank-Houston, Houston, 1984-85; v.p. loan adminstrn. Tex. Commerce Bancshares, Houston, 1985-86; sr. v.p. comml. lending Tex. Commerce Bank-Stafford, Houston, 1986-87, v.p. loan mgmt. member banks, 1987—. Kans. Banking Assn. scholar, 1980; named one of Outstanding Young Women Am., 1985. Mem. Nat. Assn. Female Execs. Republican. Roman Catholic. Office: Tex Commerce Bank-Stafford PO Box 2558 Houston TX 77002

PACE, JOHNNIE LOU, nurse admininstrator; b. Waco, Tex., Jan. 5, 1934; d. Roman and Wilma Rosalie (Sulak) Klein; m. Roy Lynn Pace, Apr. 22, 1959; children: Mark William, John Wesley, Tara, Lyne Elaine. Diploma, Providence Hosp. Sch. Nursing, Waco, 1954. RN. Staff nurse Temple (Tex.) VA Hosp., 1954-55, Waco VA Hosp., 1955-56; pvt. duty Waco Pvt. Duty RN Assn., 1956-57, 58-59, 64-69; charge nurse Hillhaven Convalescent Hosp., Waco, 1961-64, Arlington (Tex.) Community Hosp., 1969-72, All Saints Episcopal Hosp., Ft. Worth, 1974; dir. nurses Arlington Villa Sr. Citizens, 1974—. Democrat. Roman Catholic. Home: 114 Linda Ln Euless TX 76039 Office: Arlington Villa 2601 W Randol Mill Rd Arlington TX 76012

PACE, NORMA, economist, consulting firm executive. Grad., Hunter Coll., 1941; grad. study, Columbia U.; Ph.D. (hon.), Mich. Tech. U., 1975, Poly. Inst., N.Y., 1976, Cedar Crest Coll., 1977, Grove City Coll., 1980, City U. N.Y., 1981. Staff Econometric Inst.; with U.S. Economics Corp. (bus. adv. cons. service), 1944-71, pres., 1969-71; v.p., dir. indsl. econs. Lionel D. Edie & Co., N.Y.C., 1971-73; sr. v.p. Am. Paper Inst.; asst. devel. visual aids for teaching econs. Columbia Visual Lab.; dir. Sears, Roebuck & Co., Ga. Pacific Corp., Englehard Corp., Hasbro Co., 3M Co., A. O. Smith Co.; gov. U.S. Postal Service;. Trustee Com. for Econ. Devel. Named to Hunter Coll. Hall of Fame, 1973. Mem. U.S. C. of C. Address: 290 Madison Ave New York NY 10017

PACEK, CYNTHIA DIANNE, nurse, administrator; b. Worcester, Mass., Sept. 27, 1938; d. Laurence and Florence Dorothy (Haddad) Chrzsiewski; m. Richard Joseph Pacek, Aug. 29, 1959; children: Michael, Daniel, Nancy. Diploma in nursing, Worcester City Hosp., 1959; BS, Anna Maria Coll., Paxton, Mass., 1978, MBA, 1983. Registered nurse. Instr. Worcester City Hosp. Sch. Nursing, 1960-61, staff nurse, 1961-65, 67-73, clin. supr., 1965-67; head nurse St. Vincent Hosp., Worcester, 1973-80, clin. dir., 1980-87; dir. clin. services Med. Assocs., Chelmsford, Mass., 1987—. Mem. Auburn (Mass.) Personnel Bd. 1985-86, Women's Guild Our Lady of Providence , Auburn Bd. Health, 1986—; chmn. clin. network group div. Harvard Community Network. Mem. Am. Assn. Ambulatory Nurse Adminstrs., Mass. Assn. Nursing Execs. (membership com. 1984-85, legis. com. 1986—), Nurse Assn. of Am. Coll. Ob-Gyn, Worcester Diocesan Council Cath. Nurses, Worcester City Hosp. Alumni Assn., Anna Maria Alumni Assn. Democrat. Roman Catholic. Home: 104 Bryn Mawr Ave Auburn MA 01501

PACE-OWENS, SYLVIA, nurse practitioner, clinical administrator; b. St. Joseph, Mo., Oct. 16, 1936; children—Laura, Sara, Alan. B.S. in Nursing, U. Tex.-Galveston, 1960. R.N.; lic. ob-gyn nurse practitioner. Ob-gyn nurse practitioner Harris County Health Dept., Houston, 1975-78, Planned Parenthood, Houston, 1978-79; ob-gyn nurse practitioner Reproductive Services, Houston, 1979-80, clinic dir., 1980-82; clin. coordinator in vitro fertilization/embryo transfer program U. Tex. Med. Sch., Houston, 1982-84; IVF/G.I.F.T. nurse coordinator The Woman's Hosp. Tex., 1984—. Contbr. chpt. to Human In Vitro Fertilization and Embryo Transfer (Quigley and Wolfe), 1984; also articles on in vitro fertilization and embryo transfer program. Named Hon. Faculty Assoc., U. Texas Sch. Nursing, Houston, 1982—. Mem. Americ Fertility Soc., Am. Nurses Assn., Tex. Nurses Assn., Nurses Assn. of Am. Coll. Ob-Gyn. (cert. Ob-gyn nurse practitioner 1981), Primary Council of Nurse Practitioners, Hockaday Alumnae Assn., Kappa Kappa Gamma Alumnae. Episcopalian. Office: Baylor Coll Medicine Baylor Population Program Dept Ob-Gyn #1 Baylor PLaza Houston TX 77030

PACETTI, SHIRLEY ANN, educator, interpreter, consultant; b. Baton Rouge, Oct. 8, 1936; d. William Seward and Lena Beatrice (Davis) Smith; children: Robert Reynolds, Kenneth M., Rebecca P., Mark C. AAS, Houston Community Coll., 1987. Cert. interpreter for deaf, speech communications cons. Free-lance interpreter Houston, 1954—; exec. sec. Geosource, Inc., Houston, 1981-83; vocat. communications specialist Tex. Rehab. Commn., Houston, 1983—; adj. prof. Houston Community Coll., 1983—; cons. Tex. Commn. for Deaf, Austin, 1984—. Bd. dirs. Hear-Say, Houston, 1985-86, Deaf Council of Greater Houston, 1983-85, Gov.'s Com. on Aging, 1967-71. Shirley Ann Pacetti Day named in her honor Mayor of Houston, 1986. Mem. Nat. Rehab. Assn., Am. Deafness and Rehab. Assn., Coalition for Barrier Free Living, Tex. Soc. Interpreters for Deaf (pres. bd. dirs. 1967-77), Greater Houston Interpreters for Deaf (bd. dirs. 1985-87, pres. 1988-89), Nat. Assn. Female Execs., Delphian Soc. (pres. 1972). Democrat. Baptist. Home and Office: 2601 Bellefontaine Apt A 301 Houston TX 77025

PACHOLSKI, AUDREY PHYLLIS, university official, consultant; b. Concord, Mass., May 16, 1961; d. Stanislaus Stephen and Audrey Phyllis (Paulhus) P. B.S., Mankato State U., 1985. Publicist Mankato State U., Minn., 1983-85, ann. giving officer, 1985—; cons. pub. relations and motivational speaker Bd. dirs. Mankato Area Coalition for Affordable Housing, 1985—; big sister YMCA program. Mem. Minn. Valley Civitan Club, Internat. Festival Com., Mankato Merely Players, Nat. Soc. Fund Raising Execs., Nat. Assn. Female Execs., Mankato Area C. of C. (ACT 2000 arts adv. com. 1985-86). Democrat. Roman Catholic. Lodges: Toastmasters, Zonta (jr. bd. 1985-86), Civitan (pres.-elect Minn. Valley chpt., internat. festival com.). Avocations: acting, singing, writing, painting, pub. speaking. Home: 609 S 4th St Mankato MN 56001 Office: Mankato State U PO Box 101 Mankato MN 56001

PACK, PHOEBE KATHERINE FINLEY, civic worker; b. Portland, Oreg., Feb. 2, 1907; d. William Lovell and Irene (Barnhart) Finley; student U. Calif., Berkeley, 1926-27; B.A., U. Oreg., 1930; m. Arthur Newton Pack, June 11, 1936; children: Charles Lathrop, Phoebe Irene. Layman referee Pima County Juvenile Ct., Tucson, 1958-71; mem. pres.'s council Menninger Found., Topeka; mem. Alcoholism Council So. Ariz., 1960—; bd. dirs. Kress Nursing Sch., Tucson, 1957-67, Pima County Assn. for Mental Health, 1958—, Ariz. Assn. for Mental Health, Phoenix, 1963—, U. Ariz. Found., Casa de los Niños Crisis Nursery; co-founder Ariz.-Sonora Desert Mus., Tucson, 1975—, Ghost Ranch Found., N.Mex.; bd. dirs. St. Mary's Hosp., Tucson, Tucson Urban League, Tucson YMCA Youth Found. Mem. Mt. Vernon Ladies Assn. Union (state vice regent, 1962-84),Mt. Vernon One Hundred (founder), Nature Conservancy (life), Alpha Phi. Home: Villa Compana Apt 415 6653 E Carondelet Dr Tucson AZ 85710

PACK, SUSAN JOAN, advertising copywriter; b. N.Y.C., June 15, 1951; d. Howard Meade and Nancy (Buckley) P. BA summa cum laude, Princeton U., 1973. Market researcher Case & McGrath Inc., N.Y.C., 1977-78; copywriter Laurence Charles & Free, N.Y.C., 1978-83, Warwick Advt., N.Y.C., 1983-85; sr. copywriter Saatchi & Saatchi Compton, N.Y.C., 1985—. Mem. Princeton (N.J.) U. Library Council, 1985—; trustee Pack Found. for Med. Research, N.Y., 1983—; bd. dirs. The Poster Soc., N.Y., 1985-87. Recipient 4 Clio awards, 1981, 1 Clio award, 1982.

PACKARD, BARBARA BAUGH, physician scientist administrator, physiologist; b. Uniontown, Pa., Mar. 10, 1938; d. Walter Ray and Yolande (Ciarlo) Baugh; m. Lawrence Arthur Krames, Nov. 24, 1963 (div. 1971); m. John E. Packard III, July 14, 1979. B.S., Waynesburg Coll., 1960; M.S., W. Va. U., 1961, Ph.D., 1964; M.D., U. Ala.-Birmingham, 1974. Physiologist myocardial infarction br. Nat. Heart Inst., Bethesda, Md., 1967-71; research assoc. U. Ala.-Birmingham, 1971-74; med. intern Johns Hopkins Hosp., Balt., 1974-75; sr. med. scientist adminstr. cardiac disease br. div. heart and vascular disease Nat. Heart, Lung, and Blood Inst., Bethesda, Md., 1975-79, assoc. dir. cardiology, 1979-82, dir. div. heart and vascular diseases, 1980-86, assoc. dir. for sci. program ops., 1986—. Mem. editorial bd. Jour. Soviet Research in Cardiovascular Diseases, 1980-84, Jour. Urban Cardiolgy, 1988—. Served with USPHS, 1975—. Recipient Commendation medal USPHS, 1978, Outstanding Service medal, 1986, Meritorious Service medal, 1986, 88. Fellow Am. Coll. Cardiology; mem. Am. Physiol Soc., Am. Heart Assn., Johns Hopkins Med. and Surgical Soc., Sigma Xi. Home: 10401 Grosvenor Pl Rockville MD 20852 Office: Nat Heart Lung & Blood Inst Bethesda MD 20892

PACKARD, KATRINA BERNIECE DANNHAUS, planner; b. Freeport, Tex., Feb. 2, 1953; d. Harvey Dean Walter Henry and Wilma Berniece (Adams) Dannhaus; m. Steven DeWitt Packard, Aug. 7, 1971 (div. Dec. 1979); 1 son, Jason DeWitt. A.A. with honors, Coll. of Mainland, Texas City, Tex., 1979; B.A. cum laude, U. Houston, 1982; J.D. U. Houston, 1986. Cert. peer counselor, alcoholism counselor. Legal sec. Dist. Atty., Huntsville, Tex., 1971-72; adminstrv. sec. Sam Houston State U., Huntsville, 1972-74, Pierce, Goodwin, Flanaga, Houston, 1974-75; legal sec. Vinson & Elkins, Houston, 1975-77; exec. dir. Bay Area Commn. Drugs and Alcohol, Houston, 1977-79; planner Houston-Galveston Area Council, Houston, 1979-85; assoc. Wood, Lucksinger & Epstein, Houston, 1986-88; atty. Jenkens & Gilchrest, 1988—. Del. White House Conf. on Children, 1970, White House Conf. on Youth, 1971; com. chmn. Tex. White House Conf., Austin, 1970; v.p. Tex. Youth Conf., Austin, 1968-71, state counselor, 1969; mem. Leadership Inst. Tex.; bd. dirs. Recovery Ctr., Inc., 1978-80, Clear Lake Social Service Ctr., 1980, U. Houston/Clear Lake Cultural Ctr., 1980, Tex. Community Services, 1978, Four C's Clinic, LaMarque, Tex., 1979-80, Women's Ctr., Coll. of Mainland, 1980; mem. Children's Council Tex., 1978-80, Assn. Vol. Coordinators, 1978-80, Galveston County Assn. Social Service Dirs., 1978-80. Mem. Golden Key, Phi Theta Kappa, Phi Delta Phi. Home: 13126 Trailhollow St Houston TX 77079

PACKER, KATHERINE HELEN, librarian, educational administrator; b. Toronto, Ont., Can., Mar. 20, 1918; d. Cleve Alexander and Rosa Ruel (Dibblee) Smith; m. William A. Packer, Sept. 27, 1941; 1 dau., Marianne Katherine. B.A., U. Toronto, 1941; A.M.L.S., U. Mich., 1953; Ph.D., U. Md., 1975. Cataloguer William L Clements Library, U. Mich., 1953-55, U. Man. (Can.) Library, Winnipeg, 1956-59; cataloguer U. Toronto Library, 1959-63; asst. prof. Faculty Library Sci., 1967-75, assoc. prof., 1975-78, prof., dean, 1979-84, prof. emeritus, 1984—; head cataloguer York U. Library, Toronto, 1963-64; chief librarian Ont. Coll. Edn., Toronto, 1964-67; Can. Council Library Schs. rep. to Adv. Bd. on Sci. and Tech. Info., NRC Can., 1976-78. Author: Early American School Books, 1954. Recipient Disting. Alumnus award U. Mich., 1981. Mem. Can. Library Assn. (Howard Phalin award 1972), Phi Kappa Phi. Home: 53 Gormley Ave, Toronto, ON Canada M4V 1Y9 Office: U Toronto, Faculty Library and Info Sci, 140 Saint George St, Toronto, ON Canada M5S 1A1

PADBERG, HELEN SWAN, violinist; b. Shawnee, Okla., May 3, 1919; d. Frank P. and Birdie B. (Rudell) Swan; A.A., Stephens Coll., 1938; Mus.B., U. Okla., 1940; Mus.M., Northwestern U., 1941; student Jacques Gordon; m. Frank Padberg, Feb. 6, 1943; children—Frank, Kristen. Solo performances and concerts, 1932—; mem. faculty string quartet and symphony soloist Stephens Coll., 1937-38; violinist Oklahoma City Symphony Summer Concerts, 1940; soloist Northwestern U. Symphony, 1941; USO performer, 1941-43; violinist Nat. Orchestral Assn. and Am. Youth Orch., N.Y.C., 1944-46; tchr. strings Maywood (Ill.), 1946-47; asst. concertmaster West Suburban Symphony, Chgo., 1947-48; mem. Chgo. Women's Symphony, Chgo. Civic Orch. and chamber music groups, 1947-51; violinist Ark. String Trio, 1952-58; concertmaster Ark. Symphony and Little Rock Philharmonic, 1953-57, Marjorie Lawrence TV Series, Ark., 1953-54; pvt. tchr. violin, Little Rock, 1953-66; accompanist and performer on piano, harp. Pres., Ark. Med. Soc. Aux., 1962-63, historian, 1963—; co-founder Little Rock Chamber Music Soc., 1954; pres. bd. dirs. Vis. Nurse Assn. of Pulaski County, Ark., 1967-69; chmn. Women Assocs. Internat. Vis. Ctr. Chgo., 1988—. Mem. Am. Harp Soc., Chgo. Harp Soc. (sec. 1979-84), Am. Fedn. Musicians, Am. Opera Soc. of Chgo. (v.p. and program chmn. 1981-82, pres. 1984-87), Pi Kappa Lambda, Mu Phi Epsilon, Pi Beta Phi (pres. Little Rock Alumnae Club). Presbyterian. Clubs: Aesthetic (pres. Little Rock); Womens' Athletic of Chgo. Home: 175 E Delaware Pl Chicago IL 60611

PADDEN, LORRAINE KAY, electrical engineer; b. Ekalaka, Mont., Nov. 9, 1960; d. Benjamin Folsom and Dorothy (Brewer) P.; m. Robert W. Chin, June 6, 1987. BSEE, S.D. Sch. of Mines and Tech., 1983. Tester Grand Electric Coop., Buffalo, S.D., 1980-81; engring. apprentice Marathon Pipeline Co., Powell, Wyo., 1982; engr. Shell Oil Co., Houston, 1983-84; assoc. facilities engr. Shell Western Exploration and Prodn. Inc., Houston, 1984-87, facilities engr., 1987—; tutor Gulf Coast Alliance for Minority Engrs., Houston, 1983-87. Mem. Power Engring. Soc. of IEEE (sec.-treas. 1982-83, Outstanding Service award 1983, Certs. of Merit 1983-87), Soc. Petroleum Engrs., Instrumentation Soc. Am. Methodist. Home: PO Box 820269 Houston TX 77282 Office: Shell Western Exploration & Prodn Inc PO Box 576 Houston TX 77001

PADDOCK, SUSAN C., educational administrator, consultant, researcher; b. Madison, Wis., Sept. 23, 1947; d. Robert H. and Elizabeth I. (Church) P. BA, U. Wis.-Madison, 1969; MA in Teaching, U. Mass., 1971; PhD, U. Oreg., 1977. Info. specialist U. Mass., Amherst, 1970-71; tchr. Atlantic City Pub. High Schs., 1971-74, Eugene (Oreg.) Pub. Schs., 1974-76; grad. research assoc. U. Oreg., Eugene, 1976-77; faculty research assoc. Ariz. State U., Tempe, 1977-81, dir. advanced pub. exec. programs, 1981—; acting dir. staff devel., State of Ariz., Phoenix, 1982-83; cons. Ark. Dept. Edn., Little Rock, 1980-86, Scottsdale Pub. Schs., Ariz., 1982-83, Dorothy Garste Ctr., 1987. Author: (monograph) Community Education Leadership Series, 1981, Collaborative C.E. Training, 1977; co-author: Education Policy and Management, 1980; co-editor: Education Equity and Leadership Jour. 1979-83; contbr. chpts. to books, articles to profl. jours. Trainer and leader Ariz. Cactus-Pine Girl Scouts U.S., 1982-86; sec. Library Bd., Tempe, 1982-86; bd. dirs. Ariz. Foster Care Review Bd., 1982-87, Tempe Pub. Library, 1983-86; elder Univ. Presbyn. Ch., Tempe, 1984-86. Mem. Am. Soc. Tng. (com. mem. 1983-85), Nat. Community Edn. Assn. (com. chmn. 1980-81), Ariz. Community Edn. Assn. (pres. 1981-82). Am. Soc. Pub. Adminstrs., Am. Ednl. Research Assn., Nat. Cert. Pub. Mgr. Consortium (chmn. 1982-83), Internat. Personnel Mgmt. Assn. (chpt. bd. dirs. 1987—), Western Social Sci. Assn., Phi Delta Kappa, Alpha Gamma Delta (adv. Tempe chpt. 1986-88). Democrat. Office: Arizona State Univ Sch of Pub Affairs Adv Pub Exec Program Tempe AZ 85287-0503

PADEN, BETTY BURNS, education educator; b. Evanston, Ill., July 9, 1937; d. Joseph Ferdinand and Estelle (Taggart) Burns; m. Alvin Robert Paden, Aug. 18, 1962; children: Renee Lynn, Tina Jo. AA, Kendall Coll., 1958; BA, Roosevelt U., 1961, MA, 1963; EdD, Loyola U., Chgo., 1970; JD, No. Ill. U., 1979. Bar: Ill. 1980. Tchr. Chgo. Pub. Schs., 1961-67; editor, writer Scott Foresman Pub. Co., Glenview, Ill., 1967-68; instr. Loyola U., 1968-70; cons., author Addison-Wesley Pub. Co., Scott Foresman Pub. Co., Lyon and Carhahan Pub. Co., Tangley Oaks Pub. Co., Harper Row Pub. Co., 1967-82, Chgo. Bd. Edn., State of Ill., Chgo. Consortium of Colls. and Univs., 1973-82; prof. elem. edn. Northeastern Ill. U., Chgo., 1970—, assoc. chair elem. edn. dept., 1972-77; sole practice, Evanston, Ill., 1980—. Author, editor: More Power and Moving Ahead, Open Highways Series, 1968, What Are They Up To? and What Does It Take?, 1971, What a Week!, Carmen Takes a Bow, Jamila, The Young America Basic Reading Program, 1973, The Ruby Pin Mystery, 1976, Truth is Stranger Than Fiction, 1981, What is Big? What is Small?, Ann's Suprise, Make a Clown, 1983. Alderman City of Evanston; bd. dirs. Evanston Zoning Bd. Appeals, Evanston Community Devel. Corp. Named Woman of Yr., NAACP, 1983; Kalm scholar, 1957-58; Com. Organized Research, Northeastern Ill. U. grantee, 1974-75, UNI grantee, 1985-86; UNI Found. fellow, 1984, UNI Kellogg fellow, 1984. Mem. ABA, Ill. Bar Assn., Chgo. Bar Assn., Internat. Reading Assn., Assn. Supervision and Curriculum Devel., Assn. Tchr. Educators. Office: 5500 N St Louis Ave Room 3019 Chicago IL 60625

PADEN, CAROLYN EILEEN BELKNAP, dietitian; b. Takoma Park, Md., Dec. 10, 1953; d. Donald Julius and Lydian Allyne (Plyer) Belknap; m. Raymond Louis Paden, Dec. 29, 1985. BS in Home Econs. cum laude, Southern Coll., 1977; MS in Nutrition, Loma Linda (Calif.) U., 1983. Registered dietitian. Dietitic tech. Loma Linda U. Med. Ctr., 1978-82, nutritional support dietitian, 1982-84; clin. dietitian Mercy Meml. Med. Ctr., St. Joseph, Mich., 1984-86, chief clin. dietitian, 1986—; instr. dietetics Andrews U., Berrien Springs, Mich., 1986—; researcher nutritional status of hospitalized patients Mercy Meml. Med. Ctr., St. Joseph, 1986, 87; cons. nutritional support various Berrien County hosps., 1984—. Mem. Am. Dietetic Assn., Am. Soc. Parenteral and Enteral Nutrition. Adventist. Home: 195 Knott Rd Niles MI 49120 Office: Mercy Meml Med Ctr 1234 Napier Ave Saint Joseph MI 49085

PADGETT, GERALDINE WETHERINGTON, educator; b. Ft. Lauderdale, Fla., June 4, 1950; d. James Barney and Geneva Ethel (McKenzie) Wetherington; m. Wayne H. Padgett, June 23, 1972; children: Stacey Michelle, Brian Wayne. BA in Elem. Edn., Palm Beach Atlantic Coll., 1972; MEd, U. Louisville. Clk. Broward County License Tag Bur., Ft. Lauderdale, 1969-71; tchr. Spencer County Elementary, Taylorsville, Ky., 1978-86, Westward Elementary Sch., West Palm Beach, 1987, Wynnebrook Elem. Sch., West Palm Beach, 1987—. Mem. com. on edn. Harvey Sloane Gubernatorial Candidate, Louisville, Ky., 1981. Mem. Internat. Reading Assn., Palm Beach County Reading Council, Phi Kappa Phi. Democrat. Baptist. Club: Homemakers (v.p. 1980-82) (Taylorsville). Home: 820 Mimosa Ct West Palm Beach FL 33416

PADGETT, MARTHA WADE, retail buyer, consultant; b. Lynchburg, Va., Oct. 22, 1954; d. Winston Irvin and Helen Gertrude (Worsham) P. Student, Longwood Coll., 1973-75; BS, Va. Poly. Inst. and State U., 1977. Mgmt. trainee Leggett Dept. Store, Manassas, Va., 1977-78; coordinator BARS/MIR Leggett Dept. Store, Westminster, Md., 1978, divisional mgr., 1978-82; divisional mgr. Leggett Dept. Store, Dover, Del., 1982-84, Lynchburg, 1984-87; mktg. cons. Sta. WJJS Radio, Lynchburg, 1988—. Mem. Rape Companion Program. Mem. Nat. Assn. Female Execs., Kappa Omicron Phi. Home: 1300 I Weeping Willow Dr Lynchburg VA 24501

PADILLA, ALMA J., chemist; b. Peñaranda, Nueva Ecija, Philippines, Apr. 29, 1944; came to U.S., 1966; d. Gil V. and Lydia (Justo) P. BS in Chemistry, U. Santo Tomas, Philippines, 1963; MS in Chemistry, Northeastern U., 1969. Registered chemist, Philippines. Research trainee indsl. research div. Nat. Inst. Sci. Tech., Manila, 1963-64; tchr. chemistry, math, physics U. Santo Tomas High Sch., Manila, 1964-66; teaching asst. Northeastern U., Boston, 1966-69; from asst. scientist to assoc. scientist organic chemistry dept. Polaroid Corp., Cambridge, Mass., 1969-78, assoc. scientist to scientist black & white photog. lab, 1978-84, scientist polymer dept., magnetics group, 1984-85; scientist PB Diagnostic Systems, Cambridge, Mass., 1985—. Mem. Am. Chem. Soc. Roman Catholic.

PADILLA, GERALDINE VALDES, research scientist, educator, dean; b. Manila, Philippines, Feb. 28, 1940; d. Jose Mariano and Ruby Pilar (Baugh) Valdes; (parents Am. citizens); m. Gilbert J. Padilla, June 30, 1966 (dec. Jan. 1985); children: Mark J., Mathew L. BA, Assumption Coll., Manila, 1962; MA, Ateneo U., Manila, 1965; PhD, UCLA, 1971. Research asst. Ateneo U., Manila, 1964-65, UCLA, 1967-68; instr. Calif. State U., Dominguez Hills, Calif., spring 1970, Los Angeles, 1981-86, thesis adv., 1982-88; dir. nursing research City of Hope Nat. Med. Ctr., Duarte, Calif., 1970-85; research scientist, 1986-87, assoc. dean research, UCLA, 1987—; cons. Nat. Cancer Inst., Bethesda, Md., 1983—, Luth. Hosp. Soc. So. Calif., 1983—; mem. cancer control grant rev. com. USPHS Nat. Cancer Inst., 1983-87. Author: Interacting with Dying Patients, 1975; contbr. articles to profl. jours. Mem. Am. Psychol. Assn., Sigma Theta Tau. Democrat. Roman Catholic. Office: UCLA Sch Nursing 10833 Le Conte Ave Le Conte CA 90024-1702

PADILLA, LORRAINE MARIE, insurance company executive; b. Bklyn., Mar. 24, 1952; d. Amerigo L. and Helen M. (Mosca) Muratore; m. Samuel P. Padilla, Aug. 21, 1977; 1 child, Adam L. BS in Math., NYU, 1973. CLU., chartered fin. cons. Contract's actuarial specialist N.Am. Reassurance Co., N.Y.C., 1973-75; regional mgr. pension sales The Phoenix, N.Y.C., 1975—; instr. pension retirement planning and employee benefits Nat. Inst. Fin., N.J., 1980-85. Nat. Merit and Regents scholar, 1969. Mem. Gen. Agts. and Mgrs. Assn., Nat. Life Underwriters, Women Life Underwriters, Chartered Life Underwriters, Snug Harbor Cultural Ctr., N.Y. Mus. Natural History. Republican. Roman Catholic. Home: 40 Mallow St Staten Island NY 10309 Office: The Phoenix 888 7th Ave 44th fl New York NY 10106

PADZENSKY, ROCHELLE G., bookkeeping service executive; b. Chgo., July 4, 1936; d. Edward H. and Mary B. (Battock) Kreisman; m. Herbert R. Padzensky, June 17, 1956; children—Leslie Jay, Lori Beth. Bookkeeper, Lincoln Finance Co., Denver, 1955-56; teller Colo. Indsl. Bank, Denver, 1956-57, Peoples Bank, Cedar Rapids, Iowa, 1957-58; supr. mktg. research surveys Frank Magid Assocs., Denver, 1969-72; savs. supr. Colo. Fed. Savs., Denver, 1973-78; sec. Perkin-Elmer Data Systems, Denver, 1978-79; v.p. KHL Corp., Denver, 1979-85; owner, pres. Books Plus, 1985—. Named Outstanding Student, Savs. and Loan League, Denver, 1976, 77. Mem. Nat. Assn. Female Execs. Democrat. Jewish. Home: 3792 S Sebring Ct Denver CO 80237

PAGE, ANNE EICHELBERGER, violinist; b. Chattanooga, Mar. 5, 1953; d. Edward Lee and Martha Nell (Douthitt) Eichelberger; m. Joseph Thomas Page, June 10, 1978; children: Andrew Joseph, Hannah Carol. MusB, Fla. State U., 1975; MusM, Yale U., 1977, M in Mus. Arts, 1978. Violinist Atlanta Chamber Players, 1978—, Atlanta Opera Orch., 1980—, Atlanta Virtuosi, 1984—, Lullwater String Quartet, Atlanta, 1984—; concertmaster Atlanta Pops Orch., 1984—; violin teaching affiliate Emory U., Atlanta, 1978-79; music history faculty affiliate Mercer U., Atlanta, 1978-79; performer Eastern Music Festival, Greensboro, N.C., 1976, 77, numerous recordings and television programs, 1978—; performed with Atlanta New Music Ensemble, Carnegie Hall, N.Y.C., 1982; toured Spain and Italy with Atlanta Virtuosi, 1988. Mem. Ch. of Christ. Address: 1136 Gunnison St Clarkston GA 30021

PAGE, ANNE RUTH, educator, education specialist; b. Norfolk, Va., Apr. 13, 1949; d. Amos Purnell and Ruth Martin (Hill) Bailey; m. Peter Smith Page, Apr. 24, 1971; children: Edgar Bailey, Emmett McBrannon. BA, N.C. Wesleyan Coll.; student, Fgn. Lang. League; postgrad., N.C. State U.; student, Overseas Linguistic Studies, France, Spain, Eng., 1978, 85, 86. Cert. tchr., N.C. Tchr. Cary (N.C.) Sr. High Sch., 1971-72; tchr., head dept. Daniels Middle Sch., Raleigh, N.C., 1978-83; tchr., head gifted, talented dept. Martin Middle Sch., Raleigh, N.C., 1983—; dir. student group Overseas Studies, Am. Council for Internat. Studies, France, Spain, Eng., 1982, 84, 86; bd. dirs. N.T.M. Inc., Washington; participant Mentor Program, Wake County Pub. Schs., 1988. Sunday sch. tchr. Fairmont United Meth. Ch., Raleigh, 1983-85. Mem. Alpha Delta Kappa. Democrat. Club: Weswyn. Home: 349 Wilmot Dr Raleigh NC 27606 Office: Martin Middle Sch GT 1701 Ridge Rd Raleigh NC 27607

PAGE, BRENDA DEE, personnel director; b. Grand Rapids, Mich., May 17, 1955; d. Benjamin F. and Mary Dell (Parsons) Pratt; m. John R. Page, Oct. 4, 1980. BA in Psychology cum laude, DePauw U., 1977; MS in Indsl. Relations with honors, Purdue U., 1979. Employment rep. Inland Steel Co., Chgo., 1979-80; coordinator EEO Gen. Motors Corp., Marion, Ind., 1981-82, labor relations rep., 1982-83, engr. mfg., 1983-84, staff asst. personnel, 1984-85; supr. labor relations Cadillac div. Detroit, 1985-86, personnel adminstr., 1986-87; mgr. salaried human resources Cadillac div. GMC, Detroit, 1987—. Sponsor Jr. Achievement, Grant County, Ind., 1982-84; bd. dirs. Minority Tng. Council, Marion, 1983-85. Mem. Indsl. Relations Assn. Detroit, Am. Mgmt. Assn. Republican. Methodist. Office: Gen Motors Corp 2860 Clark St Detroit MI 43232

PAGE, JOYCE ANN, human resources executive; b. Franklin, Pa., Oct. 17, 1943; d. Edward John Lukasik and Rosemary (Bennett) Lukasik; m. Constantine Page, Aug. 28, 1976; children: Christopher Page, Gregory Page. MusB, Sherwood Music Sch., 1965; student, U. Chgo., 1961-65; postgrad., Loyola U., Chgo., 1966. Tchr. music Wurlitzer Co., Chgo., 1970-71; adminstrv. asst. to pres. Pain and Sutherlin, Inc., Chgo., 1971-73; dir. personnel OmRon Corp. of Am., Chgo., 1973-76; adminstrv. asst. to head Lyric Opera, Chgo., 1979-81; owner, pres. Page Bus. Services, Inc., Chgo., 1981—; cons. Women Employed, Chgo., 1985-87. Mem. Nat. Assn. Female Execs., Nat. Assn. Women Bus. Owners, Chgo. Assn. Commerce and Industry. Republican. Roman Catholic. Office: Page Bus Services Inc 32 W Washington Suite 402 Chicago IL 60602

PAGE, LINDA KAY, state official; b. Wadsworth, Ohio, Oct. 4, 1943; s. Frederick Meredith and Martha Irene (Vance) P. Student Franklin U., 1970-75, Sch. Banking, Ohio U., 1976-77; cert. Nat. Personnel Sch., U. Md.-Am. Bankers Assn., 1981; grad. banking program U. Wis.-Madison, 1982-84. Asst. v.p., gen. mgr. Bancohio Corp., Columbus, Ohio, 1975-78, v.p., dist. mgr., 1979-80, v.p., mgr. employee relations, 1980-81, v.p., div. mgr., 1982-83; commr. of banks State of Ohio, Columbus, 1983-87, dir. Commerce, 1988—; guest speaker, lectr. various banking groups. Bd. dirs. Clark County Mental Health Bd., Springfield, Ohio, 1982-83, Springfield Met. Housing, 1982-83; bd. advisers Orgn. Indsl. Standards, Springfield, 1982-83; trustee League Against Child Abuse, 1986—; treas bd. trustees Ohio Housing Fin. Agy., 1988. Recipient Leadership Columbus award Sta. WTVN and Columbus Leadership Program, 1975, 82, Outstanding Service award Clark County Mental Health Bd., 1983. Mem. Nat. Assn. Bank Women (pres. 1980-81), Bus. and Profl. Women's Club, LWV, Conf. State Bank Suprs. (bd. dirs. 1984-85), dist. chmn. 1984-85), Ohio Bankers Assn. (bd. dirs. 1982-83). Democrat. Lodge: Zonta. Avocations: tennis; animal protection; matchbook collecting, reading, golf. Home: 1330 Erickson Ave Columbus OH 43227 Office: Dept Commerce Div of Banks 2 Natiowide Plaza Columbus OH 43215

PAGE, MARJORIE EILEEN, county officia.; b. Stratton, Nebr., July 21, 1920; d. Coral and Ruby Eleanor (Clark) Brouse; m. Harold Ray Page, May 18, 1947; 1 child, James Edward. Student pub. schs., Littleton, Colo. Clk. Clerk & Recorder's Office, Littleton, Colo., 1941-48, dep. clk., 1948-56, clk., recorder, 1956—. Bd. dirs. Met. Mental Health Assn., Arapahoe chpt., 1963-65; active various fund raising orgns.; mem. Sewell Found. Aux. Named Woman of Yr., Englewood Bus. and Profl. Women's Club, 1962-63; Disting. Service award, Nat. Assn. Counties, 1982; Clk. of Yr., Nat. Assn. County Recorders and Clks., 1982, others. Mem. Colo. Assn. County Clks. and Recorders (sec.-treas.), Nat. Assn. County Recorders and Clks. (pres. 1974-75), Nat. Assn. Counties (dir. 1985-87), Englewood Bus. and Profl. Women's Club, Centennial C. of C. Lutheran. Republican. Club: Zonta. Avocations; hiking; cooking; collecting antiques. Home: 5 Robincrest Ln Littleton CO 80123 Office: Arapahoe County Clerk and Recorder 5334 S Prince St Littleton CO 80166

PAGE, RUTH, dancer; b. Indpls., Mar. 22, 1899; d. Lafayette and Marian (Heinly) P.; m. Thomas Hart Fisher, Feb. 8, 1925; m. Andre Delfan, May 16, 1983. Studied under, Enrico Cecchetti, Monte Carlo, 1925; student, Tudor Hall, N.Y.C.; hon. L.H.D., Ind. U., 1983, DePaul U., Chgo., 1984, U. Ill., 1985, Lincoln Coll., 1985. Dancer, with Pavlowa at age of 15; performed leading role in J. Alden Carpenter's The Birthday of the Infanta produced by Chgo. Opera Co., 1919; later in N.Y.C.; toured U.S. as prin. dancer with Adolph Bolm's Ballet, later appeared in London, with Mr. Bolm; premier danseuse, 2d Music Box Revue, N.Y.C., 1921-23; premiere danseuse, Chgo. Allied Arts performances, 1924, 25, 26, Municipal Opera Co., Buenos Aires, Ravinia Opera Co., 1926-31; dancer with Diaghilev's Ballet Russe de Monte Carlo, 1925; guest soloist with Met. Opera Co., 1926-28; guest artist at enthronement ceremonies for Emperor Hirohito, Japan, 1928; performed series of Am. dances before Sophil Soc., Moscow, 1930; ballet dir., Chgo. Opera, 1934-37, 42-43, 45; dir., Fed. Theatre Dance Project, Chgo., 1938-39; S.Am. tour with first dance group as co-dir., Page-Stone Ballet, 1940, guest choreographer with Bentley Stone; dancer: Frankie and Johnny for Ballet Russe de Monte Carlo, 1945; guest choreographer, dancer: The Bells for Ballet, Russe de Monte Carlo, 1946, Billy Sunday, 1948, Impromptu au Bois, and Revanche, Les Ballets des Champs-Elysees, 1951, Royal Festival Ballet, Vilia, 1953; co-dir., Les Ballets Americains, Theatre des Champs Elysees, Paris, 1950; ballet mistress, Chgo. Lyric Opera, 1954-69; choreographer, dir. Ruth Page's Chgo. Opera Ballet, 1956-66, Ruth Page's Internat. Ballet, 1966-70; pres. Ruth Page Found. Sch. of Dance, Chgo., 1971—; choreographer: Merry Widow Ballet, 1956, Susanna and the Barber, 1957, Salome, 1957, Triumph of Chastity, 1958, El Amor Brujo, 1958, Camille, 1958, Carmen, 1959, Fledermaus, 1960, Concertino, 1961, Mefistofela, 1962, Bullets or Bon-Bons, 1965, Nutcracker, 1965-76, Carmina Burana, 1966, Bolero, 1967, Dancer's Ritual, 1968, Alice in the Garden, 1970, also Alice in Wonderland and Alice Through the Looking Glass at Pitts. Ballet Theatre, 1971, Catulli Carmina, 1973, Chain of Fools, 1973; restaged Die Fledermaus, PBS prodn., 1986; lectr. tour: Ruth Page's Invitation to the Dance, 1971-72; Author: Class, A Selection of Notes on Dance Classes Around the World, 1916-1980, 1985. Contbr. to mags. Recipient award Adult Council Greater Chgo., 1963, citation outstanding service Ballet Guild Chgo., Mahariski award Columbia U., 1977, Ill. Assn. Dance Cos. award for outstanding service to dance, 1978, Community Arts Found. award, 1978, Dance Mag. award, 1980, medals of merit Mayors Daley, Byrne, Chgo., Ill. Gubernatorial award, 1985, Peabody award for Merry Widow prodn., PBS, 1985, Ruth Page Week at Ravinia, 1985. Mem. Chgo. Nat. Assn. Dance Masters (hon.). Clubs: Arts (Chgo.), Friday (Chgo.), Racquet (Chgo.). Address: Ruth Page Found Sch Dance 1016 N Dearborn St Chicago IL 60610 *

PAGE, SALLY JACQUELYN, university official; b. Saginaw, Mich., July, 1943; d. William Henry and Doris Effie (Knippel) P.; B.A., U. Iowa, 1965; M.B.A., So. Ill. U., 1973. Copy editor, C.V. Mosby Co., St. Louis, 1965-69; edit. cons. Edit. Assos., Edwardsville, Ill., 1969-70; research adminstr. So. Ill. U., 1970-74, asst. to pres., affirmative action officer, 1974-77; civil rights officer U. N.D., Grand Forks, 1977—, lectr. mgmt., 1978—; polit. commentator Sta. KFJM, Nat. Public Radio affiliate, 1981—. Contbr. to profl. jours. Chairperson N.D. Equal Opportunity Affirmative Action Officers, 1987-88; pres., Pine to Prairie council Girl Scouts U.S.A., 1980-85 ; mem. employment com. Ill. Commn. on Status of Women, 1976-77; mem. Bicentennial Com. Edwardsville, 1976, Bikeway Task Force Edwardsville, 1975-77; mem. Civil Service Rev. Task Force, Grand Forks, 1982, civil service commr., 83, chmn., 1984, 86. Mem. AAUW (dir. Ill. 1975-77), Coll. and Univ. Personnel Assn. (research and publs. bd. 1982-84) Am. Assn. Affirmative Action, Soc. Research Adminstrs., M.B.A. Assn. Republican. Presbyterian. Home: 3121 Cherry St Grand Forks ND 58201 Office: Univ ND Grand Forks ND 58202

PAGE, SARA MARIE, social worker; b. Wheeling, W.Va., Oct. 25, 1940; d. Dominic R. and Josephine L. (Giardino) Page; 1 child, Eve Marie; BA cum laude, Muskingum Coll., 1963; MSW, Case Western Res. U., 1965. Lic. clin. social worker. Sr. psychiat. social worker Akron (Ohio) Child Guidance Ctr., 1965-71; chief social worker, children's unit Ga. Mental Health Inst., Atlanta, 1972-75, program dir., children's unit, 1975-77; pvt. practice psychiat. social work, Atlanta; field instr. grad. social work Western Res. U., U. Ga. Mem. Nat. Assn. Social Workers, Acad. Cert. Social Workers, Atlanta Mental Health Assn. Home: 5465 Mt Vernon Pkwy NW Atlanta GA 30327 Office: 6111 Peachtree Dunwoody Rd Suite F-103 Atlanta GA 30328

PAGELS, CARRIE FANCETT, psychologist, educator, consultant; b. Newberry, Mich., Jan. 5, 1958; d. William Henry and Ruby Evelyn (Skidmore) F.; m. Jeffrey D. Pagels. B.A. in Psychology, Lake Superior State Coll., 1978; student Whittier Coll., 1976-77; M.A. in Sch. Psychology, U. S.C., 1981; Ph.D. in Sch. Psychology, 1984. Lic. psychologist., cert. sch. psychologists; Cert. sch. psychologist, III, S.C. Research asst. U. S.C., Columbia, 1979-80, 81-83; instr., 1983; instr. Lake Superior State Coll., Sault Ste. Marie, Mich., 1981; sch. psychologist III Head Start Program, Columbia, 1983-86, Charleston, 1987— ; child psychotherapist Counseling and Readjustment Services, Columbia, 1985—; psychologist Children's Hosp., Columbia, 1983—; clin. asst. prof. U. S.C. Sch. Medicine, Columbia, 1984—; sch. psychologist Berkeley County Schs., 1986-87; pvt. sch. psychologist, North Charleston, 1987—; cons. Richland Meml. Hosp., Columbia, 1983, Divorce Mediation Project, Columbia, 1982, Life Satisfaction Grant, Columbia, 1979-81. Contbr. chpt. to book. Campaign aide Democratic party, U.S. Senate race, Sault Ste. Marie, Mich., 1978. Stephenson scholar, 1978; NIMH fellow, 1980-81. Mem. Am. Psychol. Assn., Nat. Perinatal Assn., S.C. Assn. Sch. Psychologists, Nat. Assn. Female Execs. Democrat. Episcopalian. Avocations: writing fiction; computers; reading; aerobics. Home: 8425 Deerwood Dr Charleston Heights SC 29418 Office: Richland Meml Hosp Div Neonatology Columbia SC 29210

PAGELS, ELAINE HIESEY, historian of religion, educator; b. Palo Alto, Calif., Feb. 13, 1943; d. William McKinley and Louise Sophia (Boogaert) Hiesey; B.A., Stanford, 1964, M.A., 1965; Ph.D., Harvard, 1970; m. Heinz R. Pagels, June 7, 1969. Asst. prof. history of religion Barnard Coll., Columbia, 1970-74, from asso. prof. to prof., chairperson dept. religion, 1974-82; Harrington Spear Paine prof. religion Princeton U., 1982—. Nat. Endowment Humanities grantee, 1973; Mellon fellow Aspen Inst. Humanistic Studies, 1974, Hazen fellow, 1975; Rockefeller fellow, 1978-79; Guggenheim fellow, 1979-80; MacArthur prize fellow, 1981-87. Mem. Soc. Bibl. Lit., Am. Acad. Religion. Episcopalian. Club: Bibl. Theologians. Author: The Johannine Gospel in Gnostic Exegesis, 1973, The Gnostic Paul, 1975, The Gnostic Gospels, 1979, Adam, Eve and The Serpent, 1988.

PAGLIO, LYDIA ELIZABETH, editor; b. Providence; d. Victor and Lydia Anne (DiPrete) P. B.A., N.Y. U., 1970. Researcher Young Pres. Orgn., 1970-71; editorial asst. Sport mag., N.Y.C., 1971-72; assoc. editor True Experience, also True Love mags., N.Y.C., 1972-73; editor True Experience mag., 1973-81; assoc. editor Dell Pub., N.Y.C., 1983; editor Dell Pub., 1983-84, sr. editor, 1984-87, dir. Candlelight Ecstasy Romances, 1984-87; sr. editor Zebra Books, Pinnacle Books, 1987—; dir. publicity Dancer's World, Springfield, Mass., 1978-80. Pres., sec., mem. exec. com. West Side Community Recycling Corp. 1979-81. Mem. Editorial Free-lance Assn. (dir. 1984), Sigma Delta Chi. Home: 41 W 82d St New York NY 10024 Office: Zebra Books 475 Park Ave S New York NY 10016

PAIGE, RUTH ULLMANN, psychologist; b. Germany, May 4; came to U.S., 1938, naturalized, 1946; d. Adolf and Else (Heumann-Abraham) Ullmann; B.A., Bklyn. Coll., 1956; M.S. (scholar), CUNY, 1957; postgrad. U. Kans., Lawrence, 1957-60; Ph.D., U. Oreg., Eugene, 1978; m. Albert B. Paige, Mar. 20, 1954; children—David, Elizabeth, Rebekah. Teaching and research asst. counseling psychology U. Kans., 1957-58; sch. psychologist, Shawnee, Kans., 1958-59; remedial reading instr., also pvt. practice, Lawrence, 1957-63; psychologist Lawrence-Douglas County Mental Health Clinic, 1959-63; psychology research asst. Menninger Clinic, Topeka, 1963; psychology research asst. VA Hosp., Leavenworth, Kans., 1964-65; counselor Group Processes, Inc., Seattle, 1969-72; psychologist intern Snohomish County Mental Health Clinic, Everett, Wash., 1973-74, Highline-West Seattle Mental Health Ctr., 1974-75; dir. Counseling Ctr. programs North Seattle Community Coll., 1979-86; pvt. practice clin. psychology, Seattle, 1985—; psychologist, cons. Terrap, Bellevue, Wash., 1987—; cons. family mediation King County Family Ct., 1978-86; instr. Lane Community Coll., 1972-73; vol. instr. U. Oreg., 1972-73. Mem. Am. Psychol. Assn., Western Psychol. Assn., Wash. State Psychol. Assn. (pres. 1985), Assn. Women in Psychology, Counseling and Guidance Dirs. Assn. Wash. Community Colls. (pres. 1981-82), N.W. Family Therapy Inst. Contbr. articles to profl. jours. Home: 13436 NE 47th St Bellevue WA 98005 Office: Nordstrom Med Tower 1229 Madison Suite 890 Seattle WA 98104

PAINE, MERLYN LANSING, environmental services administrator; b. San Mateo, Calif., Apr. 30, 1949; d. Stuart Douglas Lansing and Margaret (Sharrah) P.; m. James Julian Rhode, June 10, 1988. BA, Stanford U., 1971; MS, Oregon State U., 1978. Cert. energy auditor. Research asst. marine biology U. Calif., Santa Barbara, 1967-68; research asst. anthropology Stanford (Calif.) U., 1970-71, asst. dir. social and political issues program, 1973-75; comprehensive planner natural resources Deschutes County, Bend, Oreg., 1978-80; project mgr. and assoc. Ctr. 4 Engring., Redmond, Oreg., 1980-82; prin. planner CH2M Hill, Anchorage, 1982; project mgr., engr. Alaska Power Authority, Anchorage, 1983-84; regional environ. coordinator and section chief Alaska Dept. Transp. and Public Facilities, Anchorage, 1984—; Preceptor, instr. women/minorities course Stanford U., 1975, natural resources Salem (Oreg.) Pub. Schs., 1978. Contbr. articles to profl. jours; choral mem. Anchorage Civic Opera, 1984-86. V.p. Russian Jack Condominium Assn., Anchorage, 1982-88; vol. KSKA pub. radio sta., Anchorage, 1984-87, Clean Air Coalition, Anchorage, 1986-88; research assoc. Ecology Action, Palo Alto, Calif., 1976, Covelo (Calif.) Citizens' Group, 1977. Scholar Calif. Scholarship Fedn., 1966-67; grantee Newhouse Found., 1970-71. Mem. Alaska Assoc. Environ. Profls. (founder and dir. 1984-87), Calif. Assoc. Environ. Profls., Nat. Assoc. Environ. Profls., Audubon Soc., Stanford Alumni Assoc., Anchorage (pres. 1984-86). Office: Alaska Dept Transp PO Box 196900 4111 Aviation Dr Anchorage AK 99519-6900

PAINE, SALLY JANE, computer asisted telecommunications company executive; b. Haverhill, England, Apr. 4, 1938; came to U.S., 1974, naturalized, 1983; d. William Vinter Gurteen and Mary Cooper; m. G. Eustis Paine, Sept. 13, 1975. Owner, Boutique, England, 1962-65; pres. Anchor Foods, Virgin Islands, 1977-81; corp. sec. The Wine Exchange Ltd., Phila., 1984—. Republican. Mem. Ch. of England. also: Wex France, 1 Ave de Verdun, 33500 Libourne France also: Wine Exchange UK Ltd, Asphalte House Palace St, London SW1 E5HS, England

PAINTER, JUDY ANN, advertising executive; b. Huntington, N.Y., July 23, 1952; d. Joseph Albert and Shirley Arlene (Stephens) P. B.A. in English, SUNY, 1981. Adminstrv. asst. Marsteller, N.Y.C., 1981-82; sr. writer Arrow Electronics, Melville, N.Y., 1982-83; Kopf & Isaacson, Melville, 1983-84; assoc. creative dir. Foote, Cone & Belding, N.Y.C., 1984—. Mem. L.I. Advt. Club (bd. dirs. 1986—, named Best on L.I. 1984). Republican. Home: 276 Moriches Rd Saint James NY 11780 Office: Foote Cone & Belding/LKP 101 Park Ave New York NY 10178

PAINTER, SARA ANN, hospital executive; b. Atlantic City, Sept. 5, 1937; d. Ethel Margaret Buchanan; m. Howard Twaddell Painter Jr., Sept. 19, 1964; children: Cynthia Louise, Lee-Ann Cheryl; stepchildren: Howard T. III, Gary Bruce. Diploma in nursing, Presby. Sch. Nursing, 1958; BS in Nursing, U. Pa., 1963, MS in Nursing, 1979; cert. in nursing adminstrn., Villanova, 1985. Instr., staff RN Presbyn. Med. Ctr., Phila., 1958-72, coordinator patient care, 1979-81, dir. nursing, 1981-83, asst. adminstr. for nursing, 1983-85; staff RN Riddle Meml. Hosp., Media, Pa., 1972-75; asst. instr. Sch. Nursing, Widener U., Chester, Pa., 1976-77; project cons. New Ralston House, Phila., 1986; cons., adminstr. nursing Nat. Technomics, West Chester, Pa., 1986; v.p. patient care service Good Samaritan Hosp., Pottsville, Pa., 1986—; preceptor, guest lectr. Nursing adminstrn. master's program Widener U., 1982-84; guest lectr. hosp. adminstrn. program, Temple U., Phila., 1983-84. Mem. adv. com. Area Vocat.-Tech. Sch., Marlin, Pa., 1987—, Franklin Acad., Pottsville, 1987—; mem. devel. com. Am. Heart Assn., Pottsville, 1987—. Honored by Chapel of Four Chaplains, 1984. Mem. Am. Orgn. Nurse Execs., Pa. Orgn. Nurse Execs. (ea. region), Presbyn. Sch. Nursing Alumni Assn. (pres. 1968-71, 81-83). Democrat. Presbyterian. Office: Good Samaritan Hosp Tremont and E Norwegian Sts Pottsville PA 17901

PAIR, ANNIE LEE, naval officer; b. Emporia, Va., Jan. 14, 1951; d. Henderson and Rosa (Ingram) P. BA in English, Va. Poly. Inst., 1973; MS in mgmt., USN Postgrad. Sch., 1983. Commd. ensign USN, 1974, advanced through grades to lt. comdr., 1984; personal services officer Amphibious Base, USN, Little Creek, Va., 1974-76; program mgr. to chief naval tech. tng. Millington, Tenn., 1976-77; asst. dir. technical services Naval Electronics System Security Engrs. Ctr. Washington, 1978-81, asst. for appraisal to Chief Naval Ops., 1983-86; commdg. officer Mil. Entrance Processing Sta. Cin., 1986—; asst. mgr. Foodmaker, Richmond, Va., 1977-78; sales assoc. Sampson and Assocs., Richmond, Va., 1978. Active ARC, Big Bros.-Big Sisters Am. Mem. Nat. Assn. Female Execs., Nat. Assn. Accts. Home: 5027 Hawaiian Terr Cincinnati OH 45223 Office: Mil Entrance Processing Sta 550 Main St Cincinnati OH 45202

PAISS, DORIS BELL, educational and psychological consultant, lecturer, educator; b. Phila., Nov. 19, 1929; d. Simon and Sarah (Freedman) Cohen; m. Lee Paiss, July 26, 1953; children—Jana, Michael. B.F.A., Barnard Coll., 1954; postgrad. Los Angeles City Coll., 1962-63; M.A., Columbia U., 1963, Ph.D. in Philosophy of Ancient Civilizations, 1976, degree in Geriatrics in Abnormal Psychology, 1978. Active Jewish education, 1963-86; edn. dir. M.D. Hoffman Regional Hebrew High Sch., Phila., 1973-83; coordinator Daroff Campus of Sr. Adult Studies, Raymond and Miriam Klein br. Jewish Community Ctr., Phila., 1982-85, mem. faculty Daroff Campus Adult Studies, 1978-85; cons. Life Care and Retirement, 1985-88; designing support and edn. programs for stress related memory loss; lectr. on stress, memory, time mgmt., devel. human potential, Phila., 1976-87, guest lectr. Columbia U., U. Wis., U. Calif.-Santa Barbara, Oberlin Coll., Rochester Inst. Tech., Rutgers U., U. Tampa, Coalition for Jewish Edn., writers' confs., community service orgns., indsl. seminars; mem. faculty Inst. Awareness, 1980-83, Satinsky Inst. for Blind, 1980-85; free-lance writer and producer comml., indsl. and edn. films, 1950-70. Recipient numerous awards. Mem. Nat. Assn. Female Execs., Am. Film Inst. Democrat. Jewish. Avocations: research on memory; show music.

PALACIOS, MARIANA ALICIA, pharmaceutical company executive; b. Havana, Cuba, Aug. 21, 1946; d. Jose Rosendo and Mariana (Fornaris) P.; m. William D. Zacek, Apr. 16, 1971 (div. Dec. 1984); m. Timothy W. Abbott, Apr. 22, 1988. BS, Barry U., 1966; MS, U. Miami, 1969; MBA, Rensselaer Poly. Inst., 1982. Research biologist Sterling Drug Inc., Rensselaer, N.Y., 1969-79, clin. research assoc., 1979-82, clin. coordinator; dir. licensing and acquisitions/internat. N.Y.C., 1985-87, dir. cardiovascular medicines/internat., 1987—. Contbr. articles to profl. jours. Mem. Licensing Execs. Soc., Pharm. Advt. Council. Republican. Office: Sterling Drug Inc 90 Park Ave New York NY 10016

PALADINO, GELSA (JELSA PALAO), singer-songwriter, educator; b. N.Y.C., Nov. 2, 1944; d. Rocco and Genevieve (Fascigone) P. Student, John Powers Modeling Sch., Dick Grove Music Sch., Tom Selden Acting Workshops, Am. Acad. Dramatic Arts; studies with Clark McClellan, Nancy Nash, Robert Edwards, Buddy Kaye. Owner Gelsa Music; recording artist Poplar Records, Laurel Records, Laurie Records, Madison Records, 1958-61; tchr. Cen. Juvenile Hall, McClarran Hall for abused children, Los Angeles, 1984-85. Appeared in various TV musical variety shows including Am. Bandstand, Fantasy Show, Ted Steele's Bandstand, Rosey Greer Show; composed spl. material for Sarah Vaughn, Frank Sinatra, Al Jarreau, Liza Minelli, and others; contbg. editor Songwriters Market, 1984-85, Music Connection Mag., 1983-84. Benefit performer numerous armed forces shows, City Hope, Muscular Dystrophy, Boys' Club, Lighthouse for Blind, VA hosps., Orgn. Rehab. Tng., various homes for aged. Recipient Women Achievement award Am.-Italian Assn., 1976. Mem. AFTRA, Am. Guild Variety Artists, Am. Fedn. Musicians U.S.-Can., Nat. Acad. Rec. Arts and Scis., Screen Actors Guild, B.M.I. Home: 6541 Kester Ave #205 Van Nuys CA 91411

PALANCA, TERILYN, information management consultant; b. Chicago Heights, Ill., Aug. 15, 1957; d. Raymond Anthony and Barbara Jean (Schweizer) P. BA, Coll. William and Mary, 1979; MBA, Rutgers U., 1983. Chief auditor, mgr. Williamsburg Hilton, Va., 1979-81; corp. auditor RCA Corp., Princeton, N.J., 1982-83; EDP cons. Price Waterhouse & Co., N.Y.C., 1983-84; data base adminstr. Chubb & Son, Inc., Warren, N.J., 1984-85; cons., tech. mgr. Applied Data Research, Inc., Princeton, N.J., 1985-88, cons., acct. mgr. Oracle Corp., Iselin, N.J., 1988—. Mem. Assn. of Inst. for Cert. Computer Profls. (cert. in data processing), Am. Mgmt. Assn., Nat. Assn. Female Execs. Republican. Avocations: Masterwork Chorus, pianist, literature, hiking, animal aid. Office: Oracle Corp 120 Wood Ave South Suite 401 Iselin NJ 08830

PALEY, RENÉE E., service executive; b. Portsmouth, Va., Jan. 3, 1945; d. William Eisnitz and Eleanor (Schoolman) Wishengrad; m. Howard S. Paley, Mar. 21, 1965 (separated); children: Marisa Anne, William Martin. Student, Antioch Coll., 1961-62; BA in English Lit., NYU, 1965; postgrad., Hunter Coll., 1966-68. Asst. photo editor Modern Photography Mag., N.Y.C., 1965-66; English tchr. Jamaica (N.Y.) High Sch., 1967-68; reporter Community Newspapers, Glen Cove, N.Y., 1974-80; editor The Westbury (N.Y.) Times, 1980, The Roslyn (N.Y.) News, 1980-81, Glen Cove Record-Pilot, 1981-84; community relations coordinator The Community Hosp. at Glen Cove, 1984-86, dir. community relations, 1986—; newsletter editor Twin Rinks, Roslyn, 1975, Robert Half Internat., San Francisco, 1985—; travel editor Blvd. Mag., Greenvale, N.Y., 1986—; v.p. Hyphenates, Roslyn, 1985—. Scriptwriter, location coordinator Word of Mouth, 1986; copywriter radio advertisements, 1985-87. Mem. adv. com. Glen Cove Sr. Citizens, 1985—, vice chmn., 1988; mem. adv. com. Glen Cove Interagency Council, 1984—; pres. Greater Roslyn United Civic Assn., 1977, North Park Civic Assn., 1975. Mem. Soc. Profl. Journalists, Am. Soc. Hosp. Mktg. and Pub. Relations, Nat. Assn. Female Execs., Nassau-Suffolk Hosp. Council Pub. Relations, Healthcare Pub. Relations Assn. Greater N.Y. Club: L.I. Press. Office: Community Hosp Glen Cove St Andrews Ln Glen Cove NY 11542

PALIT, HELEN MABEL VERDUIN, social service agency administrator; b. Detroit, May 12, 1948; d. Cornelius Bos and Helen Estelle (Masenhimer) Ver Duin; m. Satyajit Joy Palit, May 17, 1980. BA in Sociology, Psychology, Art, Tex. Tech. U., 1978, postgrad. in Sociology, 1979; PhD (hon.), Iona Coll., 1988. Comml. truck driver Lubbock-Amarillo Armored Service, Lubbock, Tex., 1974-75; jr. acct. Philips Petroleum Norway, Stavanger, 1975; producer, co-owner St. Nicholas Film Co., Lubbock, 1979-82; dir. Community Soup Kitchen, New Haven, Conn., 1980-82; vol. coordinator Planned Parenthood Assn., Oklahoma City, 1980; exec. dir., founder City Harvest Inc., N.Y.C., 1982—; mem. Select Com. on Hunger U.S. Ho. of Reps., 1985—, Inst. for Non-Profit Mgmt. Columbia U., 1988—. Nominated Esquire Mag. 400 Men and Women under 40, 1985, 10 Americans Who Made a Difference Better Health and Living, 1987. Home: 36 Riverview Trail Croton-On-Hudson NY 10052 Office: City Harvest Inc 135 W 26th St New York NY 10001-1807

PALLADINO, DOLORES, educational reading specialist; b. Wilkes-Barre, Pa., Nov. 5, 1936; d. John and Anna (Phillips) Wanat; widowed; children: JoAnna, Mimi, Rafe, Alan. BS in Elem. Edn., Bloomsburg (Pa.) U., 1959; MA in Reading, William Paterson Coll., 1977. Elem. tchr. Allentown (Pa.) Sch. Dist., 1959-62, West Milford (N.J.) Sch. Dist., 1962-65; reading tchr., remedial lab. dept. head Sarasota (Fla.) Vocat. Ctr., 1977—. Author booklets on Vocational Resume Writing. Leader Girl Scouts Am., Parsippany, N.J., 1974-75; den mother Boy Scouts Am., Sarasota, 1978-79; com. mem. Big Bros./Big Sisters, Sarasota, 1980-81. Named Tchr. Yr., Sarasota Vocat. Ctr., 1984. Mem. Am. Vocat. Assn., Fla. Vocat. Assn. (Outstanding Vocat. Tchr. 1985, bd. dirs. 1987—), Sarasota Vocat. Assn. (pres. 1984-85, Officer's award 1985), Fla. Spl. Needs Assn. (pres. 1987—), Internat. Reading Assn., Phi Delta Kappa. Democrat. Roman Catholic. Home: 3209 Riviera Dr Sarasota FL 34232 Office: Sarasota Vocat Tech Ctr 4748 Beneva Rd Sarasota FL 33583

PALLADINO, LUCY JO, psychologist, communications executive; b. N.Y.C.; m. Arthur A. Cormano, July 1, 1979; children: Julia, Jennifer. BS summa cum laude, Fordham U., 1972; MA, Ariz. State U., 1975, PhD, 1978. Lic. psychologist, Ariz. Tchr. N.Y.C. schs., 1972-74; psychology intern Good Samaritan Hosp., Phoenix, 1974-75, psychology assoc., 1977-78; psychology fellow Southwestern Med. Sch., Dallas, 1976-77; pvt. practice psychology Tucson, 1979-86; dir. Media Research Assocs., Encinitas, Calif., 1986—; mgr. Good Health Communications, Tucson, 1983—; lectr. in field. Scriptwriter and producer ednl. TV program Caring, Relaxercise, Coping. Recipient Small Business Innovation Research award Dept. Health and Human Services, 1985; Tucson Community Cable Corp. grantee, 1985. Mem. Am. Psychol. Assn., Assn. Ind. Video and Filmmakers, North County Psychol. Assn., Phi Beta Kappa. Home: 1626 Linda Sue Ln Encinitas CA 92024

PALLADINO-CRAIG, ALLYS, art gallery director; b. Pontiac, Mich., Mar. 23, 1947; d. Stephan Vincent and Mary (Anderson) Palladino; m. Malcolm Arnold Craig, Aug. 20, 1967; children—Ansel, Reed, Nicholas. B.A. in English, Fla. State U., 1967; grad., U. Toronto, Ont.,Can., 1969; M.F.A., Fla. State U., 1978. Editorial asst. project U. Va. Press, Charlottesville, 1970-76; instr. English Inst. Franco Americain, Rennes, France, 1974; adj. instr. Fla. State U., Tallahassee, 1978-79; dir. Four Arts Ctr. Fla. State U., Tallahassee, 1979-82, Univ. Gallery Fla. State U., Tallahassee, 1982—; curator Nocturnes and Nightmares. Author various exhbn. catalogues, 1982-87; Editor Athanor I-VIII, 1980—; paintings represented in Fla. Ho. of Reps., Fla. Dept. Natural Resources. Individual artist fellow Fla. Arts Council, 1979. Mem. Fla. Art Mus. Dirs. Assn., Am. Assn. Mus., Fla. Cultural Action Alliance, Phi Beta Kappa. Democrat. Home: 1410 Grape St Tallahassee FL 32303

PALM, JODY IONA, writer; b. Evanston, Ill., Mar. 21, 1953; d. Ralph D. and Charlene (Ferris) P. BA, No. Ill. U., 1978. Acctg. clk. Am. Hosp. Supply Corp., Evanston, 1979-80, incentive investment plan adminstr., 1980-83, documentation coordinator, 1984-85; data processing standards bus. analyst CNA Ins. Co., Chgo., 1985-86; sr. tech. writer Cyborg Systems, Inc., Chgo., 1986—. Pub. relations rep. Japanese Cultural Ctr., Chgo., 1987—. Mem. Soc. Tech. Communication (pub. relations com. 1987—), Chgo. Dance Coalition. Office: Cyborg Systems Inc 2 N Riverside Plaza 12th Chicago IL 60606

PALMA, DOLORES PATRICIA, urban planner, consultant, lecturer, author; b. Bklyn., Jan. 20, 1951; d. Anthony Michael Resse and Eleanor Dorothea (Palma) Graffeo; m. Doyle G. Hyett, Apr. 12, 1986. BA, CUNY, Bklyn., 1972; M of Urban Planning, U. Mich., 1974. Student intern Mich. Mcpl. League, Ann Arbor, 1973-74; park planner Metro Bd. Parks and Recreation, Nashville, 1975; preservation planner Metro. Hist. Commn., Nashville, 1976; sr. community planner Metro Planning Commn., Nashville, 1977-79; exec. dir. Metro Hist. Zoning Commn., Nashville, 1980-82; asst. dir. Mid-Atlantic Regional Office, Nat. Trust for Hist. Preservation, Washington, 1983, dir. Office of Neighborhood Conservation, 1984, project dir. Urban Demonstration Program Nat. Main St. Ctr., 1984-87; pres. Hyett-Palma Inc. 1985—, Hyett-Palma Publs. 1988—; del. Nat. Assn. Neighborhoods Platform Conv., 1979; cons. in field. Neighborhood Reinvestment Council, Nashville, 1978; mayoral appointee Neighborhood Housing Services, Nashville, 1979-82; dir. Restore the U.S. Capitol Campaign, 1983. Author: Salaries, Wages and Fringe Benefits in Michigan Cities and Villages, 1973; Nashville: Conserving a Heritage, 1977; Neighborhood Commercial Buildings: A Survey and Analysis of Metropolitan Nashville, 1983; Business Enhancement for Downtown Poughkeepsie, N.Y., 1987; Future Directions for Seward, Alaska, 1987; Action Agenda for Gay Street, Knoxville, 1987; Agenda for Economic Enhancement of Haymarket Lincoln, Nebraska, 1987; Management of Downtown Palmer, Alaska, 1988; Successful Business Recruitment Strategies in the U.S., 1988, Business Clusterine: How to Leverage Sales, 1988, Strategic Thinking for Commercial District Enhancement: A Video Script, 1988, Business Plans for Business Districts, 1988, Business Clustering: How to Leverage Sales, 1988; project dir.: A Market and Design Study for the Broadway National Register Historic District, 1982; author studies, pamphlet, articles; contbr. newsletters; editor Edgefield News, Nashville, 1979-80. Publicity dir. Hist. Edgefield, Inc., 1979; hon. mem. Tenn. State Legislature, 1980. Woodlawn scholar Nat. Trust for Hist. Preservation, 1976; named one of Outstanding Young Women of Am., 1985. Office: PO Box 65881 Washington DC 20035

PALMER, ADA MARGARET, computer executive; b. Arkansas City, Kans., Feb. 8, 1940; d. Mark Lloyd Palmer and Eunice Elizabeth (Thompson) Palmer Schnitzer; A.A., Colo. Woman's Coll., 1960; B.A., George Washington U., 1962. Adv. sr. programmer Merrill Lynch, N.Y.C., 1969-72; systems analyst Tchrs. Ins. & Annuity, N.Y.C., 1972-77; systems specialist N.Y. Times, N.Y.C., 1977-81; computer cons. Applied Systems Resources, Inc., N.Y.C., 1981-82; asst. sec. Mfrs. Hanover Trust, N.Y.C., 1982—. Mem. Bus. and Profl. Women, AAUW, George Washington U. Alumni Assn. of N.Y.C. (planning com.). Republican. Presbyterian. Home: 201 W 85th St Apt 11 A New York NY 10024

PALMER, ALTA BRITTON, educational administrator; b. Yazoo City, Miss., June 14, 1935; d. william Henry and Alma (Woods) Britton; m. Alvin Carroll Palmer Jr., Mar. 19, 1955; children: Laura Jean Palmer Moloney, Pamela Joan Palmer Randle, William Alvin, James Britton. BS, La. State U., 1959, MS, 1959, EdD, 1975. Cert. sch. system supt., La. Tchr. East Baton Rouge (La.) Parish Schs., 1957-69; owner, bd. dirs. Baton Rouge Reading Clinic, Inc., 1969-79; project officer La. Dept. Edn., 1979-81, dir. bur. devel., 1981-84; asst. supt. St. Tammany Parish Pub. Schs., Covington, La., 1984—; cons. in field. Mem. Internat. Reading Assn., Supr. and Curriculum Devel., La. Reading Council, Gov's. Learning Adv. Council. Baptist. Club: Pilot Internat. (pres. Baton Rouge chpt. 1969). Lodge: Order of Eastern Star. Home: 613 W 17th Ave Apt H Covington LA 70434

PALMER, CAROL ANN, psychotherapist, writer; b. Stamford, Conn., Sept. 20, 1949; d. Theodore Barclay and Mary Joan (Rekosz) P. BA in English, Skidmore Coll., 1981. Editorial asst. Internat. Brotherhood Elec. and Electronics Engrs., N.Y.C., 1970-71; artists rep. Quinlan Artwork, Ltd., N.Y.C., 1971-73; picture researcher, sect. mgr. The Bettmann Archive, N.Y.C., 1973-74; advocate MFY Legal Services, N.Y.C., 1976-77; dir. research capital punishment project NAACP Legal Def. Fund, N.Y.C., 1977-84; compliance officer SEC First Realty Res., N.Y.C., 1984-85; stockbroker N.Y.C., 1985; psychotherapist Morgan Stanly & Co., Bklyn., 1986—; co-producer, co-host tv program Cable Investors Digest, N.Y.C., 1984-86; counselor AIDS, N.Y.C., 1986—. Pitney Bowes scholar 1967. Mem. Nat. Coalition to Abolish the Death Penalty (bd. dirs. 1977—), Nat. Assn. Female Execs., Am. Assn. for Counseling and Devel. Democrat. Roman Catholic. Home: 64 3d Pl Brooklyn NY 11231

PALMER, DEBRA KAY, accountant; b. Ft. Myers, Fla., Oct. 7, 1959; d. Irving Jacob Buchman and Jeannie Maxine (Kelly) Beigler; m. James Buckingham Palmer II, Nov. 26, 1977. AA in Acctg., Hillsborough Coummunity Coll., 1987. Clk. Taronc Bus. Machines, Tampa, Fla., 1974-75; sec., bookkeeper Dial Fin., Tampa, 1975-76, Gen. Fin., Tampa, 1976-78; pvt. practice interior design Northdale Interiors, Tampa, 1978-80; bookkeeper, sec. Brown Automatic Sprinklers, Tampa, 1981-86, acctg. mgr., 1986—. Mem. Nat. Assn. Women Constrn. (pres. 1987—, Rookie of Yr. 1982). Republican. Methodist. Home: 5405 Hopedale Dr Tampa FL 33624 Office: Brown Automatic Sprinklers 3010 N 38th St Tampa FL 33605

PALMER, DIANA FRANCES, rancher, horse breeder; b. Belfast, Ireland, Sept. 29, 1944; came to U.S., 1965; d. Denis Osborne and Joan (McAlister) Vero; m. Michael M. Murphey, June 15, 1967 (div. 1973); 1 child, Ryan; m. Charles Michael Palmer, May 31, 1975; 1 child, Jeremy. Grad. pvt. sch., London. Exec. sec. Nems Enterprises Ltd., London, 1964-65, A&M Records, Los Angeles, 1966-70; sec.-treas. L. J. & M. Land Co., Austin, Tex., 1973-88, cons., 1988—; rancher, horse breeder Leander, Tex., 1982—; cons. Vero and Everitt Co., Atherstone, Eng., 1979-86. Adult leader Williamson County 4-H Hoofpicks, Georgetown, Tex., 1980-88; treas. Forest North Recreation Assn., Austin, 1980-81. Mem. Am. Quarter Horse Assn., Palomino Horse Breeders Assn., Capital Area Quarter Horse Assn., Capital Area Quarter Horse Assn. (bd. dirs. 1987-88). Democrat. Episcopalian. Home: Rt 12 Box 917 Leander TX 78641

PALMER, ELIZABETH ANN, lawyer; b. Hartford, Conn., Aug. 19, 1956; d. Kalman Poliner and Helen (Pious) Palmer. B.A. cum laude, Wesleyan U., Middletown, Conn., 1978; J.D., Boston U., 1981, LL.M., 1984. Bar: Conn. 1981, Mass. 1982, U.S. Dist. Ct. Conn. 1982, U.S. Dist. Ct. Mass. 1984. Spl. dep. asst. state's atty. Office Chief State's Atty., Wallingford, Conn., 1981-82; tax examiner Mass. Dept. Revenue, Boston, 1984; staff tax acct. Peat Marwick Mitchell & Co., Hartford, 1985; assoc. tax counsel Beneficial Mgmt. Corp., Peapack, N.J., 1985-86; tax cons. Price Waterhouse, N.Y.C., 1987—. Alumni admissions interviewer Wesleyan U., 1978—; mem. Wesleyan Alumni Fund, 1982—. Johnston Trust scholar Wesleyan U., 1974-76. Mem. ABA. Home: 134 Clover St Middletown CT 06457

PALMER, JANET JOYCE, business educator, author, consultant; b. Providence, R.I., Feb. 26, 1941; d. John Frank and Esther Blanche (Nietupski) Anisewski; m. John Bergin Palmer, Oct. 9, 1964; 1 child, April Jayne. B.S., Bryant Coll., 1962; M.A., Tchrs. Coll. Columbia U., 1963; Ed.D., Ariz. State U., 1982. Instr., Bryant Coll., North Smithfield, R.I., 1963-67; psychology instr. Cape Cod Community Coll., West Barnstable, Mass., 1969-71; bus. tchr., chmn. Nauset Regional High Sch., North Eastham, Mass., 1970-78; grad. teaching asst. Ariz. State U., Tempe, 1978-82; asst. prof. Western Ky. U., Bowling Green, 1982-87, assoc. prof. Lehman Coll. CUNY, Bronx, 1987—; freelance speaker, 1982; cons. Co-author: Office Automation: A Systems Approach, 1987; contbr. articles to profl. jours. Mem. Data Processing Mgmt. Assn. (Outstanding Service Bd. Mem. award 1984—, v.p. 1984, pres. 1984, bd. dirs. 1987-88), Office Systems Research Assn. (nat. sec. 1984), Am. Soc. for Tng. and Devel., Nat. Bus. Edn. Assn., Eastern Bus. Edn. Assn, Delta Pi Epsilon. Roman Catholic. Avocations: reading; travel; tennis; cross-country skiing. Home: 3647 Johnson Ave Riverdale NY 10463 Office: CUNY Lehman Coll Bedford Park Blvd W Bronx NY 10468-1589

PALMER, JEANNETTE URSULA, counselor, educator; b. Calif., June 21, 1941; d. Edward and Jeannette (Wilkox) Jaurszewski; div.; 1 child, Michelle. BA in History and Edn., Salve Regina Coll., 1963; postgrad., Colo. State Coll., 1968; MS in Rehab. Counseling, U. Ariz., 1973; postgrad., U. Tex. Health Sci. Ctr., 1979, North Tex. State U., 1980, East Tex. State U., 1983—. Lic. profl. counselor, Tex. Tchr. pub. sch. system, New Eng., Colo., 1963-69; substitute tchr. Amphitheatre Dists., Tanque Verde Dists., Tucson, Ariz., 1969-70; counselor, coordinator intern Rehab. Dept. U. Ariz., 1971; asst. dir., counselor Goodwill Rehab. Ctr., Winston-Salem, N.C., 1972-73; program coordinator, instr. Eastfield Coll., Mesquite, Tex., 1973—; cons. to def. attys., 1971-72, Tex. Commn. for the Deaf, Tex. Edn. Agy., Guatemala Dept. Edn., Parent Edn. Groups, So. Bapt. Conv., Tex. Soc. Interpreters for Deaf; adj. prof. Sch. Allied Health of Southwestern Med. Sch. U. Tex., 1975-76; pres. Tex. Cultural Alliance, 1987, 88. Mem. Am. Assn. Counseling and Devel. Democrat. Club: Quota. Home: 1242 N Selva Dallas TX 75218 Office: Eastfield Coll 3737 Motley Dr Mesquite TX 75150

PALMER, LINDA CONNER, telecommunications manufacturer's sales representative; b. Lexington, Ky., Aug. 5, 1949; d. Walter Thomas and Anna Mark (Hendrix) Conner; m. Jeffrey Taylor Palmer, June 20, 1981. B.S. in Edn., No. Ill. U., 1971; student Morton Jr. Coll., 1967-69. Substitute tchr. Pub. Schs., DuPage County, Ill., 1971-72; asst. office mgr. B.A.M. Agy., Chgo., 1972-73; adminstrv. asst. Budget Rent-A-Car, Chgo., 1973-76, Mesirow & Co., Chgo., 1976-77; account mgr. Tellabs, Inc., Lisle, Ill., 1977-81, Oakland, Calif., 1981-86; area sales mgr. Reliable Electric/Utility Products, Oakland, 1986—; ptnr. Palmer & Assocs., mktg., 1984—. Republican. Roman Catholic.

PALMER, MARILYN JOAN, educator; b. Mahoning County, Ohio, Mar. 3, 1933; d. Rudolph George and Marian Eleanor Wynn; phys. therapy cert. UCLA, 1954, B.S., 1955; M.A. in Philosophy, Ohio State U., 1969; postgrad. U. Okla., 1981—; m. Richard Palmer, Nov. 10, 1956 (dec. 1987); children—Ricky, Larry, Kevin. Phys. therapist Neil Ave. Sch. for Handicapped, Columbus, Ohio, 1968-69; instr. philosophy Ohio State U., Columbus, 1969; instr. English, Youngstown (Ohio) State U., 1970-71; writer, editor The Economy Co., ednl. publs., Oklahoma City, 1977-81; grad. asst. in English, U. Okla., Norman, 1981—; free-lance editing and cons. Fund-raiser Easter Seal Soc., 1965-68; den mother Boy Scouts Am., 1966, 67. Dept. Energy grantee, 1976. Mem. AAUP, Am. Phys. Therapy Assn., Soc. for Women in Philosophy, Alpha Xi Delta (nat. editor Quill 1984-86). Editor: Kindergarten Keys Teacher's Guidebook, 1982, author parochial supplement, 1982. Office: 760 Van Fleet Oval Norman OK 73069

PALMER, NINA, public relations executive; b. Roaring Spring, Pa., Aug. 19, 1947; d. George Joseph and Helen Louise (Camp) P.; m. William Victor Sweeney, June 15, 1968; 1 child, Megan McDonnell. BA, Knox Coll., 1968; MA, U. Iowa, 1970. Research assoc. Carl Byoir & Assocs., N.Y.C., 1976-77, account exec., 1978-80, v.p., account supr., 1981-84, sr. v.p., mgmt. group supr., 1985-86; sr. v.p., gen. mgr. Doremus Porter Novelli, N.Y.C., 1986-87; exec. v.p., gen. mgr. Doremus Publ. Relations, N.Y.C., 1987—; bd. dirs. Doremus & Co., N.Y.C., 1988—. Recipient Pub. Relations Soc. Am. Silver Anvil awards Internat. Assn. Bus. Communicators, 1984. Mem. Pub. Relations Soc. Am. (silver anvil award 1979, 83). Home: 3 Peter Cooper Rd 8G New York NY 10010 Office: Doremus Pub Relations 120 Broadway New York NY 10271

PALMER, PATRICIA ANN TEXTER, English language educator; b. Detroit, June 10, 1932; d. Elmer Clinton and Helen (Rotchford) Texter; m. David Jean Palmer, June 4, 1955. B.A., U. Mich., 1953; M.Ed., Nat. Coll. Edn., 1958; M.A., Calif. State U.-San Francisco, 1966; postgrad. Stanford U., 1968, Calif. State Coll.-Hayward, 1968-69. Chmn. speech dept. Grosse Pointe Univ. Sch. (Mich.), 1953-55; tchr. South Margerita Sch., Panama, 1955-56, Kipling Sch., Deerfield, Ill., 1955-56; grade level chmn. Rio San Gabriel Sch., Downey, Calif., 1957-59; tchr. newswriting and devel. reading Roosevelt High Sch., Honolulu, 1959-62; tchr. English, speech and newswriting El Camino High Sch., South San Francisco, 1962-68; chmn. English as 2d lang. dept. South San Francisco Unified Sch. Dist., 1968-81; dir. English as 2d lang. Inst., Millbrae, Calif., 1978—; adj. faculty New Coll. Calif., 1981—; Calif. master tchr. English as 2d lang. Calif. Council Adult Edn., 1979-82; cons. in field. Recipient Concours de Francais Prix, 1947; Jeanette M. Liggett Meml. award for excellence in history, 1949. Mem. Internat. Platform Assn., Calif. Assn. Tchrs. English to Speakers Other Langs., TESOL, Nat. Assn. for Fgn. Student Affairs, Computer Using Educators, AAUW, U. Mich. Alumnae Assn., Nat. Coll. Edn. Alumnae Assn., Ninety Nines (chmn. Golden West chpt.), Chi Omega, Zeta Phi Eta. Club: Peninsula Lioness (pres.). Home: 2917 Franciscan Ct San Carlos CA 94070 Office: 450 Chadbourne Ave Millbrae CA 94030

PALMER, ROSE, foundation director, nurse; b. Pitts., Oct. 14, 1943; d. William Woodrow and Marion (Kuhn) Robbins; m. Anthony Joseph Palmer, (div. 1977); children: Tony, Kim; m. Alvin Phelps, 1985; stepchildren: Todd, Craig, Dean, Ryan, Mindy. AS in Nursing, Community Coll. Allegheny County, 1979; student in Bus. Adminstrn. and Communications, Carlow Coll., 1988. RN, Pa. Dir. SUPPORT, Pitts., 1979—. Legis. chair Allegheny County Transit Council, Pitts., 1985-87; candidate 45th legis. dist. Pa. Ho., 1988. Recipient Take Charge award Clairol, 1988. Mem. ABA (adv. bd. Child Support Advocacy Project 1987—), Nat. Child Support Coalition (treas. 1986—), Am. Acad. Family Mediators (assoc. 1986—), Family Mediation Council of Western Pa. (legis. com., bd. dirs.), Joint Family Law Council Pa., NOW, Women's Agenda Pa. Office: SUPPORT 429 Forbes Ave Suite 1617 Pittsburgh PA 15219

PALMER, RUTH MARIE BUEHRER, educational administrator; b. Newark, Feb. 11, 1924; d. John Herman and Matilda Anne (Rose) Buehrer; m. Robert Field Palmer. BS, State Coll., Newark, 1941; MA, Seton Hall U., 1949. Kindergarten tchr. Hawkins St. Sch., Newark, 1944-66; project coordinator Burnet St. Sch., Newark, 1966-71; vice-prin. Chancellor Ave. Sch., Newark, 1977-78; cen. office coordinator Bd. Edn., Newark, 1971-77, 78-83, supr., 1983—; adminstr. Title I summer program, Bd. Edn., Newark, 1970-77; instr. Newark StateColl., 1949-50, Head Start program, Newark, 1966-67; rep. State Dept. Edn. Four-State Conf., 1967. Pres. Home Sch. Assn. Hawkins St. Sch., 1958-59; panelist Nat. Conf. Parents and Tchrs., Phila. 1968; vol. Fair Haven Library, 1987. Recipient Leadership and Contbns. to Edn. award Benedetto Croce Soc., Newark, 1977. Mem. Essex County Edn. Assn. (pres. 1976-80, dist. service award 1987),N.J. (treas. 1969-71), NEA (Urban Task Force 1968-69), N.J. Assn. Childhood Edn., 1952, N.J. Edn. Assn. (treas. 1969-71). Republican. Home: 84 Hance Rd Fair Haven NJ 07704

PALMER, SHARON-JOY, inventor, designer; b. S.I., N.Y., Oct. 16, 1947; d. James Murdock Palmer and Lillian Elinore (Nelson) Daniels; 1 child, Cameron Nelson. Student, Wayne U., Chgo., 1966-68, Dade Jr. Coll., 1969-73, U. N.Mex., 1980-82; BS in Fin., Liberty U., 1985, BS in Ch. Ministries, 1988. Dental asst. Francis J. Byron Jr., DDS, S.I., N.Y., 1966-69; flight attendant Delta Airlines, Miami, 1969-77; realtor D.W. Hyder and Assocs., Albuquerque, 1976-78; sales rep. Postique of Colo., Denver, 1976-78; dir. Combanc Internat., Inc., Albuquerque, 1976-80; mfr.'s rep. Innovative Mktg. Concepts, Albuquerque, 1977-79; developer, owner Angel Skye Investments, Ltd., Angel Fire, N.Mex., 1979-82; econ. adv. Am. S.S.T. Corp., Parkersburg, W. Va., 1982-85; chmn., pres. S.E.E.D. Internat., Inc., Albuquerque, 1980-87; Ptnr. Angel Skye Investments, 1980—, Carlton Engring., Albuquerque, 1985—; bd.dirs. Asia Enterprise Ltd., Tokyo, 1983—, Condoc-Paraguay Ltd., Asuncion, 1983—, Victory Internat. Inc., Panama City, Republic of Panama, 1983—, S.E.E.D. Kenya Ltd., Nairobi, 1980—, Mountains Herbs and Spices, Albuquerque, 1980—, E.N. Enterprises Inc., Canby, Oreg., 1977—. Inventor agrl. energy efficient growth chamber, 1982. Agrl. devel. liaison Embassy Kenya, Washington, 1983; mem. various childrens' hosps., Miami, 1973, Westside Assn., Coralles, N.Mex., 1980. Mem. Am. Dental Assts. Assn., Better Bus. Bur., Bd. Realtors. Republican. Baptist. Clubs: Angel Fire Country, Rio Rancho (N.Mex.) Country. Home: 1725 Brenda Rd Rio Rancho NM 87124 Office: SEED Internat Inc 2116 Leonard St Rio Rancho NM 87124

PALMER-HASS, LISA MICHELLE, state agency official; b. Nashville, Sept. 4, 1953; d. Raymond Alonzo Palmer and Anne Michelle (Jones) Davies; m. Joseph Monroe Hass, Jr. BS in Bus. Adminstn., Belmont Coll., 1975; AA in Interior Design, Internat. Fine Arts Coll., 1977. Sec. to pres. Hermitage Elect. Supply Corp., Nashville, 1981-83; sec. to dir. Tenn. Dept. Mental Health and Mental Retardation, Nashville, 1984-86; transp. planner Tenn. Dept. Transp., Nashville, 1986—; interior designer Lisa Palmer Interior Designs, Nashville, 1977-84. Mem. Nat. Arbor Day Found. Mem. Profl. Secs. Internat. (cert.). Republican. Mem. Disciples of Christ Ch. Club: Nashville Striders. Office: Tenn Dept Transp Environ Planning Office 505 Deaderick St Suite 900 Nashville TN 37219

PALMER-MALLEY, JANIS V., educational administrator; b. Ft. Mitchell, Ky., Sept. 20, 1950; d. Charles B. and Ethel V. (Voss) Palmer; m. Alfred Dever Malley, Mar. 20, 1983. B.S. in Sociology, No. Ky. U., 1972, cert. in teaching, 1973. Tchr. social studies Erlanger Bd. Edn., Ky., 1973-75; founder, dir., owner Little Red Sch. House, Erlanger, 1975—. Officer Humane Edn. Auxillary, Ft. Mitchell, 1983—. Mem. Ky. Assn. Sch. Adminstrs., No. Ky. Assn. Sch. Adminstrs., Ky. Assn. Children Under Six, No. Ky.. Alumni Assn., Big Sisters Am., Friends Animals, People for Ethical Treatment of Animals. Republican. Lutheran. Avocations: animal welfare work; tennis; swimming; children's welfare. Office: Little Red Sch House 4104 Dixie Hwy Erlanger KY 41018

PALMORE, MARY KATE, obstetrician-gynecologist; b. Chgo., July 24, 1952; d. Richard Eugene and Mary Kate (Mann) P.; B.A. in Biology, Hampton Inst., 1974; M.D., Rush Med. Coll., 1978. Community rep. Chgo. Dept. Human Resources, summers 1976, 76; resident in ob-gyn Presbyn.-St. Luke's Med. Center, Chgo., 1978-82, also adj. attending staff, instr. Rush Med. Coll., 1981-82; obstetrician and gynecologist Kaiser Permanente of Tex., Dallas, 1982-86; asst. instr. dept. ob-gyn U. Tex. Health Sci. Ctr. at Dallas, 1986-87; attending physician dept. ob-gyn Michael Reese Health Plan, Chgo., 1987—; mem. exec. com. C.V. Roman Med. Soc., 1984-86. Bd. dirs., v.p. community affairs and pub. relations Girls Clubs of Dallas, 1984—. Mem. Am. Med. Women's Assn., AMA, Nat. Med. Assn., Alpha Kappa Alpha. Democrat. United Methodist. Office: 2545 S Martin Luther King Dr Chicago IL 60616

PALUSIAK, MARY ELLEN, educator, consultant; b. Chgo., Dec. 12, 1958; d. Chester and Julia Helen (Piatek) P. BS in Edn., Eastern Ill. U., 1980; MA in Edn., U. Tex., Austin, 1985. Elem. tchr. Pflugerville (Tex.) Ind. Sch. Dist., 1980-84, Lake Travis Ind. Sch. Dist., Austin, 1984—; reading cons. Lake Travis Ind. Shc. Dist., Austin, 1986—; pvt. tutor; cons. remedial reading and sci. Austin Pub Schs., 1986—; mem. adv. bd. to supt., stipend rev. com., pay schedule rev. com., and discipline bd., 1987—. Author (curriculum): Texas Economics, 1986, Beaker Fever, 1987, Gems Galore, 1988, (handbook) Using Newspapers in the Classroom, 1983. Mem. Assn. Tex. Profl. Educators (local pres. 1986-87), Tex. Fedn. Tchrs. (localv.p. 1987-88), Tex. Assn. for Improvement of Reading, Nat. Assn. Female Execs. Republican. Roman Catholic. Home: 1411 Gracy Farms Ln #66 Austin TX 78758 Office: Lake Travis Elem Sch 607 N Ranch Rd 620 Austin TX 78734

PALUSKA, ANNETTE SUE, advertising, public relations and marketing analyst; b. Columbia, Mo., Nov. 4, 1949; d. James Edward and Denise (Boutlier) P. AA, Marymount Coll., 1970; BS, U. Ill., 1971, MA summa cum laude, 1972; postgrad., UCLA. Advt. and pub. relations assoc. dir. Krannert Ctr. for Performing Arts, Champaign-Urbana, Ill., 1971-72; stat. dept. head Coca Cola Co. Latin Am., Coral Gables, Fla., 1972; copywriter Beber Silverstein Ad Agy., Coral Gables, 1973; advt. cons. various firms, Miami, Fla., 1974-76; employee trainer Victoria Sta., Miami, 1977-80; mktg. mgr. Haney & Assocs., Woodland Hills, Calif., 1983, Alba Industries, Los Angeles, 1985-86; analyst City Govt. of Santa Monica, Calif., 1986-88; direct mktg. cons. Donhill Trading Co., Beverly Hills, Calif., 1985—. Author articles The Good Life, 1985; contbr. articles to profl. jours. Vol. Los Angeles Venereal Disease Inf. Council, 1982, Betty Clooney Found. for Brain Injured, Los Angeles, 1985—; program adminstr. Local City Govts., Santa Monica & Los Angeles, 1986-88; speaker Nat. Coalition to Reduce Car Crash Injuries, Washington, 1986—; lobbyist for airbag safety. Mem. Women in Communications, UCLA Pub. Relations Club.

PAMPUSCH, ANITA M., academic administrator; b. St. Paul, Aug. 28, 1938; d. Robert William and Lucille Elizabeth (Whaley) P. BA, Coll. of St. Catherine, St. Paul, 1962; MA, U. Notre Dame, 1970, PhD, 1972. Tchr. St. Joseph's Acad., St. Paul, 1962-66; instr. philosophy Coll. of St. Catherine, St. Paul, 1970-76, assoc. acad. dean, 1979, acad. dean, 1979-84, pres., 1984—; Am. Council Edn. fellow Goucher Coll., Balt., 1976-77; bd. dirs. St. Paul Cos.; head Women's Coll. Coalition, 1988. Author: (book rev.) Philological Quarterly, 1976. Mem. adv. com. Instl. Leadership project, Columbia U., 1986—; dist. chmn. Rhodes Scholarship Selection com., Mo., Neb., Minn., Kans., N.D., S.D., 1987—; exec. com. Women's Coll. Coalition, Washington, 1985—. Mem. Council for Ind. Colls. (bd. dirs. 1987—), Am. Phil. Assn., Women's Econ. Roundtable, St. Paul C. of C. (bd. dirs. 1986—), Phi Beta Kappa. Roman Catholic. Clubs: St. Paul's Athletic (St. Paul), Women's (Mpls.). Office: Coll of St Catherine Office of the Pres Saint Paul MN 55105

PANEHAL, ALEXANDRIA LEE, federal agency adminstrator; b. Cleve., July 3, 1954; d. Robert James and Francine M. (McAllister) P. BS, Georgetown U., 1976; M of Policy Adminstrn., Harvard U., 1982. Chief of research Cleve. City Council, 1976-80; housing asst. specialist Cuyahoga County Dept. Community Devel., Cleve., 1982-83; regional housing officer U.S. AIO, Washington, 1983-84, Bangkok, 1984, Tegucigalpa, Honduras, 1985-87; acting dir. Regional Housing and Urban Devel. Office for Cen. Am. U.S. AIO, Miami, Fla., 1987—. campaign mgr. Ohio House Reps., Lakewood, 1974, 76, 78, candidate 1980. George Gund Found. scholar, 1981. Home and Office: USAID/Tegucigalpa APO Miami FL 34022

PANEK, JERI HERNDON, computer/public relations exec.; b. Salt Lake City, June 15, 1939; d. Norman C. and Geraldine E. (Griffin) Herndon; ed. U. Utah; m. Larry H. Panek, Sept. 20, 1958 (div.); 1 son, Larry Brad. Public relations asst. Univac, Salt Lake City, 1961-69; dir. communications U. Utah, Salt Lake City, 1969-73; coordinator communications Sperry-Univac, Salt Lake City, 1973-74; electronic data processing communications coordinator Singer Bus. Machines Internat. Div., Brussels, Belgium, 1974-76; public relations and corp. planning mgr. Beehive Internat., Salt Lake City, 1977-80; program mgr., sales rep. Digistar computer graphics Evans & Sutherland Computer Corp., Salt Lake City, 1980—. Mem. Public Relations Soc. Am. (chmn. membership com., editor newsletter, chpt. treas. 1968—, v.p., immediate pas pres.), Assn. Computing Machinery (mem. conf. and symposia com. 1972-74), Internat. Planetarium Soc., Planetarium Assn. Can., C. of C. (aviation com.). Home: 1754 So Oak Springs Dr Salt Lake City UT 84108 Office: 580 Arapeen Dr Salt Lake City UT 84108

PANEK-MERTENS, THERESA ANN, nurse; b. Irvington, N.J., Dec. 7, 1954; d. Walter Felix and Josephine Theresa (Dziedzic) P.; m. Carl R. Mertens, Mar. 19, 1988. BSN, Rutgers U., 1978. Cert. Emergency Nurse, Advanced Cardiac Life Support. Staff nurse emergency dept. Irvington Gen. Hosp., 1978-80, Beth Israel Med. Ctr., Newark, 1980-84; asst. head nurse emergency dept. Beth Israel Med. Ctr., 1984-88; nurse educator of emergency dept. Newark Beth Israel Med. Ctr., 1988—; relief supr. Irving Gen. Hosp., 1979-80. Cheerleader coach for football cheerleaders, 1970-78; active Police Athletic League. Mem. Nat. Assn. Female Execs., Emergency Nurses Assn., Am. Nurse's Assn., Rutgers Coll. Nursing Alumni Assn. Republican. Roman Catholic. Home: Rd3 Box 624 Howell NJ 07731 Office: Newark Beth Israel Med Ctr 201 Lyons Ave Newark NJ 07112

PANELA, DEBRA LYNNE, interior and fashion designer, management consultant; b. Honolulu, July 28, 1961; d. Sixto Quindag and Emilia Morales (Tehero) P. BS in Dance Choreography, Brigham Young U. Mgr. office David G. Stringer AIA and Assocs., Ltd., Honolulu, 1982; mgr. office, paralegal Gima & Harrison, Honolulu, 1982-84; owner, fashion and interior designer, mgmt. cons. The Tangy Mango, Honolulu, 1980—; dir. mktg. and pub. affairs D'Image Internat. of Hawaii, Honolulu, 1985-86; adminstrv. asst. to house counsel Gentry Cos., Honolulu, 1986; paralegal Law Offices of Steven Guttman, 1986-88, Boccuto, Gilbert, Jeynes & Hurd, 1988—; pres., chief exec. officer, chmn. bd. Another Brainstorm Corp. and subs. Artis Gratis and Hawaii Parasearch, 1988—; chair Standards Com. of Hawaii Assn. Legal Assts., 1988—; instr. aerobics and exercise. Choreographer numerous mini-musicals, opera The Magic Flute. Pres. Young Women's Orgn., Ch. of Jesus Christ of Latter Day Saints, Honolulu, 1981-82. Named 1st Princess, Miss Filipinas Hawaii Am. 1986. Mem. Nat. Assn. Female Execs., Am. Bus. Women's Assn., Hawaii Assn. Legal Assts. Mormon. Avocations: dance, music, theatre, fine arts, fitness.

PANFILLI, RHONDA RHEA, nurse, consultant; b. Galveston, Tex., Aug. 12, 1950; d. Archie Frank and Loraine Ann (Novelli) P. BS in Nursing, U. Tex., Arlington, 1976; MS in Nursing, Wayne State U., 1983. RN, Mich., Tex. Community resource asst., project coordinator Region IX Edn. Service Ctr., Wichita Falls, Tex., 1976; staff nurse St. Paul Hosp., Dallas, 1977-78; nurse emergency room Sinai Hosp., Detroit, 1978-83; clin. nurse specialist Harper Hosp., Detroit, 1983—; ednl. cons. Region IX Edn. Service Ctr., 1977-79; mem. part-time faculty Wayne State U., Detroit, 1985. Author: (trainer's manual) Bilingual Health Nutrition Education, 1979; contbr. articles to profl. jours. Solicitor funs United Way Campaign, Detroit, 1983. Research grantee Tex. Title IV, Wichita Falls, 1978, Abbott Labs., Chgo., 1986; Wayne State U. scholar, 1980-81. Mem. Am. Nurses Assn., Mich. Transcultural Nursing Soc. (co-chair 1984-86), North Am. Nursing Diagnosis Assn., Mich. Nursing Diagnosis Assn. (bd. dirs. 1985), Wayne State U. Alumni Assn. (solicitor funds 1983—), Sigma Theta Tau. Club: Dearborn Racquet (Mich.). Home: 18091 Muirland Detroit MI 48221 Office: Harper Hosp Nursing Service 3990 John R Detroit MI 48201

PANG, MAY FUNG YEE, actress; b. N.Y.C., Oct. 24, 1950; d. Jack Fee and Linda (Lim) Pang. Student pvt. schs., N.Y.C. Asst. to John Lennon and Yoko Ono, 1970-76; asst. Island Records, N.Y.C., 1977-78; music pub. United Artists Music, N.Y.C., 1981-83; appeared in films Hot Shot, Heartburn, Laser Man, Fatal Attraction; TV roles in The Equalizer, Our Family Honor, Choices, Kate & Allie, Cagney & Lacey, Search For Tomorrow, Another World, Loving; appeared in music videos: Fashion (David Bowie), Satisfaction Guaranteed (The Firm), Oh Yeah (Bill Withers); prodn. co-ordinator Mind Games, Walls and Bridges, Rock 'N Roll (John Lennon); Fly, Feeling the Space (yoko Ono). Author: Loving John, 1983. Mem. Screen Actors Guild, AFTRA, Musicians Union Local 47. Roman Catholic. Avocations: photography; travel.

PANICCIA, PATRICIA LYNN, television news reporter and anchor, lawyer; b. Glendale, Calif., Sept. 19, 1952; d. Valentino and Mary (Napoleon) P.; m. Jeffrey McDowell Mailes, Oct. 5, 1985. BA in Communication, U. Hawaii, Honolulu, 1977; JD, Pepperdine U., Malibu, Calif., 1981. Bar: Hawaii 1981, Calif. 1982, U.S. Dist. Ct. Hawaii 1981. Law clk. Hon. Samuel P. King U.S. Dist. Ct., Honolulu, 1980; newswriter Sta. KTLA-TV, Los Angeles, 1981-83; reporter, anchor woman Sta. KEYT-TV, Santa Barbara, Calif., 1983-84; reporter Sta. KCOP-TV, Los Angeles, 1984—; instr. communications law Pepperdine Sch. Law, 1987—; profl. surfer, 1977-81. Mem. ABA (law and media com. 1987— , vice chmn. young lawyers div. media com. 1987-88, Nat. Conf. Com. Lawyers and Reps. of the Media, 1987—, mem. young lawyers sect. Law and Media Com., vice chmn. 1987—), Calif. State Bar (mem. com. on fair trial and free press 1983-84, pub. affairs com. 1985-87), Hawaii Bar Assn., Radio TV News Assn., Phi Delta Phi (historian 1980-81). Avocations: surfing, skiing, piano, guitar. Office: Channel 13 News 915 N La Brea Ave Los Angeles CA 90038

PANKEY, VINETA MARVALENE, real estate broker; b. Virgil City, Mo., Aug. 2, 1948; d. Gilbert and Nada Susan (Lee) P. BS in Edn., SW Mo. State U., 1970; MA, U. Tulsa, 1973. Cert. tchr. Mo.; lic. real estate broker. Tchr. State Fair Community Coll., Sedalia, Mo., 1974-75, Benton County R-1 Schs., Lincoln, Mo., 1974-77; instr. Cottey Coll., Nevada, Mo., 1978-79; sales assoc. Century 21-Gayla Realty, Nevada, 1981-83; art therapist, supr. Nevada State Sch. and Hosp., 1978-81; tchr. Miami R-1 Schs., Amoret, Mo., 1982-85; broker, owner Rainbow Realty, Nevada, 1984—; sales rep. L.A.W. Publs., Addison, 1987—; sales rep. Am. Home Shield, Dublin, Calif. Area coordinator, mem. state fine arts com. Mo. Spl. Olympics, Joplin, Nevada, Mo., 1979—; program coordinator Vernon County Emergency Preparedness, Nevada, 1981-82; sec. Five County Bd. Realtors, 1984-85; treas. Kans. Art Therapy Assn., Emporia, Kans., 1983-85; active Vernon County Child Abuse Council, 1980—; bd. dirs. Area XII Special Olympics (treas. 1986-87). Alumni scholar SW Mo. State Alumni Assn., Springfield, 1967; named one of Outstanding Young Women Am., 1983. Mem. Nat. State Assn. Realtors, Vernon County Bus. Profl. Women (historian 1986-87), Constnl. Rights Activist. Home: 506 S Chestnut Nevada MO 64772 Office: Rainbow Realty 111 E Cherry PO Box 672 Nevada MO 64772

PANNELL, DEBORAH DENISE, pharmaceutical company manager; b. Chgo., Jan. 19, 1952; d. Richard Ivanhoe and Naomi Elizabeth (Thomas) P. BA in Econs., Rutgers U., 1975. Research planner United Way of Cen. Jersey, New Brunswick, 1975-76; prodn. supr. Johnson & Johnson Corp., New Brunswick, 1976-80; mgmt. trainee Burlingtin, Ind., Raeford, N.C., 1980-81; prodn. supr. Halston Fragrance, Dayton, N.J., 1981-85; materials mgr. Altana, Inc., Melville, N.Y., 1985—. Mrm. Am. Planning & Inventory Control Soc. (sec. 1986—), Nat. Women Execs. Home: 1000 Grand Concourse #&B Bronx NY 10451 Office: Altana Inc 60 Baylis Rd Melville NY 11747

PANNULLO, DEBORAH PAOLINO, quality assurance director; b. Providence, Apr. 2, 1953; d. Joseph and Lena (Wilde) Paolino; m. Michael J. Pannullo, Apr. 23, 1971 (div. 1973); 1 child, Melissa Jean. BA in Econs., R.I. Coll., 1977; cert. in mfg. mgmt., Bryant Coll., 1982, MBA, 1987. Payroll analyst Bostitch/Textron, East Greenwich, R.I., 1977-79, cost analyst, 1979-80, U.S. mfg. coordinator, 1980-82, quality circles mgr., 1982-85; productivity mgr. Stanley-Bostitch, East Greenwich, 1985-87, dir. quality assurance, 1987—. Named outstanding Woman of Yr. WMCA, 1985. Mem. Nat. Assn. Female Execs., Am. Soc. Quality Assurance, Internat. Assn. Quality Circles (pres. 1984-85, bd. dirs. R.I. chpt. 1985—), Jr. Achievement (bus. cons. 1986—), Delta Mu Delta. Roman Catholic. Home: 17 Hawkins St Greenville RI 02828 Office: Stanley-Bostitch Rt 2 East Greenwich RI 02818

PANOS SCHMITT, A(THANASIA) NANCY, marketing educator; b. Great Falls, Mont., Oct. 2, 1951; d. Alexander H. and Katherine (Papadrikopoulos) Panos; m. Gary Allen Schmitt, June 14, 1974; 1 son, Kyle Christopher. BS, U. Utah, 1974, MBA, 1979; MS, Va. Tech., 1976. Research specialist U. Utah, Salt Lake City, 1977-78; market adminstr. Mountain Bell Telephone Co., Salt Lake City, 1979-80; assoc. prof., chairperson mktg. dept. Westminster Coll., Salt Lake City, 1980—; owner, pres. Mktg./Mgmt. Inc., Salt Lake City, 1982—. Mem. Am. Mktg. Assn., Western Mktg. Assn., Salt Lake C. of C., Phi Beta Lambda, Phi Eta Sigma, Phi Sigma. Democrat. Greek Orthodox. Lodge: Zonta. Office: Westminster Coll Sch Bus 1840 S 1300 East Salt Lake City UT 84105

PANOZZO, DIANE JEAN, business executive; b. Chgo., Dec. 16, 1937; d. Anthony Muffy and Genevieve Phyllis (Coffero) P. B.A., Coll. St. Francis, Joliet, Ill., 1959. Mgr., Variety Personnel Service, Chgo., 1959-71; adminstrv. asst. Finn. Industries div. Potlatch Forests, Inc., Chgo., 1971-72; exec. asst. to chmn., pres. Chemetron Corp., Chgo., 1972-79; adminstrv. asst. Price Waterhouse & Co., Chgo., 1979-80; adminstrv. sec. Chgo. Sch. Fin. Authority, 1980-81; v.p. fin. Jonpir, Inc., Hinsdale, Ill., 1981-85; exec. asst. to chmn. Telemedia, Inc., Chgo., 1981—. Home: 1455 Sandburg Terr Apt 1602 Chicago IL 60610 Office: 310 S Michigan Ave Chicago IL 60604

PANTANO, LYNN THERESA, clinical psychologist; b. Detroit, Sept. 1, 1949; d. Guy Dewey and Lois Ulin (Buchanan) Pantano; B.A. in Psychology with honors, Wayne State U., 1971, M.A. (grad. scholar), 1975, Ph.D. in Clin. Psychology, 1979; m. Kenneth Andrew Skuzenski, July 20, 1979. Neuropsychology clin. asst. Harper Hosp., Detroit, 1971-72, neuropsychology intern, 1975-76; psychology clin. asst. Lafayette Clinic, Detroit, 1972-74, psychology intern, 1974-75; psychologist, unit coordinator Northeast and Northwest Centers, Detroit Psychiat. Inst., 1976-79, Northwest Center, Northville Regional Psychiat. Hosp., Detroit, 1979-81; psychologist Alt. Living Service, Southgate (Mich.) Regional Center, 1981-82; dir. psychology Kingswood Hosp., Ferndale, Mich., 1982—; clin. psychologist E. Pointe Mental Health Assn., Harper Woods, Mich., 1981—; asst. adj. prof. psychiatry Coll. Osteo. Medicine, Mich. State U., Lansing., 1982—; adj. prof. psychology Wayne State U., Detroit, 1987. NSF grantee, 1970, USPHS grantee, 1971-72. Mem. Am., Midwestern, Eastern, Mich. psychol. assns., Internat. Neuropsychology Soc., Gerontol. Soc. Am., Phi Beta Kappa, Psi Chi. Roman Catholic. Contbr. articles in field to profl. publs. Home: 19228 Linville Ave Grosse Pointe Woods MI 48236 Office: 19959 Vernier Harperwoods MI 48225

PANZA, GEORGENE ANGELA, insurance company executive; b. Bklyn., Mar. 9, 1950; d. Ben and Marian Delores (Boccio) Sfraga; m. James Panza, July 1, 1984; 1 child, Andrea L. Cardamone. BA in Psychology, Hofstra U., 1971. Diplomate Internat. Claims Assn. Claims/sr. claims examiner N.Y. Life Ins., N.Y.C., 1971-76, 78-79, claims/sr. claims analyst, 1979-81, mgr., 1981—, exec. asst., 1981-82, asst. v.p., 1982-84, corp. v.p., 1984— , service product dir., 1985-86. Trustee, treas. Washington Green Assn., 1985—. Hofstra U. scholar, 1967-71. Mem. Am. Mgmt. Assn., Nat. Assn. Female Execs., Life Office Mgmt. Assn. (chmn. ordinary ins. services com.). Avocations: tennis, horseback riding, dancing. Office: NY Life Ins Co 51 Madison Ave New York NY 10010

PANZARINO, MICHELE ALLISON, retail company executive; b. N.Y.C., July 8, 1960; d. Hilmore Bernard (stepfather) and Jacquiline Ardrey (Feldstein) Albert; m. Joseph Frances Panzarino, July 24, 1982. AA in Acctg., CCNY, 1980; BA, Pace U., 1982. Controller Byford Imports, Inc., N.Y.C., 1983-85, treas., 1986-88, trustee, also bd. dirs.; treas., children's wholesaler Victor B. Handal and Bros., Inc., N.Y.C., 1988. Mem. Nat. Assn. Female Execs., Pace Univ. Alumni Assn. Home: 72 Bogota St Staten Island NY 10314 Office: Victor B Handal 277 5th Ave New York NY 10016

PAOLELLA, MARY LYNDA, systems analyst; b. Miami, Fla., Feb. 10, 1963; d. Bruce Conrad and Patricia Ann (Woodfin) Bartlam; m. Christopher Joseph Paolella, Aug. 24, 1985; 1 child, Katherine Elyse. BS in Math., Mary Washington Coll., 1985. Systems analyst Advanced Tech., Inc., Dumfries, Va., 1985—. Mem. Nat. Assn. Female Execs. Republican. Presbyterian.

PAOLINI, SHIRLEY JOAN, university dean, humanities educator; b. Cleve.; d. James Francis and Ann Dorothy (Jurist) Burke; m. Maurizio Paolini; children: Kenneth, Marco, Angela, Laura. BA, Mt. St. Mary's Coll., 1954; postgrad. U. Lausanne, Switzerland, 1954-55; MA, Calif. State U.-Fullerton, 1966; PhD, U. Calif.-Irvine, 1973. Asst. dir. edn. Nat. Systems Corp., Newport Beach, Calif., 1971-73; dir. planning Chaminade U., Honolulu, 1975-78; asst. prof. English, asst. specialist U. Hawaii, Manoa, 1977-78; art reach dir. Anchorage Arts Council, Anchorage, 1978-79; asst. dean acad. affairs Alaska Pacific U., Anchorage, 1979-80, dean continuing edn., 1980-82, dean univ. affairs, 1982-83, dean spl. programs, 1983-85; cons. Hawaii State Govts., Honolulu, 1977-78, Alaska Ednl. Agys., 1979—; chmn. dir. of humanities chmn.; dean sch. arts and scis.; dean sch. arts and scis. Barry U., Miami Shores Fla., 1988—. Author: Confessions of Sin and Love, 1982. Editor: North American School of Conservation, 1971-73, Studies in Interdisciplinarity, 1987—. Contbr. articles to various publs. Recipient French Govt. award, Los Angeles Consulate, 1954, Faculty Research award Alaska Pacific U., 1987; Swiss Govt. fellow U. Lausanne, 1954-55. Mem. Am. Comparative Lit. Assn., MLA, Internat. Comparative Lit. Assn., Council for Adult and Exptl. Learning (co-mgr. Alaska region, 1985-87), Philol. Assn. Pacific Coast, Am. Assn. Italian Studies and Australian Studies, World Affairs Council (Anchorage chpt.). Democrat. Roman Catholic. Clubs: La Mirada Womens (v.p. 1965-66) (Calif.). Office: Barry U Sch Arts & Scis 11300 NE 2d Ave Miami Shores FL 33161

PAOLUCCI, ANNE ATTURA, playwright, poet, English and comparative literature educator; b. Rome; d. Joseph and Lucy (Guidoni) Attura; m. Henry Paolucci. B.A., Barnard Coll; M.A., Columbia U., Ph.D., 1963. Mem. faculty English dept. Brearley Sch., N.Y.C., 1957-59; asst. prof. English and comparative lit. CCNY, 1959-69; univ. research prof. St. John's U., Jamaica, N.Y., 1969—; prof. English St. John's U., 1975—, acting head dept. English, 1973-74, chmn. dept. English, 1982—, dir. doctor of arts degree program in English; Fulbright lectr. in Am. drama U. Naples, Italy, 1965-67; spl. lectr. U. Urbino, summers 1966-67, U. Bari, 1967, univs. Bologna, Catania, Messina, Palermo, Milan, Pisa, 1965-67; disting. adj. vis. prof. Queens Coll., CUNY; bd. dirs. World Centre for Shakespeare Studies, 1972—; spl. guest Yugoslavia Ministry of Culture, 1972; founder, exec. dir. Council on Nat. Lits., 1974—; mem. exec. com. Conf. Editors Learned Jours.-MLA, 1975—; del. to Fgn. Lang. Jours., 1977—; mem. adv. bd. Commn. on Tech. and Cultural Transformation, UNESCO, 1978—; vis. fellow Humanities Research Centre, Australian Nat. U., 1979; rep. U.S. woman playwright Inter-Am. Women Writers Congress, Ottawa, Ont., Can., 1978; organizer, chmn. profl. symposia, meetings; TV appearances; hostess Mags. in Focus, Channel 31, N.Y.C., 1971-72; mem. N.Am. Adv. Council Shakespeare Globe Theatre Center, 1981—; mem. Nat. Grad. Fellows Program Fellowship Bd., 1985—; mem. Nat. Garibaldi Centennial Com., 1981; mem. Nat. Grad. Fellows Program, 1985—. Author: (with H. Paolucci) books, including Hegel On Tragedy, 1962, From Tension to Tonic: The Plays of Edward Albee, 1972, Pirandello's Theater: The Recovery of the Modern Stage for Dramatic Art, 1974, Poems Written for Sbek's Mummies, Marie Menken, and Other Important Persons, Places, and Things, 1977, Eight Short Stories, 1977, Sepia Prints, 1985; 2nd edit. 1986; plays include Minions of the Race (Medieval and Renaissance Conf. of Western Mich. U. Drama award 1972), Cipango!, 1985; pub. as book, 1985, 86, videotape excerpts, 1986; The Actor in Search of His Mask, 1987, Italian tranl. and prodn.; poems Riding the Mast Where It Swings, 1980; contbr. numerous articles, revs. to profl. jours.; editor, author: introduction Dante's Influence on American Writers, 1977; gen. editor: tape-cassette series China, 1977, 78; founder, gen. editor: tape-cassette series Rev. Nat. Lits, 1970—, CNL/Quar. World Report, 1974—. Bd. dirs. Italian Heritage and Culture City-wide Com., 1986—; Pres. Reagan appointee Nat. Grad. Fellows Program Fellowship Bd., 1985-86, Nat. Council Humanitites, 1986—. Recipient Notable Rating for Mags. in Focus series N.Y. Times, 1972, Woman of Yr. award Dr. Herman Henry Scholarship Found., 1973, Amita award, 1970, award Women's Press Club N.Y., 1974, Order Merit, Italian Republic, 1986; named Cavaliere Italian Republic, 1986, One of 10 Outstanding Italian Am. Women in Washington Ambassador Rinaldo Petrignani, 1986; Columbia U. Woodbridge hon. fellow, 1961-62; Am. Council Learned Socs. grantee Internat. Pirandello Congress, Agrigento, Italy, 1978. Mem. Internat. Shakespeare Assn., Shakespeare Assn. Am., Renaissance Soc. Am., Renaissance Inst. Japan, Internat. Comparative Lit. Assn., Am. Comparative Lit. Assn., MLA, Am. PEN, Hegel Soc. Am., Dante Soc. Am. (v.p. 1976-77), Pirandello Soc. (pres. 1978—), Nat. Soc. Lit. and Arts, Nat. Book Critics Circle. Office: Saint John's U Jamaica NY 11439

PAPA, PHYLLIS MARYANN, ballet dancer and director, choreographer, educator; b. Trenton, N.J., Jan. 30, 1950; d. Armando Carmen and Mary (Grace) P.; m. Thomas E. de Ment Jr., Sept. 2, 1979; children: Janelle and Tamra (twins), Chenée. Student, Royal Ballet Centre, 1955-62, Am. Ballet Ctr., N.Y.C., 1962-65, Harkness House for Ballet Arts, N.Y.C., 1965-68. Dancer Princeton (N.J.) Ballet Co., 1963-68, Harkness Youth Co., N.Y.C., 1965-68, Am. Ballet Theatre, N.Y.C., 1968-70, Royal Danish Ballet, Copenhagen, 1970-72; founder, artistic dir. Mercer Ballet (formerly West Jersey Ballet Co.), Mooretown, N.J., 1972—, Ballet Concertante, Mooretown, 1975—; founder Am. Internat. Ballet, Inc., N.Y.C., 1979—, choreographer, prin. dancer S.E. Asia tour, 1980; artistic dir. Atlantic City Ballet, 1981—; founding dir. Atlantic Contemporary Ballet Theatre; tchr. Royal Dance Centre, Royal Ballet Centre, Mercer County Community Coll.; cons. in field. Artistic dir., ballet mistress, prin. dancer Stars of Am. Ballet, N.Y.C.; prin. dancer Atlanta Ballet Co., 1978—; prin. dancer, ballet mistress Ballets Elan, 1980; choreographer over 25 ballets for regional and profl. cos. Grantee N.J. State Council of Arts and Nat. Endowment on Arts, 1975-76, 82.

PAPA-LEWIS, ROSEMARY, educator; b. Los Angeles, Dec. 12, 1950; d. Ralph Michael and Josephine (Sirchia) Papa; children: Jessica, Giselle, Sofia. BA, Calif. State U., Los Angeles, 1972; MA, Calif. State U., Northridge, 1977; EdD, U. Nebr., 1983. Lic. tchr., Calif., Nev., Nebr.; counselors lic. K-12, Calif., Nev., Nebr.; adminstr.'s lic. K-12, Calif., Nev., Nebr. Tchr. pub. elem. and secondary schs., So. Calif., 1971-78; prin. St. Mary's Sch., Bellevue, Nebr., 1979-84; chief adminstr. Holy Name Sch., Omaha, 1984-85; vis. asst. prof. U. New Orleans, 1985-86; assoc. prof. Calif. State U., Fresno, 1986—. Contbr. articles to profl. jours. Mem. Nat. Profs. Edn. Adminstrn., Calif. Prof. Edn. Adminstrn., Calif. Educators Research Assn., Am. Ednl. Research Assn., Am. Soc. Curriculum Devel., Phi Delta Kappa, Delta Kappa Gamma. Democrat. Roman Catholic. Home: 5639 N Bond Fresno CA 93710 Office: Calif State U at Fresno Sch of Edn Dept Advanced Studies Fresno CA 93740-0003

PAPALIA, DIANE ELLEN, human development educator; b. Englewood, N.J., Apr. 26, 1947; d. Edward Peter and Madeline (Borrin) P.; m. Jonathan Finlay, June 19, 1976; 1 child, Anna Victoria Finlay. A.B., Vassar Coll., 1968; M.S., W.Va. U., 1970, Ph.D. (NSF fellow), 1971. Asst. prof. child and family studies U. Wis., Madison, 1971-75; assoc. prof. U. Wis., 1975-78, prof., 1978—, coordinator child and family studies, 1977-79; adj. prof.

psychology in pediatrics U. Pa. Sch. Medicine, 1987. Author: (with Sally W. Olds) A Child's World: Infancy through Adolescence, 1975,, 4th edit., 1987, Human Development, 1978, 3d edit., 1986, Psychology, 1985, 2d. edit. 1988; contbr. articles to profl. jours. Am. Council on Edn. fellow, 1979-80; U. Wis. grantee. Fellow Gerontol. Soc.; mem. Am. Psychol. Assn., Soc. Research in Child Devel., Nat. Council Family Relations, Psi Chi.

PAPANDREA, LORNA, data processing executive; b. Bay Shore, N.Y., Feb. 20, 1960; d. Richard William and Bernadette (Munn) Davidson. Grad. high sch., Bay Shore. Sr. sec. Digital Equipment Corp., N.Y.C., 1981-82, adminstrv. asst., 1982-83, rep. customer service, 1983-84, rep. software mktg., 1984-85, specialist bus. accounts, 1985-86, specialist software, 1986—; facilatator Actualizations, Inc., N.Y.C., 1984-85. Mem. Vic D'Amore Dance, Deer Park, N.Y., 1985-87, Big Sisters Am. Mem. Nat. Assn. Female Execs. Republican. Mem. Christian Ch. (Disciples of Christ). Home: PO Box 725067 Atlanta GA 30339 Office: Digital Equip Corp 360 Interstate N Pkwy Atlanta GA 30339

PAPAROTTI, JUDIE L., credit company executive; b. San Francisco, June 3, 1938; m. William G. Paparotti, July 6, 1958; children: Dinaa Lynn, William Mitchell, Monette Cherise, Lisha Ann. Grad. pub. sch.s, Los Gatos, Calif. Mgr. Bay Counties Credit Bur., San Jose, Calif., 1963-84; owner Calif. Pacific Credit Services, San Jose, 1985—. Mem. Nat. Assn. Female Execs., Internat. Consumer Credit Assn., Calif. Assn. Residential Lenders, Better Bus. Bur., San Jose C. of C. Office: Calif Pacific Credit Services 1099 N Fourth St San Jose CA 95112

PAPE, PATRICIA ANN, social worker, psychotherapist; b. Aurora, Ill., Aug. 2, 1940; d. Robert Frank and Helen Louise (Hanks) Grover; divorced; Scott Allen, Debra Lynn. BA in Sociology, Northwestern U., 1962; MSW, George Williams Coll., 1979. Cert. addictions counselor, social worker, sch. social worker, Ill. Pvt. practice family counseling 1979—; coordinator community resources DuPage Probation Dept., Wheaton, Ill., 1977-80; dir. The Abbey Alcoholism Treatment Ctr., Winfield, Ill., 1980-81; prin. Pape & Assocs., Wheaton, 1982—; dir. alcoholism counselor tng. program Coll. of DuPage, Glen Ellyn, Ill., 1982—; Chgo. affiliate Employee Assistance Program, 1982—; cons. Luth. Soc. Services Ill., 1979-82. Contbr. articles to profl. jours. Mem. alcohol drug task force Ill. Synod Luth. Ch. Am., Chgo., 1985—. Named Woman of Yr., Entrepreneur Women in Mgmt., Oak Brook, Ill, 1986. Mem. Assn. Labor-Mgmt. Adminstrs. Cons. Alcoholism (women's issues com. 1984—), Acad. Cert. Social Workers, Am. Assn. Marriage Family Therapists, Ill. Alcoholism Counselors Alliance, Ill. Alcoholism Drug Dependence Assns., Nat. Assn. Soc. Workers, Women in Mgmt. Home: 519 Byron Ct Wheaton IL 60187 Office: Pape & Assocs 628 S Prospect Wheaton IL 60187

PAPE, PATRICIA JEAN, insurance company consultant, personnel consultant; b. Willimantic, Conn., Jan. 31, 1958; d. Robert Joseph and Mary Louise (Campbell) P. BS in Psychology cum laude, U. Hartford, 1983, postgrad., 1987—. Supr. career continuation services Cigna Corp., Hartford, Conn., 1983-85; mgr. planning and systems devel. Cigna Corp., Phila., 1985-87; sr. cons. Cigna Corp., Hartford, 1987-88, asst. dir., 1988—; outplacement cons., Phila., Hartford, 1985—. Co-author, editor co. manual, 1987. Mem. Am. Soc. Personnel Adminstrs., Phila. Fin. Assn., Nat. Assn. Female Execs., U. Hartford Alumni Assn. Republican. Home: 174 Mott Hill Rd East Hampton CT 06424 Office: Cigna Corp N 87 Hartford CT 06152

PAPERNOW, PATRICIA LEE, psychologist; b. San Diego, Apr. 29, 1946; d. Leon Neil and Felicia (Liebow) P.; m. Robert G. Lee (div.); stepchildren: Phyllis, Pam; 1 child, Michelle. BA magna cum laude, Harvard U., 1969; MA in Psychology, Goddard Coll., 1976; EdD, Boston U., 1980. Edn. dir. The Sanctuary, Cambridge, Mass., 1971-73; faculty Policy Tng. Ctr., Boston, 1977-81; dir. Community Tng. Resources, Cambridge, 1973-77; staff psychologist ACT, Waltham, Mass., 1977-80; dir. Charles River Gestalt Ctr., Newton, Mass., 1981-87; pvt. practice psychology Cambridge, 1981—; organizational cons. and lectr. in field. Contbr. articles to profl. jours. Mem. Stepfamily Assn. Am. (research chmn.), Am. Psychol. Assn., Mass. Psychol. Assn., Am. Orthopsychiat. Assn., Gestalt Inst. Cleve. Home and Office: 1 Arnold Circle Cambridge MA 02139

PAPPALARDO, FRANCINE PATRICIA, nursing educator; b. Lawrence, Mass., Mar. 17, 1949; d. Gaetano Carmelo and Josephine Mary (Consoli) Sciacca; m. Thomas Domenico Pappalardo, May 1, 1971; children: Anthony Guy, Dina Christine, Angela Marie. BSN, Boston Coll., 1970. RN, Mass. Staff nurse Bon Secours Hosp., Methuen, Mass., 1970-71; instr. practical nursing Greater Lawrence Tech. Coll., West Andover, Mass., 1971—; asst. prof. No. Essex Community Coll., Haverhill, Mass., 1982—. Bd. dirs. NE Ind. Living Program, Lawrence, Mass., 1976—. Mem. Nat. League for Nursing, Council Practical Nurse Educators. Republican. Roman Catholic. Club: Arba Sicula (N.Y.C.). Office: No Essex Community Coll Elliot Way Haverhill MA 01830

PAPPAS, DEBRA ANN, commodities trader; b. Chgo., Aug. 11, 1961; d. Robert Emory and Karyn Ann (Bambach) McGee; m. George C. Pappas, May 1, 1988. Grad. high sch., Des Plaines, Ill. Lic. real estate assoc. Asst. to oral surgeon Dr. Eugene C. Lekan, Park Ridge, Ill., 1979-82; commodities trader Murlas Commodities, Inc., Chgo., 1984—; pres. Deban Commodities, Inc., Chgo., 1984—; dir. research, trader Murlas Commodities, Inc., Chgo., 1987—; cons. commodities Murlas Commodities, Inc., Chgo., 1984—. Contbr. articles to profl. jours. Mem. Am. Horses Assn., U.S. Dressage Fedn., Ill. Dressage Assn. Roman Catholic. Club: Chgo. Merc. Office: Murlas Commodities Inc 200 W Adams St 1st Floor Chicago IL 60606

PAPPAS, DESPINA K., restaurateur; b. Patmos, Greece, Apr. 21, 1932; came to U.S., 1935, naturalized, 1953; d. John Nick and Margaret (Miaoulis) Kleoudis; m. John Dan Pappas, Sept. 25, 1955 (dec. Apr. 1978); children—Viki Joan Pappas Moustoukas, Margaret Denise Pappas Minetos, Dennis John. Grad. high sch. Office sec. Straus-Frank Co., Houston, 1950-56; sec. City of Houston, 1956-60; owner-mgr. Rustic Oak Restaurant, Hempstead, Tex., 1978—. Mem. Bus. and Profl. Women Hempstead, Nat. Restaurant Assn., Tex. Restaurant Assn., Houston C. of C., Philoptohos Soc. Lodge: Daus. of Penelope (sec. 1976-78, dir. 1981-83). Home: 2018 Greengrass St Houston TX 77008 Office: Rustic Oak Restaurant 735 10th St Hempstead TX 77445

PAPPAS, EVA, psychologist, psychoanalyst; b. N.Y.C., 1942. BA, Pace U., 1962; MA, NYU, 1965, PhD, 1973. Lic. psychologist, N.Y. Tchr. pub. schs. N.Y.C., 1963-65; counselor P.A.L. Project, N.Y.C., 1965-66; instr. psychology dept. edn. Adelphi U., N.Y.C., 1966-69; sr. staff psychologist Goldwater Meml. Hosp., N.Y.C., 1973-76; fellow Postgrad. Ctr. for Mental Health, N.Y.C., 1976-78, assoc. staff, 1976-80, staff, 1980-83, co-teaching staff, 1982-83, assoc. supervisory staff, 1983-85, psychologist, psychoanalyst, supr. in pvt. practice, 1976—. Mem. adv. council Queens Coll. Ctr. Byzantine Studies, 1984-88. Mem. Am. Psychol. Assn., Nat. Registry Health Service Providers in Psychology, N.Y. Soc. Clin. Psychologists (minority groups relations com. 1980-81, employment com. 1981-82), Greek-Am. Behavioral Scis. Inst. (exec. bd., treas. 1983-85). Office: 81 Irving Place Suite 1-B New York NY 10003

PAPPAS, LEAH AGLAIA, civic worker, political consultant, educator; b. Ogden, Utah, Mar. 23, 1936; d. George Thomas and Maria (Harames) P. BA, Coll. St. Mary of the Wasatch, 1959. Tchr. Bishop Gorman High Sch., Ogden, Utah, 1959-64; with Dist. Atty.'s staff, Ogden, Utah, 1972-75; tchr. Weber State Coll., Las Vegas, 1985; civic worker various charitable orgns., Ogden and Las Vegas, 1955—; cons. numerous polit. campaigns, Ogden, Las Vegas and Boston. Alt. del. Chgo. Nat. Conv., vol. Sen. Robert Kennedy campaign, 1968; supr. campaign Sen. Edward Kennedy, Boston, 1970-76; campaign worker Sen. Paul Laxalt, Las Vegas, 1974, Gov. Jerry Brown, Los Angeles, 1978; mgr. campaign office Pres. Ronald Reagan, Ogden, 1984; campaign staff George Bush for Pres. campaign, Ogden, 1988. Greek Orthodox. Home: 1323 Marilyn Dr Ogden UT 84403

PAPPAS, TONI H., public relations executive; b. Hoboken, N.J., June 14, 1943; d. John Edward and Elfrieda (Peter) Farley; m. William Pappas, Aug. 28, 1971. BA in English, Rutgers U., 1970; postgrad., Bank St. Coll., 1972-73. Tchr. All Souls Sch., N.Y.C., 1975-77, Educate Child Ctr., Manchester, N.H., 1975-77; owner Pappas Assocs., Manchester, 1977—; mem. N.H. Ho. Reps., Concord, 1985—. Bd. dirs. Manchester YMCA, 1982—, del. N.H. Constl. Conv., 1984; commr. N.H. Commn. Status of Women, 1984-86; N.H. state chmn. Statue of Liberty/Ellis Island, 1986; pres. Manchester Palace Theater, 1986-88. Recipient Handicapped Awareness award Easter Seal N.H./Vt., 1986, Voting Accessibility award Granite State Ind. Living Found., 1986; named Legislator of Yr. N.H. Rehab. Assn., 1985. Mem. Nat. Order Women Legislators, Nat. Fedn. Rep. Women, N.H. Alliance Safety Belts (bd. dirs. 1985—). Lutheran. Home: 432 Hanover St Manchester NH 03104

PAQUETTE, CAROL JEAN, travel agency executive, travel consultant; b. Brockton, Mass., May 27, 1939; d. Bruce Cameron and Marjorie Wilder (Augustine) Soderholm; m. Robert Louis Paquette; children: Janice Lynn, Tracy Ann. Cert., Grace Downs Air Career, N.Y.C., 1958. Cert. Am. Soc. Travel Agts. Revenue acct. N.E. Airlines, Boston, 1958-59; travel agt. Louis Benjamin Travel, Brockton, Mass., 1959-60; mgr. Brockton Travel, Brockton, Mass., 1962-67, Holiday Travel, Brockton, Mass., 1967-72, Boufides Travel, Brockton, Mass., 1977-86, Cushman Travel, Brockton, Mass., 1986—. Coach Youth Athletic Assn., West Bridgewater, 1977-85. Republican. Episcopalian. Home: 268 Crescent St West Bridgewater MA 02379 Office: Cushman Travel 1776-R Main St Brockton MA 02401

PARAMOURE, IRENE MARZELLA, mathematics educator; b. Ocala, Fla., Oct. 21, 1940; d. Marvin Leon Williams and Narlie (Doyle) Williams Campbell; m. Clifford G. Paramoure, Jr., June 9, 1959 (div. 1968); children—Michelle, Reginald G. B.S., Trenton State Coll., 1974, M.Ed., 1976, postgrad., 1976-78. Cert. elem. tchr., N.J. Basic skills math. tchr. Trenton Bd. Edn., N.J., 1973—, mem. curriculum com., 1984—; day care supr., summer camp dir. East Trenton Day Care and Community Ctr., 1975-85; math. tutor Mercer County Community Coll., Trenton, 1983-84. Acting sec. Community Ednl. Adv. Council, Hamilton Twp., N.J., 1982—; clk. Gen. Election Bd., Mercer County, N.J., 1983—; mem. Exec. Plus Women's Orgn., Trenton, 1985—. Mem. N.J. Ednl. Assn., Tchrs. Ednl. Assn., NEA, Nat. Assn. Female Execs., Zeta Phi Beta (chpt. parliamentarian 1978—). Democrat. Methodist. Avocations: reading; travel; aerobics. Home: 47 N Johnston Ave Trenton NJ 08609

PARDEE, MARGARET ROSS, violinist, violist, educator; b. Valdosta, Ga., May 10, 1920; d. William Augustus and Frances Ross (Burton) P.; diploma Inst. Mus. Art, Juilliard Sch. Music, 1940, grad. diploma, 1942, diploma Juilliard Grad. Sch., 1945; m. Daniel Rogers Butterly, July 5, 1944. Instr. violin and viola Manhattanville Coll. Sacred Heart, N.Y.C., 1942-54, Juilliard Sch., N.Y.C., 1942—, Meadowmount Sch. Music, Westport, N.Y., 1956-84, 88—, Bowdoin Coll. Music Festival and Sch., Maine, summer 1987; faculty Estherwood Sch. and Summer Festival, 1984-86; concert master Great Neck (L.I.) Symphony, 1954-85; adj. assoc. prof. music Queens Coll., Flushing, N.Y., 1978—; adj. assoc. prof. Adelphi U., Garden City, N.Y., 1979-83; adj. prof. SUNY, Purchase, 1980—debut N.Y. Town Hall, 1952; toured U.S. as soloist and in chamber music groups; soloed with symphony orchs. in Miss., N.J., D.C. and N.Y.; mem. jury for internat. competitions; guest artist prof. 1st Internat. Festival for Young Violinists, Caracas, Venezuela, 1988. Bd. dirs. Meadowmount Sch. Music. Mem. Soc. for Strings (dir. 1965-86), Associated Music Tchrs. League N.Y. (cert.), N.Y. State Music Tchrs. Assn. (cert.), Music Tchrs. Nat. Assn., Am. Fedn. Musicians, Viola Research Soc. Office: care Juilliard Sch Lincoln Ctr Plaza New York NY 10023

PARDINEK, MARY THERESE, engineer; b. Gary, Ind., Feb. 28, 1958; d. Benjamin Joseph and Joyce Annette (Desatnik) P. BS in Engring., Purdue U., 1984. Inspector U.S. Nuclear Regulatory Commn., Arlington, Tex., 1980-81; cons., asst. to v.p. U.S. Gypsum Co., Chgo., 1984; engr. Tenech Engring., East Chicago, Ill., 1985-86; prin. Corp. Engring. Assocs., Hammond, Ind., 1986—; instr. Sam Core Devel., Chgo., 1987—; cons. Small Bus. Devel. Corp., Chgo. 1987—; speaker SBA, Hammond, 1987—. Contbr. articles to profl. jours. Mem. Chgo. C. of C. (mem. labor/mgmt. com. 1987), Hammond C. of C. (bd. dirs. environ. com.), Lake County, Ind. Local Emergency Planning Commn.Subcommittee. Home: 1113 Chicago Ave Hammond IN 46327

PARDOE, SUSAN MEREDITH, manufacturing executive; b. New Castle, Pa., May 6, 1948; d. Stephen C. and Frances E. (Simonsic) Meredith; m. Lawrence J. Pardoe, Apr. 28, 1972 (div. Oct. 1983). BS in Journalism cum laude, Ohio U., 1970; cert. exec. devel. program, U. Houston, 1982. Mktg. rep. advt. Chem. Abstract Services, Columbus, Ohio, 1970-71; free-lance copywriter, editor Hudson, Ohio and Los Angeles, 1971-76; mgr. advt. Automatic Sprinkler Corp. Am., Cleve., 1976-79; mgr. mktg. communications Norton Co., Akron, Ohio, 1979-82, dir. communications, 1982—. Mem. Internat. Advt. Assn., Bus. and Profl. Advertisers Assn. Office: Norton Co PO Box 350 Akron OH 44309

PARDUE, DANA BAUGH, interior designer; b. Nashville, Dec. 24, 1959; d. John Thomas Jr. abd Nell (Apple) B. Student, Seminole Coll., 1983. Sr. designer Packer & Assocs., Brentwood, Tenn., 1984-86; co-owner, sr. interior designer Maddux-Pardue Design Cons., Brentwood, 1986—. Chmn. Heart Gala Heart Assn., Nashville, 1987. Named one of Outstanding Young of Am., 1985, Best Interior Designer, 1984, 85, Young Careerist, 1985. Mem. Nashville Home Builders Assn., Bus. Profl. Women Assn. Republican. Office: Maddux-Pardue Design Cons 5121 Md Way Suite 207 Brentwood TN 37027

PARDUE, MARY LOU, biology educator; b. Lexington, Ky., Sept. 15, 1933; d. Louis Arthur and Mary Allie (Marshall) P. B.S., William and Mary Coll., 1955; M.S., U. Tenn., 1959; Ph.D., Yale U., 1970; D.Sc. (hon.), Bard Coll., 1985. Postdoctoral fellow Inst. Animal Genetics, Edinburgh, Scotland, 1970-72; assoc. prof. biology MIT, Cambridge, 1972-80; prof. MIT, 1980—; summer course organizer Cold Spring Harbor Lab., N.Y., 1971-80; mem. rev. com. NIH, 1974-78, 80-84, mem. nat. adv. gen. med. scis. council, 1984-88 ; mem. sci. adv. com. Wistar Inst., Phila., 1976—; mem. health and environ. research adv. com. U.S. Dept. Energy, 1987—. Mem. editorial bd. Chromosoma, Molecular and Cellular Biology, Cell Biol. Internat. Reports, Jour. Cell Biology Biochemistry; mem. editorial bd. mem. Annual Rev. of Cell Biology; contbr. articles to profl. jours. Recipient Esther Langer award Langer Cancer Research Found., 1977; grantee NIH, NSF, Am. Cancer Soc. Fellow AAAS, Nat. Acad. Scis., Am. Acad. Arts and Sci.; mem. Genetics Soc. Am. (pres. 1982-83), Am. Soc. Cell Biology (council 1977-80, pres. 1985-86), Phi Beta Kappa, Phi Kappa Phi. Home: 321 Harvard St Unit 208 Cambridge MA 02139 Office: MIT Dept Biology 16-717 77 Massachusetts Ave Cambridge MA 02139

PARENT, LOIS BURBANK, social worker, educator; b. Barre, Vt., Sept. 18, 1931; d. Richard Henry and Helen Urana (Dean) Burbank; m. Arthur Joseph Parent, Sept. 17, 1959; children: James, Anthony, Joseph, Helen Charles Parent. BS in Edn., Castleton Tchrs. Coll., 1953; MSW, U. Pitts., 1956. Social worker Mont Alto Sanatorium, So. Mountain, Pa., 1956-57, Westfield (Mass.) Sanatorium, 1958-59; social worker therapist Ariz. Children's Home, Tucson, 1959-64, Burlington (Vt.) Dept. Welfare, 1966-68; psychiat. social worker Med. Ctr. Hosp. Vt., Burlington, 1969-77; pvt. practice therapist Burlington, 1977—. Mem. Nat. Assn. Social Workers, Clin. Social Workers Vt. (pres. 1987), Nat. Assn. Female Execs. Home: RFD Box 780 Starksboro VT 05487 Office: 267 Pearl St Burlington VT 05401

PARENTI, LINDA SUZANNE, investment firm consultant; b. Dayton, Ohio, July 13, 1960; d. Frank V. and Adele M. (Cekun) Parenti. BS in Bus. Adminstrn. cum laude, U. Dayton, 1982, MBA 1987. Asst. to pres. James Investment Research, Inc., Alpha, Ohio, 1982-86; fin. cons. Shearson Lehman Bros., Inc., N.Y.C., 1986—; fin. chmn. Miami Valley Rep. Club, 1988. Recipient award of outstanding service U. Dayton, 1982. Mem. U. Dayton Alumni Assn. (Dayton chpt.), Bus. and Profl. Woman's Club (2d v.p. 1988, Outstanding Young Career Woman of 1987), Nat. Right to Life, Alpha Xi Delta (life mem.). Club: U. Dayton Pres. Roman Catholic. Office: Shearson Leahman Bros Inc 300 Gem Plaza 3rd & Main Sts Dayton OH 45402

PARGANOS, ANGELA, radio executive; b. Queens, N.Y., July 29, 1964; d. Ernest and Valeria Ann (Hundzienski) P. Research analyst Storer Communications, N.Y.C., 1982-84; sr. research analyst Blair TV, N.Y.C., 1984-87; research dir. Sta. WRXL-FM/WRNL-AM, Richmond, Va., 1987-88, Donahue Research, Inc., Radio TeleMail Inc., Richmond, 1988—. Home: 4651 A Briary Rd Richmond VA 23224 Office: Donahue Research & Mktg Inc Radio TeleMail Inc 4507 Patterson Ave Richmond VA 23226

PARHAM, RUBY INEZ MYERS, civic worker, former educator; b. Tamaha, Okla., Nov. 4, 1914; d. Ola T. and Bursha Bell (Culver) Myers; B.S. in Edn., Northeastern State Coll., 1940, M.Teaching, 1955; m. Rufus K. McCollum, Dec. 31, 1937 (dec. Oct. 1966); m. Jewell A. Parham, June 10, 1973 (dec. Sept. 1987); stepchildren—Bill, Donal E., Ann (Mrs. Everett George), Garry. Tchr. rural schs., Haskell County, Stigler, Okla., 1934-38, Adair County, Stilwell, Okla., 1946-50, Cherokee County, Tahlequah, Okla., 1939-46, 50-66; tchr. Westville (Okla.) Jr. High Sch., 1966-77, ret., 1977. Vol., pres. Tahlequah City Hosp. Aux., 1982-83, 84-85, 85-86; vice chmn. Bapt. Women's Missionary Union, also past pres.; chmn. Nutrition Site Council, Tahlequah; mem. project council Cookson Hills Community Action Found., Inc.; adv. com. Helping Hands; precinct worker Republican party Recipient Oklahoma Bankers award, 1965. Mem. Nat., Okla. edn. assns., Tahlequah Sr. Citizens (bd. dirs.), Nat. Ret. Tchrs. Assn., Okla. Ret. Tchrs. Assn., Am. Assn. Ret. Persons, Am. Legion Aux., Northeastern State U. Alumni Assn. (life), Nat. Wildlife Assn., sr. Citizens Tahlequah, Kappa Kappa Iota (royal high lady Tahlequah, Okla., 1953-55), Delta Kappa Gamma. Clubs: Rebekah (noble grand 1959-60, jr. noble grand 1960-61, lodge dep. 1961-63, musician), Order Eastern Star (worthy matron 1979, organist, chmn. edn. com.). Home: 215 S College St Tahlequah OK 74464

PARIS, KATHERINE WALLACE, museum consultant; b. Kansas City, Mo., Feb. 6, 1930; d. Julian Lee and Eva Katherine (Wright) Wallace; m. John Lyn Paris, 1950; children: Nicole, Christopher, Deirdre. AA, Stephens Coll., 1948; BA, Carnegie Mellon U., 1949, MA, 1950. Adminstr. tour programs, docent The Nelson-Atkins Mus. of Art, Kansas City, 1962-69; curator, registrar Columbus (Ohio) Mus. Art, 1970-78; guest curator Philbrook Art Ctr., Tulsa, 1978-79; exec. dir. Beaumont (Tex.) Art Mus., 1980-85; mus. cons. Katherine Wallace Paris, Cons., Houston, 1986—; mem. visual arts & archtl. panel Tex. Commn. on Arts, Austin, Tex., 1982-84; art mus. rep. Ohio Mus. Assn., Cleve., 1976-78. Author (curator) Victorian Staffordshire Figures, 1976, Gloria dell' Arte, 1979; editor (curator) The Frederick W. Schumaker Collection, 1978, Catalog of the Collection (Columbus Mus. Art), 1979. Mem. Tex. Arts Alliance; mem. long-range planning com., major instns. task force Tex. Commn. on Arts; invited participant Future Directions for Tex. Mus. com. Tex. Hist. Commn. Mem. Internat. Council Mus., Am. Assn. Mus. (accredation vis. com. 1976—, chmn. registrars standing profl. com. 1976-78), Mountain-Plains Mus. Assn., Tex. Assn. Mus. Office: 20511 Atascocita Shores Dr Atascocita TX 77346-1627

PARIS, LUCILLE MARIE, educator; b. Cleve., Apr. 8, 1928. BA, U. Calif., 1950, MA, 1952; ED.D., Columbia U., 1960. Educator Contra Costa Coll., Richmond, Calif., 1954-55, Ball State U., Muncie, Ind., 1955-57, Columbia U., N.Y.C., 1957-58, William Paterson Coll., Wayne, N.J., 1959—. Exhibitions: Jersey City State Coll. 1985, Am. Abstraction N.J. State Mus. 1985, Chubb World Head Quarters 1985, Rutgers U. Walters Gallery 1984, Bronx Mus., Newark Mus., San Francisco Mus., Oakland Mus.

PARIS, MARY JANE, infosystems specialist, personnel consultant; b. Gloversville, N.Y., Jan. 9, 1948; d. Carl Mario and Jane Ruth (Albini) Balzano; m. Donald Joseph Paris, Aug. 31, 1968 (div. Jan. 1982); children: Timothy Scott, Daniel John. AA, Fulton-Montgomery Community Coll., 1967; postgrad., Housatonic Community Coll., Bridgeport, Conn., 1986-88. Adminstrv. asst. Elizabeth Shelton Elementary Sch., Shelton, Conn., 1982; adminstrv. asst., peer counselor Women's Ctr. Housatonic Community Coll., Bridgeport, Conn., 1982-83; customer service rep. Olsten Services, Trumbull, Conn., 1983, sales, acctg. rep., 1983-85, asst. mgr., 1985-87, br. mgr., 1987—; with direct mktg. dept. Joyce Beverage Co., Norwalk, Conn., 1982-83. Mem. PTA, Shelton, 1977—; chair crafts, membership coms. Welcome Wagon, Huntington-Shelton, 1978-82; asst. coach Shelton Youth Soccer League, 1980; speaker, mem. YWCA, Bridgeport, Conn., 1984—; mem. St. Vincent De Paul Soc., Shelton, 1986—; lector, spl. minister St. Joseph's Ch., Shelton. Mem. Assn. Records Mgrs. and Adminstrs. (chair hospitality 1984-86, treas., 1986—, Chpt. Mem. of Yr., 1985, 86), Assn. Info. Systems Profls., Women's Network of Greater Bridgeport (corr. sec., 1985-86, membership com. 1986-87),. Republican. Roman Catholic. Office: Olsten Services 925 White Plains Rd Trumbull CT 06611

PARISH, MARION ROBBINS, speech and language pathologist; b. Houston, Feb. 2, 1944; d. Walter Alvis and Maude Marion (Robbins) P.; B.A., U. Tex., Austin, 1966; M.A., Our Lady of Lake Coll., 1967. Speech pathologist Corpus Christi (Tex.) Speech and Hearing Center, 1966; instr., supr. undergrads. Our Lady of Lake Coll., San Antonio, 1967-72; dir./owner Speech Pathology Assocs., Houston, 1972—; founder, dir. Parish Children's Sch., 1982—; cons. in field. Contbr. chpt. to Prospering In Private Practice. Active, Jr. League Houston. Mem. Houston Area Assn. Communication Disorders, Am. Speech-Lang.-Hearing Assn. (mem. legis. council), Tex. Speech-Lang.-Hearing Assn. (past pres.), Orton Soc., Houston Assn. for Communication Disorders (past pres.). Office: 11059 Timberline Houston TX 77043

PARISI, BONNIE LEE, clinical social worker; b. Columbia, S.C., July 1, 1946; d. Dominick George and Barbara Pauline Parisi; B.A. in Psychology, Sacred Heart Coll., Belmont, N.C., 1970; M.S.W., U. S.C., 1978. Social worker Guilford County Mental Health Center, Greensboro, N.C., 1970-74; clin. social worker Upper Savannah Health Dept., Greenwood, S.C., 1978-79; outreach services coordinator, vol. services coordinator. Tri-County Mental Health Center, Dillon, S.C., 1979-87; dir. social work Coastal Carolina Hosp., Conway, S.C., 1987—; trainer, group facilitator Partners-In-Parenting, Greenwood, 1978-79; mem. steering com., conf. group facilitator White House Conf. on Families, 1980. Registered social worker. Mem. Nat. Assn. Social Workers (clin. social work register, diplomate), Acad. Cert. Social Workers, S.C. Assn. Social Workers (com. on inquiry), S.C. Social Welfare Forum, S.C. Soc. Clin. Social Workers. Club: Dillon Pilot (chaplain 1981-92, v.p. 1982-83). Home: 14 Night Heron Crescent Myrtle Beach SC 29577 Office: 7010 Waccamaw Med Park Rd Conway SC 29577

PARISI, PAULA ELIZABETH, writer, photographer, editor; b. N.Y.C., Feb. 27, 1960; d. Alfred John and Patricia Ann (Delucas) P. BA, Rutgers U., 1982; photography classes, Phila. Coll. Art, 1978-82. Reporter TVSM Inc./The Cable Guide, Horsham, Pa., 1982-84; assoc. editor Home Viewer Publs., Phila., 1984-85, mng. editor, 1985-87; home video cable TV, technology editor The Hollywood Reporter, Los Angeles, 1987—. Contbr. articles to Billboard, Film & Video Prodn., Mix, Hollywood Reporter, Phila. Enquirer; photographs published in Phila. Inquirer, Washington Jour., Miami Herald, Circus, Us, Sixteen, others. Republican. Roman Catholic. Office: The Hollywood Reporter 6715 Sunset Blvd Los Angeles CA 90028

PARIZO, MARIE JEAN, accountant; b. Montpelier, Vt., June 24, 1956; d. Bert Sylvester and Glendeen Jean (Cary) P.; m. Donald Roger Vincent, July 9, 1980 (div. May 1985). AS, BS, Castleton State Coll., 1978. Clk. Vt. Dept. Edn., Montpelier, 1973-74; clk. registrar's office Castleton (Vt.) State Coll., 1974-78; trust clk. Dartmouth Nat. Bank, Hanover, N.H., 1978-79; bookkeeper Creare Products Inc., Lebanon, N.H., 1979-80; acctg. supr. A.M. Peisch & Co. CPAs, White River Junction, Vt., 1980—; instr. acctg. Lebanon Coll., Fall 1984; instr. personal income taxes Lebanon Coll., Fall 1986. Tutor Hanover High Sch., 1983; vol. West Cen. Services Inc., Lebanon, 1983-84; mem. The Friends of Hopkins Ctr. and Hood Mus. Art, Hanover, 1986-87. Mem. Nat. Assn. Female Execs. Home: PO Box 1367 White River Junction VT 05001 Office: AM Peisch & Co CPA Gilman Office Ctr White River Junction VT 05001

PARK, ANNE, retail executive; b. Seoul, Korea, Feb. 11, 1958; arrived in U.S., 1970; d. Joong Ho and Choong Shik (Mihn) P. BFA in fashion design, Pratt Inst., Bklyn., 1980. Asst. designer Charles James Esquire, N.Y.C., 1977-79; sales rep. Diane Pernet, N.Y.C., 1979-80; talent mgr. La Rocka Modeling Agy., N.Y.C., 1980; buyer Burghard's, N.Y.C., 1980-82; v.p. sales

OLA Designs, N.Y.C., 1982-85; v.p. merchandising Et Vous, N.Y.C., 1985—. Grantee scholarship Connell Rice and Sugar Co., N.J., 1976-80.

PARK, GLADYS JAYNAR, nurse; b. Waialua, Hawaii, Apr. 17, 1931; d. Joseph Ponciano and Alice (Sales) Jaynar; m. David Tai Young Park, Dec. 12, 1953; children—Sandra Eai Lan, Lawrence Jaynar. R.N., Queen's Hosp. Sch. Nursing, Honolulu, 1953; B.S. in Nursing, U. Hawaii, 1960, M.P.H., 1973. Staff nurse Queen's Hosp., Honolulu, 1953-54; pvt. duty nurse, Honolulu, 1954-55; staff pub. health nurse Hawaii Dept. Health, Honolulu, 1955-64, supr. chest clinic, 1964-66, project supr., 1966-68, pub. health nursing supr., 1968-73, comprehensive health planning coordinator, 1974-77; comprehensive health planning officer, 1977—; mem. Honolulu Home Care Adv. Com., Honolulu, 1973-77; mem. Western Ctr. Health Planning Interim Adv. Bd., San Francisco, 1975-76; mem. Hawaii Bd. Audiology and Speech Pathology, Honolulu, 1979-82; mem. Govs. Adv. Com. Long Term Care, Honolulu, 1982-85; mem. Hawaii Sr. Ctr. Med. Adv. Com., 1975-77. Trustee Palama Settlement, Honolulu, 1974-82; sec. Palolo Community Council, Honolulu, 1966-68; chmn. Palolo Community Action Program, 1966-68. Mem. Queen's Sch. Nursing Alumnae Assn. (sec. 1954-55, 88—), Hawaii Nurses Assn. (membership chmn. 1966-68), Am. Pub. Health Assn., Hawaii Pub. Health Assn. (pres. 1981), Am. Sewing Guild (sec. Honolulu chpt. 1988—), Phi Kappa Phi. Clubs: Waialua '49 (sec. 1979—); Gen. Fedn. Women's (corr. sec. 1979) (Honolulu). Office: State Health Planning and Devel Agy 335 Merchant St #214E Honolulu HI 96813

PARK, JONI GLORIA ZACCARA, publishing company executive, educator; b. N.Y.C., July 24, 1933; d. Pasquale J. and Deveda (Pelligrini) Zaccara; m. Ivan Clinton Park, Oct. 15, 1955; children: Kristin D. Travers, Torri Leigh, Scott Alan, Kimberly Dana. BA, Wilson Coll., 1955; postgrad., Godard Coll., 1975. Cert. tchr., Fla., N.J. Tchr. Jacksonville (Fla.) Pub. Sch., 1955-56, Glen Rock (N.J.) Pub. Sch., 1972-73, Ind. Day Sch., Tampa, Fla., 1975-77; vol. coordinator Dept. Juvenile Justice, Annapolis, Md., 1977-78; sales rep. R.L. White Publs., Danbury, Conn., 1978-82; sales mgr. Homes Mag., Danbury, 1982, ops. mgr., 1982—; radio interviewer Fairleigh Dickinson U., Teaneck, N.J., 1969-73. Trustee Town of Brookfield (Conn.) Library, 1983—. Mem. Wilson Coll. Alumnae Assn. (pres. class of 1955). Democrat. Mem. Soc. of Friends. Home: 71 Indian Trail Brookfield CT 06804 Office: Homes Mag PO Box 246 Danbury CT 06813

PARK, ZAIDA ANN, nurse; b. Lyons, N.Y., Apr. 15, 1940; s. Ralph Vernon and Olive Ruth (Eaton) Harris; m. Roswell Park, Apr. 20, 1985; m. John F. Guest, Jr., Sept. 1, 1962 (div. Nov. 1973); children: John, Michele. Student William Smith Coll., 1958-59; RN, Genesee Hosp. Sch. Nursing, 1962. Pvt. duty nurse Wayne County Hosps., N.Y., 1962-65; charge nurse Newark Wayne Community Hosp., N.Y., 1965-66; charge nurse E.J. Barber Hosp., Lyons, N.Y., 1966-73; office nurse Marvin Bergman, MD, Lyons, N.Y., 1968-70; supr. Clifton Springs Hosp., N.Y., 1973-76; office nurse Yung Soo Pang, M.D., Lyons, N.Y., 1975-76; occupational health nurse Borden, Inc., Lyons, N.Y., 1976-86; adminstrv. asst. Park Pkg., 1986—; instr. ARC, 1978—. Treas., United Way, Wayne County 1976-78; sec. United Presbyterian Women, Lyons, 1972-76; founder, pres. Lyons Coop. Nursery Sch., 1968-70. Mem. Genesee Hosp. Alumna, Am Nurses Assn., Am Occupational Health Nurses Assn. Republican. Presbyterian. Avocations: sailing, crafts. Office: PO 70 Lyons NY 14489

PARKAS, IVA RICHEY, educator, historian, curator, paralegal; b. Comanche County, Tex., June 28, 1907; d. Andrew Jackson and Pearl Lucretia (Kennedy) Richey; grad. Wayland Coll., 1927; B.A., Tex. Tech. U., 1935; M.Litt., U. Pitts., 1950; postgrad. UCLA, 1960, Pa. State U., 1961, U. Calif., Berkeley, 1962, Duquesne U., 1963, Carnegie-Mellon U., 1968; m. George Eduardo Parkas, May 5, 1945. Curator, historian Fort Pitt Blockhouse, Pitts., 1946-52, asst. curator-historian, 1964-84; tchr. U.S. history Pitts. sr. high schs., 1953-72; paralegal Allegheny County (Pa.) Law Dept., 1977-82. Del., White House Conf. on Children and Youth, Washington, 1960, 70, World Food Conf., Rome, 1974; U.S. Congl. Sr. Citizens intern, Washington, 1984. Named Disting. Alumnae, U. Pitts., 1978; recipient Valley Forge Classroom Tchr.'s medal, 1960. Henry Clay Frick Ednl. fellow; NDEA grantee; Greater Pitts. Air Force Squadron scholar, Pitts. Press scholar, 1960. Mem. NEA (life), AAUW (pres. Pitts. br. 1974-76), Hist. Soc. Western Pa., Western Pa. Council Social Studies (pres. 1969-71,), DAR (regent Pitts. chpt. 1987-89), U. Pitts. Alumnae Assn. (bd. dirs. 1978—, v.p. 1984), Pa. Retired Pub. Sch. Employees Assn. (chairperson Am. revolution bicentennial 1974-76), Western Pa. Hist. Soc., Allegheny County Bicentennial Commn., Delta Kappa Gamma, Phi Alpha Theta. Editor: So Your Children Can Tell Their Children, 1976. Contbr. articles on hist. subjects to newspapers, mags. Home: 5520 Fifth Ave Pittsburgh PA 15232

PARKE, JANET DIANE, interior designer; b. Winnemucca, Nev., Aug. 20, 1930; d. Willard Virdell and Lois (Carlson) Booth; m. Jack Evan Parke, June 11, 1950; children- Deborah Diane Parke Smith, Cary Evan, James Robert. B.A., Brigham Young U., 1950. Interior designer Brunson Homes, Reno, Nev., 1972-74, Bakers Interiors, Reno, 1976-81, Tristan Parke Interiors, Reno, 1981-86. Designer showcase homes. Bd. dirs. Nev. Jr. Miss, 1969-79; hostes Miss Nev., Reno, 1974-77; com. mem. Congressman Jim Santini, Reno. Mem. AIA (assoc.), Nev. Home Builders Assn. (assoc.), Sigma Nu (pres. White Rose chpt. 1952-53). Democrat. Mormon. Lodges: Order Ea. Star, Daus. of Nile. Office: Tristan Parke Interiors 26 Hillcrest Dr Reno NV 89509

PARKE, MADELYN SARA (MINDY), insurance executive, educator; b. N.Y.C., Oct. 6, 1951; d. Edwin Daniel and Muriel (Cohen) P.; divorced; 1 child, Howard Silverman. BS cum laude, Queens Coll., 1972, MS magna cum laude, 1976. Educator N.Y.C. Bd. Edn., 1977-85; technician CIGNA Fin. Services, Tarrytown, N.Y., 1985-86; supr. Presdl. Life Ins., Nyack, N.Y., 1987—; tchr. Adult Edn., Pearl River, N.Y., 1987—; craftsperson Country Charm, Nyack, 1987—. Bd. dirs. Friday Nite Alternative, Pearl River, 1987. Recipient Regents scholarship, N.Y., 1968. Mem. Nat. Assn. Female Execs. Lodge: B'nai Brith (sec. Pomona Friendship N.Y. chpt. 1982).

PARKER, ADRIENNE NATALIE, art educator, art historian, lecturer; b. N.Y., May 23, 1925; d. Benjamin and Bertha (Levine) Lefkowitz; m. Norman Richard Parker, July 22, 1945; children: Dennis, Jonathan W., Steven L. BA cum laude, Hunter Coll., 1945; MFA, Montclair Coll., 1975; postgrad., Instituto Des Artes, San Miguel, Mex., 1987. Instr. art, English Granby High Sch., Norfolk, Va., 1945-46; instr. art Mahwah (N.J.) Bd. Edn., 1970-75, Daus. of Miriam Home for the Aged, Clifton, N.J., Fedn. Home, Paterson, N.J.; instr. art, history Bergen Community Coll., Paramus, N.J., 1980—. Exhibits include art painting N.J. Art Educators, Bergen County Art Educators, N.J. Tercentenary (first place); fiber arts Pine Library; painting, silversmithing, one-man weaving Bergen Community Coll. Editor Fairlawn High Sch. PTA, Thomas Jefferson Jr. High Sch.; pres. The Community Sch., Fairlawn, 1983-86, bd. dirs. Mem. N.J. Art Educators, Bergen County Art Educators, Wood Stock Art Assn., Fairlawn Art Assn., Hunter Coll. Alumni Assn. (bd. dirs. no. N.J. chpt), Palisade Guild Spinners and Weavers (founder, editor, charter), Phi Beta Kappa. Home: 3827 Fairlawn Ave Fair Lawn NJ 07410

PARKER, ALLISON, association executive; b. Monterey, Calif., Dec. 9, 1962; d. Charles Marvin and Sue (Williams) P. Student, Longwood Coll., 1981, No. Va. Community Coll., 1982. Dir. services U.S. Health, Inc., Greenbelt, Md., 1981-84; dir. conv. services Free Congress Found., Washington, 1984-85; exec. asst. The Hill Group, Washington, 1985-86; exec. Assn. Mgmt. Group, Washington, 1986—. Fellow Am. Soc. Assn. Execs., Nat. Assn. for Female Execs. Republican. Office: Assn Mgmt Group 3299 K St NW 7th Floor Washington DC 20007

PARKER, ANNE VEREEN, furniture executive; b. Rockingham, N.C., Mar. 18, 1937; d. F. Lee Sr. and Gladys Elizabeth (Fields) P. Student, Kings Bus. Coll., 1956. Clk. typist Jefferson Standard Life, Greensboro, N.C., 1955-56; office mgr. Thomas P. Heritage Archtl. Engr., Greensboro, 1956-62; v.p., treas. Kindleys Office Furniture, Inc., Greensboro, N.C., 1962—. Vol. Red Cross, Greensboro, 1973-74, Am. Cancer Soc., Greensboro, 1980-88, Guilford County Dem. Party, Greensboro, 1987-88, Greensboro Urban Ministry, 1987-88. Mem. Nat. Assn. Female Execs., Inc., Nat. Assn. Profl. Saleswomen, Nat. Mus. Women in the Arts, Guilford Coutny Dem. Women, Christian Women's Assn. Baptist. Home: 3741 Sagamore Dr Greensboro NC 27410 Office: Kindleys Office Furniture Inc 513 S Elm St Greensboro NC 27406

PARKER, BETTYE JEAN, real estate professional; b. Rossville, Ga., May 31, 1931; d. Leonard Virgle and Azalea (Miller) Burroughs; m. Edwin Carroll Parker, Oct 13, 1947; children: Elaine Parker Phibbs, Eileen Parker Sands, Edwin Paul, Susie Parker Deal, Polly Parker Wagoner. Diploma in bus., Edmondson Bus. Coll., 1947; student, U. Chattanooga, 1947-49, U. Tenn., Chattanooga, 1969-71. Tchr. Hamilton County Sch System, Chattanooga, 1963-68; prin., real estate broker Bettye Parker Realty Inc, Chattanooga, 1970—; pvt. practice real estate devel. and bldg. constrn. Chattanooga, 1951—; mem. legis. com. Chattanooga Bd. Realtors, 1987—, Multiple Listing Service com., 1988. Exec. rep Hamilton County Health Adv. Commn., 1981—; vice chmn. Scenic Cities Beautiful Commn., (Give a Hoot award) 1985—; chmn. bd. dirs. N.E. YMCA, Chattanooga, 1985-87, treas., 1988; mem. signs and billboards task force com. Chattanooga Venture, 1986—; mentor U. Tenn.-Chattanooga Pilot Project for High Sch Srs., 1987; advisor Youth in Govt. club Cen. High Sch., 1987; vol. chmn. Students Staying Straight-Project 714 Brown Mid. Sch., 1987—; life mem. nat., state, local PTA's. Mem. Tenn. Assn. Realtors (profl. standard com. 1980-88), Am. Bus. Women's Assn. (pres. Lake Chickomauga chpt. 1979-80, Woman of Yr. award 1979), Small Bus. Council (steering com. 1986-88), Greater Chattanooga Area C. of C. (bd. dirs. 1980-83, Disting. Citizen of Yr. award 1983), North 58 C. of C. (pres. 1981, sec. 1988), Chamber Outstanding Service award 1987). Methodist. Club: Tenn. Valley Patriots (v.p. 1986-87). Lodge: Civitan (pres. Riverland chpt. 1982—, Honor Key-Dist. Ms. Civitan award Appalachian dist. Riverland chpt. 1980, 83-84, Club Builder award, 1982, Citizen of Yr. award 1982, 87, dir. 1987—, lt. gov. Appalachian dist. 1988—). Office: Bettye Parker Realty Inc 4819 Hwy 58 N Chattanooga TN 37416

PARKER, BONNIE ST. CLAIR, federal relations liason; b. Bethesda, Md., Jan. 13, 1954; d. Lloyd Dale and Bonnie Ruth (Reed) St. Clair. BS, U. Md., 1976, MA, 1984. Staff asst. Architect of Capitol, Washington, 1977-78; staff asst. U.S. Senate Select Com. on Ethics, Washington, 1978-80, chief clk., 1980-83, dep. staff dir., 1983, staff dir., 1983-87, staff adminstr., 1987-88; fed. relations liason The Tobacco Inst., Washington, 1988—. Episcopalian. Home: 3630 39th St NW A 529 Washington DC 20016 Office: The Tobacco Inst 1875 I St NW Washington DC 20007

PARKER, BOOTS FARTHING, management consultant, public relations executive, political consultant; b. Boone, N.C., Dec. 25, 1929; d. Joseph Edward and Polly Ida (Harmon) Farthing; student Ohio State U., 1948; m. Paul Hixson, Dec. 31, 1949 (dec. 1968); m. 2d, W. Dale Parker, Sept. 13, 1968; 1 adopted dau., Jacquelyn Susan. With Greenpark Hotel, Blowing Rock, N.C., and Sea Ranch Hotel, Ft. Lauderdale, Fla., 1947-48, O'Neil Co., Akron, Ohio, 1948-67; chief Firestone's United Trading Co., also ofcl. hostess, chief of protocol Firestone Internat., Monrovia, Liberia, 1958-61; with Holiday Inns. Am., F.W. Woolworth, Fla., 1967-72; pres. Multiple Services, Titusville, Fla., 1972—; ptnr. 3 gold mining ops. including California Creek, Can. Former mem. Democratic Exec. Com. Recipient International. Humanitarian award, London, 1972, Disting. Service award Fla. Sheriff's Assn., 1976; hon. col. Ala. State Militia; named hon. navy recruiter U.S. Navy Dept., 1977. Mem. N.Y. Vets. Police Assn., Va. Sheriffs Assn. Clubs: Royal Oak Golf and Country, Order of Does, Fla. Fraternal Order Police. Avocation: collecting rare and valuable space artifacts. Home: PO Box 246 Dale/Boots Dr Boone NC 28607 Office: PO Box 1441 Titusville FL 32781

PARKER, DEBORAH ANSONIA, manufacturing company executive, oral surgery specialist; b. Washington, Dec. 3, 1953; d. William C. Robinson Sr. and Virginia A. (Brent) Wildy; m. Johnnie L. Parker Sr., Nov. 24, 1972; children: Johnnie L. Jr., Dana A., Kevin Thomas. Cert., Cortez Bus. Coll., 1971. Cert. dental technician. Substitute tchr. Prince George's County (Md.) Schs., 1980-84; dental technician various dentists, Md. and D.C., 1984—; pres. New Concept Mfg. Ltd., Clinton, Md., 1985—; cons. Martin Marietta Corp., U.S. govt., 1986—. Dir. activities Clinton Boys and Girls Clubs, 1981-85; coordinator travel Boy Scouts Am., Clinton, 1986—. Fellow Nat. Assn. Female Execs. Home: 6305 Den Lee Dr Clinton MD 20735 Office: New Concept Mfg Ltd 9015 Woodyard Rd Suite 105 Clinton MD 20735

PARKER, DEBORAH L. ROBERTS, counselor; b. Meridian, Miss., Mar. 15, 1952; d. Bernice (Roberts) Pringle; m. Curtis Edward Parker, Nov. 25, 1972; 1 child, Shana. BS, U. So. Miss., 1978; MEd, Miss. State U., 1980. Lic. profl. counselor; nat. cert. counselor. Asst. PBX op., with client admissions dept. Weems Mental Health Ctr., Meridian, 1972-75, counselor children's services, 1981-86; career facilitator Meridian Pub. Schs., 1978-80; dir. gov.'s youth grant Lauderdale County Juvenile Ctr., Meridian, 1980-81; adolescent counselor, case mgr. Laurel Wood Psychiat. and Recovery Ctr., Meridian, 1986—. Active Permanency Planning Task Force, 1986, Commn. for Children and Youth Juvenile Justice Task Force, 1987—; bd. dirs. Miss. juvenile justice adv. com., 1985—. Named one of Outstanding Young Women of Am., 1983. Mem. AAUW, Am. Assn. for Counseling and Devel., Am. Assn. Clin. Mental Health Counselors, Alpha Lamda Delta, Delta Sigma Theta. Roman Catholic. Home: 411-45th Ct Meridian MS 39301 Office: Laurel Wood Psychiat & Recovery Ctr Hwy 39 N Meridian MS 39303

PARKER, EDNA G., judge; b. Johnston County, N.C., 1930; 1 child, Douglas Benjamin. Student, N.J. Coll. for Women (now Douglass Coll.); B.A. with honors, U. Ariz., 1953; postgrad., U. Ariz. Law Sch.; LL.B., George Washington U., 1957. Law clk. U.S. Ct. Claims, 1957-59; atty.-advisor Office of Gen. Counsel, Dept. Navy, 1959-60; trial atty. civil and tax div. Dept. Justice, 1960-69; adminstrv. judge Contract Appeals Bd., Dept. Transp., 1969-77; spl. trial judge U.S. Tax Ct., 1977-80, judge, 1980—. Mem. ABA, Fed. Bar Assn., D.C. Bar, D.C. Bar Assn., Women's Bar Assn., Nat. Assn. Women Lawyers (D.C. chpt.), Nat. Assn. Women Judges. Office: US Tax Ct 400 2d St NW Washington DC 20217

PARKER, ELINOR MILNOR, editor; b. Jersey City, Mar. 20, 1906; d. Charles Wolcott and Emily (Fuller) P.; A.B., Bryn Mawr Coll., 1927. Gen. asst. The Bookshop, Morristown, N.J., 1928-38; head children's books, then asst. mgr. Scribner Book Store, N.Y.C., 1938-53; editor trade books Charles Scribner's Sons, 1953-79, dir., 1966-79, asst. sec., 1970-79, v.p., 1973-79, editorial cons., 1979—. Mem. Nat. Soc. Colonial Dames. Episcopalian. Club: Cosmopolitan (N.Y.C). Author: Cooking for One, 1949; Some Dogs, 1950; Entertaining Singlehanded, 1952; Most Gracious Majesty, 1953. Compiler: A Birthday Garland, 1949; 100 Story Poems, 1951; 100 Poems About People, 1955; I Was Just Thinking, 1959; 100 More Story Poems, 1960; The Singing and the Gold, 1962; Poems of William Wordsworth, 1964; Here and There, 1967; Four Seasons Five Senses, 1974; Poets and the English Scene, 1975; Echoes of the Sea, 1977; Letters and Numbers for Needlepoint, 1978. Home: 30 E 72d St New York NY 10021

PARKER, HARRIET MASHBURN, retired university administrator; b. Jackson County, N.C., June 26, 1935; d. Avery Richard and Lydia (Higdon) Mashburn; B.S.Ed., Western Carolina U., 1957; m. Grady C. Parker, Sept. 3, 1955; children—Greg, Doug, Tony. Asst. registrar Western Carolina U., 1957-69, registrar, 1970-87. Named Boss of Yr., Western Carolina chpt. N.C. Assn. Ednl. Office Personnel, 1979, Dist. Boss of Yr., 1980; cert. tchr. bus., health and phys.edn., N.C. Mem. Am. Assn. Collegiate Registrars and Admissions Officers (hon.), So. Assn. Collegiate Registrars and Admissions Officers, Carolinas Assn. Collegiate Registrars and Admissions Officer, N.C. State Employees Assn., AAUW (pres. 1982-86), Jackson County C. of C., Jackson County Bus. and Profl. Women (pres. 1982-83), Camp Lab Parent-Tchr. Orgn. Baptist. Club: Order Eastern Star (grand marshal, past matron, dist. dep.). Home: Route 66 Box 40 Cullowhee NC 28723

PARKER, JERI, educator, writer, consultant; b. Rexburg, Idaho, Oct. 28, 1939; d. Elbert and Shirley (Stoddard) P.; B.A., Brigham Young U., 1957; M.A., U. Utah, 1970, Ph.D. (Pres. Research fellow), 1973; postgrad. Am. U., Beirut, summer 1962, U. Grenoble, summer 1963, U. Cambridge U., 1983. Dir. Women's Center, Westminster Coll., Salt Lake City, 1975-79; dir. Summer Writing Workshop, U. Utah, Salt Lake City, 1980-81, instr. English, 1979-83; tech. writing cons. Exxon, Chevron, Shell Oil, U.S. Navy, NASA, others; mem. bd. advs. Network Publs., Odyssey House, 1979. Mem. Delta Kappa Gamma, Phi Kappa Phi. Mormon. Club: Literary. Author: Uneasy Survivors: Five Women Writers, 1975, also tech. writing manuals for engrs.; contbr. theatre revs., poems, short stories to various publs. Home and Office: The Carriage House 956 Browning Ave Salt Lake City UT 84105

PARKER, JOAN, public relations executive; b. N.Y.C., Oct. 13, 1935; d. Albert and Elizabeth (Durgin) P.; m. Francis Shea (div. 1964); 1 child, Sarah Young; m. Dale Coenen; children: Stephen, Alison. Student, Hood Coll., 1953-55, Tobé Coburn Sch., 1956. Asst. to pub. relations dir. Elizabeth Arden, N.Y.C., 1956-57; acct. exec. Rowland Co., N.Y.C., 1958-60; owner pub. relations firm N.Y.C., 1969-81; dir. consumer products pub. relations N.W. Ayer Pub. Relations Co., N.Y.C., 1981-82, dir. pub. relations, 1982—. Dir. House of Vision, Chgo., 1983-85, Wolverine Worldwide, Grand Rapids, Mich., 1983—. Mem. Pub. Relations Soc. Am. (acad. counselor), Tobé Coburn Alumni Assn. (Most Disting. Alumni 1980), Fashion Group. Office: Ayer Pub Relations 260 Madison Ave New York NY 10016

PARKER, JUDITH KOEHLER, science educator; b. Dalhart, Tex., May 12, 1940; d. James Albert and Mildred Zimlich K.; B.S., St. Louis U., 1962; M.A., Washington U., 1979; m. Gerald E. Parker, Dec. 30, 1964; children—James E., G. Michael. Head bacteriologist St. Louis U. Hosp., 1962-63; bacteriologist N.Mex. Pub. Health Dept., 1963-64; instr., head bacteriologist St. Louis U. Hosp., 1964-66; med. technologist S.W. Med. Center, St. Louis County, Mo., 1966-72; adj. instr. Maryville Coll., Sunset Hills, Mo., 1981-83, mgr. sci. lab., 1983—; propr. Splty. Retail Shop, 1981-84. Bd. dirs. Spl. Sch. St. Louis County, 1982-88, pres., 1983-87; Bonhomme Democratic committeewoman, 1979-86; mem. Mo. State Dem. Com., 1980—; del. Nat. Dem. Conv., 1980. Mo. State Conv., 1980, 84. Recipient Civic award Maryville Coll., 1983. Mem. Am. Soc. Clin. Pathologists (affiliate), Mo. Assn. Children with Learning Disabilities, CORO Women in Leadership, Gamma Pi Epsilon, Pi Lambda Theta, Phi Dalta Kappa. Roman Catholic. Home: 11812 Bayberry Des Peres MO 63131

PARKER, KATHLEEN, television personality, producer; b. Pasadena, Calif., Dec. 3, 1955; d. Spelts Higgins and Lorraine Rita (Hodonicky) P. AA, Saddlebruck Coll., 1983; B, San Diego State U., 1986. Radio news broadcaster Par Broadcasting Co., Oceanside, Calif., 1985-86; TV anchorwoman Calif. Oreg. Broadcasting, Medford, Oreg., 1986-88; TV anchorwoman, producer Bangor (Maine) Communications, 1988—. Club: Collie of Am. Home: PO Box 46 East Vasselboro ME 04935 Office: Bangor Communications Sta WVII-TV 371 Target Indsl Circle Bangor ME 04401

PARKER, LAURA LEE, graphic designer, marketing communications professional; b. Denver, Feb. 2, 1947; d. Harry Arthur and Sarah Geneva (Jones) Steinbach; student Colo. Inst. Art, San Francisco Acad. Art, San Francisco Art Inst. Graphic designer Wells Fargo Bank, San Francisco; ptnr. Ariel, San Francisco; prin., art dir., designer Laura Parker Design, San Francisco. Editor, Vermissa Herald, 1982-84. Recipient Cert. of Merit award Paper Works Competition, 1987, 1st place prize Nat. Assn. Fund Raising Counsel; award of excellence Nat. Assn. Art Dirs. and Designers. Mem. San Francisco Art Dirs. Club (bd. dirs.), Am. Inst. Graphic Artists. Clubs: Adventuresses of Sherlock Holmes (N.Y.C.) (Hon. Miss Miles); Scowrers and Molly Maguires (San Francisco), Commonwealth. Home: 3150 Franklin St #11 San Francisco CA 94123 Office: Laura Parker Design 1235 Deharo St San Francisco CA 94107

PARKER, LENORE, organization executive; b. Rome, N.Y., Mar. 21, 1933; d. Anthony and Ena (Rizzuto) La Gatta; m. James F. Parker, Jan. 25, 1957 (dec. 1985); 1 son, Donald. B.S., Fordham U., 1955. Dir. pub. relations Am. Med. Ctr. of Denver, 1963-67; exec. dir. Am. Council for Emigres in Professions, N.Y.C., 1967-78; exec. dir. YWCA of City N.Y., 1978—; bd. dirs. ECF Mgmt. Inc. Contbr. chpts. to books, articles to profl. jours. Bd. dirs. Am. Immigration and Citizen Conf., N.Y.C.; chmn. Women Execs. in Human Services, N.Y.C., Community Council Greater N.Y.; treas. Pvt. Industry Council, N.Y.C., 1984—.

PARKER, LYNDA MICHELE, psychiatrist; b. Phila., Sept. 28, 1947; d. Albert Francis and Dorothy Thomasinia (Herriott) P.; B.A., C. W. Post Coll., 1968; M.A. (Martin Luther King Jr. scholar 1968-70), N.Y.U., 1970; M.D., Cornell U., 1974; postgrad. N.Y. Psychoanalytic Inst., 1977-82. Intern, N.Y. Hosp., N.Y.C., 1975; resident in psychiatry Payne Whitney Clinic, N.Y.C., 1975-78; psychiatrist in charge day program Cabrini Med. Center, N.Y.C., 1978-79, attending psychiatrist, 1978—; admitting psychiatrist inpatient psychiat. treatment Payne Whitney Clinic, N.Y.C., 1978—, supr. psychiatry residents, 1978—, supr. long-term psychotherapy, 1980-82; attending psychiatrist N.Y. Hosp., Cornell Med. Center, 1979—; practice medicine specializing in psychiatry, N.Y.C., 1979—; instr. psychiatry Cornell U. Med. Coll., 1979-86, asst. prof., 1986—; instr. psychiatry, N.Y. Med. Coll., 1978—; psychiat. cons. Bldg. Service 32BJ Health Fund, 1983—, Inwood House, N.Y.C., 1983-86, Time-Life Inc., 1986—, Ind. Med. Examiners, 1986—, Epilepsy Inst., 1986-87, asst. med. dir., 1987-88, med. dir., 1988—; ind. med. examiner Rep. Health Care Rev. Scis. Mem. Am. Psychiat. Assn., Am. Womens Med. Assn. Episcopalian. Office: 219 E 69th St #1J New York NY 10021

PARKER, MARGARET MARY, insurance company executive; b. Richmond, Va., Feb. 23, 1951; d. Vincent Nathan and Margaret Mary (Hargadon) P. B of Applied Studies magna cum laude, U. Richmond, 1986. Sec. law The Life Ins. Co. of Va., Richmond, 1969-77, staff asst. law, 1978-80, legal asst., 1980-83, sr. legal asst., 1983-85, asst. sec., 1985-86, dir. govt. relations, asst. sec., 1986—. Mem. Nat. Assn. Legal Assts., Richmond Assn. Legal Assts. (1st v.p. 1983-85, pres. 1985-87). Roman Catholic. Home: 10000 Bellona Ct Richmond VA 23233 Office: The Life Ins Co of Va 6610 W Broad St Richmond VA 23230

PARKER, MARION DEAN HUGHES, home care service executive; b. Greenwich, Conn., July 21, 1911; d. Walter A. and Marion K. (Dean) Hughes; B.A., UCLA, 1932; m. Conkey P. Whitehead, Nov. 14, 1929 (div. Aug. 1933); m. Andrew Granville Pierce III, Oct. 21, 1933; m. Willard Parker, Oct. 5, 1939 (div. 1951); 1 child, Walter van Eps. Actress appearing in Broadway prodns. New Faces, Three Waltzes, I Must Love Someone, on tour in The Women, The Man Who Came to Dinner, Lady in the Dark; various night club engagements; appeared in motion picture All About Eve; TV appearances; owner, mgr. Marion Parker's Guys & Dolls, Scottsdale, Ariz., 1951-59; mng. dir., purchasing agt. shipboard gift and accessory shops Am. Export Lines, 1960-64; dir. spl. events ITT, N.Y.C., 1965-66; exec. dir. Assn. Operating Room Nurses, N.Y.C., 1966-68; pres. Home Care-Ring Service, N.Y.C., 1968—; staff Park East Real Estate; asst. to v.p. in charge devel. Bennett Coll., Millbrook, N.Y., 1970; pub. relations cons., 1970—. Mem. Women's Nat. Republican Club, N.Y.C., Manhattan East Rep. Club, N.Y.C.; sustaining mem. Rep. Nat. Com., 1981—. Mem. Screen Actors Guild, Actors Equity. Address: 301 E 78th St New York NY 10021

PARKER, MARY EVELYN, state treasurer; b. Fullerton, La., Nov. 8, 1920; d. Racia E. and Addie (Graham) Dickerson; m. W. Bryant Parker, Oct. 31, 1954; children: Mary Bryant, Ann Graham. BA, Northwestern State Coll., La., 1941; diploma in social welfare, La. State U., 1943. Social worker Allen Parish, La., 1941-42; personnel adminstr. War Dept., Camp Claiborne, La., 1943-47; editor Oakdale, La., 1947-48; exec. dir. La. Dept. Commerce and Industry, Baton Rouge, 1948-52; with Mut. of N.Y., Baton Rouge, 1952-56; chmn. La. Bd. Pub. Welfare, Baton Rouge, 1950-51; commr. La. Dept, Pub. Welfare, Baton Rouge, 1956-63, La. Div. Adminstrn., 1964-67; treas. State of La., 1968-87. Chmn. White House Conf. on Children and Youth, 1960; pres. La. Conf. on Social Welfare, 1959-61; mem. Democratic Nat. Com., 1948-52; bd. dirs. Woman's Hosp., Baton Rouge; trustee Episcopal High Sch., Baton Rouge Gen. Hosp. Found.; mem. adv. council Coll. Bus., Tulane U., New Orleans. Named Baton Rouge Woman of Yr., 1976. Baptist. Home: 9309 Hill Trace Ave Baton Rouge LA 70809 *

PARKER, NAIDA LOUISE, town clerk; b. Boston, Oct. 31, 1948; d. Armand L. Marois and Naida C. (Backman) Chapman; m. John D. Parker, Feb. 14, 1976. Diploma, Boston Bus. Sch., 1970. Exec. sec. New Bedford

(Mass.) Ceta Consortium, 1979-80; sec. to selectman Town of Marion, Mass., 1980-82; assessors clk. Town of Rochester, Mass., 1982-85, town clk., 1984—. Mem. Mass. Town Clks. Assn., Tri County Clks. Assn. Home: 661 Walnut Plain Rd West Wareham MA 02576 Office: Town of Rochester 560 Rounseville Rd Rochester MA 02770

PARKER, RUBY BRASTOW, telecommunications executive; b. Boston, June 11, 1947; d. Richard Brastow and Ruby (Stoddard) P. B.A., U. Mass., 1969; M.S., Central Conn. Coll., 1973. Tchr. Hartford Pub. Sch., Conn., 1969-74; counselor Haverhill Pub. Sch., Mass., 1974-81; with computer prodn. support dept. Honeywell, Waltham, Mass., 1981-83, telecommunications project analyst, 1983-86, mgr. data network adminstrn. and planning, 1986—. Fellow NOW. Home: 10 Washington Ave Billerica MA 01821 Office: Honeywell 200 Smith St Waltham MA 02154

PARKER, SARA ANN, state librarian; b. Cassville, Mo., Feb. 19, 1939; d. Howard Frankline and Vera Irene (Thomas) P. B.A., Okla. State U., 1961; M.L.S., Emporia State U., Kans., 1968. Adult services librarian Springfield Pub. Library, Mo., 1972-75, bookmobile dir., 1975-76; coordinator Southwest Mo. Library Network, Springfield, 1976-78; library developer Colo. State Library, Denver, 1978-82; state librarian Mont. State Library, Helena, 1982—; cons. and lectr. in field. Author, editor, compiler in field; contbr. articles to profl. jours. Sec., Western Council State Libraries, Reno, Nev., 1984-86, mem. Mont. State Data Adv. Council, 1983—, Mont. Telecommunications Council, 1985, WLN Network Council, vice chmn., 1984-87, Kellogg ICLIS Project Mgmt. Bd., 1986—. Inst. Ednl. Leadership Ednl. fellow, 1982. Mem. ALA, Chief Officers State Library Agys., Mont. Library Assn. (bd. dirs. 1982—), Mountain Plains Library Assn. (sect. chmn. 1980, pres. 1987—). Club: Montana (Helena). Home: 135 Seventh Ave Helena MT 59601 Office: Mont State Library 1515 E Sixth Ave Helena MT 59620

PARKER, SHERRY, advertising executive; b. Los Angeles, July 18, 1945; d. Robert Lowell and Rosanna (Crane) P. BA, Occidental Coll., 1968; cert. de la langue Française, Univ. de Lausanne, France, 1969. Account coordinator Dixon and Parcels, N.Y.C., 1969-72; advt. account exec. J. Walter Thompson, San Francisco, 1972-82; exec. v.p. advt. D'Arcy Masius Benton and Bowles, San Francisco, 1982—. Named one of 75 women to take over corp. Am. Working Woman Mag., 1985. Democrat. Congregational. Home: 30 Almaden Ct San Francisco CA 94118 Office: D'Arcy Masius Benton & Bowles 433 California St San Francisco CA 94104

PARKER, SUE TERRY, communications executive; b. Ely, Nev., Aug. 2, 1951; d. DeLile and Sybil (Oxborrow) Terry; m. Patrick Micheal McDonald, Oct. 1, 1977 (div.); 1 child, Jacqueline; m. Rick L. Parker, Dec. 7, 1980. BS, U. So. Calif., 1973; MBA, U. Nev., 1985. Asst. acct. Sun Valley (Idaho) Co., 1975-77; bus. mgr. Group W Cable, Reno, 1983-84, TCI Cable, Pocatello, Idaho, 1984—. Mem. Profl. Women's Networking. Republican. Mormon. Club: Las Literas (Pocatello). Home: 2798 Kootenai Pocatello ID 83201 Office: TCI Cable 735 Yellowstone Ave Pocatello ID 83201

PARKER, SUZANE WARD, data processing company executive; b. Peoria, Ill., Aug. 10, 1952; d. George Edward and Adlean (Sledge) Ward; m. Ronald Willis Parker, Aug. 25, 1973; 1 child, Brandon Russell. BA in History Edn., Western Ill. U., 1974; postgrad., N.Y. Inst. Tech., Westbury, 1985—. High sch. tchr. Nyack (N.Y.) Schs., 1975-77; personnel adminstrn. specialist IBM Corp., Sterling Forest, N.Y., 1977-79, personnel staff asst., 1979-80, personnel recruiting specialist, 1980-82, adminstrv. asst. to site gen. mgr., 1982, personnel counselor, 1982-84, mgr. adminstrn. and office automation, 1984-86; mgr. equal opportunity and edn. IBM Corp., Tarrytown, N.Y., 1986-87, mgr. compensation and benefits, 1987—. Chmn. adv. council Graham-Windom Sch., Hastings-on-Hudson, N.Y., 1986—. Mem. Am. Mgmt. Assn., Nat. Assn. Female Execs., Coalition 100 Black Women, Delta Sigma Theta (v.p. Rockland County alumnae chpt. 1986-87). Home: 3 Enterprise Ct Nanuet NY 10954

PARKER, TERRY MARIE, lawyer, city official; b. Higginsville, Mo., Apr. 16, 1948; d. Elvis Wyatt and Lola Mae (Jennings) P.; B.A., U. Mo., Kansas City, 1970; J.D., U. Kans., 1973; M.P.A., Ariz. State U., 1984; m. Robert David Sparks, Jan. 3, 1980. Admitted to Kans. bar, 1973; staff atty. Ariz. Legis. Council, Phoenix, 1973-78; mgmt. asst., mgmt. and budget dept. City of Phoenix, 1978-80, cable communications officer Office Cable Communications, 1980-87, contract adminstr. div. Pub. Works, City of Phoenix, 1987—. Mem. Am. Bar Assn., Internat. Soc. Pub. Telecommunications Profls. (pres.), Kans. Bar Assn., Internat. City Mgmt. Assn., Ariz. Mcpl. Mgmt. Assts. Assn., Am. Soc. Public Adminstrn., Nat. Assn. Telecommunications Officers and Advisors (exec. com.), Women in Cable (dir. Ariz. chpt.). Club: Soroptomists Internat. Office: 101 S Central Ave Suite 400 Phoenix AZ 85004

PARKER, TREELA M(AY), army non-commissioned officer; b. Wise County, Va., Aug. 21, 1954; d. James Hobert and Bonnie F. (Begley) P. A.A., Cecil Community Coll., 1974; BS in Social Psychology with distinction, Park Coll., Parksville, Mo., 1983; MA in behavioral scis. Catholic U. Am., 1987. Enlisted as pvt. 1st class U.S. Army, 1975, advanced through grades to sgt. 1st class, 1984; legal clk. Hdqrs. 1st Maintenance Bn., Ludwigsburg, W. Ger., 1976-78; ops. specialist 235th Signal Detachment, Fort Monmouth, N.J., 1978-79; asst. noncommissioned officer-in-charge 209th Mil. Intelligence Bn., Yong San Seoul, Korea, 1979-80, Army community services Hdqrs. Installation Support Activity, Fort Monmouth, 1980-81; adminstrv. asst. to dir. of personal info. systems directorate Mil. Personnel Ctr., Alexandria, Va., 1981-83; chief top secret repository NATO Subregistry Army Materiel Command, Alexandria, 1983-87, also asst. instr. for phys. fitness test, 1984-86; recruiter U.S. Army, Carlisle, Pa., 1987—; mem. promotion selection bds., 1984-86, Soldier of Yr./Quarter Bds., 1984-86. Author NATO Subregistry Newsletter, 1984-86. Decorated Legion of Merit. Mem. Women's Army Corps Vet. Assn., Phi Theta Kappa. Avocations: horseback riding; reading; writing prose and poetry; dancing; theatre. Office: US Army Recruiting Office Suite 47 MJ Mall Carlisle PA 17013

PARKER, VIRGINIA ANNE, ranch administrator; b. Brockton, Mass., Apr. 24, 1918; d. John and Jennie (Krusas) Salus; student Bryant Stratton Coll., Boston, 1938, Columbia U., 1941; m. John Glendon Parker, Feb. 1942 (div. 1952); one dau., Deborah Anne. Sales supr. Reuben H. Donnelley Corp., N.Y.C., 1944-46; traveling sales rep. Elizabeth Arden Inc., N.Y.C., 1946-47; advt. salesperson Park East Pub. Co., N.Y.C., 1947-48; point of sale display work Parker Kleinhans Assos. and V.A. Parker Co., N.Y.C., 1950-55; merchandising coordinator WGBS Radio Sta., Miami, 1957-59; lighting cons. Verd-A-Ray Corp., Miami, 1960-63; string writer, advt. salesperson Palm Beach Post Times, Fla., 1963-65; advt. salesperson Avon Park Sun, Fla., and Sebring News, Fla., 1965-67; sales mgr. radio sta. WJCM, Sebring, and advt. salesperson radio sta. WIPC, Lake Wales, Fla., 1967-69; office mgr., trustee asst., exec. sec. Griffith Ranch Inc., Okeechobee, Fla., 1969-80, semi-ret., 1980, now vol. worker with retarded and handicapped, also with ret. vol. sr. programs Nu-Hope. Mem. Bus. and Profl. Women Miami (2d v.p., rec. sec. 1958-60, state award for nat. security 1960), Parents Without Ptnrs. Fla. (news editor 1962-63). Club: Advt. Miami. Address: 415 Mat-Lo Ave PO Box 1112 Sebring FL 33871

PARKER-MCGEHEE, SYLVIA JO, comptroller; b. Tacoma, Feb. 15, 1960; d. David Coleman and Minnie (Eliot) Parker; m. Michael Lawrence McGehee, Sept. 30, 1983; 1 child, James. AS in Data Processing, Ft. Steilacoom Community Coll., Tacoma, 1982. Bookkeeper OK Tire, Port Orchard, Wash., 1975-76; proof op. Kitsap County Bank, Port Orchard, Wash., 1976-77; bookkeeper Groff Electric, Inc., Tacoma, 1977-79; accounts receivable bookkeeper U. Travel Agy., Seattle, 1982-85; comptroller Reston (Va.) Travel Agy., Inc., 1986—; with Barghausen Cons. Engrs., 1988—. Mem. Bus. and Profl. Women, Data Processing Mng. Assn. (treas. 1982). Home: 15421 SE 177th Pl Renton WA 98058 Office: Barghausen Cons Engrs 18215 72d Ave S Kent WA 98032

PARKES, SUSAN CAROL, lawyer; b. Nashville, July 9, 1955; d. Thomas Theodore and Peggy Ann (Taylor) P. B.A. in Polit. Sci., Miss. U. for Women, 1977; J.D., U. Tenn., 1980. Bar: Tenn. 1980. Assoc. firm Ahles & Kinnard, Lebanon, Tenn., 1980-83; sole practice law, Lebanon, 1983—; counsel Inter-Agy. Youth Council, Lebanon, 1983—. Chmn. Lebanon chpt. March of Dimes, 1982. Mem. ABA, Tenn. Bar Assn., Wilson County Bar Assn., Nashville Women's Bar Assn., Phi Delta Phi. Democrat. Methodist. Home: 1425 Alhambra Dr Lebanon TN 37087 Office: 202 E Gay St Lebanon TN 37087

PARK-HAGEMAN, SALLY HOPE, home economist educator; b. Choteau, Mont., May 14, 1952; d. John G. and Betty M. (Grover) Park; m. Wayne E. Hageman, Dec. 28, 1985. BS, Mont. State U., 1975. Cert. family community leadership trainer. Tchr. Big Horn Sch. Dist. #1, Byron, Wyo., 1976-79; asst. houseware dept. Odegards Dept. Store, Billings, Mont., 1980; extention agt. S.D. Cooperative Extention Service, Brookings, S.D., 1981—; mem. policy bd. Family Community Leadership of S.D. Columnist: Hot Springs Star, Edgemont Herald-Tribune, Custor Chronicle; editor 2 county newsletters. Mem. bd. dirs. Western Jr. Home Econs. Show, S.D. Advocacy for Women, Rapid City, S.D., 1984—. Mem. AAUW, Bus. and Profl. Women (Young Careerist of Month 1982), S.D. Extension Home Economist Assn. (bd. dirs. we. dist. 1981-83, v.p., past bd. dirs.). Republican. United Methodist.

PARKIN, SHARON KAYE, bookkeeper; b. Portland, Oreg., Nov. 21, 1940; d. Charles Edward and Beulah Elizabeth (Foraker) King; m. Russell Jerome Gartrell, Aug. 5, 1960 (div. Dec. 1971); children—Mark Russell, William Edward; m. Jack Edgar Parkin, Feb. 21, 1975. Student, Portland State U., 1959-60. Timekeeper, Sears, Roebuck & Co., Redmond, Wash., 1971-77; bookkeeper, acct. Bristol Bay Area Health Corp., Dillingham, Alaska, Mental Health Corp., Bellingham, Wash., 1977-78, 82; bookkeeper Whatcom Counseling, 1978-80, Charlie's Marine, Juneau, Alaska, 1980-81, L & M Supplies, Dillingham, 1983—; owner, pres. Parkin Bookkeeping, 1984—; notary public State of Alaska, 1983—. Democrat. Mem. Christian Ch. Avocations: boating; fishing; hunting; traceling; crochet. Home: PO Box 515 Dillingham AK 99576 Office: L & M Supplies PO Box 550 Dillingham AK 99576

PARKINSON, ANTOINETTE (TONI), public relations executive; b. Camden, N.J., Oct. 1, 1943; d. Anthony Vincent and Enes Marie (Guidarini) Parassio; divorced; children: Kim, Kris, Kraig. Grad., Peirce Sch. Bus. Adminstrn., 1963; BS in Pub. Relations, Pacific Western U., 1987. Adminstrv. asst., copywriter Neighborhood Publs., Collingswood, N.J., 1982-85; instr. Canterbury Press, Phila., 1983-85, v.p. nat. sales, 1984-85, pres., 1985; community liaison coordinator O'Brien Kreitzberg, Merchantville, N.J., 1985-86; pub. info. officer Camden County Solid Wate Mgmt., Camden, 1985-86; dir. mktg. Consolidated Fin. Mgmt., Clementon, N.J., 1986—; pub. relations cons. IACREOT, Camden, 1987, Atlantic Beach Real Estate, Stone Harbor, N.J., 1986—, Ea. Resource Mgmt., Inc., Haddonfield, N.J., 1987; owner, pres. Parkinson Pub. Relations. Project coordinator (video) Recycling-The Winners Circle, 1987; columnist newspaper Camden County Record, 1986—;. Candidate Haddon Township Commrs., 1983, 87; press coordinator Hart for Pres. Campaign, Camden County, 1983; mem. Haddonfield Township PTA, 1983-86; bd. dirs. Robin's Nest, Woodbury, N.J., 1986—; chair friends of Haddonfield Symphony, 1983-87. Mem. Pub. Relations Soc. Am., Pub. Relations Profls. of South Jersey, Nat. Assn. Female Execs., Cherry Hill C. of C., South Jersey C. of C., Am. Heart Assn. Home: 653 W Crystal Lake Ave Haddonfield NJ 08033 Office: Consol Fin Mgmt 211 Gibbsboro Rd Clementon NJ 08021

PARKINSON, MARIA LUISA, entertainment employment executive; b. Burbank, Calif., July 27, 1951; d. Roy Wilbur (Parky) and Serafina Antonia (Sorzano) P. AA, Pasadena City Coll., 1973; student, Acad. Stage and Cinema Arts, Los Angeles, 1973-76, The Living History Center, Augoura, Calif. Career counsleor Apple One Employment Agy., Marina Del Rey, Calif., 1977-80; career counselor Good People, Inc., Los Angeles, 1980-83, Friedman Personnel Agy., Inc., Los Angeles, 1983-84; owner Parkinson Entertainment Agy., Hollywood, Calif., 1984—; lectr. in field, 1978—. sponser Latin Legal Ctr., Santa Monica, 1987—; charter mem. Mus. Contemporary Art. Mem. Am. Film Inst., Women in Show Bus. (publicity chair), Acad. Sci. Fiction, Fantasy and Horror Films, Hollywood C. of C. (exec. com.), Entertainment Council, 1984—, Bd. Govs. Count Dracula Soc. Democrat. Roman Catholic. Office: Parkinson Entertainment Agy 6525 Sunset Blvd 3d Floor Hollywood CA 90028

PARKS, BLANCHE CECILE, human resources professional; b. Leavenworth, Kans., Feb. 2, 1949; d. Nile Eugene Sr. and Fern (Dickinson) Williams; m. Sherman A. Parks Jr.; children: Michael A., Stacy M. B in Edn., Washburn U., 1971, M in Edn., 1976, postgrad. in ednl. adminstrn., 1983-84. Tchr. Topeka Pub. Schs., 1971-76, reading specialist, 1979-84; ins. regulator Kans. Ins. Dept., Topeka, 1984-85, consumer rep., 1985-87, asst. to sec. human resources, 1987—. Named one of Outstanding Young Women of Kans. Jaycee Women, 1984, 85, one of Outstanding Young Women Am., 1985. Mem. Jr. League of Topeka, Jack and Jill Am., Kans. C. of C. (leadership award 1985), Phi Kappa Phi, Phi Delta Kappa, Alpha Delta Kappa, Delta Kappa Gamma, (life) Delta Sigma Theta (v.p. 1980-82). Republican. Mem. A.M.E. Ch. Home: 3744 S E Fremont Topeka KS 66612

PARKS, CHRISTI DEAN, marketing professional; b. Alton, Ill., Sept. 17, 1955; d. Floyd Calloway and Norma (Gimmeson) Dean; m. Thomas Charles Parks, Aug. 13, 1977. BA, Evangelical Coll., 1977. Continuity writer Sta. KTTS-Radio, Springfield, Mo., 1976-77; dir. pub. relations Ill. Dist. Assemblies of God, Carlinville, 1977-78; account exec. Suburban Newspapers of Greater St. Louis, Alton, Ill., 1978-81; mktg. asst. Alton Sq. div. May Ctrs., Inc., 1981-82; dir. mktg. May Ctrs., Inc., St. Louis, 1982-85, Paramount Group, Inc., St. Louis, 1985—; cons. small retail Ctr. for Bus. and Industry, Lewis Clark Community Coll., Godfrey, Ill., 1986—. Mem. choir, Sunday sch. tchr. and counselor youth Assemblies of God Ch. Mem. Internat. Council Shopping Ctrs. (cert. dir. mktg.), St. Louis Pub. Relations and Advt. Club, St. Louis Radio Assn., Am. Assn. Univ. Women (sec. Wood River, Ill. chpt. 1984-85). Home: 773 Condit St Wood River IL 62095 Office: Paramount Group Inc 514 Northwest Plaza Saint Louis MO 63074

PARKS, JACKELEE ANTHONISE, small business owner, graphoanalyst; b. Chgo., Oct. 16, 1935; d. Herbert Frank and Dorothy Irene (Lougren) Anthonise; m. James M. Parks (div. 1958); 1 child, Joel David Parks. Student, U. Houston, U. Nev., 1984, Holistic Health Assn., 1978-82. Cert. shorthand reporter, Tex., graphoanalyst; registered profl. reporter, securities dealer. Mem. traveling group Spotlighters Melodrama, Houston, 1954-55; dir. vols. Civil Def., Houston, 1954-55; owner, operator German Shepherd Kennels, Houston, 1955-57; singer, dancer Theatre, Inc., Houston, 1956-57, Joyce Roland Dancers, Houston, 1957-58; exec. sec. Pan Am. Ins. Co., Houston, 1958-60; ins. investigator Internat. Service Ins. Co., Houston, 1960; exec. sec. Atlantic Refining, J. Ray McDermott, Houston, 1961; owner, operator Parks Reporting, Livingston, Tex., 1962—; parapsychologist 1975—, graphoanalyst, 1982—; rep. Nat. Assn. Securities Dealers, 1984—. Den Mother Cub Scouts, Boy Scouts Am., Houston. Mem. Internat. Graphoanalysis Soc., Ecumenical Soc. Psychorientology, Nat. Shorthand Reporters Assn., S.W. Writers, Tex. Graphoanalysts, Tex. Shorthand Reporters Assn., Houston Shorthand Reporters Assn. Mem. Unity Ch. Club: Westwood Civic. Home: PO Box 539 Livingston TX 77351 Office: Parks Reporting PO Box 539 Livingston TX 77351

PARKS, JANET ELAINE, pharmacist; b. Watertown, S.D., Oct. 20, 1946; d. Dale O. and Della E. (Horn) P. B.S., S.D. State U., 1970; M.B.A., U. Minn., 1981. Registered pharmacist, Minn., Iowa, Wis. Staff pharmacist St. Luke's Hosp., Duluth, Minn., 1970-81; fin. cons. Parks & Parks, Marshall, Minn., 1981-82; pharmacy cons. J. Parks, Mason City, Iowa, 1982-85; night pharmacist St. Joseph Mercy Hosp., Mason City, 1982-85; dir. pharmacy Tomah Meml. Hosp., Wis., 1985-86; pharmacy cons. Tomah Care Ctr., 1985-86; mgr. pharmacy computer ops. St. Nicholas Hosp., Sheboygan, Wis., 1986—; fin. cons. Methodist chs. Mem. AAUW, Am. Soc. Hosp. Pharmacists (region sec. 1975), Nat. Assn. Future Women (photographer 1984), Nat. Assn. Female Execs., Phi Kappa Phi, Rho Chi. Methodist. Avocations: nature photography; needlecraft; cross-country skiing; bicycling; personal computers. Home: 1628 N 28th St Sheboygan WI 53081 Office: St Nicholas Hosp Sheboygan WI 53081

PARKS, JULIA ETTA, educator; b. Kansas City, Kans., Apr. 5, 1923; d. Hays and Idella Long; B.Ed., Washburn U., 1959, M.Ed., 1965; Ed.D., U. Kans., 1980; m. James A. Parks, Aug. 10, 1941; 1 child, James Hays. Tchr., Lowman Hill Elem. Sch., 1959-64; faculty Washburn U., Topeka, Kans., 1964—, prof. edn. 1981—, mem. pres.'s adv. council, 1981-84, chair edn., phys. edn., health and recreation div., multicultural com., dept. edn., 1986—; lectr., Topeka Pub. Schs. Mem. acad. sabbatical com., Washburn U., 1987—, vis. teams Nat. Council for Accreditation of Tchr. Edn., 1974-86. Bd. dirs. Children's Hour, 1981-84, Mulvane Art Center, 1974-78; judge, All Kans. Spelling Bees, 1982-86; sec. Brown Decision Sculpture Com., 1974-85. Author: (books) What's so Funny?, The Reading Program: An Historical Perspective 1938-1982; contbr. articles to profl. jours. Mem. Washburn U. Alumni Assn. (recipient Teaching Excellence award 1983), Internat. Reading Assn., Kans. Inst. Higher Edn. (mem. pres. adv. council, 1981-83), Kans. Reading Assn., Kans. Reading Profls. Higher Edn., Delta Kappa Gamma, Phi Delta Kappa. Methodist. Club: Links (pres. 1982-84, chairperson scholarship com. 1984—), Topeka Back Home Reunion (historian). Office: Washburn U Dept Edn 1700 College Ave Topeka KS 66621

PARKS, KARYN ANN, architect; b. Tulsa, June 14, 1955; d. Lloyd Lee and Mary Ellen (Scott) P.; m. Michael James Pickard, July 8, 1978 (div. Feb. 1986). BArch, Ariz. State U., 1978. Draftsman Brock & Craig Architects, Mesa, Ariz., 1978-79; project mgr. Dwayne G. Lewis Architects, Inc., Phoenix, 1979-82; pres., prin. Karyn A. Parks Architect, Inc., Scottsdale, Ariz., 1982—. Vol. Tempe Home Service, Ariz., 1986-87. Mem. AIA, Women Execs. Assn. Met. Phoenix. Republican. Home: 1605 E Diamond Dr Tempe AZ 85283 Office: Karyn A Parks Architect Inc 6535 E Osborn Suite 404 Scottsdale AZ 85251

PARKS, MARY IRENE, bookseller, antiques dealer; b. Asheboro, N.C., Apr. 19, 1919; d. Carl Clifton and Revella Rose (Strickland) Rollins; m. Albert Lee Parks, July 3, 1938; children—Albert Lee, Jr. (dec.), Rachel Yvonne White, Teresa Diana Cooper, Candace Susan Kirk, James Michael, Cynthia Revella Whitley. Bookseller Grandpa's House, Troy, N.C., 1963—. Baptist. Office: Grandpa's House Hwy 27 Rt 3 Box 292 Troy NC 27371

PARKS, MELANIE ANN, financial analyst; b. Pueblo, Colo., July 6, 1958; d. William Thomas and Barbara Jean (Chatham) Leonard; m. Floyd Mason Parks, Feb. 17, 1979. Student, U. So. Colo., 1976-78; BS in Mgmt., U. Utah, 1981. Dept. mgr. Grand Cen. Stores, Salt Lake City, 1981-82; asst. mgr. House of Fabrics, Denver, 1982; color analyst Stretch and Sew Fabrics, Denver, 1982-84; receptionist, sec. Westam. Mortgage Co., Denver, 1984, budget analyst, 1984-85, pricing coordinator, 1985-86, jr. acct., 1986, fin. analyst, 1986—. Vice-chairperson Rep. precinct, Salt Lake City, 1981-82. Mem. Am. Bus. Womens Assn., Nat. Assn. Female Execs. Baptist. Office: Westam Mortgage Co 7900 E Union Ave Suite 500 Denver CO 80237

PARKS, PATRICIA JEAN, foundation administrator, educator; b. Boone, Iowa, Feb. 10, 1936; d. William James and Kathryn Julia (Dunn) Conway; m. James Francis Parks, Aug. 26, 1961; children: Martha, Michael, James, Patricia, Peter, Halligan, Tom, Patrick, Fabiola, Enriqueta. BA, Clarke Coll., 1957. Math. tchr. Milw. Pub. Schs., 1957-81; founder, pres. Family Unity Internat., Milw., 1981-87, Elm Grove, Wis., 1987—. Ward chair various polit. campaigns, Milw. Recipient Disting. Alumni award Clarke Coll.

PARLE, RITA THERESE, mental health center executive; b. Omaha, May 28, 1924; d. Harry Vincent and Mary Hiltrude (McEvoy) P. BA, Dunbarton Coll., 1973; MA, Cath. U. of Am., 1974; EdD, George Washington U., 1985. Joined Visitation Order of Holy Mary, 1945. Superioress Visitation Order of Holy Mary, Bethesda, Md., 1967-70; various positions Sears, Roebuck and Co., Md. and Washington, 1970-75; adminstrv. asst. Counseling Ctr. George Washington U., Washington, 1976-78; clinic dir. Mid-Nebr. Community Mental Health Ctr., Broken Bow, 1978-80; exec. dir. Mid-Plains Ctr. for Profl. Service, Grand Island, Nebr., 1980—. Author: Wife Abuse Factors in Semi Rural Nebr., 1985. Mem. Nebr. Assn. Mental Health Providers (pres. 1987—). Home: 35 Chantilly St Grand Island NE 68803

PARLETT, DEBORAH ANN, service executive; b. Balt., Sept. 13, 1957; d. Alvin Harry and Rosalie Amanda (Bricker) P.; m. Timothy Wayne Lewis, Jan. 29, 1977. AA, Essex Community, 1976; BA in Acctg., Loyola Coll., 1977; MS in Fin., U. Balt., 1983. Auditor Wooden and Benson CPA's, Towson, Md., 1977-79; auditor in charge Schnepfe and Co., CPA's, Lutherville, Md., 1979; asst. audit officer Mercantile Bankshares, Balt., 1979-82; asst. dir. fin. services The Arundel Corp., Towson, 1983-85; controller Md. Mgmt. Co., Balt., 1985-87; mgr. Marriott Corp., Washington, 1987—. Mem. Nat. Assn. Accts., Am. Inst. CPA's, Md. Assn. CPA's, Greater Bd. Realtors. Democrat. Methodist. Office: Marriott Mgmt Corp One Marriott Dr Washington DC

PARMESE, BARBARA JEAN, medical organization executive, consultant; b. Hackensack, N.J., Sept. 21, 1954; d. Jack and Rose (Lodato) Insinga; m. Vincent James Parmese, Oct. 6, 1984. BS, Trenton State Coll., 1976; postgrad. William Paterson Coll., 1979-80. Health record analyst Hackensack Med. Ctr., 1976-79; quality assurance analyst Englewood Hosp., N.J., 1979-80; quality rev. mgr. Assn. Profl. Health Care Rev., Saddle Brook, N.J., 1980-82, asst. dir., 1982-83, exec. dir., 1983-85; assoc. exec. dir. North Jersey Physicians Rev., Parsippany, 1985—; mem. reimbursement adv. com. N.J. Dept. Health, Trenton, 1986. Mem. Am. Mgmt. Assn. Home: 487 Kaplan Ave Hackensack NJ 07601 Office: North Jersey Physicians 120 Littleton Rd Parsippany NJ 07054

PARNELL, DIANA DEANGELIS, dermatologist; b. Tacoma, Wash., May 18, 1940; d. Fulvio Garibaldi and Ruth Margaret (Nordlund) DeAngelis; m. Francis W. Parnell, Feb. 27, 1965; children—Cheryl Lynn, John Francis, Kathleen Diana, Alison Anne, Thomas William. B.S., Pa. State U., 1961; M.D., Georgetown U., 1965. Diplomate Nat. Bd. Examiners, Am. Bd. Dermatology. Intern, Univ. Hosps., U. Wis., Madison, 1965-66, resident in dermatology, 1966-69; dermatologist Univ. Health Service, U. Wis., Madison, 1969-70; practice medicine specializing in dermatology, Greenbrae, Calif., 1970-76, 78—, Ridgewood, N.J., 1976-78; corp. med. cons. indsl. dermatology, 1976-79; v.p. Parnell Med. Corp., Greenbrae, 1980—; pres. Parnell Pharms., San Rafael, Calif.; clin. instr. medicine U. Wis. Sch. Medicine, Madison, 1969-70; clin. instr. dermatology U. Calif. Sch. Medicine, San Francisco, 1970-76, 87; mem. staff Marin Gen. Hosp., Greenbrae, 1970—, Ross Gen. Hosp. (Calif.), 1970-75, 78-84, Valley Hosp. Ridgewood, N.J., 1976-78. Fellow Am. Acad. Dermatology; mem. Pacific Dermatol. Assn., San Francisco Dermatol. Soc., Am. Soc. Dermatol. Surgery, Nat. Women's Polit. Caucus, Delta Delta Delta. Democrat. Roman Catholic. Home: PO Box 998 Ross CA 94957 Office: 599 Sir Francis Drake Blvd Greenbrae CA 94904

PARNESS, ARLYNE ELLEN, manufacturing company executive; b. Bklyn., Sept. 4, 1942; d. Joseph and Ann (Rosenbaum) Paull; m. Melvyn H. Parness, Nov. 26, 1964; children: Bari Lisa, Caryn Blaine. BS, NYU, 1964. Cert. elem. tchr. Tchr. Bd. Edn. N.Y.C., 1964-68, Bd. Edn. East Ramapo, N.Y., 1975-85; regional mgr. OPI Products Inc., Monsey/Chestnut Ridge, N.Y., 1985—. V.p. Bnai Zion Nat. Women's League, N.Y.C., 1980—; pres. Bnai Zion (Dr. Harris J. Levine chpt.), 1977—. Mem. Nat. Assn. Women Execs. Democrat. Jewish.

PARNES-SHARKEY, MARA ILISE, advertising executive; b. Ft. Hood, Tex., Nov. 28, 1961; d. Edmund Ira Parnes and Betty Faye (Brant) Warshaw; m. Keith Seldon Sharkey, Mar. 4, 1984. BA in Advt., U. Fla., 1983. Account exec. Weiss and Assocs., Inc., Miami, Fla., 1983—; mktg. advisor Bus. Vols. for Arts, Miami, 1986—. Advisor B'Nai B'Rith Youth Orgn., Miami, 1984-86; pub. relations com. Greater Miami Jewish Fedn., 1986—. Mem. Nat. Assn. Female Execs., Advt. Fedn., Mensa. Republican. Jewish. Office: Weiss and Assocs Inc 9500 S Dadeland Blvd Miami FL 33156

PARR, CAROLYN MILLER, judge; b. Palatka, Fla., Apr. 17, 1937; d. Arthur Charles and Audrey Ellen (Dunklin) Miller; m. Jerry Studstill Parr, Dec. 12, 1959; children: Kimberly Susan, Jennifer Parr Turek, Patricia Audrey. BA, Stetson U., 1959; MA, Vanderbilt U., 1960; JD, Georgetown U., 1977; LLD (hon.), Stetson U., 1986. Bar: Md. 1977, U.S. Tax Ct. 1977, D.C. 1979, U.S. Supreme Ct. 1983. Gen. trial atty. IRS, Washington, 1977-

81, sr. trial atty. office of chief counsel, 1982; spl. counsel U.S. Dept. Justice, Washington, 1982-85, judge U.S. Tax Ct., Washington, 1985—. Mem. ABA, Fed. Bar Assn., Md. Bar Assn., Women's Bar Md., Nat. Assn. Women Judges. Republican. Office: US Tax Ct 400 2nd St NW Washington DC 20217

PARR, DORIS ANN, financial institution executive, consultant; b. Fergus Falls, Minn., July 10, 1933; d. Henry Fritzolf and Esther Marie (Ahlgren) Peterson; m. Mark Hoffman, 1949 (div. 1960); children: Cynthia Lee Davis, David Alan; m. Harold R. Parr, 1961 (div. 1974). Student Am. Savs. and Loan Inst., 1965-66, Pioneer Nat. Title Ins. Co., 1969, Menlo Coll., 1975. Comml. loan officer Savbank Service Corp., Seattle, 1975-77; exec. v.p., mgr. Sound Savs. & Loan, Seattle, 1976-78; v.p. Queen City Savs. & Loan, Seattle, 1978-82; v.p., mgr. State Savs. & Loan Assn., Dallas, 1983-84; pres. Nat. Real Estate Mortgage Services Inc., Dallas, 1984—; instr. real estate law San Francisco City Coll., 1975. Recipient 1st Pl. Speech trophy Am. Savs. & Loan Inst., 1964. Mem. Assn. Profl. Mortgage Women (program chmn. Seattle chpt. 1969-70, program chmn. San Jose chpt. 1973-74, pres. 1975-76, Woman of Yr. 1979), U.S. Savs. and Loan League (consumer affairs and secondary market com.), Nat. Assn. Females Execs., Fed. Home Loan Bank Bd. (maj. comml. loan underwriter). Organized and managed 1st U.S. minority savs. and loan assn. Home: 5767 Caruth Haven Ln Dallas TX 75206

PARRINELLO, DIANE DAVIES, educator; b. West Warwick, R.I., Oct. 17, 1939; d. Stanley Duane and Catherine Margaret (Heelan) Davies; m. John Richard Parrinello, Apr. 28, 1962; children: Gregory, Timothy, Bethany, Matthew. BA, U. Rochester, 1961; MS in Edn., Nazareth Coll., 1987. Cert. tchr., N.Y. Biochem. research asst. Syracuse (N.Y.) U., 1962-64; presch. tchr. Jewish Community Ctr., Syracuse, 1964-65; co-owner, mgr. Spl. Creations, Rochester, N.Y., 1979-84; tchr. Winton Rd. Nursery Sch., Rochester, 1983—. Mem. women's council Meml. Art Gallery, Rochester, 1972—; coach Brighton Little League, Rochester, 1975-82; leader Camp Fire Girls, Inc., Rochester, 1975-78; bd. dirs., coach Brighton Soccer League, 1975-85; co-founder Brighton Girls Soccer League, 1976. Mem. Nat. Assn. for Edn. Young Children (Rochester chpt.). Republican. Roman Catholic. Home: 334 San Gabriel Dr Rochester NY 14610 Office: Winton Rd Nursery Sch 220 Winton Rd South Rochester NY 14610

PARRIS, NINA GUMPERT, curator, writer, researcher; b. Berlin, Ger., Sept. 11, 1927; came to U.S., 1937, naturalized, 1944; d. Martin and Charlotte (Blaschko) Gumpert; m. Arthur Parris, Feb. 13, 1949 (div. 1974); children—Carl Joseph, Thomas Martin. B.A., Bryn Mawr Coll., 1968; M.A., U. Pa., 1969, Ph.D., 1979. Teaching fellow U. Mich., Ann Arbor, 1969-70; lectr. Phila. Coll. Art, 1970-71; research asst. Phila. Mus. Art, 1970-71; curator, lectr. U. Vt. Robert Hall Fleming Mus., Burlington, 1971-79; chief curator Columbia Mus., S.C., 1979—. Author: Prints, Paintings and Drawings in Collection of Robert Hall Fleming Mus., 1979, (collection catalogue) S.C. Collection Columbia Mus., 1985, (exhibition catalogue) Through a Master Printer, 1985, The South Carolina Collection of the Columbia Museum, 1987;columnist, State newspaper, Columbia, 1984—. Bd. dirs. Photography Cooperative, Montpelier, Vt., 1977-79, Chittenden Arts Council, Burlington, Vt., 1976-78. Woodrow Wilson fellow, 1968, Univ. fellow Ford Found., 1968-72; grantee NEA, NEH, S.C. Com. Humanities, Vt. Council Arts. Mem. Am. Assn. Museums (pres. curator's com. 1985-87, v.p. 1983-85), Art Mus. Com. Internat. Council Mus., New Eng. Assn. Mus., Southeastern Mus. Assn. Office: Columbia Mus 1112 Bull St Columbia SC 29201

PARRISH, CYNTHIA JOYCE, bank executive, accountant; b. Rock Hill, S.C., Nov. 26, 1955; d. William Kelly and Margaret Elizabeth (Robinson) P.; m. Michael Eugene Ritcher, Aug. 21, 1977 (div. Dec. 1983). BS, Winthrop Coll., 1976; MBA, U. Mo., 1983. Auditor Monsanto Co., St. Louis, 1976-78, area acctg. supr., 1978-81, acctg. supr., 1981-84, acctg. supt., 1984-86; asst. v.p. security services Bankers Trust, N.Y.C., 1987-88, v.p. security services, 1988—. Hotline counselor, treas. advs. bd. Women's Self Help Ctr., St. Louis, 1984-86. Mem. Nat. Assn. Accts. Episcopalian. Home: 2314 Mountain Ave Scotch Plains NJ 07076 Office: Bankers Trust Co PO Box 3343 Ch St Sta New York NY 10008

PARRISH, DIANE SCHMIDT, lawyer; b. Sedalia, Mo., Mar. 1, 1952; d. Richard R. and Vivian J. (McAtee) Schmidt; m. Steven C. Parrish, Jan. 16, 1982; 1 dau., Amanda; m. Ken D. Percy, June 1, 1974 (div. 1980). A.A., Johnson County (Kans.) Community Coll., 1972; B.S. in Dental Hygiene, U. Mo.-Kansas City, 1974; J.D., U. Kans.-Lawrence, 1979. Bar: Mo. 1979, U.S. Dist. Ct. Mo. 1979, U.S. Ct. Appeals (8th cir.) 1983. Assoc., Shook, Hardy & Bacon, Kansas City, Mo., 1979-83. Editor Kans. Law Rev., 1978-79. Mem. Central Exchange, Kansas City, Mo.; chmn. Leawood Plan Commn.; deacon Country Club Christian Ch. Mem. ABA, Mo. Bar Assn., Kans. City Athenaeum, Order of Coif. Democrat. Mem. Disciples of Christ.

PARRISH, MARY ANNE, advertising executive; b. Virginia Beach, Va., Jan. 21, 1953; d. Elijah and Maria Upchurch (Roberson) P.; m. Philip Michael Hadfield Semsch, May 21, 1980 (div. 1981). A.A. in Bus. Adminstrn., Palm Beach Jr. Coll., 1973; B.A. in Journalism, U. Md., 1978. Asst. to v.p. Richard A. Viguerie Co., Falls Church, Va., 1978-79; asst. fundraising dir. Connally for Pres., Arlington, Va., 1979-80; cons. CBS, Rockville, Md., 1980-82; pres. Zeta Media Systems Corp./Copyworks div., Falls Church, 1982-84, Zeta Media, Inc., Juno Beach, Fla., 1984—; dir. Listworks, Inc., Fairfax, Va., 1981; chmn. bd. S. Tigre & Assocs., Washington, 1982—. Mem. Direct Mail Mktg. Assn., Capitol Flyers (sec. 1982—). Home: PO Box 7247 Port Saint Lucie FL 34985 Office: Zeta Media Inc 901 US Hwy 1 Suite 7 Juno Beach FL 33408

PARRISH, MICKEY JOYCE, oil company executive, accountant; b.Kosciusko, Miss., Dec. 6, 1945; d. Hosea Holcomb and Lavada (Ferguson) Lewis; children: Randall, Matthew; m. D. Russell Parrish, June 28, 1975. BS, La. Tech. U., 1979, postgrad., La. Tech. U., 1988. Exec. dir. Sherer, Underwood, Mayhall, Jasper, Ala., 1972-75; exec. asst. Richard Rubin, M.D., P.A., Decatur, Ala., 1975-76; acct. La. Tech. U., Ruston, La., 1979-80; gen. mgr. Big State Ranch-Baron Oil, Ruston, 1980-87; owner, prin. Parrish & Assocs., Ruston, 1982—; lectr. in field. Mem. troop leadership council Boy Scouts Am., 1980-85; trustee Stephen Bufton Meml. Edn. Fund, 1985—; mem. Mayor's Commn. for Women, Ruston, La., 1986—,(pres. 1986-87); chmn. pub. relations Ruston Peach Festival, 1987. Mem. Nat. Assn. Women Bus. Owners, Nat. Speaker's Assn., Nat. Assn. Accts., Nat. Assn. Female Execs., Am. Mgmt. Assn., Nat. Fedn. Ind. Bus. Owners, Am. Bus. Women's Assn. (nat. pres. 1987), 1 of Top Ten Bus. Women 1984, trustee Steven Bufton Meml. Fund, trustee, 1985—, dist II v.p. 1985-86, nat. pres. 1987—, nat. first up 1986-87), Ruston C. of C. (leadership devel. com. 1987—), Women in Bus. (com. chmn.) Baptist.

PARRISH, NANCY ELAINE BUCHELE, lawyer, state senator; b. Cedar Vale, Kans., Nov. 9, 1948; d. Julian Milton and Vergie May (Bryant) Buchele; BS in Edn., Kans. State U., 1970; MS in Spl. Edn., U. Kans., 1974; JD magna cum laude, Washburn U., 1984; m. James Wesley Parrish, Jan. 31, 1970; children: Leslie Elgin, Tyler Jonathan. Tchr., Topeka Public Schs., 1970-75; spl. edn. tchr. Topeka State Hosp., 1975-81; mem. Kans. Senate, 1980—; mem. edn. task force Council of State Govts., 1981-84; adv. bd. Boy's Club of Topeka, Kans. Action for Children; mem. fiscal affairs task force Nat. Council State Legislatures, 1985—; policy chmn. Senate Minority Party, 1985—. Bd. dirs. Family Service and Guidance Ctr., Topeka. Active Golden City Forum, Jr. League Topeka. Mem. ABA, Kans. Bar Assn., Topeka Bar Assn., Office: State Capitol Bldg Room 403 Topeka KS 66612 also: 700 Jackson Suite 200 Topeka KS 66603

PARRISH, SHAREN DENISE, civil engineer; b. Opa Locka, Fla., Aug. 17, 1959; d. Frank Junior and Alice Lee (Baldwin) Brown; m. Anthony Parrish, Aug. 20, 1983; 1 child, Anthony. A.A. in Bus. Adminstrn., Fla. State U., 1978; B.S. in Civil Engring., U. Fla., 1982. Lic. engr. intern. Civil engr. Post, Buckley, Schuh & Ternigan, Cons. Engrs., Miami, Fla., 1982; profl. engring. intern Dept. Transp. Fla., Miami, 1982; service planner engr., Fla. Power and Light, Miami, 1983—. Mem. Harris Chapel Methodist Ch., Ft. Lauderdale, Engring. Leadership Circle, U. Fla., Gainesville, 1981—. Mem. Nat. Tech. Assn. (founding pres. S. Fla. 1984-85, treas. 1985—, leadership award 1985), Fla. Engring. Soc., ASCE, Fla. Blue Key, Alpha Kappa Alpha (Soror of Yr. 1982). Democrat. Baptist. Club: Silhouette. Avocations: jogging; swimming; dancing. Home: 3345 NW 23rd Ct Lauderdale Lakes FL 33312

PARRISH, VIRGINIA ELLEN, educator. d. John Richard and Wila Nina (Bonino) Parrish; m. Donald Rogers, June 8, 1969 (div. 1978); children: Jonathan, Hilary; m. William Haes, Dec. 15, 1978 (div. 1987). BA with honors, Rutgers U., 1970. Cert. secondary tchr., N.J. Tchr. French and English West Deptford (N.J.) Twp. Bd. Edn., 1970-71; proofreader Valdosta (Ga.) Daily Times, 1971-72; tchr. French Limestone (Maine) Jr. Sr. High Sch., 1973-74; fin. aid clk. Glassboro (N.J.) State Coll., 1977-78; inside claims adjuster Reliance Ins. Co., Haddonfield, N.J., 1978-79; tchr. English Haddonfield Bd. Edn., 1979-80, Woodstown (N.J.)-Pilesgrove Regional Bd. Edn., 1980-81; tchr. French and English Monroe Twp. Bd. Edn., Williamstown, N.J., 1981—, coordinator exchange student program Eurolangues, Internat, N.Y.C., 1981—. Author: (poem) Note to My Brother, 1986 (3d place award 1986); contbr. articles to profl. jours. Mem. Am. Fedn. Tchrs., Societé Culturelle Franco-Américaine de South Jersey. Home: 27 Fairmount Dr Glassboro NJ 08028 Office: Oak Knoll Sch Bodine Ave Williamstown NJ 08094

PARROTT, BETTY JANE, mechanical engineer; b. Milw., Feb. 25, 1951; d. Warren Howard and Kathryn Ann (Mauer) Podolske; m. Albert T. Parrott, June 16, 1984; children: Darlene Anita, Sharlene Annette. BS in Elec. engring., U. Wis., Milw., 1973, MBA, 1987. Engr. Milw. Metal Products Co., 1973—, v.p., 1984—. Mem. Soc. Women Engrs., Soc. Automotive Engrs., Beta Gamma Sigma. Christian Scientist. Club: Milw. Dog Tng. Office: Milw Metal Products Co 8000 W Florist Ave Milwaukee WI 53218

PARROTT, BONNIE FRANCINE, automobile dealership official; b. Miami Beach, Fla., July 29, 1953; d. Meyer and Edith (Klein) London; m.Timothy W. Parrott, Oct. 29, 1972 (div. Apr. 1983); children: Melinda Sara, Michael Kevin, Lisa Beth. Student, Miami-Dade Community Coll., 1971-72. Lic. ins. agt., Fla. Fin. mgr. Potamkin Dodge & Volkswagon, Hialeah, Fla., 1984—; cons. SE Bank, 1984—, Homestead Bank, 1984—, Barnett Bank, Miami, 1987—, Consol. Bank, 1988—. Mem. Pierpointe IC Homeowners Assn. Mem. Nat. Assn. Female Execs., Am. Soc. Notaries, Homestead C. of C. Democrat. Jewish. Club: Pembroke Lakes Golf and Racquet, Sheraton Internat. Home: 11935 NW 12th St Pembroke Pines FL 33026 Office: Potamkin Dodge & Volkswagon 1350 W 49th St Hialeah FL 33012

PARRY, CAROL JACQUELINE, banker; b. Chgo., Apr. 12, 1941; d. Ralph G. and Estelle (Hoffman) Newman. B.A., Tufts U., 1964; M.S.W., U. Conn., 1969; postgrad., Harvard U., 1984. Dir. program planning N.Y.C. Agy. for Child Develop., N.Y.C., 1971-72; cons. McKinsey & Co., N.Y.C., 1972-74; asst. commr. Spl. Services for Children, N.Y.C., 1974-77; v.p., dist. head Chem. Bank, N.Y.C., 1978-80, sr. v.p., div. head, 1981-86, sr. v.p. nat. expansion program, 1985, sr. v.p. comml. sector, chmn. regional bank, 1985—, head private banking, 1987—. Bd. dirs. N.Y. Urban Coalition, Nat. Child Labor Com. Channel 13 adv. bd.; chmn. N.Y. State Juvenile Justice Bd. Recipient Big WEAL award Women's Equity Action League, 1984. Home: 60 E 8th St New York NY 10003 Office: Chem Bank 277 Park Ave New York NY 10172 *

PARRY, LOIS IRENE, cosmetic company executive; b. Indpls., Mar. 12, 1945; d. Hilbert Edward and Mary Olive (Lanman) Roth; m. Edward Hayden Parry, Nov. 5, 1966 (div. 1981); children: Jeffrey Alan, Matthew Edward, Jennifer Lynne. Student, Butler U., 1962-65, John Herron Art Ins., 1963-65, Ind. U., 1980-81. Dept. mgr. L.S. Ayres & Co., Indpls., 1980-81, asst. buyer, 1981-82, assoc. buyer, 1982; territory mgr. Charles of the Ritz Group, N.Y.C., 1982-85; acct. exec. Lancome/Cosmair, N.Y.C., 1985—. Pres. West Grove Elem. Sch. PTO, 1979; bd. dirs. White River Coalition, Greenwood, Ind., 1980-81. Mem. Delta Theta Tau-Nu Tau (pres. 1980-81). Republican. Avocations: reading, watercolors, fitness. Home: 5488 W Walnut Dr Greenwood IN 46142 Office: Lancome/Cosmair 575 Fifth Ave New York NY 10017-2450

PARRY, NANCY, surgeon; b. Salt Lake City, Dec. 20, 1940; d. Nathaniel Edmunds and Dortha Nell (Harris) P.; B.S., U. Utah, 1963; M.D., U. Calif., Irvine, 1967. Intern, Latter-Day Saints Hosp., Salt Lake City, 1967-68; gen. practice medicine and surgery, Anaheim, Calif., 1969—; mem. staff Martin Luther Hosp., Anaheim, Anaheim Meml. Hosp., West Anaheim Community Hosp.; originator, developer, pres. Parry Devel. Co., Sun Valley, Idaho, Maui, Hawaii, Lancaster, Anaheim and Carlsbad, Calif., Salt Lake City, 1973—; developer, mng. gen. partner Med. Arts East, Anaheim, 1974—; developer Parry Profl. Bldg.; pres. Breast Inst.; pres. Profl. Edn. Services, Anaheim, 1975—; mem. gen. practice com. Martin Luther Hosp. Bd. dirs. Martin Luther Hosp. Found., 1982—. Orange County Med. Assn. Found. Diplomate Am. Bd. Family Practice. Fellow Acad. Family Physicians; mem. Am. Coll. Emergency Physicians, AMA, Am. Women Med. Assn., Orange County Women in Bus. (dir.), Calif. Med. Assn., Orange County Med. Assn. Address: 1801 W Romneya Dr #601 Anaheim CA 92801

PARRY, PATRICIA GILMAN, hospital executive, consultant; b. N.Y.C., Jan. 9, 1942; d. Max and Gertrude (Weinberg) Gilman; m. Michael Nroman Kahn, Dec. 23, 1962 (div. June 1973); children: Jennifer Lynn, Jason David; m. John Edward Parry, Aug. 28, 1977. BA in History, CCNY, 1963; postgrad. in non-profit mgmt., New Sch. for Social Research, 1987. Grants adminstr. SUNY, New Paltz, 1978-80; dir. sponsored funds SUNY, Purchase, 1980-81; dir. devel. Ulster Assn. for Retarded Citizens, Kinsgston, N.Y., 1983-86, Cornwall (N.Y.) Hosp., 1987—; cons. PGP Assocs., Cornwall, 1986—. Pres. Ulster County Ballet Guild, New Paltz, 1980-82; bd. dirs. Amos and Sarah Holden Home, Newburgh, N.Y., 1987—. Mem. Nt. Assn. Fund Raising Execs., Nat. Assn. Hosp. Devel., Nat. Assn. Female Execs. Democrat. Jewish. Home: 68 Laurel Ave Cornwall NY 12518 Office: Cornwall Hosp Laurel Ave Cornwall NY 12518

PARRY, RANDINE ELIZABETH, psychologist; b. Hartford, Conn., Sept. 6, 1947; d. William Brown and Mary Elizabeth (Caton) P.; m. Stanley A. Cruwys; children—Robert W. Parry-Cruwys, Brendon C. Parry-Cruwys. A.B., Mt. Holyoke Coll., 1968; Ph.D. (USPHS fellow, 1968-72), U. Chgo., 1977. Staff psychologist behavior analysis research lab., dept. psychiatry, U. Chgo., 1971-74, dir. fluency clinic, 1974-77; dir. psychology Walter Fernald State Sch., Waltham, Mass., 1977-80, chief psychologist, 1980—; lic. psychologist SE Counseling Assocs., Norwood, Mass., 1980-82; vis. asst. prof. Northeastern U., Boston, 1977-80; cons. Human Resource Inst. of Franklin, Mass., 1979-81. Contbr. papers to profl. confs. Active NOW, 1974—, chmn. ERA com., Chgo. chpt., 1974-77; mem. Women's Polit. Caucus, 1977—, ACLU, 1978—, Nat. Abortion Rights Action League, 1977—, Friends of Family Planning, 1981—, Belmont Day Sch. Parents Assn., 1984—, Friends of Sturbridge Village, 1981—, N.E. Aquarium, Mus. Fine Arts, Mus. Sci., Boston, 1979—; bd. dirs. Waverley Oaks Child Devel. Center, 1984-86. Mem. Am. Psychol. Assn., Eastern Psychol. Assn., New Eng. Psychol. Assn., Mass. Psychol. Assn., Assn. for Applied Behavior Analysis, Assn. for Advancement of Behavior Therapy, Assn. for Advancement of Psychology, Assn. for Women in Psychology, Boston Behavior Therapy Interest Group. Home: 15 Cherry Oca Ln Framingham MA 01701 Office: Walter Fernald State Sch Dept Psychology 200 Trapelo Rd Waltham MA 02154

PARRY, RUTH ELAINE, health science specialist; b. Salisbury, Md., Apr. 10, 1952; d. Robert Owen and Margaret Elsie (Elburn) P. BA, Washington Coll., Chestertown, Md., 1974; MA, Conn. Coll., 1981; M in Adminstrv. Sci., Johns Hopkins U., 1983. Human factors scientist BDM Services Co., Ft. Ord, Calif., 1975-76; research coordinator sch. pub. health Johns Hopkins U., Baltimore, 1980-83; research assoc. sch. medicine U. Md., Balt., 1983-87; health sci. specialist VA Med. Ctr., Perry Point, Md., 1987—. Contbr. articles to profl. jours., 1983, 84, 88. Research and devel. com. mem. Md. High Blood Pressure Commn., 1983-86. Mem. Nat. Assn. Female Execs., U. Md. Law Sch. Student Bar Assn. (v.p. evening class 1989). Democrat. Home: 9900-I Tailspin Ln Baltimore MD 21220 Office: VA Med Ctr HS R&D Spl Projects Office #152 Perry Point MD 21902

PARSON, MARY JEAN, management consultant; b. Houston, July 26; d. Guy Virgil and Ursula (Clark) P. BA, Birmingham-So. Coll., 1956; MFA, Yale U., 1959. Dir. spl. projects Am. Nat. Theatre & Acad., 1959-60; bus. mgr. Mineola (N.Y.) Playhouse, 1962; asst. to pres. Nat. Performing Arts, Inc., N.Y.C., 1963; dir. exhibits Better Living Ctr. World's Fair, Flushing, N.Y., 1964-65; with ABC, N.Y.C., 1965-80, dir. planning, devel., 1975-79, dir. planning, corp. relations, 1979-80; v.p. planning and adminstrn. Blair TV/Radio, N.Y.C., 1980-83; owner Creative Planning & Communications, Teaneck (N.J.), Birmingham (Ala.), 1983—; cons. in field, 1983—; adj. prof. Yale U., Fordham U. Grad. Sch. Bus., Birmingham-So. Coll., U. Ala.-Birmingham. Author: An Executive's Coaching Handbook, 1986, The Single Solution, 1987, Managing the One Person Business, 1988; (with Matthew J. Culligan) Back to Basics: Planning, 1985; contbg. editor Savvy mag., 1986; contbr. articles to Working Woman mag., New Woman mag., 1987. Bd. dirs. NCCJ, N.Y.C., 1977-81; bd. advisors UN Assn. N.Y., N.Y.C., 1978-82, Ptnrship Birmingham, 1986—; chair rehearsal Festival of Arts, Birmingham, 1987—. Recipient citation Birmingham C. of C. Festival of Arts, 1964, Disting. Alumni award Birmingham-So. Coll., 1986. Mem. Internat. Radio and TV Soc. (chair coll. conf. 1978-81, nat. bd. 1982-84), Am. Women in Radio and TV (treas., pres. N.Y.C. chpt. 1972-74, v.p. nat. bd. 1975-77, award 1977), Women's Network. Club: The Lambs (N.Y.C.). Office: Creative Planning and Communications 3008-1 13th Ave S Birmingham AL 35205

PARSONS, CHRISTINE THOMAS, computer and infosystems engineer, consultant; b. Winston-Salem, N.C., July 9, 1957; d. Emory Augustus and Mary (Mitchell) Thomas; m. Stephen Charles Parsons, Aug. 30, 1980; 1 child, Patrick Thomas. BS in Applied Physics, Appalachian State U., 1978; MS in Computer and Information Science, U. Ala., Birmingham, 1983. Physicist So. Research Inst., Birmingham, Ala., 1979-81; systems analyst So. Co. Services, Birmingham, 1981-84; engring. systems analyst So. Co. Services, Atlanta, 1984—; cons. in field; instr. Samford U., Birmingham. Contbg. author to profl. jours. Bd. dirs. Blackwell Bend Homeowners Assn., Atlanta, 1986, bd. dirs. Summerford Homeowners Assn., Atlanta, 1987. Acad. Achievement scholar Appalachian State U., 1977. Mem. Atlanta Lawn and Tennis Assn, Sigma Pi Sigma, Gamma Beta Phi. Home: 3471 Summerford Ct Marietta GA 30062 Office: Southern Co Services 64 Perimeter Ctr E Atlanta GA 30346

PARSONS, DEBRA DEANNA, trucking company executive; b. Ft. Smith, Ark., July 12, 1957; d. Gail Dean and Lerene Marie (Houpt) P. BS in Journalism, Kans. State U., 1980. Sales exec. Sta. KWIK-AM, Pocatello, Idaho, 1980-81, Sta. KIFI-TV, Pocatello, 1981-82; sales mgr. Sta. KSEI-AM, Pocatello, 1982-83, Sta. KUJ-FM-AM, Walla Walla, Wash., 1983; mgr. nat. accounts ANR Freight System, Portland, Oreg., 1986-87; regional dir. sales Matlack, Inc., Portland, 1987—. Bd. dirs. Wade Park Estates, Portland. Soprano Portland Symphonic Chorale, 1986—. Named one of Outstanding Young Women Am., 1982. Mem. N.W. Chem. Assn., Council Logistic Mgmt. (v.p. 1987-88, pres. 1988—), Doll Artisans Guild. Republican. Lodge: Civitans (chairperson 1980-83). Office: Matlack Inc 8101 NE 11th St Portland OR 97211

PARSONS, GAIL, accountant; b. Salt Lake City, Mar. 12, 1946; d. Paul Eugene and Virginia (Jarvis) P.; B.S. in Acctg., U. Utah, 1969; m. Carl Andersen Heyes, July 25, 1975. CPA, Utah. Staff acct. Hansen, Barnett & Maxwell, C.P.A.'s, Salt Lake City, 1969-75; controller Timberhaus Ski Shops, Inc., Park City and Snowbird, Utah, 1975-76; pvt. practice as cert. public accountant, Salt Lake City, 1976—. Mem. Am. Inst. CPA's, Utah Am. Woman's Soc. CPA's, Utah Assn. CPA's, Am. Woman's Soc. CPA's. Home and Office: 5641 Oakdale Dr Salt Lake City UT 84121

PARSONS, LEONA MAE, health services administrator; b. Newark, Ohio, Sept. 13, 1932; d. Enos Andrew and Emma Mae (Simmers) Chew; RN, Andrews U., 1960; BS in Nursing, So. Missionary Coll., 1980; MBA, Rollins Coll., 1986; m. David J. Parsons, June 14, 1953; children—Davona Joy, Cynthia Carol, David J. Operating room supr. Bongo Hosp., Angola, Africa, 1961-68; dir. nurses Bongo Mission Hosp., Angola, 1968-75; nurse in charge refugee camps S. African Govt., Windhoek, S.W. Africa, 1975-76; matron, dir. nurses Windhoek (S.W. Africa) State Hosp., 1976-79; asst. v.p. Fla. Hosp., Orlando, 1980-87; v.p. patient services, Hays Meml. Hosp., San Marcos, Tex., 1987—. Mem. adv. bd. Seminole Community Coll., 1981-87; adv. com. Seminole Community Coll. co-op., Seminole County Child Abuse Prevention. Mem. Assn. Seventh-day Adventist Nurses (bd. dirs. 1981-87), Nat. League Nurses, Fla. League Nurses, Fla. Nurses Assn., Coalition Childbirth Educators (bd. dirs.), Fla. Hosp. Assn., Fla. Orgn. Nurse Execs., Nat. Perinatal Assn., Fla. Perinatal Assn., Loma Linda Med. Soc. Aux., Fla. Med. Soc. Aux., Am. Orgn. Nurse Execs., Tex. Orgn. Nurse Execs., Tex. Nurses Assn., Am. Soc. Psychoprophylaxis in Obstetrics, Fla. Soc. Hosp. Nursing Service Adminstrs., Nat. Assn. Female Execs., S. African Nurses Assn., Orange County Med. Soc. Aux. (bd. dirs.), Am. Med. Assn. Aux.

PARSONS, PATRICIA ANN HUDSON, educator; b. Byron, Mich., Jan. 17, 1951; d. Donald Robert and K. Lucille (Wakeman) Hudson; B.A., Spring Arbor Coll., 1973; M.A., Central Mich. U., 1983; m. J. Mark Parsons, Oct. 14, 1972; children—Caleb Joseph, Jordan Donald. Tchr., Evart (Mich.) High Sch., 1974-75; media specialist Evart Public Schs., 1975-81, elem. sch. tchr., 1981-82, K 12 media specialist, 1982—. Adv. bd. REMC2, 1985-88. Mem. ALA, Mich. Library Assn., Evart Edn. Assn., Mich. Edn. Assn., NEA, Mich. Assn. Media In Edn. (regional chmn. 1985—, cert. com. 1988), 7-County Media Selection Com., Mich. Cheerleading Coaches Assn. (dir. 1978-80, v.p. 1980-81, 82-83, state championship com. mem. 1979-83). Methodist. Club: Evart Sports Boosters. Contbr. articles to profl. publs. Home: 624 N Main St Evart MI 49631 Office: Evart Pub Sch 321 Hemlock Evart MI 49631

PARSONS, PATTY LEIGH, lawyer; b. Pocomoke City, Md., Feb. 20, 1954; d. E. Carmel Wilson (stepfather) and Evelyn Gay (Carter) Parsons-Wilson; m. Harry Dorman McKnett, May 24, 1980 (div. Dec. 1987). BA in Psychology, U. Md., Balt., 1976; JD, U. Balt., 1979. Bar: Md. 1981, U.S. Ct. Appeals (4th cir.) 1984. Residential counselor U. Md., Balt., 1973-76; adminstr. Juvenile Law Clinic, Balt., 1979-80; legal asst. Edelman & Rubenstein P.A., Balt., 1979-81; labor atty. Edelman & Rubenstein, P.A., Balt., 1981-85; labor atty. Abato, Rubenstein and Abato, P.A., Balt., 1985-87, ptnr., 1988—; Drug counselor Open Arms Community Counseling Ctr., Balt., 1972-73. Recipient Md. Poetry Soc. award, 1972; Outstanding Adv. award, U. Balt., 1977-78. Mem. Md. State Bar Assn. (adv. bd. labor sect.), ABA (developing labor law com., labor and employment sect.), Indsl. Relations Research Assn., Coalition of Labor Union Women. Democrat. Home: 2 Quimper Ct 1A Baltimore MD 21208 Office: Abato Rubenstein and Abato 2360 W Joppa Rd Lutherville MD 21093

PARTON, DOLLY REBECCA, singer, composer, actress; b. Sevier County, Tenn., Jan. 19, 1946; d. Robert Lee and Avie Lee (Owens) P.; m. Carl Dean, May 30, 1966. Country music singer, rec. artist, composer, actress, radio and TV personalit, star ABC-TV series Dolly, 1987—; owner theme park Dollywood. Radio appearances include Grand Ole Opry, WSM Radio, Nashville, Cass Walker program, Knoxville; TV appearances include Porter Wagoner Show, from 1967, Cass Walker program, Bill Anderson Show, Wilburn Bros. Show, Barbara Mandrell Show; rec. artist, Mercury, Monument, RCA record cos.; star movie Nine to Five, 1980, The Best Little Whorehouse in Texas, 1982, Rhinestone, 1984; albums include Here You Come Again (Grammy award 1978), Real Love, 1985, Just the Way I Am, 1986, Portrait, 1986, Think About Love, 1986, Trio (with Emmylou Harris, Linda Ronstadt) (Grammy award 1988), 1987, Heartbreaker, Great Balls of Fire; composer numerous songs including Nine to Five. Recipient (with Porter Wagoner) Vocal Group of Yr. award, 1968; Vocal Duo of Yr. award All Country Music Assn., 1970, 71; Nashville Metronome award, 1979; Am. Music award, 1984; named Female Vocalist of Yr., 1975, 76; Country Star of Yr., Sullivan Prodns., 1977; Entertainer of Yr., Country Music Assn., 1978; People's Choice award, 1980, 88; Female Vocalist of Yr., Acad. Country Music, 1980; Dolly Parton Day proclaimed, Sevier County, Tenn., designated Oct. 7, 1967, Los Angeles, Sept. 20, 1979; recipient Grammy awards for best female country vocalist, 1978, 81, for best country song, 1981, for best country vocal performance with group, 1987; co-recipient (with Emmylou Harris and Linda Ronstadt) Acad. Country Music award for album of the yr., 1987. Address: care Creative Artists Agy Inc 1888 Century Park E Suite 1400 Los Angeles CA 90067

PARTRITZ, JOAN ELIZABETH, lawyer, educator; b. Chgo., July 16, 1931; d. Norman John and Florence May (Russell) P. A.B., Ball State U., 1953; M.A., Whittier Coll., 1963; J.D., Loyola U., Los Angeles, 1977. Bar: Calif. 1977, U.S. Dist. Ct. (cen. dist.) Calif. 1981, U.S. Ct. Appeals (9th cir.) 1984, U.S. Supreme Ct. 1985. Copy writer Nelson Advt. Service, Los Angeles, 1953-53; speech, hearing therapist Port Hueneme Sch. Dist., Calif., 1953-54; math. tchr. Montebello Sch. Dist., Calif., 1954-77; comedy writer Foster Prodns., Los Angeles, 1980-83; prof. Calif. State U., Los Angeles, 1978—; assoc. Parker & Dally, Pomona, Calif., 1977—; dir., speaker Inservice Law Seminars, Pomona, 1977—; cons. Foxtail Press, Inc., Whittier, Calif., 1978—. Author: California Modern Mathematics, 1960. Vol. ACLU, Los Angeles, 1981—. NSF grantee, 1965, 66, 69; recipient Nat. Jurisprudence award, 1976. Mem. ABA (tort com. 1978-80, ins. com. 1978—). Assn. Univ. Attys., Calif. Tchrs. Assn. (salary chmn. 1970-71, keynote speaker 1979), La Habra Art Assn. (first prize Water Color Show 1979, 87), AAUW, NOW (speakers bur. 1984—), Women's Political Caucus, Women Trial Lawyers Assn. Democrat. Home: 10515 S Portada Dr Whittier CA 90603 Office: Parker & Dally 281 S Thomas 5th Floor Pomona CA 91766

PASACHOFF, NAOMI, writer; b. N.Y.C., Jan. 27, 1947; d. Isaac and Anna (Jacobson) Schwartz; m. Jay M. Pasachoff, Mar. 31, 1974; children: Eloise Hilary, Deborah Donna. AB magna cum laude, Harvard U., 1968; AM, Columbia U., 1969; PhD, Brandeis U., 1974. Editor Houghton Mifflin Co., N.Y.C., 1970-71; with Berkshire Community Coll., Pittsfield, Mass., 1974; vis. asst. prof. Skidmore Coll., 1974-77, Rensselaer Polytech. Inst., Troy, N.Y., 1977-78; writer Scott, Foresman and Co., Williamstown, Mass., 1978—. Author (with others): Playwrigths, Preachers, and Politicians, 1975, Physical Science, 1983, Earth Science, 1983, Basic Judaism for Young People: Torah, 1986, Basic Judaism for Young People: Isreal, 1986, Basic Judaism for Young People: God., 1987; contbr. articles to Encyclopedia Britannica Yrbk. of Sci. and Future, World Book. Home and Office: 1305 Main St Williamstown MA 01267

PASACRETA, JEANNIE VIRGINIA, nurse, educator; b. Norwalk, Conn., Dec. 2, 1956; d. Eugene Joseph Pasacreta and Virginia (Raymond) Johnson. BSN, Villanova U., 1978; MSN, Columbia U., 1982. RN, Conn., N.Y. Staff nurse Meml. Sloan-Kettering Cancer Ctr., N.Y.C., 1978-79, psychiat. nurse clinician, 1986—; staff nurse Hall Brooke Hosp., Westport, Conn., 1979-82, coordinator nursing care, 1982-83; psychiat. nurse clinician Danbury (Conn.) Hosp., 1983-86; supr., nurse cons. Anuk, Inc., Stamford, Conn., 1979-81; pvt. practice psychotherapy, Norwalk, 1983—; clin. instr. Sch. Nursing, Columbia U., N.Y.C., 1987—; cons., clin. supr. Women's Crisis Ctr., Norwalk, 1983—, bd. dirs., 1987; presenter in field. Contbr. articles to profl. jours. Mem. Am. Nurses Assn. (cert. clin. specialist in adult psychiat. community mental health nursing), Conn. Nurses Assn., Oncology Nursing Soc. Republican. Roman Catholic. Home: 24 Davenport Ave Westport CT 06880 Office: Sloan-Kettering Cancer Ctr Dept Nursing 1275 York Ave New York NY 10021

PASAKARNIS, PAMELA ANN, worldwide diagnostics company executive; b. Pittsfield, Mass., May 11, 1949; d. Richard W. and Regina (Piskorski) Turner; m. Donald L. Pasakarnis, May 25, 1974; children: Seth M., Casey L. BA, Northeastern U., 1972; M.T., New Eng. Deaconess Hosp., Boston, 1973. Staff med. technologist New Eng. Deaconess Hosp., 1972-75, supr. clin. chemistry, 1975-77; tech. product supr. Corning Med. Co., Medfield, Mass., 1977-83, product mgr. clin. instrumentation, 1983-85; mgr. mktg. communications CIBA Corning Diagnostics Corp., Medfield, 1985-88, mgr. mktg. ops., 1988—. Mem. Am. Assn. Clin. Chemists, Clin. Lab. Mgrs. Assn., Biomed. Mktg. Assn., Am. Mgmt. Assn. Republican. Avocations: winemaking; fashion design; interior decorating; needlework. Home: 3 Partridge Ln Walpole MA 02081

PASCHAL, ANNE BALES, educator; b. Runnels County, Tex., Oct. 10, 1929; d. Wirt Samuel and Lora Louise (Corum) Bales; B.S. Angelo State U., 1970, M. Sch. Adminstrn., 1983; m. Bill Paschal, Dec. 16, 1946; children—William Douglas, Susan Louise Paschal Spates, Paul Neal. Tchr. math. Central High Sch., San Angelo, Tex., 1970—; workshop presenter; dir. Concho Educators Fed. Credit Union, 1975-80, pres. bd., 1979-80. Recipient Leadership and Scholarship award Angelo State U., 1970. Acad. Excellence awards, 1968, 69, Leadership and Achievement award Angelo U., 1969, 70; named Outstanding Tchr., Central High Sch., 1977, Tchr. of Yr., 1978. Mem. Nat. Council Tchrs. of Math., San Angelo Council Tchrs. of Math (v.p. 1975), NEA, Tex. Tchrs. Assn., (local treas. 1978-79), Tex. State Classroom Tchrs. Assn. (treas. 1978-79), Kappa Delta Pi, Delta Kappa Gamma, Pi Mu Epsilon, Sigma Tau Delta, Alpha Chi, Phi Delta Kappa. Republican. Home: 801 W Ave D San Angelo TX 76901 Office: 100 Cottonwood St San Angelo TX 76901

PASCHALL, PAMELA GENELLE, financial analyst; b. Pasadena, Calif., June 18, 1949; d. James Edward and Mary Anita (Butler) P. BS, U. So. Calif., 1976; MBA, U. Conn., 1988. Asst. dir. fiscal services Pasadena (Calif.) Unified Sch. Dist., 1972-78; staff acct. George C. Troutman, C.P.A., Louisville, 1978-80; sr. staff acct. Celanese Water Soluble Polymers Co., Louisville, 1980-82; supr. gen. acctg. Celanese Splty. Resins Co., 1983; mgr. fin. analysis Celanese Internat. Co., N.Y.C., 1984-86; mgr. acctg., ins. and credit Hoechst Celanese Corp., 1988—. Mem. Ky. Soc. C.P.A.s, Nat. Acctg. Assn., Am. Inst. C.P.A.s. Home: 1700 Rally Dr Virginia Beach VA 23454

PASCHKE PATTERSON, KAREN ANNE, journalist, author, public relations consultant; b. Pitts., Mar. 7, 1948; d. Frederick John, Jr., and Gladys Mary (Steinhardt) Killmeyer; m. John H. Patterson, Sept. 6, 1987; children by previous marriage: Jesse Frank, Joshua Kane. Student speech and drama Penn Hall Jr. Coll., 1966-67; BA in Broadcast and Sociology, Marquette U., 1970. Assoc. editor Nat. Safety Council, Chgo., 1970-72; editor, research asst. U.S. Savs. and Loan League, Chgo., 1972; editor, dir. pub. relations Nat. Eye Research Found., Chgo., 1972-73; editorial dir. Red Bud Publs., Columbus, Ohio, 1974-76; pres., creative dir. Pace Media, Columbus, 1976-83; dir. communications Price Waterhouse, Columbus, 1983-85; dir. pub. relations and devel. Med. Ctr. Hosp., Chillicothe, Ohio, 1985-87; pres. Pace Communications, Chillicothe, 1987—; cons.; freelance writer, contbr. trade and comml. publs.; books include: Construction: Principles, Materials and Methods, 1972; City Slicker's Guide to Self Sufficiency, 1981-82; Heavenly Herbs, 1982; Borden: A Price Waterhouse Perspective, 1984; also novels, 1979-80. Recipient Communicators award Gt. Lakes Regional Com., 1983. Mem. Nat. Soc. Fund Raising Execs., Ohio Assn. for Hosp. Devel., Ohio Soc. for Hosp. Pub. Relations, Nat. Assn. Female Execs., Pub. Relations Soc. Am., Women in Communications, Internat. Assn. Bus. Communicators, Ohio Hosp. Assn., Hosp. Assn. Central Ohio, Zeta Phi Eta. Clubs: Penn Hall Alumni, Marquette U. Alumni. Office: Pace Communications 36 N Walnut St Chillicothe OH 45601

PASCHKES, MITZI ELLEN, cataloger, librarian; b. Newark, Sept. 15, 1953; d. Harold and Carole (Weiss) Binder; m. Mark J. Paschkes, Jan. 29, 1984; 1 child, Alison Rose. B.A., Rutgers U., 1975; M.L.S., U. Tenn., 1976; A.A.S., Houston Community Coll., 1982. Temporary asst. reference librarian Fairleigh Dickinson U., Rutherford, N.J., 1977-78; sr. reference librarian Ridgewood Pub. Library (N.J.), 1978-80; from asst. librarian to librarian Bernard Johnson Inc., Houston, 1980-81; from cataloging asst. to asst. cataloger Harris County Pub. Library, Houston, 1982—. Author: Catalogue to the Lawson D. Franklin Manuscript Collection, 1976. Mem. N.J. Library Assn., Spl. Libraries Assn., Nat. Assn. Female Execs. Office: Harris County Pub Library 49 San Jacinto 200 Houston TX 77002

PASCHYN, LISA JASEWYTSCH, financial executive; b. Cleve., Aug. 10, 1954; d. Walter and Joan (Halchak) J.; m. Oleh Roman Paschyn; children: Larissa I., Christina M. Student, Cleve. Inst. Music, 1975; BA, Cleve. State U., 1976. Cons. Dunn & Bradstreet, Cleve., 1975-80; statis. mgr. IRS, Cleve., 1980; mgr. Navy Fed. Credit Union, Cleve., 1980—. Dir. (album) MRIA..., 1977; author credit union tng. manual, 1984. Mem. Nat. Banking Inst., Internat. Credit Assn. NE Ohio, Ohio Credit Union League. Office: Navy Fed Credit Union 1240 E 9th St Cleveland OH 44130

PASCOE, ELIZABETH JEAN, magazine editor; b. Cloquet, Minn.; d. Truman Archie and Floride (Vos) P. Student, Hamline U., 1949-51; BS, U. Wis., 1955. Staff writer Medical Economics, Oradell, N.J., 1960-61, 1967-70; fin. editor Medical Economics, Oradell, 1978-79; fin. researcher Time Mag., N.Y.C., 1962-66; editor "Right Now" column McCall's Mag., N.Y.C., 1973-76; free lance writer N.Y.C., Denver, 1970-78; sr. editor Women's Day Mag., N.Y.C., 1979—. Co-author: The Women's Day Book of Family Medical Questions, 1979. Bd. dirs. Rush Dance Co., N.Y.C., 1982; county Dem. comwoman., N.Y.C., 1975. Mem. Am. Soc. Mag. Editors. Office: Woman's Day CBS Mags 1515 Broadway New York NY 10036

PASIC, MARY ROSE, principal; b. Crested Butte, Colo., Oct. 19, 1937; d. John Louis and Rose Mary (Kuretich) P. BA, Mt. St. Mary's Coll., 1959, MS in Edn., 1966. Cert. tchr., Calif. Tchr. Los Angeles Unified Sch. Dist., 1959-73, asst. prin., mem. tng. and demonstration, 1973-78, prin., 1978—. Holder numerous offices Jrs. League Crippled Children, Los Angeles, 1961-72. Mem. Mt. St. Mary's Coll. Alumnae Assn., Euclan, Phi Delta Kappa (chmn. membership UCLA chpt. 1983-84), Delta Kappa Gamma (pres. 1975-76, scholar 1975), Kappa Delta Pi (sec. So. Calif. Alumni chpt. 1984-85).

PASKI, VICKI LYNNE, insurance agent, professional billards player; b. Lansing, Mich., Oct. 16, 1955; d. Martin John Roesch and Virginia Mary (Sands) Balgoyen; m. Stephen Carl Frechen, June 13, 1975 (div. Sept. 1980); m. Robert Bernard Paski, July 15, 1986; 1 child, Michael Robert. AA in Bus. cum laude, Lansing Community Coll., 1976. V.p. Harry O. Culp Ins. Agy., Inc., Grand Ledge, Mich., 1973—; v.p. Centennial Property and Casualty, Lansing, 1986—. Columnist: Billiard Digest; guest appearance ESPN Sports Network, 1983. Recipient Nat. 9 Ball Champion award NPCA Classic Cup, 1982. Mem. Nat. Assn. Ins. Women, Profl. Ins. Agts., Women's Profl. Billiard Assn. (v.p. 1985—). Office: Harry O Culp Ins Agy Inc 219 E Jefferson St Grand Ledge MI 48837

PASLAWSKY, JEAN MARIE, telecommunications trainer and consultant; b. Pottsville, Pa., Sept. 18, 1957; d. Joseph Anthony and Eleanor Marie (Baddick) P. BA in English, Secondary Edn., Immaculata Coll., 1979. Tchr. English Muhlenberg (Pa.) Sr. High Sch., 1979-80; bus./credit analyst Dun & Bradstreet, Inc., Phila., 1980-82; regional coordinator promotion, trainer sales dept. Durawood/Sears Kitchen Cabinets, Trevose, Pa., 1982-84; telecom system coordinator, trainer Standard Telecom, Phila., 1984-86; ind. telecom system coordinator/trainer Willow Grove, Pa., 1986—. Active Cath. Charities Appeal, Phila., 1983—; instr. Confraternity of Christian Doctrine program St. David's Parish, Willow Grove, 1985—; vol. Hatboro YMCA, 1982-83, Montgomery County Spl. Olympics. Mem. Am. Soc. for Tng. and Devel., Immaculata Coll. Alumnae Assn. (pres. 1983-85, assoc. editor, staff writer newspaper 1984-86, past pres. 1985-87, coordinator telecom fund raising telethon 1985-87, alumnae bd. govs. del. 1983—), Nat. Assn. Female Execs., Alpha Psi Omega, Lambda Iota Tau. Home and Office: 8 Knock-N-Knoll Circle Willow Grove PA 19090

PASQUARIELLA, SUSAN KINGSLEY, librarian; b. Newark, Feb. 11, 1944; d. William and Gertrude (Kruessel) Kingsley; m. Bernard Guy Pasquariella, Sept. 29, 1973. B.A., Skidmore Coll., 1966; M.S., Columbia U., 1972, D.L.S., 1981. Research asst. Sloan Kettering Inst., N.Y.C., 1967-70, Cornell Med. Ctr., N.Y.C., 1970-71; indexer, reference librarian Columbia U., N.Y.C., 1972-75, sr. librarian, 1975-79, head librarian, 1979—, dir. info. services Ctr. Population and Family Health, 1979—; cons. Recipient George Virgil Fuller award Columbia U., 1978; mem. working group on computerization Population Info. Network for Africa. Mem. Assn. Population/Family Planning Libraries and Info. Ctrs. (officer 1976—), UN Population Info. Network, Population Info. Network Africa (mem. working group on computerization), ALA, Spl. Libraries Assn., Med. Library Assn. (cert. 1974, 83). Contbr. articles to profl. jours. Home: 200 Cabrini Blvd New York NY 10033 Office: Columbia U Ctr Population and Family Health 60 Haven Ave New York NY 10032

PASQUARIELLO, ANGELA CATHERINE, health care administrator; b. Buffalo, N.Y., June 29, 1955; d. Julius and Maria (Cervera) P. BS in Pharmacy, Albany Coll., 1978; MBA, Union Coll., 1984, postgrad., 1987—. Pharmacist CUS Pharmacy, Inc., Schenectady, N.Y., 1978-85; mgr. A.W. Lawrence, Schenectady, 1985; mgr. prescription drug programs Empire Blue Cross and Blue Shield, Albany, N.Y., 1985-87; pharmacist Electronic Data Systems, Albany, 1987—; mem. CUS Pharmacy Adv. Panel, Woonsocket, R.I., 1981-84, N.Y. State Tech. ad hoc Pharmacy Adv. Panel, Albany, N.Y., 1982-86. Mem. Alumni Assn. Albany Coll. Pharmacy (Outstanding Young Alumni 1979, 2d v.p. 1985-86, 1st v.p. 1986-87, bd. dirs. 1987-88). Roman Catholic. Home: 345 Dolan Dr Schenectady NY 12306 Office: Electronic Data Systems 220 Washington Ave Exit Albany NY 12203

PASQUESI, PENNY ROSE, corporate administrator; b. Chgo., Nov. 15, 1948; d. Dante Jerome and Rose (Venturi) P. BS, St. Louis U., 1970. Tchr. various schs., Ill., 1970-74; with Electronic Data Systems Corp., 1978—; dir. corp. communications Electronic Data Systems Corp., Dallas, 1983-86; regional dir. pub. affairs Washington, 1986—. Election judge Com. to Re-elect Jane Byrne, Chgo., 1983; mem. communications com. USO, Washington, 1986—. Mem. Pub. Relations Soc. Am. Office: Electronic Data Systems 6430 Rockledge Dr Bethesda MD 20817

PASS, CAROLYN JOAN, dermatologist; b. Balt., May 14, 1941; d. Isidore Earl and Rhea (Koplowitz) P.; B.S., U. Md., 1962, M.D., 1966; m. Richard Malcolm Susel, June 23, 1963; children—Steven, Gary. Rotating intern USPHS Hosp., Balt., 1966-67; med. resident St. Agnes Hosp., Balt., 1967-68; dermatology resident and fellow U. Md. Sch. Medicine Hosps., 1968-71; pvt. practice specializing in dermatology, Balt. and Ellicott City, Md., 1971—; mem. staff James Lawrence Kernan, St. Agnes, South Baltimore Gen., Lutheran Gen. and Bon Secours hosps.; vol. dermatology clinics U. Md., St. Agnes hosps.; asst. clin. prof. dermatology U. Md. Sch. Medicine, 1978—; mem. exec. com. adv. bd. Nat. Program in Dermatology, 1975. Diplomate Am. Bd. Dermatology. Mem. AMA, Med. and Chirurgical Faculty Md., Balt. City Med. Soc. (del. 1974), Am. Women's Med. Assn., Am. Acad. Dermatology (award exhibit 1970), Soc. Investigative Dermatology, Md. Dermatology Soc. (sec.-treas. 1974-76, pres. 1976-77), Soc. Contemporary Medicine and Surgery, U. Md. Sch. Medicine Alumnae Assn. (bd. dirs.). Jewish. Clubs: Suburban Country (Balt.); Country Garden. Gourmet. Home: Timberlane 8410 Park Hts Ave Pikesville MD 21208 Office: Pine Heights Med Center Suite 301 1001 Pine Heights Ave Baltimore MD 21229

PASSAMANECK, RANDI LEA, medical technologist; b. Richmond, Va., May 18, 1942; d. Yale and Ann (Berman) P.; B.S. in Med. Tech., U. N.C., 1964; postgrad. Johns Hopkins Hosp., 1972-73. Research technologist USPHS Hosp., Balt., 1964-65; lab. scientist U. Md. Hosp., Balt., 1965-72, tech. and adminstrv. specialist, 1973-74; lab. assoc. Johns Hopkins Hosp., Balt., 1972-73; dir. tech. services ARC Blood Services, Chesapeake region, Balt., 1974-85; tech. services specialist ARC, Washington, 1985—. Bd. dirs. Mid-Atlantic Assn. Blood Banks, 1976-81, pres., 1979-80; mem. tech. workshop com. Am. Assn. Blood Banks, 1976-78; v.p. Washington-Balt. Blood Study Group, 1975-76; mem. tech. adv. com. ARC, 1982-84. Mem. Am. Soc. Clin. Pathologists, Am. Soc. Med. Tech., Internat. Soc. Blood Transfusion, Md. Soc. Med. Tech., Pa. Assn. Blood Banks, Regulatory Affairs Profls. Soc. Democrat. Jewish. Office: ARC 17th and D Sts NW Washington DC 20006

PASTEN, LAURA JEAN, veterinarian; b. Tacoma, May 25, 1949; d. Frank Larry and Jean Mary (Slavich) Brajkovich; student Stanford U., 1970; BA in Physiology, U. Calif., Davis, 1970, DVM (regents scholar), 1974; postgrad. Cornell U., 1975. Veterinarian, Nevada County Vet. Hosp., Grass Valley Calif., 1975-80; pvt. practice vet. medicine, owner Mother Lode Vet. Hosp., Grass Valley, 1980—; affiliate staff Sierra Nevada Meml. Hosp.; lectr. in field. Bd. dirs. Sierra Services for Blind. Mem. AVMA, Calif. Vet. Med. Assn. (ethics com.), Mother Lode Vet. Assn., Am. Animal Hosp. Assn. (Mother Lode Vet. Hosp. cited for excellence), Nat. Ophthal. Soc., Nat. Pygmy Goat Assn., Nat. Appaloosa Soc., Nat. Assn. Underwater Instrs., Denver Area Med. Soc., Internat. Vet. Assn. Am., Endurance Riding Soc. Republican. Lutheran. Club: Grass Valley Bus. Women. Author: (with Dr. Muller) Canine Dermatology, 1970; contbr. articles to profl. jours. Home: 15978 Shebley Rd Grass Valley CA 95945 Office: 11509 La Barr Meadows Rd Grass Valley CA 95949

PASTERNACK, MARCIA ANNE, librarian; b. Buffalo, Jan. 27, 1945; d. Sidney Charles and Sylvia Rochelle (Bornstein) Pasternack. Student, SUNY-Geneseo, 1963-65; B.A., Daemen Coll., 1967; M.L.S., SUNY-Buffalo, 1970. Catalog librarian Kent State U. (Ohio), 1970-71; asst. librarian N.Y. State Library, Albany, 1973—. Co-founder Fund for a Democratic Majority, Washington, 1983; mem. So. Poverty Law Ctr., Montgomery, Ala., 1984, Infant Formula Action Coalition, Mpls., 1983, Impact, Washington, 1984, Statue of Liberty/Ellis Island Found., 1983—, ACLU, People for the Am. Way, Nat. Planned Parenthood Assn., N.Y. Easter Seal Soc., Freedom to Read Found., Nat. Urban League, 1986—, Americans for Separation of Ch. and State, 1986—, N.Y. Library Staff Devel. Com., 1986—; Mem. No. Ohio Tech. Services Librarians, N.Y. Library Assn., ALA. Democrat. Jewish. Club: Library Sch. Alumni Assn. Office: NY State Library Empire State Plaza Albany NY 12230

PASTINE, MAUREEN DIANE, university librarian; b. Hays, Kans., Nov. 21, 1944; d. Gerhard Walter and Ada Marie (Hillman) Hillman; m. Jerry Joel Pastine, Feb. 5, 1966. A.B., in English, Ft. Hays State U., 1967; M.L.S., Emporia State U., 1970. Reference librarian U. Nebr.-Omaha, 1971-77; undergrad. librarian U. Ill., Urbana, 1977-79; reference librarian, 1979-80; univ. librarian San Jose State U.-Calif., 1980-85; dir. libraries Wash. State U., Pullman, 1985—; mem. adv. bd. Foothill Coll. Library, 1983-85; led ednl. delegation librarians to People's Republic of China, 1985, Australia/New Zealand, 1986. Co-author: Library and Library Related Publications: A Directory of Publishing Opportunities, 1973; asst. compiler: Women's Work and Women's Studies, 1973-74, 1975; compiler procs. Teaching Bibliographic Instruction in Graduate Schools of Library Science, 1981; contbr. articles to profl. publs. Recipient Disting. ALumni Grad. award Emporia State U., 1986. Mem. ALA (chmn. World Book-ALA Goal awards jury 1984-85), Assn. Coll. and Research Libraries (editorial adv. bd. BIS Think Tank 1982-85, chmn. bibliographic instrn. sect. 1983-84, editorial bd. Choice 1983-85, chmn. Miriam Dudley Bibliographic Instrn. Librarian of Yr. award com. 1984-85, mem. task force on librarians as instrs. 1986—), Library Administrn. and Mgmt. Assn. (chmn. stats. sect. com. on devel., orgn., planning and programming 1982-83, sec. stats. sect. exec. com. 1982-83, mem. at large 1986—), ALA Library Instrn. Round Table (long range planning com. 1986—), ALA Library Research Round Table, Wash. Library Assn., Pacific Northwest Library Assn., Phi Kappa Phi, Beta Phi Mu. Home: SE 760 Ridgeview Ct Pullman WA 99163 Office: Washington State U Director of Libraries Pullman WA 99164-5610

PASTOR, MILLIE A., interior designer; b. Wayne County, Mich.; d. Martin Joseph and Bessie B. Kloka; student U. Detroit, 1947-48; m. Robert Henry Pastor, Sept. 29, 1951; children—Robert Henry, George H., Patricia C., Karen M. BSNE, RN, Mercy Coll., 1951. Founder, pres. Pastor Interiors, Inc., Bloomfield Hills, Mich., 1965—; cons. URI, Nashville; cons., speaker, mem. nat. women's bd. Northwood Inst. Pres., Project Hope, 1973-75; commr. Mich. Am. Revolution Bicentennial, 1972-78; bd. dirs. March of Dimes, 1980-82, Christ Child Soc., 1960-68, Mich. Artrain, Women's Com. Hospice Care, Salvation Army, Women's Com. of Detroit Symphony Orch., Mich. Opera; pres. Am. Lung Assn. Southeastern Mich.; active Boys and Girls Club Met. Detroit. Recipient Outstanding Contbn. award March of Dimes, 1977-79, Outstanding Fund Raising Vol. award Nat. Soc. Fund Raising Execs., 1982; named Women of Yr., Boys Town of Italy, 1980. Mem. Nat. Home Fashions League (Image Maker award Mich. chpt. 1979, v.p.), Am. Soc. Interior Designers, Design Lighting Inst., Detroit Zool. Soc., Orch. Hall Assn. Founders Soc., Mich. Cancer Soc. Republican. Studio: Grand Traverse Br 7769 Deepwater Dr Village MI 49610

PASTUSZAK, SOPHIE KATHERINE, advertising executive, coordinator; b. Brantford, Can., May 13, 1960; d. Sophie (Lyp) P. Policy issue clk. Can. Foresters, Brantford, 1979-85, asst. editor, 1985-86, editor, adv. exec., 1986—, graphics co-ordinator, 1985—; Editor: The Canadian Forester mag. Mem. Life Communication Assn., Can. Direct Mktg. Assn., Internat. Assn. Business Communicators. Mem. Liberal party. Roman Catholic. Office: Can Foresters, PO Box 850, Brantford CAN NBT 553

PATAKY, MARIE ANN, accountant; b. Wilkensburg, Pa.; d. John Andrew and Elizabeh Ann (Koczka) P.; B.S. in B.A., Robert Morris Coll., 1974; A.S. in Data Processing, Community Coll. Allegheny County, Pitts., 1970. Auditor, Peat, Marwick, Mitchell & Co., Pitts., 1974-76; tax acct. G.L. Roteman & Assos., Pitts., 1976-77; acctg. cons. Career & Life Planning Inst., Pitts., 1977-78; tax acct. Westinghouse Electric, Pitts., 1978-80; internal auditor Johnson & Johnson, New Brunswick, N.J., 1980-81; tax supr. Interpublic Group of Cos., Inc., N.Y.C., 1981—; fin. cons., dir. Contrarian Investment Inst., Princeton, N.J., 1981—; pres. Princeton Fin. Plans, 1985—. Treas., Children's Hosp. Fund., 1979-80. C.P.A., Pa., cert. fin. planner, Pa.; Robert Morris scholar, 1972-74. Mem. Am. Inst. C.P.A.s, Pa. Inst. C.P.A.s, Nat. Assn. Accts., Assn. M.B.A. Execs., Am. Women's Soc. C.P.A.s, Inst. Cert. Fin. Planners, Internat. Inst. Fin. Planning. Club: Toastmistress (treas. 1979-80). Address: Box 1442 Palmer Sq Princeton NJ 08542

PATANELLI, DOLORES JEAN, physiologist; b. Elkhart, Ind., July 20, 1932; d. Michael and Concetta (Robina) P. BA, NYU, 1955, MS, 1958, PhD, 1962. Asst. to med. dir. population council Rockefeller U., N.Y.C., 1956-62; research fellow Merck Inst. Therapeutic Research, Rahway, N.J., 1963-72; reproductive physiologist Ctr. Population Research, Contraceptive Devel. Br. Nat. Inst. Child Health, Bethesda, Md., 1972—; mem. regional health adv. commn. Health, Edn. and Welfare, N.Y.C., 1970-78; mem.membership com. Soc. Study Reproduction, 1973-75, nominating com., 1980-81. Editor: (book) Hormonal Control of Male Fertility, 1978; inventor (with others) Spiroxenone, 1972. Mem. N.Y. Acad. Scis., Endocrine Soc., Am. Assn. Anatomists, Am. Soc. Andrology, Am. Fertility Soc., Sigma Xi. Office: Nat Inst Child Health Ctr Population Research 6130 Executive Blvd Rm 600F Bethesda MD 20892

PATCH, LORRAINE MARIE, investment systems manager; b. Revere, Mass., Feb. 21, 1947; d. William Albert and Mary Rita (Gelardi) P.; B.A. magna cum laude in Mgmt. (Coll. Profl. Studies prize 1978), U. Mass., Boston, 1978; M.B.A., Suffolk U., 1981; Ed.M., Harvard U., 1986, postgrad.; 1 son, Derek Scott Burke. Benefits coordinator, money market bookkeeper State St. Bank and Trust Co., Boston, 1968-76; freshmen adv. U. Mass., Boston, 1976-77; customer service rep. First Nat. Bank Boston, 1977-78; analyst investment systems group TMI Systems Corp. (now SEI Corp.), Lexington, Mass., 1980-81, staff cons., sect. mgr., 1981-82, mgr. investment mgmt. dept., 1983-86; tng. coordinator Money Mgmt. Systems, Waltham, Mass., 1987-88; free-lance cons., Natick, Mass., 1988—. Mem. search com. for chancellor U. Mass., 1979, Spl. Edn. Adminstrn., Natick; coordinator Spl. Edn. Parents Adv. Council of Natick. Mem. Female Execs. Assn., Assn. Data Processing Trainers, Smithsonian Associates, Women in Mgmt. Network Assn. (co-founder 1981, treas. 1981-83), Am. Soc. Profl. and Exec. Women, AAUW, U. Mass. Alumni Assn. Suffolk U. Alumni Assn., NOW. Home: 30 Bradford Rd Natick MA 01760

PATCHIS, PAULINE, handwriting expert; b. Pawtucket, R.I., Apr. 17, 1940; d. Alexander P. Patchis and Rose E. (Acquaviva) Jankowski. Grad., Warwick Police Acad., 1967. Cert. document examiner, R.I. Exec. sec. to personnel dir. Ciba-Geigy Pharm. Co., Cranston, R.I., 1963-65; various ranks, then detective Warwick (R.I.) Police Dept., 1967-71; cons. jury selection, graphoanalyst Patchis and Wayne, Warwick, 1971—; lectr., instr. various orgns., New England area, 1971—. Contbr. articles to profl. jours. Mem. Nat. Forensic Ctr., Mass. Police Fraudulent Check Assn., Internat. Graphoanalysis Assn. Home and Office: 67 S Fair St Warwick RI 02888

PATE, CHRISTINE NELSON, mortgage banker; b. Atlanta, Feb. 18, 1950; d. Julian Cary and Helen Clyde (Taylor) Pate. Student, St. Mary Coll., Raleigh, N.C., 1967-69, U. So. Fla., 1969-71. Loan processor Tampa (Fla.) Savs. & Loan Assn., 1969-73; owner, mgr. C.P. Smith Inc., Orlando, Fla., 1973-77; asst. sec., supr. Suburban Coastal, Tampa, 1979-82; asst. area v.p. Residential Fin. Corp., Tampa, 1982-84; asst. regional v.p. Great So. Mortgage Corp., Tampa, 1984-86; asst. v.p. Citizens and So. Mortgage Corp. Fla., Tampa, 1986—. Pres., v.p. Berkley Sq. Condo Assn., Tampa, 1985—; active Am. Cancer Soc., Tampa; contbr. Tampa Bay Performing Arts Ctr., 1985—. Recipient award Am. Legion, 1967. Mem. Mortgage Bankers Assn., Nat. Assn. Female Execs., Tampa Bd. Realtors, Savs. and Loan League, DAR. Republican. Episcopalian. Office: Citizens and So Mortgage Corp Fla 10050 N Florida Ave Suite 305 Tampa FL 33612

PATE, JACQUELINE HAIL, data processing company manager; b. Amarillo, Tex., Apr. 7, 1930; d. Ewen and Virginia Smith (Crosland) Hail; student Southwestern U., Georgetown, Tex., 1947-48; children—Charles (dec.), John Durst, Virginia Pate Edgecomb, Christopher. Exec. sec. Western Gear Corp., Houston, 1974-76; adminstr., treas., dir. Aberrant Behavior Ctr., Personality Profiles, Inc., Corp. Procedures, Inc., Dallas, 1976-79; dist. adminstrn. mgr. Digital Equipment Corp., Dallas, 1979—. Active PTA, Dallas, 1958-73. Mem. Internat. Assn. Facility Mgrs., Metrocrest Profl. Womens Assn., Daus. Republic Tex. Methodist. Home: 3519 Casa Verde #268 Dallas TX 75234 Office: 14131 Midway Rd Suite 800 Dallas TX 75244-3608

PATE, JENNIFER ROSE, social worker; b. Guthrie, Okla., Jan. 14, 1949; d. Diehl Leon and Jean Elizabeth (Wilson) Craven; m. James Walter Pate, Dec. 20, 1970; children: Jamie Mae, Robin Elizabeth, Brice Walter. Student, U. Okla., 1966-70; BS in Health Services Adminstrn., U. Houston, Clear Lake City, Tex., 1978. Cert. social worker, Tex., life ins. agt., Tex. Social worker Salvation Army, Freeport, Tex., 1979-81, 86—; social worker, mentally handicapped-mentally retarded liasion specialist Gulf Coast Mental Health/Mental Retardation Service, Freeport, 1982-83; clerical adminstrv. asst. Lake Jackson (Tex.) Library, 1983-84; del. Nat. Social Work Conv., San Antonio, 1979. Mem. task force on environment and air pollution Houston/Galveston (Tex.) Area Council, 1979-83; mem. panel com. Brazosport (Tex.) Community Food Pantry, 1986; adv. bd. United Way Brazoria County, Freeport, 1986—; charter mem. Gov. Clement's Com., 1982; leader, service chmn. Girl Scouts U.S., Freeport, 1972-85; active Cerebral Palsy Found., Rainbow Orgn. for Girls; adminstrv. bd. Freeport 1st Meth. Ch., 1988—. Mem. AAUW (edn. com. 1979-85), United Meth. Women (life). Republican. Home: 1504 W 10th Freeport TX 77541 Office: Salvation Army 1618 N Ave J Freeport TX 77541

PATE, JOAN SEITZ, judge; b. Islip, N.Y.; d. Anthony and Frances Kowalski; m. Raymond Seitz (div.); children—Laura, Cherryl; m. Howard M. Pate, Dec. 9, 1961; stepchildren—Patricia, Barbara, Marsha, Peggy. B.A., Ariz. State U.; J.D., U. Ariz., 1974. Bar: Ariz. 1974, D.C. 1976, Ky. 1978; C.P.A., Ariz., Ky. Pvt. practice acctg. Phoenix, 1956-69; trial atty. U.S. Dept. Justice, Washington, 1974-78; ptnr. Goldberg & Simpson, Attys., Louisville, 1978-83; spl. trial judge U.S. Tax Ct., Washington, 1983—. Contbr. articles to profl. jours. Mem. ABA, Fed. Bar Assn. (bd. dirs. 1983-87), Ky. Bar Assn., Ariz. Bar Assn., D.C. Bar Assn., Ky. Soc. C.P.A.s, Order of Coif. Home: 1325 18th St NW Apt 304 Washington DC 20036 Office: US Tax Ct 400 2d St NW Washington DC 20217

PATE, PATTY KAY, business owner; b. Phoenix, Aug. 16, 1958; d. Marilyn J. (Velting) Pate. Real estate license, Lane Coll., 1985. Various positions Phoenix, 1976-80; asst. mgr. Sizzler Steak House, Eugene, Oreg., 1980-81; co-owner Precision Hairworks, Eugene, 1981-83; campaign mgr. Hall for Oreg. Ho. Reps., Eugene, 1984; owner Full of Hot Air, Eugene, 1984—. Mem. 29th St. Traffic Task Force, Eugene, 1982; pres. City of Eugene's Women's Commn., 1981—, Pres.'s Council, 1984-85; staff Mondale-Ferraro Nat. Campiagn, Oreg., 1984; co-leader ACLU Gay Rights Task Force, Corvallis, 1987. Mem. NOW, Nat. Women's Polit. Caucus. Democrat. Office: Full of Hot Air 273 Coburg Rd Eugene OR 97401

PATE-COMBS, PAULETTE MICHELLE, technical illustrator, graphic designer; b. Dayton, Ohio, Jan. 30, 1957; d. Benny Lawson and Sylvia Jeanne (Christian) Pate; m. Keith Erick Combs, July 17, 1985; 1 child, Corrahn LaMarr Pate. Tech. illustration assoc., Sinclair Community Coll., 1985. Parish sec. officer adminstr., Westwood Luth. Ch., Dayton, 1978-81; receptionist United Health Services, Dayton, 1981; clk. typist Mil. Personnel, Wright-Patterson AFB, Ohio, 1981, editorial asst. Mil. Specifications and Standards div., 1981-83, tech. illustrator aide, 1983-84, tech. equipment illustrator, 1984—, co-chmn. EEO com. Directorate of Support Systems Engring., 1983-84, chmn., 1984-86, dep. for engring., 1985—; freelance graphic artist, Dayton, 1978—; comdr. equal employment opportunity counselor Aeronautical Systems Div., 1986. Del. Nat. Blacks in Govt. Assembly, Washington, 1984, 85, 86, 87; hospitality com. chmn. Greater Dayton chpt. Blacks in Govt., Dayton, 1985, 1st v.p. program com., 1988; newsletter artist, 1985; dir. Parish Emergency Food Service, Westwood Luth. Ch., 1979-81; kickoff runner Combined Fed. Campaign, Wright-Patterson AFB, 1982, 83, 84, 87; 2d v.p., membership com. chairperson Greater Dayton Chpt. Blacks in Govt., 1987; mem. Art Ctr. Dayton, 1986, 87, 88. Recipient various award Wright-Patterson AFB, 1983-85. Mem. Greater Dayton chpt. of Blacks in Govt. (panel mem. tips on rising to the top 1984, corr. sec. 1986), Nat. Assn. for Women in Careers (founding mem. and 1st v.p. Dayton chpt.), Am. Bus. Women's Assn. Democrat. Lutheran. Club: Sashay Prodn. Modeling Co. (model 1985—) (Dayton). Avocations: graphic designing; painting; flower arranging; camping; bowling. Office: Specifications and Standards Div ASD/ENES Wright-Patterson AFB OH 45433

PATEL, MARILYN HALL, judge; b. Amsterdam, N.Y., Sept. 2, 1938; d. Lloyd Manning and Nina J. (Thorpe) Hall; m. Magan C. Patel, Sept. 2, 1966; children: Brian, Gian. B.A., Wheaton Coll., 1959; J.D., Fordham U., 1963. Mng. atty. Benson & Morris, N.Y.C., 1963-65; sole practice N.Y.C., 1965-67, San Francisco, 1971-76; atty. Dept. Justice, San Francisco, 1967-71; judge Alameda County Mcpl. Ct., Oakland, Calif., 1976-80, U.S. Dist. Ct. (no. dist.) Calif., San Francisco, 1980—; adj. prof. law Hastings Coll. of Law, San Francisco, 1974-76. Author: Immigration and Nationality Law, 1974; also numerous articles. Mem. bd. of visitors Fordham U. Sch. of Law. Mem. ABA (litigation sect., jud. adminstrn. sect.), ACLU (former bd. dirs.), NOW (former bd. dirs.), Am. Law Inst., Am. Judicature Soc. (bd. dirs.), Calif. Conf. Judges, Nat. Assn. Women Judges (founding mem.), Internat. Inst. (bd. dirs.), Advs. for Women (co-founder). Democrat. Office: US Dist Ct 450 Golden Gate Ave PO Box 36060 San Francisco CA 94102

PATEL, THELMA GRAFSTEIN, lawyer, educator; b. N.Y.C., Mar. 14, 1922; d. George and Anna (Silver) Grafstein; m. Sam Patel, Feb. 2, 1946; children—Daniel, Andrew. B.A., Bklyn. Coll., 1946; M.A., Queens Coll., 1965; J.D., Hofstra Univ., 1980. Bar: N.Y. 1980. Tchr. Hewlett-Woodmere Schs. (N.Y.), 1957-77; sole practice, Woodmere, 1980-81; atty. DC 37 Mcpl. Employees Legal Services, N.Y.C., 1981-84; cons. Am. Film Inst., 1969-75; lectr. New Sch. Social Research, N.Y.C., 1969-72, Ctr. Understanding, N.Y.C., 1969-74; lectr.-demonstrator N.Y. State Communication Assn., 1969-71. Dir. record Folkways Call of Freedom, 1962; dir. films, 1962-77; editor booklets, children's stories, poems. Vol. YMCA, Lawrence, N.Y., 1954-55, Temple Beth El Nursery Sch., Cedarhurst, N.Y., 1956-57; negotiator Union Contracts, N.Y.C., 1940-75. Recipient N.Y. State Tchr. of Yr. award N.Y. State Dept. Edn. and Bd. Regents, 1973; Nat. Tchr. of Yr. Honor Roll award, 1973; Resolutions of Congratulation award N.Y. Senate/Assembly, 1974. Mem. Hewlett-Woodmere Faculty Assn. (pres. 1969-72), ABA, N.Y. State Bar Assn., Nassau County Bar Assn. Democrat. Jewish. Home and Office: 113 Longworth Ave Box 142 Woodmere NY 11598

PATERSON, SHEILA, advertising agency executive; b. N.Y.C., Oct. 10, 1940; d. John and Sarah Agnes (Duncan) P. AB, Syracuse U., 1962; MBA, Pace U., 1975. Market research interviewer Procter and Gamble, Cin., 1962-63; media asst. to media supr. Dancer Fitzgerald Sample, N.Y.C., 1964-68; media planner to assoc media dir. Ted Bates (now Backer Spielvogel Bates, Inc.), N.Y.C., 1968-73, v.p., media dir., 1973-75, v.p., acct. exec., 1975-76, v.p., account supr., 1976; sr. v.p., exec. v.p. Backer Spielvogel Bates, Inc., N.Y.C., from 1976. Office: Backer Spielvogel Bates Inc 1515 Broadway New York NY 10036 *

PATERSON, VICKI SWITZER, nurse; b. Vestaburg, Mich., Sept. 16, 1939; d. Harvey Mahlon Switzer; m. Charles Olds Paterson, Sept. 1960 (div. Mar. 1972); children: Suzanne Marie Paterson Asbury, George Thomas; m. Ronald Jean Rousseau, Nov. 29, 1986. Diploma in nursing, Henry Ford Hosp. Sch. Nursing, 1960; BS, Western Mich. U., 1972; MPH, U. Mich., 1976; student, Cornell U., 1982, cert. in community health nursing, 1984. RN, Tenn. Pub. health nurse Kalamazoo County Dept Pub. Health, 1971-75; dir. nursing Macomb Oakland Regional Ctr., Mt. Clemons, Mich., 1976-79; nurse cons. Mich. State Dept. Pub. Health, Lansing, 1979-81, coordinator div. tng., 1981-82; head nurse hosp. based home care VA Med. Ctr., Memphis, 1983-86; nurse cons. Mich. Dept. Mental Health, Lansing, 1986; rehab. coordinator, nurse cons. Memphis, 1987—. Mem. Am. Pub. Health Assn., Am. Nursing Assn., Tenn. Nurses Assn. Office: 4352-C Stage Rd Memphis TN 38128

PATERSON-BERWICK, SHEENA, newspaper editor and publisher; b. Bridge of Allan, Scotland, May 8, 1942; came to U.S., 1982; d. James and Jean (Kelly) Michie; m. Keith Berwick, Jan. 24, 1987; children: Karen Jan Paterson, Paul Scot Paterson. Assoc., London Coll. Music and Speech, 1959. Mng. editor Weekend Mag., Montreal, Que., Can., 1973-74, editor in chief, 1974-76; insight editor The Toronto Star, Ont., Can., 1977-78; editor Saturday Toronto Star, Ont., Can., 1978-81, asst. mng. editor, 1981-82; assoc. editor Los Angeles Herald Examiner, 1982-87; pres., publisher Am. Collegiate Network, Santa Monica, Calif., 1987—. Club: Los Angeles Athletic. Home: 2935 Goodview Tr Los Angeles CA 90068 Office: Am Collegiate Network Grand American Inc 3110 Main St Santa Monica CA 90405

PATKOWSKI, IRENE, registered nurse; b. Cleve., Dec. 5, 1956; d. Jerzy and Regina (Kuligowski) P. BSN, Ursuline Coll., Ohio, 1983. RN, Ohio. Psychiat. staff nurse Met. Gen. Hosp., Cleve., 1983-85; fitness technician One Fitness Ctr., Cleve., 1985; psychiat. staff nurse Mt. Sinai Hosp., Cleve., 1985—; lectr. in field. Mem. Gestalt Inst. Cleve., Reebok Profl. Instr. Alliance, Sigma Theta Tau (Iota Psi chpt.). Avocations: raising plants, collecting antiques, bicycling, yoga, swimming. Home: 12700 Lake Ave #901 Lakewood OH 44107

PATMAN, JEAN ELIZABETH, journalist; b. Lincolnshire, Eng., Dec. 12, 1946; came to U.S., 1955, naturalized, 1967; d. Donald Geoffrey and Regina (Iwanir) P.; m. Lou Schwartz. BA in English, CCNY, 1967. Stringer Newsweek mag., N.Y.C., 1966-67; copygirl, then asst. to entertainment editor N.Y. Post, 1964-70; successively copy editor, spl. sects. editor, night city editor Reporter-Dispatch, White Plains, N.Y., 1970-74; assoc. editor United Feature Syndicate, N.Y.C., 1974-75; successively copy editor, asst. news editor, news editor, Sunday editor Newsday mag., L.I., N.Y., 1975-80, exec. news editor, 1980-83, fgn. editor, 1984-85; mag. cons. Los Angeles Times, 1986, asst. view editor, 1987—. Mem. Newswomen's Club, Sigma Delta Chi. Created team that won 1985 Pulitzer prize for international reporting. Office: Los Angeles Times Times Mirror Sq Los Angeles CA 90053

PATNOAD, MARTHA SMITH, college administrator; b. Wakefield, R.I., Sept. 21, 1946; d. Edwin Jr. and Helen (Gould) S.; m. Brian P. Martin, Aug. 17, 1968 (div. 1973); m. Edward Raymond Patnoad; 1 child, Aimee Catherine. BS, U. R.I., 1968, MS, 1976. Extension home economist Coop. Extension U. R.I., Kingston, 1972-80, state program leader, 1980-85; dept. chmn. Coll. Resource Devel. U. R.I., Kingston, 1985—. Contbr. articles to profl. jours. Mem. adv. com. Wood River Health Services, Inc., Hope Valley, R.I., 1981-82; mem. St. Joseph's Ch. Parish Council, Hope Valley, 1984-86; bd. dirs. Chariho Child Services, Hopkinton, R.I., 1981-82. Mem. Am. Home Econs. Assn. (cert.), R.I. Home Econs. Assn., Nutrition Council R.I. (pres. 1982-83), New England Assn. Extension Home Economists (pres. 1978-80), Epsilon Sigma Phi (pres. 1983-84). Home: PO Box 363 Wyoming RI 02898 Office: Univ RI Colle Resource Devel Woodward Hall Kingston RI 02881

PATON, DAWNA LISA, marketing executive; b. Melrose, Mass., Oct. 7, 1955; d. Charles D. and Constance (Conaxis) P. BS, MIT, 1977, MS, 1979. Air quality scientist Environ. Research and Tech., Concord, Mass., 1979-81; product mgr. Software Arts, Wellesley, Mass., 1981-82, market research mgr., 1982-85; market mgr. Pugh-Roberts Assoc., Cambridge, Mass., 1985-86; v.p. mktg. and sales Intec Controls, Foxboro, Mass., 1986—. Author Professional Dynamo, 1986, Paragon Control, 1986; contbr. articles to profl. jours. Mem. Am. Assn. Female Execs., N.Y. Acad. Scis., Nat. Geographic Assn., Sigma Xi. Office: Intec Controls 132 Central St 203B Foxboro MA 02035

PATRICK, CATHERINE LYNN, accountant; b. Sacramento, June 10, 1957; d. William Lawrence and Lucille Beverly (Miller) P. BS in Acctg., Calif. State U., 1979; MS in Tax, Golden Gate U., Sacramento, 1987. CPA, Calif.; cert. fin. planner. Sales mgr. Macy's Dept. Store, Sacramento, 1978-80; staff position Alexander Grant Co., Sacramento, 1980, jr. staff, 1981, sr. staff, 1981-82, supr., 1983-84, tax mgr., 1985—; speaker in field. Mem. Sacramento Prodn. Credit Assn., Calif. Fedn. Rep. Women. Mem. Am. Inst. CPA's, Calif. Soc. CPA's, Cert. Fin. Planners Assn., Am. Mgmt. Assn. Republican. Methodist. Home: 351 Del Verde Condo #6 Sacramento CA 95833 Office: Grant Thornton 555 Capitol Mall Suite 302 Sacramento CA 95814

PATRICK, GEORGIA O'BRIEN LAKAYTIS, communications executive; b. Dallas, July 2, 1945; d. Jack Dallas and Jane (Childs) O'Brien; B.J., U. Mo., 1967; m. Thomas Donald Patrick, Oct. 23, 1981. Tech. writer Mo. Regional Med. Programs, Columbia and Kansas City, 1967-69; public relations dir. Center for Student Life, U. Mo., Columbia, 1969-76; communications dir. Am. Home Econs. Assn., Washington, 1976-81; exec. v.p. The Communicators, Inc., Washington, 1981—. Mem. Pub. Relations Soc. Am., Counselors Acad., Washington Bus. Communicators (v.p. 1981-82), Council of Communications Mgmt. Contbr. articles to profl. jours.; leader seminars and workshops for nat. and internat. orgns. Home: Blue Ridge Acres Box 11 Harpers Ferry WV 25425 Office: The Communicators Inc 966 Hungerford Dr Suite 14 Rockville MD 20850

PATRICK, JANE AUSTIN, association executive; b. Memphis, May 27, 1930; d. Wilfred Jack and Evelyn Eudora (Branch) Austin; m. William Thomas Spencer, Sept. 11, 1952 (div. Apr. 1970); children: Anthony Duke, Tonilee Candice Spencer Hughes; m. George Milton Patrick, Oct. 1, 1971. Student Memphis State U., 1946-47; BSBA, Ohio State U., 1979. Service rep. So. Bell Telephone and Telegraph, Memphis, 1947-52; placement dir. Mgmt. Personnel, Memphis, 1965-66; personnel asst. to exec. v.p. E & E Ins. Co., Columbus, Ohio, 1966-69; Ohio exec. dir. Nat. Soc. for Prevention of Blindness, Columbus, 1969-73; regional dir. Ohio and Ky. CARE and MEDICO, Columbus, 1979—; lectr., cons. in field. Mem. choir 1st Community Ch., Columbus, Ohio State Univ. Hosp.'s Service Bd.; bd. dirs. Columbus Council on World Affairs, 1981—, sec., 1983—. Recipient commendations Nat. Soc. Prevention Blindness and Central Ohio Lions Eye Bank, 1973, Nat. Soc. Fund-Raising Execs., 1984, 85, Plaques for Service award Upper Arlington Pub. Schs., 1986. Mem. Non-Profit Orgn. Mgmt. Inst. (pres.), Nat. Soc. Fund-Raising Execs. (cert., nat. dir.), Pub. Relations Soc. Am. (cert., membership com. chairperson), Ins. Inst. Am. (cert.), Mensa Internat., Columbus Dental Soc. Aux., Alpha Gamma Delta, Epsilon Sigma Alpha. Home: 2511 Onandaga Dr Columbus OH 43221 Office: 280 N High St Suite 1520 Columbus OH 43215

PATRICK, JANET CLINE, medical society administrator; b. San Francisco, June 30, 1934; d. John Wesley and Edith Bertha (Corde) Cline; m. Robert John Patrick Jr., June 13, 1959 (div. 1988); children—John McKinnon, Stewart McLellan, William Robert. B.A., Stanford U., 1955; postgrad. U. Calif.-Berkeley, 1957, George Washington U., 1978-82. English tchr. George Washington High Sch., San Francisco, 1957, K.D. Burke Sch., San Francisco, 1957-59, Berkeley Inst., Bklyn., 1959-63; placement counselor Washington Sch. Secs., Washington, 1976-78, asst. dir. placement, 1978-81; mgr. med. personnel service Med. Soc. D.C., 1981—. Chmn. area 2 planning com. Montgomery County Pub. Schs. (Md.), 1974-75; mem. vestry, corr. sec., Christ Ch., Kensington, Md., 1982-84, vestry, sr. warden, 1984-85, vestry, chmn. ann. giving com., 1986-88. Mem. Employment Mgmt. Assn., Met. D.C. Med. Group Mgmt. Assn., Phi Beta Kappa. Republican. Episcopalian. Club: Jr. League (Washington). Home: 5206 Carlton St Bethesda MD 20816 Office: Med Soc DC 1707 L St NW Washington DC 20036

PATRICK, JUNE CAROL, psychiatrist; b. Charlotte, Mich., Aug. 29, 1932; d. John and Rachel Irene (Towe) Granstrom; m. Robert Bruce Patrick, Aug. 28, 1955 (dec. Jan. 1981); 1 child, Kathleen Ann. BA, U. Mich., 1954, MA, 1956; DO, Mich. State U., 1978. Diplomate Am. Bd. Psychiatry and Neurology. Staff psychiatrist Milw. County Mental Health Complex, Milw., 1982—; practice medicine specializing in psychiatry Milw. Psychiatric Hosp., Wauwatosa, Wis., 1982—; asst. clin. prof. psychiatry and mental health scis. Med. Coll. of Wis., Milw., 1983—. Mem. NOW, AMA, Am. Psychiat. Assn, Wis. Psychiat. Assn. (women's com. chmn. 1985-86), Am. Osteo. Assn. office: Milw Psychiat Hosp 1220 Dewey Ave Wauwatosa WI 53213

PATRICK, SUZANNE DOROTHY, financial analyst; b. Johnson City, Tenn., Oct. 6, 1955; d. John Francis deValangin and Dorothy (Sztankay-Burget) F. Cert. Institut d'Etudes Politiques, Paris; BA in European Studies, Randolph-Macon Woman's Coll., 1977; MA in Govt., Georgetown U., 1986. Econ. research asst. Am. Enterprise Inst., Washington, 1977-78; internat. program mgr. Naval Air Systems Command, 1979-83; fgn. aviation programs br. head Staff of Chief Naval Ops., Washington, 1983-85; congl. advisor USN, 1985-87; fin. advisor Sanford C. Bernstein & Co., N.Y.C., 1987—. Contbr. articles to naval quarterly. Served to lt. (j.g.) USN, 1984—. Named one of Washington Women of Yr., Washington Woman Mag., 1985, Outstanding Young Women Yr., 1986; Gearge C. Marshall scholar. Roman Catholic. Home: 170 E 88th St New York NY 10128 Office: Sanford C Bernstein & Co 767 Fifth Ave New York NY 10153

PATRICK, TANDY CAROL, lawyer; b. Lexington, Ky., May 21, 1954; d. Walter and Nancy (Shinnick) P. MusB, U. Ky., 1974; JD, U. Louisville, 1978; MBA, Bellarmine Coll., 1984. Bar: Ky. 1979, U.S. Ct. Appeals (6th cir.) 1979, U.S. Dist. Ct. (we. dist.) Ky. 1979. Assoc. atty. Wyatt, Tarrant and Combs, Louisville, 1978-82, Morgan and Pottinger, Louisville, 1982-83; counsel Capital Holding Corp., Louisville, 1983-84; assoc. atty. Greenbaum Doll and McDonald, Louisville, 1984—. Mem. ABA, Ky. Bar Assn. (corp., banking, bus. and real property law sects.). Democrat. Club: Victory Athletic (Louisville) (v.p. 1985—). Home: 2381 Valley Vista Rd Louisville KY 40205 Office: Greenebaum Doll & McDonald 3300 First National Tower Louisville KY 40202

PATRIE, CHERYL CHRISTINE, educator; b. Dobbs Ferry, N.Y., June 8, 1947; d. Edward F. and Antoinette C. (Patrie) P. B.A. in Edn., U. Fla., 1969; M.S. in Edn., U. Miami, 1979. Cert. assoc. master tchr., Fla. Tchr. Marion County Sch. Bd., Ocala, Fla., 1970, Dade County Sch. Bd., Miami, Fla., 1974—; bldg. union steward United Tchrs. Dade, 1979—; faculty council Lorah Park Elem. Sch., Miami, 1979—, dropout prevention com., 1985, career lab. cons., 1983-85, Human Growth and Devel. cons., 1983—, comprehensive plan com., 1984—, phys. fitness co-chmn., 1984—; coordinator Quality Instrn. Incentives Program, 1984—; vol. Dade County Elem. Sch. Day Task Force, 1987—; mem. Dade County Elem. Sch. Day Task Force, 1987—. Mem. Crisis in Inner City task force United Tchrs. Dade, Miami, 1984-85. Named Tchr. of Yr., Lorah Park Elem. Sch., 1986. Mem. United Tchrs. Dade. (Disting. Service award 1984). Home: 1127 Robin Ave Miami Springs FL 33166 Office: Lorah Park Elem 5160 NW 31st Ave Miami FL 33142

PATRIS, DIANE SUE, small business owner; b. Massillon, Ohio, Dec. 14, 1945; d. John Bennie and Nell L. (Finefrock) Cullen; m. Robert Edward Patris, Mar. 25, 1946; children: Stacy Lyn, Rob. BS, Ohio State U., 1967; postgrad., Ashland Coll., 1987. Cert. tchr., Ohio. Instr. Hoover High Sch., North Canton, Ohio, 1967-70; instr. community edn. Jackson Twp. Community Edn., Massillon, 1977-87, cons. bus., 1983—; owner Contemporary Secretarial Service, Massillon, 1981—; instr. adult evening sch. Hoover High Sch., North Canton, 1968-77; instr. Wayne Gen. & Tech. Coll. U. Akron, Orrville, Ohio, 1978-85; mem. adv. com. Wayne Gen. & Tech. Coll., Orrville, 1979-85, Bus. Office Skills Specialists, Massillon, 1986-87. Team counselor Jackson Baseball Assn., Massillon, 1982—; chmn. publicity com. Jackson Athletic Booster Club, Massillon, 1986—; chmn. membership com. Sauder Elem. Sch. PTA, Massillon. Methodist.

PATRON, JUNE EILEEN, govt. ofcl.; b. N.Y.C., May 15; d. Irving B. and Mollie Patron; A.B. in Govt. with honors, Clark U., Worcester, Mass., 1965; M.A., Am. U., 1967. With U.S. Dept. of Labor, 1966—, head Black Lung benefits program, 1976-79, asst. adminstr. pension and welfare benefit programs, 1979-84, assoc. dir. pension and welfare benefit programs, 1984-88, dir. program services, 1988—; mem. Sr. Exec. Service. Recipient various awards Dept. Labor. Office: 200 Constitution Ave NW Washington DC 20210

PATRYN, ELAINE LILLIAN, real estate broker, life and health insurance salesperson; b. Phila., Sept. 14, 1937; d. Frank and Lillian Helen (Genga) Borgioni; divorced; 1 child, Steven James. B.S., Chestnut Hill Coll., 1959; postgrad. in acctg. and bus. law St. Joseph's Coll., Phila., 1960-61, Coll. for Fin. Planning, Denver, 1986. Engring. asst. Gen. Electric Co., Phila., 1959-61, math. technician, Santa Barbara, Calif., 1961-62, Reseda, Calif., 1964-65, King of Prussia, Pa., 1966-67; math. technician Space Tech. Lab., Redondo Beach, Calif., 1962-64; real estate broker Patryn Realty Corp., Ocala, Fla., 1980—; instr. Gold Coast Sch. Real Estate, Ocala, 1983-84. Mem. AAUW (treas. 1980-81), Nat. Assn. Female Execs. (dir. Marion County network 1985-86). Republican. Roman Catholic. Home: 525 Emerald Rd Ocala FL 32672 Office: Patryn Realty Corp 6661 SE Maricamp Rd Ocala FL 32672

PATTEN, LINDA FRANK, banker; b. Chgo., Sept. 5, 1949; d. Eugene T. and Annette (Fell) Frank; B.A., St. Olaf Coll., 1971; M.B.A., So. Meth. U., 1977; m. Clark W. Patten, May 17, 1975; children: Jennifer Lin, Allyce Karin. Successively computer programmer, mgr. adminstrn., personnel cons., mgr. staffing Res. Life Ins. Co., Dallas, 1975-77; compensation analyst-internat., Bank of Am., San Francisco, 1977-78, tng. officer South, Los Angeles, 1979-80; head mgmt. tng., 1980-81, asst. v.p., head tng. dept., 1981-82, v.p. human resource planning and adminstrn., San Francisco, 1982-83; v.p., mgr. personal banking div. tng. Crocker Bank, San Francisco, 1983-86; v.p. personnel, adminstrn. The Fox Group of Cos., Foster City, Calif., 1986-87; ptnr. the Patten Group, Oakland, 1986—. Served with U.S. Army, 1970-74. Decorated Army Commendation medal with oak leaf cluster. Mem. Am. Soc. for Tng. and Devel., Internat. Assn. Personnel Women, Am. Compensation Assn., Nat. Assn. Female Execs. Republican. Lutheran. Home: 3545 Perada Dr Walnut Creek CA 94598

PATTEN, MAURINE DIANE, psychologist; b. Peoria, Ill., Aug. 30, 1940; d. Maurice H. and Esther Ann (Wilkenson) Foote; m. C. Alfred Patten, Aug. 26, 1961; children: Paul A., Bethany M. BS, Bradley U., 1961; MS, Chgo. State U., 1971; EdD, No. Ill. U., 1977. Lic. psychologist, Ill. Tchr. Elementary Schs., Skokie and Manhattan, Ill., 1961-63; dir. Southwest Coop Presch., Chgo., 1970-74; tchr. spl. edn. Dekalb County (Ill.) Spl. Edn. Assn., 1974-76, asst. dir., 1978-80; resource tchr. Sycamore (Ill.) Sch. Dist., 1976-78; asst. prof. Chgo. State U., 1980-81; psychologist Sycamore, 1981—; Cons. Arthur Andersen & Co., St. Charles, Ill., 1981—; profl. devel. workshops coordinator, 1981—. Fellow Am. Psychol. Assn., Ill. Psychol. Assn., Am. Pain Soc., Nat. Assn. Neurolinguistic Programming, Am. Registry of Lic. Psychologists and Mental Health Providers, Am. Soc. Profl. and Exec. Women. Methodist. Home: 530 Calvin Park Blvd Rockford IL 61107 Office: 964 W State St Sycamore IL 60178

PATTERSON, ANNE, textile executive; b. Teaneck, N.J., June 13, 1956; d. Charles Symon and Helen Ann (Jindra) Finke; m. Wesley J. Patterson, Nov. 27, 1982. BS, U. Wis., Menomanie, 1978; MBA, Fairleigh Dickinson, 1982; student, N.C. State U. Lab. technologist Manhattan Industries, Glen Rock, N.J., 1978-79; lab. technologist U.S. Testing Co., Inc., Hoboken, N.J., 1979-81, supr., 1981-82, mgr., 1982-83, asst. v.p., 1983-85, v.p., 1985—. Recipient N.J. People to Watch award, 1987; named U. Wis. Menomonie Disting. Young Alumnus, 1987. Mem. Am. Soc. Testing and Materials, Am. Assn. Textile Chemists and Colorists (com chmn. 1986—, sec. met. section 1987—), Am. Apparel Mfrs. Assn. (mem. apparel quality com.), Nat. Bus. Woman's Assn., Textile Inst., Textile Quality Control Assn., Indsl. Fabrics Assn. Democrat. Home: 17 Cross Ridge Cir Marlboro NJ 07746 Office: US Testing Co Inc 1415 Park Ave Hoboken NJ 07030

PATTERSON, DAWN MARIE, educator, consultant; b. Gloversville, N.Y., July 30; d. Robert Morris and Dora Margaret (Perham) P.; m. Robert Henry Hollenbeck, Aug. 3, 1958 (div. 1976); children: Adrienne Lyn, Nathaniel Conrad. BS in Edn., SUNY, Geneseo, 1962; MA, Mich. State U., 1973, PhD, 1977; postgrad., U. So. Calif. and Inst. Edl. Leadership. Librarian Brighton (N.Y.) Cen. Schs., 1962-67; asst. to regional dir. Mich. State U. Ctr., Bloomfield Hills, 1973-74; grad. asst. Mich. State U., Ann Arbor, 1975-77; cons. Mich. Efficiency Task Force, 1977; asst. dean Coll. Continuing Edn., U. So. Calif., Los Angeles, 1978-84; dean continuing edn. Calif. State U., Los Angeles, 1985—; pres. Co-Pro Assocs. Mem. Air Univ. Bd. Visitors, 1986—, Commn. on Extended Edn. Calif. State U. Calif., 1988—; Hist. Soc., Los Angeles Town Hall, Los Angeles World Affairs Council. Dora Louden scholar, 1958-61; Langworthy fellow, 1961-62; Edn. Professions Devel. fellow, 1974-75; Ednl. Leadership Policy fellow, 1982-83. Mem. AAUW (pres. Pasadena br. 1985-86), Am. Assn. Adult and Continuing Edn.

(charter), Nat. Univ. Continuing Edn. Assn., Calif. Coll. and Mil. Educators Assn. (pres.), Los Angeles Airport Area Edn. Industry Assn. (pres. 1984), Kappa Delta Pi, Phi Delta Kappa. Republican. Unitarian. Club: Fine Arts of Pasadena. Lodge: Zonta. Office: 5151 State University Dr Los Angeles CA 90032

PATTERSON, DEBRA GOLDBERG, public relations executive; b. Atlanta, Dec. 18, 1960; d. Joel Goldberg and Carole Louise (Brockey) Goldberg; m. William Christopher Patterson, Nov. 6, 1958. AB in Journalism, U. Ga., 1983. Asst. acct. exec. McKenzie Gordon & Potter, Atlanta, 1983-86; acct. exec. McKenzie & Assocs., Atlanta, 1986—. Mem. Young Careers The High Mus. of Art, Atlanta, 1983-85, Bus./Profl. Women's Div. Atlanta Symphony, 1984-85, steering com. Young Profls. Am. Jewish Com., Atlanta, 1985—, Support Campaign Exodus, Inc., Atlanta, 1986—; auction chmn., com. mem. Crescendo Ball, Cystic Fibrosis Found., 1988. Mem. Pub. Relations Soc. Am. (assoc. mem. 1983-85), Alpha Delta Pi. Office: McKenzie & Assocs Inc 600 W Peachtree St Suite 1550 Atlanta GA 30308

PATTERSON, ELIZABETH JOHNSTON, U.S. Congresswoman; b. Columbia, S.C., Nov. 18, 1939; d. Olin DeWitt and Gladys (Atkinson) Johnston; B.A., Columbia Coll., 1961; postgrad. in polit. sci. U. S.C., 1961, 62, 64; m. Dwight Fleming Patterson, Jr., Apr. 15, 1967; children—Dwight Fleming, Olin DeWitt, Catherine Leigh. Pub. affairs officer Peace Corps, Washington, 1962-64; recruiter VISTA, OEO, Washington, 1965-66; state coordinator Head Start and VISTA, OEO, Columbia, 1966-67; tri-county dir. Head Start, Piedmont Community Actions, Spartanburg, S.C., 1967-68; adminstrv. asst. Congressman James R. Mann, Spartanburg, 1969-70; mem. Spartanburg County Council, 1975-76; mem. S.C. State Senate, 1979-86; mem. 100th Congress from 4th S.C. Dist., 1987—. Trustee, Wofford Coll.; bd. dirs. Charles Lea Center, Spartanburg Council on Aging; pres. Spartanburg Democratic Women, 1968; v.p. Spartanburg County Dem. party, 1968-70, sec., 1970-75. Mem. Bus. and Profl. Women's Club, Alpha Kappa Gamma. Methodist. Office: Longworth Ho Office Bldg Rm 1641 Washington DC 20515 also: PO Box 5564 Spartanburg SC 29304

PATTERSON, GRENAY JAN, communications executive; b. Bklyn., Sept. 1, 1962; d. Grant George and Mary Evelyn (Faison) Patterson. BS, Boston U., 1984. Communications coordinator Bloomingdales, N.Y.C., 1985-86; tech. sport specialist U.S. Sprint, N.Y.C., 1986-87; asst. to dir. telecommunications Peat, Marwick, Main & Co., N.Y.C., 1987—. Vol. Pratt Area Community Counsel, Bklyn., 1987; founder, chmn. internship program com. on minorities Pub. Relations Soc. Am., N.Y.C., 1985; admissions advisor alumni schs. com. Boston U., 1987. Fellow Nat. Assn. Female Execs.; mem. Women/Men in Telecommunications. Baptist.

PATTERSON, JANET DOERR, banker; b. Rochester, Minn., Oct. 7, 1941; d. Rudy Ernest and Mary Leone (Wilkes) Doerr; student U. Iowa, 1959-61; m. Walter Patterson, Apr. 22, 1978. Dir. mktg. The Drovers Nat. Bank of Chgo., 1976-78; dir. mktg. Lawndale Trust and Savs. Bank, Chgo., 1978, v.p. comml. banking group, 1978-79, pres., chief exec. officer, 1979-83; pres., chief exec. officer Bank of Chgo., 1983-85; sr. v.p. Lawrence & Allen, 1985—. Episcopalian. Club: Econ. of Chgo. Office: One Energy Ctr Naperville IL 60566

PATTERSON, KATHERINE HULEN, pharmacist; b. Caracas, Venezuela, Dec. 21, 1947; d. Joseph T. and Antoinette (deLarroque) H.; m. Gary Wayne Patterson, May 31, 1969; children—Katherine Denise, Gary Wayne. B.F.A., U. Miss., 1969; B.S., U. Houston, 1980. Pharmacist, mgr. Superex Drugs, Houston, 1980-81, Walgreen Drugs, Houston, 1981-84, Gordon Drugs, Houston, 1984—. Mem. Spring Branch PTA, Houston, 1974—; sec. Spring Shadows Women's Club, 1973-74; rep. Spring Shadows Civic Assn., 1976-77. Mem. Am. Pharm. Assn., Tex. Pharm. Assn., Harris County Pharm. Assn. (bd. councillors 1984-86), Alpha Delta Pi. Republican. Roman Catholic. Clubs: U. Miss., Real Estate Investment (Houston). Avocations: swimming; tennis; reading; cooking. Home: 2819 Shadowdale Dr Houston TX 77043

PATTERSON, LUCY PHELPS, educator; b. Dallas, Tex., June 21, 1931; d. John C. and Florence L. (Harllee) Phelps; A.B., Howard U., 1950; M.S.W., U. Denver, 1963; m. Albert S. Patterson, Nov. 25, 1950; 1 son, Albert Harllee. Tabulating machine operator supr. Dept. Commerce, Bur. Census, Washington, 1950-52, Dept. Navy, Bur. of Ships, Washington, 1952-54; caseworker dept. public welfare Dallas, 1954-61, casework supr., 1963-68; dir. Interagy. Project, Dallas, 1968-71; exec. dir. Dallas County Child Care Council, 1971-73; planning dir. Community Council of Greater Dallas, 1973-74; asst. prof. and field work coordinator N. Tex. State U., 1974-78; Ethel Carter Branham prof. Bishop Coll., Dallas, 1978—, dir. social work, 1978—; cons. to Creative Learning Center, Rhodes Terrace Pre-sch., Head Start Consultation Register, Inst. Urban Studies, So. Meth. U. Councilwoman, City of Dallas, 1973-80; chairwoman Nat. Afro-Am. History & Culture Commn., 1985—; mem. adminstrv. bd., chairwoman bd. ch. and soc. com. St. Paul United Meth. Ch., 1987—. Recipient Outstanding Woman award Women's Center of Dallas, 1978, Public Service award Elite Newspaper, 1978; named Mother of Yr., 1979. Mem. Nat. Assn. Social Workers, Acad. Cert. Social Workers, Council on Social Work Edn., Tex. Assn. Coll. Tchrs., Nat. Assn. Black Social Workers, Dallas County Mental Health Assn., NOW, Tex. Black Polit. Caucus, Tex. Assn. of Women Elected Ofcls., Women's Council of Dallas County, LWV, Nat. Council of Negro Women, Council on Consumer Edn., Nat. Polit. Congress Black Women, Exec. Women in Govt., Alpha Kappa Alpha. Republican. Club: Altrusa. Weekly columnist Post Tribune, 1973-80, The Dallas Weekly, 1973-80. Home: 2779 Almeda Dr Dallas TX 75216 Office: 3837 Simpson Stuart Rd Dallas TX 75241

PATTERSON, LYDIA ROSS, industrial relations specialist, consulting company executive; b. Carrabelle, Fla., Sept. 3, 1936; d. Richard D. Ross and Johnnie Mae (Thomas) Kelley; m. Edgar A. Corley, Aug. 1, 1964 (div.); 1 child, Derek Kelley; m. Berman W. Patterson, Dec. 18, 1981. BA, Hunter Coll., 1958. Indsl. relations specialist U.S. Dept. Energy, N.Y.C., 1966-68; regional dir./mgr. Div. Human Rights State of N.Y., N.Y.C., 1962-66, 68-76; v.p. Bankers Trust Co., N.Y.C., 1976-87; pres., chief exec. officer Extend Cons. Services, N.Y.C., 1985—; v.p., mgr. Merrill Lynch and Co. Inc., N.Y.C., 1987—; seminar speaker Columbia U., Wharton Sch. Bus., Harvard U., Duke U., Cornell U., 1976-85; bd. dirs. Project Discovery Columbia U.; mem. Bus. Policy Rev. Council, Exec. Leadership Council. Bd. dirs. Project Discovery Columbia U., 1988. Mem. Am. Soc. Personnel Adminstrn., N.Y. and Nat. Urban League, Employment Mgrs. Assn., Fin. Women's Assn. (govt./community affairs com. 1986-87), Nat. Assn. Black Women (bd. dirs. Women's Ctr. 1978—), Women's Ctr. Edn. Advancement (bd. dirs. 1978—), Employment Dissemination of Information Group Awareness Edn. Solving of Problems (bd. dirs. 1979—). Office: Merrill Lynch and Co Inc World Fin Ctr South Tower New York NY 10080-1105

PATTERSON, MARILYN JEAN, petroleum services company executive; b. Dallas, Nov. 2, 1943; d. J.D. and Mary Lois (Powell) Williams; m. Richard Lester Patterson, Aug. 19, 1967 (div. 1979); 1 child, Corbett Layne Patterson. BS in Edn., Abilene Christian U., 1966. Tchr. sch. systems, Abilene and Dallas, 1966-70; polit. liason customer relations R.S. Tapp & Co., Lubbock, Tex., 1976-80; exec. v.p. Increased Energy Corp., Coleman, Tex., 1981-83; pres. Increased Resources Corp., Abilene, 1983-84, PetroScis. Internat. Inc., Abilene, 1984—; commd. by Gov. of Tex. to bus. devel. and jobs creation task force; cons. in field. Contbr. articles to profl. jours., lectr. profl. confs. Mem. spl. task force Disabled Children Christian Homes, Abilene, 1985—; vice chmn. of bd. Christina Homes of Abilene, chmn. capital campaign Abilene Christian Schs., 1985—, exec. bd. trustees, 1985—; adminstrv. bd. Christian Homes of Abilene, 1985—; apptd. strategic econ. policy commn. task force Study Trad. Industry in Tex.; mem. exec. com. Taylor County Reps. Named in Portrait in Oil, Abilene Reporter News, 1985. Mem. Soc. Profl. Well Log Analysts, Nat. Assn. Female Execs., Tex. Found. Women's Resources (Leadership Tex. 1986), Tex. Women's Alliance (steering com. Taylor County chpt.). Clubs: Women's, Women for Abilene, Desk and Derrick, Republican Women; South Plains Republican (founder); Christian University (Abilene). Avocation: cooking. Home: 1657 Morrow Ln Abilene TX 79601 Office: PetroScis Internat Inc 833 Vista Ln Abilene TX 79606

PATTERSON, MARJORIE SCOTT SELLERS, librarian; b. Decatur, Ala., Apr. 18, 1925; d. Clyde R. and Eula W. (Lewis) Scott; student Kansas City Met. Jr. Coll., Park Coll.; m. Leonard S. Sellers, Nov. 25, 1943 (div.); children—Carol, Steve, Mark; m. Thomas W. Patterson, 1983. Substitute and library asst. Oak Park Sr. High Sch., North Kansas City, Mo., 1968-71; periodicals bank coordinator Kansas City Regional Council for Higher Edn., 1971-74; co-founder, dir. Mid-Am. inter-library services, interlibrary loans librarian Park Coll., Parkville, Mo., 1974-81; founder Access to Info. Services Assos., 1981—; owner, operator Bell Rd. Barn Book, rare and out-of-print books, 1981-83; sec. Internat. Libray Exchange Ctr., 1986—. Editor: The LOANER newsletter, 1974-80, Mid-Am. Shelflist newsletter, 1981—, The Dusty Shelf, 1986—, Family Focus newsletter, 1984—. Sec. Emerald-Hodgson Hosp Aux., 1987—; mem. N. Central Evaluation Com. Mem. Mo. Library Assn., Mountain Plains Library Assn., Oral History Assn., Park Coll. Hist. Soc., U. of the South Friends of the Library, Park Coll. Friends of the Library, Internat. Library Exchange Ctr. Methodist. Address: care Gen Delivery Sewanee TN 37375

PATTERSON, P. J., accountant; b. Pana, Ill., June 7, 1950; d. Gordon G. and Doris (Stolte) Moore. Cert. tax practitioner. Acct. ADM, 1971-73, Ford Motor Co., 1973-74; asst. controller Union Iron Works, Decatur, Ill., 1974; acct. Caterpillar Co., Decatur, 1975; pvt. practice acctg., owner Patterson Acctg., Decatur, 1975—; speaker Networking Women convs., 1983-86. Bd. dirs. Boys Club, Decatur, 1985-87, Decatur Area Arts Council, 1985-87, 87—, Decatur Advantage, 1986, YWCA, Decatur, 1983-86. Mem. Ind. Accts. Assn. (treas. 1984), Nat. Assn. Income Tax Practitioners (pres. 1984—), Nat. Assn. Tax Practitioners, Nat. Assn. Income Tax Practitioners (pres. cen. Ill. chpt. 1984—), Assn. Bus. Women Am. (treas. 1982), Nat. Assn. Female Execs. (bd. dirs. 1983-86), Decatur C. of C. (Outstanding Bus. of Yr. award 1983). Republican. Baptist. Club: Decatur. Home: 315 Shoreline Pl Decatur IL 62526 Office: Patterson Acctg 1212 E Pershing Decatur IL 62526

PATTERSON, PAMELA JANE, audiologist; b. Passaic, N.J., Feb. 26, 1951; d. Robert and Marian M. Patterson. BS, Ohio State U., 1973, postgrad., 1973-74; MA, Kent State U., 1976. Audiologist E.N.T. Head and Neck Surgeons, Columbus, Ohio, 1975-76; audiologist Arnold D. Rubenfield M.D. & Assocs., New Kensington, Pa., 1976-80, bus. mgr., 1978-80; dir. audiological services Hearing Cons. for Industry, New Kensington, 1977-80; audiologist Cen. Ohio Hearing Aid Ctr., Reynoldsburg, 1980-83; pres. Micro Hearing Systems, Inc., Columbus, 1984—. Mem. Am. Speech and Hearing Assn., Auditory Soc. of Am., Ohio Hearing Aid Soc. Republican. Presbyterian. Home: 157 N Oak St London OH 43140 Office: Micro Hearing Systems Inc 15 Norton Rd Columbus OH 43228

PATTERSON, PEGGY JEAN, real estate broker; b. Macon County, N.C., Nov. 10, 1940; d. Jay B. and Agnes Aletha (Saunders) Moore; student Southwestern Tech. Coll., 1974; m. Morris Patterson, Aug. 23, 1970; children—Kenneth Douglas, Aletha Darlene. Sec., John Phelan Real Estate, Highlands, N.C., 1973-74; broker Jones Real Estate, Franklin, N.C., 1974-75; owner, pres., sec. Patterson Realty, Inc., Franklin, 1977—. Mem. adv. com. South Western Tech. Coll. Recipient Membership award Franklin Area C. of C., 1980; Beautification award Franklin Garden Club, 1980. Mem. C. of C. (dir. 1980), Better Bus. Bur., N.C. Assn. Realtors (dir. 1981—), Franklin Bd. Realtors (sec. 1979, pres. 1981), Nat. Assn. Female Execs., Nat. Assn. Realtors. Republican. Baptist. Clubs: Merchants Assn., Bus. and Profl. Women's. Home: 14 Pine Rd Otto NC 28763 Office: 146 Palmer St Franklin NC 28734

PATTERSON, POLLY REILLY (MRS. W. RAY PATTERSON), civic worker; b. Wilkinsburg, Pa.; d. Thomas L. and Margaret (Coughey) Reilly; m. W. Ray Patterson, Sept. 2, 1943. Student, U. Pitts. With Bell Telephone Co. of Pa., Pitts., 1925-71, beginning as clk., successively various mgmt. positions, 1935-64, assoc. pub. relations staff, 1965-71. Asst. treas. Allegheny County (Pa.) Soc. for Crippled Children, 1962-66, v.p., 1966-70; mem. nat. ho. of dels. Nat. Soc. for Crippled Children and Adults, 1965-67; mem. Allegheny County United Way, 1972—; bd. dirs. Jr. Achievement, Inc. of S.W. Pa., 1950-71, Pitts. YWCA, 1964-72, Pa. Soc. Crippled Children and Adults, 1960-68. Named Pitts. Advt. Woman of Yr., 1958, one of Pitts.'s Ten Outstanding Women, Pitts. Sun Telegraph, 1959; recipient Crystal Prism award Am. Advt. Fedn., 1972, 75. Mem. Assn. Pitts. Clubs (bd. dirs. 1946-81, pres. 1953), Altrusa Internat. (pres. Pitts. club 1950-51), Pitts. Advt. Club (v.p., sec. 1929-69), Pitts. Bus. and Profl. Women's Club, Telephone Pioneers. Home: 402 Olympia Rd Pittsburgh PA 15211

PATTERSON, SHIRLEY ABBOTT, artist, writer; b. Buffalo, Dec. 13, 1923; d. Walter DeForest and Eleanor Agnes (Flinn) Abbott; m. Ralph Gordon Patterson, Sept. 25, 1948; children: Lois Elaine (dec.), Brian Alan. Diploma, Albright Sch. Fine Art, Buffalo, 1944; BS, SUNY, Buffalo, 1945. Cert. tchr., N.Y. Tchr. art Griffith Inst. and Cen. Sch., Springville, N.Y., 1945-46; critic tchr. art Kenmore (N.Y.) Pub. Schs., 1946-49; pvt. practice art tchr. Wilmington, Del., 1958-70; founder, mgr. Today's Artists, Wilmington, 1974-77; freelance writer, artist Wilmington, 1977—; advisor exhbn. U. Del., Newark, 1979, advisor books, 1981, lectr., 1983, 86; critic Studio Group, Inc., Wilmington, 1985-87; juror Del. Camera Club, 1986, 87, 88. Contbr. numerous stories to children's mags., 1955-67; contbr. book revs. to News Jour. Co., 1975-77; represented in numerous pub. and pvt. collections. Recipient Artist of Yr. award Wilmington Christmas Com., 1976. Mem. AAUW (group leader 1960-64), Nat. League Am. Pen Women (br. pres. 1978-80, First Prize Painting award 1977, 79, 81, 83, 85, First Prize Short Story award 1981, Writer's scholarship 1983), Studio Group, Inc. (pres. 1978-80), Pa. Watercolor Soc. (signature, hon.), Ky. Watercolor Soc., Del. Artists Register, Delta Zeta (chpt. pres. 1943-44, alumni chpt. pres. 1982-83). Republican. Mem. Unitarian Ch. Home and Office: 3405 S Rockfield Dr Wilmington DE 19810

PATTERSON, VANESSA LEIGH, development executive. m. Stanley M. Patterson, Sept. 23, 1965; 1 child, Lee E. II. BA, SUNY, Albany, 1964; postgrad., Memphis State U., 1983-85. Project coordinator Holiday Inns, Inc., Memphis, 1978-79; supr., research corp. strategies div. Holiday Corp., Memphis, 1979-85; dir. research and records Fairleigh Dickinson U., Rutherford, N.J., 1985—. Mng. editor Strategic News Review newsletter, Holiday Corp., 1984-85, Biomed. Research Zone Com. newsletter, 1985. Mem. Biomed. Research Zone com. of Memphis Ctr. City Commn., 1984-85, com. on info. tech. of William Carlos Williams Ctr. for Performing Arts, Rutherford, 1985-86. Mem. Am. Soc. Info. Scientists, Nat. Assn. Female Execs. (network dir. 1981-85), Council for Advancement and Support of Edn. Unitarian. Office: Fairleigh Dickinson U The Castle Rutherford NJ 07070

PATTERSON, VIVIAN ROGERS, banker; b. Wake County, N.C., June 2, 1924; d. Lattie Raymond and Dala Earnal (Prince) Rogers; B.S.C., N.C. Coll., 1951, M.S.C., 1961; postgrad. Stonier Grad. Sch. Banking, Rutgers U., 1978, Cannon's Trust Sch., U. N.C., 1981; m. Cecil L. Patterson, Apr. 1, 1956. With Mechanics and Farmers Bank, Durham, N.C., 1944—, asst. v.p., 1967-68, v.p., 1968—, corp. sec., 1979—, trust officer, 1980—; mem. adv. council Sch. Bus., N.C. Central U., Durham; dir. REMCA, Inc. Past mem. fin. com. Harriet Tubman br. YWCA, Durham; past sec., 1st v.p. Durham chpt. Am. Cancer Soc.; past unit leader Durham United Fund; pres. bd. dirs. Durham YWCA; sec., bd. dirs. Durham chpt. ARC; mem. vestry St. Titus Episcopal Ch., Durham; Ch. Women del. Gen. Conv., Episcopal Ch., 1973, lay del., 1982; mem. Hist. Commn. Durham. Mem. Am Inst. Banking, Nat. Assn. Bank Women, Durham Council Estate Planning, Durham Bus. and Profl. Women's Club, NAACP, Durham C. of C. (downtown task force), N.C. Central U. Alumni Assn., Delta Sigma Theta. Clubs: Lawson St. Community, Downtown. Home: 409 Lawson St Durham NC 27707 Office: PO Box 1932 Durham NC 27702

PATTISON-LEHNING, BARBARA JEANNE, educational ombudsman, marketing consultant; b. Tacoma, Wash., Jan. 2, 1936; d. Richard Stanley and Elizabeth June (Miller) Bennatts; m. Thomas Wesley Lehning, Aug. 26, 1983; children: Mark, Scott, Kimberly, Trishawn. BA in Communications, U. Wash., 1972; MBA, Seattle, 1979. Promotion dir. Sta. KIRO-TV, Seattle, 1960-67; editor TV Guide, Seattle, 1967-73, legis. asst. Seattle councilman, 1973-76; chmn. internat. conf. Assn. for Children with Learning Disabilities, Seattle, 1976; ombudsman Wash. State Parent Community Relations Project, Seattle, 1976—; cons. Rising Star Enterprise, Seattle, 1983—; small business owner, 1984—. Author, producer various video tapes and brochures. Political Strategist, Re-elect Councilwoman V. Galle, Seattle, 1984, Re-elect Councilwoman J. William, 1984; county coordinator Re-elect State Supt., King County, 1984. Recipient Award of Merit, Wash. State Spl. Edn., 1983; named Outstanding Citizen, Wash. Assn. Children, 1982. Mem. Wash. Press Assn. (sec. 1982-83, pres. 1983-84, cons., Woman of Achievement award 1984), Wash. Soc. for Intelligence Tng. (fund-raiser 1986, cons.), Wash. Generals, Gov.'s Com. Employment of Handicapped (chmn. pub. relations and edn. coms. 1982-85, bd. dirs.), Women of Variety (sec., v.p. 1982—), Seattle C. of C. (small bus. com. 1986, activist 1984—). Democrat. Home: 9319 42d Ave NE Seattle WA 98115

PATTON, ANNIE MOSS, human resource management specialist, consultant; b. Ocilla, Ga., Aug. 12, 1951; d. Willie B. and Kathleen Moss; m. Phillip W. Patton, June 5, 1982. BS, Mercy Coll. of Detroit, 1974; postgrad., U. Mich., 1980-81, U. Detroit, 1981-82; MBA, Calif. State U., San Bernardino, 1987. Cert. med. technoloigst, nuclear medicine technologist. Supr. med. tech. Comprehensive Diagnostic Lab., Detroit, 1974-75; research asst. Hutzel Hosp., Detroit, 1975-76; supr. med. tech. Sci. Med. Lab., Detroit, 1976-79; asst. dept. mgr. Detroit Osteo. Lab., 1979-80; dept. mgr. VA Med. Ctr., Allen Park, Mich., 1980-82; dept. mgr., dir. edn. VA Med. Ctr., Los Angeles, 1982-85; emergency nuclear medicine technologist, mgmt. cons. San Bernardino, Calif., 1984—; cons. Best Nuclear Inc., Reseda, Calif., 1984-86. Mem. NAACP, Am. Soc. Med. Technologists, Am. Soc. Clin. Pathologists, Soc. Nuclear Medicine, Nat. Assn. Female Execs. Democrat. Roman Catholic. Home and Office: 1554 W Windsor St San Bernardino CA 92407

PATTON, CONNIE GARCIA, educator; b. Luarca, Spain, Nov. 7, 1941; d. Antonio Garcia and Palmira Garcia (Lavin) Mendez; BA, U. N.Mex., 1964, MA, 1966; PhD U. Kans., 1988; m. Michael G. Patton, July 5, 1970; children: Michael Anthony, Ryan Blake. Instr., Peace Corps, 1964-66; asso. prof. fgn. lang. Emporia (Kans.) State U., 1966—; chmn. fgn. langs. dept., 1984-86; court translator Lyon County Courthouse, 1974—. Bd. dirs. Sexual Offense Services, 1974-78; v.p. Big Bro.-Big Sister, 1977-79. Ford Found. grad. fellow, 1963-66; KNEH grantee, 1986, 87, NEH grantee, 1976, 78; recipient Xi Phi Outstanding Faculty award, 1976, 77, LA&S Outstanding Tchr. award, 1986; named Outstanding Young Kansan, Jaycees, 1977. Mem. Am. Assn. Tchrs. Spanish and Portuguese, MLA, MALAS (sec.-treas.), Midwest Assn. of Latin Am. Studies, AAUP, P.E.O., Sigma Delta Pi. Lodge: Rotary. Author: Spanish Vocabulary Units, 1975; Castles in Spain, 1984. Home: 2919 Monterey Dr Emporia KS 66801 Office: 1200 Commercial St Emporia KS 66801

PATTON, KAREN LYNN, university building services superintendent; b. Dayton, Ohio, Apr. 11, 1946; d. Irving and Dorothy Ellen (Baker) Atkins; m. Donald Lee Patton, Aug. 28, 1966; children: Tara-Lynne, Troy. BA, Ball State U., 1969, MA, 1973. Lic. vocat. tchr. Tchr. Indpls. Pub. Schs., 1969-70; instr. Ball State U., Muncie, Ind., 1975-76; prodn. supr. Chevrolet div. Gen. Motors Corp., Muncie, 1976-81; owner Patton Bookkeeping and Tax Services, Muncie, 1981-83; supt. bldg. services Ball State U., Muncie, 1983—; tng. dir. phys. plant Ball State U., 1983—, newsletter editor, 1986—. Author: P.P. Custodial Handbook, 1985. Com. mem. Pride Task Force, Muncie, 1986—; adv. com. Assn. Physical Plant Adminstrn. on Staffing Guidlines; bd. dirs. Muncie Boy's Clubs. Mem. Am. Bus. Women's Assn. (v.p., program chmn., membership chmn. 1982—), Assn. Colls. and Univs. Bldg. Services Supervisors (exec. bd., membership chmn. 1987, conf. co-chmn. 1986—). Home: 19101 N Elizabeth Ln Muncie IN 47303 Office: Ball State U Phys Plant Muncie IN 47306

PATTON, RITA JONES, career planning administrator; b. St. Louis, Aug. 11, 1946; d. Alphonzo and Desma L. (Hill) Jones; divorced; children: Desma M., J. Kirk. BA, Lane Coll., 1968; MEd, U. Mo., St. Louis, 1976. Tchr. St. Louis Pub. Schs., 1968-69, career counselor, 1971-82; personnel interviewer, recruiter hotel div. Loew's Corp., N.Y.C., 1969-71; pres., owner Rita Patton & Assocs., St. Louis, 1983—. Recipient Bus. Entrepreneur of Yr. award Minority Bus. Devel., St. Louis, 1984, Minority Bus. of Yr. award St. Louis Met. Minority Supplier Devel. Council, Inc., 1986, Outstanding Services in Bus. award Iota Phi Lambda, St. Louis, 1986. Mem. Mo. Assn. Personnel Cons., Inst. Temp. Services, Regional Commerce and Growth Assn., Alpha Kappa Alpha. Office: Rita Patton & Assocs 4660 Maryland Saint Louis MO 63108

PAUL, CYNTHIA ROSE CECHINI, management consultant; b. Grand Rapids, Minn., May 18, 1958; d. Norman Lino and Rosella Mae (Edoff) Cechini; m. Howard Roger Paul, Sept. 8, 1984. BA in Bus. Adminstrn., Ft. Lewis Coll., 1980; MBA, U. Denver, 1982. Zone mgr. Lincoln Mercury div. Ford Motor Co., St. Louis, 1982-83; sr. cons. Fails Mgmt. Inst., Denver, 1983—; bd. dirs. NORCO Devel., Denver. Tutor Vol. Tutors Am., Denver, 1980-82; donor Bonfils Blood Ctr., Denver, 1976—. Home: 12890 W 16th Dr Golden CO 80401 Office: Fails Mgmt Inst 90 Madison Suite 600 Denver CO 80206

PAUL, EVE W., lawyer; b. N.Y.C., June 16, 1930; d. Leo I and Tamara (Sogolow) Weinschenker; m. Robert D. Paul, Apr. 9, 1952; children: Jeremy Ralph, Sarah Elizabeth. B.A., Cornell U., 1950; J.D., Columbia U., 1952. Bar: N.Y. 1952, Conn. 1960, U.S. Ct. Appeals 2d cir. 1975, U.S. Supreme Ct. 1977. Assoc. Botein, Hays, Sklar & Herzberg, N.Y.C., 1952-54; sole practice Stamford, Conn., 1960-70; staff atty. Legal Aid Soc., N.Y.C., 1970-71; assoc. Greenbaum, Wolff & Ernst, N.Y.C., 1972-78; v.p. legal affairs Planned Parenthood Fedn. Am., N.Y.C., 1979—. Contbr. articles to legal and health publs. Trustee Cornell U., Ithaca, N.Y., 1979-84; mem. Stamford Planning Bd., Conn., 1967-70; bd. mem. Stamford League Women Voters, 1960-62. Harlan Fiske Stone scholar Columbia Law Sch., 1952. Mem. ABA, Conn. Bar Assn., N.Y. County Lawyers Assn., Stamford Bar Assn., Assn. Bar City N.Y., Phi Beta Kappa, Phi Kappa Phi. Office: Planned Parenthood Fedn 810 7th Ave New York NY 10019

PAUL, GRACE, retired medical technologist, author; b. Liberal, Kans., Mar. 12, 1908; d. David and Myrtle Helen (Brewer) P.; student Tulsa U., 1930-36, Auburn U., 1948, Columbia U., 1949-51. Med. technologist St. Johns Hosp., Tulsa, 1930-36, VA Hosp., Wadsworth, Kans., 1947-48; plant quarantine insp. U.S. Dept. Agr., N.Y.C., 1948-51; claims examiner Social Security Adminstrn., Balt., 1956-71; market research interviewer Response Analysis, Princeton, N.J., 1973-76. Vol. worker United Way of Temple (Tex.), 1974-84, Cultural Activities Center, Youth Services Bur., Ret. Sr. Vol. Program; active CAC Humanities Council of Temple, 1972-86. Served with WAC, 1944-46. Recipient Jefferson award for Central Tex., 1983; named Outstanding Vol. in Temple Chs., 1985. Mem. Am. Soc. Med. Technologists, Entomol. Soc. Am., Internat. Platform Assn. Presbyn. Club: Business and Professional Women's. Author: Your Future in Medical Technology, 1962; A Short Course in Skilled Supervision, 1965; contbr. to Environ. Engr.'s Handbook, vol. III, 1975. Home: 18 Carlton Rd Hutchinson KS 67502

PAUL, LINDA EDWARDS, loss prevention representative; b. Kansas City, Mo., Sept. 23, 1951; d. J.T. and Mary (Skorupan) Edwards; m. Kevin Charles Paul, Aug. 28, 1982. BS in Edn., Cen. Mo. State U., Warrensburg, 1973, MS in Edn., 1978. Safety research instr. Cen. Mo. State U., Warrensburg, 1973-74; driver edn. instr. Winnetonka High Sch., Kansas City, Mo., 1976-81; traffic safety instr. Ill. State U., Normal, 1981-82; traffic safety cons. Community Edn. Services, Independence, Mo., 1986-88; loss prevention rep. Halls Merchandising Inc., Kansas City, 1988—; summer sch. instr. Olathe Sch. Dist., Olathe, Kans., 1975-79; substitute instr. Shawnee Mission Sch. Dist., Shawnee Mission, Kans., 1982-88, Grandview Sch. Dist., Grandview, Mo., 1982-88; substitute/summer sch. instr. Raytown Safety Ctr., Raytown, Mo., 1983-88, adult edn., sch. bus trainer, 1986-88. Contbr. articles to profl. jours. Adv. bd. Mo. Student Safety Program, Jefferson City, 1976-88, Nat. Safety Town Ctr., Cleve., 1980-88. Mem. Am. Driver and Safety Edn. Assn. (bd. dirs. 1979-81, 1986—), Mo. Driver and Safety Edn. (treas. 1977-78, v.p. 1978-79, pres. 1979-80), Alpha Xi Delta (province pres. 1985—). Presbyterian. Office: Halls Merchandising Inc Crown Ctr 200 E 25th St Kansas City MO 64198-2598

PAUL, ROSLYN CROOG, computer systems analyst; b. New Haven, July 14, 1942; d. Herbert Bernard and Belle (Brown) Croog; children: Bradley Jordan, Katie Miriam. AS, Quinnipiac Coll., 1962; BS, Fla. Internat. U.,

1982. Analyst, programmer DBA Systems, Inc., Melbourne, Fla., 1982-84; system mgr. DBA Systems, Inc., Fairfax, Va., 1984-86; mem. tech. staff MRJ, Inc., Oakton, Va., 1986—. Office: MRJ Inc 10455 White Granite Dr Oakton VA 22124

PAULEY, JANE, television journalist; b. Indpls., Oct. 31, 1950; m. Garry Trudeau; 3 children. B.A. in Polit. Sci, Ind. U., 1971; D. Journalism (hon.), DePauw U., 1978. Reporter Sta. WISH-TV, Indpls., 1972-75; co-anchor WMAQ-TV News, Chgo., 1975-76, The Today Show, NBC, 1976—; prin. writer, reporter NBC Nightly News, 1980-82; co-anchor Early Today, 1982-83. Office: Today Show care NBC 30 Rockefeller Plaza New York NY 10020 *

PAULIN, ANNE MEREDITH, medical salesman; b. Richmond, Va., Dec. 15, 1954; d. Lehan Bernard and Thelma Monroe (Sutton) Paulin. BA in Polit. Sci., Agnes Scott Coll., 1977. Territory mgr. Kendall Co. div. Colgate Palmolive, Atlanta, 1979-81; cardiopulmonary system specialist Baxter Travenol Labs, Atlanta, 1981-83; terr. mgr. Acutecare div. Becton-Dickinson (formerly Deseret div. Warner Lambert), Atlanta, 1983—; pres., owner Hermelon, Atlanta, 1982—. Contbr. articles to profl. jours. Mem. Atlanta Ballet, Soc., 1983-87, Atlanta Ballet Guild, 1982-87; mem. Jr. Com. Atlanta Symphony Orch., 1980—; bd. dirs. Terpsichore, 1983; bd. dirs., v.p. City Ctr. Dance Theatre, 1981-83; mem. High Mus. Art, 1973—, High Mus. Art Young Careers, 1983-87, King and Queen County Hist. Soc., 1971-88, Arts Festival of Atlanta, 1984-88, Jr. League of Atlanta, 1988—; charter mem. New High Mus. Art, 1982-88; mem. jr. com. Shepherd Spinal Ctr., 1983—, Atlanta Bot. Gardens The Club, 1984—, jr. com. 1986—. Named Charles A. Dana Found. scholar, 1976. Mem. Nat. Assn. Female Execs., Atlanta Hist. Soc., Current Historians, Ga. Trust for Historic Preservation, Arts Festival Soc., High Mus., Alpha Sigma Beta. (pres. 1976—). Roman Catholic.

PAULIN, LORI ANN, business analyst; b. San Francisco, Sept. 15, 1960; d. William John and Margaret (Rocks) Peck; m. Thomas John Paulin, Aug. 20, 1983. BA, BS, San Francisco State U., 1982. Personnel rep. Bank of Calif., San Francisco, 1982-84; adminstrv. asst. San Francisco State U., 1983-84; coordinator, account mgmt. Hewlett Packard Corp., Brisbane, Calif., 1984-86, systems analyst, 1986-87; bus. analyst Hewlett Packard Corp., Mountain View, Calif., 1987—. Roman Catholic.

PAULING, MARY JANE, education administrator; b. Boston, Oct. 29, 1943; d. Alphonso and Marian (Wooton) Williams; m. Clifford Hill Jr. (div. 1976); children: Karen, Clifford III, Christine; m. Isaiah Pauling; 1 child, Tenil. BS in Community Services Adminstrn., Empire State Coll., 1977; MS in Health Care Mgmt., Iona Coll., 1982. Sec. Riverside Ch., N.Y.C., 1965; mgr. order dept. Carlee Corp., Rockleigh, N.Y., 1968-73; exec. dir. Nyack (N.Y.) Community Child Devel. Ctr. Inc., 1973—. Pres. Lakeside Sch. Unitied Sch. Dist., Spring Valley, N.Y., 1984—, Conashaugh Lakes Community Assn, Milford, Pa., 1982—. Mem. Nat. Assn. Edn. Young Children, Rockland Council Young Children, Westchester-Rockland Program Devel. Com. (chmn. personnel com.). Democrat. Roman Catholic.

PAULSEN, VIVIAN, editor; b. Salt Lake City, May 10, 1942; d. Paul Herman and Martha Oline (Blattman) P. B.A., Brigham Young U., 1964, postgrad., 1965; postgrad., U. Grenoble, France, 1966. Cert. tchr., Utah. Tchr. French Granite Sch. Dist., Salt Lake City, 1966-67; assoc. editor New Era mag., Salt Lake City, 1970-82; mng. editor Friend mag., Salt Lake City, 1982—. Contbr. numerous articles to mags. Am. Field Service scholar, 1959; grad. fellow Brigham Young U., 1964-66. Mem. Soc. Children's Book Writers. Republican. Mem. Ch. of Jesus Christ of Latter-day Saints. Office: The Friend 50 E North Temple Salt Lake City UT 84150

PAULSON, CAROL ALICE, accounting firm administrator; b. Ambrose, N.D., Apr. 5, 1930; d. Louis J. and Mathilda J. (Anderson) P. Exec. dir. Rexall Drug Co., Los Angeles, 1948-69; adminstrv. mgr. Peat, Marwick, Main & Co., Los Angeles, 1970—. Organist Hollywood Lutheran Ch., Los Angeles, 1956-88. Recipient Woman of Yr. award YWCA, Los Angeles, 1983. Republican. Avocations: music; reading; traveling. Home: 1011 E California Ave Glendale CA 91206 Office: Peat Marwick Main & Co 725 S Figueroa St Los Angeles CA 90017

PAULSON, DANNELLE LYNNE, nurse; b. Escanaba, Mich., Apr. 14, 1954; d. Daniel Ernest and Gertrude Marie (Wunder) Wellman; m. Steven Michael Paulson, June 13, 1975. BS in Nursing, No. Mich. U., 1978. Staff nurse St. Francis Hosp., Escabana, 1979-80; asst. head nurse St. Francis Hosp., Escabana, Mich., 1980-81; staff nurse SCU St. Francis Hosp., Escabana, 1983-85; charge nurse ICU Portage View, Hancock, Mich., 1981-83; staff nurse Mercy Hosp., Cadillac, Mich., 1985; asst. supr. ICU Gwinnett Hosp. System, Lawrenceville, Ga., 1985-87; instr. basic life support Ga. chpt. Am. Heart Assn., 1981—, advanced cardiac life support system, 1982. Mem. Am. Assn. Critical Care Nurses (cert. 1986, Atlanta Chpt. hospitality com. 1985-87). Democrat. Home: 4207 125th St W Savage MN 55378 Office: Gwinnett Med Ctr 1047 Wayne Dr Snellville GA 30278

PAULSON, JEANNETTE LEE, cultural affairs director; b. Pasadena, Calif., May 23, 1940; d. Leo E. and Lucille J. (Bartholama) Butts; m. Guy William Paulson, Aug. 27, 1960 (div. Mar. 1983); children: Bradley William, Kelly Colleen, Holly Ileene. BS, Chaminade U., 1978; postgrad., U. Hawaii. Story teller Artist-in-the-Schs. Program, Dept. Edn. States of Oreg. and Hawaii, 1968-78; program dir. Jackson County Mental Health Assn., Medford, Oreg., 1973-74; producer, writer ednl. TV State of Hawaii, Honolulu, 1975-79; film producer, v.p. mktg. Farm House Films, Inc., Honolulu, 1978-80; community relations officer East-West Ctr., Honolulu, 1980-83, film festival coordinator, 1983—. Author: Touching a Season of Time, 1975; producer, writer (film) Taro Tales, 1979 (Best of West award 1979). Mem. adv. council Communications Dept. Chaminade U., 1986—; vol. Hawaii's Thousand Friends, Honolulu, 1983—; founder, dir. Storytelling Guild of So. Oreg., 1964-75; founder, Children's Festival So. Oreg., 1966-73. Mem. Nat. Press Women (pres. Hawaii chpt. 1984-85), Women in Communications Inc. (v.p. 1982-85, Headliner award 1984). Democrat. Congregationalist. Office: East-West Ctr 1777 East-West Rd Honolulu HI 96848

PAULSON, LORETTA NANCY, psychoanalyst; b. Los Angeles, Nov. 5, 1943; d. Frank Morris and Rose (Kaufman) Fargo; m. Glenn Lewis Paulson, Dec. 27, 1970 (div. 1984). BA, U. So. Calif., 1966; MS in Social Work, Columbia U., 1969; cert. psychoanalyst, C.G. Jung Inst., N.Y.C. Cert. clin. social worker, N.Y., Conn. Pvt. practice psychoanalysis N.Y.C. and Wilton, Conn., 1976—; faculty, supr., mem. inst. tng. bd., mem. evaluations com. C. G. Jung Inst., N.Y.C., 1986—. Mem. Internat. Assn. for Analytical Psychology, Nat. Assn. for Accreditation of Psychoanalysis (accreditation and evaluation com.), Nat. Assn. Social Workers (diplomate in clin. social work), N.Y. Assn. for Analytic Psychology (program com.). Democrat. Office: 6 Turtleback Rd Wilton CT 06897 Office: 334 W 86th St #1A New York NY 10024

PAULSON, PATSY ANN, educator, consultant; b. Ottawa, Kans., Mar. 30, 1943; d. George Franklin and Hazel Annette (Howell) Hamilton; m. Jimmy Rex Sneed, 1961 (div. 1976); children: Cheryl Lynn, Joyce Rene, James Kevin, Toby Donell; m. Maurice Edgar Paulson, June 25, 1977. AA, Coll. of DuPage, 1983; BA, Nat. Coll. Edn., 1985. Instr. Sunergos Inst., Downers Grove, Ill., 1971-75; bus. mgr. Profl. Rolfing Practice, Downers Grove, Ill., 1975-83; cons. Downers Grove, Ill., 1983—; tchr. Coll. of DuPage, Glen Ellen, Ill., 1984—; co-founder Phoenix Rising, Wheaton, Ill., 1984—. Author: (with others) Living On Purpose, 1987. Office: Phoenix Rising PO Box 3088 Glen Ellyn IL 60138

PAULSTON, CHRISTINA BRATT, linguistics educator; b. Stockholm, Sweden, Dec. 30, 1932; came to U.S., 1951; d. Lennart and Elsa (Facht) Bratt; m. Rolland G. Paulston, July 26, 1963; children: Christopher-Rolland, Ian Rollandsson. B.A., Carleton Coll., 1953; M.A. in English and Comparative Lit., U. Minn., 1955; Ed.D., Columbia U., 1966. Cert. tchr., Minn. Tchr. Clara City and Pine Island High Schs., Minn., 1955-70, Am. Sch. of Tangier, Morocco, 1960-62, Katrineholm Allmanna Laroverk, Katrineholm, Sweden, 1962-63, East Asian Library, Columbia U., N.Y.C., 1963-64; asst. instr. Tchrs. Coll., Columbia U., 1964-66; instr. U. Punjab, Chandigarh, India, summer 1966, Pontificia Universidad Catolica Del Peru, Lima, 1966-67; cons. Instituto Linguistico de Verano, Lima, 1967-68; asst. prof. linguistics U. Pitts., 1969-75, prof., 1975—, asst. dir. English Lang. Inst., 1969-70, dir. English Lang. Inst., 1970, acting dir. Lang. Acquistion Inst., fall 1971, acting chmn. dept. gen. linguistics, 1974-75, chmn., 1975—. Author books and numerous articles on linguistics. Recipient research award Am. Ednl. Research Assn., 1980; Fulbright-Hays grantee, Uruguay, 1985. Mem. Assn. Tchrs. of English to Speakers of Other Langs. (2d v.p., conv., chmn. 1972, exec. com. 1972-75, research com. 1973-75, 78-80, chmn. 1973-75, 1st v.p., pres. 1976), Linguistics Soc. Am. (com. linguistics and pub. interest 1973-77), Internat. Assn. of Tchrs. of English as a Fgn. Lang., Am. Council on Teaching of Fgn. Langs., MLA (exec. com. lang. and soc. 1975-76), Ctr. Applied Linguistics (trustee 1976-81, exec. com. 1980, publs. com. 1981, research com. 1981), Eastern Competitive Trailriding Assn. Democrat. Episcopalian. Office: U Pitts Linguistics Pittsburgh PA 15260

PAULU, FRANCES BROWN, international center administrator; b. Hastings, Minn., June 22, 1920; d. Thomas Andrew and Florence Ida (Tuttle) Brown; m. Burton Paulu, June 29, 1942; children: Sarah Leith Paulu Boittin, Nancy Jean Paulu Hyde, Thomas Scott. BA magna cum laude, U. Minn., 1940, postgrad. sch. social work, 1942-44. Case worker Family Welfare Assn. Mpls., 1943-45; interviewer Community Health and Welfare Council, Mpls., 1963; sch. social worker Project Head Start, Mpls., 1966; program dir. Minn. Internat. Ctr., Mpls., 1970-72, exec. dir., 1972—; mem. tourism adv. com. City of Mpls., 1976-83; mem. adv. council Minn. World Trade Ctr., 1984-86. Pres. UN Rally, 1970-72; chmn. Mpls. Charter Commn., 1972-74; bd. dirs. Urban Coalition of Mpls., 1967-70; dir. Minn. World Trade Week, 1977-81; participant Intercultural Communication Project, Japan, 1974; mem. mgmt. team Minn. Awareness Project, 1982—. DeWitt Jennings Payne scholar, 1939-40; recipient Nat. People to People Disting. Membership award, 1987. Mem. Nat. Council for Internat. Visitors (officer and/or exec. com. mem. 1975-81, leader fact-finding team North Africa, Middle East, India 1978), Nat. Assn. for Fgn. Student Affairs, People to People Internat., LWV (pres. Mpls. 1967-69), UN Assn. Minn. (adv. council 1979—), Mpls.-St. Paul Com. on Fgn. Relations, Phi Beta Kappa, Alpha Omicron Pi, Lambda Alpha Psi. Home: 5005 Wentworth Ave Minneapolis MN 55419 Office: Minn Internat Center 711 East River Rd Minneapolis MN 55455

PAULUS, NORMA JEAN PETERSEN, lawyer; b. Belgrade, Nebr., Mar. 13, 1933; d. Paul Emil and Ella Marie (Hellbusch) Petersen; LL.B., Willamette Law Sch., 1962; LL.D., Linfield Coll., 1985; m. William G. Paulus, Aug. 16, 1958; children—Elizabeth, William Frederick. Sec. to Harney County Dist. Atty., 1950-53; legal sec., Salem, Oreg., 1953-55; sec. to chief justice Oreg. Supreme Ct., 1955-61; admitted to Oreg. bar, 1962; of counsel Paulus and Callaghan, Salem, mem. Oreg. Ho. of Reps., 1971-77; sec. state State of Oreg., Salem, 1977-85; of counsel firm Paulus, Rhoten & Lien, 1985-86; dir. Pacific Northwest Bell, 1985—; adj. prof. Willamette U. Coll. Law, 1985. Fellow Eagleton Inst. Politics, 1971; mem. Pacific NW Power Planning Council, 1987—; adv. com. Defense Adv. Com. for Women in the Service, 1986, Nat. Trust for Hist. Preservation, 1988—; trustee Willamette U., 1978—; bd. dirs. Benedictine Found. of Oreg., 1980—,Oreg. Grade. Ctr., 1985—, Mid Willamette Valley council Camp Fire Girls, 1985—, Oreg. Innovation Network, 1985—; overseer Whitman Coll., 1985—; bd. cons. Goodwill Industries of Oreg.; mem. Salem Human Relations Commn., 1967-70, Marion-Polk Boundary Commn., 1970-71; mem. Presdl. Commn. to Monitor Philippines Election, 1986. Recipient Distinguished Service award City of Salem, 1971; Path Breaker award Oreg. Women's Polit. Caucus, 1976; named One of 10 Women of Future, Ladies Home Jour., 1979. Woman of Yr., Oreg. Inst Managerial and Profl. Women, 1982, Oreg. Women Lawyers, 1982, Woman who Made a Difference award Nat. Women's Forum, 1985. Mem. Nat. Soc. State Legislators (dir. 1971-72), Oreg. State Bar, Nat. Order Women Legislators, Women Execs. in State Govt., Women's Polit. Caucus Bus. and Profl. Women's Club (Golden Torch award 1971), Zonta Internat., Delta Kappa Gamma. Office: 750 Front St NE Salem OR 97301

PAUTH, PATRICIA RUTH, librarian; b. Rochester, N.Y., Feb. 14, 1936; d. Frank Alvin and Ruth Rose (Vose) P.; student Wittenberg U., Springfield, Ohio, 1953-56. Library asst. periodicals dept. Rush Rhees Library, U. Rochester (N.Y.), 1956-59; with Price Waterhouse, N.Y.C., 1959—, purchasing asst., 1959-63, reference librarian, 1963-72, asst. librarian, 1972-74, head librarian, 1974-85, mgr. info. services, 1985—. Mem. Spl. Libraries Assn., Am. Soc. for Info. Sci., DAR, Union Street Gardens Assn. (past treas., pres.). Home: 376 Union St Brooklyn NY 11231 Office: 153 E 53d St New York NY 10022

PAUTSCH, DELORES ALMA, retired business executive; b. Fond du Lac, Wis., Oct. 30, 1928; d. William Frederick and Alma Pauline (Schmidt) Mielke; student Fond du Lac Bus. Coll., 1945-46; m. Milton Gustave Pautsch, Nov. 5, 1949; children: Floyd A., Joy Faye, Bonnie Mae and Betsy Mae (dec.)(twins). With Nat. Rivet Co., 1946-47, Johnson Truck Service, 1947-49, Milt's Service Sta., 1949-52, Nash Waupun, 1952-57, Peters Oil Co., 1957-62; self-employed floral designer, 1963-75; owner, pres. Pautsch Distbg. Co., Waupun, Wis., 1975-85; with Scientia, Houston, 1985-87; ret., 1987. Home: 734 S Madison St Waupun WI 53963

PAVEL, LINDA JOYCE, medical technologist, epidemiology coordinator; b. Pickstown, S.D., July 18, 1951; d. Rudolph John and Helen (Fuchs) P.; m. Glenn Willian Custard, 1973 (div. 1974). BS in Biology and Chemistry, U. S.D., 1973. With U.S. Govt. Indian Health Service, 1976—, staff med. technologist, Wagner, S.D., 1976, Chinle, Ariz., 1976-79, asst. lab. supr., Pine Ridge, S.D., 1979-81, supervisory med. technologist, Eagle Butte, S.D., 1981-83, Poplar, Mont., 1983-87, staff tech. Indian Health Service, Parker, Az., AIDS coordinator, 1988, co-founder Lapaz County epidemiology team, coordinator epidemiology team, Fort Peck Indian Reservation, Poplar, 1985-87; condr. mgmt. course, 1986, condr. hematology course, 1979, cons. tchr., Eagle Butte and Poplar, 1981-87; AIDS coordinator Colo. River Service Unit, Parker, Ariz., 1988—; substitute instr. in bacteriology Navajo Community Coll., Tsaile, Ariz., 1978. Tchr., Ch. of Christ Mission, Many Farms, Ariz., 1977-78; co-founder Roosevelt County Epidemiology Team, Mont., 1986; founder Lapaz County Epidemiology team, 1988; mem. Wagner Indian Health Service Com. on Alcoholism, 1976. Recipient various awards Indian Health Service. Mem. Am. Soc. Clin. Pathologists, Nat. Assn. Female Execs. Avocations: reading, gardening, writing. Home: Rural Rt 1 Box 21 Parker AZ 85344 Office: Colo River Service Unit Indian Health Rural Rt 1 Box 12 Parker AZ 85344

PAVELKA, ELAINE BLANCHE, mathematics educator; b. Chgo.; d. Frank Joseph and Mildred Bohumila (Seidl) P.; B.A., M.S., Northwestern U.; Ph.D., U. Ill. With Northwestern U. Aerial Measurements Lab., Evanston, Ill.; tchr. Leyden Community High Sch., Franklin Park, Ill.; prof. math. Morton Coll., Cicero, Ill.; speaker 3d Internat. Congress Math. Edn., Karlsruhe, Germany, 1976. Recipient sci. talent award Westinghouse Elec. Co. Mem. Am. Edn. Research Assn., Am. Math. Assn. 2-Year Colls., Am. Math. Soc., Assn. Women in Math., Can. Soc. History and Philosophy of Math., Ill. Council Tchr. of Math., Ill. Math. Assn. Community Colls., Math. Assn. Am., Math. Action Group, Ga. Center Study and Teaching and Learning Math., Nat. Council Tchrs. of Math., Sch. Sci. and Math. Assn., Soc. Indsl. and Applied Math., Northwestern U. Alumni Assn., U. Ill. Alumni Assn., Am. Mensa Ltd., Intertel, Sigma Delta Epsilon, Pi Mu Epsilon. Home: PO Box 7312 Westchester IL 60153 Office: Morton Coll 3801 S Central Ave Cicero IL 60650

PAVINO, MARIBEL KOKSENG, human resources professional; b. Cebu, Philippines, June 18, 1946; came to U.S., 1967; d. Vincent Tan and Connie (Uytengsu) Kokseng; m. Theodore Cowan Pavino, Sept. 20, 1969; children: Katherine Margaret, Karen Marjorie. AA in Secreterial Sci., St. Theresa's Coll., Cebu, 1966, BS in Bus. Mgmt., 1966. Sec. Cravens Dargan and Co., Los Angeles, 1967-70; ins. counselor Precision Ins. Cos., Manila, 1971-75; internat. ticketing officer Philippine Air Lines, Manila, 1975; regional adminstrv. sec. Comml. Union Ins. Cos., Los Angeles, 1975-81, regional adminstrv. supr., 1981-84, adminstrv. and personnel mgr., 1984—; Treas. Ins. Personnel Mgmt. Forum, 1986, chairperson, 1987. Mem. Personnel and Indsl. Relations Assn., Am. Soc. Personnel. Roman Catholic. Office: Comml Union Ins Cos 520 S Lafayette Park Pl Los Angeles CA 90057

PAVKOV, JANET RUTH, health care facility administrator; b. Wadsworth, Ohio, Aug. 7, 1939; d. George and Helen Rose (Pamer) P.; RN, Mansfield (Ohio) Gen. Hosp., 1960; BS in Tech. Edn., U. Akron, 1972, MA in Family Life, 1976; cert. in nursing home adminstrn., Ohio State U., 1983. Lic. social worker; lic. nursing home adminstr., counselor. Charge nurse obstet. dept. Mansfield Gen. Hosp., 1960; gen. practice office nurse P.O. Staker, M.D., Mansfield, 1961; operating room nurse Akron (Ohio) Gen. Hosp., 1961-70; charge nurse obstet. dept. Wayne Gen. Hosp., Orrville, Ohio, 1970-71; nursing faculty mem. North Cen. Tech. Coll., Mansfield, 1972-74, asst. chairperson nursing program, 1973-74; instr. St. Thomas Hosp. Sch. Nursing, Akron, 1974-77; nurse epidemiologist Alum Crest Nursing Home, Columbus, 1978-84, nursing supr., 1978-80; nursing home adminstr. Am. Health Care Facilities, Springfield, Ohio, 1986—; vol. nurse and camp counselor Webster Springs (W.Va.) Camp, 1960-75, Palisades Camp, Pacific Palisades, Calif., 1963, Camp Massanetta, Harrisonburg, Va., 1978-79, 86; vol. nurse Prescott (Ariz.) Pines Camp, 1967, Oakwood Camp, Syracuse, Ind., 1968, Presbyn. Camp, Portland, Oreg., 1970; cons. McNeil Pharms., Spring House, Pa., 1982, 84, Assn. Developmentally Disabled Intermediate Care Facility forMentally Retarded, Columbus, 1983-85, Alum Crest Nursing Home, 1979-85; mem. ARC Vol. Nurse Div., 1958—, Nat. Council Nursing Home Nurses, 1979-84, Nat. Council Family Relations, 1975-84, Retired Sr. Vol. Program adv. council, 1975-77; instr. lic. practical nurse program Warren (Ohio) Pub. Schs., 1972; active Ohio Dist. 6 Mental Health Older Adult Council, 1977-84; staff nurse Eastland Care Ctr., Columbus, 1981-84; adminstr.-on-call nursing services Kimberly Pkwy. Group Home, Columbus, 1983-84, coordinator patient assessment and nursing services, 1983-84; counselor, shift leader emergency services Columbus Area Community Mental Health Ctr., Columbus, 1977-86, coordinator geriatric services, 1977-87, mem. quality assurance and peer rev. com., 1978-87; mem. adv. bd. home health care div. Health Care Personnel Assn., Inc., 1983-86; sec. Specialized Health Adminstrv. Resource Enterprises, 1983-85; chairperson Franklin County Mental Health Bd. Older Adult Task Force, 1984-87; mem. adv. com. Program 60 Ohio State U., 1984-87; workshop and seminar leader; lectr. in field. Editor: Ohio Gerontol. Soc. newsletter, 1984-85; mem. editorial adv. bd. Jour. Long Term Care Adminstrn., 1985-87; editorial asst. Ohio chpt. Am. Coll. Health Care Adminstrs. newsletter, 1985-87; contbr. articles to profl. jours. Instr. Sunday sch. Apostolic Christian Ch., 1958-83; mem. exec. com. Internat. Christian Friendship Group, 1965-79, mem. missionary com., 1980-83. Recipient Bronze medal Brit. Med. Soc., 1983, Staff award Franklin County Mental Health Bd., 1985. Mem. Am. Coll. Long Term Care Adminstrs., Am. Home Econs. Assn., Gerontol. Soc. Am., Ohio Gerontol. Assn., Cen. Ohio Geriatric Nurses Assn. (mem. program and planning com. 1979—, chairperson publicity com. 1980-81, sec. 1979-81, sec.-treas. 1981-84, mem. edn. com. 1983—), Mansfield Gen. Hosp. Alumnae Assn. (sec. 1960-61). Home: 169 G Brandywine Dr Westerville OH 43081 Office: Seminole Villa Care Ctr 1365 W Seminole Ave Springfield OH 45506

PAVLICK, PAMELA KAY, nurse; b. Topeka, Aug. 16, 1944; d. Cy Pavlick and June Lucille (Arnold) Dull. Diploma nursing, St. Luke's Hosp., Kansas City, Mo., 1966; BA in Psychology magna cum laude, U. North Fla., 1982, MS in Health Adminstrn. summa cum laude, 1987. RN, Mo., Ill., Fla.; cert. ins. rehab. specialist; lic. rehab. providor, Fla. Clin. instr. St. Luke's Hosp., Kansas City, 1966-69; instr. lic. practical nursing Springfield (Ill.) Sch. Bd., 1969-71; nursing supr. Jacksonville Beach (Fla.) Hosp., 1971-74; nurse pub. health State of Fla., Ocala, 1974-79; med. rep. Traveler's Ins., Jacksonville, Fla., 1979-85; nurse cons. Aetna Life & Casualty, Jacksonville, 1985—. Mem. Am. Nurses Assn., Am. Assn. Rehab. Nurses, Nat. Assn. Rehab. Providers, Phi Kappa Phi, Nat. Assn. Rehab. Providors. Republican. Episcopalian. Home: 1848 Willowood Dr Jacksonville FL 32225 Office: Aetna Life & Casualty PO Box 2200 Jacksonville FL 32203

PAVLIK, ELSA M., civic worker; b. Cleve., Apr. 6, 1943; d. Heinrich Sebastian and Olga Mary (Trampush) Felgemacher; m. Thomas Chester Pavlik Sr., Nov. 19, 1966; 1 child, Thomas Chester, Jr. BA, Case Western Res. U., 1967. V.p. Glor-el Real Estate Devel. Corp., Cleve., 1983-86. Editor On Cue, 1982—. Mem. adv. bd. Fairmount Theatre of the Deaf, Cleve., 1982—, Cath. Social Services Cleve., 1986—; trustee Cleve. Heritage Parks Assn., 1974-76, Beck Ctr. for The Cultural Arts, Lakewood, Ohio, 1985—, Hist. Sites Found., Cleve., 1985—. Mem. Nat. Assn. for Female Execs., Susan B. Anthony Soc. Women Space, Internat. Platform Assn., Great Lakes Shakespeare Festival (pres. women's com. 1979-81, I Will award 1982, 86). Republican. Roman Catholic. Clubs: Women's City Cleve. (pres. 1987—), Coll. Club West (Rocky River). Office: Women's City Club Cleve 850 Euclid Ave Cleveland OH 44114-3760

PAVLOV, HELENE, physician, educator; b. Phila., Aug. 1, 1946; d. Al and Sylvia Pavlov; m. Harvey Zeichner, Sept. 4, 1983. A.B., Temple U., Phila., 1968, M.D., 1972. Diplomate Am. Bd. Radiology. Intern, Lenox Hill Hosp., N.Y.C., 1972-73; resident in radiology Germantown Hosp., Phila., 1973-76; fellow Hosp. for Spl. Surgery, N.Y.C., 1976-77, attending radiologist, 1983—; asst. prof. Cornell U., N.Y.C., 1977-83, assoc. prof. radiology, 1983—; asst. attending N.Y. Hosp., N.Y.C., 1977-83, assoc. attending, 1983—. Author: Atlas of Knee Menisci, 1983, The Running Athlete Roentgenograms and Remedies, 1987; mem. editorial bd. Contemporary Orthopaedics; bimonthly columnist Contemporary Orthopaedics; reviewer sci. jour., contbr. chpts. and articles on radiology, orthopedic surgery and sports medicine to profl. publs. Mem. Radiol. Soc. N.Am., Internat. Skeltal Soc., Am. Roentgen Ray Soc., Am. Coll. Radiology (alt. del. to N.Y. state chpt.), Am. Assn. Women Radiologists, N.Y. Roentgen Ray Soc. Office: Hosp for Spl Surgery 535 E 70th St New York NY 10021

PAXTON, ALICE ADAMS, interior architect and designer; b. Hagerstown, Md., May 19, 1914; d. William Albert and Josephine (Adams) Rosenberger; m. James Love Paxton Jr., June 26, 1942 (div.); 1 child, William Allen II. Student, Peabody Inst. Music, Balt., 1937-38; grad., Parson's Sch. Design, N.Y., 1940; studied portrait painting with J. Laurie Wallace, 1944-46; studied with Augustus Dunbier, 1947-48, Sylvia Curtis, 1949, Milton Wolsky, 1950, Frank Sapousek, 1951. Free-lance work archtl. renderings and interior design, N.Y., 1937-40; interior designer, designer spl. furnishings, muralist Orchard and Wilhelm, Omaha, 1940-42; tchr. art classes Alice Paxton Studio, Omaha, 1957-64; tchr. mech. drawing, archtl. rendering and mech. perspective Parson's Sch. Design, N.Y., 1937-40. Designer: (interior) Chapel Boys' Town, Nebr., 1942; one-woman show of archtl. renderings Washington County Mus. Fine Arts, Hagerstown, 1944; exhibited group shows at Joslyn Mus., Omaha, 1943-44, Ann. Exhbn. Cumberland Valley Artists, Hagerstown, 1945; represented permanent collections at No. Natural Gas Co. Bldg., Omaha, Swanson Found., Omaha; also pvt. collections; vol. designer, decorator: recreation room Omaha Blood Bank, ARC, 1943, recreation room Creighton U., 1943, lounge psychiat. ward Lincoln (Nebr.) Army Hosp., 1944; planner, color coordinator: Children's Hosp., Omaha, 1947, painted murals, 1948, decorated dental room, 1950; designed Candy Stripers' uniforms; painted and decorated straw elephant bag presented to Mrs. Richard Nixon, 1960; contbr. articles and photographs to Popular Home mag., 1958. Co-chair camp and hosp. coms. ARC, 1943-45, mem. county com. to select and send gifts to servicemen, 1943-46; mem. Ak-Sar-Ben Ball Com., Omaha, 1946-48, Nat. Mus. Women in the Arts, The Md. Hist. Soc.; judge select Easter Seal design, Joslyn Mus., 1946; mem. council Girl Scouts U.S., Omaha, 1943-47; spl. drs. chmn. Jr. League, Omaha, 1947-48, chair Jr. League Red Cross fund dr., 1947-48; bd. dirs., vol. worker Creche, Omaha, 1954-56; chmn. Jr. League Community Chest Fund Dr., 1948-50; co-chair Infantile Paralysis Appeal, 1944; numerous vol. profl. activities for civic orgns., hosps., clubs, chs., also community playhouse. Recipient three teaching scholarships Parson's Sch. Design, 1937-40, presdl. citation ARC activities, 1946, 1st prize Ann. Midwest Show Joslyn Mus., 1943. Mem. Associated Artists Omaha (charter), Am. Security Council (nat. adv. bd.), Internat. Platform Assn., U.S. Hist. Soc., Nat. Mus. Women in Arts (charter), Md. Hist. Soc. Republican. Episcopalian. Club: Fountain Head Country. Home: 300 Meadowbrook Rd Hagerstown MD 21740

PAXTON, DORIS HALL, real estate executive; b. Ft. Worth, June 23, 1931; d. Allon Killough and Ruth Augusta (McRae) Hall; m. James Robert Paxton, Aug. 14, 1954; children—Mary McRae, Ruth Hall, Martha Ellen Paxton Lemons, Jane Stratton Paxton Bonnet, Sarah Elizabeth, Rebecca Lee. BS, U. Tex., 1952. Field rep. Am. Cancer Soc., Austin, Tex., 1953-54; broker, owner 1st Realty, Palestine, Tex., 1975—; owner Diet Ctr. of Palestine. Founder, Wesley Communicty Ch. Mem. Palestine Bd. Realtors (bd. dirs. 1981—), Phi Beta Kappa. Mem. Wesley Community Ch. Clubs:

Harvey Woman's, Lit. Forum (v.p. 1970-71, pres. 1971-72, 88-89) (Palestine). Home: 126 Meadowbrook Dr Palestine TX 75801 Office: First Realty 1000 N Church Palestine TX 75801

PAXTON, LAURA BELLE-KENT, English language educator, management professional; b. Lake Charles, La., Feb. 8, 1942; d. George Ira and Gladys Lillian (Barrett) Kent.; m. Kenneth Robert Paxton Jr., Jan. 2, 1962. BA, McNeese U., Lake Charles, 1963, MA in English, 1972; EdD, East Tex. U., 1983. cert. English, social studies instr., principal, superintendent, ednl. adminstr. Ariz. Tchr. Darrington (Wash.) High Sch., 1966-70; English instr. Maricopa Community Coll. Dist., Phoenix, 1974-85; migrant program instr. Phoenix Union High Sch. Dist., 1984-88; English instr. Embry-Riddle Aeronautical U., Luke AFB, Ariz., 1985-87; sales rep. Merrill Lynch Realty, Phoenix, 1985-88; co-owner Paxton Mgmt. Co., Phoenix, 1985—; Editor Ariz. corr. courses, 1987-88; presenter migrant worker program confs., 1987—; reviewer Prentice-Hall, 1985. Author: (books) A Handbook for Middle Eastern Dancers, 1978, The Kent Family History from 1787 to 1981, 1981, A Handbook of Home Remedies, 1981; contbr. articles, poems to mags., profl. jours. Mem. Everett, Wash. Opera Guild, 1966-70, Ariz. State U. Opera Guild, Tempe, 1978-80; mem. City of Darrington Council, 1969-70; ESL instr. Friendly House, Phoenix, 1978-79. Mem. NEA, Ariz. Edn. Assn., Ariz. English Assn., Ariz. Sch. Adminstrs., Ariz. Assn. Supervision and Curriculum Devel., Assn. Sch. Bus. Officials Internat., AWARE, Classroom Tchrs. Assn., Pre-Legal Soc. of McNeese U., Pi Kappa Delta, Alpha Delta Kappa. Home: 8415 N 32d Ave Phoenix AZ 85051

PAXTON, TERRICE ALLEN, geologist; b. San Bernardino, Calif., June 3, 1946; d. Byron William Jr. and Gleynna Phyllis (Bromley) Allen; m. William Dent Paxton III, Dec. 22, 1967; children: William Dent IV (dec.), Dana Kristen. BS in Geology with honors, Calif. State U., San Diego, 1977. Uranium exploration geologist Uranerz USA, INc., Casper, Wyo., 1977-79; chief mine geologist Lucky Mc Mine Pathfinder Mines Corp., Gas Hills, Wyo., 1979-81; exploration geologist Gulf Oil subs. Chevron USA, Midland, Tex., 1981-85; sr. geologist Conoco, Inc., Midland, Tex., Lafayette, La., 1985-88; project geologist Geo-Sec Inc., San Bernadino, Calif., 1988—. Mem. Am. Assn. Petroleum Geologists. Home: PO Box 9622 Canyon Lake CA 92380 Office: Geo-Sec Inc 237 S Waterman Ave San Bernardino CA 92408

PAYAD, AURORA TORRES, real estate broker; b. Cavite, Philippines, Jan. 12, 1938; came to U.S., 1978; d. Isidro Paglinawan and Felicidad (Torres) P. LLB, Lyceum of the Philippines, 1959; MPA, U. Philippines, 1967; MPA, PhD in Pub. Adminstrn., U. So. Calif., 1975. Admitted to Philippine bar, 1960. Tng. specialist and professorial lectr. Local Govt. Ctr., Manila, 1975-76; asst. prof. U. Philippines, Manila, 1976-78; Pepperdine U., Los Angeles, 1979-81; lectr. U. So. Calif., Los Angeles, 1978-81; assoc. prof. Calif. State U., San Bernardino, 1981-85; owner D'Avon Gift Ctr., 1986—; pres. RB Realty Corp., 1987-88; mem. editorial bd. Calif. Manila Times, 1987-88; pub. Manila Times Weekly, 1988—; owner Dawn Towers Advt. Agy, 1988—; corp. sec. Calif. Manila Times Pubs., Inc., 1987-88; mgmt. cons. Filipino Internat. Nurses Assn., Inc., 1988—, Filipino Internat. Nurses Assn., Inc. Author: Organization Behavior in American Public Administration: An Annotated Bibliography, also various short stories, research papers. Club advisor Pub. Adminstrn. Club, San Bernardino, 1983; v.p., treas. Jr. Women's Club, San Bernardino, 1983. Grad. fellow U. Philippines, 1965-67; U.S. AID-Nat. Econ. Council grantee, 1970-72; Ford Found. dissertation grantee, Bangkok, Thailand, 1973-74. Mem. Am. Soc. Pub. Adminstrn. (exec. com. sect. on profl. and organizational devel.), Acad. Polit. Sci., Calif. State Assocs.

PAYNE, BARBARA CASTEEL, lawyer; b. Houston, Jan. 23, 1940; d. Bryon Wharton Casteel and Sydell Louise (Sterling) Dodson; m. Thomas Nelson Payne, Oct. 5, 1957; children—Gary Allen, Melanie Rhea, Dina Dae, Deidre Dee. B.A. summa cum laude in Psychology, U. Bridgeport (Conn.), 1979; J.D., Hofstra U., 1981. Bar: Conn. 1983, U.S. Tax Ct., U.S. Dist. Ct. Conn. Sole practice, Wilton, Conn., 1983-84, Stamford, Conn., 1986—; atty. ITT, Tempe, Ariz., 1984-85; assoc. Law Offices of David Wallman, 1985-86; sole practice, 1986—; legis. cons., Phoenix, 1984. Dana scholar, 1979. Mem. ABA, Conn. Attys. Title Ins. Co., Assn. Trial Lawyers Am., Conn. Bar Assn. (lawyers and community sect.), Stamford/Darien Bar Assn. (chmn. lawyers community com.). Club: Toastmasters (ednl. v.p.). Democrat. Congregationalist. Home: 35 W Brother Dr Greenwich CT 06830 Office: Barbara C Payne Atty at Law 733 Summer St Stamford Ct 06901

PAYNE, BEULAH ELLEN, education center administrator; b. Bedford, Va., Oct. 23, 1926; d. Johnson E. and Mary Odell (Bowman) Penn; m. William Emanuel Payne, Aug. 26, 1948; children: Gerard E., Lucinda P. Reid. Student, Roanoke Coll.; AA in Early Childhood, Va. Western Coll.; cert. in child care, Cen. Va. Community Coll. Dir., tchr. Total Action Against Poverty, Roanoke, Va., 1966-72; dir. ctr. Bedford Head Start Program, 1972—. Treas. United Way, 1972-73; project chmn. Keep Bedford Beautiful, 1979-84; founder Black History Mus.; mem. Bedford Housing Authority Commn., 1980—, Democratic Com., Voters League, 1966—, Youth Orgn. NAYCE, 1972—. Mem. NAACP (sec. Bedford chpt. 1982—). Baptist. Club: Good News (Bedford). Lodge: Order Eastern Star (past matron). Home: 2001 Wilson St Bedford VA 24523

PAYNE, CONNIE SUE, nurse; b. Charleston, W.Va., Sept. 24, 1946; d. John Foster and Felicia Eilene (Ranson) Trent; m. Manuel Franklin Miller, Apr. 7, 1968 (div. Nov. 1973); m. Gene Douglas Payne, Jan. 31, 1987; children: Rhonda Faye Miller, Tara Lynn Miller. Diploma, Jackson Meml. Hosp. Sch. Nursing, 1968; cert. in Neurosurg. Nursing, The Meth. Hosp., Houston, 1980; BSN, Prairie View A&M, 1983. Cert. neurosurg. RN. Staff nurse Jackson Meml. Hosp., Miami, Fla., 1968, U.S. Army Hosp., Camp Kue, Okinawa, Japan, 1969, Winchester (Va.) Meml. Hosp., 1970, Brevard Hosp., Melbourne, Fla., 1970-73; head nurse in neurology, orthopedics Holmes Regional Med. Ctr., Melbourne, Fla., 1973-79; staff nurse neurosurg. intermediate care unit, The Meth. Hosp., Houston, 1979-80; liaison nurse The Inst. for Rehab. and Research, Houston, 1981-83, dir. outpatient services, 1983-86; sr. rehab. cons. Am. Internat. Health and Rehab. Services, Houston, 1987—. Mem. Am. Assn. of Neurosci. Nursing (S.E. Tex. chpt.), World Fedn. Neurosci. Nursing, Am. Assn. Neurosci. Nursing, Assn. Rehab. Nurses, Nat. Assn. Rehab. Profls. in the Pvt. Sector. Democrat. Baptist. Office: AIHRS 2200 N Loop W Suite 400 Houston TX 77018

PAYNE, DEBORAH ANN, infosystems specialist; b. Weisbauden, Fed. Republic of Germany, Oct. 14, 1952; came to U.S., 1954; d. Robert Roswell and Paulene Ruth (Boone) P.; m. Dale Bruce Rickard, Dec. 22, 1974 (div. Mar. 1982). Student, U. Hawaii, 1970-72; BA in Psychology, U. Okla., 1974; postgrad., Midwestern State U., Wichita Falls, Tex., 1979-80. Counselor Travelers Aid Soc., Oklahoma City, 1974-75; fin. aid counselor Allstate Bus. Coll., Dallas, 1976-79, dir. grad. placement, 1980-81; fin. aid counselor Midwestern State U., 1979-80; corp. tng. specialist AMF, Inc. subs. Minstar, Inc., Garland, Tex., 1981-85; computer tng. specialist Glendale, Calif., 1985-86; dist. sales mgr. AMF Bowling Cos., Inc. div. AMF, Inc., Houston, 1986-87; computer systems specialist Garland, 1987—. Mem. AAUW, Am. Bus. Women's Assn., Networking Women, Delta Gamma Alumnae Assn. Republican. Mem. Ch. Religious Sci. Office: AMF Bowling Cos Inc div AMF Inc 911 S Jupiter Rd Garland TX 75042

PAYNE, DEBORAH ANNE, medical company officer; b. Norristown, Pa., Sept. 22, 1952; d. Kenneth Nathan Moser and Joan (Reese) Dewhurst; m. Randall Barry Payne, Mar. 8, 1975. AA, Northeastern Christian Jr. Coll., 1972; B in Music Edn., Va. Commonwealth U., 1979. Driver, social asst. Children's Aid Soc., Norristown, Pa., 1972-73; mgr. Boddie-Noell Enterprises, Richmond, Va., 1974-79; retail food saleswoman Hardee's Food Systems, Inc., Phila., 1979-81; supr. Cardiac Datacorp., Phila., 1981—. Mem. Nat. Assn. Female Execs., Delta Omicron (pres. Alpha Zi chpt. 1978-79, pres. Epsilon province 1980-85, chmn. Ea. Pa. alumni div. 1986—, Star award 1979). Republican. Office: Cardiac Datacorp 1429 Walnut St 2d Floor Philadelphia PA 19102

PAYNE, JUNE PATRICIA, editor; b. Albuquerque, May 20, 1930; d. Stanley Thomas and Effie (Pierce) P. B.A., Ariz. State U., 1952. Assoc. editor Ariz. Beverage Jour., Phoenix, 1952-64; asst. editor state desk Ariz. Republic, Phoenix, 1964; editorial asst., editor Bur. Publs., Ariz. State U., 1964-81, editor community relations, 1981-85, asst. dir. univ. publs., 1985—. Editor newspaper ASU Insight, 1983-85; mem. editorial bd. Jour. of American Indian Edn., 1976-81. Mem. Photographic Soc. Am., Ariz. Press Women, Women in Communications Inc. Club: Phoenix Press. Home: 4733 E Cambridge St Phoenix AZ 85008 Office: Ariz State U Publ Design Ctr Matthews Hall 102 Tempe AZ 85287

PAYNE, LORRAINE MARIE, marketing professional; b. Sherbrooke, Que., Can., Dec. 8, 1952; d. Marcel Joseph and Betty Cecilia (Larson) Gregoire; m. Robert Michael Payne, July 7, 1971 (dec. 1979); children: Jason Robert, Cory Steward; m. Patrick J. McKenna, Aug. 3, 1985. Student, Grant McKewan Coll., Edmonton, Alta., Can., 1975-77. Sr. copywriter Woodwards Ltd., Edmonton, 1977-79; advt. dir. Grove Pub., Edmonton, 1980-81; sr. dir. Mary Kay Cosmetics, Can., 1981-82; pub. affairs cons. Alta. Govt. Pub. Affairs Bur., Edmonton, 1982-86; v.p., ptnr. Williams & Wilson's PR Ltd., Edmonton, 1986; founder, ptnr. Saxby Payne & Cook Inc. - Strategic Communications, Edmonton, 1986—; dir. pub. relations Edmonton Heritage Festival Assn., 1986-87; chmn. pub. relations Edmonton C. of C. Centennial '87 Com., 1987—. Author (column) Paynefully Thought Over, Edmonton Examiner, 1977-79; contbr. articles to profl. jours. Bd. dirs. Uncles at Large, Edmonton, 1980-82. Mem. Can. Pub. Relations Soc. (accredited), Am. Mktg. Assn. (exec., founder No. Alta. chpt.). Progressive Conservative. Roman Catholic. Club: Toastmasters (founder Edmonton chpt. 1984). Office: Saxby Payne & Cook Inc, 1600 Royal LePage Bldg, Edmonton, AB Canada T5J 3N9

PAYNE, MILDRED LYNETTE, educator; b. Houston, Oct. 14, 1945; d. Norman Emory and Clara LaVerne (Nunalee) Payne. B.A., Baylor U., 1967; postgrad. Sam Houston State U., 1968-70; M.Ed., U. Houston, 1974, postgrad., 1978-80. Lic. ednl. diagnostician, tchr., Tex. Tchr., North Forest Ind. Sch. Dist., Houston, 1967-76, ednl. diagnostician, 1976-78, dir. spl. edn., 1978-81; project dir. Harris County Dept., Houston, 1981-83; agt. State Farm Ins., Houston, 1983-84; counselor Woodland Hills Elem. Sch., Humble Ind. Sch. Dist. (Tex.), 1984-87; tchr. gifted and talented students Aransas County Ind. Sch. Dist., Rockport, Tex., 1987—. Author: Zingo, Creative Reading Activities, Book 1, 1976; Zingo, Creative Reading Activities, Book 2, 1976. Mem. Council for Exceptional Children (pres. 1981-83), Tex. Adminstrn. Spl. Edn. (regional coordinator 1978-81), Gulf Coast Adminstrn. Spl. Edn. (sec. 1979-80), Delta Kappa Gamma. Democrat. Mem. Unity Ch. Christianity. Home: HCR Box 251-D Rockport TX 78382

PAYNE, ROBERTA KAY, government service administrator; b. Rock Springs, Wyo., Oct. 8, 1938; d. Walter John and Lavon (Wade) Anderson; m. George Willard Grayson, Dec. 28, 1959 (div. July 1961); m. Richard Noel Payne, Aug. 19, 1961; children: Alan Lee, Ricky Jay, Jimmy Dean. Grad. high sch., Riverside, Calif., 1956. Teletype operator U.S. Dept. Defense, San Bernardino, Calif., 1956-60, procurement agent, 1960-66; procurement agent U.S. Dept. Defense, Ankara, Turkey, 1966-67; communications specialist U.S. Dept. Defense, Corona, Calif., 1967-69; contract specialist U.S. Dept. Defense, Portsmouth, N.H., 1969-71; contract negotiator U.S. Dept. Defense, Ridgecrest, Calif., 1972-81; supr. contracting officer U.S. Dept. Defense, Norfolk, Va., 1981-83, Atlanta, 1983-87; dir. contracts U.S. Dept. Defense, Ft. McPherson, Ga., 1987—; sec., treas. Bankers Internat. Corp., Atlanta. Chmn. Billy Graham Orgn., Kern County, Calif., 1981; counsellor Christian Broadcasting Network, Virginia Beach, 1983-84. Republican. Home: 2069 Cedar Hill Dr Riverdale GA 30269 Office: Ft McPherson Bldg 184 East Point GA 30330

PAYNE, ROSLYN BRAEMAN, finance company executive; b. Kansas City, Mo., Apr. 30, 1946; d. Aaron and Sophie (Pincus) Braeman; m. Lisle Warren Payne, Dec. 27, 1973; children: Matthew, Andrew. BBA, U. Mich.; MBA, Harvard Bus. Sch. Intern, 1st National Bank of Chgo., 1968, Coopers & Lybrand, N.Y.C., 1969; v.p., prin. Eastdil Realty, N.Y.C., San Francisco, 1970-81; group v.p., gen. mgr. Genstar Corp., San Francisco, 1981-85; pres., chief operating officer Fed. Asset Disposition Assn., San Francisco, 1986-88; pres. Jackson Street Ptnrs., Ltd., San Francisco, 1988—; bd. dirs. Fin. Center Bank, San Francisco, First Am. Fin. Corp.Mem. Bay Area Mortgage Assn. (pres. 1981-82), Women's Forum West (dir., treas. 1981-83), Real Estate Research Council, Urban Land Inst., Lambda Alpha (dir.). Clubs: Peninsula Golf and Tennis, Menlo Circus.

PAYNE-PARSONS, SHARON LEE, management consultant; b. Chgo., Aug. 10, 1945; d. Steve and Shirley Florence (Johnson) Sawchuk; m. Edward Shier Parsons Jr., Feb. 14, 1981; Kimberly, Katharine, David. BS, U. Nev., 1977. Media dir. O'Brien Advt., Reno, 1978-81; ptnr. Mgmt. Devel. Associates, Reno, 1981—. Pres. Nev. Alliance for the Arts, Reno, 1985—; treas. Nev. Alliance Arts Edn., Las Vegas, 1985—; panelist Am. Orch. Symphony League, Salt Lake City, 1986. Recipient Gov.'s Arts award Nev. State Council on the Arts, 1985. Mem. Reno Ad Club. Office: Mgmt Devel Assocs 135 N Sierra St Reno NV 89501

PEACE, LISA BURK, systems programmer; b. San Diego, Jan. 31, 1960; d. Curtis R. and Karen (Schwab) Burk; m. Robert Dale Peace, June 1, 1985. A.A., Chipola Jr. Coll., Fla., 1980; B.S., U. West Fla., 1982. Computer systems analyst I, State of Fla., Tallahassee, 1982-83, II, 1983-84; programmer/analyst R.J. Kelly & Assocs., Tallahassee, 1985; systems programmer N.W. Regional Data Ctr., Tallahassee, 1985—. Editor bull. Capital Chatter, 1985-86. Vol., Leon County Humane Soc., 1985. Mem. Am. Bus. Women's Assn. (bull. chmn. 1985—, corr. sec. 1986-87), Nat. Assn. Female Execs., Internat. Platform Assn., Nat. Systems Programmers Assn. Democrat. Avocations: sewing; knitting; jogging. Office: 2048 E Paul Dirac Dr Tallahassee FL 32304

PEACE, MIRIAM SISKIN, cytotechnologist, lawyer; b. Winnipeg, Man., Can., Feb. 13, 1931; d. David L. and Rissa (Ghitter) Siskin; cert. Sch. of Cytology, Med. Coll. of Ga., 1951; L.L.B., John Marshall Sch. Law, 1972; children—Brian Smiley, Carl Smiley, Janice Smiley Hazlehurst, Vickie Smiley Sholes, Rissa Peace. Cytologist Med. Coll. of Ga., Augusta, 1951-52, Grady Hosp., Atlanta, 1956-57; supr. St. Joseph's Infirmary, Atlanta, 1957-62, Peace Labs., Atlanta, 1962-69; cytotechnologist Peachtree Lab., Atlanta, 1969-86; supr. Piedmont Hosp., Atlanta, 1979—; admitted to Ga. bar, 1973; individual practice law, Atlanta, 1974-75. Precinct co-chmn. Andrew Young campaign for Congress, 1970, 72. Mem. Am. Soc. Clin. Pathologists (registered cytotechnologist, charter mem.), Am. Soc. for Cytotechnology, State Bar of Ga. Democrat. Jewish. Home: 4717 Roswell St NE Apt D7 Atlanta GA 30342 Office: 1968 Peachtree Rd NW Atlanta GA 30309

PEACHEY, GEORGIA A., government official; b. Bklyn., Feb. 16, 1928; d. Alfred Archer and Dorothy (Abrams) P. AA, N.Y. Community Coll., 1974; BA, Hunter Coll., 1980. Clerical asst. NIH, H.Y.C., 1955-60, IRS, H.Y.C., 1960-61; personnel asst. FDA, Bklyn., 1961-72; specialist devel. and staffing HHS, N.Y.C., 1972-80; mgr. equal employment fed. women's and hispanic employment programs U.S. Army C.E., N.Y.C., 1980-85, acting chief EEO officer, 1985-87, chief EEO officer, 1987—; leader, speaker Bklyn. Coll., 1982—, workshop leader 1985—; leader, speaker Hunter Coll., CUNY, 1982—. Mem. adv. bd. Bklyn. Pub. Library, 1986—. Recipient Vol. Community Service award Pres. U.S., 1983, N.Y. Community Service award N.Y. Fed. Exec. Bd., 1983, Nat. Sojourner Truth award Nat. Assn. Negro Bus. and Profl. Womens Club, 1984, numerous others. Mem. Fed. Employed Women (pres. N.Y.C. chpt. 1985—, leader, speaker), Image (women's chmn. 1982-86, nat. pres.'s award 1983), Internat. Tng. Communication (numerous offices and workshops), Am. Mgmt. Assn. Home: 47 McKeever Pl Apt 8D Brooklyn NY 11335

PEAK, LORI MARIE, travel agency executive, education administrator; b. Alliance, Ohio, Feb. 8, 1953; d. Frank Nick and Violet Richie (Polidan) Salaski; children: Anthony, Jessica. Cert. secretarial skills Mott Community Coll., Flint, Mich., 1972, A.A., 1973; Religious tng. permit Diocese of Lansing, Mich., 1973; A.A., Henry Ford Community Coll., Dearborn, Mich., 1979; B.S. in Elem. Edn./Spl. Edn., Wayne State U., 1982, postgrad., 1987. Dental technician pvt. dental office, Flint, 1969-73; Emergency room tech. St. Joseph Hosp., Flint, 1973-75; dental technician in oral surgery, hygenist, instr., USN, Cherry Point, N.C., 1975-76; boatswainmate USN, N.C., 1976-77; sales exec. Tiara Exclusives, Dunkirk, Ind., 1978-79; dist. sales mgr. Wright Air Lines, Cleve., 1982-85; pres., owner Peak Travel Industries, Detroit, 1983—; leasing analyst fin. div. Stroh's Brewery, Detroit, 1985-86; gen. mgr. Advanced Copier Services, Inc., Detroit, 1986-87; team ednl. coordinator Boysville Mich. Inc., Detroit, 1987—; instr. Pontiac Bus. Inst., Farmington Hills, Mich., 1984-85, Dorsey Sch. Bus., Roseville, Mich., 1986-87; subs. teacher Garden City (Mich.) Sch. Dist., 1982-85. Served as petty officer USN, 1975-77. Mem. Nat. Assn. Female Execs., Dist. Area Sales Mgr. Assn., Detroit Women in Travel Assn., Detroit Passenger and Traffic Orgn., Detroit/Windsor Interline Club, Pi Lambda Theta. Home: 109 Fisher Ct Clawson MI 48017

PEALER-WENZEL, DEANNA RUTH, lawyer; b. Danville, Pa., Oct. 9, 1952; d. Harlan Dean and Ruth (Appleman) Pealer; m. Francis G. Wenzel, Jr., Aug. 30, 1980. B.A., Mansfield U., 1974; J.D., Dickinson Sch. Law, 1977. Bar: Pa. 1977. Claims atty. Nationwide Ins. Co., Harrisburg, Pa., 1977-79; sole practice, Bloomsburg, Pa., 1979—, dist. atty. Columbia County, 1988 ; spl. master Columbia County Ct., Bloomsburg, 1982—; bd. dirs. Susquehanna Legal Services Inc. Chmn., Columbia County Heart Fund Drive, Bloomsburg, 1980; bd. dirs. North Central Pa. chpt., Am. Heart Assn., Williamsport, 1980-83; mem. adv. bd. Children and Youth Services Agy., Columbia County, Pa., 1981-82; bd. dirs. Columbia County YMCA, Bloomsburg, 1983; co-chmn. publicity Bloomsburg Hosp. Aux., Bloomin Follies, Bloomsburg, 1984; crusade chmn. Am. Cancer Soc., 1985. Mem. ABA, Pa. Bar Assn., Columbia-Montour Bar Assn. (law day chmn. 1981-83, treas. 1984-85), Bloomburg Hist. Preservation Soc. (bd. dirs. 1986—), Bloomsburg Theatre Ensemble (bd. dirs. 1987—). Democrat. Methodist. Club: Soroptimist. Home: 455 Market St Bloomsburg PA 17815 Office: 455 Market St Bloomsburg PA 17815

PEARCE, JANE, psychiatrist; b. Austin, Tex., Jan. 13, 1914; d. James Edward and Belinda (Doppelmayer) P.; student Radcliffe Coll., 1931-32; B.A. cum laude, U. Tex., Austin, 1934; M.D., U. Chgo., 1941, Ph.D., 1941; student Washington Sch. Psychiatry, 1947-48; grad. William A. White Inst., N.Y.C., 1944-49; student Inst. Individual Psychology, Chgo., 1936-41; children from previous marriage—Sarah, Robert, Paul, Christopher. Intern, Harriet Lane Hosp., Balt., 1942, Albany (N.Y.) Hosp., 1942-43, resident in psychiatry, 1943; resident N.Y. State Psychiat. Inst., N.Y.C., 1943-44, 48-49; pvt. practice psychoanalysis, N.Y.C., 1944—; tng. analyst William Alanson White Inst., 1946-57, faculty, 1950-57; co-founder, asst. dir., research dir., supr. Sullivan Inst. Research in Psychoanalysis, N.Y.C., 1957-77; mem. faculty N.Y. U., 1951-53; co-founder, clin. dir. North Side Center, N.Y.C., 1945-46. Diplomate Am. Bd. Psychiatry and Neurology. Fellow Am. Assn. Social Psychiatry; mem. AMA, Am. Psychiat. Assn., Physicians for Social Responsibility, Phi Beta Kappa, Sigma Xi, Kappa Kappa Gamma. Democrat. Author: (with Saul Newton) The Conditions of Human Growth, 1963; contbr. articles to profl. jours. Home: 332 W 77th St New York NY 10024 Office: 332 W 77th St New York NY 10024

PEARCE, JOAN DELAP, research company executive; b. Oakland, Calif., June 13, 1930; d. Robert Jerome and Wilhelmina (Reaume) DeLap; m. Gerald Allan Pearce, June 18, 1953; 1 child, Scott Ford. Student, U. Oreg., 1948-55. Research assoc. deForest Research, Los Angeles, 1966-78; dir. research Walt Disney Prodns., Burbank, Calif., 1978; assoc. dir. deForest Research, Los Angeles, 1978—; lighting dir. Wilcoxen Players, Beverly Hills, Calif., 1955-60, Theatre 40, Los Angeles, 1960-66. Bd. advisors Living History Ctr., Marin County, Calif., 1982—, Hist. Oaks Found., Agoura Hills, Calif., 1988—. Mem. Am. Film Inst. Democrat. Avocations: photography; travel; theater; swimming. Home: 2621 Rutherford Dr Los Angeles CA 90068 Office: deForest Research Service Inc 1645 N Vine St Suite 701 Los Angeles CA 90028

PEARCE, MARTHA VIRGINIA, educator; b. Wilmington, Del., Sept. 26, 1929; d. Alva Elmer and Mary Rickards (Clark) P.; B.S., Columbia U., 1958; M.S., Boston U., 1965; Ed.D., Ariz. State U., 1980. Faculty asso. Ariz. State U., Tempe, 1977-81, asst. prof. aero. tech., 1981-87, assoc. prof., 1987—. Served with Nurses Corps, USN, 1954-75. Mem. Nat. Assn. Flight Instrs., Soaring Soc. Am., Ninety-Nines, Inc., Ariz. Adult Edn. Assn., Pi Lambda Theta, Alpha Eta Rho. Home: 2331 E Aspen Dr Tempe AZ 85282 Office: Ariz State U Tempe AZ 85287

PEARCE, MARY MCCALLUM (MRS. CLARENCE A PEARCE), artist; b. Hesperia, Mich., Feb. 17, 1906; d. Archibald and Mabel (McNeil) McCallum; A.B., Oberlin Coll., 1927; student John Huntington Inst., 1929-34, Cleve. Inst. Art, 1935-37, 54, Dayton Art Inst., 1946-49; m. Clarence A. Pearce, June 30, 1928 (dec.); children—Mary Martha (Mrs. William B. Robinson), Thomas McCallum. One woman shows at Cleve. Women's City Club, 1959, 69, Cleve. Orch., 1967, Cleve. Playhouse Gallery, 1968, 71, 76, 87, Van Wezel Hall, 1979, Sarasota (Fla.) Library, 1979, Hilton Leech Gallery, Sarasota, 1979, 80, 81, 86 Fed. Bank, Sarasota, 1980; exhibited in group shows at Oberlin Art Mus., Akron Art Inst., Grand Rapids (Mich.) Art Gallery, Dayton (Ohio) Art Inst., Smithsonian Inst., Birmingham Mus. of Art, Am. Watercolor Soc., Cleve. Mus. Art, Foster Harmon Galleries, 1986, many others: represented in pvt. collections: tchr. art, supr. pub. schs., Mayfield Heights, Ohio, 1927-28, Maple Heights, Ohio, 1928-30, Chagrin Falls, Ohio, 1938-39. Named best woman artist Ohio Watercolor Soc., 1955; recipient Bush Meml. award Columbus Gallery Fine Arts, 1962; nat. 1st prize for drawing Nat. League Am. Penwomen, 1966, 68; Littlehouse award Ala. Watercolor Soc., 1967; Wolfe award Columbus Gallery Fine Arts, 1971; awards Longboat Key Art Center, 1973, 75, 79-86; award Southeastern Art Soc., 1975; Merit award Art League Manatee County, 1977, 78, 3d prize, 1985; 3d prize Sarasota Art Assn., 1977, 78, Merit award, 1981, 85; 1st prize Venice (Fla.) Art League, 1979, 81, 82, 83, 86, 87, 2d prize, 1979, 80, 81, 3d prize, 1978, merit award, 1985; 1st prize Hilton Leech Gallery, 1981, 85, 1st prize Venice Art League, 1987, 1st prize Friends of Arts and Scis., numerous others. Mem. Nat. League Am. Pen Women (treas. 1962), Am. (assoc.), Ala., Fla. watercolor socs. Republican. Congregationalist. Home: 5400 Ocean Blvd Apt 1401 Sarasota FL 34242

PEARCY, CYNTHIA FERRIS, nurse, cons.; b. Providence, May 31, 1946; d. William Frances and Marcella Rose Ferris; R.N., Grace Hosp., Detroit, 1967; divorced; children—Shawn Michael, Ryan Robert. Staff nurse Grace Hosp., 1967-68; head nurse ICU, Martin Place Hosp., Warren, Mich., 1968-69; charge nurse intensive cardiac care S. Macomb Hosp., Warren, 1971-73; head nurse intensive care stepdown St. Joseph Health Network, Mt. Clemens, Mich., 1975-80, edn. coordinator critical care services, 1980-85, dir. guest relations, 1985—; also instr. coronary care. Mem. Nat. Assn. Female Execs., Internat. Platform Assn., Am. Mgmt. Assn., Am. Heart Assn. (1st v.p. Macomb County div.), Am. Assn. Critical Care Nurses. Roman Catholic. Home: 37342 Glenbrook Mount Clemens MI 48043 Office: 215 North Ave Mount Clemens MI 48043

PEARLMAN, FLORENCE SADOFF, social worker; b. N.Y.C., Dec. 26, 1928; d. Sam and Eva (Brunstein) Sadoff; BA, Barnard Coll., 1950; MSW, Wurzweiler Sch. Social Work, 1971; m. Donald Pearlman, June 22, 1947 (div. Feb. 1971); children: David J., Erica Lee (dec.). Editorial staff profl. jours., 1951-54; alumnae sec. Briarcliff Coll., Briarcliff Manor, N.Y., 1966-67; psychiat. social worker Westchester County (N.Y.) Mental Health Clinics, 1971; supr. Alcoholism Clinic, Yonkers, 1974-75, sr. social worker, 1986—. Mem. coms. Planned Parenthood-World Population, 1965-75, bd. dirs., 1966-72; active Planned Parenthood Westchester, 1962-80; bd. dirs. Assoc. Alumnae of Barnard Coll., 1975-78. Mem. Acad. Cert. Social Workers (diplomate in clin. social work), Nat. Assn. Social Workers, Amateur Chamber Music Players, Am. Orthopsychiat. Assn. Democrat. Jewish. Club: The Bohemians. Home: 17 Cedar Road S Katonah NY 10536

PEARLMAN-SHNIDERMAN, ANNETTE REBA, elementary educator; b. N.Y.C., Sept. 8, 1935; d. Ruben and Fay (Fenster) Pearlman; m. E. Stanley Shniderman, June 24, 1961; children: Alisa Randi, Brian Scott. BA, kindergarten primary, elem. credential, U. Calif., Los Angeles, 1957. Tchr. Los Angeles Unified Sch. Dist., 1957-62, Las Virgenes Unified Sch. Dist., Calabasas, Calif., 1967-87. Grantee Calif. State Bd. Edn., 1987. Mem. Las Virgenes Edn. Assn. (W.H.O.O. award 1986), Calif. Tchrs. Assn., Nat. Tchrs. Assn. Democrat. Jewish. Clubs: Friendship Havarah, Pioneer Women (v.p. 1960-62). Home: 7146 Pomelo Dr West Hills CA 91307 Office: Round Meadow Sch 5151 Round Meadow Rd Hidden Hills CA 91302

PEARSALL, ROSELLEN DEE, insurance executive; b. Ft. Dix, N.J., Aug. 15, 1945; d. Raymond Donald and Rosemary (Dannenberg) P. BS in Nursing, U. Ky., 1967. RN U. Ky. Med. Ctr., Lexington, 1967-68; RN Cardiac Care Unit Cedars of Lebanon Hosp., Los Angeles, 1968-69; rehab. nurse cons. Employers Ins. of Wausau, Los Angeles, 1969-76; asst. v.p. rehab. services Fremont Compensation Ins. Co., Los Angeles, 1976—; ins. adv. bd. Casa Colina Inc., Pomona, Calif., 1984—. Recipient Cert. Achievement in Bus. and Industry Los Angeles YWCAs, 1978, 80. Mem. Nat. Assn. Rehab. Profls. in the Pvt. Sector (legis. chair Calif.), Nat. Rehab. Assn. (pres. So. Calif. chpt. 1979-80, Outstanding Achievement award 1981), Rehab. Nurses Soc. (founding pres. 1972-74, Outstanding Services award 1980, Greatest Support award 1984-85), Ins. Rehab. Study Group. Club: Los Angeles Athletic. Office: Fremont Compensation Ins Co 1709 W 8th St Los Angeles CA 90017

PEARSON, BELINDA KEMP, economist, consultant; b. Kansas City, Mo., Apr. 14, 1931; d. William Ewing and Margaret Norton (Johnson) Kemp; m. Carl Erik Pearson, Sept. 15, 1953; children—Erik, Frederick, Margaret. B.A., Wellesley Coll., 1952; M.A., Tufts U., 1954, Ph.D., 1958. Research asst. Harvard U., Cambridge, Mass., 1954-55; instr. econs. Suffolk U., Boston, 1956-59; lectr. econs., Wellesley Coll., Mass., 1964-65; econ. analyst, asst. econs. Seafirst Bank, Seattle, 1966-79, v.p., 1974-85; chief economist, 1979-85; dir. Lektor, Inc., Bellevue, Wash., 1984—, pres., 1987—; mem. Wash. Gov.'s Council Econ. Advisors, Olympia, 1979—; dir. Pacific N.W. Regional Econ. Conf., 1979—, chair, Seattle Conf., 1987; mem. econ. devel. edn. council Assn. Wash. Bus., Olympia, 1983—; mem. bd. regents Wash. State U.-Pullman, 1985—, mem. investment com., 1986—; mem. Wash. State Library Commn., Olympia, 1976-84. Fulbright scholar London Sch. Econs., 1952-53. Mem. Am. Econ. Assn., Nat. Assn. Bus. Economists (chmn. arrangements 1982 ann. meeting), Seattle Economists Club (pres. 1973-74), Mcpl. League. Club: City (Seattle) (chmn. reports com. 1986—). Office: Lektor Inc 305 108th Ave NE Suite 100 Bellevue WA 98004

PEARSON, GLORIA, financial planner, stockbroker; b. Bklyn., May 5, 1920; d. Maurice Benjamin and Esther (Krauss) Green; m. Henry Pearson, Aug. 31, 1947; children: Laurence Drew, James Elliot, Robert Allen. Student, Bklyn. Coll., 1938-42; degree in bus., Colby Bus. Coll., Bklyn., 1942-44; cert. fin. planner, Coll. for Fin. Planning, 1980. Registered investment advisor. Rep. Profl. and Exec. Planning, Long Beach, N.Y., 1957-60; ptnr., v.p. W.R. Reich and Co., N.Y.C., 1960-63; rep. Edwards and Hanly, Hewlett, N.Y., 1963-69; account exec. Herzfeld and Stern, Hollywood, Fla., 1970-84; fin. planner FSC Corp., Hollywood, Fla., 1984—. Mem. Internat. Assn. for Fin. Planners (bd. dirs. 1982-86, bd. dirs. S. Fla. chpt. 1982-85), Inst. Cert. Fin. Planners, Stock Brokers Assn.

PEARSON, LINDA LEVIN, real estate executive; b. Cin., Apr. 9, 1944; d. Robert Morton and Lucille (Rosenbaum) Levin; m. Robin H. Pearson, Sept. 3, 1966; children: Lara Allison, Gregory Sidney. BS, Syracuse U., 1966; postgrad., Ariz. State U., 1966-68; MSW, Ind. U.-Purdue U. at Indpls., 1970. Social worker Cuyahoga County Welfare Dept., Cleve., 1966; cons. social work Laredo (Tex.) Ind. Schs., 1969; social worker Cleve. VA Hosp., 1970-71; pvt. practice marital and family therapy Cleve., 1971-72; owner Lindie Ltd., Cleve., 1982—; real estate agt. Callahan Realty, Cleve., 1985—; conductor seminars in field; lectr. in field. Author: Complete Entertaining Notebook, 1982. Bd. dirs. Mt. Sinai Med. Ctr. Aux., Cleve., 1970—; jury commr. Shaker Mcpl. Ct., Ohio, 1982—; trustee Council on Human Relations, Cleve., 1980-86; com. mem. Jewish Community Fedn., Cleve., 19000; chair urban studies Cleve. State U., 1984—; mem. adv. com. A.A. Levin. Margaret Sanger Seminar scholar, 1967, 68. Mem. Nat. Assn. Social Workers, Acad. Family Mediators (cert. divorce and family moderator 1984—), Nat. Council Jewish Women. Democrat. Jewish. Home: 22400 Shaker Blvd Shaker Heights OH 44122

PEARSON, LOUISE MARY, retired manufacturing company executive; b. Inverness, Scotland, Dec. 14, 1919 (parents Am. citizens); d. Louis Houston and Jessie M. (McKenzie) Lenox; grad. high sch.; m. Nels Kenneth Pearson, June 28, 1941; children—Lorine Pearson Walters, Karla. Dir. Wauconda Tool & Engring. Co., Inc., Algonquin, Ill., 1950-86; reporter Oak Leaflet, Crystal Lake, Ill., 1944-47, Sidelights, Wilmette, Ill., 1969-72, 79-82. Active Girl Scouts U.S.A., 1955-65. Recipient award for appreciation work with Girl Scouts, 1965. Clubs: Antique Automobile of Am. (Hershey, Pa.); Veteran Motor Car (Boston); Classic Car of Am. (Madison, N.J.). Home: 125 Dole Ave Crystal Lake IL 60014

PEARSON, P. A. (LEE), marine consultant; b. Phoenix, June 23, 1939; d. David Samuel and Margaret (Holtzman) Hamburger; divorced; 1 child, Stuart Deene. Student, Glendale Coll., 1963-64, Yacht Design Inst., 1975-76. Surveyor, cons. Lenders Yacht Mfrs. Ins. Co., 1974—; prin. Pearson Enterprises, Seabrook, Tex., 1974-79, 1982—. Served as instr. USCG Aux. Mem. Soc. Naval Architects/Marine Engrs., Soc. Small Craft Designers, Am. Boat and Yacht Council. Democrat. Office: Pearson Enterprises PO Box 580547 Houston TX 77258

PEARSON, SUSAN WINIFRED, educational administrator; b. Wasco, Calif., Oct. 8, 1941; d. Gerald Thomas and Maxine (Jensen) P.; B.S., Tex. Christian U., 1963, M.Ed., 1971; Ed.D., U. Houston, 1982. Tchr. history, chmn. dept. Spring Branch Ind. Sch. Dist., Houston, 1963-68; personnel asst. Tenneco Inc., Houston, 1969-70; grad. asst. Tex. Christian U., 1970-71; dir. student activities Navarro Jr. Coll., Corsicana, Tex., 1972-73; dir. counseling services North Harris County Coll., Houston, 1973-84, div. head bus., communications and fine arts, developmental studies and counseling, 1984-86, dean instrn./student services, 1986—. Mem. Am. Personnel and Guidance Assn., Am. Coll. Personnel Assn., Nat. Assn. Women Deans, Adminstrs. and Counselors, So. Coll. Personnel Assn., Tex. Assn. Women Deans, Adminstrs. and Counselors, Tex. Assn. Coll. and Univ. Student Personnel Adminstrs., Phi Kappa Phi, Delta Gamma. Presbyterian. Author articles in field. Office: 20000 Kingwood Dr Kingwood TX 77339

PEASE, CAROL HELENE, oceanographer; b. Bay City, Mich., Dec. 29, 1949; d. George Olson and Mernabelle Hattie (Laabs) P.; m. Alexander Jeffrey Chester, June 16, 1974 (div. May, 1978). Student, U. Mich., 1968-71; BS in Math., U. Miami, Coral Gables, Fla., 1972; MS in Phys. Oceanography, U. Wash., Seattle, 1975, MS in Meteorology, 1981, postgrad., 1985. Research asst. Arctic Ice Dynamics Joint Experiment, U. Wash., Seattle, 1972-75; oceanographer Pacific Marine Environ. Lab., Nat. Oceanic and Atmospheric Adminstrn., Seattle, 1975-78, sea ice project leader, 1978—. Contbr. articles to profl. jours. Mem. Arboretum Found., Seattle, 1975—, Seattle Art Mus., 1978—, Nat. Women's Polit. Caucus, Seattle, 1984—; sustaining mem. Friends of KUOW, KCTS Found., Seattle, 1978, 82. Recipient performance awards NOAA, 1977, 82, 85, 87, 88, Adminstr.'s award, 1988. Mem. AAAS, Assn. Women in Sci., Am. Geophys. Union, Am. Meteorol. Soc. (session chair symposium meterology and oceanography N.Am. high latitudes 1984, mem. standing com. on polar meteorology and oceanography 1985—, chmn. 1987—, session chair, co-convener conf. on polar meteorology and oceanography 1988). Clubs: Corinthian Yacht (Seattle). Lodges: Valkyrien (sec. 1978-81), Daughters of Norway. Office: Pacific Marine Environ Lab 7600 Sand Point Way NE Seattle WA 98115

PEASE, ELEANOR THOMPSON (MRS. DONALD CARGILL PEASE), lawyer; b. Bucyrus, Ohio, Mar. 28, 1923; s. Edgar William and Mary (Biss) Thompson; m. Donald Cargill Pease, Sept. 9, 1949; 1 child, William Thompson. B.A., Vassar Coll., 1944; J.D., Yale U., 1946. Bar: U.S. Dist. Ct. D.C., U.S. Ct. Appeals (D.C. cir.) 1947. Corp. lawyer E.I. Dupont Co., 1947-49. By-laws chmn. Jr. League, Wilmington, Del., 1951-53, bd. dirs., 1951-53, mag. chmn., 1959-60, edn. com., 1961-62; pres. Jr. League of Wilmington Sustainers Garden Club, 1969-70; by-laws chmn., bd. dirs. Del. Soc. Prevention Cruelty to Animals, 1950-52; day chmn. Winterthur Mus. Jr. League docents, 1955-61; del., class rep. Vassar Alumnae Council, 1954; parliamentarian Girl Scouts, Wilmington, 1957, 59; pres. Del. Vassar Club, 1960-62; area chmn. United Fund, 1960-62; exec. com. Women's Coll. Info. Program, 1961; docent Del. Art Mus., 1961-63; mem. Cts. Task Force Del. Agy. to Reduce Crime, 1968-71. Bd. dirs. Vol. bur. Del. Welfare Council, 1950-52, Friends of John Dickinson Mansion, 1979-80. Mem. Del. Hist. Soc., Nat. Trust for Hist. Preservation, Nat. Soc. Colonial Dames Am. (bd. mgrs. 1973-79, pres. Del. chpt. 1976-79), Roger Williams Family Assn. Republican. Presbyterian. (deacon). Home: 804 Princeton Rd Westover Hills Wilmington DE 19807

PEASE, VERLE ANTOINETTE, language and theatre arts educator; b. San Antonio, Aug. 15, 1954; d. Gordon Franklin and Dorothy Lee (Curtis) P. BA magna cum laude, Trinity U., San Antonio, 1975; MFA, U. Tex., 1978. Cert. English and French tchr., cert. drama and speech tchr. English, French and drama tchr. West Campus South San Antonio High Sch., 1978-79; real estate sales agt. Michael Proctor, Realtor, San Antonio, 1980—; drama and speech tchr. Kirby (Tex.) Jr. High Sch., 1981-82; English, drama and speech tchr. Jefferson High Sch., San Antonio, 1982-85; English and theatre arts tchr. Holmes High Sch., San Antonio, 1986—; dir. one-act play competition West Campus South San Antonio High Sch., 1979; co-dir. one-act play competition Jefferson High Sch., 1982-85. Active Trinity U. Summer Theatre, San Antonio, 1975, U. Tex. Summer Theatre Prodn., Austin, 1978. Recipient Morton Brown award, 1977-78; Minnie Stevens Piper Found. scholar, 1971-75; Pres.'s scholar Trinity U., 1972-75. Mem. Assn. Tex. Profl. Educators, San Antonio Bd. Realtors, Alpha Lambda Delta, Alpha Chi, Kappa Delta Pi. Presbyterian. Home: 9710 Gemini San Antonio TX 78217

PECARICH, PAMELA JAE, accountant; b. Grand Island, Nebr., Nov. 11, 1943; d. A.J. and Lorraine Hanway; student U. Calif.-Berkeley, 1961-62; B.S. with honors, Calif. State U., 1969; postgrad. in acctg. U. Wash., 1971-72; m. Frank J. Pecarich, Apr. 13, 1965; 1 son, Jason Dean. C.P.A. Sr. cons. revenue and taxation com. Calif. State Assembly, 1969-74; cons. U.S. Adminstrv. Conf., Washington, 1974-75; dir. Office Policy and Planning, Commodity Futures Trading Commn., 1975-77; staff dir. subcom. on oversight U.S. Ho. of Reps. Ways and Means Com., 1977-81, chief tax policy analyst, 1981-84; ptnr. nat. tax directorate Coopers & Lybrand, Washington, 1984—. Mem. Am. Soc. Pub. Adminstrn., Beta Alpha Psi, Beta Gamma Sigma, Phi Kappa Phi. Home: 1468 Highwood Dr McLean VA 22101 Office: Coopers & Lybrand 1800 M St NW Washington DC 20036

PECK, ANN, television producer, writer, educator; b. N.Y.C., Mar. 17, 1945; d. Harris Beaver and Shulamit (Shohan) P. BA, Radcliffe Coll., 1966; EdM, Harvard U., 1978. Prodn. asst. Graphic Curriculum, Inc., N.Y.C., 1967-68; assoc. producer Take Two, Inc., N.Y.C., 1968-71, Documentary Unit ABC News, N.Y.C., 1971-74; producer Instrnl. TV Ctr., Ramat Aviv, Israel, 1974-77, Pub. Broadcasting Assocs., Cambridge, Mass., 1979-81, 85-87; sr. staff producer Nathan/Tyler, 1988—; freelance writer, producer WGBH, CTW, CBS Cable, 1981-86; vis. lectr. Dartmouth Coll., Hanover, N.H., 1984-85. Writer, producer: (films) Other People's Garbage, Margaret Mead: Taking Note for Odyssey, Looking and Clues for The Ring of Truth. Vis. scholar Grad. Sch. of Edn. Harvard U., 1985. Mem. Women in Film and Video (program chair 1984-85). Home: 6 Ellsworth Ave Cambridge MA 02139

PECK, ANNE ELLIOTT ROBERTS, trust banker; b. N.Y.C., Dec. 17, 1935; d. James Ragan and Jane Ziegler (Elliott) Roberts; B.A. with honors in English, Wellesley Coll., 1957; M.A. with honors in Comparative Lit., Columbia U., 1966; postgrad. Villanova U., 1978-80, U. Bridgeport, 1988; m. George Linn Davis, May 29, 1955 (div. Aug. 1967); children—James Roberts, Elliott Britton, George Linn Jr., William Vaughn (dec.); m. 2d, Robert Gray Peck 3d, Oct. 24, 1969; children—Andrew Adams, Matthew Canfield Roberts. Contbg. editor "Newsfront" mag., 1960-63; English tchr. The Masters Sch., Dobbs Ferry, N.Y., 1963-65; sports feature writer Westchester-Rockland newspapers, Gannett chain, White Plains, N.Y., 1969—; corr., weekly column Knickerbocker News-Union Star, Capital Newspapers, Hearst chain, Albany, N.Y., 1971-73; public and exec. tax preparer H & R Block, Inc., Wayne, Pa., 1976-79; bookkeeper Shop of John Simmons, Bryn Mawr, Pa., 1979; sr. estate planning trust officer Provident Nat. Bank-Trust div. PNC Fin. Corp., Phila., 1981-86; v.p. new bus. devel. div., trusts and investments dept. Mellon Bank (east) 1986—; asst v.p., trust officer People's Bank, Stamford, Conn., 1988—. Mem. Mus. Art and Sci., Schenectady, N.Y., 1960-68; bd. dirs. Scarsdale (N.Y.) Jr. League, 1960-61; asst. producer Poetry, Channel 25-TV, N.Y.C.; bd. dirs., legis. chmn. Greenacres Sch. PTA, 1968-69; legis. chmn. AAUW, Albany-Schenectady, N.Y. br.; public relations chmn. Planned Parenthood League, Schenectady; sec., parliamentarian N.Y. State Legis. Forum, 1971-73; pres. Career Group W, Phila., 1983—; editor directory St. David's Ch., 1976, mem. exec. com. every-member canvass, 1977; fair gates-keeper Episcopal Ch., 1974-80, rep. Merion Deanery, 1982—; on-screen TV panel moderator Access, Channel 17, Albany-Schenectady-Troy, N.Y.; maj. gift solicitor Planned Parenthood Southeastern Pa., 1975-76; mem. plant sale exec. com. Haverford Sch., 1976, 77; Republican pollchecker Tredyffrin Twp., 1978, 79; majority insp. of elections Tredyffrin Twp. E-2, 1980—. Recipient prize Coll. Bd. Contest Mademoiselle mag., 1954; Prix de Paris, Vogue mag., 1957. Mem. DAR (bd. mgrs.-pub. relations Phila. chpt., treas. 1983, Phila. Bicentennial Celebration com. 1987), AAUW (dir. Schenectady 1971-73, legis. chmn. Valley Forge br.), N.Y. State Women's Press Club (Capital dist. br.), Jr. League Phila. (sustaining; edn. com., child abuse center com., bicentennial cookbook com., Waterworks Restoration com., 1984), Career Group Phila. (pres. 1983-85). Republican. Clubs: Schenectady Curling, Valley Forge Council Republican Women, Mohawk Golf (Schenectady); Shendrock Shore (Rye, N.Y.); Merion Cricket (Haverford, Pa.); Acorn (Phila.), Little Acorns Investment, Career Group (founder, chair 1984-85), Jeptha Abbott Crap (Bryn Mawr, Pa.), Wellesley Alumnae (Phila.), Little (Egg) Harbor Yacht (Beach Haven, N.J.), Jr. League of Phila. (sustaining mem. Waterworks com.). Home: PO Box 356 100 Steeplechase Rd Devon PA 19333 Office: Mellon Bank (East) 2 Mellon Ctr 5th Floor Philadelphia PA 19102

PECK, DIANNE KAWECKI, architect; b. Jersey City, June 13, 1945; d. Thaddeus Walter and Harriet Ann (Zlotkowski) Kawecki; BA in Architecture, Carnegie Mellon U., 1968; m. Gerald Paul Peck, Sept. 1, 1968; children: Samantha Gillian, Alexis Hilary. Architect, P.O.D. Research & Devel., 1968, Kohler-Daniels & Assos., Vienna, Va., 1969-71, Beery-Rio & Assocs., Annandale, Va., 1971-73; ptnr. Peck & Peck Architects, Occoquan, Va., 1973-74, Peck, Peck & Williams, Occoquan, 1974-81; corp. officer Peck Peck & Assos., Inc., Woodbridge, Va., 1981—. Work pub. in Am. Architecture, 1985. Vice pres. Vocat. Edn. Found., 1976; chairwoman architects and engrs. United Way; mem. Health Systems Agy. of No. Va., commendations, 1977; mem. Washington Profl. Women's Coop.; chairwoman Indsl. Devel. Authority of Prince William, 1976, vice chair, 1977, mem., 1975-79; developer research project Architecture for Adolescents, 1987-88. Recipient commendation Prince William Bd. Suprs., 1976, State of Art award for Contel Hdqrs. design, 1985. Mem. Prince William C. of C. (dir.). Republican. Roman Catholic. Club: Soroptimist. Research on inner-city rehab. Office: 1924 Opitz Blvd Woodbridge VA 22191

PECK, ELLIE ENRIQUEZ, state administrator; b. Sacramento, Oct. 21, 1934; d. Rafael Enriquez and Eloisa Garcia Rivera; m. Raymond Charles Peck, Sept. 5, 1957; children—Reginaldo, Enrico, Francisca Guerrero, Teresa, Linda, Margaret, Raymond Charles, Christina. Student polit. sci. Sacramento State U., 1974. Tng. services coordinator Calif. Div. Hwys., Sacramento, 1963-67; tech. and mgmt. cons., Sacramento, 1968-78; expert examiner Calif. Personnel Bd., 1976-78; tng. cons. Calif. Personnel Devel. Center, Sacramento, 1978; spl. cons. Calif. Commn. on Fair Employment and Housing, 1978; community services rep. U.S. Bur. of Census, No. Calif. counties, 1978-80; spl. cons. Calif. Dept. Consumer Affairs, Sacramento, 1980-83, project dir. Golden State Sr. Discount Program, 1980-83; asst. chief of staff and dir. spl. programs for Calif. Lt. Gov., 1983—; mem. Sacramento Community Services Planning Council, 1987—; chairperson Calif. Suprs.' Forum, 1966. Trustee, Stanford Settlement, Inc., Sacramento, 1975-79, hon. life trustee, 1979—; bd. dirs. Sacramento Emergency Housing Center, 1974-77; v.p. Comision Femenil Nacional, Inc., 1987—; del. Democratic Nat. Conv., 1976; mem. Sacramento County Democrat Cen. Com., mem. exec. bd. Calif. Dem. Central Com. Recipient numerous awards, including Outstanding Community Service award Comuicaciones Unidos de Norte Atzlan, 1975, 77, Outstanding Service award, Chicano/Hispanic Dem. Caucus, 1979, Vol. Service award Calif. Human Devel. Corp., 1981. Mem. Nat. Women's Polit, Caucas, Mexican-Am. Polit Assn, Hispanic C. of C. Club: Hispanic Dem. Sacramento County (v.p. 1982-83). Author U.S. Office Consumer Edn. publ., 1982, Calif. Dept. Consumer Affairs publ., 1981. Home: 2667 Coleman Way Sacramento CA 95818

PECK, MARYLY VANLEER, college president, chemical engineer; b. Washington, June 29, 1930; d. Blake Ragsdale and Ella Lillian (Wall) VanLeer; m. Jordan B. Peck, Jr., June 15, 1951; children: Jordan B. III, Blake VanLeer, James Tarleton VanLeer, Virginia Ellaine.; m. Walter G. Ebert, Sept. 3, 1983. Student, Ga. Inst. Tech., 1948, 53-58, Duke U., 1947-48; B.Ch.E., Vanderbilt U., 1951; M.S.E., U. Fla., 1955, Ph.D., 1963. Chem. engr. Naval Research Lab., Washington, 1951-52; chem. engr. Med. Field Research Lab., Camp LeJeune, N.C., 1952; asso. research and instr. U. Fla., Gainesville, 1953-55; chem. engr., research asso. Ga. Tech. Expt. Sta., Atlanta, 1956-58; lectr. Ga. State Coll., Atlanta, 1957-58; lectr. math. East Carolina Extension, Camp Lejeune, 1959; sr. research engr. Rocketdyne div. N.Am. Aviation Co., 1961-63; self-employed as lectr. 1963; assoc. prof. Campbell Coll., Buie's Creek, N.C., 1963-66; prof. Campbell Coll., 1966; acad. dir. St. John's Episcopal Sch., Upper Tumon, Guam, 1966-68; chmn., prof. phys. scis. U. Guam, Agana, 1968-73; dean Coll. Bus. and Applied Tech. U. Guam, 1973-74, dean Community Career Coll., 1974-77; pres. Cochise Coll., Douglas, Ariz., 1977-78; systems planning analyst Urban Pathfinders, Inc., Balt., 1978-79; dean undergrad. studies U. Md. Univ. Coll., College Park, 1979-82; pres. Polk Community Coll., Winter Haven, Fla., 1982—. Founder, pres. Guam Acad. Found., 1972-77; bd. dirs. Cochise Coll. Found., 1977-78, Turnaround, Inc. 1986—; founding mem. Prince George's Ednl. TV Cable Coalition; mem. Prince George's Cable TV Ednl. Adv. Group, 1980-82, Polk County Council Econ. Edn., 1982; sec. Polk Community Coll. Found., 1982—; mem. Polk County Coordinating Council Vocat. Edn., 1982—, PRIDE Adv. Council; vice chmn. Fla. State Job Tng. Coordinating Council, 1983—. Recipient Golden Plate of Achievement Dell Webb Corp., 1962; NSF fellow, 1961-63. Mem. Am. Inst. Chem. Engrs., Am. Chem. Soc., Soc. Women Engrs. (nat. v.p. 1962-63), Nat. Soc. Profl. Engrs., Am. Assn. for Higher Edn., Am. Assn. Community and Jr. Colls., Am. Assn. Univ. Adminstrs., AAUW, Sigma Xi, Tau Beta Pi (women's badge 1950), Chi Omicron Gamma, Phi Kappa Phi, Delta Kappa Gamma. Episcopalian. Club: Rotarianne. Home: 601 14th Street NE Winter Haven FL 33881-4310 Office: Polk Community College 999 Avenue H NE Winter Haven FL 33881-4299

PECK, SUSAN, data processing executive; b. Bklyn., Aug. 31, 1948; d. Cornelius Lawrence and Loretta Agnes (Freligh) Cleary; m. Richard Carl Peck, Mar. 7, 1972; 1 child, Mary Catherine. BS in Speech, St. John's U., 1970. Lic. real estate salesman, N.Y. Speech therapist, dept. chair, tchr. Christ the King Elem. Sch., Commack, N.Y., 1970-72; supr. purchase planning Estee Lauder, Inc., Melville, N.Y., 1973-78; staff analyst Gen. Instrument Corp., Hicksville, N.Y., 1978-83; systems analyst ADP, Melville, 1983-85; mgr. info. systems R. A. Rodriguez, Inc., Garden City, N.Y., 1985-87; dir. personal computer ops., liaison healthforce Career Employment Services, Inc., East Meadow, N.Y., 1987—; v.p. Richard Peck Ltd., Shirley, N.Y., 1982—. Lector, extraordinary minister of eucharist St. Joseph the Worker Roman Cath. Ch., East Patchogue, N.Y., 1980-82; vol. Brookhaven (N.Y.) County Task Force, 1987. Touro Coll. Law scholar, 1987. Mem. Nat. Assn. for Female Execs., Mensa. Republican. Office: Career Employment Services Inc 1975 Hempstead Turnpike East Meadow NY 11554

PECKENPAUGH, ANN DREESEN, executive search consultant; b. Gary, Ind., Nov. 15, 1954; d. Donald Hugh and Mary Frances (Dreesen) P. BA with high distinction, U. Mich., 1976; MBA, Harvard U., 1980. Assoc. dir. MBA admissions Harvard Bus. Sch., Boston, 1980-82; search dir. Debra Radabaugh Assocs., Menlo Park, Calif., 1982-84; pres. Peckenpaugh & Co., San Francisco, 1984-87; v.p. David Powell, Inc., Woodside, Calif., 1987—. Home: 1225 Washington St San Francisco CA 94108 Office: David Powell Inc 29995 Woodside Rd Suite 150 Woodside CA 94062

PEDERSEN, AMANDA B., lawyer; b. New Haven, Conn., Sept. 20, 1944; d. Gerald P. Norton, Sept. 25, 1971; children: Jeremy, Elizabeth, Adam. A.B., Vassar Coll., 1966; J.D., George Washington U., 1972. Bar: D.C. Asst. gen. counsel Cost of Living Council, Washington, 1974; assoc. Bergson Borkland Margolis & Adler, Washington, 1975-78, ptnr., 1979-81; dep. dir. Bur. Consumer Protection, FTC, Washington, 1982—, acting dir., 1985-86; mem. hearing com. Bd. Profl. Responsibility, D.C. Ct. Appeals, 1978-83. Mem. Adminstrv. Conf. U.S., ABA. Office: Fed Trade Commn 7th St & Pennsylvania Ave Washington DC 20580

PEDESCLEAUX, GAIL, systems analyst; b. Cleve., June 20, 1949; d. Alfonso and Belle (Pindard) P. BA in English, Cen. Mich. U., 1971. Sr. rater, account analyst The Travelers Ins. Co., Southfield, Mich., 1972-79; asst. ops analyst The Travelers Ins. Co., Hartford, Conn., 1979; account analyst The Travelers Ins. Co., Garden City, N.Y., 1979-81; comml. underwriter Am. Internat. Group, N.Y.C., 1981-83, system analyst, 1985-87, bus. analyst, 1988—; supr., sr. underwriter Fireman's Fund, N.Y.C., 1983-84; supr. bus. accounts The Continental Ins. Co., N.Y.C., 1984-85; system analyst Tokio Marine Mgmt., N.Y.C., 1987-88; mentor Brandeis program Am. Internat. Group, 1986. Author: (poems) A-Brief-Moment-in-Time, 1985 (recipient Silver award 1986). Mem. Nat. Ins. Industry Assn. Home: 2410 Village Dr Avenel NJ 07001

PEDIGO, SKIP COOLEY, public relations exec.; b. Sharon, Tenn., May 30, 1933; d. Ocie D. and Nellie Lee (Garrett) Cooley; m. Jerry L. Pedigo, Dec. 10, 1977; 1 child, Alison. BA, Calif. State U., 1970. Copywriter/account supr. Chris Art Studio, Costa Mesa, Calif., 1971-73, mktg. dir. Pacific City Bank, Huntington Beach, Calif., 1973; promotion/mktg. dir. for Westminster (Calif.) Mall, Homart Devel. Co., 1974-76; editor Orange Coast mag., Newport Beach, 1976-78, Sr. Life mag., Newport Beach, 1978, HomeBuyer's Guide, Newport Beach, 1979; pres. Pedigo Public Relations, Newport Beach, 1979-80; owner/ptnr. Coombe & Pedigo Pub. Relations, Newport Beach, 1980—; owner Pedigo Pub., Huntington Beach, 1985—; lectr. in field. Bd. dirs. The Rap Ctr., Tustin, Calif., 1973-74; mem. spl. events bd. City of Huntington Beach, 1979. Contbr. articles to profl. jours. and consumer publs. Mem. C. of C., Nat. Council Shopping Ctrs., Calif. Press Women, Women Can Win, Nat. Assn. Female Execs., Orange County Coast Assn., Am. Soc. Profl. and Exec. Women, AAUW. Contbr. articles to profl. jours. and consumer pubs. Home: 6652 Luciento Dr Huntington Beach CA 92647 Office: 180 Newport Ctr Dr Suite 180 Newport Beach CA 92660

PEEBLES, LINDA M(AE), photographer; b. Toledo, May 3, 1950; d. William Russell Duckett and Gertrude LaVerne (Jones) Gruber; m. Ray Randall Peebles II, June 20, 1970; children: Nedra Allyn, Karla Marie. Student, St. Petersburg (Fla.) Jr. Coll., 1968-69, U. Toledo, 1969-71. Various positions WSPD-TV (formerly WTVG-TV), Toledo, 1970-76; sr. billing clk. Owens-Corning Fiberglass, Toledo, 1976-78; owner, photographer Peebles Photography, Sylvania, Ohio, 1979—. Trustee Sylvania Community Services, 1986—, Latchkey Program Sylvania; bd. dirs. First United Meth. Christian Nursery Sch., pres. 1985-86, 86—; adminstrv. bd. First United Meth. Ch., 1986—, Sylvania. Mem. Profl. Photographers Am., Prof. Photographers of N.W. Ohio (treas., v.p. 1983-87), Profl. Photographers of Ohio (N.W. Ohio rep. 1987-88, pres. 1988—). Club: Highland Meadows Golf (Sylvania). Office: Peebles Photography 6625 Maplewood Sylvania OH 43560

PEEKENSCHNEIDER, JOY LYNNE, oil company executive; b. Davenport, Iowa, June 19, 1946; d. Lloyd E. Tucker and Juanita M. (Ouverson) Manning; m. Gene H. Peekenschneider; children: Nicole Joy, Lindsey Marie. BA in Acctg. and Bus. Adminstrn., Marycrest Coll., Davenport, 1987. Legal sec. Atty. Edward N. Wehr, Davenport, 1969-70; sec. U.S. Steel Co., Davenport, 1970, Ford Mktg., Davenport, 1970-71; v.p., sec. Peekenschneider Oil Co., Inc., Dixon, Iowa, 1971—. Mem. Dixon Meml. Park Bd., 1972-75. Mem. Kappa Gamma Pi. Home: Box 55 Dixon IA 52745

PEEL, DEBRA LEE THORSON, auditor; b. Sumter, S.C., Mar. 28, 1961; d. Leonard R. and Maxine Elaine (Durkee) Thorson; m. Anthony J. Peel, June 9, 1984. BS in Acctg., U. Ala., Birmingham, 1984. CPA, Ala. Auditor Ernst & Whinney, Birmingham, 1984—. Cons. bus. Jr. Achievement, Birmingham, 1986; youth counselor Luth. Ch. of Bestavia Hills, Birmingham, 1986—. Mem. Nat. Assn. Accts. (bd. dirs. 1985—), am. Inst. CPA's., Ala. Soc. CPA's., Am. Soc. Women Accts. (chairperson 1986—). Office: Ernst & Whinney 1800 First Nat So Natural Bldg Birmingham AL 35203

PEERENBOOM, SHARON KATHLEEN, state agency administrator; b. Salem, Oreg.. BA, U. Portland, 1979; MA in Mgmt., Willamette U., 1982. Analyst Oreg. Dept. Transp., Salem, 1983-85; analyst-project mgr. Oreg. Div. Adult and Family Services, Salem, 1986—. Mem. Nat. Assn. Female Execs.

PEETZ, MICHELE MARY, healthcare executive; b. Northampton, Mass., July 3, 1954; d. Michael Harold and Shirley Mae (Biladeau) McLaughlin; m. Raymond G. Peetz, Mar. 16, 1954; children: Ryan Matthew, Jennifer Lyn. BS cum laude, U. Mass., 1976. Real estate mgr. Kamins of Amherst, Mass., 1975-77; asst. nurse practitioner Amherst Med. Ctr., 1977-79; substitute tchr. Belcherteron (Mass.) Schs., 1980-82; office supr. Quality Care, Springfield, Mass., 1984; service dir. Norrell HealthCare, Sarasota, Fla., 1984-86; mem. ops. task force Norrell HealthCare, Sarasota, 1985-86, br. mgr., 1987—; tng. and devel. mgr. Norrell HealthCare, Atlanta, 1986-87. Home: 2532 Parma Ave Sarasota FL 33581 Office: Norrell Health Care 3663 Bee Ridge Rd Sarasota FL 33583

PEGO, TERESA, coating company executive; b. N.Y.C., Nov. 18, 1936; d. Jose Fernandez and Maria Teresa (Rocafort) P.; m. Paul C. Christensen, May 15, 1965 (div. 1983); children: Kirstine, Erik; m. Joseph A. Gross, Aug. 9, 1985. Grad. high sch., N.Y.C. Supr. Equitable Life Assurance, N.Y.C., 1955-68; setter Slide Ctr., Rutherford, N.J., 1982-87; owner Floortec Inc., Carlstadt, N.J., 1985—. Contbr. articles to profl. jours. Episcopalian. Office: Floortec 333 Hackensack St Carlstadt NJ 07072

PEI, PHYLLIS CECILE, pollution control administrator; b. Shanghai, People's Republic of China, Nov. 10, 1953; came to U.S., 1970; d. Y.K. and Claudia (Lee) P.; m. Sanders B. Cox, June 14, 1986. BA in Chemistry, U. Dallas, 1975, MBA in Bus., 1980; MA in Biochemistry, U. Tex. Health Sci. Ctr., 1977. Purchasing buyer, supr. Mostek Corp., Dallas, 1980-82; chem. support sec. HEAD Signetics Corp., Albuquerque, 1982-84; mgr. environ. affairs Signetics Corp., Sunnyvale, Calif., 1984-85; mgr. pollution control Sandia Nat. Labs., Albuquerque, 1985—. Vol. Project Share, Albuquerque, 1987—; mem. Albuquerque/Bernalillo County Air Quality Control Bd., 1988—. Mem. Hazardous Waste Fedn. (bd. dirs. 1986-87, pres.-elect 1987—), N.Mex. Hazardous Waste Mgmt. Soc. (chairperson program com. 1982-83, treas. 1986-87, chairperson membership com. 1987—). Office: Sandia Nat Labs PO Box 5800 Div 3314 Albuquerque NM 87185

PEIFFER, ELIZABETH ANNE, computer systems analyst, consultant, auditor; b. Syracuse, N.Y., Dec. 5, 1954; d. Robert Victor and Marion Alice (Jagelle) P.; m. Gerald Lee Brickey, June 9, 1978. BA in Econs., Acctg. and Psychology, Coll. Holy Cross, 1976. CPA, Oreg., Ill.; cert. info. systems auditor. Mem. audit staff Arthur Young & Co., Chgo., 1976-78; sr. auditor, computer auditor Arthur Young & Co., Portland, Oreg., 1978-80; corp. auditor EDP Orbanco Fin. Services Corp., Portland, Oreg., 1980-82, systems audit mgr., 1982-83, asst. v.p., asst. dir. auditing, 1983-84; computer audit mgr. Coopers & Lybrand, Portland, 1984—; instr. Concordia Coll., Portland, 1986-87; cons. 1000 Friends of Oreg., Portland, 1981; lectr. in field. Developer, editor EDP ednl. materials. Econ. adviser Portland Energy Commn., 1980; fundraiser Northwest Artists Workshop, Portland, 1984; adviser St. Mary's Acad., Portland, 1986—. Mem. Am. Inst. CPA's, Inst. Internal Auditors (bd. dirs. 1988—), Oreg. Soc. CPA's (chair 1987-88, bd. dirs. 1988—), EDP Auditors Assn. (chpt. pres. 1985-86, regional asst. v.p. 1986-88, regional v.p. 1988—), Phi Beta Kappa. Office: Coopers & Lybrand 2700 1st Interstate Tower Portland OR 97201

PEIRCE, CAROL MARSHALL, educator; b. Columbia, Mo., Feb. 1, 1922; d. Charles Hamilton and Helen Emily (Davault) Williams; m. Brooke Peirce, July 12, 1952. A.B., Fla. State U., 1942; M.A. (McGregor fellow, DuPont fellow), U. Va., 1943; Ph.D. (Harvard tutor, Anne Radcliffe traveling fellow), Harvard U., 1951. Head English dept. Fairfax Hall, Waynesboro, Va., 1943-44; instr. English Cedar Crest Coll., Allentown, Pa., 1944-46, Harvard U., 1952-53; asst. dean instrn. Radcliffe Coll., Cambridge, 1950-53; head English extension home study U. Va., Charlottesville, 1953-54; asst. dir. admissions Goucher Coll., Towson, Md., 1956-62; chmn. dept., prof. English U. Balt., 1968—, gen. edn. core coordinator, 1985-87, Disting. teaching prof. Coll. Liberal Arts, 1981-82, chmn. humanities div., 1972-79; chmn. bd. New Poets Series, 1975-85; vis. scholar Lucy Cavendish Coll., U. Cambridge, Eng., 1977-78. Author: (with Brooke Peirce) A Study of Literary Types and an Introduction to English Literature from Chaucer to the Eighteenth Century, 1954, A Study of Literary Types and an Introduction to English Literature from the Eighteenth Century to the Present, 1954; editor: (with Lawrence Markert) On Miracle Ground: Second Lawrence Durrell Conference Proceedings, 1986; contbr. essays to: Poe and Our Times, 1986, Critical Essays on Lawrence Durrell, 1987; assoc. editor: Deus Loci: The Lawrence Durrell Journal, 1986—. Mem. Edgar Allen Poe Soc. (dir. 1973—), Lawrence Durrell Soc. (nat. pres. 1980-82), MLA, Md. Assn. English Depts., Phi Beta Kappa, Chi Delta Phi, Phi Alpha Theta, Phi Kappa Phi. Home: 705 Warren Rd Cockeysville MD 21030 Office: U Balt Dept English Baltimore MD 21201

PEIRCE, ELLEN RUST, law educator; b. Washington, May 5, 1949; d. Wentworth W. and Ethel M. (Byrne) P.; m. Daniel A. Graham, June 10, 1978; 1 child, William. B.A., Bryn Mawr Coll., 1971; J.D., Duke U., 1976. Bar: N.Y. 1977, D.C. 1977, N.C. 1979. Assoc., Mudge Rose Guthrie & Alexander, N.Y.C., 1976-78, Powe Porter Alphin & Whichard, Durham, N.C., 1978-80; assoc. prof. law U. N.C. Sch. Bus. Adminstrn., Chapel Hill, 1980-85, assoc. prof., 1986—; legal cons. IBM, 1983-84, various software cos., N.C.; counsel SSI, Durham, 1978-84. Contbr. articles and chpts. to legal jours.; editor Duke Legal Research and Writing, 1975-76; reviewer legal pub. cos. Research grantee Dept. Transportation, 1987. Mem. ABA, N.Y. State Bar Assn., D.C. Bar Assn., N.C. Bar Assn., Am. Bus. Law Assn., Southeastern Regional Bus. Law Assn. (sec. 1981-82, v.p. 1982-83, pres.-elect 1983-84, pres. 1984-85). Episcopalian. Home: 1 Southampton Pl Durham NC 27705 Office: U NC Sch Bus Adminstrn Chapel Hill NC 27514

PEISER, JUDITH LOUISE, film maker, executive director media products and special events; b. Cleve., June 4, 1945; d. Louis Ephraim and Celia (Kabakoff) P. BA, U. Ill, 1967; MA, Memphis State U., 1970. Co-founder, exec. dir. Ctr. for So. Folklore, Memphis, 1972—. Author: American Folklore Films and Videotapes: An Index, A Catalogue, vol. II, Images of the South: Visits with Eudora Welty and Walker Evans; editor films including Gravel Springs Fife and Drum, 1971, Ray Lum: Mule Trader, 1972, Black Delta Religion, 1974, Mississippi Delta Blues, 1974; editor, producer films Green Valley Grandparents, 1972, Fannie Bell Chapman: Gospel Singer, 1975; producer films Four Women Artists, 1977, Leon "Peck" Clark: Basketmaker, 1978, Hush Hoggies Hush: Tom Johnson's Praying Pigs, 1979, Bottle Up & Go, 1980, If Beale Street Could Talk, 1983. Active Leadership Memphis; mem. Memphis, Shelby County Film, Tape and Music Commn., 1985—. Recipient over 50 film awards including Am. Film Festival, Ann Arbor Film Festival, Athens Internat. Film Festival, Balt. Film Festival, Chgo. Internat. Film Festival, Columbus Film Festival, Council on Internat. Non-theatrical Events, Festival die Popoli, Midwest Film Conference, Sinking Creek Film Celebration; named Woman of Achievement, City of Memphis, 1985, one of 272 people under 40 who are changing Am., Esquire Mag., 1984. Mem. Am. Folklore Soc., Tenn. Folklore Soc. Democrat. Jewish. Office: Ctr So Folklore 1216 Peabody Memphis TN 38104

PEKAR, CATHERINE DUSEK, nurse; b. Chgo., Aug. 4, 1951; d. Anton J. and Rose Mary (Zielonka) Dusek; B.S. in Nursing, St. Xavier Coll., Chgo., 1973; M.S.N., Loyola U., Chgo., 1978; R.N.; m. Dennis J. Pekar, May 28, 1978. Staff nurse birth unit and women's ambulatory care clinic Rush-Presbyn.-St. Luke's Med. Center, Chgo., 1973-75; maternal/child health instr. Meml. Hosp. DuPage County, Elmhurst, Ill., 1975-77; head nurse, clin. nursing instr. U. Chgo. Med. Center, 1977-80; adminstrv. dir. maternal/child nursing St. Joseph Hosp., Chgo., 1980-87, cons. women's health care, also mem. adv. bd. for women's health, 1988; cons. Ill. Div. of Services for Crippled Children; instr. LaMaze childbirth edn., 1980—, CPR instr. Am. Heart Assn., 1980— . Mem. Internat. Childbirth Edn. Assn., Am. Nurses Assn., Nurses Assn. of Am. Coll. Ob-Gyn (vice-chair Ill. sect.), Parent and Child Edn. Soc., Midwest Parentcraft Center, Ill. Soc. Nurse Adminstrs., Ill. Nurses Assn. (dist. program chmn. 1976-77), Sigma Theta Tau. Roman Catholic.

PELÁEZ, ARMANTINA R., religious educator; b. Havana, Cuba, Apr. 21, 1948; came to U.S., 1962; d. Armando and Argentina (Pérez) P. BA, Ladycliff Coll., Highland Falls, N.Y., 1973; MA in Religious Edn., Fordham U., 1977; Cert. Tng. in Psychoanalysis and Psychotherapy, Weschester Inst., 1987. Asst. child care worker St. Joseph's Home of Peekskill (N.Y.), 1968-70; assoc. dir. religious edn. St. Joseph's of Palisades Parish, Western N.Y. and N.J., 1973-75; sec. evangelization Diocese of Paterson (N.J.) Roman Cath. Ch., 1975-80; Hispanic Apostolate coordinator, asst. adminstr. to vicar of Hispanic ministries 1980-84; spl. catechetical project coordinator Cath. Conf. U.S. Dept. Edn., Washington, 1984—; vol. team mem. pastoral Hispanic youth ministry St. Augustine's Parish, Union City, N.J., 1979—; cons. Latin Am. Program Wilson Ctr., Washington, 1982, Ctr. for Applied in Apostolate, 1981; authorized instr. parent and tchr. effectiveness tng., N.J.; psychotherapist Palisade Counseling Ctr., Rutherford, N.J., 1982—, Lakeland Counseling Ctr., Dover, N.J., 1985-87. Contbr. numerous articles in English and Spanish. Chmn., nat. bd. dirs. Nat. Planning Council, 1974-75. Mem. Nat. Assn. for Women Religious, Found. of Thanatology (assoc.), Am. Soc. Psychical Research, Las Hermanas Nat. Orgn. (N.Y. coordinator 1970-72, N.Y. Upstate coordinator 1972-73, N.J. coordinator 1978-79), Nat. Assn. Advancement of Psychoanalysis and Am. Bds. for Accreditation and Certification Inc., Nat. Counseling and Devel. Assn. Clubs: N.Y. Road Runners, N.Y. Race Walking; N.J. Shore Athletic, N.J. Athletics Congress. Office: 1312 Massachusetts Ave NW Washington DC 20005

PELAGALLI, MARY PERRIN, computer software company executive; b. Passaic, N.J., Dec. 4, 1954; d. George Edward and Eileen Clare (McGinnis) Perrin; m. Paul Pelagalli, July 8, 1978. BA magna cum laude, SUNY, Albany, 1977. Editor Jour. Reading Behavior, Albany, 1978-80; analyst Computing Ctr. SUNY, Albany, 1981-82; pub. relations officer N.Y. State Social Services, Albany, 1982-83; dir. publs. The Software Group, Ballston Lake, N.Y., 1983-84, dir. original equipment mgr. sales and devel., 1985-87; mktg. rep. IBM, Albany, 1987—; guest lectr. SUNY, Albany, 1987. Author: Enable System Overview, 1984; editor: Enable Documentation, 1984. Mem. Tax Execs. Inst. (guest speaker 1987), Sigma Delta Pi. Democrat. Roman Catholic. Home: 109 Fernbank Ave Delmar NY 12054 Office: IBM 80 State St Albany NY 12207

PELHAM, FRAN O'BYRNE, writer, teacher; b. Phila., Oct. 16, 1939; d. Frederick Thomas and Frances Rebecca (Johns) O'Byrne; m. Donald Lacey Pelham; children: Mary Frances, Michael. BA, Holy Family Coll., 1967; M in English Edn., Trenton U., 1974; postgrad., U. Pa. Cert. secondary tchr. Tchr. Sch. Dist. Bristol (Pa.) Twp., 1967-70; feature writer various publs., Phila. and others, 1980—; prof., dir. Writing Ctr. Holy Family Coll., Phila., 1982—; dir. tech. communications Internat. Chem. Co., Phila., 1985—; speaker, workshop leader various orgns. Author: Search for Atocha Treasure, 1988, Philadelphia for Children, 1988; contbr. articles to mags. Bd. dirs. Home and Sch. Assn., Jenkintown, Pa., 1983; mem. Jenkingown Arts Festival, 1984, Campus Ministry Team Holy Family Coll., Phila., 1986—, Phila. Children's Reading Roundtable, Phila. Recipient Citation Mayor's Commn., 1988. Mem. Nat. League Am. Pen Women (br. pres. 1982-84), Phila. Writers' Conf. (bd. dirs. 1982-86), Pi Lambda Theta. Republican. Roman Catholic. Office: Internat Chem Co 2628 N Mascher St Philadelphia PA 19133

PELL, MARY CHASE (CHASEY), civic worker; b. Binghamton, N.Y., May 23, 1915; d. Charles Orlando and Mary (Lane) Chase; m. Wilbur F. Pell, Jr., Sept. 14, 1940; children: Wilbur F., Charles Chase. BA, Smith Coll., 1937. Case worker Binghamton State Hosp., 1937; sociology tchr. Charles W. Wilson Meml. Hosp., Johnson City, N.Y., 1938; commentator travel and industry, sta. WSVL, Shelbyville, Ind., 1962-67. Contbr. articles to publs. Chmn. Ind. Fund Raising Com. for Smith Coll., Indpls., 1961; bd. dirs. Nat. Mental Health Assn., 1961-79, pres. 1976-77; pres. Ind. Mental Health Meml. Found., Indpls., 1964-65, Mental Health Assn. Ind., Indpls., 1962-63; commr. Ind. Mental Health Planning Commn., Indpls., 1964-65; mem. Central Ind. Task Force on Mental Health Planning, 1965-66; mem. Ind. Com. on Nursing, Indpls., 1965-66, Central Ind. Regional Mental Health Planning Com., 1968; chmn. Manpower Conf. on Mental Health, Washington, 1969; del. Ind. Republican Conv., 1951; vice chmn. Shelbyville Rep. Com., 1951; sec. Ind. Com. for Rockefeller, 1969-70; pres. Indpls. Smith Coll. Club, 1969-70; participant Nat. Health Forum of Nat. Health Council, N.Y.C., 1971; pres. Mental Health Assn. Ill., Springfield, 1975; mem. Gov.'s Commn. for Revision of Mental Health Code Ill., 1975-76; v.p. for N.Am., World Fedn. for Mental Health, 1977-87; bd. dirs. Vis. Nurse Assn. Evanston (Ill.), 1975-87, v.p. 1981-84, pres., 1984-86; community mental health adviser Jr. League of Chgo., 1979-83; mem. Ill. Guardianship and Advocacy Commn., 1978-86, chmn., 1981; mem. adv. com. to sect. on psychiatry and the law, Rush-Presbyn.-St. Luke's Med. Ctr., Chgo., 1978-86; gov. Task Force on Future of Mental Health in Ill., 1986-87; mem. home health adv. com. to Dept. Pub. Health, State of Ill., 1982-87; pres. Mental Health Assn. Chgo., 1983-84; pres. Smith Coll. Alumnae of Chgo., 1984-86; mem. Women's Bd. Northwestern U., Aux. of Evanston and Glenbrook Hosps., University Guild of Evanston, Jr. League Evanston, pres. Ind. Lawyers' Wives, Indpls., 1959-60; treas. Nat. Lawyers' Wives, 1961-62; mem. commn. to rev. and revise Ill. Mental Health Code, 1987—. Recipient Outstanding Citizen award Shelby County C. of C., 1959-60, Outstanding Vol. of Yr. award Indpls. Jr. League, 1962, Leadership award Mental Health Assn. Ind., 1971, Arts and Humanities award, Shelbyville Rotary Club, 1981; named One of Ten Most Newsworthy Women In Ind., Indpls. News, 1962, Disting. Leader in Vol. Mental Health Movement, Ill. Ho. of Reps., 1976, Miss. Col., 1976, Ala. Lt. Gov., 1980. Presbyterian. Clubs: Fortnightly (Chgo.); Garden of Evanston, Jr. League of Evanston. Home: 1427 Hinman Ave Evanston IL 60201

PELL, PYRMA DAPHNE TILTON, civic worker; b. N.Y.C., Feb. 5, 1909; d. Newell Whiting and Mildred Olive (Bigelow) Tilton; student Queens Coll., London, 1921-26, Kunst Akademie, Vennia, Austria, 1927-28; m. John Howland Gibbs Pell, Sept. 3, 1929; children—Sarah Gibbs, John Bigelow. Active in preservation and restoration Fort Ticonderoga, N.Y., 1950—, also coordinator spl. events, 1950—; treas. Friends of Chung Ang U., Korea, 1965-71, recipient spl. award, 1971. Recipient First award Historic Preservation, Garden Club Am., 1973. Mem. Am. Acad. Poets (co-founder), Colonial Dames Am., Assn. Churchill Fellows of Westminster Coll., Alpha Xi Delta. Christian Scientist. Club: Colony. Other: Pelican Place Bellevue Ave Newport RI 02840

PELLEGRINO, DONNA MARIE, educator; b. Camden, N.J., June 23, 1953; d. Rocco Frank and Concetta (Perfetto) P.; m. Karl M. Wielgus, June 8, 1984. Cert. RN, Our Lady of Lourdes, 1976; BA, Rutgers U., 1979; EdM, Temple U., 1980, EdD, 1985. Mgr. Medox, Phila., 1981-83; adminstr. Temp. Nursing Service, Phila., 1983-84; pres. Unltd. Productivity Assn., Moorestown, N.J., 1984—; asst. prof. Temple U., Phila., 1985—, Beaver Coll., Glenside, Pa., 1986—; cons. Lausanne Inst., Unionville, Pa., 1986—, Am. Dairy Assn., Phila., 1987. Bd. dirs. LWV, Moorestown, 1985—; mem. Childbirth Edn. Assn., South Jersey, 1985—, Caesarean Prevention Movement, 1986—. Democrat. Baptist. Home and Office: 315 S Lenola Rd Moorestown NJ 08057

PELLERIN, ANNETTE MONKS, insurance underwriter; b. El Cajon, Calif., Aug. 30, 1963; d. Gerald Paul and Ruth Ellen (Brock) Monks; m. William Louis Pellerin, Jan. 4, 1986; 1 child, Blake Thomas. BA in Speech Communication, U. Houston, 1985. Underwriter Jerry Monks-Mr. Ins., Houston, 1978—; v.p. Tax Service Inc., instr. aerobics, Houston, 1985—; coach cheerleading Marian Christian High Sch., Houston, 1982—. Tchr. St. Vincent de Paul Sunday sch., Houston, 1986—; Rep. precinct worker, Houston, 1986—. Mem. Aerobic Fitness Assn. Am. (cert.), Nat. Assn. Female Execs., Profl. Bail Agts. of U.S. (asst. to pres.). Home: 8423 Lorrie Houston TX 77025 Office: Mr Ins 4189 Bellaire Blvd #201 Houston TX 77025

PELLERIN, BEVERLY JEAN, product manager; b. Meriden, Conn., Nov. 2, 1951; d. George William and Dorothy Marie (Wayland) P. B.S.Ed., U. Conn., 1973. Band tchr. Valley Regional High Sch., Deep River, Conn., 1973-75; office mgr. Consol. Cigar Co., Glastonbury, Conn., 1975-80; foreman I and II, 1980-82; product mgr. Marshall Industries, Wallingford, Conn., 1983—. Mem. Nat. Assn. Female Execs. Roman Catholic. Club: Goebel Collectors. Avocations: horseback riding, aerobics, reading. Home: 532 Main St Portland CT 06480

PELLEY-FERULLO, SHARON LEE, administrative executive; b. Framingham, Mass., Dec. 16, 1957; d. Richard A. Pelley and Ruth E. (Mercer) Dusseault; m. Michael F. Ferullo, Nov. 16, 1985; children: Christopher A. Pelley, Michael John Ferullo. BA in Psychology, Framingham State Coll., 1984. Sec. Sun Life Assurance Co., Wellesley, Mass., 1976-78; field sales sec. Ransco Industries, Inc., Medway, Mass., 1984-87; prin. Computerized Bus. Services, Franklin, Mass., 1987—. Home: 264 Dailey Dr Franklin MA 02038

PELLICCIOTTI, PATRICIA M., financial analyst, management consultant; b. Phila.. V.p., dir. regional sales EGR Commnications Inc., N.Y.C., 1975-77; pres. Pellicciotti Assocs., Northfield, N.J., 1977-83; registered rep. IDS/Am. Express, Mpls., 1981-85; v.p. Herzog, Heine, Geduld Inc., N.Y.C., 1984-85; pres. Fin. Cons. Group Inc., Phila., 1985—; registered rep. Rothschild Registry Inc., N.Y.C., 1986—; Founder, bd. dirs. Woman to Woman Seminars. Producer, hostess radio talk show WWDB-FM Woman to Woman, Phila.; author: Renting Money. Bd. dirs. Girl Scouts U.S. Mem. Mktg. Communications Execs. Internat. (past v.p.), Nat. Assn. Securities Dealers (registered rep.), Nat. Econ. Round Table, SBA (adv. Pres. Carter's Interagy. Task Force for Women, cons. Active Corp Execs.). Club: Toastmasters. Office: Fin Cons Group PO Box 59317 Philadelphia PA 19102

PELLMAN, RENEE GREENBERG, psychotherapist; b. N.Y.C., May 12, 1936; d. Irving and Dorothy (Sherman) Greenberg; m. Frederic E. Freedgood, 1988. B.A., Brandeis U., 1954; M.A., Columbia U., 1958; Ph.D., Rutgers U., 1980; children—Amy, David. Diplomate in clin. social work; cert. supr. mediators. Pvt. practice psychotherapy, sex therapy, N.Y.C., 1965—; sr. psychotherapist Bronx-Lebanon Hosp. Center, Dept. Psychiatry, N.Y.C., 1966-69; clin. supr., asst. dir. Big Brothers Residence, N.Y.C., 1969-71; cons. Office of Child Devel., U.S. Govt., 1969-73; clin. supr. Youth Services, Jewish Family Service, N.Y.C., 1971-76; sr. family therapist Family Mental Health Clinic, Jewish Family Service, N.Y.C., 1971-76; lectr. and cons. in field. Fellow Am. Orthopsychiatry, Acad. Cert. Social Workers, N.Y. State Soc. Clin. Social Work; mem. Am. Group Psychotherapy Assn., Am. Assn. Family Counselors and Mediators, Inc., Eastern Assn. Sex Therapists, Eastern Group Psychotherapy Assn. Contbr. articles to profl. publs. Office: 111 E 80th St Apt 7B New York NY 10014

PELOSI, LORRAINE MARY, educational administrator; b. N.Y.C., Apr. 8, 1941; d. Joshua and Elizabeth Orgel (Deming) Esposito; BS, Pace Coll., 1971; m. William Demarest, Jan. 13, 1962 (dec. 1969); children: William, Susan, Robert; m. Andrew Pelosi, Apr. 7, 1971; children: Gina, Nicole. Pvt. tutor, Thornwood, N.Y., 1969; nursery sch. asst. Pace Little Sch./Pace Cottage, Pleasantville, N.Y., 1970; tchr. emotionally disturbed Pleasantville (N.Y.) Cottage Sch., 1970-73; founder, dir., tchr. Gingerbread Nursery Sch., St. Petersburg, Fla., 1972—; founder, dir. Wellington Sch., St. Petersburg, 1974; founder, past pres. Gingerbread Nursery Sch., Seminole, Fla., 1978—; pres. Gingerbread-Wellington Schs., St. Petersburg, 1975—; founder Gingerbread Nursery Sch. Azalea, St. Petersburg, 1982-85, Gingerbread-Wellington Sch.-Bardmoor, Seminole, 1983; founder, v.p. Gingerbread Sch., Carillon, 1987. Lectr., cons. Mem. Redeemer Luth. Chanod Choir, LaVictoria Mission, Santo Domingo, 1987, 88. Mem. So. Assn. Children Under Six Pinellas Assn. Children Under Six, Pinellas Assn. Acad. Non-Public Schs., Women's Forum (treas.). Home: 931 79 St S Saint Petersburg FL 33707 Office: 4355 Central Ave Saint Petersburg FL 33713

PELOSI, NANCY, congresswoman; b. Balt., 1941; d. Thomas J. D'Alesandro Jr.; m. Paul Pelosi; children: Nancy Corinne, Christine, Jacqueline, Paul, Alexandra. Grad., Trinity Coll. Former chmn. Calif. State Dem. Com., 1981; committeewoman Dem. Nat. Com., 1976, 80, 84; elec. to U.S. Congress from 5th dist. Calif. 1987; fin. chmn. Dem. Senatorial Campaign Com., 1987. Office: Offices of House Members care The Postmaster Washington DC 20515

PELTIER, LINDA JEANNE, lawyer, educator; b. St. Louis, Nov. 29, 1948; d. Louis Cook and Louisa Harriet (Russell) Peltier; m. James Edward Britain, June 23, 1979. BA in Polit. Sci., Bucknell U., 1970; JD, George Washington U., 1973. Bar: D.C. 1973, Pa. 1975, U.S. Ct. Claims 1974. Assoc. Fried, Frank, Harris et al, Washington, 1973-74; staff atty. Susquehanna Legal Services, Williamsport, Pa., 1974-77; asst. prof. law U. Ky., Lexington, 1977-79; asst., then assoc. prof. law New Eng. Sch. Law, Boston, 1979-82; assoc. prof. law, U. Cin., 1982-86, adj. prof., 1986-87; chmn. univ. jud. council, 1983-86; mem. support group Ctr. for Law and Human Values, N.Y.C., 1983—; coordinator, creator Hunger and Law Conf., Cin., 1983, other confs. Contbr. articles to profl. jours; editor-in-chief Vol. 41, George Washington U. Law Rev., 1972-73. Ending hunger briefing leader The Hunger Project, San Francisco, 1984; mem. mental health/mental retardation adv. bd. Union-Snyder Community Counseling Service, Lewisburg, Pa., 1975-77; advisor Law Explorer Posts 100/830, Williamsport, Pa. and Lexington, Ky., 1975-79. Jr. Year Abroad grantee Inst. Am. Univs., France, 1968-69. Mem. ABA. Democrat. Episcopalian. Home: 108 Beaufort Ln Columbus OH 43214 Office: U Cin Coll Law Cincinnati OH 45221

PELTON, SANDRAANN ZIRKELBACH, physical therapist, health care administrator; b. Erie, Pa., Nov. 11, 1955; d. Robert Eugene Zirkelbach and Lois Marie (Weber) Calhoun; 1 dau., Tiffany Louise. B.S. in Phys. Therapy, U. Tex. Med. Br., Galveston, 1977. Lic. phys. therapist Tex. Bd. Phys. Therapy Examiners. Phys. therapist Rutherford Gen. Hosp., Mesquite, Tex., 1977-78; dir. phys. therapy Fairfield (Tex.) Meml. Hosp., 1978-79; regional dir. phys. therapy TPT, Inc., Houston, 1979-81, v.p. phys. therapy, 1981-82, exec. v.p., 1983-84, pres., 1984-85; owner, pres. RCSA, 1985—; mem. adv. com. Houston Community Coll., 1982-85. Mem. Am. Phys. Therapy Assn., Tex. Phys. Therapy Assn. (chmn. pub. relations com.), Nat. Assn. Female Execs., U. Tex. Med. Br. Alumni Assn., Republican. Roman Catholic. Home: 1622 Plantation Richmond TX 77469 Office: RCSA 10701 Corporate Dr Suite 190 Stafford TX 77477

PELTON, VIRGINIA LUE, small business owner; b. Utica, Kans., Apr. 15, 1928; d. Forrest Selby and Nellie (Simmons) Meier; m. Theodore Trower King, Jr., Oct. 27, 1956 (div. 1970); m. Harold Marcel Pelton, July 11, 1970; children: Mary Virginia Joyner, Diana Jean. Student, Kans. State U., 1946-47, Ft. Hays U., 1947-48, Washington U., St. Louis, 1950-51. Instr. Patricia Stevens Modeling Sch., Kansas City, Mo., 1948-50; model various cos., Calif. and N.Y., 1951-53; fashion cons. Giorgio, Beverly Hills, Calif., 1967-68, Charles Gallay, Beverly Hills, 1975-77, Dorso's, Beverly Hills, 1977-79; buyer, mgr. giftware Slavick's, Laguna Hills, Calif., 1980-83; owner P.J. Secretarial Services, Laguna Hills, 1980—; v.p. H.P. Fin. Inc., Laguna Hills, 1983—. Editor Profl. Network newsletter, 1980—. Sec. Leukemia Soc. Am., Santa Ana, 1985—; mem. Laguna Beach Art Mus., 1986—. Mem. Profl. Network Assn. (sec. 1986—), Market Plus The Consumer Network, Saddleback C. of C., Kappa Delta. Republican. Methodist. Club: Laguna Hills. Home: 24942 Georgia Sue Dr Laguna Hills CA 92653

PELZ, CAROLINE DUNCOMBE, retired educational administrator; b. White Plains, N.Y.; d. David Sanford and Helena (Ebert) Duncombe; A.B., Barnard Coll., 1940; m. Edward Joseph Pelz, July 11, 1942; children—Caroline Pelz Elbow, Margaret L. (dec.), Patricia Pelz Hart, Sanford M. Adjustments supr. R.H. Macy & Co., N.Y.C., 1940-42; admissions interviewer Barnard Coll., 1960-63; alumni sec. Allen-Stevenson Sch., N.Y.C., 1967-70, admissions asst., 1969-70; adminstrv. asst. Ednl. Records Bur., N.Y.C., 1970-72; dir. admissions Grace Church Sch., N.Y.C., 1972-87. Trustee Barnard Coll., 1963-67. Mem. Barnard Coll. Alumnae Assn. (pres. 1963-66), Woman's Nat. Farm and Garden Assn. (scholarship chmn. N.Y.C. met. br. 1981—), English-Speaking Union. Republican. Episcopalian. Home: Box 395 S Main St Berlin NY 12022 Other: 55 E 87th St New York NY 10128

PEMBERTON, JANETTE MATTHEW, language educator; b. Trinidad, W.I.; came to U.S., 1961, naturalized, 1974; d. Cecil E. and A. Elaine Matthew; m. Sandi Macpherson Pemberton. BA, Howard U., 1965, MA, 1967; D of Arts, Cath. U. Am., 1978. Asst. instr. Howard U., Washington, 1967; instr. Bowie State Coll., 1968; asst. prof. Prince George's Community Coll., 1968-71, assoc. prof. dept. English, 1971-82, prof., 1982—, mem. acad. standards and regulations com., 1979, chmn. Afro-Am. studies com., 1976-78, mem. affirmative action com., 1973-74; guest instr. Cath. U. Am., Washington, 1975-78. Author: Transcendatalism and the Promise of Educational Reform, 1980, The Teaching of Afro-American Poetry: An Aesthetic Approach, 1978, Discussions on Aristotle's Ethics: Implications for Teachers and Administrators, 1980. Nat. Teaching fellow, 1968; recipient Teaching award Cath. U. Am., 1975, Community Leadership award, 1976, Disting. Women's award, 1980, Outstanding Service and Achievement award, 1981, medal of honor, 1985; named to Hall of Fame for contbns. to edn., 1985, Bd. Govs., ABI, 1986. Mem. Washington Soc. Performing Arts, Nat. Symphony Orch., Internat. Platform Assn., Nat. Council Tchrs. English, Edn. Writers Assn., MLA, Am. Assn. Advancement of Humanities, AAUP, Nat. Soc. Lit. and Arts. Seventh-day Adventist. Office: PO Box 1326 Bethesda MD 20817

PEMBERTON, JOANNE JODY, legal administrator; b. Norwalk, Conn., Feb. 19, 1952; d. Joseph J. Jr. and Sandra J. (Constantino) Smith; m. Frank R. Pemberton, Apr. 8, 1978. BS in Elem. Edn., Western Conn. State U., 1973; postgrad., U. New Haven, 1975-77. With adminstrn. research and devel. Pitney Bowes Inc., Stamford, Conn., 1975-80; mgr. office Starting Line, Saratoga Springs, N.Y., 1980-82; v.p. AMI, Computer Cons., Saratoga Springs, 1982-85; administr. legal Ferrara, Jones and Sipperly, Saratoga Springs, 1985—. Mem. Nat. Bus. Women's Leadership Assn., Saratoga County Mock Trial Program (co-ordinator 1986—), Nat. Assn. Female Execs., Saratoga Springs C. of C. (chmn. exec. dialogue com. 1982—). Republican. Roman Catholic. Home: 27 Northway Ct Saratoga Springs NY 12866 Office: Ferrara Jones and Sipperly 179 West Ave PO Box 396 Saratoga Springs NY 12866

PENA, ANTONIA MURILLO, physician, radiologist; b. San Diego, July 18, 1946; d. Blas and Elvira (Murillo) Pena. B.A., Loma Linda U., Riverside, Calif., 1968; M.D., 1973. Diplomate Nat. Bd. Radiology. Intern, White Meml. Med. Ctr., Los Angeles, 1973-74, resident, 1974-77; radiologist Paradise Valley Hosp., National City, Calif., 1978-79; neuroradiology fellow Los Angeles County-U.So. Calif. Med. Ctr., 1977-78, 79-80; radiologist Arlington Radiology Med. Group, Riverside, Calif., 1980—; attending staff Riverside Gen. Hosp. U. Med. Ctr., 1980—; assoc. staff Parkview Community Hosp., 1980—; med. dir. Magnetic Resonance Imaging Ctr., Parkview Community Hosp., 1985—; cons. radiologist Computerized Diagnostic Med. Group of Riverside, 1980—; cons. Veitch Student Health Ctr., Riverside, 1980—. Mem. Radiol. Soc. N.Am., Am. Coll. Radiology, Calif. Radiol. Soc., AMA, Calif. Med. Assn., Am. Assn. Women Radiologists, Inland Radiology Soc., Am. Soc. Neuroradiology (sr.), Riverside County Med. Soc. Republican. Seventh-Day Adventist. Office: 9851 Magnolia Ave Riverside CA

PEÑA, HEATHER MARIA, internist; b. North Hampton, Mass., Sept. 30, 1955; d. Cesareo Dennis and Eloise Verna (Morrison) P. BS summa cum laude, Tufts U., 1977; MD, Harvard U., 1981. Intern, resident in internal medicine UCLA Hosp. and Clinics, 1981-84; staff physician Woodview Calabasas (Calif.) Hosp., 1983—, Oceanview Med. Group at Pritikin Long Ctr., Santa Monica, Calif., 1984—. Mem. Am. Heart Assn. Epidemiology Council. Mem. Am. Coll. Physicians (assoc.), Harvard Med. Hamilton-Hunt Soc., Phi Beta Kappa. Democrat. Office: Oceanview Med Group 1910 Ocean Front Walk Santa Monica CA 90405

PENA, MICHI E., technical consultant; b. Chgo., July 16, 1955; d. Severo George and Mildred M. (Salmeron) P.; B.A., North Park Coll., 1975; M.B.A., Roosevelt U., 1978; cert in acctg, Northwestern U., 1988. Office mgr., bookkeeper Airways Broadcasting Sales, Niles, Ill., 1974-76; systems engr. IBM, Chgo., 1977-82; sr. systems engr. Paradyne Corp., Des Plaines, Ill., 1982-87; systems cons. Micro Tempus Corp., 1987. Mem. Data Processing Mgmt. Assn., Nat. Assn. Female Execs., NOW, ACLU, Sierra Club. Home: 645 W Fullerton Pkwy Chicago IL 60614 Office: 625 N Michigan Ave Suite 500 Chicago IL 60611

PEÑA, MIRIAM, metallurgical engineer; b. East Chicago, Ind., Sept. 18, 1961; d. Pedro Thomas and Armanda (Miranda) P. BSE, Purdue U., 1984; MS in Mgmt., Marion Coll., 1987. Metall. trainee LaSalle Steel Co., Hammond, Ind., 1980-81; metall. engr. Sherry Labs., Muncie, Ind., 1984—. Mem. Am. Soc. for Metals (asst. sec. 1985-86), Soc. of Women Engrs., Nat. Assn. for Female Execs. Home: 1705 Norfield Dr Muncie IN 47304 Office: Sherry Labs 2203 S Madison Muncie IN 47302

PENCE, JUDITH ANN, oboist; b. Springfield, Ohio, Apr. 1, 1933; d. Lowell David and Thelma Marcellite (Kelsey) Isenbarger; B.M., Butler U., 1955; M.A., Ball State U., 1966; m. Homer Charles Pence, July 16, 1955; children—Terry Alan, Kristin Ilona. Oboist, Indpls. Symphony Orch., 1955-56, 71-85, soloist, 1972; instr. music Ball State U., 1958-70, Butler U., 1972-78; oboist Musical Arts Quintet, 1960-70, Sebago Long Lake Region Chamber Music, summers 1972 ; recitalist Carnegie Hall, 1963, 66; rec. artist Musical Arts Quintet, Indpls. Symphony Orch. Mem. Internat. Conf. Symphony and Opera Musicians.

PENDALL, MARIA HELGA, sales executive; b. Vienna, Austria, July 27, 1944; d. Francis Joseph and Helga Maria (Landesman) P. BA in English, Le Moyne Coll., 1968; postgrad., SUNY, Cortland, N.Y., 1968, 69. Cert. secondary edn. tchr., N.Y. Tchr. pub. schs. Syracuse, N.Y., 1968-72; sales rep. Atlantic-Richfield Co., Buffalo, 1972-73, Hills Bros. Coffee, Syracuse, 1973-79; sales supr. M&M/Mars Co., Syracuse, 1979—. Republican. Roman Catholic. Home: 8240 E Seneca St Manlius NY 13104 Office: M&M/Mars Co High St Hackettstown NJ 07840

PENDELL, JUDYTH WICKETT, insurance company executive; b. New Haven, Conn., Nov. 9, 1942; d. Kenneth Melvin and Anne Amrein (Crandall) Wickett; m. Thomas Gerow Pendell, Nov. 25, 1961 (div. Apr. 1979); children: Robert Gulian, Stephanie Wickett; m. Warren Bailey Azano, Jan. 16, 1988. BA, Vassar Coll., 1978; student, SUNY, Albany, 1978-80; M in Pub. and Pvt. Mgmt., Yale U., 1982. Commentator, producer Sta. WKIP Radio, Poughkeepsie, N.Y., 1974-80; mgr., dir. pub. policy issues analysis Aetna Life and Casualty, Hartford, Conn., 1982-87, asst. v.p. law, communications and pub. affairs, 1987—; mem. ins. adv. com. Inst. Civil Justice RAND Corp., Santa Monica, Calif., 1984—. Chmn. Dutchess County Exec.'s Task Force Emergency Housing, Poughkeepsie, 1980; pres., bd. dirs. Family Counseling Services, Poughkeepsie, 1969-73; bd. dirs. United Way of Dutchess County, Poughkeepsie, 1976-80, N.Y. State United Way, Albany, 1978-80. Mem. Issues Mgmt. Assn. Episcopalian. Club: Vassar (Hartford) (scholarship treas. 1985-87). Office: Aetna Life and Casualty 151 Farmington Ave Hartford CT 06107

PENDERGRAFT, KATRINA JONES, rehabilitation specialist; b. Atlanta, Feb. 19, 1959; d. Bernard Franklin and Virginia Inez (Stroud) Jones; m David William Pendergraft, Feb. 14, 1987. BS in Psychology, N. Ga. Coll., 1981; MA in Rehab. Counseling, U. Ga., 1985. Cert. ins. rehab. specialist and vocat. evaluator. Rehab. counselor Boatner Rehab. Counseling Services, Dalton, Ga., 1983-84; counsleor, evaluator Singer Vocat. Services Ctr., Atlanta, 1984-85, 85-86; rehab. specialist Underwriters Adjusting Co., Atlanta, 1985; indsl. specialist Union Meml. Hosp., Balt., 1986—; cons. in field; speaker in field. Mem. Vocat. Evaluation Work Adjustment Assn. (ethics chairperson 1984-86, state chpt. pres. 1986, mem. chairperson 1986—). Democrat. Club: Padonia Health and Fitness. Office: Union Meml Hosp 201 E Univ Pkwy Baltimore MD 21218

PENDLETON, BARBARA JEAN, banker; b. Independence, Mo., Aug. 14, 1924; d. Elmer Dean and Martha Lucille (Friess) P. Student, Cen. Mo. State Coll., 1942; D of Bus. Adminstrn. (hon.), Avila Coll., 1986. V.p. Grand Ave. Bank, Kansas City, Mo., 1962-76, exec. v.p., 1976-79; vice chmn. City Bank & Trust Co., Kansas City, 1979-82, chmn., 1982-83; exec. v.p. United Mo. Bank of Kansas City, 1983—; bd. dirs. City Bancshares, Inc., Kansas City. Vice chmn., mem. def. adv. com. Women in the Service, Washington, 1967-69; trustee City of Kansas City Employee Retirement Fund, Kansas City, 1985—. Recipient Matrix award Press Women, 1963, Wohelo award Campfire, Inc., 1979. Mem. Nat. Assn. Bank Women (pres. 1972-73), Am. Humanics, Inc. (hon.). Club: Cen. Exchange (Kansas City) (pres. 1983-84). Office: United Mo Bank Kansas City 1010 Grand Ave PO Box 226 Kansas City MO 64141

PENDLETON, CAROLYN M., banker; b. Park City, Utah, May 17, 1941; d. Charles Henry and Sarah Madge (Petersen) John; children—Rick L. Dowden, Randy S. Dowden. Student U. So. Calif., UCLA, El Camino Coll. With Crocker Bank, Los Angeles, 1966-72, br. mgr., 1972-75, ops. officer, 1975-79, asst. v.p., account officer, 1979-81; asst. v.p. product devel. First Interstate Bank, Los Angeles, 1981-83; sr. v.p., mgr. comml. banking services Calif. Fed. Savs. & Loan, Los Angeles, 1983—; banking advisor So. Calif. Regional Occupational Ctr., Torrance, Calif., 1973-81; instr. Jr. Achievement, Los Angeles, 1981-83; bd. govs. AIB, Los Angeles, 1971-75. Recipient Leadership award, YWCA, 1980. Mem. Nat. Assn. Female Execs, Nat. Assn. Bank Women, Big Sisters of Los Angeles. Republican. Mem. Ch. of Jesus Christ of Latter-day Saints. Club: Los Angeles Athletic. Avocation: running. Office: Calif Fed Savs & Loan 5680 Wilshire Blvd Plaza East Los Angeles CA 90036

PENDLETON, GAIL RUTH, newspaper editor, writer; b. Franklin, N.J., May 8, 1937; d. Waldo A. and Ruby (Bonnett) Rousset; m. John E. Tyler, Mar. 10, 1956 (div. 1978); children: Gwenneth, Victoria, Christine; m. Jeffrey P. Pendleton, Oct. 1, 1978. BA, Montclair (N.J.) State Coll., 1959; M in Div., Princeton (N.J.) Theol. Sem., 1973. Ordained minister Presbyn. Ch., 1974. Tchr. Epiphany Day Sch., Kaimuki, Oahu, Hawaii, 1956-58; editor Women's Sect. Daily Record, Morristown, N.J., 1959-62, reporter, 1963-65; tchr. Hardystown Twp. Sch., Franklin, 1968-69; asst. pastor First Presbyn. Ch., Sparta, N.J., 1973-74; reporter N.J. Herald, Newton, 1976-78, editor lifestyle sect., 1978—. Recipient Ruth Cheney Streeter award Planned Parenthood N.W. N.J., 1985. Mem. N.J. Press Assn. (family sect. layout award 1985, 87, 2d feature columns award 1986). Lodge: Zonta. Office: NJ Herald 2 Spring St Newton NJ 07860

PENDLETON, SYDNEY HARRISON, nurse researcher, writer; b. Pitts., Dec. 28, 1939; d. Dudley Digges and Mary Sutherland (Harrison) P.; student Wellesley Coll., 1956-58; diploma Episcopal Hosp. Sch. Nursing, Phila., 1961; B.S.N., U. Pa., 1963; M.Ed., Tchrs. Coll., Columbia U., 1971, Ed.D. (USPHS spl. predoctoral fellow), 1975; adopted children—Jennifer Page, Elizabeth Stockton, Beverly Sutherland. Staff nurse Bryn Mawr Hosp., 1961-62; asst. instr. Sch. Nursing, Hosp. U. Pa., 1962-64; instr. Women's Med. Coll. Hosp. Sch. Nursing, 1965-66; pvt. duty nurse, 1966-76; asso. prof. nursing, area coordinator adult health and illness grad. program La. State U., 1976-78; asso. prof., clin. coordinator rehab. nursing U. Ala., Birmingham, 1978-83; assoc. prof. Sch. Nursing, U. Mo.-Kansas City, 1983-87; nursing cons. and writer, Prairie Village, Kans., 1987—. Bd. dirs. Village de L'est Improvement Assn., New Orleans, 1977-78; founding mem. bd. dirs. and treas. Ala. Friends of Adoption, 1979-81. N.Y. State Regents fellow, 1968-69; USPHS trainee, 1963, 66-68. Fellow Am. Anthrop. Assn., Soc. Applied Anthropology; mem. Am. Nurses Assn., Am. Med. Writers Assn., Nat. Writers Union, The Author's League, Internat. Womes Writing Guild, Council Nurse Researchers, Nat. League Nursing, Nurses Coalition for Action in Politics, NOW, Nat. Women's Polit. Caucus, Kappa Delta Pi, Phi Delta Kappa, Pi Lambda Theta. Episcopalian. Author: (with others) Guia Para Investigaciones sobre el Dessarrollo de la Enfermeria en America Latina, 1974; contbr. articles to profl. publs. Home: 3112 W 73d St Prairie Village KS 66208

PENDLETON, THELMA BROWN, physical therapist, health service administrator; b. Rome, Ga., Jan. 30, 1911; d. John O. and Alma (Ingram) Brown; diploma Provident Hosp. Sch. Nursing, 1931; cert. Loyola U., 1942, Northwestern U., 1946; m. George W. Pendleton, Mar. 2, 1946; 1 son, George William. Pediatric nurse Rosenwald Found., Chgo., 1931-32; staff nurse Vis. Nurse Assn., Chgo., 1932-45; chief phys. therapy Provident Hosp., Chgo., 1946-55; phys. therapy cons. Parents Assn., Inc., Chgo., 1956-60; cons. United Cerebral Palsy of Greater Chgo.'s Pipers Portal Schs., 1961-63, dir., 1963-64; dir. phys. therapy services LaRabida Children's Hosp. and Research Center, Chgo., 1964-75; mem. nat. com. Joint Orthopedic Nursing Adv. Services, 1947-55; clin. supr., instr. programs in phys. therapy Northwestern U. Med. Sch., Chgo., 1947-55, 64-75; cons. United Cerebral Palsy, 1970-75; lectr. Japanese service com. on Cerebral Palsy, 1970; mem. Ill. Phys. Therapy Exam. Com., 1952-62. Recipient cert. of commendation CSC Cook County (Ill.), 1961, Citation of Merit, Wands Cerebral Palsy Unit, 1961. Mem. Am., Ill. phys. therapy assns., Provident Hosp. Nurses Alumni Assn. Democrat. Clubs: Tu-Fours Bolivia. Author: Low Budget Gourmet, 1977; (booklet) Patient Positioning, 1981; contbr. articles on phys. therapy to profl. jours.; contbr. to Am. Poetry Anthology. Address: 2631 S Indiana Ave Chicago IL 60616

PENFOLD, PATRICIA MARIE, sales executive; b. Brighton, Colo., Feb. 2, 1951; d. Joseph Eugene and Elaine Mildred (Yeager) Sigg; m. Jon Eric Penfold, Aug. 21, 1971; children: Eric Michael, Joey Keith. BS, U. No. Colo., 1973. Tchr. various schs., Wiggins, Colo., 1975; acctg. clk. to export coordinator Monfort of Colo., Greeley, 1975—. Office: Monfort of Colo PO Box G Greeley CO 20632

PENLAND, EULA EILEEN, personnel executive; b. St. Louis, Nov. 3, 1931; d. William and Eula Aura (Covington) Mummert; m. Robert Samuel Penland, Feb. 19, 1983; children by previous marriage—Ralph E., Frances Eileen, Pamela Darlene. Student Del Mar Coll., 1949, Victoria Coll., 1969, U. N.Mex., 1972. Bookkeeper, Tarrant Wholesale Distbrs., Corpus Christi, Tex., 1963, Zarsky Lumber Co., Corpus Christi, 1963-64; with Tex. Employers Ins. Co., Corpus Christi, 1965; with E. I. DuPont De Nemours & Co., Inc., Victoria, Tex., 1965-71; exec. sec. The Heil Co., Huntsville, Tex., 1977-78; personnel dir. Continental Savings Assn., Angleton, Tex., 1978—; cons. in field. Editor newsletter Continental Express, 1980-84; contbr. articles to profl. jours. Volunteer, Sheriff's Campaign, Angleton, 1980, United Way, 1982—; leader Camp Fire Girls, 1961-62; den mother Boy Scouts Am., Houston, 1958-59. Nat. Honor Soc. scholar, 1948. Mem. Am. Soc. Personnel Assn., Inst. Fin. Edn., others. Democrat. Unitarian. Office: Continental Savs Assn 4500 Bissonnet Bellaire TX 77401

PENN, PATSY SHARON, construction company executive, federal contract administrator; b. Rockville, Ind.; d. B. Franklin and Edith May (Hutson) Market; m. Robert Eugene Penn, Jan. 18, 1964; 1 child, Brookelyn Shane. M. Cosmetology, Smart Appearance Beauty Acad., Terre Haute, Ind., 1967. Owner, mgr. stylist Hair Fashions by Patsy, Rockville, Ind., 1969-79; contract adminstr. Penn & Penn Gen. Contractors, Rockville, 1977-79; owner, operator Midway Construction Co., Rockville, 1981—; organizer, project estimator, Midway Construction Co., Rockville, 1981—, contract adminstr., 1981—, sec., bookkeeper, 1981—, legal council Dept. of Interior Contract Appeals, 1983-84. Monitering of legis. request Pres. of the U.S., Washington, 1984. Home: Rural Route 4 US 36 W Rockville IN 47872 Office: Midway Constrn Co Rural Route 4 US 36 W Rockville IN 47872

PENN, SUSAN BERLAND, community volunteer; b. N.Y.C.; s. Harry and Sherle Joy (Peters) Berland; m. Deane Arnold Penn, Mar. 28, 1970; children: Jonathan Jay, Stacey Helene. BA in Psychology and Sociology, U. Pa., 1969; MBA in Marketing and Finance, Columbia U., 1971. Sr. research analyst NBC, N.Y.C., 1971-74; media cons. polit. polling Penn & Schoen, Inc., N.Y.C., 1984-86; assoc. realtor Schlott Realtors, Alpine, N.J., 1986-87. Arbitrator Better Bus. Bur., Paramus, N.J., 1986-87; trustee Alpine Bd. Edn., 1985—, co-chmn. curriculum and pub. relations coms.; program chmn. Young Leadership United Jewish Appeal, Bergen County, N.J., 1987, 88, nat. cabinet mem. 1987, 88; co-chmn. after sch. enrichment programs Alpine Sch., 1981-88; chmn. Alpine Recreation Com., St. Jude's Bikeathon, 1983-84; pres. Alpine Home and Sch. Assn. (PTA), 1983-86, Bergen County Med. Soc. Aux., 1980-81, v.p. fashion show com., 1979-80; mem. Alpine Environ. Commn., 1987, 88; bd. dirs. women's div. United Jewish Community, Bergen County, 1986-88, co-chmn. spring luncheon women's div., 1986. Mem. Orgn. for Rehabilitation through Tng. (v.p. membership 1975-77), Sisterhood Temple Sinai (v.p. programming 1988). Republican. Clubs: Alpine Country, U. Pa. Metro N.J. (bd. dirs.). Home: Buckingham Dr Alpine NJ 07620

PENNA, CAROLYN MARIE, legal association administrator, lawyer; b. Flushing, N.Y., Aug. 23, 1952; d. Gilbert Russell Jr. and Lovetta (MacNaughton) Hoffman; m. Joseph N. Penna, May 6, 1978; 1 child, Justin Scott. BA, CUNY, 1974; JD, N.Y. Law Sch., 1984. Supr. communications Hosp. for Spl. Surgery, N.Y.C., 1978-81; editor of court decisions Am. Arbitration Assn., N.Y.C., 1981-86, regional v.p., 1986—; commr. Bergen County State Superior Ct., Hackensack, N.J., 1986-87. Contbr. articles to profl. jours. Mem. ABA, N.Y. State Bar Assn., N.J. State Bar Assn., Assn. Bar City N.Y., Bergen City Bar Assn., Morgan Horse Assn. of N.J. Lutheran. Office: Am Arbitration Assn 140 W 51st St New York NY 10020

PENNELL, FRANCES, management consultant; b. Boston, Aug. 6, 1951; d. Walter Francis and Helen (Redmond) P.; B.S., Simmons Coll., 1973; M.P.H. in Health Adminstrn., Columbia U., 1978; M.B.A. in Fin., N.Y.U., 1983. Emergency room med. technologist Martha's Vineyard Hosp., Mass., 1973; med. technologist, ednl. in-service coordinator Park Med. Lab., Brookline, Mass., 1974-76; mgmt. cons. Macro Systems, Inc., Silver Spring, Md., 1977; program and fin. analyst N.Y.C., Health and Hosp.'s Corp., 1978-80; mgr. Coopers & Lybrand, N.Y.C., 1980-84, ptnr., 1985—; sr. v.p. Comprehensive Cancer Care Corp., 1984-85. Mem. Hosp. Fin. Mgmt. Assn., Am. Soc. Clin. Pathologists (registered med. technologist). Contbr. articles on health care industry to profl. jours. Home: 105 W 70th St Apt 5R New York NY 10023

PENNER, LUELLA MARIE, computer company administrator; b. Newton, Kans., Feb. 11, 1946; d. Otto R. and Metha (Wiebe) P. BA in Psychology, U. Kans., 1969; MA in Edn. Counseling, U. Mo., Kansas City, 1972; MBA, James Madison U., 1986. Adminstr. counselor Christian Ctr., Syria, Va., 1973-83; instr. Germanna Community Coll., Locust Grove, Va., 1974-84; sales Real Estate III, Charlotteville, Va., 1984-86; gen. mgr., sales Cedar Systems, Ltd., Charlotteville, 1986—. Group leader various religious orgns., Va., 1975-83; chair, bd. dirs. Christian Ctr., Syria, 1984—. Home: 23 Spring Ct Charlottesville VA 22901

PENNICK, LORAINE ANNE, accountant; b. New Haven, Mar. 18, 1954; d. Rocco W. Sr. and Mary C. (Cassella) Gargano; m. Edward David Pennick, July 12, 1980; 1 child, Victoria Lee. BS summa cum laude, U. New Haven, 1976; AS, So. Conn. State U., 1974; MBA, U. New Haven, 1987; C.P.A., Conn. Lic. real estate broker, Conn. Property mgr. Crestwood Mgmt., West Haven, Conn., 1973-78; sr. tax acct. Deloitte Haskins & Sells, New Haven, 1978-84; tax planning So. New Eng. Telephone Co., New Haven, 1984; tax mgr. LIGHTNET, New Haven, 1984-86; mgr. of acctg. and taxation SNET Systems, Inc., New Haven, 1986—; instr. Becker C.P.A. rev. course, Fairfield, Conn., 1982-86. Treas., RESPOND, New Haven, 1982-85; commr. West Haven Fair Rent Commn., 1982-84. Mem. Conn. Soc. C.P.A.s, Am. Inst. C.P.A.s, Conn. Estate and Tax Planning Council, Greater New Haven Jaycees (controler 1983-84, treas. 1985-86). Roman Catholic. Home: 430 Barton Dr Orange CT 06477 Office: SNET Systems Inc 367 Orange St New Haven CT 06511

PENNINGTON, JUDITH CAROL RUSH, biologist; b. Tylertown, Miss., July 26, 1945; d. David Harmon Rush and Nell Marie (Dunaway) Carnes; m. Carlos Harrison Pennington, Aug. 12; children: Jennifer Denise, Cathryn Haley. BS, Southeastern La. U., 1967, MEd, 1971; postgrad., La. State U., 1984—. Cert. med. technologist, secondary sch. tchr., La., Tex., Tenn. Med. technologist Navarro County Meml. Hosp., Corsicana, Tex., 1973-74; biol. lab. technician Veterinary Toxicology and Entomology Research Lab., USDA, College Station, Tex., 1974-75; tech. asst. Tex. A&M U., College Station, 1974-75; instr. Southeastern La. U., Hammond, La., 1976-77; med. technologist Hammond State Sch., 1976-77, Mercy Regional Med. Ctr., Vicksburg, Miss., 1977-78; chemist Waterways Experiment Sta. U.S. Army C.E., Vicksburg, 1978-80, biologist Waterways Experiment Sta., 1980-85, research biologist Waterways Experiment Sta., 1985—. Judge St. Francis Elem. Sch. Sci. Fair, Vicksburg, 1982; co-chair Women's Week Workshop Waterways Experiment Sta., Vicksburg, 1983; publicity com. South Park Elem. Sch. PTO, Vicksburg, 1983; judge paper presentation, Miss. Jr. Acad. Scis., Clinton, 1984. Mem. Internat. Assn. Aquatic Vascular Plant Biologists, Am. Med. Technologists, Southeastern Biol. Control Working Group, Kappa Delta Pi (Zeta Kappa chpt.). Democrat. Methodist. Club: Toastmasters (adminstrv. v.p. 1983-84). Office: WESES-R USAE Waterways Experiment Sta PO Box 631 Vicksburg MS 39180-0631

PENNINGTON, MARGARET ANGELA, financial consultant, art consultant; b. Birmingham, Ala., Sept. 20, 1942; d. George Frederick and Regina Angela (Moreno) Kirchoff; B.A., U. Tenn., 1963; M.S.W., Smith Coll., 1965; m. Gerald Lee Pennington. Faculty dept. psychiatry Emory U., Atlanta, 1966-69; asso. dir. St. Jude's House, Atlanta, 1969-72; asso. dir. public affairs Mental Health Assn., Atlanta, 1972-73; community orgn. cons. Ga. Dept. Human Resources, Atlanta, 1974-75; fine art cons. Rentar Industries, N.Y.C., 1975-85; v.p. Shannsongs, Inc., 1985—; pres. Marpal, Inc., Nokomis, Fla., 1980-86; v.p. Penn-Products, Venice, Fla., 1982—. Bd. dirs. New Coll. Music Festival, Sarasota, Fla., 1982-86, Sarasota-Manatee Jewish Family Service, 1986-88; v.p. women's div. Sarasota-Manatee Jewish Fedn., 1986—; co-chmn. Venice div. Combined Jewish Appeal, 1984-87, chmn. Womens' Div. Sarasota-Manatee Counties, 1986—; charter mem. Venice Jewish Community Ctr.; bd. dirs. Manatee Community Coll. Found., 1986-88. Recipient awards, grants: Vocat. Rehab. Adminstrn., Nat. Found., Gen. Tire and Rubber Co., Wallace Silver Co., SCV. Mem. Nat. Assn. Social Workers, Acad. Cert. Social Workers, Am. Craft Council, Nat. Soc. Magna Charter Dames, Smith Coll. Alumnae Assn., DAR, Colonial Dames XVII Century, Women's Am. O.R.T., Pi Beta Phi. Jewish. Clubs: Hadassah, The Oaks, Plantation Golf and Country. Home and Office: 2207 Casey Key Rd Nokomis FL 34375

PENNINGTON, MARY ANNE, art museum director art educator; b. Franklin, Va., Apr. 12, 1943; d. James Clifton and Martha Julia (Futrell) P.; m. Walter Joseph Shackelford, Nov. 26, 1981. Student East Carolina U., 1962; BFA, Va. Commonwealth U., 1965, MFA, 1966; postgrad. Cameron U., 1970, East Carolina U., 1972, U. N.C., Chapel Hill, 1980. Instr. art Presbyn. Coll., Clinton, S.C., 1966-69; tchr. art in Pitt County, 1970-71, Greenville City (N.C.) Sch. Systems, 1971-73; instr. art Pitt Community Coll., 1972-73; coordinator visual arts and humanities program, Ludwigsberg, Fed. Republic Germany, 1974-76; vis. artist-in-residence Salt Pond Art Ctr., Blacksburg, Va., summer, 1978; asst. prof. art Pembroke State U., N.C., 1976-80; exec. dir. Greenville Mus. Art, 1980-87, dir. The Lauren Rogers Mus. of Art, Laurel, 1987—; judge art competition, 1980—; speaker N.C. Dept. Corrections, 1980-87; guest lectr. art Converse Coll., Spartanburg, S.C., summer, 1966. Author: Application of Industrial Sand Casting to Sculpture, 1966, Handbook to the Collection of the Lauren Rogers Mus. Art; also articles. Bd. dirs. Pitt-Greenville Arts Council; program coordinator Pitt-Greenville Leadership Inst., 1982-87. Recipient Vol. award N.C. Gov., 1981; 2 N.C. Arts Council scholarship awards, 1980, 87, N.C. Disting. Women award, 1986. Mem. Am. Assn. Mus., Southeastern Mus. Conf., Inc., N.C. Mus. Council (bd. dirs. 1986-87), Miss. Mus. Assn., Miss. Inst. Arts and Letters. Office: The Lauren Rogers Mus of Art PO Box 1108 Laurel MS 39441

PENNY, JANE CLARK, environmental engineer; b. Urbana, Ill., June 18, 1956; d. James Gordon and Janice Elizabeth (Winters) Clark; m. Michael David Penny, Aug. 13, 1977; children: Jared Clark, Claudia Michelle. BS, U. Ill., 1978, postgrad., 1979-80. Registered profl. engr., Ill. Engr. technician Clark, Dietz Engrs., Urbana, 1974-78; project engr. CRS Group Engrs., Urbana, 1978-83; environ. engr. Chanute AFB, Rantoul, Ill., 1983-86, Air Force Regional Civil Engrs., Atlanta, 1986—. Mem. Nat. Soc. Profl. Engrs., Air Force Assn., Soc. Am. Mil. Engrs. (treas. 1984-86, Outstanding Young Engr. 1984-85), Chi Epsilon. Republican. Home: 503 Ryan Pl Stone Mountain GA 30087 Office: Air Force Regional Civil Engrs 77 Forsyth St Suite 291 Atlanta GA 30335-6801

PENNY, JOSEPHINE B., retired banker; b. N.Y.C., July 7, 1925; d. Charles and Delia (Fahey) Booy; student Columbia U., Am. Inst. Banking; grad. Sch. Bank Adminstrn. U. Wis., 1975; m. John T. Penny, July 15, 1950 (div.); children—John T., Charleen Penny DeMauro, Patricia Penny Paras. With Prentice-Hall, N.Y.C., 1942-43; with Trade Bank & Trust Co., 1943-52, 61-70; with Nat. Westminster Bank U.S.A., 1970-85, v.p., dep. auditor, 1978-85. Mem. Bank Adminstrn. Inst. (chpt. dir. 1983-85), Inst. Internal Auditing, Nat. Assn. Bank Women (chpt. chmn. 1980-81). Home: 1-N Old Nassau Rd Jamesburg NJ 08831

PENNY, LINDA LEA, social work administrator; b. Big Spring, Tex., Aug. 6, 1943; d. Charlie Nichol and Bonnie Wayne (Tartt) Farrar; 1 child, Larry Lee II. B in Social Work, Tex. Woman's U., 1975, MA in Sociology, 1977; diploma Inst. for English Speaking Students, Internat. Grad. Sch., U.

Stockholm, 1978. Cert. social worker. Coordinator human resources Catholic Charities, Fort Worth, 1975-76; program specialist Tex. Dept. Human Resources, Austin, 1977; program specialist/ombudsman Tex. Gov.'s Com. on Aging, Austin, 1978-80; project dir., tng. dir. Ctr. for Pub. Interest, Dallas, 1980-82; dir. social work dept. Presbyn. Hosp., Dallas, 1982-84, Meml. Hosp., Cleburne, Tex., 1984-86; coordinator Johnson County Health Dept. Indigent Health Program, Cleburne, 1986—; pvt. cons./trainer, Cleburne, 1980—; ptnr., cons. Gormet Basket, Cleburne, 1985-86. Bd. dirs. Johnson County Family Crisis Ctr., Cleburne, 1985-86; allocations com. Johnson County United Way, Cleburne, 1985-86. Samuel E. Ziegler Found. fellow, Dallas, 1976-77. Mem. Tex. Soc. Hosp. Social Work Dirs., Am. Bus. Women's Assn., Nat. Assn. Female Execs., Assn. Ind. Real Estate Owners, Am. Mensa. Democrat. Lutheran. Avocations: real estate investments; refinishing antiques; collecting glassware. Home: 1305 N Wood St Cleburne TX 76031 Office: Johnson County Health Dept PO Drawer E Cleburne TX 76031

PENROSE, CYNTHIA C., health plan administrator, consultant; b. Manila, Philippines, Nov. 24, 1939; came to U.S., 1940; d. Douglas Lee Lipscomb Cordiner and Jane (Sturgeon) Edises; m. Douglas Francis Penrose, July 11, 1959 (div. 1981); children—Vicki Lynn, Lee Douglas; m. Alan Harrison Magazine, Aug. 30, 1984. B.A., U. Calif.-Berkeley, 1963; M.B.A., U. Santa Clara, 1977. Cert. social services. Vice pres and dir. employment Resource Ctr. for Women, Palo Alto, Calif., 1973-78; bus. planner Raychem Corp., Menlo Park, Calif., 1979; adminstrv. mgr. Electric Power Research Inst., Palo Alto, 1979-83; dir. ops. Utility Data Inst., Washington, 1984-85; dir. ops. Randmark, Inc., 1986-87; coordinator mkt. devel. for Mid-Atlantic States Kaiser Foundation Health Plan, Washington, 1987—; sr. ptnr. MB Assocs., Washington, 1983—; bd. dirs. and treas. Unique Enterprises, Washington, 1985-87; sec. Wesley Property Mgmt. Co., 1987—; bd. dirs. Wesley Housing Devel. Corp., 1988—. Bd. dirs., v.p. LWV, Berkeley and Palo Alto, 1966-73; chmn. program adv. council Resource Ctr. for Women, Palo Alto, 1980-83; mem. Affirmative Action Adv. Com. Palo Alto, 1975-76. Mem. Exec. Women's Roundtable (Washington, founder), Peninsula Profl. Women's Network (v.p. 1981-82), Women in Energy, Am. Soc. Assn. Execs., Wed. Group, AAUW (Bicentennial br. sec. 1986-88, bd. dirs. Washington div. 1988—), LWV. Democrat. Episcopalian. Avocations: swimming; nutrition and health; reading. Home: 1302 Chancel Pl Alexandria VA 22314 Office: Kaiser-Permanente 4200 Wisconsin Ave Washington DC 20016

PENSIERO, SHERREN ELIAS, educator; b. Washington, Pa., Nov. 22, 1947; d. Nasime Abraham and Alexandria Martha (Thomas) Elias; m. Daniel Victor Pensiero, June 24, 1972; children: Lisa Danielle, Tara Nicole. BS in Edn., Calif. (Pa.) State Coll., 1968, MEd, 1987. Cert. tchr., Pa. Tchr. English Hopewell Area Schs., Aliquippa, Pa., 1968-72; tchr. reading and speech Somerset (Pa.) Area Schs., 1972—; tchr. pub. speaking Westmoreland County Community Coll. for Kids, Youngwood, Pa., 1988—; poetry workshop site coordinator Pa. Council on the Arts, Somerset, 1974-83. Mem. NEA, Pa. State Edn. Assn., Somerset Area Edn. Assn., Somerset County Reading Tchrs. Assn., Phi Delta Kappa. Republican. Club: Somerset Music. Lodge: Elks. Office: Somerset Jr Sr High Sch South Columbia Ave Somerset PA 15501

PENTA, IRENE PLATT (MRS. WALTER E. PENTA), nurse, club woman; b. Concord, N.H., Jan. 2, 1920; d. Frank Bishop and Ida Louisa (Cable) Platt; student Portland Jr. Coll., 1939; R.N., Dr. Drummond's Hosp. Nursing Sch., Portland, Maine, 1942; m. Walter E. Penta, Sept. 25, 1943; 1 son, Donald Platt. Nurse, Maine Med. Center, Portland, 1942-43, Mercy Hosp., Portland, 1943, Boston City Hosp., 1943-44, Beth Israel Hosp., Boston, 1944, Mass. Gen. Hosp., Boston, 1944, Deaconess Hosp., Boston, 1943, Meth. Hosp., Dallas, 1944-45, Med. Arts, Dallas, 1944-45, So. Bapt. Hosp., Dallas, 1944-45. Sec., Woman's Aux. Maine Med. Assn., Portland, 1955-56, v.p., 1956-57, pres.-elect, 1957-58, pres., 1958-59, bd. dirs., 1955—, internat. health chmn., 1967-69; v.p. Ladies of Kiwanis, Portland, 1958, pres., 1959, bd. dirs., 1957—, welfare chmn., 1968-69, activities chmn., 1972-74; active Hosp. Aux. Maine Med. Center; mem. organizational com. Tri-State Health Careers Research Group, Portland, 1960-61; rural health chmn. region one, Women's Aux. to AMA, 1960—, internat. health chmn. Maine Women's Aux., 1968-71. Mem. Am., Maine nurses assns., Dr. Drummonds Hosp. Alumni Assn. (pres. 1964-66, 82-86), Nat. Soc. Daus. Founders and Patriots Am. (treas. Me. chpt. 1987-88), Internat. Platform Assn., Wives' Wing Aerospace Med. Assn., Maine Hist. Soc., Victoria Soc. of Maine Women, Am. Water Ski Assn., Nat. Soc. Women Descs. Ancient and Hon. Arty. Company (v.p. Maine chpt. 1973—, color bearer 1975—). Congregationalist (pres. Jr. Guild 1956). Club: Woodfords (Portland). Home: 316 Woodford St Portland ME 04103

PENTECOST, PEGGIE C., real estate contractor, interior designer; b. Gross Pointe, Mich., Oct. 21, 1951; d. Richard Rudolph Papes and Barbara Joy (Kading) Stadtmiller; m. Kyle Lee Pentecost, May 24, 1975; children: Blair. BS in Bus. and Commerce, U. Houston, 1981. Interior designer Continental Designers, Inc., Houston, 1981-85, Designsource, Inc., Houston, 1985-87, Pemberton Devel., Inc., Houston, 1987—. Bd. dirs. St. Anne's Guild, Houston, 1985. Mem. Houston Bd. Realtor's, Profl. Women's Exchange Group of Houston, River Oak Bus. Women's Exchange Club, Women's Sailing Assn. Republican. Roman Catholic. Office: Pemberton Builders Inc PO Box 270625 Houston TX 77277

PENWELL, JOANNE ALBERTA MARGARET, educator; b. Pitts., Apr. 7; d. Henry J. and Alberta May (Ing) Reis; m. Stanley Curtiss Campbell, Dec. 27, 1955 (dec. 1956); 1 son, Scott Jeffrey; m. Richard McMaster Penwell, Oct. 31, 1959; children—Steven Richard, Shawn Michael. B.S.N., M.S.N., U. Pitts.; M.Ed., John Carroll U., 1983. R.N., Pa., Ohio. Operating rm. nurse Presbyn. Hosp., Pitts.; faculty Presbyn. Univ. Hosp., Pitts., U. Pitts., 1958-61, Central Sch. Practical Nursing, Cleve., 1973; prof. nursing Lakeland Community Coll., Cleve./Mentor, Ohio, 1973—; cons. Geauga Community Hosp., 1976-79, Madison Hosp., 1980; dir. Home Health Care, Inc., Mentor, 1983. Mem. Am. Nurses Assn., Nat. League Nursing, Geauga Nurses Assn. (treas. 1970-73), Sigma Theta Tau. Republican. Episcopalian. Clubs: Russell Women's, Chagrin Jr. Women's, Episcopal Ch. Women. Office: Lakeland Community Coll Rt 306 Mentor OH 44060

PÉPIN, LUCIE, Canadian legislator; b. St. Jean d'Iberville, Que., Can., Sept. 7, 1936; d. Jean and Thérèse (Bessette) P.; children: Natalie, Sophie. Student, U. Montreal, Que., McGill U., Montreal. Nurs; mem. Can. Ho. of Commons, 1984—. Mem. Cercle Univ. d'Ottawa. Mem. Liberal Party. Roman Catholic. Club: Can. Office: 666 Confederation Bldg, Ottawa, ON Canada K1A 0A6 *

PEPKA, KATHLEEN MARY, sales and marketing executive; b. Niagara Falls, N.Y., Feb. 2, 1949; d. Edmund Francis and Casmera Josephine (Nowak) Olszowka; m. Leon Michael Pepka, Aug. 16, 1968 (div. Aug. 1986); children: Cheri, Deanna. AA, Saddleback Coll., 1982; BS, U. La Verne, 1985. Dir. merchandising W.R. Grace Properties, Newport Beach, Calif., 1975-79; mgr. mktg. Campeau Corp., Newport Beach, 1979-82; v.p. sales and mktg. Mission Viejo (Calif.) Co., 1982—. Mem. Inst. Residential Mktg., Nat. Sales and Mktg. Council, Home Builders Council, So. Calif. Sales and Mktg. Council, Bldg. Industry Assn. (treas. Sales and Mktg. council 1982, v.p. 1983, pres. 1984; Pres.'s Achievement award 1981, 83, Major Achievement in Merchandising Excellence 1984-86, Mktg. Dir. of Yr. 1986). Republican. Roman Catholic. Home: 25101 Meadowbrook Mission Viejo CA 92692 Office: Mission Viejo Co 26137 La Paz Rd Mission Viejo CA 92691

PEPPER, ADELINE, author, photographer; b. Madison, Wis.; d. John William and Emmeline (Able) P.; BA, U. Wis. Med. writer AMA, ACS; asst. advt. mgr. Mead Johnson & Co., Evansville, Ind., publicity dir. Com. on Care of Children in Wartime, Evansville, 1945; radio advt. writer Knox Reeves, Inc., Mpls.; pub. relations Pa. R.R. Centennial, 1946; advt. writer L. W. Frohlich Agy., N.Y.; med. advt. writer and designer E. R. Squibb & Sons, Ciba Pharm.; owner Pep, Inc., advt. service, 1956—. Vice pres. council Union County Extension Service, Rutgers U., 1980-81. Mem. N.Y. Acad. Scis., Theta Sigma Phi, Phi Kappa Phi. Author: Tours of Historic New Jersey (N.J. Tercentenary medal 1964), 1965, rev. edit., 1973; N.J. vol. Fodor's Guide to the U.S.A., 1966; The Glass Gaffers of New Jersey (award N.J. Assn. Tchrs. English 1972, award of Merit Am. Assn. State and Local History 1972), 1971. Contbr. articles on travel, history, and decorative arts to mags. and major met. newspapers.

PEPPER, CAROL ANNE, banker; b. Chelsea, Mass., Apr. 28, 1962; d. Charles Edward and Anne Lucille (Colella) P. BA cum laude, Bryn Mawr Coll., 1984; postgrad., Columbia U., 1986—. Fin. analyst Salomon Brothers, Inc., N.Y.C., 1984-86; asst. treas. Morgan Guaranty Trust Co., N.Y.C., 1986—. Republican. Roman Catholic. Home: 17 Douglass St Brooklyn NY 11231

PEPPLE, RUTH ANN, real estate executive; b. Keokuk, Iowa, Apr. 27, 1943; d. John William and Doris Elizabeth (Kiser) P. BA, U. Iowa, 1965; postgrad., U. Mo., 1975-76. Lic. real estate broker, Mo., Fla. Dir. spl. activities Hallmark Cards, Kansas City, Mo., 1965-70; personnel interviewer K.C. Power and Light Co., Kansas City, 1970-71; dir. ops. Intercommunity Relocations Inc., Kansas City, 1971-79, v.p., 1979-84; v.p. Equitable Realty Network, Inc., Orlando, Fla., 1984-85, chief operating officer, 1986-87; chief operating officer Travelers Realty Network, Orlando, 1987—; guest speaker various relocation seminars, nat. Mem. Mensa, Employee Relocation Council. Roman Catholic. Club: Ski (Orlando). Office: Travelers Realty Network 5850 TG Lee Blvd Orlando FL 32872

PERALTA, GRETCHEN CATHERINE, nurse, homecare executive; b. Long Beach, Calif., Aug. 15, 1947; d. Nicholas Arnold and Mildred Lillian (Schneider) Smith; m. Ronald Michael Peralta, June 22, 1975; children: David Christian, Joshua Warren. Lic. vocat. nurse, Cerritos Coll., 1969; diploma registered nurse, LAC-USC Sch. Nursing, Los Angeles, 1973; AA, San Francisco City Coll., 1975; community coll. teaching credential, Calif. State U., 1980. RN, Calif. Staff nurse burn ICU LAC-USC Ctr., Los Angeles, 1969-74, staff nurse med. emergency admitting unit, 1975-83; staff nurse trauma/surg. ICU San Francisco Gen. Hosp., 1974-75; v.p. edn. and quality assurance Lifeline Homecare, Downey, Calif., 1981—; chairperson, pres. adv. com. Soc. Nutritional Support, 1986—; speaker, lectr. various profl. assns., 1981—. Contbr. articles to profl. jours. Sec. Am. Heart Assn., Downey, 1987—. Mem. Nat. Intravenous Therapy Assn. (pres. local chpt. 1986—), Am. Soc. Parenteral and Enteral Nutrition, Nat. Intravenous Nurse Assn. (pres. Los Angeles chpt. 1986—, dist. leader 1987—). Republican. Lodge: Rotary. Home: 8903 Guatemala Downey CA 90242 Office: Lifeline Homecare 12130 S Paramount Blvd Downey CA 90242

PERDUE, JEANNE MARIE, chemist; b. Tonawanda, N.Y., June 21, 1958; d. Raymond Frank and Ruth Ann (Brady) Jay; m. Stephen H. Weinstein, June 7, 1980 (div. May 1981); m. Charles Franklin Perdue, Jr., June 30, 1984; children: Charles Edward, Daniel Stephen; 1 stepchild, James Mitchell. BS in Chemistry, SUNY, Albany, 1980; postgrad., U. Houston, 1982-86. Chemist Texaco Oil Co., Houston, 1980—. Booth chmn. Notre Dame Ch. Bazaar, Houston, 1985-86; Texaco coordinator Teamwalk-March of Dimes, Houston, 1985-86. Recipient Bausch and Lomb award, 1976, Citizenship award Genesee County chpt. DAR, 1976. Mem. Soc. Petroleum Engrs. (tech. editor 1986—), Nat. Assn. Female Execs. Republican. Roman Catholic. Club: Texaco Employees (pres. 1985-86). Home: 7303 Carvel Circle Houston TX 77072 Office: Texaco Oil Co E&P Tech Div 3901 Briarpark Houston TX 77042

PEREBOOM, MARGARET GAMBLE, psychologist; b. Lusk, Wyo., May 30, 1928; d. George D. and Cecile (Durst) Gamble; m. Andrew Clinton Pereboom, Feb. 11, 1952; children—Joanne, Drew. B.A., UCLA, 1950; M.A., Tex. Tech U., 1963; Ph.D., U. Tex., 1972. Lic. psychologist, La. Psychologist Greater Baton Rouge Cerebral Palsy Ctr., 1962-72; asst. prof. La. State U. Spl. Edn., Baton Rouge, 1973, adj. asst. prof. psychol. dept., 1987—; psychologist Margaret Dumas Mental Health Ctr., Baton Rouge, 1974-78; pres. Edn. and Psychol. Services, Inc., Baton Rouge, 1977—; owner Associated Psychol. Services, Baton Rouge, 1980—; guest lectr. Win With Women, La., 1982; workshop leader River Region Stress Reduction, Assertiveness Tng.; bd. dirs. Agenda for Children, Baton Rouge, La. Council Child Abuse, Baton Rouge; past pres Baton Rouge Youth; chmn. Govs. Commn. Children and Youth, Baton Rouge, 1984-85; bd. dirs. Friends Pub. Edn., East Baton Rouge Sch. Bd., 1979-82; legis. lobbyist La. Women's Polit. Caucus, Older Women's League; chairwoman La. Women in Politics, 1987. Fellow Am. Acad. Cerebral Palsy and Devel. Medicine; mem. Am. Psychol. Assn., Soc. Pediatric Psychology, Council for Exceptional Children, LWV, Sigma Pi Sigma, Psy Chi. Democrat. Mem. Unitarian Ch. Office: Associated Psychol Services 4256 Perkins Rd Baton Rouge LA 70808

PEREIRA, CECELIA, educational program coordinator; b. Oakland, Calif., June 14, 1940; d. Frank Andrew and Thelma (Pederson) McEneany; m. Nicola Mario Pereira Jr., May 4, 1963; children: Nicola Mario III and Paul Andrew. BA, U. Calif., Berkeley, 1962; MA, San Diego State U., 1986. Cert. adminstrv. services, Calif. Community Coll. supr., gen tchr. Tchr. Mt. Aviat Acad., Childs, Md., 1971-73, Punahou Sch., Honolulu, 1975, St. John Vianney Sch., Kailua, Hawaii, 1975-77; instr. MiraCosta Adult High Sch. Diploma Program, Oceanside, Calif., 1980-84, ednl. coordinator, 1984-87, coordinator non-credit programs, 1987—; com. mem. San Diego Adminstrv. Women in Edn., 1986—; regional coordinator Competency Based Adult Edn. Staff Devel., Sacramento, Calif., 1987—. Mem. San Diego Zool. Soc., 1978—; San Diego Museum of Art, 1978—. Mem. Assn. of Calif. Adminstrs., San Diego Council of Adminstrv. Women in Edn., Calif. CBAE Inst., San Diego County Adult Edn. Adminstrs. Assn. Home: 4894 Alondra Way Carlsbad CA 92008 Office: MiraCosta Adult High Sch Diploma Program Bldg 1331 Camp Pendleton CA 92005

PEREIRA, JORGINA ANTUNES, associate technical specialist; b. Rio De Janeiro, Brazil, Aug. 12, 1944; came to U.S., 1974; d. Rafael and Maria Dolores Antunes Pereira; BA, Social Service Sch. Rio De Janeiro, 1970; BGS with emphasis in Computer Sci., Roosevelt U., 1978, M.S. in Info. Systems, 1985; m. Mark Louis Branham, Dec. 31, 1980. Head social work programs Paroquia Santa Cruz De Copacabana, Rio De Janeiro, 1971-73; participant council of internat. program Jane Addams Grad. Sch. Social Work, U. Ill., Chgo., 1974-75; trainee No. Trust Bank, Chgo., 1977-78, programmer, 1978-79, sr. programmer, 1979-80, tech. analyst, 1980-82, systems analyst, 1982-84; sr. systems analyst Montgomery Ward, 1984-86, assoc. tech. specialist, 1986—. Pres. Council of Internat. Program for Social Workers, Chgo., 1979-81, 85—. Mem. Data Processing Mgmt. Assn. (bd. dirs.), Franklin Honor Soc. Home: 665 W Roscoe Chicago IL 60657 Office: 1 Montgomery Ward Plaza Chicago IL 60671

PERELLA, SUSANNE BRENNAN, librarian; b. Providence, Mar. 19, 1936; d. Laurence J. and Harriet E. (Delaplane) Brennan. B.A., U. Conn., 1960; M.L.S., U. Mich., 1967. Head M.B.A. Library, Univ. Conn., Hartford, 1964-66; asst. librarian Cornell Univ. Grad. Sch. Bus., Ithaca, N.Y., 1967-72; head reader's services FTC Library, Washington, 1972-79; library dir. FTC Library, 1979—. Mem. Law Librarians Soc., Spl. Libraries Assn., Am. Assn. Law Libraries, Fed. Library and Info. Network (exec. adv. council 1985-87). Office: Fed Trade Commn 6th & Pennsylvania Ave NW Washington DC 20580

PERETTI, LINDA MARIE, film producer; b. Seattle, Feb. 24, 1946; d. Roger Joseph and Charlotte Mary (Reinhardt) Pagni; m. Mark Anthony Peretti, Aug. 16, 1969 (div. 1975). BA in Edn., Seattle U., 1968; MA in Childhood Edn., U. Wash., 1974. Cert. elem. and secondary edn. tchr., Wash. Tchr. elem. schs. Kent, Wash., 1970-76; dir. Northline UniServ Council, Bothell, Wash., 1976-80; field rep. Wash. Edn. Assn., Federal Way, 1980-81; gen. mgr. Lyric Theatre, Des Moines, Wash., 1981-82; freelance producer Seattle, 1982-86; exec. producer Dirs. Group, Inc., Seattle, 1986—; tchr. elem. schs. Fallon, Nev., 1969-70, Renton, Wash., 1968-69. Fund raiser N.W. Kidney Found., Seattle, 1984-87; del. State Dem. Conv., 1980, Dem. Legis. Dist. Caucus, 1982, 84; v.p. Seattle chpt. ladies aux. Italian Club, 1985-87; v.p. Des Moines, Wash. chpt. Lyric Theatre 1986-87; sec. Parkview Homes Bd., Seattle, 1986-87. Named Tchr. of Yr. Kent C. of C., 1974-75; recipient Excellence award Kent Edn. Assn., 1976, Creative Leadership in Women's Rights award Wash. Edn. Assn., 1979. Mem. Wash. Film and Video Assn. (v.p. 1987-88), Assn. Ind. Commercial Producers. Roman Catholic. Home: 2018 1/2 Taylor Ave N Seattle WA 98109 Office: Dirs Group Inc 1201 1st Ave S Suite 200 Seattle WA 98134

PEREZ, AGNES CECILLE, chemical engineer; b. Kingston, Jamaica, Sept. 13; came to U.S., 1971; d. Ivanhoe Perez and Brusena Thomas. BS, St. Francis Coll., Bklyn., 1976, Poly. Inst. N.Y., 1983. Engr. Xerox Corp., Webster, N.Y., 1985—. Tutor sci. and math. program for students, Rochester, N.Y., 1984—; advisor Jr. Achievement, Rochester, 1986—. Mem. Am. Inst. Chem. Engrs. Home: 471 Webster Ave Rochester NY 14609

PEREZ, ANA C., principal; b. Douglas, Ariz., Nov. 15, 1954; d. Henry F. and Aurelia (Torres) P. BA in Edn., Ariz. State U., 1976, MA of Edn., 1980, cert. in adminstrv., 1984. Cert. elem. tchr. 1976, spl. edn. tchr., 1976, elem. prin., 1984, Ariz. Tchr. Mesa (Ariz.) Unified Sch. Dist. #4, 1976-80, program specialist, 1980-84, prin., 1984—; Cons. Mesa Unified Sch. Dist. #4, 1980, 85-86; rep. Assn. Severe Handicapped. Author numerous curriculum programs. Bd. dirs., sec. Ariz. State Spl. Olympics, Tempe, Ariz. Named Outstanding Educator League of United Latin Am. Citizens, 1985, Outstanding Elem. Sch. Prin. League of United Latin Am. Citizens, 1988. Mem. Council for Exceptional Children, Mesa Assn. Retarded Citizens (Educator of the Yr. award 1984), E. Valley Civitan, Phi Kappa Phi, Phi Delta Kappa. Office: Mesa Unified #4 Parkway Sch 1753 E 8th Ave Mesa AZ 85204

PEREZ, JOSEPHINE, psychiatrist, educator; b. Tijuana, Mex., Feb. 10, 1941, naturalized, 1968. B.S. in Biology, U. Santiago de Compostela, Spain, 1971; M.D., 1975. Clerkships in internal medicine, gen. surgery, otorhinolaryngology, dermatology and venereology Gen. Hosp. of Galicia (Spain), 1972-75; resident in gen. psychiatry U. Miami (Fla.), Jackson Meml. Hosp. and VA Hosp., Miami, 1976-78; practice medicine specializing in psychiatry, marital and family therapy, individual psychotherapy, Miami, Fla., 1979—; nuclear medicine technician, EEG technician, supr. Electrographic Labs., Encino, Calif., 1963-71; emergency room physician Miami Dade Hosp., 1975; attending psychiatrist Jackson Meml. Hosp., 1979—, asst. dir. adolescent psychiat. unit, 1979-83; mem. clin. faculty U. Miami Sch. Medicine, 1979—, clin. instr. psychiatry, 1979—. Mem. AMA (Physicians' Recognition award 1980, 83, 86), Am. Assn. for Marital and Family Therapy (cert. clin. mem., treas. 1982-84, pres.-elect 1985-87, pres. 1987—), Am. Psychiat. Assn., South Fla. Psychiat. Soc., Am. Med. Women's Assn. Office: 921 SW 27th Ave Suite 2A Miami FL 33135

PEREZ, JULIE ANNA, audio engineer; b. Miami, Sept. 2, 1961; d. Miguel Angel and Dorothy Elizabeth (Hedford) P. MusB, U. Miami, 1984. Audio engr. Ron Miller Quartet, Miami, 1980-84, Orange Bowl Com., Miami, 1982-84, Off The Wall Sound Co., Miami and Ft. Lauderdale, Fla., 1982-83, NBC, Inc., N.Y.C., 1984—; owner Jota-Pe, N.Y.C., 1986—; judge 1987 Emmy awards. Editor Music Engring. Tech. newsletter, 1983. Mem. Pub. Citizen Consumer Activists, Washington, 1987; contbr. Planned Parenthood Fedn. Am., 1986—; judge Emmy Awards, 1987, 88. Recipient Down Beat award Down Beat mag., 1982. Mem. Audio Engring. Soc., Nat. Acad. TV Arts and Scis. (Emmy nominee 1986), Nat. Assn. Female Execs., Nat. Assn. Broadcast Employees and Technicians, Women in Music, Nat. Acad. Recording Arts and Scis. Democrat. Home: 67-25 Dartmouth St 3G Forest Hills NY 11375 Office: NBC Inc 30 Rockefeller Plaza Rm 670D New York NY 10112

PÉREZ, LAURAN BARBARA SCHMID, accountant, educator; b. Austin, May 1, 1953; d. Caspar Johann and Laura Frances (King) Schmid; m. Frank Edward Pérez, Nov. 20, 1982. BBA, U. Tex., 1981; MBA, Pan Am. U., Brownsville, Tex., 1988. CPA, Tex. Auditor U. Tex. System Adminstrn., Austin, 1981-82; acct. Garcia, Marren & Co., CPAs, Brownsville, 1982-84; instr. acctg. Tex. Southmost Coll., Brownsville, 1985—. Mem. Am. Inst. CPAs, Tex. Soc. CPAs, Profl. Women Speak (fin. chair 1985—), Tex. Jr. Coll. Tchrs. Assn., Tex. Southmost Coll. Faculty Assn., Phi Beta Chi. Republican. Episcopalian. Office: Tex Southmost Coll 80 Fort Brown Brownsville TX 78520

PEREZ, NYDIA ESTHER, physician; b. N.Y.C., Dec. 10, 1950; d. Sixto Mercado and Secundina (Couvertier) Ortiz. M.D., Columbia U., N.Y.C., 1979. Diplomate Nat. Bd. Med. Examiners; cert. advanced cardiac, trauma life support physician. Intern, St. Lukes Hosp., N.Y.C., 1979-80; med. dir. Harlem Hosp., N.Y.C., 1980-82; family practitioner Margaretville Meml. Hosp. (N.Y.), 1982-83, East Harlem Council for Human Services, N.Y.C., 1983-84; Andes Town doctor, 1982-83; emergency room physician No. Dutchess Hosp., Rhinebeck, N.Y., 1984—. Mem. N.Y. State Med. Soc. Democrat. Roman Catholic. Home: Barrytown NY 12507 Office: PO Box 692 Rhinebeck NY 12572

PEREZ, PAULINA GANDY, nursing consultant; b. Centralia, Ill., Apr. 11, 1945; d. A. P. and Theda (Copple) Gandy; m. Eric Douglas Perez, Aug. 28, 1965; children: Bryan, Mark Scott. BS in Nursing, Tex. Woman's U., Denton, 1966. RN, Tex.; cert. childbirth educator. Staff nurse premature nursery St. Joseph Hosp., Houston, 1966; head nurse nursery Sharpstown Gen. Hosp., Houston, 1966-67; nurse in pvt. ob/gyn. practice Houston, 1967-74, nurse clinician, 1974-80; pres. Childbirth & Family Edn., Inc., Houston, 1980—; childbirth cons. Houston, 1981—; cons. numerous workshops, univs., assns.; condr. seminars in field; lectr. in field. Contbr. articles to profl. jours. Mem. med. adv. bd. Parents of Prematures, Houston, Parents of Premature and High-Risk Infants, Inc., N.Y.C.; bd. dirs. Premature, Inc., Houston, Internat. Childbirth Edn. Assn., Mpls. Office: Childbirth & Family Edn Inc 11832 Westheimer St Houston TX 77077

PEREZ-WOODS, ROSANNE HARRIGAN, nursing educator, child development consultant; b. Miami, Fla., Feb. 24, 1945; d. John Henry and Rose (Hnatow) Harrigan; m. Helio C. Perez, May 29, 1965 (div. 1978); m. David C. Woods, Apr. 12, 1986; children: Dennis James, Michael Helio, John Henry. BS, St. Xavier Coll. Chgo., 1965; MSN, Ind. U.-Indpls., 1974; EdD, Ind. U., Bloomington, 1979. Cert. pediatric nurse practitioner Nat. Bd. Pediatric Nurse Practitioners and Assocs. Staff nurse, evening charge nurse Mercy Hosp., Chgo., 1965-66; nursing educator Chgo. State Hosp., 1966-67; pediatric nurse practitioner Marion County Health and Hosp. Corp., Indpls., 1974-75; lectr. Ind. U.-Indpls., 1974-75, asst. prof. nursing, 1975-77, project dir. prenatal nursing program, 1978-85, assoc. prof., 1980-82, prof., chmn. dept. pediatrics, family and women's health Sch. Nursing, 1982-85, adj. prof. pediatrics Sch. Medicine, 1982-85; chief nursing sect. James Whitcomb Riley Hosp. Child Devel. Program, Indpls., 1982-85; Niehoff chair and prof. maternal child health Loyola U. Marcella Niehoff Sch. Nursing, 1985—; ednl. cons. Author: Immunological Concepts Applied, 1978, Protocols for Perinatal Nursing practice, 1981; contbr. articles to profl. jours. Named Nurse of Yr., March of Dimes, 1978. Mem. Am. Nurses Assn., Ind. State Nurses Assn., Nurses Assn. of Am. Coll. Ob-Gyn. (pres. cert. corp.), Nat. Perinatal Assn. (bd. dirs.), Adult Edn. Assn. Am., Am. Nurses Found., Ind. U. Alumni Assn., AAAS, Sigma Xi, Pi Lambda Theta, Sigma Theta Tau. Republican. Roman Catholic. Lodge: Soroptomists. Home: 3909 S Blanchan Brookfield IL 60513 Office: Loyola U 6525 N Sheridan Rd DH 411 Chicago IL 60626

PERFALL, ALISON ELLEN, advertising sales executive; b. New Hyde Park, N.Y., July 26, 1956; d. Arthur G. Perfall and Beryl Shiela (Howell) Ahrens; BBA, U. Wis.-Whitewater, 1978; MBA, Hofstra U., 1984. Classified telephone sales rep. Newsday, Inc., Melville, N.Y., 1978-80, classified spl. projects telephone sales rep., 1980-82, coop. advt. telephone sales rep., 1982, classified-automotive advt. sales rep., 1982-83, coop. advt. sales rep., 1983-84; nat. advt. account exec. Times Mirror Nat. Mktg., N.Y.C., 1984-86, nat. account exec./travel, 1984-86, nat. account exec./classified-recruitment advt., 1986, mgr. recruitement advt. Million Market Newspapers/Times Mirror Nat. Mktg., Los Angeles, 1987—. Mem. Execs. South Bay, Nat. Assn. Female Execs., Alpha Sigma. Episcopalian. Club: Advt. of Los Angeles. Office: Million Market Newspapers Times Mirror Nat Mktg 11601 Wilshire Blvd Suite 1820 Los Angeles CA 90025

PERGERICHT, FRANCES LEE, lawyer; b. Cleve., June 4, 1952; d. Joseph and Ann Pergericht; m. Roman G. Kuperman, Feb. 24, 1982; 1 child, Natalie Jill. B.A. magna cum laude, Case Western Res. U., 1974; J.D., Washington U., St. Louis, 1978. Bar: Ill. 1981, N.H. 1979. Law clk. presiding justice U.S. Dist. Ct. No. Dist. Ill., Chgo., 1979-81; assoc. Jenner & Block, Chgo., 1981-83; asst. regional atty Dept. Health and Human Services, Chgo., 1983—. Topics editor Washington U. Law Quar., 1977-78.

Mem. Chgo. Bar Assn., Chgo. Council Lawyers, Phi Beta Kappa. Office: Dept Health and Human Services 300 S Wacker Dr Chicago IL 60606

PERIGYI, JO-ANN KATHERINE, nursing administrator; b. New Haven, Mar. 2, 1953; d. Arthur John Kelleher and Helen Katherine (Grady) Rohne; m. Carl Alexander Perigyi, July 14, 1984. A, Norwalk Community Coll., 1977; BS in Nursing magna cum laude, U. Bridgeport, 1986. Lic. practical nurse Jersey Shore Med. Ctr., Neptune, N.J., 1972-75; nursing asst., RN BentleyGardens, West Haven, Conn., 1975-78; staff nurse., mgr. patient care Park City Hosp., Bridgeport, Conn., 1978-85; intake facilitator Hosp. Home Health Care Conn., New Haven, 1986; from asst. dir. nurses to dir. nurses Regis Multi Health Ctr. Inc., New Haven, 1986—. Mem. Am. Mgmt. Assn. Roman Catholic. Home: 654 Oldfield Rd Fairfield CT 06430

PERINE, MARTHA LEVINGSTON, banker; b. Mobile, Ala., June 27, 1948; d. George H. and Martha C. (Matthews) Levingston; m. David A. Perine, June 14, 1969; children: David Andrew Jr., Alissa Lynette, Alison Lynette. BS in Bus. Adminstrn., Clark Coll., 1969; MA in Econs., Washington U., St. Louis, 1971. Mgmt. trainee Fed. Res. Bank of St. Louis, 1971-72, adminstrv. asst., 1973-74, asst. mgr., 1975-77, mgr., 1977-78, asst. v.p., 1978-81, v.p., 1981-83, v.p., controller, 1983—. Mem. allocation com. United Way, St. Louis, 1987—, Conf. Edn.'s Statewide Task Force on Tchr. Edn., 1987-88; vol. United Negro Coll. Fund, chairperson ann. fundraising dinner 1984, 86, co-chair, 1983, 85; bd. mgrs. Monsanto br. YMCA, St. Louis, 1981—, v.p. fin., 1983; sec. Jackson Park PTO, St. Louis, 1982-83, pres., 1983-84, treas., 1985-86; pres. Brittany Woods PTO, St. Louis, 1986-87, treas., 1987-88; fin. sec., bd. dirs. Holy Met. Missionary Bapt. Ch. Mem. Nat. Assn. Bank Women Inc., NAACP (life), Iota Phi Lambda (v.p. 1987—). Democrat. Office: Fed Reserve Bank St Louis 411 Locust St Saint Louis MO 63166

PERINE, MAXINE HARRIET, educator; b. Worth County, Mo., May 11, 1918; d. Robert Rozwell and Della Dale (Martin) P.; B.S. in Edn., Central Mo. State U., 1944; M.A., Columbia U., 1954, profl. diploma, 1960, Ed.D., 1977. Tchr., Worth County schs., 1935-44, Kansas City (Mo.) public schs., 1944-59; reading cons. Kansas City (Mo.) public schs., 1959-64; editor Holt, Rinehart, Winston, N.Y.C., 1964; mem. faculty U. Mich., Flint, 1964—, prof. edn. specializing in reading, 1972-86, prof. emeritus, 1986—; vis. scholar Columbia U., 1978; chair World Congress of Reading, Dublin, 1982; speaker. Mem. Internat. Reading Assn., AAUP, Kappa Delta Pi (chpt. founding counselor 1980—, internat. com. constn. and bylaws 1982-84), Delta Kappa Gamma (named Woman of Distinction 1972). Presbyterian. Author, editor in field. Office: 1321 E Court St Flint MI 48503

PERKINS, ANNE SCARLETT, state legislator; b. Balt., Sept. 29, 1937; d. William George and Anne (Edelen) Scarlett; m. Thomas P. Perkins III; children: Anne, Virginia, Robert. AB, Boston U., 1959; JD, U. Balt., 1979. Staff atty. Md. Advocacy Unit for Developmentally Disabled, Balt., 1979-81; elected mem. Md. Gen. Assembly, Annapolis, 1979—; adj. prof. Goncher Coll., Towson, Md., 1983. Recipient Disting. Service award Greenmount West Community Assn. and Balt. Braille Assn., 1981, Ann London Scott award for Legis. Excellence NOW, 1982, Award for Outstanding Legis. Leadership Md. Assn. for Housing and Redevel. Agys., 1983, Md. Victims Assistance Network award, 1984, Cert. Merit Md. Common Cause, 1984, Award for helping to eliminate domestic violence House of Ruth, 1985, Spl. award Women's Housing Coalition, 1985, Spl. awards Md. Child Care Assn., 1985, 86, Leadership award Gov.'s Housing Initiative Celebration Com., 1986, Coop. Statesman award Md. Coop. Law Coalition, 1986, Legis. Excellence award House of Ruth, 1986, The Peabody Conservatory medallion, 1987. Democrat. Episcopalian. Home: 4110 Greenway Baltimore MD 21218

PERKINS, CHERYL ALICE, computer programmer; b. Forest, Miss., July 17, 1956; d. Richard and Fannie Mae (Gresham) Gray; m. Kevin Isaac Perkins, Nov. 29, 1978; 1 child, Karl. BBA, Marian Coll., 1986. Mail carrier U.S. Post Office, Indpls., 1978-79; advanced sales asst. Jefferson Nat. Life Ins., Indpls., 1979-82, programmer, analyst I, 1982-85; programmer Ind. Vocat. Tech. Coll., Indpls., 1985—. Presidential scholar, 1978; Freedom of Choice grantee, 1978. Torchbearer United Way Greater Indpls., 1984-85; mem. com. United Charities, 1984-85; bd. dirs. Dyslexia Remedial Assn., 1985. Mem. Nat. Council Negro Women (liaison 1980-85), Data Processing Mgmt. Assn., Nat. Assn. Female Execs., Aglow Christain Women's Internat. (rec. sec. 1987—), Love Christian Fellowship, Agape Neighborhood Bible Fellowship (dir.). Home: 4710 E 46th St Indianapolis IN 46226 Office: Ind Vocat Tech Coll 1 W 26th St Indianapolis IN 46226

PERKINS, DEBRA ANN, computer company executive; b. New London, Conn., Aug. 25, 1961; d. Ronald Sprague and Ann Elizabeth (Fallon) P. Student, Monmouth Coll., 1987. Lab. technician Drs. Kline and Kline, New London, 1979-81; asst. clk. banking Legislature State of Conn., Hartford, 1981-82; adminstrv. asst. Conn. Marine Trades Assn., Hartford, 1982-83; scheduler Guglielmo for Congress, East Lyme, Conn., 1983; coordinator service Lanier Harris Corp., Hartford, 1983-84; nat. mgr. Ashton-Tate, Torrance, Calif., 1984-87; dir. Support Our Systems Inc., Red Bank, N.J., 1987—; cons., trainer Office Automation Assn., Hartford, 1983-85. Justice peace Town of Waterford, 1981; counselor Nat. Teenage Reps., Washington, 1982-83; sec. Waterford Rep. Town Com., 1980, Waterford Week Com., 1979; active Council Employment Disabled, 1986—. Mem. Nat. Assn. Female Execs., Time Mgmt. Educators, Assn. Documentation Specialists (exec. com. 1987—, columnist quar. pub. 1987), Hartford Area Trainers. Roman Catholic. Office: Support Our Systems Inc 10 Mechanic St Red Bank NJ 07701

PERKINS, DIANE ARONBERG, agricultural products manager; b. Richmond, Va., Aug. 2, 1952; d. Eliot and Fannie (Hirsohn) Aronberg; m. Robert R. Perkins, May 23, 1976; children: Debra, Kimberly. BS in Bus. Edn., Va. Commonwealth U., 1974, MS in Acctg., 1975. CPA, Va.; cert. data processing. Instr. Va. Commonwealth U., Richmond, 1975-76; acct. Coopers & Lybrand, Richmond, 1976-78; electronic data processing auditor Va. Power, Richmond, 1978-80; sr. data processing controls analyst Philip Morris USA, Richmond, 1980-86, mgr. purchasing, inventory info., 1986—. Mem. Nat. Assn. Accts. (v.p. Richmond-Jackson chpt. 1981-82), Am. Inst. CPA's (cert. 1977), Inst. Internal Auditors. Club: La Leche League (treas. 1985-88). Office: Philip Morris USA PO Box 26603 Richmond VA 23261

PERKINS, ESTHER ROBERTA, literary agent; b. Elkton, Md., May 10, 1927; d. Clarence Roberts and Esther Crouch (Terrell) P.; student West Chester State Tchrs. Coll., 1945-47, U. Del. Acct., E. I. duPont de Nemours & Co., Inc., Wilmington, Del., 1947-65; records specialist U. Del., 1966-78; partner Holly Press, Hockessin, Del., 1977-83; owner Esther R. Perkins Lit. Agy., Childs, Md., 1979—; author's agt. Mem. Cecil County Arts Council. Mem. Authors Guild, Nat. Assn. Female Execs., Nat. Writer's Club, DAR, Romance Writers of Am. Republican. Methodist. Author: Backroading Through Cecil County Maryland, 1978; Things I Wish I'd Said, 1979; Canal Town, Historic Chesapeake City, Maryland, 1983. Home and Office: PO Box 48 Childs MD 21916

PERKINS, (DARRYL) JOY, personnel service executive; b. Batesville, Ark., June 14, 1949; d. Richard Long and Royce June (Jeffery) Dunn; m. Van Ray Perkins, Sept. 4, 1970. B.A. in History and English, U. Tex.-Arlington, 1973. Cert. personnel cons. Cons., Adminstrv. Support Group, Inc., Dallas, 1973-74, cons., 1974-77, office mgr., 1977-84, v.p., 1984, pres., 1984-85; v.p. Diversified Human Resources Group, Inc. (merger), 1985—. Mem. Tex. Assn. Personnel Consultants (dir. 1982-85, pres. 1985-86), Metroplex Assn. Personnel Consultants (dir. 1980-81, pres. 1982-83), Nat. Assn. Personnel Cons. (dir. 1987—). Republican. Office: Adminstrv Support Group Inc 900 Providence Tower East Dallas TX 75244

PERKINS, KATHRYN DIANE, financial monitor; b. Urbana, Ill., Jan. 4, 1957; d. Harold Eugene and Leora Stephan (O'Kelly) P.; 1 child, Stacey. Student, Ill. Wesleyan U., 1975-76, Parkland Coll., 1979-87. Exec. sec. Champaign (Ill.) Comprehensive Employment and Tng. Act. (CETA) Consortium, 1978-81; fin. monitor Champaign County Mental Health Bd., Urbana, 1981-87; fiscal monitor Ill. Coalition Against Domestic Violence, Springfield, 1987—. Coach Rantoul (Ill.) Girls' Softball League, 1986-87; mem. fin. com. Champaign County Child Devel., Inc., 1980-82; vol. March of Dimes, Fisher, Ill., 1980-81, Muscular Dystrophy, Champaign, 1979-81. Mem. Nat. Assn. Female Execs. Methodist. Home: 1821 Seven Pines Rd #5 Springfield IL 62704 Office: Ill Coalition Against Domestic Violence 937 S 4th Springfield IL 62703

PERKINS, MARIAN EMILY, lawyer; b. Chgo., Aug. 8, 1959; d. Toussaint and Thelma (Tillman) P. B.B.A., Howard U., 1981, J.D., 1985. Bar: Ill. Law clk. FAA, Washington, 1980, NAACP Legal Def. Fund, Washington, 1982, Office of D.C.Bar Counsel, 1983; legis. intern Office of City of Chgo., Washington, 1984; atty. Chgo. Transit Authority law dept., 1985—. Vol. polit. campaigns, 1981—. Mem. Delta Sigma Theta. Democrat. Unitarian-Universalist. Avocations: playing the violin; tennis; reading; jogging.

PERKINS, MARSHA ANNE, computer software systems executive; b. Ft. Clayton, Canal Zone, Panama, Jan. 25, 1956; d. Clarence Oliver and Barbara Joan (Bohannon) P. BA, Purdue U., 1977. Mgr. trainee Osco Drug Co., West Lafayette, Ind., 1977-79; br. mgr. G.E. Credit Corp., Stamford, Conn., 1979-82, Indpls. Morris Plan, 1983-85; credit mgr. Cellular One of Indpls., 1985-86; loan originator Old Stone Mortgage Corp., Indpls., 1986-88; dir. origination systems mktg. Data-Link Systems, Inc., South Bend, Ind., 1988—. Dir. vol. tng. Ransburg Y.M.C.A., Indpls., 1985-87. Named one of Outstanding Young Women of Am., Outstanding Young Women of Am., 1985, 86, 87. Mem. Am. Bus. Women's Assn. (pres. 1980-81), Met. Indpls. Bd. Realtors, Assn. Profl. Mortgage Women, Indpls. Jaycees (v.p. 1987-88, Richard E. Rowland Meml. award 1987), Ind. Jaycees (sec. 1987-88, John H. Armbruster Meml. award 1987), Castleton Jaycees (pres. 1985-86). Roman Catholic. Home: 3145 Mountain Maple Ct South Bend IN 46628

PERKINS, MARTHA LOUISE, banker; b. Elkton, Ky., Aug. 24, 1915; d. Sterling and Sallie (Chesnut) P.; student public schs., Elkton. With Elkton Bank & Trust Co., 1937—, past pres., now chmn. bd., dir. Mem. adminstrv. bd. Petrie Meml. Methodist Episcopal Ch.; treas. City of Elkton, 17 yrs.; treas. Todd County Bd. Edn., 25 yrs. Address: Elkton Bank Trust Co Public Sq Elkton KY 42220

PERKINS, MARY LYNN, educator; b. Grenada, Miss., Jan. 23, 1954; d. Ralph Jamison and Myrtice Yvonne (Vanlandingham) P. BE, U. Miss., 1975, MEd, 1976. Cert. tchr. Tchr. Calhoun County Sch. System, Calhoun City, Miss., 1976—; pvt. tutor, Calhoun City, 1975-83; cheerleader sponsor Calhoun City Mid. Sch., 1979-80, social studies chair for Insructional Mgmt. Program, 1987—. Com. mem. Nat. Library Week Calhoun City Pub. Library, 1985—, chair 1987—; mem. publicity div. Calhoun County chpt. Am. Cancer Soc., Pittsboro, Miss., 1986-87, mem.-at-large, 1987-88; dist. III edn. dept. chmn. Miss. Fedn. Women's Clubs, Jackson, Miss., 1985-86, free enterprise dept. chmn. 1986-87. Named Outstanding Young Educator Calhoun City Jaycees, 1978; named one of Outstanding Young Women Am., 1984. Mem. Miss. Assn. Educators, Nat. Edn. Orgn., Phi Kappa Phi, Kappa Delta Pi. Baptist. Club: New Century (Calhoun City) (com. mem. 1985—, pres. 1988—). Home: Rt 1 Box 210 Calhoun City MS 38916-9741 Office: Calhoun City Mid Sch PO Box 559 Calhoun City MS 38916

PERKINS, NANCY JANE, industrial designer; b. Phila., Nov. 5, 1949; d. Gordon Osborne and Martha Elizabeth (Keichline) P.; student Ohio U., 1967-68; B.F.A. in Indsl. Design, U. Ill., Champaign, 1972. Indsl. designer Peterson Bednar Assos., Evanston, Ill., 1972-74, Deschamps Mills Assos., Bartlett, Ill., 1974-75; dir. graphic design Cameo Container Corp., Chgo., 1975-76; indsl. design cons. Sears Roebuck & Co., Chgo., 1977-88; cons. indsl. design, 1988—; founder Perkins Design Ltd., indsl. design cons. co., 1979—; adj. prof. grad. design Seminar U. Ill. at Chgo., 1982, 88, instr. undergrad. design, 1984, 1988; adj. prof. Ill. Inst. Tech., 1987; instr. Inst. Design Ill. Inst. of Tech., Chgo., 1987; juror Annual Design Rev. Industrial Design mag., 1986; keynote speaker Soc. Automotive Engrs., 1980, Women in Design, 1982, 84, Meadow Club, 1983, U. Ill. Disting. Alumni Lecture Series, 1983, Human Factors Soc. Interface '85, 1985. Contbr. articles to profl. jours.; profiled in Industrial Design mag., 1986. Co-leader Cadette troop DuPage County council Girl Scouts U.S.A., 1978-79. Recipient Outstanding Alumni award U. Ill. Alumni Jour., 1981. Mem. Indsl. Designers Soc. Am. (treas. Chgo. chpt. 1977-79, vice chmn. 1979-80, chmn. 1981, dist. membership 1982, ann. conf. com. 1983, publs. com. 1985-86, dir. at large 1987—). Patentee marine, automotive and consumer products. Home and Office: 1111 N Dearborn #606 Chicago IL 60610

PERKINS, TANYA GOODMAN, public relations specialist, writer; b. Savannah, Ga., Apr. 24, 1954; d. Melvin and Annette (McTier) Goodman; m. Eric Glenn Perkins, June 16, 1984 (separated). BA in Sociology and Journalism, George Washington U., 1976; cert. in journalism, U. Calif., Berkeley, 1980. Reporter, copy editor The Evansville (Ind.) Press, 1980-81; pub. relations specialist Delta Sigma Theta, Inc., Washington, 1982; editor Raven Corp., Washington, 1982-83; sr. philatelic programs specialist U.S. Postal Service, Washington, 1984-87, media relations rep., 1987—. Assoc. editor Black Ethnic Collectibles mag.; contbr. articles to newspapers and mags. Vol. spokesperson Carter-Mondale, campaign, 1976. Mem. Women in Advt. and Mktg., Delta Sigma Theta. Roman Catholic. Office: US Postal Service 475 L'Enfant Plaza SW Washington DC 20260-2157

PERKINS-CARPENTER, BETTY LOU, business executive; b. Rochester N.Y., Jan. 22, 1931; d. Edward C. and Bertha M. (Loeser) Kalmn; m. Floyd F. Perkins, Jan. 31, 1951 (div. 1979); children—Cheryl Lee, F. Scott; m. Marcellus Chipman Carpenter, Oct. 10, 1981. BS in Phys. Edn. Adminstrn., Empire State Coll., N.Y., 1979; MS in Early Childhood Edn. Adminstrn., Nova U., 1983. Tchr., coach Rochester YWCA, 1954-59, Perkins Swimming Sch., Penfield, N.Y., 1959-64; pres. Perkins Swim Club, Inc., Rochester, 1964—, Perkins Fit By Five, Inc., Rochester, 1969—, Child Fitness Prodns., Inc.d/b/a Sr. Fitness Prodns., Rochester, 1983—, Fit By Five Franchise Corp., Rochester, 1984—; diving coach Olympic Games, Montreal, 1976; mem. adv. com. N.Y. State Task Force Phys. Fitness and Sports, 1978-82; bd. dirs. U.S. Olympic Diving Com., 1976-80; cons. European sports facilities, 1969-83, Pres.'s Council on Phys. Fitness and Sports, 1986—; mem. adv. com. Community Savs. Bank, Rochester, 1976-79. Author: The Fun of Fitness-A Handbook for the Senior Class, 1988; Am. editor: Teaching Babies to Swim, 1979; contbr. articles to profl. jours. Exec. producer audio-visual instructional materials. Served with USAF, 1948-51. Recipient Gold medal Inst. Achievement of Human Potential, Brazil, 1973; Mike Malone Meml. Diving award, 1977; Cady Diving award, 1977; named to Monroe County Athletes Hall of Fame, Rochester, 1979; named Sports Woman of Yr., U.S. Olympic Diving Commn., 1979. Mem. U.S. Diving Assn. (life, numerous offices), Rochester Assn. Edn. of Young Children, Nova U. Alumnae Assn., Genesee Valley Sports Medicine Council, AAUW. Republican. Club: Oak Hill Country (Rochester). Lodge: Order Eastern Star (life). Avocations: swimming; cross-country skiing; reading; travel. Office: Perkins Swim Club 1606 Penfield Rd Rochester NY 14625

PERKINSON, DIANA AGNES ZOUZELKA, rug import company executive; b. Prostejov, Czechoslovakia, June 27, 1943; came to U.S., 1962; d. John Charles and Agnes Diana (Sincl) Zouzelka; m. David Francis Perkinson, Mar. 6, 1965; children—Dana Leissa, David. B.A., U. Lausanne (Switzerland), 1960; M.A., U. Madrid, 1961; M.B.A., Case Western Res. U., 1963; cert. internat. mktg. Oxford (Eng.) U., 1962. Assoc. Allen Hartman & Schreiber, Cleve., 1963-64; interpreter Tower Internat. Inc., Cleve., 1964-66; pres. Oriental Rug Importers Ltd., Cleve., 1979—; treas. Oriental Rug Designers, Inc., Cleve., 1980—; sec., treas. Oriental Rug Cons., Inc., Cleve., 1980—; chmn. Foxworthy's Inc. subs. Oriental Rug Importers Ft. Myers, Naples, Sanibel, Fla.; dir. Beckwith & Assocs., Inc., Cleve., Dix-Bur Investments, Ltd. Trustee, Cleve. Ballet, 1979, exec. com., 1981; mem. Cleve. Mayor's Adv. Com.; trustee Diabetes Assn. Greater Cleve.; chmn. grantsmanship Jr. League of Cleve., 1982; mem. mem. Cleve. Found.-Women in Philanthropy, 1982; trustee Diabetes Assn. Greater Cleve. Mem. Women Bus. Owners Assn., Oriental Rug Retailers Am. (dir. 1983). Republican. Roman Catholic. Clubs: Cleve. Racquet, Recreation League (Cleve.). Home: Ravencrest 14681 County Line Rd Cleveland OH 44022 also: Stratford at Pelican Bay Crayton Rd Naples FL 33940 Office: Oriental Rug Importers Ltd Inc 23533 Mercantile Rd Beachwood OH 44122

PERKS, BARBARA ANN MARCUS, psychologist; b. Wilson, Pa., July 1, 1937; d. Alfred M. and Lillian (Reibman) Marcus; B.S., Pa. State U., 1959; M.A., Columbia U., 1963; cert. in ednl. psychology Oxford (Eng.) U., 1965; postgrad. U. Oreg., U.S. Internat. U.; Ed.D., U. B.C., 1984; m. Anthony Manning Perks, Sept. 9, 1963. Tchr. gifted Hamden (Conn.) Sch. Dist., 1959-62; reading cons. Oxfordshire County, Littlemore, Eng., 1964-65; sch. psychologist Vancouver (B.C., Can.) Sch. Bd., 1972-76; supr. student tchrs. U. B.C., Vancouver, 1977-78, cons. Research Center, 1978-79, ednl. psychologist, child and family unit child psychiatry Health Scis. Centre Hosp., 1979-81, lectr., 1977—; instr. psychology Langara Coll., 1985; pvt. practice counseling and teaching, Vancouver, 1984—, counseling and sch. psychology, Burnaby, B.C., 1985—. Recipient Can. Daus. League award; Provincial Council of B.C. award, 1981, U. B.C. awards, 1980; Jonathan Rogers award, 1984; Univ. fellow, Dr. MacKenzie Am. Alumni scholar U. B.C., 1976; U. B.C. summer scholar, 1982; cert. psychologist, B.C. Mem. Am. Psychol. Assn., B.C. Psychol. Assn., Assn. Humanistic Psychology, Nat. Assn. Sch. Psychology, Am. Ednl. Research, N.Am. Soc. Adlerian Psychology, Am. Orthopsychiat. Assn., Mortar Bd., Pi Sigma Alpha, Pi Lambda Theta, Kappa Delta Pi. Clubs: Figure Skating (Vancouver, B.C., New Haven, Conn., Allentown, Pa.). Author research papers. Home: 4570 Glenwood Ave, North Vancouver, BC Canada V7R 4G5

PERLBERG-MONTAÑO, TREYCE DARLENE, quality assurance manager; b. Tucson, July 20, 1960; d. Elroe Julias and Audrey Etta (Davis) Geier; m. Robert Andrew Perlberg, Oct. 22, 1983 (div. Feb. 1987); m. Gilbert S. Montaño, Aug. 21, 1987. Cert. in Acctg., Sociology, Bus. Law, Bus. Planning, Tucson Coll. Bus., 1986. Quality assurance mgr. Tremy Turbines, Tuscon, 1983-86, Xytec Mfg., Inc., Tuscon, 1986—; pres. Bus. Card Internat., Tucson, 1983—, pres., founder of Perlberg Pl., Tucson, 1983—, founder of Pet Finders, Tucson, 1983-86, pres., founder of Bus. Consultations Unltd., 1984—, pres., v.p. Nail Studio, 1987—. Served with USAF, 1978-82. Mem. Nat. Assn. for Female Execs. (life, cert. 1983, 84, 85, 86, 87), Am. Entrepenuer Assn. (life), Smithsonian Instn. (life), Am. Legion. Lutheran. Lodge: Elks (sec. local chpt. 1982-85). Home: 6231 E 15th St Tucson AZ 85711 Office: Tucson Med Ctr 5301 East Grant Rd Tucson AZ 85713

PERLESS, ELLEN, advertising executive; b. N.Y.C., Sept. 9, 1941; d. Joseph B. and Bertha (Messinger) Kaplan; m. Robert L. Perless, July 2, 1965. Student, Smith Coll., 1958-59, Bard Coll., 1959-62. Copywriter Doyle, Dane Bernbach, N.Y.C., 1964-70, Young & Rubicam, N.Y.C., 1970-74; creative supr. Young & Rubicam, 1974-76, v.p., creative supr., 1977, v.p., assoc. creative dir., 1978, sr. v.p., assoc. creative dir., 1979-84; v.p., assoc. creative dir. Leber Katz Ptnrs., 1984-85, sr. v.p., creative dir., 1986-87, sr. v.p., sr. creative dir., 1987—. Recipient Clio award, 1979, 83, Andy award, awards Art Dirs. Club N.Y. Mem. One Club for Art and Copy. Club: Northeast Harbor Fleet of Maine. Home: 37 Langhorne Ln Greenwich CT 06831 Office: FCB/Leber Katz Ptnrs 767 Fifth Ave New York NY 10153

PERLMAN, BARBARA ANN, sales professional; b. Newark, Feb. 1, 1964; d. Jerome Sanford Perlman and Susan Gloria (Riegelhaupt) Meiselman. BS in Mktg., Pa. State U., 1986; postgrad., Seton Hall U., 1987—. Sales rep. CF AirFreight div. Consol. Freightways, Inc., Elizabeth, N.J., 1986-87, account exec., 1987-88; asst. sales mgr. CF AirFreight div. Consol. Freightways, Inc., Elizabeth, 1988—. Mem. Nat. Assn. Female Execs., Lakeland Traffic Assn. (chairperson 1986—, bd. govs. 1988—). Home: 11 Stanford Dr 2A Bridgewater NJ 08807

PERLMAN, CAROLE SHOOLMAN, small business owner; b. Washington, Dec. 9, 1947; d. Robert Benjamin and Rae (Plimack) Shoolman; m. Philip Stewart Perlman, Aug. 20, 1967 (div. 1975). AA, Balt. Jr. Coll., 1967. Librarian Bloomington (Ind.) Tribune, 1967-68; service rep. Social Security Adminstrn., Bloomington, 1968-71, Columbus, Ohio, 1971-73; hosp. rep. Blue Cross of Cen. Ohio, Columbus, 1973-76; sales rep. Sherwood Med. Corp., St. Louis, 1976-79, Stryker Corp., Kalamazoo, 1979-81; sr. territory mgr. Air-Shields Vickers, Hatboro, Pa., 1982-87; owner Social Graces, Inc., Columbus, 1987—. Active Museum Jr. Council, Columbus, 1986-87, chairperson poster sales com. 1987-88, pres.-elect 1988—. Mem. Updowntowners Columbus C. of C. (mem. social com. 1988—). Democrat. Jewish. Home: 4842 Hewn Timber Ln Columbus OH 43230

PERLMAN, CINDY LOU, chinaware company executive; b. N.Y.C., Jan. 30, 1957; d. Harold H. Perlman and Joanne Betty Perlman Schwartz. A.A.S., Fashion Inst. Tech., 1976, student, 1982-83; student Mudelein Coll., 1979-81; cert. Dale Carnegie, Chgo., 1980. Facility supr. J&P Hayman's, N.Y.C., 1976-78; mgr. Midwest dist. Omniform div. John Meyer, Norwich, Conn., 1978-81; br. mgr. Nutri/System, N.Y.C., 1982-83; designer liaison Rego Internat., N.Y.C., 1984—. Active Deborah Heart Fund, N.Y.C., 1970—; vol. worker with deaf. Mem. Inst. Bus. Designers, Am. Soc. Interior Designers, Resources Council, Nat. Assn. Female Execs. Avocations: horses; computers.

PERLMAN, RHEA, actress; b. Bklyn., Mar. 31; m. Danny DeVito, Jan. 8, 1982; children: Lucy Chet, Gracie Far, Jake. Grad., Hunter Coll. Has appeared in numerous Broadway plays; founder Colonades Theatre Lab., N.Y.C.; various roles in TV movies include I Want to Keep My Baby!, 1976, Stalk the Wild Child, 1976 Intimate Strangers, 1977, Having Babies II, 1977, Mary Jane Harper Cried Last Night, 1977, Like Normal People, 1979, Drop Out Father, 1982, The Ratings Game (cable), 1984; TV series include Taxi, 1978-82, Cheers, 1982—;. Recipient Emmy award for Outstanding Supporting Actress in a Comedy Series, 1984. Office: Triad Artists c/o J Kimball 10100 Santa Monica Blvd 16th Floor Los Angeles CA 90067 *

PERLMUTTER, DIANE F., consultant; b. N.Y.C., Aug. 31, 1945; d. Bert H. and Frances (Smith) P. Student, NYU, 1969-70; AB in English, Miami U., Oxford, Ohio, 1967. Writer sales promotion Equitable Life Assurance, N.Y.C., 1967-68; adminstrv. asst. de Garmo, Inc., N.Y.C., 1968-69, asst. account exec., 1969-70, account exec., 1970-74, v.p., account supr., 1974-76; mgr. corp. advt. Avon Products, Inc., N.Y.C., 1976-79, dir. communications Latin Am., Spain, Can., 1979-80, dir. brochures, 1980-81, dir. category merchandising, 1981-82, group dir. motivational communications, 1982-83, group dir. sales promotion, 1983-84, v.p. sales promotion, 1984, v.p. internat. bus. devel., 1984-85, area v.p. Latin Am., 1985, v.p. advtg. and campaign mktg., 1985-87, v.p. U.S. operational planning, 1987; cons. N.Y.C., 1987—; chairperson ann. meeting Direct Selling Assn., Washington, 1982; v.p. Nat. Home Fashions League, N.Y.C., 1975-76. Founding bd. mem. Am. Red Magen David for Israel, N.Y.C., 1970-75; pres. adv. council Miami Sch. Bus., 1986—; mem. Miami Sch. Applied Scis., 1978-81. Mem. Advt. Women of N.Y., Women in Communications, Miami U. Alumni Assn. (pres., chair 1986), Beta Gamma Sigma. Jewish. Club: Atrium (N.Y.C.).

PERLMUTTER, DONNA, newspaper music and dance critic; b. Phila.; d. Myer and Bessie (Krasno) Stein; m. Jona Perlmutter, Mar. 21, 1964; children—Aaron, Matthew. B.A., Pa. State U., 1958; M.S., Yeshiva U., 1959. Music and dance critic Los Angeles Herald Examiner, 1975-84, Los Angeles Times, 1984—; dance critic Dance Mag., N.Y.C., 1980—; music critic Opera News, N.Y.C., 1981—, Ovation Mag., N.Y.C., 1983—; panelist, speaker various music and dance orgns. Mem. Music Critics Assn. Home: 10507 Le Conte Ave Los Angeles CA 90024

PERLMUTTER, FELICE DAVIDSON, social work administration educator; b. N.Y.C., Nov. 2, 1931; d. Samuel and Helen (Newman) Davidson; m. Daniel D. Perlmutter; children: Shira, Saul, Tova. BA in English with honors, NYU, 1953; MSW, U. Conn., 1955; PhD, Bryn Mawr Coll., 1969. Program dir. Jewish Community Ctr. Staten Island, Staten Island, N.Y., 1955-58; psychiat. social worker Inst. Juvenile Research, Champaign, Ill., 1958-60; prin. investigator, exec. dir. Champaign Youth Council, Human Relations Commn., 1960-64; lectr. Bryn Mawr (Pa.) Coll., 1968; asst. prof. U. Pa., Phila., 1969-73; assoc. prof. Temple U., Phila., 1973-75, prof., 1975—; pvt. practice family mediation Phila., 1981—; cons. Pa. Dept. Pub. Welfare, Harrisburg, 1974-78, 86; mem. rev. panel NIMH, Rockville, Md., 1977-82. Editor: A Design for Social Work Practice, 1974, Leadership in Social Administration, 1980, Mental Health Promotion and Primary Prevention, 1982, Human Services at Risk, 1984, Alternative Social Agencies: Administrative Strategies, 1988; mem. editorial bd. profl. jours.; contbr. articles on mental health and social work to profl. jours. Vol. local services Fedn. Jewish Agys., Phila., 1978—; bd. dirs. Jewish Community Relations Council, Phila., 1980—, Acad. Family Mediators, 1982-86; vol. policy com. United Way, Phila., 1986—. NIMH fellow, 1965-68, Lurie fellow, 1967-68, NSF fellow, 1972; Fulbright sr. scholar, 1987. Fellow Am. Orthopsychiat. Assn. Democrat. Jewish. Office: Temple U Broad and Columbia Philadelphia PA 19122

PERLOFF, JEAN MARCOSSON, lawyer; b. Lakewood, Ohio, June 25, 1942; d. John Solomon and Marcella Catherine (Borngen) Marcosson; m. William Harry Perloff, Dec. 26, 1968. B.A. magna cum laude, Lake Erie Coll., 1965; M.A. in Italian, UCLA, 1967; J.D. magna cum laude, Ventura Coll. Law, 1976. Bar: Calif. 1976. Assoc. in Italian U. Calif.-Santa Barbara, 1967-70; law clk., paralegal Ventura County Pub. Defender's Office, Ventura, Calif., 1975; sole practice, Ventura, 1976-78; co-prin. Clabaugh & Perloff, A Profl. Corp., Ventura, 1979-82; sr. jud. atty. to presiding justice 6th div. 2d Dist. Ct. Appeals, Los Angeles, 1982—; instr. Ventura Coll. Law, 1976-79. Pres., bd. dirs. Santa Barbara Zool. Gardens, 1987—. Mem. ABA, Calif. State Bar, Ventura County Bar Assn., Calif. Women Lawyers, Women Lawyers Ventura County, Ventura County Criminal Def. Bar Assn. (pres. 1979), Mar Vista Bus. and Profl. Women, Kappa Alpha Sigma. Democrat. Home: 1384 Plaza Pacifica Santa Barbara CA 93108 Office: 2d Dist Ct of Appeals 1280 S Victoria Ventura CA 93003

PERLOV, DADIE, association executive; b. N.Y.C., June 8, 1929; d. Aaron and Anna (Leight) Heitman; m. Norman B. Perlov, May 29, 1950; children—Nancy Perlov Rosenbach, Jane, Amy Perlov Schenkein. BA, NYU, 1950; postgrad., Adelphi U., 1963, Vanderbilt U., 1973. Cert. assn. exec., 1978. Exec. dir. Operation Open City, N.Y.C., 1962-64; field services dir. Nat. Council Jewish Women, N.Y.C., 1968-74; exec. dir. N.Y. Library Assn., N.Y.C., 1974-81, Nat. Council Jewish Women, N.Y.C., 1981—; cons. HEW, 1975-76; mem. bd. Nat. Assembly for Social Policy, 1970-74, 81-83; pres.-elect Internat. Council Library Assn. Execs., 1973-74; exec. mem. Conf. of Pres., 1981—. Contbr. articles to profl. jours. Dem. committeewoman, 1966; mem. N.Y. Zool. Soc., 1959—, adv. bd. Nat. Inst. Against Prejudice and Violence, 1985—, profl. adv. com. for Hornstein Program in Jewish communal service, Brandeis U., 1986—; bd. visitors Pratt Inst., Bklyn., 1980-84; bd. dirs. Pres.'s Council on Handicapped, 1981—. Recipient Recognition award N.Y. Library Assn., 1978; cert. N.Y. State Legislature, 1978; named N.Y. State Exec. of Year, 1980. Mem. Am. Soc. Assn. Execs. (evaluator 1980—, bd. dirs. 1987—, Excellence award 1983), N.Y. Soc. Assn. Execs. (pres. 1985), Global Perspectives in Edn. (dir.), LWV (chpt. pres. 1960-62), Nat. Orgn. Continuing Edn. (council), Audubon Soc., N.Y. Citizens Council on Libraries (dir. 1981-84), Am. Arbitration Assn. (mem. panel).

PERLS, RAE DEZETTEL, psychologist; b. Chgo., Mar. 31, 1937; d. Louis Max and Marcella (Klasky) Dezettel; m. Stephen Rudolph Perls, June 20, 1956; children: Robert Alan, Nancy Lynn. Student, Antioch Coll., 1954-58; BA, U. Chgo., 1959; MA, U. N.Mex., 1970, PhD, 1973. Lic. psychologist, N.Mex. Counselor Albuquerque Pub. Schs., 1970-71; clin. intern Drs. Hudson and Backer Ltd., Albuquerque, 1971-73; pvt. practice psychology Albuquerque, 1973—; cons. psychologist, The Abortion Clinic, Albuquerque, 1973-78, VA Speech Dept., Albuquerque, 1973-76, Albuquerque Pub. Schs., 1978—; lectr. various orgns., workshops. Author: (with others) Handbook of Short Term Group Psychotheries, 1983. Chmn. Rape Crisis Ctr., Albuquerque, 1979, Edn. task force City of Albuquerque, 1970's; mem. Jewish Family Service Bd., Albuquerque, 1987—. Fellow Am. Group Psychotherapy Assn. (past chmn. nominating com., chmn. elect affiliate assembly), Am. Orthopsychiat. Assn.; mem. Am. Psychol. Assn. Democrat.

PERMAR, MARY ELIZABETH, real estate investor; b. Augusta, Ga., Mar. 18, 1956; d. Philip Howard and Doris (Maxwell) P. BS in Architecture, Clemson U., 1978; MArch, U. Ill., 1981, MBA, 1982. V.p., sec., treas. Assn. Student Chpts., AIA, Washington, 1978-79; with The Prudential Realty Group, 1982—; investment mgr. The Prudential Realty Group, Chgo., 1982-85; dir. acquisitions and sales The Prudential Realty Group, Newark, 1985-87; dir. acquisitions The Prudential Realty Group, Chgo., 1988—. Mng. editor CRIT The Archtl. Student Jour., 1978-79. Tutor Program for Underprivileged Children, Chgo., 1982-85. Charles G. Rummel fellow U. Ill. Sch. Architecture, 1979-82. Mem. Execs. Club Chgo., Western Soc. Engrs. Republican. Presbyterian. Office: The Prudential Realty Group One Prudential Plaza Suite 3300 Chicago IL 60601

PERNICK, SANDRA ROSE, business executive; b. Chgo., Oct. 7, 1944; d. Karl and Diana (Matlin) Witt; m. Steven L. Pernick, Oct. 11, 1964; children—Kevin Michael, Kelly Andrew. B.A., Roosevelt U., Chgo., 1964. Corr. Time, Inc., 1964-66; tchr. emotionally handicapped children Chgo. Pub. Schs., 1966-68; pres. bd. dirs. Orchard Village, Skokie, Ill., 1976—; pres. Direct Response Corp., Des Plaines, Ill., 1981—. Mem. mental health com. Nat. Council Jewish Women. Mem. Am. Telemarketing Assn. (bd. dirs. 1986—, pres. 1988), Chgo. Assn. Direct Mktg. (legis. com. 1986—), Nat. Assn. Retarded Citizens, Ill. Assn. Retarded Citizens. Office: The Direct Response Corp 1865 Miner St Des Plaines IL 60016

PERNSTEINER, CAROL ANN, hotel executive; d. Alvin Anton and Lillian Therese (Spreen) P. B.A., Marquette U., 1969. With The Sheraton Corp., 1971—, front office mgr. Sheraton Washington, D.C., 1979-81, resident mgr. Sheraton St. Louis Hotel, 1981—. Capt. Operation Brightside, St. Louis, 1984-86. Recipient Pres.'s award The Sheraton Corp., Washington, 1979, Divisional Pres.'s award The Sheraton Corp., St. Louis, 1985. Mem. Adminstrv. Mgmt. Soc., Am. Hotel and Motel Assn. Republican. Avocations: violin; piano. Home and Office: Sheraton Saint Louis Hotel 910 N 7th St Saint Louis MO 63101

PEROTTI, ROSE NORMA, lawyer; b. St. Louis, Aug. 10, 1930; d. Joseph and Dorothy Mary (Roleski) Perotti. B.A., Fontbonne Coll., St. Louis, 1952; J.D., St. Louis U., 1957. Bar: Mo. 1958. Trademark atty. Sutherland, Polster & Taylor, St. Louis, 1958-63, Sutherland Law Office, 1964-70; trademark atty. Monsanto Co., St. Louis, 1971-85, sr. trademark atty., 1985—. Honored with dedication of faculty office in her name, St. Louis U. Sch. Law, 1980. Mem. Mo. Bar Assn., Bar Assn. Met. St. Louis, ABA, Am. Judicature Soc., Smithsonian Assocs., Friends St. Louis Art Museum, Mo. Bot. Garden. Office: Monsanto Co 800 N Lindbergh Blvd Saint Louis MO 63167

PERRAULT, DOROTHY ANN JACQUES, small business owner, nurse; b. New Orleans, Aug. 25, 1937; d. Alvin Joseph and Dorothy (Angelety) Jacques; m. Harry Joseph Perrault Jr., Oct. 24, 1959; children: Harry J. Perrault III, TroyLynne Ahmed, Sabrina. BSN, Dillard U., 1960. RN. Head nurse Sara Mayo Hosp., New Orleans, 1960; supr. Flint Goodridge Hosp., New Orleans, 1960-64; relief supr. Charity Hosp., New Orleans, 1964-69, nursing instr., 1969-70, supr., 1970-71, 1971-77, asst. dir., 1969-77; owner, adminstr. Perrault Kiddy Kollege, Inc., New Orleans, 1972—; pres. Deli Deluxe Catering Service, The Fashion Korner, New Orleans; dir. Coalition Child Care, New Orleans, Nat. Assn. for Edn. Children, New Orleans, La. Fedn. Child Care, New Orleans. Author: Louisiana: Pelican State, 1980, also editor, Blissful Stages; playwright America, Our Country, 1987. Bd. dirs. Am. Security Council, New Orleans, 1979—, Pvt. Industry Council, New Orleans, United Negro Coll. Fund, New Orleans, 1986—; mem. exec. com. La. Leauge Good Govt., New Orleans, 1979; past pres. Nurses' Fedn. Charity Hosp. Recipient Thomas Jefferson award Am. Inst. for Pub. Service, 1978, Achievement in Child Care Mayor of New Orleans, 1987, La. Gov.'s award, 1986, numerous others; named Distinguished Alumni, Dillard U., 1985, one of Outstanding Bus. Women of Yr., Nat. Council of Negro women, 1988. Mem. Dillard U. Profl. Orgn. Nurses (pres. 1988), Dillard U. Nat. Alumni Assn. (pres. 1981-83), Nat. Assn. Female Execs., Nat. Assn. Mgrs., New Orleans C. of C., Nat. Black Bus. League, Zeta Phi Beta. Democrat. Roman Catholic. Club: Estelle Hubbard. Lodge: Knights of Peter Claver. Office: Perrault Kiddy Kollege Perrault Plaza 6201 Chef Menteur Hwy New Orleans LA 70126

PERRAULT, PATSY ANN, advertising agency executive; b. Darrouzett, Tex., Mar. 30, 1939; d. Carson Lee and Mamie (Allen) Altmiller; m. Ronald Ray Weaver, Sept. 3, 1960 (div. July 1979); children—Leanne Weaver, Douglas Weaver; m. Thomas Burt Perrault, July 25, 1981. B.S., West Tex. State U., 1961, M.A., 1964. Program dir. Sta. KFMK, Houston, 1971-74; media buyer McCann-Erickson, Houston, 1974-77; media planner Smith, Smith, Baldwin & Carlberg, Houston, 1977-78; media supr. Rives Smith, Baldwin & Carlberg, Houston, 1978-80; media mgr. Houston Coca-Cola Bottling, 1980-81; v.p., media dir. W. B. Doner, Houston, 1981-83; ptnr., exec. v.p. Taylor Brown & Barnhill, Houston, 1983—. Mem. adv. bd. bus. mktg. dept. Stephen F. Austin U. Mem. Houston Advt. Fedn., Assn. Women Radio & TV, Alpha Delta Pi. Republican. Mem. Assembly of God Ch.

PERRETTA, NANCY VROOMAN, medical insurance company representative; b. Oneonta, N.Y., Oct. 17, 1940; d. Harold Clute and Beatrice Evelyn (Thomas) Vrooman; m. Francis A. Perretta, Nov. 17, 1962; 1 child, Helenarose. Student, Stetson U., 1958-59; BA, Keuka Coll., 1962; postgrad., Wroxton (Eng.) Abbey, 1970; MS in Edn., SUNY, Onetona, 1973. Editor women's news Daily Star, Onetona, 1958; tchr. elem. grades Onetona Pub. Schs., 1962-63, Cooperstown (N.Y.) Cen. Schs., 1965-66, Onetona Jr. High Sch., 1966-78; dir. women's news Sta. WDOS, Onetona, 1964-65; sales rep. Met. Life Ins. Co., Traverse City, Mich., 1978-80; account exec. Devoe Ins. Agy., New Milford, Conn., 1980-82, Crowe Ins. Agy., Stroudsburg, Pa., 1982-85; mktg. rep. Blue Cross Northeast Pa., Stroudsburg, 1985—; area news reporter Sta. WNFB-TV, Binghamton, N.Y., 1964-65. Bd. dirs. Ctr. for Devel. Disabilities, Stroudburg, 1986-88; v.p. Pocono Raceway Ambassadors, Stroudsburg, 1988—; pres. Monroe unit Am. Cancer Soc., Stroudsburg, 1988. Mem. Nat. Assn. Females Execs., Pocono Mtns. C. of C. (bd. dirs. 1986—), Exec. Womne's Council (co-chmn. 1987—), LWV (past bd. dirs. Onetona and Stroudsburg). Republican. Roman Catholic. Clubs: Torch, Shawnee Country, Glen Brook Country (Stroudsburg). Home: Rd 4 PO Box 4006 Stroudsburg PA 18360 Office: Blue Cross Northeast Pa 701 Main St Stroudsburg PA 18360

PERRETTI, SERENA, judge; b. Passaic, N.J., Oct. 3, 1928; d. Peter N. and Jessie (Ingram) P.; A.B., Vassar Coll., 1948; J.D. with honors, Rutgers U., 1954; postgrad. dept. religious studies Seton Hall U., 1982; m. Richard S. Benson, Mar. 27, 1962; children: Thane, Serena, Peter. Admitted to N.J. bar, 1955; individual practice law, Passaic, 1955-76; U.S. magistrate, Newark, 1976-87; judge criminal law div. Superior Ct. N.J., Newark, 1987—; panelist, participant seminars. Sec., Passaic County Ethics Com., 1969, mem., 1969-71, 75-76; mem. Passaic Bd. Edn., 1956-59. Mem. Passaic County Bar Assn. (sec. 1976, trustee 1973-76), Assn. Fed. Bar N.J. Republican. Mem. United Ch. of Christ. Mng. editor Rutgers Law Rev., 1953, editor-in-chief, 1954; contbr. articles to profl. publs. Office: Essex County Courts Bldg Newark NJ 07102

PERRI, AUDREY ANN, lawyer; b. Oxnard, Calif., Feb. 2, 1936; d. Zafon Audry and Francis May (Sandblom) Hartman; m. Frank Perri, Aug. 10, 1958; children—Michael, Michelle. B.A., U. Redlands, 1958; J.D., U. LaVerne, 1976. Cert. family law specialist State Bar Calif. Tchr. English as fgn. lang., Reykjavic and Akureyre, Iceland, 1962-63; tchr. English and govt. various high schs., Calif., Ill., 1958-76; dep. dist. atty. San Bernardino County, 1976-80, dist. atty., 1976-81; ptnr. law firm Covington & Crowe, Ontario, Calif., 1981—. Articles editor: Jour. Juvenile Justice Law Rev., 1975-76. Mem., host, chmn. Internat. Exchange Program, 1965-84; com. mem. Upland (Calif.) City Council, 1970; mem. Dem. State Central Com., 1981-82; bd. dirs. NCCJ, 1977-82. Mem. Inland Counties Women at Law (founding pres. 1980-81), Calif. Women Lawyers (dir. 1980-84, 1st v.p. 1984), San Bernardino County Bar Assn. (mem. com. 1977-84, dir. 1981-83, 84-87), ABA, Calif. State Bar (conf. del. 1977-86, exec. com. 1985—), AAUW (pres. Ontario-Upland br. 1969-70). Home: 8373 Camino Sur Cucamonga CA 91730 Office: Covington & Crowe PO Box 1515 Ontario CA 91762

PERRIE, TRUC-CHI THI HUYNH, scientist; b. Saigon, Vietnam, Nov. 11, 1954; came to U.S., 1973; d. Vi Huu Huynh and Truan Thi Pham. BS in Ceramic Engring., Alfred U., 1977, MS in Ceramic Engring., 1978; PhD in Materials Sci., MIT, 1987. Technician quality control Corhart Refractories Co., Buckhannon, W.Va., 1976; research engr. Globe Union, Glendale, Wis., 1977; devel. scientist, cons. Corning Glass Works, Raleigh, N.C., 1983-87; research scientist Nat. Research Council, Halifax, N.S., Can., 1988—. Translator Vietnamese Assn. at Raleigh, 1983—. Hitachi Found. fellow, 1979-82. Mem. Am. Ceramic Soc., Phi Kappa Phi. Presbyterian. Office: Nat Research Council, Atlantic Research Lab, 1411 Oxford St, Halifax, NS Canada B3H 3Z1

PERRIN, SARAH ANN, lawyer; b. Neoga, Ill., Dec. 13, 1904; d. James Lee and Bertha Frances (Baker) Figenbaum; LL.B., George Washington U., 1941, J.D., 1964; m. James Frank Perrin, Dec. 24, 1926. Bar: D.C. 1942. Assoc. atty. Mabel Walker Willebrandt, law office, Washington, 1941-42; atty. various fed. housing agys., 1942-69, asst. gen. counsel FHA, Washington, 1959-60, asst. gen. counsel HUD, Washington, 1960-69; sec. Nat. Housing Conf., Washington, 1970-80; research cons. housing and urban devel., Palmyra, Va., 1970—; acting sec. Nat. Housing Research Council, Washington, 1973-80; bd. dirs. Nat. Housing Conf., 1972—. Trustee Found. for Coop. Housing, 1975-80; mem. Blue Ridge Presbytery Div. Mission, Presbyterian Ch., 1979-80. Mem. Am. Bar Assn., Fed. Bar Assn., Women's Bar Assn. D.C. (pres. 1959-60), Nat. Assn. Women Lawyers, George Washington Law Assn., Charlottesville Area Women's Bar Assn., Fluvanna County Bar Assn., Phi Alpha Delta (internat. pres. 1955-57), Fluvanna County Hist. Soc. (pres. 1973-75, exec. com. 1985—). Lodge: Order Eastern Star. Home: Solitude Plantation Palmyra VA 22963

PERRONE, GINA FERNOW, hearing instrument specialist; b. Phila., Aug. 29, 1947; d. Ralph Edward and Katherine (Fernow) Gordy; m. Preston I. Perrone, Dec. 19, 1969; children—Carl, Scott. Student U. Miami, 1966-68, Katharine Gibbs Sch., 1968, NYU, 1968. Adminstrv. analyst IBM Corp., 1970-79; office mgr. Greiner Engring., Orlando, 1979-81; sales mgr. The Colony Beach & Tennis Resort, Longboat Key, Fla., 1982-83; sales ops. mgr. Electone, Inc., Orlando, 1983-85; telemktg. mgr. Omni Bus. Systems, Inc., Melbourne, Fla., 1985-86; sales mgr. Gulf Atlantic Hearing Aid Ctrs. Inc., Melbourne, 1986-87; mktg. mgr. Health One, Inc., 1987. Langston-Hughes Poetry scholar, 1968. Mem. Am. Mgmt. Assn., Am. Soc. Profls. and Exec. Women, Fla. Hearing Aid Soc., Telemktg. Mgrs. Assn. Home: 345 Cathedral Oak Dr Vero Beach FL 32963 Office: Gulf Atlantic Hearing Aid Ctrs 1700 W New Haven Ave Melbourne FL 32904

PERRONE, KIMBERLY MARIA, retail executive; b. Hoboken, N.J., Aug. 2, 1959; d. Salvatore and Maria (Gervase) P. BA, Lehigh U., 1982. Asst. buyer Lord & Taylor, N.Y.C., 1982, br. asst. buyer, 1982-83, div. mgr., 1983-84; assoc. buyer Bonwit Teller, N.Y.C., 1984-85, sportswear buyer, 1985-87; nat. sales mgr., merchandiser Ungard Ter GFT USA Corp., N.Y.C., 1988—. Mem. Am. Women for Econ. Devel., Phi Beta Kappa. Republican. Roman Catholic. Home: 31 Arrowhead Dr Upper Saddle River NJ 07458 Office: GFT USA Corp 650 5th Ave New York NY 10019

PERRY, ANNE MARIE LITCHFIELD, educator; b. LaJunta, Colo., May 20, 1943; d. Robert Silas and Anne (Kennedy) Hovey; m. Franklin Haile Perry, Dec. 21, 1968; children: Kristina Marie, Tad Kennedy. BEd, Drake U., 1966; MA, U. Tex., 1969; PhD, Tex. A&M U., 1977. Grade sch. tchr., San Antonio, 1966-67, Austin, 1967-68; research assoc. Research and Devel. Ctr., U. Tex., Austin, 1968; grad. asst., instr. Tex. A&M U., 1969-70; kindergarten tchr., 1970-72; instr. U. St. Thomas, 1973-74; spl. edn. tchr., supr. Cypress-Fairbanks Ind. Sch. Dist., Houston, 1974-77, supr. gifted/talented, bilingual, English lang. devel. programs, 1977-80; mem. adj. grad. faculty U. Houston, 1979-80; lower sch. dir. curriculum and ednl. resources Kinkaid Sch., Houston, 1980-86, dir. young writers workshops, 1985—; tchr. Klein (Tex.) Intermediate Sch. Dist., 1986—; cons. gifted/talented edn., 1978—; cons. teaching of writing, 1985—; vis. asst. prof. Tex. A&M U., 1988. Author, photographer: Riders Ready, 1985; editor: Travels in Mexico and California (A.B. Clarke), 1988. Named Tchr. of Yr., Hancock Elem. Sch., 1975. Mem. NEA, Nat. Council for the Social Studies, Tex. Assn. for Gifted and Talented, Tex. Computer Educators Assn., Tex. Joint Council of Tchrs. of English, Tex. State Tchrs. Assn. Presbyterian.

PERRY, ANNE WATERS, home economics educator; b. Rebecca, Ga., Feb. 12, 1933; d. Thomas McArthur and Emmie Louise (Haynie) Waters; m. Charles Eugene Perry, July 25, 1954; children: Connie, Cathy, Cindy, Chuck. BS, Ga. State Coll. for Women, 1954; M of Home Econs., U. Ga., 1961. Tchr. home econs. Bacon County, Alma, Ga., 1954-56, Berrian County, Nashville, Ga., 1956-67; tchr. elem. sch. Jefferson (Ga.) City Sch. System, 1957-58; tchr. home econs. Winder (Ga.) City System, 1958-60; tchr. secondary sch. Burke County, Midville, Ga., 1962-63, tchr. elem. sch., 1964, county extension agt., 1965—. Dir. Burke County 4-H Activities, Waynesbor, 1965-87; vice-chairperson Burke County Bd. Edn., 1985-87; adminstrv. chairperson Midville Meth. Ch. Mem. Am. Home Econs. Assn., Nat. Assn. Extension Home Economists (disting. service award 1979), Am. Home Econs. Assn., Ga. Home Econs. Assn., Ga. Assn. Extension 4-H Agts. (bd. dirs. 1986-87, award 1986), Ga. Assn. Extension Home Economists (sec. 1986, Disting. Service award 1977), Ga. Home Econs. Assn., Epsilon Sigma Phi (past pres., disting. service award). Democrat. Club: Midville Woman's (pres.), Midville Garden (pres.). Home: Rt 1 PO Box 146 Midville GA 30441 Office: Coop Extension Service Burke County Office Park W 6th St Waynesboro GA 30830

PERRY, BARBARA BENNETT, manufacturing company executive; b. Hackensack, N.J., Oct. 9, 1945; d. Richard Bacon and Frances Edith (Wright) Bennett; m. Edward Earl Perry, Sept. 25, 1982. AS, Endicott Jr. Coll., Beverly, Mass., 1965; BBA, Ga. State U., 1971; MBA, MIT, 1981. Research analyst Citizens & So. Nat. Bank, Atlanta, 1972-74; research cons. First Pa. Bank, Phila., 1974-76; dir. research Bank Mktg. Assn., Chgo., 1976-79; asst. to chmn. Bennett Box & Pallet Co., Inc., Ahoskie, N.C., 1979-81, v.p. mktg., 1981-86, pres., chief exec. officer, 1986—, also bd. dirs. Author: Pace II, 1976, Bank Market Experience, 1976, 77; editor numerous books. Active Adminstrn. bd. Ahoskie United Meth. Ch., 1983-86. Mem. Southeastern Lumber Mfg. Assn. (by-products com. 1982-83, 86-87), Mortar Bd. Soc., Beta Gamma Sigma, Alpha Iota Delta, Delta Psi Omega. Republican. Office: Bennett Box & Pallet Co Inc N Railroad St Ahoskie NC 27910

PERRY, BLANCHE BELLE, physical therapist; b. New Bedford, Mass., Sept. 2, 1929; d. Joseph Rudolph and Beatrice (Faria) Andrews; B.S., Ithaca (N.Y.) Coll., 1951; M.A., Assumption Coll., Worcester, Mass., 1978; m. Louis Perry, Nov. 26, 1953; (dec. 1980); children—Marcia, Susan, Tracey, Evelyn. Office and hosp. phys. therapist, Mass. and N.Y., 1961-65; dir. rehab. services St. Luke's Hosp., New Bedford, 1967—; profl. adv. com. Vis. Nurse Assn. Wareham, 1980; corporator New Bedford Five Cents Savs. Bank./Chmn. Mattapoisett Sch. Com., 1970; vice chmn. Mass. Sch. Commn. Area IV, 1972-75; sec. Old Colony Regional Vocat. Sch. Com., 1973—; trustee Abner Pease Scholarship Found.; chmn. com. opportunity ctr. CARF, New Bedford, 1987. Grantee Elks Nat. Found., 1965. Mem. Am. Phys. Therapy Assn., Nat. Rehab. Adminstrs. Assn., Delta Kappa Gamma. Republican. Club: Mattapoisett Women's. Home: 41 Aucoot Rd Mattapoisett MA 02739 Office: 101 Page St New Bedford MA 02740

PERRY, CAROLE JOAN, educator, manufacturing executive; b. Bklyn., Aug. 12, 1942; d. Allen and Ruth (Dworkin) Marcus; B.A., Bklyn. Coll., 1964; M.S., Richmond Coll., 1974; m. Lawrence Perry, Aug. 29, 1966; children—Jeffrey, Lori. Tchr., Public Sch. 244, Bklyn., 1954, Gladstone St. Sch., Azusa, Calif., 1966-68, sci. enrichment tchr., 1967-68; tchr. Public Sch. 22, S.I., N.Y., 1972; v.p. Avant-Guard Devices, Bklyn., 1972—, Rapidcircuit, Inc., 1972—, also dir. product mktg.; v.p., sec. Designalarm, Inc., 1982—; sec. Microtech Industries, Bklyn., 1982—; pres. Media Mentors, Inc., S.I., 1986—; electronics tchr. S.I. Public Schs., 1982—. Leader, Brownies, S.I., 1976-77. Elected Amateur Radio Operator of the Year, 1987. Mem. Am. Radio Relay League (chmn. ednl. task force). Club: S.I. Tennis. Author tech. articles on energy saving devices, also articles on teaching radio in pub. schs. Office: Media Mentors Inc PO Box 1646 Staten Island NY 10314

PERRY, CARRIE SAXON, mayor, state representative; b. Hartford, Conn.. Student, Howard U. Mayor, Hartford, Conn., State rep. 7th Assembly Dist. (Conn.), exec. dir. Amistad House Inc., Conn., adminstr., Community Renewal Team of Greater Hartford, Ambulatory Health Care Planning Inc., Hartford, Hartford Community Trainers, Conn. Welfare Dept.; mem. Exec. Bd. Greater Hartford Black Dems.; regional dir. Nat. Orgn. Black Elected Women Legislators, Nat. Black Caucus of State Legislators; corporator Oak Hill Sch. for the Blind, Hartford Pub. Library, Conn. Black and Hispanic Urban. Inst.; mem. steering com. Our Neighborhood and St. Monica's Bldg. Fund, nominating chair permanent com. status Hartford Women, Fed. Dem. Women. Named Women of Yr. YMCA; recipient Outstanding Community Service award Black People's Union U. Hartford. Mem. NAACP (life), Nat. Orgn. 100 Black Women (pres. Hartford chpt.). Home: 203 Ridgefield St Hartford CT 06141 Office: Office of the Mayor 550 Main St Hartford CT 06103

PERRY, CHARLOTTE MARIE, marketing professional; b. Augusta, Ga., Feb. 24, 1959; d. Alexander Bache and Martha Louise (Mills) P. BS in Biology, Stanford U., 1981. Sales rep. ICL Sci., Fountain Valley, Calif., 1983-84, tech. rep., 1984-86; regional mgr. V-Tech., Inc., Pomona, Calif., 1986-87, mktg. mgr., 1987—. Mem. Nat. Assn. Female Execs., Stanford Profl. Women, Mktg. Com. Stanford Annual Fund, Stanford U. NOW (regional chair, events coordinator 1986—), Orange County Wine Soc., Order of the Palate. Republican. Clubs: Orange County (Calif.) Stanford Jrs. (charter), Stanford of Orange County; Los Angeles County Stanford Jrs., Stanford of Los Angeles. Home: 177 Covina Ave Apt A Long Beach CA 90803 Office: V-Tech Inc 270 E Bonita Pomona CA 91767

PERRY, CYNTHIA JO, small business owner; b. Grand Rapids, Mich., Nov. 10, 1946; d. Russell M. and Frances O. (Fritz) Gray; m. Glen E. Perry Jr., Aug. 18, 1967; children: Jeff, Angie. Grad. high sch., Rockford, Mich. Keyliner Printco, Inc., Greenville, Mich., 1975-77; keyliner, typesetter Trails-A-Way, Greenville, 1980-81; printer ArrowSwift Printing, Greenville, 1980-81, typesetter, 1983-84; keyliner Greenville Printing Co., 1981-83; owner The Scribe, Greenville, 1984—; sec., instr. reading, tchr. music Greenville Pub. Schs., 1974-84. V.p. Cedar Crest (Mich.) PTA, 1978-80, pres., 1980-82. Mem. Greenville C. of C. (staff com. 1987). Republican. Baptist. Office: The Scribe 120 E Washington Greenville MI 48838

PERRY, CYNTHIA SHEPARD, diplomat; b. Terre Haute, Ind., Nov. 11, 1928; d. George William and Flossie (Phillips) N.; m. James O. Shepard, Nov. 2, 1946 (div. June 1970); children: Donna Ross, James O. Jr., Milo Kent, Mark; m. James O. Perry Sr., Mar. 20, 1971; children: Paula Lucille, James O. Jr. BS in Polit. Sci., Ind. State U., 1967, DCL (hon.), 1987; EdD, U. Mass., 1972; LLD (hon.), U. Md., 1984. Sec. Nichols Investment Corp., Terre Haute, 1956-61; ednl. rep. Ohio region IBM Corp., Terre Haute, 1962-68; dir. tchrs. corps U. Mass., Amherst, 1968-71; assoc. prof. edn. Tex. So. U., Houston, 1971-74, dean internat. student affairs, 1978-82; cons., lectr., U. Nairobi U.S. Peace Corps, Kenya, 1974-76; staff devel. officer UN Econ. Com. for Africa, Addis Ababa, Ethiopia, 1976-78; chief edn. and human resources div. Agy. for Internat. Devel., Washington, 1982-86; U.S. ambassador to Sierra Leone, Freetown, 1986—. Contbr. articles to profl. jours. Recipient Disting. Alumni award U. Mass., 1981, Ind. State U., 1987. Mem. Nat. Bus. and Profl. Women, Internat. Council for Ednl. Devel. (bd. dirs. 1984—), Altrusan Soc. (bd. dirs. 1981-82), Delta Sigma Theta (pres. 1982-83). Republican. Office: Am Embassy/Freetown Dept of State 2201 C St NW Washington DC 20520

PERRY, ELIZABETH DALE, real estate management executive; b. Ft. Worth, Jan. 3, 1959; d. Bob Dale and Sarah Elizabeth (Henry) Perry. BBA of Internat. Bus. and Fin., U. Tex., 1981. Lic. real estate broker, Tex. Asst. property mgr. PLG Mgmt./D&L Investments, Houston, 1981—; owner Perry Ventures, 1987—. Vol. Houston Proud, Big Bros./Big Sisters of Houston; sec. bd. dirs. Gethsemane Sch. for Little Children, 1987—. Mem. Houston Bd. Realtors, Ex-Students Assn. U. Tex. (life), Houston Jr. C. of C. Methodist. Office: Perry Ventures 2223 West Loop South #550 Suite 2100 Houston TX 77027

PERRY, ELYCE DORATHY, medical technologist; b. Chgo., Oct. 18, 1945; d. Roy Earl and Dorothy Mary (Ziegler) Hall; B.S., Coll. St. Francis, Joliet, Ill., 1967; m. Allan E. Perry, Nov. 21, 1970; children—Mara Elan, Max Joshua. Bench technologist St. James Hosp., Chicago Heights, Ill., 1967-69; mem. staff St. Francis Hosp., Blue Island, Ill., 1968—, chem. supr., 1972-73, tech. supr., 1973—; saleswoman McNulty Real Estate, 1979-83; dir. SuPer Industries, Inc., 1983—; tchr. immunology, 1971-72, 73-77; mem. adv. bd. dept. phlebotomy Moraine Valley Community Coll., Palos Hills, Ill., 1986—. Chmn. com. Cub Scout Council Boy Scouts Am., 1987; bd. dirs. Reach Out, Blue Island, 1987—. Mem. Am. Soc. Clin. Pathologists. Roman Catholic. Home: 2505 Burr Oak St Blue Island IL 60406 Office: 12935 Gregory St Blue Island IL 60406

PERRY, JACKLYN JOY, commercial real estate broker; b. Springdale, Ark., Sept. 20, 1961; d. Jack D. and Joan R. (Hobson) P. AA, U. Ark., 1981. Sec. Olympic Properties, Dallas, 1983-84; leasing agt. Gwin Slaughter Realty, Dallas, 1985-86; owner, broker J.P. Realty, Dallas, 1986—. Mem. Dallas C. of C., North Dallas Network of Career Women, Women in Indsl. Real Estate, Dallas Bd. Realtors, Am. Lung Assn.. Home: 11655 Audelia #602 Dallas TX 75243 Office: 4301 Alpha Rd Suite 102 Dallas TX 75244

PERRY, JEAN LOUISE, educator; b. Richland, Wash., May 13, 1950; d. Russell S. and Sue W. Perry. B.S., Miami U., Oxford, Ohio, 1972; M.S., U. Ill., Urbana, 1973, Ph.D., 1976. Cons. ednl. placement office U. Ill., 1973-75, adminstrv. intern Coll. Applied Life Studies, 1975-76, asst. dean, 1976-77, assoc. dean, 1978-81; asst. prof. dept. phys. edn., 1976-81; assoc. prof. phys. edn. San Francisco State U., 1981-84, prof., 1984—, chmn. dept., 1981—. Named to excellent tchr. list U. Ill., 1973-79. Mem. AAHPERD (fellow research consortium, pres. 1988-89), Am. Assn. Higher Edn., Am. Ednl. Research Assn., Nat. Assn. Phys. Edn. in Higher Edn., Nat. Assn. Girls and Women in Sports (guide coordinator, pres.), Delta Psi Kappa, Phi Delta Kappa. Home: 3216 Sun Valley Ave Walnut Creek CA 94596

PERRY, JOYCE LEE, real estate appraiser; b. Thomasville, N.C., May 1, 1945; d. Wesley Sherrill and Dorothy Mae (Hilton) Wood; m. John Roy Perry, Jr., Sept. 12, 1976. B, Ashemore Bus. Coll., 1964. Bookkeeper Brokers, Inc., Thomasville, 1964-72; payroll and bookkeeping Myrtle Desk Co., High Point, N.C., 1972-77, Car-Del Furniture, High Point, 1977-79; real estate appraiser Perry Appraisals, Thomasville, 1979—. Mem. N.C. Assn. Realtors, Nat. Assn. Realtors, Thomasville Bd. Realtors, Nat. Assn. Review Appraisers, Am. Assn. Cert. Appraisers , Internat. Inst. Valuers. Democrat. Methodist. Home and Office: 802 Lakeview Dr Thomasville NC 27360

PERRY, KIMBERLY JEAN, environmental engineer; b. Meadville, Pa., Mar. 8, 1955; d. Robert Russell and Nancy Jean (Maurer) P. BA, Vassar Coll., 1977; MS, Va. Poly. Inst. and State U., 1979. Engr. Sverdrup & Parcel & Assocs., Inc., St. Louis, 1979-81; quality assurance auditor Monsanto Co., St. Louis, 1981-86, sr. environ. engr., 1986—. V.P., 1st Unitarian Ch., St. Louis, 1985-86, pres., 1986-87. U.S. EPA fellow, 1978-79. Mem. Am. Chem. Soc., Water Pollution Control Fedn., Soc. Quality Assurance. Office: Monsanto Co 800 N Lindbergh F2WJ Saint Louis MO 63167

PERRY, LESLIE KAREN, communications executive; b. Colorado Springs, Colo., Mar. 31, 1946; d. Abe and Lottie (Obodov) Mogilner; m. Robert Leland Perry, Aug. 26, 1968 (div. May 1982); 1 child, Rachel Tamsen. BA in Russian, U. Wyo., 1973. Editor technical Water Resources Research Inst., Laramie, Wyo., 1973-76; pres. World of Toys and Hobbies, Grand Island, Neb., 1977-86; cons. telecommunications Dial-Net Inc., Grand Island, Neb., 1987—; cons. Rich Bros.Co., Sioux Falls 1985-86, Midwest Distbrs., Juniata, Neb. 1982-84; bd. dirs. Conestoga Mall Merchants Assn., Grand Island 1979-86. Contbr. articles to profl. jours. Chairperson Retail Task Force/Grand Visions Council 1987-88; dir. Visions from Heartland, central Neb. 1985-86, Children's Village 1987-89. Mem. Grand Island Trade Assn. (pres. 1985-86), Grand Island C. of C. (bd. dirs. 1985—), Pres.' Club, Grand Island Indsl. Found., Women's Networking. Democrat. Jewish. Home: 2717 SunnyBrooke Rd Grand Island NE 68801 Office: Dial Net Inc 105 N Wheeler Grand Island NE 68802

PERRY, MARGARET, librarian; b. Cin., Nov. 15, 1933; d. Rufus Patterson and Elizabeth Munford (Anthony) P. A.B., Western Mich. U., 1954; Cert. d'etudes Francaises, U. Paris, 1956; M.S.L.S., Catholic U. Am., 1959. Young adult and reference librarian N.Y. Pub. Library, N.Y.C., 1954-55, 57-58; librarian U.S. Army, France and Germany, 1959-63, 64-67; chief circulation U.S. Mil. Acad. Library, West Point, N.Y., 1967-70; head edn. library U. Rochester, N.Y., 1970-75, asst. prof., 1973-75, assoc. prof., 1975-82, asst. dir. libraries for reader services, 1975-82, acting dir. libraries, 1976-77, 80; dir. libraries Valparaiso U., Ind., 1982—, assoc. prof., 1982—; mem. Task Force on Coop. Edn., Rochester, 1972. Author: A Bio-bibliography of Countee P. Cullen, 1903-1946, 1971, Silence to the Drums: A Survey of the Literature of the Harlem Renaissance, 1976, The Harlem Renaissance, 1982, The Short Fiction of Rudolph Fisher, 1987; also numerous short stories; contbr. articles to profl. jours. Bd. dirs. Urban League, 1978-80. Recipient 1st prize short story contest Armed Forces Writers League, 1966; 2nd prize Frances Steloff Fiction Prize, 1968; seminar scholar Schloss Leopoldskron, Salzburg, Austria, 1956. Mem. ALA, Amateur Chamber Music Assn., Chamber Music Am., NOW, Delta Kappa Gamma. Democrat. Roman Catholic. Home: 1200 Wood St Valparaiso IN 46383 Office: Valparaiso U Henry F Moellering Library Valparaiso IN 46383

PERRY, MARGARET N., academic administrator; b. Waynesboro, Tenn., Apr. 23, 1940; m. Randy L. Perry; 2 children. BS in Home Econs., U. Tenn., Martin, 1961; MS in Nutrition, U. Tenn., Knoxville, 1963, PhD in Biochemistry, 1965. NDEA fellow depts. food sci. and nutrition U. Tenn., Knoxville, 1961-64, part-time instr. dept. food sci. Coll. Home Econs., 1963-64, asst. prof. food sci. and food systems adminstrn., asst. to dean, 1966-68, asst. dean Coll. Home Econs., 1967-68, assoc. dean, 1968-73, dean for grad. studies, assoc. prof., 1973-79; assoc. v.p. for acad. affairs Tenn. Tech. U., 1979-86, dir. Joe L. Evins Appalachian Ctr. for Crafts, 1982-83; chancellor U. Tenn., Martin, 1986—; part-time dietitian Ft. Sanders Presbyn. Hosp., Knoxville, 1964-65; mem. exec. com. Council Grad. Schs. in U.S., Washington, 1974-77, chair nominating com., 1977; mem. exec. com. So. Conf. Grad. Schs., 1975-78; bd. dirs. Knoxville Early Child Devel. Ctr., 1975-78, corr. sec., 1976-77; apptd. mem. team Am. educators to visit and study univs. in Iraq, 1977; mem. Tenn. planning com. Identification Women in Higher Edn. Programs, Am. Council on Edn., 1978—, chair, 1979-81, mem. Nat. Forum on Women in Higher Edn., Athens, Ga., 1978, mem. Commn. on Women in Higher Edn., Washington, 1979-82, resource person Nat. Forum on Women in Higher Edn., Princeton, N.J., 1981; rep. to N.E. U. Tech., Shenyang, Peoples Republic China, 1984; lectr. in field. Mem. editorial bd.: Grad. Programs and Admissions Manual, 1975-78; contbr. articles to profl. publs. Mem. U. Tenn. Alumni Bd. Govs., 1969-71; chair Tenn. Tech. U. United Way Drive, 1979-82, dept. leader, 1983-86; mem. adv. com. Univ. Day Care Ctr., 1984-86; tchr. Sunday sch. Collegeside Ch. of Christ, 1979-86; bd. dirs. Putnam County United Way, 1981-85. Nat. Endowment for Arts grantee, 1979-83. Mem. Profl. and Organizational Devel. Networks in Higher Edn., Inst. Food Technologists, Am. Home Econs. Assn., Tenn. Home Econs. Assn., Am. Men and Women in Sci., Omicron Nu, Sigma Xi, Phi Kappa Phi, Omicron Delta Kappa, Delta Kappa Gamma. Club: U. Tenn. at Knoxville Faculty (bd. dirs. 1974-77). Home: Chancellor's Residence Martin TN 38238 Office: Univ of Tenn at Martin Office of the Chancellor 325 Administration Bldg Martin TN 38238-5009 *

PERRY, MARSHA GRATZ, legislator, professional skating coach; b. Niagara Falls, N.Y., Dec. 9, 1936; d. William Henry and Margaret Edna (Barr) Gratz; m. Robert X. Perry Jr., Jan. 14, 1961; children: Robert, Margarett, David. Student, Elmira Coll., 1954-57; BILR, Cornell U., 1959. Coll. recruiter Inmont, N.Y.C., 1959-61; skating dir. City of Bowie (Md.), 1971—; skating coach Benfield Pines Ice Rink, Millerville, Md., 1974—; mem. Md. Ho. of Dels.; summer hockey coach Washington Capitals, Landover, Md., 1986, 87. v.p., dist. dir., planning zoning dir. Crofton (Md.) Civil Assn., 1974-86; pres. West County Fedn. of Community Assn. Hazardous Adv. Council, 1986-87; mem. Substance Adv. Council, Md., 1982-87. Named Citizen of Yr. Crofton Civic Assn., 1986. Mem. Assn. Women Legislators. Home: 1605 Edgerton Pl Crofton MD 21114 Office: Md Ho of Dels Lowe Bldg Room 215 Annapolis MD 21401

PERRY, MARTHA ANN, insurance company executive; b. Mpls., Nov. 26, 1951; d. Warren Arden and Harriet Ann (Mott) P. AA in Risk Mgmt., Ins. Inst. Am., 1986. Library asst. Idaho State Library, Boise, 1969-70; policy coder Farmers Home Mut. Ins. Co., Mpls., 1970-71; sec. Berman Buckskin Co., Mpls., 1971-73; underwriting asst. Royal Ins., Mpls., 1973-79; sales asst. Nordstrom Agy., Inc., Mpls., 1979-80; adminstrv. asst. Corroon & Black, Mpls., 1980-81, Johnson & Higgins, Mpls., 1981-82; captive analyst Rollins Burdick Hunter, Chgo., 1982-86; v.p. FNP Risk Services, Inc., Chgo., 1986—. Vol. Rep. Hdqtrs., Boise, 1967-68; contbr. Anti Cruelty Soc., Chgo., 1983-87. Mem. Ins. Distaff Execs. Assn., Chgo. Nat. Assn. of Ins. Women. Republican. Lutheran. Home: 1700 N North Park Ave #5-P Chicago IL 60614 Office: FNP Risk Services Inc 111 N Canal Suite 955 Chicago IL 60606

PERRY, MATILDA TONI, lawyer; b. Decatur, Ill., d. Nathan Otis Perry and Elizabeth May Armstrong; m. Donald Harry Rubin, May 9, 1982, children: Michael, Deborah, Nikki, Brenda, Tom. BA, U. Nev., 1972; JD, U. Calif., Berkeley, 1975. Bar: Calif. 1975, U.S. Supreme Ct. 1980. Atty. State of Calif., Long Beach, 1975-77; dep. county counsel County of Orange, Calif., 1977-83; assoc. Rutan & Tucker, Costa Mesa, Calif., 1983-85; ptnr. Rutan & Tucker, Costa Mesa, 1986—. Mem. ABA, Calif. Bar Assn., Orange County Bar Assn., County Counsel Assn. (sch. law study sect.), Irvine Bus. and Profl. Women Assn. (program chmn. 1985). Office: Rutan & Tucker 611 Anton Blvd Suite 1400 Costa Mesa CA 92626

PERRY, NANCY ESTELLE, psychologist; b. Pitts., Oct. 30, 1934; d. Simon Warren and Estelle Cecelia (Zaluski) Reinhard; m. John Cleveland; children: Scott, Karen, Elaine; BS, Ohio State U., 1956, MA in Psychology, 1969, PhD in Psychology (EPDA fellow), 1973.Nurse, various locations, 1956-63; sch. psychologist Public Schs. Columbus (Ohio), 1970-72; human devel. specialist Madison County (Ohio) Schs., 1972-75; pvt. practice clin. psychology, cons. psychology, Worthington, Ohio, 1975-80; tchr. U. Wis. Sch. Nursing, Milw., 1980-88, Milw. Devel. Center, 1980-83; pvt. practice Assoc. Mental Health Services, 1983-87; dir., pvt. practice Glendale Clinic for Stress Mgmt. and Mental Health Clinics, 1987—. Ohio Dept. Edn. grantee, 1973-76. Mem. Wis. Psychol. Assn., Am. Psychol. Assn., Internat. Soc. Hypnosis, Internat. Soc. Study of Multiple Personality and Associated Disorders, Am. Assn. Marriage and Family Therapists. Home: 2210 Charter Mall Mequon WI 53092 Office: 5227 N Ironwood Rd Milwaukee WI 53217

PERRY, NANCY JO, investment company executive; b. Olean, N.Y., Dec. 12, 1931; d. Thomas Bronson and Doris Marjory (Bacon) White; student Gustavus Adolphus Coll.; grad. Bethesda Hosp. Sch. Nursing, St. Paul, 1952; m. Charles Robert Perry, Apr. 9, 1955; children—Elizabeth Perry Sewell, Charles Thomas, Nancy Marie. Asst. head nurse U. Colo. Gen. Hosp., 1953-55; co-owner, dir. Perry Gas Co., Perry Energy Co., Odessa, Tex., 1967-82; v.p. Perry Investments, Perry Found., 1982—; past sec.-treas. Perry Energy Co., Perry Gas Processors, Perry Gas Transmissions, Inc., PGP Gas Products, Inc., Rockies Oil and Gas Corp. Bd. dirs. Odessa Council on Alcoholism, Task Force on Women; bd. dirs. Our New Beginnings, halfway house for recovering alcoholic women, sec., 1982-86; pres. bd. dirs. West Tex. Pastoral Counseling Center; gov.'s appointee Tex. Commn. on Alcohol and Drug Abuse, 1985—. Presbyterian (elder). Home: 9 San Miguel Sq Odessa TX 79762 Office: PO Box 6268 Midland TX 79711-0268

PERRY, PRISCILLA ROSENFELD, community, political and media relations consultant; b. Brockton, Mass., July 2, 1932; d. Michael Louis and Lena Sylvia (Altman) Rosenfeld; m. Morton L. Perry, Apr. 6, 1958 (div. June 1974); children—Pamela, Aaron; m. 2d, Eugene H. Man, Sept. 15, 1976. B.Ed., U. Miami, 1955, M.A., 1971. Assoc. dir. Anti-Defamation League, B'nai B'rith Fla. Regional Office, Miami, 1954-58; coordinator urban affairs project U. Miami, Coral Gables, Fla., 1968-71, instr. dept. human relations, 1968-70, assoc. dir. Ctr. for Urban and Regional Studies, 1971-73, dir. ctr., 1973-75, founder and dir. Inst. for Study Aging, 1975-80; cons. community, polit. and media relations, South Miami, Fla., 1980—. Editor, Miami Interaction, 1968-75; contbr. articles to prof. jours. Founder, League of Working Mothers, Miami-Dade County, Fla., 1972; chmn. health planning council Environ. Health Planning Com., Miami, 1978; dir. Sta.-WLRN-TV, Miami-Dade County, 1979—. Bd. dirs. Greater Miami C. of C. New World Com., 1983, action com., 1983—; charter bd. dirs. Area Agy. on Aging/United Way Dade County, 1980-82; mem. Miami Mayor's Com. on Budget; mem. Dade County Commn. on Status of Women. Recipient Women in Bus. and Industry award YWCA, 1983; Adminstrn. on Aging grantee U. Miami, 1976-79, 77. Mem. Fla. Council on Aging (trustee 1979), So. Gerontol. Soc. (v.p. 1979-80; founding mem.), Council Univ. Insts. for Urban Affairs, Am. Soc. Pub. Adminstrn., Am. Inst. Planners, Gerontol. Soc. Democrat. Jewish. Home and Office: Priscilla R Perry and Assocs 5740 SW 64th Pl South Miami FL 33143

PERRY, ROSE THERESA, printing and direct mail compnay executive; b. Maple Shade, N.J., Apr. 10, 1961; d. Thaddeus Anthony and Mary Sophie (Hatala) Nowakowski; m. Kenneth Allen Perry, Nov. 27, 1982. BA in Communications, Glassboro (N.J.) State Coll., 1982. Advt. intern Serpente & Assocs., Mt. Laurel, N.J., 1981; editing supr. Lehigh ROCAPPI, Inc., Pennsauken, N.J., 1982-84; mfg. mgmt. trainee Donnelley/ROCAPPI, Inc., Cherry Hill, N.J., 1984-86, supr. in-house and offsite typesetting, 1986-87; planning, art mgr. Hibbert Group, Trenton, N.J., 1987—; dreative cons. Jazz Dir., 1987. Writer publicity city council and mayoral campaigns, Burlington, N.J., 1980-87. Garden STate scholar, 1979-82. Mem. Nat. Assn. Female Execs., Gamma Tau Sigma. Democrat. Roman Catholic. Office: Hibbert Group 21 Muirhead Ave Trenton NJ 08638

PERRY-JONES, WILMA JEANNE, social services administrator; b. Sedan, Kans., Jan. 3, 1952; d. Earl Austin and Wilma Magnolia (Powers) Perry; m. Thomas Frank Jones IV, July 14, 1979 (div. July 1987); 1 child, Thomas Frank Jones V. Student, Kansas City (Kans.) Community Jr. Coll., 1969, Baker U., Baldwin, Kans., 1970-71, Drew U., Madison, N.J., 1971; BA in History and Polit. Sci., Ariz. State U., 1972, teaching cert., 1975; MA in Spl. Edn., U. Nev. at Las Vegas, 1980. Lic. alcohol and drug abuse counselor. Tchr. automobile shop class Clark County Community Coll., Las Vegas, 1975-77, Spring Mountain Youth Camp, Mt. Charleston, Nev., 1975-80; probation officer Clark County Juvenile Ct. Services, Las Vegas, 1981—; tchr. adult edn. Clark County Sch. Dist., Las Vegas, 1986—; counselor Community Action Against Rape, Las Vegas and Mt. Charleston, 1981—; substance abuse counselor, program administr. Bur. Alcohol and Drug Abuse, Mt. Charleston and Carson City, Nev., 1982—. Master plan com., 1980-82, co-chair town adv. bd., 1980—; co-founder, sec. Evergreen Alliance, Mt. Charleston, 1985—; rep. Clark County Dem. Cen. Com., 1984-86. Emergency med. technician, vol. firefighter City of Mt. Charleston, 1976-80, dispatcher Mt. Charleston fire dept., 1987—; rep. Nev. State Dem. Cen. Com., 1984-86; del., 1984, 86, 88. Mem. Clark County Pub. Employees Assn. Methodist. Home: 1225 Aspen Mount Charleston NV 89124 Office: Spring Mountain Youth Camp Angel's Peak Mount Charleston NV 89124

PERSHING, DIANA KAY, financial investment executive; b. Battle Creek, Mich., Jan. 17, 1943; d. James Harry and Frances Virginia (Garrett) Prill; m. Robert Geroge Pershing, Sept. 16, 1961; children: Carolyn Frances, Robert James Lester. Student, Kent (Ohio) State U., 1967. Real estate sec. Village Realty, Glen Ellyn, Ill., 1975-76, rep. real estate, 1976-77; real estate sales Crown Realty, Glen Ellyn, 1977-79; corp. sec. Teltend Inc., St. Charles, Ill., 1979—, also bd. dirs.; pres. DKP Prodns. Inc., Villa Park, Ill., 1985—, also bd. dirs. Mem. Nat. Assn. Female Execs., Nat. Acad. Rec. Arts and Scis., Nat. Assn. Ind. Record Distbrs. Office: DKP Prodns 739 N Harvard Villa Park IL 60181

PERSICO, CYNTHIA KAYE, management consultant; b. Jacksonville, Fla., Aug. 28, 1962; d. Anthony John Persico and Barbara Ellen (Stephens) Childers. BA, Jacksonville U., 1984; M of Health Sci., U. Fla., 1986. Cert. rehab. counselor, employee assistance profl. Counselor Youth Crisis Ctr., Jacksonville, Fla., 1984-85, Clin. Research and Support, Gainesville, Fla., 1984-85, Transitions, Gainesville, 1985-86; hall dir. U. Fla., Gainesville, 1985-86; v.p. Resource Employee Assistance Programs, Inc., Jacksonville, 1986—; instr. Fla. Community Coll. Bd. dirs. Unitarian Universalist Ch., Jacksonville, 1986—. Mem. NOW, Nat. Assn. Female Execs., Assn. Bus. Profl. Women, Assn. Labor-Mgmt. Asminstrs. Cons. Alcoholism (sec. 1986—), Mental Health Assn., Fla. Women Bus. Owners, Fla. Occupational Programs Com. Home: 1537 Talbot Ave Jacksonville FL 32205 Office: Resource EAP Inc 1541 Riverside Ave Jacksonville FL 32204

PERSILY, NANCY ALFRED, business executive; b. Albany, N.Y., July 24, 1943; d. Nathan Charles and Shirley (Jasper) Alfred; m. Andrew A. Persily, June 9, 1968 (dec.); children: Nathaniel Alfred, Meredith Mallis. BS, Cornell U., 1964; MPH, Yale U., 1966. Resident Montefiore Hosp., Bronx, N.Y., 1965-66; spl. asst. to pres. Mt. Sinai Med. Ctr., N.Y.C., 1966-70; prof. Fla. Internat. U., Miami, 1973-77; dir. planning and mktg. Mt. Sinai Med. Ctr., Miami Beach, Fla., 1977-82; pres. Persily Assocs., Miami, 1982—; adj. prof. Bernard Baruch Coll., N.Y.C., 1970-72; adj. assoc. prof. Sch. Medicine U. Miami, 1979—. Author, editor: Hospitals and the Aged, 1983; contbr. articles to profl. publs. Pres. Agys. Concerned with the Elderly, Miami, 1978—; chmn. health council South Fla. Tech. Adv. Com. on Rehab., Miami, 1983. USPHS trainee, Yale U., 1964, faculty trainee, UCLA, 1967. Fellow Am. Pub. Health Assn. (sect. council 1980-81, bd. govs., action bd.); mem. Soc. for Hosp. Planning and Mktg. (edn. com. 1982-84), Gerontol. Soc. Am., Am. Hosp. Assn., Am. Mktg. Assn., Cornell U. Alumni Assn. (v.p). Democrat. Jewish. Home: 7600 SW 125th St Miami FL 33156 Office: Persily Assocs 1450 Madruga Ave Suite 304 Coral Gables FL 33146

PERSING, JENNIFER IRENE, visual director; b. Topeka, Kans., June 22, 1961; d. Morris Elwood and Melba Irene (Cunning) Persing. Student Platt Coll., 1981, Mo. Western State Coll., 1981. Textile mgr. Frenn's Fabric, Topeka, Kans., 1978-80; design cons. Furniture City, St. Joseph, Mo., 1980-81; fashion cons., visual dir. J.C. Penney Co., Kansas City, Mo., 1981-84; visual dir. Einbenders, Inc., St. Joseph, Mo., 1984—; fashion cons. Visual Novations, Kansas City, 1983-86, free-lance design cons., 1984—, interior designer, 1984—; asst. producer bridal showsings, J.C. Penney Co., 1982-84, producer bridal showings, Einbenders, 1984—; model various civic-benefit events. Mem. Nat. Assn. Female Execs., Nat. Assn. Display Industries. Christian Ch. Office: Visual Novations 6735 Holmes Kansas City MO 64131

PERSKY, MARLA SUSAN, lawyer; b. Pitts., Feb. 15, 1956; d. Bernard and Elaine (Matus) Persky; m. Craig Heberton IV, May 20, 1984. B.S., Northwestern U., 1977; J.D., Washington U., 1982. Bar: Ill. 1982. Asst. dir. med. records Chgo. Lake Shore Hosp., 1978; sales/mktg. rep. Colgate-Palmolive Co., Chgo., 1978-79; mem. firm Lurie Sklar & Simon, Chgo., 1982-86; corp. counsel Baxter Healthcare Corp., Deerfield, Ill., 1986—. Sr. editor Urban Law Ann., 1981-82; contbr. articles to profl. jours. Mem. Chgo. Bar Assn., Ill. Bar Assn. (writing contest award 1983), ABA (vice chmn. medicine and law com. 1984-86), Am. Soc. Law and Medicine, Am. Acad. Hosp. Attys. Democrat. Office: Baxter Healthcare Corp One Baxter Pkwy Deerfield IL 60015

PERSON, DOROTHY EVELYN, genealogy educator; b. Battle Ground, Wash., Mar. 19, 1924; d. Ivan Llewelyn and Claire Inez (Spencer) Wooldridge; m. Vernon Lyle Person, Nov. 26, 1944; children: Pamela Rae, Renee Arlene, Timothy Ivan. AA, Clark Coll., 1960; BA, U. Portland, 1963, MA, 1968. Cert. tchr., Wash. Elem., jr. high tchr. Hockinson Sch., Brush Prairie, Wash., 1961-81, retired, tchr. lacemaking, Vancouver, Wash., 1982; tchr. genealogy Clark Coll., Vancouver, 1983—. Author: From a Forest Clearing, 1978, Leaves From Family Tree, 1978, Spencer Citings, 1986; co-author: Pioneer Stories, 1986. Pres. PTA, Battle Gound, 1962; judge Clark County Fair, 1973-85, Wash. County Fair, Oreg., Skamania Fair, Wash. Scholar Vancouver PTA, 1960. Mem. Ft. Vancouver Hist. Soc. (mem. com. 1965-66, 85), Clark County Geneal. Soc. (lectr. 1980—), DAR (chpt. regent 1987—), Daughters of Pioneers (pres., sec. 1972-80). Clubs: Clark County Quilters (v.p. 1982-83), Volcano Lacemakers (pres., sec. 1981-87) (Vancouver); Columbia Stitchery Guild. Republican. Avocations: history and genealogy, needlework, lacemaking, quilting, sewing. Home: 30200 NE 123 Pl Battle Ground WA 98604

PERYON, MARY CHARLEEN D., special education consultant; b. Milw., Apr. 29, 1931; d. Raymond James Dolphin and Violet Selma Solheim Dolphin Berendes; m. Robert Edward Peryon, Nov. 21, 1953; children: Anne Marie Peryon Noonan, Robert Louis, Lynne Marie. BA in Biology, Clarke Coll., Dubuque, Iowa, 1953; cert. med. tech., St. Anthony Hosp. Sch. Med. Technology, Rockford, Ill., 1954; MEd in Clin. Reading, U. Guam, 1972; PhD in Spl. Edn., Utah State U., 1979. Cert. tchr. Ill., Iowa; cert. cons. Iowa; cert. sch. adminstr. Utah. Tchr. sci. LaGrange (Ill.) Schs., 1966-68, Washington Sr. High Sch., Mangiloa, Guam, 1968-70; asst. prof. edn. U. Guam, Mangiloa, 1970-71; reading specialist Dept. Edn. Territory of Guam, Agana, 1971-73, state curriculum cons., 1973-75; assoc. prof. reading and spl. edn. U. Guam, Mangiloa, 1975-85; assoc. prof. reading and learning disabilities Clarke Coll., Dubuque, 1985-86; spl. edn. cons. Keystone Area Edn. Agy., Dubuque, 1986—; cons. in field. Author: Distar Teacher Aide's Handbook, 1974; co-author Reading Specialist's Handbook, 1973; mem. edit. bd. U. Guam Press, Manigloa, 1983-85. Recipient spl. award U.S. Dept. Def. Sch. Dist., Manila, 1976, Internat. Reading Assn. of Newark, 1975. Mem. Internat. Reading Assn. (pres. Guam chpt. 1973-74, Pacific area chair 1973-75), Phi Delta Kappa (historian 1977-78, 83-84), Chi Omicron Gamma (pres. 1982-83). Roman Catholic. Home: PO Box 127 Cascade IA 52033 Office: Keystone Area Edn Agy 1473 Central Ave Dubuque IA 52001

PESCHEL, MAZIE, psychotherapist; b. Corsicana, Tex., Jan. 15, 1949; d. Billy C. Hoffman and Elise (Gay) Brinkley; m. Cecil W. Peschel, June 29, 1968; children: Cinnamon Wimberly, Barkley Wayne. BS in Psychology, U. Houston, 1979, MSW, 1981. Cert. social worker. Youth lay minister St. John's Meth. Ch., Richmond, 1974-78; owner, psychotherapist Peschel Psychosocial Services, Richmond, Tex., 1979—; therapist Belle Park Psychiatric Hosp., Houston, 1980-82; workshop leader Family Services, Stafford, Tex., 1980-82; seminar leader Peschel & Assocs., Richmond, 1980—; cons. Youth Opportunities Unlimited, Richmond, 1982-84; psychology instr. Wharton County Jr. Coll., Richmond, 1983-85; field instr. U. Houston, 1985-86; interviewer, advocate Sta. KFRD, 1986. Creator stress mgmt. tapes, 1986—. Dir. children's choir St. John's Meth. Ch., Richmond, 1973-86; cert. lay speaker Tex. Meth. Conf., Houston, 1978—; chmn. Ft. Bend County Health Fair, Rosenberg, Tex., 1985-86; pres. Rosenberg/Richmond Helping Hands Inc., 1985—; pres. Ft. Bend County Health Council, Rosenberg, 1986—; adv. council sec. Tex. Commn. for Alcoholism and Drug Abuse. Recipient Vol. of Yr. United Way, 1981, Community Service award Ft. Bend County Women's Refuge, 1985. Mem. Nat. Assn. Social Workers, Harris County Biofeedback Soc., Am. Group Psychotherapy Assn., N. Am. Assn. Christians in Social Work (Tex. chpt. state rep. 1985—). Office: Peschel Psychosocial Services 1601 Main Suite 401 Richmond TX 77469

PESIKOFF, BETTE S., lawyer; b. N.Y.C., Oct. 9, 1942; d. Stephen and Ethel (Barrett) Schein; m. Richard B. Pesikoff, June 7, 1964; children—David, Joshua, Daniel. BS, NYU, 1963, MA, 1964; JD, U. Houston, 1974. Bar: Tex. 1974. Tchr. pub. schs., N.Y.C., 1964-68; sole practice law, Houston, 1977—; lectr. various profl. groups. Mem. ABA (sec. family law sect. 1985-86), State Bar Tex., Houston Bar Assn. (exec. com. family law sect. 1980-81, sec. family law sect. 1985-86), Democrat. Jewish. Club: Baylor Faculty Wives. Office: 3816 W Alabama Suite 200 Houston TX 77027

PESYNA, GAIL MARLANE, medical products company manager; b. Pitts., June 16, 1948; d. Theodore F. and Marjorie B. (Wootton) P. AB, Wells Coll., 1970; MS, Cornell U., 1973, PhD, 1975. Sci. cons. Com. on Sci. and Tech., U.S. Ho. Reps., Washington, 1975-78; budget examiner Office Mgmt. and Budget, Exec. Office of the Pres., Washington, 1978-80; mem. profl. staff Pres.'s Commn. for a Nat. Agenda for the '80s, Washington, 1980-81; program specialist DuPont Cen. Research and Devel. Ctr., Wilmington, Del., 1981-83; ter. mgr. DuPont Pharms., Birmingham, Ala., 1983-84; health econs. specialist DuPont Pharms., Wilmington, 1984-86; dist. mgr. DuPont Med. Products, Claremont, Calif., 1986-87, Hoffman Estates, Ill., 1987—. Contbr. articles to profl. jours. Mem. adv. com. NSF, Washington, 1981—; com. mem. NRC, Washington, 1985-87. Mem. AAAS (adv. com. 1981-87), Sigma Xi, Phi Beta Kappa. Democrat.

PETCH, SHARON LU, set designer; b. Johnstown, Pa., Nov. 23, 1954. Grad. high sch., Johnstown. Tax assessor Johnstown Per Capita, 1972-74; welder Bethlehem Steel, Johnstown, 1974-75; office mgr. Richland Mall, Johnstown, 1975-79, mktg. dir., 1979-81; pres., owner Fantasy Folks, 1981—; free-lance stylist Columbus, Ohio, 1981-82; free-lance designer L.I. and N.Y.C., 1982-83; free-lance designer, artist, writer Columbus, 1982—. Mem. Nat. Assn. Female Execs. Home and Office: 6824 Centennial Dr Reynoldsburg OH 43068

PETER, LILY, plantation operator, writer; b. Marvell, Ark.; d. William Oliver and Florence (Mowbrey) P. B.S., Memphis State U., 1927; M.A., Vanderbilt U., 1938; postgrad. U. Chgo., 1930, Columbia U., 1935-36; L.H.D., Moravian Coll., Bethlehem, Pa., 1965, Hendrix Coll., Conway, Ark., 1983; LL.D., U. Ark., 1975. Owner, operator plantations, Marvell and Ratio, Ark.; writer poetry, feature articles pub. in S.W. Quar., Delta Rev., Cyclo Flame, Etude, Am. Weave, others; mem. staff S.W. Writers Conf., Corpus Christi, Tex., 1954—, sponsor Ark. Writers' Conf. Chmn., Poetry Day in Ark., 1953—; chmn., sponsor music Ark. Territorial Sesquicentennial, 1969. Author: The Green Linen of Summer, 1964; The Great Riding, 1966; The Sea Dream of the Mississippi, 1973; In the Beginning, 1983. Bd.

dirs. Ark. Arts Festival, Little Rock, Grand Prairie Festival Arts; chmn. bd. Phillips County Community Center, 1969-73; hon. trustee Moravian Music Found. Recipient Moramus award Friends of Moravian Music, 1964, Disting. Alumni award Vanderbilt U., 1964, Gov.'s award as Ark. Conservationist of Year, Ark. Wildlife Fedn., 1975, Whooping Crane award Nat. Wildlife Fedn., 1976; named Poet Laureate Ark., 1971, Democrat Woman of Year, 1971, 1st Citizen of Phillips County, Phillips County C. of C., 1985, Most Disting. Woman of Ark., Ark. C. of C., 1985. Mem. DAR, (hon. state regent), Nat. League Am. Pen Women, Ark. Authors and Composers Soc., Poets' Roundtable Ark., poetry socs. of Tenn., Tex., Ga., Met. Opera Assn., So. Cotton Ginners Assn. (dir. 1971—), Big Creek Protective Assn. (chmn. 1974—), Sigma Alpha Iota (hon.). Democrat. Episcopalian. Clubs: Pacaha (Helena, Ark.); Woman's City (Little Rock). Home: Route 2 Box 69 Marvell AR 72366

PETERMAN, DONNA COLE, corporate communications executive; b. St. Louis, Nov. 9, 1947; d. William H. and Helen Cole; B.J., U. Mo., 1969; M.B.A., U. Chgo., 1984; m. John Andry Peterman, Feb. 7, 1970. Editor, employee publs. Edison Bros. Stores, Inc., St. Louis, 1969-72; dir. public relations Ron Katz & Assocs., St. Louis 1972-73; editor St. Louis Realty & Investment, 1973-74; chmn. statewide polit. campaign Citizens for Ashcroft, Mo., 1974; asst. media dir. DeKalb County, Ga., 1975; writer Atlanta Mag., 1975; dir. internal communications, exec. speechwriter Sears Roebuck and Co., Atlanta, 1976-80; dir. public affairs Seraco Group-Homart Devel. Co., Chgo., 1980-82; dir. corp. editorial services Sears Roebuck and Co., Chgo., 1982-83, dir. corp. communications, 1983-85; first v.p., dir. corp. communications Dean Witter Fin. Services Group Inc., N.Y.C., 1985-86, sr. v.p., dir. corp. communications, 1986-88, sr. v.p., mng. dir. Hill and Knowlton, Inc., 1988—. Bd. dirs. Trust Inc. Mem. Internat. Assn. Bus. Communicators, Public Relations Soc. Am., Nat. Assn. Corp. Real Estate Execs., Kappa Tau Alpha, Alpha Chi Omega. Republican. Roman Catholic. Clubs: Huguenot Yacht, City Midday, Columbia Yacht. Office: Hill nad Knowlton Inc One Illinois Ctr 111 E Wacker Dr Chicago IL 60601

PETERS, B. JEANNE, management consultant; b. Chgo., May 26, 1940; d. James William and Evelyn (Short) Hill; children—Lisa L., Krylyn G. B.A., No. Ill. U., 1962; postgrad. U. Ill., Northwestern U. Tchr., ednl. writer suburban sch. dists. Ill., 1962-74; pres. Affirmative Action Cons., Wheeling, Ill., 1974-77; employee relations adminstr. Motorla, Inc., 1977-78, corp. mgr. compliance programs, 1978-79, corp. dir. affirmative action and compliance, 1979-83, dir. tng., 1984-85; v.p. Phoenix Assocs., Inc., 1986—; tech. adv. mem. U.S. Employer Del. ILO, 1981-83, 86. mem. mgmt. devel. bd. Ariz. Dept. Adminstrn., 1984—; pres. bd. trustees 1st UU Ch. Phoenix, 1986—. Unitarian. Home: 7811 E Beryl Dr Scottsdale AZ 85258 Office: 500 E Thomas Rd Phoenix AZ 85012

PETERS, BARBARA NANCY, highway safety administrator; b. White Plains, N.Y., Aug. 19, 1956; d. Henry S. and Barbara A. (Hannigan) P. BS in Edn., SUNY, Oneonta, 1978; MS in Spl. Edn., Coll. New Rochelle, 1979. Cert. tchr., N.Y. Tchr. spl. edn. White Plains Pub. Schs., 1978-79; tng. technician Westchester County Traffic Safety Dept., White Plains, 1979-81, instr. def. driving, 1983—, freedom of info. officer, 1986—. Editor newsletter, Westchester County Traffic Safety Dept., 1987—. Recipient Child Safety Program award Nat. Assn. Counties, 1981, Occupant Restraint Program award Nat. Assn. Counties, 1985, Corp. Community Seat Belt Program award Nat. Assn. Counties, 1987. Mem. N.Y. State Assn. Traffic Safety Bds. (regional v.p. 1985-86, 1st v.p. 1986-88), N.Y. State Soc. Profl. Engrs. (scholastic guidance com. 1987—), Nat. Assn. Female Execs., TRANSCOM (pub. info. com. 1986—), N.Y. State Women in Traffic Safety (govs. council, regional dir. 1988—). Roman Catholic. Home: 295 Columbus Ave White Plains NY 10604 Office: Westchester County 148 Martine Ave White Plains NY 10601

PETERS, BERNADETTE (BERNADETTE LAZZARA), actress; b. Queens, N.Y., Feb. 28, 1948; d. Peter and Marguerite (Maltese) Lazzara. Student, Quintano Sch. Young Profls., N.Y.C. Ind. actress, entertainer 1959—. Appeared on TV series All's Fair, 1976-77; frequent guest appearances on TV including (ABC movie of week) David, 1988; films include The Longest Yard, 1974, Silent Movie, 1976, Vigilante Force, 1976, W.C. Fields and Me, 1976, The Jerk, 1979, Pennies from Heaven, 1981 (Golden Globe Best Actress award), Heart Beeps, 1981, Tulips, 1981, Annie, 1982, Slaves of New York, 1988; stage appearances include The Most Happy Fella, 1959, Gypsy, 1961, This is Google, 1962, Riverwind, 1966, The Penny Friend, 1966, Curly McDimple, 1966, Johnny No-Trump, 1967, George M!, 1968, Dames at Sea, 1968, La Strada, 1969, W.C., 1971, On the Town, 1971, Tartuffe, 1972, Mack and Mabel, 1974, Sally and Marsha, 1982, Sunday in the Park with George, 1983, Song and Dance, 1985, Into the Woods, 1987; rec. artist: (MCA Records) Bernadette Peters, 1980, Now Playing, 1981. Recipient Drama Desk award for Dames at Sea, 1968, Drama Desk award nomination, 1987; Tony award nominee, 1971, 74, 85, Tony award for Song and Dance, 1986, Theatre World citation for George M!, 1968, Drama Desk award, 1986, Drama League award, 1986. Office: care Richard Grant & Assocs 8500 Wilshire Blvd Suite 520 Beverly Hills CA 90211

PETERS, CAROL BEATTIE TAYLOR (MRS. FRANK ALBERT PETERS), mathematician; b. Washington, May 10, 1932; d. Edwin Lucius and Lois (Beattie) Taylor; B.S., U. Md., 1954, M.A., 1958; m. Frank Albert Peters, Feb. 26, 1955; children—Thomas, June, Erick, Victor. Group mgr. Tech. Operations, Inc., Arlington, Va., 1957-62, sr. staff scientist, 1964-66; supervisory analyst Datatrol Corp., Silver Spring, Md., 1962; project dir. Computer Concept, Inc., Silver Spring, 1963-64; mem. tech. staff, then mem. sr. staff Informatics Inc., Bethesda, Md., 1966-70, mgr. systems projects, 1970-71, tech. dir., 1971-76; sr. tech. dir. Ocean Data Systems, Inc., Rockville, Md., 1976-83; dir. Informatics Gen. Co., 1983—. Mem. Assn. Computing Machinery, IEEE Computer Group. Home: 12321 Glen Mill Rd Potomac MD 20854 Office: 6011 Executive Blvd Rockville MD 20852

PETERS, ELLEN ASH, state supreme court chief justice; b. Berlin, Mar. 21, 1930; came to U.S., 1939, naturalized, 1947; d. Ernest Edward and Hildegard (Simon) Ash; m. Phillip I. Blumberg; children: David Bryan Peters, James Douglas Peters, Julie Kris Peters. BA with honors, Swarthmore Coll., 1951, LLD (hon.), 1983; LLB cum laude, Yale U., 1954, MA (hon.), 1964, LLD (hon.), 1984; LLD (hon.), U. Hartford, 1983, Georgetown U., 1984, Conn. Coll., 1985, N.Y. Law Sch., 1985, Colgate U., 1986, Trinity Coll., 1987, Bates Coll., 1987, Wesleyan U., 1987, DePaul U., 1988; HLD (hon.), St. Joseph Coll., 1986. Bar: Conn. 1957. Law clk. to judge U.S. Circuit Ct., 1954-55; prof. law Yale U., 1956-78, adj. prof. law, 1978-84; assoc. justice Conn. Supreme Ct., Hartford, 1978-84; chief justice Conn. Supreme Ct., 1984—; bd. dirs. Conf. Chief Justices. Author: Commercial Transactions: Cases, Texts, and Problems, 1971, Negotiable Instruments Primer, 1974; contbr. articles to profl. jours. Bd. mgrs. Swarthmore Coll., 1970-81; trustee Yale New Haven Hosp., 1981-85, Yale Corp., 1986—; conf. of Chief Justices, 1984—; hon. chmn. U.S. Constitution Bicentennial Com., 1986—; mem. Conn. Permanent Commn. on Status of Women, 1973-74, Conn. Bd. Pardons, 1978-80, Conn. Law Revision Commn., 1978-84. Recipient Ella Grasso award, 1982, Jud. award Conn. Trial Lawyers Assn., 1982, citation of merit Yale Law Sch., 1983, Pioneer Woman award Hartford Coll. for Women, 1988. Mem. ABA, Conn. Bar Assn., Am. Law Inst. (council). Office: Conn Supreme Ct Drawer Z Station A Hartford CT 06106

PETERS, FRANCES BARBARA, textile research scientist; b. Lowell, Mass., Nov. 8, 1936; d. Teotonio Medina and Barbara (Sperling) Davis; m. Frank Charles Peters, Jan. 6, 1964; children—Charles Frank, Deborah Lee. B.S. in Textile Chemistry, Lowell Technol. Inst., 1961; postgrad. U. Mo., 1974-75; M.S. in Plastics, U. Lowell, 1978. Tech. dir. U. Lowell Research Found., 1974-79, vis. lectr. U. Lowell, 1978-79; mgr. fabrics lab. NIKE, Inc., Exeter, N.H., 1979-81; research textile technologist U.S. Army Research and Devel. Labs., Natick, Mass., 1981-85; dir. finishes, fiber and fabrics Foss Mfg. Co., Haverhill, Mass., 1985-86; cons. 1986—. Contbr. articles to profl. jours. Assoc. The Textile Inst., Manchester, Eng., 1982. Mem. Am. Assn. Textile Chemists and Colorists (corp. rep. 1977-79), ASTM, TAPPI, Am. Assn. Textile Tech. (mem. exec. council 1980—, sec., 1982-84, chmn. 1984-86). Roman Catholic. Clubs: Toastmasters (sgt. at arms 1985), Colonial Treasure Hunters (editor 1983—). Avocations: metal detecting; archaeology; museums; traveling. Home: 12 Blodgett St Lowell MA 01851

PETERS, JANET J., clothing manufacturing company executive; b. Reading, Pa., Oct. 6, 1930; d. James Hubert and Dorothy Mary (Knoblanch) McElfatrich; m. Henry A. Peters; 1 child, Lisa Renee. Student June McAdam Coll. Vice pres. Vanity Fair Mills, Wyomissing, Pa.; v.p. VF Corp., Wyomissing, Pa. Chmn. Mother's Day Luncheon Mother's Day Council Am., N.Y.C., from 1980; bd. dirs., fundraiser Reading Community Coll., 1983—; active Factory for Sr. Citizens, Fleetwood, Pa., 1983—. Office: VF Corporation 1047 N Park Rd Wyomissing PA 19610 *

PETERS, JUDITH ROCHELLE, educator, administrator; b. Phila., July 16, 1951; d. John Bernard and Priscilla Jo (Johnson) P.; B.S. (Senatorial scholar), Pa. State U., 1973; postgrad. Temple U. Sch. Pharmacy, 1975-77; M.B.A., H.H.S.A., Cornell U., 1977. Supr., lifeguard Phila. Dept. Recreation, 1971-74; pharmacy intern Needle & Boonin, Zachian Bros. and Bell Family Pharmacies, Phila., 1976-79; mgr., partner Adero Pharmacy, Phila., 1980-83; sci. specialist Phila. Bd. Edn.; exec. dir. Urban Health Network Inc., 1984, YMCA of West Phila., 1985—. Vol., Big Sisters Am., ARC, Phila.; elder Lombard Central Presbyterian Ch. USA, Phila. Mem. Nat. Assn. Health Services Execs., Am. Public Health Assn., Pa. Assn. Notaries, Internat. City Mgmt. Assn., United Presbyn. Women. Club: United Soul Ensemble.

PETERS, JUDY GALE, manufacturing company official, educator; b. Matoaka, W.Va., Dec. 13, 1941; d. Thomas Delbert and Vicie Clarice (Mundy) Hankins; m. Jesse Everitt Lobdell, Jr., Dec. 2, 1963 (div. Jan. 1975); 1 child, Jesse Everitt III; m. Kenneth Rae Peters, June 6, 1975 (div. Dec. 1984) 1 child, Kenneth Phillip. BS, Radford Coll., 1964. Tchr. county schs., Licking County, Ohio, 1964-73; with Hydrostrut Co., Newark, Ohio, 1974-76; buyer Anchor Coupling Co., Hebron, Ohio, 1976-78; expeditor Diebold Inc., Hebron, 1978-80, buyer, 1980—. Advisor 4-H Club Band, Licking County, 1965-67. Named Tchr. of Yr., Northridge Local Schs., 1972. Mem. Am. Choral Dirs., Diebold Mgmt. Club, Nat. Assn. Female Execs., Am. Soc. Profl. and Exec. Women. Club: Utica Music Boosters (Ohio). Lodge: Phythias. Avocations: reading, writing, dancing, bowling. Home: 3525 Johnstown Utica Rd Utica OH 43080

PETERS, LUANN, personnel consultant; b. Wichita, Kans., May 17, 1954; d. Dwight Henry and Mildred Pearl (Shoemaker) Tjaden; m. Joseph Noeker Monaghan II, Sept. 18, 1977; 1 child Nicholas Joseph; m. Stanley Cornelius Peters, May 14, 1986. Grad. high sch., Wichita, Kans., 1972. Sec., receptionist Personnel Services, Inc., Wichita, 1973-74, adminstrv. asst., 1974-75, personnel cons., 1975-77, temp. div. mgr., 1977-85, v.p., 1985—; judge Office Edn. Assn., Wichita, 1985-86. Mem. Am. Soc. Personnel Adminstrn. Republican. Home: 720 Brookfield Wichita KS 67206 Office: Personnel Services Inc 345 Riverview Suite 409 Wichita KS 67203

PETERS, MARY KATHERINE, computer education center administrator; b. Erie, Pa., Mar. 25, 1957; d. Jack Steven and Joan Marcia (Witkowski) P. Grad. high sch., Erie. Personal banking rep. Marine Bank, Erie, 1979-82; savings officer, tng. specialist Colony Savings Bank, Erie, 1982-85; instr., coordinator Control Data Multiskill Ctr., Erie, 1985-87; job developer, counselor Greater Erie Community Action Com., Erie, 1987—. Democrat. Roman Catholic. Home: 503 E 13th Erie PA 16503 Office: Greater Erie Community Action Com 18 W 9th St Erie PA 16501

PETERS, MERCEDES, psychoanalyst; b. N.Y.C.; B.S., L.I. U., 1945; postgrad. Columbia U., 1944-45; M.S., U. Conn., 1953; tng. in psychotherapy Am. Inst. Psychotherapy and Psychoanalysis, 1960-70; grad. Postgrad. Center Mental Health; postgrad. Union U. Grad. Sch., 1987—. Social worker various agys., pub. instns., 1945-63; staff affiliate, sr. psychotherapist Community Guidance Service, 1960-75; affiliate Postgrad. Center for Mental Health, 1974-76; pvt. practice psychotherapy, Bklyn., 1961—. Certified psychoanalyst Am. Examining Bd. Psychoanalysis; certified mental health cons. Fellow Am. Orthopsychiat. Assn.; mem. Nat. Assn. Social Workers, LWV, NAACP, Brooklyn Heights Mus. Soc. Office: 142 Joralemon Brooklyn NY 11201

PETERS, ROBERTA, soprano; b. N.Y.C., May 4, 1930; d. Sol and Ruth (Hirsch) P.; m. Bertram Fields, Apr. 10, 1955; children: Paul, Bruce. Ed. privately; Litt.D., Elmira Coll., 1967; Mus. D., Ithaca Coll., 1968, Colby Coll., 1980; L.H.D., Westminster Coll., 1974, Lehigh U., 1977; D.F.A., St. John's U., 1982. Author: Debut at the Met; Met. Opera debut as Zerlina in Don Giovanni, 1950; recorded numerous operas; appeared motion pictures; frequent appearances radio and TV; sang at Royal Opera House, Covent Garden, London, Cin. Opera, summers 1952-53, 58, Vienna State Opera, Munich Opera, West Berlin Opera, Salzburg Festival, debuts at festivals in Vienna and Munich; concert tours in U.S., Soviet Union, Scandinavian countries, Israel, China, debut, Kirov Opera, Leningrad, USSR, sang at Bolshoi Opera, Moscow. Named Woman of Yr. Fedn. Women's Clubs, 1964; honored spl. ceremony on 35th anniversary with the Met. Opera Co., 1985. Home: Scarsdale NY 10583 Office: ICM Artists Ltd 40 W 57th St New York NY 10019

PETERS, ROXANNE LEIGH, nurse practitioner, consultant; b. Gillette, Wyo., Sept. 11, 1954; d. Leonard Andrew and Margaret Rose (DeGering) McCullough; m. Michael James Thiry, Dec. 27, 1975 (div. Aug. 1978); m. John Peters, Oct. 28, 1978; 1 child, Mandi. BA in Nursing, Augustana Coll., Sioux Falls, S.D., 1976. RN, Wyo.; cert. nurse practitioner, physicians asst. Nurse Crook County Meml. Hosp., Sundance, Wyo., 1976-77; nurse practitioner So. Nev. Meml. Hosp., Las Vegas, 1978, Advanced Health Systems, Sundance, 1978-82; v.p. Med. Emergency Rescue Cons., Sundance, 1981—; bus. mgr., patient edn. coordinator N.W. Wyo. Med. Ctr., Sundance, 1986—; cons. Parachute Med. Ruscue Service, Kalamazoo, Mich., 1981, Refugee Relief Internat., Boulder, Colo., 1983—. Treas., trustee Crook County Sch. Dist., Sundance, 1982-85; chmn. Crook County unit Am. Cancer Soc., Cheyenne, Wyo., 1983-88; trustee Bd. Coop. Ednl. Services, Gillette, 1982-85, vice chmn., 1984-85; bd. dirs. Crook County Family Violence and Sexual Assault Services, 1985—, also vice chmn., vol. trainer; commr. Wyo. Commn. for Women, 1983—; speaker Adolescent Drug/Alcohol Community Group, 1987—. Kellogg Found. grantee, 1977. Fellow Wyo. Assn. Physician Assts. (bd. dirs. 1978); mem. Am. Acad. Physicians Assts. Republican. Home: PO Box 1070 Sundance WY 82729 Office: NE Wyo Med Ctr 301 Main St Sundance WY 82729

PETERS, SALLY ANN, English language educator; b. N.Y.C., Oct. 17, 1938; d. Joseph Herman and Sophia (Selwyn) Goldberg; m. Victor Ervin Vogt, June 30, 1973 (div. Mar. 1983); m. Edward Hargrave Peters, Feb. 1, 1958 (dec. Nov. 1967); children: Scott Philip, Jeffrey Hargarve, Douglas Michael. AB magna cum laude with distinction in English, Temple U., 1960; MA, U. So. Fla., 1970; PhD, Fla. State U., 1973. Teaching fellow Fla. State U., Tallahassee, 1971-73; asst. prof. English, supr. tchr. prep. program Yale U., New Haven, Conn., 1973-79, dir. faculty writing workshop, 1979; freelance writer, cons. Middletown, Conn., 1979—; vis. asst. prof. English Wesleyan U., Middletown, 1984—; lectr. univs., libraries, convs., lit. discussion groups, others, 1973—; cons. Aetna Life and Casualty Co., Hartford, Conn., 1980, Darome, Inc., Stamford, Conn., 1981, Nat. Jr. Achievement, Stamford, 1982, People Mgmt. Inc., Simsbury, Conn., 1984—. Author articles, biog. profiles, poetry, 1976—, nat. scholarship exams, Jr. Achievement, 1982. Pierson Coll. fellow Yale U., 1978-79; Conn. Humanities scholar, 1987-88, 88-89. Mem. AAUP, Bernard Shaw Soc., Am. Soc. Tng. and Devel., Phi Kappa Phi. Office: Wesleyan U Grad Liberal Studies Program Middletown CT 06457

PETERS, TERESA WIDNER, office automation consultant, microcomputer specialist; b. Knoxville, Tenn., June 11, 1959; d. Johnny Mack Widner and Wanda Faye (DeMarcus) Widner Rule; m. H. Wesley Peters, Mar. 18, 1982; 1 child, Erica Renee. BS in Mgmt.-Office Systems Concentration with honors, U. Tenn., 1985. Mktg. rep. Word Processing Systems, Inc., Oak Ridge, Tenn., 1985-86; service rep. Manpower Temporary Services, Knoxville, 1986; office automation cons. U. Tenn., Knoxville, 1986—. Mem. Adminstrv. Mgmt. Soc. (v.p. mgmt. devel. greater Knoxville chpt. 1987-88), Nat. Assn. Female Execs. Club: Knoxville Ski. Home: PO Box 22073 Knoxville TN 37933 Office: U Tenn 915 Volunteer Blvd Suite 500 Knoxville TN 37916

PETERS, VERA CONSTANCE ASTER HESS, real estate executive; b. Bklyn., Apr. 3, 1945; d. Charles H. and Erna Anna (Schoen) Aster; student LDS Bus. Coll., 1958, U. Utah, 1961; m. Ted Peters, Nov. 23, 1980; children by previous marriage—Troy Dee, Tyrone Chad. Legal sec., office mgr. Gordon I. Hyde, Salt Lake City, 1969-71; adminstrv. asst. Flying Diamond Oil Corp., Salt Lake City, 1971-74, also exec. sec. to chmn. bd.; sec. treas. Shuhart Industries, Inc., Salt Lake City, 1974-77; Realtor, 1977-80; broker, 1980—; product mgr. System One Direct Access, 1987—; owner, pres. Market Realty, Inc., 1980-85. Mem. Nat. Assn. Realtors, Salt Lake Bd. Realtors, Women's Council Realtors, LWV. Lutheran. Home: 501 Esplanade #104 Redondo Beach CA 90277 Also: 1120 E 400 N Bountiful UT 84010

PETERSEN, GEORGETTE DIANE DOUNIS, nurse practitioner; b. Washington, July 9, 1958; d. Peter George and Demetra (Pavlos) D. BA in Nursing, Jamestown Coll., 1980; MS in Nursing, Cath. U. Am., 1985. RN; cert. adult nurse practitioner, emergency nurse. Nurse, Leland Meml. Hosp., Riverdale, Md., 1980, Prince Georges Gen. Hosp., Cheverly, Md., 1981-83, Shady Grove Adventist Hosp., Rockville, Md., 1983-87; adult nurse practitioner The Pain Treatment Ctr., Lanham, Md., 1987; adult nurse practitioner Met. Med. Assocs. Md., 1988—; staff and charge nurse Health Care Network, Washington Conv. Center, 1983-84, D.C. Armory, 1983—, R.F.K. Stadium, 1984—. Mem. Nurse Practitioners Assn. D.C. Greek Orthodox. Home: 7883 Butterfield Dr Elkridge MD 21227 Office: 1501 E Belvedere Ave Baltimore MD 21239

PETERSEN, MARGARET HASBROUCK, painter, sculptor, fashion and accessory designer, ceramicist; b. Yakima, Wash., Oct. 11, 1940; d. Ralph Louis and Evelyn Mae (Williams) Johnson; m. Orval L. Petersen, Feb. 9, 1979; children by previous marriage—Tracy Fredrick Kemp, Dana Kenneth Price. Student U. Colo., Foothills Coll., Yavapai Coll.; also various profl. workshops, seminars. Owner, operator Hasbrouck Petersen Inc.—Fine Arts Plus, Sedona, Ariz., 1965—; guest speaker in field, Eng., Germany, U.S. One-woman show Ratliff-Williams Gallery, Sedona, 1986; group shows include Sedona Art Ctr., Tulac Ctr. for Arts, No. Ariz. U.; represented in pvt. collections U.S. and abroad. Recipient numerous art awards and honors, including award of excellence AWA Exhibit, No. Ariz. U., 1985; 1st place in Watercolor Sedona Art Ctr., 1985. Mem. Ariz. Watercolor Assn., Sedona Art Galleries and Assocs., Sedona Art Ctr. Artists and Craftsmen's Guild (past pres.).

PETERSEN, MARGARET SARA, civil engineering educator; b. Moline, Ill., Apr. 28, 1920; d. Charles and Alvena Catherine (Fischer) P. BSCE, U. Iowa, 1947, MS in Mechanics, Hydraulics, 1953. Registered profl. engr., Iowa. Hydraulic engr. Waterways Experiment Sta. U.S. Army C.E., Jackson, Miss., 1947-52; hydraulic engr. Mo. River Div. U.S. Army C.E., Omaha, 1953-55; hydraulic engr. Little Rock (Ark.) Dist. U.S. Army C.E., 1955-64; chief wave dynamics section Waterways Experiment Sta. U.S. Army C.E., Vicksburg, Miss., 1964; proj. engr. Water Resources Planning Br. Sacramento (Calif.) Dist. U.S. Army C.E., 1964-68, chief investigating section Sacramento Dist., 1968-75, chief Marysville Lake investigation sect. Sacramento Dist., 1975-77; assoc. prof. civil engring. Dept. Civil Engring. U. Ariz., Tucson, 1981—; cons. in field. Auhtor: Water Resource Planning and Development, 1984, River Engineering, 1986; contbr. articles to profl. jours. Recipient U. Iowa Disting. Alumni award, 1987. Mem. ASCE (various coms.), Am. Water Resources Assn., Internat. Assn. for Hydraulic Research, Permanent Internat. Assn. Navigation Congresses, Internat. Water Resources Assn., Sigma Xi, Chi Epsilon. Home: PO Box 42168 Tucson AZ 85733

PETERSEN, MARIE ANNE, magazine publisher; b. Chgo., Nov. 21, 1942; d. Chester William and Hazel Alice (Gilso) Reinke; m. William Neil Petersen, Aug. 17, 1963 (div. 1975); children: Elaine Myrtice, Edward William; m. Lyle N. Clapper, Jan. 1, 1980; children: Jeffrey Leland, Anne Reinke; stepchildren: John Scott, Susan Louise. Student, Augustana Coll., Rock Island, Ill., 1960-63; EdB, Northeastern U., 1964. Writer Pack-o-Fun mag., Park Ridge, Ill., 1976-77, editor, 1977-78; asst. to pub., circulation dir. Crafts 'n Things mag., Park Ridge, Ill., 1978-82, pub., 1982—. Host TV show The Crafts 'n Things Show. Mem. Hobby Industry Am., Soc. Craft Designers. Office: Crafts 'n Things 14 Main St Park Ridge IL 60068

PETERSEN, SUSAN JANE, publishing company executive; b. Akron, Ohio, Oct. 9, 1944; d. Christian Henry and Sue Elizabeth (Wigand) P.; m. Bruce S. Harris, Aug. 5, 1973; 1 child, Petersen Nathanial. B.A., Vassar Coll., 1966; M.F.A., N.Y.U., 1969. Vice pres. advt. and promotions Pocket Books, N.Y.C., 1978-80; v.p., mktg. dir. Ballantine, N.Y.C., 1980-82; exec. v.p. Ballantine Delrey Fawcett Books, N.Y.C., 1981-82, pres., 1982—; exec. v.p. Random House, Inc., N.Y.C., 1987—. Mem. Assn. Am. Pubs. (bd. dirs. 1985—), Com. Vis. Harvard U. Press. Lutheran.

PETERSEN, SUZANNE JAQUES, travel agency executive; b. Austin, Tex., July 20, 1938; d. John Earl and Margaret (Holliday) Jaques; m. Edward Laurence Petersen, Feb. 9, 1957 (div. Dec. 1979); children: John Alan, Christopher Lawerence, Todd Edward. Student, Howard Payne Coll., 1956-57, U. Md. extension, Bitburg, Fed. Republic of Germany, 1961-64; grad., Am., Continental, Pan Am. and Cruise Line Internat.; cert., Pan Am. Tariff Sch., 1974. Cert. cruise counselor Cruise Line Internat. Assn. V.p. E.L. Petersen Tours, Irving, Tex., 1966-73; with sales dept. Alpha Travel, Dallas, 1973-76; mgr. Airport Freeway Travel, Irving, 1976-79; pres., owner The Travel Emporium, Irving, 1979-84, Gt. Expectations Travel Agy., Irving, 1985—; pub. speaker Successful Females in Bus. Ownership, Christian Women in Home and Bus. Leadership; cons. in designing and implementing new travel agys. Mem. master planning com. Plymouth Park Bapt. Ch., Irving, 1984-86, pres. choir, 1973-74, 84-87, pres. emeritus, 1987—; active Boy Scouts Am., Irving, 1966-76; past mem. Irving Symphony League. Mem. Nat. Assn. Retail Travel Agts., Nat. Assn. Female Execs., Irving C. of C., Am. Soc. Travel Agts., Network of Profl. Women (charter), Women's Quilting and Wine Tasting Soc. (pres. 1972-73). Democrat. Home: 1624 Oak Meadow Dr Irving TX 75061 Office: Gt Expectations Travel Agy 122 W Carpenter Freeway Suite 420 Irving TX 75062

PETERSEN, TONI, information manager; b. N.Y.C., May 13, 1933; d. Joseph John and Julia (Fiore) De Rosa; m. Norman R. Petersen, Jan. 28, 1956; children—Kristen A., Mark A., Joanna. B.A., Bklyn. Coll., 1956; M.L.S., Simmons Coll., Boston, 1963. Cataloger Clark Art Inst., Williamstown, Mass., 1971; exec. editor RILA (Internat. Repertory of Lit. of Art), Williamstown, Mass., 1972-80; dir. Art and Architecture Thesaurus, Santa Monica, Calif., 1980—, Bennington College Library, 1980-86. Contbr. articles on indexing and documentation of art data to profl. jours. Mem. Art Libraries Soc. N.Am. (chmn. 1985-86), Soc. Am. Archivists, Am. Library Assn. Home: 51 Bulkley St Williamstown MA 01267 Office: Art and Architecture Thesaurus Getty Art History Info Program 401 Wilshire Blvd Santa Monica CA 90401

PETERSEN, MRS. WILLIAM J. (BESSIE RASMUS PETERSEN), orgn. exec., club woman; b. Cherokee, Iowa, June 30, 1902; d. Andrew John and Singni (Nystedt) Rasmus; B.A., State U. Iowa, 1926, M.A., 1930; m. William John Petersen, Sept. 25, 1937. Speech pathologist Rockefeller Found. Mental Hygiene Clinic for Iowa, Iowa City, 1926-28; instr. speech, phonetics U. Iowa, 1928-37; organizer, dir. U. Iowa, Articulatory Speech Clinic, 1928-37; lectr., speech pathology U. Nebr., summers 1931, 37, 38, 39, 40, 41; lectr. Butler U., summer 1937; cons. spl. edn. Iowa Dept. Pub. Edn., 1948-50; asst. dir. Iowa State Hist. Soc. Tours, 1948—. Mem. com. White House Conf. on Spl. Edn., 1929. Mem. Girl Scout Council, 1938-41. Mem. Needlework Guild of Am. (pres. 1939), AAUW (pres. 1940), Iowa Speech and Hearing Assn., Iowa Bus. and Profl. Women's Club, Iowa State Hist. Soc., League Women Voters Iowa Fedn. Women's Clubs, Sigma Xi, Chi Omega. Mem. Order Eastern Star. Club: University. Home: 329 Ellis Ave Iowa City IA 52240

PETERSON, BARBARA JOYCE, artist, doll artist and designer; b. Lewiston, Idaho, Oct. 17, 1943; d. Clarence Vard and Emma (McGarrah) Jackson; m. James John Peterson, June 4, 1965 (div. 1980); children—Sandra Renae, Jason John. Artist Designer Keepsake Originals, Springdale, Ark., 1976—. Original porcelain doll designer: The Farmer, 1978 (award 1978), Grandmother, 1979 (award 1979), Albert and Emma, Bundle of Joey, 1985. Mem. United Fedn. Doll Clubs (awards 1978, 79, 86). Club: N.W. Ark. Heirloom Doll. Avocations: photography. Home: 103 Lakeview Dr

Springdale AR 72764 Office: Keepsake Originals PO Box 784 418 E Emma St Springdale AR 72765

PETERSON, BECKY ANN, home health care service administrator; b. Freeport, Ill., Feb. 23, 1951; d. Donald Theodore Olson and Evelyn Ada (Dodge) Olson Hollenberg; m. H. Edwin Skaggs, Aug. 7, 1971 (div. Feb. 1982); children: Julie Ann, Kathy Jean; m. John Howard Peterson, Jan. 8, 1983; stepchildren: Kristina Lynn, Caryn Sue. Cert. in respiratory care, Swedish Am. Hosp., Rockford, Ill., 1973. Unit sec. Swedish Am. Hosp., 1971-72, respiratory therapist, 1972-74; respiratory therapist Pekin (Ill.) Meml. Hosp., 1974-75, St. Francis Hosp./Med. Ctr., Peoria, Ill., 1977-79, Rockford (Ill.) Meml. Hosp., 1979-83; respiratory therapist, rehab. therapist Northwest Community Hosp., Arlington Heights, Ill., 1983-85; dir. respiratory care dept. Home Med. Equipment Co., Northbrook, Ill., 1985-87, ops. mgr., 1988—. Mem. Am. Assn. Respiratory Care, Ill. Soc. Respiratory Care (co-chairperson program com. 1984-87, elections com. 1982-84, mem. edn. com. 1982-83, rep. chpt. VI 1981-83, mem. exec. council 1981-83, vice chmn. home care com., other offices), Nat. Bd. Respiratory Care (cert.). Methodist. Home: 526 Commanche Trail Wheeling IL 60090 Office: Home Med Equipment Co 2855 Shermer Rd Northbrook IL 60062

PETERSON, CAMILLE M., service executive; b. N.Y.C., Oct. 29, 1938; d. Charles Joseph and Vivian (Thompson) Murrow; m. Charles R. Peterson; children: Steven Michael, Eric Vincent. Cert. in Nursing, New Rochelle (N.Y.) Hosp. Sch. Nursing, 1961; student, Iona Coll., 1967-69. Staff nurse post anesthesia unit Miami Valley Hosp., New Rochelle, 1961-65; office mgr. Heimlich Med. Group, New Rochelle, 1963-65, Rye (N.Y.) Med. Group, 1965-67; asst. head nurse post anesthesia unit New Rochelle Hosp., 1966-69, asst. dir. home health care, 1969-72, asst. dir. extended care facility, 1970-72; mgr. utilization Miami Valley Hosp., Dayton, Ohio, 1972-73; cons. Blue Cross SW Ohio, Cin., 1973-79; v.p. accountemps div. Robert Half of Dayton, 1979—; cons. Mont City Joint Vocat. Schs., Dayton, 1979—, Miami U., Oxford, Ohio, 1981; lectr. various profl. orgns., colls. Mem. adminstrv. campaign staff Dayton United Way, 1986-88. Mem. Exec. Women Internat. (treas. 1985-87), Dayton Exec. Women's Network, Dayton Assn. Personnel Consultants (treas. 1985-87). Presbyterian. Office: Robert Half of Dayton Inc 28 N Wilkinson St Dayton OH 45402

PETERSON, CHERYL COX, writer, computer consultant; b. Altus, Okla., Sept. 30, 1957; d. Clyde Robert and Sheila Anita (Petersen) Reid Cox; m. Dale Robert Peterson, Nov. 25, 1981; children: Jewel Diane, Joshua Daniel. Student, Brigham Young U., 1976-77, Utah Tech. Coll., 1977-78. Staff writer Databus, Tampa, St. Petersburg, Fla., 1987. Contbr., columnist Portable Companion, Redwood City, Calif., 1983-84, Ahoy!, N.Y.C., 1984-87, Computer Shopper, Titusville, Fla., 1984—; contbr. articles to Power/Play, West Chester, Pa., 1984-85, Commodore Microcomputers, West Chester, 1984-85, CompuServe's Online Today, Columbus, Ohio, 1985—. Mem. Nat. Assn. Female Execs., Fla. Freelance Writers Assn. Republican. Mormon.

PETERSON, DONNA C., State senator. B.A. in Anthropology, U. Minn.; married; 2 children. Mem. Minn. Ho. of Reps., 1981-82; mem. Minn. Senate, 1982—. Mem. Democratic-Farmer-Labor Party. Office: Minn State Capitol Bldg State Senate Saint Paul MN 55155 Address: 2824 38th Ave S Minneapolis MN 55406 *

PETERSON, DOROTHY FAYE, accountant; b. Lake Preston, S.D., Oct. 29, 1921; d. John Howard and Bertha Faye (Holm) Payne; student Merritt Bus. Coll., 1939; secretarial cert. Healds Bus. Coll., 1944; m. Lennard Martin Peterson, Apr. 15, 1950; children—Cristine Ann, Scott Martin. Analyst, U.S. Govt. Air Transport Command, Alameda, Calif., 1943-47; exec. sec., investigator Montgomery Ward, Oakland, Calif., 1947-50; tax acct. Watkins & Klee, Mendocino, Calif., 1951-61; pvt. practice tax acctg. and enrolled agt., Mendocino, Calif., 1961—. Sec. Mendocino-Little River Cemetery Dist., 1964—; fin. officer Mendocino City Community Services Dist., 1974—; trustee Mendocino Sch. Dist., 1958-61; commr. Mendocino County Civil Service Commn., 1962-65; trustee Mendocino Presbyn. Ch., 1970-74. Mem. Nat. Enrolled Agts. Assn., Nat. Soc. Accts., Calif. Enrolled Agts. Assn., Mendocino Bus. and Profl. Council (treas. 1976-80), Soroptomists Internat. of Ft. Bragg. Democrat. Presbyterian. Office: 10540 Lansing St Mendocino CA 95460

PETERSON, ESTHER, consumer advocate; b. Provo, Utah, Dec. 9, 1906; d. Lars and Annie (Nielsen) Eggertsen; m. Oliver A. Peterson, May 28, 1932; children: Karen Kristine, Eric N., Iver E., Lars E. A.B., Brigham Young U., 1927; M.A., Columbia Tchrs. Coll., 1930; M.A. hon. degrees, Smith Coll., Bryant Coll., Carnegie Inst. Tech., Montclair Coll., Hood Coll., Maryhurst Coll., Simmons Coll., Northeastern U., U South Utah, Western Coll. Women, Oxford, Ohio, Mich. State U., U. Mich., U. Utah, Williams Coll., Georgetown U., Temple U. Tchr. Branch Agr. Coll., Cedar City, Utah, 1927-29, Utah State U., Winsor Sch., Boston, 1930-36, Bryn Mawr Summer Sch. for Women Workers in Industry, 1932-39, asst. dir. edn. Amal. Clothing Workers Am., 1939-44, Washington legis. rep., 1945-48; legis. rep. indsl. union dept. AFL-CIO, 1958-61; dir. Women's Bur., U.S. Dept. Labor, 1961-64, asst. sec. labor for labor standards, 1961-69; exec. vice chmn. Pres.'s Commn. on Status of Women, 1961-63, Interdeptl. Com. Status Women, 1963-65; chmn. Pres.'s Com. Consumer Interests, 1964-67, spl. asst. to President for consumer affairs, 1964-67; legis. rep. Amal. Clothing Workers Am., Washington, 1969-70; consumer adviser Giant Food Corp., 1970-77; spl. asst. to Pres. for consumer affairs 1977-80; chmn. Consumer Affairs Council, 1979-80; mem. Fed. Commn. on Fed. Paperwork, 1975-77; lectr. Bd. dirs. Internat. Med. Services for Health, 1987, United Srs. Health Coop., 1987, Center Sci. in Public Interest, Common Cause; hon. chmn. Nat. Com. Household Employment, 1964; mem. Women's Nat. Democratic Club; NGO rep. of Internat. Orgn. Consumers Union at Econ. and Social Council UN, 1985—. Decorated Presdl. medal of Freedom, 1981. Mem. AAUW, Am. Newspaper Women's Club (asso.), Am. Home Econs. Assn. (hon.), Nat. Consumers League (pres. 1974-76, hon. pres. 1981), Phi Chi Theta (hon.), Delta Sigma Theta (hon.). Home: 7714 13th St NW Washington DC 20012

PETERSON, HAZEL AGNES, consulting petroleum geologist; b. Houston; d. Howard Lynn, Sr., and Carrie Rice (Brown) P.; BA in Geology, N.Y. U., 1939; MA in Geology, U. Tex., 1942; postgrad. various univs. Jr. subsurface geologist Shell Oil Co., Houston, 1942; subsurface geologist Texaco, Houston and Tulsa, 1942-44, Sun Oil Co., Dallas and Corpus Christi, Tex., 1944-52; supervising geologist Seaboard Oil Co. of Del., Dallas, 1952-54; pvt. practice cons. petroleum geologist, Dallas, Commerce and Denton, Tex., 1952—; asst. prof. East Tex. State U., Commerce, 1958-78; former water resources adv. City of Commerce. Mem. City of Commerce Planning and Zoning Commn., 1977-82, Bicentennial com. of the City of Denton, 1986-88. Research grantee, U.S. Nat. Park Service, 1959-61; faculty research grantee East Tex. State U., 1960s. Mem. Am. Assn. Petroleum Geologists (cert. petroleum geologist), Dallas Geol. Soc., Dallas Geneal. Soc., DAR (regent 1983-85, parlimentarian 1985-88, state chmn. Tex. Woman's U. nursing scholarship fund 1985-91), Tex. State Soc. DAR, Huguenot Soc. of Founders of Manakin (parliamentarian Tex. state br.), Soc. New Eng. Women, Delta Zeta, Sigma Xi (hon.). Methodist. Club: Panhellenic. Research profl. fields and local history; contbr. articles to various publs. Home and Office: 820 Hillcrest Denton TX 76201

PETERSON, JIMMIE RUTH, savs. and loan exec.; b. Tenaha, Tex., Jan. 7, 1922; d. Fred Sue and Jimmie Jewell (Currie) Stillwell; student Garner Bus. Sch. and Inst. Fin. Edn., New Orleans, 1974-75; m. Oscar Isidore Peterson, Dec. 15, 1941; 1 son, Fred Stillwell. With Central Savs. and Loan Assn., New Orleans, 1950—, loan clk., cashier, 1950-66, asst. v.p., 1966-71, v.p., 1971-73, exec. v.p., 1973-74, pres., 1974-78, dir., 1971—, chmn. bd. dirs., 1978-81, cons., 1981—. Tchr., St. Bernard United Meth. Ch., 1955-75; cubs den mother Pack 277 New Orleans Area council Boy Scouts Am., Chalmette, La., 1960-69; mem. Urban League Task Force, New Orleans. Mem. Home Builders Assn. Greater New Orleans (dir., 1978-81; dir. Ladies Aux. 1979; recipient Spike award 1979, 80, Spikette award 1979), New Orleans Realtors (dir. Women's Council 1979), Internat. House (World Trade Center, New Orleans), U.S. League of Savs. and Loan Assns., La. State League Savs. Assns., League of Savs. and Loan-Homestead Assn. Met. New Orleans, Greater New Orleans Exec. Assn., Inst. Fin. Edn. Democrat. Clubs: Carolyn Park Garden (Chalmette), Pandora Carnival (New Orleans), Order Eastern Star, Daus. of Desert, Daus. of Nile, Jerusalem Temple Clownettes. First woman to serve on bd. dirs. Central Savs. and Loan Assn. and on bd. of Home Builders Assn. Greater New Orleans; winner nat. and local flower shows. Office: 710 Canal St New Orleans LA 70130

PETERSON, KATHY MARIE, real estate executive; b. Burlington, Colo., Apr. 11, 1951; d. Marvin W. and Shirley M. (Revert) James; m. Dennis E. Wuthier, Aug. 13, 1972 (div. 1979); 1 child, Stacy M.; m. Kent M. Peterson, May 9, 1981. BBA, Colo. State U., 1972; BBA in Real Estate, Colo. U., 1981. Real estate adminstr. United Banks of Colo., Inc., Denver, 1978-83; property mgr. Silverado Banking, Denver, 1983-84; property mgr. Field Real Estate Co., Denver, 1984-85, v.p. leasing, 1985, v.p. property mgmt., 1985-88, sr. v.p. property mgmt., 1988—; Sec. Colo Bus Energy Conservation, Denver, 1982-83. Mem. Bldg. Owners and Mgrs. Assn. (ednl. com. 1987—), Bldg. Owners and Mgrs. Internat., Soc. Real Property Adminstrn., Women in Comml. Real Estate. Republican. Baptist. Home: 1150 Lafayette St Denver CO 80218 Office: Field Real Estate Co 210 University Blvd Suite 600 Denver CO 80206

PETERSON, LOIS IRENE, transportation company executive; b. Falun, Kans., Mar. 25, 1935; d. Robert Theodore and M. LaVerne (Oleen) Dauer; m. Gerald L. Peterson, Mar. 13, 1955 (dec. May 1971); children: Dennis G., Linda Diane Peterson Johnson, Barbara Lynn Peterson Denny. Grad., Bell and Howell Internat. Acctg. Sch., Chgo., 1974; student, Brown-Mackie Coll., Salina, Kans., 1983. Co-owner Gerald's IGA Store, Falun, 1960-66; co-owner Gerald's Trucking Service, Falun, 1966-71, pres., 1972—; sec.-treas. Wheat State Carriers Inc., Salina, 1985-88; asst. office mgr. Eldon's IGA Stores, Inc., McPherson, Kans., 1966-71; asst. office mgr. Smoky Hill Feedlot, Inc., Falun, 1971-86; speaker in field. Treas. Rural Water Dist. #1, Kans., 1972-75; bd. dirs. Falun Drainage Assn., 1979. Mem. Kans. Motor Carriers Assn. (bd. dirs. 1979-82, 84—, Safety awards 1977-80, 82-88), Am. Trucking Assn. (state del. 1980-82). Avocations: photography, travel, reading, sewing. Home: Box 8 Falun KS 67442 Office: Gerald's Trucking Service Falun KS 67442

PETERSON, MARGARET MARY, radiation therapist, consultant; b. Newark, July 25, 1948; d. Andrew Joseph and Margaret Mary P.; student in X-ray tech. USPHS Hosp., S.I., N.Y., 1966-68; student in radiation tech. Los Angeles County/U.So. Calif. Med. Center, 1969-70; AA in Bus. Adminstrn., San Mateo City Coll., 1978, U. Phoenix, 1982; MA in Pub. Adminstrn. and Organizational Change, Calif. State U., Hayward, 1987. Staff technician, dosimetrist Los Angeles County/U. So. Calif. Med. Center, 1969-71; dosimetrist City of Hope Nat. Med. Center, Duarte, Calif., 1971-74; radiation therapy technologist So. Bay Hosp., Redondo Beach, Calif., 1974-76; dept. mgr., dosimetrist Peninsula Hosp. and Med. Center, Burlingame, Calif., 1976-81; clin. cons. ATC Med. Technology, Sunnyvale, Calif., 1981-82; locum tenens technologist, 1982-86; intern Hayward Edn. Fund, 1986; info. mgmt. intern City of Sunnyvale, 1986-87; applications specialist ADAC Labs., Milpitas, Calif., 1988—; cons. in field. Supervisory com. Peninsula Hosp. Credit Union, 1979-83, mgmt. steering com., 1980-81, vice chmn., 1981. Grantee, State of Calif., 1980-83; lic., cert. radiology and radiation therapy. Mem. Am. Assn. Med. Dosimetrists (pres., 1979-81), Assn. Univ. Radiol. Technologists, Am. Soc. Radiol. Technologists, Calif. Soc. Radiol. Technologists (joint rev. com. therapeutic radiologists com. on tech. and edn. com. Am. Assn. Med. Dosimetrists), Am. Soc. for Pub. Adminstrn. (mcpl. mgmt. assts. of Northern Calif. 1986-88), No. Calif. Soc. Radiation Therapy Technologists (pres.). Home: 645 Topaz St Redwood City CA 94061

PETERSON, MARJORIE ANN, communications consultant, educator; b. Sioux Falls, S.D., Aug. 10, 1940; d. Charles Henry and Marion Mattie (Duis) Brother; m. Wayne Roger Erickson, Nov. 1960 (div.); 1 son, David Charles; m. 2d, David Glenn Peterson, Aug. 6, 1977. B.A. in Speech Communication, Bethel Coll., 1970; postgrad. in pub. adminstrn., U. Okla., 1981—. Instr. speech and debate Bethel Coll., St. Paul, 1970-72; freelance cons., writer, audio-visual producer, St. Paul, 1972-80; tchr. adult edn. Temple U., European div., 1981-83; organizational devel. cons. U.S. Army, Ansbach, W.Ger., 1983; master tchr. Big Bend Community Coll., European div., 1983-84; conf. planner, publs. editor Nat. Assn. Alcoholism and Drug Abuse Counselors, 1984-87; tech. writer, editor Jaycor, 1985; free-lance editor, communications cons., 1985— . Bd. dirs., treas. Employment Support Ctr., Washington, 1984—. Author: How to Finish Your Own Home, 1979; contbr. articles to profl. jours. Dir., sec. People Inc., St. Paul, 1974-80; commr., task force chmn. Planning Commn., Arden Hills, Minn., 1976-80; chmn. Bd. Appeals, Arden Hills, 1974-76; active Park and Recreation Com., Arden Hills, 1974-76; elder Central Presbyn. Ch., St. Paul, 1975-79, New York Ave Presbyn. Ch., Washington, 1986-87; gov., speaker, discussion group chmn. Am. Women's Activities, Germany, 1982-84, area conf. planner, 1982-84. Recipient Ansbach Mil. Community Exceptional Service award, 1984. Mem. Women in Communications, Inc. (chmn. audio-visual seminar 1978, v.p. membership com. Washington chpt. 1987-88), Am. Soc. Pub. Adminstrs., Pi Kappa Delta (spl. distinction 1970). Republican. Presbyterian. Address: 943A S Rolfe Arlington VA 22204

PETERSON, MARTHA ANGELL, banker; b. Nebr., Mar. 28, 1945; d. Robert Geyer and Barbara Patricia (Bartlett) Angell; m. Carroll Floyd Peterson, Feb. 5, 1972; children: Andrew Lars, Wyatt Angell. BS in Acctg. magna cum laude, U. So. Calif., 1967. CPA, Calif. Supr. Ernst & Whinney, Los Angeles, 1967-72; sr. mgr. Ernst & Whinney, San Francisco, 1972-84; v.p., mgr. fin. reporting and acctg. Crocker Nat. Bank, San Francisco, 1985, 1st v.p., mgr. fin. planning and analysis, 1985-86; sr. v.p., chief fin. officer, treas. Midland Am. Corp., San Francisco, 1986; sr. v.p., chief fin. officer, treas. Bracton Corp., San Francisco, 1986—, also bd. dirs. Chmn. Graphic Arts Council, San Francisco, 1985—; bd. dirs. Jr. League, San Francisco, 1985-86; v.p., treas. Hearing and Speech Ctr., San Francisco, 1975-81. Price Waterhouse & Co. scholar, 1967; named Outstanding Career Woman, Bus. and Profl. Women, 1974. Mem. Fin. Execs. Inst., Am. Inst. CPA's (mem. task force 1983-84), Calif. Soc. CPA's, St. Vincent de Paul Soc. (treas., bd. dirs. 1984—), Beta Alpha Psi, Phi Kappa Phi, Beta Gamma Sigma. Club: St. Francis Yacht (San Francisco). Office: Bracton Corp 100 Spear St 10th Floor San Francisco CA 94105

PETERSON, MARY LOUISE, trucking company executive; b. New Orleans, Dec. 20, 1940; d. Edmond Adam's and Dorethea (Fletcher) Peterson; children—DeVon Daniel, Danita Daniel, Michelle Johnson, Mitchel Johnson. Owner, mgr. Agee's 24 Hour Moving & Storage Co., Los Angeles, also All Day All Night Moving & Storage Inc. Home: 1837 S Bronson St Los Angeles CA 90019 Office: Agee's 24 Hour Moving & Storage 806 W 47th St Los Angeles CA 90037

PETERSON, MILDRED OTHMER (MRS. HOWARD R. PETERSON), lecturer, writer, librarian, civic leader; b. Omaha, Oct. 19, 1902; d. Frederick George and Freda Darling (Snyder) Othmer; m. Howard R. Peterson, Aug. 25, 1923 (dec. Feb. 9, 1970). Student, U. Iowa, 1919, U. Nebr., 1921-23, Northwestern U., 1935, U. Chgo., 1943, Am. U. Switzerland, 1985. Asst. purchasing agt. Met. Utilities Dist., 1920-21; asst. U. Nebr. Library, 1921-23; tchr. piano, dir. choir Harlan, Iowa, 1924-26; dir. pub. relations and gen. asst. Des Moines Pub. Library, 1928-35; broadcaster weekly book programs Sta. WHO, Des Moines, and other Iowa radio stas.; columnist, writer Mid-West News Syndicate, Des Moines Register and Tribune; editor Book Marks, 1929-35; writer for Drug Topics, Drug Trade News, others, No. Ill., 1935; writer, spl. asst. ALA, Chgo., 1935-59, Chgo. Tribune, 1941-59; travel writer Hyde Park Herald, 1974—; lectr. SS. Rotterdam of Holland Am. Line, 1971; lectr. tours U.S., Can., Mexico, 1970—; internat. lectr. on travel, fgn. jewelry and internat. relations, 1940—; del. 1st Assembly Librarians Ams., Washington, 1947. Contbr. articles to newspapers, periodicals, encys. and yearbooks. Chmn. India Famine Relief, 1943; a founder Pan Am. Council, 1939, v.p., 1982—, numerous other coms.; a founder, 1st pres. Pan Am. Bd. Edn., 1955-58, Internat. Visitors Center, 1952-56, hon. life dir., 1986; rep. Chgo. at State Dept. Conf. on Community Services to Fgn. Visitors; a founder COSERV (Nat. Council for Community Services to Internat. Visitors), Washington, 1957; mem. exec. bd., awards com. Mayor's Com. on Chgo. Beautiful; mem. Ill. Gov.'s Com. on Ptnrs. of the Americas, São Paulo, Brazil and Ill. sister states; mem. U.S. Dept. State conf. for Partners of Am., Domenican Republic, 1985, Little Rock, 1986, Jamaica, 1987 (Superior Service award 1987); mem. chancellor's com. U. Nebr.; former bd. dirs. council, troop leader Girl Scouts U.S.; mem. council, and mission bd. Hyde Park Union Ch., also 75th, 100th and 110th anniversary coms.; bd. dirs. YWCA, Chgo. Lung Assn.; women's bd. Camp Brueckner-Farr, Grad. Bapt. Student Center.; mem. exec. council Friends of Channel 11; chairwoman Hyde Park Christmas Seals Campaign, 1985-86, 87— (Outstanding Service award 1987). Decorated Uruguayan medal, 1952; Internat. Eloy Alfaro medal, 1952; Order of Carlos Manuel de Cespedes Cuba; Order of Vasco Nuñ ez de Balboa Panama; cited by Chgo. Sun, Ill. Adult Edn. Council, 1953; recipient scholarship in Latin-Am. field U. Chgo. and Coordinator Inter-Am. Affairs, U.S. Govt., 1943, world understanding merit award Chgo. Council on Fgn. Relations, 1955, Disting. Service award Hospitality Center, 1958, Disting. Service medal U. Nebr., Disting. Service medal U. Nebr. Alumni Assn., 1963, Disting. Achievement award, 1975, Ambassador of Friendship award Am. Friendship Club, 1963, merit award YWCA, 1964; Disting. Service award, 1975; Civic salute WMAQ radio, Chgo., 1965; Disting. Service award Pan-Am. Bd. Edn., 1966; also founders award, 1968; Laura Hughes Lunde Meml. award Citizens Greater Chgo., 1968; Friendship award Philippine Girl Scouts, 1971; Disting. Service award OAS, 1971; named Woman of Yr. Friends of Chgo. Sch. and Workshop for Retarded, 1975; Disting. Service trophy Fedn. Latin Am. Orgns., 1976; Merit Award WTTW-TV, Chgo., 1983. Fellow Am. Internat. Acad. (life mem.); mem. Nat. Council Women U.S., Chgo. Council for USA-USSR Friendship, English Speaking Union, Japan-Am. Com., U.S.-China Friendship Assn. (bd. dirs. 1987—), Internat. House Assn. (v.p.), Pan-Am. Bd. Edn. (founder, pres., Merit award), U.S. Capitol Hist. Soc., Ill. Hist. Soc., Nebr. Hist. Soc., Chgo. Hist. Soc., Hyde Park Hist. Soc. (charter mem. award 1978), Field Mus. Natural History, Mus. Sci. and Industry, Lincoln Park Zool. Soc., Citizenship Council Met. Chgo., Oriental Inst., Am. Heritage Council, ALA, Ill. Library Assn. (local arrangements com. of nat. conf. 1976, 78, 85), Internat. Fedn. Library Assns. (local arrangements com. 1985), Soc. Woman Geographers (pres. Chgo. chpt., v.p. internat. council 1987—), Council Fgn. Relations (speakers bur.), Nat. Assn. Travel Ofcls. (Chgo. Tribune rep.), Library Internat. Relations (ball com. 1969—), U. Nebr. Alumni Assn. (past pres. local chpts.), U. Nebr. Found., U. Chgo. Internat. House Assn. (v.p. 1976—), Art Inst. Chgo., U. Chgo. Service League (past bd. mem., now bd. dirs. Camp Brueckner-Farr Aux.), Am. Legion Aux. (mem. state bds. Iowa and Ill.), AAUW, League Women Voters, Children's Benefit League, United Negro Coll. Fund Bd., Renaissance Soc., Peruvian Arts Soc., Hispanic Soc. Chgo., Chgo. Acad. Scis. (woman's bd.), Chgo. Chamber Orch. Assn., John G. Shedd Soc., Japan Am. Soc., Friends Chgo. Pub. Library, Chgo. Symphony Soc., Citizens Greater Chgo., Found. for Ill. Archaeology, Cook County Hosp. Aux., Lyric Opera Guild, Crossroads Student Center, Internat. Platform Assn., Exec. Service Corps Chgo., Friends of Grant Park Concerts, Chgo. Council for USA-USSR, Friendship U. Ill., Chgo. Internat. Programs, Alpha Delta Pi (past pres. local alumnae chpts., editor Adephean 1938-39, woman of year award U.S. and Can. 1955), Xi Delta. Clubs: Mem. Order Eastern Star, South Shore Country, College, Quadrangle, Ill. Athletic, University of Chicago Dames, Iowa Authors, Lakeside Lawn Bowling, Hyde Park Neighborhood, Travellers Century. Address: 5834 Stony Island Ave Chicago IL 60637

PETERSON, MONICA MONIQUE DOROTHY, actress, singer, writer. Drama cert., Neighborhood Playhouse, N.Y.C., 1960, Jeff Corey Sch. Acting, 1966; student Sch. Music and Dance, Covent Gardens, London, 1970; AA, Santa Monica Coll., 1983; BA, U. So. Calif., 1986. Editorial sec., writer Look mag., N.Y.C., 1964-65, asst. mgr. mag. advt., 1965-66; contract actress 20th Century Fox Film Studio, Hollywood, Calif., 1967-70; freelance actress, singer, performer 1968—; advt. mgr. Women in Film, Los Angeles, 1981-82; legal firm asst. Encino, Calif., 1984-86; freelance writer, assignment writer Los Angeles Times, 1987—; singer, actress, performer Agy. William Norris, London, Spain, Italy,. Script analyst, editor, asst. casting dir. Inner City Cultural City, Los Angeles, 1974-76. Recipient Hollywood Star of Tomorrow award ABC, 1968, Overseas award USO, 1969, Two Thousand Women of Achievement award, Foremost Women in Communication Am. Pub. Co. Mem. Screen Actor's Guild (v.p. minority com. 1969-71, rep. Image award 1969-72), Women in Film, AFTRA. Democrat. Roman Catholic.

PETERSON, NADEEN, advertising agency executive; b. McKeesport, Pa., Dec. 3, 1934; d. Michael James and LaVerna Peal (Long) Powell; m. Robert Glenn Kilzer, Dec. 24, 1966; 1 son, Douglas Robert; m. 2d, Peter A Schweitzer, Dec. 31, 1977. Student, U. Fla., 1952-53. Copywriter Ellington & Co., N.Y.C., 1961-64; v.p., assoc. creative dir. Tatham-Laird, N.Y.C., 1964-65, Foote, Cone & Belding, Inc., N.Y.C., 1966-69; v.p., sr. assoc. creative dir. Norman, Craig & Kummell, N.Y.C., 1969-70, sr. v.p., creative dir., 1975-77; sr. v.p., creative dir. Doyle, Dane, Bernbach, Inc., N.Y.C., from 1978; sr. v.p. Saatchi & Saatchi DFS Compton, N.Y.C., exec. v.p., creative dir., exec. v.p., exec. creative dir., 1987—. Recipient Matrix award, 1977. Office: Saatchi & Saatchi DFS 375 Hudson St New York NY 10014 *

PETERSON, NANCY ANN, real estate broker; b. Fargo, N.D., Sept. 18, 1947; d. Simar Kristian and Rhoda Alice (Anderson) Nelson; m. John William Peterson, Oct. 26, 1967 (dec. Aug. 1979); 1 child, Dauvin John. BS, Moorhead State U., 1979; student Real Conservatorio, Madrid, Spain, 1981. Cert. comml. investment mgr. Owner, pres. Circle Realtors Inc., Fargo, 1971—; bd. dirs. Town & Country Realty; Honorarium prof. Classical Guitar Moorhead State U. Bd. dirs. Plains Art Mus., Moorhead, Minn., 1983—, pres., 1987—; mem. devel. council Moorhead State U., 1987; treas. O'Rourke-Plains Mus., Moorhead, 1984-85, v.p., 1986-87; pres. O'Rourke-Plains Arts Assn., 1987-88; pres. Plains Art Mus., 1987-88. Mem. Nat. Assn. Realtors, Fargo-Moorhead Bd. Realtors, Women's Council Realtors (pres. 1977), Fargo-Moorhead Home Builders, Linden Assoc. Lodge: Zonta. Avocations: classical guitar, fishing, scuba diving, skiing. Office: Circle Realtors Inc 1220 Main Ave Fargo ND 58103

PETERSON, PATTI MCGILL, college president; b. Johnstown, Pa., May 20, 1943; d. Earl Frampton and Helen Gertrude (Hershberger) McGill; m. Luther D. Peterson, Aug. 31, 1968; 1 son, Lars-Anders. B.A. in Polit. Sci., Pa. State U., 1965; M.A. in Polit. Sci., U. Wis., 1968, Ph.D. in Polit. Sci. and Ednl. Policy, 1974; cert. advance study, Harvard U., 1977; D.Litt (hon.), Le Moyne Coll., 1983. Asst. prof. polit. sci., dean of freshman women Schiller Coll., Ger., 1968-69; asst. prof. polit. sci. SUNY-Oswego, 1971-72, asst. to pres., adj. prof., 1972-77, v.p. acad. services and planning, assoc. prof., 1978-80; pres., prof. govt. Wells Coll., Aurora, N.Y., 1980-87, St. Lawrence U., Canton, N.Y., 1987—; mem. commn. on govt. relations Am. Council Edn.; pres. Assn. Colls. and Univs. N.Y., 1984-86; mem. N.Y. State Edn. Dept. Commr.'s Adv. Council on Postsecondary Edn.; pres. Women's Coll. Coalition, 1983-85; vis. prof. Syracuse U., (N.Y.), 1974-75. Author numerous articles in field. Trustee Nat. Women's Hall of Fame; dir. SML Properties Corp., Security Mut. Life Ins. Co., OnBank; trustee Northwood Sch., Sta. WCNY-TV-FM. Carnegie fellow Harvard U., 1977. Mem. Am. Council Edn., Am. Assn. Higher Edn., Middle States Assn. Colls. and Schs. (cons., chmn.). Home: Taylor House Aurora NY 13026 Office: St Lawrence U Canton NY 13617

PETERSON, POLLY WIETZKE, education educator; b. Flint, Mich., May 15, 1939; d. Mark Carl and Mary (Jones) Wietzke; m. David Leon Peterson, Aug. 30, 1962; children: David, Pirkko. BS, U. Mich., 1961; MA, Mich. State U., 1963, PhD, 1973. Tchr. U. Mich. Children's Psychiat. Hosp., Ann Arbor, 1961-62, asst. dir. sch., 1964-66; master tchr. dept. ednl. psychology U. Mich., Ann Arbor, 1964-66; asst. prof. psychology U. Miami, Coral Gables, Fla., 1966-68; asst. prof. pediatrics, dir. edn. div. U. Miami, Fla., 1968-76; cons. Grupo Alfa, Casolar, Manzanillo, Mexico, 1977; EdD practicum advisor Nova U., Ft. Lauderdale, Fla., 1978—, sr. faculty Ctr. for Advancement Edn., 1980—; exec. dir. Grand Traverse Area Child Care Council, Northwestern Mich. Coll., 1987-88. Contbr. articles to profl. jours., 1976—. Profl. pres. Ft. Lauderdale (Fla.) Jr. League, 1973, active Jacksonville, 1988—; bd. dirs. Pub. TV of South Florida, 1976-79; vol. abuse prevention programs pub. schs., Mich., 1985-87; chmn. Benzie (Mich.) Family Advs., 1983-86; pres. bd. United Way, Benzie County, Mich., 1987-88. Mich. Dept. Pub. Health grantee, 1984, 85. Mem. Nat. Reading Assn., Nat. Assn. Educators Young Children, Council Exceptional Children, Delta Delta Delta. Republican. Congregationalist. Home: 2746 Holly Point W Orange Park FL 32073

PETERSON, ROSE MARIE, health science association administrator; b. Mobile, Ala., Nov. 10, 1949; d. Roosevelt and Ella Mae (Lewis) Bendolph;

m. Paul Douglas Peterson; 1 child, Douglas Aundre. Student in pre-law, S.D. Bishop State Jr. Coll., 1977-78; student, U. South Ala., 1978-82. With pub. relations dept. Med. Ctr. U. South Ala., Mobile, 1977-82; exec. dir. Sickle Cell Disease Assn. of Gulf Coast Ala., Inc., Mobile, 1982—; sec. U. South Ala. Comprehensive Sickle Cell Ctr.; counselor Ladies Aux., Mobile, 1983—; mem. community health com. Mobile County, 1983—; mem. Lower Ala. Genetics Task Force, 1984—. Bd. dirs., chair personnel com. Mobile Pre-Sch. for the Sensory Impaired; mem. task force Urban League, Mobile, 1985. Recipient Dr. Martin Luther King Humanitarian award 1st Congl. Dist. Voters League, 1984, Community Service award Tri-County Sickle Cell Anemia Assn., 1984-85; named Hon. Lt. Col. Aide, Gov. George C. Wallace, 1985. Mem. Ala. Assn. Sickle Cell Disease (chair budget and fin. com., treas. 1983—), Mobile County Health Edn. Roundtable, Ala. Pub. Health Assn. Democrat. Roman Catholic. Lodge: Knights of Peter Claver (jr. dau. Mobile chpt. 1983—). Home: 258 Rickarby Mobile AL 36606 Office: Sickle Cell Disease Assn of Gulf Coast Ala Inc 2261 Costarides St Mobile AL 36617

PETERSON, THERISIA LEE, commercial real estate broker; b. Pasadena, Calif., Oct. 19, 1941; d. Nathan Davis and Bonny May (Williams) Whitman; m. Harold Kenneth Peterson, Oct. 14, 1973 (div. Mar. 1980); 1 dau. Lauren Elizabeth. BS in Econs., U. Nev., 1964. Purchaser Nev. Dept. Motor Vehicles, Carson City, 1960-67; job devel. and placement specialist Nev. Dept. Human Resources, Carson City, 1967-70; bus. mgr. Nev. League Cities, Carson City, 1970-73; office mgr. econs. dept. U. Nev., Reno, 1973-75; owner T&P Investments, Reno, 1975—; from sales assoc. to ptnr. Lucini & Assocs., Reno, 1977-83, cons. real estate investments, 1978—; comml. div. mgr., cons. Keystone Realty, Reno, 1983-85; broker, owner Comml. Investment, 1985—; real estate brokerage and cons.; instr. Realty 500, Reno, 1980-83. Chmn. Nev. affiliate Am. Heart Assn., 1982-84, pres. No. Div., 1980-82, sec. No. Div., 1979-80, SW region rep. Nev. affiliate, 1984-86; subcom. chmn. Easter Seals, 1981—, Am. Lung Assn., 1985—; bd. dirs. Community Runaway and Youth Services, v.p. 1986—. Recipient Devoted Service award Am. Heart Assn., 1983, Ann. Million Dollar Club awards, 1978—. Mem. Realtors Nat. Mktg. Inst. (cert. Comml. Investment Mem. 1981—, grader, mem. other coms., governing counsellor 1985—), Nat. Assn. Realtors, Nev. Assn. Realtors (Grad. Realtors Inst., 1979, Omega Tau Rho award 1984), Real Estate Securities and Syndications, Internat. Real Estate Fedn., Reno Bd. Realtors. Republican. Lutheran. Lodge: Soroptomist (dir. 1979-81). Avocations: skiing, water skiing, hiking and camping, reading, piano. Home: 959 Nixon Ave Reno NV 89509 Office: 401 Ryland St Suite #300 Reno NV 89502

PETERSON, VICKI JENKINS, clinical social worker; b. Wichita; d. William Harvard and Emelyne Bess (Gumm) Jenkins; m. Richard Herbert Peterson, Oct. 4, 1980; children—Erin, Michael, Chris. B.A., Duke U., 1971; M.S.W., U. N.C., 1980. Clin. social worker Western Carolina Ctr., Morganton, N.C., 1975-80, coordinator child and family services, 1980-83; exec. dir. Hospice Burke County, Morganton, 1983-84; dir. mktg. Mountain MicroSystems, Morganton, 1984-86 ; clinical instr. sch. social work East Carolina U., Greenville, N.C., 1986—; instr. Western Piedmont Community Coll., 1985-86 ; cons. Morganton Area Psychologists and Attys., 1982-84; cons., trainer N.C. State Dept. Social Services. Steering com. Burke Soup Kitchen, Morganton, 1985-86 ; pres. bd. dirs. 1st Presbyn. Preschool Program, Morganton, 1985-86 ; pres. Durham Rape Crisis Ctr., N.C., 1975; lay reader St. Marys Episc. Ch., Morganton, 1983-86, St. Timothy's Episc. Ch., Greenville, 1987—; mem. program planning com., Greenville Community Shelter, 1987—. Named Outstanding Young Woman in Am. 1981, Outstanding Staff Mem. Western Carolina Ctr. 1982. Mem. Nat. Assn. Social Workers, Am. Assn. Mental Deficiency, N.C. Assn. Social Workers Mental Health, Assn. Retarded Citizens. Democrat. Episcopalian. Avocations: reading, travel. Home: 1900 E 6th St Greenville NC 27858 Office: East Carolina U Sch Social Work Greenville NC 27834

PETERSON, VIRGINIA ANNE, insurance agent; b. Cameron, Mo., Jan. 23, 1932; d. Earl D. Bratcher and Freda Mac (Cline) McMahon; m. E. Duane Peterson (div.); children: Mitchel D., Cynthia A. Springer, Marty Jo Lindsey. CPCU. Underwriter R.B. Jones and Sons, Kansas City, Mo., 1961-66, R.B. Miller Ins., Kansas City, 1966-70; mgr. Wernall Ins., Kansas City, 1972-78; owner Virginia Peterson Ins., Independence, Mo., 1978—. Hon. fellow HST; mem. City of Independence Parks and Recreation Neighborhood Council, 1975-80. Mem. Harry S. Truman (hon. fellow). Democrat. Mem. Christian Ch. Club: One by One's Sq. Dancing (Independance) (treas. 1981). Home and Office: 16104 E Pacific Independence MO 64050

PETERSON-VITA, ELIZABETH ANN, psychologist; b. N.Y.C., Apr. 16, 1955; d. Donald Arthur and Adelphine Rose (Lippman) Peterson; m. James Paul Vita, June 10, 1978. B.A., NYU, 1975; M.A., L.I. U., 1977, Ph.D., 1984. Lic. psychologist, N.Y. Psychology intern Northport VA Med. Ctr., N.Y., 1978-79; clin. psychologist L.I. Cons. Ctr., Rego Park, N.Y., 1979-85; clin. psychologist J.F.K. Med. Ctr., Edison, N.J., 1980, Northport VA Med. Ctr., 1980-85; instr. in clin. psychiatry SUNY-Stony Brook, 1985—; staff psychologist South Oaks Hosp., Amityville, N.Y., 1985—; dir. internship tng. South Oaks Hosp., 1985—; cons. to psychology and psychiatry services Northport VA Med. Ctr., 1985—; pvt. practice psychology, Amityville and West Islip, N.Y., 1985—. cons. Four Winds Hsop., Katonah, N.Y., 1988—. Mem. Am. Psychol. Assn. (accreditation com.), N.Y. Neuropsychology Group, N.Y. Acad. Sci., N.Y. Soc. Clin. Psychologists, Nat. Register of Health Service Providers in Psychology. Presbyterian. Avocations: theatre; film arts; art history; creative writing. Home: 74 Brandy Ln Wappinger Falls NY 12590 Office: 735B Montauk Hwy West Islip NY 11795

PETILLO, M. JOANN, analytical chemist, researcher; b. Balt., May 30, 1959; d. Frank and Carmen Marta (Fimiani) P. B.S. in Biology, Loyola Coll., Balt., 1981; postgrad. U. Balt. Analytical chemist Ecol. Analysts, Sparks, Md., 1982-83, Martin Marietta Corp., Balt., 1983-84; lab. mgr. Arundel Corp., Towson, Md., 1984—. Mem. Am. Concrete Inst., Soc. Applied Spectroscopy, Materials Research Soc., ASTM, Smithsonian Assocs., Nat. Assn. Female Execs. Democrat. Roman Catholic. Lodge: Sons of Italy. Avocations: jogging; raquetball; bicycling; piano. Home: 1612 Pinnter Rd Lutherville MD 21093 Office: The Arundel Corp 6806 Greenspring Ave Baltimore MD 21209

PETITTI, ALDA MARIA, accountant; b. Fayal, Azores, Portugal, Dec. 15, 1953; came to U.S., 1962; d. Francisco I. and Natalie (Lopes) Furtado; m. Kenneth Charles Petitti, Sept. 7, 1974; children: Lauren Francis, Margo Allison. BS in Acctg., So. Mass. U., 1979; MS in Taxation, Bentley Coll., 1987. CPA, Mass. Sr. staff mgr. J.G. Hodgson & Co., New Bedford, Mass., 1979-82, tax mgr., 1982-85, tax ptnr., 1985—; bd. dirs. New Bedford 5Savs. Bank. Tax columnist Business Digest. Active New Bedford Steering Com., 1986—, bd. dirs. Waterfront Hist. Assn., New Bedford, 1985—. Mem. Nat. Assn. Female Execs., Am. Inst. Cert. Pub. Accts. Home: 305 Hawthorn St New Bedford MA 02740 Office: JG Hodgson & Co 700 Pleasant St New Bedford MA 02740

PETKOFF, RUTH LINKSMAN, educator; b. Bklyn., Nov. 27, 1924; d. Morris and Miriam (Schiff) Linksman; B.A., L.I.U., 1946; M.A. in Ednl. Adminstrn., Fed. City Coll., Washington, 1975; Ed.D. in Ednl. Adminstrn., Va. Poly. Inst. and State U., 1984; m. Leonard Petkoff, Apr. 20, 1969; children—Marcy, Carrie. Contract adminstr. Linochine Products Co., N.Y.C., 1949-59; v.p. Boraca Corp., P.R., 1959-69; instr. lang. and culture, Seoul, Korea, 1969-71; cons. continuing edn. women Fed. City Coll., also U. Va., Falls Church, 1973-74; career counselor Washington Opportunities Women, 1973-75; career devel. coordinator Arlington (Va.) Career Center, 1974-76; supr. CETA Tng. Center, Arlington, 1975-87; dir. Employment Tng. Ctr., 1987—; co-dir. Career Edn. Project Handicapped, 1975-76; lectr. vocat. rehab. Trinity Coll., Washington, 1978—; mem. Arlington Coalition Career Edn., 1979—; also Title IX Coordinating Com.; mem. vocat. com. Va. Mental Health and Mental Retardation Services Bd.; cons. in field Mem. Am. Vocat. Assn., Nat. Skill Center Adminstrs. Assn., Adult Edn. Assn., Nat. Assn. Female Execs., Nat. Employment and Tng. Assn., Va. Employment and Tng. Assn. (pres. 1981), Va. Vocat. Assn. (v.p. 1981), Arlington Bus. and Profl. Women, Women's Am. ORT. Author curriculum materials, papers in field. Office: 818 S Walter Reed Dr Arlington VA 22204

PETRAITIS, CAROL SARAH, editor; b. N.Y.C., July 11, 1952; d. Arnold Irving Goldstein and Helen Paula (Kaplan) Smith; m. Peter Steven Petraitis, Apr. 21, 1976; children: Daniel Louis, Robert Steven. BA, U. Calif., San Diego, 1974. Pub. relations asst. Brookhaven Nat. Lab., Upton, N.Y., 1974-79; bus. mgr. Field mag., Oberlin, Ohio, 1979-80; field rep. Easter Seal Soc., Cape Cod, Mass., 1980-81; freelance writer, editor Phila., 1981-83; asst. editor Jour. Econ. History, Phila., 1983—. Bd. dirs. Spruce Hill Community Assn., Phila., 1980-82, v.p., 1983-84, exec. v.p., 1985-86, treas., 1987, West Phila. Partnership, 1985—. Democrat. Jewish. Home: 516 S Melville St Philadelphia PA 19143

PETRAKIS, JULIA WARD, small business owner; b. Englewood, N.J., Mar. 24, 1936; d. William Davis and Elizabeth (Shaw) Ticknor; children by previous marriage: Elizabeth Anne Stam Kinnunen, Allan Conrad III; m. Peter L. Petrakis, Jan. 2, 1988. BA in Biochemistry, Radcliffe Coll., 1958. Ct. reporter Miller Reporting, Washington, 1979-81; sec. Whittaker Corp., Arlington, Va., 1981-82; adminstrv. asst. Entre Computers, Tysons Corner, Va., 1982-84; bus. owner Facts on Line, Annapolis, 1984—; cons., instr. in field. interviewer Harvard-Radcliff Colls., Cambridge, Mass., 1984-85; vol. Cancer Drive, Heart Drive, Annapolis, 1986, 88; dir. Cape St. Claire Security Fund, Anapolis, Md., 1988. Mem. Md. Fedn. Art, Nat. Assn. Realtors. Home and Office: Facts OnLine 1236 River Bay Rd Annapolis MD 21401

PETRAS, KATHLEEN MARY SHAFER, health industry executive; b. Chgo., Dec. 29, 1948; d. James Albert and Irene Jeanne (Yurcega) Shafer; m. Kenneth Allan Petras, Sept. 24, 1983. BS in Speech Edn., Northwestern U., 1970. Benefits counselor Hosp. Service Corp., Chgo., 1970-73; personnel rep. Am. V. Mueller div. Baxter-Travenol, Chgo., 1973-74, inventory coordinator, 1974-77, product mgr., 1977-82, sr. product mgr. urology, 1982-83, market mgr.-cardiovascular, 1984-87; dir. mktg., Bioprods. for Medicine div. FCS Labs., Tempe, Ariz., 1987—. Roman Catholic. Home: 1002 S Lagoon Dr Gilbert AZ 85234 Office: Bioprods for Med div FCS Labs 2405 S Industrial Park Dr Tempe AZ 58281

PETRAUSKAS, HELEN O., automobile manufacturing company executive; b. 1944; married. BS, Wayne State U., 1966, JD, 1971. Chemist, group supr. Sherwin-Williams Co., 1966-71; various positions Ford Motor Co., Dearborn, Mich., 1971-79, asst. dir. emissions and fuel economy cert., 1979-80, dir. emissions and fuel economy cert., 1980-82, exec. dir. environ. and safety engrng. and research staff, 1982-83, exec. dir. engrng. and tech. staffs, 1983, corp. v.p. environ. and safety engring., 1983—. Office: Ford Motor Co Environ & Safety Engring The Am Rd Dearborn MI 48126 *

PETREY, KATHERINE GOSSICK, lawyer; b. Oak Ridge, July 27, 1948; d. Ben Rogers and Jean Elizabeth (Koehler) Gossick; m. Kenneth Doyle Petrey, Jan. 6, 1973; 1 child, Samuel Harlan. B.A., U. Ky., 1970, J.D., 1974. Bar: Ohio. Assoc. Squire, Sanders & Dempsey, Cleve., 1974-84, ptnr., 1984—. Trustee Panta Rhei, Inc.; mem. women's com. Cleve. Playhouse; mem. Greater Cleve. Growth Assn., Citizens League Cleve. Mem. Nat. Assn. Bond Lawyers, Ohio Bar Assn., Greater Cleve. Bar Assn., Legal Aid Soc. Cleve., Soc. Collectors, Cleve. Mus. Art, Cleve. Zool. Soc. Democrat. Clubs: Cleve. Garden Ctr. Avocations: gardening, tennis, antiques. Office: Squire Sanders & Dempsey 1800 Huntington Bldg Cleveland OH 44115

PETRIE, MARY ELIZABETH, real estate manager; b. Tripoli, Libya, July 17, 1960; came to U.S., 1967; d. Richard S. and Mary Theresa (McGeever) P. Student, Annhurst Coll., Woodstock, Conn., 1979-81; BA, Elms Coll., Chicopee, Mass., 1983. Property mgr. Realty Mgmt. Assocs., Willimantic, Conn., 1978-84; mgr. Century 21 Evans-Wentworth, Willimantic, 1984—. Mem., emergency med. technician Lebanon, Conn. Vol. Fire Dept., 1986—; sec., treas. Tri-County Women's Softball League, Lebanon, 1984—, property mgr. St. Francis Parish Council, mem. Republican Town Com. Mem. Nat. Assn. Realtors, Conn. Assn. Realtors, Willimantic Bd. Realtors. Roman Catholic. Office: Century 21 Evans-Wentworth 1125 Main St Willimantic CT 06226

PETRIGAC, MAIDA YVONNE, mayor; b. Cleve., Nov. 15, 1932; d. Jay Milton and Helen Elizabeth (Spencer) Boyd; m. Edward George Petrigac, June 18, 1955; children: Velinda, Brenda, Mark, Vanessa. Student, Fenn Coll., Cleve., 1951-52, Dyke Spencerian Coll., Cleve., 1952-53. Bookkeeping sec. Lakewood (Ohio) Printing, 1953-55, Pilkey Realty, Lakewood, 1955-57; sec., treas., statutory agt. E & C Auto Parts, North Olmstead, Ohio, 1977-85; counicIperson City of North Olmsted, 1978-85, mayor, 1986—. Active local PTA; v.p. recreation commn. City of North Olmsted, 1972; Parkwood Homeowners Assn. Recipient life mem. Ohio PTA; named One of Most Interesting Persons Cleveland Mag., 1987, Woman of Yr. North Olmsted Rep. Club. Mem. Cuyahoga County Mayors and City Mgrs. Assn. (mem. exec. bd.), NE Ohio Coordinating Agy., Cleve. Growth Assn., United Martial Arts Black Belt Assn. (hon. black belt), LWV, North Oldmsted C. of C., West Tech. Alumni (hall of fame). Presbyterian. Home: 26653 Sweetbriar Dr North Olmsted OH 44070 Office: City of North Olmsted 5200 Dover Center Rd North Olmsted OH 44070

PETRIKIN, KATHLEEN MARIE, personnel executive; b. Chgo., May 2, 1955; d. Raymond William and Barbara Elaine (Justeson) Richardson; m. James Ronald Petrikin. BS in Psychology and Sociology, MacMurray Coll., 1977; MA, U. Tulsa, 1987, postgrad., 1987—. Word processor Arthur Andersen & Co., Chgo., 1977-78; sales asst., new account supr. Dean Witter Reynolds, Inc., Tulsa, 1978-79, sales asst., new account supr. Bus. Resources and Exec. Search, Tulsa, 1979, dir. personnel State Fed. Savs. and Loan, 1979-85; rep. Agrico Chem. Co., Tulsa, 1985-87; cons. Cambridge Court Services, Ltd., Tulsa, 1987-88; dir. human resources Okla. Practice Touch-Ross and Co., Tulsa, 1988—. Leader Girl Scouts U.S.A., 1962-84. Recipient Award of Appreciation Girl Scouts U.S.A., Jacksonville, Ill., 1975. Mem. Inst. Fin. Edn. (pres. 1981-84), Tulsa Personnel Assn., Am. Soc. Personnel Adminstrn. Democrat. Roman Catholic. Lodge: Kiwanitas (bd. dirs. Tulsa 1982). Home: 6277 S Yorktown Pl Tulsa OK 74136 Office: One Williams Ctr Suite 2400 Tulsa OK 74172

PETRINOVIC, RUTH CHAVES, ballet educator, choreographer; b. Great Neck, N.Y., Jan. 29, 1931; d. Alvaro da Silva Ferreira and Mildred (Byron) Chaves; m. Frano John Petrinovic, May 15, 1953 (div. 1980); children—Robert Francis, Alexis Alvaro. B.A., The Principia, Elsah, Ill., 1952. Dir. Imperial Studios, Ft. Lauderdale, Fla., 1963-73; founder, dir. Atlantic Found. for Performing Arts, Ft. Lauderdale, 1973-82; dir. ballet Greater Miami Opera, Fla., 1978-82; asst. dir. research and tng. Harkness House for Ballet Arts, N.Y.C., 1966-68, dir. research and tng., 1968-70; composition dir. Marin Ballet, San Rafael, Calif., 1983-87; dir. Sch. the Richmond (Va.) Ballet, 1987—; mem., master tchr. Fla. State Dance Assn., 1980-82. Choreographer: (ballets) 14 one-act ballets including Romeo and Juliet, Carmina Burana, 1974—; 3 full-length ballets including Nutcracker, Cinderella, 1974-81; ballet for opera including Adriana Lecouvreur, Turandot, 1978-82. Mem. Pacific Regional Ballet Assn. (pres. 1983, bd. dirs. 1984). Avocations; travel; theatre; music. Office: Sch Richmond Ballet 614 N Lombardy St Richmond VA 23220

PETRITS, NANCY ANN, military officer; b. Royal Oak, Mich., Dec. 1, 1959; d. Paul John and Shirley Jean (Burke) P. BA in Radio-TV, U. Ariz., 1983. Commd. 1st lt. USAF, 1984; officer maintenance 2951 Combat Logistics Support Squadron, McClellan AFB, Calif., 1984-87; officer in charge 35 Aircraft Maintenance Unit, Kunsan AB, Korea, 1987—; advanced through grades to capt. USAF, 1985; guest lectr. in field. Active United Way, McClellan AFB, 1984-85. Home: 8130 Broadway F-2 Tucson AZ 85710 Office: 8th A6S 35 AMU MAAMA APO SF San Francisco CA 96264

PETRO, VIVIAN HAZEL, wallcovering sales company executive; b. Plainfield, N.J., Nov. 13, 1921; d. Victor and Hazel (Vaughn) Petersen; student Pasadena Bus. Coll., 1943-44, Middlesex County Coll., 1972-73; m. Albert R. Petro, Aug. 3, 1947; children—Robert, Edward, Donna. Office mgr. Central Cutter Corp., Somerset, N.J., 1965-73; head dept. teller tng. Franklin State Bank, 1973-78; pres. Wallpaper Factory, Point Pleasant, N.J., 1978—; instr. banking to Spanish-speaking class Union County Coll., 1977. State Commr. N.J. Bd. Pharmacy, 1973-78; pres. scholarship com. Assn. PTAs of Edison, 1965-68; pres. Edison (N.J.) Republican Club, 1967-68; pres. PTA, Stelton Sch., Thomas Jefferson Jr. High Sch., Edison; pres. Edison Council PTA, 1968-69; mem. Women's Referral Network Step-Up. Club: Midstreams Women's (sec.). Office: 2700 Bridge Ave Point Pleasant NJ 08742

PETROCCHI, LINDA ANN, banker; b. Ft. Worth, Jan. 8, 1958; d. Till A. and Jane E. (Bushmiller) P. MusB, Tex. Christian U., 1979; MA, NYU, 1982. Pvt. practice piano tutoring Ft. Worth, 1978-81; educator creative arts various locations, N.Y.C., 1982-85; mgmt. assoc. Citibank, Bklyn., 1985-87; office mgr. Bruce Kelly/David Varnell Landscape Architects, N.Y.C., 1987—. Author: Me and Mom. Mem. Am. Mgmt. Assn., Nat. Assn. Bank Women, Inc., Nat. Assn. Female Execs. Office: Bruce Kelly/David Varnell Landscape Architects 1220 Broadway Suite 302 New York NY 10001

PETRONE, AUGUSTA HENDERSON, educator, civic worker; b. Cambridge, Mass., Mar. 10, 1937; d. Ernest and Mary (Stephens) Henderson; m. Joseph Carlton Petrone, June 23, 1958. BA, Smith Coll., 1958; diplome, Sorbonne, Paris, 1962. English tchr. Seminary High Sch., Alexandria, Va., 1964-65, Kyunghi High Sch., Seoul, Korea, 1965-66, Sudo Women's Tchrs. Coll., Seoul, 1965-66; French tchr. Marshalltown Community Coll., Iowa, 1973-74; Reagan spokesman TV round-table, Geneva, 1976; Reagan chmn. Marshall County, Iowa, 1975-76, 79-80; Reagan-Bush co-chmn. State Iowa, Des Moines, 1983-84; coordinator Dutch's Dollies (161 costumed supporters of "Dutch" Reagan); observer UNESCO Gen. Conf., 1983; mem. presdl. del. Malagasy Republic, 1985; Del. to Rep. Nat. Conv., 1980, 84. Contbg. author: The Feel of Korea, 1966; weekly columnist Korea Times, 1966. Troop leader North Atlantic council Am. Girl Scouts, Fontainebleau, France, 1960; social welfare aide ARC, Fort Hood, Tex., 1962-63; adult advisor Young Reps., Marshalltown, 1972-80; nat. com. woman Iowa Young Reps., 1974-75. Mem. Capitol Hill Club, Women's Nat. Rep. Club. Episcopalian. Home: 1608 W Main St Marshalltown IA 50158

PETROSHIUS, SUSAN MARIE, marketing educator; b. Waukegan, Ill., Oct. 23, 1952; d. Lawrence Joseph and Hazel Florence (Ward) Petroshius; m. Kenneth Evan Crocker, Aug. 23, 1980. A.B., Syracuse U., 1973; M.S. in Bus. Adminstrn., U. Mass., 1978; Ph.D., Va. Poly. Inst. and State U., 1983. Service rep. Ill. Bell Telephone Co., Highland Park, 1974-76; instr. mktg. Va. Poly. Inst. and State U., Blacksburg, 1979-81; asst. prof. mktg. Bowling Green State U. (Ohio), 1981—. Contbr. articles to various publs. Mem. Am. Mktg. Assn., Assn. for Consumer Research, Am. Psychol. Assn., Acad. Mktg. Sci., Nat. Assn. Female Execs., NOW, Alpha Kappa Psi, Beta Gamma Sigma, Phi Kappa Phi. Home: 560 Candyce Ct Perrysburg OH 43551 Office: Bowling Green State U Dept of Mktg Bowling Green OH 43403

PETROVICH, JUDY M., stock broker; b. Elmira, N.Y., Oct. 14, 1945; d. Harry E. and Ruth M. (O'Brien) Harvey; m. Anthony Petrovich, Mar. 26, 1976 (div. Oct. 1979); children: Deborah Avramiis, Jamie Graves, Suzanne Graves. Agent Allstate Ins. Co., Latham, N.Y., 1973-78; dist. mgr. Sentry Ins., Morristown, N.Y., 1976-80; dist. sales mgr. Merrill Lynch, Sarasota, Fla., 1981-84; stock broker, v.p. Dean Witter Reynolds, Sarasota, 1984-87, EF Hutton, Sarasota, 1986—. Mem. NOW, Nat. Assn. Bus. Women. Club: Misty Creek Country (Sarasota); Toastmaster Internat. (Albany, N.Y.) (edn. v.p. 1978-80). Home: 4403 Charing Cross Rd Sarasota FL 33583

PETRY, BARBARA LOUISE, elementary educator; b. Canton, Ohio, Jan. 8, 1954; d. Glenn Griffin and Mary Lucille (Bamberger) Cross; m. Thomas Alan Petry Sr., July 23, 1983; 1 child, Thomas Ala Jr. BA, BS, U. Tampa, 1975; MEd, U. Akron, 1978; cert. tchr. of gifted, Ashland Coll., 1988. Tchr. Our Lady of Peace, Canton, 1975-78; prin. St. Paul Sch., Canton, 1978-82; tchr. Canton City Schs., 1984—. Mem. Jr. League of Canton, Kappa Delta Pi, Phi Delta Kappa. Republican. Roman Catholic. Home: 34 Bentley Dr North Canton OH 44709

PETRY, BETH SOUTHARD, accountant; b. Noblesville, Ind., Aug. 24, 1957; d. K. Charles and Helen Louise (Morris) Southard; m. Davied Alan Petry, May 30, 1982. BS in Acctg., Ball State U., Muncie, Ind., 1978; MBA, SUNY, Albany, 1986. CPA, Ind. Staff acct. Fowler, Suttles & Co., Indpls., 1978-81; sr. acct. Bollam, Sheedy, Torani & Co., Albany, 1981-85; audit mgr. Ernst & Whinney, Indpls., 1985—; bd. dirs. entrpreneurial adv. bd. Ball State U, Muncie. Vol. Pan Am. Games, Indpls., 1987; vol. Jr. Achievement, 1986-87. Mem. Nat. Assn. Female Execs. (dir. 1982—), Network Women in Bus., Women's Bus. Initiative Assn. (corp. fund raising com. 1987), Am. Inst. CPA's, Ind. CPA's Soc. (mem. benefit com. 1986—), Phi Gamma Nu (co-chmn. 1977-78). Republican. Home: 324 Nelson Circle Noblesville IN 46060 Office: Ernst & Whinney 1 Indiana Sq Suite 3400 Indianapolis IN 46204

PETRY, RUTH VIDRINE, educator; b. Eunice, La., Jan. 20, 1947; d. Adea and Ruth Alice (Fox) Vidrine; m. Carson Clinton Petry, June 19, 1976. BA, La. Coll., 1971; MEd, McNeese State U., 1984. Cert. tchr., La. Jr. high sch. tchr. Jefferson Davis Parish, Jennings, La., 1970-72; high sch. tchr. St. Tammany Parish, Mandeville, La., 1972-73, Jefferson Parish, Gretna, La., 1973-81; jr. high tchr. Acadia Parish, Crowley, La., 1981-87; lang. arts tchr. Crowley Jr. High Sch., 1981-87; writing assessment coordinator Crowley Jr. High Sch., 1984-85, mem. faculty inservice team, chmn. spelling bee, 1983-88; co-chmn. interim self study Crowley Jr. High Sch. So. Assn., 1985-86. Co-sponsor Nat. Jr. Hon. Soc., 1984-88. Mem. Nat. Council Tchrs. English, Associated Profl. Educators La., Delta Kappa Gamma (pres. XI chpt. 1988—). Republican. Baptist. Home: 206 Bruce Lafayette LA 70503

PETTEBONE-LONG, KATHLEEN, editor, publisher; b. Louisville, Apr. 28, 1945; d. John Elliott II and Elsie Mae (Gyles) Pettebone; m. 2d, R. Eugene Long II, June 29, 1974. Student Meredith Coll., 1963-65; B.A., U. Md., 1967; postgrad. Radcliffe Coll., 1970, Harvard U., 1972-73; postgrad. U. Pa. Wharton Sch., 1977-79. Asst. editor Naval Inst., 1968-70; asst. dir. pub. relations, instr. Anne Arundel Community Coll., Arnold, Md., 1970-71; asst. editor Nutrition Today, 1973-74; sr. book editor Robert J. Brady Pub. Co., a Prentice-Hall Co., 1974-77, acting mng. editor, 1975-76; pres., chief exec. officer KPL & Assocs., Annapolis, Md., 1976—; dir. pub. activities Nat. Inst. Child Support Enforcement, Univ. Research Corp., Washington, 1979-81; mng. editor, pub. BioSci. mag. Am. Inst. Biol. Scis., Arlington, Va., 1981-84; exec. editor, pub. Computer Graphics News mag. Scherago Assocs. Pub., Inc., N.Y.C., 1984-85; guest lectr. publs. specialist program George Washington U., 1977-82; cons. publs. Author: The History and Fundamentals of Child Support Enforcement, 1980; Paternity Establishment: Who Does It Benefit, 1981; author filmstrip: (with P. Semler-Carlson) Child Support Enforcement; Program Basics, 1980; contbr. articles to jours.; editor numerous books, including: Junks and Sampans of the Yangtze (Assn. Am. Univ. Press award 1971), 1971; Rape: Victims of Crisis, 1974; Current Medical Abbreviations, 1977; The Madness in Sports, 1977; author teaching aids for Nutrition Today. Mem. Soc. Scholarly Pub. Council Biology Editors (chmn. com. on pub. policy 1984-86), Am. Soc. Tng. and Devel., Washington Book Pubs., The Word Guild, Balt. Pubs. Assn., AAUW, NOW, Meredith Coll. Alumni Assn. Democrat. Methodist. Clubs: Chesapeake Bay Yacht Racing Assn., Indian Landing Boat, Jr. League of Balt. Lodge: DAR. Office: KPL & Assocs 7875 Americana Circle #102 Glen Burnie MD 21061 also: 1515 Broadway 10th Floor New York NY 10036

PETTI, ANNMARIE, entrepreneur, former oil company executive; b. Yonkers, N.Y., Jan. 8, 1955; d. John B. and Santa (Conte) P.; m. Ralph Pane. BBA cum laude in Acctg., Pace U., 1976; MBA in Fin., St. Joseph's U., 1985. Various mgmt. positions Mobil Corp., N.Y. and Pa., 1976-87; co-owner, pvt. practice in consumer service bus. Mem. Pace U. Alumni Assn., Pace U. Soc. Acctg.

PETTIETTE, ALISON YVONNE, lawyer; b. Brockton, Mass., Aug. 16, 1952; d. David and Loretta (LeClair) Waters; Student Sorbonne, Paris, 1971-72; B.A., Sophie Newcomb Coll., 1972; M.A., Rice U., 1974; J.D., Bates Coll., 1978. Bar: Tex. 1979, U.S. Dist. Ct. (so. dist.) Tex. 1980, U.S. Ct. Appeals (5th cir.) 1981. Ptnr. Harvill & Hardy, Houston, 1979-83; sole practice, Houston, 1983-84; assoc. O'Quinn & Hagans, Houston, 1984-86, assoc. Jones & Granger, Houston, 1986—; editor Houston Law Rev. U. Houston, 1976-78. Exercise instr. YWCA, Houston, 1976-81, U. St. Thomas, Houston, 1982—. NDEA fellow Rice U., Houston, 1972-74; Woodrow Wilson scholar, Tulane U., New Orleans, 1972. Mem. ABA, Assn. Trial

Lawyers Am., Tex. Trial Lawyers Assn., Houston Trial Lawyers Assn., Phi Delta Phi, Phi Beta Kappa. Office: Jones & Granger 10000 Memorial 8th Floor Houston TX 77024

PETTIGREW, DANA MARY, musician; b. Oklahoma City, Jan. 15, 1951; d. Richard Clester and Alice Butler (Sargent) P.; children: Marilyn Yvonne, Lonnie Dean Jr. Student, Oklahoma City U., 1966-68. Profl. performance musician Oklahoma City, 1965—; ind. agt. Pettigrew Ins. Agy., Oklahoma City, 1975—. Ch. organist Pa. Ave. Christian Ch., 1979—. Life Underwriter Tng. Council fellow, 1984. Mem. Oklahoma City Health Underwriters Assn. (bd. dirs., sec. 1986—, v.p. 1987, pres.-elect 1988), Oklahoma City Life Underwriters Assn. (bd. dirs. 1984-85), Musicians Exchange, Nat. Assn. Female Execs., Oklahoma Country Music Assn., Profl. Ins. Agts. Assn. Democrat. Mem. Christian Ch. Lodge: Kiwanis (sec. 1988, pianist1987—). Home: 12009 Briar Lake Ct Oklahoma City OK 73170 Office: 9636 N May Ave Suite 200 Oklahoma City OK 73120

PETTIGREW, KAREN BETH, lawyer; b. Lubbock, Tex., July 26, 1948; d. Jim Moore and Wanda Beth (Chastain) P. B.A. with honors, Tex. Tech. U., 1970; J.D., So. Meth. U., 1974. Bar: Tex. 1974, U.S. Tax Ct., U.S. Dist. Ct. (so. and no. dists.) Tex. Staff mem. U.S. Senator John G. Tower, Dallas, 1970-71; law clk. U.S. Dept. Justice, Tax Div., Dallas, 1973-74; atty. Andrews & Kurth, Houston, 1974-80, Wyckoff, Russell, Dunn & Frazier, Houston, 1980-82, Morris, Tinsley & Snowden, Houston, 1982-84, Thelen, Marrin, Johnson & Bridges, Houston, 1984-86, ptnr., 1986—. Del. Tex. Rep. Conv., 1984; bd. dirs. Tex. Tech. U. Century Club, Houston, 1983-86, Bellaire Christian Ch., Houston, 1983; bd. dirs. Houston Red Raider Club, 1981—, v.p., 1986—; mem. Ladies Go-Texan com., 1984-86, Skybox com., 1985-86, Internat. com., 1987—, Houston Livestock Show and Rodeo (life mem.); trustee Theatre Under the Stars, 1987—. Acad. scholar Tex. Tech. U., 1966-70, So. Meth. U. Sch. Law, 1971-74. Mem. Houston Bar Assn., Tex. Bar Assn., ABA, Order of Coif, Phi Delta Phi, Phi Kappa Phi, Alpha Lambda Delta, Phi Alpha Theta, Phi Sigma Alpha. Republican (del. state conv. 1984). Mem. Disciples of Christ (deaconess 1983-86, pulpit com. 1986-87). Home: 3650 Glen Haven Houston TX 77025 Office: Thelen Marrin Johnson & Bridges 1700 Texas American Bldg Houston TX 77002

PETTIGREW, L. EUDORA, university administrator; b. Hopkinsville, Ky., Mar. 1, 1928; d. Warren Cicero and Corrye Lee (Newell) Williams; children: Peter W. Woodard, Jonathan R. (dec.). B.Mus., W.Va. State Coll., 1950; M.A., So. Ill. U., 1964, Ph.D., 1966. Music/English instr. Swift Meml. Jr. Coll., Rogersville, Tenn., 1950-51; music instr., librarian Western Ky. Vocat. Sch., Paducah, 1951-52; music/English instr. Voorhees Coll., Denmark, S.C., 1954-55; dir. music and recreation therapy W.Ky. State Psychiatric Hosp., Hopkinsville, 1956-61; research fellow Rehab. Inst., So. Ill. U., Carbondale, 1961-63, instr., resident counselor, 1963-66, coordinator undergrad. ednl. psychology, 1963-66, acting chmn. ednl. psychology, tchr. corps instr., 1966; asst. prof. dept. psychology U. Bridgeport, Conn., 1966-79; prof., chmn. dept. urban and met. studies Coll. Urban Devel. Mich. State U., East Lansing, 1974-81; assoc. provost, prof. U. Del., Newark, 1981-86; pres. SUNY Coll. at Old Westbury, 1986—; cons. for research and evaluation Hall Neighborhood House Day Care Tng. Project, Bridgeport, 1966-68, coordinator for edn. devel., 1968-69; cons. Bridgeport Public Schs. lang. devel. project, 1967-68, 70; cons. research/evaluation U.S. Eastern Regional Lab., Edn. Devel. Center, Newton, Mass., 1967-69; assoc. prof. U. Bridgeport, 1970, Center for Urban Affairs and Coll. of Edn., Mich. State U., East Lansing, 1970-73; cons. Lansing Model Cities Agy., Day Care Program, Lansing, Mich., 1971; trustee L.I. Community Found.; program devel. specialist Lansing Public Schs. Tchr. Corps program, 1971-73; cons. U. Pitts., 1973, 74, Leadership Program, U. Mich. and Wayne State U., 1975, Wayne County Public Health Nurses Assn., 1976, Ill. State Bd. Edn., 1976-77; lectr. in field; condr. workshops in field; cons. in field. Tv/radio appearances on: Black Women in Edn, Channel 23, WKAR, East Lansing, 1973, Black Women and Equality, Channel 2, Detroit, 1974, Women and Careers, Channel 7, Detroit, 1974, Black Women and Work: Integration in Schools, WITL Radio, Lansing, 1974, others.; Contbr. articles to profl. jours. Named Outstanding Black Educator NAACP, 1968; Outstanding Woman Educator Mich. Women's Lawyers Assn. and Mich. Trial Lawyers Assn., 1975; recipient Diana award Lansing YWCA, 1977, others. Mem. Nat. Assn. Acad. Affairs Adminstrs., AAAS, Phi Delta Kappa. Office: SUNY Coll at Old Westbury Box 210 Old Westbury NY 11568

PETTIJOHN, JOYCE LORRAINE, pharmacist, educator; b. Portland, Oreg., Jan. 7, 1955; d. Elzo Irving and Verona Muriel (McKittrick) Pettijohn; B.S. with honors in Pharmacy, Oreg. State U., 1978; postgrad. in bus. adminstrn. U. Puget Sound, 1980-81. Pharmacy extern St. Vincent's Hosp., Portland, 1977; pharmacy intern Lakeshore Clinic Pharmacy, Kirkland, Wash., 1978; staff pharmacist Evergreen Pharm. Services, Kirkland, 1979-80, sr. staff pharmacist, 1981—; dir. Health Products, Inc., Kirkland, 1981-85. Lic. pharmacist, Wash., Calif., Oreg. Mem. Am. Pharm. Assn., Wash. Pharm. Assn., Seattle Women's Network, Internat. Platform Assn. Office: 402 6th St S Kirkland WA 98033

PETTINGILL, KATHLEEN ANNE, lawyer; b. Washington, Mar. 13, 1955; d. Stuart Anderson and Margaret Elizabeth (Larkin) P.; m. Gene Allan Wimmer, Sept. 14, 1985. BA magna cum laude, Allegheny Coll., 1977; M in Social Sci. Adminstrn., Case Western Res. U., Cleve., 1982, JD, 1982. Bar: Ohio 1982. Clk. to presiding judge Ohio Ct. Appeals (8th dist.), Cleve., 1983-84; legal asst. Chessie System R.R.'s, Cleve., 1985-86; assoc. Goldfarb & Reznick, Cleve., 1986-87; sole practice Cleve., 1987-88; staff atty. Baker & Hostetler, Cleve., 1988—. Chair pastoral search com. Olmsted Community Ch., 1987-88. Mem. ABA, Ohio State Bar Assn., Cleve. Bar Assn., Sierra Club (mem. exec. com. 1983-84, membership com. chair 1983-84, v.p. 1984), Phi Beta Kappa. Club: Nature Conservancy (Nags Head, N.C.). Home: 444 Nobottom Rd Berea OH 44017 Office: Baker & Hostetler 3200 National City Center Cleveland OH 44114

PETTIS, SHIRLEY NEIL, business executive, former congresswoman; b. Mountain View, Calif.; d. Harold Oliver and Dorothy Susan (O'Neil) McCumber; m. Jerry Pettis, (dec. 1975); children—Peter Dwight, Deborah Neil; m. B.B. Roberson, Feb. 6, 1988. Student Andrews U., U. Calif.-Berkeley. Co-founder, mgr. Magnetic Tape Duplicator, Hollywood, Calif., 1951-64; Audio-Digest Found., Glendale, Calif., 1951-55; sec., treas. Pettis, Inc., Hollywood, 1958-64; mem. 94-95th Congresses from Calif. 37th Dist.; dir. corp. bds. Kemper Group, 1979—. Mem. Pres.'s Arms Commn. Control and Disarmament Commn., 1981-83; trustee U. Redlands, 1979-82; v.p., pres. Women's Research and Edn. Inst., Washington, 1979-82. Mem. DAR. Republican. Clubs: Congressional, Capitol Hill. Home: 12315 Ridge Circle Los Angeles CA 90049

PETTIT, JULIA MARIE CANTWELL, health services facility administrator; b. Portsmouth, Va., Oct. 27, 1955; d. John Roger and Virginia (Gallagher) Cantwell; m. Peter Dudley Pettit, Mar. 27, 1983; 1 child, Gregory William. Student, Old Dominion U., 1974-78, Va. Commonwealth U., 1978-83. Coordinator emergency room Chesapeake (Va.) Gen. Hosp., 1977-83; dir. ops. Med-Systems Assocs./PHCMS Inc., Portsmouth, Va., 1984-87; v.p. Med-Systems Assocs.-Profl. Health Care Mgmt. Services Inc., Portsmouth, Va., 1987-88; founder, pres. Mgmt. Assn. Physicians and Staff, Inc., Chesapeake, Va., 1988—. Instr. swimming Spl. Olympics, Va., 1987. Mem. Am. Mgrs. Assn., Nat. Assn. Female Execs., Tidewater Hosp. Account Mgrs. Assn. Office: Mgmt Assn Physicians & Staff Inc Chesapeake VA 23320

PETTIT, KATHY ROBIN, college admissions administrator; b. Queens, N.Y., Jan. 29, 1956; d. Garrett John and Joan (Storm) G. BS, Cornell U., 1978; MS with distinction, Calif. State U., Fresno, 1982. Asst. mgr. ranch Sahaptin Farm, Winona, Minn., 1978-79; mgr. ranch George Minic Appaloosas, Fresno, 1979, Charly's Quarter Horses, Fresno, 1979-81; asst. merchandiser J.C. Penney Co., Fresno, 1981-83; sales rep. Paul Revere Co., Fresno, 1983-84; admissions rep. Westland Coll., Clovis, Calif., 1984-86, Heald 4C's Coll., Fresno, 1986—; area rep. courses div. Werner Erhard & Assocs., Fresno, 1987—. Mem. AAUW, Profl. Saleswomen Assn., Fresno Women's Trade Club, Cornell U. Alumni Assn., Calif. State U.-Fresno Alumni Assn., Phi Kappa Phi. Republican. Office: Heald 4C's Coll 255 W Bullard Fresno CA 93704

PETTIT, MARGARET ESTA, broadcasting executive; b. Provo, Utah, July 22, 1926; d. Howard Hammil and Edith Susan (Cummins) Cain; student public schs.; m. Claud Martin Pettit, July 30, 1948; children—Ruth Elaine, Paul Martin. Co-owner, office supr. Sta. KEOS, Flagstaff, Ariz., 1960-61; co-owner, bookkeeper Sta. KWIV, Douglas, Wyo., 1965-74; co-owner, bookkeeper, program dir., office supr. Sta. KCMP, Brush Colo., 1976-82; dir. Custom Broadcasting Co., Denver; sec.-treas., dir. Ranchland Broadcasting Co.; dir., v.p. Better Day, Inc., Arvada, Colo. Bd. dirs. Jefferson Park Community Activity Assn., Denver, 1981-84, North Fed. Recreation, Denver, 1984—. Mem. Model T Ford Club. Baptist. Home and Office: 8320 W 66th Ave Arvada CO 80004

PETTIT, WENDY JEAN, advertising agency executive; b. Gary, Ind., Oct. 6, 1945; d. Wendell E. and Ethel (Binkley) Pettit. B.A., MacMurray Coll., 1967; M.S.B.A., Ind. U., 1978. Acctg. clk. J. Walter Thompson USA, Chgo., 1967-68, adminstrv. asst., 1968-72, personnel asst., 1973-74, fin. analyst, 1974-78, office services asst., 1978-79, acctg. dept. mgr., 1979—. Bd. dirs. Miller Citizens Corp., Gary, 1979-86, treas., 1979-82. Named Career Woman of the Year, Bus. and Profl. Women, Gary, 1967. Mem. Nat. Assn. Female Execs., Am. Mgmt. Assn., LWV. Methodist. Avocations: singing; piano; cooking. Home: 8000 Oak Ave Gary IN 46403 Office: J Walter Thompson USA Inc 875 N Michigan Ave Chicago IL 60611

PETTUS, MARY CATHERINE, public relations executive; b. Bellingham, Wash., Apr. 18, 1947; d. Edgar Raymond and Catherine Amanda (Selander) May; m. Drew Douglas Pettus, Dec. 22, 1970. BA in History, Western Wash. U., 1970. Store mgr. Portland Art Mus., 1970-74; store cons. Corcoran Gallery of Art, Washington, 1974-75, devel. cons., 1977; store cons. Phillips Collection, Washington, 1976; owner Mary Pettus & Assocs., Washington, 1978—. Mem. Am. Inst. Wine and Food (chair regional chpt. 1986—). Democrat. Lutheran. Home: 720 A St NE Washington DC 20002 Office: Mary Pettus and Assocs Inc 3242 Jones Ct NW Washington DC 20007

PETTY, CAROL, computer systems analyst; b. Schenectady, N.Y., Nov. 10, 1950; d. John Stewart Petty and Jane Beverley (Robertson) Taylor. BS, U. Rochester, 1972; MA, U. Mich., 1976; MBA, St. Joseph's U., 1984—. Tchr. elem. sch. North Rose-Wolcott (N.Y.) Schs., 1972-78; tchr. 6th grade math Soule Rd. Middle Sch., Liverpool, N.Y., 1978-80; tchr. 7th and 8th grade math. Veron-Verona-Sherrill Jr. High, N.Y., 1980-81; assoc. systems analyst Unisys, Syracuse, N.Y., 1981-82; sr. systems analyst Unisys, Devon, Pa., 1982-85; project systems analyst Unisys, Radnor, Pa., 1985—. Mem. Nat. Assn. Female Execs., Pi Lambda Theta. Clubs: Living Well; Kirkwood Fitness. Office: Unisys 240 Radnor Chester Rd Radnor PA 19087

PETTY, JOYCE JONES, instructor, real estate broker; b. Little Rock, Jan. 1, 1945; d. Albert Lee and Julia Anna (Weekly) Jones; m. Pruitt Gordon Petty, Aug. 10, 1969; children: Pruitt Jr., Nicholas, Marc. BA, Philander Smith, 1966; MEd, Cleve. State U., 1979. Cert. work study coordinator, Cleve. Bd. Edn.; lic. real estate broker, Ohio. English tchr. Cleve. Bd. Edn., 1966-70, transition team leader, 1971-78; real estate agt. Heights Realty, Cleve. Heights, Ohio, 1972-79; work study coordinator Cleve. Bd. Edn., 1979—; real estate broker J. Petty Realty, Inc., Cleve. Heights, 1979—; drama dir., newspaper advisor Cen. Jr. High Sch., Cleve., 1966-74; honor soc. advisor Harry E. Davis Jr. High Sch., Cleve., 1982-86. Youth dir. First Bapt. Ch., Little Rock, 1964-66; active Beachwood PTA. Mem. Cleve. Area Bd. Realtors, Alpha Kappa Alpha. Democrat. Club: FNO Bridge (Cleve.). Home: 25830 Annesley Rd Beachwood OH 44122 Office: 2000 Lee Rd Suite 1 Cleveland Heights OH 44118

PETTY, PRISCILLA HAYES, writer, newspaper columnist, consultant; b. Nashville, Aug. 22, 1940; d. Anderson Boyd and Margaret Louise (Lauper) Hayes; m. Gene Paul Petty, Jan. 10, 1961; children—Eric, Damon, Boyd. B.A. in English, Vanderbilt U., 1962; student Russian Inst., Dartmouth Coll., 1965. Cert. tchr., Ohio. Tchr. English, Cin. Suburban Pub. Schs., 1962-65, head dept. English, tchr., 1971-79; newspaper columnist Cin. Enquirer, 1978—, also syndicated newspaper columnist Gannett News Service, Washngton, 1982—; cons. Arthur Andersen & Co., 1981-82; writer United Western Corp., 1982. Author: History of a Boardsman (oral history), 1979, Under a Lucky Star: The Story of Frederick A. Hauck, 1986. Mem. Cin. Council World Affairs; chmn. Cin. Media-Bus. Exchange, 1983; founder, pres. bd. trustees Cin. Oral History Found., 1984—. Named Outstanding Tchr., Project Teach, Ohio Edn. Assn., 1978; recipient WICI Great Lakes Regional Communicators' award; Pulitzer Prize nominee for Harvard Bus. Rev. article. Mem. Women in Communications (Outstanding Communicator of Yr. 1985), Oral History Assn., Sigma Delta Chi. Club: Woman's City (Cin.). Home: 229 Oliver Rd Cincinnati OH 45215

PETTYJOHN, CAROL LAVONNE, genetic engineering company executive; b. Maple Creek, Sask., Can., May 13, 1940; came to U.S., 1948, naturalized, 1986; d. Glenn C. Pettyjohn and Ruth I. (Cox) Savchenko; m. Thomas Edward Hatfield, June 13, 1958 (div. 1964); 1 child, Tamra R.; m. Dan Franklin Black, Oct. 1, 1964 (div. 1971); children—Kelley S., Anthony G. Student Memphis State U., 1958-59, San Diego State U., 1960, Bapt. Meml. Hosp. Sch. Nursing, 1957-59, Atlanta Law Sch., 1963, U. Maine, 1976, Coll. DuPage, 1984. Staff nurse Erlanger Hosp., Chattanooga, 1961-62, DeKalb Gen. Hosp., Decatur, Ga., 1962-63; med. cons. Prudential Ins. Co., Atlanta, 1964-67, employment interviewer, 1967-71; personnel mgr. Montgomery Wards, Jacksonville, Fla., 1972-75; office mgr. Drs. Wildstein, Kaiser, Schlemann, Springvale, Maine, 1975-78; pres., owner Options Agy., Sanford, Maine, 1978-81; controller, product mgr., div. mgr. Immuno Genetics, Inc., Eldora, Iowa and Vineland, N.J., 1981-86; chief exec. officer, pres. PanoGen, Inc., 1986—; bus. cons. Sanford Fire Dept., 1979-81, Drs. Harrigan, Pollard, Peterlein, Schlemann, Kaiser, Buell, Bellevaun, 1978-81. Area coordinator NOW, Jacksonville, Fla., 1974-75, Portland, Maine, 1975-79; softball coach Little League, Sanford, 1977-82; mem. LWV, Sanford, 1978-79; bd. dirs. Big Bros./Big Sisters, Biddeford, Maine, 1979-80. Mem. Nat. Assn. Female Execs. (network dir. 1985—), Nat. Agri-Mktg. Assn. (bd. dirs. 1987), Livestock Conservation Inst., Nat. Swine Improvement Fedn. (bd. dirs.). Democrat. Club: Eldora Ambassador. Avocations: reading, softball, chess, music, fishing. Office: PanoGen Inc PO Box 496 Airport Rd Eldora IA 50627

PETYKIEWICZ, SANDRA DICKEY, editor; b. Detroit, Sept. 23, 1953; d. James Fulton and Alice Diane (Nowak) Dickey; m. Edward W. Petykiewicz, Oct. 17, 1981. BA, Cen. Mich. U., Mt. Pleasant, 1975. Reporter Big Rapids (Mich.) Pioneer, 1975, Midland (Mich.) Daily News, 1975-77; reporter Saginaw (Mich.) News, 1977-79, feature editor, 1979-80, asst. metro editor, 1980-81; copy editor Washington Post, 1981-82; asst. city editor Balt. News Am., 1982-83; metro editor Jackson (Mich.) Citizen Patriot, 1983-87, editor, 1987—; bd. dirs. Mich. Associated Press, 1987-88. Mem. Associated Press Mng. Editors, Am. Soc. Newspaper Editors, Bus. Profl. Women's Club (editor newsletter 1985-86, Young Career Woman of Yr. award 1984), Sigma Delta Chi.

PETZEL, FLORENCE ELOISE, educator; b. Crosbyton, Tex., Apr. 1, 1911; d. William D. and A. Eloise (Punchard) P.; Ph.B., U. Chgo., 1931, A.M., 1934; Ph.D., U. Minn., 1954. Instr., Judson Coll., 1936-38; vis. instr. Tex. State Coll. for Women, 1937; asst. prof. textiles Ohio State U., 1938-48; asso. prof. U. Ala., 1950-54; prof. Oreg. State U., 1954-61, 67-75, 77, prof. emeritus, 1975—, dept. head, 1954-61, 67-75; prof., div. head U. Tex., 1961-63; prof. Tex. Tech U., 1963-67; vis. prof. Wash. State U., 1967. Effie I. Raitt fellow, 1949-50. Mem. Seattle Art Mus., Oreg. Art Mus., Textile Mus., Met. Opera Guild, San Francisco Opera Assn., Portland Opera Assn. Sigma Xi, Phi Kappa Phi, Omicron Nu, Iota Sigma Pi, Sigma Delta Epsilon. Author Textiles of Ancient Mesopotamia, Persia and Egypt, 1987; contbr. articles to profl. jours. Home: 730 NW 35th St Corvallis OR 97330

PETZOLD, CAROL STOKER, state legislator; b. St. Louis, July 28; d. Harold William and Mabel Lucille (Wilson) Stoker; m. Walter John Petzold, June 27, 1959; children: Ann, Ruth, David. BS, Valparaiso U., 1959. Tchr. John Muir Elem. Sch., Alameda, Calif., 1959-60, Parkwood Elem. Sch., Kensington, Md., 1960-62; legis. aide Md. Gen. Assembly, Annapolis, 1975-79; legis. asst. Montgomery County Bd. Edn., Rockville, Md., 1980; community sch. coordinator Parkland Jr. High Sch., Rockville, 1981-87; mem. Ho. Dels., Annapolis, 1987—. Editor Child Care Sampler, 1974, Stoker Family Cookbook, 1976. Pres. Montgomery Child Care Assn., 1976-78; mem. Md. State Scholarship Bd., Balt., 1978-87, chmn. 1985-87; chmn. Legis. Com. Montgomery County Commn. for Children and Youth, 1979-84; mem., v.p. Luth. Social Services Nat. Capitol Area, Washington, 1980-86. Recognized for outstanding committment to children U.S. Dept. HEW, 1980. Mem. AAUW (honoree Kensington br. 1971, honoree Md. div. 1981), Women's Polit. Caucus (chmn. Montgomery County 1981-83), Women's Caucus Md. Legislature, LWV. Democrat. Lutheran. Home: 14113 Chadwick Ln Rockville MD 20853 Office: Md House Delegates Lowe House Office Bldg Annapolis MD 21401

PEUGH, SARAH LOUISE PEARSON (MRS. WALTER STEPHEN PEUGH, SR.), freelance writer; b. Houston, Miss., Oct. 4, 1924; d. Edd Monroe (dec.) and Mattie (Shivers) (dec.) Pearson; student Trevecca Coll., 1941-43, Miss. state Extension, 1964, Auburn U., 1970, student Itawamba Jr. Coll., 1970; m. Walter Stephen Peugh, Sr., Dec. 20, 1947; children—Sarah Peugh Franks, Mary Jo Peugh Ayres, Steve Jr., Bob. Clk., teller First Nat. Bank, Phila. and San Diego, 1944; owner Town House Restaurant, Aberdeen, Miss., 1952-62; owner, grad., bridal cons. Wedding Services, Aberdeen, 1969-76; columnist Aberdeen Examiner, 1970-74, 77; Aberdeen News Herald, 1974-75. Exec. sec. ARC, Aberdeen, 1972-73, bd. dirs. 1973-77; bd. dirs. Miss. YMCA, 1974-78, Miss. for Ednl. TV, 1978-80; chmn. Council Clubs and City Beautiful Commn., 1974-76; area rep. Keep Miss. Beautiful, 1974-76; initiator Butterfly scholarship Miss. Fedn. Women's Clubs, 1978, Amblin scholarship, 1976, organizer 1st Juniorette Club, 1974. Miss. YMCA, Youth Gov. scholarship, 1977. Named Most Outstanding Woman, Jr. Aux. Charity Ball, Aberdeen, 1972. Mem. Aberdeen C. of C., Miss. Press Women (Woman of Achievement 1987), Miss. Fedn. Women's Clubs (Outstanding Woman of Yr. 1981), Nat. Fedn. Press Women, Miss. Poetry Soc. (organizer North Branch, Miss. chpt. 1979), Public Relations Assn. of Miss., N.E. Miss. Tourism Council, Am. Legion Aux. Clubs: Woman's (pres. 1973-74), Home and Garden, Gourmet (founder), Miss. Fashion Women (founder, exec. dir.). Editor: The Glencoe Story, 1967, Clubwoman Mag., The Miss. Clubwoman, 1984-88; mem. editorial bd. Lyric Miss., 50th Anthology; contbr. poetry to various publs. Address: 205 Hillcrest St Aberdeen MS 39730

PEVEAR, ROBERTA CHARLOTTE, state legislator; b. Bethel, Maine, July 4, 1930; d. Frank Albert Sr. and Thirza Estella (Hickford) Gibson; m. Edward Gordon Pevear, Aug. 21, 1971. Diploma in Comml. Art, Gould Acad., 1947. Sec. Wilner Wood Products, South Paris, Maine, 1947-50; sec. export dept. Whitaker Cable, North Kansas City, Mo., 1951-56; sec. br. and dist. Anheuser-Busch, Inc., Kansas City, Mo., 1957-59; legal sec. Johnson & Johnson, New Brunswick, N.J., 1960-65, St. John, Ronder & Bell, Kingston, N.Y., 1966; sec., adminstrv. asst. Sears-Roebuck & Co., Overland Park, Kans., 1967-70, Exeter, N.H., 1971-77; salesman Avon Products, Hampton Falls, N.H., 1978-86; mem. ho. reps. State of N.H., 1979—; Commr. Rockingham Planning Commn., N.H., 1979—, N.H. Planning Com., 1985—; clk. Environment and Agrl. Com. N.H. Ho. Reps., 1983—; del. mem. Rockingham County, 1979—, exec. bd., 1984-88; chmn. Rockingham County Home, 1987-88. Civil Def. dir., Hampton Falls, N.H., 1980—. Recipient Community Citizen award Hampton Falls Grange, 1982, Seacoast Retired Sr. Service award, 1985. Mem. Nat. Order Women Legislators, N.H. Order of Women Legislators, DAR. Clubs: Hampton Monday; Gen. Fedn. Women's. Home: 27 Drinkwater Rd Hampton Falls NH 03844 Office: NH Ho Reps State House LOB Room 303 Concord NH 03301

PEVELER, SARAH KATHRYN FESSLER, personnel official; b. Mt. Vernon, Ill., Feb. 21, 1947; d. Floyd Roscoe and Mildred Faye (Carson) Fessler; B.A., Emory U., 1969; postgrad. U. South Sch. Theology, 1980-84; m. R. David Peveler, June 14, 1969 (div. Aug. 1981). Tng. dir. Ill. Shore council Girl Scout U.S.A., Wilmette, Ill., 1970-73, Abnaki council, Brewer, Maine, 1973-75, tng. dir., dir. field services Shawnee council, Martinsburg, W.Va., 1976-77; personnel dir. Seamen's Ch. Inst. N.Y. and N.J., N.Y.C., 1978-82; personnel dir. Trinity Ch., N.Y.C., 1982—; owner, propr. The Uncommon Resume, cons. firm. Personnel com. Greater N.Y. council Girl Scouts U.S.A.; mem. Episcopal Women's Caucus; mem. clergy compensation com. Episcopal Diocese of N.Y. Mem. Am. Soc. Personnel Adminstrn., N.Y. Personnel Mgmt. Assn., Phi Mu. Office: 74 Trinity Pl New York NY 10006

PEWITT, EDITH MARIE, educational administrator; b. Greenville, Tex., Feb. 27, 1926; d. Charles Ambrose, Jr. and Beulah Edna (King) Hendrix; m. Edgar Lee Pewitt, Feb. 23, 1945; children—Edith Pamela Pewitt Chatagnier, Robert Lewis, II, Edgar Lee. B.S., Tex. Women's U., 1961; M.Ed., N. Tex. State U., 1964, Ed.D., 1967. Supr. sch. lunches to tchr. Grapevine Ind. Sch. Dist., Tex., 1958-66; research asst., lab. instr. to asst. prof. edn. N. Tex. State U., 1966-68; coordinator curriculum Edn. Service Ctr., Region XI, Ft. Worth, 1968-70; cons. Novato Unified Sch. Dist., Calif., 1970-71, adminstrv. asst., 1971-72; staff devel. coordinator Ptnrs. in Career Edn., Arlington, Tex., 1972-74; tchr. high sch. sci., instructional leader, coordinator Career Planning Acad., Ft. Worth Ind. Sch. Dist., 1974-88; prin. B.H. Carroll Ctr. for New Lives, Ft. Worth Independent Sch. Dist., 1988—, cons. in field. Mem. NEA, Adminstrv. Women in Edn. (membership chmn. 1980-81), Assn. Supervision and Curriculum Devel., Soc. Study Edn., Nat. Aci. Tchrs. Assn., Tex. Tchrs. Assn., Tex. Assn. Supervision and Curriculum Devel., Ft. Worth Public Schs. Adminstrs. Assn., LWV, Kappa Delta Pi (past chpt. pres.), Phi Delta Kappa. Methodist. Home: 303 Ridge Rd Grapevine TX 76051 Office: 3908 McCart Fort Worth TX 76110

PEYTON, MARY JOHANNA, secondary educator; b. Salt Lake City, Apr. 15, 1946; d. John Edward and Ellen Bernice (Michaud) P. B in Music, U. Mont., 1968, M in Music Edn., 1969. Cert. secondary tchr., Calif. Elem. instr. music Ceres (Calif.) Unified Sch. Dist., 1969-71, instr. jr. high music, 1971-75, instr. jr. high English, 1975-84, instr. jr. high econs., 1984-86, coordinator career edn., 1984—, instr. ind. study, 1986—, cons. various edn. orgns., 1984—; trainer career edn. Nat. Diffusion Network, U.S. Dept. Edn., Washington, 1985—. Producer, writer film Project Ceres, 1985; speaker in field. Mem. NEA, Calif. Tchrs. Assn., Calif. Career Edn. Assn., Ceres Unified Tchrs. Assn. (faculty rep. 1969—, negotiations team 1979—, 2d v.p. 1980, negotiations chair 1984—). Republican. Roman Catholic. Home: 3128 Scenic Dr Modesto CA 95355

PFAFF, FRANCOISE SIMONE-LOUISE, educator; b. Paris, Oct. 15, 1946; came to U.S., 1971; d. René Jason and Hélène Thérèse Pfaff. BA, U. Paris, 1970, MA, 1971, PhD, 1975. Tchr. Collè de Juilly, France, 1970-71; teaching asst. Bates Coll., Lewiston, Maine, 1971-72; lectr. French, Lit. and Film of France and Francophone Africa Howard U., Washington, 1972-73, instr., 1974-76, asst. prof., 1976-80, assoc. prof., 1980-88, prof., 1988—; tchr. Cours de Petits Champs, Paris, 1973-74. Author: The Cinema of Ousmane Sembene, A Pioneer of African Film, 1984, 25 Black African Filmmakers, 1988; contbr. articles to profl. jours. A.W. Mellon Fund grantee, 1977, 78, 86, faculty research grantee Howard U., 1978, 79. Mem. Coll. Lang. Assn., African Lit. Assn. Roman Catholic. Office: Howard U Dept Romance Langs Washington DC 20059

PFAFFENROTH, SARA BEEKEY, educator; b. Reading, Pa., Dec. 2, 1941; d. Cyrus Ezra and Viola Bessie (Sweigart) Beekey; A.B., Bryn Mawr Coll., 1963; M.A., Ind. U., 1964; m. Peter Albert Pfaffenroth, June 26, 1966; children—Elizabeth Kilmer, Peter Cyrus, Catherine Genevieve. Instr. English, Northwestern Mich. Coll., Traverse City, 1964-66, Middlesex County Coll., Edison, N.J., 1966-88; prof. English, County Coll. of Morris, Randolph, N.J., 1968—; grants cons., 1979-82, dir. internat. edn. County Coll. of Morris, 1988—. Recipient poetry award Bryn Mawr Arts Council, 1963, Gertrude Saucier Hist. Poetry award, 1970; mid-career fellow Princeton U., 1983-84. Mem. N.J. Poetry Soc. (trustee), MLA, Coll. English Assn., Jane Austen Soc. N.Am. Lutheran. Editor anthologies: Beyond Tether, 1975; A Palette of Poets, 1976; Endless Waters Welling Up, 1977; From Rim to Rim, 1978; Crystal Cadences, 1980. Home: Box 429 Chester NJ 07930 Office: County College of Morris Randolph NJ 07801

PFEIFFER, ISOBEL LORRAINE, education educator; b. Warsaw, Ind., Aug. 30, 1921; d. Franklin Otis and Ethel Faun (Shilling) R.; m. Robert Thomas Pfeiffer, June 9, 1945. BA, Manchester Coll., 1942; MA, Ind. U., 1948; PhD, Kent (Ohio) State U., 1966. Tchr. Warsaw Jr. High Sch., 1942-45, 46-48, South San Francisco (Calif.) High Sch., 1945-46, West Aurora (Ill.) Schs., 1948-49; instr. Aurora Coll., 1949-51; tchr. Martinsville (Ind.)

Schs., 1951-53, East Lansing (Mich.) Schs., 1953-56, Tallmadge (Ohio) Schs., 1956-57; tchr., dean of girls Kent Schs., 1957-66; prof. U. Akron, Ohio, 1966-82, West Ga. Coll., Carrollton, 1982—; cons. instrnl. supervision, Cuyahoga County, Ohio, 1970-72, U. Akron Ednl. Research and Devel. Ctr., 1978-82; adviser Northeastern Ohio Sch. Supervisors Assn., Akron, 1972-80. Author: Supervision of Teachers, 1982; contbr. articles to profl. jours. Mem. AAUW (pres. 1961-63), Council of Profs. of Instrnl. Supervision, Ga. Assn. for Supervision and Curriculum Devel. (editor newsletter 1983-84), Delta Kappa Gamma (pres. local chpt. 1970-72), Phi Delta Kappa (chpt. editor 1984-85). Home: 85 Camp Ln Carrollton GA 30117 Office: West Ga Coll Dept Ednl Leadership Carrollton GA 30118

PFEIFFER, JANE CAHILL, former broadcasting company executive, consultant; b. Washington, Sept. 29, 1932; d. John Joseph and Helen (Reilly) Cahill; B.A., U. Md., 1954; postgrad., Cath. U. Am., 1956-57; LHD (hon.), Pace Coll., 1978, U. Md., 1979, Manhattanville Coll., 1979, Amherst U., 1980, Babson Coll., 1981; m. Ralph A. Pfeiffer, Jr., June 3, 1975. With IBM Corp., Armonk, N.Y., 1955-76, sec. mgmt. rev. com., 1970, dir. communications, 1971, v.p. communications and govt. relations, 1972-76, bus. cons., 1976-78; chmn. NBC, Inc., N.Y.C., 1978-80; bus. cons., 1980—; dir. Ashland Oil Co., Chesebrough-Ponds, Inc., Internat. Paper Co., J.C. Penney Co., Ashland Oil Co. Mem. pres.'s adv. com. White House Fellows, 1966, Pres.'s Gen. Adv. Commn. on Arms Control and Disarmament, 1977-80, Pres.'s Commn. Mil. Compensation; Trustee Rockefeller Found., U. Md., Carnegie Hall, U. Notre Dame. White House fellow, Washington, 1966; Achievement award Kapppa Kappa Gamma, 1974-80; Eleanor Roosevelt Humanitarian award N.Y. League for Hard of Hearing, 1980; Disting. Alumna award U. Md., 1975; NOW Humanitarian award, 1980. Mem. Council on Fgn. Relations, Overseas Devel. Council. Club: Econ. of N.Y. Office: 90 Field Point Circle Greenwich CT 06830

PFEIFFER, SOPHIA DOUGLASS, lawyer; b. N.Y.C., Aug. 10, 1918; d. Franklin Chamberlin and Sophie Douglass (White) Wells; m. Timothy Adams Pfeiffer, June 7, 1941; children—Timothy Franklin, Penelope Mersereau Keenan, Sophie Douglass. A.B., Vassar Coll., 1939; J.D., Northeastern U., 1975. Bar: R.I. 1975, U.S. Ct. Apls. (1st cir.) 1980, U.S. Supreme Ct. 1979. Editorial researcher Time, Inc., N.Y.C., 1940-41; writer Office War Info., Washington, 1941-43, N.Y.C., 1943-45; editorial staff Nat. Geog. Mag., Washington, 1958-59, 68-70; editor Turkish Jour. Pediatrics, Ankara, 1961-63; staff atty. R.I. Supreme Ct., Providence, 1975-76, chief staff atty., 1977-86. Contbr. in field. Pres., Karachi Am. Sch. (Pakistan), 1955-56; chair, Brunswick Village Review Bd., 1986—. Home: 15 Franklin St Brunswick ME 04011

PFEUFFER, SYLVIA REICHEL, medical consulting company; b. San Antonio, Feb. 28, 1949; d. Charles Luther Sr. and Ethel (Nichols) Peters; m. Alvin Moore Jr., Mar. 9, 1965 (dec. 1976); 1 child, Leslie Dawn Moore; m. Jimmy Nicholas Pfeuffer, Dec. 17, 1977. BSBA, Southwestern U., 1982; postgrad., S.W. Tex. State U., 1985—. Analyst health record Santa Rosa Med. Ctr., San Antonio, 1976-78; dir. med. records Luth. Gen. Hosp., San Antonio, 1978-83; divisional dir. San Antonio Children's Ctr., 1984-85; chief exec. officer Med. Record Cons. Service, San Antonio, 1985—; instr. mgmt. practicum Incarnate Word U., San Antonio, 1983; instr. leadership Sanyo Program, San Antonio, 1978-83. Speaker Explorers Club, San Antonio, 1979-83. Mem. Am. Med. Record Assn. (cert.), Nat. Assn. Quality Assurance Profls. (assoc. editor jour. 1983-85), Tex. Med. Record Assn., Nat. Assn. Female Execs. Republican. Baptist. Home: 7335 Karankawa San Antonio TX 78223

PFLAGER, RUTH WOOD, communications coordinator, retired; b. Springfield Mass., Mar. 3, 1917; d. Walter Guy and Mabel (Munson) Wood; B.S., U. Mass., 1938; postgrad. Northwestern U., 1939-40; m. Miller S. Pflager, Aug. 31, 1940; children—Sandra P. Wischmeyer, Charlene P. Balistrere, William Wood, Jessie Pflager Avery. Program chmn., v.p. Radio and TV Council Greater Cleve., Inc., 1973-75, pres., 1975-77, exec. dir., 1977-79. Mem. Communications Commn., Greater Cleve. Interchurch Council, 1972—, vice chmn. 1981-82, chmn., 1983—; chmn. Community Mental Health Inst., 1981-82; communications coordinator Ch. Women United in Cleve., 1974-82, bull. editor, 1974-78, honor award, 1980; chmn. media concerns Ch. Women United in Ohio, 1979-81; chmn. TV Tune-In, 1981—. Recipient Outstanding Service award Radio-TV Council, 1977. Mem. AAUW (br. pres. 1977-79, com. on women Ohio div. 1979-81, chmn. media concerns task force), Am. Council Better Broadcasts (life mem., sec. 1979-80 v.p. 1980—), Nat. Assn. Better Broadcasting, Nat. Citizens Com. for Broadcasting, Orange Hist. Soc. Methodist. Club: Women's City (mem. mental health com. 1974—) (Cleve.). Home: 360 Strickler Ave Waynesboro PA 17268 Office: 2230 Euclid Ave Cleveland OH 44115

PFUND, ROSE TOSHIKO, academic administrator; b. Honolulu, July 22, 1929; d. Toichi and Kame (Gibo) Omine. BA, U. Hawaii, 1951, MEd, 1978; PhD, U. Pitts., 1985. Sci. and tech. editor Water Research Ctr. U. Hawaii, Honolulu, 1966-72, info. coordinator Sea Grant Coll. Program, 1973-79, acting assoc. dir. Sea Grant Coll. Program, 1981-83, assoc. dir. Sea Grant Coll. Program, 1984—; mem. adv. com. Marine Affairs Hawaii State Legis., Honolulu, 1985-86, U. Hawaii Communications Council, Honolulu, 1987—. Editor Sea Grant Quar., 1979—. Contbr. articles to profl. jours. Mem. ESEA Title III/IV adv. council, Hawaii, 1970-79; pres. Hawaii PTA, Honolulu, 1976-78; state rep. com. status and role women United Meth. Ch., So. Calif.-Hawaii region, 1976-80, organizer, chair Asian Women's Caucus, 1977-80; mem. task force Gov.'s Ocean Resources Tourism Devel., 1987—. Hawaii state legis. grantee, 1975—. Mem. Am. Fisheries Soc., Am. Soc. Pub. Adminstrn. (nat. council 1987—, planning and evaluation com. 1987-88, chpt. devel. com. 1988—), Acad. Polit. Sci., Western Govtl. Research Assn. Office: U Hawaii Sea Grant Program 1000 Pope Rd MSB 220 Honolulu HI 96822

PHAIR, PATRICIA ANTOINETTE, banker; b. N.Y.C., Mar. 24, 1941; d. Thomas Francis Donohue and Mildred Mary (Raia) Tate; m. Craig G. Chanslor, Apr. 16, 1960 (div. Mar. 1974); 1 child, Dione; m. Richard G. Phair II, Oct. 28, 1977. BA in Social Psychology, U. Nev., 1971; JD, Old Coll. Sch., 1985. Escrow sec. First Am. Title Co., Reno, 1972-74; escrow sec. First Comml. Title, Inc., Reno, 1974-77, title officer, 1977-78; loan processor State Mortgage Co., Reno, 1978-79, br. mgr., 1979-83; real estate loan officer Security Bank of Nev., Reno, 1983-86; consumer, comml. loan dept. supr. First Fed. Savs. and Loan, Reno, 1986—. Mem. Bus. and Profl. Women (treas. 1987—). Republican. Clubs: Reno Kennel (sec. 1978-80); Bonanza Kennel (pres. 1985-86)(Carson City). Office: First Fed Savs and Loan Assoc One California Ave Reno NV 89501

PHARES, MARGUERITE LINTON, ballet educator, artistic director; b. Columbus, Ohio, Mar. 4, 1917; d. Henry Jehu and Viola Alice (Carmean) Linton; m. Hugh Kinzel Phares, Jr., June 6, 1941; children—Hugh III, Lisa Elaine. B.S. in Music Edn., Ohio State U., 1939. Profl. dancer, N.Y.C., 1939-41; ballet tchr. various schs. Glendale, Calif., 1941-43, Mt. Vernon, N.Y., 1944-47; prin. Marguerite Phares Sch. of Dance, Sacramento, Calif., 1947—; artistic dir. Theatre Ballet of Sacramento, 1967—; choreographer ballets: Cinderella, 1977, 78; Sleeping Beauty, 1980, 85; Romeo and Juliet, 1984; regional dir. Internat. Ballet Competition, Jackson, Miss., 1981, regional field judge, Sacramento, 1982-83. Recipient Outstanding Tchr. Plaudit award Nat. Dance Assn., 1978; sleceted to represent Calif. in Young Americans Nat. Dance Festival. Mem. Pacific Regional Ballet Assn. Honor Co. (sec. 1977-79, pres. 1980-81), Delta Zeta (pres. 1954-55). Republican. Office: Marguerite Phares Sch Dance 4430 Marconi Ave Sacramento CA 95821

PHARIS, CLAUDIA CECILIA, small business owner; b. Phila., May 30, 1944; d. Clyde Anthony and Eula Mae (Faulkner) P. Student, Trinity Coll., Washington, 1962-65; BS in Physics, U. Hawaii, 1971; MBA, Harvard U., Boston, 1983. Policy analyst HUD, Washington, 1971-78, Office Mgmt. and Budget, Exec. Office of Pres., Washington, 1978-79; staff rep. budget com. Congressman William Gray, U.S. Ho. of Reps., Washington, 1979-80, U.S. Senate, Washington, 1980-81; dep. mng. dir. City of Phila., 1981; with strategic planning dept. 1st Nat. Bank Boston, summer 1982; exec. v.p. Royal Bus. Sch., N.Y.C., 1983-86; pres. Edu-Net, Media, Pa., 1987—; cons. State of Oregon, Salem. Harvard U. Grad. Sch. Design Loeb fellow. Club: Century (Boston). Home and Office: 420 Vernon St Media PA 19063

PHARIS, RUTH MCCALISTER, banker; b. San Diego, Feb. 13, 1934; d. William L. and Mary E. (Beuk) McC.; grad. Del Mar Coll., Corpus Christi, Tex., 1975-79; m. E. Edwin Pharis, Mar. 14, 1953; children—Beth, Tracey, Todd. Asst. cashier Parkdale State Bank, Corpus Christi, 1970-72, asst. v.p., 1972-76, v.p., 1976-79: v.p. Cullen Center Bank & Trust, Houston, 1979-81, sr. v.p., 1982—; instr. Am. Inst. Banking, 1977-79. Mem. adv. council Houston Community Colls. Mem. Am. Soc. Personnel Adminstrs., Bank Adminstrn. Inst. (v.p. Coastal Bend chpt. 1979), Nat. Assn. Bank Women (ednl. chmn. Coastal Bend group), Am. Inst. Banking (rep.), Tex. Bankers Assn. (council 1983-84), Coastal Bend Personnel Soc. (v.p.), Houston Personnel Assn., Corpus Christi C. of C. (mem. women's com. 1976-79). Republican. Baptist. Club: Order Eastern Star. Home: 5102 Wightman Ct Houston TX 77069 Office: 600 Jefferson St Houston TX 77001

PHARO, GWEN MCRAE, management consultant, government affairs specialist; b. Lafayette, Ala., Aug. 5, 1927; d. Wesley Talmadge and Mary Louise (Tyson) McRae; m. Milam Bernard Pharo, June 23, 1951 (div. Sept. 1979); children—Milam Randolph, Mark Langston. Student Cottey Jr. Coll. for Women, 1945-46, U. Houston, 1946-48, Exec. Sch. of Protocol, 1981. Adminstrv. asst. to dep. adminstr. Gen. Services Adminstrn., Dallas, 1950-51; advt. copy writer Bonwit Teller, Phila., 1951; civic worker, Dallas, 1952-74; mng. ptnr. Maley, Pharo & Holloman, Inc., Dallas, 1974; corp. v.p. for nat. and internat. pub. relations Intercontinental Translations, Austin, Tex., 1975-81; Washington rep. O.I.L. Energy, Inc. subs. Kidde, Inc., Dallas; cons. to pub. Tex. Tribune, Austin, 1979-82; fin. cons. Americans For The High Frontier, 1987-88; cons. Physicians Who Care, 1987—; pub. relations cons. Tex. Free Enterprise Found., also dir. Press liaison and advance worker for state and nat. candidates, 1960's and 1970's; co-chmn. Reagan for Pres. Com., Dallas, 1968; mem. del. selection com. 3d Congl. Dist., mem. del.-at-large selection com. state conv., 1968-76; del. to dist. and state conv., Dallas, 1980; mem. Dallas Council on World Affairs; pres. Park Cities Republican Women's Club, 1966, 67; served on Presdl. Rank awards for Sr. Exec. Service, Dallas, 1983; pres. Pub. Affairs Luncheon Club, Dallas, 1965-66; pres. Dallas Health and Sci. Mus. Guild, mem. adv. com. Mus. Bd. Govs.; charter mem. Dallas chpt. Freedoms Found. at Valley Force; charter mem. Fair Campaign Practices Com.; mem. Dallas Council World Affaris; bd. dirs. Rosalind Kress Haley Library, Dallas Bapt. U., So. Hearing Found., New Orleans. Named Dame of the Sovereign Order of St. John, San Francisco, 1988. Mem. League of Rep. Women, Fgn. Policy Assn., Internat. Assn. Drilling Contractors, Am. League Lobbyists, Internat. Platform Assn., Tex. Ind. Producers and Royalty Owners, Tex. State Soc., Coolidge Soc., English Speaking Union. Episcopalian. Clubs: Tex. Breakfast, Capitol Hill, Monday (Washington); Chaparral, Public Affairs Luncheon, Sci. Place (Dallas). Home: 6310A Bandera Dallas TX 75225

PHELAN, CAROLE MARY ROSS, minister, writer; b. Sydney, New South Wales, Australia, Dec. 30, 1925; came to U.S., 1962; d. Henry James and Elizabeth Maud (Shaw) Stevens; m. Christopher Joseph Phelan, Dec. 23, 1953; 1 child, Colin Michael Ross. BBA, Clarks Coll., London, 1942; DD, Philpots Sem., London, 1956. Sec. to dir. Archers Film Prodns., London, 1943-45; editorial asst. Hutchinson & Co., London, 1945-50; sec. to gen. mgr. Kemsley Newspapers, London, 1951-53; tchr. Philpots Sem., 1956-62; dir. edn. Universal Mind Sci. Ch., Long Beach, Calif., 1971-72; adminstr. Mountain View, Calif., 1972-74; treas.-sec., minister, tchr. Aquarian Horizon Centre, Los Angeles, Cupertino and Santa Barbara, Calif., 1975-86; pres., sec., minister, tchr. Los Angeles, 1987—. Author: Why Meditation?, 1988; contbr. articles on self-devel. and metaphysics to profl. jours. Home and Office: Aquarian Horizon Centre 10760 Rose Ave Suite 304 Los Angeles CA 90034

PHELAN, F. ADELE, foundation executive; b. Denver, Nov. 15, 1935; d. Frank Adam and Della Catherine (Pigotti) Muto; B.A. in English, Webster Coll., 1959; M.A. in English (Woodrow Wilson fellow), St. Louis U., 1962; M.A. in Ednl. Psychology (NDEA Inst. fellow), U. Minn., 1974; m. Gerry Phelan, Oct. 9, 1971. Chmn. English dept. Machebeuf High Sch., Denver, 1961-67; mem. faculty English dept. Loretto Heights Coll., Denver, 1967-68, dir. counseling, 1968-70, dean of students, 1970-74, pres., 1975-83; dir. programs Piton Found., 1983-85; pres. Clayton Found., 1985—; asst. to dean of students U. Denver, 1974-75; dir. 1st Interstate Bank of Denver. Mem. Colo. Bd. Ethics; mem. council Public TV-Channel 6; trustee Kent Denver Country Day Sch.; bd. dirs. Mile Hi council Girl Scouts U.S.; bd. dirs. Webb-Waring Lung Inst. NDEA Inst. fellow, 1966; recipient Ann. Salute to Women award, 1982. mem. Women's Forum Colo. Lodge: Rotary (Denver). Office: 3801 Martin Luther King Blvd Denver CO 20205

PHELAN, JANE CHESTER, technical writer; b. Hartford, Conn., May 4, 1945; d. Ebbe Carl and Ruth Emma (Chester) Blomstrand; m. Clifford James Phelan, Sept. 4, 1965. BA, Cen. Conn. State U., 1972; postgrad. St. Joseph Coll. Child care worker Child & Family Services, Hartford, Conn., 1966-69; dir. Home Care Services, 1973; with Travelers Ins. Co., 1973-88, sr. tech. writer, 1982—. Mem. Women in Communications, Soc. Tech. Communications. Office: 632 Country Club Rd Avon CT 06001

PHELAN, MARY BENEDICT, religious organization administrator, researcher, consultant; b. Galesburg, Ill., Mar. 4, 1902; d. John Francis and Ellen Victorine (Malone) P. BA, Clarke Coll., 1924; MA, U. So. Calif., 1928; PhD, Cath. U. Am., 1941; LittD (hon.), Loras Coll., 1967; LLD (hon.), U. Dubuque, 1969, Clarke Coll., 1974. Tchr., adminstr. Burbank (Calif.) Pub. Schs., 1925-31; prof., chmn. dept. psychology and edn. Mundelein Coll., Chgo., 1934-57; pres. Clarke Coll., Dubuque, Iowa, 1957-69; corp. rep. Sisters of Charity, B.V.M., Dubuque, Iowa, 1970-79; editor, researcher, cons. Sisters of Charity, B.V.M., Dubuque and Chgo., 1970—; mem. Gov.'s. Commn. on Status of Women, Des Moines, 1964-68; cons. HEW div. Coll. Support, Washington, 1968, 69; various commns. Arts, religion. Author: Report of the President for Twelve Years, 1969 (Merit award 1969). Contbr. articles to profl. jours. Vol. letter writter Amnesty Internat., Nederland, Colo., 1970—, tutor Lit. Vols. Chgo., 1975—. Recipient George Washington Honor Medal award Freedoms Found., 1965, Disting. Civil Service award Dubuque Area C. of C., 1967, 1970 Annual Alumni Achievement award in Edn. Cath. U. Am., 1970; Mary Benedict Hall named in her honor Clarke Coll., 1974. Mem. Am. Psychol. Assn. (emeritus mem.). Home: 6364 N Sheridan Rd Chicago IL 60660

PHELAN, PHYLLIS WHITE, psychologist; b. Harrisonburg, Va., Aug. 12, 1951; d. Shirley Lewis and Jean Elwood (Driver) White; m. Kenneth Edward Phelan, May 21, 1983. BA with honors, Coll. William and Mary, 1973, MA, 1977; PhD, U. Minn., 1984. Lic. cons. psychologist. Intern Ramsey Mental Health Ctr., St. Paul, 1983-84; psychologist Mental Health Clinics of Minn. P.A., St. Paul, 1983-84, Harley Clinics, Mpls., 1983-84; psychologist, dir. eating disorders program Primary Health Care, Bloomington, Minn., 1984-87; pvt. practice psychology St. Paul, 1987—; exec. dir. Eating Disorders Inst. for Edn. and Research, St. Paul, 1987—; instr. Continuing Edn. program, U. Minn., 1983-84, clin. asst. prof. dept. psychiatry, 1986—. Contbr. articles to profl. jours. Coll. of William and Mary scholar, 1975-77; U. Minn. fellow 1981, 82-83. Mem. Am. Psychol. Assn., Minn. Psychol. Assn., Minn. Psychologists in Pvt. Practice, Minn. Women Psychologists. Home: 942 Summit Ave Saint Paul MN 55105 Office: 570 Asbury St Saint Paul MN 55105

PHELPS, CHARLOTTE MAE, health educator; b. Plymouth, Mass., Aug. 10, 1931; d. Lewis Edward and Eleanor (Buswell) Billings; m. Richard H. Phelps, Sept. 3, 1955; children: Elisabeth, Richard. BS, U. Vt., 1954; MS in Nursing, U. Md., 1973. Faculty instr. U. Vt., Burlington, 1954-57, St. Joseph's Sch. Nursing, Marshfield, Wis., 1961-63, St. Agnes Nursing Sch., Balt., 1963-65, Frederick (Md.) County Community Coll., 1968-72; faculty instr. Garland County Community Coll., Hot Springs, Ark., 1973-78, dir. health scis. dept., 1978—. Active ARC, YWCA, Hot Springs; also serves on numerous health delivery bds., state, local coms. Recipient Clara Barton Medal ARC, 1978. Mem. Am. Nurses Assn. (Polit. Action Com.), Ark. State Nurses Assn. (pres. 1978-80), Nat. League for Nursing (site visitor), Sigma Theta Tau. Republican. Methodist. Home: 113 Grand Ridge Dr Hot Springs AR 71901 Office: Garland County Community Coll 1 College Dr Hot Springs AR 71913

PHELPS, DIANA JAYNE, nurse; b. Louisville, Sept. 25, 1941; d. James Windsor and Victoria Burt (Sappio) Deeble; R.N., St. Mary's Sch. Nursing, 1962; m. Marshall Lyons Phelps, Jan. 25, 1963; children: Peter Marshall, Deborah Lynn, Sarah Victoria, Rebecca Lynn. Charge nurse pediatrics Meml. Hosp., Worcester, Mass., 1964-66; nursery and pediatric nurse Grossmont Hosp., La Mesa, Calif., 1968-72; water safety instr. San Diego and Tustin, Calif., 1974-77; exec. dir. Orange County Apple Sch., Costa Mesa, Calif., 1977-80; child birth educator Shaw Health Center, Los Angeles, 1980—; lectr. in field. Chmn. bd. dirs. Orange County Apple Sch., 1977-80; adv. Com. on Pub. Health and Safety, 1981; vol. aide program Elem. Sch. Reading, La Mesa, 1972-73; pres. San Diego chpt. Children's Asthma Research Inst. & Hosp., 1970-72. Recipient Pub. Service award Am. Acad. Husband-Coached Childbirth, 1976. Mem. Am. Cultural Assn. (v.p. 1980-81), Internat. Profl. Assn. (pres. 1979), La Leche League Internat., Internat. Childbirth Educators Assn., Soc. for Protection of Unborn Through Nutrition, Nat. Assn. Parents and Profls. for Safe Alternative in Childbirth. Author: How Natural Childbirth Can Protect You and Your Baby, 1979; producer: Welcome to Our World, movie, 1976. Address: 1401 Bryan Ave Tustin CA 92680

PHELPS, ELIZABETH MATHER, documentation specialist; b. Balt., Sept. 21, 1944; d. Ellsworth and Anne Marjorie (Grove) P. Student, U. Wis., 1962-63; BA, Southwestern U., 1966; postgrad., George Washington U., 1968. Adminstrv. asst. U.S. Govt., Washington, 1967-71; service rep., taxi driver, trainer, drivers safety commn. Greater Houston Transp. Co., 1972-78, also bd. dirs.; illustrator, editor Strode Publishers, Huntsville, Ala., 1979-80; tech. editor Superior Tech. Services, Huntsville, 1980-82; sr. tech. editor Kendrick & Co., Washington, 1982-83; sr. tech. editor SEMCOR, Inc., Arlington, Va., 1983-84, prodn. mgr., 1984-86; prodn. mgr. Eldyne, Inc., Arlington, 1986—; bd. dirs. Fed. Credit Union, Greater Houston Transp. Co., 1972-78. designer book jackets, 1979-80; editor various technical pubs. vol. coordinator Twickenham Repertory Co., Huntsville, 1980, stage mgr., 1979-81; set decorator Huntsville Little Theater, 1981; vol. Wordstage Reader's Theater Arlington County Arts Program, 1985. Mem. Nat. Assn. Female Execs. Republican. Presbyterian. Office: Eldyne Inc 2231 Crystal Dr Suite 201 Arlington VA 22202

PHELPS, ERIN MARGARETTA, psychologist; b. Waynesville, Mo., Jan. 23, 1951; d. Richard Clayton and Ellen Margaretta (Beasley) P.; m. Richard Allen McElroy, Aug. 8, 1982. BA, Douglass Coll., 1973; EdM, Harvard U., 1974, EdD, 1981. Cons. Project Zero, Cambridge, Mass., 1979-83; lectr. Harvard U. Grad. Sch. Edn., Cambridge, 1979-84; sr. research assoc., tech. dir. Murray Research Ctr. of Radcliffe Coll., Cambridge, 1981—. Contbr. articles to profl. jours. Active town meetings, Arlington, Mass., 1987—. Mem. NOW (Boston chpt.), Soc. Research in Child Devel., Phi Beta Kappa. Office: Radcliffe Coll Murray Research Ctr 10 Garden St Cambridge MA 02138

PHELPS, FLORA L(OUISE) LEWIS, editor, anthropologist, photographer; b. San Francisco, July 28, 1917; d. George Chase and Louise (Manning) Lewis; student U. Mich. AB cum laude, Byrn Mawr Coll., 1938; AM, Columbia U., 1954; m. C(lement) Russell Phelps, Jan. 15, 1944; children—Andrew Russell, Carol Lewis, Gail Bransford. Acting dean Cape Cod Inst. Music, East Brewster, Mass., summer 1940; assoc. analyst social sci., U.S. Govt., 1942-44; co-adj. staff instr. anthropology Univ. Coll., Rutgers U., 1954-55; mem. editorial bd. Américas mag. OAS, Washington, 1960—, sr. editor, 1963-71, editor English edit., 1971-74, mng. editor, 1974-82, contbg. editor, 1982—; N.J. vice chmn. Ams. Dem. Action, 1950; mem. Dem. County Com. N.J., 1948-49. Mem. AAAS, Am. Anthrop. Assn., Anthrop. Soc. Washington, Latin Am. Studies Assn., Soc. for Am. Archaeology, Soc. Woman Geographers. Author articles in field of anthropology, art, architecture, edn., travel; contbr. Latin Am. newspapers. Home and Office: 3618 Albemarle St NW Washington DC 20008

PHELPS, JEANNIE GERALDINE, educator; b. Eustis, Fla., July 12, 1940; d. Curtis Myrle and Lorene (Collins) Shockley; m. Dale L. Phelps, Oct. 4, 1958; children: Karen, Kelly, Kandi. BS, Fla. Southern U., 1982; MBA, Webber Coll., 1984; EdD, Nova U., 1988. Mktg., sales dir. AMI, Coral Gables, Fla., 1973-81, The Beck Group, Cin., 1981-84; prof. Valencia Community Coll., Orlando, Fla., 1984—; tchr. Osceola High Sch., Kissimmee, Fla., 1984-87, Dr. Phillips High Sch., Orlando, 1987—; cons. in field. Mem. Assn. Exec. Females, Mktg. Assn., Alpha Delta Kappa. Baptist. Home: 702 Paul St Kissimmee FL 32741

PHELPS, SUZANNE, educational administrator; b. Tyler, Tex., Sept. 12, 1946; d. Julius Carl and Charm (Moseley) Norris; divorced, 1978; children: Melissa, Jennifer. BA, Baylor U., 1967, MS in Edn., 1980; postgrad., Tex. A&M U. Tchr. Midway Schs., Waco, Tex., 1967-68, Clear Creek Schs., League City, Tex., 1968-69, Jefferson County Schs., Denver, 1971-74, Robinson Schs., Waco, 1975-79, Temple (Tex.) Schs., 1979-80; edn. cons. Region XII Edn. Service Ctr., Waco, 1980-83; supr. math. Bryan (Tex.) Schs., 1983-85, dir., 1985—; mem. adv. com. Tex. Edn. Agy., Austin, 1985—. Tchr. First Baptist Ch., Bryan, 1984—. Mem. Assn. of Tex. Profl. Educators (treas. 1981-82, sec. 1982-83, v.p. 1983-84, chair legisl. com. 1984-85), Assn. of Supr. and Curriculum Devel., Bryan C. of C. (Leadership Brazos, 1986-87), Phi Delta Kappa, Delta Kappa Gamma. Home: 2913 Burning Tree Bryan TX 77802 Office: Bryan Ind Sch Dist 101 N Texas Ave Bryan TX 77801

PHELPS, VADA JO, town official; b. Laramie, Wyo., Aug. 30, 1943; d. Joseph Marion and Zula Alsetta (Curtis) Throneburry; m. Bobby Eugene Andrews, Feb. 11, 1962 (dec. Feb. 1976); children: Terri Lynelle, Joel Douglas; m. Robert Lee Phelps, Sept. 20, 1979. BBA, U. Denver, 1986, MBA, 1988. Office mgr. Prudential Nat. Co., Denver, 1961-64; policy clk. Conn. Mut. Life Ins. Co., Denver, 1964-68; computer operator Genuine Auto Parts Co., Denver, 1969-70; bookkeeper Summit County Schs., Frisco, Colo., 1970-71; office mgr. B.D.F. Constrn. Co., Frisco, 1972-76; town clk.-treas. Town of Frisco, 1976—. Mem. accountability com. Summit Schs., Frisco, 1973-75. Mem. Internat. Inst. Mcpl. Clks. (cert. mcpl. clk.), Colo. City Clks. Assn. (2d v.p. 1986-87, 1st v.p. 1987—), Colo. Mcpl. Fin. Officers Assn., Mcpl. Treas. Assn., U. Denver M.E.C. Alumnae, Epsilon Sigma Alpha Internat. (Woman of Yr. award 1980). Republican. Mem. Church of Christ. Club: TOPS (Frisco). Avocations: travel, reading, education. Home: 334 Emily Ln PO Box 313 Frisco CO 80443 Office: Town of Frisco 1 Main St Box 370 Frisco CO 80443

PHELPS-MUNSON, ROSE CHRISTINE, nurse, art consultant; b. N.Y.C., June 6, 1931; d. Knud Larsen and Mary (Nardel) Larsen Bernstein; m. Neil Phelps-Munson, Apr. 23, 1960 (div. 1968); children: Marcus, Dale C. Degree in nursing, Flower Fifth Ave. Sch. Nursing, N.Y.C., 1951; BS in Nursing, Hunter Coll., 1955. Nurse various hosps., N.Y.C., 1951-57; operating room nurse USMC Hosp., Bethesda, Md., 1959-61, Seattle, 1962-64; gen., clin. nurse Global Assocs., Kwajalein, Marshall Isles, 1965-67; newspaper art, publicity dir. Global Assocs., Mich., 1968; spl. duty nurse West Palm Beach, Fla., 1969-74; operating room nurse Stanford (Calif.) U. Hosp., 1974—; gallery owner, cons. The Art Connection, Palo Alto, Calif., 1981—. Served to lt. USN, 1957-59. Mem. Com. For Recognition Nursing Achievement (negotiating com. 1982—). Republican. Club: Stanford Singles (Palo Alto). Office: The Art Connection 765 #27 San Antonio Rd Palo Alto CA 94303

PHEND, JULIE MARIE, academic director; b. Wausau, Wis., July 9, 1948; d. Ralph Martin and Mary Edith (Kaufman) Oldenburg; m. John Lee Phend; children: Jennifer Noelle, Nicholas Jonathan. BA in Speech and Drama, Valparaiso U., 1970; MS in Edn., U. Wis., 1976. Tchr. Elgin (Ill.) Pub. Schs., 1971-74; tchr. drama Episc. Day Sch., Bristol, Va., 1974-76, Total Action Against Poverty, Roanoke, Va., 1976-78; tchr. drama North Cen. Coll., Naperville, Ill., 1979—, dir. noncredit programs, 1983—. Author: Courses for Children, 1987; short stories. Bd. dirs., officer publicity Summer Pl. Theatre, Naperville, 1983-86; mem. retreat com. 1st Congl. Ch., Naperville, 1986-88, tchr. Sunday Sch., 1986-88. Mem. ICCHE, Learning Resources Network, Ill. Theatre Assn. Office: North Cen Coll Ctr for Continuing Edn Naperville IL 60566

PHERRIN, KATHERINE HEIDI, educator; b. Evanston, Ill., Oct. 21, 1952; d. Gerald Patrick and Mary Olive (Baker) Horan; m. John Patrick Pherrin, Mar. 4, 1978; children: John Patrick II, David Gerald. AA, Fullerton Coll., 1972; BA, Calif. State U., Fullerton, 1975; MA, U.S. Internat.

U., 1986. Cert. elem. and secondary sch. tchr. Substitute tchr. Santa Ana Unified Sch. Dist., 1980-87; sales rep. Allied Distbg. Co., Gardena, Calif., 1978-80; staff advisor Roosevelt Sch. Adv. Com., Santa Ana, 1985—; advisor, cons. Bilingual and Bicultural Com., Santa Ana, 1985—; tutor Calif. State U., Santa Ana, 1986—; tchr. trainer English as a Second Language Capacity Bldg. Team, 1983, 87, Santa Ana, 1987—. Active Santa Ana Sch. Bd. campaign, 1984; vol. Reagan/Zschau Rep. Election Rally, Costa Mesa, Calif., 1986; religious edn. tchr. Santiago De Compostela Ch., El Toro, Calif., 1986—, auction chair, fundraiser, 1987. Roman Catholic. Club: Family Fitness Ctr. (Costa Mesa and Labuna Niguel). Office: Santa Ana Unified Sch Dist 1405 French St Santa Ana CA 92701

PHILBRICK, MARGARET ELDER, artist; b. Northampton, Mass., July 4, 1914; d. David and Mildred (Pattison) Elder; m. Otis Philbrick, May 23, 1941 (dec. Apr. 1973); 1 child, Otis. Grad., Mass. Sch. Art, Boston, 1937; student, De Cordova Mus., Lincoln, Mass., 1966-67. Juror art shows; exhibited one woman show, Bare Cove Gallery, Hingham, Mass., 1979, Greenwich Garden Ctr., Cos Cob, Conn., 1981; retrospective exhbn. graphics, Ainsworth Gallery, Boston, 1972; exhibited 40 yr. retrospective, Westenhook Gallery, Sheffield, Mass., 1977, 50 yr. retrospective, 1985; group shows, Boston Printmakers, 1948—, USIA tour to Far East, 1958-59, Boston Watercolor Soc., 1956-82, Pratt Graphic Art Ctr., N.Y.C., 1966, New Eng. Watercolor Soc., 1982—; represented in permanent collections, Library of Congress, Washington, Boston Pub. Library, Nat. Bezalel Mus., Jerusalem; artist, designer: Wedgwood Commemorative Plates, Stoke-on-Trent, Eng., 1944-55; illustrator books. Recipient purchase Library of Congress, 1948; recipient 1st graphics Acad. Artist, Springfield, Mass., 1957, Multum in Parvo Pratt-2d Internat. Miniature Print Exhbn., 1966, 1st prize in floral Miniature Art Soc. Fla., 1986, Ralph Fabri award. Mem. NAD (Ralph Fabri 1977), Boston Printmakers (exec. bd. 1951—Presentation Print), Kent Art Assn., Acad. Artists, New Eng. Watercolor Soc. Home: Main St Sheffield MA 01257 Office: Westenhook Gallery Main St Sheffield MA 01257

PHILIPPBAR, DEBORAH DEBARR, retail executive, financial consultant; b. Grafton, W.Va., Dec. 18, 1951; d. Perry J. DeBarr and Mary Angela (Bevilocke) Stephenson; m. Mark Davies Philippbar, Feb. 28, 1986; 1 child, Kristan Angela. Student, Blue Ridge Coll., 1970-71, SUNY, Binghamton, 1981-83. Cert. fin. cons., ins. broker, N.Y., Conn., Va., Md., D.C. Fin., ins. cons. Binghamton, 1978-81; owner Faces and Things, Binghamton, 1980-82, Twice But Nice, Binghamton, 1980-82; fin. cons. Pat Ryan and Assocs., Chgo., 1983-86; bus. mgr. Tony March Buick, Hartford, Conn., 1986—; dir. tng. F&I Alternatives, Inc., Springfield, Mass., 1988—; credit cons., Hartford, 1986—. Nat. Assn. Female Execs., Nat. Orgn. Fin. and Ins. Specialists. Republican. Baptist.

PHILLIPS, ALMA FAYE, lawyer; b. Pitts., Aug. 31, 1925; d. Alexander Harvey and Jean (Ginsberg) Weinberger; m. Leonard Phillips, Mar. 24, 1946 (dec. Oct. 1985); children: Robin, Susan, Nancy. B.A., U. Calif.-Berkeley, 1972; J.D., San Francisco Law Sch., 1977. Bar: Calif. 1979. Sole practice, Oakland, Calif., 1979—; pro tem judge Alameda County Mcpl. Ct., Oakland-Piedmont-Emeryville Jud. Dist. (Calif.), 1983—; mem. Voluntary Legal Services Program. Past pres., life mem. PTA, Oakland; bd. dirs. Oakland Pub. Library Assn. Mem. Alameda County Bar Assn. (client's relation com., lawyers referral com., fee arbitration com.), Calif. Bar Assn. Club: Highlands Country (Oakland) (pres., dir. 1983—); Athletic (dir. Alameda County). Office: 1 Kaiser Plaza Suite 2225 Oakland CA 94612

PHILLIPS, BARBARA FROMM, organizational development specialist; b. Washington, May 18, 1944; d. Seymour Martin and Frances Sylvia (Goldstein) Fromm; m. Lawrence Bennett Phillips, Aug. 29, 1965 (div. 1969); m. Craig Alan Rogers, Nov. 14, 1986. BA in Psychology and Math., Temple U., 1965; MA in Sci., Tech. and Pub. Policy, George Washington U., 1977. V.p. mktg. Cambridge Communications Corp., Washington, 1968-71; dep. dir. studies Am. Soc. Internat. Law, Washington, 1971-73; legis. corr. U.S. Congress, Washington, 1973-74; environ. analyst, mgr. Smithsonian Instn.'s Ctr. for Natural Areas, Washington, 1974-75; lobbyist Bechtel Corp., Washington, 1975-79, Barbara Phillips & Assocs., Washington, 1979-82; gen. mgr. Retail Comml. Enterprise, McLean, Va., 1982-83; organizational devel. specialist Louis Berger Internat., Inc., Washington, 1983—; Legal adviser Wis. Ave Corridor Com., Georgetown and Washington, 1976. Mem. Nat. Assn. for Female Execs., Women in Govt. Relations, Soc. for Internat. Devel. Home: 2810 Lorcom Ln Arlington VA 22207 Office: Louis Berger Internat Inc 1819 H St NW #900 Washington DC 20006

PHILLIPS, BARBARA RUTH, insurance company executive; b. Kansas City, Mo., Oct. 30, 1936; d. William Earl Daugherty and Ruth Augusta (Schultze) Woolfolk; divorced; 1 child, Hunter L. BS, U. Mo., 1961. Cert. tchr., Mo., Calif. Previously high sch. tchr. Mo. and Calif., 1958-62, 65-67; underwriting liaison The Travelers Ins. Group, San Francisco, 1963-64; claims adminstr. Conn. Gen. Ins., Seattle, 1964-65; adjuster Unigard Ins. Group, 1968-70; casualty claims dir. Zurich-Am. Ins. Group, Los Angeles, 1970-74; regional asst. to sales supt. Republic Nat. Life Ins., Los Angeles, 1974-82; corp. risk mgr. Rogers Group Inc., Nashville, 1983-87; dir. risk mgmt. Equitable/Equicor/Hosp. Corp. Am., Nashville, 1987—. Previously active Encino (Calif.) Hist. Park Found.; currently active Nashville Civil Justice Reform, Zoo Booster Assn., YWCA. Mem. Am. Soc. Safety Engrs., Risk Ins. Mgrs. Soc. (sec. Nashville 1987-88, 1st v.p. 1988—), Am. Mgmt. Assn., Nat. Assn. Ins. Women (cert. profl. ins. woman), Nat. Assn. Female Execs. Office: Equitable-Equicor-HCA 1801 West End Ave Nashville TN 37203

PHILLIPS, COLETTE ALICE-MAUDE, public relations consultant, educator; b. St. Johns, Antigua, W.I., Sept. 20, 1954; d. Douglas Alfred Richard and Ionie Alice-Maude (Francis) P. AS, Grahm Jr. Coll., Boston, 1974; BS summa cum laude, Emerson Coll., Boston, 1976, MS, 1979. Editor in chief Govt. of Antigua, St. John's, news corr. Radio Antilles, Montserrat, W.I., TV talk show host Antigua Broadcasting Service, St. Johns, 1977-78; dir. pub. relations Patriot's Trail council Girl Scouts U.S.A., Boston, 1980-84; dir. pub. relations Cablevision of Boston, 1984-85; cons. pub. relations Royal Sonesta Hotel, 1985-87; instr. Stone Hill Coll., North Easton, Mass., 1982-85, Emerson Coll., 1984-86, Antioch Coll., 1986; pres. APR Co., 1985—. Mem. pub. info. com. Am. Cancer Soc., Boston, 1978—, chmn. 75th Anniversary com., 1987-88; v.p. Horizon for Youth, 1986—; mem. exec. com. Mus. Fine Arts Council, 1988, co-chair membership com.; cabinet mem. Finnegan for Boston Com., Boston, 1983; trustee Friends Boston Ballet, 1987—; bd. dirs. Urban League Eastern Mass., 1980—, Metro Council Ednl. Opportunity, Boston, 1981—, AIDS Action Com., 1987-88. Recipient Outstanding Alumni award Emerson Coll., 1983, United Way Agy. award for outstanding achievement in communication, 1981; named 100 Most Powerful in Boston Herald, 1987, one of 100 Most Influential Blacks in Blston, 1986, 87, 88, one of Ten Outstanding Young Leaders in Boston Jaycees, 1988, Faces to Watch in '88 Boston Mag. Mem. Pub. Relations Soc. Am., Mass. Assn. Mental Health (bd. dirs. 1984-87). Methodist. Home and Office: 41 Colborne Rd Brighton MA 02135 Office: Cablevision of Boston 28 Travis St Boston MA 02134

PHILLIPS, DARLENE ANN, infection control manager; b. Springfield, Mass., July 24, 1951; d. Walter Theodore and Ann Christine (Morris) Kurman; m. George Stanley Phillips, Oct. 23, 1943. BS in Nursing, St. Anselm Coll., 1973; grad. course in surveillance, prevention and control of nosocomial infections U. Iowa, 1981; MS in Health Sci., Quinnipiac Coll., 1984. RN, Conn. Staff nurse gynecology Yale New Haven Hosp., 1974-75, staff nurse post-anesthesia care unit, 1975-81, staff nurse ambulatory surgery, 1977-80, infection control coordinator, 1981-83; nurse epidemiologist Holyoke Hosp., Mass., 1983-87; mgr. infection control Bay State Med. Ctr., Springfield, Mass., 1987—. Recipient Otis Clapp award Am. Assn. Occupational Health Nursing, 1985. Mem. Assn. Practitioners Infection Control (New Eng. preceptor 1986-87), Area Health Edn. Ctr. Pioneer Valley, Nat. Assn. Female Execs., Sigma Theta Tau. Roman Catholic. Avocations: needlework, landscaping. Home: 158 Edgewood Rd West Springfield MA 01089 Office: Baystate Med Ctr 759 Chestnut St Springfield MA 01199

PHILLIPS, DOROTHY KAY, lawyer; b. Camden, N.J., Nov. 2, 1945; d. Benjamin L. and Sadye (Levinsky) Phillips; children—Bethann P., David M. Schaffzin. B.S. magna cum laude in English Lit., U. Pa., 1964; M.A., Family Life and Marriage Counseling and Edn., NYU, 1975; J.D., Villanova U., 1978. Bar: Pa., N.J., U.S. Dist. Ct. (ea. dist.) Pa., U.S. Dist Ct N.J., U.S. Ct. Appeals (3d cir.), U.S Supreme Ct. Tchr., Haddon Twp. High Sch. (N.J.), and Haddon Heights High Sch. (N.J.), 1964-70; lectr., counselor Marriage Council of Phila., marriage and family life counselor Marriage and Family Life Assocs., Willingboro, N.J., lectr. U. Pa. and Hahnemann Med. Schs., profl. cons., lectr. Lankenau Hosp., Phila., 1970-75; atty. Adler, Barish, Daniels, Levin & Creskoff, Phila., 1978-79, Astor, Weiss & Newman, Phila., 1979-80; ptnr. Romisher & Phillips, P.C., Phila., 1981-86; ptnr., Law Office of Dorothy K. Phillips, 1986—; guest speaker on domestic relations issues on radio and TV shows; featured in newspaper and mag. articles. Mem. Rosenbach Found., Art Alliance, Phila.; bd. dirs. Philadanco; mem. Bus. and Profl. Women's Coalition of Fedn. Jewish Agys. Greater Phila., Bus. Women's Network. Mem. ABA, Assn. Trial Lawyers Am., Pa. Trial Lawyers Assn., Pa. Bar Assn., N.J. Bar Assn., Phila. Bar Assn. (chmn. early settlement program 1983-84, mem. rules drafting com. custody rules, vol. bar diabetes 10K run, 1984-85), Phila. Trial Lawyers Assn., Montgomery County Bar Assn., Camden County Bar Assn., Tau Epsilon Rho Law Soc., Lawyers Club. Office: 220 S 16th St Suite 600 Philadelphia PA 19102

PHILLIPS, DOROTHY REID, library technician; b. Hingham, Mass., Apr. 21, 1924; d. James Henry and Emma Louise (Davis) Reid; m. Earl Wendell Phillips, Apr. 22, 1944; children—Earl W., Jr., Betty Herrera, Carol Coe. Cert., Durham Vocat. Sch., 1952; B.S. in Comml. Edn., N.C. Central U., 1959; postgrad. U. Colo., 1969; M.Human Relations, Webster Coll., 1979; postgrad. Grad. Sch. Library Sci., U. Denver, 1983. Vocat. nurse Meml. Hosp., U. N.C., Chapel Hill, 1955-59; vol. work, Cairo, Egypt, 1965-67; library technician Base Library, Lowry AFB, Colo., 1960-65, Fitzsimons Med. Library, Aurora, Colo., 1976—; mem. Denver Mus. Natural History, Denver Art Mus., Mariners. Mem. AAUW (chpt. community rep. 1982-83, state chmn. edn. found. 1982-84, pres. Denver br. 1984-86), Altrusa Internat. (corr. sec. Denver 1982-83, bd. dirs. 1984-85, pres. Denver chpt. 1988), Friends of Library, Colo. Library Assn., Council Library Technicians, Federally Employed Women, Delta Sigma Theta (corr. sec. Denver 1964-66). Democrat. Presbyterian. Home: 3085 Fairfax St Denver CO 80207 Office: Fitzsimmons Army Med Ctr Med Tech Library Aurora CO 80045

PHILLIPS, EDITH BELLE, library science educator; b. Shelby, Mich., Mar. 24, 1921; d. Boyd Earl and Jessie Beatrice (Rankin) Crowl; m. Clarence Albert Phillips, June 19, 1943 (dec. 1981); children: Jonathan Kirk (dec.), Sara Grace (dec.). B.A., Eastern Mich. U., 1942; postgrad. Wayne State U., 1942-45, U. Chgo., 1945; M.L.S., U. Mich., 1949. Jr. librarian U. Mich., Ann Arbor, 1945-49; librarian Chgo. Jewish Acad., 1951-52; cataloger and asst. dir. Kent County Library, Grand Rapids, Mich., 1953-55; asst. sch. librarian Pub. Schs., Grandville, Mich., 1958-62; head catalog and book selection coordinator Library of Mich., Lansing, 1962-68; assoc. prof. library sci., 1968—, acad. program coordinator, 1983-86; del. Mich. White House Conf., Lansing, 1979; mem. Mich. Interorganization Council on Continuing Library Edn. (sec. 1986—); tchr. A-J Seminar, Southfield, Mich., 1981; cons. City of Detroit, 1982, Gale Research Co., Detroit, 1982-83; mem. adv. com. Oakland Community Coll., Farmington Hills, Mich., 1983-85. Author: (with others) Managment and Use of State Documents in Indiana, 1970. Editor: (with others) Background Reading in Building Library Collection, 1979. Mem. Friends of Detroit Pub. Library, 1970—, Founders' Soc., Inst. of Arts, Detroit, 1977—; Mem. AAUP, Assn. for Library and Info. sci. Edn. (liaison rep. 1979-84), ALA, Mich. Library Assn. (chmn. library edn. caucus 1982-84), Women's Nat. Book Assn. (pres., bd. dirs. Detroit), LWV (bd. dirs. Southfield 1981-84), ACLU (bd. dirs. Detroit 1981—), Kappa Delta Pi, Pi Gamma Mu. Avocations: reading; theatre; hiking; swimming. Office: Wayne State U. 106 Kresge Library Library Sci Program Detroit MI 48202

PHILLIPS, ELIZABETH JOAN, marketing company executive; b. Cleve., July 8, 1938; d. Joseph Tinl and Helen Walter; m. Erwin Phillips, June 1956 (div. 1960); 1 son, Michael A. B.A., Fordham U., 1980. Account exec., David Cogan Mgmt., N.Y.C., 1969-77; account exec. N.F.L. Films, N.Y.C., 1977-78; mgr. sports programs Avon Products, N.Y.C., 1978-83; v.p. Needham, Harper & Steers (now Needham, Harper Worldwide), N.Y.C., 1983-86; v.p. Ted Bates Event Mktg., N.Y.C., 1986-87; pres. Custom Event Mktg. subs. Ted Bates Advt.(now Backer, Spielvogel, Bates Worldwide) 1987—. adj. prof. NYU, N.Y.C., 1987—. Mem. exec. com. Vanderbilt YMCA, N.Y.C., 1976-84; ofcl. 1984 Olympic Games, Los Angeles, 1984; referee Women's Olympic Marathon, Los Angeles, 1984; pres. Met. Athletics Congress, N.Y.C., 1980-83. Mem. Women's Sports Found. (bd. advisors 1983—). Club: N.Y. Road Runners (v.p., mem. exec. com. 1976—, pres. 1970—). Office: Custom Event Mktg Inc 1515 Broadway New York NY 10036

PHILLIPS, ELIZABETH LOUISE (BETTY LOU), author; b. Cleve.; d. Michael N. and Elizabeth D. (Materna) Suvak; m. John S. Phillips, Jan. 27, 1963 (div. Jan. 1981); children—Bruce, Bryce, Brian; m. 2d, John D.C. Roach, Aug. 28, 1982. B.S., Syracuse U., 1960; postgrad. in English, Case Western Res. U., 1963-64. Cert. elem. and spl. edn. tchr., N.Y. Tchr. pub. schs., Shaker Heights, Ohio, 1960-66, sportswriter Cleve. Press, 1976-77; spl. features editor Pro Quarterback Mag., N.Y.C., 1976-79; freelance writer specializing in books for young people, 1976—. Author: Chris Evert: First Lady of Tennis, 1977; Picture Story of Dorothy Hamill (ALA Booklist selection), 1978; American Quarter Horse, 1979; Earl Campbell: Houston Oiler Superstar, 1979; Picture Story of Nancy Lopez, (ALA Notable book), 1980; Go! Fight! Win! The NCA Guide for Cheerleaders (ALA Booklist), 1981; Something for Nothing, 1981; Brush Up on Your Hair (ALA Booklist), 1981; Texas ... The Lone Star State, 1987, Who Needs Friends? We All Do!, 1989; also contbr. articles to young adult and sports mags. Mem. Soc. Children's Book Writers, Delta Delta Delta. Republican. Roman Catholic. Home: 4 Random Rd Englewood CO 80110

PHILLIPS, FRANCES ISABELLE, educational adminstrator; b. Newark, Feb. 5, 1912; d. William Webster and Susan Isabelle (Snyder) P.; diploma Newark State Coll., 1933; B.Ed., Rutgers U., 1938, M.Ed., 1949. Tchr., N.J. elem. schs., 1933-48; tchr. of deaf, Newark, 1948-59; chmn. dept. edn. Gallaudet Coll., Washington, 1959-65; dir. spl. edn. West Essex Area Schs., Essex County, N.J., 1965-67; asso. prof. Paterson State Coll., 1967-68; coordinator programs for deaf and hearing impaired, Hackensack, N.J., 1968-73, Bergen County Spl. Services Sch. Dist., 1973-74; mem. Gov.'s Ad Hoc Com. on Deaf Edn., 1968-74; adv. bd. N.J. Assn. Children with Hearing Impairment. Recipient Outstanding Alumni award Kean Coll., 1970. Mem. AAUW, Am. Assn. for Mental Retardation, Conf. Ednl. Adminstrs. Serving the Deaf (hon.), Conv. Am Instrs. of the Deaf, Assn. for Supervision and Curriculum Devel., Nat. Assn. Edn. Young Children, NEA (life), Kappa Delta Pi. Club: Montclair (N.J.) Music. Home: 97 Haddon Pl Upper Montclair NJ 07043

PHILLIPS, GENEVA FICKER, editor; b. Staunton, Ill., Aug. 1, 1920; d. Arthur Edwin and Lillian Agnes (Woods) Ficker; m. James Emerson Phillips, Jr., June 6, 1955 (dec. 1979). B.S. in Journalism, U. Ill., 1942; M.A. in English Lit., UCLA, 1953. Copy desk Chgo. Jour. Commerce, 1942-43; editorial asst. patents Radio Research Lab., Harvard U., Cambridge, Mass., 1943-45; asst. editor adminstrv. publs. U. Ill., Urbana, 1946-47; editorial asst. Quar. of Film, Radio and TV, UCLA, 1952-53; mng. editor The Works of John Dryden, Dept. English, UCLA, 1964—. Bd. dirs. Univ. Religious Conf., Los Angeles, 1979—. UCLA teaching fellow, 1950-53, grad. fellow 1954-55. Mem. Assn. Acad. Women UCLA, Friends of Huntington Library, Friends of UCLA Library, Renaissance Soc. So. Calif., Samuel Johnson Soc. of So. Calif., Assocs. of U. Calif. Press., Conf. Christianity and Lit., Soc. Mayflower Descs. Lutheran. Home: 213 First Anita Dr Los Angeles CA 90049 Office: UCLA Dept English 2225 Rolfe Hall Los Angeles CA 90024

PHILLIPS, JAYNE ANNE, writer; b. Buckhannon, W. Va., July 19, 1952; d. Russell Randolph and Martha Jane (Thornhill) Phillips; m. Mark Brian Stockman, May 26; 1 son, Theo Thornhill; stepsons—Ben, Noah. B.A. in English, W.Va., U., 1974; M.F.A., U. Iowa, 1978. Teaching fellow M.F.A. Program U. Iowa, Iowa City, 1977-78; lectr. Humboldt State U., Arcata, Calif., 1978-79; fellow Fine Arts Work Ctr., Provincetown, Mass., 1979-80, Bunting Inst., Radcliffe Coll., Cambridge, Mass., 1980-81; asst. prof. English, Boston U., 1982-83. Author: (short stories) Black Tickets, 1979, limited edits. Fast Lanes, 1984; Machine Dreams, 1984, How Mickey Made It, 1981, Counting, 1978, Sweethearts, 1976. Recipient Sue Kaufman award Am. Acad. and Inst. Arts and Letters, 1980; fellow Nat. Endowment for Arts, 1978, 85. Mem. Authors Guild, PEN. Democrat. Office: care E P Dutton 2 Park Ave New York NY 10016

PHILLIPS, JOAN RYAN, florist; b. Louisville, May 9, 1941; d. John Lawrence and Lucile Graham (Wymond) Ryan; m. Richard Blankinship, Apr. 10, 1960 (div. 1974); m. Robert Edward Phillips, Oct. 26, 1974; children—Kimberly Graham, Jacquelin Ryan. Student Christian Coll., Columbia, Mo., 1959-61, St. Petersburg Jr. Coll., Fla., 1965-66. Owner, mgr. Northeast Florist, St. Petersburg, 1967-75, Maas Bros. Florist, St. Petersburg, 1975—, Clearwater, Fla., 1978-82. Bd. advisers St. Petersburg Vocat. Tech. Inst., 1984—. Recipient Golden Circle award Florist Transworld Delivery, 1984—. Home: 940 Eden Isle Dr NE Saint Petersburg FL 33704 Office: Maas Bros Florists 124 2d St N Saint Petersburg FL 33701

PHILLIPS, JOYCE MARTHA, human resources executive; b. Bridgeport, Conn., Dec. 18, 1952; d. Stephen and Shirley B. (Howard) Tabory; m. Glenn L. Phillips, July 14, 1974. BA in English, Fairfield (Conn.) U., 1974; MS in Indsl. Relations, U. New Haven, 1982. Tchr. English and reading Fairfield Woods Jr. High Sch., 1975; asst. to v.p. mktg. Bunker Ramo Corp., Trumbull, Conn., 1975-76; rep. in investor relations Gen. Electric Co., Fairfield, 1976-77, specialist in manpower relations, 1977-79; specialist in employee benefits Gen. Electric Co., Bridgeport, Conn., 1979-80, specialist in employee relations, orgn. and staffing, 1980-84; mgr. hdqrs. personnel and office services Armtek Corp., New Haven, 1984-87, dir. compensation and benefits, 1987—. Counsel Fairfield U. Alumni Adv. Council, U. New Haven Alumni Adv. Council. Mem. Conn. Personnel Assn., Pvt. Industry Council Greater New Haven Area (bd. dirs. 1986—, mem. exec. com. 1987—), Human Resources Exec. Roundtable (exec.). Office: Armtek Corp 500 Sargent Dr New Haven CT 06536

PHILLIPS, JULIA MAE, physicist; b. Freeport, Ill., Aug. 17, 1954; d. Spencer Kleckner and Marjorie Ann (Figi) Phillips. BS, Coll. William and Mary, 1976; PhD, Yale U., 1981. Mem. tech. staff AT&T Bell Labs., Murray Hill, 1981—. Editor: Heteroepitaxy on Silicon Technology, 1987; contbr. articles to profl. jours. Mem. APS, Materials Research Soc. (sec. 1987-88), Sigma Xi, Phi Beta Kappa. Office: AT&T Bell Labs 600 Mountain Ave Murray Hill NJ 07974

PHILLIPS, JULIE ANNE, artist; b. Independence, Mo., Feb. 2, 1953; d. Robert Joseph and Margaret Elizabeth (Williams) Brown; married, 1971 (div. 1983). Student, Longview Community Coll., Lee's Summit, Mo., 1976, Cen. Mo. State U., Warrensburg, 1977. Profl. relations rep. Blue Cross Blue Shield, Kansas City, 1971-83; acct. exec. Prime Health, Overland Park, Kans., 1983-85; artist Lee's Summit, 1984—; instr. Blue Springs Coll., Blue Springs, Mo., 1985—; sec. on board ICCS, Kansas City, 1986—; v.p. Biotronics, Inc., North Kansas City, 1987—. mktg. cons., 1987. Mem. Tri-County Art League, 1984-87. Mem. Female Execs., Independence C. of C. (com. pres.), Phi Sigma Pi, (hon.) Delta Sigma Pi. Democrat. Roman Catholic. Club: Tri-County. Home: S-5A Lake Lotawana Lee's Summit MO 64063 Office: 2701 Rockcreek Pkwy North Kansas City MO 64117

PHILLIPS, KAREN BORLAUG, economist; b. Long Beach, Calif., Oct. 1, 1956; d. Paul Vincent and Wilma (Tish) Borlaug. Student Cath. U. P.R., 1973-74; B.A., U. N.D., 1977, B.S., 1977; postgrad. George Washington U., 1978-80. Research asst. research and spl. programs adminstrn. U.S. Dept. Transp., Washington, 1977-78, economist, office of sec., Washington, 1978-82; profl. staff mem. (majority) Com. Commerce, Sci., Transp., U.S. Senate, Washington, 1982-85, tax economist (majority) com. on fin., 1985-87, chief economist (minority) senate com. on fin., 1987—. Contbg. author studies, publs. in field. Recipient award for Meritorious Achievement, Sec. Transp., 1980, Spl. Achievement awards, 1978, 80, Outstanding Performance awards, 1978, 80, 81. Mem. Am. Econ. Assn., Women's Transp. Seminar, Tax Coalition, Transp. Research Forum, Blue Key, Phi Beta Kappa, Omicron Delta Epsilon. Republican. Lutheran. Office: 205 Dirksen Senate Office Bldg Washington DC 20510

PHILLIPS, LINDA JANE, software engineer; b. Pitts., Mar. 12, 1948; d. Henry Albert and Frances Helen (Moore) P.; BS in Math, U. Mass., Amherst, 1971; postgrad. Rensselaer Poly. Inst. Tchr. Stoneleigh-Burnham Sch., Greenfield, Mass., 1971-73, Assabet Valley Regional Vocat. High Sch., Marlborough, Mass., 1973; supr. software devel. Gerber Sci. Instruments, South Windsor, Conn., 1974-78; mgr. design software Gerber Systems Tech., Inc., South Windsor, 1979-80; dir. software engring. Nova Robotics, East Hartford, Conn., 1981-84; supr. CAD/CAM tech. Pratt and Whitney, East Hartford, Conn., 1984—. Gerber rep. to working com. Initial Graphics Exchange Specification, Nat. Bur. Standards, Gaithersburg, Md., 1980. NSF grantee, 1979. Mem. Am. Nat. Standards Inst., ASME (main com. Y14 on engring. drawing and related documentation practices, chair Y14.26 subcom. for computer aided preparation of product definition data 1988-91), Nat. Assn. Female Execs., Computer and Automated Systems Assn. (sr.), Soc. Mfg. Engrs./CASA (sr.), The Computer Mus. (Boston) (founding), Alpha Gamma Delta. Office. 400 Main St 105-18 East East Hartford CT 06108

PHILLIPS, LINDA LOU, pharmacist; b. Mason City, Iowa, Sept. 3, 1952; d. Reece Webster and Bettye Frances (Martin) Phillips. B.S. in Polit. Sci., So. Meth. U., 1974; B.S. in Pharmacy, U. Ark., 1976; M.S. in Pharmacy, U. Houston, 1980. Registered pharmacist, Tex. Pharmacy intern Palace Drug Store, Forrest City, Ark., 1976-77; pharmacy resident Hermann Hosp., Houston, 1978-79; dir. pharmacy Alvin Community Hosp., (Tex.), 1979-80; relief pharmacist Twelve Oaks Hosp., Houston, 1980; cons. pharmacist Health Facilities, Inc., Houston, 1980-81; pharmacy supr. Meth. Hosp., Houston, 1981—. Mem. Am. Pharm. Assn., Am. Soc. Hosp. Pharmacists, So. Meth. U. Alumni Assn., Ark. Alumni Assn., Arts Symposium of Houston, Am. Cancer Soc., Young Republicans, Rho Chi, Pi Sigma Alpha. Republican. Methodist. Club: Girls' Cotillion (bd. dirs. 1983-85). Home: 7400 Bellerive #403 Houston TX 77036 Office: Meth Hosp Pharmacy 6565 Fannin Houston TX 77030

PHILLIPS, LISA RUSTEEN, small business owner; b. Nov. 7, 1964; d. Samuel W. Jr. and Betty (Aumeier) P. Owner Exotic Jungle Pet, Morgantown, W.Va., 1983—, Exotic Imports Wholesale, Morgantown, W.Va., 1986—. Mem. Nat. Assn. Female Execs. Home: 1197 Herman Ave Morgantown WV 26505 Office: Exotic Jungle Pet Ctr 1716-D Mileground Morgantown WV 26505

PHILLIPS, LOIS GAIL, exotic bird breeder; b. Detroit, June 21, 1939; d. John Patrick and Leona Victoria (Wagner) P.; BS in Chemistry, Fresno (Calif.) State U., 1962. Radiol. chemist Nat. Canners Assn., Berkeley, Calif., 1963-64; tchr. Progress Sch., Long Beach, Calif., 1966-67; vol. Peace Corps tchr., Nepal, 1967-69; univ. extension tchr. Nepal tng. programs, Davis, Calif., 1969-71; nursery employee Valley Gardens, Woodland, Calif., 1971-74, Farrell's Garden Center, Sonoma, Calif., 1974-75; mgr. 7-Eleven Store, Petaluma, Calif., 1977-85; chemist, Chem. Waste Mgmt. div., 1985-87, Clearwater Environ., Santa Rosa, 1987—; owner Bodega Birds, Petaluma. Bd. dirs. Sonoma County People Econ. Opportunity, 1978-83, sec. to bd., 1978-79. Mem. ACLU, Am. Fedn. Aviculture, Nat. Audubon Soc., Sierra Club. Home: 1821 Lakeville St Apt 55 Petaluma CA 94952 Office: 1791 Marlow Santa Rosa CA 95401

PHILLIPS, LOIS PLOWDEN, travel agency owner; b. Ft. Gaines, Ga., Dec. 30, 1927; d. Leonard Dale and Helen (Lindsay) Plowden; m. James Henry Phillips, Aug. 25, 1956 (div. Feb. 1959); 1 child, Jaye Dale. Student Ga. State Coll. for Women, 1946-48. Adminstrv. asst. U.S. Air Force, Warner Robins, Ga., 1950-56; asst. buyer Mut. Buying Syndicate, N.Y.C., 1957-59; owner, operator Junior Vogue, Macon, Ga., 1960-69; mgr. Lee-Roi, Atlanta and Highland, N.C., 1971-73; mgr., buyer Isakson's, Atlanta, 1974-76; owner, mgr., pres., Mercury Travel, Inc., Atlanta and Marietta, Ga., 1977—. Mem. Am. Soc. Travel, Prost Exec. Women. Republican. Clubs: Idle Hour (Macon, Ga.). Avocations: travel; gardening. Office: Mercury Travel Service Inc 1325 Johnson Ferry Rd Marietta GA 30067

PHILLIPS, MARGARITA GÓMEZ, microbiologist; b. Jerez, Zacatecas, Mex., July 20, 1942; came to U.S., 1964, naturalized, 1972; d. José Gómez and Guadalupe Lamas (de la Torre) Lozano; diploma Adult Tech. Sch.,

1967; B.A. in Microbiology, U. S. Fla., 1972; m. Perry Lineal Phillips, Jan. 13, 1962; 1 son, José. Med. lab. technician Manatee Meml. Hosp., Bradenton, Fla., 1967-68; med. technologist Community Hosp., New Port Richey, Fla., 1973-74, head microbiology, 1974-75, asst. to mgr., 1975-80; microbiologist Smith Kline Clin. Labs., Tampa, Fla., 1980-82; chief technologist, mgr. Internat. Clin. Labs., Inc., New Port Richey, 1982-87; dir. lab. services, Centro Espanol Meml. Hosp., Tampa, 1987—. Mem. Am. Soc. Clin. Pathologists, Am. Soc. Microbiology, Am. Soc. Med. Technology, Soc. Applied Anthropology, Nat. Cert. Agy. Lab. Personnel, Fla. Assn. Blood Banks, U. South Fla. Alumni Assn. Democrat. Roman Catholic. Home: 912 Linwood Terr Lutz FL 33549 Office: Centro Espanol Meml Hosp 4801 N Howard Ave Tampa FL 33603-1484

PHILLIPS, MARILYN CHENAULT, legal administrator; b. Mt. Vernon, Ill., Oct. 21, 1949; d. Nathan Bullock and Marguerite (Woodberry) Chenault; m. Tom Dee McFall, Aug. 29, 1969; children—Shannon, Nathan; m. 2d, Troy David Phillips, Aug. 14, 1981; stepchildren—Todd, Brittany. B.S. with honors, Okla. State U., 1970. Adminstrv. asst. Opticks, Inc. div. G. D. Searle, Dallas, 1977-78; office adminstr. Baker, Glast, Riddle, Tuttle & Elliott, Dallas, 1978-81; dir. adminstrn. Haynes and Boone, Dallas, 1981—; lectr. instr. So. Meth. U. Sch. Law, Dallas, 1981—, paralegal program, 1981—. Lou Wentz scholar Coll. Bus., Okla. State U., Stillwater, 1969-70, also C.V. Richardson scholar, 1969-70; named Outstanding Office Mgmt. Grad., 1970. Mem. Nat. Assn. Legal Adminstrs. (dir. of adminstrn. sect. 1979-85, large firm adminstrn. sect. 1985—, com. mem. 1986-88, int. issues com. 1988—, instr. law office adminstrn. course 1984, 87, pres. Dallas chpt. 1985-86), VS Legal Users Group (nat. bd. dirs. and v.p. 1985—), Wang Legal Adv. Council. Methodist. Home: 7038 Midbury St Dallas TX 75230 Office: Haynes and Boone Law Firm 3100 First RepublicBank Plaza Dallas TX 75202

PHILLIPS, MARION GRUMMAN, author, civic worker; b. N.Y.C., Feb. 11, 1922; d. Leroy Randle and Rose Marion (Werther) Grumman; student Mt. Holyoke Coll., 1940-42; B.A., Adelphi U., 1981; m. Ellis Laurimore Phillips, Jr., June 13, 1942; children—Valerie Rose (Mrs. Adrian Parsegian), Elise Marion (Mrs. Edward E. Watts III), Ellis Laurimore III, Kathryn Noel (Mrs. Philip Zimmermann), Cynthia Louise (Mrs. Kenneth Gleason Jr.). Civic vol. Mary C. Wheeler Sch., 1964-68, Historic Ithaca, Inc., 1972-76, Ellis L. Phillips Found., 1960—; bd. dirs. North Shore Jr. League, 1960-61, 64-65, 68-69, Family Service Assn. Nassau County, 1963-69, Homemaker Service Assn. Nassau County, 1959-61; writer; books include: (light verse) A Foot in the Door, 1965; The Whale-Going, Going, Gone, 1977; Doctors Make Me Sick (So I Cured Myself of Arthritis), 1979; editor: (with Valerie Phillips Parsegian) Richard and Rhoda, Letters from the Civil War, 1982; editor Jr. League Shore Lines, 1960-61, The Werthers in America-Four Generations and their Descendants, 1987; A B-Tour of Britain, 1986; contbr. articles on fund raising to mags. Episcopalian. Clubs: Hanover Garden, Creek, Mt. Holyoke of N.Y., PEO Sisterhood. Home: Point of View RR1 Box 274 Sharon VT 05065

PHILLIPS, MARLENE ELAINE, psychotherapist; b. Bklyn., Dec. 25, 1939; d. Boris Abraham and Ethel Claire (Kritz) Newman; divorced; children: Fred Stewart, Lori Michelle, Randi Sue. BA, Calif. State U., Fullerton, 1981, MS, 1983; postgrad., U.S. Internat. U., 1983—. Cert. hypnotherapist, Calif. Ptnr., psychotherapist Saddlebock Counseling & Psychotherapy Assocs., Laguna Hills, Calif., 1985—; Chairperson med. legal com. Adam Walsh Childrens Resource Ctr., Orange, Calif., 1985—. Contbr. articles to mags. Mem. Am. Assn. Profl. Hypnotherapists, Am. Psychol. Assn., Am. Soc. Behavioral Medicine, Am. Soc. Psychosomatic Medicine, Calif. Assn. Marriage and Family Therapists, Calif. State Psychol. Assn., Orange County Psychol. Assn., Saddleback Valley C. of C. Office: Saddleback Counseling & Psychotherapy Assocs 23521 Paseo de Valencia #302A Laguna Hills CA 92653

PHILLIPS, MARTHA HUGGINS, home economist; b. Lake City, S.C., Jan. 17, 1950; d. James Allison Jr. and Julia Louise (Baker) Huggins; m. Floyd Terry Phillips, Mar. 25, 1972 (div. 1983); children: Hayden Nicole, Nicholas Terry. BS in Home Econs., Limestone Coll., 1971; MEd in Personnel Services, Clemson U., 1977. Tchr. Dist. 7 Schs., Spartanburg, S.C., 1971-72; asst. county extension agt. Clemson Extension Service, Spartanburg, 1972-75; assoc. county extension agt. Spartanburg and Gaffney, S.C., 1975-82; sr. assoc. extension agt. Gaffney, 1982-85, sr. county extension agt., 1985—; del. S.C. to White House Conf. on Aging, 1981. Founder Parents of Preschoolers Charles Lea Ctr. for Mentally Handicapped, 1982—; chmn. legis com. McCarthy PTO; mem. Cannon United Meth. Women; tchr. Sunday sch. class; sec. Cherokee County Social and Health Orgns. Council, 1979, mem. project com., 1980-81, vice-chmn., 1983, chmn., 1984—, chmn. healthy mother/healthy baby network; chmn. nominating com. Am. Lung Assn., S.C., 1984, mem. Broad River adv. bd., 1984—, mem. program com., 1985, mem. state planning com., 1985. Recipient State Communications award S.C. Assn. Extension Home Economists, 1974, Young Career Woman award Spartanburg County, 1976; named Outstanding Home Economist of Yr. Piedmont dist. S.C. Assn. Extension Home Economists, 1979. Mem. Nat. Assn. Extension 4-H Agts. (jr. editor news and views so. region), S.C. Assn. Extension 4-H Agts. (participant state meeting 1983, pres. 1988, editor newsletter), Nat. Exec. Devel. Inst., Epsilon Sigma Phi (initiation com. 1980-81, screening and selection com. 1981-83). Democrat. Club: Town and Country Garden. Home: 280 Bramblewood Ln Spartanburg SC 29302 Office: Clemson Extension Service PO Box 700 Gaffney SC 29342

PHILLIPS, MIRIAM ERNESTINE, civic worker; b. Haverhill, Mass., Mar. 11, 1918; d. William B. and Ermina Floride (Coburn) Faulcon; m. Oscar George Dudley Phillips, Dec. 19, 1954; children: Peter Joshua, Miriam Elaine. BA in Edn., U. Mass.-Boston, 1985; MA in English, U. Mass., Boston, 1987. Adminstrv. asst. Am. Bapt. Chs. of Mass., Boston, 1948-58. Contbr. articles to religious publs. Nat. denominational v.p. Church Women United, 1974-77, Northeast regional v.p., 1977-80, other nat. and state offices; mem.-at-large Gen. Council, Am. Bapt. Chs. USA, 1969-71, rep. to gen. bd., 1971-78, Participant study tour to People's Republic of China, 1978; mem. exec. com. Bd. Nat. Ministries; rep. to Nat. Council Chs., 1969-72, del. to World Council Chs., 1968; v.p. Am. Bapt. Chs. Mass., 1972, 73, 1st v.p., 1987—, chmn. ann. meeting com., mem. personnel com., mem. communications com.; nat. chmn. communications Am. Bapt. Women USA, 1964-68; trustee Mass. Bible Soc.; trustee Andover Newton Theol. Sch., 1969—, sec. bd. dirs., mem. coms.; commr. Medford Housing Authority, Mass., 1972—, chmn., 1974-75; co-founder Medford br. NAACP, chmn. press and publicity; bd. dirs. Middlesex-Cambridge Lung Assn., Family Service Assn. of Greater Boston, Resthaven Home. Recipient Valiant Woman award Ch. Women United, 1979. Avocation: travel. Home: 94 Monument St Medford MA 02155

PHILLIPS, NANCY CHAMBERS, social worker; b. Danville, Ky., Oct. 11, 1941; d. Alvia Jackson and Virginia Oradell Chambers; m. Eldon Franklin Phillips, Nov. 27, 1968 (div. 1984). BA, Georgetown Coll., 1962; MSW, U. Denver, 1968; postgrad. Tulane U., 1981-85. Tchr., Hazard (Ky.) High Sch., 1962; social worker Ky. Dept. Econ. Security, 1964-71; rehab. counselor Ky. Bur. Vocat. Rehab., 1971-72; team leader Cath. Social Services, Bureau, Ky., 1972-74; instr. U. Cin., 1972-77; vis. asst. prof. Fla. Internat. U., 1977-79; asst. prof. social work Idaho State U., Pocatello, 1979-81; research asst. Child Welfare Tng. Ctr. Region VI, Tulane U., New Orleans, 1981-83; village mgr. Countryside Village, Belle Chasse State Sch., New Orleans, 1983-85; asst. supr. case mgmt. services Office Mental Retardation/Developmental Disabilities, Dept. Health and Human Resources, Greater New Orleans Regional Service Ctr., 1985-86; social work cons. Depelchin Children's Ctr., Houston, 1986-87; cons. Vis. Nurses Assn. of Brazoria County, Inc., 1986—, Nat. Med. Care, Inc., dialysis services div. S.W. Houston Dialysis Ctr.; med. social worker Dialysis Services div. Bio-Med. Applications of S.W. Houston, S.W. Houston Dialysis Ctr., 1987—; former mem. profl. adv. bd. Fla. Soc. Autistic Children, South Fla. Soc. Autistic Children, adv. council Ohio State U. Community Edn. Unit. Formerly active children's subcom. Dade and Monroe Counties Mental Health Bd., United Family and Children's Services, Family and Child Advocacy in Action Group. Recipient ednl. stipend Ky. Dept. Econ. Security, 1966-68, Nat. Cert. Recognition, South Fla. Soc. Autistic Children, 1979, Disting. Service award, 1979; named Ky. col. Mem. Nat. Assn. Social Workers. Home: 10950 Westbrae Pkwy Apt 1206 Houston TX 77031 Office: SW Dialysis Ctr 10850 S Gessner Houston TX 77071

PHILLIPS, NANCY PATRICIA, real estate appraiser; b. Oakland, Calif., Nov. 16, 1955; d. Richard LeRoy and Helen Elizabeth (Phillips) Fulgham; m. William Wane Phillips, Mar. 8, 1980. BA, U. Calif., Santa Barbara, 1978. Designated real estate appraiser. Intern Santa Barbara County Assessor, Calif., 1978; appraiser Great Western Sav. and Loan, San Jose, Calif., 1978-80, Trident Advisors Inc., Monterey, Calif., 1980-82, Nancy Phillips, RM R.E. Appraiser, Monterey, 1982—. Mem. Am. Inst. Real Estate Appraisers (dir. 1984—, v.chmn. nat. candidate guidance com. 1986-87, co-vice chmn. nat. admissions appraisal reports subcom. 1987—, regional mem. SW regional grievance com. 1984—), Soc. Real Estate Appraisers (candidate), Pacific Grove Heritage Soc. Republican. Lodge: Soroptimist (Carmel). Office: 555B Hertiage Harbor Monterey CA 93940

PHILLIPS, NORMA JEAN, association executive; b. Denver, Mar. 17, 1938; d. Norman Clyde and Mary Asunda (Fantoni) Collins; m. Harold Ray Phillips, Sept. 30; children: Harold Ray Jr., Allen, Dean Robert (dec.); m. Eudene Pfeiffer (div.). With Bank of Am., Escondido, Calif., 1956-65; receptionist, bookkeeper graybill Med. Clinic, Escondido, 1965-69; sec. treas. Harold Phillips Corp., Escondido, Calif., 1969—. Pres., Mothers Against Drunk Driving San Diego County, 1982-88, Nat. Mothers Against Drunk Driving, 1985—, MADD/Nat. Council for Chpt. Affairs, 1985-86; numerous TV and radio appearances, 1982—; mem. Presdl. Commn. on Drunk Driving, 1986, Nat. Commn. Against Drunk Driving, 1986. Recipient Outstanding Safety Vol. award Safety Engrs. San Diego, 1985, One of Outstanding Women San Diego County, ARC Orgn., 1985, One of San Diegans to Watch in '86, San Diego Mag., 1986. Club: Country Friends (Rancho Sante Fe).

PHILLIPS, REBECCA MINA, publishing company executive; b. Chgo., Sept. 11, 1955; d. Clifford Oren and Harriett Juanita (Rhoades) Dudley; m. Jonathan Lee Phillips, Aug. 5, 1977; children: Aubrey, Jonathan M., Robert. Student, No. Ark. Community Coll., 1975-76. Sec., bookkeeper New Leaf Press, Inc., Green Forest, Ark., 1975—. Troop leader Girl Scouts Am., Green Forest, 1986—; vol. ARC, 1986-87. Republican. Mem. Assembly of God. Office: New Leaf Press Inc PO Box 311 Green Forest AR 72638

PHILLIPS, RUTH C., financial executive; b. Odum, Ga., June 17, 1935; d. Robert P. and Edna (Britt) Culpeper; m. Wiley Paul Phillips, Aug. 9, 1954; 1 child, Dorothy Kay. Attended Manatee Community Coll. and Bradenton (Fla.) Bus. Sch. With Peacock TV, Bradenton, 1953-55, Wyman Green & Blalock, Bradenton, 1955-66; fin. officer, asst. computer specialist Deschamps & Gregory Inc., Bradenton, 1966—. Mem. Nat. Assn. Female Execs., Credit Women's Assn. (sec.-treas. Bradenton area 1966-68). Democrat. Mem. Church of God. Office: Deschamps & Gregory Inc 1812 Manatee Ave W Bradenton FL 34205

PHILLIPS, STEPHANIE LYNN, accountant; b. Honolulu, May 2, 1957; d. Wayne Robert Jr. and Joyce (Hefner) P. BBA, S.W. Tex. State U., 1979. CPA, Tex. Auditor State Comptroller Pub. Accts., Houston, 1979-80; tax ptnr. Melton & Melton, CPA's, Houston, 1980—. Vol. Act for 8, Houston, 1986-88. Mem. Am. Inst. CPA's, Tex. Soc. CPA's, Houston Soc. CPA's, West Houston C. of C. Methodist. Home: 9222 Keegans Wood Dr Houston TX 77083 Office: Melton & Melton CPA's 10333 Richmond Suite 500 Houston TX 77042

PHILLIPS, SUSAN E., government official; b. June 23, 1945; d. Fred Nathan and Gertrude (Goldberg) P. B.A., U. Mass., 1967; M.B.A., Va. Poly. Inst., 1985. Tchr. Newton Pub. Schs., Mass., 1968-72; mfr.'s rep. Boston, 1972-76; dir. research and publs. Conservative Caucus Found., Vienna, Va., 1977-82; cons. grants and contracts Dept. Edn., Washington, 1982, dir. intergovtl. relations, 1982-83; dir. Inst. Mus. Services, Washington, 1983-85; assoc. dir. office Presdl. Personnel, Washington, 1985—; mem. Pres.'s Adv. Council on the Arts and Humanities, 1983-85; mem. Fed. Adv. Council on the Arts, 1983-85. Com. mem. Hosp. Relief Fund of the Caribbean, Washington, 1982—, chmn. Interagy. com. on Women's Bus. Enterprise, 1986—. Mem. Exec. Women in Govt., Republican Women's Fed. Forum, Nat. Women's Economic Alliance. Office: Office Presdl Personnel The White House 1600 Pennsylvania Ave NW Washington DC 20500

PHILLIPS, SUSAN M., university administrator; b. Richmond, Va., Dec. 23, 1944; d. William G. and Nancy (Meredith) P. B.A., Agnes Scott Coll., 1967; M.S., La. State U., 1971, Ph.D., 1973. Asst. prof. La. State U., 1973-74; asst. prof. U. Iowa, 1974-78; Brookings Econ. Policy fellow 1976-77; econ. fellow Directorate of Econ. and Policy Research, SEC, 1977-78; assoc. prof. fin. dept. U. Iowa, 1978-83, assoc. v.p. fin. and univ. services, 1979-81; commr. Commodities Future Trading Commn., 1981-83, chmn., 1983-87; v.p. fin. and univ. services U. Iowa, Iowa City, 1987—; Bd. dirs. Iowa Resources Corp. Contbr. articles in field to profl. jours. Bd. govs. Chicago Mercantile Exchange; trustee Agnes Scott Coll. Office: U Iowa VP Fin and U Services 101 Jessup Hall Iowa City IA 52242

PHILLIPS, VIOLET ROSECRANS, school business executive; b. Moravia, N.Y., Jan. 15, 1935; d. Albert H. and Olive A. (Shelter) Rosecrans; m. Donald E. Phillips, Nov. 21, 1953; children: Bonnie Steger, Roger W., James E. AS, Tompkins-Cortland Community Coll., Dryden, N.Y., 1985. Ednl. sec. Moravia Cen. Sch., 1956-79, asst. bus. mgr., 1979-84; shared bus. mgr. Cortland-Madison BOCES, 1984-85; bus. exec. Trumansburg (N.Y.) Cen. Sch., 1985—. Mem. Internat. Assn. Sch. Bus. Ofcls., N.Y. State Assn. Sch. Bus. Ofcls., Cen. N.Y. Assn. Bus. Ofcls., Nat. Assn. Ednl. Office Personnel, N.Y. State Assn. Ednl. Secs. (past pres. conf. chmn., regioan dir., membership dir.). Republican. Methodist. Club: Philomath (Moravia) (pres. 1979-80). Home: RD #2 Box 179 Locke NY 13092

PHILLIPS, VIRGINIA LYNN, real estate sales executive; b. Paris, Tex., Oct. 11, 1955; d. Ornie V. and Sarah Lue (Womack) Mantooth; m. R. Wesley Phillips III, Oct. 18, 1975; 1 child, Ievane Destinie. Student, El Centro Jr. Coll., 1971-72, Tulsa Jr. Coll., 1976-77, U. Tulsa, 1977-78. Acct., owner Computerized Acctg. Service, Tulsa, 1976-86; real estate broker, assoc. Merrill Lynch Realty, Tulsa, 1986—. Treas. Tulsans Against Property Tax Discrimination, 1985—. Mem. Nat. Assn. Realtors (bd. dirs. Tulsa chpt. women's council 1987—), Real Estate Assocs. Tulsa, SE Tulsa Homeowners Assn. (bd. dirs.), Shadow Mountain Homeowners Assn., Okla. U. Alumni of Tulsa (treas. 1985-87). Republican. Lutheran. Home: 7311 E 62d St Tulsa OK 74133 Office: Merrill Lynch Realty 8121 S Harvard Tulsa OK 74136

PHIPPS, JEANNE KAY, data systems executive; b. Villas, N.J., Mar. 25, 1943; d. Clifford Perry and Catherine (Amos) Chew; m. Jerry Dean Phipps, Aug. 23, 1965; children: Russell Dean, Penny Lynn. AA, Ky. Mt. Bible Inst., Vancleve, 1964; BS in Bus., Grand Canyon Coll., Phoenix, 1976; MBA, Ariz. State U., 1983. Licensed real estate agt., Ariz. Personnel specialist The Travelers Ins. Co., Phoenix, 1971-77; personnel asst. Gen. Semiconductor, Tempe, Ariz., 1977-79; instr. Glendale (Ariz.) Community Coll., 1979—; realtor John Hall & Assocs., Phoenix, 1981—; pres. Quality Data Systems, Phoenix, 1984—. Mem. Adv. Bd. Maricopa County Skill Ctr., Phoenix, 1978-79. Mem. Ariz. Affirmative Action Assn., Phoenix Personnel Mgmt. Assn., Phoenix Bd. of Realtors, Profl. Devel. Club (program chairperson 1979). Republican. Methodist. Club: Moon Valley Women's. Home: 13401 N Coral Gables Phoenix AZ 85023

PHLEGM, VELMA ELAINE, insurance company executive; b. Coldspring, Tex., Sept. 13, 1950; d. Frank Kevin and Mary Jane (Jackson) P.; m. Richard H. Williams, Aug. 4, 1970 (div. June 1982); children: Keta Dawn Williams, Verlynn Elaine Williams. BS in Criminology, Sam Houston State U., Huntsville, Tex., 1972. Asst. to dir. Williams & Son's Mortuary, Huntsville, 1970-74; dir. Community Day Facility, Huntsville, 1970-72; underwriter, sales Allstate Ins. Co., Houston, 1972-78; underwriter Am. Gen. Ins. Co., Houston, 1978-80, Bayly, Martin & Fay Ins. Agy., Houston, 1980-82; owner, mgr. V.E. Phlegm Ins. Agy., Houston, 1982-87. Mem. United Negro Coll. Fund, Houston, 1983-87, Rainbow Coalition, Houston, 1984-87. Recipient Honor Ring, Allstate Ins. Co., 1978. Mem. Ind. Agent's Assn., Ins. Women's Assn., Nat. Assn. Female Execs., Nat. Thoroughbred Assn., Thoroughbred Assn. Tex., Tex. Women's Assn. for Paramutual Betting, Minority Businessmen Assn., Keepers of the Flame, Assn. for Research & Enlightenment, Calif. Astrology Assn., Nat. Assn. Minority Bus. Women. Democrat. Clubs: Lone Star Trail (Coldspring); Riders. Home: 5734 D E Hampton Dr Houston TX 77039 Office: V E Phlegm Ins Agy PO Box 11083 Houston TX 77293-1083

PHOENIX, NANCY M., non-profit organization administrator; b. Appleton, Wis., Nov. 25, 1951; d. Edward Peter and Eunice Margaret (Schmeichel) Jochman. BS in Communications, Pub. Adminstrn., U. Wis., Green Bay, 1979. Fin. officer Youth Devel. Tng., Green Bay, Wis., 1977-78; acting dir. Youth Resources Council, Green Bay, 1978-79; exec. dir. Vol. Ctr., Green Bay, 1980—; bd. dirs. John W. Karn Day Care Ctr., Green Bay; adv. com. U. Wis. Social Work, Green Bay, Tech. Sch. Vol. Services, Green Bay; mem. planning commn., Wis. Vol. Tng. Inst. Mem. nominations com. United Way of Brown County, Green Bay, 1985—. Recipient Super Producer award Community Programming Network, Green Bay, 1985. Mem. Bay Area Mgrs. of Vol. Services (sec. 1985-87, coordinator Harriet Naylor Vol. Adminstrn. award), Assn. for Vol. Adminstrn., Mgmt. Women, Nat. Assn. of Female Execs., Human Service Vol. Coordinators of Wis. (bd. dirs. 1986, chair edn. com., editor newsletter 1987-88), Brown County Jaycees (named outstanding boss 1984), U. Wis. Alumni Assn. Office: Vol Ctr 411 St John St Green Bay WI 54301

PHOX, PAMELA INEZ, artist; b. N.Y.C., Mar. 26, 1953; d. James Alfred and Phyllis Evadney (Bowman) P. BFA, U. Denver, 1975. art and artist's coordinator Inter-Dimensions, Outer Expressions, 1976, Soc. Please Let it Be So, Denver, 1978; lectr. in field. Exhibited in group shows at Harriet Tubman House Gallery, 1983, Emmanuel Gallery, 1983, U. No. Colo., 1979, Colo. Springs Fine Arts Ctr., 1983, U. Denver, 1984, Gallery Bwana, 1985, Zach's Restaurant, 1985, Ariz. State U., 1986, Ariz. Western Coll., 1986; one woman shows include: Harpo's, Denver, 1985, Boettcher Concert Hall, 1985, U. No. Colo., 1985; work exhibited in permanent collections at Rasputin Gallery, Denver, Wesley Box, Denver. Recipient Best of 1982 award Visual Arts Category Denver Black C. of C., Outstaninding Contributions to the Arts award Eden Theatrical Workshop, 1982. Mem. Am. Crafts Council, Black Umbrella, Denver Area Women Artists. Studio: 2128 Lafayette St Denver CO 80205

PHYFER, MARY ALEXANDER, academic administrator; b. Redbank, N.J., Dec. 9, 1943; d. Emmett Cox and Frances Pauline (Murphy) Alexander; children: Cynthia, Benjamin. BS, Duke U., 1966; MS, St. Louis U., 1981; postgrad., U. Miss., 1986—. Staff, charge nurse VA Hosp., Columbia, S.C., 1966-68; nurse various orgns., Va., Mo., 1969-72; instr. nursing edn. Three Rivers Community Coll., Poplar Bluff, Mo., 1974-79, 1981; interim dir. nursing edn. Three Rivers Community Coll., Poplar Bluff, 1981-82, dir. nursing and allied health, 1982-86, interim v.p., 1986, v.p., 1986—. Bd. dirs., treas. Haven House, Inc., Poplar Bluff, Mo., 1985—. Named Career Woman of Yr. Bus. and Profl. Women's Club, 1984, Leaders for the 80's Am. Assn. Women in Community and Jr. Colls., 1986. Mem. Mo. Assn. Community and Jr. Colls., Mo. Vocat. Assn., Nat. League for Nursing, Mo. League for Nursing, Mo. Council Assoc. Degree Nursing (pres. 1985-86), Sigma Theta Tau, Kappa Delta Pi. Home: 2011 Snider Rd Poplar Bluff MO 63901 Office: Three Rivers Community Coll Three Rivers Blvd Poplar Bluff MO 63901

PIAGGI, CLAIRE MARIE, newspaper publisher; b. North Adams, Mass., Dec. 22, 1931; d. George Frederick and Rose Marie (Perreault) Rhodes; m. Edmund V. Piaggi, Sept. 10, 1960; children: Denise Marie, Wayne Victor. Grad. high sch., North Adams, 1950. Bookkeeper, office mgr. various cos., North Adams, 1950-61; progressively bookkeeper, bus. mgr., gen. mgr., then pub. The Transcript (Berkshire Newspapers), North Adams, 1961—. Mem. adv. bd. Mark Hopkins Sch., North Adams, 1974-79; bd. dirs. North Berkshire United Way, 1978-85, Berkshire Hills Conf., 2 yrs.; pres. Santa Fund, North Adams, 16 yrs.; mem. Parents Against Deadly Drugs, North Adams, 1987—. Mem. Mass. Newspaper Pubs. Assn. (bd. dirs. 1981—), Berkshire City Traffic Assn. (bd. dirs., pres. 1972—), North Berkshire Profl. & Bus. Women's Club (Woman of Yr. 1982), North Berkshire C. of C. (bd. dirs., pres. 1982—). Home: 240 Ashland St North Adams MA 01247 Office: The Transcript 124 American Legion Dr North Adams MA 01247

PIANETTI, CATHERINE NATALIE, occupational therapist; b. Rock Spring, Wyo., June 4, 1909; d. Anthony and Anna Mary (Picco) P.; diploma Seattle Pacific Coll., 1932; B.A. in Edn., Central Wash. U., 1938; postgrad. U. Wash., 1940; cert. of proficiency in occupational therapy Mills Coll., 1945. Tchr., Wash. Public Schs., 1936-45; chief occupational therapist Marion (Ind.) VA Hosp., 1948-50, 54-69; head occupational therapist NP sect. Walter Reed Army Hosp., 1950, Valley Forge Army Hsop., 1952-53; chief occupational therapist Downey (Ill.) VA Hosp., 1953-54; ret., 1969; lectr. Ball State U., Purdue U., Marion and Anderson colls. Bd. dirs., sec., v.p. Family Service Orgn.; bd. dirs., treas., v.p. Grant County Mental Health Assn.; bd. dirs. Blind Assn., Retarded Children Assn. Served from 1st lt. to capt., Womens Med. Specialists Corps., U.S. Army, 1950-53. Recipient Excellence in Communications with Pub. award, 1969, Mgrs. commendation on retirement, 1969. Mem. Am., Ind. occupational therapy assns., Am. Legion Aux. (1st and 2d vice comdr. Rainier Valley Post 139, 1971-72, comdr. 1976, comdr. Service Girls Post 1977, comdr. 1st Seattle Dist. 1978-79), 20 and 4, 8 and 40 (pres. 1976, chmn. 1979—), Pioneers of Columbia, Nat. Assn. Fed. Employees. Roman Catholic. Clubs: Seattle Womens Century (publicity chmn. rec. sec. Past Pres.'s Assembly 1974-75, treas. 1975-77, v.p. 1976-78, pres. 1979-81), DAV, Gen. Fedn. Womens' Clubs. Contbr. articles to profl. jours. Home: 4221 47th Ave S Seattle WA 98118

PIANO, EVELYN MARLENE, banker; b. Seattle, Mar. 2, 1950; d. Anthony and Evelyn (Gelinas) P.; m. Douglas W. Behrens, July 23, 1983. BA, Clark U., 1972; MBA, Columbia U., 1978. Devel. assoc. Clark U., Worcester, Mass., 1972-76; product mgr. Citicorp, N.Y.C., 1978-81; advt. mgr. First Bank System, Mpls., 1981-82, dir. product devel., 1982-84; v.p. mktg. First Bank System, Duluth, 1984—. Vice chmn. Neighborhood Housing, Duluth, 1986; bd. dirs. Duluth Conv. and Visitors Bur., 1985—. Mem. Duluth C. of C., Leadership Duluth. Office: First Bank Duluth 130 W Superior St Duluth MN 55802

PIANTADOSI, JEANETTE KEMCHICK, business executive; b. Point Pleasant, N.J., Sept. 2, 1954; d. Patrick John and Gloria E. (Stensland) Kmiechick; m. Roger Anthony Piantadosi, Aug. 4, 1975 (div. Mar. 1982); m. William J. Collard, Mar. 12, 1982 (div. June 1988). B.A. in Sociology magna cum laude, Am. U., 1977, M.Ed., 1979; postgrad. Va. Poly. Inst. and State U., 1980, George Washington U., 1981, UCLA Extension, 1983; postgrad. in pub. adminstrn. U. So. Calif., 1985—. Dir. fin. aid Am. U., Washington, 1977-81; legis. aide to Rep. Patricia Schroeder, Washington, 1981-82; dir. fed. and state relations Systems Research, Inc., Washington, 1981-84; v.p. mktg. Sigma Systems, Inc., Los Angeles, 1982-84; v.p. The Wyndgate Group, Sacramento, 1984—. Recipient Meritorious Service award Am. U., 1977, 80; Gen. U. scholar, 1975-76, Mathas scholar, 1975-77; Charles Revson fellow, 1981-82. Mem. Nat. Assn. Women Deans, Adminstrs. and Counselors (chmn. div. govt./agy. spl. programs 1984). Democrat. Roman Catholic. Home: 464 Wyndgate Rd Sacramento CA 95864 Office: The Wyndgate Group 9310 Tech Center Dr Suite 230 Sacramento CA 95826

PIAZZA, MARGUERITE, opera singer, actress, entertainer; b. New Orleans, May 6, 1926; d. Albert William and Michaela (Piazza) Luft; m. William J. Condon, July 15, 1953 (dec. Mar. 1968); children: Gregory, James (dec.), Shirley, William J., Marguerite P., Anna Becky; m. Francis Harrison Bergtholdt, Nov. 8, 1970. MusB, Loyola U., New Orleans; MusM, La. State U.; MusD (hon.), Christian Bros. Coll., 1973; LHD honoris causa, Loyola U., Chgo., 1975. Singer N.Y.C. Ctr. Opera, 1948, Met. Opera Co., 1950; TV artist, regular singing star Your Show of Shows NBC, 1950-54; entertainer various supper clubs Cotillion Room, Hotel Pierre, N.Y.C., 1954, Las Vegas, Los Angeles, New Orleans, San Francisco, 1956—; ptnr. Sound Express Music Pub. Co., Memphis, 1987—; bd. dirs. Cemrel, Inc. Appeared as guest performer on numerous mus. TV shows. Nat. crusade chmn. Am. Cancer Soc., 1971; founder, bd. dirs. Marguerite Piazza Thanksgiving Gala for the Benefit of St. Jude's Hosp., 1976; bd. dirs. Memphis Opera Co., World Literacy Found., NCCJ; v.p., life bd. dirs. Memphis Symphony Orch.; nat. chmn. Soc. for Cure Epilepsy. Decorated Mil. and Hospitaller Order of St

Lazarus of Jerusalem; recipient service award Chgo. Heart Assn., 1956, service award Fedn. Jewish Philanthropies of N.Y., 1956, Sesquicentennial medal Carnegie Hall; named Queen of Memphis, Memphis Cotton Carnival, 1973, named Person of Yr. La. Council for Performing Arts, 1975, named Woman of Yr. Nat. Am. Legion, named Woman of Yr. Italian-Am. Soc. Mem. Nat. Speakers Assn., Woman's Exchange, Beta Sigma Omicron, Phi Beta. Roman Catholic. Clubs: Memphis Country, Memphis Hunt and Polo, New Orleans Country, New Orleans City.

PICARDI, SHIRLEY MAE, university administrator; b. Margaretville, N.Y., Feb. 20, 1948; d. Clifford Daniel and Edna Rose (Moore) Ives; A.B. summa cum laude in chemistry, Radcliffe Coll., 1970; S.M., M.I.T., 1972, Ph.D. in Food Sci., 1976, S.M. in Mgmt., 1981; m. Anthony Charles Picardi, Sept. 4, 1970. Indsl. liaison officer M.I.T., Cambridge, 1976-79, asst. dir. Indsl. Liaison Program, 1979-80, spl. asst. to v.p. for resource devel., 1981, sec. Alumni Assn. 1981-85, bursar, 1985—; lectr. in field. NSF grad. fellow, 1970-73; Nestle Co. fellow, 1973-74; Nutrition Found. fellow, 1974-75; Alfred P. Sloan fellow, 1980-81. Mem. Inst. Food Technologists, Phi Beta Kappa, Sigma Xi. Contbr. articles to profl. jours. Office: Bursar's Office MIT Room E19-215 Cambridge MA 02139

PICARIELLO, JEANNE MELINDA, military officer, nurse; b. Washington, Nov. 20, 1952; d. Ciro James and Theresa Ann (Carifio) P. BS in Nursing, U. Md., Balt., 1975; M in Cardiovascular Nursing, U. Wash., 1980. RN. Commd. 1st lt. U.S. Army, 1971, advanced through grades to maj., 1986; staff nurse burn unit U.S. Army Med. Ctr., Ft. Sam Houston, Tex., 1975-78; asst. head nurse intensive care unit U.S. Army Med. Activity, Ft. Campbell, Ky., 1978-79; asst. head nurse critical care unit, cardiac rehab. coordinator U.S. Army Med. Ctr., Ft. Lewis, Wash., 1980-82; health fitness nurse U.S. Army War Coll., Carlisle, Pa., 1982-84; program dir. Army corp. fitness project U.S. Army Pentagon, Washington, 1984-86, coordinator health promotion programs, 1986-87; coordinator health promotion, med.-surg. nurse 97th Gen. Hosp., V Corps, Frankfurt, Fed. Republic of Germany, 1987—. Vol. U.S. Soldiers' and Airmen's Home, Washington, 1985-86; active Befriend a Child Big Sister program Fairfax (Va.) Dept. Social Services, 1985—. 1st woman selected to train with U.S. Modern Pentathlon team, Ft. Sam Houston, 1975—. Mem. Am. Coll. Sports Medicine, Fedn. Orgn. Profl. Women (bd. dirs. 1986—). Roman Catholic. Club: D.C. Masters Swim Team. Home: care of 1770 Plunkett St #209 Hollywood FL 33020

PICCIANO, JACQUELINE LUCILLE, medical librarian; b. Los Angeles, July 19, 1928; d. Frank Booth and Margaret Mary (Metzler) Chambers; m. Eugene Michael Picciano, Dec. 31, 1955; children—Louis, Eugene, Stephen, Michael. BA, Trinity Coll., Washington, 1946-50; MSLS, Cath. U., Washington, 1952; MBA, Rutgers U., 1986. Reference librarian Nat. Library Medicine, Washington, 1951-56; librarian of sci. library Hoffmann LaRoche Inc., Nutley, N.J., 1956-57; librarian Acad. Medicine N.J., Bloomfield, 1960-71; librarian Am. Jour. Nursing Co., N.Y.C., 1971-81; library systems coordinator Read More Publs., N.Y.C., 1982-84; head access dept. Cornell U. Med. Coll., N.Y.C., 1984—; editor Internat. Nursing Index, N.Y.C., 1971-81; mem. Interagy. Council on Library Resources for Nursing, 1969-81, 84—, chmn. pro tem, 1983, pres., 1985-86; hosp. library cons., 1964—; mem. adv. com. N.Y./N.J. Regional Med. Library, N.Y.C., 1971-81, chmn., 1974-75, chmn.-elect governance council, 1977-78; mem. legis. com. Consumer Health Info. Task Force, 1988—. Contbr. articles to profl. jours. Trinity Coll. scholar, 1946; fellow Cath. U., 1950. Mem. METRO (N.Y. State 3 R's program), Med. Library Assn. (cert., nat. by-laws chmn. 1979-82, nominating com. 1978, 83; pres. N.Y./N.J. chpt. 1974-75, chmn. program com. 1972-73, 82-84, chmn. govtl. relations com. 1985—), AAUW (1st v.p. Bloomfield br. 1983-84, 86—), ALA (dir. div. 1968-71, by-laws chmn. 1972-73), Am. Soc. Info. Sci. (chmn. hospitality com. ann. meeting 1980, program com. 1984—). Roman Catholic. Home: 380 Essex Ave Bloomfield NJ 07003 Office: Cornell U Med Coll Library 1300 York Ave New York NY 10021

PICHE, STEPHANIE EMILIE, sales executive; b. Hialeah, Fla., Dec. 9, 1959; d. Joseph Etienne and Audrey Jane (Kurtz) P.; m. Ronald James Dennis, Apr. 1, 1982 (div. Feb. 1987); 1 child, Joseph David. BS, U. Nev., 1981. R.N., Nev., Utah; lic. real estate agt., Utah. Publisher's asst. Nev. Messenger, Las Vegas, 1974-76; sec. circulation Las Vegas Sun Newspaper, 1976-77; medical asst. Drs. Jacobs and Modaber, Las Vegas, 1977-79; lab asst. Sunrise Hosp., Las Vegas, 1979-81; nurse Dr. David Peterson, Orem, Utah, 1981-82; assoc. realtor Century 21, Provo, Utah, 1982-83; v.p. sales and mktg. Zion Worldwide Enterprises, Provo, Utah, 1983-84; mgr. regional sales Digital Tech. Internat., Orem, Utah, 1984—; cons. publishing groups, Buffalo 1984—. Area dir. fundraising. Am. Cancer Assn., Orem 1983-84. Mem. Buffalo Assn. Female Exec. (dir. 1987—), Nat. Assn. Female Exec. Republican. Roman Catholic. Clubs: Aviation (pres. 1976-77), Ski (sec. 1977-78). Home: 1095 C Youngs Rd Williamsville NY 14221 Office: Digital Tech Internat 500 W 1200 S Orem UT 84058

PICKARD, CHARLENE WILLHOIT, banker; b. Japan, Feb. 24, 1952; came to U.S., 1955; d. Charles Henry and Eva Maudine (Barnes) Willhoit. Student, Wichita State U., 1974-76. Investor remittance clk. Bank IV Wichita (Kans.), N.A., 1974-76, supr. tng., 1976-79, mgr. real estate collections, 1979-85, mgr. real estate ops., 1985-86, officer real estate ops., 1986, officer, mgr. real estate, installment and escrow ops., 1986—; bd. dirs. Parallax Program Inc., Wichita, 1986—, chmn. fin. devel., 1985-87. Pres. area A Citizens' Participation Assn., Wichita, 1986-88. Lodge: Lioness (pres. 1986-87). Home: 478 Pamela St Wichita KS 67212 Office: Bank IV Wichita NA PO Box 1069 Wichita KS 67201

PICKERING, AVAJANE, specialized education facility executive; b. New Castle, Ind., Nov. 5, 1951; d. George Willard and Elsie Jean (Wicker) P. BA, Purdue U., 1974; MS in Spl. Edn., U. Utah, 1983, postgrad., 1985—. Tchr. Granite Community Edn., Salt Lake City, 1974-79; tchr. coordinator Salt Lake City Schs., 1975-85; co-dir., owner Specialized Ednl. Programming Service, Inc., Salt Lake City, 1976—; adj. instr. U. Utah, Salt Lake City, 1985—. Rep. del. Utah State Conv., also county conv.; vol. tour guide, hostess Temple Square, Ch. Jesus Christ of Latter-Day Saints, 1983—. Mem. Council for Exceptional Children, Assn. Children and Adults with Learning Disabilities, Delta Kappa Gamma. Home: 1595 S 2100 E Salt Lake City UT 84108 Office: 2022 S 2100 E Suite 201 Salt Lake City UT 84108

PICKETT, BETTY HORENSTEIN, psychologist; b. Providence, R.I., Feb. 15, 1926; d. Isadore Samuel and Etta Lillian (Morrison) Horenstein; m. James McPherson Pickett, Mar. 10, 1952. A.B. magna cum laude, Brown U., 1945, Sc.M., 1947, Ph.D., 1949. Asst. prof. psychology U. Minn., Duluth, 1949-51; asst. prof. U. Nebr., 1951; lectr. U. Conn., 1952; prof. assoc. psychol. scis. Bio-Scis. Info. Exchange, Smithsonian Instn., Washington, 1953-58; exec. sec. behavioral scis. study sect. exptl. psychology study sect. div. research grants NIH, Washington, 1958-61; research cons. to mental health unit HEW, Boston, 1962-63; exec. sec. research career program NIMH, 1963-66, chief cognition and learning sect. div. extramural research program, 1966-68, dep. dir., 1968-74, dir. div. spl. mental health programs, 1974-75, acting dir. div. extramural research program, 1975-77; asso. dir. for extramural and collaborative research program Nat. Inst. Aging, 1977-79; dep. dir. Nat. Inst. Child Health and Human Devel., Bethesda, Md., 1979-81; acting dir. Nat. Inst. Child Health and Human Devel., 1981-82, dir. Div. Research Resources, 1982—; mem. health scientist adminstr. panel Civil Service Commn. Bd. Examiners, 1970-76, 81—. Contbr. articles to profl. jours. Mem. Am. Psychol. Assn., Eastern Psychol. Assn., Psychonomic Soc., Assn. Women in Sci., AAAS, Phi Beta Kappa, Sigma Xi. Home: 1320 21st St NW Washington DC 20036 Office: Bldg 31 Room 5B/03 Bethesda MD 20892

PICKETT, NANCY ELIZABETH, government council executive, consultant, trainer; b. Barksdale AFB, La., Nov. 7, 1948; d. Richard Dewey and Evelyn (Weis) P.; m. Wendell Alfred Smith III, May 31, 1968 (div. 1976); children—Melinira Lynne, Wendell Alfred, IV. B.A., Nicholls State U., 1970, MEd, 1972. Tchr. St. Charles Sch. Bd., Luling, La., 1970-71; counselor, coordinator River Parishes Council Govt., Convent, La., 1973-74, exec. dir., Boutte, La., 1974-86; exec. asst. Centec Corp., New Orleans, 1986-87; vocat. rehab. cons. Crawford Health and Rehab., Metairie, La., 1987—; pres. pvt. industry council, LaPlace, La., 1981-83; pvt. practice trainer, cons., Boutte, La., 1979—; mem. adv. bd. La. Family Planning Program, New Orleans, 1976—. Editor: Directory Community Resources, 1977. Del. White House Conf. Families, Mpls., 1978, La. Gov.'s Conf. Libraries, Baton Rouge, 1978; founding bd. dirs. St. Charles Community Theatre, Luling, La., 1979-84; bd. dirs., v.p. S.E. La. Girl Scout Council, New Orleans, 1978-83. Nat. Merit scholar, 1966. Mem. Am. Soc. for Tng. and Devel. (bd. dirs., treas. 1984, chmn. position referral 1983), Nat. Assn. Female Execs. (charter), Service Delivery Area Dirs. Assn. Office: Crawford Health and Rehab 3337 N Hullen Suite 301 Metairie LA 70002

PICKETT, OLIVIA KREDEL, librarian; b. Charleston, S.C., Dec. 8, 1942; d. Frederick Evert and Constance (Orme) Kredel; m. Robert William Pickett, Mar. 17, 1985. AB, Duke U., 1964; MA, Middlebury Coll., 1966; MLS, U. Md., 1972. Assoc. librarian U. Md., College Park, Md., 1972-75; tech. services librarian Nat. League of Cities, Washington, 1975-79, mgr. mcpl. reference service, 1979-84, staff assoc. III, 1984—. Contbr. articles in profl. field. Mem. Spl. Libraries Assn. (sect. chmn. 1985-86), Beta Phi Mu. Clubs: Toastmasters, Rockville, Md. (pres. 1985), Potomac Appalachian Trail, 1975—. Home: 10404 Burnt Ember Dr Silver Spring MD 20903 Office: Nat League of Cities 1301 Pennsylvania Ave Washington DC 20004

PICKFORD, SHIRLEY ROBERTA CLAY, computer and financial consultant; b. London, Aug. 17, 1949; d. Thomas R. and Maisey D. (Clay) P.; children—Clay, Christina. B.A. cum laude, Boston U., 1969; M.A., Brandeis U., 1972; Ph.D., Tex. A&M U., 1977. C.P.A., Fla.; lic. realtor, mortgage broker, securities broker, prin. ins. agt., Fla. Owner, fin. cons. Fin. Planning for Women Inc., Orlando, Fla., 1972-86, Integrated Fin. Services Internat. Inc., Orlando, 1977—, also bd. dirs.; asst. prof. acctg. U. Central Fla., Orlando, 1977-81; assoc. prof. Fla. Atlantic U., Boca Raton, 1982-85; owner, computer cons. COMPSOL, Inc., Orlando, 1982—, also dir.; cons. Fla. Dept. Law Enforcement, 1978-80. Author: Accounting Principles, 1980-82. Fla. Dept. Law Enforcement grantee, 1980, 81. Mem. Am. Inst. CPAs, Am. Acctg. Assn., Electronic Data Processing Assn., Phi Kappa Phi, Beta Gamma Sigma, Alpha Beta Sigma, Fla. Exec. Women (founder, pres. 1980-81). Avocations: running; reading; music.

PICKUP, PATRICIA ANN, computer consultant; b. Phila., Jan. 17, 1959; d. Harry Charles and Kathryn Theresa (McQuiston) P. Student, Johns Hopkins U., 1977-81. Analyst Progrm Ctr. for Forensic Econs., Phila., 1982-83, Nat. Property Analysts, Phila., 1983-85, Trilog/CIGNA, Phila., 1985-86, EZ Ware Corp., Phila., 1986-87; cons. Pecon, Phila., 1987—; freelance cons., Phila., 1982—. Past active United Cerebral Palsy Assn., Girl Scouts of U.S. Mem. AAUW, Phila. Area Computer Soc., Phila. Osborne Group, Computer Profls. for Social Responsibility, Women and Math., Mensa, Nat. Assn. Female Execs., Johns Hopkins U. Alumni Assn.

PICOLOGLOU, SUSAN MARIE, geneticist, molecular biologist; b. Mpls., Dec. 5, 1946; d. Walter A. and Enid J. (Evans) Burton; m. Basil Picologlou, Aug. 12, 1972; children: Aliki, Elizabeth. BA, U. Minn., 1967; MS, Purdue U., 1971, PhD, 1975. Contbr. articles to sci. jours. Mem. Genetics Soc. Am., Am. Soc. Microbiology, Gamma Sigma Delta. Home: 1315 Gilbert St Downers Grove IL 60515 Office: U Ill Dept Biol Scis Box 4348 Chicago IL 60680

PICONE, EDITH, real estate company executive; b. Bklyn., Jan. 24, 1917; d. Amedeo and Domenica (Smilari) Moretti; m. John Picone, Jan. 24, 1952 (dec.); children—John Jr., Peter, Elisa. Grad. high sch., Bklyn. Buyer, Goldsmith Bros., N.Y.C., 1934-51; mgr. Bellmore Liquor Co., Greenwich, Conn., 1951-72; pres. John and John, Inc., Greenwich, 1972-77; gen. ptnr. PIC Assocs., Greenwich, 1977—. Republican. Roman Catholic. Lodge: Order Eastern Star (Matron 1949-52). Avocations: travel; cooking; philately.

PICOTTE, SUSAN CARROLL, lawyer; b. Brighton, Mass., Sept. 2, 1954; d. John Dennis, Jr., and Patricia (Curran) Carroll; m. William Burgess Picotte, Aug. 12, 1978; children: David Hunter, Philip Burgess. B.A. in Econs. magna cum laude, Russell Sage Coll., 1976; J.D., Union U., Albany, N.Y., 1979. Bar: N.Y. 1980, U.S. Dist. Ct. (no. dist.) N.Y. 1980, U.S. Dist. Ct. (we. dist.) N.Y. 1985, U.S. Supreme Ct. 1988. Legal clk. O'Connell & Aronowitz, P.C., Albany, 1978-79; assoc. firm Cooper, Erving & Savage, Albany, 1979-82, ptnr., 1983-86; ptnr. Cooper, Erving, Savage, Nolan & Heller, Albany, 1987—. Bd. dirs., 1st v.p. Council Community Services N.E. N.Y., Albany, 1980-86; trustee Shaker Heritage Soc., 1983-86; mem. Jr. League Troy, Inc., 1981-86; bd. dirs. University Found. Albany, Inc., 1987—. Mem. ABA, N.Y. State Bar Assn., Albany County Bar Assn. (dir. 1983—), N.Y. State Women's Bar Assn., Emma Willard Sch. Alumnae Assn. (dir. 1982-88, v.p. 1988—). Club: Hudson River (Albany), Steuben Athletic (Albany). Office: Cooper Erving Savage et al 39 N Pearl St Albany NY 12207

PIECH, RUTH DIANE, nurse; b. Saltsburg, Pa., Mar. 26, 1935; d. Paul Emerson and Ruth Catherine (Williams) Almes; m. Bernard John Piech; children: John Paul, Mark Daniel. Cert. in nursing, Shadyside Hosp. Sch. Nursing/U. Pitts., 1956. Registered nurse Pa., Ohio, Tex. Staff nurse St. Clair Meml. Hosp., Mt. Lebanon, Pa., 1959, charge nurse, 1959-60; spl. duty nurse Carmi (Ill.) Gen. Hosp., 1961-64; office nurse MacGregor Med. Clinic, Houston, 1965-70; I.V. nurse McKeesport (Pa.) Hosp., 1970-71; staff nurse Mansfield (Ohio) Gen. Hosp., 1971-73; office nurse, pediatric nurse specialist MacGregor Med. Assn., Houston, 1973—, referral coordinator, 1987; med. adv. bd. Hosp. Mgmt. Systems Soc., Houston, 1987-88. Recipient Danforth Found. award, 1953. Mem. Am. Nurses Assn., Tex. Nurses Assn., Am. Assn. Physician's Nurses. Democrat. Lutheran. Lodge: Daughters of the Nile. Home: 6706 Stiller Dr Missouri City TX 77489 Office: MacGregor Med Assn 2550 Holly Hall Houston TX 77054

PIEL, ELEANOR JACKSON, lawyer; b. Santa Monica, Calif., Sept. 22, 1920; d. Louis Harris and Blanche Melicent (Virden) Jackson; student U. Calif. at Los Angeles, 1936-39; B.A., U. Calif.-Berkeley, 1940, LL.B., 1943; postgrad. U. So. Calif., 1940-41; m. Gerard Piel, June 24, 1955; 1 dau., Eleanor Jackson. Bar: Calif. 1943, N.Y. 1957. Law clk. U.S. Dist. Ct., San Francisco, 1939, 44; dep. atty. gen. State of Calif., 1944; clk. U.S. Senate Civil Service Com., 1945; legal adviser Supreme Command Allied Powers, Japan, 1945-48; practice law, Los Angeles, 1948-55; atty. Legal Aid. Soc., N.Y.C., 1957-58; practice in N.Y.C., 1957—; mem. com. on bicentennial U.S. cont. U.S. Ct. Appeals (2d cir.). Trustee, NYU, Med. Ctr., 1967—. Fellow ABA (life), Com. Public Justice; mem. Assn. Bar. City N.Y. (mem. spl. com. to revise criminal code 1970-83, com. on penology 1971-76, grievance com. 1973-76) N.Y. Bar Assn., N.Y. County Lawyers Assn., Am. Arbitration Assn. (comml. arbitration com.). Clubs: Cosmopolitan, Women's City (counsel). Home: 1115 5th Ave New York NY 10128 Office: 36 W 44th St New York NY 10036

PIEPER, JANET LEAH, university administrator; b. Norfolk, Nebr., Feb. 12, 1932; d. Walter Arthur Arnold and Alma Eulalia (Heintzelman) Steffen; B.Sc., U. Nebr., 1954; postgrad. Omaha U., 1957-58, Butler U., 1965-66; M.A., U. Nebr., 1969, Ph.D., 1976; m. Donald R. Pieper, June 20, 1954; children—David Richard, James Steffen, Steven Donald. Math., English and journalism tchr. Stanton (Nebr.) High Sch., 1954-56; instr. English, Omaha U., 1956-58; asst. dir., editor Study Commn. Undergrad. Edn., U. Nebr., Lincoln, 1972-75, adminstrv. asst. to dean, 1976-78; dir. dept. personnel State Nebr., Lincoln, 1978-83; dir. personnel and employee relations Calif. Poly. State U., San Luis Obispo, 1984—. Chmn., Savs. Bond Dr. State Employees, 1978-81. AAUW Ednl. Found. Project grantee, 1979-80, AAUW individual project grantee, 1973-74, Johnson fellow, 1971-72. Mem. AAUW (edn. chmn. state div. 1968-79), Nat. Assn. State Personnel Execs., Internat. Personnel Mgmt. Assn., Mortar Bd. Alumni Assn. (pres. 1978-79), Phi Beta Kappa, Pi Lambda Theta, Pi Mu Epsilon, Delta Phi Alpha, Gamma Phi Beta, PEO. Club: Sweet Adelines. Home: 119 Searidge Ct Shell Beach CA 93449 Office: Calif Poly State U Adminstrn Bldg San Luis Obispo CA 93407

PIEPER, PATRICIA R., artist, photographer; b. Paterson, N.J., Jan. 28, 1923; d. Francis William and Barbara Margareth (Ludwig) Farabaugh; student Baron von Palm, 1937-39, Deal (N.J.) Conservatory, summers 1939, 40, Utah State U., 1950-52; m. George F. Pieper, July 1, 1941 (dec. May 3, 1981); 1 dau., Patricia Lynn. One-woman shows: Charles Russell Mus., Great Falls, Mont., 1955, Fisher Gallery, Washington, 1966, Tampa City Library, 1977, 78, 79, 80, 81, 83, 84, Center Place Art Ctr., Brandon, Fla., 1985; exhibited in group shows: Davidson Art Gallery, Middletown, Conn., 1968, Helena (Mont.) Hist. Mus., 1955, Dept. Commerce Alaska Statehood Show, 1959, Joslyn Mus., Omaha, 1961, Denver Mus. Natural History, 1955, St. Joseph's Hosp. Gallery, 1980, 82, 84-86; represented in pvt. collections. Pres. Bell Lake Assn., 1976-78, 79. Winner photog. competition Gen. Telephone Co. of Fla., 1979; recipient Outstanding Service award Bell Lake Assn., 1987; photography winner in top 100 out of 8,000 Nat. Wildlife Fedn. competition, 1986. Mem. Pasco County (Fla.) Water Adv. Council, 1978—, chmn., 1979-82, 83-84, 86-88; gov.'s appointee to S.W. Fla. Water Mgmt. Dist., Hillsborough River Basin Bd., 1981-82, 84-87, vice chair, 1987; active Save Our Rivers program, 1982-84, 85-86, chmn., 1986; pres. Bell Lake Assn., 1986, 87; adv. bd. Tampa YMCA, 1979-80. Mem. Nat. League Am. Pen Women (v.p. Tampa 1976-78, Woman of Yr. award 1977-78), Tampa Art Mus., Retired Officer's Wives Assn., Land O' Lakes C. of C. (dir. 1981-82, outstanding service award 1980), Fla. Geneal. Soc., West State Archaeol. Soc.; distaff mem. Retired Officer's Assn., MacDill AFB, 1982—. Clubs: Lutz, Land O' Lakes Women's. Home and Studio: PO Box 15 Land O' Lakes FL 34639

PIEPHO, SUSAN BRAND, chemist; b. Pound Ridge, N.Y., Apr. 28, 1942; d. Byron Alexander and Katherine F. (Brammer) Brand; B.A. summa cum laude with honors in Chemistry, Smith Coll., 1964; M.A. in Sci. Edn., Columbia U., 1965; Ph.D. in Phys. Chemistry (NDEA fellow 1968-70, A.T. Gwathmey Meml. award 1970), U.Va., 1970; m. Edward Lee Piepho, June 13, 1964. Secondary sch. tchr., N.Y.C. and Charlottesville, Va.,1965-67; asst. prof. chemistry Sweet Briar (Va.) Coll., 1971-73; postdoctoral research asso. U. Va., 1973-75; NATO postdoctoral fellow Oxford (Eng.) U., 1975-76; postdoctoral fellow U.So. Calif., 1976; asst. prof., then asso. prof. chemistry Randolph-Macon Woman's Coll., Lynchburg, Va., 1977-81; assoc. prof. chemistry Sweet Briar Coll., 1981-84, prof., 1984—, chmn. chemistry dept., 1983-86; visiting prof. chemistry U. Va., 1986-87. NSF grantee, 1979, 82, 83, 86-89; visiting professorships for women, NSF, 1986-87. Mem. Am. Chem. Soc., Am. Phys. Soc., AAAS, AAUP, ACLU (chmn. Lynchburg chpt. 1977-81), Common Cause (coordinator Amherst County, Va. 1979-82), Phi Beta Kappa, Sigma Xi. Democrat. Episcopalian. Club: Village Garden (treas. 1980-82, v.p. 1986-88, pres. 1988-89). Author (with Paul N. Schatz) Group Theory in Spectroscopy: With Applications to Magnetic Circular Dichroism, 1983, also papers in field. Home: Box AM Briarhurst Dr Sweet Briar VA 24595 Office: Sweet Briar Coll Dept Chemistry Sweet Briar VA 24595

PIERCE, ANNE-MARIE B., headmistress; b. Grenoble, Isere, France, Sept. 9, 1943; came to U.S., 1961; d. Joseph and Andreé Georgette (Hauguenauer) Bernheim; m. Robert L. Pierce, Mar. 21, 1964; 1 child, Eric. BA, U. Calif., Berkeley, 1965; MA, Hayward State U., 1973. Head fgn. lang. dept. Head-Royce Sch., Oakland, Calif., 1965-75; head fgn. lang. dept. San Francisco U. High Sch., 1975-79, dir. pub. events, 1980—; headmistress Ecole Bilingue, Berkeley, 1980—. Co-author radio instrn. A Touch of France, 1980—. Named to Cum Laude Soc. Head-Royce Schs., 1982. Mem. Am. Assn. Tchrs. French, Assn. French Schs. in Am. (founder, pres. 1985-86, 87—), Fgn. Lang. Assn. No. Calif., Calif. Assn. Ind. Schs. (exec. bd. dirs. 1985-88), Nat. Assn. Female Execs. Democrat. Home: 536 Parker Ave San Francisco CA 94118 Office: Ecole Bilingue 1009 Heinz St Berkeley CA 94710

PIERCE, CYNTHIA JANE, sales professional, nurse; b. Knoxville, Tenn., July 21, 1948; d. Franklin Brewer and Viola Joy (White) P.; m. Tommy Brewer, July 3, 1971 (div. June 1973). Student, John C. Calhoun Jr. Coll., 1966-68; A in Nursing, Mid. Tenn. State U., 1976. Supr. Giles County Hosp., Pulaski, Tenn., 1976-77; staff nurse Clinic for Woman, Huntsville, Ala., 1977-79; surg. nurse Humana Hosp., Huntsville, 1979-81, John Muir Mem. Hosp., Walnut Creek, Calif., 1981-82; supr. surgery St. Mary's Hosp., Reno, 1983-85; scrub nurse Sr. Stancel M. Riley, Huntsville, 1985-86; surg. nurse St. Mary's Hosp., Knoxville, 1986-87; sales rep. Pierce's Nu-Stock, Pulaski, 1987—. Mem. Assn. Operating Room Nurses. Democrat. Methodist. Home and Office: 1358 Pierce Ln Pulaski TN 38478

PIERCE, DELILA FRANCES, judge; b. St. Cloud, Minn., Jan. 21, 1934; d. Lawrence August and Alvina Elizabeth (Hechtel) Pierskalla. BS, U. Minn., 1957, JD cum laude, 1958. Bar: Minn. 1958. Assoc. Robert L. Ehlers, St. Paul, Minn., 1958-59; ptnr. Mitchell & Pierce, Mpls., 1959-65; sole practice, Mpls., 1966-73; referee Family Ct., Dist. Ct., Hennepin County, Minn., Mpls., 1973-74; judge Hennepin County Mcpl. Ct., Mpls., 1974-83, Dist. Ct. Minn. (4th jud. dist.), 1983—; mem. adv. bd. Genesis II, Mpls., 1975-76. Fellow Am. Acad. Matrimonial Lawyers; mem. Am. Judges Assn., Nat. Assn. Women Judges, ABA, Am. Judicature Soc., Minn. State Bar Assn., Hennepin County Bar Assn., Minn. Dist. Judges Assn., Minnesota County Judges Assn. (bd. dirs. 1984-87), Hennepin Hist. Soc., Mpls. Soc. Fine Arts. Office: Dist Ct Minn 4th Dist Hennepin County Govt Ctr Minneapolis MN 55487

PIERCE, ELIZABETH GAY (MRS. WILLIAM CURTIS PIERCE), civic worker; b. N.Y.C., Mar. 26, 1907; d. Martin and Julia (Stone) Gay; A.B., Barnard Coll., 1929; m. William Curtis Pierce, June 19, 1929; children—Martin Gay, Elizabeth Gay (Mrs. Joseph S. Stout, Jr.), Josiah. Vol. worker Boston City Hosp., 1929-30, Community Service Soc., N.Y.C., 1931-32; mem. dependent children's sect. Welfare Council, N.Y.C., 1939-40; chmn. house com. North Shore Holiday House, Huntington, L.I., 1944, pres., 1945; co-chmn. thrift shop com. Knickerbocker Hosp., N.Y.C., 1957-64; mem. exec. com. of women's com. Legal Aid Soc., N.Y.C., 1958-59; mem. Women's Aux. Knickerbocker Hosp. (exec. com. 1960-64); adv. trustee Maine Citizens for Hist. Preservation, 1983-87; trustee Jones Mus. Ceramics and Glass, 1985—. Mem. Soc. Colonial Dames in State N.Y. (bd. mgrs., 1962-67, corr. sec. N.Y. 1965-67, pres. 1967-70), Nat. Soc. Colonial Dames Am. (pres. 1972-76), Soc. for Preservation New Eng. Antiquities (Maine council, former chmn. Marrett House), Mayflower Soc. N.Y. (sec. 1985-88), Daus. Founders and Patriots), Nat. Grange. Episcopalian. Club. Colony. Home: Box 352 Route 1 West Baldwin ME 04091

PIERCE, J LEA, direct mail advertising consultant; b. Des Moines, Oct. 7, 1957; d. Richard Eugene and L. Ann (O'Bleanus) P. B.S., MacMurray Coll., 1978; M.A., Sangamon State U., 1979. Reporter Record-Herald, Indianola, Iowa, 1979-80; asst. pres. sec. NOW, Springfield, Ill., 1980; copywriter Scott, Foresman & Co., Glenview, Ill., 1981-82; sr. copywriter Bradford Exchange, Niles, Ill., 1982-84; v.p., creative dir. PDM, Inc., Northfield, Ill., 1984-85; founder, owner Lea Pierce, Wordsmith, Evanston, Ill., 1985—; co-founder, prin. Sisters of Cinema, TV and Film Scriptwriting, 1985—; creative cons. L.E. Kelley Mktg., Bloomington, Minn., 1983—. Mem. Nat. Assn. Female Execs., Chgo. Assn. Direct Mktg. (creative exchange membership com.), Womens' Direct Response Group, NOW (founder South Lake chpt. 1981, pres. North Lake chpt. 1981-82, fundraising coms. Ill. 1982-85, Ill. polit. action com. 1983-85). Democrat. Home and Office: 1617 South Blvd Evanston IL 60202

PIERCE, JANIS VAUGHN, insurance executive, consultant; b. Memphis, Dec. 23, 1934; d. Jesse Wynne and Dorothy Arnette (Lloyd) Vaughn; B.A. (univ. scholar), U. Miss., 1956, M.A., 1964; m. Gerald Swetnam Pierce, May 27, 1956; children—Ann Elizabeth Swetnam, John Willard. High sch. tchr., 1957-58; mem. faculty Memphis Univ. Sch., 1964-66, Memphis State U., 1968-75; agt. Aetna Life Ins. Co., Memphis, 1977-80, career supr., 1980—, mgr., 1983, supr. prime/career, 1984, chmn. Aetna Women's Task Force, 1980-85; coordinator agy. tng. Specialist Union Central Life Ins. Co., Memphis, 1985—; v.p., dir. Consultants System, Inc., bus. cons., 1975-84, pres., 1984—. Pres., Women's Resources Center, Memphis, 1974-77; sec. Tenn. chpt. Women's Polit. Caucus, 1975-76; bd. dirs., treas., mem. exec. com. Memphis YWCA, 1979—; mem. Memphis Area Transit Authority, 1982—, chmn. fin. and adminstrn. com., 1983—; pres., bd. dirs. The Support Ctr. Memphis, 1986—, Support Ctrs. Am., 1987—; mem. Tenn. adv. com. U.S. Civil Rights Commn., 1980-85, steering com. Big Break, 1978; mem. adv. bd. Porter Leath Children's Ctr., 1984—, bd. dirs. 1986—. Named Aetna Regionnaire, 1977-82, First Year Top Achiever, 1977; mem. Leadership Memphis, 1981. C.L.U. Mem. Million Dollar Roundtable, 1978, 79, Women Leaders Roundtable, 1978—. CLU. Mem. Nat. Assn. Life Underwriters, Tenn. Life Underwriters Assn., Am. Pub. Transp. Assn. (governing bds. com. 1985—, sec. 1987—, mem. task force transp. for the handicapped, 1987), Women's Life Underwriters Conf. (bd. dirs., pres. 1985), Memphis Life Underwriters Assn. (bd. dirs. 1982, edn. chmn. 1982, pub. service com.

1983, law and legis. chmn. 1984, pres. 1986), Memphis PTA (council 1971-72), Memphis Soc. CLUs, LWV, AAUW, Mortar Bd. (regional coordinator 1972-78), Memphis C.L.U. Assn., C. of C. (ambassador 1980), Mortar Bd., Alpha Lambda Delta, Sigma Delta Pi. Republican. Episcopalian. Club: Le Bonheur (dir.), Memphis State U. Women's (pres. 1978). Home: 4743 Park Ave Memphis TN 38117 Office: Union Cen Life Ins 860 Ridge Lake Blvd #360 Memphis TN 38119

PIERCE, MARIANNE LOUISE, scientific and healthcare products company executive, real estate developer, consultant; b. Atchison, Kans., Apr. 22, 1949; d. James Arthur and Marian Louise (Patton) P.; m. Woodrow Theodore Lewis Jr., June 23, 1973 (div. June 1981). Student, Barnard Coll.; AB, Columbia U., 1970, MBA, 1975. Dep. dir. N.Y. Model Cities, N.Y.C., 1971-73; assoc. corp. fin. Citibank Mcht. Banking, N.Y.C., 1975-77; sr. assoc. Booz Allen Hamilton, N.Y.C., 1977-82; dep. biotechnology dir. Ciba Geigy A.G., Basel, Switzerland, 1982-85; pres. Life Scis. Assocs., Ltd., N.Y.C.; Conn.; Basel; Adelaide, Australia, 1985—; founder, pres. The Patton Cos., 1986—; bd. dirs. Patton Group, N.Y.C. Author: (pamphlet) Developing Biotechnology Strategies for Multinational Corporations, 1985. Mem. Brit. Biotech. Assn., Comml. Devel. Assn. Democrat. Office: Life Scis Assocs Ltd 33 Old Mill Rd New Milford CT 06776

PIERCE, MILDRED LOUISE, librarian; b. Fulton County, Ga., Nov. 30, 1928; d. John Oliver Pierce and Florence Idella (Carr) Sansted; m. Harry Eugene Springer, Oct. 17, 1967; 1 son, Jesse Ladd. B.S. in Edn., SUNY-Geneseo, 1951; M.A. in Librarianship, U. Denver, 1955. Library asst. SUNY-New Paltz, 1951; elem. librarian Hastings Pub. Schs., Hastings-on-the Hudson, N.Y., 1951; library grad. student aide Denver Pub. Library, 1954-55; children's bookmobile librarian Alexander Mitchell Pub. Library, Aberdeen, S.D., 1955-56; librarian Mineral County Sch. Dist., Hawthorne, Nev., 1956-64; adult edn. tchr. Clark County Sch. Dist., Las Vegas, 1964-65; tech. librarian RADSAFE, Reynolds Elec. and Engring. Co., Mercury, Nev., 1965-67; reference cons. Mother Lode Library System, Auburn, Calif., 1967-68; dir. Tech. Info. Service, Hawthorne, 1976—. Author: Nevada Rockfinder, 1970; columnist An Ounce of Prevention, 1973-75; editor Wordwebs, 1979-81. Founder, trustee Walker-Wassuk Arts Alliance, Hawthorne, 1977; founder trustee Preservation Mineral County Courthouse and Flag Chowder and Marching Soc., 1982; candidate Nev. Senate, 1976, Nev. Assembly, 1978, 80. Mem. ALA, NEA, Nev. State Tchrs. Assn., Mineral County Tchrs. Assn., Mineral County Council on Alcohol and Drug Abuse, Nev. Alliance for the Arts, Kappa Delta Pi. Republican. Episcopalian. Home: 674 I St PO Box 1721 Hawthorne NV 89415 Office: Tech Info Service PO Box 1721 Hawthorne NV 89415

PIERCE, SANDRA MARIE, industrial relations specialist; b. Woodstock, Ill., Feb. 26, 1947; d. Kenneth Eugene and Dorothy Margaret (Ritzert) Casey; m. Steven J. Pierce, Sept. 4, 1965; children: Brett Pierce, Rebecca Pierce. BS in Indsl. Tech., So. Ill. U., 1985. Personnel mgr. Guardian Electric Mfg., Woodstock, 1972-79; dir. indsl. relations and material procurement Rae Corp., McHenry, Ill., 1979—. Mem. adv. council Dept. Commerce and Community Affairs, State of Ill.; chmn. pvt. industry council CETA, McHenry, 1981—, JTPA, McHenry, 1985—. Mem. Soc. Mfg. Engrs. (sr.), Am. Prodn. and Inventory Control Soc., McHenry C. of C. (chmn. legis. adv. council 1986—). Republican.

PIERCE, SHARON VALERIUS, financial executive; b. Sharon, Pa., Dec. 7, 1951; d. Carl Elston and Clara Colleen (Morgan) Valerius; m. Walter Lee Pierce, June 26, 1970 (div.); 1 child, Christina. BBA, Fla. Internat. U., 1978. CPA, Fla. Sr. acct. Laventhol & Horwath, Miami, Fla., 1979-81; audit mgr. Deloitte Haskins & Sells, Orlando, Fla., 1981-85; v.p. fin. Delta Capital Corp., Orlando, 1985—, The Charles J. Givens Orgn., Orlando, 1985—. Mem. Am. Inst. CPA's, Nat. Assn. Accts., Fla. Inst. CPA's. Republican. Presbyterian. Office: Delta Capital Corp 520 Crown Oak Centre Dr Longwood FL 32750

PIERCY-PONT, ANN LISA, military officer, educational technologist; b. Tacoma, Nov. 15, 1951; d. Jeff Johnston and Leatha Annabelle (Feeler) Piercy; m. Larry Thomas Moore, Feb. 5, 1970 (div. Dec. 1972); m. Steven Pont, Nov. 23, 1974. AA, Fla. State U., 1974, BA, 1976; MA, Calif. State U., Sacramento, 1981. Cert. USAF tng. instr., 1978. Commd. 2d lt. USAF, 1976, advanced through grades to maj., 1987; occupational analyst Occupational Measurement Ctr., Lackland AFB, 1976-77; instructional system devel. advisor, tng. evaluation officer 323 Flying Tng. Wing, Mather AFB, Calif., 1977-81; E-3 systems instructional system devel. tng. advisor 552 Airborne Warning and Control Wing, Tinker AFB, Okla., 1981-85; chief exportable edn. br., dep. dir. nonresident programs div. sch. systems and logistics, chief evaluation and tech. br. ops. and plans div. Air Force Inst. of Tech., Wright-Patterson AFB, Ohio, 1985—. Mem. Air Force Assn., Am. Soc. Tng. and Devel., Nat. Soc. for Performance and Instrn., Assn. for Edn1. Communications and Tech., NOW (del. 1980). Roman Catholic. Home: 1005 Meadowlark Dr Enon OH 45323 Office: AFIT/XPX Wright-Patterson AFB OH 45433-6583

PIERONEK, JOANN F., nurse; b. Hamtramck, Mich., July 9, 1939; d. Joseph and Mary (Socha) Winiarski; m. Richard Michael Pieronek, Oct. 14, 1961; children: Catherine Frances, Thomas Joseph, Patricia Marie. BSN, Mercy Coll., 1961; MSN, Wayne State U., 1975, postgrad. Staff Pieronek Photographics, Hamtramck, 1955—; assoc. prof. Mercy Coll., Detroit, 1975-86, dean div. of nursing, 1986—; cons. phys. assessment Mercy Hosp., Port Huron, Mich., 1982. Author, editor: (slide/tape) NDC Program, 1980; author: (research) Informed Consent, 1975. Mem. com. nat. alumni, Detroit, 1987, quality evaluation/med. staff com., Detroit, 1987. Recipient Sci. award Bausch and Lomb, Rochester, N.Y., 1957; Wayne State U. scholar, 1974; Mercy Coll. grantee, 1980. Mem. Am. Nurses Assn., Mich. Nurses Assn., Nat. Assn. Pro Life Nurses, Mich. Soc. Instructional Tech., Mich. Assn. Colls. of Nursing, Grosse Pointe Woods (Mich.) War Meml. Assn., Mercy Coll. Alumni Assn. Roman Catholic. Home: 1557 Lochmoor Blvd Grosse Pointe Woods MI 48236 Office: Mercy Coll of Detroit 8200 W Outer Dr Detroit MI 48219

PIERPONT, GLENNA GAIL, energy/gas pipe line co. exec.; b. Bellville, Tex., Mar. 21, 1950; d. Steve A and Eunice S. Gindorf; B.S., Stephen F. Austin State U., 1972; m. William G. Pierpont, June 25, 1972. With, Transco Energy Co., 1973—, mgr. employee relations and personnel adminstrn., Houston, Tex., 1983—. Mem. Houston Personnel Assn., Sigma Kappa (nat. officer). Republican. Presbyterian. Home: 4206 Southwestern St Houston TX 77005 Office: Transco Energy Co PO Box 1396 Houston TX 77251

PIERSANTE, DENISE, marketing executive; b. Detroit, Jan. 9, 1954; d. Joseph Lawrence and Virginia (Grunwald) P.; m. Wilfred Lewis Was II, June 7, 1975 (div. 1981). BA in Communications, Mich. State U., 1978. Tchr. Northwestern Ohio Community Action Commn., Defiance, 1979-80, counselor, 1980-82, job developer, 1982-83; job developer Pvt. Industry Council, Defiance, 1983, job developer coordinator, 1983-84, dir. pub. relations and job devel., 1984-86; market master North Market, Columbus, Ohio, 1986-87; dir. mktg. Richard S. Zimmerman Jr., Columbus, 1987—; cons. Small Bus. Mgmt., Archbold, Ohio, 1985-87; promotion dir. Miss N.W. Ohio Pageant, Defiance, 1985-87; promotion dir. Gallery Jazz Series, 1988, organizer, Prism Awards Competition, 1987; scholarship auction, 1988; pub. relations coordinator Defiance County Social Service Agys., 1981—; author of various grants. Editor Job Tng. Partnership Act newsletter, 1984-86, (newsletter) North Market Soc., 1986-87. Defiance County Social Service Agys. newsletter, 1981-86; Value/Style Community News, 1987—. Organizer Auglaize River Race, Defiance, 1985. Nat. Merit scholar, 1972; recipient Am. Legion Citizenship award, 1969, 72. Mem. Pub. Relations Soc. Am., Nat. Assn. Female Execs., Am. Mktg. Assn., Jaycees (Jaycee of Month 1985). Club: Bus. and Profl. Women (Defiance); Corps de Ballet (Columbus); Conductors (Columbus); Operation Operatics (Columbus). Home: 2363 Meadow Village Dr Worthington OH 43085 Office: 100 S 3d St Suite 414 Columbus OH 43215

PIERSON, KATHLEEN MARY, child care center administrator, consultant; b. Detroit, Apr. 17, 1949; d. Peter and Elsa (Stanke) Kornberger; m. David Alan Pierson, Aug. 23, 1980 (div. Nov. 1981). A.S., Macomb Coll., Mich., 1974; B.S., Central U. Mich., 1976. Model, Detroit, 1970-74, also piano player, lounges; horse jockey, Detroit, 1974-78; recreation therapist Rehab. Inst., Detroit, 1978-81; exec. dir. Kreative Korners, Warren, Mich., 1981—, founder Kreative Korners Adult Day Care Ctr., 1987; cons. low income child care centers Mich., 1986—. Bd. dirs. Macomb Coll., Warren, Mich., 1984—. Guest of Honor, Mich. Opportunity Soc., 1985, Easter Seal Soc., 1976; speaker United Found., 1987, 88. Mem. South Warren Community Orgn., Nat. Exec. Female Assn., Internat. Platform Assn. (speech competition). Lutheran. Avocations: Doberman breeding; playing classical music; horseback riding. Home: 34160 Ryan Rd Sterling Heights MI 48077 Office: Kreative Korners Inc 22021 Memphis St Warren MI 48091

PIERZCHALA-DESMOND, ANNE MARIE, chemist; b. San Francisco, Mar. 4, 1956; d. Andrew Matthew and Julia (Guidotti) Pierzchala; m. Dennis Patrick Desmond, Sept. 27, 1986. BS, U. Nev., 1978. Analytical chemist Western Testing Labs., Sparks, Nev., 1979-80; analytical and research chemist U.S. Bur. Mines, Reno, 1980—, asst. fed. women's program mgr., 1982-84, fed. women's program mgr., 1984-87; chairperson women's week Interagy. EEO Counsel, Reno, 1984-85. Vol. counselor Planned Parenthood of no. Nev., Reno, 1982—; vol. United Blood Services, Reno, 1987. Mem. Pi Mu Epsilon, Phi Kappa Phi. Democrat. Roman Catholic. Home: 965 Gear St Reno NV 89503

PIGNATELLI, DEBORA BECKER, vocational counselor, state legislator; b. Weehawken, N.J., Oct. 25, 1947; d. Edward and Frances (Fishman) Becker; m. Michael Albert Pignatelli, Aug. 22, 1971; children: Adam Becker, Benjamin Becker. AA, Vt. Coll., 1967; BA, U. Denver, 1969. Exec. dir. Girl's Club Greater Nashua, N.H., 1975-77; dir. tenant services Nashua Housing Authority, 1979-80; vocat. counselor Comprehensive Rehab. Assocs., Bedford, N.H., 1982-85; specialist job placement Crawford & Co., Bedford, 1985—; mem. N.H. Ho. of Reps., Concord, 1986—; mem. Children, Youth and Elderly Com.; del. Am. Council of Young Polit. Leaders, Fed. Republic Germany, 1987. Mem. Nashua Peace Ctr., 1980—; asst. coach Little League Baseball, Nashua, 1987—; mem. steering com. Gephardt for U.S. Pres. campaign, N.H., 1987-88; del. to Dem. Nat. Conv., 1988. Mem. Nat. Order Women Legislators, N.H. Order Women Legislators. Democrat. Office: NH Legislature Main St Concord NH 03301

PIGOTT, IRINA VSEVOLODOVNA, educational administrator; b. Blagoveschensk, Russia, Dec. 4, 1917; came to U.S., 1939, naturalized, 1947; d. Vsevolod V. and Sophia (Reprev) Obolianinoff; m. Nicholas Prischepenko, Feb. 1945 (dec. Nov. 1964); children—George, Helen. Grad. YMCA Jr. Coll., Manchuria, 1937; B.A., Mills Coll., 1942; cert. social work U. Calif.-Berkeley, 1944; M.A. in Early Childhood Edn., NYU, 1951. Dir.-owner Parsons Nursery, Flushing, N.Y., 1951-59; dir. Montessori Sch., N.Y.C., 1966-67; dir., tchr. Day Care Ctr., Harlem, 1967-68; dir.-owner East Manhattan Sch. for Bright and Gifted, N.Y.C., 1968—; organizer, pres., exec. dir. Non-Profl. Children's Performing Arts Guild, Inc., N.Y.C., 1961-65, 87—. Organizer Back Yard Theatre, Bayside, N.Y., 1959-61. Democrat. Greek Orthodox. Avocations: music, dance, theatre, art, sports. Office: East Manhattan Sch 208-210 E 18th St New York NY 10003

PIKE, JOAN ELIZABETH, sales executive; b. Columbus, Ohio, Aug. 20, 1956; d. Eugene Charles and Sally Ann (Jedlicka) Herzog; m. James Frederick Pike, Sept. 27, 1980; children: Mary Elizabeth, Madeleine Ann. BS, Mich. State U., 1978. Registered dietitian. Renal dietitian Hurley Med. Ctr., Flint, Mich., 1979-81; clin. specialist Flint Osteo. Hosp., 1981-82; chief clin. dietitian Greater Flint Health Maintenance Orgn., 1983-87; med. sales rep. Mead Johnson div. Bristol Myers, Flint, 1982-83, 87—; clin. advisor Kith Haven, Inc., Flint, 1981-84; mem. Genesee County Nutrition Council, Flint, 1981-87. Author: Exterior Designs Weight Management Program, 1986; diet manual Greater Flint Health Maintenance Orgn., 1985. Mem. edn. com. Flint and Swartz Creek Community Schs., 1985-87; mem. Nature Conservancy, Portland, 1987—. Mem. Maine Dietetic Assn., Am. Dietetic Assn., Jr. League Portland, Phi Eta Sigma. Home and Office: 12 Ludlow St Portland ME 04103

PIKE, PRISCILLA RAE, small business owner; b. Los Angeles, Dec. 7, 1930; d. Raymond Bruce and Amy Elizabeth (Dunaway) Linganfield; student schs. Glendale, Calif.; m. William F. Pike, Aug. 7, 1949; children: Pamela R. Pike Plowman, Lauri E. Pike Miller, Gary W., Thomas C. Various positions Ventura County (Calif.) dist. atty's office, superior ct.; county clk. Ventura County Bd. Suprs., 1970-75; hearing reporter Calif. Coastal Commn., Ventura, 1977-87; founder Priscilla Pike Ct. Reporter Services, Ventura, Walesnburg, Colo., 1978—; ct. reporter coordinator Pacific Career Coll., West Los Angeles, Calif.; conf. planner, author; participant confs. U.S., Can. Bd. dirs. Friends of Commn. for Women Ventura County. Mem. Nat. Ct. Reporters Assn., Calif. Ct. Reporters Assn., Nat. Assn. Female Execs. Christian Scientist. Republican. Office: 3639 E Harbor Blvd Suite 203-A Ventura CA 93001

PILAO, LEONORA CARRIAGA, health care administrator; b. Lucena City, Philippines, Feb. 20, 1951; came to U.S., 1973, naturalized, 1981; d. Norberto Pamposa and Natalia Laloon (Carriaga) P.; B.S. in Nursing, U. of the Philippines, 1972; postgrad. in gerontology Rutgers U., 1976, U. Pa., 1980; postgrad. in philosophy Manhattan Sch. Practical Philosophy and Econs., 1984—. Head nurse Senator Convalescent Center, Atlantic City, 1973-74; nursing supr. Senator Manor Nursing Home, Atlantic City, 1974-75; dir. in-service edn. Shore Manor Nursing Home, Atlantic City, 1975-76, asst. dir. nursing, 1976-77; dir. nursing services SCA Intermediate Care Facility, Atlantic City, 1977-86, alternate adminstr., 1979-86, adminstr. King David Care Ctr. Atlantic City, 1986—; mgmt. cons. Golden Crest Convalescent Center, Atlantic City, 1978-80, 85—; chmn. com. investigating impact of casino industry to health care delivery Atlantic County, 1980; participant Kellogg Found. nursing adminstrn. tng. program U. Pa., 1982, Soviet-Am. Gerontol. Nursing Study Tour, 1982; guest speaker civic orgn. Mem. Am. Nurses Assn., N.J. Assn. In-Service Edn. and Tng., N.J. League of Nursing, Nat. Assn. Female Execs. Condr. research on efficacy of influenza vaccine among elderly, 1980. Office: 166 S South Carolina Ave Atlantic City NJ 08401

PILIA, PATRICIA ANN, pathology educator, researcher; b. East Orange, N.J., May 10, 1948; d. Frank Joseph and Catherine Vivian (Moretti) P. BA, Boston U., 1970; MS, Med. U. of S.C., 1978, PhD, 1980. Supr. lab. research Med. U. S.C., Charleston, 1973-83, asst. prof. pathology and lab. medicine, 1983—. Contbr. articles to profl. jours. Postdoctoral fellow Nat. Kidney Found., 1980-82; recipient Julia P. Aptner award Assn. Women in Sci., 1980. Mem. Am. Soc. Nephrology, Electron Microscopy Soc. of Am., Sigma Xi, Am. Assn. Pathologists, Southeastern Electron Microscopy Soc., S.C. Electron Microscopy Assn., Assn. Women Sci., AAAS, Am. Assn. U. Women. Republican. Roman Catholic. Office: Med U SC 171 Ashley Ave Charleston SC 29425

PILIERE, DIANE FRANCINE, business executive; b. Camden, N.J., July 21, 1940; d. John and Mary (DiSalvio) P. B.S. in Social Sci., St. Joseph's U., 1970; M.S. in Bus. and Psychology, Miami U., 1973; doctoral candidate Pace U. Adminstr., RCA Corp., Camden, N.J., 1958-72; mgmt. devel. specialist Gen. Dynamics, Groton, Conn., 1973-77; dir. Singer Electronics Systems div., Wayne, N.J., 1977—. Bd. dirs. John C. Crystal Ctr., N.Y.C., 1982—, CETA Industry Council, Paterson, N.J., 1981-82. Recipient Tribute to Women in Industry award YWCA Ridgewood (N.J.), 1982. Mem. Am. Soc. Tng. and Devel., Am. Mgmt. Assn. Home: 180 Walnut St Montclair NJ 07042 Office: Singer Electronics Div 164 Totowa Rd Wayne NJ 07474-0975

PILIPUF, SHARON, commercial services executive; b. Chgo., Jan. 29, 1964; d. Nick Michael and Patricia Dale (Resepa) P. Student, Coll. DuPage, 1982, No. Ill. U., 1982-84; BA in Mktg., North Cen. Coll., 1987. Adminstr., mgr. Pilipuf-Grist & Assocs., Elk Grove, Ill., 1984—. Researcher, creative dir. Advt. Campaigns, 1987. Mem. Nat. Assn. Female Execs., Sigma Chi little sisters. Republican. Roman Catholic. Office: Pilipuf-Grist & Assocs 2550 United Ln Elk Grove IL 60007

PILL, CYNTHIA JOAN, social worker; b. N.Y.C., Mar. 30, 1939; d. Alfred and Edna (Strauss) Fruchtman; B.S. cum laude, Jackson Coll., Tufts U., 1961; MS, in Social Work, Simmons Coll. 1963; PhD in Social Work, 1988; m. Robert Pill, July 29, 1961; children—Laura, Daniel, Karen. Registered clin. social worker. Clin. social worker Concord (Mass.) Family Service, 1965-78; coordinator family life edn. Family Counseling Service, Newton, Mass., 1979-83; pvt. practice clin. social work, Newton, Mass., 1979—; co-founder, clin. social worker Remarriage Counseling Collaborative, Newton, Mass., 1981-87; cons. Hospice of the Good Shepherd Inc., 1979-84. Vol. coordinator Hospice at Home, Sudbury, Mass., 1986—. Lic. ind. clin. social worker. Mem. Mass. Acad. Clin. Social Work, Inc., Nat. Assn. Social Workers, Soc. Family Therapy and Research, Nat. Assn. Social Workers, Register Clin. Social Workers. Contbr. to profl. publs. Address: 14 Mason Rd Newton Center MA 02159

PILLING, JANET KAVANAUGH, lawyer; b. Akron, Ohio, Sept. 5, 1951; d. Paul and Marjorie (Logue) Kavanaugh; m. Martin Jolles, Mar. 6, 1987; 1 child, Madeleine Sloan Langdon. B.A., Ohio Wesleyan U., 1973; J.D., U. Mo., 1975; LL.M., Villanova U., 1985. Bar: Pa. 1976, U.S. Tax Ct. 1976, U.S. Dist. Ct. (ea. dist.) Pa. 1976. Atty., Schnader, Harrison, Segal & Lewis, Phila., 1976-83; gen. counsel Kistler-Tiffany Cos., Wayne, Pa., 1983—. Mem. ABA, Phila. Bar Assn., Pa. Bar Assn., Montgomery County Estate Planning Council, Chester County Estate Planning Council, Phi Beta Kappa, Phi Delta Phi. Office: Kistler Tiffany Cos Suite 706 987 Old Eagle School Rd Wayne PA 19087

PILOT-PETERS, NORMA LOU, principal, educator, choir director; b. Mt. Clemens, Mich., Nov. 27, 1942; d. Arthur Louis and Elsie Lydia (Kempf) Ploetz; m. Louis Otto Peters Jr., Dec. 26, 1982; 1 stepchild, Mark Andrew. BA, Concordia Coll., 1966; Grad., Nat. Tchr's. Coll., Evanston, Ill., 1974; postgrad., Alverno Coll., 1981, U. Wis., Milw. Tchr. Elm Grove (Wis.) Luth. Sch., 1964-65; kindergarten tchr. Resurrection Luth. Sch., Chgo., 1966-67; tchr. Milw. Pub. Schs., 1967-68, 1969-78; tchr. Mo. Pub. Schs., University City, 1968-69; prin., founder, tchr. Holy Comforter Luth. Sch., Balt., 1978-81; prin. St. Peter's Christian Day Sch., Balt., 1981—; founder, master tchr., organizer Primary Individualized Learning Ctr., Allen Field Sch., 1969-71; mem. Md. Synod Lay Profl. Com., Balt., 1986-87. Mem. Luth. Prins. Conf., Balt., 1978—, speaker, 1982; founder, project dir. Learning Early to Achieve Potential Pre-Sch. Pub. Schs., Milw., 1971-76; speaker alternative edn. conf. Webster Coll., Webster Grove, Mo., 1971, Wis. Reading Conv., Milw., 1971, Luth. Spl. Edn. Dist., St. Louis, 1969; pres. Village Luth. Council; charter mem. Village Luth. Ch., Milw., 1967—. Mem. Am. Luth. Edn. Assn., Milw. Tchrs. Assn. Assn., Assn. Early Childhood Edn. Home: 3704 Delverne Rd Baltimore MD 21218 Office: St Peter's Christian Day Sch 7910 Belair Rd Baltimore MD 21236

PILOUS, BETTY SCHEIBEL, nurse; b. Cleve., July 30, 1948; d. Raymond W. and Dorothy E. (Groth) S.; m. Lee Alan Pilous, Sept. 11, 1970; 1 child. Diploma in nursing Huron Rd. Hosp., Cleve., 1970. RN, Ohio; student St. Joseph's Coll.; cert. med.-surg. nurse, nursing adminstr. Nurse Huron Rd. Hosp., Cleve., 1970-71, Hillcrest Hosp., Cleve., 1974-77; head nurse, relief supr. Oak Park Hosp., Oakwood, Ohio, 1977-81; head nurse med.-surg. Bedford Hosp., Ohio, 1981-87; dir. med.-surg. nursing Meridia Euclid Hosp., Euclid, Ohio; instr. ARC, Am. Heart Assn.; mem. nursing standatds com. Community Hosp. of Bedford. Mem. health and safety com. Twinsburg Schs., Ohio, 1984—, mem. curriculum com., 1981-83; chairperson standards com. Community Hosp. of Bedford; counselor jr. high youth 1st Congl. Ch., Twinsburg. Mem. Ohio Hosp. Assn., Nat. League Nursing, Southeast Cleve. Mid Mgrs. Networking Group. Lodge: Order Eastern Star. Avocations: aerobics, hiking. Office: Euclid Hosp 18901 N Lake Shore Blvd Euclid OH 44143

PINCH, PATRICIA ANN, insurance agent; b. Port Hueneme, Calif., Oct. 8, 1947; d. William Claude and Lois (Monroe) Pinch; m. Vincent J. Lupo, Apr. 6, 1973 (dec. 1975). B.S. in Med. Tech., Med. Coll. Va., 1969. Human cytogenetic researcher Bklyn. Hosp., 1970-72; animal genetic researcher Mt. Sinai Hosp., N.Y.C., 1972-74; med. tech. supr., owner Vee-Jay Clin. Labs., Bklyn., 1974-86; supr. G.J.L. Clin. Lab., Amityville, N.Y., 1986-87; dist. agt. Prudential Ins., 1987—. Mem. Am. Soc. Clin. Pathologists. Roman Catholic. Office: 124 Kime Ave North Babylon NY 11703

PINDALE, KAREN LEIGH, finance professional; b. Bessemer, Ala., Apr. 14, 1960; d. Robert Edward and Shirley Anne (Posey) P. BSBA, U. Ala., Huntsville, 1983; postgrad., U. Ala., 1985-86. Adminstrv. asst. Intergraph Corp, Huntsville, 1984-85; research asst. dept. fin. U. Ala., Tuscaloosa, 1985-86; sales asst. to v.p. Howard, Weil, Labouisse, Friedrichs subs. Legg, Mason, Wood, Walker, Huntsville, 1986—. Mem. Assn. MBA Execs., Nat. Assn. for Female Execs., U. Ala.-Huntsville Alumnae Assn., Kappa Delta Alumnae Assn. Office: Howard Weil Labouisse Friedrichs 2705 Artie St Suite 40 Huntsville AL 35805

PINE, LOIS ANN HASENKAMP, nurse; b. Cheyenne, Wyo., Feb. 21, 1950; d. Clifford Norbert and Julie Adda (Younglund) Hasenkamp; m. Julius William Pine Jr., Feb. 16, 1974; children: Margaret Ann, Julius William III, Lawrence Michael. BS, U. Wyo., 1976, postgrad., 1986—. RN. From staff nurse to charge nurse Ivinson Meml. Hosp., Laramie, Wyo., 1976-86. Mem. St. Lawrence Council of Cath. Women, Laramie, 1980—, St. Cecilia's Group, Laramie, 1980—, Albany County PTA, Laramie, 1985—, Crisis Pregnancy Program; asst. den header Cub Scouts. Mem. Nurses Assn. Am. Coll. of Ob-Gyns. (sect. vice chmn. 1980-86), Am. Acad. Pediatrics (perinatal pediatrics dist. VIII sect.), Nat. Assn. Neonatal Nurses (charter), Rebel Bowling Leauge, Sigma Theta Tau. Democrat. Avocations: reading, knitting, crocheting, bowling, basketball. Home: 1614 Whitman Laramie WY 82070

PINEDA, MARIANNA, sculptor, educator; b. Evanston, Ill., May 10, 1925; d. George and Marianna (Dickinson) Packard; m. Harold Tovish, Jan. 14, 1946; children: Margo, Aaron, Nina. Student, Cranbrook Acad. Art, summer 1942, Bennington Coll., 1942-43, U. Calif.-Berkeley, 1943-45, Columbia U., 1945-46, Ossip Zadkine Sch. Drawing and Sculpture, Paris, 1949-50. instr. sculpture Newton Coll. Sacred Heart, 1972-75, Boston Coll., 1975-77; vis. assoc. prof. Boston U., 1974, 78, 83, 84, 85, 86, 87. Exhibited solo shows: Walker Art Ctr., Mpls., 1952, Currier Gallery, Vt., 1954, De Cordova Mus., Lincoln, Mass., 1954, 63, 64, 72, 86, Premier Gallery, Mpls., 1963, Swetzoff Gallery, Boston, 1953, 56, 64, Honolulu Acad. Art, 1970, Alpha Gallery, Boston, 1972, Newton Coll., (Mass.), 1972, Bumpus Gallery, Duxbury, Mass., 1972, Contemporary Art Ctr., Honolulu, 1982, Pine Manor Coll., 1984; group shows: Galerie 8 Paris, 1950, Met. Mus. Art, N.Y.C., 1951, Whitney Mus. Am. Art, N.Y.C., 1953, 54, 55, 57, 59, Boston Arts Festival, 1957, 58, 60, 62, 63, 65, Pitts. Internat., 1958, Mus. Modern Art., N.Y.C., 1960, Art Inst. Chgo., 1959, 61, Nat. Inst. Arts & Letters, 1961, World's Fair, 1964, De Cordova Mus., 1963, 64, 1972, 75, 87, Sculptors Guild, N.Y.C., 1967-87, Pine Manor Coll, Mass., Pa. State U., 1974, Simmons Coll., 1980, SUNY-Buffalo, 1983, Fitchburg Mus. Art, Mass., 1984, Nat. Acad. Design, 1985, 86, Newton Art Ctr., 1985, Boston U. Art Gallery, 1986, Shulman Scuplture Pk., White Plains, N.Y., 1986, Fed. Res. Gallery, Boston, Port History Mus., Phila., 1987, Judi Rotenberg Galler, Boston, 1987, 88, A.I.R. Gallery, N.Y.C., 1988, Alchemie Gallery, Boston, 1987, Nat. Acad. Design, NY.C., 1985, 86, 87, Boston Artist Union Invitational, 1986, Brockton Art Ctr., Ma., 1987, Bunting Inst., Fed. Reserve Gallery, Boston, 1986, others; represented permanent collections, Walker Art Ctr., Mus. Fine Arts, Boston Williams Coll., (Mass.), Dartmouth coll., Hanover, N.H., Addison Gallery, Andover, Mass., Munson-Williams-Proctor Inst., Ithaca, N.Y., Fogg Art Mus., Cambridge, Mass., Radcliff Coll., Boston Pub. Library, Wadsworth Athenaeum, Hartford, Conn. State of Hawaii, NAD, 1983, 84, 85; commd. work, Twirling, Bronze figure group, East Boston Housing for Elderly, The Spirit of Lili'uokalani bronze, Hawaii State Capitol. Home: 380 Marlborough St Boston MA 02115 Office: care Judi Rotenberg 130 Newbury St Boston MA 02116

PINES, LOIS G., state legislator; b. Malden, Mass.; m. Joseph Pines; 2 children. BA, Barnard Coll., 1960; JD, U. Cin. Law Sch., 1963. Corp. tax atty. 1964-72; alderman City of Newton, Mass., 1971-73; mem. Mass. Ho. of Reps., 1973-78; regional dir. New England Fed. Trade Commn., 1979-81; mem. Mass. State Senate, 1986—. Address: 40 Helene Rd Newton MA 02168 *

PINGREE, DIANNE, publisher, video producer; b. Dallas, B.F.A. magna cum laude, So. Meth. U., 1976; A.A. summa cum laude, Richland Coll., 1974; m. Harlan Pingree. Freelance journalist, 1974-76; editor, pub. Tex. Woman Mag., Dallas, 1977-80; pres. Tex. Woman, Inc., Dallas, 1980-85; owner, operator Dianne Pingree & Assocs., Dallas, 1985—. Recipient Women Helping Women award Women's Center Dallas, 1980. Mem.

Women in Communications (Matrix award 1979), Exec. Women Dallas (sec., bd. mem. 1981-85, 87-88, v.p. 1982, pres. 1983-84), Dallas Communications Council, Dallas Press Club (Gridiron Show award 1982), Tex. Hist. Assn., Dallas Hist. Assn., Dallas Com. Foreign Visitors, AAUW, Sigma Delta Chi. Office: 5551 Yale Blvd Dallas TX 75206

PINKERTON, HELEN JEANETTE, health care executive; b. Chattanooga, Mar. 17, 1956; d. Jesse Robert and Irene Louise (Boyd) Pinkerton. BS, U. Tenn.-Knoxville, 1979, MPH, 1980. Intern, Southeast Regional Health Dept., Chattanooga, 1979, Alex B. Shipley Health Dept., Knoxville, 1980; coordinator hypertension Alton Park Health Ctr., Chattanooga, 1981—; council mem. Task Force on Prevention of Handicapping Conditions, Chattanooga, 1984—. Contbr. to Tenn. Hypertension Control Manual, 1984. Chaplain Joyful Noise, Chattanooga, 1974—; mem. Bapt. Student Union, Community Services Club, 1986—; dir. youth group, 1983-85, task force on prevantion of handicapping conditions, 1984-86, Chattanooga Jaycees. Doak scholar, 1977. Mem. Tenn. Soc. Pub. Health, Nat. Assn. Female Execs., Women Network Inc., Hypertension Coalition (chmn. 1984—), Alton Park C. of C. (council mem. 1982-86), Alpha Kappa Alpha, Gamma Sigma Sigma. Democrat. Avocations: walking, reading, singing, jogging. Home: 4103 Dayton Blvd Apt D-80 Chattanooga TN 37415 Office: Alton Park Health Ctr 100 E 37th St Chattanooga TN 37410

PINKHAM, ELEANOR HUMPHREY, university librarian; b. Chgo., May 7, 1926; d. Edward Lemuel and Grace Eleanor (Cushing) Humphrey; AB, Kalamazoo Coll., 1948; MS in Library Sci. (Alice Louise LeFevre scholar), Western Mich. U., 1967; m. James Hansen Pinkham, July 10, 1948; children—Laurie Sue, Carol Lynn. Pub. services librarian Kalamazoo Coll., 1967-68, asst. librarian, 1969-70, library dir., 1971—; vis. lectr. Western Mich. U. Sch. Librarianship, 1970-84; mem. adv. bd., 1977-81, also adv. bd. Inst. Cistercian Studies Library, 1975-80. Mem. ALA (chair coll. library sect. 1988-89), AAUP, Mich. Library Assn. (pres. 1983-84, chmn. acad. div. 1977-78), Mich. Library Consortium (exec. council 1974-82, chmn. 1977-78, Mich. Librarian of Yr 1986), OCLC Users Council, Beta Phi Mu. Home: 2519 Glenwood Dr Kalamazoo MI 49008 Office: 1200 Academy St Kalamazoo MI 49007

PINKHAM, ROBIN REMICK, financial executive; b. Bridgeport, Conn., May 5, 1944; d. Irving Grant and Theresa Helena (Busci) Pinkham; A.B. in English, Conn. Coll. Women, 1965; postgrad. N.Y. Inst. Fin., 1965-66. Registered investment advisor. With Paine, Webber, N.Y.C., 1965-68, Scudder, Stevens & Clark, N.Y.C., 1969-72, Wood Walker, N.Y.C., 1972-73; asst. treas. pension fund investment mgr. Nat. Forge Co., N.Y.C., 1973-87; 1st v.p. E.F. Hutton, 1987—. Vol., Lighthouse for the Blind, 1966-68. Mem. N.Y. Soc. Security Analysts, Fin. Analysts Fedn. Republican. Home: 245 E 63d St Apt 1127 New York NY 10021 Office: 17 Battery Pl Suite 314 New York NY 10004

PINKNEY, NAOMI DUPREE, educator; b. Pitt County, N.C., July 13, 1931. BS in Elem. Edn., Winston-Salem (N.C.) U., 1954; MA in Adminstrv. Supervision and Spl. Edn., Columbia U, 1967. Tchr. St. Paul (N.C.) Elem. Sch., 1955-58, Elem. Sch., Rockaway, N.Y., 1958-59; tchr. spl. edn. Staten Island (N.Y.) Devel. Ctr., 1968-74, asst. prin., supr. tchrs., 1974; tchr. N.Y. Dept. Spl. Edn., 1959—, N.Y.C. Pub. Schs.; dir. youth, bd. dirs. Mt. Lebanon Bapt Ch., 1974-87. Office: 2760 Victory Blvd Staten Island NY 10314

PINNELL-STEPHENS, JUNE ALICIA, information broker, consultant; b. Dayton, Ohio, June 11, 1948; d. Earl Emery and Helen Marie (Fedash) Pinnell; m. Dennis James Stephens, Jan. 3, 1982. BA, Pomona Coll., 1971; MLS, U. Wash., 1972. Cert. librarian, Wash., cert. tchr., Alaska. Children's librarian King County Library System, Seattle, 1972-76; coordinator children's services Bellingham (Wash.) Pub. Library, 1976-80; librarian Mat-Su Community Coll., Palmer, Alaska, 1980-82; newsroom librarian Daily News-Miner, Fairbanks, Alaska, 1982-83; prin. Borealis Research, Fairbanks, 1983-85; sr. research assoc. ASK* Info. Search, Fairbanks, 1985-87; prin. Profl. Info. Resources, Fairbanks, 1987—; librarian Fairbanks North Star Borough Pub. Library, Fairbanks, 1988—; adj. faculty Western Wash. U., Bellingham, 1978-79; instr. U. Alaska, Palmer, Kodiak, Fairbanks, 1980-81, 84; chmn. Alaska We the People Project, Fairbanks, 1984—; cons. Northwest Arctic Sch. Dist., Kotzebue, Alaska, 1985-87. Contbr. articles to profl. jours.; editor: AkLA Intellectual Freedom Manual, 1985. Mem. library com. Mayor's Transition Task Force, Fairbanks, 1985; del. Dem. Dist. Conv., Fairbanks, 1986; mem. gov.'s celebration commn. U.S. Constitutional Bicentennial, 1986—; bd. dirs. Fairbanks Symphony Assn. Mem. Alaska Library Assn. (chmn. IFC 1984-85, v.p., pres. 1985-87), Wash. Library Assn. (chmn. Children's and Young Adults Service Interest Group 1976-78, 2d v.p. 1979-80), ALA (chmn. Wash. membership com. 1979-80), Pacific Northwest Library Assn. (chmn. Intellectual Freedom Interest Group 1986—), Alaska Civil Liberties Union (bd. dirs. 1987—), Dance Amnium. Home and Office: 3140 Roden Ln Fairbanks AK 99709

PINO, LITA VAZQUEZ, marketing consultant; b. Havana, Cuba, Jan. 1, 1951; came to U.S., 1960; d. Eugenio A. and Maria Teresa (Garcia-Montes) Vazquez; m. J. Pino, 1969 (div. 1981); children—George, Lianne. B.B.A. with honors, U. Miami, 1972, postgrad., 1980. Project specialist U. Miami (Fla.), Coral Gables, 1977-80; coordinator copywriting Cons. Pharm. Advt., Key Biscayne, Fla., 1980-81; mng. cons. M.E.T.A., Pub. Relations Cons., Miami, Fla., 1981-82; mktg. project mgr. Paramount Internat. Coin Corp., Miami, 1982-83; mktg. mgr. Interval Internat., South Miami, 1983-84; with Mgmt. Consultants of South Fla., 1984—. Mem. Am. Mktg. Assn., Nat. Assn. Female Execs., Am. Mgmt. Assn. Republican. Roman Catholic. Home: 11400 SW 94th Ave Miami FL 33176 Office: Mgmt Cons South Fla 9951 SW 108th St Miami FL 33176

PINSKER, ESSIE LEVINE, sculptor, former advertising and public relations executive; b. N.Y.C.; d. Harris and Sophia (Feldman) Levine; m. Sidney Pinsker; children: Susan Harris, Seth Howard. BA, Bklyn. Coll.; postgrad., Columbia U., NYU, New Sch. for Social Research, Art Students League, 1955, Cambridge (Eng.) U., 1985. Former buyer Ohrbach's, N.Y.C., Arkwright, N.Y.C.; former editor Woman's Wear Daily, N.Y.C.; former press. dir. Am. Symphony Orch., N.Y.C.; pres. Essie Pinsker Advt. Assocs., Inc., N.Y.C., 1960-82; guest editor Teen Merchandiser mag., Infant's and Children's Rev.; editor travel, beauty and fashion Woman Golfer mag.; lectr., instr. Fashion Inst. of Tech.; contbg. journalist N.Y. Times. One-woman shows include Bodley Gallery, N.Y.C., 1981, Vorpal Gallery, N.Y.C., 1987; exhibited in group shows at Met. Life, N.Y.C., 1969, Huntington (N.Y.) Art League, 1977, C.W. Post Ctr., Old Westbury, N.Y., 1978, North Shore Arts Ctr., Manhasset, N.Y., 1980, Allied Artists of Am., N.Y.C., 1980, Lever Bros., N.Y.C., 1982, Knickerbocker Artists, N.Y.C., 1982, Cadme Gallery, Phila., 1984, River Gallery, Westport, Conn., 1984, Clark Whitney, Lenox, Mass., 1985, Images Gallery, South Norwalk, Conn., 1987, Arco Internat. Art Fair, Madrid, 1988, Konstmassan Internat. Art Fair, Stockholm, 1988, Galleri Atrium, Stockholm, 1988, Galerie Atrium, Marbella, Spain, 1988; represented in permanent collections Everson Mus., Syracuse, N.Y., Aldrich Mus. Contemporary Art, Ridgefield, Conn., Okla. Art Ctr., Oklahoma City, Minn. Mus. Art, St. Paul, Mus. Arts and Scis., Daytona Beach, Fla., Vassar Mus., Poughkeepsie, N.Y., Nat. Art Inst., Warsaw, Poland, New Sch., N.Y.C., Pace U., N.Y.C., Necca Mus., Brooklyn, Conn., Lincoln Ctr. Fordham U., N.Y.C., Hinkhouse Collection, Eureka (Ill.) Coll.; represented in corp. collections Devon, Inc., N.Y.C., Judy Bond, Inc., N.Y.C., Regina Porter, Inc., N.Y.C., Paramount Group, Los Angeles, Joseph P. Day Realty Corp., N.Y.C., Rubenstein Planning Corp., N.Y.C., Queensboro Steel Corp., Wilmington, N.C., Southerland Tours, St. Croix, V.I.; exec. producer film Pupae (Cine Eagle award). Recipient Knickerbocker Artist's 24th ann. exhbn. sculpture award, Met. Life sculpture award. Mem. Nat. Mus. Women in the Arts, Internat. Sculpture Ctr., Artist's Equity, Fashion Group N.Y., Advt. Women N.Y., Fashion Coalition N.Y. Address: 8 Peter Cooper Rd New York City NY 10010

PINSKER, PENNY (PANGEOTA) COLLIAS, television producer; b. Miami, Fla., Aug. 22, 1942; d. Theodore Peter and Agatha Madge (Bridgeman) Collias; m. Lewis Harry Pinsker, Oct. 22, 1968. Grad. high sch., Miami, Fla. Operator So. Bell Telephone Co., Miami, 1960-67; asst. dir. pub. affairs Sta. WCKT-TV, Miami, 1968-70; dir. public affairs Sta. WOR-AM, N.Y.C., 1971-78; reporter documentary and consumer affairs Sta. WTFM, N.Y.C., 1978-81; dir. editorials and sta. services Sta. WWOR-TV, N.Y.C. and Secaucus, N.J., 1981 . Author, editor: (resource directory) Sta. WOR on Crime, 1982 (recipient George Washing Medal Honor Freedom Found.), The Changing Family, 1982 (recipient Broadcast Media award San Francisco State U., Emmy nominated), A Child is Missing, 1983 (recipient Broadcast Media award San Francisco State U., Emmy nominated), Taking the High Out of High School, 1984 (recipient Broadcast Media award San Francisco State U, Angel award Religion Media , Bronze medal Internat. TV and Film Soc.). Media advisor N.J. Crime Prevention Officers Assn.; mem. communication com. Am. Heart Assn. N.J. Affiliation; bd. dirs. Queensboro Soc. Prevention Cruelty Children, 1978-83; pub. mem. N.J. Gov.'s Task Force on Child Abuse and Neglect, 1988—. Recipient disting. service award N.J. Speech-Lang.-Hearing Assn., 1987, community service award Urban League Hudson County, 1986. Mem. Nat. Broadcast Editorial Assn. (bd. dirs. 1986-87), Nat. Broadcast Assn. Community Affairs, Nat. Assn. Female Execs., Advt. Council N.J. (bd. trustees 1986—). Home: Winterwood Farm 270 Kingwood-Locktown Rd Flemington NJ 08822 Office: Sta WWOR-TV 9 Broadcast Plaza Secaucus NJ 07094

PINSKY, ELISABETH, English language professional; b. Yonkers, N.Y., Mar. 11, 1947; d. Jesse Myles and Thelma F. (Weiss) Eisen; m. Stephen Howard Pinsky, June 16, 1968; children: Seth, Kira. BS, NYU, 1969; M Reading, Hofstra U., 1973. Elem. tchr. P.S. 27, Yonkers, 1968-70; reading specialist Tenafly (N.J.) High Sch., 1978-81, Eden Prairie (Minn.) Cen. Mid. Sch., 1981—; mem. Dist. Reading Com. Eden Prairie Schs., 1986—, Dist. Assurance Mastery Com., Eden Prairie. Mem. Internat. Reading Assn., Minn. Reading Assn. Home: 4615 Gaywood Dr Minnetonka MN 55345 Office: Eden Prairie Schs 8025 School Rd Eden Prairie MN 55344

PINTEN, MARLENE JUNE, educator, association administrator; b. Ashland, Wis., July 29, 1932; d. Arthur Emery and Monica Gertrude (Fromholz) P. B.A., Coll. St. Scholastica, 1954; M.A., U. Minn., 1965. Tchr., Pulaski High Sch. (Wis.), 1954-55, Stanbrook Hall, Duluth, Minn., 1955-59, Acad. Holy Angels, Richfield, Minn., 1959-61; social worker Cath. Welfare Services, Mpls., 1961-64; sch. counselor Burnsville High Sch. (Minn.), 1964-66, Lincoln Sr. High Sch., Bloomington, Minn., 1966-74, dir. guidance, 1975-82; pres. Am. Sch. Counselor Assn., Alexandria, Va., 1982-83, cons., 1983-84; counselor Jefferson Sr. High Sch., Bloomington, Minn., 1984—; adv. bd. Campus Access for Disabled Student-Closer Look, Washington, 1983—; bd. dirs. Higher Edn. and the Handicapped, Washington, 1981-83; adv. bd., trustee Citizens Scholarship Found. Am., Concord, N.H., 1983—. Guest editor Nat. Assn. Secondary Sch. Prins. jour NASSP Bull., 1987; contbr. articles to profl. jours. and newsletters. Chmn. Bloomington Youth Commn. City Council (Minn.), 1971; treas., bd. dirs. Family Edn. Ctr., Edina, Minn., 1973-75; adv. bd. Community Resources div. United Way, Greater Hennipen County, Mpls., 1984-87; bd. dirs. Bloomington Scholarship Found., 1974-76, Citizens Scholarship Found.-Midwest, St. Peter, Minn., 1976-80. Recipient Outstanding Community Service award Lions Club, Bloomington, 1974; Leadership and Service award Bloomington Counselors Assn., 1980; Marjorie Quandt award Coll. St. Scholastica, 1982; Outstanding Service award City of Bloomington, 1975. Mem. Am. Assn. Counseling and Guidance (senate 1982, 84 bd. dirs. 1982-83, service award 1983), Am. Sch. Counselor Assn. (governing bd. 1981-84, leadership award 1983), Minn. Sch. Counselor Assn. (bd. dirs. 1971-81, pres. 1978-80, disting. service award 1976-78, leadership award 1980), Minn. Personnel and Guidance Assn. (bd. dirs. 1976-80), AAUW, World Future Soc., Delta Kappa Gamma. Democrat. Roman Catholic. Office: Jefferson Sr High Sch 4001 W 102d St Bloomington MN 55431

PINTO, EMILIE ANNA, corporate executive; b. Vienna, Austria, Sept. 5, 1956; came to U.S., 1961; d. Donald Vincent and Emilie (Cervenka) P.; m. Forest Selby Schmeling, May 10, 1986. BA in Graphic Design, U. Louisville, 1978, BS in Mktg., 1980. Playing pro, mgr. Okolona Racquetball Club, Louisville, 1980-81; mgr. purchasing Fridays Restaurants, Louisville and Washington, 1981-84; nat. event coordinator Corp. Sports Battle, Washington, 1984-85; nat. dir. Challenge Bus. Enterprises, Louisville, 1985—. Local, state and nationally ranked women's racquetball player, 1978-81. Democrat. Roman Catholic. Office: Challenge Bus Enterprises 330 B Distillery Commons Lexington Rd at Payne St Louisville KY 40206-1919

PIOMELLI, MARIA-ROSARIA, architect; b. Naples, Italy, Oct. 24, 1937; d. Alberto and Giuseppina (Trapanese) Angrisano; came to U.S., 1957; B.Arch., M.I.T., 1960; M.Art Accademia d'Arte, Naples, 1955; m. Sergio Piomelli, M.D., Apr. 25, 1956; children—Ascanio Alberto, Fosca Francesca. Designer, Warner Burns Toan & Lunde, Architects, N.Y.C., 1963-69; asso. architect E.H. Grosmann Architect, Rotterdam, Netherlands, 1969-70; project architect I.M. Pei & Partners, N.Y.C., 1971-74; prin. Rosaria Piomelli, Architect, N.Y.C., 1971-79; tchr. design and bldg. systems tech. Pratt Inst., CCNY, 1971-76, chmn. faculty Pratt Inst. Sch. Architecture, Bklyn., 1975-79; dean Sch. Architecture, CCNY, 1980-83; disting. prof. U. Calif.-Berkeley Sch. Architecture, 1984; organizer exhibit Women in Architecture, 1974. Chmn., N.Y.C./AIA Equal Opportunity Com., 1973-75. Recipient HEW design award for Brown U. Sci. Library, 1966; Mudd Found. design award for Oberlin Coll. Learning Center, 1973. Mem. AIA (dir. exec. com. N.Y. chpt. 1977-79). Home: 390 W Broadway New York NY 10012

PION, BARBARA JEAN, investment consultant; b. Springfield, Mass., July 6, 1960; d. Robert Alfred and Marion Grace (Whelan) P. BA cum laude, Boston Coll., 1982. Reconcilement clk. Bradford Trust Co., Boston, 1981-82; supr. adjustment dept. Shawmut Bank of Boston, 1982-83, supr. control dept., 1982-84; portfolio/account adminstr. Brandes Investment Mgmt., Inc. (formerly Brandes Investment Counsel), San Diego, 1985—. Mem. Zool. Soc. of San Diego, 1986—, The Cousteau Soc., San Diego, 1985—; alumni admissions bd., Boston Coll. Mem. Nat. Assn. Female Execs., Am. Assn. Profl. and Exec. Women, Nat. Abortion Rights Action League, Alpha Kappa Delta. Club: Boston Coll. of San Diego. Home: 11075 Canyon Point Ct San Diego CA 92126 Office: Brandes Investment Counsel 12760 High Bluff Dr #160 San Diego CA 92130

PIONE, NONA SMITH, small business owner; b. New Bedford, Mass., Mar. 20, 1943; d. Standish Lyman and Grace (Coughlan) Smith; m. Nicholas René Pione; children: Anthony, Nicholas, Arthur. BS in Pub. Relations, Boston U., 1966. Model Copley Seven Models, Boston, 1961-65; weather girl Channel 7 News, Boston, 1963; owner René Coiffeurs, Inc., Boston, 1964-75, Nona Wig Imports, Boston, 1965-70; direct distbr. Amway Corp., Winchester, Mass., 1972-83; sr. mgr. Calif. Trim, Inc., Fairhaven, Mass., 1984-85; owner Hawaiian Sun, Inc., Fairhaven, 1985—; facilitator Pacific Inst. Self Image Seminars, Brockton, Mass., 1983—; owner Classique Designs, Buzzards Bay, Mass., 1986—; cert. color analyst Crown Assocs., Brockton, 1982-84; judge, mistress of ceremonies over 100 local and state beauty pageants. Named Miss Mass. Miss Am. Pageant 1961. Mem. Suntanning Assn. for Edn., Am. Bus. Women's Assn., Nat. Assn. Female Execs., New Bedford C. of C. Roman Catholic. Home: 614 Washington St Fairhaven MA 02719 Office: Hawaiian Sun Inc 84 Huttleston Ave Fairhaven MA 02719

PIONTEK, BARBARA MARIE, nursing administrator; b. St. Paul, Dec. 4, 1948; d. Edward and Eleanor (Keidrowski) P. Cert. lic. practical nurse, Mpls. Vocat. Inst., 1970; AA in Nursing, Normandale Community Coll., 1976; BS in Health Services Adminstr., Coll. of St. Francis, Joliet, Ill., 1984, MS in Health Services Adminstrn., 1986. RN. Lic. practical nurse Fairview Southdale Hosp., Edina, Minn., 1970-76, RN in coronary care unit, 1976-80, edn. and tng. specialist, 1980-85, quality assurance coordinator, 1985-86; asst. dir. nursing services Fairview Ridges Hosp., Burnsville, Minn., 1986—. Mem. Am. Coll. Healthcare Execs., Nat. Assn. Female Execs. Roman Catholic. Home: 900 W 89th St Bloomington MN 55420 Office: Fairview Ridges Hosp 201 E Nicollet Blvd Burnsville MN 55337

PIPER, KATHLEEN BRYANT, music educator; b. North Little Rock, Ark., Feb. 28, 1941; d. Madison Horace and Lorene Macel (Smith) Bryant; m. Thomas Milton Piper, Aug. 21, 1959; 1 child, Thomas Milton Jr. Student, U. Ark., Little Rock, 1959-62, 69-70; BA in Comprehensive Music, U. Ark., Monticello, 1982; student, U. Cen. Ark., 1961. Organist First Bapt. Ch., Little Rock, 1958; clk.-typist Library U. Ark., Little Rock, 1960; asst. organist Trinity Episcopal Cathedral, Little Rock, 1959-61; clk. Electronic Supply, Little Rock, 1961; organist, choir dir. Highland Heights Presbyn. Ch., Little Rock, 1961; organist 28th St. Meth. Ch., Little Rock, 1962-64; clk.-typist Ark. Library Commn., Little Rock, 1964; organist Gardner Meml. Meth. Ch., North Little Rock, 1964; piano tchr. Monticello, 1970—; substitute organist Park Hill Christian Sci. Ch., North Little Rock, 1970, United Meth. Ch., Newport, Ark., 1971-72, Wood Ave. Presbyn. Ch., Monticello, 1982-87; organist and choir dir. St. Luke's Episc. Ch., N. Little Rock, 1965-70; substitute tchr. Tuckerman Pub. Schs., 1972, Monticello Schs., 1985-86; choir dir. and substitute organist, St. Paul's Episc. Ch., Newport, 1975-77; chmn. Jr. Festival Nat. Fedn. Music Clubs, Monticello Ctr., S.E. Dist., 1984—; counselor Ark. Fedn. Music Clubs, S.E. Dist., 1984—; mem. U. Ark. at Little Rock Choir, 1959-62, U. Ark. at Little Rock U. Select Madrigals, 1960-61. Contbg. mem. Statue of Liberty Ellis Island Found., 1985-86; council mem. Tuckerman Fine Arts Council, 1978-80; active various charitable orgns.; active Boy Scouts Am., Little League; orgnl. chmn. Tuckerman PTO, 1972, pres., 1972-74, reporter, 1975-77, parliamentarian, 1977-80. Recipient Maxine Alexander award Ark. Jaycee Aux., 1974-75, Sparkette Quar. award, 1973, Dist. V.p. award, 1972-73, div. assistance award, 1971-72, Road Runner of Yr., 1970-71, others; U. Ark. scholar, 1961; Minnie L. Moore scholar, 1959-60, 61; Delta Kappa Gamma Soc. scholar, 1959, others. Mem. Am. Coll. Musicians, Nat. Guild Piano Tchrs., Music Tchrs. Nat. Assn., Ark. Music Tchrs. Assn., Ark. Jaycee Aux. (dist. v.p. 1972-73), Tuckerman Jaycee Aux. (pres. 1972-73), Nat. Fedn. Music Clubs, Ark. Fedn. Music Clubs (chmn. Nat. Music Week 1987, Southeast Dist. sec. 1987), Monticello Music Club (pres. 1986-87, v.p. 1983-85, sec. and parliamentarian 1987—), Ark. Archaeol. Soc. Episcopalian. Club: Monticello Music (pres. 1986-87). Address: 382 E Willis St Monticello AR 71655

PIPER, PAT KATHRYN, state senator; b. Delavan, Minn., July 16, 1934; d. Claire I. and Geneva R. (Tibodeau) P. BA, Coll. St. Teresa, Winona, Minn., 1962; MA, Cath. U., 1972. Tchr. St. Augustine Sch., Austin, Minn., 1956-58, St. Francis Sch., Rochester, Minn., 1958-60, St. James (Minn.) Sch., 1960-61; catechist St. Catherine Sch. Ctr., Luverne, Minn., 1961-63, catechist, dir., 1964-67; catechist Area Ctr., Hayfield, Minn., 1963-64; dir. St. Ann's Ctr., Slayton, Minn., 1967-69, Christian Edn. Ctr., Austin, 1969—; mem. Minn. Ho. of Reps., 1982-84, 84-86, Senate State of Minn., 1986—. Contbr. articles to profl. jours. Active United Way, YMCA, Council for Hanicapped, Salvation Army. Mem. LWV, Bus. and Profl. Women. Mem. Democratic Farm Labor Party. Roman Catholic. Lodge: Zonta. Home: 800 1st Dr NW Austin MN 55912 Address: 301D 4th Ave NE Austin MN 55912

PIPITONE, PHYLLIS L., psychologist, educator, author; b. Chgo.; m. S. Joseph Pipitone, Aug. 28, 1948 (dec.); children: Guy, Daniel, Paul; m. Thomas A. Cox, Jan. 3, 1980. Student Chgo. Conservatory Music, 1941-44, Peabody Conservatory Music, 1945, Chgo. Tchrs. Coll., 1946-47, So. Meth. U., 1951-52; MA, U. Akron (Ohio), 1967; PhD, Kent (Ohio) State U., 1974. With B.S. & H. Advt. Agy., Chgo., 1941-43; instr. piano and theory Music Acad. Chgo.; psychologist, instr. U. Akron and Kent State U., 1970-79; pvt. practice psychology, Akron, 1967—; lectr. in field in U.S and abroad. Served with WAC, AUS, 1944-46. NIMH grantee, 1974, HEW Child Devel. fellow, 1974. Mem. Am. Psychol. Assn., Nat. Assn. Sch. Psychologists, Mensa, Council Exceptional Children, Am. Hypnosis Soc., Kent Psi Research Group, Study/Dreams (assoc.), Am. Soc. Psychical Research. Clubs: Tuesday Musical, Weathervane Theatre Women's Bd., Akron Women's City, Wadsworth Women's. Home: 224 Pheasant Run Wadsworth OH 44281

PIPKORN, DONNA ELIZABETH, retired small business executive; b. Oshkosh, Wis., Apr. 29, 1921; d. Guy Plummer and Lillian (Marks) Grundy; m. Homer W. Pipkorn, June 20, 1952 (dec.); 1 child, Homer "Skip" W. BS in Edn., U. Wis., Oshkosh, 1943. Tchr. elem. schs. Manitowoc, Wis., 1943-46, Oshkosh, 1946-52; prin. Pipkorn Fuel & Supply Co., Oshkosh, 1957-70; sec.-treas. Pipkorn's, 1985—. Active del. Wis. Reps.; local chpt. chmn. ARC, 1984-85, bd. dirs., 1979—, vol. Mercy Hosp., also local chpt. blood bank; sec. Winnebago land chpt. United Cerebral Palsy, also pres. and sec. of vols.; docent Paine Arboreteum, 1977—; mem. Wis. Red Cross Territorial Disaster Team. Mem. Ladies Benevolent Soc. (sec.), Winnebago County Ret. Tchrs. Assn., Wis. Ret. Tchrs. Assn., Friends of Paine Art Ctr. and Arboreteum, U. Oshkosh Ret. Alumni Assn., Friends of Oshkosh Mus., Campfire Girls, Nat. Assn. Retired People (Oshkosh Friends of Srs.), Winnebago Rep. Women. Episcopalian. Clubs: Twentieth Century (hon., bd. dirs. Oshkosh chpt., parliamentarian 1978-79, treas 1985—), Oshkosh Country, Power Boat. Home: 1255 Merritt Ave Oshkosh WI 54901

PIRACHA, GWENDOLYN CARTER, training coordinator; b. Galveston, Tex., Apr. 7, 1947; d. Walter Laurent and Della (Pete) Carter; m. Mansoor Asghar Piracha, April 11, 1986. BS, Tex. So. U., 1971, MS, 1977. Mgmt. trainee Sears, Roebuck & Co., Dallas, 1971-72; acct. Gen. Electric, Dallas, 1972-74; guidance counselor Opportunity Industrialization Ctr., Phoenix, 1974-75; edn. counselor League United Latin Am. Citizens, Houston, 1975-76; dir. Housing Assistance Payment Program, Houston, 1976-78; dir. tng. Labor Recruitment Program, Houston, 1978-79; campaign coordinator McConn for Mayor, Jim Hightower for R.R. Commn., Houston, 1979-80, tng. coordinator City of Houston, 1980—. Creator tng. programs. Mem. Nat. Soc. Tng. Developers, The Tng. and Devel. Council, Nat. Forum Black Adminstrs., Nat. Assn. Female Execs., Am. Mgmt. Assn., Nat. Assn. Housing and Redevel. Offls., Tex. Assn. Housing and Redevel. Offls. Democrat. Muslim. Home: 12713 Ann Louise Rd Houston TX 77086

PIRSCH, CAROL MCBRIDE, customer relations administrator, state senator; b. Omaha, Dec. 27, 1936; d. Lyle Erwin and Hilfrie Louise (Lebeck) McBride; student U. Miami, Oxford, Ohio, U. Nebr., Omaha; m. Allen I. Pirsch, Mar. 28, 1954; children—Pennie Elizabeth, Pamela Elaine, Patrice Eileen, Phyllis Erika, Peter Allen, Perry Andrew. Former mem. data processing staff Omaha Public Schs.; former mem. wage practices dept. Western Electric Co., Omaha; former legal sec., Omaha; former office mgr. Pirsch Food Brokerage Co., Inc., Omaha; former employment supr. U.S. West Communications, Omaha, now supr. customer relations; mem. Nebr. Senate, 1979—. Bd. dirs. U. Nebr. at Omaha Parents Assn., Nebr. Developmental Disabilities Council, Crisis Line; past pres., bd. dirs. Nebr. Coalition for Victims of Crime. Recipient Golden Elephant award; Outstanding Legis. Leadership award Nat. Orgn. Victim Assistance, Keystoner of the Month award. Mem. Orgn. U.S. West Women, Nat. Order Women Legislators, Tangier Women's Aux., VASA, Pilot Internat. Assn. Clubs: Omaha Women's, N.W. Civic, Benson Republican Women's, Bus. and Profl. Rep. Women. Office: State Capitol Lincoln NE 68509

PIRT, NANCY EILEEN, lawyer; b. Pitts., Apr. 6, 1952; d. John Joseph and Helen Marie (Giza) P. B.A. cum laude in Speech and Hearing Therapy, U. Pitts., 1974; J.D., Duquesne U., 1979; M.P.H., Harvard U., 1986. Bar: Pa. 1979. Law clk. Office of Public Defender, Pitts., 1976-77; sr. law clk. Superior Ct. Pa., Pitts., 1977-83; sole practice, Pitts., 1979-87; atty. EPA, Washington, 1987—; mem. bd. arbitrators Allegheny County, Pitts., 1981-84; mem. Com. for More Women Judges, Pitts., 1984; mem. Gov.'s/MBA Commn. on the Unmet Legal Needs of Children, 1986. Mem. editorial staff Duquesne Law Rev. U. Pitts. scholar, 1970-71; contbr. articles to profl. jours. Pa. Higher Edn. Assistance Agy. scholar, 1970-71. Mem. ABA, Allegheny County Bar Assn. Home: 2861 Schoolhouse Circle Silver Spring MD 20902 Office: 499 S Capitol St SW FOSD (EN397F) Washington DC 20460

PISCITELLO, DENISE EMILY, advertising executive; b. San Fernando, Calif., May 25, 1948; d. Robert Francis and Dorothy (Johnson) Werner; m. Charles Michael Piscitello, Mar. 5, 1946; children: Michael Carmelo, Charles Robert. AA, Los Angeles Valley Coll., 1968; BA, Calif. State U., Northridge, 1970. Prodn. artist Audio Magnetics, Gardena, Calif., 1970-71, Glenco, Sepulveda, Calif., 1971-73, Typo Grafix Inc., Reseda, Calif., 1973-75; graphic artist Indsl. Electronic Engrs., Van Nuys, Calif., 1975-77, graphic artist, 1977-82, advt. mgr., 1982—. Roman Catholic. Office: Indsl Electronic Engrs 7740 Lemona Ave Van Nuys CA 91405

PISESKY, SHARON ROZELLA VIOLET, educational administrator; b. Edmonton, Alta., Can., Dec. 8, 1942; d. William and Elswet (Nikiforuk) Yurchuk; m. Rudolph Pisesky, Aug. 10, 1963; children: Leann Marie, Katherine GayAnne. BS in Home Econs. Edn., U. Alta., 1963, MEd, 1971. Cert. tchr., Alta. Lectr. U. Alta., Edmonton, 1965-69; high sch. tchr.

Edmonton Cath. Schs., 1969-73, cons. in home econs., 1974-79, practical arts supr., 1979—; guest lectr. U. Alta., 1973-74. Author: (learning materials) What's To Eat, 1977. Trustee Newman Theol. Coll., Edmonton, 1985—; chmn. bd. trustees Edmonton Pub. Library, 1984—; co-chair tactics Decore for Liberal Leader, Edmonton, 1987, zone chmn. mayoral campaign, 1983, 86; dep. election campaign chair Liberal Party Alta., 1978-80, campaign co-chair, 1984; mem. Edmonton South Liberal Constituency Assn., pres., 1984. Mem. Can. Home Econs. Assn. (Ruth Binnie award 1987), Alta. Home Econs. Assn. (pres. 1979-80), Home Econs. Specialists Council (pres. 1974-75), Bus. Edn. Specialists Council, Alta. Tchrs. Assn. Roman Catholic. Office: Edmonton Cath Sch Bd, 9807 106th St, Edmonton, AB Canada T5J 1C2

PITCHER, HELEN IONE, advertising executive; b. Colorado Springs, Colo., Aug. 6, 1931; d. William Forest Medlock and Frankie La Vone (Hamilton) Tweed; m. Richard Edwin Pitcher, Sept. 16, 1949; children: Dushka Myers, Suzanne, Marc. Student, U. Colo., 1962-64, Ariz. State U., 1966, Maricopa Tech. Coll., 1967, Scottsdale Community Coll., 1979-81. Design draftsman Sundstrand Aviation, Denver, 1962-65; tech. illustrator Sperry, Phoenix, 1966-68; art dir. Integrated Circuit Engring., Scottsdale, Ariz., 1968-71, dir. advt., 1981—; advt. artist Motorola Inc., Phoenix, 1971-74; pres. Pitcher Tech. Pubs., Scottsdale, 1974-81. Profl. advisor Paradise Valley Sch. Dist., Phoenix, 1984—; mem. bd. advisors graphic arts dept. Ariz. State U., Tempe. mem. Nat. Audio Visual Assn., Bus. Profl. Advt. Assn. (treas. 1982-86), Direct Mktg. Club. Democrat. Mem. Ch. Christ. Home: 13681 N Pima Rd PO Box 2313 Scottsdale AZ 85252 Office: Integrated Circuit Engring Corp 15022 N 75th St Scottsdale AZ 85260

PITKIN, PATRICIA A., library administrator; b. Rochester, N.Y., Oct. 6, 1951; d. Patrick and Marie E. (Perrotta) Albanese. B.A., SUNY-Geneseo, 1973, M.L.S., 1974. Database mgr., original cataloger Rochester Inst. Tech., 1974-75, head library systems dept., 1975-79, head automated and tech. services, 1979-81, acting dir. Wallace Meml. Library, 1981-83, dir. Wallace Meml. Library, 1983—. Mem. Dataphase Users Group (pres. 1985), ALA. Home: 800 E River Rd Rochester NY 14623 Office: Rochester Inst Tech Wallace Meml Library 1 Lomb Memorial Dr Rochester NY 14623-0887

PITOU, PENNY, travel agency owner, professional skier; b. Bayside, L.I., N.Y., Oct. 8, 1938; d. Augustus and Eualie (Schaefer) Pitou; m. Egon Norbert Zimmermann, Feb. 19, 1961; children—Christian Egon, Kim Erik; m. Milo L. Pike, Sept. 1, 1981. Student Middlebury Coll., 1957. Cert. profl. ski instr., 1965. Operator, co-dir. Penny Pitou Ski Sch., Gunstock, N.H., 1961-68. Blue Hills, Mass., 1963-68; ski fashion cons. White Stag, 1960-70, Montgomery Ward, J.C. Penney; coach girl's ski team Laconia High Sch., N.H., 1965-66; owner Penny Pitou Travel, Inc., Laconia, N.H., 1974—, Concord, N.H., 1979—, Plymouth, N.H., 1985—, Wolfeboro, N.H., 1985—, Portsmouth, N.H., 1986—; bd. dirs. Laconia People's Nat. Bank, 1967-68. Appeared various TV programs including What's My Line, To Tell the Truth, The Today Show; appeared numerous mag. covers; speaker various orgns. Chmn. bd. advisors Wildcat Winners Circle, U. N.H., 1981—; bd. dirs. Odyssey House, Portsmouth, 1985—, Lakes Region Conservation Trust, N.H., 1984—. Recipient numerous awards including two silver medals Winter Olympics, Squaw Valley, Calif., 1960, New Eng. Council award, 1960, Nat. Ski Hall of Fame award, 1961; named Woman of Yr., Mademoiselle mag., 1965; rep. Pres. Gerald Ford as head of presl. del. at Olympics, Innsbruck, Austria, 1976. Home: 196 Potter Hill Rd Gilford NH 03246 Office: Penny Pitou Travel Inc 55 Canal St Laconia NH 03246

PITT, JANE, medical educator; b. Frankfurt, Fed. Republic Germany, Aug. 25, 1938; came to U.S., 1939.; d. Ludwig Friederich and Vera (Aberle) Ries; m. Martin Irwin Pitt, Aug. 12, 1962 (dec. 1980); children: Jennifer, Eric Jonathan; m. Robert Harry Socolow, May 25, 1986; stepchildren: David, Seth. BA, Radcliffe U., 1960; MD, Harvard U., 1964. Diplomate Am. Bd. Pediatrics. Resident Children's Hosp. Med. Ctr., Boston, 1964-66; fellow Tufts U. Med. Sch., Boston, 1966-67, Harvard U. Med. Sch., Boston, 1967-70; asst. prof. SUNY Downstate Sch. Medicine, N.Y.C., 1970-71; instr. Columbia U. Coll. Physicians and Surgeons, N.Y.C., 1971-72, asst. prof., 1972-76, assoc. prof., 1976—; mem. instl. rev. bd. Columbia Health Scis. Campus, N.Y.C., 1982—. Reviewer Jour. of Infectious Diseases, New Eng. Jour. Medicine, 1976—; contbr. articles to profl. jours. Grantee NIH, 1974, 78. Fellow Infectious Disease Soc.; mem. NIH (grantee study sects.), Pediatric Infectious Disease Soc., Soc. Pediatric Research. Democrat. Jewish. Home: 34 Westcott Rd Princeton NJ 08540 Office: Columbia U Coll Physicians Surgeons 630 W 168th St New York NY 10032

PITTA, PATRICIA JOYCE, psychologist; b. N.Y.C., July 3, 1947; d. John Joseph and Mildred (Gioiosa) P.; m. Eric Eugene Kirk; children: Eric Jon, Kevin. BA, Queens Coll., 1968; MS, Hunter Coll., 1972; PhD, Fordham U., 1975. Recreational therapist Roosevelt Hosp., N.Y.C., 1968-73, psychology intern, 1973-74; staff psychologist NYU Med. Ctr., 1974-78, clin. instr., 1975—; pvt. practice psychology Manhasset, N.Y., 1977—; chief psychologist St. John's Episc. Hosp., Smithtown, N.Y., 1978-79; cons. North Shore U. Hosp., Manhasset, 1979-84; mem. faculty L.I. family therapy div. Inst. Psychoanalysis; lectr. in field. Contbr. articles to profl. jours., newspapers. Mem. Am. Psychol. Assn., Nassau County Psychol. Assn. (bd. dirs. 1987—, pvt. practice com. 1986—), Working Women of Manhasset, L.I. Ctr. for Bus. and Profl. Women, Assn. Retarded Children (bd. dirs. 1988—). Office: 35 Bonnie Heights Rd Manhasset NY 11030

PITTARI, LINDA, brokerage firm executive; b. Bklyn., Nov. 22, 1944; d. Edward and Grace Pittari; B. Profl. Studies with distinction, Pace U., 1978; M.S. in Human Resource Mgmt., New Sch. Social Research, 1982. Sec., Merrill Lynch, N.Y.C., 1962-72, exec. sec., 1972-76, tng. adminstr., 1976-78, adminstrv. mgr., 1978-80, asst. v.p., mgr. mgmt. resources, 1980-82, v.p., mgr. manpower resources, 1982-83, v.p., mgr. mgmt. resources and devel., 1985—. Cert. profile assessment center adminstr. Devel. Dimension Internat. Mem. Career Planning and Adult Devel. Network, Am. Soc. Tng. and Devel. Office: 800 Scudders Mill Rd Plainsboro NJ 08536

PITTENGER, KAREN DENISE, advertising company executive; b. Nashville, Oct. 10, 1954; d. J.H. Pittenger and Ruby M. (Woodson) Haralson; m. Glenn Lewis Arnold, Jan. 15, 1977 (dec. June 1984); 1 child, Jason Lewis Pittenger Arnold. BA, Purdue U., 1975; postgrad., Butler U., 1987—. Art dir., creative dir. Art Emporium, Indpls., 1975-76; pres. Pittenger Studio, Indpls., 1976-83; v.p. Haynes & Pittenger Direct, Indpls., 1983—; tchr. Free U., Indpls., 1981; v.p., owner Spl. Projects, Indpls., 1983—. Creator: (direct mktg. stratagies) Child Support (Top Echo award 1984), Drunk Driving (Echo awards 1984-87), Gen. Electric (Top 5 Caples award 1988). Mem. hospice com., bd. dirs. St. Vincent Stress Ctr., Indpls., 1985-87, v.p. adv. bd., 1987-88, sec. 1985-87; mgr. direct mktg. Rep. Gov.'s campaign for Ind., 1988. Recipient Award of Excellence Beckett Paper Co., 1980, Addy award Advt. Club of Indpls., 1984, 85, 86; named one of Outstanding Young Women Am., 1982. Mem. Direct Mktg. Assn. (creative guild, numerous awards), Am. Inst. Graphic Designers. Office: Haynes and Pittenger Direct 303 N Alabama St Indianapolis IN 46204

PITTMAN, SANZEE GLEE, nurse, educator; b. Shattuck, Okla., Feb. 15, 1948; d. Loyd Edwin and Jacquiline Genevieve (Woods) Wanger; m. Harry Lee Pittman, Feb. 21, 1970 (div. Feb. 1983); children: Eric Loyd, Zaneta Zoe, Jarrod Heath, Damara Grace. Student, Cen. Okla. State U., 1983-86, St. Mary of the Plains Coll., 1987—. RN. Staff nurse Mercy Hosp., Oklahoma City, 1969-70, San Diego, 1970, Newman Meml. Hosp., Shattuck, 1971-73; clk.-typist Army-Air Force Exchange Hdqrs., Camp Mercy, Okinawa, 1973; staff nurse Spohn Hosp., Corpus Christi, Tex., 1975-78, asst. head nurse, 1976-78; staff nurse Bay Gen. Hosp., Chula Vista, Calif., 1979-82; instr. High Plains Area Vocat. Tech. Sch. of Practical Nursing, Woodward, Okla., 1983-87, coordinator practical nursing, 1988—, chmn. staff devel., 1987; asst. supr. Newman Meml. Hosp., 1971-73; advisor Health Occupations Students of Am., 1985—. Navy family ombudsman USS Belleau Wood LHA3, San Diego, 1979-82; mem. Sur Pac Ombudsman, San Diego, 1979-82; mem. worship com., ch. pianist Fargo (Okla.) United Meth. Ch., 1982—. Mem. Am. Vocat. Assn., Okla. Vocat. Assn. (Outstanding New Tchr. Mem. 1987), Am. Nurses Assn., Okla. Nurses Assn., Health Occupations Edn. Assn., Okla. Health Occupations Edn. Assn. (tchr., chmn. legis. com. 1986). Republican. Home: Box 274 Fargo OK 73840 Office: High Plains Area Vocat Tech 3921 34th St Woodward OK 73801

PITTS, DEBORAH KRUEGER, management consultant; b. Jamestown, N.D., Mar. 11, 1956; d. Lester James and Phyllis Jean (Koenig) K.; B.A. in Biology, U. Calif.-Santa Barbara, 1978; M.H.A., Duke U., 1980. Cardiopulmonary clk. Cottage Hosp., Santa Barbara, 1978; patient account rep. Durham (N.C.) County Hosp., 1979-80; health adminstrn. fellow Duke U. Hosp., Durham, 1980-81; v.p. Amherst Assocs., Atlanta, 1981-84, Tampa, 1984-88. Vol. Imola State Hosp., Napa, Calif., 1973-74; big sister St. Vincents Sch. for Mentally Handicapped, Santa Barbara, 1974-78; fund raiser Duke U. Health Adminstrn. Dept., 1980—; assoc. coordinator Catholic Young Adults, Durham, 1980-81; bd. dirs., vice chmn., chmn. fin., chmn. planning coms. Hospice of Pinellas County, St. Petersburg, Fla., 1984-88; v.p., Partners for Tampa Theatre, 1987-88. Calif. State Scholar, 1974; scholar. Am. Bus. Women's Assn., Loyal Order of Moose, Napa, Calif. Mem. Am. Coll. Healthcare Execs., Healthcare Fin. Mgmt. Assn., Am. Hosp. Soc. for Mktg. and Planning, Sun Coast Adminstrs. Group, Bay Area Healthcare Planners Assn., Alpha Delta Pi (v.p., pres. 1977; Violet award 1978), Phi Sigma Kappa (little sister). Roman Catholic.

PITTS, ELAINE RUTH HALLEAD (MRS. PAUL ELBERT PITTS), engineering executive; b. Chgo., June 20, 1917; d. Harry Albert and Ethel Mae (Waring) Hallead; m. Paul Elbert Pitts, Aug. 25, 1945. Student, Art Inst. Chgo., 1947-48, Ill. Inst. Tech., 1948-49, NYU, 1976-78. Packaging engr. Aldens, Inc., Chgo., 1943-46; sr. packaging engr. Spiegel, Inc., Chgo., 1946-52; mgr. package engring. Sperry & Hutchinson Co., Chgo., 1953-59, mgr. consumer relations, N.Y.C., 1959-70, dir. consumer affairs, N.Y.C., 1970, v.p. corp. relations, N.Y.C., 1970-79; ptnr. Dalton/Pitts Assocs., San Mateo, Calif., 1979—; lectr. MIT, Cambridge, U. Wis., Purdue U., Lafayette, Ind., UCLA, Ill. Inst. Tech., U. Ill.; mem. packaging adv. bd. Ariz. State U., Tempe. Mem. nat. adv. bd. Distributive Edn. Clubs Am., 1962-80, vice chmn., 1964, chmn., 1965; bd. dirs. S and H Found., 1974-79. Mem. Secs. Guild Chgo. Boys' Clubs (pres. 1963), Bus. and Profl. Women's Club, Soc. Packaging and Handling Engrs. (chpt. pres. 1957, nat. chmn. bd. 1966-67), Office Edn. Assn. (bd. dirs.), Soc. Women Engrs. (exec. com. 1968-69, 77-80, trustee 1982—), Am. Women in Radio and TV (v.p. 1969-70, pres. 1973-74, found. bd. dirs. 1982-87), Pub. Relations Soc. Am. (chmn. pub. affairs sect. 1985, bd. dirs. 1986-88), U.S. C. of C. (consumer affairs com.). Home: 1081 Beach Park Blvd Apt. 214 Foster City CA 94404 Office: 307 S B St San Mateo CA 94401

PITTS, JOANNE PATRICIA, software engineer, systems analyst; b. Riverside, Calif., Jan. 9, 1953; d. Otis Kemp and Margaret Louise (Schaffer) P. BA in Math., BS in Computer Sci., U. Calif., Irvine, 1974; MBA in Mgmt., Calif. State U., Fullerton, 1987. Computer programmer Rockwell Internat., Anaheim, Calif., 1974-76, Los Angeles, 1976-77; lead software engr. Anaheim, 1978—, Seal Beach, Calif., 1987—; software analyst Computer Sci. Corp., Santa Ana, Calif., 1977-78. Sponsor Immigration and Refugee Ctr. St. Anselm's, Garden Grove, Calif., 1979-82; soprano in ch. choir. Mem. Am. Mgmt. Assn., Nat. Mgmt. Assn., Nat. Assn. Female Execs., Beta Gamma Sigma. Democrat. Episcopalian. Home: 12292 Lesley St Garden Grove CA 92640 Office: Rockwell Internat 2600 Westminster Blvd Mail Code SJ62 Seal Beach CA 90740

PITTS, LINDA MANESS, accountant, educator; b. Longview, Tex., July 29, 1959; d. Bob and JoRuth (Edwards) Maness; m. Brandon Charles Pitts, Nov. 26, 1983; children: Brett Michael, Reed Mackenzie. BBA, U. Tex., 1981. CPA, Tex. Mem. audit staff Ernst & Whinney, Dallas, 1981-83, audit sr., 1983-85, audit mgr., 1985-86; pvt. practice acctg. Richardson, Tex., 1986—; acctg. instr. So. Meth. U., Dallas, 1987—. Mem. Jr. League Dallas; com. chmn. Dallas Heart Assn. Ball. Mem. Tex. Soc. CPAs, Delta Delta Delta (chmn. alumnae com.). Methodist. Office: 1702 N Collins Blvd Suite 209 Richardson TX 75080

PITTS, MARGARET JANE, chemist; b. Spokane, Wash., Aug. 10, 1923; d. Herbert Ryder and Gladys (Burchett) P. BS in Chemistry, Wash. State U., 1946. Chemist, Electrometall. Co., Spokane, 1943-44, div. indsl. research Wash. State U., Pullman, 1945-46, Haynes Stellite Co., Kokomo, Ind., 1946-51, Pacific NW Alloys, Spokane, 1951-53, Pitts. Testing Labs., Portland, 1954-56, Boeing Co., Seattle, 1956-60, U. Wash., Seattle, 1960-63, Comml. Chems., Inc., Seattle, 1964-65, Puget Sound Naval Shipyard, Bremerton, Wash., 1966-77, Naval Undersea Warfare Engring. Station, Keyport, Wash., 1977-86. Mem. Am. Chem. Soc., ASTM, AAUW, Federally Employed Women, Bus. and Profl. Women, Iota Sigma Pi, Alpha Delta Pi. Home: 2100 3rd Ave #1601 Seattle WA 98121-2303

PITTS, WENDY JO, bank executive; b. St. Louis, Mar. 18, 1956; d. Joseph Max Michaels and Joan Eleanor (Weiss) Gutmann; m. Robert Brantson Pitts, Apt. 20, 1980 (div. Jan. 1988). Student, Ohio U., 1974-77. Supr. ops. No. Trust Co., Chgo., 1977-79; customer service rep. internat. banking Chase Manhattan Bank, N.Y.C., 1980-81; customer service rep. Allied Irish Bank, N.Y.C., 1981-82; br. mgr., officer United Counties Trust Co., Cranford, N.J., 1982-87, CenTrust Savs. Bank, Orlando, Fla., 1988—. Mem. Winter Park (Fla.) C. of C. Republican. Jewish. Home: 2498 Timberline Dr Winter Park FL 32792 Office: CenTrust Savs Bank 2295 Lee Rd Winter Park FL 32798

PIVA, LILLY BELLE, former county and city labor union official; b. Gatesville, Tex., Aug. 11, 1918; d. William Wesley and Lillie Emaline (Lawrence) Payne; m. Francis Peter Piva, Jan. 21, 1937; children—Francis Anthony, Robert Lewis, Nicholas Dean. Student Tacoma Community Coll., 1968. Riveter Boeing Aircraft, Tacoma, 1942-43; cook mgr. Tacoma Sch. Dist., 1950-59; staff rep. Am. Fedn. State, County and Mcpl. Employees Council II, Seattle, 1962-78, staff rep. local 120, 1962-78; v.p. Central Labor Council, Tacoma, 1976-78. Bd. dirs. United Way Pierce County, Tacoma, 1967-72; commr. Tacoma Housing Authority, 1978-82; union counsellor Community Services AFL-CIO, Tacoma, 1967; committeeperson Democratic party, Tacoma, 1985; mem. adv. bd. Vocat. Tech. Inst., Tacoma, 1986; sec. Tacoma/Pierce County Nat. Council Sr. Citizens, 1986; v.p.-elect, Meth. Women of Mason Ch., 1988—. Recipient Certs. of Appreciation, Supt. Pub. Instrn., State Wash., 1985, Dem. Nat. Com., Washington, 1982. Democrat. Methodist. Clubs: 1918 Club, Candidates Forum (vice-chmn.) (Tacoma). Avocations: bowling. Home: 2410 N Stevens St Tacoma WA 98406

PIVETTA, RAPHAELA, artist, entrepreneur; b. Piacenza, Italy, July 3, 1948; d. Antonio Pietro and Luisa Rita (Magistrali) P.; m. Charles McKenna. BA, McGill U., 1971; cert., Art Students League of N.Y., 1978. Dir. Cornelia St. Cafe Inc., N.Y.C., 1977—. Music corr. Il Mucchio Selvaggio, 1980-82; sculptor A Pleasant Square, N.Y.C., 1987. Mem. Nat. Assn. of Women Bus. Owners, Nat. Assn. Female Execs., Arts Students League of N.Y. Office: Cornelia St Cafe Inc 29 Cornelia St New York NY 10014

PIVNICKA, BARBARA MILLIKEN, public relations executive; b. Fremont, Nebr., Apr. 24, 1953; d. James Dale and Jane (Little) Milliken; m. Richard J. Pivnicka, Sept. 24, 1977. BA in English and Art History magna cum laude, U. San Francisco, 1975. Dir. pub. relations Schwabacher/Frey Inc., San Francisco, 1977-79; dir. mktg. and pub. relations Beier and Gunderson, Oakland, Calif., 1979-83; dir. pub. relations Servamatic Systems Inc., San Ramon, Calif., 1983-86; mgr. pub. relations The Roulac Group Deloitte Haskins and Sells, San Francisco, 1986—. Editor Servamatic Jour., 1983, Roulac Register Newsletter, 1986—. Dir. Sanctuary for the Homeless, San Francisco, 1986—, The Support Ctr., San Francisco; mem. Arthritis Found., San Francisco, 1986—; mem. exec. com. Learning Through Edn. in the Arts project, 1987—. Mem. Internat. Assn. Bus. Communicators, Am. Mgmt. Soc., Sales and Mktg. Execs. Assn. Republican. Roman Catholic. Home: 5530 Moraga Ave Piedmont CA 94611 Office: Roulac Group Deloitte Haskins Sells 50 California St Suite 1300 San Francisco CA 94111

PIWKO, BARBARA ANTOINETTE, sales executive, manager outpatient billing; b. Buffalo, Apr. 14, 1948; d. Henry Peter and Antoinette Christine (Frygman) P. BA in Bus. Mgmt. and Econs., Empire State Coll., Albany, N.Y., 1985. Sr. clk. typist Erie County Med. Ctr., Buffalo, 1971-83, supr. patient billing, 1983-85, mgr. outpatient billing, 1985—; telemarketer Valco Sales Co., Kenmore, N.Y., 1980—; v.p. Civil Service Employees Assn., Buffalo, 1976-86; pres. Peaks Tng., Inc., Buffalo, 1987—. Com. woman Dem. Party, Town Tonawanda, 1985; 5 gallon donor Bloodmobile, Buffalo, 1982. Mem. The Exec. Female. Roman Catholic. Club: 600 Bowling. Home: 212 Wilson St Buffalo NY 14212 Office: Erie County Med Ctr 462 Grider St Buffalo NY 14212

PIXTON-GAEDE, JUNE DORIS, English language educator, drama coach; b. Santa Ana, Calif., June 12, 1930; d. Andrew Cunliffe and Ruth Mathilda Maria (Ruff) Pixton; m. Edward Lee Gaede, July 25, 1959 (div. Dec. 1976); 1 child, Bruce Andrew. BA, U. Calif., Berkeley, 1951; MA, Calif. State U., Bakersfield, 1975. Cert. tchr., Calif. Tchr. North High Sch., Bakersfield, Calif., 1961—; bd. dirs. Motley Theatre Co., Bakersfield. Bd. dirs. Bakersfield Community Theatre, 1974-83, Calif. State U. Theatre, Bakersfield, 1977. Mem. Nat. Council of Tchrs. of English, Calif. Tchrs. English (bd. dirs. 1984-88), Calif. Tchrs. Assn., Kern Council Tchrs. English (pres. 1984-88). Republican. Lutheran. Home: 606 Ray St Bakersfield CA 93308 Office: North High Sch 300 Galaxy Bakersfield CA 93308

PIZZOLATO, MARY ANN ROSE, chemical engineer; b. Newark, Apr. 23, 1953; d. Benjamin and Jennie (Lombardino) P.; B.S.Ch.E., Rutgers U., 1976. Process engr. FMC Corp., Carteret, N.J., 1976, asst. area supr., 1977-78; chem. engr. Gulf Oil Co.-U.S.A., Phila., 1978-80, sr. refining analyst, Houston, 1980-84, feedstock coordinator, 1984-85; ptnr. Scarlett O's doll shop, Humble, Tex., 1984-86; founder The Doll Hosp, Spring, Tex., 1987—. George Auchter scholar, 1974-76; Ross scholar, 1974-76. Mem. Am. Inst. Chem. Engrs., Tex. chpt. Rutgers Alumni Assn., Rutgers Engring. Soc., Nat. Assn. Female Execs., Soc. Women Engrs. Roman Catholic. Home: 7503 Live Oak Dr Humble TX 77396 Office: 118C Midway St Spring TX 77373

PLACEK-ZIMMERMAN, ELLYN CLARE, educator, consultant; b. Chgo., Sept. 3, 1951; d. Clarence Joseph and Jerrine LaMarr (Ruhlow) Placek; m. Allan John Zimmerman, Aug. 10, 1974; 1 child, Alissa Jan. B.S., No. Ill., 1973, M.S., 1977, C.A.S., 1978, Ed.D., 1982. Tchr. Arlington Heights Pub. Sch., Ill., 1973-75, 75-76, dir. library and learning ctr., 1976-81, tchr. lang. arts and reading jr. high sch., 1981-84, tchr. kindergarten, 1984-86; dir. Ill. State grant "At Risk Program" for pre-sch. children, Cary Pub. Schs., 1986-87. mem. part-time faculty Coll. of Edn., Roosevelt U., Chgo., 1983-84, 88—; tchr. jr. high sch. studies, 1988; cons. in field; mem. steering com. Curriculum'90 Conf., De Kalb, Ill., 1985; lectr. in field; mem. registration com. Fall conf. IASCD, 1987; supr. student tchrs. Ill. State U., Normal, 1986, Roosevelt U., Chgo., 1988—. Contbg. author: Feeling Good About Food. Sec. Scarsdale Estates Homeowners Assn., Arlington Heights, 1983; hon. life mem. PTA. Mem. Ill. Assn. for Supervision and Curriculum Devel. (triple I arrangements com. 1988, registration com. for fall conf. 1987), Ill. Assn. Tchrs. of English (cons., speaker conf. 1984), Ill. Women Adminstrs. (publicity com. conf. 1985). Avocation: playing guitar, calligraphy. Home: 402 E Orchard Arlington Heights IL 60005 Office: Arlington Heights Pub Sch Dist 25 301 W South St Arlington Heights IL 60005 also: Roosevelt U 430 S Michigan Ave Chicago IL 60605

PLACETTE, BRENDA JANETTE, advertising executive; b. Teague, Tex., Oct. 1, 1940; d. James Bernard and Elsie Clytee (Wren) Gilliam; m. Raymond Placette, July 1, 1975 (div. 1979); children: Karla Brandt, Alison Groves, Eva Zubel. Student, Alvin Jr. Coll., 1971, Wharton Jr. Coll., 1973, Coll. Mainland, 1983. Trainer classified sales Houston Post, 1961-64; editor, ad dir. Gulf Internat. Trader, Houston, 1964-67; ad. dir. Fort Bend Mirror, Stafford, Tex., 1967-71; owner, pub. Fort Bend Suburbia, Rosenberg, Tex., 1972-77; dir. operations and mktg. Fort Bend Suburbia, Rosenberg, 1977-80; ad. dir. Tex. City Sun, 1980—. Mem. Options Galveston County (founder, pres. 1985), Citizens Devel. Com. (dir. 1985-88), Gulf Coast Future Issues Council (dir. 1986-87), Galveston C. of C. (vice-chair 1986), Tex. Women Advt. (founder 1987), Internat. Newspaper Advt. and Mktg. Exec., Tex. Newspaper Advt. Mgrs. Assn., Bus. and Profl. Women Found. (dir. 1986). Republican. Office: Texas City Sun 624 4th Ave N Texas City TX 77590

PLAEHN, CONNIE JO, banker; b. Grundy Ctr., Iowa, Feb. 9, 1953; d. Paul Leroy and Darlene (Lampe) P. BA, Luther Coll., 1975; M in Mgmt., Northwestern U., 1985. CPA, Ill. Mgr. pub. relations and mktg., auditor, Office of Investigations and Audits Chgo. Bd. Trade, 1975-80; office mgr. Contifin. div. Conticommodities, Chgo., 1980-82; cons. Akroyd and Smithers, PLC, London, 1982-84; mgr. brokerage office Morgan Futures Corp., London, 1984-86; sales mgr. tng. program design Morgan Guaranty Trust, N.Y.C., 1986-87, v.p. domestic taxable fixed income, sales mgr., 1987—. Mem. Am. Inst. CPA's. Home: 252 W 17th St New York NY 10011

PLAKANS, SHELLEY SWIFT, social worker, psychotherapist; b. Boston, Aug. 29, 1943; d. William Nye and Phyllis (Childs) Swift; m. John Joseph Guinan Jr. (div. 1975); children: Ashley, Lindsey; m. John Plakans. AB, Wheaton Coll., 1965; MEd, Fitchburg (Mass.) State Coll., 1977; MSW, Simmons Sch. of Social Work, Boston, 1987. Lic. social worker, Mass. Staff psychologist Ayer (Mass.) Guidance Ctr., 1978-81; family therapist North Shore Community Health Ctr., Salem, Mass., 1984-85; psychotherapist Boston-North Shore Assocs., Salem, 1985—; clinician Caldwell Sch., Fitchburg, 1977-79; counselor Couryner, Guinan & Murray Counseling Assocs., Concord, Mass., 1979-81; social worker North Shore Children's Hosp., Salem, 1986—. Mem. Marblehead (Mass.) Hist. Soc., 1986-87; mediator Lynn (Mass.) Youth Resource Bur., 1986-87. Mem. Nat. Assn. Social Workers, Mass. Acad. Clin. Social Work, Inc. Office: Boston-North Shore Assocs 1 Cambridge St Salem MA 01970

PLANT, MARETTA MOORE, public relations executive; b. Washington, Sept. 4, 1937; d. Henry Edwards and Lucy (Connell) Moore; m. William Voorhees Plant, June 14, 1959; children—Scott Voorhees, Craig Culver, Suzannah Holliday. B.S. in Bus. Adminstrn., U. Ark., 1959. Owner, mgr. Handcrafts by Maretta, Westfield, N.J., 1966-73; photographer M-R Pictures, Inc., Allendale, N.J., 1973-77; communications asst. United Way-Union County, Elizabeth, N.J., 1977-79; pub. relations cons. Creative Arts Workshop, Westfield, 1977-81, Coll. Adv. Cons., 1983—; community relations coordinator Raritan Bay Health Services Corp., Perth Amboy, N.J., 1979-81; dir. pub. relations St. Elizabeth Hosp., Elizabeth, 1981-86; dir. mkgt./communications Somerset Med. Ctr., Somerville, N.J., 1986—. Trustee Bridgeway House, Elizabeth, 1982-86; mem. pub. relations com. N.J. Hosp. Assn., Princeton, 1982-83; committeewoman Union County Republican Com., Westfield, 1983-85. Mem. Pub. Relations Soc. Am., Nat. Fedn. Press Women, N.J. Press Women, Nat. Assn. Female Execs., Am. Soc. Hosp. Mktg. and Pub. Relations (council mem. Region II, membership com.), N.J. Hosp. Mktg. and Pub. Relations Assn. (corr. sec. 1984-86, pres. 1986—), Internat. Platform Assn., U. Ark. Alumni Assn., Summit-Westfield Assn., Delta Gamma. Clubs: Coll. Women's (Westfield); Soroptomists Internat. (charter). Home: 118 Effingham Pl Westfield NJ 07090 Office: Somerset Med Ctr Rehill Ave Somerville NJ 08876

PLANTE, LAURI ANN, corporate recruiter; b. Norfolk, Va., Mar. 8, 1958; d. Robert A. LaBella and Norma (Caputo) Redmond; m. Mark J. Plante, Apr. 4, 1981; 1 child, Kelly Ann. Student, Thomas A. Edison State Coll., 1987—. Account rep. Kelly Services, Cherry Hill, N.J., 1981-83; sr. human resource adminstr. City Fed. Savs. and Loan Assn., Hillsborough, N.J., 1983-86; corp. recruiter Travelers Mortgage Services, Cherry Hill, 1986—. Mem. Adv. bd. Burlington County Coll., Pemberton, N.J., 1984-85, Haddonfield (N.J.) Bd. Edn., 1987-88. Mem. Am. Soc. for Personnel Adminstrn., Tri-State Personnel Assn. (treas. 1983-84, v.p. 1984-86, bd. dirs. 1986-87). Office: Travelers Mortgage Services 2339 Rt 70 W Cherry Hill NJ 08034

PLANTHOLD, MILDRED ANN, association executive, mayor; b. St. Louis, Mar. 3, 1913; d. Frederick F. and Amanda-Marie Ann (Rook) P.; student N.Y. U., 1935-36, Washington U., St. Louis, 1936-37; m. Louis Cardinal Michie, Apr. 23, 1955 (dec.). Instr. speech Chautauqua (N.Y.) Summer Schs., 1937-38; speech instr. Notre Dame Acad., Quincy, Ill. and Belleville, Ill., also women's editor St. Louis Register, 1940-41; ch. editor St. Louis Globe-Democrat, 1941-43, women's editor, fashion and food editor, 1941-56; exec. sec. Allied Florists of Greater St. Louis, 1956-78; exec. sec. Profl. Florists of Mississippi Valley, 1978-83. Mem. adv. com. hort. div. East Central Coll., Union, Mo., 1976-86; mayor Town of Piney Park (Mo.), 1954-58, 79-83; bd. trustees Scenic Regional Library System, 1971-73. Named St. Louis Woman of Achievement, 1948; recipient award Am. Meat Inst., 1950; Sterling trophy Netherlands Flower-Bulb Inst., 1965; John Walker award Soc. Am. Florists, 1982. Mem. Nat. Fedn. Press Women (life, pres. 1969-71),

Mo. Press Women (life, pres. 1975-77), Women in Communications (30 yr. commendation 1980), Soc. Am. Florists Assn. Exec. Div. (chmn. 1966-70). Author, dir. documentary film on convent life, 1953. Home: 1651 Michie Ln Saint Clair MO 63077

PLATNICK, ELLEN SHEILA, cosmetics manufacturing company administrator; b. N.Y.C., Feb. 10, 1952; d. Leonard Howard Platnick and Bernice Morin Manis. BA, Am. U., 1974; cert., Coll. Para-legal Studies, 1975. Adminstrv. sec. Combined Properties, Washington, 1975-80; adminstrv. asst. Marsh and McLennan, N.Y.C. and Washington, 1980-84, B.H. Kreuger, Fairlawn, N.J., 1985-87; mgr. ops. Manhattan Ice Inc., N.Y.C., 1987-88; dir. sales Dri Mark Products, Inc., Port Wash., N.Y., 1988—. Mem. Nat. Assn. Female Execs., Nat. Assn. Chain Drug Stores, Cosmetic Exec. Women, Ind. Cosmetic Mfrs. Distbrs. Democrat. Jewish. Home: PO Box 3 Northport NY 11768 Office: Dri Mark Products Inc Harbor Park Dr Port Washington NY 11050

PLATTI, RITA JANE, educator, draftsman, author; b. Stockton, Calif., Aug. 29, 1925; d. Umbert Ferdinand and Concettina Maria (Natoli) Strangio; m. Elvin Carl Platti, July 27, 1955; 1 child, Kimberley Jane. Student, Dominican Coll., 1943-45; AB in Math, U. Pacific, 1947, postgrad., 1947-52, 68. Cert. secondary tchr., Calif. Farmer Escalon, Calif., 1943—; tchr. math St. Mary's High Sch., Stockton, 1947-49, 52, 54; chem. analyst Petri Winery, Escalon, 1949; draftsman Kyle Steel Co., Stockton, 1950-52; pvt. practice as draftsman Stockton, 1952-66; tchr. math Montewma Sch., Stockton, 1956-57, Davis Elem. Sch., Stockton, 1957-58; with rental bus. 1958-81; tchr. math Amos Alonzo Stagg High Sch., 1961-80; tchr. math. Humphreys Coll., 1981-82, math tchr., 1981-83; tchr. math Hamilton Jr. High Sch., 1984—; real estate agt., 1979—. Author: Math Prociciency Plateaus, 1979; author, pub. Math Proficiency Plateaus Series, 1979-86. Mem. NEA, Calif. Tchrs. Assn. Democrat. Roman Catholic.

PLATUS, LIBBY, artist, sculptor; b. Los Angeles, Aug. 18, 1939; d. Benjamin Lyon and Gertrude Goldman; children—Julie Linda, Diana Lisa. B.A., UCLA, 1961. Group shows include Richmond (Calif.) Designer Craftsmen, 1971, E. B. Crocker Gallery, Sacramento, 1973, Comsky Gallery, Beverly Hills, Calif., 1973, Galeria del Sol, Santa Barbara, Calif., 1973, Laguna Beach (Calif.) Mus. Art, 1973, Riverside (Calif.) Art Center, 1974, Calif. State U. Northridge, Los Angeles, 1974, Calif. State U., Fullerton, 1974, Calif. Design '76, Los Angeles, 1976, Cleve. Mus. Art, 1977; represented in collections: Tex. Christian U., Faberge Hdqrs., N.Y.C., numerous other public and pvt. collections; commd. works: Big Canyon Country Club, Newport Beach, Calif., Carolando Hyatt Hotel, Orlando, Fla., Mc Culloch's Silver Lakes Resort Hotel, Victorville, Calif., Blue Cross So. Calif., Los Angeles; lectr., condr. workshops numerous internat., nat., regional and state meetings, including World Craft Conf., Kyoto, Japan, 1978, Vienna, Austria, 1980, Glasgow (Scotland) Sch. Art, 1980, 84, Loughborough Coll. Art, Eng., 1980, 84, Konstfackskolan, Sweden, 1984, Goldsmith's Coll., Eng., 1984; Taideteo Ilinen Korkeakoulo, Finland, 1984; juror regional exhbn. Fairbanks Art Assn., Alaska, 1984; mem. Los Angeles Olympics 1984 Cultural and Fine Arts Commn., 1980-84, Los Angeles Olympics 1984 Citizens Adv. Commn. 1980-84; mem. Los Angeles County Museum Art Costume Council, adv. bd. Crafts Report Edn. Fund; mem. Craft and Folk Art Mus. Contemporary Craft Council. Recipient Graphic Achievement award Fox River Paper Corp., 1974; winner Tex. Christian U. Nat. Invitational Fiberwork Competition, 1977. Mem. Artists Equity (adv. bd. Los Angeles chpt. 1981—), Women In Bus., Am. Crafts Council, Handweavers Guild Am., Women's Caucus for Art. Home and Office: PO Box 55026 Sherman Oaks CA 91413-0026

PLAYER, THELMA B., librarian; b. Owosso, Mich.; d. Walter B. and Grace (Willoughby) Player; B.A., Western Mich. U., 1954. Reference asst. USAF Aero. Chart & Info. Center, Washington, 1954-57; reference librarian U.S. Navy Hydrographic Office, Suitland, Md., 1957-58; asst. librarian, 1958-59; tech. library br. head U.S. Navy Spl. Project Office, Washington, 1959-68, Strategic Systems Project Office, 1969-76. Mem. Spl. Libraries Assn., D.C. Library Assn., AAUW, Canterbury Cathedral Trust in Am., Nat. Geneal. Soc., Internat. Soc. Brit. Genealogy and Family History, Ohio Geneal. Soc., Royal Oak Found., Daus. of Union Vets. of Civil War, Friends Folger Library. Episcopalian. Home: 730 24th St NW Washington DC 20037

PLAZA, EVA M., lawyer; b. Torreon, Coahuila, Mex., Feb. 13, 1958; d. Sergio and Eva (Torres) P. BA cum laude, Harvard U., 1980; JD, U. Calif., Berkeley, 1984. Intern Congressman Richard White, Washington, 1978, U.S. Dept. of State, Washington, 1979; paralegal Grambling Mounce, El Paso, Tex., 1980-81; law clerk Pub. Advocates, San Francisco, 1982-83; trial atty. U.S. Dept. Justice, Washington, 1984-86; assoc. Arent, Fox, Kintner, Plotkin, Washington, 1986—. Legal adv. bd. Dem. Nat. Com., Washington, 1986—. Mem. ABA, Tex. Bar Assn., Pa. Bar Assn., D.C. Bar Assn., Hispanic Bar Assn. (pres. D.C. chpt.). Democrat. Roman Catholic.

PLECENIK, JEANNE TODD, accountant; b. Paterson, N.J., Nov. 16, 1955; d. David Robert and Eileen Rose (Crisbacher) McDougall; m. Richard Michael Plecenik, Sept. 25, 1982; children: Richard David, Karen Elizabeth. BBA in Pub. Acctg. magna cum laude, Pace U., 1981; postgrad., Marist Coll., 1987—. CPA, N.Y. Sales asst. Merrill Lynch, Pierce, Fenner & Smith, N.Y.C., 1976-77; exec. asst. The Barbuda Devel. Co., N.Y.C., 1977-80; staff acct. Arthur Young & Co., N.Y.C., 1981-83; prin. Jeanne T. Plecenik, CPA, Wappingers Falls, N.Y., 1983—; adj. lectr. Dutchess Community Coll., Poughkeepsie, N.Y., 1984—. Mem. Am. Woman's Soc. CPA's, N.Y. State Soc. CPA's, Nat. Alliance Homebased Businesswomen (treas. 1987—). Roman Catholic. Home: 11 Helen Ave Wappingers Falls NY 12590 Office: PO Box 582 Hughsonville NY 12537

PLEMING, LAURA CHALKER, educator; b. Sheridan, Wyo., May 25, 1913; d. Sidney Thomas and Florence Theresa (Woodbury) Chalker; B.A., Long Beach State Coll. (now Calif. State U., Long Beach), 1953, M.A. in Speech and Drama, 1954; postgrad. U. So. Calif., 1960-63; Rel.D., Sch. Theology, Claremont, Calif., 1968; m. Edward Kibbler Pleming, Aug. 25, 1938; children—Edward Kibbler, Rowena Pleming Chamberlin, Sidney Thomas. Profl. Bible tchr., 1953—; lectr. Calif. State U., Long Beach, 1960-66, U. So. Calif., 1963-65; Bible scholar for teaching Scriptures Program, First Ch. of Christ Scientist, Boston, 1970-75; free-lance Bible lectr., tchr., resource person for adult seminars, 1954—; active in summer teaching for young people, 1963-68, 86-87; tchr. adult edn. Principia Coll., summers 1969-71; tour lectr. to Middle East, yearly, 1974—; mem. archaeol. team, Negev, Israel. Mem. Am. Acad. Religion, AAUP, Soc. Biblical Lit. and Exegesis, Am. Schs. Oriental Research, Inst. Mediterranean Studies, Religious Edn. Assn., Internat. Congress Septuagint and Cognate Studies, Internat. Platform Assn., Phi Beta, Zeta Tau Alpha, Gamma Theta Upsilon. Republican. Christian Scientist. Author: Triumph of Job, 1979; editor Bibleletter Rev., 1968, 76, 81, 8-84. Home: 2999 E Ocean Blvd Apt 2020 Long Beach CA 90803

PLESHETTE, SUZANNE, actress, writer, producer, designer; b. N.Y.C., Jan. 31; d. Eugene and Geraldine (Rivers) P.; m. Thomas Joseph Gallagher, III, Mar. 16, 1968. Student, Syracuse U., Finch Coll., Neighborhood Playhouse Sch. of Theatre. designer home furnishings and bed linens. Debut in Truckline Cafe; star in Broadway prodns. Compulsion, The Cold Wind and the Warm, The Golden Fleecing, The Miracle Worker, Special Occasions; star TV series Bob Newhart Show, 1972-78, Suzanne Pleshette is Maggie Briggs, 1984; starred in TV series Bridges to Cross, 1986—; star 30 feature films including: The Birds, Forty Pounds of Trouble, If It's Tuesday This Must Be Belgium, Nevada Smith, Support Your Local Gunfighter, Hot Stuff, Oh God! Book II, 1980; TV movies including: Flesh and Blood, Starmaker, Fantasies, If Things Were Different, Help-Wanted Male, Dixie Changing Habits, One Cooks, The Other Doesn't, For Love or Money, Kojak, The Belarus File, A Stranger Waits, Command in Hell; writer, co-creator, producer two TV series.

PLESKO, SUSAN MARIE, educator; b. Superior, Wis., Nov. 28, 1945; d. Ernest Duane and Betty Jane (Meyers) Wittkopf; m. Forrest Joseph Plesko, Nov. 30, 1968; 1 child, Forrest V. BA, Calif. State U., Long Beach, 1972, MA, 1975. Cert. tchr. Calif., Minn., Wis. Freelance writer Santa Monica, Calif., 1976-79; advt. exec. Westmoreland, Larson & Hill Agy., Duluth, Minn., 1979-80; lectr. U. Wis., Superior, 1983-84, U. Minn., Duluth, 1984—; dir. writing ctr. U. Wis., Superior, 1987—; faculty advisor U. Minn., Duluth chpt. Delta Chi Omega, 1984—. Contbr. more than 45 articles to nat. mags. Home: 1913 Garfield Ave Superior WI 54880

PLEWINSKI, TERESA MARIA SAUER, physician; b. Poland; d. Gustav and Jadwiga (Bedynski) Sauer; naturalized, 1974; M.D., Wroclaw and Warsaw Med. Sch., 1951, Ph.D., 1966; m. Gustav L. Plewinski, Apr. 5, 1949; children—Magdalena, Michael. Intern, resident in internal medicine Columbus Hosp., N.Y.C., 1969-73; dep. surgeon-in-chief Children's Hosp., Warsaw, Poland, 1958-67; pediatric surgeon-in-chief Regional Hosp., Ho, Ghana, 1968; attending physician Cabrini Med. Center, N.Y.C., 1973—. Recipient Physician's Recognition award AMA, 1972, 75, 78. Fellow A.C.P., Am. Acad. Family Practice; mem. N.Y. Acad. Scis., Polish Inst. Arts and Scis. in Am. Research and publs. in med. field. Home: 10 Waterside Plaza New York NY 10010 Office: 242 E 19th St New York NY 10003

PLIAKOS, SUSAN PATRICE, industrial engineer; b. St. Louis, Mar. 17, 1957; d. Harry George and Georgia (Lazanas) P. BIndslE., Purdue U., 1979; MBA, Lindenwood Coll., 1985. Indsl. engr. Owens-Ill. Glass Co., Toledo, 1979-80; indsl. engr. McDonnell-Douglas Corp., St. Louis, 1980-84, sr. indsl. engr., 1984—. Mem. Inst. Indsl. Engrs., Computer Automatic Systems Assn. Home: 1 Lake Pembroke Saint Louis MO 63135 Office: McDonnell-Douglas Corp PO Box 516 Dept E133 Bldg 101A Saint Louis MO 63135

PLIMPTON, PAULINE AMES, civic worker; b. N. Easton, Mass., Oct. 22, 1901; d. Oakes and Blanche Ames; B.A., Smith Coll., 1922; m. Francis T.P. Plimpton, June 4, 1926; children: George Ames, Francis T.P., Oakes Ames, Sarah Gay. Pres., House of Industry, 1940-48; bd. dirs. Inst. World Affairs, 1940-74, Pub. Edn. Assn., 1933-44; chmn. United Campaign Fund for Planned Parenthood of Manhattan and Bronx, 1946-49; chmn. Planned Parenthood Fedn. Am. campaign, 1959-60, bd. dirs. 1959-67, 70-73; chmn. United Campaign, 1964; bd. dirs. Planned Parenthood of N.Y.C., 1965-74; rep. Western Hemisphere region Internat. Planned Parenthood Fedn., 1970-73; fund raiser Ladies' Aux. Philharm. Symphony Soc. N.Y., N.Y. Legal Aid Soc., ARC; mem. adv. council Friends of the Columbia Libraries, 1986-89. Recipient Planned Parenthood award for devoted service, 1969, Republican. Unitarian. Clubs: Cosmopolitan, River (N.Y.C.); Ausable (Adirondacks). Contbg. author, editor, compiler Orchids at Christmas, 1975, The Ancestry of Blanche Butler Ames and Adelbert Ames, 1977, Oakes Ames: Jottings of a Harvard Botanist, 1979, The Plimpton Papers: Law and Diplomacy, 1985, A Window on Our World: More Plimpton Papers, 1988. Home: 131 E 66th St New York NY 10021 also: 168 Chichester Rd West Hills Huntington NY 11743

PLITT, JANE RUTH, consultant; b. Suffern, N.Y., Mar. 19, 1948; d. George and Rose (Wollowitz) Plitt; m. James Terrence Bruen, Sept. 1, 1973; children—Brett Plitt Bruen, Beth Plitt Bruen. B.S., Cornell U., 1969. Staff asst. labor relations Rochester Telephone Corp., N.Y., 1969-71, mgr. labor relations, 1971-73, mgr. staff devel., 1973; exec. dir. NOW, Chgo., 1973-75; cons. Cresap, McCormick & Paget, Chgo., 1975-76; cons. tng., Rochester, 1977-79; adj. faculty Cornell U. Sch. Indsl. and Labor Relations, Rochester Inst. Tech., 1977—; bus. service ombudsman N.Y. State Dept. Commerce, Rochester, 1978-79; pres. JP Assocs., Rochester, 1979—, arbitrator, 1979—; adv. bd. dirs. Community Savs. Bank, Rochester, 1981-83; del. White House Conf. on Small Bus., 1986; regional coordinator N.Y. State Small Business Network. Small bus. columnist Rochester Democrat, 1988, Rochester Chronicle, 1988; contbr. articles to profl. jours. Chmn. Rochester Charter Commn., 1981; del. Dem. Nat. Conv., 1971; campaign mgr. city ct. campaign, Rochester, 1983; bd. dirs. Rochester Ednl. TV and Radio, 1983—; pres., bd. dirs. Women's Career Ctr., Rochester Women's Network, 1977—; pres. Rochester Small Bus. Council, 1987—. Named Best Ombudsman, N.Y. State Dept. Commerce, 1979, Small Businessperson of Yr., 1986. Mem. Nat. Assn. Women Bus. Owners (pres. Rochester chpt., 1987-88), Indsl. Relations Research Assn., Rochester C. of C. Address: JP Assocs 165 West Ave Rochester NY 14611

PLITT, JEANNE GIVEN, librarian; b. Whitehall, N.Y., Aug. 27, 1927; s. Charles Russell and Anna Marie (Noyes) Given; student St. Lawrence U., 1945-47; A.B., U. Md., 1940; postgrad. Am. U., 1960-61; M.L.S., Cath. U. Am., 1968; m. Ferdinand Charles Plitt, Jr., Jan. 19, 1952; children—Christine, Marie, Charles Randolph. Library asst. Spl. Services div. U.S. Army, 1949-51; tchr. secondary schs., Md. and Va.; reference librarian Alexandria (Va.) Library, 1967-68, asst. dir., 1968-70, dir., 1970—; chmn. librarians' tech. com. Council Govts., Washington, 1971-72, 80-81; chmn. No. Va. Library Networking Com. Active Little Theatre Group, Alexandria. Recipient Alexandria Pub. Service award, 1964, 74. Mem. ALA, Va. Library Assn. (legis. com. 1988—), Manuscript Soc., PTA, U. Md., Cath. U. alumni assns., Alexandria Assn., Urban League, Alexandria Hist. Soc. (dir. 1974—). Roman Catholic. Club: Zonta (sec. chpt. 1972-73, dir. 1988—). Office: Alexandria Library 717 Queen St Alexandria VA 22314

PLODZIEN, CAROL ANNA, educator; b. Chgo., Oct. 7, 1948; d. Joseph Thomas and Elizabeth Ann (Hempel) P. B.S., No. Ill. U., 1971; M.S., George Williams Coll., 1979. Tchr. phys. edn. William Fremd High Sch., Palatine, Ill., 1971—. Author: (with June E. Meyer) Thinking Straight, 1983, Excelling in Sports Though Thinking Straight; The Right Choices for Coaches and Athletes, 1988; contbr. articles to profl. jours. Named Coach of Yr., Mid-Suburban League North, 1983-84. Mem. Ill. Girls Basketball Assn. (pres. 1979-80), Ill. Coaches Assn. for Girls' and Women's Sports, Women's Basketball Coaches Assn. (200th Victory award), Nat. Wildlife Fedn., Nat. Audubon Soc. Office: William Fremd High Sch 1000 S Quentin Rd Palatine IL 60067

PLONA, MARY FEBRONIA, nun, nursing home administrator; b. Gardner, Mass., Oct. 2, 1912; d. Alexander and Alexandra (Wiski) Plona. R.N., St. Catherine's Hosp. Sch. Nursing, Bklyn., 1944; B.S. in Nursing, St. Joseph Coll., West Hartford, Conn., 1959. Joined Daus. of Mary of Immaculate Conception, Roman Catholic Ch., 1936. Nurse, New Britain Meml. Hosp. (Conn.), 1944-54; adminstr. Our Lady of Rose Hill Home, New Britain, 1954-63, St. Lucian's Home for Aged, New Britain, 1965—. Bd. dirs. Sancta Maria Hosp., Cambridge, Mass., 1973-76, Monsignor Bojnowski Manor, New Britain, 1974—. Mem. Con. Soc. Gerontology, Conn. Assn. for Non Profit Facilities for Aging (bd. dirs. 1967-74, 76—), Cath. Hosp. Assn. (New Eng. Conf.), Cath. Nurses (bd. dirs. Hartford chpt. 1960), New Britain Council Cath. Nurses (bd. dirs. 1960), St. Catherine's Hosp. Nurses Alumnae Assn., Nat. Geriatric Soc., Nat. Council on Aging, New Britain Area Conf. of Chs. Address: 532 Burritt St New Britain CT 06053

PLOPA, PATRICIA ANN, clinical psychologist; b. Detroit, Jan. 9, 1949; d. John and Jane (Miarecki) Gorski; m. Jeffrey David Plopa, Aug. 24, 1973; 1 dau., Lisa Michelle. B.A., Mich. State U., 1971; M.A., U. Detroit, 1976, Ph.D., 1977. Instr., U. Detroit, 1971-73; psychol. examiner, therapist Adult Psychiat. Clinic, Detroit, 1972-74; psychol. intern Children's Ctr. of Wayne County, Detroit, 1973-74, Sinai Hosp., Detroit, 1974-75; therapist, research asst. U. Detroit Psychology Clinic, 1972-77; therapist Project Headline: Family Counseling Ctr., Eastwood Clinic, Detroit, 1976-77; clin. psychologist Adult/Youth Devel. Services, Farmington, Mich., 1977-83; pvt. practice Maple Clinic, Birmingham, Mich., 1977-83, Northland Clinic, Southfield, Mich., 1980—; bd. dirs. Northland Clin., 1985—; cons. Marriage Growth Ctr., 1983—, St. Owen's Pastoral Minstry Program, Birmingham, 1987—; adj. faculty dept. psychology U. Detroit, 1986—. Mich. State Trustees scholar, 1967-71; U. Detroit teaching fellow, 1971-73. Mem. Mich. Soc. Clin. Psychologists (exec. com. council 1981-83, directory editor 1981-83), Mich. Psychol. Assn. (continuing edn. com. 1981-85), Mich. Soc. Psychoanalytic Psychology (program planning com. 1981-82), Am. Psychol. Assn., Nat. Register Health Service Providers in Psychology, Assn. for the Advancement of Psychoanalysis (program planning com. 1981-83), Phi Beta Kappa. Home: 4655 Pickering Rd Birmingham MI 48010 Office: 17117 W Nine Mile Rd Suite 1221 Southfield MI 48075

PLOTKIN-ZINBARG, ROBERTA J., communications executive; b. Bklyn., June 12, 1936; d. Max and Dorothy (Wolkofsky) Goldman; m. Donald Plotkin, Sept. 9, 1962 (dec.); m. Eugene Zinbarg, Sept. 27, 1987. BS in Math., Queens Coll., 1957; MS in Math., Loyola U., Los Angeles, 1968. Data analyst Rocketdyne div. N. Am. Aviation, Canoga Park, Calif., 1957-59; programmer analyst System Devel. Corp., Santa Monica, Calif., 1959-63; systems engr. IBM Corp., Santa Monica, 1963-64; sr. programmer analyst Control Data Corp., Los Angeles, 1964-65; mem. tech. staff Informatics, Inc., Van Nuys, Calif., 1965-67; sr. engr., scientist Douglas Aircraft Co., Long Beach, Calif., 1967-70; sr. product mgr. McDonnell Douglas Automation Co., Long Beach, 1970-72; prin. systems analyst Western Union Info. Systems, Mahwah, N.J., 1972-75; mgr., network engr. ITT-USTS, Secaucus, N.J., 1975—; cons. Med. Group, Santa Monica, Calif., 1966-68, Pulmonary Dept., N.Y. Hosp., 1975, ACLU, N.Y., 1980-83, mem. 1977—. V.p. donor plans Hadassah Lenox Hill Chpt., N.Y., 1983-86, v.p. fundraising, 1986—. Mem. Nat. Assn. Female Execs. Democrat. Jewish. Home: 500 E 77 St #3225 New York NY 10162

PLUCKER, CHARLOTTE ANN, writer; b. Rochelle, Ill., Oct. 8, 1955; d. Allen Dean Braddy and Shirley June (Taylor) McKinley; m. Jeffrey Lee Plucker, Mar. 7, 1986. Student, Kishwaukee Jr. Coll., 1974-80; BA in Journalism, No. Ill. U., 1987. Mgmt. asst. Wurlitzer Co., DeKalb, Ill., 1977-78; sales rep. Ammons Music Co., Pine Bluff, Ark., 1979; research asst. Peavey Commodities, DeKalb, 1980, Consorcio Panamericano de Inversionistas, S.A., San Jose, Costa Rica, 1980-81; co-owner, adminstr. Meier & Assocs., Inc., Chgo. and DeKalb, 1981-84. Editor: Precious Metals Trading Handbook, 1983, Investment Strategies for Financial Security, 1984; author (column) Trader's Notebook, 1983. Troop leader aide Girl Scouts U.S., Sycamore, Ill., 1988. Mem. No. Ill. U. Alumni Assn. Home: 610 Emmert Sycamore IL 60178

PLUE, MARILYN TROTTER, insurance company executive; b. Worcester, Mass., Oct. 2, 1931; d. Cecil Arnold and Clara L (Schunke) Trotter; m. Bradford B. Plue, Mar. 27, 1954. Grad. exec. sec. with honors, Salter Secretarial Sch., Worcester, 1950. Cert. profl. sec. With Motors Ins. Corp., N.Y.C., 1952-66; pres. Banner Personnel Cons., Inc., Worcester, 1966-68; trust adminstr. Bowditch, Gowetz and Lane, Worcester, 1968-69; employment supr. Paul Revere Life Ins. Co., Worcester, 1969-71, employment mgr., 1971-73, mgr. personnel adminstrn., 1973-80, dir. personnel adminstrn., 1980-81, asst. treas., dir. human resources adminstrn., 1981-84, asst. treas., dir. compensation and benefits, 1984-85, 2d v.p., asst. treas. compensation and benefits, 1985—. Bd. dirs., corporator Vis. Nurse Assn., Worcester; mem. med. and bus. adv. com. Cen. Mass. Bus. Group on Health, affirmative action com. United Way Cen. Mass.; mem. Boston Mus. Fine Arts, Worcester Art Mus., Peabody Mus., Worcester Sci. Ctr., Friends of Sturbridge Village. Mem. Am. Businesswomen's Assn. (Woman of Yr. 1973, Boss of Yr. 1972), Am. Soc. Personnel Adminstrn. (dist. dir. western Mass. 1983-86), Cert. Profl. Sec. Assocs. of New England, Am. Compensation Assn., Personnel Mgmt. Assn. Cen. Mass. Home: 10 Jefferson Dr Auburn MA 01501 Office: Paul Revere Life Ins Co 18 Chestnut St Worcester MA 01608

PLUMB, BARBARA LOUISE, editor; b. Pitts., Apr. 22, 1934; d. Earle Alfred and Louise (Graham) Brown; m. William Lansing Plumb, Oct. 8, 1955 (div.); 1 child, Christian Chamberlain. Student, Denison U., 1951-53; BA, Cornell U., 1955. Editorial asst. Woman's Day, N.Y.C., 1955; copywriter Eves Advt. Agt., San Diego, 1955, Walker Scott Dept. Store, San Diego, 1956-57; tchr. English Brit. Sch., Milan, 1957-59; asst. editor Interiors Mag., N.Y.C., 1959-60, assoc. editor, 1961-62; reporter N.Y. Times, 1962-70; editor architecture and environ. Am. Home Mag., N.Y.C., 1970-73; sr. editor Charles Scribner's Sons, N.Y.C., 1973-75, Pantheon Books, N.Y.C., 1975-80; sr. editor Workman Pub., N.Y.C., 1975-82, cons. editor, 1982—; editor At Home Vogue Mag., N.Y.C., 1975-82, editor Living column, 1982—. Home: 108 E 86th St New York City NY 10028 Office: Vogue Mag 350 Madison New York City NY 10017

PLUMB, PAMELA PELTON, former mayor, councilwoman; b. St. Louis, Oct. 26, 1943; d. Frank E. and Dorothey-Lee (Culver) Pelton; m. Peter Scott Plumb, June 11, 1966; children: Jessica Culver, David Scott. BA, Smith Coll., 1965; MA, NYU, 1967. Tchr., Master's Sch., Dobbs Ferry, N.Y., 1967-69; exec. dir. Greater Portland (Maine) Landmarks, 1969-71; engaged in civic and vol. work, 1971-79; mem. Portland City Council, 1979—, mayor, 1981-82; vice chmn. Peoples Heritage Savs. Bank. Bd. dirs. Tom's of Maine, pres., 1987-88. Nat. League Cities, 1983—, 2d v.p., 1985-86, 1st v.p., 1986-87, pres., 87—. Recipient Doric Dames's Bullfinch award for preservation, 1979, Greater Portland Landmark's Preservation award, 1980, Deborah Morton award Westbrook Coll., Portland, 1982, Neal W. Allen award Greater Portland C. of C., 1982; named Portland and Maine Outstanding Young Woman, Jaycees, 1979. Democrat. Office: City Hall 389 Congress St Portland ME 04101

PLUMER, JANICE ANN, grants management specialist; b. Mineola, N.Y., July 12, 1954; d. Peter James and Maria Ann (DiPietro) Rubertone; m. Arnold Plumer, Mar. 22, 1986. BA in Communication Arts, Molloy Coll., 1976; MS in Speech Pathology and Audiology, Adelphi U., 1977. Program asst. for childhood immunization HEW, N.Y.C., 1976-77, coordinator trust fund, 1977-80; assoc. state rep. N.Y. Dept. Edn., N.Y.C., 1980-86, counselor equal opportunity, 1980-86, specialist grants mgmt., 1986—; mgr. fed. women's program, chair N.Y. Fed. Exec. Bd., N.Y.C., 1984—. Named Outstanding Young Woman of Yr. Molloy Coll., 1985. Mem. Nat. Rehab. Assn., Nat. Orgn. Female Execs., NOW. Democrat. Roman Catholic. Home: 240 E 27th St #11C New York NY 10016 Office: US Dept Edn 26 Federal Plaza Rm 4104 New York NY 10278

PLUMMER, EDNA MAE, business woman; b. Conrad, Iowa, May 29, 1921; d. Elmer Leonard and Fern (Haggin) Schultz; diploma in bus. Spencerian Coll., Louisville, 1942; m. Kenneth (dec.); 1 son, Jerald D. Plummer. Stenographer, Monarch Equipment Co., Louisville, 1942-45; sec. Army Air Forces, Louisville, 1945-46, L&N R.R., Louisville, 1946; with Chevrolet Motor div. Gen. Motors Corp., Louisville, 1946—, cashier, sec., 1974—. Mem. nat. bd. advisors Am. Biog. Inst. Mem. Am. Bus. Women's Assn. (Woman of Yr. 1979-80, corr. sec. River City chpt. 1976, sec. 1977, v.p. 1978, pres. 1979), Ky. Women's C. of C. (mem. legis. com. 1979-80, exec. bd. 1980—, sec. 1981-82, pres. 1983-84). Democrat. Mem. Christian Ch. Club: Woodson Bend Resort.

PLUMMER, ORA BEATRICE, nursing consultant; b. Mexia, Tex., May 25, 1940; d. Macie Idella (Echols); B.S. in Nursing, U. N.Mex., 1961; M.S. in Nursing Edn., UCLA, 1966; children—Kimberly, Kevin, Cheryl. Nurses aide Bataan Meml. Meth. Hosp., Albuquerque, 1958-60, staff nurse, 1961-62, 67-68; staff nurse, charge nurse, relief supr. Hollywood (Calif.) Community Hosp., 1962-64; instr. U. N.Mex. Coll. of Nursing, Albuquerque, 1968-69; sr. instr. U. Colo. Sch. Nursing, Denver, 1971-74; asst. prof. U. Colo. Sch. Nursing, Denver, 1974-76; staff asso. III Western Interstate Commn. for Higher Edn., Boulder, Colo., 1976-78; dir. nursing Garden Manor Nursing Home, Lakewood, Colo., 1978-79; ednl. coordination Colo. Dept. Health, Denver, 1979—. Active Colo. Cluster of Schs.-faculty devel.; mem. adv. bd. Affiliated Children's and Family Services, 1977; mem. state instl. child abuse and neglect adv. com., 1984—; mem. planning com. State Wide Conf. on Black Health Concerns, 1977; mem. staff devel. com. Western Interstate Commn. for Higher Edn., 1978, minority affairs com., 1978, coordinating com. for baccalaureate program, 1971-76; active minority affairs U. Colo. Med. Center, 1971-72; mem. ednl. resources com. public relations com., rev. com. for reappointment, promotion, and tenure U. Colo. Sch. Nursing, 1971-76. Mem. Am. Nurses Assn., Colo. Nurses Assn. (affirmative action comm. 1977, 78, 79), Phi Delta Kappa. Contbr. articles in field to profl. jours. Office: 4210 E 11th Ave Denver CO 80013

PLUMMER, SHEILA YVONNE, child care professional; b. Alton, Ill., Mar. 12, 1948; d. Wallace Monroe and Mary Elizabeth (Johnson) Hyndman; m. Alvin A. Plummer, Apr. 17, 1976; children: Ustan, Novia, Alexander. Student, So. Ill. U., Carbondale, 1966-68; BS in Edn., So. Ill. U., Edwardsville, 1971; MEd in Spl. Edn., U. Mo., 1974, EdS in Ednl. Adminstrn., 1980. Cert. tchr. spl. edn. K-12, Mo.; cert. secondary prin. 9-12, Mo. Resource tchr. Alton Pub. Schs., 1971-72; educator DuPage Sch. for Boys, Naperville, Ill., 1972-73; spl. edn. tchr. Mid Mo. Mental Health Ctr., Columbia, 1974-75; instr. Columbia (Mo.) Coll., 1975-77; spl. edn. cons., Mo. Dept. Elem. and Secondary Edn., Jefferson City, 1977-80; spl. edn. tchr., ednl. supr. Mo. Tng. Sch. for Boys, Boonville, 1981-83; adult edn. tchr. Columbia Pub. Schs., 1984-85; pres. Kids Individualized Devel. Systems,

Inc., Ashland, Mo., 1985—; mgr., founder Midway K.I.D.S. Child Care Ctr., Columbia, 1986—. Author: Young New Members Handbook, 1981. Asst. youth dir., Sunday sch. tchr. Progressive Bapt. Ch., Columbia, 1980-87; chairperson bd. dirs. Rockbridge Child Devel. Ctr., Columbia, 1980-83, Andersen-Hayes Child Care Ctr., Columbia, 1981-83, Progressive Day Care Ctr., Columbia, 1982—; v.p. Field Sch. PTA, Columbia, 1987. Named one of Outstanding Young Women Am., 1980. Mem. Assn. for Edn. of Young Children (2d v.p. 1986—). Democrat. Baptist. Office: Midway KIDS Child Care Ctr 6401 W Hwy 40 Columbia MO 65203

PLUNKETT, ANNE MARIE CECILIA, banker; b. Rochester, Minn., July 15, 1932; d. Eugene and Anna (Regan) Leddy; B.A., Manhattanville Coll., Purchase, N.Y., 1953; postgrad. Fordham U., 1953-54; m. Richard Harding Plunkett, July 12, 1958; children—Pamela, Patricia, Richard Harding, Julianne, Maureen. Instr. socio-econ. problems St. Marys Sch. Nursing, Rochester, 1957-58, 65-66; chmn. bd. Rochester Bank & Trust Co., 1973-82; v.p., sec. Midwest Video Electronics, Inc., Rhinelander, Wis., 1972-79; dir. Medelco, Inc., 1973-78. Pres., Olmsted County Lawyers Wives, 1959-60; leader Girl Scouts U.S.A., 1969-72; vol. tchr. St. Johns Religious Edn., 1972-75; founder Southeastern Minn. Regional Arts Council, 1973; chmn. Minn. Arts Bd., 1974-75; co-chairperson Minn. Bicentennial Commn., 1975-76; v.p., mem. finance com. United Way, Olmsted County, 1978, bd. dirs., 1976-78; chmn. subcom. on elementary edn. Rochester Sch. Dist. 535 Citizens Adv. Com. on Ednl. Facilities, 1976-77; bd. dirs., v.p. Friends of Mayowood, 1987-88; coordinator Minn. Aesthetic Environment Program for Olmsted County, 1977; co-founder condrs. com. Rochester Symphony Orch., 1977; mem. Pres.'s Forum, Minn. Bible Coll., Rochester, 1977-79; mem. exec. com. Rochester Pres.'s Council, Coll. St. Teresa, Winona, Minn., 1977-78; adv. com. Agrl. Interpretative Center, Fairmont, Minn., 1979; 1st Dist. coordinator vol. activities Vice Pres. Walter F. Mondale, 1968; del. State Conv. from Olmsted County, Minn. Democratic party, 1974, 76, 78; nat. treas. U.S. Sen. Wendell R. Anderson Vol. Com., 1977-83; bd. dirs. AAU Rochester Swim Club, Family Consultation Center, Rochester YWCA, 1969-70, Lourdes High Sch. Devel. Fund; vol. Mondale for Pres. campaign, 1984; mem. Gov.'s Task Force Women's History Interperative Ctr., 1985—. Recipient Outstanding Vol. medal St. Marys Hosp., 1967, plaque of appreciation Olmsted County Bicentennial Commn., 1976, medallion and cert. of recognition Minn. Bicentennial Commn., 1976, cert. of appreciation Gov.'s Aesthetic Environ. Program, 1977. AAUW Ednl. Found. grantee, 1976. Mem. AAUW (founder Dayton Benefit for Scholarships 1955, dir. Rochester br. 1955-56, 75-77), Hospitality Inst. Tech. and Mgmt. (bd. dirs.), Rochester Banks Clearing House Assn. (chairperson 1977-78), Audubon Soc. (bd. dirs. Zumbro Valley chpt. 1987-88, v.p. 1988—), Needlework Guild (v.p. 1986—) Assoc. editor jour. The Loon, 1987—. Home: 2918 SW 15th Ave Rochester MN 55902 Office: Rochester Bank & Trust Co Box 6478 Rochester MN 55903

PLUNKETT, MELBA KATHLEEN, manufacturing company executive; b. Marietta, Ill., Mar. 20, 1929; d. Lester George and Florence Marie (Hutchins) Bonnett; student public schs.; m. James P. Plunkett, Aug. 18, 1951; children—Julie Marie Plunkett Hayden, Gregory James. Co-founder, 1961, since sec.-treas., dir. Coils, Inc., Huntley, Ill. Mem. U.S. C. of C., U.S. Mfg. Assn., Ill. C. of C., Ill. Notary Assn. Roman Catholic. Home: Route 1 Sleepy Hollow Rd West Dundee IL 60118 Office: 11716 Algonquin Rd Huntley IL 60142

POBANZ, RITA BERNADETTE, nurse; b. Bklyn., Oct. 16, 1941; d. John Daniel and Mary Robert (Simpson) Grady; A.D.N. with honors, Eastern N.Mex. U., 1974; B.S.N., SUNY, 1987; m. Kenneth Walter Pobanz, June 5, 1960; children—Karen, Stephen. Staff nurse Gerald Champion Hosp., Alamogordo, N.Mex., 1974; critical care staff, charge nurse, intensive care instr. Hampton (Va.) Gen. Hosp., 1974-79, patient edn. coordinator, 1978-79, critical care coordinator, 1980-82; critical care supr. Holy Cross Hosp., Austin, Tex., 1979-80; asst. dir. nursing Coliseum Park Nursing Home, Hampton, 1982-85; head nurse, trauma and plastic surgery U. Cin. Hosp., 1985—. Office chmn. Family Services, USAF, 1961-62, publicity chmn., 1962-64; hosp. vol. ARC, 1967-70; den leader Cub Scouts Am., 1970, C.P.R. instr. Am. Heart Assn., 1979-81. Mem. Am. Assn. Critical Care Nurses (sec. Tidewater chpt. 1981, pres.-elect. Tidewater chpt. 1982), Nat. League Nursing, Carolina-Va. Soc. Critical Care Medicine, Phi Theta Kappa. Home: 3152 Shorewalk Rd Maineville OH 45039 Office: U Cin Hosp Mail Drop 725 5 West St Cincinnati OH 45267

POCOCK, JENNIE ANN, artist; b. Tokyo, Dec. 1, 1950; came to U.S., 1958; d. Donald Allen and Namiko (Endo) Pocock; ed. U. Mich., 1969-73. Archtl. sec., word-processing operator Ayres, Lewis, Norris & May, Ann Arbor, Mich., 1972-76; archtl. sec., word processor Prentice & Chan, Ohlhausen, Architects and Planners, N.Y.C., 1976-84; adminstrv. sec. Beyer Blinder Belle, Architects and Planners, 1984-87, adminstrv. mgr., 1987—; exhibited works group shows, 1977-81; works represented permanent collections.

PODD, MARSHA DIANNE, small business owner, nurse; b. Washington, Apr. 14, 1951; d. John Francis and Gretchen (Green) P. BS in Child Devel., U. Calif., Davis, 1973; AA in Nursing, De Anza Coll., 1978. RN, Calif. Nurse Palo Alto (Calif.) Med. Clinic, 1973-78, St. Joseph Hosp., Orange, Calif., 1979-80, Diet Ctr., Petaluma, Calif., 1981—; nurse Petaluma Valley Hosp., 1980-86; cons. Diet Ctr., Rexburg, Idaho, 1984-85; co-founder Health in Motion Prodns., 1987—. Nurse Vietnam Refugee Placement, Hamilton AFB, 1980. Recipient award for one of top ten fastest growing Diet Ctrs. in U.S. and Can., 1987. Mem. Bay Area Diet Ctr. Assn. (pres. 1984, treas. 1987—), U. Calif. Aggie Alumni Assn. Republican. Home: 1108 Susan Way Novato CA 94947

PODGOR, ELLEN SUE, lawyer; b. Bklyn., Jan. 30, 1952; d. Benjamin and Yetta (Shilensky) Podgor. BS magna cum laude, Syracuse U., 1973; JD, Ind. Sch. Law-Indpls., 1976; MBA U. Chgo., 1987. Bar: Ind. 1976, N.Y. 1984, Pa. 1987. Instr., Ind. U.-Purdue U.-Indpls., 1975-76; law clk. Kroger, Gardis & Regas, Indpls., 1975-76; dep. prosecutor Lake County Prosecutor's Office, Crown Point, Ind., 1976-78, asst. county atty., 1981-83; ptnr. Nicholls & Podgor, Crown Point, Ind., 1978-87, instr. Temple U. Sch. Law, 1987—. Assoc. editor: Ind. Law Rev., 1975-76; contbr. articles to legal jours. Del., Ind. Democratic State Conv., 1982; bd. dirs. Lake County chpt. Am. Cancer Soc., 1982-83. Mem. ABA, Ind. Bar Assn., Lake County Bar Assn., Nat. Assn. Criminal Def. Lawyers, Women Lawyers Assn. Lake and Porter County (past pres.), Democrat. Jewish. Home and Office: 457B Newgate Ct Bensalem PA 19020

PODLES, ELEANOR PAULINE, state senator; b. Dudley, Mass., June 6, 1920; d. Francis and Pauline Magiera; student U. N.H.; m. Francis J. Podles, June 28, 1941; children: L. Patricia Podles Barrett, Elizabeth Lee Podles Keegan. Mem. N.H. Ho. of Reps., 1976-80; selectman City of Manchester, 1976-81; v.p. City of Manchester, Manchester, 1978-79; mem. N.H. Senate, 1980—; asst. majority whip, mem. fin. com., chmn. public affairs com., public instns. health and welfare com. Del., N.H. Republican Conv., 1976, 78, N.H. Constl. Conv., 1984; v.p. N.H. Senate, chair jud. com., vice chair exec. com., senate fin. com., health and human services for pub. insts. com.; pres. Manchester Rep. Women's Club, 1979-80; bd. dirs. St. Joseph's Community Service, Manchester Vis. Nurse Assn.; state chmn. Am. Legis. Exchange Council. Mem. Am. Legis. Exchange Council, Orgn. Women Legislators, Manchester Vis. Nurse Assn. Club: Manchester Country. Address: 185 Walnut Hill Ave Manchester NH 03104

PODURGIEL, MADELAINE MARY, nursing educator; b. Jewett City, Conn., Aug. 17, 1942; d. Stanley Joseph and Helen Mary (Luty) Kilbosa; children: Rebecca, Bernard, Debra, Jennifer. Cert. RN, Joseph Lawrence Sch., 1963; BS in Nursing, St. Louis U., 1966; MS in Nursing, Boston U., 1974; PhD in Edn., U. Conn., 1983. Staff nurse Hartford (Conn.) Hosp., 1967-68, faculty nursing dept., 1968-69, dir. nursing edn. and research, 1987—; faculty nursing dept. Rochester (Minn.) State Jr. Coll., 1970-72; faculty nursing dept. Mohegan Community Coll., Norwich, Conn., 1974-78, coordinator continuing edn., 1978-81; dir. nursing continuing edn. U. Conn., Storrs, 1981-87; cons. dept. staff devel. Hartford Hosp., 1984-85, dept. nursing edn. and research U. Conn. Health Ctr., Farmington, 1985-87. Coordinator cardiac program Am. Heart Assn., Norwich, 1976-80. Recipient award Nat. Univ. Continuing Edn. Assn., 1987; grantee U. Conn. Research Found., 1985-86. Mem. Am. Assn. Critical Care Nurses (program com., co-founder local chpt. 1976-80), Conn. Nurses Assn. (cons. to continuing edn. 1982-87), Internat. Assn. Near-Death Studies (cons.). Democrat. Roman Catholic. Office: Hartford Hosp Seymour St Hartford CT 06115

PODUSLO, SHIRLEY ELLEN, neuroscientist; b. Richeyville, Pa., Dec. 24, 1941; d. Joseph Poduslo and Helen Kondor. BS, Ohio State U., 1963; M, Johns Hopkins U., 1976, PhD, 1980. Biology tchr. Woodbridge (N.J.) Sr. High Sch., 1963; asst. Albert Einstein Coll. Medicine, N.Y.C., 1964-73; asst. Johns Hopkins U. Sch. Medicine, Balt., 1973-76, asst. prof., 1976-84, assoc. prof., 1984—. Contbr. articles to profl. jours. Grantee Kroc Found., 1979-82, NIH, 1980—, Multiple Sclerosis Soc., 1980-86. Mem. Am. Soc. Neurochemistry, Soc. for Neuroscience, Am. Soc. for Cell Biology, Am. Soc. Biological Chemists. Office: Johns Hopkins U Sch Medicine 600 N Wolfe St Baltimore MD 21205

POE, MERRY REX, insurance agency executive; insurance agent; b. Geneva, Ohio, Oct. 8, 1957; d. Glenn George and Ethel (Horvath) Rex; m. Gregory Scott Poe, July 25, 1981. B.S., Miami U., Oxford, Ohio, 1980. Lic. property, casualty, life, accident and health agt., Ohio; lic., registered rep. Nat. Assn. Securities Dealers. Underwriter trainee Shelby Mut., Ohio, 1980-81; adminstrv. asst. Johnson & Higgins, Cleve., 1981-82; agt. Planned Ins. Counseling, Inc., Chesterland, Ohio, 1982—, v.p., 1982-88; ind. ins. agt. Rex-Poe Ins. Agy., Inc., 1988—, v.p., 1988—. Mem. Profl. Ins. Agts. Assn. Republican. Presbyterian. Office: Rex-Poe Insurance Agy Inc 12200 Sperry Rd Chesterland OH 44026

POE, (LYDIA) VIRGINIA, reading educator; b. Bklyn., Jan. 19, 1932; d. Harold Waldemar and Lydia Beatrice (Doswell) Lind; m. Harold Weller Poe, Sept. 11, 1954; children: Michael Lind, David Harold, Timothy Claude. BA, Beloit Coll., 1954; MEd, U. Southwestern La., 1961, EdS, 1972; EdD, U. So. Miss., 1983. Cert. tchr., Fla., La., Ill., Wis. Elem. tchr. Caroline Brevard Sch., Tallahassee, 1961-64; supervising tchr. Fla. State U., Tallahassee, 1962-64; elem., supervising tchr. Hamilton Lab. Sch., Lafayette, La., 1965-67; assoc. prof. reading U. Southwestern La., Lafayette, 1968—, head Dept. Curriculum and Instr., 1987—; co-originator field experiences U. Southwestern La., 1970—; observer in elem. sch. Ecole de Charlemagne, Nancy, France, 1967; cons. Lafayette Parish Schs., 1968—. Contbr. to book: Reading Research Review, 1984; contbr. articles profl. jours., 1985-87; presenter papers to profl. orgns. 1968—. Organizer Conf. on Women in Politics, Lafayette, 1976 (recipient scholarship 1974); treas. State of La. ERA United, 1977; organizer, pres. First Luth. Ch. Day Care Ctr., Lafayette, 1977-80. Recipient research grant, U. Southwestern U., 1986-87. Mem. Internat. Reading Assn., Am. Reading Assn., Coll. Reading Assn., AAUW, (fellowship contribution 1976), United Fedn. Coll. Tchrs., Phi Delta Kappa, Phi Kappa Phi, Kappa Delta Pi, Beta Sigma Phi. Democrat. Lutheran. Office: U Southwestern La USL Box 42051 Lafayette LA 70504

POETHIG, EUNICE BLANCHARD, clergywoman; b. Hempstead, N.Y., Jan. 16, 1930; d. Werner J. and Juliet (Stroh) Blanchard; m. Richard Paul Poethig, June 7, 1952; children—Richard Scott, Kathryn Aileen, Johanna Klare, Margaret Juliet, Erika Christy. B.A., De Pauw U., 1951; M.A., Union Theol. Seminary, 1952; M.Div., McCormick Theol. Sem., 1975, S.T.M., 1977; Ph.D., Union Theol. Seminary, 1985. Ordained to ministry Presbyterian Ch., 1979; missionary United Presbyn. Ch. USA to United Ch. of Christ in Philippines, 1956-72; mem. faculty Ellinwood Coll. Christian Edn., Manila, 1957-61; mem. faculty, campus ministry Philippine Women's U., Manila, 1962-68; editor New Day Pubs., Manila, 1969-72; curriculum editor Nat. Council Chs., Manila, 1962-72; assoc. exec. Presbytery Chgo., 1979-85; exec. Presbytery of Western N.Y., 1986—; speaker United Presbyn. Women, 1973, 76, 79, 81, 85; mem. Council Execs., Ill. Council Chs., 1980-85. Author: Bible Studies in Concern, Response, A.D., 1975, Good News Women, 1987. Editor Hymn book-series: Everybody, I Love You, 1971-72, 150 Plus Tomorrow, 1982, 85. Mem. organizing bd. Asian Center Theology and Strategy, Chgo., 1974; bd. dirs. Ch. Women United, Chgo., 1974-79; trustee McCormick Theol. Sem., Chgo., 1974-75. Recipient Walker Cup, DePauw U., 1951. Nettie F. McCormick fellow in Old Testament Hebrew, McCormick Sem., Chgo., 1975. Mem. Soc. Bibl. Lit., Soc. Ethnomusicology, Am. Schs. Oriental Research, Witherspoon Soc. Office: Presbytery of Western NY 2450 Main St Buffalo NY 14214

POETKER, FRANCES LOUISE, florist; b. Cin., Apr. 16, 1912; d. Charles Benjamin and Louise (Johnston) Jones; BA, Vassar Coll., 1933; MA, U. Cin., 1934; m. Joseph G. Poetker, Aug. 10, 1937. Buyer Mabley & Carew Dept. Store, Cin., 1933-35; owner Jones the Florist, Cin., 1942-85, chmn., 1980, cons., 1986—; owner, cons. flower shop Pogue's L.S. Ayres, Cin.; lectr. in field; dir. Cin. Bell Telephone Co.; co-chmn. flower decorations Winter Olympics, 1980 (silver medal); dir. profl. flower shows, N.Y. and France, commentator wedding shows; mem. Nat. Eisenhauer People to People expedition to China, 1987; cons. Cin. Zool. Botanical Gardens 1st flower and plant show. Mem. spl. dirs. com. Cin. Park Bd.; mem. honors com. U. Cin.; founding mem. Nat. Mus. Women in the Arts, 1986, charter mem.; mem. Friends of Taft Mus., Cin. Mus. Natural History; friend of Nat. Arboretum Wildlife Protection Inst. Am.; mem. program com. Cin. Hist. Soc.; pres.'s com. Xavier U., Cin.; exec. com. Cin. Opera; Coll. Club of Cin. (hon mem.1986); v.p. Air Pollution Control League Cin.; adv. bd. Civic Garden Ctr.; bd. dirs. Bethesda Hosp., Cin.; mem. Cin. Beautiful Com. Recipient award of appreciation Dept. Agr., 1962, Sylvia award floral excellence, 1976; Belle Skinner Clark fellow, 1930; named Woman of Year, Cin. Enquirer, 1978; named to Floricultural Hall of Fame, 1967; commd. for World Book Identification and Symbolism of Plant Materials in Porcelain Collection Taft Mus. Cin., 1987. Mem. Am. Hort. Soc. (dir., chmn. 1982 conv., chmn. decorations N.Y.C. nat. meeting 1987, Frances Jones Poetker award named for), Soc. Am. Florists (1st Century award 1982), Florists Transworld Delivery Assn. (commentator 1942), Am. Acad. Florists (dir. emeritus), Allied Florists Assn. Cin., Profl. Florist Commentators Internat. (Tommy Bright award 1982), MacDowall Soc., McMicken Soc., N.C. Florists Assn. (mem. nat. com. on capital formation and estate taxation), Hillside Trust, Nature Conservency, Am. Music Scholarship Assn. (bd. dirs. 1987), English Speaking Union (Cin. chpt.). Lutheran. Clubs: Travel (pres., dir.), Women's, Symphony (lectr.), Banker's (Cin.); Garden of Am. (mem.-at-large), Town. Co-author: Wild Wealth, 1971; co-author The Herbalist; newspaper columnist Fun With Flowers, 1949; contbr. articles to mags.; designer food pictures for Gourmet mag; panelist weekly TV program Sunday Soul; actress, designer 3 syndicated movie shorts for Soc. Am. Florists; subject of various mag. articles. Home and Office: 1059 Celestial St Cincinnati OH 45202

POGO, BEATRIZ TERESA GARCIA-TUNON, cell biologist, virologist, educator; b. Buenos Aires, Argentina, Dec. 24, 1932; came to U.S., 1964, naturalized, 1976; d. Dario and Maria Teresa (Vergnory) Garcia-Tunon; m. Angel Oscar Pogo, Jan. 13, 1956; children: Gustavo, Gabriela. B.S., Lycee No. 1, Buenos Aires, 1950; M.D., Sch. Medicine, Buenos Aires, 1956; D.M.Sci., 1961. Intern Univ. Hosp., Buenos Aires, 1956-57; asst. Inst. Histology and Embryology, Buenos Aires U., 1957-59; fellow Sloan Kettering Meml. Hosp., N.Y.C., 1959-60, Rockefeller U., N.Y.C., 1960-61; asst. prof. cell biology Inst. Cell Biology, Cordoba U., Argentina, 1962-64; research assoc. Rockefeller U., N.Y.C., 1964-67; asst. Pub. Health Research Inst., N.Y.C., 1967-69, assoc., 1969-73, assoc. mem, 1973—; prof. exptl. cell biology and microbiology Mt. Sinai Sch. Medicine, CUNY, 1978—, acting dir. ctr. for exptl. cell biology, 1987—. Contbr. articles to profl. jours. Damon Runyon Fund fellow, 1964-65; grantee Am. Cancer Soc., 1970-73, 79-80, 84-85, NIH, 1975—. Mem. Am. Assn. for Cancer Research, N.Y. Acad. Sci., Am. Soc. Cell Biology, Harvey Soc., Am. Soc. Virology, Assn. for Women in Sci. (v.p. met. N.Y. chpt. 1981-83, pres. 1984-86), Am. Microbiol. Soc. Home: 237 Nyac Ave Pelham NY 10803 Office: Mt Sinai Sch Medicine 1 Gustave Levy Pl New York NY 10029

POGODIN, ARLYNE, data processing executive, consultant; b. Chgo., Jan. 21, 1947; d. Arnold M. and Bertha (Erkes) P.; B.A., DePaul U., 1980. Timekeeper Morris Handler Co., Chgo., 1964-70; comptroller, v.p. Lazar & Assocs. of Ill., Chgo., 1970-77; corp. sec., comptroller Interior Alterations, Inc., Chgo., 1977-86; pvt. practice fin. systems and computer analysis, 1986—; pres. Rly and Assos. Inc.,Chgo. Clubs: Mt. Sinai Hosp. Service, De Paul Century.

POGOS, ELLEN, financial consultant; b. Vilno, U.S.S.R., Mar. 16, 1953; came to U.S., 1962; d. Fred Pogos and Rose (Zelman) Rathaus. BA in Sociology, Ohio State U., 1977, MBA, 1983. With Merrill Lynch, Columbus, Ohio, 1977-80; fin. cons. Merrill Lynch, N.Y.C., 1983-84, Columbus, 1984—. Active Jr. League, Columbus, 1988—; mem., vol. Columbus Jewish Fedn., 1987. Mem. Pacesetters (Achievement award 1983). Jewish. Home: 576 Jasonway Ave Columbus OH 43214 Office: Merrill Lynch 100 E Broad St Columbus OH 43215

POGOZELSKI, BERNADETTE, occupational health specialist; b. Jersey City, Feb. 10, 1955; d. Vincent Frank and Mary Grace (Marchitto) P. BS, Bloomsburg U., 1977; MS, Temple U., 1981. Cert. indsl. hygienist, occupational hearing conservationist. Tchr., instrnl. guide Pennsbury Sch. Dist., Yardley, Pa., 1977-78, Harford County Bd. Edn., Belair, Md., 1978-80; indsl. hygienist Space Systems div. Gen. Electric Co., King of Prussia, Pa., 1981-82, Am. Newspaper Pubs. Assn., Reston, Va., 1982-85, Celanese Research Co., Summit, N.J., 1985-86; indsl. hygiene and environ. coordinator Hoechst Celanese Corp., Summit, 1986-87; supr. indsl. hygiene and safety Hoechst Celanese Va. Chems., Portsmouth, 1987—; cons. Towne Labs., Somerville, 1986-87, The Pitts. Press. Mem. Am. Soc. Safety Engrs., Am. Indsl. Hygiene Assn., Nat. Assn. Female Execs., Am. Acad. Indsl. Hygiene (diplomate), Bloomsburg U. Alumnae Assn. Roman Catholic. Club: Allentown (Pa.) Hiking. Home: 1521 Heritage Ave Virginia Beach VA 23464 Office: Hoechst Celanese Va Chems 801 Water St Portsmouth VA 23704

POGUE, ANNALEE, chemist; b. Visalia, Calif., June 30, 1945; d. Richard Lee and Anna Vivan (Palm) P. BA, San Jose State U., 1967. Chemist Monolithic Dielectrics, Burbank, Calif., 1966-68; mgr. materials U.S. Capacitor Corp., Burbank, 1968-71; emgr. tech. sales Sel-Rex Corp., Santa Ana, Calif., 1971-72; mgr. materials div. Cladan Inc., San Marcos, Calif., 1972-73; pres. Ann Pogue & Assoc. Inc., Solana Beach, Calif., 1972—. Bd. dirs. Solana Beach Town Council, 1974-81; sec. San Dieguito Citizens Planning Group, Solana Beach, 1975-76; chmn. local coastal plan com. City of Solana Beach. Mem. Cons. Chemist Assn. (treas. 1982-87—), Women in Bus. (support group 1986, bd. dirs. 1987-89), Am. Ceramic Soc., Am. Chem. Soc., Internat. Soc. Hybrid Microelectronics, Sierra Club (SCCOPE treas. 1986, Susan B. Miller award 1985, nat. computer chmn., regional vice chmn. for conservation, treas. Calif. chpt.), San Diego Land Conservancy (bd. dirs. 1986-88). Republican. Presbyterian. Home and Office: 258 Barbara St Solana Beach CA 92075-1232

POGUE, MARY ELLEN (MRS. L. WELCH POGUE), youth and community worker; b. Fremont, Nebr., Oct. 27, 1904; d. Frank E. and Mary (Coe) Edgerton; m. L. Welch Pogue, Sept. 8, 1926; children: Richard Welch, William Lloyd, John Marshall. BFA, U. Nebr., 1926; studied violin with Harrison Keller, Boston, 1926-28, Kemp Stillings Master Class, N.Y.C., 1936-37. Mem. Potomac String Ensemble, 1947-80. Historian, Gov. William Bradford Compact, 1966—; vice chmn. Montgomery County (Md.) Victory Garden Ctr., 1946-47; pres. Bethesda Community Garden Club, 1946-48; bd. dirs. Montgomery County YWCA, 1946-50, 52-55. Recipient Outstanding Service award Bethesda United Meth. Ch., 1984, Cert. of Appreciation, Bethesda Community Garden Club, 1985, Outstanding Contbns. award Soc. Mayflower Descs. in D.C., 1985. Mem. Mayflower Soc. (dir. D.C. 1950—), PEO (pres. 1957-59), Mortar Bd. Alumnae (pres. 1965-67, award 1986), Nat. Geneal. Soc., Nat. Soc. Women Descs. Ancient and Hon. Arty. Co., Welcome to Washington Internat. Club, Ind. Agy. Women (assoc.), Delta Omicron Music. Methodist. Club: Capital Speakers. Editor: Favorite Recipes of Mary Edgerton of Aurora, Nebraska, 1963; compiler, editor Edgerton Coe History, 1965. Home: 5204 Kenwood Ave Chevy Chase MD 20815

POHL, GAIL PIERCE, trade association executive, editor; b. Stigler, Okla., Nov. 18, 1938; s. William James and Kathleen Louise (McConnell) Pierce; m. Lee W. Pohl, July 7, 1962; 1 dau., Leslie Kathleen. B.A. in Journalism, U. Okla., 1960. Statehouse reporter Okla. Bus. News, Oklahoma City, 1960-66, news editor, 1966-72; editor Jour. Am. Ins., Chgo., 1973-77; pub. relations assoc. Alliance of Am. Insurers, Chgo., 1972, dir. publs., 1977-78, dir. policy communications, 1978-79; exec. dir. Self-Service Storage Assn., Eureka Springs, Ark., 1981—. Contbr. articles and news stories to various publs. Pres., Parent's Orgn., 1st Montessori Sch. Atlanta, 1980-81, trustee, 1980-81. Recipient 1st place award for Jour. Am. Ins. mag. Nat. Mut. Ins. Communicators, 1977, Mag. Honor award, 1978; 1st prize for news story Chgo. Assn. Bus. Communicators, 1978, honor award for feature article, 1978. Mem. Chgo. Ins. Women (bd. dirs. 1978-79), Women in Communications, Inc., Bus. and Profl. Women (pres. 1985—), bd. dirs. Eureka Springs chpt.), Am. Soc. Assn. Execs. Clubs: Beaver Lake Sailing (Ark.). Home: 270 Spring St Eureka Springs AR 72632 Office: Self-Service Storage Assn PO Box 110 16 First St Eureka Springs AR 72632

POHLY, SHEILA RIMLAND, educational psychologist; b. N.Y.C., Oct. 10, 1946; d. Selig and Anne (Liberman) Rimland; student Russell Sage Coll., 1963-65; B.S. with distinction, Cornell U., 1967, M.S., 1968; permanent cert. sch. psychologist N.Y. State, Columbia U. Tchrs. Coll., 1971; Ph.D. in Psychology, SUNY, Stony Brook, 1979; m. Lawrence M. Pohly, Aug. 20, 1967; children—Michael Brian, Robert Scott. Instr. SUNY, Stony Brook, 1978-79; adj. faculty C.W. Post Coll., L.I. U., 1980—; sch. psychologist, gifted and talented program Northport-East Northport (N.Y.) Union Free Sch. Dist., 1980—; pvt. practice psychology, 1983—; cons. sch. dists. Active Citizens-Profl. Adv. Com. on Gifted Edn., Roslyn Pub. Schs., 1981-83; mem. alumni interviewing com. Cornell U., 1981—; mem. sch. bd. local Temple Sch., 1980-84. Mem. Am. Psychol. Assn., Nassau County Psychol. Assn., Nat. Assn. Gifted Children, Orton Soc., Cornell U. Alumni Assn., Phi Kappa Phi, Omicron Nu. Contbg. author writings to profl. publs., papers to profl. confs. Home: 3 Meadow Rd Old Westbury NY 11568 Office: 110 Elwood Rd Northport NY 11768

POINSETT, LINDA KAY, real estate executive; b. Cape Girardeau, Mo., July 12, 1950; d. Loren A. and Lois Marie (Morrison) Huffman; m. Michael Poinsett, Sept. 3, 1970 (div. Feb. 1974); m. Ronald Howard Silverman, Oct. 3, 1982. BS, U. South East Mo., 1970. Real estate broker Murdoch & Coll, Inc., St. Louis, 1981. Mem. beautification com. Downtown St. Louis, 1985, 86 (Better Downtown award 1985); bd. dirs. Downtown St. Louis, Inc., 1986-87. Mem. Regional Commerce and Growth Assn., Comml. Real Estate Women (sec. 1981), Ambassadors of St. Louis, Nat. Assn. Female Execs., Nat. Assn. Indsl. and Office Park Developers. Avocations: reading; movies; travel. Office: Murdoch & Coll Inc 314 N Broadway Saint Louis MO 63102

POITRAS, NANCY LOU, secondary educator; b. Hartford, Conn., May 24, 1944; d. Louis N. and Carolyn (Philbrick) P. BS in Social Sci., Cen. Conn. State Coll., 1966, MS in History, 1975; MA in Am. Studies, Pepperdine U., 1986. Cert. secondary tchr. Tchr. Berlin (Conn.) Pub. Schs., 1967-81; employee K-Mart Corp., Wethersfield, Conn., 1981-82; dept. chmn. history Parish Hill High Sch., Chaplin, Conn., 1982—; field researcher Berlin High Sch. and U. Conn. Alternative Edn., 1973, 74-81, Parish Hill High Sch. and U. Conn. Human Rights assessment for Conn. Dept. Edn., 1985-86; workshop participant for revision Human Rights Manual Dept. State, 1982-83, cons. State of Conn. Manual on Human Rights, 1986. Adult leader girls Tri-Hi-Y YMCA Youth Club, Berlin, 1967-72; state conv. rep. Conn. Edn. Assn., Berlin, 1967-81, contract negotiator local level, 1973-79, grievance negotiator local level, 1979-80, local pres., 1980-81. Recipient Am. Studies fellow Ea. Coll., St. Davids, Pa., 1978, Pepperdine U., 1981, 85, endowment study fellowship, Conn. Council Humanities, 1988, Am. Studies Alumni fellow Ea. Coll., 1987; Julian Virtue fellow Pepperdine U., 1982. Mem. Nat. Hist. Soc. (founding), Nat. Trust for Hist. Preservation, Conn. Council for Social Studies, Nat. Council for Social Studies (research com. 1983-87), Alumni Assn. Cen. Conn. State U., Alumni Assn. Pepperdine U. Republican. Roman Catholic. Club: Womens Bus. and Profl. of Hartford. Office: Parish Hill High Sch Parish Hill Rd Chaplin CT 06235

POKORNI, ORYSIA, musician; b. Ternopil, Ukraine, Aug. 4, 1938; came to U.S., 1951; d. Gregory and Olha (Moroz) Danylkiw; m. Paul Pokorni, Jan. 25, 1958; children: Daniel, Mark. Student, Cosmopolitan Sch. Music, 1962; AA, Truman Coll., 1984. Mgr. Internat. Theatre of Chgo., 1963—; asst. office mgr. Ravenswood Hosp., Chgo., 1980-83; radio announcer WEDC, Chgo., 1965-66; choir dir. Moloda Dumka Children's Choir, Chgo., 1981-85. Accompanist various choirs and soloists, 1960—; composer songs;

music arranger for children's plays. Tchr. St. Nicholas Saturday Sch., Chgo., 1966-85; active Ukrainian Women's League, Chgo., 1985. Mem. Ukrainian Congress Com. (chmn. spl. events 1984—). Home and Office: 4520 N Richmond Chicago IL 60625

POKORNOWSKI, BARBARA KAREN, travel agency owner, computer consultant; b. Landstuhl, Fed. Republic of Germany, Jan. 16, 1959; d. Ronald Felix and Joan Barbara (Krygier) P. BA, U. Notre Dame, 1980; MBA, Loyola U., Chgo., 1982; AAS, Coll. of DuPage, Glen Ellyn, Ill., 1983, AA, 1984. Cert. computer cons., cruise cons. Med. asst. Cen. Dupage Internists, Carol Stream, Ill., 1974-77, acct., 1973—; owner, mgr. Fun 'N Travel, Wheaton, Ill., 1978—, computer cons. DKP Enterprises, Wheaton, Ill., 1982—. Mem. Am. Soc. Travel Agts., Assn. Retail Travel Agts., Pacific Asia Travel Assn., Winfield (Ill.) Hist. Soc., U. Notre Dame Alumni Assn., Loyola U. Alumni Assn. Republican. Roman Catholic. Clubs: Dominic (Naperville, Ill.); Scuba Divers (Chgo.), Notre Dame. Home: 26 W 260 Blair St Winfield IL 60190 Office: Fun 'N Travel 1411 E Roosevelt Rd Wheaton IL 60187

POLAN, NANCY MOORE, artist; b. Newark, Ohio; d. William Tracy and Francis (Flesher) Moore; A.B., Marshall U., 1936; m. Lincoln Milton Polan, Mar. 28, 1934; children—Charles Edwin, William Joseph Marion. One-man shows Charleston Art Gallery, 1961, 67, 73, Greenbrier, 1963, Huntington Galleries, 1963, 66, 71, N.Y. World's Fair, 1965, W.Va. U., 1966, Carroll Reese Mus., 1967; exhibited in group shows Am. Watercolor Soc., Allied Artists of Am., Nat. Arts Club, 1968-74, 76-77, 86, 87, Pa. Acad. Fine Arts, Opening of Creative Arts Center W.Va. U., 1969, Internat. Platform Assn. Art Exhibit, 1968-69, 72, 73, 74, 79, 85, 86. Allied Artists W.Va., 1968-69, 86, Joan Miro Graphic Exhbn., Barcelona, Spain, 1970, XXI Exhibit Contemporary Art, La Scala, Florence, Italy, 1971, Rassegna Internazionale d'Arte Grafica, Siena, Italy, 1973, 79, 82, Opening of Parkersburg (W.Va.) Art Center, 1975, Internat. Platform Assn. Ann. Exhbn., 1979, others. Hon. v.p. Centro Studi e Scambi Internazionale, Rome, Italy, 1977; life mem. Huntington (W.Va.) Mus. Art. Recipient Acad. of Italy with Gold medal, 1979; recipient Norton Meml. award 3d Nat. Jury Show Am. Art, Chautauqua, N.Y., 1960; Purchase prize, Jurors award, Watercolor award Huntington Galleries, 1960, 61; Nat. Arts Club for watercolor, 1969; Gold medal Masters of Modern Art exhbn., La Scala Gallery, Florence, 1975, gold medal Accademia Italia, 1984, 1986, diploma Internat. Com. for World Culture and Arts, 1987, many others. Mem. DAR, Allied Artists W.Va., Internat. Platform Assn. (3d award-painting in ann. art exhbn. 1977), Allied Artists Am. (asso.), Huntington Galleries, Tri-State Arts Assn. (Equal Merit award 1978), Sunrise Found., Pen and Brush (Grumbacher golden palette mem.; Grumbacher award 1978), Am. Watercolor Soc. (asso.), Am. Fedn. Arts, Nat. Arts Club, Leonardo da Vinci Acad. (Rome), W.Va. Watercolor Soc. (charter), Accademia Italia, Sigma Kappa. Episcopalian. Club: Vero Beach Arts (Fla.). Address: 2 Prospect Dr Huntington WV 25701 Other: 2106 Club Dr Vero Beach FL 32963

POLASCIK, MARY ANN, ophthalmologist; b. Elkhorn, W.Va., Dec. 28, 1940; d. Michael and Elizabeth (Halko) Polascik; B.A., Rutgers U., 1967; M.D., Pritzker Sch. Medicine, 1971; m. Joseph Elie, Oct. 2, 1973; 1 dau., Laura Elizabeth Polascik. Jr. pharmacologist Ciba Pharm. Co., Summit, N.J., 1961-67; intern Billings Hosp., Chgo., 1971-72; resident in ophthalmology U. Chgo. Hosp., 1972-75; practice medicine specializing in ophthalmology, Dixon, Ill., 1975—; pres. McNichols Clinic, Ltd.; cons. ophthalmology, Dixon Devel. Ctr.; mem. staff Katherine Shaw Bethea Hosp., Dixon, Dixon Developmental Ctr. Hosp. Bd. dirs. Sinissippi Mental Health Ctr., 1977-82; bd. med. dirs. Winnebago Ctr. for Blind. Mem. AMA, Ill. Med. Soc., Ill. Assn. Ophthalmology, Am. Assn. Ophthalmology, Alpha Sigma Lambda. Roman Catholic. Clubs: Galena Territory, Dixon Country. Office: 120 S Hennepin Ave Dixon IL 61021

POLCAR, GERTRUDE ELIZABETH, judge; b. Cleve., Oct. 10, 1916; d. Martin and Gertrude M. (Jirele) Polcar; student Leland Stanford Jr. U., 1934-36; A.B. in Law, U. Chgo., 1938, J.D., 1940. Admitted to Ohio bar, 1941, U.S. Supreme Ct. bar, 1981; individual practice law, Parma, 1942-44, 50-56, 60-71; asst. atty. gen. of Ohio, 1945-49, 57-59; councilman City of Parma, 1960-68; mem. Ohio Ho. of Reps. from Dist. 51, 1969-71; judge Parma Mcpl. Ct., 1972—, presiding and adminstrv. judge, 1976-77, 82-83, 88—; v.p.-at-large Greater Cleve. Safety Council. Mem. Republican State Central Com. from 20th Dist., 1954-64; mem. South Ridge Civic Assn.; dir.-at-large Friends of Parma Libraries, 1981—. Recipient superior jud. service awards Supreme Ct. Ohio, 1975-86. Mem. Ohio, Cuyahoga County, Parma bar assns., Bar Assn. Greater Cleve., Cleve. Women Lawyers' Assn., Ohio Mcpl. Judges Assn. (trustee), Greater Cleve. Mcpl. Judges Assn. (pres. 1982), Ohio Jud. Conf., Am. Judges Assn., Parma Area Hist. Soc. Clubs: Order Eastern Star, Ladies Oriental Shrine N.Am. Home: 7060 Ridge Rd Parma OH 44129 Office: 5750 W 54th St Parma OH 44129

POLEMITOU, OLGA ANDREA, accountant; b. Nicosia, Cyprus, June 28, 1950; d. Takis and Georgia (Nicolaou) Chrysanthou. BA with honors, U. London, 1971; PhD, Ind. U.-Bloomington, 1981. CPA, Ind. Asst. productivity officer Internat. Labor Office/Cyprus Productivity Ctr., Nicosia, 1971-74; cons. Arthur Young & Co., N.Y.C., 1981; mgr. Coopers & Lybrand, Newark, 1981-83; mgr. Bell Atlantic, Phila., 1983—; chairperson adv. council Extended Day Care Community Edn., West Windsor Plainsboro, 1987-88. Contbr. articles to profl. jours. Bus. cons. project bus. Jr. Achievement, Indpls., 1984-85; chairperson adv. council Community Edn., West Windsor, Plainsboro, N.J., 1987-88, chairperson adv. council. Mem. Nat. Assn. Female Execs., Nat. Trust for Hist. Preservation, Ind. CPA Soc., N.J. CPA Soc., Am. Inst. CPAs., Princeton Network of Profl. Women. Avocations: water skiing, tennis. Home: PO Box 401 Princeton Junction NJ 08550 Office: Bell Atlantic 1880 John F Kennedy Blvd Philadelphia PA 19103

POLEN-DORN, LINDA F., communications executive; b. Cleve., Mar. 23, 1945; d. Stanley M. and Mildred K. Neuger; m. Samuel O. Dorn; children: Lanelle, Brian, Adam, Dawn. Student, U. Iowa, 1963-66; BA cum laude, U. Miami, 1967. Dir. pub. relations Muscular Dystrophy Assn., Miami, 1967-71; cons. pub. relations Miami, 1971-75; writer, cons. Jack Cory & Assocs., Ft. Lauderdale, Fla., 1976-79; supr. account Maizner & Franklin, Ft. Lauderdale, 1980-86; v.p. communications Glendale Fed. Savs. & Loan Assn., Ft. Lauderdale, 1987—. Vice chmn. govt. task force, 1986. Mem. Mus. Art Ft. Lauderdale, Philharmonic Soc., Pub. Relations Soc. Am., Internat. Assn. Bus. Communicators, C. of C. Office: Glendale Fed Savs and Loan Assn 301 E Las Olas Blvd Fort Lauderdale FL 33301

POLEVOY, NANCY TALLY, lawyer, social worker; b. N.Y.C., May 27, 1944; d. Charles H. and Bernice M. (Gang) Tally; m. Martin D. Polevoy, Mar. 19, 1967; children: Jason Tally, John Gerald. Student, Mt. Holyoke Coll., 1962-64; BA, Barnard Coll., 1966; MS in Social Work, Columbia U., 1968, JD, 1986. Bar: N.Y. 1987. Caseworker unmarried mothers' service Louise Wise Services, N.Y.C., 1967, caseworker adoption dept., 1969-71; caseworker Youth Consultation Service, N.Y.C., 1968-69; asst. research scientist, psychiat. social worker dept. child psychiatry NYU Med. Ctr., N.Y.C., 1973-81; adv. ct. apptd. spl. advs. Manhattan Family Ct., N.Y.C., 1981-82; matrimonial assoc. Ballon, Stoll & Itzler, 1987, Herzfeld & Rubin, P.C., 1987—; cons. social work, 1981-86. Contbr. articles on early infantile autism to profl. jours. Recipient French Govt. prize, 1963. Mem. Assn. of City of N.Y. Bar Assn., N.Y. State Bar Assn., Nat. Assn. Social Workers, Acad. Cert. Social Workers, Alumni Assn. Columbia U. Sch. Social Work. Home: 1155 Park Ave New York NY 10128 Office: Herzfeld & Rubin 40 Wall St New York NY 10005

POLICASTRO, ANNE, nurse; b. Queens, N.Y., Mar. 11, 1955; d. Michael A. and Anna (Dintino) P. Diploma in nursing, Beth Israel Sch. Nursing, 1978; BS in Nursing, Pace U., 1987. RN. Staff nurse Beth Israel Med. Ctr., N.Y.C., 1978-83, utilization rev. examiner, 1983-85, supr. quality assurance, utilization rev., 1985-87, mgr. quality assurance, asst. dir. utilization rev., 1987—. Mem. Nat. Assn. Quality Assurance Profls., N.Y. Assn. Quality Assurance Profls., Sigma Theta Tau. Office: Beth Israel Med Ctr 16 St and 1st Ave New York NY 10003

POLINSKY, JANET NABOICHECK, state legislator; b. Hartford, Conn., Dec. 6, 1930; d. Louis H. and Lillian S. Naboicheck; BA, U. Conn., 1953; postgrad. Harvard U., 1954; m. Hubert N. Polinsky, Sept. 21, 1958; children—Gerald, David, Beth. Mem. Waterford 2d Charter Commn. (Conn.), 1967-68, Waterford Conservation Commn., 1968-69; Waterford rep. Town Meeting, 1969-71, SE Conn. Regional Planning Agy., 1971-73; mem. Waterford Planning and Zoning Commn., 1970-76, chmn., 1973-76; mem. Waterford Dem. Town Com., 1976—, del. State Dem. Conv., 1976, 78, 80, 82, 84, 86; mem. Conn. Ho. of Reps. from 38th Dist., 1977—, asst. majority leader, 1981-83, chmn. appropriations com., 1983-84, 87-88, ranking mem., 1985-86, minority whip, 1985-86. Trustee Eugene O'Neill Meml. Theatre Ctr., 1973-76, 81—; corporator, Lawrence and Meml. Hosps., 1987—; mem. New Eng. Bd. Higher Edn., 1981-83; mem. fiscal affairs com. Eastern Conf. Council of State Govts., 1983—. Named Woman of Yr., Waterford Jr. Women's Club, 1977, Nehantic Women's Bus. and Profl. Club, 1979, Legislator of Yr., Conn. Library Assn., 1980. Mem. Order Women Legislators, Delta Kappa Gamma (hon.). Home: 19 E Neck Rd Waterford CT 06385 Office: State Capitol Hartford CT 06106

POLINSKY, LINDA CAROLYN, educational association executive; b. Freeport, Tex., Oct. 13, 1949; d. Orion Oswald Barnes and Gene Clair (Usrey) Chapmon; m. Donald Jay Hearn, Jan. 31, 1971; m. David Loren Polinsky, June 5, 1982; children: Dinah Leigh Hearn, Andrew Orion Morris. BS in Acctg., Calif. State U., Sacramento, 1985; postgrad. in bus. adminstrn., Calif. State U., 1985—; BS in Mgmt. Info. Systems, McGeorge Sch. Law, Sacramento, 1985. Owner, developer All Occasion Catering, Auburn, Calif., 1974-77; co-owner, mgr. The Kitchen, Auburn, 1977-79; ptnr., developer Community Alcohol Diversion, Auburn, 1981-82; v.p. Pacific Ednl. Services Inc., Auburn, 1982-85, owner, pres., 1985—. Treas. Com. to Re-elect Judge Young, Auburn, 1982; bd. dirs. Placer Women Ctr., Auburn, 1982; mem. Jud. Adv. Council, Auburn, 1986—, Dist. Atty.'s Domestic Violence Task Force, Auburn, 1987. Mem. AAUW, Nat. Assn. Female Execs., Auburn Bus. and Profl. Women (pres. 1987-88), Women in Leadership, Calif. Elected Women's Assn. Research and Edn. Democrat. Lodge: Soroptimist Internat. Office: Pacific Ednl Services Inc 11484 C Ave Auburn CA 95603

POLITE, EDMONIA ALLEN, consultant; b. Washington, June 22, 1922; d. Thomas Samuel and Narcissus Bertha (Porter) Allen-Sylvester; m. George Frederick Polite, Jan. 5, 1941; 1 child, Frederick Gartrell. BA, Roosevelt U., 1958; MEd, Loyola U., Chgo., 1966; PhD in Adminstrn. and Supervision, Purdue U., 1973; DDiv, Ea. U., Tampa, Fla., 1971, DEd in Psychology, 1972. Dir. Media Ctr., Chgo., 1958-69, 73-81; instr. media scis. Purdue U. West Lafayette, Ind., 1969-73; pres. Cons. Inc., Chgo. and Orlando, Fla., 1974—; dir. Community Tutoring Ctr., Chgo., 1974-80; dir. workshop U. Cen. Fla., 1987; cons. Lake Region Conf., Detroit, 1966, Librarians, Inc., Chgo., 1970-71. Author: In Passing, 1970, People Who Help Us, 1982. Founder South End Parents Council, Chgo., 1960, Humanitarian Profls., Chgo., 1974, Orlando, 1983—; bd. dirs. Salem House, Chgo., 1980—. Recipient Outstanding Service award Lions Club, Chgo., 1975, Outstanding Educator award Fla. Agrl. and Mech. U. Alumni Assn. Mem. Nat. Assn. Club Women (dir. archives 1980—), Ill. Audio Visual Assn., Phi Delta Kappa. Club: Successful Progressors (Orlando) (pres. 1983—). Avocations: writing, community service, counseling. Home and Office: PO Box 580459 Orlando FL 32858

POLITE, MARIE ANN, special education educator; b. Savannah, Ga., Jan. 26, 1954; d. Lucius Sr. and Leola (Denegal) Levett; m. Alan Polite, Sept. 1, 1972; children: Sharmona Melissa, Nakisha Kenyatta. Cert. tchr., Ga. Learning disabilities specialist Savannah (Ga.)-Chatham Bd. Edn., 1976—, Royce Reading Ctr., Savannah, 1980-85; summer employment counselor Savannah-Chatham Bd. Edn., 1986—; tng. cons. Ga. Employees Assn., 1986, MAP to Success Cons. Firm, Savannah, 1985—; talk show host Sta. WSOK Radio, Savannah, 1986—. Commr. Savannah Housing Authority, 1987—. Named one of Outstanding Young Women Am., 1980; recipient Outstanding Service award Savannah Police Dept., 1982. Mem. Am. Mgmt. Assn., Am. Soc. for Pub. Adminstrs., Ga. Fedn. Tchrs. (v.p. 1983—), Savannah Fedn. Tchrs. (pres. 1983-86), Savannah Women's Network (bd. dirs. 1987—), Ga. Fedn. Bus. and Profl. Women (dist. dir. SE Ga. 1986-88, pres. Port City chpt. 1983-84), Nat. Polit. Congress Black Women, Action Together (pres.), Phi Delta Kappa. Democrat. Presbyterian. Lodge: Zonta. Home: 10446 Gray Fox Way Savannah GA 31406

POLITY, LEDDY S., preschool director; b. Wrightsville, Pa., Nov. 6, 1936; d. Michael Kenneth and Vivian Lentz (Birnstock) Smith; m. Richard Milton Polity, Sept. 15, 1956; children: Karen, Bruce, Jennifer. Student, Gettysburg (Pa.) Coll., 1954-56, Kean Coll., 1966-74. Cert. early childhood edn. Tchr. Little Folks Nursery Sch., Woodbridge, N.J., 1966-67; co-founder, tchr. Presbyn. Nursery Sch., Matawan, 1967; dir. Presbyn. Nursery Sch., 1982—; cons. community services bd. Brookdale Community Coll., 1977-82; workshop presentor, various community groups statewide. Contbr. articles to profl. jours.; appeared as TV panelist on N.Y. and N.J. talk shows. Mem. Sch. Aged Child Care Task Force, N.J. Dept. Human Services, 1983; ad hoc citizens adv. bd., N.J. Bur. of Licensing, 1981, 85, 86-87; Sunday sch. tchr., Cross of Glory Luth. Ch., Aberdeen, 1963-73, Sunday Sch. supt., 1974-76, vacation sch. dir., 1976-78; coordinator, Girl Scouts of U.S., Matawan, 1976-79; apptd. to Gov's. Child Care Adv. Council of N.J., 1984—. Mem. N.J. Shore Chpt. Assn. for Edn. of Young Children (pres. 1976-78), N.J. Assn. for Edn. of Young Children (lit. chmn. 1978-80, 1st v.p. 1980-82, state pres. 1982-84, exec. bd. advisor 1984-86), Assn. for Edn. of Young Children (state conf. planner, 1980, 81, 82). Home: 144 Idlebrook Ln Matawan NJ 07747 Office: Presby Nursery Sch 33 Hwy 34 Matawan NJ 07747

POLK, EDWINA ROWAND, engineer, surveyor; b. Lakeland, Fla., Jan. 30, 1921; d. Charles Adrian and Edith Ruth (Gramling) Rowand; m. Virgil Isaac Polk, Jan. 2, 1949; 1 child, Edith. B.S. in Math., Fla. So. Coll., 1942; postgrad. The Citadel, 1943. Registered land surveyor, Fla. Draftsman U.S. Navy, Charleston, S.C., 1942-45; tchr. math. Brandon High Sch., Fla., 1945-46; draftsman Food Machinery, Lakeland, 1946-49; draftsman designer, 1949-63; designer Polk County, Bartow, Fla., 1963-76, asst. county engr., 1976—; tchr., mem. tech. com. Polk Community Coll., Winter Haven, Fla., 1966-69. Mem. Fla. Soc. Profl. Land Surveyors. Democrat. Baptist. Avocations: history; antiques; cooking. Home: 302 Ariana St Lakeland FL 33803 Office: Polk County Engring 168 W Main St Bartow FL 33830

POLK, MARY JO MCCRACKEN, state official; b. Quitaque, Tex.; d. Leon and Lockwood McCracken; B.B.A., U. Tex., El Paso, 1967; m. D. Wade Polk, May 15, 1948; children—Linda, Paul, Laura. Elem. and kindergarten tchr., 1967-78; mem. Tex. Ho. of Reps., 1979-84, mem. energy com., jud. affairs com., urban needs com., steering com., mem. ways and means com., chmn. human services com., chmn. select com. on teenage pregnancy; exec. asst. to commr. Tex. Dept. Human Services, 1984—. Bd. dirs. Runaway Center and Sch. for Teen-Age Parents. Mem. Nat. Conf. State Legislatures (human resources com.), Tex. Tchrs. Assn. (life), Tex. Elected Women. Democrat. Methodist. Home: 2409 Versailles Cedar Park TX 78613 Office: 701 W 51st St Austin TX 78769

POLK, MELANIE ROSA, engineering scheduler; b. Houston, Sept. 13, 1955; d. John H. and Ramona (Smith) P. Student Pearl River Jr. Coll., Poplarville, Miss., 1973-74, Jackson County Jr. Coll., Pascagoula, Miss., 1974-75, U. Houston, 1979-82. Prodn. control scheduler Ingalls Shipyard, Pascagoula, 1976-78; sr. engring. scheduler Brown & Root, Houston, 1978-84; sr. engring. scheduler Litton Data Systems, Pascagoula, 1984-85, sr. engring. scheduler, New Orleans, 1985-86; sr. research and devel. scheduler Litton Guidance and Control, Woodland Hills, Calif., 1986—, sr. performace measurement analyst. Contbr. to Best Loved American Poems, 1979, 80. Mem. Assn. Profl. Planners and Schedulers (treas. 1979-80), Nat. Assn. Female Execs. Avocations: scuba diving, sky diving, modeling, acting, traveling. Office: Litton Guidance and Control 5500 Canoga Ave Woodland Hills CA 91367

POLKOW, LINDA ROSE, rehabilitation services administrator, occupational therapist; b. N.Y.C., Apr. 8, 1953; d. John Hans and Leonore (Hamburger) Schiff; m. Melvin Samuel Polkow, June 22, 1975; children: Eric Daniel, Jessica Gail. BS, NYU, 1975, postgrad. in pub. adminstrn., 1981—. Lic. occupational therapist. Dir. occupational therapy Burke Rehab. Ctr., White Plains, N.Y., 1975-84; rehab. services coordinator Barnert Meml. Hosp. Ctr., Paterson, N.J., 1984-86; pvt. cons. physicians offices Children's Aid Soc., N.Y., N.J., 1986-87; info. and referral specialist community outreach and pub. relations Health and Welfare Council Bergen County, Hackensack, N.J., 1988—; vis. guest lectr. various colls. and univs. Contbr. articles to profl. publs. Mem. Jewish Community Ctr., Paramus, N.J., 1982—; mem. aux. Bergen City Med. Soc., 1987—, Hackensack Med. Ctr., 1987—; vol. Health & Welfare Council Bergen County, 1988—; bd. govs. Jewish Community Ctr., Paramus, N.J., 1985—; mem. Yarneh Parents Assn., Aux. Paramus. Mem. Am. Occupational Therapy Assn., Vis. Nurses Assn. (utilization reviewer Westchester and White Plains chpts. 1980-84. Democrat. Jewish. Avocations: tennis, biking, camping, travel, reading.

POLLACK, BETTY GILLESPIE, health care executive; b. Oak Park, Ill., Apr. 4, 1940; d. Leon H. and Elta F. Gillespie; B.A., Whittier coll., 1962; M.S., Columbia U., 1964; m. David Pollack, Dec. 18, 1971; 1 son, Michael Alan. Community organizer, Boston, 1964-66; faculty mem. Grad. Sch. Social Welfare, U. Calif., Berkeley, 1967-71; exec. dir. Calif. chpt. Nat. Assn. Social Workers, Millbrae, 1971-81; pres., chief exec. officer Vis. Nurse Assn., Santa Clara County, Calif., 1981—; mem. exec. com. Assn. United Way Agencies, 1982-85, chmn. Cert. Assn. Execs. Study Course, 1981. Mem. No. Calif. Soc. Assn. Execs. (sec.-treas. 1980-82, pres.-elect 1982-83, pres. 1983-84, program chmn. 1984-85, chmn. nominating com. 1985-86), Peninsula Profl. Women's Network (sec. 1981-82, chmn. networking conf. 1981, pres. ednl. fund 1981-82), No. Calif. Coalition Vis. Nurse Assns. (v.p. 1983-85, pres. 1985), Bay Area Profl. Women's Network (mem. newsletter com. 1980-81), Am. Soc. Assn. Execs., LWV. Democrat. Home: 316 Sycamore St San Carlos CA 94070 Office: 2025 Gateway Pl Suite 260 San Jose CA 95110

POLLACK, FLORENCE ZAKS, executive relocation and conference management company executive; b. Washington, Pa.; d. Charles and Ruth (Isaacson) Zaks; divorced; children—Melissa, Stephanie. BA, Flora Stone Mather Coll., Western Res. U., 1961. Pres., treas. Exec. Arrangements, Inc., Cleve., 1978—. Lobbyist Ohio Citizens Com. for Arts, Columbus, 1975-83; mem. Leadership Cleve., 1978-79; trustee Jr. Com., Cleve. Orch., Cleve. Ballet, Dance Cleve., Jr. Com. of No. Ohio Opera Assn., Cleve. Opera, Shakers Lakes Regional Nature Ctr., Cleve. Music Sch. Settlement, Playhouse Sq. Cabinet, Cleve. Ctr. Econ. Edn., Cleve. Conv. and Visitors Bur. Named Idea Woman of Yr., Cleve. Plain Dealer, 1975; named to Au Courrant list Cleve. Mag., 1979, named to Cleve.'s 100 Most Influential Women, 1985, 88, named one of 1988 Trendsetters Cleveland Woman mag. Mem. Cleve. Area Meeting Planning. Clubs: Skating, University, Women's City, Playhouse. Avocations: arts, travel, reading. Office: Exec Arrangements Inc 13221 Shaker Sq Cleveland OH 44120

POLLACK, JANE MYRA, federal agency administrator; b. N.Y.C., July 16, 1951; d. Samuel M. and Sarah (Orshansky) P.; m. Vincent E. Meehan, May 1, 1983; 1 child, Richard Paul. BA, SUNY, Stony Brook, 1972; MBA, Fordham U., 1987. Postal supr. U.S. Postal Service, N.Y.C., 1975-79; mgmt. assoc. U.S. Postal Service, Boston, 1980-83, mgr. retail sales and services, 1983—. Active vol. Huntington's Disease Soc. Am. (N.Y. State chpt.). Mem. Nat. Assn. Female Execs., Mktg. Club. Democrat. Jewish. Home: 11 Riverside Dr New York NY 10023

POLLACK, LANA, state senator; b. Ludington, Mich., Oct. 11, 1942; d. Abbie and Genevieve (Siegel) Schoenberger; m. Henry Pollack, 1963; children—Sara (dec.), John. B.A., U. Mich., 1965, M.A., 1970; postgrad. Am. U., Am. Acad. Performing Arts, 1976.Instr. Washtenaw Community Coll., 1975-81; sr. adminstr. John Howard Compound Sch., Zambia, 1970-71; chmn. Ann Arbor Democratic Party (Mich.), 1975-77; mgr. campaign for State Senate, 1978, campaign for 2d Congl. Dist., 1980; regional coordinator gubernatorial campaign, 1981; mem. Mich. State Senate, 1983—. Trustee, Ann Arbor Bd. Edn., 1979-82. Democrat. Office: 465 Farnum Bldg Lansing MI 48909 also: 2065 Columbia Ann Arbor MI 48104

POLLACK, MARY LOUISE, hotel executive; b. Phila., Nov. 15, 1949; d. Edward Latshaw and Mary Louise (Dempsey) Gruber; m. Stephen J. Pollack, May 15, 1977 (div. 1981). BA in English, Duke U., 1971; postgrad. Hotel Sch., Cornell U. Cert. tchr., Pa. Travel agt. G & O Travel, N.Y.C., 1977-80; sales mgr. Halloran House, N.Y.C., 1980-81; regional dir. Halloran Hotels, N.Y.C., 1981-83, nat. dir. sales, 1983-84; assoc. dir. mktg. Treadway Hotels and Resorts, Saddle Brook, N.J., 1984-85, dir. mktg., 1985-86, v.p. mktg., 1986-87, also bd. dirs.; dir sales, mktg. Eastern region Prime Mgmt., Fairfield, N.J., 1987—; dir. Somerset Hotels, N.J., Treadway Inns Corp. Mem. Hotel Sales Mgrs. Assn. Internat., U.S. Tour Operators Assn., Am. Bus Assn., Meeting Planners Internat., Nat. Passenger Traffic Assn. (hotel com. 1986), Am. Soc. Travel Agts., Travel Industry Assn. Am. (planning com. 1983-84), Nat. Tour Assn. (conv. com. 1982-84, membership com. 1984, cert. com. 1986, mktg. com. 1987), Pa. Travel Council (program chmn. for 1st Gov.'s Conf. on Travel 1983, mem. mktg. com. 1983).

POLLACK, NANCY ELLEN BLEIER, manufacturing executive; b. Bklyn., May 20, 1941; d. Benjamin Sydney and Selma (Karger) Bleier; children: Bonnie, Michael. Student, U. R.I., 1959-60; BS in Edn., Hofstra U., 1962; cert. in interior design, Willsey Inst., Hempstead, N.Y., 1974. Tchr. Westwood Sch., West Islip, N.Y., 1962-63; with sales dept. Howard Printz, Inc., Freeport, N.Y., 1971-75; owner, pres Nancy Designs Ltd., Rockville Centre, N.Y., 1975—; ptnr. Original Impressions Ltd., Rockville Centre, N.Y., 1978—; cons. Wallcovering Distbrs. Assn., N.Y.C., 1986—. Contbg. designer and stylist various wallcovering books, 1982-86. Trustee Rockville Centre C. of C., 1977-81; bd. dirs. Temple B'nai Sholom, 1981—. Mem. Decorating Products Dealers Assn. N.Y. Office: Nancy Designs Ltd 434 Sunrise Hwy Rockville Centre NY 11570

POLLARD, ANNIE RANDOLPH, educator; b. Greenville, N.C., Feb. 11, 1943; d. Frank and Laura (Teel) Randolph; m. Percy Edward Pollard Sr., May 22, 1965; children: Tracie Anita, Percy Jr. BS, Va. State U., 1970; MA in Teaching, Fairleigh Dickinson U., 1984; student in ednl. mgmt. and policy, Fordham U., 1984—. Cert. biol. scis. and computer edn. tchr. Chem. analyst Gen. Aniline and Film Corp., Binghampton, N.Y., 1970-73; tchr. earth sci., biology and gen. math. Montgomery County Pub. Schs., Rockville, Md., 1973-81; sales rep. Equitable Life Co., Fairfield, N.J., 1980; tchr. biology and computer scis. Teaneck (N.J.) Pub. Schs., 1981—; cons., instr. computer camp Va. State U., Petersburg, summers 1985—. Author: Planning a Residential Computer Camp, 1985, also brochures. Bd. dirs. YWCA, Binghampton, 1969-70; liaison Broad St. Community Action Com., Endicott, N.Y., 1968; v.p. Broad St. Elem. Sch., Endicott, 1968-69; adv. fundraiser Shady Grove Adventist Hosp., Rockville, 1975-76; judge Montgomery County Bd. Elections, Rockville, 1978-79; Stephen minister Franklin Lakes United Meth. Ch., N.J. Recipient Spl. Tchr. and Outstanding Achievements awards Carver High Sch. Mem. NEA, N.J. Edn. Assn., Teaneck Tchrs. Assn., Nat. Assn. Female Execs., Nat. Found. for Improvement Edn. (founder), Nat. Assn. Black Coll. Alumni, North N.J. Alumni Assn. of Va. State U., Coalition of 100 Black Women (co-chair 1986—), Alpha Kappa Alpha (workshop leader), Alpha Phi Alpha (workshop leader). Democrat. Baptist. Home: 8 Monroe Dr Mahwah NJ 07430 Office: Teaneck Bd Edn 1 Merrison Pl Teaneck NJ 07666

POLLARD, BETTE SILVER, systems analyst; b. Knoxville, Iowa, July 24, 1945; m. Harvey B. Pollard. AB, U. Calif., Berkeley, 1965; MS, U. Chgo., 1966. Systems analyst NIH, Bethesda, Md., 1983—. V.p. bd. dirs. Montgomery County Dept. Recreation, Rockville, Md., 1981-82; pres. Fox Hills Civic Assn., Potomac, Md., 1982-83. Mem. Women in Computing, U. Chgo. Alumni Assn. (treas. 1981-82). Office: NIH Westwood Bldg Room 1A07 Bethesda MD 20892

POLLARD, BOBBIE JEAN, librarian, educator; b. Anguilla, Miss., June 16, 1942; d. J.D. and Delia (Washington) Thornton; m. Wilbert B. Pollard, Apr. 27, 1974; 1 dau., Abiola. B.A. in English Lit., Jackson (Miss.) State U., 1964; M.L.S., Atlanta U., 1965; M.A. in Edn., NYU, 1974. Librarian, acting br. librarian Bklyn. Pub. Library, 1965-70; assoc. prof. library sci. Baruch Coll., N.Y.C., 1970-78, 79—; sr. librarian U. Benin, Benin City, Nigeria, 1968. Rockefeller Found. scholar, 1965-66; Profl. Staff Congress grantee, CUNY, 1983-84. Mem. ALA, Assn. Coll. and Research Libraries (chmn. N.Y.C. area 1983-84), Library Assn. CUNY (chmn. Inst.) 1976, Nat. Assn. Female Execs., Beta Phi Mu, Alpha Kappa Mu. Democrat. Baptist. Home: 245 E 93rd St Apt 4A New York NY 10128 Office: Baruch Coll Library 156 25th St New York NY 10025

POLLARD, DUBENA RENÉE, operations analyst, educator, model, professional beauty consultant; b. Jacksonville, Fla., Feb. 12, 1961; d. Dessie B. and Zellene (Hugley) P. BA, U. Fla., 1983. Tchr. Dept. Edn. State of Fla., 1983—; dormitory coordinator, counselor Edward Waters Coll., Jacksonville, 1983; communications analyst Blue Cross/Blue Shield, Jacksonville, 1984-86, ops. analyst, 1986—; model Jacksonville, 1986—; activities and publs. dir. Christian Devel. Ctr., Inc., 1987—; beauty cons. Jacksonville, 1988—. Role model for We Care program Jacksonville Urban League; modeling instr. Tots N'Teens Theater of Jacksonville. Nat. Assn. Female Execs., Nat. Council Negro Women, Gamma Sigma Sigma. Democrat. Club: Toastmasters (Jacksonville) (pres. 1986—).

POLLARD, HINDA GREYSER, management educator, lawyer; b. Boston, Sept. 2, 1937; d. Morris and Gladys (Koven) Greyser; m. Alan Payson Pollard, Sept. 5, 1960; children—Daniel Lincoln, John Franklin. A.B. magna cum laude, Tufts U., 1959; J.D, Boalt Hall Sch. Law, U. Calif.-Berkeley, 1964; student (sponsored State Dept.) Helsinki, Finland, 1964-65, Moscow, USSR, 1965-66. Bar: R.I. 1978, U.S. Dist. Ct. 1978. Teaching assoc. Harvard Bus. Sch., Boston, 1959-60; instr. Fisher Jr. Coll., Attleboro, Mass., 1976-79; asst. prof. mgmt. dept. Bryant Coll., Smithfield, R.I., 1979-83, assoc. prof., 1983—, chmn. dept., 1981—, coordinator internship program, 1981—, Small Bus. Inst. coordinator, 1983—; mem. Small Bus. Inst. Dirs.' Assn., 1982—; sole practice law, Providence, 1978—. Author articles in field; contbr. to profl. report. Divisional Keyperson, United Way, Smithfield, 1983. Boalt Hall scholar, 1961-62. Mem. ABA (labor and employment sect.), Acad. of Mgmt., AAUW (Bryant Coll. instl. rep. 1981—), Nat. Soc. for Internships and Experiential Edn., Indsl. Relations Research Assn., Phi Beta Kappa. Home: 567 Wayland Ave Providence RI 02906 Office: Bryant Coll Smithfield RI 02917

POLLARD, MARILYN BERGKAMP, utility company executive; b. Fowler, Kans., July 7, 1937; d. Frank Henry and Mary Magdalene (Kuhl) Bergkamp; 1 child, Darin. Student, U. Colo., Denver, 1962, U. Denver, 1968, Metro State Coll., Denver, 1969, Colo. Women's Coll., Denver, 1977. Ins. underwriter Laurin Jones Agy., Dodge City, Kans., 1955-60; legis. asst. State of Kans., Topeka, 1960-61; various positions Denver, 1961-76; asst. to pres. Pub. Service Co. of Colo., Denver, 1976-86, asst. to chmn. bd., chief exec. officer, pres., 1986—. Mem. Nuclear Energy Women, 1979—, Private Industry Council, Denver, 1984—; bd. dirs. Denver Jr. Achievement, 1979—, Colo. Found. Dentistry for Handicapped, 1985—, Am. Humanics, Denver, 1985—, Artreach, Denver, 1987—, Denver Civitan Club; incorporator, co-chmn. Colo. for Sensible Energy Policy, Denver, 1982; vice chmn. Denver Salvation Army, 1979—. Recipient Downtown Denver Career Woman award, 1974, Outstanding Achievement in Pub. Relations award, 1972. Club. Denver Press (bd. dirs. 1977-78). Office: Pub Service Co Colo 550 15th Denver CO 80201

POLLICK, MONIKA FORYSIAK, market developer; b. Poland, Nov. 29, 1962; came to U.S., 1963; d. Vick Andrew and Eugenia (Merana) F. BS, Montclair State Coll., 1984. Account rep. Ricoh Am., Maywood, N.J., 1984-85; bus. mgr. Fette Ford Inc., Clifton, N.J., 1985-86, after-market sales specialist, 1986-87; ednl. services rep. ITT Ednl. Services, N.Y.C., 1987; mkt. developer Dealer Services Network Inc., Palisades Park, N.J., 1987—; mgmt. cons. Montclair (N.J.) State Coll., 1984. Mem. Nat. Assn. Female Execs. Republican. Roman Catholic. Home: 353 Maplewood Ave Clifton NJ 07013 Office: Dealer Service Network Inc 21 Fairview St Palisades Park NJ 07656

POLLITT, GERTRUDE STEIN, psychotherapist, clinical social worker; b. Vienna, Austria; came to U.S., 1949, naturalized, 1951; d. Julius and Sidoni (Brauch) Stein; m. Erwin P. Pollitt, Jan. 13, 1951 (dec. Aug. 1977). Social Service course Brit. Council, London, 1943-44; BA, Roosevelt U., 1954; MA, U. Chgo., 1956; LHD (hon.) World U., Ariz., 1986. Cert. Chgo. Inst. Psychoanalysis, 1963, cert. clin. social worker, 1987. Resident social worker Anna Freud Residential Nursery Sch., Essex, Eng., 1944-45; dep. dir. UN, U.S. Zone, Germany, 1945-48; psychiat. social worker Jewish Children's Bur., Chgo., 1955-63; pvt. practice as psychotherapist and/or clin. social worker, Glencoe, Ill., 1961—; cons. Winnetka (Ill.) Community Nursery Sch., 1962-63, North Shore Congregation Nursery Sch., 1966-69, Oakwood Home for Aged, Highland Park (Ill.) High Sch., 1979-80; instr. profl. devel. programs Chgo. Inst. for Psychoanalysis, 1982, Sch. Social Service Adminstrn., U. Chgo.; mem. faculty profl. devel. program Sch. Social Service Adminstrn., U. Chgo.; cons., supr. ongoing profl. study groups on clin. issues, 1984—. Contbr. articles to profl. jours. Bd. dirs. Glencoe Youth Service, Menninger Found. Fellow Am. Orthopsychiat. Assn.; mem. Nat. Assn. Social Workers (chmn. pvt. practice com. 1965-70), Ill. Soc. Clin. Social Workers (bd. dirs.), Acad. Cert. Social Workers. Home and office: 481 Oakdale Ave Glencoe IL 60022

POLLITT, KATHA, writer, poet, educator; b. N.Y.C., Oct. 14, 1949; d. Basil Riddiford and Leanora (Levine) P.; m. Randy Cohen, June 6, 1987. BA, Harvard U., 1972; MFA, Columbia U., 1975. Lit. editor The Nation, N.Y.C., 1982-84, contbg. editor, 1986—; jr. fellow council of humanities Princeton (N.J.) U., 1984; lectr. The New Sch., N.Y.C., 1986-87, Poetry Ctr. 92d St YMHA and YWHA, N.Y.C., 1986-88. Author: Antarctic Traveller, 1982 (Circle award Nat. Book Critics 1983); poetry appeared in The New Yorker, The New Republic, Poetry, and others; contbr. articles to jours. Recipient I.B. Lavan Younger Poet's award Acad. Am. Poets, 1984; Fulbright grantee, 1985; grantee N.Y. Found. of the Arts, 1987; Guggenheim fellow, 1987. Mem. Am. PEN Club. Democrat. Home: 317 W 93rd St New York NY 10025

POLLOCK, ANN DELPHINE, real estate executive; b. Flagstaff, Ariz., Dec. 15, 1946; d. Thomas Elmer and Dorothy Oldham (Peach) P.; m. Nick Charles King, Aug. 31, 1968 (div.); children:Nick Charles, Justin Keith; m. Guy R. Householder II, Nov. 28, 1987. Student U. Ariz., 1963-65; BS in Mktg., No. Ariz. U., 1968. Lic. real estate broker, Ariz. Adminstrv. sec. Coldwell Banker & Co., Phoenix, 1969-76; office mgr. Rierson, Ledbetter & Assocs., Phoenix, 1976-79; asst. v.p. Community Devel. Corp., Scottsdale, Ariz., 1979-80; sales assoc. No. Ariz. Realty, Flagstaff, 1980-82; broker, ptnr. Kinsey-Pollock, Inc., Flagstaff, 1982-87; ptnr. Cave-Pollock Realty & Mgmt., Inc., Flagstaff, 1987—. Mem. ann. fundraising com. No. Ariz. U., Flagstaff, 1981—, mem. pres.'s screening com. for dean, 1982; mem. steering com. R. Kimball for Corp. Commr., Flagstaff, 1982; bd. dirs. Flagstaff Pine Country Pro-Rodeo, Inc.; mem. adv. bd. Salvation Army, Flagstaff Corps. Mem. No. Ariz. Bd. Realtors (treas. 1986-87, pres.-elect 1987-88), Flagstaff C. of C. (dir. 1980-86). Republican. Episcopalian. Home: 2001 N Navajo Dr Flagstaff AZ 86001 Office: Cave-Pollock Realty & Mgmt Inc 518 N Beaver St Flagstaff AZ 86001

POLLOCK, LOIS ANN, infosystems specialist; b. Chgo.; m. Paul K. Pollock. BA, Beloit (Wis.) Coll., 1976. Programmer Outboard Marine Corp., Beloit, 1978-79, jr. systems analyst, 1979-80, programmer, analyst, 1980-82; project mgr. Warner Electric Co., South Beloit, Ill., 1982-84, mgr. systems devel., 1984, mgr. info. resources, 1984—; mem. DCN com. Dana Corp., Toledo, 1985—; mem. adv. com. Blackhawk Tech. Inst., Beloit, 1987—. Mem. Vol. Action Ctr., Beloit, 1985—; mem. citizens computer com. City of Beloit, 1986-87; mem. Radug/Decus steering com., Rockford, Ill., 1987. Recipient Conwell-Huffer Math. prize Beloit Coll., 1976. Mem. Computer and Automated Systems Assn., Data Processing Mgmt. Assn. Office: Warner Electric Co 449 Gardner St South Beloit IL 61080

POLLOCK BORAWSKI, MARY MACALPINE, accountant; b. Hartford, Conn., Dec. 22, 1953; d. Woolsey MacAlpine and Margaret (Stoeke) P.; m. David Francis Borawski, July 4, 1981 (div. Apr. 1986). BA in English, Cen. Conn. State U., 1984. Jr. acct. TeleConcepts, Inc., Newington, Conn., 1980-86; sole proprietor Loretta Recycling, Wethersfield, 1985—; mgr. Pollock & Hallsted Partnership, Wethersfield, 1982—; acct. Interstate Ford Truck Sales, Inc., Hartford, 1986-87; office mgr. O'Connell & Co. CPA, Hartford, 1987—. Model interviewer trade publ. Celebrity Model, 1984; contbr. recipe book Now You're Cooking Connecticut, 1985. Mem. Hartford Architecture Conservancy, Hartford. Mem. Nat. Assn. Female Execs. Home: 303 Brimfield Rd Wethersfield CT 06109

POLLOCK O'BRIEN, LOUISE MARY, public relations executive; b. Tarentum, Pa., Mar. 14, 1948; d. Louis P. and Amelia M. (Ballay) Pollock; m. Vincent Miles O'Brien. BS, Ind. U. of Pa., 1970. Tchr. Archbishop Wood High Sch., Warminster, Pa., 1970-75; spokesperson, publicist Calif. Olive Industry, Fresno, 1976-78; account exec. Ketchum Pub. Relations, N.Y.C., 1979-81, account supr., 1982-83, v.p., 1984, v.p., group mgr., 1985-88; sr. v.p., group mgr. 1988—; mem. pub. relations adv. com. Mayor's Vol. Action Com., N.Y.C., 1986; mem. food service adv. bd. L.I. City Coll., Bklyn., 1987-88. V.p., fundraiser West 76th St. Block Assn., N.Y.C., 1982. Mem. Internat. Foodservice Editorial Council (v.p., bd. dirs. 1984-85). Democrat. Office: Ketchum Pub Relations 1133 Avenue of the Americas New York NY 10036

POLON, LINDA BETH, educator, writer, illustrator; b. Balt., Oct. 7, 1943; d. Harold Bernard and Edith Judith Wolff; m. Marty I. Polon, Dec. 18, 1966 (div. Aug. 1983); m. Robert Dorsey, Apr. 13, 1986 (Nov. 6, 1986). B.A. in History, UCLA, 1966. Elem. tchr. Los Angeles Bd. Edn., 1967—; writer-illustrator Scott Foresman Pub. Co., Glenview, Ill., 1979—, Frank Schaffer Pub. Co., Torrance, Calif., 1981-82, Learning Works, Santa Barbara, Calif., 1981-82; editorial reviewer Prentice Hall Pub. Co., Santa Monica, Calif., 1982-83. Author: (juvenile books) Creative Teaching Games, 1974; Teaching Games for Fun, 1976; Making Kids Click, 1979; Write up a Storm, 1979; Stir Up a Story, 1981; Paragraph Production, 1981; Using Words Correctly, 3d-4th grades, 1981, 5th-6th grades, 1981; Whole Earth Holiday Book, 1983; Writing Whirlwind, 1986; Magic Story Starters, 1987. Mem. Soc. Children's Book Writers. Democrat. Home: 1515 Manning Ave Apt 3 Los Angeles CA 90024 Office: Los Angeles Bd of Edn 980 S Hobart Blvd Los Angeles CA 90006

POLSKY, CYNTHIA HAZEN, art administrator, publisher, artist; b. N.Y.C., Feb. 28, 1938; d. Joseph and Lita Hazen; m. Leon B. Polsky, Apr. 19, 1957; children—Alexander M., Nicholas A. Student Art Students League, 1957-60, New Sch. for Social Research, 1957-60; B.A., Marymount Coll., 1978; M.B.A., Fordham U., 1981. Pres. Octagon Communications Internat., N.Y.C. One-woman shows include Los Angeles, Houston, East Hampton, N.Y., Wichita, N.Y.C., 1968-77; represented in permanent collections Corcoran Mus., Washington, Fogg Mus., Cambridge, Mass., Cornell U., Herbert F. Johnson Mus., Rockefeller U., Storm King Art Ctr., N.Y., Israel Mus., Jerusalem. Trustee Met. Mus. Art, N.Y.C., Asia Soc.; v.p., trustee Storm King Art Ctr.; mem. adv. com. dept. art and archaeology Columbia U., N.Y.C., Ctr. U.S.-China Arts Exchange, Sackler Mus., Washington. Office: Octagon Communications Internat Inc 110 E 59th St New York NY 10022

POLSTON, JANICE, educator; b. Avon Park, Fla., Dec. 8, 1953; d. Oliver Samuel and Lucille (Dampier) P. AA, Santa Fe Community Coll., 1975; BA in Edn., U. Fla., 1976, postgrad., 1977; MS, Nova U., 1986. Cert. elem. tchr., Fla. Tchr. Woodlawn Elem. Sch., Sebring, Fla., 1976-80, Sebring Mid. Sch., 1980—. Troop leader, service team mgr. Girl Scouts U.S., Sebring, 1978-82. Mem. Alpha Delta Kappa (historian, chmn. altruistic com. 1982-84, recording sec. 1984-86, pres.-elect 1986—). Democrat. Baptist. Club: Highlands County Gator. Home: 1308 Hotiyee Ave Sebring FL 33870 Office: Sebring Mid Sch 500 E Center St Sebring FL 33870

POLVOGT, ALENE, accountant, investment counselor; b. Dallas, Oct. 5, 1923; d. Carl W. and Bennie (Lowry) P.; B.B.A., So. Meth. U., 1976. Pvt. practice acctg., Dallas, 1974—; mem. faculty U. Tex., Dallas, 1980—. Mem. Am. Inst. C.P.A.s, Tex. Soc. C.P.A.s. Republican. Presbyterian. Home and Office: 5841-A Sandhurst St Dallas TX 75206

POMAR, BARBARA HELEN, financial consultant and planning company executive; b. Oakland, Calif., Dec. 11, 1945; d. Miguel Joseph and Helen Isabell (Laws) P. AA, Santa Ana Coll., Calif., 1965; BS, Salisbury State Coll., 1982. Sec. Rollmet Inc., Santa Ana, 1969-72, asst. purchasing mgr., personnel, 1978-80; reporter/TV talk show hostess Teleprompter TV, Newport Beach, Calif., 1972-75; sec. Tesoro Petroleum, Beverly Hills, Calif., 1975; sec., adminstrv. asst. US Life Savs. & Loan, Los Angeles, 1975-78; clerical counselor Manpower Inc., Salisbury, Md., 1982-83; fin. sales and ins. Gray Ins., Salisbury, 1983; fin. cons. Del. Fin. Services, Salisbury, 1984; owner, fin. cons. Salisbury Securities, 1984—; cons. Delmarva Fin. Network, Salisbury, 1987. Chmn. Delmarva Ski Show, Salisbury, 1984-86. Mem. AAUW (corr. soc. 1988—), Salisbury C. of C., Inst. Cert. Fin. Planners, Internat. Assn. for Fin. Planning. Republican. Roman Catholic. Clubs: Salisbury Ski (pres. 1986-87). Office: Salisbury Securities 212 E Main Salisbury MD 21801

POMEROY, CAROLINE SAUNDERS, infosytems specialist; b. Hartford, Conn., Feb. 14, 1960; d. Walter Saunders and Dorothy Ann (Entwistle) P. BA, Lehigh U., 1982; MBA, Rensselaer Poly. Inst., Hartford, Ct., 1986. System mgr. New Departure Hyatt Gen. Motors, Bristol, Conn., 1983-85; software cons. Hamilton Standard United Tech. Corp., Windsor Locks, Conn., 1985-87; sr. bus. analyst Lotus Devel. Corp., Cambridge, Mass., 1987—. Advisor Jr. Achievement, Bristol, Conn., 1983-84; bd. govs. Lehigh U., Bethlehem, Pa., 1987—, young alumni rep., 1986—. Mem. Am. Prodn. and Inventory Control Soc. (rep. Hamilton Standard). Republican. Protestant. Club: Conn. Sports.

POMEROY, MARY DELIA, social worker; b. N.Y.C., Apr. 23, 1955; d. Richard Wayne and Ruth (Fairchild) P. BA in Psychology, Conn. Coll., 1977; Min Social Work, Fordham U., 1980. Social work Cath. Guardian Soc., Bklyn., 1980-82, LAMM Inst. Long Island Coll. Hosp., Bklyn., 1982—. Democrat. Prsbyterian (deacon). Home: 305 89th St #7C Brooklyn NY 11209

POMPA, SUSAN JOY, medical products executive; b. Chgo., Oct. 14, 1951; d. Hy I. and Evelyn (Cohn) Kaplan; 1 child, Nicole. Student, Met. Sch. Bus., Chgo., 1970-71. With med. records dept. Swedish Covenant Hosp., Chgo., 1971-74; dir. med. records Northwestern U. Med. Assocs., Chgo., 1974-75; research assoc. Am. Med. Records Assn., Chgo., 1975-76; dir. med. records HMO Rush Presbyn. St. Lukes Hosp., Chgo., 1977; pres., chief exec. officer S.J. Kaplan & Assocs., Inc., Lincolnwood, Ill., 1980—; cons., research assoc. health care grants, 1976—; cons. graphic arts dept. Niles West High Sch., Skokie, Ill., 1985. Patentee in field. Mem. Am. Med. Record Assn. (cert.). Office: SJ Kaplan & Assocs 7215 N Kildare Lincolnwood IL 60646

POND, PHYLLIS JOAN, state legislator; b. Warren, Ind., Oct. 25, 1930; d. Clifford E. and Rosa E. (Hunnicutt) Ruble; B.S., Ball State U., Muncie, Ind., 1951; M.S., Ind. U., 1963; m. George W. Pond, June 10, 1951; children—William, Douglas, Jean Ann. Tchr. home econs., 1951-54; kindergarten tchr., 1961—; mem. Ind. Ho. of Reps. from 15th Dist., 1978-82, from 20th Dist., 1982—, majority asst. caucus chmn. Del. Ind. State Rep. Conv., 1976, 80, 84; alt. del. Rep. Nat. Conv., 1980. Mem. AAUW. Lutheran. Club: New Haven Woman's.

PONDER, ADELAIDE WALLACE, editor; b. Madison, Ga., Apr. 16, 1925; d. Leonard Dewey and Anne Fitzpatrick (Douglas) Wallace; m. William Graham Ponder, Nov. 5, 1923; children: Anne Douglas Ponder Rice, Mary Graham Ponder Foster, Douglas Ponder Suto, William Jr. AB, Wesleyan Coll., 1946. With pub. relations dept. Ga. State Dept. Commerce, Atlanta, 1947; advt. copywriter J.P. Allen, Atlanta, 1947-48; editor Madisonian, Madison, Ga., 1957—, co-publisher, 1967—; journalism instr. U. Ga., Athens, 1976. Contbr. feature articles to newspapers. Vice chmn. bd. trustees Morgan County Found., Inc., Madison, 1974—; trustee Madison-Morgan Cultural Ctr., 1975—, Wesleyan Coll., Macon, Ga., 1980-87; vice chmn. Ga. Heritage Trust Commn., Atlanta, 1976—; bd. mgrs. Ga. Trust for Hist. Preservation, Atlanta, 1983—. Mem. Nat. Soc. Newspaper Editors, Press Inst. (chmn. 1976), Ga. Press Assn., Women in Communications, Pi Delta Epsilon (Medal of Merit, 1976), Colonial Dames of Am in the State of Ga. (chair patriotic service com. 1974-81, v.p. 1981-84). Episcopalian. Club: Cracker Crumble (chair 1988—). Home: 782 S Main St Madison GA 30650 Office: Madisonian 131 W Jefferson Madison GA 30650

PONDER, CATHERINE, clergywoman; b. Hartsville, S.C., Feb. 14, 1927; d. Roy Charles and Kathleen (Parrish) Cook; student U. N.C. Extension, 1946, Worth Bus. Coll., 1948; B.S. in Edn., Unity Ministerial Sch., 1956; 1 son by previous marriage, Richard. Ordained to ministry, Unity Sch. Christianity, 1958; minister Unity Ch., Birmingham, Ala., 1956-61; founder, minister Unity Ch., Austin, Tex., 1961-69, San Antonio, 1969-73, Palm Desert, Calif., 1973—. Mem. Assn. Unity Chs., Inc. (hon. D.D. 1976), Internat. New Thought Alliance, Internat. Platform Assn. Clubs: Bermuda Dunes Country, Racquet (Palm Springs, Calif.); Los Angeles. Author: The Dynamic Laws of Prosperity, 1962; The Prosperity Secret of the Ages, 1964; The Dynamic Laws of Healing, 1966; The Healing Secret of the Ages, 1967; Pray and Grow Rich, 1968; The Millionaires of Genesis, 1976; The Millionaire Moses, 1977; The Millionaire Joshua, 1978; The Millionaire from Nazareth, 1979; The Secret of Unlimited Prosperity, 1981; Open Your Mind to Receive, 1983; Dare to Prosper!; The Prospering Power of Prayer, 1983; The Prospering Power of Love, 1984; Open Your Mind to Prosperity, 1984, The Dynamic Laws of Prayer, 1987. Office: 73-669 Hwy 111 Palm Desert CA 92260

PONNÉ, NANCI TERESA, publisher; b. Chgo., May 10, 1958; d. Joseph Anthony and Irene Theresa (Nasadowski) P. BA, DePaul U., 1980. Actress, model Chgo., 1978—; pub. Chgo. Talent Directory, 1985—; speaker in field. Vol. Dems. to Re-elect Mayor Washington, 1987. Named Miss Chgo., recipient Spl. Judges award Miss America Scholarship Pageant, 1981-82. Mem. Women in Film, Women's Advt. Club of Chgo., Chgo. Advt. Club, New Chgo. Coalition, Theatre Chgo. Affiliates, Entrepreneurs Assn., Nat. Assn. Female Execs. Roman Catholic. Home: 2215 E 83d St Chicago IL 60617 Office: Chgo Talent Directory 230 N Michigan Ave Chicago IL 60601

PONSER, MARILYN RUTH, real estate administrator; b. Newark, Ohio, May 29, 1952; d. Verlin and Freda Evelyn (Davis) Mathis; m. Gene Walter Ponser, Feb. 3, 1970; children: Rick Walter, Wanda Lynn. Student, Cen. Ohio Tech. Inst., 1974. Realtor Archie L. Brown REal Estate, Newark, 1974—; weatherization aide Licking Econ. Action Devel. Study, Newark, 1983-87, energy auditor, 1985—, weatherization program dir., 1987—. Treas. Hazelwood PTA, Newark, 1980-82, pres., 1982-84. Mem. Nat. Bd. Realtors, Ohio Bd. Realtors, Licking County Bd. Realtors, Nat. PTA, Lincoln PTA. Office: Archie L Brown Real Estate 221 W Church St Newark OH 43055

PONTIUS, CAROL YVONNE, rehabilitation counselor; b. Reedsburg, Wis., Jan. 21, 1959; d. Martin Edward and Marlene Levita (Luetkens) Koenecke; m. Dale Edwin Pontius, July 26, 1985. BA in Psychology, La. State U., 1981; MA, Rollins Coll., 1986. Cert. addictions profl., Fla. Psychiat. technician Mid-Continent Hosp., Olathe, Kans., 1981-82; asst. dir. Drug Abuse Edn. Ctr., Olathe, 1981-82; probation officer Johnson County, Olathe, 1982-83; probation officer, investigator Fla. Dept. Corrections, Orlando, 1983-85; dir. Neighborhood Watch Program Orlando Crime Commn., 1985-86; program counselor Straight, Inc., Orlando, 1986-87, assoc. dir., 1987—. Vol. Spouse Abuse, Inc., Orlando, 1985, Greenpeace, Washington, 1986—. Mem. Am. Assn. for Counseling and Devel., Am. Mental Health Counselors Assn., Fla. Alcohol and Drug Abuse Assn., Psi Chi, Mu Sigma Rho, Alpha Xi Delta. Republican. Lutheran. Home: 3316 Clay Ave #18 Orlando FL 32804 Office: Straight Inc 2400 Silverstar Rd Orlando FL 32803

PONTIUS, GERALDINE CAROL, architect, visual artist; b. Greensburg, Pa., Jan. 24, 1947; d. Paul Edward and Doris Norma (Hesselmeyer) P. BA in Math., Barnard Coll., 1968; MArch, Columbia U., 1974. Registered profl. architect. Designer James Stewart Polshek & Ptnrs., N.Y.C., 1975; design architect John Young/Urban Deadline Architects, N.Y.C., 1976; sr. design architect I.M. Pei & Ptnrs., N.Y.C., 1977-82; pvt. practice architecture, N.Y.C., 1981—; project design architect Kohn Pederson Fox Assocs., N.Y.C., 1982-86; prof. Columbia U. Summer Session, N.Y.C., 1980-86, Parsons Sch. of Design, N.Y.C., 1981-83. Sr. project designer Hyatt Regency Hotel, Greenwich, Conn. (winner AIA award, 1985-86). Prin. works include collaboration for dance stage set Art on the Beach, 1983, Archtl. Drawings, Fifth St. Gallery, 1977-80. Ind. Exhbns. Program grantee, Artists' Space, 1977, 78; recipient Grand Prize AIA Jour. Drawing Contest, 1982. Mem. AIA, Archtl. League. Presbyterian. Club: Barnard Coll. (N.Y.). Avocation: ballet. Home: 310 Greenwich St #14A New York NY 10013 Office: 30 W 26th St 12th fl New York NY 10010

POOL, DEANNA, educator, satellite engineering group comptroller; b. Rabat, Morocco, North Africa, Apr. 21, 1942; came to U.S., 1975; d. Joseph and Perla (Dery) Amar; m. David Lynn Pool, Oct. 5, 1964; children—Nathaniel Dan, Michael Messod, Joel Eli. Student Universite de Rabat, 1960-61; diploma in Hispanic culture Centro Cultural Espanol, Madrid, Spain, 1964. Chief comml. liaisons and fgn. markets dept. Ministry of Commerce, Industry, Mines & Merchant Marine, Rabat, 1961-62; asst. to dir. fin. Caisse de Depot, 1962-64; co-owner, Marshall Tool and Die, Kansas City, Mo., 1975-77, Bio-Safe, Kansas City, 1977-80; co-owner, comptroller Satellite Engring. Group, Kansas City, 1980—; lectr. in Morocco, Honduras, Philippines, 1960-75; guest lectr., U. Mo.-Kansas City, 1984—; lectr. in field. Mem. Mo. Conservation Soc., Soc. Prevention Cruelty to Animals. Jewish. Advocations: Antiques; embroidery; reading. Home: 114 Hackberry Lee's Summit MO 64063 Office: Satellite Engring Group 6114 Connecticut Kansas City MO 64120

POOL, MADONNA COOPER, health company administrator; b. Santiago, Cuba, May 30, 1952; came to U.S., 1956; d. Clarence Jasper Sr. and Joan Kathleen (Cooper) Pool. BS in Psychology, U. Utah, 1974. Systems engr. Electronic Data Systems, San Francisco, 1977-79; with medicare dept. Optimum Systems Inc., Sunnyvale, Calif., 1979-80; account rep. systems AZ/NV Phoenix, 1980-81; account coordinator health care Bradford Nat. Corp., N.Y.C., 1981-82; cons. Empire Blue Cross/Blue Shield, N.Y.C., 1982-84, specialist nat. mktg., 1984-86; mgr. bus. systems Middletown, N.Y., 1986—. Republican. Office: Empire Blue Cross/Blue Shield 100 Crystal Run Rd Middletown NY 10940

POOLE, ALMA LOUISE, federal agency administrator; b. Kansas City, Mo., Apr. 27, 1939; d. Elder Luther W. and Alma C. (McWilliams) S.; m. George Lee Poole Sr., May 14, 1955; children: George Jr., Angela, Virgil, Terry Poole. BA, Mid Am. Nazarene Coll., 1984. Cert. Air Traffic Controller. Tax examiner IRS, Kansas City, 1968-72; air traffic controller FAA, Burlington, Iowa, 1972-75, Emporia, Kans., 1975-76, Kansas City, 1976-81; equal employment opportunity specialist FAA, Olathe, Kans., 1981-85, air traffic control tng. specialist, 1985-86; personnel staffing specialist FAA, Kansas City, 1986—; investigator FAA, 1982—. Author One PK's Opinion, 1986. Vol. Planned Parenthood, Kansas City, 1976-80, United Auto Workers Women Vols., 1979-83, Women United, 1981-84, Big Bros./Big Sisters, Kansas City, 1977-83; sec. A. Philip Randolph Inst., Kansas City, 1983-85. Recipient Spl. Service award Fed. Exec. Bd., Kansas City, 1982, Community Service award So. U., 1984, Mgrs. award Fed. Women Program, Washington, 1985. Mem. Am. Bus. Women (pres. 1982-84), Negro Bus. and Profl. Women (chairperson 1987—). Democrat. Pentacostal. Club: We're On Our Way Investment (pres. 1986—). Home and Office: 7504 E 119th Terr Grandview MO 64030

POOLE, ANN, interior designer; b. Akron, Ohio, Dec. 19, 1944; d. Don S. and Alice (Miller) P. Student, Purdue U., 1962-63; diploma, Art Inst. of Pitts., 1967. Interior designer Interior Furnishings, Inc., Akron, 1968; instr. interior design Art Acad. Mich., Detroit, 1969, Art Inst. of Ft. Lauderdale (, Fla., 1969-71; interior designer Delta Design Assocs., Ft. Lauderdale, N.Y.C., 1971-72; pvt. practice interior design Ft. Lauderdale, 1973-79; pres. design dir. A/Design Internat., Ft. Lauderdale, 1979—. Mem. Internat. Soc. Interior Design, Interior Design Guild of Fla. Democrat. Unitarian. Office: A/Design Internat 2485 E Sunrise Blvd Fort Lauderdale FL 33304

POOLE, GERTRUDE MARGARET, accounting educator; b. N.Y.C., Oct. 26, 1939; d. Robert John and Gertrude Amelia (Toulman) P.; B.B.A., Pace U., 1974; M.B.A., Rutgers U., 1982. Mgr. mdse. acctg. Reader's Digest, N.Y.C., 1965-74; staff acct. Coopers & Lybrand, N.Y.C., 1974-75; sr. acct. SS&O C.P.A.s, Perth Amboy, N.J., 1975-77; tax and internal audit sr. Church & Dwight, Piscataway, N.J., 1977-78; chief acctg. and control div. Fed. Res. Employee Benefits System, N.Y.C., 1978-82; asst. prof. Sch. Bus. Adminstrn., Monmouth Coll., West Long Branch, N.J., 1982—. C.P.A., N.Y., N.J. Mem. NOW (chmn. speaker's bur. Monmouth chpt. 1974-75), N.J. Soc. C.P.A.s, Am. Inst. C.P.A.s, Nat. Assn. Female Execs., LINK, Am. Soc. Women Accts. Roman Catholic. Home: 2006 F St South Belmar NJ

07719 Office: Monmouth Coll Sch Bus Adminstrn West Long Branch NJ 07764

POOLE, PAMELA, publishing executive; b. Junction City, Kans., Nov. 30, 1945; d. Willis Ray and Dorothy Lou (Morris) P. BA, Baylor U., 1967; MS, East Tex. State U., 1973. Tchr. Plano (Tex.) Ind. Schs., 1967-73; cons. Rand McNally & Co., Chgo., 1973-80; regional mgr. Riverside Pub. Co., Chgo., 1980-84; sales mgmt. Merrill Pub. Co., Dallas, 1984—. Fulbright Found. scholar, 1970. Mem. Tex. State Tchrs. Assn. (life), Fulbright Alumni Assn., Baylor U. Alumni Assn. (life), Delta Kappa Gamma, Alpha Delta Kappa. Republican. Baptist. Office: Merrill Pub Co PO Box 831122 Richardson TX 75083

POOLE, SHERYL LYNN, college administrator; b. Mineola, N.Y., Oct. 30, 1960; d. Walter Thomas and Barbara (Brown) Schoen; m. Christopher Alan Poole, Dec. 6, 1986. BA, Smith Coll., 1982; MEd, U. Vt., 1986. Coordinator pediatric units Mass. Gen. Hosp., Boston, 1982-84; admissions counselor U. Vt., Burlington, 1984-85, asst. to v.p., 1985-86; asst. to dean Fisher Jr. Coll., Boston, 1985, asst. to pres., 1986-87; mgr. corp. classroom Boston U., 1987—; cons. Mus. Sci., Boston, 1987. Disabled Am. Vets. scholar 1982; named one of Outstanding Young Women Am., 1986. Mem. Am. Assn. Higher Edn., Nat. Assn. Women Deans, Adminstrs., Counselors, Nat. Assn. Student Personnel Adminstrs., Am. Coll. Personnel Assn., Psi Chi. Republican. Methodist. Office: Boston Univ Corp Classroom 110 Cummington St Boston MA 02215

POOLEY, BRIDGET KAY, marketing professional; b. Little Rock, Aug. 18, 1958; d. Richard Lewis and Catharine Loraine (Harris) P. AB, U. Calif., Berkeley, 1983. Compliance adminstr. Charles Schwab and Co., San Francisco, 1983-84; mktg. rep. Consol. Capital, Emeryville, Calif., 1984-87; midwest regional mktg. dir. Sierra Capital, San Francisco, 1987—. Chmn. Calif. State Spl. Olympics, Berkeley, 1984-85, No. Calif. Band Party, Berkeley, 1985-86; bd. dirs. Spinsters of San Francisco, 1987-88. Mem. Internat Assn. Fin. Planners, Inst. Cert. Fin. Planners, Nat. Assn. Profl. Execs., Young Profl. Women's Assn. Home: 2675 Monterey Oakland CA 94602 Office: Sierra Capital One Market Plaza San Francisco CA 94111

POOR, SUZANNE DONALDSON, advertising and public relations executive; b. Somers Point, N.J., Oct. 6, 1933; d. James Watt and Roberta (Radford) Donaldson; m. Richard Sumner Poor, Mar. 19, 1955 (div. Sept. 1983); children—Jonathan Scott, Jeffrey Sumner, Sara Suzanne. A.B., Mt. Holyoke Coll., 1955; M.A., Montclair State Coll., 1975; postgrad NYU, 1977-83, Drew U. 1987—; photography student New Sch. Social Research, 1979-82. Reporter, copy writer WFLB, WFLB-TV, Fayetteville, NC., 1955-56; dir. public relations Montclair YMCA, N.J., 1965-69; dir. public relations Girl Scouts Greater Essex County, Montclair, 1969-74; assoc. pub. relations dept. Nat. League Nursing, N.Y.C., 1974; freelance public relations, photography, Montclair, 1974-76; dir. communications Insts. Religion and Health, N.Y.C., 1976-78; ptnr., pres. Miller/Poor Assocs., Verona, N.J., 1978—. Pres. bd. trustees Doubletree Gallery, Montclair, 1977-79; trustee Friends of N.J. Network. Mem. Am. Soc. Mag. Photographers, Am. Woman's Econ. Devel. Corp., Nat. Assn. Female Execs., Exec. Women N.J. (bd. dirs. 1980-83), Ad Club NJ (bd. govs. 1983—, editor Ad Talk, 1982—. Democrat. Episcopalian. Avocations: bicycling, swimming, tennis, furniture restoration. Home: 30 Plymouth St Montclair NJ 07042 Office: Miller/Poor Assocs 280 Bloomfield Ave Verona NJ 07044

POOS, DENISE MARIE, electric utility engineer; b. Arlington, Va., Dec. 18, 1958; d. Frank William and Catherine J. (Kolakoski) P. B.S. in Mech. Engring., Ga. Inst. Tech., 1982. Mech. design engr. trainee Nottingham & Assocs., McLean, Va., 1977-81; fuels engr. West Tex. Utilities Co., Abilene, 1982-87, engr. trainee Test and Balance Corp., 1988— . Sci. fair judge Jr. League of Abilene, 1985, 86. Mem. Tex. Soc. Profl. Engrs. (bd. dirs. Abilene chpt. 1986-87), Soc. Women Engrs., ASME. Republican. Roman Catholic. Avocations: swimming; softball; reading. Home: 16108 Northglenn Dr Tampa FL 33618 Office: Test and Balance Corp 3912 W Humphrey St Tampa FL 33614

POPCHAK, BARBARA JO, educational adminstrator; b. Clairton, Pa., Feb. 12, 1941; d. John Francis and Barbara Lucille (Demchak) P. BS, Carlow Coll., 1969; MEd, Xavier U., Cin., 1976. Cert. Montessori tchr., tchr., Pa. Tchr. parochial schs. Pitts., 1962-76; founder, dir., adminstr. Mt. Lebanon Montessori Sch., Pitts., 1976—; vis. supervising tchr. Montessori Tchr. Tng., N.Y.C., Boston, Pitts., 1980—; founder Master Degree Tchr. Tng. Ctr., 1979; workshop presenter various parents groups, Pitts., 1975—. Recipient award for 10 Years excellence Mt. Lebanon Parents Group, 1987; grantee Cath. Daus. Am., 1972, Carlow Coll., 1979. Mem. Am. Montessori Soc. (cons. 1979—), Greater Pitts. Montessori SOc. (chmn. 1980-83), Pa. Assn. for Edn. Young Children. Republican. Roman Catholic. Home: 1817 Mary St Pittsburgh PA 15228

POPE, BARBARA M. HARRAL, editor; b. Lubbock, Tex., Jan. 26, 1937; d. Leonard Paul and Olivette (Stuart) Harral; m. John Rowell Toman (div. 1963); 1 child, Stuart Rowell. BS in Edn., Tex. Christian U., 1959; MLS, U. Hawaii, 1968; postgrad., Golden Gate U., 1980-82. Tchr. pub. elem. schs., various cities, Tex. and Hawaii, 1959-66; contracts abstractor, indexer Champlin Oil Co., Ft. Worth, 1963-64; adminstrv. asst. engring. Litton Industries, Lubbock, Tex., 1964-65; mgr. research library Hawaii Employers' Council, Honolulu, 1968-72; dir. med. library U. S.D.-Sacred Heart Hosp., Yankton, 1977-79; editor, adminstrv. coordinator book div. ABC-Clio, Inc., Santa Barbara, Calif., 1981-88; freelance research/editorial cons. Albuquerque, 1988—; research cons. Thailand Hotel, Tuche-Ross Assocs., Honolulu, 1974—, Sacred Heart Hosp., Yankton, S.D., 1978, Mt. Marty Coll., Yankton, 1978. Vol., contbr. Boy's Ranch, Amarillo, Tex., 1987—; mem. Lobero Theater Group, Santa Barbara, 1975-76; mem., treas. Yankton Med. Aux., 1977-79. Mem. Spl. Libraries Assn., Med. Libraries Assn., ALA, Am. Soc. Info., Sci., Tex. Christian U. Alumni Assn., Delta Delta Delta. Republican. Episcopalian. Home: 9300 Seabrook Albuquerque NM 87111 Office: PO Box 26356 Albuquerque NM 87125

POPE, BARBARA SPYRIDON, federal agency administrator; b. Pitts., Nov. 10, 1951; d. Gus Arthur and Katherine (Soumas) Spyridon; m. James Selkirk Pope, Nov. 24, 1984; 1 child, James Cantwell. BA, Vanderbilt U., 1973; postgrad., George Washington U., 1977-80. Indsl. counsellor Litton Industries, Pascagoula, Miss.; staff asst. SBA, Washington, 1974-79, exec. asst. to gen counsel, employee devel. specialist, 1980-82, acting chief of staff, spl. asst., 1982-86, dep. asst. sec. def. force mgmt. and personnel (family support, edn. and safety), 1986—. Mem. adv. bd. Charles Edison Youth Meml. Found., Washington, 1978-81. Scottish Rite fellow, George Washington U., 1979; named one of Outstanding Young Women Am., 1981. Mem. Downtown Jaycees, Washington (bd. dirs. 1984-86). Republican. Greek Orthodox. Home: 408 Constitution Ave Washington DC 20002-0002 Office: Office Sec Def Family Support & Edn & Safety The Pentagon Washington DC 20301

POPE, BECKY LYNN, banker; b. Edgewater, Fla., Feb. 19, 1953; d. William Albert and Ella (Moore) P. AA, Daytona Beach Community Coll., 1973; BS, Fla. So. coll., 1975. Cert. tchr.; FHA direct endorsement underwriter; lic. mortgage broker. Supr. corr. lending Security 1st Fed. Savs. and Loan Co., Daytona Beach, Fla., 1978-84; office mgr., underwriter CityFed Mortgage Corp., Orlando, Fla., 1984-85; v.p. adminstrn. Colony 1st Mortgage Corp., Orlando, 1985—. Mem. Assn. Profl. Mktg. Women (dir. 1986-87), Nat. Assn. Female Execs. , Mortgage Bankers Assocs. Methodist. Club: Cracker Country Cloggers (New Smyrna Beach) (chmn. bd., instr.). Home: 699 Raleigh Ct Deltona FL 32738

POPE, DONNA, government official; b. Cleve., Oct. 15, 1931; d. John Emil and Marie Josephine (Thiel) Kolnik; m. Raymond Pope, Oct. 21, 1951; children: Candace Pope Wooley, Cheryl Ann. Student public schs. Supr. election ofcls. dept. Cuyahoga County Bd. Elections, Cleve., 1965-68; mem. Ohio Ho. of Reps., 1972-81, minority whip; dir. U.S. Mint, Washington, 1981—. Mem. Exec. Women in Govt. Roman Catholic. Office: Dept of the Treasury US Mint 633 3rd St NW Washington DC 20220

POPE, INGRID BLOOMQUIST, artist, sculptor; b. Arvika, Sweden, Apr. 2, 1918; came to U.S., 1928; d. Oscar Emanuel and Gerda (Henningson) Broström; m. Howard Richard Bloomquist, Feb. 14, 1941 (dec. Nov. 18, 1982); children: Dennis Howard, Diane Cecile Connelly, Laurel Ann Shields; m. Marvin Hoyle Pope, Mar. 9, 1985. BA cum laude, Manhattanville Coll., 1979, MA in Humanities, 1981; MA in Religion, Yale Div. Sch. Yale U., 1984. Exhibitions include Manhattanville Coll., Greenwich Art Soc., Greenwich Arts Council, Yale Div. Sch., First Ch. Round Hill, Scarsdale Congl. Ch. (N.Y.), Ch. of Sweden, N.Y.C. Past bd. mem. N.Y.C. Mission Soc., Greenwich YMCA, Greenwich Acad. Mothers' Assn.; trustee First Ch. Round Hill, Greenwich; pres. Church Women United, 1988—. Republican. Clubs: Field, Yale (N.Y.C.); Greenwich. Home: 538 Roundhill Rd Greenwich CT 06831

POPE, JOAN, physical scientist, researcher; b. N.Y.C., Sept. 30, 1948; d. James Francis and Norma (Newman) P. BS, SUNY, Oneonta, 1970; MS, U. R.I., 1976; postgrad., SUNY, Buffalo, 1976-80. Cert. profl. geologist, Ind. Tchr. Elbridge (N.Y.) Elem. Sch., 1970-71, Oneonta Jr. High Sch., 1971-72; research scientist U. R.I., Kingston, 1972-74; geologist U.S. Army Corps Engrs., Buffalo, 1974-77, coastal geologist, 1977-83; research physical scientist Waterways Exptl. Sta., Vicksburg, Miss., 1983-86, supervisory physical scientist, 1986-88, chief, coastal structures and evaluation br. at Coastal Engring. Research Ctr., 1988—; mgr., instr. tng. courses U.S. Army Corps Engrs., 1983—. Contbr. articles to sci. jours. Mem. ASCE (vice chmn. Conf. Coastal Sediments), Permanent Internat. Assn. Navigation Congresses, Soc. Econ. Paleontolotists and Mineralogists, Am. Shore and Beach Preservation Assn. Club: Toastmasters (sec.-treas.) (Vicksburg). Office: US Army Engrs Waterways Exptl Sta Vicksburg MS 39180

POPE, MARALEE OSTERMEIER, communications executive; b. Wilmington, Ohio, Oct. 27, 1954; d. Leonard George and Jay (Fender) O. BS in Mktg. Mgmt., Miami U., Oxford, Ohio, 1976. Sales rep. Mead Corp., Bridgeview, Ill., 1976-80; account exec. Ill. Bell, Chgo., 1980-82; account exec., industry cons. AT&T Info. Systems, Chgo., 1983-85, account exec., cons. major account mgmt., 1986—; guest speaker Printers Industry Assn., 1979, Chgo. Sci. Analysts, 1983, Pub. Utility Analysts of Chgo., 1983. Pres. Big Bros./Big Sisters Orgn., Oxford, 1973-76; hostess Council for Internat. Programs, Chgo., 1985; pledge sec. St. Giles Episcopal Ch., Northbrook, Ill., 1985-86; mem. St. Veronica's Alter Guild, Northbrook, 1982-87. Mem. Pi Sigma Epsilon (regional dir. 1975-76, v.p. 1975-76, Exec. Scholar 1974-87), Zeta Tau Alpha (Miami Pageant rep. 1976). Office: AT&T 10 S Riverside Plaza Chicago IL 60606

POPE, NANCY MCCARTHY, manufacturing company representative; b. Pitts., Dec. 23, 1961; d. William B. and Margaret (O'Keefe) McC.; m. Frederick J. Pope. BS in Mktg., Pa. State U., 1983; cert., Dale Carnegie Courses, Hackensack, N.J., 1984, 85; postgrad., Pa. State U., 1987. Inside sales rep. Microamerica, Moonachie, N.J., 1984-85, mgr. inside sales, 1985-86; outside sales rep. UARCO, Deep River, Conn., 1987—. Mem. Nat. Assn. Female Execs. Home: 41 E Pattagansett Rd Apt 1d Niantic CT 06357

POPE, REBECCA, special education educator; b. Lexington, Ky., Aug. 7, 1948; d. Charles B. and Vela (Moran) Reid; m. W. David Pope, Aug. 16, 1969 (div. Feb. 1981); children: Mark Andrew David, Michael Charles. BA, Asbury Coll., 1969; cert. supr., East Tex. U., 1984; MEd, Western Ky. U., 1978. Cert. tchr. elem. edn., Ky. Tchr. music Fayette County (Ky.) Sch. Dist., 1969-70, tchr. elem. sch., 1970-72; clin. diagnostician Western Ky. U., Bowling Green, 1977-78; coordinator spl. edn. for most handicapping conditions Richardson (Tex.) Ind. Sch. Dist., 1978-81, spl. edn. tchr. emotionally disturbed, 1981—, cons., 1980; lectr. in field. Group leader Mental Health-Mental Retardation, Austin, Tex., 1976-77; in-hospl program for new parents of handicapped children, Austin, 1976-77. Recipient Outstanding Achievement in Spl. Edn. award Richardson Ind. Sch. Dist., 1983. Mem. NEA, Tex. Edn. Assn., Council for Exceptional Children (state student rep. 1977-78), Council for Children with Behavior Disorders, Phi Delta Kappa. Democrat. Methodist. Club: Asbury Coll. Fine Arts (v.p. 1967-68, pres. 1968-69). Home: 14679 Reforma Dallas TX 75240 Office: RISD-Spring Creek Elem Sch 7667 Roundrock Rd Dallas TX 75248

POPE, SUZETTE STANLEY, accountant; b. Florala, Ala., Sept. 15, 1925; d. Raymond T. and Vashti Viola (Williams) Stanley; m. W. Norelle Pope, June 22, 1947; children—Stephanie Suzanne, Brently Preston. A.S., Miami-Dade Community Coll., 1967; B.B.A. magna cum laude, U. Miami, 1969, M.B.A., 1971; Ed.S., U. Fla., 1976. Staff acct. Stuzin C.P.A.s; supr. acctg. staff Dade County Pub. Schs., Miami, Fla., 1969-75, chief acct. acctg. div., 1976-83, accounts payable div., 1983—. Contbr. articles to profl. publs. Bd. dirs. United Manpower Service, Inc., Miami, 1976-80; bd. dirs. United Home Care Service, 1981—; trustee Bay Oaks Home, 1981—. Named Outstanding Adminstr., Dade County Pub. Schs., 1982, Outstanding Bus. Woman Dade County, 1983, Outstanding Woman Vol., 1984, OUtstanding Bus. Woman of Dade County, 1984, Outstanding Woman Vol. of Dade County, 1985. Mem. Assn. Sch. Bus. Officials, Fla. Support Adminstr. Assn., Southeastern Assn. Sch. Bus. Ofcls., Fla. Assn. Sch. Bus. Ofcls., Fla. Fedn. Bus. and Profl. Women, Fla. Sch. Fin. Council, Am. Soc. Women Accts. (v.p. 1982-83), AAUW, Coral Gables Bus. and Profl. Womens Club (v.p. 1984-85, del. state conv. 1985—, nat. conv. 1986—, 1st v.p., 1985-86, pres. 1986-87, bd. dirs. dist. 12, Woman of Yr. 1987, recipient Justice Cup award 1985), Fla. Assn. Sch. Adminstrs. (bd. dirs. 1986-88), Fla. Support Adminstrs. Assn. (bd. dirs. 1982—, pres. 1987-88), Fla. Sch. Fin. Officers Assn., SE Assn. Sch. Bus. Officials (bd. dirs. 1981-83). Democrat. Baptist. Lodge: Soroptomist (bd. dirs. So. region 1984—, del. 1981—, treas. 1986-88, chmn. tng. awards program 1982-84). Home: 3925 NW 4th Terrace Miami FL 33126 Office: Dade County Pub Schs Room 602 1450 NE 2d Ave Miami FL 33132

POPE-MASSETTI, AUDREY LAURA, government agency director; b. St. Cloud, Minn., Apr. 4, 1951; d. Wheeler Henry and Laura Catherine (Scheeler) Pope; m. Richard Paul Massetti, Aug. 13, 1984. BA in Astrophysics, St. Cloud State U., Minn., 1980, BS in Geology, 1980; MS in Geodesy, Ohio State U., 1986. Ins. rep. Lincoln Nat. Life Ins. Co., Mpls., 1974-76; group ins. cons. Prudential Ins. Co., Mpls., 1976-78; geodesist defense mapping agy. Dept. Defense, Cheyenne, Wyo., 1982-86, Kwajalein, Marshall Islands, 1987—; geodetic cons. RCA Corp., Kentron Corp., Global Assn., FAA, MIT, et al. Kwajalein, 1987—. Vol. Micronesian Handicraft Assn., Kwajalein, 1987—. Academic grantee St. Cloud State U., 1970-73. Mem. Am. Congress on Surveying and Mapping. Roman Catholic. Club: Yacht (Kwajalein), Scuba (Kwajalein).

POPIELARZ, BEVERLY, advertising executive; b. Borger, Tex., Aug. 24, 1949; d. Leighton J.F. and Delores Martina (Rinker) Helm; m. Robert Philip Seppey, Aug. 14, 1975 (div. Dec. 1980); m. Donald Thomas Popielarz, Jan. 16, 1983; 1 child, Rachel Katherine. BA, Occidental Coll., 1971. V.p., personnel dir. Ogilvy & Mather, Los Angeles, 1971-83; sr. v.p., dir. human resources, ops. Foote Cone & Belding, Los Angeles, 1983—. Mem. Los Angeles Advt. Club. Office: FCB Los Angeles 11601 Wilshire Blvd Los Angeles CA 90025

POPOVICH, HELEN, university president; b. El Paso, Tex., Nov. 19, 1935; m. James E. Popovich, Oct. 4, 1967 (dec. Apr. 1976); 1 son, Peter Edward; m. Donald G. MacConnel, Oct. 14, 1984. B.A., U. Tex.-El Paso, 1955, M.A., 1958; Ph.D., U. Kans., 1965. Asst. prof. to assoc. prof., assoc. dean U. South Fla., Tampa, 1965-78; dean, v.p., acting pres. Winona State U., Minn., 1978-83; pres. Fla. Atlantic U., Boca Raton, 1983—. Bd. dirs. Winona LWV, 1980-82, Boca Raton United Way, 1983—, Med. Investment Trust Fund, 1985—; mem. Minn. Humanities Commn., St. Paul, 1980-83. Mem. Am. Assn. Higher Edn., Delta Kappa Gamma, Phi Delta Kappa.

POPP, CHARLOTTE LOUISE, health development center administrator, nurse; b. Vineland, N.J., July 26, 1946; d. William Henry and Elfriede Marie (Zickler) P. Diploma in Nursing, Luth. Hosp. of Md., Balt., 1967; BA in Health Edn., Glassboro (N.J.) State Coll., 1972; MA in Human Devel., Fairleigh-Dickinson U., 1981. Cert. Sch. Nurse, N.J., Health Educator, N.J. Charge nurse Newcomb Hosp., Vineland, N.J., 1967-71; supr. Vineland Rehab. Ctr., 1971-72; charge nurse Bridgeton (N.J.) Hosp., 1972-73; dir. inservice edn. Millville (N.J.) Hosp., 1973-76; dir. hosp. inservice edn. State of N.J., Vineland Devel. Ctr., 1976-78, program asst., 1978-87, dir. habilitation planning services, 1987—, lead program coordinator, 1981—; exam proctor State of N.J. Bd. Nursing, Newark, 1973—. Editorial Review Bd.: (jour.) Nursing Update, 1973-77. Instr. basic life support, Am. Heart Assn., bd. dirs. Tri-county chpt., 1979-83, South Jersey chpt., 1983—. Mem. Am. Nurses Assn., N.J. State Nurses Assn., Am. Assn. for Mental Retardation, South Jersey Inservice Exchange (life), Lutheran Hosp. of Md. Alumni Assn., Glassboro State Coll. Alumni Assn., Fairleigh-Dickinson U. Alumni Assn. Lutheran. Office: Vineland Devel Ctr 1676 E Landis Ave Vineland NJ 08360

POPP, VIRGINIA GAIL, real estate developer; b. Balt., Sept. 10, 1944; d. LaMar John and Virginia Margaret (McComas) Campbell; m. Richard Lyell Guy, 1962 (div. 1964); children: Richard Jr., James (dec.); m. Lawrence Joseph Popp Jr., Feb. 10, 1973 (div. 1988); 1 child, JoElla; 1 stepchild, John. Grad. high sch., Towson, Md. Credit corr. Humble Oil Co., Balt., 1963-68; typist Charles J. Cirelli and Son, Inc., Severna Park, Md., 1969-70, from bookkeeper to adminstrv. asst., 1970-80, v.p., 1980—, also bd. dirs.; bd. dirs. Cirelli Constrn. Co., Severna Park. Mem. Chpt. 81 Parents Without Ptnrs., Inc. Mem. Ch. of the Brethren Lodge: Ladies Aux. of the Moose.

POPPEN, JANET KLAWITER, accountant; b. Kansas City, Mo., Oct. 24, 1941; d. Harold Julius and Selma Elizabeth (Hilmer) Klawiter; divorced; children: Gavin, Ann. BA, U. Mo., Columbia, 1963; BS in Bus. Adminstrn., U. Mo., St. Louis, 1981. CPA. Staff acct. Lester Witte Co., St. Louis, 1981-82; tax sr. Rubin Brown Gornstein, St. Louis, 1982-84; tax supr. KMG Main Hurdman, St. Louis, 1984-86; ptnr. Poppen and Duncan, St. Louis, 1986—. Officer Citizen's Adv. Council Lindberg Sch. Dist., St. :Louis, 1983-84. Mem. Am. Inst. CPA's, Mo. Soc. CPA's, St. Louis Soc. CPA's (treas. alliance 1987-88), Nat. Assn. Women Bus. Owners, Kirkwood C. of C. Mem. United Ch. Christ. Office: Poppen and Duncan 117 N Kirkwood Rd Suite 129 Saint Louis MO 63122

POPPER, PAMELA ANNE, investment banker; b. Columbus, Ohio, Oct. 24, 1956; d. Edwin D. and Eleanor Ida P. Student Ohio State U. Assoc. dir. Conservatory of Piano, Columbus, 1974-79; v.p. The Window Man, Columbus, 1979-81; pres. Popper Brace Scott, Columbus, 1981-87; pres., chief exec. officer, The Popper Group, 1985—; v.p., dir. Hamilton Fin. Corp., Columbus, 1983—; chmn. Netcare Found., 1986—; pres., chief exec. officer Hamilton Capital Corp. Corp., 1987—; bd. dirs. Shelter One Group Corp., 1986—, Kaiser Devel., 1987—. Trustee Neoteric Dance Theatre, Columbus, 1985-87, Netcare Found., Columbus, 1985—, Columbus Contemporary Dance Theatre, 1987—; dir.; bd. dirs. Treemar Retreat, South Webster, Ohio, 1986—, Ballet Met., Columbus, 1976-79; mem. ways and means com. Am. Heart Assn., Columbus. Recipient Vol. award Netcare Corp., 1984; profl. sales awards. Mem. Nat. Assn. Profl. Saleswomen. Republican. Home: 338 Bristol Woods Ct Worthington OH 43085 Office: Popper Group 659 F Park Meadow Westerville OH 43081

POPPETT, THERESA MARY, realtor, optician; b. Monterrey, Mex., Oct. 3, 1939; came to U.S., 1963, naturalized, 1985; d. Jose and Gue Sam (Chan) Yuen; m. George Thomas Poppett, Oct. 28, 1972. Student, Skyline Coll., Los Angeles City Coll., Santa Monica Coll. Lic. real estate agt., optician, Calif. With various optical cos. Calif., 1972-83; sec. Los Angeles Bar Assn., 1983-86; real estate assoc. Merrill Lynch Realty Co., Marina Del Rey, Calif., 1986—; co-mgr., optician Rips Eyeglasses Unltd., Los Angeles, 1986—; mgr. optician Nu Vision Optical, Santa Monica, Calif., 1987—. Mem. Venice/Marina Del Rey Bd. Realtors, Rancho Pk. Women's Golf Assn., Mex. Am. Women's Golf Assn.

POPRICK, MARY ANN, psychologist; b. Chgo., June 25, 1939; d. Michael and Mary (Mihalcik) Poprick; B.A., De Paul U., 1960, M.A., 1964; Ph.D., Loyola U., Chgo., 1968. Intern in psychology Elgin (Ill.) State Hosp., 1961-62; staff psychologist, 1962; staff psychologist Ill. State Tng. Sch. for Girls, Geneva, 1962-63, Mt. Sinai Hosp., Chgo., 1963-64; lectr. psychology Loyola U. at Chgo., 1964-67; asst. prof. Lewis U., Lockport, 1967-70, assoc. prof., 1970-75, chmn. dept., 1968-72 (on leave 1972-73); postdoctoral intern in clin. psychology Ill. State Psychiat. Inst., Chgo., 1972-73; pvt. clin. practice David Psychiat. Clinic, Ltd., South Holland Ill., 1973-87; pvt. practice, South Holland, Ill., 1987—; assoc. sci. staff Riveredge Hosp., Forest Park, Ill., 1975-76; mem. sci. staff dept. psychiatry Christ Hosp., Oak Lawn, Ill., 1983—. Co-chmn. commn. on personal growth and devel. Congregation of 3d Order St. Francis of Mary Immaculate, Joliet, 1970-71; clin. resource person Cath. Archdiocese of Chgo., 1977-88 . Mem. Am. Psychol. Assn. (rep. from Ill. 1985-88), Calif., Ill. (sec.-treas. acad. sect. 1975-77, mem. student devel. com. 1975-77, chmn. acad. sect. 1977-78, 78-79, mem. program com. 1977-78, sec. 1979-81, pres.-elect 1981-82, pres. 1982-83, past pres. 1983-84, chmn. program com. 1981-82, awards com. 1983-86), Midwestern psychol. assn., Soc. for Sci. Study Religion, AAAS, Chgo. Assn. Psychoanalytical Psychology, Kappa Gamma Pi, Psi Chi (sec. 1964-65, pres. 1965-66). Home: 547 Marquette Ave Calumet City IL 60409 Office: 16284 Prince Dr South Holland IL 60473

POQUETTE, NELL FARNHAM, construction management company executive; b. DeFuniak Springs, Fla., Jan. 16, 1932; d. Thomas D. and Mary Katherine (Mixon) Farnham; m. Vernon Lyle Lipp, May 19, 1951 (div. Jan. 1964); children—Angela Yvette Lipp Marstiller, Desiree Renee Lipp Wiltsey, V. Lyle Lipp II; m. Harold Francis Poquette, Sept. 9, 1978; stepchildren: Lee Francis Poquette, Gregory Brian Poquette. Student Rollins Coll. Various real estate positions, Orlando, Fla., 1968-75; v.p. Comml. Food Brokers Inc., Clearwater, Fla., 1977-86. Democrat. Mormon. Avocations: biking, walking, cooking, handcrafts.

PORADA, EDITH, archeologist, educator; b. Vienna, Austria, Aug. 22, 1912. Ph.D., U. Vienna, 1935. Mem. faculty Queens Coll., 1950-58; mem faculty Columbia U., 1958—, prof. art history and archaeology emeritus, 1982—; hon. curator seals and tablets Pierpont Morgan Library, 1956—. Author: Alt Iran, 1963, The Art of Ancient Iran, 1965; also monographs, articles. Recipient award for disting. achievement Archaeol. Inst. Am., 1977; Guggenheim fellow, 1983-84. Fellow Am. Acad. Arts and Scis., Brit. Acad. (corr.), Austrian Acad.; mem. Am. Philos. Soc. Office: Columbia U 757 Schermerhorn Hall New York NY 10027

PORCELLA, MICHELLE, graphic artist; b. Elizabeth, N.J., Sept. 6, 1962; d. Sylvester and Lois (Ferguson) Manto; m. George Alston Porcella Jr., July 4, 1986. BFA, B in Bus., Kean Coll., 1985. Pres. Creative Inspiration Inst., Edison, N.J., 1986—; designer WLMW Assocs., W. Orange, N.J., 1982-85, Novel Lithographers, Pt. Reading, N.J., 1984-85; asst. art dir. The Cherenson Group, Livingston, N.J., 1985-86, The Enthusiastic Theatre Co.; cons. Alivening Pubs., Far Hills., N.J., Land-o-Lakes, Fla., 1983—; art dir. Champagne Theatre Prodns., Redbank, N.J., 1986—; v.p. Nat. Escort Valet Co. Mem. Artists League of Cen. N.J. (publicity dir. 1987), Artists Equity. Home: 215 Parsonage Rd Edison NJ 08837

PORLIER, LINDA KAY, professional speaker and sales communications company executive; b. Seattle, Jan. 28, 1948; m. Terry Lamont Porlier, Sept. 21, 1967. BBA, U. Wash., 1970. Prin., POKO Internat., Ltd., Seattle, 1971-80; mgr., tng. exec. Dale Carnegie Courses, Seattle, 1980-84; pres. Porlier Tng. Systems Inc., 1985—; cons. in communications, human relations, sales tng., improved decision making, career blueprinting and developing motivation by design, 1985—; profl. speaker and workshop presenter in field. Sec., King County Republican Women's Commn. 1984; candidate for Wash. State Senate, 1982; Mem. Seattle C. of C. (roundtable facilitator 1986). Republican. Mem. Christian Ch. Lodge: Zonta (chmn. 1988—).

PORRAS, JUANITA ANA, nurse; b. Dallas, Feb. 11, 1955; d. Silverio and Maria Esther (Bonilla) P. AAS in Nursing, El Centro Coll., 1981, AAS in Legal Assistance, 1984; BS, U. Dallas, 1986. Nurse asst. Baylor U. Med. Ctr., Dallas, 1986, grad. nurse, 1981; acctg. lab. tutorial asst. El Centro Coll., Dallas, 1983-87; staff nurse Walnut Place, Dallas, 1987—. Vol. ARC., Dallas, 1978—. Named Outstanding Young Woman Am., 1986; recipient Humane award N. Shore Animal League, 1978-79. Mem. Dallas Mus. Art, Dallas Assn. Legal Assts., U. Tex. Alumni Assn., Phi Theta Kappa. Democrat. Mem. Seventh Day Adventists. Home: 4710 Travis Dallas TX 75205

PORT, APRIL MICHELLE, education teacher; b. Carmel, Calif., Apr. 12, 1952; d. John Yard and Naomi (Bishop) P. BA in History, Dominican Coll., 1975, MS in Spl. Edn., 1977; cert., U. San Francisco, 1985. Instr. Napa (Calif.) Coll., 1977; tchr. health impaired San Lorenzo (Calif.) Unified Sch. Dist., 1978; tchr. spl. day class Tamalpais Union High Sch. Dist., Larkspur, Calif., 1978-81; program specialist Marin County Office Edn., San Rafael, Calif., 1981-83, tchr. spl. day class, 1983—, mgr. summer sch. program, 1986; instr. grad. course Dominican Coll., San Rafael, 1984-85; cons. Quercus Corp., Castro Valley, Calif., 1986—. Mem. Calif. Tchrs. Assn., Phi Delta Kappa. Democrat. Home: 12 Margarita Terr Novato CA 94947 Office: Marin County Office Edn 1111 Las Gallinas San Rafael CA 94913

PORTER, CLARA LOU, management consultant; b. Tonopah, Nev., Feb. 13, 1940; d. Ernest Clarence and Lois Gail (Titus) Hildebrand; m. Jimmy O'Neal Porter, Nov. 15, 1957 (div. 1979); children: James Douglas, John Barrett, Barbara Dianne, Robyn Louise, Jeffrey O'Neal. Student, U. Nev., 1976-77, Clark County Community Coll., 1981-85; BBA in Mktg., Nat. U., Las Vegas, 1988. Machine bookkeeper 1st Nat. Bank, Las Vegas, 1957-58, 63-65; supr. machine bookkeepers Alaska Nat. Bank, Fairbanks, 1960-61; asst. dir. personnel So. Nev. Meml. Hosp., Las Vegas, 1966-77; bus. mgr. Emergency Assocs., Las Vegas, 1978-82; prin. C. Porter Med. Mgmt. Cons., Inc., Las Vegas, 1982—; owner Secretarial Support Services Nev., 1983—; bd. dirs. Exec. Suites of Am. Democrat. Baptist. Home: 127 Victory Rd Henderson NV 89015 Office: 2810 W Charleston Blvd F-62 Las Vegas NV 89102

PORTER, DIXIE LEE, insurance executive, consultant; b. Bountiful, Utah, June 7, 1931; d. John Lloyd and Ida May (Robinson) Mathis. B.S., U. Calif. at Berkeley, 1956, M.B.A., 1957. Personnel aide City of Berkeley (Calif.), 1957-59; employment supr. Kaiser Health Found., Los Angeles, 1959-60; personnel analyst U. Calif. at Los Angeles, 1961-63; personnel mgr. Reuben H. Donnelley, Santa Monica, Calif., 1963-64; personnel officer Good Samaritan Hosp., San Jose, Calif., 1965-67; fgn. service officer AID, Saigon, Vietnam, 1967-71; gen. agt. Charter Life Ins. Co., Los Angeles, 1972-77, Kennesaw Life Ins. Co., Atlanta, from 1978, Phila. Life Ins. Co., San Francisco, from 1978; now pres. Women's Ins. Enterprises, Ltd.; cons. in field. Co-chairperson Comprehensive Health Planning Commn. Santa Clara County, Calif., 1973-76; bd. dirs. Family Care, 1978-80, Aegis Health Corp., 1977—, U. Calif. Sch. Bus. Adminstrn., Berkeley, 1974-76; mem. task force on equal access to econ. power U.S. Nat. Women's Agenda, 1977—. Served with USMC, 1950-52. C.L.U. Mem. C.L.U. Soc., U. Calif. Alumni Assn., U. Calif. Sch. Bus. Adminstrn. Alumni Assn., AAUW, Bus. and Profl. Women, Prytanean Alumni, The Animal Soc. Los Gatos/Saratoga (pres. 1987—), Beta Gamma Sigma, Phi Chi Theta. Republican. Episcopalian. Home and Office: PO Box 64 Los Gatos CA 95031

PORTER, DONNA JUNE, interior designer; b. Alva, Okla., June 24, 1937; d. Floyd Robert and Elsie Martha (Schick) Paris; b. Max. E. Walters, Aug., 1959 (div. 1981); m. Jerry R. Porter, Sept. 21, 1983; children—Terri Sue, Bradford Paris. B.S., Okla. State U., 1959; postgrad., 1970; Kansas City Art Inst., 1979. Tchr., Jefferson County Schs., Denver, 1962-64, Shawnee Mission Schs., Kans., 1964-66; dir. restaurant design Frontier Foods, Stillwater, Okla., 1967-72; dir. design Great Am. Restaurant Co., Kansas City, Mo., 1972-80; owner, designer D.J. Interior Design, Kansas City, 1980—. Bd. dirs. Kansas City Conv. and Vis. Bur., 1975-78, Kansas City Met. Parents Anonymous, 1984— (pres. bd. dirs.), The Crittenton Ctr., 1988. Recipient Key to City Mayor Cin., 1976. Mem. Interior Design Excellence Com., Nat. Assn. Women Bus. Owners, Friends of Art, Profl. Sources Greater Kansas City, Historic Kansas City Soc., Chi Omega (Outstanding Chi Omega, Okla. 1974, Chi Omega of Yr., Kans. City, 1981) Nat. Dir. extension 1979-82, PEO (chaplain 1979-81). Democrat. Mem. Disciples of Christ Ch. Clubs: Carriage (exec. com.), Chi O Mothers (pres.) (Kansas City). Avocation: tennis. Home and Office: 812 W 59th Terr Kansas City MO 64113

PORTER, ELISABETH SCOTT (LEEZEE), businesswoman, political worker; b. Mar. 23, 1942; d. Buford and Mary (Lowe) Scott; 1 child, Erin Lee; m. Julian Grenfell. Student, Sweet Briar Coll., Pan Am. Bus. Sch. Pres. Antique and Contemporary Leasing, Inc., Washington; founder, dir. Women's Nat. Bank, Washington; mem. Bd. Trade, Washington, Allied Bd. Trade, N.Y.C. Mem. fin. com. Diocese of Washington; mem. adv. bd. WAMU-FM, Washington; founder, profl. mem. Potomac chpt. Inst. Bus. Designers; active PTA; vestry mem. Grace Episcopal Ch., Washington; mem. Georgetown Citizens Assn.; mem. adv. bd. Elk Hill Farm, Va., Urban League; Democratic co-chmn. Women's Campaign Fund, Washington; mem. Dem. Women's Council; mem. bd. Women's Campaign Research Fund; trustee Maret Sch., Washington. Mem. Washington C. of C., Nat. Assn. Women Bus. Owners, Georgetown Bus. and Profl. Orgn., Capitol Hill Assn. Bus. and Profls. Office: Antique and Contemporary Leasing Inc 709 12th St SE Washington DC 20003

PORTER, HELEN VINEY (MRS. LEWIS M. PORTER, JR.), lawyer; b. Logansport, Ind., Sept. 7, 1935; d. Charles Lowry Viney and Florence Helen (Kunkel) V.; m. Lewis Morgan Porter, Jr., Dec. 26, 1966; children: Alicia Michelle, Andrew Morgan. A.B., Ind. U., 1957; J.D., U. Louisville, 1961. Bar: Ind. and Ill. 1961, U.S. Supreme Ct. 1971. Atty. office chief counsel Midwest regional office IRS, Chgo., 1961-73; assoc. regional atty. litigation center Equal Employment Opportunity Commn., Chgo., 1973-74; practice in Northbrook, Ill., 1974-79, 80—; ptnr. Porter & Andersen, Chgo., 1979-80, Porter & Porter, Oakbrook Terrace, Ill., 1986—; lectr. Law in Am. Found., Chgo., summer, 1973, 74; assoc. prof. No Ill Coll Law (formerly Lewis U. Coll. Law), Glen Ellyn, Ill., 1975-79. Lectr. women's rights and fed. taxation to bar assns., civic groups. Recipient Disting. Alumni award U. Louisville Sch. of Law, 1986, President's award Nat. Assn. of Women Lawyers, 1985. Fellow Am. Bar Found., Ill. State Bar Found.; mem. Women's Bar Assn. Ill. (pres. 1972-73), ABA (chmn. standing com. gavel awards 1983-85, bd. editors jour. 1984—), Fed. Bar Assn. (pres. Chgo. chpt. 1974-75), Ill. Bar Assn. (del. 1972-78), Nat. Assn. Women Lawyers (pres. 1973-74). Home: 225 Maple Row Northbrook IL 60062 Office: Two Mid America Plaza Suite 800 Oak Brook Terrace IL 60181

PORTER, JOYCE MAXINE, communication company professional; b. Overton, Tex., Apr. 4, 1936; d. John William and Dovie Lee (Still) Driver; m. Billy Don Porter, May 5, 1955 (div. 1978); children: Randal Lee, Perry Don, Patti Lynn Webster. Grad. high sch., Tyler, Tex. With So. Bell, Longview, Tex., 1971—. Republican. Roman Catholic. Home: 301 W Hawkins Longview TX 75605

PORTER, KAREN MOORE, federal agency administrator; b. Kittanning, Pa., Dec. 29, 1949; d. Kenneth J. Moore; m. James R. Porter, Nov. 13, 1976 (div. July 1981). Sec. Nat. Limestone Inst., Washington, 1970-72, Robert L. Hines Cons. Firm, Washington, 1972-74; legal sec. Collier, Shannon, Rill & Scott, Washington, 1974-80; legal sec., office mgr. deKieffer, Berg & Creskoff, Washington, 1980; confidential asst. to gen. counsel Exec. Office of Pres. U.S. Trade Rep., Washington, 1981-83, confidential asst. to dep. U.S. Trade Rep., 1983—. Mem. Beta Sigma Phi (sec. 1983, v.p. 1984, pres. 1985). Republican. Lutheran. Office: US Trade Rep 600 17th St NW Washington DC 20506

PORTER, MARY FAITH, security administrator; b. Muskegon, Mich., May 13, 1958; d. Maurice Raymond and LaVeryl Cornelia (Wade) P. B.A., Mich. State U., 1980; A.A., Muskegon Community Coll., 1978; postgrad., U. Houston. Cert. security trainer; cert. protection profl. Ops. mgr. security dept. The Methodist Hosp., Houston, 1981—, chairperson mktg. com., 1983-84. Instr. trainer defensive driving Tex. Safety Assn., Austin, 1982; instr. trainer CPR, Am. Heart Assn., Houston, 1982; mem. Methodist Hosp. com. of United Way, Houston, 1983. Recipient Scholarship, State Mich., Lansing, 1976. Mem. Am. Soc. Indsl. Security (edn. com. 1983-84), Am. Acad. Security Educators and Trainers, Texas Gulf Coast Crime Prevention Assn., NOW, Alpha Phi Sigma. Office: Meth Hosp 6565 Fannin St Houston TX 77030

PORTER, MAXIENE HELEN GREVE, civic worker; b. Los Angeles; d. Henry Chris and Meyerl (Dixon) Greve; student U. So. Calif., 1928; m. Wellington Denny Palmer, Nov. 18, 1929 (dec. Mar. 1933); children—Virginia Palmer Stanhagen, Wellington Denny; m. 2d, Dale R. Porter, May 17, 1941. Accounting clk. Inglewood (Calif.) Sch. System, 1948-51; dep. tax collector City of San Luis Obispo (Calif.), 1963-65; acctg. clk. San Luis Obispo County Schs., 1965-66; asst. innkeeper Holiday Inn, Darien, Conn., 1967, Alexandria, Va.; innkeeper Holiday Inn, Falls Church, Va., 1973—; asst. gen. mgr. Darien Motor Lodge Assos.; tax cons. H & R Block, 1975-79, office mgr., 1976. Officer, Native Daus. Golden West, 1953—, state pres., 1959-60; chmn. various coms. Calif. Fedn. Womens Clubs, 1960-63; v.p. Bus. and Profl. Women, 1936-37; sec. Inglewood Coordinating Council, 1945-47, pres., 1947-48; pres., various other offices West Ebell Club, Los Angeles, 1947, 60-63; mem. public relations com. YWCA, Fairfax County, Va., 1967-68, Fairfax Hosp. Aux., 1967-68, spl. pub. com. Smithsonian Assn., 1967-68; sec.-treas. Pinecrest Citizens Assn., 1968, v.p., 1974; chmn. finance com. Va. Commn. Status of Women, 1973-75; docent vol. chmn. Green Spring Farm Park, Fairfax County, 1979-80; treas. Greater Falls Church Republican Womens Club, 1968-70, v.p., 1973-74, pres., 1975-76; treas. Va. Fedn. Rep. Women, 1968—, parliamentarian, 1976-80; vice-chmn. Va. Nixon Inaugural Com., 1968-69; treas. Va. Women for Nixon, 1968; mem. Fairfax County Nixon for Pres. Com., co-chmn. Fairfax County Ladies for Lin—Gov.'s Campaign, 1969; mem. Fairfax County Rep. Com., 1968—, dist. chmn., 1974—, sec., 1975-76. Mem. Fairfax County C. of C. (legis., edn., polit. activities coms. 1973-74), Nat. Trust for Historic Preservation, Nat. Hist. Soc., Va., Metro (mem. program com., v.p. 1972-73) motel assns., Am. Mgmt. Assn., Fairfax Cultural Assn. (membership com. mem. 1969—). Clubs: Toastmistress (treas. No. Va. 1975, organizer, charter pres. Falls Church 1977-78, pres., 1983-84 council extension chmn. 1977-78, council treas. 1979-80, council sec. 1980-81, council v.p. 1981-82, council pres. 1983—, parliamentarian 1983-84 editor council newsletter 1978-79, regional awards chmn. 1984-85), Annandale Women's, No. Va. Fedn. Women's (registration chmn. 1980, conservation and energy com., scholarship com. 1982-84, pub. affairs chmn. 1984-86), Nat Genealogy Soc., Maine Hist. Soc., Maine Geneal. Soc., Piebscot Hist. Soc., Kittery Hist. Soc., Harpswell Sounders, Merriconeag Grange. Lutheran. Home: PO Box 11464 Alexandria VA 22312 also: Orr's Island ME 04066

PORTER, NADINE SUMPTER, science educator; b. Mt. Pleasant, Pa., May 27, 1944; d. A. Guy and Lois (Messner) Nicholls; m. James Robert Sumpter, May 7, 1966 (div. 1978); children—Kristin Joy, Kerry Susanne; m. Verleon H. Porter, Mar. 15, 1980. B.S., Pa. State U., 1965; M.S., Tex. A&M U., 1969; Ed.D., U. Houston, 1980. Cert. tchr., Tex. Research asst. Parke Davis & Co., Ann Arbor, Mich., 1966-67; research asst. Tex. A&M U., College Station, 1969-70; biology instr. Coll. DuPage, Glen Ellyn, Ill., 1971-72; instr. Houston Community Coll., 1973-77; teaching fellow U. Houston, 1977-79; tchr. chemistry Kinkaid Sch., Houston 1979—; tech. writer New Sci. Prospects, Houston, 1981-87, pres., 1987-88; v.p. Vapor Recovery & Compression Equipment, Inc., 1984—; profl. mem. Project SERAPHIM; lectr. in field. Contbg. editor Enhanced Energy Recovery newsletter, 1982; contbr. articles to profl. jours. Zone chmn. March of Dimes, Houston, 1982-84; block capt. Am. Heart Assn., 1986-88; Rep. candidate for Dist. 135 Tex. Ho. of Reps., 1988. Mem. Nat. Sci. Tchrs. Assn. Met. Houston Chem. Tchrs. Assn. (sec. 1982-84, safety chmn. 1985-86, chmn. 1987-88), Am. Chem. Soc., Associated Chemistry Tchrs. Tex., Houston Assn. Biology Tchrs. (chmn. 1985-86), Iota Sigma Pi. Home: 2818 Kismet St Houston TX 77043 Office: Kinkaid Sch 201 Kinkaid Sch Dr Houston TX 77024

PORTER, PAMELA KAY, personnel and administration director; b. Slaton, Tex., Jan. 8, 1956; d. James Richard and Marsa (Swope) Porter; m. John David Hammit, Dec. 31, 1976 (div. 1980). Student McMurry Coll., 1974-75; student in Bus. Mgmt., Tex. Tech. U., 1975-77. With pub. relations University City Country Club, Lubbock, Tex., 1976; adminstrv. asst. Permian Basin Regional Planning Commn., Midland, Tex., 1977-79, dir. personnel and adminstrn., 1981-87; exec. dir. Southwestern Bell Mobil Systems, Midland-Odessa, Tex., 1987—; personnel asst. HNG Oil, Midland, 1979-80; mgmt. trainee U.S. CSC, Dallas, 1979. Panelist TV interview, 1983. Active United Way campaigns, Midland and Odessa, 1980-83; officer, coordinator Permian Basin Housing Fin. Corp., Midland and Odessa, 1982-83; nat. consumer arbitrator Better Bus. Bur., 1987; vol. Big Bros./Big Sisters, 1985-87. Recipient certs. of achievement U.S. Civil Service, 1979-80, personnel dept. Midland Coll., 1981; Outstanding Achievement award Bd. Dirs. Permian Basin Regional Planning Commn., 1983. Mem. Nat. Assn. Regional Councils (fed. briefings Washington 1981, 82, 83), Tex. Assn. Regional Councils (conv. chmn. 1983), Bus. and Profl. Women (officer 1982-83, pres. 1985-86; Best Speaker award 1983), Permian Basin Personnel Assn. (bd. dirs. 1987), Am. Bus. Women, Beta Sigma Phi, Xi Pi Kappa. Democrat. Methodist. Office: Southwestern Bell Mobil Systems Inc PO Box 6191 Midland TX 79711

PORTER, SYLVIA, writer; b. Patchogue, L.I., N.Y., June 18, 1913; d. Louis and Rose (Maisel) Feldman; m. Reed R. Porter, 1931; 1 dau., Cris Sarah; 1 stepson, Sumner Campbell Collins; m. James F. Fox, 1979. B.A. magna cum laude, Hunter Coll., 1932; student, Grad. Sch. Bus. Adminstrn., N.Y. U.; 16 hon. degrees. Founder weekly news letter (Reporting on Governments); assoc. N.Y. Post, 1935-77, N.Y. Daily News, 1978—; syndicated columnist Los Angeles Times Syndicate; chmn. Sylvia Porter Orgn., Inc., 1987—. Editor-in-chief: Sylvia Porter's Personal Finance Mag.; author: How to Live Within Your Income, 1948, Sylvia Porter's Income Tax Guide, pub. annually 1960—, How to Get More for Your Money, 1961, Sylvia Porter's Money Book-How to Earn It, Spend It, Save It, Invest It, Borrow It, and Use It to Better Your Life, 1975, paperback edit., 1976, Sylvia Porter's New Money Book for the 80's, 1979, paperback edit., 1981, Sylvia Porter's Your Own Money, 1983, Love and Money, 1985. Named one of Am.'s 25 Most Influential Women World Almanac, 1977-82, Woman of the Decade Ladies Home Jour., 1979. Mem. Phi Beta Kappa. Office: Sylvia Porter's Personal Fin Mag 380 Lexington Ave New York NY 10017

PORTER, VERNA LOUISE, lawyer; b. Los Angeles, May 31, 1941. B.A., Calif. State U., 1963; J.D., Southwestern U., 1977. Bar: Calif. 1977, U.S. Dist. Ct. (cen. dist.) Calif. 1978, U.S. Ct. Appeals (9th cir.) 1978. Ptnr. Eisler & Porter, Los Angeles, 1978-79, mng. ptnr., 1979-86, sole practice, 1986—; judge pro-tempore Los Angeles Mcpl. Ct., 1983—; mem. subcom. on landlord tenant law, panelist conv., mem. real property law sect. Calif. State Bar, 1983; speaker on landlord-tenant law to real estate profls., including San Fernando Bd. Realtors. Editorial asst., contbr. Apt. Owner Builder; contbr. to Apt. Bus. Outlook, Real Property News, Apt. Age. Mem. ABA, Los Angeles County Bar Assn., Los Angeles Trial Lawyers Assn., Landlord Trial Lawyers Assn. (founding mem., pres.), da Camera Soc. Republican. Office: 500 S Virgil Ave Suite 360 Los Angeles CA 90020

PORTERFIELD, RITA ELAINE, banker; b. Hooker, Okla., July 30, 1947; d. Frank Emery and Elsie Gertrude (Brown) Loveland; m. Marion Arthur Crow, Aug. 8, 1962 (dec. Feb. 1965); 1 child, Roberta Sue Crow Jones; m. Clifford Porterfield, Jr., Nov. 13, 1965 (dec. Oct. 1978); children—Buddy Wayne, Paula Jean; m. Gary Gayle Hix, Feb. 14, 1985 (div. Apr. 1987). Grad. Draughn's Bus. Coll., 1972. Office mgr. Millco Moving Service, Amarillo, Tex., 1973-77; bookkeeper Edwards Tires & Auto, Weatherford, Tex., 1977-78; computer operator Liberty State Bank, Tahlequah, Okla., 1981-83, asst. cashier, 1983-85, asst. v.p., 1985—. Co-chmn. Eastern Okla. March of Dimes, Tahlequah, 1984-86. Mem. Nat. Assn. Bank Women (chmn. edn. and tng. com. 1985-86, sec.-treas. 1987-88), Nat. Assn. Female Execs. Republican. Baptist. Club: Ladies Aux. Lodge: Sertoma. Avocations: boating; camping; bowling. Office: Liberty State Bank 130 S Muskogee PO Box 1068 Tahlequah OK 74465

PORTNOY, FERN C., foundation director; b. N.Y.C., Aug. 5, 1945; d. Seymour Chagrin and Leah (Stein) Miller; m. Norman Portnoy, Dec. 24, 1964 (div.); 1 child, Rachael Laura; m. John Edward Moye, Dec. 22, 1982; children: Kelly, Mary, Megan. BS, U. Pitts., 1965, MEd, 1966; PhD, U. Colo., 1976. Instr. Quinsigamond Community Coll., Worcester, Mass., 1967-68; research assoc. Worcester Youth Guidance Ctr., 1967-68, U. So. Calif. Sch. Medicine, Los Angeles, 1968-69; instr. West Los Angeles Coll., 1970, Community Coll. Denver, 1970-71; psychologist Denver Pub. Schs., 1971-72; chief exec. officer U. Med. Ctr. Child Care Ctr., Denver, 1972-74, The Piton Found., Denver, 1975-87; owner Tabor Travel, Denver, 1987—; pres. Portnoy & Assocs. Inc., Denver, 1987—; bd. dirs. Council on Founds., Washington, Ind. Sector, Washington, Gary Energy Corp., Denver, Nat. Equity Fund, Chgo. Contbr. articles to profl. publs. Pres. Women's Forum, 1980; commr. State Colo. Supreme Ct. Nominating Com., 1984—; dir., founder Women's Bank, Denver, 1977, Women's Found. Colo., 1986; bd. dirs. Pub. Edn. Coalition, Denver, 1985—, Blue Cross/Blue Shield Colo., Denver, 1987—. Recipient Boucher award Mortgage Bankers Assn., 1984, Big Sisters award Big Sisters of Colo., 1986, Pub. Service award U. Colo. Grad. Sch. Pub. Affairs, 1986. Mem. Women and Founds. Corp. Philanthropy, Internat. Women's Forum (pres. 1982—). Democrat. Jewish. Club: Denver. Office: Portnoy and Assocs 461 Race St Denver CO 80206

PORUCZNIK, MARY ANN, writer, editor, advertising and public relations consultant; b. Chgo., May 4, 1948; d. John Charles and Anna J. (Malec) P. B.A., St. Xavier Coll., Chgo., 1970; postgrad. Northwestern U., 1971-73, Triton Coll., 1981-82. Editor publs. CAC Ins. Co., Chgo., 1972-75, asst. dir. advt. and sales, 1975; advt. and sales promotion CNA Ins. Co., Chgo., 1975-77; dir. mktg. services N.Am. Co. Life and Health Ins., Chgo., 1977-81; gen. ptnr. Taurus Communications, Oak Park, Ill., 1981-86; profl. writer, Oak Park, 1986—. Mem. Ind. Writers Chgo. (bd. dirs. 1986, exec. sec. 1987-88), Nat. Assn. Female Execs., Direct Mktg. Assn., VFW Aux., NOW (west suburban newsletter editor 1985-87, pres. 1987—, Ill. NOW Times editor 1987), 19th Century Women's Club (chmn. literature dept. 1987—), Feminist Writers' Guild, Nat. Writers' Union. Avocations: filet crochet, camping, cooking, bridge, music. Address: 133 LeMoyne Pkwy Oak Park IL 60302

POSEY, ELSA, dance educator, artistic director; b. Huntington, N.Y., June 27, 1938; d. Jack Moody and Martha Edna (Kimmich) P.; children—Theo A. D. Novak, Thayer A. C. Novak. Student, Met. Opera Ballet Sch., N.Y.C., 1952-54, Ballet Russe de Monte Carlo, N.Y.C., 1954-56, Sch. Am. Ballet, N.Y.C., 1955-60, Am. Ballet Theatre Sch., N.Y.C., 1954-60, Dance Dept. 92d St., N.Y.C., 1952-58, Dance Notation Bur., N.Y.C., 1966. Co-dir. All About Dance Co., Huntington, N.Y., 1969-76; dir. Posey Dance Co., Huntington, 1976-79, artistic dir., 1980—; artistic dir. L.I. Ballet, Northport, N.Y., 1979-80; bd. dirs. Performing Arts Resources, Inc., pres. Posey Sch. of Dance, Inc., Northport, 1953—, also dir., pres. Dance Edn. Services of L.I., Inc., 1969—, also dir.; dir. Am. Dance Guild, Inc., N.Y.C.. Author: At Ease with Dance, 1979. Mem. Am. Dance Guild (founding mem., pres. 1983-84), Congress on Research in Dance, Nat. Coalition for Edn. in Arts, N.Y. Found. for Arts and Artists Roster, Dance Critics Assn., Soc. Dance History Scholars, NEA (dance movement specialist), Nat. Dance Assn. (chmn. studio service com.), Am. Alliance Phys. Edn., Recreation and Dance. Avocation: sailing. Office: Posey Sch Dance PO Box 254 Northport NY 11768

POSEY, GAYLE DAVIS, accountant; b. Memphis, Mar. 11, 1960; d. Arthur Gerald and LaVerne (Knight) Davis; m. William Harold Posey, Sept. 7, 1985. B in Accountancy, Miss. State U., 1982. CPA, Ark., Miss., Tenn. Sr. acct. Deloitte, Haskins and Sells, Memphis, 1982-85; mgr. Arthur Young and Co., Little Rock, 1985-88; corporate fin. CCX Network, Inc., Conway, Ark., 1988—. Treas., bd. dirs. Treatment Homes, Inc., Little Rock, 1987. Mem. Am. Inst. CPA's, Ark. Soc. CPA's, Nat. Assn. Female Execs. Office: CCX Network Inc 301 Indsl Blvd Conway AR 72032

POSEY, GLENNIS BAILEY, educator; b. Arab, Ala., July 19, 1936; d. Loyd Marion and Iva Irene (Maze) Bailey; m. Donald S. Posey, May 27, 1957; 1 child, Donald Loyd. B.S., Florence State U., 1957, M.A., 1962. Tchr. Lauderdale Bd. Edn., Florence, Ala., 1957-58, Winston County Bd. Edn., Double Springs, Ala., 1959—, chmn. bus. dept., 1973—; adviser Future Bus. Leaders Am., Ala., 1957—. Mem. Double Springs Library Bd., 1960-68, Double Springs Recreation Bd., 1978-84. Mem. Ala. Vocat. Assn. (v.p. 1985-86; named Outstanding Bus. Edn. Tchr. 1983, Outstanding Vocat. Tchr. Ala. 1983), Tenn. Valley Bus. Tchrs. Assn., NEA, Data Processing Mgmt. Assn., Delta Pi Epsilon, Alpha Delta Kappa. Republican. Mem. Ch. of Christ. Club: Double Springs Study. Avocations: tole painting; crocheting. Home: PO Box 244 Double Springs AL 35553 Office: Winston County Vocat Ctr PO Box 146 Double Springs AL 35553

POSEY, LISA ANNE, merchandiser; b. Atlanta, Apr. 24, 1962; d. Marshall Lyne and Deanna (Dyson) P. BA, Radcliffe Coll., 1984. Asst. merchandiser Ralph Lauren Women's Wear, N.Y.C., 1985-87, merchandiser, 1987-88; mdse. mgr. Brit. Khaki, N.Y.C., 1988—. Democrat. Episcopalian. Office: Brit Khaki 214 W 39th St New York NY 10010

POSNER, KATHY ROBIN, communications executive; b. Oceanside, N.Y., Nov. 3, 1952; d. Melvyn and Davonne Hope (Hansen) P. BA in Journalism, Econs., Manhattanville Coll., 1974. Fin. planner John Dreyfus Corp., Purchase, N.Y., 1974-80; corp. liaison Gulf States Mortgage, Atlanta, 1980-82; dir. promotion Gammon's of Chgo., 1982-83; coordinator trade show mktg. Destron, Chgo., 1983-84; pres. Postronics, Chgo., 1984-87; exec. Martin E. Janis & Co., Chgo., 1987—. Editor: How To Maximize Your Profits, 1983; contbg. editor Internat. Backgammon Guide, 1974-84, Backgammon Times, 1981-84. Bd. dirs. Chgo. Beautification Com., 1987, Concerned Citizens for Action, Chgo., 1987; mem. steering com. Better Boys Found.; campaign mgr. Brown for Alderman, Chgo., 1987. Mem. Women in Communication, Am. Soc. Profl. and Exec. Women, Mensa, NOW. Republican. Jewish. Clubs: Cavendish North (bd. dirs. 1984-87), Gammon's of Chgo. (bd. dirs. 1980-83, editor newsletter 1982-83), The Turf. Home: 5415 N Sheridan Rd Chicago IL 60640

POSNER, MARY MCCLEARY, marketing and advertising executive; b. Kansas City, Mo., Mar. 21, 1939; d. Glenn Avann and Julia Porter (Quinby) McCleary; student Ohio Wesleyan U., 1957-59; A.B., U. Mo., 1961; M.A., Ind. U., 1962; postgrad. N.Y.U., 1967-69; m. Alan Kent Posner, Dec. 27, 1965. Public relations supr. AT&T, N.Y.C., 1962-68; sr. v.p. Harshe-Rotman & Druck, Inc., N.Y.C., 1968-79; pres., owner Posner McCleary Inc., Columbia, Mo., 1979—; Charles Waldo Haskins assoc. N.Y.U. Sch. Bus. and Pub. Adminstrn. Vice-chmn. Ind. Coll. Fund N.Y., Inc., 1986-87; bd. dirs. Westchester County chpt. ARC, 1986—; trustee Ohio Wesleyan U., 1973-83, mem. exec. com., 1980-83, mem. orgn. com., 1980-83; chmn. student affairs com., 1981-83; mem. N.Y. Dist. Council, U.S. SBA, 1972-76; mem. N.J. Dist. Export Council, 1980-81; mem. fundraising com. U. Mo. Law Sch. Found., Columbia; mem. regional panel Pres.'s Commn. on White House Fellowships, 1985-86. Recipient Disting. Non-Alumni award U. Mo. Sch. Law, 1985. Mem. Internat. Public Relations Assn., Assn. Pvt. Enterprise Edn., Nat. Adv. Council of U.S. Small Bus. Adminstrn. Republican. Office: Posner McCleary Inc 303 West Blvd S Columbia MO 65203

POSNIAK, SALLIE CECELIA, retail designer; b. Appleton, Wis., Mar. 2, 1934; d. Joseph Benjamin and Rebecca (Begin) P. Student, Ray Vogue Art Sch., Chgo., 1952-53, Chgo. Art Inst., 1954-57. Trimmer Marshall Fields, Chgo., 1957-58, asst. designer, 1958-61, designer, 1961-67, master designer, 1967-86, mgr. cen. design, 1986—. Office: Marshall Fields 111 N State St Chicago IL 60690

POSPISIL, EVA SUE, systems engineer; b. Hobbs, N. Mex., May 6, 1953; d. Earl Lee and Ruby Pearl (Bryan) Holdridge; m. Charles Henry Beecroft, Oct. 2, 1971 (div.); m. Francis Joseph Pospisil, Oct. 10, 1980. AS, Baylor U., 1977; BS, NYU, 1983; MS in Sci. Counseling Psychology, Am. Technol. U. with honors, 1985, MS in Mgmt. Sci. with honors, 1986. Med. technician, instr. Acad. Health Sci., Fort Sam Houston, Tex., 1971-81; med. technician Darnall Army Community Hosp., Fort Hood, Tex., 1982-84; program analyst DOIM, Fort Hood, 1984-88; systems engr. Northern Telecom, Richardson, Tex., 1988—; instr. Cen. Tex. Coll., Killeen, 1985-88; product verification engr. Northern Telecommunications, Inc., Richardson, Tex., 1988—; owner, mgr. SUEDE, Copperas Cove, Tex., 1985—; research mgr. Cen. Tex. Coll., Killeen, 1984-85; cons. Mary Kay Cosmetics. Served with U.S. Army, 1971-81. Mem. Am. Med. Technicians, Tex. Assn. Counseling and Devel., Nat. Assn. Underwater Diving Instrs., Nat. Assn. Parachute Clubs, Nat. Assn. Hangliding Assn., Copperas Cove C. of C., Epsilon Delta Phi. Democrat. Roman Catholic. Club: Fort Hood Parachute. Avocations: skydiving, scuba diving, water and snow skiing, racquetball. Home: 1329 Kesser St Plano TX 75023

POST, EDITH, sch. counselor; b. N.Y.C., Mar. 22, 1920; d. Samuel and Sarah (Bucholtz) Dolitzky; B.S., Boston U., 1941, M.S.W., 1943; m. Milton Macy Post, Sept. 8, 1946; chidlren—Andrea Post Rae, Judith Post Yudkoff. Sch. adjustment counselor South Hadley Public Schs., 1966-72; coordintor community-family resources Mt. Holyoke Coll. Learning Devel. Center, 1972-77; counselor Holyoke (Mass.) Public Schs., 1977-81, tchr. support team, 1981-82; pvt. practice counseling, 1982—; cons. Incorporator, Holyoke Vis. Nurse Assn., 1962—; bd dirs. Pioneer Devel. Center, 1978-82; mem. Sch. Improvement Council, Holyoke Pub. Schs., 1985—. Lic. ind. clin. social worker, Mass. Mem. Holyoke Tchrs. Club, Mass. Tchrs. Club, NEA, Nat. Assn. Social Workers, Acad. Cert. Social Workers, Mass. Acad. Psychiat. Social Workers, Delta Kappa Gamma. Home: 1319 Northampton St Holyoke MA 01040

POST, JACKIE EDITH, business executive; b. Lakewood, Ohio, Nov. 17, 1928; d. Sidney Walter and Della N. (Korver) Jackson; 1 child by previous marriage, Deborah Downs Cottingham Dryer. BS cum laude, Miami U., Oxford, Ohio, 1950. Sec. to Henry Laribee Laribee & Cooper, Medina, Ohio, 1955-69; sec. to Baya M. Harrison Harrison, Greene, Mann, Davenport et al, St. Petersburg, Fla., 1970-72; corp. sec., sec. to chmn. bd. Jack Eckerd Corp., Clearwater, Fla., 1972—. Mem. Exec. Women Internat. (v.p., pres.-elect), Beta Gamma Sigma, Delta Zeta. Republican. Home: Largo FL 34644 Office: Jack Eckerd Corp PO Box 4689 Clearwater FL 34618

POSTER, CAROL, electronics executive, writer; b. N.Y.C., Aug. 5, 1956; d. William Shakespeare and Constance (Hammett) P.; m. David Chris Allen, July 1986. BA summa cum laude, Hollins Coll., 1977; postgrad., Ind.U., 1978-79, U. So. Miss., 1979, Athens, Greece, 1973-74. Founder, dir. Necessary Repertory, Roanoke, Va., 1976-77; DIR. Almost Street Theatre, Salt Lake City, Utah, 1985-86; dir. Off Broadway theatres, N.Y.C., 1977-78; assoc. instr. Ind. U. Dept. of English, Bloomington, Ind., 1978-79; teaching asst. U. So. Miss, Hattiesburg, 1979-80; software writer Cen. Data Corp., Rockville, Md., 1980-81; assoc. programmer Sperry Corp., Salt Lake City, Utah, 1981-83, sci. programmmer, 1983-84; owner Amaryllis Software, 1984—; judge Ariz. Authors Assn. poetry contest, 1987; lectr. various colls., univs., workshops, confs. Assoc. editor: The Sports Guide, 1988—; author: Selected Poems of Jacques Prevert, (trans.), and numerous other poems and articles. Mem. Computer Profls. for Social Responsibility, 1986—, Greenpeace, 1984—, Zero Population Growth (officer), 1982—. Recipient 2d prize Utah Original Writing Competition, 1986, Excellence award Cen. Data Corp., 1981. Mem. IEEE, Assn. for Computing Machinery, Poets and Writers, Associated Writing Programs. Office: Amaryllis Software 535 Parkview Dr Park City UT 84060

POSTER-ELLIS, DALE L., county government administrator; b. N.Y.C., June 16, 1953; d. Harvey Harold and Regina (Solomon) Poster; m. Gary Warren Ellis Jr., Sept. 28, 1980; 1 child, Hanna Faye. AB cum laude, Boston U., 1975; M in Pub. Adminstrn., Fla. Internat. U., 1979. Legal advocate San Francisco Lawyers Com. Urban Affairs, 1974; social worker Chelsea (Mass.) Jewish Nursing Home, 1975-76, North Miami Gen. Hosp., Miami, Fla., 1976-77; instrl. asst. Miami-Dade Community Coll., Miami, 1977-78; grad. advisor Fla. Internat. U., Miami, 1978-79; Presdl. mgmt. intern U.S. Office Personnel Mgmt., Washington, 1979-80; budget examiner U.S. Office Mgmt. and Budget, Washington, 1980-82; sr. budget analyst Metro-Dade County Govt., Miami, 1982-87; adminstr. Metro Dade County Mgr.'s Office, Miami, 1987—; network mem. Young Women's Christian Assn., Miami, 1983—; speaker Women of Work, Dade County Pub. Schs., 1985—. Contbr. articles to profl. jours. Mem. Nat. Women's Polit. Caucus, Washington, 1979-82; crisis counselor Switchboard of Miami, 1986—. Mem. LWV, Presl. Mgmt. Alumni Group, Metro-Dade Women's Assn. (chair com. 1986—), YMCA, Phi Kappa Phi. Democrat. Office: Metro-Dade County 111 NW 1st St Suite 2710 Miami FL 33128

POSTER-TAYLOR, TERRI LEE, temporary employment company executive; b. Boston, Oct. 2, 1952; d. Harold Bernard and Sarah Lillian (Cristol) Poster; m. Barry Millman, Feb. 23, 1975 (div. Feb 1979); m. Clark Martin Taylor, Oct. 19, 1985. Student, Boston Conservatory of Music, 1970-73. Beauty advisor Revlon Co., N.Y.C., 1975-77; mktg. rep. V.H. Monette & Co., Smithfield, Va., 1977-78; sales mgr. Vidal Sassoon, Inc., Los Angeles, 1978-81; account exec. Sarvis & Assocs., Jacksonville, Fla., 1981-82; v.p., owner Exchange & Commissary Sales, Jacksonville, 1982-83; area mgr. Assoc. Temporary Staffing, Jacksonville, 1983-85; pres., owner Easy Info, Inc., Jacksonville, 1985-86; br. mgr. Ablest Temporary Services, Jacksonville, 1986-88, area mgr., 1988—; speaker in field. Mem. Am. Soc. for Personnel Adminstrs., Adminstrv. Mgmt. Soc. (pres. 1985-86), Northeast Fla. Women Bus. Owners, Jacksonville C. of C. (chmn. area council main event, sec. Arlington council 1988, bd. dirs. 1988, chmn. pub. relations com. Ambassadors 1988), Hadassah. Republican. Jewish. Lodge: Civitan (bd. dirs. Jacksonville 1985-86). Office: Temporaries Inc 8130 Baymeadows Way W Suite 103 Jacksonville FL 32216

POSTON, CAROL OLIVER, communications company executive; b. Cin., Jan. 20, 1942; d. Robert Hall and Jeanette Dorothy (Piccirillo) Oliver; m. Charles A. Poston, Oc. 27, 1973; 1 child, C. Oliver. BA in English, U. Cin., 1964, BS in Edn., 1965; MEd in Human Resources Devel., Xavier U., 1980; PhD in Human Behavior and Orgn. Devel., Union Grad. Sch., 1988. Supr. engring. AT&T Communications, Cin., 1965-70, supr. corp personnel, 1870-77, mgr. staff nmktg., 1977-81, mgr. nat. account, 1981-83, asst. v.p. nat. mkts., 1983-87, dir. mng., client edn. learning systems for future, 1988—; lectr. Miami U., Oxford, Ohio, 1985—. Mem. Internat. Teleconferencing Assn. (speaker), Am. Soc. Tng. and Devel. (speaker), Nat. Retail Mchts. Assn. (speaker), Paper Industry Mgmt. Assn., Am. Iron Inst., Sales and Mktg. Execs., Cin. Bus. and Profl. Women Cin., Nat. Assn. Female Execs., Cin. Symphony (women's com.), Cin. C. of C. Home: 795 Woodbine Ave Cincinnati OH 45246 Office: AT&T Communications 11311 Cornell Park Dr Suite 200 Cincinnati OH 45242

POSTON, EDITH HUFFMAN, real estate executive; b. Hickory, N.C., Jan. 25, 1914; d. George W. and Ada (Arney) Huffman; m. George R. Poston, Nov. 17, 1956 (dec. 1977). BA, Lenoir-Rhyne Coll., 1934; MA, U. N.C., Greensboro, 1947; postgrad., U. Chgo., 1952-53. Tchr. Lowell (N.C.) Pub. Schs., 1934-42, Hickory Pub. Schs., 1942-45; instr. edn. The Woman's Coll. U. N.C., Greensboro, 1945-47, asst. prof. edn., 1947-52, assoc. prof. edn., 1953-57; pres. Superior Properties, Inc., Gastonia, N.C., 1967—. Mem. Alpha Psi Omega, Pi Lambda Theta. Episcopalian. Club: UC Book (Gastonia) (pres. 1971-73). Home: 1211 Oakwood Ave Gastonia NC 28052 Office: Superior Properties Inc 392 N Edgemont Ave Gastonia NC 28054

POSTON, ERSA HINES, management consultant; b. Paducah, Ky., May 3, 1921; d. Robert S. and Adele (Johnson) Hines; AB, Ky. State Coll., 1942; MSW, Atlanta U., 1946; LLD, Union Coll., 1971, Fordham U., 1978; DHL, Mercy Coll., 1980. Community orgn. sec. Hartford (Conn.) Tb and Health Assn., 1946-47; teen-age program dir. Westside br. YWCA, N.Y.C., 1947-48, adult dir., 1948-49; asst. dir. Clinton Community Ctr., N.Y.C., 1949-50; dir., 1950-53; field sec. N.Y.C. Welfare and Health Council, 1953-55; field project supr. N.Y.C. Youth Bd., 1955, asst. dir. program rev., 1955-57; area dir. N.Y. State Div. for Youth, 1957-62, youth work coordinator, 1962-64; confidential asst. to Gov. Rockefeller, 1964; dir. N.Y. State Office Econ. Opportunity, 1964-67; pres. N.Y. State CSC, 1967-75, commr., 1975-77; commr. U.S. CSC, 1977-79; vice-chmn. U.S. Merit Systems Protection Bd., 1979-83; pres. Poston Pub. Personnel Mgmt. Cons., Chevy Chase, Md., 1983—; former mem. Internat. CSC, Nat. Commn. to Study Goals for State Colls. and Univs.; mem. adv. council Federally Employed Women; chmn. Pres.'s Adv. Council Intergovtl. Personnel Policy; trustee Med. Coll. Pa.; bd. dirs. Pub. Pvt. Ventures; v.p. Nat. Urban League; U.S. del. UN Gen. Assembly, 1976; vice presiding officer U.S. Commn. on Observance of Internat. Woman's Yr. Bd. govs. Albany Med. Ctr. Hosp.; bd. dirs. Whitney M. Young Meml. Found. Recipient Achievement awards Bklyn. club Nat. Assn. Negro Bus. and Profl. Women's Clubs, Dutchess of Paducah award, Dau. of Paducah plaque; named Ky. col.; Disting. Alumni award Ky. State Coll., Disting. Service award Greater N.Y. chpt. Links; Woman of Yr. award Cen. Jersey club Nat. Assn. Negro Bus. and Profl. Women's Clubs, Achievement award Phi Delta Kappa, Populus Dei award Mercy Coll.; Woman of Year award Utility Club; Outstanding Woman of Year award Iota Phi Lambda; Nat. Achievement award Nat. Assn. Negro BPW Clubs, 1967; Outstanding Service award 26th A.D. Rep. Orgn. Queens County; Trail Blazer award Jamaica Club Nat. Assn. Negro BPW Clubs; Benjamin Potoker Brotherhood award, 1970; named 1970 Woman of Year, BPW Club Albany; Equal Opportunity Day award Nat. Urban League, 1976; Spl. award Psi Nu chpt. Omega Psi Phi, 1977; Disting. Public Servant award Capital Press Club, 1978, IPMA Stockberger award, Ottawa, Can., 1987; Founders' Day award Alpha Kappa Alpha, 1978; First award Nat. Black Personnel Assn., 1978; named to N.Y. State Women's Hall of Fame, 1980; many others. Mem. Nat. Assn. Social Workers, Acad. Cert. Social Workers, Nat. Acad. Public Adminstrn., Am. Soc. Public Adminstrn., Internat. Personnel Mgmt. Assn. (Exec. Bd. award Nat. Capital area 1979, hon. life mem., Walter Stockberger award 1987), Nat. Council Negro Women, Links, Girlfriends, Inc., Lambda Kappa Mu (hon.; Achievement award Nu chpt.), Alpha Kappa Alpha (outstanding awards Bklyn. chpt. 1960, 65). Office: 4701 Willard Ave #924 Chevy Chase VA 20815

POST REILLY, CONSTANCE, governmental administrator; b. Danbury, Conn., Oct. 30, 1949; d. Christian Charles and Constance Rosetta (Attanasio) Post; m. Kevin Christopher Reilly, Apr. 24, 1982; 1 child, Maura. BA, Culver-Stockton Coll., 1971; postgrad., Ala. A&M U., 1977-78. VISTA vol. Huntsville-Madison County (Ala.) Community Action Agy., 1972-74; asst. dir. ESAA program Ala. A&M U., Normal, 1974-77, dir. tutorial program, 1977-79; cons. Cons. & Research SErvices, Inc., Huntsville, 1979; research and grants adminstr., econ. devel. dir. City of Mt. Vernon, N.Y., 1980-86; dep. exec. dir. Mt. Vernon Urban Renewal Agy., 1986—. Bd. dirs. Huntsville-Madison County CAC, 1973-74; sec. bd. dirs. Area 7 Community Council, 1974-78, Huntsville Commn. on Human rights, 1975-79, Mt. Vernon Community Action Group, 1980—, Mt. Vernon Indsl. Devel. Corp., 1980—; asst. sec. Mt. Vernon Indsl. Devel. Agy., 1986—; dep. exec. dir. Mt. Vernon Urban Renewal Agy., 1986—. Mem. Delta Sigma theta. Roman Catholic. Home: 115 Overlook St Mount Vernon NY 10552 Office: City of Mt Vernon City Hall Mount Vernon NY 10550

POSZE, MARY ELLEN GENS, travel agency executive; b. Lorain, Ohio, Oct. 25, 1935; d. George F. and Mabel (Strehle) Gens; m. Alex Richard Posze, Aug. 22, 1953 (div. Dec. 1980); children—Jennifer Lynn, Vanessa Elizabeth. Student Baldwin-Wallace Coll., 1965, Miami U., Oxford, Ohio, 1961-63, Kans. State U., 1960. Student Union acct. Kans. State U., Manhattan, 1960; office mgr., asst. to nat. adminstr. Phi Kappa Tau, Oxford, 1960-63; Realtor, Taft-Hossfeld, Inc., Berea, Ohio, 1965-75; pres., chief exec. officer Village Sq. Travel, Cleve., 1975—; mem. U.S. Congl. Adv. Bd., Washington, 1985. Mem. Greater Balt. Com., Inc., 1983—. Mem. Am. Soc. Travel Agts., Cleve. Advt. Club, Soc. Travel Agts. in Govt., Assn. Retail Travel Agts., Ohio Bd. Realtors, Cleve. Area Bd. Realtors (trustee), Council Smaller Enterprises, Sales and Mktg. Execs. Cleve., Women's City Club, Greater Cleve. Growth Assn., Berea C. of C. (trustee 1977—), Jacksonville C. of C. Home: 249 Stanford Rd Berea OH 44017 Office: Village Sq Travel Inc 433 W Bagley Rd Berea OH 44017

POTASEK, MARY JOYCE, physicist, researcher; b. Mpls., Oct. 27, 1945; d. Chester and Millie P.; m. Karl W. Beeson, Jan. 22, 1977; 1 child, Jessica Elizabeth. BA in Math., Coll. St. Catherine, 1967; MS in Physics, U. Ill., 1970, PhD, 1974. Research asst. U. Ill., Urbana, 1970-74; research scientist Internat. Bus. Machines, Watson Research Ctr., Yorktown Heights, N.Y., 1974-75; NSF, AAUW postdoctoral fellow Princeton (N.J.) U., 1975-78; NATO postdoctoral fellow Max Planck Inst., Gottingen, West Germany, 1978-80; mem. tech. staff AT&T Bell Labs., Murray Hill, N.J., 1980—. Contbr. articles to profl. jours. Mem. AAAS, Optical Soc. of Am., Am. Phys. Soc. Home: 197 Dodds Ln Princeton NJ 08540 Office: AT&T Bell Labs 600 Mountain Ave Murray Hill NJ 07974

POTASH, JANICE SUE, accounting educator; b. Ft. Knox, Ky., Mar. 24, 1955; d. Robert S. and Madeline J. (Kirschner) Kraft; m. Steven Robert Potash, May 28, 1978; 1 child, Jamie Rebecca. BS in Bus. cum laude, Miami U., Ohio, 1977; MBA, Xavier U., 1982. CPA, Ohio. Staff acct., auditor Arthur Andersen & Co., Cin., 1977-78; acctg. supr. Children's Hosp. Med. Ctr., Cin., 1978-81; asst. prof. acctg. Miami U., Hamilton, Ohio, 1982-84, Marian Coll., Indpls., 1985—. Campaign worker jud. polit. campaigns, Cin., 1972—; mem. Women's Am. ORT, Cin., 1982-85, Indpls., 1986—; advisor Explorer post Boy Scouts Am., Kokomo, Ind., 1984. Mem. Am. Acctg. Assn., Am. Inst. CPA's, Ohio Soc. CPA's, Acctg. Research Assn., Am. Woman's Soc. CPA's, Ind. CPA Soc., Am. Soc. Women Accts. Republican. Jewish. Office: Marian Coll 3200 Cold Spring Rd Indianapolis IN 46222

POTENZA, DAISY MCKASKLE, newspaper executive; b. Houston, Mar. 5, 1906; d. George Washington and Dora Amy (Crump) McKaskle; student Sinclair Bus. Coll., 1925, Massey's Bus. Coll., 1924-26, U. Houston; m. Julius Orian Potenza, Sept. 26, 1928; 1 dau., Marjorie Ann (Mrs. William L. Hale) (dec.). With Houston Chronicle, 1926—, adminstrv. asst. to editor-in-chief, 1930-79, adminstrv. asst. to sr. v.p. and cons., 1979-87. Exec. sec. Houston Endowment, Inc., 1968-69; bd. dirs. Pin Oak Charity Horse Show, 1978, 79, 80, 81, 82, 83, 84. Recipient award United Fund, 1967—; tribute for exec. service to Chronicle, 1983; outstanding ticket sales awardee Pin Oak Charity Horse Show, Tex. Children's Hosp., 1975-83, 84. Mem. Nat., Tex. press women, Women in Communications, Press Club Houston (hon. life). Methodist. Club: Farm and Ranch. Home: 2405 San Felipe Rd Houston TX 77019 Office: 801 Texas Ave Houston TX 77002

POTTENGER, MARITHA SUSAN, publishing executive, astrologer; b. Tucson, May 21, 1952; d. Henry Farmer and Zipporah (Pottenger) Dobyns. BA, U. Calif., Berkeley, 1974; MA, Calif. Sch. Profl. Psychology, 1976. Librarian asst. U. Calif. Grad. Social Scis. Library, Berkeley, 1971-74; cons. Los Angeles, 1976—; editorial dir. ACS Pubs., San Diego, 1983—; cons. Astro Computing Services, San Diego, 1986—. Author: (book) Encounter Astrology, 1978, Healing with the Horoscope, 1982, Complete Horoscope Interpretation, 1986. Mem. Nat. Council for GeoCosmic Research, Am. Fedn. of Astrologers, Fraternity of Canadian Astrologers, NOW, Internat. Soc. for Astrological Research. Office: ACS Pubs Inc PO Box 16430 San Diego CA 92116-0430

POTTER, ELAINE CLARKE, sociology educator; b. Warren, Ohio, Jan. 31, 1935; d. Scot Butler Clarke and Lucy Jean (Spiers) Kellers; m. Ralph Miles, Potter, July 13, 1957; 1 child, Russell Alan. B.A. magna cum laude, Case Western Res. U., 1970; M.A., Kent State U., 1972. Office mgr. McGovern/Shriver Hdqrs., Euclid, Ohio, 1972; instr. sociology Ursuline Coll. for Women, Pepper Pike, Ohio, 1973-74; instr. sociology and soc. sci. Cuyahoga Community Coll., Parma, Ohio, 1975—. Mem. Am. Sociol. Assn., AAUP, North Central Sociol. Assn., Sociologists for Women in Soc., ACLU, NOW, Women's Internat. League for Peace and Freedom (pres. Cleve. chpt. 1975-76), Women Space (v.p. 1980), Phi Beta Kappa, Tri Beta. Democrat. Unitarian. Club: Sierra. Avocations: hiking; reading. Home: 2618 Brainard Rd Pepper Pike OH 44124 Office: Cuyahoga Community Coll West Campus 11000 Pleasant Valley Parma OH 44130

POTTER, EMMA JOSEPHINE HILL, educator; b. Hackensack, N.J., July 18, 1921; d. James Silas and Martha Loretta (Pyle) Hill; A.B. cum laude with honors in Classics (scholar), Alfred (N.Y.) U., 1943; A.M., Johns Hopkins U., 1946; m. James H. Potter, Mar. 26, 1949. Tchr. Latin, Balt. County Public Schs., 1943-44; instr. French, Spanish, Balt. Poly. Inst., 1950-83; instr. Spanish adult edn. classes, 1946-48; treas. Bruno Potter Inc., acctg. Trustee James Harry Potter Gold Medal, ASME. Mem. Johns Hopkins U., Alfred U. alumni assns., Internat. Platform Assn. Democrat. Roman Catholic. Club: Johns Hopkins U. Faculty. Home: 419 3d Ave Avon by the Sea NJ 07717

POTTER, EVELYN GOODWIN, executive recruiter; b. Dumont, N.J.; d. Russell M. and Marie (Hermida) Goodwin; B.A., U. Mich., 1949; m. Neil Potter, June 30, 1950; children—Eugene, Jill. Exec. sec. Office Bd. Trustees, SUNY, N.Y.C., 1950-52; asst. to dir. Profl. Exam. Service, Am. Public Health Assn., 1953-54; dir. public relations SUNY Downstate Med. Center, Bklyn., 1954-75, asst. to pres., 1967-75; v.p. univ. relations Clark U., Worcester, Mass., 1975-77; v.p. The Cantor Concern, N.Y.C., 1977—; cons. health careers N.Y.C. Bd. Edn., 1963-69; mem. com. on health careers Empire State Health Council, 1964—; public relations com. Council Higher Ednl. Instns. in N.Y.C., 1961-69; bd. dirs. N.Y.C. Health Planning Agy., 1974-75, West Midwood Assn., 1964-65. Recipient certificate of merit Acad. Hosp. Public Relations, 1972, Award Community Agys. Public Relations Assn., 1975. Mem. Assn. Am. Med. Colls., Nat. Assn. Sci. Writers, Am. Coll. Pub. Relations Assn. (citation of merit 1959, 72), Met. Coll. Pub. Relations Assn., Health and Welfare Pub. Relations Soc. (charter mem., dir., chmn. publs. com.), Nat. Assn. Corp. and Profl. Recruiters, Council Advancement and Support Edn. Club: Boston Press. Author: Medical Education in Brooklyn-The First 100 Years, 1960. Home: Westbourne Alger Ct Bronxville NY 10708 Office: The Cantor Concern 171 Madison Ave New York NY 10016

POTTER, JENNIFER LEE, real estate broker; b. Santa Monica, Calif., Oct. 25, 1957; d. Jed Denton Potter and Nanette (Macy) Duquette; m. Robert Emil Langlois, Aug. 1, 1986; children: Lisa, Cody, Ryan. Grad. high sch., New Hall, Calif. Salesperson Coldwell Banker Real Estate, Newhall, 1976-80, Valencia (Calif.) Realty, 1980-86; broker J. Potter & Assocs., Hemet, Calif., 1986—. Mem. Nat. Assn. Realtors, Calif. Assn. Realtors, Hemet-San Jacinto Bd. Realtors, San Jacinto C. of C. Republican. Office: J Potter & Assocs 25120 San Jacinto St Suite M Hemet CA 92383

POTTER, NANCY DUTTON, psychologist; b. St. Joseph, Mo., Jan. 16, 1946; d. Paul Vernon and Rosa Lee (Hatfield) Dutton 1 child, Blakeslee Ann. BA, Pitzer Coll., 1968; MA, U. Kans., 1971; Ph.D., U. Mo., 1974; postgrad., Georgetown U., 1977-79. Lic. psychologist, D.C., Va. Chief clin. psychology Keesler AFB Med. Center, Miss., 1976-77; clin. psychologist Malcolm Grow Med. Center, Andrews AFB, Md., 1977-78; assoc. dir. Georgetown U. Counseling Ctr., Washington, 1978-79, acting dir., 1979-80, dir. internship tng., 1978-81; pvt. practice psychology Va., 1978—; chmn. ethics and profl. affairs Va. Acad. Clin. Psychology, Va., 1987—. Bd. dirs. Family Counseling Agy., Biloxi, Miss., 1976. Served to maj. USAF, 1974-88. Mem. Am. Psychol. Assn., Am. Personnel and Guidance Assn., No. Va. Soc. Clin. Psychologists (v.p. 1984-86, pres. 1986-88). Home: 7400 Carath Ct Springfield VA 22153 Office: 8987 Cotswold Dr Burke VA 22015

POTTER, TANYA JEAN, lawyer; b. Washington, Oct. 30, 1956; d. John Francis and Tanya Agnes (Kristof) P. BA, Georgetown U., 1978, JD, 1981. Bar: D.C. 1982, U.S. Ct. Appeals (D.C. cir.), U.S. Ct. Appeals (fed. cir.), U.S. Dist. Ct. (D.C. dist.), U.S. Ct. Internat. Trade. Assoc. Ragan and Mason, Washington, 1981—; mediator D.C. Superior Ct., 1986—. Author: Practicing Before the Federal Maritime Commission, 1986. Mem. exec. council Washington Opera's Jr. Com., 1983—, chmn. com. 1988; mem. internat. com. ARC, Washington, 1986—; auction chmn. Young Friends of ARC, Washington, 1985-86; mem. benefit com. Vincent T. Lombardi Cancer Ctr., Washington, 1985—; del. Georgetown U. Nat. Law Alumni Bd. Dirs., 1986—. Recipient Community Service Recognition award ARC, Washington, 1986. Mem. ABA, Bar Assn. of D.C. (exec. council ad law sect. 1985—, moderator adminstrv. law symposium 1986—). Roman Catholic. Clubs: Pisces, Georgetown U. Met. (bd. govs. 1986—) (Washington). Office: Ragan and Mason 900 17th St NW Washington DC 20006

POTTS, BARBARA JOYCE, mayor, radiology technician; b. Los Angeles, Feb. 18, 1932; d. Theodore Thomas and Helen Mae (Kelley) Elledge; m. Donald A. Potts, Dec. 27, 1953; children—Tedd, Douglas, Dwight, Laura. A.A., Graceland Coll., 1951; grad., Radiol. Tech. Sch., 1953. Radiol. technician Independence Sanitarium and Hosp., Mo., 1953, 58-59; radiol. technician Mercy Hosp., Balt., 1954-55; city council mem.-at-large City of Independence, Mo., 1978-82, mayor, 1982—; chmn. Mid-Am. Regional Council, Kansas City, Mo., 1984-85; bd. dirs. Mo. Mcpl. League, Jefferson City, Mo., 1982—, v.p., 1986-87, pres. 1987; chmn. Mo. Commn. on Local Govt. Cooperation, 1985—. Mem. Mo. Gov.'s Conf. on Edn., 1976, Independence Charter Rev. Bd., 1977; bd. dirs. Hope House Shelter for Abused Women, Independence, 1982—; pres. Child Placement Services, Independence, 1972—; trustee Independence Regional Health Ctr., 1982—, Nat. Women's Polit. Caucus, LWV. Recipient Woman of Achievement award Mid-Continent Council Girl Scouts Am., 1983, 75th Anniversary Women of Achievement award, Mid-Continent Council Girl Scouts, 1987; Jane Adams award Hope House, 1984; Community Leadership award Comprehensive Mental Health Services, Inc., 1984. Mem. Reorganized Ch. of Jesus Christ of Latter-Day Saints. Home: 18508 E 30th Terr Independence MO 64057 Office: City of Independence 111 E Maple St Independence MO 64051

POULIOT, ASSUNTA GALLUCCI, business school owner and director; b. West Warwick, R.I., Aug. 14, 1937; d. Michael and Angelina (DeCesare) G.; Gallucci; m. Joseph F. Pouliot, July 4, 1961; children—Brenda, Mark, Jill, Michele. B.S., U. R.I., 1959, M.S., 1971. Bus. tchr. Cranston High Sch., R.I., 1959-61; bus. dept. chmn. Chariho Regional High Sch., Wood River Junction, R.I., 1961-73; instr. U. R.I., Kingston, 1973-78; founder, dir. Ocean State Bus. Inst., Wakefield, R.I., 1977—; dir. Fleet Nat. Bank, 1985—; bd. mgrs. Bank of New Eng., 1984-85; speaker in field. Pres. St. Francis Women's Club, Wakefield, 1975; sec. St. Francis Parish Council, Wakefield, 1980; mem. Econ. Devel. Commn., Wakefield, 1981-85; mem. South County Hosp. Corp., Wakefield, 1978—; fin. dir. Bus. and Profl. Women's Club, Wakefield, 1982-84. Mem. R.I. Bus. Edn. Assn. (newsletter editor 1979-81), New Eng. Bus. Coll. Assn. (sec. 1984-86, pres. 1985-87), R.I. Assn. Career and Tech. Schs. (treas., bd. dirs. 1979-86), Eastern Bus. Edn. Assn. (conf. leader), Nat. Bus. Edn. Assn. (conf. leader), Assn. Ind. Colls. and Schs. (conv. speaker, pub. relations com., govt. relations com.), R.I. Women's Golf Assn. (exec. bd., tournament co-chmn.), Phi Kappa Phi, Delta Pi Epsilon (pres., newsletter editor). Roman Catholic. Club: Point Judith Country. Avocations: golf; gardening. Home: 137 Kenyon Ave Wakefield RI 02879 Office: Ocean State Bus Inst 1 High St PO Box 377 Wakefield RI 02880

POULOS, CLARA JEAN, nutritionist, biologist; b. Los Angeles, Jan. 1, 1941; d. James P. and Clara Georgie (Creighton) Hill; Ph.D. in Biology, Fla. State Christian U., 1974; Ph.D. in Nutrition, Donsbach U., 1979; D in Nutritional Medicine, John F. Kennedy U., 1986; Cert. in Diabetes Edn.; m. Themis Poulos, Jan. 31, 1960. Dir. research Leapou Lab., Aptos, Calif., 1973-76, Monterey Bay Research Inst., Santa Cruz, Calif., 1976—; nutrition specialist, Santa Cruz, 1975—; dir. nutritional services, health enhancement, lifestyle planning, Santa Cruz, 1983—; instr. Santa Cruz Extention U. Calif. and Stoddard Assocs. Seminars; cons. Biol-Med. Lab., Chgo., Nutra-Med Research Corp., N.Y., Akorn-Miller Pharmacal, Chgo., Monterey Bay Aquaculture Farms, Threshhold Lab., Calif., Resurrection Lab., Calif. Recipient Najulander Internat. Research award, 1971, Wainwright Found. award., 1979, various state and local awards. Fellow Internat. Coll. Applied Nutrition, Am. Nutritionist Assn., Internat. Acad. Nutritional Consultants; mem. Am. Diabetes Assn. (profl., pres. Santa Cruz chpt., sec. No. Calif. chpt.), AAAS, Internat. Platform Soc., Am. Public Health Assn., Calif. Acad. Sci., Internat. Fishery Assn. (health asct.), Clubs: Toastmistress, Quota. Author: Alcoholism—Stress - Hypoglycemia, 1976; The Relationship of Stress to Alcoholism and Hypoglycemia, 1979; assoc. editor Internat. Jour. Bio-social Research, Health Promotion Features; contbr. articles to profl. jours. Office: 1595 Soquel Dr Suite 222 Santa Cruz CA 95065

POULSEN, FERN SUE, public relations consultant; b. Chgo., Sept. 29, 1959; d. Herman and Renee (Greenberg) Bass; m. Gregory Carl Poulsen, May 5, 1953. Ba, N. Ill. U., 1981. Corporate communications staff coordinator Centel Corp., Chgo., 1981-86; mgr. special events Network Mktg. Group, Oak Brook, Ill., 1986-88; pres. Poulsen Promotions, Chgo., 1988—. Vol. Easter Seal Soc. and March of Dimes, Chgo., 1987-88, Penny Pullen Campaign Com., Park Ridge, Ill., 1981-83, Am. Cancer Soc., Des Plaines, Ill., 1983; exec. advisor Jr. Achievement, Chgo., 1982-83; active Lincoln Park Cen. Assn., Chgo., 1988. Named Outstanding Woman Student Leader N. Ill. U. Women's Faculty, 1980. Mem. Internat. Assn. Bus. Communicators, Ad-Net Chgo., Omicron Delta Kappa, Phi Beta Kappa. Home and Office: Poulsen Promotions 2201 N Cleveland Chicago IL 60614

POULTON, ROBERTA DORIS, nurse, consultant; b. Balt., Oct. 19, 1943; d. Charles Robert and Mary Doris (Guercio) P. Nursing diploma Md. Gen. Hosp., 1964. Staff nurse Md. Gen. Hosp., Balt., 1964-67, Project Hope, Columbia, 1967, Tunisia, 1969-70; staff nurse St. Agnes Hosp., Balt., 1968-69, team leader, 1972-83, staff nurse-preceptor, 1983-88, head nurse pediatric emergency room and ambulatory services, 1988—; cons., Girl Scouts U.S.A., Balt., 1972—, Bapt. Conv. Md., 1963—. Vol. CPR instr. ARC, Balt., 1972—. Mem. Am. Nurses Assn., Md. Nurses Assn., Am. Assn. Critical Care Nurses, Appalachian Trial Conf. Democrat. Baptist.

POUNDS, JANET LYNN, chemist; b. Dallas, Nov. 29,. 1944; d. Truman Edward and Marilynn (Carlton) P.; BA in Chemistry, La. State U., 1966, MS in Organic Chemistry, 1969; divorced; 1 dau., Kristina. Grad. teaching asst. La. State U., 1966-69; tchr. sci. Baker (La.) Jr. High Sch., 1969-70; instr. chemistry So. U., Baton Rouge, 1972-77; research chemist PPG Industries, Corpus Christi, Tex., 1977-80, research chemist, Barberton, Ohio, 1980-85, sr. research chemist, Barberton, 1985—. NIH fellow, 1978. Mem. NOW (La. legis. coordinator 1973-74, ERA coordinator 1974-75), Am. Chem. Soc. Episcopalian. Clubs: Akron All-Breed Dog, Akron Ski. Home: 3097 Baughman Rd Clinton OH 44216 Office: PO Box 31 Barberton OH 44203

POUSSAINT, RENEE FRANCINE, journalist; b. N.Y.C., Aug. 12, 1944; d. Christopher Wallace and Bobbie (Vance) P.; m. Henry J. Richardson III, Sept. 10, 1977. B.A., Sarah Lawrence Coll., 1966; M.A., UCLA, 1971; postgrad., Yale Law Sch., 1966-67, Ind. U., 1971-72; student, Sorbonne, Paris, 1964-65; hon. doctorate, Mt. Vernon Coll., Washington, 1985; cert., Columbia U. Journalism Sch., Michele Clark Fellowship Program for Minority Journalists, 1972. Program dir. AIESEC, N.Y.C., 1968-69; editor African Arts Mag., Los Angeles, 1969-71; reporter WBBM-TV, Chgo., 1974-76, CBS Network News, Chgo., Washington, 1976-78; anchorperson WJLA-TV, Washington, 1978—; dancer Jean Leon Destine Troupe, N.Y.C., 1966; translator U. Calif. Press, Los Angeles, 1970; tutor Operation Rescue, Washington, 1981—. Hon. dir. Nat. Kidney Found., Washington, 1981—; citizen advisor YWCA, Nat. Capitol Area, 1983—; co-chmn. Nat. Capital Area Lung Assn., 1982; membership chmn. Arthritis Found., 1981-82. Recipient Reporting award Ill. Mental Health Assn., 1976; recipient Reporting award Nat. Assn. Media Women, 1977, Broadcasting Excellence award AAUW, 1979, Emmy awards, 1979, 80, 81, 82, Broadcast award NAACP, 1980, Whitney Young Meml. award Washington Urban League, 1983. Mem. AFTRA, NAACP (life), Capitol Press Club. Office: WJLA-TV 4461 Connecticut Ave NW Washington DC 20008 *

POWELL, ANICE CARPENTER, librarian; b. Moorhead, Miss., Dec. 2, 1928; d. Horace Aubrey and Celeste (Brian) Carpenter; student Sunflower Jr. Coll., 1945-47, Miss. State Coll. Women, 1947-48; B.S., Delta State Coll., 1961, M.L.S., 1974; m. Robert Wainwright Powell, July 19, 1948; children—Penelope Elizabeth, Deborah Alma. Librarian, Sunflower (Miss.) Pub. Library, 1958-61; tchr. English, Isola (Miss.) High Sch., 1961-62; dir. Sunflower County Library, Indianola, Miss., 1962—; mem. adv. council State Instl. Library Services, 1967-71; mem. adv. bd. library services and constrn. act com. Miss. Library Commn., 1978-80, mem. pub. library task force, 1986—. Mem. ALA, Miss. Library Assn. (exec. dir. Nat. Library Week 1975, steering com. 1976, chmn. right to read com. 1976, chmn. legis. com. 1979, chmn. intellectual freedom com. 1975, 80, mem. legis. com. 1973-86, chmn. membership com. 1982, pres. 1984, chmn. nominating com. 1986; Peggy May award 1981, co-chmn. right-to-read com. 1987), AAUW, Sunflower County Hist. Soc. (pres. 1983-87), Miss. Literacy Assn., Delta Council, Sunflower County Literacy Council (treas.). Methodist. Home: Box 310 Sunflower MS 38778 Office: Sunflower County Library 201 Cypress Dr Indianola MS 38751

POWELL, ANNABELLE COUNCIL, geology educator, geoscience resources company executive; b. Burlington, N.C., Nov. 23, 1953; d. Thomas Edward and Annabelle (Council) P.; m. Russell E. Guy, July 12, 1986. B.A., Wellesley Coll., 1975; Ph.D., Oxford U., Eng., 1980. Asst. to curator Mus. of Basel, Switzerland, 1980; asst. prof. geology Rutgers U., New Brunswick, N.J., 1981-82; founder, pres. Geosci. Resources, Inc., 1982—; mem. bd. advisors Love Sch. Bus. Elon Coll., N.C., 1986—. Mem. Geol. Soc. Am., Am. Assn. Petroleum Geologists, Soc. Econ. Paleontol. Mineralogists. Republican. Avocations: piano; organ; flying. Home: 2911 S Fairway Burlington NC 27216

POWELL, BARBARA, clinical psychologist; b. Dexter, Mo., Apr. 25, 1929; d. Clarence Albert and Ethel (Mohrstadt) P.; B.A., Wellesley Coll., 1950; M.A., Columbia U., 1967; Ph.D., Fordham U., 1975; m. Richard W. O'Neill, Jan. 3, 1953 (div. 1966); children—Richard W., Susan P., Jennifer A., Julia K.; m. 2d, Charles J. McCarthy, May 13, 1967 (div. 1978); m. 3d, David S. Burt, June 16, 1983. Copywriter, Parade mag., 1951-52, McCall's, 1952-53; publicity dir. Silvermine Guild Art, New Canaan, Conn., 1964-66; reporter Bridgeport (Conn.) Post, 1964-69; psychologist Dunlap & Assos., Darien, Conn., 1966-67; dir. Guidance Center for Women, U. Conn., 1968-69; intern N.Y. Hosp., Westchester, 1972-73; psychologist St. Mary's in-the-field, Valhalla, N.Y., 1973-77, Behavior Therapy Inst., White Plains, N.Y., 1975-78; pvt. practice clin. psychology, Rowayton, Conn., 1976—; lectr. U. Conn., 1976-77; co-founder, assertive tng. leader Woman's Place, Darien. USPH grantee, 1970-71. Mem. Am. Psychol. Assn., Am. Assn. Marriage and Family Therapists, Am. Assn. Advancement Behavior Therapy, Soc. Clin. and Exptl. Hypnosis, Phi Beta Kappa, Sigma Xi. Author: Careers for Women after Marriage and Children, 1965; How to Raise a Successful Daughter, 1979; Overcoming Shyness, 1979; The Complete Guide to Your Child's Emotional Health, 1984; Alone, Alive and Well, 1985; Good Relationships Are Good Medicine, 1987. Address: 20 Covewood Dr Rowayton CT 06853 also: Mansion Beach PO Box 1036 Block Island RI 02807

POWELL, BARBARA JOAN, psychologist, educator; b. Williamsville, Ill., June 30, 1933; d. Fred Alonzo and Bertha (Hanner) P. BA in Psychology, Washington U., St. Louis, 1957, PhD, 1964; MA in Psychology, George Washington U., 1960. Diplomate Am. Bd. Profl. Psychology; lic. psychologist, Kans. Dir. psychol. services Malcolm Bliss Mental Health Ctr., St. Louis, 1969-74; staff psychologist VA Med. Ctr., Lexington, Ky., 1974-77; staff psychologist VA Med. Ctr., Kansas City, Mo., 1977—, prin. investigator alcohol research program, 1981—; acting assoc. chief of staff for research and devel. div., chief psychology VA Med. Ctr., Kansas City, 1986—; prof. Kansas U. Med. Ctr., Kansas City, 1977—; assoc. prof. med. psychology Washington U. Med Sch., St. Louis, 1973-74; assoc. prof. U. Ky. Med. Sch., Lexington, 1974-77; co-chmn. Lt. Gov.'s Task Force on Mental Health Delivery, Mo., 1974. Author: A Layman's Guide to Mental Health Problems and Treatments, 1981; co-author: Psychiatric Diagnostic Interview, 1981; contbr. 92 articles to profl. jours. Recipient awards Nat. Inst. Alcoholism and Alcohol Abuse, 1974, VA Merit Rev., 1976, 81, VA Coop. Studies, 1979, Burroughs Wellcome Co., 1984. Fellow Am. Psychol. Assn. (vis. scientist 1972); mem. Midwest Psychol. Assn., Assn. for Med. Edn. and Research in Substance Abuse, Soc. Psychologists in Addictive Behaviors, Soc. VA Psychologists. Home: 12516 W 105 Terr Overland Park KS 66215 Office: VA Med Ctr 151 4801 Linwood Blvd Kansas City MO 64128-2295

POWELL, BEVERLY ANN, utilities company executive; b. Balt., Apr. 11, 1938; d. William Thomas and Margaret Amelia (Hancock) Ballantine; m. John P. Powell, May 29, 1955 (div. 1971). Student, Catonsville Community Coll., Balt., 1974-76, Harvard U., 1983. Clk. Balt. Gas and Electric Co., 1956-59, programmer/analyst, 1959-70, systems project leader, 1971-78, pub. affairs rep., 1978-80, sr. pub. affairs rep., 1980-83, supr. employee policies and compensation, 1983-85, dir. pub. affairs, 1985—. Mem. cen. com. Anne Arundel County, Md. Reps., 1978. Recipient Twin award Annapolis (Md.) YWCA and Anne Arundel County, 1986. Mem. Md. and D.C. Utilities Assn., Md. C. of C. (legis. com. 1985—). Methodist. Home: 6240 Woodland Rd Linthicum Heights MD 21090 Office: Balt Gas and Electric Co PO Box 1475 Baltimore MD 21203

POWELL, CAROL CHRISTINE, restaurant owner; b. Seattle, Feb. 15, 1941; d. Benjamin Olaf and Lois Carol (Smith) Michel; m. William Fred Roth, Apr. 8, 1961 (div. Dec. 1972); children: Christine Roth, Fred Roth, Traci Roth; m. George Benjamin Powell, Dec. 22, 1972; children: Kathy Powell Rank, George Powell Jr. Grad., Franklin High Sch., Seattle, 1959. Dishwasher Happy Chef, Cherokee, Iowa, 1978; dishwasher, waitress Randall's Cafe, Cherokee, 1978-79, mgr., 1979-82; owner, operator The Food Broker, Cherokee, 1983—. Mem. adv. com. Cherokee Sch. Mem. Assn. Consumer Preferred Bus., Cherokee C. of C. Democrat. Home: 320 N 6th St Cherokee IA 51012 Office: The Food Broker Hwy 59 S Cherokee IA 51012

POWELL, DIANA KEARNY, lawyer, poet; b. Washington, Apr. 15, 1910; d. William Glasgow and Alice Van Voorhees (Joline) P.; LL.B., Columbus U., 1940, LL.M., 1942; A.A., George Washington U., 1945; postgrad. Law Sch. Georgetown U., 1957. Admitted to D.C. bar, 1940, U.S. Supreme Ct. bar, 1959; practice law, Washington; contbr. poetry to various mags., 1930—; poetry recitations. Precinct chmn. Republican Party, 1965-68, co-chmn., 1972-75; mem. various campaign coms.; sec. Sodality Holy Name Soc. of St. Matthew's Cathedral, 1978-81, chmn. workshop com., 1975-81, 83-86, pres., 1981-83; mem. Republican Presdl. Task Force, 1982. Recipient various local and nat. poetry awards Nat. League Am. Pen Women; cert. of appreciation Anchor Mental Health Assn., 1975. Mem. ABA, Nat. Assn. Women Lawyers, Internat. Platform Assn., Saintpaulia Internat. Roman Catholic. Author: Selected Poems, 1986. Assoc. editor: Washington Vistas, 1953.

POWELL, DOROTHY JEAN, banker; b. Nocona, Tex., Nov. 15, 1927; d. Arthur William and Bertie Belle (McMurtry) McNabb; student Kilgore Coll., 1945-46, Joliet (Ill.) Jr. Coll., 1965-68, Lewis U., 1969-71; m. Robert E. Powell, Apr. 16, 1948; children—Elizabeth Joyce, Patrick Vernon. Clk., First Nat. Bank, Longview, Tex., 1946-47; teller, bookkeeper Cleveland Nat. Bank (Tenn.), 1947-49; sec. to dean students Lewis U., Lockport, Ill., 1965-67; v.p., cashier Heritage First Nat. Bank, Lockport, 1967-82, pres., 1982—, dir., 1978—. Pres. bd. govs. Salem Village, Joliet. Mem. Nat. Assn. Bank Women (state chmn. Ill. group 1976-77), Zonta Internat., Am. Soc. Profl. and Exec. Women, Lockport Bus. and Profl. Women's Club (pres. 1976-77), Lockport Area Devel. Commn. Home: 706 State St Lemont IL 60439 Office: 800 State St Lockport IL 60441

POWELL, ERNESTINE BREISCH, retired lawyer; b. Moundsville, W.Va., Feb. 16, 1906; d. Ernest Elmer and Belle (Wallace) Breisch; student Dayton YMCA Law Sch., 1929; m. Roger K. Powell, Nov. 15, 1935; children—R. Keith (dec.), Diane L.D., Bruce W. Admitted to Ohio bar, 1929; tax analyst tax dept. Wall, Cassell & Groneweg, Dayton, Ohio, 1929-31; practiced law, 1931-40; gen. counsel for Dayton Jobbers and Mfrs. Assn., 1931-41; mem. firm Powell, Powell & Powell, Columbus, Ohio, 1944-86, ret. Ohio chmn. Nat. Woman's Party, Washington, 1950-51, nat. chmn., 1953, hon. nat. chmn. Pres. vol. activities com. Columbus State Sch., 1960-61, mem. bd. trustees, 1957-59. Mem. Nat. Assn. Women Lawyers, Am., Ohio, Columbus bar assns., Nat. Soc. Arts and Letters (pres. Columbus chpt. 1963-64), Nat. Lawyers Club (charter mem.), Nat. Mus. Women in Arts (charter mem.). Co-author: Tax Ideas, 1955; Estate Tax Techniques, 1956—. Editor-in-chief: Women Lawyers Jour., 1943-45. Office: 1382 Neil Ave PO Box 8010 Columbus OH 43201

POWELL, JOY LEE (LEE, BOK SIN), antique dealer, importer; b. Pyong-Yang, Korea, Jan. 29, 1936; came to U.S., 1956, naturalized, 1962; d. Yong Joon and Chun Jai Lee; m. Jimmy Wayne Powell, Sept. 24, 1960; children—Chn Jai Lee, Miran Victoria. Student Internat. Speech Coll., Pusan, Korea, 1952; Nat. U. Pusan, 1953-55, McMurry Coll., Abilene, Tex., 1956-58; B.A., Wayland Baptist U., Plainview, Tex., 1966; postgrad. Central State Coll., Okla., 1967-68. Cert. antique appraiser and consultant. Nurse, Ruk Med. Sch., Pusan, 1950-53, news announcer Pusan Radio Sta., Korea, 1953; sec., choir organizer chaplain's office U.S. Army div. Hqdrs., Pusan, 1954-56, Meth. Mission, Pusan, 1955-56, U.S. A.S.C. Office, Floydada, Tex., 1958, Am. U., Washington, 1958-60; with Washington Post, U.S. Acad. Sci., 1960; survey taker Pub. Schs. Plainview, Tex., 1965-66; tchr. Oklahoma City Sch. Systems, 1968-70; owner Internat. Antiques, Fairfax, Va., 1973—. Contbr. articles to profl. jours., Contbr. (poetry) New Voices in American Poetry, 1978. Contbr. poems and essays to Korean periodicals. Mem. Mang Hiang, Internat. Platform Assn., NOW, Nat. Trust for Hist. Preservation, Smithsonian Assocs. Nat. Hist. Preservation. Mem. Nat. Bus. Assn., Better World Soc., Women's Mus., World Affairs Council Washington, Nat. Assn. Female Execs., Internat. Student House. Avocations: art; painting; music; writing; swimming. Home and Office: PO Box 185 Chantilly VA 22021

POWELL, LOUISA ROSE, psychologist; b. Highland Park, Mich., Oct. 10, 1942; d. Albert and Mildred Loraine (Bos) Feldman; B.S., Roosevelt U., 1966; M.S., U. Chgo., 1969, Ph.D., 1973; m. Philip Melancthon Powell, Dec. 29, 1962; children—David, Aaron, Robert. Intern in psychology VA Hosp., Newington, Conn., 1973-75; instr. So. Conn. State Coll., New Haven, 1975-76; psychologist Austin (Tex.) Evaluation Ctr., 1979-80, 81-82; dep. dir. gen. clin. services Austin Child Guidance and Evaluation Ctr., 1982-86; sch. psychologist San Rafael (Calif.) Schs., 1980-81; instr. S.W. Tex. State U., San Marcos, 1978-79; adj. prof. dept. psychology U. Tex., Austin, 1984—, clin. coordinator learning abilities Child-Family Practicum Ctr., 1986-87; pvt. practice psychology. Chmn. Cub Scouts Pack No. 54, 1977-78; v.p. pub. affairs Austin Alliance for Mentally Ill, 1987-88; mem. Nat. Alliance for Mentally Ill, Tex. Alliance for Mentally Ill; bd. dirs. Capital Area Mental Health Ctr., 1985-86; cellist Austin Community Orch. Lic. psychologist, health services provider, Tex. Fellow Am. Orthopsychiat. Assn.; mem. Am. Psychol. Assn., Southwestern Psychol. Assn., Tex. Psychol. Assn., Capital Area Psychol. Assn. (sec. 1985, 86), Am. Assn. Marital and Family Therapy (assoc.), Soc. Research in Child Devel., Central Tex. Assn. Gifted Children (co-v.p. 1984-85), Am. Group Psychotherapy Assn. (assoc.). Democrat. Home: 3910 Edgerock Dr Austin TX 78731 Office: 3724 Jefferson St Suite 209 Austin TX 78731

POWELL, MARCIA L., communications consultant, television personality, author; b. Opelika, Ala., Apr. 19; d. Clyde L. and Leonora (Stowe) P.; m. George Winship, May 21, 1963 (div. 1967); m. 2d John J. Gallagher, Apr. 27, 1969 (div. 1971). A.B. in Journalism, U. Ga., 1962; postgrad. N.Y. Sch. Interior Design, 1968-69, New Sch. Social Research, 1970, NYU, 1979. Club editor Phoenix Gazette, 1962-64; asst. account exec. Edward Gottlieb & Assocs., N.Y.C., 1964-65; pub. relations specialist Parsons-Jurden Corp., N.Y.C., 1965-66; Eastern editor Housewares Buyer Mag., N.Y.C., 1966-67; home editor Electricity on the Farm, N.Y.C., 1967-73; owner Marcia Powell Enterprises, N.Y.C., 1973—; founding ptnr. RTI Communications, N.Y.C., 1979—; communications dir. J.O.S. Enterprises Inc., Des Moines, 1981-87. Co-author: The Honeymoon Handbook, 1980; Beauty Is My Business, 1982; The Look of Success, 1982; The Real You, 1987. Bd. dirs. Found. for Facially Disfigured, Des Moines, 1981-87. Recipient Feature Writing award Ariz. Press Women, 1963, Hist. Feature award, 1964; Editorial Excellence award Am. Assn. Home Appliance Mfrs., 1972, 73. Mem. Am. Soc. Journalists and Authors, Women in Communications, Inc. (N.Y. pres. 1969-70), Nat. Acad. TV Arts and Scis., Am. Women in Radio and TV, Authors Guild, Authors League of Am., Cosmetic Exec. Women, Publicity Club N.Y., Fashion Group, Am. Home Econs. Assn., Home Economists in Bus., Soc. Profl. Journalists, Alpha Xi Delta (N.Y. pres. 1967-68, 75th ann. cons. 1968, pub. relations counsel 1965-67).

POWELL, MARY LOUISE WELLS, psychologist, educator; b. Asheville, N.C., July 7, 1935; d. John Kendall and Beatrice (Rice) Wells; A.B., U. N.C., 1957, M.S., 1964, Ph.D., 1976; m. Elton George Powell, June 21, 1969. Tchr., Myers Park High Sch., Charlotte, N.C., 1957-58; editorial research asst. Time, Inc., N.Y.C., 1959-60; recreation and program dir. Spl. Services U.S. Forces Europe, Germany and France, 1960-62; resident adviser undergrad. women U. N.C., Chapel Hill, 1963-64, research asso. and asst. to project coordinator State/Fed. Inst. for Profl. Devel., 1964-66; prof. organizational indsl. personnel psychology Appalachian State U., Boone, N.C., 1967—. NDEA fellow, 1966; NASA fellow, 1981. Mem. Am. Psychol. Assn., Southeastern Psychol. Assn., N.C. Assn. Counseling and Devel., So. Mgmt. Assn., N.C. Coll. Personnel Assn., N.C. Vocat. Guidance Assn., Am. Soc. Personnel Adminstrn. (accredited personnel diplomate, tng. and devel.), Am. Soc. Tng. and Devel., Organizational Behavior Teaching Soc., Acad. of Mgmt., AAUW, Pi Delta Phi. Home: 200 Anne Marie Dr Boone NC 28607 Office: Appalachian State U 112-A Smith Wright Hall Boone NC 28608

POWELL, PEGGY JEAN, public relations executive; b. La Grande, Oreg., June 29, 1933; d. Kenneth Gladstone and Clara Gertrude (Hercher) LaViolette; m. Donald Allan Powell, Sept. 14, 1957; children: Anthony Forrest, Alison Carol. BA, U. Calif., Berkeley, 1956; postgrad, Wayne State U., 1967. Writer Mademoiselle Mag., N.Y.C., 1955-56; reporter Berkeley Daily Gazette, 1956-57, Vancouver (B.C., Can.) Sun, 1957-59; freelance writer Calif., 1960-75; pvt. practice pub. relations cons. Irvine, 1975-85; ptnr. Investor Communication Systems, Irvine, 1985—; bd. dirs. Shareholder Communication Systems. Contbr. numerous articles to profl. and entertainment jours. Mem., docent, patron Newport Harbor Art Mus., Newport Beach, Calif., 1972-84; bd. dirs. Campus View Homeowners Assn., Irvine, 1976. Recipient Golden Orange award Orange County (Calif.) Advt. Fedn., 1981. Mem. Pub. Relations Soc. Am., Orange County Chpt. Pub. Relations Soc. Am. (3 Excellence awards 1984, 2 Excellence awards 1985), Publicity Club Am., U. Calif. Berkeley Alumni Assn., Prytanean Alumni Assn., Alpha Gamma Delta. Democrat. Unitarian. Office: Investigator Communication Systems 4400 MacArthur #930 Newport Beach CA 92660

POWELL, RITA ELAINE, sales professional; b. Clarkson, Ky., Aug. 8, 1939; d. Alfie Lee and Della Francis (Alvey) P. Student, U. Louisville. Buyer Gen. Electric Supply, Louisville, Ky., 1967-73, sales rep., 1973—. Vol. Kidney Found of Ky., Louisville, 1975-78, 88. Republican. Baptist. Home: 1507 Dawn Dr Louisville KY 40216 Home: Gen Electric Supply 4200 Leghorn Dr Louisville KY 40218

POWELL, ROSALIE, home economist; b. Milw., Oct. 24, 1947; d. William and Daisy P.; B.S., U. Wis., Stout, 1969, M.S. in Home Econs. Edn., 1974. Extension home economist U. Wis. Extension, Langlade County, 1969-74; Waukesha County, 1976—; instr. U. Wis.-Stout, Menomonie, 1975-76; asst. prof. dept. family devel. U. Wis. Extension, 1976-81, assoc. prof., 1981-87, chmn. family devel. dept., 1984—, prof., 1987—. Mem. Am. Home Econs. Assn., Wis. Home Econs. Assn., Nat. Assn. Extension Home Economists, Wis. Assn. Extension Home Economists, Soc. Nutrition Edn., Wis. Consumers League, Bus. and Profl. Women (chpt. pres. 1970-72), Am. Council on Consumer Interests, Gamma Sigma Sigma (nat. pres. 1975-77), Epsilon Sigma Phi. Club: Waukesha Altrusa. Home: 403 Sheffield Rd Waukesha WI 53186 Office: 500 Riverview Ave Waukesha WI 53188

POWELL, SANDRA THERESA, timber company executive; b. Orofino, Idaho, Jan. 9, 1944; s. Harold L. and Margaret E. (Thompson) P. B.S. in Acctg., U. Idaho, 1966. C.P.A., Idaho. Acct., Weyerhaeuser Co., Tacoma, Wash., 1966-67; with Potlatch Corp., 1967—, asst. sec., San Francisco, 1981, sec., asst. treas., 1981—. Mem. Am. Inst. C.P.A.s, Idaho State Bd. Accountancy, Idaho Soc. C.P.A.s, Am. Soc. Corp. Secs. Inc. Office: Potlatch Corp PO Box 3591 San Francisco CA 94119

POWELL, SARA JORDAN, musician, religious worker; b. Waller, Tex., Oct. 6, 1938; d. Samuel Arthur and Mable Ruth (Ponder) Jordan; m. John Atkins Powell, June 24, 1967; 1 child, Marc Benet. B.A., Tex. So. U., 1960; M.R.E., U. St. Thomas, Houston, 1979. Tchr., Chgo. Bd. Edn., 1961-68, Houston Ind. Sch. Dist., 1968-73; youth dir. Gospel Music Workshop Am., Detroit, 1972-76; dir. talent and fine arts Ch. of God in Christ, Memphis, 1974—, dir., cons. ch. hist. mus. and fine arts center, 1980—; mem. nat. reference com. One Nation Under God, Virginia Beach, Va., 1979—; regional sponsor Yr. of the Bible, Washington, 1983; soloist Savoy Record Co., 1972-79; counselor Mike Barber Prison Ministries, 1987—. Bd. dirs. talent coordinator Charles Harrison Mason Edn. Found., 1975—; bd. dirs. James Oglethorpe Patterson Fine Arts Scholarships, 1974—; music and talent dir. Juneteenth U.S.A., 1985—. Recipient 1st Pl. award Record Album, Savoy Record Co., 1972. Best Female Vocalist, Gospel Music Workshop Am., 1973, 74, 75, Gold record, 1978; letter of appreciation Cook County Dept. Corrections, Chgo., 1978; Silver Plate award Assembly of God Ch., Calcutta, India, 1978; letter of appreciation for White House performance, Washington, 1979. Mem. Houston PTA, Houston Peoples Workshop (dir. 1981—), Women in Leadership (adv. bd. 1985—). Home: 9203 McAvoy Dr Houston TX 77074

POWELL, SHARON LEE, social welfare organization administrator; b. Portland, Oreg., July 25, 1940; d. James Edward Carson and Betty Jane (Singleton) Powell. BS, Oreg. State U., 1962; MEd, Seattle U., 1971. Dir. outdoor edn. Mapleton (Oreg.) Pub. Schs., 1962-63; field dir. Totem Girl Scout Council, Seattle, 1963-68, asst. dir. field services, 1968-70, dir. field services, 1970-72; dir. pub. relations Girl Scout Council of Tropical Fla., Miami, 1972-74; exec. dir. Homestead Girl Scout Council, Lincoln, Nebr., 1974-78, Moingona Girl Scout Council, Des Moines, 1978—. Pres. agy dirs. assn. United Way of Cen. Iowa, 1987—; mem. priorities com. United Way of Cen. Iowa, Des Moines, 1986—; mem. priority goals task group United Way Found., Des Moines, 1985—; capt. Drake U. Basketball Ticket Dr., Des Moines, 1983—. Mem. Assn. Girl Scout Execs. (chair nat. conv. 1985-87, nat. bd. dirs. 1985-87, mem. nat. nominating com. 1982-84, nat. treas. 1987-90), AAUW, Urbandale C. of C. (bd. dirs.), Des Moines Obedience Tng. Club, Des Moines Golden Retriever Club, Chi Omega Alumni Assn. Democrat. Roman Catholic. Club: Altrusa (Des Moines) (treas. 1983-85, community service chair 1986-87). Office: Moingona Girl Scout Council 10715 Hickman Rd Des Moines IA 50322

POWELL, SUSIE LEE JOHNSON, nurse; b. Metter, Ga., Dec. 1, 1926; d. James Casbin and Adna (Mixon) Johnson; m. Sam E. Powell, Sept. 14, 1947; children: David, Mike, Jim, Vicki, Susan. Grad., Baroness Erlanger Sch. Nursing, 1948. RN. Staff nurse T.C. Thompson Childrens Hosp., Chattanooga, 1948-50, Baroness Erlanger Hosp., Chattanooga, 1950-56; surg. nurse Hutcheson Meml. Tri-County Hosp., Ft. Oglethorpe, Ga., 1956-64, Emory U. Hosp., Atlanta, 1964-68, Atlanta Hosp., 1968-76, Decatur (Ga.) Hosp., 1976—. Baptist. Club: Lake Capri Women's (Lithonia, Ga.). Home: 2685 Paces Landing Conyers GA 30207

POWER, SUSAN ANN, data processing executive; b. Indpls., May 19, 1947; d. David E. and Mary L. (Holland) P.; m. Stephen A Mattox, Nov. 27, 1968 (div. June 1978); children: Stephen A. Mattox Jr., David E. Mattox. Student, Purdue U., 1965-66, Ind. U., Indpls., 1967, Butler U., 1980-83. Programmer, analyst SMC Pneumatics, Inc., Indpls., 1978-80, mgr. data processing, 1980-83, mgr. mgmt. info. services, 1983-86; v.p. B Fulgenzi & Co., Inc., Indpls., 1987—; pres. Tech. Expertise Corp., Indpls., 1983—. Charter contbr. Ellis Island Found., N.Y.C., 1984; preferred mem. U.S. Senatorial Club, Washington, 1984—. Mem. Data Processing Mgmt. Assn., Nat. Assn. Female Execs., Internat. Soc. Wang Users, Ind. Wang User's Group (1st pres. 1980-81). Republican. Club: Continental Dance (Indpls.). Home: 8461 Westport Ln Indianapolis IN 46234 Office: B Fulgenzi & Co Inc 7457-61 W 10th St Indianapolis IN 46214-2517

POWER-BARNES, MARIE RUTH, public relations and marketing executive, photographer; b. Trenton, N.J., Jan. 30, 1958; d. Robert Bruce and Mai Norma (Ulesoo) Power; m. Kenneth George Barnes, Aug. 5, 1978. B.A. in Journalism summa cum laude, Rider Coll., 1980. Campaign assoc. Delaware Valley United Way, Lawrenceville, N.J., 1980-82; dir. pub. relations and mktg. Hamilton Hosp., N.J., 1982—. Contbr. articles, cover feature story to profl. jours. and mags.; author, editor, graphic designer. Mem. Am. Soc. Hosp. Pub. Relations and Mktg., N.J. Hosp. Pub. Relations and Mktg. Assn. (regional coordinator, Percy award 1983-86), Nat. Assn. Female Execs., Am. Coll. Healthcare Mktg., Am. Mktg. Assn., Sigma Delta Chi, Phi Beta Kappa, Alpha Epsilon Zeta. Lutheran. Office: Hamilton Hosp Whitehorse-Hamilton Square Rd Hamilton NJ 08690

POWERS, CAROL DIANE, educator; b. Cheverly, Md., Dec. 5, 1950; d. Fred J. and Iris G. (Taylor) Walker; m. James Roy Powers, Aug. 26, 1972. BA, Salisbury (Md.) State U., 1972; MA, Middlebury Coll., 1976; postgrad., U. Md., 1982-83. Tchr. Riverdale Bapt. Schs., Upper Marlboro, Md., 1974-78, Montrose Christian Sch., Rockville, Md., 1978-79; tchr. Spanish Thomas W. Pyle Jr. High Sch., Bethesda, Md., 1979-81, Rock Creek Forest Elem. Sch., Chevy Chase, Md., 1981-82, Parkland Jr. High Sch., Rockville, 1983-86, Banneker Jr. High Sch., Burtonsville, Md., 1986-87, John F. Kennedy Sr. High Sch., Silver Spring, Md., 1987—. Sec. Westleigh Civic Assn., Gaithersburg, Md., 1980-83, Ashton (Md.) Oaks Homeowners Assn., 1984—. Office: John F Kennedy Sr High Sch 1901 Randolph Rd Silver Spring MD 20902

POWERS, CHARLOTTE DRAK, telecommunications analyst, consultant; b. Petersburg, Va., Sept. 24, 1944; d. Churchill Gibson Sr. and Charlotte Francis (Pond) Drake; m. Jerry Milton Powers, Sr., Feb. 27, 1965 (div. 1980); children: Christie Elaine, Jerry Milton, Jr. Grad. high sch., Colonial Heights, Va. Clk. Market Rambler, Inc., Petersburg, 1963-64, Bottled Gas Corp. of Va., Colonial Heights, 1964-67; receptionist Carolina Exchange Service, Columbia, S.C., 1968-70; PBX operator Thalheimers Bros., Inc., Raleigh, N.C., 1972-73; trainer, telephone call dir. Amoco Oil Co., Raleigh, 1973-76, supr., telephone call dir., 1976-84; sales authorization sr. credit rep. Amoco Oil Co., Des Moines, 1984, telecommunications analyst, 1984-87; advisor Gold Leaf chpt. Am. Bus. Women's Assn., Raleigh, 1983; cons. edn. dept. State of Iowa, 1987; lectr. in field;. Fundraiser Raleigh Dem. Party, 1982; ch. counselor, 1985. Named Boss of Yr. Am. Bus. Women's Assn. Gold Leaf chpt., 1983. Mem. Nat. Bus. Woman's Assn., Telemktg. Assn. Iowa, Amoco User Group, MidWest SL-1 User Group, Iowa Telecommunications User Group. Republican. Methodist. Lodge: Order of Eastern Star. Home: 4218 Plymouth Dr #104 West Des Moines IA 50265 Office: Amoco Oil Co 4300 Westown Pkwy West Des Moines IA 50265

POWERS, CHRISTINE ELIZABETH, pharmaceutical company executive; b. Greenfield, Mass., Dec. 25, 1953; d. Richard Frederic and Jeanne Elizabeth (Day) Powers; B.S. in Chem. Engring., Worcester, Poly. Inst., 1975; postgrad. No. Ill. U. Process engr. Clairol, Inc., Stamford, Conn., 1975-77, prodn. planner, 1977; process engr. Armour-Dial Co., Montgomery, Ill., 1977-78; project engr. Baxter HealthCare Corp., Deerfield, Ill., 1978-81, prodn. supr., 1981-83, process engr., 1983-85, prodn. supt., 1985—. Mktg. adviser Jr. Achievement Stamford, 1976-77. Mem. Am. Inst. Chem. Engrs., Soc. Women Engrs., Am. MBA Execs. Republican. Unitarian. Home: 703 Drae Ct Wheeling IL 60090 Office: Baxter HealthCare Corp PO Box 490 Round Lake IL 60073

POWERS, COLETTE MARGARET, special education administrator, b. Chgo., Mar. 9, 1912; d. Alois J. and Mary H. (Wagner) Gaul; m. Thomas J. Powers (dec.); children: Colette D. Powers Foley, Richard J., Dolores R. Powers Fisher. BS in Commerce, DePaul U., 1934. Cert. tchr., Ill. Founder West Suburban Assn. for the Retarded, Lombard, Ill., 1955—, from asst. dir. to dir., 1967—. Author West Suburban Assn. for the Retarded Newsletter. Named Disting. Alumni, Alvernia High Sch., 1980, Woman of the Yr., City of Lombard, 1981. Roman Catholic. Lodge: Rotary (Medal of Merit award 1983). Office: West Suburban for the Retarded 1027 E Division St Lombard IL 60148

POWERS, HELEN ANN, banker; b. Marshall, N.C., June 18, 1925; d. Robert L. and Bertha (Ramsey) P. Student banking sch., U. Wis., 1965-67. Adminstrv. asst. to plant mgr. Am. Enka Corp., N.C., 1944-60; personnel officer The Bank of Asheville, N.C., 1960-62, asst. cashier, 1962-65, v.p., cashier, 1965—; instr. extension classes Western Carolina Coll., Cullowhee, 1957-60. Mem. Am. Inst. Banking (bd. dir.), Nat. Assn. Bank Auditors and Controllers (bd. dirs.). Episcopalian. Home: 116 Midland Dr Lake View Asheville NC 28804

POWERS, JUDYTH GLADSTEIN, microcomputer consultant; b. Bridgeport, Conn., Nov. 25, 1955; d. Arnold S. and Alice (Greenburg) Gladstein; m. Thomas H. Powers Jr., Jan. 5, 1975 (div. 1982). BFA, Md. Inst., 1977. Assoc. Cain Bros., N.Y.C. and Shattuck, N.Y., 1983-86; decision support analyst Paramount Pictures, N.Y.C., 1986-88, decision support cons., 1988—. Mem. N.Y. Personal Computer Soc., Amnesty Internat. Democrat. Office: Paramount Pictures 1 Gulf and Western Plaza New York NY 10023

POWERS, KAY CARSON, marketing executive; b. Monticello, Ark., Mar. 22, 1947; d. Frank Jr. and Eloise (Groves) Carson; m. Lonnie Austin Powers, July 3, 1969. BA in Journalism, U. Ark., 1969; MBA, Simmons Coll., 1986. Cert. Pub. Relations Counselor. Tchr. Fayetteville (Ark.) Pub. Schs., 1969-70; assoc. editor Squire Publs., Shawnee Mission, Kans., 1970-72; editor Ark. Bankers Assn., Little Rock, 1973-76; info. mgr. Ark. Dept. Local Services, Little Rock, 1976-78; v.p. Leavitt and Assocs., Little Rock, 1978-79; pres. Kay Powers Communications, Inc., Little Rock, Boston, 1979-86; mktg. mgr. Caravan for Commuters, Inc., Boston, 1987—. Mem. jour. adv. com. U. Ark., Fayetteville, 1980-83. Recipient Woman of Achievement award Ark. Press Women, 1981. Mem. Pub. Relations Soc. Am. (state sec. 1983-84). Democrat. Home: 16 Concord Sq #1 Boston MA 02118

POWERS, NONA, custom framing company executive; b. St. Anthony, Idaho, Feb. 24, 1942; d. Russell H. and Della S. (Mathis) Smith; m. Joe M. Powers, Jan. 2, 1963; children—Kira L., Joe Marvin. A.A. in Art, San Diego City Coll., 1973; B.A. cum laude in Art, San Diego State U., 1976, M.A. in Art, 1978. Instr. San Diego State U., 1976-77; custom framer Potpurri, San Diego, 1978-81; owner, mgr. Monterey Custom Framing, San Diego, 1981—; lectr. in field; color cons. Bainbridge, London, Can. and Am. Br., 1984. Featured in art and framing mags. including Art Bus. News; columnist Decor mag., 1988. Pres. Edison Elem. Sch. PTA, 1975; trustee Religious Sci. Ch. Ctr., San Diego, 1980. Mem. Profl. Picture Framers Assn. of San Diego (numerous framing awards), Profl. Picture Framers Assn. Guild (nat. media rep. 1987), La Mesa C. of C. Lodge: Soroptimists. Office: Monterey Custom Framing 4703 Spring St La Mesa CA 92041

POWLEY, ANN MARIE, manufacturing company executive; b. Los Angeles, Dec. 20, 1945; d. Leo Joseph and Ethel Louise (Fitzgerald) Greenhalgh; student Santa Monica (Calif.) Coll., UCLA. Field support officer C.O.R.D.S. program AID mission to Vietnam, 1968-71; adminstrv. asst. Manzuno & Assocs., Inc., Malibu, Calif., 1972-75; supr. sales adminstrn. TRW Datacom Internat., Inc., Los Angeles, 1975-77; nat. logistics mgr. Computer Communications, Inc., Torrance, Calif., 1978-80; materiel mgr. data systems services div. Eaton Corp., Los Angeles, 1981-84; dir. Homestead Enterprises Inc., Los Angeles, 1985—; purchasing mgr. UCLA, 1986—. Mem. Nat. Assn. Ednl. Buyers, Nat. Assn. Purchasing Mgrs. (cert. purchasing mgr.), Am. Mgmt. Assn. Home: 2613 Patricia Ave Los Angeles CA 90064

POYNTER, MARION KNAUSS, publishing executive; b. Poughkeepsie, N.Y., Apr. 17, 1926; d. Louis Eugene and Rose (Arndt) Knauss; m. Nelson Paul Poynter, May 4, 1970 (dec. 1978). A.B., Vassar Coll., 1946. Librarian, Time, Inc., N.Y.C., 1949-51; research analyst U.S. Govt., Washington, 1952-60; editorial research analyst St. Petersburg Times, Fla., 1961-63, editorial asst./editorial writer, 1963-70, contbg. editor, 1970-78; dir. Times Pub. Co., 1970—, Poynter Inst. for Media Studies, 1970—; dir. Nat. Inst. for Citizen Edn. in Law, 1984—; trustee Florida House, Washington, 1981—. Mem. Women in Communications, Internat. Press Inst. Home: The Meadows Rt 5 Box 303 Warrenton VA 22186

PRACHT, IRENA, manufacturing company executive; b. Council Grove, Kans., Dec. 24, 1927; d. Berend Hiram and Amanda (Anderson) Bicker; student Kans. Agrl. Coll., 1945-46; B.S., Kans. State Coll., Emporia, 1949; m. Harold Ray Pracht, Oct. 23, 1948; children—Rae Ann Pracht Lowery, Gregory Ray, Rena Rochelle Pracht Coby, Glen Frederick. Bookkeeper, Eby Constrn. Co., Wichita, 1951-52; partner Bell Sewing Centers, Tex., N.Mex., 1954-62, Tri State Sewing Machine Distbrs., Council Grove, Kans., 1962-68; staff acct. Mize, House & Reed C.P.A.s, Topeka, 1968-69; staff acct., gen. ledger supr., controller Farah, Inc., El Paso, 1969—; partner Pracht Enterprises, El Paso, 1975—; sec. treas. Vernon Investment Corp., El Paso, 1971—; v.p. dir. Tex. Pure Products, El Paso, 1981-86; Timber Made Playsets, Inc., El Paso, 1986—. C.P.A., Tex. Mem. Tex. Soc. C.P.A.s, Theta Sigma Upsilon, Xi Phi. Home: 364 McCune Rd El Paso TX 79915 Office: 8889 Gateway West El Paso TX 79925

PRAEGER, HELENE CAROL, lawyer; b. N.Y.C., Sept. 6, 1944; d. Irving and Ruth (Rosenblum) Schechtman; m. Donald Lewis Praeger, June 1, 1976 (div.); 1 child, Denton. A.B., Queens Coll., CUNY, 1966; J.D., N.Y. Law Sch., 1970. Bar: N.Y. 1971, U.S. Dist. Ct. (so. and ea. dists.) N.Y. 1974, U.S. Ct. Appeals, 2d cir.) 1975. Assoc. Family Ct. br. Legal Aid Soc. Bklyn., 1970-72; assoc. litigation dept. Finley, Kumble, Heine, Underberg & Grutman, N.Y.C., 1972-74, Emil, Kobrin, Klein & Garbus, N.Y.C., 1974-76; sole practice law, Poughkeepsie, N.Y., 1976-85, N.Y.C., 1986—. Bd. dirs. Mill St. Loft. Mem. ABA, N.Y. State Bar Assn., N.Y.C. Bar Assn., Mid-Hudson Women's Bar Assn.

PRAGER, KAREN JEAN, psychologist, educator; b. Cleve., Sept. 20, 1952; d. Morton David and Lois Margery (Lurie) P.; m. George Gregory Eaves, May 18, 1985. BA, U. of Tex., Austin, 1973, MA, 1975, PhD, 1977. Lic. psychologist, Tex. Counselor Community Coll. of Phila., 1977-78; sr. clinician St. Clare's Hosp. Community Mental Health Ctr., Denville, N.J., 1978-79; assoc. prof. U. of Tex. at Dallas, Richardson, 1986—, acting coll. master Sch. Gen. Studies, 1987. Contbr. articles to profl. jours. V.p. bd. dirs. Citizen's Devel. Ctr., Irving, Tex., 1985—; chairperson membership com. Dallas Hadassah, Tamar Group. Mem. Am. Psychol. Assn., Am. Assn. Marital and Family Therapy, Am. Ednl. Research Assn. Office: U of Tex at Dallas Dept Psychology PO Box 830688 Richardson TX 75083-0688

PRÄGER-BENETT, NANCY ANN, artist; b. N.Y.C., Mar. 17, 1943; d. Sigmund Godfrey and Eleanor Pauline Prager; student MA program Syracuse U., 1961-62; BFA, Accademia de Belle Arte, Florence, Italy, 1965; B.A., Cooper Union Coll., 1968; m. Barry Lawrence Benett, June 19, 1966; children—Lara Christina, Andrew Bernard, Ariane Alison. Work exhibited in pvt. individual shows, also mus. and univ. group shows, U.S., Italy, France, Can., Turkey, Am. embassy, Turkish Mission to UN; represented pvt. and corp. collections, U.S., Italy, Eng., Turkey, France, Can.; tchr. Black Emergency Cultural Coalition, Met. Mus., N.Y. prison systems; dir. devel. and pub. relations, .world Children's Day, Found. Mem. Bd. TV Arts and Scis.; chmn. bd. Mannes Coll. Music; co-dir. program for disabled children Met. Mus. Art, 1987—. Recipient Prix de Paris, 1975, Grand Prix Humanitaire de France, 1976. Mem. Acad. TV Arts & Scis., Am. Ballet Theatre II, Georgetown U. Sch. of Languages and Linguistics, Amalfi Coast Consortium; mem. Am.-Scandinavian Found., Les Surindependants Societaire, Graphic Art Assn., Smithsonian Assocs., Met. Mus., Am.-Italian Found. for Cancer Research. Presbyterian. Club: Saltaire Yacht (dir. 1972-80, gov.). Work noted in Artist USA Bicentennial, N.Y. Art Yearbook, Nouvelle Littaire, Art News Mag., Arts Mag.; author: Turkish Costumes in the Collection of the Costume Institute Metropolitan Museum of Art.

PRAHL, MARGARET MARSHALL, lawyer; b. Lincoln, Nebr., Nov. 28, 1938; d. Walter E. and Lucy (Heim) Marshall; m. Jerry C. Prahl, Aug. 21, 1960; children—Paula Jean, Jay Marshall, David Andrew. B.A., U. Nebr., 1960; J.D. with honors, U. S.D., 1981. Bar: Iowa 1981, S.D., 1982, U.S. Dist. Ct. (no. and so. dists.) Tchr. Iowa, 1981. English, Lincoln Pub. Schs. (Nebr.), 1960-62; course writer U. Nebr., Lincoln, 1962; copywriter Griffith Advt., Sioux City, Iowa, 1972-73; cons. prin. clients Briar Cliff Coll., Sioux City, 1978, Rosetti Archtl. Assocs., Detroit, 1979; ptnr. Eidsmoe, Heidman, Fredregill, Patterson & Schatz, Attys., Sioux City, 1981—. Editor-in-chief S.D. Law Rev., 1980-81. Mem. Sioux City City Council, 1973-77; pres. Sioux City LWV, 1968-70, bd. dirs., 1968-71; bd. dirs. LWV of Iowa, 1971-73; organizer, bd. dirs. Sioux City Vol. Bur., 1970-73, Siouxland Ctr. for Women, Sioux City, 1974-86; bd. dirs. Siouxland Community Blood Bank, Sioux City, 1978—, Tax Research Conf., Sioux City, 1978—, Sanford Community Ctr., Sioux City, 1979—, Marian Health Ctr., Sioux City, 1981—, chmn. 1986—. Named Woman of Yr., Sta.-KMEG-TV, Sioux City, 1973, Woman of Excellence, 1985. Mem. Woodbury County Bar Assn., Iowa Bar Assn., S.D. Bar Assn., ABA, Sioux City C. of C. (chmn. bd. 1987—), Club: Jr. League (bd. dirs. 1969-71) (Sioux City). Office: Gleysteen Harper Eidsmoe Heidman & Redmond Attys PO Box 3086 Sioux City IA 51102

PRATHER, LENORE LOVING, state supreme court justice; b. West Point, Miss., Sept. 17, 1931; d. Byron Herald and Hattie Hearn (Morris) Loving; m. Robert Brooks Prather, May 30, 1957; children: Pamela, Valerie Jo, Malinda Wayne. B.S., Miss. State Coll. Women, 1953; LL.B., U. Miss., 1955. Bar: Miss. 1955. Practice with B. H. Loving, West Point, 1955-60, sole practice, 1960-62, 65-71, assoc. practice, 1962-65; mcpl. judge City of West Point, 1965-71; chancery ct. judge 14th dist. State of Miss., Columbus, 1971-82; supreme ct. justice State of Miss., Jackson, 1982—; v.p. Conf. Local Bar Assn., 1956-58; sec. Clay County Bar Assn., 1956-71. Mem. Miss. State Bar. Assn., Miss. Conf. Judges, DAR. Episcopalian. Clubs: Pilot, Jr. Aux. Columbus. Office: Miss Supreme Ct PO Box 116 Jackson MS 39205

PRATHER, SUSAN LYNN, public relations executive; b. Melrose Park, Ill.; d. Horace Charles and Ruth Anna Paula (Backus) P.; divorced. BS, Ind. U., 1973, MS, 1975. Arts administr. Lyric Opera Chgo., 1975; jr. account exec. Morton H. Kaplan Assocs., Chgo., 1976-78, sr. account exec., 1978-81; account supr. Ketchum Pub. Relations, Chgo., 1981-83, v.p., 1983-87, v.p., group mgr., 1985-87; v.p., dir. pub. relations Cramer-Krasselt, Chgo., 1987—; cons. Skil Corp., Creda, Inc., Michael Reese Health Plan, Velamints, Citicorp Global Payments Div., Walter R. Kuenle & Co., Kellogg Co., Battle Creek, Mich., 1985—, Village of Rosemont, Ill., 1977—. Singer various recitals; founder, dir. Chgo. Sports Hall of Fame, 1978-81. Chmn. spl. projects Jr. Governing Bd. Chgo. Symphony Orch., 1986—, mem. archives com., 1986—, long term planning com., 1987—, press advance team Papal Visit to Chgo., 1978, White House Press Advance Team, Chgo., 1976-80. Mem. Pub. Relations Soc. Am. (bd. dirs. Chgo. chpt. 1987—), Internat. Pub. Relations Assn. Lutheran. Clubs: Publicity (Chgo.) (bd. dirs. 1986—, Merit award 1982, Golden Trumpet award 1987). Home: 3950 N Lake Shore Dr Chicago IL 60613

PRATNICKI, TANIA MARIE, automotive executive; b. Detroit, Oct. 12, 1955; d. Leon Wyncinty and Ruth Ann (Campbell) P.; m. Andrew Gerard Young, May 6, 1988. BA, U. Detroit, 1977; MA, Cen. Mich. U., 1983. Foreman trim dept. Chrysler Corp., Warren, Mich., 1977-79; supr. warehouse service and parts Chrysler Corp., Center Line, Mich., 1979-80, supr. procurement, 1980-82; office mgr. Chrysler Packaging Plant, Brownstown, Mich., 1982-83; strategic analyst service and parts div. Chrysler Corp., Center Line, 1983-84; warehouse mgr. Chrysler Chgo. Parts Depot, Itasca, Ill., 1984-86; tng. coordinator Chrysler Mfg. St. Louis Assembly II, Fenton, Mo., 1986, area mgr. paint dept., 1987-88, launch coordinator, executive, 1988—; lectr. Madonna Coll., Livonia, Mich., 1984-88. Mem. Chrysler Mgmt. Club, Nat. Sorority, Phi Alpha Theta, Sigma Sigma Sigma (pres. Detroit Alumnae group 1982-84). Roman Catholic. Home: 14365 Willowbend Park Chesterfield MO 63017 Office: Chrysler St Louis Assembly Plant 1050 Dodge Dr Fenton MO 63026

PRATO, NANCY RUTTER HENRY, insurance consultant; b. Burlington, Vt., Feb. 4, 1935; d. William Rutter and Marjorie (Hodge) Henry; m. Raymond C. Prato, May 21, 1960; 1 child, William Henry (dec.). AS in Risk Mgmt. Cert. ins. cons. Asst. mgr. Arthur Murray Dance Studios, New Haven, 1954-60; numerous sales positions 1960-75; sales rep. Sentry Ins., Concord, Mass., 1975-80; comml. agt. Mathog Group Ins., New Haven, 1980-83; sr. sales rep. A.A. Watson, Inc., Wethersfield, Conn., 1983-86; owner Nancy Henry Prato Ins. Mgmt. and Cons. Services, Hamden, Conn., 1987—; lectr. in field. Mem. Nat. Assn. Female Execs., Ind. Ins. Agts. Am., Underwriters Trng. Council. Republican. Home and Office: 80 Blue Trail Hamden CT 06518

PRATT, DEBRA KAY, commercial development company executive; b. Bakersfield, Calif., July 29, 1955; d. Richard Eugene and Cleta Rose (Salyards) Bird; m. Stephen I. McTaggart, Jan. 31, 1987. R.N., Bakersfield Jr. Coll., 1974; student Long Beach State U., 1974-75, U. So. Calif., 1976. Sales agt. Fireside Realty, Bakersfield, 1977-78, Contempo Realty, Cupertino, Calif., 1979-80; broker Re/Max Realtors, Los Gatos, Calif., 1980-81; owner, pres. R.B. Malcolm Co., Los Gatos, 1981-83, Lazarion, Inc., Scottsdale, Ariz., 1983—; investment cons. Tower Corp., Grand Cayman, B.W.I., 1980-83, Cayman Mgmt. Co., 1980-83; prodn. coordinator West Heuco Corp., El Paso, Tex., 1982-83. Author poems. Mem. Scottsdale Spl. Olympics program, 1984-85. Mem. Calif. Assn. Realtors, Internat. Real Estate Exchangors, Scottsdale C. of C. Republican. Avocations: water skiing; sailing; travel; reading; writing. Office: Lazarion Inc 4440 N Civic Ctr Plaza Scottsdale AZ 85251

PRATT, E(LLEN) MARCELLA MORIN, designer; b. Trail, B.C., Can. (parents Am. citizens); d. Francis George and Rose Delima (Bousquet) Morin; student extension courses Wash. State Coll.; grad. Normal Coll., Victoria, B.C.; m. George Collins Pratt, Sept. 22, 1946. With art dept. Universal Internat. Pictures 1935-46; now home designer and decorator, Calif., Wash. Mem. Assistance League So. Calif., Canadian Red Cross (life), Navy League of the U.S. (life), Mary and Joseph League (life), Eisenhower Med. Aux. (founder, life mem.), Palm Desert, Calif., Desert Mus., Nat. Mus. of Women in the Arts (charter). Republican. Home: Box 427 Cathedral City CA 92234

PRATT, FRANCINE G. ESPOSITO, social work administrator; b. Ft. Worth, Nov. 3, 1948; d. Philip Anthony and Mary Ruth (Baker) Esposito; m. Michael Everett Welch, Sept. 3, 1966 (div. Dec. 1973); 1 child, Robin Michelle; m. Michael Lee Pratt Sr., Jan. 1, 1981; 1 stepchild, Michael Lee Jr. Student, North Tex. State U., 1974-75; AA, Tarrant County Jr. Coll., 1985; BSW, U. Tex., Arlington, 1987. Cert. social worker, Tex. From sec. to advt. dir. The Ft. Worth Press, 1966-67, from sec. to pub., 1975-76; from sec. to franchise dir. Radio Shack, Ft. Worth, 1967-68; from sec. to pres. Wesco Refractories, Ft. Worth, 1968-71; youth counselor Youth Services Bur. of Tarrant County, Ft. Worth, 1971-74; info. specialist United Way, Ft. Worth, 1974-75; personnel specialist Tex. Coll. Osteopathic Medicine, Ft. Worth, 1976-80; program dir. bus. adminstrn. The Bridge Assn., Inc., Ft. Worth, 1980-84; exec. dir. Northside Inter-Ch. Agy., Inc., Ft. Worth, 1984—; Mem. Tex. Council Juvenile Justice, Austin, 1972-74, Yo Soy Adv. Council, Ft. Worth, 1984—; vol. Ctr. West Adv. Council, Ft. Worth, 1986—; trustee Tarrant County Youth Collaboration, Ft. Worth, 1984—. Mem. housing com. Community Devel. Council, Ft. Worth, 1984—, Tarrant County Housing Coalition, 1986-87; vol. Dem. Party Work, Ft. Worth, 1984. Recipient Vol. Appreciation award, Vol. Connection/KXASTV-Channel 5; scholar AAUW, 1985, First United Meth. Ch., 1986, Nat. Soc. Fundraising Execs., 1987. Mem. The Bridge Assn. (treas. 1972-74, Vol. Appreciation award 1972-74, 79), Emergency Assistance of Tarrant County (tng. com. chmn. 1981). Office: Northside Inter-Ch Agy Inc 506 NW 15th St Fort Worth TX 76106

PRATT, KELSEY WARD, purchasing agent; b. Keene, N.H., June 13, 1958; d. Robert and Mimi (Steady) Ward; m. William Parker Pratt, July 10, 1982. Student, U. N.H., 1976-78. Owner Clothes Horse, Brentwood, N.H., 1976-78; night mgr. Music World, Manchester, N.H., 1978-80; treas., mgr. Video World Ltd., St. Thomas, V.I., 1980-83; buyer U. Tex., Dallas, 1983-87; owner, pres. Beauty and the Beast, McKinney, Tex., 1985—; purchasing rep. Electronic Data Systems Corp., Richardson, Tex., 1987—. Author: Dark Days, 1978. Mem. N.H. Hist. Soc., 1975-80; vol. Tex. Humane Soc., 1983—. Mem. Nat. Assn. of Purchasing Mgmt., Nat. Assn. Ednl. Buyers, Nat. Wildlife Fedn., U.S. Humane Soc. Republican. Club: Brentwood 4-H (pres. 1974-78). Home: 501 N Bradley McKinney TX 75069

PRATT, MARGARET WADE, information science executive; b. Kansas City, Mo., Apr. 5, 1925; d. Walter Wesley and Leone (Smith) P.; B.A., Washburn U., 1945; postgrad. in law Southwestern U. Dir. maternal and child health studies George Washington U., Washington, 1962-73; dir. maternal and child health studies project Minn. Systems Research, Inc., Washington, 1974-75; pres., project dir. Info. Sciences Research Inst., Vienna, Va., 1976—. Mem. Am. Public Health Assn., Assn. MCH Program Dirs.

PRATT, MARTHA LEE, nurse; b. Chattanooga, Tenn., Mar. 25, 1957; d. Joseph Hilliard and Thelma (Lee) Anders; m. Frank Martin Pratt, Jr., Dec. 9, 1977; children: Jessica Kristin, Andrew Brett. B.S. in Nursing, U. Ala.-Birmingham, 1979. Nurse's aide Univ. Hosp., Birmingham, 1977-79, staff nurse, 1979-80, charge nurse of burn dressing team, 1980—, speaker Burn Ctr., 1980—; researcher Robert Wood Johnson Found., Birmingham, 1985-88. Tchr. Valley Creek Baptist Ch., Hueytown, Ala., 1984-85. Recipient Clin. Excellent in Nursing U. Ala. Hosp., 1988. Mem. Am. Burn Assn., Nat. Burn Prevention Com. Democrat. Avocations: horseback riding, boating, camping, reading. Home: 149 Greenridge Rd Hueytown AL 35023 Office: University Hosp 619 S 19th St JT Room 1010A Birmingham AL 35233

PRATT, MILDRED INEZ, educator; b. Henderson, Tex., Oct. 15, 1928; d. R. P. and Eula (Thirkill) Sirls; B.A., Jarvis Coll., 1951; M.A., Butler U., 1952; M.A., Ind. U., 1955; Ph.D., U. Pitts., 1969; m. Theodore A. E.C. Pratt, Nov. 24, 1964; children—Awadagin, Menah. Program dir. All Nations Found., Los Angeles, 1956-59, Rouge Ecorse United Center, Ecorse, Mich., 1959-63; asst. prof. U. Pitts., 1963-69; prof. social work Ill. State U., Normal, 1969—; faculty Cath. U., Rio de Janeiro, Brazil, 1972-73, Fed. U., Rio de Janerio, 1972-73. Mem. Council on Social Work Edn. Contbr. articles to profl. jours. Home: 1405 W Hovey Ave Normal IL 61761 Office: Ill State U Dept of Sociology & Anthropology Normal IL 61761

PRATT, ROSALIE REBOLLO, harpist, educator; b. N.Y.C., Dec. 4, 1933; d. Antonio Ernesto and Eleanor Gertrude (Gibney) Rebollo; Mus.B., Manhattanville Coll., 1954; Mus.M., Pius XII Inst. Fine Arts, Florence, Italy, 1955; Ed.D., Columbia U., 1976; m. George H. Mortimer, Esquire, Apr. 22, 1987; children—Francesca Christina Pratt Ferguson, Alessandra Maria Pratt Jones. Prin. harpist N.J. Symphony Orch., 1963-65; soloist Mozart Haydn Festival, Avery Fisher Hall, N.Y.C., 1968; tchr. music public schs., Bloomfield and Montclair, N.J., 1962-73; mem. faculty Montclair State Coll., 1973-79; prof. Brigham Young U., Provo, Utah, 1985-87, coordinator grad. studies dept. music, 1987—; coordinator grad. studies dept. music. Fulbright grantee, 1979; Myron Taylor scholar, 1954. Mem. Am. Harp Soc. (Outstanding Service award 1973), AAUP (co-chmn. legis. relations com. N.J. 1978-79), Internat. Assn. of Music for the Handicapped (co-founder, exec. dir., jour. editor), Coll. Music Soc., Music Educators Nat. Conf., Phi Kappa Phi, Sigma Alpha Iota. Co-author: Elementary Music for All Learners, 1980; contbr. articles to Music Educators Jour., Am. Harp Jour., others. Editor procs. 2d, 3d and 4th Internat. Symposia Music Edn. for Handicapped, 1981, 83, 85. Office: Brigham Young U Harris Fine Arts Ctr Provo UT 84602

PRATT, SANDRA KAY, sporting goods store executive; b. Durant, Okla., Feb. 8, 1959; d. Kenneth Jacob and Jessie Willene (Waggoner) Evans; m. Gary Stephen Pratt, May 20, 1978. BS in Acctg., Southeastern Okla. State U., 1988. Clk. Gordon's Jewelers, Oklahoma City, 1976, 1st Nat. Bank Midwest City, Okla., 1977; sales person Sheplers, Inc., 1976-77; stenographer Okla. State Welfare Dept., Oklahoma City, 1977-79; resident mgr. Nat. Corp. for Housing Ptnr., Washington, 1979-82; owner, pres. Pratt's Outdoor Sports, Durant, 1984—. Conco award scholar 1987. Mem. Durant Jaycee's (chmn. 1985), Durant Women of Today, Durant Ducks, Unltd., Bryan County Primitive hunters (sec. 1987—), Okla. Archery Assn., Nat. Field Archery Assn. Democrat. Baptist. Home: 112 Meadowlark Ln Durant OK 74701 Office: Pratt's Outdoor Sports 3702 W Main St Durant OK 74701

PRATT, SUZANNE GARRETT, physician; b. La Grange, Ga., Mar. 9, 1948; d. Roswell and Susie Turner (Keller) Garrett; m. Frank Graham Pratt III, Sept. 18, 1971; children—Frank Graham, Edward Garrett. BS summa cum laude, U. Ga., 1970; MD, Med. Coll. Ga., 1973. Diplomate Am. Bd. Ob-Gyn. Resident Med. Coll. Ga., Augusta, 1973-77; physician D.D. Eisenhower Army Med. Ctr., Ft. Gordon, Ga., 1977-79; practice medicine specializing in ob-gyn, Rome, Ga., 1980—; coordinator ob-gyn family practice residency program Floyd Med. Ctr., Rome, 1983-84. Nat. Merit scholar U. Ga. Found., 1966-70. Fellow Am. Coll. Obstetricians and Gynecologists; mem. Floyd-Polk-Chattooga Med. Soc. (sec. 1982-84), AMA, Ga. Soc. Obstetricians and Gynecologists, Med. Assn. Ga., Endometriosis Assn. (bd. dirs., v.p. edn. and community relations1987-88), Zodiac, Phi Beta Kappa, Phi Kappa Phi. Avocation: reading. Home: 3 Hill Dale Ln SW Rome GA 30161 Office: Three Rivers Ob-Gyn 909 N 5th Ave Rome GA 30161

PREBULA, DAWN O., catering executive; b. Butler, Pa., Mar. 8, 1951; d. Donald O. and Ann (McDowell) Oesterling; m. Gary J. Prebula, Aug. 2, 1969; 1 child, Illya Eric. Student, U. Pa., 1969-72, U. So. Calif., 1973-75. Asst. to dir. events U. So. Calif., Los Angeles, 1972-75; catering mgr. Univ. Hilton, Los Angeles, 1975-76; catering mgr. Los Angeles Hilton, 1976-78, dir. catering, 1982—; catering mgr. Los Angeles Marriott, 1978-80; dir. catering Amfac Hotel, Los Angeles, 1980-82; instr. UCLA, 1986; lectr. Calif. State Poly U., Pomona, 1983—; advisor culinary arts program Los Angeles Trade Tech. Coll., 1984—. Mem. Women in Bus. (dir. 1982-83, v.p. 1985, pres. 1987), Brit. Am. C. of C., Assn. Catering Execs. (pres. 1982-84). Home: 3807 Evans St Los Angeles CA 90027

PRECUP, ALICEMARIE VERONICA, managing editor; b. N.Y.C., Apr. 28, 1945; d. C. Benedict and Alice Isabelle (Fanelli) Mauro; B.A., George Washington U., 1967; m. Ronald G. Precup, Dec. 19, 1964; children—Ronald G., Elizabeth Anne, Margaret Joy. Secondary sch. tchr. D.C. Pub. Sch., 1967-68; references editor Ralph Nader Congress Project, Washington, 1972; prodn. editor Am. Personnel & Guidance Assn., Washington, 1972-75, Am. Inst. Biol. Scis., Washington, 1975-81; editorial cons. Am. Inst. Biol. Scis., Nat. Acad. Scis., Smithsonian Instn. Press, 1982-84; publs. mgr. Nat.-Am. Wholesale Grocers Assn., 1983; mng. editor pub. services U.S. Pharmacopeia, 1983—. Mem. St. Agnes Choir, 1972—, Arlington (Va.) Met. Chorus, 1973—; cantor St. Agnes Parish, 1978—. Mem. Council Biology Editors, Smithsonian Assocs., Soc. for Scholarly Pub., Nat. Assn. Female Execs., Internat. Platform Assn., NOW. Democrat. Roman Catholic. Contbr. articles to profl. jours. Address: 4123 N Richmond St Arlington VA 22207

PREIK, MICHELLE LETITIA PETRUNA, engineer; b. McKees Rocks, Pa., Sept. 11, 1951; d. Charles P. and Elizabeth L. (Butler) Petruna. BS in Metall. Engring., U. Pitts., 1973. Quality assurance engr. Westinghouse Electric Corp., Pitts., 1974-77, process devel. engr., 1977-78, materials devel. engr., 1979; quality assurance engr. Parsons, Brinckerhoff, Quade & Douglas,

Pitts., 1979-81; sr. quality assurance engr., cons. Energy Cons., Inc., Pitts., 1981-83; sr. quality assurance engr. Battelle Meml. Inst., Columbus, Ohio, 1983-85; quality assurance mgr. McGraw-Edison Power Systems, Zanesville, Ohio, 1985-88; cons. Zanesville, 1988—. Mem. Am. Soc. Quality Control (sr. mem., officer Pitts. and Columbus sect. 1976-83), Am. Soc. Metals. Home and Office: 3100 Lisa Ln Zanesville OH 43701 Also: 9498 Babcock Blvd Allison Park PA 15101

PREISKEL, BARBARA SCOTT, lawyer, association executive; b. Washington, July 6, 1924; d. James and B. Beatrix Scott; m. Robert H. Preiskel, Oct. 28, 1950; children: John S., Richard A. BA, Wellesley Coll., 1945; LLB, Yale U., 1947. Bar: D.C. 1948, N.Y. 1948, U.S. Supreme Ct. 1960. Law clk. U.S. Dist. Ct., Boston, 1948-49; assoc. Poletti, Diamond, Roosevelt, Freidin & Mackay, N.Y.C., 1949-50; assoc. Dwight, Royall, Harris, Hoegel & Caskey, N.Y.C., 1950-54, cons., 1954-59; cons. Ford Found. Fund for the Republic, N.Y.C., 1954; dep. atty. Motion Picture Assn. Am., Inc., N.Y.C., 1959-71, v.p., legis. counsel, 1971-77, sr. v.p., gen. atty., 1977-83; sole practice N.Y.C., 1983—; bd. dirs. Gen. Electric Co., Fairfield, Conn., Mass. Mut. Life Ins. Co., Springfield, Textron, Inc., Providence, Am. Superstores Co., Wilmington, Del., The Washington (D.C.) Post Co. Mem. Pres.'s Commn. on Obscenity and Pornography, 1968-70, Am. Arbitration Assn., 1971-87, N.Y.C. Bd. Ethics, 1976—, Inst. Civil Justice, 1984-86, Citizens Com. for Children, N.Y.C., 1966-72, 85—, Child Adoptive Service of State Charities Aid Assn., N.Y.C., 1961-68, Hillcrest Ctr. for Children, N.Y.C., 1958-61, Fedn. Protestant Welfare Agys., N.Y.C., 1959-61, 64—, N.Y. Philharm. Soc., 1971—, Am. Women's Econ. Devel. Corp., 1981—, Med. Edn. for South African Blacks, Inc., Washington, 1985—; bd. dirs. Wiltwyck Sch., N.Y.C., 1950—, chmn. bd., 1969-78; successor trustee Yale Corp., New Haven, 1977—; trustee Ford Found., N.Y.C., 1982—, Am. Mus. of Moving Image, 1986—; mem. distbn. com. N.Y. Community Trust, Inc., N.Y.C., 1978—; chmn. council advisors Hunter Coll. Sch. Social Work, 1985—; mem. Dumpson chair com., Fordham U., N.Y.C., 1981—. Recipient meritorious award Nat. Assn. Theatre Owners, 1970, 72, Alumni Achievement award Wellesley Coll., 1975, Tribute to Women in Internat. Industry award YWCA, 1984, Elizabeth Cutter Morrow award YWCA, 1985. Mem. ABA, Bar Assn. City N.Y. (exec. com. 1972-76), ACLU (bd. dirs.). Episcopalian. Clubs: Cosmopolitan, Yale (N.Y.C.); Wellesley. Office: 36 W 44th St New York NY 10036

PRENTICE, ANN ETHELYND, academic library and information administrator; b. Grafton, Vt., July 19, 1933; d. Homer Orville and Helen (Cooke) Hurlbut; divorced; children—David, Melody, Holly, Wayne. A.B., U. Rochester, 1954; M.L.S., SUNY, Albany, 1964; D.L.S., Columbia U., 1972; Litt.D. (hon.), Keuka Coll., 1979. Lectr. sch. library and info. sci. SUNY, Albany, 1971-72; asst. prof. SUNY, 1972-78; prof., dir. grad. sch. library and info. sci. U. Tenn., Knoxville, 1978-88; assoc. v.p. library and information resources U. South Fla., Tampa, 1988—. Author: Strategies for Survival, Library Financial Management Today, 1979, The Library Trustee, 1973, Public Library Finance, 1977, Financial Planning for Libraries, 1983, Professional Ethics for Librarians, 1985; editor Public Library Quar., 1978-81; co-editor: Info. Sci. in its Disiplinary Context, 1988; assoc. editor Library and Info. Sci. Ann., 1987—. Cons. long-range planning and personnel Knoxville City County Library, 1980, 85-86, Richland County, S.C. Library System, 1981, Upper Hudson Library Fedn., N.Y., State Library Ohio, 1986; Trustee Hyde Park (N.Y.) Free Library, treas., 1973-75, pres., 1976; trustee Mid-Hudson Library System, Poughkeepsie, N.Y., 1975-78. Recipient Disting. Alumni award SUNY/Albany, 1987. Mem. ALA, Am. Mgmt. Assn., Am. Soc. Info. Sci. (exec. bd. 1986-89), AAUP, Assn. Info. Mgrs., Assn. for Library and Info. Sci. Edn. (pres. 1986), Am. Printing History Assn. Home: 11516 Foxford Dr Knoxville TN 37922 Office: 6314 Chauncy St Tampa FL 33647

PRENTICE, MARY LEA, media educational administrator; b. Plymouth, Ill., May 16, 1930; d. Clyde J. and Mary R. (Huddleston) Ware; B.S., Western Ill. U., 1958; NDEA scholar Purdue U., summer 1966; M.S. (Delta Kappa Gamma scholar), Ill. State U., 1974; postgrad. U. Mo., 1982; postgrad. (scholar) Photographer's Edn. Workshop, St. Cloud State U., summer 1982; m. Richmond Ellis Prentice, Aug. 4, 1950; children—Rodney Ellis, Gina Luan. Tchr. elem. sch., Hancock County, Ill., 1950-55; library asst. Streator (Ill.) Elem. Schs., 1956-57; media supr. Pikeland Community Unit No. 10 Schs., Pittsfield, Ill., 1961—; mem. North Central Accreditation Visitation Teams, 1965—; cons. Library Book Selection Service, Inc., 1977-84. Bd. dirs. Pittsfield Public Library, 1975—; bd. dirs. West Cen. Ill. area Gt. River Library System, 1982—, v.p., 1986-87. Mem. NEA, Ill. Assn. Media Educators, Western Ill. Audiovisual Assn., Div. Sch. Media Specialists, Assn. Ednl. Communications and Tech. (presentor internat. conf. 1987), Ill. Assn. Edn. Communications and Tech. (treas. 1982—), Delta Kappa Gamma (pres. Sigma chpt. 1988—). Methodist. Contbr. articles to profl. jours. Office: Pittsfield High Sch Pittsfield IL 62363

PRESKA, MARGARET LOUISE ROBINSON, university president; b. Parma, N.Y., Jan. 23, 1938; d. Ralph Craven and Ellen Elvira (Niemi) Robinson; m. Daniel C. Preska, Jan. 24, 1959; children: Robert, William, Ellen. B.S. summa cum laude, SUNY, 1957; M.A., Pa. State U., 1961; Ph.D., Claremont Grad. Sch., 1969; postgrad., Manchester Coll., Oxford U., 1973. Instr. LaVerne (Calif.) Coll., 1968-75, asst. prof., asso. prof., acad. dean, 1972-75; instr. Starr King Sch. for Ministry, Berkeley, Calif., summer, 1975; v.p. acad. affairs, equal opportunity officer Mankato (Minn.) State U., 1975-79, pres., 1979—; dir. No. States Power Co., Norwest Bank, Mankato. Pres. Pomona Valley chpt. UN Assn., 1968-69, Unitarian Soc. Pomona Valley, 1968-69, PTA Lincoln Elem. Sch., Pomona, 1973-74; mem. Pomona City Charter Revision Commn., 1972; chmn. The Fielding Inst., Santa Barbara, 1983-86; bd. dirs. Elderhostel Internat., 1983—, Minn. Agrl. Interpretive Ctr. (Farmam.), 1983—; nat. pres. Campfire, Inc., 1985-87; chmn. Gov.'s Council on Youth, Minn., 1983-86, Minn. Edn. Forum, 1984; mem. Gov.'s Commn. on Econ. Future of Minn., 1985—, NCAA Pres.'s Commn., 1986—, Minn. Brainpower Compact, 1985; commr. Midwest Gov.'s Econ. Devel. Council, 1986; bd. dirs. Am. Assn. State Colls. and Univs. Carnegie Found. grantee Am. Council Edn. Deans Inst., 1974; recipient Outstanding Alumni award Pa. State, Outstanding Alumni award Claremont Grad. Sch.; named one of top 100 alumni, SUNY, 1985. Mem. AAUW, LWV, Women's Econ. Roundtable, Mpls./St. Paul Com. on Fgn. Relations., Am. Council on Edn., Am. Assn. Univ. Adminstrs. Unitarian. Clubs: Benedicts Dance, Zonta. Lodge: Rotary. Home: 10 Sumner Hills Mankato MN 56001 Office: Mankato State U Office of Pres Box 24 Mankato MN 56001

PRESLAR, MARY ELVA, bank administrator; b. Houston, Aug. 13, 1943; d. Charles M. and Zora E. (Mauney) Medford; m. W. Charles Preslar Jr., May 31, 1975. BS cum laude, U. Tex., Dallas, 1983. Benefit plan adminstrn Tyler Corp., Dallas, 1975-81; benefit planning and devel. First Republic Bank Corp., Dallas, 1983—. Mem. SW Pension Conf., Internat. Found. of Cert. Employee Benefit Specialists, Nat. Assn. Female Execs., U. Tex.-Dallas, Alumni Assn., Ducks Unlimited (com. mem.). Democrat. Methodist. Office: First Rep Bank Corp PO Box 660020 Dallas TX 75266-0020

PRESLEY, DANA CLARE, data processing executive; b. Detroit, Apr. 11, 1945; d. Charles Frederick and Joanne (Stenehjem) Korby; m. Roland Dennis Presley, Nov. 7, 1964. BBA, Ea. Mich. U., 1980, MLS, 1988. Cert. systems profl., legal asst. Info. systems supr. Midland Nuclear Project Bechtel Power Corp., Ann Arbor, Mich., 1980-84; sr. systems analyst U. Mich. Hosps., Ann Arbor, 1984-85; quality assurance mgr. People's Community Hosp. Authority, Wayne, Mich., 1985-87; dir. data processing Chelsea (Mich.) Community Hosp., 1987—. Recipient Bronze Quality Improvement award Bechtel Power Corp., 1982, Silver Quality Improvement award Bechtel Power Corp., 1983. Mem. Assn. Systems Mgmt. (treas. 1982-84), Hosp. Info. Systems Assn. Office: Chelsea Community Hosp 775 Main St Chelsea MI 48118

PRESLEY, DELIA ANN, public relations executive; b. Paul's Valley, Okla., Aug. 18, 1957; d. Don Featherstone and Betty Anne (McCulley) P. B.A., S.W. Tex. State U., 1979. Field rep. Am. Cancer Soc., Bryan, Tex., 1979-80, dist. exec. dir., Midland, Tex., 1980-82, area pub. info. dir., Midland, 1981-82, area dir. pub. info. and crusade, Dallas, 1982-85; freelance pub. relations cons., 1985—; cons. Fairhill Pvt. Sch., 1983. Artfest vol. 500, Inc., 1983; mem. Community Gold II, Midland, 1981; vol. United Way, Dallas, 1982, employee campaign coordinator, 1983; judge Golden Herald awards Dallas Times Herald, 1984. Recipient awards Am. Cancer Soc. Tex. Div., Inc., 1981-84. Mem. Sigma Delta Chi, Pub. Relations Soc. Am. Republican. Presbyterian. Home and Office: 6673 Santa Anita St Dallas TX 75214

PRESLEY, VIVIAN MATHEWS, junior college administrator; b. West Point, Miss., Oct. 12, 1952; d. Beatrus and Lula (Butler) Mathews; m. Dwight Presley, Sept. 12, 1971; 1 child, Julian. BA, Miss. State U., 1973, MA, 1975, Cert. Edn. Specialist, 1978, EdD, 1983. Counselor Coahoma Jr. Coll., Clarksdale, Miss., 1975-80, title III coordinator, 1981-82, asst. to pres., 1982-83, v.p., 1983—. Vice chairperson Miss. State Council on Vocat. Edn., Jackson, Miss., 1984. Named One of Outstanding Young Women of Am., 1981, 84, 85. Mem. Nat. Assn. Female Execs., Assn. Univ. Women, Nat. Council for Resource Devel., Psi Kappa Psi, Delta Sigma Theta. Democrat. Methodist. Home: 122 Crestline Apt 1301 Clarksdale MS 38614 Office: Coahoma Jr Coll Rt 1 Box 616 Clarksdale MS 38614

PRESS, LINDA JEANNE, commercial real estate agent; b. Rockville Centre, N.Y., Nov. 19, 1953; d. James W. and Virginia (Oxenchuk) P. Student Nassau Community Coll., SUNY-Farmingdale, C.W. Post Coll. Gen. mgr. Controlled Sheet Music Service Inc., Copiague, N.Y., 1974-80; sales adminstr. Modern Main Food Products, Garden City, N.Y., 1980-83; mktg. mgr. DCA, N.Y.C., 1983; v.p. Richheimer Coffee subs. Wechsler Coffee Co., Moonachie, N.J., 1984-88; salesperson Greiner Maltz, 1987—; bd. dirs. Music Jobbers Assn., 1979-80. Mem. Nat. Assn. Female Execs. Avocations: skiing; bicycling. Office: 7600 Jericho Turnpike Woodbury NY 11726

PRESSEL, PAMELA FAYE, health care administrator; b. Storm Lake, Iowa, Aug. 8, 1945; d. Merle Claude and Vera Maude (Van Buskirk) Pressel; m. N. Goeddel, Feb. 4, 1966 (div. June 1983); children: Sarah Elizabeth, Heather Lorien. BS in Bus. Adminstrn., U. Phoenix, 1984. Sec., Vis. Nurse Service, Denver, 1967-71, acctg. clk., 1977-78; acct. Rx Home Health, Wheat Ridge, Colo., 1978-80; adminstr. Ptnrs. Extended Care, Lakewood, Colo., 1981—; asst. adminstr. Ptnrs. Home Health, Lakewood, 1981-83, adminstrv./v.p., 1983-86; v.p., treas. Health Care Ptnrs., Nashville, 1983—; br. mgr. Total Pharm. Care, Inc., 1987—. Author: You Can Get Well at Home, 1986. Chair, Denver Sch. Bilingual Com., 1976-77; del. Colo. Democratic Conv., 1976; mem. Alameda Music Boosters, Lakewood, 1986—, Alameda PTSA, 1986—. Mem. Am. Fedn. Home Health Agys. (regional dir. 1983-85), Am. Soc. Profl. and Exec. Women, Exec. and Profl. Women's Council, Denver C. of C., Lakewood C. of C. Democrat. Methodist. Avocations: photography. Home: 6215 W 1st Ave Lakewood CO 80226 Office: 2505 W 2d Ave Suite 12 Denver CO 80219

PRESSLEY, JOYCE CAROLYN, clinical research analyst; b. Edneyville, N.C., Jan. 11, 1953; d. Merrimon Lewis and Barbara Lee (Gilliam) P. A.B. in Chemistry, Psychology, U. N.C., 1975; M.P.H. in Health Adminstrn., U. S.C., 1980. Asst. dir. emergency med. service Centralina Council of Govts., Charlotte, N.C., 1976-78; dir. emergency med. services Area IV EMS Program, Research Triangle, N.C., 1980-81; clin. research analyst Duke U., Durham, N.C., 1981—; bd. dirs. Carolina Cinema Corp. Author abstracts; contbr. articles to profl. jours. Docent bd. dirs. N.C. Mus. Art, Raleigh, 1984-85, chmn. library com.; del. N.C. Rep. Party, Chapel Hill, 1976-78. Acad. trainee HEW, 1978-80. Mem. Am. Heart Assn., S.C. Student Pub. Health Assn. (pres. 1978-79), Triangle Cultural Arts Com., N.C. Art Soc., Duke Faculty Club, LWV. Club: Duke Mgmt. Avocations: tennis, art. Home: 1016 Minerva Ave Durham NC 27701 Office: Duke U Box 3860 Durham NC 27710

PRESSLY, BARBARA, state legislator; b. Chgo., May 13, 1937; d. C. David and Esther (Rustado) Brown; m. George Byrne Pressly, 1960; children: Patricia, George Jr., Robert. BS, U. Ill., 1959. Former mem. N.H. Ho. of Reps.; mem. Hillsborough County Exec. Com.; alderman-at-large Nashua, N.H.; mem. N.H. State Senator. Mem. Nashua Hist. Dist. Commn.; deaconess First Congl. Ch., Nashua, 1980-83. Mem. Kings Daus. Benevolent Soc. Democrat. Address: 80 Concord St Nashua NH 03060

PRESSMAN, LISA JO, entrepreneur; b. Brookline, Mass., Jan. 7, 1963; d. Larry and Barbara (Karas) P. Student, Pedigree Inst., 1981. Owner Grooming by Lisa, Lynn, Mass., 1981—, Las Vegas East Casino, Lynn, 1983—; pres., owner TLC Videos Inc., Lynn, 1987—. Sponsor Girls Club Career Exploration Program, Lynn, 1982—; advisor North Shore Animal Relief Assn., Swampscott, Mass., 1983; pres. Am. Field Service Internat. and Intercultural Program, Lynn and N.Y.C., 1981—; advisor fireworks com. Muscular Dystrophy Assn., Lynn and Danvers, Mass., 1986-88. Recipient Citizenship award City of Lynn. Mem. North Shore C. of C., Mass. Dog Groomers Assn., Nat. Dog Groomers Assn., Nat. Fedn. Ind. Businesses. Democrat. Jewish. Home and Office: 30 Red Rock St Lynn MA 01902

PRESSMAN, THELMA, microwave company executive, consultant; b. N.Y.C., Apr. 10, 1921; d. William and Ida (Neckrich) Rosenson; m. Morris Pressman, May 17, 1942; children: Paul, Richard. Student, UCLA, 1073-77. Cert. coll. instr., Calif. Supr. new product testing Waste King Corp., Los Angeles, 1959-69; cons. Microwave div. Amana Corp., 1969-77; pres., owner Microwave Cooking Ctr., Encino, Calif., 1969—; dir. consumer edn. and services Sanyo Electric, Inc., 1971-87; instr., cookware designer Microwave Cooking Ctr., Encino, 1969—; microwave instr. Calif. State U., Northridge; currently spokesperson for Procter & Gamble Bounty Microwave Paper Towel, The Glass Packaging Inst. Author: The Art of Microwave Cooking, 1983 (selected by Library of Congress to be used as talking book for the blind, 1984), Microwave Cooking/Meals in Minutes, 1982, Microwave Magic, 1985, The Great Microwave Dessert Book, 1985; also New Product Cookbooks for Sears Roebuck & Co., 1977—; microwave columnist Bon Appetit mag., 1979-82; articles for newspapers and mags. throughout U.S. mem. Mayor's adv. council, Los Angeles, 1979. Recipient plaque Atlanta Microwave Profls., 1983, trophy Sanyo Electric, Inc., 1985. Mem. Internat. Microwave Power Inst. (editor jour. 1975-77), Elec. Women's Round Table (pres. 1978-79), Am. Women in Radio and TV, Internat. Assn. Cooking Profls., AFTRA. Club: Hadassah (Beverly Hills). Home and Office: 17728 Marcello Pl Encino CA 91316

PRESTAGE, JEWEL LIMAR, political scientist; b. Hutton, La., Aug. 12, 1931; d. Brudis L. and Sallie Bell (Johnson) Limar; m. James J. Prestage, Aug. 12, 1953; children—Terri, James, Eric, Karen, Jay. B.A., So. U., Baton Rouge, 1951; M.A., U. Iowa, 1952, Ph.D., 1954. Assoc. prof. polit. sci. Prairie View (Tex.) Coll., 1954-55, 56; assoc. prof. polit. sci. So. U., 1956-57, 58-62, prof., 1962—, chairperson dept., 1965-83, dean pub. policy and urban affairs, 1983—; Chairperson La. adv. com. to U.S. Commn. on Civil Rights, 1975—; mem. nat. adv. council on women's ednl. programs U.S. Dept. Edn., 1980—; vis. prof. U. Iowa, 1987-88. Author: (with M. Githens) A Portrait of Marginality: Political Behavior of the American Woman, 1976; contbr. articles to profl. jours. Rockefeller fellow, 1951-52; NSF fellow, 1964; Ford Found. postdoctoral fellow, 1969-70. Mem. Am. Polit. Sci. Assn. (v.p. 1974-75), So. Polit. Sci. Assn. (pres. 1975-76), Nat. Conf. Black Polit. Scientists (pres. 1976-77), Alpha Kappa Alpha. Home: 2145 77th Ave Baton Rouge LA 70807 Office: So Univ Box 9222 Baton Rouge LA 70813

PRESTON, ELAINE VICTORIA, lawyer; b. Erie, Pa., July 1, 1949; d. Joseph Henry and Celia (Tatara) Prezwicki; m. Kenneth Isaacson, Sept. 29, 1979; 1 dau., Mariel Preston. B.A. in English, Villa Maria Coll., 1971; M.Ed., Edinboro U., 1972; J.D., Duquesne U., 1979. Bar: Pa. 1979, U.S. Supreme Ct. 1983. Continuity asst. WSEE-TV, Channel 35, Erie, Pa., 1970-71; pub. relations asst. Model Cities Program, Erie, 1971; tchr. McDowell Sr. High Sch., Millcreek, Pa., 1972-76; residential/comml. real estate salesperson Stevens & Co., Realtors, Erie, 1976; law clk. Watzman & Elovitz, Pitts., 1978; law clk. U.S. Dist. Ct. (we. dist.) Pa., 1978-79; pvt. practice law, Pitts., 1979—. Dir. debate team, theatre club, McDowell Sr. High Sch., Erie, 1973-76; mem. philosophy com. Millcreek Long Range Planning Bd., Erie, 1975-76; mem. Legal Rights of Women, Pitts., 1979—. Mem. ABA, Pa. Bar Assn., Pa. Trial Lawyers Assn., Allegheny County Bar Assn., Assn. Trial Lawyers Am., Duquesne Women Law Students Assn., Alice Maynell Lit. Soc., Order Barristers, Pi Alpha Delta, Kappa Gamma Pi. Democrat. Office: 1100 Lawyers Bldg 428 Forbes Ave Pittsburgh PA 15219

PRESTON, FRANCES W., performing rights organization executive. children: Kirk, David, Donald. Hon. degree, Lincoln (Ill.) Coll. With BMI (Broadcast Music, Inc.), Nashville, from 1958, v.p., 1964; sr. v.p. performing rights BMI, N.Y.C., 1985, exec. v.p., chief exec. officer, 1986, pres., chief exec. officer, 1986—. Mem. Film, Entertainment and Music Commn. Adv. Council State of Tenn.; mem. Leadership Nashville, John Work Meml. Found.; trustee Country Music Found., Inc.; 1st woman mem. Rotary, Nashville; mem. Commn. White House Record Library, Carter adminstrn.; mem. Pres.'s Panama Canal Study Com., Carter adminstrn.; bd. dirs. Rock & Roll Hall of Fame; founding mem. Black Music Assn.; mem. adminstrv. council CISAC (Internat. Confedn. of Socs. of Authors and Composers); v.p. Nat. Music Council; hon. trustee Nat. Acad. Popular Music. Recipient Women's Equity Action League (WEAL) Achievement Award; named to Gospel Music Hall of Fame; Country Music Assn.'s Irving Waugh Award of Excellence. Mem. Country Music Assn. (lifetime mem. bd., past chmn. bd., past pres., dir.), Nashville Symphony Assn. (past sec., dir.), Nat. Acad. Recording Arts and Scis. (past dir. Nashville chpt.), Nashville Songwriters Assn. (life mem.), Gospel Music Assn. (lifetime mem. bd., past chmn. bd., past pres., dir.), Am. Women in Radio and TV (past dir.). Presbyterian. Office: care BMI 320 W 57th St New York NY 10019

PRESTON, LOYCE ELAINE, educator; b. Texarkana, Ark., Feb. 25, 1929; d. Harvey Martin and Florence (Whitlock) P.; student Texarkana Jr. Coll., 1946-47; B.S., Henderson State Tchrs. Coll., 1950; certificate in social work La. State U., 1952; M.S.W., Columbia U., 1956. Tchr. pub. schs., Dierks, Ark., 1950-51; child welfare worker Ark. Dept. Public Welfare, Clark and Hot Spring counties, 1951-56, child welfare cons., 1956-58; casework dir. Ruth Sch. Girls, Burien, Wash., 1958-60; asst. prof. spl. edn. La. Poly. Inst., Ruston, 1960-63; asst. prof. Northwestern State Coll., Shreveport, La., 1963-73; asst. prof. La. State U., Shreveport, 1973-79; ret., 1979. Chpt. sec. La. Assn. Mental Health, 1965-67, Gov's. adv. council, 1967-70; mem. Mayor's Com. for Community Improvement, 1972-76. Mem. AAUW (dir. Shreveport br. 1963-69), Acad. Cert. Social Workers, Nat. Assn. Social Workers (del. 1964-65, pres. North La. chpt., state-wide com. 1968-69), La. Conf. Social Welfare, La. Fedn. Council Exceptional Children (pres. 1970-71), La. Tchrs. Assn. Home: 9609 Hillsboro Dr Shreveport LA 71118

PRESTON, MARY LEE, educator; b. New Willard, Tex., Nov. 20, 1931; d. Damon and Angeline Fletcher Hunter; B.S., Tex. So. U., 1972, M.A.Ed., 1981; m. Foster Preston, Dec. 5, 1950; children—Angie, Alfred, Annie, Foster, Rosemary, Ava, Sherry, Michael, Mona. Clk., Community Chapel Pre-Need Funeral Plans, Houston, 1966-81; instructional coordinator Dunbar Elem. Sch., Houston, 1978-80; 4th grade tchr. and chairperson Anson Jones Sch., Houston Ind. Sch. Dist., 1980—; tchr. vol. Adult Basic Edn. and Gen. Edn. Diploma, 1958-82; edn. cons. Martin Luther King Jr. Community Center, 1979-82, treas. bd. dirs., 1980-81. Pres., Dunbar Alliance Parents, Tchr. Assos. and Patrons, 1975-81; chmn. bd. Purpose, Inc., 1970-74; supr. Shaklee Corp.; bd. dirs., ednl. dir. Haitian Cultural Foyer, 1986-87; interdenom. networking missionary, 1985—. Named Tchr. of Yr., Anson Jones Sch., 1982, 83. Mem. NEA, Nat. Assn. Female Execs., Tex. State Tchrs. Assn., Houston Tchrs. Assn., Tex. So. Reading Club, Select Houston Execs., Literacy Advance Houston. Baptist. Lodges: Order Eastern Star (sec.). Home: 3401 Oakdale St Houston TX 77004

PRESTON, SUSAN BETH, insurance brokerage executive; b. Sparta, Wis., Jan. 9, 1953; d. David Clayton and Mary Douglas (Wade) Hinshaw; m. Alan Robert Preston, May 18, 1974. Student Mich. State U., 1971-73. Personal line broker's asst. CSE Ins. Co., San Francisco, 1976-77; comml. broker's asst. A. Mason Blodgett & Assocs., San Francisco, 1977-79, ins. broker, life agt., 1979—, v.p. sales, 1987—. Bd. dirs. Camp Fire, Inc., San Francisco, 1980-85, chmn. nominating com., 1982-85; mem. Prison Law Office Bd. of San Quentin, 1984-85. Mem. Profl. Ins. Agts., San Francisco Ins. Women. Methodist. Home: 10 Cavalla Cay Novato CA 94949 Office: A Mason Blodgett & Assocs 1625 Van Ness St San Francisco CA 94109

PRESTON, VERA ALMA, educator; b. Oklahoma City, May 30, 1942; d. Joe Lafayette and Liberty (Bennett) P.; B.S., Okla. State U., 1962; M.A. (grad. asst.), U. Maine, 1969; m. Norman Bruce Callahan, Oct. 14, 1964 (div. 1976); children—Melissa, Mark. Vol., Peace Corps, Baños, Tungurahua, Ecuador, 1962-64; tchr. Gaithersburg (Md.) High Sch., 1964-65, Edgewood (Md.) High Sch., 1965; instr. math. West Chester (Pa.) State Coll., 1967; part-time math. instr. Berkshire Community Coll., 1973-76; tchr. Zebulon (N.C.) High Sch., 1978-81; tchr. math. Red Rock (Okla.) Pub. Sch., 1982-84, Central Jr. High Sch., Bartlesville, Okla., 1984-86; tchr. Sci. Acad., Lyndon B. Johnson High Sch., Austin, Tex., 1986-87; instr. math. Austin Community Coll., Austin, 1987—; del. Equity Conf., Albuquerque, 1982. Tchr., Sunday sch. Unity Ch., 1978-81; organizer, 1st pres. Family Centered Parents, Inc., Wilmington, Del., 1970; organizer Literacy Vols. Am., Pittsfield, Mass., 1976. Mem. Nat. Council Tchrs. of Math., Okla. Council Tchrs. of Math. (dir. 1982-85), Women and Math. Edn. (bd. dirs. 1986—, pres. 1987—), Assn. Supervision and Curriculum Devel., Kappa Delta Pi. Home: 9513 Blue Creek Ln Austin TX 78758-5801

PRESTON, WENDY ANN, research pharmacist; b. Oneonta, N.Y., July 17, 1956; d. Keith Gerald and Cynthia Mary (Wescott) P. BS, Albany Coll. Pharmacy, 1979; PhD, Purdue U., 1984. Registered pharmacist, N.Y. Group leader formulations research Lederle Labs. div. Am. Cyanamid Co., Pearl River, N.Y., 1984-87, group leader, 1987—. Contbr. articles to profl. jours. Vol. Rockland County Jail Ministry, New City, N.Y., 1986-87; mem. Nat. Right to Life Com., Inc., Washington, 1986—; bd. dirs. Rockland Pregnancy Counseling Ctr., 1986—. USP fellow U.S. Pharmacopeial Conv., 1983-84. Mem. Am. Assn. Pharm. Scientists, Am. Pharm. Assn., Nat. Assn. for Female Execs. Republican. Baptist. Club: Lederle Employees Recreation Assn. Winter Tennis (Pearl River) (pres. 1987-88). Home: 8 Lenox Ct #804 Suffern NY 10901 Office: Lederle Labs div Am Cyanamid Co N Middletown Rd Pearl River NY 10965

PRESTRIDGE, PAMELA ADAIR, lawyer; b. Delhi, La., Dec. 25, 1945; d. Gerald Wallace Prestridge and Peggy Adair (Arender) Martin. BA, La. Poly. U., 1967; M in Edn., La. State u., 1968, JD, 1973. Bar: U.S. Dist. ct. (mid. dist.) La. 1975, U.S. Dist. Ct. (so. dist.) Tex. 1982, U.S. Ct. Appeals (5th cir.) 1982, U.S. Dist. Ct. (ea. dist.) Tex. 1984. Law clk. to presiding justice La. State Dist. Ct., Baton Rouge, 1973-75; ptnr. Breazeale, Sachse & Wilson, Baton Rouge, 1975-82, Hirsch & Westheimer P.C., Houston, 1982—. Counselor Big Bros., Big Sisters, Baton Rouge, 1968-70; legal cons., bd. dirs. Lupus Found. Am., Houston, 1984—; bd. dirs. Quota Club, Baton Rouge, 1979-82, Speech and Hearing Found., Baton Rouge, 1981-82. Named one of Outstanding Young Women Am., 1980; named Outstanding Profl. Woman Houston, 1984. Mem. ABA, La. Bar Assn., Tex. Bar Assn., Houston Bar Assn., Assn. Trial Lawyers Am., Phi Alpha Delta, La. State U. Student Bar Assn. Democrat. Episcopalian. Home: 908 Welch Houston TX 77006 Office: Hirsch & Westheimer PC 700 Louisiana #2550 Houston TX 77002

PRETLOW, CAROL JOCELYN, fashion and communications consultant; b. Salisbury, Md., Nov. 9, 1946; d. Kenneth H. and Vivian Virginia (Hughes) P. B.A., Fisk U., 1976; M.A., Norfolk State U., 1982; postgrad. Antioch Law Sch., 1984-85. Fashion columnist The Smithfield Times (Va.), 1977-80; talk show hostess Sta. WAVY-TV, 1978-81; fashion editor Tidewater Life Mag., 1979; reporter, asst. news dir. Sta. WNSB News, Norfolk, Va., 1980-81; press sec. Com. to Elect Fred D. Thompson Jr. Treas. Isle of Wight County, 1981; ind. fashion cons., Smithfield, Va., 1982—; fashion reporter Sta. WRAP Radio, Norfolk, 1986-87; adj. prof. communication Paul D. Camp Community Coll., Franklin, 1986-87; entertainment fashion editor Citizens Press Am. Newspaper, Portsmouth, Va.; fahion publicist, cons. Carrie's House of Fashion, Smithfield, Va.; ind. fashion cons., publicist, Smithfield, 1987—. Va. Coordinator Sesquitricentennial Celebration, Isle of Wight County, 1984. Home: RR3 Box 697 Smithfield VA 23430

PREUITT, JUDIETH CHENOWETH, management information services executive; b. Paris, Tenn., Oct. 31, 1943; d. Clarence Fredrick and Margaret Carline (Kesterson) Chenoweth; m. Emmett Clyde Preuitt, Nov. 9, 1963; children: Janice Carolyn, Pamela Gayle. BSBA in Bus. Mgmt., U. Ozarks, 1986. Programmer analyst Defense Depot Memphis Tenn., 1962-78; systems, programming supr. Rheem Mfg. Co., Ft. Smith, Ark., 1978-86; v.p. mgmt. info. services Harris Meth. Health Services, Ft. Worth, 1986—.

Republican. Methodist. Home: Rt 1 Box 6080 Azle TX 76020 Office: Mgmt Info Services 701 Fifth Ave Suite B-1 Fort Worth TX 76104

PREVOST, MARY LYNN, lawyer, executive policy analyst; b. Decatur, Ill.; d. Raymond Lynn and Edith Lydia (Munro) Braden; children: Denise, Nancy, Jeffrey. BA, Evergreen State Coll., 1979; JD, U. Puget Sound, 1982. Bar: Wash. 1982. Legal intern Owens, Weaver, Davies, Mackie & Lyman, Olympia, Wash., 1981; mgmt. analyst State of Wash., Olympia, 1982; staff cons. Office Fin. Mgmt., State of Wash., Olympia, 1982-85, exec. policy analyst, 1985-86, on spl. assignment for comparable worth study Office of Gov., 1985-87; exec. policy analyst Office of Gov. State of Wash., Olympia, 1986—; mem. adv. com. Highline Community Coll. Legal Asst. Program, Midway, Wash., 1977-78; student coordinator Wash. Bar Assn. Conf. on Adoption Legislation, Tacoma, 1981. Program coordinator Rotary Internat. Dist. Conf., Olympia, 1980. Evergreen Found. scholar, 1979. Mem. Wash. Bar Assn. (legis. com. 1987—, Centennial com. 1988—, task force on minorities in the profession 1988—), ABA, Governmental Lawyers (pres. 1986-87), Wash. Women Lawyers. Methodist. Office: Office of Gov Ins Bldg MS AQ-44 Olympia WA 98504

PREZIOSO, SALLY ANNE, human resources manager; b. Belleville, N.J., Sept. 14, 1955; d. Salvatore Sabino and Nancy Theresa (Palmisano) P. Student, Teesside Poly., Middlesbourough, Eng., 1975-76; BA, William Paterson Coll., 1977; MA in Personnel Psych., Fairleigh Dickinson U., 1982, postgrad., 1982—. Caseworker Essex County Welfare, Newark, 1977-79; interviewer Varityper div. of AM Internat., East Hanover, N.J., 1979-82, employment mgr., 1982-84, mgr. compensation and benefits, 1984—. Vol. Somerset Hills Handicapped Riders, Bedminster, N.J., 1987. Mem. Am. Compensation Assn., Am. Soc. Personnel Adminstrs., Morris County C. of C., Computer Industries Personnel Assn. Office: Varityper div AM Internat 11 Mt Pleasant Ave East Hanover NJ 07936

PRICE, ALICE L., literary agency executive, writer, consultant; b. Charlottesville, Va., Feb. 3, 1949; d. Robert Huntington and Alice Isabel (Valle) Knight; 1 child, Rita Michael. BA, UCLA, 1982, MBA, 1982. Owner, mgr. Rocky Mt. Housing, Denver, 1972-74; organizational cons., Los Angeles, 1977-82, Don't Ask Computer Software, Inc., Los Angeles, 1982-83; lit. agt. Peter Livingston Assocs., Boulder, Colo., 1983—; cons. ABC TV, Los Angeles, 1978—, Lorimar Prodns., Los Angeles, 1977-79, Foote, Cone & Belding/Honig, Los Angeles, 1980, Microsystems Cons. Group, Los Angeles, 1980-82; guest lectr. Colo. Lang. Arts Soc., 1986; vol. writing tchr. Boulder County Pub. Schs., 1984—; fed. and state election judge, 1986-87; expert witness in pub. cases, 1987. Co-author: (with Gillian Rice) Together Again, 1987; contbg. author: The World's Great Contemporary Poems, 1981; contbg. author, editor: How to Get a Man to Make a Commitment, 1985; editor: Gray Eagles, 1986, Rebecca Wood's Encyclopedia of Whole Foods, 1986; seminar leader: "How to Get your Book Published, 1987—. Dem. del., Colo., 1972, 76; Colo. State Arbitrator 20th Judicial Dist., 1988—. Mem. Ind. Lit. Agts. Assn., Inc., Am. Film Inst., Sierra Club, Colo. Chautauqua Assn., Denver Art Mus., Boulder Hist. Soc., Colo. Authors' League, Phi Beta Kappa, Psi Chi, Pi Gamma Mu. Club: Pres.'s. Office: 2978 Eagle Way Boulder CO 80301

PRICE, ANDREA RENEE, hospital administrator; b. Flint, Mich., June 16, 1959; d. Clifford and Clara (Jones) P. BA in Lit., Sci. and Arts, U. Mich., 1981; MHA, Tulane U., 1984. Adminstrv. resident D.C. Hosp. Assn., Washington, 1983-84; mgr. ambulatory care services DataCom Systems Corp., Washington, 1984-85; admission/registration interviewer George Washington Hosp., Washington, 1985; adminstrv. fellow Children's Hosp., Washington, 1985-86, asst. to exec. v.p., 1986, acting dir. planning and mktg., 1986-87, asst. v.p. adminstrv. services, 1986—; speaker in field; preceptor George Washington Sch. Bus., 1987; presiding officer Am. Coll. Healthcare Execs., Chgo., 1988, bd. dirs., chair, corp. sponsor women's forum, 1987—. Mem. Lupus Found., Washington, 1983—. Recipient Excellence in Healthcare Industry award Bus. Exchange Network, Washington, 1987. Mem. Am. Pub. Health Assn., Am. Soc. Healthcare Risk Mgmt., Nat. Assn. Health Services Execs. (bd. dirs. D.C. chpt., sec. 1987, membership chair, mem. program com.), Alpha Kappa Alpha, Zeta Chi Omega. Democrat. Baptist. Home: 47 Mich Ave NE Washington DC 20002 Office: Children's Hosp Nat Med Ctr 111 Mich Ave NW Washington DC 20010

PRICE, BONNIE BURNS, political science educator; b. San Diego, June 26, 1940; d. Jack and June (Chandonia) Burns, stepdau. Lois (Maus) Burns; m. John Paul Price, Sept. 2, 1961; 1 child, Jacqueline. Student, Am. U., 1961; BA in Polit. Sci., Albright Coll., 1962; MA in Polit. Sci., U. Pa., 1966; PhD in Polit. Sci., Temple U., 1979. Secondary tchr. Daniel Boone Sch. Dist., Athol, Pa., 1962-63, Muhlenberg Sch. Dist., Laureldale, Pa., 1963-66; instr. polit. sci. Albright Coll., Reading, Pa., 1966-67, adj. instr. history, 1969; asst. prof. history Kutztown (Pa.) U., 1970; prof. polit. sci. Reading Area Community Coll., 1970-87, acting v.p. acad. affairs, 1987—; chief cons. Orgnl. Techs., Inc., Reading, 1980-87. Bd. dirs. Muhlenberg Sch. Dist., 1975-87, Planned Parenthood of North East Pa., Trexlertown, 1987. Lilly fellow U. Pa., Phila., 1983-85; grantee Pa. Pub. Commn. for Humanities, 1980. Mem. Am. Soc. Pub. Adminstrn., Pa. Polit. Sci. Assn., Am. Fedn. Tchrs., Berks Assn. Supervision and Curriculum Devel., AAAS, ACLU (bd. dirs. Berks chpt. 1979-87). Democrat. Home: 3414 Poinciana Ave Reading PA 19650 Office: Reading Area Community Coll 10 S 2d St Reading PA 19605

PRICE, CHERYL AVIS, librarian; b. Oak Park, Ill., Mar. 14, 1944; d. Minor Carr and Malvina D. P.; B.S., Mo. Valley Coll., 1966; M.A., No. Ill. U., 1971; M.A.L.S., Rosary Coll., 1977. Jud. liaison specialist DuPage County Govt., Wheaton, Ill., 1971-73, county law librarian, 1973-79; polit. sci./law librarian No. Ill. U., DeKalb, 1979-81, internat. documents and law librarian, 1981-83, gen. reference librarian, 1983-85. Bibl. Inst. coordinator Ill. Inst. Tech., Chgo., 1986—. Mem. AAUW, ALA, Am. Law Librarians Assn.

PRICE, DONNA, chemist, educator; b. Balt., Oct. 23, 1913; d. William Mitchell and Emma Deisha (Feddeman) P. AB in Chemistry, Goucher Coll., 1934, DSc (hon.), 1974; PhD in Phys. Chemistry, Cornell U., 1937. Instr. Rockford (Ill.) Coll., 1938-40; fellow in chem. physics Harvard U., Cambridge, Mass., 1940-41; fellow in chem. kinetics U. Chgo., 1942; research chemist Hercules Powder Co., Wilmington, Del., 1942-48; chemist to supr. chemistry U.S. Naval Ordnance Lab., Silver Spring, Md., 1949-60, acting div. chief, 1961-62; sr. research chemist U.S. Naval Surface Warfare Ctr., Silver Spring, Md., 1963-86; sr. scientist Advanced Technol. and Research, Inc., Burtonsville, Md., 1987—; cons. Am. Marietta Co., Seattle, 1955; lectr. Lawrence Livermore (Calif.) Nat. Lab., 1959, Ministry of Supply, U.K., London, 1959, U.S. Naval Surface Weapons Ctr., Silver Spring, 1981-82; chmn. adv. com. explosives and propellants Naval Ordnance Lab., 1955-61; mem. propellant hazardous assessment panel Strategic Systems Project Office, 1972—, editorial adv. bd. Combustion and Flame, 1974-77. Contbr. articles to profl. jours. Mem. Common Cause, Washington, 1950—. Fellow Cornell U., Goucher Coll., 1935, 36. Fellow AAUW; mem. Smithsonian Assocs., Combustion Inst., Am. Chem. Soc., Am. Phys. Soc. Democrat. Home: 3706 Manor Rd #2 Chevy Chase MD 20815

PRICE, ELAINE DENISE, accountant; b. Long Beach, Calif., Sept. 15, 1955; d. Ralph Amaya and Angie (Sanchez) Price. BA of Bus. Adminstrn., Calif. State U., Fullerton, 1977; postgrad., U. So. Calif. Audit sr. Moss and Adams, Los Angeles, 1977-81; supr. Brigante and Johnson, Torrance, Calif., 1981-84; tax mgr. Laventhol and Horwath, Los Angeles, 1984—. Mem. Nat. Assn. Women Bus. Owners, Latin Bus. Assn. Republican. Roman Catholic. Office: Laventhol and Horwath 3699 Wilshire Blvd Los Angeles CA 90010

PRICE, FAYE HUGHES, mental health consultant; b. Indpls.; d. Twidell W. and Lillian Gladys (Hazlewood) Hughes; AB with honors (scholar 1939-43), W.Va. State Coll., 1943; postgrad. social work (scholar) Ind. U., 1943-44; MSW, Jane Addams Sch., U. Ill., 1951; student summer insts. U. Chgo. 1960-65; m. Frank Price, Jr., June 16, 1945; 1 dau., Faye Michele. Supr. youth activities Flanner House, Indpls., 1945-47; program dir. Parkway Community House, Chgo., 1947-56, dir., 1957-58, dir. social services mental health div. Chgo. Dept. Health, 1958-61, dir. community services, 1961-65, asso. dir. planning and devel., 1965-69, regional program dir., 1969-75, asst. dir. mental health, 1975, acting dir., 1976, asst. dir. bur. mental health, 1976-86; cons. various health, welfare and youth agencies; field instr. U. Ill., U. Chgo., Atlanta U., George Williams U.; lectr. Chgo. State U., U. Ill., other profl. workshops, seminars and confs. Active mem. Art Inst. Chgo., Bravo chpt. Chgo. Lyric Opera, Chgo. Urban League, Southside Community Art Center, Chgo., Chgo. YWCA, 9800 Parnell Ave. Block Club, Chgo., DuSable Mus., Chgo.; trustee Episc. Charities and Community Services of Chgo. Bd. Episcopal Charities Chgo.; mem. bd. cannon Samuel J. Martin Found. Recipient scholarship Mt. Zion Baptist Ch., 1938-39, Fisk U., 1943; Mother-of-Year award Chgo. State Women's Club, 1975. Mem. Nat. Assn. Social Work, Acad. Certified Social Workers, Ill. Welfare Assn., Ill. Group Psychotherapy Soc., Nat. Conf. on Social Welfare, Council on Social Work Edn., Center for Continuing Edn. of Ill. Mental Health Insts., Nat. Assn. Parliamentarians, Am. Assn. Parliamentarians, Alpha Gamma Pi, Alpha Kappa Alpha, NAACP, U. Ill. Alumni Assn., Nat. Council Negro Women, Urban League, Municipal Employees Soc. Chgo. Episcopalian. Clubs: Jack and Jill of Am. Assocs., Links, Inc. (nat. dir. trends and services) (Chgo.), Les Cameos Social, Chums. Address: 9815 S Parnell Ave Chicago IL 60628

PRICE, HOLLISTER ANNE CAWEIN, airline project administrator, interior design consultant; b. Memphis, Feb. 11, 1954; d. Madison Albert Cawein and Billie Jeanne (Roberts) Stewart; m. James H. Price, Jr., Oct. 21, 1978 (div. 1985). BA in Journalism Memphis State U., 1988. Office mgr. Bruce Motor Co., Memphis, 1975-76; br. mgr. Central States Agy., Memphis, 1976-78; facility coordinator Fed. Express Corp., Memphis, 1978-86, corp. interior designer, project mgr., 1986—; design cons. Smart Shoppes, Inc., Hardy and Trumann, Ark., 1985-86; Fed. Express dept. coordinator interior design student interns Memphis State U. Dept. leader Ch. Sch. Edn. Program, Central Ch., 1984-85; mem. Arts Services League for Greater Memphis Area, 1986—; active Very Spl. Arts Council for Handicapped, Memphis, 1987—. Mem. Nat. Assn. Female Execs., Delta Gamma Alumnae. Republican. Episcopalian. Club: Duration (Memphis). Avocations: scuba diving, horseback riding, biking, antique collecting. Office: Fed Express Corp Dept 1870 PO Box 727 Memphis TN 38194

PRICE, JEANNINE ALLEENICA, clinical psychologist; b. Cleve., Oct. 29, 1949; d. Q. Q. and Lisa Denise (Wilson) Ewing; m. T. R. Price, Sept. 2, 1976. B.S., Western Res. U., 1969; M.S., Vanderbilt U., 1974. Cert. alcoholism counselor, Calif. Health Service coordinator Am. Profile, Nashville, 1970-72; exec. dir. Awareness Concept, San Jose, Calif., 1977-80; mgr. employee assistance program Nat. Semiconductor, Santa Clara, Calif., 1980-81; mgmt. cons. employee assistant programs. Mem. Gov.'s Adv. Council Child Devel. Programs. Mem. Am. Bus. Women's Assn., Nat. Assn. Female Execs., AAUW, Coalition Labor Women, Calif. Assn. Alcohol counselors, Almaca. Author: Smile a Little, Cry a Lot; Gifts of Love; Reflection in the Mirror. Office: 728 N 1st St San Jose CA 95112

PRICE, JOYCE MARIE COMBEST, lawyer; b. Pachuta, Miss., July 17, 1945; d. Tommy and Marie (Edmonson) Combest; m. James Price, Feb. 23, 1974; 1 child, Dorian Jade. BS, Tougaloo (Miss.) Coll., 1967; MA, Chgo. State U., 1979; JD, DePaul U., Chgo., 1984. Bar: Ill. 1984, U.S. Dist. Ct. (no. dist.) Ill. 1984, U.S. Ct. Appeals (7th cir.) 1984. Research technician U. Chgo. Hosps., 1967-69; tchr. Chgo. Pub. Schs., 1969-74, math coordinator, 1974-77, coordinator regional service, 1977-80, dir. tchr. incentives, 1980-85, adminstr. resource devel., 1985-86; asst. atty. Chgo. Bd. Edn., 1986—; cons. 38th Sch. Dist., 1974-78; lectr. in field. Contbg. author: Pre-Algebra Curriculum, 1974, Math Curriculum Guide, 1975; editor: Math Objectives (K-8), 1976. Sec. bd. dirs. Faulkner Sch., Chgo., 1980. Mem. ABA, Ill. Bar Assn., Chgo. Bar Assn., Am. Judiciary Soc., Alpha Kappa Alpha. Democrat. Baptist. Home: 5201 S Cornell Ave Chicago IL 60615 Office: Chgo Bd Edn Law Dept 1819 W Pershing Rd Chicago IL 60609

PRICE, KAY, public television producer; b. Reedsburg, Wis., June 25, 1943; d. Lionel Norman and Emily Therese (Diehl) P.; m. Greg Mulcahy, Aug. 14, 1964 (div. 1984); 1 child, Lisa. BA in Communications, U. Wis., Green Bay, 1980. Free-lance writer Wis., 1967—; pub. TV producer Price Detective & Video Services, Sauk City, Wis., 1982—; pvt. investigator Sauk City, 1985—; judge writing contest U. Baraboo, Wis., 1987. Producer (TV) pub. service spots, Madison, 1986, four shows on bicentennial of constitution, Madison, 1987; contbr. articles to newspapers. Fund raiser Sauk City Library, 1985, Am. Cancer Soc., Sauk City, 1986; pres. August Dereleth Soc., Sauk City, 1981, bd. dirs.7. Mem. Women in Communications, Wis. Regional Writers Assn. Republican. Roman Catholic. Home and Office: Price Detective & Video Services 100 Jefferson St Sauk City WI 53583

PRICE, LUCILE BRICKNER BROWN, civic worker; b. Decorah, Iowa, May 31, 1902; d. Sidney Eugene and Cora (Drake) Brickner; B.S., Iowa State U., 1925; M.A., Northwestern U., 1940; m. Maynard Wilson Brown, July 2, 1928 (dec. Apr. 1937); m. 2d, Charles Edward Price, Jan. 14, 1961 (dec. Dec. 1983). Asst. dean women Kans. State U., Manhattan, 1925-28; mem. bd. student personnel adminstrn. Northwestern U., 1937-41, personnel research Sears Roebuck & Co., Chgo., 1941-42, overseas club dir. ARC, Eng., Africa, Italy, 1942-45; dir. Child Edn. Found., N.Y.C., 1946-56. Participant 1st and 2d Iowa Humanists Summer Symposiums, 1974, 75. Del. Mid Century White House Conf. on Children and Youth, 1950; mem. com. on program and research of Children's Internat. summer villages, 1952-53; mem. bd. N.E. Iowa Mental Health Ctr., 1959-62, pres. bd., 1960-61; mem. Iowa State Extension Adv. Com., 1973-75; project chmn. Decorah Hist. Dist. (listed Nat. Register Historic Places); trustee Porter House Mus., Decorah, 1966-78, emeritus bd. dirs., 1982—; participant N. Cen. Regional Workshop Am. Assn. State and Local History, Mpls., 1975, Midwest Workshop Hist. Preservation and Conservation, Iowa State U., 1976, 77; mem. Winneshiek County (Iowa) Civil Service Commn., 1978-87; rep. Class of 1940 Northwestern U. Sch. Edn. and Social Policy, 1986—. Recipient Alumni Merit award Iowa State U., 1975; award for outstanding contbns. to community, state and country Iowa State U., 1988. Mem. Am. Coll. Personnel Assn., (life), Am. Overseas Assn. (nat. bd.; life), AAUW (life mem., mem. bd. Decorah; recipient Named Gift award 1977), Nat. Assn. Mental Health (del. nat. conf. 1958), Norwegian-Am. Mus. (life, Vesterheim fellow), Winneshiek County Hist. Soc. (life, cert. of appreciation 1984), DAR, Pi Lambda Theta, Chi Omega. Designer, builder house for retirement living. Home: 508 W Broadway Decorah IA 52101

PRICE, MARILYN JEANNE, fund raising and management consultant; b. N.Y.C., Jan. 24, 1948; d. George Franklin and Mary Anastasia (Barnishin) Lawrence; student Temple Bus. Sch., 1964-66; student U. Md., 1973-74; 1 child, Kimberly Jean. Asst. to sr. printing and paper buyer ARC, Washington 1965-67; conf. planner for classified mil. confs. Nat. Security Indsl. Assn., Washington, 1967-69; fund devel. office asst. Nat. Urban Coalition, Washington, 1970; direct mail/membership coordinator Common Cause, Washington, 1970-72; mgr. direct mail fund raising Epilepsy Found. of Am., Washington, 1973-76; exec. v.p. Bruce W. Eberle & Assocs., Vienna, Va., 1977-81; pres. Response Dynamics, Inc., Vienna, Va., 1981-83; v.p. The Best Lists, Inc., Vienna, 1981-83; pres. The Creative Advantage, Inc., Fairfax, Va., 1983—, Creative Mgmt. Services, Inc., Fairfax, 1987—; cons. in field. Asst. to Young Citizens for Johnson, 1964; vol. Hubert Humphrey campaign, 1968, George McGovern campaign, 1972. Recipient Silver Echo award, Direct Mail/Mktg. Assn. Internat. competition for mktg. excellence, 1980. Mem. Nat. Soc. Fund Raisers, Direct Mail Mktg. Assn., Non-Profit Mailers Fedn., Assn. Direct Response Fundraising Council (bd. dirs., treas.), Direct Mktg. Club. Home: 9614 Lindenbrook St Fairfax VA 22031 Office: The Creative Advantage 9401 Lee Hwy Suite 205 Fairfax VA 22031

PRICE, MELISSA LEE, media production executive; b. Columbia, S.C., Nov. 17, 1954; d. Thomas Hart and Margaret Melissa (Fletcher) P. BA in Art, U. S.C., 1978, M of Media Art, 1982. Grad. teaching asst. U. S.C., Columbia, 1979-81; media cons. Francis Marion Coll., Florence, S.C., 1981-86; pres. Mystery Prodn., Columbia, 1986-87; dir. mktg. Miscellaneous Imports, Columbia, S.C., 1987—; instr. Florence-Darlington (S.C.) Tech. Coll., 1986, Benedict Coll., Columbia, 1987—. Producer: (film) The Parade's Gone By, 1978 (Film South award 1978). Fundraiser Florence County Boy Scouts Am., 1984, Bruce Hosp., Florence, 1985, Florence County YMCA, 1986; statistician U. S.C., 1972—. Mem. Assn. Multi-Image, Soc. Motion Picture and TV Engrs. Office: Mystery Prodn 727 Meadow St Suite 1 Columbia SC 29205

PRICE, N. LEIGH, bank executive; b. Malin, Oreg., Feb. 6, 1941; d. Clarence Loraine and Nina Ellen (Kamping) P.; children: Brian, Leigh Ann. BA in Psychology, UCLA, 1980, MBA in Mgmt., 1982. Analyst Standard Oil Co., Tulsa, 1967-69; programmer/analyst Honeywell, Inc., Mpls., 1969-73; sr. systems analyst Fabri-Tek, Inc., Mpls., 1974-77; pres. Price & Assocs., Mpls., 1978-79; sr. cons. MRG Assocs., Los Angeles, 1981-83; exec. v.p., chief operating officer Prescription Health Services, Los Angeles, 1984-85; v.p., mgr. First Interstate Bank, Los Angeles, 1985—. Del. Minn. Democratic Conv., 1972; chmn. Parent/Sch. Bd. Council, Edina, Minn., 1975; pres. Friends Los Angeles Opera, 1980-81; v.p. Guild Opera Co., Los Angeles, 1983-85; exec. v.p. Opera Guild So. Calif., 1984-85, pres., 1985-87. Unitarian. Office: First Interstate Bank of California 1200 W 7th St Los Angeles CA 90017

PRICE, REINE IRENE, educational administrator; b. Natchitoches, La., Sept. 6, 1950; d. Robert Lee and Neva Lucille (Uhl) Merriam; m. Michael Clinton Price, Aug. 11, 1973; children—Autumn Irene, Gabriel Clinton. B.S. in Edn., Bowling Green State U., 1971; M.S. in Edn., U. Central Ark., 1982; MEd in gifted edn. U. Ark., 1986. Cert. elem. tchr., Ark., cert. biology, gifted and reading specialist, cert. elem. prin. and supr. Tchr. Oregon Pub. Schs., Ohio, 1971-72, Immaculate Conception Sch., North Little Rock, Ark., 1974-77; dir. plan edn. North Little Rock Br., 1973-74; reading specialist U. Central Ark., Conway, 1982-83; reading specialist Dardanelle Pub. Schs., Ark., 1983-84, coordinator spl. services, 1984-85; prin. East End Elem. Sch., Bigelow, Ark., 1985-87, Wilson Elem. Sch. Little Rock Dist., 1987—; tutor, Mayflower, Ark., 1981-83; cons. in field; program developer, coordinator Spl. services 1st Gifted Preschool tied to pub. sch. in Ark., 1984-85; mem. Ark. Gov.'s Sch. Staff, summer 1986. Ch. organist Brumley Baptist Ch., Conway, Ark., 1976-81, youth dir., 1977-80. Mem. Internat. Reading Assn., North Central Reading Assn. Council (sec. 1985-86), Agate Council Educators, Prin.'s Roundtable, Ark. Assn. Ednl. Adminstrs., Ark. Gifted and Talented Edn. (bd. dirs., v.p. membership 1986—), Assn. Supervision and Curriculum Devel., Women's Missionary Union (pres. 1978-79, sec. 1979-80), Kappa Delta Pi, Phi Delta Kappa. Democrat. Lodge: Order Eastern Star. Avocations: sewing; needlework; crafts; boating; reading. Home: RR 1 Box 152 Houston AR 72070 Office: Wilson Elem Sch 4015 Stannus Rd Little Rock AR 72204

PRICE, ROSALIE PETTUS, artist; b. Birmingham, Ala.; d. Erle and Ellelee (Chapman) Pettus; A.B., Birmingham-So. Coll., 1935; M.A., U. Ala., Tuscaloosa, 1967; m. William Archer Price, Oct. 3, 1936. Painter in watercolors, casein, oil and acrylic; one man shows include: Samford U., 1964, Birmingham Mus. of Art, 1966, 73, 82-83, Town Hall Gallery, 1968, 75, South Central Bell, 1977; instr. Birmingham (Ala.) Mus. Art, 1967-70, Samford U., 1969-70. Bd. dirs. Birmingham Mus. of Art, 1950-54, vice chmn., 1950-51; bd. trustees Birmingham Music Club, 1956-66, rec. sec., 1958-62; mem. Springfield (Mo.) Art Mus. Recipient purchase award Watercolor USA, 1972; named to Watercolor USA Honor Soc., 1986. Mem. Nat. Watercolor Soc., Nat. Soc. Painters in Casein and Acrylic (W. Alden Brown Meml. award 1970, Joseph A. Cain Meml. award 1983), Birmingham Art Assn. (pres. 1947-49, Little House on Linden purchase award 1968), So. Watercolor Soc., Watercolor Soc. Ala. (sec. 1948-49), La. Watercolor Soc., Pi Beta Phi. Episcopalian. Clubs: Jr. League of Birmingham (chmn. art com. 1947-50), Window Box Garden. Home: 300 Windsor Dr Birmingham AL 35209 Office: 2132 20th Ave S Birmingham AL 35223

PRICE, SUSAN JOHNSON, psychotherapist; b. N.Y.C., Sept. 9, 1941; d. Herbert W. and Lois (Vaughn) Johnson; m. Stephen M. Price, Apr. 26, 1941; children: Angela, Michael. BA, Muskingam Coll., 1964; MSW, Rutgers U., 1976. Cert. clin. social worker, psychotherapist. Intern Ednl. Alliance, N.Y.C., 1975-76; psychotherapist Counseling and Human Devel. Ctr., N.Y.C., 1975-77; pvt. practice psychotherapy N.Y.C., 1977—. Author: The Female Ego, 1985; co-author: No More Lonely Nights: Overcoming the Hidden Fears that Keep You From Getting Married, 1987; columnist Glamour Mag. Mem. Internat. Assn. Transactional Analysis, Assn. Clin. Social Work Psychotherapists, Nat. Assn. Social Workers. Episcopalian. Home: PO Box 110 Lake Placid NY 12946 Office: 360 E 55th St Suite 4L New York NY 10022

PRICE-LEE FATT, PATRICIA ANN, automobile leasing consultant; b. Danville, Va., June 19, 1954; d. William Oliver and Bessie Carolyn (Keene) P. Cert. data entry Braxton Bus. Sch., Richmond, Va., 1973; cert. computer ops. data analysis Mgmt. Info. Systems Office, San Antonio, 1980. Ordained to ministry Ch. Gospel Ministry, 1986, ordained bishop, 1988. With data entry dept. Va. Dept. Taxation, Richmond, 1985; telephone surveyor Stan Parris Campaign for Gov., Richmond, 1985; telephone sec. Sleepy Time & Wakeup, Richmond, 1984; writer, salesman, pres. Sister Starfire & Co., Richmond, 1982—; automobile leasing cons. Trans Leasing, Richmond, 1986—; beauty cons. Avon, Richmond, 1981; distbr. Amway, Richmond, 1980-83; radio/telephone operator FCC, Richmond, 1983—. Contbr. to World of Poetry, 1985 (Golden Poet award 1986, 87), American Poetry Anthology, 1986. Fund raiser Crop Walk for Hunger, Richmond, 1982, Elks Lodge 15, 1985; chpt. mem. Muscular Dystrophy Assn., 1987—; mem. Crusade for Voters, Richmond, 1982, Friendship Force of Richmond, 1987—; voters registrant Office of City Registrar, Richmond, 1983; mem. Republican Presdl. Task Force, 1985—, Muscular Dystrophy Assn. Served with U.S. Army, 1979-81. Recipient Unsung Hero award Met. Bus. Shoppers Guide, Richmond, 1985. Mem. Internat. Platform Assn., Nat. Assn. Female Execs. (network dir. 1985), Liberian Aux. Assn. (hon. internat. hostess 1983—), NAACP (vets. affairs and armed forces com. 1982), Nat. Com. to Preserve Social Security and Medicare, Smithsonian Assocs., Songwriters of Am. (life), Internat. Platform Assn. Republican. Buddhist. Club: Dollywood Ambassador. Avocations: photogrpahy; theater; aerobics; reading; stamp collecting. Home: 225 Laurel Fork Dr Richmond VA 23225

PRICHARD, ELIZABETH ROBINSON, social worker, civic worker; b. N.Y.C., Oct. 20, 1915; d. Harold Grant and Kathryn Virginia (Robinson) P.; B.A., Adelphi U., 1943; M.S., Columbia U. Sch. Social Work, 1947. Home service worker ARC, Bklyn. and N.Y.C., 1943-45, 47-48; social worker N.Y. U., Bellevue Pilot Home Care Project, N.Y.C., 1948-49; asst. dir. social service Columbia-Presbyn. Med. Center, N.Y.C., 1949-54, dir. social services, 1954-81; asst. prof. clin. social work Coll. Physicians and Surgeons, Columbia U., 1957-81; mem. profl. adv. bd. for social work Found. Thanatology, 1970—, mem. exec. com., 1974—. Trustee, Empire State chpt. Myasthenia Gravis Found., 1981—, nat. bd. dirs., 1986—; participant seminar on death Columbia U.; lectr. Brookdale Inst. Aging, Columbia U. Ret. Faculty Projet; mem. New York County Democratic Com. Mem. Nat. Assn. Social Workers, Acad. Cert. Social Workers, Nat. Conf. Social Welfare, Internat. Conf. Social Welfare, Am. Pub. Health Assn., AAAS, N.Y. Acad. Scis., Columbia U. Sch. Social Work Alumni Assn. (mem. student liaison com. and internat. host program, 1984—). Clubs: Women's City (health and mental health coms. 1981—), City. Editor 6 books, including 5 books on death and dying; contbr. articles on social work and care of terminally ill to profl. publs. Address: 510 E 86th St Box 44 New York NY 10028

PRICOLO, EDITH MARIE, design engineer; b. Merced, Calif., Nov. 8, 1936; d. Tony and Edith Cecelia (Silva) Azevedo; m. Danny Ralph Pricolo, Feb. 19, 1955; children: Dennis, Dina, Danette, Damien. Student San Jose State U., 1953-54. Sales clk. J.J. Newberry store, San Jose, 1967; integrated circuit fabrication worker Fairchild Semicondr., Mountain View, Calif., 1967-68, integrated circuit mask designer, 1969-73; integrated circuit mask designer Advanced Microdevices, Sunnyvale, Calif., 1973-84, integrated circuit mask design engr., 1984—. Designer bipolar microprocessor AM 2901, 1975. Steering com. mem. Fleming Ave Homeowners Assn., San Jose, 1979-81; funding chmn., counselor Contact 24 hour crisis hotline, San Jose, 1985; tchr. Confrat. of Christian Doctrine, 1973-74; active San Jose Symphony Aux. Mem. Nat. Assn. Female Execs. Avocations: refinishing furniture, dancing, photography, sewing. Home: 168 Clareview Ave San Jose CA 95127 Office: Advanced MicroDevices (Semicondr) 901 Thompson Pl Sunnyvale CA 94088

PRIDGEN, MARY DEE, law educator; b. Washington, July 23, 1949; d. Delmas Courtland and Mary Yearley (Hiss) P.; m. David James Newson, July 3, 1982 (div. 1985); m. Kenichi Matsuno, Nov. 22, 1987. BA, Cornell U., 1971; JD, NYU, 1974. Bar: D.C. 1977. Law clk. U.S. Dist. Ct. (D.C.),

Washington, 1974-76; instr. Cath. U., Washington, 1976-77; atty. Legal Research and Services for Elderly, Washington, 1977-78, FTC, Washington, 1978-82; prof. U. Wyo. Coll. of Law, Laramie, 1982—; cons. Nat. Consumer Council, London, 1983. Author: Consumer Protection and the Law, 1986; contbr. articles to profl. jours. Pres. Laramie chpt. ACLU, 1985—; mem. Citizen's Com. on Cable TV, 1987. Mem. Soc. Am. Law Tchrs., U. Faculty Assn., Phi Beta Kappa, Order of the Coif. Democrat. Office: U Wyo Sch Law Laramie WY 82071

PRIDGEN, MICHELLE LYNN, educator; b. St. Louis, July 31, 1954; d. Edward and Doris Jean (Fleming) Stewart; m. Kivy Leon Pridgen, Aug. 26, 1974 (dec.); children—Kivy Leon II, Janee Danese-Michelle. B.S.A., St. Louis U., 1977; student Washington U. St. Louis, 1982; cert. Internat. Air Acad., St. Louis, 1985. Substitute tchr., schs., Fla. and Ill., 1977-80; med. officer mgmt. staff, med. asst. Sunbay Med. Office Bldg. Humana Corp., St. Petersburg, Fla., 1980-82; tchr. Cahokia Sch. Dist., Ill., 1982-86; airlines reservations operator Internat. Airline Acad., St. Louis, 1985. Founder, group leader Centreville Young Astronauts Program, 1986. Nat. Merit scholar, 1972. Mem. Nat. Assn. Female Execs, Am. Automobile Assn. Inst. Cert. Travel Agts. (exam. proctor), Pinellas County Fla. Med. Wives Aux. Club, 1980-82. Democrat. Avocations: Travel; poetry; writing; cooking; miniaturist; music. Home: 810 S 55th St Centreville IL 62207

PRIESAND, SALLY JANE, clergywoman; b. Cleve., June 27, 1946; d. Irving Theodore and Rosetta Elizabeth (Welch) P. B.A. in English, U. Cin., 1968; B.Hebrew Letters, Hebrew Union Coll.-Jewish Inst. Religion, 1971, M.A. in Hebrew Letters, 1972; D.H.L. (hon.), Fla. Internat. U., 1973. Ordained rabbi, 1972. Student rabbi Sinai Temple, Champaign, Ill., 1968, Congregation B'nai Israel, Hattiesburg, Miss., 1969-70, Congregation Shalom, Milw., 1970, Temple Beth Israel, Jackson, Mich., 1970-71; rabbinic intern Isaac M. Wise Temple, Cin., 1971-72; asst. rabbi Stephen Wise Free Synagogue, N.Y.C., 1972-77; assoc. rabbi Stephen Wise Free Synagogue, 1977-79; rabbi Temple Beth El, Elizabeth, N.J., 1979-81, Monmouth Reform Temple, Tinton Falls, N.J., 1981—; chaplain Lenox Hill Hosp., N.Y.C., 1979-81. Author: Judaism and the New Woman, 1975. Mem. commn. on synagogue relations Fedn. Jewish Philanthropies N.Y., 1972-79, mem. com. on aged commn. synagogue relations, 1972-75; mem. task force on equality of women in Judaism pub. affairs com. N.Y. Fedn. Reform Synagogues, 1972-75; mem. com. on resolutions Central Conf. Am. Rabbis, 1975-77, com. on cults, 1976-78, admissions com., 1983—; chmn. Task Force on women in rabbinate, 1977-83, chmn. 1977-79, mem. exec. bd., 1977-79; mem. joint commn. on Jewish edn. Central Conf. Am. Rabbis-Union Am. Hebrew Congregations, 1974-77; mem. task force on Jewish singles Commn. Synagogue Relations, 1975-77; mem. N.Y. Bd. Rabbis, 1975—, Shore Area Bd. Rabbis, 1981—; mem. interim steering com. Clergy and Laity Concerned, 1979-81; bd. dirs. NCCJ, N.Y.C., 1980-82, Jewish Fedn. Greater Monmouth County, trustee; trustee Planned Parenthood of Monmouth County, also chair religious affairs com., Brookdale Ctr. for Holocaust Studies, Monmouth Campaign for Nuclear Disarmament; v.p. Interfaith Neighbors, 1988—. Cited by B'nai B'rith Women, 1971; named Man of Yr. Temple Israel, Columbus, Ohio, 1972, Woman of Yr. Ladies Aux. N.Y. chpt. Jewish War Vets., 1973, Woman for All Seasons N. L.I. region Women's Am. ORT, 1973; recipient Quality of Life award Dist. One chpt. B'nai B'rith Women, 1973, Medallion Judaic Heritage Soc., 1978, Eleanor Roosevelt Humanities award Women's div. State of Israel Bonds, 1980; named Extraordinary Women of Achievement NCCJ, 1978. Mem. Hadassah (life), Central Conf. Am. Rabbis, NOW, Am. Jewish Congress, Am. Jewish Com., Assn. Reform Zionists Am., B'nai B'rith Women (life), Jewish Peace Fellowship, Women's Rabbinc Network. Home: 10 Wedgewood Circle Eatontown NJ 07724 Office: 332 Hance Ave Tinton Falls NJ 07724

PRIETO, CORINE, geophysicist; b. El Paso, Tex., Sept. 26, 1946; d. Manuel M. and Angela (Zapata) P. BS in Physics and Math., U. Tex., El Paso, 1968; MS in Applied Physics, U. Toronto, Ont., Can., 1974. Geophysicist Mobil Oil Corp., Dallas, 1968-71, sr. geophysicist, 1973-76; exploration supr. Superior Oil Co., Houston, 1976-82; pres. Integrated Geophysics Corp., Houston, 1982—. Named Houston Bus. Woman of Yr., Tex. Exec. Women, 1983. Mem. Soc. Exploration Geophysicists, Geophysical Soc. Houston (chmn. potential fields sect. 1980-83), Nat. Assn. Rep. Women in Tex. Office: Integrated Geophysics Corp 1502 Augusta Dr Suite 390 Houston TX 77057

PRIMAVERA, JOANNE MARTINA, vocational education administrator; b. Langley, Wash., Sept. 17, 1940; d. Victor and Anna Ethel (Peters) P.; m. Donald E. McClain, Sept. 10, 1960 (div. Mar. 1967). BS in Home Econs. Edn., U. Wash., 1964, MEd, 1972; PhD in Vocat. Edn. Adminstrn., U. Mo., 1978. Cert. home economist. Home econs. tchr. Mukilteo (Wash.) Sch. Dist., 1965-68, Fed. Way (Wash.) Sch. Dist., 1968-75; asst. dir. U. Mo. Curriculum Devel. Lab., Columbia, 1976; research asst. Ellis & Assocs., College Park, Md., 1977; vocat. edn. adminstr. Renton (Wash.) Vocat. Tech. Inst., 1977—. Contbr. articles to profl. jours. Bd. dirs. King County YMCA, Seattle, 1979-82, Child and Family Resource Ctr., Seattle, 1985—; community rep. Puget Power, Bellevue, 1981; mem. policy council Head Start, King County, 1985-87. U.S. Dept. Edn. fellow, 1975-77. Mem. Nat. Council Vocat. Adminstrs. (bd. dirs. 1985—), Nat. Restaurant Assn., Wash. Council Vocat. Adminstrs. (pres. 1981-82), Wash. Vocat. Assn. (pres. 1983-84), Wash. Home Econs. Assn. (pres. 1988). Club: Bellevue Athletic. Home: 14615 NE 40th #J-2 Bellevue WA 98007

PRIMKA, MARGARET DAWN, savings and loan executive; b. Princeton, N.J., Sept. 21, 1959; d. Edward John Jr. and Sally (Branin) P. BS in Human Resources, U. Del., 1982. Mgr. customer service People Express Airlines, Newark, 1983-87; acct. exec. Citicorp, Iselin, N.J., 1987—; sales agt. Century 21, North Bruswick, N.J., 1986. Recipient Top Sales award Century 21, 1986. Mem. N.J. Realtors Assn., Alpha Sigma Alpha. Republican.

PRIMO, MARIE NASH, shopping centers official; b. Clarksburg, W.Va., Dec. 10, 1928; d. Frank and Josephine (DiMaria) Nash; student pub. schs. Clarksburg; m. Joseph C. Primo, Sept. 27, 1953; 1 dau., Joan E. Sec., Nat. Bank Detroit, 1945-46; exec. sec. Cutting Tool Mfrs. Assn., Detroit, 1946-50; adminstrv. asst. Irwin I. Cohn atty., Detroit, 1950-84; mgr. Bloomfield (Mich.) Shopping Plaza, 1959—; North Hill Center, Rochester Hills, Mich., 1957—; Drayton Plains Shopping Center (Mich.), 1958-84; South Allen Shopping Center, Allen Park, Mich., 1953-77, Huron-Tel Corner, Pontiac, Mich., 1977—; officer, dir., numerous privately held corps. Mem. steering com., treas. Univ. Liggett Antiques Show, 1971-76, advisory com., 1977-80; mem. parents' com. Wellesley Coll., 1979-1981. Mem. Founders Soc. Detroit Inst. Arts, Women's Econ. Club, Mich. Humane Soc., Detroit Sci. Center, Detroit Zool. Soc., Smithsonian Assos., Hist. Soc. Mich., Grosse Pointe War Meml. Assn., Grosse Pointe Pub. Library Assn., Mich. Opera Theatre Guild. Roman Catholic. Home: 1341 N Renaud Rd Grosse Pointe Woods MI 48236 Office: 1631 1st National Bldg Detroit MI 48226

PRINCE, ANTOINETTE ODETTE, visual artist, art educator; b. Watertown, N.Y., Mar. 18, 1946; d. Clarence Oliver and Marion Eva (Moffatt) Odette; m. George Mather Prince, Aug. 5, 1976 (div. 1981). Grad., Boston Mus. Sch., 1981-82; postgrad., Harvard U., 1986—. Painting instr. Boston Mus. Sch., 1981-82, 86, Tufts U. Exptl. Coll., Medford, Mass., 1986; dir. Loading Dock Gallery, 1982-83; painting instr. Cambridge (Mass.) Art Assn., 1983-85, instr. painting, drawing and art, 1984—; freelance painting instr. 1984-86; coordinator Art Talk, Cambridge Art Assn., 1983-85, bd. dirs. Recipient Traveling Scholars award Mus. Fine Arts, 1982; Pub. Action for Arts grantee, 1985. Home: 20 St Lukes Rd Allston MA 02134

PRINCE, CAROL ANN, controller; b. Sheffield, Ala., June 11, 1953; d. Fred Lonnie and Mary Lucille (Crockett) P. BA, U. North Ala., 1975, cert., 1976, BS, 1979. CPA, Ala. CPA Robbins, Crews and Assocs., Florence, Ala., 1979-84; controller Florence City Bd. Edn., 1984—. Mem. Am. Inst. CPAs (past pres. North Ala. chpt.), Ala. Soc. CPAs, Ala. Assn. Sch. Bus. Officials. Home: 2104 Gusmus Ave Muscle Shoals AL 35661 Office: 541 Riverview Dr Florence AL 35630

PRINCE, FRANCES ANNE KIELY, civic worker; b. Toledo, Dec. 20, 1923; d. John Thomas and Frances (Pusteoska) Kiely; student U. Louisville, 1947-49; A.B., Berea Coll., 1951; postgrad. Kent Sch. Social Work, 1951, Creighton U., 1969; M.P.A., U. Nebr., Omaha, 1978; m. Richard Edward Prince, Jr., Aug. 17, 1951; children—Anne, Richard III. Instr. flower arranging Western Wyo. Jr. Coll., 1965, 66; editor Nebr. Garden News, 1983—. Chmn., Lone Troop council Girl Scouts U.S.A., 1954-57, trainer leaders, 1954-68, mem. state camping com., 1959-61, bd. dirs. Wyo. state council, 1966-69; chmn. Community Improvement, Green River, Wyo., 1959, 63-65, Wyo. Fedn. Women's Clubs State Library Services, 1966-69, U.S. Constitution Bicentennial Commn. Nebr. 1987—, Omaha Commn. on the Bicentennial 1987—; mem. Wyo. State Adv. Bd. on Library Inter-Co-op., 1965-69, Nat. sub com. Commn. on the Bicentennial of hte U.S. constitution; bd. mem. Sweetwater County Library System, 1962—, pres. bd., 1967-68; adv. council Sch. Dist. 66, 1970—; bd. dirs. Opera Angels, 1971, fund raising chmn., 1971-72, v.p., 1974—; bd. dirs. Morning Musicale, 1971—; bazaar com. Children's Hosp., 1970-75; docent Joslyn Art Mus., 1970—; mem. Nebr. Forestry Adv. Bd., 1976—; citizens adv. bd. Met. Area Planning Agy., 1979—; mem. Nebr. Tree-Planting Commn., 1980—;Recipient Library Service award Sweetwater County Library, 1968; Girl Scout Services award, 1967; Conservation award U.S. Forest Service, 1981; Plant Two Trees award, 1981; Nat. Arbor Day award, 1982; Pres. award Nat. council of State Garden Clubs, 1986. Mem. AAUW, New Neighbors League (dir. 1969-71), Ikebana Internat., Symphony Guild, Omaha Playhouse Guild, ALA, Nebr. Library Assn., Omaha Council Garden Clubs (1st v.p. 1972, pres. 1973-75, mem. nat. council 1979—), Internat. Platform Assn., Nat. Trust for Hist. Preservation, Nebr. Flower Show Judges Council, Nat. Council State Garden Clubs (chmn. arboriculture 1985—), Nebr. Fedn. Garden Clubs (pres. 1978-81). Mem. United Ch. of Christ. Clubs: Intermountain (dir. 1963-69), Garden (dir. 1970-72, pres. 1972-75). Author poetry. Editor Nebr. Garden News, 1983—. Home: 8909 Broadmoor Dr Omaha NE 68114

PRINCE, JACQUELYNNE BOLANDER, nurse, consultant; b. Norfolk, Va., July 4, 1955; d. Jack C. Bolander and Particia (Loud) Bolander Melvin; m. John Martine Prince, Jr., Oct. 1, 1977; children—Emily Alene, John Ryland. B.S., Med. Coll. of Va., 1978; M.S., Tex. Woman's U., 1985. Registered critical care nurse. Staff nurse Med. Coll. of Va., Richmond, 1978-80; asst. nurse coordinator Parkland Hosp., Dallas, 1980-82, supr., 1982-83; head nurse N.C. Meml. Hosp., Chapel Hill, 1983-85; coordinator critical care edn. Wise Appalachian Regional Hosp., Wise, Va., 1985-86; coordinator continuing edn. Norton (Va.) Community Hosp., 1986—; cons. in field. Contbr. articles to profl. publs. Advanced Cardiac Life Support instr. Am. Heart Assn., Dallas, Chapel Hill, N.C., 1980—; chmn. bd. dirs. Wise Sch. Dance; v.p. PTA. Mem. Assn. Critical Care Nurses (bd. dirs.), Am. Nurses Assn., North Atlantic Nursing Diagnosis Assn., N.C. Meml. Collaborator Practice Com., Wise County Med. Soc. Auxilliary (pres.). Baptist. Club: Parkland Woman's (project service chmn. 1980-83). Avocations: skiing, quilting, reading, running. Home: 704 Ridge Ave Norton VA 24273 Office: Norton Community Hosp 100 15th St NW Norton VA 24273

PRINCE, VIVIEN JANE SCHAPIRA, craft import company executive, author; b. Nairobi, Kenya, Nov. 10, 1946; came to U.S., 1977; d. Norbert Nathan Schapira and Doris (Wareham) Bolton; m. William Kenneth Plenderleith, Mar. 1969 (div. Mar. 1974); 1 child, Bruce William; m. Allan Fredrick Prince, Feb. 11, 1976; 1 child, Fiona Claudine. Student Kianda Coll., Newspaper Inst. of N.Y., Inst. Children's Lit. Sec., dep. prin. Univ. Coll., Nairobi, 1965-66, Daly & Figgis, Advocates, Nairobi, 1968-70; instr., owner Riding Establishment, Nairobi, 1967; sec. Archer & Wilcock, Advocates, Nairobi, 1972-74, Hamilton Harrison & Mathews, Advocates, Nairobi, 1974; exec. asst., sec. Wilkinson Sword, Nairobi, 1975-76; owner, mgr. Kenyan Craft Importing and Mgmt., Roxbury, Conn., 1983; lectr. in field; pvt. trainer, 1970-73; lady jockey, Nairobi, Gt. Britain, 1969-74, 84. Author: Kenya: The Years of Change, 1986. Organizer Kenya Fund, Roxbury, 1982—. Named 1st hon. treas. Lady Jockeys' Assn. of Gt. Britain, 1972. Mem. Nat. Assn. Female Execs., Newspaper Inst. Am. Mem. Ch. of Eng. Avocation: breeder Pembroke Welsh Corgi dogs. Home: 23 Fox Run Woodbury CT 06798

PRINCIPAL, VICTORIA, actress; b. Fukuoka, Japan, Jan. 3, 1945; d. Victor and Ree (Veal) P.; m. Harry Glassman, 1985. Attended, Miami-Dade Community Coll.; studied acting with, Max Croft, Al Sacks and Estelle Harman. Worked as model, including TV comml. appearances; film debut in The Life and Times of Judge Roy Bean, 1972; other movie appearances include Vigilante Force, Earthquake, I Will I Will For Now, The Naked Ape, The Mistress, 1987; TV film appearances include Last Hours Before Morning, 1975, Fantasy Island, 1977, The Night They Stole Miss Beautiful, 1977, Pleasure Palace, 1980, Not Just Another Affair, 1982; became theatrical agt., 1975; appeared in TV series Dallas, 1978-87; other TV appearances include Sixty Years of Seduction. Author: The Body Principal, The Beauty Principal, The Diet Principal. Office: care John Kimble Triad 10100 Santa Monica Blvd Los Angeles CA 90067

PRINGLE, BARBARA CARROLL, state legislator; b. N.Y.C., 1939; d. Nicholas Robert and Anna Joan (Woloshinovich) Terlesky; m. Richard D. Pringle, Nov. 28, 1959; children: Christopher, Rhonda. Student, Cuyahoga Community Coll. With Dunn & Bradstreet, 1957-60; precinct committeewoman City of Cleve., 1976-77; elected mem. Cleve. City Council, 1977-81, Ohio Ho. Reps., 1982—; mem. Ohio Ho. Reps. pub. utilities, ins., econ. devel., small bus., aging, and housing coms.; chair Fin.-Edn. subcom. 116th Gen. Assembly; mem. Ohio Power Siting Bd.; appointed vice chmn. ins. com. Econ. Affairs and Fed. Relations, Hwy. and Pub. Safety Com. Vol. Cleve. Lupus Steering Com.; vol. various community orgns. Mem. Nat. Order Women Legislators. Democrat. Address: 708 Timothy Lane Cleveland OH 44109

PRINGLE, DORA ROBERTA, nurse; b. Waldwick, N.J., Sept. 23, 1921; d. James Arthur and Olive May (Conklin) Lamb; m. Fulton Knight Singleton I, Oct. 24, 1942 (dec. 1959); children: Fulton Knight II, Diane J., William Edward, Pamela Ann; m. William Broadbent Pringle, Oct. 12, 1971 (dec.); 1 stepchild, Janice Pringle. Grad., Bklyn. Meth. Sch. Nursing, 1942; BS in Health Care Adminstrn., U. Santa Monica, 1984. RN, N.J. With Pascack Valley Hosp., Westwood, N.J., 1975—; rehab. nurse community health care projects Pascack Valley Hosp., Westwood, 1983—. Advocate pub. hearings N.J. Legis. Newworking Com., Trenton, 1984-86; adv. bd. Hayden Rehab. Agy., 1983-86. Mem. N.J. Assn. R.N.'s (chmn. legis. con. 1984—), Nat. Assn. Rehab. Nurses (mem. legis. com. 1986—), N.J. Assn. Rehab. Profls. Pvt. Sector, N.Y. Neurosci. Nurses. Republican. Methodist. Club: Pascack Valley Hosp. Stroke Recovery (coordinator). Home: 79 Riverdale St Hilsdale NJ 07642 Office: Pascack Valley Hosp Old Hook Rd Westwood NJ 07675

PRINTZ, BONNIE ALLEN, painter, photographer; b. Luray, Va., Apr. 12, 1946; d. Robert Leonard Jr. and Mildred Allen (Ward) P.; m. Daniel Alexander Gorski, June 26, 1971 (div. 1987); children: Kalika Theodora, Elektra Printz. BFA, Va. Commonwealth U., 1968; MA, Hunter Coll., 1970. Tech. asst. Mus. Modern Art, N.Y.C., 1968-70; faculty mem. Md. Inst. Coll. Art, Balt., 1972—; exhbns. include McIntosh/Drysdale Gallery, Washington, 1987, Open Space Gallery, Victoria, B.C., Can., 1978, Art Fair, Internat. Fair of Contemporary Art, Bologna, Italy, 1978, Corcoran Gallery of Art, Washington, 1979, 82, Polaroid Collaboratory, Victoria, 1979, Balt. Mus. Art, 1979, 80, 83, 85-86, William Penn Meml. Mus., Pa. State Women in the Arts, 1979, 80, 82, Va. Mus. Fine Arts, Richmond, 1980, 83, Pa. State Women in the Arts Invitational Exhbn., 1980, 82, 83. Profl. fellow in photography Va. Mus. Fine Arts, 1979-80; Alliance Ind. Colls. of Art grantee, 1985; Mellon grantee Md. Inst. Coll. Art, 1986; 1st place award Pa. Women in Arts, 1982; Yaddo, Saratoga Springs, N.Y., 1988. Lutheran. Home: 1104 Regester Ave Baltimore MD 21239 Office: Md Inst Coll of Art 1300 W Mt Royal Ave Baltimore MD 21217

PRIOLEAU, ELIZABETH STEVENS, writer, educator, public affairs executive; b. Richmond, Va., Nov. 14, 1942; d. Hugo Osterhaus and Adeline (Howle) Stevens; A.A., Bennett Coll., Millbrook, N.Y., 1962; B.S., U. Va., Charlottesville, 1966, M.A., 1972; Ph.D., Duke U., 1980; m. Philip Gendron Prioleau, Apr. 3, 1972. Asst. feature editor Charlottesville Daily Progress, 1963-64; instr. English, Fairleigh Dickinson U., 1980; lit. cons. Am. Jour. Dermatopathology, 1980—, John Barnes Prodns., 1980-81; public affairs dir. Marcel Breuer Assocs., N.Y.C., 1981-83; vis. scholar Inst. Research in History, 1981. Recipient Jean Besselievre Boley prize for fiction, 1963. Mem. MLA, Ind. Scholars in Lang. and Lit., Victorian Soc. Am., Lychnos Hon. Soc. Author: Circle of Eros, 1983. Contbr. articles to profl. jours. Home and Office: 1230 Park Ave New York NY 10028

PRIOR, DEBORAH ANN, insurance agent; b. Weisbaden, Fed. Republic Germany, Jan. 19, 1953; came to U.S., 1955.; d. Eugene Joseph and Ruth (Meskill) P. Contract analyst Aetna Life & Casualty, Hartford, Conn., 1976-84; asst. admininstr. Aetna Life & Casualty, Hartford, 1984-86; ins. agt. New York Life, Rocky Hill, Conn., 1986-88; prin. Prior Planning Fin. Services, 1988—. Republican. Home: 43 Valley Crest Dr Wethersfield CT 06109 Office: Prior Planning 43 Valley Crest Dr Wethersfield CT 06109

PRISK, PATRICIA, nurse, computer programmer and analyst; b. Troy, N.Y., Nov. 6, 1944; d. Harold George and Mary Alice (Murphy) Connor; m. William Prisk; children: William, Sandra, Kimberly, Rebecca, Sharon. Student, Hudson Valley Community Coll., 1962; RN, Samaritan Hosp. Sch. Nursing, 1965. Staff nurse Samaritan Hosp., 1965, Mt. Sinai Hosp., Hartford, Conn., 1966-69, Johnson Meml. Hosp., Stafford Springs, Conn., 1972-74; supr. Riverside Health Care Center, 1974-76; dir. nursing Middletown (Conn.) Health Care Center, 1976-81, staff nurse, 1981-82; staff nurse Lorraine Manor, Hartford, 1981-81; computer programmer Aetna Life and Casualty Co., Hartford, 1982-83; programmer analyst Hartford Ins. Co., 1983—; lectr., cons. in field. Mem. Conn. Assn. Health Care Facilities. Office: 1 Hartford Plaza Hartford CT

PRISOCK, KAY WHITT, import-export company executive; b. Houston, Miss., June 9, 1935; d. Kay and Rita Lee (Dill) Whitt; m. Lee V. Prisock, Apr. 14, 1959; 1 child, Kerry Lee. BS, Houston Hosp., 1958. Owner Jack & Jill Nursery and Kindergarten, Jackson, Miss., 1962-78, Bengal Imports, Jackson, 1965-71, North Am. Import & Export, Jackson, 1971—. Author cookbook, 1985. Candidate for senate State of Miss., 1976. Mem. Miss. Nurses Assn. Home: 4710 Old Canton Rd Jackson MS 39211 Office: Prisock Profl Bldg Corner North and Fortification Sts Jackson MS 39211

PRITCHARD, GAYLE SOPHIA, hospital human resources executive; b. Clovis, N.M., Dec. 23, 1943; d. Blanchard Lewis and Grace Virginia (Ott) P. BBA, West Tex. State U., 1976. Bookkeeper P.K. Supply, Inc., Amarillo, Tex., 1964-66; sec. Amarillo Hosp. Dist., 1964-68; sec. High Plains Bapt. Hosp., Amarillo, 1968-70, personnel coordinator, 1970-72, dir. personnel, 1972-85, v.p. human resources, 1985—; bd. dirs. Amarillo Fed. Credit Union. Adv. com. Amarillo Comprehensive Alcoholism Treatment, 1974-77; trustee Don Harrington Discovery Ctr., Amarillo, 1975-77; adv. bd. United Way Info. and Referral Service, Amarillo, 1981-83; bd. dirs. Children's Learning Ctrs., Amarillo, 1983-86. Mem. Am. Soc. Personnel Adminstrn., Tex. Soc. Hosp. Personnel Adminstrn. (bd. dirs. 1973-76), Panhandle Personnel Assn. (pres. 1983-84). Presbyterian. Office: High Plains Bapt Hosp 1600 Wallace Blvd Amarillo TX 79106

PRITCHARD, LOIS RUTH BREUR, engineer; b. Paterson, N.J., Mar. 26, 1946; d. George L. and Ruth Margaret (Farquhar) Breur; m. Bruce N. Pritchard, Aug. 10, 1968 (div. May 1982); children: John Douglas, Tiffany Anne; m. Robert H. Krause. Student, Keuka Coll., 1964-65; BS in Chemistry cum laude, Fairleigh Dickinson U., 1980; postgrad., Stevens Inst. Tech. With research and devel. dept. UniRoyal, Wayne, N.J., 1966-68, Jersey State Chemical Co., North Haledon, N.J., 1968-69, Inmont, Clifton, N.J., 1969; from chemist to sr. analyst Lever Bros., Edgewater, N.J., 1976-80; process engr. Bell Telephone Labs., Murray Hill, N.J., 1980-84, RCA, Somerville, N.J., 1984-86; sr. engr. electron beam lithography ops. Gain Electronics Corp., Somerville, 1986—; presenter profl. papers for profl. confs. Patentee package design. Troop leader, trainer, cons. Bergen County council Girl Scouts U.S., 1969-80, troop leader Morris Area council, 1980-83, head com. Mt. Olive twp., 1980-81; den leader, den leader coach, trainer Boy Scouts Am., 1973-76. Mem. IEEE, Components, Hybrids, and Mfg. Tech. Soc. (semicondr. tech. subcom. electronic components conf. program com. 1981-86), Soc. Photo-Optical Instrumentation Engrs., Am. Soc. for Quality Control, Soc. Women Engrs., Am. Chem. Soc., Am. Inst. Chemists, Assn. Women in Sci., AAAS, AAUW, Nat. Assn. for Female Execs., Mensa, Phi Omega Epsilon. Republican. Episcopalian. Home: 80 Lozier Rd Budd Lake NJ 07828

PRITCHARD-PULLINS, MARY LOU, home health care executive; b. Akron, Ohio, Dec. 13, 1948. Exec. dir. Buckeye Home Health Service Inc., Zanesville, Ohio, 1983—; seminar leader Nat. Assn. Home Health Care, Washington, 1987. Bd. dirs. Athens County Dept. Human Services, 1985, 86, 87; area coordinator Ohio Spl. Olympics, S.E. Ohio, 1987; vol. Planned Parenthood S.E. Ohio, 1985, 86, 87. Republican. Roman Catholic. Home: 32 Grosvenor St Athens OH 45701 Office: 860 Bethesda Dr Zanesville OH 43701

PRITT, MARILYN HARKINS, mortgage loan executive; b. Cleve., July 27, 1953; d. Wayne George and Ruth Naomi (Thiel) Harkins; m. James Bruce Pritt, May 28, 1972; children: Amy Lynn, Sara Beth. Student, Davis & Elkins Coll., 1971-72, Glenville State Coll., 1973-75. Lic. real estate agent, W.Va. Sec., W. Va. Bd. Regents, Charleston, 1978-79; computer operator McDonough-Caperton, Charleston, 1979-80; mortgage loan officer Home Mortgages, Inc., Charleston, 1980-82, mortgage br. mgr. 1982-83; mortgage loan officer Reliable Mortgage Co., Charleston, 1983-85; mortgage loan originator Magnet Mortgages, Inc., 1985—; fin. con. Area Real Estate Firms, Charleston, 1980—. Named to Million Dollar Club Home Mortgages, Inc., 1982-83, Best Loan Originator, Reliable Mortgage Co., 1983-84, 22 Million Dollar Loan Originator Reliable Mortgage Co., 1984-85. Mem. Women's Council of Realtors, Kanawha Valley Bd. Realtors. Republican. Avocations: aerobics, walking, cooking. Home: 122 Timberlake Circle Scott Depot WV 25560 Office: Magnet Mortgages Inc PO Box 167 Scott Depot WV 26650

PRIVOTT, JO A., real estate agent; b. Ahoskie, N.C., Jan. 19, 1953; d. Joseph and Ethel Faye (Minton) Andrusia; m. Steven David Privott, June 25, 1972 (div. Apr. 1983); 1 child, David Joseph. Grad., Realtor's Inst. Va., 1985. Sales assoc. Hometown Properties, Inc., Herndon, Va., 1984-87; sales assoc., assoc. broker Merrill Lynch Realty, Herndon, 1987; assoc. broker RE/MAX, 1988—. Mem. Realtors Active in Politics, Fairfax, Va., 1985—. Mem. No. Va. Bd. Realtors (speakers program 1986-88, profl. edn. subcom. 1987, profl. courtesy 1987), Nat. Assn. Realtors (instr. mid-yr. conv. 1987), Va. Assn. Realtors, Realtors Nat. Mktg. Inst. (council course promo subcom. 1987-88, council spl. events com. 1987-88), Women's Council Realtors. Republican. Home: 7 Awsley Ct Sterling VA 22170 Office: RE/MAX 20 Pidgeon Hill Dr #201 Sterling VA 22170

PROBASCO, PEGGY, lawyer; b. Ogden, Utah, Aug. 13, 1952; d. Robert Vere and Dorleen Elfrieda (Oppliger) P.; m. John Matthias Verburg, Dec. 18, 1972 (div.). Student, Weber State Coll., 1971-72, Utah State U., 1972-74, U. Utah, 1977-79; BA in Philosophy, U. Mont., 1980, JD, 1983. Bar: Mont. 1983. Unit mgr. Univ. Med. Ctr., Salt Lake City, 1975-81; inventory controller U. Mont., Missoula, 1981-82, research asst. Sch. Law, 1981-82; legal intern Petersen & Berndt, Missoula, 1982, Robinson, Doyle & Bell, Hamilton, Mont., 1982-83; assoc. Law Office of Gerald D. Schultz, Hamilton, 1983-86; staff atty. Dist. XI Human Resource Council, Inc., Missoula, 1985—; dep. county atty. Ravalli County, 1986-87; city judge, Stevensville, 1985-86; rep. Women's Law Caucus, Missoula, 1980-83; researcher Rocky Mountain Natural Resource Clinic, Missoula, 1981-83. Del. Utah Dem. Conv., Salt Lake City, 1972; candidate Mont. Ho. of Reps., 1984. Mem. ABA, Mont. Bar Assn., Assn. Trial Lawyers Am., Am. Judicature Soc., Mont. Magistrates Assn. (dist. chmn.), LWV, Phi Delta Phi. Lodge: Soroptimists (1st v.p.). Home: 629 N 5th West Missoula MT 59802 Office: 617 S Higgins Missoula MT 59801

PROBST, WILMA COHEN, government administrator; b. Perth Amboy, N.J., Sept. 28, 1944; d. Bernard and Ida (Stolz) Cohen; m. Peter S. Probst, May 14, 1967 (div. 1974). BA, Conn. Coll. Women, 1966. Research asst. Hist. Evaluation and Research Orgn., Washington, 1966-67; asst. dir. Washington Met. Area Jobs Council, 1968; chief program devel. Mayor's Econ. Devel. Com., Govt. Washington D.C., 1969, program analyst Mayor's Manpower Adv. Com., 1972-73; mgmt. cons. Internat. Paper Co., Inter-Am. Devel. Bank, Am. Tech. Assistance Corp., Tegucigalpa, Honduras, 1970-71; dir. alcohol abuse program, sr. staff assoc. Nat. League Cities, U.S. Conf.

Mayors, Washington, 1973-76; mgmt. analyst, intergovt. relations specialist U.S. Comm. Fed. Paperwork, Washington, 1976-77; policy coordination specialist U.S. Dept. Energy, Washington, 1977-82, intergovtl. relations mgr., 1984—; mgr. state govt. relations Panhandle Eastern Corp., Houston, 1982-83; pub. affairs cons. Houston, 1983-84; mem. tech. adv. com. Two-Way Express Transit Demonstration Project Washington Met. Area Council Govts., 1968. Contbr. numerous articles to various profl. jours. Precinct capt. Bd. Edn. Elections, Washington, 1968; co-chmn. subcom. employment D.C. Com. Status Women, 1974-75, task force consumer credit, 1973-74; mem. steering com. Mayor's Community Coordinated Child Care Program, Washington, 1968, Houston Ballet Guild, 1983-84, Alexandria (Va.) Environ. Policy Commn., 1986-88; bd. dirs., v.p. Brighton Sq. Neighborhood Assn., 1986-87; bd. dirs. U.S. Govt. Women's Assn. Honduras, 1970-71. Mem. Nat. Energy Resources Orgn. (v.p. 1981-82, treas. 1982), U.S. Jaycees (nat. adv. council op. THRESHOLD 1975-76), Washington Area State Govt. Relations Group, Houston C. of C. (govt. relations com. 1983-84), Houston Assn. Homebuilders (govt. relations com. 1984). Club: Tex. State Soc. (Washington). Office: US Dept Energy RW-233 1000 Independence Ave SW Washington DC 20585

PROCHNOW, VIRGINIA WILMA, insurance agent; b. Yakima, Wash., Mar. 30, 1935; d. Leonard M. and Wilma Louise (Radsek) P. AA, Yakima Valley Coll., 1955; BA cum laude, Pacific Luth. Univ., Tacoma, 1957. Pvt. practice music edn. Yakima, 1957—; ins. agt., securities rep. Luth. Brotherhood, Yakima, 1984—; dir. Daniel Pollack Summer Music Program, Yakima, 1977-85. Trustee Allied Arts Assn. Yakima, 1968-71, Yakima Community Concerts, 1965-66; treas. Coll. Concert Series, 1969-85; pres. Ladies' Music Club, 1974-75; organist Cen. Luth. Ch., Yakima, 1957—, dir. handbell choir, 1980—. Named to Leaders' Club Luth. Brotherhood, 1984, Exec. Club, 1985, 86, 87; recipient Quality Service award Nat. Assn. Fraternal Ins., 1987. Mem. Life Underwriters Assn. (Sales Achievement, Quality Achievement award 1985, 86), Fraternal Orgn. Ins. Counselors, Am. Guild Organists, Wash. State Music Tchrs. Assn. (state v.p. 1966-67, organ chmn., 1980-85). Home: 1420 S 34th Ave Yakima WA 98902 Office: Luth Brotherhood Chinook Tower 402 E Yakima Ave Suite 780 Yakima WA 98901

PROCIDANO, MARY ELIZABETH, psychologist, educator; b. New Rochelle, N.Y., Apr. 1, 1954; d. John D'Arge and Dorothy Diane (Utter) P.; m. Stephen Anthony Buglione, Aug. 9, 1986; 1 child, Daniel Stephen. BS summa cum laude with honors, Fordham U., 1976; PhD, Ind. U., 1981. Lic. psychologist. Research asst. Fordham-Yale Prison Research Project Fordham U., 1974-76; research asst. N.Y. State Psychiat. Inst., 1975; teaching asst. psychology Ind. U., Bloomington, 1976-79, assoc. instr., 1979-80; intern in clin. psychology Inst. of Living, Hartford, Conn., 1980-81; asst. prof. Fordham U., Bronx, N.Y., 1981—, also advisor, mem. various coms., asst. chair psychology dept., 1984-87, research assoc. Hispanic Research Ctr., 1984—, chair Inst. Rev. Bd. for Protection of Human Subjects, 1986—; mem. exec. com. psychology dept. Fordham U.; mem. Fordham Coll. Council. Contbr. articles to profl. and scholarly jours. Mem. Am. Psychol. Assn., Eastern Psychol. Assn., Assn. for Advancement of Behavior Therapy, Phi Beta Kappa, Psi Chi, Sigma Xi. Roman Catholic. Office: Fordham Univ Dept Psychology Bronx NY 10458

PROCOPE, ERNESTA GERTRUDE, insurance broker; b. Bklyn., Feb. 9; d. Clarence and Elvira Forster; m. John L. Procope, July 3, 1954. Student, Bklyn. Coll., Coll. Ins., Pohs Inst. Ins.; LLD (hon.) Adelphi U., Marymount Manhattan Coll., 1987, HHD (hon.) Morgan State U., 1978. Pres. E.G. Bowman Co. Inc., N.Y.C., 1953—, also chief exec. officer; dir. Avon Products, Inc., Chubb Corp., Columbia Gas Systems Inc.; panelist corp. governance and advancement of women Women's Bur., U.S. Dept. Labor, 1981; ambassador 10th Anniversary Independence Celebration, Republic of Gambia, 1975. Trustee N.Y. Zool. Soc., Cornell U., dir. adv. council Gov.'s office Mgmt. and Productivity, 1984—, Bus. Adv. Bd., 1984—. Recipient achievement award Thelma T. Johnson Meml. Scholarship Fund, 1972, bus. achievement award Interracial Council for Bus. Opportunity, 1973, Community Service award F & M Schaefer Brewing Co., 1974, Sojourner Truth award Negro Bus. and Profl. Women's Club, Inc., 1974, Bus. Achievement award Nat. Bus. League, 1976, Catalyst award Women Dirs. of Corps., 1977; honored as disting. black woman in corp. role Nat. Council Negro Women, Inc., 1981, also others. Mem. Nat. Assn. Ins. Brokers, Nat. Assn. Ins. Women, Women's Forum, Alpha Kappa Alpha (hon.). Presbyterian. Club: Cosmopolitan. Office: EG Bowman Co Inc 97 Wall St New York NY 10005

PROCTER, CAROL ANN, cellist; b. Oklahoma City, June 26, 1941; d. Leland Herrick and Alice (McElroy) P.; student Eastman Sch. Music, 1958-60; MusB, New Eng. Conservatory of Music, 1963, MusM, 1965. Cellist Springfield (Mass.) Symphony Orch., 1961-65, Cambridge (Mass.) Festival Orch., 1961-65, Boston Symphony Orch. and Boston Pops Orch., 1965—; cellist New Eng. Harp Trio; viola da gambist Curtisville Consortium, Stockbridge, Mass., 1974—; solo viola da gambist Boston Symphony Orch., 1976, 81, 85, Boston Pops Orch., 1980, 87. Mem. Japan Philharm. Cultural Exchange, 1969-70. Recipient Fulbright award, 1965; Fromm fellow, 1965. Mem. Assn. for Responsible Communication, Mu Phi Epsilon. Office: Boston Symphony Orch Symphony Hall Boston MA 02115

PROCTOR, BARBARA GARDNER, advertising agency executive, writer; b. Asheville, N.C.; d. William and Bernice (Baxter) Gardner; B.A. Talladega Coll., 1954; m. Carl L. Proctor, July 20, 1961 (div. Nov. 1963); 1 son, Morgan Eugene. Music critic, contbg. editor Down Beat Mag., Chgo., from 1958; internat. dir. Vee Jay Records, Chgo., 1961-64; copy supr. Post-Keyes-Gardner Advt., Inc., 1965-68, Gene Taylor Assos., 1968-69, North Advt. Agy., 1969-70; contbr. to gen. periodicals, from 1952; founder Proctor & Gardner Advt., Chgo., 1970—, now pres., chief exec. officer. Mem. Chgo. Urban League, Chgo. Econ. Devel. Corp. Bd. dirs. People United to Save Humanity, Better Bus. Bur. Cons. pub. relations and promotion, record industry. Recipient Armstrong Creative Writing award, 1954; awards Chgo. Fedn. Advt. Clubs, N.Y. Art Dirs. Club. Woman's Day; Frederick Douglas Humanitarian award, 1975; named Chgo. Advt. Woman of Year, 1974. Mem. Chgo. Media Women, Nat. Assn. Radio Arts and Sci., Women's Advt. Club, Cosmopolitan C. of C. (dir.), Female Execs. Assn., Internat. Platform Assn., Smithsonian Instn. Assos. Author TV documentary Blues for a Gardenia, 1963. Office: Proctor & Gardner Advt 111 E Wacker Dr Chicago IL 60601 *

PROCTOR, JEANETTA STARR, educational administrator; b. Winnsboro, Tex.; d. Robert Dorman Proctor and Jeanetta Beth (Ingram) Henrix. B.S. cum laude, Tex. Woman's U., 1979. Art dir. Oak Cliff Tribune, Dallas, 1964-68; continuity dir., producer, promotion mgr. KDTV-Channel 39, Dallas, 1968-73; owner Arabian Horse Farm, Susarr Farm, Lewisville, Tex., 1977-81; transp. supr. Lewisville Ind. Sch. Dist., 1981—; sec., pres.-elect North Tex. Assn. for Pupil Transp., Tex. Assn. Pupil Transp. Mem. Tex. State Tchrs. Assn., Alpha Chi, Alpha Kappa Delta. Democrat. Club: Humane Soc. (Lewisville). Avocations: building raquetball; tennis; animal rights. Home: 8005 Westover Dallas TX 75231

PROCTOR, PATRICIA ANN PEZANOWSKI, accountant; b. North Tarrytown, N.Y., Apr. 4, 1958; d. Joseph and Joan (Strieder) Pezanowski; m. Alan S. Proctor, Oct. 4, 1981. BS in Acctg., U. Bridgeport, 1980; cert. in computer literacy, So. Meth. U., 1986. Acct. Briar Electric, Inc., Croton-on-Hudson, N.Y., 1980-81; acct., cash mgmt. analyst Exxon Office Systems Co., Stamford, Conn., 1981-83; sr. staff acct. United Technologies Bldg. System, Irving, Tex., 1983-85; fin. acct. Dresser Industries, Inc., Dallas, 1985—. Volleyball coach YMCA, Arlington, Tex., 1985; recruiter U. Bridgeport, 1985—. Mem. Nat. Assn. of Accts., Am. Soc. Women Accts., Am. Bus. Womens Assn., U. Bridgeport Alumni Assn., U. Bridgeport Acctg. Roundtable, Omega Phi Alpha. Republican. Roman Catholic. Office: Dresser Industries Inc 1600 Pacific Dallas TX 75201

PROEFROCK, VICKI GAITHER, psychometrist; b. Bloomington, Ill., Sept. 18, 1947; d. Harold Victor and Grace Lucille (Phelps) Gaither; m. David Wayne Proefrock, June 20, 1970; children—Amy, Benjamin. Student Western Ill. U., 1965-66, Memphis State U., 1976-78; B.A., Augusta Coll., 1982. Med. technician Mercy Hosp., Urbana, Ill., 1967-72; med. technician Med. Coll. Ga., Augusta, 1972-74, psychometrist, 1980—; research chemist U. Tenn. Ctr. Health Scis., Memphis, 1975-80. Contbr. articles to profl. jours. Vice pres. Augusta Coll. Women, 1983-84; mem. ways and means com. Assn. Parents of Gifted, Columbia County, Ga., 1983-84; chmn. Friends of Ezekiel Harris, mem. Columbia County Democratic Com., 1982—; mem. Ga. Dem. Com., 1982—; mem. adv. bd. ga. Regional Hosp., Augusta, 1984—; mem. Community Leadership Program, Columbia, 1986—. Recipient de Treville award for hist. article Richmond County Hist. Soc., 1982, Modern Traditional Homemaker award State of Ga., 1987, Golden Key award Augusta Coll. Found. for Community Service, 1987; named to Outstanding Young Women Am., U.S. Jaycees, 1983, 84; named Modern Traditional Homemaker for State of Ga.; nat. merit scholar Western Ill. U., 1965. Mem. Augusta Area Psychol. Assn. (assoc.), Hist. Augusta, Augusta Coll. Alumni Assn. (bd. dirs. 1983—, Golden Key award 1987). Unitarian. Avocations: aerobic dancing; baking; historical research. Home: 4684 Oakley Pirkle Rd Martinez GA 30907 Office: Med Coll Ga Dept Pediatrics BIW 848 Augusta GA 30912

PROFIT, LORETHA SPURS, educator; b. Monroe, La., Aug. 15, 1947; d. James and Willie Mae (Kiper) Spurs; B.A., N.E. La. U., 1976; m. Simon Profit, Jr., June 6, 1966; children—Anthony Simeon, Adriane Sirena, Simon, III. Asst. mgr. Nelsons Drive In and Motel, Monroe, 1966-68, mgr., 1970-73, co-owner, 1980-84; substitute tchr., vol. tutor Ouachita Prish Sch. Bd., Monroe, 1968-69; paraprofl. Swayze Elem. Sch., Monroe, 1973-76; tchr. 2d grade Woodlawn Elem. Sch., W. Monroe, 1976—. Mem. NEA, La. Assn. Educators, Ouachita Assn. Educators (faculty rep.), Assn. Supervision and Curriculum Devel., Northeast La. Reading Assn., Classroom Tchrs. Assn., Internat. Platform Assn., Breeze Gospel Group, Delta Sigma Theta. Club: Order Eastern Star. Home: 4005 Gaston St Monroe LA 71203 Office: 5946 Jonesboro Rd Monroe LA 71291

PROJANSKY, LINDA FAITH, personnel executive; b. Chgo., Sept. 17, 1951; d. Morris and Marion Olga (Stern) P. BA in Sociology, U. Ill., Chgo., 1974; MS in Indsl. Relations, Loyola U., Chgo., 1981. Caseworker Ill. Dept. Pub. Aid, Chgo., 1974-76; social worker Ill. Dept. Children and Family Services, Chgo., 1976-78; employment interviewer Rush Presbyn.-St. Luke's Med. Ctr., Chgo., 1978-80; mgr. asst. regional personnel Wausau Ins. Co., River Forest, Ill., 1980-82; mgr. regional personnel West Orange, N.J., 1982-84; mgr. human resources Campbell-Mithun, Inc., Chgo., 1984—. Mem., tutor Lakeview Citizens Council, Chgo., 1987. Mem. Internat. Assn. Personnel Women (v.p. communications 1986-87), Bus. Tng. Edn. Adv. Mktg. Com., Rehab. Inst. of Chgo. (chair mktg. subcom.). Office: Campbell-Mithun Inc 737 N Michigan Ave Chicago IL 60611

PROPP, GAIL DANE GOMBERG, computer consulting company executive; b. N.Y.C., Mar. 22, 1946; d. Oscar and Goody (Rosenburgh) Dane; B.A. in Econs., Barnard Coll., 1965; m. Ephraim Propp; children—Eric Wesley, David Marc, Anna Michelle. Instr., programmer IBM Corp., N.Y.C., 1965-66; systems and programmer analyst R.S. Topas Co., N.Y.C., 1966-67; dir. systems and programming Abercrombie & Fitch Co., N.Y.C., 1967-69; dir. corp. data processing and MIS, 1969-77; founder, 1977, since pres. Met Data Systems, Inc., N.Y.C., 1977—; founder, pres. Datatype Internat. Inc, 1982—; assoc. dir. Burns Archive of Hist. Med. Photographs, N.Y.C., 1979—. Bd. overseers Bar-Ilan U., Israel. Mem. Internat. Council Computers in Edn., Women in Info. Processing, Assn. Systems Mgmt., Data Processing Mgmt. Assn., Assn. Systems Mgmt., Assn. Inst. Certification Systems Profls., Photog. History Soc. Am., Photog. Historic Soc. N.Y. Author articles in field. Office: 919 3d Ave New York NY 10022

PROPST, ANNABETH LADNY, statistician; b. Chgo., June 7, 1950; d. Howard E. and Lee Ann (Ladny) P.; m. Joseph R. Compton, Nov. 1, 1969 (div. Aug. 1973); children: Raymond Nelson, Heidi Ann. BS in Mgmt., No. Ill. U., 1976, MS in Applied Scis., 1978. Asst. liaison engr. Borg Warner Corp., Dixon, Ill., 1977-80, mfg. engr., 1980-82, plant statistician, 1982-84; sr. quality assurance engr. Amerock Corp., Rockford, Ill., 1984-86; sr. cons. JDQ Cons., Inc., Rockford, 1986-87; cons. Process Mgmt. Inst., Mpls., 1987—. Book reviewer Technometrics, 1986—. Advisor Jr. Achievement, Dixon, 1983-84, Rockford, 1985-86; cons. Project Bus., Rockford, 1986. Mem. Am. Soc. for Quality Control (chair conf. 1986—, newsletter pub. 1987—), Am. Statis. Assn. (SPES adv. bd. 1986—), Beta Gamma Sigma, Pi Mu Epsilon, Omicron Delta Kappa. Republican. Presbyterian. Home: 732 Parkview Ave Rockford IL 61107 Office: Process Mgmt Inst Inc 4801 E Bush Lake Rd Minneapolis MN 55435

PROSSER, DOWA DAYLE, marketing executive; b. Hemingway, S.C., July 4, 1953; d. Doward and Maude (Lambert) P.; m. Dean Lee Grussing, June 1979 (div. Mar. 1983). AS, Lake Sumter Community Coll. From catering sec. to convention services mgr. Atlanta Cen. Ramada Inn, 1976-78; program inst. Rainbow's End Drug Prevention Ctr., Tavares, Fla., 1979-81; catering coordinator Kiawah Island Co., Charleston, S.C., 1981; asst. food and beverage controller Am. Seafood Exchange, Cape Canaveral, Fla., 1983-84; regional sales mgr. Mission Inn Golf and Tennis Resort, Howey-in-the-Hills, Fla., 1984-85; dir. sales and mktg. The Lakeside Inn of Mt. Dora, Fla., 1985-86; asst. dir. sales and mktg. Sheraton Charleston Hotel, 1986—. Mem. Meeting Planners Internat., Cen. Fla. Soc. Assn. Execs., Va. Soc. Assn. Execs., Carolinas Soc. of Assn. Execs., S.C. Soc. Assn. Execs. Republican. Methodist. Home: 83 Ashley Ave Apt D Charleston SC 29401

PROST, MARY ROSE, law enforcement officer, lawyer; b. Detroit, June 11, 1947; d. John Peter and Aileen Theresa (Moroney) McGuinness; m. Patrick Francis Prost, Oct. 16, 1969 (div. Jan. 1986); 1 dau., Megan. B.A., Duquesne U., 1969; J.D., U. Detroit, 1980. Bar: Mich. 1981, U.S. Ct. Appeals (6th cir.) 1983, U.S. Supreme Ct. 1988. Police officer Detroit Police Dept., 1971-83, 3d dep. chief, 1983-86; 2d dep. chief, 1986— . Bd. dirs. Federated Council Domestic Violence Programs, Hazel Park, Mich., 1982; bd. dirs. Mcpl. Pub. Safety Consortium. Mem. Mich. Assn. Chiefs of Police, Mich. Bar Assn. Office: Detroit Police Dept 1300 Beaubien St Detroit MI 48226

PROTERO, DODI, soprano; b. Toronto, Can., Mar. 13, 1935; came to U.S., 1965; d. Stewart and Dorothy (Flaherty) McIlraith; ed. in Europe. Soprano with Vienna State Opera, Salzburg Festival, Glyndebourne Festival, Rome Opera, San Carlo Opera, Can. Opera, Vancouver Opera, San Antonio Opera, Pitts. Opera Co.; prof. voice U. Ill., Urbana, 1976-87; assoc. dir. voice Opera and Music Theater Inst. of N.J. Montclair State Coll., 1987—; tchr. pvt. voice students, N.Y.C., 1975—; prof. voice Banff (Alta.) Sch. Fine Arts. Can. Council fellow, 1965, 69, 73. Mem. Nat. Assn. Tchrs. of Singing, Equity, AFTRA, Am. Guild Musical Artists, Screen Actors Guild, Ill. State Music Tchrs. Assn. Recorded for Phillips Records on Epic Label; appeared in movie, Vienna City of My Dream, 1958. Home: 257 Central Park W Apt 12H New York NY 10024

PROUDFIT, CAROL MARIE, pharmacologist; b. Cin., Nov. 22, 1937; d. Robert James and Edna Carolyn (Hettesheimer) Lavell; m. Herbert K. Proudfit, Sept. 12, 1970 (div. 1981); 1 child, Amanda. BS, U. Cin., 1959; PhD, U. Kans., 1971; MBA, Rosary Coll., 1986. Lectr. Triton Coll., River Grove, Ill., 1974, Northwestern U., Evanston, Ill., 1975, U. Ill. Med. Ctr., Chgo., 1975—; sr. scientist AMA, Chgo., 1976—; reviewer drug monographs U.S. Pharmacopeia, Washington, 1984-87. Author (12 chpts.) Drug Evaluations, 1980, 83, 86; contbr. articles to profl. jours. Pres. Sounds of Joy Choristers, Oak Park, Ill., 1980-83; print chmn. Oak Park Camera Club, 1977-1979. Mem. Drug Info. Assn., Am. Fertility Soc., Am. Soc. Clin. Pharmacologists and Therapeutics, Am. Diabetes Assn. Office: Am Med Assn 535 N Dearborn St Chicago IL 60610

PROUDFIT, DONNA MAE, marketing executive; b. Washington, Iowa, Nov. 28, 1951; d. Donald Eugene and Virginia Ruth (Warden) P. BS in Journalism, Iowa State U., 1974. Asst. dir. pub. relations St. Luke's Hosp., Cedar Rapids, Iowa, 1974-78; from adminstrv. asst. to v.p. LaCrosse (Wis.) Luth. Hosp., 1978-85; v.p. mktg. Franciscan Health Services Washington, Tacoma, 1985—. Mem. allocations com. United Way, Tacoma, 1986—; bd. dirs. Pierce Co. Diabetes Assn., Tacoma, 1985—; mem. Tacoma Art Museum, 1986—, Jr. League. Named one of Outstanding Young Women in Am., 1984. Mem. Am. Mktg. Assn. (Distbn. award 1986), Internat. Assn. Bus. Communicators, Am. Soc. for Bus. Communications, Iowa State U. Alumni Assn. (bd. dirs. 1984—). Republican. Methodist. Office: Franciscan Health Services of Washington PO Box 2197 Tacoma WA 98401

PROUT, JOANNE CONNIE, marketing professional; b. Breda, The Netherlands, Nov. 19, 1949; came to Can., 1953; d. Adrian and Gertrude (Vreugde) Vanden Enden; m. Barry Leonard Prout; children: Barry John, Gavin, Nicole. Grad. high sch., Chatham, Ont., Can. Adminstrv. asst. N.Am. Life Ins., Toronto, 1970-73, automobile plan rep. McNaughton & Ward Ins., Surrey, B.C., 1973-74; br. clk. N.Am. Life Ins., Burnaby, B.C., 1974-75; sales rep. London Life Ins. Cos., Oshawa, Ont., 1985-87; mktg. mgr. The Employment Centre, Oshawa, 1987—. Trustee Durham Region Roman Cath. Sch. Bd., Oshawa, 1982-85; founder, exec. dir. 3d Thursday Women's Breakfast Network Durham Region, 1986—; founder, pres. St. Theresa Sch. Polit. Action Com., Whitby, Ont. Club: Whitby Curling (bd. dirs. 1987—).

PROVENCHER RYDER, FRANCES NORMA, public relations executive; b. Exeter, N.H., Apr. 22, 1947; d. Roger Arthur and Josette Marguerite (Camus) Provencher; m. Benjamin C. Ryder, Apr. 12, 1969 (div. Mar. 1979); 1 child, Tiffany Nicholas. BA, U. N.H., 1969. Clk. typist, editorial asst. U.S. Embassy, Moscow, 1964-65; asst. editor Durham (N.H.) Advertiser, 1965-69; assoc. editor Kaman Aerospace Corp., Bloomfield, Conn., 1970-71; publs. editor The Hartford Ins. Group (Conn.), 1974-76; pub. relations cons. Fran Ryder Assocs., Farmington, Conn., 1976-78; pub. relations account exec. Shailer Davioff Rogers, Inc., Fairfield, Conn., 1978-80; sr. account exec. Creamer Dickson Basford, Inc., Hartford, Conn., 1980-83; account group mgr., account exec. Spiro & Assocs., Phila., 1983-84, v.p., assoc. pub. relations dir., 1984-85; sr. v.p. pub. relations LSGE Advt. Inc., Avon, Conn., 1985-87; v.p. corp. communications Wondriska Assocs., Farmington, Conn., 1987—. Translator: The Cogito in Edmund Husserl's Phenomenology, 1969. Founder, The Art Guild, 1975; bd. dirs. Parent's Assn., Hartford Sch. Ballet, 1982-83, U. Conn. Found., 1986—. Recipient Gold Quill awards Internat. Assn. Bus. Communicators, 1974. Mem. Pub. Relations Soc. Am. (accredited; bd. dirs. 1980—, mem. Counselors Acad. 1982—, assembly del. 1987—, spl. commendation 1985). Republican. Congregationalist. Home: 38 Tunxis Village Farmington CT 06032 Office: 11 Talcott Notch Rd Farmington CT 06032

PROVENSEN, ALICE ROSE TWITCHELL, artist, author; b. Chgo.; d. Jay Horace and Kathryn (Zelanis) Twitchell; m. Martin Provensen, Apr. 17, 1944; 1 dau., Karen Anna. Student, Chgo. Art Inst., 1930-31, U. Calif., Los Angeles, 1939, Art Student League, N.Y., 1940-41; D.H.L. (hon.), Marist Coll., 1986. With Walter Lanz Studios, Los Angeles, 1942-43; OSS, 1944-45. Exhibited (with Martin Provensen), Balt. Mus., 1954, Am. Inst. Graphic Arts, N.Y., 1959, Botolph Group, Boston, 1964; books represented in Fifty Books of Yr. Selections, Am. Inst. Graphic Arts, 1947, 48, 52 (The Charge of the Light Brigade named Best Illustrated Children's Book of the Yr., N.Y. Times 1964, co-recipient Gold medal Soc. Illustrators 1960); Author, illustrator: books including Karen's Opposites, 1963, Karen's Curiosity, 1963, What is a Color?, 1967, (with Martin Provensen) Who's In the Egg, 1970, The Provensen Book of Fairy Tales, 1971, Play on Words, 1972, My Little Hen, 1973, Roses are Red, 1973, Our Animal Friends, 1974, The Year at Maple Hill Farm, 1978, A Horse and a Hound, A Goat and a Gander, 1979, An Owl and Three Pussycats, 1981, Town and Country, 1984, Shaker Lane, 1987; illustrator: (with Martin Provensen) children's books including Mother Goose Book, 1976, Old Mother Hubbard, 1977, A Peaceable Kingdom, 1978, The Golden Serpent, 1980, A Visit to William Blake's Inn, 1981, Birds, Beasts and the Third Thing, 1982, The Glorious Flight (Caldecott medal), 1984, The Voyage of the Ludgate Hill, 1987; also textbooks.

PROVENZALE, MARYELLEN KIRBY, judge, educator; b. Chgo., Dec. 21, 1938; d. Cornelius A. and Hanora (O'Sullivan) Kirby; children: Donald J. Jr., James P., John G., Patrick L. BA, Mundelein Coll., 1960; JD, DePaul U., 1977. Bar: Ill. 1977, U.S. Dist. Ct. (no. dist.) Ill. 1978. Asst. state's atty. DuPage County, Wheaton, Ill., 1977-85; assoc. judge Ill. 18th jud. cir. DuPage County, Wheaton, 1985—; instr. Criminal Law Coll. of DuPage, Glen Ellyn, Ill., 1987—; adj. prof. U. Ill. Police Tng. Acad. 1985, Nat. Law Inst., FBI Acad., Quantico, Va., 1985. V.p. Oak Creek Homeowners Assn., Downers Grove, Ill., 1974; mem. criminal justice adv. com., Coll. DuPage, Glen Ellyn, 1984—. Recipient award Glen Ellyn Family Shelter, 1984, Presdl. Excellence award State's Atty, DuPage County, 1979; presenter of Yr. Presdl. Excellence award, 1981. Mem. ABA, DuPage County Bar Assn., DuPage Assn. Women Lawyers. Roman Catholic. Home: 1225 Candlewood Dr Downers Grove IL 60515 Office: DuPage County 18th Jud Cir 201 Reber St Wheaton IL 60187

PROVIS, DOROTHY L., artist, sculptor; b. Chgo., Apr. 26, 1926; d. George Kenneth Smith and Ann Hart (Day) Smith Guest; m. William H. Provis, Sr., July 28, 1945; children: Timothy A., William H., Jr. Student Sch. Art Inst., Chgo., 1953-56, U. Wis.-Milw., 1967-68, 69-70. Sculptor Port Washington, Wis., 1963—; pres. bd. dirs. West Bend Gallery of Fine Arts, Wis., 1984-86, bd. dirs., 1987-89; speaker, presenter in field. Author, lobbyist Wis. Consignment Bill, Madison, 1979; panelist Women's Caucus for Art Conf., Phila., 1983; mem. adv. bd. Percent for Art Pro., 1985-87, Wis. Arts Bd. Wis. Arts Bd. Designer-Craftsmen grantee, NEA, 1981. Mem. Coalition of Women's Art Orgns. (del. to continuing com. Nat. Women's Conf. 1979, panelist conf. 1981, v.p. for membership/nominations, 1981-83, pres. 1983-85, nat. pres. 1985-87, v.p. communications 1987—, CWAO newsletter 1985—), Wis. Painters and Sculptors (pres. 1982-84, editor newsletter 1982-85), Wis. Women in Arts (legis. liaison 1978-80), Artists for Ednl. Action (corr. 1979-85), Wis. Designer Craftsmen, Women's Caucus for Art (presenter Nat. Sculpture conf. 1987, panelist, nat. women's conf. com. 1977-87), Chgo. Artists Coalition, Internat. Sculpture Ctr. Home and Studio: 123 E Beutel Rd Port Washington WI 53074

PROVOST, ELEANOR, county judge; b. Schenectady, N.Y., Aug. 22, 1947; d. Roger and Evelyn (Palme) P.; m. Albert H. Costa, Aug. 5, 1978. BA, U. Calif., Berkeley, 1969; JD, New Eng. Sch. Law, 1975. Bar: Calif., 1976. Dep. dist. atty. Tuolumne County, Sonora, Calif., 1977-82; judge Justice Ct. (4th jud. dist.) Tuolumne County, Groveland, Calif., 1982—. Mem. civic adv. bd. Sonora Community Hosp., 1984—; pres. Friends of Library, Sonora, 1987. Mem. Calif. Judges Assn., Calif. Women Lawyers. Democrat. Office: 4th Justice Ct PO Box 496 Groveland CA 95321

PROVOST, RHONDA MARIE, nurse anesthetist; b. Qunicy, Mass., Sept. 13, 1948; d. John Stanley and Roberta Adelaide (Tangstrom) P. RN, Qunicy City Hosp. Sch. Nursing, 1969, Nurse Anesthetist, 1971; BS, George Washington U., 1982. Cert. registered nurse anesthetist. Staff anesthetist, instr. Children's Hosp. Med. Ctr., Boston, 1971-77; staff anesthetist George Washington U. Med. Ctr., Washington, 1977-78; dir. Sch. of Anesthesia, New Eng. Med. Ctr. Hosp., Boston, 1978-79; staff anesthetist Kaiser-Permanente Med. Group, Redwood City, Calif., 1979—, chief anesthetist, 1988—; freelance anesthetist Pregnancy Counseling Ctr., San Jose, Calif., 1983-84, Plastic Reconstructive Ambulatory Ctr., Los Altos, Calif., 1984-85; treas. Specific Publs., Inc., 1983. Co-author: Indoor Exercise Book, 1981, Advanced Indoor Exercise Book, 1982, Feeling Fit in Your Forties, 1986; also articles; TV race commentator 2d Ann. Manila Internat. Marathon, 1983. Sec. bd. dirs. Grant Ave. Condominium Owners Assn., Palo Alto, Calif., 1984, v.p. bd. dirs., 1985. Mem. Am. Assn. Nurse Anesthetists, Calif. Assn. Nurse Anesthetists. Roman Catholic. Avocations: triathletics, piano, snow skiing, water skiing, horseback riding. Home: 107 Lilac Ln Saint Helena CA 94574 Office: Kaiser-Permanente Hosp 1110 Veteran's Blvd Redwood City CA 94063

PROVUS, BARBARA LEE, management consultant; b. Washington, Nov. 20, 1949; d. Severn and Birdell (Eck) P.; m. Fred W. Wackerle. Student N.Y. U., 1969-70; B.A., Russell Sage Coll., 1971; postgrad. Smith Coll., 1971; M.S.I.R., Loyola U., Chgo., 1979. Cons. exec. search and corp. mgmt. devel. Booz, Allen & Hamilton, Inc., Chgo., 1973-80; mgr. mgmt. devel. Federated Dept. Stores, Inc., Cin., 1980-82; v.p. Lamalie Assos., Inc., Chgo., 1982-86; prin. Sweeney Shepherd Bueschel Provus Harbert & Mummert, Inc., 1986—. Bd. dirs. Ill. Cancer Council. Mem. Human Resources Planning Soc., Anti-Cruelty Soc., Nat. Assn. Women Bus. Owners, Nat. Assn. Corp. and Profl. Recruiters. Club: Executives (Chgo.). Home: 3750 N Lake Shore Dr Chicago IL 60613 Office: Sweeney Shepherd Bueschel et al 1 S Wacker Dr Suite 2740 Chicago IL 60606

PRUETT, BARBARA ANN, nurse; b. Ft. Benning, Ga., Feb. 9, 1942; d. Frank Lewis and Margaret Lavata (Lane) Macomber; m. James Curtis Ammerman, Feb. 29, 1962 (div. 1964); m. 2d, John Kenneth Pruett, Sept. 3, 1965; children—Thomas Alan, Afton Elizabeth, Patrick Macomber. Diploma, J.F. Drake State Tech. Coll., Huntsville, Ala., 1979; A.S. Nursing, Calhoun Coll., 1982. R.N. Staff nurse Quality Care Nursing Service, Huntsville, Ala., 1979-81, Big Spring Manor, Huntsville, 1981-82, Kimberly Nursing Home, Huntsville, 1983-86, Bagwell Chiropractic Clinic, Huntsville, 1986-88; guidance counselor Faith Christian Acad., Huntsville, 1988—. Vol. worker Am. Cancer Telethon, Huntsville, 1965; vol. nurse Hospice Huntsville, 1979-81, Choose Life, 1985—; dir. nursing service ARC, Huntsville, 1979-83; dir. Women's Missionary Union, Southside Baptist Ch., 1985-86. Clubs: Mended Hearts, Touch (Huntsville). Democrat. Home: 1008 Edgewood Ave Huntsville AL 35801 Office: Faith Christian Acad 4315 Spartacus Dr Huntsville AL 35805

PRUETT, SHARON HENSON, petroleum landman; b. Houston, Jan. 8, 1941; d. V. Earl and Foy Lorene (Morton) Henson; diploma, Durham Bus. Coll., 1965; B.S. with honors, East Tex. State U., 1977, now postgrad.; children—Kevin Wayne, Nancy Caroline, Donna Lorene. Sec., Tex. Dept. Human Resources, Pittsburg, 1972-74; med. eligibility worker Tex. Dept. Human Resources, Quitman, 1974-79, proposal devel. specialist, regional planner, dir. data sect. Paris, 1979-80; ind. petroleum land rep., Tyler, Tex., 1980—; cons. Tex. Child Welfare Bds., 1980, Study of Child Welfare Staffing Issues, 1980—. Wood County Rep. Gov.'s Com. on Aging, 1974; sec. ARC, 1973; active PTA. Mem. East Tex. Assn. Petroleum Landmen, Am. Soc. for Public Adminstrn., Nat. Assn. Female Execs., Acad. Polit. Sci., NOW, East Houston Athletic Assn., Pi Sigma Alpha. Contbr. articles to profl. jours. Address: PO Box 764 Quitman TX 75783

PRUITT, ANITA C., medical records technician; b. Cleve., July 23, 1946; d. Lewis F. and Geneva (Manley) Nalls; m. Melvin Wheeler, June 4, 1966 (div.); children: Keith D., Lauren M., Michael J.; m. Robert Pruitt, Oct. 17, 1987. AS, Cuyahoga Community Coll., Cleve., 1976. Med. records technician Mt. Sinai Hosp., Cleve., 1976-78; coordinator med. corr. Kaiser Health Plan, Cleve., 1978—. Vol. Cleve. Area Project LEARN, Literacy Coalition Inc., Laubach Literacy Action, Hunger Project, Nat. Polit. Congress of Black Women. Mem. Am. Med. Records Assn. (cert.), Ohio Med. Records Assn., N.E. Ohio Med. Records Assn. (chair pub. relations com. 1988). Democrat. Episcopalian. Office: Kaiser Med Services 50 Severance Circle Cleveland OH 44118

PRUITT, DOROTHY J. GOOCH, educational administrator; b. Granville County, N.C., June 10, 1935; d. Edgar N. and Lorine (Henley) Gooch; m. William Leonard Pruitt, July 22, 1958. BS, East Carolina U., 1956; MEd, U. N.C.-Chapel Hill, 1971; sixth yr. cert. Nova U., 1984, EdD, 1985. Home econs. tcr. Granville County Schs., Oxford, N.C., 1956-69; cons. State Dept. Pub. Instrn., Raleigh, N.C., 1972-82; prin. Granville County Schs., 1982—. Bd. dirs. N.C. Sch. Bd. Assn., Raleigh, 1980-82; chmn. Granville County Bd. Edn., 1979-82; v.p. Jr. Woman's Club, Oxford, 1965-66 (named Club Woman of Yr. 1965). Named Granville County Prin. of Yr., 1987-88. Mem. N.C. Assn. Sch. Adminstrs., Am. Sch. Curriculum Devel. Assn., Am. Sch. Curriculum Assn., Am. Ednl. Research Assn., N.C. Future Homakers of Am. (hon.), Alpha Delta Kappa (corr. sec. 1970). Baptist. Home: 106 Country Club Dr Oxford NC 27565 Office: Granville County Schs 223 College St Oxford NC 27565

PRUITT, KATHY LEE, systems analyst; b. Roanoke, Va., Feb. 4, 1954; d. Lewis Edward and Mary Ivalee (Furrow) Pruitt. Grad. high sch., Roanoke. Keynote operator Wometco, Roanoke, 1972-74, Atlantic Cos., Roanoke, 1974-75; with Community Hosp. of Roanoke Valley, 1975-88, programmer, 1983-84, programmer, analyst, 1984-86, systems analyst, 1987-88; systems engr. Computer Task Group, Roanoke, 1988—. Mem. Am. Mgmt. Assn., Nat. Assn. Female Execs. Democrat. Baptist. Office: Computer Task Group Inc 4502 Starkey Group SW Suite 200-A Roanoke VA 24014

PRUTZMAN, PENELOPE ELIZABETH, educator; b. Vancouver, Wash., Apr. 25, 1944; d. Delbert Daniel and Jessie May (Lowry) P. BA in Sociology, CUNY, 1975; diploma, Grand Diplôme Cooking Sch. Tchr. Mt. Carmel-Holy Rosary Sch., N.Y.C., 1968—. Active Vol. Services for Children, N.Y.C., 1980-83. Recipient 10 Yr. Service to Cath. Schs. of Harlem award Office of Supt. Sch. Archdiocese of N.Y., 1979, 20 Yrs. to Cath. Sch. award Archdiocese of N.Y., 1986; named one of Outstanding Elem. Tchrs. of Am., 1974. Mem. Fedn. Cath. Tchrs. (exec. council 1974—, negotiating com., Cert. of Honor 1982), Nat. Cath. Edn. Assn., Reading Reform Found. Democrat. Episcopalian. Home: 35-25 34 St C44 Astoria NY 11106 Office: Mt Carmel-Holy Rosary Sch 371 Pleasant Ave New York NY 10035

PRYATEL, HOLLY ANN, compensation and benefits executive; b. South Bend, Ind., Apr. 1, 1948; d. Frank John and Lillian May (Holley) P. B in History, Am. U., 1971, MBA, 1977. Cert. compensation profl., employee benefits specialist. Employee relations specialist COMSAT, Washington, 1978-79, personnel info. specialist, 1979-81, supr. personnel systems and records, 1981-82, compensation cons., 1982-83; mgr. compensation and benefits Ctr. Naval Analyses, Alexandria, Va., 1984-88, Dialcom, Inc., Rockville, Md., 1988. Contbr. article to profl. jour. Mem. Washington Personnel Assn. (v.p. 1988—), Washington Tech. Personnel Forum, Nat. Council of Career Women (career day com. 1984, nominating com. 1988), Washington Area Recreation and Employee Services Council (v.p. 1979). Republican. Lutheran. Home: 14905 Bradwill Ct Rockville MD 20850 Office: Dialcom Inc 6120 Executive Blvd Rockville MD 20852

PRYOR, ANNIE RUTH, nurse, real estate broker; b. Ariton, Ala., Oct. 25, 1936; d. Homer and Fannie (Kelley) Pryor. A.A., Wilson Coll., 1954; R.N., Grant Hosp. Sch. Nursing, 1957; continuing edn. U. Chgo., 1960, West Valley Coll., 1981. Cert. perioperative nurse. Operating room nurse U. Chgo. Hosp., 1957-65, head nurse, 1965-66, supr. clin. instrn., 1966-67; operating room nurse Sequoia Hosp., Redwood City, Calif., 1967-68; office nurse, asst. to pvt. physician, Carmel, Calif., 1968-69; operating room nurse Los Gatos Community Hosp., Calif., Good Samaritan Hosp., San Jose, Calif., 1968-75; owner, broker Vasona Properties & Investments, Campbell, Calif., 1982—. Mem. O'Connor Hosp. Aux., San Jose, 1973—; sponsor Explorer project Post 850, Boy Scouts Am., 1983—; mem. adv. council Sta. KRON-TV, San Francisco. Mem. Nat. Assn. Realtors, Calif. Assn. Realtors, Calif. Assn. Operating Room Nurses, Nat. Assn. Operating Room Nurses, Republican. Baptist. Avocations: painting; tennis; knitting. Home and Office: Vasona Properties & Investments 671 Division St Campbell CA 95008

PRYOR, KAREN WYLIE, biologist, writer; b. N.Y.C., May 14, 1932; d. Philip Gordon Wylie and Sally Ondeck; m. Taylor A. Pryor, June 25, 1954 (div. 1973); children: Tedmund, Michael, Gale; m. Jon M. Lindbergh, May 14, 1983. BA in English, Cornell U., 1954; postgrad., U. Hawaii, 1957-59, NYU, 1977-79, Rutgers U., 1979-82. Founder, curator Sea Life Park Oceanarium, Honolulu, 1960-71; copywriter Fawcett-McDermott, Honolulu, 1973-76; drama critic Honolulu Advertiser, 1971-75; free lance writer 1963—, marine mammal cons., 1970—; sci. advisor U.S. Tuna Found., Washington, 1976-82; cons. NSF, NASA, Nat. Geographic Soc., 1976—; commr. Marine Mammal Commn., Washington, 1984-87. Author: Nursing Your Baby, 1963, rev. edit. 1973, Lads Before the Wind: Adventures in Porpoise Training, 1975, Don't Shoot the Dog! The New Art of Teaching and Training, 1984 (Excellence in Media award Am. Psychol. Assn. 1984), How to Teach Your Dog to Play Frisbee, 1985; contbr. articles to profl. jours. Mem. Internat. Marine Amimal Trainers Assn., Authors Guild, Marine Mammal Soc. (charter mem.), Soc. Women Geographers, Soc. Marine Mammalogy. Club: Cosmopolitan (N.Y.). Home: 44811 SE 166 St North Bend WA 98045

PRYOR, SUSAN ROBERTS, interpreter; b. Norfolk, Va., May 9, 1959; d. Benjamin Irving and Marie Celeste (Kemp) R. BS in History, Radford U., 1981. Visitor aide Col. Williamsburg Found., Williamsburg, Va., 1981-83; craft interpreter Col. Williamsburg Found., Williamsburg, 1983-84, skilled craft interpreter, 1984—. Contbr. articles to profl. jours. Mem. Am. Assn. for the History of Medicine. Home: 142 King Henry Way Williamsburg VA 23185 Office: Col Williamsburg Found Pasteur & Galt Apothecary Shop Williamsburg VA 23185

PRZELOMSKI, ANASTASIA NEMENYI, newspaper editor; b. Cleve., Dec. 11, 1918; d. Ernest Nicholas and Anna (Ress) Nemenyi; m. Edward Adrian Przelomski, July 4, 1946. A.B., Youngstown State U., 1939; M.Ed., U. Pitts., 1942. Tchr. Youngstown Pub. Sch., Ohio, 1939-42; reporter Vindicator, Youngstown, 1942-57, asst. city editor, 1957-73, city editor, 1973-76, mng. editor, 1976—. Named Woman of Yr., Youngstown Bus. and Profl. Women's Club, 1977, bus. category Woman of Yr., YWCA, 1986; recipient Community Service award Youngstown Fedn. Women's Clubs, 1981, Woman of Yr. award YWCA, 1983; named to Ohio Woman's Hall of Fame, 1986. Mem. AP Mng. Editors Assn., UPI Ohio Editors Assn. (bd. dirs. 1984—), Ohio Assn. AP, Ohio Soc. Newspaper Editors, Youngstown State U. Alumni Assn. (trustee 1978-83) Catholic Collegiate Assn., Phi Kappa Phi. Republican. Roman Catholic. Home: 2261 Cordova Ave Youngstown OH 44504 Office: The Vindicator Printing Co Vindicator Sq PO Box 780 Youngstown OH 44501-0780

PRZYBYLOWICZ, CAROLYN LYON, controller, personnel administrator; b. Clare, Mich., Jan. 18, 1947; d. Aaron Eugene and Alice Marie (Fall) Prout; m. Stanley George Lyon, July 13, 1968 (dec. May 1971); children: Lori Anne Lyon, Jamie Lynn Lyon; m. Dennis Karl Hunt, Jan. 1975 (div. Nov. 1977); 1 child, Julie Marie Hunt Przybylowicz; m. Arthur Roy Przybylowicz, Nov. 3, 1979. Cert. acctg., Lansing Bus. U., 1965. Bank teller Citizens Bank & Trust, Rosebush, Mich., 1965-68; bookkeeper, sec. Doyle & Smith P.C., Lansing, Mich., 1968-74; legal sec. Foster, Swift, Collins & Coey P.C., Lansing, 1974-79; mgr. office ARC, Lansing, 1979-81; controller, personnel adminstr. Mich. Protection & Advocacy Service, Lansing, 1981-88; bus. adminstr. White, Beekman, Przybylowicz, Schneider & Baird, P.C., Okemos, Mich., 1988—. Vol. bookkeeper Citizens Alliance to Uphold Spl. Edn., Lansing, 1977-79; coordinator bingo IHM Sch., Lansing, 1979-80; mem. St. Casimir Christian Service, Lansing, 1981-84, chairperson, 1983-84; bd. dirs. Immaculate Heart of Mary Sch., Lansing, 1977-80. Democrat. Roman Catholic. Office: White Beekman Przybylowicz Schneider & Baird PC 2214 University Park Dr Suite 200 Okemos MI 48864

PUBANZ, JAN CHRISTINA, small business owner; b. San Bernardino, Calif., Apr. 13, 1950; d. Harold James Dixon and Jane Anna (Bedford) Kennedy; m. Charles Freitas III, Oct. 12, 1975 (div. 1985); children Corey James, Ka'le Elihu; m. Charles Louis Pubanz, Apr. 11, 1987. Student, U. Hawaii, Hilo, 1972-73. Lic. real estate agt., Hawaii. Co-owner Calif. Steel Erection Co., Huntington Beach, Calif., 1968-72, Structural Steel Erection Co., San Leandro, Calif., 1968-72; prodn. sec. Crane Hoist Engring. Co., San Leandro, 1971-72; payroll bookkeeper Crane Hoist Engring. Co., Downey, Calif., 1972-73; bookkeeper Herk's Tavern, Hilo, Hawaii, 1973-74; advt. rep. Hawaii Tribune-Herald, Hilo, 1974-78; sales rep. Burke Concrete Co., Hilo, 1979-80; advt.-promotions mgr. Sure Save Super Markets, Hilo, 1980-81; pres., owner Big Island Roofing, Inc., Hilo, 1981—. Mem. Nat. Assn. Female Execs., Nat. Fedn. Ind. Bus., Constrn. Industry Legis. Orgn., Hawaii Island Contractors' Assn., Kanoelehua Area Indsl. Assn. (bd. dirs. 1987—), Nat. Roofing Contractors Assn. Democrat. Club: Big Island Press. Home: 786-A Ko'ele St Hilo HI 96720 Office: Big Island Roofing Inc 424 Kanoelehua Ave Hilo HI 96720

PUCCINO, SUZANNE, wholesale travel executive; b. Bklyn., May 9, 1957; d. John Joseph Puccino and Roslyn (Newmark) Rubin; m. Marc Neil Hildebrand, Mar. 16, 1980. Cert., New Sch. Social Research, 1978; student, Queens Coll. Reservationist, then ops. supr. Arthur Frommer Internat., N.Y.C., 1976-82; gen. mgr. Lotus Tours, N.Y.C., 1982-84; dir. ops. Fantasy Holidays, Inc., Jericho, N.Y., 1984-86; pres. All State Bus Travel Corp., Bklyn., 1986—. Recipient award CORE, Bklyn., 1984. Mem. Am. Soc. Travel Agents, Nat. Tour Assn., Bklyn. C. of C. Democrat. Club: Flushing Meadow (sec. 1980-83). Home: 77-14 113th St Forest Hills NY 11375 Office: All State Tours Inc 26 Court St Brooklyn NY 11242

PUFF, JEAN ELLINGWOOD, civic worker; b. Evanston, Ill., July 25, 1924; d. Lloyd and Margaret (Brown) Ellingwood; B.S. in Nursing, Northwestern U., 1947; m. Henry B. Puff, June 10, 1950; children—James Raymond, Margaret Elizabeth. Nurse, student health service, Northwestern U., Evanston, Ill., 1947-48; Pres. Gov. Wentworth Arts Council, N.H., 1973-81 ; bd. dirs. Wolfeboro (N.H.) Playhouse, 1975—; vol. Delta Gamma vision screening, Buffalo, 1960-65, Buffalo Philharmonic, 1959-69; mem. Huggins Hosp. Aid (Wolfeboro). Mem. Evanston Hosp. Alumni Assn., Northwestern U. Alumni Assn., Republican Women's Fedn., Delta Gamma. Presbyterian. Clubs: Lakes Region Tennis. Home: Box 743 Springfield Point Wolfeboro NH 03894

PUGH, CLAUDIA ANN, accountant; b. San Bernardino, Calif., May 31, 1947; d. Claude Aaron and Loyce Lillian (Brown) Norton; m. Lloyd Douglas Martin, Feb. 26, 1966 (div. Nov. 1975); children: John Eric, Christopher Scott; m. William Reibert Pugh, Dec. 6, 1975. AS Magna Cum Laude, Lord Fairfax Coll., Middletown, Va., 1986. Sales rep. Sta. WFFV-FM radio, Middletown, 1974-75; sales clk. Winchester (Va.) Book Gallery, 1975-76; acctg. clk. Southland Corp., 1976; owner, ptnr. Bayliss Market and Gift Shop, Winchester, 1976-81; asst. to controller Arthur Fulton, Inc., Stephens City, Va., 1982-83; sec. treas. Pugh Enterprises, Inc., Wincester, 1983—; sec., treas. Borror and Pugh Enterprises, Inc., Winchester, 1984—; pres. Uniglobe Ultimate Travel Inc., Winchester, 1988—. Mem. Nat. Assn. Female Execs. Democrat. Club: Exchange (Shenandoah Valley). Home: 1889 Wayland Dr Winchester VA 22601 Office: Uniglobe Ultimate Travel Inc 121 Weems Ln Winchester VA 22601

PUGH, MARTHA GREENEWALD, lawyer; b. Washington, Feb. 1, 1913; d. Eugene Ludwig and Mary Martha (Curtis) Greenewald; m. Wallace R. Pugh, Aug. 29, 1935 (div. 1945); children—John Clifford, William Wallace; m. 2d, Wallace R. Pugh, Aug. 29, 1975. B.A. in Physics, U. Colo., 1934; M.S. in Physics, U. Mich., 1936; J.D., Seton Hall U., 1961. Bar: D.C. 1964, U.S. Ct. Appeals (D.C. cir.) 1964, N.J. 1965, U.S. Dist. Ct. N.J. 1965, U.S. Ct. Customs and Patent Appeals 1966, U.S. Ct. Appeals (3d cir.) 1966, U.S. Supreme Ct. 1977, U.S. Patent Office 1947. Instr. physics NYU, N.Y.C., 1941-43; mem. patent staff Bell Telephone Labs., Murray Hill, N.J., 1943-67; patent agt. Gulton Industries, Metuchen, N.J., 1957-58; patent agt., Summit, N.J., 1958-64; sole practice, Summit, 1964-81; ptnr. Mathews, Woodbridge, Goebel, Pugh & Collins, Morristown, N.J., 1981—. Author article Jour. Patent Office Soc. Mem. Coalition for Nuclear Freeze, 1983—. Mem. N.J. Bar Assn. (chmn. patent sect. 1976-77), Union County Bar assn. (trustee 1976-78), ABA, N.J. Patent Law Assn. (2d v.p. 1984, treas. 1985, sec. 1986, 1st v.p. 1987, pres.-elect 1988), Am. Patent Law Assn., Nat. Assn. Women Lawyers, Women Lawyers of Union County, Nat. Soc. Inventors (council), Mortar Bd., Sigma Pi Sigma, Kappa Beta Pi, Pi Beta Phi. Democrat. Unitarian. Club: Green Mountain. Office: Mathews Woodbridge Goebel Pugh & Collins 22 Park Pl PO Box 112M Morristown NJ 07960

PUGH, NELDA JORDAN, business administrator educator; b. Birmingham, Ala., Aug. 5, 1935; d. Gordon Brookins and Nell (Jones) Jordan; m. Tillman William Pugh Jr., Dec. 18, 1954; children—Gordon Irwin, Tillman W., III (dec.). B.S., Samford U., 1955; M.A., U. Ala., 1961; postgrad., Cumberland Sch. Law, 1970-1972; Ed.D., Nova U., 1981. Instr. Jefferson County, Birmingham, 1965-69; educator Jefferson State Coll., Birmingham, 1969—; speaker Civic orgns., Birmingham, 1980—; active Ala. Symphony Assn., 1985—; capt. Heart Sunday Drive, Birmingham, 1988; sponsor Women on the Way, Birmingham, 1979-83; coordinator Ala. Bus. Communication Assn., 1983. Editor newsletter Jordans Journeys, 1980—; textbook editor. Seminar coordinator Winners Circle, Jamaica, 1981, YMCA, Birmingham, 1980. Mem. Nat. Bus. Law Assn., Am. Bus. Communication Assn. (proceedings reviewer 1984), Nat. Bus. Edn. Assn., Women's Com. of 100 for Birmingham, Inc., Depta Pi Epsilon. Republican. Baptist. Club: Internat. Toastmistress (treas., pres., v.p., sec., del., 1976—). Avocations: genealogy, needlework. Home: 3723 Brookwood Rd Birmingham AL 35223-1538 Office: Jefferson State Coll 2601 Carson Rd Birmingham AL 35215

PUGLIESE, BARBARA WIERCIOCH, research and analysis co. exec.; b. Lowicz, Poland, Apr. 1, 1941; came to U.S., 1949, naturalized, 1959; d. Henryk and Ludwika (Gostkiewicz) Wiercioch; B.A. cum laude in Math., Conn. Coll. for Women, 1963; m. William Pugliese, Aug. 15, 1973. Programmer, mathematician Naval Underwater Systems Center, New London, Conn., 1959-63, ops. research analyst, 1963-67; sr. systems analyst (sonar-tactics) Marine Research Lab., Raytheon Corp., New London, 1967-69; sr. v.p., mgr. effectiveness analysis dept., plank owner Analysis and Tech., Inc., North Stonington, Conn., 1969-81; pres. BWP Cons., 1981—; cons., instr., lectr. on mil. ops. research, navy tactics, tactical and strategic measures of effectiveness and performance exercise/operational design and analysis. NSF grantee, 1962-63. Mem. Mil. Ops. Research Soc., Am. Def. Preparedness Assn., Nat. Security Indsl. Assn., U.S. Naval Inst., Am. Mgmt. Assn. Republican. Contbr. articles on naval ops. to profl. jours.

PUGLIESE, RANADA MARIE, nurse; b. Cleve., Sept. 22, 1950; d. Joan Lee Green; divorced; 1 child, Kathryn Marie. AA, Los Angeles Valley Coll., 1974; student, Pepperdine U., 1981-82, U. San Francisco, 1985. Nurse emergency and ICU St. Joseph Hosp., Burbank, Calif., 1968-76; asst. dir. emergency services Brotman Hosp., Los Angeles, 1976-78; clin. instr. Stanford (Calif.) U., 1978-80; dir. emergency services White Meml. Hosp., Los Angeles, 1980-82; coordinator base sta. UCLA, Los Angeles, 1982-84; program dir. Calstar, 1984-87. Mem. Emergency Nurses Assn. (pres. local chpt. 1987-78), Flight Nurse Assn., Critical Care Nurses Assn.

PUGLISI, ANGELA AURORA, educator, consultant, artist; b. Messina, Italy, Jan. 28, 1949; came to U.S., 1954, naturalized, 1980; d. Vittorio and Carmela (Alizzi) P. B.A. cum laude, Dunbarton Coll., 1972; M.F.A., Cath. U., 1974, M.A. in Art History, 1976, M.A. in Modern Langs and Lit., 1977, Ph.D. in Comparative Lit., 1983. Art instr. Cath. U., Washington, 1974-84, lectr. modern langs., 1984-85; cons., writer U.S. Dept. Edn., Washington, 1983-85; faculty fine arts Georgetown U. Sch. Continuing Edn., Washington; asst. to dean Am. U., 1988—; various exhbns. of works, 1972-84. Author poetry: Nature's Canvas, 1984, Homage, 1984, Sonnet I, 1985, Primavera, 1986, Ocean Waves, 1986, Sand Dunes, 1986, The Sun's Journey, 1986, Prelude, 1987, Jet d'Eau, 1987; Woodland Revisited, 1988; art work in pvt. collections. Founding mem. Italian Cultural Ctr., Washington; bd. dirs. Edn. Enterprises. Mem. Nat. Assn. Female Execs., Nat. Mus. of Women in Arts (charter), Corcoran Gallery Art Assocs. Republican. Roman Catholic. Avocations: writing, sculpting.

PULITANO, CONCETTA NORIGENNA, corporate professional; b. Sicily, Italy, June 16, 1941; came to U.S., 1947, naturalized, 1948; d. Umberto and Benedetta (Triassi) Norigenna; student public schs., North Miami, Fla.; m. Francis Joseph Pulitano, Dec. 29, 1962; children: Maria Anne, Margaret Theresa, Angela Marie. Sec., Ka-Line Pool Products, Hialeah, Fla., 1959-61, Westinghouse, Balt., 1961, Bendix Communications, Balt., 1961-63; student council moderator, sec., learning center coordinator Cathedral Sch., Balt., 1974-83; sec., word processor operator Md. Agy., Balt., 1983-85, adminstrv. asst., 1988—; exec. sec. Comp-U-Staff, Inc., 1985-88; adminstrv. asst. Md. Agy., Balt., 1988—. Democrat. Roman Catholic. Club: Valley Country.

PULITZER, EMILY S. RAUH (MRS. JOSEPH PULITZER, JR), museum administrator; b. Cin., July 23, 1933; d. Frederick and Harriet (Frank) Rauh. A.B., Bryn Mawr Coll., 1955; student, Ecole du Louvre, Paris, France, 1955-56; M.A., Harvard, 1963. Mem. staff Cin. Art Mus., 1956-57; asst. curator drawings Fogg Art Mus., Harvard, 1957-64, asst. to dir., 1962-63; curator City Art Mus., St. Louis, 1964-73; mem. painting and sculpture com. Mus. Modern Art, 1975—; chmn. visual arts com. Mo. Arts Council, 1976-81; co-chmn. fellows Fogg Art Mus.; mem. bd. Inst. Mus. Services, 1979-84; commr. St. Louis Art Mus., 1981—, vice chmn., 1988—. Bd. dirs. 1st St. Forum, St. Louis, 1980—, Mark Rothko Found., 1976—, Arts in Transit Com., East-West Gateway Coordinating Council, 1987—. Mem. Am. Fedn. Arts (dir. 1976—). Home: 4903 Pershing Pl Saint Louis MO 63108

PULLEN, LETTIE MAE, health facility administrator; b. Forest, Va., Aug. 21, 1937; d. Victor John Henry and Mary Frances (Younger) Jones; m. Thomas Pullen Jr., Nov. 11, 1961; children: Jerri P. Jones, Jackie P. Carson, Carol A., Thomasena V., JoAnn. Grad. high sch., Bedford, Va., 1958. Cert. site mgr. Bedford Nutrition Ctr., Lynchburg, Va., 1977—. Columnist Bedford Bulletin, 1984, actress Little Town Players, 1985—; singer Bedford Choral Soc., 1985—. Dir. pledge ctr. Muscular Dystrophy Assn., Bedford, 1980—; outreach worker Total Action Against Poverty, 1969-72, Lynchburg Community Action Group, 1973-77. Democrat. Baptist.

PULLEN, PENNY LYNNE, state legislator; b. Buffalo, Mar. 2, 1947; d. John William and Alice Nettie (McConkey) P.; B.A. in Speech, U. Ill., 1969. TV technician Office Instructional Resources, U. Ill., 1966-68; community newspaper reporter Des Plaines (Ill.) Pub. Co., 1967-72; legislative asst. to Ill. legislators, 1968-77; mem. Ill. Ho. of Reps., 1977—, chmn. ho. exec. com., 1981-82, minority whip, 1983-87, asst. minority leader, 1987—; mem. Pres.'s Commn. on AIDS Epidemic, 1987-88; mem. Ill. Goodwill Del. to Republic of China, 1987; del. Rep. Nat. Conv, 1984; mem. Republican Nat. Com., 1984—. Del. Atlantic Alliance Young Polit. Leaders, Brussels, 1977; summit conf. observer as mem. adhoc Women for SDI, Geneva, 1985; active Maine Twp. Mental Health Assn.; mem. Nat. Council Ednl. Research, 1983—. Recipient George Washington Honor medal Freedoms Found., 1978, Dwight Eisenhower Freedom medal Chgo. Captive Nations Com., 1977, Outstanding Legislator awards Ill. Press Assn., Ill. Podiatry Soc., Ill. Coroners Assn., Ill. County Clks. Assn., Ill. Hosp. Assn., Ill. Health Care Assn.; named Ill. Young Republican, 1968, Outstanding Young Person, Park Ridge Jaycees, 1981, One of 10 Outstanding Young Persons, Ill. Jaycees, 1981. Mem. Am. Legis. Exchange Council (dir. 1977—, exec. com. 1978-83, 2d vice chmn. 1980-83), DAR. Lodge: Kiwanis. Home: 2604 W Sibley St Park Ridge IL 60068 Office: 22 Main St Park Ridge IL 60068

PULLIS, SUZANNE JULIET, sales professional; b. Tripoli, Lebanon, Feb. 10, 1953; came to U.S., 1954; d. Alphonse and Jasmin (Wirr) Telfeian; m. William Joseph, Nov. 30, 1985. BA in Journalism, Rider Coll., 1975. Talk show host Sta. WEIM Radio, Fitchburg, Mass., 1976-78; news announcer Sta. WCSH Radio, Scarborough, Maine, 1978-79; news dir. Sta. WLOB-FM, Portland, Maine, 1979-80; exec. dir. Nat. MS Soc., Portland, 1980-82; exec. dir. Orange County chpt. Nat. MS Soc., Orange, Calif., 1982-84; dir. sales rental div. Sunrise Co., Palm Desert, Calif., 1984-87, dir. rental div., group sales dir., 1987—. Mem. Hotel Sales Mktg. Assn., Soc. Travel Execs., Meeting Planners Internat., So. Calif. Soc. Assn. Execs. Republican. Home: 76-210 Honeysuckle Dr Palm Desert CA 92260 Office: Sunrise Co 76-300 Country Club Dr Palm Desert CA 92260

PULTI-GOLDSCHMIDT, ASHA, producer; b. Bombay; d. Umanath G. and Shashikala Puthli; m. Marc Goldschmidt, 1974 (div. 1981); 1 child, Jannu. BS, MS, U. Baroda, India, 1965. Rec. artist CBS Internat., London, 1973-74, Phonogram Records, Fed. Republic Republic, 1980-82; founder, producer, writer Top of World Prodns., N.Y.C., 1984—; pres. Promotional Internat. Network, N.Y.C., 1987—. Vocalist Science Fiction, CBS, 1971 (Down Beat award 1972); songwriter, singer The Devil Is Loose, 1977 (Oscar Del Successo award 1978); featured actress N.D.R. TV, Hamburg, Fed. Republic Germany, 1973, Mcht.-Ivory Prodns., N.Y.C., 1973, Titanus Prodns., Italy, 1979. Bd. dirs. Indian-Am. Forum for Edn., 1986—; co-founder Gandhi Peace Ctr., 1986. Recipient Gold Record CBS, 1978; key to city City San Remo (Italy), 1979; plaque Girl Scouts U.S., 1986. Mem. AFTRA, Nat. Assn. Female Execs., Council Indo-U.S. Relations (founding). Home and Office: 230 Central Park W New York NY 10024

PULTON, JANIS, trucking company executive; b. Newark, June 19, 1949; d. Joseph and Lucille (Bragaglia) La Capra; div.; 1 child, Lisa; m. Paul J. Vallone. BS in Mktg., Fairleigh Dickinson U., 1975. Advt. asst. F.A.O. Schwarz, N.Y.C., 1975-76; gen. mgr. Consolidated Truck Service, South Kearny, N.J., 1976-85; pres., owner Direct Express and Transfer Inc., Jersey City, 1985—. Sec. Physicians Spouses of St. Clares Riverside Med. Ctr., Denville, N.J. Mem. N.J. Assn. Women Bus. Owners. Roman Catholic. Home: 8 Arrowhead Rd Convent Station NJ 07961

PUMPHREY, JANET KAY, editor; b. Balt., June 18, 1946; d. John Henry and Elsie May (Keefer) P. A.A. in Secondary Edn., Anne Arundel Community Coll., Md., 1967, A.A. in Bus. and Pub. Adminstrn., 1976. Office mgr. Anne Arundel Community Coll., Arnold, Md., 1964—; mng. editor Am. Polygraph Assn., Severna Park, Md., 1973—, archives researcher, 1973—. Editor: (with Albert D. Snyder) Ten Years of Polygraph, 1984; (with Norman Ansley) Justice and the Polygraph, 1985. Mem. Am. Polygraph Assn. (affiliate), Md. Polygraph Assn. (affiliate), Nat. Assn. Female Execs.,

Internat. Platform Assn., Anne Arundel County Hist. Soc., Alumni Assn. Anne Arundel Community Coll. Republican. Methodist. Avocations: travel, poetry, gardening. Home: 3 Kimberly Ct Severna Park MD 21146 Office: Am Polygraph Assn PO Box 1061 Severna Park MD 21146

PUND, MARGARET ANN, academic administrator; b. Huntingburg, Ind., June 18, 1952; d. Adrian Frank and Anna Mae (Schaeffer) P. BA, Ind. State U., 1974; MA, Ball State U., 1984. Caseworker Marion County Dept. Pub. Welfare, Indpls., 1975-76; extension agt. Coop. Extension Service Purdue U., Tell City, Ind., 1976-81, Indpls., 1976—. Mem. Broad Ripple Village Assn., Indpls. Mem. Ind. Extension Agts. Assn. (pres. youth section, 1983-84, bd. dirs. 1983-84), Nat. Assn. Extension Agts. (Disting. Service award 1987). Roman Catholic. Office: Purdue Univ Coop Extension Service 9245 N Meridian Suite 118 Indianapolis IN 46260

PURCELL, ANN MARIE C., medical industrial company marketing manager; b. Harvey, Ill., Feb. 20, 1957; d. Carlo Leo and Lucille Lillian (Colletti) Allegro; m. Fredrick William Purcell, June 29, 1980; children: Carly Allegro, Gianna Cecile. B.S., Loyola U. Chgo., 1979; postgrad. Keller Grad. Sch. Mgmt., 1981—. Lab. instr. Loyola U., Chgo., 1977-79; research technician Travenol Labs., Inc., Morton Grove, Ill., 1979-80, research asst., 1980, research assoc., 1980-81; product specialist Fenwal Labs. div. Travenol Labs., Inc., Deerfield, Ill., 1981-85, product mgr., 1985—. Mem. Women's Aux. to Dental Soc. Loyola U. Dental Sch., Nat. Assn. Female Execs., Phi Kappa Omega Alumnae (a founder), Tri Beta. Roman Catholic. Home: 1921 Tano Ln Mount Prospect IL 60056

PURCELL, ELAINE IRENE (SCHOCK), banker; b. Pottsville, Pa., Nov. 13, 1946; d. Salem Henry and Ethel Mae (Howells) Schock; m. Jerome James Purcell, June 27, 1969 (div. July 1984). BS in Math., Bloomsburg U., 1968; JD, Duquesne U., 1981; MBA in Fin. and Acctg., Columbia U., 1983. Cert. tchr., Pa. Math. tchr. Pottsville Area High Sch., 1968-69, Keystone Oaks Sch. Dist., Pitts., 1969-81; credit trainee 1st Nat. Bank Chgo., 1983-84; corp. banking officer 1st Nat. Bank Chgo., N.Y.C., 1984-86, asst. v.p., 1987—. Mem. Women in Cable, Pa. Bar Assn., Nat Assn. Female Execs., Internat. House, Bklyn. Acad. Music. Office: 1st Nat Bank Chgo 153 W 51st St New York NY 10019

PURCELL, JOYCE M., organization administrator; b. Las Vegas, N. Mex., Apr. 20, 1949; d. John Donald and Helen Marie (Griffin) P.; 1 child, W. Daniel Schneider. BA, U. N.Mex., 1975, MA, 1977. Staff asst. Coll. Pharmacy, U. N.Mex., 1970-71; authorizations analyst VA, 1971-73; claims analyst Social Security Adminstrn., 1974-75; staff asst. VA Hosp., Albuquerque, 1977-78; cons. Los Alamos Pub. Schs., 1977-78; natural resources and space and sci. analyst Senate Budget Com., Washington, 1977-83; sr. program officer Space Sci. Bd., Nat. Acad. Scis., 1983—. Mem. Am. Communication Assn., Am. Soc. Tng. and Devel., Am. Geophys. Union, Women in Aerospace. Office: 2101 Constitution Ave NW Washington DC 20418

PURCELL, MARY LOUISE GERLINGER, educator; b. Thief River Falls, Minn., July 17, 1923; d. Charles and Lajla (Dale) Gerlinger; student Yankton Coll., 1941-45, Yale Div. Sch., 1949-50, NYU, summer 1949; MA (alumni fellow), Tchrs. Coll. Columbia, 1959, EdD, 1963; m. Walter A. Kuyawski, June 9, 1950 (dec. July 1954); children—Amelia Allerton, Jon Allerton; m. 2d, Dale Purcell, Aug. 26, 1962. Teen-age program dir., YWCA, New Haven, 1945-52; dir. program in family relations, asst. prof. sociology and psychology Earlham Coll., Richmond, Ind., 1959-62, conf. coordinator undergrad. edn. for women, 1962; chmn. div. home and community Stephens Coll., Columbia, Mo., 1962-73, chmn. family and community studies, 1962-78, dir. Learning Unltd., continuing edn. for women, 1974-78, developer course The Contemporary Am. Woman, 1962, cons., 1962; prof., Auburn (Ala.) U., 1978—, head dept. family and child devel., 1978-84, spl. asst. to v.p. acad. affairs, 1985-86. chmn. search com. for v.p. acad. affairs, 1984, spl. asst. to v.p. acad. affairs, 1985—; vis. prof. Ind. U. Summer Sch., 1970. Cons. student personnel services, Trenton (N.J.) State Coll., 1958-59, 61. Recipient Alumni Achievement award Yankton Coll., 1975. Mem. AAUW, Am. Home Econs. Assn. (chmn. family relations and child devel. sect. 1986—, bd. dirs.), Groves Conf. on Family, Nat. Council Family Relations (dir., chmn.-elect affiliated councils, 1981-82, chmn., 1982-83, nat. program chmn. 1977, chmn. film awards com., chmn. spl. emphases sect., bd. dirs., Ernest G. Osborne award for excellence in teaching 1979), Delta Kappa Gamma. Presbyterian. Contbr. articles to coll. bulls., jours. Home: 2408 Heritage Dr Opelika AL 36801 Office: Auburn U 278B Spidle Hall Auburn AL 36830

PURCELL, MARY THOMPSON, occupational health nurse, nurse; b. Livermore, Calif., Oct. 12, 1963; d. William Elbert and Bridget Theresa (Maguire) Thompson; children: Courtney, Theresa. BS, U. San Francisco, 1985, postgrad., 1986—. RN, Calif. Nurses aide Hacienda Health Care, Livermore, 1980-82, Staff Builders Health Care, Hayward, Calif., 1983; staff nurse Meml. Hosp., San Leandro, Calif., 1985-86; occupational health nurse Intel Corp., Livermore, 1986—. Recipient Alta Bates Hosp. scholarship, 1983. Mem. Am. Assn. Female Execs., Am. Assn. Occupational Health Nurses, Calif. Nurses Assn., AAUW. Democrat. Roman Catholic. Office: Intel Corp 250 N Mines Rd Livermore CA 94550

PURCELL, MICKI NOLAN, personnel service executive; b. Washington, Apr. 13, 1953; d. Bernard A. and Theresa (Hagan) Nolan; m. Joseph F. Purcell, Apr. 21, 1979; children: Jennifer, Anthony. Ed. pub. schs., Bowie, Md. V.p. Washington Internat. Secretarial Exchange, 1973-79; pres. MNP Personnel Service, Beverly Hills, Calif., 1979-88, Newport Beach, Calif., 1988—. Mem. Nat. Assn. for Personnel Cons. Republican. Roman Catholic. Home: 2800 Casiano Rd Bel Air CA 90077 Office: MNP Personnel Service 3100 W Oceanfront Newport Beach CA 92663

PURDY, BARBARA JOYCE, trust company executive; b. Glens Falls, N.Y., Oct. 28, 1938; d. J. Floyd and Mary Ruth (Bennett) Sleight; m. Richard H. Purdy, July 16, 1960; children: Christine Purdy Wichers, Cynthia, Douglas R. Student, Adirondack Community Coll., Glens Falls, 1976-86, Empire State Coll., Saratoga Springs, N.Y., 1987—. Clk., sec. Glens Falls Nat. Bank, 1956-60, clk. to adminstrv. asst., 1974-84, trust ops. officer, 1984-86, asst. trust officer, 1986—; Mem. Estate Planning Council, Northeastern N.Y., 1984—. Mem. Nat. Assn. Bank Women (past bd. dirs.), Nat. Assn. Female Execs. Republican. Lodge: Zonta (Glens Falls) (treas. 1986—). Office: Glens Falls Nat Bank & Trust Co 250 Glen St Glens Falls NY 12801

PURDY, HELEN CARMICHAEL, librarian; b. Miami, Jan. 17, 1920; d. James B. and Alice Cornelia (Brown) C.; m. Joseph Lynn Purdy, Feb. 12, 1946 (div. Aug. 1971). AB, U. Miami-Coral Gables, 1943; MS, Fla. State U.-Tallahassee, 1957. Asst. dept. head U.S. Censorship, Miami, 1944-45; library asst. catalog dept. U. Miami, Coral Gales, 1946-56, cataloger, 1957-60, Fla. cataloger, 1961-77/78, head archives and spl. collections dept., 1978, 79—, senator Faculty Senate, 1967-71, mem. council, 1969-71; mem. Women's Adv. Com. on Acad. Affairs, Coral Gables, 1972-81. Mem. Citizens Crime Watch, Miami, 1980—; mem. Republican Nat. Com., Washington, 1981—; mem. Republican Party of Fla., Tallahassee, 1983—. Mem. ALA, Southeastern Library Assn., Fla. Library Assn. (div. vice chmn. 1958-59, chmn. 1959-60), Soc. Fla. Archivests, Miami Pioneers. Beta Phi Mu. Episcopalian. Lodge: Zonta Internat. Home: 5824 SW 50th St Miami FL 33155 Office: Univ Miami Library Coral Gables FL 33124

PURE, MELINDA ALICE, business manager; b. San Bernardino, Calif., Sept. 17, 1960; d. Kenneth Walter and Marian Lucille (Bown) P. BA in Mgmt., cert. computers and programming, Calif. State U., San Bernadino, 1983. Bus. mgr. Bruggeman, Smith & Peckham, Attys. (now Smith & Peckham), San Bernardino and Rancho Cucamonga, Calif., 1983—. Mem. Employer's Adv. Council, San Bernadino, 1984—. Mem. ABA (assoc.), Assn. Legal Administrators, Alumni Assn. Calif. State U. San Bernadino (life), Nat. Assn. Female Execs. Republican. Presbyterian. Office: Smith & Peckham 524 N Mountain View Ave San Bernardino CA 92401-1295

PURICELLI, MARJORIE GIBSON, retired government official, consultant; b. Opelika, Ala., Jan. 11, 1923; d. Frederick Meyer and Lottie Belle (Hearn) Gibson; student U. Ala., 1965, 66, Macon Jr. Coll., 1968-71; m. Russell Antonio Puricelli, May 17, 1984; children by previous marriage: William Guy Walter, Ralph Gibson Walter. Contract negotiator trainee Robins AFB, Ga., 1966 68, contract negotiator, 1968-71; fin. analyst HUD, Birmingham and Washington, 1971-75; contract price analyst U.S. Army, Washington, 1976-77; contract price analyst U.S. Marine Corps, Albany, Ga., 1977-80, head contracts support br., contracts div. Marine Corps Logistics Base, Albany, Ga., 1980-84, br. head value analysis engrng. data mgmt. br., office competition advocate, 1984-86; ret., 1986; v.p. MARCON Cons.; ptnr. Amare Stained Glass Co. Vice pres. Woman's Caucus, HUD, 1975. Recipient Sustained Superior Performance award U.S. Marine Corps, 1978. Mem. Nat. Contract Mgmt. Assn., Fed. Mgrs. Assn. Home: 466 Church St NE Dawson GA 31742

PURKEY, RUTH ELANE, insurance agency executive; b. Upper Sandusky, Ohio, Apr. 4, 1936; d. Charles William Henry and Avah Alice (Wilson) Butcher; m. Wallace D. Purkey, Jr., Apr. 17, 1955; children: Robin Sue Purkey VanGorder, Justin Neal. Grad. high sch., Millbury, Ohio. Ins. agt. Purkey Ins. Agy., Northwood, Ohio, 1967—, v.p., sec., treas., 1976—; speaker on youth substance abuse to various groups and orgns. Mem., v.p. PTA Genoa Schs., Ohio, 1968-70; club adviser 4-H Clubs Am., Ottawa County, Ohio, 1968-73; bd. dirs., treas. Friends of Library of Genoa, 1972-75; chmn. Village Bikeway Com., Genoa, 1972-76; facilitator Parents Helping Parents, Inc., Toledo, 1985—, mem. exec. bd., 1986; cons. Wood County Juvenile Ct. Adv. Bd., 1985—, Wood County Schs. Without Drugs Community Action Bd., 1987—; mem. Nat. Fedn. Parents for Drug-Free Youth, 1983—; mem. exec. bd. Chem. Abuse Reduced through Edn. and Services Agy. of Lucas County, 1988—; mem. Parents Resource Inst. Drug Edn., 1986—, Region V of U.S. Atty.'s Force Prevention Drug and Alcohol Abuse, 1987. Recipient Jefferson award, 1988. Mem. Profl. Ins. Agts., Nat. Assn. Female Execs., Fedn. Women's Clubs (bd. dirs. Genoa 1973-76). Republican. Methodist. Club: Belle Ami (Genoa) (sec. 1969-70, v.p. 1972-73). Avocations: distance swimming, cross-country skiing, American Indian pottery. Home: 1524 Red Bud Dr Northwood OH 43619 Office: Purkey Ins Agy Inc 3040 Woodville Rd Northwood OH 43619

PURSELL, DIANE LYN, office manager; b. Portsmouth, Va., Sept. 24, 1959; d. William P. and Barbara J. (Lines) P. Grad. high sch., Frenchtown, N.J. Sr. credit reporter Hunterdon County Credit Bur., Flemington, N.J., 1977-82; sr. planning clk. Hunterdon County Planning Bd., Flemington, 1982-84; legal sec. Reed, Strauss & Tauriello, Flemington, 1984-85; adminstrv. asst., cons. Program Dynamics, Inc., Flemington, 1981—; office mgr. Withum, Smith, & Brown, CPA's, Somerville, N.J., 1985—. Contbr. articles to profl. jours. Democrat. Mem. United Ch. of Christ. Home: 191 Main St Flemington NJ 08822 Office: Withum Smith & Brown 981 Rt 22 Box 580 Somerville NJ 08876

PURSELL, JULIE CROW, corporate communications administrator, media consultant, journalist; b. Nashville, Feb. 26, 1936; d. William Russell and Eleanor Farrell (Weber) Crow; m. William Whitney Pursell, Apr. 26, 1965; children—Ellen Pursell Spicer, Margaret, Laura, Bill, 1 stepchild, Sharon. Student Vanderbilt U., 1953-55, Peabody Coll., 1958-60, U. Tenn., 1961-62. Reporter, feature writer, The Tennessean, Nashville, 1958-65; freelance writer, Nashville, 1965-73; art-home editor Nashville Banner, 1973-80; asst. to mayor City of Nashville, 1980-84; asst. to chmn. Earl Swensson Assocs., Nashville, 1984-86; dir. corp. communications, Yearwood Johnson Stanton & Crabtree, Inc., 1986—. Editor: Symphony Guild newsletter, 1966-68; contbg. writer, editorial bd. Tenn. Architect mag., 1985—; contbg. writer, Nashville! mag. Dir. publicity Vietnam Veterans Day Salute, Nashville, 1981; mem. adv. bd. Nashville Pub. TV, 1981—; dir. publicity Metro Courthouse Day, Nashville, 1982, Historic Belmont Assn., 1988; mem. adv. bd. Belmont Coll. Dept. Communications Arts, Nashville, 1983—; co-dir. grand opening Riverfront Park, Nashville, 1983. Mem. Nashville C. of C. (mem. cultural affairs com. 1984-86), Pub. Relations Soc. Am. (bd. dirs. 1984, 86), Tenn. State Mus. Assn. Inc., AIA (affiliate mem.), Assn. for Preservation of Tenn. Antiquities, Kappa Delta. Roman Catholic. Clubs: Exchange of Nashville; Savage of London (affiliate). Avocations: art; historic preservation; urban planning; travel; history. Home: 895 S Curtiswood Ln Nashville TN 37204 Office: Earl Swensson Assocs Inc 2100 W End Ave Nashville TN 37203

PURSGLOVE, BETTY MERLE, small business owner; b. Pitts., Sept. 15, 1923; d. Earle E. and Merle A. (Smith) Baer; m. Larry A. Pursglove, June 30, 1944; children: Diana, Kathleen, Merry, Tanya, Yvonne. BS in Physics, U. Pitts., 1944; postgrad., Carnegie-Mellon U., 1947-49, W. Va. U., 1949-51, Mich. State U., 1968-69. Micro-pilot plant operator Minn. Mining and Mfg., St. Paul, 1944-46; cons. research chemist Food Mach Co., Pitts., 1947-49; computer coder Dow Chem. Co., Midland, Mich., 1954; asst. entomologist pvt. collections, Midland, 1955-56; instr. chemistry Cen. Mich. U., Midland, 1958; head chem. dept. Midland Hosp., 1958-64; chem., physics tchr. parochial schs., Bay City, Mich., 1964; prin., chief exec. officer Crypticlear Inc. (tech. writing and computer programming), Lansing, Mich., 1965—. Author: Family Tales, 1980. Troop leader Midland Girl Scouts, Girl Scout U.S., 1953-63. Mem. Sigma Xi, Sigma Pi Sigma.

PURTLE, CAROL JEAN, art historian, educator; b. St. Louis, Feb. 20, 1939; d. Clarence Philipp and Rose Bertha (Kloeppel) P.; BA magna cum laude, Maryville Coll., St. Louis, 1960; MA, Manhattanville Coll., Purchase, N.Y., 1966; PhD, Washington U., St. Louis, 1976. Joined Religious of Sacred Heart, Roman Cath. Ch., 1963; tchr. Acad. Sacred Heart, St. Charles, Mo., 1964-66, Grand Coteau, La., 1966-68; lectr. art history Maryville Coll., St. Louis, 1969-75; instr. art history Washington U., 1970-76; asst. prof. art and coordinator art history Memphis State U., 1977-82, assoc. prof., 1982—; coordinator nat. symposium 600 Years Netherlandish Art, Memphis, 1982; project dir. Internat. Research Conf. on Tradition and Innovation in Study No. European Art, U. Pitts., 1985. Author: The Marian Paintings of Jan Van Eyck, 1982, also articles. Bd. dirs. Acad. Sacred Heart, New Orleans, 1971-73; trustee Acad. Sacred Heart, Grand Coteau, La., 1982-85. Recipient M. Spalding Young award Maryville Coll., 1960, Ann. Scholarship award 1960, Alumni Profl. Achievement award, 1987, Faculty Devel. award Memphis State U., 1980, 85-86; Advanced Research fellow Belgian-Am. Endl. Found., 1974-75, NDEA fellow, 1968-71, 76, NEH fellow, 1982, 88, Danforth Assoc., fellow, 1979—, Coolidge research fellow, 1985; faculty research grantee Memphis State U., 1983. Mem. Coll. Art Assn. Am., Southeastern Coll. Art Conf., Mid-West Art History Soc., Historians of Netherlandish Art (pres. 1983-85), Assocs. for Religion and Intellectual Life, Delta Epsilon Sigma. Home: 767 Mount Moriah Apt 32 Memphis TN 38117 Office: Memphis State U Dept Art Jones Hall Memphis TN 38152

PURUCKER, MARY IRENE, librarian, consultant; b. Lynn, Mass., Feb. 12, 1934; d. Frederick George and Mary Agnes (Sweeney) Mahoney; m. Frederick J. Purucker Jr., June 23, 1955; children—Katherine Ann, John David. A.A., Boston Coll., 1955; A.B. in English, UCLA, 1963, M.L.S., 1964. Librarian, Los Angeles Pub. Library, 1964-65; librarian, media specialist Santa Monica/Malibu United Sch. Dist., Malibu, Calif., 1965-83, tchr. English, John Adams Jr. High Sch., Santa Monica, 1983-85; librarian Lincoln Middle Sch., Santa Monica, 1985—; lectr. UCLA Grad. Sch. Library Info Sci., Los Angeles, 1981—; lectr. Loyola-Marymount, Los Angeles, 1984-86. Mem. Calif. Lit. Project Cadre, 1985—. Mem. Mariposa County Fish Camp Town Planning Adv. Council (Calif.), 1978-83. Michael J. Harding scholar Boston Coll., 1952. Mem. ALA, Nat. Council Tchrs. English, Calif. Library Assn., Calif. Media Library Educators Assn., Children's Lit. Assn. Roman Catholic. Office: Lincoln Middle Sch Library 1501 California Ave Santa Monica CA 90403

PUSEY, ELLEN PRATT, home economist; b. Milford, Del., Aug. 27, 1928; d. Algeo Newell and Ruby Newton (Boorman) Pratt; B.S., U. Md., 1950, M.S., 1951; m. William W. Pusey, June 12, 1950; children—William W., Patricia A., Cynthia L., Daniel N. Camp dietitian N.Y. Herald Tribune Fresh Air Fund Camps, 1947; supr. cafeteria Roosevelt Hosp., N.Y.C., 1948; supt. sch. cafeterias, Seaford, Del., 1964; field faculty home economist Md. Coop. Ext. Service, Wicomico County, Md., 1967—. Chmn. lower shore council Am. Lung Assn., Md., 1978-79. Mem. Am. Home Econs. Assn., Md. Home Econs. Assn., Nat. Assn. Extension Home Economists, Md. Assn. Extension Home Economists, Tri-County Home Econs. Assn., U. Md. Coll. Home Econs. Alumni Assn. (dir.), Nutrition Jour. Club of Eastern Shore, Phi Kappa Phi, Alpha Xi Delta. Presbyterian. Club: Soroptimists (pres. 1978) (Salisbury, Md.). Home: 301 W Federal St Snow Hill MD 21863 Office: PO Box 1836 Salisbury MD 21801

PUSKAR, KATHRYN ROSE, nurse, educator; b. Akron, Ohio, Apr. 7, 1946; d. Stanley William and Virginia (Roberts) McKavish; m. George Paul Puskar, Aug. 28, 1969; 1 child, Stacey. Diploma in nursing, Johnstown Mercy Sch. Nursing, 1966; BS, Duquesne U., 1969; MS in Nursing, U. Pittsburgh, 1971, MPH, 1978, DrPH, 1981. RN. Mem. faculty U. Ill., Chgo., 1976-78; cons. Westmoreland Coll., Greensburg, Pa., 1976; clin. specialist McKeesport (Pa.) Hosp., 1971-73; dir. mental health clinic Frick Hosp., Mt. Pleasant, Pa., 1974-76; asst. prof. U. Pitts., 1980—; cons. Southwood Hosp., 1984-86, VA Med. Ctr., Pitts., 1985—. Contbr. articles to profl. jours.; editor profl. jour. Cons. Newcomers Club, Pitts., 1985-87. NIMH fellowship. Mem. Am. Nurses Assn. (cert. psychiat. specialist), Pa. Nurses Assn., Sigma Theta Tau. Republican. Roman Catholic. Home: 1795 Robson Dr Pittsburgh PA 15241 Office: U Pitts Sch Nursing 367 Victoria Pittsburgh PA 15261

PUTNAM, BARBARA DEYO, nurse; b. Brattleboro, Vt., Oct. 28, 1926; d. Harold E. and Grace B. (Thomas) Deyo; m. Richard B. Putnam, Jr., Dec. 11, 1949; children—Richard B., III, Alan E., Jeffrey S. Nurse Springfield Hosp. Tng. Sch. for Nurses, 1945-48. Operating rm. staff nurse Brattleboro (Vt.) Meml. Hosp., 1948-51, asst. night supr., 1961-68, coordinator discharge planning, 1980-88 ; office nurse ob-gyn, 1968-72; pub. health nurse Brattleboro Pub. Health Nursing, 1973-78. Staff vol. ARC, nurse, 1985—; den mother Boy Scouts Am.; pres. PTA, Academy Sch., Brattleboro, 1960; co-organizer Brattleboro chpt. United Ostomy Assn., Inc.; active Vt./New Hampshire chpt. Continuity of Care, Am. Assn. Continuity Care, rses Assn., Nat. Rifle Assn., Brattleboro Sportsmen, Am. Assn. Ret. Persons.

PUTNAM, BONNIE BEAN, marketing executive; b. Rockville Centre, N.Y., Dec. 20, 1955; d. David Charles and Betty Lou (Simonin) Bean; m. William Shields Putnam, Oct. 29, 1978. A.B. in Econ., Duke U., 1978, A.B. in Can. Studies, 1978, M.B.A., 1983. Material and acctg. mgmt. assoc. Western Elec. Co., Winston-Salem, N.C., 1978-79, material planning specialist, Greensboro, N.C., 1979-80; rate design adminstr. GTE of S.E., Durham, N.C., 1980-83; market research analyst Northern Telecom, Research Triangle Park, N.C., 1983, product mgr., 1983-84, mgr. market research and bus. planning, 1984-85, mgr. contract services, San Ramon, Calif., 1985-86, regional mktg. mgr., 1987, dir. product mktg., 1988—. Author research papers. Bd. dirs. Fuqua Sch. Bd., Durham, 1985—. Exec. scholar GTE of S.E., 1981. Mem. Am. Mktg. Assn., Women in Telecommunications. Republican. Avocations: cooking, alpine skiing, interior design. Home: 1908 Cedar St Durham NC 27707 Office: Northern Telecom Dept 2210 PO Box 13010 Research Triangle Park NC 27709

PUTNAM, CAROLINE JENKINS (MRS. ROGER LOWELL PUTNAM), civic worker; b. Glymont, Md., Nov. 16, 1892; d. Thomas Canfield and Eleanor (Compton) Jenkins; student Mt. St. Agnes Acad., 1905-07; LL.D., Newton Coll. Sacred Heart, 1967, St. Mary's Coll., 1959, Regis. Coll., 1952, St. Michael's Coll., 1956; L.H.D., Am. Internat. Coll., 1950, Manhattanville Coll., 1959; L.H.D. (hon.), Duquesne U., 1969; m. Roger Lowell Putnam Oct. 9, 1919; children—Caroline Canfield, Roger Lowell, William Lowell, Anna Lowell (Mrs. Everett P. Tomlinson), Mary Compton (Mrs. Charles W. Chatfield), Michael Courtney Jenkins. Mem. Springfield (Mass.) Housing Authority, 1952-62; mem. advisory bd. Mass. Commn. Against Discrimination, Springfield, 1949—; mem. Comm. for Study of De Facto Segregation Pub. Schs. of Mass., 1964-65; mem. Mass. sub-com. under Nat. Commn. on Civil Rights, 1959-64; pres. Catholic Scholarships for Negroes, Inc., 1946—. Recipient Nat. Human Relations award NCCJ, 1976; Jefferson award for outstanding pub. service, 1982. Mem. Kappa Gamma Phi (hon.). Democrat. Roman Catholic. Home: 101 Mulberry St Springfield MA 01105

PUTNAM, FRANCES ISENBERGER, educator, computer school administrator; b. Hilight, Wyo., July 10, 1924; d. Claude Francis and Helen Isabel (Sinclair) Isenberger; m. Harry Gordon Putnam, Feb. 14, 1942; children—Frances Teckla, Barbara Lynne Heffelfinger, Harry Putnam III, Kathleen Doris. B.E., San Diego State U., 1961, M.A., 1965. Life cert. elem. tchr., life cert. guidance and counseling, Calif. Tchr. Campbell and Converse County Schs., Wyo., 1941-54, Las Vegas Pub. Schs., 1955-59; tchr. Chula Vista City Schs., Calif., 1960-68, resource tchr. for gifted, 1968-78, head tchr. for gifted, 1978-84, cons. gifted program and computer sci., 1984—; owner, operator Computer Scholar of Chula Vista, 1984—. Author ednl. materials and computer programs. Recipient Am. Freedom Found. award, 1965. Mem. Chula Vista Assn. Gifted Children (auditor 1982—, Honored Tchr. 1982), Computer Using Educators of Calif., Computer Using Educators of San Diego County, South Bay Ret. Tchrs. Assn., MENSA, Delta Kappa Gamma. Democrat. Presbyterian. Avocations: travel; reading; computer science. Home: 764 Brightwood Ave Chula Vista CA 92010 Office: Computer Scholar of Chula Vista 764 Brightwood Chula Vista CA 92010

PUTNAM, KATHRYN ANNETTE, automobile dealership executive; b. Altus, Okla., Oct. 5, 1953; d. John Carlis and Mary Kathryn (Phelps) P. BE in Spl. Edn., S.W. Mo. State U., 1976. Office mgr. Putnam Lincoln-Mercury, Ft. Smith, Ark., 1978-84, v.p., 1984—; sec., treas., co-owner Sallisaw (Okla.) Ford, 1984, Sallisaw Chrysler, 1985, Perrin Tractors, Ft. Smith, 1986; co-owner Brunwick Pl., Ft. Smith, 1984. Lodge: Zonta (pres. Ft. Smith 1985). Office: Putnam Lincoln-Mercury 4515 Towson Ave Fort Smith AR 72901

PUTNAM, NANNETTE SUDDETH, music promotions director; b. Clovis, N.Mex., Oct. 26, 1957; d. William T. and Marlene O. (Tranyham) Suddeth; m. Miron Walter (Dub) Putnam, Jr., Nov. 26, 1982; 1 stepchild, Melissa. AA in Bus. Adminstrn., Tarrant City Jr. Coll., Ft. Worth, 1977; student, J.R. Powers Modeling Sch., Ft. Worth, 1984, Ogle Sch. Hair, Arlington, Tex., 1985. Lic. facialist. Product distbn. analyst Motorola, Inc., Austin, 1977-82; office mgr. Ribigital, Inc., Ft. Worth, 1982-83; pres., owner The Word Market, Inc., Ft. Worth, 1983-84; exec. asst. Stas. KPLX/KLIF Radio, Arlington, 1984-86; dir. spl. events Spl. Promotions, Inc., Nashville, 1986—; owner, pres. Everybody's Talking; instr. J.R. Powers Modeling Sch., 1984-86; pvt. practice make-up artist, Ft. Worth and Nashville, 1984-86; cons. The Brownstone Devel. Corp., Ft. Worth, 1984-85. Nominated Most Outstanding Young Woman in Am., 1982. Mem. Nat. Assn. Female Execs. Mem. Assembly of God Ch. Lodge: Order of Rainbow. Home: 158 Woodmont Blvd Nashville TN 37205 Office: Spl Promotions Inc 918 19th Ave S Nashville TN 37212

PUTNAM, ROSEMARY WERNER, special education educator; b. Chgo., June 8, 1940; d. Louis and Zelda (Wolock) Werner; m. Robert David Putnam, June 15, 1963; children: Jonathan, Lara. BA, Swarthmore Coll., 1962; MA, U. Mich., 1977. Cert. tchr., Mass., Va., Mich. Translator U.S. Govt., Washington, 1962-63; jr. librarian New Haven Free Pub. Library, 1964-66; tchr. McLean (Va.) High Sch., 1977-79, Medford (Mass.) High Sch., 1979-80, Krebs Sch., Lexington, Mass., 1980-82; aide Wellesley (Mass.) High Sch., 1982-83; tchr. Wellesley Middle Sch., 1983-85; dir. lang. program Wellesley High Sch., 1985—. V.p. Temple Isaiah Sisterhood, Lexington, 1986-87; sec. Lexington Bicentennial Band, 1987. Mem. Mass. Tchrs. Assn. Democrat. Jewish. Home: 15 Diana Ln Lexington MA 02173

PUTNAM, SANDRA RAE, human resources administrator; b. Lincoln, Nebr., Jan. 1, 1948; d. Robert Merritt and Helen Elizabeth (Harrison) P. Cert., Laval U., Quebec, Can., 1967; BA in French, D'Youville Coll., 1969; cert., L'Institut Catholique, Paris, 1972; MEd, SUNY, Buffalo, 1975. Cert. secondary educator, N.Y. Tchr. fgn. lang. Nichols Sch./Nottingham Acad., Buffalo, 1969-74; research asst. VA Hosp., Palo Alto, Calif., 1974-75; dir. career counseling D'Youville Coll., Buffalo, 1975-83; coordinator human resources Goldome Realty Credit Corp., Buffalo, 1983; mgr. tng. and devel. Vis. Nursing Assn., Buffalo, 1983-85; mgr. human resources devel. Home Club, Inc., Fullerton, Calif., 1985—. Mem. Am. Soc. for Tng. and Devel. Democrat. Roman Catholic.

PUTNEY, MARY ENGLER, federal auditor; b. Overland, Mo., May 1, 1933; d. Bernard J. and Marie (Kunkler) Engler; children: Glennon (dec.), Pat Michael, Michelle. Student Fontbonne Coll., 1951-52; AA, Sacramento

City Coll., 1975; BS in Bus., Calif. State U., 1981; CPA, Calif. Asst. to acct. Mo. Research Labs., Inc., St. Louis, 1953-55, sec. to controller, 1955-56, adminstrv. asst. to pres., 1958-60; sec. to mgr. Western region fin. Gen. Electric Co., St. Louis, 1960-62; sec. to regional v.p. agrl. loans Crocker Nat. Bank, Sacramento, 1962-67, asst. credit analyst No. region, 1967, sec. to v.p. and mgr. capital office, Sacramento, 1967-72; student tchr. Sacramento County Dept. Edn., 1979-81; acctg. technician East Yolo Community Services Dist., 1983; mgmt. specialist USAF Logistics Command, 1984; staff auditor office Insp. Gen., U.S. Dept. Transp., 1984—. Mem. Sacramento Community Commn. for Women, 1978—, rec. sec., 1980-81, bd. dirs., 1980—; mem. planning bd. Golden Empire Health Systems Agy. Mem. Nat. Assn. Accts. (dir., newsletter editor), Fontbonne Coll. Alumni Assn., AAUW (fin. officer 1983—), Assn. Govt. Accts. (chpt. officer), Am. Soc. Women Accts., Beta Gamma Sigma, Beta Alpha Psi. Roman Catholic. Club: Arden Hills Swim and Tennis. Home: 2616 Point Reyes Way Sacramento CA 95826 Office: US Dept of Tng/Office Insp Gen Room 287 PO Box 1915 Sacramento CA 95809

PUTTERMAN, FLORENCE GRACE, painter, printmaker; b. N.Y.C., Apr. 14, 1927; d. Nathan and Jean (Feldman) Hirsch; m. Saul Putterman, Dec. 19, 1947. B.S., NYU, 1947; M.F.A., Pa. State U., 1972. Founder, pres. Arts Unlimited, Selinsgrove, Pa., 1969—; curator Milton Shoe Collection, 1970—; artist in residence Title III Program Cultural Enrichment in Schs. Program, 1969-70; instr. Lycoming Coll., Williamsport, Pa., 1972-74, Susquehanna U., Selinsgrove, PA, 1984—. Exhibited one-woman shows, Everson Mus., Syracuse, N.Y., 1976, Hagerstown, Md., 1978, Stuhr Mus., Grand Island, N.B., 1979, Muhlenburg Ctr. for the Arts, Pa., 1985, Harmon Gallery, Fla., 1985, The State Mus. of Pa., 1985-86, Segal Gallery, N.Y., 1986, Canton Inst. Fine Arts, Ohio, 1986, Fla. Biennial Polk Mus., Lakeland, Fla., 1987, Artists Choose Artists, Tampa Mus., 1987, Auburn Works on Paper, 1987, Ala.; group shows, Library Congress, Soc. Am. Graphic Artists, Ball State Drawing Ann., Muncie, Ind., Arts Club N.Y., Colorprint, U.S.A., Smithsonian Traveling Exhbn., Boston Printmakers, N.C. Print & Drawing, Chautauqua Nat., U. Dallas Nat. Print Invitational, Segal Gallery, Rutgers Drawing, Polk Mus., Tampa Mus., Sichaun Fine Art Inst., Mickelson Gallery, Harmon Gallery, Mus. Art U. Ariz., 1988. Bd. dirs. Fetherston Found. Recipient award Silvermine Guild Conn. Appalachian Corridors, Arena, 1976; recipient Gold medal of honor Audubon Artists ann. competition; grantee Nat. Endowment Arts; Whitehead award Boston Printmakers, 1985, Shellenberg award Artists Equity, 1985, award N.C. Print & Drawing, 1985, award Chautauqua Nat., 1985, Johnson & Johnson award 3rd Ann. Nat. Printmaking Council of N.J., 1985, PUrchase award N.J. State Mus., 1987; Va. Ctr. for the Creative Arts fellow 1983-84. Mem. Soc. Am. Graphic Artists, Nat. Assoc. of Women Artists, Boston Printmaker, Audubon Artists, Los Angeles Printmaking Soc. Home: 3 Fairway Dr Selinsgrove PA 17870

PUTZ, CHRISTINE, financial executive, accountant; b. Palmer, Mass., Feb. 4, 1950; d. Anthony Charles and Stephanie Veronica (Niemiec) P. Student Salem State Coll., Springfield Tech. Coll.; B.S. in Bus. Adminstrn., Western New Eng. Coll., 1979. Chief acct. Wing Meml. Hosp., Palmer, 1969-79; field acct. Hillhaven Corp., Lexington, Mass., 1979-83; fin. dir. Bus. Mgmt., Malden, Mass., 1983-87; cons. Melrose VNS, Mass., 1983-87; hosp. controller Psychiatric Inst. Am. Hosp., 1987—. Mem. Healthcare Fin. Mgmt. Assn., Nat. Assn. Female Execs. Roman Catholic. Avocations: outdoor activities; sports reading; work. Office: Nashua Brookside Hosp Nashua NH 03061

PUTZRATH, RESHA MAE, toxicologist; b. Camden, N.J., Sept. 9, 1949; d. Franz Ludwig and Pearl (Robins) P.; m. Lawrence Smedley Olson, May 13, 1978. BA in Physics cum laude, Smith Coll., 1971; MS in Biophysics, U. Rochester, 1974, PhD in Biophysics, 1978. Diplomate Am. Bd. Toxicology. Research fellow Med. Sch. Harvard U., Boston, 1977-79, fellow Sch. Pub. Health, 1979-81; cons. U.S. Environ. Protection Agy., Washington, 1981-82; assoc. scientist Nat. Acad. Scis., Washington, 1982-83; sr. assoc. ENVIRON Corp., Washington, 1983-86, project mgr., 1986—; mem. faculty Found. for Advanced Edn. in Scis., NIH, Rockville, Md., 1982-86; exec. dir. Acad. Toxicol. Scis., Washington, 1983-84; mem. FDA Planning Bd., Washington, 1984-86. Author: Elements of Toxicology and Chemical Risk Assessment, 1986. Nat. evaluator NSTA-NASA Space Shuttle Student Involvement Project, Washington, 1982-86. Mem. Am. Coll. Toxicology, Biophys. Soc., ASTM, Environ. Mutagen Soc., Assn. for Women in Sci. (mem. exec. bd. Washington chpt. 1982—, v.p. 1982-83, pres. 1985-87), Phi Beta Kappa. Home: 3223 N St NW Washington DC 20007 Office: ENVIRON Corp 1000 Potomac St NW Washington DC 20007

PYE, CASSANDRA WALKER, lobbyist; b. Washington, Sept. 29, 1959; d. William and Ella (Sanders) Walker; m. Kelvin E. Pye, Apr. 7, 1983. Student, Hood Coll., Frederick, Md., 1977-79; BA, George Washington U., 1981; postgrad., Brandeis U., 1981-82; postgrad. in law, U. Md., 1984-86; postgrad., McGeorge Sch. Law, Sacramento, 1987—. Coordinator programs, lobbyist Nat. Student Ednl. Fund, Washington, 1981-82; coordinator polit. programs Nat. Women's Polit. Caucus, Washington, 1982-83; fed. lobbyist Food Mktg. Inst., Washington, 1983-86; sr. govtl. affairs rep. Calif. Grocers Assn., Sacramento, 1986—; assoc. mem. Nat. Conf. on Weights and Measures, Washington, 1983-86; bd. dirs. Washington Area State Relations Group, Washington, 1984-86. Exec. dir. Litter-Free Washington Com., 1985; chair D.C. Litter and Solid Waste Commn., 1986; bd. dirs. Sacramento Family Services Agy. Recipient cert. of appreciation D.C. Litter and Solid Waste Commn., 1986. Mem. Coalition of 100 Black Women (chair conf. com.), Sacramento Black Women's Network, Capitol Women's Network, Women in Advocacy, Family Services Agy. of Sacramento (bd. dirs.). Republican. Mem. Christian Meth. Episcopal Ch.

PYLES, MITZI ANN, state pageant director, clothing company executive; b. Fayetteville, N.C., Dec. 6, 1954; d. Arthur and Elizabeth (Gentry) Collins; m. Steven Michael Pyles, Sept. 17, 1984; children: Valerie, Dallas, Breanna. Student, Nat. Bus. Sch., Va., 1978. Dressmaker, owner Specially Handmade by Mitzi, Martinsville, Va., 1981-82, Designs by Mitzi, Vinton, Va., 1982-87; acct. Vogue Cleaners, Inc., Roanoke, Va., 1984—; pres. D.B.M. Prodns., Inc., Goodview, Va., 1986—; state pageant dir. Roanoke, 1987—; cons. in field. Mem. Nat. Assn. Female Execs. Baptist. Club: Christian Women's (telephone chmn. 1981-82). Lodge: Moose. Home and Office: 4205 Lynnbrook Dr Wilmington NC 28405

PYNE, VICKI ROSE, human resources director; b. N.Y.C., Sept. 27, 1952; d. Carlo and Sylvia (Roffis) Kunstler; m. Martin Pyne, Mar. 12, 1977; Douglas William Pyne. BA magna cum laude, Ithaca (N.Y.) Coll., 1974. Cert. tchr., N.Y. Personnel assoc. Doubleday & Co., Inc., N.Y.C., 1974-77; employment mgr. Brentano's, Inc. subs. MacMillan & Co., Inc., N.Y.C., 1977-78; asst. personnel mgr. Underwriter Labs., Inc., Melville, N.Y., 1979-80; dir. human resources Citicorp Credit Services, Inc., Hunt Valley, Md., 1980-87; dir. human resources dist. services div. Citicorp, Inc., Hunt Valley, Md., 1987—; lectr., visiting faculty Adelphi U., 1984-86. Mem. Greenlawn (N.Y.) PTA, 1986—. Mem. Am. Soc. Personnel Adminstrs., Am. Compensation Assn., Phi Alpha Theta, Gamma Delta Pi. Democrat. Jewish. Office: Citicorp Credit Services Inc 200 International Circle Hunt Valley MD 21031

PYNES, NINA, restaurant exec.; b. Syracuse, N.Y., June 25, 1936; d. Samuel and Palma (Quinto) Collette; student Syracuse U., 1955-60, grad. advanced acctg. course, 1983, advanced arts and craft courses, 1984; m. Buddy Pynes, Nov. 9, 1967; children—Patricia, Mitchell. Owner, operator Big M Supermarket, Weedsport, N.Y., 1962-65; owner, pres., acct. Soo Lin Restaurant, Inc., DeWitt, N.Y., 1967—. Mem. N.Y. State Restaurant Assn., N.Y. State Sheriffs Assn., Everson Mus., Central N.Y. Tavern Keepers. Office: Soo Lin Restaurant Erie Blvd E De Witt NY 13214

PYPLACZ, BONITA MARIE, financial analyst; b. Cranbrook, B.C., Can., June 5, 1959; d. Stanley A. and Wilma (Michalsky) P.; m. John Nicolas Shaske, Feb. 8, 1986. BS in Physics and Math., U. of B.C., Vancouver, 1981, MS in Econ. Planning, 1984. Planning asst. Sunshine Coast Regional Dist., Sechelt, B.C., 1984; econ. devel. officer Regional Dist. Nanaimo, B.C., 1984; mgr. Sunshine Coast Employment Agy., Sechelt, 1985; mgr., analyst North Fraser Investment Corp., Mission, B.C., 1985—. Mem. Econ. Devel. Assn. of B.C. (treas. 1987—). Conservative. Roman Catholic. Office: North Fraser Investment Corp, 33179 Second Ave, Mission, BC Canada V2V 1J9

PYSZ, JEAN ANN, personnel executive; b. Taunton, Mass., May 1, 1947; d. Paul J. and Adela (Baran) Ladebauche; student Fisher Jr. Coll., 1982-85, Stonehill Coll., 1984; 1 son, Mark Richard. Sec. to dist. mgr. Prudential Ins. Co., Taunton, 1965-66; sec. to personnel mgr. Raytheon Co., North Dighton, Mass., 1967-75; exec. sec. to mgr. corporate audit Motorola Inc., Phoenix, 1977-79; asst. to corporate dir. employee relations Robertson Factories, Inc., Taunton, 1979-82, dir. personnel, 1982-88, adminstrv. asst. to pres., 1988—. Team capt. United Way, 1982-85;, co-chmn. Greater Taunton United Way, 1988-89;, chmn. of indsl. com. United Way, Taunton, 1988; officer Miss Taunton Scholarship Pageant, 1979—; co-dir., 1980, dir., 1987; chmn. Jobs for Bay State Grads., 1984-85, co-chmn. 1986-87; active Taunton Employment of Handicapped 1984—. Mem. Taunton Area C. of C. (chmn. peronnel com. 1984-85), Nat. Assn. Female Execs., Taunton Mgmt. Club (exec. bd. 1984-85, 1st v.p. 1985-86, pres. 1987-88). Ballet instr., 1963-65. Home: 8 McSoley Ave Taunton MA 02780 Office: 33 Chandler Ave Taunton MA 02780

QUACKENBUSH, POLLY MARIE, counselor, educator; b. Boise, Idaho, Jan. 10, 1931; d. Howard E. and Helen M. (Woods) Packenham; divorced; children: Karl J., Kathleen M., Robert C. BS in Edn., U. Idaho, 1952; MS in Counseling/Guidance and Organizational Mgmt., Ea. Wash. U., 1980. Instr. Inst. for Extended Learning Life Skills Programs Community Colls. Spokane, Wash., 1981—, counselor, 1984—; Lectr., presenter Action Womens' Exchange, Spokane, 1987, Jr. League Spokane, 1987, Womens' Health Conf., Spokane, 1987, Women in Constrn., 1987; developer career transition curriculum; mem. Women's Commn. Task Force on Edn. Mem. AAUW, NOW, Wash. Women United (past mem. bd. dirs.), YWCA, Nat. Assn. Female Execs. Office: Inst for Extended Learning W 3305 Ft George Wright Dr Spokane WA 99204-5228

QUADT, SUZANNE MARIE, sales and marketing executive; b. Phila., May 2, 1947; d. George Joseph and Mary Anne (Poniatowski) Cummings; m. Robert Paul Quadt, Aug. 3, 1968; David Paul, Rachel Anne. BA in Govt. Politics, George Mason U., 1977; MBA in Mktg., Marymount Coll., 1982. Dir. sales, mktg. Info. Concepts, Inc., Washington, 1982-83; sales, sr. mkt. planner, devel. Hazeltine Corp., Reston, Va., 1984-86; v.p. internat. sales and mktg. Computers Anywhere, Inc., McLean, Va., 1986-87; dir. fed. mktg. Bus. Computer Solutions, Inc., Vienna, Va., 1987; owner, pres. Internat. Advantage, Inc., Vienna, 1988—; cons. various bus., not-for-profit and polit. orgns., Washington; bd. dirs. Health Systems Agy., No. Va., 1982; chmn. Group Residential Facilities Commn., Fairfax, Va., 1979-81; mem. criminal adv. bd. NOVA Planning Dist. Commn., 1977-78. Campaign worker, local, state, nat. campaigns, Va., 1970-82; campaign mgr. Barbara Weiss for State Dele., Va., 1977; chmn., Minority Affairs Standing com., Fairfax, 1972-79, Dem. Party Steering com., 1972-79; bd. dirs., Fedn. Civic Assns., Fairfax County, 1975-76; v.p., bd. dirs., YWCA, 1976-77, chmn. pub. policy and social action com., 1978-79. Mem. World Trade Council, Washington Trade Assn., Va. Trade Assn., Internat. Trade Assn., Fairfax County C. of C., Nat. Assn. Female Execs., Am. Mktg. Assn., Am. Electronics Assn., Nat. Mus. Women in the Arts, Delta Epsilon Sigma. Roman Catholic. Office: Internat Advantage Inc 8375 Leesburg Pike Suite 133 Vienna VA 22180

QUALLS, CORETHIA, archaeologist; b. Sparta, Tenn., Jan. 17, 1948; d. Malcolm Talmadge and Lucille (Jackson) Qualls. BA, Marlboro Coll., 1970; MPhil, Columbia U., 1980, PhD, 1981. Exec. curator Mus. of Archaeology of Staten Island, 1981; asst. prof. St. John's U., S.I., 1981-82; cons. curator Queens Mus., N.Y., 1982-83; cons. curator Kuwait Nat. Mus., 1984-86; curatorial advisor for archaeology, Bahrain Nat. Mus., 1987—; archaeologist Columbia U., 1970-74, NYU Inst. Fine Arts, 1972-73, 84, Johns Hopkins U., 1974, Fulbright prof. archaeology, 1985-86. Dir. excavations Hamad Town, Bahrain, 1985-86. Editor: Seals of the Marcopoli Collection, vol. 1, 1984; contbr. articles to profl. jours. Columbia U. fellow, 1970-74; Am. Schs. Oriental Research fellow, 1973-74. Mem. Am. Inst. Archaeology, Am. Oriental Soc., Am. Schs. Oriental Research, Inst. Nautical Archaeology, Brit. Sch. Archaeol. in Iraq, Oriental Club of N.Y.C., Egypt Exploration Soc., Am. Soc. Profl. and Exec. Women. Roman Catholic.

QUALLS-SULKOWSKI, SUSAN JANE, athletics educator; b. Detroit, Nov. 20, 1954; d. Roy A. and Mary Susanne (Comer) McLalin; m. 2d Mard Edward Sulkowski, Feb. 18, 1984; m. Cecil O. Qualls, Apr. 23, 1977 (div.). B.S. in Social Sci., Eastern Mich. U., 1976, B.S. in Phys. Edn., 1976; M.S. in Athletic Adminstrn., Mich. State U., 1983. Cert. tchr., Mich. Teller, Mfrs. Bank, Detroit, 1973-76; coach, tchr. Flushing High Sch. (Mich.), 1976-78; coach, tchr. Detroit County Day Sch., Birmingham, Mich., 1978-83 , athletic dir., 1979—. Active Easter Seals, March of Dimes. Mem. Detroit Field Hockey Assn. (pres. 1981-83), Met. Conf. Athletic League (sec. Birmingham 1979-83), Nat. Volleyball Assn., Mich. High Sch. Athletic Assn. (ski com. 1983—), Delta Psi Kappa (treas. 1974-76). Home: 26150 W 12 Mile Rd Apt 59B Southfield MI 48034

QUAM, JEAN KATHLEEN, social work educator; b. Fargo, N.D., Oct. 16, 1948; d. Frederick Wallace and Lois May (Partenheimer) Q. BA, Moorhead (Minn.) State U., 1970; MSW, U. Nebr., 1972; PhD, U. Wis., 1981. Social worker Linn County Social Services to Handicapped, cedar Rapids, Iowa, 1972-75, U. Iowa Hosps., Iowa City, 1975-87; asst. prof. Moorhead STate U., 1976-77; asst. prof. I. Minn., Mpls., 1980-85, assoc. prof., 1985—. Author: Social Work: An Introduction, 1985. Fulbright fellow, 1987. mem. Nat. Assn. Social Workers (v.p. Minn. chpt. 1983-85). Home: 4900 Thomas Ave S Minneapolis MN 55410 Office: U Minn Sch Social Work 400 Ford Hall Minneapolis MN 55455

QUARLES, MARY VIRGINIA, education union consultant; b. Nashville, Nov. 12, 1940; d. Chester Lew and Virginia Estelle (Cooper) Q. BA, Miss. Coll., 1962; MA, Fla. State U., 1970. Tchr. recruiter Brevard County Schs., Titusville, Fla., 1962-76; dir. Fontana/Chaffey UniServ, Calif., 1976-78, Cen. Wis. UniServ Council-West, Wausau, Wis., 1978—. Older children dir. Park Ave. Bapt. Ch., Titusville, Fla., 1970-73; Sunday Sch. dir. Calvary Bapt. Ch., Schofield, Wis., 1985-86, 1st Bapt. Ch., Wausau, 1986—. Experienced Tchr. fellow Fla. State U., 1970. Mem. Indsl. Relations Research Assn., Fla. chpt. AAUW, Teaching. Profession div. NEA (bd. dirs. 1974-76), Sigma Tau Delta. Democrat. Home: 726 N 1st Ave Wausau WI 54401 Office: Cen Wis UniServ Council-West PO Box 1606 Wausau WI 54402-1606

QUARNSTROM, DORIS ELLEN, illustrator, graphic designer; b. Tuckasegee, N.C., Apr. 22, 1943; d. Frank Lee and Cannie (Owen) Ammons; m. John Franklin Quarnstrom; children: David Patrick, Erik Stephen. BA in Fine Arts, Calif. State U., Long Beach, 1977, MA in Illustration, 1986. Cert. bio-med. illustrator. Illustrator Price Assoc., Raymon Film Prodn., Sy Wexler Film Prodn., U. So. Calif. Sch. Medicine, 1977-78; art dir. Hancock Lab., 1978-79; free lance artist 1980-82; owner Creative Endeavors, El Toro, Calif., 1982—; cons. Nat. Soc. Prevent Blindness, Orange County, Calif., 1985-87. Illustration West-80 (Best In West, 1981), Prevent Blindness poster, 1985 (community service 1987); publisher Consumer Guide Med. Care Orange County, 1985 (commendation county 1985). Mem. So. Calif. Women Advtg. (v.p. edn., 1984-86), Soc. Illustrators Los Angeles, (Illustration award, 1980-83). Democrat. Mem. Ch. Religious Science. Club: Toastmasters.

QUATTLEBAUM, DOROTHY EVELYN CLEWIS (MRS. WALTER EMMETT QUATTLEBAUM, JR.), investment exec.; b. Unadilla, Ga., Nov. 1, 1924; d. Otis Clyde and Mabel (DuPree) Clewis; student Puttman Bus. Sch., 1953, Chipola Jr. Coll., 1962-64; m. Walter Emmett Quattlebaum, Jr., Oct. 19, 1946; children—Walter Emmett III, Amalia Ann. Sec.-treas. Sneads Telephone Co., 1948-55, Cottondale Telephone Co., 1954-55, Grand Ridge Telephone Co., 1954-55; sec.-treas., dir. Tri-County Telephone Co., Inc., Bonifay, Fla., 1955-62; asst. to stock analyst Quattlebaum Investments, Bonifay, 1962—. Methodist (pres. Wesleyan service guild 1957, 58). Address: PO Box 36 Bonifay FL 32425

QUEEN, LIL MAMIE, consultant; b. Roxboro, N.C., Nov. 26, 1944; d. Eddie and Mable (Bolton) McGhee; m. Glenn Mike Queen, May 16, 1969; 1 child, Varek Michael. AA, Strayer Coll., 1974; BS, U. San Francisco, 1982; postgrad., Antioch Law Sch., 1983. Ct. reporter Dept. Justice, Los Angeles, 1975-82; fed. agt. Dept. Def., Washington, 1982—; pres., owner Queen and Assoc. Cons., Seabrook, Md., 1984—; pres., owner Queen Pub. Co., Harbor City, Calif., 1979-82; instr. 1st Class Inc., Washington, 1986—. Mem. Assn. Fed. Investigations (v.p. 1986, sec. 1985), Women in Fed. Law Enforcement (newsletter editor 1984). Democrat. Baptist. Home and Office: PO Box 729 Seabrook MD 20706

QUELLAND, JUDITH ANN, photographer; b. Mpls., Jan. 29, 1948; d. Norman Roger and Ethel Lorraine (Sanford) Q. Lab technician Thomas C. Nelson, D.D.S., Winter Park, Fla., 1969-71; with Quelland Gallery, Winter Park, 1971-73; office staff Hugh Houston, D.D.S., Winter Park, 1974-75; asst. mgr. So-Fro Fabrics, Hagerstown, Md., 1976-78; mgr. Photography of Dale, Hagerstown, 1978-83, owner Valley Studio, Hagerstown, 1983—. Assoc. mem. Miss Md. Scholarship Found., Hagerstown, 1986—. Recipient cert. of merit Triangle Profl. Photographers Assn., Pitts., 1981. Mem. Profl. Photographers Am., Southeastern Profl. Photographers Assn., Md. Profl. Photographers Assn. (Candid Photograph of Yr. award 1982, Hartig Meml. award for most creative photograph 1982). Republican. Methodist. Office: Valley Studio 104 Valley Mall Hagerstown MD 21740

QUERY, JOY MARVES NEALE, medical sociology educator; b. Worcestershire, Eng.; came to U.S., 1952; d. Samuel and Dorree (Oakley) Neale; children: Jonathan, Margo, Evan. A.B., Drake U., 1954, M.A., 1955; postgrad., U. Syracuse, 1955-56; Ph.D., U. Ky., 1960. Tchr. secondary schs. Staffordshire, Eng., 1947-52; dep. prin. Smethwich Hall Girls' Sch., Staffordshire, 1948-52; instr. U. Ky., 1956-57, asst. prof., 1960; asso. prof. sociology and psychology Transylvania Coll., Lexington, Ky., 1961-66; asso. prof. N.D. State U., Fargo, 1966-68; prof. sociology and psychology N.D. State U., 1969-75, also chmn. sociology and psychology depts., 1969-70; chmn. sociology and anthropology dept. 1968-73; prof. div. psychiatry behavioral sci., dept. neurosci. U. N.D. Sch. Medicine, Fargo, 1975—; on sabbatical leave Yale U., 1974-75. Mem. bd. adv. editors Sociological Inquiry jour., 1987-89; contbr. articles and papers to profl. jours. Field dir. Girl Scouts U.S.A., 1953-55; mem. Lexington Civil Rights Commn., 1960-66; bd. dirs. Fargo-Moorhead Family Service Agy., 1967-70; mem. Mayor's Coordinating Council for Youth, Fargo-Moorhead, 1976—; pres. Hospice of Red River Valley, 1986-87. Fellow Internat. Assn. Social Psychiatry; mem. Am. Sociol. Assn., N.D. Mental Health Assn. (pres. Red River Valley chpt.), AAUP, Midwest Sociol. Soc. (dir. 1970-73, 75-78), Alpha Kappa Delta. Unitarian. Home: 1202 N Oak St Fargo ND 58102 Office: U ND Sch Medicine 1919 Elm St N Fargo ND 58102

QUIAZON, VIOLETA P., registered nurse; b. Santo Tomas, Pangasinan, Philippines, Jan. 3, 1951; came to U.S., 1976; BSN, Philippine Women's U., Manila, 1975; MS, U. Calif., San Francisco, 1988. RN, Tex., Calif.; cert. critical care registered nurses. Staff, charge nurse Refugio (Tex.) County Hosp., 1976-78; staff, charge nurse San Francisco Gen. Hosp., 1978-85, acting head nurse, 1985-86, staff critical care unit (part-time), 1986—. Mem. Am. Heart Assn. Mem. Am. Assn. Critical Nurses, Filipino Nurses Assn. Home: 423 Quartz Ln Vallejo CA 94589 Office: San Francisco Gen Hosp 1001 Potreio Ave San Francisco CA 94589

QUICK, JAN MARY, educational association executive; b. St. Louis, Aug. 17, 1950; d. Robert J. and Beatrice B. (Lowitsky) Uhler; m. John Joseph Quick, Sept. 6, 1969 (div. Mar. 1986); children: Robert Scott, Megan Elizabeth; m. James Richard Leuthauser, June 18, 1988. BA in Sociology and Psychology, U. Mo., 1976, postgrad. Tng. coordinator St. Louis County Govt., 1976-81; sr. staff devel. rep. McDonnell Douglas Automation, St. Louis, 1983-85; sr. trainer Citicorp., St. Louis, 1985-86; pres. The Corp. Learning Ctr., St. Louis, 1986. Contbr. articles to profl. jours. Mem. Citizen's Adv. Counsel, St. Louis, 1988. Mem. Am. Soc. Tng. and Devel., Open Door Soc. (bd. dirs. 1986-88). Home: 12364 Oak Hollow Dr Saint Louis MO 63141 Office: The Corp Learning Ctr 12364 Oak Hollow Dr Saint Louis MO 63141

QUICK, SHARON WELLS, real estate executive, developer; b. Bethesda, Md., Apr. 13, 1945; d. John Ashley and Alicia (Kenyon) Wells; m. Michael K. Mann, Sept. 6, 1966 (div. July 1971); 1 child, Amy C.; m. Winston C. Fulton, Sept. 3, 1984. BA, U. Wis.-Madison, 1965; postgrad. Oxford U., Eng., 1965-67, Purdue U., 1974-77. Cert. real estate broker. Pres. Shaman & Assocs. Ltd., London, 1967-71; vis. lectr. U. Aberystwyth, Wales, 1971-73; sales assoc. Livesay Realty, Lafayette, Ind., 1977-79; owner, pres. The Wells Agy., Lafayette, 1979—; investment cons. Mem. Realtors Polit. Action Com., 1980—, Nat. Trust for Hist. Preservation. Mem. Internat. Council Shopping Ctrs., Women in Bus., Midwest Real Estate Exchangors, Nat. Assn. for Female Execs., Farm and Land Inst., Internat. Exchangors, Nat. Bd. Realtors, Smithsonian Instn., Nat. Fedn. Independent Bus., Nat. Assn. Indsl. and Office Parks, C. of C. Lafayette. Republican. Presbyterian. Office: The Wells Agy 200 Ferry St Suite C Lafayette IN 47901

QUIGLEY, BEHNAZ ZOLGHADR, educator, consultant; b. Tehran, Iran, Nov. 17, 1944; came to U.S., 1968, naturalized, 1978; d. Hamid and Behjat (Shoaibi) Zolghadr; m. Herbert Gerald Quigley, Aug. 24, 1968; children: Narda, Paran. Diploma in Edn., Tchrs. Tng. Coll., Tehran, 1964; BA, U. Tehran, 1968; MBA, U. D.C., 1975; PhD, U. Md., 1987. Tchr. secondary sch. Ministry of Edn., Tehran, 1964-68; instr. in bus. Strayer Coll., Washington, U. D.C., Prince George's (Md.) Community Coll., U. Md., College Park, 1975-88; asst. prof. bus. adminstrn. Mt. Vernon Coll., Washington, 1976-87, assoc. prof., 1987—, chmn. dept. bus. adminstrn., 1978—; aide to chief economist Iranian Econ. Mission, 1974; freelance cons. World Trade Assocs., Distbn. Systems, co-owner, freelance cons. Univ. Systems Assocs., Inst. Curriculum Devel., Mid. East Inst., 1975—. Author several books; coeditor: Management Systems: Contemporary Perspectives; contbr. articles to profl. jours. Faculty devel. grantee Mt. Vernon Coll., Mid. East Inst. Mem. Nat. Assn. Female Execs. (bd. dirs. Washington area chpt.), Assn. MBA Execs., Am. Acctg. Assn., Acad. Mgmt., Am. Soc. for Pub. Adminstrn., U. D.C. Alumni Assn., U. Md. Alumni Assn. Democrat. Home: 5 Canfield Ct Potomac MD 20854 Office: 2100 Foxhall Rd Washington DC 20007

QUIGLEY, LAURA ANNE, lawyer; b. Washington, Oct. 28, 1950; d. Edward Joseph and Violet (DeMint) Q.; m. Clem Leo Hyland. BA in Econs., Coll. William and Mary, 1972, JD, 1975; M Law in Taxation, Georgetown U., 1981. Bar: Fla. 1983. Judge clk. Fairfax (Va.) Cir. Ct., 1975-76; ptnr. Soutzos & Pierson, Vienna, Va., 1976-80; assoc. Furey, Doolan and Abell, Chevy Chase, Md., 1981-82, DeWolf, Ward and Morris, PA, Orlando, Fla., 1983—; adj. prof. George Mason U., Fairfax, 1981; lectr. Nat. Bus. Inst., Fla., 1983—, Women's Bus. Ednl. Council, Inc., Fla., 1986, Longwood C. of C., Fla., 1986, Valencia Community Coll., Fla., 1985—, U. Cen. Fla., 1987, Small Bus. Devel. Ctr., Fla., 1987, Koivu, Ruta & Felsing, Fla., 1985-86. Contbr. articles to law jours. Tutor Madiera (Va.) High Sch. Legal Program, 1979-80; legal community coordinator George Mason U., Va., 1979. Mem. Fla. Bar Assn. (bd. cert. tax lawyer 1985, co-chmn. internat. tax for internat. law section 1986—), Orange County Bar Assn. (vice chmn. tax com. 1986-87, chmn. 1987), Internat. Tax Roundtable, Employment Benefits Council of Cen. Fla., Cen. Fla. Assn. Women Lawyers. Republican. Roman Catholic. Office: 200 E Robinson St Suite 1475 Orlando FL 32801

QUIGLEY-WOLF, ANNA MARIE HELEN, organizational development consultant; b. Phila., Aug. 15, 1950; d. William Joseph, Jr. and Elizabeth (Harkins) Ailes. BA, Point Park Coll., Pitts., 1972; postgrad. Temple U., Phila.; MA, Antioch U., Phila., 1984. Ednl. resource specialist Community Coll. Phila., 1972-74; edn. coordinator Penn Mut. Life Ins. Co., Phila., 1974-76, human resource cons., 1976-81; adminstr. orgn. devel. RCA Service Co., Cherry Hill, N.J., 1981-85; mgr. orgn. devel. and compensation The Lehigh Press, Inc., Pennsauken, N.J., 1985—; chmn. Women's Resource Group, Phila., 1980-81; speaker in field. Mem. Orgn. Devel. Network, Am. Soc. Tng. and Devel., Nat. Assn Female Execs., Human Resource Planning Soc., Am. Compensation Assn. Office: Cooper Pkwy Bldg W North Park Dr and Airport Hwy Pennsauken NJ 08109

QUILL, CAROLYN JOY, federal agency administrator; b. Phila., Dec. 1, 1944; d. Edward Yee and Irene Devore (Lee) Q.; m. Marshall Sheldon Galinsky, Apr. 4, 1971 (div. Dec. 1977). AB, Bryn Mawr Coll., 1966. Program specialist HEW, Washington, 1966-68, mgmt. intern, 1968-71, mgmt. analyst, 1971-74; long range planner Office of Regional Dir. HEW,

San Francisco, 1974-77; sr. program analyst Office Insp. Gen., U.S. Dept. Health and Human Services, San Francisco, 1977-85, sr. evaluator Office Insp. Gen., U.S. Dept. Health and Human Services, Phila., 1985-87, dep. regional insp., 1987—. Mem. Old City Civic Assn., Phila., 1986. Mem. Nat. Assn. Female Execs., Mensa. Democrat. Mem. Soc. of Friends. Office: US Dept Health and Human Services Office Insp Gen 3535 Market St Philadelphia PA 19104

QUIMBY, SALLY CROSBY, nursing adminstrator; b. Washington, Nov. 19, 1946; d. Lowell Horace and Millicent Winn (Childs) Quimby. B.S. in Nursing, La. State U., 1975; M.S. in Nursing, Med. Coll. Ga., 1980. Asst. head nurse E. Jefferson Hosp., Metairie, La., 1976; head CCU St. Joseph Hosp., Savannah, Ga., 1977-78, asst. supr. CCU, 1978-80, supr., 1980; dept. head ICU El Camino Hosp., Mountain View, Calif., 1980—; planner CCU for computer monitoring system, 1978-79; instr. CPR, 1978-80. Task force organizer Save Our Satellite, 1977. Named outstanding Graduating Nursing Student, La. State U., 1975. Mem. Am. Nurses Assn., Am. Assn. Critical Care Nurses, Calif. Soc. Nursing Service Adminstrs. (program com. 1985-86), AAUW. Sigma Theta Tau. Democrat. Methodist. Home: 725 Mariposa #305 Mountain View CA 94041 Office: 2500 Grant Rd Mountain View CA 94042

QUINLAN, KELLY JEAN, social services adminstrator, consultant; b. Saugus, Mass., Oct. 12, 1962; d. Frederick James and Elizabeth Mae (Kudera) Q. BS in Criminal Justice summa cum laude, U. New Haven, 1984. Intern World Prison Poetry Ctr., New Haven, 1983-84; substitute tchr. Saugus Pub. Schs., 1982-84; adminstrv. asst. Peabody (Mass.) Mcpl. Light Plant, 1985-86, cons., 1986—; project adminstr. IUE/The Work Connection Inc., Saugus, 1986—; participant in seminars N.E. Pub. Power, Peabody, 1985. Mem. adv. com. World Prison Poetry Ctr., 1986; developer creative writing program Salem (Mass.) House Correction, 1984—. Recipient Link award North Shore Assn. for Volunteerism, 1987. Mem. Nat. Assn. for Female Execs., Am. Pub. Power Assn. (energy services com. 1986), Alpha Lambda Delta. Democrat. Roman Catholic. Home: 6 Third St Saugus MA 01906

QUINLAN, LIZ (ISADORA) W., public relations executive; b. N.Y.C., Dec. 30, 1937; d. A. Ralph and Mary Ella (Darbee) Wexler; m. Robert J. Quinlan, Aug. 6, 1966. A.B., Vassar Coll., 1959. Assoc. editor Macmillan Pubs., N.Y.C., 1962-65, Reader's Digest Almanac, N.Y.C., 1965-67; publs. editor Assn. of Jr. Leagues, N.Y.C., 1968-72, 76-80, dir. communications, 1980—; cons. pub. relations, N.Y.C., 1972-80; mem. rev. com. Ind. Sector/Ad Council Nat. Voluntarism Ad Campaign, 1982-83; rep. to subcom. of Presdl. Task Force for Pvt. Sector Initiatives, 1982. Contbr. articles to mags., and assn. jours. Mem. governing com. Off-the-Record Series, Fgn. Policy Assn., N.Y.C., 1977-85. Recipient cert. of merit Art Dirs.' Club, 1970. Pub. Relations Soc. Am., Mem. Women in Communications, Alumnae/Alumni of Vassar Coll. (dir. 1982-86, pres. 1986—), DAR (Maj. Jonathan Lawrence chpt.). Episcopalian. Club: Vassar of N.Y. (dir. 1972-79, pres. 1976-79). Home: 200 East End Ave New York NY 10128 Office: Assn of Jr Leagues Inc 660 First Ave New York NY 10016

QUINLIN, MARGARET MARY CAMPBELL, publisher; b. Pitts., May 15, 1951; d. John Joseph and Marie Josephine (Campbell) Q.; m. Jack J. McDowell, Nov. 7, 1981. BA, Albertus Magnus Coll., 1974; MBA, Emory U., 1987. Jours. editor Elsevier North-Holland Publ. Co., N.Y.C., 1974-75, supervising desk editor, 1976-77, aquisitions editor, 1977-78; series editor Allyn and Bacon Inc., Newton, Mass., 1979-82; med. editor Butterworths Publ. Co., Stoneham, Mass., 1982-83; editorial dir. allied health and edn. Aspen Pubs. Inc., Rockville, Md., 1983-88; v.p., exec. editor Peachtree Pubs. Ltd., Atlanta, 1988—. Contbr. articles to profl. jours. Mem. corp. adv. bd. Am. Speech/Lang. and Hearing Found., Rockville, 19856. Recipient pub. awards. Mem. Soc. Scholarly Publs. (chair newsletter subcom., mem. publs. com.), Assn. Info. Mgrs., Am. Med. Pubs. Assn., Assn. Am. Pubs. (profl. and scholarly pub. div.). Democrat. Home: 164 Fifth St NE Atlanta GA 30308 Office: Peachtree Pubs Ltd 494 Armour Cir NE Atlanta GA 30308

QUINN, BARBARA ANN, athletics administrator; b. Freehold, N.J., Jan. 13, 1933; d. Walter Stanley and Mary (Craig) Harris; B.S. in Health and Phys. Edn., Ursinus Coll., 1955; M.A., Trenton State Coll., 1968. Dir. phys. edn. for girls Charles Ellis Sch., Newtown Square, Pa., 1956-60; instr. phys. edn. Pennsbury Schs., Yardley, Pa., 1960-63, Exeter Twp. High Sch., Reading, Pa., 1963-66, Hartwick Coll., Oneonta, N.Y., 1966-68; asst. prof. phys. and health edn. Madison Coll., Harrisonburg, Va., 1968-71; instr. phys. edn. Whitemarsh Jr. High Sch., Plymouth Meeting, Pa., 1971-74; dir. women's intercollegiate athletics U. Nev., Las Vegas, 1974-76; dir. women's intercollegiate athletics Simpson Coll., Indianola, Iowa, 1977-78; dir. women's athletics U. N.C., Asheville, 1978-81; dir. women's intercoll. athletics SUNY, Cortland, 1981-84; fitness dir. St. Joseph's Hosp., Asheville, N.C., 1985—; site dir. Western Region, Women's U.S. Olympic Basketball Trials, Las Vegas, 1976, U.S. Volleyball Assn. Coaches Clinic, Simpson Coll., 1977; chmn. selection com. Va. State Lacrosse Tournament, 1970-71; mem. selection com. So. Dist. Lacrosse Tournament, 1970-71; coach So. dist. team U.S. Women's Lacrosse Assn. Nat. Tournament, 1971; mem. women's soccer com. Nat. Collegiate Athletic Assn. 1982-84, chmn. NE region; participant 5th Nat. Inst. Girls' Sports Advanced Basketball Coaching, 1969. Mem. AAHPER (sec. coll. div. N.Y. State chpt. 1967), Va. Women's Lacrosse Assn. (chmn. nominations com. 1970-71), Nat. Assn. Coll. Athletic Dirs., N.Y. Assn. Intercollegiate Athletics for Women (chair ethics and eligibility com. 1982). Address: RD 3 Box 238 Bear Branch Rd Mars Hill NC 28754

QUINN, BETTY NYE, educator; b. Buffalo, Mar. 22, 1921; d. Fritz Arthur and Alma (Svenson) Hedberg; A.B., Mt. Holyoke Coll., 1941; A.M., Bryn Mawr Coll., 1942, Ph.D., 1944; m. John F. Quinn, Sept. 21, 1950. Analyst, U.S. Army, 1944-46, CIA, 1947; instr., asst. prof. Vassar Coll., Poughkeepsie, N.Y., 1948-59, dir. pub. relations, 1952-59, assoc. prof., 1959-68; prof. classics Mt. Holyoke Coll., South Hadley, Mass., 1968—. Am. Acad. Rome fellow, 1942-43; Am. Philos. Soc. grantee, 1952. Mem. Am. Philos. Assn., Mediaeval Acad. Am., Classics Assn. New Eng. (pres. 1970-71) Vergilian Soc. Am. Republican. Lutheran. Home: 27 W Parkview Dr South Hadley MA 01075 Office: Mount Holyoke Coll Dept of Classics South Hadley MA 01075

QUINN, CHRISTINE AGNES, radiologist; b. Cleve., Sept. 23, 1946; d. Paul Leo and Estelle Christine Q.; B.A., Marquette U., 1967; M.D., Med. Coll. Pa., 1971; m. Paul C. Janicki, July 11, 1970; children—Sarah Christine, Megan Alexandra. Intern, St. Luke's Hosp., Cleve., 1971-72; resident in diagnostic radiology Cleve. Clinic Found., 1972-75, radiologist, 1975-81; radiologist Marymount Hosp., Cleve., 1981—. Diplomate Am. Bd. Radiology. Mem. Radiol. Soc. N. Am., Am. Coll. Radiology, Soc. Nuclear Medicine, Ohio Med. Soc., Cuyahoga County Med. Soc., AMA. Contbr. to CRC Handbook Series, Vol. II, 1977; contbr. articles to profl. jours. Home: 2781 Sherbrooke Rd Shaker Heights OH 44122 Office: 12300 McCracken Rd Cleveland OH 44125

QUINN, DOREEN ANN, metal processing executive; b. Gary, Ind., May 11, 1957; d. Walter Edward and Delores Marie (Gadbury) Cisowski; m. Robert Steven Quinn, Nov. 20, 1982; children: Courtney, Aaron, Sydney, Eamonn, Margaret. BS in Social Work, U. Evansville, 1978. Compliance checker Midwest div. Nat. Steel Corp., Portage, Ind., 1979-80, turn supr., 1980-81, supr. labor relations, 1981-82, plant security guard, 1982-83, supr. labor relations, 1983-87, supr. safety employee relations, 1987-88, coordinator employee relations, 1988—; supervisory com., dirs. Midwest Steel Employees Fed. Credit Union, Portage, Ind., 1983—, bd. dirs., 1988—. Mem. Midwest Steel Suprs. Assn., Midwest Steel Employees Assn. Republican. Roman Catholic. Home: 2700 Walnut Ln Hobart IN 46342 Office: Midwest Div Nat Steel Rt 12 Portage IN 46368

QUINN, JANE BRYANT, journalist; b. Niagara Falls, N.Y., Feb. 5, 1939; d. Frank Leonard and Ada (Laurie) Bryant; m. David Conrad Quinn, June 10, 1967; children—Matthew Alexander, Justin Bryant. B.A. magna cum laude, Middlebury Coll., 1960. Assoc. editor Insiders Newsletter, N.Y.C., 1962-65, co-editor, 1966-67; sr. editor Cowles Book Co., N.Y.C., 1968, editor-in-chief Bus. Week Letter, N.Y.C., 1969-73, gen. mgr., 1973-74; syndicated financial columnist Washington Post Writers Group, 1974—; contbr. fin. column to Women's Day mag., 1974—; contbr. NBC News and Info. Service, 1976-77; bus. corr. WCBS-TV, N.Y.C., 1979, CBS-TV News, 1980-87; contbg. editor Newsweek mag., 1978—. Author: Everyone's Money Book, 1979, 2d edit., 1980. Mem. Phi Beta Kappa. Office: Newsweek Inc 444 Madison Ave New York NY 10022

QUINN, JULIA PROVINCE, civic worker; b. Franklin, Ind., Feb. 23; d. Oran Arnold and Lillian (Ditmars) Province; B.A., Franklin Coll., 1937; M.S., Smith Coll. Sch. Social Work, 1939; m. Robert William Quinn, Jan. 21, 1942; children: Robert Sean, Judith Ditmars. Caseworker, student supr. Community Service Soc., N.Y.C., 1939-44; caseworker community research Family Service Soc., New Haven, 1946; social worker in research, dept. preventive medicine Yale U. Sch. Medicine, New Haven, 1946-49; research asst. dept. preventive medicine Vanderbilt U. Sch. Medicine, Nashville, 1969-70. Bd. dirs. Tenn. Bot. Gardens and Fine Arts Center, 1976-81, Friends of J. F. Kennedy Center, 1976-81, Family and Children's Service, Nashville, 1977-83, Friends of Cheekwood, 1966-81, Nashville Symphony Assn., 1978-85, Tenn. Performing Arts Found., 1979—; active Friends of the Tenn. Performing Arts Ctr., 1985—, charter mem., 1986—; bd. dirs. Nashville Opera Assn., 1983—, chmn. pub. relations, 1985—, Nashville Opera Guild (charter mem., bd. dirs. 1987); chmn. pub. relations Friends of Cheekwood, 1966-68, 72-74, 76-78, Tenn. Performing Arts Found., 1978-85, Family and Children's Service, 1978-83; mem. adv. bd. Vanderbilt Center for Fertility and Reproductive Research, 1981-85; charter mem., bd. dirs. Nashville Opera Guild, 1987—. Recipient Nashville Vol. Activist award Cain-Sloan and Germaine Monteil, 1979. Mem. Nat. Assn. Social Workers, Acad. Cert. Social Workers, Ladies Hermitage Assn., Vanderbilt Med. Center Aux., Nashville Opera Assn. Guild, Nashville Area C. of C. (cultural affairs com. 1979-85). Democrat. Presbyterian. Clubs: Smith Coll., Centennial (Nashville); Vanderbilt Garden, Vanderbilt Woman's. Contbr. articles to social work and med. jours. Home: 508 Park Center Dr Nashville TN 37205

QUINN, KAREN LEE, advertising executive; b. Berwyn, Ill., June 24, 1955; d. Walter Richard Foote and Jane Claire (Scheffer) Grape; m. Gregory Mathias Quinn, Aug. 14, 1977. BSBA, Ill. State U., 1977; MS in Advt., U. Ill., 1980. Account coordinator Young & Rubicam, Chgo., 1978-79; sales rep. Barron's Bus. and Fin. Weekly subs. Dow Jones and Co., Chgo., 1979-80; mgr. advt. New Eng. Barron's Bus. and Fin. Weekly subs. Dow Jones and Co., 1980-84, mgr. advt. N.Y., 1984-85, mgr. advt. Eastern U.S., 1985—. Dir. Pleasantville (N.Y.) Music Theater, 1986. Kraft Corp. fellow U. Ill., 1977. Mem. Nat. Investor Relations Inst., Bus. Profl. Advt. Assn. (awards chmn. 1982-84). Republican. Presbyterian. Home: 180 S State Rd Briarcliff Manor NY 10510 Office: Barron's/Dow Jones & Co 420 Lexington Ave Suite 2540 New York NY 10017

QUINN, MARY HOPE, financial analyst; b. N.Y.C., Feb. 14, 1941; d. Frank Edward and Catherine Agnes (Berrill) Q. A.B., Mt. St. Agnes Coll., 1964; Ed.M., U. Ga., 1973; M.B.A., Loyola Coll., Balt., 1976. Chartered fin. analyst. Instr. Mt. de Sales High Sch., Macon, Ga., 1964-69; adminstr. St. Vincent's Acad., Savannah, Ga., 1970-72, Mercy High Sch., Balt., 1973-75; v.p. Mercantile Trust Co., Balt., 1976-83; dir. fin. Sisters of Mercy, Silver Spring, Md., 1984—; Trustee Loyola Coll., Balt., 1982—, Mt. Aloysius Jr. Coll., Cresson, Pa., 1980—; mem. pastoral council Archdiocese of Balt., 1977-80; mem. sch. bd. St. Vincent's Acad., Savannah, Ga., 1974-80; bd. dirs. Mount St. Agnes Ctr., Balt., 1977-82; mem. investment com. Sisters of Mercy Nat. Office, Silver Spring, 1980—. R. J. Reynolds fellow, 1970. Mem. Fin. Analysts Fedn., Fin. Mgmt. Assn., Assn. Governing Bds. of Colls. and Univs., Washington Soc. Investment Analysts, Washington Assn. Money Mgrs., Phi Kappa Phi, Kappa Delta Pi, Alpha Sigma Nu. Democrat. Roman Catholic. Home: 1111 University Blvd W Silver Spring MD 20902 Office: Sisters of Mercy of the Union 1320 Fenwick Ln Silver Spring MD 20910

QUINN, PATRICIA ANNE, university administrator; b. Rochester, N.Y., Sept. 25, 1948; d. Harold Joseph and Marion Elizabeth (Loucks) Q.; m. Martin Finkenstaedt, July 10, 1982. BA in History, BA in English with honors, U. Rochester, 1970; MA, SUNY, Binghamton, 1972, PhD, 1985. Instr. Broome Community Coll., Binghamton, 1975-78; acad. advisor SUNY, Binghamton, 1976-78, dir. continuing edn. for women ctr., 1978-82; coordinator adult opportunity U. of Wis., Eau Claire, 1982—. Author: Better Than The Sons of Kings, 1987; contbr. articles to profl. jours. Program coordinator Wis. Humanities com., Eau Claire, 1987. Fulbright-Hayes fellow, Fed. Republic Germany, 1973-74, Germanistic Soc. Am. fellow, Fed. Republic Germany, 1973-74; named one of Outstanding Young Women, Am., 1979. Mem. AAUW (corp. rep. 1985-87, reader, cons. 1986-87, bd. internat. fellows 1987—), Am. Hist. Assn., Internat. Ctr. Medieval Art, Inst. Internat. Forecastors, World Future Soc., Eau Claire C. of C. (Ptnrs. in Edn. award 1986). Democrat. Office: U Wis Adult Opportunity Office Eau Claire WI 54701

QUINN, RITA MARIE, lawyer; b. Boston, Aug. 31, 1929; d. Joseph Patrick and Helen Veronica (Griffin) Sullivan; m. Robert Clarke Quinn, Apr. 11, 1953 (dec. 1969); children: Deborah, Susan, Michael, Maureen, Robert, Stephen. BA, U. Mass., 1974; JD, Suffolk U., 1985; Cert. in Mgmt., Simmons Coll., 1987. Owner, mgr. Atlantic Coast Vending CO., Sommerville, Mass., 1969-77; manpower specialist U.D. Dept. Labor, Boston, 1977-82; chief contract ops. Def. Logistics Agy., Burlington, Mass., 1982—. Mem. Arlington (Mass.) Town Meeting, 1987—. Mem. Mass. Bar Assn., Nat. Contracts Mgmt. Assn. Home: 205 Jason St Arlington MA 02174 Office: Def Logistics Agy DCASR 495 Summer St Arlington MA 02210

QUINN, SALLY, journalist; b. Savannah, Ga., July 1, 1941; d. William Wilson and Bette (Williams) Q.; m. Benjamin Crowninshield Bradlee, Oct. 20, 1978; 1 child, Josiah Quinn Crowninshield Bradlee. Grad., Smith Coll. Reporter, Washington Post, 1969-73, 74—; co-anchorperson CBS Morning News, N.Y.C., 1973-74. Author: We're Going to Make You a Star, 1975, (novel) Regrets Only, 1986. Address: 3014 N St NW Washington DC 20007

QUINN, TRUDY LEE, communications executive; b. Rock Hill, S.C., July 28, 1952; d. Joseph Erskine and Amelia Rose (Ford) Q.; m. John Merrill Stoudemayer, Nov. 5, 1978 (div. May 1983). BA in Sociology, Furman U., 1974. Supr. bus. office So. Bell, Columbia, S.C., 1974-75, supr. spl. services, 1975-76, account mgr., 1976-78; mgr. corp. planning Atlanta, 1978-79; mgr. corp. communications Columbia, 1980-84; staff mgr. CCNC Bellsouth Services, Atlanta, 1984-86, staff mgr. network planning, 1986—. Bd. dirs. Friendship Ctr., Columbia, 1984. Mem. Phi Beta Kappa. Home: 66 Sycamore Sta Decatur GA 30030 Office: Bellsouth Services 675 W Peachtree St NE Atlanta GA 30375

QUINTANA, MARIA DEL ROSARIO, laboratory supervisor; b. Havana, Cuba, Mar. 23, 1958; came to U.S., 1970; d. Manuel and Juana Maria (Alfonso Q.; m. Efren Leal, Dec. 23, 1978 (div. Oct. 1985); 1 child, Aymee Marie. AA, Miami-Dade Community Coll.-North, 1978; BS in Med. Tech., Fla. Internat. U., 1980. Med. technician Jackson Meml. Hosp., Miami, 1979-80; med. technologist Cedars Med. Ctr., Miami, 1980-85; toxicologist Cen. Med. Lab., Inc., Miami, 1985-87; chemistry/toxicology supr. Nat. Health Labs., Miami, 1987—. Mem. Nat. Assn. Female Execs., Am. Soc. Clin. Pathologists (cert. med. technologist). Roman Catholic.

QUINTILIAN, ELLEN MARIA, organizational development and education consultant; b. Balt., May 26, 1952; d. Julian Joseph and Laura (Kucinski) Q.; m. Andrew Lee Davidson, July 30, 1977 (div. Sept. 1981). AA, Cantonsville Community Coll., 1972; BS, Ohio State U., 1974, MS, 1977, PhD, 1986. Tng. supr. The Nisonger Ctr., Columbus, Ohio, 1974-75; asst. dir. med. edn. St. Elizabeth Med. Ctr., Dayton, Ohio, 1977-80; dir. edn. services Miami Valley Hosp., Dayton, 1980-82; project cons. Ross div. Abbott Labs., Columbus, 1983-84; cons., instr. Sinclair Community Coll., Dayton, 1980-85; group facilitator Merrell Dow Pharms., Cin., 1984-85; pvt. practice cons. Dayton, 1985-87; dir. orgn. devel. Multicare Med. Ctr., Tacoma, 1987—; nutrition cons. Assn. Developmentally Disabled, Columbus, 1975; edn. cons. Springfield (Ohio) Community Hosp., 1978, Family Practice Residency, Dayton, 1980; script cons. Network for continuing Med. Edn., N.Y.C., 1978-79. Active Freedom of Choice Bd., Dayton, 1982-83; vol. St. Joseph Treatment Ctr., Dayton, 1987; cast mem. Greene Meml. Hosp. Follies, Xenia, 1987. Senatorial scholar State Md., Balt., 1970; named One of Outstanding Young Women of Am., 1982. Mem. Nat. Assn. Female Execs., Am. Dietetic Assn., Am. Soc. Tng. Devel., Phi Kappa Phi. Democrat. Presbyterian. Club: Pilot. Lodge: Zonta.

QUIRING, SUSAN M., state agency administrator; b. Wichita, Kans., Jan. 13, 1952; d. J. Melvin and Virginia (Ready) Q. BA, Ottawa U., 1973; MS, Kans. State U., 1977, PhD, 1984. Extension home economist Kans. Cooperative Extension Service, Larned, Kans., 1973-76, Olathe, Kans., 1977-85; housing specialist Tex. Agrl. Extension Service, College Station, Tex., 1985—. Contbr. articles to profl. jours. Counselor Am. Inst. Foreign Studies, several countries, 1981, 82, 85; sponsor LABO-4-H Japanese Exchange Program, 1979, 82; mem. exec. bd. Cedar House-Transitional Living, Olathe, 1980-85; speaker Christian Womsn' Club, 1980-84. Recipient Nat. Consumer Edn. award Texize Co., 1981, Communications award Kans. Assn. Extension Home Economists, 1982; Dist. Service award Kans. Assn. Extension Home Economists, 1985. Mem. Kans. Home Economics Assn. (sec. 1982-84, chmn. conv. 1981-82),Tex. Assn. Extension Specialists (various coms. 1985—), Elec. Women's Round Table (sec. treas. 1986—), Am. Soc. Interior Designers, Coll. Educators in Home Equipment, Beta Sigma Phi (social chmn. 1986). Republican. Baptist. Office: Tex Agrl Extension Service Spl Services 201-A College Station TX 77843

QUIRK, DONNA HAWKINS, financial analyst; b. Chgo., Sept. 29, 1955; d. Martin Francis and Monica Mae (Hesslau) Hawkins; m. John James Quirk, Dec. 5, 1981; children: Martin Patrick, Mary Kathleen. B.S. in Commerce, DePaul U., Chgo., 1977, M.B.A., 1982. With Jewel Food Stores, Melrose Park, Ill., 1977—, acctg. mgr., 1980-85, fin. analyst, 1985—. Mem. Assn. M.B.A. Execs., Nat. Assn. Female Execs., Beta Gamma Sigma, Delta Mu Delta. Roman Catholic. Avocations: reading; ceramics; sports. Home: 5046 N Mason Ave Chicago IL 60630 Office: Jewel Food Stores 1955 W North Ave Melrose Park IL 60160

QUIRK, KATHLEEN MARY, developer, fundraiser; b. Chgo., Dec. 21, 1956; d. James Lawrence and Marilyn Ann (Oberklaner) Q.; m. William B. Kelley, Aug. 15, 1987. BS, Iowa State U., 1979; MA, Cen. Mich. U., 1985. Field rep. Am. Heart Assn., Des Moines, 1979-81, asst. field services dir., 1981-83, field services dir., 1983-86; exec. dir. Am. Heart Assn., Cheyenne, Wyo., 1986-88; dir. devel. Am. Heart Assn., Phoenix, 1988—. Mem. Soc. for Heart Assn. Profl. Staff (chmn. edn. com. 1981-82), C. of C. (liason com. 1986—). Democrat. Unitarian. Office: Am Heart Assn 1445 E Thomas Phoenix AZ 85014

QUISENBERRY, SHARRON SUE, entomologist, educator; b. Kirksville, Mo., Apr. 19, 1945; d. Thomas Leonard and Bonnie P. (Hays) Grogan; B.S. (NSF and Regents scholar), N.E. Mo. State U., 1966; postgrad. Thiel Coll. (NSF scholar), 1972; M.A., Hood Coll., 1975; M.S., U. Mo., 1977, Ph.D., 1980; m. Larry D. Quisenberry, Oct. 8, 1965. Tchr. sci. high schs. Lewis County, Mo., 1966-67, Macon County, Mo., 1968-69, Prince George's County, Md., 1969-74; devel. specialist Research and Devel. Center for Cognitive Learning, U. Wis., Madison, 1974-75; asst. prof. entomology Iowa State U., Ames, 1980-82; asst. prof. entomology La. State U., Baton Rouge, 1982-85, assoc. prof., 1985—. Recipient Leonard Haseman Recognition award U. Mo., 1979. Mem. Am. Registry Profl. Entomols. (mem. gov. council), Entomol. Soc. Am., Sigma Xi, Delta Sigma Gamma. Subject editor: Jour. Entomol. Soc. Contbr. articles to entomol. jours. Office: Dept of Entymology 418 Life Science Bldg 70803 Louisiana State Univ Baton Rouge LA 70803

RABIN, JANICE SHEPARD, transportation company executive, consultant; b. Franklin, N.C., Oct. 5, 1954; d. Roy Lyle and Helen Ruth (Duvall) Shepard; m. Ronald Stuart Rabin, Fed. 14, 1982. Student, DeKalb Community Coll., 1973-74. Sec. Lincoln Nat. Life Ins. Co., Atlanta, 1973-74; rate analyst Textile Traffic Assn., Atlanta, 1974-79; transp. supr. Firestone Tire & Rubber Co., Atlanta, 1979-85; program planning mgr. F.H. Trapper, Inc., Iselin, N.J., 1985—. Mem. Nat. Assn. of Female Execs., Internat. Assn. Quality Circles (treas. 1984-85), Delta Nu Alpha. Democrat. Baptist. Home: 35 Carmel Ct Old Bridge NJ 08857

RABIN, SAMANTH BLAKE, brokerage house executive; b. N.Y.C., Nov. 21, 1950; d. Max and Pearl (Wise) Fisher; m. Sander Marc Rabin, Dec. 18, 1976; children: Chopin Margaux, Karden Harley. Student, Boston U., 1968-72. Receptionist Schaeffer, Dale & Tavrow, N.Y.C., 1973-75; office mgr. Ivan S. Fisher, Esq., N.Y.C., 1975-76; mng. clk. Stroock, Stroock & Lavan, N.Y.C., 1976-79, Botein, Hays & Sklar, N.Y.C., 1979-83; v.p., dir. adminstrn. Paine Webber Inc., N.Y.C., 1983—. Mem. Assn. Legal Asminstrs., ABA. Jewish. Office: Paine Webber Inc 120 Broadway Legal 5th Floor New York NY 10271

RABINOWITZ, MARGARET GOLDNER, business manager; b. Phila., June 1, 1964. Student, Boston U., 1984; BA, U. Pa., 1987, MEd, 1987. Fundraiser Boston U., Mass., 1982-84; asst. mgr. AIA Bookstore, Phila., 1984; bus. mgr. Atkin, Voith & Assocs., Phila., 1984—; tchr. Germantown Friends Sch., Phila., 1988—. Author: (poetry) Collected Sonnets, 1986. Mem. Found. for Architecture; friend Phila. Mus. Art, Mus. Modern Art. Democrat. Jewish. Home: Garden Ct Apts #510 349 S 47th St Philadelphia PA 19143 Office: Atkin Voith & Assocs 125 S 9th St Philadelphia PA 19107 also: Germantown Friends Sch Philadelphia PA 19107

RABURN, JOSEPHINE, librarian, educator; b. Norman, Okla., Dec. 6, 1929; d. Albert E. and Josephine D. (Hudson) Riling; m. James Winston Raburn, Sept. 29, 1950; children: Catherine Anne Heller, Dora Lynn Greenleaf. BS, U. Okla., 1950, MLS, 1964, PhD, 1981. Library asst. Spl. Services, Ft. Sill, Okla., 1962-63, reference, adminstrv. librarian, 1964-66; reference and circulation librarian Morris Sweatt Tech. Library, 1966-67; spl. instr. U. Okla. Sch. Library Sci., 1966-67; reference librarian Cameron Agrl. and Mech. Jr. Coll., 1967-68; instr. Cameron U., Lawton, Okla., 1968-72, asst. prof., 1972-81, assoc. prof., 1981-85, prof., 1985—, dept. chmn., 1982-83, head lang. arts div., 1983-87; trustee Lawton Pub. Library, 1973-86; pres. bd., 1973-76, also systems analyst; adv. com. library tech. asst. program Rose State Coll., Oklahoma City, 1986-88; cons., lectr. in field. Contbr. articles to profl. jours., chpts. to books. Mem. mammography bd. Meml. Hosp., 1979-81, sec., 1979-80. Recipient Disting. Faculty award Cameron U., 1976; Helen Olander scholar, 1979. Mem. ALA, Okla. Library Assn. (sec. Sequoyah children's book award com. 1985-86, chmn., 1987-88), Okla. Orgn. Ednl. Tech., Assn. Ednl. Communications and Tech., Adolescent Lit. Assn., AAUW, Friends of Library, Beta Phi Mu (pres. Lambda chpt. 1973), Phi Kappa Phi, Delta Kappa Gamma (pres. Xi chpt. 1986-88), Alpha Delta Kappa. Democrat. Methodist. Home: 511 NW 40th St Lawton OK 73505 Office: Cameron U Lawton OK 73505

RACCAH, DOMINIQUE MARCELLE, publisher; b. Paris, Aug. 24, 1956; arrived in U.S., 1964; d. Paul Mordechai and Colette Bracha (Madar) R.; m. Raymond W. Bennett, Aug. 20, 1980; children: Marie, Lyron, Doran. BA, U. Ill., Chgo., 1978; MS, U. Ill., Champaign-Urbana, 1981. Research analyst Leo Burnett Advt., Chgo., 1980-81, research supr., 1981-84, assoc. research dir., 1984-87; pub., owner Fin. Sourcebooks, Naperville, Ill., 1987—. Author Financial Sourcebooks' Sources, 1987. Mem. Am. Mktg. Assn., Chgo. Book Clinic, Chgo. WOmen in Publishing, Psychometric Soc., Nat. Assn. Female Execs. Democrat. Jewish. Home: 26 N Webster St Naperville IL 60540 Office: Fin Sourcebooks PO Box 313 Naperville IL 60566

RACENET, LAUREL KAY, nurse; b. St. Johnsbury, Vt., June 25, 1957; d. Joseph Ernest and Joyce Carolyn (Salt) R. BS in Nursing, Tex. Christian U., 1979. Cert. critical care nurse. Night shift charge nurse med.-surg. unit Northeastern Vt. Regional Hosp., St. Johnsbury, 1979, night and evening charge nurse spl. care unit, 1979-81; clin. nurse progressive care unit Providence Hosp., Anchorage, 1981-85, asst. unit mgr., 1985—, asst. dir. documentation council, 1987—; ins. basic life support Am. Heart Assn., Anchorage, 1984—, advanced cardiac life support Alaska Heart Assn., Anchorage, 1983—. Mem. Am. Assn. Critical Care Nurses (cert., pres. Anchorage chpt. 1986-87), Alaska Sled Dog and Racing Assn. Republican. Baptist. Home: 3041 Brookridge Circle Anchorage AK 99504 Office: Providence Hosp Progressive Care Unit 3200 Providence Dr Anchorage AK 99502

RACHELLE, TAMAR, dancer; b. Ithaca, N.Y., May 17, 1959; d. Seymour and Rita Barbara (Liss) Smidt. Grad. high sch., Winston-Salem, N.C. Dancer Israel Ballet, Tel Aviv, 1977; corps dancer Pitts. Ballet Theatre, 1978-80, soloist, 1980-86, prin., 1986—. Mem. Am. Guild Musical Artists (bd. govs. 1987—). Office: Pitts Ballet Theatre 2900 Liberty Ave Pittsburgh PA 15201

RACITI, DOMENICA GRACE, publishing company executive; b. N.Y.C., June 2, 1928; d. Joseph and Marie (DiBiase) Raciti. B.Ed., SUNY-New Paltz, 1948; M.Ed., Columbia U., 1953, profl. diploma, 1956. Tchr. 1st grade, White Plains, N.Y., 1948-53; remedial reading tchr., Bogota, N.J., 1953-55; reading specialist Bd. Coop. Ednl. Services, White Plains, 1955-63; lang. arts cons. Northeastern U.S., 1963-65; nat. curriculum coordinator Am. Book Co., 1965-68, dir. mktg. services, N.Y.C., 1968-70, exec. editor lang. arts, 1970-73, v.p., dir. mktg., 1973-75; v.p., gen. mgr. for reading and lang. arts Houghton Mifflin Co., Boston, 1975-81, v.p., editorial dir. langs., 1981—. Mem. Internat. Reading Assn., Nat. Council Tchrs. English. Office: Houghton-Mifflin Co 1 Beacon St Boston MA 02108

RACY, JANET LOUISE, fashion executive, consultant; b. Bklyn., Jan. 3, 1952; d. Albert John and Louise Elsie (Bressmer) R. A.A.S., Fashion Inst. Tech., 1973; B.A., Queens Coll., 1977; M.A., NYU, 1978. Designer Rivets, N.Y.C., 1973-74, Goulder Co., N.Y.C., 1974-75; free-lance designer, cons. fashion, N.Y.C., 1973-82; fashion coordinator Assoc. Dry Goods, N.Y.C., 1978-82, fashion dir., 1982-86 ; mktg. dir. Gear Inc., N.Y.C., 1982; cons. NYU, 1977—, lectr. fashion merchandising and design, 1977—, adj. prof. fashion merchandising, 1978—, dir. fashion merchandising Harper's Bazaar Mag., 1987—. Recipient Community Service award NYU, 1978, Spl. Recognition award Distributive Edn. Clubs Am., 1983; Tobé scholar Inst. Retail Mgmt., NYU, 1977. Mem. Fashion Group, Fashion Rountable, Met. Mus. Art. Contbg. editor Textile Fabrics and their Selection.

RADAZAR, PAMELA ANNE, nurse; b. Fitchburg, Mass., June 8, 1944; d. Alvah Michael Reida and Sirkka Margaret (Anttila) Kao; m. Dennis Alan Joaquin, 1967 (div. 1973); children: Joshua, Amy, Sebastian; m. Yahya Radazar, Oct. 1983 (dec. Sept. 1987). BA in English, Philosophy, Calif. State U., Los Angeles, 1966; RN diploma with honors, Leominster (Mass.) Hosp., 1976; BS in Nursing cum laude, Fitchburg (Mass.) State Coll., 1982; MS magna cum laude, Lesley Coll., 1986. Substitute tchr. Fitchburg Pub. Schs., 1966-67; social worker N.Y.C. Dept. Social Services, N.Y.C., 1967-68; news correspondent The Lowell (Mass.) Sun, 1969-71; nurse lab., delivery Leominster Hosp., 1976-77; inservice coordinator Birchwood Manor Nursing Home, Fitchburg, 1977, asst. dir. nursing, 1977-78, dir. nursing, 1978-80; dir. nursing Naukeag Hosp., Ashburnham, Mass., 1980-84; asst. dir. nursing Beech Hill Hosp., Dublin, N.H., 1984-87, dir nursing, 1987—, chair utilization rev. com., 1985—; mem. adv. council allied health majors Mass. Regional Vocat. Sch., Fitchburg, Mass., 1977-84; with Area Speakers Bur., Fitchburg, 1980-84, vice chair Quality Assurance Program, 1988; cons. Quality Healthcare Resources, Inc. subs. Joint Commn. on Accreditation of Hosps. Vol. Family Planning, Fitchburg, 1981-82; del. Intercity Mgmt. Council, Fitchburg, 1980-84. Mem. Nat. Assn. Female Execs., Tri-City Nursing Home Assn. (pres. 1978-80), Nat. Nurses Assn., N.H. Nurses Assn. (program com. 1985—), Greater Fitchburg C. of C., N.H. Orgn. Exec. Nurses, N.H. Quality Assurance Assn. Office: Beech Hill Hosp Old Harrisville Rd Dublin NH 03461

RADCLIFFE, FLORENCE JACKSON, author, educational consultant; b. Richmond, Va., June 1, 1924; d. Wiliiam Alexander and Lucy (Braxton) Jackson; m. Andrew Leo Radcliffe (dec. Apr. 1962); children: Andrea Radcliffe Blagburn, Iris Radcliffe Lewis, Jacqueline. BS, Miner Tchrs. Coll., 1939; MA, NYU, 1951. Pub. sch. tchr. Washington, 1942-53; instr., supr. student tchrs. D.C. Tchrs. Coll., Washington, 1953-60, asst. prof., 1960-66; prin. Nat. Elem. Sch., Washington, 1966-74, ret.; asst. to asst. supr. pub. schs. Washington, 1974-80; ednl. cons., site visitor Office of Edn., Washington, 1986; site visitor U.S. Dept. Edn., 1986-88. Author: Jump Rope Rhymes, 1968, Simple Matter of Justice, 1985; contbr. articles to profl. jours.; editor The Columbian, 1963-54, The Pilot, Classroom Tchrs. Assn. publ., 1960-62. Chairperson Commn.'s Youth Council, Washington, 1957-60; camp dir. Phyllis Wheatley YWCA, Washington, 1957-60, pres. 1963-66; chairperson adv. bd. Sacred Heart Sch., Washington, 1983—; sec. Optempetry Bd., Washington, 1983—; bd. dirs. NCA Epilepsy, Washington, 1982—. Recipient awards Wheatley YWCA, 1966, Patterson Elem. Sch., Washington, 1974, Edmonds/Peabody Sch., Washington, 1970, D.C. Pub. Schs., 1980, numerous others. Mem. NEA (sec. D.C. chpt. 1956-60), Nat. Elem. Prin. Assn., Nat. Supervision/Curriculum Devel. Assn., Phi Delta Kappa (1st Baselius 1986). Democrat. Roman Catholic. Clubs: Apronstrings Social, Dem. Women's (Washington). Home: 4708 Blagden Ave NW Washington DC 20011

RADCLIFFE, SUSAN KEACH, educational program director; b. Nashua, N.H., Mar. 1, 1944; d. Stanley Jordan and Lola Burton (Rawson) Keach; 1 child, Alison Chase Radcliffe. Student, Bates Coll., 1960-62; BA, Upsala Coll., 1964; MA, U. Md., 1973. Tchr. Vail-Dean Sch., Elizabeth, N.J., 1965-66; tchr. English Onslow County Schs., Swansboro, N.C., 1966-68; librarian Prince George's County Schs., Hyattsville, Md., 1968; advisor, counselor U. Md., College Park, Catonsville, 1971-73; counselor Harford Community Coll. PREP, Aberdeen Proving Ground, Md., 1973-75; asst. prof. psychology Harford Community Coll., Bel Air, Md., 1975-77; specialist, coordinator instl. research Howard Community Coll., Columbia, Md., 1981-86, dir. research and personnel, 1986-87, exec. dir. research and personnel, 1987—; Pres. Md. Community Coll. Research Group, 1986-87; cons. microcomputer tng. Am. Mgmt. Assn. and others. Contbr. numerous articles to profl. jours. Active Green Mountain String Band. Office: Howard Community Coll Little Patuxent Pkwy Columbia MD 21044

RADDIN, VERONICA FIRTKO, educator; b. Bklyn., Mar. 12, 1944; d. Joseph Stephen and Veronica Mary (Berczel) Firtko; m. Thomas Albert Raddin, July 1, 1972; children: Alexander Thomas, Andrew James. BA, Rutgers U., New Brunswick, N.J., 1966; MA in Teaching, Brown U., 1967. Tchr. Morris Sch. Dist., Morristown, N.J., 1967—. Bd. dirs. Welcome Wagon of the Mendhams and Harding, Mendham, N.J., 1987—; mem. Love the Children Adoptive Parents' Assn., 1987, Nat. Trust for Historic Preservation, 1987—. Mem. NEA, N.J. Edn. Assn., Tchrs. Assn. Morris. Club: Mendham (N.J.) Racquet and Swim. Home and Office: 2 Mountainside Rd Mendham NJ 07945

RADER, (M.) ELIZABETH, accountant; b. Knoxville, Tenn., May 7, 1951; d. Charles Edward and Eleanor (Wall) R.; m. Donald Floyd McKee. BA, Rice U., 1973; MBA, Tulane U., 1975. CPA, Tex., N.Y. From staff auditor to audit mgr. Arthur Andersen & Co., Houston, 1975-81; securities profl., acctg. fellow U.S. SEC, Washington, 1981-83; audit mgr. nat. office Touche Ross & Co., N.Y.C., 1983-84, audit ptnr. Fin. Services Ctr., 1984—; exchange exec. Pres.'s Commn. on Exec. Exchange, 1983-84. Thomas J. Watson fellow, 1973-74; recipient John Burnis Allred award Tex. Soc. CPA's, 1975. Mem. Am. Inst. CPA's, Am. Acctg. Assn. (SEC liaison com. 1985-86), Fin. Women's Assn. of N.Y., Phi Beta Kappa, Beta Gamma Sigma. Methodist. Club: Roton Point (Rowayton, Conn.). Office: Touche Ross & Co One World Trade Ctr 93d Floor New York NY 10048

RADICE, ANNE-IMELDA, museum director; b. Buffalo, Feb. 29, 1948; d. Lawrence and Anne (Marino) R. A.B., Wheaton Coll., (Mass.), 1969; M.A., Villa SchiFanoia, Florence, Italy, 1971; Ph.D., U. N.C., 1976; M.B.A., Am. U., 1984. Asst. curator Nat. Gallery of Art, Washington, 1972-76; archtl. historian U.S. Capitol, Washington, 1976-80, curator Office of Architect, 1980-85; dir. Nat. Mus. Women in the Arts, 1985—. Contbr. articles to profl. jours. Home: 2311 Connecticut Ave NW Washington DC 20024 Office: Nat Mus Women in Arts New York Ave and 13th St NW Washington DC 20005

RADIN, LAURA LEVINE, state official; b. N.Y.C., Aug. 24, 1944; d. Samuel Archie and Ray (Tessler) L; m. Kalman David Radin, June 15, 1965 (div. 1972). B.S., CCNY, 1965; M.A., Columbia U., 1978. Employment interviewer N.Y. State Dept. Labor, N.Y.C., 1965-67, vocat. counselor, 1967-70, supervising interviewer, 1970-76, employement security mgr., 1976-80; environ. programs specialist Port Authority of N.Y. and N.J., N.Y.C., 1984, hazardous materials specialist, 1984, asst. mgr. Lincoln Tunnel, 1986, mgr. pub. services div. Tunnels Bridges and Terminals Dept., 1984—. Co-author: Creativity: A Human Resource, 1984. Mem. Women's Equity-Port Authority N.Y. and N.J., Women's Transp. Sem., City Coll. Alumni Assn. Bronx High Sch. Sci. Alumni Assn. Democrat. Jewish. Avocations: piano playing; tennis; skiing; travel. Office: Port Authority NY and NJ One World Trade Ctr Room 71W New York NY 10048

RADLEY, VIRGINIA LOUISE, educational administrator; b. Marion, N.Y., Aug. 12, 1927; d. Howard James and Lula (Ferris) R. B.A., Russell Sage Coll., 1949, L.H.D., 1981; M.A., U. Rochester, 1952; M.S., Syracuse U., 1957, Ph.D., 1958. Instr. English Chatham (Va.) Hall, 1952-55; asst. dean students, asst. prof. English Goucher Coll., 1957-59; dean freshmen, asst. prof. English Russell Sage Coll., 1959-60, assoc. dean, assoc. prof. English, 1960-61, prof. chmn. dept., 1961-69; dean coll., prof. English Nazareth Coll., Rochester, N.Y., 1969-73; provost for undergrad. edn., central adminstrn. State U. N.Y., Albany, 1973-74; exec. v.p., provost Coll. Arts and Scis., State U. N.Y., Oswego, 1974-76; acting pres. Coll. Arts and Scis., State U. N.Y., 1976-78, pres., 1978—; vis. prof. Syracuse U., summer 1957-59, Nazareth Coll., summer 1965; cons. N.Y. State Dept. Edn.; Chmn. commn. on women Am. Council on Edn., 1978-81; mem. commn. on higher edn. Middle States Assn., 1979-86;. Author: Samuel Taylor Coleridge, 1966, Elizabeth Barrett Browning, 1972, also articles. Mem. MLA (chmn. regional sect. Romanticisn 1969), English Inst., Pi Lambda Theta. Republican. Home: Shady Shore SUNY Oswego NY 13126

RADSPINNER, DIANA BRAIDEN, academic communications specialist; b. N.Y.C., Jan. 25, 1942; d. William Patrick and Margaret Mary (Smith) Braiden; m. Frank Hanly Radspinner, Dec. 22, 1978. BS, SUNY, Oswego, 1963; MA, U. Calif., San Francisco, 1972. Tchr. Smithtown (N.Y.) Unified Sch. Dist., 1963-65; tchr., adminstr. Berkeley (Calif.) Unified Sch. Dist., 1965-78; coordinator cable communications Dallas Ind. Sch. Dist., 1978—; cons. State of Calif., Sacramento, 1971-74, Infomart, Dallas, 1985-87. Mem. steering com. Metroplex Closeup, Dallas, 1983—, Shakespeare in the Park, Ft. Worth, 1985—; mem. City of Dallas Mayoral Task Force, 1984-86; mem. com. Am. Cancer Soc., Dallas, 1985—. Recipient 1st Place Ethnic Expression award Nat. Fedn. Local Cable Program Assn., 1986-87, Crystal award Warner-Am. Express, 1985—. Mem. Tex. Computer Edn. Assn. (bd. dirs.), Dallas Adminstrv. Assn., Women in Communications.

RADUKA, SHARLENE EDITH, manufacturing company executive; b. Rockville Centre, N.Y., Dec. 19, 1952; d. Frank and Edith (Rosenau) R. BS in Indsl. Engring., Rutgers U., New Brunswick, 1974; MBA, Rutgers U., Newark, 1979; CPIM, 1986. Cert. practitioner inventory mgmt. Indsl. engr. Union Carbide Corp., Bound Brook, N.J., 1974-78; indsl. engr. Thomas & Betts Corp., Raritan, N.J., 1979-81, fin. analyst, 1982-83, project leader, 1984-86, project mgr., 1987—. Nat. mem. The Smithsonian Assocs., Washington; contbr. The Statue of Liberty Ellis Island Found., Inc., N.Y.C., 1984-86. Fellow Am. Inst. Indsl. Engrs.; mem. Am. Prodn. and Inventory Control Soc., Rutgers U. Alumni Assn. Presbyterian. Home: 29 Redbud Rd Piscataway NJ 08854 Office: Thomas & Betts Corp 1001 Frontier Rd Bridgewater NJ 08807

RAEDER, MYRNA SHARON, educator, lawyer; b. N.Y.C., Feb. 4, 1947; d. Samuel and Estelle (Auslander) R.; m. Terry Oliver Kelly, July 13, 1975; 1 child, Thomas Oliver. B.A., Hunter Coll., 1968; J.D., NYU, 1971; LL.M., Georgetown U., 1975. Bar: N.Y. 1972, D.C. 1972, Calif. 1972. Spl. asst. U.S. atty. U.S. Atty.'s Office, Washington, 1972-73; asst. prof. U. San Francisco Sch. Law, 1973-75; assoc. O'Melveny & Myers, Los Angeles, 1975-79; assoc. prof. Southwestern U. Sch. Law, Los Angeles, 1979-82, prof., 1983—. Prettyman fellow Georgetown Law Ctr., Washington, 1971-73. Author: Federal Pretrial Practice, 1987. Mem. ABA (chmn. com. on fed. rules and criminal procedure criminal justice sect. 1987, trial evidence com. litigation sect. 1980—), Assn. Am. Law Schs. (com. on sects. 1984-87 , chairperson women in legal edn. sect. 1982), Order of Coif, Phi Beta Kappa. Office: Southwestern U Sch Law 675 S Westmoreland Los Angeles CA 90005

RAEZER, SALLIE STEWART, software company executive; b. N.Y.C., May 11, 1951; d. John Larry and Margaret Ann (Thompson) Stewart; m. John Raezer, Aug. 18, 1984; children: John Kenneth, Julie Rebecca. BA, Bucknell U., 1973. Programmer to systems analyst Sperry Univac, Blue Bell, Pa., 1973-75; systems analyst Prudential Ins. Co. Am., Dresher, Pa., 1975-76; systems engr. Datapoint Corp., Bala-Cynwyd, Pa., 1976-78; v.p., bus. design architect Finpac Corp., Narberth, Pa., 1978—, bd. dirs., sec.; founder SR Investment Co., Narberth, Pa., 1984—. Mem. Soc. Indsl. and Applied Math., Bucknell U. Alumni Assn. (trustee 1978-83). Club: Island Heights (N.J.) Yacht. Home: 107 Foxhall Ln Narberth PA 19072 Office: Finpac Corp Windsor and Forrest Aves Narberth PA 19072

RAFAEL, RUTH KELSON, archivist, librarian, consultant; b. Wilmington, N.C., Oct. 28, 1929; d. Benjamin and Jeanette (Spicer) Kelson; m. Richard Vernon Rafael, Aug. 26, 1951; children—Barbara Jeanette Rafael Martinez, Brenda Elaine. B.A., San Francisco State U., 1953, M.A., 1954; M.L.S., U. Calif.-Berkeley, 1968. Tchr. San Francisco Unified Sch. Dist., 1956-57; librarian Congregation Beth Sholom, San Francisco, 1965-83; asst. archivist Western Jewish History Ctr. of Judah L. Magnes Mus., Berkeley, Calif., 1968, head archivist, librarian, 1969—; cons. Inst. Righteous Acts, Berkeley, 1982-83, NEH, Washington, Congregation Sherith Israel, San Francisco, Mount Zion Hosp., San Francisco, Benjamin Swig archives project, San Francisco, Camp Swig, Saratoga, Calif. Author: Continuum, 1976, rev. edit., 1977; (with Davies and Woogmaster) (poems) Relatively Speaking, 1981; Western Jewish History Ctr.: Archival and Oral History Collections, Judah L. Magnes Meml. Mus., 1987, Second Hand, Maybe, Ghetto, No, The Californians, 1986; contbg. editor Western States Jewish Hist., 1979—. Mem. exec. bd. Bay Area Library Info. Network, 1986—. Bur. Jewish Edn. scholar, San Francisco, 1983; NEH grantee, 1985. Mem. Soc. Am. Archivists, ALA, Soc. Calif. Archivists, Calif. Library Assn., No. Calif. Assn. Jewish Librarians (pres. 1975-76), Jewish Arts Council of the Bay (bd. dirs. 1981-83), Spl. Libraries Assn. Office: Western Jewish History Ctr Judah L Magnes Mus 2911 Russell St Berkeley CA 94705

RAFAELS, DIANE, marketing director; b. Kingsport, Tenn., Aug. 7, 1940; d. John Claude and Sarah Katherine (Piety) Catron; m. David Michael Deans, Oct. 25, 1957 (div. Sept. 1975) children—Juliana Susan, Leslie Gloria; m. Umberto Rafaels, Mar. 28, 1985. A.A., Sullins Coll., Bristol, Va., 1959. Cert. mktg. dir. Assoc. account exec. Ehrich-Manes Advt., Bethesda, Md., 1974-76; asst. mall mgr. Kettler Bros., Gaithersburg, Md., 1976-79; mktg. dir. Farber Co., Pompano Beach, Fla., 1979-80, Springfield Mall, Va., 1980-83; communications mgr. MD-IPA, Rockville, Md., 1983; dir. mktg. Chas. E. Smith Cos., Arlington, Va., 1983—; mem. adv. bd., dir. MD-IPA, Rockville; cons., Publicity & Media Resources, Falls Church, Va. Contbr. articles to profl. jours. and mags. Chmn. communications com. Fairfax County Arts Council, Va., 1982-83; publicity com. Internat. Children's Festival-Wolftrap, Vienna, Va., 1982-83, mktg. com. chair, 1985-86. Recipient Vol. Recognition awards Fairfax County Fire Dept., 1983, N. Va. Lung Assn., 1983, United Way, 1982-83. Mem. Internat. Council Shopping Ctrs., Women in Advt. and Mktg., Washington Ad Club, Fairfax County C. of C. (communications com. 1981-84), Arlington County C. of C. (communications com. 1984-85), Montgomery County C. of C. (communications com. 1983). Democrat. Methodist. Clubs: Jr. Women's of Rockville (pres. 1972-73), Jr. Clubs (Md. state dir. 1974-76), Contemporary (v.p. 1984-86). Avocations: reading, needlework. Office: Chas E Smith Cos 1735 Jeff Davis Hwy Arlington VA 22202

RAFE, KATHLEEN BERNADETTE, behavioral communication consultant; b. Phila., June 10, 1952; d. John Louis Rutowski and Nancy M. Brooke; m. Stephen C. Rafe, Dec. 31, 1983; children: Gary Eugene, Timothy John. Grad., Middlesex County Coll., Edison, N.J., 1981. Project mgr. Coll. of Medicine and Dentistry, Piscataway, N.J., 1980-82; owner Key Comp, Parlin, N.J., 1980-83; co-owner, exec. mgr., behavioral cons. Starfire Enterprises, Warrenton, Va., 1983—; asst. hydrotherapist Children's Specialized Hosp. Mountainside, N.J., 1988; substitute tchr. Fauquier County, Va. schs.; speaker Venezula Tng. Club. Contbr. photographs to mags. Vol. Handicapped Riders Assn., Bedminster, N.J., 1984-86, Children's Specialized Hosp., Mountainside, N.J., 1986—. Mem. Animal Behavior Soc. Mem. Christian Ch. Home: Rt 1 Box 327 F Warrenton VA 22186 Office: Starfire Enterprises PO Box 3119 Warrenton VA 22186

RAFF, BEVERLY STEIN, foundation administrator; b. N.Y.C., Nov. 15, 1933; d. Samuel and Rose (Deutsch) Stein; m. Joseph Raff, Apr. 11, 1954; children: Marla Lynn, Garry Scott. BS, Bellevue Sch. Nursing, 1955; MA, NYU, 1967, PhD, 1976. Asst. prof. SUNY, Farmingdale, 1967-71; assoc. prof. Adelphi U., Garden City, N.Y., 1971-78; v.p. profl. edn. March of Dimes Birth Defects Found., White Plains, N.Y., 1978—; bd. dirs. NCC Certification Corp. Co-author Maternity Nursing, 1982; mem. editorial bd. Issues in Health Care of Women, N.Y.C., 1985—. Bd. dirs. Alliance of Genetic Support Group, Washington, 1985, Family Aide, Inc., Hicksville, N.Y., 1985-87. Mem. Nurses Assn. of Am. Coll. Ob-Gyns. (vice chair dist. II 1982-84), Am. Nurses Assn. (councils, coms. 1985-87, Perinatal Nurse of Yr. 1986), Nat. Perinatal Assn. Office: March of Dimes Birth Defects Found 1275 Mamaroneck Ave White Plains NY 10605

RAFF, SANDRA BETH, internist; b. N.Y.C., June 9, 1947; d. Edward and Claire (Barcham) R. BA, NYU, 1967; MD, N.Y. Med. Coll., 1971. Rotating intern Beth Israel Med. Ctr., N.Y.C., 1971-72, resident-in-internal medicine, 1972-74; asst. prof. internal medicine U. Ala. Sch. Medicine, Tuscaloosa, 1976-77, U. Conn. Sch. Medicine, Hartford, 1977-79; practice medicine specializing in diabetes and endocrinology Cromwell, Conn., 1980-84, Middletown, Conn., 1984—; attending physician Middlesex Meml. Hosp., Middletown, 1978—; instr. clin. medicine NYU Sch. Medicine, 1974-76; cons. Elmcrest Psychiat. Hosp., Portland, Conn., 1983—; physician advisor Conn. Peer Rev. Orgn., 1984—; bd. dirs. M.D. Health Plan, New Haven. Contbr. articles to med. jours. Bd. dirs. Greater Middletown Chorale, 1986-88. Mem. AMA, ACP, Am. Soc. Internal Medicine, Am. Diabetes Assn. (diabetic camp com. 1980—), Psi Chi, Delta Phi Epsilon. Office: 520 Saybrook Rd Middletown CT 06457

RAFFALOW, JANET TERRY, law librarian; b. Burbank, Calif., Oct. 11, 1947; d. Melvin and Honey (Sobel) Whitney; m. Richard Elliott Raffalow, June 9, 1984. BA, UCLA, 1968, MLS, 1969, cert. in pub. adminstrn., 1980. Cert. community coll. tchr., Calif. Young adult librarian Los Angeles Pub. Library, 1969-70; librarian Calif. Atty. Gen.'s Library, Los Angeles, 1970-78, supervising librarian, 1978—. Vol. Pub. TV-KCET, Los Angeles, 1973—; vice chmn. Los Angeles Jr. C. of C., 1979-81; vol. citizens commn. Los Angeles Olympic Organizing Com., 1982-84; mem. City of Hope. Mem. Los Angeles Law Librarians Assn. (long range planning com.), Am. Assn. Law Libraries (cert.), So. Calif. Assn. Law Libraries, UCLA Library Sch. Alumni Assn. Democrat. Jewish. Club: Sunshines of Cedars Sinai, (v.p. 1971-73). Office: Calif Atty Gen's Library 3580 Wilshire Blvd Room 701 Los Angeles CA 90010

RAFFERTY, GENEVIEVE KENNEDY, social service agy. adminstr.; b. Davenport, Iowa, Jan. 21, 1922; d. Thomas Cyril and Mabel Veronica (Finefield) Kennedy; B.A., St. Ambrose Coll., 1942; postgrad. U. Iowa, 1972; m. Daniel J. Rafferty, Aug. 22, 1942 (dec. 1984); children—Daniel D., Michele M., Genevieve, Thomas K., Eileen M., Margaret M., Sheila M. Real estate saleswoman Manhard Realty, Moline, Ill., 1950-59; substitute tchr., Rock Island, Ill., 1963-67; head start tchr. Rock Island-Scott County Dept. Social Services, 1966; public welfare worker Scott County Dept. Social Services, Davenport, Iowa, 1967-72; exec. dir. Info., Referral and Assistance Service, Rock Island, 1972—; chair Rock Island Housing Authority; mem. Quad-City Council on Crime and Delinquency, 1977-80; mem. Rock Island County Council on Alcoholism, 1976-82; chairperson CETA Adv. Bd., 1982-84, bi state metropolitan planning comn. 1986—; steering com., Quad-City Vision for the Future, 1987; bd. dirs. Quint-City Drug Abuse. Named Social Worker of Yr. Quad-City, Nat Assn. Social Workers, 1973. Mem. Nat. Assn. Social Workers, Iowa Council Info. and Referral Providers, Nat. Conf. Social Welfare, Ill. Welfare Assn., NOW, Ill. Alliance Info. and Referral Services (dir.). Republican. Roman Catholic. Office: 2002 3d Ave Rock Island IL 61201

RAGAN, ELIZABETH HOFFMAN, retired business executive; b. Albemarle, N.C., Nov. 11, 1916; d. Joseph Filson and Lilly Bassett (Carter) Hoffman; cert. bus. adminstrn. High Point Coll., 1937; m. Herbert Tomlinson Ragan, Oct. 14, 1939 (div. Sept. 1985); 1 son, Herbert Tomlinson. Head bond dept. Sunflower Ordnance Works, Hercules Powder Co., DeSota, Kans., 1942-45; sec.-treas. Ragan-Carmichael, Inc., High Point, N.C., 1956-74, Staple Products, Inc., High Point, 1956-74, R & C Holding Co., Inc., High Point, 1956-74, sec. Ragan Hardware Co., Inc. (merger), High Point, 1974-82; trustee Ragan-Hardware, Inc., Profit Sharing Trust and Pension Trust, 1974-82. Cellist, N.C. Symphony, 1932-35. Mem. adv. bd. Maryfield Nursing Home, 1975-79; bd. visitors High Point Coll., 1979-82; mem. exec. bd. Friends of Guilford Coll. Library, 1980-82. Democrat. Mem. Soc. of Friends (organist, choir dir.), High Point Hist. Soc. (dir. 1977-81, pres. 1979-80). Author, compiler: The Lineage of the Amos Ragan Family, 1976. Home: 1825 Country Club Dr High Point NC 27260

RAGLAND, ALWINE MULHEARN, judge; b. Monroe, La., July 28, 1913; m. LeRoy Smith, 1947 (dec.); children—LeRoy, Caroline Smith Christman; m. 2d, L. Percy Ragland, Mar., 1978. A.A., Principia Coll., St. Louis; J.D., Tulane U., 1935. Bar: La. 1935. Sole practice, Tallulah, La., 1935-74; mem. firm Mulhearn & Smith, 1972-74; judge 6th Jud. Dist. Ct., Lake Prvidence, La., 1974—; atty. for inheritance tax collector Madison Parish, La., 1968-74; former city atty., Delta, La.; temporary judge La. Ct. Appeals (2d cir.), 1976. Charter bd. dirs. Silver Waters council Girl Scouts U.S.A.; past pres. Band Boosters Assn. Tallulah High Sch., Tallulah High Sch. PTA; past dist. dir., past bd. dirs, lay reader 1st Ch. Christ Scientist, Vicksburg, Miss.; past bd. dirs. Delta Christian Sch. Mem. ABA, La. Bar Assn., 6th Jud. Bar Assn., Am. Judges Assn., La. Judges Assn., Am. Judicature Soc., La. Council Juvenile and Family Ct. Ct. Judges (past pres.), Nat. Council Juvenile Ct. Judges, So. Juvenile Ct. Judges, Assn. Trial Lawyers Am., La. Trial Lawyers Assn., Family Conciliation Cts. and Services, Nat. Juvenile Ct. Service Assn., La. Conf. Social Welfare, Practicing Law Inst., Nat. Assn. Women Judges, La. Assn. Def. Counsel. Home and Office: PO Box 392 Lake Providence LA 71254

RAGLAND, LEGORA ELAINE, insurance executive; b. Phila., Dec. 25, 1939; d. Sherman and Lillian Kate (Ward) Gauthney; m. Raymond Ragland Jr., Sept. 29, 1962; children: Raymond III, Steven Andrew, Phillip Sherman. AS in Acctg., Temple U., 1961. Acctg. clk. Penn Mut. Life Ins. Co., Phila., 1957-61; exec. sec. Gen. Electric Co., Phila., 1961-65; project dir. Wynnefield Residents Assn., Phila., 1972-75, asst. dir., 1975-77, exec. dir., 1977-80; salesman, investment cons. N.Y. Life Ins. Co., Phila., 1980—; cons. in tax, acctg., investment, 1962—; ins. counselor Innovative Fin. Services, Phila., 1986—, Employee Communications Systems, Dallas, 1987—. Mem. affiliate funding com. United Way, PHila., 1986—; pres. Wynnefield Devel. Corp., Phila., 1981-85; pres. adv. council Wynnefield Cultural Ctr., bd. dirs. Wynnefield Residents Assn., 1980—. Baptist. Club: Nat. Pinochle Social and Civic. Home: 5102 Overbrook Ave Philadelphia PA 19131

RAGLAND, LINDA KYKER, publishing company owner; b. Johnson City, Tenn., July 1, 1951; d. Calvin Allen Kyker and Buena Rose (Elliott) Lentz; m. Kenneth Wayne Van Dyke, Aug. 22, 1969 (div. 1979); m. Joe Frank Ragland, Sept. 5, 1981. Student, State Area Vo-Tech, Blountville, Tenn., 1972-74, Columbus (Ga.) Coll., 1986. Regional sales tng. mgr. Allstate Ins. Co., Charlotte, N.C., 1974-84; realtor Showcase Realty, Columbus, Ga., 1984; mgr. TMC Long Distance, Columbus, 1985; sales Windsor Pub., Columbus, 1985; owner Ragtime Pub., Columbus, 1987—. Mem. Christian Edn. com., Columbus, 1985—; treas. Symphony Women, Columbus, 1987; candidate Columbus Tax Commr., 1984. Mem. Advt. Club of Columbus, Columbus Area Network For Profl. & Exec. Women (bd. dirs. 1986—), LWV, Southern Bicycle League. Presbyterian. Club: Chattahoochee Cycling (Columbus). Home and Office: 1803 Buena Vista Rd Columbus GA 31906

RAGONE, THERESE VICTORIA, transportation executive; b. Bklyn., Oct. 13, 1935; d. James Vincent and Celeste Marie (Pizzani) R.; m. Harold Anthony Castellano, Sept. 15, 1956 (div. 1971); children: Michele, Harold Jr., James, Suzanne, Victoria. Student, Suffolk Community Coll. Single copy rep. Newsday, Inc., Melville, N.Y., 1978-79, single copy supr., 1979-81, transp. field supr., 1981-82, asst. transp. foreman, 1982—. Home: 175 Main Ave 114 Wheatley Heights NY 11798 Office: Newsday Inc Pinelawn Rd Melville NY 11747

RAGONETTI, MARCIA L., marketing professional; b. Auburn, Nebr., June 5, 1950; d. Harold G. and Marcille (Poppe) Lortscher; m. Thomas J. Ragonetti, Dec. 30, 1971; 1 child, Peter. AB with distinction, Cornell U., 1972, MA in Teaching, 1973. Tchr. Ithaca (N.Y.) Pub. Schs., 1973-74; asst. dir. pub. info. Simmons Coll., Boston, 1974-75; mgr. pub. relations/advt. Cabot, Cabot & Forbes, Boston, 1975-77; dir. advt./mktg. Van Schaack & Co Realtors, Denver, 1977-81; pres., owner Copy By Design, Denver, 1981—; mem., solo artist Opera Colo., 1982—; trustee, bd. dirs., chmn. mktg. com. Young Audiences, Inc., Denver, 1986—. Grantee Denver Lyric Opera Guild, 1986, Met. Opera Nat. Council, 1984. Mem. Cornell U. Alumni Assn. (chmn. secondary schs. com. 1981-83), Denver Advt. Fedn., Denver Vocal Arts Ensamble (co-founder), Cornell U. Nat. Council, Phi Beta Kappa, Phi Kappa Phi. Methodist.

RAGSDALE, DOROTHY HELEN, human resources consultant; b. Jackson, Ill., Jan. 7, 1951. BBA in Personnel Mgmt. Mktg., Loyola U., 1972. Human resources rep. Inland Steel, Chgo., 1973-85; personnel rep. Inland Steel, East Chicago, Ind., 1985; mgr. employment div. Softsheen Product, Chgo., 1985-87; mgr. relocation Moran, Stahl & Boyer, N.Y.C., 1987—; mgr. HR devel. Bell & Howell; cons. Roosevelt U., Chgo., 1986. Mem., panelist Youth Motivation merit Com., Chgo., 1973-85; mem., bd. dirs. vocat. adv. council Chgo. City Coll., 1979-81. Am. Industry and Steel Inst. fellow, 1982-84. Mem. Midwest Coll. Placement Assn.

RAHBAR, ZITA INA, health insurance executive; b. Kaunas, Lithuania, Mar. 15, 1937; came to U.S. 1949; d. Stasys and Ona (Eitkeviciute) Carneckas; m. Vytautas Dudenas, June 20, 1960 (div. 1965); m. 2d, Darius Rahbar, Mar. 26, 1970. B.A. St. Xavier Coll., Chgo., 1957; postgrad. in physiology U. Chgo., 1957-59, M.B.A., 1978. Mng. editor Lyons & Carnahan div. Meredith Corp., Chgo., 1960-68, mgr. program planning, 1968-73; exec. cons. George S. May Co., Chgo., 1973-75; sr. cons. planning Blue Shield Assn., Chgo., 1975-76, dir. corp. planning Blue Shield/Blue Cross Assn., 1976-78, sr. dir. program devel. and implementation, 1978-81, v.p. mktg. Blue Cross Calif., Los Angeles and Oakland, Calif., 1981-87; pres., Creative Mktg. Solutions, 1987—. Bd. dirs. Bethune Ballet, Los Angeles, 1982—; mem. com. Orgn. Women Execs., Los Angeles, 1982—; co-founder Women in Pub., Chgo., 1965; mem. NOW, Town Hall Calif., Chgo. Council Fgn. Relations, World Affairs Council Los Angeles. Fellow U. Chgo., 1957-58. Mem. Am. Mgmt. Assn., Am. Mktg. Assn., AAAS, Republican. Roman Catholic. Home: 912 Blue Spring Dr Westlake Village CA 91361

RAHDERT, ELIZABETH ROSE QUANZ, pharmacist, clinical psychologist; b. Evanston, Ill., May 13, 1935; d. Carl Peter and Josephine Anne (Kirk) Quanz; student Albert Ludwigs Universitat, Freiburg, W.Ger., 1955-56; B.S. in pharmacy, Purdue U., 1958, M.S. in Psychology, 1975, Ph.D. in Psychology (David Ross fellow), 1980; m. June 7, 1958 (div. 1982); children—David A., Diana M. Research pharmacologist asst. in biomed. research Dow Chem. Co., Indpls., 1959-61; asst. dir. spl. edn. Greater Lafayette (Ind.) Area Spl. Services, 1976-77; psychology intern VA Hosp., Danville, Ill., 1979-80; asst. prof. clin. pharmacy Purdue U., 1980-86; clin. psychopharmacologist treatment research br. Div. Clin. Research, Nat. Inst. Drug Abuse, Rockville, Md., 1985—. Bd. dirs. Family Service Agy., Tippecanoe County, Ind., 1971-75; bd. dirs. Tippecanoe County Youth Services Bur., 1973-76, pres. bd., 1974-76. Mem. Am. Psychol. Assn., Ind. Psychol. Assn., Am. Pharm. Assn., Ind. Pharmacists Assn., Am. Soc. Hosp. Pharmacists, Ind. Soc. Hosp. Pharmacists, Am. Assn. Colls. Pharmacy, AAUW, Kappa Epsilon. Office: Nat Inst Drug Abuse Div Clin Research 5600 Fishers Ln Rockville MD 20857

RAHEEL, MASTURA, textile scientist, educator; b. Lahore, Pakistan, Mar. 1, 1938; d. Sultan Mohamad and Firdous Dean; M.S., Punjab U., 1959, Okla. State U., 1962; Ph.D., U. Minn., 1971; m. Akbar Javed Raheel, Jan. 25, 1959; children—Seemal, Salman. Asst. prof., head dept. textiles and clothing Home Econs. Coll., Lahore, Pakistan, 1960-77; lectr. textiles and clothing U. Minn., 1977-78; vis. prof. Ind. U., Bloomington, 1978; asst. prof. textile sci. U. Ill., Urbana, 1978-84, assoc. prof., 1984—, chmn. div. textiles, apparel and interior design, 1987—. Ford. Found. fellow, 1960-62, 68-71, research award grantee, 1979—. Mem. Am. Coll. Profs. Textiles and Clothing, Am. Assn. Textile Chemists and Colorists, Am. Home Econs. Assn., Coll. International de L'enseignement Textile, Omicron Nu, Sigma Xi. Contbr. research articles to profl. and tech. jours. Home: 1904 S Vine St Urbana IL 61801 Office: U Ill 239 Bevier Hall Urbana IL 61801

RAHM, KAREN ELIZABETH LANE, business executive; b. Bklyn., Apr. 21, 1944; d. Gilbert H. and Joan Elizabeth (Dean) Lane, Jr.; A.A., Packer Collegiate Inst., 1962; B.A. magna cum laude, Allegheny Coll., 1964; M.A., Ind. U., 1966; m. Carl Michael Rahm, Feb. 3, 1968; 1 son, Christopher Michael. Economist, Fed. Res. Bank of N.Y., 1966-70; planning devel. officer Econ. Devel. Adminstrn., Seattle, 1970-71; successively urban economist, asst. dir. econ. devel., dir. econ. devel. Seattle Dept. Community Devel., 1971-77; mgr. planning div. King County, Seattle, 1977-81; dir. Wash. State Planning and Community Affairs Agy., Olympia, 1981-83; sec. Wash. State Dept. Social and Health Services, 1983-85; sr. dir. portfolio devel. Glacier Park Co. subs. Burlington No., Inc., Seattle, 1986-87, v.p., 1987—; Bd. dirs. Pacific Med. Ctr.; trustee Children's Home Soc. Washington, 1986—; bd. dirs. Alki Found., 1987—mem. Wash. Corrections Standards Bd., 1981-83; mem. Wash. State Housing Fin. Commn., 1983, Wash. State Adv. Commn. on Intergovtl. Relations, 1982-84. Mem. Seattle Bd. Freeholders, 1974-75, Wash. Commn. Constl. Alternatives, 1976; chmn. Women Execs. in State Govt., 1985. Mem. Council State Community Affairs Agys. (sec. 1983), LWV, Lambda Alpha. Office: 1011 Western Ave Seattle WA 98104

RAIFORD, SHERI STORY, interior designer, consultant; b. Oak Ridge, Tenn., May 18, 1947; d. Marion Delmar and Helen Winagene (Nichols) Story; m. David Carlton Raiford, Feb. 2, 1974. BS in Interior Design, U. Tenn., 1969. Designer Goodstein Hahn Shore and Binkley, Knoxville, Tenn., 1971-72; project designer Assoc. Space Design, Inc., Atlanta, 1973-77; sr. assoc. Thompson Ventulett Stainback & Assocs., Atlanta, 1977—. Home: 2942 Shady Creek Ln Marietta GA 30062 Office: Thompson Ventulett Stainback & Assocs 12th Floor N CNN Ctr Atlanta GA 30303

RAIMONDO, BEVERLY NICKELL, data processing company executive; b. Lexington, Ky., Feb. 24, 1946; d. William Rice and Frances Louise (Jinkins) Nickell; m. Anthony Neal Raimondo, Apr. 24, 1976; children: Christa Nickell, Laurel Dana. BA in Edn., U. Ky., 1968, MSLS, 1969; postgrad. Xavier U., 1974-78. Librarian, IBM Corp., Lexington, 1969-75, edn. coordinator, 1975-79, mgr., 1979-81, project mgr., 1982-84, adminstrv. asst., 1984-86, plans and controls mgr. 1987; seminar instr. U. Ky. Community Edn., Lexington, 1981-83. Co-chmn., March of Dimes Mother's March, Lexington, 1984; mem. Fayette County Schs. task force for excellence in edn., 1984-85; mem. Blue Grass Trust for Historic Preservation, 1981—, Leadership Lexington, 1983-84; bd. dirs. Lexington Children's Theatre, 1985—, pres. 1987—88; bd. dirs. YWCA, 1987—. Recipient IBM IPD Achievement award, 1982. Mem. Profl. Women's Forum, Ky. Library Assn., U. Ky. Alumni Assn., Beta Phi Mu (pres. 1974). Republican. Christian Science. Clubs: Cotillion, Spindletop Hall. Avocations: boating; reading; spectator sports. Home: 1327 Strawberry Ln Lexington KY 40502

RAIMONDO, MICHELE CARMELA, speech therapist; b. Jersey City, Aug. 9, 1951; d. James Frank and Carmela H. (Marchitelli) R. BA, Montclair State Coll., 1973. Speech therapist Union City (N.J.) Bd. Edn., 1975-81, 85—; program dir. N.J. Spl Olympics, Piscataway, 1981-85; chairperson, event dir. Bergen County Spl. Olympics, Ridgefield Park, N.J., 1985-87; chairperson curriculum Union City Speech Dept., 1986; instr. sign lang. Girl Scouts U.S., Paramus council, 1986—. Troop leader Girl Scouts U.S., Bergen County Council, 1985—, trainer, 1986—, service unit program task force, Paramus council, 1987—, chmn. service unit, Ridgefield Park, N.J., 1986—. Mem. Union City Edn. Assn. (bldg. rep. 1985-87), N.J. Edn. Assn., NEA. Democrat. Roman Catholic. Home: 143 Church St Lodi NJ 07644 Office: Jefferson Sch 3400 Palisade Ave Union City NJ 07087

RAINES, JEAN WALKER, health care educator and administrator; b. Roxboro, N.C., Mar. 9, 1940; m. James G. Raines, Sept. 23, 1961; children: Teresa, Jennifer. RN, Meml. Hosp. Sch. Nursing, Danville, Va., 1961; BS magna cum laude, Christopher Newport Coll., 1986. RN, Va. Staff nurse Riverside Hosp., Newport News, Va., 1961-65, supr. nurses, 1965-71, in-service instr., 1971-76, dir. dept. staff devel., 1976-86; dir. co. care Riverside Healthcare Assn., Newport News, 1986-88, dir. corp. staff devel., 1986—; v.p. Raines Constrn., Ltd., 1977—; cons. in field. Mem. editorial staff The Riverside Nurse, 1984—; contbr. articles to profl. jours. Pilot mem. United Way Va. Peninsula, Newport News, 1985-86; mem. Am. Heart Assn. Recipient Presdl. plaque Va. Chpt. Am. Soc. for Healthcare Edn. and Trg., 1980, Disting. Mem. award Va. Chpt. Am. Soc. for Helthcare Edn. and Trg., 1981. Mem. Am. Soc. for Healthcare Educators (pres. Va. chpt. 1980, chairperson 1983-85), Nat. Assn. for Occupational Health Nurses, Nat. Assn. for Exec. Women, Peninsula C. of C. Methodist. Office: Riverside Healthcare Assn 606 Denbigh Blvd Suite 301 Newport News VA 23602

RAINES, JOAN BINDER, literary agent; b. N.Y.C., July 25, 1931; d. Samuel Lawrence and Shirley (Cooper) Binder; student Columbia U.; m. Theron Raines, July 29, 1971; 1 son, Keith B. Korman. Office mgr. Raines Agy., N.Y.C., 1968, agt., 1969—, ptnr., 1974—. Contbr. articles to N.Y. Daily News Sunday Mag., St. Anthony Messenger. Mem. Soc. Authors' Reps., Authors Guild (assoc.). Office: 71 Park Ave New York NY 10016

RAINES, JO-ANN RYAN, real estate salesperson; b. N.Y.C., June 4, 1948; d. James Henry Ryan and Vevette Yvonne (Morales) Ryan Lewis; m. Rudolf Lawrence Raines, June 14, 1980; children: Aisha, Dana, Felicia, Christopher. B.A. in Social Scis., St. John's U., Jamaica, N.Y., 1969; M.A. in Adult Edn. Columbia, U., 1976; cert. in mktg. and mgmt. Trenton State Coll., 1984. Lic. in real estate sales, N.J. Ednl. cons. N.Y. Telephone, N.Y.C., 1969-76; staff mgr. AT&T, Bedminster, N.J., 1976-84; real estate salesperson Bea M. Scott Realty, East Orange, N.J., 1985-88, Coldwell Banker Real Estate, Livingston, N.J., 1988—; career cons., South Orange, N.J., 1985—. Mem. South Orange/Maplewood Awareness Council, 1982—; bd. dirs. Gardens Nursery Sch., N.Y.C., 1978-81, Assn. Retarded Citizens for Essex County, N.J., 1983—. Mem. Nat. Assn. Female Execs., Nat. Assn. Realtors, Phi Delta Kappa, Sigma Delta Pi, Delta Sigma Theta (v.p. chpt. 1968-69). Democrat. Roman Catholic. Avocations: reading; aerobics; travel. Home: 357 Irving Ave South Orange NJ 07079 Office: Coldwell Banker Real Estate Livingston Mall Eisenhower Pkwy Livingston NJ 07039

RAINEY, GAIL RICHARDS, medical laboratory executive; b. Milford, Conn., Aug. 18, 1932; d. James Gardner and Isabel Lavica (Capps) R. AB cum laude, Adelphi U., 1957; A. in Gen. Studies, SUNY, Bklyn., 1961. Supr. lab. E.R. Marino, Bklyn., 1961-65; owner, dir. Rainey Med. Lab., Orleans, Mass., 1965—. Chmn. com. Nauset Regional Sch., Orleans, 1971-75, Orleans Bd. Health, 1985—. Mem. Nat. Assn. Female Execs., Assn. Med. Technologists, Am. Assn. Bioanalysts, Bus. and Profl. Women (named Woman of Yr. 1985, 86). Democrat. Home and Office: PO Box 975 Orleans MA 02653

RAINEY, KAY GODBEY, city official; b. Ft. Worth, Jan. 18, 1946; d. Paschal Lee and Ester Katherine (Williams) Godbey; m. Billy King Rainey, Nov. 29, 1975; children—Tammy Denise Black, Shelly Rae Ramos. AAS, Tarrant County Jr. Coll., 1985; B in Career Arts Dallas Bapt. U., 1987, postgrad. U. Tex., Arlington, 1988—. Cert. mcpl. clk., Tex. peace officer. Ct. clk. City of Ft. Worth, 1966-68; transcriber for ct. reporters, Dallas and Tarrant Counties, 1970-75; sec. City of Euless Police Dept., Tex., 1975-81; city sec. Euless, 1981—; speaker, instr. police report writing Tex. A&M U., Tarrant County Jr. Coll. Police Acad., 1979-81; speaker IBM, various computer groups, Tex., Calif., 1983—, North Tex. State U. Ctr. for Community Services, Denton, 1984, 87—. Recipient Disting. Service awards Euless Police Dept., 1976, 79. Mem. Internat. Inst. Mcpl. Clks. Advanced Acad. (com. on technol. devel. 1984—), Tex. Mcpl. Clks. Assn. Inc. (trustee officer, 1987—), Bus. and Profl. Women, Assn. Record Mgrs. and Adminstrs., North Tex. City Secs. Assn. (pres. 1986). Baptist. Avocations: reading, hiking. Home: PO Box 1344 Euless TX 76039 Office: PO Box 1344 Euless TX 76039-3595

RAINEY, MARY CATHERINE, home economics educator; b. Wilmette, Ill., Feb. 27, 1941; d. Clarence Wager and Clarissa (Devney) R. BS, St. Mary's Coll., Notre Dame, Ind., 1963; MA, Mich. State U., 1967, PhD, 1971. Vol. U.S. Peace Corps, Philippines, 1963-65; program assoc. Asia Soc., N.Y.C., 1971-72; dir. bilingual edn. U. Guam, Agana, 1972-74; dir. non-formal edn. info. ctr. Mich. State U., East Lansing, 1974-76; dir. family study ctr. Okla. State U., Stillwater, 1976-78; dir. ctr. for family Am. Home Econs. Assn., Washington, 1978-79; sr. research assoc. Creative Assocs., Inc., Washington, 1979-80; prof. family ecology, dir. Sch. for Home Econs. U. Akron, Ohio, 1980—; cons. in field. Contbr. articles to profl. jours. Mem. AAAS, Am. Home Econs. Assn., Assn. for Women in Devel., Assn. Adminstrs. Home Econs., Comparative and Internat. Edn. Soc., Nat. Council Adminstrs. Home Econs., Nat. Council on Family Relations, World Future Soc., Groves, Phi Delta Kappa, Kappa Omicron Phi. Democrat. Roman Catholic. Home: 3636 Sparrow Pond Circle Bath OH 44313 Office: Univ Akron 215 Schrank Hall South Akron OH 44325

RAINEY, MARY LOUISE, chemical company executive; b. Flagler, Co., Jan. 20, 1943; d. Paul Redmond and Frances Gilbert (Yoder) Barnett; m. Joseph Matthew Rainey, Aug. 11, 1967; 1 child, Jessica Louise. BA, Knox Coll., 1964; PhD, U. Md., 1974. Tchr. math. Cardozo High Sch., Washington, 1967-69, Walt Whitman High Sch., Bethesda, Md., 1969-71; research specialist analytical Dow Chem., Midland, Mich., 1974-79, group leader research, 1979-83, group leader regulatory issues, 1983-88, mgr. health, environ. and regulatory affairs, 1988—. Office: Dow Chem Co 1803 Bldg Midland MI 48640

RAINS, JACQUELINE LYNN, management consultant; b. Burbank, Calif., Nov. 30, 1960; d. Lyndon Carroll and Beth Luine (Pierce) Rains; m. Michael John Dias, July 28, 1984 (divorced). AA cum laude, La. Valley Jr. Coll., 1979; BA magna cum laude, Calif. State U., Northridge, 1981; MBA cum laude, Pepperdine U., 1987. Office mgr. sales Val Corp./Am. Energy Savs., Northridge, 1980-81, Harold Ring & Assocs., Encino, Calif., 1981-82; energy services sales specialist Honeywell, Inc., Commerce, Calif., 1982-84; supr. Exec. Life, West Los Angeles, Calif., 1984-85; owner, mgmt. cons. Mgmt. Trends, Los Angeles, 1984—; cons. Tiger Enterprises, Los Angeles, 1983—, Hope Chapel, Venice, Calif., 1984-86; contract adminstr. Channel One Video, Venice, 1985, Stewart & Stevenson Services, Inc., Beverly Hills, Calif., 1986—. Campaign worker Mondale/Ferraro, Van Nuys, Calif., 1983, Jimmy Carter/Walter Mondale, Van Nuys, 1979. Mem. Adminstrv. Mgmt. Soc. (Speaker award 1985), Nat. Assn. Female Execs., Calif. Assn. Sch. Transp. Ofcls. Democrat. Avocations: singing, acting, dancing, racquetball, swimming.

RAINS, MARY JO, banker; b. Konawa, Okla., Oct. 27, 1935; d. Albert Wood and Mary Leona (Winfield) Starns; student Okla. Sch. Banking, 1969, Seminole Jr. Coll., 1970-72, E. Central State U., 1978-79, Okla. State U., 1987, Pontotoc County Adult Vocat. Tech. Ctr., 1987; diploma Am. Inst. Banking, 1981, 83; m. Billy Z. Rains, June 17, 1956; 1 son, Nicky Z. Accounting div. Universal C.I.T., Oklahoma City, 1953-56; cashier Okla. State Bank, Konawa, 1957—, now sr. v.p. Sec., 1st Baptist Ch., Konawa, 1969-79, mem. budgeting com., 1982—. Mem. Okla. Bankers Assn. (dir. women's div. 1974-76), Konawa C. of C., Am. Legion. Club: Order Eastern Star. Home: Rural Rt 2 PO Box 28 Konawa OK 74849 Office: PO Box 156 Konawa OK 74849

RAINS, PATRICIA JANE, learning disabilities educator; b. Portland, Oreg., Mar. 26, 1934; d. Lawrence Marion and Mary Leticia (Roberts) R. A.B. in Edn., Cascade Coll., 1960; BS in Elem. Edn., Portland State U., 1962, diploma Inst. Children's Lit. Cert. tchr. Tchr. Lynch Sch. Dist. 28, Portland, Oreg., 1960-70; tchr. high sch. learning ctr. Tillamook Edn. Service Dist., Oreg., 1970-79, Nehalem Learning Ctr., 1979—, sch. dist. 56, Nehalem, 1983-86; vol. adult tutor Portland Community Coll., 1969-70. Author: Land Series Program, 1957-86. Active Sweet Adelines; pres. Wesleyan Fellowship, Tillamook. Summer sch. scholar, Tillamook Ednl. Service and Oreg. State Dept., 1971; chmn. ch. and soc. com. Inter-religious and Ecumenical Concerns, Religion and Race, Status and Role of Women. Mem. NEA, Tillamook Edn. Tchrs. Assn. (del., pres. 1970-86), Oreg. Ednl. Assn. (del. 1960-86), Council of Exceptional Children, Nat. Assn. Female Execs., Oreg. Sheriff's Assn. (hon.). Republican. Club: Internat. Tng. in Communication (pres. council 2, 1979). Avocations: travel; bowling; handicrafts; singing; teaching Sunday Sch. kindergarten. Home: PO Box 122 Netarts OR 97143 Office: Nehalem Lower Elem Sch PO Box 190 Nehalem OR 97131

RAITA, DEBORAH RUTH, management professional; b. Cin., Dec. 7, 1951; d. Aaron Paul and Ruth Marilla (Ingraham) Raita; m. Paul Edwin Smith, Aug. 25, 1973 (div. 1978). BA in English, Ohio U., 1973; MA in Pub. Adminstrn., Ohio State U., 1980. Systems analyst directorate of supply ops. Def. Constrn. Supply Ctr., Columbus, Ohio, 1973-78; analyst systems automation ctr. Def. Logistics Agy., Columbus, 1978-80, program analyst, 1980-85, computer specialist system automation ctr., 1985-86, chief justification and analysis, systems automation ctr., 1987; chief systems and procedures, office of policy and plans Defense Logistics Agy., Columbus, 1987—. Vol. supr. WOSU-AM-FM radio and TV stas., Columbus, 1982—, warehouse mgr. Auction 34, 1984-85; soprano Columbus Symphony Chorus, 1985. Mem. Nat. Assn. Female Execs., Phi Beta Kappa. Democrat. Buddhist. Club: Saturday Music (Columbus). Home: 528 Arden Rd Columbus OH 43214 Office: Def Constrn Supply Ctr 3990 E Broad St Columbus OH 43216-5000

RAITT, BONNIE LYNN, singer, musician; b. Burbank, Calif., Nov. 8, 1949. Student, Radcliffe Coll. Performer blues clubs, East coast; concert performer tours in Britain, 1976, 77; albums include: Bonnie Raitt, 1971, Give It Up, 1972, Takin' My Time, 1973, Streetlights, 1974, Home Plate, 1975, Sweet Forgiveness, 1977, The Glow, 1979, Green Light, 1982, Nine Lives, 1986. Office: PO Box 626 Los Angeles CA 90078

RAJAGOPAL, SHAKUNTALA, pathologist; b. Kerala, India, Oct. 1, 1940; d. K.V. and Retnamma (Pillai) Sivaraam; grad. Womens Coll., Trivandrum, Kerala, 1956; M.B., B.S., Med. Coll., Trivandrum, 1963; m. K.G. Rajagopal, Jan. 21, 1963; children—Devi, Nimmi, Molly. Resident in pathology West Suburban Hosp., Oak Park, Ill., 1964-69; pathologist, dir. labs., Westlake Community Hosp., Melrose Park, Ill., 1970—; demonstrator in pathology Northwestern U. Med. Sch., Chgo., 1967-75; med. dir. Triton Coll., 1972—; mem. AIDS task force Met. Health Care Council Chgo. Troup leader Girl Scouts U.S.A., 1978-79. Fellow Coll. Am. Pathologists, Am. Soc. Clin. Pathologists (continuing med. edn. award); mem. AMA, Chgo. Med. Soc. (continuing med. edn. com. 1986—), Am. Assn. Blood Banks, Am. Cancer Soc., Kerala Assn. Chgo. (pres. women's aux. 1977-79; v.p. 1980-81, sec. 1984). Hindu. Clubs: Woodfield Racquet. Home: 1868 Prestwick Dr Palatine IL 60067 Office: 1225 Superior St Melrose Park IL 60160

RAJOTTE, MARGIE CARTER, interior designer; b. Nashville, Sept. 25, 1941; d. William Franklin and Bessie Mae (Spears) Carter; m. William B. McKenzie, Mar. 4, 1959 (div. 1980); 1 child, Leah McKenzie; m. Richard W. Rajotte, Apr. 16, 1982. Student, Nashville Tech., 1962-68. With 1st Am. Bank, Nashville, 1959-69; broker Medlin Realty, Nashville, 1974-82, Barnes Realty, Nashville, 1982—; cons. Marlo's Gifts and Interiors, Brentwood, Tenn., 1982—; pres. Marlo's Inc., Brentwood, 1988—. Mem. Nat. Assn. Female Execs., Brentwood Network, Bus. Women of Am., Nashville Bd. Realtors. Republican. Home: 1622 Vineland Dr Brentwood TN 37027 Office: Marlo's Inc PO Box 1609 Brentwood TN 37027

RAJSKY, MARIANNE PATRICIA, English language educator; b. Butte, Mont., Apr. 16, 1940; d. Patrick John and Elsie Elisabeth (Garlisch) Whelan; m. Harry Chester Rajsky, Oct. 15, 1966; 1 child, Patrick Louis Rajsky. BA, U. Mont., 1962; post grad., U. Boston, 1965; MA, N. Ariz. U., 1970. Cert. secondary edn. tchr. English tchr. Rancho High Sch., Las Vegas, Nev., 1963-79, Valley High Sch., Las Vegas, Nev., 1979-83; English tchr., English dept. coordinator Roy Martin Jr. High Sch., Las Vegas, Nev., 1983-88; English tchr. Woodbury Jr. High Sch., Las Vegas, 1988—; mem. curriculum, Clark County Sch. Dist., 1986—. Editor: Roy Martin's Writing Handbook, 1987; co-author: Composition I Basic Syllibus and Test, 1987. Mem. aux. vols. Humana-Sunrise Hosp., Las Vegas, 1982—, community concerts, 1984—, Las Vegas Symphony Choir, 1963-66. Mem. Nat. Council Tchrs. of English, S. Nev. Tchrs. of English, Nev. Council Tchrs. of English, S. Nev. Tchrs. of English (sec. 1987—), Delta Delta Delta, Delta Kappa Gamma. Democrat. Roman Catholic. Office: Woodbury Jr High Sch 3875 E Harmon Ave Las Vegas NV 89121

RAKHMAN, SUSAN ANN SMALL, surgical sciences educator, health facility administrator, nurse; b. Wilmington, Del., Apr. 30, 1949; d. Claude Wilbur and Judith Ann (Kolodzjiej) Small; m. Jacob J. Rakhman, May 3, 1981; children—Joshua Josef, Benjamin Baron. Diploma, St. Elizabeth's Hosp. Sch. of Nursing, Brighton, Mass., 1970. RN; cert. operating room nurse. Mem. ICU staff St. Elizabeth's Hosp., Brighton, 1970-71; staff nurse operating room Mass. Eye and Ear Infirmary, Boston, 1970-71; sr. staff nurse operating room, specialized in cardiovascular NYU Med. Ctr., N.Y.C., 1972-77; operating room supr. N.Y. Infirmary, N.Y.C., 1977-79; instr. surg. scis., operating room supr. N.Y. Coll. of Podiatric Medicine (affiliated with Foot Clinics N.Y.), N.Y.C.; lectr., cons. Am. Podiatry Assn. Clin. Conf., N.Y.C., 1984; Podiatric Research Ctr. and Skills Lab.; cons. on office procedures to podiatrists in pvt. practice; lectr. on laser safety in surgery N.Y. Coll. Podiatric Medicine. Contbr. articles to profl. jours.; contbr. Am. Poetry Anthology. Mem. Assn. Operating Rm. Nurses (voting del. ann. congress 4 yrs.), Am. Soc. Lasers in Medicine and Surgery. Democrat. Jewish. Home: 72 Grandview Blvd Yonkers NY 10710 Office: N Y Coll Podiatric Medicine Foot Clinics NY 53 E 124th St New York NY 10035

RALAY, VOAHIRANA, retail executive; b. Washington, June 5, 1965; d. Roger Flavien and Jeanne R. Student, Montgomery Coll., 1982-83. Sales rep. Frontier Fruit & Nut Co., Kensington, Md., 1980-81; artist and sales rep. Cordially Yours, Kensington, 1981-82; sales rep., asst. mgr. Benetton Inc., Kensington, 1982-84; supr. Benetton Inc., Washington, 1984-85; regional dir. Benetton-Bel Ami, San Francisco, 1985—. Mem. Malagasy Alliance, Am. Malagasy Club. Home: 265 Fell St #105 San Francisco CA 94112 Office: Benetton Bel Ami 1969 Union St San Francisco CA 94123

RALIS, PARASKEVY, art educator, artist; b. N.Y.C., Sept. 16, 1951; d. Harry and Katerina (Koumi) R. AA, Miami-Dade Community Coll., 1970; BFA, Fla. Internat. U., 1973; MS, Nova U., 1977. Tchr. Miami (Fla.) Park Elem. Sch., 1973-80; instr. visual arts, photography Am. Sr. High Sch., 1980-81; tchr. Holmes Elem. Sch., 1981-84, Horace Mann Jr. High Sch., 1983-85; instr. visual arts, photography R.R. Moton South Ctr. for the Expressive Arts, 1984—. Prin. works include Twenty-first M. Allen Hortt Meml. Exhbn., Contempory Reflections of the 19th Century, 1979, Media Plus, 1980, Inception, 1981, Artspace, 1982, Class Impressions, 1983, Southern Exposure, 1986; exhibited in group shows at Met. Mus. Art and Art Ctr., Coral Gables, Fla., 1986, Broward Community Coll. Fine Arts Gallery, 1985, Mus. Art, Ft. Lauderdale, 1979, 84, North Miami Mus. and Art Ctr., 1983, Fla. Internat. U., 1980, Nat. Exhibit Am. Art, Chautauqua, N.Y., 1985. Mem. Dade County Art Tchrs. Assn. (bd. dirs., publicity chmn., Pres.'s award 1984). Greek Orthodox. Home: 6791 SW 57th Terr Miami FL 33143 Office: RR Moton S Ctr for Excellence 18050 Homestead Ave Perrine FL 33157

RALPH, DEBORAH MALONE, social services administrator, educator; b. N.Y.C., Aug. 4, 1951; d. Richard Ernest Sr. and Lottie Mae (Richardson) Malone; m. Hilroy Walton Ralph, Aug. 2, 1975; children: Jamaal, Marcus. BS with honors, SUNY, Buffalo, 1972; MSW, Columbia U., 1974. Lic. social worker, N.Y. Psychiat. social worker Arthur C. Logan Meml. Hosp., N.Y.C., 1974-77; asst. exec. dir. Community Participation Ednl. Program, N.Y.C., 1976-79; acting social work supr. Bronx Lebanon Hosp., N.Y.C., 1979-84; supr. clin. services Dept. Juvenile Justice City N.Y., 1979—, mem. Com. Women's Concerns, 1985; adj. prof. Coll. New Rochelle, N.Y.C., 1979—, adj. mem. faculty CCNY Sophie Davis Sch. Biomed. Edn., 1978-79; vis. prof. Tchr.'s Coll. Inst. Urban Minority Edn. Columbia U., N.Y.C., 1986, guest speaker Sch. Social Work, 1985; mem. field work adb. bd. Sch. Social Work NYU, 1986—. Columbia U. scholar, 1972; recipient Innovations award Dept. Juvenile Justice Ford Found., Boston, 1986. Mem. Nat. Assn. Social Workers (cert.), Assn. Black Social Workers, Nat. Juvenile Detention Assn., N.Y. State Juvenile Detention Assn. Office: NYC Dept Juvenile Justice Non-Secure Detention 365 Broadway New York NY 10013

RALSTON, SUSAN SCHOFIELD, psychologist; b. Argentia, Nfld., Can., Aug. 8, 1949; came to U.S., 1950; d. Thomas Jones and Beulah (Doyle) Schofield; m. David Thomas Ralston, June 8, 1986. BS in Psychology, UCLA, 1971; MS in Spl. Edn., U. So. Calif., 1972; PhD, U.S. Internat. U., San Diego, 1982. Program dir. child unit Coll. Hosp., Long Beach, Calif., 1980-82, Charth Hosp. of Long Beach, 1982-86, Los Altos Hosp., Long Beach, 1986—; pvt. practice psychology Long Beach, 1982—. Mem. Am. Psychol. Assn., Long Beach Psychol. Assn., Los Angeles Psychol. Assn. Office: 540 El Dorado Suite 101 Pasadena CA 91101

RAMANATHAN, ROHINI BALAKRISHNAN, banker; b. New Delhi, India, Nov. 4, 1952; came to U.S., 1972, naturalized, 1984; d. Mayuram Srinivasa Venkata and Gnanam (Sundaresan) Subramanian; m. Balakrishnan Ramanathan, July 4, 1977; children—Karthik Shankar, Ashwin Kalyan. B.A. with honors, Jesus and Mary Coll., New Delhi, 1972; M.S., Federal City Coll., 1974; Ed.D., Boston U., 1979. Sr. media intern Federal City Coll., Washington, 1973-75; media specialist Fashion Inst. Tech., N.Y.C., 1979-80; sr. mgmt. cons. N.Y.C. Health and Hosps., 1981-82; mgr. computer based tng. Chem. Bank, N.Y.C., 1983-88; dir. computing ctr. St. Johns U., Jamaica, N.Y., 1988—; pres., creative dir. Images Internat. Contbr. articles to profl. jours. Editor, broadcaster news programs. Bd. dirs. ethnic fellowships Queens Coll. Grad. Library Sch., N.Y., 1980-83. N.Y.C. Police Commisioner's Asian Am. Adv. Council (co-chmn.); trustee Carnatic Music Acad. of N.A., N.Y.C., 1979-80. Mem. Asian Indian Women in Am. (founder 1981, editor News 1981-83), Fedn. Indian Assns. (chmn. publicity 1980-82, v.p. N.Y.C. 1986-87), Bharathi Soc. (sec. 1979-80, pres. 1988-89), Avocations: Vocal South Indian classical and other Indian light music; writing; sports. Home: 171 Harris Dr Oceanside NY 11572 Office: Saint Johns U Grand Central & Utopia Pkwys Jamaica NY 11439

RAMBO, SYLVIA H., federal judge; b. Royersford, Pa., Apr. 17, 1936; d. Granville A. and Hilda E. (Leonhardt) R.; m. George F. Douglas, Jr., Aug. 1, 1970. B.A., Dickinson Coll., Carlisle, Pa., 1958; J.D., Dickinson Sch. Law, Carlisle, Pa., 1962; LL.D. (hon.), Wilson Coll., Chambersburg, Pa., 1980. Bar: Pa. 1962. Atty. trust dept. Bank of Del., Wilmington, 1962-63; pvt. practice Carlisle, 1963-76; public defender, then chief public defender Cumberland County, Pa., 1976; judge Ct. Common Pleas, Cumberland County, 1976-78, U.S. Dist. Ct. Middle Dist. Pa., Harrisburg, 1979—; asst. adj. prof. law Dickinson Sch. Law, 1973, 76, 77; mem. Gov. Pa. Com. Crime and Delinquency. Mem. Am. Bar Assn., Nat. Assn. Women Lawyers, Nat. Assn. Women Judges, Pa. Bar Assn., Pa. Trial Lawyers Assn., Phi Alpha Delta. Democrat. Presbyterian. Office: US Dist Ct PO Box 868 Harrisburg PA 17108

RAMBOW, VIRGINIA JOAN, veterinarian; b. Battle Creek, Mich., Nov. 4, 1946; d. Larry Russell and Rosamond Newton (Patten) R.; m. Richard Dale Bohn, June 30, 1973 (div. 1983); children: Heidi Marie, Heather Patten. BA, Keene State Coll., 1968; DVM, Mich. State U., 1971; postgrad., U. Minn., 1978-79, MIT, 1980-81. Lic. veterinarian, Mass., N.H., Minn. Gen. practice vet. medicine Mass., 1972-77, Minn., 1977-79, N.H., 1979-80; relief veterinarian Mass. and N.H., 1981—; pres. New Eng. Vet. Relief Services, Hollis, N.H., 1983—. Co-editor articles in field. Mem. AVMA, N.H. Vet. Med. Assn. (editor newsletter 1985—, chmn. pub. relations 1984-87, sec. 1985-87), Mass. Vet. Med. Assn., Minn. Vet. Med. Assn. Club: Boston Beanstalks. Office: New Eng Vet Relief Services PO Box 814 Hollis NH 03049

RAMEH, CLEA ABDON, foreign language educator; b. Recife, Pernambuco, Brazil, Jan. 9, 1927; came to U.S., 1965; d. Abdon Salomao and Josefina Jorge R. BA, U. São Paulo, Brazil, 1947, licentiate, 1948, especialization, 1955; MS in Linguistics, Georgetown U., 1962, PhD in Linguistics, 1970. Tchr. English State Schs., São Paulo, 1951-63; instr. eng. research asst. U. São Paulo, 1963-65; instr. portuguese Georgetown U., Washington, 1969-70, asst. prof. portuguese, 1970-75, assoc. prof. portuguese, 1975—, chmn. dept. portuguese, 1979-87; vis. prof. U. São Paulo, 1975, Cath. U., 1975; tchr. Seminar Tchrs. Foreign Languages, Rio De Janeiro, 1975; chmn. Georgetown U. Round Table on Languages and Linguistics, 1976. Co-author: Português Contemporâneo I, 1966, 67, 71, 72, 75, 78, 83, 86, Português Contemporâneo II, 1967, 69, 71, 73, 78, 83, 86; editor Semantics, Theory and Application (Georgetown U. Round Table on Lang. and Linguistics), 1976. Fulbright Travel grantee, 1959; Gulbenkian Found. grantee, 1980, 81; OAS scholar, 1960-62, 66-68. Mem. Am. Council Teaching Foreign Languages, Modern Language Assn. (del. assembly 1978-80, exec. bd. div. Luso-Brazilian language and literature 1981-85), Am Assn. Tchrs. Spanish and Portuguese, Greater Washington Assn. Tchrs. Foreign Languages (v.p. 1980-81, pres. 1981-83). Roman Catholic. Office: Georgetown U Dept Portuguese 37 & O Sts NW Washington DC 20057

RAMELL, GUNILLA CHRISTINA, energy policy analyst; b. Gothenburg, Sweden, Apr. 23, 1946; came to U.S., 1966, naturalized, 1978; d. Victor K. A. and Alice Linnea (Hornberg) Ramell; B.A. summa cum laude, UCLA, 1970; M.A., Harvard U., 1974. Govt. relations analyst Atlantic Richfield Co., Los Angeles, 1974-77; communications program mgr. Internat. Paper Co., N.Y.C., 1977-78; public affairs specialist Indsl. Indemnity Co., San Francisco, 1978-80; sr. analyst Wholesale Rate Dept., Pacific Gas & Electric Co., San Francisco, 1980-87; teaching fellow Harvard U., 1971-74. Mem. com. No. Calif. Democratic Party, 1981; United Way sponsored exec., 1982. Alfred P. Sloan Found. fellow, 1972; Washington internship fellow office of Sen. Charles E. Goodell. Mem. Calif. Soc. Mcpl. Fin. Officers, San Francisco Mcpl. Forum, Issues Mgmt. Assn. (founding), Swedish Women's Ednl. Assn. (bd. dirs. 1983-85). Democrat. Club: Commonwealth, Harvard of San Francisco (bd. dirs. 1982-87), Harvard of N.Y.C. Home: 2323 Larkin St San Francisco CA 94109 Office: San Francisco Bus Times 325 Fifth St San Francisco CA 94107

RAMEY, AVA LORRAINE, policewoman, detective; b. Northumberland County, Va., Mar. 21, 1951; d. Homer Albert and Marilyn Orenette (Corbin) Campbell; m. Kenneth Lee Howard, Apr. 5, 1972 (div. Mar. 1981); m. Randall Russell Ramey, Aug. 6, 1981; children—Ryan Randall, Robert Ryan. Student Radford Women's Coll., 1969-70, D.C. U., 1970-72, U. Md., 1974-76. Tour guide Landmark Services, Washington, 1970-71; store detective Hecht Co., Washington, 1971-72; policewoman, detective Washington Met. Police Dept., 1972—; owner, dir. Lord Mayor Acad., Capital Children's Mus., Washington, 1984—; owner Mattapony Video, specializing in children's videos, Md., 1986—. Author: (children's book) Tarsha, 1975. Served with USAR, 1977-80. Named among Top Ten Coll. Girls in Am., Glamour mag., 1969. Mem. Exec. Female, Black Women in Law Enforcement, Com. Police Parents (pres. 1983-84). Avocation: white water rafting. Office: Lord Mayor Acad 800 3d St NE Washington DC 20002

RAMEY, MARIANNE CLIFFORD, civil engineer; b. Peoria, Ill., Nov. 12, 1957; d. Lloyd Samuel and Lois Lucille (Staat) C.; m. Timothy J. Ramey, Aug. 22, 1981. BSCE, Purdue U., 1978; MBA, U. Houston, 1982. Registered profl. engr., Tex., Va., Md., Mo., Calif. Staff engr. Turner, Collie & Braden Corp., Houston, 1979-80; sr. engr. Espey, Huston & Assocs., Houston, 1980-84; regional dir. Washington office The Nielsen-Wurster Group, Inc., Fairfax, Va., 1984-86; regional dir., regional civil engr. Marriott Corp., 1986—. Mem. Harris County Mcpl. Utility Dist. 119 Bd. of Dirs., Houston, 1982-84. Mem. ASCE, Project Mgmt. Inst., Soc. Mktg. Profl. Services. Republican. Lutheran. Home: 12203 Hollow Tree Ln Fairfax VA 22030 Office: Marriott Corp Dept 934 46 One Marriott Dr Washington DC 20058

RAMIRES, ELAINE GRACE, costume designer; b. San Francisco, Sept. 17, 1956; d. Ernesto Fernando and Rowena Winifred (Smith) R. BA, U. Calif., Santa Barbara, 1978; MFA, UCLA, 1982. Free-lance costumer and costume designer Los Angeles, 1982—. Costumer 1984 Olympic opening and closing ceremonies, Los Angeles, 1984, (TV shows) He's the Mayor, Liberty Weekend, Fame, The Slap Maxwell Story, numerous plays Los Angeles rea, 1982—. Project leader Community Affairs Bd., U. Calif., Santa Barbara, 1975—. Recipient Critics award Drama League, Los Angeles, 1984. Mem. Motion Picture Costumers, Nat. Assn. Broadcast Employees in TV.

RAMÍREZ, MARÍA DE LOURDES, sales executive; b. Ponce, P.R., Sept. 30, 1956; d. José M. and Ilia (García) R. BS in Pub. Communications, Boston U., 1978. Communications cons. Pub. Communicators, San Juan, P.R., 1978-84; adminstrv. asst. Dept. Consumer Affairs, City of N.Y., 1984-86; acct. exec. N. American Bolt and Screw Co., Inc., N.Y.C., 1986—; mfr.'s rep. AMV Enterprises, Inc., Caguas, P.R., 1986—. Assoc. mem. Am. Mus. Natural History, N.Y.C., 1986—. Recipient Outstanding Service award EEOC, N.Y.C., 1985. Mem. Nat. Assn. Female Execs., Boston U. Alumni Assn. Home: PO Box 592 Murray Hill Station NY 10156

RAMIST, ROSELYN BARBARA, lawyer; b. N.Y.C., Aug. 31, 1939; d. Charles and Sophie (Bussel) Prager; m. Leonard E. Ramist, Aug. 2, 1964 (div. 1971); 1 child, Joanne Sharon. BA, Syracuse U., 1961; JD, U. Pa., 1964. Bar: Pa. 1967. Law clk. Ct. of Common Pleas, Phila., 1970-73; asst. dist. atty. Phila. County, Phila., 1973-74; trust officer Gilard Bank, Phila., 1974-79; v.p., sr. trust officer Commonwealth Nat. Bank, Lancaster, Pa., 1979-86; assoc. Richard G. Greiner Esq., Lancaster, 1986—; speaker bus. orgns. Bd. dirs. Lancaster YWCA, 1983-88, Arthritis Found. Cen. Pa., 1981—, also pres. 1987—, Planned Parenthood Lancaster, 1983—; mem. budget rev. and allocations com. Lancaster United Way, 1984—; campaign chmn. Donald Weaver for Lancaster County Controller, 1985; mem. Lancaster County Women's Task Force, 1986—. Mem. Lancaster Bar Assn., Pa. Bar Assn., Estate Planning Council Lancaster. Home: 2812 Southwick Dr Lancaster PA 17601 Office: Richard G Greiner Assocs 600-A Eden Rd Lancaster PA 17601

RAMO, VIRGINIA M. SMITH, civic worker; b. Yonkers, N.Y.; d. Abraham Harold and Freda (Kasnetz) Smith; B.S. in Edn., U. So. Calif., D.H.L. (hon.), 1978; m. Simon Ramo; children—James Brian, Alan Martin. Nat. co-chmn. ann. giving U. So. Calif., 1968-70, vice chmn., trustee, 1971—, co-chmn. bd. councilors Sch. Performing Arts, 1975-76, co-chmn. bd. councillors Schs. Med. and Engring.; vice-chmn. bd. overseers Hebrew Union Coll., 1972-75; bd. dirs. The Muses of Calif. Mus. Sci. and industry, UCLA Affiliates, Estelle Doheny Eye Found., U. So. Calif. Sch. Medicine; adv. council Los Angeles County Heart Assn., chmn. com. to endow Chair in cardiology at U. So. Calif.; vice-chmn., bd. dirs. Friends of Library U. So. Calif.; bd. dirs., nat. pres. Achievement Rewards for Coll. Scientists Found., 1975-77; bd. dirs. Les Dames Los Angeles, Community TV So. Calif.; bd. dirs., v.p. Founders Los Angeles Music Center; v.p. Los Angeles Music Center Opera Assn.; v.p. corp. bd. United Way; v.p. Blue Ribbon-400 Performing Arts Council; chmn. com. to endow chair in gerontology U. So. Calif.; vice chmn. campaign Doheny Eye Inst., 1986. Recipient Service award Friends of Libraries, 1974; Nat. Community Service award Alpha Epsilon Phi, 1975; Disting. Service award Am Heart Assn. 1978; Service award U. So. Calif.; Spl. award U. So. Calif. Music Alumni Assn., 1979; Life Achievement award Mannequins of Los Angeles Assistance League, 1979; Woman of Yr. award PanHellenic Assn., 1981; Disting. Service award U. So. Calif. Sch. Medicine, 1981; U. So. Calif. Town and Gown Recognition award, 1986; Asa V. Call Achievement award U. So. Calif., 1986; Phi Kappa Phi scholarship award U. So. Calif., 1986. Mem. UCLA Med. Aux., U. So. Calif. Pres.'s Circle, Commerce Assos. U. So. Calif., Cedars of Lebanon Hosp. Women's Guild (dir. 1967-68), Blue Key, Skull and Dagger.

RAMON, SHARON JOSEPHINE, personnel management executive, real estate salesperson; b. Chgo., Nov. 8, 1947; d. Edward Albert and Helen Josephine (Tomaszewski) Mazur; m. Kevin John Ramon, Aug. 4, 1979. BA, U. Ill.-Chicago, 1969. Caseworker, ct. aide Social Service Dept. of Cir. Ct. Cook County, Chgo., 1969-71; investigator aide U.S. Civil Service Commn., Chgo., 1971-72, personnel staffing specialist, 1972-74, personnel mgmt. specialist, 1974-80; mgmt. cons. U.S. Office Personnel Mgmt., Chgo., 1980-82, personnel mgmt. specialist, 1982-83, personnel staffing specialist, 1983-86; salesperson First United Realtors, Barrington, Ill., 1987—. Recipient Certs. of Spl. Achievement, U.S. Office Personnel Mgmt., 1980, Cert. of Appreciation, 1981. Mem. Nat. Assn. Female Execs., AAUW. Roman Catholic. Office: First United Realtors 115 S Hough St Barrington IL 60010

RAMOS, LINDA MARIE, endoscopy technician; b. San Jose, Calif., July 8, 1961; d. Albert Sequeira and Catherine Marie (Souza) Vieira; m. John Bettencourt Ramos, June 12, 1982. AA, De Anza Coll., 1986; BA, St. Mary's Coll. Calif., Moraga, Calif., 1988. Endoscopy technician O'Connor Hosp., San Jose, 1979—; instr. aerobic 1st Lady Spas, Mountain View, Calif. Contbr. articles to profl. jours. Vol. O'Connor Hosp., 1975-79; active campaign Santa Clara City Council, 1980-81. Fellow Irmandade Da Festa Do Espirito Santo (sec. 1974-82, queen 1975-76), No. Soc. Gastrointestinal Assts., Luso Am. Fraternal Fedn. (state youth pres. 1979-80, youth leader Oakland, Calif., chpt. 1979-87, scholar, 1979, founder, organizer Mountain View-Santa Clara chpt. 1980, pres. local region 1980-84, state 20-30 pres. 1984-85). Republican. Roman Catholic. Home: 1101 Civic Center Dr 10 Santa Clara CA 95050 Office: O'Connor Hosp 2105 Forest Ave San Jose CA 95126

RAMPEL, MARION ELLA, psychologist; b. N.Y.C., June 22, 1924; d. Terrell Bertram King and Ella Josephine (Winternitz) Bergen; m. Guy G. Rampel, Apr. 2, 1944 (div. 1963); children: Carol, Guy, Susan (dec.), Paul, Mark. BA in Math., NYU, 1945; MEd in Guidance, Rutgers U., 1963, EdD in Psychology, 1967. Lic. psychologist, N.Y., N.J. Interviewer employment NYSES, Mt. Vernon, N.Y., 1958-60; dean women, assoc. prof. Westminster Choir Coll., Princeton, N.J., 1965-66; asst. prof. edn. St. John's U., Jamaica, N.Y., 1967-72; staff psychologist St. Vincent's Hosp., Harrison, N.Y., 1970-75; sr. staff psychologist St. Vincent's Hosp., Harrison, 1975-79, supervising psychologist, 1979-85, dir. dept. psychology, 1985—; clin. asst., prof. psychiatry N.Y. Med. Coll., Valhalla, 1980—, cons. oncology edn., 1983-87; Research cons. Cogent Assocs., Princeton, 1972-81, N.Y.C. Bd. Edn., 1980-85; cons. Family Service Eastchester, N.Y., 1980-85. Bd. dirs. Domestic Violence Housing, Pleasantville, N.Y., 1987—. Mem. Am. Psychol. Assn. (N.Y. State, N.J., Westchester County chpts.). Republican. Presbyterian. Office: St Vincent's Hosp 240 North St Harrison NY 10528

RAMSAY, JANICE SUSAN, computer programer, analyst.; b. Nashville, Ark., Aug. 20, 1952; d. Reginald Carlyle and Jesse Evelyn (Hill) R. BA in English, Ariz. State U., 1977. With data ops. Maricopa County Govt., Phoenix, 1973-82, programmer analyst I, 1982-84, programmer analyst II, 1984-86; sr. programmer analyst Peralta Community Colls., Oakland, Calif., 1986—. Author: Recovery Techniques, 1984, User-Friendly FAMS, 1985. Active Sierra Club, World Wildlife. Mem. Assn. for Women in Computing, No. Calif. Profls. Home: 1715 Grand St Alameda CA 94501 Office: Peralta Community Colls 501 5th Ave Oakland CA 94606

RAMSAY, PATRICIA LEYDEN, academic support administrator; b. Virginia, Minn., Oct. 5, 1935; d. Ralph Calvin Leyden and Marion (Imo) Kelly; m. O. Bertrand Ramsay, Apr. 12, 1962; 1 child, C. Sean. AA, Stephens Coll., 1954; BA, U. Mo., 1956; MA, Ind. U., 1957. Instr. fgn. langs., dir. lang. lab. Mary Baldwin Coll., Staunton, Va., 1957-59; asst. prof., dir. lang. lab. U. Pacific, Stockton, Calif., 1960-62; instr. ESL Kendall Coll., Evanston, Ill., 1964-65; media asst. Eastern Mich. U., Ypsilanti, 1974-80, supr. instructional support ctr., 1980-86, coordinator instructional support ctr., 1986—; mem. planning com. Instructional Support Ctr., Eastern Mich. U., 1978-80. Pres. bd. trustees 1st Unitarian Ch., Ann Arbor, Mich., 1976-78. Mem. Internat. Assn. Learning Labs., Nat. Assn. Devel. Edn., Assn. Edn. Communications Tech., Midwest Coll. Learning Ctr. Assn., Mich. Assn. Computer Users in Learning, Phi Theta Kappa, Phi Beta Kappa. Office: Eastern Mich U ISC 102 Univ Library Ypsilanti MI 48197

RAMSEUR, DIANNA LOU BROOKS, elementary educator, geriatric consultant; b. Bluefield, W.Va., July 5, 1954; d. Rex L. and Lola B. (Little) Brooks; m. Franklin F. Ramseur III, Jan. 19, 1945; children: Franklin F. IV, John Braxton, Leann Brook. AB, Seminole Community Coll., Sanford, Fla., 1974; BA in Edn., U. Cen. Fla., 1976. Cert. elem. tchr., Fla. Tchr. Washington Shores Elem. Sch., Orlando, Fla., 1976-79; kindergarten tchr. Lake Mary (Fla.) Elem. Sch., 1980-86; geriatric coordinator Lyman Learning Ctr., Lake Mary, Fla., 1986—, also cons., 1986—; cons. Orangewood Christian Sch., Maitland, Fla., 1986-87, Lyman Learning Ctr., Lake Mary, 1987—. Active local chpt. Am. Heart Assn., 1985—. Presbyterian. Home: 210 Colonial Lake Longwood FL 32750

RAMSEY, CAROL SUZANNE, physician; b. Stockton, Calif., Dec. 23, 1946; d. William Howard and Pauline (Crawford) R. BA in Speech, Calif. State U., Hayward, 1968; MA in Speech, Pa. State U., 1973, postgrad., 1975-77; DO, Phila. Coll. Osteopathic Medicine, 1981. Diplomate Am. Bd. Internal Medicine. Substitute tchr. San Leandro, San Lorenzo Sch. Dist., Calif., 1968-69; instr. speech Pa. State U., Altoona, 1970-77; staff physician Humana Med. First, Glen Burnie, Md., 1984-85; intensive care physician Ch. Hosp., Balt., 1984-87; pvt. practice medicine Balt., 1985-87; occupational medicine physician CMC, Balt., 1987; assoc. med. dir. North Arundel Hosp. Life Ctr., Occupational Med. Ctr., Glen Burnie, Md., 1987—. Serves as capt., flight surgeon USAFR, 1983—. Home: PO Box 19049 Baltimore MD 21284 Office: 200 Hospital Dr Suite LL-10 Glen Burnie MD 21061

RAMSEY, CHRISTINA URBAN, federal agency administrator; b. Petersburg, Va., Mar. 8, 1941; d. Adolph and Otelia Loretta (Blaha) Urban; divorced; 1 child, Ann Kendall Ramsey Delorier. BS in Edn., James Madison U., 1962; MS in Earth Scis., Va. State U., 1972. Tchr. Chesterfield County Schs., Chester, Va., 1962-64; tchr., head sci. dept. Chesterfield County Schs., Matoaca, Va., 1964-74; environ. specialist Dept. of the Army, Ft. Lee, Va., 1974-78, Alexandria, Va., 1978-80; chief environ. br. Army NG, Washington, 1980-82; dep. dir. environ. planning Office of Sec. Defense, Washington, 1982—. Recipient NSF award 1968. Mem. Office Sec. Def. Profl. Women, Dept. Defense Speakers Bur., Nat. Assn. Women Execs. Office: Office Sec of Def 206 N Washington St Suite 200 Alexandria VA 22314

RAMSEY, CONNIE HOMAN, purchasing services executive; b. Sedalia, Mo., May 7, 1959; d. Arthur Lee and Dorothy Jane (DeHaven) Homan; m. Gary Kent Ramsey, June 3, 1984. BA in Bus. Adminstrn., Stephens Coll., 1981. Mgmt. trainee Joskes Dept. Stores, Dallas, 1981-83; mgmt. info. systems/data processing buyer Placid Oil Co., Dallas, 1983—. Mem. Dallas Mus. Art, 1985-87, Kimbell Art Mus., Ft. Worth, 1986-87, Met. Mus. Art, N.Y.C., 1987. Mem. Nat. Assn. Female Execs. Republican. Baptist. Club: Stephens Alumnae (pres. 1985-86). Home: 1001 Liberty #122 Dallas TX 75204 Office: Placid Oil Co 3900 Thanksgiving Tower Dallas TX 75201

RAMSEY, DONNA MOORE, medical technologist, college administrator; b. Toledo, Jan. 13, 1941; d. Wendle Adolphus and Thelma Grace (Wilson) Moore; children: James Albert, Wendle Scott. B.S. in Zoology, Ohio U., Athens, 1962; diploma med. tech., Mercy Hosp., Toledo, 1963; M.Ed. in Supervision/Coordination Vocat. and Tech. Edn., Rutgers U., 1976. Med. technologist, instr. Mercy Hosp., 1963-65, Mt. Carmel Hosp., Columbus, Ohio, 1965-69; med. technologist Doctor's Hosp., Columbus, 1970-71; instr. med. lab. tech. Columbus Tech. Inst., 1972-73; instr. vocat. and tech. edn. Middlesex County (N.J.) Bd. Edn., 1974; med. tech. coordinator Rutgers U. Med. Sch., 1974-75; supr. med. lab. Douglass Coll., Rutgers U., 1976; asst. prof. med. tech. Cuyahoga Community Coll., Cleve., 1976-81, program dir. med. assisting/med. lab. tech., 1981-84, div. head math. and techs., 1984—; panelist med. assisting edn. Ohio Acad. Family Physicians; critiquer, surveyor Nat. Accrediting Agy. for Clin. Lab. Scis. Fipse grantee, 1983; cons. North Cen. Assn., Ohio. Mem. Am. Soc. Clin. Pathologists, Am. Assn. Med. Assts., Am. Soc. Med. Technologists, Am. Vocat. Assn., Ohio U. Alumni and Friends (sec. arts and scis.), Minorities and Women Higher Edn. (state adv. bd.), Leaders For 80's, Kappa Delta Pi. Office: 11000 Pleasant Valley Rd Parma OH 44130

RAMSEY, ELIZABETH M(APELSDEN), physician, placentologist; b. N.Y.C., Feb. 17, 1906; d. Charles Cyrus and Grace (Keys) Ramsey; grad. Bishop's Sch., LaJolla, Calif.; B.A., Mills Coll., 1928; fellow Inst. Internat. Edn., Hamburg, Germany, 1928-29; M.D., Yale U., 1932; D.Sc., Med. Coll. Pa., 1965; m. Hans Alexander Klagsbrunn, Jan. 27, 1934. Intern, asst. resident New Haven Hosp., 1932-34; asst. pathology Yale U., 1933-34; asso. pathology George Washington U., 1934-41, professorial lectr., 1941-55; asst. chief Office Med. Info., NRC, 1942-45; guest investigator dept. embryology Carnegie Inst., Washington, 1934-51, research asso. and pathologist, 1951-63, staff mem. placentalogy and pathology, 1963-71, research asso., 1976—; Mamie A. Jessup vis. prof. ob-gyn. U. Va. Sch. Medicine, 1972-76; Bartholomew Mosse Meml. lectr. Rotunda Hosp., Dublin, Ireland, 1970; professorial lectr. ob-gyn. Georgetown U. Sch. Medicine, 1981—. Bd. dirs. Nat. Symphony Orch., 1949—, 2d v.p., 1952-55, mem. exec. com., 1955-64, 67-68, 73-79, chmn., 1955-61, pres. women's com., 1950-52; trustee Cathedral Choral Soc., 1967-81, 83—. Recipient Alumna of Year citation Bishop's Sch., 1960, Lewis prize Am. Philos. Soc., 1970, diplome d'Honneur, Federation Internationale de Gynecologie Infantile et Juvenile, 1972. Hon. fellow Chgo. Gynec. Soc.; mem. Audubon Naturalist Soc. Central Atlantic States (dir. 1961-64), Am. Assn. Anatomists (exec. com. 1963-66, v.p. 1974-76), Am. Coll. Obstetricians and Gynecologists (hon. asso., recipient disting. service award 1976, named to Hall of Fame 1985), Am. Gynecol. Soc. (hon.), Perinatal Research Soc. (charter), Soc. Gynecologic Investigation (hon., recipient Pres.'s Disting. Scientist award 1987), AAAS, Acad. Med. Scis. (Cordoba, Argentina) (acad. fgn. corr.), Soc. Perinatal Obstetricians, Phi Beta Kappa, Sigma Xi. Episcopalian. Club: City Tavern. Author: The Placenta of Laboratory Animals and Man, 1975; (with Martin W. Donner) Placental Vasculature and Circulation, 1980; The Placenta, Human and Animal, 1982; mem. editorial bd. Placenta Tropholalast Research. Contbr. to profl. jours. Home: 3420 Q St NW Washington DC 20007 Other: Salem Farm Route 1 Box 600 Purcellville VA 22132

RAMSEY, JOANNE MARIE, data processing executive; b. Long Branch, N.J., Oct. 13, 1945; d. Erwin P. and Erna M. (Green) Forrest; B.S., Monmouth Coll., 1967; M.S., Stevens Inst. Tech., 1971; 1 dau., Cheryl. Mem. tech. staff Bell Telephone Labs., Holmdel, N.J., 1967-71; programmer analyst Cooper Electric Supply Co., Middletown, N.J., 1971-73; sr. programmer Insco Systems Corp., Neptune, N.J., 1973-78; programmer analyst Internat. Flavors & Fragrances, Hazlet, N.J., 1978-80; project mgr. E.R. Squibb & Sons, Inc., East Brunswick, N.J., 1980—. Mem. Am. Prodn. and Inventory Control Soc., Nat. Assn. Female Execs. Home: 424 E Highland Ave Atlantic Highlands NJ 07716 Office: 25 Kennedy Blvd East Brunswick NJ 08816

RAMSEY, NANCY ROCHESTER, property manager; b. San Antonio, Dec. 29, 1949; d. James C. and Wilma F. (Brown) Rochester; divorced; children: Ryan, James, Jeremiah. Student, Acad. of Real Estate. Resident mgr. Barry Gillingwater Mgmt. Co., San Antonio, 1980-82; resident mgr., property mgr. Selig Hunt Property Services, Austin, Tex., 1982-84; property mgr. Compass Property Mgmt. Co., San Antonio, 1984; dist. dir., property mgr. Eugene Burger Mgmt. Corp., Austin and San Antonio, 1985—. Mem. Austin Apt. Assn., Exec. Female Assn. Republican. Baptist. Home: 2650 Thousand Oaks San Antonio TX 78232 Office: Eugene Burger Mgmt Corp 14800 San Pedro Suite 124 San Antonio TX 78232

RAMSEY, PAMELA PRATT, advertising executive; b. Columbus, Ohio, Aug. 27, 1961; d. John Eli and Leona Mae (Longshore) Pratt; m. Bruce Mitchell Ramsey, May 21, 1983. Student, U. Fla., 1979-81; BBA with honors, Fla. Atlantic U., 1983. Account exec., media buyer, copywriter, account supr. Mktg. Cons., Inc., West Palm Beach, Fla., 1981-84; dir. account services Lawrence, Prather & Welsh, West Palm Beach, Fla., 1984-85; v.p., dir. account services Hanna, Ramsey & Coats, Inc., West Palm Beach, Fla., 1985—. Mem. communications com. Pvt. Sector Initiatives, West Palm Beach, 1983-84, Adopt-A-Family, West Palm Beach, 1986—. Mem. Am. Mktg. Assn., Ad Club Palm Beaches (pub. service com. 1983-84), Nat. Assn. for Female Execs., West Palm Beach C. of C. (communications com. 1983-84), Beta Gamma Sigma. Home: 7791 Nemec Dr S West Palm Beach FL 33406 Office: Hanna Ramsey & Coats Inc 215 Fifth St Suite 105 West Palm Beach FL 33401

RAMSEY, SALLY ANN SEITZ, state official; b. Columbus, Ohio, Feb. 15, 1931; d. Albert Blazier and Mildred (Dodson) Seitz; m. Edward Lewis Ramsey, Apr. 11, 1953 (div. 1962); children—Edward Lewis, Sylvia Ann Mitchell. B.A., Ohio State U., 1952, M.A., 1955, postgrad., 1963-66; postgrad. St. Mary Coll.-Xavier, Kans., 1962. Research engr., then sr. research engr. N.Am. Aviation, Inc., Columbus, Ohio, and Downey, Calif., 1962-67; legis. intern State of Ohio, 1964-65; research and info. officer Ohio Dept. Urban Affairs, Columbus, 1967-68; adminstrv. specialist Ohio Dept. Devel., Columbus, 1968; assoc. planner, then sr. planner Div. State Planning, Fla. Dept. Adminstrn., Tallahassee, 1968-76; econ. analysis supr., then econ. analyst Fla. Dept. Commerce, 1976—; congl. campaign cons., 1966. U.S. Econ. Devel. Adminstrn. fellow, 1978-79. Mem. Fla. Econs. Club, Am. Soc. for Pub. Adminstrn., Internat. Graphoanalysis Soc., Kappa Kappa Gamma,

Pi Sigma Alpha. Episcopalian. Club: Forest Meadows Athletic. Home: 2429 Merrigan Pl Tallahassee FL 32308 Office: Fla Dept Commerce 107 W Gaines St Tallahassee FL 32301

RANCK, EMILY WILLETT, insurance company representative; b. Leominster, Mass., May 27, 1957; d. Hurd C. and Dorothy (Bachman) Willett; m. Gary N. Ranck, May 19, 1984. Cert., So. Sem., 1977, Am. Inst. Paralegal Studies, 1980; BS, U. Lowell, 1985. Mgr., trainer Gaitwood Farm, Littleton, Mass., 1977-80; exec. sec. to pres. 1st Bank, Lowell, Mass., 1980-85; assoc. mgr. Met. Life and Affiliated Cos., Marlboro, Mass., 1985—, territorial rep. for sales adv. council, 1987—. Mem. Nat. Assn. Life Underwriters, Nat. Assn. Female Execs. Congregationalist. Office: Met Life and Affiliated Cos 180 Boston Post Rd Marlboro MA 01752

RANCOUR, JOANN SUE, nurse; b. Elyria, Ohio, Nov. 10, 1939; d. Joseph and Ann (Donich) Sokol; diploma M.B. Johnson Sch. Nursing, 1960; B.S. in Profl. Arts, St. Josephs Coll., N. Windham, Maine, 1981; student in psychology Alfred Adler Inst., Chgo., 1976—, Lorain County Community Coll., 1973-75, Ursuline Coll., Cleve., 1976, Baldwin Wallace Coll., 1982; m. Richard Lee Rancour, July 29, 1961; children—Kathleen Ann, Donna Marie. Staff nurse Elyria Meml. Hosp., 1960-62, 72-75, head nurse psychiat. unit, 1975-79; sec.-treas. Alfred Adler Inst. Cleve., 1978-79; nurse Lorain County Juvenile Detention Home, Elyria, 1980; nurse VA Med. Center, Brecksville, Ohio, 1981—; mem. Cleve. VA nursing bioethics com. Active PTA, yearbook com., 1969-70, co-chmn. ways and means, 1971; Democratic poll worker, 1971-72; sec. St. Mary's Confrat. Christian Doctrine Program, 1970-71. Mem. Am. Nurses Assn. (cert. generalist practitioner psychiat. and mental health nursing practice), Ohio Nurses Assn., Nurses Orgn. of VA (NOVA), N.Am. Soc. Adlerian Psychology. Roman Catholic. Home: 205 Denison Ave Elyria OH 44035

RAND, JOELLA M., nursing college administrator; b. Akron, Ohio, July 9, 1932; d. Harry S. and Elizabeth May (Miller) Halberg; m. Martin Rand; children: Craig, Debbi Stark. BSN, U. Akron, 1961, MEd in Guidance, 1968; PhD in Higher Edn. Adminstrn., Syracuse U., 1981. Staff nurse Akron Gen. Hosp., 1953-54; staff-head nurse-instr. Summit County Receiving, Cuyahoga Falls, Ohio, 1954-56; head nurse psychiat. unit Akron Gen. Hosp., 1956-57; instr. psychiatric nursing Summit County Receiving, Cuyahoga Falls, 1957-61; head nurse, in-service instr. Willard (N.Y.) State Hosp., 1961-62; asst. prof. Alfred (N.Y.) U., 1962-76, assoc. prof., assoc. dean, 1976-78, acting dean, 1978-79, dean, 1979—; cons. N.Y. State Regents Program for Non-Collegiate Sponsored Instrn., 1984, Collegiate Programs for N.Y. State Dept. Edn., 1985. Recipient Teaching Excellence award Alfred U., 1977, Mary E. Gladwin Outstanding Alumni award Akron U. Coll. Nursing, 1983. Mem. N.Y. State Council of Deans (treas. 1984—), Genesee Regional Consortium (v.p.), Sigma Theta Tau (treas. Alfred chpt. 1984-85), Genesee Valley Nurses Assn. (chair 1984-86). Office: Alfred U Coll Nursing PO Box 517 Alfred NY 14802

RAND, MARTHA ELIZABETH, mental health clinician; b. N.Y.C., Nov. 30, 1950; d. Arthur and Jean (MacNeish) R.; m. David Louis Ryzman, Apr. 20, 1985. BA, CUNY, 1972; cert. in dance and movement therapy, Inst. of Sociotherapy, N.Y.C., 1978; MA, New Sch. for Social Research, N.Y.C., 1982; diploma, Swedish Inst., 1985. Adj. prof. Queensborough Community Coll., Queens, N.Y., 1978, 80; dep. dir. communications and spl. projects N.Y. State Spl. Prosecutor for Health, Social Service and Welfare, N.Y.C., 1978-79; instr. phys. edn. YWCA., N.Y.C., 1981-82; instr. Human Relations Ctr. New Sch. for Social Research, 1980-82; ptnr. Help Yourself Assocs., N.Y.C. and Montclair, N.J., 1981—; recreation dir. Coler Hosp., N.Y.C., 1985-86; staff clinician intermediate care program eating disorders unit St. Clare's Hosp., Boonton, N.J., 1986; ptnr. Lively Earth Yoga Studio, N.Y.C., 1984-85. Mem. Am. Massage Therapy Assn.

RANDALL, CINDY, television production executive; b. San Diego, Dec. 31, 1956; d. Barney L. and Doris K. (Klink) Jones; m. David J. Randall, Feb. 25, 1980 (div. 1987). Student in English, San Diego State U., 1974-76. Newspaper columnist Beach Cities Newspapers, Manhattan Beach, Calif., 1977; mng. editor Z Channel mag., Los Angeles, 1977-78; newspaper editor, writer, founding staff mem. L.A. Weekly, Los Angeles, 1979-81; freelance writer Warner Bros. Pictures, Los Angeles, 1982-85; prodn. co. exec. On the Scene Prodns., Inc., Los Angeles, 1986—; writer, producer NBC Teletex Project, 1981-82. Actress Odyssey Theatre, Los Angeles, 1985; majorette Pasadena (Calif.) Doo-Dah Parade, 1986. Office: On the Scene Prodns Inc 5900 Wilshire Blvd 14th Floor Los Angeles CA 90036

RANDALL, CLAIRE, church executive; b. Dallas, Oct. 15, 1919; d. Arthur Godfrey and Annie Laura (Fulton) R. A.A., Schreiner Coll., 1948; BA, Scarritt Coll., 1950; DD (hon.), Berkeley Sem., Yale U., 1974; LHD (hon.), Austin Coll., 1982; LLD, Notre Dame U., 1984. Assoc. missionary edn. Bd. World Missions Presbyterian Ch., U.S., Nashville, 1949-57; dir. art Gen. Council Presbyterian Ch., U.S., Atlanta, 1957-61; dir. Christian World Mission, program dir., assoc. dir. Ch. Women United, N.Y.C., 1962-73; gen. sec. Nat. Council Ch. of Christ in U.S.A., N.Y.C., 1974-84; pres. Ch. Women United, N.Y.C., 1988—. Mem. Nat. Commn. on Internat. Women's Yr., 1975-77, Martin Luther King Jr. Fed. Holiday Commn., 1985. Recipient Woman of Yr. in Religion award Heritage Soc., 1977; Empire State Woman of Yr. in Religion award State of N.Y., 1984; medal Order of St. Vladimir, Russian Orthodox Ch., 1984. Democrat. Presbyterian. Home: 155 W 68th St New York NY 10023 *

RANDALL, GERALDINE MARGARET, lawyer; b. Wayne, Mich., Oct. 27, 1943; d. Anthony and Nellie Olga (Navickas) Gronos; m. Gale Randall, Sept. 1962 (div. 1967); 1 child, Laurelyn Gaye. AB in Math., U. Calif., Berkeley, 1970; JD, U. Calif., Davis, 1973. Bar: Calif. 1973; Atty. Pacific Gas and Electric Co., San Francisco, 1973-74; labor counsel Kaiser Industries, Oakland, Calif., 1974-76, Bank of Am., San Francisco, 1976-77; arbitrator, mediator, [illegible] San Anselmo, Calif., 1977— ; commr. Los Angeles City Employee Relations Bd., 1985—. Contbr. articles to profl. jours. Regents scholar U. Mich., 1961; recipient 1st place Traynor Calif. State Moot Ct. Competition, 1971; 1st place Western region Jessup Internat. Moot Ct. Competition, 1972; Mem. State Bar Calif., ABA, Indsl. Relations Research Assn., Soc. Profls. Dispute Resolution (regional v.p. 1982-84), Nat. Acad. Arbitrators, Phi Beta Kappa. Office: PO Box 1540 San Anselmo CA 94960

RANDALL, JUDIE LYN, real estate appraiser; b. Zumbrota, Minn., Sept. 4, 1952; d. Lawrence George and Norma Rose (Poppe) R. BS in Home Econs., Mankato State Coll., 1974. Appraiser Midwest Fed. Savs. Assn., Mpls., 1977-80, United Mortgage Inc., Bloomington, Minn., 1980—. Mem. Soc. Real Estate Appraisers, Nat. Assn. Rev. Appraisers. Lutheran. Office: United Mortgage Corp 8300 Norman Center Dr Suite 1000 Bloomington MN 55437

RANDALL, LINDA L., nurse; b. Williamson, W.Va., Nov. 5, 1945; d. Opal Ferne (Chapman) C.; diploma St. Mary's Hosp. Sch. Nursing, Huntington, W.Va., 1966; postgrad. W.Va. U., 1969, Marshall U., 1971, St. Joseph's Coll., North Windham, Maine, 1978, U. Central Fla., 1982—; cert. emergency nurse; m. Steven Edward Randall, Oct. 12, 1974. Charge nurse ICU and CCU, St. Mary's Hosp., Huntington, 1966-68; supr. ICU and CCU, Drs. Meml. Hosp., Huntington, 1968-73; team leader CCU, Community Hosp., Springfield, Ohio, 1973-74; charge nurse Urbana (Ohio) Care Center, 1974, dir. nursing services, 1974-78; dir. nursing services The Palms Health Care Center, Sebring, Fla., 1978-79; asst. head nurse, emergency and employee health services Ringling Bros., Barnum & Bailey Circus World, Orlando, Fla., 1979-80; asst. charge nurse emergency dept. Halifax Hosp. Med. Center, Daytona Beach, Fla., 1980-82; supr. operating room and post anesthesia Daytona Beach (Fla.) Gen. Hosp., 1982-83; head nurse emergency dept. Community Hosp. of Bunnell (Fla.), 1983-84; charge nurse emergency dept. Fla. Hosp. Med. Ctr., Orlando, 1984-86; occupational health nurse Repco Inc., Orlando, 1986—; mem. trauma staff Daytona Beach Internat. Speedway, 1981-86; program dir. SW div. W.Va. Heart Assn., 1969-73; bd. dirs. Ohio Hi-Point Joint Vocat. Sch. Allied Health Fields. Recipient Dr. Frist Humanitarian award Hosp. Corp. of Am., 1984. Mem. Nat. League Nursing, Am., Fla. nurses assns., Emergency Dept. Nurses Assn., Am. Heart Assn. (basic life support instr. 1981, advanced cardiac life support 1982), Am. Assn. Critical Care Nurses, Am. Assn. Occupational Health Nurses, Fla. Assn. Ocupational Health Nurses, Defenders of Wildlife, Fla. Audubon Soc., Fla. Wildlife Found., Nat. Audubon Soc., Nat. Wildlife Found., Fla. Wildlife Assn., Cousteau Soc. Republican. Roman Catholic. Home: 435 Tulane Dr Altamonte Springs FL 32714

RANDALL, LOLLY (PRISCILLA), manufacturers' representative; b. Boston, Aug. 15, 1952; d. Raymond Victor and Priscilla (Richmond) R.; m. Harold Glen Middleton, Dec. 7, 1983; 1 child, Priscilla Eva. B.Arts and Scis., U. Colo., 1973. Asst. to dir. pub. relations Pepsi Cola Co., Mpls., 1975; sales rep. DiCosta Knits, Ltd., San Francisco, 1975-76, Lilli Ann Corp., San Francisco, 1976-78; owner Lolly & Co., Seattle, 1978—; dir. 6100 Bldg. Assn., Seattle, 1981. Mem. Pacific N.W. Toy Assn. (pub. relations officer 1981-82, founding mem. 1981). Republican. Episcopalian. Avocations: volunteer work in field of recovering alcoholics, skiing. Home: 418 SW 189th St Seattle WA 98166 Office: Lolly & Co 6100 4th Ave S #255 Seattle WA 98108

RANDALL, LYNN ELLEN, librarian; b. Chgo., Oct. 10, 1946; d. Ward W. and Hazel A. (Nettles) R. BA, King's Coll., 1970; MA, Seton Hall U., 1973; MLS, Rutgers U., 1978. Librarian, N.J. Inst. Tech., Newark, 1970-75; library dir. N.E. Bible Coll., Essex Fells, N.J., 1975-81; reference librarian Seton Hall U., South Orange, N.J., 1983-85; dir. library services Berkeley Sch., West Paterson, N.J., 1985—; instr. Morris (N.J.) County Coll., 1981-83. Mem. Union County (N.J.) Heritage Commn., 1975-76. Mem. Middle States Assn. Bible Colls., Am. Assn. Bible Colls. (evaluator 1977, 79, 84), ALA, N.J. Library Assn. (chair automated library services com. 1986-88, conf. program 1987—, editor newsletter 1982-84, 87—), N.J. Library Network (pres. Region II 1987—), Assn. Coll. and Research Libraries (com.). Co-author: N.J. Online Directory, 1983. Editor N.J. Libraries, fall 1984, spring 1986. Home: 173 Ridge Rd Apt #H7 Cedar Grove NJ 07009

RANDALL, MARION STANTON, motel executive; b. Ogden, Utah; d. Charles Benjamin and Marian (Savyer) Stanton; m. Edmund W. Baker, Aug. 21, 1948 (div. 1976); children—Jeffrey Alan, Roger Edmund, Laurel Terese, Lisa Diane Baker Barbeau and Maureen Louise (dec.) (triplets), Douglas Owen; m. 2d Raymond L. Randall, June 20, 1981. A.B. in Psychology, Marygrove Coll., Detroit, 1943. Adminstrv. sec., sec. to labor mgmt. bd. Ohio Employment Services, Akron, 1943-45; exec. sec. asst. to exec. tech. editor Govt. Labs., Akron, 1945-48; exec. sec.-adminstrv. asst. Eastman Kodak, Chgo., 1948-49; exec. sec. to exec. dir. in-patient psychiatry U. Minn. Hosps., Mpls., 1949-50; exec. sec. in personnel and field support systems Hughes Aircraft, Culver City, Calif., 1950-55; owner, operator Surfside Motel, Port Hueneme, Calif., 1974-84; legal cons. motels. Exec. sec. Minor League Baseball, West Covina, Calif., 1967. Mem. AAUW (editor chpt. bull. 1968-70, chpt. v.p. programs 1971-72), So. Calif. Psychiat. Research. Club: Mary and Joseph League (Los Angeles).

RANDALL, PATRICIA LORENE, clinical social worker; b. Springfield, Mo., Nov. 14, 1942; d. James Joseph and Bertha (Sperandio) R. B.A. in Sociology, Mt. St. Scholastica Coll., 1964; M.S.W., St. Louis U., 1966. Staff mem., clin. social worker Family and Personal Support Ctrs. of Greater St. Louis, 1966-80, dir. Clayton (Mo.) Ctr. office, 1981-87, v.p. for Special Services, St. Louis, 1987—. Del. gov.'s adv. bd. Mo. White House Conf. on Families, 1979-80; chmn. St. Louis County Schs. Agys. Com. on Youth, 1969-71; mem. Block Partnership, 1971-72, mem. St. Francis Xavier Parish Council, 1982-83; bd. dirs. New Life Styles Orgn., 1981-84; mem. Children's Mental Health Services Council, 1981—, Christian Life Community Group St. Louis. Cert. Acad. Cert. Social Workers. Mem. Nat. Assn. Social Workers (del. state bd. 1977-79), Am. Assn. Marriage and Family Therapy (approved supr.), Am. Group Psychotherapy Assn., Mo. Assn. Social Welfare. Roman Catholic. Lodge: Soroptimists. Home: 21 W Rose Webster Groves MO 63119 Office: Family Ctrs of Greater St Louis 2650 Olive St Saint Louis MO 63103

RANDALL, RUTH EVELYN, state official, educator; b. Underwood, Iowa, Mar. 4, 1929; d. Oluf and Lillie Martha (Bondo) Larsen; m. Robert Dale Randall (dec.); children—Robert, Mark, Diane. Teaching cert., Dana Coll., Blair, Nebr., 1949; B.S., U. Omaha, 1961; M.S., U. Nebr.-Omaha, 1968, Ed.S., 1972; Ed.D. in Ednl. Adminstrn., U. Nebr.-Lincoln, 1976. Various teaching positions Iowa and Nebr., 1949-67; elem. prin. Omaha Pub. Schs., 1967-75; asst. prin. Horace Mann Pub. Sch., Omaha, 1976-78; asst. supt. Rosemount Ind. Sch. Dist., Minn., 1978-81, dep. supt., 1981, supt., 1981-83; commr. of edn. State of Minn., St. Paul, 1983—; mem. Tandy Ednl. Grants Rev. Bd., planning group for Nat. Bd. Cert. of Profl. Tchrs., Carnegie Corp., Minn. State High Sch. League; mem. Nat. Bd. for Profl. Teaching Standards; lectr. in field. Mem. editorial adv. bd. Electronic Learning mag., T.H.E. Journal; contbr. articles to profl. jours. Mem. exec. com. Minn. Acad. Excellence Found., adv. council for Mentally Retarded and Physically Handicapped, Higher Edn. Adv. Council, Horace Mann League of U.S., Minn. Women's Edn. Council, Jr. Achievement Bd., Citizens League, Sci. Mus., Blue Ribbon Campaign for Child Survival, Elem. Sch. Ctr., Minn. Permanent Sch. Fund. Adv. com., Sta. KTCA Channel Two, Luth. Women's Caucus, Commn. on New Luth. Ch.; bd. dirs. Luth. Brotherhood Mut. Fund Bd., mem. North Cen. Regional Edn. Lab. Bd., Nat. Adv. Panel Ctr. on Effective Secondary Schs.; trustee Tchrs. Retirement Assn.; mem. nat. adv. bd. Pub. Agenda Found.; mem. edn. adv. council Carnegie Corp., N.Y.; sec. Minn. Bd. Edn.; ex-officio mem. Minn. Indian Affairs Council; mem. Minn. High Tech. Council; mem. adv. bd. Bush Pub. Schs. Exec. Fellows; mem. Edn. Commn. of States; mem. bd. advisors Close Up, Young Writer's Contest Found. (hon.); bd. dirs. Global Perspectives in Edn. Inc., Council Chief State Sch. Officers, 1987—, SEARCH Inst., Agy. for Instrnl. Tech., Minn. Job Tng. Ptnrship. Iowa Farm Bur. scholar Dana Coll., 1947-49; Franklin E. and Orinda M. Johnson fellow U. Nebr.-Lincoln, 1975-76; Bush Pub. Schs. Exec. fellow, 1980-81; recipient appreciation award Apple Valley C. of C., 1983, Award U. Nebr. Lincoln, 1983, Disting. Alumnus award Dana Coll., 1984. Mem. Council of Chief State Sch. Officers (bd. dirs.), Am. Forum (bd. dirs.), Minn. Valley Bus. and Profl. Women's Club (Woman of Yr. 1982), Minn. Assn. Supervision and Curriculum Devel. (award for contbns. to Am. Edn. 1988), Minn. Assn. Sch. Adminstrs., Adminstrv. Women in Edn. Minn., LWV, AAUW, Upper Midwest Women in Edn. Adminstrn., Nat. PTA (life), Omaha Edn. Assn. (Human Relations award 1978), Women Execs. in State Govt. (founding), Nat. Council Adminstrv. Women in Edn., Am. Edn. Research Assn., Am. Assn. Sch. Adminstrs., Assn. Supervision and Curriculum Devel., Minn. Council for Gifted and Talented, Minn. Women's Econ. Roundtable, Minn. Soc. Fine Arts, Travelers Soc., U. Nebr.-Omaha Alumni (Achievement award 1987, recipient distinguished alumnus award, 1987), U. Nebr. Alumni Assn. (life), Dana Coll. Alumni Assn., Phi Delta Kappa, Delta Kappa Gamma. Mem. Democratic Farm Labor Party. Lutheran. Home: 8738 Summer Wind Bay Woodbury MN 55125 Office: Edn Dept 712 Capitol Sq Bldg 550 Cedar St Saint Paul MN 55101

RANDISI, ELAINE MARIE, apparel manufacturing executive; b. Racine, Wis., Dec 19, 1926; d. John Dewey and Alveta Irene (Raffety) Fehd; A.A., Pasadena Jr. Coll., 1946; B.S. cum laude (Giannini scholar), Golden Gate U., 1978; m. John Paul Randisi, Oct. 12, 1946 (div. July 1972); children—Jeanine Randisi Manson, Martha Randisi Cheney, Joseph, Paula Randisi Small, Catherine Randisi Tateo, George, Anthony (dec.). With Raymond Kaiser Engrs., Inc., Oakland, Calif., 1969-75, 77-86, corp. acct., 1978-79, sr. corp. acct., 1979-82, sr. payroll acct., 1983-86, acctg. mgr., Lilli Ann Corp., San Francisco, 1986—; corp. buyer Kaiser Industries Corp., Oakland, 1975-77; lectr. on astrology Theosophical Soc., San Francisco, 1979—; mem. faculty Am. Fedn. Astrologers Internat. Conv., Chgo., 1982, 84. Mem. Speakers Bur., Calif. Assn. for Neurologically Handicapped Children, 1964-70, v.p. 1969; bd. dirs. Ravenwood Homeowners Assn., 1979-82, v.p., 1979-80, sec., 1980-81; mem. organizing com. Minority Bus. Fair, San Francisco, 1976; pres., bd. dirs. Lakewood Condominium Assn., 1984-87. Mem. Am. Fedn. Astrologers, Nat. Assn. Female Execs., Calif. Scholarship Fedn. (life), Alpha Gamma Sigma (life). Mem. Ch. of Religious Science (lic. practioner). Initiated Minority Vendor Purchasing Program for Kaiser Engrs., Inc., 1975-76. Home: 742 Wesley Way Apt 1-C Oakland CA 94610 Office: Lilli Ann Corp 2701 16th St San Francisco CA 94103

RANDLE, ELLEN EUGENIA FOSTER, opera, classical singer, educator; b. New Haven, Conn., Oct. 2, 1948; d. Richard A.G. and Thelma Lousie (Brooks) Foster; m. Ira James William, Mar. 7, 1947 (div. 1972); John Willis Randle, Feb. 12, 1938. Student, Calif. State Coll., Sonoma, 1970; studied with Boris Goldovsky, 1970; student, Grad. Sch. Fine Arts, Florence, Italy, 1974; studied with Tito Gobbi, Florence, 1974; student, U. Calif., Berkeley, 1977; BA in World History, Lone Mountain Coll., 1976, MA in Performing Arts, 1978; studied with Madam Eleanor Steber, Graz, Austria, 1979; studied with Patricia Goehl, Munich, Fed. Republic Germany, 1979. instr. East Bay Performing Art Ctr., Richmond, Calif., 1986, Chapman Coll., 1986. Singer opera prodns. Porgy & Bess, Oakland, Calif., 1980-81, La-Traviata, Oakland, 1981-82, Aida, Oakland, 1981-82, Madame Butterfly, Oakland, 1982-83, The Magic Flute, Oakland, 1984, numerous others; performances include TV specials, religious concerts, musicals; music dir. Natural Man, Berkeley, 1986. Recipient Bk. Am. Achievement award. Mem. Music Tchrs. Assn., Nat. Council Negro Women, Nat. Assn. Negro Musicians, The Calif.-Nebraskan Orgn., Inc. Democrat. Mem. African Methodist Episcopal Zion Ch. Home: 5314 Boyd Ave Oakland CA 94618

RANDLETT, MARY WILLIS, photographer; b. Seattle, May 5, 1924; d. Cecil Durand and Elizabeth (Bayley) Willis; m. Herbert B. Randlett, Oct. 19, 1950 (div.); children—Robert, Mary Ann, Peter, Susan. B.A., Whitman Coll., Walla Walla, Wash., 1947. Freelance photographer, 1949—; one-woman shows: Seattle Sci. Center, 1971, Western Wash. State U., 1971, Seattle Art Mus., 1971, Art Gallery of Greater Victoria, 1972, Alaska State Mus., 1972, others; group shows: Am. Soc. Mag. Photographers, 1970, Whatcom Mus., Bellingham, Wash., Henry Gallery, Seattle, 1971, 74, Royal Photog. Soc., 1979, Heard Mus., Phoenix, 1979, others; works represented in permanent collections Met. Mus., Nat. Collection of Fine Arts, Nat. Portrait Gallery, Washington State Library, Manuscript div. U. Wash., Pacific Northwest Bell, Seattle, Swedish Med. Center, Seattle; works appeared in books: The Master and His Fish (Roderick Haig-Brown), 1982; Theodore Roethke: The Journey to I and Otherwide (Neal Bowers), 1982; Mountain in the Clouds (Bruce Brown), 1982; Masonry in Architecture (Louis Redstone), 1982; Writings and Reflections from the World of Roderick Haig-Brown, 1982; Pike Place Market (Alice Shorett and Murray Morgan), 1982; The Dancing Blanket, (Cheryl Samuel), 1982, Collected Poems of Theodore Roethke, 1982; Poetry: An Introduction (Miller and Greenberg), 1983; Spires of Form (Victor Scheffer), 1983; Assault on Mount Helicon (Mary Barnard), 1983; New as a Wave (Eve Triem), 1983; Sketchbook: A Memoir of the '30's and the Northwest School (William Cumming), 1983; Good Intentions (Jane Adams), 1985; Blackbirds of the Americas (Gordon Orians and Tony Angell), 1985; Historic Preservation in Seattle (Larry Kreisman), 1985; Down Town Seattle Walking Tours (Mary Randlett and Carol Tobin), 1986; Seattle, the Seattle Book, 1986; When Orchids were Flowers (Kate Knap Johnson), 1986; others; works also appeared in newspapers and mags. Nat. Endowment for Arts grantee, 1976; recipient Wash. State Gov.'s award for spl. commendation for contbns. in field of photography, 1983. Mem. Am. Soc. Mag. Photographers. Home: Box 10536 Bainbridge Island WA 98110

RANDO, RAE, manager; b. Paterson, N.J., Apr. 12, 1956; d. Frank J. and Rachel R. (Turpstra) R.; m. Dimitri Voicechovski, Nov. 6, 1976; 1 child, Nikolai Aleksei. B.S. in Bus. Adminstrn. candidate Thomas A. Edison State Coll., 1985—; cert. Katharine Gibbs Sch., 1974-76. Tenant/landlord adminstr. Claridge House, Verona, N.J., 1976-79, Paragon Enterprises, West Orange, N.J., 1979-81; account rep. Sci. Mgmt., Parsippany, N.J., 1981-82, mgr. temporary services, 1982-86, mgr. major accounts, 1986-88, br. mgr., 1988—. Canvas vol. Greenpeace, 1980—; trustee North Jersey Psychotherapeutic Inst., 1983-85 , treas., 1984-85. Avocations: astronomy, skiing, birding, wildlife conservation. Roman Catholic. Home: Jennings Rd Milton NJ 07438 Office: Sci Mgmt Corp 2001 Rt 46 Waterview Plaza Parsippany NJ 07054

RANDOLPH, DEBORAH JEAN GREENWAY, data processing executive; b. Anderson, S.C., Sept. 17, 1951; d. Charles Corbett and Ruth Marcelia (Ham) Greenway; m. Randall Scott Randolph, June 14, 1980; 1 child, Jordan Vance. BA in Journalism, U. S.C., 1973, BS in Computer Sci., 1979. Data processing supr. Giant Cement Co., Columbia, S.C., 1973-78; data processing mgr. Greater Carolinas Ins. Co., Columbia, 1979-80; asst. dir. data processing Providence Hosp., Columbia, 1980-85; dir. computer services Richland Sch. Dist. 2, Columbia, 1985—. Named Outstanding Young Woman in Am., 1985. Mem. Nat. Assn. for Female Execs., Data Processing Mgmt. Assn., Common IBM Users Group. Democrat. Methodist. Home: 4010 Linwood Rd Columbia SC 29205 Office: Richland Sch Dist Two 6831 Brookfield Rd Columbia SC 29206

RANDOLPH, WILLENE JOYCE, computer specialist; b. Lebanon, Ill., Feb. 7, 1935; d. Rudolph Mitchell and Cleo (Gant) Davis; m. Scott Roosevelt Randolph, Feb. 2, 1952; children—Craig, Teresa, Keith and Kathy (twins). B.A., Stephens Coll., 1985. Sec., USAF, Scott AFB, Ill., 1958-63, computer programmer, 1963-69; computer specialist U.S. Army, St. Louis, 1969-72; data processing instr. State Community Coll., East St. Louis, Ill., dir. computer services/plan and research 1976-81; data processing mgr.Bd. Edn., 1981-82; computer systems analyst, program mgr. Fed. Govt., U.S. Army, St. Louis, 1982—; mem. Ford Found. Adv. Bd., 1984—, St. Louis Community Coll. adv. bd., 1986-87. Pres., Jack and Jill Am., East St. Louis, 1979; editor newsletter St. Paul Bapt. Ch., East St. Louis, 1982—; precinct committeewoman East St. Louis Precinct 33, 1983. Recipient Outstanding Performance award USAF, 1963; Fed. Women's Program Mgr. of Year award, 1984-86; Spl. Act award U.S. Army, 1982-84; award of Merit Top Ladies of Distinction, 1984. Mem. Blacks in Govt. (v.p. 1984-85), Federally Employed Women (workshop presenter), Data Processing Mgrs. Assn., Ill. Bus. Edn. Assn., St. Louis Fed. Women's Program Council. Republican. Avocations: travel, reading. Home: 490 N 33d St East Saint Louis IL 62205 Office: US Army ALMSA 210 N Tucker Blvd Saint Louis MO 63188

RANFT, LISA MARIE, marketing executive; b. Queens, N.Y., Mar. 8, 1960; d. Francis Edward and Teresa Veronica (McGrath) R.; m. Robert Lawton Shimer, July 21, 1984. B.A. in Econs., Columbia U., 1983. Fin. analyst IBM, Princeton, N.J., 1983, sr. planner, 1984, product adminstr., Montvale, N.J., 1984-85, mktg. rep., West Orange, N.J., 1986—. Recipient Outstanding Achievement awards IBM, 1984-85. Mem. Nat. Assn. Female Execs., Barnard Coll. Alumni Assn., Peddie Sch. Alumni Assn. Club: [illegible]. Avocations: tennis; travel; reading. Home: 969 Bloomfield Ave Unit A12 Glen Ridge NJ 07028

RANGELL, SYDELLE RAY, television producer; b. Bklyn., July 25, 1931; d. Morris and Pauline (Kaiser) R.; M.A. magna cum laude, Bklyn. Coll., 1954. Former producer Jack Tinker & Ptnrs., Tinker Dodge Delano; v.p., exec. producer Needham Harper & Steers Inc., N.Y.C., 1971-83; exec. TV producer Dancer, Fitzgerald, Sample, N.Y.C., 1983-87, free-lance producer, 1987—. Recipient numerous awards.

RANKAITIS, SUSAN, artist; b. Cambridge, Mass., Sept. 10, 1949; d. Alfred Edward and Isabel (Shimkus) Rankaitis; m. Robbert Flick, June 5, 1976. B.F.A. in Painting, U. Ill., 1971; M.F.A. in Visual Arts, U. So. Calif., 1977. One person shows Los Angeles County Mus. Art, 1983; one person shows Internat. Mus. Photography, George Eastman House, 1983, Min Gallery of Tokyo, 1988; represented in permanent collections U. Ill., Santa Monica Coll., Ctr. for Creative Photography, UCLA, Mus. Modern Art, Santa Barbara Mus. Art, Los Angeles County Mus. Art, Mpls. Inst. Arts, San Francisco Mus. Modern Art, Security Pacific Bank, Mus. Modern Art, Lodz, Poland; assoc. prof. art Chapman Coll.; overview panelist visual arts Nat. Endowment for Arts, 1983, 84; mem. steering com. U. So. Calif. Friends of Fine Arts, 1983-84. Bd. dirs. Friends of Photography, 1985-88, mem. adv. bd. trustees. Nat. Endowment for Arts fellow, 1980; Chapman research fellow 1984-87; Graves award in the humanities, 1985. Mem. Coll. Art Assn., Los Angeles Inst. Contemporary Art, Los Angeles County Mus. Art, Friends of Photography, Center Creative Photography, Calif. Council Fine Arts Deans. Studio: 707 E Hyde Park Blvd Inglewood CA 90302

RANKIN, DIANNE MARY, financial planner; b. Mineola, N.Y.; d. David Jay and Rose Mary (Ruggerio) Keller; B.A., U. Louisville (Deans scholar), 1969, postgrad., 1976—; m. Eric Lynn Rankin, Nov. 18, 1972. CPA, N.J.; cert. fin. planner; registered investment adviser. Stewardess, Pan Am. Airways, 1969-72; material controller RCA, Somerville, N.J., 1972-75; pvt. practice acctg., Flemington, N.J., 1975—; investment adv. SEC, 1982; instr. tax preparation, Flemington, 1976-78. Mem. Delaware Twp. Mcpl. Utilities Authority, 1979—. Author: Financial Planning, 1984, Tax Reform, 1987.

Mem. Nat. Soc. Public Accts., Nat. Tax Tng. Inst. Address: RD 2 Ferry Rd Flemington NJ 08822

RANKIN, JUDITH TORLUEMKE, professional golfer; b. St. Louis, Feb. 18, 1945; d. Paul W. and Waneta (Clifton) Torluemke; student public schs., Eureka, Mo.; m. Walter Rankin, June 12, 1967; 1 son, Walter. Profl. golfer; pres. Ladies Profl. Golfers Assn., 1976-77; golf commentator, ABC Network Golf, Midland, Tex., 1984—, ABC-TV Network, 1984-88. Recipient Vare trophy for lowest scoring average, 1973-76; Victor award for Female golfer, 1976; leading money winner, 1976-77; first woman to win more than $100, 000 in one year, 1976. Author: Natural Way to Golf Power. Address: 2405 Culpepper Midland TX 79701

RANKIN, MARLENE OWENS, personnel executive, clinical social worker; b. Cleve., Apr. 19, 1939; d. James Cleveland (Jesse) and Minnie Ruth (Solomon) Owens; m. Stuart McLean Rankin, Nov. 19, 1961; 1 son, Stuart Owen. B.S. in Social Welfare, Ohio State U., 1961; A.M. (M.S.W.), U. Chgo., 1978. Cert. social worker. Caseworker, Cook County Dept. Pub. Aid, Chgo., 1961-66; social worker Project Learn, Chgo., 1968-69; social service planner Chgo. Com. Urban Opportunity, OEO, Chgo., 1969-72, planning coordinator, Model Cities, 1972-74; social service planner Gov.'s Office Human Relations Chgo., 1974-75; therapist United Charities Chgo., 1978-81; dir. personnel, 1981—. Bd. dirs. Hyde Park Neighborhood Club, Chgo., 1982—; mem. Personnel Dir. Group United Way, Chgo., 1982—, City Chgo. Bd. Ethics, 1987—. Mem. Acad. Cert. Social Workers, Ohio State U. Alumni Assn. (bd. dirs. 1985—). Democrat. Methodist. Office: United Charities of Chgo 14 E Jackson Blvd Chicago IL 60604

RANKIN, PEGE BETTY, retired educator; b. Twin Falls, Idaho, July 23, 1919; d. Marion P. and Margaret (Conway) Betty; B.A., U. Calif.-Berkeley, 1941; postgrad. U. Calif.-Berkeley, Calif. State Coll., Savannah State Coll., San Francisco State Coll.; M.Ed., U. San Francisco, 1976; m. Herbert E. Rankin, June 5, 1941; children—Greg Robert, Todd Conway. Tchr. contract bridge San Francisco Bay area, 1950-69; pres., officer Oakland Pub. Schs. (Calif.), 1967—; tchr. journalism Skyline High Sch., Oakland, 1967—; tchr. guide European coll. tours, summers 1970—. Chmn. div. fund Am. Cancer Soc., 1958; organizer, condr. Mental Health Bridge Charity, 1961; mem. Friends of Herrick Hosp., Friends of Berkeley Library, Wall Street Jour., Monterey Aquarium, All Calif., Oakland Mus., San Francisco Commonwealth Club; mem. adv. bd. Invest in America. Named Outstanding Tchr. Journalism, Calif. PTA; Newspaper Fund fellow, 1969. Mem. AAUW, Am. Contract Bridge League, Oakland Press Honor Assn., Women in Communications (scholarship chmn. 1973), Columbia Scholastic Press Assn., Journalism Educators No. Calif. (v.p. 1980), San Francisco Opera Guild (bd. dirs. 1981—), Calif. Acad. Sci., M.H. de Young Meml. Mus., Smithsonian Assocs., Alpha Chi Alpha. Republican. Methodist. Club: Fannie Hill Ski (San Francisco). Home: 752 Cragmont Ave Berkeley CA 94708 Office: 12250 Skyline Blvd Oakland CA 94619

RANKIN, RACHEL ANN, media specialist; b. High Point, N.C., Mar. 8, 1937; d. Benjamin Carl and Anne Jane (Robinson) Mixson; m. Thomas M. Rankin, July 30, 1961; 1 dau., Roxanne. A.A., Mars Hill Coll., 1957; B.A., Wake Forest U., 1959; M.L.S., U. S.C., 1977. Caseworker, Rockingham County Welfare, Reidsville, N.C., 1959-61; tchr. Reidsville & Rockingham County Schs., Reidsville, Wentworth, 1961-65, Berlin Am. Sch. (W.Ger.), 1967-69, Albemarle County Schs., Charlottesville, Va., 1970-72, Lexington County Schs., Ballentine, S.C., 1973-76; teaching asst., student tchr. supr. Sch. Edn., U. S.C., Columbia, 1976-77; sch. media specialist Montgomery County Schs., Rockville, Md., 1977—. Vice-pres. Berlin Am. PTA, 1967-68; del. European Conf. PTA's, Garmisch, West Germany, 1968; mem. planning com. N.C. Cherry Blossom Ball, Ct., Washington, 1983. Named Most Outstanding Tchr., Jackson Burley Sch., Charlottesville, Va., 1972; ofcl. citation Ho. of Dels., Md. Gen. Assembly, 1983. Mem. NEA (life), Internat. Assn. Sch. Librarians (charter, del. 1983), Am. Assn. Sch. Librarians (del. Montgomery County 1982), ALA, Md. Ednl. Media Orgn., Montgomery County Ednl. Media Specialists Assn. (treas. 1981-82, newsletter editor 1979-80), Montgomery County Edn. Assn., Montgomery County Ednl. Media Specialists Assn. (pres. 1983-84), N.C. State Soc. of Washington (bd. govs. 1984-86), Internat. Platform Assn., Delta Kappa Gamma (sec. Sigma chpt. 1988—). Democrat. Presbyterian. Club: N.C. Soc. (Washington). Home: 2912 Bluff Point Ln Silver Spring MD 20906 Office: Paint Branch High Sch Old Columbia Pike Burtonsville MD 20866

RANKIN, RUBY DEIONE, youth program administrator; b. Port Gibson, Miss., Mar. 18, 1960; d. John Henry and Mary Lou (Harris) R.; 1 child, Carlanza Deiontá. BS, Alcorn State U., 1981, MS, 1983; postgrad., Miss. State U. Records mgmt. specialist Grand Gulf Nuclear Power Sta., Port Gibson, Miss., 1983-84; 4-H youth agt. Miss. Coop. Extension Service, DeKalb, Miss., 1984—. Mem. choir Wall Hill Bapt. Ch., Lorman, Miss., 1977-84, Brown Ridge Bapt. Ch., DeKalb, 1984-87; vol. Riley-Kemper Hosp., DeKalb, 1987; active local PTA. Mem. Miss. Extension Youth Agts., NAACP. Home: PO Box 64 DeKalb MS 39328 Office: Miss Coop Extension Service PO Box 339 DeKalb MS 39328

RANNEY, HELEN MARGARET, physician, educator; b. Summer Hill, N.Y., Apr. 12, 1920; d. Arthur C. and Alesia (Toolan) R. A.B., Barnard Coll., 1941; M.D., Columbia, 1947; Sc.D., U. S.C., 1979. Diplomate: Am. Bd. Internal Medicine. Intern Presbyn. Hosp., N.Y.C., 1947-48; resident Presbyn. Hosp., 1948-50; practice medicine specializing in internal medicine, hematology N.Y.C., 1954-70; asst. physician Presbyn. Hosp., 1954-60; instr. Coll. Phys. and Surg. Columbia, 1954-60; asso. prof. medicine Albert Einstein Coll. Medicine, 1960-64, prof. medicine, 1965-70; prof. medicine SUNY-Buffalo, 1970-73; prof. medicine U. Calif.-San Diego, 1973—, chmn. dept. medicine, 1973-86. Fellow AAAS, A.C.P.; mem. Am. Soc. for Clin. Investigation, Am. Soc. Hematology, Harvey Soc., Am. Assn. Physicians, Nat. Acad. Sci., Inst. Medicine, Am. Acad. Arts and Scis., Phi Beta Kappa, Sigma Xi, Alpha Omega Alpha. Home: 6229 La Jolla Mesa Dr La Jolla CA 92037

RANSOHOFF, PRISCILLA BURNETT, psychologist, educator; b. Pitts., June 16, 1912; d. Levi Herr and Clara Amelia (Brown) Burnett; B.S., U. Pitts., 1941; M.A., Columbia U., 1952, Ed.D., 1954; m. James Hampton Johnston, Aug. 4, 1934; 1 dau., Priscilla Burnett; m. 2d, Nicholas Sigmund Ransohoff, Nov. 27, 1947. Dir. rehab. Monmouth Med. Center, Long Branch, N.J., 1944-54; pres. Cons. Assocs., Inc., Long Branch, 1954-64; v.p. Dale-Elliot Mgmt. Cons., N.Y.C., 1958-60; edn. adviser U.S. Army Electronics Command, Ft. Monmouth, N.J., 1964-78; organizational effectiveness staff officer U.S. Army Communications Materiel Readiness Command, Ft. Monmouth, 1978—; co-adj. prof. Ocean County Community Coll., Toms River, N.J.; co-adj. instr. Monmouth Coll., West Long Branch, N.J., Brookdale Community Coll., Lincroft, N.J. Founder, pres., chmn. bd. Monmouth Rehab. Workshop, Red Bank, N.J., 1954-58; vice chmn. N.J. del. Women's Conf., Houston, 1977. Recipient CECOM Comdr.'s Internat., 1982; Woman of Yr. award Zonta, 1984; cert. practitioner neuro linguistic programming. Mem. Orgn. Devel. Network, Internat. Platform Assn., Federally Employed Women (pres. 1973, 74, chpt. pres. 1984—), Internat. Tng. in Communication Club, Assn. U.S. Army (sec., adv. com. to nat. exec. bd., 3 yrs.), Def. Preparedness Assn., Assn. U.S. Army (sec., drug and alcohol com. Ft. Monmouth chpt., suicide prevention and intervention counicl, human resource com.), Pi Lambda Theta, Kappa Delta Pi, Delta Zeta. Lodges: Zonta Internat. (bd. dirs. Monmouth County chpt.), Order of Eastern Star. Home: 13 River Ave Monmouth Beach NJ 07750 Office: Aviation Research and Devel Activity Fort Monmouth NJ 07703

RANSOM, MARGARET PRISCILLA, government official; b. Jackson, N.C., Sept. 17, 1947; d. Lister and Argentina (Lockhart) R.; BS, N.C. A&T State U., 1969; M.A., Central Mich. U., 1981. IRS agt. various locations, 1969-76, exempt orgns. analyst, Washington, 1976-82, group mgr., Balt., 1982—. Recipient Communications and Services to Public award IRS, 1971, Disting. performance award, 1982, 85, 86, 87, group award for program accomplishments, 1983, 87. Mem. Nat. Assn. Female Execs., Assn. Improvement of Minorities in Internal Revenue Service, Federally Employed Women, Profl. Mgrs. Assn., Delta Sigma Theta.

RAO, CAROLINE A.C., service executive; b. Inverness, Scotland, Nov. 20, 1961; came to U.S., 1968; d. V.V. and Annie Nellie (Ensell) R. BS, Wagner Coll., 1984. Placement counselor Office Force div. Adia Internat., N.Y.C., 1984-85; supr., then sr. account rep. Kelly Services, Inc., N.Y.C., 1985-87; resident br. mgr. Kelly Services, Inc., Monroeville, Pa., 1987—; job cons. Jericho Project, N.Y.C., 1984. Active Covenant House, N.Y.C., 1986—, Planned Parenthood, N.Y.C., 1986—. Democrat. Episcopalian. Home: 5841 Walnut St Apt 33 Pittsburgh PA 15232 Office: Kelly Services Inc 303 Jonnet Bldg Monroeville PA 15146

RAPHAEL, ELLEN S., educational administrator; b. Boston, Oct. 27, 1954; d. Gale L. and Doris M. (Miller) R. Student, Vassar Coll., 1972-74; AB, Brown U., 1978; M of Pub. Policy, Harvard U., 1982, PhD in Pub. Policy, 1988. Cert. tchr., Mass., R.I. Math. lab. coordinator Newton (Mass.) North High Sch., 1974-76; spl. asst. to dean of student life Brown U., Providence, 1979-80, acting asst. dir. of health services, 1980, planning cons., 1980-81; sr. advisor, asst. dean of freshmen Harvard U., Cambridge, Mass., 1982-84; assoc. dir. Mass. Edn. Loan Authority, Boston, 1984-86, acting exec. dir., 1986-87; asst. dean for fin. and adminstrn. Coll. Liberal Arts, Boston U., 1987—; instr. Sch. Govt. Harvard U., 1983. Democrat. Jewish. Home: 246 Hampshire St #3 Cambridge MA 02139 Office: Boston U Coll Liberal Arts 725 Commonwealth Ave Boston MA 02215

RAPIN, LYNN SUZANNE, psychologist, consultant, educator; b. Sault Ste. Marie, Mich., Nov. 26, 1946; d. John Floyd and Ruth Antoinette (Martin) R.; m. Robert K. Conyne; children: Suzanne, Zachary. BA, Fla. State U., 1968; MEd, U. Ill., 1970, PhD, 1973. Lic. psychologist, Ohio, Ill. Resident dir. U. Ill., Champaign-Urbana, 1970-73, assoc. dir. unit one living ctr. coll. arts. and scis., 1971-73; asst. prof. edn. Ill. State U., Normal, 1973-78, assoc. prof. edn., 1978-80; pvt. practice psychology Cin., 1980—; staff psychologist Student Counseling Ctr., Ill. State U., 1973-76, coordinator ednl. programs., 1976-80; adj. assoc. prof. U. Cin., 1981—; cons. in field. Contbr. articles to profl. jours. and chpts. to books. Bd. dirs. Personal Assistance Telephone Help, 1979-81. Ill. State U. grantee 1975-79, State of Ill. grantee, 1978-79. Mem. Am. Psychol. Assn., Am. Assn. Counseling and Devel., Am. Coll. Personnel Assn., Assn. for Specialists in Group Work, Assn. for Counselor Edn. and Supervision. Home and Office: 1134 Cryer Ave Cincinnati OH 45208

RAPOPORT, BONNIETHEL, health administrator; b. North Hollywood, Calif., Dec. 5, 1955; d. Robert and Isabella Gibson (Carnahan) R. BS, Calif. State U., Northridge, 1978; MBA, U. Alaska, 1980. Head dept. Dutch Boy Paints, Northridge, 1976-78; research coordinator program devel. Fairbanks (Alaska) Native Assn., 1979-81; sr. analyst planning and markets Mapco Alaska Petroleum, North Pole, 1981-83; chief budget and mgmt. Fairbanks North Star Borough, 1983-86; exec. dir. Alaska Crippled Children and Adults, Inc., Fairbanks, 1986—. Mem. gen. bd., coach Interior Youth Basketball, Fairbanks, 1983—, v.p., 1987—; interior rep. health and social services grant rev. bd. State of Alaska, 1983-87; chairperson United Way Tanana Valley Dirs., 1986—; mem. Barrier Free Access Rev. Com., Alaska, 1988—. Named Vol. of Yr. Gov. of Alaska, 1981. Club: Quota. Home: PO Box 2771 Fairbanks AK 99707

RAPOZA-RIEGEL, CYNDIE MARIE, property manager; b. Honolulu, Sept. 10, 1953; d. Joseph Edward and Betty Marie (Himan) Rapoza; m. Richard Alan Riegel, Feb. 5, 1977; children: Jana Marie, Brian David. BA, LaVerne (Calif.) Coll., 1975. Mgr. bookstore LaVerne Coll., 1976-81; dir. pub. relations Compiler Systems, Sierra Madre, Calif., 1981-82; family day care provider Riegel Family Day Care, Pasadena, Calif., 1982-88; property mgr. Riegel Properties, Pasadena, 1988—. Editor: Hastings Ranch Nursery Sch. newsletter, Pasadena, 1985-86. Block capt., com. chmn. Upper Hastings Ranch Assn., Pasadena, 1984—, sec. 1985-86, pres. 1987—; pres. Women Attentive To Children's Happiness, Pasadena, 1986—. Democrat. Home and Office: 1130 Medford Rd Pasadena CA 91107

RAPP, DORRIE LOUISE, clinical psychologist; b. Chgo., Sept. 14, 1949; d. Edward Thomas and Louise Kathryn (Leisten) Tholke; B.A., U. Ill., Chgo., 1970; Ph.D., Cambridge U., Eng., 1977, diploma in clin. psychology, 1981. Diplomate Am. Bd. Neuropsychology. Psychologist, Spastics Soc., London, 1976-79; asst. dir. psychol. services Moss Rehab. Hosp., Phila., 1981-83; pvt. practice, 1983—; neuropsychologist Drucker Brain Injury Ctr., 1984-85. Lic. psychologist, Pa., Vt. Fellow Am. Acad. Cerebral Palsy and Devel. Medicine (Richmond Cerebral Palsy Center award 1980); mem. Am. Psychol. Assn., Pa. Psychol. Assn., Phila. Soc. Clin. Psychologists, Brit. Psychol. Soc., Nat. Acad. Neuropsychologists, Nat. Head Injury Found., Phila. Clin. Neuropsychology Group, Internat. Neuropsychology Group. Inventor drool control electronic device, 1979; author: Brain Injury Casebook, 1986; contbr. articles in field to profl. publs.

RAPP, MARJORIE LENORE (GREEN), financial manager; b. Elmhurst, Ill., June 5, 1932; d. DeWitt Clinton and Ruth Marion (Mueller) Green; B.A. with honors, U. Chgo., 1951, M.A. with honors, 1954; postgrad. U. Colo.; m. Alan Dean Rapp, June 14, 1953; children—Jeffrey Clinton, Martha Coralynne, David Cyril. Gen. mgr. Sark Aviation, Colorado Springs, Colo., 1961-64; North Union Devel. Co., also LaSalle Devel. Co., Colorado Springs, 1964-76; v.p., chief fin. officer Janus Corp., Colorado Springs, 1964-70; v.p., treas. Med. and Data Services, Inc., Colorado Springs, 1977-78; founder, 1978, owner Pandora Enterprises, Colorado Springs, 1978—; mng. gen. ptnr. Soda Creek Land Co., 1983—, Perkins-Shearer Bldg. Partnership, 1988—; gen. ptnr. RMD Enterprises, 1985—, R&N Enterprises, 1985—(all Colorado Springs); seminar tchr., 1975—. Dir. Candy-Stripe program St. Francis Hosp., Colorado Springs, 1967-68; asst. to minister music First Presbyn. Ch., Colorado Springs, 1967-75; genealogy research librarian Penrose Public Library, Colorado Springs, 1971-73; pres. guild Colorado Springs Choral Soc., 1962-63; treas., bd. dirs. Colo. Opera Festival, 1978-81. Mem. Earthwatch, Nat. Trust Historic Preservation, Nat. Geneal. Soc. New Eng. Hist. and Geneal. Soc., Soc. Preservation New Eng. Antiquities, Colo. Geneal Soc., Pikes Peak Geneal. Soc., Colorado Springs Fine Arts Ctr., Friends of the Pikes Peak Library Dist., Friends of the Pioneers Mus., Friends of White House Ranch, Opera Council of 500, Arthritis Found., Cheyenne Mountain Zoo Vol. Assn., Smithsonian Assocs., Am. Assn. Ret. Persons, AAUW, DAR, Mayflower Soc., Meml. Hosp. Aux. (life), Quadrangler Alumni Assn. (life), El Paso County Med. Aux., Phi Beta Kappa. Republican. Clubs: Colorado Springs Country, Plaza (founder). Address: 4807 Avondale Circle Colorado Springs CO 80917

RAPP, SUE CAROL STORER, small business owner, writer; b. Springfield, Ohio, Aug. 24, 1939; d. John Earl and Irene Mae (Beedy) Storer; m. William H. Johnson, June 24, 1958 (div. 1961); m. Thomas Alan Rapp, Feb. 3, 1962; 1 child, Tami Sue. Grad. high sch., Bellefontaine, Ohio. Bookkeeper United Telephone Co., Bellefontaine, 1957-58; exec. sec. Barber Colman Co., Rockford, Ill., 1958-64; supr., head cashier Laurentide Fin., Seaside, Calif., 1962-63; office mgr. Certified Water Co., Byron, Ill., 1981-82; owner, operator Rapp's Water Treatment, Byron, 1982—. Author: From Somewhere Within, 1986, (poetry) Seasons of Love, 1988; author short stories, numerous poems; composer songs; freelance writer Ogle County Life, Oregon, Ill., 1988—; author polit. and social reform papers. Com. chair Rockford area Muscular Dystrophy Assn., 1983—. Mem. Nat. Water Quality Assn., Ill. Writers, Inc., World of Poetry (12 Certificate of Merit awards, Golden Poet award 1985, 86), Am. Poetry Assn., Byron C. of C.

RAPPAPORT, MARGARET M., psychologist, author, consultant; b. Buffalo, Nov., 16, 1941; d. Leo J. and Marie L. (Fischle) Williams; m. Herbert Rappaport, Oct. 21, 1967; children—Amanda, Alexander. B.A., U. Buffalo, 1967; M.A., SUNY, 1969; Ph.D., U. Colo., 1971. Adj. faculty Temple U., Phila., 1974-1984; exec. dir. Inst. for Parent/Child Services, Phila., 1978—; pvt. practice clinician Rappaport Assocs., Phila., 1974—; prof., researcher Univ. Dar es Salaam, Tanzania, 1970-74; program dir. Frontrunners, 1978—; child care/devel. cons. to media especially TV, 1984—; program dir. First Steps, 1986—. Author books and articles on parenting and family life, monographs on existential psychology. Mem. NOW, AAUP, Nat. Assn. for Edn. of Young Children, Del. Valley Assn. for Edn. of Young Children. Republican. Club: Phila. Cricket (Pa.). Home: 509 E Sedgwick St Philadelphia PA 19119

RAPPAPORT-FRIEDMAN, LAURY FAE, psychotherapist; b. N.Y.C., Apr. 25, 1953; d. Sol and Renee (Fink) R.; m. Neil Louis Friedman. BA in Art Therapy cum laude, SUNY, Buffalo, 1975; MEd in Art and Expressive Therapy, Lesley Coll., Cambridge, Mass., 1979; PhD in Psychology and Spirituality, Union Grad. Sch., Cin., 1987. Registered art therapist. Art therapist DeVeaux Sch., Niagara Falls, N.Y., 1975-76; instr. psychotherapy SUNY, Buffalo, 1976; pvt. practice psychotherapy Cambridge, 1977-78, 83—; expressive arts therapist Greater Lawrence (Mass.) Day Treatment Ctr. for Adults, 1979-80; expressive arts therapist, supr. Perspective Day Treatment Ctr., Wakefield, Mass., 1979-84; cons., expressive arts therapist Community Group, Wakefield, 1980-84; cons., staff mem. Spring Hill Inst., Ashby, Mass., 1984—, co-exec. dir., 1986—; expressive arts therapist Shore Collaborative, Medford, Mass., 1977-78, Danvers State Hosp., Hathorne, Mass., 1977-78; vol. West Seneca (N.Y.) State Sch., 1975; adj. faculty expressive therapies program Lesley Coll. Grad. Sch., 1981—; lectr. in field. Exhibited in shows at Gallery 219, Buffalo, 1974, Lesley Coll., 1978; contbr. articles to profl. jours. Art dir. community outdoor mural projects, Buffalo, 1975-76. Mem. Am. Art Therapy Assn. (cert. art therapist), Creative Arts Therapy Coalition, Assn. Humanistic Psychology. Home: 11 Donnell St Cambridge MA 02138 Office: Spring Hill Inst 678 Massachusetts Ave Cambridge MA 02139

RASBERRY, SHAROL BARTA, accountant, management company executive; b. Red Cloud, Nebr., Oct. 15, 1947; d. Allen James and Orfa Irene (Copley) Barta; m. Robert E. Rasberry, Dec. 29, 1968; children: Kimberly, Robert E. BBA, U. Nebr., 1969. CPA, Kans. Tax prin. Arthur Young & Co., Wichita, Kans., 1969-79; dir. taxes CWG Enterprises, Wichita, Kans., 1979-80; exec. v.p. fin. Capital Enterprises, Wichita, 1980—. Bd. dirs. YWCA, 1978, Accent on Kids, 1983—, Wichita area council Girl Scouts U.S., 1986—, Leadership 2000, 1986; treas. Wichita Jr. League, 1985—. Mem. Am. Inst. CPAs, Kans. Soc. CPAs, Wichita C. of C., Beta Gamma Sigma. Republican. Avocation: skiing. Home: 8501 Tipperay Wichita KS 67206 Office: Capital Enterprises Inc 300 N Main St Suite 200 Wichita KS 67201

RASHAD, JOHARI MAHASIN, employee development specialist; b. Washington, Mar. 13, 1951; d. Henry and Millie Lucerita (Adams) Jones; children: Chekesha W. Rashad. BA, Howard U., 1976, postgrad., 1984—; MA, U. D.C., 1981. With U.S. Customs Service, 1976; data standardization specialist U.S. Civil Service Commn., 1977-79; personnel mgmt. specialist U.S. Office of Personnel Mgmt., Washington, 1979-86; with U.S. Coast Guard, 1986—; pres. Rashad Assocs. Cons., Washington, 1987—. Author: poetry, (R)evolutions, 1982, Woman, Too, 1984; author: Federal Jobhunting Simplified, 1979; Washington corr. Changing woman Mag., 1986—. Vol. various charitable orgns., cdnl. orgns. Recipient numerous certs. of appreciation local civic orgns. Mem. Am. Soc. Tng. and Devel., AAUW, Internat. Communication Assn., Washington Ind. Writers, Downtown Jaycees (dir. 1985-87, v.p. individual devel. 1988—), SCA Alumnae Assn. (pres. 1978-82).

RASMUSSEN, CAREN NANCY, hospital executive; b. Fort Riley, Kans., July 7, 1950; d. Stanley Junior and Katherina Wilhelmina (Wagner) R. A.A.S., Grand Rapids Jr. Coll., 1970; B.S., U. Md., 1977. Med. sec., Walter Reed Army Med. Ctr., Washington, 1970-72, sec. procurement, 1972-76, contract specialist, 1976-79, 81-84; contract specialist Kadena Air Base, Okinawa, 1979-81; procurement analyst Walter Reed Med. ctr., 1984—. Fellow Nat. Assn. Female Execs.; mem. Nat. Contract Mgmt. Assn. Democrat. Avocations: photography; stamp collecting; gardening; travel. Home: 17514 Longview Ln Olney MD 20832 Office: Contracting Div Walter Reed Army Med Ctr Washington DC 20307

RASMUSSEN, ELAINE LINDA, school system administrator; b. Cedar Falls, Iowa, Oct. 31, 1942; d. Niels Christian and Blanche Henrietta (Patterson) R. BA in Music Edn., U. No. Iowa, 1964, MA in Music Edn., 1967, MEd, 1976, EdS in Edn., 1981. Tchr. Waterloo (Iowa) Community Schs., Pacific area, 1964-66, 67-69, Overseas Sch. System, U.S. Dept. Def., 1969-74; tchr. New Hartford (Iowa) Community Schs., 1976-79, dist. supr., 1980-85; adminstrv. intern Cedar Falls (Iowa) Community Schs., 1979-80; dist. supr. Independence (Iowa) Community Schs., 1985—. Mem. Wapsie Riverfest/Celebrate 4 Com., Independence, 1986—, Independence Ambassadors Club, 1987—. Mem. Am. Assn. Sch. Adminstrs., U. No. Iowa Adminstrs. Assn., Iowa Assn. Sch. Adminstrs. (mem. profl. relations com. 1983—), Iowa Assn. Sch. Bds. (mem. supr.'s search com. 1986—), Iowa Assn. for Sch. and Curriculum Devel., Independence Area C. of C. (bd. dirs. 1986—), Phi Delta Kappa. Lutheran. Office: Independence Community Schs 1207 First St W Independence IA 50644

RASMUSSEN, EVIE WEBB, financial institution executive; b. Wurzburg, Franken, Federal Republic of Germany, June 18, 1952; came to U.S., 1956; d. Robert Daniel and Rosemarie Franziska (Scheidermeier) Webb; m. Terry James Rasmussen, Dec. 29, 1973; 1 child, John Robert. Student, Mt. Hood Community Coll., Portland, Oreg., 1983-84, Claremont Coll., Pamona, Calif., 1984-86. Clk. Unishops Inc., Portland, Oreg., 1969-71; teller Tigard (Oreg.) Community Fed. Credit Union, 1980-81; auditor Nat. Credit Union Adminstrn., Portland, 1981-83; chief exec. officer United Assn. NW Federal Credit Union, Portland, 1983—. Vol. Portland Easter Seals, 1986—, Nat. Fedn. for Blind, 1987. Credit Union Nat. Assns. scholar 1984. Mem. Nat. Assn. Female Execs., Credit Union Womens Assn., Oregon Credit Union League (scholarship com. 1983—, budget com. 1986—, bd. dirs, dir.-at-large, 1987, bd. dirs. Columbia chpt. 1985—), Smithsonian Assocs. Club: Toastmasters (Portland) (treas. 1987—). Office: United Assn NW Fed Credit Union 2111 NE 43d Ave Portland OR 97213

RASMUSSEN, JULIE SHIMMON, educator, cellist; b. Aberdeen, S.D., June 3, 1940; d. George Barr and Clara (Lange) Shimmon; m. Frederick Robert Rasmussen, Apr. 1, 1961 (div. May 1971). B.Music, Ind. U., 1963; M.Ed., U. Fla., 1967. Cert. tchr., Fla. Coordinator music Bradford County Sch. Bd., Starke, Fla., 1965-68; tchr. Duval County Sch. Bd., Jacksonville, Fla., 1968-69, community edn., 1972-79, program devel., 1979—; master tchr. Clay County Sch. Bd., Orange Park, Fla., 1969-72; facilitator, mem. planning com. Duval County Sch. Bd., Jacksonville, 1985-86. Grant writer in ednl. areas, 1979—. Com. mem. Jacksonville Community Council, Inc., 1973; cellist Jacksonville Symphony, 1963-65; tech. asst. Arts Assembly of Jacksonville, Inc., 1979-82; mem. Cummer Art Gallery, Jacksonville, 1983; bd. dirs. YWCA, 1986; active Resource Devel. Assistance Program Com. for Vol. Jacksonville, 1986. Recipient Little Red Schoolhouse award Fla. Dept. Edn., 1977-78, Sense of Community award Duval County Community Edn., 1979; Internat. String Congress grantee Musician's Union, 1961. Mem. Fla. Ednl. Research Assn., Pi Kappa Lambda, Phi Delta Kappa, Kappa Delta Pi (parliamentarian 1985-86). Democrat. Lutheran. Club: Pilot. Avocations: physical fitness; jogging; swimming; cycling; psychology. Home: 3946 St John's Ave Jacksonville FL 32205 Office: Duval County Sch Bd Adminstrn Bldg 1701 Prudential Dr Jacksonville FL 32207

RASMUSSEN, VIRGINIA MARIE, preschool educator; b. Jefferson, Iowa, Nov. 16, 1947; d. James Edward and Margaret Jeanne (Gannon) McDermott; m. James Leo Rasmussen, June 3, 1972; children: Adrienne, Allison, Rian, Arynn, Regis. BA, Clarke Coll., 1969. Cert. tchr., Iowa. Math tchr. Dow City (Iowa) Community Sch., 1969-74; substitute tchr. Manilla (Iowa) Community Sch., 1974—; tchr. Prime Time Preschool, Manilla, 1980—, dir. curriculum, 1980. Pres. Crawford County Family and Home Council, Denison, 1977; mem. sch. bd. Manilla Community Sch., 1978; leader Crawford County 4-H, Manilla, 1985; sec. Community Betterment Council, 1987; choir dir. Sacred Heart Ch., Manilla, 1986, CCD tchr. 1987. Recipient Leadership award Gov. Iowa, 1984. Mem. AAUW, Manilla C. of C. (v.p. 1987—), Altar Soc. Democrat. Roman Catholic. Club: Golf (pres. 1982). Home and Office: 579 8th St Manilla IA 51454

RAST, STEPHANIE ANNE, military officer; b. Waco, Tex., July 30, 1946; d. Earle Henderson Jr. and Beverly Ann (roberts) R.; m. Johnny C. Cather, June 24, 1971 (div. Jan. 1976); 1 child, Steven Jonathan. BA, San Diego State Coll., 1967; MBA, So. Ill. U., 1986. Commd. U.S. Army, 1967, advanced through grades to lt. col., 1984; platoon leader WAC Basic Tng. Co., Ft. McClellan, Ala., 1967-69; commd. comdr. WAC Co., Ft. Lee, Va., 1969-71; recruiting officer Recruiting Main Sta., Des Moines, 1971-72; housing officer U.S Army Garrison, Ft. Hamilton, N.Y., 1972-74; combat devel. project officer U.S. Army Q.M. Sch., Ft. Lee, 1974-78; supply and maintenance officer 652d Engr. Battalion, Ft. Shafter, Hawaii, 1978-79; contracting officer Def. Subsistence Region Europe, Zweibruecken, Fed. Republic Germany, 1979-82; ops. officer U.S. Army Western Commissary

Region, Ft. Lewis, Wash., 1982-84; logistics staff officer Hdqrs. Dept. Army, The Pentagon, Washington, 1984-85; comdr. Def. Contract Adminstrn. Services Mgmt. Area, Cedar Rapids, Iowa, 1985-88; student U.S. Army War Coll., Carlisle Barracks, Pa., 1988—. Mem. Nat. Contract Mgmt. Assn. (pres. Ea. Iowa chpt. 1987-88), Armed Forces Communications and Electronics Assn., Assn. U.S. Army, Beta Gamma Sigma. Lodge: Sertoma Internat. Home: 553 Craig Rd Carlisle PA 17013 Office: US Army War Coll Barracks Carlisle PA 17013

RATCLIFF, SUELLEN, empoyment manager; b. Peoria, Ill., Nov. 6, 1956; d. Harold Boardman and Betty Lee (Swisher) R. BA in Psychology, Baylor U., 1978. Employment coordinator Fox and Jacobs, Dallas, 1979-81; recruiter A.D.P., Dallas, 1982; mgr. recruiting Uccel Corp., Dallas, 1982-87, area employment mgr. Digital Equipment Corp., Dallas, 1987—. Vol. Children's Mental Health and Retardation, Peoria, summers 1974-78. Mem. S.W. High Tech. Coop. Office: Digital Equipment Corp 4851 LBJ Freeway Suite 1100 Dallas TX 75244

RATCLIFFE, SHIRLEY PENDLETON, real estate broker, communications executive; b. Blountville, Tenn., Mar. 30, 1932; d. Paris Lee and Elizabeth Armetta (Gammon) Pendleton; m. Robert Issac Ratcliffe, Jan. 26, 1952 (div. Apr. 1970); children—Paula, Louise, Darby. Student U. Ky., 1952, East Tenn. U., 1962-63; grad. Grad. Realtors Inst. Lic. broker, Tenn., Va., N.C. Broker, Pendleton Real Estate, Blountville, 1970—; v.p. Mount Empire Devel. Co., Kingsport, Tenn., 1971-74, Pendleton Land Co., Blountville, 1975—; pres. Tenn. Radio Telephone, Kingsport, 1982—; Cell-Tel of Knoxville, Kingsport, 1985—; chmn. Cellular One, Tri-Cities, Washington, 1984-85; pres. Ragtime Investments, Kingsport, 1978—. Vol. Contact Concern, Kingsport, 1978—; mem. Sullivan County Republican Exec. Bd., Tenn.; bd. dirs. Sullivan County LWV. Methodist. Clubs: Ridgefields Country, Ridgefield Garden. Lodge: Order Eastern Star. Avocations: golf; tennis; bridge. Home: 536-B Fleetwood Ct Kingsport TN 37660 Office: Pendleton Real Estate PO Box 253 Main St Blountville TN 37617

RATEKIN, CHRISTINE MARIE, real estate executive; b. Houston, Aug. 17, 1963; d. Glenn Earl and Maria Clelia (Ballio) R. BA in Pub. Relations, La. State U., 1985; postgrad., U.Tex., Arlington. Aast. dir. ops. Gulf Coast Mgmt. Corp., Shreveport, La., 1983-84; exec. asst. to v.p. Bill Hanna Ford, Inc., Shreveport, 1984-85; adminstrv. asst. to gen. mgr. United Cable TV, Bossier City, La., 1985-86; exec. asst. dir. ops. SENCA Real Estate Devel. Co., Ft. Worth, 1986—, sec., treas., 1986—. Activist God in Our Schs., Dallas, 1987. Recipient Silver medal in Tennis, Brazil, 1977. Mem. Nat. Assn. Female Execs., Am. Mgmt. Assn., Nat. Notary Assn., Assn. Legal Secs. Republican. Roman Catholic. Home: 7800 Youree Dr #269 Shreveport LA 71105

RATH, MARI KAYE, litigation consultant; b. Elgin, Ill., Sept. 10, 1958; d. Lester Herman and Marsilia Marie (Parrucci) R. BBA, Western Ill. U., 1979. CPA, Ill. Acct. Arthur Andersen & Co., Chgo., 1980-81; exec. litigation cons. Peterson & Co., Chgo., 1981—. Named one of Outstanding Young Women of Am., 1987. Mem. Am. Inst. CPA's, Ill. Soc. CPA's, Ill. Auctioneers Assn. (sec.-treas. 1988—), Nat. Auctioneers Assn. Roman Catholic. Home: 38 W 196 US 20 Elgin IL 60123 Office: Peterson & Co 310 S Michigan Suite 1900 Chicago IL 60604

RATH, MARLENE FRIEDEL, public relations specialist; b. Cleve., Sept. 27, 1961; d. Robert William and Mary Eileen (Sailor) R. BS in Pub. Relations, Kent State U., 1983. Communications coordinator employment Precision Metalforming Assn., Richmond Heights, Ohio, 1984—. Vol. pub. relations staff Nat. Safety Town Ctr., Cleve., 1984-85. Mem. Am. Soc. Assn. Execs., Nat. Assn. Female Execs., Greater Cleveland Soc. os Assn. Execs., Kent State Alumni Assn. Home: 41 Trenton Sq Euclid OH 44143 Office: Precision Metalforming Assn 27027 Chardon Rd Richmond Heights OH 44143

RATHER, LUCIA PORCHER JOHNSON, library administrator; b. Durham, N.C., Sept. 12, 1934; d. Cecil Slayton and Lucia Lockwood (Porcher) Johnson; m. John Carson Rather, July 11, 1964; children: Susan Wright, Bruce Carson. Student, Westhampton Coll., 1951-53; A.B. in History, U. N.C., 1955, M.S. in Library Sci., 1957. Cataloger Library of Congress, Washington, 1957-64; bibliographer Library of Congress, 1964-66, systems analyst, 1966-70; group head MARC Devel. Office, 1970-73, asst. chief, 1973-76, acting chief, 1976-77, dir. for cataloging, 1976—; Chmn. standing com. on cataloguing Internat. Fedn. Library Assns., 1976-81; sec. Working Group on Content Designators, 1972-77; chmn. Working Group on Corp. Headings, 1978-79, Internat. ISBD Rev. Com., 1981-87. Co-author: the MARC II Format, 1968. Recipient Margaret Mann award, 1985. Mem. ALA, Phi Beta Kappa. Democrat. Presbyterian. Home: 10308 Montgomery Ave Kensington MD 20895 Office: Library of Congress 10 1st St SE Washington DC 20540

RATHJÉ, JUDY CHRISTINE, health science facility administrator; b. Bklyn., Nov. 4, 1952; d. James A. and Margaret Agnes Smith; 1 child, Sheri Christine. AAS in Nursing, Hudson Valley Community Coll., Troy, N.Y., 1973; BS in Nursing and Psychology, SUNY, Albany; postgrad. in bus. adminstrn., Calif. Coast U. RN. Scrub nurse, 1st asst. dr. Metin Koluksuz, Schenectady, N.Y., 1974-77; staff nurse, relief head nurse St. Clare's Hosp., Schenectady, 1973-77; dir. rev. programs Profl. Standards Rev. Orgn., Inc., Albany, 1977-79; quality assurance coordinator Martha's Vineyard Hosp., Oak Bluffs, Mass., 1979-80; sr. nurse St. Peter's Hosp., Albany, 1980-84; nurse mgr. Rensselaer Poly. Inst., Troy, 1982-84; dir. nursing and patient services Samaritan Hosp., Troy, 1984-88; program coordinator, adj. faculty Cornell U., Albany, 1985-87; dir. nursing consultative services Hosp. Assn. N.Y. State, Albany, 1988—; cons. in health care mgmt. Mem. Am. Orgn. Nurse Execs., Am. Mgmt. Assn., Bus. and Profl. Women's Assn., Northeastern N.Y. Nursing Services Adminstr.'s Assn., Nat. League for Nursing. Democrat. Office: Hosp Assn NY State Albany NY 12207

RATHKE, SHEILA WELLS, advertising and public relations executive; b. Columbia, S.C., Aug. 9, 1943; d. Walter John and Elizabeth Marie (McLaughlin) Wells; m. David Bray Rathke, Sept. 1966 (div. Apr. 1977); 1 child, Erinn Michele. BA summa cum laude, U. Pitts., 1976, postgrad., 1976-77. Loan coordinator Equibank, Pitts., 1961-65; office mgr. U.S. Steel Corp., Pitts., 1966-70; v.p., gen. mgr. Burson-Marsteller, Pitts., 1977—; adviser Exec. Report Mag., Pitts., 1986—; instr. Slippery Rock Coll., Pitts., 1984-85. Trustee U. Pitts., 1974-80; bd. dirs. Vocat. Rehab. Inst., Pitts., 1986—. Named one of Outstanding Young Women of Am., 1977. Mem. Nat. Investor Relations Inst. (program chmn. 1984-85), Internat. Assn. Bus. Communicators (First Place award 1979), Alpha Sigma Lambda (charter). Home: 15 Marquette Rd Pittsburgh PA 15229 Office: Burson-Marsteller One Gateway Ctr Pittsburgh PA 15222

RATKIN, MARILYN LEE, health care coordinator; b. St. Louis, Mo., Jan. 21, 1944; d. Samuel Louis and Mamie (Bachman) Lewin; m. Gary Alan Ratkin, June 12, 1966; children—Kimberlee Jill, Stephani Lyn. Student Northwestern U., 1962-64; B.A. with honors, Washington U., 1966; M.B.A., U. Mo., 1980. Cert. tchr., real estate agt. Elem. tchr. Flynn Park Sch., St. Louis, 1966-67; elem. tchr. Hebron Sch., Pitts., 1967-68; travel agt. Frosch Travel, Houston, 1975; real estate agt. Ira E. Berry, St. Louis, 1981-82; health care coordinator Health Fair, St. Louis, 1982-85; project head Maritz, Inc., 1986—. Editor: (cookbook) Life-Saving Recipes, 1970; coordinator, author: Office Personnel Manual, 1981, also brochure. Bd. dirs., mem. div. pub. edn. com. Am. Cancer Soc., St. Louis, 1981—; mem. alumni council Northwestern U., 1985—program dir. Maritz Motivation, 1986—. Recipient Leadership award Jewish Community Ctr., San Antonio, 1973, Program award Am. Cancer Soc., 1980. Mem. Am. Mktg. Assn., Women's Commerce Assn., Beta Gamma Sigma. Jewish.

RATKOVICH, CYNTHIA, lawyer; b. Chgo., May 22, 1957; d. Steve and Mildred (Evans) Ratkovich. B.S., Purdue U., 1979; J.D., U. Iowa, 1982. Bar: Ill. 1982. Paralegal, sec. Sonnenschein, Carlin, Nath & Rosenthal, Chgo., summer 1979; filing clk. Norus Property Co., Chgo., summer 1979, law clk., summer 1980; sec., asst. mgr. L.J. Sheridan & Co., Chgo., summer 1981; in-house counsel Thomas F. Seay, Chgo., summer 1982, 83, ltd. rep., prin., 1982—; counsel CNA Ins. Co., Chgo., 1983-87; atty. Met. Life Ins. Co., 1987—. Mem. ABA, Ill. State Bar Assn., Chgo. Bar Assn., Alpha Lambda Delta, Phi Kappa Phi, Beta Gamma Sigma, Purdue U. Alumni Assn. Serbian Orthodox. Office: Met Life Ins Co 2021 Spring Rd Suite 440 Chicago IL 60521

RATLIFF, DONNA LEE, corporate treasurer; b. Manhattan, N.Y., Nov. 21, 1946; d. Josiah William and Edith Mae (Pernuzzi) Davis; m. Ronald Wayne Ratliff, Apr. 16, 1966; children: Lisa Ann, Colleen Marie, Brock Wayne. Bookkeeper Downtown Motors, Canton, Ohio, 1964-65, title clk., 1965-66; credit clk. 1st Nat. Bank Pa., Erie, 1971-73, loan asst., 1973-76, internal auditor, 1976-78; acctg. mgr. Budget Rent-A-Car, Houston, 1978-79; sec.-treas. Gill Services, Inc., Houston, 1979-84; controller Santa Fe Supply Co., Inc., Houston, 1984-85; treas. GNI Group Inc., Webster, Tex., 1985—. Pres. Greengate Swim Team, Spring, Tex., 1984. Mem. Nat. Assn. Female Execs., Nat. Notary Assn. Home: 6619 Lynngate Dr Spring TX 77373 Office: GNI Group Inc 202 Medical Ctr Blvd Webster TX 77598

RATLIFF, DOROTHY ANN, sales executive; b. Jackson, Miss., Oct. 8, 1952; d. Sylvester and Gertrude (Rogers) R.; 1 child, Charles Couser. AA, Oakland Community Coll., 1983. Sales mgr. Shifren Willen, Bloomfield, Mich., 1970-72; engring. asst. Gen. Motors Corp., Pontiac, Mich., 1972-79; sr. sales dir. Mary Kay Cosmetics, Dallas, 1979-82; exec. sales rep. Don Massey Rolls Royce, Plymouth, Mich., 1984-87, asst. sales mgr., 1987—; speaker motivational women's career workshop, 1979-84. Pres. Antioch Nursing Guild, Pontiac, 1972; chair fundraising gubernatorial campaign State of Mich., 1986-87. Club: Crest of Cadillac Motor Car Co. Office: Don Massey Rolls Royce Cadillac 40475 Ann Arbor Rd Plymouth MI 48170

RATLIFF, LEIGH ANN, pharmacist; b. Long Beach, Calif., May 20, 1961; d. Harry Warren and Verna Lee (Zwink) R. D in Pharmacy, U. Pacific, 1984. Registered pharmacist, Calif., Nev. Pharmacist intern Green Bros. Inc., Stockton, Calif., 1982-84, staff pharmacist Thrifty Corp., Long Beach, Calif., 1984-85, head pharmacist, 1986-87, pharm. buyer, 1987—. Mem. Nat. Assn. Female Execs., Am. Pharm. Assn., Am. Inst. History Pharmacy, Calif. Pharmacist Assn., Lambda Kappa Sigma. Republican. Methodist. Avocations: creative writing, horseback riding, fishing, house plants, painting. Home: 3913 Virginia Rd #301 Long Beach CA 90807 Office: Thrifty Corp 3424 Wilshire Blvd Los Angeles CA 90010

RATLIFFE, SHARON ANN, communications and English language educator; b. Dearborn, Mich., Sept. 23, 1939; d. Harold LaVerne and Evalyn June (Ahrens) R. BA, Western Mich. U., 1963; MA, Wayne State U., 1965, PhD, 1972. Cert. coll. instr. and supr., Calif. Assoc. prof. Western Mich. U., Kalamazoo, 1965-76; prof. Ambassador Coll., Pasadena, Calif., 1976-78; instr. Golden West Coll., Huntington Beach, Calif., 1978—; cons. in field. Author: (with Ernest Stech) Working In Groups, 1976, Effective Group Communication, 1984; (with Deldee Herman) Self-Awareness, 1982; (with Wes Bryan) One To One, 1984; (with David D. Hudson) Skill-Building For Communication Competence, 1988 (with David D. Hudson) Communication for Everyday Living: Integrating Speaking, Listening, and Thinking Skills, 1989; editor: Michigan Speech Association Curriculum Guide Series; Communication Edn.; assoc. editor The Speech Communication Tchr., 1986—; mem. editorial bd. Communication Edn.; contbr. articles to profl. jours. Recipient Master Tchr. award Nat. Inst. for Teaching Excellence, 1986, 87. Mem. Am. Fedn. Tchrs., Calif. Speech Assn. (exec. bd., exec. sec.), Cen. States Speech Assn. (v.p., chair states adv. council, exec. com., Outstanding Young Tchr. award), Mich. Speech Assn. (pres., exec. sec., chair research com., hon. life mem., Disting. Service award), Nat. Council Tchrs. English, Nat. Assn. for Devel. Edn. (mem. task force on speaking and listening skills), Speech Communication Assn. (chair instructional devel. div., chair ednl. policies bd.), Com. on Exit Competencies for Community Coll. Students (adminstrv. com., del. legis. council, participant state conf., chair pre-service div. Nat. Devel. Conf. Tchr. Educators in Communication), Western Speech Communication Assn. (del., legis. council). Home: 9 Badger Pass Irvine CA 92714 Office: Golden West Coll 15744 Golden West St Huntington Beach CA 92647

RATNER, LILLIAN GROSS, psychiatrist; b. N.Y.C., Aug. 18, 1932; d. Herman and Sarah (Widelitz) Gross; B.A., Barnard Coll., 1953; postgrad. U. Lausanne (Switzerland), 1954-56; M.D., Duke U., 1959; m. Harold Ratner, Feb. 4, 1961; children—Sanford Miles, Marcia Ellen. Intern, Kings County Hosp., Bklyn., 1959-60, resident, 1967-70, fellow in child psychiatry, 1969-70, psychiatrist devel. evaluation clinic, 1970-72; resident Jewish Hosp. Bklyn., 1960-62, fellow in pediatric psychiatry, 1962-63; physician in charge pediatric psychiat. clinic Greenpoint (N.Y.) Hosp., 1964-67; pvt. practice psychiatry, Great Neck, N.Y., 1970—; clin. instr. psychiatry Downstate Med. Center, Bklyn., 1970-74, clin. asst. prof., 1974—; lectr. in psychiatry Columbia U., 1974—; psychiat. cons. N.Y.C. Bd. Edn., 1972-75, Queens Children's Hosp., 1975—; mem. med. bd. Camp Sussex (N.J.), 1963—, Saras Center, Great Neck, N.Y., 1977—. Diplomate Am. Bd. Pediatrics, Am. Bd. Psychiatry and Neurology, Am. Bd. Child Psychiatry. Fellow Am. Acad. Pediatrics, Am. Acad. Psychiatry, Am. Acad. Child Psychiatry; mem. Am. Assn., Nassau, Bklyn. psychiat. assns., Bklyn. (sr. mem.), Nassau pediatric socs., Soc. Adolescent Psychiatry, N.Y. Council Child Psychiatry, Soc. Clin. and Exptl. Hypnosis, Am. Med. Women's Assn. (pres.-elect Nassau), AMA, N.Y., Kings County med. socs., Am. Soc. Clin. Hypnosis, N.Y. Soc. Clin. Hypnosis (pres.). Home and Office: 55 Bluebird Dr Great Neck NY 11023

RATNOFF, MARIAN FOREMAN, lawyer, retailing executive; b. Balt.; d. William Elihu and Sophia (Kuff) Foreman; m. Oscar Davis Ratnoff, Mar. 31, 1945; children—William Davis, Martha. Student, Goucher Coll., 1941-43; B.A. in Sociology, U. Chgo., 1946; M.A. in Edn., Western Res. U., 1959; J.D., Case Western Res. U., 1967. Bar: Ohio 1967. Tchr., Balt. Sch. System, 1946-50, Shaker Heights Sch. System, 1950-51; program coordinator Western Res. U., Cleve., 1960-62; assoc. law firm, Cleve., 1967-71; atty. The Higbee Co., Cleve., 1971—, asst. corp. sec., 1974—, v.p., 1981—. Contbr. articles to legal jours. Mem. many civic coms., Cleve. area, 1967—. Mem. ABA, Bar Assn. Greater Cleve., Ohio Bar Assn. Office: The Higbee Co 100 Public Sq Cleveland OH 44113

RATTA, JANICE ANN, nursing care administrator, researcher; b. Bklyn., June 16, 1960; d. Joseph Rudolph and Millicent (Mesi) R. A.A.S. in Nursing, Pace U., 1980, postgrad. Staff nurse N.Y. Infirmary-Beekman Hosp., N.Y.C., 1980-83, asst. nursing care coordinator, 1983-84, nursing care coordinator, 1984-87; assoc. adminstr. Wichita Gen. Hosp., 1987—. Mem. Am. Nurses Assn., Am. Assn. Critical Care Nurses, Am. Soc. Profl. and Exec. Women, Nat. Assn. Female Execs. Democrat. Roman Catholic. Avocations: swimming; gymnastics. Office: Wichita Gen Hosp Wichita Falls TX 76301

RATTLEY, JESSIE MENIFIELD, mayor, educator; b. Birmingham, Ala., May 4, 1929; d. Alonzo Menifield; m. Robert L. Rattley; children: Florence, Robin. BS in Bus. Edn.with hons., Hampton U., 1951; postgrad., Hampton Inst., IBM Data Processing Sch., LaSalle Extension U. Tchr. Huntington High Sch., Newport News, Va., 1951-52; owner, operator Peninsula Bus. Coll., Newport News, 1952-85; hosp. adminstr. Newport News Gen. Hosp., 1986—; elected mayor of Newport News, 1986—. Mem. Nat. League of Cities, bd. dirs., 1975, 2d v.p., 1977, 1st v.p., 1978, pres. 1979, active various coms. and task forces; active many adv. bd., coms., State Dem. Party. Recipient Cert. of Merit Daus. of Isis, 2d annual Martin Luther King, Jr. Meml. award Old Dominion U., Sojourner Truth award Nat. Assn. of Negro Bus. and Profl. Women's Clubs, Cert. of Appreciation NAACP. Office: Office of the Mayor City of Newport News 2400 Washington Ave Newport News VA 23607

RATTRAY, HELEN SELDON, newspaper editor, publisher; b. Bayonne, N.J., Sept. 29, 1934; d. Abraham Harry and Yetta (Spivack) Seldon; B., Douglass Coll., 1956; postgrad. Columbia U., 1958-60; Litt.D. (hon.), L.I.U., 1986. m. Everett T. Rattray, July 22, 1960 (dec.); children—David E., Daniel S., Bess E. Reporter East Hampton (N.Y.) Star, 1960-76, editor and columnist 1976-80, pub. 1980—; dir., sec.-treas. Graphics of Peconic. Former treas., bd. trustees Hampton Day Sch., 1969-73. Home: 17 Edwards Ln East Hampton NY 11937 Office: East Hampton Star Inc 153 Main St East Hampton NY 11937

RAUB, MARGARET, mathematics educator; b. Youngstown, Ohio, Mar. 16, 1948; d. Karl and Marie Theresa (Herrlich) R. AB, Youngstown State U., 1971; MA, Cleve. State U., 1980. Tchr. Cardinal Mooney High Sch., Youngstown, 1971-73, St. Joseph Acad., Cleve., 1973-78; tchr., mathematics dept. chmn. Strongsville (Ohio) High Sch., 1978—; instr. Capital Univ., Columbus, Ohio, 1983—. Author: (with others) Focus on Functions, 1985. Martha Holden Jennings Found. scholar, 1984; Woodrow Wilson Found. fellow, 1985, NASA Newmast fellow, 1987; recipient Presdl. award NSF, 1986. Mem. (life) Nat. Council of Tchrs. of Mathematics, Greater Cleve. Council of Tchrs. of Mathematics (bd. dirs. 1986—, pres.-elect 1988), Council of Tchrs. of Math. (NE Ohio dir. 1988—), Phi Kappa Phi, Delta Kappa Gamma. Democrat. Roman Catholic. Office: Strongsville High Sch 20025 Lunn Rd Strongsville OH 44136

RAUCH, BONNIE SUE, photographer; b. Bklyn., Feb. 27, 1944; d. Irving and Harriet (Sims) Namm; m. David Samuel Rauch, May 1, 1968 (div. Feb. 1988); children: Gregory Michael, Wendy Beth. B in Bus. Adminstrn., CUNY, 1965, MBA, 1969. Cons. Richardson-Vicks, Inc., Wilton, Conn., 1981-83; sales rep. On Target, Westbury, N.Y., 1981-83; staff photographer The Image Bank, N.Y.C., 1981—. Exhibitor Neikrug, Mari, Bridge Galleries, No. Westchester Ctr. for the Arts. Mem. Am. Soc. Mag. Photographers, Aircraft Owners and Pilots Assn., Pilots Internat. Assn. Home: Crane Rd Somers NY 10589

RAUCH, DELORES ADELE, marketing professional; b. Lafayette, Ind., Aug. 26, 1954; d. Charles Dutro and Frances Elenora (Artman) R.; m. Mirl Steven Heninger, Dec. 27, 1976 (div. 1980); m. Michael Francis Bloom, Mar. 12, 1988. BA, Purdue U., 1976. Cert. systems profl., Fla. Office administr. Bankers Life Nebr., Tampa, Fla., 1977-78; office mgr. Washington Nat., 1978; sales rep., office mgr. Ind. Life and Accident Ins. Co., 1978-79; mktg. support rep. Lanier Bus. Products, 1979-81; product test analyst Lanier/Harris, Atlanta, 1981-83; dist. mktg. support mgr. Lanier/Harris, Tampa, 1983-84; mgr. info. ctr. Honeywell, Inc., Tampa, 1984-87, mktg. support rep., 1987—; speaker in field. Mem. Assn. Info. Systems Profls. (dir. publs. 1984-85, pres. Tampa Bay chpt. 1985-87), Data Processing Mgmt. Assn. (newsletter data com. 1985-87), Soc. for Competitive Intelligence Profls., Tech. Mktg. Soc. Am. Republican. Presbyterian. Home: 7317 Willow Park Dr Temple Terrace FL 33637 Office: Honeywell Inc 10901 Malcolm Mckinley Dr M-59 Tampa FL 33612

RAUCH, KATHLEEN, systems analyst; b. Franklin Square, N.Y., Oct. 30, 1951; d. William C. and Marian (Shull) R.; B.A., U. Rochester, 1973; M.A. in L.S., U. Mich., 1974; postgrad. N.Y. U., 1981-82. Media specialist Sutton (Mass.) Sch., 1974-76; program cons. Advanced Mgmt. Research Internat., N.Y.C., 1976-79; pub. relations cons., N.Y.C., 1979; pres. N.Y. chpt. NOW, N.Y.C., 1979-80; computer programmer Blue Cross/Blue Shield of Greater N.Y., N.Y.C., 1981-82; computer programmer analyst Federal Reserve Bank of N.Y., 1983-84; systems officer Citibank, N.A., 1984-85; sr. programmer analyst Fed. Res. Bank of N.Y., 1986—. Mem. Lambda Legal Def. and Edn. Fund. Mem. Assn. for Women in Computing (v.p. membership 1984, exec. v.p. 1985, treas. 1986, mem.-at-large 1987, pres. 1988), Data Processing Mgrs. Assn., Assn. for Computing Machinery, Women's Sports Found., NOW (dir. pub. relations N.Y.C. chpt. 1978, v.p. programs 1978, chmn. bd. 1981, founding mem., sec. Service Fund, N.Y.C. chpt. 1981), Caths. for a Free Choice, Greenpeace.

RAULUK, VALERIE ANN, financial consultant, artist; b. Pitts., Jan. 22, 1956; d. Richard A. and Theresa E. (Lysien) R. BA, U. Chgo., 1978; MBA, NYU, 1980. Fin. analyst Revlon Inc., N.Y.C., 1980-82; investment banker Mabon Nugent & Co., N.Y.C., 1982-83, Morgan, Lewis, Githens & Ahn, N.Y.C., 1983-87; pvt. practice bus. consulting and art mktg. Tucson, 1987—. Office: PO Box 65108 Tucson AZ 85740-2108 Office: 6481 Foothills Dr Tucson AZ 85715

RAUSCHER, HANNAH SARAH, educator; b. Jamaica, N.Y., Aug. 16, 1925; d. Max and Jane (Schmikler) Buxenbaum; m. Norman E. Rauscher, May 14, 1952. BA, Queens Coll., 1947; BS in Edn., CCNY, 1951; EdM, Rutgers U., 1964. Bus. rep. N.Y. Telephone Co., Bklyn., 1947-51; tchr. Union Free Sch. Dist. #5, Levittown, N.Y., 1951-52, Queens Pub. Sch. 90, Richmond Hill, N.Y., 1952-56; tchr. Summit (N.J.) Pub. Schs., 1956-58, elem. reading counselor, 1958—, basic skills and lang. arts coordinator, 1986—. Co-author pamphlet Handbook of Reading Techniques, 1964. Past pres. Summit Civil Rights Comm.; Mcpl. Youth Guidance Council, YWCA, Summit Civil Rights Commn.; chmn., bd. dirs. Summit Pub. Library, 1985-86; past 1st vice chmn., sec. Rep. Com. of Union County; mem. United Way, Summit, New Providence, Berkeley Heights, N.J., Summit Comm, Drug Abuse; bd. dirs. Planning Bd., Community Pre-Sch. Recipient Stuart Reed award Summit Area YWCA, 1977. Mem. NEA, N.J. Edn. Assn., Summit Edn. Assn. (pres. 1976-78), Internat. Read Assn. (pres. 1976), Kappa Delta Pi. Republican. Club: Beacon Hill (Summit). Home: 5 Midland Terr Summit NJ 07901

RAVENS, CATHERINE ELIZABETH, public affairs specialist; b. Boston, Jan. 21, 1930; d. John Joseph and Elizabeth Mary (Pontuso) Tesorero; m. Fred Joseph Ravens Jr., June 9, 1951; children: Fred Joseph III, Margaret Perkins, David, Jean Ravens Phalen. AA, Burdett Coll., 1949, Northeastern U., 1988. With U.S. Army Corps. Engrs., Anchorage, 1951-52; sec. U.S. Army Corps. Engrs., Waltham, Mass., 1978-84; intern pub. info. U.S. Army Corps. Engrs., Waltham, 1984-85, pub. affairs specialist, 1985—. Editor Yankee Engr. newsletter U.S. Army Corps Engrs., 1988—; contbr. articles to profl. jours. Treas. St. Timothy Guild, Norwood, Mass., 1975-76; capt. tennis team, Town of Norwood, 1977-78, elections officer, 1982; com. mem. Campfire Girls Am., Norwood, 1965; asst. leader Girl Scouts U.S.A., 1973; den mother Cub Scouts Boy Scouts Am., 1972. Recipient Ofcl. Commendation U.S. Army Corps Engrs., 1982, Letters of Appreciation 1981, 83, 84. Roman Catholic. Club: Dartmouth Womens, St. Timothy Guild. Home: 72 Croydon Rd Norwood MA 02062 Office: US Army Corps Engrs 424 Trapelo Rd Waltham MA 02254-9149

RAVITCH, DIANE SILVERS, historian, educator, author; b. Houston, July 1, 1938; d. Walter Cracker and Ann Celia (Katz) Silvers; m. Richard Ravitch, June 26, 1960 (div. 1986); children—Joseph, Steven (dec.), Michael. B.A., Wellesley Coll., 1960; Ph.D., Columbia U., 1975; L.H.D. (hon.), Williams Coll., 1984, Reed Coll., 1985, Amherst Coll., 1986, SUNY, 1988. Adj. asst. prof. Teachers Coll., Columbia U., N.Y.C., 1975-78, assoc. prof., 1978-83, adj. prof., 1983—; dir. Ency. Britannica Corp. Author: The Great School Wars, 1974; The Revisionists Revised, 1977; The Troubled Crusade, 1983; The Schools We Deserve, 1985; author (with others) What Do Our 17 Year Olds Know?. Trustee N.Y. Pub. Library, N.Y.C., 1981—. Mem. Nat. Acad. Edn., Am. Acad. Arts and Scis., Soc. Am. Historians. Office: Columbia Univ Teachers Coll Box 177 New York NY 10027

RAWLINGS, MARY, escrow company executive; b. Lansing, Mich., Nov. 17, 1936; d. Frederick Thomas and Anna (Bondy) Belbeck; m. Richard M. Rawlings, Feb. 11, 1967 (div. 1985); children—Bonita Rawlings Walker, Mary Rawlings Rios, R. Patrick. Student, So. Calif. Sch. Escrows, Los Angeles, 1956-57, Pierce Coll., Woodland Hills, Calif., 1959-60. Vice pres., gen. mgr. Manhattan Mortgage Co., North Hollywood, Calif., 1962-66; mgr. San Fernando Valley Escrow Co., Calif., 1966-67; v.p., mgr. Golden West Escrow Co., Panorama City, Calif., 1967-77; pres. The Escrow Office, Inc., Woodland Hills, 1977—; bd. dirs. Escrow Agt.'s Fidelity Corp., Newport Beach, Calif., 1983-87, chmn., 1985-87; instr. Pierce Coll., 1978-80; appointed by Mayor Tom Bradley to Van Nuys Airport Citizens Adv. Council, 1987. Mem. 99's Inc. (Women Pilot of Yr. 1984), Calif. Escrow Assn. (bd. dirs. 1977—), San Fernando Valley Escrow Assn. (pres. 1977). Avocations: flying; air racing. Office: The Escrow Office Inc 21228 Ventura Woodland Hills CA 91364

RAWSON, LINDA KENNETT, lawyer; b. N.Y.C., Oct. 31, 1954; d. Kennett Longley and Eleanor S. R.; B.A. cum laude, Harvard U., 1976; J.D., N.Y. Law Sch., 1979; m. Charles Maxwell Harrison, Aug. 28, 1982. Asst. N.Y.C. Law Dept., 1977-78; asst. gen. counsel Harper & Row Pubs., Inc., N.Y.C., 1980-87; internat. cons. UN, N.Y.C., 1987—. Capt. Women's A Squash Team, 1985-86. Recipient cert. for service to law dept. Mayor of N.Y.C., 1978. Mem. N.Y. Women's Bar Assn., Nat. Acad. TV Arts and Scis., Ams. Soc., Spanish Inst., Women in Communications. Clubs: Harvard,

Radcliffe (bd. govs. 1980-82), Met. Squash Racquets Assn. (N.Y.C.); Appalachian Mountain. Contbr. chpt. to The Business of Book Pub., 1985. Office: 28 W 38th St New York NY 10018

RAY, BARBARA FRANCES, accountant; b. Pawtucket, R.I., May 11, 1938; d. Harold E. and Eva E. (St. George) Roe; m. Matthew B. Ray, Feb. 4, 1959; children: Kyle Thomas, Kristen Leigh. AS in Bus. Adminstrn., Roger Williams Coll., 1979, BS in Acctg., 1982. Mgr. purchasing NEPTCOInc., Pawtucket, 1973-86; acct. Vis. Nurse Service, Pawtucket, 1986-87, Butler Hosp., Providence, 1987—. Mem. Nat. Purchasing Mgmt. Assn., R.I. Realtors Assn. Home: 30 Gilmore St Pawtucket RI 02861 Office: Butler Hosp 345 Blackstone Blvd Providence RI 02906

RAY, CHARLOTTE KIDD, lawyer; b. Baton Rouge, Dec. 20, 1954; d. James Marion and Germaine Elizabeth (Hunt) Kidd; m. Ronald Phillip Ray, Mar. 17, 1979; children—Robert Patrick, Robyn Germaine, Ronald Phillip Jr. BS, La. State U., 1976, JD, 1978; grad. Nat. Trust Sch., Evanston, Ill., 1983. Bar: La. 1979. Trust adminstr. Fidelity Nat. Bank, Baton Rouge, 1980-81, trust officer, 1981-82, asst. v.p., trust officer, 1982-83, v.p., trust officer, 1983-87; sole practice, Baton Rouge, 1987—. Mem. ABA, La. Bar Assn., Baton Rouge Bar Assn. Republican. Episcopalian. Home: 2233 Terrace Ave Baton Rouge LA 70806 Office: 8555 United Plaza Blvd Suite 201 Baton Rouge LA 70809

RAY, JEANNE CULLINAN, lawyer, insurance company executive; b. N.Y.C., May 5, 1943; d. Thomas Patrick and Agnes Joan (Buckley) C.; m. John Joseph Ray, Jan. 20, 1968; children—Christopher Lawrence, Douglas James. Student Univ. Coll., Dublin, Ireland, 1963; A.B., Coll. Mt. St. Vincent, Riverdale, N.Y., 1964; LL.B., Fordham U., 1967. Bar: N.Y. 1967. Atty., Mut. Life Ins. Co. N.Y. (MONY), N.Y.C., 1967-68, asst. counsel, 1969-72, assoc. counsel, 1972-73, counsel, 1974-75, asst. gen. counsel, 1976-80, assoc. gen counsel, 1981-83, v.p. pension counsel, 1984-85, v.p. area counsel group and pension ops., 1985-87; v.p. sector counsel group and pension ops., 1988—; v.p. law, sec. MONY Securities Corp., N.Y.C., 1980-85; v.p. law, sec. MONY Advisers, Inc., N.Y.C., 1980—; sec. MONYCO, Inc., N.Y.C., 1980-85; v.p., counsel MONY Series Fund, Inc., Balt., 1984-87. Contbr. articles to legal jours. Cubmaster, Greater N.Y. council Boy Scouts Am., N.Y.C., 1978-84, mem. bd. rev. and scouting com., 1985—. Mem. ABA (chmn employee benefits com. Tort and Ins. Practice sect. 1981-82, v.p. legislation 1983-87, sr. vice-chmn. 1988—), Assn. Life Ins. Counsel (chmn. policyholders tax com. Tax sect. 1982—). Office: MONY Manhattanville Rd Purchase NY 10577

RAY, KAY C., rehabilitation counselor, group therapist; b. Meridian, Miss., Nov. 6, 1949; d. Charles E. and Barbara L. (Wilson) Ray. B.S., Bethune-Cookman Coll., Daytona Beach, Fla., 1971; M.A., Columbia U., 1984, M.Ed., 1984. Supr. tng. Opportunities Industrialization Ctr., Meridian, Miss., 1972-73, employment advisor, 1973-78, supr. student service, Bronx, N.Y., 1980-82; career advisor Youth Employment Tng. Program, Bronx, 1978-80; research asst. counselor psychology dept. Tchrs. Coll. Columbia U., 1984-85, teaching asst., 1984-86; group therapist and cons. Daytop Village, 1986—; vocat. rehab. counselor Samaritan Village, also cons. Samaritan Parents Assn., 1987—. Mem. Nat. Assn. Female Execs., Am. Psychol. Assn., Nat. Assn. Black Psychologists. Democrat. Baptist. Avocations: traveling, writing, bicycling, reading. Office: Samaritan Village Inc 97-99 Queens Blvd Rego Park NJ 11374

RAY, PATRICIA COOPER, manufacturing executive, office automation consultant; b. Prattsville, Ark., Mar. 19, 1932; s. Joseph Elwood and Agnes Mildred (Keesee) Cooper; m. Gene Thomas Ray, Feb. 6, 1959; children—Reynaldo, Kimberley (Mrs. Andre Landon). B.A. in Music, Tex. Woman's U., 1953, M.A., 1954. Tchr., Dallas Ind. Sch. Dist., 1954-59; landman S.W. Prodn. Co., Dallas, 1959-65; adminstrv. asst. Johnson Investment Corp., Austin, Tex., 1965-72; mgr. adminstrv. services Victor Equipment Co., Denton, Tex., 1972—; owner, operator Office Systems Cons. Mem. LWV, AAUW. Mem. Am. Mgmt. Assn., Assn. Records Mgrs. and Adminstrs., Assn. Info. System Profls., Assn. Info. and Image Mgmt., Office Tech. Mgmt. Assn., Am. Soc. Composers, Authors, Pubs. Office: PO Drawer 1007 Denton TX 76202

RAY, SHELLEY MARIA, academic director; b. Pitts., Aug. 20, 1956; d. Edward Douglas and Ruth Bennie (Young) R. Student, Bowdoin Coll., 1974-75; BA, Hampton U., 1978. Tech. marketer Beaven Cos., Chgo., 1978-84; rep. career services Computer Learning Ctr., Chgo., 1982-84; office mgr. Ameritech Mobile Communications, Schaumburg, Ill., 1984-85; dir. grad. services 1st Bus. Sch./Allied Edn., Chgo., 1985—; cons. careers. Mem. career tng. div. Urban League, Chgo., 1982—; affiliate Mayor's Adv. Bd. City Personnel, Chgo., 1986—. Recipient award Minorities in Cable and New Tech., 1982, J. H. Milestein Citizenship award B'nai B'rith, 1983. Mem. Am. Personnel and Guidance Assn., Am. Soc. for Personnel Adminstrn., Women in Communications, Midwest Coll. Placement Assn., Nat. Assn. for Female Execs. Democrat. Lutheran. Office: 1st Bus Sch 14 E Jackson Chicago IL 60604

RAYE-JOHNSON, VENDA BEVERLY, career consultant, writer; b. Massillon, Ohio, Oct. 22, 1951; d. George Raye and Josephine (Gates) Eichelberger; m. Celius L. Johnson, Jr., Oct. 24, 1984. AA, Highland Coll., 1971; BS, Kans. State U., 1973; MA, U. Mo., Kansas City, 1982. Lic. counselor, Mo. Benefits specialist Puritan Bennet Corp., Kansas City, 1975-78; tchr. English Bishop Hogan High Sch., Kansas City, 1979-81; career cons. U. Mo., Kansas City, 1981-83; pvt. practice career cons. Independence, Mo., 1983—; writer Dimensions Unltd., Kansas City, 1986—; speaker in field. Mem. Kansas City Centurions Leadership Program. Mem. Am. Assn. for Counseling and Devel., Assn. Trainers Development, Pi Lambda Theta. Club: Toastmasters (adminstrv. v.p. Independence chpt. 1987—). Home: 1515 Scott Pl Independence MO 64052

RAYFORD, KAREN LYNN, small business owner; b. Bluefield, W.Va., July 27, 1958; d. Russell Eunce and Mary M. (Bolden) Townes; m. Brett Scott Rayford, Dec. 17, 1983. Cert., Kathleen Busch Prestige Modeling Sch., Columbus, Ohio, 1978; student, Franklin U., 1980-81. Asst. buyer Holiday Boutique, Columbus, 1978-79; asst. mgr. office Granzow and Guss Architects, Columbus, 1980-81; tax acct. Dept. Taxation State of Ohio, Columbus, 1981-82; sales rep. Willis Beauty Supply, Columbus, 1982-84; owner Classic Hair Care, Inc., Cin., 1984—; receptionist, operator Ranco Controls, Columbus, 1977-80. Named one of Outstanding Young Women of Am.,1985-86. Fellow Big Bros./Big Sisters Am., Nat. Assn. for Female Execs. Club: Culture Unltd. (fellow). Home: 2102 Grandin Rd #409 Cincinnati OH 45208 Office: Classic Hair Care Inc 7733 Reading Rd Cincinnati OH 45237

RAYMOND, SUSAN GRANT, sculptor; b. Denver, May 23, 1943; d. Edwin Hendrie and Marybelle (McIntyre) G; m. Macpherson Raymond Jr., Aug. 18, 1967 (div. Mar. 1987); children: Lance Ramsay, Mariah McIntyre. BA in English, Cornell U., 1965; MA in Anthropology, U. Colo., 1968. Curator of anthropology Denver Mus. of Nat. History, 1968-71, contract artist, 1976-77, 79, 81, 83; instr. in anthropology U.S. Internat. U., Steamboat Springs, Colo., 1971-73. Sculpted monumental bronze sculpture for Littleton Colo., 1987, Vail, Colo., 1986, inspirational sculpture Childrens Hosp., 1977, diorama figures for Denver Mus. of Nat. History, 1971, 76, 77, 79, 81, 83; other prin. works include sculptures Routt Meml. Hosp, 1977, U. Denver, 1982, Craig Hosp. 1984, Lakewood Westernaires, 1984. Mem. Nat. Ski Patrol, 1965-75. Recipient Maurice Hexter award Nat. Sculpture Soc., 1984, Art Castings award N. Am. Sculpture Exhibition, 1982, Summerart award Steamboat Springs Arts and Humanities, 1984.

RAY-MORRIS, JACQUELINE, business and management consultant; b. Chester, Pa., Dec. 24, 1952; d. Haywood Filmore and Evelyn Thaw (Humphrey) Ray; m. Alton Pavaughn Morris, Aug. 22, 1981. AA, Gloucester County Coll., Sewell, N.J., 1973; BS, Hampton Inst., Va., 1976. Store asst. mgr., Bambergers, Deptford, N.J., 1976-77; hosp. asst. mgr. Service Master Mgmt., Harrisburg, Pa., 1977-78, coordinating mgr., Harrisburg, 1978-79, Alexandria, Va., 1979-82, dir. edn., Balt., 1982-84; program coordinator, tng. cons. Inst. for Type Devel., Silver Springs, Md., 1985—, N.G. Bur., 1986—, Nat. Council on the Aging, Washington, 1987—; pres. Ray-Morris Assocs., Ft. Washington, Md., 1985—; cons. Control Data Bus. Advisors, Inc., Mpls., 1984—. Bd. dirs. Old Towne Child Devel. Ctr., Alexandria, 1984—, Campfire Girls Inc., Columbia, Md., 1985—; chmn. Orgn. Devel. Cons. Unlimited, Washington, 1985—; chmn. Youth for Christ, Inc., Washington, 1984-86. Mem. Orgn. Devel. Network, Nat. Assn. Exec. Females, Nat. Soc. Notaries. Democrat. Apostolic. Avocations: designing and sewing, tennis, reading, swimming, interior decorating. Home: 2112 Old Fort Hills Ct Fort Washington MD 20744

RAYMUS, TONI MARIE, real estate executive, newspaper publisher; b. Stockton, Calif., Feb. 11, 1957; d. Antone Edward and Marie Fatima (Medeiros) R. BA, U. Pacific, 1979; postgrad., Richmond Coll., London, 1980. Gen. asst. Manteca (Calif.) News, 1977-79, asst. to pub., 1980-82, entertainment editor, 1980-82; pub. Ripon (Calif.) Record, 1982—; v.p. fin. Raymus Real Estate, Manteca, 1984—. Chairwoman Jr. Miss Scholarship Program, Manteca, 1980—; commr. Juvenile Justice Commn., Stockton, 1981-82; dir. Mateca Boys and Girls Club, 1982—. Mem. Manteca Builders Assn., Builder's Industry Assn. of Delta (dir. 1987—), Calif. Pubs. Assn., Ripon C. of C. Republican. Roman Catholic. Club: Venture (Manteca) (v.p. 1981-82). Office: Raymus Real Estate 544 E Yosemite Ave Manteca CA 95336

RAYNOLDS, ELEANOR HURRY, management consultant; b. N.Y.C., Aug. 20, 1937; d. Renwick Washington Hurry and Anna Bailey (Stoddard) Hurry Frame; m. John F. Raynolds III, Jan. 9, 1982; children—Jay C., Jennifer S. Kuhn. A.A., Bennett Coll., 1957. Coordinator coll. relations Squibb Corp., N.Y.C., 1967-68; asst. to owner Meadow Stable, 1973-77; v.p. MSL Internat. Cons., Ltd. (Hay Group), N.Y.C., 1977-81; v.p., mgr. PA Exec. Search Inc., Stamford, Conn., 1981-82; sr. v.p. Boyden Assocs., Inc., 1982-85; ptnr. Ward Howell, N.Y.C., 1985—. Adv. bd. Outward Bound. Decorated comdr. Brit. Empire. Mem. Internat. Assn. Personnel Women (adv. bd. 1979-83), Brit. Am. C. of C. (chmn. activities com., dir., pres. 1983-85, chmn. nominating com. 1985-87), Women's Forum Inc. Congregationalist. Clubs: Greenwich Field, Mayflower Soc. Home: 202 June Rd Stamford CT 06903 Office: 99 Park Ave New York NY 10016

RAYNOR, BARBARA GURWITZ, advertising agency producer; b. McAllen, Tex., Apr. 3, 1960; d. Gary Reagan and Bailey Anne (Ginsberg) Gurwitz; m. Stuart Eric Raynor, June 26, 1982. BS in Advt., U. Tex., 1981. Copywriter Anderson Advt., San Antonio, 1981-82; free-lance writer, designer Sosa & Assocs., Ed Yardang & Assocs., San Antonio, 1982-83, writer, producer Lewis & Thompson Advt., San Antonio, 1983; free-lance writer/designer/producer Cooper, Burch & Howe, Las Vegas, Nev., 1983-84; writer, producer The Pitluk Group, San Antonio, 1984-85, Thompson/Marince Advt., San Antonio, 1985—; mem. Adweek Research Panel, 1987—. Mem. Woman Am. Orgn. for Rehab. through Tng., San Antonio, 1985, Friends of Ronald McDonald House, San Antonio, 1987. Mem. Jr. League San Antonio, Jewish Fedn. Young Leadership. Democrat. Office: Thompson/Marince Advt 70 NE Loop 410 Suite 610 San Antonio TX 78216

RAZENSON, HELEN LOUISE, bank executive; b. Oceanside, N.Y., Mar. 23, 1954; d. Charles Peter and Evelyn Ruth (Marquis) Kerns; M. Charles Harvey Razenson, Apr. 9, 1978; children: William Francis, Thomas Samual. AA, Nassau Community Coll., Garden City, N.Y., 1974; BS in Acctg., N.Y. Inst. Tech., 1976; MBA, Adelphi U., 1981. Acctg. specialist, asst. v.p. fin. control div. Citibank/Citicorp, N.Y.C., 1975-85, asst. v.p., v.p. N. Am. investment bank div., 1986—. Mem. Grace Luth. Evang. Ch. Choir, North Bellmore, N.Y., 1964-86. Mem. Bethpage (N.Y.) Fire Dept. Ladies Aux. Democrat. Home: 47 Elliott Dr Hicksville NY 11801 Office: Citibank 55 Water St 42d Floor New York NY 10043

RE, ANDREA RENE, director of clinical services; b. Atlanta, Dec. 8, 1954; d. Andrew and Robbie Rene (Carson) Re; m. Robert Emery Osgood III, April 21, 1979; 1 child, Blair Carson. BA in Psychology, Ga. So. Coll., 1975, MA in Psychology, 1980; cert. pub. mgrs. program, U. Ga., 1986. Grad. asst., instr. Ga. So. Coll., Statesboro, 1975-76; planner Pineland Mental Health, Statesboro, 1976-77, dir. research, 1977-81, dir. clin. services, 1981—; site evaluator Nat. Inst. on Alcohol Abuse and Alcoholism, Statesboro, 1979-81; field reader U.S. Dept. Edn., 1983—; cons. Bulloch Alcohol and Drug Abuse Council, Statesboro, 1983—. Contbr. articles to profl. jours.; speaker to profl. orgns. Recipient Gov.'s Intern Program grant Office of the Gov., 1974, various grants Nat. Inst. Alcohol Abuse and Alcoholism, Nat. Inst. Drug Abuse, Nat. Inst. Mental Health, 1977-87, Leadership award Ga. Dept. Human Resources, 1986-87, Prevention award Concep, 1988. Mem. Ga. Coalition on Consutation, Edn. and Prevention (pres. 1986-87, sec. 1984-85, editor 1982-84), Ga. Pub. Health Assn. (liaison chair 1986—), Bulloch County United Way (bd. dirs. 1988—). Democrat. Lodge: Altrusa (charter mem., pub. relations chair 1985-87, v.p. 1988—, Community Service award 1987-88). Home: Rt 1 Box 2065 Statesboro GA 30458 Office: Pineland MH MR SA Services 21 N Zetterower Ave Statesboro GA 30458

REA, JANE STAIRHIME, purchasing executive; b. Mobile, Ala., Jan. 4, 1954; d. Richard Gene Sr. and Margaret Frances (Merriman) S.; m. William Brewer Rea III, Sept. 5, 1975; children: Elisabeth Genevieve, Joseph William. BFA, Auburn U., 1976. Salesperson Anniversary Shop, Mobile, Al., 1971-72; acctg. clk. Internat. Paper Co., Mobile, 1973; salesperson Royal Furniture Mart, Natchez, Miss., 1978-79; mall mgr. Natchez Mall, 1979; owner toy factory and fillin' sta., Natchez, 1979-82; graphic designer Catlon Petroleum, Natchez, 1981-82, print coordinator, 1982-84; mag. print coordinator B.A.S.S., Inc., Montgomery, Ala., 1984-85, purchasing dir., 1985—. Mem. S.E. Ala. Purchasing Assn. Presbyn. Home: 1532 Katrina Pl Montgomery AL 36117 Office: BASS Inc 1 Bell Rd Montgomery AL 36117

REA, JOAN, educator, consultant. d. Joseph John and Mary (Rea) Murphy; m. Hal Green, Jan. 17, 1953 (dec.); children: Kali, Philip, Diane, Pamela. BA, NYU, 1954; MA, U. Houston, 1964; PhD, U. Tex., 1970. Instr. U. Tex., Austin, 1964-68; asst. prof. Rice U., Houston, 1970-75, assoc. prof., 1975—, master, 1984—; bd. dirs. Intercultural Seminars and Adv. Service, Houston, Stages, Inc., Houston. Author: La estructura del narrador en la novela hispanoamericana contemporanea; mem. editorial bd. Latin-Am. Theatre Rev., Lawrence, Kans., 1978—; contbr. numerous articles to profl. jours. NDEA fellow 1965-68, Mellon Found. fellow 1984. Mem. Am. Assn. of University Women, Modern Lang. Assn., Carribbean Studies Assn. Office: Rice U PO Box 1892 Houston TX 77251

REA, KATHRYN POLLYANNA, management consultant, data processing consultant; b. Los Angeles, Aug. 23, 1957; d. Virginia (Robinson) Rea. BS, SUNY, Albany, 1981; Cert. in Data Processing, U. Calif., 1983. Real estate agt. Beverly Hills, Calif., 1977-80; real estate broker Beverly Hills, 1980—; pres., chmn. bd. The Consulting Edge, Inc., Beverly Hills, 1983—; instr. of data communications, systems analysis and design seminars, 1984—. Author: Data Communications For Business, 1987; contbr. articles to profl. jours. Mem. IEEE, Assn. for Computing Machinery. Office: The Consulting Edge Inc 9107 Wilshire Blvd Suite 320 Beverly Hills CA 90210

READ, DIANA ROSE, data processing executive, consultant; b. Glendale, Calif., Aug. 24, 1946; d. Michael Richard Domit and Ebba Beryl (Shipley) Ridge; m. Cecil RenÉ Sicotte, Sept. 7, 1965 (div. Apr. 1984); children: Jean Paul, Michael Roger; m. Keith Edward Read, Jan. 10, 1987. BA, St. Mary's Coll., 1987. Pres. Sun Valley Investments, Inc., Ariz., 1977—, Calif., 1978—; cons. in field. Treas. Boy Scouts Am., Martinez, Calif., 1984-85. Republican. Office: Sun Valley Investments Inc PO Box 1923 Martinez CA 94553

READ, SISTER JOEL, college president. B. in edn., Alverno Coll., 1948; M. in history, Fordham U., 1951; hon. degrees, Lakeland Coll., 1972, Wittenburg U., 1976, Marymount Coll., 1978, DePaul U., 1985, Northland Coll., 1986, SUNY, 1986. Former prof., dept. chmn. history dept. Alverno Coll., Milwaukee, Wis.; pres. Alverno Coll., 1986—; pres., Am. Assn. for Higher Edn., 1976-77; mem. Council, Nat. Endowment for the Humanities, 1977-83; bd. mem., Edn. Testing Service, Neylan Commn.; past pres., Wis. Assn. Ind. Colls. and Univs.; chmn., Commn. on the Status of Edn. for Women, Am. Assn. Colls., 1971-77; mem., Greater Milwaukee Comm.; bd. dirs., F and M Bank. First recip. Anne Row Awd., Harvard U. Grad Sch. Edn., 1980. Office: Alverno Coll Office of the Pres Milwaukee WI 53215-4020

READ, M. MARGARET, speech pathologist; b. New Castle, Ind., May 31, 1936; d. William Patrick and Mildred Margaret (Parsons) Wallace; B.S., Western Mich. U., 1958; M.S., U. Wis., 1961; postgrad. Northeastern U.; children—Jennifer Parsons, Laurie Alden. Speech therapist Lakeview-Springfield public schs., Battle Creek, Mich., 1958-60; instr. speech Tufts U., 1962-63; cons. speech and lang. therapist Cushing Hosp., Framingham, Mass., 1963-64; dir. Speech and Hearing Clinic, Kennedy Meml. Hosp., 1964-66; dir., co-owner Brockton (Mass.) Speech and Hearing Clinic, 1966-70; clin. instr. Boston U., 1966-73, 73-74; dir. Daniels Speech and Lang. Clinic, Univ. Hosp., Boston, 1966-73; instr. Boston State Coll., 1974; asst. prof. communication disorders Worcester (Mass.) State Coll., 1974-82, co-dir. Collaborative Preschool, 1975-82, dir. Communication Disorders Clinic, 1975-82; pvt. practice speech pathology, 1982—; cons. Lahey Clinic, 1983-86, Lexington (Mass.) pub. schs., 1986—; instr. human services program Boston U. Overseas, Ansbach, Ger., 1977; lectr. in field. Mem. Am. Speech-Lang.-Hearing Assn. (cert. clin. competence; legis. council 1980-88), Mass. Speech-Lang.-Hearing Assn. (officer various coms.). Democrat. Contbr. chpts. to books, articles to profl. jours. Address: 139 Day St Auburndale MA 02166

READING, BONNIE NELSON, lawyer; b. Bklyn., Nov. 13, 1943; d. Edward James Nelson and Frances (Knapp) Connor; m. Paul E. Reading, June 19, 1965 (div. July 1977); children: Eric, Christopher. BA in Russian Linguistics, Cornell U., 1964; JD, Fordham U., 1968. Bar: N.Y. 1971, Calif. 1972. Ptnr. Seltzer Caplan Wilkins & McMahon, San Diego, 1974—. bd. dirs., head scorekeeper Point Loma Little League, 1978-80, Peninsula Pony League, 1981-82, Peninsula Colt League, 1983; bd. dirs. Holiday Bowl, 1984; mem. Park and Recreation Bd. City of San Diego, 1988—. Mem. ABA (family law sect.), Am. Acad. Matrimonial Lawyers, Calif. Trial Lawyers Assn., Calif. State Bar Assn. (family law adv. com. 1980-83, family law exec. com. 1978-81, appellate rev. dept. state bar ct. 1985-87), San Diego County Bar Assn. (v.p. 1982, bd. dirs. 1979-82, chair membership com. 1978-79, clin. edn. program family law 1979, family law sect., cert. spl. sect.), San Diego Trial Lawyers Assn. (bd. dirs. 1983—), San Diego County Bar Found. (sec. 1984, bd. dirs. 1983-85), Lawyers Club (bd. dirs. 1984). Office: Seltzer Caplan Wilkins & McMahon 3003 Fourth Ave San Diego CA 92103

READING, MELISSA MARGARET, science educator; b. Tampa, Fla., Nov. 2, 1943; d. Lyle Milton and Louise Eddowes (Juckett) R.; m. Panayotis Poulos Lambropoulos, July 1, 1967 (div. 1976); m. John Irvin Castor, Aug. 6, 1977; children: Ethan Lyle Reading Castor, Emily Margaret Reading Castor. BS in Cell Biology, U. Mich., 1965; MS in Chemistry, U. Chgo., 1968, PhD in Chemistry, 1972. Research assoc. Joint Inst. Lab. Astrophysics, Boulder, Colo., 1972-75, 1978-79; asst. prof. physics U. Calif., Santa Barbara, 1975-77; sci. tchr., naturalist Livermore (Calif.) Assn. Guiding & Teaching Students, 1986—. Contbr. articles to profl. jours. Concert mgr. Valley Choral Soc., 1984-85, bus. mgr. 1986-87; vol. sci. tchr. Livermore Valley Joint Unified Schs., 1985—; mem. Growth Policy Rev. Com., 1986-87, sch. dist. sci. adv. council, 1986—. Nat. Sci. Found. fellow, 1965-70; Sandi Gamble Meml. scholar Ohlone Audubon, 1985. Mem. Am. Phys. Soc., AAAS. Democrat. Presbyterian. Home: 1240 Asti Ct Livermore CA 94550

REAGAN, MARIE ADELE, obstetrician-gynecologist; b. Pitts., Apr. 26, 1926; d. John Joseph and Marie Adele (Gallagher) R. BS, U. Pitts., 1948, MD, 1953. Diplomate Am. Bd. Ob-Gyn. Intern St. Francis Gen. Hosp., Pitts., 1953-54, mem. staff, 1957—, now sr. staff, resident in ob.-gyn., 1954-57, mem. staff, 1957—; practice medicine specializing in ob.-gyn. Pitts., 1957—. Home: 220 N Dithridge St Pittsburgh PA 15213 Office: Gynob Ltd 4221 Penn Ave Pittsburgh PA 15224

REAGAN, NANCY DAVIS (ANNE FRANCIS ROBBINS), wife of President U.S.; b. N.Y.C., July 6, 1923; d. Kenneth and Edith (Luckett) Robbins; step dau. Loyal Davis; m. Ronald Reagan, Mar. 4, 1952; children: Patricia Ann, Ronald Prescott; stepchildren: Maureen, Michael. BA, Smith Coll.; LLD (hon.), Pepperdine U., 1983; LHD (hon.), Georgetown U., 1987. Contract actress, MGM, 1949-56; films include The Next Voice You Hear, 1950, Donovan's Brain, 1953, Hellcats of the Navy, 1957; Author: Nancy, 1980; formerly author syndicated column on prisoner-of-war and missing-in-action soldiers and their families; author: (with Jane Wilkie) To Love a Child. Civic worker, visited wounded Viet Nam vets., sr. citizens, hosps. and schs. for physically and emotionally handicapped children, active in furthering foster grandparents for handicapped children program; hon. nat. chmn. Aid to Adoption of Spl. Kids, 1977; spl. interest in fighting alcohol and drug abuse among youth: hosted first ladies from around the world for 2d Internat. Drug Conf., 1985; hon. chmn. Just Say No Found. Named one of Ten Most Admired Am. Women, Good Housekeeping mag., ranking #1 in poll, 1984, 85, 86; Woman of Yr. Los Angeles Times, 1977; permanent mem. Hall of Fame of Ten Best Dressed Women in U.S.; recipient humanitarian awards from Am. Camping Assn., Nat. Council on Alcoholism, United Cerebral Palsy Assn., Internat. Ctr. for Disabled; Boys Town Father Flanagan award; 1986 Kiwanis World Service medal; Variety Clubs Internat. Lifeline award; numerous awards for her role in fight against drug abuse. Home and Office: care The White House 1600 Pennsylvania Ave Washington DC 20500

REAL, SISTER CATHLEEN CLARE, college president; b. Kewanee, Ill., June 1, 1934; d. John Thomas and Catherine Cecelia (Breen) R. BA in Math. and Chemistry, Marycrest Coll., Davenport, Iowa, 1957, LHD (hon.), 1985; MA in Math., St. Louis U., 1959; PhD in Math., U. Iowa, 1968. From asst. v.p. for acads. to pres. Marycrest Coll., 1958-75; chair dept. math. Schenectady (N.Y.) County Community Coll., 1975-77; asst. acad. dean Barat Coll., Lake Forest, Ill., 1977-79; v.p. for acads. Coll. of St. Mary, Omaha, 1979-84, acting pres., 1983-84; pres. Siena Heights Coll., Adrian, Mich., 1984—; bd. dirs. Adrian State Bank. Bd. dirs. United Way, Adrian, 1985—, Goodwill-LARC, Adrian, 1986—. Recipient Anti-Defamation award Omaha Anti-Defamation League, 1983. Mem. Am. Assn. Higher Edn. Democrat. Roman Catholic. Lodge: Zonta. Office: Siena Heights Coll Office of Pres 1247 E Siena Heights Dr Adrian MI 49221-1796

REALE, CONCETTA JEAN, nurse; b. Bronx, N.Y., Oct. 7, 1948; d. Joseph Vincent Reale and Willa Bea (Hopkins); m. Murray Glassman, Apr. 24, 1965 (div. June 1980); children: Steven Murray Glassman, Tracey Jean Glassman. Student in nursing, CUNY, 1979-81, Alfred U., 1983-84; diploma, St. James Mercy Hosp. Sch. Nursing, Hornell, N.Y., 1984. Cert. in psychiat. and mental health nursing. Staff RN St. James Mercy Hosp., 1985, Bronx Mcpl. Hosp. Ctr., 1985-87, Bath (N.Y.) VA Med. Ctr., 1987—; rape counselor Bronx Mcpl. Hosp. Ctr., 1985-86, lectr. on rape crisis intervention and schizophrenia, 1986. Mem. N.Y. State Nurses Assn. Republican. Baptist. Home: c/o Tracey Glassman 65 Central Park Ave Yonkers NY 10705

REAM, CAROLYN, job placement specialist, consultant; b. Tulsa, Feb. 17, 1920; d. John Clarence and Zelma Constance (Garner) Ghormley; m. Errol Jefferson, Sept. 15, 1951; 1 son, Eric Jeffrey. Student Okla. Sch. Bus., Accountancy, Law and Fin., 1937-38, U. Nev.-Las Vegas, 1968-69, Sacramento State U., 1974, San Diego State U., 1975. Cert. rehab. specialist. Personnel asst. U. Nev., Las Vegas, 1966-70; job devel. specialist Employment Security Dept., Las Vegas, 1970-74, State Bur. Vocat. Rehab., Las Vegas, 1974-76; counselor Nev. Indsl. Commn., Las Vegas, 1976-77, job placement specialist and pub. relations coordinator Jean Hanna Clark Rehab. Center (State Indsl. Ins. System, formerly Nev. Indsl. Commn.), 1977-84; pvt. practice cons. labor market access determinations, career devel., discriminatory employment practices against disabled, Las Vegas, 1983—; oral exam. bd. mem. State of Nev. Personnel Div., Las Vegas, 1967-84; cons., lectr. career orientation Clark County Sch. Dist., Las Vegas, 1971-73; cons., lectr. So. Nev. Meml. Hosp., Las Vegas, 1974-84; cons., advisor vocat. rehab., Tex. Inst. Rehab. and Research, Houston, 1975; cons., trainer Nev. Commn. on Equal Rights of Citizens, Las Vegas, 1975-76; cons., workshop coordinator Ohio Rehab. Services Commn., Columbus, 1978; cons., advisor Valley Hosp., Las Vegas, 1982; cons. accreditation William A. Callahan Rehab. Center, Wilsonville, Oreg., 1982; cons. accessibility for handicapped sta. KVBC-TV, Las Vegas, 1982. Writer, producer shows: Jobortunity, sta. KLAS-TV, 1973; contbr. articles to mag.; author booklets in field. Chmn.,

Econ. Opportunity Bd. Clark County Adv. Bd. on Transp. for Handicapped and Srs., Las Vegas, 1975—; bd. dirs., sec. United Way Services, Inc., 1975—, chmn. budget com.; vice chmn. So. Nev. Com. on Employment of Handicapped, 1977—, chmn., 1984-85; mem. Winchester Town Adv. Bd., 1978—; mem. adv. bd. Nev. Assn. Handicapped/Ctr. for Ind. Living, 1985—. Recipient cert. of merit, Employment Security Dept., Las Vegas, 1973, cert. of apppreciation Nev. Spl. Olympics, 1973-74, Am. Lung Assn. Nev., 1982-83, Multiple Sclerosis Soc., 1982. Mem. Nat. Rehab. Assn. (Margaret Fairbairn award job placement div. 1975, Pacific region rep. 1984—), So. Nev. Personnel Assn. (dir. 1980), Phi Mu Alumnae (coll. advisor Las Vegas 1971, treas. 1972). Democrat. Congregationalist. Home: 400 Greenbriar Townhouse Way Las Vegas NV 89121

REAMS, ELINOR PAYNE (MRS. ARTHUR A. REAMS), international educational specialist, retired government official; b. Dothan, Ala., Apr. 17, 1914; d. Alvin A. and Gladys Wise (Fritter) Payne; A.B. cum laude, Fla. State U., 1935; postgrad. George Washington U., 1940; m. Arthur Arnold Reams, Jan. 11, 1941; 1 dau., Anne Emily Reams Rapoport. Newspaper work, Panama City, Fla., 1935; mgr. Clements Ins. Agy., Miami, Fla., 1935-39; head dept. English, Redland High Sch., Dade County, Fla., 1936-40; writer confidential reports Bur. Current Information, 1940-41; editorial asst. War Dept., 1941; personnel asst. Co-ordinator Information, 1941-42; personnel officer FSA, 1942-43; mgmt. planning analyst O.W.I., 1945; mgmt. planning officer Dept. State, 1945-48, chief deptl. staff U.S. Adv. Commn. Ednl. Exchange, 1948-52, cons. internat. information adminstrn., 1952-53, Bur. Internat. Sci. and Tech. Affairs, Dept. State, 1973-75; ind. cons. U.S. govt., also pvt. orgns., 1975—; cons. Am. Council Edn., 1955-56, spl. asso. and cons. commn. edn. and internat. affairs, 1956-61, also liaison officer with UNESCO relation staff Dept. State; sr. personnel mgmt. officer Dept. State, 1961-62, chief program planning and mgmt. staff, 1962-63; fgn. affairs officer Policy Review and Research Staff, Bur. Ednl. and Cultural Affairs, Dept. State, 1963-65, asst. dir. policy review and coordination staff, 1965-67, sr. policy officer and asst. exec. dir. council on internat. ednl. and cultural affairs, 1967-70; ind. research cons., 1970—; mem. asst. sec. states com. reorgn., 1946; mem. survey mission rev. ednl. exchange activities in Europe and Near East, Dept. State, 1949; Am. Council Edn. rep. 3d gen. conf. Internat. Assn. Univs., 1960; trustee Jr. Mus. Bay County, Inc., 1976-77; pres. Friends of Bay County Pub. Libraries, Inc., 1977-78, mem. program com. diplomatic and consular officers ret., 1985—. Recipient Meritorious Service award Dept. State, 1964, Superior Service award, 1966, Superior Service Honor award, 1970. Mem. DAR, Delta Delta Delta, Phi Kappa Phi, Beta Pi Theta. Democrat. Presbyn. Clubs: Washington Golf and Country, St. Andrews Bay Yacht, Diplomatic and Consular Officers (pub. affairs and program coms.), Hidden Creek Country. Author report profl. jour. Home: The Encore Condominium 1808 Old Meadow Rd Unit 213 McLean VA 22102

REARDON, JACQUELINE MARIE, accountant; b. Phila., Jan. 25, 1963; d. Joseph Michael and Sandra Joan (Meehan) R. BBA, Loyola Coll., Balt., 1985; MS, U. Balt., 1987. Bookkeeper Robert M. Hoffman & Assocs., Balt., 1984-85; acct. JCB Inc., White Marsh, Md., 1985-87, credit supr., 1987—. Mem. Nat. Assn. Accountants, Nat. Assn. Female Execs., Sigma Iota Epsilon. Republican. Roman Catholic. Home: 1419-H Hadwick Dr Baltimore MD 21221 Office: JCB Inc 10939 Philadelphia Rd White Marsh MD 21162

REARICK, MARTHA NELL, music educator; b. Danville, Ill., Nov. 29, 1938; d. Francis George and Lilian Hartman (Brown) R. B of Music, U. Mich., 1960, M of Music, 1961. Faculty dept. music Pensacola (Fla.) Jr. Coll., 1961-63; instr. music U.So. Fla., Tampa, 1963-65, asst. prof., 1965-70, assoc. prof., 1970-80, prof., 1980—. Author: Fabric of Flute Playing, 1976; 1st flutist Fla. Gulf Coast Symphony, Tampa, 1963-78; flutist Ars Nova Wind Quintet, Tampa, 1971—; piano accompanist flute master classes, 1971—. Mem. Nat. Flute Assn. (sec. 1979-80, bd. dirs. 1980-82), Fla. Flute Assn. (v.p. 1986-88, pres. 1988—), Music Tchrs. Nat. Assn., Sigma Alpha Iota (Rose of Honor 1964). Democrat. Home: 12715 Orange Grove Dr Tampa FL 33618 Office: U S Fla Dept Music 4202 E Fowler Ave Tampa FL 33620

REAVES, JUANITA YVONNE, psychologist, researcher; b. Miami, Fla., Aug. 13, 1953; d. David Proxton and Helen (Sinquefield) R. BA magna cum laude, Spelman Coll., 1975; MS, Howard U., 1977, PhD, 1981. Lic. psychologist, D.C. Research assoc. Roy Littlejohn Assocs., Inc., Washington, 1979-81, sr. research assoc., 1981-87; chief planning and evaluation div. Commn. on Mental Health Services D.C. Govt., Washington, 1987—; asst. prof. psychology Howard U., Washington, 1986-88. Contbr. articles to profl. jours. Named one of Outstanding Young Women Am. Assn. Black Psychologists, 1978; Cath. Univ. cons. analyst grantee, Washington, 1983-84. Mem. Am. Psychol. Assn. (div. 35 psychology of women, minority fellowship 1977-79), D.C. Psychol. Assn., D.C. Assn. Black Psychologists (rec. sec. 1981-82, corr. sec. 1982-83, treas. 1986-87, pres. elect 1987-88, pres. 1988-89, Service award 1987), Nat. Council Negro Women, Washington Urban League, Spelman Coll. Alumnae Assn., Delta Sigma Theta (editor newsletter 1983-87), Psi Chi (pres. 1974-75). Democrat. Methodist. Office: St Elizabeth's Hosp 2700 Martin Luther King SE Behavioral Studies Room 204 Washington DC 20032

REAVIS, VIOLA LEA SCHUBERT, educator; b. Miami, Okla., July 11, 1927; d. Joe and Rose Lea (Van Horn) Schubert; m. Robert E. Reavis, Sept. 27, 1946; children—Edwin R., Loretta J., Kieran, Robert II. A.A., Okla. Northeastern A&M Coll., 1973; B.S., Pittsburg State U., Kans., 1975, M.S., 1961, EDS in Higher Edn., 1987 . Sec. Miami Pub. Schs., Okla., 1968-69, tchr., 1979—; tchr. Wyandotte Pub. Schs., Okla., 1977-79. Treas. Republican Women, 1975. Mem. NEA, Okla. Edn. Assn., Miami Classroom Tchrs. Assn., AAUW, Delta Kappa Gamma (scholarship 1985, 86), Beta Sigma Phi, Epsilon Sigma Alpha. Roman Catholic. Avocations: needlepoint; sewing.

REBELSKY, FREDA ETHEL GOULD, psychologist; b. N.Y.C., Mar. 11, 1931; d. William and Sarah (Kaplan) Gould; B.A., U. Chgo., 1950, M.A., 1954; Ph.D., Radcliffe Coll., 1961; m. William Rebelsky, Jan. 1, 1956 (dec. 1979); 1 son, Samuel. Counselor, U. Chgo. Orthogenic Sch., 1952-55; research asst. Kenyon & Eckhart, Inc., 1956-58; research asst. lab. human devel. Harvard U., 1959-60, teaching asst. psychology, then instr. edn., 1960-61; research asso. Speech research lab. Children's Hosp., Boston, 1960-61, M.I.T., 1961-62; mem. faculty Boston U., 1962—, prof. psychology, 1972—, dir. doctoral program in devel. psychology, 1969-74; vis. lectr. U. Utrecht (Netherlands), 1965-67; Froman prof. Russell Sage Coll., Troy, N.Y., 1972. Grantee U.S. Office Edn., 1964-65, Boston U. Grad. Sch., 1967-70, OEO, 1967-69. NIMH, 1974-76; Bunting fellow Radcliffe Coll., 1985-86; recipient Distinguished Tchr. Psychology award Am. Psychol. Found., 1970; Harbison award excellence teaching Danforth Found., 1971; Metcalf award Boston U., 1978; Disting. Career in Psychology award Mass. Psychol. Assn., 1982. Mem. AAAS, Soc. Research Child Devel. (sec. Boston 1963-65), AAUP (sec. Boston U. 1964-65, pres. 1984-85, 86-88), Am., Eastern, Mass. (chmn. program com. 1962-64) psychol. assns., Mass. Children's Lobby (pres. 1977-81), Sigma Xi, Psi Chi. Author: Child Behavior and Development: A Reader, 1969; Child Behavior and Development, 2d edit., 1973: Life: The Continuous Process, 1975; Growing Children, 1976. Address: 1 Billings Park Newton MA 02158 Office: 64 Cummington St Boston MA 02215

REBENTISCH, SUSAN WEBSTER, radio management consultant; b. Los Angeles, Apr. 24, 1943; d. Maurie E. and Judy A. (Peairs) Webster; m. Edward H. Rebentisch, Dec. 4, 1974. A.A., Parsons Sch. Design, 1965; cert. N.Y. Inst. Photography, 1982; BS in Bus. Mgmt., Mercy Coll., 1988. Office mgr. Travelworld Inc., N.Y.C., 1970-73; sales rep. Brit. Caledonia Airways, N.Y.C., 1973-74; mgr. Egyptian tours Lindblad Travel Inc., N.Y.C., 1975—; v.p., adminstrv. mgr. The Webster Group, N.Y.C., 1977—. Co-author: St. Luke's Church Sesquicentennial Celebration 1986. 4-H program asst., 1986, Coop. Extension 4-H, Mahopac, N.Y., 1982—, leader photography and communications 1979—, chmn. Putnam County 4-H Fair 1984, chmn. 4-H Publicity, 1979 , chmn. spl. events 1986-88; sr. warden St. Luke's Ch., 1986. Recipient Outstanding Leader award Kodak, 1982. Mem. S.E. Hist. Soc., Photog. Soc. Am., Nat. Assn. Female Execs., Internat. Radio and TV Soc., Delta Mu Delta Honor Soc. Avocations: photography; gardening.

REBER, BARBARA LEE, diagnostician; b. Ft. Belvoir, Va., June 23, 1947; d. Truman C. and Frances Aurelia (Smith) Goodman; m. Ron Ray Reber, Jan. 25, 1969; children: Stephanie, Amanda. BA, East Tex. State U., 1969, MEd, Tex. Christian U., 1976. Tchr. Dallas Ind. Sch. Dist., 1969; tchr. Arlington (Tex.) Ind. Sch. Dist., 1969-78, ednl. diagnostician, 1978-88; asst. prin. Little Elem. Sch., Arlington, 1988—; ednl. diagnostic cons., Arlington, 1974—. Active Council for Exceptional Children; chmn. Accent Arlington, 1984-87; mem. Leadership Arlington, 1985-86. Mem. Tex. Elem. Prins. and Suprs. Assn., Arlington Adminstrs. Assn., Arlington Elem. Adminstrs. Assn., Tex. Ednl. Diagnosticians Assn., Assn. for Children with Learning Disabilities, Delta Kappa Gamma. Republican. Methodist. Home: 901 Kristin Ln Arlington TX 76012 Office: Arlington Ind Schs 4215 Little Rd Arlington TX 76016

REBER, GLORIA LAWLER, government official; b. Iowa Falls, Iowa, Apr. 20, 1949; d. Thomas Edward and Lois Marie (Radohl) Lawler; m. Richard William Reber, Nov. 5, 1977. BA, U. Colo., 1971. Exec. asst.vets. com. U.S. Senate, Washington, 1974-76, spl. asst. to Sen. Paul Tribble, 1983—; saleswoman Golubin & Warwick Realtors, Alexandria, Va., 1976-78, mgr., broker, 1978-80; v.p., mgr. Curran Segesman Realtors, Alexandria, 1980-82. Del. Va. Rep. Conv., 1988; past mem. Alexandria Jr. Friends, Alexandria Community YWCA. Mem. Women in Govt. Relations, U. Colo. Alumnae Group, Delta Delta Delta, Sorority Alumnae Group. Roman Catholic. Club: Capitol Hill Rep. Women's. Home: 340 N Pitt St Alexandria VA 22314 Office: U S Senate Sen Paul Tribble 517 Hart Bldg Washington DC 20510

RECHT, NADYNE MARCEILLE, realtor; b. Ft. Wayne, Ind., Sept. 9, 1921; d. Donald Joseph and Gladys Marie (Bisson) Tierney; student Ind. U., Purdue, 1965-66; m. Ervin John Recht, Nov. 20, 1941; children—Diane Recht Langin, Douglas, Jeannine Recht Wells, Mark, Cynthia, Michael. Saleswoman, Daymude Albersmeyer Butler, Ft. Wayne, 1966-68; broker, supr. Daymude, Albersmeyer Brokers, Ft. Wayne, 1968-70; ptnr. Daymude & Co., 1970-73; broker, ptnr. Recht & Recht, Ft. Wayne, 1973—; treas. Multiple Listing Service, 1983-84; former chmn. Ft. Wayne Bd. Realtors. Active Amnesty Internat.; pres. Maplewood Community Assn. Mem. Civic Theater Guild, Mus. Art, Mental Health Assn., St. Francis Guild. Democrat. Roman Catholic. Club: Jefferson (v.p. 1964). Home: 6853 Woodcrest St Fort Wayne IN 46815 Office: 3330 S Calhoun St Fort Wayne IN 46807

RECHTZIGEL, SUE MARIE (SUZANNE), child care center executive; b. St. Paul, May 27, 1947; d. Carl Stinson and Muriel Agnes (Oestrich) Miller; m. Gary Elmer Rechtzigel, Aug. 20, 1968 (div. Feb. 1982); children: Brian Carl, Lori Ann. BA in Psychology, Sociology, Mankato (Minn.) State U., 1969. Lic. in child care, Minn. Rep. ins. State Farm Ind. Co., Albert Lea, Minn., 1969-73; free-lance child caretaker Albert Lea, Minn., 1973-78; owner, dir. Lakeside Day Care, Albert Lea, Minn., 1983—; asst. Hawthorne Sch. Learning Ctr., Albert Lea, 1978-83. Mem. New Residents and Newcomers Orgn., Albert Lea, 1970—, past. pres.; asst. pre-sch. United Meth. Ch., Albert Lea, 1975-78, tchr. Sunday sch., 1976-80, tchr. Bible sch., 1980-85; active Ascension Luth. Ch., 1976-80. Mem. Freeborn Lic. Day Care Assn. (v.p. 1986, pres. 1987), AAUW (home tour 1977, treas. 1980-81), Bus. and Profl. Women, YMCA, Albert Lea Art Ctr. Republican. Club: 3M Families. Home and Office: 1919 Brookside Dr Albert Lea MN 56007

RECTOR, ANNE BEST, real estate marketing executive; b. Columbia, S.C., Apr. 10, 1942; d. Fred Benjamin and Harriette (Burckhalter) Best; m. Edwin Rector, Mar. 13, 1971. B.A., Salem Coll., 1964. V.p. Manarin, Odle and Rector, Inc., Alexandria, Va., 1976-81; pres. Rector Assocs., Inc., Alexandria, 1981—. Bd. dirs. Am. Cancer Soc., Alexandria, 1979-85. Mem. Nat. Assn. Realtors, Va. Assn. Realtors (bd. dirs. 1983—), No. Va. Bd. Realtors (bd. dirs. 1988—), Alexandria C. of C. (bd. dirs. 1981-84). Office: Rector Assocs Realtors Inc 211 N Union St Suite 250 Alexandria VA 22314

REDD, JANET FAITH, librarian; b. Albany, Calif., May 24, 1945; d. Joseph Patrick and Faith Pauline (Schoen) R. B.A., U. Calif.-Berkeley, 1967, M.L.S., 1968; M.A., San Jose State U., 1974; Ph.D., Stanford U., 1980, postdoctoral scholar, 1984-86. Standard services credential, supervision-library services, Calif. Reference evening librarian asst. cataloger De Anza Coll., Cupertino, Calif., 1968-70, circulation librarian, 1970-77, acquisitions and periodicals librarian, 1978—, pres. faculty senate, 1984-85. Contbr. articles to various publs. Calif. State Scholarships fellow, 1963-68; U. Calif.-Berkeley scholar, 1963-67. Mem. ALA, Calif. Library Assn., Calif. Assn. Research Libraries, Am. Assn. Higher Edn., Assn. Coll. and Research Libraries, Am. Ednl. Research Assn., Wildlife Rescue Assn., Campanile Club, Tower and Flame, Phi Beta Kappa, Beta Phi Mu. Home: 21995 Via Regina Saratoga CA 95070 Office: De Anza Coll Learning Ctr 21250 Stevens Creek Blvd Cupertino CA 95070

REDDICK, RHODA ANNE, microbiologist; b. Waynesboro, Ga., Nov. 2, 1937; d. Loy Winfred and Eileen Elizabeth (Rhodes) R.; A.B., Ga. Coll., 1958; M.T., Emory U., 1959; M.S., Med. Coll. Ga., 1965, Ph.D., 1968; m. Robert D. Mitchum, June 20, 1970. Med. technologist Emory U. Hosp., Atlanta, 1959-61, Med. Coll. Ga., Augusta, 1961-64; postdoctoral fellow med. microbiology Centers for Disease Control, Atlanta, 1968-70; dir. diagnostic microbiology S.C. Dept. Health and Environ. Control Bur. Labs, Columbia, 1970-75, dir. Div. Lab. Improvement, 1975-82, dir. Div. Clin. Labs., 1982—; clin. asst. prof. microbiology U.S.C. Sch. Medicine, Columbia, 1976—; adj. asst. prof. lab. medicine Med. U.S.C., Charleston, 1977—; specialist Nat. Registry of Microbiology, 1971—. Named Outstanding Microbiologist in S.C., 1983. Diplomate Am. Bd. Med. Microbiology. Fellow Am. Acad. Microbiology; mem. Am. Soc. Microbiology, Am. Soc. Clin. Pathologists, Am. Public Health Assn., Conf. Public Health Lab. Dirs., Southeastern Assn. Clin. Microbiologists, S.C. Public Health Assn. Methodist. Office: PO Box 2202 Columbia SC 29202

REDDINGTON, MARTHA P., sales executive; b. New Rochelle, N.Y., May 17, 1954; d. John M. and Mary Jane (Kann) R. BA in English, Coll. of New Rochelle, 1976. Prodn. mgr. Reader's Digest, Pleasantville, N.Y., 1976-82, sales mgr., 1982-84; sales mgr. Simon & Schuster, N.Y.C., 1984-87, sales dir., 1987—. Mem. alumnae bd. dirs. Coll. New Rochelle, 1977-83; vice chmn. Holy Family Parish Council, New Rochelle, 1987—; mentor Marymount Coll., Tarrytown, N.Y., 1984—. Recipient Ursula Campus award College of New Rochelle, 1981, St. Angela award Ursuline Sch., 1987. Office: Simon & Schuster 1230 Ave of the Americas New York NY 10020

REDDITT, NINA BELLE, property management executive; b. Kinston, N.C., Apr. 26, 1923; d. Leonidus Bryan and Nina Belle (Harris) R. AA, Blackstone Coll. for Girls, 1943; BA, U. N.C., 1948. Enlisted USN, 1944, advanced through grades to chief petty officer, 1970, ret., 1977; v.p. Rampage Corp., Greenville, N.C., 1977—. Mem. women's studies adv. council, Greenville, 1984-86; sec. Pitt County Women's Commn., Greenville, 1987—. Mem. Am. Bus. Women's Assn. (pres. Triangle chpt. 1976-77, pres. Pirate Charter chpt. 1980-81, sec. 1981-82, pres. 1982-83), Women's Network, Nat. Assn. Female Execs., Fleet Res. Assn., Retired Enlisted Assn., WAVES Nat., Navy League U.S., Vietnam Vets. Am. Democrat. Mem. Christian Science Ch. Clubs: Timeless Treasures, Doll of Greenville, Intrepids of Conn. Home: 610 E 10th St Greenville NC 27858

REDDY, MARY LUCINDA, public relations executive; b. South Bend, Ind., Nov. 10, 1949; d. Charles Sheridan and Hannah Louise (Moran) R. B.A., Nazareth Coll., 1971; M.A., Ball State U., 1979. Tchr. St. Joseph Sch., Battle Creek, Mich., 1971-72, Powers High Sch., Flint, Mich., 1972-74; dir. communications Nazareth Coll., Kalamazoo, Mich., 1974-77, asst. to pres., 1979-83; dir. pub. relations and devel. Sisters of St. Joseph, Kalamazoo, 1983—. Editor newsletter Ball State U., promoter, 1978-79; author, designer Can I Not Do, 1978; editor Grapevine, 1982—, SSJ News, 1983—; contbr. articles to profl. jours. Chmn. United Way drive Nazareth Coll., 1974-77, 79-83; active Diocese Kalamazoo Communications Adv. Bd., 1981—, Nazareth Coll. Alumni Bd., 1984—. Recipient Leadership award United Way, Kalamazoo, 1979-83. Mem. Women in Communication, Inc. (scholarship com. 1984-85, workshop presenter 1982—, pres. West Mich. chpt. 1987-88), Fund Raising Inst., Sisters of St. Joseph, AAUW. Roman Catholic. Home: 5229 Amarillo Parchment MI 49004 Office: Sisters of St Joseph Gull Rd Nazareth MI 49074

REDGRAVE, LYNN, actress; b. London, Eng., Mar. 8, 1943; d. Michael Scudemore and Rachel (Kempson) R.; m. John Clark, Apr. 2, 1967; children: Benjamin, Kelly, Annabel. Ed., Queensgate Sch., London, Central Sch. Speech and Drama, London. Theatrical appearances include Midsummer Night's Dream, The Tulip Tree, Andorra, Hayfever, Much Ado About Nothing, Mother Courage, Love for Love, Zoo, Zoo, Widdershins Zoo, Edinburgh Festival, 1969, The Two of Us, London, 1970, Slag, London, 1971, A Better Place, Dublin, 1972, Born Yesterday, Greenwich, 1973; N.Y. appearances include Black Comedy, 1967, My Fat Friend, 1974, Mrs. Warren's Profession, 1975, Knock, Knock, 1976, Hellzapoppin, 1976, California Suite, 1977, St. Joan, 1977, Sister Mary Ignatius Explains It All, 1985, Aren't We All?, 1985, Sweet Sue, 1987, Twelfth Night, Stratford Conn. Shakespeare Festival, 1978, The King and I, St. Louis, 1983, (on Broadway) Sweet Sue, 1987; film appearances include Tom Jones, Girl With Green Eyes, Georgy Girl (Recipient N.Y. Film Critics award, Golden Globe award, Oscar nomination for best actress 1967), The Deadly Affair, Smashing Time, The Virgin Soldiers, Last of the Mobile Hotshots, Mrs. Warren's Profession, Don't Turn the Other Cheek, Every Little Crook and Nanny, Everything You Always Wanted to Know About Sex, The National Health, The Happy Hooker, The Big Bus, Sunday Lovers; TV appearances include: The Turn of the Screw, Centennial, 1978, The Muppets, Gauguin the Savage, Beggarman Thief, The Seduction of Miss Leona, House Calls, 1981, Rehearsal for Murder, 1982, Teachers Only, 1982, The Fainthearted Feminist (BBC-TV), 1984, My Two Loves, 1986, Home Front; co-host nat. TV syndication Not for Women Only, 1977—; nat. TV spokesperson Weightwatchers, 1984—; rec. albums: Make Mine Manhattan, 1978, Cole Porter Revisited, 1979. Named Runner-Up Actress, All Am. Favorites, Box Office Barometer 1975; recipient Sarah Siddons award as Chgo.'s best stage actress of 1977, 1978. Office: care John Clark PO Box 1207 Topanga CA 90290 *

REDGRAVE, VANESSA, actress; b. London, Jan. 30, 1937; d. Michael and Rachel (Kempson) R.; m. Tony Richardson, Apr. 28, 1962 (div.); children: Natasha Jane, Joely Kim. Student, Central Sch. Speech and Drama, London, 1955-57. Prin. theatrical roles include Helena in Midsummer Night's Dream, 1959, Stella in Tiger and the Horse, 1960, Katerina in The Taming of the Shrew, 1961, Rosaline in As You Like It, 1961, Imogene in Cymbeline, 1962, Nina in The Seagull, 1964, Miss Brodie in The Prime of Miss Jean Brodie, 1966; other plays include Cato Street, 1971, Threepenny Opera, 1972, Twelfth Night, 1972, Anthony and Cleopatra, 1973, Design for Living, 1973, Macbeth, 1975, Lady from the Sea, 1976, 78, 79; film roles include Leonie in Morgan-A Suitable Case for Treatment, 1965 (Best Actress award Cannes Film Festival 1966), Sheila in Sailor from Gibraltar, 1965, Anne-Marie in La Musica, 1965, Jane in Blow Up, 1967, Guinevere in Camelot, 1967, Isadora in Isadora Duncan, 1968 (Best Actress award Cannes Film Festival); other films include The Charge of The Light Brigade, 1968, The Seagull, 1968, A Quiet Place in the Country, 1968, Daniel Deronda, 1969, Dropout, 1969, The Trojan Women, 1970, The Devils, 1970, The Holiday, 1971, Mary Queen of Scots, 1971, Murder on the Orient Express, 1974, Winter Rates, 1974, 7% solution, 1975, Julia, 1977, Agatha, 1978, Yanks, 1978, Bear Island, 1979, Playing for Time, 1980, My Body My Child, 1981, Wagner, 1982, The Bostonians, 1984, Wetherby, 1985, Prick Up Your Ears, 1987; TV film and miniseries appearances include Snow White and the Seven Dwarfs, 1985, Three Sovereigns for Sarah, 1985, Peter the Great, 1986, Second Serve, 1986; Author: Pussies and Tigers, 1964. Bd. govs. Central Sch. Speech and Drama, 1963—. Decorated comdr. Order Brit. Empire; recipient Drama award Evening Standard, 1961, Best Actress award Variety Club Gt. Brit., 1961, 66, Best Actress award Brit. Guild TV Producers and Dirs., 1966, Golden Globe award, 1978, Acad. award for best supporting actress, 1977, Emmy award for best actress in limited series or special, 1980. *

REDLER, SHERRY PRESS, audiologist; b. N.Y.C.; d. Martin M. and Elsie (Opin) Press; B.A., Adelphi U., 1954; M.S., So. Conn. State Coll., 1971, postgrad., 1976-79; children—Michael, Steven, Lynda. Speech pathologist Roslyn (N.Y.) Public Schs., 1954-56; tchr. drama Rollins Coll., Winter Park, Fla., 1961-63; personnel counselor Internat. Bus. Assn., Pitts., 1965; speech pathologist Fairfield (Conn.) Public Schs., 1968-75, ednl. audiologist, 1976—; clin. audiologist Rehab. Center, Bridgeport, Conn., 1975-76; sign lang. instr. Bridgeport Rehab. Center, 1976-78, Staples High Sch., Westport, Conn.; instr. So. Conn. State Coll., New Haven, 1976—; lectr., cons. in field; ind. evaluator of programs for hearing impaired; author, project dir. Title IV Fed. Grant, Conn., 1976-80; mem. Conn. State Task Force to assess services provided to mentally retarded, 1981—; author, project dir. sch. audiology program, Conn., 1981. Trustee Congregation B'Nai Israel, 1985—, chmn. older adult com. Mem. com. to revise hearing screening guidelines, Conn., 1987, State Conn. com. to establish guidelines for services to hearing impaired children, 1988—. Mem. Conn. Speech and Hearing Assn. (co-chmn. com. on edn. hearing impaired 1976—), NEA, Conn. Edn. Assn., Fairfield Edn. Assn., Am. Speech and Hearing Assn., Am. Ednl. Audiology Assn. (1st v.p. 1986—, pres. 1987-88). Home: 28 Lockwood Circle Fairfield CT 06430 Office: 60 Thompson St Fairfield CT 06430

REDMAN, MICHELE THERESA, insurance company executive; b. Marin County, Calif., May 3, 1947; d. C. Thomas and Mary Kay (Irish) R. BS, U. So. Calif., 1969; cert. in elem. edn., Calif. State U., Los Angeles, 1971; postgrad., U. Hartford, 1972. Various positions Hartford Ins. Group, Pasadena, Calif., 1971-73; various positions Hartford (Conn.) Ins. Group, 1973-79, mgr. comptrollers, 1979-81, mgr. quality, asst. dir., 1981-86, dir. quality, 1987—. Solicitor Hartford Arts Council, 1983-85; organizer YWCA Conf. Women, Hartford, 1979-81; bd. dirs. N.W. Community Coll., Winsted, Conn., 1987-89. Mem. Am. Soc. Quality Control (speaker 1985, 86), Am. Mgmt. Assn. (presenter 1984-86), N.E. Quality Control Conf. (registration com. 1984-85), Ins. Inst. Am. (disting. grad. award 1984), Hartford Assn. Ins. Women (pres., Woman Yr. 1985). Democrat. Club: STAG Toastmasters (pres. 1982-84, Toastmaster Yr. 1983). Home: 66 Claire Hill Rd Burlington CT 06013 Office: Hartford Ins Group Hartford Plaza Hartford CT 06115

REDMAN, SHIRLEY LAVERNA, drilling company executive; b. Monahans, Tex., Feb. 9, 1939; d. Chester Arthur and Flossie Irene (Collum) Redman; m. David Randal Best, Feb. 1, 1959 (div. June 1972); children—Sherrie Lynn, Jane Leslie; m. Thomas Dale Kovacevich, Nov. 3, 1978 (div. May 1988). A.A., Ventura Jr. Coll., 1970; B.A., Calif. State U.-Fresno, 1984. Co-owner Pyramid Drilling Co., Inc., Manchester, Ky., 1980—; owner Spas & More, Cottonwood, Ariz., 1984—; owner, pub. The View newspaper, Cottonwood, 1985—. Recipient hon. service award YMCA, 1970, Ventura Sch. Dist., 1971. Mem. PTA (hon. life mem.). Republican. Methodist. Lodge: Women of the Moose. Avocation: art, flying.

REDMOND, GAIL ELIZABETH, petroleum company executive; b. Milw., July 28, 1946; d. George Foote and Doris Ruth (Roethke) R.; student Coll. St. Catherine, 1964-66; BS magna cum laude, Utah State U., 1968; m. John Thomas Happ, Aug. 28, 1982; stepchildren: Amy, Julie, Tammy. Tchr. pub. schs., Milw., 1968-70; staff coordinator Med. Personnel Pool, Milw., 1973-76; corp. manpower devel. mgr. Clark Oil & Refining Corp., Milw., 1976-80; sr. advisor communications, employee benefits Conoco, Inc., Ponca City, Okla., 1980-81, coordinator profl. recruiting, 1981-82, coordinator employee benefit communications, 1982-84, asst. mgr. Phase II Job Eval. Project, 1984-86, coordinator job evaluation, 1986-87; dir. employee relations and job evaluation, 1987—. Currently serving with USNR. Mem. AAUW, Naval Enlisted Res. Assn., Phi Kappa Phi. Office: Conoco Inc PO Box 1267 Ponca City OK 74603

REDMOND, LULA MOSHOURES, family therapist; b. Asheville, N.C., Feb. 3, 1929; d. Christopher John and Rosa Marie (Blankenship) Moshoures; m. John Gerald Redmond, Oct. 9, 1949 (dec. Aug. 1974); children: John Christopher, Thomas Michael, Anne Redmond Fishel. Student, Coker Coll., 1945-46; RN, Duke U., 1949; BS in Nursing, George Mason U., 1976; MS, U. Md., 1978; postgrad. Georgetown Family Ctr., Georgetown U., 1978-81. Counselor Navy Relief Soc., Hawaii, Guam, Brunswick, Maine, Washington, 1957-68; psychiat./pediatric instr. Arlington (Va.) Hosp., 1975-76; coordinator community adult edn. program Mt. Vernon Community Mental Health, Alexandria, Va., 1978-80; family therapist, edn. dir. Hospice Care Inc., Seminole, Fla., 1980-81; pvt. practitioner family therapy Clearwater, Fla., 1980—; mem. faculty Assn. for Death Edn. and Counseling Inc., Washington, 1979-83, bd. dirs., 1981—, coordinator internat. conf. 1979-81;

program case cons. Hospice Programs, 1980-83, founder, dir. Homicide Survivors Group Treatment program, 1985. Chmn. edn. com. Mental Health Assn. Pinellas County, Clearwater, 1981-82, v.p., 1982-84, chmn. bldg. com., 1983—; bd. dirs. Homicide Survivors Group Inc. Pinellas County, 1986—. Recipient Victim Services award Pinellas County Victims Rights Coalition, 1987, Nat. Service award Assn. for Death Edn. and Counseling, Inc., 1988; NIMH fellow, 1976. Mem. Am. Nurses Assn., Nat. Hospice Orgn., Sigma Theta Tau, Alpha Chi, Phi Kappa Phi. Republican. Roman Catholic. Office: Psychol Consultation and Edn Services PO Box 6201 Clearwater FL 34618

REDMOND-BRADLEY, DAWN MICHELLE, public relations consultant; b. Regina, Sask., Can., May 6, 1953; d. Frederick Wilfred and Dorothy Elizabeth (Sauer) Redmond; m. L. Thomas Bradley. Cert. tchr. Accreditation Can. Pub. Relations Society. Tchr., counselor Sask. and, Spain, 1972-78; free-lance writer, researcher Regina, 1976-80; communication and info. specialist Sask. Crop Ins. Corp., Regina, 1980-82; mgr. Continental Pub. Relations, Regina, 1982-84; dir. pub. affairs Sask. Housing Corp., Regina, 1984-86; pres. Dawn Redmond & Assocs. Ltd., Regina, 1986—. Mem. Can. Pub. Relations Soc. (pres. 1986-88), Can. Inst. Mgmt., Can. Friends of Mus. Office: 2352 Smith St, Regina, SK Canada S4T 2P6

REDO, MARIA ELAINE, gerontologist, educator; b. N.Y.C., Jan. 12, 1925; d. Ernest and Mary C. Lappano; B.S. in Edn., Fordham U., 1945; cert. in gerontology, Brookdale Sch. Social Sci., 1979; m. S. Frank Redo, June 27, 1948; children—Philip L., Martha Maria. Tchr. pvt. sch., N.Y.C., 1946-56; dir. Child Service League, Queens, N.Y., 1949-57; founder, dir. Community Concern for Sr. Citizens, Inc., N.Y.C. Dept. for the Aging, 1971-85; dir. N.Y.C. Silver Pages Directory, Silver Savers' Passport. Bd. dirs. Escort Service of Yorkville (N.Y.), 1977—, Sr. Citizen Outreach Program for Elderly, N.Y.C., 1970—; mem. Community Planning Bd., N.Y.C., 1970-77; del. Nat. Republican Conv., N.Y.C., 1976, N.Y. State White House Conf. on Aging, 1981, Nat. White House Conf. on Aging, N.Y.C., 1981; del. N.Y. State Conf. on Mid-Life and Older Women, 1983. Recipient Mayor's Cert. of Appreciation N.Y.C., 1975; Hon. Sec. of State of Mont., 1975; Franny award WPIX-TV, 1974. Mem. LWV, Roman Catholic. Club: Met. Rep. (pres. 1975-77). Contbr. tng. manuals, brochures for dept. on aging., 1973-85. Home: 435 E 70th St New York NY 10021 Office: 91 Fifth Ave 5th Floor New York NY 10003

REECE, CHERI DODSON, nurse, educator; b. Altoona, Pa., Apr. 17, 1946; d. Paul Francis and Evelyn Pearl (Brown) Dodson; diploma in nursing Western Pa. Hosp. Sch. Nursing, Pitts., 1967; B.S. in Nursing, Cedar Crest Coll., Allentown, Pa., 1969; MSN in Perinatal Nursing, Case Western Res. Univ., 1987; postgrad. in nursing Kent State U., 1979-83; 1 dau., Michelle Lynn. Nurse coll. infirmary, 1967-69; staff nurse Western Pa. Hosp., 1968; pvt. duty nurse, 1969, 78, 84-85; staff nurse Nason Hosp., Roaring Spring, Pa., 1969; instr. in-service edn. N.D. State Hosp., Jamestown, 1969-71; staff nurse Santa Clara Valley Med. Center, San Jose, Calif., 1971-72; instr. nursing San Jose Hosps. and Health Center, 1972-74; instr. nursing Kent State U., 1974-75, 78-84, Ohio Valley Hosp., Steubenville, Ohio, 1975-77; staff nurse Ashtabula (Ohio) Medicare Center, 1977-78; instr. adult edn. Ashtabula Joint Vocat. Sch., 1978-79; phys. exam. nurse Phys. Measurements, Inc., Ashtabula, 1978; grad. asst. Case Western Res. U., 1985-86; continuing edn. instr.; cons. well-baby care; staff and clin. nurse Home Health Services of Ashtabula County, 1986-87; clin. nursing faculty Cleve. State U., 1987; clin. nurse specialist Cape Fear Valley Med. Ctr., Fayetteville, N.C., 1987—. Active in campaign U.S. Rep., Am. Cancer Soc., Am. Heart Fund; patron Straw Hat Theatre; councilmatic aide Ashtabula City Council, 1981-83; head Center Shop at Ashtabula Arts Center, also patron. Mem. Nat. League Nursing, AAUW (sec. chpt. 1980-82, treas. 1983-85), Cedar Crest Coll. Alumni Assn., Alumni Assn. Claysburg-Kimmel High Sch., Harbor Music Boosters, Sigma Theta Tau. Office: Cape Fear Valley Med Ctr PO Box 2000 Fayetteville NC 28302

REECE, SHARON KAY, educator; b. Mansfield, Ohio, Jan. 29, 1951; d. William Harold and Reva Maxine (Bertsch) R. BS, Ohio State U., 1973, MEd, 1980. Tchr. Mansfield Bd. Edn., 1973—; owner Hen-Er-Ree Edn. Store, Mansfield, 1978 . Mem. United Ch. of Christ. Office: Hen-Er-Ree Inc 1339 Park Ave W Mansfield OH 44906

REED, BERENICE ANNE, art historian, artist, government official; b. Memphis, Jan. 1, 1934; d. Glenn Andrew and Berenice Marie (Kallaher) R. MFA in Painting and Art History, Istituto Pio XII, Villa Schifanoia, 1964. Cert. art tchr., Tenn. Comml. artist Memphis Pub. Co., 1955-56; arts adminstr., educator pub. and pvt. instns., Washington, Memphis, 1957-70; with fin. mgmt. service U.S. Treasury Dept., Washington, 1970—; cons. on art and architecture in recreation AIA, 1972-73; artist-in-residence St. Mary of the Woods Coll., Md., 1965; guest lectr., instr. Nat. Sch. Fine Arts, Tegucigalpa, Honduras, 1968; mem. exec. com. Parks, Arts and Leisure Project, Washington, 1972-73. Bd. dirs. Am. Irish Bicentennial Com., 1974-76; advisor Royal Oak Found. Recipient various awards for painting. Mem. Soc. Women Geographers, Nat. Soc. Arts and Letters, Ctr. for Advanced Study in Visual Arts, Art Barn Assn. (bd. dirs. 1973-83). Roman Catholic. Home: PO Box 34253 Bethesda MD 20817 Office: Dept Treasury Fin Mgmt Service 401 14th St SW Washington DC 20227

REED, CAROLYN LOUISE, computer specialist; b. Boonville, Ind., Feb. 6, 1953; d. Paul Adam Haas and Harriet Dorothy (Porter) Mohler; m. Robert Stephen Reed, Sept. 5, 1987. BA, Mo. So. State Coll., 1975. Programmer Mountain Bell, Denver, 1978-81, systems analyst, 1981—. Mem. ACLU, Nat. Assn. Realtors, Lakewood Jaycees, Data Process Mgmt. Assn. Home: 10938 W 31st Ave Lakewood CO 80215

REED, CYNTHIA JEAN, educational administrator, consultant; b. Rochester, N.Y., Nov. 24, 1956; d. Russell Roger and Jean Carolyn (Strobridge) R.; m. Douglas J. Treacy, Aug. 23, 1986. B.S. in Elem. Edn., SUNY-Oswego, 1978, M.S. in Edn., 1985; postgrad. SUNY-Cortland. Cert. elem. tchr., N.Y. Tchr., Fulton City Schs., N.Y., 1978-79; substitute tchr. Oswego and Fulton Schs., Oswego County, N.Y., 1979-80; tchr. for gifted Mexico Central Schs., N.Y., 1980-81; coordinator gifted edn. Jefferson-Lewis Bd. Coop. Ednl. Services, Glenfield, N.Y., 1981-82; tchr., coordinator gifted edn. Oswego County Bd. Coop. Ednl. Services, Mexico, N.Y., 1982-84; coordinator gifted edn. Onondaga-Cortland-Madison Bd. Coop. Ednl. Services, N.Y., 1984—. Mem. exec. com. Oswego County Environ. Mgmt. Council, 1980-81; mem. Cortland County Environ. Mgmt. Council, 1985-86. Mem. Assn. Supervision and Curriculum Devel., Advocacy for Gifted and Talented Edn., Phi Delta Kappa. Avocations: reading, hiking, camping, cooking, gardening. Office: Onondaga-Cortland-Madison BOCES 1710 Rt 13 Cortland NY 13045

REED, DENISE JEAN, restauranteur; b. Akron, Ohio, Jan. 30, 1951; d. John Davey and Gladys Mae (Bressler) Brooks; m. Earl Lee Reed, Aug. 24, 1968 (div. Sept. 1977); children: Dale Edward, David Lee; m. Richard Allen Guth, Sept. 30, 1978 (div. May 1987). AS in Restaurant Mgmt., Akron U., 1984, student, 1986—. Cook, server Deerfield (Ohio) Circle Pump, 1966-67; assembler Cleve. Electronics, Macedonia, Ohio, 1969-70; cook, server, dishwasher, prep cook, cashier East Park Restaurant, Ravenna, Ohio, 1972-80; car hop, cashier, cook, server East Park Drive-In, Ravenna, 1978-80; cook, prep cook, dishwasher Bavarian Haus I, Kent, Ohio, 1980-81; owner, operator Patterns & Pins, Ravenna, 1981-84; cook, prep cook, salead bar attendent, dishwasher Casey's Restaurant, Kent, 1982-83; asst. mgr. L&K Restaurant, Macedonia, 1984; mgr. Country Manor Family Restaurant, Kent, 1984—. Mem. Internat. Food Service Execs. Assn. (sec. U. Akron chpt. 1982-83, pres. 1983-84, scholar 1983-84), Nat. Assn. Female Execs. Democrat. Methodist. Home: 250 McKinney Blvd Kent OH 44240 Office: Country Manor Family Restaurant 427 E Main St Kent OH 44240

REED, DIANE GRAY, business information service company executive; b. Trion, Ga., Sept. 5, 1945; d. Harold and Frances (Parker) Gray; m. Harry Reed, Oct. 2, 1982. Student, Jacksonville U., 1963-64, Augusta Coll., 1972-74; BS, Ga. State U., 1981. Various mgmt. positions Equifax Services, Inc., Atlanta, 1964-72, field rep., 1972-74, tech. rep., 1974-79, mgr. systems and programs, 1979-84, dir. tech., 1984-86, asst. v.p., 1986—; presdl. adv. council Equifax Services, Atlanta, 1984—; cons. Ga. Computer Programmer Project, Atlanta, 1984-86, spkr. Oglethorpe U. Career Workshop, Atlanta, 1986. Bd. dirs. Atlanta Mental Health Assn., 1985—, Atlanta Women's Network, 1985—, United Way Bd. Bank, Atlanta, 1984-86; vol. Cobb County Spl. Olympics, Marietta, Ga., 1984-87; mem. adv. council Coll. Bus. Adminstrn. Ga. State U.; mgmt. info. systems industry adv. bd. U. Ga. Named Woman of Achievement 1987 Atlanta YWCA. Mem. Women in Info. Processing, Inst. Computer Profls. (cert.), Soc. Info. Mgmt., Internat. Women's Alliance, Ga. State Alumni, LWV. Club: Atlanta Yacht. Office: Equifax Services Inc 1600 Peachtree St NW Atlanta GA 30309

REED, DONNA LOUISE, public relations executive; b. Wichita, Kans., May 10, 1935; d. Joseph Melvin and Dorothy Yetta (Leben) Kogan; m. William Eugene Reed, Feb. 17, 1968; 1 child, Allison Lynn. Student, So. Meth. U., 1952-53, Dallas Coll. of So. Meth. U., 1955-56; BBA, U. Calif., Beverly Hills, 1986, postgrad. in bus. adminstrn., 1987—. Profl. registered parliamentarian. Pres. Preferred Printers, Inc., Dallas, 1960-68, 79—; dir. pub. relations Dallas Area Tb and Respiratory Disease Assn., 1969-71; free-lance pub. relations, 1972-78; mem. nat. pub. relations adv. by-laws com. Nat. Tb and Respiratory Disease Assn., N.Y.C., 1970-71, mem. Dallas Communications Council, 1983-84. Contbr. articles to profl. jours. Sponsor The 500, Inc.; mem. Dallas Ballet Exec. Com., Dallas Ballet Women's Com., Dallas Opera Guild, Dallas Mus. Fine Arts, Dallas Symphony Orch. League, Dallas Summer Musicals Guild, Dallas Theater Ctr. Women's Com., Dallas Rep. Forum, 1984—, Lake Highlands Rep. Women's Club, 1980—. Recipient Nat. Pub. Relations award Nat. Tb and Respiratory Disease Assn., 1970. Mem. Women in Communications (chpt. pres. 1973-74, Matrix award 1976), Women in Advt. (chpt. pres. 1972), Printing Industries Am., Am. Inst. Parliamentarians, Nat. Assn. Parliamentarians (pub. relations chairperson 1985-87), Tex. State Assn. Parliamentarians (editor Tex. Parliamentarian 1981, 2d v.p. 1983, 1st v.p. 1984, pres. 1985-86), Dallas Fedn. Women's Clubs, LWV, Phi Mu. Republican. Episcopalian. Club: Press of Dallas (Gridiron awards 1969, 72-74, 77, 80, 86). Lodges: Order Eastern Star (worthy matron 1971-72, 82-83, sec. 1987—), Daus. of Nile (queen 1979-80), Ladies Oriental Shrine of N.Am. (high priestess 1972-73), S.O.O.B., Order of the Rainbow for Girls (mother advisor 1972-73, 75-76, adult state officer 1981—), Past Matrons and Patrons Assn. Dallas (pres. 1980-81). Avocations: bridge, needlework. Office: Preferred Printers Inc 1207 Gano St Dallas TX 75215

REED, EDITH THERESA, actuary, employee benefits consultant; b. N.Y.C., Aug. 16, 1927; d. John James and Carolyn (Siebert) R. B.A., St. Joseph's Coll., 1949; postgrad. U. Mich., 1949-50. Actuarial asst. George B. Buck Cons. Actuaries, Inc., N.Y.C., 1950-57, asst. actuary 1957-74, assoc. cons. actuary, 1974-79, cons. actuary, 1979—. Fellow Conf. Actuaries in Pub. Practice; mem. Internat. Actuarial Assn., Am. Acad. Actuaries, Actuarial Soc. Greater N.Y. (formerly Actuaries Club N.Y.), Internat. Platform Assn., Nat. Assn. Female Execs., Am. Soc. Profl. and Exec. Women, Kappa Gamma Pi. Roman Catholic. Home: 300 E 40th St New York NY 10016 Office: George B Buck Cons Actuaries Inc 2 Pennsylvania Plaza New York NY 10121

REED, ELIZABETH, realtor, educator; b. Cheltenham, Eng., Nov. 29, 1949; came to U.S., 1951.; d. Stefan and Miroslawa (Dykert) Harvey; m. Thomas William Reed, May 18, 1968 (div. Oct. 1981); m. James Dale Yoakum, Aug. 16, 1986; stepchildren: Don Yoakum, Sheri Sanchez. BA, Calif. State U., Los Angeles, 1972, MA in Psychology, 1974. Cert. tchr., counselor. Keypunch operator ADP, Long Beach, Calif., 1974-77; instr. Long Beach City Coll., 1975-85; realtor Century 21 Action, Long Beach, 1977—, facilitator, 1986—. vol. counselor Cedar House for Sexually Abused Children and Their Families, 1985-86. Mem. Long Beach Dist. Bd. Realtors. Home: 218 Roycroft Ave Long Beach CA 90803 Office: Century 21 Action 3626 E Pacific Coast Hwy Long Beach CA 90804

REED, ELIZABETH ANN, nurse; b. Phila., July 14, 1943; d. Thomas B. and Ann B. (Kuzmann) R. Diploma, Thomas Jefferson U. Hosp. Sch. Nursing, Phila., 1961-64; student Temple U., 1964-68. R.N., Pa. Various nursing positions Thomas Jefferson U. Hosp., Phila., 1964-68, head nurse cardiac surgery, 1972; head nurse cardiovascular surgery Cooper Hosp., Camden, N.J., 1968-72, clin. coordinator cardiac surgery, 1972-75; head nurse clin. perfusion U. Calif.-San Francisco, 1975-76, quality assurance coordinator, 1976-78, adminstrv. nurse IV, 1978-86; operating room services supr. Pacific Presbyn. Med. Ctr., San Francisco, 1986—, dir. operating room services, 1985—; speaker numerous profl. meetings. Mem. Am. Nurses Assn., Calif. Nurses Assn., Assn. Operating Room Nurses (dir. 1977-81, dir. San Francisco chpt. 1980-84, various other offices), Nurse's Alumnae Assn. Thomas Jefferson U. Hosp. Sch. Nursing, Assn. Advancement Med. Instrumentation (dir. 1981-84). Contbg. author Alexander's Care of the Patient in Surgery, 1978, 7th edit., 1983; contbr. numerous articles and papers to profl. jours. Home: 7 Majorca Ct San Rafael CA 94903 Office: Pacific Presbyn Med Ctr PO Box 7999 (P3101) San Francisco CA 94123

REED, JANE GARSON, controller, accounting educator; b. Cleve., Jan. 11, 1948; d. Joseph John Guzowski and Irene Sophie (Dominic) Garson; m. Wayne Ellis Reed, May 17, 1969; children: Craig Michael, Kevin Matthew. BBA magna cum laude, Baldwin Wallace Coll., 1977; MBA, Case Western Res. U., 1983. CPA, Ohio. Letter carrier U.S. Postal Service, Brecksville, Ohio, 1966-76; sr. asst. acct. Deloitte, Haskins & Sells, Cleve., 1977-78; sr. corp. auditor White Motor Corp., Beachwood, Ohio, 1979-81; instr. acctg. Cuyahoga Community Coll., Parma, 1981-82; ind. contractor State of Wash., Olympia, 1982-84; dir. fin. The Montefiore Home, Cleveland Heights, Ohio, 1985-86; controller, bus. mgr. Western Res. Human Services, Inc., Akron, Ohio, 1986-87; lectr. mgmt. acctg. U. Akron, 1987-88; controller Multi-Care Mgmt. Co., Beachwood, 1988—; instr. acctg. Cuyahoga Community Coll., Parma, Ohio, 1981, 82. Fin. sec. to bd. dirs. Prince of Peace Luth. Ch., Medina, Ohio, 1978-79; mem. budget and fin. com. Wooster (Ohio) dist. office United Meth. Ch., 1983-84; mem. Brunswick High Sch. Band and Choir Boosters, 1984—; cub scout leader Boy Scouts Am., Brunswick, 1978-79; agt. Trinity High Sch. Alumni; mem. fin. com. Brunswick United Meth. Ch., 1988—, also budget com., 1988—. Mem. Am. Inst. CPA's, Am. Women's Soc. CPA's, Ohio Soc. CPA's (mem.-in-industry com. 1980-82), Nat. Assn. Accts., Soc. for Advancement Mgmt. (reactivated chpt. pres 1976-77). Methodist. Home: 1254 Hadcock Rd Brunswick OH 44212 Office: Multi-Care Mgmt 3659 S Green Rd Suite 320 Beachwood OH 44122

REED, JANNENE GRIFFITH, newspaper editor, publisher; b. Wayne, Nebr., Feb. 8, 1929; d. Frank Marion and Pearl (Stone) Griffith; m. Donald R. Reed, Apr. 5, 1953; children: Cameron Leigh, Barbara Jayne. BA, Wayne State Coll., 1951; student Kearney State Coll., 1956. Woman's feature editor Wayne (Nebr.) Herald, 1947-53; comml. artist Gen. Telephone, Chgo., 1953-55; instr. art Vermillion (S.D.) Schs., 1955-59; copywriter C.S. Wo Co., Honolulu, 1971-73; program dir. Gospel Light Publs., Glendale, Calif., 1975-78; stringer Pasadena (Calif.) Star-News, 1975-78; editor San Marino (Calif.) Tribune, 1978-80; editor, pub. Sierra Madre (Calif.) News, 1980—; Mem. steering com. Main Street program Sierra Madre; fin. chmn. Boy Scouts Am., Sierra Madre. Bd. dirs. Meth. Hosp. So. Calif., Arcadia, 1983—. Named Editor of Yr., SAR, 1982-83; SAR Community Spirit award; One Earth award Sierra Madre Environ. Action Council. Mem. Soc. Profl. Journalists, Sierra Madre C. of C., Sigma Delta Chi. Republican. Presbyterian. Lodge: Kiwanis. Office: Sierra Madre News 9 Kersting Ct Sierra Madre CA 91024

REED, JEAN SALAS, educational administrator; b. Torreon, N.Mex., Aug. 30, 1940; d. Ross Ray and Cora (Lopez) Salas; m. Cliff A. Reed, July 19, 1974. B.A. in Social Scis., Siena Heights Coll., 1969; M.A. in Ednl. Adminstrn., U. N.Mex., 1972, Edn. Specialist in Ednl. Adminstrn., 1974. Counselor Jobs for Progress, Albuquerque, 1971-72; tchr. Los Lunas Pub. Sch., N.Mex., 1972; edn. specialist N.Mex. State Dept. Edn., Santa Fe, 1973-75; prin. Harrington Jr. High Sch., Santa Fe, 1975-78, Capshaw Jr. High Sch., Santa Fe, 1978-86; asst. supt. elem. edn. Santa Fe Pub. Schs. 1986—; resident advisor Job Corp Ctr. for Women, Albuquerque, 1971-72; prin. Holy Rosary Sch., Albuquerque, 1970-71; tchr. Co. of Mary Schs., Los Angeles, 1965-70. Bd. dirs. Cancer Soc., Santa Fe, N.Mex., 1982-85. Mem. Nat. Assn. Secondary Sch. Prins., N.Mex. Sch. Adminstrs. (mem. bd. 1981-85, pres. 1986-87), N.Mex. Assn. Secondary Sch. Prins. (pres. 1981-82, honors for excellence program 1984), Phi Delta Kappa, Delta Kappa Gamma (pres. 1982-84, edn. scholar 1980). Democrat. Roman Catholic. Home: 1915 Camino Lumbre Santa Fe NM 87501 Office: Santa Fe Pub Schs 610 Alta Vista Santa Fe NM 87501

REED, JOELLEN, ombudsman; b. Winchester, Ky., May 18, 1953; d. Joe F. and Betty (Haggard) R. BS in Elem. Edn. and Early Childhood, Ea. Ky. U., 1975, MA, 1979. Tchr. elem. sch. Clark County Schs., Winchester, 1975-85; cons. Ky. Dept. Edn., Frankfort, 1985-86, dir. recognition div., 1986, ombudsman, 1986-88, liaison to edn. and humanities cabinet, 1988; advance for Gov. Wallace Wlikinson and spl. asst. to sec. Edn. and Humanity 1988—. Chmn. Clark County Heart Fund, 1970, 74, co-chmn., 1971, 77, 78; advisor Frontier Chpt. ARC, 1976-78; vol. Clark County Hosp., 1968-70; program coordinator Coll. and U. Partnership Program, 1981; asst. leader Girl Scouts U.S., 1973-74; sponsor youth club Fannie Bush Elem. Sch., 1978, ARC youth club, Leadership Ky., 1986; mem. Winchester Art Guild, Clark County Assn. for Handicapped Citizens; local chmn. Tchrs. on Target for Dems., 1983; aide Alice McDonald for Lt. Gov. Ky., 1987; mem. Dem. Women's Club Ky., 1984—, state page Dem. Nat. Convention, 1984; pres. Aplastic Anemia Found, 1981, Bapt. Young Women, 1976-81; mem. council Women's Missionary Union, 1976-81; mem. various coms. Cen. Bapt. Ch.; bd. dirs. Hospice of Clark County, 1983, Big Bros./Big Sisters of Winchester, 1981-85, Leadership Winchester, Winchester Council for the Arts, Winchester Jaycees, Leadership Ky. Alumni Assn., 1984-86. Named One of Outstanding Young Women of Am., 1984, Outstanding Young Career Woman, Clark County Bus. and Profl. Women, 1978, Outstanding Young Leader WInchester Jaycees, 1988; recipient Heart Assn. Family award State of Ky., 1977, Women of Achievement award YWCA of Lexington, 1987. Mem. Ea. Ky. U. Alumni Assn. (life), U. Ky. Alumni Assn. (assoc., bd. dirs. local chpt. 1986—), Mended Hearts, Inc., Kappa Delta Pi. Home: 526 S Maple St Winchester KY 40391 Office: Office of Gov 1st Floor Capital Plaza Tower Frankfort KY 40601

REED, KAREN ANN, academic administrator, educator; b. Alliance, Ohio, Nov. 21, 1955; d. Eugene Williams and Virginia Rose (Aebi) R.; m. Ronald L. Headley, May 24, 1980 (div. 1987). BS, Mt. Union Coll., 1977; MBA, Lake Erie Coll., 1984. Registered med. technologist, Ohio. Med. technologist Southgate Med. Labs., Maple Heights, Ohio, 1976-78, Hillcrest Hosp., Mayfield Heights, Ohio, 1978-85; program mgr., career cons. Cuyahoga Community Coll., Cleve., 1985—. Mem. Nat. Inst. Leadership Devel., 1987. Ednl. Foundations Dept. scholar U. Akron, 1987; recipient Fisher award, 1983. Mem. Am. Soc. Clin. Pathologists, Ohio Soc. Allied Health Profls. (program com. 1987—), Clevc. Area Program Dirs., Am. Assn. Women in Community and Jr. Colls., Pi Kappa Delta, Alpha Eta Soc. Republican. Methodist. Home: 17628 Winslow Rd Shaker Heights OH 44120 Office: Cuyahoga Community Coll 2900 Community College Ave Cleveland OH 44115

REED, LESLIE CASETTA, safety and health director; b. Wausau, Wis., Nov. 24, 1958; d. Duane Joseph and Margaret Rose (Major) Casetta; m. Michael Lowell Reed, Oct. 17, 1981. BS in Edn., U. Wis., Whitewater, 1981; postgrad., No. Ill. U., 1983—. Engr. safety Abbott Labs., North Chicago, Ill., 1981-82; engr. material and process Zenith Radio, Glenview, Ill., 1982-83; indsl. hygienist Occupational Safety and Health Adminstrn. div. U.S. Dept. Labor, North Aurora, Ill., 1983-86; dir. safety and health Rockford (Ill.) Products Corp., 1986-88, sr. indsl. hygienist, 1988—. Recipient community service award Rockford Fire Dept., 1986. Mem. Am. Mgmt. Assn., Am. Conf. Govtl. Indsl. Hygienists, Am. Soc. Safety Engrs., Nat. Fire Protection Assn. Roman Catholic. Home: 610 N 7th Rochelle IL 61068

REED, L'TANYA DECARLOSIS, insurance executive; b. Bessemer, Ala., June 9, 1953; d. Val Sr. and Eula Mae (Young) R. BA, Miles Coll., 1975; MA, U. Ill., 1977. Ins. claims adjuster GAB Bus. Services, Inc., Atlanta, 1978—. dir. Success Counseling Ctr., Atlanta, 1987—. Named one of Outstanding Young Women Am., 1981. mem. Atlanta Claims Assn., Nat. Assn. Female Execs., Nat. Assn. Insurance Women, Miles Coll. Alumni Assn. (sec. 1984-86, pres. 1987—, editor newsletter 1984—, Outstanding Service award 1985—). Home: 1111 Clairmont Rd Decatur GA 30030 Office: GAB Bus Services Inc 1401 W Paces Ferry Rd NW Atlanta GA 30327

REED, MARGARET ANNE, actress; b. Salinas, Calif., Nov. 15, 1956; d. Frank Joseph and Mary Dean (Biringer) R. BA, U. Calif., Santa Cruz, 1978; MFA, Cornell U., 1981. tchr., coach, N.Y.C., 1981—; actress, developer Manhattan Class Co., N.Y.C., 1983—. Appeared in plays including The Taming of the Shrew, 1981, All My Sons, 1982, The Mayor of Zalamea, 1983, Twelfth Night, 1983, The Beckett Plays, 1983; toured with John Houseman's The Acting Co., 1982-83; stars in TV series As the World Turns, 1985—. Mem. AFTRA, Actor's Equity Assn., NOW. Democrat.

REED, MARGARET CAROL, nurse; b. Frankfort, Ky., Nov. 29, 1935; d. Regis Francis and Margaret Frances (Moore) Whitehead; m. Clyde E. Reed, May 9, 1964 (div.); children—Suzanne, Rebecca Lynn. Diploma, Nazareth Sch. Nursing, 1958. Registered nurse, Ky.; lic. ins. rep., Ky. Head nurse critical care unit, intensive care unit King's Daus. Hosp., Frankfort, Ky., 1970-77; sr. regional adminstr. Ky. Peer Rev. Orgn., Louisville, 1977-81; dir. Assoc. Care Service, 1983-85; health care cons., 1985—. Pres. Franklin County (Ky.) Republican Women, 1966, 78; 4th v.p. Ky. Fedn. Rep. Women, 1979; activities dir. Good Shepherd Parish Council, 1976, 77, 78; staff senate Rep. Leadership Ky. Gen. Assembly, 1988; eucharistic minister Good Shephard Parish. Mem. Ky. Nurses Assn. (bd. dirs. polit. action com., 1979). Roman Catholic. Office: PO Box 1141 Frankfort KY 40602

REED, MARLENE MINTS, educator; b. San Antonio, Sept. 25, 1937; d. Woodie John and Heloise (Pittman) Mints; B.B.A., Baylor U., 1959; M.B.A., N.E. La. U., 1977; D.B.A., La. Tech. U., 1981; m. Bill J. Reed, Aug. 29, 1958; children—Lisa Rochelle, William Barclay. Various positions in industry, Houston, Ft. Worth, Monroe, La., and Birmingham, Ala., 1959-73; asst. prof. mgmt. N.E. La. U., 1979-81; assoc. prof. mgmt. and econs. Sch. Bus., Samford U., Birmingham, 1981—; dir. London Study Ctr. Samford U.; cons. small bus. Named Most Disting. Prof. Bus., Alpha Kappa Psi, 1982, J. Buchanan disting. tchr. Samford U., 1984. Mem. Acad. Mgmt., S.W. Small Bus. Inst. Assn., Nat. Bus. Edn. Assn., SW Decision Scis. Inst., Beta Gamma Sigma, Omicron Delta Epsilon, Delta Pi Epsilon, Pi Omega Pi, Kappa Kappa Gamma, Omicron Delta Kappa, Phi Kappa Phi. Republican. Baptist (Sunday Sch. tchr.). Home: 1582 Panorama Dr Birmingham AL 35216 Office: Samford U Sch Bus 800 Lakeshore Dr Birmingham AL 35229

REED, MARSHA LEE, personnel agency executive, consultant; b. Pitts., Sept. 8, 1953; d. Milton and Ruth (Farber) Denmark; m. David P. Reed, Sept. 4, 1977; children—Diane, Robert. B.Gen. Studies, Ohio U., 1975. Cons. Devonshire Personnel, Garden Grove, Calif., 1977-79, Mgmt. Recruiters, Miami, Fla., 1979-80; unit mgr. Dunhill Personnel, Miami, 1980-82; owner, pres. Markett Personnel, Miami, 1982—. Mem. Nat. Assn. Personnel Cons., Nat. Assn. Female Execs., Nat. Assn. Female Bus. Owners, Fla. Assn. Personnel Cons., Bus. and Profl. Women, Greater Miami Jewish Fedn., Kappa Delta (social chmn. 1973-75), Kappa Delta Alumni Assn. Democrat. Club: Hadassah (Miami). Avocations: reading; piano playing. Home: 11124 SW 132d Ct Miami FL 33186 Office: Markett Personnel PO Box 162-211 Miami FL 33116

REED, MARTHA ANN, public affairs specialist; b. Houston, Sept. 8, 1930; d. Emmett Conway and Evelyn Ysleta (Spurlock) Swain; student Tex. Christian U., 1948-50; A.A., U. Houston, 1956; m. Charles G. Reed, Apr. 20, 1974; children by previous marriage—Rebecca Hemphill Sanders, Ann Hemphill Byrns, Steven Earl. Tchr., Oakdale, La., 1956-60, Goose Creek, Tex., 1962-64; assoc. editor Oakdale Jour., 1959-62; women's editor Baytown (Tex.) Sun, 1963-70; lifestyle editor Beaumont (Tex.) Enterprise & Jour., 1970-77; dir. pub. info. Lamar u., 1977-79; spl. asst. to supt. Port Arthur (Tex.) Ind. Sch. Dist., 1979-82; pub. affairs dir. John E. Gray Inst., Beaumont, Tex., 1982-85; pub. relations coordinator McFaddin-Ward Hist. House Mus., 1985—. Mem. spl. grand jury, Jefferson County, Tex.; Sabine Oaks Sr. Citizens Home. Named Sagamore of the Wabash, 1979, Ky. Col., 1981, Adm. Nebr. Navy, 1981; named to Southeast Tex. Women's Hall of Fame, 1984. Mem. Nat. Fedn. Press Women (past pres.), Tex. Press Women (past pres.), Southeast Tex. Press Club, Internat. Assn. Bus. Communicators, Beaumont Art Mus., Beaumont Visitor and Conv. Bur., Beaumont Heritage

Soc., Lamar U. Friends of Arts, Beta Sigma Phi (hon. internat. mem.) Contbr. articles in field. Office: 1906 North St Beaumont TX 77701

REED, MARY DIANE, advertising executive; b. Santa Monica, Calif., May 30, 1941; d. Floyd Leonard and Suzanne Lucille (Bryant) Creson; m. George Edward Calkin, Feb. 3, 1957 (div. Feb. 1967); children: George, Christopher, Holly; m. William Gerald Reed, Feb. 16, 1968 (div. Dec. 1975); stepchildren: Joseph, Susan, Nancy, Steven. Student, Fullerton Jr. Coll., U. Calif., Irvine; BA in Communications with honors, Calif. Christian U. Mng. editor Huntington Beach (Calif.) Ind., 1964-71, 73-77; dir. advt. Far West Savs., Newport Beach, Calif., 1978-81, United Savs., Culver City, Calif., 1981-83; pres. United Mktg., Long Beach, Calif., 1983-85; talk show hostess Sta. KPRO, Riverside, Calif, 1985; sr. v.p. mktg. and advt. Am. Savs., Irvine, 1985—. Author: The Underground Wedding Book (Best Adult Book award 1973), The Holy Terror, 1978, The Real Thing, 1978, The Oh, What a Wonderful Wedding Book, 1984; ghost writer 6 books; contbr. numerous articles to newspapers, mags. Polit. cons. to 8 Orange County campaigns, 1978-84. Appointed Lady of the Equestrian Order of the Knights of the Holy Sepulcher by Pope John Paul II, 1987; recipient B/PAA award, 1987, and over 200 other awards; named Corporate Role Model Female Exec. Mag., 1987. Mem. Nat. Assn. Female Execs. (Named Corp. Role Model 1987), Orange County Advt. Fedn., Calif. Savs. and Loan League, Nat. Fedn. Press Women (bd. dirs., 1971, 73), Nat. Sch. Pub. Relations Assn. Democrat. Clubs: Orange County Press Women (pres. 1971, 73), Orange County Press (sec. 1969, 70). Office: Am Savs and Loan Assn 18401 Von Karman Irvine CA 92713

REED, NELDA MELINDA, wholesale executive; b. Chatsworth, Ga., Feb. 26, 1959; d. Ruben Franklin and Mary Nell (Peeples) Calfee; m. Ricky Thomas, July 4, 1976 (div. July 1986); children: Deanna Vanessa, Shawn Dedrick. Sales rep., customer service, mktg. Mica Inc., Chatsworth, 1973-80; pres. Flagship Carpets Inc., Chatsworth, 1980—. Office: Flagship Carpets Inc PO Box 1189 Chatsworth GA 30705

REED, ROSEMARY, training educator, consultant; b. Worcester, Mass., Dec. 11, 1952; d. George Albion and Rosa Mae (Duncan) R. B.S. in Speech, Emerson Coll., 1974; M.Ed., Worcester State Coll., 1976; postgrad. U. Mass., 1980; M.B.A., Anna Maria Coll., 1986. Cert. tchr., Mass. Communication instr. Suffolk U., Boston, 1976-78, 81-83, Fitchburg State Coll., Mass., 1978-80; edn. adminstr. Option Program, Haverhill, Mass., 1981-83; edn. dir. Stetson Sch., Barre, Mass., 1983-85; corp. recruiter Positions Inc., Westborough, Mass., 1985; tchr. Butler Ctr., Westborough, 1985—; tng. mgr. Future Products, Worcester, 1986-87; tng. cons. A-Z Vacuum Mart, Worcester, 1987—. Author, editor accreditation programs; mem. Barre Players. Recipient Horace Mann Teaching grant, 1987; named Tchr. of Yr., Bur. of Instl. Schs., 1988.Mem. Nat. Assn. Female Execs., Am. Soc. Tng. and Devel., Corrections Edn. Assn. Avocations: acting; reading; vegetarian cooking; program development research. Home and Office: Oak Ln Spencer MA 01562

REED, SALLY D., foundation executive; b. Lynwood, Calif., May 20, 1955; d. William H. and Sally Frances (Hayes) Gibson. A.A., Cooke County Coll., 1975; B.S.Ed., Southwestern U., 1978. Tchr. civics Killeen High Sch., Tex., 1978-81; dir. devel. Nat. Conservative Polit. Action Com., Alexandria, Va., 1981-83; founder, chmn. Nat. Council for Better Edn., Alexandria, Va., 1983—. Pres., Conservative Youth Found., Alexandria, 1984—, Profl. Educators Guild, 1984—. Author: NEA: Propaganda Front of the Radical Left, 1983; A Parent's Survival Guide to the Public Schools, 1985. Republican. Roman Catholic. Office: Nat Council Better Edn 805 Cameron St Alexandria VA 22314

REEDER, VIRGINIA LEE (FOSTER), educator; b. Tuskahoma, Okla., Jan. 25, 1929; d. Clarence William and Alice (King) Foster; m. Walter Lee Reeder, July 24, 1950; children: Ralph Wesley, Alice Jean. BA, U. Redlands, 1974; MS, Pepperdine U., 1976. Elem. tchr. Harbor City Pub. Schs., 1960-61, First Bapt. Sch., Compton, Calif., 1961-64, Compton Unified Sch., 1980—; head start tchr. Compton Community Youth Ctr., Compton, 1964-76, Charles R. Drew Sch., Compton, 1976-80; tchr. early childhood edn. Compton Coll., 1974—. Democrat. Baptist. Home: 11919 E 161st St Norwalk CA 90650

REED-GROSS, PATRICIA ELAINE, educator; b. Charleston, S.C., Dec. 17, 1952; d. David and Theodocia (Kennedy) Reed; m. Neil Gross, Sept. 26, 1980. BS, Winthrop Coll., 1974, MEd, 1976; postgrad. U. S.C., Columbia Coll., S.C., 1978—. Head spl. edn. Chester County Pub. Schs., Chester, S.C., 1976-77; spl. edn. cons. Winthrop Coll., Rock Hill, S.C., 1977-78; tchr. aphasic children S.C. Sch. for Deaf and Blind, Spartanburg, 1978-79; tchr. juvenile delinquents Spartanburg Boys' Home, S.C., 1979-80; tchr. learning disabled Springdale Sch., Camden, S.C., 1981-84; tchr. emotionally handicapped Hillcrest High Sch., Sumter, S.C., 1984-85; head tchr. autistic adults Pine Grove Sch., Elgin, S.C., 1985—; tchr. severely and profoundly retarded Dept. Mental Retardation, Columbia, 1986—; tchr. learning disabled and emotionally handicapped children Maryville Elem. Sch., Georgetown, S.C., 1987—; tchr. adult edn. Manning Correctional Instn., Columbia, 1981—; companion Columbia Area Mental Health, 1981-84. Mem. Nat. Assn. Female Execs. Baha'i. Avocations: swimming, camping. Home: PO Box 8393 Georgetown SC 29440 Office: Georgetown Pub Sch Dist Georgetown SC 29440

REED-RANDOLPH, SHIRLEY FAY, state public health administrator; b. Peoria, Ill., Sept. 19, 1936; d. Charles Edward and Ruby Fay (Williams) Sanders; m. Willard Franklyn Reed, Dec. 31, 1960 (dec. July 1971); children—Franklin Edward, Charles Thomas; m. 2d, Verdun Randolph, Oct. 16, 1982. B.S., U. Ill.-Champaign-Urbana, 1958; M.S. in Pub. Health, U. Mo.-Columbia, 1968. Continuity writer, traffic mgr. Sta. WPEO, Peoria, Ill., 1958-60; continuity writer Sta. WMAY, Springfield, Ill., 1960-61; copywriter McKay Advt. Agy., Phoenix, 1961-62; mem. pub. relations staff Motorola Semi-Conductor Products div., Phoenix, 1962-63; staff writer Ill. State Jour. and Register, Springfield, 1963-65; with Dept. Pub. Health State Ill., Springfield, 1965, adminstrv. asst. Bur. of Personal and Community Health, 1973-74, exec. asst. Office Health Services, 1974-76, chief div. local health services, 1976-79, assoc. dir., 1979—; guest lectr. Sangamon State U., Springfield, 1979—, adj. prof. health services adminstrn., mem. Health Industry Council, 1982—; preceptor dept. community health St. Louis U. Contbr. articles to profl. jours. Bd. dirs. Family Planning of Sangamon County, Inc., Springfield, 1969-71; bd. dirs. Ounce of Prevention Fund, Chgo., 1982—. Mem. Am. Pub. Health Assn. (mem. exec. bd., 1987—, editorial ady. com., 1986, governing council 1978-81, 86-91, sect. bd. 1981-83, chmn. health adminstrn. sect. 1986), Ill. Pub. Health Assn. (mem. exec. council 1969-71, sec. 1977-79, program chmn. 1980-81), Ill. Soc. Health Educators (pres. 1974-75). Methodist. Office: Ill Dept Pub Health 535 W Jefferson St Springfield IL 62761

REES, DIANE DEMURO, lobbyist, governmental and public relations affairs consultant; b. Muskegon, Mich., Jan. 8, 1939; d. Robert Guydon and Elizabeth (Hradsky) DeMuro; m. Thomas F. Rees, 1960 (div. Dec. 1984); children: Elizabeth, Dana, Andrew. BA in English, U. Colo., 1964, MA in English Lit., 1969. Reporter Colorado Springs (Colo.) Gazette Telegraph, 1959-60; reporter, librarian Star-Jour, and Chieftain, Pueblo, Colo., 1960; writer U. Colo. Conf. Bur., Boulder, 1967-73; pres. sec. to Congressman Donald G. Brotzman, Boulder, 1973-74; Repub. caucus pres. sec. Colo. Ho. of Reps., Denver, 1975-76; legis. research dir. AMAX, Inc., Golden, Colo., 1976-79; dir. state govtl. affairs AMAX, Inc., Golden, 1979-85; lobbyist, pub. relations cons. Friendly Persuasion, Boulder, 1985—; bd. dirs. Ft. Howard Corp., Green Bay, Wis.; cons. in field. Chmn. Boulder County Young Republicans, 1971; sec. Boulder County Rep. Com., 1972-73; mem. Colo. Rep. Cen. Com., 1972-80; active numerous congl., state and local Rep. campaigns; mem. exec. com. Colo. Pub. Expenditures Council, 1985—; bd. dirs. Boulder Pow Wow Rodeo, 1972-74, Colo. Mining Assn., 1982—. Mem. Internat. Rodeo Writers (sec. 1972-73, pres. 1973-75). Home and Office: 783 Cypress Dr Boulder CO 80303

REES, NORMA S., educator, university system vice chancellor; b. N.Y.C., Dec. 27, 1929; d. Benjamin and Lottie (Schwartz) D.; m. Raymond R. Rees, Mar. 19, 1960; children—Evan Lloyd, Raymond Arthur. B.A., Queens Coll., 1952; M.A., Bklyn. Coll., 1954; Ph.D., NYU, 1959. Cert. speech-language pathology, audiology. Prof. communicative disorders Hunter Coll., N.Y.C., 1967-72; exec. officer, speech and hearing scis. grad. sch. CUNY, N.Y.C., 1972-74, assoc. dean for grad. studies, 1974-76, dean grad. studies, 1976-82; vice chancellor for acad. affairs U. Wis.-Milw., 1982-85, 86—, acting chancellor, 1985-86; vice chancellor for acad. and student affairs Mass. Bd. Regent for Higher Edn., 1987—; mem. editorial bd. Jour. Speech and Hearing Research, 1980—, British Jour. Disorders of Communications, 1982—; bd. dirs. Council of Postsecondary Accreditation, Washington, 1985—. Contbr. articles to profl. jours. Trustee Citizens Govtl. Research Bur., Milw., 1985-87; mem. Task Force onw Wis. World Trade Ctr., 1985-87. Fellow Am. Speech-Lang.-Hearing Assn. (honors); mem. Nat. Assn. State Univs. and Land Grant Colls. (com. accreditation 1987—), Internat. Assn. for Study of Child Lang. Home: 120 Beaconsfield Rd Brookline MA 02146 Office: Mass Bd Regents Higher Edn 1 Ashburton Pl McCormack Bldg Room 1401 Boston MA 02108-1530

REESE, BARBARA ANN, federal employment and training program executive; b. Amsterdam, N.Y., Jan. 4, 1951; d. Arnold Alvin and Margaret Anna (Black) R.; 1 child, Evan Hamilton. AA, Fulton-Montgomery Community Coll., Johnstown, N.Y., 1971; BA in Sociology, State U. Coll., Oneonta, N.Y., 1973. Sr. welfare examiner Montgomery County Dept. Social Services, Fonda, N.Y., 1973-76; dist. dir. Green Thumb Inc., Cortland, N.Y., 1976-77, asst. dir., 1977-82, dir., 1982—. Active Cortland County Community Council, 1985, United Fund Cortland County, 1984-86; bd. dirs. YWCA, Cortland, 1987-88. Mem. Nat. Assn. Female Execs. Inc., Internat. Mgmt. Council. Episcopalian. Club: Bus. and Profl. Women (Amsterdam). Lodge: Zonta Internat. Home: 106 W Main St Cortland NY 13045 Office: Green Thumb Inc 7 Central Ave Cortland NY 13045

REESE, DANA ELIZABETH, real estate executive; b. Greenwood, S.C., Sept. 18, 1955; d. Richard Black and Jacquelyn Nenice (Hulsey) R. Grad. high sch., Greenwood. Cert. emergency med. technician. Owner Great Southern Glass Works, Crystal River, Fla., 1979—; pres. Crystal River Trading Co., 1984-87; owner, mgr. Glen Aire Apts., Crystal River, 1985—. Mem. Rainbow River Conservation, Inc., Dunnellon, Fla., 1984—, Downtown Merchants Assn., Dunnellon, 1985-86; firefighter, emergency med. technician, exec. dir. Connell Heights Vol. Fire Dept., Crystal River, 1986—. Named one of Outstanding Young Women Am., 1987. Home and Office: 129 SE Paradise Point Crystal River FL 32629

REESE, DIANE MARIE, analyst, criminal justice researcher; b. Metter, Ga., Nov. 5, 1959; d. Levy Jr. and Leola (Holloway) B.; m. James Richard Reese III, Oct. 14, 1959; children: Brandi J., Shannon Rae. BS, Savannah State Coll., 1980. Data technician Diversified Data Corp., Springfield, Va., 1981-82; messenger FBI, Washington, 1982-83; customer service rep., security agt. Sears, Roebuck & Co., Yuma, Ariz., 1984; community youth services coordinator Yuma County Juvenile Ct. Ctr., Yuma, 1984-86; analyst Diversified Data Corp., Springfield, Va., 1987; intensive probation counselor 18th Dist. Jud. Juvenile and Domestic Relations Ct. Service Unit, Alexandria, Va., 1987—. Counselor Yuma County Juvenile Ct. Ctr., 1984-86; cochmn. Yuma County Coordinating Council Task Force for Big Bros./Big Sisters, 1985-86. Mem. Nat. Assn. Female Execs., Delta Sigma Theta. Democrat. Baptist. Home: 7302 Bath St Springfield VA 22150 Office: Alexandria 18th Jud Dist 520 King St Alexandria VA 22304

REESE, ELLEN PULFORD, psychologist, writer; b. Hartford, Conn., Aug. 30, 1926; d. Alfred Ely and Katherine Cary (Cook) P.; m. Thomas Whelan Reese, Dec. 17, 1949. B.A., Mt. Holyoke Coll., South Hadley, Mass., 1948, M.A., 1954. Lic. psychologist, Mass. Research asst. Mt. Holyoke Coll., 1948-56, asst. dir. psychol. labs., 1956-64, dir. psychol. labs., 1964-69, lectr. psychology, 1970-80, assoc. prof., 1980-85, prof., 1986—; v.p. Hampshire Communications, Amherst, Mass., 1969-76. Author books including: Human Behavior, 1978; (with Beth Sulzer-Azaroff) Applying Behavior Analysis, 1982; author, dir. ednl. films including: Behavior Theory in Practice, 1965, Imprinting, 1968; mem. editorial bd. Behavior Modification, 1977—. Trustee Cambridge Ctr. Behavioral Studies, Cambridge, Mass., 1981—, Loomis Chaffee Sch., Windsor, Conn., 1973-87. Recipient award for disting. contbn. to edn. in psychology Am. Psychol. Found., 1986, award Loomis Chaffee Sch., 1987; Mt. Holyoke Coll. grantee, 1970, 71, 75, 77, 81, 83, 84, 87. Fellow Am. Psychol. Assn. (mem. exec. com. Div. 25 1973-75 77-79), Assn. for Behavior Analysis (mem. council 1981-86, pres. 1984), Animal Behavior Soc., N.Y. Acad. Scis., Sigma Xi. Office: Mount Holyoke Coll South Hadley MA 01075

REESE, KATHLEEN B., utility executive; b. Chgo., Feb. 17, 1949; d. David Jenkins and Shirley Lois (Kaltneger) B.; m. Wilson A. Reese; children—Elizabeth Alexandra, Christopher John, Melanie Suong, Sheryl Louise, Jacquelyn Cassandra. B.S., U. Wis., 1972; M.B.A., Nova U., 1984. Project specialist U. Wis., 1972-73, research asst., 1968-72; water quality control technician City of Ft. Lauderdale, Fla., 1974-75; treatment plant operator II Broward County (Fla.) Utilities Dept., Lauderdale Lakes, 1975-80, treatment plant mgr., 1980-84, spl. projects coordinator II, Pompano Beach, 1984-86, spl. project coordinator III, 1986—. Mem. Am. Water Works Assn., Am. Soc. Pub. Adminstrn., Fla. Water and Pollution Control Operators Assn., Nat. Water Well Assn., AAUW, Fla. Renaissance Guild, Nat. Assn. Female Execs. Clubs: Fla. Renaissance Guild, Eastern Star. Contbr. articles to profl. publs. Office: 2401 N Powerline Rd Pompano Beach FL 33069

REESE, KATHLEEN LEANN, marketing and promotion executive, consultant; b. Akron, Ohio, Nov. 7, 1954; d. Bruce Maynard and Margaret Ann (Gebert) R. BA in Communication, Bowling Green State U., 1977. Comml. copywriter Sta. WTOL-TV, Toledo, 1977-78; advt. specialist Andersons, Maumee, Ohio, 1978-79, pub. relations specialist, 1979-81; dir. on-air promotion Sta. KXAS-TV, Dallas, Ft. Worth, 1981-83; creative services dir. Sta. WAVY-TV, Portsmouth, Va., 1983—. Promotion coordinator Norfolk Com. for Prevention Child Abuse Celebrity Night Fundraiser, annually 1984-87; bd. dirs. Assn. Retarded Citizens, Norfolk, 1984; bd. dirs. AMC Cancer Research Ctr., Hampton Roads Chpt., 1986, 87; bd. dirs. Campus East Community Assn., 1986, 87, pres., 1986; bd. dirs., v.p. Greenbrier Civic League, 1987. Recipient Silver award Advt. Club Toledo, 1980, Promotion of Yr. award Va. Assn. Broadcasters, 1986. Mem. Broadcast Promotion Mktg. Execs. (Gold medallion, Merit award 1985), Advt. Fedn. Greater Hampton Roads, AD 2 Toledo (pres. 1980), Am. Women in Radio and TV (v.p. 1980), Kappa Delta. Avocations: writing, sailing, golf, travel. Office: WAVY TV Sta 801-Wavy St Portsmouth VA 23704

REESE, MARTHA GRACE, minister, lawyer; b. Newark, Ohio, Feb. 27, 1953; d. John Gilbert and Louella Catherine (Hodges) R.; m. William Pulliam Harman; children: Benjamin Victor Harman, Elizabeth Lang Harman. BA with high distinction, DePauw U., 1975; JD magna cum laude, Ind. U., 1980; postgrad. Christian Theol. Sem. Bar: Ind. 1980, U.S. Dist. Ct. (so. dist.) Ind. 1980, U.S. Ct. Appeals (7th cir.) 1981. Law clk. U.S. Dist. Ct. (so. dist.) Ind., 1980-82; ordained to ministry Christian Ch. (Disciples of Christ), 1988. assoc. Baker & Daniels, Indpls., 1982-83; ptnr. Wilson, Hutchens & Reese, Greencastle, Ind., 1984-86; regional adminstr. for youths and camps, The Christian Ch. in Ind. (Disciples of Christ), 1988—. Steering com. Ind. Leadership Celebration, 1983—; adminstr. for Youth, Camps and Confs. Christian Ch. of Ind., 1988—. Mem. Phi Beta Kappa. Home: 3942 N Delaware St Indianapolis IN 46205

REESMAN, DIANE MARIE, public relations company executive; b. Anaheim, Calif., Jan. 21, 1958; d. Budd Aaron and Mary Elizabeth (Fogg) R. BA in Communications, Calif. State U., Fullerton, 1983. Clk. Calif. Sports, Inglewood, 1983, sec. promotions, 1983-84; sec. Los Angeles Lakers, Inglewood, 1984-85; asst. dir. pub. relations Los Angeles Kings, Inglewood, 1985-87; rep. pub. affairs Los Angeles Dept. Water & Power, Owens Valley, Calif., 1988—. Office: 873 N Main St #227 Bishop CA 93514

REEVE, HEATHER HOUSTON, lawyer; b. Portland, June 11, 1955; d. Gerald Polk Houston and Marilyn Ada (Gleason) Lundborg; m. David Houston Reeve, Dec. 27, 1981. BA, U. So. Calif., 1979; JD, Loyola U. of Los Angeles, 1982. Bar: Calif. 1982, Wash. 1983, U.S. Ct. Appeals (9th cir.) 1982, U.S. Dist. Ct. (we. dist.) Wash. 1984, U.S. Dist. Ct. (cen. dist.) Calif. 1982. Judicial externship U.S. Dist. Ct. (cen. dist.) Calif., Los Angeles, 1981; law clk. Calif. Ct. Appeals 4th Dist., San Bernardino, Calif., 1982-83; law clk. Wash. State Supreme Ct., Olympia, 1983-84; assoc. Reed, McClure, Moceri Thonn & Moriarty, Seattle, 1984—; intern UN Non-Govt. Liaison Service, N.Y.C., 1980; mem. constn.'s com. Washington State Centennial Commn., 1986—. Editor law rev., Loyola U. of Los Angeles, 1981-82; del. Christ Episc. Ch., Diocesan Conv., Diocese of Olympia, 1987-89. Mem. exec. com. Today's Constn. and You, 1984-87. Mem. ABA, Calif. Bar Assn., Wash. State Bar Assn., Seattle-King County Bar Assn., Speaker's Bur., World Affairs Council Seattle, City Club, Phi Beta Kappa. Democrat. Episcopalian. Home: 1733 N 128th St Seattle WA 98133 Office: Reed McClure Moceri Thonn & Moriarty 3600 Columbia Ctr Seattle WA 98104

REEVES, A. SUE WINDSOR, medical service executive; b. Oxford, Miss., Mar. 1, 1947; d. Alton Eugene and Mary Emma (Haney) Windsor; m. Johnny Lafayette Reeves Jr., Nov. 1, 1969; children: Ashley Renee, Lesley Windsor, Douglas Stephens. BA in Edn., U. Miss., 1969; MEd, La. State U., 1972. Cert. tchr., La. Tchr. Jackson (Miss.) Pub. Schs., 1969-71; profl. vol. Nat. Assn. Jr. Aux., Slidell, La., 1979—; tchr. St. Tammany Parish Schs., Slidell, 1981-83; dir. infant youth services Slidell Meml. Hosp., 1984, dir. community relations, 1984-85, dir. women's ctr., 1985-87, dir. physician recruitment, 1985-87, dir. physician services, 1987—; regional physician recruitment coordinator Am. Med. Internat., New Orleans, 1986-88; mem. com. Women's Health Found. La. Project designer Vol. Coordinating Ctr., 1983, bd. dirs., 1983—. State La. grantee, 1982. Mem. Nat. Assn. Female Execs., Nat. Assn. Jr. Aux. (Martha Wise award 1984, nat. com. woman 1982-87), Phi Kappa Phi, Phi Mu. Republican. Club: Camellia (Slidell), Le Cotillion, Pinewood Country. Home: 163 W Pinewood Dr Slidell LA 70458 Office: Slidell Meml Hosp 1001 Gause Blvd Slidell LA 70458

REEVES, BETTY JEAN, accountant; b. Riverton, Wyo., June 13, 1943; d. Glen Erwin Cooper and Velva Christina (Boyd) Lanning; m. Jack D. Reeves, Feb. 4, 1962 (div. July 1985); 1 child, Kathleen Anne Reeves Gurganious; m. Earl Coats Jr., Jan. 4, 1986. BBA, U. Tex., 1978. CPA, Tex. Staff acct. Superior Oil Co., Conroe, Tex., 1978-79; owner McGee, Horne, Reeves & Co., Conroe, 1979-85, Horne & Reeves, PC, Conroe, 1985—. Mem. Am. Inst. CPA's, Tex. Soc. CPA's, Beta Gamma Sigma, Beta Alpha Psi. Republican. Office: Horne & Reeves PC 932 W Dallas Conroe TX 77301

REEVES, JANE BURNS, accountant; b. Galveston, Tex., Sept. 15, 1949; d. Robert William and Evelyn Alyne (Tomme) Burns; m. Robert Paul Reeves, Aug. 30, 1969. BA in Math., U. Tex., Austin, 1970; MS in Acctg., U. Houston, Clear Lake, 1981. CPA, Tex. Tchr. math., french McAdams Jr. High. Sch., 1971-76; tchr. math Clear Lake High Sch., 1976-79; acct. Browne, Jordan & Co., P.C., 1979-81; prin. McCollum and Reeves, P.C., Houston, 1981—; instr. grad. acctg. U. Houston, Clear Lake, 1981-82. Bd. dirs. Bay Area Council on Drugs and Alcohol, Inc., 1982-83, Houston Proud Found., 1987-89; sec. bd. dirs. 1983; fin. adv. bd. St. Bernadette Cath. Ch., 1983—; trustee Humana Hosp. Clear Lake, 1987-90. Mem. Am. Inst. CPA's, Tex. CPA's, Am. Women's Soc. CPA's, Assn. Bus. and Profl. Women (sec., treas. 1985, pres. 1986), Clear Lake Area C. of C. (chair research com. 1985-86, v.p. Fin. 1987-88, bd. dirs. 1986—), U. Houston-Clear Lake Aluni Assn. (bd. dirs. 1986—, sec., treas. 1987), Alpha Lambda Delta, Beta Alpha Psi (Outstanding Alumnus award 1984-85). Home: 4214 Lake Grove Dr Seabrook TX 77586 Office: 1100 NASA Rd One Suite 309 Houston TX 77058

REEVES, LEANNE ELYSE, telephone company executive; b. Miami, Okla., Dec. 3, 1948; d. Billy Quinn and Helen Dorothy (Skye) Kinder; m. Howard Reynold Reeves, Dec. 16, 1977; 1 child, Charla Kay. Grad. high sch., Quapaw, Okla. Service rep. Southwestern Bell, Miami, Okla., 1973-82; service mgr. Southwestern Bell, Oklahoma City, 1982-84, AT&T, Tulsa, 1984-87; systems engr., staff devel. mgr. AT&T, Piscataway, N.J., 1987—. Officer Peoria Indian Tribe Okla., 1986, 87; sponsor Oklahomans for Indian Opportunity, Quapaw, 1972; del. Nat. Congress of Am. Indians, Phoenix, 1986. Mem. Nat. Assn. Female Execs. Republican. Methodist.

REEVES, MARJORIE ANN, librarian; b. Oceanside, Calif., June 21, 1935; d. George Newton and Margaret Ida (Gleason) R. BA, Chapman Coll., 1956; MLS, U. Calif., Berkeley, 1959. Reference librarian Fresno (Calif.) State U. Library, 1959-60, serials librarian, 1960-61; librarian Chapman Coll. Library, Orange, Calif., 1961-64; head tech. services div. U. Calif. Library, Irvine, 1964-71; asst. dir. library services Oreg. State Library, Salem, 1972-74; asst. dir. tech. services Iowa State U. Library, Ames, 1974-77; rep. Northeast U.S. Coutts Library Services, Lewiston, N.Y., 1977-78; law librarian electronics/space div. TRW Inc., Redondo Beach, Calif., 1979-82; assoc. dir. Oreg. State U. Library, Corvallis, 1982—. Mem. Am. Library Assn., Oreg. Library Assn., Pacific Northwest Library Assn., Assn. Coll. and Research Libraries. Office: Oreg State U Kerr Library Corvallis OR 97331

REEVES, PATRICIA RUTH, heavy machinery manufacturing company exec.; b. Bklyn., Mar. 26, 1931; d. Maurice G. and Ethel Helen (Kessler) Der Brucke; B.A., Adelphi U., 1952; m. Cedric E. Reeves, June 22, 1952. Chief of records sect. Hydrocarbon Research, Inc., N.Y.C., 1952-65; lead sec. C.F. Braun & Co., Murray Hill, N.J., 1965-69; exec. sec. Wilputte Corp., Murray Hill, N.J., 1969-75, adminstrv. asst., 1975-79, sales coordinator, 1979-81, personnel adminstr., 1981-82; sales coordinator Krupp Wilputte Corp., Murray Hill, 1982-84; personnel adminstr. Somerset Techs., Inc. (N.J.), 1984-85, personnel mgr., 1985—. Pres., Mountain Jewish Community Center, Warren, N.J., 1976-77, bd. dirs., 1972-81. Mem. Nat. Assn. Female Execs., Women's Network Central N.J. (v.p., editor newsletter 1981-83), Am. Soc. Personnel Adminstr. (sec. 1986-88, v.p. 1988—), Community Indsl. Relations Orgn. (treas. 1985-88, pres. 1988—), AAUW. Jewish. Home: 89 Knollwood Dr Watchung NJ 07060 Office: Somerset Techs Inc Weston Canal Rd Somerset NJ 08873

REGAN, ANN KENNEDY (PAT), state legislator; b. Chgo., Mar. 21, 1923; d. Thomas Carey and Katherine (Knight) Kennedy; m. Thomas Patrick Regan; children: Kate, Thomas Joseph, Ann, Margaret. BS, Ill. Inst. Tech., 1948; MS, Ea. Mont. Coll., 1963. Tchr. Castle Rock Jr. High Sch.; mem. Mont. Ho. of Reps., 1973-74; mem. from dist. 31 Mont. State Senate, 1975-85, mem. from dist. 47, 1985—. Recipient Women of Achievement award Billings Bus. and Profl. Women. Mem. LWV, NOW, Nat. Edn. Assn., Billings, Mont. Edn. Assn. Home: 204 Mountain View Billings MT 59101 *

REGAN, ELLEN FRANCES (MRS. WALSTON SHEPARD BROWN), ophthalmologist; b. Boston, Feb. 1, 1919; d. Edward Francis and Margaret (Moynihan) R.; A.B., Wellesley Coll., 1940; M.D., Yale U., 1943; m. Walston Shepard Brown, Aug. 13, 1955. Intern, Boston City Hosp., 1944; asst. resident, resident Inst. Ophthalmology, Presbyn. Hosp., N.Y.C., 1944-47, asst. ophthalmologist, 1947-56, asst. attending ophthalmologist, 1956-84; instr. ophthalmology Columbia Coll. Physicians and Surgeons, 1947-55, asso. ophthalmology, 1955-67, asst. clin. prof., 1967-84. Mem. Am. Ophthal. Soc., AMA, Am. Acad. Ophthalmology, Assn. Research Ophthalmology, N.Y. Acad. Medicine, N.Y. State, Mass. med. socs. Clubs: River, Wellesley. Home: Tuxedo Park NY 10987 Office: Box 632 Tuxedo NY 10987

REGAN, SUZANNE MARIE, food company executive; b. Camden, N.J., May 11, 1950; d. Cornelius Joseph and Jeannette (Way) R.; B.S., U. Conn., 1972; M.B.A., Drexel U., 1978; m. Ronald L. Feldberg, Apr. 10, 1976; 1 son, Matthew Regan. Acctg. procedures analyst Campbell Soup Co., Camden, N.J., 1972-74, mktg. research analyst, 1974-77, asst. mktg. mgr. Swanson div., 1977-78, mktg. mgr. Swanson div., 1978-81, mktg. dir. Pet Food unit, 1981-85, pres., gen. mgr. Pet Food unit (Champion Valley Farms) 1985-87, gen. mgr. refrigerated deli unit, 1987—. Mem. Am. Mgmt. Assn., Nat. Assn. Female Execs. Home: 59 Woodhurst Dr West Berlin NJ 08091 Office: Campbell Pl Camden NJ 08101

REGAN, TERRI JO CONRAD, accountant; b. Champaign, Ill., Oct. 15, 1961; d. Harry William and Lillian Lendore (McNeil) C. BBA, So. Meth. U., Dallas, 1982; MBA, Pace U., 1986. CPA, N.Y., Tex. Accountant Hertz, Herson & Co., N.Y.C., 1983—. Mem. Am. Inst. CPAs, N.Y. Soc. CPAs, Nat. Assn. Female Execs. Methodist. Home: 1512 Eagle St Troy NY 12180 Office: Hertz Herson & Co 2 Park Ave New York NY 10016

REGENT, BARBARA ANN, quality assurance engineer; b. Milw., July 15, 1954; d. Walter and Betty Lou (Lindeen) Simko; m. Richard Raymond Regent, May 29, 1976. B in Chemistry, U. Wis., Milw., 1976. Instr. chemistry Milw. Area Tech. Coll., 1976-79; substitute tchr. math. and sci. Milw. Pub. Schs., 1977; exptl. chemist Delco Electronics, Oak Creek, Wis., 1978-84, reliability engr., 1984—. Organist Adoration Evang. Luth. Ch., Greenfield, Wis., 1974-85 and 1987—. Mem. Am. Radio Relay League (asst. to sect. mgr. 1984—). Club: Amateur Radio (Milw.). Home: 5003 S 26th St Milwaukee WI 53221 Office: Delco Electronics 7929 S Howell Ave Oak Creek WI 53154

REGES, MARIANNA ALICE, consumer products company executive; b. Budapest, Hungary, Mar. 23, 1947; came to U.S., 1956, naturalized, 1963; d. Otto H. and Alice M. R.; m. Charles P. Green, Feb. 15, 1975; children: Rebecca, Charles III. AAS with honors, Fashion Inst. Tech., N.Y.C., 1967; BBA magna cum laude, Baruch Coll., 1971, MBA in Stats., 1978. Media research analyst Doyle, Dane, Bernbach Advt., N.Y.C., 1967-70; research supr. Sta. WCBS-TV, N.Y.C., 1970-71; research mgr. Woman's Day mag., N.Y.C., 1971-72; asst. media dir. Benton & Bowles Advt., N.Y.C., 1972-75; mgr. research and sales devel. NBC Radio, N.Y.C., 1975-77; sr. research mgr. Ziff-Davis Pub. Co., N.Y.C., 1977-84; mgr. media research Bristol-Myers Co., 1984—. Mem. Vt. Natural Resources Council, 1977—; advisor Baruch Coll. Advt. Soc., 1975—. Mem. Am. Mktg. Assn., Am. Advt. Fedn., Media Research Dirs. Assn., Radio and TV Research Council, Beta Gamma Sigma, Sigma Alpha Delta. Home: 140 E 83d St New York NY 10028 Office: Bristol-Myers Co 345 Park Ave New York NY 10154

REGET, IONE HOZENDORF, business services company executive, enrolled agent; b. Jackson, Miss., Sept. 19, 1937; d. Glenn Frederick and Ione Belle (Lowry) Hozendorf; m. Francis John Reget, Jan. 17, 1967 (div. 1986); children—Diane Michele, Philip Francis, Michael Trahern. B.A. cum laude, U. Minn., 1959; studentColl. Fin. Planning, 1984-87; Cert. fin. planner. Pres., East Sierra Bus. Services, Inc., Bishop, Calif., 1980—; sec.-treas. Meyer Cookie Co., Inc. Soprano, Bishop Community Chorus, 1974-78; treas. Calvary Bapt. Ch., Bishop, 1975—, choir dir., 1980—; chmn.Civic Arts Commn., City of Bishop, 1984-87; bd. dirs. Inyo Council for the Arts, 1987—. Mem. Nat. Assn. Enrolled Agts., Calif. Soc. Enrolled Agts., Calif. Assn. Ind. Accts., Internat. Assn. Fin. Planners, Inst. Cert. Fin. Planners, Aircraft Owners and Pilots Assn., DAR, Mensa. Republican. Club: Playhouse 395. Home: Route 1 146 North St Bishop CA 93514 Office: 150 N Main St Bishop CA 93514 Mail Address: PO Box 448 Bishop CA 93514

REGIER, SUSAN ANNE, trust company executive; b. Clinton, Okla., Dec. 4, 1954; d. John and Shirley Anne (Leonard) R. BS in Acctg., Southwestern Okla. State U., 1977; M in Acctg., U. Okla., 1980. CPA, Okla. Internat. tax acct. Phillips Petroleum Co., Bartlesville, Okla., 1977-78; researcher, teaching asst. U. Okla., Norman, 1979-80; sr. tax acct. Grant Thornton Internat., Oklahoma City, 1981-83; v.p. Trust Co. of Okla., Oklahoma City, 1983—, Kepco Inc., Oklahoma City, 1987—; cons. Robert W. Leonard and Assocs., Houston, 1980—, Continental Ill. Bank, Chgo., 1984—, Kepco Inc., Oklahoma City., 1985-87; bd. dirs. Houston Fitness Ctr. Atlantic Richfield Corp. grantee, 1979. Mem. Am. Inst. CPA's, Okla. Soc. CPA's, Southwestern Okla. State U. Alumni Assn., U. Okla. Pres.' Ptnrs., Oklahoma City C. of C., Sigma Kappa Alumni Assn. Republican. Baptist. Club: Desk and Derrick (Oklahoma City). Home: 4400 Hemingway #229 Oklahoma City OK 73118-2244 Office: Trust Co Okla 1001 NW 63d Suite 304 Oklahoma City OK 73116 also: Kepco Inc 3535 NW 58th St Suite 450 Oklahoma City OK 73112

REGNER, BETH ELLEN, stock broker; b. Burlington, Wis., Feb. 22, 1951; d. John Lewis and Beatrice Marie (Lehsten) Regner. BS in Nursing, U. Wis., Milw., 1974; MS in Bus. Mgmt., Cardinal Stritch Coll., Milw., 1984. RN pub. health nurse Pub. Health Dept., Milw., 1974-77; from staff nurse to head nurse emergency room and cardiac rehab. unit Columbia Hosp., Milw., 1977-84; project mgr. Datacare, Inc., Milw., 1984-86; stock broker preferred stock dept. Blunt, Ellis & Loewi, Inc., 1986-87, instl. stock broker preferred stock dept., 1988—; stock broker preferred stock dept., The Milw. Co., 1987-88; vol. cardiac rehab. nurse Mt. Sinai Rehab. Program, Milw., 1977-81. Roman Catholic. Avocations: tennis, aerobics, biking, walking, traveling. Home: 2588 N Frederick Ave #311 Milwaukee WI 53211

REGNIER, JOYCE ANNE, nursing administrator; b. Ottawa County, Kans., July 22, 1940; d. Bernice Allen and Venita LoRee (Pitts) Bartley; B.S.N. cum laude, Marymount Coll., Salina, Kans., 1973; M.S., Kans. State U., 1983; N.H.A., Barton County Community Coll., 1985; m. J. Lucien Regnier, Aug. 6, 1958; children—Bernard, Douglas, Michelle. Staff nurse, charge nurse Ottawa County Hosp., Minneapolis, Kans., 1973-76; dir. nursing Kenwood View Nursing Home, Salina, Kans., 1977-79; nursing instr. Marymount Coll., Salina, 1979-81; ICU nurse, 1982-83; adminstr. Manor of Kansas City (Kans.), 1983-87; dir. nursing services Overland Park (Kans.) Manor, 1987—; pres. Premier Mgmt. Inc.; chmn. dist. I Kans. Health Care Assn.; adv. bd. vocat. tech. sch., Salina, 1977, Ottawa County Health Dept., Kans., 1976; mem. planning and coordination com. for continuing edn. for nurses, Kans. Mem. Sigma Theta Tau. Methodist. Home: 7458 Isabel Ct Kansas City KS 66112 Office: 6501 W 75th St Overland Park KS 66204

REGUERO, MELODIE HUBER, financial services professional; b. Montebello, Calif., May 10, 1956; d. Adam W. and Helen Carolyn (Antrim) H. BA in Econs. magna cum laude, UCLA, 1978; M in Bus. Taxation, U. So. Calif., 1983. CPA, Calif. Mem. tax audit staff Arthur Young & Co., Los Angeles, 1978-80; sr. mem. Singer, Lewak, Greenbaum & Goldstein, Los Angeles, 1980-82; tax supr. Coldwell Banker & Co., Los Angeles, 1983-84; fin. analyst, acquisitions specialist Coldwell Banker Residential Group, Newport Beach, Calif., 1984-86; fin. services profl. The Acacia Fin. Group, Newport Beach, Calif., 1986-88, Fin. Engring. Concepts, Inc., Orange, Calif., 1988—; treas. Champions Choice, Inc., 1980—. Active Cabaret Guild of So. Calif. Performing Arts, Costa Mesa, 1986—. Mem. Nat. Assn. Female Execs., Am. Inst. CPA's (pres. 1980—), Calif. Soc. CPA's (pres. 1980—), Newport Harbor C. of C. Republican. Club: Orange County Triathalon. Office: Fin Engring Concepts Inc 772 Town & Country Rd Orange CA 92668

REGULES, ROXANNE, school system administrator; b. Monterey, Calif., Sept. 17, 1955; d. Miguel Valenzuela Regules and Ella (Jaime) Miajara. AA, Monterey Peninsula Coll., 1974; BA, San Jose State U., 1976, MA, 1980. Cert. tchr. Spanish, sch. adminstr. Tchr. Salinas (Calif.) City Sch. Dist., 1976-78, resource tchr., 1978-82; coordinator spl. projects Santa Rita Union Sch. Dist., Salinas, 1982-86; dir. aux. and spl. projects Alisal Union Sch. Dist., Salinas, 1986—; tchr. adult edn. Monterey Peninsula Unified Sch. Dist., 1980-82, Pacific Grove (Calif.) Unified Sch. Dist., 1984-86; cons. State Dept. Edn., Sacramento, 1986-87, pvt. contracts for various sch. dists., Monterey, 1980—. Bd. dirs. Door to Hope, Salinas, 1987—; tchr. Monterey Assembly of God Ch., 1970-82, bd. dirs., 1983-86. Named Outstanding Supr. of Yr., Monterey County Youth Employment Service, 1983-84, Outstanding Educator of Yr., Salinas Woman's Jaycees, 1984; Monterey Peninsula Coll. Inst. Fgn. Studies scholar, 1973. Mem. Calif. Assn. Sch. Adminstrs., Calif. Assn. Compensatory Edn. (regional rep. 1983-86), Asilomar Regional Reading Conf. (pres.-elect 1986—, bd. dirs. 1984—), Phi Delta Kappa, Delta Kappa Gamma. Democrat. Lodge: Soroptimists. Home: 1055 Johnson Ave Monterey CA 93940 Office: Alisal Unio Sch Dist 1205 E Market St Salinas CA 93906

REHA, ROSE KRIVISKY, business educator emeritus; b. N.Y.C., Dec. 17, 1920; d. Boris and Freda (Gerstein) Krivisky; m. Rudolph John Reha, Apr. 11, 1941; children: Irene Gale, Phyllis. BS, Ind. State U., 1965; MA, U. Minn., 1967, PhD, 1971. With U.S. and State Civil Service, 1941-63; tchr. pub. schs., Minn., 1965-66; teaching assoc., part-time instr. U. Minn., Mpls., 1966-68; prof. Coll. Bus., St. Cloud (Minn.) State U., 1968-85, prof. emeritus, 1985—, chmn. bus. edn. and office adminstrn. dept., 1982-83; cons., lectr. in field. Reviewer of bus. communications and consumer edn. textbooks; contbr. articles to profl. jours. Camp dir. Girl Scouts U.S.A., 1960-62; active various community fund drives; sec., mem. relicensure rev. Com. Minn. Bd. Teaching Continuing Edn., 1984—. Recipient Achievement award St. Cloud State U., 1985, St. Cloud State U. Research and Faculty Improvement grantee, 1973, 78, 83. Mem. Am. Vocat. Assn., Minn. Econ. Assn., Minn. Women of Higher Edn., NEA, Minn. Edn. Assn. (pres. women's caucus 1981-83, award 1983), St. Cloud U. Faculty Assembly (pres. 1975-76), St. Cloud State U. Grad. Council (chmn. 1983-85), Pi Omega Pi (sponsor St. Cloud State U. chpt. 1982—), Phi Chi Theta, Delta Pi Epsilon, Delta Kappa Gamma. Jewish. Home: 1725 13 Ave SE Saint Cloud MN 56301 Office: St Cloud State Univ Coll Bus Saint Cloud MN 56301

REHAGEN-HUFF, ANDREA LEE, career consulting, outplacement company executive, consultant; b. St. Louis, Nov. 20, 1949; d. Clemens John and Margaret Mary (Sheridan) Rehagen; m. S. Michael Huff, Jan. 11, 1969; 1 child, Jeffrey Michael. B.A. in Sociology, So. Ill. U., 1971; M.A. in Counseling, Washington U., St. Louis, 1975. Career counselor State of Ill., Granite City, 1971-73; counselor RHS, Inc., St. Louis, 1973-75, Womanhelp, San Francisco, 1975-77; dir. career devel., career cons. Career Planning Services/ Woman's Way, San Rafael, Calif., 1977-80; pres., career cons. CareerWorks, San Francisco, 1980—. Mem. Am. Soc. Tng. and Devel. (chmn., founder career devel. div. 1979-81), No. Calif. Human Resources Council, Women Entrepreneurs, Career Planning and Adult Devel. Network. Democrat. Avocations: collector of early 20th century art and furnishings, collectible antique jewelry. Office: CareerWorks 100 Spear St Suite 810 San Francisco CA 94105

REHBERG, IRENE LEE, elastic materials company executive; b. Shanghai, China, Feb. 22, 1946; came to U.S., 1969, naturalized, 1982; d. Kam Yee and Chang Hing (Ho) Lee; B.S., Ohio U., 1973; 1 son, Eric Lee. Lab. specialist Fusion, Inc., Willoughby, Ohio, 1973-77; profl. chemist SCM-Gidden Metals, Cleve., 1977-78; sr. chemist Tremco, Cleve., 1978-80; v.p., dir. Elastic Materials, Inc., Brunswick, Ohio, 1980—; tchr. Chinese culture; soldering and brazing cons. Recipient award for outstanding contbn. to Lakeland Community Coll., 1974. Mem. Delta Phi Alpha. Roman Catholic. Patentee various fields. Home: 20735 White Bark St Strongsville OH 44136 Office: PO Box 828 2774 Nationwide Pkwy Brunswick OH 44212

REHM, CAROLYN, sales executive; b. Denver, May 4, 1957. Student, Richland Coll., 1975; BBA, North Tex. State U., 1979. Account exec. Comml. Printing Co., Birmingham, Ala. Active Big Sister PALS Program 1983—; mem. Coppell Mayor election com., 1985; dir. publicity Valley Ranch Bapt. Ch. 1986—, also charter mem. Named One of Outstanding Young Women Am., 1987. Republican. Office: Comml Printing Co 222 6th Ave SW PO Box 10302 Birmingham AL 35202

REHM, LISA MARIE, physical therapist; b. Inglewood, Calif., Nov. 25, 1959; d. Joseph and Verna Mae (Norman) Didone; m. Kurt Gregory Rehm, Apr. 25, 1987. BS in Biology, Santa Clara (Calif.) U., 1981; MS in Phys. Therapy, U. So. Calif., 1983. Registered phys. therapist, cert. advanced cardiac life support, Calif. Plastics service, gen. med. and orthopedic phys. therapist Santa Clara Valley Med. Ctr., San Jose, Calif., 1983-84, spinal cord injury phys. therapist, 1984-85, head injury service phys. therapist, 1985-86, cardiac rehab. phys. therapist, 1986-87, cardiac rehab. phys. therapy supr., 1987—. U. So. Calif. Dept. Phys. Therapy Meml. Fund scholar, 1982. Mem. Am. Phys. Therapy Assn. (cardiopulmonary sect.), Alpha Sigma Nu. Republican. Roman Catholic. Club: Royal Cts. Athletic (San Jose). Office: Santa Clara Valley Med Ctr 751 S Bascom Ave San Jose CA 95128

REHNKE, MARY ANN, college programs director; b. Faribault, Minn., Jan. 23, 1945; d. Wesley Arthur and Sarah Frances (Smith) Rehnke; m. Charles Orin Willis, Apr. 18, 1924. BA in English, Cornell Coll., 1967; MA in English, U. Chgo., 1968, PhD in Lit., 1974; MS in Edni Adminstrn., U. Wis., 1975. Head resident Elizabeth Waters Hall, U. Wis., Madison, 1970-73; asst. prof. English No. Ky. U., Highland Heights, 1973-82, acad. adminstr., 1976-77, dir. summer sessions, 1977-80; dir. conf. planning Am. Assn. Higher Edn., Washington, 1980-82; assoc. dean for faculty relations and acad. programs Coll. St. Catherine, St. Paul, 1982-83; assoc. dean of coll. Daemen Coll., Buffalo, N.Y., 1983-85; dir. ann. programs Council of Ind. Colls., Washington, 1986—; mem. planning com. nat. identification program Am. Council Edn., Washington, 1978-85; mem. program com. Nat. Conf. Women Student Leaders and Women of Distinction, Washington, 1985—. Author: Women in Higher Education Administration: A Brief Guide for Conference Planners, 1982; editor: Creating Career Programs in a Liberal Arts Context, 1987; editor newsletter N. Cen. Regional Women's Studies, 1978-80. Vestry mem Ch. of St. Clement, Alexandria, Va., 1982, vice chair search com., 1986-87. Named one of Outstanding Young Women Am., 1976. Mem. Am. Assn. Higher Edn. (coordinator nat. conf. roundtable 1982-86), Greater Washington Soc. Assn. Execs, Nat. Assn. Women Deans, Adminstrs. and Counselors, N.Am. Assn. Summer Sessions (research chair 1979-80), Soc. for Values in Higher Edn., Phi Beta Kappa, Phi Delta Kappa. Democrat. Episcopalian. Office: The Council of Ind Colls One Dupont Circle Washington DC 20036

REHRMANN, EILEEN MARY, legislative delegate; b. Chester, Pa., Nov. 30, 1944; d. Victor Casmir and Anne (Quinn) Marchlik; m. Joseph Anthony Rehrmann, July 3, 1965; children: William, Mary Anne, Kristine, Robert. Student, Immaculata Coll., Phila., 1962-65. Town commr. Town of Bel Air (Md.), 1979-82; mem. Md. Ho. of Dels., 1982—; del. 1980 Dem. Conv., Bel Air, 1980. Mem. Hartford Dem. Club, Dem. Women, Bel Air; pres. LWV, Hartford County, 1979. Named Outstanding State Legislator Assembly Govtl. Employees; recipient Service award Md. Troopers Assn., Appreciation award No. Md. Assn. for Retarded Children. Mem. Women Legislators of Md. (2d v.p. 1986-87), Md. Mcpl. League (pres. Bel Air area 1981, Disting. Service award). Roman Catholic. Office: 103 N Main St Bel Air MD 21014

REIBMAN, JEANETTE FICHMAN, state senator; b. Ft. Wayne, Ind., Aug. 18, 1915; d. Meir and Pearl (Schwartz) Fichman; A.B., Hunter Coll., 1937; LL.B., U. Ind., 1940; m. Nathan L. Reibman, June 20, 1943; children—Joseph M. Edward D., James E. Admitted to Ind. bar, 1940, U.S. Supreme Ct. bar, 1944; practice law, Ft. Wayne, 1940; atty. U.S. War Dept., Washington, 1940-42, U.S. War Prodn. Bd., Washington, 1942-44; mem. Pa. Ho. of Reps., 1956-66; mem. Pa. Senate, 1966—, chmn. com. on edn.; mem. Edn. Commn. of the States. Trustee emeritus, Lafayette Coll.; bd. mem., Pa. Med. Coll., Pa. Higher Edn. Assistance Agy., Pa. Council on Arts, Camphill Schs. Recipient Disting. Dau. of Pa. award and medal Gov. Pa., 1968, citation on naming of Jeanette F. Reibman Adminstrn. Bldg., East Stroudsburg State Coll., 1972; Public Service award Pa. Psychol. Assn., 1977; Jerusalem City of Peace award Govt. Israel, 1977; named to Hunter Coll. Alumni Hall of Fame, 1974. Mem. Hadassah (Myrtle Wreath award 1976), Sigma Delta Tau, Delta Kappa Gamma, Phi Delta Kappa. Democrat. Jewish. Club: Order Eastern Star. Office: 711 Lehigh St Easton PA 18042

REIBMAN-MYERS, FRANCINE LEE, business executive; b. N.Y.C., Dec. 5, 1949; d. Abe and Katherine C. (Glass) Reibman; m. Jay H. Myers, May 31, 1980; 1 child, Benjamin Alexander Reibman-Myers. B.A. cum laude, CUNY. Assoc. dir. Nat. Student Lobby, Washington, 1972-74; dir. govt. ops. Continental Mktg., Washington, 1972-74; acting dir. vets. affairs CUNY, 1974-75; chmn. bd. Culpepper, Inc., 1983—, Millburn, N.J., 1983-86; pres. Fran Reibman & Assocs., Millburn, 1976—; cons. House Select Com. on Aging, 1977-78, Triathalon Products, Inc., 1985-86, Cons. Mennen Med. Inc., 1985-87; cons., DAL Services, Inc., 1987—, U. Med. Dentistry of N.J., 1987—. Patentee rehab. gym, 1985. Candidate for N.Y. State Assembly, 1972; bd. dirs. John F. Kennedy Democratic Club, Jamaica, N.Y., 1978-84; adv. People to Rehabilitate and Integrate the Disabled, 1973-78; sec. Council on Internat. Relations for UN, 1972-73; Democratic county committee person, Queens, 1972-74; bd. govs. Queensborough Pres.'s Council for Tenants, 1972-73; mem. Carter/Mondale White House Transition Team, 1976. Mem. Am. Assn. Advancement of Med. Instrumentation, N.J. Assn. Clin. Engrs., Nat. Assn. Female Execs. (bd. dirs. 1988). Jewish. Avocations: horseback riding; golf; sailing; building; reading.

REICH, JOANNE LEE, business and marketing consultant; b. Oakland, Calif., Aug. 30, 1945; d. Herbert and Wanda Jane (Porter) R. B.A., UCLA, 1967; postgrad. Babson Coll., 1988. Programmer analyst, cons. various orgns., Los Angeles, 1969-73; sr. programmer analyst Compata, Inc., Canoga Park, Calif., 1973-75; systems engr. Data Gen. Corp., El Segundo, Calif., 1975-78; project mgr., bus. planning Honeywell Info. Systems, Billerica, Mass., 1978-82; bus. planning cons. Wang Labs., Inc., Lowell, Mass., 1982-86; project mgr., mktg. mgr. Direct Products div. Data Gen. Corp., Westboro, Mass., 1986—; market research cons. Micro Tech. Research, Chelmsford, Mass., 1984—. Mem. Am. Mgmt. Assn., Nat. Assn. Female Execs. Avocations: oil painting, drawing, community theater production activities. Office: Data Gen Corp 4400 Computer Dr Westboro MA 01580

REICH, KATHLEEN JOHANNA, librarian, educator; b. Mannheim, Germany, May 1, 1927; came to U.S., 1955, naturalized, 1958; d. Robert and Luise Charlotte Helene (Kurowsky) Weichel; 1 child, Robert Weichel. MAT in English, Rollins Coll., 1976, EdS, 1981, postgrad. U. Leipzig, U. Mainz. With Orlando (Fla.) Pub. Library, 1955-57; cataloguer, instr. U. Detroit, 1957-60, Trinity U., San Antonio, 1960-61; adminstr. Fla. Book Processing Ctr., Orlando, 1961-68; bur. chief, div. library services Fla. State Dept., Winter Park, 1968-71; assoc. prof. library sci. Rollins Coll., Winter Park, 1971—, asst. dean faculty, 1981-83, dir. overseas studies, 1983-84; head archives and spl. collections Rollins Coll., 1983—; acad. dean Prew Prep. Sch., Sarasota, Fla., 1983-85. Mem. AAUP, African Lit. Assn., Am. Water Ski Assn., Soc. Am. Archivists, Soc. Fla. Archivists, Kappa Delta Pi. Home: 211 Fawsett Rd Winter Park FL 32789 Office: Rollins Coll Winter Park FL 32789

REICH, OLIVE BUERK, artist, educator; b. Bklyn., Mar. 1, 1935; d. Percival G. and Olive (Wirth) Buerk; m. Daniel Oehler Reich, Aug. 4, 1956; children: Peter, Robin, Daniel. BA, Mt. Holyoke Coll., 1956. Painter Olive Reich Studio, Bklyn., 1970—; cons. art Union Ch., Bay Ridge, Bklyn., 1984-87, Reich Paper Co., Bklyn, 1986-88, Meta Catering Corp., Bklyn., 1987-88. Illustrator book God's Summer Cottage, 1980, Chronicle of Shelter Island Churches, 1983, Shelter Island Yacht Club, 1986. Pres. Bay Ridge Festival Arts., Bklyn, 1978-80. Mem. Nat Assn. Women Artists, Artists Equity, Contemporary Artists Guild (corr. sec. 1980-87). Clubs: Salmagundi (N.Y.C.), Catharine Lorillard Wolfe Art (1st v.p. 1982). Home: 36 79th St Brooklyn NY 11209 Office: Olive Reich Studio 7518 Third Ave Brooklyn NY 11209

REICH, SHYLA GILLER, real estate executive; b. Palm Beach, Fla., Feb. 7, 1935; d. Charles and Regina (Ravett) Giller; m. Stephen Gregory Reich, Jan. 26, 1959; children: Robert, John. BSBA, U. Fla., 1956. Broker Giller Real Estate and Constrn. Co., Palm Beach, 1956-58; broker/salesperson Huskey Realty, Orlando, Fla., 1976-81; pres. Shyla G. Reich Realty Inc., Orlando, 1981—. Bd. dirs. Better Bus. Bur., Orlando, 1986—; mem. Indsl. Devel. Commn., Orlando, 1984—; past. v.p. Fla. Symphony Soc., Orlando; past. pres. Cen. Fla. Zool. Soc., Fla. Symphony Orch. League. Recipient Outstanding Contbrn. to the Arts award Council of Arts & Scis., Orlando, 1978. Mem. Orlando Bd. Realtors (comml. investment div.), Comml. Investment Council, Orlando C. of C. (participant Leadership Orlando 1986). Democrat. Clubs: Downtown Orlando Inc.; Interlachen Country (Winter Park, Fla.); Heathrow Country (Lake Mary, Fla.). Office: 118 E Jefferson St Orlando FL 32801

REICHE, VIRGINIA CATHERINE, elementary educator; b. Lackawanna, N.Y., Apr. 21, 1941; d. Boleslau and Viola (Polanowski) Sawicki; m. Charles Ray Reiche, May 23, 1981; children: Judi, Ellen, David. BS, State U., 1964; MS in Elem. Edn. and Reading, College at Buffalo, 1972. Instr. N.Y. State United Tchrs., Albany, N.Y., 1980-84; tchr. Lackawanna City Sch. Dist., 1964—; Mem. Western N.Y. Ednl. Issues Com., Buffalo, 1979-84; facilitator, presenter Western N.Y. Tchr. to Tchr. Conf., Buffalo, 1979-80. Bd. dirs. Lackawanna Taxpayers Assn., 1986—; treas. Lackawanna Home Bur., 1982-8—; mem. Am. Legion Aux., Lackawanna, 1982—, adv. bd. Group Health Ins., Buffalo, 1985—. Named Tchr. of Yr. Lackawanna City Sch. Dist., 1980. Mem. Lackawanna Tchrs. Assn. (v.p. 1979, social activities, scholarship and sabbatical coms. 1979—), Profl. Advancement Council (negotiating team 1979—),Lackawanna Women Tchrs. Home: 20 Norfred Dr Lackawanna NY 14218

REICHELDERFER, MARGARET M., technical writer; b. Gary, Ind., Jan. 2, 1946; m. Edward L. Reichelderfer, Oct. 19, 1985. BA, U. N.Mex., 1968; MA, U. Dayton, 1969, postgrad., 1975-76; postgrad., Ill. Inst. Tech., 1980. Lectr. Ohio State U., Columbus, 1969-70; bus. systems specialist Bell Labs. AT&T, Piscataway, N.J., 1970-71; sr. tech. writer AT&T, Naperville, Ill., 1979-84; sr. product planner AT&T, Lisle, Ill., 1984-86; asst. mgr. systems group 3d Nat. Bank, Dayton, Ohio, 1972-74; sr. systems analyst 3d Nat. Bank, Dayton, 1974-76; sr. tech. writer Digital Equipment Corp., Marlboro, Mass., 1976-77; sr. sales tng. specialist NCR Corp., Dayton, 1977-79; sr. tech. cons. Personnel Scis. Inc., N.Y.C., 1986—. Author: Systems Writing, 1971, Document Converter Guide, 1986, Project Management Guide, 1987, SAMNA: The Basics, 1987. Advisor Explorer Boy Scouts Am., Dayton, 1972-76. Mem. Am. Soc. Tng. Devel. (sec. 1974-75, v.p. 1987—), Assn. System Mgmt., Soc. Tech. Writing (judge 1981), Phi Kappa Phi, Phi Beta Kappa.

REICHERT, CHERYL MCBROOM, pathologist, research consultant; b. Great Falls, Mont., Sept. 4, 1946; d. Harold and Arlyne (Cohn) R.; m. Sherwood McBroom Jr., 1964 (div. 1971); children: Scott, Cari. BS, Coll. of Great Falls, 1969; MS, U. Mich., 1971, PhD, 1974, MD, 1976. Diplomate Am. Bd. of Med. Examiners. Resident in anatomic pathology Nat. Cancer Inst., Bethesda, Md., 1977-79; resident in clin. pathology NIH, Bethesda, 1979-80, surgical pathologist, chief autopsy service, 1981-85; pathologist Sibley Meml. Hosp., Washington, 1985-86; cons. Digene Corp., College Park, Md., 1985—, Nat. Cancer Inst., Bethesda, 1985—; pathologist Columbus Hosp., Great Falls, 1987—; cons. McLaughlin Research Inst., Great Falls, 1987—; clin. assoc. prof. Uniformed Services U. of Health Scis., Bethesda, 1983-86; teaching fellow dept. biochemistry U. Mich., Ann Arbor, 1969-74; clin. researcher Nat. Inst. on Aging, Bethesda; presenter Pres. Reagan's Nat. Cancer Adv. Bd., Washington, 1983. Contbr. articles to profl. jours. Mem. profl. edn. com. Am. Cancer Soc.; bd. dirs. Ann Arbor Child Care and Devel. Served as lt. comdr. USPHS, 1977-80. Named one of Outstanding Young Women of Yr., State of Mich., 1973. Mem. U.S. Acad. Pathologists, Mont. Pathologists Soc., Galens Med. Soc., Alpha Omega Alpha. Home: 1409 4th Ave S Great Falls MT 59405

REICHGOTT, EMBER DARLENE, lawyer, state senator; b. Detroit, Aug. 22, 1953; d. Norbert Arnold and Diane (Pincich) R. B.A. summa cum laude, St. Olaf Coll., Minn., 1974; J.D., Duke U., 1977. Bar: Minn. 1977, D.C. 1978. Assoc., Larkin, Hoffman, Daly & Lindgren, Bloomington, Minn., 1977-84; counsel Control Data Corp., Bloomington, Minn., 1984-86 ; legal cons. Home Free Battered Women's Shelter, Plymouth, Minn., 1978—; mem. Minn. State Senate, 1983—. Chmn. Legis. Commn. on Econ. Status of Women, 1984—; Vice chmn. Senate Judiciary Com., 1983-86, Senate Edn. Com., 1987—; mem. exec. com. Minn. Job Skills Partnership; trustee, N.W. YMCA, New Hope, Minn., 1983—. Youngest woman ever elected to Minn. State Senate, 1983; recipient Woman of Yr. award North Hennepin Bus. and Prof. Women, 1983; Award for Contbn. to Human Services, Minn. Social Services Assn., 1983; Disting. Service award Mpls. Jaycees, 1984; named One of Ten Outstanding Young Minnesotans, Minn. Jaycees, 1984. Mem. Minn. Bar Assn., Hennepin County Bar Assn. Mem. Minn. Democratic Farmer-Labor Party (del. nat. Dem. conv. 1984, state exec. com. 1980-82). Home: 7701 48th Ave N New Hope MN 55428

REID, BONNIE LEE, junior high school principal; b. St. Louis, Jan. 30, 1937; d. William Charles Lovrenic and Fern Lee (Swingler) Reiman; m. Thomas James Fitzsimmons, Aug. 16, 1958 (div. Aug. 1966); children: Susan Lee, Scott James; m. Donald Francis Reid, Nov. 18, 1966; stepchildren: Christopher Kearns, Donald Francis Jr., Connie Ann, Britton Anthony, Douglas Nye. BE, U. Mo., 1958; MA in Adminstrn., Washington U., St. Louis, 1977, postgrad., 1978-80. Cert. tchr., Mo.; cert. secondary adminstr., Mo. Tchr. Webster Groves (Mo.) High Sch., 1958-60; tchr., dept. chmn. Parkway Sch. Dist., Chesterfield, Mo., 1971-81, asst. prin., 1982-83, assoc. prin., 1984, interim prin., 1985; prin. Parkway E. Jr. High Sch., Chesterfield, 1986—; mem. governance com. Gov.'s Conf. Edn., 1978; prin. Nat. Secondary Sch. Recognition Sch., 1986-87. Fellow Prin.'s Acad.; mem. Nat. Assn. Secondary Sch. Prins., Assn. Supervision and Curriculum Devel. (consortium sch. team leader 1986—) , Nat. Middle Sch. Assn. (conf. edn.), Mortar Bd., Mo. State Future Tchrs. Am., Parkway Ind. Community Tchrs. Assn., Greater St. Louis Tchrs. Assn., Delta Kappa Gamma, Kappa Alpha Theta, Pi Lambda Theta, Phi Sigma Iota, Kappa Epsilon Alpha, Sigma Rho Sigma. Republican. Presbyterian. Office: Parkway E Jr High Sch 181 Coeur De Ville Creve Coeur MO 63141

REID, CHARLOTTE T., business consultant, b. Kankakee, Ill., Sept. 27, 1913; d. Edward Charles and Ethel (Stith) Thompson; m. Frank R. Reid, Jan. 1, 1938 (dec. 1962); children—Patricia, Frank, Edward, Susan. Student Ill. Coll., 1931-32; LL.D. (hon.), John Marshall Law Sch., Ill. Coll., Aurora Coll. Vocalist, NBC, Chgo., 1936-39; mem. Ho. of Reps., Washington, 1962-71; mem. Commn. on FCC, Washington, 1971-76; dir. Liggett Group, N.Y.C., 1977-80, Midlantic Banks, Inc., Edison, N.Y., 1977-88 , Motorola Inc., Schaumburg, Ill., 1978-84. Mem. Presdl. Task Force on Internat. Pvt. Enterprise, 1983-85; mem. com. Def. Adv. Com. on Women in the Services, 1982-85; bd. overseers Hoover Instn., 1984—. Republican. Club: Capitol Hill (dir. 1968-82).

REID, INEZ SMITH, lawyer, educator; b. New Orleans, Apr. 7, 1937; d. Sidney Randall Dickerson and Beatrice Virginia (Bundy) Smith. BA, Tufts U., 1959; LLB, Yale U., 1962; MA, UCLA, 1963; PhD, Columbia U., 1968. Bar: Calif. 1963, N.Y. 1972, D.C. 1980. Assoc. prof. Barnard Coll. Columbia U., N.Y.C., 1972-76; gen. counsel youth div. State of N.Y., 1976-77; dep. gen. counsel HEW, Washington, 1977-79; inspector gen. EPA, Washington, 1979-81; chief legis. and opinions, dep. corp. counsel Office of Corp. Counsel, Washington, 1981-83; corp. counsel D.C., 1983-85; counsel Finley, Kumble, Wagner (now Laxalt, Washington, Perito & Dubuc), Washington, 1986—; William J. Maier, Jr. vis. prof. law W.Va. U. Coll. Law, Morgantown, 1985-86. Author: Together Black Women, 1972; contbr. articles to profl. jours. and publs. Bd. dirs. Homes and Ministries Bd. United Ch. of Christ, N.Y.C., 1978-83, vice chmn., 1981-83; chmn. bd. govs. Antioch Law Sch., Washington, 1979-81; chmn. bd. trustees Antioch U., Yellow Springs, Ohio, 1981-82. Recipient Emily Gregory award Barnard Coll., 1976, Arthur Morgan award Antioch U., 1982, Service award United Ch. of Christ, 1983, Disting. Service (Profl. Life) award Tufts U. Alumni Assn., 1988. Office: Laxalt Washington Perito et al 1120 Connecticut Ave NW Suite 1100 Washington DC 20036

REID, KATHERINE LOUISE, artist, educator; b. Port Arthur, Tex., Mar. 25, 1941; d. Clifton Commodore and Helen Ross (Moore) Reid. B.A., Baylor U., 1963; postgrad. in design and illustration, Kans. City Art Inst., 1964; M.Ed., U. Houston, 1973; cert. supervision U. Houston-Clear Lake City, 1980; postgrad. San Jacinto Coll., 1982. Cert. art educator, profl. supr., Tex. Litho reproduction artist Hallmark Cards, Kansas City, Mo., 1963-64; tchr. art high sch. Pasadena Ind. Sch. Dist. (Tex.), 1964-77, supr. art, gifted and talented and photography, 1977-85; supr. art and photography InterAct, 1985—; head crafts, asst. dir. dir. winter discovery program-ski camp Cheley Colo. Camps, Denver, Estes Park, 1967-74; staff artist, media workshop, Tex. Edn. Agy., Austin, summer 1961; art enrichment tchr. Port Arthur Ind. Sch. Dist. (Tex.), summer 1961; head crafts Camp Waluta, Silsbee, Tex., summer, 1960. Author: Through Their Eyes, 1987. Mem. Friends of Fine Arts-Baylor U., Waco, Tex., 1981—; mem. Scholastic Art awards Regional Bd., Houston, 1978-84; bd. dirs. Houston Council Student Art Awards, Inc., 1984—. Named Tchr. of Yr. Pasadena Ind. Sch. Dist., 1975; Outstanding Secondary Educator of Am., 1975; Tex. Art Educator of Yr., 1985. Mem. Tex. Art Edn. Assn. (rep., editor newsletter 1982-85, chmn. supervision div. 1982-83, v.p. membership 1978-80, chmn. pub. info. com., regional chmn. youth art month 1980-82; regional chmn. membership com. 1976-78, pres. elect 1987), Tex. Alliance for Arts Edn. (bd. vice chmn. 1984-86), Nat. Art Edn. Assn. (conv. com. 1977, 85), Houston Art Edn. Assn. (sec. 1969), Nat. Assn. for Supervision and Curriculum Devel., Delta Kappa Gamma (2d v.p. 1984-86). Baptist. Home: 106 Ravenhead Houston TX 77034

REID, LAURA MARCELLA, marketing executive; b. Vidalia, Ga., July 25, 1952; d. Robert Hugh and Lanette Marie (Haar) R. Student, Monticello Jr. Coll., 1970-71; BA, U. Ga., 1974. Bookkeeper First Nat. Bank, Vidalia, Ga., 1975-76; travel agt. Ship 'n Shore Travel, Macon, Ga., 1976-77; acting dir. of admissions, asst. dir. admissions Wesleyan Coll., Macon, 1977-79; admissions couselor Ga. Inst. Tech., Atlanta, 1979-81; market devel. mgr. Coca-Cola USA, Atlanta, 1981—; proprietor The Little House, Savannah, Ga., 1987—. Vol. DAR, Ga., 1970—, High Mus., Atlanta, 1978-86, Jr. League DeKalb County, Inc., Decatur, Ga., 1984-86, Jr. League Savannah, 1986—; bd. dirs. Hist. Savannah Found., Ga., 1988—; trustee Ga. Hist. Preservation, 1980—, Velfair Mus., 1986—; mem. jr. com. Atlanta Symphony, 1982-86. Named Hon. State Pres. Ga. Soc. CAR, 1971. Mem. Savannah Area C. of C., Nat. Assn. Female Execs., Phi Theta Kappa, Alpha Delta Pi. Episcopalian. Home: 631 E Victory Dr Savannah GA 31405 Office: The Little House 107 E Gordon St Savannah GA 31401

REID, LYNNE MCARTHUR, pathologist; b. Melbourne, Australia, Nov. 12, 1923; d. Robert Muir and Violet Annie (McArthur) R. M.D., U. Melbourne, 1946; M.D. (hon.), Harvard U., 1976. Reader in exptl. pathology London U., 1964-67, prof. exptl. pathology, 1967-73; dean Cardiothoracic Inst., 1973-76; pathologist-in-chief Children's Hosp. Med. Center, Boston, 1976—; S. Burt Wolbach prof. pathology Harvard Med. Sch., Boston, 1976—. Mem. Royal Coll. Physicians (U.K.), Royal Australian Coll. Physicians, Royal Coll. Pathologists, Royal Soc. Medicine, Royal Inst. Gt. Britain, Pathol. Soc. Gt. Britain and Ireland, Thoracic Soc., Assn. Clin. Pathologists, Brit. Thoracic and Tb Assn., Fleischner Soc., Can. Thoracic Soc., Neonatal Soc., Am. Thoracic Soc., Am. Soc. Pathologists, Fedn. Am. Socs. Exptl. Biology. Office: 300 Longwood Ave Boston MA 02115

REID, NANCI GLICK, health care professional; b. Brookline, Mass., Sept. 22, 1941; d. Robert Louis and Esther (Shostack) Green; m. Ronald Jay Coleman, July 5, 1962 (div. Sept. 1969); 1 child, Lori Sue; m. Alan Marshall Glick, Jan. 12, 1976 (div. Oct. 1978); 1 child, Staci Alison; m. Raymond Augustus Reid, Feb. 15, 1985. AS, Garland Jr. Coll., Boston, 1960; student, Harvard U. Extension, 1961, 64, 65; BS, Northeastern U., 1983. Cert. clin. lab. sci., clin. lab. specialist in cytogenetics. Research technician Children's Hosp., Boston, 1961-63; sr. research technician, med. technician New Eng. Med. Ctr., Boston, 1963-65, 67-69; cytogeneticist supr. Carney Hosp., Boston, 1969-84; instr. medicine Med. Sch. Tufts U., Boston, 1969-86; systems analyst Cognos/Coulter Corp., Waltham, Mass., 1976-77; med. technologist Milton (Mass.) Hosp, 1978-83, Mass. Eye and Ear, Boston, 1983-84; lab. mgr. Harvard Community Health Plan, Braintree, Mass., 1985-88; chairperson com. continuing edn. Harvard Community Health Plan, Boston, 1986—; quality control mgr. Oncolab Inc., Boston, 1988; presenter abstracts at 12th and 13th Internat. Hematology Soc. Confs. Contbr. articles to profl. jours. Mem. Assn. Cytogenetic Technologists (pres. 1976-78), Am. Soc. Med. Tech. (lectr.), Sigma Epsilon Rho (v.p. 1987-88, former treas.). Republican. Jewish. Clubs: Plymouth Yacht, Pythian Sisters (sec., editor 1966-67) (Sharon, Mass.). Home: 70 Flintlocke Dr Plymouth MA 02360

REID, NATALIE, language and writing specialist; b. Oakland, Calif., Mar. 8, 1947; d. Harold and Gloria (Schleifer) R.; m. Charles Edward Wood, May 19, 1985; children: DoShik Wood, Thomas Wood. BA, U. Calif., Berkeley, 1968; MA, San Francisco State U., 1974. Cert. coll. instr., Calif. Instr. ESL U. Calif., Berkeley, 1974-77; pres. Natalie Reid Assocs., San Francisco and Southborough, Mass., 1977—; cons. HUD, San Francisco, 1977—, Mortgage Bankers Assn., Washington, 1983—, Reed Services, Newton, Mass., 1986—, Gillette, Boston, 1987—. Author: America Grows Young, 1981; co-author: Dictionary of English Phrasal Usage, 1985. Mem. Nat. Assn. Female Execs.

REID, RUTH MARGARET, communications company executive, writer; b. Hartford, Conn., June 16, 1938; d. Edwin Christie and Linda Margaret (Richards) Hanford; m. Gerald J. Reid, June 13, 1959 (div. Jan. 1975); children: Margaret, Jerry, Mary Elisabeth, Tricia. Student, Trinity Coll., U. Conn.; cert., IBM Mgmt. Sch., 1986. Contract underwriting asst. The Travelers, Hartford, 1956-57; group underwriting asst. Conn. Gen., Bloomfield, Conn., 1958-59; free lance pub. relations, free lance writer Hartford, 1968-70; editor Guider Mag.-Hartford, 1970-71; communications dir. United Way of Greater Hartford, 1971-77; assoc. exec. dir. United Way Services, Cleve., 1977-85; pres. Ruth Reid & Co., Cleve., 1985—; cons. United Way of Tri-State, N.Y.C., 1987—; chmn. market research United Way of Am., Alexandria, Va., 1978-84, vice chmn. communications, 1982-84, chmn. conf.communications program, 1984. Contbr. articles to profl. jours. Campaign coordinator U.S. Rep. Toby Moffett, Suffield, Conn., 1976; active mem. Leadership Cleve., 1983—, various arts and service orgns., Cleve.; chmn. Mayor's Award for Volunteerism Pub. Relations, Cleve., 1985-86. Recipient over 100 awards for communications programs and materials, films, advt., publs., 1975—. Mem. Advt. Club. Home: 3266 Braemar Rd Shaker Heights OH 44120 Office: Ruth Reid & Co 700 W Saint Clair Ave Suite 320 Cleveland OH 44113

REID-BILLS, MAE, editor, historian; b. Shreveport, La.; d. Dayton Taylor and Bessie Oline (Boles) Reid; m. Frederick Gurdon Bills (div.); children—Marjorie Reid, Nancy Hawkins, Frederick Taylor, Virginia Thomas, Elizabeth Sharples. A.B., Stanford U., 1942, M.A., 1965; Ph.D., U. Denver, 1977. Mng. editor Am. West mag., Tucson, Ariz., 1979—. Gen. Electric fellow, 1963, William Robertson Coe fellow, 1964. Mem. Orgn. Am. Historians, Am. Hist. Assn., Phi Beta Kappa, Phi Alpha Theta. Office: American West 7000 E Tanque Verde Tucson AZ 85715

REIDLINGER, DEBORAH KAY ANNE, computer systems professional; b. Calgary, Alta., Can., June 5, 1950; d. Lawerence and Anne (Lippert) R.; m. Donald William Fraser, Sept. 2, 1978; 1 child: Cameron Scott. BSc in Math., U. Calgary, 1970; MSc in Computer Science, U. B.C., 1972. Programmer, analyst Ins. Co. B.C., Vancouver, 1973-76; systems engr. IBM Can., Vancouver, 1977-79; computer analyst B.C. Telephone Co., Vancouver, 1979-86, mgr. client computing, 1986-87, product mgr. major bus. mktg., 1988—. Office: BC Telephone, 3777 Kingsway, Burnaby Can

REIDY, MINDA GENE, data processing executive; b. New Bedford, Mass., July 21, 1960; d. Louis and Thelma (Levitt) Halberstadt; m. Richard D. Reidy, July 3, 1983; 1 child, Michael William. BSBA, Boston U., 1982, MS in Mgmt. Info. Systems, 1984. EDP auditor New Eng. Electric Systems, Westborough, Mass., 1982; sr. info. systems analyst Avco Systems Textron, Wilmington, Mass., 1983-87; software specialist Digital Equipment Corp., Waltham, Mass., 1987—. Mem. Am. Prodn. and Inventory Control Soc. (cert.; treas. So. N.H. chpt. 1986-87), Boston U. Alumni Assn. (v.p. Mgmt. Info. Systems program sect. 1986-87). Office: Digital Equipment Corp 235 Wyman St Waltham MA 02154-1265

REILING, CECILIA POWERS, hospital chaplain; b. Boston, Mar. 23, 1926; d. Edward Thomas and Delia (Hehir) Powers; m. Thomas Leonard Reiling, Nov. 11, 1960; stepchildren—Elizabeth, Kathleen, Mary, Eileen. B.A., Northeastern U., 1964, M.A., 1973; M.Ed., Boston U., 1979. Instr., advisor Chamberlayne Jr. Coll., Boston, 1964-73; instr. Bryant Coll., North Smithfield, R.I., 1973-79; chaplaincy vol. Sherrill House, Boston, 1972-79, researcher, 1977-79; program dir., v.p. College Club, Boston, 1970-72; chaplaincy vol. Martin Meml. Hosp., Stuart, Fla., 1980—. Mem. Am. Sociol. Assn., Mass. Sociol. Soc., Christian Sociol. Soc., Assn. for Clin. Pastoral Edn. Republican. Roman Catholic. Clubs: Stuart Yacht and Country (Fla.); Kittansett (Marion, Mass.). Avocations: golf, music. Home: 4264 SE Fairway E Stuart FL 34997

REILLY, CATHERINE REGINA, information manager; b. Cooperstown, N.Y., July 22, 1949; d. John Patrick and Catherine Regina (Dempsey) Reilly; B.A., Coll. of Mt. St. Vincent, 1970; M.L.S. magna cum laude, Pratt Inst., 1972. With Chase Manhattan Bank, N.Y.C., 1972—, research supr., 1975, asst. treas., mgr. research library, 1977, 2d v.p., mgr. info. center, 1981-84, bus. systems officer legal dept., 1984-85, v.p. legal dept., 1985—; chmn. Janus Seminar, 1983. Trustee Massapequa Pub. Library, 1986—; mem. WANG Legal Council, 1987—.. Mem. Nat. Info Conf. (mem. program com. 1980), Spl. Libraries Conf. (coordinator fin. insts. rountable 1979), Spl. Libraries Assn. (program chmn. N.Y. chpt. 1980-81), ALA, Am. Soc. Info. Sci., Assn. Info. Mgrs., Am. Assn. Law Librarians, Assn. Legal Adminstrs., Internat. Soc. Wang Users, Phi Beta Mu. Editor, Biz-dex, 1975-80; editor Bus. and Fin. Newsletter, 1980-82. Office: 1 Chase Manhattan Plaza New York City NY 10081

REILLY, M. SUZANNE, educational program director, consultant; b. Lakewood, N.J., June 5, 1941; d. James Russell and Margaret Katherine (Sallay) Hyres; m. Frank Richard Reilly, June 9, 1962; children: Jonathan F., Joshua J. BA, Trenton (N.J.) State Coll., 1963; MEd, Rutgers U., 1966, postgrad., 1981—; MA, Fairleigh Dickenson U., 1976. Succesively elem. tchr., title I tchr., title I head tchr., coordinator of funded programs Jackson (N.J.) Bd. Edn., 1963-84, dir. funded programs and community services, 1984-88, dir. funded programs and staff devel., 1988—; cons. Instructional Tng. Assocs., Howell, N.J., 1981—. Mem. PTO, DAV, N.J. Assn. Fed. Program Adminstrs. (pres.), Jackson Twp. Adminstrs. Assn. (pres.), N.J. Assn. Sch. Adminstrs. (exec. com.), Assn. Supervision and Curriculum Devel., N.J. Edn. Assn. (women in edn. com.), NE Coalition Ednl. Leaders. Unitarian. Club: Cruzers Soccer (Jackson). Home: RD #4 Box 611 Jackson NJ 08527 Office: Jackson Sch Dist Don Connor Blvd Jackson NJ 08527

REILLY, MAUREEN GRIFFITH, media specialist, educator; b. Jamaica, N.Y., Nov. 17, 1942; d. George Thomas and Joan Loretta (Curley) Griffith; m. Thomas Patrick Reilly, Nov. 18, 1967; children—Maryanne, Brian, Megan. B.A., Albertus Magnus Coll., 1964; M.S., Central Conn. State U., 1980, 6th yr. certification, 1985. Tchr., Levittown Pub. Schs. (N.Y.), 1964-68, Summit Pub. Schs. (N.J.), 1969, Wethersfield Pub. Schs. (Conn.), 1979; media specialist Hartford Pub. Schs. (Conn.), 1980, Lewis Mills High Sch., Burlington, Conn., 1980—, coordinator library handbook, 1981-85, coordinator video programs, 1980—; coordinator library skills curriculum Burlington Pub. Schs., 1982-83. Author: (with Betty Billman) Selected Resources for Teachers in Connecticut, 1980. Bd. dirs. Farmington Pub. Library (Conn.), 1976-80, Farmington Mus., 1976-80. Newspaper Fund scholar NYU, 1966; Pub. Sch. Coop. Libraries grantee Dept. Edn., State of Conn., 1982; Carlton W.H. Erickson award Conn. Ednl. Media Assn., 1983. Mem. ALA, Assembly on Lit. for Adolescents, Conn. Ednl. Media Assn. (sec. 1982-83, v.p. 1983-85) Albertus Magnus Coll. Alumnae Assn., LWV, Phi Delta Kappa. Democrat. Roman Catholic. Club: Red Oak Hill. Home: 9 Paper Chase Dr Farmington CT 06032 Office: Lewis Mills High Sch Library Rt 4 Burlington CT 06013

REIMER, SUSAN, health science association administrator; b. Rochester, N.Y., Feb. 19, 1951; d. Charles Blaisdell and Hester Louise (Ward) R. BS in Nursing, Vanderbilt U., 1973, MS in Nursing, 1975; MBA, Tulane U., 1985. Registered nurse, Tenn. Staff nurse VA Hosp., Nashville, 1973-74; psychiatric head nurse Hosp. Corp. Am., Nashville, 1975-76, dir. nursing, 1976-82, dir. in-patient adolescent, 1976-83, interim adminstr., 1982-83; asst. adminstr. Hosp. Corp. Am., New Orleans, 1983-84, interim hosp. exec. dir., 1984; adminstr. Psychiatric Insts. Am., New Orleans, 1984—; guest lectr. U. Tenn., Nashville, 1978-83. Bd. dirs., asst. sec. JoEllen Smith Governing Bd., New Orleans, 1984—; bd. dirs. Tulane Exec. Edn. Council, New Orleans, 1985—. Grantee NIMH, 1974. Fellow Ortho-Psychiatric Assn.; mem. Nat. Assn. Female Execs., New Orleans Mental Health Assn., Harvey Canal Indsl. Assn., Menniger Found., Tulane U. Bus. Alumni Assn. (bd. dirs. 1985—), New Orleans C. of C.. Democrat. Club: Krewe of Iris (New Orleans). Office: Jo Ellen Smith Psychiat Hosp 4601 Patterson Rd New Orleans LA 70114

REIMER, SUSAN MARTIN, lawyer; b. Long Beach, Calif., Aug. 7, 1953; d. Ival Eugene and Ernestine (Flinn) Martin; m. Robert A. Reimer, Aug. 21, 1982. Student Clemson U., 1971-73; J.D., John Marshall Law Sch., Savannah, Ga., 1979. Bar: Ga. 1979. Legal asst. Moss Creek Devel. Corp., Hilton Head, S.C., 1974-76, Sea Pines Plantation, Hilton Head Island, 1976-78, Bouhan, Williams & Levy, Savannah, 1979; assoc. Stephen E. Curry, Augusta, Ga., 1980-82; sole practice, Augusta, 1982-85; assoc. Paine, Dalis, Smith & McElreath, P.C., Augusta, 1985-86, sole practice Augusta, 1987—. Pres., dir. Central Savannah River council Girl Scouts U.S.A., 1983-86; elder Covenant Presbyterian Ch. Mem. Augusta Bar Assn. (sec.), Ga. Bar Assn., Ga. Trial Lawyers Assn., ABA, Nu Beta Epsilon (Frat. Achievement award 1979). Home: 2416 Cherokee Rd Augusta GA 30904 Office: 505 Courthouse Ln Augusta GA 30901

REIN, CATHERINE AMELIA, financial services executive, lawyer; b. Lebanon, Pa., Feb. 7, 1943; d. John and Esther (Scott) Shultz; m. Barry B. Rein, May 1, 1965. B.A. summa cum laude, Pa. State U., 1965; J.D. magna cum laude, N.Y. U., 1968. Bar: N.Y. 1968, U.S. Supreme Ct. 1971. Asso. Dewey, Ballantine, Bushby, Palmer & Wood, N.Y.C., 1968-74; with Continental Group, Stamford, Conn., 1974-85; sec., sr. atty. Continental Group, 1976-77; sec., asst. gen. counsel Continental Diversified Ops., 1978-80; v.p., gen. counsel Continental Group, 1980-85; v.p. human resources Met. Life Ins. Co., N.Y.C., 1985-88, sr. v.p. human resources, 1988—; bd. dirs. Bank of N.Y. Mem. ABA, Assn. of Bar of City of N.Y. Episcopalian. Home: 21 E 22d St 8B New York NY 10010 Office: Met Life Ins Co 1 Madison Ave New York NY 10010

REINARZ, KAREN NIELSEN, entrepreneur, publishing company executive; b. Horsens, Denmark, Apr. 6, 1941; came to U.S., 1948; d. Kurt Ejvind and Luise (Koch) Nielsen; m. Robert Charles Reinarz, Dec. 27, 1961; children: Robert Charles, Kristine Reinarz Parks. Student, U. Calif., Berkeley, 1959-60, San Diego State U., 1960-62, U. Tex., Austin, summer 1963. Model Mary Webb Davis "Living Look", Los Angeles and London, 1959-68; founder, mng. editor Mission Pub. Co., Mission Viejo, Calif., 1968—; owner Bright Ideas, Greenwich, Conn., 1975-84; v.p., sec.-treas. R.C. Reinarz and Co., Inc., San Antonio, 1981-86; ptnr., gen. mgr. C.W. Ranch Enterprises, Sisterdale, Tex., 1986—; cons. Atlantic Mgmt. Services, San Antonio, 1986—. Founder Ednl. Media Ctr. Thousand Oaks (Calif.) Sch. Dist., 1972-73; mem. fin. com. Greenwich Acad., 1981-82, chairperson renovation com., 1983; mem. gardening com. Brunswick Boys Sch., Greenwich, 1978-80. Recipient 2d pl. award Nat. Crewel Contest Phila. Mus., 1976. Republican.

REINER, MARY ELISABETH, public relations specialist; b. N.Y.C., Apr. 19, 1931; d. Francis Drake and Ethel B. (Pleis) Wells; m. John Paul Reiner, July 27, 1961; children—Mary E., Clark B. B.A., Middlebury Coll., 1953; M.A. in Anthropology, NYU, 1955; diploma Russian Inst., Columbia U., 1960, M.A. in Pub. Law and Govt., 1960. Prof. govt. Notre Dame campus St. John's U., N.Y.C., 1960-62; editor UNICEF, N.Y.C., 1973-77; info. officer U.S. Com. for UNICEF, N.Y.C., 1977-79; dir. pub. info. Internat. Human Assistance Programs, N.Y.C., 1979-81; devel. dir. Nat. Child Labor Com., N.Y.C., 1981-83; dir. resource devel. Internat. Inst. Rural Reconstrn., N.Y.C., 1984-86;dir. devel. N.Y.C. Mission Soc., 1986—. Editor newsletter News of the World's Children, 1977-79, NGO-UNICEF Newsletter, 1973-77. Nat. bd. dirs. Girl Scouts U.S.A., 1975-81; chmn. devel. World Leisure and Recreation Assn., 1980-83; del. Care, Inc., 1979-81; mem., head team of reps. at UN, World Assn. Girl Guides and Girl Scouts, 1969-78, hon. assoc. world com., London, 1978, mem. world conf. Finland, 1969, Can., 1972, London, 1975; bd. dirs. World Found. Girl Guides and Girl Scouts, 1987—. Mem. Women Execs. in Pub. Relations, Pub. Relations Soc. Am. (chpt. pub. service council 1979—), Nat. Soc. Fund-Raising Execs., Women in Communications, N.Y. Jr. League (dir. 1969-70, chmn. sustaining mems. com. 1973-74). Republican. Roman Catholic. Home: 340 E 72d St New York NY 10021 Office: 105 E 22d St New York NY 10010

REINERT, KATHLEEN HERRON, analytical chemist; b. Santa Monica, Calif., July 1, 1956; d. Thomas James and Virginia (Owen) Herron; Alumni scholar, Pomona Coll., 1974-78; m. Ted Reinert, Aug. 25, 1979; 1 child, Edward Thomas. With Beckman Instruments, 1976, U.S. Borax Research, 1977-78; analytical chemist Burroughs Corp., Carlsbad, Calif., 1978-82, microelectronics complex, San Diego, 1982-86; sr. scientist Gen. Dynamics Convair div., San Diego, 1986—. Mem. Am. Chem. Soc., Inst. Environ. Scis., ASTM, Soc. Separationists. Home: 4851 Regency Circle Oceanside CA 92056

REINERT, PAMELA ANN, social services agency administrator; b. Pipestone, Minn., Dec. 28, 1952; d. Louis Ilse Bickford and Marcella M. (Oye) Hoisington; m. Roger Leo Reinert, Mar. 14, 1970; children: Roger, Aarron, Michael, Michelle, Yolanda, Rosa, Karina, Simone. BA, S.W. Minn. State Coll., 1973; postgrad., Mankato State U., 1974; MA, Coll. St. Thomas, St. Paul, 1982. Lic. social worker. Behavior cons. Robert E. Milton Home, Redwood Falls, Minn., 1972-73; tchr. Renville Co., Olivia, Minn., 1973-74; coordinator spl. edn. Region 6E Headstart Program, Cosmos, Minn., 1974-75; therapist WCCSC, Willmar, Minn., 1975; adoption specialist Crossroads, Mpls., 1976-84; founder, exec. dir. Building Families through Adoption, Dawson, Minn., 1984—; co-founder Project Love, Willmar, 1983; cons. Grief Counseling, Mpls., 1987—. Contbr. articles to profl. jours. Treas. Nat. Coalition to End Racism, 1988—; coordinator Heal the Children, 1987—. Project Hometown Am. grantee, 1986. Mem. Nat. Assn. Social Workers, N.D. Social Workers Assn. Lutheran. Home: RR 1 Box 188 Dawson MN 56232 Office: Building Families through Adoption 7th & Chestnut Sts Dawson MN 56232

REINES, RENA RAE, special education administrator; b. N.Y.C., Dec. 6, 1940; d. Joseph and Rose F. (Greisman) R. BA in Physical Edn. with honors, Hunter Coll., 1962; MA, Stony Brook U., 1975; postgrad., Coll. New Rochelle, Caldwell Coll., C.W. Post U., Hofstra U., 1962-78. Cert. elem. tchr., N.Y. Tchr. high schs. N.Y.C., 1962-67; tchr. elem. schs. Long Island, N.Y., 1967-79, Buffalo, 1979-85; supr. spl. edn. Buffalo City Sch. Bd., 1985—; Chmn. various curriculum coms. Deer Park Sch. System, mem. various coms. Active United Way, ARC, Children's Hosp., Buffalo Zool. Assn., Am. Heart Assn., Am. Lung Assn.; rep. to P.T.A.; founder Spl. Olympics for Handicapped On L.I. Mem. Women's Equity (Buffalo chpt. v.p.), Buffalo Council Suprs. & Adminstrs., Cen. Office Educator's Assn., NEA, Buffalo Tchrs. Fedn., Assn. Children Learning Disabilities, Buffalo Council Suprs. and Adminstrs., Am. Fedn. Sch. Adminstrs., Assn. for Supervision and Curriculum Devel., Assn. Women in Phys. Edn. in N.Y. (pres.), N.Y. State Assn. Health, Phys. Edn, Recreation. Home: 180 Linwood Ave Buffalo NY 14209 Office: Buffalo Bd Edn 816 City Hall Buffalo NY 14202

REINHARD, SISTER MARY MARTHE, university executive; b. McKeesport, Pa., Aug. 29, 1929; d. Regis C. and Leona (Reese) R. AB, Notre Dame Coll.; MA, U. Notre Dame. Asst. prin. Regina High Sch., Cleve., 1960-62, prin., 1963-64; prin. Notre Dame Acad., Chardon, Ohio, 1965-72; pres. Notre Dame Coll. of Ohio, Cleve., 1973—. Campaign chairperson United Way Services, 1985, v.p.-at-large, 1987; trustee NCCJ, Cleve., 1987. Named one of 100 most influential women in Cleve. Women's City Club, 1983, one of 79 most interesting people in Cleve. The Cleve. mag., 1979. Mem. Ohio Found. Ind. Colls. (vice-chairperson 1987), Assn. Ind. Colls. and Univs. (policy com. 1987). Roman Catholic. Home: 4545 College Rd Cleveland OH 44121 Office: Notre Dame Coll 4545 College Rd Cleveland OH 44121

REINHARDT, CINDY LOU, real estate development consultant; b. Ft. Worth, Apr. 2, 1950; d. Marvin and Marjeree (Downing) R.; B.A. in Polit. Sci., S.W. Tex. State U., 1971; M. Urban and Regional Planning, Tex. A&M U., 1975. Program dir. South/West Planning Assos., Bryan, Tex., 1973-75; community planner Houston-Galveston Area Council, 1975-76; dir. planning and policy devel. Houston Housing Authority, 1976-79, dep. exec. dir., 1979-80; pres. Creative Transitions Inc., Houston, 1980-81; v.p. Realm Devel. Corp., Houston, 1982-86; adj. prof. city planning Tex. So. U., 1979-81. Vice pres. Young Democrats Tex., 1972. Mem. Am. Inst. Cert. Planners (charter), Am. Planning Assn. (chmn. profl. devel. com. Tex. chpt. 1980-82). Home and office: 4235 Case Houston TX 77005

REINHART, KAY ELLEN, arts marketing professional; b. Port Washington, Wis., Sept. 20, 1946; d. John L. and Betty (Morrison) Rahmlow; m. Carl F. Reinhart III, Nov. 25, 1967 (div. 1972); m. Charles E. Ziff, May 29, 1976; 1 child, Emily Lambert Ziff. Student, U. Wis., Madison, 1964-66; BFA, U. Wis., Milw., 1969. Exec. asst. Nikolais-Louis Found., N.Y.C., 1969-71; art editor Harcourt Brace Jovanovich, N.Y.C., 1972-79; mgr., talent coordinator Ziff Mktg. Inc., Brooklyn Heights, N.Y., 1981—; owner, artist Open East Pottery, Brooklyn Heights, 1975—. Editor (screenplay) The Winning Sky; (novel) This Ascending Dust, 1983. Mem. Conn. Craftsmen, Greenpeace, Coop. Am. Office: Ziff Mktg Inc 118 Willow St Brooklyn NY 11201

REINHART, KELLEE CONNELY, journalist; b. Kearney, Nebr., Dec. 15, 1951; d. Vaughn Eugene and Mary Jo (Mullen) Connely; m. Stephen Wayne Reinhart, June 15, 1974; children: Keegan Connely, Channing Mullen. B.A., U. Ala., 1972, M.S., 1974. Advt. copywriter Stas. WTBC-AM, WUOA-FM, 1970-72; asst. mgr. Ala. Press Assn., 1972-74; asst. to the editor Antique Monthly mag., 1974-75, mng. editor, 1975-77; editorial dir. Antique Monthly and Horizons mags., 1977—. Mem. Soc. Profl. Journalists, Am. Soc. Mag. Editors, Art Table, Sigma Delta Chi. Office: 1305 Greensboro Ave Tuscaloosa AL 35401

REINING, BETH LAVERNE (BETTY), public relations consultant, journalist; b. Fargo, N.D.; d. George and Grace (Twiford) Reimche; student N.D. State Coll., U. Minn., Glendale Community Coll., Calif. State Coll., Carson; 1 dau., Carolyn Ray Toohey Hiett; m. Jack Warren Reining, Oct. 3, 1976 (div. 1984). Originated self-worth seminars in Phoenix, 1970-76; owner Janzik Pub. Relations, 1971-76; talk show reporter-hostess What's Happening in Ariz., Sta. KPAZ-TV, 1970-73; writer syndicated column People Want to Know, Today newspaper, Phoenix, 1973; owner JB Communications, Phoenix, 1976-84; owner, pres. Media Communications, 1984—; freelance writer; tchr. How to Weigh Your Self-Worth courses Phoenix Coll., Rio Solado Community Coll., Phoenix, 1976-84; muralist, works include 25 figures in med. office. Founder Ariz. Call-A-Teen Youth Resources, Inc., pres., 1975-76, v.p., 1976-77, now bd. dirs. Recipient awards including 1st pl. in TV writing Nat. Fedn. Press Women, 1971-88, numerous state awards in journalism Ariz. Press Women, 1971-76, Good Citizen award Builders of Greater Ariz., 1961. Mem. Ariz. Press Women, No. Ariz. Press Women (pres. 1983), Nat. Fedn. Am. Press Women, Pub. Relations Soc. Am., Phoenix Pub. Relations Soc., Nat. Acad. TV Arts and Scis., Phoenix Valley of Sun Convention Bur., Verde Valley C. of C. (bd. dirs., tourism chmn. 1986-87, Best Chair of Yr. award 1986), Phoenix Metro C. of C. Cottonwood C. of C. (chmn. of Yr. award, 1986). Inventor stocking-tension twist footlet, 1962. Club: Phoenix Press. Office: PO Box 10509 Phoenix AZ 85064 Address: PO Box 10509 Phoenix AZ 85016

REINOLD, CHRISTY DIANE, school counselor, consultant; b. Neodasha, Kans., July 21, 1942; d. Ernest Sherman and Faye Etta (Herbert) Wild; m. Willaim Owen Reinold, Dec. 20, 1964; children: Elizabeth, Rebecca. BA Edn., Calif. State U., Fresno, 1964, MA in Edn. and Psychology, 1964. Cert. counselor, family wellness instr.; lic. mental health counselor, Fla. Tchr. Clovis (Calif.) Unified Sch. Dist., 1965-66, Santa Clara (Calif.) Unified Sch. Dist., 1966-67, Inst. Internat. Chateaubriand, Cannes, France, 1968-69; tchr., vice prin. Internat. Sch., Siliema, Malta, 1969-70; elem. sch. counselor Duval City Schs., Jacksonville, Fla., 1977-82, Lodi (Calif.) Unified Sch. Dist., 1982—; cons. Calif. Dept. Edn.; mem. Calif. Commn. on Tchr. Credentialing, Sacramento, 1986—. Chmn. bd. dirs. Oak Crest Child Care Ctr., Jacksonville, 1979-81. Mem. AAUW (by-laws chmn. 1980—, 3d v.p. 1974, 1st v.p. 1980), Am. Sch. Counselor Assn., Calif. Sch. Counselor Assn. (legis. chmn. 1985—, newsletter editor 1985—), Calif. Assn. Counseling and Devel., Lodi Pupil Personnel Assn. (pres. 1986-87), Fla. Sch. Counselors Assn., Lodi Pupil Personnel Assn. (pres. 1986-87). Republican. Home: 1180 Northwood Dr Lodi CA 95240

REINSCHMIEDT, ANNE TIERNEY, nurse; b. Washington, Mar. 6, 1932; d. Edward F. and Frances (Palmer) Tierney; m. Edwin Ruben Reinschmiedt, Sept. 20, 1959 (div. 1961); 1 child, Kathleen Frances Tierney. BS, Cen. State U., Edmond, Okla., 1975. Nurse San Jose (Calif.) Hosp., 1952-55; adminstrv. asst. Hominy (Okla.) Hosp., 1961-63; nurse Jackson County Dept. Health, Altus, Okla., 1963-65; adminstr. Propp's Inc., Oklahoma City, 1965-80; nursing homes cons. Propps & Self, Oklahoma City, 1965—; operator, pres. Shamrock Health Care Ctr., Bethany, Okla., 1981—; cons. in field. Author: Recovery Room Procedures, 1958. Mem. Jackson County (Okla.) Draft Bd., 1965-70. Served to lt. USN, 1955-59. Mem. Am. Nurses Assn., Nat. Assn. Residential Care Facilities, Okla. Assn. Residential Care Facilities (bd. dirs. 1983-85, pres. 1981-87), Beta Sigma Phi, Phi Alpha Delta. Republican. Roman Catholic. Office: Shamrock Health Care Box 848 Bethany OK 73008

REINSTEIN, NAOMI SHERRY, national credit manager; b. Bronx, N.Y., Mar. 10, 1940; d. Isidor and Rhoda Hilda (Schwaidelson) Zurin; m. David H. Reinstein; children: Patti Carol De Lorenzo, Fran Laurie. BA, Hunter Coll., 1960. Credit clk. S.A. Schonbrun, Palisades Park, N.J., 1977-79; credit mgr. Comprehensive Video, Northvale, N.J., 1979-83; nat. credit mgr. Onkyo USA Corp., Ramsey, N.J., 1983—; chairperson Riemer Reporting, Cleve., 1985-86. Mem. N.J. Credit Mgrs. Assn. Home: 10 Fletcher Ct Spring Valley NY 10977 Office: Onkyo USA Corp 200 Williams Dr Ramsey NJ 07446

REISINGER, SANDRA SUE, journalist, lawyer; b. Washington Court House, Ohio, Feb. 27, 1946; d. Dale E. and Elinor Jean (McMurray) R. B.S., Ohio State U., 1968, M.A., 1969; J.D., U. Dayton (Ohio), 1980. Bar: Ohio 1980. Teaching asst. Ohio State U., 1968-69; with Dayton Daily News, 1969-81, asst. mng. editor, 1976-81; mng. editor The Miami News, 1981—. Mem. ABA, Associated Press Mng. Editors Assn. (bd. dirs. 1982-87, exec. com. 1987—). Office: The Miami News PO Box 615 Miami FL 33152

REISLER, HELEN BARBARA, publishing and advertising executive; b. N.Y.C., June 21; d. George and Elizabeth Lois (Schultz) Gottesman; B.S., in Edn., N.Y. U., 1954; M.S. in Edn. and Reading, L.I. U., 1978; m. Melvin Reisler, June 5, 1955; children—Susan O'Brien, Karen, Keith. Elem. tchr., N.Y.C., 1954-78; instr. grad. sch., adj. lectr. L.I. U., Bklyn., 1978; account exec. N.Y. Yellow Pages, Inc., N.Y.C., 1979, personnel mgr., 1979, adminstrv. dir., 1980-83, v.p. personnel, 1983-84, v.p. adminstrn./personnel, 1984-85, also dir.; staff specialist sales and market support Southwestern Bell Publs., 1985-88, NY. mgr. pub. relations and recruitment N.Y. Yellow Pages/Mast Advt. and Pubs., Inc. of Southwestern Bell, 1988—; recruiter Northeast Region, N.Y. area community relations rep.; moderator weekly cable TV show New York Business Forum, N.Y.C., 1983—. Named Ptnr. in Edn., N.Y.C. Bd. Edn., 1984. Mem. Sales Execs. Club N.Y. (bd. dirs., reception, membership and mem. relations coms., chmn. youth edn., v.p. 1987—), Execs. Assn. Greater N.Y. Clubs: NYU, Heritage Hill Top Hatters, Sales Execs. (v.p.). Profiled in various bus. publs. Lodge: Rotary. Home: 47 Plaza St Park Slope Brooklyn NY 11217 Office: Southwestern Bell Publs 91 Fifth Ave New York NY 10003

REISMAN, JUDITH A., educational institute executive; b. Hillside, N.J., Apr. 11, 1935; M.A. in Speech Communication, Case Western Res. U., 1976, Ph.D. in Speech Communication, 1980. Faculty dept. anthropology and sociology and sch. of edn. Haifa U., Israel, 1981-83; research prof. sch. edn. Am. U., Washington, 1983-85; founder Inst. Media Edn., 1985—; cons., reviewer grant proposals audio-visual drug programs for youth Dept. Edn., 1987; research design cons. Alcohol and Tobacco Media Analysis in Mainstream Mags. Dept. HHS, 1987-88; cons., field reviewer Drug Free Youth Sch. Candidates Dept. Edn., 1988; lectr.; expert witness. Contbr. articles to profl. jours. Co-recipient Scholastic Mag. awards: Dukane award, 1982, Gold Camera award, 1982, Silver Screen award 1982, Filmstrip of Yr. award, 1981-82, Silver Plaque award, 1982, Family Service Assn. Am. 1st pl. award local TV series, 1974; Best of 1965 award, 1965. Mem. AAAS, Am. Assn. Composers, Authors and Pubs., Internat. Communication Assn., N.Y. Acad. Scis., Soc. Sci. Study Sex, Nat. Black Child Devel. Inst. Office: Inst Media Edn PO Box 7404 Arlington VA 22207

REISMAN, LAURA JAN, respiratory therapy program manager; b. Hartford, Conn., May 25, 1955; d. Hyman Bernard and Renee (Cain) R.; m. Erol Martin Beytas, Aug. 1, 1987. Student, U. Hartford, 1974-77; AS, Manchester (Conn.) Community Coll., 1980; BS in Pub. Health, U. N.C., 1984. Registered respiratory therapist. Respiratory care practitionaer Duke U. Med. Ctr., Durham, N.C., 1980—, asst. dir. pulmonary rehab. program, 1985—. Cantor Judea Reform Congregation, Durham, 1986—. Mem. Nat. Bd. Respiratory Care, Am. Assn. Respiratory Care (chmn.-elect pulmonary rehab. and continuing care sect. 1986—), Am. Assn. Cardiovascular and Pulmonary Rehab. (charter, bd. dirs. 1986-87), N.C. Thoracic Soc., Better Breathers Club (co-founder). Democrat. Home: 4625 Pinedale Dr Durham NC 27705 Office: Duke U Med Ctr Box 3911 Durham NC 27705

REISS, DALE ANNE, investment company executive, accountant; b. Chgo., Sept. 3, 1947; d. Max and Nan (Hart) R.; m. Jerome L. King, Mar. 5, 1978; 1 child, Matthew Reiss. BS, Ill. Inst. Tech., 1967; MBA, U. Chgo., 1970. CPA, Ill. Cost acct. First Nat. Bank, Chgo., 1967; asst. controller City Colls. of Chgo., 1967-70; dir. fin. Chgo. Dept. Pub. Works, 1970-72; prin. Arthur Young & Co., Chgo., 1972-80; sr. v.p., controller Urban Investment & Devel. Co., Chgo., 1980-85, mng. ptnr. Kenneth Leventhal & Co., Chgo., 1985—; bd. dirs. Urban Diversified Properties, com. chmn. Assn. Real Estate Cos. Active Lincoln Park Zool. Soc.; fund raiser Grad. Sch. of U. Chgo.; bd. dirs., treas. Info. Tech. Research Ctr.; bd. dirs. Mus. Sci. and Industry; Urban Land Inst. Mem. Nat. Assn. Real Estate Cos., Fin. Execs. Inst., Am. Inst. CPA's. Clubs: Econ., Metropolitan, Chgo. Yacht. Office: Kenneth Leventhal & Co 500 W Madison St Suite 3300 Chicago IL 60606

REISS, ELAINE SERLIN, advertising agency executive, lawyer; b. N.Y.C., Oct. 27, 1940; d. Morris and Dorothy (Geyer) Serlin; m. Joel A. Reiss, Sept. 1, 1963; children: Joshua Adam, Naomi Lee. B.A., N.Y. U., 1961, LL.M., 1973; LL.B., Columbia U., 1964. Bar: N.Y. 1965. Mgr. legal dept. Doyle Dane Bernbach Advt., 1965-68; mgr. legal clearance dept., then v.p., mgr. legal dept. Ogilvy & Mather, Inc., N.Y.C., 1968-78; sr. v.p., mgr. legal dept. Ogilvy & Mather, Inc., 1978-82, gen. counsel, sec. U.S. bd. dirs., 1982—, exec. v.p., 1985—; industry adv. seminar series on children Georgetown U. Law Sch., 1978-79; mem. part-time faculty NYU Tisch Sch. Arts, 1982—. Recipient Matrix award in advt. N.Y. Women in Communications, 1987. Mem. Am. Assn. Advt. Agencies (chmn. legal com. 1979-81), ABA (com. on corp. law depts.), Assn. Bar City N.Y., Legal Aid Soc. (bd. dirs.). Office: 2 E 48th St New York NY 10017

REITER, ELAINE MARY, state agency administrator; b. Ellsworth, Minn., July 21, 1928; d. Jacob Nicholas and Esther Suzanne (Kappes) R.; B.S. in Bus. Adminstrn., Marquette U., Milw., 1953; M.Ed. in Counseling, U. Mo., Columbia, 1967, M.P.A., 1976. Personnel asst. Square D Co., Milw., 1953-56; exec. asst. Psychol. Service Corp., St. Louis, 1957-63; services mgr. Psychol. Assos., St. Louis, 1963-64; counselor Mo. Employment Service, St. Louis, 1964-68; dep. dir. Mo. Office Aging, Jefferson City, 1968-72; cons. adult services to State of Mo., 1973-76; regional adminstr. Mo. Div. Family Services and Aging, 1977-81, alternative services adminstr. Mo. Div. Aging, 1981—; bd. dirs. Mo. Green Thumb, 1978, Nat. Com. for the Prevention of Elder Abuse, 1988—; mem. nat. protective services task force Adminstrn. Aging, 1982; del. White House Conf. Aging, 1971. Recipient various service awards. Mem. Am. Public Welfare Assn. (chmn. membership Mo. chpt. 1976-77), Mo. Assn. Social Welfare (dir. 1975-82, exec. com. 1976-79, chmn. aging task force 1975-80, chmn. Kansas City div. 1981-82), AAUW, Geront. Soc., Mo. Assn. Prevention Adult Abuse, Mid-Am. Congress Aging. Roman Catholic. Club: Lakewood. Lodge: Zonta. Office: Div of Aging 2701 W Main PO Box 1337 Jefferson City MO 65102

REITER, ELIZABETH, marketing professional; b. Chgo., Dec. 23, 1956; d. George and Eugenia (Francuz) Mosarski; m. Hershel Reiter, May 16, 1980. AA with honors, Mayfair City Coll., 1976; BS in Commerce, DePaul U., 1983. Acct. Freeman United Coal Mining Co., Chgo., 1980-83, market analyst, 1983-87; asst. mktg. mgr. United Coal Mining Co., Chgo., 1987—; registered sales rep. First Investors Corp., Des Plaines, Ill., 1984-85; cons. Nat. Coal Assn., Washington, 1983—, Clarity Cons., Chgo., 1985—. Vol. Chgo. Bus. Youth Motivation Program, 1985—, Bus. Vols. for Arts, Chgo., 1986—. Mem. Nat. Assn. Security Dealers, Nat. Assn. Female Execs., Women in Mining (pres., chmn. bd. Chgo. chpt.), Phi Theta Kappa (pres. Chgo. chpt. 1975-76). Roman Catholic. Office: Freeman United Coal Mining Co 222 N LaSalle St Chicago IL 60601

REITER-DYAS, MARJORIE HOPE, hospital administrator; b. Newark, Mar. 9, 1957; d. Sydney Howard and Constance (Rohr) Reiter; m. Timothy John Dyas, May 17, 1987. BA, Brandeis U., 1979; postgrad., Harvard U., 1979-82; MPH, Boston U., 1984. Adminstrv. asst. Boston City Hosp., 1979-81; dept. asst. Beth Israel Hosp., Boston, 1981-82; intern Organ Transplantation Task Force Mass. Dept. Pub. Health, Boston, 1983-84; tchr. Temple Beth Elohim, Wellesley, Mass., 1982-85, Temple Sinai, Summit, N.J., 1985—; coordinating mgr. Gouverneur Hosp., N.Y.C., 1985-87; adminstr. dept ob-gyn Saint Barnabas Med. Ctr., Livingston, N.J., 1987—; cons. DIY-601, Boston, 1984-85. Founding mem. Moonlighters, Boston, 1980-85. Mem. Am. Pub. Health Assn., Am. Council on Transplantation, Nat. Assn. Female Execs., Mass. Pub. Health Assn., N.J. Hosp. Assn., N.J. Pub. Health Assn., Health Policy Adv. Com., Back Bay Neighborhood Assn., Nat. Council Jewish Women (past treas.). Democrat. Club: Masterworks Chorus. Home: English Village 14 Apt 2C Cranford NJ 07016 Office: St Barnabas Med Ctr Old Short Hills Rd Livingston NJ 07039

REITER-SCOTT, GAYLA DENISE, labor union official, government official; b. Beloit, Kans., Sept. 12, 1945; d. Gail Francis and Vivian Maxine (Lagle) R.; m. Stephen C. Chappell, Apr. 10, 1976 (div. 1980); m. Wilfred Joseph Scott, July 4, 1982; 1 child, Layla Diana Scott (dec.), BS magna cum laude, Portland State U., 1967; cert. Chemeketa Community Coll., 1973; labor studies credential San Francisco City Coll., 1982; grad. trade union program Harvard U., 1987. Pub. affairs specialist Social Security Adminstrn., San Francisco, 1974-75, mgr., 1975-80, claims specialist, 1980-87; sr. personnel specialist, U. Calif., Davis, 1987-88; pres. local 3172, Am. Fedn. Govt. Employees, San Francisco, 1979-86, exec. v.p. Nat. Council 220, 1982—, pres. regional council 147, San Francisco, 1982-87; chief litigator, 1982—; del. San Mateo County Labor Council, Calif., 1982—. Co-editor Union Line from Region Nine, 1980-87 (outstanding Regional Paper 1983). Co-dir., fundraiser SIRS Hunger Project, San Francisco, 1982; legis. chmn. Calif. adv. council SIDS Found., 1984—, pres. 1988—; co-chmn. combined fed. campaign United Good Neighbors, San Francisco, 1984-86; chmn. Nat. Legis. Polit. Action Comm., 1984—, regional chmn. 1980-84. Recipient Gov.'s award State of Oreg., 1971, Superior Achievement award Social Security Adminstrn., Seattle, 1973, Nat. SIDS Found. Congrl. Leadership award 1986; named to San Mateo Womens Hall of Fame. Mem. Am. Fedn. Govt. Employees (nat. polit. action coordinator for Calif., Nev., Ariz. 1984-87, legis. rep. Congl. testimony 1982—; del., com. chmn. nat. conv. Cleve., 1984; del., 1st v.p. officer no. council of locals 1982-86; nat. leadership award 1982), ACLU, NOW, Women Execs. San Francisco (v.p., publicist 1975—), Coalition Labor Union Women, LWV (moderator various ednl. TV programs, redevel. com., 1988—), Phi Beta Kappa (v.p. Outstanding Speaker award 1967), Alpha Sigma Omega (Outstanding Woman award 1966). Democrat. Clubs: Masters Swim Program, Soroptimist (pres., v.p. 1976-80), Women's Spiritual Network.

REITH, KATHRYN MARGARET, association administrator, writer; b. Oklahoma City, Oct. 7, 1956; d. John Langan and Charlotte (Robinson) R. BA in Anthrpology magna cum laude, Brown U., 1978. Adminstrv. asst. Kodaly Mus. Tng. Inst., Watertown, Mass., 1978-80; asst. promotion Pub. Broadcasting Assocs., Boston, 1980-81; copy editor Internat. Data Corp., Framingham, Mass., 1982-83; dir. communications U.S. Rowing Assn., Phila. and Indpls., 1983-85; press officer Hands Across Am., Indpls., 1986; dir. ops. Women's Sports Found., N.Y.C., 1987—; press officer Pan Am. Games, Indpls. 1987. Contbr. articles to profl. jours. Mem. Am. Canoe Assn., (co-opted mem. Council 1987). Democrat. Club: Riverside Boat, (Cambridge, Mass.)(sec. 1983). Office: Women's Sports Found 342 Madison Ave New York NY 10173

RELKIN, EVELYN MARDER, health care organization administrator; b. N.Y.C., Nov. 11, 1935; d. Louis and Bertha (Sumberg) Marder; divorced; children: Gary, Keith, Jonathan. BA in Journalism, Pace U., 1972; MA in Psychology, Marist Coll., Poughkeepsie, N.Y., 1982; postgrad., Walden U., Mpls., 1987. Zone staff specialist The Upjohn Co., White Plains, N.Y., 1972-82; tng. dir. Read's Co., Yorktown, N.Y., 1982-83; career counselor Pace U., White Plains, 1983-85; v.p. Counseling Home Care Services, N.Y.C., 1985—. Mem. Am. Assn. for Counseling and Devel., Nat. Assn. for Home Care, Profl. Journalism Soc., Nat. League Nursing, N.Y. Bus. Group on Health. Office: Counseling Home Care Services 902 Broadway New York City NY 10010

REMICK, LEE (MRS. WILLIAM RORY GOWANS), actress; b. Quincy, Mass.; d. Frank E. and Margaret (Waldo) R.; m. William A. Colleran, Aug. 3, 1957 (div. 1969); children: Kate, Matthew; m. William Rory Gowans, Dec. 18, 1970. Student, Barnard Coll., 1953. Broadway debut in Be Your Age, 1953; other plays include: Anyone Can Whistle, 1964, Wait Until Dark, 1966, Bus Stop, London, 1974, I Do, I Do, 1983, Follies in Concert, 1985; films include: A Face in the Crowd, 1956, The Long Hot Summer, 1957, Anatomy of a Murder, 1959, Wild River, 1959, Sanctuary, 1960, Experiment in Terror, 1961, Days of Wine and Roses, 1961, The Wheeler Dealers, 1962, Baby The Rain Must Fall, 1963, Hallelujah Trail, 1965, No Way to Treat a Lady, 1967, The Detective, 1968, Hard Contract, 1969, Loot, 1972, A Delicate Balance, 1973, Hennessy, 1974, The Omen, 1976, Telefon, 1977, The Europeans, 1979, The Competition, 1980, Tribute, 1980; appeared in TV prodns.: Jennie, Lady Randolph Churchill, 1975; TV mini-series Wheels, 1978; TV mini-series Ike, 1979, Haywire, 1980, The Women's Room, 1981, The Letter, 1982, Mistral's Daughter, 1984, Rearview Mirror, 1984, The Snow Queen, 1985, Toughlove, 1985, Follies in Concert, 1986, Of Pure Blood, 1986, Eleanor in Her Own Words, 1986, Nutcracker, 1987, Money, Murder, Madness, 1987, The Vision, 1988. Address: care Internat Creative Mgmt 8899 Beverly Blvd Los Angeles CA 90048

REMINGTON, STEPHANIE JOLENE, consultant, marketing executive; b. St. Joseph, Mo., Feb. 16, 1954; d. Charles Wesley and Patricia Lee (Smith) R.; m. Robert Steven Juenger, July 30, 1977 (div. Aug. 1980); m. John A. Tatroe, II, Oct. 4, 1986. Student, Colo. State U., 1972-74, FuJen U., Taipei, Taiwan, 1975; BEd, U. Mo., 1977; postgrad., Cornell U., 1981-82. Mgr. restaurant Hospitality Foods, Columbia, Mo., 1974-80; food and beverage asst. Alameda Plaza Hotel, Kansas City, Mo., 1980; food and beverage dir. Raphael Hotel, Chgo., 1981-83; sales mgr. Tech.-Am., Elwood, Kans., 1984-85; owner, cons. Remington Assocs., Phoenix, 1985—. Mem. SW Ariz. Assn. Teleprofls. (pres. 1987—), Am. Telemktg. Assn., Better Bus. Bur., Assn. Female Execs. Democrat. Home: 3754 E Shangri La Rd Phoenix AZ 85028 Office: Remington Assocs 9830 N 32d St Suite C-203 Phoenix AZ 85028

REMSEN, ANN TRAPANI (MRS. FRANK TALLARICO), educator; b. Bklyn.; d. S. James and Helen I. (Marx) Trapani; B.S., Bklyn. Coll., 1941; M.S., Hofstra U., 1959; postgrad. State U. Tchrs. Coll., Genesco, N.Y., 1959; Ph.D., N.Y. U., 1974; m. John Remsen, Nov. 1936; 1 dau., Charlene Remsen Haroche; m. 2d, Frank Tallarico, Aug. 9, 1967. Tchr., Hicksville Sch. System, 1955-56; tchr. West Hampstead Pub. Schs., 1956-58, remedial reading tchr. elementary grades, 1958-59; reading clinician Hofstra U., 1957-58; dist.-wide reading cons. elementary and jr. high sch. Syosset Sch. System, 1959-62, developmental reading tchr. South Woods High Sch., 1960; asst. prof., supr. student tchrs. St. John's U., Jamaica, N.Y., 1962-85, sec. interdeptl. com. on linguistics; numerous lectures; cons. CAUSE, 1972-73; sec. Nassau Reading Council, 1964-65; tchr. Peace Corps Workers for Jamaica B.W.I., summer 1965; cons. project LAWYER, Westbury Sch. System, 1970-71. Pres. Albany Ave. Sch. PTA, 1954-55; tchr. rep. PTA Bd., 1958-59. Mem. NEA, West Hempstead Tchrs. Assn. (past treas.), Internat. Reading Assn., St. John's U. Faculty Assn. (sec., dir. 1974-81), Kappa Delta Pi (adviser). Home: 63A Independence Ct Yorktown Heights NY 10598

RENCEHAUSEN, LINDA MARY, industrial hygienist; b. Springfield, Mass., Feb. 1, 1950; d. Victor Frank and Lorraine Ruth (Perusse) Antienowicz; m. Walter William Rencehausen, Apr. 16, 1970; 1 child, Will. BS in Microbiology, Ariz. State U., 1977. Microbiology technician Armour-Dial, Phoenix, 1976; histology technician Phoenix Meml. Hosp., 1977-78; soils technician U.S. Forest Service, Flagstaff, Ariz., 1979; secondary sch. tchr. Logan (N.Mex.) Schs., 1980-81, Ft. Sumner (N.Mex.) Schs., 1981-83; industrial hygienist Westinghouse Electric Co., Carlsbad, N.Mex., 1984—. Served with USMC, 1968-70. Mem. Am. Soc. Safety Engrs., Am. Indsl. Hygiene Assn., Am. Chem. Soc. (div. chem. health and safety). Republican. Roman Catholic. Home: 2835 Western Way Carlsbad NM 88220 Office: Westinghouse Electric PO Box 2078 Carlsbad NM 88221

RENDE, ANN HIGGINS, real estate executive, educator; b. Geneva, N.Y., Nov. 4, 1942; d. James Edward and Margaret (Proechel) Higgins; m. Alexander Dominick Rende, June 29, 1968; children: Marguerite, Kathleen. BS, N.Y. State U., 1964. Tchr. Port Jefferson (N.Y.) Schs., 1964-65, New Rochelle (N.Y.) Schs., 1965-67, Bd. Coop. Services, South Westchester, N.Y., 1967-70; assoc. realtor Century 21, Pelham, N.Y., 1985—. Dir. New Rochelle Community Theatre, 1972-77; charter mem., dir. Pel Players, Pelham, 1971-75; pres. Pelham Children's Theatre, 1974-77. Mem. Westchester Bd. Realtors, N.Y. State Bd. Realtors, Nat. Bd. Realtors, Pelham Jr. League (sustaining, v.p. community affairs 1982-83), Jr. League N.Y. State (chmn. pub. affairs com. 1983-85), Alpha Psi Omega. Democrat. Roman Catholic. Home: 4472 Boston Post Rd Pelham Manor NY 10803 Office: Century 21 123 Wolfs Ln Pelham NY 10803

RENDL-MARCUS, MILDRED, artist, economist; b. N.Y.C., May 30, 1928; d. Julius and Agnes (Hokr) Rendl; BS, NYU, 1948, MBA, 1950; PhD (Dean Bernice Brown Cronkhite fellow 1950-51), Radcliffe Coll., 1954; m. Edward Marcus, Aug. 10, 1956. Economist, Gen. Electric Co., 1953-56, Bigelow-Sanford Carpet Co., Inc., 1956-58; lectr. econs. evening sessions CCNY, 1953-58; research investment problems in tropical Africa, 1958-59; instr. econs. Hunter Coll. CUNY, 1959-60; lectr. econs. Columbia U., 1960-61; research econ. devel. Nigeria, W. Africa, 1961-63; sr. economist Internat. div. Nat. Indsl. Conf. Bd., 1963-66; asst. prof. Grad. Sch. Bus. Adminstrn., Pace Coll., 1964-66; asso. prof. Borough of Manhattan Community Coll., City U. N.Y., 1966-71, prof., 1972-85; vis. prof. Fla. Internat. U., 1986; prin. MRM Assos., Rendl Fine Art; corp. art econ. cons.; fine arts appraiser; participant Internat. Economical Meeting, Amsterdam, 1968, Econs. of Fine Arts in Age of Tech., 1984, Internat. Economic Assn. North Am., Laredo, Tex., 1987-88, Soc. Southwestern Economists, San Antonio, 1988. Exhibited New Canaan Art Show, 1982, 83, 84, 85, New Canaan Soc. for Arts Ann., 1983, 85, New Canaan Arts, 1985, Stamford Art Assn., 1987; symposium participant Sienna, Italy, 1988; contbr. articles to Women in the Arts newsletter, 1986-87, Coalition Womens Art Orgns., 1986-87. Bd. dirs. N.Y.C. Council on Econ. Edn., 1970— ; mem. program planning com. Women's Econ. Roundtable; participant Eastern Econ. Assn., Boston, 1988. Recipient Disting. Service award CUNY, 1985. Fellow Gerontol. Assn.; mem. Internat. Schumpeter Econs. Soc. (founding), Am. (vice chmn. ann. meeting 1973), Met. (sec. 1954-56) econ. assns., Indsl. Relations Research Assn., Audubon Artists and Nat. Soc. Painters in Casein (assoc. 1987-88) Allied Social Sci. Assn. (vice chmn. conv. 1973), AAUW, N.Y.C. Women in Arts, Women's Econ. Roundtable, N.Y. U. Grad. Sch. Bus. Adminstrn. Alumni (sec. 1956-58). Clubs: Radcliffe; Women's City (art and landmarks com.). Author: (with husband) Investment and Development of Tropical Africa, 1959, International Trade and Finance, 1965, Monetary and Banking Theory, 1965; Economics, 1969; (with husband) Principles of Economics, 1969; Economic Progress and the Developing World, 1970; Economics, 1978; also monographs and articles in field. Econ. and internat. research on industrialization less developed areas, internat. debtor nations and workability of buffer stock schemes; columnist economics of art Women in Art. Home: 928 West Rd New Canaan CT 06840 Office: PO Box 814 New Canaan CT 06840 also: 7441 Wayne Ave Miami Beach FL 33141

RENEE, PAULA, artist; b. Hackensack, N.J., Mar. 3; d. Paul and Helen (Boyko) Wilk; m. Robert F. Handschuh, June 19, 1954 (div. Dec. 1968); children: Kim, Dawn; m. Thomas D. Murray, Jan. 4, 1969 (div. Dec. 1975); m. Samuel R. Hazlett, June 6, 1978 (div. Apr. 1986). Student, Fairleigh Dickenson U., 1973-77, Ramapo State Coll., 1973, Rockland Community Coll., 1970-71, Thomas A. Edison Coll., 1978. Artist self-employed, Tenafly, N.J., 1978-84; artist self-employed Palasades, N.J., 1984-87, Nyack, N.Y., 1987—; artist-in-residence Bergen Community Coll., Hackensack, 1978-79. Artist: tapestry work exhibited in Shuttle Spindle and Dyepot mag., 1981-86. Home: Rivercrest 103 Gedney St 1H Nyack NY 10960

RENEKER, MAXINE HOHMAN, librarian; b. Chgo., Dec. 2, 1942; d. Roy Max and Helen Anna Christina (Anacker) Hohman; m. David Lee Reneker, June 20, 1964 (dec. Dec. 1979); children: Sarah Roeder, Amy Johannah, Benjamin Congdon. BA, Carleton Coll., 1964; MA, U. Chgo., 1970. Asst. reference librarian U. Chgo. Libraries, 1965-66, classics librarian, 1967-70, asst. head acquisitions, 1970-71, personnel librarian, 1971-73; personnel/bus. librarian U. Colo. Libraries, Boulder, 1978-80; asst. dir. sci. and engring. div. Columbia U., N.Y.C., 1981-85; assoc univ. librarian for pub. services Ariz. State U. Libraries, Tempe, 1985—; acad. library mgmt. intern Council on Library Resources, 1980-81. Contbr. articles to profl. jours. Research grantee Council on Library Resources, Columbia U., 1970-71. Mem. ALA, Am. Soc. Info. Sci., Associated Info. Mgrs., Phi Beta Kappa, Beta Phi Mu. Home: 7637 E Ironwood Dr Scottsdale AZ 85258 Office: Univ Libraries Ariz State U Tempe AZ 85287

RENFRO, MAXINE JUNE, consumer shows producer; b. Grand Rapids, Mich., Feb. 11, 1927; d. Archie Dennis and Gertrude Fern (Nelson) Korb; m. Robert David Kaley, Mar. 1947; 1 child, Mark; m. Harry Edward Renfro, June 1, 1959; children: Daniel Nelson, Todd Ryan, Kevin Dennis. Grad. high sch., Traverse City, Mich. From sec. to treas. Indpls. Boat, Sport and Travel Show, 1972-86, pres., 1986—; pres. Renfro Prodns., Indpls., 1985—. Pres. Fishers, Ind. council PTA, 1968, United Meth.

Women, 1980-83; treas. United Meth. Ch., Fishers, 1977-79. Recipient cert. of appreciation Ind. Wild Turkey Fedn., 1983, cert. of appreciation Ind. Bass Fedn., 1986, 87, 88. Mem. Internat. Sport Show Producers Assn., Internat. Assn. Travel Exhibitors, Am. Fishing Tackle Manufacturers Assn. Republican. Office: Indpls Boat Sport Travel Show 2511 E 46th St #V-1 Indianapolis IN 46205

RENGSTORFF, VIVIAN ALICE, educational administrator; b. Jersey City, Aug. 10, 1947; d. George Henry and Vivienne Alice (Salzman) R. BA, Gustavus Adophus Coll., St. Peter, Minn., 1971; MEd, U. Minn., 1982, postgrad., 1984—. Cert. tchr., Minn. Tchr. Fred Moore Jr. High, Anoka, Minn., 1971-84, asst. prin. Coon Rapids (Minn.) Jr. High. Author:(workbook) Fitting In: A Mental Health Workbook, 1978. Mem. Adminstrv. Women in Edn., Nat. Assn. Secondary Sch. Prins., Minn. Assn. Secondary Sch. Prins., Phi Kappa Phi. Democrat. Lutheran. Home: 15122 Zuni St NW Ramsey MN 55303 Office: Coon Rapids Jr High Sch 11600 Raven St NW Coon Rapids MN 55433

RENICK, CYNTHIA LEE, marketing professional; b. Kansas City, Mo., Aug. 21, 1951; d. Lawrence Wayne and Dortha Lee (Brownlee) Durbin; m. William G. Renick, Dec. 26, 1969 (div. Apr. 1978); children: Sybil Lee, Douglas Walter. Grad. high sch., Raytown, Mo. Customer service rep. Fireman's Fund Ins. Co., Kansas City, 1970-72; mktg. rep. Womack & Assocs., Kansas City, 1972-73, 75-79, Robert E. Miller Agy., Kansas City, 1979-83; sr. mktg. specialist Marsh & McLennan, Inc., Kansas City, 1983-85; v.p., mgr. major accounts mktg. Alexander & Alexander, Inc., Kansas City, 1985-87; corp. search cons. Morgan Hunter Corp. Search, Overland Park, Kans., 1988—. Mem. Ins. Women Greater Kansas City (pres.1988, bd. dirs. 1986-87), Kansas City Women's C. of C. Baptist. Club: Investors Extrodinaire (recording ptnr. 1986-87). Home: 5906 Northern Raytown MO 64133 Office: Morgan Hunter Corp Search 6800 College Blvd Overland Park KS 66211

RENICK, SUSAN GARNER, school system administrator; b. Birmingham, Ala., Nov. 30, 1945; d. John Chester and Eloise (Fisher) Garner; m. Robert Renick, Oct. 2, 1975 (div. Nov. 1984). BS, U. Montevallo, 1969; MA with honors, U. Ala., 1975; Cert., U. No. Colo., 1976, Fla. Internat. U., 1979. Cert. exceptional student edn. adminstr., Fla. Tchr. vocat. edn. Jefferson County Pub. Schs., Hewitt-Trussville, Ala., 1969, reading tchr. for mentally retarded, 1974-75; tchr. learning disabilitites Dade County Pub. Schs., Miami, Fla., 1975-77, specialist exceptional student placement, 1977-78, dir. exceptional student, 1978—; ednl. cons. emotionally disturbed children Charter Hosp., Miami, 1987; awards chmn. Broader Opportunities for Learning Disabled, 1986-87; bd. dirs. Fla. Diagnostic Learning Resources Ctr., Miami; various appointments Fla. Dept. Edn. Com. mem. Miami-Metro Action Plan, 1986—; mem. Greater Miami Drug Council, 1987; chmn. North Cen. area campaign United Way, 1987. Recipient Awards of Appreciation, 1975—. Mem. Fla. Assn. Sch. Adminstrs., Council Exceptional Children (com. mem. Spl. Olympics, Birmingham area 1973-75), Assn. for Children with Learning Disabilities, Dade Assn. Sch. Psychologists, Fla. Council Adminstrs. Spl. Edn., U. Montevallo Alumni Assn., Family Christian Assn. Am., Phi Delta Kappa (hon.). Democrat. Office: Dade County Pub Schs Norht Area Exceptional Student Dept 19340 NW 8th Ct Room 12 Miami Springs FL 33166

RENKAR-JANDA, JARRI J., paint manufacturing executive; b. Chicago Heights, Ill., Feb. 26, 1951; d. Eugene N. and RoseMarie (Morgenson) Zar; m. Leonard F. Renkar (div.); 1 child, Sandra R.; m. James E. Janda. Student, Northeastern Ill. U., 1978, Harper Jr. Coll., 1978, Mundelein Coll., 1979-80. Acctg. clk. Wittek Mfg., Chgo., 1970-73; credit clk. McKesson Chem., Chgo., 1973, purchasing agt., 1973-76; product supply mgr. Gen. Paint and Chem., Cary, Ill., 1976-78; purchasing mgr. Glidden Coatings and Resins, Chgo., 1978-80, Columbus and Oakwood, Ga., 1980-84, Paint div. Ace Hardware Corp., Matteson, Ill., 1984—; materials mgr. Paint div. Ace Hardware Crop., Matteson, Ill. Counselor Shelter for Battered Women, Gainesville, Ga., 1982. Mem. Chgo. Paint and Coating Assn. (buyers com. 1985-87), Chgo. Soc. Coatings (mfg. com. 1986-87), Chgo. Paint and Coatings Assn. (golf com. 1986-88). Office: Ace Hardware Corp Paint div 21901 S Central Ave Matteson IL 60443

RENKEN, ANNE CHRISTINE, service executive; b. Rochester, N.Y., Jan. 12, 1960. BS in Restaurant and Hotel Mgmt., Purdue U., 1982. Mgr. convention sales Tysons Corner Marriott, Vienna, Va., 1982-84; mgr. sales St. Louis Airport Marriott, 1984-85; dir. sales Trumbull (Conn.) Marriott, 1985-88; dir. Stouffer Hotels and Resorts, N.Y.C., 1988—. Named Outstanding Young Woman of Am., 1986; recipient Service award U.S. Dept. Justice, 1986. Mem. Meeting Planners Internat., Women in Sales, Conn. Bus. Network, Sales Exec. Club N.Y., Sales and Mktg. Execs. N.Y., Fairfield Network Exec. Women, Alpha Phi. Club: Purdue Alumni. Home: 245 Unquowa Rd #122 Fairfield CT 06430 Office: Stouffer Hotels and Resorts 19 W 44th St Suite 514 New York NY 10036

RENNEBOHM, ANITA CAROL, secretarial service executive; b. Omak, Wash., Aug. 7, 1943; d. Lester and Ida Ellen (Moomaw) Waggoner; children—Pamelia Carol McClellan, Lisa Lynn McClellan, Krista Anne Carlson; m. Ronald Albert Rennebohm, May 28, 1982. Grad. CTC Bus. Edn. Systems, 1970. Bus. fin. mgr. automobile dealership, 1970-72; legal asst. to Harry B. Platis, Atty., Lynnwood, Wash., 1972-82; owner, operator ACR Enterprises, Inc., Lynnwood 1982-83. Mem. Snohomish County Women Bus. Owners Assn., South Snohomish County C. of C., Secretarial Services Assn., Executive Suite Network. Office: Lynnwood Exec Ctr Inc 3400 188th SW #324 Lynnwood WA 98037

RENNER, BRENDA LORETTA, auto dealer; b. Greeneville, Tenn., July 22, 1950; d. U.L. and Ida Belle (Blazer) R. BS, East Tenn. State U., 1972, postgrad., 1984-85. Bus. mgr. Cocke County Meml. Hosp., Newport, Tenn., 1973-76; bus. mgr. and corp. sec.-treas. Bewley Oldsmobile-Subaru, Inc., Greeneville, Tenn., 1976—. Dir. Tenn.-Caroline Fair Assn., Newport, Tenn., 1983-86. Named Bus. Mgr. of Quar., Subaru Top Achievement Recognition Club, 1982. Mem. Nat. Assn. Female Execs., Oldsmobile Bus. Mgmt. Club, Jaycees (v.p. Cocke County 1985-86, v.p. Greeneville, 1987-88), Epsilon Sigma Alpha (Tenn. state pres. 1986-87, named Outstanding Mem. 1981, 84). Republican. Methodist. Avocations: travel, reading. Home: 317 Bird Circle Greenville TN 37743 Office: Bewley Oldsmobile-Subaru Inc 535 Tusculum Blvd Greeneville TN 37743

RENNER, HELEN LOUISE, counselor; b. Independence, Mo., Jan. 12, 1943; d. Walter Red Breckenridge and June Jeannetta (Combs) Gambrill; m. Robert Louis Renner, June 4, 1961; children—Lori Ann, Scott Robert. Student U. Md., 1972-73, Park Coll., 1977; cert. of completion Inchbald Sch. Design, London, 1975; B.A., La. Tech. U., 1983, M.A. in Guidance and Counseling La. State U., 1985, MSW La. State U., 1987. Program dir. Recreation Ctr., Rickenbacker AFB, Ohio, 1977-79, Skyclub Recreation Ctr., Barksdale AFB, La., 1980; sec. La. Tech. U., Barksdale AFB, 1980-81; mgr. So. Gallery, Shreveport, La., 1981—; psychiat. social worker, Charter Forest Hosp., 1988—. Counselor Ctr. for Displaced Homemakers, Shreveport, 1984-87 , Hospice of La., Shreveport, 1984—, Open Ear Crisis Line, Shreveport, 1984-85. Named Outstanding Young Women Am., 1968, one of 2000 Notable Am. Women; recipient Cert. of Achievement Upper Heyford Anglo-Am. Com., Eng., 1968. Mem. Nat. Assn. Social Workers, Am. Mental Health Counselors Assn., Am. Assn. for Counseling and Devel., AAUW, Phi Kappa Phi. Republican. Clubs: Officers Wives (Barksdale AFB); Questers. Home: 406 Kenshire Ct Shreveport LA 71115

RENNER, JACQUELINE MARIE, marketing professional; b. N.Y.C., Feb. 15, 1958; d. Ernest John and Patricia Aurora (Romano) R. BA in Chemistry, U. Pa., 1979; MBA, NYU, 1984. Research chemist Olin Corp., New Haven, 1979-81; comml. devel. mgr. Olin Corp., Stamford, Conn., 1981-85, product mgr., 1985-87; comml. dir. Johnson Matthey, West Deptford, N.J., 1987—. Patentee novel functional fluids, 1981. Robert Bosch fellow, 1984-85. Mem. Am. Chem. Soc., Comml. Devel. Assn., Sigma Xi. Office: Johnson Matthey 2001 Nolte Dr West Deptford NJ 08066

RENNER, MELINDA LEE SWETT, association executive; b. Atlanta, May 12, 1946; d. James Alexander and Dorothy Ellen (Sigman) Lee; m. Roy Albert Swett, Jr., July 5, 1965 (div. 1970); m. Stephen Alan Renner, Aug. 4, 1979 (div. 1984). Student Ga. So. Coll., 1965-66; B.A., Emory U., 1968, M. Librarianship, 1969; specialist in library service Atlanta U., 1976; postgrad. in legal research and info. sci. Catholic U., 1980-82. Group chief supr. So. Bell Telephone & Telegraph, Atlanta, 1967-69; serials and microforms librarian DeKalb Community Coll., 1969-75, pub. services librarian, 1975-77; asst. to program coordinator U.S. Nat. Commn. on Library and Info. Sci., White House Conf. on Libraries and Info. Services, Washington, 1977; library program officer tng. and profl. devel. USIA, Washington, 1977-81; tech. info. cons. Nat. Council on Radiation Protection and Measurements, Bethesda, Md., 1981; library and tech. info. mgr. Atomic Indsl. Forum, Washington, 1981-82, assoc. tech. mgr. Nat. Environ. Studies Project, 1982-85, mgr. spl. projects, 1985-87; editor NESP Newsletter, 1982-87; dir. ops. Utility Data Inst., Washington, 1987—; contbg. editor Pub. Utilities Reports/Analysis of Investor-Owned Electric and Gas Utilities, 1985, 86 edits. Contbr. articles to profl. jours. Mem. adv. bd. Friends of Libraries, Washington, 1981-83; advisor House of Ruth, home for battered women, Washington 1982-85; mem. adv. bd. Sta. WETA-TV, Atlanta, 1975-77, Sta. WAMU-FM, Washington, 1986—; active Arthritis Found., Columbia Hist. Soc., Nat. Mus. for Women in the Arts, Smithsonian Assocs., Ga. State Regents scholar, 1964; Emory U. scholar, 1966-68; HEW fellow, 1968-69, 75. Mem. D.C. Library Assn. (exec. bd. 1982-84, treas. 1982-84), ALA (standing com. on library edn. 1980-81, chmn. Nat. Library Week 1981-82), Soc. for Risk Analysis, Ga. Library Assn. (govtl. affairs chmn. 1975-77), Am. Soc. for Info. Sci., Elec. Women's Round Table, Greater Washington Soc. Assn. Execs., Women in Energy, Nuclear Energy Women, Spl. Libraries Assn., NOW, Nat. Abortion Rights Action League, Planned Parenthood, Mensa, Phi Beta Kappa, Eta Sigma Phi, Beta Phi Mu. Home: 3711 Windom Pl NW Washington DC 20016 Office: Utility Date Inst 1700 K St NW Suite 400 Washington DC 20006

RENNICK, KYME ELIZABETH WALL, lawyer; b. Columbus, Ohio, Dec. 27, 1953; d. Robert Leroy and Julie (Allison) Wall; m. Ian Alexander Rennick, Oct. 15, 1983; 1 child, Daniel Alexander. BA, Centre Coll., 1975; MA, Ohio State U., 1978; JD, Capital U., 1982. Bar: Ohio 1982, U.S. Dist. Ct. (no. and so. dists.) Ohio 1983. Legal intern Ohio Dept. Natural Resources, Columbus, 1981-83, gen. counsel, 1983-86, chief counsel, 1986—. Editor: Baldwin's Ohio Revised Code Annotated, Title 15 Conservation of Natural Resources, 1984. Mem. ABA, Columbus Bar Assn. Presbyterian. Office: Ohio Dept Natural Resources Fountain Sq Bldg D-3 Columbus OH 43224

RENNINGER, KATHARINE STEELE, artist; b. Phila., Feb. 26, 1925; d. John Stewart and Katherine Frick Steele; m. John Snowden Renninger, Nov. 17, 1951; children: Ann, Molly, Sally, Patrick. BFA, Moore Coll. of Art, Phila., 1946. mem. community arts, spl. projects panels Pa. Council on the Arts, Harrisburg, 1973-79; chmn. Bucks County Council on the Arts, Doylestown, Pa., 1974, 75, 78. Works exhibitions shown in Washington, Phila., Lambertville, 1967-88. Bd. dirs. Planned Parenthood, Bucks County, 1976—. Recipient awards Nat. Soc. Casein Painters, 1973, 74, 82, Am. Acad. Arts and Letters, 1979, Allied Artists Am., 1981, 85. Republican. Episcopalian. Home and Studio: 148 N State St Newtown PA 18940

RENNINGER, MARY KAREN, librarian; b. Pitts., Apr. 30, 1945; d. Jack Burnell and Jane (Hammerly) Gunderman; m. Norman Christian Renninger, Sept. 3, 1965 (div. 1980); 1 child, David Christian. B.A., U. Md., 1969, M.A., 1972, M.L.S., 1975. Tchr. English West Carteret High Sch., Morehead City, N.C., 1969-70; grad. asst. instr. English U. Md., College Park, 1970-72; head network services Nat. Library Service, Library of Congress, Washington, 1974-78, asst. for network support, 1978-80; mem. fed. women's program com. Library of Congress, Washington, 1977-79; chief library div. Library of Congress, Va., 1980—, mem. Fed. Library com., 1980—, mem. exec. adv. bd., 1985—; mem. USBE personnel subcom., 1982-84; bd. regents Nat. Library of Medicine, 1986—; fed. librarian task force for 1990 White House Conf. on Libraries, 1986—. Co-chmn. VA edn. research and devel com., 1987—. Recipient Meritorious Service award Library of Congress, 1974; Spl. Achievement award Library of Congress, 1976, Performance award VA, 1982, 83, 84, 85, 86, 87 Adminstr.'s Commendation, 1985, Spl. Contbn. award, 1986. Mem. ALA, Library Tech. Assn., Med. Library Assn. (govt. relations com. 1985—), D.C. Library Assn., NOW, Phi Beta Kappa, Alpha Lambda Delta, Beta Phi Mu. Home: 840 College Pkwy Rockville MD 20850 Office: Library Div (142D) VA 810 Vermont Ave NW Washington DC 20420

RENNIX, CHERYL STROUP, bank manager; b. Phila., June 25, 1959; d. William V. and Wilma C. Stroup. Cert. in French, Sorbonne U., Paris, 1979; BA in Spanish, French; cert. multilingual bus. govt. studies, Temple U., 1981. Translator, export asst. Syntex Dental Products, Valley Forge, Pa., 1982-83; specialist internat. trade Mellon Bank East, Phila., 1983, from coordinator to supr. letter credit, 1983-84, from trainee credit analysis to asst. officer cash mgmt., 1984-86; asst. v.p. cash mgmt. Midlantic Nat. Bank South, Cherry Hill, N.J., 1986; mgr. cash mgmt. mktg. Midlantic Nat. Bank South, Pennsauken, N.J., 1986—; cons. Midlantic Nat. Bank South, 1987—; mem. steering com. ADP, Ann Arbor, Mich., 1986-88. Author: A Compendium of Modern Business Spanish Terms, 1981. Mem. Amnesty Internat., NOW, Nat. Assn. Corporate Cash Mgrs., Greenpeace, Planned Parenthood, Sigma Delta Pi. Office: Midlantic Nat Bank South 1070 Thomas L Busch III Meml Hwy Pennsauken NJ 08110-0204

RENOUD, DOROTHY IDA, publishing company executive; b. Far Rockaway, N.Y., Aug. 11, 1933; d. Herbert William and Elizabeth (Fischer) Owen; m. David Francis Renoud, Jan. 18, 1958; children—David, Douglas. Sales service mgr. Reinhold Pub., N.Y.C., 1951-61; circulation dir. United Tech. Pub., Garden City, N.Y., 1961-80; v.p. Coastal Communications, N.Y.C., 1980—. Recipient Fraundorf award Long Beach Fire Dept., N.Y., 1979. Mem. Nat. Bus. Circulation Assn. (bd. dirs. 1981—). Avocation: camping. Home: 527 W Chester St Long Beach NY 11561 Office: Coastal Communications Corp 488 Madison Ave New York NY 10022

RENSE, PAIGE, editor, publishing company executive. Student, Calif. State Coll., Los Angeles. Writer Cosmopolitan, 1967-68; assoc. editor Archtl. Digest (Knapp Communications Corp., 1970-72; editor-in-chief Archtl. Digest (Knapp Communications Corp.), Los Angeles; sr. v.p. Knapp Communications Corp., Los Angeles. Recipient Nat. Headliner Women in Communications award, 1983; named Woman of Yr. Los Angeles Times, 1976. Office: Archtl Digest 5900 Wilshire Blvd Los Angeles CA 90036 *

RENSIN, KATHERINE KALLET, speech and language pathologist; b. Syracuse, N.Y., July 4, 1943; d. Joseph Ralph and Sylvia (Radman) K.; m. Howard Malcolm Rensin, June 13, 1964; children—Joseph, Samuel, David, Deborah. B.A., Vanderbilt U., 1963; M.S., Syracuse U., 1964. Lic. speech lang. pathologist, Md.; cert. in learning disabilities. Speech pathologist Washington Hosp. Ctr., 1964-65; speech/lang. pathologist, Silver Spring, Md., 1965—, cons. learning disabilities, 1974—; dir. learning disability program Hebrew Acad., Silver Spring, 1978-81; cons. Bd. Jewish Edn., Silver Spring, 1978-83; dir. lang. devel. Children's Learning Ctr., Silver Spring, 1976-84. Vice pres. Stonegate Sch. PTA, Silver Spring, 1979-80, pres., 1980-81; Cub Scout leader Boy Scouts Am., Silver Spring, 1973-83. Mem. Am. Speech, Hearing, Lang. Assn., Md. Speech, Hearing Lang. Assn., Assn. Children with Learning Disabilities. Democrat. Club: Synagogue (chmn. membership 1980-84, bd. trustees 1979-85). Avocations: bridge; tennis; swimming; horseback riding.

RENTER, LOIS IRENE HUTSON, librarian; b. Lowden, Iowa, Oct. 23, 1929; d. Thomas E. and Lulu Mae (Barlean) Hutson; B.A. cum laude, Cornell Coll., Iowa, 1965; M.A., U. Iowa, 1968; m. Karl A. Renter, Jan. 3, 1948; children—Susan Elizabeth, Rebecca Jean, Karl Geoffrey. Tchr. Spanish, Mt. Vernon (Iowa) High Sch., 1965-67; head librarian Am. Coll. Testing Program, Iowa City, Iowa, 1968—; vis. instr. U. Iowa Sch. Library Sci., 1972—. Mem. Am. Soc. Info. Sci., ALA, Spl. Libraries Assn., Phi Beta Kappa. Methodist. Home: 1125 29th St Marion IA 52302 Office: Box 168 Iowa City IA 52243

RENTERIA, ESTHER G., public relations executive; b. East Los Angeles, Calif., May 1, 1939; d. Oliver Jay and Violet Gatfield; AA, East Los Angeles Coll., 1958; BA, Calif. State U., Los Angeles, 1974; m. Martin Renteria, Feb. 13, 1971; children: Christopher, David. Reporter, Alhambra (Calif.) Post Advocate, 1959-61; reporter, soc. editor East Los Angeles Tribune & Gazette, 1962-68, desk editor, newswriter Sta. KNX, Los Angeles, 1968; asso. producer, hostess-moderator Ahora! TV Series, Public Broadcasting Sta. KCET, 1969-70; public info. dir. East Los Angeles Coll., 1970-83; pres. Esther Renteria Pub. Relations, Inc., 1983—; producer Sta. KNXT TV Series: Bienvenidos and The Siesta is Over, 1970-74, ednl. cons. bilingual edn. series Juntos, 1979-82; sec., dir. Future Broadcasting Corp., 1980—; v.p. Trojan Security Services, Inc. Public relations dir. Los Angeles Street Scene Festival, 1978—; mem. steering com. Nat. Hispanic Media Coalition. Named one of Most Influential Hispanics in U.S., one of 100 Top Women Communicators in U.S. Mem. Hispanic Pub. Relations Assn. (pres., v.p., bd. dirs.), Hispanic Acad. Media Arts and Scis (bd. dirs. Hollywood chpt.), Bilingual Found. of Arts, Latin Bus. Assn. Democrat. Roman Catholic. Club: Job's Daus. (life). Home: 301 Dochan Circle Montebello CA 90640 Office: 5400 E Olympic Blvd Los Angeles CA 90022-5113

RENTZ, AUDREY LOUISE, student development educator; b. Peekskill, N.Y., May 1, 1941; d. Joseph F. and Julia U. Rentz. AB, Coll. of Mt. St. Vincent, 1963; MS, Pa. State U., 1965; PhD, Mich. State U., 1969. Prof. coll. student personnel Bowling Green State (Ohio) U., 1974—. Office: Bowling Green State U Dept of Coll Student Personnel Bowling Green OH 43403

RENTZEL, JEAN M., electronics executive; b. Hanover, Pa., Nov. 15, 1936; d. Charles Frances and Dorothy Alice (Myers) Gouker; m. Walter Elmer Rentzel, Nov. 13, 1954 (div. June 1971); 1 child, David Allen. Student, San Diego State U. Various secretarial postions Pa., 1958-75; prodn. planner G.A. Techs., San Diego, 1978-83, logistic service rep. Sorrento Electronics div., 1983—. Chair membership Rep. Federated Women, San Diego, 1982-85, advocate, 1984. Mem. Soc. Indsl Engrs., Am. Nuclear Soc., San Diego Engring. Soc., Tech. Mktg. Soc. Am., Nat. Assn. Female Execs. Home: 13114 Dana Vista Poway CA 92064

REOHR, JANET RUTH, psychologist, educator; b. Auburn, N.Y., Apr. 25, 1948. BS, SUNY, Cortland, 1970; MEd, Boston U., 1975, EdD, 1978. cert. tchr., N.Y. Elem. sch. tchr. Commack (N.Y.) Sch. Dist., 1970-71; jr. high tchr. Newark Jr. High Sch., 1971-73; asst. dir. parks and recreation Camillus (N.Y.) Recreation Dept., 1973-74; adminstrv. asst. humanistic, devel. and organizational studies Boston U., 1976-78; instr. psychology No. Essex Community Coll., Haverhill, Mass., 1978-79, Northeastern U., Boston, 1979-80; cons. Beacon Research Assocs., Boston, 1979; assoc. prof. psychology Jr. Coll. Albany, N.Y., 1980—, chair social sci. div., 1985—; cons. tng. div. N.Y. State Dept. Civil Service, Albany, 1981-82. Contbr. articles to profl. jours. Chair Educators for Social Responsibility Albany Chpt., 1981-86. Mem. Am. Psychol. Assn., Internat. Soc. Study Personal Relationships, Assn. Women in Psychology, Ea. Psychol. Assn. Roman Catholic. Home: 732 Morris St Albany NY 12208 Office: Jr Coll Albany 140 New Scotland Ave Albany NY 12208

REPASKY, B. NADINE, temporary service firm executive; b. New Castle, Pa., Jan. 22, 1931; d. John Donald and Beulah Mae (Balmer) Bartlett; m. Robert Stephen Repasky, 1952 (div. 1961); children—Timothy Gene, Mark Douglas, Suzan Rene. A.A., New Castle Bus. Sch., 1952. With Martin Marietta Aerospace Co., Orlando, Fla., 1961-81, cost control analyst, 1975-81; founder Temp World, Inc., Orlando, 1981-87; owner Repasky Enterprises Real Estate Investments, 1987—; del. White House Conf. Small Bus., 1986. Coordinator Salvation Army drive Martin Marietta Aerospace Co., Orlando, 1973, adviser Jr. Achievement, 1975; coordinator Foster Children's Christmas gift giving, Orlando, 1983; sponsor-coordinator Foster Children's ann. picnic, Orlando, 1984; speaker on success Women's Network, Orlando, 1985. Named Small Bus. Person of the Year, Orlando, 1986. Mem. Citrus Club Orlando, Am. Bus. Women's Assn. (treas. 1983-84, chpt. Woman of Yr. award 1984), Nat. Assn. Female Execs., Better Bus. Bur., Orlando Area C. of C., U.S. C. of C. Republican. Methodist. Avocations: golf; fishing; biking; tennis; swimming. Office: Temp World Inc 7000 Lake Ellenor Dr Suite 123 Orlando FL 32809

REPETTI, BRIDGET BERNADETTE, real estate professional; b. N.Y.C., Feb. 21, 1934; d. Hugh Hugo and Madeline (Black) Rudden; m. Gregory G. Repetti Jr., Oct. 6, 1956; children: Gregory, Mark. Student, St. John's U., 1951-54. Media buyer Ralph H. Jones Co., N.Y.C.; office mgr. Gt. Lakes Canvas Co., Milw., 1965-66; sales rep. Crib Diaper Service, Milw., 1967-68, Baker Realty, Inc., Akron, Ohio, 1969-71, Marting Realty, Inc., Akron, 1971-79; broker, owner, sales rep. Repetti Realty, Inc., Akron, 1979—. Rep. United Cerebral Palsy, Akron, 1987; fund raiser Children's Hosp., Akron, 1987. Mem. Women's Council Realtors (pres. Akron chpt. 1981, state pres. 1984), Akron Area Bd. Realtors (treas. 1986, v.p. 1987, pres. elect 1988). Republican. Roman Catholic. Clubs: Silver Lake Country, Cascade. Office: Repetti Realty Inc 1755 W Market St Akron OH 44313

REPETTI, SUSAN LEONARD, lawyer; b. Boston, Jan. 4, 1956; d. Jerome M. and Virginia R. (Curley) Leonard; m. James R. Repetti, Aug. 16, 1980; 1 child, Jane Elizabeth. B.A. in Econs., Wellesley Coll., 1977; student London Sch. Econs., 1975-76; J.D., Boston Coll., 1980; LL.M., Boston U., 1984. Bar: Mass. 1980, U.S. Dist. Ct. Mass. 1981, U.S. Tax Ct. 1982. Assoc. law firm Sullivan & Worcester, Boston, 1980—; lectr. Mass. Continuing Legal Edn., 1985, 87. Editor Boston Coll. Law Rev., 1979-80. Alumnae liaison Wellesley Coll. AC-CESS Assocs., 1981-85; mem. Wellesley Coll. Career Assocs., 1980—. Durant scholar, 1977. Mem. ABA, Mass. Bar Assn., Boston Bar Assn., Order of Coif, Phi Beta Kappa. Roman Catholic. Club: Hyannisport. Office: Sullivan & Worcester 1 Post Office Sq Boston MA 02109

REPPERT, NANCY LUE, county official; b. Kansas City, Mo., June 17, 1933; d. James Everett and Iris R. (Moomey) Moore; student Central Mo. State U., 1951-52, U. Mo., Kansas City, 1971-75; cert. legal asst., Rockhurst Coll., Kansas City, Mo., 1980; cert. risk mgr., 1979; m. James E. Cassidy, 1952 (div.); children: James E., II, Tracy C. With Kansas City (Mo.) chpt. ARC, 1952-54, N. Central region Boy Scouts Am., 1963-66, Clay County Health Dept., Liberty, Mo., 1966-71, City of Liberty, 1971-80; risk mgr. City of Ames (Iowa), 1980-82; risk mgr. City of Dallas, 1982-83; dir. Dept. Risk Mgmt., Pinellas County, Fla., 1984—; mem. faculty William Jewell Coll., Liberty, 1975-80; vis. prof. U. Kans., 1981; seminar leader, cons in field. Lay minister United Meth. Ch., 1965—; dir. youth devel. Hillside United Meth. Ch., Liberty; co-chmn. youth dir. Collegiate United Meth. Ch. scouting coordinator Palm Lake Christian Ch., Exec. Fellow U. South Fla., mem. Council of Ministries; advancement chmn. Mid-Iowa Council Boy Scouts Am., membership chmn. White Rock Dist. council, health and safety chmn. West Central Fla. council, 1985—; scouting coordinator Palm Lake Christian Ch., 1987—; skipper Sea Explorer ship, 1986—. Recipient Order of Merit, Boy Scouts Am., 1979, Living Sculpture award, 1978,79; Service award Rotary Internat., 1979; Exec. fellow U. South Fla., 1988. Mem. Am. Mgmt. Assns., Internat Platform Assn., Risk and Ins. Mgrs. Soc., Public Risk and Ins. Mgmt. Assn., Am. Soc. Profl. and Exec. Women, Am. Film Inst., U.S. Naval Inst., Nat. Assn. Female Execs., Nat. Inst. Mcpl. Law Officers. Author: Kids Are People, Too, 1975. Pearls of Potentiality, 1980; also articles. Home: Blind Pass Marina 9555 Blind Pass Rd St Petersburg Beach FL 33706 Office: 315 Court St Clearwater FL 33516

RESCH, JAN ROBERTSON, bank officer; b. Effingham, Ill., Feb. 12, 1932; d. Cheswold Lindley and Della (Calhoun) Robertson; m. Dewey L. Resch, Oct. 29, 1950; 1 child, Donald. AAS in Banking and Fin., Lincoln Trail Coll., 1982; student, DePaul U., 1984-87. News broadcaster Effingham Broadcasting Co., Newton, Ill., 1952—; recorder, dep. cir. clk. Jasper County, Newton, 1954-61; teller First Nat. Bank Newton, 1961-64, head bookkeeper, proof operator, gen. ledger, 1964-70, teller, 1970-72, asst. cashier, 1972-76, sec., receptionist, 1976-82, internat bank auditor, asst. trust officer, 1982—; instr. banking and fin. Lincoln Trail Coll., Robinson, Ill. 1982—. Bd. dirs. Jasper County Am. Cancer Soc., Newton; mem. Jasper Jobs Inc., Newton, 1986—, Jasper Post #20 Legion Aux., Newton, 1952—, Heartland Hospice, Effingham, 1986—. Mem. Ill. Banking Assn., Ill. BankPac. Democrat. Methodist. Office: First Nat Bank Newton 204 W Washington Newton IL 62448

RESCH, MARY LOUISE, child therapist, social services counselor; b. David City, Nebr., Oct. 26, 1956; d. Ernest John and Mary Jean (Roelandts) Cermak; m. Eugene Joseph Resch, Apr. 28, 1979. BS in Psychology, SUNY, Albany, 1984; MS in Counseling and Edn. with high honors, U. Wis., Platteville, 1986. Enlisted U.S. Army, 1974, advance through ranks to sgt., 1982; bomb disposal tech. U.S. Army, Ft. Riley, Kans., 1977-79, Platteville, 1982-85; bomb disposal instr. U.S. Army, Indian Head, Md., 1979-80; resigned U.S. Army, 1985; intern in family advocacy Army Community Service, U.S. Army, Ft. Belvoir, 1986; sr. counselor, child therapist Community Crisis and Referral Ctr., Inc., Waldorf, Md., 1986-87, also adolescent suicide specialist; instr. family advocacy Army Community Service, Ft. Belvoir, 1986; human services cons., mil. family specialist Devel. Asst. Corp., Washington, 1986-87; on-site adminstr. USDA Grad. Sch., Washington. Mem. Nat. Assn. Female Execs., Am. Assn. for Counseling and Devel., Am. Mental Health Counselors Assn., Mil. Educators and Counselors Assn., Nat. Organ. for Victim Assistance, Va. Counselors Assn. Democrat. Lutheran. Home: 6552 China Grove Ct Alexandria VA 22310 Office: Community Crisis and Referral Ctr Inc Tri County Fed Savs & Loan Bldg Waldorf MD 20601 Office: Walter Reed Army Med Ctr 6825 16th St NW Washington DC 20307

RESNICK, ALICE ROBIE, judge; b. Erie, Pa., Aug. 21, 1939; d. Adam Joseph and Alice Suzanne (Spizarny) Robie; m. Melvin L. Resnick, Mar. 20, 1970. Ph.B., Siena Heights Coll., 1961; J.D., U. Detroit, 1964. Bar: Ohio 1964, Mich. 1965, U.S. Supreme Ct. 1970. Asst. county prosecutor Lucas County Prosecutor's Office, Toledo, 1964-75, trial atty., 1965-75; judge Toledo Mcpl. Ct., 1976-83, 6th Dist. Ct. Appeals, State of Ohio, Toledo, 1983—; instr. U. Toledo, 1968-69. Trustee Siena Heights Coll., Adrian, Mich., 1982—; organizer Crime Stopper Inc., Toledo, 1981—; bd. dirs. Toledo-Lucas County Safety Council; bd. dirs. Guest House Inc. Mem. Toledo Bar Assn., Lucas County Bar Assn., Nat. Assn. Women Judges, Am. Judicature Soc., Toledo Women's Bar Assn. Ct. of Appeals Judges Assn., Toledo Mus. Art, Internat. Inst. Toledo. Roman Catholic. Home: 2407 Edgehill Rd Toledo OH 43615 Office: 6th Dist Ct Appeals 800 Jackson St Toledo OH 43604

RESNICK, CYNTHIA BILT, speech and language pathologist; b. Bklyn., Mar. 8, 1946; d. Murray and Helen Francis (Rubin) Bilt; B.A. cum laude, Marymount Manhattan Coll., 1976; M.S. in Speech Pathology, Tchrs. Coll., Columbia U., 1978; m. Jerry Resnick, June 17, 1967 (dec. 1972). Trainee in speech and language clin. pathology Marymount Manhattan Coll., N.Y.C., 1975, Columbia U., N.Y.C., 1976-77, Kennedy Child Study Center, N.Y.C., 1977, Beth Abraham Hosp., Bronx, N.Y., 1977; speech and language clinician L.I. Jewish-Hillside Med. Center, New Hyde Park, N.Y., 1977; tchr. speech and hearing handicapped Good Shepherd Sch., Inwood, N.Y., 1977-78; mem. staff Bur. Speech Improvement, N.Y.C. Bd. Edn., 1978; speech/lang. pathologist and coordinator of speech/lang. services Lorge Sch., N.Y.C., 1978-80 Summit Sch., N.Y.C., 1980; speech/lang. cons. Forest Hills Nursing Home, 1980-85; speech/lang. cons. Coll. Nursing Home, Flushing, N.Y., 1983-85; pvt. practice, Rego Park, N.Y., 1981—. Recipient hon. mention for acad. excellence in speech sci., Marymount Manhattan Coll., N.Y.C., 1976; citizenship award Roosevelt Prep. Sch., Stamford, Conn., 1963. Mem. Am. (cert.), N.Y. State speech and hearing assns., Mass. Speech Lang. Hearing Assn., Speech Communication Assn., Internat. Assn. Logopedics and Phoniatrics. Address: 94-11 59 Ave Suite A7 Rego Park NY 11373

RESNICK, JUDY SUE, data processing executive; b. Bklyn., Nov. 12, 1956; d. Joseph L. and Rhoda L. (Harris) Kluger; m. Ira A. Resnick, Mar. 14, 1976; children: Bryna, Frayda, Adina, Rivka, Mordechai, Yosef. BS in Acctg., Bklyn. Coll., 1978. Acct. N.Y.C. Tchrs. Retirement System, 1979-81; computer programmer State Ins. Fund, N.Y.C., 1981-87. Union rep. Profl. Employees' Fedn., N.Y.C., 1986-87. N.Y. State Regents scholar, 1973. Jewish.

RESTANI, JANE A., federal judge; b. San Francisco, Feb. 27, 1948; d. Roy J. and Emilia C. Restani. BA, U. Calif., Berkeley, 1969; JD, U. Calif., Davis, 1973. Bar: Calif., 1973. Trial atty. U.S. Dept. Justice, Washington, 1973-76, asst. chief comml. litigation sect., 1976-80, dir. comml. litigation sect., 1980-83; judge U.S. Ct. Internat. Trade, N.Y.C., 1983—. Mem. Order of Coif, Phi Beta Kappa. Office: US Ct Internat Trade 1 Federal Plaza New York NY 10007 *

RETHERFORD, KAREN LEE, personnel director; b. Troy, Ala., Apr. 9, 1953; d. H.L. and Dorothy Levette (Perdue) Worrell; m. Danny Lane Retherford, July 7, 1973; children: Amanda Lane, Jessica Nicole. AA, Pensacola Jr. Coll., 1977; student, U. West Fla., 1983—. Sewing machine operator Vanity Fair Mills, Inc., Milton, Fla., 1971, clk. typist, 1971-72, payroll clk., 1972-73, chief payroll clk., 1973-79, mgmt. trainee, 1979-80, indsl. engr., 1980, personnel mgr., 1981—. Bd. dirs. Milton Clean Community System, 1983—, Santa Rosa Women's Adv. Council, 1987—, United Way of Santa Rosa County, 1987—; appointed by Gov. State of Fla. Region I Coordinating Council for Vocat. Adult Edn., 1985—. Mem. Fla. C. of C. (mem. Pres. Club 1985), Santa Rosa County C. of C. (sec. 1985, Pres. award 1982), Beta Sigma Phi (pres. Alpha Upsilon chpt. 1984-85). Democrat. Baptist. Office: Vanity Fair Mills Inc 1505 Vanity Fair Rd Milton FL 32570

RETHLAKE, CHERYL ANN, special education educator; b. Ft. Wayne, Ind., Apr. 22, 1958; d. Harold Anthony and Phyllis June (Warfel) R. BS in Edn., St. Francis Coll., 1980; postgrad., Ind. U. SE, New Albany, 1985, Ind. U., 1988. Learning disabled tchr. New Wash. (Ind.) Middle/High Sch., 1980-86; mentally handicapped tchr. Clarksville (Ind.) Middle Sch., 1986—. Tchr., choir leader New Wash. Christian Ch., 1987—; sponsor Fellowship Christian Athletes, New Washington, 1982-87; presenter Ind. Fedn. of Council for Exceptional Children, 1988; crafts vol. Medco Nursing Home, Clarksville. Named one of Outstanding Young Women Am., 1979. Roman Catholic. Home: 1908 Village Green Blvd #154 Jeffersonville IN 47130-5151 Office: 101 Ettles Ln Clarksville IN 47130

RETTBERG, BARBARA CAROL, chemist; b. Elizabeth, N.J., Nov. 6, 1941; d. Heinrich Wilhelm and Barbara Lilian (Brateris) R. BA, Notre Dame Coll., Staten Island, 1963; MS, Rutgers U., 1966. Technician Atlantic Powdered Metals, Elizabeth, N.J., 1964-65; sr. research analyst Merck and Co., Rahway, N.J., 1965-88. Asst. dir. Blessed Sacrament Ch. Choir, Elizabeth 1985—; bd. dirs. Choral Art Soc. N.J., Westfield, N.J. 1980—. Mem. Am. Chem. Soc., N.J. Chromatography Group. Democrat. Roman Catholic. Home: 402 Washington Ave Point Pleasant Beach NJ 08742

RETTIG, CAROLYN FAITH, educator; b. Tarentum, Pa., June 30, 1951; d. William and Jennie Annetta (Lear) Ambrose; m. Gary Alan Rettig, July 10, 1985. BS in Edn., Ind. U. Pa., 1973; MA in Student Personnel, Slippery Rock U., 1988. Cert. elem. English tchr. secondary schs. Jr. high tchr. Saxonburg and Butler, Pa., 1974-75; English tchr. Butler Area High Sch., 1975-76; assessor community needs Butler County Community Coll., Pa., 1977-78; tchr. English Butler Area Sch. Dist., 1978—; chair English Dept., Butler Intermediate High Sch., 1986—; coach speech, debate Butler Area Sch. Dist., 1979-84, curriculum writing coordinator, 1986-87; coordinated fin. aid counselor practicum Butler County Community Coll., 1988. Mem. Butler Edn. Assn., Pa. State Edn. Assn., NEA. Democrat. Lutheran. Home: 261 Fisher Rd Cabot PA 16023 Office: Butler Intermediate High Sch 151 Fairground Hill Rd Butler PA 16001

RETZER, SISTER JEANINE, head of religious order; b. Milw., Jan. 27, 1938; d. Alvin Martin and Sophie Rose (Becker) R. BA, Mt. Mary Coll., 1968; MA, St. John's U., Cleve., 1974. Tchr. Cath. Sch. Systems, Wis., Iowa and Pa., 1957-73, prin., 1966-71; dir. religious edn. St. Olaf's Parish and St. Mary's Parish, Wis., 1973-77; mem. pastoral team St. Mary's Parish, Menomonee, Wis., 1977-82; adminstr. motherhouse Mother of Sorrows Convent, Milw., 1981-82; provincial Sisters of the Sorrowful Mother, Milw., 1982—; adminstr. Gen. Lay Ministry Program, Menomonee Falls, Wis., 1980-82; mem. planning com. Gathering, Chgo., 1980; mem. Major Superior, Leadership Conf. of WOmen Religious. Mem. Cath. Health Assn., Nat. Cath. Edn. Assn., Religious Edn. Assn., Cath. Health Assn. Wis. Address: Sisters of Sorrowful Mother 6618 N Teutonia Ave Milwaukee WI 53209

RETZER, MARY ELIZABETH HELM, retired librarian; b. Balt.; d. Francis Leslie C. and Edna (Smith) Helm; B.A., Western Md. Coll., 1940; M.A., Columbia U., 1946; postgrad. George Washington U., Ind. U., U. Ill., Ill. State U., Bradley U.; Ph.D., Western Colo. U., 1972; m. William Raymond Retzer, June 28, 1945; children—Lesley Elizabeth, Apryl Christine. Mem. faculty Rockville (Md.) Bd. Edn., 1940-47, elementary supr., 1945-47; mem. staff Peoria Public Library, 1957-63, homebound librarian, 1961-63; cons. librarian Bergan High Sch., 1964-67; condr. library sci. course in reference Bradley U., 1966—; librarian Hines Elementary Sch., 1963-66, Roosevelt Jr. High Sch., 1966-69; head media center Manual High Sch., Peoria, Ill., 1969-83. Instr. water safety courses ARC, summers 1940—; pres. women's bd. Salvation Army, 1952-54; pres. Peoria Nursery Sch. Assn., 1953-54; mem. legis. action com. Ill. Congress PTA, 1955-56; mem. Crippled Children's Adv. Com., Peoria, 1957-60; active various community drives; mem. women's adv. bd. Peoria Jr. Star, 1970-73. Mem. Ill. Valley Librarians Assn. (pres. 1971-72), ALA, Ill. Library Assn., Ill. Assn. Media in Edn. (certification com. 1973—), NEA, Ill., Peoria edn. assns., Ill. Audiovisual Assn., AAUW, Internat. Platform Assn. Republican. Presbyterian. Clubs: Order Eastern Star, Ill. State U. Adminstrs., Willowknolls Country, Sarasota Yacht. Home: 1317 W Moss Ave Peoria IL 61606 also: 2221 Beneve Terr Sarasota FL 33582

RETZKE, MELANIE JAYNE, computer programmer analyst; b. Columbus, Ohio, Dec. 31, 1952; d. Franklin Albert and Dorothy Viola (Payne) R. BS in Edn., Va. Poly. Inst. & State U., 1974; postgrad., Old Dominion U., 1978-80; AS summa cum laude, Tidewater Community Coll., 1985. Tchr. Mecklenburg County Pub. Schs., Palmer Springs, Va., 1974-76; supr. aquatics Virginia Beach (Va.) YMCA, 1976-78; tchr. health and phys. edn. Holy Trinity Cath. Sch., Norfolk, Va., 1978-82; sec. Smith & Tolerton, P.C., Norfolk, 1983-85; computer programmer, analyst NIH Clin. Ctr., Bethesda, Md., 1985—; computer cons., analyst Escalation Cons., Gaithersburg, Md., 1987—. Mem. Nat. Assn. for Female Execs. Republican. Lutheran. Home: 19933 Sweet Gum Circle #32 Germantown MD 20874 Office: NIH 9000 Rockville Pike Bldg 10 Info Systems Dept Bethesda MD 20892

REUTHER, ROSANN WHITE, advertising agency executive; b. Nashville, Nov. 24, 1943; d. Wiley Butler and Mildred Elizabeth (Little) White; student George Peabody Coll., 1961-64; m. Peter Martin Reuther, Oct. 3, 1964. Advt. copywriter WHMA Radio, Anniston, Ala., 1964-65, Bapt. Sunday Sch. Bd., Nashville, 1965-72, Thomas Nelson Pubs., Nashville, 1972-73; account exec. Holder-Kennedy Pub. Relations, Nashville, 1973-74; pub. relations dir. T. Nelson, Nashville, 1974-75; pension adminstr. Wood, Bateman, Nord, Assos., Nashville, 1975-76; owner, pres. In-Vision Advt. and Pub. Relations, Nashville, 1976—; lectr. Tenn. State U., 1978-79; part-time instr. Nashville State Tech. Inst.; faculty Tenn. Entrepreneur Forum, 1984. Worker, Carter for Pres. campaign, Tenn., 1976; pres. Historic Waverly Pl. Neighborhood Assn., 1988—. Recipient Paul M. Hinkhous award of excellence in advt., 1974. Mem. Nashville Advt. Fedn. (bd. dirs. 1986-88), Am. Women in Radio and TV (pres. Nashville chpt. 1981-82, dir. dist. B, 1982-83), Hist. Waverly Place Neighborhood Assn. (pres. 1988-89). Baptist. Lodge: Sertoma (chmn. bd. dirs. Brentwood club 1986—). Home: 1908 Elliott Ave Nashville TN 37204 Office: PO Box 41161 Nashville TN 37204

REVEAL, ARLENE HADFIELD, librarian, consultant; b. Riverside, Utah, May 21, 1916; d. Job Oliver and Mabel Olive (Smith) Hadfield; children—James L., Jon A. B.S. with hons., Utah State U., 1938; grad. in librarianship San Diego State U., 1968; M.L.S., Brigham Young U., 1976. librarian, Calif. Social case worker Boxelder County Welfare, Brigham City, Utah, 1938-40; office mgr. Strawberry Inn, Strawberry, Calif., 1950-65, Dodge Ridge Ski Corp., Long Barn, Calif., 1948-65; adminstrv. asst. Mono County Office of Edn., Bridgeport, Calif., 1961-67; catalog librarian La Mesa-Spring Valley Sch. Dist., La Mesa, Calif., 1968-71; librarian Mono County Library, Bridgeport, Calif., 1971—; chmn. Mountain Valley Library System, 1987—. Author: Mono County Courthouse, 1980. Recipient John Cotton Dana award H.W. Wilson Co., 1974. Mem. Delta Kappa Gamma (pres. Epsilon Alpha chpt. 1984-88), Beta Sigma Phi (treas. Xi Omicron Epsilon chpt. 1981, 83-85, pres. 1982, 85.), Delta Phi Mu. Lodge: Rebekah (treas. 1973—). Home: PO Box 532 Bridgeport CA 93517 Office: Mono County Free Library PO Box 398 Bridgeport CA 93517

REVENTLOW, MARY ROSE, personnel executive; b. Laindon, Eng., Mar. 12, 1945; came to U.S., 1971.; d. Noel and Florence Rose (Kent) Gray; married; 1 child, Alexander. BA, Fordham U., 1988. Dir. personnel services Consolidated Analysis Ctrs., Inc., N.Y.C., 1973-75; recruiter Dime Savs. Bank of N.Y., Bklyn., 1978-81; asst. human resources dir., mgr. recruitment Goldome Bank, N.Y.C., 1981-86; asst. v.p. human resources Standard Chartered Bank, N.Y.C., 1986—; chair bus. labor adv. council Jobpath, N.Y.C., 1985, Dept. Labor, N.Y.C, 1986-87. Recipient Cert. of Merit Mayor's Office of the Handicapped, 1985, 86. Mem. Am. Soc. Personnel Adminstrs., Fgn. Bank Personnel Forum, Bank Compensation Group, N.Y. Employment and Human Resource Com. Home: 288 Hicks St Brooklyn NY 11201 Office: Standard Chartered Bank 160 Water St New York NY 10038

REVER, BARBARA L., medical educator, consultant, researcher; b. Bklyn., Dec. 18, 1947. B.A., Barnard Coll., 1969; M.P.H., U. Calif.-Berkeley, 1970; M.D., N.Y. Med. Coll., 1974. Diplomate Am. Bd. Internal Medicine, Splty. Nephrology. Intern, Los Angeles County Hosp., U. So. Calif., 1974-75; resident in internal medicine, Los Angeles County Hosp., 1975-76, Kaiser Found. Hosps., Los Angeles, 1976-77; fellow in nephrology U. Calif., Los Angeles Sch. Medicine, 1978-80, specialist inNephrology, Salinas Valley Dialysis Services, Inc., also chmn. bd.; spl. cons. Calif. State Dept. Pub. Health, summer 1970; research assoc. Dept. Community and Preventive Medicine, N.Y. Hosp. Coll., summer 1971; instr. biology and physiology Community Health Medic Tng. Program, Indian Health Service Hosp., N. Mex., summer 1972; asst. prof. medicine, asst. dir. renal transplantation div. nephrology UCLA, 1980-81. Office: 230 San Jose St Suite 30 Salinas CA 93901

REVERE, TANA KAY, regulatory coordinator; b. Canton, Ohio, Nov. 8, 1950; d. Robert John Sr. and Shirley Lorraine (Hutchman) Starkey; m. Garrett Stanley Revere Sr., Aug. 7, 1981; children: Garrett Stanley Jr., Shaylin Kay, Shandal Lorraine. Grad. high sch., Minerva, Ohio, 1968. Operator number services Ohio Bell Telephone Co., Canton, 1968-70; operator, supr. Alliance, Ohio, 1970-74; engring. clk. Canton, 1974-78; drafter Dover Elevator Corp., Horn Lake, Miss., 1978-80, Eaton Corp.; reports clk. Mountain Bell Telephone Co., Casper, Wyo., 1980-82; drafter Eaton Corp., Riverton, Wyo., 1982-85; regulatory agy. coordinator Eaton Corp., Riverton, 1985-88, sec. safety com., 1987—; sec. safety com. Eaton Corp., Riverton, Wyo., 1987—. Democrat. Episcopalian. Home: 1618 E Park Lot 14 Riverton WY 82501 Office: Eaton Corp Tech Research Park Riverton WY 82501

REVILLE, JOANN M., airport management representative; b. Buffalo, Sept. 4, 1946; d. Joseph H. and Luella (Harnick) Miller; m. Joseph M. Reville, Mar. 28, 1981; children: Kara Ann, Brittany Erin. BA in Psychology/Sociology with honors, SUNY, Buffalo, 1978, cert. in human resources mgmt., 1979; postgrad. in bus., SUNY. Exec. sec. Goodrich Tire and Rubber Co., Washington, 1964, Blue Cross Western N.Y., Buffalo, 1965-70; pub. relations asst. Gen. Motors Corp., Buffalo, 1970-73; adminstrv. asst. Erie County Dept. Mental Health, West Seneca, N.Y., 1975; grant asst. State Tchrs. Coll., Buffalo, 1976-78; exec. sec. Interstate United Corp., Tonawanda, N.Y., 1978-81; mgmt. rep. Niagra Frontier Transp. Authority, Buffalo, 1981-87. Mem. Erie County Dem. Women; notary public, election inspector Erie County. Mem. N.Y. State Airport Mgrs. Assn. (northeast chpt.), Am. Assn. Airport Execs., Alpha Kappa Delta (Zeta chpt.). Democrat. Roman Catholic. Club: Variety Women (Buffalo). Home: 85 Coolidge Rd Buffalo NY 14220 Office: Greater Buffalo Internat Airport Niagara Frontier Transp Authority Buffalo NY 14225

REVIS, FRANCES W., retired educator; b. Colbert, Okla., Dec. 10, 1910; d. Harvey R. and Ophelia (Dane) Williamson; B.S., Southeastern State Tchrs. Coll., 1931; M.A., Tex. State Coll. Women, 1950; Ed.D., Tex. Woman's U., 1958; m. Sidney M. Revis, Jan. 19, 1963. (dec. Aug. 1983). Tchr. home econs. Checotah (Okla.) High Sch., 1931-33; county dir. pub. welfare, Cotton, Logan, LeFlore counties, Okla., 1933-40; tchr. vocat. homemaking Colbert (Okla.) High Sch., 1940-57; faculty mem. Southeastern Okla. State U., Durant, 1958-76, asst. prof. home econs., 1958-65, assoc. prof., 1965-69, prof., head home econs., dept., 1969-76, prof. emeritus, 1976—. Sec.-treas. western sect., So. Regional Conf. Coll. Food and Nutrition Tchrs., 1957-76; bd. dirs. Colbert Hist. Soc. Named Outstanding Tchr., Southeastern State U., 1973-74. Mem. Am., Okla. home econs. assns., Okla. Edn. Assn., AAUP, Higher Edn. Alumni Council Okla., N.E.A., AAUW, Am., Okla. voca. assns., Am., Okla. Sch. food service assns., Ret. Tchrs. Assn., Durant Hist. Soc., Nat. Council Adminstrs. Home Econs. Soc. Nutrition Edn., Delta Kappa Gamma. Home: PO Box 70 Colbert OK 74733

REVIS-WAGNER, MARY ESTHER, restaurant executive; b. Augusta, Ga., Feb. 6, 1961; d. James Claude and Mary Edna (Miller) R.; m. Charles Kenyon Revis-Wagner, Dec. 7, 1985; stepchildren: Heyward Kenyon Wagner, Mitchell Price Wagner. BS in Adminstrv. Mgmt., Clemson U., 1983. Pvt. practice housekeeper owner, operator, Clemson, 1981-83; waitress, caterer Edgar F's Gallery and My Apt., Greenville, S.C., 1983-85; asst. mgr. sales Radio Shack Computer Ctr., Greenville, S.C., 1984-85; pres. Elaphe, Inc., Clemson, 1985—; mgr. Nick's Tavern and Deli, Clemson, 1985—. United Paperworker's Internat. Union scholar, 1979. Mem. Downtown Merchants' Assn. (ad-hoc com. 1987), Nat. Assn. Exec. Females. Clubs: Sports Car of Am., Smithsonian Assocs. Home: 121 Clemson St Clemson SC 29631 Office: Elaphe Inc 110 Sloan St Clemson SC 29631

REVUELTA, AURORA VILLANUEVA, management consultant; b. Quezon City, Philippines, Aug. 13, 1937; d. Mauro Oliveros and Leonora (Villanueva) R.; m. Michael J. Callicoat, Jan. 31, 1983. AB, Philippine Women's U., 1954; Doctorate, U. of the East, Manila, 1960. Postdoctoral research fellow NIMH, Bethesda, Md., 1968-72, research assoc., 1972-83; dir. psychiatry lab. Mt. Sinai Hosp. Sch. Medicine, N.Y.C., 1983-85; mgmt. cons. Recalli Internat. Corp., Newark, 1985—. Contbr. articles to sci. and med. jours. Named Outstanding Filipino Scientist Ministry of Sci. and Tech., 1980; recipient Citation Pres. Ferdinand Marcos, 1982. Mem. Am. Soc. Pharmacology and Therapeutics, Am. Soc. Neurochemistry, N.Y. Acad. Scis., Filipino-Asian Women's Network of Greater N.Y. (pres. 1985, Outstanding Scientist 1985). Home: 609 Parker St Forest Hill Newark NJ 07104

REY-BEAUX, MARIE AMELIE MONIQUE, management consultant, educator; b. Mauritius, Oct. 7, 1937; came to U.S., 1970; d. Henry A. Rey d'Andremont and Marie Ines (Doger de Speville) S; m. Norse A.C. Bear, Feb. 14, 1965; children: Sylvana, Norse, Daniel. Cert. in Edn., Tchr's Coll., 1960; cert. in nursing, West London Hosp., 1965; cert. in family counseling, Pa. State U., 1977, cert. in recreation, 1977; AAS in Bus. Adminstrn., No. Ky. U., 1980, BA in History, 1981, BA in Internat. Studies, 1982. Cert. elem. tchr., Ky.; RN, Ky. Tchr. Dept. Edn., Mauritius, 1960-63; property mgr. North Enterprise, Houston, 1965—; counselor mental health, Williamsport, Pa. and Ky., 1970-82; acct. Goodwill Industries, 1985—; tchr. Spring Br. Ind. Sch. Dist., 1985—; counselor home health Hospice, 1985—. Campaigner Hist. Soc. Pa. and Ky., 1970-82; fundraiser Opera, Symphony and Mus., Pa., Ky. and Houston, 1970-82, Inst. Internat. Edn., Houston, 1983-86. Recipient Disting. Service award Notable Women Tex., 1980. Mem. AAUW, Nat. Assn. Female Execs., Literacy Advance (instr. 1985-86), Gulf Coast Council Fgn. Affairs. Clubs; Newcomers, Alliance Francaise. Home: 13638 Perthshire Houston TX 77079 Office: Dawson and Dawson 4801 Woodway Dr Houston TX 77056

REYES, CANDACE MULCAHY, business administrator; b. Chgo., Feb. 16, 1946; d. Robert Emmet and Rita Helen (Schultz) Mulcahy; m. Phillip John Manzella, Aug. 18, 1964 (div. May 1967); 1 child, Janet Manzella; m. James Theodore Shell, Aug. 13, 1971 (div. May 1976); 1 child, Julia; m. Jaime Magbual Reyes, Aug. 12, 1978 (July 1987). Commodity broker Earl K. Riley, Chgo., 1968-72; acct. R.J. O'Brien, Chgo., 1974-75; commodity broker E.F. Hutton, Chgo., 1975-77; make-up artist Elizabeth Arden, Chgo., 1977-78; acct. Crocker Nat. Bank, San Francisco, 1978-80; bus. adminstr. Jaime Reyes, Casa Grande, Ariz., 1980—. Fund raiser Pinal County Med. Soc. Aux., Casa Grande, Ariz., 1983—. Fellow AMA Aux. (del. 1984), Nat. Assn. Female Execs., Pinal County Med. Soc. Aux. (pres. 1984-85), Assn. Phillippine Practicing Physicians Ariz. Aux. (sec. 1983, treas. 1982), Internat. Platform Assn. Roman Catholic. Home and Office: 1131 Avenida Fresca Casa Grande AZ 85222

REYES, MARCIA STYGLES, medical technologist; b. Winchester, Mass., July 15, 1950; d. Bernard Francis and Eleanore Cecilia (Nicgorska) Stygles; B.S. in Med. Tech., Merrimack Coll., North Andover, Mass., 1972; M.S. in Health Scs. (Kellogg Found. grantee), SUNY, Buffalo, 1977; m. Carlos Reyes, Aug. 5, 1978. Sr. med. technologist Symmes Hosp., Arlington, Mass., 1970-73; sr. microbiologist and serologist Mt. Auburn Hosp., Cambridge, Mass., 1973-75; asst. prof., clin. coordinator Quinnipiac Coll., Hamden, Conn., 1976-81; lab. supr. Canberra Clin. Labs., Meriden, Conn., 1981-86; lab. supr. Hill Health Ctr, New Haven, Conn., 1984—; cons. in med. tech. mgmt., allied health edn. Mem. Am. Soc. Clin. Pathologists, Am. Soc. Med. Tech., Conn. Soc. Med. Tech. (Speaker awards), Am. Soc. Microbiology, Am. Soc. Allied Health Profls. Home: 199 Dover St New Haven CT 06513

REYNES, WENDY WARNER, publishing company executive; b. Boston, Sept. 29, 1944; d. Philip Russell and Elizabeth (Patton) Warner; A.A., Conn. Coll., 1966; m. Jose (Tony) Antonio Reynes, III, Apr. 26, 1969; children—Jose (Tad) Antonio, Gabrielle Elizabeth. With Foote, Cone, Belding, N.Y.C., 1966-68; advt. sales rep. Cosmopolitan Mag., N.Y.C., 1968-69, Co-Ed Mag., N.Y.C., 1969-70; asst. product mgr. Avon Products, N.Y.C., 1970; advt. sales rep. Mag. Networks, N.Y.C. and Chgo., 1970-72; midwest mgr. advt. sales Girl Talk Mag., Chgo., 1972-75; div. mgr. advt. sales Pattis Group, Chgo., 1975-79; pres. Reynes & Assos., Inc., 1979—, Sales Unltd., Inc., 1985—. Bd. dirs. Multiple Sclerosis, 1974-79, St. Joseph's Sch. PTA, 1979-80, Marriage Encounter, 1976—; active Jr. League Greenwich, Conn., 1965-67, Jr. League N.Y.C., 1967-75. Mem. Agate Club (dir.), Advt. Assn., Women's Advt. Club Chgo. (co-chmn.). Clubs: Chgo. Advt., Wilmette Tennis, East Bank, Women's Advt. Chgo. Home: 460 Ash St Winnetka IL 60093

REYNOLDS, ALVA-INEZ, manufacturing company executive; b. Douglas, Ga., Oct. 31, 1933; d. Daniel Beamon and Alva (Flanders) Smith; children from previous marriage: Leon Paulk, Linda Paulk Tanner, James Paulk; m. Don Wayne Reynolds, June 13, 1973. Grad. high sch., Douglas. Order dept. sec. Steiner Co., Chgo., 1956-64; so. controller Cable Raincoats Co., Douglas, 1964-70; so. regional mgr. Sosine Mohawk Co., Statenville, Ga., 1970-78; office mgr. Pan Am. Gyro-Tex., Jasper, Fla., 1978-80; asst. gen. mgr. Gen. Laminates Corp., Jasper, 1980-86; pres., mgr. Sunshine Products Corp., Jasper, 1986-88; mgr. Suwanne Swifty Convenience Food Store, Live Oak, Fla., 1988—. Mem. Nat. Assn. Women Bus. Owners, Nat. Assn. Female Execs., Am. Assn. Retired Person, Jasper C. of C. Democrat. Baptist. Home: Rt 4 Box 99 Jasper FL 32052 Office: Sunshine Products Corp NE First St PO Box 1449 Jasper FL 32052

REYNOLDS, BARBARA LEE, advertising agency executive; b. Norman, Okla., Feb. 21, 1955; d. Richard Lee and Barbara Jean (Benz) R.; m. Donald J. Needham, Nov. 2, 1980 (div. May 1985). BA, U. Okla., 1977; postgrad. in bank mktg., U. Colo., 1981; postgrad. in banking, So. Meth. U., 1984. Mgmt. intern AT&T Long Lines, Houston, 1977-78; mktg. officer, dir. pub. relations Capital Nat. Bank, Houston, 1978-81; v.p., dir. mktg. 1st Western Bank, Houston, 1981-82; v.p., regional mktg. dir. Tex. Am. Bank, Houston, 1982-85; account supr., dir. agy. pub. relations Biederman & Co., N.Y.C., 1985-86; account supr. Bozell, Jacobs, Kenyon & Eckhardt, N.Y.C., 1986—. Bd. dirs. Dance Forum, Inc., N.Y.C., 1986—. Mem. Bank Mktg. Assn. (councilman Chgo. chpt. 1984-86, mem. nat. conv. planning com. 1986-87, treas. N.Y. chpt. 1986-87, bd. dirs. 1986—, v.p. communications 1987—, pres. N.Y.C. chpt. 1988-89), Nat. Assn. Bank Women (state conf. chmn. 1986), Pub. Relations Soc. Am. (accredited), Fin. Communications Soc. Democrat. Episcopalian. Home: 9 Carlin St Norwalk CT 06851 Office: Doyle Graf Mabley 375 Hudson St New York NY 10014

REYNOLDS, CAROLE LEE, lawyer; b. Washington; d. Vernon and Elizabeth (James) R. B.A., Am. U., 1971; M.A., New Sch. Social Research, 1973; J.D., Northeastern U., 1977. Bar: Va. 1977, D.C. 1978, U.S. Dist. Ct. (ea. dist.) Va. 1977, U.S. Dist. Ct. D.C., 1980, U.S. Ct. Appeals (4th cir.) 1977. Atty., FTC Bur. Consumer Protection, Washington, 1977—; lectr. in field. Author: The Mortgage Money Guide, How to Advertise Consumer Credit. Recipient Meritorious Service award. Episcopalian. Office: FTC Div Credit Practices Washington DC 20580

REYNOLDS, CHERYL LOUISE, lawyer; b. Burbank, Calif., Dec. 27, 1944; d. Frank Hale and Sadie Louise (Risien) Reynolds; m. Lawrence E. Myhre, Dec. 19, 1963 (div. 1973); children—Jeffrey Reynolds Myhre, Laura Louise Myhre. Student Calif. State Poly. U., 1962-64; B.A., Rutgers U., 1976; J.D., 1979. Bar: N.J. 1980. Assoc. law firm Wharton, Stewart & Davis, Somerville, N.J., 1979-80; ptnr. law firm Thiele & Reynolds, Somerville, N.J., 1980-82; group counsel Data Systems Group, The Perkin-Elmer Corp., Holmdel, N.J., 1982-85; counsel Concurrent Computer Corp., Holmdel, N.J., 1985-86; legal cons. C.L. Reynolds and Stanger, Michaelson, Reynolds, Spivak and Tobia, P.C., Long Branch, N.J., 1986—. Author: Introduction to Computer Graphics, 1976; The Self-Executing License, 1984; editor: Rutgers Jour. Computers and the Law, 1978-79, tech. cons., 1981-82; mem. adv. bd. Computer Law Reporter; contbr. articles to profl. jours. Mem. ABA, N.J. State Bar Assn., N.J. Assn. Women Bus. Owners. Republican. Unitarian. Office: 200 Ocean Ave N Long Branch NJ 07740

REYNOLDS, GARNET LULYAN, speech pathologist, communications specialist; b. California, Pa., Aug. 16, 1940; d. William Rex and Garnet Wilda (Dias) R.; m. Francis Sinko, Sept. 5, 1959 (div.); m. Charles L. Ilvento, Dec. 29, 1982. BS, Calififornia State Coll., 1960; MS, Fla. State U., 1967, PhD, 1977. Supr. Communication Disorders Dade County Pub. Schs., Miami, Fla., 1969-73; asst. prof., audiology, speech pathology Fla. State U., Tallahassee, 1974-77, Sch. Medicine, U. Miami, 1978-80; dir. clin. tng. U. Miami, Coral Gables, Fla., 1977-81; research speech pathologist VA, Miami, 1982-86; dir. The Speech-Voice-Lang. Ctr., Miami, 1982—; pres. A Positive Communication Image, Coral Gables, 1984—; cons. Am. Express-Latin Am., Coral Gables, 1985—; speech pathologist VA Hosp., Miami, 1988. Author: Speech-Facial Acceptability and Self-Concept, 1981, Foibles and Folly of Speech Therapy in Cleft Palate Speakers; editor Fla. Lang. Jour., 1980. Fundraiser Young Reps., Dade County, 1981. Recipient Dedicated Service award Nat. Council Bds. of Examiners of Speech and Hearing, 1983, Dedicated Service award Fla. Adv. Council Speech and Hearing, 1980, Outstanding Service award VA, Miami, 1984. Mem. Am. Speech, Lang., and Hearing Assn. (cert. clin. competence), Fla. Lang. Speech and Hearing Assn. (editor 1980-82), Am. Cleft Palate Assn., Am. Women in Radio and TV (sec. 1986-87, v.p. 1987—), Kappa Delta Pi, Alpha Delta Kappa. Republican. Methodist. Club: Soroptimist (pres.-elect). Home: 10725 SW 128 Terr Miami FL 33176

REYNOLDS, HELEN ELIZABETH, service executive; b. Minerva, N.Y., Aug. 30, 1925; d. Henry James and Margurite Catherine (Gallagher) McNally; m. Theodore Laurence Reynolds, Feb. 27, 1948; children: Laurence McBride, David Scott, William Herbert. BA, SUNY, Albany, 1967; MA, Union Coll., Schenectady, N.Y., 1971. Owner, mgr. Schafer Studio, Schenectady, 1970-73; co-owner, v.p. Reynolds Chalmers Inc., Schenectady, 1971—; program coordinator Schenectady County, 1980-81; adminstr. Wellspring House of Albany, N.Y., 1981—; cons., examiner N.Y. State Civil Service, Albany, 1971-81; mem. adv. council SBA, Washington, 1978-80. Mem. planning bd. Town of Niskayuna, N.Y., 1977-81, town councilwoman, 1986—; bd. dirs. HAVEN, Schenectady, 1978-81. Named Woman Vision, 1986, 87, Today's Woman, 1987, Schenectady YWCA. Mem. Antique and Classic Boat Soc. (bd. dirs. 1974—, Disting. Service award 1979), Assn. Adminstrs. Independent Housing (pres. 196-88), Inst. Real Estate Mgmt., Am. Mgmt. Assn., Lake George (N.Y.) Assn. Republican. Clubs: N.Y. State Women's Press, Albany Press. Lodge: Zonta (pres. 1981-82). Home: 2262 Cayuga Rd Schenectady NY 12309 Office: Wellspring House Albany Washington Ave Extension Albany NY 12203

REYNOLDS, JO (SCHOLZE), educational administrator; b. Sarasota, Fla., Aug. 15, 1941; d. Joseph Wendling and Frances (Amsden) Scholze; m. James Hooks Reynolds, Dec. 27, 1959 (div. May 1985); children: Jamie Jo, James Burton. AA, Palm Beach Jr. Coll., 1967; BS, Fla. Atlantic U., 1968, MEd, 1973; EdD, Nova U., 1987. Tchr. J.I. Leonard High Sch., Lake Worth, Fla., 1968-73; dean Conniston Jr. High Sch., West Palm Beach, Fla., 1973-76, Congress Middle Sch., Boynton Beach, Fla., 1976-79; asst. prin. Forest Hill High Sch., West Palm Beach, 1979-83; prin. Palm Beach pub. sch., Fla., 1983-87, Wellington Landings Community Middle Sch., Fla., 1987—; chmn. county secondary curriculum com., 1985-86. Contbr. poetry to various publs. Former Tchrs. Sarasota scholar, 1959; Selby Found. scholar and grantee, 1967. Mem. Nat. Assn. Secondary Sch. Prins., fla. Assn. Secondary Sch. Prins., Am. Assn. Sch. Adminstrs., Palm Beach C. of C. Democrat. Baptist. Office: Wellington Landings Mid Sch 1100 Aero Club Dr West Palm Beach FL 33414

REYNOLDS, KAREN DELANA, state health administrator; b. Camden, S.C., Dec. 18, 1958; d. Bennie Hilton Sr. and Delana (Branham) R. AA, Anderson (S.C.) Coll., 1979; BS, Med. U. S.C., 1982. Health info. cons. Appalachia III Pub. Health Dist., S.C. Dept. Health, Spartanburg, S.C., 1982-83; health records adminstr. S.C. Dept. Health and Environ. Control, Columbia, S.C., 1983—; auditor SysteMetrics, Inc., Santa Barbara, Calif., 1982-83; health info. cons. State Fla. Health and Rehab. Services. Mem. adv. bd. Midlands Tech. Coll., Columbia, S.C.; mem. AIDS Ednl. Task Force for S.C. Mem. Am. Med. Records Assn., S.C. Med. Records Assn. (edn. com. 1986-87), S.C. Pub. Health Assn. Home: 3700 Bush River Rd Apt #L-3 Columbia SC 29210 Office: SC Dept Health 2600 Bull St Columbia SC 29201

REYNOLDS, KARYN CHERYL, banker, consultant; b. N.Y.C., Mar. 10, 1945; d. Leonard John and Harriette (Cohen) R.; m. Elliott Wolk, Dec. 27, 1970 (div.); 1 dau., Harmony. B.S., Hofstra U., Hempstead, N.Y., 1965, M.B.A., 1977. Programmer, Control Data, Bloomington, Minn., 1967; project mgr. Phoenix Computer Tech., N.Y.C., 1968-69; pvt. practice computer applications cons., 1969-72; pres. Kth Dimension, Beechurst, N.Y., 1973-82; v.p., Chase Manhattan Bank, N.Y.C., 1982—; assoc. prof. computer applications, mgmt. sci. LIU, Greenvale, N.Y., 1976-82; assoc. prof. Hofstra U., 1978-81, 84; chmn. Kacie Trading, N.Y.C., 1972. Author poems. IBM fellow, 1978. Fellow Beta Gamma Sigma, Pi Alpha Alpha; mem. Assn. Computer Machinery. Club: Mensa (dir. 1976-77). Office: Chase Manhattan Bank 1 Chase Plaza New York NY 10081

REYNOLDS, KATHRYN ANNE, accountant; b. Kalamazoo, July 31, 1957; d. Ronald Louis and Patricia Anne (Mathers) Blaul; m. Lee Michael Reynolds, Aug. 4, 1979; children—Daniel, Stephani, Joseph. Student McHenry Community Coll., 1975-76, Knox Coll., 1976-77; B.B.A. in Acctg. magna cum laude, U. Wis.-Whitewater, 1979. C.P.A., Wis. Intern Arthur Anderson, Milw., 1979; mem. staff Baillies, Denson, Erickson & Smith, C.P.A.s, Lake Geneva, Wis., 1980-82, sr. acct., 1983-84; v.p. fin. Rubidell Recreation Inc., Elkhorn, Wis., 1984—. Rotary exchange student, France, 1973-74. Mem. Am. Inst. C.P.A.s, wis. Inst. C.P.A.s, Nat. Assn. Accts., Nat. Assn. Female Execs., Beta Alpha Psi, Phi Gamma Nu. Home: Powers Lake Rd Route 1 Box 585 Genoa City WI 53128 Office: Rubidell Recreation Inc 39 N Washington St Elkhorn WI 53121

REYNOLDS, LINDA CAROLINE, writer, educator; b. Ft. Worth, Jan. 20; d. James Daniel and Martha Caroline (Valigura) Little; B.B.A., Tex. Christian U., 1965, M.B.A., 1970. Tchr., Ft. Worth Pub. Schs., 1965-73; instr. Tarrant County Jr. Coll., 1974-75, Tex. Christian U., Ft. Worth, 1976-85; self-employed writer, lectr. and cons., Ft. Worth, 1976—. Bd. dirs. Mus. Western Transp.; active Van Cliburn INternat. Friends, Opera Guild. Mem. Am. Vocat. Assn., Am. Bus. Communication Assn., Tex. Bus. Edn. Assn., Nat. Bus. Edn. Assn. Author: Snow Country Typewriting Practice Set, 1974; Air Country Typewriting Practice Set, 1980; Gymnastics Unlimited Typewriting Practice Set, 1987; Letters PLUS, 1987; Dimensions in Personal Development, 1976; Dimensions in Professional Development, 1982, 3d edit., 1988. Office: 3817 Overton Park E Fort Worth TX 76109

REYNOLDS, LOLA SULLIVAN, lawyer; b. New Rochelle, N.Y., Apr. 25, 1955; d. James Francis and Lola Joan (Blank) Sullivan; m. Timothy Gerard Reynolds, Mar. 15, 1980; children: Timothy Gerard Jr., Terence Sullivan, Kieran Patrick. BA, Trinity Coll., Washington, 1977; JD, Fordham U., 1980. Bar: N.Y. 1981, U.S. Dist. Ct. (so. and ea. dists.) N.Y. 1981, U.S. Dist. Ct. N.J. 1981, U.S. Ct. Appeals (2d and 3d cirs.) 1984, U.S. Supreme Ct. 1984. Assoc. gen. counsel Office of Gen. Counsel, The Hearst Corp., N.Y.C., 1980—. Active Friends and Neighbors Club, Mineola, N.Y. Mem. N.Y. State Bar Assn., Assn. of Bar of City of N.Y., Guild of Cath. Lawyers, Phi Beta Kappa. Republican. Roman Catholic. Home: 185 Pomander Rd Mineola NY 11501 Office: The Hearst Corp Office Gen Counsel 959 8th Ave New York NY 10019

REYNOLDS, MARY TRACKETT, political scientist; b. Milw., Jan. 11, 1914; d. James P. and Mary (Nachtwey) Trackett; B.A., U. Wis., 1935; M.A., 1935; postgrad. (Rebecca Green fellow) Radcliffe Coll., 1935-36; Ph.D. (U. fellow, Barnard fellow), Columbia U., 1939; m. Lloyd G. Reynolds, June 12, 1937; children—Anne Reynolds Skinner, Priscilla Reynolds Roosevelt, Bruce. Research asst. Littauer Sch., Harvard U., 1938-39; instr. Queens Coll., 1939-40, Hunter Coll., 1941-42, lectr., 1945-47; assoc. in polit. sci. Johns Hopkins U., 1942-43; lectr. Conn. Coll., 1947-48, asst. prof., 1948-50; asst. prof. U. Bridgeport, 1950-51; research assoc. in econs. Yale U., 1961-67, vis. lectr. in English, 1973-82; meml. lecture Joyce Centennial, 1982. Research asst. Pres.'s Com. Adminstrn. Mgmt., 1936; sr. economist Nat. Econ. Com., 1940; adminstrn. asst. Glenn L. Martin Aircraft Co., Balt., 1942-43; editorial asst. pub. adminstrn. com. Social Sci. Research Council, 1944-45; cons. Nat. Def. Adv. Commn., 1949, Nat. Mcpl. Assn., 1956, Orgn. Econ. Cooperation and Devel., Paris, 1964, U.S. State Dept.-AID 1965. Mem. Am. Polit. Sci. Assn., Dante Soc. Am., AAUP, James Joyce Found. (editorial bd. Quar. 1985—), Conn. Acad. Arts and Scis., LWV, New Haven Hosp. Aux. (bd. dirs.), Phi Beta Kappa. Clubs: Elizabethan (Yale) (sec.-treas. 1984—, bd. incorporators 1986—); Grolier, Lawn (New Haven); Appalachian Mountain. Author: Interdepartmental Committees in the National Administration, 1940; Joyce and Nora, 1964; Source Documents in Economic Development, 1966; Joyce's Debt to Dante, 1968; Two Essays on James Joyce, 1970; Joyce and D'Annunzio, 1976; Joyce and Dante: The Shaping Imagination, 1982; A Companion to Joyce Studies, 1984; Vico, Dante and Joyce, 1987, Joyce and Pirandello, 1987; contbr. articles to profl. jours. Home: 75 Old Hartford Turnpike Hamden CT 06517 Office: Box 604 Yale Station New Haven CT 06520

REYNOLDS, NANCY BRADFORD DUPONT (MRS. WILLIAM GLASGOW REYNOLDS), sculptor; b. Greenville, Del., Dec. 28, 1919; d. Eugene Eleuthere and Catherine Dulcinea (Moxham) duPont; student Goldey-Beacom Coll., Wilmington, Del., 1938; m. William Glasgow Reynolds, May 18, 1940; children—Kathrine Glasgow Reynolds, William Bradford, Mary Parminter Reynolds Savage, Cynthia duPont Reynolds Farris. Exhibited one-woman shows: Rehoboth (Del.) Art League, 1963, Del. Art Mus., Wilmington, Caldwell, Inc., 1975, Wilmington Art Mus., 1976; exhibited group shows: Corcoran Gallery, Washington, 1943, Soc. Fine Arts, Wilmington, 1937, 38, 40, 41, 48, 50, 62, 65, NAD, N.Y.C., 1964, Pa. Mil. Coll., Chester, 1966, Del. Art Center, 1967, Met. Mus. Art, N.Y.C., 1977, Lever House, N.Y.C., 1979; represented in permanent collections: Wilmington Trust Co., E.I. duPont de Nemours & Co., Children's Home, Inc., Claymont, Del., Children's Bur., Wilmington, Stephenson Sci. Center, Nashville, Lutheran Towers Bldg., Travelers Aid and Family Soc. Bldg., Wilmington, Bronze Fountain Head, Longwood Gardens, Kennett Square, Pa. Guide, mem. research staff Henry Francis DuPont Winterthur Mus., 1955-63. Organizer vol. service Del. chpt. ARC, 1938-39; chmn. Com. for Revision Del. Child Adoption Law, 1950-52; pres. bd. dirs. Children Bur. Del.; pres., trustee Children's Home, Inc. Recipient Confrerie des Chevaliers du Tastevin Clos de Vougeot-Bourgogne France, 1960; Hort. award Garden Club Am., 1964, medal of Merit, 1976; Dorothy Platt award Garden Club of Phila., 1980; Alumni medal of merit Westover Sch., Middlebury, Conn. Mem. Pa. Hort. Soc., Wilmington Soc. Fine Arts, Mayflower Descs., Del. Hist. Soc., Colonial Dames, League Am. Pen Women, Nat. Trust Hist. Preservation. Episcopalian. Clubs: Garden of Wilmington (past pres.), Garden of Am. (past asst. zone 4 chmn.), Vicmead Hunt, Greenville Country, Chevy Chase (Washington); Colony (N.Y.C.). Contbr. articles to profl. jours. Address: PO Box 3919 Greenville DE 19807

REYNOLDS, NANCY IRENE, county registrar; b. Kansas City, Mo., Feb. 26, 1942; d. Chester Earl and Martha Louise (Laverentz) Jacobs; 1 child, Penelope Ann. Sec. to probate judge Hiawatha, Kans., 1965-66; abstractor Finley & Miller, Attys., 1967-68; clk. County Treas., Hiawatha, Kans., 1976-77; registrar deeds Brown County (Kans.), Hiawatha, 1977—; treas. Northeast Kans. Emergency Med. Tech., 1985-86, pres., 1986-87; pres. Kansas Register of Deeds Assn., 1987-88. Disaster chmn. Brown County chpt. ARC, 1984—. Mem. Hiawatha Bus. and Profl. Women's Orgn. (pres. 1985—, Woman of Yr. award 1983), Hiawatha High Sch. Alumni Assn. (treas. 1983—), Kans. Register of Deeds Assn. (treas. 1985-86). Avocations: needlecrafts, reading. Home: 608 N 3d St Hiawatha KS 66434 Office: Brown County Register of Deeds Office Courthouse Hiawatha KS 66434

REYNOLDS, PATRICIA LOU, insurance company executive; b. Columbus, Ohio, Jan. 23, 1936; d. Robert Morris and LaDonna Florence (Venerable) King; m. Harvey Noah Reynolds; children: Harvey, Patrick, Mark, David, Matthew, Anthony. Student, Mt. Carmel Nursing Sch., Columbus, Ohio, 1955, Columbus Tech. Inst., 1978. Clk. typist State of Ohio, Columbus, 1953-54; records clk. Ohio Bell Telephone Co., Columbus, 1955-56; claims examiner Nationwide Ins. Co., Columbus, 1966-67, group leader, 1967-70, unit supr., 1970-72, section supr., 1972-81; supr. Community Mut. Ins. Co., Worthington, Ohio, 1981-82; mgr. Community Mut. Ins. Co., Worthington, 1982-86, coordinator, 1986-88, mgr., 1988—; mem. adv. council Good Samaritan Med. Ctr., Zanesville, Ohio, 1986—; bd. dirs. Nationwide Credit Union, Columbus, 1979-81; com. mem. Cen. Ohio Rehab. Ctr., 1984—, chmn. 1985. Author: poetry, 1982-86. Mem. Am. Soc. Tng. and Devel. Democrat. Office: Community Mut Ins Co 6740 N High St Columbus OH 43085

REYNOLDS, PHYLLIS THURRELL, accountant; b. Wolfeboro, N.H., Sept. 15, 1955; d. Philip Emery and Patricia Josephine (Gray) Thurrell; m. Robert Gregory Reynolds, May 21, 1983. A in Bus. Adminstrn., St. Clair County Community Coll., Port Huron, Mich., 1974. Staff acct. Family Health Internat., Research Triangle Park, N.C., 1978-81, payroll and benefits acct., 1976-78, internat. travel coordinator, grants and contracts acct., 1981-83; acctg. supr. Microelectronics Ctr., Research Triangle Park, N.C., 1983—; cons. Travel, Inc., Raleigh, N.C., 1983. Mem. Nat. Assn. Female Execs. Home: 3947 Hope Valley Rd Durham NC 27707 Office: Microelectronics Ctr NC 3021 Cornwallis Rd Research Triangle Park NC 27709

REYNOLDS, SUSAN ELIZABETH, marketing professional; b. Carlisle, Pa., Dec. 12, 1950; d. Harold Kenneth and Elizabeth (Holman) R. BS, Western Mich. U., 1973, postgrad., 1974-75. Systems engr. IBM, Lansing, Mich., 1977-81; adv. regional mktg. support rep. IBM, Detroit, 1982-83, systems engring. mgr., 1984-85, area systems support mgr., 1985-86, resource programs mgr., 1986-87, area mktg. mgr., 1987; asst. to v.p. and area mgr. IBM, Southfield, Mich., 1987-88; br. mgr. IBM, Youngstown, Ohio, 1988—. Judge retriever field trials Am. Kennel Club. Recipient Grand prize photograph contest, Dog's USA, 1985. Mem. Youngstown c. of C. Republican. Lutheran. Clubs: Birmingham (Mich.) Community Women's; Wolverine Retriever (Lapeer, Mich.). Office: IBM 250 Federal Plaza E Youngstown OH 44503

REYNOLDS, VELMA SMALL, insurance sales representative; b. Wilmington, N.C., Aug. 25, 1943; d. William Thomas and Lila Elizabeth (Murphy) Small; m. Willie Charles Lanere, Oct. 19, 1964 (div. Dec. 20, 1976); children: Darren Michael Lanere, Derek Walter Lanere; m. Donald Reynolds, June 17, 1978; 1 stepdaughter, Antoinette Michelle. BS, Benedictine Coll., Atchison, Kans., 1965. Tchr. Archdiocese of Kans., Atchison, 1965-68, Atchison County Schs., Effingham, Kans., 1968-69, Atchison Unified Schs., Atchison, 1969-72; ins. rep. Ward Life Ins. Co., Oakland, Calif., 1973-76, Liberty Mut. Ins. Co., Oakland, 1976—. Mem. Nat. Assn. Exec. Women, Liberty Leaders Club. Democrat. Roman Catholic. Home: 3020 Phillips Ct Richmond CA 94806 Office: Liberty Mut Ins Co 7677 Oakport St Oakland CA 94612

REYNOLDS, W(YNETKA) ANN, university system administrator, educator; b. Coffeyville, Kans., Nov. 3, 1937; d. John Ethelbert and Glennie (Beanland) King; m. Thomas H. Kirschbaum; children—Rachel Rebecca, Rex King. BS in Biology-Chemistry, Kans. State Tchrs. Coll., Emporia, 1958; MS in Zoology, U. Iowa, Iowa City, 1960, PhD, 1962; DSc (hon.), Ind. State U., Evansville, 1980; LHD, McKendree Coll., 1984; DSc (hon.), Ball State U., Muncie, Ind., 1985, Emporia (Kans.) State U., 1987; PhD (hon.), Fu Jen Cath. U., Republic of China, 1987; D of Humane Letters (hon.), U. N.C., 1988. Asst. prof. biology Ball State U., Muncie, Ind., 1962-65; asst. prof. anatomy U. Ill. Coll. Medicine, Chgo., 1965-68, assoc. prof. anatomy, 1968-73, research prof. ob-gyn, from 1973, prof. anatomy, from 1973, acting assoc. dean acad. affairs Coll. Medicine, 1977, assoc. vice chancellor, dean grad. coll., 1977-79; prof. ob-gyn Ohio State U., Columbus, 1979-82, prof. anatomy, 1979-82, provost, 1979-82; chancellor Calif. State Univ. system, Long Beach, 1982—, prof. biology, 1982—; cons. and lectr. in field; prof. biology Calif. State U., Dominguez Hills, 1982—; prof. biol. scis. (hon.) San Francisco State U., 1982—; clin. prof. ob/gyn. U. Calif., Los Angeles, 1985—; co-chair Humanitas Council Los Angeles Ednl. Partnership, 1986—, Fed. Task Force on Women, Minorities and Handicapped in Sci. and Tech., 1987—; dir. Calif. Econ. Devel. Corp.; bd. dirs. Gen. Telephone Co. of Calif., Maytag Corp. Contbr. chpts. to books, articles to profl. jours. Active numerous civic activities involving edn.; pres. Nat. Assn. System Heads, 1987-88; bd. dirs. Am. Council for the Arts, 1986—; dir. Calif. Econ. Devel. Corp., 1984—. Recipient Disting. Alumni award Kans. State Tchrs. Coll., 1972. Fellow Calif. Acad. Scis.; mem. AAAS, Am. Assn. Anatomists, Am. Diabetes Assn., Am. Soc. Zoologists, Am. Assn. for Higher Edn. (bd. dirs. 1984—), Endocrine Soc., Perinatal Research Soc., Soc. Exptl. Biology and Medicine, Soc. Gynecologic Investigation, Sigma Xi. Office: Calif State U 400 Golden Shore Long Beach CA 90802-4275

REYNOLDS-BRYANT, WENDY LEE, advertising executive; b. Eugene, Oreg., Mar. 22, 1955; d. William Vern and Billie Eloise (Iles) Reynolds; m. Michael Howard Bryant, May 9, 1987. BFA, Va. Commonwealth U., 1977. Sec. Gann Pub. Co., Portland, Oreg., 1977-78, press operator, 1979-81; graphic artist, press operator Polk County Edn. Service Dist., Dallas, Oreg., 1978-79; graphic artist, designer Wendy's Art Studio, Portland; art dir. Roll Shutter Supply/Ja-Cor. Devel., Scottsdale, Ariz., 1983-86; pres. Reynolds Advt. Agy., Scottsdale, 1986—. Mem. pastor/parish relations com., bd. dirs. Scottsdale United Meth. Ch., 1987, AZ Walk to Emmaus Secretariat. Mem. Nat. Assn. Female Execs., Ariz. Balloon Club. Republican. Office: Reynolds Agy 1802 E Monte Cristo Phoenix AZ 85022

REYNOLDS-YOUNG, REBECCA LEE, hospital administrator; b. Houston, Sept. 24, 1955; d. Roger David and Natalie Marie (Sander) Reynold; m. Christopher Robert Young, June 20, 1981; 1 child, Christopher Joseph. BS, Seton Hill Coll., 1978; MS, Ohio State U., 1981. Cert. registered dietitian, 1981. Dir. dietary Alum Crest Nursing Home, Columbus, Ohio, 1978-82; ind. dietary service Columbus, 1981—; tchr. Nusring Home Area Tng. Ctr., Columbus, 1982—, publicity com. chmn., 1985-87; chmn. adv. bd. Nursing Home Area Tng. Ctr., Columbus, 1987—; corp. dietitian Restaurant Food Supply, Columbus, 1983-85; exec. dir., dietic services Doctors Hosps., Columbus, 1985-87; dir. nutrition services Univ. Hosps. of Cleve., 1987—. Mem. Am. Dietetic Assn., Ohio Dietetic Assn. (legislation, pub. policy co chmn., Recognized Young Dietitian of Yr. 1984), Am. Soc. Hosp. Food Adminstrs., Columbus Dietetic Assn. (pres. 1986-87), Cleve. Dietetic Assn. Presbyterian. Home: 3255 Daleford Rd Shaker Heights OH 44120

REZNIK, FELICE JILL, art director; b. N.Y.C., Jan. 14, 1956; d. Norman Daniel and Muriel (Steinberg) Rosenberg; m. Maurice Sergio Reznik, Oct. 22, 1977 (div.). BA, Queens Coll., 1977. Graphic artist Allyn Assoc., Manchester, N.H., 1978-81, U. Rochester, N.Y., 1981-83; assoc. art dir. Gero & Assoc., Phila., 1983-84; art dir. Ackerman Advt., Glen Head, N.Y., 1984—. Recipient Certs. of Merit, Best on L.I. Design award, 1985, 87. Mem. Phila. Advt. Dirs. Club (award 1984), Phila. Club of Advt. Women (Addy award 1984). Office: Ackerman Advt 31 Glen Head Rd Glen Head NY 11545

RHEE, SON-OAK, dentist; b. Seoul, Republic of Korea, Oct. 7, 1945; came to U.S., 1968; d. Enng-Ik and Bok-Nyu (Her) R. BS in Chemistry, Marymount Manhattan Coll., 1974; DDS, NYU, 1979. RN. Resident Mt. Sinai Hosp., N.Y.C., mem. staff, 1981—, cons. craniofacial team, 1983—; gen. practice dentistry N.Y.C., 1981—. Mem. First Dist. Dental Soc. Office: 150 W 58th St New York NY 10019

RHEINLANDER, MARY LINDA, assn. exec.; b. Evansville, Ind., Nov. 7, 1941; d. Clarence Joseph and Margaret Lucille (Herron) Behme; student parochial schs., also continuing edn. classes; m. Robert Edward Rheinlander, Jan. 14, 1961; children—Karen Lynn, Kristine Louise, Keith Edward, Kami Jo. Sec., Whirlpool Corp., 1960; asst. Evansville's Future, Inc., 1965-67; interviewer students Evansville Vanderburgh Sch. Corp., 1974; coordinator job placement service Ind. State U., Evansville, 1970-73; exec. sec. Ind. U. Med. Sch., Indpls., 1975-78; exec. dir. Sheet Metal Contractors Assn., Evansville, 1978—; mem. council Evansville Area Labor-Mgmt. Com.; speaker in field. Pres. Parish Council, mem. Cath. Sch. Bd. Mem. Nat. Assn. Women in Constrn., Ind. Sheet Metal Council, Nat. Assn. Sheet Metal and Air Conditioning Contractors, Nat. Assn. Female Execs., U.S. C. of C., Evansville C. of C., Ind. Lawyers Wives Assn., Evansville Lawyers Wives Assn., Am. Soc. Assn. Execs. Roman Catholic. Home: 5318 West Haven Dr Evansville IN 47712 Office: PO Box 6201 Evansville IN 47712

RHENMAN, MARY JEAN, cardiac transplant coordinator, nurse; b. Bangor, Maine, Nov. 29, 1955; d. Curtis and Mary Rita (Smith) Tackett; m. Owen Kevin McAleer, June 18, 1977 (div. Aug. 1983); children—Michael Kevin, Leah Marie; m. Birger Rhenman, Aug. 30, 1986; children: Erik, Gustav. BSN, U. Ariz., 1977. Asst. head nurse U. Med. Ctr., Tucson, 1977-79, ICU nurse, 1980-82, cardiac transplant coordinator, 1982—. Mem. planning com., nurses symposium Internat. Soc. Heart Transplantation, Cambridge, Eng., 1984—; lectr. U. Med. Ctr., Stockholm and Göteborg, Sweden, 1984. Mem. editorial bd. Progress in Cardiovascular Nursing; contbr. articles to profl. jours. Research grantee NIH, 1987. Mem. Internat. Soc. Heart Transplantation, N. Am. Transplant Coordinators Orgn., European Transplant Coordinators Orgn., So. Calif. Transplant Soc. Democrat. Roman Catholic. Home: 4273 N River Grove #233 Tucson AZ 85719 Office: U Ariz Med Ctr Dept Surgery 1501 N Campbell Ave Tucson AZ 85724

RHILE, SUSAN LOPOTEN, banker; b. Phila., June 22, 1952; d. Bernard Eliott and Anne Mary (Curran) Lopoten; m. Donald P. Clemson Sr., Mar. 5, 1972 (div. Dec. 1981); children: Donald Jr., Scott; m. Robert J. Rhile, Oct. 20, 1985. Teller PSFS, Phila., 1978-82, Progress Bank, Bridgeport, Pa., 1982; asst. mgr. Progress Bank, King of Prussia, Pa., 1982-83, mgr., 1983-84; mgr. Progress Bank, Bridgeport, Pa., 1984-86, community banking officer, 1986—. Mem. Nat. Assn. Banking Women, Montgomery County Bankers, Am. Soc. Notaries. Republican. Episcopalian.

RHINEHART, KATHERINE ANN, data systems liaison; b. New Prague, Minn., July 28, 1957; d. Melvin Emil and Beatrice Marie (Novotny) Krocak; m. Robert W. Rhinehart, June 23, 1979 (div. Nov. 1985). Student, Mankato (Minn.) State U., 1975-76, Mt. San Antonio Jr. Coll., 1977-78, Fullerton Jr. Coll., 1979-80. Teller and new accounts rep. Brentwood Savings and Loan, Diamond Bar, Calif., 1977-78; sr. savings rep. Anaheim Savings and Loan, Brea, Calif., 1978-81; checking dept. asst. mgr. Lincoln Savings and Loan, Irvine, Calif., 1981-84, branch support liaison, 1984-85; adminstrv. branch supr. San Francisco Federal Sanvings and Loan, Orinda, Calif., 1984; systems support liaison San Francisco Federal Sanvings and Loan, Orinda, 1985—. Roman Catholic. Home: 8425 E Northlake Dr Dublin CA 94568 Office: San Francisco Fed Savs and Loan 4 Orinda Way Suite 200C Orinda CA 94563

RHO, SHIN-SOON CHANG, physician; b. Korea, July 13, 1931; d. Eui-Se and Hyun-Sook (Oh) Chang; m. Yong-Myun Rho, Dec. 13, 1958; 4 sons, John I., Robert B., David S., Walter A. M.D., Korea U. Coll. Medicine, 1955. Attending physician St. Joseph's Hosp., Flushing, N.Y., 1980—, Terrace Heights Hosp., Hollis, N.Y., 1980-84, La Guardia Hosp., Forest Hills, N.Y., 1985—; practice internal medicine, Ozone Park, N.Y., 1980—. Diplomate Am. Bd. Internal Medicine. Mem. AMA, Med. Soc. County of Queens, Am. Soc. Internal Medicine. Home: 5 Randall Pl Pelham Manor NY 10803 Office: 79-20 Pitkin Ave Ozone Park NY 11417

RHOADES, NANCY ANN, air force officer; b. Fort Campbell, Ky., June 16, 1959; d. Glen Lee and Mary Josephine (Lasell) R. BS in Astro Engring., U.S. Air Force Acad., 1981; MS in Aero. and Astronaut. Engring., Stanford U., 1985. Commd. 2d lt. U.S. Air Force, 1981, advanced through grades to capt., 1985; satellite test engr. space div. Los Angeles, 1981-84; instr. dept. astronautics U.S. Air Force Acad., Colorado Springs, Colo., 1985—. Recipient Medal of Merit, Nat. Air Force Assn., 1985; named Colorado Springs Mil. Woman of Yr., Gazette Telegraph newspaper, 1987. Mem. Air Force Assn., Am. Astronautical Soc. Avocations: aerobics, long distance running, sewing. Home: 17485 Paver Way Monument CO 80132 Office: US Air Force Acad Dean Faculty Astronautics Colorado Springs CO 80840

RHOADS, GERALDINE EMELINE, editor; b. Phila., Jan. 29, 1914; d. Lawrence Dry and Alice Fegley (Rice) R. A.B., Bryn Mawr Coll., 1935. Publicity asst. Bryn Mawr (Pa.) Coll., 1935-37; asst. Internat. Students House, Phila., 1937-39; mng. editor The Woman mag., N.Y.C., 1939-42; editor Life Story mag., 1942-45, Today's Woman mag., N.Y.C., 1945-52, Today's Family Mag., N.Y.C., 1952-53; lectr. Columbia U., 1954-56; asso. editor Readers Digest, 1954-55; producer NBC, 1955-56; asso. editor Ladies Home Jour., 1956-62, mng. editor, 1962-63; exec. editor McCall's mag., 1963-66; editor Woman's Day mag., 1966-82, editorial dir., 1982-84; editorial dir. Woman's Day Resource Center, 1984—; v.p. Woman's Day mag., 1972-77, 78-84, CBS Consumer Publs., 1977-84; dir. Anchor Hocking Corp. Author: (with others) Woman's Day Help Book, 1988. Recipient award for profl. achievement Diet Workshop Internat., 1977; Elizabeth Cutter Morrow award YWCA Salute to Women in Bus., 1977; Recipient Econ. Equity award Women's Equity Action League, 1982; March of Dimes Women Editor's citation, 1982. Mem. Nat. Home Fashions League, Nat. Press Club (dir.), Fashion Group (bd. govs. 1977-79, 87-88, chmn. bd. govs. 1978-80, treas. bd. govs. 1983-85, bd. govs. 1987, bd. dirs. Found. 1980-81), Am. Soc. Mag. Editors (chmn. exec. com. 1971-73), N.Y. Women in Communications (Matrix award 1975), Advt. Women in N.Y. (bd. govs. 1983-85, 2d v.p. 1985-87, 1st v.p. 1987—, Pres.'s award 1987), Women's Forum (bd. dirs. 1985-87), YWCA Acad. Women Achievers. Home: 865 1st Ave New York NY 10017 Office: 1515 Broadway New York NY 10036

RHODEN, ROBIN LYNNE, nurse; b. Pitts., Mar. 5, 1954; d. Raymond Rudolph and Edith Claire (Ramsey) R. AA, Allegheny County Community Coll., 1976; BS in Nursing with high honors, Calif. State U., Los Angeles, 1982, MS in Nursing, 1988. RN, Calif.; cert. pub. health nurse, advanced cardiac life support. Staff nurse in operating room Shands Teaching Hosp., Gainesville, Fla., 1976-78, Cedars-Sinai Med. Ctr., Los Angeles, 1978-80; asst. head nurse Northridge (Calif.) Hosp. Med. Ctr., 1980-86; nurse mgr. supply, processing and distbn. Kenneth Norris Jr. Cancer Hosp., Los Angeles, 1987-88; head nurse operating room AMI Med. Ctr., North Hollywood, Calif., 1988; dir. surgical services Med. Ctr. North Hollywood, 1988—. Active Am. Cancer Soc., Los Angeles, 1983, Am. Diabetes Assn., 1988. Recipient award Community Leaders of Am., 1982. Mem. Assn. Operating Room Nursing (cert. 1986), So. Calif. Nursing Diagnosis Assn., Nat. Assn. Nursing Diagnosis, Nat. League for Nursing. Roman Catholic. Office: Kenneth Norris Jr Cancer Hosp 1441 Eastlake Ave Los Angeles CA 90033

RHODES, ANN L(OUISE), construction company executive; b. Ft. Worth, Oct. 17, 1941; d. Jon Knox and Carol Jane (Greene) R.; student Tex. Christian U., 1960-63. Vice pres. Rhodes Enterprises Inc., Ft. Worth, 1963-77; owner-mgr. Lucky R Ranch, Ft. Worth, 1969—, Ann L. Rhodes Investments, Ft. Worth, 1976—; pres., chmn. bd. ALR Enterprises, Inc., Ft. Worth, 1977—; pres. Sunergos Prodn. Co. div. ALR Enterprises, Inc., 1983—. Bd. dirs. Tarrant Council Alcoholism, 1973-78, hon. bd. dirs., 1978—; bd. dirs. N.W. Tex. council Arthritis Found., 1977-84; adv. bd. Stage West, 1987—; bd, dirs. Circle Theater, 1987—; exec. com. Tarrant County Republican Party, 1964-69. Recipient various service awards. Mem. Jr. League Ft. Worth, Kappa Kappa Gamma. Episcopalian. Office: Ridglea Bank Bldg Suite 908 Fort Worth TX 76116

RHODES, CHRISTINE ELISE, medical editor, writer; b. Munich, Sept. 19, 1952; came to U.S., 1954; d. Alfred H. and Martina (Donner) R.; m. E. Michael Geiger, Nov. 29, 1987. BS in Nutrition, Lehman Coll. CUNY, 1979; MS, Columbia U., 1983. Asst. editor PW Communications, N.Y.C., 1976-79; banquet mgr. Plaza Hotel, N.Y.C., 1979-80; copy editor Biomed. Info., Inc., N.Y.C., 1979-80; asst. program specialist Fed. Feeding Program/USDA, N.Y.C., 1980; editor-in-chief Jour. Practical Nursing, N.Y.C., 1982-84; sr. assoc. editor Diagnosis mag., Oradell, N.J., 1984-87; copy chief Benefit Communications Services/Equicor, Inc., N.Y.C., 1987-88; sr. editorial dir. med. communications Edelman Pub. Relations, N.Y.C., 1988—; presenter workshops in field. Democrat. Office: Daniel J Edelman Inc 1775 Broadway New York NY 10019

RHODES, CYNTHIA STRAHLER, interexchange communications company manager; b. Allentown, Pa., May 28, 1947; d. George Robert and Janet Gordon Strahler; student Ursinus Coll., 1965-66, U. Md., 1970, Lafayette Coll., 1982-88; m. Robert Wesley Rhodes, Oct. 22, 1966; children—Danielle Renee, Robert Carver. Supr. network engring. AT&T Long Lines, 1972-75, market adminstr., 1975-78, supr. spl. communications project, 1978-79, supr. service costs, Bedminster, N.J., 1979-81, staff supr. tariff planning and adminstrn., 1981-82, staff mgr. interstate tariff implementation, 1982-86, staff mgr. interstate strategic access costs, 1986—. Mem. Nat. Assn. Female Execs. Republican. Moravian. Office: 131 Morristown Rd D189 Basking Ridge NJ 07920

RHODES, ELIZABETH JANE, lighting designer; b. Clark AFB, Luzon, Philippines, June 5, 1958; d. Moffett Ritchard and Joyce Ethel (Brady) R. Student, U. Ark., 1976-78; BS in Tech. Theatre Design, Tex. Womans U., 1981. Master electrician Lighting Designer Repertory Theatre, Little Rock, 1981-82; master electrician Plaza Theatre, Dallas, 1983-86, tech. dir., 1985-86, resident lighting designer, prodn. mgr., 1986; master electrician Lyric Opera Dallas, 1984-86; lighting designer Dancers Unltd., Dallas, 1986; with lighting rental dept. Victor Duncan, Inc., Irving, Tex., 1987—; coordinator rental Duke City Studio, Albuquerque, 1987—; tech. dir. Am. Coll. Theatre Festival, Denton, Tex., 1986. Lighting designer (dance) Urban Desert, 1986, Fifth Passage, 1986, American Juke Box, 1986, Little Shop of Horrors (Best Lighting Design award 1986), 1986. Lighting designer Denton Civic Ballet, 1980, Tex. Head Injury Assn., 1986. Named one of Outstanding Young Women Am., 1980. Mem. Nat. Assn. for Female Execs.

RHODES, HELEN, art business consultant; b. Waltham, Mass., Mar. 21, 1942; d. Timothy and Janet Bernard (Smith) R.; m. Thomas Glen Regnier, May 17, 1976 (div. Dec. 1983). BA, Swarthmore Coll., 1964; postgrad., Bklyn. Coll., 1966-68. Ordained to ministry Ch. Scientology, 1976. Counselor, cons. Ch. of Scientology, N.Y.C., 1968-73; office mgr. Warren and West, N.Y.C., 1973-75; counselor Park West Mission, N.Y.C., 1975-79; exec. dir. Helen's Photo Decor, Little Rock and N.Y.C., 1979—; cons. Singer Cons. Inc., Clearwater, Fla., 1987—; rehab. cons. Riker's Island Prison, Queens, N.Y., 1975. Author (Wolof phrase book) Senegal's Native Tongue, 1965. Mem. Citizens Commn. on Human Rights, 1973—. Mem. Internat. Assn. Scientologists, Hubbard Assn. Scientologists Internat. (cert.), Nat. Assn. Female Execs. Libertarian. Home: 551 N Saturn Clearwater FL 34617 Office: Flag Service Orgn 210 S Fort Harrison Clearwater FL 34616

RHODES, MARQUERITE GOLDEN, principal, academic administrator; b. Groveland, Ga., May 31, 1917; d. Ernest A. and Pearlie (Tippens) Golden; m. Tilmon Rhodes; 1 child, Leigh T. BS, Columbia U., 1950; MA, NYU, 1957; cert. in guidance and adminstrn., Hofstra U., 1965. Cons. early childhood Div. Day Care, N.Y.C., 1961-65; guidance counselor Hempstead (N.Y.) Pub. Sch. System, 1965-69, asst. prin., 1969, prin. elem. sch., 1970-87; coordinator student teaching Hofstra U., Hempstead, 1987—. Chairperson edn. com. L.I. Urban League, 1987—, bd. dirs.; bd. dirs. Hope for Youth, Harriet Tubman Edn. for Assistance Ctr.; candidate for trustee Hempstead Pub. Schs., 1987. Recipient Martin Luther King Jr. Humanitarian award Nassau County, 1986, Community Service award Nassau County, 1986, gov.'s citation State of N.Y.; name one of Women of Yr., Nassau Suffolk Adminstrv. Women, 1986. Democrat. Club: 100 Black Women (L.I.).

RHODES, VALERIE RUTH, accountant; b. Valdosta, Ga., Oct. 25, 1961; d. Arthur and Mary Frances (Crawford) Moore. BSBA in Acctg., Boston U., 1983. Acct. mut. funds State St. Bank, Quincy, Mass., 1983-85; acct. Blue Cross/Blue Shield, Boston, 1985-86, supr. acctg. control, 1986—. Mem. Nat. Assn. for Female Execs. Home: 251 Belmont St #2B Brockton MA 02401 Office: Blue Cross Blue Shield 100 Summer St Boston MA 02110

RHODUS, IDA KATHERINE, steel company executive; b. Richmond, Ky., July 21, 1956; d. Robert Buford and Imogene (Adams) Rhodus; m. Gary Paul Howard, Dec. 9, 1983. Student Eastern Ky. U., 1973, U. Ky., 1978. Teller, Bank Commerce, Lexington, Ky., 1974-75; sales/estimator Mid State Steel Co., Lexington, 1975-78, Harry Gordon Steel Co., Lexington, 1978-81; estimator Mosher Steel Co., Houston, 1981-82, Galaxy Steel Co., Houston, 1982-84; mgr. estimating Republic Iron Works, Houston, 1984—; mgr. sales and estimating Superior Iron Works Inc, Houston, 1984-86, pres., Spectrum Metals Corp., Houston, 1986—. Named Ky. Col. Mem. Women in Constrn. (dir. 1978-82). Democrat. Home: 9449 Briar Forest 701 Houston TX 77063 Office: Spectrum Metals Corp 9219 Katy Freeway Suite 124 Houston TX 77024

RHOTEN, JULIANA THERESA, school principal; b. N.Y.C., June 28; d. Julius Joseph and Gladys Maude (Grant) Bastian; B.A., Hunter Coll., 1954; M.S., 1956; Ed.S., U. Wis., Milw., 1977; m. Marion Rhoten, Aug. 7, 1956; 1 son, Don Carlos. Tchr. elem. schs., Milw., 1957-65, reading specialist, 1965-71, adminstr., 1971-80; prin. Ninth St. Sch., Milw., 1980-83, Parkview Sch., Milw., 1983—. Mem. Assn. Supervision and Curriculum Devel., Internat. Reading Assn., Nat. Assn. Elem. Sch. Principals, Nat. Council Tchrs. English, Adminstrs. and Suprs. Council, Phi Delta Kappa, Alpha Kappa Alpha. Home: 7222 N 99th St Milwaukee WI 53224 Office: 10825 W Villard Ave Milwaukee WI 53225

RHUDE, BETH ESTHER, psychologist, clergyperson; b. Quincy, Mass., July 1, 1935; d. Clarel P. and Mary E. (MacKenzie) R.; m. Richard Morse Colgate, Aug. 3, 1974; 1 child, Cara Marie-Jean. Student, Oberlin Coll., 1954-55; BA magna cum laude, Boston U., 1957; BD, Harvard U., 1960; EdD(Pres.'s scholar), Columbia U., 1967; postgrad., Union Theol. Sem., 1960, Mich. State U., 1968. Ordained to ministry United Ch. of Christ, 1964. Asst. chaplain Mt. Holyoke Coll., South Hadley, Mass., 1960-63; grad. fellow Danforth Found., St. Louise, 1963-64; chaplain, asst. prof. U. Seven Seas, Orange, Calif., 1964-65; campus minister Riverside Ch., N.Y.C., 1965-66; lectr. psychology, counselor Queensboro Community Coll., N.Y.C., 1966-67; dean of women, lectr. religion Dickinson Coll., Carlisle, Pa., 1967-68; psychotherapist in pvt. practice N.Y.C., 1968-77, Cambridge, Mass., 1977—; asst. prof. pastoral counseling, supr. Davidson Ctr. Sch. Theology Boston U., 1977-81; vis. scholar Harvard Divinity Sch., Cambridge, 1981-83; fellow Du Bois Inst. Harvard U., Cambridge, 1983—; cons. psychologist Clergy Career Devel., Newton, Mass., 1986—; bd. dirs. United Ch. of Christ, N.Y.C., Office Ch. In Soc., Wahington, Thurman Ednl. Trust, San Francisco. Asst. dir. Ecumenical Found. Higher Edn. and Religion, N.Y.C., 1968-71; lectr. N.Y. Theol. Sem., 1972. Billings scholar, 1954-57; Ford Travel grantee, 1962, Nat. Def. Edn. Act grantee, 1965, 67-68, Danforth grantee, 1963; others. Mem. Nat. Assn. Coll. and Univ. Chaplains, Am. Psychol. Assn., Am. Assn. Women Deans and Counselors, NAACP, AAUP, AAUW, Am. Assn. Personnel and Guidance Counselors, Am. Assn. Marriage and Family Counselors, Inst. Practicing Psychotherapists, Ortho Psychiatry Assn., Nat. Campus Ministers Assn., Am. Assn. for Higher Edn., Am. Acad. Psychotherapists, Phi Beta Kappa. Home: 33 Fresh Pond Pl Cambridge MA 02138 Office: 3 Concord Ave Cambridge MA 02138

RHUE, NANCY CLIFTON, educator; b. Milford, Del., Apr. 3, 1948; d. William Carlton and Beatrice Margaret (Hudson) Clifton; m. E. Brent Rhue; children: Michael, Jonathan, Allison. BA, St. Andrew's Presbyn. Coll., 1970. Cert English tchr., Del. Tchr. English Rehoboth Jr. High Sch., Rehoboth Beach, Del., 1970-76, Lewes (Del.) Jr. High Sch., 1976-79, Cape Henlopen High Sch., Lewes, 1979—; adviser Rehoboth Jr. High cheerleaders, 1970-71, Jr. Honor soc., 1977-78, Nat. Honor Soc. Cape Henlopen High Sch., 1980—, co-adviser Student Leadership Day, 1981—, adviser acad. bowl team, 1984-87; mem. Supt.'s Adv. Council. Mem. Senator Joseph Biden Adv. Council, 1976-82; treas. state rep. campaign, Milford, 1978; mem. H. O. Brittingham Elem. Sch. PTO; ch. pianist Slaughter Neck United Meth. Ch., dir. choir 1981—, worship com. chmn. 1985—, sec. adminstrn. bd. 1972-87, sec., tchr. Sunday sch. 1976-79, dir., music dir., tchr. Vacat. Bible Sch. 1972—, United Methodist Women, 1974— (pres. 1977-78, 1988—), Friends of Milton County Library, 1987—. Named one of Outstanding Young Women Am. Milton Jaycees, 1984. Mem. NEA, Del. State Edn. Assn., Cape Henlopen Edn. Assn., United Meth. Women. Democrat. Home: RD 1 Box 135 Milford DE 19963 Office: Cape Henlopen High Sch Kings Hwy Lewes DE 19958

RIBAR, DIXIE LEE, nurse, educator; b. Albia, Iowa, June 22, 1938; d. Eugene Guy Clark and Margaret Ellen (Edwards) De Joode; m. John David Ribar, Aug. 22, 1959 (div. 1981); children: Michael, Christopher, Patrick. Diploma, St. Joseph Hosp. Sch. Nursing, Ottumwa, Iowa, 1959; BSN, U. Dubuque, 1987, postgrad. in nursing sci., 1987—. RN, Iowa; cert. emergency room nurse; cert. emergency med. technician, Iowa. Staff nurse Ottumwa Hosp., 1959-60; surg. staff nurse Jane Lamba Hosp., Clinton, Iowa, 1960-67; dur. nursing ICU-CCU Jane Lamb Health Ctr., Clinton, Iowa, 1967-79, dir. cardiac rehab., 1980-86, ednl. instr., 1986—; contractual instr. med. services Emergency Learning Resources Ctr., U. Iowa Hosp., Iowa City, 1976—, Ea. Iowa Community Coll., Davenport, Iowa, 1978—, Marycrest Coll., Davenport, 1986—; paremedic River Cities Ambulance Co., Clinton, 1987—; presenter in field. Contbr. articles to profl. jours. Bd. dirs. Clinton County Heart Assn., 1976—; coordinator emergency med. technician program Clinton Fire Dept., 1980-88; med. missionary 1st Congl. Ch. Clinton, Ghana, 1983. Mem. Emergency Nurses Assn., Iowa Emergency Nurses Assn., Am. Nurses Assn., Iowa Nurses Assn., Iowa Hosp. Assn. Republican. Roman Catholic. Home: 511 Melrose Ct Clinton IA 52732 Office: Jane Lamb Health Ctr 638 S Bluff Blvd Clinton IA 52732

RIBAROFF, MARGARET FLESHER, publishing executive; b. San Angelo, Tex., July 29, 1944; d. Charles and Helen Irene (Little) Flesher; m. Alexander Ribaroff, Dec. 11, 1976 (div. 1988). AB in Polit. Sci., Vassar Coll., 1966. Editorial asst. Harcourt Brace Jovanovich, Inc., N.Y.C., 1966-69, assoc. editor, 1969-74; producer Guidance Assocs. subs. Harcourt Brace Jovanovich, Inc., N.Y.C., 1974-76; freelance editor London, 1976-81; sr. editor Franklin Watts, Inc., N.Y.C., 1981-85; prin. Westport Pub. Group, Norwalk, Conn., 1985—; cons. young writers project Darien (Conn.) High Sch., 1986-87. Author: Mexico and The United States Today, 1985, New Leaves: A Journal for the Suddenly Single, 1987. Bd. dirs. Women's Crisis Ctr., Norwalk, 1987—. Mem. Women in Communications, Inc. (pres. Fairfield County chpt. 1986-88), The Soc. of Children's Book Writers (organizer conf. New Eng. region 1987), The Nat. Council for the Social Studies, ALA, Entrepreneurial Woman's Network (program chmn. 1987-88), Nat. Assn. Female Execs. Protestant. Office: The Westport Pub Group PO Box 149 Westport CT 06881

RIBBLE, ANNE HOERNER, information representative; b. Balt., Oct. 30, 1932; d. Jerold Kiser and Helen Blythe (Miller) Hoerner; B.A., Smith Coll., 1954; M.A., Harvard U., 1955; m. John C. Ribble, July 26, 1974; 1 dau. by previous marriage—Helen Blythe Strate. Tchr. English, Weston (Mass.) High Sch., 1955-57, tech. asst. IBM, N.Y.C., 1958-63, editor, Armonk and White Plains, N.Y., 1969-75, mgr. editorial services data processing div., White Plains, 1976-77, program adminstr. systems communications div., N.Y.C., 1977-78, staff tech. edn., fed. systems div., Houston, 1978-80, info. rep., 1980-87, staff info. systems Integration div., 1988—. Mem. Manhattan County Com., Democratic party, 1961-62; co-chmn. English Teaching Program, N.Y. Jr. League, 1965-67, honored vol., 1968, bd. dirs. 1968-69; bd. dirs. Stanley Isaacs Community Center, 1968-72; vestry Ch. of Holy Trinity, N.Y.C., 1976-78. Mem. Internat. Assn. Bus. Communicators (pres. Houston chpt. 1982), Women's Profl. Assn. (bd. dirs. 1980-81, 84-87). Home: 6200 Willers Way Houston TX 77057 Office: IBM 3700 Bay Area Blvd Houston TX 77058

RIBBY, ALICE MARIE, nurse, health care administrator; b. Lowell, Mich., Oct. 16, 1943; d. Merle Levi and Merleen Maude (Gooden) Bickford; m. Robert Allen Ribby, Nov. 25, 1961; children: Bobette Morgan, Mylie Wasylewski, Joseph R. Ribby, Barbara A. Ilten. AS in Nursing cum laude, Lansing Community Coll., 1976. RN, Mich. Nurse ICU Ingham Med. Ctr., Lansing, Mich., 1976-81; nurse hemo and peritoneal dialysis Sparrow Hosp., Lansing, Mich., 1983-84; head nurse, dir. Continuous Ambulitory Peritoneal Dialysis Program Community Dialysis Ctr., Jackson, Mich., 1984—; cons. Foote Hosp., Jackson, 1983—. Lectr. (video tape) Continuous Ambulitory Peritoneal Dialysis, 1985. Mem. Am. Assn. Critical Care Nurses. Democrat. Mem. Ch. of God.

RIBELIN, ROSEMARY BINGHAM, college bookstore and campus center administrator; b. Indpls., Ind., Aug. 8, 1933; d. Remester Alexander and Joy Dorothy (Reed) Bingham; m. Richard Grant Ribelin, Aug. 16, 1957; children—Pamela Joy, Karen Sue. Student Indpls. schs. Sec. to mgr. Phoenix Mut. Life Ins., Indpls., 1952-61, office supr., 1971-76; sec. to pres. Franklin Coll., Ind., 1976-79, bookstore/campus ctr. dir., 1979—. Leader Hoosier Capital council Girl Scouts U.S.A., 1965-75; canvasser Multiple Sclerosis Soc., Am. Cancer Soc., Am. Heart Assn., 1965-77; canvasser Channel 20 Pub. Broadcasting Service, Indpls., 1968; active com. mem. J. K. Lilly School PTA, Indpls., 1965-75, pres., 1972; canvasser United Fund, Indpls., 1968-75, pres., 1971. Moneyraiser, poll worker Republican Party, Indpls. Deacon, Sunday Sch. tchr. and supt. First Presbyn. Ch. of Franklin. Named a Go-Getter Channel 20, 1987. Mem. Philanthropic Nat. Soc., Delta Theta Tau (treas. Lambda Eta chpt. 1981-82, v.p. 1982-83, pres. 1983-85), Assn. Ind. Coll. Stores (treas. 1987—). Lodges: Daus. of Nile, Order Eastern Star, Oriental Shrine. Avocations: Hooking rugs, reading, crocheting, playing cards, embroidery. Office: Franklin Coll Bookstore Campus Ctr Franklin IN 46131

RIBNER, MURIEL S., business executive, laywer; b. N.Y.C., Mar. 8, 1924; d. Nathan Lewis and Lillian (Titan-Rubin) Solomon; B.A., N.Y. U., 1945, LL.B., 1951; m. H. J. Coman, Aug. 15, 1945 (div. 1950); m. Lloyd D. Ribner, Jan. 24, 1952 (div. 1978); children—Andrew B., Lloyd D. Soc. editor Bronxville Rev.-Press, 1941-42; AP researcher Rockefeller Pl., N.Y.C., 1942-43; admitted to N.Y. State bar, 1951; partner Ribner Bus. Systems, N.Y.C., 1954-58; pres. Estey Corp., Englewood, N.J., 1976-80; v.p. Merry Traders, N.Y.C., 1981—; bd. dirs. Starr Anne Found., 1985—; active trustee family trusts and investments. Democrat. Address: 444 E 57 St New York NY 10022

RICARDO-CAMPBELL, RITA, economist, educator; b. Boston, Mar. 16, 1920; d. David and Elizabeth (Jones) Ricardo; m. Wesley Glenn Campbell, Sept. 15, 1946; children—Barbara Lee, Diane Rita, Nancy Elizabeth. B.S., Simmons Coll., 1941; M.A., Radcliffe Coll., 1945, Ph.D., 1946. Instr. Harvard U., Cambridge, Mass., 1946-48; asst. prof. Tufts U., Medford, Mass., 1948-51; labor economist U.S. Wage Stabilization Bd., 1951-53; economist ways and means com. U.S. Ho. of Reps., 1953; cons. economist 1957-60; vis. prof. San Jose State Coll., 1960-61; sr. fellow Hoover Instn. on War Revolution and Peace, Stanford, Calif., 1968—; lectr. Health Service Adminstrn., Stanford Med. Sch., 1973-78; dir. Watkins-Johnson Co., Palo Alto, Calif., Gillette Co., Boston. Author: Voluntary Health Insurance in the U.S., 1960, Economics of Health and Public Policy, 1971, Food Safety Regulation: Use and Limitations of Cost-Benefit Analysis, 1974, Drug Lag: Federal Government Decision Making, 1976, Social Security: Promise and Reality, 1977, The Economics and Politics of Health, 1982, 2d edit., 1985; co-editor: Below-Replacement Fertility in Industrial Societies, 1987, Issues in Contemporary Retirement, 1988; contbr. articles to profl. jours. Commr. Western Interstate Commn. for Higher Edn. Calif., 1967-75, chmn., 1970-71; mem. Pres. Nixon's Adv. Council on Status Women, 1969-76; mem. task force on taxation Pres.'s Council on Environ. Quality, 1970-72; mem. Pres.'s Com. Health Services Industry, 1971-73, FDA Nat. Adv. Drug Com., 1972-75; mem. Pres. Reagan's Econ. Policy Adv. Bd., 1981—, Pres. Reagan's Nat. Council on Humanities, 1982—; bd. dirs. Ind. Colls. No. Calif., 1971-87; mem. com. assessment of safety, benefits, risks Citizens Commn. Sci., Law and Food Supply, Rockefeller U., 1973-75; mem. adv. com. Ctr. Health Policy Research, Am. Enterprise Inst. Pub. Policy Research, Washington, 1974-80; mem. adv. council on social security Social Security Adminstrn., 1974-75; bd. dirs. Simmons Coll. Corp., Boston, 1975-80; mem. adv. council bd. assocs. Stanford Libraries, 1975-78; mem. council SRI Internat., Menlo Park, Calif., 1977—. Mem. Am. Econ. Assn., Mont Pelerin Soc., Phi Beta Kappa. Home: 26915 Alejandro Dr Los Altos Hills CA 94022 Office: Hoover Instn Stanford CA 94305

RICCI, CAROLYNE YOUNGBLOOD, print shop owner; b. Westville, Okla., Jan. 11, 1951; d. Gifford Dewitt and Beatrice Louise (Owens) Youngblood; m. John James Ricci Jr., May 1, 1980 (div. June 1983); 1 child, Jared James. Student, Ea. N.Mex. U., 1969-70. File clk. Scott & White Hosp., Temple, Tex., 1971; office mgr. Dr. Gifford Youngblood, Clovis, N.Mex., 1972-75; owner Red Door Women's Wear, Clovis, 1975-77; apprentice contractor Gentry Real Estate, Clovis, 1977; office mgr. Rendering Plant, Clovis, 1980-81; ops. mgr. Sta. KMCC-TV, Clovis, 1981-83; salesperson Desert Beauty Supply, Tuscon, 1984-85; owner Pronto Printing, Tuscon, 1985—. Mem. Jr. League of Tucson, 1987—, Tucson Bus. Com. for the Arts, 1987—, Young Audiences, SW Children's Exploratory Ctr. Mem. Nat. Assn. Quick Printers, Quick Printers in Tuscon (mem. steering com. 1987), Pantano Exchange Club, Exec. Women Internat., Resources for Women, Nat. Assn. Female Execs., Tuscon C. of C., Alpha Delta Pi Alumnae (past pres.). Republican. Episcopalian. Club: TEAM (Tuscon). Home: 3245 E Broadway Tuscon AZ 85716 Office: Pronto Printing 7020 E Broadway Tucson AZ 85710

RICCIO, JANET MARIE, advertising executive; b. Bridgeport, Conn., Oct. 1, 1957; d. Victor Salvatore and Joyce (Reichert) R. B.A., Boston U., 1979. Traffic mgr. Shailer Davidoff Rogers, Inc., Fairfield, Conn., 1980-81; account exec. Savitt Tobias Balk, Inc., N.Y.C., 1981-83; v.p., account supr. Rosenfeld Sirowitz & Lawson, Inc., N.Y.C., 1983-86; sr. v.p., mgmt. supr. Laurence, Charles, Free & Lawson, Inc., N.Y.C., 1986-87; v.p. new bus. devel. Corinthian Communications, Inc. Active Planned Parenthood, N.Y. City Ballet. Roman Catholic. Avocations: travel, film prodn., sports, architecture. Office: Corinthian Communications Inc 845 Third Ave New York NY 10022

RICCIUTI, DORIS, real estate broker; b. Boston, July 16, 1924; d. Thomas Henry and Marian Pearl (Walker) Barrett; m. Salvatore Ognibene, May 3, 1947 (div. 1955); 1 child, Linda; m. James John Ricciuti, June 26, 1956; 1 child, Janice; stepchildren: Johanna, Carole, Elise, Anita. Clk. corp. DorJam Real Estate Cons., Quincy, Mass., 1982-86; prin. Ricciuti Real Estate, Quincy, 1965—. Active Boston Mus. Fine Arts. Mem. United Transp. Union (sec.-treas. 1970-81, conv. del., past alt. dist. v.p.), Am. Legion Aux. Home: 55 Tinson Rd Suite 9 Quincy MA 02169 Office: Ricciuti Real Estate 1 McIntyre Mall Quincy MA 02169

RICE, ANDREA, Spanish language educator, translator, interpreter; b. Parral, Chihuahua, Mex., May 9, 1957; came to U.S., 1970; d. James Bartley and Adelia (French) R. BA, Wichita State U., 1978; MA, Tex. Tech. U., 1981, PhD, 1987. Teaching asst. Tex. Tech. U., Lubbock, 1979-87; asst. prof. Spanish lang. Mary Washington Coll., Fredericksburg, Va., 1987—; pvt. practice in Spanish lang. translating, 1987—. Fulbright grantee, 1986. Mem. Am. Assn. Tchrs. Spanish and Portuguese, Fulbright Assn., Smithsonian Instn., Va. Head Injury Found., Sierra Club, South Cen. Modern Lang. Assn., Sigma Delta Pi, Pi Delta Phi. Home: 2526 Carriage Ln Apt 3-D Fredericksburg VA 22401 Office: Mary Washington Coll Dept Modern Fgn Langs 1301 College Ave Fredericksburg VA 22401

RICE, ARGYLL PRYOR, Hispanic studies and Spanish educator; b. Va.; d. Theodorick Pryor and Argyll (Campbell) R. B.A., Smith Coll., 1952; M.A., Yale U., 1956, Ph.D., 1961. Spanish instr. Yale U., New Haven, 1959-60, 61-63; asst. prof. Spanish, Conn. Coll., New London, 1964-67, assoc. prof., 1967-72, prof., 1972—, chair dept. Hispanic Studies, 1971-74, 77-84. Author: Emilio Ballagas: poeta o poesía, 1967. Mem. MLA, Am. Assn. Tchrs. of Spanish and Portuguese, New Eng. Council Latin Am. Studies, Phi Beta Kappa. Avocations: music, tennis. Office: Conn College New London CT 06320

RICE, BEVERLY ANN (MRS. LARRY T. RICE), department store executive; b. Evansville, Ind., Feb. 2, 1934; d. Howard H. and Grace M. (Sawin) Boegaholtz; B.S., Ind. U., 1956; m. Larry T. Rice, Aug. 6, 1961. Asst. to fashion dir. L.S. Ayres & Co., Indpls., 1956-59, buyer, designer, 1959-65, fashion dir., 1965-66, div. mdse. mgr. better apparel, 1966-69, div.

v.p., 1969-73, v.p., 1973-76, v.p., gen. mdse. mgr. apparel and small wares, from 1976; now v.p., gen. mgr. Gidding Jenny, Indpls.; mem. N.Y. Fashion Group, 1965—. Bd. fellows Northwood Inst., recipient Disting. Woman award, 1976; bd. dirs. Ind. U. Sch. Bus., Bloomington, 1985-88. Mem. Women's com. Ind. Symphony Soc. Mem. Women's C. of C., Ind. U. Alumni Assn., Indpls. Mus. Art Alliance, Alpha Omicron Pi, Beta Gamma Sigma. Presbyterian. Home: 4532 N Pennsylvania St Indianapolis IN 46205 Office: 8702 Keystone Crossing Indianapolis IN 46240

RICE, DAPHNE SWEATMAN, software developer; b. Cumming, Ga., Dec. 30, 1962; d. Crafton Lamar and Velma Grace (Moss) Sweatman; m. Keith Edward Rice, Apr. 4, 1987. Student, Gainesville (Ga.) Jr. Coll., 1982, 83, Berry Coll., Rome, Ga., 1980-81; BS in Computer Sci., U. Ga., 1984. Programmer/analyst Constrn. Data Control, Inc., Atlanta, Ga., 1984—. Mem. Marietta Jaycees (bd. dirs. 1986-87, v.p. individual devel. 1987-88, chaplain 1988—). Baptist. Home: 4770 Piney Grove Rd Cumming GA 30130 Office: Constrn Data Control Inc 3675 Crestwood Pkwy Suite 400 Atlanta GA 30136

RICE, DOROTHY PECHMAN (MRS. JOHN DONALD), medical economist; b. Bklyn., June 11, 1922; d. Gershon and Lena (Schiff) Pechman; m. John Donald Rice, Apr. 3, 1943; children: Kenneth D., Donald B., Thomas H. Student, Bklyn. Coll., 1938-39; B.A., U. Wis., 1941; D.Sc. (hon.), Coll. Medicine and Dentistry N.J., 1979. With hosp., and med. facilities USPHS, Washington, 1960-61; med. econs. studies Social Security Adminstrn., 1962-63; health econs. br. Community Health Service, USPHS, 1964-65; chief health ins. research br. Social Security Adminstrn., 1966-72, dep. asst. commr. for research and statistics, 1972-75; dir. Nat. Center for Health Stats., Rockville, Md., 1976-82; prof. Inst. Health & Aging, U. Calif.-San Francisco, 1982—. Contbr. articles to profl. jours. Recipient Social Security Adminstrn. citation, 1968, Disting. Service medal HEW, 1974, Jack C. Massey Found. award, 1978. Fellow Am. Public Health Assn. (domestic award for excellence 1978), Am. Statis. Assn.; mem. Inst. Medicine, Am. Econ. Assn., Population Assn. Am., LWV. Home: 1055 Amito Ave Berkeley CA 94705 Office: U Calif Sch Nursing N631 San Francisco CA 94143

RICE, EDGENIE HIGGINS, educational and arts consultant; b. Worcester, Mass., Feb. 8, 1942; d. Milton Prince and Alice Lord (Coonley) Higgins; A.A., Bradford Coll., 1962; cert. Ecole du Louvre, France, 1963; B.A., Boston U., 1965; m. Donald Sands Rice, Aug. 27, 1966; children—Alice Higgins, Edgenie Reynolds. Exhibits coordinator Smithsonian Inst. Traveling Exhibition Service, 1966-67; visual arts coordinator N.Y. State Council on the Arts, N.Y.C., 1967-70; asst. dir. Community Environments, N.Y.C., 1970-71; cons. Mus. Collaborative, N.Y.C., 1972; originator, dir. UN-US Mother-Child Workshop, N.Y.C., 1972-81. Bd. dirs. YWCA, N.Y.C., 1972-85, chmn. vol. com., 1979-81, exec. com., 1976-77, 78-82; mem. program com. World Mut. Service Com., 1972-76, vice chmn. program com., 1982-83, chmn. visitors service for nat. bd., 1971-72; mem. jr. council Mus. Modern Art, 1973-76; mem. grants com. Ch. of the Heavenly Rest, 1979-81; mem. benefit com. Cooper-Hewitt Nat. Mus. Design, Legal Aid Soc., YWCA-YMCA Camping Council; parents league rep. Chapin Sch., 1980-81; trustee, mem. arts and student affairs coms., acad. affairs, chmn. hon. degrees com. Clark U., Worcester, Mass., 1981—; pres. Civitas, 1982—. Clubs: Cosmopolitan, The River. Home: 1120 Fifth Ave New York NY 10128

RICE, ELIZABETH FISCHER, financial executive; b. Highland Park, Ill., Mar. 25, 1953; d. Thomas Clark and Nancy (Knight) Fischer; m. Larry Alan Rice, Feb. 25, 1984. BA, Coe Coll., 1975; MBA, Northwestern U., 1977. Fin. analyst Xerox Corp., Rochester, N.Y., 1977-81, plant controller, Oak Brook, Ill., 1981-85, program fin. mgr., Rochester, 1985—. Mem. Nat. Assn. Female Execs., Xerox Mgmt. Assn. (pres. 1987-88), Omicron Delta Epsilon, Delta Delta Delta. Republican. Episcopalian. Avocations: racquetball, running, reading. Home: 134 Beckwith Terr Rochester NY 14610 Office: Xerox Corp 1350 Jefferson Rd Henrietta NY 14623

RICE, ELLEN FRANCES, counselor; b. Gettysburg, Pa., May 14, 1941; d. John Stanley and Grace Luene (Rogers) R. BA in English, Gettysburg Coll., 1964; MA in Christian Edn., Wheaton Grad. Sch., Ill., 1966; MS in Guidance and Counseling, Nova U., 1973. Cert. tchr., Fla. Dir. Christian edn. Greenville Community Reformed Ch., Scarsdale, N.Y., 1966-69; tchr. St. Mark's Episcopal Sch., Ft. Lauderdale, 1969-70; youth dir. First United Methodist Ch., Ft. Lauderdale, 1972-74; vocat. counselor Christian Counseling Ministries, Pompano Beach, Fla., 1986-87; individual and family therapy, Pompano Beach, 1987—. Sec., bd. dirs. Ctr. of Pastoral Counseling and Human Devel., Ft. Lauderdale, 1973-78, Lago Mar Place, 1983—; vol. North Ridge Gen. Hosp. Aux., Ft. Lauderdale, 1977-81; mem. nat. bd. Med. Coll. Pa., Phila., 1976-82. Mem. Am. Assn. for Counseling and Devel., Am. Mental Health Counselors Assn., Nat. Career Devel. Assn., Delta Gamma. Clubs: Ft. Lauderdale Yacht, Lago Mar Beach. Home: 1750 S Ocean Ln Fort Lauderdale FL 33316 Office: 901 SE McNab Rd Suite 4 Pompano Beach FL 33060

RICE, FELICIA MAY, printer, publisher, artist; b. San Francisco, Sept. 12, 1954; d. Raymond Charles and Miriam Irene (Cohen) R. BA with honors, U. Calif., Santa Cruz, 1978. Fine printer, pub. Moving Parts Press, Santa Cruz, 1977—; co-dir. Printers Chappel, Santa Cruz, 1982—. Editor: For Earthly Survival by Ellen Bass, 1980 (Elliston Book award 1980), In the World's Common Grasses by William Pitt Root, 1981, In These Bodies by Katharine Harer, 1982, Blue Hooks in Weather by Christoper Buckley, 1983, before/The Rain by Robert Lundquist, 1985, Pick Up the Apples by Joan Hinchman Pera, 1986. Mem. Pacific Ctr. Book Arts, Ctr. Book Arts, N.Y. Democrat.

RICE, FERILL JEANE, writer, civic worker; b. Hemingford, Nebr., July 4, 1926; d. Derrick and Helen Agnes (Moffatt) Dalton; m. Otis LaVerne Rice, Mar. 7, 1946; children: LaVeria June McMichael, Larry L. Student, U. Omaha, 1961. Dir. jr. and sr. choir Congl. Ch., Tabor, Iowa, 1952-66; tchr. Fox Valley Tech. Inst., Appleton, Wisc., 1970-77; dir. activity Family Heritage Nursing Home, Appleton, 1972-75, Peabody Manor, Appleton, 1975-76. Editor: Moffatt and Related Families, 1981; asst. editor (mag.) Yester-Year, 1975-76; contbr. articles to profl jours. Chmn. edn. Am. Cancer Soc., Fremont County, 1962, 63, 64. Mem. Iowa Fedn. Women's Clubs (Fremont county chmn. 1964, 65, 66, 67, 7th dist. chmn. library services 1966-67), Tabor Women's Club (pres. 1962, 63, 64), Jr. Legion Aux. (founder, 1st dir. 1951-52), Fenton Art Glass Collectors Am., Inc. (co-founder 1977, sec., editor 1977-86, editor newsletter 1976-86), DAR, Mayflower Soc., John Howland Soc., Ross County Ohio Geneal. Soc., Iowa Geneal. Soc., Dallas County Mo. Geneal. Soc., Imperial Collectors Am., Tiffin Glass Collectors, Nat. Depression Glass Assn., Clay County (Ind.) Geneal. Soc., Vinton County (Ohio) Geneal. Soc., Fenton Finders of Wis. (chpt #1), Greentown Collectors. Republican. Methodist. Lodge: Order of Eastern Star (worthy matron 1959, 64), Rainbow for Girls (bd. dirs. 1964). Home: 302 Pheasant Run Kaukauna WI 54130 Office: Rice Enterprises PO Box 1056 Appleton WI 54912

RICE, GRETA JACQUELYNN, sales executive; b. Cin., Nov. 22, 1959; d. Robert and Dorothy Mae (Lindsey) R. BS, U. Cin., 1982. Lic. tchr., Ohio. Camp counselor West Cin. Summer Program, 1977, group leader, 1978, sect. leader, 1979-81; videx operator Montgomery Ward, Cin., 1982-83; tchr. multihandicapped Cin. Bd. Edn., 1982-86; sales account exec. Eastman Kodak Co., Whittier, Calif., 1985—. Recipient Kodak Regional All-Star; U. Cin. scholar. Mem. Nat. Assn. Market Developers, Nat. Assn. Exec. Women, Am. Fedn. Tchrs., Jaycees, Delta Sigma Theta (chmn. Teen Lift, 1986, chmn. Teen Pregancy Seminar, 1987—, Outstanding Service award). Democrat. Prebyterian. Office: Eastman Kodak Co 12100 Rivera Whittier CA 90606

RICE, JENNIFER SUSAN, development, public relations executive; b. Houston, Jan. 18, 1951; d. Myer and Rose (Forrest) R.; B.A. with honors, U. Tex., Austin, 1972, M.A. in Communications, 1974. Dist. exec. dir. Am. Cancer Soc., Austin, Tex., 1974-75, br. dirs., Miami, Fla., 1975-76; dir. public info./research Urban League Greater Miami, 1976-77; mental health planning cons., communications coordinator Miami Jewish Home and Hosp. for Aged, 1977-79; dir. public relations and devel. James Archer Smith Hosp., Homestead, Fla., 1979-81; assoc. dir. N.J. region Deborah Hosp. Found., Browns Mills, N.J., 1981-83; mktg. mgr. West Coast Reply-o/Kennedy Sinclair, Wayne, N.J., 1983-84; exec. dir. Ocean County Coll. Found., Toms River, N.J., 1984-87; dir. devel. Community Home Health Services Phila., 1987—. Mem. public edn. com. Am. Cancer Soc.; mem. Child Abuse Task Force, Mental Health Assn. NIMH fellow, 1972. Mem. Public Relations Soc. Am., Nat. Assn. Hosp. Devel., Nat. Soc. Fund Raising Execs., Fla. Hosp. Assn., S. Fla. Hosp. Public Relations Assn., Internat. Assn. Bus. Communicators (pres. S. Fla. chpt.), Phi Kappa Phi. Home: 7013-B McCallum St Philadelphia PA 19119 Office: Community Home Health Services Phila 21 South 12 St Philadelphia PA 19107

RICE, JOAN S., banker; b. Boston, Dec. 29, 1948; d. Robert Moran and Leona (Bruck) Slavin; m. John Winslow Rice; 1 child, Thomas Peirce. BS, U N.H., 1971. Dir. H.E.L.P. program Capitol Bank & Trust Co., Boston, 1971-74; trust officer Boston Safe Deposit & Trust Co., 1974-78; dir. planned giving Wheaton Coll., Norton, Mass., 1978-83; asst. v.p., trust officer Indian Head Banks, Portsmouth, N.H., 1983—. Bd. dirs. Children's Mus. of Portsmouth, 1986—, Portsmouth Community Found., 1983—, Portsmouth Women's Chorus, 1986—, Prescott Park Arts Festival, 1982-85, treas. 1983-85, Strawberry Bank; mem. adv. com. York County Youth Ballet, 1983—; incorporator N.H. Charitable Fund, 1985—; pres. Community Music Ctr. of Boston, 1978—, Planned Giving Group of New Eng., 1980-81, founding mem. 1978. Mem. Internat. Assn. Fin. Planners (mem. ethics com. N.H. chpt.), N.H. Estate Planning Council. Republican. Episcopalian.

RICE, JOY KATHARINE, educational policy studies and women's studies educator, psychologist; b. Oak Park, Ill., Mar. 26, 1939; d. Joseph Theodore and Margaret Sophia (Bednarik) Straka; m. David Gordon Rice, Sept. 1, 1962; children: Scott Alan, Andrew David. B.F.A. with high honors, U. Ill., Urbana, 1960; M.S., U. Wis., Madison, 1962, U. Wis., Madison, 1964; Ph.D., U. Wis., Madison, 1967. Lic. clin. psychologist. USPHS predoctoral fellow dept. psychiatry Med. Sch. U. Wis.-Madison, 1964-65, asst. dir. Counseling Ctr., 1966-74, dir. Office Continuing Edn. Services, 1972-78, prof. ednl. policy studies and women's studies, 1974—; pvt. practice psychology Madison, 1967—; mem. State Wis. Ednl. Approval Bd., Madison, 1972-73; mem. Adult Edn. Commn., U.S. Office Career Edn., Washington, 1978. Author: Living Through Divorce, A Developmental Approach to Divorce Therapy, 1985; editorial bd. Lifelong Learning, 1979-86, cons. editor Psychology of Women Quarterly, 1986— ; contbr. articles to profl. jours. Knapp fellow U. Wis.-Madison, 1960-62, teaching fellow, 1962-63. Mem. Nat. Assn. Women Deans, Counselors and Adminstrs. (editorial bd. jour. 1984—), Am. Psychol. Assn., Am. Ednl. Research Assn., Internat. Council Psychologists, Am. Assn. Continuing and Adult Edn. (meritorious service award 1978, 79, 80, 82), Wis. Psychol. Assn., Phi Delta Kappa. Unitarian. Home: 4230 Waban Hill Madison WI 53711 Office: U Wis Dept Ednl Policy Studies 243 Edn Madison WI 53706

RICE, JUDY ERWIN, insurance company executive; b. Houston, Sept. 9, 1947; d. Hal and Uva Marie (Loftis) Burton Erwin; m. Michael Allen Teague, Mar. 17, 1967 (div. Feb. 1973); children—Michael, Kathy, Jennifer, John; m. John Franklin Rice, Sept. 28, 1973. Student Stephen F. Austin U., 1966-67. Cert. ins. counselor. Personal lines clk. Liberty Mut., Houston, 1967-68, CEM Agys., Houston, 1968-72; multi-lines clk. Atkinson Bros., Houston, 1972-73, Reliable Ins. Agy., Temple, Tex., 1975-77; owner Rice Enterprises, Temple, Tex., 1977-80; account exec. Reliable Ins., Temple, 1980-86; mgr. Hendrick & Kelly Ins., Belton, Tex., 1986—. V.p. Temple Civic Ballet, Tex., 1979; bd. dirs., Cen-Tex. Zool. Soc., Waco, 1978. Mem. Fedn. Ins. Women, Nat. Assn. Female Execs., Temple Ins. Women (treas., sec. 1982), Temple Agts. Assn. (sec.-treas. 1984), Soc. of CIC. Republican. Methodist. Club: Lake Belton Yacht (sec.-treas. 1984) (Temple). Avocations: needlework; reading; gardening. Home: 209 Cole Temple TX 76501

RICE, KATHLEEN MARIE, academic administrator, consultant; b. Haverhill, Mass., Oct. 12, 1941; d. James Michael and Regina Isabel (Legare) R. BA, Northeastern U., 1967; MA, Boston Coll., 1969; EdD, columbia U., 1976. Dir. counseling Graham Jr. Coll., Boston, 1969-71; dir. transfer admissions Boston Coll., 1971-73; cons. coll. entrance exam. bd. Waltham, Mass., 1971-76; dean, prof. psychology St. Mary's Coll., Notre Dame, Ind., 1976-83; v.p. Seton Hall U., South Orange, N.J., 1984-86; v.p. student services and enrollment mgmt. Pratt Inst., Brooklyn, 1987—; mem. Northeastern U. Corp., Boston, 1976—, bd.dirs. Nat. Council, 1977—; trustee Integrity, Inc., Newark, N.J., 1986—, Sch. Arts League, City of N.Y. Author: (with others) Standards for Awarding High School Diploma, 1976; contbr. articles to profl. jours. Named one of Outstanding Women in Bus., YWCA, 1981. Democrat. Roman Catholic. Office: Pratt Inst Willoughby Ave Brooklyn NY 11205

RICE, LINDA TILLMAN, professional volunteer; b. Orlando, Fla., June 3, 1943; d. Thomas John and Stella Frances (Block) Tillman; m. James T. Rice. Student Valencia Community Coll., Orlando, 1973-74, Fla. Jr. Coll., Jacksonville, 1976-78, U. North Fla., 1983-84; student Luther Rice Sem., 1986—. Exec. sec. to mgr. advance systems engrng. Martin Marietta Aerospace Corp., Orlando, 1963-69; exec. sec. to pres., also office mgr., fashion coordinator and writer Act II Jewelry Inc., Orlando, 1969-76; legal asst., sec. Howell, Howell, Liles, Braddock & Milton, Jacksonville, Fla., 1976-78; exec. asst. to owners and developers Regency Sq. Shopping Center, Jacksonville, 1978-79; free-lance legal sec. and asst., Jacksonville, 1979-80; adminstrv. asst. to sr. v.p. human resources and labor relations Seaboard System R.R., Jacksonville, 1980-85. Hospitality chmn., v.p. Women of Jacksonville Art Mus., 1977-80, publicity chmn., 1981-82; mem. St. Luke's Hosp. Aux. and Endowment Bd., Nat. Rep. Com., Jacksonville Humane Soc. Aux. Mem. Rep. Nat. Com. Nat. Secs. Assn. (asst. treas. 1973-74, sec. 1974-75), Women's Guild Jacksonville Mus. Arts and Scis., Nat. Assn. Ry. Bus. Women (pres. 1984-85, parliamentarian 1986-87, publicity chmn. 1987-88). Recipient Dist. VI Railway Bus. Woman of Yr., 1986. Mem. Capitol Hill Women's Club. Episcopalian. Home: 10754-8 Scott Mill Rd Jacksonville FL 32223

RICE, MELANIE AILENE, singer, entertainer; b. Phila., Nov. 4, 1957; d. Anthony Joseph and Marie Rose (Ranere) R. BA in Music, Glassboro (N.J.) State U., 1980. acct. exec. The Music Plant, Absecon, N.J., 1987. Opening act for entertainers including Smokey Robinson, Shecky Greene, David Brenner; background singer Joe Piscapo, Grover Washington Jr., Bobby Rydell, others; performed for radio/TV commercials, casinos. Co-chair March of Dimes Golf Tournament, Atlantic City, N.J., 1987. Recipient John Phillip Sousa Music award, 1975; winner 1975 N.J. State Jr. Girls Golf Championship. Mem. Am. Fedn. Musicians, Assn. Research and Enlightenment. Democrat. Roman Catholic. Home: 274 Mattix Run Absecon NJ 08201

RICE, PATRICIA ANN (PATRICIA ANN RICE AVILA), general accounting manager; b. Aldrich, Mo., Aug. 24, 1946; d. William Wayne and Wilda Mae (Lowery) Rice; A.A., Southwest Baptist U., Bolivar, Mo., 1966; B.A., Southwest Mo. State U.; postgrad. Calif. State U.-Fullerton; children: Jessica Jean Rice, Clifford Wayne Rice, Jacqueline Marie, Alicia JoAnne. Office mgr. Patscheck-Veiga Constrn. Co., Tustin, Calif., 1972-75; asst. to controller Richards West Co., Newport Beach, Calif., 1976-78; acctg. supr. Warner Lambert Co., Anaheim, Calif., 1978-80, supr. fin. analysis and planning, 1980; mgr. fin. control Pepsi Cola, Torrance, Calif., 1980-82; sr. fin. adminstr. Microdata Corp., (name changed to McDonnell Douglas Computer Systems Co.), Newport Beach, Calif., 1982-86, gen. acct. mgr. Printronix, Irvine, Calif., 1986—. Bd. dirs. Real Reasons Homes for Abused Children. Mem. Nat. Assn. Female Execs., Am. Prodn. and Inventory Control Soc., Am. Mgmt. Assn., AAUW, NOW (chpt. program chmn. 1977), LaLeche League (chpt. publicity chmn. 1972-73). Democrat. Roman Catholic. Home: 29805 Rustic Oak Laguna Niguel CA 92677 Office: 30100 Town Center Dr Suite 102 Laguna Niguel CA 92677

RICE, PATRICIA BYRNE, tannery executive, taxidermy executive; b. Yuba City, Calif., July 31, 1939; d. Onslow Anthony and Margaret Pearl (Baeta) Byrne; children: Christine Marie, Deborah Lee, Michelle Lyn, Joseph F. (dec.). Student, Vallejo Jr. Coll., 1957. Apt. mgr. Metzger Bros., Columbus, Ohio, 1971-72; sec., treas. Midwest Custom Tannery, Columbus, 1972-81, pres., owner, 1981—; owner Hunters Haven Taxidermy, 1981—; owner Patti B. Rice Co., 1988—. Co-chair Ohioans for Wildlife Conservation, Columbus, 1976-77. Mem. Ohio Taxidermist Trade Register (bd. dirs. 1980-82), Ohio Assn. Taxidermists (bd. dirs. 1986, pres. 1987), Taxidermist Suppliers Assn. (sec.-treas. 1983—), Profl. Tanners Guild (v.p. 1984—), Nat. Rifle Assn., Ducks Unltd. (booklet chmn. 1984). Republican. Roman Catholic. Club: Buckeye Lady Anglers (treas. 1987). Lodge: Women of Moose (jr. regent 1964-65). Avocations: fishing, leather work, hunting. Office: Midwest Custom Tannery Inc 1765 Harrisburg Pike Columbus OH 43223

RICE, RAMONA GAIL, physiologist, phycologist, educator, consultant; b. Texarkana, Tex., Feb. 15, 1950; d. Raymond Lester and Jessie Gail (Hubbard) R.; m. Carl H. Rosen. BS, Ouachita U., 1972; MS, U. Ark., 1975, PhD, 1978; postgrad. Utah State U., 1978-80. Undergrad. asst. Ouachita U., Arkadelphia, Ark., 1970-72; grad. teaching asst. U. Ark., Fayetteville, 1972, 77-78, grad. research asst., 1973-77; asst. research scholar, scientist Fla. Internat. U., Miami, 1980-85; research coordinator, faculty Pratt Community Coll., Kans., 1985—; adj. instr. Miami Dade Community Coll., 1984-85, Wichita (Kans.) State U., 1986—. Contbr. articles to profl. jours. Judge Pratt County Sci. Fairs, Dade County Sci. Fair, Fla., 1981-85, Barber County Sci. Fairs; tchr. Sunday Sch. First Baptist Ch., South Miami, Fla., 1982-85, leader girls in action, 1982-83, youth chaperone, 1982-85; patron Pratt Community Concert Series. Grantee NSF, 1981-83, Am. Biog. Inst. Disting. Leadership award, 1987. Fla. Dept. Environ., 1981-83, EPA, 1983-85, So. Fla. Research Ctr., Everglades Nat. Park, 1983-86. Mem. AMA, Ninescah Valley Med. Soc. Aux., Pratt Higher Edn. Assn. (sec. 1987-88), Fla. Acad. Scis., AAAS, Phycological Soc. Am., Soc. Limnology and Oceanography, Sigma Xi. Democrat. Avocations: pianist, crochet, needlework, photography, reading. Office: Pratt Community Coll Dept Biol Scis Pratt KS 67124

RICE, ROBIN DIANA, advertising consultant; b. Lansing, Mich., Nov. 21, 1962; d. David Earl and Diana Kay (Parks) R. BA in Sociology, Northwestern Coll., Orange City, Iowa, 1986. Owner, mgr. Nanny Placement Services, Washington, 1983-85; free-lance writer Washington, 1984—; cons. various service orgns., Washington, 1985—; cons., lectr. Helping Hands Inc., Wilton, Conn., 1985-86. Author: The American Nanny, 1987. Mem. Nat. Assn. Female Execs., Nat. Assn. Edn. Young Children, Nanny Network (bd. dirs. 1985-87). Presbyterian. Home and Office: 4028 Argyle Terr NW Washington DC 20011

RICE, SUSAN JOETTE, nurse; b. Topeka, Nov. 15, 1946; d. Claude Harvey and Martha May (McClellan) R.; student Pasadena Nazarene Coll., 1964-66; B.S. in Nursing, Calif. State U., Los Angeles, 1969, M.S.N., 1982; postgrad Cambridge Grad. Sch. Psychology, Los Angeles, 1985—. Staff nurse Children's Hosp. Los Angeles, 1969-75, asst. head nurse, 1972-74, nurse mgr., 1974-75; nursing unit coordinator newborn and neonatal intensive care nurseries, perinatal clinician Glendale (Calif.) Adventist Med. Center, 1976-78; neonatal clin. specialist Huntington Meml. Hosp., Pasadena, 1981-85; staff nurse mental health unit Glendale Adventist Med. Ctr., 1985—. Vol. counselor Pasadena Mental Health Ctr., 1985—. Mem. Am. Assn. Critical Care Nurses, Calif. Perinatal Assn., Nat. Assn. Neonatal Nurses, Pasadena Area Psychol. Assn. Republican. Mem. Nazarene Ch. Home: 133 E Pamela Rd Monrovia CA 91016

RICE-MOORE, CHERYL LEIGH, accountant, business administrator; b. Phila., Oct. 26, 1949; d. Junius Marcus Emerson and Sylvia Lorraine (Rice) Ferguson; m. Acel Moore, Oct. 19, 1974; B.S. in Mktg. and Acctg., LaSalle Coll., 1980. Nat. pub. relations officer Nat. Assn. Black Accts., Inc., Washington, 1980; fiscal field specialist/pre-audit monitor Opportunities Industrialization Ctrs. Am., Inc., Phila., 1980-81, 86—; fiscal corp. adminstr. Gaudenzia, Inc., Phila., 1982-85; controller Hamlyn Assocs., Inc., Phila., 1985-86; vis. lectr. U. Pa. Community Wharton Edn. Program, Phila., 1981, 82, 83-84. Mem. Nat. Assn. Black Accts., Inc. (2d v.p. local chpt. 1982, 83, Eastern regional treas. 1983, 84, scholarship awards dinner chmn. local chpt. 1979, 80, 81; outstanding mem. award 1981). Baptist. Home: 6618 Greene St Philadelphia PA 19119 Office: OICS of Am Inc 100 W Coulter St Philadelphia PA 19141

RICH, DEBORAH SUE, medical company consultant; b. Columbia, Mo., Aug. 3, 1960; d. Floyd Wilford and Patricia (Scott) R. BS in Nursing, U. Mo., 1982. RN, cert. critical care nurse, Mo. Staff nurse St. Luke's Hosp., Kansas City; clin. nurse II Truman Med. Ctr., Kansas City, 1984-86; cons. med. sales, skin and wound specialist Support Systems Internat., Med. Service Inc., Charleston, S.C., 1986—. Mem. Am. Assn. Critical Care Nurses, Sigma Theta Tau. Home: 1133 Ashland Gravel Rd #1304 Columbia MO 65201 Office: Support Systems Internat Med Service Inc 612 Big Bear Blvd #521 Columbia MO 65201

RICH, HELEN WALL (MRS. ARTHUR L. RICH), music educator; b. Chester, S.C., May 4, 1912; d. George Addison and Georgia (Hardin) Wall; student Queen's Coll., 1930-32; B.S. summa cum laude, Catawba Coll., 1934; diploma in piano playing Juilliard Sch. Music, 1938; diplomas Christiansen Choral Sch., 1950, 51; m. Arthur Lowndes Rich, July 26, 1934; children—Arthur Lowndes, Ruth Anne. Instr. music Catawba Coll., Salisbury, N.C., 1934-43; univ. organist Mercer U., Macon, Ga., 1944-50, asst. prof. music, 1950-73, prof. emeritus, 1973—; organ recitalist throughout S.E.; v.p. Tudor Apts., Inc., Atlanta, 1960-73; pres. Biscayne Apts., Atlanta, 1976—. Mem. Federated Music Clubs (hon.; chmn. scholarship contest), Ga. Piano Tchrs. Guild, Nat. Assn. Schs. Music (asso.), Am. Coll. and Univ. Concert Mgrs. Assn. (asso.), Cardinal Key Soc. Mercer U. (hon.), Delta Omicron. Club: Morning Music (Macon, dir.). Home: 369 Candler Dr Macon GA 31204

RICH, JUDITH G. HEMPHILL, insurance agent, small business owner; b. Murphy, N.C., June 23, 1947; d. Ray Mauney and Mary Grace (Colwell) Hemphill; m. Sidney F. Rich, July 3, 1965 (div. 1970); 1 child, Cary R. Student Kennesaw Coll., 1977-78. Lic. ins. agt., real estate agt. Sales rep. Combined Ins. Co., Chgo., 1972-76; policy service rep. Prudential Property and Casualty Ins., Atlanta, 1976-77; sales rep. Fran Hale Ad Agy., Marietta, Ga., 1977-79, Atlantic and Pacific Life Ins., Atlanta, 1979-80; dist. sales mgr. Mut. of Omaha, College Park, Ga., 1980-84, sales rep. Hagan & Assocs., Marietta, 1984-87, also bd. dirs.; prin. Judith Hemphill Rich & Assocs., Woodstock, 1987—. Recipient awards Combined Ins., 1973, 74-75 Mut. of Omaha, 1982-83. Mem. Ins. Women of Cobb County (pub. relations chmn. 1986—, bd. dirs. 1986-87, Rookie of Yr. nominee 1987). Mem. Ch. of God. Avocation: collecting old family photographs. Office: Judith H Rich and Assoc Life Health Ins Agy Woodstock GA 30188

RICH, JUDITH S., public relations executive; b. Chgo., Apr. 14; d. Irwin M. and Sarah I. (Sandock) R. BA, U. Ill., 1960. Staff writer, reporter Economist Newspapers, Chgo., 1960-61; asst. dir. pub. relations and communications Council Profit Sharing Industries, Chgo., 1961-62; dir. advt. and pub. relations Chgo. Indsl. Dist., 1962-63; account exec., account supr., v.p., sr. v.p., exec. v.p. then nat. creative dir. Daniel J. Edelman Inc., Chgo., 1963-85; exec. v.p., dir. Ketchum Pub. Relations, Chgo., 1985—. Mem. Pub. Relations Soc. Am. (Silver Anvil award, judge Silver Anvil awards), Counselors Acad. of Pub. Relations Soc. Am. (exec. bd.). Club: Publicity (Chgo.) (7 Golden Trumpet awards). Home: 2500 N Lakeview Dr Chicago IL 60614 Office: Ketchum Pub Relations 142 E Ontario St Chicago IL 60611

RICH, MARCIA R., lawyer; b. N.Y.C., Dec. 29, 1948; d. Jack and Beatrice (Fishman) R. BA, Bard Coll., 1970; JD, Bklyn. Law Sch., 1973. Bar: N.Y. 1974, U.S. Dist. Ct. (ea. dist.) N.Y., 1976. Staff atty. juvenile rights div. Legal Aid Soc. N.Y.C., 1973-77; assoc. law asst. to justices Supreme Ct. 1st Jud. Dist., N.Y.C., 1977-87; mng. atty. Howard, Darby & Levin, 1987—. Vol. Am. Heart Assn., N.Y.C., 1979—. Mem. N.Y. County Lawyers Assn. (com. law reform 1983-86), ABA, N.Y. State Bar Assn., Assn. Law Assts. City N.Y. (exec. bd. 1980-81), N.Y. Women's Bar Assn. Office: Howard Darby & Levin 10 E 53d St New York NY 10022

RICH, MARY LYNNE, data processing consultant; b. Akron, Ohio, Dec. 13, 1941; d. Arthur Oakes and Mary Evelyn (Haberer) Wood; (div.); 1 daughter, Juli. BA, Brown U., 1963. Product mgr. Informatics, Inc., Canoga Park, Calif., 1969-75; tech. rep. Datasaab Systems, Los Angeles, 1975-78, MPG, Inc., Princeton, N.J., 1978-80; sr. cons. ICS Group, Inc., Torrance, Calif., 1980-82; pres. PFS, Inc., El Segundo, Calif., 1982—; ops. chmn. Nat. Computer Conf., 1983-84, gen. chmn., 1986; mem. program com. World

Congress on Computing, 1988-89, Localnet Show and Conf., 1988-89. Mem. Assn. for Women in Computing, Assn. Data Processing Service Orgns., Ind. Computer Cons. Assn. (bd. dirs. 1984, 86), Assn. for Computing Machinery. Republican.

RICH, SUSAN ABBY, efficiency consultant; b. Bklyn., Apr. 11, 1946; d. Milton and Jeanette (Merns) Rich. BA, Bklyn. Coll., 1967, MA, 1976, advanced cert. in adminstrn. and supervision, 1977; cert. indsl. relations UCLA, 1981. Tchr. speech, theater N.Y.C. Bd. Edn., 1967-77; employee relations supr. Crocker Nat. Bank, 1977-81; plant personnel mgr. Boise Cascade Corp., 1981-82; speaker, cons. office efficiency and productivity Get Organized, Get Rich, Playa del Rey, Calif., 1982—. Pres. Marina del Rey Singers, 1987—. Mem. Women's Referral Service (Mem. of Year award 1985), Nat. Speakers Assn. (Greater Los Angeles chpt., Bronze award 1987), The Network Group, Venice Area C. of C. (bd. dirs.). Office: Get Organized Get Rich 7777 W 91 St Suite 1154B Playa del Rey CA 90293

RICHARD, ANITA LOUISE, entrepreneur, management consultant; b. Willard, N.Y., June 22, 1951; d. Marvin Gerald and Ilene (Rosenberg) Isaacson; m. J.E. Richard, May 16, 1981; stepchildren: Christine, Chad. Student, U. Fla., 1969-70, CUNY, Bklyn., 1972-74, Barnard Baruch U., 1974-76; BA magna cum laude, Golden Gate U., 1981. Mktg. mgr. Exxon Office Systems, N.Y.C., 1976-77; program mgr. Exxon Office Systems, Dallas, 1977-78; br. mgr. Exxon Office Systems, Pasadena, Calif., 1978-79; br. sales mgr. Exxon Office Systems, Century City, Calif., 1979; mgr. regional sales program Exxon Office Systems, Marina Del Rey, Calif., 1979-81; mktg. mgr. Exxon Office Systems, San Francisco, 1981-82; product mgr. Wells Fargo Bank, San Francisco, 1984; mgmt. cons. J. Richard and Co., Montara, Calif., 1984—. Mem. Am. Mgmt. Assn., Am. Soc. for Personnel Adminstrn., Calif. Assn. for HMO's (chairperson career placement com.), Am. Compensation Assn., Group Health Assn. Am., No. Calif. Human Resource Council, No. Calif. Health Care Mktg. Assn., Practicing Law Inst. Republican. Jewish. Clubs: Los Angeles Athletic. Home and Office: 1301 Main St PO Box 779 Montara CA 94037 Office: 1301 Main St PO Box 779 Mantara CA 94037

RICHARD, BETTY BYRD, geriatric fitness educator, consultant, writer; b. Charleston, W.Va., Aug. 30, 1922; d. Ernest O'Farrell and Blanche Elizabeth (Davenport) Byrd; m. Samuel Jackson Richard, Jr., June 12, 1943 (dec. Nov. 1987); children—Caroline Byrd Richard Rossman, Samuel Jackson III. B.A. in Sociology, U. Charleston (W.Va.), 1977. Research assoc. exercise planning and design Frankel Found., Charleston, 1966-70; assoc. adminstr., 1970-79; cons. geriatric fitness W.Va. Commn. on Aging, 1979-83; dir. Gerokinetics, Charleston, 1984—; W.Va. co-originator co-dir. Preventicare program, 1970-79; coordinator 1st Appalachian Conf. on Phys. Activity and Aging, 1973; coordinator Gerokinesiatrics Conf. on Aging, 1977; author books including: Be Alive as Long As You Live, rev. edit. 1977; Age and Mobility, 1979; contbr. to Guide to Fitness After Fifty, 1977; producer gerokinetics program on audio cassette, 1980, gerokinetics slide/tape program, 1985; featured on weekly pub. TV series on exercise programs for sr. citizens, 1974-75. Recipient Gov.'s Sr. Service award, 1982. Republican. Presbyterian. Lodge: Eastern Star. Home: 321 Mountain View Dr Charleston WV 25314 Office: Gerokinetics 401 4th Ave S Charleston WV 25303

RICHARD, DARLENE DOLORAS, marketing firm executive, bank officer, writer and speaker; b. Mansfield, Ohio, Jan. 4, 1946; d. Charles Alvertis and Marjorie Elaine (Foster) Swander; m. David Allen Richard, Aug. 14, 1965 (div.). AA, Famous Artist Sch., 1964; BA in Edn., Ohio State U., 1969. Asst. to controller Johnstown Properties, Atlanta, 1978-79, adminstrv. mgr. TCG Communications, Atlanta, 1979; promotional dir. Am. Health Cons., Atlanta, 1979-82; pres. Direct Mktg./R&D, Ltd., Atlanta/Buffalo 1982—, Slight Edge Enterprises, 1983—, Marine Midland Bank, Buffalo, 1985—. Mem. Bus. Womens Advisor Com. Mem. Newsletter Assn. Am., Direct Mktg. Assn., (inner circle, telemktg. council, fin. council), Am. Inst. Banking, Am. Assn. Profl. Cons., Am. Cons. League, Am. Soc. Profl. and Exec. Women, Atlanta Profl. Women's Network, Atlanta Women Entrepreneurs, Atlanta C. of C., Printing Assn. Ga., Printing Industries of Am., Direct Mktg. Assn. of N. Tex., Southeast Direct Mktg. Club, Buffalo C. of C., Humane Soc. U.S., Kangaroo Protection Agy., Smithsonian Inst., Nat. Assn. Female Execs., AAUW, Am. Mgmt. Assn., Internat. Oceanographic Found, Creative Problem Solving Inst., Creative Edn. Found. Republican. Clubs: Seven Seas Sailing, Studio Arena Acting, Atlanta Advt. Address: Direct Mktg/R&D Ltd 95 Shoshone St Buffalo NY 14214-1019

RICHARD, SANDRA CLAYTON, academic administrator; b. Athens, Tex.; d. Chester Armendale and Lola Hybernia (Clayton) R. AA, Trinity Valley Community Coll.; BBA, U. Tex., MBA, PhD, 1968. Instr. Am. U. of Beirut, 1959-61, asst. prof., 1968-74, visiting assoc. prof., 1978-81; asst. prof. Addis Abeba U., Ethiopia, 1965-66, U. Mo., St. Louis, 1965-67; visiting assoc. prof. U. Notre Dame, 1974-77, Calif. State U., Long Beach, 1977-78; assoc. prof., chair div. bus. adminstrn. Laredo (Tex.) State U., 1981—; prodn. and inventory control cons. Mathes Mfg. Co., Athens, 1958, U.N. Indsl. Devel. Orgn., Vienna, Austria, 1968; mgmt. devel. programs Pakistan Indsl. Devel. Corp., Karachi, 1963, Beirut, Bahrain, Qatar, 1970-74, 78-81. Contbr. articles to profl. jours. Mem. Leadership Laredo, 1985—; founding bd. mem. Laredo Regional Food Bank, 1982—; bd. mem. Animal Protective Soc., Laredo, 1982—; mem. steering com. Am. for Justice in the Middle East, Beirut, 1980-81. Named Outstanding Ex-Student, Trinity Valley Community Coll., Athens, 1983; Fulbright grad. research grantee, Karachi, 1962-63. Mem. Soc. for Internat. Devel., Acad. Internat. Bus., Acad. Mgmt., Tex. Assn. Middle East Scholars, Am. Assn. Univ. Profs., Animal Air Transp. Assn., Phi Kappa Phi. Office: Laredo State Univ West End Washington St Laredo TX 78040

RICHARDELLA, LILLIE PARKER, administrative manager; b. Los Angeles, Aug. 12, 1952; d. Emmet Elwin and Darlene Margaret (Kochen) Parker; m. Roland George Richardella, May 27, 1978; 1 child, Christopher. BA, Calif. State U., Long Beach, 1973; postgrad., Cambridge (Eng.) U., 1974-76. Research asst., contract analyst Gen. Revenue Sharing, Orange County, Calif., 1977-79; assoc. exec. dir. YWCA, Oklahoma City, 1979-81; coordinator WORKHAWAII, Honolulu Job Tng. Program, Honolulu, 1983-84, acting chief planner, 1984, contracts mgr., 1985, chief of ops., 1985-86, adminstr., 1986-87; cons. Pub. Econ. Devel, Job Tng. Program, Honolulu, pvt. tng. programs. Author: (handbook, slideshow) Contributions of American Women to the Professions, 1981; project dir.: (video tape) Give Me a Break, 1986 (recipient Nat. Assn. Countries Youth Projects awd, 1986). Organizer, Mayor's Mobilization Task For Vets., Honolulu, 1985; fund raiser, treas., Lt. Govs. Conf., Honolulu, 1986; spokesperson, Network of Mktg. Women and YWCA, Honolulu, 1985-87. Recipient Fulbright scholarship, 1974, Pres'. Scholarship, Calif. State U., 1970-73. Mem. Hawaii Visitors Bur. (edn. and tng. com.), U.S. Dept. Edn. (adv. council Windward Dist. Exemplary Program), U.S. Dept. of Labor and Indsl. Relations (adv. council Sch. to Work Tranition Ctr.), Network of Mktg. Women, YWCA, Phi Kappa Phi, Nat. Women's Polit. Caucus (exec. dir. 1988), Alpha Lamda Delta. Republican. Roman Catholic. Office: Nat Women's Polit Caucus 1275 K St NW Suite 750 Washington DC 20005

RICHARDS, ALYS PRICE, educational administrator; b. Ft. Worth, Nov. 12, 1937; d. Duel Robert and Wilene (Wilson) Price; m. George Arthur Richards I, Aug. 13, 1960; children: Lyn Ann, George Arthur II. BA, So. Meth. U., Dallas, 1960. Cert. tchr., Tex. Elem. tchr. Dallas Ind. Sch. Dist., 1960-62, 65-66; mgr., owner Green & Price Co., Italy, Tex., 1972-80; bus. mgr. Dr. George Richards, Richardson, Tex., 1980—; owner, mgr. farm, Italy, 1975—; personnel asst. So. Meth. U., 1982-84, coordinator worker's compensation, 1983-84, coordinator spl. events, 1984-86, dir. spl. events, 1986—. Bd. dirs. Dallas County Dental Aux.; pres. bd. dirs. Richardson Symphony Orch., 1979-80, Richardson Symphony Orch. Guild, 1971-73, Tex. Women's Assn. for Symphony Orch., 1976-77; chmn. adminstrv. bd., council on ministries 1st United Meth. Ch., Richardson. Recipient 5-Yr. award, Richardson Symphony Orch., 1976, 10-Yr. award, Richardson Symphony Orch., 1981, cert. of appreciation Exchange Club, 1982. Mem. Alpha Delta Pi (pres. 1968-69), Zeta Phi Eta. Clubs: Richardson's Women's, Prairie Greek Garden (pres. 1976-77), Criterion Book (pres. 1977-78), Mustang, So. Meth. U. Staff. Home: 4 Forest Park Dr Richardson TX 75080 Office: So Meth U Dallas TX 75275

RICHARDS, ANN WILLIS, state official; b. Waco, Tex., Sept. 3, 1933; d. Cecil and Ona Willis; m. David Richard; children: Cecille, Daniel, Clark, Ellen. B.A., Baylor U., 1954; postgrad., U. Tex., 1957. Tchr. Austin Ind. Sch. Dist., Tex.; mgr. Sarah Weddington Campaign, Austin, Tex., 1972, adminstrv. asst., 1973-74; county commr. Travis County, Austin, 1977-82; state treas. State of Tex., Austin, 1983—; chairperson Tex. Depository Bd., Austin, from 1983; mem. State Banking Bd. Tex., from 1982; ex-officio mem. Tex. Senate Interim Com. on Agy. funds Mgmt., 1982, Joint Select Com. on State Fiscal Policy, 1982; mem. Austin Transp. Study, Tex., 1977-82, Capital Indsl. Devel. Corp., Austin, Tex., 1980-81, Spl. Commn. Delivery Human Services in Tex., 1979-81, Tex. Criminal Justice Adv. Bd., 1981-82, Pres.'s Adv. Com. on Women, 1979. Mem. com. strategic planning Dem. Nat. Com., 1983; keynote speaker Dem. Nat. Conv., 1988. Named Woman of Yr. Tex. Women's Polit. Caucus, 1981, 83. Mem. Nat. Assn. State Treas. Office: Tex State Treasury PO Box 12608 Capitol Station Austin TX 78711 *

RICHARDS, BETH ANN, convention director; b. Weatherford, Tex., Oct. 18, 1951; d. Ted Taylor and Edna Mildred (Cox) R.; m. Kurt F. Schatz, July 28, 1973 (div. 1983); children: Christian Taylor, Richard Benjamin. Student, Weatherford Coll., 1970-73, Cen. Tex. Coll., 1979-82. Stenographer Parker County Probation Office, Weatherford, 1969-70; stenographer U.S. civil Service, Ft. Wolters, Tex., 1970-73, Illesheim, Fed. Republic of Germany, 1976-79; stenographer Kelly Services, Tacoma, Washington, 1973-75; clk. sec. Centel of Tex., Killeen, 1979-80, adminstrv. supr., 1980-86; asst. dir. Annuity Bd., then purchasing agt. Support Services Dept. So. Baptist Conv., Dallas, 1986—. Mem. Nat. Assn. Female Execs., In-Plant Printing Mgmt. Assn., Nat. Assn. Printers and Lithographers, Am. Bus. Woman's Assn., Parents Without Ptnrs. 9dir. 1985-86). Baptist. Home: 1676 Choteau Circle Grapevine TX 76051 Office: So Bapt Conv Annuity Bd 511 N Akard Dallas TX 75201

RICHARDS, CHRISTINE-LOUISE, author, artist, composer, pianist; b. Radnor, Pa., Jan. 11, 1910; d. Joseph Ernest and Catherine (Fletcher) R.; student pvt. schs., art schs., N.Y.C., Munich, Ger. One-woman shows: Stockbridge, Mass., 1947, 48, 52, 53, Oneonta, N.Y., 1960, 61; group shows include: Stockbridge Art Assn., 1931-32; represented in collections, Calif., Mass., N.Y.; owner, founder, pres. Blue Star Music Pub. Co., Pittsfield, Mass., 1946—, now Morris, N.Y. Recipient Silver medal Internat. Inst. Community Service, Cambridge, Eng., gold medal Internat. Parliament U.S.A., prize of Golden Centaur, others; fellow World Literacy Acad. Mem. Phila. Art Alliance, Am. Fedn. Musicians (hon. life), Nightingale-Bamford Alumni Assn., Academia Italia delle arte e del Lavoro (2 gold medals, hon. diploma Master of Painting), Met. Mus. Art, Audubon Soc., Nat. Assn. Composers USA, Emergency Aid of Pa., Pa. Acad. Fine Arts, Nat. Mus. Women in Arts, Acad. Natural Scis., Friends of Library Bryn Mawr Coll., Phila. Mus., Friends N.Y. Pub. Library, Pa. Hort. Soc., Am. Hort. Soc., Bklyn. Bot. Gardens, Met. Opera Guild, Glimmerglass Opera Theatre, Nat. Trust, Nat. Arbor Day Found., Save the Redwoods, Doll Artisans Guild. Club: Peale (Phila.). Avocations: grand opera, dolls, photography, gardening, handicrafts. Author and Illustrator: The Blue Star Fairy Book of Stories for Children; The Blue Star Fairy Book of More Stories for Children; The Blue Star Fairy Book of New Stories for Children, 1980; Branches, 1983. Composer: (song) What Makes Me Dream of You, 1950, numerous others. Contbr. portrait to Artists U.S.A., 1970-71, 76. Address: Springslea PO Box 188 Morris NY 13808

RICHARDS, DEBORAH DAVIS, health educator, editor; b. St. Augustine, Fla., Dec. 19, 1943; d. Philip A. and Ann (Winship) Davis; m. James Lincoln Richards, June 12, 1965 (div. Aug. 1984); 1 child, Christine. BA, Wellesley Coll. (Mass.), 1965. Vol., Peace Corps, India, 1966-67, tng. assoc., 1967; clinic dir. Planned Parenthood, Washington, 1968-69; co-founder, dir. Action for Child Transp. Safety, N.Y.C., 1972-82; computer tech. analyst, Buckner News Alliance, Seattle, 1981-87; newsletter writer, editor Am. Acad. Pediatrics, Evanston, Ill., 1981—; editor Nat. Child Passenger Safety Assn., Washington, 1983-87; health educator Harborview Injury Prevention and Research Ctr., 1987—; mem. nat. hwy. safety adv. com. U.S. Dept. Transp., 1979-83; cons. Nat. Hwy. Traffic Safety Adminstrn., Washington, 1981-83. Author and narrator (ednl. film) Don't Risk Your Child's Life, 1978, revised, 1980, 83; author, editor (program manual) Protecting Our Own, 1983, rev. 1988. Mem. Nat. Child Passenger Safety Assn. (sec. bd. dirs. 1985-86, regional rep. 1981-83, 88-89). Democrat. Unitarian. Clubs: The Mountaineers, Wellesley (Seattle).

RICHARDS, FRANCES GRAY (PEGGY), grants specialist, consultant; b. Chgo., May 25, 1920; d. John and Jessie Marian (Brown) Gray; m. Paul Baker Richards, June 20, 1939; children—Nathan B., Peter G., Alison M., Jonathan T., Joel D. Student Colo. Coll., 1938-39, Ariz. State U., 1966, Denver U., 1961. Judge Archuleta County, Pagosa Springs, Colo., 1960-65; chief judge Jicarilla Apache Tribe, Dulce, N.Mex., 1960-65; exec. dir. So. Ute Community Action, Ignacio, Colo., 1965-70, field dir. Uplands Inc./OEO Rural Devel., So. Colo. and Southeastern Utah, 1970-72, econ. devel. dir. So. Ute Indian Tribe, Ignacio, 1972-77; owner, mgr. Peggy Richards & Assocs., Durango, Colo., 1977-81, 82—; grants mgmt. analyst City of Durango, 1980-81; housing mgmt. officer Indian div. HUD, 1981-82; owner, diet counselor Durango Diet Ctr., 1984—; grants cons. La Plata County, Durango, 1983—, So. Ute Indian Tribe, Ignacio, 1975-81, City of Cortez, Colo., 1979. Chmn., bd. dirs., Four Corners Sheltered Workshop, 1970-71, bd. dirs. Four Corners Industries, Inc., 1985-87; precinct chmn. Durango Dem. party, 1984-86; mem. Durango Housing Rehab. Com., 1983; mem. finance com. San Juan Hospice, 1983. Mem. Nat. Assn. Female Execs., United Indian Planners Assn., Nat. Congress Community Economic Devel., Kappa Kappa Gamma. Episcopalian. Avocations: mycology, hiking, exploring, travel. Office: Peggy Richards and Assocs 1911 B Main Ave Park Ctr Durango CO 81301

RICHARDS, HILDA, college administrator; b. St. Joseph, Mo., Feb. 7, 1936; d. Togar and Rose Avalynne (Williams) Young-Ballard. B.S. cum laude, CUNY, 1961; diploma nursing St. John's Sch. Nursing, St. Louis, 1956; M.Ed., Columbia U., 1965, Ed.D., 1976; M.P.A., NYU, 1971. Dep. chief dept. psychiatry Harlem Rehab. Ctr., N.Y.C., 1969-71; prof., dir. nursing Medgar Evers Coll., CUNY, N.Y.C., 1971-76, prof., assoc. dean, 1976-79; dean Coll. Health and Human Service, Ohio U., Athens, 1979-86; provost, v.p. for acad. affairs Indiana U., Pa., 1986—; mem. Gov.'s Council on Disabled Persons, Columbus, Ohio, 1982-84; mem. Gov.'s State Social Service Adv. Com., Columbus, 1982-86; mem. Ohio Planning Com., Am. Council Edn., 1981-86. Author: (with others) Curriculum Development and People of Color: Strategies and Change, 1983. Mem., chmn. Athens, Hocking, Vinton Community Health Bd., 1980-86; mem. Community Relations Com., Athens, Ohio, 1984-86; mem. Fair Housing Task Force, Athens County, Ohio, 1984-86; mem. exec. com., bd. dirs. Consortium for Health Edn. in Appalachia Ohio, Inc., Athens, 1982-86; mem. Indiana County Community Action, 1986—, Econ. Devel. Commn., 1986—. Recipient Rockefeller Found. award Am. Council Edn., Washington, 1976-77; USPHS trainee, NIMH, Columbia U., N.Y.C., 1963-65, Martin Luther King grantee NYU, N.Y.C., 1969-70, Gunt Found. grantee Harvard Inst. Ednl. Mgmt., Cambridge, Mass., 1981. Mem. Pa. Nurses Assn., Nat. Black Nurses Assn. (bd. dirs., 1st v.p. 1984—, editor jour.), Nat. Assn. Women Deans, Admissions and Counselors, Am. Soc. Allied Health Professions (chmn. equal representation in allied health), Am. Council Edn. (mem. exec. com. council fellows), Ohio Nurses Assn. (human rights com. and psychiat. mental health practice assembly 1982-86), Phi Delta Kappa. Democrat. Avocations: needlepoint; travel. Lodge: Zonta. Home: 3091 Warren Rd Indiana PA 15701 Office: Ind Univ of Pa 205 Sutton Hall Office of the Provost Indiana PA 15705

RICHARDS, JANE AILEEN, rehabilitation nursing consultant; b. Oakland, Calif., Oct. 19, 1948; d. John Donald and Mary Dolores (Peters) R. B.S. in Nursing, U. San Francisco, 1970; M.S. in Nursing, San Jose State U., 1976. R.N.; cert. ins. rehab. specialist. Staff nurse ICU Mills Meml. Hosp., San Mateo, Calif., 1970-73; asst. head nurse ICU, 1973-76, edn. specialist, 1976-80, mgr. acute rehab. ctr., 1980-83; rehab. nursing cons. J.R. Assocs., San Mateo, 1983—; Pres. United Cerebral Palsy Assn., Palo Alto, Calif., 1983-85, 79-81, bd. dirs., vice chmn. vol. devel. com., N.Y.C., 1983—. Mem. Assn. of Rehab. Nurses, Calif. Assn. Rehab. Profl., Nat. Rehab. Assn., Rehab. Ins. Nurse Group (pres.), Sigma Theta Tau (Alpha Gamma chpt.). Republican. Avocations: golf, camping. Home and Office: JR Assocs 456 Mariner's Island Blvd Suite 210 San Mateo CA 94404

RICHARDS, JUDITH G., business service owner; b. Kalamazoo, Oct. 20, 1939; d. Robert H. and Mary R. (Slumkoski) Richards. A.A.S., Ferris State Coll., 1960. Legal sec. Bush & Bush, Sturgis, Mich., 1965-77; owner Executives Bus. Service, Sturgis, 1978-87; pres. Exec. Suites and Services, Inc., Kalamazoo, 1987—; Mich. bus. rep. Job Tng. Coordinating Council, 1987—. Bd. dirs. ARCH Rehab. Facility, 1975-87; city commr. Sturgis City Commn., 1983-87. Methodist. Avocations: travel; sailing; gourmet cooking. Office: Exec Suites and Services Walnut Woods Centre 5955 W Main St Kalamazoo MI 49009

RICHARDS, KATHERINE MARY, librarian; b. Longview, Wash., Oct. 31, 1941; d. William Robert and Tessie Margaret (Winn) Enright; m. Joe McCall Richards, June 30, 1961 (div. 1966). B.A., Marylhurst Coll., 1964; M.L.S., Ind. U., 1968; cert., Johns Hopkins U., 1969. 73, Cath. U. Am., 1968-69, Columbia U., 1981. Asst. librarian Dental Sch. U. Oreg., Portland, 1965-67; asst. hist. librarian Med. Sch. Yale U., New Haven, 1969-70; hist. librarian Health Sci. U. Med., Balt., 1970-77; mgr. library Emergency Care Research Inst., Plymouth Meeting, Pa., 1978-79; dir. library Cooper Med. Ctr., Camden, N.J., 1979-80; assoc. librarian N.Y. Hist. Soc., N.Y.C., 1981-84; librarian Metro. Mus. Art, 1985; assoc. librarian Univ. Club, 1986—; mem. preservation com. Research Library Group, Stanford, Calif., 1983-84, mem. pub. services com., 1983-84. Author article. Sec., Trentcentun Corp., Bronx, N.Y., 1983, pres., 1983—; bd. dirs. NOW Md. State, 1975-76, Balt. chpt., 1974-76. Fellow Johns Hopkins U., 1968. Mem. ALA, Spl. Library Assn. (adv. bd. N.Y.C. 1983—, sec.-treas. Museum of Art and Humanities of N.Y.C. 1983—), Am. Printing History Assn., Am. Assn. History of Medicine. Republican. Unitarian. Home: 3001 Henry Hudson Pkwy Riverdale Bronx NY 10463 Office: Univ Club 1 West 54th St New York NY 10019

RICHARDS, KATHY MELINDA, mathematician; b. Mechanicsburg, Pa., Dec. 6, 1949; d. Harry Martin and Kathleen Mae (Skinner) Halvorsen; 1 child by previous marriage, Richard J. Diefenbeck Jr.; m. Harry Thomas Richards, May 24, 1980; children: Laura, Melinda, H. Thomas Jr. BS in Math., Stockton State Coll., 1986. Clk. FAA, Atlantic City, 1977-80, computer specialist tech. ctr., 1980-83, programmer, 1983-85, lectr. speakers bur., 1984—, systems programmer, 1985-86, mathematician, 1986—, mgr. Fed. Women's Program, 1987—. Mem. Girl Scouts U.S. Mem. Nat. Assn. Female Execs., Fed. Women's Program Com., Math. Modeling Users Group, Federally Employed Women. Lutheran. Office: FAA Tech Ctr Atlantic City Internat Airport Atlantic City NJ 08405

RICHARDS, LACLAIRE LISSETTA JONES (MRS. GEORGE A. RICHARDS), social worker; b. Pine Bluff, Ark.; d. Artie William and Geraldine (Adams) Jones; B.A., Nat. Coll. Christian Workers, 1953; M.S.W., U. Kans., 1956; postgrad. Columbia U., 1960; m. George Alvarez Richards, July 26, 1958; children—Leslie Rosario, Lia Mercedes, Jorge Ferguson. Diplomate Clin. Social Work; cert. gerontologist. Psychiat. supervisory, teaching, community orgn., adminstrv. and consultative duties Hastings Regional Center, Ingleside, Nebr., 1956-60; supervisory, consultative and adminstrv. responsibilities for psychiat. and geriatric patients VA Hosp., Knoxville, Iowa, 1960-74, field instr. for grad. students from U. Mo., EEO counselor, 1969-74, 78—, com. chmn., 1969-70, Fed. women's program coordinator, 1972-74; sr. social worker Mental Health Inst., Cherokee, Iowa, 1974-77; adj. asst. prof. dept. social behavior U. S.D.; instr. Augustana Coll., 1981-86; outpatient social worker VA Med. and Regional Office Center, Sioux Falls, S.D., 1978—; EEO counselor. Mem. Knoxville Juvenile Adv. Com., 1963-65, 68-70, sec., 1965-66, chmn., 1966-68; sec. Urban Renewal Citizens' Adv. Com., Knoxville, 1966-68; mem. United Methodist Ch. Task Force Exptl. Styles Ministry and Leadership, 1973-74, mem. adult choir, mem. ch. and society com.; counselor Knoxville Youth Line program; sec. exec. com. Vis. Nurse Assn., 1979-80; canvasser community fund drs., Knoxville; mem. Cherokee Civil Rights Commn.; bd. dirs., pub. relations, membership devel. and program devel. cons. YWCA, 1983-85. Named S.D. Social Worker of Yr., 1983. Mem. Nat. Assn. Social Workers (co-chmn. Nebr. chpt. profl. standards com. 1958-59), Acad. Cert. Social Workers, S.D. Assn. Social Workers (chmn. minority affairs com., v.p. S.E. region 1980, pres. 1980-82 exec. com. 1982-84, mem. social policy and action com.), Nebr. Assn. Social Workers (chmn. 1958-59), AAUW (sec. Hastings chpt. 1958-60), AMA Aux., Seventh Dist. S.D. Med. Soc. Aux., Coalition on Aging, NAACP (chmn. edn. com. 1983—). Methodist (Sunday sch. tchr. adult div.; mem. commn. on edn.; mem. Core com. for adult edn.; mem. Adult Choir; mem. Social Concerns Work Area). Home: 1701 Ponderosa Dr Sioux Falls SD 57103

RICHARDS, MARTA ALISON, lawyer; b. Memphis, Mar. 15, 1952; d. Howard Jay and Mary Dean (Nix) Richards; m. Jon Michael Hobson, May 5, 1973 (div. Jan. 1976); m. 2d, Richard Peter Massony, June 16, 1979 (div. Apr. 1988); 1 child, Richard Peter Massony, Jr. Student Vassar Coll., 1969-70; AB cum laude, Princeton U., 1973; JD, George Washington U., 1976. Bar: Assoc. Phelps, Dunbar, Marks, Claverie & Sims, New Orleans, 1976-77; assoc. counsel Hibernia Nat. Bank, New Orleans, 1978; assoc. Singer, Hutner, Levine, Seeman & Stuart, New Orleans, 1978-80, Jones, Walker, Waechter, Poitevent, Carrere & Denegre, New Orleans, 1980-84; ptnr. Mmahat Duffy, & Richards, 1984, Montgomery, Barnett, Brown, Read, Hammond & Mintz, 1984-86, Montgomery & Richards, 1986—; lectr. paralegal inst. U. New Orleans, 1984—. Contbr. articles to legal jours. Treas. alumni council Princeton U., 1979-81. Mem. ABA, La. Bar Assn., Fed. Bar Assn., New Orleans Bar Assn., Princeton Alumni Assn. New Orleans (pres. 1982-86). Episcopalian. Home: 1133 8th St New Orleans LA 70115 Office: Montgomery and Richards 1410 1st Nat Bank Commerce Bldg New Orleans LA 70112

RICHARDS, MILDRED RUTH, health-care administrator; b. Sterling, Colo., Feb. 5, 1933; d. Frederick and Amalia Luft; student Northeastern Jr. Coll., U. No. Colo., St. Louis U., Colo. Women's Coll.; children—Valerie Jo Richards Hettinger, Renae Ruth Richards. Co-owner Fish's Profl. Pharmacy, Sterling, 1967-70; acct. Ceres Land & Cattle Co., Sterling, 1970-75; acct. Monfort of Colo., Greeley, 1975-77; adminstr. Meml. Hosp. of Greeley, 1977-84, also bd. dirs.; adminstr. Oakhurst Towers Adult Congregate Living Community, Denver, 1987—. Trustee, No. Colo. Osteo. Hosp. Found.: active disaster com. City of Greeley. Mem. Am. Hosp. Assn., Am. Osteo. Hosp. Assn. (trustee 1981—, com. small and rural hosps. 1981—, pres. 1982, 83, 84), Colo. Hosp. Assn., Colo. Osteo. Hosp. Assn. (sec.-treas. 1980-84), N. Central Colo. Hosp. Adminstrs. Council (pres. 1982), Larimer/Weld Counties Hosp. Planning Council, Colo. Small and Rural Hosp. Task Force, TONACK (Osteo.) Assn. (sec.-treas. 1982, v.p. 1983, pres. 1984), People to People Internat./AHA goodwill ambassador to Australia and N.Z. 1981), Greeley C. of C. (city improvement com. 1984)m contract negotiator, Devel. of Craig-Meeker, Colo. Health Care/Bus. Alliance and Preferred Physician Orgn., 1985-87); adminstr. Oakhurst Towers, Denver, 1987—, Phi Sigma Alpha. Lutheran. Contbr. articles to profl. publs.ha. Lutheran. Contbr. articles to profl. publs. Office: 8030 E Girard Ave Denver CO 80231

RICHARDS, PAMELA MOTTER, lawyer; b. Columbus, Ohio, Feb. 24, 1950; d. L. Clair and Mildred Jo (Williams) Motter; m. John W. Richards, II, Mar. 1, 1975 (div. 1984); children—Christine Elizabeth, Teresa Jo. B.A., DePauw U., 1972; J.D., Ohio No. U., 1975. Bar: Ga. 1975. Assoc., Cowart, Varner & Harrington, Warner Robins, Ga., 1977-82; ptnr. Cowart, Varner, Harrington & Richards, Warner Robins, 1982-83, Cowart, Varner & Richards, 1983-84; sole practice, Robins, 1984—. Bd. dirs., sec. Kids Stuff Learning Ctrs. of Am., Warner Robins, 1983—, Warner Robins Day Care Ctr., 1976-80, Am. Cancer Soc., 1981—; v.p. Warner Robins C. of C., 1981-82, dir., 1980-82; vice chmn. Hospice of Houston County, 1986-88. Mem. State Bar of Ga., Houston County Bar Assn., ABA, Houston County Assn. for Exceptional Children (bd. dirs. 1985-88, pres. 1986-87). Club: Civitan. Office: PO Box 3044 Warner Robins GA 31099

RICHARDS, RHODA ROOT WAGNER, civic worker; b. Phila., Oct. 2, 1917; d. Edward Stephen and Rhoda Earley (Root) Wagner; student U. Pa., 1937-39; A.A., Wildcliff Jr. Coll., 1938; m. J. Permar Richards, Jr., May 18, 1940; children—Patricia A.V. Richards Cosgrave, J. Permar III. Profl. artist; founder, chmn. Hosp. Corps, Navy League Service, 1941-43; chmn. ARC

Nurses Aide Corps, Jacksonville, Fla., 1944-45, Long Beach, Calif., 1945-46; founder, chmn. Fiesta Benefits, Hahnemann Hosp., 1950-57; former chmn. jr. com. Met. Opera; bd. dirs. Phila. Lyric Opera Co.; chmn. Ring for Freedom Republican Campaign of S.E. Pa., 1960; pres. Emergency Aid of Pa., 1961-64; v.p. bd. dirs. Inglis House, Phila., 1977-82; pres. women's bd. Phila. div. Am. Cancer Soc., 1978-81, hon. life mem.; founder, chmn. Community Activities Calendar, 1970-80; gen. chmn. 1st Ann. Washington Crossing Assembly, 1978; trustee Baldwin Sch.; co-chmn. fundraising com. Ambulatory Service Pavilion, Presbyn.-U. Pa. Med. Center; vice chmn. Women's Commn. for Bicentennial, 1976; bd. dirs., mem. Appleford Commn. Parsons-Banks Arboretum; bd. dirs. St. Johns Settlement House, 1954-86, Vol. Services for Blind, Phila. div. Am. Cancer Soc., 1978-86, Phila. chpt. Lupus Found., 1980-81; mem. Delaware Valley women's bd. Freedoms Found. at Valley Forge; past v.p. women's assn., past chmn. fin. com., chmn. centennial spl. event and gen. com. for the celebration Bryn Mawr Presbyn. Ch.; hon. col. corps of cadets Valley Forge Mil. Acad. and Jr. Coll.; founder, chmn. Rittenhouse Preservation Coalition, 1982—; v.p., asst. treas. Preservation Coalition of Greater Phila.; mem. Hospitality, Phila. Style; chmn. bd. dirs. Emergency Aid of Pa. Found. Recipient Crusade award Am. Cancer Soc., 1976; spl. award for community service St. John's Settlement House, 1977; Florence A. Sanson award for patriotism, 1986; named Disting. Dau. of Pa., 1985. Mem. Phila. Mus. Art, Pa. Acad. Fine Arts, Woodmere Art Gallery, Hahnemann Hosp. Women's Assn., DAR, Daus. of the Cincinnati, Dames of Loyal Legion, Nat. Soc. Colonial Dames of XVII Centuary, Dames Sovereign Mil. Order Temple of Jerusalem, Honolulu Mus. Art, Geneal. Soc. Pa., Am. Hist. Soc., Nat. Trust for Historic Preservation, Smithsonian Instn. Clubs: Sedgeley, Cosmopolitan, Peale, Safari, Bald Peak Colony. Home: 1250 Lafayette Rd PO Box 608 Bryn Mawr PA 19010

RICHARDS, SHIRLEY ELLEN, English language educator; b. Laconia, Ind., Sept. 18, 1935; d. Robert Jesse Shields and Helen (Langdon) Stapf; m. James Iven Richards, Mar. 27, 1954; children: Jeffrey Iven, Mark James. BSE, Ind. U., 1969, M Arts for Tchrs. in English, 1974. Tchr. English Bartholomew Con. Schs., Columbus, Ind., 1969-87, adv. com. gifted, talented, 1983-87; adj. faculty Eng. instr. Ind. U., Bloomington, 1983-86. Cavanaugh scholar Purdue U. Ind., 1967. Mem. NEA, Nat. Council Tchrs. English, Ind. State Tchrs. Assn., Ind. Tchrs. Writing, Columbus Educators Assn. Home and Office: 3371 Crescent Way Columbus IN 47203

RICHARDSON, BARBARA CONNELL, transportation research scientist; b. N.Y.C., Dec. 29, 1947; d. John Joseph and Joan Marie (Tobin) Connell; m. Rudy James Richardson, Aug. 23, 1970 (div. Dec. 1984); 1 child, Anne Elizabeth. BA, SUNY, 1969; SM, MIT, 1973; PhD, U. Mich., Ann Arbor, 1982. Programmer/analyst The Phys. Review, Upton, N.Y., 1969-70; transp. planner Mass. Exec. Office of Transp. and Constrn., Boston, 1973-74; transp. research officer Greater London Council, 1974-75; assoc. research scientist and dir. transp. planning and policy Univ. Mich., Ann Arbor, 1975-86; pres. Richardson Assocs., Inc., Ann Arbor, 1983—. Contbr. numerous articles on transp. to profl. jours. Mem. AAAS, Transp. Research Bd., Am. Assn. for Advancement Sci., Assn. Advancement Automotive Medicine, Soc. Automotive Engrs., Kappa Mu Epsilon, Signum Laudis, Sigma Xi. Roman Catholic. Office: 325 E Eisenhower Pkwy Suite 301 Ann Arbor MI 48108

RICHARDSON, BARBARA KATHRYN, social worker; b. Magnet Cove, Ark., Nov. 28, 1936; d. Fred Lee and Lillian Catherine (Adkins) R.; BA, Mary Hardin-Baylor U., 1961; MSW, Washington U., St. Louis, 1965. Cert. social worker. Sec., Dyke Bros., Little Rock, 1953-55; legal sec. Donalson, Bullard & Kucera, Dallas, 1955-57; pub. welfare worker Henderson County Pub. Welfare, Hendersonville, N.C., 1961-62; child welfare worker Tex. Dept. Pub. Welfare, Belton, 1962-63, adoption worker, Tyler, 1965-66, asst. dir. child welfare, Houston, 1966-69; dir. adoptions Hope Cottage Children's Bur., Dallas, 1970-74; dir. emergency-crisis unit Dallas County Mental Health-Mental Retardation, 1974-76; ednl. contract specialist, continuing edn. bur. Tex. Dept. Human Services, 1977-81, project developer Office Research, Demonstration and Eval., 1981-88, wellness specialist Personnel div., 1988—; Dem. precinct del., Dallas, 1972. Mem. Nat. Assn. Social Workers (state dir. 1974-75), Acad. Cert. Social Workers, Council on Social Work Edn. (ho. of dels. 1980-82), Tex. Pub. Employees Assn. Home: 719 A Harris Ave Austin TX 78705 Office: Tex Dept Human Services PO Box 2960 Austin TX 78769

RICHARDSON, BOBBI, interior designer, executive; b. Evansville, Ind., July 1, 1945; d. Julius John and Anna Louise (Griggs) Steinkamp; children—Amy Griggs Richardson, Michael Lawrence Richardson. Student Lockyear Bus. Coll., 1963, U. So. Ind., Ivy Tech. Coll., 1987—. Exec. sec. Citizens Nat. Bank, Evansville, Ind., 1964-69; legal sec. Newkirk, Keane, Kowalczyk & Leal, Ft. Wayne, Ind., 1971-72; sec. Mead Johnson & Co., Evansville, 1977-78; med. staff coordinator Deaconess Hosp., Evansville, 1978-85, cons., 1985-86; exec. dir. Share-In Care, Inc., Evansville, 1985; owner, pres. Bus. Interiors, Evansville, 1985—; cons. Builders' Spltys., Evansville, 1984—. Mem. Am. Entrepreneur Assn., Nat. Assn. Female Execs., Network of Evansville Women, Women in Networking (recorder, historian 1985-87, sec. 1985-87). Republican. Roman Catholic. Avocations: skiing, reading, travel. Home and Office: Bus Interiors 10110 Lindar Ln Evansville IN 47712

RICHARDSON, BRENDA, museum administrator; b. Howell, Mich., July 15, 1942; d. Robert Burr and Helen Isabel (Wright) R. B.A., U. Mich., 1964; M.A., U. Calif.-Berkeley, 1966. Curator, asst. dir. University Art Mus., Berkeley, 1964-75, Balt. Mus. Art, 1975—. Author exhbn. catalogues: Mel Bochner, 1976, Frank Stella, 1976, Barnett Newman, 1979, Bruce Nauman: Neons, 1982, Gilbert & George, 1984, Oskar Schlemmer, 1986, Scott Burton, 1986. Recipient Disting. Alumni Lectureship, U. Calif.-Berkeley, 1973. Office: Balt Mus Art Museum Dr Baltimore MD 21218

RICHARDSON, CAROL JOAN, pediatrician; b. San Angelo, Tex., July 6, 1944; d. Giles Otto and Noreen (Bailey) R. BA, U. Tex., 1966; MD, U. Tex., Galveston, 1970. Diplomate Am. Bd. Pediatrics, sub-bd. Neonatal-Perinatal Medicine. Intern U. Tex. Med. Br. at Galveston, 1970-71, resident in pediatrics, 1971-72; asst. prof. pediatrics Med. Br. U. Tex., Galveston, 1974-78, assoc. prof., 1978-83, prof. pediatrics, ob-gyn., 1983—. Contbr. numerous articles to profl. publs., 1972—. U. Calif. San Diego fellow, 1972-74. Mem. Am. Acad. Sci., So. Perinatal Assn., Tex. Med. Assn., Tex. Pediatric Soc., Tex. Perinatal Assn. (pres. 1978-79), Alpha Omega Alpha. Democrat. Methodist. Home: 514 16th St Galveston TX 77550 Office: U Tex Med Br Dept Pediatrics Galveston TX 77550

RICHARDSON, DONNA LYNN, librarian, infosystems specialist; b. Detroit, Sept. 6, 1950; d. Samuel Johnson and Agnes Demoris (Tondee) Lewis; m. Theodore John Richardson, July 28, 1973; children: Scott Lewis, Robyn Candice. BS, Drake U., 1970; MA, U. Mich., 1972. Tchr. Highland Park Schs., Mich., 1971; librarian Pitts. Pub. Schs., 1972-73; elem. dist. librarian Dist. 64, North Chgo., Ill., 1974-79; reference librarian Father Flanagan's Boys' Home, Boys' Town, Nebr., 1979-80; acting pub. services librarian Father Flanagan's Boy's Home, Boys Town, Nebr., 1980-81, asst. dir. pub. services, 1981-82, info. services mgr., 1983-87; mem. bd. dirs. Eastern Library System, Bellevue, Nebr., treas. 1984-86. Author: (book) Youth and Family Thesaurus, 1982, (book chapter) Youth Information Resources, 1987. Mem. Jr. League of Omaha, 1983—; bd. dirs. United Methodist Community Centers, Inc., Omaha, 1980-86. Mem. Special Libraries Assn. (Omaha area chpt. provisional pres. 1980-82, pres, 1982-83), Nebr. Online Users Group, Nebr. Library Assn., Am. Library Assn. Episcopalian. Home: 8342 Bennett Ave Skokie IL 60076

RICHARDSON, DOROTHY VIRGINIA, accountant; b. Bennington, Okla., Sept. 26, 1937; d. William Lycurgus and Mittie Mae (Richardson) Ray; student Eastern Okla. A&M, 1955-56; B.B.A., U. Alaska, 1974; m. Charles Howard Richardson, Dec. 28, 1958; children—Charles Timothy, Michael Todd. Asst. acct. Peat, Marwick, Mitchell & Co., Omaha, 1975-76; gen. acct. U. Alaska Statewide System, Fairbanks, 1976; asst. bus. mgr. Geophys. Inst., Fairbanks, 1976-77; dir. grant and contract services U. Alaska, Fairbanks, 1977-80; controller Alaska Legal Services Corp., Anchorage, 1980-81; bus. mgr. div. community colls., rural edn. and extension U. Alaska, Anchorage, 1981-83; assoc. controller U. Fla., Gainesville, 1983—. Active Cub Scouts, Mothers March of Dimes, PTA; pres. Alachua County Geneal. Soc., 1984-86, Am. Cancer Soc. Served with USAF, 1957-59. Mem. Am. Inst. C.P.A.s, Soc. Research Adminstrs., Council on Govtl. Relations, Nat. Council Univ. Research Adminstrs. Office: U Fla 120 Grinter Hall Gainesville FL 32611

RICHARDSON, ELIZABETH JONAS, corporate communications consultant; b. Norfolk, Va., June 1, 1954; d. Gordon E. and Mary Elizabeth (McGown) Jonas; m. Roger David Richardson, Sept. 9, 1978; children: Lauren Christine, Erin Elizabeth. BA, Randolph-Macon Coll., 1976; MA, U. Va., 1978. Asst. dir. capitol campaign St. Paul's Coll., Richmond, Va., 1978-79; asst. v.p., asst. corp. sec., dir. investor and stockholder relations Crestar Fin. Corp., Richmond, 1979-86; v.p. corp. communications Peter Wong Assocs., Richmond, 1986-87; cons. and copywriter Richmond, 1987—; lectr. NAOTC, Washington, 1985, Fin. World Mag., N.Y.C., 1986. Dir. Gateway Homes, Richmond, 1986-87. Office: 7325 Longview Ct Richmond VA 23225

RICHARDSON, EMILIE WHITE, manufacturing company executive, investment company executive, lecturer; b. Chattanooga, July 8; d. Emmett and Mildred Evelyn (Harbin) White; B.A., Wheaton Coll., 1951; 1 dau., Julie Richardson Morphis. With Christy Mfg. Co., Inc., Fayetteville, N.C., 1952—, sec. 1956-66, v.p., 1967-74, exec. v.p., 1975-79, pres., chief exec. officer, 1980—; v.p. E. White Investment Co., 1968-83, pres., 1983—; cons. Aerostatic Industries, 1979—; v.p. Gannon Corp., 1981—; cons. govt. contacts and offshore mfg., 1981—; lectr., speaker in field. Vice pres. public relations Ft. Lauderdale Symphony Soc., 1974-76, v.p. membership, 1976-77, adv. bd., 1978—; active Atlantic Found., Ft. Lauderdale Mus. Art, Beaux Arts, Freedoms Found.; mem. East Broward Women's Republican Club, 1968—, Americanism chmn., 1971-72. Mem. Internat. Platform Assn., Nat. Speakers Assn., Fla. Speakers Assn. Presbyterian. Clubs: Toastmasters, Green Valley Country. Home: 1531 NE 51st St Fort Lauderdale FL 33334 Office: 3311 Ft Bragg Rd Fayetteville NC 28303

RICHARDSON, FRANCES KATHRYN, nursing educator; b. Mt. Sterling, Ky., Jan. 24, 1924; d. Adlai Herman and Pearl Gladys (Ponder) R. BS in Nursing, Tex. Christian U., 1970; MS in Nursing, Tex. Woman's U., 1972. Head nurse St. Joseph's Hosp., Ft. Worth, Tex., 1968-71, clin. specialist, 1971-72; prof. nursing Tex. Christian U., Ft. Worth, 1972—; cons. Psychiatric Inst., Ft. Worth, 1975—, Oakgrove Residential Ctr., Ft. Worth, 1987. Mem. Am. Nurse Assn., Am. Psychol. Assn., Nat. League Nursing, Orthopsychiat. Assn. Democrat. Episcopalian. Home: 734 Oakwood Trail Fort Worth TX 76112

RICHARDSON, GWENDOLYN KELLY, educator; b. Phila., Apr. 3, 1932; d. William Henry and Harriet Mae (Lewis) K.; m. Jennings F. Richardson, July 9, 1955 (dec. May 1979); children: Alan, Annette R. Harris. BS, Pa. State U., 1952. Cert. elem. tchr., Pa. Tchr. Sch. Dist. Phila., 1952-85, Sch. Dist. Dallas, 1985-86; securities rep. First Investor's Corp., N.Y.C., 1987—. Vol. Goode for Mayor com., Phila., 1983; women's com. Dallas Theater Ctr. Mem. Phila. Fedn. Tchrs. (sch. rep. 1981-82), Classroom Tchrs. Dallas, Delta Sigma Theta. Home and Office: 3637 Markham Dr Bensalem PA 19020

RICHARDSON, HART MIDDLETON, computer programmer; b. Sumter, S.C., Dec. 28, 1943; d. Ellis Spear Middleton and Anne Hooe (Rust) Patteson; m. Thomas W. Richardson, Jan. 23, 1965; children: Amanda Hart, Elizabeth Anne. BA in Econs., Conn. Coll. for Women, 1964. Programmer trainee Am. Nat. Bank and Trust Co., Morristown, N.J., 1966-67, programmer, 1967-69; sr. programmer Somerset Trust Co., Somerville, N.J., 1969-72; programmer analyst First Nat. Bank Cen. Jersey, Somerville, 1972-73, S.T.C. Computer Services, Raritan, N.J., 1973-78; sr. cons. Vital Computer Resources, Trenton, N.J., 1978-85; sr. programmer, analyst Baker and Taylor Co., Bridgewater, N.J., 1985—. Treas. Pattenburg United Meth. Ch., N.J., 1985-88; active Union Twp. Hist. Soc., N.J., Hunterdon Art Ctr., Clinton, N.J., Clinton Hist. Mus. Republican. Home: RD 1 Box 610 Asbury NJ 08802 Office: Baker & Taylor 652 E Main St Bridgewater NJ 08807

RICHARDSON, JEAN MCGLENN, civil engineer; b. Everett, Wash., Nov. 15, 1927; d. Clayton Charles and Marie Elizabeth (Mellish) McGlenn; BSCE, Oreg. State U., 1949; registered profl. engr., Ala., Oreg.; m. William York Richardson, II, June 11, 1949; children: William York III, Paul Kress II, Clayton McGlenn. Engr., Walter Schoel Engring. Co., Birmingham, Ala., 1950-54; office engr. G.C. McKinney Engring. Co., San Jose, Calif., 1972-74; civil design leader Harland Bartholomew & Assocs., Birmingham, 1974-78, Rust Engring. Co., Birmingham, 1978-82; owner, prin. Jean Richardson and Assocs. Inc., 1983-88; cons. engrs. Rust Internat. Corp., 1988—; FEMA, 1988—; women's engring. del. to China and USSR, Sept. 1984; counselor to female students on engring. as a career; regional chmn. Mathcounts, 1986-88; math. vol. pub. schs. Mem. NSPE, Soc. Women Engrs. (sr. sect. rep. to nat. bd.), Ala. Soc. Profl. Engrs. (pres. Birmingham br.), Alpha Phi. Republican. Episcopalian. Clubs: Inverness Country, Women's Golf Assn. Office: 1905 Indian Lake Dr Suite 3 Birmingham AL 35244

RICHARDSON, JENNIFER JANE GOODE, musician, social worker; b. LaGrange, Ga., Sept. 3, 1951; d. Thomas Earle and Jane (Mitcham) Williams; m Larry Allen Goode, March 17, 1973 (div. 1980); m. Alan Wayne Richardson, Oct. 5, 1985. MusB, Ga. State U., 1973, MusM, 1977; MSW, U. Ga., 1981. Lic. clin. social worker, music tchr., Ga. Mus. therapist Peachtree-Parkwood Hosp., Atlanta, 1977-80; intern psychotherapy Jewish Family Services, Atlanta, 1981; psychiatric social worker West Paces Ferry Hosp., Atlanta, 1982; rehab. counselor Shepherd Spinal Ctr., Atlanta, 1983-85; pvt. practice psychotherapy Ctr. For Psychiatry, Smyrna, Ga., 1985—, Brawner Psych. Inst., Smyrna, 1985-87, Phoenix, 1987—; alto singer Oakhurst Choir. Decatur, Ga., 1969-80, Third Ave. Consort, Decatur, 1978-84, Atlanta Bach Choir, 1983-84, Atlanta Vocal Consort, 1984—, All Saints Episcopal Ch. Choir, Atlanta, 1983—; alto, tenor Master Arts Sacred Singers, Atlanta, 1985—; flutist Prevailing Winds Quintet, Atlanta, 1978-80, Atlanta-Emory Orch.; ptnr. Holm, Richardson and Assocs., Atlanta, 1985—. Editor: (lit. mag.) Kudzu Revue, 1981—; contbr. article to book: J.S. Bach, 1984; feature writer Bond Community Star, Atlanta, 1979— (Community Service award 1987); contbr. articles to profl. mags., 1984-85. Mem. Appalachian Trail Conf., Harpers Ferry W.Va., 1969-79, Candler Park Neighborhood Assn., Atlanta, 1973—. Recipient John Philip Sousa award Druid Hills Band, 1969. Mem. Acad. Cert. Social Workers, Ga. Soc. Clin. Social Workers, Am. Fed. Musicians. Democrat. Episcopalian. Clubs: Caution.

RICHARDSON, KATHRYN E., quality assurance professional; b. Rochester, N.Y., July 18, 1945; d. Lyle and Christine Dietrich (Shaylor) Kingsley; m. Ronald James Richardson. BS in Chemistry, Rochester Inst. Tech., 1967. Chemistry technologist Rochester (N.Y.) Gen. Hosp., 1966-69, 1969-70, supr. clin. chemistry, 1971-79; chemistry technologist Petersburg (Va.) Gen. Hosp., 1969, M.S. Hersey (Pa.) Med. Ctr., 1971; supr. CMX Labs., Rochester, 1979-80; with customer quality assessment Eastman Kodak Co., Rochester, 1981—. Recipient Wm. Cornwell Challenge Trophy Soc. for Tech. Communications, 1984. Mem. Rochester Hosp. Assn. for Clin. Chemistry, Am. Soc. Clin. Pathologists (cert.). Episcopalian. Home: 3317 St Paul Blvd Rochester NY 14617

RICHARDSON, LYNN KAREN, lawyer; b. Trenton, N.J., Oct. 31, 1953; d. John and Joan Mae (Duenger) Richardson. B.A., Franklin and Marshall Coll., Lancaster, Pa., 1971-74; M.A., U. Tex. Med. Br.-Galveston, 1974-78; J.D., So. Tex. Coll. Law., Houston, 1976-80. Bar: Mich. 1980, U.S. Dist. Ct. (ea. dist.) Mich., 1981, U.S. Dist. Ct. (no. dist.) Calif. 1984, U.S. Ct. Appeals (6th cir.) 1981, U.S. Ct. Appeals (9th cir.) 1984, U.S. Dist. Ct. (we. dist.) Mich., 1987. Research asst. Rice U., Houston, 1976-78; research assoc. U. Mich. Sch. Pub. Health, Ann Arbor, Mich., 1980, cons. 1982; jud. law clk. U.S. Dist. Ct., Detroit, 1981-82; asst. U.S. Atty. U.S. Atty.'s Office, Detroit, 1982-84, San Francisco, 1984-87; instr. Atty. Gen.'s Adv. Inst., Washington, 1984-87; assoc. Foster, Swift, Collins & Coey, P.C., Lansing, Mich., 1987—. Author govt. documents, 1975, 80; contbr. articles to profl. jours. Mem. State Bar Assn. Mich., ABA, Fed. Bar Assn. Democrat. Presbyterian. Office: Foster Swift Collins & Coey PC 313 S Washington Sq Lansing MI 48933

RICHARDSON, MARGARET ANNE, financial administrator; b. Wichita, Kans., Oct. 3, 1923; d. Joseph John and Cecilia Mary (Switlik) Schermuly; m. Walter Leon Richardson, June 16, 1946 (dec. 1965); children: Marcia, Michael, Patrick, Anne, David, Theresa. BS in Bus. Adminstrn., Wichita State U., 1944. Staff acct. Main Hurdman, CPAs, Wichita, 1960-75; sr. acct. George V. Landis, CPA, Wichita, 1975-79; spl. projects St. Joseph Med. Ctr., Wichita, 1979-83, dir. reimbursement, 1983—. Past pres. Kans. Chpt. Arthritis Found., Wichita, mem. exec. com., 1975—; nat. trustee Arthritis Found., 1984-85, chair audit com., 1983-84. Mem. Healthcare Internal Audit Group (co-founder), Am. Inst. CPA's, Kans. Soc. CPA's, Am. Woman's Soc. CPA's, Am. Soc. Women Accts. (charter Wichita chpt.). Democrat. Roman Catholic. Home: 4022 E Morris Wichita KS 67218

RICHARDSON, MARILYN GOFF, small business owner, artist; b. Taunton, Mass., Sept. 9, 1934; d. Laurence Warren and Beatrice Cornelia (Rogers) Goff; m. Winthrop Horton Richardson Jr., July 18, 1959; children: Keith Warren, Kendra Lee. BFA, Boston U., 1956; MS, Cen. Conn. U., 1965. Cert. elem., secondary edn. tchr., Conn. Art tchr. New Britain (Conn.) Pub. Schs., 1956-63; elem. tchr. Lakeview Sch. Dist., San Angelo, Tex., 1959-60; prin. Wickettwood Arts & Graphs, Coventry, Conn., 1980—. Graphic artist: Bicentennial Cookbook, 1976, Plan of Development, 1978, Recipes from Coventry's First 275 Years, 1987, Exclusively Rhubard Cookbook, 1988; works exhibited in galleries in Taos, N.Mex., Nat. Juried Show, Women Art, 1985, Springfield, Chicopee, and Falmouth, Mass., Hartford, Glastonbury, Willimantic, and Manchester, Conn., and N.Y.C.; one-woman-shows at Casey-Greene Gallery, Willimantic, 1986, The Artery, Ellington, Conn., 1986, Gallery 24, Conn. Pub. TV, Hartford, 1988. Sec., vice chmn. Coventry Zoning bd. appeals, 1969-74; chmn. Coventry Planning and Zoning Commn., 1974-80; adv. com., supply chmn. Children's Sch. Sci., Woods Hole, Mass., 1976-81; com. mem. Booth and Dimock Meml. Library, Coventry, 1982-83; mem. Falmouth Art Guild, 1982-87, Glastonbury Art Assn., 1985—, Springfield Art Assn., 1985—, Windham Regional Arts Council, 1986—; organizing mem. Coventry Arts Commn., 1986—. Mem. AAUW (membership com. Storrs-Willimantic chpt. 1977-79, cultural com. 1985-87), Ct. Guild Craftsmen, Nat. Soc. Tole & Decorative Painters, Inc. Republican. Protestant. Home and Office: 252 Wrights Mill Rd Coventry CT 06238

RICHARDSON, MARILYN JO, mortgage company executive; b. Muncie, Ind., Apr. 20, 1947; d. Rudy Berryman and Vera Lavonne (Smedley) Weyland; m. Willie Caldwell Frazier, Feb. 18, 1974 (div. 1979); children—Kristi Irene, Jason Caldwell; m. George Emerson Richardson, Jr., Sept. 17, 1983; stepchildren—Stuart, Joyce, Judy. With Nat. First Mortage, Anaheim, Calif., 1967-71; processing supr. Mason-McDuffie So. Calif., Santa Ana, 1971-74; adminstrn. mgr. Mason-McDuffie, Berkeley, Calif., 1974-78, ptnr., 1978-82; chief adminstrn. officer Mason-McDuffie Mortgage Corp., Walnut Creek, Calif., 1982-83, chief operating officer, 1983—. Named Boss of Yr., Assn. Profl. Women No. Calif., 1984. Mem. Mortgage Assn. Am. Avocations: reading; horseback riding. Office: 141 Regent Pl Alamo CA 94507

RICHARDSON, MARTHA, nutrition analyst; b. Noble, La., Apr. 22, 1917; d. Alexander M. and Olive (Barlow) R.; A.B., U. Mo., 1938, Ph.D., 1953; M.S., Kans. State U., 1939. Dietitian, William Newton Meml. Hosp., Winfield, Kans., 1940-42, Molly Stark Sanatorium, Canton, Ohio, 1942-47; asst. dir. residence halls, instr. home econs. U. Mo., 1947-50, instr. home econs., 1951-53; head of foods and nutrition U. Utah, 1953-55; nutrition analyst Agrl. Research Service, Washington, 1955-80. Named Disting. Alumna, U. Mo., 1968. Fellow AAAS; mem. Am. Dietetic Assn., Am. Home Econs. Assn., Am. Med. Writers Assn., Am. Inst. Food Techologists, Am. Chem. Soc. Am. Assn. Cereal Chemists, Am. Forestry Assn., AAUW, N.Y. Acad. Scis., Sigma Xi, Gamma Sigma Delta, Phi Upsilon Omicron, Sigma Delta Epsilon. Contbr. articles to profl. jours. Home: 403 Russell Ave #309 Gaithersburg MD 20877

RICHARDSON, MARY ELEANORE BRZEZICKI, manufacturing company executive; b. Pittsfield, Pa., Mar. 13, 1932; d. Joseph E. and Eleanore Victoria (Battko) Bosko; student Kans. State U., Manhattan, 1952-53, Rosary Hill Coll., Buffalo, 1972, U. Pitts., 1978-79; m. Robert Edward Brzezicki, June 2, 1956 (div. Feb. 1974); children—Michael Joseph, Suzanne Marie; m. 2d, Carl Lindsey Richardson, July 9, 1983. Various secretarial positions, 1956-59, 75; engaged in real estate sales, 1972-74; freelance community corr. Buffalo Evening News, 1972-74; exec. sec. to pres. and chief exec. officer, editor corp. newsletter Struthers Wells Corp., Warren, Pa., 1975-83; owner M.E. Brzezicki Enterprises, Volant, Pa., 1983—; Warren County corr. Erie Times News, 1981-83. Exec. bd. West Falls (N.Y.) Sch. Assn., 1969-72, 2d v.p., public relations chmn. East Aurora (N.Y.) Middle Sch. Assn., 1972-73; pres. New Horizons, Warren, 1977, 80-82; bd. dirs. Warren YWCA, 1982-83. Mem. Warren Bus. and Profl. Women's Club (pres. 1982-83, Woman of Year award 1982-83), Pa. Assn. Notaries, Kappa Delta. Republican. Roman Catholic. Home and Office: RD 2 Box 122A McNulty Rd Volant PA 16156

RICHARDSON, MIDGE TURK, magazine editor; b. Los Angeles, Mar. 26, 1930; d. Charles Aloysius and Marie Theresa (Lindekin) Turk; m. Hamilton Farrar Richardson, Feb. 8, 1974. B.A., Immaculate Heart Coll., Los Angeles, 1951, M.A., 1956; postgrad., U. Calif., Santa Barbara, Duquesne U., U. Pitts. Mem. Immaculate Heart Community, Roman Catholic Ch., 1948-66; asst. to dean Sch. Arts, NYU, 1966-67; coll. editor Glamour mag., N.Y.C., 1967-74; editor-in-chief Co-Ed mag.; also editorial dir. Forecast and Co-Ed mags., N.Y.C., 1974-75; editor-in-chief Seventeen mag., N.Y.C., 1975-88; group editor-in-chief Seventeen Mag and Good Food Mag., N.Y.C., 1988—; lectr. Tishman seminars Hunter Coll., N.Y.C., 1975-77. Host, guest TV and radio programs.; Author: The Buried Life: A Nun's Journey, 1971, Gordon Parks: A Biography for Children, 1971; also articles. Bd. dirs. YMCA, N.Y.C., 1972-73, Timothy Dwight Sch., 1979-83, Girl Scout council Greater N.Y., 1979-82; life trustee Internat. House. Recipient award Outstanding Women in Pub., 1982. Mem. Am. Soc. Mag. Editors (exec. com.), Fashion Group, Women's Forum Inc. Democrat. Clubs: River, Meadow; Beach (Palm Beach). Home: 1515 S Flagler Dr West Palm Beach FL 33401 Office: Seventeen Mag 850 3rd Ave New York NY 10022

RICHARDSON, NANCY JO, nurse; b. Crawfordsville, Ind., Feb. 27, 1951; d. John E. Kenny and Helen L. (Tinder) Bahls; m. Phillip M. Benner, Aug. 23, 1969 (div. 1974); 1 child, Phillip J.; m. Richard L. Richardson, Dec. 12, 1981 (div. Jan. 1988); 1 child, April Joy; stepchildren: Brandy N., Steven L. A of Applied Sci., Parkland Coll., 1979. Registered profl. nurse. Nurses aide Douglas Nightingale Manor, Tuscola, Ill., 1969-71, dir. nurses, 1979-87; sec., bookkeeper John Kenny Constrn. Co., Champaign, Ill., 1972-79; dir. nurses Greenbrier Nursing Ctr., Champaign, 1987—; mem. adv. council Attorney Gen. Neil Hartigan's Nursing Home, 1987; mem. nursing adv. bd. Parkland Coll., 1987. Tchr. Sunday sch. Tuscola United Meth. Ch., 1986-87; leader 4-H, Camargo,Ill., 1970-74; instr. CPR Am. Heart Assn., Decatur, Ill., 1986—. Mem. Nat. Assn. Female Execs., Douglas County Bus. and Profl. Women (pres. 1986-87), Cen. Ill. Dir. Nursing Forum (organizer, pres. 1986—). Avocations: writing, reading, movies. Home: RR4 Tuscola IL 61953 Office: Greenbrier Nursing Ctr 1915 S Mattis Champaign IL 61953

RICHARDSON, RUTH DELENE, business educator; b. New Orleans, May 27, 1942; s. Daniel Edgar and Allie Myrtle (Skinner) R.; 1 child, John Daniel. B.S., Mars Hill Coll., 1965; M.S., U. Tenn., Knoxville, 1968, Ed.D. (EPDA fellow), 1974. Tchr., LaFollette (Tenn) High Sch., 1965-66; instr. Clinch Valley Coll., Wise, Va., 1967-68, U. S.C., Union, 1968-69, Tenn. Wesleyan Coll., Athens, 1969-71, Roane State Community Coll., Harriman, Tenn., 1971-73; assoc. prof., chmn. dept. bus. edn. and office adminstrn. Ala. State U., Montgomery, 1974-75; assoc. prof. U. South Ala., Mobile, 1975-80; assoc. prof. adminstrv. office services U. North Ala., Florence, 1980—; cons. career edn.; employment tester. Mem. Assn. for Bus. Communication, Nat. Bus. Edn. Assn., Ala. Friends Adoption, Profl. Secs. Internat., Delta Pi Epsilon, Omicron Tau Theta, Phi Delta Kappa, Pi Lambda Theta, Pi Omega Pi. Lutheran. Contbr. articles to profl. jours. Home: 213 Westmeade Ct Florence AL 35630 Office: U N Ala Box 5180 Florence AL 35632

RICHARDSON, RUTH GREENE, social worker; b. Washington, Mar. 30, 1926; d. Arthur Alonzo and Ruth Naomi (Conway) Greene; B.S., St. Louis U., 1948; M.S.W., Washington U., St. Louis, 1950; m. Frederick D. Richardson, June 7, 1968; 1 son, Arthur William. Exec. dir. Anna B.

Heldman Community Center, Pitts., 1962-64; assoc. dir. Hillhouse Assn., Pitts., 1964-67; assoc. dir. Dixwell House, also supr. group work services in community schs., New Haven, 1967-69; exec. dir. Three Rivers Youth Inc., Pitts., 1969—; adv. bd. Sch. Social Work, U. Pitts., 1979-80; pres. Assn. Residential Youth Care Agys., 1973-77; pres., bd. dirs. Pa. Council Vol. Child Care Agys., 1973-78; asst. v.p. Allegheny Children and Youth Services Council, 1974-76; bd. dirs. Children's Council Western Pa.; adv. council Booth Home; bd. dirs. Nat. Assn. Homes for Children, Campfire Boys and Girls, 1988. Recipient Social Assistance award Pitts. region Women's Am. ORT, 1975, Internat. Yr. of Child award region III, HEW, 1979; Jurors award Images I Pitts. Black Artists William Pitt Uniom Gallery U. Pitts, 1986. Mem. Child Welfare League Am. (co-chmn. eastern region), Nat. Assn. Social Workers, Midwest Watercolor Soc., Pa. Soc. Watercolor Painters, Black Adminstrs. in Child Welfare, Creative Lens, Visions (v.p.). Presbyterian. Paintings exhbited in Pitts. region. Home: 641 Robinwood Dr Pittsburgh PA 15216 Office: 2039 Termon Ave Pittsburgh PA 15212

RICHARDSON, SHIRLEY MAXINE, newspaper editor; b. Rising Sun, Ind., May 3, 1931; d. William Fenton and Mary (Phillips) Keith; m. Arthur Lee Richardson, Feb. 11, 1950; children—Mary Jane Hamm, JoDee Mayfield, Steven Lee Richardson. Personnel mgr. Mayhill Pubs., Knightstown, Ind., 1967-87, prodn. mgr., 1975-87, editor, 1967-87; info. staff, assoc. editor Ind. Farm Bur., Inc., 1987—. Mem. Newspaper Farm Editors of Am., Am. Agrl. Editors' Assn., Profl. Journalists of Am. Republican. Avocations: traveling; reading; boating; quilting. Home: 366 E Carey St Knightstown IN 46148 Office: 130 E Washington St Indianapolis IN 46206

RICHARDSON-FORBES, HELEN HILDA, state agency administrator; b. Detroit, July 26, 1950; d. Henry and L. Trunetta (Adams) Forbes; m. Leon Richardson (div.); 1 child, Leon Ronald Jr. BA in Edn., Human Services, U. Detroit, 1972. Cert. tchr. Mich. Substitute tchr. Detroit Bd. Edn., 1972-75; assistance payment worker State Dept. Social Services, Detroit, 1976-79; supr. assistance payment St. Dept. Social Services, Detroit, 1979-85, section mgr., 1985—; Mem. case rev. com. Mich. Dept. Social Services Gen. Assistance, 1985, 87, labor relations subcom.; mem. tng. com. Quality Initiative Task Force, Wayne County Dept. Social Services, 1984, co-chairperson task force, 1987; mem. UAW Secondary Contract Negotiations Team, 1988; mem. conf. planning com. Mich. County Social Services Assn., 1988. Coordinator Social Service United Found. Dr., Lafayette local office 1985, Social Service Black United Fund Dr. 1987, speaker Nat. Polit. Congress Black Women, 1986. Spirit of Detroit Leadership award, 1985. Mem. NOW, Am. Pub. Welfare Assn. (planning com. 1986), Nat. Assn. Female Execs. Baptist. Office: MI Dept Social Services 17330 Greydale Detroit MI 48219

RICHART, VICTORIA BETTY, agency administrator; b. N.Y.C., Nov. 1, 1937; d. Francisco Richart Cervera and Victoria (Pla Carbonell) de Richart. BA, Marymount Coll., 1960; MA, MEd, Columbia U., N.Y.C., 1979, EdD, 1982. Asst. Quaker Oats Co., N.Y.C., 1960-61; adminstr. Careers Inc., N.Y.C., 1961-63; tchr. Pub. and Pvt. Schs., N.Y. and Mex., 1963-69; sr. project assoc. Columbia U., N.Y.C., 1979-80; dir. N.H. Dept. of Edn., 1980-85; mgmt. tng. dir. Bd. of Edn. Personnel, N.Y.C., 1985-87; exec. dir. N.Y.C. Human Resource Adminstrn., 1987—; bd. dirs. Tri-Equity, Inc., Concord, N.H. Mem. Wall St. chpt. of Image, N.Y.C., 1986—. Mem. Nat. Assn. of Female Execs., Assn. for the Advancement of Internat. Edn., P.R. Educators Assn., Nat. Coalition for Sex Equity in Edn. (steering com. 1983-86), YWCA (action audit com.), Nat. Assn. Bilingual Edn., NAACP, Am. Edn. Research Adminstrn. (presentee 1983), N.H. State Bd. of Edn. (equity com. 1981-82). Home: 12 E 86th St New York NY 10028

RICHEL-SHELDON, DARLEEN MARIE, educator; b. St. Maries, Idaho, Jan. 18, 1940; d. Herbert James and Lila May (Loe) Richel; m. Clair Miller Sheldon, June 7, 1957; 1 child, Sharon LaMoyne. AA, North Idaho Coll., 1968; BS, U. Idaho, 1975, MEd in Spl. Edn., 1980. Cert. tchr., Idaho. Substitute tchr. Worley (Idaho) Pub. Schs., 1965-75, Western Benewah Pub. Sch., Plummer, Idaho, 1970-75; elem. tchr. Coeur d'Alene Indian Tribal Sch., DeSmet, Idaho, 1975—. Writer two local papers, 1968-86. Vol. telephone and mailing Kootenai County Dem. Office, Coeur d'Alene, Idaho, 1986; co-founder women's commn., Kootenai County, 1978—; mem. library commn., Kootenai County, 1986—. Mem. AAUW (telephone tree 1986—), Alpha Delta Kappa (v.p. 1984-86, pres., rec. sec. 1986—). Lodge: Grange (sec. 1963-86). Home: 1001 Emma Ave #305 Coeur d'Alene ID 83814

RICHENDOLLAR, ELIZABETH ANN, educator; b. Marion, Ohio, Apr. 27, 1946; d. Thomas Isaac and Ruth Elizabeth (Douce) Norton; m. Tommy Joe Richendollar, June 20, 1970; children: Tracie Joanne, Rebecca Renee. BS in Edn., Bowling Green (Ohio) State U., 1968. Tchr. Mt. Vernon (Ohio) City Schs., 1968-70, North Union Schs., Richwood, Ohio, 1970-72, St. Mary Sch., Marion, 1973-83, Fairmont (W.Va.) Cath. Grade Sch., 1983-86, Marion County Schs., Fairmont, 1986—. Republican. Methodist. Office: Rich-n-Vision Optical 710 Locust Ave Fairmont WV 26554

RICHEY, DOROTHY LOUISE, physical education educator; b. Mobile, Ala., Oct. 1, 1943; d. Oscar and Adeline (Morris) Richey. BS, Tuskegee Inst., 1966; MS, Ind. State U.-Terre Haute, 1967; EdD, Nova U., 1979. Instr., coach Ind. State U., 1968-72; coordination recreation, instr. Chgo. State U., 1972-74, asst. dir. athletics, 1973-74, dir. athletics, 1974-77; prof. phys. edn. Community Coll. of Allegheny County, W. Mifflin, Pa., 1978-87; asst. prof. Slippery Rock U., 1987—; ofcl. Caffifesta Games, Barbados, W.I., 1982; asst. Women's Olympic Tng. Camp, U. Ill.-Champaign, 1972; to be mgr. U.S. Olympic Festival, Durham, N.C., 1987; ofcl. USA Can. Women's Track and Field Meet, U. Ill.-Champaign, 1972, numerous other meets, competitions; mem. U.S. Olympic Com. on Coaches Edn., 1984—; lectr. in field; del. to Athletic Congress, 1980—, mem. budget and audit and records coms. Mem. Women's Track and Field Coaches Assn., Eastern Dist. Assn. Health, Phys. Edn., Recreation and Dance, Am. and Pa. Assns. Health, Phys. Edn., Recreation and Dance, Nat. Assn. Female Execs., Nat. Assn. Girls and Women in Sport (pres. 1985—), Eastern Assn. Phys. Edn. Coll. Women, Nova U. Alumni Assn., Tuskegee U. Alumni Assn., YWCA (devel. Total Woman Lifestyle Concept Program, 1988, del. U.S. Olympic Com. Ho. of Dels., del. The Athletic Congress), Nat. Women in Sport Day, Zeta Phi Beta, Delta Psi Kappa. Address: PO Box 99973 Pittsburgh PA 15233

RICHEY THIEL, VALERIE LYNNE, science administrator; b. Lawton, Okla., June 29, 1959; d. Eugene Charles and LaVerne (Bazilwich) Richey. BS cum laude in Chem. Engring., Va. Poly. Inst., 1981; MS summa cum laude in Chem. Engring., U. Tex., 1983; postgrad., U. Dayton. Assoc. technician Atlantic Research, Alexandria, Va., summer 1977; lab. technician Frederick Cancer Research Ctr., Frederick, Md., summer 1979; staff process engr. Mead Johnson, Evansville, Ind., 1983-84, 85-86, supr. prodn., 1984-85; mgr. prodn. Adria Labs., Columbus, Ohio, 1986—; speaker, coordinator Leadership Seminar Adria Labs., Columbus, 1986, Metric Seminar Adria Labs., Columbus, 1988. Vol. Big Bros.-Big Sisters, Evansville, 1983-84; mem. Humane Soc., Columbus, 1987—, Columbus Zoo, 1987—. Marshall Hahn Engring. Merit scholar Va. Poly. Inst. and State U., 1977-81. Mem. Am. Inst. Chem. Engrs., Soc. Mfg. Engrs., Am. Pharm. Assn., Tau Beta Pi, Phi Kappa Phi. Methodist. Home: 3678 Killington Ct Columbus OH 43220 Office: Adria Labs PO Box 16529 Columbus OH 43216

RICHISON, SHIRLEY HELTON, recreation sciences educator; b. Ft. Chaffee, Ark., Dec. 31, 1954; d. James Edward and Virginia (Holland) Helton; m. Joe Ray Richison III, Feb. 14, 1986. BS, Ark. Tech. U., 1977; MEd in Recreation, U. Ark., 1980, EdD in Leisure Scis., 1986. Program coordinator Ft. Smith (Ark.) Girls Club, 1977-79, asst. dir., 1980-84, aquatics dir., 1986; loan closer Surety Title/Cen. Mortgage, Ft. Smith, 1980; therapeutic recreation specialist Sparks Hosp. Psychiat. Ward, Ft. Smith, 1986; instr. Ark. Tech. U., Russellville, 1986, U. N.C., Greensboro, 1987—; cons. Gifted Eyes Leadership Program, Ft. Smith, 1985. Vol. Spl. Olympics, Fayetteville, Ark., 1986; chair Spookaree Cub Scouts, Russellville, Ark, 1986; face painter Old Fort River Festival, 1980-86; tng. leader Sebastian Co. Col. Coaches, Ft. Smith, 1984. Named one of Outstanding Young Woman in Am, 1986; recipient 500 Hr. Outstanding Vol. award ARC, 1983, Nat. Sports Found. Wonder Woman award, 1983. Mem. Nat. Recreation and Parks Assn., World Leisure and Recreation Assn., Nat. Female Execs., Bus. Profl. Women (Young Career Woman 1983-84), N.C. Recreation and Park Soc., World Leisure and Recreation Assn., Nat. Female Execs., Nat. Recreation and Parks Assn., Resort and Comml. Recreation Assn.

RICHMAN, GERTRUDE GROSS (MRS. BERNARD RICHMAN), civic worker; b. N.Y.C., May 16, 1908; d. Samuel and Sarah Yetta (Seltzer) Gross; B.S., Tchrs. Coll. Columbia U., 1948, M.A., 1949; m. Bernard Richman, Apr. 5, 1930; children—David, Susan. Vol. worker Hackensack Hosp., 1948-70; mem. bd. dirs. YM-YWHA, Bergen County, N.J., 1950-75, bd. mem. emeritus, 1975—; chmn. Leonia Friends of Bergen County Mental Health Consultation Center, 1959; founder, hon. pres. Bergen County Serv-A-Com., affiliated with women orgns. Div. Nat. Jewish Welfare Bd.; v.p. N.J. sect. Nat. Jewish Welfare Bd., 1964-71; hon. trustee women's div. Bergen County United Jewish Community; mem. adv. council Bergen County Office on Aging, 1968-83, reappointed, 1984—; mem. Hackensack Bd. Edn., 1946-51; mem. pub. relations com. Leonia Pub. Schs., 1957-58; N.J. del. White House Conf. on Aging, 1971; trustee Mary McLeod Bethune Scholarship Fund; v.p. Bergen County nat. women's com. Brandeis U., 1966-67. Recipient citation Nat. Council Jewish Women and YWCA in Bergen County, 1962; citation Nat. Jewish Welfare Bd., 1964, Harry S. Feller award N.J. Region, 1965; 14th Ann. Good Scout award Bergen county council Boy Scouts Am., 1977; Woman Vol. of Distinction, Bergen County council Girl Scouts, 1979; Human Relations award Bergen County sect. Nat. Council Negro Women, 1982; honored at testimonial United Jewish Community Bergen County, 1987. Mem. Kappa Delta Pi.

RICHMAN, JOAN F., television company executive; b. St. Louis, Apr. 10, 1939; d. Stanley M. and Barbara (Friedman) R. B.A., Wellesley (Mass.) Coll., 1961. Asst. producer WNDT, N.Y.C., 1964-65; researcher CBS News, N.Y.C., 1961-64; researcher spl. events unit CBS News, 1965-67; mgr. research CBS News (Rep. and Dem. nat. convs.), 1968; assoc. producer CBS News, 1968, producer spl. events, 1969-72; sr. producer The Reasoner Report, ABC News, 1972-75; exec. producer CBS Sports Spectacular, 1975-76; exec. producer weekend broadcasts CBS News, 1976-81, v.p., dir. spl. events, 1982-87, v.p. news coverage, 1987—. Recipient Nat. TV Acad. Arts and Scis. Emmy award for CBS News space coverage, 1970-71, 71-72; Alumnae Achievement award Wellesley Coll., 1973. Mem. Nat. Acad. TV Arts and Scis., Council on Fgn. Relations, Wellesley Coll. Alumnae Assn. (pres. class of 1961, 1966-70). Home: 133 W 81st St New York NY 10024 Office: CBS News 524 W 57th St New York NY 10019

RICHMAN, PHYLLIS CHASANOW, newspaper editor; b. Washington, Mar. 21, 1939; d. Abraham and Helen (Lieberman) C.; m. Alvin Richman, June 5, 1960 (div. 1984); children—Joseph, Matthew, Libby. B.A., Brandeis U., 1961; postgrad., U. Pa., 1961-63, Purdue U., 1966-70. Restaurant critic Washington Post, 1976—, exec. food editor, 1980—. Author: Barter, 1976, Best Restaurants, 1980, 82, 85. Mem. Washington Ind. Writers (adv. bd.), Nat. Press Club, Les Dames D'Escoffier (bd. dirs.). Home: 2118 O St NW Washington DC 20037 Office: Washington Post 1150 15th St NW Washington DC 20071

RICHMAN, SELMA, microbiologist; b. Bklyn.; d. Joseph and Leah (Kennis) R. B.S., Bklyn. Coll.; M.A., Cen. Mich. U., 1979. Successively lab. technician Queens Gen. Hosp., Jamaica, N.Y.; jr. microbiologist Cumberland Hosp., Bklyn.; asst microbiologist Queens Hosp. Ctr., Jamaica; prin. microbiologist Coney Island Hosp., Bklyn., 1965—; lectr. Scientists in Sch. program N.Y. Acad. Scis.; cons. in field. Author: Case Study on Aeromonas Hydrophila, 1982. Mem. Am. Soc. Clin. Pathologists, Am. Soc. Microbiology, Med. Mycology Soc. Am., Nat. Assn. Female Execs. Avocations: knitting; tennis; racquetball; swimming; music. Office: Coney Island Hosp 2601 Ocean Pkwy Brooklyn NY 11235

RICHMAN, VICTORIA S., real estate consultant; b. Boston, June 21, 1959; d. Justin Lewis and Susan (Kadison) R. BA, Brown U., 1981; MBA, U. Pa., 1985. Lic. in real estate sales. Pvt. investigator Pinkerton Security Service, Boston and Providence, R.I., 1980-81; bus. analyst Hibernia Nat. Bank, New Orleans, 1981-83; hotel real estate cons. Stephen W. Brener Assocs., Inc., N.Y.C., 1985—; sponsor's rep. Ann. Hospitality Investment Conf., N.Y.C., 1985—. Interviewer nat. alumni sch. program Brown U., New Orleans and N.Y.C., 1981—. Mem. Nat. Assn. Female Execs., Ednl. Inst. of Am. Hotel and Motel Assn. Clubs: Brown, Wharton (N.Y.C.).

RICHMOND, PHYLLIS ALLEN, library and information science educator; b. Boston, Jan. 5, 1921; d. Charles Francis Hitchcock and Alberta (Currie) Allen; m. James Hugh Richmond, Sept. 24, 1949 (dec. 1951). B.A., Western Reserve U., 1942; M.A., U. Pa., 1946, Ph.D., 1949; M.S. in Library Sci., Western Reserve U., 1956. Curator of history Rochester, N.Y. Mus., 1943-47; research asst. to dir. Welch Inst. Johns Hopkins U., Balt., 1952; librarian U. Rochester, N.Y., 1955-68; prof. Syracuse U., N.Y., 1969, Case Western Reserve U., Cleve., 1970-84; vis. prof. UCLA, 1985, Columbia U., 1986; speaker, U.S., Can., Europe, 1960—; cons. to profl. groups, 1965—. Author: Precis for North American Usage, 1982; co-editor Theory of Subject Analysis: A Sourcebook, 1985; mem. editorial bd. Internat. Classification, Germany, 1970—; contbr. articles to profl. jours. Mem. ALA (recipient Margaret Mann citation 1978), Am. Soc. for Info. Sci. (recipient award of merit 1972, Pioneer Info. Sci. award 1987), History of Sci. Soc., Am. Radio Relay League. Republican. Presbyterian. Home: 6628 Aintree Park Dr Apt 202 Cleveland OH 44143

RICHMOND, REBEKAH AYN, artist, graphic arts specialist; b. Ashland, Ky., July 7; d. William Orville and Julia Emily (Hatcher) R. Student, Ringling Sch. Art, Sarasota, Fla., 1960-61, U. Ky., 1961-62; degree in comml. art, Art Inst. of Pitts., 1962-64. Draftsman Ladislas Segoe and Assocs., Cin.; draftsman, graphic specialist Raymond Parish and Pine, Inc., White Plains, N.Y., 1968-71; free-lance graphic specialist Ky., 1973-77; Estes Park, Colo., 1977—. Recipient Am. Artist Profl. League award Grand Nat. Exhbn., 1984, Presentation Printmaker award 1976, 77, Silver Medal Springville Mus. Art, 1982. Mem. Acad. Artists Assn. (Gold Medal of Honor 1978, 79, Council award 1986), Hudson Valley Art Assn. (Mrs. John Newington award 1982), The Catharine Lorillard Wolfe Club (Anna Hyatt Huntington award 1979, Russell Harrington award 1980), The Print Club of Albany (John Taylor Arms Meml. Purchase prize 1978). Republican. Presbyterian. Club: The Salmagundi (N.Y.C.) (Philip Kappel award 1979, Phillip Isenberg award 1983). Home and Office: PO Box 878 Estes Park CO 80517

RICHMOND, ROCSAN, television producer; b. Chgo., Jan. 30, 1945; d. Alphonso and Annie Lou (Combest) R.; divorced; 1 child, Tina S. Student, Wilson Jr. Coll., 1963, 2d City Theatre, Chgo., 1969, Alice Liddel Theatre, Chgo., 1970. Lic. 3d class radio/telephone operator FCC. Reporter, film critic Chgo. Metro News, 1978-81; with pub. relations sect. IRMCO Corp., Chgo., 1981-82, Hollywood (Calif.) Reporter newspaper, 1985-86; exec. producer Donald Descendent's Prodns., Hollywood, 1985—. Exec. producer (TV show) Future News, 1985—. Jehovah's Witness.

RICHTER, AGNES VIGRAN, small business owner; b. Cin., Feb. 16, 1932; d. Sol and Zelda (Weinstein) Vingran; m. Stanley Richter, Aug. 9, 1953; children: Nancy, Mark A. Student, U. Cin., 1951-53. Co-owner The Two of Us Fine Jewelry, Lockland, Ohio, 1974—. Mem. Wise Temple Sisterhood, Jewish Hosp. Aux. Mem. Jewelers Am., Ohio Jewelry Assn. Republican. Jewish. Home and Office: The 2 of Us Fine Jewelry 7165 Elbrook Ave Cincinnati OH 45237

RICHTER, JACKIE WILSON, business executive; b. Hornbeck, La., Oct. 30, 1933; d. Jack Caraway and Marie (Self) Wilson; m. Clyde Joseph Richter, Dec. 12, 1952; children: Lisa Anne, Clyde Joseph, Sarah Elizabeth. Grad., Nacogdoches Bus. Coll., 1951; student, Victoria Coll., 1951, 72, Del Mar Coll., 1978-80. With R.W. Hill Co., Victoria, Tex., 1952, So. Pacific R.R., 1953-57; co-owner Richter's Precision Air Co., Victoria, 1962—, Intra-Coastal Enterprises, Corpus Christi, Tex., 1975—. Alt. del. Rep. State Conv., 80, del., 1982, 84; regional walk coordinator Collins for U.S. Senate, 1982; del. Tex. Fedn. Rep. Women Conv., 1983; v.p. Corpus Christi Rep. Women's Club, 1983-84, pres., 1984; mem. Corpus Christi Symphony Guild, Art Mus. South Tex., Art Community Ctr.; patron Harbor Playhouse. Mem. Refrigeration Engr.'s Soc. (aux. pres. 1967), Victoria C. of C., Tex. Restaurant Assn., Better Bus. Bur., Tex. Retail Grocers Assn., Nat. Soc. DAR (2d vice regent 1984-85, regent Corpus Christi chpt. 1986-88), Colonial Dames XVII Century (sec. 1983-85), Daus. Am. Colonists, Daus. Republic Tex., Photog. Soc. Ams. (Internat. Salon Silver medal, San Antonio 1981, Silver medal, Richmond, Va., 1983, Endres Silver medal 1981). Lutheran. Club: Corpus Christi Camera (past dir.). Office: PO Box 226 909 N Staples Corpus Christi TX 78403

RICHTER, ROBERTA BRANDENBURG (MRS. J. PAUL RICHTER), educator; b. Osborn, Ohio, Dec. 29; d. Warren F. and Mary M. (Davis) Brandenburg; student Miami-Jacobs Coll., 1930, Wittenberg U., 1930-31, Coll. Music, U. Cin., 1931-32, U. Dayton, 1954, 64; B.S., Miami U., Oxford, Ohio, 1958, M.Ed., 1959; postgrad. Wright State U., 1966-70; doctoral candidate Ohio State U., 1969; m. Jean Paul Richter, Oct. 6, 1934; 1 son, James Paul. Bus. mgr. T.D. Pefflcy, Inc., 1929-32; sec., prodn. mgr. Delco Products div. Gen. Motors, 1932-34; exec. sec. Meth. Union, 1932-38, LWV, 1935-38, Elder & Johnston Dept. Store, 1938-40; ct. reporter Common Pleas Ct. Montgomery County, 1940-46; adminstrv. asst. Ch. Fedn. Greater Dayton, Ohio, 1946-50; audio-visual cons. schs., chs. Twyman Films, 1950-53; legal asst. Nadlin Law Offices, 1953-58; instr. stenotype, office practice Miami-Jacobs Coll., Dayton, 1941-48; tchr. stenotype, guidance counselor Stebbins High Sch., Dayton, 1958-82; vocat. guidance coordinator Mad River Planning Dist., Montgomery County, Ohio, 1968-73. Instr. workshops in stenotype for ct. reporting Wright State U., Dayton, 1970—; 1st cellist youth div. Symphony Orch.; dir. Lang. Unlimited, Inc., Lake Forest, Ill. Supt., tchr., adviser youth div. Grace United Meth. Ch., Dayton, 1942-72, sec. adminstrv. bd., 1940—, council on ministries, 1972-74, past pres. Excel Club, circle leader, hospitality chmn., pres. homebuilders class, program chmn., laywoman chmn. Christian higher edn.; instr., counselor Camp Miniwanca, Am. Youth Found., 1949-68. Mem. Am., Ohio, Miami Valley personnel and guidance assns., Nat., Ohio bus. tchrs. assns., Am., Ohio sch. counselor assns., Nat., Ohio edn. assns., Nat. Vocat. Guidance Assn., Dayton Area Bus. Soc. (v.p. 1969-82), Nat. Shorthand Reporters Assn., Delphian Soc. (past pres.), Pub. Speaker Bur., Council World Affairs, AAUW, LWV (past pres. and treas.), Internat. Platform Assn., World Trade Club (1st woman), Greater Dayton C. of C., Bus. and Profl. Women (past pres.), Pi Omega Pi. Clubs: Order Eastern Star, Progressive Mothers (chmn. program Dayton 1969-70). Author ednl. handbooks, pamphlets. Contbr. articles to profl. jours.; lectr. in field. Home: 3865 Seiber Ave Dayton OH 45405

RICHTER, SUSAN ELIZABETH, nurse; b. Salt Lake City, Jan. 12, 1944; d. Joseph Leo and Sara Jane (Bero) Shalvoy; R.N., St. Vincent's Sch. Nursing, 1964; B.S. U. New Haven, 1984; m. Edward Frederick Richter, Jr., Nov. 6, 1965; children—Meghan, Heidi, Edward, Kathleen, Colin. Staff nurse St. Vincent's Med. Ctr., Bridgeport, Conn., 1964-71, evening supr., 1972-78, evening adminstrv. dir., 1978-82, dir. community health relations, 1982-87; dir. med. affairs Conn. div. Am. Cancer Soc., 1987—. Chmn., Community Projects Com., 1979-84; sch. vol. Assn. of Bridgeport, 1977—, bd. dirs. 1977—, chmn., 1979-80; co-leader Jr. Girl Scout Troop, 1974-77; bd. dirs. Fairfield County chpt. Am. Heart Assn., 1980-82; mem. Bridgeport Coalition on Hypertension Control, 1980-83. Mem. St. Vincent's Sch. Nursing Alumni Assn. (corr. sec. 1983—), Alpha Sigma Lambda. Republican. Roman Catholic. Clubs: St. Vincent's Med. Center Aux., Home Sch. Assn. of Assumption Sch., Am. Diabetic Assn. (rec. sec. Bridgeport chpt. 1983—), Am. Cancer Soc. (bd. dirs., exec. com. Conn. div.), Conn. Hosp. Assn., Conn. Pub. Health Assn., Am. Soc. Perspective Medicine, Nat. Ctr. Health Edn., Bus. and Industry Council, New Eng. Health Promotion Mgrs. Council, Barnum Festival Soc.

RICKARD, JAN AILEEN, communications executive; b. Portsmouth, Ohio, Nov. 29, 1956; d. John Edward and Mary Helen (Zimmerman) Dunham; m. David Wayne Rickard, Mar. 15, 1986. BBA, Taylor U., 1979. Service rep. Cin. Bell Telephone, 1979-83, computer programmer, 1983-85, acctg. staff assoc., 1985—. Youth counselor Groesbeck United Meth. Ch., Cin., 1982—, mem. adminstrv. bd., 1983—, chmn. worship com., 1986—. Home: 9983 Pebbleknoll Dr Cincinnati OH 45252 Office: Cin Bell Telephone Co 600 Vine St Cincinnati OH 45202

RICKARD, REBECCA ANN, club executive; b. Oklahoma City, Mar. 25, 1952; d. Robert Edward and Helen Clydella (Lewis) R. BA, Oklahoma City U., 1974. Desk clk. Oklahoma City Tennis Ctr., 1971-74; desk clk./saleswoman Cts. Tennis Club, Oklahoma City, 1974-76; mgr./buyer Greens Country Club, Oklahoma City, 1976-82, Walnut Crddk Country Club, Oklahoma City, 1982-86, Santa Fee Club, Oklahoma City, 1988—; advisor recreational devel. com. Oklahoma City South Jr. Coll., 1979-80. Mem. U.S. Racquet Stringers Assn. Republican. Presbyterian.

RICKARD-RIEGLE, BARBARA KATHERINE, journalist, newscaster; b. Los Angeles, May 1, 1931; d. Thomas and Katherine Elizabeth (Blackburn) Rickard; student pvt. schs., Santa Rosa, Calif.; children—Katherine, Karen, Christopher, Melissa, Richard. Editor, Phenix City (Ala.) Herald, 1957-58; news broadcaster, editor WRBL-Radio-TV, Columbus, Ga., 1958-62; polit. reporter Esquire Broadcasting Co., Sta. WQXI, Atlanta, 1962-63; news commentator Sta. WAII-TV, Atlanta, 1962-63; polit. writer, columnist Los Angeles Herald Examiner, 1963-66; Congressional news sec., Washington, 1966-67; news writer, guest broadcaster Stas. KNXT, KABC-TV, Hollywood, Calif., 1964-67; broadcaster, women's news editor Sta. KNX-CBS, 1967-71; news broadcaster, producer, reporter, bur. chief Westinghouse Broadcasting Corp., Sta. KFWB, Hollywood, 1971-87; guest broadcaster Pub. Broadcasting System, Sta. KCET, 1975—; propr., pres. Calico Feature Prodns., Anaheim, Calif., 1969—; instr. journalism Calif. State U., Fullerton, 1972-73. Republican candidate for Calif. State Assembly, 1976. Named Journalist of Year, Cypress Coll., 1980; recipient Angel of Distinction award City of Los Angeles, 1973, John Swett Journalist of Yr. award Calif. Tchrs. Assn., 1974, 79. Mem. Am. Women in Radio and TV (chpt. pres. 1982-83; chairperson bus. and industry forum Ednl. Found. 1979), Nat. Women's Polit. Caucus, Investigative Reporters and Editors, Orange County Press Club (dir. 1979—, pres. 1984-85), Women in Communications (award 1979), Pioneer Broadcasters W., Sigma Delta Chi. Author: The Long Hot Summer of 1962; Something is Missing: The Majority Sex, 1971; Dinner for One: Soupçon for Singles, 1977. Home and Office: 2512 W Chain Ave Anaheim CA 92804

RICKENBAUGH, MARY KATHERINE, insurance company executive; b. Bellevue, Ohio, June 12, 1944; d. Kent Fleet and Charlotte Mitchel (Seltzer) Dillon; student Smith Coll., 1962-63; B.A., Western Res. U., 1966; MBA, Case Western Res. U., 1983; m. Richard Carl James, Sept. 10, 1966 (div. 1984); children—Carl, Daniel; m. Donald Rickenbaugh, 1985. CPA, Ohio. Personnel asst. Fisher Foods, Inc., Cleve., 1966-69, payroll asst., 1973-75, asst. tax mgr., 1975-76, accounts payable supr., 1977; acct., C.P.A., Cohen & Co., Cleve., 1977-80; bus. mgr. Hathaway Brown, Shaker Heights, Ohio, 1980-82; fin. ops. mgr. Progressive Casualty Ins. Co., Cleve., 1982-87, asst. v.p. , 1987. Mem. Am. Inst. CPA's, Ohio Soc. CPA's, Nat. Assn. Female Execs., Republican. Episcopalian. Home: 36002 Derby Downs Solon OH 44139 Office: 6300 Wilson Mills Rd Mayfield Village OH 44143

RICKER, DEBBIE JANE, institute official; b. Tuckerman, Ark., Feb. 29, 1956; d. Orbie C. and Ruby J. (Massey) Soden; m. David E. Ricker; children: Brittany Nicole, Aaron Michael, Anthony Wade. Grad., Anderson Coll., 1980. Cert. dental asst. Dental asst. Dr. H.T. Rodgers, Anderson, Ind., 1976-79; systems mgr. Am. Accounts, Anderson, 1979-87; v.p. Internat. Collection Tng. Inst., Anderson, 1987—. Mem. Ladies Action Com. Club: Mother of Twins. Office: Internat Collection Tng Inst PO Box 880 Anderson IN 46015

RICKER, DEBRA RAE, occupational therapist; b. Los Angeles, Feb. 28, 1956; d. Melvin Buford and Marilyn Cleo (Thut) R. BS, Loma Linda (Calif.) U., 1978. Occupational therapist Patton (Calif.) State Hosp., 1978-79, Napa (Calif.) State Hosp., 1979-80, Stanislaus County Mental Health Ctr., Modesto, Calif., 1980-81, Community Rehab. Ctr., Modesto, 1981, Riverside (Calif.) Community Hosp., 1981-82, San Antonio Community Hosp., Upland, Calif., 1982-83; supr. occupational therapy Western Med. Ctr., Anaheim, Calif., 1983-84; dir. adjunctive therapy Community Psychiat. Ctrs. Santa Ana (Calif.) Psychiat. Hosp., 1985-87; dir. psychiat. services Associated Occupational Therapists, 1987—. Monthly speaker Neighbors for the Mentally Ill, Riverside, 1983-84. Mem. Am. Occupational Therapy

Assn., Occupational Therapy Assn. Calif. Republican. Mem. Seventh Day Adventist Ch. Clubs: Tyrolean Ski (San Bernadino, Calif.) (pres. 1983-84); Sailing Singles (Newport Beach, Calif.) (pres. 1984-85). Office: Los Altos Hosp 3340 Los Coyotes Diagonal Suite 12 Long Beach CA 90808

RICKIN, SHEILA ANNE, personnel executive; b. N.Y.C., Oct. 13, 1945; d. Louis and Ethel (Schmukler) Bernstein; BA, CCNY, 1966; postgrad. N.Y.U.; MBA, Pace U., 1988. Research asst. pre-baccalureate program CCNY, 1966-68; placement counselor Elaine Revell, Inc., N.Y.C., 1968; adminstr. asso. to chief exec. officer Planned Parenthood Fedn. of Am., N.Y.C., 1969-74; personnel mgr. Family Circle Mag./N.Y. Times Mag. Group, 1974-87; sr. human resources rep., Drexel Burnham Lambert, 1987—. Mem. Am. Soc. Personnel Adminstrs., Am. Mgmt. Assn., Met. N.Y. Assn. for Applied Psychology, N.Y. Human Resources Planners, N.Y. Personnel Mgrs. Assn. (program com.), Mag. Pubs. Assn. (personnel com. 1978-87). Office: Drexel Burnham Lambert 2 Broadway New York NY 10004

RIDDER, MARY ANN, insurance company executive; b. East Chicago, Ind., Dec. 21, 1942; d. Edward Joseph and Ann Theresa (Dwyer) Dolatowski; m. Richard L. Ridder, Feb. 11, 1984. B.A., Ind. U. C.L.U. Underwriter, Guarantee Res. Life, Hammond, Ind., 1963-66; field payroll coordinator Morrison Constrn. Co., Hammond, 1966-68; adminstrv. asst. to v.p. Underwriters Nat., Indpls., 1968-70; office mgr. Gregory & Appel Life Agy., Indpls., 1970-81; v.p. employee benefits div. Brougher Life Ins. Co., Greenwood, Ind., 1981-86; sr. v.p. Brougher Life Ins. Co., Indpls., 1986-87, pres., 1987—, also bd. dirs.; bd. dirs. Indpls. Mus. Art, bd. dirs., v.p. of publs. Self Ins. Inst. Am. Recipient award Polit. Sci. Dept., Ind. U., 1981, Cavanaugh award Sch. Liberal Arts, 1981. Mem. Am. Soc. C.L.U.s, Ind. U. Sch. Liberal Arts Alumni Assn. (pres. 1982-83), Gold Key Soc., Pi Sigma Alpha. Editorial adv. bd. The Self-Insurer. Contbr. articles to trade publs. Home: 1025 Collingwood Dr Indianapolis IN 46208 Office: Brougher Ins Group 525 S Meridian St Indianapolis IN 46225

RIDDLE, DIXIE LEE, wholesale company executive. Formerly v.p., then sr. v.p. Farmers Union Cen. Exchange, St. Paul, now 1st vice chmn. bd. Office: Farmers Union Cen Exchange Inc 5500 Cenex Dr Inver Grove Heights MN 55075 *

RIDDLE, DOROTHY IRENE, international management educator; b. Chgo., Jan. 12, 1944; d. Charles Wainwright and Katharine Elsie (Parker) R. BA summa cum laude, U. Colo., 1964; MBA, U. Ariz., 1981; PhD, Duke U., 1968. Asst. prof. psychology Coll. William and Mary, Williamsburg, Va., 1968-70; asst. prof. Richmond Coll.-CUNY, S.I., N.Y., 1970-72; ptnr., psychologist Alternatives for Women, Tucson, 1973-75; assoc. in clin. tng. U. Ariz., Tucson, 1976-80; prof. internat. services and cross-cultural communication Am. Grad. Sch. Internat. Mgmt., Glendale, Ariz., 1981—; chief psychologist Marana Community Clinic, Ariz., 1976-80; intercultural cons. Thunderbird Mgmt. Ctr., Glendale, 1981—; cons. UN Conf. on Trade and Devel., Geneva, 1985—, Sistema Economico Latinoamericano, Caracas, 1986—; pres. ISI Internat. Services Inst., Inc. Author: Service-led Growth: The Role of the Service Sector in World Development, 1986. Contbr. articles to profl. jours. Pres. Group Health of Ariz. (PimaCare) Tucson, 1977-79. Named Tempe All-Am. Woman, 1985. Mem. Acad. Mgmt., Am. Psychol. Assn., Acad. Internat. Bus., Services World Forum, European Found. Mgmt. Devel., Soc. Intercultural Edn., Tng. and Research. Democrat. Avocations: music; hiking. Office: Am Grad Sch Internat Mgmt Glendale AZ 85282

RIDDLES, LIBBY N., sled-dog racer, trainer and breeder; b. Madison, Wis., Apr. 1, 1956; d. Willard Parker and Mary (Reynolds) R. Grad. high sch., St. Cloud, Minn. Finished 18th place in Iditarod Sled-Dog Race, 1980, 20th place, 1981, completed and finished 1st place, 1985; finished 7th place in Kusko 300 Sled-Dog Race, 1982, 5th place, 1984. Recipient Leonard Seppala Humanitarian award Alaska Airlines, 1985, Victor awards for excellence in sports, 1985; honored by Gov. Alaska with proclamation of Libby Riddles Day, Mar. 21, 1985; named Profl. Sportswoman of Yr., Sports Found. N.Y., 1985; first woman to win 1,049 mile Iditarod Race. Home: PO Box 1438 Nome AK 99762

RIDE, SALLY KRISTEN, scientist, former astronaut; b. Los Angeles, May 26, 1951; d. Dale Burdell and Carol Joyce (Anderson) R.; m. Steven Alan Hawley, July 26, 1982 (div.). B.A. in English, Stanford U., 1973, B.S. in Physics, 1973, Ph.D. in Physics, 1978. Teaching asst. Stanford U., Palo Alto, Calif.; researcher dept. physics Stanford U.; astronaut candidate, trainee NASA, 1978-79, astronaut, 1979-87; on-orbit capsule communicator STS-2 mission Johnson Space Ctr. NASA, Houston; on-orbit capsule communicator STS-3 mission NASA, mission specialist STS-7, 1983; sci. fellow Stanford (Calif.) U., 1987—; mem. Presdl. Commn. on Space Shuttle, 1986; dir. Apple Computer Inc. Author: (with Susan Okie) To Space and Back, 1986. Office: Ctr Internat Security and Arms Control Stanford U Stanford CA 94305-1684 *

RIDENER, NORMA ANN, word processing educator; b. Pemberville, Ohio, Oct. 7, 1940; d. Louis Ernest and Mary Joanna (Maas) Rohloff; m. Martin Thomas Ridener, Jan. 24, 1936. BS in Edn. magna cum laude, Bowling Green State U., 1962; MS in Edn. with honors, U. Toledo, 1968. Adminstrv. sec. Maumee Valley Hosp., Toledo, 1962-65; word processing tchr. Penta County Vocat. Sch., Perrysburg, Ohio, 1965—; instr. office mgmt. U. Toledo Community Coll., 1985—. Organist Redeemer Luth. Ch., Toledo, 1982—. Mem. Ohio Edn. Assn., Ohio Bus. Tchrs. Assn., NW Ohio Word Processing Assn. (sec. 1981-83), Penta County Tchrs. Assn. (sec. 1968-70), Choristers Guild (sec. 1976-78), Pi Omega Pi. Home: 3455 Talmadge Toledo OH 43606 Office: Penta County Vocat Sch 30095 Oregon Rd Perrysburg OH 43551

RIDENOUR, SUZANNE SWENSON, executive search firm executive; b. Tallahassee, Feb. 15, 1943; d. Allen Edward and Margaret (Salley) Swenson; m. James Lee Ridenour, Dec. 28, 1968 (div. 1980). Student Bradley U., 1960-62. Terr. sales mgr. Am. Express Co., Chgo., 1968-69; sales rep. grocery products The Quaker Oats Co., Chgo., 1969-70; office mgr. Staff Builders Temporary Help Service, Chgo., 1970-71; placement dir. Robert Morris Coll., Chgo., 1971-76; pres. Gillick-Ridenour & Assocs., Chgo., 1976-82; pres., chief exec. officer Ridenour & Assocs., Chgo., 1982—; del. trade mission to promote export service industries Dept. Commerce, SBA, Nat. Assn. Women Bus. Owners, London, Frankfurt, Fed. Republic Germany, Madrid, 1985. Ill. del. White House Conf. on Small Bus., 1986; bd. govs. Anti-Cruelty Soc., Chgo., 1983—; bd. dirs. Chase House, Chgo., 1983-85; mem. nat. council advisers Coll. Bus. Adminstrn., Bradley U., Peoria, Ill., 1984—; mem. aux. bd. Lincoln Park Zool. Soc., Chgo., 1984—. Mem. Internat. Trade and Tourism Task Force (appointed Gov. Thompson Council Gt. Lakes Govs.' Regional Econ. Devel. Commn.), Direct Mktg. Assn. (world direct trade council, conf. program adv. com., ECHO com.), Brit. Direct Mktg. Assn., Can. Direct Mktg. Assn., European Direct Mktg. Assn., Fashion Group Inc., Mid-Am. Swedish Trade Assn. (dir.), Chgo. Assn. Direct Mktg. (officer, bd. dirs. 1979-86 , pres. 1984-85, founding trustee ednl. found. 1985—), Direct Mktg. Ednl. Found. (trustee 1985-87, chmn.), Nat. Assn. Women Bus. Owners (dep. chairperson internat. com. 1985-87 , chpt. dir. 1986-87). Republican. Office: Ridenour and Assocs 400 E Randolph St 6B Chicago IL 60601

RIDER, MARILYN ANN, stockbroker; b. Conrad, Mont., Dec. 15, 1941; d. Louis E. and Emmi V. (Markuson) Schroer; diploma acctg., Gt. Falls (Mont.) Comml. Coll., 1960; m. Joe Raunig, Jan. 2, 1960 (div. 1971); children—Christina M., Rodney B., Brett R.; m. 2d, Lloyd D. Keith, Apr. 19, 1972 (dec. July 1973); m. 3d, Bruce A. Rider, Dec. 10, 1977 (div. 1979); 1 son, Marc D. Engaged in acctg., 1960-74, 75-77; owner Keith Enterprises, Chester, Mont., 1974-75; account exec. Merill Lynch, Pierce Fenner and Smith, Spokane, from 1977, asst. v.p., fin. cons.; v.p. investments Prudential Banks, 1987—; tchr. courses in field. Mem. core team New Life. C.P.A., Wash. Mem. Wash. Soc. C.P.A.s, Am. Women's Soc. C.P.A.s. Roman Catholic. Clubs: Spokane Duplicate Bridge (dir. 1976); Pres.' of Merrill Lynch. Home: N 7927 Pine Meadow Nine Mile Falls WA 99026

RIDGE, CLAIRE LILLIAN, general contractor; b. Bklyn., Jan. 2, 1936; d. William Carl and Elizabeth Claire (Braun) Edwards; student Palm Beach Jr. Coll., 1981—; m. William J. Ridge, Nov. 6, 1968; children by previous marriage—Glenn A. Simonin, Diane C. Graziano. Lic. real estate broker; notary pub. Real estate saleswoman Provident Properties, Inc., 1965-67; owner, real estate broker Piper Realty, Inc., 1967-73; owner, builder St. Mark's Estates, Inc., Fieldcrest Homes, Inc., 1971—; owner, builder Sunshine Custom Builders, Inc. and Sunshine Builders of Palm Beach, Inc., 1977—; owner C. Ridge Realty, Inc. Mem. Singer Island Civic Assn.; mem. minority bus. enterprise staff com. Palm Beach County Commrs. Mem. North Palm Beach County Bd. Realtors, Home Builders Assn. Palm Beach County, Nat. Assn. Notaries, Nat. Assn. Women in Constrn., Palm Beach Gardens C. of C. Republican. Lutheran. Club: Frenchmen's Creek Country. Home: 1037 Morse Blvd Singer Island Riviera Beach FL 33404 Office: 1960 W 9th St Riviera Beach FL 33404

RIDGEWAY, JANICE MCCULLOUGH, librarian; b. Pelham, Ga., Apr. 17, 1949; d. John Arthur McCullough and Gladys (Ward) McCullough Sapp; m. Garry C. Horton, Mar. 21, 1970 (div.); m. Lonnie D. Ridgeway II, Feb. 17, 1979 (div.); 1 child, Leah Kathleen. Student Harvard U., summer 1968, Yale U., summer 1969; B.A., Albany State Coll., 1970; M.L.S., Emory U., 1972; postgrad. SUNY-Albany, 1975. Tchr. English, Dooly County Bd. of Edn., Vienna, Ga., 1970-71; head reference dept. Anchorage Mcpl. Library, 1972-77; co-founder, ptnr. BiblioSearch, Anchorage, 1976-79; asst. mcpl. librarian pub. services Anchorage Mcpl. Libraries, 1977-85, project mgr. for hdqrs. library, 1985-87; owner, researcher Ridgeway Research Services, Anchorage, 1979-86; constrn. mgr. Durham Developers and Builders, Inc., 1987—; dir. Anchorage Opportunity and Indsl. Ctr., 1976. Organizer Jesse Owens Games, Anchorage, Anchorage Debutant Ball; activist Anchorage Community Schs., Anchorage Community Council. Recipient Miss Albany State Coll. award, 1969-70. Mem. ALA, Alaska Library Assn. (exec. bd. 1974-75), Nat. Assn. Female Execs., Western Reserve Hist. Soc., Internat. Speakers' Platform, Alpha Kappa Mu, Beta Phi Mu. Democrat. Club: Quota. Office: Durham Developers and Builders Inc 4447 Lee Rd Cleveland OH 44128

RIDGWAY, ROZANNE LEJEANNE, foreign service officer; b. St. Paul, Aug. 22, 1935; d. H. Clay and Ethel Rozanne (Cote) R.; m. Theodore E. Deming. B.A., Hamline U., 1957, LL.D. (hon.), 1978. Entered Fgn. Service, 1957; assigned Dept. State, Washington, 1957-59, 64-67, 70-73, Am. embassy, Manila, 1959-61, U.S. Consulate Gen., Palermo, Italy, 1962-64, Am. embassy, Oslo, 1967-70; dep. chief mission Am. embassy, Nassau, 1973-75; dep. asst. sec. state, ambassador for oceans and fisheries affairs 1975-77, ambassador to Finland, 1977-80; counselor of the Dept., Washington, 1980-81; spl. asst. to sec. state 1981; ambassador to German Dem. Republic, 1982-85; asst. sec. state Europe and Can. 1985—. Recipient Profl. awards Dept. State, 1967, 70, 75, 81, Joseph C. Wilson internat. relations achievement award, 1982; named Person of Year Nat. Fisheries Inst., 1977. Office: Dept State Bur European & Can Affairs Room 6226 Washington DC 20520

RIDGWAY, VICTORIA CARMICHAEL, real estate broker, appraiser; b. Mound Bayou, Miss., Mar. 18, 1927; d. James C. and Cordelia (Lockett) Carmichael; m. Roosevelt Ridgway, Oct. 31, 1952; children: Jimmye L., Charles L., Denise R., June M. Cert. in real estate, U. Mich. Grad. Sch. Bus., 1968. lic. real estate broker, appraiser, Mich. Real estate assoc. Modern Realty Co., Flint, Mich., 1967-69; office mgr. Ridgway Electric Co., Inc., Flint, Mich., 1968-70; mgr. Flint ops. Thompson Mortgage Co., Detroit, 1969-71; broker, appraiser Roe-Vic & Assocs. Real Estate Co., Flint, 1971—; pres. assocs. group Flint chpt. Jack & Jill of Am. Inc.; fin. sec. Flint chpt. Links, Inc. V.p. Genesse County Substance Abuse Com., Flint, 1969; mem. bldg. and grounds com. United Meth. Dist., Flint, 1982—, chair allocations com. Flint United Way, 1984; region fin. sec. Nat. Black Rep. Council, St. Louis, 1985. Mem. Genesee County Bd. Real Estate (sec. 1979-81), Internat. Orgn. Real Estate Appraisers, Nat. Assn. Negro Bus. Women. Republican. Club: YWCA (corr. sec. 1984). Home: 1902 Chelan Flint MI 48503

RIDINGS, DOROTHY SATTES, communications executive, consultant; b. Charleston, W.Va., Sept. 26, 1939; d. Frederick L. and Katharine E. (Backus) Sattes; m. Donald Jerome Ridings, Sept. 8, 1962; children—Donald Jerome, Matthew Lyle. Student, Randolph-Macon Woman's Coll., 1957-59; B.S.J., Northwestern U., 1961; M.A., U. N.C.-Chapel Hill, 1968; D.Pub. Service (hon.), U. Louisville, 1985; LHD (hon.), Spalding U., 1986. Reporter Charlotte Observer, N.C., 1961-68; writer-cons. Louisville, 1968-80; editor Ky. Bus. Ledger, Louisville, 1980-83; mgmt. assoc. Knight-Ridder Inc., 1986—; mem. nat. bd. LWV U.S., Washington, 1976-86; 1st v.p. LWV U.S., 1980-82, pres., 1982-86; chair LWV Edn. Fund, 1982-86, 1st vice-chair, 1980-82, trustee, 1976-86; adj. prof. U. Louisville Night Div., 1982-83; copy editor Washington Post, summer 1967; mem. Bretton Woods Com.; mem. leadership com. Campaign for Free Speech; mem. Com. on Nat. Elections; v.p. Nat. Mcpl. League, 1985-86; bd. dirs. com. on Constl. System Child Care Action campaign, 1983-86, Nat. Com. Against Discrimination in Housing, 1982-87, Com. for Study of Am. Electorate; mem. Ind. Sector, 1983-86; mem. exec. com. Leadership Conf. Civil Rights, 1982-86; mem. adv. bd. Nat. Com. Citizen Participation in the Adminstrn. of Justice; mem. Nat. Com. U.S.-China Relations; mem. pub. affairs adv. bd. Women in Communications Inc., mem. Nat. Women's Forum. Trustee Citizens Research Found., 1982-84; mem. Gov.'s Council Ednl. Reform, 1984-85; chair Prichard Com. Acad. Excellence, 1985-86; bd. dirs. Leadership Ky., 1984-87, Louisville YWCA, 1978-80, Jr. League Louisville, 1972-74; mem. Gov.'s Commn. Full Equality, 1982-83; mem. state adv. council U.S. Commn. Civil Rights, 1975-79; mem. steering com. Task Force for Peaceful Desegregation, 1974-75; mem. session 2d Presbyn. Ch., 1972-75, 78-81, sec.-treas. ch. sch., 1972-76, mem. weekday sch. bd., 1972-75. Home: 11 Eastover Ct Louisville KY 40206 Office: PO Box 32188 Charlotte NC 28232

RIDLEY, BETTY ANN, educator, church worker; b. St. Louis, Oct. 19, 1926; d. Rupert Alexis and Virginia Regina (Weikel) Stoher; B.A., Scripps Coll., Claremont, Calif., 1948; m. Fred A. Ridley, Jr., Sept. 8, 1948; children—Linda Drue Ridley Archer, Clay Kent. Christian Sci. practitioner, Oklahoma City, 1973—; Christian Sci. tchr., 1983—; nat. bd. trustees Adventure/Unlimited; mem. Christian Sci. Bd. Lectureship, 1980-85. Found. Bibl. Research and Preservation Primitive Christianity. Mem. Jr. League Am. Home: 7908 Lakehurst Dr Oklahoma City OK 73120 Office: 3000 United Founders Blvd Suite 100-G Oklahoma City OK 73112

RIDOLFI, LORETTA B., state official; b. Trenton, N.J., Mar. 12, 1933; d. John J. and Elizabeth (Teringer) Barabas; m. Benjamin F. Ridolfi, Jr., Feb. 19, 1955; children: Cynthia, Lisa, Benjamin. BS in Pharmacy, Phila. Coll. Pharmacy and Sci., 1954; postgrad., Rutgers U., 1981. Reg. pharmacist, N.J. With various pharmacies Mercer County, N.J., 1954-80; field rep. health N.J. Dept. Health, Trenton, 1980-83, pub. health rep., 1983-84, program specialist, 1984-85, 1988—, community service officer, 1985-88. Contbr. articles to profl. jours. Chmn. Impaired Pharmacists Program of N.J., Trenton, 1987—; sec. Impaired Pharmacists Network Dist. II, 1986—; bd. dirs. Am. Cancer Soc., Mercer Co., 1983; mem. staff N.J. Drug Abuse Adv. Council, 1985. Mem. Am. Pharm. Assn., N.J. Pharm. Assn. (pres. 1980-81, Frederick B. Kilmer Meml. award 1987), Soc. Mercer County Pharmacists (pres. 1975-76, James E. Delahanty Meml. award 1984, A.H. Robins Hygeia award 1982, others), Phila. Coll. Pharmacy and Sci. Alumni Assn., Communication Workers Am. Democrat. Roman Catholic. Club: Compassionate Friends. Home: 163 Highland Ave Yardville Heights NJ 08620 Office: NJ Dept Health CN 362 Trenton NJ 08625-0362

RIECK, ANGELA MCKNETT, research and development company executive, psychologist. BS, Old Dominion U., 1975, MS, 1977; PhD, U. of Md., 1980. Mem. tech. staff Bell Labs., Piscataway, N.J., 1980-81; mgr. AT&T, Basking Ridge, N.J., 1981-86; dir. Silhouette Tech., Morristown, N.J., 1987—; instr. Drew U., Madison, N.J., 1986—; cons. The Kohl Group, 1987—. Mem. Am. Psychol. Assn., Human Factors Soc. Office: Silhouette Tech PO Box 1479 Morristown NJ 07960

RIEDEL, AMY MCLOUGHLIN, public relations executive; b. N.Y.C., Sept. 24, 1960; d. Alfred Vincent and Mary Theresa (Nelson) McLoughlin; m. George Andrew Riedel, June 4, 1983. BA in English, U. Va., 1982. Asst. account exec. Hill and Knowlton, Inc., Houston, 1982-83, account exec., 1983-84; dept. mgr. Lord & Taylor, Houston, 1984-85; pub. relations coordinator John Hancock Fin. Services, Boston, 1985-87, dir. communications services, 1987—. Office: John Hancock Fin Services 200 Clarendon St Boston MA 02117

RIEGER, BIN HUNG, teacher; b. Kota Bharu, Kelantan, Malaysia, Oct. 6, 1948; came to U.S., 1974; d. Kee Teong and Leng Yean (Tan) Teo; m. Paul Leonhard Rieger, Aug. 1, 1979; 1 child, Natasha Irina. BA, Ambassador Coll., 1978; MA, Calif. State U., Los Angeles, 1982. Cert. tchr., Calif. Temporary tchr. Zainab Secondary Sch., Kota Bharu, 1971, Islah Nat. Primary Sch., Kota Bharu, 1972-74; contract tchr. Los Angeles Unified Sch. Dist., 1979—; speaker Los Angeles Ednl. Partnership Workshop Fair, 1986. Home: 4906 Viro Rd La Canada CA 91011

RIEGER, ELLEN LUNDE, commodity exchange executive; b. N.Y.C., June 30, 1952; d. Steen and Barbara A. (Baylis) Lunde; m. Peter C. Brathauer, Aug. 17, 1974 (div. Sept. 1977); m. Thomas Muller Rieger, June 22, 1983. BA cum laude, St. John's U., N.Y.C., 1974. Banquet mgr. Princeton Club N.Y., 1975-80; asst. to ptnr. East View Co., N.Y.C., 1980-84; v.p. Windsor-Birch, Ltd., N.Y.C., 1983-86; exec. asst. to pres., Commodity Exchange, Inc., N.Y.C., 1986-87, exec. asst. to chmn., 1987—. Mem. DAR (regent Peter Minuit chpt. 1984-887, chmn. Greater N.Y. Regent's Round Table 1986-87, sec. 1987-88). Home: 1192 Park Ave New York NY 10128 Office: Commodity Exchange Inc 4 World Trade Ctr New York NY 10048

RIEGER, GERI MARIANNE, data processing executive; b. N.Y.C., Feb. 23, 1939; d. Arthur and Johanna Lina (Schmidt) R.; m. Alan L. Krakow, Aug. 22, 1969; 1 son, Jason. Adv. systems engr. IBM Corp., N.Y.C., 1961-69; adminstrv. asst. to group exec. IBM Corp., White Plains, N.Y., 1973-77; v.p. computer ops. Mfrs. Hanover Trust Co., N.Y.C., 1969-73; v.p. systems devel. Fed. Res. Bank, N.Y.C., 1977-82; v.p. computing and networking ops. Blue Cross Blue Shield, 1982—; mem. computerization bd. Multiple Sclerosis Soc., 1971-73; mem. adv. bd. U.S. Dept. of Navy ADP, 1984-86. Mem. YWCA Acad. of Women Achievers. White House fellow, 1974-75. Mem. Computer Execs. Roundtable (exec. com. 1980-88), White House Fellows Alumni Assn. (class rep. 1980-81, mem. regional bd. 1978-79), Nat. Acad. Scis. Home: Stone Hill Rd Bedford NY 10506 Office: 622 3d Ave New York NY 10017

RIEKER, ANNE ELLORA, judge, humanitarian; b. Elmira, N.Y., Sept. 27, 1923; d. Eric Wendell and Viola Della (Hinkley) Phillips; m. Thomas Henry Rieker, Nov. 6, 1943; children: Constance Anne, Carla Anne, Thomas Eric. AS, Hershey Jr. Coll., 1943; postgrad. Washburn U., 1958-59, Nat. Jud. Coll. U. Nev., 1982, 85. Dir. recreation therapy Extended Care Facility, Andover, N.J., 1967-70; exec. dir. Office on Aging, Sussex County, N.J., 1970-74; surrogate judge County of Sussex, Newton, N.J., 1975—; mem. N.J. State Juvenile Delinquency/Commn., 1987—, N.J. State and Local Expenditure and Revenue Policy Commn., 1987—, Local Govt. Policy Com. N.J. Dept. Personnel and Civil Service, 1987—. Trustee Knoll Heights Sr. Citizens Housing, Sparta, N.J., 1975-86; chmn. March of Dimes, Morristown, N.J., 1978-79; bd. dirs. Vis. Nurses Assn. Sussex County, Frankford Twp., N.J., 1983—, pres., 1988—; chmn. govt. div., Sussex County United Way, 1985—, mem. allocation com., bd. dirs., 1988—; mem. N.J. Assembly Local Govt. Affairs Adv. Council, 1988—, Sussex County Communities in Transition Planning Com., 1988, N.J. State Juvenile Delinquency Commn., 1987—, N.J. State and Local Expenditure and Revenue Policy Commn., 1987-88, Local Govt. Policy Com. to the New Jersey Dept. of Personnel, 1987—. Named Outstanding Citizen of Yr., VFW, 1975; recipient Vol. award March of Dimes, 1981, 82, 83, 84, 85. Mem. N.J. Assn. County Officers (pres. 1979-81), Nat. Coll. Probate Judges, Nat. Judges Assn., N.J. Assn. Counties (4th v.p. 1985, pres. 1987), N.J. Bar Assn. (assoc.), N.J. Assn. Elected Women Ofcls. (bd. dirs. 1981-83). Democrat. Episcopalian. Clubs: Soroptimist Internat. (v.p. 1985), Newton Country. Avocations: music; golf; handcrafts; travel. Office: Hall of Records 4 Park Pl Newton NJ 07860

RIELLO, MARIA, electronics company executive; b. Plainfield, N.J., May 15, 1960; d. Carlo and Antonia (Ragozzino) R. BS in Bus. Edn., Rider Coll., 1982, MA in Ednl. Administrn., 1987. Tchr. bus. edn. Metuchen (N.J.) Bd. Edn., 1982-84; rep. customer support Exxon Office Systems, Lyndhurst, N.J., 1984-85; corp. office automation specialist Minolta Bus. Systems, Ramsey, N.J., 1985-88, mktg. products supr., 1988—. Named Outstanding Young Women Am., 1986; Brockelbank scholar, 1979. Mem. Nat. Assn. Female Execs., Eastern Bus. Edn. Assn., Phi Beta Lambda (state sec. 1985-86), Delta Pi Epsilon, Pi Omega Pi (v.p. 1981-82), Alpha Lambda Delta. Roman Catholic. Office: Minolta Bus Systems 70 Hilltop Rd Ramsey NJ 07446

RIELY, PHYLLIS ELEANOR, microbiologist, consultant; b. Welshfield, Ohio, Jan. 25, 1918; d. Clifford James and Ethel (Corliss) Brunton; student Capital U., 1936-39; grad. Sch. Med. Tech. Huron Rd. Hosp., 1941; m. Charles T. Riely, Nov. 28, 1942 (div.); children—Terrence, Patricia, Maura, Shawn. Systems microbiologist Fairchild Hiller Co., Farmingdale, N.Y., 1960-66; life support coordinator Pall Corp., Glen Cove, N.Y., 1966-69; mgr. med. product devel. Internat. Paper Co., Tuxedo, N.Y., 1969-71; dir. med. products East-West Med. Products Co., Hauppauge, N.Y., 1971-73; mgr. biomed. regulatory affairs Pall Corp., Glen Cove, 1973-74; mgr. microbiol. devel. Marion Labs., Kansas City, Mo., 1974-81; mgr. tech. edn. Marion Sci. div. Marion Labs., Kansas City, Mo., 1981-82; biomed. cons., 1984—. Mem. Am. Soc. Microbiology, Royal Soc. Health. Republican. Methodist. Patentee in field; author book; contbr. articles to profl. jours. Home: 18002 136 Way Sun City West AZ 85375

RIETZ, BONNIE BESSE, educator; b. Devils Lake, N.D., June 2, 1948; d. Clarence Arthur and Viola Louetta (Wood) Besse; m. Timothy Charles Rietz, June 20, 1971; children: Heidi, Heather, Mindy. BS, Concordia Coll., Moorhead, Minn., 1970; postgrad., U. Minn., 1977-79, Mankato U., 1984-85, Ecoles des Langues, Montreal, 1986. French tchr. Irondale High Sch., Mpls., 1970-73; asst. office mgr. Old Nat. Bank, Spokane, Wash., 1973-74; English tchr. Manatantely Lycée, Madagascar, 1974-77; French tchr. Austin (Minn.) Community Coll., 1982-83, 85—, Am. Sch., Madagascar, 1983-84; English as 2d lang. tchr. Shaw Grade Sch., Austin, 1985-86; founder, dir. Vol. English as 2d Lang. Group, Austin, 1980-83, Amis Austin, 1982—, English Club, Madagascar, 1983-84. Pres. St. Olaf Luth. Ch., Austin, 1987—; bd. dirs. YMCA, Austin, 1982—, United Way, Austin, 1985—, Library of Austin, 1986—. Named one of Outstanding Young Women Am., 1983, People Who Make a Difference, Austin Dailey Herald, 1984, 85; recipient Human Rights award Human Rights Commn., 1986. Mem. Am. Assn. Tchrs. of French, Minn. Council Tchrs. of Fgn. Lang. (chairperson of regional reps.), Minn. Edn. Assn., French Club. Lutheran. Club: WASSO, French (pres.). Home: 610 SW 4th Ave Austin MN 55912 Office: Austin Community Coll 1200 NW 8th Ave Austin MN 55912

RIFE, SARAH JANE, marketing executive; b. Anna, Ill.; d. Charles Christopher Rife and Arlyn (McGee) Delgreco. BA, U. Va., 1979. Dir. visitor services Minn. Mus. of Art, St. Paul, 1979-80; dir. devel. Univ. Va. Art Mus., Charlottesville, 1980-82; v.p. Money Mkt. Directories, Charlottesville, 1983-87; mktg. assoc. Forstmann-Leff Assocs., Inc., N.Y.C., 1987—. Mem. Assn. Investment Mgmt. Sales Execs., Nat. Assn. State Retirement Adminstrs. (assoc.). Office: Forstmann-Leff Assocs Inc 55 E 52nd St New York NY 10055

RIFFE, CONNIE DIANNE, information systems specialist; b. Galipolis, Ohio, Sept. 14, 1957; d. Frank Eugene and Lois Marie (Noonkester) R. Student J. Sargeant Reynolds Community Coll., 1988. Sec. Dept. Info. Tech. Commonwealth of Va., Richmond, 1975-78, personnel sec., 1978-79, personnel asst., 1979, asst. personnel mgr., tng. coordinator, 1979-84, tng. & career devel. mgr., 1984—. Mem. Richmond Info. System Educators (sec. 1984, program chairperson 1986-87), Richmond Large Users Group, Data Processing Mgmt. Assn. (mem. edn. com. 1987—), Am. Soc. Tng. & Devel. Club: Richmond Volleyball. Office: Commonwealth of Va Dept Info Tech 110 S 7th St 3d Fl Richmond VA 23219

RIFKIND, ARLEEN B., physician, researcher; b. N.Y.C., June 29, 1938; d. Michael C. and Regina (Gottlieb) Brenner; m. Robert S. Rifkind, Dec. 24, 1961; children—Amy, Nina. B.A., Bryn Mawr Coll., 1960, M.D., NYU, 1964. Intern Bellevue Hosp., N.Y.C., 1964-65, resident, 1965; clin. assoc.

Nat. Inst. Child Health and Human Devel. Endocrine br. Nat. Cancer Inst., 1965-68; research assoc., asst. resident physician Rockefeller U. Hosp., 1968-71; asst. prof. medicine Cornell U. Med. Coll., N.Y.C., 1971-82, assoc. prof. medicine, 1983—, asst. prof. pharmacology, 1973-78, assoc. prof., 1978-82, prof., 1983—; chmn. Gen. Faculty Council Cornell U. Med. Coll., 1984-86, Nat. Inst. Environ. Health Scis. Rev. Com., 1985-86. Contbr. articles to profl. jours. Chmn. Friends of the Library, Jewish Theol. Sem. Am., 1984-86, mem. bd. Library Corp, 1982— ; trustee Dalton Sch., 1986—. Recipient Andrew W. Mellon Tchr.-Scientist award, 1976-78; USPHS spl. fellow, 1968-70, 71-72. Mem. Endocrine Soc., Am. Soc. Clin. Investigation, Am. Soc. Pharmacology and Exptl. Therapeutics, AAAS, Soc. Toxicology. Office: Cornell U Med Coll Dept Pharmacology 1300 York Ave New York NY 10021

RIGAS, HARRIETT BADAKER, electrical and computer engineering educator; b. Winnipeg, Man., Can., Apr. 30, 1934; came to U.S., 1956, naturalized, 1962; d. Max and Helen (Pasternak) B.; m. Anthony L. Rigas, Feb. 14, 1959; 1 child, Marc. BSEE, Queen's U., 1956; MSEE, U. Kans., 1959, PhD in Elec. Engring., 1963. Elec. engr. Biophysics, Mayo Clinic, Rochester, Minn., 1956-57; sr. research engr., aerodynamics Lockhee Missiles, Sunnyvale, Calif., 1963-66; asst. prof. Wash. State U., Pullman, 1966-71, prof., 1976, chmn. dept. elec. and computer engring. 1979-84; chmn. dept. elec. and computer engring. Naval Postgrad. Sch., Monterey, Calif., 1984-87; prof., chmn. dept electircal engring. Mich. State U., East Lansing, 1987—. Co-editor: Jour. Computers and Elec. Engring., 1982; contbr. articles to profl. jours. Recipient Disting. Engring. Service award U. Kans., 1983. Fellow IEEE (Engr. of Yr. Spokane sect. 1980, 84); mem. Soc. Women Engrs. (Achievement award 1982), Sigma Xi, Tau Beta Pi (Disting. Engr. award). Home: 1400 Sylvan Glen Rd Okemos MI 48864 Office: Mich State U East Lansing MI 48824

RIGAUD, MARIE-CLAUDE, psychiatrist; b. Port-Au-Prince, Haiti, Jan. 24, 1939; came to U.S. 1964; d. Antoine Dolbrise and Charlotte (Aarons) Saint-Jean; m. Andre Rigaud, Sept. 30, 1961; children—Carl, Ralph, J-Philippe, Cassandre, Joseph, Claudine. Bachelor, Pensionnat Sterose de Lima, Haiti, 1956; M.D., U. Haiti, 1962. Diplomate Am. Bd. Psychiatry and Neurology. Resident in pub. health, Plaisance, Haiti, 1962-63, Pont-Sonde, Haiti, 1963-64; resident in psychiatry Seton Psychiat. Inst., Balt., 1966-69, sr. staff supr., 1970-73; house physician in medicine and obstetrics Provident Hosp., Balt., 1965-66; staff psychiatrist Spring Grove State Hosp., Balt., 1969-70; med. dir. Psychiat. Day Hosp., Seton Inst., 1971-73; practice medicine, specializing in psychiatry, 1973—; psychiat. cons. to med. dept. and EAP program, Western Electric Co., Aurora, Ill., 1979-85; clin. dir. Suburban Psychiat. Assocs, Naperville, occupational cons., Lombard, Ill.; sr. psychiat. cons. Kane-Kendall Mental Health Ctr., Aurora, Ill., Cardiac Rehab. Program, Copley Meml. Hosp., Aurora; med.staff Mercy Ctr. for Health Care Services, Aurora; lectr. in field; trustee Rosary High Sch., others. Mem. ; trustee Rosary High Sch., others. Fellow Am. Psychiat. Assn.; mem. Balt. County Med. Assn., Med. and Chirurg. Faculty State of Md., Ill. Psychiat. Soc., Am. Psychiat. Soc., Md. Soc. Liaison Psychiatrists, Kane County Med. Soc., AMA, Assn. Haitian Physicians Abroad (past pres.), Women in Mgmt., Internat. Med. Council of Ill., others. Roman Catholic. Address: 103 S Highland Ave Aurora IL 60506 Office: PO Box 2816 Aurora IL 60507

RIGGINS, LOIS S., museum administrator; b. Nashville, Nov. 18, 1939; d. Percy Leon and Lula Belle Prather (Traughber) Von Schmittou; 1 son, Nicholas. B.S., Belmont Coll., 1968; postgrad., U. Western Ky., 1969-72, George Washington U., 1978. Cert. tchr., Ky., Tenn. Tchr. Ky. Pub. Schs., Adairville, 1962-71; tour supr. Tenn. State Capitol, Nashville, 1972-74; curator of extension services Tenn. State Mus., Nashville, 1975-77, curator edn., 1977-81, dir., 1981—. Chmn. Nashville Flight of Tenn. Friendship Force, Caracas, Venezuela, 1977, Tenn. Am. Revolution Bicentennial Arts Competition, 1976; bd. dirs. Zool. Soc. Mid. Tenn., 1986—, So. Folk Cultural Revival Project, 1986—. Mem. Southeastern Mus. Conf. (edn. com., rep. to Am. Assn. Mus. council, publs. advt. com. 1983), Inter Mus. Council of Nashville (chmn. edn. 1980-81), Am. Assn. Mus., Am. Assn. State and Local History (edn com. 1988—). Home: 1205 Ordway Nashville TN 37206 Office: Tenn State Mus 505 Deaderick St Nashville TN 37219

RIGGINS, ROSE, television executive; b. Princeton, N.J., July 12, 1958; d. Lee W. and Mattie (Tramnell) R. BA, Rutgers U., 1978. Stage mgr. NBC-TV, N.Y.C., 1979-83; stage mgr. ABC-TV, N.Y.C., 1983-87, assoc. dir., 1987—; assoc. dir., stage mgr. various prodn. cos., N.Y.C., 1979-88. Mem. AFTRA, Actors Equity Assn., Dirs. Guild Am., Screen Actors Guild. Club: Yacht (N.Y.C.)(sgt. at arms).

RIGGS, ANNA CLAIRE, metals service center executive; b. Danville, Ind., Jan. 22, 1944; d. Leland Wesley and Mary Alice (Miller) Cox; m. Michael Ross Riggs, Dec. 10, 1983; 1 child, Matthew. B.S. in Edn., Ind. U., 1966. Credit tng. and promotion mgr. L.S. Ayres, Indpls., 1966-74, cons., credit dept., 1984; credit ops. mgr. Burdine's, Miami, Fla., 1974-77; br. mgr. Centaur Metals, Indpls., 1977-85; gen. mgr. Copper & Brass Sales, Indpls., 1985—; promotion dir. Ind. Jersey Cattle Club. Children's choir dir. and Sun sch. tchr. United Meth. Ch., Danville, Ind. Mem. Nat. Assn. Female Execs., Am. Jersey Cattle Club, Beta Sigma Phi (pres., advisor). Avocations: travel; sewing; reading. Home: 107 Martin Dr Danville IN 46122 Office: Copper & Brass Sales 8002 Woodland Dr Indianapolis IN 46278

RIGGS, CONSTANCE KAKAVECOS, college administrator; b. Indpls., Apr. 6, 1928; d. James Eustace and Dorothy Amelia (Boren) Kakavecos; B.A., St. Mary-of-the-Woods Coll., Terre Haute, Ind., 1975; m. Kenneth Wesley Riggs, Dec. 4, 1947 (dec.); children—Ken Roger, Yvonne Denise Riggs Rench, James Cary, Vicki Catherine, Constance Amelia Riggs Reep, Jeffrey Allan. Med. edn. coordinator St. Vincent Hosp., Indpls., 1967-72; asst. to pres. Wabash Coll., Crawfordsville, Ind., 1972-78; asst. v.p. for devel. St. Mary-of-the-Woods Coll., 1978-79; asst. to pres. Rollins Coll., Winter Park, Fla., 1979—; lectr. in field. Bd. dirs. Montgomery County (Ind.) United Fund, 1973-75, Terre Haute YWCA, 1978; trustee Ind. Council for Advancement and Support of Edn., 1978. Hon. fellow Ind. Collegiate Press Assn. Mem. Fla. Freelance Writers Assn., Nat. Fedn. Press Women. Greek Orthodox. Club: Altrusa (pres. 1983-84). Author: Sam Shue and the Seven Satchels, 1976. Editor: Montgomery County Remembers, 1976; editorial bd. Vigo County Hist. Soc., 1978; columnist Orlando Sentinel, 1981—, Winter Park Outlook, 1984—, Senior Voice, 1985—. Named an Outstanding Woman in Edn. Woman's Exec. Council, 1986. Mem. Fla. Press Women, Omicron Delta Kappa. Home: 200 St Andrews Blvd Apt 3503 Winter Park FL 32792 Office: Rollins Coll Winter Park FL 32789

RIGGS, JEANETTE TEMPLETON, civic worker; b. Little Rock, Mar. 13, 1933; d. Donald M. and Fay (Templeton) Brewer; student Little Rock U., 1950-51, Tex. Coll. for Women, 1951-52; B.S., U. Ark., 1955; m. Byron Lawrence Riggs, June 1955; children—Byron Kent, Ann Templeton. Founder, Rochester (Minn.) Ballet Guild, 1970, pres., 1974; mem. establishing bd., exec. bd. Rochester Arts Council, 1972, producer, dir. T.S. Elliot's The Rock, 1970; founder, performer So. Minn. Ballet Co., 1974; sponsor Nat. Ballet Cos., Rochester, 1970-75; exec. bd. for restoration 1875 Pattern Book House, Rochester Heritage Assn., 1975-77; exec. bd. Savino Ballet Nat., 1975-78; founder, exec. bd. Citizens Action Com., 1977-79; asso., commentator Women, Cable TV Program for Women, Rochester, 1979; mem. Mayor's Com. on Drug Abuse, 1979-80; mem. Olmsted County Steering Com. for George Bush, 1979-80, a founder, mem. exec. bd. Olmsted County Republican Women's Orgn., 1979—, mem. Olmsted County Rep. Central Com., 1979—, exec. bd. issues com., 1979-80. Home: 432 SW 10th Ave Rochester MN 55901

RIGLIN, HANNAH MARGARET, medical technologist; b. Cranesville, Pa., July 5, 1953; d. Chalmer M. King and Hannah Julia (Lee) Ball; m. Kevin R. Riglin, Apr. 12, 1980 (div. Nov. 1986). BS in Med. Tech., Edinboro State Coll., 1975; MS in Ednl. Mgmt., U. Houston, 1984. Reference labe technologist No. Ohio Red Cross Blood Services, Cleve., 1977-79; supr. blood bank sect. Med. Br. U. Tex., Galveston, 1977-85, mgr. edn. and reference lab., 1985-87; tech. dir. United Blood Services, McAllen, Tex., 1987—; instr. U. Houston/Clear Lake, 1981-87. Contbr. articles to profl. jours. Vol. Grand Opera House, Galveston, 1986-87. Recipient God and Community award Girl Scouts of Am., 1970. Mem. Am. Soc. Clin. Pathology, Am. Assn. Blood Banks, So. Cen. Assn. Blood Banks. Methodist. Office: United Blood Services of Rio Grande Valley 1312 Pecan McAllen TX 78501

RIGNEY, JANE, journalist; b. Flushing, N.Y., Dec. 4, 1948; d. William J. and Janet C. (Teesink) R. B.A., U. Ill., 1971; student Juilliard Sch., 1979-81. Reporter, mag. editor Daily News-Gazette, Champaign, Ill., 1968-71; women's world editor Anchorage Daily Times, 1971-72; part-time reporter N.Y. Voice, Flushing, 1977-78; asst. dir. pub. relations Juilliard Sch., N.Y.C., 1977-81; copy editor Hudson Dispatch, Paterson, N.J., 1982-83; night copy chief N.Y. Tribune, 1983-84, dance critic, 1983-86; freelance dance critic, 1986—; freelance book editor Dance Horizons, Bklyn., 1978-87; freelance copy editor Village Voice, N.Y. Daily News, Jersey Jour., Am. Banker; also freelance writer; copy editor Time-Life Inc. (Money mag.) 1988—. Mem. Nat. Writers Union, Nat. Press Club, Editorial Freelancers Assn., Women in Communications, N.Y. Press Club, Dance Critics Assn., Soc. Profl. Journalists. Democrat. Roman Catholic. Home: 47-46 40th St Apt 1B Sunnyside Queens Village NY 11104

RIKLEEN, LAUREN STILLER, lawyer; b. Winthrop, Mass., Apr. 29, 1953; d. Joseph Stiller and Elaine Lillian (Brodie) Stiller; m. Sander A. Rikleen, May 25, 1975. Student Clark U., 1971-73; BA, magna cum laude, Brandeis U., 1975; JD, Boston Coll., 1979. Bar: Mass. 1979, U.S. Dist. Ct. Mass. 1980, U.S. Ct. Appeals (1st cir.) 1980, U.S. Supreme Ct. 1985. Asst. dir. Flaschner Jud. Inst., Boston, 1979-81; atty. enforcement div. EPA, Boston, 1981-82, Office Regional Counsel, 1982-84; asst. v.p. for negotiations Clean Sites, Inc., Alexandria, Va., 1984-87; asst. atty. gen. Mass. Dept. of the Atty. Gen., 1987—. Contbr. articles to legal publs. Mem. Wayland Planning Bd., Mass., 1980-83; mem. Met. Area Planning Council, Boston, 1980-84 . Recipient Merit award EPA, 1982. Mem. ABA (natural resources com.), Boston Bar Assn. (environment sect.), Soc. Profls. in Dispute Resolution. Democrat. Office: Mass Dept of Atty Gen One Ashburton Pl Boston MA 02108

RILEY, ADALENE BOWMAN ROSS, travel columnist, fashion show producer, public relations consultant; b. Oak Park, Ill., Dec. 14, 1919; d. Harry Bertram and Ida (Rundle) Bowman; m. George Ross, Aug. 2, 1942 (dec.); children: Nancy Lee, Lee Thornton, Lynn Louise; m. William Thomas Riley, Dec. 6, 1986. Student, San Mateo Jr. Coll., 1937-39. Internat. fashion show commentator, producer for maj. stores, designers, bus. and industry, movies and TV, 1948—; pub. relations cons., event creator various internat. firms, 1950—; travel columnist Addie's World San Mateo Times, 1969—; dir. pub. relations Bullock's No. Calif., 1970-80, v.p. pub. relations Joseph Magnin Stores Calif., Nevada, Colo., 1980-82; dir. pub. relations Shreve & Co. Jewelers, San Francisco, 1986—; lectr. in field. Founding mem. San Mateo County Soc. Crippled Children and Adults, Inc. Recipient City of San Francisco Pub. Service awards, 1959-70; San Francisco Conv. Bur. Silver Cable Car award, 1969. Mem. AFTRA (founding mem. San Francisco br.), Jr. League. Republican.

RILEY, ALICE HEISKELL, social services administrator, management consultant; b. Phila.; d. James Theodore and Alice (Heiskell) Harris; m. William L. Watkins, Dec. 19, 1946 (div. Aug. 1954); children: Teresita L. Watkins Dorrall, William L. Jr.; m. Raymond E. Riley, Nov. 11, 1962 (dec. May 1985). BA in History, Glassboro (N.J.) State Coll., 1973; MPA, Cen. Mich. U., 1978; postgrad., Princeton U., 1978-79. Adminstrv. asst. Johnson & Johnson, New Brunswick, N.J., 1966-69, community relations specialist, 1969-72; field rep. N.J. Dept. Civil Service, Trenton, 1972-73; field coordinator Div. of Youth and Family Services, Trenton, 1974-77, 1979-87, adminstrv. analyst, 1987—; asst. dep. commr. N.J. Dept. of Banking, Trenton, 1977-79; cons. Higher Edn. Assistance, Albany, N.Y., 1978—, Wanda Webster Stansbury Assoc., Trenton, 1979-84; cons. in field; banking rep. Fed. Exec. Bd. of Minority Bus. Enterprise, 1977-79. Coordinator Womens Polit. Caucus, Burlington County, N.J., 1974-77; mem. rules com. Dem. Nat. Conv., Washington, 1978. Fellow Am. Soc. of Pub. Adminstrs., Am. Mgmt. Assn., Alpha Kappa Alpha; mem. Nat. Polit. Congress, League of Women Voters (chmn. human resources 1968), Minority Womens Network (co-chair, chair 1987—), 100 Black Women of South (chair econ. devel. 1986), Sigma Iota Epsilon. Republican. Roman Catholic. Home: 255 Everly Ct Mount Laurel NY 08054 Office: NJ Dept Banking 1 S Montgomery Trenton NJ 08625

RILEY, CATHERINE IRENE, state senator; b. Balt., Mar. 21, 1947; d. Francis Worth and Catherine (Cain) R. B.A., Towson State U., 1969. Bacteriologist Balt. City Hosp., 1969-72; legis. aide Md. Ho. of Dels., Annapolis, 1973-74, del., 1975-82; mem. Md. Senate, 1982—; cons. Md. State Div. Alcoholism Control, 1973; mem. House Environ. Matters Com., 1975-82; mem. Spl. Joint Com. Energy, 1977-83, chmn. 1978-79, 1980-83; mem. So. Legis. Conf. Energy Com. 1978, Environ. Com., 1983—, vice chmn., 1985—, chair fin. com., 1987—; mem. So. Environ. Resource Council, 1978, Power Plant Siting Adv. Com., 1977—, State of Md. Energy Conservation Bd., 1978-83, Fire Safety Subcom., 1981-83; mem. BiState Cheasapeake Bay Commn., 1981-83, chmn. 1982; chmn. Forest Land Task Force, 1981-84, Budget and Taxation Senate Com., 1983-86, Subcom. Edn., Health, and Human Resources, 1983-86, Nat. Conf. State Legis. Energy Commn., 1983—; senate chmn. adminstrv. exec. and legis. review com., 1983-86, Ho. of Dels. mem. 1978-82; various state govt. coms. and subcoms.Contbr. articles to profl. jours. Mem. adv. com. State Edn. Policy Seminars Adv. Com., 1983—, Protective Services to Children and Families, 1983—; exec. bd. Balt. Area Council Boy Scouts Am., 1983—; hon. chmn. Am. Cancer Soc., 1982-83; mem. Harford County Child Protection Council, 1978-80, vice chmn. 1980; mem. Harford County Council Community Services, 1976—, Harford County legis. del., 1975-82 , chmn. 1976, 1980-82; mem. Md. Order Women Legislators, 1975—, sec. 1976-79; mem. adv. bd. Susquehanna State Park, 1975—; mem. Joppatowne Womens Club, 1975—, No. Md. Assn. for Retarded Citizens, Inc., 1975—, Upper Cheasepeake Watershed Assn., Inc., 1975—. Recipient Disting. Service award Md. State Troopers, 1980; Community Service award, United Way, 1978; Disting. Service award Jaycees, 1976; Liberty award Harford Christian High Sch., 1975; Cert. of Appreciation Md. Mcpl. League, 1984; William P. Coliton Outstanding Community Service award Johns Hopkins U., 1985; named Young Democrat of Yr. State of Md., 1975; Women of Yr. Soroptimist Club, 1980; Toll fellow, other state and civic awards. Mem. AAUW, Towson State U. Alumni Assn. (admissions council 1975—, chmn. fund drive 1980), Md. Jaycee Women, Izaak Walton League. Roman Catholic. Avocations: golf; sailing; stamp collecting. Office: State Senate 20 Office Bel Air MD 21014

RILEY, DEBORAH ANN, marketing executive; b. Pitts., June 30, 1953; d. Lionel Glen and Ethel Louise (Alexander) Davidson; m. Richard Earl Riley, May 27, 1977 (div. Dec. 1983); children: Steven Earl, Michael Glen. BA, W.Va. Wesleyan Coll., 1975. Sec., treas. Anniston Joint Venture, Inc., Dallas, 1982-85; exec. v.p. Insignia Corp., Dallas, 1985—, bd. dirs.; pres. Sports Concepts, Dallas, 1986—, bd. dirs. Mem. Glenshaw (Pa.) Players, 1975-76. Served to capt. U.S. Army, 1976-77, with Res. 1981-85. Mem. Res. Officers Assn., Nat. Assn. Female Execs., Am. Mgmt. Assn. Republican. Presbyterian. Home: 7206 Shawn Rowlett TX 75088

RILEY, DOLORES MARIE, principal; b. Ft. Thompson, S.D., Nov. 18, 1941; d. Richard LaRoche and Violet Margaret (Langdeau) Rekow; m. Michael L. Riley, Oct. 12, 1973; children: Michael, Tamara Hill, Terry Pexa, Lanny Pexa, Nicole P. BS in Elem. Edn., Black Hills State, 1977; MA in Edn., Western State Coll., 1979. Tchr. Rapid City (S.D.) Area Sch. Dist., 1977, dir. Indian edn., 1978, dir. bilingual edn., 1981-82; tchr. Logan Utah Dist., 1983-84; tchr. Salt Lake City Schs., 1984-85, elem. prin., 1985—; proposal reviewer D.C. Dept. Edn., Washington, 1977-82, 83, 85; evaluator U. N.D., Grand Forks, 1984-85; mem. S.D. State Commn. on Human Relations, 1973; cons. Hopi Tribe, Oraibi, Ariz., 1984. Fellow Utah Prins. Acad.; mem. Nat. Assn. Elem. Prins., Salt Lake Assn. Sch. Adminstrs. (treas. 1986-87), Utah Assn. Tchr. Edn., Assn. Supervision and Curriculum Devel., Phi Delta Kappa. Republican. Office: Salt Lake City Sch 400 N 200 W Salt Lake City UT 84103

RILEY, DOROTHY COMSTOCK, state chief justice; b. Detroit, Dec. 6, 1924; d. Charles Austin and Josephine (Grima) Comstock; m. Wallace Don Riley, Sept. 13, 1963; 1 child, Peter Comstock. B.A. in Polit. Sci., Wayne State U., 1946, LL.B., 1949. Bar: Mich. 1950, U.S. Dist. Court (ea. dist.) Mich. 1950, U.S. Supreme Court 1957. Atty. Wayne County Friend of Court, Detroit, 1956-68; ptnr. Riley & Roumell, Detroit, 1968-72; judge Wayne County Circuit, Detroit, 1972, Mich. Ct. Appeals, Detroit, 1976-82; chief justice Mich. Supreme Court, Detroit, 1982-83, 85—; mem. U.S. Jud. Conf. Commn. on State-Fed. Court Relations. Co-author manuals, articles in field. Mem. adv. com. Citizenship Edn. Study, 1946-50. Recipient Disting. Alumni award Wayne U. Law Sch., 1977; Headliner award Women of Wayne, 1977; Donnelly award, 1946. Mem. ABA (family law sect. 1965—; vice chmn. gen. practice sect. com. on juvenile justice 1975-80; mem. jud. adminstrn. sect. 1973—, standing com. on fed. ct. improvements), Am. Judicature Soc., Fellows Am. Bar Found., Mich. State Bar Found., State Bar Mich. (civil liberties com. 1954-58, young lawyers sect. 1956-60, family law sect. 1966—), Detroit Bar Assn. (pub. relations com. 1955-56, author Com. in Action column, Detroit Lawyers 1955, chmn. friend of ct. and family law com. 1974-75), Nat. Women Judges Assn., Nat. Women Lawyers Assn., Women Lawyers Assn. Mich. (pres. 1957-58), Karyatides, Pi Sigma Alpha. Republican. Roman Catholic. Club: Women's Econ. Office: Mich Supreme Ct PO Box 30052 Lansing MI 48909 *

RILEY, DOROTHY MARY, psychology educator; b. Darby, Pa., Aug. 8, 1938; d. William Earl and Gladys R. (Driscoll) Tynan; m. Donn C. Riley, Apr. 20, 1963; children: Paul, Michael, James. BA in Psychology, Pa. State U., 1960; MA in Counseling, Villanova U., 1972; PhD in Counseling, Psychology, U. Pa., 1981. Cert. sch. psychologist. Counselor Corestoga High Sch., Berwyn, Pa., 1972-76; project dir. Beaver Coll., Glenside, Pa., 1981-83; prof. psychology Rosemont (Pa.) Coll., 1984—. Research fellow U. Pa., 1979. Mem. Am. Psychol. Assn. (presenter 1981-86), Am. Edn. Research Assn., Eastern Psychol. Assn. (presentator 1981-86). Home: 524 Brandymede Rd Bryn Mawr PA 19010

RILEY, GAILYA NAN, educator; b. Slidell, Tex., Aug. 30, 1934; d. Homer Bedford and Lucetta Constance Winstead; BS, N. Tex. State U., Denton, 1955, MEd, 1979; m. John Howard Riley, June 4, 1955; children: John Steven, Brenda Gail, Richard Scott, Mark Allan. Tchr. schs. in Tex., 1955—; tchr. social studies, English and reading Hurst-Euless-Bedford Ind. Sch. Dist., 1968-80, secondary curriculum cons., 1980—; reviewer reader fed. grants proposals. Chmn. heritage com. Euless Bicentennial Commn., 1978-80; historian First Bapt. Ch., Euless, 1975-78; mem. facility com. City of Euless, sesquicentennial com.; mem. Tarrant County Hist. Soc. Recipient Educator medal Freedom Found., 1980; named Hurst-Euless-Bedford Tchr. of Yr., 1977; Tex. Tchr. of Yr., 1978; fellow Keizai Koho Ctr, Japan. Mem. Nat. Council for Social Studies (chmn. ho. dels., task force, exec. com., bd. dirs.), Tex. Council for Social Studies (past pres.), Assn. Suprs. and Adminstrs., Tex. Assn. Supervision and Curriculum Devel. (pres. chpt.), Nat. Council Social Studies (chairperson local arrangements 1987, chairperson local steering com. 1988, exec. com., bd. dirs., past pres.) Tex. Hist. Assn. (adv. bd.), Northeast Hist. Soc., Nat. Council for Geog. Edn., Phi Delta Kappa. Lodge: Soroptimist Internat. (past pres.). Author articles in field, sch. musicals. Home: 707 Royce Dr Euless TX 76039 Office: 1849 Central Dr Bedford TX 76021

RILEY, MATILDA WHITE (MRS. JOHN W. RILEY, JR), science adminstrator, emeritus sociology educator; b. Boston, Apr. 19, 1911; d. Percival and Mary (liff) White; m. John Winchell Riley, Jr., June 19, 1931; children: John Winchell III, Lucy Ellen Riley Sallick. A.B., Radcliffe Coll., 1931, M.A., 1937; D.Sc., Bowdoin Coll., 1972; L.H.D. (hon.), Rutgers U., 1983. Research asst. Harvard U., 1932; v.p. Market Research Co. Am., 1938-49; chief cons. economist WPB, 1941; research specialist Rutgers U., 1950, prof., 1951-73, emeritus prof., 1973—, dir. sociology lab., 1959-73, chmn. dept. sociology and anthropology, 1959-73; Daniel B. Fayerweather prof. polit. econ. and sociology Bowdoin Coll., 1974-81, prof. emeritus, 1981—; assoc. dir. Nat. Inst. on Aging, 1979—; mem. faculty Harvard, summer 1955; staff asso., dir. aging and society Russell Sage Found., 1964-73, staff sociologist, 1974-77; chmn. com. on life course Social Sci. Research Council, 1977-80; sr. research assoc. Center for Social Scis., Columbia U., 1978-80; adv. bd. Carnegie "Aging Soc." Project, 1985-87; mem. Commn. on Coll. Retirement, 1982-86; vis. prof. NYU, 1954-61; cons. Nat. Council on Aging, Acad. Ednl. Devel.; mem. study group NIH, 1971-79, Social Sci. Research Council Com. on Middle Years, 1973-77. Author: (with P. White) Gliding and Soaring, (with Riley and Toby) Sociological Studies in Scale Analysis, 1954, Sociological Research, vols. I, II, 1964, (with others) Aging and Society, vol. I, 1968, vol. II, 1969, vol. III, 1972, (with Nelson) Sociological Observation, 1974, Aging from Birth to Death: Interdisciplinary Perspectives, 1979, (with Merton) Sociological Traditions from Generation to Generation, 1980, (with Abeles and Teitelbaum) Aging from Birth to Death: Sociotemporal Perspectives, 1982, (with Hess and Bond) Aging in Society, 1983; co-editor: Perspectives in Behavioral Medicine: The Aging Dimension, 1987; Social Change and the Life Course, Vol. I. Social Structures and Human Lives (with B. Huber and B. Hess); Vol. II. Sociological Lives, 1988; editorial com.: Ann. Rev. Sociology, 1978-81; contbr. articles to profl. jours. Trustee The Big Sisters Assn. Recipient Lindback Research award Rutgers U., 1970; Social Sci. award Andrus Gerontology Center, U. So. Calif., 1972; fellow Advanced Study in Behavioral Scis., 1978-79; Matilda White Riley Award in Research Methodology established Rutgers U., 1977; Radcliffe Alumnae award, 1982, Commonwealth award 1984; Kesten Lecture award U. So. Calif., 1987; Winkleman Lectr., U. Mich., 1984; Selo Lectr., U. No. Calif., 1987; membership lectr. Am. Philos. Soc., 1987. Fellow AAAS (chmn. sect. on social and econ. scis. 1977-78); mem. Inst. Medicine of Nat. Acad. Scis. (sr.), Acad. Behavioral Medicine Research, Am. Sociol. Assn. (exec. officer 1949-60, v.p. 1973-74, pres. 1986, chmn.-elect sect. on Sociology of Aging 1988), Am. Assn. Public Opinion Research (sec.-treas. 1949-51, Disting. Service award 1983), Eastern Sociol. Soc. (v.p. 1968-69, pres. 1977-78, Disting. Career award 1986), Soc. for Study Social Biology (bd. dirs. 1986—), Am. Acad. Arts and Scis., D.C. Sociol. Soc. (co-pres. 1983-84), Sociol. Research Assn., Internat. Orgn. Study Human Devel., Phi Beta Kappa, Phi Beta Kappa Assos. Home: 4701 Willard Ave Apt 1607 Chevy Chase MD 20815 Office: NIH Nat Inst on Aging 9000 Rockville Pike Bethesda MD 20205

RILEY, PANSY SUE, academic administrator; b. Fulton, Mo., Oct. 2, 1940; d. Lawrence Fletcher and Elizabeth (Fey) Wilson; m. Henry H. Durst, Sept. 16, 1960 (div. May 1975); children: Henry Douglas, Karen K.; m. Michael B. Riley, July 30, 1975 (div. Apr. 1986); 1 child, Melanie E. Student, North Mo. State U., 1958-59. Sec. Harbison-Walker, Fulton, 1959-65; med. asst. Henry Durst, M.D., Fulton, 1965-75; fin. sec. Nat. Elect. Contractors Assn., Denver, 1977-79; adminstrv. asst. Wright-McLaughlin Engrs., Denver, 1979-80; coordinator staff MFA, Inc., Columbia, Mo., 1980-82; coordinator interim continuing edn. Sch. Engring. U. Mo., Columbia, 1982-83, adminstrv. asst. Sch. Veterinary Medicine, 1983-85, mgr. adminstrv. services Sch. Journalism, 1985—. Fundraiser Am. Cancer Soc., Columbia, 1983-85; leader Girl Scouts Am., Columbia, 1985-86. Mem. Nat. Assn. Female Execs., Beta Sigma Phi (pres. 1974-75, Woman of Yr. 1973). Presbyterian. Home: Rt 12 1655 Boris Dr Columbia MO 65203 Office: U Mo Sch of Journalism PO Box 838 Columbia MO 65205

RILEY, SARAH ANNE, supervisor; b. Balt., Oct. 23, 1946; d. Eugene John and Carroll Morley (Young) R. BA, Mt. St. Agnes Coll., 1968. Asst. registrar Loyola Coll., Balt., 1968-70; lab. scientist Med. Sch. U. Md., Balt., 1970-75; retail store mgr. Fabri-Ctrs. Am., Beechwood, Ohio, 1975-79; info. sci. tech. McCormick & Co., Inc., Hunt Valley, Md., 1979-82, assoc. info. sci., 1982-85, info. scientist, 1985-87. Mem. bd. trustees Mercy High Sch., Balt., 1983—. Mem. Md. Online Users Group (sec. 1982-84, chmn. 1985-87), Spl. Libraries Assn., Am. Soc. Microbiology, Mercy High Sch. Alumnae Assn. (chmn. 1981-84). Republican. Roman Catholic. Office: McCormick & Co Inc 202 Wight Ave Hunt Valley MD 21031

RILEY, SUE A., management consultant; b. Washington, May 24, 1929; d. Frank and Mary Concetta (Bovello) Di Prima; m. John J. Riley, Feb. 3, 1950 (div. Sept. 1970); children: Diane, John, Karen; m. John K. Thompson Jr., May 22, 1987. Student, Strayer Bus., Washington, 1947-49, Montgomery Coll., 1979-86. Legal sec. Dept. Justice, Washington, 1947-51; legal sec., office mgr. Harvey B. Steinberg, Bethesda, Md., 1964-66; legal sec., personal asst. Pierson, Ball & Dows, Washington, 1966-74; asst. to office adminstr. Wald, Harkrader & Ross, Washington, 1974-79, office adminstr., 1975-79; office adminstr. Gibson, Dunn & Crutcher, Washington, 1979-86; pvt. practice as legal mgmt. cons. Washington, 1986—. Author: How a Travel

Agency Can Best Service Your Firm, 1982. Sec. Montgomery Century Condominium, Kensington, Md., 1979, v.p., 1980. Mem. Assn. Legal Adminstrs. (chairperson membership com. 1974-76, pub. relations com. 1976-80, mem scholarship com. 1979-86, ex-officio pub. relations 1980-86, conf. leader mgmt. and adminstrn. sect. 1985-87, ann. organizer of programs and speakers). Home: 3127-7 Univ Blvd W Kensington MD 20895

RILEY-DAVIS, SHIRLEY MERLE, advertising agency executive, marketing consultant, writer; b. Pitts., Feb. 4, 1935; d. William Riley and Beatrice Estelle (Whittaker) Byrd; m. Louis Davis; 1 child, Terri Judith. Student U. Pitts., 1952. Copywriter, Pitts. Mercantile Co., 1954-60; exec. sec. U. Mich. Ann Arbor, 1962-67; copy supr. N.W. Ayer, N.Y.C., 1968-76, assoc. creative dir., Chgo., 1977-81; copy supr. Leo Burnett, Chgo., 1981-86; freelance advt. and mktg. cons., 1986—. Writer of print, radio, and TV commercials. Former bd. dirs. Epilepsy Services Chgo. Recipient Grand and First prize N.Y. Film Festival, 1974, Gold and Silver medal Atlanta Film Festival, 1973, Gold medal V.I. Film Festival, 1974, 50 Best Creatives award Am. Inst. Graphic Arts, 1972, Clio award, 1973, 74, 75, Andy Award of Merit, 1981, Silver medal Internat. Film Festival, 1982; Senatorial scholar. Mem. Women in Film, Facets Multimedia Film Theatre Orgn. (bd. dirs.), Nat. Assn. Female Execs., Greater Chgo. Council for Prevention of Child Abuse (bd. dirs.). Democrat. Roman Catholic. Avocations: dance, poetry, design.

RILLY, CHERYL ANN, cartoonist; b. Detroit, June 17, 1952; d. John Charles and Dorothy Frances (Ozanich) R. Student, Oakland Community Coll., Southfield, Mich., 1974, Art Assn., 1975. Humorist, gag writer Joan Rivers, Tom Dreesen, various other comedians, Harper Woods, Mich., 1977-84; cartoonist Tex. Gardener mag., Waco, Tex., 1984—; staff writer Contemporary Comedy, Dallas, 1982—; creator and satirist The Heeda Hooper Show Sta. WXYZ Radio, Southfield, Mich., 1983; spl. feature writer C&G Pubs., Warren, Mich., 1984-86; contbg. editor Heritage mag., St. Clair Shores, Mich., 1986-87; freelance writer, Harper Woods, 1977—. Author, editor, pub.: (Joke Books for Public Speakers) Irish Bull vol. I, 1980, vol. II, 1983; Triviallaneous, 1985; Book of Days, 1987; Contbr. articles to profl. jours. Mem. Nat. Writer's Club.

RIMA, INGRID HAHNE, economist; b. Fed. Republic of Germany, Mar. 13, 1925; d. Max F. and Hertha G. (Grunsfeld) H.; m. Philip W. Rima, June 23, 1956; children: David, Eric. BA with honors, CUNY, 1945; MA, U. Pa., 1946, PhD, 1951. Prof. econs. Temple U., Phila., 1967—. Author: Development of Economic Analysis, 1967, 2d edit., 1973, 3d edit., 1981, 4th edit., 1986, Labor Markets Wages and Employment, 1981; editor Eastern Econ. Jour. Mem. Am. Econ. Assn., Ea. Econs. Assn., History of Econs. Soc., Phi Beta Kappa. Office: Temple U Broad & Montgomery Ave Philadelphia PA 19122

RIMLAND, INGRID ANNELIESE, writer; b. Halbstadt, USSR, May 22, 1936; d. Friedrich and Evelyn (Loetkemann) Brandt; m. Woldemar Rimland, May 31, 1958 (div. 1978); children: Erwin, Rudy. BA, Wichita State U., 1971; MA, U. Pacific, 1973, EdD, 1977. Psychologist Stanislaus United Sch. Dist., Modesto, Calif., 1973-77; pvt. practice child psychologist Stockton, Calif., 1977-85; free-lance writer, speaker various locations, 1985—; cons. various sch. dists., Stockton, 1973-85. Author: The Furies and the Flame, 1984, The Wanderers, 1977 (Calif. Lit. Medal award, Gold Biennial Award 1978), Psyching out Sex, 1975; contbr. articles to mags.; book critic Sacramento Bee. Home: 2731 Lost Creek Ct Stockton CA 95207

RINALDI, KATHARINE ANNE, soil scientist; b. Woodland, Calif., Dec. 10, 1946; d. Gregory Earl and Clare Millecent (Mowers) McConnell; divorced; children: Jason MacDonald, Jesse MacDonald. BS in Soil Sci., Oreg. State U., 1983. Soil scientist trainee U.S. Forest Service Rogue River N.F., Ashland, Oreg., 1982; dist. soil scientist Alsea (Oreg.) Ranger Dist, Sinislaw N.F., 1983-85; soil scientist Bu. Land Mgmt., Las Vegas, Nev., 1987; resource asst. Las Vegas Dist. U.S. Forest Service, 1987—. Docent Kiwanis Water Conservation Park, Las Vegas, 1986—. Home: 6429 Eagle Point Rd Las Vegas NV 89108

RINALDI, RENEE ZAIRA, physician; b. N.Y.C., Dec. 10, 1949; d. John James and Concetta (Vecchio) Rinaldi; m. Kenneth Robert Ballard, June 16, 1977; children—Claudia Michele, Celeste Noelle. B.A., Barnard Coll., Columbia U., 1971; Ed.M., Harvard, 1973; M.D., N.Y. Med. Coll., 1976. Diplomate Am. Bd. Internal Medicine and Rheumatology. Intern, Met. Hosp., N.Y.C., 1976-77; resident medicine San Fernando program UCLA, Sepulveda Campus, 1977-79, adj. asst. prof. medicine, 1982-83; staff internist Olive View Hosp., Van Nuys, Calif., 1979-80; fellow rheumatology UCLA, 1980-82; practice medicine specializing in rheumatology, Los Angeles, 1983—; asst. clin. prof. medicine UCLA, 1983—. Jane Wyman Clin. fellow, 1981. Mem. So. Calif. Rheumatology Soc., Los Angeles County Women's Med. Assn., Am. Rheumatology Assn.

RINALDO, HELEN, interior designer; b. Manville, N.J., July 5, 1922; d. Zigmond and Kate (Szymanski) Ossowski; student summer and evening classes N.Y. Sch. Interior Design, 1964; student N.Y. U., 1964, Somerset County (N.J.) Coll., 1975-76; m. Nicholas Rinaldo, Feb. 7, 1948; children—Linda Ann, Lorraine Ann. Interior designer W. & J. Sloane, Red Bank and Short Hills, N.J., 1981, Lord & Taylor, Paramus, N.J., 1974; owner Rinaldo Interiors, Scotch Plains, N.J., 1959-65; designer local firms; speaker career day local sch. Mem. Hist. Commn. Twp. of Branchburg (N.J.), until 1982. Mem. Allied Bd. Trade (N.Y.C.), Internat. Platform Assn. Home and Office: 69 Partridge Ln Cherry Hill NJ 08003

RINEHART, NITA, state senator; b. Tex. BA, So. Meth. U. Mem. Wash. State Ho. of Reps., 1979-82; mem. Wash. State Senate, 1983—, vice chmn. edn. com., mem. rules, ways and means, govtl. ops. coms. Mem. LWV. Democrat. Office: Office of the State Senate State Capitol Olympia WA 98504 Other Address: 4515 51st Ave NE Seattle WA 98105 *

RING, BARBARA ANN, management consultant; b. St. Louis, Mar. 7, 1945; d. Oliver C. and Ann (McCarron) Garleb; AA in Nursing, El Camino Coll., 1964; BA, UCLA, 1967, JD, 1971; BS in Mgmt., Pacific Christian Coll., 1976; BS in Nursing, Am. Nat. U., 1980, MBA, 1982; postgrad. U. So. Calif.; 1 son, Michael Francis. With Harbor Gen. Hosp., Torrance, Calif., 1964-66, Gardena Meml. Hosp., 1967-68, UCLA Med. Ctr., 1969-70, Brotman Meml. Hosp., Culver City, 1971-73; cardiac specialist Calif. Hosp. Med. Ctr., Los Angeles, 1974-77; asst. dir. nurses Fountain Valley Community Hosp. (Calif.), 1978-79; cons. Upjohn Health Care Services, 1980-84; mgmt. cons. Ind. Contractor. Dir. Charter Counseling Ctr., De Anza, Riverside; youth camp dir. YMCA, also caravan dir. Bank Am. scholar, 1962; Westmont Coll. scholar, 1962. Mem. Am. Mgmt. Assn., Nat. Assn. Female Execs., Critical Care Nurses Assn. NOW, ACLU, Christian Bus. Women's Fellowship, Riverside C. of C. (ambassador, bd. dirs., steering com.), Jurupa C. of C. Lodge: Soroptimist.

RINK, KATHLEEN CLARE, insurance company official; b. Hinsdale, Ill., Feb. 8, 1954; d. Virgil William and Patricia Jane (Donahue) R. B.A., St. Mary's Coll., Notre Dame, Ind., 1976; J.D., DePaul U., 1979; LL.M. in Estate Planning, U. Miami, 1980. Bar: Ill. 1979; C.L.U., 1985, Chartered Fin. Cons., 1987; cert. fin. cons., Ill. Trust adminstr. State Nat. Bank, Evanston, Ill., 1981-82; assoc. dir. advanced underwriting The Equitable, Oak Brook, Ill., 1982-85; advanced underwriting cons. N.Y. Life, Bannockburn, Ill., 1985—; speaker estate planning various profl. orgns. Co-author play: Naperville Live, 1981. Mem. ABA, Ill. Bar Assn. Roman Catholic.

RINKE, LYNN THERESE, nurse, home care consultant; b. Detroit, Sept. 14, 1955; d. Leonard John and Ellen (Dakoske) R. BS in Nursing, Wayne State U., 1977; MS, U. Mich., 1980. Pub. health nurse Vis. Nurse Assn. Met. Detroit, 1977-80, nursing supr., 1980-81, dist. dir., 1981-86; dir. div. of accreditation for home care & community health Nat. League Nursing, N.Y.C., 1986-87; v.p., chief operating officer Vis. Nurse Assn. of Met. Detroit, 1987—; fellow Nat. League Nursing, Robert Wood Johnson Pub. Policy, Washington, summer 1979; intern Health Care Financing Adminstrn., HHS, Washington, summer 1980. Mem. Nat. League Nursing, Am. Pub. Health Assn., N.Y. Counties Registered Nurse Assn., Sigma Theta Tau (small research award grant Rho chpt. 1979). Roman Catholic. Home: 3345 Wincasset Apt 109 Dearborn MI 48120 Office: 7700 2d Ave Detroit MI 48202

RINKER, ROBERTA LEE, marketing professional; b. Long Beach, Calif., June 16, 1953; d. David A. Rinker and Marjorie S. (Wechsler) Hoban. Diploma, Sawyer Bus. Coll., 1972. Sec. Sheraton-Anaheim (Calif.) Hotel, 1972-74, mgr. sales, 1974-78; dir. sales, gen. mgr. Elkhorn at Sun Valley (Idaho), 1978-81; dir. sales Sheraton Hotels in Hawaii, Honolulu, 1981-83, dir. leisure sales, 1985-88, regional dir. sales, 1988—; dir. industry sales Hyatt Hotels in Hawaii, Honolulu, 1984. Mem. Am. Soc. Travel Agts., Hotel Sales Mgmt. Assn. (pres. Orange County chpt. 1978). Club: Honolulu. Office: Sheraton Hotels Hawaii 2555 Kalakaua Box 8559 Honolulu HI 96815

RINKER, RUBY STEWART, foundation administrator; b. Dayton, Ohio, June 11, 1936; d. Encle Stewart and Addie (Hamilton) Stewart-Smith; divorced; children: William Bertram Klawonn, Elizabeth Lynn Dennis, William Stewart-Bradley Klawonn; m. Marshall E. Rinker Sr., Aug. 27, 1987. MA of Adminstrn. and Supervision, Fla. Atlantic U., 1978. Human relations counselor Palm Beach County Sch. System, West Palm Beach, Fla., 1974-84; adminstrv. asst. Bohmfalk Estate, Palm Beach, Fla., N.Y.C, Newport, R.I., 1984—; hon. counselor U.S. Naval Acad., U.S. Air Force Acad. Trustee Bohmfalk Charitable Found.. Mem. Phi Delta Kappa. Home: 561 Island Dr Palm Beach FL 33480

RINSKY, JUDITH LYNN, foundation administrator; b. Sept. 12, 1941. BA in Home Econs., Montclair State Coll., 1963. Tchr. home econs. Florence Ave. Sch., Irvington, N.J., 1963-66; substitute tchr. Millburn-Short Hills Sch. System, 1978-82; coordinator sr. citizens Essex County Respite Care, East Orange, N.J., 1982-87, respite care coordinator, 1988—; member ady. com. gerontology Seton Hall U., 1984—; coordinator Mayor's Adv. Bd. Sr. Citizens, Millburn-Short Hills, 1982-87. Pres. Deerfield Sch. PTA, 1979-80, Millburn High Sch. PTA, 1983-85; co-chmn. Charles T. King Student Loan Fund dinner dance, 1981; mem. Handicapped Access Study com. 1983-85; bd. dirs. Council on Health and Human Services, 1985—. Mem. Lake Naomi Assn. (chmn. sailing com. 1981), N.J. Home Econs. Assn. Am. Home Econs. Assn., Bus. and Profl. Women Millburn-Short Hills, Notary Pub. N.J. Lodge: Millburn Rotary. Home: 23 Winthrop Rd Short Hills NJ 07078

RINZLER, CAROL GENE EISEN, lawyer, writer; b. Newark, Sept. 12, 1941; d. Irving Y. and Ruth (Katz) Eisen; m. Carl Rinzler, July 21, 1962 (div. 1976); children: Michael Franklin, Jane Ruth Amelia. AB, Goucher Coll., 1962; JD, Yale U., 1980. Bar: N.Y. 1981, U.S. Supreme Ct. 1984. Editor Charterhouse Books, Inc., N.Y.C., 1971-73, pub., 1973-74; articles editor Glamour mag., N.Y.C., 1974-77; assoc. Cahill Gordon & Reindel, N.Y.C., 1980-86; of counsel Rembar & Curtis, N.Y.C., 1986—. Author: Frankly McCarthy, 1969, Nobody Said You Had to Eat Off the Floor, 1971, The Girl Who Got All the Breaks, 1980, Your Adolescent: An Owner's Manual, 1981, How to Set Up for a Mah-jongg Game and Other Lost Arts (with J. Gelman), 1987; contbg. editor: Pubs. Weekly, 1983—; book critic, columnist Mademoiselle mag., 1981-86, Cosmopolitan mag., 1983-87; contbr. articles, columns and revs. to various publs. Mem. Friends of Scarlett O'Hara, Women's Media Group (pres. 1984-85), Nat. Book Critics Circle., PEN (exec. bd. 1986—), Assn. Bar City N.Y. (com. copyright and intellectual property 1984-87). Jewish. Club: Cosmopolitan (N.Y.C.). Home: 1215 Fifth Ave New York NY 10029 Office: Rembar & Curtis 19 W 44th St New York NY 10036

RIORDAN, FRANCIS ELLEN, linguist, educator, nun; b. Solomon, Kans., Oct. 24, 1915; d. Patrick Francis and Ella (Barret) R.; A.B., Marymount Coll., 1936; M.A., Cath. U. Am., 1945, Ph.D., 1952. Joined Sisters St. Joseph, 1937; directress St. Mary Acad., Silver City, N.Mex., 1950-51; prin. Luckey High Sch., Manhattan, Kans., 1951-53, Cathedral High Sch., Salina, Kans., 1953-57; prof. French, chmn. fgn. langs. dept. Marymount Coll., Salina, 1962-83, chmn. humanities div., 1980-83, dir. interdisciplinary program, 1973-76; mem. faculty Northwestern Coll., Orange City, Iowa, 1983-84, Ctr. for Peace Concerns, 1984—. Mem. coordinating com. State of Kans. Women's Meeting, 1977. Lang. dept. fellow Cath. U., 1948-49. Mem. Am. Assn. Tchrs. of French, Kappa Gamma Pi. Author: Concept of Love in the French Catholic Literary Revival, 1952; The Brave Walk Single File, pageant, 1959. Home: 108 N Estates Dr Salina KS 67401

RIPLEY, BEVERLY MARIE, professional service company executive; b. Boise, Idaho, June 21, 1938; d. Cecil Delmar Dicus and Edith (Adams) Dicus Aldrich; div.; 1 child, Kyle Ann. Grad. high sch., Boise. Regional mgr. Trade Wind Tours of Hawaii, Los Angeles, 1963-75; owner, mgr. The Travel Foxe, Carmichael, Calif., 1975-78; dir.ops., transp. cons. div. First Travel Corp., Van Nuys, Calif., 1978-79; v.p., gen. mgr. G.T.U., Inc., Honolulu, 1980-81; regional sales mgr. Kahala Hilton Hotel, Beverly Hills, Calif., 1982-83, Maui Inter-Continental Wailea Hotel, Los Angeles, 1983-85; ptnr. The Bill Mgrs., Laguna Hills, Calif., 1987—. Mem. Am. Soc. Travel Agts. (2d v.p. So. Calif. chpt. 1969-71), Pacific Area Travel Assn. (bd. dirs. 1968-69), Travellarians (membership chmn. Los Angeles chpt. 1963-75), Hotel Sales Mgmt. Assn., So. Calif. Soc. Assn. Execs., Meeting Planners Internat., Saddleback C. of C. Home: 27574 Lene St Mission Viejo CA 92692 Office: The Bill Mgrs 25411 Cabot Rd Suite 114 Laguna Hills CA 92693

RIPPER, RITA JO (JODY), financial executive; b. Goldfield, Iowa, May 8, 1950; d. Carl Phillip and Lucille Mae (Stewart) Ripper; B.A., U. Iowa, 1972; M.B.A., N.Y.U., 1978. Contracts and fin. staff Control Data Corp., Mpls., 1974-78; regional mgr. Raytheon Corp., Irvine, Calif., 1978-83; v.p. Caljo Corp., Des Moines, Iowa, 1983-84; asst. v.p. Bank of America, San Francisco, 1984—. Vol. and alt. del. Republican Party, Edina, Minn., N.Y.C., 1975—; vol. Cancer, Heart, Lung Assns., Edina, N.Y.C., Calif., 1974-78, 84—; Lita, 1986—. Mem. Internat. Mktg. Assn., World Trade Ctr. Assn., Acctg. Soc. (pres. 1975-76), Engring. Club of San Francisco, Mensa, Beta Alpha Psi (chmn. 1977-78), Phi Gamma Nu (v.p. 1971-72) Presbyterian. Clubs: Corinthian Yacht, Mt. Tamalpai Racquet. Home: 22 Marinero Circle #46 Tiburon CA 94920 Office: Bank of America 2 Embarcadero Ctr San Francisco CA 94111

RIPPY, FRANCES MARGUERITE MAYHEW, educator; b. Ft. Worth, Sept. 16, 1929; d. Henry Grady and Marguerite Christine (O'Neill) Mayhew; m. Noble Merrill Rippy, Aug. 29, 1955 (dec. Sept. 1980); children: Felix O'Neill, Conrad Mayhew, Marguerite Hailey. BA, Tex. Christian U., 1949; MA, Vanderbilt U., 1951, PhD, 1957; postgrad., U. London, 1952-53. Instr. Tex. Christian U., 1953-55; instr. to asst. prof. Lamar State U., 1955-59; asst. prof. English, Ball State U., Muncie, Ind., 1959-64; assoc. prof. English, Ball State U., 1964-68, prof., 1968—, dir. grad. studies in English, 1966—; editor Ball State U. Forum, 1960—; vis. asst. prof. Sam Houston State U., 1957; vis. lectr., prof. U. P.R., summers 1959, 60, 61; exchange prof. Westminster Coll., U. Oxford, Eng., 1988; cons.-evaluator North Central Assn. Colls. and Schs., 1973—, commn.-at-large, 1987—; cons.-evaluator New Eng. Assn. Schs. and Colls., 1983—. Author: Matthew Prior, 1986. Contbr. articles to profl. jours., chpt. to anthology. Recipient McClintock award, 1966; Danforth grantee, summer 1964, Ball State U. Research grantee, 1960, 62, 70, 73, 76, 87, Lilly Library Research grantee, 1978; Fulbright scholar, U. London. Mem. MLA, Coll. English Assn., Ind. Coll. English Assn. (pres. 1984-85), Johnson Soc. Midwest (sec. 1961-62), AAUP, Nat. Council Tchrs. English, Am. Soc. 18th Century Studies. Home: 4709 W Jackson St Muncie IN 47304

RISCINTO, KAREN MARIE, senior asset management specialist; b. Bronx, Oct. 12, 1958; d. James Garone and Lucille (Falce) Monge; divorced, 1984. AA in Bus. Adminstrn., Broward Community Coll., 1978; student in bus. adminstrn. and real estate, Palm Beach Jr. Coll., 1987—. Licensed mortgage broker. Field coordinator Minto Builders, Inc., Coconut Creek, Fla., 1979-81; office mgr., field coordinator Lindlar Constrn., Coral Springs, Fla., 1981-84; constrn. rep./disbursing agt. Sunrise Savs., Boynton Beach, Fla., 1984-85; fin. analyst Weitz Properties, Inc., West Palm Beach, Fla., 1985-86; staff acct. Old Port Cove Corp., N. Palm Beach, Fla., 1986-87; sr. asset mgmt. specialist MIG Realty Advisors Inc., West Palm Beach, Fla., 1987—; mem. N. Palm Beach Bd. Realtors, 1987. Mem. spl. events bd. West Palm Beach chpt. Am. Cancer Soc., 1986—, new directions, 1986—. Mem. Nat. Assn. Women in Constrn. (chmn. 1984—, leader seminars 1986-87), Nat. Assn. Mortgage Brokers. Democrat. Home: 537 W Kalmia Dr Apt #4 Lake Park FL 33403 Office: MIG Realty Advisors Inc 1645 Palm Beach Lakes Blvd West Palm Beach FL 33401

RISER, VIRGINIA MARIE, principal, educational consultant; b. La Crosse, Wis., Jan. 3, 1942; d. Frank A. and Cornelia Marie (Hurm) R. BA, State U. Iowa, 1964; MLS, Rosary Coll., 1971; PhD, U. Minn., 1981. Tchr. Oelwein (Iowa) Community Sch., 1964-66, Eastern Community Schs., Lansing, Iowa, 1966-69; library dir. Fox Lake City (Ill.) Library, 1971-72; instructional media ctr. dir., tchr. Derham Hall High Sch., St. Paul, 1972-81; instrl. developer U. Medial Sch., St. Paul and Mpls., 1976-81; prin. Assumption Sch., Richfield, Minn., 1981-84; lectr. St. Thomas Coll., Archdiocese St. Paul, U. Minn., St. Pauls and Mpls., 1973—; prin. St. Odilia Sch., St. Paul, 1984—; instrl. developer U. Minn., Archdiocese St. Pauls, Mpls., 1976—; IMC designer Archdiocese St. Paul, 1978—; tchr. supr., 1981—; speaker, cons. Parent Groups and Sch. Faculties, Upper Midwest, 1981—; Minn. rep. to Council on Am. Pvt. Edn., 1987—; adj. assoc. prof. St. Mary's Coll. Winona & Grad. Ctr., Mpls., 1987—. Contbr. articles to profl. jours. Chairperson Deaney Elem. Archdiocesan Sch. Community St. Pauls. Mem. AAUW, Archdiocesan Cath. Sch. Prins. Assn. (exec. bd. 1984—), Minn. Assn. Pvt. Sch. Adminstrs. (pres. 1987—), Deanery Prins. (chmn.), Council Am. Pvt. Edn., Jaycees (Outstanding Young Educator Lansing chpt. 1969), Phi Beta Mu. Home: 1827 Shryer Ave W Roseville MN 55113 Office: St Odilia Sch 3495 N Victoria Saint Paul MN 55126

RISHEIM, WANDA JOAN, educator, artist, pilot, real estate broker; b. July 11, 1935; d. Arthur J. and Meta C. Wands; A.B., Lincoln Christian Coll., 1961; M.S., Ft. Hays State Coll., 1963. Tchr. high schs. in Mo., Ill. and Calif., 1963-74; tchr. San Dieguito High Sch. Dist., Encinitas, Calif., 1976—; area dir. mktg. Jim Rohn Prodns., 1981; one-woman exhbn. Clayton Gallery, St. Louis, 1970; group exhbn. Art Inst. San Diego, 1974-75. Mem. Nat. Assn. Female Execs., NEA, Nat. Art Edn. Assn., Women in Sales, Women in Mgmt., Calif. Tchrs. Assn., AAUW. Club: Toastmasters. Address: 1123 Santa Helena Park Ct Solana Beach CA 92075

RISHMAGUE, SANDRA, chemist; b. Coral Gables, Fla., Apr. 8, 1964; d. Rodolphe Edouard and Frances (Lafferriere) Baboun; m. Miguel Rishmague. BS, U. Miami, Fla., 1985. Chief chemist Rishmague Rubber Co., Miami, FLa., 1985—; cons. Bandas De Colombia S.A., Bogota, Colombia, 1985—, Importadora Rishmague Ltd., Santiago, 1986—. Mem. Am. Chem. Soc. (affiliate). Republican. Roman Catholic. Home: 14553 SW 152d Pl Miami FL 33195 Office: Rishmague Rubber Co 3754 NW 54th St Miami FL 33142

RISING, SUSAN ALLSOPP, data processing executice; b. Columbus, Ohio, Jan. 30, 1954; d. George Russell and Jane Ellen (Allsopp) R. BA in Computational Math., DePauw U., 1976. Programmer Lutheran Gen. Hosp., Park Ridge, Ill., 1976-77, sr. programmer, 1977-78, programmer analyst, 1978-80; systems analyst Lutheran Gen. Health Care System, Park Ridge, Ill., 1980-86; project mgr. systems engring. Riverside Meth. Hosp., Columbus, Ohio, 1987—. Mem. Electronic Computing Health Oriented, Hosp. Mgmt. Systems Soc., Assn. Computing Machinery, Alpha Gamma Delta Internat. Frat. Republican. Episcopalian. Office: Riverside Meth Hosp 3535 Olentangy River Rd Columbus OH 43214

RISK, KATHERINE RENÉE, real estate company officer; b. Dallas, July 29, 1964; d. Jerry Wayne and Margaret Elle (Salyer) Cox; m. Gary Ray Risk (div. Aug. 1986). AA, Richland Coll., 1987; student, U. Tex, Dallas, 1987—. Lic. real estate, Tex. Personnel asst. Trans-Western Exploration, Inc., Dallas, 1981-83; adminstrv. asst. Hoyt R. Matise Co., Dallas, 1983-84; bookkeeper Park City Devel. Co., Garland, Tex., 1984-85; property mgr. Camont Assocs., Richardson, Tex., 1985—. Mem. Nat. Assn. Female Execs. Republican. Methodist.

RISLEY, EDYTH C., petroleum geologist; b. Little Rock, Oct. 12, 1928; d. Elmer J. and Lillie L. (McNeill) R.; student Randolph-Macon Woman's Coll., 1945-47; B.S., So. Meth. U., 1949; postgrad. U. Colo., 1949; M.S., Stanford U., 1951. Jr. geologist McAlester Fuel Co., Magnolia, Ark., 1949; geologist Continental Oil, Midland, Tex., 1951-56; sr. geologist, cons. McCord & Assocs., Dallas, 1957-63; sr. sci. reference librarian Dallas Public Library, 1963-75; hdqrs. staff geologist Holly Corp., Dallas, 1975-77; sr. geologist Ray Holifield & Assos., Dallas, 1977-85, cons. geologist, 1977—. Mem. Am. Assn. Petroleum Geologists (ho. of dels. 1981-84, rec. sec. 1983-84), Dallas Geol. Soc. (sec. 1979-80), West Tex. Geol. Soc., Nat. Audubon Soc., Energy Club of Dallas, Pi Beta Phi. Contbr. publs. in field. Home and Office: 2905 University Blvd Dallas TX 75205

RISNES, MARILYN LOUISE NEITZERT, teacher; b. Huron, S.D., Mar. 22, 1935; d. Herman and Lillian Julia (Delvaux) Neitzert; m. Lawrence Martin Risnes Jr., June 6, 1959 (div. Nov. 1975); children: Bruce Douglas, Wayne LeRoy, Gloria Lynn. BA, St. Cloud U., 1963; MA, St. Mary's Coll., 1978; postgrad., Hamline U. Cert. elem. tchr., reading instr. Minn. Waitress Bar Harbor Supper Club, Brainerd, Minn., 1952-55; tchr. Dist. 31 Rural Schs., Owatonna, Minn., 1954-57, Elizabeth Gardner Sch., Mound, Minn., 1957-59, Spl. Dist. No. 1, Mpls., 1968—; sales rep. Stanley Home Products, Mpls., 1962-64, World Book Ency., Mpls., 1988—; psychotherapist Internat. Transactional Analysis Inst., Mpls., 1974-76; front desk clk. Tyrol Motor Inn, Estes Park, Colo., 1987; asst. tchr. Baldwin Girls Sch., Bangalore, India, 1980; cons. Personal Dynamics Inst., Performax Systems Internat., Youth Devel. Inst., Mpls., 1980-87. Den mother Boy Scouts Am., Mpls., 1970-73. U.S. Dept. Edn. study grantee, 1972. Mem. NEA, Minn. Edn. Assn., Mpls. Edn. Assn., Minn. Fedn. Thcrs., Educators Social Responsibility, ACLU, Women Against Mil. Madness, Ams. for Legal Reform, Peace with Justice Cen. Am. Democrat. Mem. Ch. Religious Sci. Lodge: Moose. Home: 143 Cecil St SE Minneapolis MN 55414 Office: Marcy Open Sch 1042 18th AVe SE Minneapolis MN 55414

RISO, EUNICE ESTELLE, city official; b. Milford, Conn., Feb. 16, 1932; d. Thomas G. and Mildred E. (Almquist) Riso; student U. Conn., 1950-52. Recreation supr. Milford, 1953-55, Visalia (Calif.), 1955-60, Bridgeport (Conn.), 1960-62; supt. recreation Visalia, 1963-70, dir. leisure services, 1970-84, dir. adminstrn., 1984—. Vice chmn. Tulare County Commn. Status Women, 1976-80, chmn., 1980—; fund drive chmn. Golden Valley council Girl Scouts U.S.A., 1972. Mem. Calif. Parks and Recreation Soc. (dist. pres. 1967, Outstanding Recreator award 1970), AAU, Amateur Softball Assn. (commr.), Visalia C. of C. (Woman of Yr. 1984), Calif. Assn. Retarded Children (state and dist. bowling dir. 1968-74), Chi Kappa Rho (dist. pres. 1979-80), Tulare County Women's Trade Club (charter). Lodge: Soroptimist (past pres., Regional Women Helping Women award 1983, Woman of Dist. award 1987). Home: 2020 E Vassar St Visalia CA 93277 Office: 707 W Acequia Visalia CA 93291

RISO, MARIA ASSUNTA, automobile company executive; b. Francavilla, Sicily, Messina, Italy, Oct. 18, 1964; came to U.S., 1967; d. Felice Salvatore and Sebastiana (Ruvolo) R. AA in Secretarial Sci., Berkeley Sch., Ridgewood, N.J. and White Plains, N.Y., 1984; student in computer sci., Dominican Coll., 1986—. Legal sec. Atty. Robert J. Lenrow, Tenafly, N.J., 1983-84; sec. to acctg. BMW N.Am., Montvale, N.J., 1984-86, tech. info. coordinator, 1986—; computer cons. D.G. Wiggers & Son, Closter, N.J., 1986. Mem. Nat. Assn. for Female Execs. Roman Catholic. Home: 239 Livingston St Northvale NJ 07647 Office: BMW North Am Inc BMW Plaza Montvale NJ 07645

RISQUE, NANCY J., federal official; b. Paris. BA, Radford (Va.) Coll., 1968. Mem. staff Rep. Nat. Com., Washington, 1969-73; publicist Robert A. Marston & Assocs., N.Y.C., 1974-75; asst. to asst. sec. of Commerce for Tourism Dept. Commerce, Washington, 1975-77; rep. Energy Affairs dept. Am. Paper Inst., Washington, 1977-78; rep. govt. affairs Standard Oil Co. of Ohio, Washington, 1978-81; spl. asst. to Pres. for Legis. Affairs The White House, Washington, 1981-85; v.p. Russo Watts & Rollins, Inc., Washington, 1986-87; asst. to Pres. and Cabinet Sec. The White House, Washington, 1987—. Del. U.S. Del. to World Conf. to Rev. and Appraise the Achievements of the UN Decade for Women, Nairobi and Vienna, 1985-86; rep.

Presdl. Del. to Botswana Independence Day, 1986; mem. U.S. Pres.'s Interagy. Com. on Women's Bus. Enterprise, Washington, 1983. Mem. Exec. Women in Govt., The Charter 100 (founder D.C. chpt. 1983). Republican. Office: Office of the Pres 1600 Pennsylvania Ave NW Washington DC 20500

RISSER, RITA, lawyer; b. Inglewood, Calif., Apr. 15, 1953; d. Joseph Aurelius and Doris Elizabeth (Stanley) Risser; m. Ray Swartz, May 2, 1982. BA, U. Calif.-Berkeley, 1975, JD, 1978. Bar: Calif. 1979, U.S. Dist. Ct. (no. dist.) Calif. 1979. Atty., Disability Law Ctr., Campbell, Calif., 1978-79; field rep. Assemblyman John Vasconcellos, San Jose, Calif., 1979-80; atty. Law Offices of Harold A. Galloway, Santa Clara, Calif., 1980-81; sole practice law, Santa Clara, 1981-84; atty. Employment Rights Attys., San Jose, Calif., 1984—; lectr. U. Calif.-Santa Cruz, 1984—; pres. Housing for Ind. People, San Jose, 1979-84. Contbr. articles to profl. jours. Mem. Women's Concerns Task Force, Santa Clara County, 1984—. Recipient Achievement award, Calif. Women in Govt., 1981. Mem. Santa Clara County Bar Assn., Calif. Women Lawyers, ACLU, Equal Employment Opportunity Coordinators Council, Nat. Women's Polit. Caucus (pres. 1981), Nat. Speaker's Assn.. Democrat. Club: Soroptimist (pres. 1983-84). Office: Employment Rights Attys 1960 Alameda Suite 200 San Jose CA 95126

RISTEEN, DEBORAH ANN, trade journal editor; b. Viroqua, Wis., Sept. 29, 1952; d. Landon Herbert and Janice Lucille (Holmen) R. BA, Purdue U., 1974. Asst. editor KJOS Music Co., San Diego, 1975-76; mng. editor Soc. Am. Archivists, Chgo., 1977-85, Am. Soc. Clin. Pathologists, Chgo., 1985—. Vol. Ill. Citizens for Handgun Control, Chgo., 1980-81; pres. Apollo Chorus, Chgo., 1983-84; bd. dirs. The James Chorale, Chgo., 1985—. Office: Am Soc Clin Pathologists 2100 W Harrison St Chicago IL 60612

RITCH, KATHLEEN, diversified company executive; Harbor Beach, Mich., Jan. 23, 1943; d. Eunice (Spry) R.; B.A., Mich. State U., 1965: student Katharine Gibbs Sch., 1965-66. Exec. sec., adminstrv. asst. to pres. Katy Industries, Inc., N.Y.C., 1969-70; exec. sec., adminstrv. asst. to chmn. Kobrand Corp., N.Y.C., 1970-72; adminstrv. asst. to chmn. and pres. Ogden Corp., N.Y.C., 1972-74; asst. sec., adminstr. office services, asst. to chmn. Ogden Corp., N.Y.C., 1974-81, corporate sec., adminstr. office services, 1981-84, v.p., corporate sec., adminstr. office services, 1984—; part-owner Unell Mfg. Co., Port Hope, Mich., 1966-87. Mem. Am. Soc. Corporate Secs. Home: 500 E 77th St New York NY 10162 Office: Ogden Corp Two Pennsylvania Plaza New York NY 10121

RITCHARDS-ROBINSON, GLORIA RUTH, business executive, municipal official; b. Camden, N.J., May 10, 1927; d. Alexander Bakeoven and Rosella Mary Magnolia (Richardson) Evans; m. Louis Samuel Ritchards, Oct. 2, 1947 (div. Dec. 1956); children: Carolyn, Eric, Linda, Kenneth, Dennis; m. Richard Morgan Robinson, July 9, 1983. Student, Rutgers U., 1969, Camden (N.J.) Community Coll., 1969-76, American U., 1975-76, Antioch U., Phila., 1978-79, Burlington Community Coll., Cinnaminson, N.J., 1980—, Norfolk State Coll., 1975. Program specialist Social Rehab. Services, Phila., Washington, 1974-78; program analyst Dept. HHS, Health-care Fin. Adminstrn., Phila., Richmond, Va., 1978-84; dir. welfare Gen. Pub. Assistance, Palmyra, N.J., 1982-84; pres. Glo-Rich Inc., Palmyra, 1986—; dir. Defender News, Wilmington, Del., S. Jersey Area News; dir. Youth Cultural Exchange Program, Camden, 1981-84. Vol. social services cons., 1975-84; cert. day care provider, developer Smart Start program for pregnant and new teenage mothers, Camden County. Named Black Role Model, N.J. Hist. Soc., Camden, 1985, one of Outstanding Blacks in South Jersey, Black Am. Assn. Life and History, Camden, 1983. Mem. Am. Assn. Retired Persons, Nat. Assn. Female Execs., Nat. Black Caucus on Aging, Nat. Assn. Negro Bus. and Profl. Women's Clubs (3d v.p. Camden chpt. 1981- 83), Internat. Cultural Exch., VFW. Democrat. Episcopalian. Office: Glo-Rich Inc PO Box 108 Palmyra NJ 08065

RITCHIE, ELISAVIETTA ARTAMONOFF, poet, writer; b. Kansas City, Mo.; d. George Leonidovich and Jessie (Downing) Artamonoff; m. Lyell Hale Ritchie Jr., July 11, 1953 (div. May 1978); children: Lyell Kirk, Elspeth Cameron, Alexander George. Cours de Civilisation Francaise degree, U. Paris, Sorbonne, 1950-51; student, Cornell U., 1951-53; BA in English, French and Russian Studies, U. Calif., Berkeley, 1954; postgrad., Georgetown U., 1959-60; MA in French Lit., Am. U., 1976. Instr. French Am. U., Washington, 1968-74; pres. Washington Writers Pub. House, 1984-87; pres., founder The Wineberry Press., 1983—; instr. Writer's Ctr., Bethesda, Md.; lectr. workshops and translation projects, Brazil, Indonesia, Malaysia, Singapore, Thailand, Hong Kong, Japan, Korea, Philippines, New Zealand, Yugoslavia, Bulgaria. Author: Timbot, 1970, Tightening the Circle Over Eel Country (Gt. Lakes Colls. Assn. New Writer's Award), 1974, A Sheath of Dreams and Other Games, 1976, Moving to Larger Quarters, 1977, Raking the Snow, 1982 (Washington Writers Pub. House award 1981), The Problem with Eden, 1985 (Armstrong State Coll. Chapbook award); editor: Finding the Name, 1983, Dolphin's Arc: An Anthology of Poems on Endangered Marine Species, 1988; contbr. numerous poems, stories, articles to nat. and internat. publs. Mem. Com. for Poetry in Greater Washington Area. D.C. Arts Commn. grantee, 1986, 87. Mem. Washington Ind. Writers, Poetry Soc. Am. (annual awards 1973, 75), Poets and Writers Inc., Poetry Soc. Ga., Amnesty Internat. Russian Orthodox. Episcopalian.

RITCHIE, INGRID MARIA, environmental health scientist, educator; b. Munich, W.Ger., May 26, 1949; came to U.S., 1952; d. Curtis Huey and Johanna Leokadia (Kroll) Ritchie; A.S., Murray State Coll., 1969; B.S. summa cum laude, Southwestern State U., 1971; M.S., U. Minn., 1973, Ph.D. (USPHS fellow), 1980. Research scientist Air Quality Minn. Pollution Control Agy., Mpls., 1974-76, Regional Copper-Nickel Study, Mpls., 1976-79, health risk assessment Minn. Dept. Health, Mpls., 1979-82; asst. prof. Sch. Pub. and Environ. Affairs, Ind. U., Indpls., 1982—; vice chmn. Sci. and Tech. Resource Adv. Council to Minn. Joint Legis. Com. on Sci. and Tech.; mem. Indpl. Air Pollution Control Bd.; mem. task force on Kerosene heaters Underwriters Labs., Inc. Mem. Am. Pub. Health Assn., Nat. Air Pollution Control Assn. Office: Ind U BS-SPEA Room 4083 801 W Michigan St Indianapolis IN 46223

RITENOUR, PATRICIA (WAINAUSKIS), reading specialist, elementary educator; b. Pitts., July 1, 1936; d. Bernard and Sophia (Piela) Wainauskis; m. Donald William Ritenour, Oct. 18, 1980; 1 child, Mary Catherine. BS, U. Pitts., 1957, MS, 1970, MEd, 1975, cert. reading specialist, 1977. Tchr. North Hills Sch. Dist., Pitts., 1957-80, reading specialist, 1980—. Falk scholar Sophia U., 1970. Mem. NEA, Pa. Edn. Assn., North Hills Tchrs. Assn., Theta Phi Alpha. Republican. Roman Catholic.

RITSON, DONNA DIANE, communications administrator; b. Chgo., Feb. 22, 1955; d. Raymond Bernard and Elaine Marion (Englund) Nietschmann; m. Scott Campbell Ritson, Feb. 25, 1978; 1 child, Evan Ray-Bernard; 1 stepchild, Carrie Stewart. B.S. with honors, Roosevelt U., Chgo., 1983; postgrad., 1983—; cert. bus. communicator. Sec. Baxter-Travenol Labs., Deerfield, Ill., 1973-76, advt. asst., 1976-80, conv. coordinator, 1980-83; communications coordinator Angus Chem. Co., Northbrook, Ill., 1983-84, communications mgr., 1984—. Mem. Bus. Profl. Advt. Assn., Nat. Assn. Female Execs., Am. Mktg. Assn. Club: Chgo. Yacht. Avocations: skiing, sailing, scuba diving, boating. Home: 1084 Old Colony Rd Lake Forest IL 60045 Office: Angus Chem Co 2211 Sanders Rd Northbrook IL 60062

RITTENBACH, KAREN JOAN, chemical engineer; b. Colorado Springs, Colo., May 20, 1959; d. James Francis and Mary Ann (Roman) McGuire; m. Klaus Hermann Rittenbach, May 2, 1987. BS in Chem. Engring., Rutgers U., 1981. With E.I. DuPont de Nemours, Parlin, N.J., 1981—, chem. engr., 1981-83, supr., 1983-84, prodn. supr., 1984-86, product mgr., 1986—. Mem. mus. staff St. Leo's Ch., Lincroft, N.J., 1985; vol. speaker career days, local schs. Mem. Mensa, Sierra Club, NAFE. Office: EI DuPont de Nemours Cheesequake Rd Parlin NJ 08859

RITTENHOUSE, SHIRLEY BASH, university administrator; b. Champaign, Ill., Nov. 23, 1928; d. Elmer Clarence and Alice Josephine (Lee) Bash; B.S. in Chemistry with honors, U. Ill., Champaign-Urbana, 1950; m. Warren L. Rittenhouse, Nov. 29, 1975; children—Janice L. Woodward, Barbara A. Pfaller. Research asst. phys. chemistry Parke-Davis Co., Detroit, 1950-52; teaching asst. chemistry U. Ill., 1959-60, research asst. biochemistry, 1960-65, staff asst. president's office, 1965-79, staff assoc., 1979-85. Mem. Phi Beta Kappa, Iota Sigma Pi, Sigma Delta Epsilon, Kappa Alpha Theta. Home: 5 Imperial Ct Champaign IL 61820

RITTER, DEBORAH BRADFORD, lawyer; b. Boston, Nov. 4, 1953; d. Edmund Underwood and Priscilla (Rich) R. BA, Yale U., 1974; JD, Boston Coll., 1980. Bar: N.H. 1980, Mass. 1981. Assoc. McLane, Graf, Raulerson & Middleton, P.A., Manchester, N.H., 1980-82, Singer, Stoneman, Kunian & Kurland, P.C., Boston, 1983—; dir. N.H. Legal Assistance Corp., Concord, 1982-84. Sec. N.H. Performing Arts Ctr., 1980-85; bd. dirs. Yale Alumni Schs. Com., Boston, 1982—. Mem. ABA, Mass. Bar Assn., N.H. Bar Assn. Home: 413 Hammond St Chesnut Hill MA 02167 Office: Singer Stoneman Kunian & Kurland PC 100 Charles River Plaza Boston MA 02114

RITTER, LISA SHARON, advertising executive, writer; b. Los Angeles, Dec. 8, 1963; d. Barry Roy and Carol Lois (Savitsky) R. BA in English, U. Calif., Berkeley, 1985. Tour guide Universal Studios, Universal City, Calif., 1982-84; account exec. James Agy. Advt. and Pub. Relations, Los Angeles, 1985-86, v.p., 1986—; cons. Kappa Alpha Theta Career Network, nat., 1987. Mem. U. Calif. Alumni Assn. (Alumni scholar 1981-85), Phi Beta Kappa, Kappa Alpha Theta Alumni Assn. Office: James Agy Advt & Pub Relations 7455 Beverly Blvd Los Angeles CA 90036

RITTER, MARCIA KAY SOUTHARD, healthcare facility administrator; b. Cape Girardeau, Mo., Dec. 12, 1942; d. Leebert Melton and Katherine Louise Loyd; m. Ray Southard; children: Stephen Ray, Daniel Ray; m. C. John Ritter, Dec. 20, 1986; children: Robin Hackett, Emilie Clarey, John Benjamin. BS, St. Joseph's Coll., 1982; MS, Cen. Mich. U., 1986. RN, cert. nursing adminstr., Mo. Mem. nursing staff Southeast Mo. Hosp., Cape Girardeau, 1963-69, Internal Medicine Group, Cape Girardeau, 1969-72, St. Francis Hosp., Cape Girardeau, 1972-74; head nurse ICU St. Francis Med. Hosp., Cape Girardeau, 1974-76, dir. critical care, 1976-82, dir. staffing, 1982, v.p. patient care, 1982—. Mem. Mo. Orgn. Nurse Execs. (mem. state program com. 1984—), Midwest Alliance Nursing (Mo. rep. edn. for concerns on entry skills 1985-87), Mo. Nurses Assn. (chair council nursing facilitators 1983—), Mo. Orgn. Nurse Execs., Southeast Mo. Council Dirs. Nurses. Office: St Francis Med Ctr 211 Saint Francis Dr Cape Girardeau MO 63701

RITTER, MARY L., interior decorator; b. Glencoe, Ill.; children: Caroline Victoria, Mark Henry. BA, Leland Stanford Jr. U., 1948; cert. N.Y. Sch. Interior Design. Interior decorator, N.Y.C., 1951-56; model, N.Y.C., 1951-56; editorial scout numerous shelter mags. and advt. agys., N.Y.C. area, 1951-56, San Francisco area, 1956-63; interior decorator, San Francisco, 1956—; model home decorator Joseph Eichler Corp., San Francisco, 1958; cons. Earl W. Smith Devel. Corp., 1958-60, Draper Shopping Ctrs., Inc., 1959-61; instr. interior design adult edn. div. Redwood City Dept. Recreation (Calif.), 1968, West Valley Community Coll., 1976-78, Can. Coll., 1977—; rep. sculptor Richard Lippold, 1983—, Peter Lobello, 1985—. Bd. dirs. Children's Home Soc. Calif., 1966, sec. bd. dirs., 1968; chmn. internat. social services spl. event WAIF, 1976, v.p. spl. events, 1969; chmn. benefit March of Dimes, 1979; bd. dirs. San Francisco Host Com., 1979, host com. mem., 1984, chmn. dinner honoring mayor and consuls gen., 1979. Recipient Cert. Merit World Disting. Service in Field of Interior Design, London, 1968, Gold medal Pro-Am Ski Races, Sun Valley, Idaho, 1971; named as model room designer Children's Home Soc. Decorator Showhouse, 1968, San Mateo County Jr. Mus. Aux. Decorator Showcase, 1972; decor designer San Francisco City Hall, Opus I, Symphony Ball, 1984. Mem. Nat. Home Fashion League, Internat. Platform Assn., Stanford U. Alumni Assn., Calif. Palace Legion of Honor, San Francisco Mus. Art, English Speaking Union, San Francisco Ballet Guild, Am. Soc. Interior Designers (bd. dirs. 1983-84), Profl. Women's Network, Patrons of Art of Vatican Museums, Friends of Les Vieilles Maisons Françaises. Clubs: Far West Ski, Far World Ski, Menlo Park Tennis. Contbr. articles to profl. mags. Home and Office: 349 Selby Ln Atherton CA 94025

RITTER, VEDA IRENE, insurance company executive, civic worker, private investor; b. Weatherford, Tex., Aug. 11; d. Wesley Marion and Callie Ann (Hudlow) Hill; m. Chauncey Hirsch Ritter, July 16, 1943 (dec. Dec. 1981). Student, Barnes Bus. Sch., 1934-35, Denver U. Sch. Commerce, 1935-36. Assoc. Ritter Ins. Agy., Denver, 1935—, owner, 1966—; pvt. investor in stocks and bonds. Bd. dirs. Friends of Pub. Library, 1950; active vol. Vis. Nurse Assn., Denver, 1956—; 1st v.p. Republican Assocs., 1960, mem. Colo. fin. com., 1964, alt. del. Nat. Conv., 1960. Presbyterian. Clubs: Denver Press, Cherry Hills Country, Brown Palace, Denver Athletic. Lodge: Ladies of Rotary. (dir. 1950).

RITTERMAN, SHAREN BRUNEAU, audiologist; b. Boston, May 1, 1949; d. Roger Joseph and Arlene Frances (Weisend) Bruneau; A.A., Manatee Jr. Coll., 1969; M.S., U. South Fla., 1972; m. Stuart I. Ritterman, Sept. 2, 1977; 1 son, Joshua Nathaniel. Audiologist, Hillsboro County Public Schs., Tampa, Fla., 1972-75; vis. instr., clin. supr. U. South Fla., Tampa, 1975; clin. audiologist/program dir. audiology Central Fla. Speech and Hearing Clinic, Lakeland, 1976-77; speech/lang. pathologist Pasco County Schs., Dade City, Fla., 1977-83; pres. Cypher Hearing Mgmt. Services Inc. (formerly HearCare Hearing Mgmt. Services, Inc.), 1987—. Recipient cert. clin. competence Am. Speech and Hearing Assn.; cert. of registration in audiology, Fla. Mem. Fla. Speech, Lang. and Hearing Assn., Am. Speech, Lang. and Hearing Assn. Roman Catholic. Address: 181 Ellerbee Rd Wesley Chapel FL 34249

RITTMEISTER, RUTH, travel executive; b. Norway, Mar. 1, 1924; came to U.S., 1951; Asst. AEC, Oslo, Norway, 1945-49; assoc. Bob Burbark Travel, Los Angeles, 1951-54; v.p., gen. mgr. Internat. Travel Service, Honolulu, 1955-83; owner, pres. A Touch of Class Travel, Inc., Honolulu, 1984—; coordinator internat. exhibits Kaliala Hilton, Honolulu, 1967-74. Contbr. articles on travel to various mags. Commr. Mayor's Commn. on Culture and Art, Honolulu, 1977-82. Mem. Am. Soc. Travel Agts. (chmn. pub. relations com. 1968-75), Inst. Cert. Travel Agts. (charter mem.), Pacific Asia Travel Assn., Friends of the East-West Ctr. Lodge: Century (charter mem.). Home: 1650 Ala Moana Blvd Honolulu HI 96815 Office: A Touch of Class Travel Inc 1585 Kapiolani Blvd Honolulu HI 96814

RITZU, BARBARA JEAN, electronics company administrator; b. Cleve., July 25, 1951; d. Frank Charles and Laureen Catherine (Donelon) Pilny; m. Jeremy Allen Ritzu, Nov. 10, 1948; 1 child, Laura Katheryn. Cert. real estate, Lakeland Community Coll., 1986, student, 1986—. Expediter Gould Inc. Ocean Systems Div., Cleve., 1977-78, buyer, 1978-80, sr. buyer, 1980-83; sr. buyer Picker Internat. Inc., Highland Heights, Ohio, 1983-84, major subcontracts adminstr., 1984-88, mgr. subcontracts, 1988—; cons. Project Bus., Cleve., 1981-83, 86-87. Democrat. Roman Catholic. Home: 4775 Highland Dr Willoughby OH 44094 Office: Picker Internat Inc 595 Miner Rd Highland Heights OH 44143

RIVARD, PHYLLIS KELTGEN, graphic arts and printing broker, publisher; b. Mankato, Minn., Aug. 23, 1943; d. Leo M. and Catherine M. (Peters) Keltgen; student Mankato State U., 1961-64, Metro State U., 1978-79; children by previous marriage—Alan, (dec.), Daniel. With DM Printing, Inc., Mankato, Minn., 1960—, newsletter editor, 1962-80, mgr. art dept., 1962-77, instr. inservice tng., 1977-80, v.p. sales, 1977—, co-propr., 1961—; v.p. mktg. The Press, Inc., Chanhassen, Minn., 1981—; graphic arts broker, pub. Par Cons., Inc., Mpls. 1977—. Mem. All-America City Com., 1978; bd. dirs. Jr. Achievement, Mankato chpt., 1980—. Mem. Sales and Mktg. Execs. of Mpls., Minn. Women's Network, Mankato C. of C. (dir. 1977-80), Mankato State Alumni Assn. (pres. 1978-79, dir. 1976—), Printing Brokerage Assn. (Printing Broker of Yr. award). Home and Office: 1920 S First St Minneapolis MN 55454

RIVAS, JOYCE MARGARET, advertising executive; b. Abington, Pa., May 23, 1957; d. John E. and Margaret Ann (Carberry) McGovern; m. David A. Rivas, May 31, 1986. BA in Advt., Pa. State U., 1978; MBA in Mktg., Temple U., 1983. From adminstrv. to research asst. Spiro & Assocs., Phila., 1979, project dir., 1979-80, research mgr., 1980-84, dir. research, 1984-85, v.p., dir. research, 1985-87, sr. v.p. research and plans, 1987-88; sr. v.p. strategic devel. Earle Palmer Browne & Spiro, Phila., 1988—; adj. lectr. MBA program Temple U., Phila., 1985—. Bd. dirs. World Affairs Council Phila., 1986-87. Mem. Am. Mktg. Assn. (pres.-elect Phila. chpt. 1987—). Republican. Roman Catholic. Office: Earle Palmer Browne & Spiro 100 S Broad St Philadelphia PA 19110

RIVENBARK, BILLIE SUE, personnel director; b. Geneva, Ala., July 12, 1939; d. Willie Carl and Mary Edna (Cherry) Gohagan; m. William Smith Sr., Mar. 28, 1959 (div. May 1978); 1 child, William Jr.; m. William Larry Rivenbark, Mar. 30, 1984. Diploma in Bus. and Interior Decorating, Wallace Tech. Coll., Napier Field, Ala., 1959; diploma, Wallace Coll., 1976. Bookkeeper, sec. Brundidge (Ala.) Milling Co., 1959-63; personnel clk. Page Aircraft Maintenance, Inc., Fort Rucker, Ala., 1964-66, clerical specialist, 1966-72; clerical specialist Northrop Worldwide Aircraft Service, Fort Rucker, 1972-79, supr., EEO coordinator, 1979-80, supr., employee assistance program coordinator, 1980-84; supr. EEO coordinator Sikorsky Support Services, Inc., Fort Rucker, 1984—. Sponsor Ala. Alateen group, Ozark, 1979-81; mem. Ozark Job Service Improvement com., 1983, Dale Count Alcohol Abuse Service com., 1984-85, Wallace Coll. Career Adv. Council, 1987. Mem. Assn. Labor-Mgmt. adminstrs. and Consultants on Alcoholism, Wiregrass Personnel Assn., Sikorsky Mgmt. Club, Workers Compensation Claim Assn. Ala. Methodist. Home: 106 Stonebridge Ln Ozark AL 36360 Office: Sikorsky Support Services Box 69 Fort Rucker AL 36362

RIVENBARK, MELODIE LUPTON, research technician; b. Palmerton, Pa., Feb. 19, 1960; d. Dwight Keith and Marylyn Avis (Tuttleton) Lupton; m. Charles Fields Rivenbark I, Aug. 8, 1980; 1 child Charles Fields II. Student, David Lipscomb Coll., 1977-79; BA in Psychology, U. South Fla., 1985. Vet. tech. Greene Animal Hosp., Nashville, 1979-80; vet. technician Murphy Animal Hosp. Emergency Service, Tampa, Fla., 1980-82; research technician VA Hosp., Tampa, 1982-84; vet. technician Woolf Animal Hosp., Tampa, 1984-85, Central Animal Hosp., Tampa, 1985; research technician Dept Med. Microbiology and Immunology Med. Sch. U. South Fla., Tampa, 1985—; v.p. fin. Microprocessor Tech. Corp., Tampa, 1985—. Coordinator Tampa Neighborhood Watch Assn, 1985—; mem. Fla. Ave. Ch. of Christ, tchr. 1986—, visitation leader 1986—, young adult coleader 1986. Mem. Pre-Vet. Soc. (pres., v.p. 1980-84), Sigma Alpha Iota (alt. pres., sec. 1980-84). Democrat. Clubs: Dog Tng. Tampa, (jr. officer 1975-77), Civinettes (Nashville). Home: 1408 E 108th Ave Tampa FL 33612 Office: U South Fla Med Sch Dept Med Micro 12901 Bruce B Downs Blvd MDC Box 10 Tampa FL 33612

RIVERS, BONNIE MCFARLANE, brokerage house executive; b. Bronxville, N.Y., Aug. 19, 1945; d. John Andrew and Frances Darden (Sanders) McF.; (div.) 1 child, Sharon Lynn Jones; m. Alonzo Burrell Rivers, Jan. 31, 1987. Student, Emory U., 1962-63, U. Calif., 1963-64; BBA, Ga. State U., 1966. Analyst fin. Atlantic Steel Co., Atlanta, 1966-67, Minis and Co., Savannah, Ga., 1968-69; v.p. Montag and Caldwell Inc., Atlanta, 1972-79, Robinson-Humphrey Co., Atlanta, 1979-83, J.C. Bradford and Co., Nashville, 1983-85; v.p., food industry analyst Salomon Bros. Inc., N.Y.C., Atlanta, 1985—; trustee, treas. Atlanta Soc. Fin. Analysts, 1982-83. Contbr. articles to profl. jours. Fund raiser, group leader Atlanta Arts Alliance, 1976-78. Fellow Fin. Analysts Fedn.; mem. N.Y. Soc. Security Analysts Inc., Inst. Chartered Fin. Analysts, Consumer Analysts Group N.Y. Office: Salomon Bros Inc 133 Peachtree St Suite 5000 Atlanta GA 30303

RIVERS, JOAN, entertainer; b. 1937; d. Meyer C. Molinsky; m. Edgar Rosenberg, July 15, 1965; 1 child, Melissa. BA, Barnard Coll., 1958. Formerly fashion coordinator Bond Clothing Stores. Debut entertaining, 1960; mem. From Second City, 1961-62; TV debut Tonight Show, 1965; Las Vegas debut, 1969; nat. syndicated columnist Chgo. Tribune, 1973-76; creator: CBS TV series Husbands and Wives, 1976-77; host: Emmy Awards, 1983; guest hostess: Tonight Show, 1983-86; hostess The Late Show Starring Joan Rivers, 1986-87, Hollywood Squares, 1987—; originator, screenwriter TV movie The Girl Most Likely To, ABC, 1973, cable TV spl. Joan Rivers and Friends Salute Heidi Abromowitz, 1985; co-author, dir.: (films) Rabbit Test, 1978, Spaceballs, 1987; recs. include: comedy album What Becomes a Semi-Legend Most, 1983; author: Having a Baby Can be a Scream, 1974; The Life and Hard Times of Heidi Abromowitz, 1984, (autobiography) Enter Talking, 1986. Nat. chmn. Cystic Fibrosis, 1982—, benefit performer for AIDS, 1984. Recipient Cleo awards for commls., 1976, 82; named Woman of Yr., Harvard Hasty Pudding Soc., 1984. Office: care Bil Sammeth Orgn 9200 Sunset Blvd Suite 1001 Los Angeles CA 90069

RIVERS, JOAN NADIA, graphics designer; b. Santa Ana, Calif., Nov. 1, 1944; d. Hubert Murray and Alix (Bredé) Brown; m. David Allen Rivers, Sept. 3, 1965; 1 child, Kristan David. BFA, U. Tex., 1978. Staff artist Sta. KLRN/KLRU TV, Austin, Tex., 1975-78; art dir. J. Walter Thompson Co., N.Y.C., 1979-81; designer Steck-Vaughn Pub. Co., Austin, 1982-83, Tex. Instruments, Austin, 1984-85; designer, owner Rivers Graphic Design, Austin, 1985—. Author, illustrator cartoon: Word Processing and Info. Systems mag., 1980-83. Recipient Cert. Recognition Nat. Assn. Ednl. Broadcasters, 1977-78, Best of Show award Internat. Assn. Bus. Communicators, 1986, Cert. Merit Printing Industries Am., 1986. Mem. Am. Inst. Graphic Arts, Austin Graphic Arts Soc. (award of Excellence 1986), Soc. Tech. Communication (Achievement award 1986). Democrat.

RIVERS, JOYCE MANSFIELD, lawyer; b. Fairbanks, Alaska, Aug. 30, 1935; d. Ralph Julian and Carol (Caldwell) Rivers; m. John Tracy Mansfield, Sept. 15, 1956 (div. Oct. 1974); children—Eugenie Mansfield, Ralph Douglas Mansfield. B.A., Brandeis U., 1958; J.D., U. of Pacific, 1977. Bar: Calif. 1977, Alaska, 1978. Sec., tech. writer asst. for various businesses and law firms, Fairbanks, 1950-58, Los Angeles, 1959-70, Sacramento, 1971-73; legal asst. to county counsel, Sacramento, 1973-77; asst. atty. gen. civil div. Office Atty. Gen. Alaska, Anchorage, 1978-79; corp. staff atty. Alascom, Inc., Anchorage, 1979-83, legal affairs specialist, 1984—, corp. sec., 1985—; assoc. atty. firm Hughes, Thorsness, Gantz, Powell & Brundin, Anchorage, 1983-84. State coordinator NOW, Alaska, 1980-82, sec., 1985-87; chmn. ERA task force for Alaska, 1980-84; 1st v.p. Anchorage Area Democratic Council, 1982-84; mem. Spl. Citizens Com. Alaska Mini-Title IX, 1981-82; nat. del. for Alaska, White House Conf. on Families, 1980; mem. Anchorage Women's Commn., 1985—, Anchorage Sch. Dist. Sex Equity Adv. Com., 1985—. Mem. Anchorage Assn. Women Lawyers, NOW, Nat. Womens Polit. Caucus. Democrat. Home: 2741 W 42d Pl Anchorage AK 99517 Office: Alascom Inc Po Box 196607 Anchorage AK 96607

RIVERS, MARIE BIE, broadcasting executive; b. Tampa, Fla., July 12, 1928; d. Norman Albion and Rita Marie (Monrose) Bie; m. Eurith Dickinson Rivers, May 3, 1952; children—Eurith Dickinson, III, Rex B., M. Kells, Lucy L., Georgia. Student, George Washington U., 1946. Engaged in real estate bus. 1944-51, radio broadcasting, 1951—; chmn., part owner, Sta. WGUN, Atlanta, 1951-87, Sta. KWAM, KRNB, Memphis, Sta. WEAS-AM-FM, Savannah, Ga., Sta. WGOV, WAAC, Valdosta, Ga., Sta. WSWN-AM-FM, Belle Glade, Fla.; owner, chmn. Sta. WXOS, Islamorada, Fla.; chmn. The Gram Corp., Dee Rivers Group, Ocala; pres. real estate cos., Creative Christian Concepts Corp., 1985, United States K-9 Acad., Ocala, broadcast receivables cons., 1986, Deesown, Inc., Suncoast Broadcasting Inc.; owner Laser Acceptance Corp., 1988. Author: A Woman Alone, 1986; contbr. articles to profl. jours. Youth dir. Fla. Appaloosa Horse Club, 1972—. Mem. Fla. Assn. Broadcasters (bd. dirs.), Kappa Delta. Republican. Roman Catholic. Clubs: La Gorce Country (Miami Beach, Fla.); Coral Reef Yacht (Coconut Grove, Fla.); Sweetwater Country (Orlando, Fla.). Home: 7055 SW 70th Ave Ocala FL 32676 Office: GRAM Corp 2801 SW Coll Rd Suite 22 Ocala FL 32674

RIVERS, SHERRY DIANE, educational administrator, author, entrepreneur; b. Conway, Ark., Nov. 22, 1948; d. Edward Lee and Lorene Ann (Fleming) Shock; m. Pat Lee Mansfield, Feb. 6, 1970 (div. Sept. 1979); children: Jonathan Scott, Amy Christen; m. Douglas B. Rivers, Dec. 17, 1983. BSE, U. Cen. Ark., 1971, MSE, 1972; EdD, U. Ark., 1986. Classroom tchr. Ark. Schs., Hot Springs, Ark., 1971-78; edn. examiner Hot Springs Schs., 1979-80; instr. U. Cen. Ark., Conway, Ark., 1980-81; dir. spl. edn. Faulkner County Day Sch., Conway, 1979-83, Springdale (Ark.) Pub. Schs., 1983-84; asst. prof. Western Ill. U., Macomb, Ill., 1984-85; dir. spl. edn. Bi-Co. Spl. Edn. Coop., Morrison, Ill., 1984-86; dir. spl. edn., asst. curriculum dir. Clinton (Iowa) Community Schs., 1986—; Mem. adv. bd., pres. Community Providers Assn., Little Rock, 1982-83; asst. prof. spl. edn.

U. Ala., Birmingham, 1987—; ednl. cons. Vestavia Hills City Schs., Ala. Co-author: Christian Ladies in the Eighties: And Other Balancing Acts, 1986; contbr. articles to profl. jours. Pres. Rep. Women's Club, Clinton, 1987; mem. Rep. Cen.Com., Clinton, 1987. Grantee Devel. Disabilities Services, 1982-83, Found. Exceptional Children, 1985-86. Mem. Am. Assn. Sch. Adminstrs., Council for Exceptional Children, Assn., Assn. Supervision and Curriculum Devel., AAUW (program chmn. 1987), Delta Kappa Gamma, Kappa Kappa Iota. Baptist.

RIVES, SUSAN RAE, association administrator; b. Amarillo, Tex., Nov. 30, 1944; d. Forrest A. and Rubie Tom (Jordan) Gibbs; m. Ray Gilbert Besing, Aug. 1975 (div. Dec. 1980); m. Jon Matthew Rives, Mar. 4, 1983; 1 child, Tiffany. B.A., San Angelo State Coll., 1967. Sec. Cooper Airmotive, Dallas, 1972-75; simulation services adminstr. Simuflite Tng. Co., Dallas, 1981-84; mgr. office services Legion Cos., Dallas, 1985-87; mgr. admstrv. services Am. Heart Assn., 1987—. Asst. White House Advance Staff, Dallas, 1979; mem. advance publicity staff John Hill Gubernatorial Campaign, Dallas, 1979; pres. Walker Middle Sch. PTA, Dallas, 1979-80. Mem. Nat. Assn. Female Execs. Democrat. Episcopalian. Office: Am Heart Assn Nat Hdqrs 7320 Greenville Ave Dallas TX 75231

RIVETT, PATRICIA FERN, infosystems specialist; b. Calgary, Alta., Can., Feb. 6, 1947; d. Ruel Reed and Frances Lilla (Boundy) Dawson; m. Arnold Maclean Rivett, Sept. 15, 1967 (div. 1981); 1 child, Michelle. BA in English with Distinction, U. Calgary, 1971; cert. in applied info., Mount Royal Coll., 1986. Cert. Applied Info. Mgmt. Library technician U. Calgary, 1971; records clk. Husky Oil Ops., Calgary, 1980-83, info. analyst, 1983-87; analyst info. mgmt. City of Calgary, 1987—. Pastoral care Robert McClure United Ch., Calgary, 1981-82, Sunday Sch., 1981-82, outreach, 1981-82, stewardship, 1986. Mem. Assn. Records Managerial Adminstrs. (program com. 1986-87, Clara 1987), Can. Micrographics Soc. Home: 183 Maranda Close NE, Calgary, AB Canada T2A 3E7

RIVLIN, ALICE MITCHELL, economist; b. Phila., Mar. 4, 1931; d. Allan C. G. and Georgianna (Fales) Mitchell; m. Lewis Allen Rivlin, 1955 (div. 1977); children: Catherine Amy, Allan Mitchell, Douglas Gray. B.A., Bryn Mawr Coll., 1952; Ph.D., Radcliffe Coll., 1958. Mem. staff Brookings Instn., Washington, 1957-66, 69-75, 83—; dir. econ. studies Brookings Inst., 1983-87; dir. Congl. Budget Office, 1975-83; dep. asst. sec. program coordination HEW, Washington, 1966-68, asst. sec. planning and evaluation, 1968-69; Staff Adv. Commn. on Intergovtl. Relations, 1961-62; bd. dirs. UNISYS Corp. Author: The Role of the Federal Government in Financing Higher Education, 1961, (with others) Microanalysis of Socioeconomic Systems, 1961, The U.S. Balance of Payments in 1968, 1963, Systematic Thinking and Social Action, 1971, Setting National Priorities: The 1974 Budget, 1973, (with others) Economic Choices 1987, 1986; (with others) The Swedish Economy, 1987, (with others) Caring for the Disabled Elderly: Who will Pay?, 1988. MacArthur fellow, 1983. Mem. Am. Econ. Assn. (nat. pres. 1986). Office: Brookings Inst 1775 Massachusetts Ave NW Washington DC 20036

RIVLIN, RACHEL, lawyer; b. Bangor, Maine, Sept. 1, 1945; d. Lawrence and A. Sara (Rich) Lait. BA, U. Maine, 1965; MA, U. Louisville, 1968; JD, Boston Coll., 1977. Bar: Mass. 1977, U.S. Dist. Ct. Mass. 1978, U.S. Ct. Appeals (1st cir.) 1983, U.S. Supreme Ct. 1985. Audiologist Boston City Hosp., 1969-72; dir. audiology Beth Israel Hosp., Boston, 1972-74; atty. Legal Systems Devel., Boston, 1977-78, Liberty Mutual Ins., Boston, 1978-82; counsel, sec. Lexington Ins. Co., Boston, 1982-85, v.p., assoc. gen. counsel, 1985—. Mem. Boston Coll. Law Sch. Alumni Council, Newton, Mass., 1983-87, ann. fund com., 1981—, mem. ADL Civil Rights Com., Boston, 1982—, South End. Hist. Soc., Boston, 1978-84; bd. dirs. DanceArt, Inc., Boston, 1985—. Mem. ABA (vice chmn. com. on pub. regulation of ins. 1981-84, chmn. elect 1984-85, chmn. 1985-86, chmn. pub. relations 1981-84, excess surplus lines and reins. com. 1982—, vice chmn. 1986-87, chmn. elect 1987-88, chmn. 1988—, internat. ins. law com. 1982—), Boston Bar Assn. (chmn. corp. counsel com., 1987, chmn. membership com. 1978-83, subcom. on ABA model rules of profl. conduct 1980-81, council 1983-86, chmn. ins. law com. 1987—). Home: 6 Viewhill Rd. Southboro MA 01772 Office: Lexington Ins Co 200 State St Boston MA 02110

RIZZO, MARY ANN FRANCES, international trade executive, former educator; b. Bryn Mawr, Pa., Jan. 11, 1942; d. Joseph Franklyn and Armella Louise (Grubenhoff) R.; B.A. magna cum laude (N.Y. State scholar), Marymount-Manhattan Coll., 1963; M.A. (fellow), Yale U., 1965, Ph.D. (Lounsbury-Cross fellow), 1969; grad. smaller co. mgmt. program Harvard U. Bus. Sch., 1979. Instr., Romance langs. and lit. Yale U., New Haven, 1966-70; asst. prof. Finch Coll., N.Y.C., 1971-73; v.p. Joseph F. Rizzo Co., Fla., 1969-87; owner, pres., 1987—; minister of the Word coordinator, Our Lady of Perpetual Help Ch., Scottsdale, Arix., 1986—; mem. bd. adv. Assn. Internat. des Etudiants en Sciences Economiques et Commerciales, Ariz. State U. Vice chmn., charter mem. bd. regents Catholic U. Am. Mem. Am. Assn. Tchrs. of Italian, MLA, Am. Assn. Univ. Profs. Italian, Am.-Italy Soc., Il Circolo Italian Cultural Club (Palm Beach, Fla.), Fgn. Trade Council Palm Beach County (charter mem.), Ariz. World Trade Council, Scottsdale C. of C., Alpha Chi. Republican. Roman Catholic (community council 1972-74). Clubs: Harvard Bus. Sch. Greater N.Y., Yale (N.Y.C. and Phoenix); Alliance Francaise (Phoenix); Yale of Palm Beaches; Cercle Français de Palm Beach (Fla.): Ariz. Harvard Bus. Sch. Translator: From Time to Eternity, 1967; bibliographer: Italian Literature-Roots and Branches, 1976. Home: Villa Serein 2170 Ibis Isle Rd Palm Beach FL 33480 also: 5665 N 74th Pl Scottsdale AZ 85253 Office: 7436 E Stetson Dr Suite 180 Scottsdale AZ 85251 also: PO Box 1376 Lake Worth FL 33460

RIZZO, TERRIE LORRAINE HEINRICH, aerobic fitness executive; b. Oneonta, N.Y., Dec. 15, 1946; d. Steven Joseph Heinrich and Grace Beatrice (Davis) Chamberlin; m. Michael Louis Rizzo, Dec. 28, 1968; 1 child, Matthew Michael. BA, Pa. State U., 1968; MA, Johns Hopkins U., 1971. Tchr. Balt. County Sch. System, 1968-79; asst. dir. univ. relations U. Md., Catonsville, 1980-81; exec. dir. Aerobic Danse de Belgique, Brussels, 1981—; pres. Eurobics Inc., Sunnyvale, Calif., 1984—; aerobics dir. Green Valley Health Clubs, San Jose, Calif., 1985; pres. Personally Fit, 1986; cons. Belgian Ministry Sport, Sabena Airlines, others; lectr., syndicated columnist, 1986—. Author: Sittercise, 1985; contbr. articles to profl. jours. Pres. Internat. Study Group, Brussels, 1983-84. Named Marketeer of Yr. Am. C. of C. in Belgium, 1987. Mem. Internat. Dance Exercise Assn., Assn. for Fitness in Bus., Aerobics and Fitness Assn. Am., Pa. State Alumni Assn. (bd. dirs. 1979-88), Brussels and Sunnyvale C. of C., San Francisco VCB, Mensa, Pi Gamma Mu, Phi Alpha Theta. Democrat. Roman Catholic. Clubs: Am. Women's (Brussels) (dir. 1983-84); San Jose Quota (bd. dirs. 1986-87). Avocations: traveling, oenology, gourmet cooking. Home: 19755 Lanark Ln Saratoga CA 95070 Office: 108 E Fremont Ave Sunnyvale CA 94087

RIZZO-PUYA, KAREN MARIE, mortgage broker, insurance executive; b. Hempstead, N.Y., June 24, 1959; d. Salvatore John and Marie Anne (Farriella) R. AA in Fashion Mdse., Nassau Community Coll., 1978; student, Hofstra U. Mgr. floor metro 700 Entertainment Co., Franklin Square, N.Y., 1981-82; mgr. 107 No. Entertainment Co., Glen Cove, N.Y., 1982-83; agt. N.Y. Life Ins. Co., Syosset, N.Y., 1983-88; account exec. Property Asset Planning, New Hyde Park, N.Y., 1986-87; owner, pres. Property Investment Concepts, Inc., Plainview, N.Y., 1987—. Contbr. articles to profl. jours. Mem., donor Nat. Make a Wish Found. Mem. Nat. Assn. Life Underwriters, Nat. Assn. Securities Dealers (mem. securities and exchange commn. 1985-88), Nat. Assn. Women Life Underwriters (speaker 1986), N.Y. Bd. Realtors (agt. 1986-88), L.I. Networking Entreprenuers, Nat. Assn. Female Execs. Home: 850 Arthur St West Hempstead NY 11552

ROACH, ANTOINETTE VELORIES, fin. brokerage co. co. exec.; b. Meridian, Miss., July 8, 1931; d. Otha Lee and Ester (Mayatte) Ethridge; student public schs., Waco, Tex., Collinsville, Miss.; m. Billy J. Green, May 5, 1979; children—Carl Lowell Roach, Nan Roach Kurth, Mike Roach, Jackie Roach Pilkinton. Ins. and real estate salesperson, 1964-81; pres., owner, operator Lubbock Mortgage Co., Inc. (name now Guaranty Fin. Services, Inc.), Lubbock, Tex., 1976—; pres. Delta Cotton Co., 1977—; pres. Hunter & Roach Advt. Co., Lubbock, 1978—; founder Guaranty Constrn. of Miss. Inc., 1985—, Waveland, v.p., pres. Lubbock, Tex., 1985—. Mem. Nat. Assn. Fin. Cons., Nat. Assn. Female Execs. Inc., Better Bus. Bur., Sheriff Assn., Internat. Bus. Assn., Am. Alliance Small Bus. Club: Presidents of Tex. Home: PO Box 93236 Lubbock TX 79493-3236 Office: 1928 34th St Lubbock TX 79411

ROACH, DOROTHY MARIE, manufacturing executive, accountant; b. Rochester, N.Y., July 9, 1954. BBA in Acctg., John Carroll U., 1976; MBA in Fin., Case Western Res. U., 1980. CPA, Ohio. Divisional acct. Diamond Shamrock, Chardon, Ohio, 1977-78; fin. analyst Diamond Shamrock, Cleve., 1978-79, analyst fin. systems, 1979-81; fin. analyst Sherwin Williams, Cleve., 1981-84, mgr. acctg., 1984-85; mgr. fin. planning and analysis Rubbermaid, Inc., Wooster, Ohio, 1985—. instr. CPR ARC, Wooster, 1986-87; chairperson Rubbermaid fund drive United Way, Wooster, 1987; bd. dirs. Wayne County Red Cross (treas. 1987—); advisor Jr. Achievement, 1977, 85, 88. Mem. Ohio Soc. CPA's. Republican. Roman Catholic. Office: Rubbermaid Inc 1147 Akron Rd Wooster OH 44691

ROANE, DENISE MARSHA, systems engineer; b. Bklyn., June 25, 1957; d. Arnold Frances and Myrtle (Bradway) R.; m. Percy G. Johnson Jr., July 17, 1976 (div. Nov. 1982). Student, Boston U., 1975-76, 83-86, La. State U., Baton Rouge, 1977-79; BS, Lesley Coll., 1988. Stenographer South Cen. Bell, Baton Rouge, 1977, staff support supr., 1977-78, asst. mgr. electromech. systems, 1978-79, asst. mgr. staff support, 1979-80, asst. mgr. adminstrn., 1980-81, asst. mgr. electronic systems, 1981-83; service coordinator No. Telecom Inc., Framingham, Mass., 1983-84, systems engr., 1984-86; sr. systems engr. No. Telecom Inc., Waltham, Mass., 1987—. Mem. Nat. Assn. for Female Execs. Republican. Episcopalian. Office: No Telecom Inc Bay Colony Corp Ctr 1000 Winter St Waltham MA 02154

ROANTREE, DEBORAH ANNE, sales executive; b. Manhasset, N.Y., Nov. 17, 1960; d. William J. and Barbara Anne (Caffrey) R. Asst. traffic mgr. Harbor Imports Inc., Port Washington, N.Y., 1979; mgr. production Precision Reflectors Internat., Port Washington, 1980-85; pres. Aero Research Assoc. Inc., Port Washington, 1985—. Republican. Clubs: L.I. Divers Assn., Port Washington Yacht Trapshooting. Office: Aero Research Assocs Inc 1 Sintsink Dr E Port Washington NY 11050

ROASEAU, MARY LOU, financial manager; b. Richmond, Va., Aug. 27, 1955; d. Paul Eugene and Ella Mae (Johnson) Kline; m. Martin Leon Roaseau, Mar. 10, 1979. BBA, Coll. William & Mary, 1977, MBA, 1984. CPA, Va. With Newport News Shipbldg., Va., 1977—; mgr. fin. reporting Dry Dock Co. subs., 1986—; dir. Newport News Shipbuilding Employees Credit Union. Co-chairwoman United Way Campaign, 1984-86, budget panel, 1980-82, dir. internal audit Newport News Shipbuilding United Way Campaign; treas. Va. peninsula council on domestic violance, Hampton, 1985—. Mem. Newport News Shipbuilding Employees Credit Union (sec. 1982—, dir.), Peninsula Women's Network, Peninsula Young Women's Christian Assn. (Tribute to Women's Industry award 1986). Republican. Methodist. Home: 422 Dunham Massie Dr Hampton VA 23669

ROATH, ALANE ELIZABETH, sales representative; b. Aurora, Colo., July 29, 1964; d. Sterling and Marie Esther (Betts) R. BS in Mktg., SW Mo. State U., 1986. Sales rep. 3-M Co., Bloomington, Ill., 1987—. Vol. Persoinal Assistance Phone Help, Bloomington 1988. Mem. Nat. Assn. Female Execs., Am. Mktg. Assn. Home: 1906 Tracy Dr Bloomington IL 61701 Office: 3-M Co 1906 Tracy Dr Bloomington IL 61701

ROBB, LYNDA JOHNSON, writer; b. Washington, Mar. 19, 1944; d. Lyndon Baines and Claudia Alta (Taylor) Johnson; m. Charles Spittal Robb, Dec. 9, 1967; children—Lucinda Desha, Catherine Lewis, Jennifer Wickliffe. BA with honors, U. Tex., 1966. Writer, McCall's mag., 1966-68; contbg. editor Ladies Home Jour., 1968-80; lectr. bd. dirs. Reading Is Fundamental, 1968—, Lyndon B. Johnson Family Found., 1969—; mem. Woodlawn Found., White House Fellows Regional Selection Bd., Va. State council on Infant Mortality, Nat. Commn. to Prevent Infant Mortality; chmn. Pres.'s Adv. Com. for Women, 1979-81; chmn. Va. Women's Cultural History Project, 1982-85 ; bd. dirs. Nat. Home Library Found., George Marshall Found.; chmn. Va. Women's Cultural History Project, 1982—; mem. So. Govs. Task Force on Infant Mortality; mem. adv. bd. Commn. Presdl. Debates. Mem. Nat. Wildflower Research Ctr., Zeta Tau Alpha. Democrat. Episcopalian.

ROBBINS, ANN TURNER, educational administrator; b. Athens, Ala., Aug. 23, 1940; d. Frank Patterson and Ora Lee (Rose) Turner; m. James Woodrow Robbins, Oct. 28, 1956; children—James Woodrow, Joseph Howell II. B.S. in Elem. Edn. cum laude, Samford U., 1969, M.S. in Elem. Edn., 1972; advanced degree in edn. leadership U. Ala.-Birmingham, 1978. Cert. tchr. grades 1-8, cert. ednl. adminstr. kindergarten-12, Ala. Tchr. Vestavia Elem. Sch., Ala., 1969-71; tchr. Pizitz Middle Sch., Vestavia, 1972-77, tchr., adminstrv. asst., 1977-78; prin. Edgewood Elem. Sch., Homewood, Ala., 1978—. Mem. Homewood Prins. Assn. (v.p. 1984-86), Ala. Assn. Elem. Sch. Prins. (dist. v.p and pres.-elect 1986-88), Nat. Assn. Sch. Prins., Ala. Assn. Sch. Adminstrs., Ala. Council Sch. Adminstrs Suprs., Assn. Supervision and Curriculum Devel., Women Educators Network, Montevallo In-Service Ctr. (adminstr. governing bd.), Ala. Council Computer Edn., Kappa Delta Pi. Republican. Baptist. Avocations: cooking; reading; physical fitness. Office: Edgewood Elem Sch 901 College Ave Homewood AL 35209

ROBBINS, BILLIE, education educator; b. Poland, Dec. 13, 1936; came to U.S., 1946; d. Julius and Goldie (Ptasiewitch) Koziol; m. Arthur F. Robbins, June 8, 1957; children: David, Lawrence, Daniel. BS, Bklyn. Coll., 1958; MA, Queens Coll., 1965; PhD, Fordham U., 1983. Cert. tchr., N.Y. Elementary sch. tchr. N.Y.C. Bd. Edn., 1958-62, substitute tchr., 1962-70; part time instr. Hofstra U., Hempstead, N.Y., 1970-75, instr., 1975-76; instr. Adelphi U., Garden City, N.Y., 1976-80, asst. prof., 1980-86, assoc. prof., 1986—; Cons. in field, 1975—. fund raiser, sec. Great Neck Cancer Soc., 1980. Mem. TESOL, ASCD, NCTE, Alliance for Global Edn. Jewish. Home: 98 Station Rd Great Neck NY 11023 Office: Adelphi U Inst for Teaching and Ednl Studies Garden City NY 11530

ROBBINS, CARRIE F(ISHBEIN), theatrical, interior and costume designer, educator; b. Balt., Feb. 7, 1943; d. Sidney W. and Bettye A. (Berman) Fishbein; m. Richard D. Robbins, Feb. 15, 1969. B.S. and B.A., Pa. State U., 1964; M.F.A., Yale Drama Sch., 1967. Costume designer Saturday Night Live, 1985-86, (2 Tony nominations), also 19 Broadway shows, N.Y.C., 1968—, San Francisco Opera, 1980, Opera Co. of Boston, 1975, 76, 86, Hamburg State Opera (W.Ger.), 1979, Washington Opera Soc., 1975, 4 shows N.Y. Shakespeare Festival, 10 shows Lincoln Ctr. Repertory V. Beamont Theatre, 3 shows Tyrone Guthrie Theatre, Mpls., 3 shows Mark Taper Forum, Los Angeles, 9 shows various regional theatres U.S., 7 shows Chelsea Theatre Ctr., Bklyn., 3 shows John Houseman's City Ctr. Acting Co., Juilliard Sch., N.Y.C., 5 shows sta. WNET and cable TV, 5 Off-Broadway Theatres, N.Y.C.; vis. guest lectr. on costume design U. Ill., UCLA, Oberlin Coll., others; master tchr. costume design NYU, 15 yrs.; designer apparel for staff of Rainbow Room, Rockefeller Ctr., 1987. Solo exhibit art work, Cen. Falls Gallery, N.Y.C., 1980; participant group exhbns. Cooper Hewitt Mus., Pa. State U., Wright-Hepburn Gallery, N.Y.C., Scottsdale, Ariz., Cen. Falls Gallery, 1983; illustrations and calligraphy pub. annual calendar Soc. of Scribes competition, also Ms. mag.; work chosen to hang in juried show Salmagundi Club (Fine Arts Soc.), 1983, 84; original costume work photographed in books: Costume Design, 1983, Fabric Painting and Dyeing for the Theatre, 1982; original drawing reproduced Time-Life Series: The Ency. of Collectibles; designer loft conversions, comml. lobby space, studios, numerous others. Named Disting. Alumna, Pa. State U., 1979; recipient Drama Desk award, Am. Theatre Wing, N.Y.C., 1971, 72, Maharam award for design, Joseph Maharam Found., N.Y.C., 1975, Juror's Choice award for surface design, Fashion Inst. of Tech., 1980, Dramalogue Critics' award for Outstanding Achievement in Theatre, Los Angeles, 1982, Silver Medal, 6th Triennial of Theatre Design, Novisad, Yugoslavia, 1981. League N.Y. Theatres, N.Y.C., 1971-72, 73-74. Steering com. League Profl. Theatre Tng. Programs, 1977-84. Mem. Profl. Women in Theatre, Am. Women's Econ. Devel., Graphic Artists Guild, Soc. Scribes, Am. Soc. Interior Designers, United Scenic Artists Local 829. Home and Office: 11 W 30th St 15th Floor New York NY 10001

ROBBINS, CHRISTINE PATRICIA, artist, designer, creative director; b. Montclair, N.J., Jan. 9, 1954; d. Frederick James Nabkey and Rita Lewis; m. Andrew Richard Magdanz (div. Feb. 1984); m. K.C. Lambert, July 18, 1987. BA with honors, U. Wis., 1975, MA with honors, 1976; MFA, Calif. Inst. Arts, 1988. Assoc. curator Art Mus. Assn. Am., San Francisco, 1977-1981; ptnr. Max Almy Prodns., Oakland, Calif., 1981-84; exec. editor, pub. G.A.S. jour., Corning, N.Y., 1984—; artist, designer Robbins Design, San Francisco, 1980—; design ptnr. Western Influence Studios, Berkley, Calif., 1976-80; cons. fine arts design, San Francisco, 1981—, Art Programs, San Francisco, 1981-82, Calif. Arts Council, Sacramento, 1981—, Craft and Folk Art Mus., Los Angeles, 1985. Numerous internat.pub. and private collections, exhibitions and publications. Recipient 1st place Calif. State Art Exhibn., 1982, 1st place Women Design Internat., N.Y.C., 1983, 1st place internat. competition, 1983. Mem. Am. Film Inst., Glass Art Soc. (bd. dirs. 1984-88), Image Techs. (bd. advisors 1986—). Democrat. Home and Office: 365 Connecticut St San Francisco CA 94107

ROBBINS, DEBORA ROOF, financial executive; b. New Bern, N.C., Oct. 9, 1953; d. Richard E. and Shirley F. (McWharter) Roof; m. James H. Robbins Jr., Apr. 10, 1982. AA in Applied Sci., Columbus Tech. Inst., 1974; BS, Ohio State U., 1977; MBA, Ariz. State U., 1985. Sec. Motorola Semiconductor, Phoenix, 1979-81; tng. specialist, 1981-83; tng. specialist MeraBank, Phoenix, 1983, tng. supr., 1983-86, asst. tng. mgr., 1986-87, mgr. human resources, 1987—; instr. Rio Salado Community Coll., Phoenix, 1979-80; tng. officer MeraBank, Phoenix, 1985-87; asst. v.p., 1987. Mem. Nat. Assn. Bank Women, Am. Soc. Tng. and Devel. Democrat. Office: MeraBank 20002 N 19th Ave Phoenix AZ 85027

ROBBINS, EDITH R., systems analyst; b. Wilson, N.C., Oct. 18, 1945; d. Donahue Wells and Lillie Banks (Wells) Barnes; m. Andrew Robbins, Jan. 18, 1965 (div. 1970); children: Milton Donahue Wells, Felicia Antoinette Robbins Anderson. Student, Fed. City Coll., Washington, 1971-72, Prince George Community Coll., Largo, Md., 1980-81. With U.S. Postal Service, Washington, 1966—, gen. clk. contract compliance, 1972-73, appeals clk. EEO Appeals div., 1973-80, systems coordinator EEO Appeals div., 1980-82, EEO Appeals asst., EEO Appeals div., 1982-85, computer systems analyst Employee Relations div., 1985—. Mem. Nat. Assn. Female Execs., Internat. Assn. Tng. in Communications. Baptist. Club: Postal (pres. 1984). Home: 7023 Marbury Ct District Heights MD 20747 Office: US Postal Service 475 L'Enfant Plaza SW Washington DC 20260

ROBBINS, JANE BORSCH, library and information science educator; b. Chgo., Sept. 13, 1939; d. Reuben August and Pearl Irene (Houk) Borsch; married; 1 dau., Molly Warren Robbins. B.A., Wells Coll., 1961; M.L.S., Western Mich. U., 1966; Ph.D., U. Md., 1972. Asst. prof. library and info. sci. U. Pitts., 1972-73; asso. prof. Emory U., Atlanta, 1973-74; cons. to the bd. Wyo. State Library, 1974-77; asso. prof. La. State U., Baton Rouge, 1977-79; dean La. State U. (Sch. Library and Info. Sci.), 1979-81; prof., dir. Sch. Library and Info. Studies U. Wis., Madison, 1981—. Author: Public Library Policy and Citizen Participation, 1975, Public Librarianship: A Reader, 1982; contbr. numerous articles to profl. jours.; Editor: Library and Information Science Research, 1982—. Mem. ALA (councilor 1976-80), Am. Soc. Info. Sci., Assn. for Library and Info. Sci. Edn. (dir. 1979-81, pres. 1984), Wis. Library Assn. (pres. 1986). Democrat. Episcopalian. Office: U Wis Sch Library & Info Studies Madison WI 53706

ROBBINS, JANE LEWIS, educator; b. New Iberia, La., Dec. 14, 1942; d. William Lewis and Maurine (James) R. B.S., U. Okla., 1965; M.E., So. Methodist U., 1971; postgrad. Tex. Women's U., 1981, 83, 85. Tchr., Lone Grove Ind. Sch. Dist. (Okla.), 1964-65, Concord-Carlisle (Mass.) Regional Sch. Dist., 1966-67, Newton (Mass.) Pub. Schs., 1967-68, Highland Park Ind. Sch. Dist., Dallas, 1968—; instr. reading clinic So. Meth. U., 1972-75, Sch. Edn., summer 1978, adj. prof. Div. Ednl. Studies; chmn. English dept. McCulloch Middle Sch.; regional coordinator Tex. Acad. Pentathlon, 1985—. Mem. Tex. Assn. Improvement Reading, Tex. Assn. Gifted and Talented, Assn. Children with Learning Disabilities, Internat. Reading Assn. (North Tex. Council), Tex. Middle Sch. Assn., Assn. for Supervision and Curriculum Devel. Consortium, Pi Beta Phi, Delta Kappa Gamma. Republican. Episcopalian.

ROBBINS, LILLIAN CUKIER, psychology educator; b. Nancy, France, Sept. 6, 1933; came to U.S., 1943; BA, CCNY, 1954; MA, U. Ill., 1956; PhD, NYU, 1961. Cert. psychologist, N.Y. Research psychologist NYU Med. Ctr., 1962-67; asst. prof. Hunter Coll., N.Y.C., 1967-70, CCNY, 1970-71; assoc. prof. Rutgers U., Newark, 1971-76, prof., 1976—; prin. investigator Citizen's Com. for Children, N.Y.C., 1973-75. Contbr. articles to profl. jours. Chair women's issues Am. Jewish Com., N.Y.C., 1984-86. Mem. AAAS (life), AAUP (exec. council), Am. Psychol. Assn., Phi Beta Kappa. Democrat. Jewish. Home: 49 E 96 St New York NY 10128 Office: Rutgers U Newark NJ 07102

ROBBINS, LORI ANN KONENDER, data processing executive; b. Detroit, July 11, 1960; d. Robert Anthony and Margaret Ann (Clancy) K.; m. Michael John Robbins, Sept. 26, 1987. BBA, Ea. Mich. U., 1982. Mgr. account Xerox Corp., Southfield, Mich., 1983-86; mgr. dist. Compuware Corp., Farmington Hills, Mich., 1986—. Recipient scholarship State of Mich., 1978. Mem. Sigma Sigma Sigma. Home: 3624 MacNichol Trail West Bloomfield MI 48033

ROBBINS, MARTHA HELEN, corporate administrator; b. La Junta, Colo., Sept. 27, 1952; d. Richard Carl and Ruth Janet (Staman) R. BA, Drake U., 1972, M Pub. Adminstrn., 1973. Health planner Gov.'s Office for Planning and Programming, Des Moines, 1973-75, dir. health manpower project, 1975-77; dir. resources devel. Western Colo. Health Systems Agy., Grand Junction, 1977-78; planning specialist Colo. Hosp. Assn., Denver, 1978-79; chief operating officer Davis Inst. on Aging, Denver, 1979-80; asst. adminstr. The Children's Hosp., Denver, 1980-84; v.p., co-owner Med. Systems for Bus. and Industry, Inc. dba Clinicare, Denver, 1981—; corp. staff specialist Rocky Mountain Child Health Services, Inc., Denver, 1984-86; gen. and mng. ptnr. 5400 Investment Co., Denver, 1985—; v.p., co-owner Work Rite of Colo., Inc., Denver, 1985—, gen. and mng. ptnr., 1986—; instr. pub. adminstrn. Drake U., Des Moines, 1974; cons. in field, 1980—. Contbr. articles to profl. jours. Orch. mem. Des Moines Symphony, 1969-73, Des Moines Met. Operas, Indianola, Iowa, 1969-76; mem. Colo. Nursing Needs Assessment Panel, Denver, 1974-78; vice chairperson adv. bd. Colo. Hosp. Commn., Denver, 1977-78; vol. Hospice of St. John, Denver, 1987—. Named one of Outstanding Young Women of Am., 1978. Mem. Am. Soc. for Pub. Adminstrn. (chairperson task force on affirmative action Capitol chpt. 1975-77), Colo. Safety Assn., Colo. Motor Carriers' Assn., Denver C. of C., Colo. Masters Swimming Assn. Republican. Clubs: Denver Athletic. Home: 10220 W Alamo Place Littleton CO 80127 Office: MSBI/Clinicare 5400 N Washington St Denver CO 80216

ROBBINS, PAULA ANN IVASKA, university dean; b. Teaneck, N.J., Dec. 13, 1935; d. Paavo Waldemar Topias and Anna Maria Margareta (Snellman) Ivaska; m. Michael D. Robbins, 1956 (div. 1968); children—Jeffery Paul, Matthew Llewellyn. Ph.D., U. Conn., 1977. Dir. student employment Radcliffe Coll., Cambridge, Mass., 1962-64; dir. career counseling Trinity Coll., Hartford, Conn., 1970-75; instructional design assoc. Hartford Grad. Ctr., 1975-77; edn. policy fellow Inst. Ednl. Leadership, George Washington U., Washington, 1977-78; assoc. dir. grad. studies Fitchburg State Coll. (Mass.), 1977-80; mgr. software tech. writing and documentation Computervision Corp., Bedford, Mass., 1981-82; postdoctoral fellow Finnish Ministry Edn., Helsinki, 1981; vis. lectr. U. Helsinki, 1982; asst. dean Grad. Sch., U. Lowell (Mass.), 1983—; bd. dirs. Concord Mcpl. Light Plant, 1986—. Author: Successful Mid-Life Career Change, 1978. Chmn. Concord Democratic Town Com. (Mass.), 1970; del. Mass. Dem. Conv., 1970, 81, 82; mem. adv. bd. Concord-Carlisle Adult and Community Edn., 1980-88. Mem. Phi Kappa Phi, Phi Delta Kappa. Office: U Lowell Grad Sch Lowell MA 01854

ROBBINS, RIMA, journalist, public relations consultant; b. N.Y.C., Apr. 3, 1934; d. Maurice and Ruth (Ackerman) Robbins; m. Michael John Greenberg, June 10, 1954; children—Peter A., John K., Karl P. B.A. in Lit., Fla. State U., M.A. in East Asian Studies; M.S. in Journalism, Boston U. Writer, editor Career Edn. Ctr., Fla. State U., Tallahassee, 1975-77; info. specialist Fla. Dept. State, Tallahassee, 1977-80; dep. dir. pub. info. Fla.

Hosp. Cost Containment Bd., Tallahassee, 1980-81; tech. editor Planning Research Corp., Jacksonville, Fla., 1982-83; pub. relations coordinator St. Augustine Gen. Hosp. (Fla.), 1983; pres. The Shadow, St. Augustine, 1983—; adj. prof. govt., Flagler Coll., St. Augustine, 1985-86. Contbr. articles to various newspapers, newsletter, book reviews. Legislative adminstr. LWV of Fla., Tallahassee, 1974-75; mem. Leon County Democratic Women's Club, Tallahassee, 1977-80. Mem. Soc. Tech. Communication, Inc., Fla. Pub. Relations Assn., Women in Communications, Inc. (coordinator, radio documentary sect. Clarion competition 1986), Am. Med. Writers Assn., Pub. Relations Soc. Am. Democrat. Home: 9121 Gene Johnson Rd Saint Augustine FL 32086

ROBBINS, SHIRLEY KAY, manufacturing company manager; b. Anderson, Ind., June 6, 1944; d. Herschel J. and Betty J. (Davis) Musick; m. Walter Clifton Robbins, Jr., June 19, 1964; children: Kelly Jo, Kevin Clifton. Student, Internat. Bus. Coll., Ft. Wayne, Ind., 1962-63; BS, Ball State U., 1988. Stenographer Warner Gear div. Borg-Warner Automotive Transmission Systems, Muncie, Ind., 1967-74, adminstrv. asst., 1974-78, scheduling foreman, 1979-85; material handling and stores mgr. (fin. stores, trucking, service, receiving and shipping) Borg-Automotive Transmission Systems, Muncie, 1985—. Mem. Am. Bus. Womens Assn. Home: RR #2 Box 340E Muncie IN 47302 Office: Borg-Warner Automotive Transmission Systems 5401 Kilgore Muncie IN 47307

ROBBINS, YVONNE JO, respiratory therapist, educator; b. Williamsport, Pa., Oct. 4, 1953; d. Llewellyn Thomas and Lois Ella (Wilhour) Dollman; m. Paul Richard Robbins, Apr. 30, 1979; children: Elissa Brianna and Noah Thomas. B Social Work, Temple U., 1975; AS in Respiratory Therapy, Hahnemann U., 1977; postgrad., Cabrini Coll., Rosemont, Pa. Registered respiratory therapist. Staff therapist Hahneman Hosp., Phila., 1977-78; respiratory supr. The Bryn Mawr (Pa.) Hosp., 1978-79, dir. clin. edn. respiratory therapy program, 1979-83; respiratory therapy program dir. Westchester U./The Bryn Mawr Hosp., Bryn Mawr, 1983-87. Mem. Am. Assoc. Respiratory Care, Am. Heart Assoc. (instr. basic life support and advanced cardiac life support). Home: Rd #1 Box 652 Honey Brook PA 19344 Office: Westchester U/The Bryn Mawr Hosp Respiratory Therapy Program Bryn Mawr PA 19010

ROBBINS-WILF, MARCIA, English educator; b. Newark, Mar. 22, 1949; d. Saul and Ruth (Fern) Robbins; m. Leonard A. Wilf, June 21, 1970; 1 child, Orin. Student, Emerson Coll., 1967-69, Seton Hall U., 1969, Fairleigh Dickinson U., 1970; BA, George Washington U., 1971; MA, NYU, 1975; postgrad., St. Peter's Coll., Jersey City, 1979, Fordham U., 1980; MS, Yeshiva U., 1981, EdD, 1986; postgrad., Monmouth Coll., 1986. Cert. elem. tchr., N.Y., N.J., reading specialist, N.J., prin., supr., N.J., adminstr., supr., N.Y. Tchr. Sleepy Hollow Elem. Sch., Falls Church, Va., 1971-72, Yeshiva Konvitz, N.Y.C., 1972-73; intern Wee Folk Nursery Sch., Short Hills, N.J., 1978-81, dir. day camp, 1980-81, tchr., dir., owner, 1980-81; adj. prof. reading Seton Hall U., South Orange, N.J., 1987, Middlesex County Coll., Edison, N.J., 1987—; presenter numerous workshops; founding bd. dirs. Stern Coll. Women Yeshiva U., N.Y.C., 1987; adj. vis. lectr. Rutgers U., New Brunswick, N.J., 1988. Chairperson Jewish Book Festival, YM-YMHA, West Orange, N.J., 1986-87, mem. early childhood com., 1986—, bd. dirs., 1986—; vice chairperson dinner com. Nat. Leadership Conf. of Christians and Jews, 1986; mem. Hadassah, Valerie Children's Fund, Women's League Conservative Judaism, City of Hope, assoc. bd. bus. and women's profl. div. United Jewish Appeal, 1979; vol. reader Goddard Riverside Day Care Ctr., N.Y.C., 1973; friend N.Y. Pub. Library, N.Y.C., 1980—; life friend Millburn Pub. Library, N.J., 1980—. Co-recipient Am. Heritage award, Essex County, 1985; recipient Award Appreciation City of Hope, 1984, Profl. Improvement awards Seton-Essex Reading Council, 1984-86, Cert. Attendance award Seton-Essex Reading Counci, 1987. Mem. N.Y. Acad. Scis. (life), N.J. Council Tchrs. English, Nat. Council Tchrs. English, Am. Ednl. Research Assn., Coll. Reading Assn. (life), Assn. Supervision and Curriculun Devel., N.Y. State Reading Assn. (council Manhattan), N.J. Reading Assn. (council Seton-Essex), Internat. Reading Assn., Nat. Assn. for Edn. of Young Children (life N.J. chpt., Kenyon group), Nat. Council Jewish Women (vice chairperson membership com. eneving br. N.Y. sect. 1974-75), George Washington U. Alumni Coub, Emerson Coll. Alumni Club, NYU Alumni Club, Phi Delta Kappa (life), Kappa Gamma Chi (historian). Club: Greenbrook Country (Caldwell, N.J.); George Washington Univ. Home: 242 Hartshorn Dr Short Hills NJ 07078

ROBERGE, M. SHEILA, state legislator; b. Manchester, N.H.; m. A. Roland Roberge; 2 children. Ed. St. Anselm's Coll. Mem. N.H. Senate, 1985—; del., Republican Nat. Conv., 1980; Rep. nat. committeewoman from N.H. Roman Catholic. Office: NH State Capitol Bldg Concord NH 03301 •

ROBERSON, KIM ELIZABETH, nurse; b. Seattle, Sept. 20, 1955; d. Frank Tracey and Zetta Elizabeth (Jacobson) R. BS in Nursing, Seattle U., 1977. Commd. 2d lt., U.S. Army, 1977, advanced through grades to capt., 1980; asst. head nurse, Frankfurt-W.Ger., 1980-81, chief nurse Health Clinic, 1981-83, clin. staff nurse, San Francisco, 1983-85,; house supr. Seattle VA Med. Ctr., 1985-87; occupational health nurse, Boeing Aerospace Co., Seattle, 1987-88; sales assoc. Kamas Realty, Inc, 1988—; co-chairperson dept. nursing quality assurance com., 1980-81; mem. affiliate faculty Am. Heart Assn., San Francisco, 1984-85. Capt. USAR, 1985—. Avocations: kayaking, study of wines, music, reading. Home: 8730 Wabash Ave S Seattle WA 98118

ROBERSON, MARIAN HOLBROOK, volunteer association adminstrator; b. Cornwall, N.Y., Jan. 28, 1937; d. Willard Ames and Helen Hoyle (Herr) Holbrook, m. Richard Word Roberson, June 7, 1986. Student, Wellesley (Mass.) Coll., 1954-56; MusB, So. Meth. U., 1956-59. Editorial asst. Izaak Walton League of Am., Arlington, Va., 1974-76, conservation assoc., 1977-80, sr. conservation assoc., 1980-82, dir. leadership devel., 1982—. Chmn. Haiti Task Force, St. Patrick's Episc. Ch., Washington, 1984-87; bd. dirs. Hannah House Shelter for Women, Washington, 1985-87, Cathedral Choral Soc., 1985—. Mem. Assn. for Vol. Adminstrn. (chmn. pub. issues com. 1985-87, bd. dirs. 1985-87), Am. Soc. for Tng. and Devel., Am. Soc. Assn. Execs. Republican. Home: 5015 Fulton St NW Washington DC 20016 Office: Izaak Walton League of Am 1701 N Fort Meyer Dr Arlington VA 22209

ROBERSON, PATT FOSTER, mass communications educator; b. Middletown, N.Y., Dec. 3, 1934; d. Gilbert Charles and Mildred Elizabeth (O'Neal) Foster; m. Murray Ralph Roberson Jr., May 10, 1963 (dec. 1968). AA, Canal Zone Jr. Coll., 1954; BA in Journalism, La. State U., 1957, MA in Journalism, 1973; MA in Media, So. U., Baton Rouge, 1981; PhD in Mass Communications, U. So. Miss., 1985. Exec. sec. Lionel H. Abshire and Assocs., AIA, Architects, Baton Rouge, 1958-60, Murrell and Callari, AIA, Architects, Baton Rouge, 1960-63; bus. mgr. So. Rev. La. State U., Baton Rouge, 1963-69; free-lance researcher, ind. contractor Baton Rouge, 1969-74; rep. dept. info. State of La., Baton Rouge, 1974-75; assoc. prof. mass communication So. U., 1976—; reviewer Random House Pubs., N.Y.C., 1981; cons. advt. Baton Rouge Little Theater, 1971—; reporter Canal Record, St. Petersburg, Fla., 1967—; research Dictionary Literary Biography, Detroit, 1986-87; tutor, Operation Upgrade, 1978-82. Co-editor: La. State U. cookbook Tiger Bait, 1976; biographer Frank E. Gannett in Biographical Dictionary of American Journalism, 1987; contbr. articles to profl. jours.; author numerous poems; mem. editorial bd. American Journalism, 1986-87. Poll commn. East Baton Rouge Parish Govt., 1978—; pres. Our Lady Lake Regional Med. Ctr., 1971-72; bd. dir. Dist. Atty.'s Rape Crisis Commn., 1976-79; bd. dirs. Plan Govt. Study Commn., 1973-76, Selective Service System Bd. 8, Baton Rouge, 1986—; docent Greater Baton Rouge Zoo, 1974-77. Mem. AAUP (sec.-treas. La. state conf. 1988—), Assn. Edn. Journalism and Mass Communication, Women in Communications (pres. Baton Rouge chpt. 1982), Pub. Relations Assn. La., La. State U. Journalism Alumni Assn. (pres. 1977), Soc. Profl. Journalists (Sigma Delta Chi, pres. 1982 SE La. chpt.), Am. Journalism Historians Assn., La. State U. Alumni Assn. (East Baton Rouge Parish chpt. pres. 1978-80). Club: Toastmasters Internat. (Baton Rouge) (adminstrv. v.p. 1977), Pilot Internat. Home: 2801 Allen Ct Baker LA 70714 Office: So Univ Dept Mass Communications Baton Rouge LA 70813

ROBERSON, PAULA KAREN, biostatistician; b. Memphis, Nov. 26, 1952; d. Joseph Paul and Venita (Adams) R. BS, So. Meth. U., 1974; PhD, U. Wash., 1979. Math. statistician health effects research lab. U.S. EPA, Cin., 1979-81; asst. faculty mem., biostatistician St. Jude Children's Research Hosp., Memphis, 1982—, asst. dir. biostatistics, 1985—, vice chair biostats. and info. systems, 1986—; predoctoral trainee Nat. Heart, Lung and Blood Inst., 1977-79; adj. asst. prof. U. Cin., 1980-82; cons. Nat. Cancer Inst., Bethesda, Md., 1983—, U. Tenn. Ctr. for Health Scis., Memphis, 1983. Contbr. articles to profl. jours. Elder Evergreen Presbyn. Ch., Memphis, 1985-87, clk. of session, 1987. Mem. AAAS, Biometric Soc. (regional adv. bd. 1984-86), Am. Statistical Assn., Soc. Risk Analysis. Presbyterian. Office: St Jude Children's Research Hosp 332 N Lauderdale PO Box 318 Memphis TN 38101

ROBERSTON-SMITH, MARY PATRICIA (PEIRCE) (MRS. JOHN A. SMITH), college dean, administrator; b. Key West, Fla., Jan. 10, 1942; d. Robert P. and Jemeile (Seamon) Peirce; B.S. magna cum laude (Centennial Honor scholar), La. State U., 1963, M.S., 1964; M.Ed., Southeastern La. U., 1973; Ed.D., Rutgers U., 1982; postgrad. Harvard U., 1986; m. John A. Smith; children—Stephanie Dawn, Debbie, Diane, John. Young adult librarian Enoch Pratt Free Library, Balt., 1964-65, adminstrv. asst., 1965-66; instr. Balt. Jr. Coll., 1966-67; library specialist and tchr. Ednl. Media Center, Covington, La., 1967-70; instr. NASA Miss. Test Facility, 1967-68; field librarian St. Tammany Parish Sch. Bd., Covington, 1967-70; chief librarian S.E. La. Hosp., Mandeville, 1970-73, coordinator adult edn., 1972-73; asst. prof. library and learning resources Bergen Community Coll., Paramus, N.J., 1973-79, assoc. prof., 1979-81, asst. dean instructional services, 1979-81, assoc. dean instructional services, 1981-82, dean instructional services, 1982-86; v.p., dean, 1986—; tchr., cons. in planning, assessment and spl. edn.; prodn. assoc. CBS summer semester, 1974-75; mem. Gov.'s Com. Libraries, state transfer adv. bd. N.J. Dept. Higher Edn., 1986; mem. acad. council Thomas A. Edison State Coll. Staff instr. 1st Army Instr. Tng. Sch., USAR, 1975, 76, 77. Trustee Bergen County Health and Welfare Council, treas. bd., 1986—; trustee Berger County Police Acad., 1986—; chmn. fin., bd. dirs. Sherbruke Co-op; state sec.-treas., v.p., pres. Acad. Officers Assn.; chairperson team membership Mid. States Regional Accreditation. Mem. AAUW (v.p.), Gifted Child Soc. (v.p.), Mensa, Hackensack C. of C. (bd. dirs. 1986—), Delta Kappa Gamma, Kappa Delta Pi, Mu Sigma Rho, Beta Phi Mu, Alpha Lambda Delta, Kappa Delta Pi, Tau Kappa Alpha. Contbg. editor: The Special Child, 1976. Home: 427 Canterbury Dr Ramsey NJ 07446 Office: Bergen Community Coll 400 Paramus Rd Paramus NJ 07652

ROBERTO, MARY KAY, computer company executive; b. Rock Island, Ill., July 26, 1946; d. John and Antoinette (Rauker) Valsoano; m. Matthew James Roberto, May 19, 1979; 1 child, Katherine Joan. BA, Augustana Coll., 1968. Mathematician research, devel. dept. U.S. Army, Rock Island, 1968-69; systems analyst astro electronics div. RCA, Heighstown, N.J., 1969-74; mgr. tech. support UCCCorp., New Brunswick, N.J., 1974-76; mgr. nat. account sales UCCCorp., Dallas, 1977-81, dir. nat. accounts, 1981-85; v.p., gen. mgr. UCCEL Corp., Dallas, 1985-88; regional mgr. Computer Assocs. Internat., Irving, Tex., 1988—; cons. CMS Tex., Bedford, 1987—, Productivity Workshops, DeSoto, Tex., 1986—; tchr. RCA, 1979-71. Group leader United Way, Dallas, 1985; vol. Am. Cancer Soc., Ft. Worth, 1985-87; elder Ridglea Presbn. Ch., Ft. Worth, 1987—. Home: 305 High Woods Tr Fort Worth TX 76112 Office: Computer Assocs Internat Irving TX 75207

ROBERTS, ADELE MARIE (DEDE), public relations executive; b. El Paso, Tex., Sept. 6, 1941; d. George Silk and Adele Freeman (Clay) Howard; m. William Andrew Roberts III, Aug. 2, 1963 (dec. Nov. 1973); children: Janet Lynn, Sandra Kay (dec.). Student, U. Tex., 1959-60, Tex. Tech U., 1961-63. Sales promotion Southwestern Life Ins., Dallas, 1968-70, Popular Dry Goods Co., El Paso, Tex., 1970-71; acct. exec. Mithoff Advt., El Paso, 1971-74, Van Dyke & Assocs., Denver, 1974-77, Sam Lusky Assocs., Denver, 1977-79; owner, mgr. D.R. Communications, Denver, 1979-83; mktg. pub. relations dir. YWCA Met. Dallas, 1983-87; chairperson Dallas C. of C. adv. bd. Social Services & Edn. Magnet Sch., 1983-85. Copywriter various ads and videos (1st place fashion copywriting Am. Advt. Fed., outstanding pub. relations, pub. service campaign). Pub. relations chairperson Dallas welcoming com. Rep. Nat. Conv., 1983-84; v.p. pub. relations Turtle Creek of Richardson, 1984; speakers bur. Arthritis Found., 1983-87; mem. Dallas Art Mus., Dallas Arboretum. Recipient award of excellence Dallas Press Club, 1987 for annual report YWCA, award of excellence Dallas Press Club, 1987 for assn. image video, YWCA 1983-87,. Mem. Pub. Relations Soc. Am., No. Tex. Pub. Relations Soc. Am., Nat. Assn. Female Execs., Speakers Bur. and Media Com., Turtle Creek Assn. (v.p. pub. relations)Dallas C. of C. (media com.), Beta Sigma Phi (v.p. 1970-71). Club: Altrusa (Richardson, Tex.) (2nd v.p. pub. relations). Home: 7324 Skillman #201 Dallas TX 75231 Office: Arthritis Found North Texas Chpt 2824 Swiss Ave Dallas TX 75204

ROBERTS, BARBARA, state official; b. Corvallis, Oreg., Dec. 21, 1936; m. Frank Roberts, 1974; children—Mark, Michael. Mem. Multnomah County Bd. Commrs., Oreg., 1978; mem. Oreg. Ho. of Reps., 1981-85; sec. of state State of Oreg., 1985—. Mem. Parkrose Sch. Bd., 1973-83. Office: Office of Sec State 136 State Capitol Salem OR 97310 •

ROBERTS, BARBARA ANN, telephone company official; b. Milw., Feb. 21, 1929; d. Andrew Max and Ersilia (Celia) Gertrude (Comparoni) Magio; student Milw. public schs.; m. Albert Lloyd Roberts, Sept. 3, 1949; children—Marybeth, Bradley J., David L. With Wis. Telephone Co., Milw., 1961—, now group mgr. operator services; v.p., sec. Sports Dome, Inc. Mem. Bus. and Profl. Women Milw. (pres. 1979-81), Wis. Bus. and Profl. Women (dist. dir. Eastern Dist. 8 1981-82). Home: 8411 W Cheyenne St Milwaukee WI 53224 Office: 2140 Davidson Rd Waukesha WI 53186

ROBERTS, BARBARA JEAN, biologist, educator; b. Burley, Idaho, Apr. 28, 1934; d. Arthur Lincoln and Matilda Jane (Sabin) R. BA, Idaho State U., 1969, M in Teaching Biol. Sci., 1972. Cert. elem. tchr., Idaho. Sr. lab. asst. Idaho State U., Pocatello, 1970-79, lab. mat. supr., 1979—; cons. Terminally Unique Cons. Service, Pocatello, 1970—. Mem. State of Idaho Women's Commn., 1986-89, steering com. Evan for Senate, Bannock County, 1986; active Stalling for Congress, Bannock County, 1984; dir. Idaho State U. Gallery exhibit for Nat. Women's History Month, 1987. Mem. Nat. Assn. Sci. Material Mgrs., Am. Chem. Soc., Idaho Pub. Employees Assn. (chpt. v.p. 1985), Nat. Assn. Female Execs., Idaho State Univ. Profl. Women, Mortar Bd. Nat. Honor Soc., Sweet Adelines (show and pub. chair 1979-80). Democrat. Home: 1407 E Maple Pocatello ID 83201 Office: Idaho State U Biol Sci Box 8007 Pocatello ID 83209

ROBERTS, CELIA ANN, librarian; b. Bangor, Maine, Feb. 6, 1935; d. William Lewis and Ruey Pearl (Logan) R.; A.A., U. Hartford, 1957, B.A., 1961; postgrad. So. Conn. State Coll., 1963—. With catalog, acquistion and circulation depts. U. Hartford Library, 1956-65; librarian Simsbury (Conn.) Free Library, 1965; reference librarian Simsbury Public Library, 1969—. Tchr. ballet classes, 1965-66; ballet mistress Ballet Soc. Conn., Inc., 1968-70; with corps de ballet Conn. Opera Assn., 1963-64; active in prodns. Simsbury Light Opera Assn., 1964, 69. Mem. ALA, Conn. Library Assn., Simsbury Hist. Soc., Ont. Geneal. Soc., New Eng. Historic and Geneal. Soc., AAUW (past pres. Greater Hartford br.), Pro Dance, DAR (Abigail Phelps chpt.), Conn. Soc. Genealogists, Soc. Mayflower Descs. Conn., Dance Masters Am. Universalist. Office: 725 Hopmeadow St Simsbury CT 06070

ROBERTS, CHARLOTTE PAULINE, special education educator; b. Wautoma, Wis., Feb. 18, 1954; d. Linden Harley and Mildred Pauline (Kussmann) Hansel; m. Michael George Roberts, June 21, 1975; children: Brionne Elizabeth, Colin James. BS, U. Wis., Stevens Point, 1977, MEd, 1985. Cert. elem. tchr., learning disabilities specialist, Wis. Tchr. learning disabilities Stevens Point Schs., 1977—; guest speaker Internat. Council Learning Disabilities, San Diego; vol. research U. Wis., Stevens Point, 1986, 87. Bd. dirs. Community Childcare Ctr., Stevens Point, 1986-88. Mem. Stevens Point Area Tchrs. Assn. (legis. chmn. 1977—), Wis. Edn. Assn. (state del. 1977—), NEA (nat. del. 1977—). Club: Jr. Woman's (edn. chmn. 1981-85). Office: Washington Sch 3500 Prais St Stevens Point WI 54481

ROBERTS, CHERYL ANN, service representative; b. Glen Cove, N.Y., Apr. 21, 1947; d. Frank Arthur and Grace Harriet (Alexander) Taylor; m. Gerald Wayne Roberts, Dec. 15, 1966 (div. Oct. 1979); children: Lorraine Yvette, Gary Wayne. Surg. technologist, Erwin Vocat. Tech., 1975-76. Surg. technologist U. Community Hosp., Tampa, Fla., 1976-78, Ambulatory Surgery Ctr., Tampa, 1979-81; customer service rep. Durr-Fillauer Med., Tampa, 1981-82, sales rep., 1982—. Mem. Health Industry Distbrs. Assn. Republican. Baptist. Clubs: Tampa (Fla.) Sailing Squadron, Country Time Cloggers. Home: 1613 Dawnridge Ct Brandon FL 33511

ROBERTS, CONNIE MARIE, county government offical; b. San Diego, Feb. 21, 1943; d. Harold Leroy and Margaret (Hultenius) Perkins; divorced; children: Shauna, Cheryl; m. John S. Todhunter, Nov. 8, 1980. BA in Sociology, U.S. Nat. U., 1964; M in Pub. Adminstrn., San Diego State U., 1983. From social worker to div. chief dist. ops. div. Dept. Social Services County of San Diego, San Diego, 1964—. Office: County of San Diego Dept Social Services 7949 Mission Center Ct San Diego CA 92108

ROBERTS, DENA AURELIA, insurance executive; b. Ft. Wayne, Ind., Sept. 16, 1950; d. James Robert Sr. and Dena Aurelia (Arnette) Broadfoot; m. Thomas Mitchell Robert, Nov. 28, 1982; children: Jade Dorian, Ashton Noel. Student, Harding Coll., Searcy, Ark., 1972. Office desk specialist Aetna Life and Casualty, Memphis, 1972-78; claim rep. Allstate Ins. Co., Memphis, 1978—; bodily injury specialist Knoxville, Tenn., 1980—; telephone claim handler Kingsport, Tenn., 1981-84; sr. claim rep. Mobile, Ala., 1984-87; adj. instr. East Tenn. State U., 1988. Active United Way, Little Sisters. Mem. East Tenn. Claims Assn., Kappa Dleta Kappa. Republican. Mem. Ch. of Christ. Office: Allstate Ins Co PO Box 16106 Mobile AL 36616

ROBERTS, DIANA KAYE, accountant; b. Independence, Mo., Mar. 14, 1959; d. Charles Mitchell Villines and Betty Jane (Mead) Crandall; m. Robert Lee Roberts Jr., May 16, 1980; children: Valerie Marie, Rosemary Kaye. Cert. tax preparer, Mr. Tax. of Am., 1979, Nat. Tax Tng. Sch., 1981, H&R Block, 1986. Ins. agt. Mutual of Omaha, Kansas City, Mo., 1979; pres. Roberts Bookkeeping and Tax Service, Independence, 1979—. Editor Internat. Quill and Scroll, Independence, 1973-76. Mem. Bicentennial Liaison Com., Independence, 1975-76; cons. Pentecostal Ch. of God in Christ, Kansas City, 1986-88. Mem. Nat. Soc. Pub. Accts., Ind. Accts. Soc. of Mo. (sec. 1987-88), Nat. Assn. Female Execs., Concept Therapy Inst., Mo. Assn. Tax Practioners, Independence C. of C., Kansas City C. of C. Office: Roberts Bookkeeping & Tax Service Independence Acctg Services 1107 S Forest Independence MO 64050

ROBERTS, DORIS EMMA, epidemiologist, consultant; b. Toledo, Dec. 28, 1915; d. Frederic Constable and Emma Selina (Reader) R. Nursing diploma, Peter Bent Brigham Sch. Nursing, Boston, 1938; B.S., Geneva Coll., Beaver Falls, Pa., 1944; M.P.H., U. Minn., 1958; Ph.D., U. N.C., 1967. Staff nurse Vis. Nurse Assn., New Haven, 1938-40; sr. nurse Neighborhood House, Millburn, N.J., 1942-45; supr. Tb Baltimore County Dept. Health, Towson, Md., 1945-46; Tb cons. Md. State Dept. Health, 1946-50; cons., chief nurse Tb program USPHS, Washington, 1950-57; cons. div. nursing USPHS, 1958-63; chief nursing practice br. Health Resources Adminstrn., HEW, Bethesda, Md., 1966-75; adj. prof. Sch. Pub. Health, U. N.C., 1975-84; cons. WHO. Mem. Pub. Citizen, Inc. Served with USPHS, 1945-75. Recipient Distinguished Alumna award Geneva Coll., 1971; Distinguished Service award USPHS, 1971; Outstanding Achievement award U. Minn., 1983. Fellow Am. Pub. Health Assn. (v.p. 1978-79, Distinguished Service award PHN sect. 1975, Sedgwick Meml. medal 1979); mem. Inst. Medicine of Nat. Acad. Scis., Common Cause, Delta Omega. Home: 6111 Kennedy Dr Chevy Chase MD 20815

ROBERTS, DOROTHY HYMAN, apparel company executive; b. N.Y.C., Dec. 6, 1928; d. Edgar C. and Theresa M. (Marks) Hyman; B.A., Conn. Coll., 1950; m. Paul M. Roberts, June 18, 1950 (dec.); children—Lynn, Steven; m. Paul M. Cohen. With Echo Design Group, Inc. (formerly Echo Scarfs, Inc.), N.Y.C., 1950—, pres., 1978—. Mem. The Fashion Group. Office: 10 E 40th St New York NY 10016

ROBERTS, EILEEN DORIS FRAHM, graphic designer, illustrator; b. N.Y.C., June 3, 1933; d. Walter Frederick and Gertrude May (Meyer) Frahm; m. Stanton Harvey Roberts, Jr., Sept. 13, 1953; children—Jodi Lynn, Stanton Harvey, Brent Walter. Student Pratt Inst., 1951-52, SUNY-Buffalo Coll. for Tchrs., 1952-54, Albright Art Sch., 1952-54, N.Y. Sch. Interior Design, 1965, Mira Costa Coll., 1971-73, Palomar Jr. Coll., 1979, U. Calif.-San Diego, 1984. Comml. artist Art Design Assocs., Mountainview, Calif., 1959-60; illustrator Ford Found., N.Y.C., 1964-65, Evergreen Nursery, San Diego; craft coordinator Recreation Dept. City of Carlsbad, Calif., 1972; math. aide Oceanside Unified Sch. Dist., Calif., 1976-78; owner, artist Roberts Design Studio, Carlsbad, 1977—; art dir. Evergreen Nursery, San Diego, 1988—; art cons. gifted children Oceanside Pub. Schs., 1973-74. Designer, illustrator: Self-Hypnosis, A Guide To, 1983, May Centers Safety Book, 1983; painter: Misty (best of show award 1969); 1st woman contbr. to Combat Art Program USMC, Quantico, Va., 1967—. Arts and crafts assn. Prince William County Fair, Va., 1967-68; artist-in-residence Oceanside Bicentennial Com., 1975-76; chmn. Meet the Americans, Oceanside, 1975-76; mem. San Diego Art Inst. Mem. Nat. League Am. Pen Women, Artist Equity Assn., Book Publicists of San Diego. Avocations: hiking; bicycling; painting; jogging; cooking; reading. Home and Office: Roberts Design 12527 Kestrel St San Diego CA 92129

ROBERTS, ELIZABETH H., podiatrist, author; b. Bklyn. m. Nathan Wasserheit (dec.); 1 dau., Judith N. Wasserheit. D. Podiatric Medicine, L.I. U., 1943. Pvt. practice podiatry, N.Y.C., 1943—; prof. emeritus, N.Y. Coll. Podiatric Medicine; established diabetic foot clinic N.Y. Infirmary, 1949; chairperson dept. regional anatomy, M.J. Lewi Coll. Podiatric Medicine, 1954-66, chairperson dept. practice adminstrn., 1945-51. Trustee N.Y. Coll. Podiatric Medicine. Author: Manual of Practice Administration, 1949; On Your Feet, 1975, put on cassettes for blind, 1977; contbr. articles to profl. pubs. Fellow Am. Soc. Podiatric Medicine, Am. Acad. Podiatry, Am. Assn. Podiatry Adminstrn.; mem. N.Y. State Bd. Podiatry (chairperson 1979-81). Home: 210 W 90th St New York NY 10024 Office: 133 E 58th St New York NY 10022

ROBERTS, ERICA SUE, electronic data processing auditor; b. N.Y.C., Nov. 30, 1960; d. Joel S. and Rene (Farkas) Balsam; m. James J. F. Roberts, Nov. 28, 1982. B.A., NYU, 1981. Cert. info. system auditor. EDP auditing specialist Blue Cross-Blue Shield, N.Y.C., 1981; EDP auditor Dean Witter Reynolds, N.Y.C., 1982, Hazeltine Corp., Greenlawn, N.Y., 1983-84, L.I. Savs. Bank, Centereach, N.Y., 1984-85, Norton Co., Worcester, Mass., 1985-87; Ocean Spray Cranberries, Plymouth, Mass., 1987—; electronic data processing cons., Huntington, N.Y., 1982—. N.Y. State Regents scholar, 1977. EDP Auditors Assn., Nat. Assn. Female Execs., NYU Alumni Assn. Office: 225 Water St Plymouth MA 02360

ROBERTS, HELEN WYVONE, city official; b. Kirksville, Mo., Jan. 9, 1934; d. William Lawrence and Lectie Beryl (Boley) Chitwood; m. Philip C. Roberts, Jan. 9, 1952 (div. 1976); children—Christy, Cheryl, Gayla. Secretarial degree Chillicothe Bus. Sch., 1951; B.S., Lindenwood Coll., 1983. Exec. sec. McDonnel-Douglas Aircraft, St. Louis, 1962-65, Transit Homes, Inc., Greenville, S.C., 1970-76; exec. sec. City of St. Peters, Mo., 1976-79, asst. planning and devel. coordinator, 1979-81, adminstrv. asst. to city adminstr., 1981-84, purchasing agt., 1984, asst. to city adminstr., 1985—. Mem. Nat. Assn. Female Execs., Internat. Cities Mgmt. Assn., Am. Mgmt. Assn., Am. Bus. Women's Assn., Lindenwood Coll. Alumni Assn., Alpha Sigma Tau. Baptist. Avocations: horseback riding; sports; reading. Home: 329 Karen St Saint Charles MO 63301 Office: City of St Peters PO Box 9 Saint Peters MO 63376

ROBERTS, JAYNE KELLY, lawyer; b. N.Y.C., Sept. 30, 1948; d. William Frederick and Kathleen (Kelly) Mueller; m. Malcolm Jerome Roberts, Oct. 10, 1972; children—Chris, Karyn, Paul, Mark, Michael, Seth. B.A., U. Calif.-Berkeley, 1977; J.D., U. San Francisco, 1980. Bar: Calif. 1981, U.S. Dist. Ct. 1981, N.Y. 1988, U.S. Supreme Ct. 1987. Assoc., Sandvick & Martin, Oakland, 1981; sole practice, San Francisco, 1981-84 . Bd. govs. Bard Coll., Annandale on Hudson, N.Y., 1982. Mem. Am. Assn. Trial Lawyers, Calif. Assn. Trial Lawyers, San Francisco Trial Lawyers (bd. dirs.

1986—). Democrat. Office: 601 Montgomery St 19th Floor San Francisco CA 94111

ROBERTS, JEAN REED, lawyer, business executive; b. Washington, Dec. 19, 1939; d. Paul Allen and Esther (Kishter) Reed; m. Thomas Gene Roberts, Nov. 26, 1958; children—Amy, Rebecca, Nathanial. A.B. in Journalism, U. N.C., 1966; J.D., Ariz. State U., 1973. Bar: Ariz. 1974. Sole practice, Scottsdale, Ariz., 1975-84; founding ptnr. Simon, Reeves & Roberts, 1985—; legal dir., advisor to gov. Ariz.-Mex. Commn., 1980—; judge pro tem Superior Ct., Maricopa County, Ariz., 1979—. Editor: Scottsdale Bar Practice Manual, 1981. Sec. Charter 100 Phoenix, 1983-84; pres. elect Soroptimist Internat. Scottsdale, 1982—; bd. dirs. Ariz. Ctr. for Law in Pub. Interest, 1988, Ctr. for Latin Am. Studies Ariz. State U., 1988; chmn. Bd. of Adjustment, Town of Paradise Valley, 1984—. Mem. State Bar Ariz. (founder art law sect. 1979-81), Scottsdale Bar Assn. (dir. 1980-82), ABA (sec. com. mem.), Ariz. Bar Assn. (family law sect. 1988). Democrat. Jewish. Home: 6655 E Hummingbird Ln Paradise Valley AZ 85253 Office: Law Office Jean Reed Roberts 7110 E McDonald Dr Suite A-1 Scottsdale AZ 85253

ROBERTS, JEANNE ADDISON, educator; b. Washington; d. John West and Sue Fisher (Nichols) Addison; m. Markley Roberts, Feb. 19, 1966; children: Addison Cary Steed Masengill, Ellen Carraway Masengill Coster. A.B., Agnes Scott Coll., 1946; M.A., U. Pa., 1947; Ph.D., U. Va., 1964. Instr. Mary Washington Coll., 1947-48; instr., chmn. English Fairfax Hall Jr. Coll., 1950-51; tchr. Am. U. Assn. Lang. Center, Bangkok, Thailand, 1952-56; instr. Beirut (Lebanon) Coll. for Women, 1956-57, asst. prof., 1957-60, chmn. English dept., 1957-60; instr. lit. Am. U., Washington, 1960-62; asst. prof. Am. U., 1962-65, asso. prof., 1965-68, prof., 1968—; dean faculties Am. U., 1974; lectr. Howard U., 1971-72; seminar prof. Folger Shakespeare Library Inst. for Renaissance and 18th Century Studies, 1974; dir. NEH Summer Inst. for High Sch. Tchrs. on Teaching Shakespeare, Folger Shakespeare Library, 1984, 85, 86. Author: Shakespeare's English Comedy: The Merry Wives of Windsor in Context, 1979; Editor: (with James G. McManaway) A Selective Bibliography of Shakespeare: Editions, Textual Studies, Commentary, 1975; contbr. articles to scholarly jours. Danforth Tchr. grantee, 1962-63; Folger Sr. fellow, 1969-70, 88. Mem. MLA (chmn. Shakespeare div. 1981-82), Renaissance Soc. Am., Milton Soc., Shakespeare Assn. Am. (trustee 1978-81, 87—, pres. 1986-87), AAUP (pres. Am. U. chpt. 1966-67), Southeastern Renaissance Conf. (pres. 1981-82), Phi Beta Kappa, Mortar Board, Phi Kappa Phi. Episcopalian. Home: 4931 Albemarle St NW Washington DC 20016 Office: Am U Dept Lit Washington DC 20016

ROBERTS, JOAN ELLEN, arts and entertainment management consultant; b. N.Y.C., Jan. 15, 1944; d. Carl and Elizabeth (Levine) Spitz; m. Samuel Smith Roberts, Nov. 16, 1963 (div. 1973); children: Nancy Anne, Pamela Susan. Student, Boston U., 1961-63; B of Profl. Studies, Empire State Coll., 1983; MA, Montclair State Coll., 1985. Musical dir. Port Chester (N.Y.) Youth Theatre, 1963-65; various positions Elmwood Theatre, Nyack, N.Y., 1965-73; music tchr. Rockland Country Day Sch., Congers, N.Y., 1971-73; musical theatre dir. Camp Oguago, Andes, N.Y., 1978-82; mgr., adminstrv. asst. Woodstock (N.Y.) Playhouse, 1985-86; performer various clubs, resorts and restaurants, N.Y., 1972—; realtor, assoc. Yvonne B. Curran Real Estate, Kingston, N.Y., 1986—; tutor theatre Empire State Coll., New Paltz, N.Y., 1987—; cons. Byrdcliffe Theatre Festival, 1987—; tchr. Town Ramapo Cultural Ctr., Suffern, N.Y., 1971-74; house mgr. Woodstock Playhouse, summer 1984; mem. faculty Kingston Consol. Sch. Dist., 1988. Mem. Actors' Equity Assn., Phi Kappa Phi. Alpha Sigma Alpha. Jewish. Club: Woodstock Golf.

ROBERTS, JOAN I., social psychologist, educator. BA in English, U. Utah, Salt Lake City, 1957; MA in Social Psychology, Columbia U., 1960, EdD in Social Psychology, 1970. Teaching asst. in English U. Utah, Salt Lake City, 1956-57; cons. psychologist Herrold Assocs. Mgmt. Cons., N.Y.C., 1958-61; research staff mem. Makerere Coll., Kampala, East Africa, 1961-63; research assoc. Hunter Coll., N.Y.C., 1964-67; coordinator Tng. Project and Research in Intergroup Relations, Madison, Wis., 1970-73; asst. prof. dept. ednl. policy studies U. Wis., Madison, 1968-75; assoc. prof. social scis. Upstate Med. Ctr./SUNY, Syracuse, 1976-79; chairperson dept. child, family, and community studies Syracuse (N.Y.) U., 1978-80, assoc. prof. dept. child, family, and community studies, 1978-84, prof. dept. child, family, and community studies, 1985—; cultural founds. for medicine prof. Syracuse U., SUNY, Upstate Med. Ctr., LeMoyne Coll., N.Y., 1982—; prof. internat. programs abroad Syracuse U., London, 1984-85, 85-86; adj. prof. Syracuse U. Sch. Nursing, N.Y., 1976—; adj. assoc. prof. social scis. SUNY, 1979-83; project dir. Parapsychology Found. Research Grant, N.Y., 1981; project dir. model caregivers tng. project N.Y. State Dept. Social Services, 1981; lectr. and presenter of papers to various academic and profl. groups; coordinator, mem. Wis. Coordinating Council of Women in Higher Edn., 1971-74. Author: School Children in the Urban Slum: Readings in Social Science Reseach, 1966, 2d rev. edit., 1968, Group Behavior in Urban Classrooms, 1968, Scene of the Battle: Group Behavior in Urban Classrooms, 1970; Beyond Intellectual Sexism: A New Woman, A New Reality, 1976; author: (with Prof. Sherri Akinsanya) Educational Patterns and Cultural Configurations: The Anthropology of Education, Vol. I, 1976, Schooling in the Cultural Context: Anthropological Studies of Education, Vol. II, 1975. Faculty adv. com. Syracuse U.,; v.p., bd. dirs. Ctr. for a Human Future, Syracuse, 1977—; editorial bd. Alternative Lifestyles, 1977-81; editorial cons. Women and Politics, 1979—; co-pres., mem. Seneca Falls Nat. Women's Ctr. Ednl. Inst., 1983—. Mem. NOW, Am. Anthropol. Assn., Am. Psychol. Assn. (mem. Psychology and Women div.), Am. Soc. for Psychical Research, Assn. for Women in Psychology, Soc. for Applied Anthropology. Clubs: Corinthian, Brit. Univ. Women's. Lodge: Zonta. Office: Syracuse U 202 Slocum Hall Syracuse NY 13244-1250

ROBERTS, JUDITH MARIE, librarian, educator; b. Bluefield, W.Va., Aug. 5, 1939; d. Charles Bowen Lowder and Frances Marie (Bourne) Lowder Alberts; m. Craig Currence Jackson, July 1, 1957 (div. 1962); 1 son, Craig, Jr.; m. 2d, Milton Rinehart Roberts, Aug. 13, 1966 (div. 1987). B.S., Concord State Tchrs. Coll., 1965. Librarian, Cape Henlopen Sch. Dist., Lewes, Del., 1965—. Pres. Friends of Lewes Pub. Library, 1986—; chmn. exhibits Govs. Conf. Libraries and Info. Services, Dover, Del., 1978; mem. Gov.'s State Library Adv. Council, 1987—. Mem. ALA, NEA, Del. State Edn. Assn., Sussex Help Orgn. for Resources Exchange (pres. 1984-85), Del. Library Assn. (pres. 1982-83), Del. Learning Resources Assn. (pres. 1976-77). Methodist. Home: 42 DeVries Circle Lewes DE 19958 Office: Cape Henlopen High Sch Kings Hwy Lewes DE 19958

ROBERTS, KATHERINE ANN, nursing educator; b. Beaumont, Tex., Nov. 6, 1952; d. William A. and Dorothy Lee (Hall) Wood; m. Gregory Lee Roberts, Jan. 4, 1974; children—Amanda Leigh, Matthew Joseph. B.S.N., U. Tex.-Houston, 1976; M.S.N., Tex. Women's U., 1981; student Lamar U., 1971-73. Registered nurse, Tex. Staff nurse M.D. Anderson Hosp., Houston, 1976, Women-Children's Hosp., Beaumont, Tex., 1976; nursing instr. Lamar U., Beaumont, 1976-85. Tchr. Sun. Sch., First Ch. Nazarene, Beaumont, 1983-84. Mem. U. Tex. Alumni Assn., Nat. League Nursing, Am. Nurses Assn., Tex. Assn. Coll. Tchrs., Am. Cancer Soc., Am. Heart Assn., Sigma Theta Tau, Alpha Delta Pi.

ROBERTS, KATHLEEN JOY DOTY, educator; b. Jamaica, N.Y., Apr. 19, 1951; d. Alfred Arthur and Helen Caroline (Sohl) Doty; B.A. in Edn., Queens Coll., 1972, M.S. in Spl. Edn., 1974; cert. of advanced study in ednl. adminstrn. Hofstra U., 1982; m. Robert Louis Roberts, Nov. 24, 1974; children—Robert Louis, Michael Sean. Health conservation tchr. Woodside Jr. High Sch., Woodside, N.Y., 1973-77; coordinator spl. edn. dept. Ridgewood (N.Y.) Jr. High Sch., 1977-81; resource tchr. Grover Cleveland High Sch., Ridgewood, N.Y., 1981-88, mainstream coordinator, 1988—. Cert. N.Y. State Dept. Mental Hygiene; cert. sch. adminstr., math. tchr., N.Y.; lic. spl. edn. supr., ednl. adminstr., N.Y.C. Mem. NEA, N.Y. State Tchrs. Assn., Council for Exceptional Children, Soc. Mayflower Descs. AAUW, Colonial Daus. of 17th Century (pres. 1985—, nat. chmn. hist. activities com. 1988—), Nat. Soc. DAR, Phi Delta Kappa. Republican. Author: Closed Circuit Television and Other Devices for the Partially Sighted, 1971. Home: 52 Hicksville Rd Massapequa NY 11758 also: Lake Ariel PA Office: Grover Cleveland High Sch 2127 Himrod St Ridgewood NY 11385

ROBERTS, KATHY LYNN, utility company executive; b. Covington, Ga., Dec. 4, 1959; d. Willie Alfred and Ethel Genelia (Speed) R. AA in Bus. Arts, DeKalb Coll., Clarkston, Ga., 1986. Accounts payable clk. Lithonia Lighting, Conyers, Ga., 1978-81; sr. acctg. clk. Continental Group, Lithonia, Ga., 1981-85; account rep. AT&T, Atlanta, 1985—. Mem. Nat. Assn. Female Execs. Home: 1001 A Main St NW Conyers GA 30207 Office: AT&T 1960 W Exchange Pl Tucker GA 30084

ROBERTS, LILLIAN, educator, school system administrator; b. Albuquerque, Dec. 1, 1927; d. John Wagner and Mattie Rebecca (Beaty) Thomas; m. Vernie Roberts, Aug. 28, 1953 (dec. Sept. 13, 1980); children: Albert, Kenneth, Constance Marie. BA, Calif. State U., Stanislaus, 1964; MA, Fresno (Calif.) Pacific Coll., 1979. Cert. elem. tchr., Calif. Mgr., co-owner Vernie's Barber Shop and Cocktail Lounge, Merced, Calif., 1955-66; tchr. Merced City Sch. Dist., 1962-72, resource tchr., 1972-77, coordinator consolidate programs, 1977—, preschool prin., 1981—; pvt. music tchr., Merced, 1960-65; adult edn. tchr. Merced Union High Sch. Dist., 1965-66; chief attendance officer Merced City Sch. Dist., 1981—, affirmative action officer, 1981-86; adj. instr. Merced Community Coll., 1983-86, seminar leader early childhood devel., 1985. Mem. Merced County LWV, 1971—, Merced Community Concerts, 1972-79, Merced Area Dems., 1972—, Unitarian Universalists Assn. of Merced County, 1967—, Muir Trail Girl Scout Council, Merced, 1979-80, 15th Cong. Dist. Constituents Adv. Com., 1987—, Calif. State U. Acad. Adv. Council, Stanislaus, 1980, Merced Masterworks Chorale, 1980-85; proctor Merced County Acad. Decathalon. Mem. NEA, Calif. Tchrs. Assn. Merced City Tchrs. Assn., Assn. Calif. Sch. Adminstrn., Merced Sch. Employees Fed. Credit Union (credit com. 1972-77, bd. dirs 1977-84). Office: Merced City Sch Dist 444 W 23d St Merced CA 95340

ROBERTS, LOIS BACKER, engineer, consultant; b. Roanoke, Ill., Apr. 22, 1944; d. Herman Jacob and Pauline Katheryn (Behrends) Backer; m. Louis Octavio Roberts (div. 1981); 1 child, Giuletta Backer. BS in Engring., U. Ill., 1966. Registered profl. engr., Conn., N.Y., Maine, Calif. Design engr. Werner-Jensen & Adams Cons. Engrs., Stamford, Conn., 1969-73, Simonson & Simonson, Cons. Engrs., San Francisco, 1973-75; pvt. practice cons. engrs. Westport, Conn., 1976—; bd. dirs. Pub. Site and Bldg. Commn.; pres. Conn. Engrs. In Pvt. Practice, Inc., 1987—. Vol. Conn. Grand Opera Guild. Mem. NSPE, Am. Consulting Engrs. Council, Soc. Women Engrs. Episcopalian. Office: Lois Roberts PE Cons Engrs 163 Main St Westport CT 06880

ROBERTS, LORI GAYE, soft drink marketing executive; b. Manitowoc, Wis., Nov. 9, 1955; d. Albert William and Betty Lou (Brunner) Benishek; m. Ronald W. Roberts, Dec. 1985. Student U. Wis., Madison, 1973-75; B.B.A., U. Wis.-Milw., 1977. Ter. sales mgr. Coca-Cola USA, Chgo., 1977-79, sales devel. mgr., Madison, 1979-80, asst. mgr. market planning, Atlanta, 1980-84, mgr. telemarketing and direct mail, 1984—; lectr. in field. Profl. women's fund raiser Atlanta Symphony Orch., 1984; youth edn. advisor Jr. Achievement, 1981-84; counselor Rape Crisis Ctr., Madison, 1974; harpist Symphonic Orch. U. Wis., Milw., 1976; fund raiser Atlanta Symphony Orch., 1984. Mem. Sales and Mktg. Execs. (exec. mem., dir.), Am. Harp Soc. (chpt. founder., pres.), Atlanta City Women's Club (founder, dir. mktg.), Telemktg. Control Systems User Group (pres. 1987—), Pi Sigma Epsilon (nat. dir.). Clubs: Coca Cola Running, Atlanta Travel. Home: 331 Wood Ridge Dr Atlanta GA 30339 Office: Coca-Cola USA PO Drawer 1734 Atlanta GA 30301

ROBERTS, LOUISE NISBET, philosopher; b. Lexington, Ky., Apr. 21, 1919; d. Benjamin and Helen L. Nisbet; A.B., U. Ky., 1942, M.A., 1944; Ph.D. (univ. scholar 1945-46, Delta Delta Delta fellow 1946-47, AAUW fellow 1947-48), Columbia U., 1952; m. Warren Roberts, June 14, 1952; children—Helen Ward, Valeria Lamar Roberts Emmett. Instr. philosophy Fairfax Hall, Waynesboro, Va., 1943-44, Fairmount Casements, Ormond Beach, Fla., 1944-45; mem. faculty Newcomb Coll., Tulane U., 1948—, prof. philosophy, 1969-85, prof. emeritus, 1985—, head dept., 1969. Mem. So. Soc. Philosophy and Psychology, AAUW (pres. New Orleans chpt. 1986—), DAR (vice regent New Orleans chpt. 1987—), AAUP (chpt. sec.-treas. 1966-68), Phi Beta Kappa (chpt. pres. 1956-57), Delta Delta Delta. Democrat. Episcopalian. Author articles in field. Office: Newcomb Coll 1229 Broadway New Orleans LA 70118 also: Tulane U Dept of Philosophy Coll of Arts & Scis New Orleans LA 70118

ROBERTS, LUCILLE, owner fitness agency, operator; b. Leninabad, USSR, Dec. 7, 1943; came to U.S., 1943; d. Henry and Celia (Raifinoff) Spindel; m. Bob Roberts, Apr. 20, 1967; children: Kevin Van, Kirk Van. BA, U. Pa., 1964; cert. O.P.M., Harvard U., 1985. Tchr. N.Y.C. Bd. Edn., 1964-65; buyer Mays Dept. Store, N.Y.C., 1965-67; mgr. accessory mdse. Kitty Kelly Inc., N.Y.C., 1967-69; chief exec. officer Lucille Roberts Fitness Pl., N.Y.C., 1969—; cons. AWED, 1984—, N.Y. Women Bus. Owners, N.Y.C., 1983—. Author: Computercise, 1984. Mem. Nat. Multiple Sclerosis Soc., 1987—; vol. Meals on Wheels, 1986—. Named Woman Yr. Cosmopolitan mag., 1985. Mem. Young Pres. Orgn. Republican. Office: The Roberts Orgn 8A E 80th St New York NY 10021

ROBERTS, MARGOT MARKELS, business executive; b. Springfield, Mass., Jan. 20, 1945; d. Reuben and Marion (Markels) R.; children—Lauren B. Phillips, Debrah C. Herman. B.A., Boston U. Interior designer Louis Legum Furniture Co., Norfolk, Va., 1965-70; buyer, mgr. Danker Furniture, Rockville, Md., 1970-72; buyer W & J Sloane, Washington, 1972-74; pres. Bus. & Fin. Cons., Palm Beach, Fla., 1976-80, Margot M. Roberts & Assocs., Inc., Palm Beach, 1976—; v.p., dir. So. Textile Services Inc., Palm Beach. Pres. Brittany Condominium Assn., Palm Beach, 1983—; v.p. South Palm Beach Civic Assn., 1983—, South Palm Beach Pres.'s Assn., 1984—; vice chmn. South Palm Beach Planning Bd., 1983—. Mem. Nat. Assn. Women in Bus., Palm Beach C. of C. Republican. Jewish. Office: Margot M Roberts & Assocs Inc 230 Royal Palm Way Suite 211 Palm Beach FL 33480

ROBERTS, MARIE DYER, computer systems specialist; b. Statesboro, Ga., Feb. 19, 1943; d. Byron and Martha (Evans) Dyer; B.S., U. Ga., 1966; student Am. U., 1972; cert. systems profl., cert. in data processing; m. Hugh V. Roberts, Jr., Oct. 6, 1973. Mathematician, computer specialist U.S. Naval Oceanographic Office, Washington, 1966-73; systems analyst, programmer Sperry Microwave Electronics, Clearwater, Fla., 1973-75; data processing mgr., asst. bus. mgr. Trenam, Simmons, Kemker et al, Tampa, Fla., 1975-77; mathematician, computer specialist U.S. Army C.E., Savannah, Ga., 1977-81, 83-85, Frankfurt, W. Ger., 1981-83; ops. research analyst U.S. Army Contrn. Research Lab., Champaign, Ill., 1985-87; data base adminstr., computer systems programmer U.S. Army Corps of Engrs., South Pacific div., San Francisco, 1987—; instr. computer scis. City Coll. of Chgo. in Franfurt, 1982-83. Recipient Sustained Superior Performance award Dept. Army, 1983. Mem. Am. Soc. Hist. Preservation, Data Processing Mgmt. Assn., Assn. of Inst. for Cert. Computer Profls., Assn. Women in Computing, Assn. Women in Sci., Nat. Assn. Female Execs., Am. Film Inst., U. Ga. Alumni Assn., Sigma Kappa. Author: Harris Computer Users Manual, 1983.

ROBERTS, MARY BELLE, clinical social worker; b. Akron, Ohio, Sept. 27, 1923; d. Joseph Gill and Inez Wilson (Garvey) Roberts; BS, U. Mich., 1948, MSW, 1950. Cert. social worker, Md., lic. clin. social worker, Fla. Instr. dept. psychiatry U. Ala. Med. Coll., 1950-53; psychiat. social worker div. mental hygiene Ala. Dept. Pub. Health, 1950-52, acting dir., dir., 1952-53; sr. psychiat. social worker bur. mental health div. community service Pa. Dept. Welfare, 1954-55; cons. psychiat. social work community service br. NIMH, USPHS, HEW, 1955-64; pvt. practice psychiat. social work, 1964-68; caseworker Family Service, Miami, Fla., 1968-70, Family and Childrens Service, Miami, 1971-75; casework cons. United Family and Childrens Services, Miami, 1975-85, Family Counseling Services, Miami, 1985—. Home: 501 Valencia Ave #2 Coral Gables FL 33134 Office: 2190 NW 7th St Miami FL 33125

ROBERTS, MATTIE EVELYN, insurance agent, free-lance writer; b. Bivins, Tex., Apr. 13, 1935; d. Irvin and Ruby Lee (Blackwell) Lynch; m. Harold William Roberts, Sept. 25, 1954 (div. Mar. 1981); children: Sharon Kaye Roberts Landers, Danny Claude, Timmy Harold. Student, U. Conn., Ind. Life Ins. Sch., Jacksonville, Fla. Newspaper reporter, feature writer Caddo Citizen Newspaper, Vivian, La., 1978-83; community reporter Citizen's Jour., Atlanta, Tex., 1978-83; ins. agt. Ind. Life Ins. Co., Jacksonville, Fla., 1983—; ins. agt. Old Am. Ins., Kansas City, 1981-83. Contbr. articles to profl jours.; photographer front page photos. Pres. McLeod (Tex.) Community Club, 1977-80, McLeod PTA, 1980. Mem. Assn. Press Women, La. Press Women, Nat. Writers Assn., Nat. Assn. Life Underwriters. Republican. Baptist. Home: 208 E Thomas Atlanta TX 75551 Office: Ind Life Ins Co #1 Independent Dr Jacksonville FL 32202

ROBERTS, NANCY, educator; b. Boston, Jan. 25, 1938; d. Harold and Annette (Zion) Rosenthal; m. Edward Roberts; children: Valerie, Mitchell, Andrea. AB, Boston U., 1959, MEd, 1961, EdD, 1975. Elem. tchr. Sharon (Mass.) Pub. Schs., 1959-63; asst. prof. Lesley Coll., Cambridge, Mass., 1975-79; assoc. prof. Lesley Coll., 1980-83, prof., 1983—; research assoc. MIT, Cambridge, 1976-79; mem. nat. steering com. Nat. Edn. Computing Conf., Eugene, Oreg., 1979—. Author: Dynamics of Human Service Delivery, 1976, Practical Guide to Computers in Education, 1982, Computers in Teaching Mathematics, 1983, Introduction to Computer Simulation, 1983 (J.W. Forrester award 1983), Integrating Computers into the Elementary and Middle School, 1987, Computers and the Social Studies, 1988; mem. editorial bd. Jour. Ednl. Computing, 1983—; editor Computers in Edn. book series, 1984—. Mem. Computer Policy Com., Boston, 1982-84; bd. dirs. Computers for Kids, Cambridge, 1983-85. NSF grantee, 1985—. Mem. System Dynamics Soc. (bd. dirs. policy com. 1987—). Republican. Jewish. Home: 17 Fellsmere Rd Newton MA 02159 Office: Lesley Coll 29 Everett St Cambridge MA 02138-2790

ROBERTS, PAMELA MARTHA, television producer; b. Allentown, Pa., Jan. 3, 1949; d. Charles Hayward and Evelyn (Collier) R. BA, Cornell U., 1970. Freelance journalist Japan, 1970-72; potter Peters Valley Craftsmen, Layton, N.J., 1972-74; tchr. Woolman Hill Sch., Deerfield, Mass., 1974-76; TV producer The Documentary Guild, Mass., 1976. Producer (TV programs) "Will Our Children Thank Us?", 1984, A Citizens Summit, 1986, A Citizens Summit II, 1986, A Citizens Summit/Dialogue, 1986; co-producer (with Soviet TV) Gosteleradio. Home and Office: The Documentary Guild Shearer Rd Colrain MA 01340

ROBERTS, PRISCILLA WARREN, painter; b. Montclair, N.J., June 13, 1916; d. Charles Asaph and Florence (Berry) R. Student, Art Students League, 1937-39, Nat. Acad., 1939-43. Works represented collections of, Met. Mus., Cin. Art Mus., Canton Art Inst., Westmoreland County Mus. Art, Pa., I.B.M., Dallas Mus., Walker Art Center, Mpls., Butler Inst., Youngstown, Ohio. Recipient Allied Artists Zabriskie prize 1944, 46, Hallgarten prize Nat. Acad. ann. exhbn. 1945, Proctor prize 1947, popular prize Corcoran Biennial 1947, prize Westmoreland County Mus., 3d prize Carnegie Internat., Pitts., 1950. Mem. Allied Artists Am., N.A.D., Catherine Lorillard Wolfe Assn. (hon.). Address: Box 716 Georgetown CT 06829

ROBERTS, SALLY JOANN, relocation company executive; b. Terre Haute, Ind., Jan. 31, 1938; d. Frances Wayne and Berniece Ernestine (Scanlon) Hatfield; m. Ronald Leroy Roberts, June 8, 1957; children—Terri Lynn, Timothy Lee, Cynthia Ann, Christopher Allen. Student Ind. State U., 1955-57. Relocation mgr. Employee Transfer Corp., Chgo., 1977-79; mgmt. cons. C21 No. Ill. Region, Rosemont, 1979-80; v.p. Baird & Warner, Chgo., 1980-83; v.p., co-owner Profl. Relocation, Oak Brook, Ill., 1983-85; pres. Profl. Relocation, Bloomingdale, Ill., 1985—; bd. mem. I.C.R. Referral Network, Kansas City, Kans., 1981-83; mem. adv. bd. Am. Bound Pubs., Los Angeles, 1986—. Author: Homebuyers Guide, 1980, Relocation, 1981-85. Mem. Nat. Assn. Realtors (life mem. million dollar sales 1977, cons. Chgo. 1983-86), Employee Relocation Council (com. mem. 1981-85), Relocation Dirs. Council (com. mem. 1981-85), Chgo. Assn. Commerce and Industry. Republican. Lutheran. Avocations: sailing; golfing; bridge. Office: Profl Relocation Group 261 E Lake St Bloomingdale IL 60108

ROBERTS, SANDRA BROWN, realty company executive; b. Boston, May 26, 1939; d. Frederick Thomas and Christine (Peyton) Brown; m. Joseph Peter Roberts, Aug. 26, 1962 (div. May 1984); children—Christine, Joseph, Paul. B.A., Boston Coll., 1981. Lic. real estate broker, Mass. Owner, mgr. real estate, Wellesley, Mass., 1963—; pres. Riverview Realty, Wellesley, 1970—; comml. realtor, Boston, 1974—; cons. Berkshire Hathaway, New Bedford, Mass., 1983—. Founder, pres., bd. dirs. Friends of Ft. Washington, Inc.; active Friends of Boston Ballet, 1983—. Mem. New Eng. Women in Real Estate, DAR (Boston Tea Party chpt. regent 1983-84, 84-85). Navy League of U.S., New Eng. Hist. Geneal. Soc. Republican. Roman Catholic. Club: College (Boston). Lodge: Order of Crown of Charlemagne (life mem.), Order of Lafayette (bd. dirs.). Home: 52 Kenilworth Rd Wellesley MA 02181 Office: DAR Boston Tea Party Chpt 51 River St Wellesley MA 02181

ROBERTS, SUSAN BROWNING, editor; b. Summit, N.J., May 27, 1941; d. Roland Browning and Geraldine Harper (Davidson) R.; A.B., Grinnell Coll., 1963; M.A., U. Idaho, 1982; m. Louis A. Hieb, June 8, 1963 (div. June 1975); children—Matthew Alan, John Andrew. Soc. news writer New Haven Register, 1963-64; asst. young adult and teen program dir. New Haven YM-YWCA, 1964-65; reporter, sch. editor The Princeton (N.J.) Packet, 1965-70; corr. Spokane (Wash.) Daily Chronicle, Pullman, 1974-75; editor Forest Wildlife and Range Expt. Sta. U. Idaho, Moscow, 1975-84; ext. publs. editor Wash. State U., 1984—; editorial adv. Jour. Interpretation, 1982-84. Bd. deacons First Presbyn. Ch., Moscow, 1980-82; den mother Lewis Clark council Boy Scouts Am., 1976-77, 81-83, awards chmn., 1977-79, sec.-treas., 1983-84; treas., coordinator troop 344, 1985-86, chairperson, 1987. Mem. Agrl. Communicators in Edn. (awards for excellence 1979, 80, 86, Idaho state rep. 1983-84, Wash. state rep. 1986—), Am. Sociol. Assn. Democrat. Presbyterian. Office: Wash State U Agrl Info 401 Hulbert Hall Pullman WA 99164

ROBERTSHAW, JANE, lawyer; b. Houston, Nov. 20, 1952; d. John Charles and Lois Caroline R. B.A. magna cum laude with distinction in Anthropology, Colo. Coll., 1974; J.D., U. Colo., 1980. Bar: N.Mex. 1980. Mem. Sutin, Thayer & Browne, Albuquerque, 1980—. Mem. ABA, Albuquerque Bar Assn., Phi Beta Kappa, Pi Gamma Mu, Alpha Lambda Delta. Office: Sutin Thayer & Browne PO Box 1945 Albuquerque NM 87103

ROBERTSON, CHRISTINE, educator; b. Ames, Iowa, Oct. 20, 1949; d. Howard Robert and Winifred (Wolters) Cushman; m. Fred Paul Robertson, May 12, 1949 (div. Nov. 1984); children: Megan, Rusty. BS in Edn., Iowa State U., 1971; MEd, U. Cin., 1987. Cert. elem. tchr., reading specialist, gifted and talented tchr., elem. supr., Nebr., Ga., Ohio. Tchr. Johnson-Brock (Nebr.) Schs., 1972, Auburn Rural Schs., 1972-73, Cobb County Schs., Marietta, Ga., 1973-79, Cin. Pub. Schs., 1980—; tchr. LaBelle Elem. Sch., Marietta, 1974-79, Linwood Acad., Cin., 1980—; developer enrichment writing, reading program Linwood Acad., Cin., 1987—. Mem. adminstrv. bd., chmn. edn. com. St. Phillips Meth. Ch., Marietta, 1973-79, Cherry Grove Meth. Ch., Cin., 1980-87; mem. adv. council Ayer Elem. Schs, Cin., 1984-86. Martha Holden Jennings Found. scholar, 1986-87. Mem. Cin. Fedn. Tchrs, Internat. Reading Assn., Assn. Suprs. and Curriculum Devel., Ohio Valley Talented and Gifted Assn., PTA, Phi Kappa Delta. Republican. Home: 7137 Woodridge Dr Cincinnati OH 45230 Office: Linwood Acad 4900 Eastern Ave Cincinnati OH 45226

ROBERTSON, ESTELLE SPRAYBERRY, academic administrator; b. Anniston, Ala.; d. Leslie Gay and Minnie Lou (Crews) Sprayberry; m. Marion Franklin Robertson, Mar. 11, 1949; children: Susan, Scott, Keith. AA, Jacksonville (Ala.) State U., 1949, BS, 1962, MS, 1971. Cert. tchr., Ala.; cert. sch. prin., Ala.; cert. supr., Ala.; cert. supt., Ala. With sales dept. Calhoun County Bd. Edn., Anniston, 1949-61; tchr. Anniston City Bd. Edn., 1961-66, coordinator instrn., 1966-69, prin. Constantine Sch., 1969-72, prin. Tenth St. Elem. Sch., 1972—. Mem. 5th Dist. Elem. Prins. (pres.), So. Assn. Schs. and Colls. (various coms.), Alpha Delta Kappa (pres.), Kappa Delta Pi, Phi Delta Kappa. Baptist. Clubs: Camellia Garden (pres. 1966), The Supper. Lodge: Altrusa (sec., com. mem. local chpt. 1979—). Home: 220 Druid Hills Rd Anniston AL 36201 Office: Tenth St Elem Sch 1525 E 10th St Anniston AL 36201

ROBERTSON, JACLYNN RUTH, accountant; b. El Paso, Tex., July 30, 1955; d. Jack and Ramona Ruth (Thompson) Steele; m. John Dale

Robertson, July 15, 1978; children: Kara Ruth, Kyle Stewart, Kelly Dale, Kory Jack. Grad. high sch., Santa Fe, 1973. Bookkeeper N.Mex. Taxation and Revenue Dept., Santa Fe, 1973-74; acount technician N. Mex. Human Services Dept., Santa Fe, 1974-78, mem. ednl. leave com., 1974-78, mem. personnel subcom., 1978; fin. specialist N.Mex Dept. Fin. and Adminstrn., Santa Fe, 1978-81, fin. supr., 1981-85; acct. Santa Fe, 1985—. Co-author, editor N.Mex. Pub. Sch. Fin. Statistics, 1981-84. Campaign mgr. Janice Olsen for State Rep., Santa Fe, 1976; del. State Rep. Conv., 1976, 80; mem. N.Mex. Coalition for Prevention of Fetal Alcohol Symdrome, Santa Fe, 1979-81, Govs. Steering Com., 1981-82; cookie chmn. Girl Scouts of Am., Santa Fe, 1987. Republican. Mem. Ch. Religious Sci. Home and Office: 2818 Vereda Poniente Santa Fe NM 87505

ROBERTSON, MARIAN ELLA (HALL), handwriting analyst; b. Edmonton, Alta., Can., Mar. 3, 1920; d. Orville Arthur and Lucy Hon (Osborn) Hall; m. Howard Chester Robertson, Feb. 7, 1942; children: Elaine, Richard. Student, Willamette U., 1937-39; BS, Western Oreg. State U., 1955. Cert. elem., jr. high. tchr., supt. (life) Oreg.; cert. graphoanalyst. Tchr. pub. schs. Mill City, Albany, Scio and Hillsboro, Oreg., 1940-72; cons. Zaner-Bloser Inc., Columbus, Ohio, 1972-85, assoc. cons., 1985—; pres. Write-Keys, Scio, 1980—; tchr. Internat. Graphoanalysis Soc., Chgo., 1979; instr. Linn-Benton Community Coll., 1985-86. sr. intern 5th Congl. Dist. Oreg., Washington, 1984; precinct committeem. Rep. Cen. Com., Linn County, 1986, alt. vice-chair, 1986; candidate Oreg. State Legis., Salem, 1986. Mem. Altrusa Internat. (internat. chmn. 1985-86). Republican. Mem. Soc. of Friends. Home: 37929 Kelly Rd Scio OR 97374 Office: Write-Keys PO Box 54 Jefferson OR 97352

ROBERTSON, ROBERTA ANN, apartment guide publisher; b. Fairfield, Calif., Sept. 9, 1961; d. James Thomas and Valeria (Brower) R. AB in Math., Smith Coll., 1983; postgrad., U. Chgo., 1987—. Research asst. Zetetics Inc., Memphis, 1983-84; dir. research Haas Corp., Norcross, Ga., 1984-86; pub. Haas Pub. Cos., Inc., Chgo., 1986—. Mem. Nat. Assn. Female Execs., Smith Coll. Alumnae Chgo. (chmn. publicity com. 1987), Apt. and Condominium Council Greater Chgo. Republican. Presbyterian. Office: Haas Pub Cos Inc 1 S 660 Midwest Rd Suite 230 Oak Brook Terrace IL 60181

ROBERTSON, RUTH CARLSON, educational administrator; b. Oil City, Pa., Aug. 3, 1940; d. Elmer F. and Elizabeth D. (Anthony) Carlson; m. Amos G. Hollinger, Mar. 23, 1963 (div. Jan. 1980); 1 child, Mark T. Hollinger; m. A. Bruce Robertson, Jan. 2, 1986. BS in Physics, Pa. State U., 1962, PhD in Materials Sci., 1970; postgrad., Johns Hopkins U., 1962-63. Instr., then asst. prof. physics Pa. State U., Altoona, 1968-76; planning analyst Pa. State U., University Park, 1976-79; asst. chmn. dept. physics and astronomy Northwestern U., Evanston, Ill., 1979-81; mgr. chemistry dept. Princeton (N.J.) U., 1981-87; acad. planner U. Wis. System, Madison, 1987—. Mem. Am. Chem. Soc., Am. Assn. Physics Tchrs. Methodist. Office: U Wis System Office Acad Affairs 1220 Linden Dr Madison WI 53706

ROBERTSON, SANDRA DEE (GRAEN), accountant; b. Denver, Nov. 7, 1953; d. Fredrick Philip Arthur Graen and Dorothea Stone (Bell) Kohler; m. Charles E. Robertson Jr., Aug. 4, 1973 (Jan. 1985); 1 child, Daniel Philip. BS in Bus. cum laude, U. Colo., 1980. CPA, Colo. Staff acct. Brock, Cordle & Assocs., CPA's, Boulder, Colo., 1980-82; corp. tax acct. Storage Tech. Corp., Louisville, Colo., 1983-87; state tax supr. RJR Nabisco, Inc., Atlanta, Ga., 1987—. Served with U.S. Army, 1972-75. Mem. Am. Inst. CPA's, Colo. Soc. CPA's, Beta Gamma Sigma. Democrat. Club: Toastmasters. Home: 4603 Lost Mountain Ct Powder Springs GA 30073

ROBERTSON, SARA ELIZABETH, editor; b. Kansas City, Mo., July 7, 1956; d. Earl Edward Robertson Jr. and Monabelle Williams Lyda. AB, Stanford U., 1978; M in Internat. Affairs, Columbia U., 1984. Tchr. English Agy for Agrl. Research and Devel., Bogor, Indonesia, 1978-79; prodn. mgr., publicity dir. The Asia Record, Palo Alto, Calif., 1979-80; tchr. English Beijing (People's Republic China) Metallurgical Inst. Mech. and Elect. Tech., 1984-85; asst. editor Fgn. Affairs mag., N.Y.C., 1985—. Democrat. Home: 123 W 75th St #2F New York NY 10023 Office: Council on Fgn Relations 58 E 68th St New York NY 10021

ROBERTS-WRIGHT, BESSIE MARGARET SHRONTZ, nursery exec.; b. Centralia, Kans., May 23, 1905; d. Onbey Roscoe and Sarah Elizabeth (Shrontz) Roberts; student public schs., Rupert, Idaho; m. Loyd K. Wright, Feb. 6, 1924; 1 son, John Robert. Partner, treas. Kimberly Nurseries, Inc., Twin Falls, Idaho, 1924—. Sunday sch. tchr., 1946-56. Mem. Nat. Fedn. Ind. Bus., Twin Falls C. of C., Am. Nurserymen, Idaho Nursery Assn., Archaeol. Inst. Am., Twin Falls Hist. Soc. (dir.), Nat. Assn. Watch and Clock Collectors, Franklin Mint Collectors Soc., Smithsonian Soc. Republican. Methodist. Club: Daus. of Nile. Author: Me and My Other Self (autobiography), Oakley, Idaho, Pioneer Town. Home: PO Box L Kimberly ID 83341 Office: Kimberly Nurseries Inc Rt 3 Addison Ave E Twin Falls ID 83301

ROBEY, KATHLEEN MORAN (MRS. RALPH WEST ROBEY), club woman; b. Boston, Aug. 9, 1909; d. John Joseph and Katherine (Berrigan) Moran; B.A., Trinity Coll., Washington, 1933; m. Ralph West Robey, Jan. 28, 1941. Actress appearing in Pride and Prejudice, Broadway, 1935, Tomorrow is a Holiday, road co., 1935, Death Takes a Holiday, road co., 1936, Left Turn, Broadway, 1936, Come Home to Roost, Boston, 1936; pub. relations N.Y. Fashion Industry, N.Y.C., 1938-43. Mem. Florence Crittenton Home and Hosp., Women's Aux. Salvation Army, Gray Lady, ARC; mem. Seton Guild St. Ann's Infant Home. Mem. Christ Child Soc., Fedn. Republican Women of D.C. English-Speaking Union. Republican. Roman Catholic. Clubs: City Tavern, Cosmos (Washington), Nat. Woman's Republican. Home: 4000 Cathedral Ave NW Washington DC 20016

ROBICHAUD, PHYLLIS IVY ISABEL, artist, educator; b. Jamaica, West Indies, May 16, 1915; came to U.S., 1969, naturalized, 1977; d. Peter C. and Rose Matilda (Rickman) Burnett; grad. Tutorial Coll., 1933, Kingston, Jamaica, Munro Coll., St. Elizabeth, Jamaica, 1946; student Central Tech. Sch., Toronto, Ont., Can., 1960-63, Anderson Coll., Can., 1968-69; m. Roger Robichaud, July 22, 1961; children by previous marriage—George Wilmot Graham, William Henry Heron Graham, Mary Elizabeth Graham Watson, Peter Robert Burnett Graham. Sec. to supr. of Agr., St. Elizabeth, 1940-50; loans officer and cashier Confederation Life Assn., Kingston, 1950-53; tchr. art Jamaica Welfare Ltd., 1963; tchr. art recreation dept. New Port Richey, Fla., 1969-77; tchr. art Pasco Hernando Community Coll., New Port Richey, 1977—; demonstrator various organizations including West Pasco Art Guild, New Port Richey, Ace Artists, New Port Richey; propr., mgr. Band Box Dress Shop, Kingston, Jamaica, 1954-57; numerous one-woman shows of paintings including various banks, libraries, Kingston, 1963-64, 67, Toronto, 1968, New Port Richey, 1969, 70, 73, 76, Tampa, Fla., 1974, 75, 76, Omaha Cattle Company restaurant, Clearwater Fla., 1982; numerous group shows, latest being: Sweden House, Tampa, 1977-78, Chasco Fiesta, New Port Richey, 1977, Magnolia Valley Golf and Country Club, New Port Richey, 1978, W. Pasco Art Guild, New Port Richey, 1978, 79, Indian Rocks Beach, 1985, other cities in Fla.; executed murals, New Port Richey and Kingston; represented in permanent collections: New Port Richey C. of C., Magnolia Valley Golf and Country Club, also pvt. collections. Patron, St. Alban's 4H Club, 1942; sec. Sunday sch. Ch. of Eng., Kingston, 1937-39. Recipient award T. Eaton Co. of Can., 1961, cert. of merit, Mayor of New Port Richey, 1976, appreciation award New Port Richey Recreation Dept., 1977; award Fla. Heart Fund. Mem. Nat. League Am. Pen Women (v.p. Tampa br. 1978-80, dir. 1969—), West Pasco Art Guild (Blue ribbons 1978, 79), Fla. Fine Arts Guild. Republican. Roman Catholic. Address: 7032 Lenox Dr New Port Richey FL 34653

ROBICHEAU, DENISE LOUISE, apparel company executive; b. Wareham, Mass., Sept. 28, 1954; d. William Robicheau and Marie Anne (Cannizzaro) Lindenmuth; m. John D. Sullivan, Oct. 10, 1981 (div. Aug. 1985). Assoc. in Fine Arts, Gen. Studies, Miami-Dade Community Coll., 1976; BFA, Rhode Island Sch. Design, 1978. Adminstrv. asst. Carribean Rev. mag., Miami, Fla., 1970-74; adminstrv. asst. to v.p. Fla. Internat. U., Miami, Fla., 1974-76; designer M. Hoffman & Co., Boston, 1978-81; dir. mdse. and design Hoffman Apparel Internat., Boston, 1981—; cons. catalog Greenpeace, Boston, 1974-75. Organizer Chelsea (Mass.) Waterfront Neighborhood Assn., 1982-83. Recipient Raul Lovitt award, 1978, Outstanding Design award Amicale Corp. Co., 1978. Office: c/o Hoffman Cos 160 N Washington St Boston MA 02114

ROBILLARD, FLORENCE, state senator; b. Holyoke, Mass., May 30, 1926. B.S., U. Mass., Framingham. Former mem. Vt. Higher Edn. Planning Commn., Adv. Council on Comprehensive Health Edn.; mem. Vt. Senate, 1985—. Office: State Senate Office State Capitol Montpelier VT 05602 Address: Eastridge Acres Mendon VT 05701 *

ROBINETTE, SHEREE, subcontractor; b. Tampa, Fla., Mar. 12, 1957; d. William J. and Patricia Ann (Gearhart) R AA Hillsborough Community Coll., 1977; BABA U. South Fla., 1980. Mgr. Fontaine Supply, Tampa, 1977-80; owner,mgr. Tampa Accessory Corp., 1980—. Mem. Constrn. Trade Assn., Nat. Assn. Women in Constrn., Nat. Assn. Profl. Estimators . Republican. Baptist. Avocations: ballet, swimming, cycling. Office: 5700 Memorial Hwy Tampa FL 33615

ROBINS, LEE NELKEN, sociology educator; b. New Orleans, Aug. 29, 1922; d. Abe and Leona (Reiman) Nelken; m. Eli Robins, Feb. 22, 1946; children: Paul, James, Thomas, Nicholas. Student, Newcomb Coll., 1938-40; B.A., Radcliffe Coll., 1942, M.A., 1943, Ph.D., 1951. Mem. faculty Washington U., St. Louis, 1954—, prof. sociology in psychiatry; Mem. faculty Washington U., 1968—, prof. sociology, 1969—; former mem. Nat. Adv. Council on Drug Abuse, Pres.'s Commn. on Mental Health task panels; expert adv. panel mental health WHO.; Salmon lectr. N.Y. Acad. Medicine, 1983. Author 3 monographs; editor 5 books; contbr. articles to profl. jours. Recipient Research Scientist award USPHS, 1970—; Pacesetter Research award Nat. Inst. Drug Abuse, 1978; Radcliffe Coll. Grad. Soc. medal, 1979; Research grantee NIMH; Research grantee Nat. Inst. on Drug Abuse; Research grantee Nat. Inst. on Alcohol Abuse and Alcoholism. Fellow Am. Coll. Epidemiology; Mem. Am. Sociol. Assn., Internat. Sociol. Assn., Inst. of Medicine, Internat. Epidemiological Assn., Soc. Epidemiol. Research, Am. Psychopathol. Assn. (Paul Hoch award 1978, pres. 1987-88), Am. Public Health Assn. (Rema Lapouse award 1979), Soc. Life History Research in Psychopathology, Am. Coll. Neuropsychopharmacology. Office: Washington U Dept Psychiatry Med Sch Saint Louis MO 63110

ROBINS, MARJORIE MCCARTHY (MRS. GEORGE KENNETH ROBINS), civic worker; b. St. Louis, Oct. 4, 1914; d. Eugene Ross and Louise (Roblee) McCarthy; A.B., Vassar Coll., 1936; diploma St. Louis Sch. Occupational Therapy, 1940; m. George Kenneth Robins, Nov. 9, 1940; children—Carol Robins Von Arx, G. Stephen, Barbara A. Robins Foorman. Mem. Mo. Library Commn., 1937-38; mem. bd. St. Louis Jr. League, 1945, 46; mem. bd. Occupational Therapy Workshop of St. Louis, 1941-46, pres., 1945, 46; mem. bd. Ladue Chapel Nursery Sch., 1957-60, 61-64, pres. bd., 1963, 64; past regional chmn. United Fund; past mem. St. Louis Met. Youth Commn., St. Louis Health and Welfare Council; bd. dirs. Internat. Inst. of St. Louis, 1966-72, 76—82, 83—, sec., 1968, v.p., 1981; bd. dirs. Mental Health Assn. St. Louis, 1963-70, Washington U. Child Guidance and Evaluation Clinic, 1968-78; bd. dirs. Central Inst. for Deaf, 1970—, v.p., 1975-76, pres., 1976-78; bd. dirs. Met. St. Louis YWCA, 1954-63, 64-74, pres. bd., 1960-63, trustee, 1977—; mem. nat. bd. YWCA, 1967-79, nat. v.p., 1973-76; vol. tchr. remedial reading clinic St. Louis City Schs., 1968-71; trustee John Burroughs Sch., 1960-63, John Burroughs Found., 1965-80, Roblee Found., 1972—, Nat. YWCA Retirement Fund, 1979—; bd. dirs. Gambrill Gardens United Meth. Retirement Home, 1979-85, Thompson Retreat and Conf. Center, 1981-87; bd. dirs. Springboard to Learning Inc., 1980—, v.p., 1980—. Mem. Archeol. Inst. Am. (bd. dirs., treas. St. Louis chpt. 1985-87). Clubs: Vassar (sec. and pres. 1939-40), Wednesday (dir. 1968-70, 77-79, 80-81) (St. Louis). Home: 45 Loren Woods Saint Louis MO 63124

ROBINSON, ALETHA WILLIAMS, nurse, psychologist; b. Chesterfield, S.C., Sept. 27, 1934; d. John Henry and Eliza Jane (Crowley) Williams; m. Grover Snelson Robinson, Sept. 8, 1962; children: Sarah Dawn, Derek Grover. Diploma in Nursing, Presbyn. Hosp., 1958; BS in Nursing, Flora MacDonald Coll., Red Springs, N.C., 1959; MA in Counseling Psychology, George Mason U., 1979. Head nurse Presbyn. Hosp., Charlotte, N.C., 1958-59; nursing instr. Presbyn. Hosp. Sch. Nursing, Charlotte, 1959-61; health edn. advisor U.S. Agy. for Internat. Devel., Vientiane, Laos, 1962-63; vol. nurse Christian and Missionary Alliance, Vientiane, 1962-63; nursing educator WHO, Vientiane, 1964-68; counseling psychologist Nairobi, Kenya, 1979-82; marriage and family counselor Amani Counseling Soc., Nairobi, 1979-82; nursing instr. William S. Hall Psychiat. Inst., Columbia, S.C., 1983; mental health counselor Newberry Mental Health Ctr., Newberry, S.C., 1983—. Mem. Am. Psychol. Assn. (assoc.), Am. Assn. Marriage and Family Therapy (clin.), Internat. Acad. Profl. Counseling and Psychotherapy (clin.). Home: 437 Sulgrave Dr Columbia SC 29210 Office: PO Box 464 Newberry SC 29108

ROBINSON, AMY LYNN, transportation executive; b. Newark, Ohio, July 28, 1960; d. Joseph Burr and Mary Lou (Reid) R. Grad. high sch., Saline, Mich. Asst. mgr. Town & Country Fashions, Ann Arbor, Mich., 1976-78; trainee clk. Corrigan Air Freight, Ann Arbor, 1980-82; asst. mgr. C.I.C./Express Services Inc., Moonachie, N.J., 1982-85, mgr., 1985-88; mgr. cen. control Right-O-Way, Inc., Tustin, Calif., 1988—. Mem. Nat. Assn. Female Execs. Democrat. Office: Right-O-Way Inc 180 S Prospect St Tustin CA 92680

ROBINSON, ANNE FRANKLIN, health science organization executive; b. Wetumpka, Ala., Sept. 5, 1947; d. Truman Alfred and Juanita (Strickland) Franklin; m. John Philipse Robinson Jr., June 29, 1968 (div. Dec. 1983); children: John Philipse III, Truman Tucker. BA, Auburn U., 1969. Tchr. Rudyard (Mich.) High Sch., 1970-71; with logistics dept. IT&T Artic Services, Anchorage, 1971; tchr. Wetumpka (Ala.) Elem. Sch., 1975-76; dir. tng. Weight Watchers of So. Ala. and Palm Beach County, Inc., Montgomery, 1976-78, v.p tng., 1978-86, v.p. tng. and ops., 1986—, also bd. dirs. Mem. Weight Watchers Franchise Assn. (assoc.), Montgomery Area C. of C., Delta Zeta. Episcopalian. Office: Weight Watchers of So Ala and Weight Watchers Palm Beach 573 S Hull St Montgomery AL 36104

ROBINSON, BRENDA COOMBS, city official; b. Goldsboro, N.C., Dec. 16, 1947; d. Rhem Horace and Mary Kathleen (Davis) Coombs; student Meredith Coll. 1965-67; B.S. in Bus. Adminstrn. U. Central Fla. 1977, M.A. in Econs., 1979; children—Lisa Reed Donnan, Christopher Scott Donnan. Grad. asst. U. Central Fla. 1978-79; sr. planner manpower div. County of Seminole, Fla. 1979, sr. budget and mgmt. analyst 1979-81; dir. fin. City of Altamonte Springs, Fla. 1981-83; mgmt. and budget ofcl. City of Orlando, Fla., 1983-87, dep. chief adminstrv. officer, 1987—. Recipient Orlando C. of C. Gold Telephone award 1976; grad. C. of C. Leadership Program- Leadership Orlando, 1985. Mem. Govtl. Fin. Officers Assn., Beta Gamma Sigma, Omicron Delta Kappa. Democrat. Presbyterian. Home: 312 E Yale St Orlando FL 32804 Office: 400 S Orange Ave Orlando FL 32801

ROBINSON, BRENDA MARLENE, academic administrator; b. Indpls., Apr. 16, 1953; d. John Robert and Bertha Ella (Spencer) Droke; m. Charles Lewis Robinson, Aug. 23, 1975 (div. Oct. 1981); m. Robert C. Dick, June 27, 1983. BS, Ind. U., Indpls., 1981, MS, 1988. Adminstr. Meml. Clinic Indpls., 1972-77; educator Profl. Careers Inst., Indpls., 1977-78; v.p. Aristotle Coll., Indpls. and Greenwood, Ind., 1978-88; program specialist Accrediting Bur. Health Edn. Schs., Elkhart, Ind., 1982—, Assn. Ind. Colls. and Schs., Washington, 1987; cons. Allied Health Schs., 1983—; del. People-to-People Ednl. Del., People's Republic China and USSR, 1984. Mem. Am. Med. Technologists (registered), Nat. Assn. Female Execs., Am. Assn. Med. Assts. (cert.), Kappa Delta Pi. Home: 4445 N Central Ave Indianapolis IN 46205

ROBINSON, BRENDA PERRY, metals company executive; b. Richlands, Va., June 21, 1946; d. Joseph Franklin and Irene (Jessee) Perry; student public schs., Va. and Md.; m. Walter Warren Robinson, Aug. 24, 1977; 1 child by previous marriage, Lori Kay White. File clk. Tabb Brockenbrough & Ragland, Richmond, Va., 1963-64; acctg. clk. So. states R.H. Donnelley Co., Richmond, 1965; with Reynolds Metals Co., Richmond, 1966—, mgr. employee med. benefits, 1978-81, mgr. adminstrv. services, mgr. office systems implementation, 1981-84, mgr. office automation cons. and edn., 1981-86; pres. Innovative Resources, 1985—; v.p. sales Riddick Communications/MGI, 1986-87; v.p., gen. mgr. The Innovative Capitol Group, 1987; condr. seminars in field. Editor INNOVATA. Chmn. adv. council State of Va. Dept. Bus. Edn.; sec. Miss Softball Am., Richmond; co. rep. United Way, Richmond; substitute rep. Va. Nutrition Com.; project bus. cons. Jr. Achievement, 1985; mem. adv. com. Incubator Task Force, 1986, conf. speaker for Congressman Bliley, 1986; bd. dirs. Parents Anonymous, chmn. public awareness com., 1987; bd. dirs. Phoenix Halfway Ho., 1987; adv. bd. Va. Commonwealth U.; occupational edn. com. Derbyshire Bapt. Ch., chmn. computer com., Sunday Sch. tchr; adv. council occupational edn., Va. Commonwealth U. 1986. Named Boss of Yr., Am. Businesswomen's Assn., 1976. Mem. Adminstrv. Mgmt. Soc. (speakers' bur., chmn. edn. com.), Office Automation Roundtable, Va. Advanced Tech. Assn. (bd. dirs. 1984-85), Richmond Office Automation Roundtable (sec.), Women's Network. Home: 702 Sleepy Hollow Rd Richmond VA 23229 Office: 6601 W Broad St Richmond VA 23261

ROBINSON, CARLOTA NILSON, business owner; b. Austin, Minn., June 7, 1939; d. Alfred Alvin and Gwyneth Emily (Gustafsson) Norton; m. Joe B. McCawley, Jr., (div.); m. Roy E. Nilson, Oct. 10, 1970 (div.); m. Paul Robinson, Mar. 10, 1980. Grad. high sch., Austin, Minn. Dir. Sta. KICA-TV, Clovis, N.Mex., 1958; with Sta. WHOO-Radio, Orlando, Fla., 1958-59, Sta. WLCY-Radio, St. Pete, Fla., 1963-67; claims rep. Travelers Ins. Co., Orlando, Tampa; owner Creative Outlet of Fla., Inc., St. Pete, Tampa, 1967—. Author: Dream Come True Family Cookbook, 1967. Mem. advance sales and pub. relations com. Fla. State Fair, Tampa, Fla., 1967. Mem. Internat. Assn. Fairs and Expositions. Office: Creative Outlet of Fla Inc 5809-20 Ave S Tampa FL 33619-5457

ROBINSON, CATHALEEN STARN, development executive; b. Pleasantville, N.J., Nov. 20, 1940; d. Charles Sheppard and Sophie Emma (Hess) Starn; m. Neil Wentworth Robinson, Sept. 28, 1973 (dec. Oct. 1976). Grad. high sch., Pleasantville, 1958. Sec. and asst. treas. Starn's Markets Inc., Somers Point, N.J., 1959-73; pres. Robinson Enterprises, Inc., Killington, Vt., 1973—; bd. dirs. Alpine Pipeline Co. Bd. dirs. Vt. Achievement Ctr., Rutland, 1979-88; auditor towns of Sherburne, Killington, 1983-88. Baptist. Clubs: Rutland Country; Woodstock Country; Atlantic City Country;Sherburne Women's; Ch. Women United (pres. 1986, 87). Home: Robinwood-Star Rt Killington VT 05751 Office: Robinson Enterprises Inc Robinwood-Star Rt Killington VT 05751

ROBINSON, CATHERINE LAUER, government official; b. Titusville, Pa., Nov. 5, 1948; d. William A. and Frances (Zdarko) Lauer; m. James W. Robinson, May 25, 1968 (div. 1981); 1 child, Melissa C. Robinson. Student Jamestown Bus. Coll., N.Y., 1966-68, George Mason U., No. Va. Community Coll., 1972-73. Payroll clk. Cyclops Spl. Steel Co., Titusville, 1969-70; payroll specialist U.S. Dept. Navy, Washington, 1971-74; payroll liaison U.S. Dept. State, Washington, 1974-78; health liaison specialist HEW, Washington, 1978-79; grants specialist Dept. Edn., Washington, 1979-83; procurement analyst U.S. Marshals Service, McLean, Va., 1983-85, program mgr., 1985—. Recipient Outstanding Performance award U.S. Dept. Edn., 1982; Outstanding Performance award U.S. Marshals Service, 1983, 86; Outstanding Young Woman of Yr., 1983. Mem. Nat. Assn. Female Execs., Bus. and Profl. Women's Assn. Roman Catholic. Avocations: swimming, walking, sight seeing, travel. Home: 7640 Provincial Dr #302 McLean VA 22102 Office: US Marshal's Service One Tysons Corner Ctr McLean VA 22102

ROBINSON, COLLEEN MARY, personnel director; b. Camden, N.J., Feb. 25, 1954; d. Thomas Joseph Ruane and Kathryn Mary (Gattuso) Frederick; m. James Edward Robinson, May 19, 1979; 1 child, Brendan James. BA, La Salle Coll., 1976, MBA, 1983. Psychiat. technician, unit sec. Northwestern Inst. Psychiatry, Ft. Washington, Pa., 1976-79, sec. personnel, 1979-80, asst. personnel, 1980-83, dir. personnel, 1983-84; dir. personnel St. Mary Hosp., Phila., 1984—. Mem. Wyndmoor (Pa.) Community Assn., 1985, Luth. Ch. Women, Wyndmoor, 1986—. Mem. Am. Hosp. Assn. (human resources com.), Am. Soc. Personnel Adminstrn., Hosp. Assn. Pa., Phila. Hosp. Personnel Soc. (v.p. 1985-86). Democrat. Office: St Mary Hosp Frankford Ave and Palmer St Philadelphia PA 19125

ROBINSON, CORNELIA MAXINE, TV and radio producer; b. Des Moines, Mar. 3, 1951; d. Roosevelt and Thelma (Hampton) R.; children: Donovan Roosevelt, Traci Jean Bernice. BA, Columbia Coll.; postgrad., The Art Inst. Chgo. Chief exec. officer, chmn. Sta-WJYV, Chgo., 1966; newswriter, producer, editorial asst. Westinghouse Broadcasting-Sta-WIND Radio, Chgo., 1973-78; communications asst. Operation PUSH, Chgo., 1978-79; news producer Mut. Broadcasting Sta-WCFL Radio, Chgo., 1979-81; regional sales mgr. Sta-ON-TV, Mt. Prospect, Ill., 1981-84; telemktg. rep. Sta-ABC-TV, Chgo., 1984; area rep. Westinghouse Broadcasting-Group W Cable, Chgo., 1984; assoc. dir. What a Fellowship Hour, Chgo., 1977—; chmn., chief exec. officer Sta. WJTV Cable Prodns., Chgo. Bd. dirs. Columbia Coll. Alumni Assn. Mem. Women in Cable, Assn. Exec. Females, The Ctr. for New TV, Am. Women in Radio and TV (1st pres. Coll. Students in Broadcasting). Home: 1522 E 77th St Chicago IL 60619

ROBINSON, DONEITA JEAN, tax professional; b. Knoxville, Feb. 8, 1961; d. Eugene Cameron and Wahneta (Stroud) R. BA, Converse Coll., 1983. Staff acct. Telephone and Data Systems, Inc., Knoxville, 1983, Suggs and Harrelson Resort Properties, Wilmington, N.C., 1984; staff acct. KMG Main Hurdman (merged with Peat Marwick Main and Co.), Atlanta, 1984-86, sr. tax specialist, 1986-87; sr. tax specialist Peat Marwick Main and Co., Atlanta, 1987-88; tax analyst Trust Co. Bank, Atlanta, 1988—. Mem. Nat. Assn. Accts., Nat. Assn. Female Execs. Office: Trust Company Bank Trust Dept/Tax div PO Box 4655 Atlanta GA 30302

ROBINSON, ETHEL LUVENIA, air force officer; b. Chgo., Aug. 20, 1948; d. David Herman Sands and Dorothy (Boyd) Bailey; m. Clarence Jerome Robinson, Nov. 6, 1982. B.A., U. Md., 1970, M.L.S., 1971, M.A., 1975. Commd. 2d lt. U.S. Air Force, 1981, advanced through grades to capt., 1986; chief personnel utilization McGuire AFB, N.J., 1982-83; instructional analyst, Tinker AFB, Okla., 1983-85; career field mgr. Air Tng. Command, Randolph AFB, Tex., 1985—; arts specialist NEA, Washington, 1979-81. Editor reference books. Vol. mediator consumer div. Okla. Atty. Gen.'s Office, Oklahoma City, 1985. Mem. Nat. Soc. Performance and Instrn., Air Force Assn., Nat. Assn. Female Execs., Toastmasters, Tuskegee Airman Assn., Kappa Delta Pi. Avocations: antiques and collectibles. Home: PO Box 471 Randolph AFB TX 78148 Office: Hdqrs Air Tng Command Randolph AFB TX 78148

ROBINSON, FLORINE SAMANTHA, computer company executive; b. Massies Mill, Va., Feb. 4, 1935; d. John Daniel and Fannie Belle (Smith) Jackson; m. Frederick Robinson (div. 1973); children: Katherine, Theresa, Freda. BS, Morgan State U., 1976; postgrad., U. Balt., 1977-81, Liberty U., 1987. Writer, reporter Phila. Independent News, 1961-63; free lance writer, editor Balt., 1963-71; asst. mng. editor Williams & Wilkins Pubs. Inc., Balt, 1971-76; mktg. rep., then mktg. mgr. NCR Corp., Balt., 1977—; assoc. minister, trustee Christian Unity Temple, Balt., 1976—; bd. dirs. Armstrong & Bratcher, Inc., Balt. Editor: Stedman's Medical Dictionary, 1972; contbr. articles to profl. jours. Active PTA, Balt., 1963-65; bd. dirs. Howard Park Civic Assn., Balt., 1967—; leader, cons. Girl Scouts USA, 1970-73. Recipient Excellence in Research award Psi Chi, 1976. Mem. Mid-Atlantic Food Dealers Assn., Am. Soc. Notaries, Nat. Assn. Female Execs. Democrat. Club: Edelweiss. Lodge: Order Eastern Star. Home: 3126 Howard Park Ave Baltimore MD 21207

ROBINSON, GAY ELIZABETH CLARA, clergywoman; b. Stamford, Conn., Aug. 13, 1933; d. Theodore Alfred, Sr. and Elizabeth (Majher) Guilmette; student L.I.F.E. Coll., 1951-52; A.A., Orange Coast Coll., 1966; B.A., Calif. State U., 1968, M.A., 1970; postgrad., Golden State U., 1980—; m. Gary Garth Robinson, Feb. 3, 1952; children—Joy Leah Robinson, Clayton David. Asst. credit mgr. Phelps-Terkel, 1951-52; exec. adminstrv. asst. Pozzo Constrn. Co., 1952-53; ordained to ministry Internat. Ch. Foursquare Gospel, 1962; assoc. pastor Perris, Calif., 1955-58, SW Dist., 1958-60, Worldwide Mission rep. 70 countries, 1965—; pastoral staff Ch. by the Sea,

Huntington Beach, Calif., 1960-84; founder Breath of Life, 1975; instr. Dynamic Life Seminars; instr. Irvine Coll., 1976-78; SW dist. sec., 1960-78; broadcaster sta. KYMS, 1979-84; tour dir., 1977—; participant exec. mgmt. seminars, 1976-78. Mem. Republican Women's Nat. Com. Scholarship Chapman Floating Coll. of the Seas, 1966; Pepperdine U. scholar, 1951. Mem. Nat. Assn. Evangelicals, Western Psychol. Assn., United Foursquare Women (past program chmn., publicity chmn.), L.I.F.E. Alumni Assn. (past alumni sec.). Club: Temple City Jr. Women's (devotion leader, sec., 1957-60). Contbr. book revs., articles to publs. in field. Office: 24196 Alicia Pkwy Suite A Mission Viejo CA 92691

ROBINSON, GLYNNE, writer, photographer; b. Fredericksburg, Va., Feb. 23, 1934; d. Frederick Hampden and Jessie (Maguire) Robinson; children—Elizabeth, William, Katherine. A.B., Wells Coll., 1956; postgrad. in history of art Columbia U., 1957; postgrad. in journalism NYU, 1975; photography student. The New Sch., 1967, 71, of Ansel Adams, Yosemite, Calif., 1968, Paul Caponigro, Bethel, Conn., 1969-71. Cert. media specialist, N.Y.C. Bd. Edn. With news and publicity dept. Riverdale Neighborhood House, 1974-76; staff photographer, The Reporter, publ. Ethical Culture Schs., N.Y.C., 1974-76; condr. photostudy project, N.Y.C. pub. sch., 1974-75; guest lectr. U. Maine, 1979; condr. photog. workshop for jr. high sch. students sponsored by N.Y. Pub. Library, 1973; contbg. editor, co-pub. The Lakeville (Conn.) Jour., The Millerton News. Works appeared in publs. including N.Y. Times, Washington Post, N.Y. Daily News, Christian Sci. Monitor, Village Voice, San Francisco Chronicle, Los Angeles Times, Vineyard Gazette, Asia; featured in Women At Their Work, 1977; contbrg. editor The Lakeville (Conn.) Journal; author: Writers in Residence, 1981; one-woman photog. shows Soho Photo Gallery, N.Y.C., 1974, Wells Coll., 1973, N.Y. Pub. Library, 1973; participant group exhibits: Riverdale Neighborhood House, N.Y.C., 1968, Guild Hall, Easthampton, N.Y., 1970, Soho Photo Gallery, 1973, Wells Coll., 1974-75, Carnegie House, N.Y.C., 1978, Cosmopolitan Club, N.Y.C., 1976, Community Gallery Met. Mus. Art, 1976. Mem. Am. Soc. Mag. Photographers. Club: Cosmopolitan. Home: 116 E 63rd St New York NY 10021

ROBINSON, JAN, software company executive; b. Kansas City, Mo., June 8, 1945; d. Leonard Stuart and June (Barker) R.; widowed 1980. BA, U. Colo., 1966. Officer Colo. Nat. Bank, Denver, 1966-68; cons. Bank of Am., San Francisco, 1968-70, 78-80; owner Janco Systems, Kalispell, Mont., 1971-76; dir. mgmt. info. systems Shortstop Markets, Benicia, Calif., 1977-79; pres. JALAN, Spokane, 1980—; edn. administr. Am. Inst. Banking, Denver, 1967-68. computer advisor Santa Rosa (Calif.) Jr. Coll., 1979-80; dir. fin. Benicia Homeowners, 1977-79, Interplayers Theatre, Spokane, 1984-86. Mem. Kalispell C. of C., Wash. Assn. Sheriff's & Police, Assn. Wash. Cities, Nat. Assn. Female Execs., Calif. State Sheriff's Assn (assoc.). Republican. Presbyterian. Home: S 3225 Jefferson Spokane WA 99203 Office: JALAN W1500 Fourth Spokane WA 99204

ROBINSON, JANET ANDREWS, development administrator; b. Salt Lake City, Aug. 17, 1935; d. James William and Katherine (Nicol) A.; m. George Thomas Heisel, Jan. 31, 1971 (div. Aug. 1979); children—Andrea Eileen, John Michael; m. John Glass Robinson, Dec. 4, 1980 (div. Dec. 1986). B.S., U. Utah, 1957. Adminstrv. asst. St. Luke's Hosp., Phoenix, 1963-66; manpower planner Health Council of Monroe County, Rochester, N.Y., 1966-67; dir. rev. Genesee Regional Health Planning Council, Rochester, 1969-73; dir. devel. Highland Hosp., Rochester, 1980—; bd. dirs. Blue Shield Rochester; chmn. Rochester Hosp. Services Bd., Rochester, 1983-85; v.p. Highland Hosp., Rochester, 1981-84, also bd. dirs. Author manuals. Mem. exec. com. Nat. Soc. for Fund Raising Execs. (bd. dirs. 1983—), exec. com. YMCA. Republican. Roman Catholic. Club: Genesee Valley (Rochester). Avocations: squash; golf; tennis; music; art. Home: 69 Green Valley Rd Pittsford NY 14534 Office: Highland Hosp Found 1000 South Ave Rochester NY 14620

ROBINSON, JEAN RUTH, human ecology educator; b. Rockford, Ill., Dec. 9, 1925; d. Albert Eric and Eleanor (Peterson) Anderson; m. Kenneth Leon Robinson, July 10, 1954; children: James Carl, Alan Eric. B.A., Beloit Coll., Wis., 1947; M.A., Radcliffe Coll., 1951, Ph.D, 1953. Intern Vassar Coll., Poughkeepsie, N.Y., 1953-54; instr. Wells Coll., Aurora, N.Y., 1954-56, from lectr. to prof. dept. consumer econs. and housing Cornell U., Ithaca, N.Y., 1964—; dept. chmn., assoc. dean Coll. Human Ecology Cornell U., 1981—; bd. dirs., trustee Citizens Savs. Bank, 1983—. Trustee Village of Cayuga Heights, 1978-83. Named Outstanding Alumna Beloit Coll., 1977. Mem. N.Y. State Council Econ. Edn. (dir.). Lutheran. Home: 128 N Sunset Dr Ithaca NY 14850 Office: Cornell U Coll Human Ecology Dept of Consumer Econs and Housing Ithaca NY 14853

ROBINSON, JENNIFER ANNE, electrical engineer; b. North Bay, Ont., Can., May 15, 1955; d. Patrick Stephen and Lois Mary Robinson; m. Jean-Guy Michaud, Sept. 3, 1977. BEE, Carleton U., Ottawa, Ont., 1975; MEE, Carleton U., 1977. Recipient Senate Medal for Outstanding Achievement, Carleton U., Ottawa, 1975, grad. scholarship, Nat. Research Council Canada, Ottawa, 1975. Roman Catholic. Office: Bell-Northern Research, PO Box 3511 Stat C, Ottawa, ON Canada K1Y 4H7

ROBINSON, JULIE ANN, lawyer; b. Omaha, Jan. 14, 1957; d. Marvin Harold and Charlene Helen (Womack) Robinson. B.S. in Journalism, U. Kans., 1978; J.D., 1981 Bar: Kans. 1981, Mo. 1983. Law clk. Schnider, Shamberg & May, Fairway, Kans., 1981; law clk. to chief judge U.S. Bankruptcy Ct., Kansas City, Kans., 1981-83; asst. atty. U.S. Dept. Justice, Kansas City, 1983—. Reporter, writer U. Kans. Daily Kansas newspaper, 1977-78, bd. govs. U. Kans., 1987. Recipient Black Woman of Distinction award Yates br. YWCA, Kansas City, 1982. Mem. ABA, Kans. Bar. Assn., Am. Judicature Soc. (student leader award 1980), Phi Delta Phi, Delta Sigma Theta. Methodist. Office: 812 N 7th St Kansas City KS 66101

ROBINSON, KAREN MARKOFF, marketing specialist; b. Richmond, Va., Dec. 22, 1960; d. Edwin and Sondra (Gural) Markoff; m. Sherill Pace Robinson, Aug. 3, 1985; 1 child, Eli Nathaniel. BA in Liberal Arts, U. Tenn., 1981. With guest relations dept. Busch Gardens, Williamsburg, Va., 1978-81; gate mgr. Knoxville Internat. Energy Exposition 1982 World's Fair, Knoxville, 1982; with tickets, mktg. dept. Silver Dollar City Inc./Dollywood, Pigeon Forge, Tenn., 1983—. Chmn. B'Nai B'rith Youth Orgn., adv. bd. 1983-85; local com. chmn. Hadassah, 1988—. Mem. Knoxville C. of C., Nat. Assn. Female Exec., Am. Supply Assn. Ladies Aux., Women's League/Sisterhood (program chmn., treas., v.p. 1985—). Jewish. Home: 1037 Harrogate Dr Knoxville TN 37923 Office: Dollywood 700 Dollywood Ln Pigeon Forge TN 37863

ROBINSON, KATHLEEN MARIE, personnel executive; b. Milw., July 22, 1946; d. John Henry and Dorothy Ellen (Dunlavy) Robinson. B.S., U. Cin., 1968, M.A., 1970. Head resident U. Wis., Oshkosh, 1970-72, U. Tenn., Knoxville, 1972-73; asst. to dir. Opportunities Indsl. Ctr., Springfield, Ohio, 1975-78; EEO supr. Internat. Harvester, 1978-81; sr. personnel mgr., mgr. compensation and staff relations Citicorp., Denver and Phoenix, 1982-85, compensation and benefits analyst, St. Louis, 1985-87, mgr. human resources, 1987—. Bd. dirs. Springfield Urban League, Project Woman, Springfield. Mem. Am. Compensation Assn. (cert.), U. Cin. Alumni Assn., Alpha Chi Omega. Office: Citicorp 670 Mason Ridge Ctr Dr Saint Louis MO 63141

ROBINSON, KATHY, association director; b. Des Moines, Jan. 24, 1953; d. Watson and Margaret (Langford) Turner; m. Vernon V. Robinson II, July, 1970 (div. 1977); children: Vernon V. III, Doria D.L.L. AA, Contra Costa Coll., 1978; BA, J.F. Kennedy U., 1982. Licensed children's ctr. operator, Calif. Various social service positions Richmond, Calif., 1975-78; tchr. Yellow Brick Road Presch., Richmond, 1977-79, Head Start Program, North Richmond Neighborhood House, 1978-81; dir. Richmond Infant Care Ctr. II, Richmond, 1981-82; site supr. Southside Community Ctr. Richmond Headstart Program, 1982-83; asst. dir., program cons. One-of-a-Kind Children's Ctr., 1985; tchr. after sch. program YWCA, Richmond, 1979-81; dir. child and family services dept. YWCA, Oakland, 1983-85; dir. YM-Care Program West Contra Costa YMCA, Richmond, Calif., 1985—; adj. prof. Contra Costa Community Coll., 1987—; organizer girls' teen club YWCA/Parks and Recreation, Richmond, 1976-78; tutor ESL program Wilson Elementary Sch., 1982; organizer single mothers' group YWCA/Contra Costa Children's Council, 1981-83. mem. Parent and Faculty Club Richmond Unified Sch. Dist., 1971—, parent vol. program, 1971-79, impact com. Oakland Community Child Care, 1983-84, bd. dirs. Creative Learning Ctr., 1985. Mem. Nat. Exec. Bus. Women's Assn., Oakland Early Childhood Assn., Calif. Assn. of Compensatory Edn. (scholar 1977), Gifted Children's Assn. of West Contra Costa. Office: West Contra Costa YMCA 4197 Lakeside Dr Suite 150 Richmond CA 94806-1942

ROBINSON, LILIEN FILIPOVITCH, educator; b. Ljubljana, Yugoslavia, Feb. 7, 1940; d. Milenko and Branka Filipovitch; B.A. with distinction, George Washington U., 1962, M.A., 1965; Ph.D., Johns Hopkins U., 1978; m. David Robinson, June 8, 1974. Grad. teaching fellow George Washington U., 1962-64, lectr. in art history, 1964-65, asst. prof. art history, 1965-71, asso. prof., 1971-76, prof., 1979—, chmn. dept. art, 1976—. Mem. Coll. Art Assn. Am., Phi Beta Kappa, Omicron Delta Kappa, Delta Gamma. Author: Contemporary Criticism on 19th Century European Art. Serbian Orthodox. Office: George Washington U Art Dept Washington DC 20052

ROBINSON, LOIS HART, public relations executive; b. Freeport, Ill., Aug. 9, 1927; d. Seril N. and Cora (Stabenow) Hart; m. Noel M. Henze, Nov. 15, 1947 (div. 1964); m. Jack Fay Robinson, July 16, 1968; children—Susan Henze Bentley, Cynthia Henze Berkeley, Charles Henze. Student Oakton Community Coll., 1976-77, Northwestern U., 1977-81. Med. sec. Freeport Meml. Hosp., 1945-47; sec. No. Ill. Corp., 1947-49; adminstrv. asst. to supt. schs. Community Sch. Dist. 303, St. Charles, Ill., 1962-68; exec. sec. Bell & Howell Co., Chgo., 1969-73, supr. corp. relations, 1973-79, mgr. corp. communications, 1979-85, mgr. corp. communication services, 1985—; pres., dir. Bell & Howell Found., 1983—. Recipient Effie award Am. Mktg. Assn., 1983. Mem. Chgo. Women in Philanthropy, Corp. Volunteerism Council. Mem. Internat. Assn. Bus. Communications. Congregationalist. Home: 2614 Lincolnwood Dr Evanston IL 60201

ROBINSON, LORI JEAN, social services administrator; b. Los Angeles, Aug. 20, 1954; d. Florence (Silberberg) Robinson. AA, El Camino Coll., 1975; student, UCLA, 1976; BA, San Francisco State Coll., 1979. Dance instr. Calif. Rehab. Ctr., Norco, 1976; phys. edn. tchr. Notre Dame Acad., Los Angeles, 1976-77; dance instr., counselor St. Elmo Village, Los Angeles, 1973-77; group supr. Hillcrest Juvenile Hall, San Francisco, 1979; therapist Schick Ctrs., San Francisco, 1980; asst. dir. Northrop U. Resident Services, Los Angeles, 1981-82; sec. cons. Glide Meml., San Francisco, 1983-84; program dir. Potrero Hill Neighborhood House Social Devel. Ctr., San Francisco, 1984—. Choreographer Glide Dance Troupe "Dance for My Father", 1984, "Unmasked Potential", 1987, dancer, 1980—. Mem. festival com. St. Elmo Village Los Angeles, 1970-77; vol. Glide Found., Community, San Francisco, 1980—, Martin Luther King Rally, Glide Family, Civic Ctr., San Francisco, 1986—, 5th Congl. seat Open Forum, San Francisco, 1987; singer peace rally H.B. Barnum's Life Choir, Rose Bowl, Pasadena, Calif., 1982; counselor, telephone aid Living with Kids, San Francisco, 1985—; mem. legis. com. Devel. Disabilities Council San Francisco, 1986—; mem. program com. Glide Meml. Ch., 1983—; mem. Devel. Disabilities Council, San Francisco, 1985—. Democrat. Jewish. Office: Potrero Hill Neighborhood House 953 DeHaro St San Francisco CA 94107

ROBINSON, LOUISE WILSON, nursing administrator; b. O'Donnel, Tex., Feb. 3, 1943; d. Woodrow and Velma Mae (Gillham) Wilson; m. Tommy E. Robinson (div. Nov. 1973). Diploma in nursing, Meth. Hosp. Sch. Nursing, Lubbock, Tex., 1967; BS in Nursing, St. Louis U., 1981; BS in Data Processing, Washington U., St. Louis, 1983. Cert. nursing adminstr.; cert. peri-operative nurse; cert. Nat. assoc. dir. nursing. Staff nurse Meth. Hosp., Lubbock, 1967-69, Holy Cross Hosp., Austin, Tex., 1969-73; commd. 1st lt. USAF, 1973, advanced through grades to maj., resigned, 1984; dir. surg. services Pendleton Meml. Meth. Hosp., New Orleans, 1984-86; with spl. patients services Slidell (La.) Meml. Hosp., 1986-88; assoc. dir. nursing PeriOperative Services Touro Infirmary, New Orleans, 1988—; pres. Cornerstone Found. Cons., 1984—. Contbr. articles on computers to profl. jours. Cons. Fannie Williams Mid. Sch., New Orleans, 1986;. Mem. Am. Nurses' Assn., Assn. Operating Room Nurses. Home: 419 Eden Isles Dr Slidell LA 70458

ROBINSON, LYNN BROWN, marketing educator; b. Mobile, Ala., July 29, 1938; d. Samuel and Carolyn D. (Greenfield) B.; m. John Kenneth Robinson, Feb. 27, 1963; children—Jennifer Kay, John Kenneth Jr. B.B.A., Emory U., 1960; M.B.A., U. Ala., 1965, Ph.D., 1972. Asst. prof. to prof. U. South Ala., Mobile, 1968—, dir. grad. studies Coll. Bus., 1977-80, chmn. dept. mktg. and transp., 1983—; v.p. Engineered Textile Products, Inc. Bd. dirs. St. Mary's Home for Children, Ala. Easter Seal Soc. Mem. Am. Mktg. Assn., So. Mktg. Assn., Sales and Mktg. Execs. Internat., Beta Gamma Sigma. Office: Univ So Ala Dept Mktg & Transp Mobile AL 36608

ROBINSON, MARION SWETT, banker; b. Boston, Aug. 3, 1947; d. Albert Hersey and Mary (Stewart) Swett m. Lawrence R. Robinson III, June 30, 1979; 1 son, Albert Hersey. BA, Wellesley Coll., 1969; MBA, Stanford U., 1979; MA, Stanford Food Research Inst., 1979. Sr. asst. dir. Morgan Grenfell & Co. Ltd., London, 1970-77; asst. v.p. Mfrs. Hanover Trust, N.Y.C., 1979-80; v.p. Bankers Trust Co., N.Y.C., 1980—; bd. dirs., sec. Internat. Swap Dealers Assn. Class corr. Stanford Bus. Sch., 1979—; nat. com. The Friends of Wellesley Coll. Athletics, 1986—; trustee New Canaan Congl. Ch. Republican. Club: Fairfield Villages Wellesley (devel. fund chmn.). Office: 1 Bankers Trust Plaza New York NY 10015

ROBINSON, MARY BETH, academic program administrator; b. Hinsdale, Ill., Sept. 2, 1943; d. Lee Fulton and Freda Margaret (Doehle) Higman. BA, UCLA, 1965; MA, Stanford U., 1974; PhD, Ohio State U., 1978. Secondary tchr. Berkeley (Calif.) Unified Sch. Dist., 1966-75; teaching evaluator Ohio State U. Sch. Vet. Med., Columbus, 1975-78; lectr., curriculum evaluator Calif. State Poly. U., Pomona, 1978-80; program evaluator Sch. Dist. Phila., 1980-81; coordinator field edn., tchr. edn., sch. edn. Stanford (Calif.) U., 1982-86; reading specialist East Side Union High Sch. Dist., San Jose, Calif., 1986-87; German dept. chair, sch. program evaluation Centinela Valley Union High Sch. Dist., Lawndale, Calif., 1987—; instl. program evaluator Commn. on Tchr. Credentialing, Sacramento, 1987—. Mem. Calif. Council on Tchr. Edn., Nat. Assn. Female Execs., Friends of Stanford U. Sch. Edn., Assn. Supervision and Circiculum Devel., Phi Delta Kappa. Democrat. Episcopalian. also: 1249 Via Romero Palos Verdes Estates CA 90274

ROBINSON, MARY LOU, U.S. district judge; b. Dodge City, Kans., Aug. 25, 1926; d. Gerald J. and Frances Strueber; m. A.J. Robinson, Aug. 28, 1949; children: Rebecca Aynn Gruhlkey, Diana Ceil, Matthew Douglas. B.A., U. Tex., 1948, LL.B., 1950. Bar: Tex. 1949. Practice law Amarillo, 1950-55; judge County Ct. Potter County, Tex., 1955-59; judge (108th Dist. Ct.), Amarillo, 1961-73; assoc. justice Ct. of Civil Appeals for 7th Supreme Jud. Dist. of Tex., Amarillo, 1973-77; chief justice Ct. of Civil Appeals for 7th Supreme Jud. Dist. of Tex., 1977-79; U.S. dist. judge No. Dist. Tex., Amarillo, 1979—. Named Woman of Year Tex. Fedn. Bus. and Profl. Women, 1973. Mem. Nat. Assn. Women Lawyers, ABA, Tex. Bar Assn., Amarillo Bar Assn., Delta Kappa Gamma. Presbyterian. Office: Box F 13248 Amarillo TX 79189 *

ROBINSON, MILDRED ELAINE, educator; b. Eastover, S.C., July 30, 1945; d. Jim and Betty (Grooms) R. BA, Benedict Coll., 1966; MEd, U. S.C., 1975, Edn. specialist, 1979. Tchr. Kershaw County Schs., Camden, S.C., 1966-71; tchr. Richland Sch. Dist. I, Columbia, S.C., 1971—, law related edn. instr., 1986-87; English lang. instr. Richland County Sch. Dist. II, Columbia, 1980-85. Former chairperson policy bd. Lower Richland Health Ctr. Mem. Nat. Edn. Assn. (del. 1978—, Cert.), S.C. Edn. Assn., Richland County Edn. Assn. (sec. 1983-84, Cert. 1984), Nat. Council Negro Women. Democrat. Home: Rt 1 Box 283 Eastover SC 29044

ROBINSON, MIRIAM PIGOTT, accountant; b. Picayune, Miss., June 17, 1951; d. Maurice and Grace (Preston) Pigott; m. Rucks Hilton Robinson, Aug. 26, 1972; children: Timothy, Andrew, Maria. AA, Pearl River Jr. Coll., 1971; BS in Acctg., U. So. Miss., 1973. CPA, Miss. Acctg. clk. U. So. Miss., Hattiesburg, 1973-74; tax preparer H&R Block, Pascagoula, Miss., 1976-79; acct. Nat. American Cos., Gautier, Miss., 1979-81; staff acct. Wolfe, McDuff, Mallett & Co., Pascagoula, 1981-84; pvt. practice acctg. Pascagoula, 1984—. Den leader Cub Scouts, Gautier, 1983; tchr. CCD St. Mary's Catholic Ch., Gautier, 1984, St. Ann's Catholic Ch., Hurley, 1987-88. Mem. Am. Inst. CPA's, Miss. Soc. CPA's, Am. Bus. Women's Assn. (Citation 1986). Office: 1702 Jackson Ave Pascagoula MS 39567

ROBINSON, NELL BRYANT, nutrition educator; b. Kopperl, Tex., Oct. 15, 1925; d. Basil Howell and Lelia Abiah (Duke) Bryant; m. Frank Edward Robinson, July 14, 1945 (dec.); 1 child, John Howell Robinson. B.S., N. Tex. State U., 1945; M.S., Tex. Woman's U., 1958, Ph.D., 1967. Registered dietitian, Tex. Tchr. Comanche High Sch., Tex., 1945-46, Kopperl High Sch., Tex., 1946-48; county extension agt. Agrl. Extension Service, Tex., 1948-56; prof. nutrition Tex. Christian U., Fort Worth, 1957—, chmn. dept. nutrition and dietetics, 1985—. Contbr. chpt. to book. Named Top Prof., Tex. Christian U. Mortar Bd., 1978. Mem. Am. Dietetic Assn. (del., council on edn., ethics com. 1985—), Am. Home Econs. Assn., Tex. Dietetic Assn. (pres., 1972-73, Disting. Dietitian 1981), Tex. Home Econs. Assn. (pres. 1978-80, Home Economist of Yr. 1975). Club: Fort Worth Women. Lodge: Order Eastern Star. Home: 5729 Wimbleton Way Fort Worth TX 76133 Office: Tex Christian U PO Box 32869 Fort Worth TX 76129

ROBINSON, PATRICIA ANN, marketing educator, business consultant; b. Tallulah, La., Sept. 30, 1952; d. Roosevelt Martin and Lorene Robinson. BA, Tarkio (Mo.) Coll., 1973; MBA, Prarie View (Tex.) A&M U., 1978; MS, Tex. So. U., 1980; PhD, Okla. State U., 1986. Cert. elem. tchr. Catalogue inventory specialist Montgomery Ward & Co., Kansas City, Mo., 1974-77; fiscal affairs asst. Prairie View (Tex.) A&M U., 1977-78; adminstrv. asst., instr. Tex. So. U., 1978-82; grad. asst. Okla. State U., Stillwater, 1970-84; cons. Kate's McGehee (Ark.) Tng. Ctr., 1985-86; asst. prof. mktg. U. Ark., Fayetteville, 1984-87, U. Akron, Ohio, 1987-88; cons. Kate's McGehee (Ark.) Training Ctr., 1975-76. Recipient Acad. Advising Service award U. Ark., 1986. Mem. Am. Collegiate Retailing Assn., Am. Home Econs. Assn., Am. Mktg. Assn., Consumer Research Assn., So. Mktg. Assn., Internat. Assn. Black Bus. Educators, Acad. Internat. Bus., Midsouth Mktg. Assn., Midwest Mktg. Assn., Ohio Home Econs. Assn., Southwestern Mktg. Assn., Pi Sigma Epsilon, Beta Gamma Sigma (first v.p.), Durcury Honorary Soc. Democrat. Baptist. Home: 1609 Hampton Knoll Dr Akron OH 44313 Office: U Akron Dept Mktg Coll Bus Adminstrn Mktg Dept Akron OH 44325

ROBINSON, PATRICIA NEIL, manufacturing company executive; b. Coleman, Tex., Apr. 20, 1939; d. Paul Brown and Mary Anita (Forman) Smith; divorced; children: Michael Dan, Mark Alan, Misty Dawn. Grad. high sch., Coleman, 1956. Stenographer Dept. Pub. Welfare, Coleman, 1957-60; acct. Choate Enterprises, Abilene, Tex., 1965-68; owner Robinson Acctg., Abilene, 1968-71; v.p. ABCO Industries, Inc., Abilene, 1974—. Sponsor Abilene-Cooper Rodeo Club, 1985—; chmn. com. W. Tex. Fair and Rodeo, Abilene, 1986—. Mem. Nat. Assn. Women in Constrn., Nat. Assn. Credit Mgrs., Am. Assn. Sheriff Posses and Riding Clubs, Nat. Assn. Female Execs., Tex. Bus. Council (charter), Taylor County Sheriff Posse. Republican. Baptist. Home: 3202 Chimney Circle Abilene TX 79606 Office: ABCO Industries Inc PO Box 268 Abilene TX 79604

ROBINSON, PATTIE JANE, small business owner; b. Roanoke, N.C., Nov. 16, 1955; d. Jessie and India Marie (Highe) R. BA in Sociology, Vassar Coll., 1978. Adminstrv. asst. premiums dept. Sieko Time Corp., N.Y.C., 1979-81; asst. mgr. merchandising Stride Rite Shoes, Macy's, N.Y.C., 1981-82; asst. mgr. promotions Remy Martin Amerique, Inc., N.Y.C., 1982-86; pres. Amenity Enterprises, Inc., Bklyn., 1986—. Mem. Am. Mgmt. Assn., Meeting Planners Network, Nat. Assn. Female Execs. Home and Office: 912 Schenectady Ave Brooklyn NY 11203

ROBINSON, PEGGY MADSEN, administrative librarian, archivist; d. Carl Westergard and Margaret (Kennedy) Madsen. A.A., Stephens Coll.; B.A., Loretto Heights Coll., 1973; M.L.S., U. Denver, 1973, archival cert., 1975. Asst. librarian Loretto Heights Coll., Denver, 1973-77, art curator, 1974-77; adminstrv. librarian U.S. Dept. Army, Germany, 1977-79; tech. process intern Jefferson County Sch. Dist., Denver, 1980, archivist, 1981-82; dir. N.E. Colo. Regional Library, Wray, 1983-84; head librarian Periodicals dept. U. So. Colo., 1984—; adminstrv. librarian Friends of Children-Viet Nam Internat. Adoption Orgn., Denver, 1984—; instr. English U. Without Walls, Denver, 1973-77. Mem. ALA, Colo. Library Assn. Mountain Plains Library Assn., Soc. Scholarly Pub., SLA, AAUW (rep. commn. women, publicity chair), Wyoming Hist. Soc. (v.p. Washakie chpt.), U. Denver Alumni Assn. (sec.), Stephens Coll. Alumni Assn. (pres.), Citizen Ambassador China, 1985.

ROBINSON, ROB, publishing company executive; b. Chgo., June 17, 1955; d. Joseph Ross and Charlotte Evelyn (Harchanko) R. BA, No. Ill. U., 1977. Account exec. Meldrum & Fewsmith, Inc., Chgo., 1978-81; sales rep. Jack O'Grady, Inc., Chgo., 1981-82, Leigh Communications, Inc., Chgo., 1982; sales rep. Midwest region Modern Metals Pub. Co., Chgo., 1982-83; regional sales mgr. Morgan-Grampian Pub. Co., Chgo., 1983-86, Cahners Pub. Co., Des Plaines, Ill., 1986—; bd. dirs. Am. Advt. Fedn. 6th Dist. Mem. Electronic Young Tigers, Women in Electronics (bd. dirs. 1985—), Bus. and Profl. Advt. Assn. (co-chmn., benefit officer, bd. dirs.), Women's Ad Club of Chgo. (co-chmn. ADDY com. 1982—, co-chmn. ednl. benefit 1980—, officer, bd. dirs.), Surface Mount Tech. Assn. (officers, bd. dirs.), Sigma Kappa (1st v.p. 1976-77, chpt. historian 1975-76). Democrat. Roman Catholic. Clubs: Chgo. Area Runners Assn.; The Athletic Congress. Home: 1111 N Dearborn St Chicago IL 60610 Office: Cahners Pub Co 1350 E Touhy Ave Des Plaines IL 60018

ROBINSON, RONYA DELL, software company executive; b. Atlanta, Sept. 23, 1944; d. Parker Morrill and Byrona (Dell) R. BA, U. Calif., Berkeley, 1974, MA, 1977. Tech. writer Arthur G. McKee & Co., San Francisco, 1970-72; tech. writer, lexicographer Search Group, Inc., Sacramento, 1976-77; mgr. customer service Softlab, Inc., San Francisco, 1979-86, v.p. ops., 1986—; bd. editors Berkeley Linguistics Soc., 1975-77. Co-author: Dictionary of Criminal Justice Terminology, 1977. Mem. Nat. Assn. Female Execs. Democrat. Office: Softlab Inc 188 The Embarcadero Bayside Plaza 7th Floor San Francisco CA 94105

ROBINSON, SALLY WINSTON, artist; b. Detroit, Nov. 2, 1924; d. Harry Lewis and Lydia (Kahn) Winston; B.A., Bennington Coll., 1947; student Cranbrook Acad. Art, 1949; grad. Sch. Social Work, Wayne U., 1948, M.A., 1972; M.F.A., Wayne State U., 1973; m. Eliot F. Robinson, June 28, 1949; children—Peter Eliot, Lydia Winston, Suzanne Finley, Sarah Mitchell. Psychol. tester Detroit Bd. Edn., 1944; pyschol. counselor and tester YMCA, N.Y.C., 1946; social caseworker Family Service, Pontiac, Mich., 1947; instr. printmaking Wayne State U., Detroit, 1973—. One person shows U. Mich., 1973, Wayne State U., 1974, Klein-Vogol Gallery, 1974, Rina Gallery, 1976, Park McCullough House, Vt., 1976, Williams Coll., 1976, Arnold Klein Gallery, 1977; exhibited group shows Bennington Coll., Cranbrook Mus., Detroit Inst. Art, Detroit Artists Market, Soc. Women Painters, Soc. Arts and Crafts, Bloomfield Art Assn., Flint Left Bank Gallery, Balough Gallery, Detroit Soc. Women Painters, U. Mich., U. Ind., U. Wis., U. Pittsburg, Toledo Mus., Krannert Mus.; represented in permanent collections, Detroit, N.Y.C., Birmingham, Bloomfield Hills; tchr. children's art Detroit Inst. Art, 1949-50, now artistic advisor, bd. dirs. drawing and print orgn. Bd. dirs. Planned Parenthood, 1951—, mem. exec. bd., 1963—; bd. dirs. PTA, 1956-60, Roeper City and Country Sch., U. Mich. Mus. Art, 1978; trustee Putnam Hosp. Med. Research Inst., 1978; mem. Gov.'s Commn. Art in State Bldgs., 1978-79; mem. art and devel. coms. So. Vt. Art Ctr., 1987-88; mem. vol. com. Marie Selby Gardens. Mem. Detroit Artists Market (dir. 1956—), Bennington Coll. Alumnae Assn. (regional co-chmn. 1954), Detroit Soc. Women Painters, Birmingham Soc. Women Painters (pres. 1974-76), Bloomfield Art Assn. (program co-chmn. 1956), Founders Soc. Detroit Inst. Art. Unitarian (mem. Council 1963—). Clubs: Village Women's (Birmingham, Mich.); Women's City (co-ordinator art shows 1950) (Detroit); Garden Clubs Am. (Bennington, Vt., Sarasota, Fla.); Cosmopolitan (N.Y.C.). Home: 7 Monument Circle Old Old Bennington VT 05201 also: 708 Pine Run Dr Osprey FL 33559

ROBINSON, SANDRA LAWSON, physician, state department administrator; b. New Orleans, Mar. 22, 1944; d. Alvin James Lawson and Elvera (Stewart) Martin; m. Carl Robinson; children—Michael, Carla. B.A., Howard U., 1965, M.D., 1969; M.P.H., Tulane U., 1977. Intern in pediatrics

Children's Hosp. Nat. Med. Ctr., Washington, 1969-70, resident in pediatrics, 1970-71; resident in pediatrics, fellow in ambulatory care U. Calif.-San Francisco, San Francisco Gen. Hosp., 1971-72; coordinator minority affairs La. State U. Med. Ctr., 1979; med. dir. Neighborhood Health Clinics, New Orleans, 1973-77; dir. ambulatory care and outpatient services Charity Hosp., New Orleans, 1977-81; dir. ambulatory care service Children's Hosp. New Orleans, 1981-84; sec. and state health officer La. Dept. Health and Human Resources, Baton Rouge, 1984—; clin. asst. prof. pediatrics La. State U. and Tulane U. Schs. Medicine, 1974—; adj. asst. prof. Tulane U. Sch. Pub. Health and Tropical Medicine, 1977—. Recipient Region V award Howard U. Alumni; Outstanding Community Service award Black Orgn. Leadership Devel.; Outstanding Service award Tangipahoa Voters League; Scroll of Merit Nat. Med. Assn.; Woman's Day Honor award Mt. Zion United Meth. Ch.; named Woman of Yr. Tulane Women's Assn., 1987. Mem. New Orleans Med. Soc., Pediatric Soc. of New Orleans, Tulane Women's Assn., Orleans Parish Women's Med. Assn., New Orleans Grad. Med. Assembly, Ambulatory Pediatric Soc., Nat. Med. Assn., La. Women's Network, Inc., Assn. State and Terr. Health Ofcls., Nat. Women's Forum, Delta Sigma Theta (Community Service award, Pub. Service award). Democrat. Roman Catholic. Avocations: skiing; reading. Office: Dept Health and Human Resources PO Box 3776 Baton Rouge LA 70821

ROBINSON, SARAH BONHAM, artist, art educator, therapist; b. Somerville, N.J., Mar. 16, 1939; d. Robert Daniel and Eleanor Cammann (McMurtry) Bonham; m. Bruce Mitton Robinson, Aug. 28, 1961 (div. 1975); children—Christopher Day, David Brooke, Megan Louise, Andrew Cornell. B.A., Wilson Coll., 1961; M.F.A., U. Pa., 1962; art edn. cert. Kean Coll., 1979. Asst. art instr. Wilson Coll., Chambersburg, Pa., 1960-61; art educator Newark Acad., Livingston, N.J., 1966-68; adj. instr. Rutgers U., New Brunswick, N.J., 1967; art therapist J.E. Runnells, Berkeley Heights, N.J., 1974; creative arts therapist dept. psychiatry Elizabeth Gen. Med. Ctr. (N.J.), 1974—, dir. activity therapy, 1976—, clin. chief partial hosp., 1978-85, chmn. quality assurance psychiatry 1980-83, asst. dir. rehab. services, 1983-87; art therapy cons. Children's Specialized Hosp., Mountainside, N.J., 1976—. Producer, editor film strip: Changes, 1974. Illustrator: Miller-Cory Colonial Cooking, 1975. Paintings exhibited in eastern U.S., 1960—, including World's Fair 1965. Artist, Miller-Cory Hist. Orgn., Westfield, N.J., 1969-79; artist, mem. Sane, Union County, N.J., 1969—. Woodrow Wilson fellow, 1961. Mem. Am. Assn. Partial Hosps., N.J. Assn. Partial Hosps. (regional chmn. 1983-87, founder), N.J. Assn. Rehab. Facilities, N.J. Psychiat. Rehab. Assn. Democrat. Episcopalian. Home: 235 Sinclair Pl Westfield NJ 07090 Office: Elizabeth Gen Med Ctr 925 E Jersey St Elizabeth NJ 07201

ROBINSON, TERI SKINNER, information systems specialist; b. Buffalo, May 26, 1956; d. Carlton Philip and Shirley (Moore) Skinner; m. James C. Robinson Jr., Apr. 26, 1986. BA, U. Fla., 1977; MBA, Rollins Coll., Winter Park, Fla., 1985. Asst. in computer sci. U. Fla., Gainesville, 1977-79; data processing mgr. Piezo Tech., Orlando, Fla., 1979-82; sr. cons. mgmt. cons. services Price Waterhouse, Orlando, 1982-84, mgr. mgmt. cons. services, 1984-86; employee information systems mgr. Red Lobster, Orlando, 1986-87; point of sale systems mgr. Gen. Mills Restaurants, Orlando, 1987—. Mem. Jr. League of Orlando-Winter Park, 1987. Mem. Am. Prodn. and Inventory Control Soc., Data Processing Mgmt. Assn. Democrat. Methodist. Office: General Mills Restaurants 6770 Lake Ellenor Dr Orlando FL 32809

ROBINSON, VIRGINIA BATCHELOR, medical sales representative; b. Buffalo, May 13, 1955; d. Lee and Lillion (Pressley) Batchelor; m. David Edward Robinson III; m. Tyonna Maria. AA, Erie Community Coll., 1975; BA, Empire State U., 1980. Prodn. log clk., pub. relations asst. Sta. WKBW- TV, Buffalo, 1974-78; social welfare examiner Erie County Dept. Social Services, Buffalo, 1981; sales rep. Gen. Mills, Buffalo, 1981-84; mktg. cons., acct. exec. Sta. WBLK-FM, Buffalo, 1984-86; acct. exec. Sta. WHTT-AM, FM, Buffalo, 1986-87; med. sales rep. Mead Johnson, Buffalo, 1987—. Mem. Nat. Assn. Female Execs. Democrat. Home and Office: 295 LaSalle Ave Buffalo NY 14215

ROBISON, ANN GREEN, columnist; b. N.Y.C., Nov. 19, 1904; d. Boris and Mary (Sugarman) Green; B.A., U. Maine, 1924, L.H.D., 1975; M.A., Columbia U., 1934; cert. Women's Inst., Jewish Theol. Sem. Am.; LL.D. (hon.), U. East Asia, 1982; m. Adolf Robison, Aug. 28, 1927 (dec. Aug. 1988); children—Peter Jordan, Michael Douglas. Tchr. French, English, algebra, dramatics Mattanawcook Acad., Lincoln, Maine, 1924-25, New Rochelle, N.Y., 1925-39; v.p. Robison-Industries, Inc., 1966-88; treas. Robison-Anton Co., 1959-83; lectr. on world affairs. Columnist for weekly periodical, 1965—. Accredited observer UN for Nat. Council Jewish Women, 1946-52, for AAUW, 1950-51; attended all gen. assemblies UN, 1946-52; broadcaster from Paris to U.S., concerning UN assemblies, 1948, 51; mem. UN com. Synagogue Council Am.; sec. Nat. Jewish Community Relations Adv. Council, 1972, v.p., 1973-75; v.p. Jewish Fedn. for Community Services Bergen County, 1973-78, chmn. county campaign, 1973-77; lectr. tour Israel, 1962, Republic South Africa, 1969. Mem. membership com., mem. interfaith and univ. com. Am.-Israel Cultural Found.; sec. Am.-Israel Public Affairs Com., 1973-76. Hon. chmn., officer woman's div. United Jewish Appeal Teaneck; exec. com., adv. com. dept. Hebraica and Judaica, chmn. spl. com. on scholarships and grants Rutgers U.; mem. president's adv. com. on Bergen in Israel, Bergen Community Coll.; bd. dirs. Community Mus. Bergen County; bd. dirs., telethon com. Easter Seal Assn.; bd. dirs., chmn. internat. com. Bergen County Women's Republican Club. Recipient medal of merit Fairleigh Dickinson U., 1963; Woman of Yr., United Jewish Appeal, 1964, Brandeis award Zionist Orgn. Am., 1972, award Jewish War Vets., 1972; AAUW fellowship named Ann Robison; honors Bergen Community Coll., 1985, Sutton Ensemble, 1985. Hon. fellow Hebrew U., Jerusalem, 1975. Mem. AAUW (1st v.p. charge program No. Valley br. 1968-70, 81-83, chmn. fellowship com., internat. affairs com.), Nat. Council Jewish Women (nat. dir., exec. com. 1965-75, life bd. dirs. 1981—; nat. chmn. internat. affairs, 1968-74, dir. Teaneck, rep. various confs.; del. Triennial Conv. Internat. Council Jewish Women in London, 1965, Jerusalem, 1968, Toronto, 1972, Australia 1975, U.S. 1978, Israel, 1981; internat. chmn. resolutions 1968-74, v.p. 1972-78, editor internat. newsletter), Am. Assn. Jewish Edn. (governing council), YM-YWHA Bergen County (dir. 1967-82; 1st woman yr. award 1970), Am. Assn. UN (trustee), Internat. Platform Assn., Bergen and Passaic Counties Lung Assn. (sec., bd. mem., exec. com., chmn. program), Am. Lung Assn. of N.J. (rep. dir., v.p., chmn. public relations adv. com. 1973—, mem. com. contracts and qualifications and nominating com. 1969—, exec. com. 1971—, mem. resolutions com. 1980 conv., elected to Nat. Hall of Fame 1980), UN Assn., Am. Orgn. UN, Hadassah (life), Brandeis U. Women's Assn. (life), Internat. Assn. U. Pres. (asso.), Town and Gown Soc. Fairleigh Dickinson U., Phi Beta Kappa, Phi Kappa Phi. Club: Teaneck College. Contbr. reports, articles on UN sessions, also UN News for Women Broadcasters. Weekly columnist On the Go in Jewish Standard; editor mag. Internat. Council Jewish Women. Home: 554 S Forest Dr Teaneck NJ 07666

ROBISON, BARBARA ANN, newspaper editor; b. Portland, Oreg., July 15, 1933; d. Louis Keith and Marjorie (Work) R.; 1 child, Nancy. Student, Coll. Idaho, 1951-54, U. Utah, 1968-70. Reporter Caldwell (Idaho) News Tribune, 1951-54; sports editor LaGrande (Oreg.) Evening-Observer, 1954-55; reporter Idaho Daily Statesman, Boise, 1955-57; asst. women's editor Tacoma (Wash.) News Tribune, 1958-59; lifestyle editor Salt Lake Tribune, 1967—. Mem. Salt Lake Exchange Club, 1986—. Episcopalian. Home: 4210 Caroleen Way Salt Lake City UT 84124 Office: Salt Lake Tribune Box 867 Salt Lake City UT 84110

ROBISON, BARBARA JANE, tax accountant; b. Bkln., Oct. 17, 1924; d. Matthews and Sara (Birnbaum) Brilliant; m. Morris Moses Robison, Aug. 30, 1945; 1 child, Susan Kay. BS, Ohio State U., 1945; MBA, Xavier U., 1976. CPA. Acct. Antenna Research Lab. Inc., Columbus, Ohio, 1948-51; office mgr. Master Distributors, Inc., Columbus, 1951-57; treas. Antlab Inc., Columbus, 1957-69; tax acct. AccuRay Corp., Columbus, 1969-76, tax mgr., 1976—. Mem. Am. Inst. CPA's, Ohio Soc. CPA's, Am. Soc. Women Accts. (pres. 1978-79), Columbus chpt. Am. Payroll Assn. Home: 1888 Jewett Rd Powell OH 43065 Office: Accuray Corp 650 Ackerman Rd Columbus OH 43202

ROBISON, JUDY ANN, university program administrator; b. Little Rock, Ark., Dec. 29, 1951; d. Earl D. and Louise (Denison) R. BSE, U. Cen. Ark., 1973; MS, So. Ill. U., 1975; postgrad., Tex. Woman's U., 1984—. Chartered cert. home economist. County agt. cooperative ext. service U. Ark., Fayetteville, 1974-75; instr. home econs. cooperative ext. service U. Ark., Waldron, 1975-78; 4-H program specialist U. Ark., Little Rock, 1978—; program presentor various 4-H club orgns., Chgo., 1984, Mobile, Ala., 1984, Orlando, Fla., 1981, Louisville, 1981. Recipient Dist. Service award, Pulaski County Farm Bur., 1982. Mem. Ark. Assn. Ext. 4-H Agts. (Dist. Service award 1986), Nat. Assn. Ext. 4-H agts. (Dist. Service award 1982, Regional Communications award 1982), Ark. Home Econs. Assn., Nat. Home Econs. Assn., Ark. Assn. Cooperative Ext. Specialists, Epsilon Sigma Phi, Delta Zeta. Methodist. Office: Univ of Ark Cooperative Ext Service 1201 McAlmont Little Rock AR 72203

ROBISON, JUDY KAY, nursing home administrator; b. Rosebud, Tex., Mar. 26, 1947; d. Edwin Jerry and Mildred Nadine (Tawater) Slovacek; m. James Harold Cunningham, Mar. 19, 1971 (div. Aug. 1976); 1 child, Jena Cassidie; m. Donnie Ray Robison, Dec. 20, 1976 (div. July 1982). Student LaSalle Extension U., 1966, U. Tex., 1976; AAS, McLennan Community Coll., 1980. Designer Green Flower Shop, Rosebud, 1961-65; exec. sec. Gary Job Corps Ctr., San Marcos, Tex., 1965-74; asst. adminstr. Rosebud Med. Services, 1975-77, adminstr., 1977-82; Community adminstr. Hosp. Assn. of Tex., Inc., Rosebud, 1982—. Mem. Med. Products Research Panel, 1985—; adv. bd. Foodservice Research Ctr., 1984, Temple Jr. Coll., Tex., 1982, 85, R-L Ind. Sch. Dist., 1979—; TV telethon coordinator Easter Seal Soc., 1985. Recipient Friend to Edn. award Tex. State Tchrs. Assn., 1986. Mem. Am. Coll. Nursing Home Adminstrs. Club: Rosebud Ex-Students (sec., treas. 1982—). Avocations: music, horticulture, tennis, skiing, dancing. Home: 530 E Ave G Rosebud TX 76570 Office: Community Hosp Assn Tex Inc Heritage House Corner of College and Ave F Rosebud TX 76570

ROBISON, PAULA JUDITH, flutist; b. Nashville, June 8, 1941; d. David Victor and Naomi Florence R.; m. Scott Nickrenz; Dec. 29, 1971; 1 child, Elizabeth Hadley, Amadea. Student, U. So. Calif., 1958-60; B.S., Juilliard Sch. Music, 1963. Soloist with various maj. orchs., including N.Y. Philharmonic, co-dir. chamber music, Spoleto Festivals, Charleston, S.C. and Spoleto, Italy (Recipient First prize Geneva Internat. Competition 1966); commd. flute concertos by Leon Kirchner, Toru Takemitsu, Oliver Knussen, Robert Beaser. Recipient Adelaide Ristori prize, 1987; named Musician of Month, Musical Am., 1979; Martha Baird Rockefeller grantee, 1966. Mem. Chamber Music Soc. Lincoln Center (founding). Office: care Shaw Concerts 1900 Broadway New York NY 10023

ROBLE, CAROLE MARCIA, accountant; b. Bklyn., Aug. 22, 1938; d. Carl and Edith (Brown) Dusowitz; m. Richard F. Roble, Nov. 30, 1969. MBA with distinction, N.Y. Inst. Tech., 1984. CPA, Calif., N.Y. Comptroller various orgns., 1956-66; staff acct. ZTBG CPA'S, Los Angeles, 1966-67; sr. acct. J.H. Cohn & Co., Newark, 1967-71; lectr. New School, Queens Coll., Empire State Coll., Touro Coll., N.Y. Inst. Tech., N.Y., 1971-82; prin. Carole M. Roble, CPA, South Hempstead, N.Y., 1971—; guest appearances various N.Y. radio and TV stats.; speaker and moderator Found. for Accounting Edn., N.Y., 1971-87. Treas. Builders Devel. Corp. of L.I., Westbury, N.Y., 1985; dir. Women Econ. Devels. of L.I., 1985-87. Recipient Sisterhood citation Nat. Orgn. Women, 1984, 85, cert. of Appreciation Women Life Underwriters, 1988, Women in Sales, 1982, 84; named top Tax Practitioner Money Mag., 1987. Mem. Am. Acct. Assn.(auditing sect.), Am. Inst. CPA's, Am. Soc. Women Accts. (pres. N.Y. chpt. 1980-81), Am. Woman's Soc. CPA's, Nat. Conf. CPA Practitioners (L.I. chpt. trustee 1981-82, sec. 1982-83, treas. 1983-84, v.p. 1984-85, 1st v.p. 1985-86, pres. 1986-87, nat. nomination com. 1983-86), Calif. Soc. CPAs, N.Y. State Soc. CPAs (Nassau chpt. bd. dirs. 1981-86, bd. profl. devel. 1982-86, various com. positions 1977-86), Delta Mu Delta. Home and Office: 626 Willis St South Hempstead NY 11550

ROBLEDO, ANGELA LEE, insurance executive; b. Whittier, Calif., Jan. 19, 1960; d. Rodolfo and Betty Lee (Fanning) R. BA in Sociology, Whittier Coll., 1982. Adminstr. asst. sales Calif. Western Life Ins. Co., Sacramento, 1982-84; rep. mktg. Corroon & Black/James Burpo Ins., Sacramento, 1984-85; account exec. Whittaker Health Services, Inc., Orange, Calif., 1985-86; specialist health sales, cons. CNA Ins. Cos., Brea, Calif., 1986—. Speaker, panelist conf. Calif. Commn. on Aging, Sacramento, 1987. Mem. Nat. Assn. Exec. Women, Nat. Assn. Life Underwriters. Democrat. Roman Catholic. Office: CNA Ins Cos 1800 E Imperial Hwy Brea CA 92621

ROBLIN, NANCY ROSAN, corporate executive; b. Milford, Conn., June 25, 1944; d. Richard A. and Helen (Marshall) Rosan; m. Richard O. Roblin; children: Pamela Roblin Andrews, Tyler Tujin (adopted). AB cum laude, Vassar Coll., 1966; M in Music, Boston U., 1976. Dir. music Grace United Ch., Frederick, 1976-82; account mgr. A.G. Fishkin Assoc., Rockville, Md., 1983-84; sr. staff specialist Planning Research Corp., McLean, Va., 1984-86; sr. staffing cons. Comsat Corp., Clarksburg, Md., 1986—; coordinator music dept. Frederick Community Coll., 1978-80; dir. The Frederick Singers, 1976-81; dir., founder The Frederick Chorale, 1977—. Chmn. music Frederick Arts Council, 1976-78; creative dir. numerous civic events, 1976—; conductor, keyboardist Concerts for Western Md. civic groups and chs. throughout the state. Mem. Am. Choral Dirs. Assn. (life, chairperson community choirs com. 1985—), Employment Mgmt. Assn., Pi Kappa Lambda. Home: 605 W Second St Frederick MD 21701 Office: Comsat Corp 22300 Comsat Dr Clarksburg MD 20871

ROBLYER, KATHLEEN ANNE CASEY, minister, nurse; b. Los Angeles, May 11, 1955; d. Donald F. and Marie A. (Round) Casey; m. Dwight A. Roblyer, Nov. 29, 1985. AA in Nursing, De Anza Coll., Cupertino, Calif., 1976; BS in Nursing, SUNY, Albany, 1981; MDiv, Golden Gate Bapt. Theol. Seminary, Mill Valley, Calif., 1985, postgrad., 1986—; MS, U. Calif., San Francisco, 1987. RN; ordained to ministry Bapt. Ch., 1983. Nurse clin. cancer research ctr. M.D. Anderson Hosp. and Tumor Inst., Houston, 1977-79; nurse emergency dept. Kaiser-Permanente Hosp., Santa Clara, Calif., 1979-81; emergency specialist Emergency Specialists Corp., San Jose, Calif., 1981-83; coordinator Cambodian ministries 19th Ave. Bapt. Ch., San Francisco, 1982-84, asst. pastor, 1984-85; nurse emergency dept. and ICU St. Mary's Hosp., San Francisco, 1983-85; nurse emergency dept. Community Hosp. Los Gatos (Calif.)-Saratoga, 1985-87; ethnic missions cons. Pikes Peak Park Bapt. Ch., Colorado Springs, Colo., 1987—; cons. for outreach and leadership devel. programs, First Bapt. Ch., Cupertino, 1985-87; mem. metro evangelism adv. council Home Mission Bd. So. Bapt. Conv., Atlanta, 1985-87. Editor: In God's Image, 1983-84. Bd. dirs. S.E. Asian Sch. Theology, Mill Valley, 1984-87; active Laubach Literacy Action. Named Outstanding Young Woman of Am., 1982-84. Mem. Nat. Assn. for Female Execs., Internat. Assn. Women Ministers, So. Bapt. Women in Ministry, Council on Nursing and Anthropology. Democrat. Office: Pikes Peak Park Bapt Ch 3725 El Morro Rd Colorado Springs CO 80910

ROBSON, KAREN JOHNSON, communications and marketing executive; b. Ft. Smith, Ark., Dec. 1, 1953; d. Woodrow W. and Licia (Louvier) Johnson.; 1 child, Heath. BA, La. State U., 1975, postgrad., 1987—. Regional adminstr. U.S. Housing, Shreveport, La., 1978-80; property mgr. Univ. Property Mgmt., Bossier City, La., 1979-80; site adminstr. Wichita Fall Hist. Soc., Wichita Falls, Tex., 1981; dir. communications Am. TV and Communications, Shreveport, 1981-84, dir. mktg. and communications, 1984—. Producer advt. and pub. relations campaigns on cablevision, 1985-87. Mem. La. State U. Med. Ctr. task force, Shreveport, 1984; Friend Child Find, 1985; coordinator Mid South Cable TV Polit. Action Com., Shreveport, 1985—; mem. Leadership Council Shreveport, 1985—. Named Pub. Affairs Mgr. of Yr. Time Inc., 1985. Mem. Pub. Relations Soc. of Am. (bd. 1985—), Sales and Mktg. Execs. Democrat. Roman Catholic. Office: ATC 6529 Quilen Rd Shreveport LA 71108

ROCCA, MARY FRANCES, dentist; b. Berkeley, Calif., Apr. 27, 1957; d. Carlo Richard and Dorothy Teresa (Kotula) R.; m. Eric Jerome Grigsby, June 29, 1985. BS, U. San Francisco, 1980; DDM, Boston U., 1984. Assoc. dentist Rochester Dental Group, Rochester, Minn., 1986-86; gen. practice dentistry Rochester, 1986—; mem. adv. council to med. services rev. bd. Dept. Labor and Transp. State Minn., St. Paul, 1985—. Co-chmn. Women of Achievement Awards Com., Rochester, 1976-87; vol. Amigos de las Americas, Honduras, 1979. Mem. ADA, Zumbro Valley Dental Soc. (bd. dirs. 1987—), Nat. Assn. Bus. and Profl. Women, Acad. Gen. Dentistry, Minn. Dental Assn., Rochester C. of C. Leadership 2000. Democrat. Home: 1815 35th St NE Rochester MN 55904 Office: Downtown Dental Care 212 First Ave SW Rochester MN 55902

ROCHA, MARILYN EVA, clinical psychologist; b. San Bernardino, Calif., Oct. 23, 1928; d. Howard Ray Gonding and Laura Anne (Johanson) Walker; m. Hilario Ursala Rocha, Mar. 25, 1948 (dec. Feb. 1971); children: Michael, Sherry, Teri, Denise. AA, Solano Jr. Coll., 1970. BA, Sacramento State U., 1973, MA, 1974; PhD, U.S. Internat. U., 1981. Psychologist, Naval Drug Rehab. Ctr., U.S. Navy, San Diego, 1975-85, chief psychologist, 1983-84; staff clin. psychologist Calif. Youth Authority No. Reception Ctr. Clinic, 1985—; dir. Self-Help Agys., San Diego. Author short story. Vol. counselor Hamonium, San Diego, 1976-77; SMRC Planning Group Scripps/Miramor Ranch, 1982-85; leader Vacaville council Cub Scouts Am., Calif., 1957-62, 4-H, also Brownie's. Mem. Calif. Scholastic Fedn., PTA (hon. life), Am. Psychol. Assn., Am. Assn. Suicidology, Bus. and Profl. Women, Delta Zeta. Democrat. Unitarian. Home: 4919 Gastman Way Fair Oaks CA 95628

ROCHE, CELESTE PAULA, management consultant; b. Bronxville, N.Y., Sept. 8, 1962; d. John Dennis and Pauline (Redyk) R. Student, Marymount Coll., 1980-81; BBA, Pace U., 1985. Compensation/benefits analyst Pepsico Inc., Purchase, N.Y., 1984; mgmt. trainee Gen. Motors, N. Tarrytown, N.Y., 1984, prodn. supr., 1985-86; cons. in mfg. Mgmt. Alternatives, Detroit, 1986; cons. in work flows Scheduling Corp. Am., Oak Brook, Ill., 1986-88; internal analyst Bank of N.Y., 1988—. Mem. Nat. Assn. Female Execs., AAUW. Republican. Roman Catholic. Office: Scheduling Corp Am 2215 York Rd Oak Brook IL 60521

ROCHE, SISTER DENISE ANN, college president; b. Buffalo, Sept. 17, 1942; d. Vincent Joseph and Mary Elizabeth (Crehan) R. B.A., D'Youville Coll., 1967; M.A., Boston U., 1968; Ph.D., U. Mass., 1977. Tchr., Our Lady of Fatima Grade Sch., L.I., N.Y., 1964-66; instr. D'Youville Coll., Buffalo, 1968-71, asst. prof., 1975-78, assoc. dean for continuing studies, 1978-79, pres., 1979—; teaching assoc. U. Mass.-Boston, 1972-75; mem. adv. bd. Business First, Buffalo, 1985—. Trustee Marygrove Coll., Detroit, 1981—; bd. dirs. Lafayette Gen. Hosp., Buffalo, 1980—, ARC, Buffalo, 1979—; chmn. coll. and univ. div. United Way Appeal, Buffalo, 1983—; mem. Task Force on Acute Care in Erie County, Buffalo, 1981-82, Erie County Legis. Task Force on Unemployment, Buffalo, 1984—. Named Citizen of Yr. N.Y. Soc. Profl. Engrs., 1984; recipient Pub. Service award SUNY-Buffalo Alumni Assn., 1985. Mem. Ind. Coll. Fund N.Y., Western N.Y. Consortium Higher Edn. (v.p.), Western N.Y. Regional Edn. Ctr. for Econ. Devel. Roman Catholic. Club: Zonta. Home: 320 Porter Ave Buffalo NY 14201 *

ROCHEROLLE, EUGENIE KATHERINE, composer, lyricist, pianist, educator; b. New Orleans, Aug. 24, 1936; d. Gustave Joseph and Katherine Lucille (Schlegel) Ricau; m. Didier Andre Rocherolle, May 14, 1960; children—Valerie, Laurent, Damien, Justin. B.A. in Music, Sophie Newcomb Coll. Tulane U., 1958. Composer, lyricist 44 anthems for chorus, 3 band works, 1 work for band and chorus; composer 22 books for piano; composer musicals, chamber works, string orch. work, radio commls.; performance of Vignette for flute and piano, Kennedy Ctr., Washington, 1988; commd. piano solo Clavier Mag., 1983; commd. anthem Wilton Congregational Ch. (Conn.), 1976; featured Am. composer and judge Audrey Thayer Meml. Piano Competition, Avon, Conn., 1986; guest composer Anne Arundel State Music Teachers Assn., Annapolis, Md., 1987, Del. State Music Tchrs. Assn., Dover, Del., 1987, Piano Festival, Anderson (S.C.) Coll., 1988, Hartford chpt. Conn. State Music Tchrs. Assn., 1986; featured composer Profl. Devel. for Piano Tchrs, Montgomery (Md.) Coll., 1988, featured composer Profl. Devel. for Piano Tchrs., Montgomery Coll, Rockville, Md., 1988, Piano Festival Concerto Competition and Concert Series, Anderson Coll., S.C., 1988; Mem. Women's Republican Club, Wilton, 1980—, exec. bd., 1982-86; mem. exec. bd., sec. Wilton Orch., 1983-86. Mem. Nat. League Am. Penwoman (co-state chmn. music 1983-85, v.p. Pioneer br. 1986-88 , 1st prize-choral competition 1986, competition for piano composition for the left hand prizewinner 1988), Nat. Fedn. Music Clubs (judge jr. festivals 1982—), ASCAP, Conn. Composers Inc., sec. Wilton Orch. 1983-86). Roman Catholic. Clubs: DAR (chaplain Drum Hill chpt. 1982-86, Drum Hill chpt. vice regent 1987—); Shubert of Fairfield County (bd. dirs. 1986-88).

ROCHESTER, JANET H., systems documentation writer; b. London, Oct. 25, 1943; came to U.S., 1969; d. Frederick and Hazel Diamond (Gray) Williams; m. Michael Ian Brambley, Sept. 10, 1966 (div. Apr. 1980); m. Haydon Rochester Jr., Apr. 23, 1982. BSc, London U., 1966, Diploma in Edn., 1967; MS, Drexel U., 1983. Tchr. high sch. chemistry Inner London Edn. Authority, 1967-68, Merchantville (N.J.) Sch. Dist., 1970-72, Gloucester City (N.J.) Sch. Dist., 1972-73; asst. editor Biological Abstracts, Phila., 1973-76; info. specialist Systems Research Co., Phila., 1976-81; sr. member engrng. staff Electronics Systems Div. RCA, Moorestown, N.J., 1983—. Contbr. articles to profl. jours. Mem. IEEE, Soc. Tech. Communication (sr. mem.), Nat. Assn. Female Execs. Republican. Lutheran.. Club: Am. Assn. U. Women, (pres. 1984-86, editor st. newspaper). Office: RCA-ESD Borton Landing RD Moorestown NJ 08057

ROCHIRA, NANCY MARY, public housing administrator; b. Lawrence, Mass., May 1, 1944; d. Walter Richard and Anna (Kuchuruk) Kibildis; m. Joseph Rochira, Nov. 25, 1962 (dec. Jan. 1984); 1 child, Teresa Anne. Cert. McIntosh Bus. Sch., 1962, pub. housing mgr., 1979; lic. real estate rep. State N.H., 1985; student N.H. Coll., 1975, 77, U. N.H., 79, 85, Castle Jr. Coll., 1984, Inst. for Practicing Real Estate, 1985, 87, Quantum Ednl. Acctg., 1987, Computer Support Services Tng., 1987. Receptionist, exec. sec. Supervisory Union, Atkinson, N.H., 1961-68; sales assoc. Salem-Derry Cable Co., Salem, N.H., 1971; asst. to mgr. Lancelot Assos., Salem, 1974; exec. dir. Salem Housing Authority, 1974—, sec. bd. commrs., 1974—. Area leader Heart Fund, 1980-81; mem. Salem Assn. Retarded Citizens, Salem, 1975—; mem. adv. com. Town and Country Theatre, 1985; Greater Salem Human Services Council, 1984; sec. Help the Handicapped Club, 1975—. Recipient Cert. of Recognition, Green Thumb Nat. Farmers Union, 1980, Cert. of Recognition, N.H. Housing Commn., 1978, Cert. Recognition Am. Cancer Soc., 1985. Mem. N.H. Assn. Exec. Dirs., N.H. Assn. Housing Authorities (sec.-treas. 1987—), Nat. Assn. Female Execs., Nat. Assn. Housing and Redevel. Ofcls. (cert. 1987). Avocations: swimming; gardening; cooking. Home: 117 Haverhill Rd Salem NH 03079

ROCHLIN, IRMA S., state legislator; b. Bklyn., Apr. 28, 1924; d. Matthew and Lillian Rebecca (Gold) Silverstein; divorced; children: Rolinda Schonwald, Tamara Gottstein, Raquel Rochlin, Debby Liberman. Student, U. Miami, Fla., 1940-41, Fla. State Coll. for Women, 1941-42; RN cert., John Hopkins Sch. Nursing, Balt., 1945; postgrad., Humboldt State Tchrs. Coll., 1957-58, Merritt Hosp., Oakland, Calif., 1969. Pvt. practice in Nursing Swannanoa, N.C., 1946; operating room supr. Michael Reese Hosp., Chgo., 1947; chair Women's div. Broward County State of Israel Bonds, Fla., 1976-84; elected mem. Fla. Ho. of Reps., Hallandale, 1984—; mem. Ho. of Reps. com. corrections, probation and parole, 1985—, regulatory reform, com. on youth; vice chmn. Health and Rehab. Services Fla. Ho. of Reps. Mem. profl. adv. com. Parents Without Ptnrs., 1985; chair Broward County Commn. on Status of Women, 1982-88; sr. summer intern Congressman William Lehman, Washington, 1976; vice chair Hallandale Land Use Planning Com., 1977-78; mem. Hallandale Planning and Zoning Bd., 1979-84, Gov.'s Comm. on Prison Health, 1985-86; active Concerned Dems., Children's Consortium, Women's Advocacy of Majority-Minority. Served to 2d lt. Med. Services Corp., U.S. Army, 1945-46. Recipient Outstanding Legislator award Fla. chpt. Am. Assn. on Mental Deficiency, 1984, Cert. Appreciation Broward County Bd. of County Commrs., 1984, Proclamation of Appreciation City of Hallandale, 1984, Cert. Appreciation Foster Grandparents of Broward County, 1984, Plaque Hollywood Jewish Fedn., 1985, Cert. Appreciation Am. Lung Assn., 1985, Outstanding Achievement Fla. State Acupuncture Assn., 1986, Cert. Achievement Dept. Corrections State of Fla., 1986; named to Fla. Women's Hall of Fame, 1986. Mem. Am. Assn. Ret. Persons, NOW (Broward County chpt.), Gwen Cherry Women's Polit. Caucus, Hallandale C. of C., Women's Advocacy the Majority-Minority, Women's Profl. Network. Clubs: Gulfstream Dem. Women's; Hills Dem. (charter mem.). Lodge: Order of Orchid. Office: 646 E Hallandale Beach Blvd Hallandale FL 33009-4422

ROCHWARGER, MICHELLE, business consultant; b. Buffalo, Mar. 7, 1955; d. Leonard and Arlene Joan Rochwarger. BA, U. Wis., 1977; MBA, U. San Francisco, 1981. Corp. loan officer Wells Fargo Bank, San Francisco, 1981-83, asst. v.p., tng. mgr., 1983-85; fin. services cons. Omega, San Francisco, 1985-87; pres. Rochwarger and Assocs., San Francisco, 1987—. Bd. dirs. Big Bros./Big Sisters of San Francisco, 1983-86, Florence Crittendon Soc., San Francisco, 1984-86, Ct. Appointed Spl. Advs., San Francisco, 1983-85. Recipient Community Support award United Way, 1984. Mem. Nat. Soc. Performance and Instrn., San Francisco Advt. Club. Democrat. Jewish. Office: Rochwarger and Assocs 2040 Polk St Suite 281 San Francisco CA 94109

ROCKEFELLER, REGINA STRAZZULLA, lawyer; b. Boston, Mar. 31, 1951; d. Philip and Anne Lenore (Silvestro) Strazzulla; m. Godfrey Anderson Rockefeller Jr., Aug. 3, 1974; children: Victoria Hamilton, Lisa Anderson. Lang. cert., U. Dijon, France, 1970; BA in Polit. Sci. magna cum laude, Tufts U., 1973; JD cum laude, Boston Coll., 1976. Bar: Mass. 1977, Fla. 1977, U.S. Dist. Ct. Mass. 1977. Ptnr. Hutchins & Wheeler, Boston, 1976—; bd. dirs. Strazzulla Bros. Co., Inc., Fort Pierce, Fla. Trustee Waltham (Mass.) Weston Hosp. and Med. Ctr., 1980—; bd. dirs. Hospice West, Inc., Waltham, 1984—. Mem. ABA, Mass. Bar Assn. (chmn. health law sect. 1986-87), Fla. Bar Assn., Nat. Health Lawyers Assn. Club: Prouts Neck Country (Maine); Tufts (Boston). Office: Hutchins & Wheeler 1 Boston Pl Boston MA 02108

ROCKLEN, KATHY HELLENBRAND, lawyer, banker; b. N.Y.C., June 30, 1951; d. Samuel Henry and Sheila (Kurzrok) Hellenbrand; m. R. Michael Rocklen, Aug. 26, 1972 (div. June 1978). BA, Barnard Coll., 1973; JD magna cum laude, New England Sch. Law, 1977. Bar: N.Y. 1978, U.S. Dist. Ct. (so. and ea. dists.) N.Y. 1982, U.S. Dist. Ct. (no. dist.) Calif. 1985. Assoc. Weiss, Rosenthal, N.Y.C., 1977-79; interpretive counsel N.Y. Stock Exchange, N.Y.C., 1979-81; asst. counsel Bradford Nat. Corp., N.Y.C., 1981-84; asst. v.p. E.F. Hutton & Co. Inc., N.Y.C., 1984, v.p., 1985, 1st v.p., 1986; v.p., gen. counseland sec. S.G Warburg (U.S.A.) Inc., N.Y.C., 1986—. Office mgr. Com. to elect Charles D. Breitel Chief Judge, N.Y., 1973. Named one of Outstanding Young Women in Am., 1976. Mem. ABA, N.Y. State Bar Assn., N.Y. Women's Bar Assn., Assn. of Bar of City of N.Y. (second century com. 1982-85, sec. second century com. 1985-86, sex and law com. 1982-85, young lawyers com. 1979-82, corp. law com. 1986—, spl. com. on drugs and law 1986—). Club: Athletic and Swim (N.Y.C.). Home: 153-29 82d St Howard Beach NY 11414 Office: SG Warburg (USA) Inc 787 7th Ave New York NY 10019

ROCKMAN, ILENE FRANCES, librarian, teacher, consultant; b. Yonkers, N.Y., Nov. 9, 1950; d. Leon and Margaret (Klein) R. B.A., UCLA, 1972; M.S. in L.S. U. So. Calif., 1974; M.A., Calif. Poly. State U., 1978; Ph.D., U. Calif.-Santa Barbara, 1985. Librarian, Wash. State U., Pullman, 1974-75, Calif. Poly. State U., San Luis Obispo, 1975—; adj. prof. Cuesta Coll., San Luis Obispo, 1982-85; abstracter Women Studies Abstracts, Rush, N.Y., 1976—. Contbr. articles to profl. jours.; editor, Reference Services Rev., 1987—; co-author: BLISS--Basic Library Information Sources and Services, 1985. Active Mozart Festival, San Luis Obispo, 1981—, KCBX-FM Pub. Radio, San Luis Obispo, 1983—. Del. Democratic Nat. Conv., 1984. Recipient scholarship Calif. PTA, Los Angeles, 1973. Mem. ALA, Calif. Library Assn. (mem. council 1983-86), Assn. Coll. and Research Libraries, Am. Ednl. Research Assn., Total Library Exchange (pres. 1979-80), Library Assocs. Calif. Poly. State U. (exec. sec. 1981-83). Home: 654 Rancho Dr San Luis Obispo CA 93401 Office: Calif Poly State U San Luis Obispo CA 93407

ROCKOFF, SHEILA G., nursing educator; b. Chgo., Mar. 15, 1945; d. Herbert Irwin and Marilyn (Victor) R.; m. Richard J. Applebaum, Aug. 4, 1985 (div. Dec. 1987). A.D.N., Long Beach City Coll., 1966; B.S.N., San Francisco State Coll., 1970; M.S.N., Calif. State U.-Los Angeles, 1976. R.N., pub. health nurse, nursing instr., Calif. Staff nurse Meml. Hosp., Long Beach, Calif., 1966-67, Mt. Zion Med. Ctr., San Francisco, 1967-69; instr. nursing Hollywood Presbyn. Med. Ctr., Los Angeles, 1970-74; nursing supr. Orthopedic Hosp., Los Angeles, 1974-76; instr. nursing Ariz. State U., Tempe, 1976-78; nurse supr. Hoag Meml. Hosp., Newport Beach, Calif., 1977-78; nurse educator U. Calif.-Irvine and Orange, Calif., 1978-80, Santa Ana Coll. (Calif.), 1980—, Rancho Santiago Community Coll., Santa Ana Campus ; nurse cons. Home Health Care Agy., Irvine, 1983; educator/cons. Parenting Resources, Tustin, Calif., 1985—. Mem. Calif. Nurses Assn. (chmn. com. 1970-73), Am. Heart Assn., Nat. League for Nursing, Am. Cancer Soc., Phi Kappa Phi. Democrat. Jewish. Home: 13834 Comanche Tustin Ranch CA 92680 Office: Rancho Santiago Community Coll 17th at Bristol Santa Ana CA 92706

ROCKS, JUDITH ANN, orchestra administrator; b. Cleve., Jan. 13, 1939; d. Harold Worden and Virginia (White) Tredway; m. James Engel Rocks, June 30, 1973. BS in Biology and Psychology, Baldwin-Wallace Coll., 1962; MA in Ednl. Psychology, Northwestern U., 1979; MS in Indsl. Relations, Loyola U., Chgo., 1985; cert. mgmt. seminar, Am. Symphony Orch. League, 1987. Dir. phys. therapy Cleve. Clinic, 1970-72; instr. allied health sci. U. Ill., Chgo., 1972-74; assoc. instr. Sch. Phys. Therapy Northwestern U., Chgo., 1974-80; dir. phys. therapy Martha Washington Hosp., Chgo., 1983-85; mgr. health care dept. Columbus Hosp., Chgo., 1986-87; gen. mgr. Chgo. Chamber Orch., 1987—; chairperson various coms. Chgo. Symphony Orch., 1978—; pub. relations dir. and archivist Goodman Theatre Inner Circle Bd., Chgo., 1986—. Soloist Cleve. Civic Ballet, 1954-57; freelance writer Parma Sun Post, 1970; contbr. articles to profl. jours. Mem. Am. Symphony Orch. League, Chgo., Music Alliance (spl. events planning com. 1987—), AAUW, Psi Chi, Phi Delta Kappa, Alpha Sigma Nu. Home: 446 Oakdale Chicago IL 60657

ROCKWELL, ELIZABETH DENNIS, fin. planner; b. Houston; d. Robert Richard and Nezzell Alderton (Christie) Dennis. Student Rice U., 1939-40, U. Houston, 1938-39, 40-42. Purchasing agt. Standard Oil Co., Houston, 1942-66; asst. sec. Heights Savs. Assn., Houston, 1967-70, asst. v.p., 1970-75, v.p. mktg., 1975-82; sr. v.p., fin. planner Oppenheimer & Co., Inc., Houston, 1982—; 2d v.p. Desk and Derrick Club Am., 1960-61; instr. Coll. of Mainland, Texas City, Tex.; instr. Downtown Coll. and Continuing Edn. Ctr., U. Houston; mem. Dean's adv. bd. U. Houston, alumni bd. 1987—, treas., 1988. Bd. dirs. ARC, Houston Heights Assn., 1973-77, 85—; active Houston Jr. League, 1986-87. Named Outstanding Woman of Yr., YWCA. Mem. Am. Savs. and Loan League (state dir. 1973-76, chpt. pres. 1971-72; pres. S.W. regional conf. 1972-73; Leaders award 1972), Savs. Inst. Mktg. Soc. Am. (Key Person award 1974), Inst. Fin. Edn., Fin. Mgrs., Soc. Savs. Instns., U.S. Savs. and Loan League (com. on deposit acquisitions and adminstrn.), Spring Branch Meml. C. of C., Internat. Platform Assn., Houston Heights Assn. (charter, dir. 1973-77), Houston North Assn., Harris County Heritage Soc., Rice U. Bus. and Profl. Women, River Oaks Bus. Womens Exchange Club, U. Houston Bus. Womens Assn. (pres. 1986). Club: Forum. Author articles on retirement planning and tax options. Home: 3617 Yoakum Blvd Houston TX 77006 Office: Oppenheimer & Co Inc 333 Clay St Suite 4700 Houston TX 77002

ROCKWELL, SALLY JEAN, nutritionist; b. Astoria, Oreg., Feb. 23, 1933; d. James Patrick and Lorita Agnes (McManamna) Campbell; divorced; children: William, Kenneth, Kelli. BS, U. Wash., 1981; postgrad., Union Grad. Sch., Cin., 1985—. Prin. Nutrition Survival Services, Seattle, 1981—; cons. State of Alaska, Metlakatla Indian Reservation, J.B. Naturopathic Coll.; mem. adv. bd. Oreg. State Dept. Mental Health, Coalition for Alternatives in Nutrition and Health; instr. U. Wash. Exptl. Coll., Seattle, 1982—; founder Food Allergy Support Teams, 1982. Author: The Rotation Game, 1981, Coping with Candida, 1984, Sally Rockwell's Allergy Recipes, 1985; creator (audio cassette tapes) Overcoming Allergies, Conquering Candida, 1987, (video tape) Rotation Diet & What's Left to Eat?, 1988; editor Allergy Alert Newsletter, 1982—. Mem. Women's Bus. Exchange (Bus. Woman of Month 1985), Women Entrepreneurs Network, Am. Acad. Environ. Medicine, Am. Holistic Med. Soc., Soc. for Nutrition Edn. Home and Office: 4703 Stone Way North Seattle WA 98103

ROCQUE, BERNICE L., administrator; b. Norwich, Conn., Aug. 28, 1950; d. Michael William and Gabrielle Jean D'Arc (Picard) Janovicz; m. Christopher Grey Rocque, Jan. 12, 1973. BA, U. Conn., 1972; MLS, Syracuse U., 1975. Circulation asst. Conn. Coll. Library, New London, 1972-74; young adult/reference librarian Simsbury Pub. Library (Conn.), 1976-79; supr. corp. library and info. services Texaco Inc., Harrison, N.Y., 1979-80, coordinator corp. library and info. services, 1980-81, coordinator corp. library network, 1981-83, area coordinator info. analysis and devel., 1983-86, area coordinator tng. and devel., 1986—; mem. Westchester adv. council Grad. Sch. Library and Info. Sci., Pratt Inst., Bklyn., 1980-86. Pres. Pine Hill Manor Condominium Assn., Stamford, 1983—, treas., 1981-83, v.p., 1979-80; Texaco team mem. Westchester Women's Indsl. Tennis Assn., 1982—; gov. Texaco Forum, 1981-83. Gaylord Bros. Co. scholar, 1974-75. Mem. Am. Soc. Tng. Devel., Spl. Libraries Assn., Beta Phi Mu. Home: 57 Pinewood Trail Trumbull CT 06611 Office: Texaco Inc Corp Services Dept 2000 Westchester Ave White Plains NY 10650

RODABAUGH, MARY JANE, education educator emeritus; b. Napoleon, Ohio, Aug. 2, 1917; d. Daniel and Sophia Wilhemina (Ruetz) Gorman; B.A., B.S. in Edn., Capital U., Columbus, Ohio, 1939; M.A., Ohio State U., 1945; m. James H. Rodabaugh, Nov. 9, 1946. Tchr. social studies and English, Mt. Zion (Ohio) High Sch., 1939-43; tchr., chmn. history dept. Columbus Sch. for Girls, 1955-63; instr. Kent (Ohio) State U., 1963-65, asst. prof., 1965-67; instr. Miami U., Oxford, Ohio, 1967-69, asst. prof. dept. tchr. edn., from 1969, now prof. emeritus. John Hay fellow Williams Coll., 1965. Mem. Am. Assn. Ret. Persons (state legrs. com.), Ohio Council Social Studies, LWV, AAUW, Phi Delta Kappa. Author: (with James H. Rodabaugh) Nursing in Ohio: A History, 1951; (with Parker LaBach) Common Learnings: Core and Interdisciplinary Team Approaches, 1969. Home: 7 Chestnut Hill Oxford OH 45056

RODAWAY, SHIRLEY JEAN, diversified company executive; b. Denver, Oct. 9, 1947; d. Robert Edward Mitchell and Barbara V. Thorne. BS in Botany, Calif. State Poly. U., 1969, MS in Biology, 1971; PhD in Plant Physiology, Mich. State U., 1977. Postdoctoral research fellow Inst. for Cancer Research, Phila., 1977-81; sr. research plant biologist Am. Cyanamid Co., Princeton, N.J., 1981—. Contbr. articles to profl. jours. Mem. Am. Soc. Plant Physiologists, AAAS, Plant Growth Regulant Soc. Am. Office: Am Cyanamid Co PO Box 400 Princeton NJ 08540

RODDICK, ELLEN HAWLEY, communications consultant, author; b. Bronxville, N.Y., Feb. 13, 1936; d. Harrison Arnold and Mary Elizabeth (Henrici) R.; m. Karl W. Haffenreffer, Mar. 11, 1961 (div. July 1965); m. Walter W. Meade, Nov. 2, 1967; 1 child, Luke Harrison. BA, Wellesley Coll., 1958. Free-lance writer 1966—; columnist Cosmopolitan mag., N.Y.C., 1975-81; owner Write/Action, Yorktown Heights, N.Y., 1983-86; pres. Ellen Roddick Inc., Bodega Bay, Calif., 1986—. Author: (fiction) Together, 1979, Holding Patterns, 1981; (nonfiction) Young Filmmakers, 1969 (N.Y. Pub. Library prize 1969), Writing that Means Business, 1984, Everyone Can Write: Thinking Skills for Writing (Activities Kit for grades 4-8), 1987; contbr. articles to mags., profl. jours. Vol. various activities including pro-environ. and anti-nuclear activities. Mem. Am. Soc. Tng. and Devel., Women in Communications, Authors Guild, Inst. of Noetic Scis. Club: Wellesley (No. Calif.). Office: Ellen Roddick Inc PO Box 548 Bodega Bay CA 94923

RODDY, ANNETTE A., substance abuse counselor; b. East Chicago, Ind., Sept. 21, 1962; d. Modesto Alicea and Felicita Rodriguez. BS in Pub. Health, Ind. U., 1984. Field experience worker Bloomington (Ind.) Hosp., 1984; instr.'s aide Stone Belt Ctr., Bloomington, 1983-84; psychiatric technician Tri-City Commn. Mental Health, East Chicago, 1985-86; activities coordinator, counselor asst., intake coordinator Franklin Blvd. Community Hosp., Chgo., 1986-87, counselor, 1987—; counselor, intake coordinator Cen. Community Hosp., Chgo., 1987; substance abuse counselor Our Lady of Mercy, Dyer, Ind., 1987—; co-chairperson alumni assn. of adolescent chem. dependency program Our Lady of Mercy Hosp., Dyer, Ind. Mem. Am. Coll. Healthcare Execs., Nat. Assn. Female Execs., Alpha Angel. Roman Catholic. Home: 521 Emlyn Pl East Chicago IN 46312

RODEHEAVER, OLAH ANITA, county official; b. Houston, Sept. 27, 1923; d. Charles Lee and Olah Hunter (West) Robertson; m. James Harvey Rodeheaver, Nov. 1, 1943; children—Margaret Dianne Rodeheaver Dupont, Nancy Ruth Rodeheaver Luksa. Grad. John H. Reagan High Sch., Houston, 1941. Exec. asst. to clk. Harris County, Houston, 1961-78, clk., 1979—; mem. faculty Internat. Ctr. Election Law and Adminstrn., 1985. Bd. dirs. New Directions, Inc., Houston, 1982—; mem. adv. panel Fed. Elections Commn., 1987, adminstrv. bd. Collins United Methodist Ch., Houston, 1984—. Recipient Outstanding Achievement to Community and Mankind award Ethel Ransom Literary Club, 1985. Mem. Internat. Assn. Clks. Recorders, Election Ofcls. and Treas. (past pres., 2d v.p. 1985), County and Dist. Clks. Assn. Tex. (co-chmn. legis. com. 1979—), Nat. Assn. Counties. Democrat. Lodge: Order Eastern Star. Avocations: fishing; crocheting; enjoying children and grandchildren. Home: 4514 Mountwood St Houston TX 77018 Office: County Clk PO Box 1525 1001 Preston St Houston TX 77251

RODENBAUGH, MARCIA LOUISE, educator; b. Pitts., Nov. 11, 1942; d. F. Thomas and Lucy Indiana (Fry) Wimer; m. John Anthony Lee, Mar. 21, 1964 (div. Nov. 1971); m. Richard Allan Rodenbaugh, Aug. 3, 1975; stepchildren—Ken, Tiffany, Tricia. B.A. in Edn., Westminster Coll., New Wilmington, Pa., 1964, M.Ed. in Remedial Reading, 1966. Tchr., North Hills Sch. Dist., Pitts., 1964-70, Central Bucks Schs., Doylestown, Pa., 1970—. Author children's books: Marci Books (set of 6), 1983—. Pres. Maple Leaf Day Care Ctr. Bd., Warminster, Pa., 1971; pres. Wesley Coll. Parents Assn., Dover, Del., 1985-86. Mem. Pa. Edn. Assn., NEA, Central Bucks Edn. Assn., Nat. Assn. Female Execs., AAUW. Republican. Presbyterian. Avocations: skiing; sailing; writing; piano; church choir. Home: 7-16 Aspen Way Doylestown PA 18901 Office: Central Bucks Sch Dist 315 W State St Doylestown PA 18901

RODENBUSH, REBECCA LYNN, financial consultant; b. Benton, Ill., Sept. 11, 1948; d. Kenneth Monroe and Anne (Shapkoff) R.; m. Lawrence Wayne Shook, Sept. 6, 1969 (div. Sept. 1973); 1 child, Jennifer Anne. BA, San Diego State U., 1972. Fin. analyst Univ. Hosp. of U. Calif., San Diego, 1974-77; personnel cons. M. David Lowe, Houston, 1978-81; fin. cons. Dean Witter Reynolds, San Diego, 1981-83, Sutro and Co., San Diego, 1983-84, Merrill Lynch, San Diego, 1984—. Mem. Rep. Nat. Com. Mem. Zoolog. Soc. San Diego. Methodist. Office: Merrill Lynch 701 B St 24th Floor San Diego CA 92101

RODERICK, SUE SCHOCK, medical executive; b. Muskogee, Okla., Oct. 28, 1937; d. Willie Orville and Dona Leona (Gordon) Perry; m. Kenneth Robert Schock, Nov. 22, 1955 (div. 1971); m. John Kenneth Roderick, Aug. 9, 1981. BS with distinction, San Jose (Calif.) State U., 1970; MS, San Jose State U., 1973; M in Pub. Adminstrn., U. So. Calif., 1982, D in Pub. Adminstrn., cert. in gerontology, 1984. cert. tchr., Calif. Sr. citizens dir. City of San Jose, 1968-72; chief gerontology Kings View Mental Health, Visalia, Calif., 1972-74; cons. on aging State of Calif., Sacramento, 1974-76; dir. edn. Calif. Assn. Health Facilities, Sacramento, 1976-77; exec. dir. Hilhaven Found., Tacoma, Wash., 1977-83; pres. Med. Ednl. Services Devel., Alameda, Calif., 1979—; asst. v.p. planning and research Am. Bapt. Homes of the West, Oakland, Calif., 1984—; cons. St. Mary's Hosp., San Francisco, 1973-74, Hillsdale Manor, Inc., San Mateo, Calif., 1973—, St. Peter's Adult Day Care Ctr., San Leandro, Calif., 1973—; bd. dirs. St. Peter's Adult Day Care Ctr., San Leandro, Alameda County Adult Day Care Ctr., San Leandro, 1984; co-founder, dir. Shades of Gray: Perspectives in Aging, Alameda, 1987. Contbr. articles to profl. jours. Bd. dirs. Alameda County Adult Day Health Care Council, Oakland, 1985—. Chi Kappa Rho scolar San Jose State U., 1970, U. So. Calif.-Gerontology Ctr. scholar, 1971-74. Mem. Am. Soc. on Aging, Intercare, Am. Assn. of Homes for Aging, Am. Coll. of Health Care Adminstrs., Calif. Specialists on Aging, Calif. Assn. of Homes for Aging. Democrat. Home: 3406 Redhook Lane Alameda CA 94501 Office: Am Bapt Homes of the West 400 Roland Way Oakland CA 94621

RODGER, GINETTE, professional association executive, nurse; b. Amos, Que., Can., Mar. 18, 1943; d. Joseph and Blanche (Gagnon) Lemire; m. William James Rodger; children: Robert, Philippe, Sabrina. Diploma in nursing, U. Ottawa, 1964, B.S. in nursing, 1966; M.Nursing Adminstrn., U. Montreal, 1971; D.Sci. h.c., U. N.B., 1985. Gen. duty nurse Ottawa Gen. Hosp., Ont., 1964-65; asst. dir. nursing St. Vincent Hosp., Ottawa, summer 1965; gen. duty nurse Queen Mary Hosp. and Jewish Gen. Hosp., Montreal, Que., summer 1966, Hotel-Dieu Hosp., Amos, summer 1967, Queen Mary Hosp., summer 1968; adminstrv. asst. Hosp. Notre-Dame, Montreal, 1968-72; gen. duty nurse Hosp. Notre-Dame, 1972-73, nurse researcher, 1973, asst. dir. nursing, 1973, in-charge nursing research, 1973-74, dir. nursing, 1974-81; exec. dir. Can. Nurses Assn., Ottawa, 1981—. Mem. Can. Council Hosp. Accreditation, 1972-86, chmn., 1981-82; nat. dep. dir. St. John Ambulance for Health Care Program, 1981-86; mem. nat. com. tng. Order of St. John, 1981-86; mem. service adv. com. Victorian Order of Nurses for Can., 1981—; mem. nat. health com. Can. Red Cross Soc., 1981—; mem. Que. council Order of St. John, 1975-81, v.p., 1976-79; pres. Assn. St. John, 1976-79; chmn. nursing edn. com. Que. Ministry Edn., 1978-80; mem. Fedn. Que. Health and Social Affairs Adminstrs., 1975-81; mem. com. essential services Que. Ministry Labor, 1978-80; mem. group dirs. nursing Montreal Univ. Hosps., 1980-81. Decorated Serving Sister Can. Order St. John Ambulance, 1979; recipient Vigor prize Que. Fedn. Health Services Adminstr., 1981; officer St. John Ambulance, 1981; Ryerson fellowship award Ryerson Poly. Inst., 1984—. Mem. Can. Coll. Health Service Execs., Can. Nurses Assn., Can. Hosp. Assn., Ordre des infirmieres et infirmiers du Quebec, Coll. Nurses Ont., Registered Nurses Assn. Ont., Am. Soc. Hosp. Nursing Service Adminstrn., Can. Nurses Found. (sec.-treas. 1981—), Med. Research Council Can., Can. Nurses Protective Soc. (chief exec. officer, treas.). Office: Can Nurses Assn, 50 The Driveway, Ottawa, ON Canada K2P 1E2

RODGERS, CATHERINE A., corporation manager, hazard management specialist; b. Chgo., Mar. 26, 1955; d. Edward Francis and Nancy Anne (Freer) R.; m. Steven Edward Emick, June 5, 1982; 1 child, Jennifer Leigh. BA in Phys. Edn., U. Calif. State, Chico, 1976; MA in Hazard Mgmt., U. Calif. State, 1978; MBA in Mgmt. and Fin., Golden Gate U., 1984; postgrad., U. Santa Clara, 1987—. Cert. paramedic; lic. tchr., Calif. Neuroanatomy research asst. Nat. Inst. of Health, Bethesda, Md., 1974; paramedic Butte County, Chico, Calif., 1977; instr. Butte (Calif.) Jr. Coll., 1978; safety engr. IBM Corp., San Jose, Calif., 1978-80; emergency response mgr. IBM Corp., San Jose, 1980-82, 2d level hazard mgr., 1982-84, site chem. ops. mgr., 1984-85; corp. hdqrs. program mgr. IBM Corp., Purchase, N.Y., 1985-86; v.p. SEECAR, Inc., Morgan Hill, Calif., 1986—; chmn. Gov.'s Earthquake Preparedness Task Force Office of Emergency Services, Sacramento, 1976-87; bd. dirs. ARC, 1977—; mem. Santa Clara County Disaster Preparedness for Bus. and Industry, 1985. Author: As Feeings Grow, 1983, Second Thoughts, 1987. Instr. Am. Red Cross, Los Altos, Calif., Am. Heart Assn., Los Altos, 1972-78. Named Woman of Yr. Santa Clara County, 1983. Mem. Am. Soc. Indsl. Security, Aircraft Owner's and Pilot's Assn., Nat. Assn. Female Execs. Republican. Roman Catholic. Office: IBM Corp 5600 Cottle Rd San Jose CA 95193

RODGERS, DEBORAH LYNN, corporate manager; b. Sacramento, June 10, 1957; d. Earl and Patricia Ann (Shannon) Rodgers; divorced; children: Michelle, Anthony. BS, U. Mary Hardin-Baylor, Belton, 1979; postgrad., Tex. Women's U. Cert. tchr., Tex. Research technician M.D. Anderson Hosp. and Tumor Inst., Houston, 1980, research technician human lymphocyte antigen, 1980-81; biochem. asst. HEM Research Inc., Rockville, Md., 1981-87; sr. research assoc. Georgetown U., Washington, 1982, UCLA - Tissue Typing Lab, Los Angeles, 1982-84; founder, owner OCS Labs., Denton, Tex., 1984-85, v.p., c.e.o., 1985—. Mem. Immaculate Conception Ch., Denton Communications Commn., 1987—, lector 1986-87, lay ministry 1986—. Mem. Am. Soc. Histocompatibility and Immunogenetics, Nat. Assn. Female Exec., AAAS. Roman Catholic. Office: OCS Labs PO Box 2067 Denton TX 76202

RODGERS, KATHERINE JEAN, insurance company associate, consultant; b. Jacobs Creek, Pa., Mar. 6, 1934; d. Francis E. and Charlotte (Kelly) Semko; m. Robert James Rodgers, Jan. 4, 1953; children—Cecilia, Robert James, Elizabeth, Eileen, Jeanine, Kathleen. Student in med. tech. Franklin Sch. Sci. and Arts, 1953. Floating cor. Beneficial Ins. Co., Phila., 1974-75, asst. to mgr. 1975; corr. Penn Mut. Life Ins. Co., Phila., 1975-76, annuity technician, 1976-78, research analyst, 1978-82, sr. mktg. info. analyst, 1982-87; info. assoc., 1987—; owner Target Assocs., Marlton, N.J., 1983—. Contbr. poetry to various publs. Dir. membership Women's Resource Group, Penn Mut. Life Ins. Co., 1981-83. Fellow Life Mgmt. Inst.; mem. Am. Mktg. Assn. (treas. chpt. 1982-85, dir. 1985-87, v.p. communications 1987-88), Nat. Assn. Female Execs., Network of Women in Computer Tech., N.J. Assn. Women Bus. Owners, Am. Bus. Communications Assn., NOW. Office: Penn Mut Life Ins Co Independence Sq Philadelphia PA 19172

RODGERS, MARY COLUMBRO, university chancellor, English language educator; b. Autora, Ohio, Apr. 17, 1925; d. Nicola and Nancy (DeNicola) Columbro; m. Daniel Richard Rodgers, July 24, 1965; children: Robert, Patricia, Kristine. A.B., Notre Dame Coll., 1957; M.A., Western Res. U., 1962; Ph.D., Ohio State U., 1964; postgrad. Fulbright scholar, U. Rome, 1964-65; Ed.D., Calif. Nat. Open U., 1975, D.Litt., 1978. Tchr. English Cleve. elem. schs., 1945-52, Cleve. secondary schs., 1952-62; supr. English student tchrs. Ohio State U., 1962-64; asst. prof. English U. Md., 1965-66; assoc. prof. Trinity Coll., 1967-68; prof. English D.C. Tchrs. Coll., 1968—; pres. Md. Nat. U., 1972—; chancellor Am. Open U., 1965—. Author numerous books and monographs; (latest works include) A Short Course in English Composition, 1976, Chapbook of Children's Literature, 1977, Comprehensive Catalogue: The Open University of America System, 1978-80, Open University of America System Source Book, V, VI, VII, 1978, Essays and Poems on Life and Literature, 1979, Modes and Models: Four Lessons for Young Writers, 1981, Open University Structures and Adult Learning, 1982, Papers in Applied English Linguistics, 1982, Twelve Lectures on the American Open University, 1982, English Pedagogy in the American Open University, 1983, Design for Personalized English Graduate Degrees in the Urban University, 1984, Open University English Teaching, 1945-85: Conceptual History and Rationale, 1985, Claims and Counterclaims Regarding Instruction Given in Personalized Degree Residency Programs Completed by Graduates of California National Open University, 1986, The American Open University, 1965 t0 1985: History and Sourcebook, 1986, New Design II: English Pedagogy in the American Open University, 1987, The American Open University, 1965 to 1985: A Research Report, 1987, The American Open University and Other Open Universities: A Comparative Study Report, 1988, others. Fellow Catholic Scholars; mem. Am. Open U. Acad., Poetry Soc. Am., Nat. Council Tchrs. English, Am. Ednl. Research Assn., Pi Lambda Theta. Roman Catholic. Home and Office: Coll Heights Estate 3916 Commander Dr Hyattsville MD 20782

RODGERS, NANCY LUCILLE, corporate executive; b. Denver, Aug. 22, 1934; d. Francis Randolph and Irma Lucille (Budy) Baker; student public schs.; m. George J. Rodgers, Feb. 18, 1968; children by previous marriage: Kellie Rae, Joy Lynn, Timothy Francis, Thomas Francis. Mgr., Western Telearm, Inc., San Diego, 1973—; pres. Rodgers Police Patrol, Inc., San Diego, 1977-80; br. mgr. Honeywell Inc., Protection Services div., San Diego, 1979—; pres. Image, Inc., Image Travel Agy., Cairo, Egypt, 1981-83, Western Solar Specialties, 1979-80; founder, pres. Internat. Metaphysicians Associated for Growth through Edn., San Diego, 1979; founder, dir. Point Loma Sanctuary, 1983-86; co-founder, producer Zerciee Prodns. Unltd., 1986—, co-founder, producer, dir. mktg., 1986—. Bd. dirs. Cen. City Assn. Named Woman of Achievement Cen. City Assn., 1979. Mem. Nat. Assn. for Holistic Health, Am. Bus. Women's Assn. (Woman of Yr. 1980), Am. Union Metaphysicians, Philae West (co-owner, mgr.). Republican. Clubs: Am. Bashkir Curly Registry, Bashkir Curly Breeder.

RODGERS, SALLY ANN, accountant; b. Alliance, Ohio, Sept. 27, 1940; d. Forrest LeRoy and Elizabeth Ann (Meinzen) Albright; m. John Dixon Tuttle, July 6, 1968 (div. June 1970); 1 child, Melanie; m. John Albert Rodgers, Nov. 16, 1974; adopted Melanie. Student, Akron U., 1966-72. Bookmobile librarian Rodman Pub. Library, Alliance, 1960-62; acctg. clk. E.W. Bliss Co., Canton, Ohio, 1962-67; bookkeeper Met. Contract, North Canton, Ohio, 1967-74; staff acct. Bruner, Cox et al, Canton, 1974-84; owner Rodgers & Assocs. formerly Record Mgmt. Services, Canton, 1984—. Mem. Am. Inst. CPA's, Ohio Soc. CPA's (chairperson mem. com. 1984-87), Am. Soc. Women Accts. (com. chairperson 1985—, v.p. 1985-87, pres. 1987—), Network, Inc. Democrat. Presbyterian. Lodge: Eastern Star. Office: Rodgers & Assocs 4445R 20th St NW Canton OH 44708

RODGERS-BURTON, JOAN CASSANDRA, educational administrator; b. Phila., July 3, 1940; d. John Coleman and Lucille Lutrecia (Holloman) Rodgers; children: Edmond Durant, Marian Renne Burton. BA in Sociology, York Coll., Jamaica; MA in Urban Studies Adminstrn., Queens Coll., Flushing, N.Y.; postgrad., Southampton Coll., 1977. Statis. asst. Allied Purchasing Corp., N.Y.C., 1958-61; map router Texaco Touring, N.Y.C., 1963-65; sec. fiscal office sec. Qualicap Corp., Queens, 1966-67; asst. head start program N.Y.C. Bd. Edn., Queens, 1967-68, spl. ed. tchr., 1968-72, unit coordinator, 1973-82, learning disablities specialist, 1982-87, supr. spl. edn., 1982-87; lead supr. spl. edn. N.Y.C. Bd. Edn., Bklyn., 1987—; prin. Pub. Sch. 80, Queens, 1988—; adj. lectr. Kingsborough Community Coll., Bklyn., 1977-83; cons. Urban Edn. Inc., N.Y.C., 1975-77; site supr. Summer Youth Program of N.Y.C., Queens, 1979-80. tchr. Mt. Oliver Ch., N.Y.C., 1977-78. Mem. Council for Exceptional Children, Assn. of Black Educators of N.Y., NAACP, Laurelton Fedn. of Black Assocs. Democrat. Roman Catholic. Home: 234-03 139 Ave Laurelton NY 11422

RODIN, JUDITH SEITZ, psychology educator; b. Phila., Sept. 9, 1944; d. Morris and Sally R. (Winson) Seitz; m. Nicholas Niejelow, Feb. 12, 1978. A.B., U. Pa., 1966; Ph.D., U. Columbia, 1970. Asst. prof. psychology N.Y. U., N.Y.C., 1970-72; assoc. prof. Yale U., 1973-78, prof., dir. grad. studies, 1979-84, Philip R. Allen prof. psychology, medicine and psychiatry, 1984—; chmn. John D. and Catherine T. MacArthur Found. Research Network on Health-Promoting and Health-Damaging Behavior, 1984—. Author: (with S. Schachter) Obese Humans and Rats, 1974, Exploding the Obesity Myths, 1982; editor: Appetite Jour, 1979—; contbr. articles to profl. jours. Fellow Woodrow Wilson Found., 1966-68, John Simon Guggenheim Found., 1986-87; grantee NSF, 1975—, NIH, 1979—. Fellow Am. Psychol. Assn. (bd. sci. affairs 1979-82), AAAS, Soc. Behavioral Medicine; mem. Inst. Med, Acad. Behavioral Medicine Research, Eastern Psychol. Assn. (exec. bd. 1980-83, pres. div. 38 health psychology 1982-83, Outstanding Contbn. award 1980, Disting. Sci. award 1977), Phi Beta Kappa, Sigma Xi (pres. Yale chpt. 1986-87). Office: Yale U Box 11A Yale Station New Haven CT 06520

RODLIN, JUDITH, psychologist, educator; b. Phila., Sept. 4, 1944; d. Morris and Sally (Winson) R.; m. Nicholas G. Nielelow, Feb. 12, 1978; 1 child, Alexander. AB, U. Pa., 1966; PhD, Columbia U., 1970. Asst. prof. psychology NYU, N.Y.C., 1970-72; asst. prof. psychology Yale U., New Haven, 1972-75, assoc. prof., 1975-79, dir. grad. studies, 1978-83, prof. psychology, 1979-83, prof. psychiatry, 1980, Philip R. Allen prof. psychology, 1984. Chief editor Appetite Jour., 1979—; assoc. editor Personality and Social Psychology Bull., 1976-79; mem. editorial bd. Internat. Jour. of Obesity, 1977, Health Psychology, 1981—, Behavioral Medicine, 1978-84. Chmn. John D. and Catherine T. MacArthur Found. Research Network on Health-Promoting and Health Damaging Behavior, 1984—. Fellow NSF, 1971. Fellow AAAS Inst. Medicine; mem. Eastern Psychol. Assn. (pres. 1982-83), Am. Psychol. Assn. (pres. div. 38 health psychology 1982-83, Outstanding Contbn. award 1980, Disting. Scientific award for an Early Career Contbn. to Psychology 1977). Home: 10 Maple St Stratford CT 06497 Office: Yale Univ Dept Psychology 2 Hillhouse Ave New Haven CT 06484

RODMAN, ANGELA FAYE, telecommunications research executive; b. Arlington, Va., Apr. 3, 1963; d. John Ivan and Wanda Faye (Smith) Slane; m. Edward Ford Rodman, Oct. 12, 1985. AS in Info. Systems/Computer Sci. with high honors, Chattanooga State Tech. Community Coll., 1983; BS in Math., Momouth Coll., 1987. Tech. assoc. AT&T Bell Labs., Holmdel, N.J., 1983-84; staff technologist Bell Communications Research, Red Bank, N.J., 1984-87, sr. staff technologist, 1987—. Music software developer (book) Animation, Games and Sound for the IBM PC, 1983. Mem. Digital Equipment Computer Users Soc., Phi Theta Kappa. Republican. Episcopalian.

RODMAN, CYNTHIA WILLETT, food products executive; b. Norfolk, Va., Feb. 21, 1960; d. David B. and Carol (Willett) R. AB, Mt. Holyoke Coll., 1982. Brand asst. Procter & Gamble Co., Cin., 1982-83, asst. brand mgr., 1983-85; product mgr. Kellogg Co., Battle Creek, Mich., 1985-87, group product mgr., 1987—. Club: Mt. Holyoke of Western Mich.(sec.). Home: 3704 Tartan Circle Portage MI 49002

RODMAN, ELLEN RENA, broadcasting executive; b. Boston, July 5, 1940; d. Samuel and Edith (Aronson) Blumsack; m. William Bryant Rodman, Sept. 2, 1962; children—Pamela Beth, Keith Andrew. B.S., Simmons Coll., 1962; M.A., Columbia U., 1964; Ph.D., NYU, 1980. Dir. theatre arts various pvt. schs., N.Y.C., 1970-74; features writer N.Y. Daily News, N.Y. Times and McCalls mag., N.Y.C., 1974-79; children's entertainment reviewer N.Y. Times, 1974-79; dir. children's info. services NBC, N.Y.C., 1980-82, dir. corp. info. services NBC, 1982-84; dir. corp. communications Westinghouse Broadcasting and Cable, Inc., 1984-85; v.p. corp. communications Children's TV Workshop, 1985-86; ptnr. LN Productions, 1987—, dir. Nat. Assn. for Industry-Edn. Coop., Washington, 1983-87. Author: (with Richard Flaste) The N.Y. Times Guide to Children's Entertainment, 1976; contbr. chpts. to books, articles to profl. jours., mags. Mem. Women in Communications, Am. Women in Radio and TV, Internat. Radio and TV Soc., Nat. Assn. Broadcasters (children's TV com. 1983-84). Office: 50 Riverside Dr Suite 3B New York NY 10024

RODMAN, IRENE BETTY, association executive; b. Bklyn., Nov. 5, 1924; d. Frederick Sheldon Clark and Frances (Rice) Emmont; m. Warren Edward Rodman, June 27, 1943; children—Warren Lee, Donald Edward, Justin Leslie, Barbara Lynn. Profl. trainer N.Y.S. Quarterhorse Assn., Ghent, Buskirk, N.Y., 1952-76; teacher, coordinator Cottage Crafts Handspuns, Greenwich, N.Y., 1976-79; mgr. admissions Bennington Mus., Inc., Old Bennington, Vt., 1980-83; dir. caretaker Historic Preservation Old Bennington, 1983-85; exec. dir. Am. Cancer Soc., Hudson Falls, N.Y., 1986—; dir. Goodrich Quarter Horse Farms, Buskirk, 1965-70; cons. Peter Mattison Tavern, Shaftsbury, Vt., 1977-85, Mus. Old Bennington, 1978—. Recipient Am. Biog. Inst. Commemorative Medal of Honor. One-woman shows at Loveland Mus., Colo., 1984, Autumn Retreat Festival, Colo., 1984; represented in permanent collections at Bennington Mus., Inc., Peter Matteson Tavern. Contbr. articles to profl. publs. Co-author: Herbs to Infinity, 1979. Mem. Co. Mil. Historians, Chapman Mus., Hyde Collection, Inc., Bennington Mus., Inc., N.Y. State Quarter Horse Assn. (treas. 1958-68). Republican. Methodist. Avocations: collecting military miniatures; writing; snowshoeing; gardening. Home: Box 126 RD#3 Kenyon Rd Greenwich NY 12834

RODMAN, SUE ARLENE, wholesale Indian crafts company executive, artist; b. Fort Collins, Colo., Oct. 1, 1951; d. Marvin F. and Barbara I. (Miller) Lawson; m. Alpine C. Rodman, Dec. 13, 1970; 1 child, Connie Lynn. Student Colo. State U., 1970-73. Silversmith Pinel Silver Shop, Loveland, Colo., 1970-71; asst. mgr. Traveling Traders, Phoenix, 1974-75; co-owner, co-mgr. Deer Track Traders, Ltd., Loveland, 1975-85, exec. v.p., 1985—. Author: The Book of Contemporary Indian Arts and Crafts, 1985. Mem. Rep. Presdl. Task Force, 1982—; mem. U.S. Senatorial Club, 1982-87, Civil Air Patrol, 1969-72, 87—, personnel officer, 1988—. Mem. Internat. Platform Assn., Nat. Assn. Female Execs., Indian Arts and Crafts Assn. Baptist. Club: Crazy Horse Grass Roots (S.D.). Avocations: museums, recreation research, fashion design, reading, flying. Office: Deer Track Traders Ltd PO Box 448 Loveland CO 80539

RODMANN, DOROTHY ELLEN, association adminstr.; b. Washington, Feb. 1, 1930; d. Michael Albert and Georgie Rebecca (Stant) Peters; B.A., George Washington U., 1954, postgrad., 1954-55; m. Horst Rodmann, June 7, 1958; children—Leslie Ann, Karen Lynn. Adminstr. asst. Am. Polit. Sci. Assn., Washington, 1954-58; personnel asst. NEA, Washington, 1959-69, personnel assoc., 1969-71, employment mgr., 1971-72; personnel mgr. Nat. League Cities-U.S. Conf. of Mayors, Washington, 1972-76; personnel dir. Am. Chem. Soc., 1977—. Mem. Washington Personnel Assn., Conf. Instl. Adminstrs., Greater Washington Soc. Assn. Execs., Alpha Delta Pi. Home: 8428 Georgian Way Annandale VA 22003 Office: 1155 16th St NW Washington DC 20036

RODOVICH, ARLENE GUYOTTE, administrator, small business owner; b. Springfield, Mass., Mar. 21, 1935; d. Walter L. Guyotte and Dorothy (Hawley) Bigelow; m. Robert F. Rodovich, Sept. 30, 1955; children: Heidi E. Pacheco. AA, Greenfield (Mass.) Community Coll., 1977. Cert. property mgr. Sec., bookkeeper Gordon E. Ainsworth Assocs., South Deerfield, Mass., 1954-60; from jr. clk. to dir. U. Mass. Property and Inventory Control, Amherst, 1966—; owner Conway (Mass.) Bus. Service, 1958—. Author: (manual) Property Management, 1972. Chmn. fin. com., zoning bd. appeals, Conway, 1975—. Mem. Nat. Property Mgmt. Assn. (v.p. profl. devel. 1987—, v.p. fin. 1988, Property Person of Yr. 1984, Property Person of Yr. ea. region 1986), Mass. Fedn. Bus. and Profl. Women (2d v.p. 1986—, 1st v.p. 1987-88, pres.-elect 1988—). Home: Ashfield Rd Conway MA 01341 Office: U Mass Goodell Bldg Amherst MA 01341

RODRIGUES, NANCY DURDEN, marketing executive; b. Albany, Ga., Oct. 8, 1955; d. Gene R. and Dorothy (Whitfield) Durden; m. Ruy V. Rodrigues, Jan. 25, 1986. BA in Bus. Adminstn., U. N.M., 1975. Pub. affairs mgr. Sta. WCBD-TV, Charleston, S.C., 1976-78; exec. asst. Kiawah Island Resort, Charleston, S.C., 1978-80; exec. asst. Boca Raton (Fla.) Hotel & Club, 1980-81, regional sales mgr., 1981; dir. sales & conf. service The Boca Beach Club, 1982-83; dir. mktg. Grand Bay Hotel, Coconut Grove, Fla., 1983-84; dir. mktg. and special projects Rosewood Hotels Inc., Dallas, 1984-86; v.p. RVR and Assocs., Dallas, 1986—. Mem. Hotel Sales Mgmt. Assn., Meeting Planners Internat. Republican. Episcopalian. Home: 733 Terrell Crossing Marietta GA 30067

RODRIGUES, PHYLLIS MARIE, account systems engineer; b. Hilo, Hawaii, Feb. 3, 1958; d. Daniel and Julia (Rubella) R. Student, U. Granada (Spain), 1979; BA in Math., Beloit Coll., 1980; MBA, U. Wis., 1982. Mktg. research asst. Gen. Mills, Inc., Mpls., 1979; mktg. asst. Ralston-Purina, St Louis, 1981; systems engr. IBM, N.Y.C. and San Francisco, 1982—. Presdl. scholar Beloit Coll., 1976-80; advanced grad. fellow U. Wis., 1980-82. Mem. Nat. Assn. Female Execs., MBA Assn. Office: IBM 425 Market St San Francisco CA 94105

RODRIGUEZ, ISIDORA HERNANDEZ, retail executive; b. Velasco, Oriente, Cuba, May 15, 1928; came to U.S., 1966; d. Pedro and Angela (Perez) Hernandez; children: Angela, Pedro. Designer Ellen Terri Fashions, Hialeah, Fla., 1972-81; pres. Dora Originals, Hialeah, 1981—. Republican. Roman Catholic. Home: 730 E 46th ST Hialeah FL 33013 Office: Dora Originals 1050 SE 5th St Hialeah FL 33010

RODRIGUEZ, ROSEMARIE JEAN, marketing professional; b. New Brunswick, N.J., Mar. 16, 1955; d. Eleuterio Huerta and Rose Marie (Sframeli) R.; m. Joseph Louis Rivera, May 30, 1987. BA in History, Rutgers U., 1978. Exec. sec. mktg. ops. AT&T Long Lines, Bedminster, N.J., 1980-82, trainer computer software ops., 1982-84; human factors analyst AT&T Communications, Basking Ridge, N.J., 1984—; cons. human factors analyst Bus. Markets Group, Basking Ridge, N.J., 1986—. Author: Wordstar Trainer's Guide, 1983, Wordstar-Practical Applications, 1983. Mem. Human Factors Soc., Hispanic Assn., Soc. for Info. Display. Office: AT&T Communications 295 N Maple Ave Basking Ridge NJ 07920

RODRIGUEZ-OLIVIERI, MARIA DEL CARMEN, psychologist; b. San Juan, P.R., June 16, 1953; d. J. Pablo and Sarah (Olivieri) Rodriguez; m. F. Solano (div. Oct. 1987). BA, U. P.R., 1975, MA, 1978; PhD, NYU, 1985. Psychologist P.R. Legal Services Corp., Rio Piedras, 1978-79; sch. psychologist N.Y.C. Bd. Edn., Bklyn., 1982-83; assoc. psychologist N.Y. State Psychiat. Inst., N.Y.C., 1985-86; field supr. N.Y.C. Bd. Edn., 1986-87; sr. psychologist Lincoln Youth Achievement Ctr., Bronx, N.Y., 1987—; adj. instr. Puerto Rican studies Lehmann Coll. CUNY, Bronx, 1980, 83-85; coordinator 1st Hispanic Psychology Symposium at N.Y. State Psychiat. Inst., 1985-86; cons. in field. Contbr. articles to profl. jours. Mem. Am. Psychol. Assn., Am. Orthopsychiatry Assn., P.R. Psychol. Assn. Home: 105 Pinehurst Ave #66 New York NY 10033 Office: Lincoln Youth Achievement Ctr 966 Prospect Ave Bronx NY 10459

RODRIGUEZ ORENSTEIN, ROSA MARIA, lawyer; b. Juarez, Chihuahua, Mexico, Jan. 5, 1956; came to U.S., 1961, naturalized, 1975; d. Alejo and Carmen (Montalvo) Rodriguez; m. James David Orenstein, May 20, 1979; children: Louis Thomas, Sara Lucia. BA in Econs., Stanford U., 1978; JD, U. Calif., Berkeley, 1981. Bar: Tex. 1982. Ptnr., Gardere & Wynne, Dallas, 1982—. Mem. Dallas Hispanic C. of C., ABA, Tex. Bar Assn., Mexican Am. Bar Assn., Dallas Bar Assn. (mem. minority participation com.). Democrat. Roman Catholic. Office: Gardere & Wynne 717 N Harwood 15th Floor Dallas TX 75201

ROE, DONNA JENSEN, sales executive; b. Akron, Ohio, Nov. 22, 1930; d. John Davidson and Helen Graves (Shipley) Miller; student Kent State U., 1949-51; C.P.S., Ariz. State U., 1962; A.A., Phoenix Coll., 1974; postgrad. Grad. Sch. Bus., U. Wis.-Madison, 1980; m. Robert B. Roe, July 5, 1975 (dec.); children—Pamela, Christopher. Community, communication specialist Sperry Flight Systems, Phoenix, 1957-76; appointments sec. Gov. Wesley Bolin, State of Ariz., Phoenix, 1977-78; corr. sec. Gov. Bruce Babbitt, State of Ariz., Phoenix, 1978; asst. to dir. Ariz. Dept. Econ. Security, Phoenix, 1978-79; asst. exec. dir. Samaritan Med. Found., Phoenix, 1979-82; dir. catering sales Camelback Inn, Scottsdale, Ariz., 1983—. Mem. exec. bd. Theodore Roosevelt Council, Inc. Boy Scouts Am., 1977—, mem. Western Arts Assocs., Scottsdale Artists' Sch. (bd. dirs. 1988). Mem. Ariz. Soc. Assn. Execs., Phoenix Art Mus. League, Phoenix Symphony Guild, Ariz. Women in Food and Wine (bd. dirs. 1987), Am. Culinary Inst., CPS Soc. Ariz. Republican. Presbyterian. Home: 77 E Missouri Ave Phoenix AZ 85012

ROE, RAMONA JERALDEAN, lawyer, state official; b. Gassville, Ark., May 27, 1942; d. Roy A. and Wanda J. (Finley) R. B.A., U. Ark., 1964; J.D., U.Ark.-Little Rock, 1976. Bar: Ark. 1976, U.S. Dist. Ct. (ea. and we. dists.) Ark. 1979. Mng. ptnr. Roe & Hunt, Rogers, Ark., 1977-78; sole practice, Rogers, Ark., 1978-81, Little Rock, 1982-84; assoc. Richardson & Richardson, Little Rock, 1981-82; dep. exec. dir. Ark. Workers' Compensation Commn., Little Rock, 1984—. Contbr. articles to profl. jours. Recipient Am. Jurisprudence awards U. Ark. Sch. Law, 1971-72, Corpus Juris Secundum award, 1971, Hornbook award, 1971, Am. Judicature award, 1972. Mem. AAUW (treas. 1980), Bus. and Profl. Women (chpt. treas.-v.p. 1978-80), Delta Theta Phi (clk. of rolls 1973-74, tribune 1974-75), Mensa, Lambda Tau, Internat. Platform Assn. Methodist. Office: Ark Workers' Compensation Commn Justice Bldg Little Rock AR 72201

ROEBLING, MARY GINDHART, bank executive; b. West Collingswood, N.J.; d. I.D., Jr. and Mary W. (Simon) Gindhart; m. Siegfried Roebling (dec.); children: Elizabeth (Mrs. D.J. Hobin), Paul. Student bus adminstrn., econs. and fin., U. Pa., econs. and fin., NYU; LLD (hon.), Ithaca Coll., 1954; DS in Bus. Adminstrn. (hon.), Bryant Coll.; DSc (hon.), Muhlenberg Coll.; HHD (hon.), Wilberforce U.; DFA (hon.), Rider Coll.; DCS (hon.), St. John's U.; LHD (hon.), Marymount Coll., Rutgers U., 1987. Former chmn. bd. Nat. State Bank N.J., Women's Bank, Denver, now chmn. emeritus; chmn. N.Y. World's Fair Corp., 1964-65; dir. Companion Life Ins. Co., N.Y. Mem. adv. com. U.S. commr. gen. for Expo '67; nat. bd. dirs. U.S.O.; pub. gov. Am. Stock Exchange, 1958-62; mem. Regional Adv. Com. on Banking Policies and Practices; econ. ambassador State N.J. Chmn., N.J. Citizens for Clean Water, 1969-70; mem. Ann. Assay Commn., 1971, Nat. Bus. Council on Consumer Affairs; mem. adv. com. N.J. Museum. Life trustee George C. Marshall Research Found., N.J. Dental Service Plan; mem. nat. adv. council Nat. Multiple Sclerosis Soc.; trustee Invest-in-America; adv. bd. Assn. U.S. Army, civilian aide emeritus to Sec. Army, First Army; bd. govs. Del. Valley Council; chmn. N.J. Savs. Bond Com.; mem. 4th dist. Adv. Council Naval Affairs; bd. govs. Swedish Hist. Found.; nat. bd. Jr. Achievement Inc.; emeritus mem. def. adv. com. on women in services Dept. Def.; civilian aide to Sec. Army First Army Area; citizens adv. council Com. on Status of Women; bd. dirs. Am. Mus. Immigration; chmn. N.J. Hospitalized Vets.'s Service; comptroller Trenton Parking Authority; founder Donnelly Meml. Hosp. Women's Com. Decorated Royal Order Vasa (Sweden); commendatore Order Star Solidarity (Italy); recipient Brotherhood award NCCJ; Nat. Assn. Ins. Women award; Distinguished Service award Marine Corps League; Golden Key award N.J. Fedn. Jewish Philanthropies; Spirit of Achievement award women's div. Albert Einstein Coll. Medicine; Holland award N.J. Fedn. Women's Clubs; Outstanding Civilian Service medal Dept. Army, 1969; Humanitarian award N.J. chpt. Nat. Arthritis Found., 1970; Four Chaplains award, 1969; Trenton chpt. Nat. Secs. Boss of Year award, 1969, Internat. Boss of Year award, 1972; Golden Plate award Am. Acad. Achievement; Jerusalem Holy City of Peace award State of Israel; Dept. of Def. medal for Disting. Pub. Service, 1984; others. Mem. Nat. Def. Transp. Assn. (life mem.), U.S. Council of I.C.C. (trustee), N.J. Conf. Christians and Jews, Swedish Colonial Soc., League Women Voters, Am. Inst. Banking, N.J. Investment Council, Am. Bankers Assn., Soc. Mayflower Descs., Colonial Daus. 17th Century, Trenton C. of C., N.J. Firemen's Mut. Benevolent Assn. (hon. life), DAR, Geneal. Soc. Pa., Bus. and Profl. Women's Club, Daus. Colonial Wars, Pilgrim John Howland Soc. Clubs: Zonta, Trenton Country; Colony (N.Y.C.), Sea View Country, Contemporary (Trenton), Greenacres Country (Lawrenceville); Overseas Press (assoc.); Am. Newspaper Women's (asso.), 1925 F Street (Washington). Mailing Address: 120 Sanhican Dr Apt 3C Trenton NJ 08618

ROEBUCK, JANET, history educator, administrator; b. Rotherham, Eng., Sept. 1, 1943; came to U.S., 1968; d. Ernest and Olive (Dean) Roebuck. B.A. in History, U. Wales, 1964; Ph.D. in History, U. London, 1968. Asst. prof., assoc. prof. history U. N.Mex., Albuquerque, 1968-79, prof., 1979—, also chmn. dept.; cons. NEH, Ednl. Testing Service, various pub. houses; mem. nat. screening com. for Fulbright program. Author: The Making of Modern English Society from 1850, 1973, 82; The Shaping of Urban Society, 1974; Urban Development, 1979; contbr. articles to hist. jours. Office: U N Mex Dept History Albuquerque NM 87131

ROEDELL, MARY LOU, small business owner; b. Waynoka, Okla., Nov. 1, 1926; d. William Dexter and Sarah Ruth (Compton) McNeely; m. Floyd J. Roedell, Aug. 15, 1948; 1 child, Alison Ann Sheehan. AB, Northwestern State U., 1948. Tchr. Avard (Okla.) Pub. Schs., 1947-48; documents librarian Okla. A&M Coll. Library, Stillwater, 1948-52; engring. aide Boeing Aircraft, Wichita, 1952-58; founder, dir. First United Meth. Pre-Sch., Wichita, 1966-72; bookkeeper R.R. Savs. and Loan, Wichita, 1978-81; owner A Quilt Shoppe Etc., Kechi, Kans., 1982—. Mem. Prairie Quilt Guild, Sigma Sigma Sigma. Republican. Methodist. Home: 6501 Rockwood Rd Wichita KS 67206

ROEHM, MARYANNE EVANS, university dean; b. Vigo County, Ind., Nov. 29, 1925; d. Herbert and Fern Evans; m. Joseph L. Roehm, Aug. 10, 1947. BS, Ind. State U.-Terre Haute, 1953, MS, 1957; MS in Nursing, Ind. U., Bloomington, 1965, EdD., 1966. Instr. nursing, asst. dir. Sch. Nursing, Union Hosp., Terre Haute, 1946-55; assoc. dir. edn. Sch. Nursing, St. Anthony Hosp., Terre Haute, 1957-64; asst. and assoc. prof. nursing Ind. State U., 1966-70, dir. continuing edn., 1970-78, dean Sch. Nursing, 1977—; mem. Ind. State Bd. Nursing Registration and Nursing Edn., 1978-81, pres., 1980-81; mem. adv. com. hypertension project Vigo County Health Dept., 1981; mem. health occupations adv. com. Ind. Vocat. Tech. Coll., 1970—. Mem. Vigo County Home Citizens Com., Ind., 1970—; mem. Vigo County Blood Donor Council, 1980; vice precinct committeeman Vigo County. Recipient Outstanding Leadership award Ind. div. Am. Cancer Soc., 1982. Mem. Ind. State Nurses Assn. (Cert. of Recognition 1978, named Outstanding Nurse Educator 1959), Ind. League for Nursing, Am. Nurses' Assn., AAUP, Am. Assn. Coll. Deans, Midwest Alliance on Nursing, Ind. Council Baccalaureate and Higher Degree Deans and Dirs., Ind. Council Assoc. Degree Deans and Dirs. Home: Route 22 Box 561 Terre Haute IN 47802

ROELKER, NANCY LYMAN, history educator; b. Warwick, R.I., June 15, 1915; d. William Greene and Anna R. (Koues) Roelker; A.B., Radcliffe Coll., 1936; Ph.D., Harvard U., 1953. Tchr. history Winsor Sch., Boston, 1941-63; asst. prof. history Tufts U., 1963-65, asso. prof., 1965-69, prof., 1969-71; prof. European history Boston U., 1971-80; adj. prof. Brown U., 1979—. John Simon Guggenheim fellow, 1965-66; recipient medal for disting. achievement Radcliffe Coll., 1970, Metcalf prize Boston U., 1974, Gold medal City of Paris, 1985. Mem. Am. Hist. Assn., (v.p. research div. 1975 78, chmn. internat. activities com., U.S. del. to Internat. Congress Hist. Scis. 1982—), Soc. French Hist. Studies (pres. 1977-78), Am. Soc. Reformation Research, Am. Acad. Arts and Sci. Author: The Paris of Henry of Navarre, 1958; Editor, translator In Search of France, 1963, From Wilson to Roosevelt: American Foreign Policy 1913-1945, 1963; Queen of Navarre, Jeanne d'Albret, 1528-1572, 1968. Contbr. articles to profl. jours. Home: 777 Love Ln East Greenwich RI 02818 Office: Brown U Box N Providence RI 02912

ROEMER, ELIZABETH, educator, astronomer; b. Oakland, Calif., Sept. 4, 1929; d. Richard Quirin and Elsie (Barlow) R. B.A. with Honors (Bertha Dolbeer scholar), U. Calif. at Berkeley, 1950, Ph.D. (Lick Obs. fellow), 1955. Tchr. adult class Oakland pub. schs., 1950-52; lab technician U. Calif. at Mt. Hamilton, 1954-55; grad. research astronomer U. Calif. at Berkeley, 1955-56; research asso. Yerkes Obs. U. Chgo., 1956; astronomer U.S. Naval Obs., Flagstaff, Ariz., 1957-66; asso. prof. dept. astronomy, also in lunar and planetary lab. U. Ariz., Tucson, 1966-69; prof. U. Ariz., 1969—; astronomer Steward Obs., 1980—; Chmn. working group on orbits and ephemerides of comets commn. 20 Internat. Astron. Union, 1964-79, 85—, v.p. comm. 20, 1979-82, pres., 1982-85, v.p. commn. 6, 1973-76, 85—, pres., 1976-79; Mem. adv. panels Office Naval Research, Nat. Acad. Scis.-NRC, NASA. Recipient Dorothea Klumpke Roberts prize U. Calif. at Berkeley, 1950, Mademoiselle Merit award, 1959; asteroid (1657) named Roemera, 1965; Benjamin Apthorp Gould prize Nat. Acad. Scis., 1971; NASA Spl. award, 1986. Fellow AAAS (council 1966-69, 72-73), Royal Astron. Soc. (London); mem. Am. Astron. Soc. (program vis. profs. astronomy 1960-75, council 1967-70, chmn. div. dynamical astronomy 1974), Astron. Soc. Pacific (publs. com. 1962-73, Comet medal com. 1968-74, Donohoe lectr. 1962), Internat. Astron. Union, Am. Geophys. Union, Brit. Astron. Assn., Phi Beta Kappa, Sigma Xi. Office: U Ariz Lunar and Planetary Lab Tucson AZ 85721

ROES, NANCY BENNETT, controller; b. Freeport, N.Y., Jan. 9, 1954; d. John Joseph and Elizabeth Anne (Howell) Bennett; m. Nicholas A. Roes, Nov. 26, 1977. BS, U. Bridgeport, 1976. Bookkeeper North Atlantic Ins. Co., Syossett, N.Y., 1976-79; chief fin. officer NAR Assocs., Saddle River, N.J., 1977—; office mgr. Ridgewood (N.J.) Ford, 1979-84; mgr. bus. Higgins Buick, Ridgewood, 1984—; cons. Winfo., Hohokus, N.J., 1979—, Tchr. Update, Inc., Belmont, Mass., 1983—, NAR Prodn., Barryville, N.Y., 1986; office mgr. Pistilli Ford, Paramus, N.J. Office: NAR Assocs PO Box 205 Saddle River NJ 07458

ROESCHLAUB, JEAN MARIAN CLINTON, restaurant chain executive; b. Berkeley, Calif., June 1, 1927; d. Clifford E. and Nelda M. (Patterson) C.; m. David J. Davis III, June 26, 1946 (dec. 1963); children: David J. Davis IV, Diane Davis Ciardy, Burce Clinton Davis; m. Ronald Curtis Roeschlaub, Jan. 9, 1965; 1 child, Ronald W. AA, Stephens Coll., 1944. Civilian cons. on loan Q.M. Gen., 1944-45; co-owner, exec. v.p. Clinton's Restaurants, Inc., operators Clinton's Cafeterias, Los Angeles, 1944—; bd. dirs. Glendale Fed. Savs. and Loan Assn. Chmn. bd. curators Stephens Coll.; bd. dirs., mem. exec. com. Assistance League of So. Calif.; mem. aux. bd. Braille Inst. Am., Los Angeles. Mem. Nat. Restaurant Assn., Calif. State Restaurant Assn. Republican. Presbyterian. Clubs: Orphanage Guild, Los Angeles Country, Los Angeles Athletic. Home: 222 Monterey Rd #1606 Glendale CA 91206 Office: 515 W 7th St Los Angeles CA 90014

ROESS, ALICE GABRIELLE, investment executive; b. St. Petersburg, Fla., May 20, 1943; d. William Rhinelander and Martha Alice (Kithcart) Wood; m. Martin John Roess, Jr., Nov. 21, 1981; 1 child, Florence Alice Roess. B.A. in Real Estate, Eckerd Coll., St. Petersburg, Fla., 1988. Cert. real estate broker, property mgr., Fla. Property mgr. Kuhlman & Gentry, St. Petersburg, Fla., 1977-78; condominium mgr. Isla Del Sol, St. Petersburg, 1978-80; pres. Guaranty Mgmt., Assocs., Inc., St. Petersburg, 1982-83, Tour Hosts Mgmt., Inc., St. Petersburg, 1983—; v.p. Ocean Club of Palm Beach, St. Petersburg, 1983—; supervisory mgmt. cons. A. Clinton Brooks & Co. Inc., St. Petersburg, 1980-86; sec.-treas. Lenders Nationwide Mortgage Corp., St. Petersburg, 1984-86; pres. The Gabrielle Corp., St. Petersburg, 1984—. Mem. Nat. Soc. DAR, Tampa Mus. Fine Arts, St. Petersburg Mus. Fine Arts, Nat. Assn. Realtors, Inst. Real Estate Mgmt., Community Assns. Inst., St. Petersburg Bd. Realtors, Fla. Assn. Realtors. Mensa. Republican. Episcopalian. Clubs: Intertel, Ocean (Palm Beach Shores). Home: PO Box 40070 Saint Petersburg FL 33743-0070 Office: 1301 66th St N PO Box 40070 Saint Petersburg FL 33743

ROESSER, JEAN WOLBERG, state legislator; b. Washington, May 8, 1930; d. Solomon Harry Wolberg and Mary Frances Brown; m. Eugene Francis Roesser, Aug. 3, 1957; children: Eugene Jr., Mary, Anne. BA, Trinity Coll., Washington, 1961; postgrad. in Econs., Cath. U. of Am., 1951-53. Congl. relations asst. U.S. Info. Agy., Washington, 1954-58; news reporter for Montgomery County Council Suburban Record, 1983-86; elected mem. Md. Gen. Assembly, Annapolis, 1986—; mem. Md. Ho. Dels. constl. and adminstrv. law com., spl. com. on Drug and Alcohol Abuse; mem. Md. Gen. Assembly Women's Legis. Caucus. Contbr. articles to polit. jours. Former pres. Montgomery County Fedn. Rep. Women, Potomac Women's Rep. Club; former 3d v.p. Md. Fedn. Rep. Women; ; founding mem. Montgomery County Arts Council. Mem. West Montgomery County Assn., Germantown Citizen's Assn., Gaithersburg C. of C., Upper Montgomery County C. of C., Germantown C. of C., Potomac C. of C. Republican. Roman Catholic. Home: 10830 Fox Hunt Ln Potomac MD 20854 Office: Maryland Gen Assembly Lowe House Office Bldg Annapolis MD 21401

ROESSLER, P. DEE, lawyer, municipal judge; b. McKinney, Tex., Nov. 4, 1941; d. W.D. and Eunice Marie (Medcalf) Powell; m. George L. Roessler, Jr., Nov. 16, 1963; (div. Dec. 1977); children: Laura Diane, Trey. Student Austin Coll., 1960-61, 62-64, Wayland Bapt. Coll., 1961-62; B.A., U. West Fla., 1968; postgrad. East Tex. State U., 1975, U. Tex.-Dallas, 1977; J.D., So. Meth. U., 1982. Bar: Tex. 1982, U.S. Dist. Ct. (ea. dist.) Tex. 1983, U.S. Dist. Ct. (no. dist.) Tex. 1983. Tchr., Van Alstyne Ind. Sch. Dist., Tex., 1968-69; social worker Dept. Social Services, Fayetteville, N.C., 1971-73, Dept. Human Services, Sherman and McKinney, Tex., 1973-79, 81; assoc. atty. Abernathy & Roeder, McKinney, Tex., 1982-85, Ronald W. Uselton, Sherman, 1985-86, program coordinator Collin County Community Coll., McKinney, 1986—; judge City of McKinney Mcpl. Ct., 1986—; mem. Collin County Shelter for Battered Women, 1984-86, chmn., 1984-85; v.p. Collin County Child Welfare Bd., 1985—, pres. 1986—; Republican jud. candidate Collin County, 1986; chmn. bd. Tri County Consortium Mental Health Mental Retardation, 1984-85; mem. Tex. Area 5 Health System Agy., 1979; mem. Collin County Mental Health Adv. Bd., 1978-79. Mem. Collin County Bar Assn., Collin County Women's Bar (chmn. 1984-85). Baptist. Avocations: dancing, tennis, golf, reading, writing. Home: 2118 Chippendale St McKinney TX 75069 Office: Collin County Community Coll 2200 University McKinney TX 75069

ROFFEY, LEANE ELIZABETH, insurance company systems analyst programmer; b. Chgo., Mar. 17, 1949; d. Joseph Andrew and Ethel Antoinette (DeSalvo) Accomando; m. Arthur Roffey, 1972 (div. 1973). B.A., Wayne State U., 1972. Indsl. cons. Computype Corp., Ann Arbor, Mich., 1976-77; project leader Manufacturing Data Systems, Ann Arbor, 1978-80; info. mgmt. supr. First Variable Life Ins. Co., Little Rock, 1980-82; programmer/analyst First Pyramid Life, Little Rock, 1982-83, Ark. Blue Cross and Blue Shield, Inc., Little Rock, 1983-85, Am. Security Life Ins. Co., San Antonio, 1985—. Fellow Life Mgmt. Inst.; mem. Mensa, Phi Theta Kappa. Republican. Episcopalian. Avocations: vocal coach, classic car restoration, auto racing.

ROGALSKI, ADRIENNE ALICE, cell biologist, educator; b. Chgo., Aug. 2, 1953; d. Edward Joseph and Viola Veronica (Komen) R.; B.A., U. Chgo., 1975; Ph.D., U. Ill., 1981. Sr. research technician U. Chgo., 1975-76; research asst., Univ. fellow U. Ill., 1976-81; NIH fellow U. Calif., San Diego, 1981-85; asst. prof. dept. anatomy U. Ill.-Chgo., 1985—. Pew Scholar Biomed. Scis., 1987—. Mem. Am. Soc. Cell Biology, AAAS, N.Y. Acad. Scis., Sigma Xi. Office: U Ill Chgo Dept Anatomy & Cell Biology Box 6998 808 S Wood St Chicago IL 60680

ROGALSKI, LOIS ANN, speech and language pathologist; b. Bklyn., Dec. 17, 1947; d. Louis J. and Filomena Evelyn (Maro) Giordano; B.A., Bklyn. Coll., 1968; M.A., U. Mass., 1969; Ph.D., N.Y. U., 1975; m. Stephen James Rogalski, June 27, 1970; children—Keri Anne, Stefan Louis, Christopher James, Rebecca Blair. Speech, lang. and voice pathologist Rehab. Center of So. Fairfield County, Stamford, Conn., 1969, Sch. Health Program-P.A. 481, Stamford, 1969-72; pvt. practice speech, lang. and voice pathology, Scarsdale, N.Y., 1972—; cons. Bd. Coop. Ednl. Services, 1976-79, Handicapped Program for Preschoolers for Alcott Montessori Sch., Ardsley, N.Y., 1978—; research methodologist Burke Rehab. Center, 1977. Mem. profl. adv. bd. Found. for Children with Learning Disabilities, 1978—. Lic. speech and lang. pathologist, N.Y. State; Rehab. Services Adminstrn. fellow, 1968-69; N.Y. Med. Coll. fellow, 1972-75. Bd. dirs. United Way of Scarsdale-Edgemont, 1988—. Mem. N.Y. Speech and Hearing Assn., Westchester Speech and Hearing Assn., Am. Speech, Hearing and Lang. Assn. (cert. clin. competence), Council for Exceptional Children, Assn. on Mental Deficiency, Am. Acad. Pvt. Practice in Speech Pathology and Audiology (bd. dirs., treas. 1983-87, pres. 1987—), Internat. Assn. Logopedics and Phoniatrics, Sigma Alpha Eta. Contbr. articles to profl. jours. Office: PO Box 1242 Scarsdale NY 10583

ROGELL, IRMA ROSE, harpsichordist; b. Malden, Mass.; d. M. Edward and Sara (Freedman) Rose; A.B., Radcliffe Coll.; student Wanda Landowska; m. Bernard C. Rogell (dec. 1964); children—Gerald, Gillian, Michael. Profl. debut Boston Jordan Hall, 1960; N.Y. debut, 1961; soloist with symphony orchs. including: Boston Symphony Orch., Brazil Symphony; European concert tours; radio-TV appearances; rec. artist Titanic Records, Protone; mem. faculty CUNY, 1973-78, Ethical Culture Sch. of N.Y.; guest lectr.-recitalist at various colls. and univs.; vis. faculty mem. Longy Sch. Music, Cambridge, Mass. Mem. Coll. Music Soc., Piano Tchrs. Congress N.Y. (sec.). Jewish. Club: Harvard (N.Y.C.). Home and Studio: 31 Devon Rd Newton Center MA 02159

ROGERS, AILENE KANE, educator; b. Jamaica, N.Y., Jan. 17, 1938; d. Daniel H. and Helen (Shirkey) Kane; B.A., Middlebury Coll., 1959; M.S., Am. U., 1963; m. Edward Lee Rogers, Nov. 18, 1961; children—Ruth, John, Helen, Daniel. Asst. dir. program Student Conservation Assn., Charlestown, N.H., 1959-60; dir., 1960; teaching asst. Am. U., Washington, 1961-62, naturalist Nat. Park Service, 1966-68; tchr. sci. Hauppaugue (N.Y.) Middle Sch., 1972-73; tchr. sci. Oak Grove Coburn Sch., Vassalboro, Maine, 1974-75, head sci. dept., 1976-79; tchr. sci. lower sch. Nat. Cathedral Sch., Washington, 1979-82, tchr. sci. upper sch., 1982—; counselor Sci. Camp, The Potomac Sch., McLean, Va., summers 1982—, dir. sci. camp, 1986—; lectr. Young Assoc. Program Smithsonian Inst., Jan., Feb., 1988. Founder Setauket Environ. Ctr., 1970, bd. govs., 1970-72; bd. dirs. Student Conservation Program, 1970-79; cons. Sch. Wide Environ. Edn. Program, N.Y.C., 1978; cons. edn. programs Nat. Geog. Soc., 1980—; founder, chmn. Pittston (Maine) Conservation Commn., 1975-78; co-pres. McLean High Sch. Student-Parent-Tchr. Assn., 1982-84. NSF grantee, 1962. Mem. Nat. Parks and Conservation Assn., Student Conservation Assn., Nature Conservancy (dir. Maine chpt. 1976-78). Club: The Grange (Pittston, Maine). Home: 6601 Jerry Pl McLean VA 22101 Office: Nat Cathedral Sch for Girls Mount Saint Albans Washington DC 20016

ROGERS, ALICE BRADSHAW, public relations and advertising executive; b. Dayton, Tex., Sept. 18, 1911; d. William Benjamin and Mannie Willis (Davis) Bradshaw; m. Evert A. Rogers, Aug. 17, 1934 (div. May 1950); children—Jane Rogers Matthews, Elizabeth Rogers Bannister, Nancy Lynn Rogers Stephanow. Student U. Tex., 1927-29, U. Houston, 1953, 59. Sec., Henry L. Doherty, stocks and bonds, 1930-33, L.E. Norton Real Estate, 1933-34, Fisk Electric Co., 1934-37; sec.-treas. Art Engraving Co., 1937-49, pres., 1949-50; pres. Advt. Arts Bldg. Corp., 1952-54, Houston Tradetypers, 1955-57, Goodwin-Dannenbaum Advt. Agy., 1957; dir., sec.-treas., pres. Art Engraving Co., Inc.; dir., pres. Advt. Arts Bldg. Corp.; pub. relations dir. Houston Youth Symphony, 1962-64; bus. relations dir. Better Bus. Bur., Houston; community club awards dir. Houston Chronicle, 1963-64; activities coordinator Houston Club, editor, bus. mgr. The Houston Clubber, 1964-83. Mem. adv. bd. Achievement Rewards Coll. Scientists Found.; dist. chmn. publicity bd. Girl Scouts U.S.A., 1946-50; mem. publicity com. United Fund, 1952-54; mem. advt. program com. Pin Oak Horse Show, Houston Fat Stock Show. Mem. Advt. Fedn. Am. (dir. 10th dist. 1955-81, Sterling Silver award 1978), Houston Advt. Fedn. (Outstanding Woman of Yr. award 1981, Alice B. Rogers Edn. Fund established 1982), Houston Soc. Assn. Execs., Houston Advt. Club (hon. life, v.p., dir., sec.-treas., Disting. Service mem., Silver medal award 1979), Harris County Heritage Soc., Houston C. of C., Gamma Alpha Chi. Clubs: Press (life) (Houston); Mothers (Zeta Tau Alpha). Home: 2501 Lazy Hollow Apt 110B Houston TX 77063

ROGERS, AMY, management consultant; b. Wilmington, Del., May 14, 1947; d. Samuel and Dorothy (Chassen) R. BA in Govt., Am. U., 1969; MSW, Yeshiva U., 1975. Cert. social worker, N.Y. Social worker psychiat. Kings Psychiat. Ctr., N.Y.C., 1975; exec. asst. city council mem. Henry Berger, N.Y.C., 1977; dir. home healthcare services People Care, N.Y.C., 1978-79; exec. asst. Nat. Jewish Archives Broadcasting, N.Y.C., 1982-84; dir. tng. and devel. dept. fin. N.Y.C., 1984—; cons. Amy Rogers Assocs., N.Y.C., 1980-83; trainer sales Bloomingdales, N.Y.C., 1983-84. Mem. People for Am. Way, N.Y.C., 1985-87, Nat. Abortion Rights Action League, N.Y.C., 1985-87. Named Hon. Citizen Md., Gov. Tawes, 1964; recipient Americanism medal, Am. Legion, 1964. Mem. Am. Soc. Tng. and Devel. (Chat. award 1987). Democrat. Home: 760 W End Ave New York NY 10025

ROGERS, BONNIE JEAN, real estate salesperson; b. Hartley, Iowa, May 24, 1947; d. Albert and Katherine Lucille (DeLaney) Tapp; m. James Edward Rogers Apr. 23, 1967 (dec. May 1974); children: Jason Eric, Kelly Renea. Grad. high sch., Scottsdale, Ariz. With engrng. dept./ Western Electric Co., Sunnyvale, Calif., 1965-74; pvt. investigator San Jose, Calif., 1975-77; pvt. practice real estate sales person San Jose, 1978-82; real estate sales person Century-21, Campbell, Calif., 1982—; chairperson communications dept. San Jose Real Estate Bd., Calif., 1986, mem. local govt. relations com., 1986-87. Mem. Calif. Assn. Realtors (vice chmn. communications for No. Calif. 1986, state dir. 1982-86). Home: 6393 Bancroft Way San Jose CA 95129 Office: Century 21 Advance 2315 S Bascom Ave Campbell CA 95008

ROGERS, BRENDA GAYLE, educational administrator, educator, consultant; b. Atlanta, July 27, 1949; d. Claude Thomas and Louise (Williams) Todd; m. Emanuel Julius Jones, Jr., Dec. 17, 1978; children: Lavelle, Brandon. BA, Spelman Coll., 1970; MA, Atlanta U., 1971, EdS, 1972; PhD, Ohio State U., 1975; postgrad. Howard U., 1980, Emory U., 1986. Program devel. specialist HEW, Atlanta, 1972; research assoc. Ohio State U., Columbus, 1973-75; asst. prof. spl. edn. Atlanta U., 1975-78, program adminstr., 1978—, CIT project dir., 1977—; tech. cons. Dept. Edn., Washington, 1978, 80, 82, 85, 86; due process regional hearing officer Ga. State Dept Edn., Atlanta, 1978-84, adv. bd., 1980-84. Mem. Ga. Assessment Project com.; Atlanta Pub. Schs. Adv. Council, 1986—, Hidden Lake Civic Assn., Decatur, Ga., 1978—; bd. dirs. SW Montessori Sch., Atlanta, 1980, Malibu Civic Assn., College Park, Ga., 1977-78; mem. Grady Meml. Hosp. Community Action Network, Atlanta, 1982-83. Recipient disting. service award Atlanta Bur. Pub. Safety, 1982, award Atlanta Pub. Sch. System, 1980, 82, 83; fellow Ohio State U., 1972-74, Howard U., 1980; mem. Assn. for Retarded Citizens, Council for Exceptional Children: Phi Delta Kappa, Phi Lambda Theta. Democrat. Roman Catholic. Avocation: gourmet cooking. Office: Atlanta U 233 James P Brawley Atlanta GA 30314

ROGERS, CINDY MARIE, accountant; b. Harlingen, Tex., June 29, 1959; d. William M. and Bettye (Waters) R. BBA summa cum laude, Tex. A&M U., 1981. CPA, Tex. Audit staff Arthur Andersen & Co., San Antonio, 1981-83, audit sr., 1983-85, audit mgr., 1985-86; dir. fin. reporting Harte-Hanks Communications, Inc., San Antonio, 1986-88, dir. operational fin., 1988—. Allocations vol. United Way, San Antonio, 1987-88. Mem. Am. Inst. CPA's, Tex. Soc. CPA's, Nat. Assn. of Accts (treas. 1983-84). Republican. Roman Catholic. Club: Los Amigos Ski. Office: Harte-Hanks Communications Inc 7710 Jones Maltsberger San Antonio TX 78216

ROGERS, DOLORES MCMANUS, training company executive; b. Bellflower, Calif., Mar. 31, 1936; d. Joseph John and Thelma Joanne (Hinds) McManus Miller; m. Michael Creighton Rogers, Nov. 26, 1971; children—Michael Creighton II, Eric Grinnell, Blake Lawrence. m. Clinton Lewis Byers, Jr., Aug. 2, 1958 (div. Mar. 1971). B.S., UCLA, 1957. Sales promotion staff Georgia Bullock, Inc., Los Angeles, 1957-62, v.p. sales promotion, 1962-66; dir. sales promotion Travilla, Los Angeles, 1966-71; owner, mgr. Exec. Assocs., Sherman Oaks, Calif., 1975—. Bd. dirs. Coldwater Counseling Ctr., Studio City, Calif., 1974-76; rec. sec. Las Donas, Los Angeles, 1979—. Mem. Am. Soc. Tng. and Devel., Fashion Group, AAUW. Republican. Episcopalian. Clubs: Sherman Oaks C. of C., UCLA Alumni Assn., Kappa Kappa Gamma. Avocations: cooking; reading; travel; golf; needlework. Home: 3906 Stone Canyon Rd Sherman Oaks CA 91403 Office: Executive Assocs 15015 Ventura Blvd Sherman Oaks CA 91403

ROGERS, DOROTHY SARA, college adminstrator; b. Melrose, Mass., Feb. 1, 1929; d. Robert J. and Sadie (Gardner) Nathan; m. Alan David Rogers, Jan. 21, 1951; children—Joan Rogers Leopold, Leslie S. B.S., Simmons Coll., 1950; student NYU, 1965, N.H. Coll., 1962. Trainee, service exec. Jordan Marsh Co., Boston, 1950-51; buyer sportswear and dresses Rogers Co., Inc., Manchester, N.H., 1952-55; fashion cons. Internat. Shoe Corp., St. Louis and Manchester, 1955-56; promotion cons. Pandora Industries, N.Y.C. also Manchester, 1956-57; fashion dir. Manchester Union Leader Corp., 1959-60; cons. sales tng. and fashion promotion The Lynch Co., Manchester, 1957-58; instr. distributive edn. City of Manchester, 1955-72; asst. prof. principles of mktg. and retailing N.H. Coll., 1972-74, dir. coop. edn., 1976-83, dir. career devel. ctr., 1983—; cons. New Eng. Mut. Life Ins. Co., Boston, 1981-83. Author: Retailing Cases for Analysis, 1979, Faskin: A Marketing Approach, 1983, Retailing: New Perspectives, 1988. Prin., ptnr. RG Cons., Manchester, N.H., 1976—; speaker various assns.; cons. Northeastern U., Boston, 1980, 1984; mem. Com. for Internat. Student Exchange, U.S. Dept. State, 1980. Author: Fashion: A Marketing Approach, 1983, Retailing: New Perspectives, 1988. Mem. Coop. Edn. Assn., New Eng. Assn. Coop. Edn. and Field Experience, Nat. Soc. Internships and Exptl. Edn., Am. Mktg. Assn., Nat. Retail Merchants Assn., Am. Collegiate Retailing Assn., N.H. Com. for Vocat. Edn. (dir.), AAUP, N.H. Women in Higher Edn., Eastern Coll. Personnel Officers. Republican. Jewish. Office: New Hampshire Coll 2500 N River Rd Manchester NH 03104

ROGERS, EVELYN EICHEL, psychologist; b. Bklyn., Nov. 26, 1956; d. Simon and Maria (Ungerleider) Eichel; married. BA, SUNY, Stony Brook, 1978; MA, Hofstra U., 1980, PhD, 1982. Research assoc. Am. Mgmt. Assn., N.Y.C., 1979-81, asst. to dir. research, 1981-82; mgmt. devel. assoc. PepsiCo, Purchase, N.Y., 1982-83, mgr. mgmt. devel., 1983-84; mgr. mgmt. devel. Pepsi Cola Corp., Purchase, 1984-86; mgr. human resource planning and ops. Young and Rubicam, N.Y.C., 1986-87, dir. people devel. and info., 1987—; supr. Hofstra U. grad. intern program, N.Y.C., 1986—. Mem. Am. Psychol. Assn., Human Resource Planning Soc. (membership com. 1986—, newsletter editor 1988—). Jewish. Home: 11 River Rd 101 Palmer Point Cos Cob CT 06807

ROGERS, GINGER (VIRGINIA KATHERINE MCMATH), dancer, actress; b. Independence, Mo., July 16, 1911; d. William Eddins and Lela Emogene (Owens) McMath; m. Edward Jackson Culpepper (div.); m. Lew Ayers (div.); m. Jack Briggs (div.); m. Jacques Bergerac (div.); m. G. William Marshall (div.). Ed. pub. schs. Began as a child dancer, 1926; appeared in motion pictures, 1930—; starred in Broadway prodn: Girl Crazy, 1929-30; danced with Fred Astaire in Flying Down to Rio, 1933, has co-starred with Astaire in numerous motion picture prodns. including Roberta, Shall We Dance, Top Hat, Gay Divorcee, Follow the Fleet, Swing Time; other movie appearances include Teenage Rebel, Twenty Million Sweethearts, Change of Heart, Chance at Heaven, The Sap from Syracuse, Sitting Pretty, Young Man of Manhattan, Star of Midnight, Top Hat, In Person, Golddiggers of 1933, Stagedoor, Vivacious Lady, Having a Wonderful Time, O Men O Women, Harlow, Carefree, The Story of Vernon and Irene Castle, Bachelor Mother, Fifth Avenue Girl, Primrose Path, Lucky Partners, Kitty Foyle (Acad. award for Best Actress, 1940), Tom, Dick and Harry, Roxy Hart, The Confession, The Major and The Minor, Tales of Manhattan, Once Upon a Honeymoon, Lady in the Dark, Tender Comrade, I'll Be Seeing You, Week-end at the Waldorf, Heartbeat, Magnificent Doll, It Had to Be You, Barkleys of Broadway, Perfect Strangers, Storm Warning, The Groom Wore Spurs, We Are Not Married, Monkey Business, Forever Female, Dreamboat, Twist of Fate, Black Widow; TV appearances include Perry Como Show, Bob Hope Show; star stage plays Hello Dolly, 1965, Mame, 1969; dir. play Babes in Arms, 1987.

ROGERS, GLENNA JOAN, media relations executive; b. Terre Haute, Ind., May 25, 1947; d. Glenn Norman and Joan (Smith) Felling; m. George E. Rogers, May 25, 1975. BE, Ind. State U., 1970. Real estate assoc. Meneely-Williams, Terre Haute, 1980-85; corp. conf. coordinator Unidynamics Corp., Stamford, Conn., 1982-85; media relations exec. GTE Corp., Stamford, Conn., 1985—; bd. dirs. GTE Employees Assn. Mem. Westchester/Fairfield County Meeting Planners. Mem. Delta Gamma. Republican. Presbyterian. Club: Century. Home: 1330 High Ridge Rd Stamford CT 06903

ROGERS, HARRIET ROWLEY, health and physical education educator; b. Utica, N.Y., Sept. 3, 1908; d. Henry Waite and Lulu Cornelia (Childs) Rowley; m. Raymond H. Rogers, June 25, 1932; children: Raymond M., Merrilyn H., Don R. B Phys. Edn., NYU, 1929; BS in Health and Phys. Edn., U. Cin., 1932, MA in Edn., 1933. Instr. U. Cin., 1929-33, Duke U., Durham, N.C., 1939-42, Cooperstown High Sch., N.Y., 1956-72, summer session Oneonta State U., N.Y., 1965, Montgomery County Community Coll., Gloversville, N.Y., 1967; mem. sch. community com. Cooperstown Central Sch., 1983—. Contbr. articles to local history publs. Town historian Middlefield, N.Y., 1967—; pres., curator, bd. dirs. Middlefield Hist. Assn., 1965—; pres. bd. trustees Meth. Ch. Recipient Community Service award Cooperstown VFW Aux., 1980, Merit award Regional Conf. Hist. Agy., 1980. Fellow Am. Sch. Health Assn.; mem. N.Y. State Ret. Tchrs. Assn., Otsego County Ret. Tchrs. Assn., DAR (regent 1976-79, historian 1980—), Dau. Founders and Patriots Am. Delta Kappa Gamma (pres. 1975-76). Republican. Club: Criterion. Lodges: Red Creek Valley Grange (lectr. 1945-47, sec. 1965-75, treas. 1983-86, 87—). Co-author: Bicentennial History Main Street Cooperstown, N.Y., 1988. Avocations: swimming, volunteering, jogging, writing,; hist. research. Home: 63 B Chestnut St Cooperstown NY 13326

ROGERS, HELEN EVELYN WAHRGREN, newspaperwoman; b. Tacoma, Jan. 24, 1924; d. John Sigurd and Emma Elina (Carlson) Wahrgren; B.A., U. Wash., Seattle, 1946; m. Charles Dana Rogers, July 24, 1948. Mem. editorial staff Holiday mag., Phila., 1946; civilian public relations writer, Ft. Lewis, Wash., 1946-47; asst. society editor Tacoma News Tribune-Sunday Ledger, 1947-51, radio-TV editor-columnist, 1951-86. Author: What's Your Line? vol. I: Delila Sprague Sherburne Harrington: Her Ancestors and Descendants. Mem. Newspaper Guild, Wis. Geneal. Soc., Tacoma-Pierce County Geneal. Soc., U. Wash. Alumni Assn. Democrat. Lutheran. Home: 2906 N 24th St Tacoma WA 98406 Office: 2906 N 24th St Tacoma WA 98406

ROGERS, IRENE, librarian; b. Yonkers, N.Y., Oct. 12, 1932; d. Franklyn Harold and Mary Margaret (Nealy) R.; B.S. in Edn., New Paltz State Tchrs. Coll., 1954; M.L.S. (N.Y. State Tng. grantee), Columbia U., 1959. Tchr., West Babylon (N.Y.) Sch. System, 1954-57, Yonkers Sch. System, 1957-58; reference librarian Yonkers Pub. Library, 1959-67, adult services coordinator, 1967-73, asst. library dir., 1973—. Mem. Mayor's Adv. Com. Consumer Edn., Yonkers, 1970—; active United Way of Yonkers; mem. curriculum adv. com., report card revision com. Office Supt. Schs., 1982; mem. Yonkers unit Am. Cancer Soc. West Library System grantee, 1966. Mem. ALA, Westchester, N.Y. library assns. Club: Soroptimist (pres. 1978-79, 80-81, sec. dist. I North Atlantic region), Bus. and Profl. Women's (Yonkers). Home: 41 Amackassin Terr Yonkers NY 10703 Office: 7 Main St Yonkers NY 10701

ROGERS, JANSIE, art and decorating company executive; b. Lenoir, N.C., Feb. 22, 1939; d. Raymond L. and Ruth (Henley) Setzer; m. G.R. Walter Rogers, June 23, 1963; (div. July 1984); children: Rob, Sharon. BA, James Madison U., 1961. Cert. custom decorator. Pub. sch. tchr., Baltimore County, Md., 1960-63, Perryville, Md., 1975-77; custom decorator Transart Industries, Woodstock, Ga., 1977-78, design dir., 1978-82, nat. dir. Trans Designs, Woodstock, 1982—. Bd. dirs. YMCA, Nat. Multiple Sclerosis Soc., Arthritis Found. Recipient awards including trips abroad, mink coats, diamonds TransDesigns, 1977-86. Mem. The Female Exec., Am. Bus. Women's Assn., LWV, Howard County C. of C. Democrat. Avocations: tennis, racquetball. Home and Office: 7554 Weatherworn Way Columbia MD 21046

ROGERS, JOAN CAROL, occupational therapist, educator; b. Buffalo, July 31, 1941; d. Andrew Stephen and Antoinette Marie (Stopinski) R. BS, Canisius, 1966; MA, U. So. Calif., 1968; PhD in Philosophy, U. Ill., 1975. Asst. clin. prof. SUNY, Buffalo, 1969-72; asst. prof. U. So. Calif., Los Angeles, 1974-77; assoc. prof. U. N.C., Chapel Hill, 1978-84; prof. U. Pitts., 1984—; faculty assoc. Geriatric Edn. Ctr. Pa., Pitts., 1985—. contbr. articles to profl. jours. Third Brookdale Visiting scholar Brookdale Inst. Columbia U., 1983. Fellow Am. Occupational Therapy Assn. (Eleanor Clarke Slagle lectr. 1983, research acad. award 1984); mem. Gerontol. Soc. Am., Am. Psychol. Assn. Roman Catholic. Office: U Pitts WPIC 3811 O'Hara St Pittsburgh PA 15213

ROGERS, JUDITH W., state judge. AB cum laude, Radcliffe Coll., 1961; LLB, Harvard U., 1964; LLM, U. Va., 1988. Bar: D.C. 1965. Law clk. Juvenile Ct. D.C., 1964-65; asst. atty. D.C., 1965-68; trial atty. San Francisco Neighborhood Legal Assistance Found., 1968-69; atty. U.S. Dept. Justice, 1969-71; gen. counsel Congl. Commn. on Organization of D.C. Govt., 1971-72; coordinator legis. program Office of Dep. Mayor D.C., 1972-74, spl. asst. to mayor for legis., 1974-79, asst. city adminstr. for intergovtl. relations, 1979, corp. counsel, 1979-83; assoc. judge D.C. Ct. Appeals, 1983—; mem. D.C. Law Revision Commn., 1979-83, Mayor's Commn. on Crime and Justice, 1982, vis. com. Harvard Law Sch., 1984—; trustee Radcliffe Coll., 1982—; mem. grievance com. U.S. Dist. Ct. for D.C., 1982-83. Bd. dirs. Wider Opportunities for Women, 1972-74, Friends of the D.C. Superior Ct., 1972-74. Mem. ABA, Phi Beta Kappa. Office: DC Ct of Appeals 500 Indiana Ave NW Washington DC 20001

ROGERS, JUDY, social worker; b. Newark, Jan. 29, 1943; d. John Oliver and Grace (Daniels) R.; A.B. with honors in Sociology, Dickinson Coll., 1965; M.S.W., N.Y.U., 1970; 1 child. Kimani. Coordinator social rehab., anti-recidivism project, Jersey City. 1967-68; therapist Bklyn. Psychiat. Centers, 1970-72; counselor VIP Med. Assocs., N.Y.C., 1972-73; clin. coordinator Harlem Center for Child Study, Harlem Hosp., N.Y.C., 1973—, co-chmn. staff devel. com., 1983-85, coordinator day treatment programs child adolescent psychiatry div., 1988—; therapist family support demonstration project Psychiat. Inst. N.Y.; field instr. Sch. Social Work, Columbia U.; mem. profl. adv. com. James Weldon Johnson Mental Health Center, 1980-86. First v.p. Parents Assn., Hunter Coll. Elem. Sch. 1981-82, pres. Black Parents Group, 1982-84; treas. Black Task Force on Child Abuse; active Operation Crossroads Africa, 1963, U.S. Youth Council, 1966-68. Recipient Gaylord H. Patterson Meml. prize for sociology, 1965. Mem. Nat. Assn. Social Workers (bd. dirs. N.Y.C. chpt., chmn. child and family advocacy com.), Nat. Assn. Black Social Workers. Office: 121 W 128th St New York NY 10027

ROGERS, KAREN BROWN, financial planning executive; b. Dallas, Apr. 6, 1960; d. Donald Eugene and Janice Ellen (Rademacher) Brown; m. Mark Elliott Rogers, Oct. 4, 1986. BBA in Acctg., Tex. Tech U, 1982. CPA, Tex. Sr. auditor Coopers & Lybrand, Dallas, 1982-84; fin. planning mgr. STB Systems, Inc., Richardson, Tex., 1984—. Mem. Am. Inst. CPA's, Am. Women's Soc. CPA's, Dallas Chpt. Am. Women's Soc. CPA's, Tex. Soc. CPA's, Dallas Chpt. Tex. Soc. CPA's, The 500, Inc., Beta Alpha Psi, Gamma Phi Beta Alumni. Republican. Methodist. Club: Prestonwood Newcomers (Dallas). Office: STB Systems Inc 1651 N Glenville Suite 210 Richardson TX 75081

ROGERS, KAREN GAIL, state agency administrator; b. Winnemucca, Nev., Sept. 18, 1955; d. Arthur M. and Meryde G. (Brown) English; m. William L. Ware, June 9, 1973 (div. 1979); children: Bill, Brandon, Jason,; m. Michael D. Rogers, Sept. 6, 1980; 1 stepchild, Paula. AA, No. Community Coll., Winnemucca, 1985. Inventory machine operator Automated Inventorier of Hawaii, Honolulu, 1977-78; acct. maintenance supply clk. U.S. Commissary, Schofield Barracks, Hawaii, 1978; dispatcher Humboldt County Sheriff's Dept., Winnemucca, 1979; youth supr. Humboldt County Juvenile Probation Dept., Winnemucca, 1979-80; program aide Humboldt County and UNR (4-H program), Winnemucca, 1980-81; adminstrv. aide Nev. Dept. of Transp., Winnemucca, 1982-84, mgmt. asst., 1984—. Treas.

Winnemucca Little League Baseball, 1985-87; den leader Winnemucca Cub Scouts, 1981. Mem. DAR (mem. Reno chpt.), Internat. Rainbow for Girls (hon.), Nat. Assn. Female Execs., Cert. Profl. Secs., No. Nev. Hist. Soc., Humbodt County Genealog. Soc., Beta Sigma Phi (sec. 1980-87). Republican. Lodge: Order of Eastern Star. Home: PO Box 745 Winnemucca NV 89445 Office: Nev State Dept of Transp PO Box 326 Winnemucca NV 89445

ROGERS, KATE ELLEN, educator; b. Nashville, Dec. 13, 1920; d. Raymond Lewis and Louise (Gruver) R.; M.A. in Fine Arts, George Peabody Coll., 1947; Ed.D. in Fine Arts and Fine Arts Edn., Columbia U., 1956. Instr., Tex. Tech. Coll., Lubbock, 1947-53; co-owner, v.p. Design Today, Inc., Lubbock, 1951-54; student asst. Am. House, N.Y.C., 1953-54; asst. prof. housing and interior design U. Mo., Columbia, 1954-56, assoc. prof., 1956-66, prof., 1966-85,. emeritus, 1985—, chmn. dept. housing and interior design, 1973-85; mem. accreditation com. Found. for Interior Design Edn. Research, 1975-76, chmn. standards com., 1976-82, chmn. research, 1982-85. Nat. Endowment for Arts research grantee, 1981-82. Mem. Interior Design Educators Council (pres. 1971-73, chmn. bd. 1974-76, chmn. research com. 1977-78), Am. Soc. Interior Designers, (hon.), Am. Home Econs. Assn., Soc. Archtl. Historians. Democrat. Author: The Modern House, USA, 1962; editor Jour. Interior Design Edn. and Research, 1975-78.

ROGERS, KATHARINE MUNZER, educator; b. N.Y.C., June 6, 1932; d. Martin and Jean (Thompson) Munzer; B.A. summa cum laude, Barnard Coll., 1952; Fulbright scholar, Newnham Coll., Cambridge U., 1952-53; Ph.D., Columbia U., 1957; m. Kenneth C. Rogers, Aug. 4, 1956; children—Margaret, Christopher, Thomas. Instr. English, Skidmore Coll., Saratoga Springs, N.Y., 1954-55, Cornell U., 1955-57; lectr. to prof. English, Bklyn. Coll., 1958—; mem. doctoral faculty City U. N.Y. Mem. MLA. Author: The Troublesome Helpmate: A History of Misogyny in Literature, 1966; William Wycherley, 1972; Feminism in Eighteenth Century England, 1982. Editor anthologies: The Signet Classic Book of 18th and 19th Century British Drama; Selected Writings of Samuel Johnson, 1981; co-editor: (with William McCarthy) The Meridian Anthology of Early Women Writers: British Literary Women from Aphra Behn to Maria Edgeworth, 1987. Contbr. articles to profl. jours. Home: 6202 Perthshire Ct Bethesda MD 20817 Office: Dept English Bklyn Coll Brooklyn NY 11210

ROGERS, KAY FRANCES KIRBY, educator; b. Hickory, N.C., Nov. 19, 1940; d. Rufus Fredrick and Lois Pauline Kirby; m. John Thomas Rogers Jr., July 19, 1970. BA, Furman U., 1963; MA, Appalachian State Univ., 1969; Ednl. Specialist degree, U. N.C., Charlotte, 1984. Tchr. Montclaire Sch., Charlotte, N.C., 1963-69, 72-74, Frankfurt (Mil.) Schs., Germany, 1969-70, Druid Hills Sch., Charlotte, 1970-72, Amay James Sch., Charlotte, 1974-83, Sharon Sch., Charlotte, 1983—. Mem. Am. Assn. U. Women, Phi Delta Kappa. Republican. Baptist. Home: 2730 Rothwood Dr Charlotte NC 28211 Office: Sharon Sch 4330 Foxcroft Rd Charlotte NC 28211

ROGERS, LESLIE LOUISE, banker; b. Detroit, Aug. 20, 1952; d. William Edward and Eulalla Louise (Griffith) R.; m. Richard Van Buren Manix, July 13, 1984; children: Catherine Griffith, James Leighfield. BA, U. Mich., 1973. Bus. analyst Dun and Bradstreet, Inc., N.Y.C., 1974-76; asst. treas. Bankers Trust Co., N.Y.C., 1976-79; v.p. Marine Midland Bank, N.A., N.Y.C., 1979-87, Generale Bank, N.Y.C., 1987—. Mem. Greenacres Oil Purchasing Consortium, Scarsdale, N.Y.; mem. Hitchcock Presbyn. Ch., Scarsdale. Mem. Nat. Assn. Female Execs., Nat. Assn. Bank Women, U. Mich. Alumnae Club, U. Mich. Alumni Club N.Y. Republican. Home: 102 Greenacres Ave Scarsdale NY 10583 Office: Generale Bank-NY Br 12 E 49th St 22d Floor New York NY 10017

ROGERS, LISA (BOONE), marketing executive; b. Deoles, France, Oct. 27, 1958; d. Albert G. and Phyllis Frances (Venneman) R. BA in Journalism, U. S.C., 1980. Mktg. asst. Fripp Island (S.C.) Co., 1980-82; dir. sales Seabrook Island Co., Charleston, S.C., 1982-83; dir. advt. Vail (Colo.) Assocs., Inc., 1983-86; v.p. mktg. Trammell Crow Co., Atlanta, 1986—. Mem. Atlanta High Mus., All Saints Ch. Mem. Nat. Assn. Exec. Women, Club Mgrs. Assn. Am. Republican. Episcopalian. Office: The Vinings Club 2859 Paces Ferry Rd Suite 200 Atlanta GA 30339

ROGERS, LISA HENNING, college administrator; b. Jersey City, Aug. 22, 1959; d. George Frank and June Phyllis (Fegely) Henning; m. Leo Paul Rogers Jr., May 27, 1984. BA, Coll. of William and Mary, 1981, postgrad.; MSW in Adminstrn., Rutgers U., 1983. Asst. coordinator Rutgers U., New Brunswick, N.J., 1981-83; ednl. rep. March of Dimes, Fairfield, N.J., 1983-84; dir. facilities Coll. of William & Mary, Williamsburg, Va., 1984—; cons. Child Devel. Resources, Williamsburg, 1984—. Surrogate Union County Gary Hart for President, Elizabeth, N.J., 1984; vol. Big Sisters Program, Williamsburg, 1985—; mem. Chisel Run Homeowners Assn., Williamsburg. Recipient Garden State scholar State of N.J., 1977-81, George Anderson Meml. scholar Coll. of William & Mary, 1977-78, Chubb Found. scholar Chubb & Son, Inc., Short Hills, N.J., 1977-81. Mem. Am. Coll. Personnel Assn. (bd. dirs. 1980-81), Assn. of Coll. Unions Internat., Psy Chi, Kappa Delta Pi. Democrat. Lutheran. Home: 5406 Trudy Ln Williamsburg VA 23185 Office: Coll William & Mary Campus Ctr Williamsburg VA 23186

ROGERS, MARGARET GAY, insurance executive; b. Ketona, Ala., Mar. 25, 1937; d. James Elbert and Margaret Louis (Nolde) Haigler, Jr.; student Massey Bus. Coll., 1957; m. Douglas Earl Rogers, June 30, 1975. Tng., inventory clk. Goodwill Industries, Ft. Wayne, Ind., 1959; with Ala. Title Co., Inc., Birmingham, 1963, file clk., asst. bookkeeper, 1965, policy clk., asst. bookkeeper, 1966, asst. bookkeeper, exec. asst. to pres., 1975—. Supporter numerous civic orgns. Mem. Nat. Fraternal Soc. of the Deaf. Republican. Lutheran. Home: 111 2d St Robinwood Birmingham AL 35217 Office: 2233 2d Ave N Birmingham AL 35203

ROGERS, MARIANNE, labor association political executive; b. Passaic, N.J., Sept. 8, 1954; d. Bart and Adele R.; m. Frank Preston Drozak, Apr. 6, 1984. Student, Mary Washington Coll., 1972-73, Monmouth Coll., 1973-76. With personal staff Gov. Brendan Byrne, N.J., 1975-76; legis. asst. Congressman Leo Zefretti, N.Y., 1976-78; with Com. on Merchant Marine and Fisheries U.S. Ho. of Reps., Washington, 1978-80; nat. dir., asst. to pres. Seafarers Internat. Union of N.Am., Camp Springs, Md., 1980—; mem. com. on polit. edn. AFL-CIO, Washington, 1980—, exec. bd. Md. and D.C. sects. Mem. Rep. Nat. Labor Adv. Com., Labor Adv. Council Dem. Nat. Commn. Mem. U.S. Navy League, Nat. Women's Polit. Caucus. Roman Catholic. Clubs: Nat. Propeller, Nat. Democratic, Capitol Hill. Office: Seafarers Internat Union N Am AFL-CIO 5201 Auth Way Camp Springs MD 20746

ROGERS, MARIANNE EDITH, insurance broker, insurance agency executive; b. Clinton, Mass., Mar.4, 1948; d. George Milton and Marion (Hayes) R. B.A., Clark U., 1970. CPCU Broker, corp. officer George M. Rogers Ins. Agy., Inc., Boylston, Mass., 1972—, corp. clk., 1984—, pres., 1986—. Bd. dirs., mem. human rights com. Worcester Area Assn. Retarded Children (Mass.), 1981—; area coordinator for South Worcester County, Mass. Spl. Olympics, 1984-85; bd. dirs. Worcester Foothills Theatre Co., 1981-82, Little Theatre Stage Co. Inc., Worcester, 1983-84; mem. exec. com. March of Dimes, Worcester, 1983-84; mem. adv. bd. Occupational Tng. Ctr., Worcester, 1984—; mem. diocesan communications com. Episcopal Diocese of Western Mass., 1979; mem. vestry, lay reader Episcopal Ch. of the Good Shepherd, Clinton, Mass. Named Outstanding Young Leader, Worcester Jaycees, 1982. Mem. Soc. C.P.C.U.s (edn. coordinator Central Mass. chpt. 1980-84, chpt. tchr. 1981-84, chpt. pres. 1983-84), Profl. Ins. Agts. New Eng. (Mass. steering com., bd. dirs., chmn. community relations com. 1984-88, chmn. award com. 1988—; Presdl. citation 1985), Ind. Ins. Agts. Worcester County (bd. dirs. 1982-84). Republican. Club: Worcester Exec. Home: 1053 Pleasant St Worcester MA 01602 Office: George M Rogers Ins Agy Inc 545 Main St Boylston MA 01505

ROGERS, MARTHA, marketing educator; b. Tallahassee, Apr. 30, 1952; d. John Lewis and Ruby Ann (Madsen) R. BA magna cum laude, Birmingham So. Coll., 1974; MA, U. New Orleans, 1979; PhD, U. Tenn., 1983. Advt. copywriter Loveman's, Birmingham, Ala., 1973-74; advt. copywriter Maison Blanche, New Orleans, 1974-76, copy chief advt. dept., 1976-78, advt. dir., 1978; asst. prof. mktg. Bowling Green (Ohio) State U., 1981—; instr. Meadows-Draughon Coll., New Orleans, 1976, U. Tenn., 1981; speaker in field; cons. Elder-Tech Market Assocs, 1983-85, Whitman Ford, Temperance, Mich., 1984-85, Am. Assn. Advt. Agys., N.Y.C., 1985—, Aspen Grill & Cafe, 1985-86, Am. Hair Replacement Systems, Cleve., 1986—, others. Recipient Seklemian Advt. award Seklemian Found., 1975, 76; Karl A. Bickel fellow, 1979-80, 80-81; named Master Tchr. Bowling Green State U., 1987. Mem. Acad. Mktg. Sci., Am. Acad. Advt., Am Advt. Fedn. (edn. com. Toledo chpt. 1984-86), Am. Collegiate Retailing Assn., Am. Mktg. Assn., Assn. Educators in Journalism and Mass Communication, Nat. Advt. Rev. Bd., Phi Beta Kappa, Phi Kappa Phi, Kappa Tau Alpha. Office: Bowling Green State U Dept Mktg Bowling Green OH 43403-0266

ROGERS, NATALIE H., psychotherapist, consultant; b. Bklyn., Oct. 19, 1938; d. Leo and Rose (Kessler) R.; m. harold S. Herbstman, Sept. 20, 1969; 1 child, Colette Hinda Herbstman. AA, N.Y. Tech. Coll., 1975; BA, Baruch Coll., 1977; MS, Columbia U., 1979. Cert. social worker. Artistic dir. Dove Theatre Co., N.Y.C., 1967-73; pres. Talk Power Tng. Seminars, N.Y.C., 1976—; pvt. practice psychotherapy N.Y.C., 1980—; mem. faculty CUNY, Omega Inst. Skiros (Greece) Ctr., Open Ctr., 1975-87, developer Theatre Program for Skiros Ctr., 1984-87; communications cons. to various orgns., corps. and polit. clients, 1975-79; presenter numerous seminars. Author: Talk Power How to Speak Without Fear, 1982. Recipient Disting. Alumni award N.Y. Tech. Coll., 1983; recipient grant Nat. Council on the Arts, 1970, N.Y. State Council on the Arts, 1971; fellow Cornel Med. Coll., 1981. Mem. Assn. for the Advancement of Behavior Therapy, Nat. Assn. of Social Workers, N.Y. State Soc. Clin. Social Work Psychotherapists, Soc. for the Exploration of Psychotherapy Integration. Democrat. Jewish. Home: 333 E 23d St New York NY 10010

ROGERS, PATRICIA DIANNE, elementary educator; b. Walnut Ridge, Ark., Dec. 18, 1943; d. Jack Boggs and Vivian Vallaree (Meadows) Reed; m. Bennie Mack Rogers, Aug. 21, 1965; 1 child, Michael Alan Rogers. AA, Hinds Jr. Coll., 1963; BA in Edn., U. Miss., 1965; MEd, Miss. State U., 1979. Elem. tchr. Bearss Acad., Jackson, Miss., 1966-67, Pearl (Miss.) Elem. Sch., 1967-71; kindergartem tchr. Alta Woods Bapt. Ch., Jackson, 1972-74; elem. tchr. Pearl Upper Elem., 1974—; mem. ann. staff Pearl Upper Elem., 1983—, spelling bee chmn., 1986. Past pres. South Jackson Music Club; block capt. Neighborhood Watch Program, Jackson. Mem. Miss. Profl. Educators, Alpha Delta Kappa (chaplain 1986—). Baptist. Home: 1526 Wood Glen Dr Jackson MS 39204 Office: Pearl Upper Elem 180 Mary Ann Dr Pearl MS 39208

ROGERS, PEGGY PODUSKA, computer marketing; b. Memphis, June 16, 1943; d. Ben F. and Lily (Reid) Poduska; m. Don Carlton Rogers, Nov. 22, 1969. BS in Econ., Auburn U., 1961-64, MBA, 1964-65. Faculty, sch. econ. Auburn U., Auburn, Ala., 1966; systems eng. IBM Corp., Montgomery, Ala., 1966-75; distribution industry mktg. exec. IBM Corp., Atlanta, Ga., 1975-77; systems engrng. mgr. IBM Corp., Atlanta, 1977-79, bus. planning exec., 1979-83, software mktg. exec., 1983-86, distribution industry mktg. exec., 1986—. Mem. Friends of Zoo Atlanta, 1978—; mem. Mt. Paran/ Northside Civic Assn., Atlanta, 1986; mem. Whitewater Creek Neighborhood Assn., Atlanta, 1986—. Mem. Auburn Alumni Assn., Omicron Delta Epsilon, Phi Kappa Phi. Episcopalian.

ROGERS, RUTH LOTTE, fashion consultant; b. Vienna, Austria, Dec. 31; came to U.S., 1938; d. Arnold and Elsie (Zemanek) Karplus; m. Martin C. Rogers, 1938 (div. 1950); m. Hans C. Altmann, Oct. 8, 1965; children: Susan Friedman, Victoria Thorson. Diploma, Kunst Gewerbe Akadamie, Vienna. Design cons. Herzmansky, Vienna, White Stag, N.Y.C., Koret of Calif., N.Y.C.; exec. v.p. R.R.J. Industry, N.Y.C.; now pres. Ruth Rogers Enterprises Internat., N.Y.C.; cons. Oxford Industries, Inc., The Forgotten Woman Stores; cons. Met. Mus. Costume Inst., N.Y.C.; panelist Am. Woman's Econ. Devel. Corp., N.Y.C.; lectr. Shenkar Coll., Tel-Aviv, Israel, Fashion Inst. Tech., N.Y.C. Author fashion and color forecast Burlington Industry; columnist: Knit Notes. Mem. Fashion Group Inc. (chairperson knits com. forecasting trendbook), Fashion News Workshop, Designers Group Nat. Knitwear and Sportswear Assn. (exec. com.), Woman's Fashion Network (charter). Avocations: painting, skiing, art. Home: 71 Park Ave New York NY 10016 Office: Ruth Rogers Enterprises Internat 71 Park Ave New York NY 10016

ROGERS, SHARON J., library administrator; b. Grantsburg, Wis., Sept. 24, 1941; d. Clifford M. and Dorothy L. (Beckman) Dickau; m. Evan D. Rogers, June 15, 1962 (div. Dec. 1980). BA summa cum laude, Bethel Coll., St. Paul, 1963; MA in Library Sci., U. Minn., 1967; PhD in Sociology, Wash. State U., Pullman, 1976. Lectr., instr. Alfred (N.Y.) U., 1972-76; assoc. prof. U. Toledo, 1977-80; assoc. dean Bowling Green (Ohio) State U. Libraries, 1980-84; librarian George Washington U., Washington, 1984—; bd. dirs. Washington Research Library Consortium, 1987—. Author: Science of Knowledge, 1987; contbr. articles to profl. jours. Bd. dirs. ACLU, Toledo, 1978-84, Universal Serials and Book Exchange, 1987—, also treas; bd. dirs. Washington Research Library Consortium, 1987—; bd. dirs., treas. Online Computer Library Ctr. Users Council, 1985—. Jackson fellow U. Minn., 1964-65; NSF trainee Wash. State U., 1969-72. Mem. ALA (exec. council 1987—), Assn. Coll. and Research Libraries (pres. 1984-85), Am. Sociol. Assn., Washington Research Library Consortium (bd. dirs. 1987—), Universal Serials and Book Exchange (bd. dirs., treas. 1987), Online Computer Learning Ctr. (user's council 1985—). Office: George Washington U Gelman Library 2130 H St NW Washington DC 20052

ROGERS, SHARON MARIE, community education administrator; b. Phila., July 22, 1960; d. Glenn Howard Borden and Jean Marie (Kaczorowski) Borden Costello; m. Alfred Pepper Rogers, Jan. 9, 1982; 1 child, Matthew Ryan. BSBA, Phila. Coll. Textiles and Sci., 1981. Spl. projects engr. Caron Internat., Rochelle, Ill., 1981, supr. dyehouse lab., 1982-83, mgr. quality control, 1983-84, mgr. quality assurance , 1984-85; coordinator plant safety Aigner, An Avery Internat. Co., Rochelle, 1986-87, supr. mfg., 1985-87; asst. coordinator community edn. and services Kishwaukee Coll., Malta, Ill., 1987—, adv. council mem., 1987-88; advisor Rock Valley Jr. Achievement, Rochelle, 1984-85; dir. Rochelle Community Child Care Ctr., Rochelle, 1985, 87-88; student recruiter Phila. Coll. Textiles and Sci., 1983—; speaker profl. confs., civic orgns. Contbr. articles to profl. jours. Com. mem. Hillcrest Zoning Bd., Ill., 1984-88; mem. adv. bd. community child care com. Rochelle Area C. of C., 1985; bd. dirs. Rochelle Area Community Chest, 1986-87. Recipient Presdl. award Pres. Richard Nixon, Washington, 1974, Frank Leslie Honor award Textile Vets. Assn., Phila., 1981, Rochelle Young Career Woman award Rochelle Bus. and Profl. Women, 1983; W. W. Smith Found. acad. scholar, Phila., 1980-81, Manpower Found. scholar, Milw., 1980-81. Mem. Nat. Fedn. Bus. and Profl. Women (pres. Rochelle chpt. 1985-86), Ill. Fedn. Bus. and Profl. Women (program chmn. 1985, assoc. dir. 1985-86, dist. VI program award 1985), Am. Assn. Textile Chemists and Colorists (reception chair 1984 Internat. Tech. Conf. and Exhbn. 1982-84), Internat. Assn. Quality Circles (v.p. Kishwaukee Valley chpt. 1983), U.S. Jaycees (sec. Rochelle chpt. 1985). Democrat. Clubs: Young Adults (mem. steering com. 1985), La Leche League, Faith Luth. Ch. Women (Rochelle) (sec. 1988). Avocations: counted cross-stitch, gardening, camping, swimming. Home: 829 N 10th St Rochelle IL 61068 Office: Kishwaukee Coll Rt 38 & Malta Rd Malta IL 60150-0500

ROGERS, SUSAN (SUE), data processing consultant; b. Jonesboro, Ark., Aug. 22, 1949; d. Eric J. Jr. and Suzanne (Payne) R.; m. Joseph Edward Aldrich, July 3, 1974 (div. Mar. 1985). BS in Math, U. Ark., 1975. Cert. computer programmer. Chief programmer State Ark. Dept. Fin. and Adminstrn., Little Rock, 1973-76; programmer, analyst Dillards Dept. Stores, Little Rock, 1976-77; mem. profl. staff Cutler-Williams Inc., Dallas, 1977-79; sr. tech. cons. Sterling Software (formerly Informatics Gen.), Dallas, 1979-86; pvt. practice cons. Dallas, 1986-87; programmer, analyst Fed. Res. Bank, Dallas, 1988—. Exhibitions at State Fair of Tex., 1985-87, Plano Art Assn., 1985, Arlington Art Assn., 1986, North Lake Coll., 1987. Vol. arts and crafts program Dallas County Juvenile Detention Ctr. Mem. Tex. Designer and Craftsmen (exhibition 1986), Craft Guild of Dallas, Bead Soc. of Dallas, North Tex. Enamelist Guild, Direct Jewelers Assn., North Tex. Herb Club, Mensa. Office: 2925 Seymour Dallas TX 75229

ROGERS, VERA ROSALIE, veterinarian; b. Cedar Rapids, Iowa, July 3, 1938; d. Martin V. and Victoria (Kopecek) Polehna; m. L. Wayne Rogers, June 13, 1940; children: Briana Lee, Bard Layne. BS, Kans. State U., 1960, DVM, 1962, MS, 1968. Research assoc. Wash. State U., Pullman, 1962-63; research assoc. Kans. State U., Manhattan, 1963-64, anatomy instr., 1964-67; asst. prof. Ahmadu Bello U., Zaria, Nigeria, 1967-70; clinician Canton (Ohio) South Animal Hosp., 1970-73, Bench Animal Hosp., Boise, Idaho, 1974-76, Relief Vet. Service, Boise area, 1976-84; assoc. prof, dir. animal health tech. N.E. Mo. State U., Kirksville, 1984—; tchr. Boise Sch. System, 1976-80; admissions com. mem. Wash. State U., Pullman, 1982-84. Treas. Homedale (Idaho) PTA, leader Girl Scouts U.S.A., Homedale, 1974-77, Boy Scouts Am., Homedale, 1980-81; pres. bd. dirs. Community Health Clinics, Nampa, Idaho. Pet Food Inst. grantee, 1966. Mem. AVMA, Mo. Vet. Med. Assn., N.E. Mo. Vet. Med. Assn.AAUW, Beta Sigma Phi. Office: NE Mo State U BT 257 Kirksville MO 63501

ROGERS, VIRGINIA MARIE BUXTON, industrial psychologist; b. Phila., May 18, 1952; d, Robert Stevens and Dorothy Louise (Miller) B.; B.S., Pa. State U., 1974; M.A., U. Md., 1977, Ph.D., 1979. Research cons. Personnel Decisions Research Inst., Washington, 1978-79; personnel research specialist BP Am., Cleve., 1979-81, staff tng. assoc., 1981-83, mgr. exec. assessment and devel., 1983-88, mgr. exec. tng. and devel., 1988— . Lic. psychologist, Ohio. Mem. Am. Psychol. Assn. (indsl. organizational psychology). Home: 11687 River Ridge Strongsville OH 44136 Office: BP Am 34-4156-B BP Am Bldg 200 Public Sq Cleveland OH 44114

ROGERS-NAPIER, OLIVE VERNA, artist; b. Linwood, N.J., Oct. 2, 1902; d. George Herbert and Mary Margaret (Sutton) Rogers; m. Walter Simpson Napier, Dec. 9, 1941. Student, Sch. Indsl. Arts, Trenton, N.J., 1921, Graphic Sketch Club, Phila., 1923-24; grad., Pa. Mus. and Sch. Indsl. Art, 1925, Beaux Arts Inst. of Design, 1925. art critic, lectr., demonstrator, juror, Nev. and Calif., 1955—. One-man show includes Internat. Bldg., San Francisco, 1965-66; exhibited in group shows Oakland (Calif.) Art Mus., 1950-60, 62-68, Cunningham Meml. Galleries, Bakersfield, Calif., 1955-62, 64-67, M. H. deYoung Meml. Mus., San Francisco, 1956-60, Nat. Fine Arts Gallery, Smithsonian Inst., Washington, 1960, Fukuoka, Japan and Oakland, Calif., 1964, Crocker Galleries, Sacramento, 1964-67, Mills Coll., Oakland, 1964, Assn. Western Mus. traveling shows, 1964-66, 67-69, Haggin Galleries, Stockton, Calif., 1967; represented in pvt. collections. Mem. adv. bd. Ann. San Francisco Art Festival, 1954-66, v.p., 1958-59, treas., 1960-66; chmn. artists' adv. bd. Northern sect. Calif. State Expn. and Fair, 1961-70, chmn. emeritus, 1971—. Mem. Soc. Western Artists (pres. 1959, bd. dirs. 1955-61), Nat. League Am Pen Women (1st prize water color competition 1959, 1st v.p. 1958, 62), Marin Soc. Artists (bd. dirs. 1958-61, 65, artists' adv. council 1967-68), East Bay Artists Assn. (adv. bd. 1955-71), Hayward Art Assn., Santa Cruz Art League, Oakland Art Assn., Oakland Museums Assn., Humane Soc. Marin, Nat. Fedn. Wildlife, de Young Mus. Soc., Patrons of Art and Music. Lodge: Order of Eastern Star.

ROGERSON, LYNDA GAIL, career consultant; b. Bangor, Maine, Sept. 2, 1948; d. John Albin and Helen Julia (Domagala) Nelson; m. Michael Mont Rogerson, Oct. 21, 1978; children: Katelyn Mae, Sarah Grace; 1 child by previous marriage, Lara Lyn Lambert. B.A., U. Colo.-Colorado Springs, 1971, M.A., 1978; postgrad. U. No. Colo., 1985—. Librarian's asst. U. Colo., Colorado Springs, 1971-73; asst. librarian Kaman Scis. Corp., Colorado Springs, 1973-74; Vets. cert. officer Pikes Peak Community Coll., Colorado Springs, 1974-80, career devel. specialist, 1980-83; career cons. Lynco Assocs., Colorado Springs, 1977—; adv. bd. Workout Ltd., Colorado Springs, 1983—. Bd, dirs., 1978-83. Mem. Am. Soc. Tng. and Devel. (v.p. position referral service), Adminstrv. Mgmt. Soc. (v.p. programming), Colo. Employment Counselors Assn. (adv. bd. 1982-83), Nat. Voc. Guidance Assn., Nat. Assn. Female Execs., Bus. and Profl. Women, Am. Assn. for Counseling and Devel., Colo. Assn. Counseling and Devel. Republican. Lutheran. Home and Office: 2930 Marilyn Rd Colorado Springs CO 80909

ROGGE, RENA WOLCOTT, librarian; b. Bklyn., Nov. 3, 1920; d. Ralph Stratton and Mona Florence (Shannon) Wolcott; m. Carl Frederick Rogge Jr., Aug. 4, 1942; 1 son, Carl Frederick Rogge. B.A., Elmira Coll., 1941; M.L.S., Rutgers U., New Brunswick, N.J., 1966; M.A.L.S., New Sch. Social Research, N.Y.C., 1972, D. Info. Services, Nova Univ., 1987. Sec. Sch. Dist. South Orange, Maplewood, N.J., 1958-65; head reference librarian Cranford (N.J.) Pub. Library, 1966-68; readers' advisor Jersey City, 1968-69; reference librarian Newark State Coll., Union, N.J., 1969—; reference coordinator, asst. dir. for info. services Kean Coll. Library, sec. faculty senate, 1978-79, archivist faculty senate, 1979—, chmn. constn. revision, 1982—, grad. research com. 1983—. Recipient Outstanding Pub. Employee award, State of N.J., 1972, merit Award, 1983; online research grantee, Kean Coll. N.J., 1979. Mem. N.J. Library Assn., Am. Soc. Indexers, N.J. State Coll. Librarians' Assn., Kean Coll. Fedn. Tchrs. (exec. com.). Club: Elmira Coll. Home: 27 Bodwell Terr Millburn NJ 07031 Office: Kean Coll Nancy Thompson Library Morris Ave Union NJ 07083

ROGGOW, DIANE LYNN, telecommunications manager; b. Cochabamba, Bolivia, Feb. 9, 1957; came to U.S., 1963; d. Zelma Joy (Divers) R.; m. Kim Lance Thorne, May 20, 1978 (div. April 1983). BBA, U. Denver, 1988. Adminstrv. asst. Mobile Premix Concrete, Inc., Denver, 1978; adminstr. Mr. Steak, Inc., Denver, 1979; regional account coordinator AT&T Teletype Corp., Denver, 1980-85; adminstrv. mgr. US Sprint, Denver, 1986—. Mem. Nat. Assn. Female Execs. Republican. Home: 4107 Walnut #2-N Kansas City MO 64111 Office: 8140 Ward Parkway Kansas City MO 64114

ROGOVIN, SHEILA ANNE, psychologist; b. N.Y.C, Feb. 28, 1931; d. Irving Benjamin and Eva (Klein) Ender; m. Mitchell Rogovin, Jan. 31, 1954; children: Lisa Shea, Wendy Meryl, John Andrew. BS, Queens Coll., 1952; PhD, Am. Univ., 1979. Gen. practice psychology Silver Springs, Md., 1977—; with youth and family services Montgomery County Health Dept., Silver Spring, 1973-77. Mem. Am. Psychol. Assn., Am. Group Psychotherapy Assn., Am. Personnell and Guidance Assn., Md. Psychol. Assn., D.C. Psychol. Assn. Office: 8720 Georgia Ave Suite 206 Silver Spring MD 20910

ROGOZINSKI, TINA MARIE, pharmaceutical company marketing executive; b. Oklahoma City, Dec. 10, 1962; d. Leonard Peter and Mildred Helen (Little) R. B.S. in Internat. Mktg., Quinnipiac Coll., 1984, cert. in export mktg., 1983. Advt. coordinator Healthkraft, Inc., Danbury, Conn., 1983-85; mktg. mgr. Tishcon Corp., Westbury, N.Y., 1985-87; owner Unistar Mktg. Group Inc., 1986—; prin. Unistar Mktg. Group, Inc., 1987—. Contbr. poems to mags. Conn. State scholar, 1980. Mem. Nat. Assn. Female Execs., Am. Women Entrepreneurs, Internat. Platform Assn. Avocations: writing; tennis; skiing. Home: PO Box 10194 Westbury NY 11590 Office: Unistar Mktg Group 30 Charm City Dr Jefferson NY 11776

ROHDE, JEAN CATHERINE, social worker; b. N.Y.C., June 27, 1948; d. John Francis and Nancy Anastasia (Robuck) R. BA cum laude, Fairleigh Dickinson U., 1970; MSW, NYU, 1975; postgrad., Columbia U., 1979—, Psychoanalytic Inst. for Clin. Social Workers, 1978-79. Group leader Manhattan Psychiat. Ctr., N.Y.C., 1972-73, supr., 1975-77, coordinator outpatient program, 1977-79; program asst. Council on Social Work Edn., N.Y.C., 1980-81; research assoc. Indsl. Social Welfare Ctr., Columbia U. Sch. Social Work, N.Y.C., 1981-82; lectr. dept. sociology Barnard Coll., 1982-84; research assoc. runaway and homeless youth project Council on Accreditation of Services for Families and Children, 1983-84; social worker, supr. field placement Spl. Ednl. Services Program, condr. stress workshops for disabled coll. students, L.I. U., 1985—; presentations on treatment of mentally ill. Mental Hygiene scholar, 1973-75; NIMH trainee, 1979-80. Mem. Council on Social Work Edn., Nat. Assn. Social Workers, Acad. Cert. Social Workers, Am. Orthopsychiat. Assn. Home: 52 W 56th St Apt 4R New York NY 10019

ROHLAND, PAMELA, reporter; b. Danville, Pa., Apr. 13, 1958; d. Robert Maurice and Janet Avalon (Berry) R.; m. Robert Lee Keeler, May 30, 1981 (div. Mar. 1987). BS, Kutztown U., Pa., 1980, MS, 1981. Editor Spring-Ford Reporter, Royersford, Pa., 1983-85; reporter Reading (Pa.) Eagle-Times, 1985—; part-time book reviewer Phila. Inquirer, 1987—. State coordinator Experiment in Internat. Living, Brattleboro, Vt., 1985—, vol. 1979—; mem. Ches-Mont BPW, Phoenixville, 1984-85. Davidnoff scholar, Wesleyan U., Conn., 1986.

ROHM, JESSICA DEE, public relations and marketing firm executive; b. N.Y.C., Feb. 26, 1956; d. Edward J. and Tereza Ann (DiPiazza) Zive; m. Eberhard Heinrich Rohm, Sept. 22, 1984. BA, Barnard Coll., 1977. Pres. Jessica Dee Communications, N.Y.C., 1977—. Office: Jessica Dee Communications Inc 160 E 56th St New York NY 10022

ROJAS, KRISTINE BRIGGS, insurance underwriter; b. Pocatello, Idaho, July 25, 1947; d. Fergus Jr. and Shirley (Tanner) B.; m. Anthony Sanchez Rojas Jr., June 4, 1966 (div. Nov. 1979); children: Anthony Ted, Nancy Kristine. Student, Idaho State U., 1965-66. Ops. clerical coordinator Farmers Ins. Group, Pocatello, 1971-81; service rep. All Seasons Ins. Agy., Ventura, Calif., 1982; sr. comml. underwriting asst. Royal Ins. Co., Ventura, 1982-85; sr. comml. lines underwriter Andreini & Co., Ventura, 1985-88; comml. account service rep. Frank B. Hall, Inc., Oxnard, Calif., 1988—. Editor (bulletin) News Waves, 1985-87; artist various works specializing in charcoal portraits. Mem. Ins. Women Ventura County (treas. 1987-88, v.p. 1988-89, dir. 1986-87), Nat. Assn. Ins. Women, Nat. Assn. Female Execs. Republican. Baptist. Home: 564 Merritt Ave Camarillo CA 93010 Office: Frank B Hall Inc 2500 Vineyard Oxnard CA 93030

ROKS, MARTY JANETTE, telecommunications executive; b. Dyess, Ark., May 15, 1942; d. Marvin Edward and Delma Mae (Crownover) Turman; m. John Roks, Feb. 3, 1960 (div. Jan. 1970); 1 child, Flora Leigh Bettencourt. AS, Miramar Coll.; BA, Nat. U., BBA, MBA. Entertainer Foxey Lady Agy., Fullerton, Calif., 1974-75; coordinator spl. projects Nat. U. Alumni Assn., San Diego, 1981-82; v.p. Rosjum Mining Corp., San Diego, 1983-84; prin. Unipeg Enterprises, Lemon Grove, Calif., 1983-84; acad. asst. continuing edn., conf. facilities, telecommunications Nat. U., Inglewood, 1984-86; ind. contractor Traditional Industries, El Cajon, Calif., 1985. Vol. San Diego Navy League, 1982. Recipient Letter of Commendation, State Atty. Gens. Office, 1985. Mem. Telecommunication Assn., Assn. MBA Execs., Nat. Assn. Female Execs., Nat. U. Alumni Assn., Antique Aircraft Assn. (v.p. 1980). Democrat. Mem. Ch. of Christ. Home: 15 H St Encinitas CA 92024

ROLAND, LISA JOY, bank training director; b. Newark, Oct. 30, 1956; d. Jack and Natalie (Molin) R. Student, Inst. Internat., Madrid, 1977; BA, Douglass Coll., 1978; postgrad., Kean Coll., 1980. Cert. Spanish tchr., N.Y. Tchr. Union (N.J.) High Sch., 1978-81; customer service mgr. People Express Airlines, Newark, 1981-82, corp. tng. mgr., 1982-84; city mgr. O'Hare Airport People Express Airlines, Chgo., 1984-86; sr. tng. mgr. Citibank N.Am., N.Y.C., 1986-87, asst. v.p., dir. teller tng., 1988—; cons. Nancy Weed Assocs., San Francisco, 1986-87. Gymnastics instr. Summer Enrichment Program, Union; mgr. Cabaret Theatre Soc., New Brunswick. Mem. Am. Soc. Tng. and Devel. Democrat. Jewish. Home: 110 Kingsberry Dr Somerset NJ 08873

ROLFE, ELAINE ANDERSON, accountant; b. Kansas City, Mo., July 10, 1936; d. Harold Joseph and Marguerite (Snyder) Anderson; m. Robert Edward Rolfe, Dec. 22, 1956 (div. Aug. 1982); children: Harold Edward, Frank Edwin. B.S., U. Tex.-Dallas, 1981. Assoc. analyst ARCO Oil and Gas Co., Dallas, 1981—. Mem. Am. Inst. CPAs, Tex. Soc. CPAs (Dallas chpt.). Home: 3439 Northaven Rd Dallas TX 75229

ROLLANS, MARY ANN, university official, consultant; b. Fort Smith, Ark., Sept. 23, 1946; d. Ronald R. and Mary Josephine (Korkames) Hobaica; m. David Carter Rollans, Aug. 10, 1968; children—Mary Alicia, Carrie Ann, Russell David. B.A., Ark. Tech. U., 1968; M.A., U. Central Ark., 1974; Ed.D., U. Ark., 1986. Cert. tchr., Ark. Tchr. Russellville High Sch., Ark., 1968-70; instr. Capital City Bus. Coll., Russellville, 1971-76; pub. relations rep. Ark. Employment Security Div., Russellville, 1976-79; affirmative action officer, grant coordinator Ark. Tech. U., Russellville, 1980—; profl. devel. cons., 1980—. Mem. Russellville Planning Commn., 1979-85; mem. bd. edn. Cath. Diocese of Little Rock, 1978-82; bd. dirs. Ark. River Valley Arts Ctr., Russellville, 1980-83. Recipient Ark. Merit award, 1978. Mem. Bus. and Profl. Women (pres. 1981-82, Young Career Woman award 1968, 70), Ark. Council Women in Higher Edn., Russellville C. of C. (bd. dirs. 1984-85), Ark. Tech. U. Alumni Assn. (bd. dirs. 1980-83), Delta Kappa Gamma (sec. 1978-79; doctoral fellow 1983-84). Avocations: water skiing, camping, running, boating, fishing. Home: 2017 Skyline Dr Russellville AR 72801 Office: Ark Tech U N Arkansas Ave Russellville AR 72801

ROLLIN, BARBARA KLEINBERG, real estate professional; b. N.Y.C., July 18, 1941; d. Lawrence L. and Hermia (Rosen) Hyams; m. David K. Kleinberg, Aug. 22, 1963 (div. Sept. 1980); children: Julie, Michael; m. Dennis S. Rollin, May 13, 1981 (dec. Sept. 1985). BA in English Lit., Queens Coll., 1962; MA in English Lit., Hunter Coll., 1964; postgrad., U. Md., 1965-67. Tchr. English Trumansburg (N.Y.) High Sch., 1963-65; instr. gourmet cooking, creative writing Prince Georges Community Coll., Largo, Md., 1976-78; realtor Century 21 Award Realty, Crofton, Md., 1978-81, Long & Foster Real Estate, Crofton, Md., 1981—; instr. Bowie, Md., 1983; tng. dir. Crofton, 1985-86. Mem. editorial bd. Realtor Mag., Fairfax, Va., 1985-86. Named to Disting. Sales Club, Anne Arundel County, 1980—; U. Md. fellow, 1966. Mem. Anne Arundel County Bd. Realtors, Prince Georges County Bd. Realtors. Democrat. Jewish. Home: 1716 Tipton Dr Crofton MD 21114 Office: Long & Foster Real Estate 1151 Maryland Rt 3 Gambrills MD 21054

ROLLINS, BARBARA ANN, social service administrator; b. Waterloo, Iowa, May 31, 1949; d. Willie Andrew and Mary Jane (Young) Simpson; m. Herschel Mark Epps, Aug. 26, 1972 (div. Oct. 1985); children: Dawn Denise, Sharon Marie, Shaun Andrew; m. Stephen Warren Rollins. BA in Journalism, Speech Pathology, U. No. Iowa, 1974, postgrad., 1983-84. Mng. editor The Iowa Bystander, Des Moines, 1974-75; reporter Radio Sta. KCBC, Des Moines, 1976-77; contract compliance officer, personnel officer Iowa Dept. Transp., Ames, 1976-79; credit mgr. City of Jackson, Miss., 1979-82; investigator commerce dept. State of Minn., St. Paul, 1984-86; exec. dir. Putting it All Together, St. Paul, 1986—. Dir. youth choir New Hope Baptist Ch., St. Paul, 1986-87; chair Integration Review Com., St. Paul, 1987. Mem. Minn. Assn. Vol. Social Service Agy., Nat. Assn. Female Execs. Democrat. Office: Putting it All Together 60 N Kent St Saint Paul MN 55102

ROMAIN, MARGARET ANN, accountant; b. Mercer, Pa., Jan. 1, 1940; d. Peter Paul and Susie Ann (Murcko) Kutcher; m. Joseph Romain Jr.; children: Lucretia Ann, Kimberly Rose, Annette Marie. Student, Youngstown State U., 1957-58, 68-69, LaSalle Extension U., Pa. State U., Alliance Coll. Cert. graphoanalyst. Bookkeeper Mort-Bohn & Assocs., CPA, 1960-62, D.G. Reed & H. Hudson, PA, 1962-64; asst. office mgr. J.V. McNicholas Transfer Co., 1965-66; ptnr. Reed-Romain & Assocs., 1966-70; pvt. practice acctg. 1970-76; ptnr. Romain-Pendel & Assocs., 1976-78, R-P Computer Services, 1976-80, Romain Pendel Office Rental, 1976-80; pvt. practice acctg. 1978—. Editor: Pennsylvania Accountant, 1980-84. Asst. treas. St. John's Episcopal Ch., 1974-75, mem. exec. bd. Episcopal Churchwomen, 1977-78. Mem. Nat. Soc. Pub. Accts., Nat. Assn. Enrolled Agts. (sec. Pa. chpt. 1972-73), Pa. Soc. Pub. Accts. (state sec. 1978—), Pa. Soc. Enrolled Agts. (pres. 1972-74, exec. dir. 1975—), Internat. Graphoanalysis Soc. Democrat. Clubs: Saddlemates Saddle (Transfer, Pa.) (treas. 1979), Quota, Baldwin Organ (Sharon, Pa.) (pres. 1969); Butler Area Dairy Goat, 4-H Leader, Shenango Valley C. of C.

ROMAKER, JANET JUNE, newspaper editor, columnist; b. Toledo, Nov. 4, 1952; d. Charles Edward and Barbara Ann (Russell) Romaker; BS, Bowling Green State U., 1974. Reporter, The Blade Newspaper, Toledo, 1974-75, 76-79, asst. regional editor, 1979, regional editor, 1979-88, columnist, 1985—, roving editor, 1988—; editor Swanton (Ohio) Enterprise Newspaper, 1976; faculty Sch. Journalism, Bowling Green State U., 1982-83, 87; mem. panel humor writing workshop U. Toledo, Nov. 1986; lectr. in field. Chmn. fund drive Am. Heart Assn., 1980. Mem. Soc. Profl. Journalists (treas. 1981-82), Ohio Newspapers Women's Assn. (1st place newswriting category 1982, 1st place critical writing category, 1987), Sigma Delta Chi. United Methodist. Club: Toledo Press. Office: 541 N Superior St Toledo OH 43660

ROMAN, CAMILLE, writer, English language educator; b. LaPlatta, Md., Feb. 18, 1948; d. Arthur Robert and LaNelle (Bugg) R.; m. Chris D. Frigon, Aug. 9, 1975. B.A., U. Mich., 1970; M.A., Boston Coll., 1983, postgrad. Brown U., 1985—. Writer, copy editor Quincy (Mass.) Patriot Ledger, 1969-72; community relations dir. Cambridge (Mass.) Pub. Library, 1972-73; editorial cons., Cambridge, 1973-76; publicity coordinator G.K. Hall & Co., Boston, 1976-78; editorial cons., Boston, 1978—; instr. English, Aquinas Jr. Coll., Newton, Mass., 1978-85. Author: Women Alive! (poetry), 1983; editor: (with Chris Frigon) Twayne Music Series, 1983—; contbr. articles revs., essays and poetry to newspapers, mags., jours., newsletters, TV and radio programs. Bd. dirs. Cambridge YWCA, 1970-72. Recipient John Cotton Dana award ALA, 1973. Mem. MLA, Women in Communications (v.p. Boston 1973-74, Edward Bernays award 1975), D.H. Lawrence Soc., Phi Theta Kappa (adv. 1982-85). Office: Brown U Dept English Box 1852 Providence RI 02912

ROMAN, DINA MARIA, sales representative; b. Forest Hills, N.Y., Mar. 28, 1961; d. Robert and Marta Marie (Lanfrit) R. BS, Fordham U., 1983. Rep. sales The Procter & Gamble Distbg. Co., Jericho, N.Y., 1983-85; v.p. sales and mktg. Am. Sunwear Co., N.Y.C., 1985-86, cons., 1986-87; with advt. sales N.Y. Times, N.Y.C., 1987—; tennis instr. jr. devel. program Bay Terrace (N.Y.) Racquet Club, 1986—. Dir. Queens Borough free clinic program N.Y.C. Dept. Parks and Recreation/Nat. Jr. Tennis League, Flushing Meadow Park, N.Y., 1980-81. Mem. Nat. Assn. for Female Execs., U.S. Tennis Assn. Republican. Roman Catholic.

ROMAN, PATRICIA NEWTON, nursing administrator; b. Camden, N.J., Sept. 18, 1957; d. Adelbert Forbes and Margaret Mary (Coogan) Newton; m. B. Kent Roman, Feb. 5, 1983. BS in Nursing, Am. U., 1979. RN, N.Y., Washington. Staff nurse neurosurgery Georgetown Med. Ctr., Washington, 1979-83; staff nurse surgical ICU Mount Sinai Hosp., N.Y.C., 1983-85, nurse clin. resource coordinator, 1985-86; quality assurance coordinator N.Y. Infirmary subs. Beekman Downtown Hosp., N.Y.C., 1986—. Coordinator Brooklyn Heights InterFaith Shelter for the Homeless, Bklyn., 1985—; mem. block assn., Bklyn., 1985—. Recipient Record of Commendation, Georgetown U. Hosp., Washington, 1980. Mem. Nurses for Quality Assurance. Roman Catholic. Home: 90 Bergen St Brooklyn NY 11201 Office: NY Infirmary-Beekman Hosp 170 William St New York NY 10038

ROMAN, VALERIE ANN, data processing executive; b. Saugus, Mass., July 24, 1956; d. George Anthony and Esther (Theodore) Anthonakes; m. Anthony Michael Roman, Oct. 2, 1982; 1 child, Matthew Michael. BA, Wellesley Coll., 1978. Chief dept. consumer expenditures, system analysis and design Census Bur., Washington, 1978-85; dir. data processing City of Cambridge, Mass., 1985—. Mem. Nat. Assn. Female Execs., Assn. System Mgrs., Mass. Mcpl. Data Processing Assn., Phi Beta Kappa. Home: 32 Blossom Rd Windham NH 03087 Office: City of Cambridge 795 Massachusetts Ave Cambridge MA 02139

ROMANANSKY, MARCIA CANZONERI, book company executive; b. Bklyn., Apr. 22, 1941; d. Nicholas C. and Ellen (Zukas) Canzoneri; m. Robert Edward Romanansky, June 1, 1963. B.A. in History, Coll. of Misericordia, Dallas, Pa., 1962; M.L.S., Pratt Inst., 1969; M.A. in Edn., Seton Hall U., 1973; postgrad. Fairleigh Dickinson U., 1980—. Acquisitions librarian St. Peter's Coll., Jersey City, 1963-68; sch. librarian Roselle High Sch. (N.J.), 1968-72; selection librarian Baker & Taylor, Somerville, N.J., 1972-74, chief librarian, 1974-80, asst. mgr. program services, 1980-81, mgr. program services, 1981-87, dir. pub. library mktg., 1987—. Contbr. articles to profl. jours. Mem. publicity com. Showhouse, Aux. Muhlenberg Hosp., Plainfield, N.J., 1982, 84. Mem. ALA (tech. services com. 1982-84), Beta Phi Mu. Home: 994 Oakland Ave Plainfield NJ 07060 Office: 652 Main St Bridgewater NJ 08807

ROMANO, JANET BOCCHINO, lawyer; b. Newark, N.J., June 26, 1947; d. John Giacomo and Connie (Zoppi) B.; m. Mario Giovanni, July 25, 1970; children: Gabriella, Franca. BA, Montclair (N.J.) State Coll., 1969; JD, Seton Hall Law Sch., Newark, 1975. Bar: N.J. 1975, U.S. Dist. Ct. N.J. 1975. Ptnr. Romano & Romano, Verona, N.J., 1975—. Pres. Essex Fells (N.J.) PTA, 1981; v.p. Essex Fells Bd. Edn., 1985, pres. 1986. Mem. Assn. Trial Lawyers Am., N.J. State Bar Assn., Essex County Bar Assn., U.S. Dist. Ct. Hist. Soc. Club: Fells Brook. Home: 110 Devon Rd Essex Fells NJ 07044 Office: Romano & Romano 573 Bloomfield Ave Verona NJ 07044

ROMANOFF, MARJORIE REINWALD, educator; b. Chgo., Sept. 29, 1923; d. David Edward and Gertrude (Rosenfield) Reinwald; student Northwestern U., 1941-42, 43-45; B.Ed., U. Toledo, 1947, M.Ed., 1968, Ed.D., 1976; m. Milford M. Romanoff, Nov. 6, 1945; children—Bennett Sanford, Lawrence Michael, Janet Beth (dec.). Tchr., Old Orchard Elem. Sch., Toledo, 1946-47, McKinley Sch., Toledo, 1964-65; substitute tchr., Toledo, 1964-68; instr. Mary Manse Coll., Toledo, 1974; instr. children's lit. Sylvania (Ohio) Bd. Edn., 1977; supr. student tchrs. U. Toledo, 1968-73, 85—, instr. advanced communications, 1977, researcher, 1973-74, instr. Am. Lang. Inst., 1978—; adj. asst. prof. elem. edn. Bowling Green (Ohio) State U., 1978—. Presenter numerous workshops and demonstrations in children lit. and analysis of tchr. behavior, 1976—; mem. research com. Am. Language Inst. U. Toledo, 1985—, also asst. prof. elem.edn. in lang. arts 1985—. Trustee Children's Services Bd., 1974-76; pres. bd. Cummings Treatment Center for Adolescents, 1978-80; mem. Crosby Gardens Adv. Bd., 1976-82, Community Planning Council, 1980-84 , Citizens Rev. Bd. of Juvenile Ct., 1979—; mem. allocations com. Mental Health and Retardation Bd., 1980-81; mem. Bd. Jewish Edn., 1976—, pres., 1982-84; mem. Jewish Family Service, 1978-85, v.p., 1980-85; bd. dirs. Family Life Edn. Council, 1984—, sec., 1988—. Named One of Ten Women of Yr. St. Vincent's Hosp. Guild, 1985. Mem. Tchrs. English to Speakers Other Langs., Am. Assn. Supervision and Curriculum Devel., Am. Edn. Research Assn., Nat. Soc. for Study Edn., Toledo Assn. Children's Lit., Nat. Council Jewish Women, Orgn. Rehab. and Tng., Hadassah (chpt. pres. regional bd. 1961-64), Northwestern U. Alumni Assn., Phi Kappa Phi, Phi Delta Kappa, Kappa Delta Pi (pres./faculty adv. 1971-75), Pi Lambda Theta (chpt. pres. 1978-80, nat. com. 1979-84). Democrat. Home: 2514 Bexford Pl Toledo OH 43606 Office: U Toledo CEC 1006 Toledo OH 43606 Office: Bowling Green State U Coll Edn Bowling Green OH 43402

ROMANO-KOENIG, RAE, insurance broker, underwriter; b. Bklyn., Sept. 16, 1953; d. Dominic Romano and Frances Lillian Carow; m. John Edward Koenig, Sept. 14, 1986. Cert. ins. broker, N.Y. Rep., broker Jo-Mil Ins. Agy., Glen Cove, N.Y., Citation Agy., Garden City, N.Y., Donald A. Hall Agy., Valley Stream, N.Y.; comml. acct. exec. Bern-Ed Agy., East Meadow, N.Y., 1987—. Active Franklin Square Rep. Club, L.I., N.Y.; musician L.I. Mummers String Band. Mem. Young Ins. Profls. Methodist.

ROMAN-OLEKSY, LISA MARIE, personnel specialist; b. Cleve., Apr. 14, 1964; d. Paul R. Roman and Rozlynd Louise (Sobczak) Smith. Student in mktg., Cuyahoga Community Coll., Cleve., 1984—. Adminstrv. asst. Mass. Casualty, Beachwood, 1983-84; sr. info. specialist Christian & Timbers, Beachwood, 1984-87; mgr. Office Mates 5, Euclid, Ohio, 1987—. Mem. Nat. Assn. Female Execs., Carnegians. Roman Catholic. Office: Office Mates 5 26250 Euclid Ave Euclid OH 44132

ROMANS, KATHLEEN DOBROZSI, lawyer; b. Middletown, Ohio, Apr. 10, 1949; d. Andrew Joseph and Mary M. (Raterman) D.; m. Michael Frank Romans, Aug. 28, 1970; children: Katharine, Juliann, Mary Emily. BS in Edn., Miami U., Oxford, Ohio, 1973; JD, U. Dayton, 1983. Bar: Ohio 1983. Tchr. Archdiocese of Cin., Middletown, 1970-75, Middletown City Schs., 1975-78; asst. prosecuting atty. Butler County Prosecutor, Hamilton, Ohio, 1983—; bd. dirs. Legal Assistance, Hamilton, 1985—. Bd. dirs. John XXIII PTO, 1985-87, Neighborhood Watch of Middleton, 1988—, Family Service of Middleton, 1988—. Mem. Ohio State Bar Assn., Middletown Bar Assn. (sec. 1984), Butler County Bar Assn. Democrat. Roman Catholic. Home: 4130 Rosedale Rd Middletown OH 45042 Office: Prosecutor's Office 300 N Fair Ave Hamilton OH 45011 also: 56 S Main St Middletown OH 45044

ROMANT-SOLIS, JANICE ANNE, sales and marketing executive; b. New Orleans, Oct. 24, 1944; d. Salvador and Lorraine (Demazelier) Romant; m. Ray E. Solis, Jan. 30, 1965; children: Ray E. Solis Jr., Janice Lorraine, John Charles. AA, Skyline Jr. Coll., 1974, BA, San Francisco State U., 1976, postgrad., 1976. Employment counselor Employment Devel. Dept., San Mateo, Calif., 1966-73, career developer, 1966-75; with research and stats. dept. Employment Data and Research, San Francisco, 1973-75; fund developer for social service programs Ala. County Tng. and Employment Bd./Assn. Community Action Programs, Hayward, Calif., 1975-78; work incentive program counselor, pres. Fashion Dynamics Inc., Foster City, Calif., 1982-86; pres. mktg. and sales Solex Enterprise, Inc., Foster City, Calif., 1986—. Creator "Calif. Kid of Yr." award "Pros for Kids" San Mateo, 1986; fund raiser, chairperson Leukemia Curathon, Ctr. For Ind. Disabled, Mexican Earthquake Relief Fund San Francisco, 1983-86. Named Bus. Woman of Yr. award Am. Bus. Women's Assn. Burlingame, Calif., 1985; elected to San Mateo County Hall of Fame Bd. of Trustees Redwood City (Calif.), 1986. Mem. Nat. Speakers Assn., Nat. Assn. Female Execs., Am. Bus. Women's Assn. (speaker), Direct Sales Assn. Am. (speaker, trainer, cons.), Foster City (Calif.) C. of C., San Jose (Calif.) C. of. C. Democrat. Roman Catholic. Office: Fashion Dynamics 1155 Triton Dr Suite D Foster City CA 94404

ROMBERG, LESLIE HOLMES, international marketing management company executive; b. Bklyn., Aug. 11, 1941; d. Alton Butler and Margaret Nichol (Arnett) H.; m. Jon Word Blaschke, Aug. 20, 1966 (div. June 1968); m. Conrad Louis Romberg, Jan. 6, 1985; 1 stepdaughter, Allison Romberg. Student, Baylor Coll. Dentistry, 1959-60, U. Tulsa, 1962-64; BS in Chemistry and Biology, Cen. State U., Edmond, Okla., 1966; PhD in Biochemistry, U. Okla., 1968. Head internat. ops. New Eng. Nuclear Corp., Boston, 1969-77 (name now DuPont-NEN); sales engr. Tracor Analytic, Des Plaines, Ill., 1977-79; internat. mktg. and product mgr. Zoecon Industries, Dallas, 1979-80; owner, operator Tex-Am. Internat., Dallas, 1980—; ptnr. Twin Assocs. Engring. Cons., Olten, Switzerland. V.p. Richardson Unitarian Ch., 1985-86, pres., 1986-87, bd. dirs. 87—, sec. 1988-89; founder, bd. dirs. Greenhill Alumnae Parents Assn., 1987-88; founder Greenhill Former Parents' Assn., 1988. Mem. Dallas C. of C., Rowlett C. of C. (exec. com.), North Dallas Network Career Women. Republican. Home and Office: PO Box 549 Rowlett TX 75088

ROME, FLORENCE MILES, author; b. Chgo., Sept. 24, 1910; d. Maurice David and Rose Miles; student, U. Ill., 1927-29; m. Harold Rome, Feb. 3, 1939; children—Joshua David, Rachel Miles. Author: The Scarlett Letters, 1971; The Tattooed Men, 1975, Arlene Francis, 1978; contbr. articles and short stories to profl. jours. Home: 150 E 69th St #14S New York NY 10021

ROMEI, LURA KNACHEL, magazine editor; b. Mansfield, Ohio, Nov. 17, 1947; d. Dale Conrad and L. Blanche (Nichols) Knachel; m. Richard Dale Romei, Sept. 13, 1968 (div. 1978); children: Christopher Dale, Craig Steven. B Music Edn., Otterbein Coll., 1970; Assoc., Lakeland Community Coll., 1974. Contract programmer Hunter Mfg. Co., Solon, Ohio, 1974; programmer Better Meat Products Co., Cleve., 1974-76, Childers Products Co., Beachwood, Ohio, 1976-77; analyst, programmer Cuyahoga County Data Ctr., Cleve., 1977-79; analyst, programmer Penton Pub., Cleve., 1979, assoc. editor Modern Office Tech., 1979-84, editor Modern Office Tech., 1984—. Author over 180 articles; editor over 280 articles. Mem. Am. Soc. Bus. Press Editors, Sigma Delta Chi. Methodist. Office: Penton Pub 1100 Superior Ave Cleveland OH 44114

ROMENSKI, KATHRYN B., physical therapy administrator; b. Pawtucket, R.I., Aug. 13, 1948. BS in Phys. Therapy, Boston U., 1970. Staff phys. therapist Allied Services for the Handicapped, Scranton, Pa., 1970-71, asst. chief phys. therapist, 1971-74, chief phys. therapist, 1974-77, dir. patient services, 1977-79, dir. phys. therapy, 1979—; mem. Allied Services Fed. Credit Union, 1970—, treas., 1974-75, pres., 1984-86; mem. profl. adv. bd. Allied Services Home Health Div., 1985—, Civic Ballet Co., 1985—. Mem. Am. Phys. Therapy Assn. (ho. of dels. 1973, 86), Pa. Phys. Therapy Assn. (mem. nominating com. 1977-78, state conv. com. 1979, chair nominating com. 1986—), Am. Mgmt. Assn., Nat. Rehab. Assn., Am. Acad. Orthotics and Prosthetics, Nat Rehab. Adminstrs. Assn., Internat. Rehab. Inst., Nat. Assn. Female Execs., Nat. Assn. Mgmt.

ROMEO, JOANNE JOSEFA MARINO, mathematics educator; b. Youngstown, Ohio, Nov. 21, 1943; d. Joseph James and Ann Marie (Bonamase) Marino; m. John Homer Romeo, Aug. 14, 1965; children: Christopher, Chrisanne, Jonathan. BS, Ohio State U., 1965; postgrad., Youngstown State U., 1969-70; MS, Purdue U., 1974; postgrad. in computer sci., U. Tenn., Knoxville, 1974. Substitute tchr. Columbus, Ohio, 1964-65; tchr. geometry, math. and French Hamilton Sch. Dist., Columbus, Ohio, 1965-66; tchr. gifted children Bluegrass Elem. Sch., Knoxville, Tenn., 1976-77; tchr. math. and sci. Webb Sch., Knoxville, 1977-85, also developer computer sci. program, 1977-85; headmistress Greenbrier Acad., Sevierville, Tenn., 1985-86; instr. math. State Tech. Inst. Knoxville, 1986-88. Dir. religious edn. Sacred Heart Parish, Knoxville, 1979—. Mem. Nat. Council Tchrs. Math., Nat. Cath. Edn. Assn., Nat. Council Parish and Religious Coordinators and Dirs., Nat. Sci. Tchrs. Assn., Ohio State U. Alumni Assn., Purdue U. Alumni Assn., Alpha Gamma Delta. Republican. Home: 1708 Capistrano Dr Knoxville TN 37922 Office: Sacred Heart Parish Ctr 711 Northshore Dr Knoxville TN 37919 also: PO Box 22990 Hardin Valley Rd Knoxville TN 37933-0990

ROMEO, NANCY C., health care executive; b. Queens, N.Y., Apr. 22, 1956; d. John Salvatore and Christine Marie (LaSala) Romeo; divorced; 1 child, Maria Elizabeth. BS in Nursing, Hartwick Coll., 1978; M in Pub. Adminstrn., Pace U., 1986. Staff nurse Peekskill (N.Y.) Community Hosp., 1973-78, No. Westchester Hosp., Mt. Kisco, N.Y., 1978-80; pediatric nurse Westchester County Med. Ctr., Vahalla, N.Y., 1980-82; staff supr. MARRS Extended Care Facility, Shrub Oak, N.Y., 1984-85; supr. home health care Westchester County Health Dept., Peekskill, 1982-85; supr. home health care West Jersey Home Health Care, Marlton, N.J., 1985-86, dir. patient services, 1986; dir. quality assurance Found. Health Preferred Plan, Short Hills, N.J., 1986—, v.p., 1987—; lectr. in field; career advisor Hartwick Coll., Oneonta, N.Y., 1987—, mem. career planning adv. panel. Recipient Achievement award Nat. Assn. Counties, 1985. Mem. Nat. Assn. Female Execs., Am. Coll. Health Care Execs., Am. Coll. Utilization Rev. Physicians, Nat. Assn. Quality Assurance Profls., Soc. Ambulatory Profls., Home Health Assembly N.J., N.Y. Nurses Assn., N.J. Home Health Assembly. Republican. Roman Catholic. Home: 238 Elmwood Ave Maplewood NJ 07040 Office: Found Health Preferred Plan 748 Morris Turnpike Short Hills NJ 07078

ROMERO, DONNA SUSANNE, accountant; b. Denver; d. Donald Peter and Maxine Anna (Porreco) James; m. Joseph Daniel Romero, Mar. 14, 1972; 1 child, Lora M. BA, U. Colo., 1975. CPA, Alaska. Acct. David L. Rosen, CPA, Anchorage, 1976-77; sr. acct. Burnett and Meyer, CPA's, Anchorage, 1977-79, Price Waterhouse, Paris, 1979-82; mgr. Price Waterhouse, Anchorage, 1982-85; sr. mgr. Price Waterhouse, N.Y.C., 1985-86, Anchorage, 1986—. Bd. dirs. ARC, Anchorage, 1984-85. Mem. Am. Inst. CPA's, Alaska Soc. CPA's, Nat. Assn. Female Execs., Anchorage Estate Planning Council, Alaska Erisa Forum. Office: Price Waterhouse 101 W Benson Blvd Anchorage AK 99503

ROMERO, ELIZABETH RIVERA, public health nurse; b. Manila, Jan. 10, 1958; came to U.S., 1973; d. Vivencio Delapaz and Erlinda (Magalona) Rivera; m. Oscar Dedios Romero, Feb. 14, 1978; 1 child, Sherilynn R. B.S. in Nursing cum laude, San Francisco State U., 1980. R.N., Calif. Staff nurse St. Lukes Hosp., San Francisco, 1980-85; pub. health nurse St. Mary's Hosp., San Francisco, 1984-85, Kimberley Home Patient Care, Pinole, Calif., 1984-87, utilization rev. case mgr. Brookside Hosp., San Pablo, Calif, 1987—. Mem. Am. Nurses Assn., Calif. Nurses Assn., Golden Gate Nurses Assn., Am. Heart Assn. (Contra Costa chpt.), Filipino Nurses Assn. of Calif., Calif. Scholarship Fedn. Roman Catholic. Avocations: dancing; travel; camping; photography.

ROMERO, JOSIE TORRALBA, mental health executive, social worker; b. Piedras Negras, Mex., Sept. 24, 1944; d. Amado Torralba Mann and Isabel (Flores) Torralba; m. Arturo Romero, May 6, 1967; children: Diana Isabel, Arturo Romero Jr. AA, Gavilan Coll., 1972; BA, San Jose State U., 1976, MSW, 1979. Lic. clin. social worker, Calif. Bilingual tchr. aide Gilroy (Calif.) Unified Sch. Dist., 1968-69; mental health community worker Santa

Clara County Mental Health, Gilroy, 1969-78; minority program specialist Santa Clara County Mental Health, San Jose, Calif., 1978-80; so. county ctr. dir. Santa Clara County Mental Health, Gilroy, 1980-82; asst. dir. community mental health Santa Clara County Mental Health, San Jose, 1982-84, regional dir., 1984—; pvt. practice psycho-therapist San Jose, 1984—; cons., trainer in field, San Jose, 1978—; bd. dirs. Hispanic Inst. Family Devel., 1984-86. Contbr. articles to profl. jours. Bd. dirs. Gardener Health Ctr., San Jose, 1984-86; mem Hispanic Women Polit. Assn., Gilroy, 1984. Mem. Bay Area Assn. Spanish Speaking Therapists, Nat. Orgn. Spanish Speaking Health and Mental Health Therapists, Assn. Raza Mental Health Adminstrs. (bd. dirs. advocates 1970-78), Nat. Assn. Social Workers. Democrat. Roman Catholic. Office: Cen Mental Health Ctr 2221 Enborg Ln San Jose CA 95128

ROMIJN, ELIZABETH KUIZENGA, English as a second language teacher; b. Waukesha, Wis., Oct. 29, 1947; d. Henry Bernard and Grace Elizabeth (Abney) Kuizenga; m. Jacob Herman Romijn, June 24, 1968 (div. 1979); children: Rebecca Alie, Tamara Betty. Tchr. English as 2d lang. Mission Community Coll. Ctr., San Francisco, 1969—, Mission Lang. & Vocat. Sch., San Francisco, 1970-74; workshop presenter, 1979-82. Author (with others), pub.: (textbook) Live Action English, 1979, 85, 88 (cassette set), 1986. Office: 1400 Shattuck Ave #7-62 Berkeley CA 94709

RONALDER, NINA WALKER, geologist; b. Fort Worth, July 1, 1955; d. John and Virginia (Stiles) Walker; m. Ronnie Lee Ronalder, Dec. 30, 1978; children—Katrina Michelle, Stephen Christian. B.S., Baylor U., 1977; M.S., U. Tex.-Arlington, 1982. Geologist Mobil Exploration Producing Services Inc., Dallas, 1979-81, prodn. geologist, Houston, 1982-84, Midland, Tex., 1985, staff ops. engr., 1986, reservoir geologist, 1987, team leader Devel. Studies Prodn. Geology Team, 1988—; assoc. instr. geology Tarrant County Jr. Coll., Ft. Worth, 1978-79. Mem. Am. Assn. Petroleum Geologists, Soc. Petroleum Engrs., West Tex. Geol. Soc., AAUW, Baylor Alumni Assn., Chi Omega. Baptist. Office: Mobil Producing Tex and New Mexico Inc PO Box 633 Midland TX 79702

RONAN, ELENA VINADÉ (MRS. WILLIAM JOHN RONAN) real estate broker; b. Havana, Cuba; d. Ricardo Poblet and Virtudes (Alpérez-Inclán) Vinadé; B.A., N.Y. U., 1943; m. William John Ronan, May 29, 1939; children—Monica Ronan Nourie, Diana Ronan Quasha. Broker Douglas, Elliman, Gibbons & Ives, N.Y.C., 1976-88, broker Sotheby's Internat. Realty, 1988— ; pres. Comillas Corp., N.Y.C., 1982—. Clubs: Cosmopolitan; Maidstone (East Hampton, L.I.); Knickerbocker; Winged Foot Golf; Creek. Home: 655 Park Ave New York NY 10021 Office: 575 Madison Ave New York NY 10021

RONDEAU, DORIS JEAN, entrepreneur, consultant; b. Winston-Salem, N.C., Nov. 25, 1941; d. John Delbert and Eldora Virginia (Klutz) Robinson; m. Robert Breen Corrente, Sept. 4, 1965 (div. 1970); m. Wilfrid Dolor Rondeau, June 3, 1972. Student Syracuse U., 1959-62, Fullerton Jr. Coll., 1974-75; BA in Philosophy, Calif. State U.-Fullerton, 1976, postgrad., 1976-80. Ordained to ministry The Spirit of Divine Love, 1974. Trust real estate clk. Security First Nat. Bank, Riverside, Calif., 1965-68; entertainer Talent, Inc., Hollywood, Calif., 1969-72; co-founder, dir. Spirit of Divine Love, Capistrano Beach, Calif., 1974—; pub., co-founder Passing Through, Inc., Capistrano Beach, 1983—; instr. Learning Activity, Anaheim, Calif., 1984—; chmn. bd., prin. D.J. Rondeau, Entrepreneur, Inc., Capistrano Beach, 1984—; co-founder, dir. Spiritual Positive Attitude, Inc., Moon In Pisces, Inc., Vibrations By Rondeau, Inc., Divine Consciousness, Expressed, Inc., Capistrano Beach. Author, editor: A Short Introduction To The Spirit of Divine Love, 1984; writer, producer, dir. performer spiritual vignettes for NBS Radio Network, KWVE-FM, 1982-84; author: Spiritual Meditations to Uplift the Soul, 1988. Served with USAF, 1963-65. Recipient Pop Vocalist First Place award USAF Talent Show, 1964, Sigma chpt. Epsilon Delta Chi, 1985, others. Mem. Hamel Bus. Grads., Smithsonian Assocs., Am. Mgmt. Assn., Nat. Assn. Female Execs. Avocations: long-distance running, body fitness, arts and crafts, snorkeling, musical composition.

RONGO, LUCILLE LYNN, medical center executive; b. N.Y.C., Sept. 15, 1958; d. Vincent Frank and Lucy Ann (Guilano) R. B.S., Mercy Coll., Dobbs Ferry, N.Y., 1984. Asst. supr. accounts receivable Montefiore Med. Ctr., Bronx, 1978-81, asst. mgr. accounts payable, 1981-83, payroll mgr., 1983-87, spl. funds mgr., 1987—. Mem. Nat. Assn. Female Execs., Am. Payroll Assn. Avocations: drying, preserving and framing flowers; collecting miniatures; art; dance, skiing. Home: 4219 Baychester Ave Bronx NY 10466 Office: Montefiore Med Ctr 111 E 210th St Bronx NY 10466

RONHOVDE, VIRGINIA SEDMAN, political and civic worker; b. Missoula, Mont., Dec. 17, 1909; d. Oscar Alfred and Harriet Laura (Rankin) Sedman; student U. Mont., 1925-27; B.A., Wellesley Coll., 1929; M.A., Columbia U., 1930; postgrad., 1930-33; postgrad. (Columbia U. fellow) U. Berlin, 1933-35; m. Andreas G. Ronhovde, Apr. 7, 1936; children—Erik Sedman, Andrea Rankin, Nora Montana Ronhovde Hohenlohe, Kent McGregor. Instr. sociology and labor problems Rutgers U., 1935-36; salesman Boss and Phelps, Inc., Simmons Properties, Washington, 1954-76. Sec., League Rep. Women, Washington, 1969-71, bd. dirs., 1971-73, 75-77, 1st v.p., 1973-75; del. Nat. Fedn. Rep. Women Conv., Dallas, 1975; del., mem. permanent orgn. com. Rep. Nat. Conv., 1976; mem. cen. com. D.C. Rep. Com., 1976-80, 80-84, alt. nat. committeewoman, 1980-84; mem. Missoula Design Rev. Bd. Mem. Missoula Rep. Women's Club, Kappa Kappa Gamma. Episcopalian. Home: 600 Beverly Ave Missoula MT 59801

RONSTADT, LINDA MARIE, singer; b. Tucson, July 15, 1946; d. Gilbert and Ruthmary (Copeman) R. Rec. artist numerous albums including Evergreen, 1967, Evergreen Vol. 2, 1967, Linda Ronstadt, The Stone Poneys and Friends, Vol. 3, 1968, Hand Sown, Home Grown, 1969, Silk Purse, 1970, Linda Ronstadt, 1972, Don't Cry Now, 1973, Heart Like a Wheel, 1974, Different Drum, 1974, Prisoner In Disguise, 1975, Hasten Down the Wind, 1976, Greatest Hits, 1976, Simple Dreams, Blue Bayou, 1977, Living in the U.S.A, 1978, Mad Love, Greatest Hits Vol. II, 1980, Get Closer, 1982, What's New, 1983, Lush Life, 1984, For Sentimental Reasons, 1986, Trio (with Dolly Parton, Emmylou Harris), 1986, 'Round Midnight, 1987, Canciones de Mi Padre, 1987; starred in Broadway prodn. of Pirates of Penzance, 1981, also in film, 1983, off Broadway as Mimi in La Boheme, 1984. Recipient Am. Music award, 1978, Grammy awards, 1975, 76, 87, (with Emmylou Harris and Dolly Parton) Acad. of Country Music award, 1987. Office: care Peter Asher Mgmt Inc 644 N Doheny Dr Los Angeles CA 90069

ROOD, KATHRYN ANN (MINETT), businesswoman; b. Clinton, Ind., Apr. 21, 1927; d. Thomas Everett and Francis Ann (Dyrval) Minett; student Terre Haute Comml. Coll., 1944-45; m. Robert Enoch Rood, Jan. 29, 1946; children—Robert Thomas, Larry Warren, Ronald Irvin, Richard Alan (dec.). Sec., Lammers Paint and Glass Co., Terre Haute, Ind., 1945-46; office mgr., corp. sec. Eurich Home Improvement Inc., Saginaw, Mich., 1969-78, also dir.; sec.-treas., mem. exec. com. Saginaw County Republican Com. from 1979-81; cons., bus. counseling K.A.R. Enterprises, 1987—. Mem. Saginaw Human Planning Commn., 1975—, sec., 1975-76, chmn., 1977-78, 85-86; jury commr. Mich. State, 1979—; bd. dirs. Civic Center, Saginaw, 1980—, Neighborhood Housing Services, 1978—, Saginaw Networking & Women's Bus. Alliance, 1988—. Recipient award Saginaw Neighborhoods Inc., 1980. Mem. LWV (v.p. chpt. 1969-71, chpt. bull. editor 1969-74, county fin. chmn., 1969-74). Clubs: Bus. and Profl. Women's, (pres. 1986-88), Saginaw Rep. Women's. Lodge: Order Eastern Star. Home and Office: 2712 Morgan Saginaw MI 48602 Also: PO Box 6635 Saginaw MI 48608

ROOKER, CASSANDRA JEAN, nurse; b. Nashville, Dec. 27, 1950; d. William Roy and Dorothy Clair (Shelton) R.; m. Phillip Wayne Trusty, Dec. 30, 1973 (div. Mar. 1976). Student, Rutherford Hosp., Murfreesboro, Tenn., 1970, Memphis State U., 1978-80; diploma in nursing, St. Joseph Hosp., Memphis, 1983. Cert. psychiat./mental health nurse. Clin. lab. technician Rutherford Hosp., Murfreesboro, Tenn., 1970-73, Murfreesboro, 1970-77; clin. lab. technician New Vaughn Meml. Hosp., Selma, Ala., 1974-75, Freeman Labs., Nashville, 1975-76, Bapt. Meml. Hosp., Memphis, 1977-83; nurse St. Joseph Hosp., Memphis, 1983-85, Eastwood Hosp., Memphis, 1985—; co-therapist Dept. of Human Services, Memphis, 1985—, Psychology Group, Memphis, 1987—. Youth dir. Winchester Heights Christian Ch., Memphis, 1985—; vol. Hospice of Memphis Inc., 1980-83. Republican. Mem. Disciples of Christ Ch. Home: 4640 Oak Forest Way #2 Memphis TN 38118 Office: Eastwood Hosp 3000 Getwell Rd Memphis TN 38118

ROONEY, CAROL BRUNS, dietitian; b. Milw., Dec. 20, 1940; d. Edward G. and Elizabeth C. (Lemke) Bruns; m. George Eugene Rooney Jr., July 1, 1967; children: Steven, Sean. BS, U. Wis., 1962; MS, U. Iowa, 1965. Intern VA Med. Ctr., Hines, Ill., 1962-63; resident in dietetics VA Med. Ctr., Iowa City, 1963-65; dietitian nutrition clinic VA Med. Ctr., Hines, 1965-67, 69-70, chief clin. dietetics, 1970-71, chief adminstrv. dietetics, 1971-73; clin. dietitian VA Med. Ctr., Memphis, 1967-68; asst. chief dietetic service Zablocki VA Med. Ctr., Milw., 1974-85, chief dietetic service, 1985—; adj. lectr. Loyola U. Coll. Dentistry, Maywood, Ill., 1969-72; investigator nutrition VA/Med. Coll. Wis., Milw., 1975—, co-dir. ann. clin. nutrition symposium, Milw., 1979—; chairperson task force on ration allowance VA, Washington, 1977-84, mem. dietetic service spl. interest users group, Washington, 1983-85, chairperson tech. adv. group region IV, 1986; mem. dietetic intership adv. bd. St. Luke's Hosp., Milw., 1983-87; lectr., speaker in field, 1965—. Author videocassette, 1976; editor: Nutrition Principles and Dietary Guidelines for Patients Receiving Chemotherapy and Radiation Therapy, 1980; contbr. articles to profl. jours., 1978—. Mem. profl. edn. com. Milw. South unit Am. Cancer Soc., 1976-86, bd. dirs. Milw. South unit, 1984-86, Milw. div., 1986—, Wis. div., 1978—, del. to Milw. div., 1984-85, mem. organizational and expansion com. Milw. div., 1986—, profl. edn. com. Milw. div., 1986-87, Wis. div., 1987—, mem. taking control com. Wis. div., 1987—; mem. med. adv. com. YMCA Met. Milw., 1985—. Recipient Disting. Service award Am. Cancer Soc. Milw. South unit, 1980, Women of Achievement award Girl Scouts Milw. Area, 1987; Paralyzed Vets. Am. research grantee, 1981-83. Mem. Am. Dietetic Assn. (registered, practice group 1980—, mgmt. responsibilities in gerontol. nutrition, dietetics in phys. medicine and rehab. 1983—, nat. media spokesperson 1983—, Outstanding Service award 1983-87), Wis. Dietetic Assn. (co-chairperson div. mgmt. practice 1976-77, chairperson 1977-78, bd. dirs. 1981-83, 87—, council on practice 1982-83, coordinating cabinet 1984—, pres.-elect 1987—, Wis. Medallion award 1986), Milw. Dietetic Assn. (community nutrition and clin. dietetics and research coms. 1975-76, chairperson ad hoc com. for nutrition and oncology patient 1976-79, clin. dietetics and research study group 1981—, chairperson 1983-85, pres. 1982-83, by-laws com. 1983-84, chairperson policies and procedures com. 1983—, pub. relations com. 1983-87, chairperson nominating com. 1984-85). Home: 18230 LeChateau Dr Brookfield WI 53005 Office: Zablocki VA Med Ctr 5000 W National Ave Milwaukee WI 53295

ROONEY, MARY FRANCES, lawyer; b. Chgo., Nov. 1, 1952; d. Francis A. and Cele M. (Looney) R. BA, Marquette U., 1974; JD, John Marshall Sch. Law, Chgo., 1981. Bar: Ill. 1981. Project analyst City of Milw., 1975; adminstrv. asst. to lt. gov. Ill., Chgo., 1976; staff asst. Ill. Senate, Chgo. and Springfield, 1977-82, legis. asst., 1982-83, parliamentarian, legal counsel, 1983-84; atty. Richard S. Jalovec & Assocs., Chgo., 1985—; parliamentarian, legal counsel Ill. Dem. Party, Chgo. and Springfield, 1983-84; legal counsel Waste Mgmt. of N.Am., Oak Brook, Ill., 1986— . Pres. Dem. Party of Rogers Park and Edgewater, Chgo., 1983-84; mem. Chgo. Area Pub. Affairs Council, 1983-84; fundraiser Dem. Nat. Com., 1984—; asst. Ill. counsel Walter Mondale Presdl. Campaign, 1984; gen. counsel Ill. Com. to elect Albert Gore Pres., 1988. Mem. ABA, Ill. State Bar Assn., Chgo. Bar Assn. Home: 1041 W North Shore Ave Chicago IL 60626 Office: Waste Mgmt of N Am 3003 Butterfield Rd Oak Brook IL 60521

ROOSEVELT, SELWA S., federal protocol chief; b. Kingsport, Tenn., Jan. 13, 1929; m. Archibald B. Roosevelt, Sept. 1, 1950; 1 stepchild, Tweed. B.A., Vassar Coll., 1950. Reporter, columnist Washington Star, 1954-58; spl. asst. to head Kennedy Ctr. Performing Arts, 1961; feature writer Washington Post, 1961; writer Family Circle Mag., 1976-82. contbg. editor Town & Country, 1976-82; contbr. articles to profl. mags. and newspapers. Mem. adv. bd. Duke U. Comprehensive Cancer Ctr.; chmn. Blair House Restoration Project. Recipient Outstanding Civilian Service medal Dept. Army, 1983, Betty Ford award Susan Komen Found., Dallas, 1985; honored by the Ripon Soc. in their Salute to Republican Women, 1987. Mem. Folger Shakespeare Library. Republican. Methodist. Clubs: "F" Street (Washington); Colony (N.Y.). Office: Dept State 2201 C St NW Room 1232 Washington DC 20520

ROOT, JOAN SCHIMPF, civic worker, museum trustee; b. Phila., Jan. 25, 1926; d. Henry Leonard and Josephine Abbott (Sibson) Schimpf; B.A., Skidmore Coll., 1947; m. Stanley W. Root, Jr., Sept. 3, 1949; children—Henry W., Louise A., Walter W. (dec.). Chmn. mus. guide program Phila. Mus. Art, 1971-74, exec. com. Friends of Mus., 1975-77, pres. women's com., 1977-80, ex-officio mem. bd. trustees, 1977-80, trustee, mem. exec. com., 1980—; port warden, mem. exec. com. Phila. Maritime Mus., 1979-86; bd. dirs. Friends Ind. Nat. Hist. Park, 1975-78, mem. capital projects com., 1980, mem. intern selection com., 1981-83; mem. trustee com. Mus. Council Phila., 1981; exec. com. U.S. Assn. Mus. Vols., 1980-82; bd. dirs. Goldie Paley Design Ctr., Phila. Coll. Textiles and Sci., 1982-85; mem. Morris Arboretum Mem. Council, U. Pa., 1985—; trustee Fairmount Park Council Hist. Sites, 1985—. Mem. Internat. Council Mus., Am. Assn. Mus., Vol. Com. Art Mus., Eastern Nat. Parks and Monuments Assn., Am. Craft Council, Nat. Trust Historic Preservation. Republican. Episcopalian. Clubs: Acorn, Sedgeley. Address: 16 Hounds Run Ln Blue Bell PA 19422

ROOT, NINA J., librarian; b. N.Y.C., Dec. 22; d. Jacob J. and Fannie (Slivinsky) Root; B.A., Hunter Coll.; M.S. in L.S., Pratt Inst.; postgrad. U.S. Dept. Agr. Grad. Sch., 1964-65, City U. N.Y., 1970-75. Reference and serials librarian Albert Einstein Coll. Medicine Library, Bronx, N.Y., 1958-59; asst. chief librarian Am. Cancer Soc., N.Y.C., 1959-62; chief librarian Am. Inst. Aeros. and Astronautics, N.Y.C., 1962-64; head reference and library services sci. and tech. div. Library of Congress, Washington, 1964-66; mgmt. cons. Nelson Assocs., Inc., N.Y.C., 1966-70; chmn. dept. library services Am. Mus. Natural History, N.Y.C., 1970—; free-lance mgmt. cons. and library planning, 1970—. Trustee Barnard Found., 1984—; mem. library adv. council N.Y. State Bd. Regents, 1984—, trustee Metro, 1987— . Recipient Meritorious Service award Library of Congress, 1965. Mem. ALA (preservation com. 1977-79, chmn. library/binders com. 1978-80, chmn. preservation sect. 1980-81, mem. council 1983-86), Spl. Libraries Assn. (sec. documentation group N.Y. chpt. 1972-73, 2d v.p. N.Y. 1975-76, treas. sci. and tech. group N.Y. 1975-76, mus. arts and humanities div. program planning chairperson-conf. 1977), AAAS, Am. Sci. Info. Sci., Archons of Colophon (convener 1978-79), Soc. History of Natural History (N. Am. rep. 1977-85), N.Y. Acad. Scis. (mem. publs. com. 1975-80, archives com. 1976-78, search com. 1976). Club: Grolier (mem. exhbn. com. 1977-79, admissions com. 1979-81, library com. 1988—). Home: 400 E 59th St New York NY 10022 Office: Library Am Mus Natural Hist Central Park W at 79th St New York NY 10024

ROOTS, LINDA LEE, lawyer; b. N.Y.C., Apr. 4, 1949; d. Howard S. and Lenora M. (Mitchell) R.; 1 child, Jade L. BA summa cum laude, Queens Coll., 1973; JD, St. John's Sch. Law, 1980. Tng. specialist N.Y. Community Tng. Inst., N.Y.C., 1974-77; cons. Donchian Mgmt. Services, N.Y.C., 1977-80; asst. dep. atty. gen. N.Y. State Dept. Law, N.Y.C., 1980-82; assoc. Robinson, Silverman, Pearce, Aronsohn & Berman, N.Y.C., 1982-88; ptnr. Roots & Branch P.C., N.Y.C., 1988—; co-chmn. Third World Lawyers Caucus, N.Y. State Dept. Law, 1981-82. Co-chmn. PTA Lewis Armstrong Middle Sch., Queens. Recipient plaque Third World Lawyers Caucus. Mem. Macon B. Allen Black Bar Assn., St. Johns Law Sch. Alumni Assn., Black Am. Law Student Assn. Alumni Group. Home: 24-37 95th St East Elmhurst NY 11209

ROPER, MARGARET ELIZA, personnel director; b. Richmond, Va., May 28, 1956; d. Robert Joseph Roper and Margaret (Jones) Galbreath. BA, East Carolina U., 1980. Supr. mfg. Burlington Industries, Raeford, N.C., 1980-82, mgr. dept. mfg., 1982-83; mgr. personnel-tng. Goshen Rubber Co., Snow Hill, N.C., 1983-87; personnel mgr. Aeroquip Corp., Middlesec, N.C., 1987—. Republican. Episcopalian. Home: 1216-C Manassas Ct Raleigh NC 27609 Office: Aeroquip Corp PO Box 369 Middlesex NC 28580

ROPER, RUTH, manufacturing company administrator; b. Laurens, S.C., Mar. 24, 1954; d. Robert Hudgens Jr. and Virginia Caroline (Wier) R. BA in English, Winthrop Coll., 1975; MBA, Clemson U., 1986. Tchr. S.C. Pub. Schs., Laurens, 1975-79; supr. prodn. Cryovac div. W. R. Grace & Co., Simpsonville, S.C., 1979-81, mgr. materials, 1981-83, mgr. personnel, 1983-84; sr. fin. analyst Duncan, S.C., 1984-86; supt. mfg. Simpsonville, 1986—. Bd. dirs. Old Ninety-Six council Girl Scouts U.S., Greenville, S.C., 1986—. Mem. S.C. Vocat. Rehab. (bd. dirs. 1985—), Univ. Ridge Assn. (bd. dirs. 1984-85). Presbyterian. Club: Tryon Hunt (N.C.). Home: 212 W Prentiss Ave Greenville SC 29605 Office: Cryovac div W R Grace & Co Maple St Simpsonville SC 29361

ROQUEMORE, NANCY GWEN, magazine editor; b. Atlanta, Jan. 15, 1949; d. Robert Lee Roquemore and Helen (Davis) Cox. BA in English, Ga. Southwestern Coll., 1973; MLS, Atlanta U., 1978. Tchr., librarian Lee Crest Acad., Fayetteville, Ga., 1973-75; librarian Clayton County, Riverdale, Ga., 1975-80; photo librarian Atlanta Jour.-Constn., 1980-81, typesetter mag., 1981-82, copy editor mag., 1982-84, assoc. editor mag., 1984—. Lodge: Order Eastern Star (worshipful master 1981-82). Office: Atlanta Weekly 72 Marietta St Atlanta GA 30303

RORISON, MARGARET LIPPITT, reading consultant; b. Wilmington, N.C., Feb. 6, 1925; d. Harmon Chadbourn and Margaret Devereux (Lippitt) R.; A.B., Hollins Coll., 1946; M.A., Columbia U., 1956; Diplôme de langue, L'Alliance Française, Paris, 1966; postgrad. U. S.C., 1967-70, 81—. Market and editorial researcher Time, Inc., N.Y.C., 1949-55; classroom and corrective reading tchr. N.Y.C. public schs., 1956-65; TV instr. ETV-WNDT, Channel 13, N.Y.C., 1962-63; grad. asst., TV instr. U. S.C., Columbia, 1967-70; instrnl. specialist in reading S.C. Office Instrnl. TV and Radio, S.C. Dept. Edn., Columbia, 1971-81; reading cons. S.C. Office Instructional Tech., 1982—. Active Common Cause. Mem. Internat. Reading Assn., Am. Ednl. Research Assn., Assn. Supervision and Curriculum Devel., Nat. Soc. Study of Edn., AAUW. Phi Delta Kappa, Delta Kappa Gamma. Episcopalian. Author instrnl. TV series: Getting the Word (So. Ednl. Communications Assn. award 1972, Ohio State award 1973, S.C. Scholastic Broadcasters award 1973), Getting the Message, 1981. Home: 1724 Enoree Ave Columbia SC 29205

RORKE, MARCIA LYNNE, research firm executive; b. Albany, N.Y., Nov. 17, 1942; d. Gerald Dean and Bernice Elizabeth (Ferguson) Bouton; m. Jerome Alan Grad, Sept. 1966 (div. Jan. 1971); m. John Joseph Rorke, III, May 3, 1980; children: Blys Lien Grad, John Joseph. BA, U. Denver, 1969, MA, 1975. Pres., Mohawk Research Corp., Rockville, Md., 1979—; research asst. dept. mass communications U. Denver, 1967-69; instr. dept. history Trinity Coll., Burlington, Vt., 1971-72; research asst. spl. edn. program U. Vt., Burlington, 1971-73; writer/editor Behavior Assocs., Tucson, Ariz., 1973-74; research social scientist Social Systems Research and Evaluation Div. and Ctr. for Social Research and Devel., Denver, 1975-79; treas., dir. Inventors Council Chgo., 1983-86; dir. Ind. Bus. Assn. Ill., 1983-86; cons. The World Bank, Washington, 1977-79, U.S. AID, Dept. State, Washington, 1978, Entrepreneurship Inst., Columbus, Ohio, 1977-79, Owens-Corning Fiberglas, Granville, Ohio, 1977-78, Coler Engring. Co., N.Y.C., 1977-81. Contbr. articles to profl. jours. Mem. alumni exec. bd. Am. Field Service Internat. Scholarships, N.Y.C., 1971-73, exchange student scholar, 1960. Mem. Lic. Execs. Soc., AAAS, Tech. Transfer Soc., Inventors Council of Chgo. Office: Mohawk Research Corp 915 Willowleaf Way Rockville MD 20854

ROSADO, PEGGY MORAN, actress, singer, dancer, educator; b. Canton, Ohio, Apr. 16, 1946; d. Clarence Ellsworth and Mabel Cecilia (Kearns) Moran; student Northwestern U.; B.S., Kent State U.; M.A., Hunter Coll., 1969; student Arthur Mitchell's Dance Theatre of Harlem, 1971, Am. Ballet Theatre, 1972-74; m. Richard Robert Garcia di Magpiong, Apr. 7, 1979. Dir., lead dancer New World Dancers Inc., N.Y.C., 1971—; dance tchr. performing arts program Franklin K. Lane High Sch., Bklyn., 1970-71; dance tchr., choreographer Lincoln Sq. Community Center, N.Y.C., 1971-76, 81—; tchr. singing La Guardia High Sch., Lincoln Ctr., 1985—, stage dir., Opera Workshop choreographer, 1986— ; emergency dancer Arthur Mitchell's Dance Theatre of Harlem, 1976—; student head NBC Theatre Workshop, N.Y.C., 1960-61; film appearances Serpico, Dog Day Afternoon, Nunzio, Prince of the City, Ragtime, So Fine, Cotton Club; TV series Fame; choreographer New World Journey, 1971, The Creation, 1982, Glück's Orfeo and Euridice, La Guardia High Sch., 1987, Purcell's Dido and Aeneas, 1988. Mem. Actors Equity Assn., Screen Actors Guild, AFTRA, AGVA, Assn. Am. Dance Cos., Am. Indian Community House. Roman Catholic. Home and Office: 345 W 58th St New York NY 10019

ROSAMOND, PATRICIA ANN, construction company executive; b. Columbia, S.C., June 19, 1947; d. Joseph William and Ethel Alice (Frossard) Ludwig; m. Denver Wade Rosamond, July 17, 1965; children: Jill Ann, Joy Christine. Student, Queens Coll., 1976-78. Inter co. sales Anixter Bros., Inc., St. louis, 1971-72; adminstrv. asst. Rodgers Builders, Inc., Charlotte, N.C., 1972-75, project mgr., 1975-78, v.p., 1978-82, exec. v.p., 1982-87; pres. Rodgers Builders, Inc., Charlotte, 1987—. Appointed mem. pvt. Industry Council, 1984-85; bd. dirs. Hornet's Nest Girl Scout Council, Charlotte, 1985-86, U. N.C.-Charlotte Athletic Found., 1986—, Mercy Hosp. South Adv. Council, Pineville, 1987—. Mem. Carolinas Assn. Gen. Contractors (bd. dirs. 1986—), Mecklenburg Gen. Contractors (bd. dirs. 1987—). Office: Rodgers Builders Inc 5701 N Sharon Amity Rd Charlotte NC 28215

ROSAMOND, SANDRA PAULINE (SANDI), educator; b. Oklahoma City, July 22, 1947; d. Benjamin Franklin and Opal Pauline (Wilson) Creason; m. Marvin Lee Cooke, Dec. 23, 1967 (div. 1979); 1 child, Francis Wesley Cooke; m. Freedus Edward Rosamond, Mar. 17, 1984. BS in Edn., Cen. State U., Okla., 1969; MS in Family Relations and Child Devel., Okla. State U., 1977, postgrad., 1986—. Cert. educator, vocat. educator, Okla. Tchr. Oklahoma City Pub. Schs., 1969-70, Ctr. Sch. Dist., Kansas City, Mo., 1970-72; adminstrv. asst. Grad. Sem., Phillips U., Enid, Okla., 1974-75; tchr. pre-sch. Meml. Dr. United Meth. Ch., Tulsa, 1975-77; officer probation Juvenile Bur. Okla. Dist. Ct., Tulsa, 1977-81, fiscal officer, 1981-82; tchr. Liberty Mounds Schs., Mounds, Okla., 1982-83; tchr. L.E. Rader Juvenile Ctr., Sand Springs, Okla., 1983-86, chairperson tchrs., 1983-86, tchr. intensive treatment, 1986—; owner Sandi's Crochet Originals; grant reader Okla. State Bd. Edn., Oklahoma City, 1985. Contbr. articles to profl. jours. Chairperson, with curriculum devel. sexuality com. Okla. United Meths., Oklahoma City, 1974-77, bd. dirs. placement and adoption bd., 1975-78; mem. rewrite com. Okla. State Dept. Vocat./Tech. Edn. in Home and Community Services, 1988. Mem. NEA, Nat. Assn. Vocat. Edn. for Spl. Needs Persons, Am. Vocat. Assn., Sand Springs Edn. Assn. (rep. 1985-87, Bldg. Tchr. of Yr. 1987), Omicron Nu, Beta Sigma Phi. Democrat. Office: LE Rader Juvenile Ctr Intensive Treatment Program Rt 4 Box 9 Sand Springs OK 74063

ROSAR, VIRGINIA WILEY, librarian; b. Cleve., Nov. 22, 1926; d. John Egbert and Kathryn Coe (Snyder) Wiley; m. Michael Thorpe Rosar, April 8, 1950 (div. Feb. 1968); children: Bruce Wiley, Keith Michael, James Wilfred. Attended, Oberlin Coll., 1944-46; BA, U. Puget Sound, 1948; MS, C.W. Post Coll., L.I.U., Greenvale, N.Y., 1971. Cert. elem. music teacher, N.Y.; cert. sch. library media specialist. Music programmer Station WFAS, White Plains, N.Y., 1948; prodn. asst. NBC-TV, N.Y.C., 1948-50; tchr. Portledge Sch., Locust Valley, N.Y., 1967-70; librarian Syosset (N.Y.) Schs., 1970-71, Smithtown (N.Y.) Schs., 1971—; pres. World of Realia, Woodbury, N.Y., 1969-86; founder Cygnus Pub., Woodbury, 1985-87. Active local chpt. ARC, 1960-63, Community Concert Assn., 1960-66, Leukemia Soc. Am., 1978—. Mem. Suffolk Sch. Library Media Assn., AAAS, N.Y. Acad. Scis., Am. Mus. Natural History (assoc.), Am. Library Assn., L.I. Alumnae Club of Pi Beta Phi (pres. 1964-66). Republican. Presbyterian. Home: 10 Warrenton Ct Huntington NY 11743

ROSBERGER, ANNE WALDMAN, psychotherapist; b. N.Y.C., Nov. 23, 1932; d. Joseph and Susan (Wagner) Waldman; B.A., Bklyn. Coll., 1953; M.S., Columbia U., 1955; postgrad Yeshiva U., 1977—; m. Henry Rosberger, Oct. 12, 1958; children—Daniel, Richard. Sr. caseworker, supr. Salvation Army Family Service Bur., N.Y.C., 1955-59; field instr., 1968-69; chief cons., supr. Widows Consultation Center, N.Y.C., 1971-76; pvt. practice psychotherapy, N.Y.C., 1958—; exec. dir. Bereavement and Loss Center of N.Y., N.Y.C., 1976—; cons. St. Vincent's Hosp. Hospice, N.Y.C., 1979—; lectr. in field. Contbr. articles to profl. jours. Mem. Nat. Assn. Social

Workers, Acad. Cert. Social Workers, Columbia U. Sch. Social Work Alumni Assn. (dir.), Alpha Kappa Delta. Office: 170 E 83d St New York NY 10028

ROSCHE, CHRISTINE, health educator; b. Linz, Austria, Apr. 30, 1951; d. Fred Richard and Gertrude (Susan) R. BA in Psychology, Stanford U., 1976; MPH, San Jose State U., 1983. Coordinator Community Preventive Medicine, Stanford, Calif., 1979-81; sr. health edn. specialist Control Data Corp., San Jose, Calif., 1983-86; health promotion edn. specialist Berkson Clinic, Los Altos, Calif., 1986—; cons. YMCA, Palo Alto, 1985—, Cardiovascular Research, Los Altos, 1986—, Stanford Heart Disease Prevention Program. Author: Taking Charge of Your Stress, Decode the Insurance Puzzle; contbr. articles to profl. jours. Mem. Assn. Fitness in Bus., Am. Soc. Tng. and Devel., Am. Pub. Health Assn., Calif. Health Practitioners Assn., Trager Inst. Democrat. Roman Catholic. Home: 10441 Pharlap Dr Cupertino CA 95014 Office: 774 Montrose Ave Palo Alto CA 94301

ROSE, DEBORAH JANE, financial planner; b. San Francisco, Apr. 14, 1954; d. Leonard L. Rose and Charlene (Reynolds) Lewis. BS summa cum laude, U. Houston, 1983. Asst. mgr. Home Savs., Houston, 1977-79; mgr. bus. devel. Commonwealth Savs., Houston, 1979-80; self-employed pension cons. Houston, 1980-82; regional pres. Gibraltar Savs., Houston, 1982-86; v.p. br. adminstrn. BancPlus, Houston, 1986-87; fin. planner CM Alliance, Houston, 1988—. Mem. speakers bur. Houston Livestock Show and Rodeo, Houston, 1986—. Mem. Fedn. Houston Profl. Women (dir. ways and means com. 1987), Am. Bus. Women Assn. (program chmn. 1984), Houston C. of C. (life, vice. chmn. membership com. 1985-87), Leadership Houston Class VI (grad.). Republican. Lodge: Kiwanis (Houston). Home: 8323 Wilcrest #8004 Houston TX 77072 Office: CM Alliance 4265 San Felipe 7th Floor Houston TX 77027

ROSE, DENISE BEYE, ins. co. official; b. Portsmouth, Va., Oct. 22, 1953; d. Fred Lewis and Donna Kathleen (Luing) Beye; B.A., U. Ark., 1974; m. Andy Murray Rose, Nov. 23, 1979. With Nationwide Ins., Denver, 1974-75; with Ins. Co. of N.Am., 1975-77, bond underwriter, Dallas, 1976-77; resident mgr. states of Tenn., Ky., Lawyers Surety Corp., Nashville, 1977-85, ind. agy. mgr. Allstate Ins. Co., 1985-87; sr. mktg. mgr. Nat. Grange Mut. Ins. Co., 1987—. Cert. profl. ins. woman, cert. ins. counselor licensed agt. Mem. Nat. Assn. Ins. Women, Tenn. Ins. Assn., Insurers of Tenn., Surety Assn. Nashville, Profl. Ins. Agts. Tenn., Nat. Assn. Female Execs., Ark. Alumni Assn. Republican. Baptist. Club: 1752 (v.p. 1980, pres. 1981, sec.-treas. 1982-84, treas. 1985-86). Home: 4019 Moss Rose Dr Nashville TN 37216

ROSE, DENISE FARAH, program analyst; b. Bklyn., June 24, 1962; d. Donald Charles and Marcelle Helen (Farah) R. BA, Furman U., 1984. Researcher Nat. Ctr. Mcpl. Devel., Washington, 1983-84; product adminstr. Unisys, McLean, Va., 1984-85; data analyst Planning Research Corp., McLean, 1985-88; sr. program analyst Am. Automobile Assn., Falls Church, Va., 1988—. Mem. McLean Jr. Women's Club. Mem. Nat. Assn. Female Execs. Club: Toastmasters (adminstrv. v.p. McLean chpt. 1986—). Home: 1725 Cy Ct Vienna VA 22180 Office: Am Automobile Assn 8111 Gatehouse Rd Falls Church VA 22047

ROSE, DIAN JORDAN, training program coordinator; b. Waco, Tex., Dec. 19, 1962; d. Frank Clifton and Ruby Lee (Warren) Jordan; m. Kenneth E. Rose, Jan. 10, 1987. AA in Journalism, Eastern Okla. State Coll., 1987; student, U. Okla., 1987—. Paste-up artist, writer Jour. Newspaper, Broken Bow, Okla., 1981-83; news anchorwoman Sta. KLOP TV, Broken Bow, 1983-85; nontraditonal coordinator Kiamichi Area Vo-Tech. Sch., Idabel, Okla., 1985—. Contbr. articles to profl. jours. Vol. Southeastern Shelter Battered Women, Idabel, 1985-87. Mem. Am. Vocat. Assn., Okla. Vocat. Assn., Okla. Women Edn. Adminstrn., Vocat. Equity Council, McCurtain County Pub. Resource Assn. (domestic violence task force) Bus. and Profl. Women's Club (pres. elect, pub. relations chmn. 1986, Young Careerist 1987). Home: 104 Banbury Ln Idabel OK 74745 Office: Kiamchi Area Vo-Tech Sch Rt 3 Box 177 Idabel OK 74745

ROSE, EDITH SPRUNG, lawyer; b N.Y.C., Jan. 7, 1924; d. David L. and Anna (Storch) Sprung; m. David J. Rose, Feb. 15, 1948; children Elizabeth Rose Stanton, Lawrence, Michael. B.A., Barnard Coll., 1944; LL.B., Columbia U., 1946. Bar: N.Y. 1947, N.J. 1973. Adminstr., Practising Law Inst., N.Y.C., 1947-48; ptnr. Smith, Lambert, Hicks & Miller, Princeton, N.J., 1974-88; counsel to Drinker, Biddle & Reath, Princeton, 1988—. Mem. ABA, N.J. Bar Assn., Princeton Bar Assn., Women's Law Caucus of Mercer County. Club: Princeton (N.Y.C.). Home: 201 Lambert Dr Princeton NJ 08540 Office: PO Box 627 1 Palmer Square Princeton NJ 08540

ROSE, ELAINE OLGA, small business owner, artist; b. Pawtucket, R.I., Mar. 31, 1943; d. Thomas and Olga Ann (Rabchenuk) Graiko; m. Guiteau Lanoue, 1984; children: Tamara, Nicole Lanoue. Student, U. Tenn., 1974. Supr. claims Chesapeake Life Ins., Balt., 1973-75; supr. ins. Kelsey-Seybold, Houston, 1975; pres. Artist's Touch, Inc., Houston, 1976—. Pub. posters Westheimer Festival, 1979—; exhibitor Internat. Art Exhbn., N.Y.C., 1984—; numerous commns. Recipient cert. for contbn. Houston Sch. for Deaf, 1981-82, Merit award Notable Women Tex., 1984, Tex. Star award Channel 8 Auction, 1987. Mem. Art League Houston, Water Color Soc. (so. chpt.), Profl. Picture Framers Assn., Art Dealers Assn., Nat. Artists Equity Assn., Nat. Mus. Women in Arts. Republican. Mem. Assemblies of God. Office: Artists Touch Inc 8800 K Bissonnet St Houston TX 77074

ROSE, ELIZABETH (PATRICIA H. BURKE), author; b. N.Y.C., Sept. 18, 1941; d. William James and Bernadine S. (Ryan) Burke; children: Kimberly, Dana. Nurse, Lenox Hill Hosp. Sch. Nursing, 1962; BA summa cum laude, U. Redlands, 1976. Asst. head nurse emergency room N.Y.C., 1963-66; head nurse San Pedro (Calif.) Hosp., 1968-69; pub. Butterfly Pub. Co., Santa Monica, 1985; radio and TV personality Los Angeles, 1985—; founder Candidiasis Anonymous, Santa Monica, 1985; cons. health profls.. Author: Lady of Gray: Healing, 1985, Candida-Nightmares Chemical Epidemic, (audio cassettes) Healing Candida I through IV; contbr. articles to profl. jours. Mem. UCLA Alumni Assn. (life), Independent Writers So. Calif., Womens Nat. Book Assn., Pubs. Mktg. Assn., Cousteau Soc., Los Angeles County Mus. Art., Better Word Soc., Nat. Abortion Rights League, Can. Abortion Rights League. Clubs: Los Angeles Blue Book, Sierra. Office: Elizabeth Rose Prodns 2210 Wilshire Blvd Suite 845 Santa Monica CA 90403

ROSE, EUNICE MARGOLIS, singer; b. Cleve., Jan. 9, 1935; d. Marvin and Florence (Eglin) Margolis; m. Norman Rose, Feb. 12, 1961; 1 child, Heidi Margolis. Student, Cleve. Inst. Music, 1953-54, Cleve. Coll., 1953-54, Rosary Hill, 1969-70, Villa Maria, 1971-72. With The Tracey Twins; solo act Euni Tracey Presents; agt., coordinator Fenby/Stein Talent Agy., Farmington Hills, Mich., 1976-83. Tracey Twins appeared in TV shows, clubs, theaters and fairs; (as Euni Tracey) appearance on cable TV program Time for a Story, 1987 (Philo T. Farnsworth award), Yankee Doodle Sings Again; recs. include Tonight You Belong to Me; solo appearances in schs. Children's programmer Southfield (Mich.) Pub. Library, 1974-76; pres. Friends of the Southfield Pub. Library, 1982—; mem. 2001 Com. for City of Southfield, 1983; dir. Temple Emanu-El Youth Choir, Oak Park, Mich., 1972—, Southfield Youth Chorus, 1981-83. Democrat. Jewish. Home and Office: 16300 N Park Dr #707 Southfield MI 48075

ROSE, GAIL ELAINE, wholesale trade company manager; b. Chgo., Sept. 14, 1949; d. Edward Vincent and Ollove Lorraine (Ruska) Ruzicka. A.A.S., Morton Coll., 1969; B.A., Nat. Coll. Edn., Evanston, Ill., 1984. Dental asst. Merrill Shepro, D.D.S., LaGrange Park, Ill., 1968-71; dental asst. instr. Morton Coll., Cicero, Ill., 1969-71; dental asst. Bernard C. Marker D.D.S., Niles, Ill., 1971-73; adminstrv. asst. KYB Corp. Am., Oak Brook, Ill., 1973-78, adminstrv. mgr., Lombard, Ill., 1978-87, dir. adminstrv. dept., 1987—. Mem., assoc. Ill. Sheriffs' Assn., 1982-86; mem. Republican Nat. Com., Washington, 1980—. Mem. Am. Mgmt. Assn., Internat. Platform Assn., Nat. Assn. Female Execs., Japan Am. Soc. Chgo. Roman Catholic. Lodge: Women of Moose. Avocations: phys. fitness, bicycling, reading. Office: KYB Corp Am 901 Oak Creek Dr Lombard IL 60148

ROSE, JANET SHIRLEY, nurse, educator; b. Holdenville, Okla., May 22, 1938; d. Audrey (Moses) Rose. B.S., Barry U., 1981. R.N.; cert. emergency and trauma nurse. Staff nurse psychiatry Norton Meml. Infirmary, Louisville, 1959-60; asst. head nurse psychiatry Cleve. Clinic Hosp., 1960-63; head nurse intensive care Winter Haven Hosp. (Fla.), 1963-70; office mgr. for physician, Winter Haven, 1970-72; supr. nursing Lake Wales Hosp. (Fla.), 1972-73; staff nurse emergency dept. Parkway Regional Med. Center, North Miami Beach, Fla., 1973-83, nursing educator, 1983-86, hospice utilization rev. nurse, 1986—. Mem. Nat. Assn. Female Execs., Nat. Assn. Educators, Emergency Dept. Nurses Assn. (sec., dir. edn. 1981-83), Nat. Emergency Dept. Nurses Assn., Am. Nurses Assn., Fla. Nurses Assn., Am. Assn. Critical Care Nurses. Republican. Episcopalian. Office: 100 N Biscayne Blvd Miami FL 33132

ROSE, JOANNA SEMEL, cultural board member; b. Orange, N.J., Nov. 22, 1930; d. Philip Ephraim and Lillian (Mindlin) Semel; m. Daniel Rose, Sept. 16, 1956; children: David S., Joseph B., Emily, Gideon G. Cert. Shakespeare Inst., U.K., 1951; BA summa cum laude, Bryn Mawr Coll., 1952; postgrad. St. Hilda's Coll., Oxford U., 1953. Chmn. adv. bd. Partisan Rev., N.Y.C.; former pres. bd. dirs. current bd. dirs. Paper Bag Players, N.Y.C.; current bd. dirs. Poets and Writers, Inc., N.Y.C., Guild Hall, East Hampton, N.Y., Nat. Dance Inst., N.Y.C., British Inst., N.Y.C., Musical Theatre Works, N.Y.C., Eldridge St. Project, N.Y.C., Ctr. for Visual History, N.Y.C., Am. Friends of St. Hilda's Coll.; Assoc. fellow Berkeley Coll., Yale U. Bryn Mawr European fellow Oxford U., 1952-53. Clubs: Cosmopolitan, Bryn Mawr (N.Y.C.). Home: 895 Park Ave New York NY 10021

ROSE, JULIE BETH, small business owner, fashion design educator; b. Houston, Aug. 23, 1960; d. Michael Laurence Rose and Mary Ann (Hayutin) Rolfe. AAS in Jewelry Design, Fashion Inst. Tech., N.Y.C., 1981. Sales rep. Morris Berger, Inc., N.Y.C., 1981; designer Jenay Jewelry, N.Y.C., 1981; prin. Julie Rose...Jewelry, N.Y.C., 1981—; mem. faculty Parsons Sch. Design, N.Y.C., 1986—. Mem. Nat. Orgn. Female Execs., Women's Jewelry Assn. Jewish. Club: China. Office: 301 W 45 Suite 2B New York NY 10036

ROSE, LISA, interior designer; b. N.Y.C., Jan. 22, 1950; d. Marte and Elisabeth (Carradonna) Previti; B.S., Cornell U., 1971; student N.Y. Sch. Interior Design, 1975. Asst. designer Braswell-Willoughby, N.Y.C., 1976-78; designer Jay Spectre Inc., N.Y.C., 1978-80; pres. Aubergine Interiors Ltd., N.Y.C., 1980—. Interior design projects pub. by various publs., including N.Y. Times, Interior Design, House Beautiful, Cosmopolitan, Maison Francaise, Home mag., Design mag., Diversion mag., Ladies Home Jour., Designer mag. Mem. Internat. Soc. Interior Designers, Women Bus. Owners, Women in Design.

ROSE, ROSEMARY S. CATHERINE, business executive, financial consultant; b. Antigo, Wis., Jan. 2, 1931; d. Ernest J. and Rose F. Slizewski; 1 child, Ted R. Secretarial cert. Bryant-Stratton Sch., Milw., 1953; real estate course Spencerian Sch., Milw., 1964-65; Am. Inst. Paralegal Studies, 1985-86. Lic. real estate broker, Wis. Adminstrv. asst. H. R. Salen, Waukesha, Wis., 1951-55; owner, operator Country Motel, Brookfield, Wis., 1955-65; co-owner Al's Super Service, Lannon, Wis., 1960-65; exec. sec. E.P. Hoyer, New Berlin, Wis., 1967-70; owner, operator Sanitation Service Inc., Menomonee Falls, Wis., 1970-74, North Twin Supper Club, Phelps, Wis., 1975-79; exec. sec., v.p. systems O.L. Schilffarth Co. div. Crown Industries, Milw., 1979-82; adminstr. food service Meurer Bakeries of Milw., 1984; owner R-Service Co., Germantown, Wis., 1980—; exec. housekeeper Park East Hotel, Milw., 1984-85; office mgr. Cedar Disposal, Inc., Menomonee Falls, 1985-87; gen. mgr., Hotel Rogers, Beaver Dam, Wis., 1983-84; broker, prin. Alrose Realty Co., 1964—; adminstr. A-1 Service Co., Inc., Germantown, 1987—; mem. Research Bd. of Advisors Nat. Div. Am. Biographical Inst., Inc. Mem. Internat. Platform Assn., Nat. Assn. Female Execs., Nat. Rifle Assn. Home: N105 W15750 Hamilton Ct Germantown WI 53022 Office: A-1 Services Co N 104 W 13075 Donges Bay Rd Germantown WI 53022

ROSE, SHIELA ANNE, technical products consultant; b. Missoula, Mont., Feb. 27, 1954; d. Robert Sayre and Coralie Mae (Segraves) R. Student, U. Mont., 1972-73; B.A. in Spl. Studies in Counseling and Nutrition, Graceland Coll., Iowa, 1976; postgrad. in counseling, Mont. State U., 1978-79. Records specialist Gallatin County, Mont., 1978-79; prodn. supr. High Country News, Bozeman, Mont., 1979-81; prodn. specialist Insty-Prints, Bozeman, 1981-82; press supr. Star Printing, Gillette, Wyo., 1982-83; owner Rose Enterprises, Wright, Wyo., 1983—; tech. writing/publs. cons. space div. Morton Thiokol Inc. Wasatch Ops., Brigham City, Utah, 1987—; tech. writing cons. printer products div. Eaton Corp., Riverton, Wyo., 1986—; bus. plan cons. Diamond "L" Industries Inc., Gillette, 1986—, Allstar Video Inc., Gillette, 1985; subcontractor Amax Coal Co., Gillete, 1986—; tech. services/drafting cons. Thunder Basin Coal Co., Wright, Wyo., 1983-86. Active Nat. Coalition Against Sexual Assault. Mem. Am. Inst. Design and Drafting (state sec. 1984-85, asst. editor D&D News 1983-84, co-chair nat. editorial and pub. relations com.), Soc. for Tech. Communications, NOW, AAUW, Women in Bus. (v.p. 1987), Nat. Assn. Female Execs., Associated Photographer's Internat., Wright Area C. of C., Douglas Area C. of C. Avocation: graphic arts/photography Office: Rose Enterprises PO Box 119 Wright WY 82732

ROSE, SUSAN CAROL, restaurant executive, consultant; b. Rochester, N.Y., Jan. 29, 1942; d. Frederick Raymond Smith and Grace Eunice (Read) Smith Drum; m. Larry Anthoney Rose, Jan. 5, 1963 (div. Jan. 1976); children: John David, Karen Michelle Haines, Patricia Anne. Student, Monroe Community Coll., Rochester, 1959-60; cert. exec. steward, Innisbrook Resort, 1976; student, St. Petersburg Jr. Coll., Tarpon Springs, Fla., 1978-80, Pinellas Voc. Tech., 1987—. With Blue Cross-Blue Shield, Rochester, 1959-67; from coffee service mgr. to exec. steward Innisbrook Resort, Tarpon Springs, 1974-84; catering team supr. Bon Appetit Restaurant, Dunedin, Fla., 1984, Bounty Caterers, Dunedin, 1984; asst. mgr. trainee Wendy's Internat., Largo, Fla., 1984; store mgr. Long John Silver's, Largo, 1984-85; exec. steward, banquet chef, room service mgr., cons. Sandestin Beach Hilton, Destin, Fla., 1985; day mgr. Shells Restaurant, Clearwater, Fla., 1986-87; sous chef, kitchen mgr. Saltwaters Seafood Grille, Palm Harbor, Fla., 1987; exec. steward Adam's Mark Caribbean Gulf Resort, Clearwater Beach, 1987—. Mem. Nat. Assn. Female Execs., Hospitality Industry Assn., Smithsonian Inst. Assocs., Holiday Inn Priority Club, Internat. Travel Club, Clearwater Jaycees. Democrat. Roman Catholic. Home: 1162 Jackson Clearwater FL 33515 Office: Adam's Mark Caribbean Gulf Resort Gulfview Blvd Clearwater Beach FL 34616

ROSE, SUSAN JEAN, accountant; b. Ft. Worth, June 26, 1951; d. Theodore Warren and Dora Jean (Britt) Thompson; m. Billy L. Rose, Feb. 10, 1944 (div. Sept. 1982); 1 child, Melanie Marie. BBA in Acctg., U. Tex., Arlington, 1985. Acctg. mgr. Collier Cobss & Assocs. of Dallas, Inc., 1985—. Flautist Garland Community Orch., 1983—; sec. Gatewood Homeowner's Assn., Garland, Tex., 1986-87, bd. dirs., 1987—. Mem. Dallas Assn. of Credit Mgmt. (chair 1987), Beta Alpha Psi, Beta Gamma Sigma. Club: Toastmasters (sec. 1974-75). Home: 4817 Rollingwood Ct Garland TX 75043 Office: Collier Cobb & Assocs 5750 Pineland Dr Suite 308 Dallas TX 75231

ROSE, VELMA ANNETTE, accountant; b. Aurora, Colo., Dec. 18, 1953; d. William Wood and Marcella Aga (Sheifer) Middleton. BS in Acctg. magna cum laude, U. Colo., 1976, MBA, 1977. CPA, Colo. Sr. auditor Arthur Anderson & Co., Oklahoma City, 1977-80, Peat, Marwick, Mitchell & Co., Denver, 1980-82; mgr. audit Lehman, Butterwick & Co., Lakewood, Colo., 1982-84; controller Regional Transp. Dist., Denver, 1984, fin. dir., 1984-86; dir. budget Denver Pub. Schs., 1986-87, exec. dir. budgetary services, 1987—; mem. fin. policies and procedures com. Colo. Bd. Edn., 1986—; bd. dirs. Colo. Sch. Dists. Self Ins. Pool. Clarinetist Jewish Community Ctr. Orch., Denver, 1980-86. Mem. Am. Inst. CPA's, Colo. Soc. CPA's, Govt. Fin. Officers Assn., (reviewer mem. budget awards program 1985—), Council Great City Schs. Bus. Ofcls., Colo. Assn. Sch. Execs. (bd.dirs. 1987—). Democrat. Jewish. Home: 1928 S Cherry St Denver CO 80222 Office: Denver Pub Schs 900 Grant St Denver CO 80203

ROSELL, SHARON LYNN, physics and chemistry educator, researcher; b. Wichita, Kans., Jan. 6, 1948; d. John E. and Mildred C. (Binder) R. BA, Loretto Heights Coll., 1970; postgrad., Marshall U., 1973; MS in Edn., Ind. U., 1977; MS, U. Wash., 1988. Cert. profl. educator, Wash. Assoc. instr. Ind. U., Bloomington, 1973-74; instr. Pierce Coll. (name formerly Ft. Steilacoom (Wash.) Community Coll.), 1976-79, 82, Olympic Coll., Bremerton, Wash., 1977-78; instr. physics, math. and chemistry Tacoma (Wash.) Community Coll., 1979—; instr. physics and chemistry Green River Community Coll., Auburn, Wash., 1983-86; researcher Nuclear Physics Lab., U. Wash., Seattle, 1985—. Mem. Am. Assn. Physics Tchrs. (rep. com. on physics for 2 yr. coll. 1986-87, v.p. 1987-88, pres. 1988—, Wash. chpt.), Am. Chem. Soc., Internat. Union Pure and Applied Chemistry (affiliate). Democrat. Roman Catholic. Home: 1204 N 7th Apt A Tacoma WA 98403 Office: Tacoma Community Coll 5900 S 12th Tacoma WA 98465

ROSEN, CAROLE ELAINE, communications executive; b. N.Y.C., Oct. 21, 1933; d. Harry Perdesco and Elsie Anna (Zilke) Hoagland; div.; children: Deborah Elizabeth, Robert Alexander. Student, Columbia U., 1950. With TV prodn. MGM TV, Culver City, Calif., 1960-61; writer, syndicator, prodn. Winters/Rosen, Inc., Los Angeles, 1964-73; prodn., TV syndication Rosen, Inc., Los Angeles, 1973-80; pub. relations, mktg. Bombard Soc., Ltd., Century City, Calif., 1980-82; cons. Hemphill/Harris, Inc., Encino, Calif., 1982—; cons. Herbert M. Piken Assocs., Studio City, Calif., Am. Scandinavian Student Exchange, Newport Beach, Calif. Mem. Am. Assn. Travel Editors. Office: Hemphill Harris Inc 16000 Ventura Blvd #200 Encino CA 91436

ROSEN, JAYNE HALPERN, corporate executive; b. N.Y.C., Nov. 10, 1944; d. Max J. and Rosalind Halpern; m. Paul I. Rosen, June 21, 1970. Student U. Wis., 1962-63; B.S., Boston U., 1966. Assoc. editor Pyramid Pubs., 1966-67; assoc. dir. beauty clinic Good Housekeeping, 1967-68; asst. beauty editor Seventeen Mag., N.Y.C., asst. fashion editor Town & Country, N.Y.C., 1968-72; assoc. fashion editor Bride's Mag., N.Y.C., 1972-76; owner Jayne Rosen Pub. Relations, N.Y.C., 1976-81; dir. pub. relations Charles of the Ritz Group, Ltd., N.Y.C., 1981-83; now creative dir., promotions and mktg. J.R. Prodns. Mem. Fashion Group, Cosmetic Exec. Women.

ROSEN, KAREN, interior designer; b. N.Y.C., Jan. 14, 1946; d. Leon D. and Beatrice (Willett) Miller; 1 child, Meredith Lauren. Student Boston U., 1964-66; B.S. in Elem. Edn., NYU, 1968; cert. N.Y. Sch. Interior Design, 1971. Pres., KMR Design Group, Inc., full service design firm, N.Y.C., 1973—; color cons. to various mfrs. and showrooms in design field; interior design work ranges from residential to pub. and comml.; designer custom furnishings; guest lectr. various coll. and real estate courses; numerous radio and TV appearances; work featured in several major design mags. and newspapers. Recipient S.M. Hexter award for best residential interior, 1981. Mem. Am. Soc. Interior Designers (assoc.), Internat. Soc. Interior Designers. Office: KMR Design Group Inc 27 E 63d St Suite 1B New York NY 10021

ROSEN, LUCY GAIR, marketing and public relations professional, photographer; b. Sterling, Ill., Apr. 23, 1960; d. William Maurice Clithero and Suzanne (Grace) Gair; m. Brett Randall Rosen, Oct. 22, 1960 (div. Oct. 1985). B in Mktg., U. N.Mex. Owner, operator Nova Photography, Albuquerque, N.Mex., 1978-80; with salesdept. Sta. KZIA, Albuquerque, N.Mex., 1980-81, Rosen and Assocs., Albuquerque, N.Mex., 1981-86; v.p., creative dir. Rosen and Assocs., N.Y.C., 1986—; dir. pub. relations Alzheimers disease and related disorders, Albuquerque, 1983-85; fundraiser Animal Humane Assn., Albuquerque, 1986—. Mem. social action com. Stephen Wise Free Synagogue, 1986-87. Recipient award for photo exhibit of homeless in N.Y.C., United Jewish Appeal, 1987, Stephen Wife Free Synagogue, 1986; various other awards for photography. Mem. Pub. Relations Soc. Am., Nat. Assn. Female Execs., Albuquerque Jaycees (dir. pub. relations1985-86). Democrat. Jewish. Club: YMCA Photo. Home: 101 W 90th 16-A New York NY 10024

ROSEN, MARCELLA JUNG, advertising executive; b. N.Y.C., Sept. 29, 1934; d. Leo and Irma (Rothschild) Jung; m. E. David Rosen, Dec. 22, 1962 (dec. Feb. 1982); children: Burt, Lisa. BA, Barnard Coll., 1951-55; MA, Columbia U., 1957. Research assoc. Cunningham and Walsh, N.Y.C., 1957-62; account exec. Doyle Dane Bernbach, N.Y.C., 1962-63, Smith Greenland, N.Y.C., 1963-64; dir. mktg. services Altman Stoller, N.Y.C., 1964-66; mktg. cons. Marcella Rosen Assoc., Inc., N.Y.C., 1967-70; pres. Trager-Rosen, N.Y.C., 1970-77; v.p. assoc. mktg. services N.W. Ayer, N.Y.C., 1977-78; sr. v.p., mng. dir. media services N.W. Ayer, Inc., N.Y.C., 1978—; bd. dirs. Audit Bur. Circulation, N.Y.C., 1985—. Guest editor: (mag.) Media Decisions, 1981. Mem. Communal Planning Com., N.Y.C., 1985—; bd. dirs. Overseas United Jewish Appeal-Fedn., N.Y.C., 1986—. Recipient Matrix award Women in Communications, N.Y.C., 1986; named one of 25 Who Count in TV View Mag., N.Y.C., 1985. Mem. Adv. Research Found. (bd. dirs. 1984—), Internat. Radio TV Soc. (bd. dirs. 1983—), Am. Assn. Advt. Agencies (chmn. Media Policy Com. 1986—), Coalition Leading Women's Orgn. (chmn. 1985—), Barnard Coll. Bus. and Profl. Women (pres. 1980), Women's Forum (bd. dirs. 1983-85). Office: N W Ayer Inc 1345 Ave of the Americas New York NY 10105

ROSEN, MARTHA GRUBER, social services administrator; b. N.Y.C., Jan. 26, 1925; d. Morris and Annie (Mostel) Gruber; m. Irving Rosen, Apr. 12, 1945; 1 child, Shelley Frances. Student, Hunter Coll., 1941-45. Acct., legal sec. N.Y.C., 1946-66; founder, parent Assn. Advancement Blind and Retarded Inc., Jamaica, N.Y., 1955-67, exec. dir., 1967-86, mgr. program devel., office, 1986—; mem. comptroller's com. Inter-Agy. Council, N.Y.C., 1987—. Founder 1st day sch. blind retarded children, 1967, 1st residence blind retarded, 1974; vol. Cancer Care, ARC Assn. Retarded Children, USA for Africa, Help All Needy in Distress, 1987—, Hadassah Stuyvesant Group. Recipient Outstanding Contbn. spl. award S.E. Council, Queens, N.Y., 1981, Outstanding Leadership award Community Council, 1984, Our Town Thanks You award, 1986, merit award St. Albans C. of C., 1978; named Women Achiever YMCA, 1986. Lodge: B'nai B'rith. Home: 601 E 20th St New York NY 10010 Office: Assn Advancement Blind and Retarded Inc 164-09 Hillside Ave Jamaica NY 11432

ROSEN, MAXINE DIANE, advertising executive, creative director; b. Newark, Mar. 6, 1950; d. Melvin B. and Barbara Z. (Weinberg) Cohen; m. Robert N. Rosen, Aug. 1, 1972 (div. 1979). BS in TV/Film, Boston U., 1972; postgrad., Sch. Visual Arts, N.Y.C., 1975-76. Art dir. McCann-Erickson, N.Y.C., 1975-76; sr. art dir. Young & Rubicam, N.Y.C., 1977-81; v.p. art, supr. William Esty, N.Y.C., 1981-82; v.p., sr. art dir. J. Walter Thompson, N.Y.C., 1983; sr. v.p., creative dir. Ted Bates Inc., N.Y.C., 1984—. Democrat. Jewish. Office: Ted Bates Advt NY 1515 Broadway New York NY 10036

ROSEN, PHYLLIS, art dealer, appraiser; b. Boston, May 31, 1937; s. Samuel and Lillian (Smith) Bornstein; student U. Heidelberg, Germany, 1956-58; m. Theodore Rosen. Dir., Obelisk Gallery, Inc., Boston, 1961—, Parker 470 Gallery, Boston, 1971-74, Harcus Krakow Rosen Sonnabend Gallery, Boston, 1972-74, Sculpture to Wear, Inc., N.Y.C., 1973-76; appraiser, cons. 20th Century art, Appraisal Services, 1976—. Office: 90 Commonwealth Ave Boston MA 02116

ROSEN, SHERRILL LYNN, lawyer; b. Denver, Jan. 26, 1955; d. Maynard Charles and Sandra Marilyn (Collinger) R. B.S. in Journalism, U. Colo., 1975; J.D., U. Mo., 1978. Bar: Mo. 1979, U.S. Dist. Ct. (we. dist.) Mo. 1979. Pub. relations asst. Bicentennial Horizons of Am. Music, St. Louis, 1975-76; legal researcher Ctr. Research and Social Behavior, U. Mo.-Columbia, 1976-77; staff Ind. Legal Services Assn., Columbia, 1976-77, dir., 1977-78; atty. Legal Aid Western Mo., Kansas City, 1978-82; sole practice, Kansas City, 1982—; lectr. Rockhurst Coll., 1982—; lectr. Sch. Law U. Mo., Kansas City, 1987; cons. Adult Abuse Remedies Coalition, Columbia, 1978-80. Bd. dirs. Housing Assistance, Inc., Kansas City, 1984-86, sec., 1985; vice chmn. Jackson County Bd. Domestic Violence Shelters, 1984-85, sec., 1986—. Recipient Vol. award Central Mo. Counties Human Devel. Corp., 1978; Criminal Justice award Rose Brooks Ctr., Inc., 1981; Margit Lasker award, 1982. Mem. ABA (exec. mem. family law sect., domestic violence com. 1984—, co-chmn. 1985-86, chmn. 86-87), Mo. Bar Assn. (family law com.), Kansas City Bar Assn. (adv. com. family law com. 1983—), Sigma Delta Chi, Kappa Tau Alpha. Office: 906 Grand Suite 600 Kansas City MO 64106

ROSENBAUM, ARLENE, direct marketing services executive; b. Bklyn., Feb. 17, 1944; d. Milton and Clara (Spector) Pollack; m. Steven Alan Rosenbaum, Apr. 5, 1964; children—Laura Ellen, Michelle Lynn. B.S., CCNY, 1964. Software programmer Gen. Foods, White Plains, N.Y., 1966-71; pres., cons. Starline Systems, Inc., New City, N.Y., 1972—; v.p. Magi, Elmsford, N.Y., 1983-85, pres., 1985—. Mem. Direct Mktg. Assn. Office: Magi 3 Westchester Plaza Elmsford NY 10523

ROSENBAUM, BELLE SARA, personal property appraiser, interior designer, educator; b. N.Y.C., Apr. 1, 1922; d. Harry and Hinda (Sits) Heimowitz; m. Jacob H. Rosenbaum, Mar. 12, 1939; children—Linda Zelinger, Simmi Brodie, Martin, Arlene Levene. Cert. N.Y. Sch. Interior Design, 1945. Sr. mem. Am. Soc. Appraisers, Washington, 1979—; tchr./Judaica, Yeshiva U., 1984—; pres. Jarvis Designs, Inc., Union City, N.J., 1955-75, Design Assocs., BLS., Monsey, N.Y., 1970-78; v.p. Lord & Lady Inc., Union City, 1955-70, Cardio-Bionic Scanning, Inc., Spring Valley, N.Y., 1975-78; v.p., treas. Rapitech Systems, Inc., 1985. Author of short stories, 1947-48; contbr. articles on interior design to profl. jours. Bd. dirs. Migdal Ohr Schs., 1971—. Named Woman of Valor State of Israel, 1960. mem. Internat. Soc. Artists (founding mem.), Yeshiva of North Jersey Women (hon. pres. 1955). Clubs: Amit Women (pres. 1955-57) (N.J.), AMI Women (treas. 1948-78), Community Synogogue-Monsey (v.p. 1982—). Avocations: collector of art, antiques, Judaica, artist, gardening, communal and charity work.

ROSENBAUM, JOAN HANNAH, museum director; b. Hartford, Conn., Nov. 24, 1942; d. Charles Leon and Lillian (Sharasheff) Grossman; m. Peter S. Rosenbaum, July 1962 (div. 1970). A.A., Hartford Coll. for Women, 1962; B.A., Boston U., 1964; student, Hunter Coll. Grad Sch., 1970-73; cert., Columbia U. Bus. Sch. Inst. Non Profit Mgmt., 1978. Curatorial asst. Mus. Modern Art, N.Y.C., 1966-72; dir. mus. program N.Y. Council on Arts, N.Y.C., 1972-79; cons. Michal Washburn & Assocs., N.Y.C., 1979-80; dir. Jewish Mus., N.Y.C., 1980—; mem. adv. bd. Pub. Ctr., N.Y.C. Bd. dirs. Artists Space, 1980—; pres. Council Jewish Mus., 1986; mem. policy panel Nat. Endowment for Arts, 1982-83. European travel grantee Internat. Council Mus., 1972. Mem. Am. Assn. Mus. (cons. 1979—), N.Y. State Assn. Mus. (v.p. 1983—). Office: Jewish Mus 1109 Fifth Ave New York NY 10128

ROSENBERG, AMY GOFF, actuary; b. Worcester, Mass., July 10, 1955; d. Julius L. and Doris (Katz) Goff; m. Barry David Rosenberg, May 29, 1977; children: Jennifer Beth, Jeffrey Matthew, Rachel Laura. BS, Tufts U., 1977. Actuarial asst. Paul Revere Ins. Group, Worcester, 1977-80, assoc. actuary, 1980—. Designer computer software. V.p. Dysautonomia Found., Worchester County, 1986—. Mem. Soc. Actuaries, Am. Acad. Actuaries, Phi Beta Kappa. Office: Paul Revere Life Ins Co 18 Chestnut St Worcester MA 01608

ROSENBERG, JO, psychiatric social worker, psychoanalyst; b. Albany, N.Y., June 12, 1948; d. Irving H. and Madeline P. Rosenberg; B.A., Goucher Coll., Towson, Md., 1970; M.S., Columbia U., 1973; psychoanalysis cert. (fellow 1975-79), Postgrad. Center Mental Health, N.Y.C., 1979, postgrad. N.Y.U., 1981—. With maternal and child health dept. Bronx (N.Y.) Mcpl. Hosp. Center, 1973-76, coordinator emergency services children dept. child psychiatry, 1976-79; field work instr. N.Y.U. Sch. Social Work, 1977-79; sr. psychiat. social worker div. child and adolescent psychiatry N.Y. Hosp.-Cornell Med. Center, Westchester div., White Plains, N.Y., 1979-82, social work coordinator, 1982—; faculty Cornell U. Med. Sch., 1982—pvt. practice psychoanalysis and psychotherapy, N.Y.C. Fellow N.Y. State Soc. Clin. Social Work Psychotherapists; mem. Nat. Assn. Social Workers, Acad. Cert. Social Workers, Am. Orthopsychiat. Assn., Am. Group Psychotherapy Assn. Contbr. articles on group therapy to profl. jours. Home: 145 Woodland Ln White Plains NY 10607 Office: NY Hosp White Plains NY 10605

ROSENBERG, SHELI ZYSMAN, lawyer, financial management executive; b. N.Y.C., Feb. 2, 1942; d. Stephen B. and Charlotte (Laufer) Zysman; m. Burton X. Rosenberg, Aug. 30, 1964; children: Leonard, Marcy. BA, Tufts U., 1963; JD, Northwestern U., 1966. Bar: Ill. 1966. Ptnr. Schiff, Hardin & Waite, Chgo., 1973-80; sr. v.p., gen. counsel Equity Fin. Mgmt., Chgo., 1980—, Equity Groups Investment Inc., Chgo., 1988—; gen. counsel Delta Queen Steamboat Co., New Orleans, 1985—; bd. dirs., v.p., sec., gen. counsel Great Am. Mgmt. & Investment, Chgo., 1984—; bd. dirs. NuCorp Energy Inc., Digicon Inc., The Chgo. Network.

ROSENBERG-BLATT, ELLEN PHYLLIS, lawyer; b. N.Y.C., Feb. 27, 1953; d. Harold and Sarah (Levy) Rosenberg; married, Sept. 3, 1978; children: Hal Jared, Shira Beth. AB in Criminology, U. Calif., Berkeley, 1974; JD, Am. U., 1978. Bar: D.C. 1978, Calif. 1979, Md. 1985. Law clk. to presiding justice U.S. Dist. Ct. D.C., 1978-79; assoc. Malcolm & Daly, Newport Beach, Calif., 1979-80; trial atty. U.S. Dept. Energy, Washington, 1980-85; ptnr. Blatt & Rosenberg-Blatt, Balt., 1985—. V.p. Associated Jewish Charities, Balt., 1985-87. Office: Blatt & Rosenberg-Blatt 1101 St Paul #403 Baltimore MD 21201

ROSENBERGER, JUDITH BRAILEY, psychotherapist, psychoanalyst; b. Columbus, Ohio, Mar. 24, 1943; d. Lester George and Helen Cornelia (Castle) Brailey; B.S., Purdue U., 1965; M.A., U. Mich., 1967, Ph.D., 1973; M.S.W., Hunter Coll., 1976; cert. psychoanalysis, Postgrad. Ctr. for Mental Health, 1982; m. Ernst H. Rosenberger, June 10, 1978; children: John Brailey, Anne Elizabeth. Intern in counseling, student services counseling center, U. Mich., Ann Arbor, 1967-70; counselor Wayne State U., Detroit, 1970-71; lectr. Herbert N. Lehman Coll., City U. N.Y., 1971-82; pvt. practice psychotherapy and psychoanalysis, N.Y.C., 1978—; faculty Postgrad. Center for Mental Health, N.Y.C., 1985—; summer faculty Smith Coll. Sch. Social Work, 1984, 85; asst. prof. Hunter Coll. Sch. Social Work, 1985—; invited presenter, Mary Gottesfeld lectr. Hunter Coll., 1987; presenter at confs. Assn. Children and Adults with Hearing Disabilities, 1988, Am. Orthopsychiat. Conf., 1988. Profl. project dir. Profl. Staff Congress, Bd. Higher Edn. research project, 1977-79; invited presenter, trustee, bd. dirs. Gateway Sch. of N.Y., 1987—; bd. dirs. Postmasters Program in Clin. Social Work, 1986—. Cert. psychologist, Mass.; cert. social worker, N.Y. Mem. Am. Psychol. Assn. (div. psychoanalysis), AAUP, Acad. Cert. Social Workers, N.Y. Soc. Clin. Social Work Psychotherapists, Nat. Assn. Social Workers, Postgrad. Psychoanalytic Soc., Nat. Assn. Advancement Psychoanalysis, Am. Orthopsychiat. Assn. (bd. dirs. 1988—), Assn. Children and Adults with Learning Disabilities (bd. dirs. 1988—). Author: The Identity Experience of College Women: Some Contributing Factors, 1973; Women Who Aspire to be Police Officers, 1979. Office: 315 E 68th New York NY 10021

ROSENBLATT, LOUISE MICHEL, emerita educator; b. Atlantic City, Aug. 23, 1904; d. Samuel and Jennie (Berman) R.; B.A. with honors, Barnard Coll., 1925; certificat d'etudes francaises, U. Grenoble, France, 1926; D.Comparative Literature, U. Paris, 1931; postgrad. in Anthropology, Columbia U., 1932-34; m. Sidney Ratner, June 1932; 1 son, Jonathan. Instr., English, Barnard Coll., 1927-38; asst. prof. English Bklyn. Coll., 1938-48; asso. chief Western European sect., chief central reports sect. Bur. Overseas Intelligence, Office War Info., 1943-45; prof. English edn. N.Y. U., 1948-72, prof. emerita, 1972—; vis. prof. Rutgers U., 1972-75; mem. faculty insts. in English, Northwestern U., Mich. State U., U. Pa., U. Ala., U. Alta. (Can.), Auburn U., U. Mass., 1978—; cons. in field. Franco-Am. Exchange fellow, 1925-26; Guggenheim fellow, 1942-43; recipient N.Y. U. Great Tchr. award, 1972; Nat. Council Tchr. English Disting. Service award, 1973; Russell award for disting. research, 1980; Leland Jacobs award for Lit., 1981. Mem. MLA, Am. Soc. Aesthetics, AAUP, Nat. Council Tchrs. English, Nat. Conf. Research in English, Am. Comparative Literature, Internat. Comparative Lit. Assn., Phi Beta Kappa. Author: L'Idee de l'Art pour l'Art, 1931, reprinted, 1976; Literature as Exploration, 1938, 3d rev. edit., 1976, 4th edit., 1983; (with William S. Gray) Reading in an Age of Mass Communication, 1949; Research Development in the Teaching of English, 1963; The Reader. The Text. The Poem: The Transactional Theory of the Literary Work, 1978; (with Robert Parker) Developing Literacy, 1983; (with Charles Cooper) Researching Response to Literature, 1984; (with Patricia Demers) The Creating Word, 1985, Writing and Reading: The Transactional Theory, 1988; also articles on lit. theory, theory of composition, criticism, teaching of lit. Home: 11 Cleveland Ln Princeton NJ 08540

ROSENBLITH, JUDY FRANCIS, psychology educator; b. Salt Lake City, Mar. 20, 1921; d. John Edward and Mary Louise (Slack) Francis; m. Walter A. Rosenblith, Sept. 27, 1941; children—Sandra Y., Ronald F. Student Occidental Coll., 1938-40; A.B., UCLA, 1942; M.A., Radcliffe Coll., 1950, Ph.D., 1958. Asst. prof. psychology Simmons Coll., 1951-52; New Eng. supr. Nat. Opinion Research Center, 1953-57; teaching fellow social relations Harvard U., 1948-50, Grad. Sch. Edn., 1953-56, instr., 1956-57, lectr., 1962-63; asst. prof. psychology Brown U., 1957-61, asst. mem. to mem. Inst. Life Scis., 1961-75, sr. research investigator div. biol. and med. scis., 1975-77; assoc. psychology dept. psychiatry Harvard Med. Sch., 1961-64, clin. assoc., 1965-67; assoc. prof. Wheaton Coll., Norton, Mass., 1965-68, prof. psychology, 1968-84, prof. emerita, 1984—; mem. maternal and child health research adv. com. Nat. Inst. Child Health and Human Devel., 1974-78. Author: (with Judith Sims Knight) In the Beginning: Development in the First Two Years, 1985. Adv. editor Contemporary Psychology, 1979-80; sr. editor: The Causes of Behavior: Readings in Child Development and Educational Psychology, 3 edits., 1962, 66, 72. Named Meneely Prof., Wheaton Coll., 1972-74; N.Y. Acad. Scis. fellow, 1976; grantee NIMH, 1958-60, Neurol. Diseases and Blindness, 1961-64, Child Health and Human Devel., 1966-70, Grant Found., 1971-77. Fellow Am. Psychol. Assn. (mem. bd. social and ethical responsibility for psychology 1977-81, mem. pub. info. com. 1981-84) mem. Soc. for Research in Child Devel. (sec. 1965-69, chmn. conv. arrangements 1979-81), Internat. Assn. Cross-Cultural Psychology, Internat. Assn. Applied Psychology, Internat. Soc. Study of Behavioral Devel., Psychonomic Soc., New Eng. Psychol. Assn., Eastern Psychol. Assn., Sigma Xi. Home: 164 Mason Terr Brookline MA 02146 Office: Wheaton Coll Norton MA 02766

ROSENBLOOM, GLENDA GENE, health science association administrator; b. Aledo, Ill., Dec. 17, 1941; d. Mary (Amy) Wise; m. Alan M. Rosenbloom. BS in Acctg., U. Ill., Champaign, 1965. CPA, Ill. Audit supr. Peat Marwick Mitchell and Co., Chgo., 1965-72; sr. dir. Medicare provider payments Blue Cross Assn., Chgo., 1972-82; mgr. cons. Ernst & Whinney, Los Angeles, 1982-83; dir. prospective payments, asst. v.p. Am. Med. Internat., Beverly Hills, Calif., 1983—. Mem. Hosp. Fin. Mgmt., Am. Inst. CPA's, Fedn. of Am. Health Systems (chmn. Medicare/Medicaid com. 1985—). Republican. Office: Am Med Internat PO Box 6454 Woodland Hills CA 91365

ROSENBLUM, BETH ANN, civic activities director; b. Cleve., Feb. 14, 1939; d. Jack Maurice and Edith Louise (Kessner) Bassett; m. Stanley Theodore Rosenblum, Aug. 31, 1958; children: Janis Roskoph, Steven, Karen, Lisa. BS, Cleve. State U., 1978. Various civic positions City of University Heights (Ohio), 1955-81; substitute tchr. Beachwood, Cleveland Heights and University Heights, Ohio, 1979-80; realtor Stuart E. Wallace & Assoc., East Cleve. Suburbs, Ohio, 1979-80; substitute tchr. Agnon Sch., Beachwood, Ohio, 1975-80, tchr. phys. edn., tchr., 1980-85; recreation dir. City of Beachwood, Ohio, 1981—, sr. adult activities dir., 1987—; coordinator NE Ohio Community Edn. Assn., Cleveland and Columbus, 1987—. Mem. Beachwood Boosters, PTA, Cleveland Heights, University Heights and Beachwood, 1963-85, Civic League, Beachwood, Friends of the Library, Beachwood; leader Cleveland Heights council Girl Scouts U.S., 1967-80, cert. volleyball ofcl., Ohio High Sch. Athletic Assn., 1975—. Mem. Cleve. Women's Phys. Edn., Recreation Assn., Ohio Parks and Recreation Assn., Ohio Community Edn. Assn., Ohio High Sch. Athletic Assn., Cleve. Volleyball Ofcls. Assn. Democrat. Jewish. Office: City of Beachwood Dept of Recreation 2700 Richmond Rd Beachwood OH 44122

ROSEN-DEROSE, DIANE, sales executive; b. Burbank, Calif., June 20, 1961; d. Daniel B. and Leona H. (Rasch) Rosen; m. Joseph D. DeRose, Sept. 20, 1986. Student, Golden Gate U., 1981. Account services Holiday Inn's, Inc., San Francisco, 1980-83; sales rep. Hertz Corp., San Francisco, 1983-85, tng. mgr., 1985-87; mgr. sales adminstrn. and tng. Hertz Corp., Park Ridge, N.J., 1987—. Editor: (newsletter) Sales/Training News. Mem. Am. Soc. Tng. and Devel., Bay Area Passenger Traffic Assn. Office: Hertz Corp 225 Brae Blvd Park Ridge NJ 07656

ROSENE, LINDA ROBERTS, organizational consultant, researcher; b. Miami, Fla., Nov. 1, 1938; d. Wilbur David and Dorothy Claire (Baker) Roberts; m. Ralph W. Rosene, Aug. 3, 1957; children: Leigh, Russ, Tim. MA, Fielding Inst., 1981, PhD in Clin. Psychology, 1983. Lic. clin. psychologist. Counselor Rapid City (S.D.) Regional Hosp., 1978-81, Luth. Social Services, Rapid City, 1978-83; v.p. Target Systems Inc., Dallas and Irving, Tex., 1983-85, cons., 1985—; cons. S.W. Home Furnishing Assn., Dallas, 1984, Northwestern Bell, Omaha, 1985; presenter, developer seminars gest-Accor Retail Assn. of Can., Am. Assn. Med. Assts. Pub. Profl. Furniture Merchants mag. Bd. dirs. Assn. Children with Learning Disabilities, S.D., 1983-84, West River (S.D.) Alcoholism Services, 1983-84, Health Adv. Com. of Head Start, S.D., 1980-84, St. Martins Acad., S.D., 1971-75; mem. Rapid City Mayor's Commn. on Racial Conciliation, 1971-73, Nat. Trust for Hist. Preservation; charter mem. Nat. Mus. Women in the Arts. Research grantee Nat. Luth. Ch., 1981. Mem. Am. Psychol. Assn., N.C. Psychol. Assn., Aircraft Owners and Pilots Assn., Am. Soc. Tng. and Devel., S.W. Home Furnishing Assn., Internat. Platform Assn. Unitarian. Avocations: bicycling, racquetball, music, birdwatching, flying. Home: 300 Shinoak Valley Irving TX 75063

ROSENFELD, SELMA, television producer; b. N.Y.C., June 21, 1924; d. Louis and Freida Sovel; m. Sidney N. Rosenfeld, May 25, 1963; children: Kenneth, Louis, Brian, Gary. BA, Bklyn. Coll., 1949; postgrad., Pa. State U., 1974. Cert. English, Spanish and elem. tchr. Tchr. Northeastern Sch. Dist., Mt. Wolf, Pa., 1961-63, 69-77; TV producer Cable TV 4, York, Pa., 1984—. Co-producer TV series The Emerging Woman, 1984-85, TV show In Focus, 1988; producer, host TV series On-The-Go, 1986. Chmn. First Night/York, 1987, Strand Capitol's Corp.-Bus. Campaign, 1986-87, casting Com. York Little Theatre, 1983—; bd. dirs. Hist. Soc. York, 1985—, YWCA, 1980-83, Citizens for the Arts in Pa., 1986—, Strand-Capitol Performing Arts Ctr., 1986—, Women's Network York, 1983—, chmn. program com., 1988—; mem. spl. events com. United Way, 1988—; mem. Pa. Arts Coalition, 1987—; mem. citizens adv. com. Jr. League York, 1986—. Recipient Vol. of Yr. award York C. of C., 1988, Jefferson Liberty Bell award York County Bar Assn. adv. com., 1986; named Outstanding Community Leader Cen. Pa. chpt. Women in Communications, 1985. Democrat. Jewish. Home: 119 S Harlan St York PA 17402

ROSENHEIM, CHRISTINE LABODA, health management consultant; b. N.Y.C., June 22, 1952; d. Henry Oliver and Olga Caroline (Chupurdy) Laboda; m. Thomas Rosenheim, May 19, 1973; children: Brad Erik, Randy Thomas. AA in Nursing, Queensborough Community Coll., 1972; BS in Health Care Adminstrn., Stockton State Coll., 1976. RN., N.J., N.Y. Staff nurse N. Shore Med. Ctr., Manhassett, N.Y., 1972-73, W. Jersey Hosp., Voorhees, N.J., 1973-79; nurse Everrett R. Curran Jr. M.D., Cherry Hill, N.J., 1979-83, Valley Rehab. Co., Hammonton, N.J., 1983-85; nurse auditor Consolidated Rehab. Co., Haddon Heights, N.J., 1986-87; pres. Medi Fax Cons., Atco, N.J., 1987—. Editor: Pediatric Press, 1982. Chairperson Cub Scouts Am., Atco 1986-87; v.p. Waterford Twp. Home and Sch. Assn., Atco 1985-87. Mem. Emergency Dept. Nurses Assn., S. Jersey Claims Assn., Nat. Assn. Female Exec. Home: 807 Linden Ave Atco NJ 08004 Office: Medi-Fax Cons 152 Atco Ave Atco NJ 08004

ROSENHEIM, MARGARET KEENEY, former university dean, social work educator; b. Grand Rapids, Mich., Sept. 5, 1926; d. Morton and Nancy (Billings) Keeney; m. Edward W. Rosenheim, June 20, 1947; children: Daniel, James, Andrew. Student, Wellesley Coll., 1943-45; J.D., U. Chgo., 1949. Bar: Ill. 1949. Mem. faculty Sch. Social Service Adminstrn., U. Chgo., 1950—, assoc. prof., 1961-66, prof., 1966—, Helen Ross prof. social welfare policy, 1975—, dean, 1978-83; vis. prof. U. Wash., 1966, Duke U., 1984; acad. visitor London Sch. Econs., 1973; cons. Pres.'s Commn. Law Enforcement and Adminstrn. Justice, 1966-67, Nat. Adv. Commn. Criminal Justice Standards and Goals, i972; mem. Juvenile Justice Standards Commn., 1973-76; trustee Carnegie Corp. N.Y., 1979-87, Children's Home and Aid Soc. of Ill., 1981—; dir. Nat. Inst. Dispute Resolution, 1981—, Nuveen Bond Funds, 1982—. Editor, contbr.: Justice for the Child, 1962, reprinted. 1977, Pursuing Justice for the Child, 1976; Contbr. articles and book revs. to profl. jours. Ford Found. grantee, 1967-68, 84-85. Mem. Chgo. Bar Assn. Address: 5805 Dorchester Ave Chicago IL 60637

ROSENSOHN, MINDY SHANNON, newscaster, news editor; b. Casper, Wyo., Feb. 5, 1955; d. Greer Pierson Streetman and Patricia Ann (Wulff) Ivey; m. Daniel Lasker Rosensohn, Oct. 27, 1979 (div. Feb. 1987); children: Patricia Andrea, Elizabeth Susan Lasker. BA, Eastern Ky. U., Richmond, 1977. News reporter, producer, air personality Sta. WEKU-FM-TV, Richmond, 1974-76; air personality Sta. WWKY, Winchester, Ky., 1976; news reporter, air personality Sta. WVLK-AM-FM, Lexington, Ky., 1976-77; gen. assignment-govt. affaris reporter Sta. WLEX-TV, Lexington, 1977-79; news anchor, producer, investigative researcher Sta. WHAS-TV, Louisville, 1979-80; news anchor, news editor Sta. WLEX-TV, Lexington, 1981—; owner, breeder Sun Rose Farm, Lawrenceburg, Ky., 1982-87; coordinator Eastern Ky. U. Alunmi Career Network, Richmond, 1985—. Mem. com. Lexington YWCA Women of Achievement Program, 1981—, Ky. Atty. Gen. Child Abuse Prevention Program, Frankfort, 1985; bd dirs. Eastern Ky. U. Cath. Neuman Ctr., Richmond, 1983-85; chmn. Bluegrass chpt. March of Dimes, Lexington, 1985; trustee Ky. chpt. Leukemia Soc. Am., 1986-87; vol. Head Start Lexington Community Action Agy., 1988. Named one of Outstanding Young Women of Am., 1984; Broadcasting Excellence award Associated Press, 1982. Mem. Soc. Profl. Journalists (pres. elect 1986-87, pres. 1988), Sigma Delta Chi, Kappa Delta Tau. Democrat. Episcopalian. Office: Sta WLEX-TV Russell Cave Pike Lexington KY 40591

ROSENSTOCK, FRANCYNE NORA, public relations executive, writer; b. N.Y.C., Jan. 29, 1951; d. Max Samuel and Gloria Corinne (Weisser) R. BA, U. Miami, 1974; M in Pub. Adminstrn., U. Hartford, 1980. Polit. pub. relations cons. Avon, Conn., 1980-82; prin. Showriter Assocs., Ellenville, N.Y., 1982—; dir. pub. relations Orange County Rural Devel. Adv. Corp., Goshen, N.Y., 1986-88; asst. to exec. dir. Orange County Renal Devel. Adv. Corp., Goshen, 1988—; county coordinator Community Housing Resource Bd., Orange County, N.Y., 1986-88. Pres. Wawarsing Women's Democrat. Club, Ellenville, 1985-87; pub. relations chmn. Conn. Women's Polit. Caucus, 1981-82; mem. Town Wawarsing Dem. Com., Ellenville, 1986—, Ellenville Charter Commn., 1987—, Ellenville Human Rights Commn., 1988—. Democrat. Jewish. Home: PO Box 52 Ellenville NY 12428

ROSENSTOCK, JUDITH DEAN, educational adminstrator, consultant; b. Syracuse, N.Y., Sept. 17, 1947; d. Jacob A. and Pearl (Rugg) Naistadt; m. Harvey Allan Rosenstock, May 9, 1982; children: Benjamin Leipzig, Deborah Elise Leipzig, Amara, Aaron and Marc Rosenstock. Student Boston U., 1965-67; BS, NYU, 1969; MS, Va. Commonwealth U., 1973; PhD, Syracuse U., 1980. Counselor, Overbrook State Hosp., Cedar Grove, N.J., 1968-69; asst. dir. St. Joseph's Adolescent Unit Program, Syracuse, 1970-71; tchr. learning disabled B.O.C.E.S., Syracuse, 1969-73; Child Find coordinator Syracuse Sch. Dist., 1975-76; N.Y. state adminstrv. intern N.Y. State Edn. Agy., Syracuse, 1975-76; asst. prof. U. Houston Clear Lake, 1979-84; dir. Teaching and Learning Ctr. Tex., Houston, 1983—; trainer, cons. N.Y. State Dept. Edn., Albany, 1976-77; cons. Bur. Indian Affairs, Washington, 1978; accreditation mem. Nat. Council for Accreditation of Tchr. Educators, Washington, 1982—; field reader Office Spl. Edn. and Rehab., Washington, 1983. Author: (with Harvey Rosenstock) Helping Parents Cope with Quarreling Siblings, 1983, Play: Important at Any Age, 1984, Your Stay in the Hospital, 1984; Childhood Friendships, 1985. Bd. dirs. I. Weiner Sch., Houston, 1983, Beth Jacob, Galveston, Tex., 1978; D. Miller Found. Dr. Ivan Vasey fellow, 1967; Center on Human Policy fellow, Syracuse, 1971; Va. Commonwealth U. fellow, Richmond, 1974; Bur. Edn. of Handicapped fellow, Washington, 1975. Mem. Council for Exceptional Children, Council for Assoc. of Sch. Exec. Adminstrs., Profs. Sch. Adminstrn., Phi Delta Kappa. Jewish. Office: Teaching and Learning Ctr Tex PO Box 35553 Houston TX 77035

ROSENTHAL, CAROL A., financial planner; b. Ephrata, Pa., Mar. 22, 1942; d. James Whiteside and Marian Isabel (Shiffer) Magruder; m. Albert L. Rosenthal, July 31, 1969; children: Robert, Jill, Bruce. BA, Rider Coll., 1973, AA, 1962. Exec. sec. RCA Labs., Princeton N.J., 1962-69; fin. planner Albert L. Rosenthal, M.D., P.A., Lawrenceville, N.J., 1969—. Pres., Friends of N.J. State Mus., Trenton, 1983-85, v.p. fine arts, 1980-83; bd. dirs. McCarter Assocs., Princeton, 1985—, Shakespeare 70, 1985—, Princeton Art Assn., 1988—; v.p., bd. dirs. Old Barracks, Trenton, N.J., 1986—; founder Friends of Morven, Princeton, 1987—. Mem. Mus. Modern Art, Friends of Phila. Mus., Newark Mus., Trenton City Mus. Office: Albert L Rosenthal MD PA 74 Franklin Corner Rd Lawrenceville NJ 08648

ROSENTHAL, CHRISTINE GIGLIO, writer, editor; b. Bklyn., Dec. 22, 1949; d. Vincent and Victoria (Roberto) Giglio; B.J., L.I. U., 1971; m. Peter Rosenthal, Mar. 16, 1978; 1 son, Joel. Asso. editor Woman's World Mag., N.Y.C., 1972-74; publs. editor public relations dept. St. Vincent's Hosp., N.Y.C., 1975-76; editor Teen Beat Mag., N.Y.C., 1976-77; publs. editor Physicians Planning Service, N.Y.C., 1978; public info. specialist N.Y.C. Dept. Transp., 1978-79; reporter City Life Newspaper, 1980-81; pub. relations dir. Central Queens YM & YWHA, Forest Hills, N.Y., 1982-88; lectr. in field. Home: 68-19 Groton St Forest Hills NY 11375

ROSENTHAL, ELLEN, military officer; b. Cleve., July 6, 1953; d. Ray Lee and June (Gibbs) Brown; m. Mark Louis Rosenthal, Mar. 20, 1977; 1 child, Erin. BS in Edn., Cleve. State U., 1974; MBA, Golden Gate U., 1984. Commd. ensign USN, 1975, advanced through grades to lt. comdr., 1984; imagery analyst Def. Intelligency Agy., Washington, 1975-77; watch officer Fleet Ocean Surveillance Info. Ctr., Norfolk, Va., 1977-79; adminstrv. officer, course coordinator Fleet Intelligence Tng. Ctr., Norfolk, 1979-82; internal control officer Naval Mil. Personnel Command, Washington, 1984-86; cost analyst, budget officer Naval Ctr. for Cost Analysis, Washington, 1986-87; exec. officer Fleet Area Control and Surveillance Facility, Va. Capes, Virginia Beach, Va., 1987—. Jewish.

ROSENTHAL, EVELYN DAOUD, business executive; b. Bellaire, Ohio; d. Azeez Joseph and Nora (Yarbroudi) Tanous; m. Joseph Daoud, Feb. 6, 1932 (dec. Dec. 1963); children: Joseph A. III, Patricia, Alex; m. Milton Rosenthal, Dec. 5, 1975. Student, St. John's U., 1928-31; LLB, U. Miami, 1949. Bar: N.Y., 1932. Sole practice Lawrence, N.Y., 1932; exec. sec. Joseph Daoud and Sons, Atlantic City, 1933-39; v.p. Joseph Doaud and Sons, Miami Beach, Fla., 1931-41; v.p., dir. Joseph Doaud Inc., Miami Beach, 1941-79; owner Rosenthal Outdoor Advt. Co., Miami Beach; pres. Almond Garden Apts., 1974—. Pres. St. Patrick's PTA, Miami Beach, 1955-56, bd. dirs. 1953-56, Barry Coll. Aux. 1954-56, 1952-57, Community Chest Dade County (Fla.) 1951-57, chief dir. fund drive, Miami Beach, 1950-60, Visiting Nurses Assn. Dade County, 1956, St. Francis Hosp. Aux., Miami Beach, 1954-57, Friends Bethany Home Dependent Teenage Girls, Miami 1966-67, Miami Beach Lib., 1948—, also trustee; mem. endowment com. St. Jude's Research Children's Hosp., Memphis 1966—; sec. Miami Beach Pub. Library, 1956-60, bd. mem. adv. com. 1986, mem. adv. bd.; trustee, mem. Clients Council Legal Services Miami Beach, 1952-59, pres. Fedn. Med. Ctr., 1982-84. Named Woman Yr., Civic League, Miami Beach 1956. Mem. ABA, N.Y. Bar Assn., Friends Bass Mus., Am. Assn. Ret. Persons., Patrician Club (mem bd. 1954-57), Syrian Lebanese Inst., Miami C. of C., Iota Tau Tau, Kappa Bet Pi. Home and Office: 1777 Michigan Ave #107 Miami Beach FL 33139

ROSENTHAL, MARTHA NEWMAN, dir. ballet school; b. N.Y.C., Oct. 8, 1956; d. Norman and Janice (Newman) R.; m. Adorno Sclano, Mar. 2, 1978 (div.). B.A., Sarah Lawrence Coll., 1978. Jr. copywriter McCann-Erickson, Inc., N.Y.C., 1978-80; office mgr. Ed Libonati Prodns. Inc., N.Y.C., 1980-82; dir. spl. events and pub. relations Sch. Am. Ballet, N.Y.C., 1982-85; spl. cons., assoc. dir. of jr. council and new ballet audiences of Am. Ballet Theatre, N.Y.C., 1986, asst. dir., 1986-87; dir. Sch. Classical Ballet of Am. Ballet Theatre, N.Y.C., 1987—. Writer, editor, designer newsletters, 1982; writer, designer mailing pieces, 1982; editor, designer advt. jour., 1985. Club: Doubles. Avocations: travel, languages, cultural institutions. Office: American Ballet Theatre 890 Broadway New York NY 10003

ROSENTHAL, SALLY JANE, computer systems administrator; b. Toronto, Ont., Can., Feb. 25, 1963; came to U.S., 1968; d. Brian and Shirley Ann (Woodgate) Wallace; m. Ronald Barton Rosenthal, Dec. 31, 1985. BS in Criminal Justice, Calif. State U., Long Beach, 1985. Coordinator projects Word Processors, Long Beach, 1983-85; systems supr. Della Femina, Travisano and Ptnrs., Los Angeles, 1986—; cons. in field, Los Angeles,

1986—. Mem. Nat. Assn. Female Execs. Office: Della Femina McNamee WCRS Inc 5900 Wilshire Blvd #1900 Los Angeles CA 90036

ROSENTHAL, YONINA KOLLER, education and training consultant; b. Los Angeles, May 24, 1934; d. Irving M. and Doris S. Koller; m. David Walter Rosenthal, July 6, 1952; children—Gabriella, Albert, Aliza, Oren. B.A., Boston U., 1955; M.Ed., Rutgers U., 1963; Ph.D., U. N.C., 1974. Instr., U. N.C., 1965-71, Louisberg (N.C.) Coll., 1974, N.C. State U., 1975; ptnr. E. F. R. Assocs., 1975-81; program coordinator dept. human resources Duke U. Med. Ctr., 1979-81; tng. dir. Boston Counseling Assocs., 1981; mem. staff dept. staff devel. and edn. Melrose-Wakefield Hosp., Melrose, Mass., 1982-85; tchr. Boston Ctr. Adult Edn., 1981-83; instr. New Eng. Hosp. Assembly, 1982, adj. prof. Mass. Bay Community Coll., 1981-85, Israel Inst. Technology, 1986—. Mem. Gov.'s Adv. Bd. N.C.-Israel Vis. Scholars program, 1979-81; mem. N.C. Council on Social Legislation, 1979-81; mem. N.C. Council Woman's Orgn., 1978-81; mem. Glenwood Task Force, City of Raleigh, 1976-81. Mem. Am. Soc. Tng. and Devel., AAUW, Am. Soc. Health Care Edn. and Tng., U.N.C. N.C. Alumni Assn., Am. Mgmt. Assn., Boston U. Alumni Assn., LWV. Club: Hadassah. Home: 233 Clark St Brookline MA 02146

ROSENZWEIG, CAROL BARBARA, writer, art publisher; b. N.Y.C.; d. Sidney and Sadie (Greenberg) Kupersmith; m. Saul Louis Rosenzweig, Feb. 11, 1961; children: Davy, Laurance. BA, Pa. State U., 1951. Acct. exec., v.p. Pub. Relations Research Inc., Pitts., 1951-60; freelance writer St. Louis, Los Angeles, Palm Springs, Calif., 1961-80; pres. Rosebranch, Inc., Los Angeles, 1980-86, Artist Editions Ltd., Beverly Hills, Calif., 1985—; v.p. R.Z. Group, Inc., Los Angeles, 1986—. Author: (TV shows) House Husband, 1983, 21 Days of America, 1985 (Heritage award), Women of the World, 1987. Chmn. emeritus Young Talent award com. Los Angeles County Mus. Art, 1985—; pres. Carol and Saul Rosenzweig Family Found., Los Angeles, 1987. Mem. Women in Film, Royal TV Soc., Modern and Contemp. Art Council (bd. dirs. 1976-85). Jewish. Club: Mountaingate (Los Angeles). Office: RZ Group Inc 1082 Westwood Bld Los Angeles CA 90024

ROSE-ROSENSWEIG, RHONDA, brokerage house executive; b. Los Angeles, Dec. 19, 1956; d. Alvin Frederick and Jacqueline Ann (Davidson) R.; m. Philip Eugene Rosensweig. Real estate broker Rose Realty, Miami, Fla., 1977-84; account exec., stock broker Prudential Bache Securities, Santa Barbara, Calif., 1984-85, Miami, 1985—. Vol. Women's Abuse Ctr., Miami, 1985-86; dep. treas. Joshua Soc., Miami, 1986-87. Democrat. Office: Prudential Bache Securities SE Fin Ctr Miami FL 33131

ROSETT, JACQUELINE BERLIN, financial executive; b. N.Y.C., Aug. 28, 1945; s. Marshall Hamilton and Lenore (Berlin) Rosett. BS in Physics, Columbia U., 1967. With George B. Buck Inc., N.Y.C., 1967-68; pres. Jacqueline Rosett Assocs., N.Y.C., 1968—; cons. in internat. investments. Photographer: The African Ark, 1974. Vol. counselor N.Y.C. Opera Guild, 1982—; mem. Diamond Club San Diego Zool. Soc., 1975—. Mem. Am. Soc. Profl. and Exec. Women, Nat. Assn. Female Execs., Bronx Zoological Soc. Democrat. Jewish. Club: Camerata (events chmn.). Office: Jacqueline Rosett Estate & Trust 300 E 74th St New York NY 10021

ROSEVEAR, PAMELA ADELE, airline executive, restaurant consultant; b. Corvallis, Oreg., Nov. 26, 1953; d. Reginald, III, and Tomoko (Nonoue) R.; m. Robert Keith Suder, May 27, 1984. Student in Advanced Japanese, U. Hawaii, 1975, 77-78; BS, U. Oreg., 1977; postgrad. in Advanced Japanese, El Camino Community Coll., 1985, 86. Flight attendant Braniff Internat. Airline, Dallas, 1978-81; mgr. Wendy's Inc., Houston, 1982; mgr., trainer Hungry Tiger, Houston, 1982-84; flight attendant Hawaii Express, Los Angeles, 1983; trainer, interpreter Chyuiitsuya Co., Tokyo, 1983, cons., 1983—; v.p. passenger services and inflight, Air Am., Los Angeles, 1984—. Mem. Mortar Board, Kappa Alpha Theta. Republican. Mem. United Ch. of Christ. Avocations: marathon running, cooking, education. Home: 530 24th St Hermosa Beach CA 90254 Office: Air Am 5534 Westlawn Los Angeles CA 90066

ROSHER, JERELENE, cytotechnologist; b. Safety Harbor, Fla., Jan. 29, 1945; d. John Louis and Alberta (Crockam) R.; A.A., Indian River Community Coll., 1966; grad. Bethune-Cookman Coll., 1984. Cytotechnologist, Halifax Hosp. Med. Center, Daytona Beach, Fla., 1967-78; supr. cytology dept. Assn. Med. Labs., Ormond Beach, Fla., 1978-83; practical nurse North Miami Gen. Hosp., 1985-86, RN, Meml. Hosp. Ormond Beach, 1987—. Cert. cytotechnologist. Mem. Fla. State Soc. Cytology, Am. Soc. Clin. Pathologists. Baptist.

ROSLANSKY, PRISCILLA FENN, microbiologist; b. Rochester, N.Y., Nov. 24, 1925; d. Wallace Osgood and Clara Bryce (Comstock) Fenn; m. John Dale Roslansky, June 20, 1953; children: Louise, John Wallace, William Fenn, Clara Ruth. BA, Smith Coll., 1947; MA, Radcliffe Coll.-Harvard U., 1948; PhD, U. Rochester, 1952. Clin. lab. technician, Calif., N.J., part-time, 1952-59; research assoc. U. Calif., Berkeley, 1953-55; NIH fellow, Copenhagen, 1959-60; research assoc. U. Ill., Urbana, 1960-63; research assoc. Marine Biol. Lab., Woods Hole, Mass., 1964-68, 75-79, research on ultrastructure of nerves, also bd. dirs., 1987—; research assoc. U. Saarlandes, Homburg-Saar, Fed. Republic Germany, 1968-69; clin. lab. technician Falmouth Med. Assocs., 1969-75, fellow Bunting Inst. of Radcliffe Coll., 1981-83; dir. research Assocs. of Cape Cod, 1983-86, resident scientist, 1986—. V.p. Woods Hole Community Assn., 1976; mem. Woods Hole Civic Assn., 1967-68. Contbr. articles to profl. jours. Mem. Am. Soc. Microbiology, LWV (bd. dirs. 1979—), Sigma Xi. Club: Woods Hole Women's. Home: 57 Buzzards Bay Ave Woods Hole MA 02543

ROSNESS, BETTY JUNE, advertising and public relations agency executive; b. Oklahoma City, Mar. 4, 1924; d. Thomas Harrison and Clara Marguerite (Stubblefield) Pyeatt; student Oklahoma City U., 1940-41; m. Joseph H. Rosness, Aug. 5, 1960; children—Melody L. Johnson (dec.), Michael C., Randall L., Melinda Rosness Mason, John C. Continuity dir. Sta. KFBI, Wichita, Kans., 1957-58; sales exec. Sta. KFH, Wichita, 1958-60; U.S. senatorial press sec., 1961-66; dir. advt. and public relations Alaska State Bank, Anchorage, 1966-68; prin. Rosness Advt. Assocs., Goleta, Calif., 1968—; bd. dirs. Fin. Corp. Santa Barbara (Calif.), Santa Barbara Savs. & Loan. Pres., Goleta Valley Girls Club, 1972-75, Ret. Officers Womens Assn., 1970; v.p. Santa Barbara Symphony Assn., 1977-80; bd. dirs. Channel City Womens Forum, 1976—, Goleta Valley Community Hosp.; Chmn. U. Calif. at Santa Barbara Affiliates, Pvt. Industry Council Santa Barbara County, 1985-86; bd. dirs. Cancer Found., Santa Barbara, 1978-82, founding mem. Goleta Beautiful, Club West Track and Field; mem. allocations com., bd. dirs. United Way, Santa Barbara; founding mem., bd. dirs. Children's World of Hospice; mem. evangelism com. Good Shepherd Lutheran Ch. Named Woman of Year, Santa Barbara County, 1978, Affiliate of Yr., U. Calif.-Santa Barbara, 1983-84. Mem. Greater Santa Barbara Advt. Club. (past v.p.), Goleta Valley C. of C. (past dir.), Santa Barbara C. of C. (bd. dirs. 1982-86), Goleta Valley C. of C. Address: 669 Larchmont Pl Goleta CA 93117

ROSS, BELLA, manufacturing company executive; b. Regensberg, Fed. Republic of Germany, Aug. 21, 1947; came to U.S., 1951; d. Samuel and Lola (Kapelushnek) Rothkopf; m. John David Ross, Mar. 15, 1970; children: Steven J., Daniel A. BA, Yeshiva U., 1969. Cert. tchr., N.Y. Tchr. London, 1970-72; pres. J.B. European Antiques, North Brunswick, N.J., 1972-73, J/B Ross, New Brunswick, N.J., 1973—. Author articles and booklet on furniture selection. Capt. fund raising com. Bill Bradley for Gov., Princeton, N.J. Recipient Furniture USA Design award, Furniture World, 1974, 75, 76, 77, 78, 79, 80, Rosco award Resources Council, N.Y.C., 1978. Jewish. Club: Princeton Jewish Ctr. Office: J/B 409 Joyce Kilmer Ave New Brunswick NJ 08901

ROSS, BETTY GRACE, medical distributing company executive; b. N.Y.C., July 14, 1931; d. Philip and Nancy Anna (Meredith) Boccella; R.N., Presbyn. Hosp., 1952; student Ariz. State U., 1960-62; m. Robert W. Ross, Mar. 1, 1968 (div. July 1976). Sr. operating rm. nurse Roosevelt Hosp., N.Y.C., 1953-58, pvt. surg. nurse, neurosurgery group, 1958-59, orthopedic surgery group, 1960-64; mem. sales staff Zimmer U.S.A., Phoenix, Ariz., 1964-71, owner, distbr. Zimmer Ross Assocs., Phoenix, 1971—, Zimmer-Ross Ltd., 1978—; instr. operating room nursing Englewood (N.J.) Hosp. 1960. Mem. Assn. Operating Room Nurses Phoenix (charter mem.), Maricopa Mental Health Assn., Bloomfield Coll. Alumni Assn. Republican. Club: Century. Home: 5713 Cattletrack Rd N Scottsdale AZ 85253 Office: 1232 E Missouri St Phoenix AZ 85014

ROSS, BLANCHE SHIRLEY, communications executive; b. Atlanta, Dec. 3, 1924; d. Sam A. and Lena (Clein) Goldstein; m. Chester M. Ross; 1 child, Dorien. BA, Sarah Lawrence Coll., 1976. Nat. pres. Brandeis U., 1957-60, nat. v.p. women's com., 1960-63, mem. nat. women's bd., 1957—; chmn. N.Y. women's div. United Jewish Appeal, 1966-68; pres. N.Y. Assn. New Ams., 1976-80; pres., chief exec. officer Ross Assocs. Speakers Bur., Inc., N.Y.C., 1980—. Chmn. legal and def. and edn. fund Buddy award NOW, 1987; co-chmn. N.Y. Women's Forum Nat. Meeting, 1987. Office: Ross Assocs Speakers Bur Inc 250 W 57th St Suite 2122 New York NY 10107

ROSS, CAROL D(RING), financial director; b. Los Angeles, Dec. 1, 1944; d. Buddy and Ruth C. (Lawrence) Burlingame; m. Bruce C. Ross, Apr. 2, 1977; children: Andrew, Tiffany. Student, UCLA, 1963-66; MBA, Pepperdine U., 1979. Internal auditor Planning Research, Westwood, Calif., 1966-68; acct. Calif. Aero Dynamics, Van Nuys, Calif., 1968-69; pvt. practice acctg. 1969-74; office mgr. J.M. Carden Sprinkler, Los Angeles, 1974-77; chief fin. officer Am. Dietary Lab., Burbank, Calif., 1977; v.p., co-owner Ziegler Ross, San Francisco and Los Angeles, 1982-87; dir. fin. Westridge Sch. for Girls, Pasadena, Calif., 1988—; dir. bus. services Internal Edn. Found., Los Angeles, 1977-81; speaker Continuing Legal Edn.; bd. dirs. Ziegler Ross. Author: Part-Time Employment, 1979; author/editor (newsletter) L.O.G.I.C. Chmn. personnel commn. Glendale (Calif.) Community Coll., 1980—. Mem. ABA, Nat. Assn. Accts. Unitarian. Office: Westridge Sch 324 Madeline Dr Pasadena CA 91105

ROSS, CAROLYN THAYER, lawyer; b. Cin., June 5, 1948; d. Edward Miller and Carolyn (Warner) Thayer. BA, U. Pa., 1970; JD, Boston Coll., 1975. Bar: Mass. 1975, Ga. 1980, U.S. Dist. Ct. Mass. 1976, U.S. Supreme Ct. 1983. Tchr. Springside Sch., Phila., 1970-72; assoc. Abraham & Pappas, Boston, 1975-76, Bowker, Elmes, Perkins, Mecsas & Gerrard, Boston, 1976-81; sole practice, Boston, 1981-82, 87—; v.p., gen. counsel Yankee Oil & Gas Inc., Boston, 1982-84; sr. v.p., gen. counsel Yankee Cos., Inc., 1984-87; of counsel Boston Investors Fund, Inc., 1987—. Home: 60 Temple St Boston MA 02114

ROSS, CATHERINE LOUISE, marketing executive; b. Cin., Feb. 23, 1956; d. Paul Anthony and Aurelia Jean (O'Gallagher) R. BS in Secondary Edn., BA in History summa cum laude, U. Cin., 1978; MBA, U. Pa., 1985. Seasongood fellow Nat. Mcpl. League, Cin., 1977; mgmt. analyst office of the city mgr. City of Cin., 1978-83; J.E. Webb fellow The Smithsonian Inst., Washington, 1984; asst. product mgr. The Drackett Co., Cin., 1985—. Mem. Am. Mktg. Assn., Wharton Alumni Assn., U. Cin. Alumni Assn. Home: 3764 Drake Ave Cincinnati OH 45209 Office: The Drackett Co 201 E 4th St Cincinnati OH 45202

ROSS, CHARLOTTE PACK, suicidologist; b. Oklahoma City, Oct. 21, 1932; d. Joseph and Rose P. (Traibich) Pack; m. Roland S. Ross, May 6, 1951 (div. July 1964); children: Beverly Jo, Sandra Gail. Ed. U. Okla., 1949-52, New Sch. Social Research, 1952-53. Cert. tchr. Exec. dir. Suicide Prevention and Crisis Ctr. San Mateo County, Burlingame, Calif., 1966—; pres., exec. dir. Youth Suicide Nat. Ctr., Washington, 1985—; pres. Calif. Senate Adv. Com. Youth Suicide Prevention, 1982-84; speaker Menninger Found., 1983, 84; instr. San Francisco State U., 1981-83; conf. coordinator U. Calif., San Francisco, 1971—; cons. univs. and health services throughout world. Contbg. author: Group Counseling for Suicidal Adolescents, 1984; Teaching Children the Facts of Life and Death, 1985. Mem. editorial bd. Suicide and Life Threatening Behavior, 1976—. Mem. regional selection panel Pres.'s Commn. on White House Fellows, 1975-78; mem. CIRCLON Service Club, 1979—, Com. on Child Abuse, 1981—; founding mem. Women for Responsible Govt., co-chmn., 1974-79. Recipient Outstanding Exec. award San Mateo County Coordinating Com., 1971; Koshland award San Francisco Found., 1984. Mem. Internat. Assn. Suicide Prevention (v.p. 1985—), Am. Assn. Suicidology (sec. 1972-74), bd. govs. 1976-78, accreditation com. 1975—, chair region IX, 1975-82), Assn. United Way Agy. Execs. (pres. 1974), Assn. County Contract Agys. (pres. 1982). Club: Peninsula Press Club. Office: 1811 Trousdale Dr Burlingame CA 94010

ROSS, CLO S., manufacturing executive; b. Muncie, Ind., July 9, 1939; d. Floyd and Hazel (Duncan) Stephens; divorced; children: Kim, Lori. BA, Marywood Coll., 1982; MBA, Nova U., 1985. V.p. operations Clairson Internat., Ocala, Fla., 1979—; instr. Nova U., Ft. Lauderdale, 1986—; lectr. Am. Mgt. Assn., Atlanta, 1987—. Mem. Am. Soc. Personnel Assn. Lodge: Altrusa (pres. 1981-82). Home: 2309 SE 19th Cir Ocala FL 32671 Office: 3101 SE College Rd Ocala FL 32674

ROSS, DIANA, singer, actress, entertainer, fashion designer; b. Detroit, Mar. 26, 1944; d. Fred and Ernestine R.; m. Robert Ellis Silberstein, Jan. 1971 (div. 1976); children: Rhonda, Tracee, Chudney; m. Arne Naess, Oct. 23, 1985; 1 son: Ross Arne. Grad. high sch. Pres. Diana Ross Enterprises, Inc., fashion and merchandising, Anaid Film Prodns., Inc., RTC Mgmt. Corp., artists mgmt., Chondee Inc., Rosstown, Rossville, music pub. Lead singer until 1969, Diana Ross and the Supremes; solo artist, 1969—; albums include Diana Ross, 1970, 76, Everything Is Everything, 1971, I'm Still Waiting, 1971, Lady Sings The Blues, 1972, Touch Me In The Morning, 1973, Original Soundtrack of Mahogany, 1975, Baby It's Me, 1977, The Wiz, 1978, Ross, 1978, 83, The Boss, 1979, Diana, 1981, To Love Again, 1981, Why Do Fools Fall In Love?, 1981, Silk Electric, 1982, Swept Away, 1984, Eaten Alive, 1985, Chain Reaction, 1986; films include Lady Sings the Blues, 1972, Mahogany, 1975, The Wiz, 1978; NBC-TV spl., An Evening With Diana Ross, 1977, Diana, 1981, numerous others. Recipient citation Vice Pres. Humphrey for efforts on behalf Pres. Johnson's Youth Opportunity Program, citation Mrs. Martin Luther King and Rev. Abernathy for contbn. to SCLC cause, awards Billboard, Cash Box and Record World as worlds outstanding singer, Grammy award, 1970, Female Entertainer of Year NAACP, 1970, Cue award as Entertainer of year, 1972, Golden Apple award, 1972, Gold medal award Photoplay, 1972, Antoinette Perry award, 1977, nominee as best actress of year for Lady Sings the Blues Motion Picture Acad. Arts and Scis., 1972, Golden Globe award, 1972; named to Rock and Roll Hall of Fame, 1988. Office: RTC Mgmt PO Box 1683 New York NY 10185 also: care Shelly Berger 6255 Sunset Blvd Los Angeles CA 90028 *

ROSS, DORIS G., civic worker; b. Thompsonville, Conn.; d. Philip A. and Eva (Saffir) Sisitzky; student Barnard Coll., Max Reinhardt Drama Workshop, N.Y. U. Radio Workshop, Lee Strasberg Theatre Inst., Royal Acad. Dramatic Arts; m. Lewis H. Ross, Jan. 4, 1942; children—Phyllis, Allyne. Dir. New Eng. Zionist Youth Com., 1943-45; dir. theatre arts Manchester Inst. Arts and Scis., 1947-48; pres. Manchester Girls Clubs, 1950-51, dir., 1949-53, 54-58, 59-69, chmn. nat. adv. bd. Girls Clubs Am., 1955-57, v.p., 1956-57, pres., 1957-59, chmn. 15th Ann. Conf., 1960, first acting chmn. past pres. com., 1974, 1st pres. past pres. club, 1975-77, chmn. 15th ann. conf., 1960, chmn. silver jubilee com., 1969-70, chmn. directions and social concerns com., 1978-79, founder Children's Creative Theatre, 1978, chmn., 1979-81; hon. mem., 1981—; exec. com. Girls Clubs N.Y., 1970-73, bd. dirs., 1970-73, sustaining dir., 1973—, co-chmn. long range planning com., 1970-71; 1st pres. Theatre Art Players, Temple Emanuel, N.Y.C., 1970-71; trustee Actors Studio, 1978-82, 84, conceived Actors Studio Achievement awards celebration, 1981; dir. Manchester Settlement Assn., 1951-54, Manchester Vis. Nurses Assn., 1955-61; del. Nat. Soc. Welfare Assembly, 1957-59, White House Conf. on Children and Youth, 1960, voting del. nat. council state coms., 1960, mem. N.H. state exec. com., 1960, N.H. state sub-com. on Leisure Times Activities chmn., 1960; charter colleague Nat. Assembly Nat. Voluntary Health and Welfare Orgns., Inc., 1976—, mem. Nat. Juvenile Justice Program Collaboration, Mem. Pres.'s Citizens Adv. Com. on Fitness of Am. Youth, 1958-60; mem. exec. com. Gov.'s Com. on Children and Youth, 1961-63; Gov.'s rep. to Pres.'s Conf. on Youth Fitness, 1962; pres. Manchester Garden Club, 1963-64; dir. Opera League New Hampshire, Inc., 1964-69; trustee Actors Studio, 1978-82. Mem. Hadassah (pres. Manchester chpt. 1943-44, dir. Manchester chpt. 1942-49, New Eng. regional v.p. 1944-46). Address: 985 Fifth Ave New York NY 10021

ROSS, ELEANORA (BETSY), consultant, speaker, writer, counselor; b. Washington, Iowa; d. Roy Lloyd and Erna Machan (Spera) Miller; m. Robert E. Anderson (div. Jan. 1971); children—R. Daryl, Rebecca, David; m. William Wayne Ross, June 26, 1972 (dec. Aug. 1975). B in Gen. Studies with honors, U. Iowa, 1979, M in Div., 1983; founder, dir. Ray of Hope, Inc., Iowa City, Iowa, 1976—. Author: After Suicide: A Ray of Hope, 1986; producer (videotapes): After Suicide: A Unique Grief Process, 1980; Survivorship After Suicide, 1984. Grantee Ella Lyman Cabot Trust, 1983, Kaltenborn Found., 1984 ; recipient Edn. awards P.E.O., 1974, 82, Bus. and Profl. Women, 1984. Mem. Assn. for Death Edn. and Counseling, Am. Assn. Suicidology, Am. Assn. Retired Persons, Omicron Delta Kappa. Avocations: dancing, drama, poetry and fiction writing, music, travel. Office: Ray of Hope Inc PO Box 2323 Iowa City IA 52244

ROSS, ELISE JANE, newspaper executive; b. Manchester, Conn., Aug. 29, 1943; d. Harry and Sophia J. (Osher) R. B.A., NYU, 1965. Programmer Met. Life Ins. Co., N.Y.C., 1965-68; systems analyst Bache, N.Y.C., 1968-70; mgr. systems and programming Omniswitch, Inc., Lake Success, N.Y., 1970-73; sr. v.p. info. systems N.Y. Times, N.Y.C., 1973—. Jewish. Office: The New York Times 229 W 43rd St New York NY 10036

ROSS, EUNICE LATSHAW, judge; b. Bellevue, Pa., Oct. 13, 1923; d. Richard Kelly and Eunice (Weidner) Latshaw; m. John Anthony Ross, May 29, 1943 (dec. Jan. 1978); 1 child, Geraldine Ross Coleman. B.S., U. Pitts., 1945, LL.B., 1951. Bar: Pa. 1952. Atty., Pub. Health Law Research Project, Pitts., 1951-52; atty. jud. asst., law clk. Ct. Common Pleas, Pitts., 1952-70; adjunct law prof. U. Pitts., 1967-73; dir. family div. Ct. Common Pleas, Pitts., 1970-72; judge Ct. Common Pleas of Allegheny County, Pitts., 1972—; mem. Bd. Jud. Inquiry and Rev., Commonwealth of Pa., Gov's Justice Commn., 1972-78. Author: (with others) Survey of Pa. Public Health Laws, 1952. Contbr. articles to legal publs. Com. person for 14th ward, vice chmn. Democratic Com., Pitts., 1972; exec. com. bd. trustees U. Pitts., 1980-86; adv. bd. Animal Friends, Pitts., 1973—; bd. mem. The Program, Pitts., 1983-87, Pitts. History and Landmarks FDTN., West Pa. Hist. Soc., West Pa. Conservancy. Recipient Disting. Amumna award U. Pitts., 1973, Medal of Recognition, 1987; named Girl Scout Woman of Yr., Pitts. council Girl Scouts U.S., 1975; cert. of Achievement Pa. Fedn. Women's Clubs, 1975, 77. Mem. Allegheny County Bar Assn. (vice chmn., exec. com. young lawyers sect. 1956-59), Pitts. Bus. and Profl. Women's Club, Pa. State Trial Judges Conf. Home: 1204 Denniston Ave Pittsburgh PA 15217 Office: 802 City-County Bldg Pittsburgh PA 15219

ROSS, GAIL SHARON, pediatric psychologist, educator; b. Paterson, N.J., Nov. 19, 1946; d. Samuel Michael and Matilda (Gershon) R.; B.A. magna cum laude with honors in Psychology, Barnard Coll., 1968; M.A., U. Chgo., 1969; Ph.D., Harvard U., 1978; m. Robert Jay Schwartz, Jr.; children—Matthew Alexander, Michael Benjamin, Alexandra Ross. Assoc. in research in psychology Yale U., New Haven, 1976-78; research assoc. in psychiatry and pediatrics Cornell U. Med. Coll., N.Y.C., 1978-80, instr. psychiatry and pediatrics, 1980, asst. prof. pediatrics, 1982—, staff psychologist Perinatology Center, N.Y. Hosp., N.Y.C., 1978—, research dir. perinatal follow-up program, 1986—; dir. Early Childhood Direction Center of Manhattan and Bronx, 1980-82. NDEA Title IV fellow, 1968-69; NIMH grantee, 1972-76; N.Y. State Developmental Disabilities grantee, 1979-82. Mem. Am. Psychol. Assn., Am. Acad. Scis., N.Y. Acad. Scis., Soc. Research in Child Devel., Am. Assn. Women in Psychology, Phi Beta Kappa, Phi Delta Kappa. Contbr. articles to profl. jours.; research in devel. of normal and highrisk infants. Office: Perinatology Ctr 525 E 68th St New York NY 10021

ROSS, GLORIA FRANKENTHALER, artist; b. N.Y.C., Sept. 5, 1923; d. Alfred and Martha (Lowenstein) Frankenthaler; m. John J. Bookman; children: Alfred Frankenthaler Ross, Beverly Ross, Clifford Ross. BA, Mt. Holyoke Coll., 1943. Owner, operator Gloria F. Ross Tapestries, N.Y.C., 1963—; collector Gloria F. Ross Collection Contemporary Navajo Weaving Denver Art Mus., 1983; mem. Churro Sheep Project U. Utah, Logan; lectr. Internat. Tapestry Symposium, Australian Bicentennial, Fashion Inst. Tech., N.Y., Harvard Club, Shared Horizons, Santa Fe. Exhibited in group shows at Feigen Gallery, Chgo. and N.Y., Pace Edits., N.Y., The Ringling Mus., Sarasota, Fla., Lausanne Biennale, Kauffman Gallery, Houston; represented in permanent collections at IBM, J.C. Penney Co., Tougaloo (Miss.) Coll. Art Mus., Kennedy Internat. Airport, N.Y., Bank of Tokyo, N.Y., Citibank, N.Y.; commd. tapestries for Westinghouse Broadcasting Co., Phila., Winters Bank, Dayton, Ohio, Fed. Courthouse, Portland, Oreg., Mazza Gallery Prudential Ins. Co., Washington; collaborator tapestries with various artists. Chmn. Child Devel. Ctr., N.Y.C., 1960's; trustee Mt. Holyoke Coll., South Hadley, Mass., 1986—; active numerous civic groups, N.Y.C. Mem. Am. Craft Council, ArtTable, Cooper Hewitt, Met. Mus. Modern Art, Mus. Natural History, Textile Mus., Mt. Holyoke Coll. Art Mus.

ROSS, HAZEL, health science association administrator; b. Bklyn., Oct. 29, 1934; d. Leo and Mae (Press) Leudesdorff; m. Harold B. Rosenthal (div. 1982); children: Donna Jean, Michael A., Robert F. Grad. high sch., Tilden. V.p. Recco Home Care Service, Inc., Massapequa, N.Y., 1977—, Recco HealthCare Services, Massapequa, 1984—, Cert. Mgmt. Corp., Massapequa, 1986—; mem. N.Y. State Health Adv. Commn., Albany, 1984-86. Organizer congl. campaign J. Halpern, Long Island, N.Y.; founder Laurelton Block Assn.. Long Island; pub. relations person Jackson Presdl. campaign, Long Island; pres. Marine Park Civic Assn., Bklyn. Mem. N.Y. State Assn. of Health Care Providers (legis. chair 1978-82), N.Y. State Assembly Com. on Home Care (Tallon com. 1982-84), Nat. Assn. for Health Care. Office: Recco Healthcare Assn 524 Hicksville Rd Massapequa NY 11758

ROSS, JANICE KOENIG, artist, educator; b. Harrisburg, Pa., May 2, 1926; d. Paul Lindenmuth and Edna Rachel (Lowe) Koenig; m. Conrad H. Ross, Apr. 19, 1954; children—Katherine Ann, Joseph Aaron, Lucie Rachel. B.A., Pa. State u., 1947; M.F.A., U. Ill., 1954. Prof. art Tuskegee U., Ala., 1968—; artist in residence art studies abroad Program U. Ga., Cortona, Italy, 1984; lectr. in field; Fulbright-Hays Cross Cultural Study Tour Traditional Arts and Crafts of Pakistan participant, 1986. Art work included in regional and nat. group and solo exhibitions, pvt. and pub. collections. NEH fellow 1981; grantee Com. for Humanities in Ala., 1982. Mem. Coll. Art Assn., Southeastern Womens Caucus for Art (sec.-treas. 1978-80), Womens Caucus for Art (nat. bd. mem. 1988-90), Studio 218 (founder; pres. 1980-82, 84-86, sec.-treas. 1982-84). Democrat. Unitarian. Home: 447 Wrights Mill Rd Auburn AL 36830 Office: Tuskegee U Art Dept Tuskegee AL 36088

ROSS, JOAN KENNEDY, municipal official; b. York, S.C., Aug. 29, 1947; d. Wade Edward and Josephine (Gill) Kennedy; children: Curtis Alan Ross, Brian Ashley Ross. BA, St. Augustine Coll., 1969; M in Urban Adminstrn., U. N.C., Charlotte, 1982. Speech therapist Wake County Schs., Raleigh, N.C., 1969-70; tchr. Balt. City Schs., Raleigh, 1970-74; program coordinator Project 70001, Gary, Ind., 1974-76; adminstrv. intern City Mgr.'s Office, Charlotte, N.C., 1979-80; analyst intern Budget and Evaluation dept. City of Charlotte, 1980; adminstr. Charlotte-Mecklenburg Utility, Charlotte, N.C., 1980-83; adminstrv. officer Charlotte Parks and Recreation Dept., 1983—; lectr. Ind. U. N.W., Gary, 1975-76; cons. Mirosaun, Charlotte, 1987—. Author: The Politics of Agenda, 1982. Bd. dirs., treas. Charlotte Civic League, 1980—; chair Black Women's Health Project, Charlotte, 1985—; sec. Westside Coalition, Charlotte, 1986—; mem. Black Polit. Caucus, Charlotte, 1986—. Mem. Nat. Recreation & Parks Assn., Nat. Assn. Female Execs., N.C. Recreation and Parks Soc., Carolina Assn. Black Women Entrepreneurs, Leadership Charlotte. Democrat. Presbyterian. Home: 2900 Remington St Charlotte NC 28216 Office: Charlotte Parks and Recreation Dept 310 N Kings Dr Charlotte NC 28204

ROSS, JUDITH PARIS, life insurance executive; b. Boston, Dec. 23, 1939; d. Max and Ruth Paris; ed. Boston U., 1961, UCLA, 1978; grad. Life Underwriting Tng. Council, 1978; 1 son, Adam Stuart. Producer, co-host Checkpoint TV show, Washington, 1967-71; hostess Judi Says TV show, Washington, 1969; brokerage supr., specialist impaired risk underwriting Beneficial Nat. Life Ins. Co. (now Nat. Benefit Life), Beverly Hills, Calif., 1973-82, dir. Salary Savs. program for West Coast, 1982-87; ins. and benefits specialist, cons. Alliance Assocs., 1987—; mktg. dir. Brougher Ins. Group, 1982-87; ins. and benefits specialist Alliance Assocs., Beverly Hills, 1987—; featured speaker ins. industry seminars. Active local PTA, Boy Scouts Am., Beverly Hills local politics; mem. early childhood edn. adv. com. Beverly Hills Unified Sch. Dist., 1977. Mem. Nat. Assn. Life Underwriters, Calif. Assn. Life Underwriters (dir. W. Los Angeles 1980—, v.p. chpt. 1982—, chmn. pub. relations), West Los Angeles Life Underwriters Assn. (v.p. fin. 1983-84). Office: Alliance Assocs 449 S Beverly Dr #206 Beverly Hills CA 90212

ROSS, KATHERINE BALL, editor; b. Washington, Feb. 25, 1944; d. Frederic Joseph and Juelda (Watson) Ball; m. John Munder Ross, Aug. 17, 1974; 1 son, Matthew Munder Ball Ross. B.A., Wellesley Coll., 1965. Assoc. editor, articles Redbook Mag., N.Y.C., 1970-76, sr. editor, 1976-78, contbg. editor, 1978-80; articles editor Mademoiselle Mag., N.Y.C., 1980-83, assoc. editor, 1983-87; dir. spl. features Self Mag., N.Y.C., 1987-88; editor-in-chief Hearst Spl. Pubs., N.Y.C., 1988—. Mem. Am. Soc. Mag. Editors, Women's Media Group, Women in Communications, Soc. Profl. Journalists. Home: 277 West End Ave New York NY 10023 Office: Hearst Spl Pubs 1700 Broadway New York NY 10019

ROSS, KATHLEEN ANNE, college president; b. Palo Alto, Calif., July 1, 1941; d. William Andrew and Mary Alberta (Wilburn) R. B.A., Ft. Wright Coll., 1964; M.A., Georgetown U., 1971; Ph.D., Claremont Grad. Sch., 1979. Cert. tchr., Wash. Secondary tchr. Holy Names Acad., Spokane, Wash., 1964-70; dir. research and planning Province Holy Names, Wash. State, 1972-73; v.p. acads. Ft. Wright Coll., Spokane, 1973-81; research asst. to dean Claremont Grad. Sch., Calif., 1977-78; assoc. faculty mem. Harvard U., Cambridge, Mass., 1981; pres. Heritage Coll., Toppenish, Wash., 1981—; cons. Wash. State Holy Names Schs., 1971-73; coll. accrediting assn. evaluator N.W. Assn. Schs. and Colls., Seattle, 1975—; dir. Holy Names Coll., Oakland, Calif., 1979—; cons. Yakima Indian Nation, Toppenish, 1975—; speaker, cons. in field. Author: (with others) Multicultural Pre-School Curriculum, 1977; Cultural Factors in Success of American Indian Students in Higher Education, 1978. Chmn. Internat. 5-Yr. Convocation of Sisters of Holy Names, Montreal, Que., Can., 1981; TV Talk show host Spokane Council of Chs., 1974-76. Recipient E.K. and Lillian F. Bishop Founds. Youth Leader of Yr. award, 1986; Holy Names medal Ft. Wright Coll., 1981; Disting. Citizenship Alumna award Claremont Grad. Sch., 1986; named Yakima Herald Repub. Person of the Yr. 1987; numerous grants for projects in multicultural higher edn., 1974—. Mem. Pub. Policy Commn., Nat. Assn. Ind. Colls. and Univs., Nat. Catholic Edn. Assn. (N.W. regional assoc. 1974-82), Am. Assn. Higher Edn., Soc. Intercultural Edn., Tng. and Research, Sisters of Holy Names of Jesus and Mary. Roman Catholic. Office: Heritage Coll Route 3 Box 3540 Toppenish WA 98948

ROSS, KATHLEEN B. HENRICH, marketing manager, dental hygienist, consultant; b. Providence, Dec. 25, 1947; d. Daniel Ernest Baker and Virginia Mary (Furey) Bidle; m. Clarence Dean Ross, Oct. 11, 1985. B.S. in Dental Hygiene, U. R.I., 1970. Dental hygienist various dental offices, Mass., Fla., Mo., Minn., Ga., 1970—; research cons. Forsyth Dental Research Ctr., Boston, 1970-72, Monsanto Co., St. Louis, 1973-79; instr. dental hygiene Forest Park Jr. Coll., St. Louis, 1975-76; ednl. cons. Dental Sci. Systems, Reston, Va., 1982-85; ednl. cons. Teledyne Water Pik, Ft. Collins, Colo., 1977-85, dir. continuing edn., 1985-86, dental profl. mktg. mgr., 1986—; pres. Candy Baker, Inc., Atlanta, 1981—. Mem. Am. Dental Hygiene Assn., Ga. Dental Hygiene Assn., Internat. Dental Health Found., Internat. Assn. for Dental Research, Internat. Platform Assn. Home and Office: 4322 Sprucebough Dr Marietta GA 30062

ROSS, KENDRA ANN, nursing educator; b. Coldwater, Mich., Oct. 6, 1940; d. Clyde Kenneth and Betty Ann (Barnes) Dryer; m. William Alexander Reid Wilson, Apr. 21, 1962; children—Kendra Ann, Laura, Bill; m. 2d, Stuart Charles Ross, June 18, 1982. B.S. in Nursing, U. Mich., 1962; M.S. in Nursing, No. Ill. U., 1979. Head nurse, med.-surg. ICU, Annapolis Hosp., Wayne, Mich., 1962-65, evening supr., instr. medication course for practical nurses, 1965-68; practical nurse coordinator Ann Arbor Practical Nurse Center, 1963-64; instr. staff devel. Borgess Hosp., Kalamazoo, 1970-71; instr. assoc. degree nursing program Kalamazoo Valley Community Hosp., 1970-71; instr. diploma nursing program Copley Sch. Nursing, Aurora, Ill., 1975-78; clin. specialist, nurse practitioner-neurology, cons. neurol. nursing, tchr. practitioner Rush-Presbyn.-St. Luke's Med. Center, Chgo., 1980-82; instr. assoc. degree nursing program Coll. Dupage, Glen Ellyn, Ill., 1982-84; instr. diploma nursing program St. Joseph Med. Ctr., Joliet, Ill., 1984—; instr., course developer Pharmacotherapeutics Coll. Dupage, Glen Ellyn, Ill., 1984, physical assessment adult client correlating normal and abnormal findings and nursing diagnosis. Co-author: Fundamentals of Nursing: A Learning Guide, 1987. Mem. bd. Dupage County Health Dept., Wheaton, Ill., 1975; active local councils Girl Scouts U.S., 1948-51, 71-73; co-founder Naperville chpt. Nat. Assn. Learning Disabilities, 1971-75. Mem. Soc. Nursing Profls., Nat. League Nursing, DAR. Republican. Congregationalist. Home: 104 Foxcroft St Naperville IL 60565

ROSS, KHADIJA ELIZABETH RUSSELLA, escrow finance specialist; b. Bremerton, Wash., June 27, 1949; d. Donald Alonzo Ross, Jr. and Geraldine Russella (Kent) Ross Osorio; m. Francis A. Dahmer, Jr., Mar. 1968 (div. 1976); 1 child, Cory. BA, Ga. So. Coll., 1976; MEd, U. Wash., 1982. Dir. ESL program Army Community Services, Ft. Stewart, Ga., 1975-76; asst. store mgr. K-Mart, San Jose, Calif., 1982-83; income property loan adminstr. Westside Fed. Savs. & Loan, Seattle, 1984-85, asset mgr., liquidations, loan servicing specialist Fed. Savs. and Loan Ins. corp., Seattle, 1985-86; sr. escrow officer Ticor Title Ins. Co., Seattle, 1986—; admitted Wash. State Supreme Ct., ltd. practice officer, 1984. Mem. Seattle Art Mus., Seattle Sci. Ctr., Greenpeace. Served with U.S. Army, 1967-68. Mem. Nat. Assn. Female Execs., Alumni Assn. U. Wash., NOW, Mensa. Shi'ite Moslem. Avocations: writing, traveling, studying. Office: Ticor Title Ins Co 1008 Western Seattle WA 98104-1032

ROSS, LEABELLE I. (MRS. CHARLES R. ROSS), retired psychiatrist; b. Lorain, Ohio, Feb. 11, 1905; d. Charles E. and Harriet (Dobbie) Isaac; A.B., Western Res. U., 1927, M.D., 1930; m. Charles R. Ross, Sept. 23, 1941; children—Charles R., John Edwin. Surg. intern Lakeside Hosp., Cleve., 1931-32; resident obstetrics and gynecology Iowa State U. Hosp., 1932-33; resident obstetrics and surgery N.Y. Infirmary, N.Y.C., 1933-34; pvt. practice, Cleve., 1935-40; staff physician Cleve. State Hosp., 1938-42; dir. student health Bowling Green (Ohio) State U., 1942-45; psychiatrist Bur. Juvenile Research, Columbus, Ohio, 1946-47; psychiat. cons., 1948-51; psychiatrist Mental Hygiene Clinic, Columbus VA, 1951-55; dir. med. services Juvenile Diagnostic Center, 1955-59, acting supt., 1958, 61-62, dir. psychiat. services, 1959-62, clin. dir., 1962-70. Mem. Am. Psychiat. Assn., Ohio Psychiat. Assn., Am. Group Psychotherapy Assn., Tri-State Group Psychotherapy Soc., Neuropsychiat. Assn. Central Ohio, Assn. Physicians Div. Mental Hygiene and Correction (pres. 1963-64), Alpha Sigma Rho, Nu Sigma Phi. Club: Soroptimist. Home: 1289 Gold Ridge Rd Sebastopol CA 95472

ROSS, LINDA SUE, financial manager; b. Chgo., Feb. 26, 1949; d. Donald and Vadys (Ellis) R. BBA, East Tex. State U., 1971; MBA, U. Tex., 1980. CPA, Tex., Ga. Staff acct. Travis & Ramsey, Dallas, 1971-74, Vantage Cos., Dallas, 1974-76; acctg. supr., tax acct. Tex. Instruments Inc., Dallas, 1976-79; sr. profitability analyst, sr. fin. analyst No. Telecom, Inc., Richardson, Tex., 1979-82, mgr. non-direct distbn. market control, 1982-83; br. fin. mgr. Atlanta, 1983-86; fin. mgr., controller No. Telecom, Inc., Atlanta, 1986-87; cons. fin. Atlanta, 1987—; instr. applied econs. Jr. Achievement, Atlanta, 1986. Active Atlanta Zool. Soc., 1987. Named one of Outstanding Young Women in Am., 1985. Mem. Am. Inst. CPAs, Ga. Soc. CPAs (various coms. 1985—), Ga. State Bd. Pub. Acctg., Tex. State Bd. Pub. Acctg. Home and Office: 2941 Cravey Dr Atlanta GA 30345

ROSS, LOIS LINA, manufacturing and distributing company executive, new products marketing consultant; b. Boston, Nov. 5, 1947; d. Harry and Esther (Kashuck) Sadow; m. Paul M. Ross, Aug. 25, 1968; children—Gregory, Nicole. Student, Boston U. Asst. office mgr. Waldoroth Label Mfg., Mattapan, Mass., 1965-67, mem. union labor relations com., Stop & Shop, Hyde Park, Mass., 1967-68; office and personnel mgr. Friends Baked Beans, Malden, Mass., 1968-69; community relations rep. McDonalds Restaurant, Syracuse, N.Y., 1978-80; pres., owner Your Hats Desire, Inc., Manlius, N.Y., 1981—; speaker Syracuse U., 1984. Recipient Super Achiever award Admanco Mfg., 1984. Mem. Am. Camping Assn., Advt. Specialty Inst., Women Bus. Owners, Syracuse C. of C. Democrat. Jewish. Clubs: Women's Am. (Syracuse). Avocations: bridge, aerobics, tennis, theater. Office: Your Hats Desire Inc 116 Fayette St PO Box 434 Manlius NY 13104

ROSS, MADELYN ANN, newspaper editor; b. Pitts., June 26, 1949; d. Mario Charles and Rose Marie (Mangieri) R. B.A., Indiana U. of Pa., 1971; M.A., SUNY-Albany, 1972. Reporter Pitts. Press, 1972-78, asst. city editor, 1978-82, spl. assignment editor, 1982-83, mng. editor, 1983—; instr. Community Coll. Allegheny County, 1974-81. Adv. com. Task Force Leadership Pitts., 1985; v.p. Press Old Newsboys Charity Fund. Democrat. Roman Catholic. Clubs: Women's Press, Pitts. Press. Office: Pitts Press 34 Blvd Allies Pittsburgh PA 15230

ROSS, MARILYN LOUISE, intermurals and recreation director, consultant; b. Winston-Salem, N.C., Mar. 30, 1948; d. Herman Lee and Mattie Marie (Gauldin) Sheets; m. Gary Raymond Ross, Dec. 29, 1971 (div.). BS, MEd, Western Carolina U., 1971. Cert. tchr., N.C. Coach Charlotte (N.C.) Latin Sch., 1971-74; dir. intramurals U. Pitts., 1974—. Recipient 1st place award World Games Orgn., 1985. Mem. Nat. Intramural Recreation Assn. Club: Nat. Racquetball. Home: 750 Washington Rd #909 Pittsburgh PA 15228 Office: U Pitts 148 Trees Hall Pittsburgh PA 15261

ROSS, MARY COWELL (MRS. JOHN O. ROSS), lawyer; b. Oklahoma City, Okla., Oct. 1, 1910; d. Sears F. and Elizabeth (Van Zwaluwenburg) Riepma; A.B., Vassar Coll., 1932; LL.B., Memphis State U., 1938; LL.D., U. Nebr., 1973; m. Richard N. Cowell, Mar. 1, 1946 (dec. Jan. 1953); m. 2d, John O. Ross, Mar. 31, 1962 (dec. June 1966). Bar: Tenn. 1938, D.C. 1944, N.Y. 1947. Atty. U.S. Govt., Washington, 1940-44; pvt. practice Cromelin & Townsend, Washington, 1944-46, Royall, Koegel & Rogers and predecessors, N.Y.C., 1946-61; individual practice law, 1961—; treas., dir. 39 E. 79th St. Corp., 1966-73; treas., dir. 795 Fifth Ave. Corp., 1977—; mem. adv. com. N.Y. Commn. on Estates, 1965-67. Bd. dirs. Silver Cross Day Nursery, N.Y.C., 1963-70, Cunningham Dance Found., 1969-72, Central Park Community Fund, 1977-81; trustee U. Nebr. Found., 1966—, bd. dirs., 1974-79; hon. trustee Nebr. Art Assn. Mem. Am. Bar Assn., N.Y. Women's Bar Assn. (pres. 1955-57, dir. 1957-63, 74-80, adv. council 1963—), Bar Assn. City N.Y. (surrogate cts. com. 1961-65, library com. 1965-78, com. on profl. responsibility 1972-75), Nat. Assn. Women Lawyers (assembly del. 1962-64, 73-74, UN observer 1965-67, v.p. 1967, chmn. 1971 ann. conv., distinguished service award 1973), Vassar Coll. Alumnae Assn., Phi Alpha Delta, Delta Gamma, Dinner Dances, Inc. (bd. govs. 1979—). Address: 2 E 61st St Apt 2404 New York NY 10021

ROSS, NANCY L., advertising agency executive; b. Dixon, Ill., July 20, 1940; d. Oscar Kenneth and Louise (Taylor) Welty; m. Stuart C. Ross, Nov. 9, 1963 (div. May 1981); children: Elizabeth Ann, Julia Kay, Ellen Marie. BA in Edn., Shimer Coll., Mt. Carroll, Ill., 1962. Tchr. Dakota (Ill.) Jr. High Sch., 1962-63; employment counselor Ill. State Employment Service, Ottawa, 1963-65; tchr. Serena (Ill.) High Sch., 1967-68; employment counselor AvailAbility, LaGrange, Ill., 1968-70; account rep. Donnelley Directory, Chgo., 1975-88; account exec. The Source, Crystal Lake, Ill., 1988—. Trustee Shimer Coll., 1984—; evangelism com. Brookfield (Ill.) United Meth. Ch., 1971, council on ministries, 1976-80, adminstrv. bd., 1976-80. Named one of Outstanding Young Women in Am., 1976. Mem. Shimer Coll. Alumni Assn. (pres. 1984-88). Republican. Club: United Meth. Women (Brookfield) (pres. 1976, v.p. 1974-76, chmn. ways and means com. 1970-71). Home and Office: 610 Preston Dr #327 Bolingbrook IL 60439

ROSS, PATRICIA LYNN, technical services manager; b. Columbus, Ohio, Feb. 25, 1953; d. Edgar James and Mary Alice (Stack) R.; m. Bryan Lee Hart, Mar. 18, 1978 (div. April 1981); m. James Michael Istok, April 29, 1985; 1 child, Aubrey Anne. BS in Dietetics, Ind. State U., 1974; MS in Foods and Nutrition, Ill. State U., 1976. Registered dietitian. Grad. asst. Ill. State U., Normal, 1975-76; chief home economist Golden DIPT/DCA, Millstadt, Ill., 1976-78; home economist, food technologist Ponderosa, Inc., Dayton, Ohio, 1978-82, product assurance specialist, 1983-84; food research supr. Wendy's Internat., Inc., Dublin, Ohio, 1982-83; foodservice product mgr. Southland Corp., Dallas, 1984—. Mem. Am. Dietetics Assn., Inst. of Food Technologists, Am. Home Economists Assn., Female Execs. in Am., Delta Gamma. Republican. Home: 214 Willowbrook Dr Duncanville TX 75116 Office: Southland Corp 3806 McKinney Ave Dallas TX 75204

ROSS, PATTI JAYNE, physician; b. Sharon, Pa., Nov. 17, 1946; d. James J. and Mary N. Ross; B.S., DePauw U., 1968; M.D., Tulane, U., 1972; m. Allan Robert Katz, May 23, 1976. Asst. prof. U. Tex. Med. Sch., Houston, 1976-82, asso. prof., 1982—, dir. adolescent obstetrics and gynecology, 1976—, also dir. phys. diagnosis; speaker in field. Bd. dirs. Pituitary Found., 1982—; mem. Rape Council. Diplomate Am. Bd. Ob-Gyn. Mem. Tex. Med. Assn., Harris County Med. Soc. So. Perinatal Assn., Houston Obstetric and Gynecologic Soc., Assn. Profs. Obstetrics and Gynecology, Soc. Adolescent Medicine, AAAS, Am. Women's Med. Assn., Orgn. Women in Sci., Sigma Xi. Roman Catholic. Clubs: River Oak Breakfast, Profl. Women Execs. Contbr. articles to profl. jours. Office: 6431 Fannin St Houston TX 77030

ROSS, REBECCA ANN, sales executive; b. Jackson, Miss., Apr. 10, 1952; d. Robert Bryan and Betty Lou (Mize) R. B.S. in Bus. Adminstrn., U. So. Miss., 1974. Buyer, McRaes Dept. Stores, Jackson, 1974-76, Sanger Harris Dept. Store, Dallas, 1976-78; sales mgr. Internat. Playtex Co., Dallas, 1978-83; regional sales mgr. Rush Hampton Industries, Inc., Dallas, 1983-84; sales mgr. So. region Liz Claiborne Hosiery div. Kayser-Roth Hosiery Inc., Dallas, 1984-85; sales mgr. LDS Metromedia, Dallas, 1985-87, Clay Desta Communications, Dallas, 1987—. Active mem. USA Film Festival. Mem. Nat. Assn. Female Execs. Home: 18040 Midway Rd #201 Dallas TX 75252

ROSS, ROBERTA MAYE, diversified company executive; b. Santa Paula, Calif., Jan. 9, 1928; d. Theodore Arthur and Minnie Thelma Stangland; student Ventura Jr. Coll., 1946; Calif. State U., Los Angeles, 1952-56; B.A., LaVerne U., 1972; m. John Paul Ross, June 20, 1959; children—Theodore David, Victoria Lou. Office mgr. Southport Engring. Co., Los Angeles, 1949-57; controller Framing Contractors Ltd. also Trent Meredith Inc., Oxnard, Calif., 1957-60; owner Adminstrv. Assts., Oxnard, Calif., 1960-78, sr. partner, 1978-81, sec.-treas., 1981—, pres., 1986; sec.-treas. Victoria Land Co. Inc. Gard Trucking, Inc., C-D Woodworks Inc., Santa Paula, Calif.; v.p. OSW & F Inc. Cert. profl. sec. Mem. Profl. Secs. Internat., Am. Soc. Women Accts. Clubs: Mediodia Bus. and Profl. Women's Altrusa (gov. Dist. 11, 1985-87). Address: Adminstrv Assts Inc 416 N A St Oxnard CA 93030

ROSS, SHEILA MAUREEN HOLMES, sales manager; b. San Jose, Calif., Nov. 1, 1951; d. Douglas F. and Mary A. (Zager) Murphy; B.A., San Jose State U., 1973; m. Lawrence Richard Ross, Dec. 20, 1981; 1 child, Vanessa Katherine Ross. Exec. sec. J.M. Mfg., Santa Clara, Calif., 1972-74; mktg. coordinator Chick, Orthopedic/Hosmer-Dorrance, Campbell, Calif., 1974-75; mgr. mktg. adminstrn. Consol. Video Systems, Sunnyvale, Calif., 1975-83; regional mgr., Pacific dist. sales mgr. ADDA Corp., Los Gatos, Calif., 1977-84, N.W. regional mgr., 1983-84; broadcast sales mgr. Aurora Systems, San Francisco, 1984-86; dir. U.S. sales Vertigo Systems Internat., Inc., Vancouver, B.C., Can., 1986-87; sales mgr., Digital F/X, Inc., Santa Clara, Calif., 1987—. Soc. Motion Pictures and TV Engrs. Home: 28 Dartmouth Pl Danville CA 94526

ROSS, SUSAN JULIA, lawyer; b. Phila., July 24, 1943; d. Herbert Joseph and Susan Eshleman (Reese) R.; B.A., magna cum laude, U. Pa., 1965, J.D. magna cum laude, 1969; postgrad. N.Y. U. Law Sch., 1972-75. Bar: N.Y., 1971, N.Mex., 1976; assoc. Dewey, Ballantine, Bushby, Palmer & Wood, N.Y.C., 1969, 71-76; ptnr. Natelson & Ross, Taos, N.Mex., 1976—; vis. assoc. prof. law U. Oreg., 1978; dir. Beneficial Corp., Wilmington, Del., 1979—. Trustee Millicent Rogers Mus., Taos. Thouron-U. Pa. fellow, Oxford U., 1969-70; Am. Scandinavian Assn. fellow, Stockholm U., 1970. Mem. Phi Beta Kappa, Order Coif. Contbr. in field articles to jours.

ROSS, SUSAN SANDBERG, corporate executive; b. Kansas City, Mo., Sept. 5, 1940; d. Maurice Heilig and Lola Frances (Brown) Sandberg; m. Thomas Ernest Ross, July2, 1960; children: Wendy Allison, Thomas Ernest Jr., Carrie Frances. Student, Iowa State U., 1958-60, La Salle U., Chgo., 1970. Dir. sales Mary Kay Cosmetics, Ft. Lee, Va., 1973-75; pres. The Ribbon Place, Inc., Albuquerque, 1978—. Author: Amateur Athletic Registration System, 1980. Sec. N.Mex. AAU, Albuquerque, 1976-79; pres. N.Mex. TAC, Albuquerque, 1982-84; nat. registration chmn. The Athletic Congress, Indpls., 1979—; mem. Albuquerque Conv. and Visitors Bur. Recipient Pres.'s award The Athletics Congress, 1981. Republican. Christian Scientist. Office: The Ribbon Place Inc 141 C Wyoming NE Albuquerque NM 87123

ROSS, SUZANNE IRIS, fund raising executive; b. Chgo., Feb. 2, 1948; d. Irving and Rose (Stein) R. BA in Secondary Edn., Western Mich. U., 1971. Dir. youth employment Ill. Youth Services Bur., Maywood, Ill., 1978-79; exec. dir. Edn. Resource Ctr., Chgo., 1979-82; asst. dir. devel. Art Inst. Chgo., 1982-83, mgr. govt. affairs, 1983-84, dir. govt. affairs, 1984-85; v.p. devel. Spertus Coll. Judaica, Chgo., 1985—; lectr. Sch. Art Inst., Chgo., 1982-85, Ill. Fire Inspectors Assn., Mt. Prospect, Ill., 1982-84, Episcopalian Archdiocese, Chgo., 1984, Nat. Soc. Fund Raising Execs. and Donor's Forum, Chgo., 1987; instr. DePaul U. Sch. for New Learning, 1987, Columbia Coll., Chgo., 1980—. Mem. adv. council Citizens Com. on Media, Chgo., 1978-80; adv. panelist Chgo. Office Fine Arts, 1981-82; mem. adv. council Greater Chgo. Food Depository, 1984-85; exec. com. Chgo. Coalition Arts in Edn., 1981-82; mem. info. services com. Donors' Forum Chgo., 1986—, mem. adv. bd. Chgo. Moving Co., 1987—. Mem. Nat. Soc. Fund Raising Execs., Am. Assn. Mus., Am. Council Arts, Ill. Arts Alliance. Democrat. Jewish. Avocation: attending cultural events. Home: 3709 N Janssen #2RB Chicago IL 60613 Office: Spertus Coll Judaica 618 S Michigan Ave Chicago IL 60605

ROSS, VELMA JEAN, realtor; b. Lancaster, Pa., June 22, 1934; d. Jacob Kauffman Shenk and Ida (Bare) Brubaker; m. Daniel Webster Ross, Oct. 10, 1959; children: David Wendel, Janet Marie Miller. BA, Goshen Coll., 1959. Tchr. Oxford (N.J.) Cen. Sch., 1966-70; owner, dir. Bambi Pre-Sch. and Day Care Ctr., Sarasota, Fla., 1973-80; assoc. First Realty Century 21, Sarasota, 1983-84, Merrill Lynch Realty-Boomhower, Sarasota, 1984-85, RE/MAX Realty I, Sarasota, 1985—. Treas. Samaritan Ctr. of Sarasota, Inc., 1986—; bd. dirs. Mennonite Econ. Devel. Assocs., Sarasota, 1986—. Recipient Excellence award Amer-First Savs. and Loan, 1987. Mem. Realtors Nat. Mktg. Inst. (cert.), Women's Council Realtors, Sarasota Bd. Realtors, Fla. Assn. Realtors, Nat. Assn. Realtors. Republican. Mennonite. Home: 800 Ben Franklin Dr Unit 102 Sarasota FL 34236 Office: RE/MAX Realty I 130 N Tamiami Trail Sarasota FL 34236

ROSS, VIRGINIA R., business executive; b. Los Angeles; d. Roy Renwick and Olivia Marie (Macbride) Wilson; B.S., U. Redlands; M.A., Calif. State U.; children—Will, Brian, Darrell, Leslie. Writer-editor, fiber artist, 1965-70; product mgr. A Stitch 'n' Time, San Marino, Calif., 1970-75; product mgr. research and devel. Hazel Pearson Handicrafts, Industry, Calif., 1976-81. Editor, REC, Inc., Arcadia, Calif., 1983-86. Mem. Am. Crafts Council, Surface Design Assn. Republican. Presbyterian.

ROSS-DENNSTEDT, CAROL FRANCES, management; b. Marlboro, Tenn., Oct. 12, 1944; d. Overton and Cornelia (Summar) Perry; m. Barry A. Ross, June 5, 1965 (div. Mar. 1977); 1 child, Philip O.; m. Douglas M. Dennstedt, Jan. 1, 1988. BS, Mid. Tenn. State U., 1968. Adminstrv. asst. Irwin Mgmt. Co., Columbus, Ind., 1972-77; confidential asst. U.S. Dept. of Interior, Washington, 1977-81; spl. asst. U.S. Dept. Transp., Washington, 1981-83; asst. v.p. Tricorp., Ltd., Denver, 1983—. Mem. dir.'s com. Denver Ctr. Performing Arts, 1985—; bd. dirs. Salton Sea Environ. Com., Habitat, Calif., 1986—. Mem. Nat. Assn. Female Execs. Episcopalian. Home: 6377 Mountain View Dr Parker CO 80134 Office: Tricorp Ltd 1050 17th St Suite 900 Denver CO 80265

ROSSER, BARBARA ANN ALLEN, broadcasting executive, real estate executive; b. Detroit, Feb. 12, 1952; d. Perry Ellsworth and Dorothy Ann (Craig) Allen; m. James Jeffery Rosser, Aug. 27, 1977; 1 child, Tyler Craig. Student, St. Mary's Coll., Notre Dame, Ind., 1970-73, U. Fla., 1973-74. News anchor, dir. pub. affairs Sta. WBBH-TV, Ft. Myers, Fla., 1974-76; news anchor Sta. KTUL-TV, Tulsa, 1976-78; corr., anchor NBC Network Radio, N.Y.C., 1978-79; anchor, reporter Sta. WRC-TV, Washington, 1979-82, Sta. WFSB-TV, Hartford, Conn., 1982-85; free-lance TV reporter and anchor Boston, 1985-88; free-lance real estate broker Andover, Mass., 1986-88; freelance broadcaster, comml. talent, pub. relations Birmingham, Ala., 1988—. Mem. steering com. Greater Lawrence Found., 1986—. Recipient Columbia Dupont award, 1984. Roman Catholic. Home and Office: 3235 Dell Rd Birmingham AL 35223

ROSSI, CHERYL ANN, manufacturing executive; b. Phillipsburg, N.J., Oct. 13, 1957; d. Frank John and Lillian Theresa (Serafino) R. BA, Moravian Coll., 1980, postgrad., 1984—; postgrad., East Stroudsburg (Pa.) U., 1981. Cert. tchr., N.J.; lic. real estate broker, N.J. Secondary tchr. Belvidere (N.J.) High Sch., 1980-81, Phillipsburg High Sch., 1981-82; adminstrv. aide Manpower Temp. Services, Easton, Pa., 1982-84; adminstr. customer service Iscar Metals, Inc., Hackettstown, N.J., 1984-86; aerospace contract adminstr. Ametek-Aerospace Products, Sellersville, Pa., 1986—. Profl. advisor Bethlehem (Pa.) Tchr.-Edn. Com., 1980—. Mem. NEA, N.J. Edn. Assn., N.J. Assn. Realtors, Phi Alpha Theta, Phi Mu Epsilon. Democrat. Roman Catholic. Clubs: Sister of Swiss (Phillipsburg), Mac Travel (Easton). Home: 465 Thomas St Phillipsburg NJ 08865 Office: Ametek-Aerospace Products 900 Clymer Ave Sellersville PA 18960

ROSSI, MARIE THERESA, marketing company executive; b. N.Y.C., Apr. 19, 1939; d. Dominick and Theresa (Marino) Porco; B.A., Coll. New Rochelle (N.Y.), 1960; m. Louis F. Rossi, June 11, 1960 (dec.); children: Donna, Laura. Cert. assn. exec. Dir. alumnae relations Coll. New Rochelle, 1973-75, dir. ann. giving/estate planning, 1975-77; dir. sales and mktg. Aero-Vend, Inc., Portchester, N.Y., 1977-80; pres. Organized Bus. Techniques, Inc., OBT, Inc., Valhalla, N.Y., 1979—. Bd. dirs. Coll. New Rochelle. Mem. Valhalla C. of C. (pres. 1980-81), Meeting Planners Internat., Women in Sales Assn. (founder 1979), Sales and Mktg. Execs. Westchester (bd. dirs., exec. dir. 1980-83, pres. 1987-88), Am. Soc. Assn. Execs., Sales Exec. Club N.Y. Roman Catholic. Author articles in field. Office: 8 Madison Ave Valhalla NY 10595

ROSSI, RUTH ANNE, lawyer; b. Yonkers, N.Y., June 1, 1944; d. Anthony Joseph and Winnie (Semple) DeMartino; children by previous marriage: Anthony, Christine. AA, Dutchess Community Coll., 1979; AB, Vassar Coll., 1981; JD, Fordham U., 1986. Bar: N.Y. 1987. Asst. dir. Associated Colls. Mid-Hudson Area, Poughkeepsie, N.Y., 1976-78; writer, producer Culinary Inst. Am., Hyde Park, N.Y., 1978-79; asst. to exec. dir. Nat. League Nursing, N.Y.C., 1981-83; asst. to pres. Res. Group Mut. Funds, N.Y.C., 1984-85; law clk. Spengler Carlson Gubar Brodsky and Frischling, N.Y.C., 1985-86, assoc., 1986—; cons. Community Environ. Designs Young, Poughkeepsie, 1979-80. Mem. ABA, Assn. of Bar of City of N.Y., N.Y. State Bar Assn., Westchester Bar Assn., N.Y. NOW, Phi Beta Kappa. Democrat. Home: 5 Bacon Ct Bronxville NY 10708

ROSSINI, CARLOTTA, advertising executive; b. N.Y.C., Apr. 21, 1944; d. Luigi and Hulda (Lefridge) R. Student, Columbia U., 1963-64. Mgmt. trainee InterPub. Group of Cos., N.Y.C., 1966; media planner Wunderman, Ricotta & Kline Inc., N.Y.C., 1967; pres. Rossini/Steven Assocs., N.Y.C., 1967-70; v.p., supr. mgmt. Ogilvy & Mather Advt., N.Y.C., 1970-86; pres. Carlotta Rossini & Assocs., Inc., N.Y.C., 1986—. Recipient Addy award Am. Advt. Fedn., 1968, Effie award Am. Mktg. Assn., 1981, named to Outstanding Young Women Am., U.S. Jaycees, 1977. Mem. NOW, ACLU.

ROSSINI, PAULETTE JANE, private club executive; b. Waterbury, Conn., Feb. 15, 1948; d. Paul David and Bertha (Hudon) R. AS, Post Coll., Waterbury, 1968. Acctg. clk. Peter Paul Co., Naugatuck, Conn., 1968, Waterbury Read Mix Concrete Co., 1969-70; office mgr. Perazzini Constrn. Co., Inc., 1970-79; operating engr. Tilcon/Tomasso Co., New Britain, Conn., 1979-80; comptroller Tumble Brook Country Club, Bloomfield, Conn., 1980—. Trustee Chris Brown Scholarship Fund, New Haven, 1987-88, CATS Boys Gymnastics Assn., Cheshire, Conn., 1987-88. Emil Manweiler scholar, 1966. Mem. Nat. Assn. Women in Constrn. (past pres., rec. sec., treas., com. chmn. Hartford chpt., Woman of Yr. award, 1979, past chmn. nat. com.), Internat. Assn. Hospitality Accts. Roman Catholic. Home: 86 Woodland St Naugatuck CT 06770 Office: Tumble Brook Country Club 376 Simsbury Rd Bloomfield CT 06002

ROSS-JACOBS, RUTH ANN, golf and country club executive, b. Milw., Mar. 10, 1934; d. Arthur Theodore and Mary Marilyn (Digert) Kamman; m. Warren Ross, Aug. 9, 1957 (div. Sept. 1972); 1 child, Michael Edward; m. Albert Jacobs, June 28, 1973 (dec. Apr. 1978). B.S., U. Miami, Coral Gables, Fla., 1958; M.S., Wayne State U., 1961; postgrad. U. Wis., 1967-69. R.N., Fla., Wis., Mich. Staff nurse Lafayette Clinic, Detroit, 1958-59; instr. Milw. Inst. Tech., 1962-67; dir. inservice edn. St. Mary's Hosp., Milw., 1963-69; cons. Hearthside Rehab., Milw., 1968-69; owner Peddler Stores, Milw., 1969-72; pres. Jacobs & Densmore Ltd., Toronto, Ont., Can., 1978-83; v.p. Vaughn Ltd., Toronto, 1978—; pres. Glen Road Leasing Ltd., Toronto, 1978-79, Evnor Apts. Ltd., Toronto, 1978-79, Norman Lathing Ltd., Toronto, 1978-79; v.p. Elgin Mills Investments Ltd., Toronto, 1978-80. Author: Inservice Education, 1967; Nursing Procedures, 1969. Pres. PTO, Boca Raton, Fla., 1973-76; mem. Republican Nat. Com., Washington, 1984—; mem. Inner Circle, Washington, 1984—, Security and Intelligence Found, 1986—. Recipient stipend NIH, Bethesda, Md., 1959. Mem. Pres. Club USO 1986—, Sigma Theta Tau. Republican. Lutheran. Club: Boca Raton, President's. Avocations: real estate investments; travel; charity. Home: 23 Gloucester, Toronto, ON Canada M4Y 1L8 Office: 2000 S Ocean Blvd Penthouse K Boca Raton FL 33432

ROSSMAN, JANET, architectural interior designer; b. Lansing, Mich., Feb. 13, 1954; d. Elmer Chris and Jean Elizabeth (Schell) R.; m. Farzad Moazed. BA with High Honors, Mich. State U., 1976. Designer Tilton & Lewis Assocs., Inc., Chgo., 1977-79, Swanke Hayden Connell & Ptnrs., N.Y.C., 1979-81, Bonsignore Brignati & Mazzotta Architects, N.Y.C., 1982-84; dir. design, assoc. SPGA Group, Inc., N.Y.C., 1984—; instr. Design Edn. Ctr., Lansing, 1975-76. Fellow Mus. Modern Art, N.Y.C., 1979—. Mem. Am. Soc. of Interior Designers (chair. 1973-76, editor Collage 1973-76), Inst. Bus. Designers, Nat. Assn. for Female Execs., Omicron Nu. Republican. Club: Atrium, Landmark. Home: 76 Waters Edge Rye NY 10580 Office: SPGA Group Inc 65 Bleecker St New York NY 10012

ROSSNAGEL, SUSAN GAIL, infosystems specialist; b. Elizabeth, N.J., Oct. 10, 1954; d. John Joseph and Irene (Novak) Ruschak; m. David W. Rossnagel, May 27, 1978 (div. Apr. 1985). BS, Kean Coll., 1978; MBA, Monmouth Coll., 1984. Systems analyst Herman's Sporting Goods, Carteret, N.J., 1972-82; methods and process analyst Bradford Data Services, N.Y.C., 1982-84; project dir. Am. Internat. Group, N.Y.C., 1984—. Mem. Nat. Assn. Female Execs., Delta Mu Delta. Roman Catholic. Home: 618 E 1st Ave Roselle NJ 07203 Office: Am Internat Group 16-99 John St New York NY 10038

ROSSNER, JUDITH, novelist; b. N.Y.C., Mar. 31, 1935; d. Joseph George and Dorothy (Shapiro) Perelman; m. Robert Rossner (div.); children: Jean, Daniel; m. Mort Persky (div.). Student, City Coll. N.Y., 1952-55. Author: novels To the Precipice, 1966, Nine Months in the Life of an Old Maid, 1969, Any Minute I Can Split, 1972, Looking for Mr. Goodbar, 1975, Attachments, 1977, Emmeline, 1980, August, 1983; also short stories. Address: care Julian Bach Agy 747 3rd Ave New York NY 10017 *

ROSSOW, RACHEL LEE WHEELER, mental health nursing consultant; b. Long Beach, Calif., Mar. 20, 1939; d. Robert Edward and Leila Palestine (Jacobsen) Wheeler; m. Carl Joseph Rossow, Dec. 27, 1964; children: Rachel Marie, Robert, Susan, Eddy, Ellen, Dina, Simone, David, Patrick, Charlie, Mary, Maria, Benjamin, Christa Lee, Roy, Jose Luis, Christopher, Michael, Aaron. BS, Salve Regina Coll., 1960, DHL, 1984; MS in Nursing, Cath. U. Am., 1973. Head nurse Medfield State Hosp., Harding, Mass., 1960-61; novice Discalced Carmelite Monastery, Barrington, R.I., 1961-63; nurse/therapist Edgemeade (Md.) Residential Sch., 1963-64, Extension Vols., Hanesville, Ky., 1965-66; pres. Alpha and Omega, Inc., Ellington, Conn., 1974—; cons. for children Conn. Dept. of Children and Youth Services, 1987—. Writer various booklets; contbr. articles to profl. jours. Mem. Conn. Gov's. Com. on Employment of Handicapped, 1983-85; sec. Conn. Commn. on Children and Youth, 1985—; chair Community Health Commn., Ellington, 1974-81; bd. dirs., sec. Community Child Guidance Clinic, Manchester, Conn., 1974-79; mem. bd. of Fin., Ellington, 1984—; mem. Dem. Town Com., Ellington, 1972—, chair, 1988—. Recipient Spl. award Conn. Assn. Retarded Citizens, 1981, Family of Yr. award Greater Vernon (Conn.) Jaycees, 1981, Gt. Am. Family Community award, 1982, others. Roman Catholic. Home: 15 1/2 Lanz Ln Ellington CT 06029

ROSS-RHOADES, VICKI ANN, accountant; b. St. Ansgar, Iowa, Apr. 27, 1957; d. Darwin Ross and Alice Josephine (Wirth) Rhoades; m. Steven James Ross, Sept. 18, 1982; 1 child, Forrest Lee Ross. BS, Mankato State U., 1979. CPA, Minn. Staff acct. Clapper, Kitchenmaster & Co., CPA's, Waseca, Minn., 1980, Goldfein, Silverman & Olson, CPA's, Mpls., 1980-81; prin. Henry S. Krigbaum, Ltd., CPA's, Bemidji, Minn., 1982—. Treas. Paul Bunyan Playhouse, Bemidji, 1982—. Mem. Am. Inst. CPA's, Minn. Soc. CPA's, Jaycee Women (bd. dirs. Bemidji 1982), N.W. Minn. Woodland Owner's Assn. (treas. 1983-85). Lutheran. Home: Box 368 Pennington MN 56663 Office: Henry S Krigbaum Ltd 315 5th St Bemidji MN 56601

ROSS TALBOT, SYLVIA, religious organization administrator. m. Frederick Hilborn Talbot. Student, Inter-Am. U., Puerto Rico, Yale U. Former Minister of Health, Guyan; pres. Ch. Women United in U.S.A., 1987—. Office: Ch Women United in the USA 475 Riverside Dr Room 812 New York NY 10115 *

ROSS-WALDO, DIANE LOUISE, nurse, sales marketing consultant; b. Madison, Wis., Dec. 28, 1955; d. Delwin F. and Darlene L. (Wagner) R.; m. Michael N. Stark, Aug. 14, 1977 (div. Dec. 1980); 1 child, Jennifer; m. Dale K. Waldo, May 24, 1987. Diploma in nursing, U. Wis., 1978. RN, Wis. Staff nurse Madison Gen. Hosp., 1978-79; nurse clinician U. Wis. Hosp., 1979-82; oncology nurse clinician Mt. Sinai Med. Ctr., Milw., 1982-83; dir. ops. Stein Med. Clinic, Milw., 1983-85; nurse cons. Smith-Nephew Med. Clinic, Milw., 1985-86; dir. clin. service, mktg. Home Care Med., Inc., Milw., 1986—. Mem. Southeastern Wis. Oncology Nursing Soc. (pres. 1984—), Am. Cancer Soc. (profl. edn. com.), Oncology Nursing Soc. (speaker's com.). Lutheran. Home: N2W31920 Twin Oaks Dr Delafield WI 53012 Office: Franciscan Home Health Inc 9450 N 107th St Milwaukee WI 53224

ROST, RITA ELLEN, computer science educational consultant; b. Hackensack, N.J., May 24, 1947; d. Frederick Nachbaur and Regina T. (Cassidy) Nuscher; m. Gary Engel, Aug. 23, 1969 (div. 1980); 1 child, Carolyn Michelle; m. Robert E. Rost, July 22, 1980. BA in Math., St. Francis Coll., Loretto, Pa., 1969; MA in Human Devel., Fairleigh Dickinson U., 1982. Cert. tchr., N.J. Tchr. Schor Jr. High Sch., Piscataway, N.J., 1972-75; mgr. AT&T, Piscataway, 1975-76; account exec. Program Products, Inc., Montvale, N.J., 1976-78, TSI Internat., Norwalk, Conn., 1978-80; mgr. Advanced Systems, Inc., Arlington Heights, Ill., 1980-84, AT&T IS, Altamonte Springs, Fla., 1984-86, AT&T C, South Plainfield, N.J., 1986-87; prof. Somerset County Coll., Rariton, N.J., 1986-87; cons. Auxco Computer Enterprises, Inc., Maitland, Fla., 1987—. Author: 3B5 System Admin, 1986, 3B15 Administration, 1986, AFP Architecture, 1987. Mem. Usenix. Democrat. Roman Catholic. Office: Auxton Computer Enterprises Inc 851 Trafalgar Ct Maitland FL 32751

ROSTOW, ELSPETH DAVIES, political science educator; b. N.Y.C.; d. Milton Judson and Harriet Elspeth (Vaughan) Davies; m. Walt Whitman Rostow, June 26, 1947; children: Peter Vaughan, Ann Larner. AB, Barnard Coll., 1938; AM, Radcliffe Coll., 1939; MA, Cambridge (Eng.) U., 1949; LHD (hon.), Lebanon Valley Coll.; LLD (hon.), Austin Coll., 1982, Southwestern U., 1988. Lectr. Am. studies Barnard Coll., N.Y.C., 1939-41, instr. govt., dir. Am. studies, 1941-43, instr. hist., 1945-46; mem. social sci. faculty Sarah Lawrence Coll., Bronxville, N.Y., 1945-47; lectr. history Cambridge U., Eng., 1949-50, 58-59; research assoc. dept. econs. and social sci. MIT, Cambridge, 1950-52, asst. prof., 1952-61, 65; assoc. prof. hist. Am. U., Washington, 1961-69; lectr. history Georgetown U., Washington, 1961-62; assoc. prof. govt. U. Tex., Austin, 1969-76, acting dir. Am. studies, 1970-71, chmn. comparative studies, 1972-74, acting dean div. gen. and comparative studies, 1974-75, dean div. gen. and comparative studies, 1975-77, prof. govt., 1976—, dean Lyndon B. Johnson Sch. Pub. Affairs, 1977-83, Stiles prof. Am. studies, 1985—; mem. Pres.'s Adv. Com. for Trade Negotiations, 1978-82, Pres.'s Commn. for a Nat. Agenda for the Eighties, 1979-81; research assoc. OSS, Washington, 1943-45; Geneva corr. London Economist, 1947-49; mem PhD com. for Lyndon B. Johnson Sch. Pub. Affairs, U. Tex., 1985-86; lectr. Air War Coll., 1963-81, Army War Coll., 1965, 68, 69, 78, 79, 81, Nat. War Coll., 1962, 68, 74, 75, Indsl. Coll. Armed Forces, 1961-65, Naval War Coll., 1971, Fgn. Service Inst., 1974-77, Dept. State, Europe, 1973; bd. dirs. World Affairs Forum, 1960-61, U.S. Inst. of Peace, 1988—. Author: Europe's Economy After the War, 1948, (with others) America Now, 1968, The Coattailess Landslide, 1974; editor (with Barbara Jordan): The Great Society: A Twenty-Year Critique, 1986; columnist Austin Am. Statesman, 1985—; contbr. (with others) articles, revs., poems to scholarly jours., newspapers, mags. Trustee, mem. nominating com. Sarah Lawrence Coll., 1952-59; faculty advisor Hogg Found., 1984—; mem. strategic task force Huston-Tillotson Coll., 1985—, Coll. Bd.'s Presdl. Search Com., 1985-86, bd. visitors and govs. St. John's Coll., 1986—, bd. advisors ctr. internat. edn. Southwest Tex. State U., 1986—, Hogg Found. adv. com. to Austin Groups for Elderly, 1986—; bd. dirs., trustee Overseas Edn. Fund, 1961-74; bd. dirs. Barnard Coll., 1962-66, Lyndon Baines Johnson Found., 1977-83; trustee The Coll. Entrance Exam. Bd., 1978-82; bd. dirs. Salzburg Seminar, 1981—; bd. dirs. Tex. Art Alliance, 1976-79; vis. scholar Phi Beta Kappa, 1984-85. Recipient award Air U., ; Fulbright lectr., USIA participant, 1983-84. Mem. Nat. Acad. Pub. Adminstrn., Am. Enterprise Inst. (adv. com. on competing in changing world economy 1984—), Tex. Philos. Soc. (pres. 1987), Phi Beta Kappa, Phi Nu Epsilon (hon.), Mortar Bd. (hon.), Omicron Delta Kappa. Club: Headliners (Austin). Home: One Wild Wind Point Austin TX 78746 Office: Drawer Y University Station Austin TX 78713

ROSVOLD, VIRGINIA RAE, marketing director; b. New Haven, Oct. 7, 1949; d. Haldor Enger and Mary Winifred (McKinnon) R.; m. Richard Ingram Skinner, Nov. 29, 1986. BA, Allegheny Coll., Meadville, Pa., 1971; MSW, U. Md., 1974. Therapist, coordinator of family services and continuing edn. Carroll County Mental Health Bur., Westminster, Md., 1975-80, coordinator clin. services, 1980-82; dir. community edn. Psychiat. Inst. Montgomery County, Rockville, Md., 1982-86; dir. mktg. Psychiat. Inst. Montgomery County, Rockville, 1986—; clin. supr. Human Affairs Internat., Rockville and Salt Lake City, 1985-87; owner EAP bus.; cons. in field. Recipient First Place Mktg. Project award Nat. Assn. Pvt. Psychiat. Hosps., 1987, Outstanding Mktg. Dir. award Psychiat. Inst. Am., 1988. Mem. Am. Mktg. Assn., Nat. Assn. Social Workers, Assn. Labor-Mgmt. Adminstrs. and Cons. on Alcoholism, Assn. Employee Assistance Program Practitioner. Home: 4004 Ashland Brooke Way Olney MD 20832 Office: Psychiat Inst of Montgomery County 14901 Broschart Rd Rockville MD 20850

ROTBERG, IRIS COMENS, public policy analyst; b. Phila., Dec. 16, 1932; d. Samuel Nathaniel and Golda (Shuman) Comens; m. Eugene H. Rotberg, Aug. 29, 1954; children: Diana Golda, Pamela Lynn. BA, U. Pa., 1954, MA, 1955; PhD, Johns Hopkins U., Balt., 1958. Research psychologist Pres.'s Commn. on Income Maintenance Programs, Washington, 1968-69, Office Planning, Research and Evaluation, Office Econ. Opportunity, Washington, 1970-73; dep. dir. compensatory edn. study Nat. Inst. Edn., Washington, 1974-77, dir. Office Planning and Program Devel., 1978-82; program dir. NSF, Washington, 1985-87; tech. policy fellow Com. on Sci., Space and Tech., U.S. Ho. of Reps., Washington, 1987—. NSF fellow, 1956-58. Home: 7211 Brickyard Rd Potomac MD 20854

ROTERT, DENISE ANNE, occupational therapist, army officer; b. Sioux Falls, S.D., Nov. 18, 1949; d. Leonard Joseph and Irene Winnifred (Jennings) R.; B.S., U. Puget Sound, 1971; M.A., U. No. Colo., 1975. Commd. 2d lt. Med. Specialist Corps, U.S. Army, 1970, advanced through grades to maj., 1983; staff occupational therapist Tripler Army Med. Center, Honolulu, 1973-76, officer in charge occupational therapy sect. Ireland Army Hosp., Fort Knox, Ky., 1976-77; clin. supr. occupational therapy sect. Letterman Army Med. Center, Presidio of San Francisco, 1977-79; chief instr. occupational therapy asst. course Acad. Health Scis., Ft. Sam Houston, Tex., 1979-84; chief occupational therapy Tri-Service Alcohol Recovery Dept., Naval Hosp., Bethesda, Md., 1984—. Mem. Am., Occupational Therapy Assn., D.C. Occupational Therapy Assn., World Fedn. Occupational Therapists. Roman Catholic. Office: Occupational Therapy Tri-SARD NHBETH Bethesda MD 20814

ROTH, ANN, costume designer. Student, Carnegie-Mellon U. Designer costumes for theatre and film prodns., 1958—; Broadway shows include Maybe Tuesday, Make a Million, Gay Divorcee, A Far Country, Purlie Victorious, This Side of Paradise, A Case of Libel, The Last Analysis, The Odd Couple, The Impossible Years, Play It Again Sam, They're Playing Our Song, Tiny Alice, What the Butler Saw, Fun City, 6 Rms Riv Vu, The Best Little Whorehouse in Texas, Lunch Hour, Present Laughter, The Misanthrope, Open Admissions, Arms and the Man, Hurlyburly, Design for Living, Biloxi Blues, numerous others; films The World of Henry Orient, A Fine Madness, Up the Down Staircase, Pretty Poison, Sweet November, Midnight Cowboy, Jenny, The Owl and the Pussycat, The People Next Door, Klute, Day of the Locust, California Suite, The Island, Honky Tonk Freeway, Only When I Laugh, Rollover, The World According to Garp, The Man Who Loved Women, Silkwood, The Survivors, Places in the Heart, also others; also designed costumes for various regional repertory theatres including costumes Am. Conservatory Theatre, Am. Ballet Theatre, Am. Shakespeare Festival, Kennedy Center, Mpls. Opera, San Francisco Opera. Office: care United Scenic Artists 575 5th Ave New York NY 10176

ROTH, ANNEMARY T., regulatory law official; b. Phila.; d. Theodore H. and Annemary Roth. BS, Franklin U., 1974; BA, Calif. U., 1974, MS, 1988. With U.S. Treasury-ATF, 1967—; sr. inspector U.S. Treasury-ATF, Lansdale, Pa., 1982—. Author: Inexpensive Craft Projects for Groups, 1972; contbr. articles to profl. jours.; editor newsletter Interchange, 1968-71, Sacred Heart Devotion News, 1966-76. Dir. religious edn. St. James Ch., Elkins Park, 1961—; coordinator N. Penn Regional Catholic High Sch. Mem. Soc. Fed. Labor Relations Profl., Fed. Employed Women Assn., Christian Profl. Women, Nat. Treas. Employees Union, Assn. Phila. Dirs. Religious Edn., Lansdale Bus. Profl. Women, Nat. Fedn. Christian Life Communities. Republican. Roman Catholic. Clubs: Abington Country, Nat. Young Adult, YOC Soc. Home: Box 202 Lansdale PA 19446 Office: US Treasury Bur ATF 100 W Main St Lansdale PA 19446

ROTH, EDITH ELIZABETH, account executive, securities trader, political campaign consultant; b. Budapest, Hungary, June 2, 1935; came to U.S., 1949; d. Edmond and Mary (Bertalan) Rockenstein; m. Mickey Moshe Roth, Apr. 9, 1964; children: Leonora Rose, Adrienne Haddassah. BA, Cleve. State U., 1981; MA, Kent State U., 1982. Coordinator re-entry women's program Cleve. State U., 1981; pvt. practice campaign cons., Ohio, 1982—; div. mgr. First Investors Corp., 1985—; co-owner Imagination in Plastic, Cleve., 1982—. Trustee Heights Community Congress, Cleveland Heights, Ohio, 1977-80; chairperson Severance Devel. Commn., Cleveland Heights, 1978; pres. Millikin Neighbors, Inc., Cleveland Heights, 1978-82; mem. fin. com. City Council, Cleveland Heights, 1979-81. Mem. Pi Sigma Alpha. Clubs: Cleveland Heights Democratic. Home: 3691 Blanche Rd Cleveland Heights OH 44118 Office: Dean Witter Reynolds Inc 24400 Chagrin Blvd Beachwood OH 44122

ROTH, JANE RICHARDS, judge; b. Phila., June 16, 1935; d. Robert Henry Jr. and Harriett (Kellond) Richards; m. William V. Roth Jr., Oct. 9, 1965; children: William V. III, Katharine K. BA, Smith Coll., 1956; LLB, Harvard U., 1965. Bar: Del. 1965, U.S. Dist. Ct. Del. 1966, U.S. Ct. Appeals (3d cir.) 1974. Adminstrv. asst. various fgn. service posts U.S. State Dept., 1956-62; assoc. Richards, Layton & Finger, Wilmington, Del., 1965-73, ptnr., 1973-85; judge U.S. Dist. Ct. Del., Wilmington, 1985—. Trustee Hist. Soc. Del., Wilmington; mem. Chesapeake Bay Girl Scouts Council, Wilmington; hon. chmn. Del. chpt. Arthritis Found., Wilmington; bd. dirs. U. Del Library Assocs., Newark, Del. Recipient Nat. Vol. Service citiation Athritis Found., 1982. Mem. Fed. Judges Assn., Del. State Bar Assn. Republican. Episcopalian. Office: US Courthouse Lockbox 12 844 King St Wilmington DE 19801

ROTH, LINDA LOU, secondary educator; b. W.Palm Beach, Fla., Jan. 4, 1947; d. Emory Perry and Kathleen Annette (Hampton) Wall; m. Larry Ernest Roth, Sept. 11, 1965; children: Lawrence Scott, Ronald Perry. BS in Maths. and Physics, Cen. Mich. U., 1975, MA in Maths., 1980, cert. tchr. computer sci., 1986. Cert. tchr., Mich. Various positions Mich. and Miss., 1963-72; tchr. Midland (Mich.) Pub. Schs., 1976—; cons. Curriculum Devel., Computer Literacy Workshop Leader, Midland, 1984—; spkr. in field. Host family Mich. Little League, Midland, 1984; statistician Explorers Open Class Men's Softball Team, Midland, 1986—; chairperson Curriculum Council Gifted/Talented Com., Midland, 1986; mem. Writing Network, Midland, 1987—. Candidate Tchr. in Space, NASA, 1985. Mem. Nat. Edn. Assn., Midland City Edn. Assn., Mich. Assn. of Computer Users in Learning, Nat. Assn. Investment Clubs (local sec.), Delta Kappa, Kappa Mu Epsilon, Midland Apple Users. Republican. Club: Jobs Daughters (guardian 1967-68). Office: Midland High Schs 1301 Eastlawn Midland MI 48640

ROTH, REGINA SARAH, psychologist; b. Lake Forest, Ill., Mar. 6, 1950; d. Richard James and Shirley (White) R.; A.B. with honors, Conn. Coll., 1972; M.A., NYU, 1974, Ph.D. (NIMH trainee), 1976; postdoctoral student Northwestern U. Med. Hosp. Inst. Psychiatry, 1978-79. Staff cons. clin. div. Worthington Hurst & Assocs., Chgo., 1977-78; psychology postdoctoral trainee Hines (Ill.) VA Hosp., 1979; psychology postdoctoral trainee West Side VA Hosp., Chgo., 1979-80; pvt. practice clin. psychology, 1980—. Mem. Am. Psychol. Assn., Ill. Psychol. Assn., Nat. Register Mental Health Service Providers, Chgo. Assn. Psychoanalytic Psychology, Am. Group Psychotherapy Assn. Home: 3001 S King Dr Apt 508 Chicago IL 60616 Office: 1701 E Lake Ave Suite 445 Glenview IL 60025

ROTHBERG, JOAN O., advertising agency executive; b. Newark, Aug. 29, 1941; d. Abraham and Nettie (Rasnick) Oxman; m. Robert R. Rothberg, Sept. 1, 1963; 1 dau., Abra C. A.B., Vassar Coll., 1961; M.B.A., Harvard U., 1963. Asst. advt. media mgr. Scott Paper Co., 1963-65; v.p. SSC&B Advt. Inc., N.Y.C., 1965-72; sr. v.p., dir. Ted Bates & Co. Inc., N.Y.C., 1973-81; exec. v.p. Ted Bates/N.Y. Inc. (now Backer, Spielvogel, Bates, Inc.), 1981—; dir. Progressive Corp. Trustee Westminster Civic League. Recipient Tribute to Women in Internat. Industry award Nat. YWCA, 1981; Ford Found. fellow; Fulbright grantee Mex. *

ROTHBERG, JUNE SIMMONDS, university administrator, nursing educator; b. Phila., Sept. 4, 1923; d. David and Rose (Protzel) Simmonds; m. Jacob Rothberg, Sept. 7, 1952; children: Robert, Alan. Diploma in nursing, Lenox Hill Hosp., 1944; B.S., N.Y. U., 1950, M.A., 1959, Ph.D. (NIH fellow), 1965. USPHS traineeship N.Y. U., 1957-59; sr. public health nurse Bklyn. Vis. Nurse Assn., 1951-53; prin. investigator in nursing, homestead study project Goldwater Hosp. and N.Y. U., 1959-61; instr. N.Y. U., 1964-65, asst. prof., 1965-68, assoc. prof., 1968-69, project dir. grad. program rehab. nursing, 1964-69, prof., 1969-87, prof. emeritus, 1987—; dean Adelphi U., Garden City, N.Y., 1969-85; v.p. acad. adminstrn. Adelphi U., 1985-86; dir., chmn. compensation com. Quality Care, Inc.; cons. to various ednl. and service instns.; cons. region 2 Bur. Health Resources Devel., HHS.; speaker on radio and TV; dir. Ipco Corp. Contbr. articles to profl. jours. Mem. pres's council N.Y. U. Sch. Edn., 1973-75; treas. Nurses for Polit. Action, 1971-73; trustee Nurses Coalition for Action in Politics, 1974-76; bd. visitors Duke Med. Center, 1970-74; mem. governing bd. Nassau-Suffolk Health Systems Agy., 1976-79; leader People-to-People Internat. med. rehab. del. to, People's Republic of China, 1981; mem. com. for the study pain disability and chronic illness behavior Inst. Medicine, 1985-86, com. on ethics in rehabilitation Hastings Ctr., 1985-87; trustee Paget's Disease Found., 1987—. Recipient Disting. Alumna award NYU, 1974, recognition award Am. Assn. Colls. Nursing, 1976, Achievers award Ctr. for Bus. and Profl. Women, 1980. Fellow Am. Acad. Nursing (governing council 1980-82); mem. Nat. League Nursing (exec. com. council of baccalaureate and higher degree programs 1969-73), Am. Nurses Assn. (joint liaison com. 1970-72), Commn. Accreditation of Rehab. Facilities, Am. Congress Rehab. Medicine (pres. 1977-78, chmn. continuing edn. com. 1979-86), Am. Assn. Colls. Nursing (pres. 1974-76), L.I. Women's Network (pres. 1980-81), Kappa Delta Pi, Sigma Theta Tau, Pi Lambda Theta. Home: 305 Elm St West Hempstead NY 11552 Office: Adelphi Univ Sch Nursing Garden City NJ 11530

ROTHCHILD, NINA, state official; b. N.Y.C., Mar. 5, 1930; d. Robert Lee and Mary Todd (McCall) Peek; m. Kennon Rothchild, Sept. 22, 1951; children—Kennon, Mary Todd, Sally. A.B. magna cum laude, Smith Coll., 1951. Mem. community faculty Met. State U., St. Paul, 1973-76; exec. dir. Council Econ. Status of Women, St. Paul, 1976-82; commr. employee relations State of Minn., St. Paul, 1983—. Author: Sexism in Schools: A Handbook for Action, 1973. Mem. Mahtomedi Bd. Edn. (Minn.), 1970-76; bd. dirs. St. Paul YWCA, 1977-82; v.p., bd. dirs. Planned Parenthood of Minn., St. Paul, 1972-78; del. Internat. Women's Yr. Conv., Houston, 1977; founder, bd. dirs. Minn. Women's Consortium, St. Paul, 1981—. Recipient Outstanding Achievement award Adminstrv. Women in Edn., St. Paul, 1978; Outstanding Leadership in Govt. award St. Paul YWCA, 1981; Disting. Service to State Govt. award Nat. Govs. Assn., 1984. Mem. NOW, Minn. Women's Polit. Caucus, Minn. Women's Econ. Roundtable, Minn. Working Women 9 to 5, LWV, Phi Beta Kappa, Sigma Xi. Office: Employee Relations 520 Lafayette Saint Paul MN 55155

ROTHENBERG, SAUNDRA HAMM, day care center administrator, business executive; b. N.Y.C., May 30, 1943; d. Harold and Etta (Isaacs) Hamm; m. Max P. Rothenberg, Feb. 21, 1965; children: Dana, Jordan. BA, Bklyn. Coll., 1965; BRE, Tchrs. Inst. for Women, N.Y.C., 1964. Tchr., Ramaz Sch., N.Y.C., 1963-65, N.Y.C. Pub. Schs., 1965-67, Hebrew Acad., Miami Beach, Fla., 1967-68, Dade County Pub. Schs., North Miami Beach, Fla., 1968-70; prin., adminstr. Red and White Sch. House, Hollywood, Fla., 1972-87, Golden Glades Day Sch., Opa Locka, Fla., 1980—; regional field cons. For the State of Fla. for Am. Mizrachi Women, 1987—; lectr. in field. Bd. dirs. Hillel Day Sch., North Miami Beach, 1970-84, Hebrew Acad., Miami Beach, 1984-86, Cen. Agy. Jewish Edn., Dade County, 1985—, Touro Coll., 1987—; chmn. scholarship dinners Hillel Day Sch. and Hebrew Acad., chmn. jour. dinner Shaaray Tefilah; mem. adv. bd. Broward County 4-H, Fla., 1975-77, Broward Assn. Children Under Six, 1980—, Broward County Kindergarten and Nursery Assn., 1980—; pres. southeast Fla. council Amit Women, 1983-87, pres. Galil chpt. Am. Mizrachi Women, North Miami Beach, 1969-72, pres. Vered chpt., North Miami Beach, 1972-83, pres. SE Fla. council, 1983—; del. So. Fla. Community Relations Bd., 1984-85, 1987—; alt. del. Internat. Conf. on Women, Nairobi, Kenya, 1985. Recipient numerous awards including Am. Mizrachi Women; Builders award Hillel Community Day Sch., 1981; Community Service award Shaaray Tefliah, 1983; Key to City Miami Beach Service award, 1985, Mayor's Service award, 1985. Mem. Dade Fedn., South Broward Fedn., Women's Study Group North Miami Beach (chmn. 1980-84). Jewish. Avocations: travel, tennis; bowling; swimming; gourmet cooking. Home: 1320 NE 172d St North Miami Beach FL 33162

ROTHENBERG, SUSAN, artist; b. Buffalo, Jan. 20, 1945; d. Leonard M. and Adele (Cohen) R.; m. George Trakas, May 1, 1971-1976, 1 dau., Maggie. B.F.A., Cornell U., 1966. One-woman shows of paintings include Willard Gallery, N.Y.C., 1976, 77, 79, 81, 83, Univ. Art Mus., Berkeley, Calif., 1978, Walker Art Center, Mpls., 1978, Greenberg Gallery, St. Louis, 1978, Mayor Gallery, London, 1980, Akron (Ohio) Art Mus., 1981-82, Stedelijk Mus., Amsterdam, 1982, Los Angeles County Mus., 1983, San Francisco Mus. Art, 1983, Carnegie Inst. Mus. Art, Pitts., 1984; numerous group shows, 1974—, including Mus. of Modern Art, N.Y.C., 1980, Padiglione d'Arte Contemporanea di Milano, Italy, 1980, Clarke-Benton Gallery, Santa-Fe, 1980, Indpls. Mus. Art, 1980, Yarlow/Salzman Gallery, Toronto, 1980, Tex. Gallery, Houston, 1981, Young Hoffman Gallery, Chgo., 1981, Inst. Contemporary Art, Richmond, Va., 1981, Kunsthalle, Basel (Switzerland), 1981, Willard Gallery, N.Y., 1983, Los Angeles County Mus. Art, 1983, Inst. Contemporary Art, Boston, 1983, Barbara Krakow Gallery, Boston, 1984, Des Moines Art Ctr., 1985, A.P. Giannini Gallery, San Francisco; group exhbns. include A.M. Sachs Gallery, N.Y.C., 1974, Willard Gallery, 1975, 76, Inst. for Art and Urban Resources, Long Island City, N.Y., 1977, Mus. Modern Art, N.Y., 1977, Cleve. Mus. Art, 1978, Albright-Knox Art Gallery, N.Y., 1978, Whitney Mus. Am. Art, 1979, Renaissance Soc. of U. Chgo., 1979, Clarke-Benton Gallery, Santa Fe, 1980, Audrey Stohl Gallery, 1980, Tex. Gallery, Houston, 1981, Univ. Art Mus., Santa Barbara, 1981,

Akron Art Mus., 1981, Art Inst. Chgo., 1982, Sidney Janis Gallery, 1982, Paula Cooper Gallery, N.Y., 1983, Fogg Art Mus., Harvard U., 1984, CDS Gallery, 1984, N.Y. Pub. Library, 1985, Seattle Art Mus., 1985, Daniel Weinberg Gallery, 1985,Barbara Mathes Gallery, 1986, Butlre Inst. Am. Art, Youngstown, Ohio, 1986, 1st Bank of Mpls., 1986-87, Mus. Fine Arts, Boston, 1986-87; represented in permanent collections, Mus. Modern Art, N.Y.C., Mus. Fine Arts, Houston, Whitney Mus. Am. Art, N.Y.C., Albright-Knox Art Gallery, Buffalo, Walker Art Center, Des Moines, Iowa., Akron Art Mus., Stedelijk Mus., Carnegie Inst. Mus. Art, Dallas Mus. Fine Art. Guggenheim fellow, 1980. Office: care Gagosian Gallery 521 W 23rd St New York NY 10011

ROTHERMEL, JANIS MARGUERITTE, sales professional; b. Camden, N.J., June 23, 1951; d. George Sanford and Margueritte Lenore (Kephart) R. Student, Rutgers U., Camden, 1971; BTh cum laude, St. Joseph's U., Phila., 1988. Observer comml. service N.J. Bell, Pleasantville, 1972-74, rep. customer sales, 1974—. Contbr. articles to profl. jours. Mem. Atlantic City Med. Ctr. Aux., Atlantic City Women's C. of C., Children's Seashore House Aux., Alpha Sigma Lambda. Roman Catholic. Club: Le Chambertin Wine (Somers Point, N.J.). Lodge: Zonta (pres. local chpt. 1988—). Home: 37 N 30th Ave Longport NJ 08403 Office: NJ Bell Rd 3 Black Horse Pike and Fire Rd Pleasantville NJ 08232

ROTHMAN, DEANNA, electroplating company executive; b. Bklyn., Sept. 20, 1938; d. Frank Philip and Elsie (Goldstein) Dukofsky; m. Edward Rothman, Dec. 8, 1956 (div. July 1984); children: Jeffrey Scott, Michele Dawn, Robert Jay; m. Ronald Friedman, Aug. 17, 1986. B.A., Bklyn. Coll., 1968. Exec. Bronzemaster Co., Bklyn., 1969-80, Perma Plating Co. Inc., Bklyn., 1980-84; pres. Duratron Finishing Corp., Bklyn., 1984—. Sec. Tenants Assn., S.I., 1973-77; v.p. Orgn. Rehab. and Tng., Woodmere, N.Y., 1978-80. Mem. Masters Electroplating Assn., Am. Metal Finishers, Nat. Assn. Female Execs., NOW. Republican. Jewish. Avocations: painting; collecing art deco; dance; theatre. Home: 755 Flanders Dr North Woodmere NY 11581 Office: Duratron Finishing Corp PO Box 789 East NY Sta Brooklyn NY 11207

ROTHMAN, ESTHER POMERANZ, social agency executive, psychologist; b. N.Y.C., Nov. 25, 1919; d. Max and Anne (Reiner) Pomeranz; m. Arthur M. Rothman, Apr. 13, 1946; 1 dau., Amy. B.A., Hunter Coll., 1942; M.A., Columbia U., 1944; M.A., CCNY, 1946; Ph.D., NYU, 1958. Cert. psychologist, N.Y. Tchr., N.Y.C. Bd. Edn., 1944-57, prin., 1957-80; exec. dir. Glie Youth Program, N.Y.C., 1980-85; exec. dir. Correctional Edn. Consortium, 1985—; research psychologist Tchrs. Hot Line, N.Y.C., 1972-74. Author: Angel Inside Went Sour, 1972; Troubled Teachers, 1974; co-author: Disturbed Child, 1967. Mem. Citizens Com. for Children, N.Y.C., 1972—. Recipient Valley Forge Freedom award, 1976. Fellow Am. Assn. Orthopsychiatry (sec. 1976-79); mem. Am. Psychol. Assn. Home: 200 E 16 St New York NY 10003 Office: Correctional Edn Consortium 29-10 Thomson Ave Long Island NY 11101

ROTHMAN, JUDITH LEE, editor-in-chief; b. N.Y.C., Nov. 17, 1940; d. William and Beatrice (Schwartz) R. BA, CUNY, Queens, 1962; student, CBS Sch. Mgmt., N.Y.C. and Boston, 1979-80, Hennig/Jardim Mgmt. Sch. for Women, N.Y.C., 1979-81. Legal sec. Kaufman, Taylor & Kimmel, N.Y.C., 1962-64; editor Fairchild Publs., N.Y.C., 1964-71; prodn. asst. Paramount Pictures, N.Y.C., 1971; editor coll. div., Prentice-Hall, Inc., Englewood Cliffs, N.J., 1973-78; pub. humanities div., Holt Rhinehart & Winston Publs., N.Y.C., 1978-80; editorial dir. CBS Edn. Pub., N.Y.C., 1980-81; sr. editor Random House, Inc., N.Y.C., 1981-84; editor-in-chief Harper & Row, Inc., N.Y.C., 1984—; cons. Assn. Am. Publishers, N.Y.C., 1981-82. Mem. Nat. Women's Book Assn. (Women Who Make A Difference award 1987). Democrat. Jewish. Office: Harper & Row Inc 10 E 53d St New York NY 10022

ROTHROCK, JANE CLAIRE, nursing educator; b. Abington, Pa., Mar. 20, 1948; d. John Richard and Dorothea Ethel (Leser) Lynch; m. Joseph Rothrock, III, Apr. 17, 1977. BSN, U. Pa., 1974, MSN, 1978; DNSc, Widener U., 1987. Staff nurse Hosp. U. Pa., Phila., 1969-71, staff developer, 1971-74; dir. operating room Grad. Hosp., Phila., 1974-76; clin. instr. U. Pa., Phila., 1976-77; dir. operating room, Bryn Mawr Hosp., Pa., 1978-79; assoc. prof. Delaware County Community Coll., Media, Pa., 1979-88, prof., 1987—; pres. Quest RN Inc., Wallingford, Pa., 1985—; mem. adv. bd. Edn. div. Am. Sterilizer Co., Erie, Pa., 1984-87. Bd. dirs. Community Mental Health Ctr., Chester, Pa., 1980—. Author: Chesapeake Odysseys, 1984; editor: The RN First Assistant, 1986; contbr. articles to profl. jours. Assn. Operating Rm. Nurses scholar, 1974, 85-86, 86-87. Mem. Am. Nurses Assn., Pa. Council Operating Rm. Nurses (pres. 1984-86), Assn. Operating Rm. Nurses (bd. dirs. 1987—, edit. bd. 1983-86, research com. 1986-87), Soc. Research in Nursing Edn. Republican. Methodist. Clubs: Pine Ridge Garden, Jr. Womens. Avocations: sailing, skiing, needlework. Office: Delaware County Community Coll Rt 252 Media PA 19063

ROTHSCHILD, AMALIE RANDOLPH, filmmaker, producer, director; b. Balt., June 3, 1945; d. Randolph Schamberg and Amalie Getta (Rosenfeld) R.; B.F.A., R.I. Sch. Design, 1967; M.F.A. in Motion Picture Production, N.Y. U., 1969. Spl. effects staff in film and photography Joshua Light Show, Fillmore E. Theatre, NYC, 1969-71; still photographer TWA Airlines Pub. Relations Dept., Village Voice newspaper Rolling Stone magazine, Newsweek magazine, After Dark, N.Y. Daily News, numerous others, 1968-72; co-founder, partner New Day Films, distbn. coop., 1971—; owner, operator Anomaly Films Co., NYC, 1971—; mem., co-founder Assn. of Independent Video and Filmmakers, Inc., NYC, 1974, bd. dirs., 1974-78; instr. in film and TV, N.Y. U. Inst. of Film and TV, 1976-78; cons. in field to various organizations including Youthgrant Program of Nat. Endowment for Humanities, Washington, 1973-76; motion pictures include: Woo Who? May Wilson, 1969; It Happens to Us, 1972; Nana, Mom and Me, 1974; Radioimmunoassay of Renin, Radioimmunoassay of Aldosterone, 1973; Conversations with Willard Van Dyke, 1981; Richard Haas: Work in Progress, 1984; editor: Doing It Yourself, Handbook on Independent Film Distribution, 1977. Mem. Community Planning Bd. 1, Borough of Manhattan, N.Y.C., 1974-86. Recipient spl. achievement award Mademoiselle mag., 1972; independent filmmaker grant, Am. Film Inst., 1973; film grantee N.Y. State Council on the Arts, 1977, 85, 87, Nat. Endowment Arts, 1978, 85, 87, Md. Arts Council, 1977, Ohio Arts and Humanities Councils, 1985. Mem. Internat. Film Seminars (trustee 1975-80), Independent Cinema Artists and Producers (bd. dirs. 1976-84), Univ. Film and Video Assn., N.Y. Women in Film. Democrat. Address: 135 Hudson St New York NY 10013 also: Via delle Mantellate 19, Rome 00165, Italy

ROTHSCHILD, DIANE, advertising agency executive; b. Apr. 11, 1943; d. Morton Royce and Marjorie Jay (Simon) R.; 1 child, Alexandra Rothschild Spencer. B.A., Aldephi U., 1965. Copywriter Doyle Dane Bernbach Advt., Inc., N.Y.C., 1967-73, v.p., 1973-79, sr. v.p., assoc. creative dir., 1979-85, exec. v.p., creative dir., 1985-86; pres. Grace and Rothschild, N.Y.C., 1986—. Recipient maj. advt. awards. Mem. YWCA Acad. Women Achievers. Office: Grace and Rothschild 767 3d Ave New York NY 10017

ROTHSTEIN, BARBARA JACOBS, federal judge; b. Bklyn., Feb. 3, 1939; d. Solomon and Pauline Jacobs; m. Ted L. Rothstein, Dec. 28, 1968; 1 child, Daniel. B.A., Cornell U., 1960; LL.B., Harvard U., 1966. Bar: Mass. bar 1966, Wash. bar 1969. Individual practice law Boston, 1966-68; asst. atty. gen. State of Wash., 1968-77; judge Superior Ct., Seattle, 1977-80; judge Fed. Dist. Ct. Western Wash., Seattle, 1980-87, chief judge, 1987—; faculty Law Sch. U. Wash., 1975-77, Hastings Inst. Trial Advocacy, 1977, N.W. Inst. Trial Advocacy, 1979—. Recipient Matrix Table Woman of Year award, 1980. Mem. Am. Judicature Soc., ABA (judicial sect.), Phi Beta Kappa, Phi Kappa Phi. Office: US Dist Ct 411 US Courthouse 1010 5th Ave Seattle WA 98104

ROTHSTEIN, MARILYN SIMON, advertising and writing agency executive; b. Bklyn., May 11, 1953; d. Leo and Freida (Hammer) Simon; m. Alan Miles Rothstein, Jan. 24, 1976; children—Sharyn Pamela, Marisa Shana. B.A., NYU, 1974. Staff writer Seventeen Mag., N.Y.C., 1974-77; copy supr. Gabriel Industries, N.Y.C., 1977-78; copywriter Mintz & Hoke, Avon, Conn., 1978-81; owner Rothstein Advt. Writers, Avon., 1981-84; pres. Simon Advt. & Writing, Inc., Avon, 1984—. Recipient awards for advt. and copywriting Advt. Club Greater Hartford, Advt. Club Western Mass., Conn. Art Dirs. Club; Retail Advt. Conf. TV award of Merit, Nat. Com. on Films for Safety. Mem. Women in Communications (program chmn. Central Conn. chpt. 1981-83, v.p. 1983-84, pres. 1984-85, co-chmn. northeast regional conf. 1988), NOW. Club, Advt. Club of Greater Hartford, Probus of Greater Hartford. Home: 592 Lovely St Avon CT 06001 Office: Simon Advt & Writing Inc 152 Simsbury Rd PO Box 756 Avon CT 06001

ROTHWEILER, THERESA MARIE, nursing care services executive; b. Neola, Iowa, Feb. 18, 1929; d. Robert Francis and Margaret (Burns) Cavanaugh; m. George Anton Rothweiler, Jr., Sept. 12, 1953; children—Beatrice, Gregory, Steven, Paul, Joan. B.S.N., Lorretto Heights Coll., 1951; M.S., U. Minn., 1972; Ph.D., U. Minn., 1980. Nurse, St. Anthony Hosp., Denver, 1952-53; asst. head nurse Miller Hosp., St. Paul, 1953-54; nurse educator Anoka Ramsey Community Coll., Coon Rapids, Minn., 1972-74; nurse educator Gustavus Adolphus Coll. St. Peter, Minn., 1975-80; asst. prof. nursing U. Minn., Mpls., 1980-87; pres. Health ProNursing Service, Inc., 1987—; founder Profl. Stress Mgmt. Inc., 1985; lectr. in field. Mem. Washington County Community Health, 1977-82. Mem. Minn. Nurses Assn. (edn. commn. 1979-81, 83-86, dist. bd. dirs. 1977-83), C. of C. (govt. affairs chair, Cottage Grove 1988—), Sigma Xi, Sigma Theta Tau. Lodge: Rotary (community service chair 1988—).

ROTOLO, GWEN ELIZABETH PARDUN, interior designer; b. Oak Park, Ill., Sept. 27, 1940; d. Eugene Stewart Pardun and Elizabeth Ruth (Hafner) Pardun/Quitsch; divorced; children: Donna Marie, Michael Eugene, Elise Suzanne. AS in Interior Design, Harper Coll., 1974; student, Art Inst. of Chgo., 1958-60. Interior designer Color Councellors, Evanston, Ill., 1971-72, J.C. Penney, Schaumburg, Ill., 1972-73, Hillside Design, Saugus, Mass., 1974-77, Drexel/Heritage Showcase, Burlington, Mass., 1978-80, Homer's Furniture, Skokie and Palatine, Ill., 1980-85; prin. interior design Interiors by Gwen, Schaumburg, 1985—. Mem. Internat. Soc. Interior Designers, Am. Soc. Interior Designers, Ill. Design Soc., Harper Interior Design Assn. Home and Office: 130 Century Ct Schaumburg IL 60193

ROUDYBUSH, ALEXANDRA, novelist; b. Hyres, Cote d'Azur, France, Mar. 14, 1911; d. Constantine and Ethel (Wheeler) Brown; student St. Paul's Sch. for Girls, London; m. Franklin Roudybush, 1942. Journalist, London Eve. Standard, 1931, Time mag., 1933, French News Agy., 1935, CBS, 1936, MBS, 1940; White House corr. MBC Radio, 1940-48; author: Before the Ball Was Over, 1965; Death of a Moral Person, 1967, Capital Crime, 1969; House of the Cat, 1970; A Sybaritic Death, 1972; Suddenly in Paris, 1975; The Female of the Species, 1977; Blood Ties, 1981. Mem. Crime Writers Am. and Brit. Democrat. Episcopalian. Clubs: Am. Woman's (Paris); Miramar Golf (Porto, Portugal).

ROUGHSEDGE, CAROLYN DUNN, advertising agency executive; b. Rocky Ford, Colo., July 9, 1944; d. Joseph Michael and Frances (Barnes) Dunn.; m. Robert Roughsedge, Nov. 29, 1968 (div. Nov. 1978); 1 son, Michael Caine. BA, Manhattanville Coll., 1966. Casting sec. Grey Advt., N.Y.C., 1966-67; TV producer Savage Friedman, N.Y.C., 1967-68; v.p., owner Steppingstone Prodns., N.Y.C., 1968-77; TV producer CBS Records, N.Y.C., 1977-78; v.p., dir. broadcast prodn. Needham, Harper & Steers, Los Angeles, 1978-83; v.p., dir. broadcast prodn. Needham, Harper & Steers, N.Y.C., from 1983, to sr. v.p.; sr. v.p., dir. broadcast prodn. Saatchi & Saatchi DFS Compton, N.Y.C., now exec. v.p., dir. broadcast prodn. Office: Saatchi & Saatchi DFS Compton 375 Hudson St New York NY 10174 *

ROUKEMA, MARGARET SCAFATI, congresswoman; b. Newark, Sept. 19, 1929; d. Claude Thomas and Margaret (D'Alessio) Scafati; m. Richard W. Roukema, Aug. 23, 1951; children—Margaret, Todd (dec.), Gregory. B.A. with honors in History and Polit. Sci, Montclair State Coll., 1951, postgrad. in history and guidance, 1951-53; postgrad. program in city and regional planning, Rutgers U., 1975. Tchr. history, govt., public schs. Livingston and Ridgewood, N.J., 1951-55; mem. 97th-100th Congresses from 5th N.J. Dist., 1981—; vice pres. Ridgewood Bd. Edn., 1970-73; bd. dirs., co-founder Ridgewood Sr. Citizens Housing Corp. Trustee Spring House, Paramus, N.J.; trustee Leukemia Soc. No. N.J., Family Counseling Service for Ridgewood and Vicinity; mem. Bergen County (N.J.) Republican Com.; NW Bergen County campaign mgr. for gubernatorial candidate Tom Kean, 1977. Mem. Bus. and Profl. Women's Orgn. Clubs: Coll. of Ridgewood, Ridgewood Rep. Office: 303 Cannon House Office Bldg Washington DC 20515 *

ROULEAU, CAROLYN FERNAN, systems coordinator; b. Miami, Fla., Jan. 1, 1950; d. Philip A. and Joanne Fernan; m. Kenneth E. Rouleau, Mar. 3, 1973 (div. Feb. 1980); children: Tiffany Ann, Joseph Philippe. Student Fla. Atlantic U., 1969-71, Fla. Internat. U., 1972-73, U. Miami, 1985—. Coordinator, Conservation Found. Air Quality Workshop, Miami, Fla., 1970-71; field systems coordinator Arthur Young & Co., Miami, 1971—; dir. Colleen Mine, Balt., 1983—; owner, mgr. External Systems Service, 1986—. Patron, Greater Miami Opera; trustee Miami Ch. Religious Sci., 1987—. Mem. Nat. Assn. Female Execs., Bus. and Profl. Women's Club, LWV, Greater Miami C. of C. (marine industry com.), Greater Miami Opera Guild, Dade County, Beta Gamma Sigma. Avocations: sailing, golfing, gardening.

ROULEAU, WINIFRED JOSEPHINE, real estate associate; b. Bellingham, Wash., Nov. 17, 1931; d. George Earle and Gladys J. (Knutson) Chandler; m. Gerald Vincent Rouleau; 1 child, Gerald Remi. Sec. Seattle First Nat. Bank, Toppenish, Wash., 1951-52, Seattle, 1952-54; acct. Chandler Dist. Ct., Toppenish, 1954-63; real estate assoc. Countryman Real Estate, Eugene, Oreg., 1973-79, Stan Wiley Real Estate, Eugene, 1979-80, Gordon Brunton Realty, Eugene, 1980—. Bd. trustees United First Meth. Ch., Eugene, 1986—. Mem. Eugene Bd. of Realtors (life), Blanche Markum Guild, Oreg. State U. Moms Club (sec. 1985-86), Daughters of Nile. Home: 4315 Inwood Ln Eugene OR 97405 Office: Gordon Brunton Realty 1601 Willamette Eugene OR 97401

ROUMILLAT, L. FLORETTA, microbiologist, researcher; b. East Point, Ga., Oct. 25, 1941; d. Ulysses Charles and Luna Lee (Foreman) R. BS, Ga. State U., 1969; MS, Tulane U., 1970; PhD, U. Ga., 1980. Lab. aide Ga. State Pub. Health Dept., Atlanta, 1961-62; lab. dir. Atlanta Diagnostic Lab., Decatur, 1970-71; lab. technologist Ctrs. for Disease Control, Atlanta, 1962-69, technologist, 1971-80, research biologist, 1980-82, research microbiologist, 1982—; cons. Consults, Inc., Lawrenceville, Ga., 1986—. Author clin. microbiol. research and various related articles, 1980-84. Mem. Sigma Xi. Home: 1670 Stanwyck Terr Tucker GA 30084 Office: Ctrs for Disease Control 1600 Clifton Rd Atlanta GA 30333

ROUNDS, H. PAULINE MICHAL, animal breeder; b. Princeton, N.J., Nov. 30, 1948; d. Edward Vincent and Helen Miranda (Drake) Michal; m. John McCarthy Rounds, Dec. 19, 1970. BA in Art and Psychology, Calif. State U., Chico, 1970. Founder, owner Windigo Enterprises, Tustin, Perris, Calif., 1971—; area rep. Greater Lake Mathews Rural Trails Assn., 1987—; exec. officer Riverside Conty Trails Task Force, 1988. Named to many nat. rankings, showing and honor rolls for breeding, 1981-87. Mem. Tenn. Walking Horse Breeders and Exhibitors Assn. (Versatility champion 1983, Supreme Versatility champion 1984), Pacific Coast Walking Horse Assn. (v.p. 1982-84). Home and Office: 15598 Multiview Dr Perris CA 92370

ROUNDS, MARTHA GILTNER, fitness and nutrition counseling company executive; b. Joplin, Mo., Apr. 12, 1919; d. Frank Phillips and Berry Frances (Barnes) Giltner; m. Francis Joseph Rounds; children—Berry R. Lane, Kevin T., Tracy A. B.S. in Bus., Miami U., Oxford, Ohio, 1941. Buyer John Shillato Co., Cin., 1941-44, Stix, Baer & Fuller, St. Louis, 1945-49; owner, pres. Martha Rounds Slimnastics, St. Louis, 1962—, Martha Belle, Ltd., St. Louis, 1975—, Martha Rounds Acad. for Children, St. Louis, 1983—; dir. Mark Twain State Bank, Bridgeton, Mo. Bd. dirs. Delta Gamma Found., 1953-57, U.S. Nat. Sr. Olympics, 1986-87; mem. aux. bd. St. Louis U. Hosps., 1967-75, Nat. WOmen's Forum, 1987; co-chmn. Salvation Army Tree of Lights project, 1976-77; mem. pres.' adv. cabinet Girl Scouts U.S., 1980. Recipient Shield award Delta Gamma Found., 1983; named Woman of Yr., Nat. Fedn. Bus. and Profl. Women's Club, 1979, Bus. Person Of Yr., Brentwood, Mo.'s C. of C. 1987). Home: 12 Southcote St Brentwood MO 63144 Office: Martha Belle Ltd 1801 Parkridge Brentwood MO 63144

ROUNTREE, ELIZABETH COFFEE, librarian; b. Alto, Ga., July 13, 1937; A.B. in English, Piedmont Coll., 1958; M.A., U. Ill., 1959; Diploma Advanced Studies Librarianship, Emory U., 1971; M.P.A. U. New Orleans, 1984. Dir., Piedmont Coll. Library, 1959-65, N.E. Ga. Regional Library, 1965-72, Brunswick-Glynn County Regional Library, 1972-77; asst. librarian New Orleans Pub. Library, 1977-83; dir. St. Tammany Parish Library, 1984—. Contbr. articles to profl. jours. Mem. ALA, La. Library Assn., Greater New Orleans Library Club, Beta Phi Mu. Address: Saint Tammany Parish Library 310 W 21st Ave Covington LA 70433

ROUP, BRENDA JACOBS, nurse, army officer; b. Petersburg, Va., July 8, 1948; d. Eugene Thurman and Sarah Ann (Williams) Jacobs; m. Clarence James Roup, May 8, 1976. B.S.N., Med. Coll. Va., Richmond, 1970; M.S.N., Cath. U. Am., 1977. Commd. 2d lt. U.S. Army, 1970, advanced through grades to lt. col., 1986; chief infection control Brooke Army MEDCEN, San Antonio, 1983-86; chief infection control Walter Reed MEDCEN, Washington, 1986—; nurse con. in infection control to U.S. Army Surgeon Gen., 1986—. Mem. Assn. Practitioners in Infection Control, Assn. Mil. Surgeons, Sigma Theta Tau. Avocations: reading; swimming; cooking. Office: Walter Reed Army Med Ctr 16th St Washington DC 20307

ROURKE, KELLI KALÍ, saving and loan executive; b. Bellingham, Wash., Dec. 21, 1958; d. Paul J. and Marie H. (Baskett) Priestley; m. Daniel Jeremiah Rourke III, Oct. 4, 1986; 1 child, Devin Jemarié. Diploma, Charles C. Sch., Tulsa, 1976. Closing coordinator Zenith Mortgage Co., Austin, Tex., 1977-78, Mason-McDuffie Mortgage Co., Austin, 1978-80; br. mgr., closing officer Austin Title Co., 1980-83; asst. v.p., escrow closing officer Travis Title Co., Austin, 1983; reg. account exec. for cen. Tex. PMI Mortgage Ins. Co., Austin, 1983-86; mktg. dir., closing officer Security Title Co., Austin, 1986-87; closing mgr. statewide ops. First Fed. Savs. and Loan Assn. of Austin, 1987—. UPI scholar, 1976; McMahon Sch. Journalism scholar, 1976. Mem. Nat. Assn. Female Execs., Nat. Assn. Profl. Mortgage Women (v.p. Austin Assn. 1988), Womens Council Realtors, Austin Ctr. Theaters. Republican. Methodist. Office: First Fed Savs and Loan Assn 200 E 10th St Austin TX 78701

ROUSE, ARLENE ELIZABETH, social worker; b. N.Y.C., Nov. 14, 1934; d. Fleming William and Janice Elizabeth (Kollock) Prince; divorced. BA, Hunter Coll., 1957, MSW, 1961. Lic. social worker, N.Y. Caseworker ARC, Washington, 1962-63, Inwood House, N.Y.C., 1963-65; sr. caseworker Floyd Patterson House, N.Y.C., 1965-66; psychiat. social worker Bellevue Psychiat. Hosp., N.Y.C., 1966-69; sch. social worker N.Y.C. Bd. Edn., Bklyn., 1969—. Sec. scholarship com. Medgar Evers Coll., N.Y.C., 1972-76. Mem. Nat. Assn. Black Social Workers, Am. Cancer Soc., Zeta Phi Beta. Methodist. Home: 185 Hall St New York NY 11205

ROUSE, DORIS JANE, physiologist, research administrator; b. Greensboro, N.C., Oct. 3, 1948; d. Welby Corbett and Nadia Elizabeth (Grainger) R.; m. Blake Shaw Wilson, Jan. 6, 1974; 1 child, Nadia Jacqueline. B.A. in Chemistry, Duke U., 1970, Ph.D. in Physiology and Pharmacology, 1980. Tchr. sci. Peace Corps, Tugbake, Liberia, 1970-71; research scientist Burroughs Wellcome Co., Research Triangle Park, N.C., 1971-76; sr. physiologist Research Triangle Inst., 1976-83; ctr. dir. Research Triangle Inst., 1983—, also dir. NASA tech. application team, 1980—; adminstr. ANSI Tech. Adv. Group for Wheelchairs, N.Y.C., 1982-86; adj. asst. prof. Sch. Medicine U. N.C., 1983—. Mem. adv. bd. Assn. Retarded Citizens, Arlington (Tex.), 1981—; bd. dirs. Simon Found., Chgo., 1983—; mem. adv. bd. Western Gerontology Soc., San Francisco, 1982-85; mem. spl. rev. com. small bus. applications NIH, 1983—; mem. Nat. Forum on Tech. and Aging. Recipiet Group Achievement award NASA, 1979. Mem. Rehab. Engring. Soc. N.Am. (chmn. wheelchair com. 1981-86), Am. Soc. on Aging, Rehab. Engring. Soc. N.Am., Tech. Transfer Soc., Nat. Space Soc. Club: Triangle Dive. Home: 2410 Wrightwood Ave Durham NC 27705 Office: Research Triangle Inst PO Box 12194 Research Triangle Park NC 27709

ROUSE, ELOISE MEADOWS, foundation executive; b. Shreveport, La., July 22, 1931; d. Curtis Washington and Lucille Eloise (Loyd) Meadows; m. Dudley Lee Rouse, Aug. 26, 1952; children: Deborah L. Lee, Elizabeth M. B of Music Edn., Baylor U., 1952. Tchr. 1st grade Brentwood Elem. Sch., Austin, Tex., 1953-55; v.p., dir., mem. grants rev. com., trustee The Meadows Found., Dallas, 1979—. Mem. honor bd. New Horizons Ranch and Ctr. Home for Troubled Youth, Goldthwaite, Tex.; mem. exec. bd. Meadows Sch. of the Arts, So. Meth. U., Dallas; mem. exec. com., bd. dirs. Dallas Summer Musicals; bd. dirs., mem. exec. com. Nat. Wildflower Research Ctr.; mem. adv. com. Baylor U. Sch. Music; chair, mem. host com. Conf. S.W. Founds.; mem. landscape devel. com. Dallas Garden Ctr.; active Dallas Mus. Art, Wadley Guild, Dallas Summer Musicals Guild; mem. exec.'s Bible class 1st Bapt. Ch. Dallas, past Sunday sch. tchr., past mem. music com. Mem. Nat. Trust Hist. Preservation, Park Cities Hist. Soc., Internat. Platform Assn., DAR, Women's Tennis Assn., Council on Founds., Independent Sector. Clubs: Village Gardeners' Garden (former 1st v.p.), Marianne Scruggs Garden (crystal charity ball com.), Dallas Country, Dallas Women's, Lancers (Dallas); Pontre Vedra (Fla.) Inn and Club, Tournament Players (Ponte Vedra). Office: The Meadows Found 2922 Swiss Ave Dallas TX 75204

ROUSE, SUE THOMPSON, emerita educator; b. Ulman, Mo., Aug. 28, 1920; d. Clyde Waldo and Retta (Darr) Thompson; A.B., Harris Tchrs. Coll., St. Louis, 1942; M.A., U. N.C., Chapel Hill, 1950; Ed.D. (fellow 1960), George Peabody Coll., Nashville, 1963; postgrad. U. Minn.; m. Linwood I. Rouse, Aug. 29, 1945 (div.). Elem. sch. tchr., Mo. and N.C., 1947-59; mem. faculty U. S.C., Columbia, 1961—, prof. edn., 1974-86, disting. prof. emerita, 1986—; cons. infield. Chmn., S.C. Commn. Ministry for Christian Ch. (Disciples of Christ), 1973-80; mem. regional bd. Christian Chs. in S.C., 1979-83, moderator, 1980-82; pres. Regional Assembly Christian Chs. in S.C., 1977-78; mem. nat. adv. com. ministry Christian Ch., 1978-82, nat. bd. dirs. Div. Homeland Ministries, 1981-87, Ch. Women's Coordinating Council, 1987—. Served with USCGR, 1943-46. Fellow Am. Assn. Mental Defiency; mem. NEA (life), S.C. Edn. Assn., Council Exceptional Children, S.C. Psychol. Assn., S.C. Mental Health Assn., Nat. Audubon Soc., Delta Kappa Gamma, Phi Delta Kappa. Democrat. Author articles in field, chpts. in books.

ROUSE, TERRIE SUZITTE, museum director, consultant; b. Youngstown, Ohio, Dec. 2, 1952; d. Eurad R. and Florence (Wilcox) R.; 1 child, Malcolm Adam. BA, Trinity Coll., 1974; MS in Profl. Studies, Cornell U., 1977; certificate Internat. Affairs, Columbia U., 1979, MA, 1979. Mgr., curator Adam Clayton Powell St. Office Bldg., N.Y.C., 1979-81; sr. curator Studio Museum Harlem, N.Y.C., 1981-86; dir. museum N.Y.C. Transit Exhibit-Transit Authority, Bklyn., 1986—; advisor Bellevue Hosp. Art Bd., 1981—. Contbr. articles to profl. jours. Named Outstanding Young Women Am., 1981-83. Mem. Am. Assn. Museums, (assessor 1981—), Art Table. Home: 409 Edgecombe Ave #11D New York NY 10032 Office: NYC Transit Authority 81 Willoughby St #802 Brooklyn NY 11201

ROUSH, ANNE FRANCES, social worker; b. Carroll, Iowa, Nov. 20, 1930; d. Lawrence James and Frances Xavier (Whalen) Lane; R.N., Mercy Hosp. Sch. Nursing, Des Moines, 1951; B.S., St. Louis U., 1953; M.S.W., U. Hawaii, 1968; m. Howard Patrick Roush, Aug. 6, 1955; children—Mary Frances, Louise Catherine, Jenny Elizabeth, Frederick Lawrence, Martin Louis. Head nurse Barnes Hosp., asst. in nursing Washington U., St. Louis, 1953-54; instr. St. Marys Hosp. Sch. Nursing, Tucson, 1955-56; psychiat. social worker So. Ariz. Mental Health Center, Tucson, 1968—, mental health treatment team leader, 1982—; field instr. Sch. Social Work Ariz. State U., Tempe; cons., co-founder, mem. bd. COPE, 1975-81. Recipient Field Instr. award, 1982. Mem. Nat. Assn. Social Workers (chmn. nominations com. Ariz chpt. 1982-84), Acad. Cert. Social Workers. Mem. Holy Resurrection Orthodox Ch. Research in manpower in social work, 1968. Home: 6260 N Oasis St Tucson AZ 85704 Office: 1930 E 6th St Tucson AZ 85719

ROUSH, DIANE Y., sales executive; b. Pontiac, Mich., Sept. 12, 1942; d. Preston and Phyllis Eleanor (Baldwin) Yost; m. Lester G. Knickerbocker, Aug. 24, 1963 (div. 1975); 1 child, Russell Glen Knickerbocker; m. Thomas Roush, Feb. 24, 1977 (dec. Feb. 1984). BA, Albion Coll., 1964. Tchr. Albion (Mich.) Pub. Schs., 1964-65, Benton Harbor (Mich.) Pub. Schs., 1965-66, St. Joseph (Mich.) Pub. Schs., 1967-68, 74-78; office mgr. Mainstreet Boardwalk Complex, Pentwater, Mich., 1982; owner Sunshine Emporium, Pentwater, 1983-85; mfrs.' rep. Vanguard Sales Agy., Grand Rapids, Mich., 1984-87; co-owner Personal Touch, Saugatuck, Mich., 1987—. Chmn. bd. dirs. Alamo Teen Ctr., Stevensville, Mich., 1970-74; commr. Lincoln Twp. (Mich.) Parks and Recreation Bd., 1970-76. Mem. Nat. Assn. Female Execs. Episcopalian. Club: Lakeshore Jr. Women's (Stevensville). Home and Office: 1011 State St Saugatuck MI 49453

ROUSH, SALLY FAYE, human resources executive; b. Denver, Mar. 28, 1947; d. Wilbur James and Mary Ellen (Kastle) Ziege; children: Claire Ellen, Beth Louise. Student, Lewis and Clark Coll., 1965-66; BA in Sociology, U. Denver, 1969; postgrad., U. Colo., 1972-74. Asst. personnel officer Colo. Dept. Edn., Denver, 1970-72; personnel dir. U. Colo., Denver, 1974-81, San Diego State U., 1982—; presenter numerous workshops, panels human resource mgmt., affirmative action topics. Vol. transport com. Project Wildlife, San Diego, 1986—. Mem. Coll. and Univ. Personnel Assn. (San Diego chpt.), Campus Concerns for Women, Scripps Ranch Community Assn., U. Denver Alumni Assn. (admissions council 1986—), San Diego Zool. Soc. Democrat. Office: San Diego State U Office Personnel Dir San Diego CA 92182

ROUSSELL, VANESSA LYNN, communications company adminstrator; b. New Orleans, Dec. 20, 1952; d. Dorothy Roussell. BS, Vanderbilt U., 1973. Asst. dial service adminstr. South Cen. Bell, New Orleans, 1974-75, adminstr. dial service, 1975-76; staff specialist Birmingham, Ala., 1976-81; mgr. New Orleans, 1981-83; product mgr. Bell South Services Co., Inc., Birmingham, 1983-87, group product mgr., 1987—; product mgr., cons. Dept. Def., Washington, 1987. Named one of Outstanding Young Women Am., 1977. Mem. Birmingham C. of C. (women's forum). Democrat. Baptist. Home: 3436 Loch Haven Dr Birmingham AL 35216

ROUTZANN, LINDA KAY, electrical engineer; b. Butler, Pa., Aug. 12, 1959; d. William Gordon and Twila Mae (Bartlett) Ferry; m. Douglas Vernon Routzahn, July22, 1978; 1 child, Erin Lynne. BEE, Case Western Res. U., 1981. Engr. systems quality Cleve. Electric Illuminating Co., 1981-84, engr. lead quality, 1984-86, staff analyst to sr. v.p. nuclear group, 1985-86, engr. lead audit, 1986-87, engr. simulator ops., 1987—; tech. spokesperson U.S. Council for Energy Awareness, Washington, 1985—; tech. coordinator emergency plan orgn. Perry (Ohio) Power Plant, 1985-87, tech. spokesperson, 1987—; speakers bur. Cleve. Electric Illuminating Co., Cleve., 1981—. Mem. Community Committment Program, 1986—. Recipient Cert. of Merit, Cleve. YWCA, 1985. Home: 940 Mineral Springs Rd Ashtabula OH 44004 Office: Cleve Electric Illuminating Co PO Box 97 Perry OH 44081

ROVELSTAD, MATHILDE VERNER, library science educator; b. Kempten, Germany, Aug. 12, 1920; came to U.S., 1951, naturalized, 1953; d. George and Therese (Hohl) Hotter; m. Howard Rovelstad, Nov. 23, 1970. Ph.D., U. Tubingen, 1953; M.S. in L.S, Catholic U. Am., 1960. Cataloger Mt. St. Mary's Coll., Los Angeles, 1953; sch. librarian Yoyogi Elem. Sch., Tokyo, 1954-56; mem. faculty Cath. U. Am., 1960—, prof. library sci., 1975—; vis. prof. U. Montreal, 1969. Author: Bibliotheken in den Vereinigten Staaten, 1974; translator Bibliographia, an Inquiry into its Definition and Designations (R. Blum), 1980, Das Bibliotheken in den Vereinigten Staaten von Amerika und in Kanada, 1988; contbr. articles to profl. jours. Research grantee German Acad. Exchange Service, 1969. Mem. ALA (internat. relations com. 1977-80), Internat. Fedn. Library Assns. and Instns. (standing adv. com. on library schs. 1975-81), Assn. for Library and Info. Sci. Edn. Home: 11 Banbury Rd Gibson Island MD 21056 Office: Catholic U Am Sch Library & Info Sci Washington DC 20064

ROVET, JOANNE FRANCES, psychologist; b. Montreal, Que., Can., Feb. 24, 1946; d. David George and Jane (Adelman) Rigler; B.Sc. magna cum laude, York U., 1968; Ph.D., U. Toronto, 1974; m. Ernest Rovet, Dec. 26, 1967; children—Benjamin, Heather, Jennifer. Postdoctoral fellow Hosp. Sick Children, Toronto, 1975-78, research asso., 1978-83, asst. prof., 1983-86; asst. prof. spl. edn. Ont. Inst. Studies in Edn., 1986—, asst. prof. pediatrics U. Toronto, 1986—. Recipient Lionel Charlesworth prize York U., 1965; York U. scholar, 1964, Can. Council doctoral fellow, 1971-73, Med. Research Council postdoctoral fellow, 1975-78, Ont. Mental Health Found. fellow, 1981-82; Health and Welfare Can. research scholar, 1983-88. Mem. Soc. Research Child Devel., Soc. for Behavioral Pediatrics, Internat. Neuropsychol. Soc., Am. Psychol. Assn., Can. Psychol. Assn., Ont. Bd. Examiners Psychology, Turner Syndrome Soc. (dir., chmn. of fundraising com.). Contbr. articles to profl. jours. Home: 399 Glengrove Ave, Toronto, ON Canada M5N 1W8 Office: 555 University Ave, Toronto, ON Canada M5G 1X8

ROVNER, ILANA DIAMOND, federal judge; b. 1938; m. Richard N. Rovner. AB, Bryn Mawr Coll., 1960; postgrad., U. London King's Coll., 1961, Georgetown U., 1961-63; JD, Ill. Inst. Tech., 1966. Bar: Ill. 1972, U.S. Dist. Ct. (no. dist.) Ill. 1972, U.S. Ct. Appeals (7th cir.) 1977, U.S. Supreme Ct. 1982. Judicial clk. to presiding justice U.S. Dist. Ct. (no. dist.) Ill., Chgo., 1972-73; chief pub. protection U.S. Atty.'s Office, Chgo., 1973-77; dep. gov., legal counsel Gov. James R. Thompson, Chgo., 1977-84; dist. judge U.S. Dist. Ct. (no. dist.) Ill., Chgo., 1984—. Recipient Spl. Commendation award U.S. Dept. Justice, 1975, 76, Ann. Nat. Law and Social Justice Leadership award The League to Improve the Community, 1975, Ann. Guardian Police award, 1977, Profl. Achievement award Ill. Inst. Tech. Chgo. Kent Coll. Law, 1986; named Today's Chgo. Woman of Yr., 1985, Woman of Yr., The Chgo. Woman's Club, 1986; honored by Midwest Women's Ctr., 1986, Judaica Service award Spertus Coll., 1987. Mem. ABA, Ill. State Bar Assn., Chgo. Bar Assn. (Def. of Prisoners Com. Commendation 1987), Women's Bar Assn. Ill., Fed. Bar Assn. (following offices with Chgo. chpt. judicial selection com. 1977-80, treas. 1978-79, sec. 1979-80, 2d v.p. 1980-81, 1st v.p. 1981-82, pres. 1982-83, nat. 2d v.p. 7th cir. 1984, v.p. 7th cir. 1986), Chgo. Council Lawyers, The Decalogue Soc., Kappa Beta Pi. Office: US Dist Ct 219 S Dearborn St Chicago IL 60604

ROWCLIFFE, JUDY LESLIE, public relations executive; b. Pasadena, Calif., Mar. 29, 1954; d. Theodore Harry and Irene Patricia (Hamblin) R.; m. Christopher Barnett Godchaux, Nov. 30, 1985. AA, Citrus Coll., 1974; BA, Calif. State U., Fullerton, 1976. Asst. account exec. Daily & Assocs., Los Angeles, 1979-80, account exec., 1980-81; account supr. Edelman Pub. Relations, San Francisco, 1981-83, v.p., 1983—. Contbg. author: Women's Guide to Travel. Office: Edelman Pub Relations 550 California St #1160 San Francisco CA 94104

ROWE, DOROTHY ISDELL, social services administrator; b. Springfield, Mo., Sept. 1, 1929; d. Robert Harold and Gladys Pearl (McConnell) Isdell; m. Melvin E. Rowe, Nov. 25, 1950; children: Jerry, Robert David, Melinda Jean, Dana Melanie. Student, Ferrum Coll., 1947-48; BS, Am. U., 1950; postgrad., Mt. San Antonio Coll., 1983, Chaffey Coll., 1984-86. Personnel clk. Dept. Def., Washington, 1948-50, USAF, San Bernardino, Calif., 1951-52; sec. Calif. ANG, Ontario, 1953-62; title clk. Adams, Porter, Radigan & Marys, Arlington, Va., 1965-67; sec./supr. research div. U.S. Army, Washington, 1967-68; case worker, surp. San Bernardino Couty, 1971—; cons. Geneal. Group, Ontario, 1980-83. Co-author: Isdell-Kidd, Ireland and USA, 1985. Chmn. PTA Mothersingers, Ontario, 1960-62. Mem. Welfare Suprs. Assn. (sec. 1986-87), Irish-Am. Cultural Inst., So. Calif. Geneal. Soc., Ohio Geneal. Soc., DAR (regent/registrar Ontario-Upland 1980—, cert. 1984, 85, 88), First Families of Ohio, Daughters of Union Veterans of Civil War, Provincial Families of Md., Hereditary Order of Descendants of the Loyalists & Patriots of Am. Revolution. Home: 9095 Helena Ave Montclair CA 91763

ROWE, DOROTHY LEE, educator; b. Huntington, W.Va., Oct. 30, 1920; d. McKinley Leander and Mabel Mae (Ferris) Rowe; B.S. in Edn., Ohio U., 1941; postgrad. Harvard Grad. Sch. Edn., 1953, Purdue U., summer, 1956; M.A., U. Chgo., 1958; postgrad. Bowdoin Coll., summer, 1962. Tchr. math. Chesapeake, Ohio, 1941-43, Ironton (Ohio) High Sch., 1943-46, Gallia Acad. High Sch., Gallipolis, Ohio, 1946-58; instr. math. Miami U., Oxford, Ohio, 1958-73, sr. instr., 1973-78, prof. emeritus math. and stats., 1978—. Nat. adv. bd. Am. Security Council, 1978-88; sustaining mem. Republican Nat. Com., 1971-87; Ford Found. fellow, 1952-53; Gen. Electric fellow, summer, 1956; NSF fellow, 1957, 58, summer 1962. Mem. AAUW, AAUP, Math. Assn. Am., NEA, Nat. Ret. Tchrs. Assn., Ohio Ret. Tchrs. Assn., Pi Lambda Theta, Pi Mu Epsilon, Delta Kappa Gamma, Kappa Delta Pi. Republican. Presbyterian. Address: 4741 Nottingham Court Ashland KY 41101

ROWE, ELIZABETH WEBB, administrative assistant; b. Canton, Ohio, Dec. 2, 1957; d. Thomas Dudley and Verity Elizabeth (Voight) Webb O'Brien; m. David Lee Rowe, June 21, 1986. AB, Mt. Holyoke Coll., 1979. Legal asst. Willkie Farr & Gallagher, N.Y.C., 1979-82, legal asst. supr., 1983-88, adminstrv. asst., 1988—; legal asst. Community Law Offices, N.Y.C., 1980-82; clerical asst. 17th Precinct Police Detective, N.Y.C., 1981-82. Chair homeless shelter St. Bartholomew's Ch., N.Y.C., 1984-85; vol. Breakfast Feeding Program, 1983—, mem. Community Ministry Council, 1986-88; mem. N.Y. Jr. League, Pres.'s Council, 1988—; rep. Mt. Holyoke Coll. Alumnae Fund, 1986—. Home: 167 E 67th St Apt 6-E New York NY 10021-5916 Office: St Bartholomew's Ch 109E 50th St New York NY 10022

ROWE, GENEVA LASSITER, psychotherapist, counseling center administrator; b. Atlanta, Aug. 11, 1927; d. Hoyt Cleveland and Tinie (Gresham) Lassiter; m. Fred Earnest Rowe, May 3, 1958; children: Carol, Vickie, Randall. BA, Oglethorpe U., 1968; MSW, U. Ga., 1970; PhD, Fla. State U., 1978. Accredited Acad. Cert. Social Workers; lic. marriage and family therapist, Ga.; approved AAMFT supr., 1986. Alcohol and drug counselor Georgian Clinic, Atlanta, 1968; outpatient counselor DeKalb Guidance Clinic, Atlanta, 1969; protective services supr. DeKalb Family and Children Services, Decatur, Ga., 1970-72; outpatient therapist Cen. DeKalb Mental Health Ctr., 1972-75; marriage and family therapist Fla. State U., 1977; lectr. sociology Oglethorpe U., 1978-81; psychotherapist, clin. supr., dir., owner N.E. Counseling Ctr., P.C., Atlanta and Lawrenceville, Ga., 1978—; clin. supr. master's students in practicum Ga. State U., 1980—; approved AAMFT supr., 1986—; allied health profl. CPC Parkwood Hosp., 1987—. Fellow Am. Orthopsychiat. Assn., Internat. Council Sex Edn. and Parenthood; mem. Am. Assn. Marriage and Family Therapy (clin. mem., approved supr.), AAUW, Ga. Assn. Marriage and Family Therapy (pub. relations chmn. 1984-86), Gwinnett County C. of C., Young Women of Arts. Methodist. Home: 2005 Woodsdale Rd NE Atlanta GA 30324 Office: NE Counseling Ctr PC 2995 Lawrenceville Hwy Lawrenceville GA 30245

ROWE, MAE IRENE, investment company executive; b. Gardner, Mass., Dec. 6, 1927; d. Clifford Wesley and Mertie (Moore) Mann; m. Willard Chase Rowe, June 18, 1951 (div. 1979); children—Gail B. Rowe Simons, Bruce C. B.A. with high honor, Am. Internat. Coll., 1949. Cert. real property adminstr. Social worker City of Montague, Turners Falls, Mass., 1949-51; mgr. Park Investment Co., Cleve., 1979—. Pres., v.p., bd. dirs. Park Ridge Counseling Service, Ill., 1972-76; clk. Village of Kildeer, Ill., 1977; bd. dirs. Maine Township Mental Health Service, Park Ridge, 1975-76; trustee Heathermore Condominium Assn., 1987, pres. 1988. Mem. Cleve. Bldg. Owners Mgrs. Assn. (mem. edn. com. 1983—), Bldg. Owners Mgrs. Assn. Internat., Soc. Real Property Adminstrs. (cert.), LWV (v.p., mem. city adv. com. 1973-76), Am. Mensa Soc. Republican. Unitarian. Club: Cleve. Racquet. Lodge: Kiwanis (bd. dirs.) Avocations: tennis. Home: 34108 Chagrin Blvd Apt 5103 Moreland Hills OH 44022 Office: Park Investment Co 907 Park Bldg Cleveland OH 44114

ROWE, MARGARET STEED, hospital supply manager; b. Los Angeles, July 5, 1947; d. Robert Franklin and Margaret Anne (Martin) Steed; m. Charles R. Rowe, III, July 9, 1977; 1 dau., Courtney Renee. B.S., Calif. State U.-San Diego, 1970; M.S., U. Mo.-Columbia, 1975. Dietetic intern Colo. State U., 1970-71; adminstrv. dietitian U. Mo., Columbia, 1971-74, teaching asst., 1974-75; food systems mgr. Am. Dietary Products div. Am. Hosp. Supply Corp., Santa Ana, Calif., 1975-82, dietary systems mgr., 1982-83; nat. dietary systems mgr., McGaw Park, Ill., 1983-84, nat. systems mgr., 1984-85, dir. planning, 1985-86, region mgr., 1986-87; dir. ops. Hosp. Supply Div. Baxter Internat., McGaw Pk, 1987-88; speaker profl. confs. Mem. Am. Dietetic Assn., Dietitians in Bus. and Industry, Women in Bus. Home: 1448 Lawrence Ave Lake Forest IL 60045 Office: Hosp Supply Div Baxter Internat McGaw Park IL 60085

ROWE, MARY P., university administrator, educator. married; children: Katherine, Susannah, Timothy. BA in History, Swarthmore Coll., 1957; PhD in Econs., Columbia U., 1971; LLD (hon.), Regis Coll., 1975. With World Council of Chs./Office of UN High Commr. for Refugees, Salzburg and Vienna, Austria, 1957-58; research asst. Nat. Bur. Econ. Research, N.Y.C., 1961; economist planning bd. Office of Gov., V.I., 1962-63; freelance cons. Nigeria, 1963-66, Boston, 1967-69; cons., sr. economist with Ctr. for Ednl. Policy Research, Harvard U. OEO, Cambridge, Mass., 1970; cons., sr. economist with Abt Assocs. OEO, 1970, tech. dir. with Mass. Early Edn. Project, Harvard U., 1971-72; cons. economist with Abt Assocs. U.S. Dept. Labor, 1971; dir. Carnegie Corp. Grant Radcliffe Inst., Cambridge, 1972; spl. asst. to pres. MIT, Cambridge, 1973—, adj. prof. Sloan Sch. Mgmt., 1985—. Mem. editorial bd. Negotiation Jour., 1985—, Alternative Dispute Resloution Report, 1987—; contbr. articles to profl. jours. Trustee Cambridge Friends Sch., 1969-75; mem. bd. advisors Brookline Children's Ctr., 1971-76; mem. Cambridge Friends Meeting and Com. on Clearness, 1971-78, New Eng. Concerns Com., 1973—, Mass. Policy Adv. Com. on Child Abuse/Neglect, 1977-79, Mass. State Youth Council, 1978-83; mem. Mass. State Employment and Tng. Council, 1975-83, chair, 1980-83; mem. nat. adv. Com. Black Women's Ednl. Policy and Research Network Project/Wellesley Coll. Ctr. for Research on Women, 1980-83; bd. dirs. Bay State Skills Commn., 1980-81, Wellesley Women's Research Ctr., 1984-87; sec. bd. dirs. Bay State Skills Corp., 1981—; mem. panel on employment disputes Ctr. for Pub. Resources, 1986—. Mem. Am. Econs. Assn., Soc. Profls. in Dispute Resolution (chair com. on ombudspersons 1982—), Calif. Caucus Coll. and Univ. Ombudsmen, Univ. and Coll. Ombudsman Assn., Corp. Ombudsman Assn. (pres. 1985-87). Office: MIT 77 Massachusetts Ave Room 10-213 Cambridge MA 02139

ROWE, MARY SUE, accounting professional; b. Melrose, Kans., Aug. 31, 1940; d. Gene and Carmen (Glidewell) Woffard; m. Edward Rowe, Nov. 27, 1985; children from previous marriage: Denise, Dynell, Dalene, Denette. Student, MTI Bus. Coll., 1968, Calif. State U., Fullerton, 1969; cert. bus. mgmt., San Bernardino, 1986. Variou bookkeeping and secretarial 1968-76; asst. mgr., acct. RM Dean Contracting, Chenango Forks, N.Y., 1976-80; acctg. asst. Hemet (Calif.) Unified Sch. Dist., 1981-86; dir. acctg. Desert Sands Unified Sch. Dist., Indio, Calif., 1986—. Mem. Parent without Ptnrs., N.Y. and Calif., 1976-84; bd. dirs. Family Services Assn., Hemet, 1982-83. Mem. Riverside Assn. Chief Accts. (co-chmn. 1986-88), Calif. Assn. Sch. Bus. Ofcls., Nat. Assn. Female Execs., Desert Schs. Mgmt. Assn. Republican. Home: 41080 Grand Teton Hemet CA 92344 Office: Desert Sand Unified Sch Dist 82-879 Hwy 111 Indio CA 92201

ROWE, SANDRA MIMS, newspaper executive editor; b. Charlotte, N.C., May 26, 1948; d. David Lathan and Shirley (Stovall) Mims; m. Gerard Paul Rowe, June 5, 1971; children—Mims Elizabeth, Sarah Stovall. B.A., E. Carolina U., Greenville, N.C., 1970. Reporter to asst. mng. editor The Ledger-Star, Norfolk, Va., 1971-80, mng. editor, 1980-82; mng. editor The Virginian-Pilot and The Ledger Star, Norfolk, Va., 1982-84, exec. editor, 1984-86, v.p., exec. editor, 1986—; mem. nominating jury for Pulitzer Prize in Journalism, 1986, 87; mem. Nieman Selection Com., 1987—. Bd. dirs. Hampton Rds. YMCA, 1987—. Named Woman of Yr. Outstanding Profl. Women of Hampton Rds., 1987. Mem. AP Mng. Editors, Am. Soc. Newspaper Editors, Va. Press Assn. (bd. dirs. 1985—), Am. Press Inst. (adv. bd. 1984—). Episcopalian. Home: 1020 Baldwin Ave Norfolk VA 23507 Office: The Virginian-Pilot The Ledger Star 150 W Brambleton Ave Norfolk VA 23510

ROWE, SUELLEN, accountant; b. Bremen, Ind., Sept. 9, 1956; d. Paul Otho and Patricia Ruth (Minnick) R. BBA cum laude, Hanover (Ind.) Coll., 1978. CPA. Staff auditor Ernst & Whinney, South Bend, Ind., 1979-1980, advanced staff auditor, 1980-81, sr. auditor, 1981-82; sr. internal auditor Wickes Cos., Wheeling, Ill., 1982-83, supervising sr. internal auditor, 1983-85, mgr. controls evaluation and audit, 1985-88; dir. fin. analysis and control Wickes Mfg. Co., Southfield, Mich., 1988—. Mem. Mus. of Sci. & Industry, 1984—; choir mem. St. Paul United Ch. Christ, 1982-88; treas. United Religious Community, 1982, Discovery Hall Assocs., 1982; bd. fin. Zion United Ch. of Christ, 1982, tchr., mem. choir 1980-82. Mem. Am. Inst. CPA's. Republican. Home: 6725 Colby Ln Birmingham MI 48010 Office: Wickes Mfg Co 26261 Evergreen Rd PO Box 999 Southfield MI 48037

ROWELL, REBECCA EARLENE, foundation executive; b. Moultrie, Ga., Feb. 9, 1954; d. Lawrence George and Stella Earlene (Wilson) R.; m. Charles Everett Lamkin. BS, U. Ga., 1976, MS, 1977. Cert. speech-lang. pathologist, Ga. Speech pathologist Iredell County Sch. System, Statesville, N.C., 1977-80; head speech pathologist Easter Seal Speech and Hearing Ctr., Brunswick, Ga., 1980-82, dir., 1982—; instr. Brunswick Jr. Coll., 1981. Dir., referee Golden Isles Wheelchair Tennis Tournament, Brunswick, 1982-87; sec. Golden Isles Tennis Assn., 1983—. Mem. Am. Speech-Lang.-Hearing Assn., Ga. Speech-Lang.-Hearing Assn. Democrat. Episcopalian. Club: Brunswick Woman's. Office: Easter Seal Speech and Hearing Ctr 2228 Starling St Brunswick GA 31520

ROWE-MAAS, BETTY LOU, real estate investor; b. San Jose, Calif., Apr. 2, 1925; d. Horace DeWitt and Lucy Belle (Spiker) Rowe; children: Terry Lee, Clifford Lindsay, Craig Harrison, Joan Louise. Real estate investor, Saratoga, Calif., 1968—. Mem. Nat. Trust Hist. Preservation, Smithsonian Instn., San Jose Mus., Saratoga Mus., San Francisco Mus., Los Gatos Mus., San Jose Symphony, Moltalvo; bd. dirs. Valley Inst. Theatre Arts; San Francisco Ballet, City Ctr. Ballet of San Jose and Cleve., Music and Arts Found.; mem. Route 85 Task Force, 1978—, treas., 1984-88; mem. Saratoga Good Govt., 1970—; treas. Traffic Relief for Saratoga. Mem. LWV. Republican. Clubs: Commonwealth of Calif. (life), Saratoga Country. Home: 20360 Saratoga Los Gatos Rd Saratoga CA 95070

ROWEN, ROSE LEE, mathematician; b. Chgo., Feb. 11, 1917; d. Benjamin and Sarah (Browdy) Greenberg; widowed; children: William Edward, Celia Rowen Barash. AA, Woodrow Wilson Coll., 1936; BA, NYU, 1945. Cert. med. tech. With Army Map Service, Washington, 1947-49, Bur. Standards, Washington, 1949-50, Joint Chief of Staff, Washington, 1950-52; with aircraft and space divs. Hughes Aircraft Co., Culver City, Calif., 1953-60; with Horton project Aero. Corp., Los Angeles, 1961-63; earthquake researcher UCLA, 1963-65; with space contracts Hughes Aircraft Co., Hawthorne, Calif., 1965-67; with Watkins-Johnson, Gaithersburg, Md., 1976—. Contbr. over 50 articles on math., physics, and computer sci. to profl. jours. Mem. Soc. Applied Math., Am. Math. Soc., Soc. Women Engrs., Pi Mu Epsilon, Sigma Pi Sigma. Democrat. Lutheran. Club: Cosmos. Home: 1060 Pipestem Pl Potomac MD 20854

ROWEN, RUTH HALLE, musicologist, educator; b. N.Y.C., Apr. 5, 1918; d. Louis and Ethel (Fried) Halle; m. Seymour M. Rowen, Oct. 13, 1940; children: Mary Helen Rowen, Louis Halle Rowen. B.A., Barnard Coll., 1939; M.A., Columbia U., 1941, Ph.D., 1948. Mgmt. ednl. dept. Carl Fischer, Inc., N.Y.C., 1954-63; assoc. prof. musicology CUNY, 1967-72, prof., 1972—, mem. doctoral faculty in musicology, 1967—. Author: Early Chamber Music, 1948, reprinted, 1974; (with Adele T. Katz) Hearing-Gateway to Music, 1959, (with William Simon) Jolly Come Sing and Play, 1956, Music Through Sources and Documents, 1979, (with Mary Rowen Obelkevich) Instant Piano, 1979, 80, 83; contbr. articles to profl. jours. Mem. ASCAP, Am. Musicol. Soc., Music Library Assn., Coll. Music Soc., Nat. Fedn. Music Clubs (nat. musicianship chmn. 1962-74, nat. young artist auditions com. 1964-74, N.Y. state chmn. Young Artist Auditions 1981, dist. coordinator 1983), N.Y. Fedn. Music Clubs (pres.), Phi Beta Kappa. Home: 115 Central Park W New York NY 10023

ROWLAND, CAROLE ANN, air force officer; b. Oskaloosa, Iowa, Mar. 30, 1952; d. Willis Marion and Majorie Ann (Lamb) R. B.S. in Edn., Northeast Mo. State U., 1975, M.A. in Phys. Scis., 1976; grad. Squadron Officer Sch., Montgomery, Ala., 1985. Prof. sci. Northeast Mo. State U., Kirksville, 1975-76; asst. maintenance supr. Davis-Monthan AFB, Ariz., 1978-81; chief equipment allowance sect. Hdqrs. TAC, Langley AFB, Va., 1981-84; equipment maintenance squadron officer-in-charge maintenance br. 363 Tactical Fighter Wing, Shaw AFB, 1984-85, maintenacne supr., 1985-86, comdr., 1986; dep. comdr. for maintenance Det 4 81 Tactical Fighter Wing, Norvenich Air Base, Germany, 1986—; officer's club rep., 1985-86; resident cons. for mil. women Davis-Monthan AFB, Ariz., 1980-81. Editor film Grand Canyon Adventure, 1975; also articles; mural artist. 4-H leader, Sumter, S.C., 1985-86; base donation organizer ARC, Tucson, 1978-81. Served to capt. USAF, 1976—. Mem. Nat. Assn. Female Execs., Fed. Women's Program (program and publicity com.), Nat. Wildlife Fedn. (life), Nat. Parks and Conservation Assn. (life), Alpha Sigma Tau, Sigma Zeta. Avocations: photography, basketball, racquetball, art, softball

ROWLAND, JEFFIE LANDERS, artist; b. Murray Cross, Ala., July 10, 1924; d. Eli Jefferson and Pearl Dorsey (Baskin) Landers; B.S., Jacksonville (Ala.) State Tchrs. Coll., 1945; postgrad. U. Ga., Athens; pupil of Lamar Dodd; m. Jack Lamb Rowland, Dec. 23, 1947; children—Mary Jane, Nancy Eugenia, Alice Alden. Elem. sch. tchr., Athens, 1947-48, 1st schs. art supr., 1948-52; 1st schs. art supr. Clarke County schs., Athens, 1952-62; art cons. North Ga. elem. schs., 1962-80; chmn. docents U. Ga. Mus. Art, Athens, 1978—, sch. coordinator for docents program, 1981—, also mem. bd. Friends of Mus.; illustrator Belle Meade Fox Hunt, 1985-86; one-woman show Jacksonville State Tchrs. Coll., 1948; group exhbns. include High Mus. Art, Atlanta, S.E. Art Assn., Nat. Exhbn. St. Herbert's Ch., Madison, N.J., 1987; works featured Chronicle of the Horse mag., 1987, Doysboro Jour. newspaper, 1988. Mem. show com. Renfrew Hunter-Jumper Shows. Recipient Belle Meade Fox Hunt Hammerhead award, 1982, Staff award, 1983; other art awards. Mem. DAR, Arts Alliance, Greater Atlanta Dressage Assn. (coordinator Pony club). Republican. Presbyterian. Club: Belle Meade Fox Hunt (Thomson, Ga.). Author articles in field; book: Fox Hunt Cartoons, 1983. Address: Beech Haven Athens GA 30606

ROWLAND, LISA ANN, health care executive; b. Chattanooga, Aug. 13, 1955; d. Charles Edward and Patricia Louise (Leonard) Chambers; m. Kenneth N. Rowland, Mar. 15, 1975 (div. Jan. 1982); 1 child, Jamie Christine. Student, Erlanger Sch. Nursing, 1973-74, U. Tenn. Chattanooga, 1973-74, Chattanooga State Community Coll., 1978—. Teller supr. First Tenn. Bank, Chattanooga, 1979-85; pvt. duty coordinator Home Health Care of East Tenn., Chattanooga, 1985-87, mem. adv. bd., 1985—; pvt. duty coordinator Valley Home Health Care, Jasper, Tenn., 1985-87, community edn. coordinator, 1987—; Mem. adv. bd. A-Med. Health Services, Chattanooga, 1986—. Fund raiser Multiple Sclerosis, Chattanooga, 1982—, Children's Miracle Network Telethon, Chattanooga, 1986, Arthritus Found., Chattanooga, 1986, Diabetes Assn., Chattanooga, 1987; mem. Chattanooga Ballet Guild, 1985—, Women of the Ch. of God, 1985—; mem. adv. bd. Ballet Tenn., 1987—. Fellow Chattanooga Wellness Council, In Home Services Council, Nat. Assn. for Feamale Execs., Greater Chattanooga Home Health Assn. (creator logo 1987, conf. planning, in home services council 1987). Office: Home Health Care of E Tenn 6237 Vance Rd Suite 1 Chattanooga TN 37421

ROWLAND, PATRICIA BRITTINGHAM, accountant, real estate executive; b. Guyton, Ga., July 14, 1941; d. Kenneth L. and Faye (McClelland) Brittingham; student DeKalb Coll., U. Ga.; m. J.D. Rowland; children—Philip Charles, Debora Faye, Jeffrey Allan. Various corp. sec.-treas. and controller positions, 1970-78; pres. Charles S. Roberts & Co., Atlanta, 1978-82; corp. sec. Spalding & Co., Securities Brokers, Atlanta, 1980-81; acct., salesperson Adams Realty, Inc., Royston, Ga., 1982-84; assoc. broker Pinehurst Realty Co., Lavonia, Ga., 1984-86; broker, co-owner Watermark Realty Co., Lavonia, 1986—. Democrat. Episcopalian. Home: 155 Teepee Ln Lavonia GA 30553 Office: Watermark Realty Co PO Box 613 Lavonia GA 30553

ROWLANDS, GENA, actress; b. Cambria, Wis., June 19, 1936; d. Edwin Merwin and Mary Allen (Neal) R.; m. John Cassavetes; children: Nicholas, Alexandra, Zoe. Student, U. Wis., Am. Acad. Dramatic Art, N.Y.C. Theatrical appearance include The Middle of the Night, 1956; films include The High Cost of Loving, 1958, Lonely Are The Brave, 1962, A Child is Waiting, 1962, Spiral Road, 1962, Faces, 1968, At Any Price, 1970, Minnie and Moscowitz, 1971, Woman Under the Influence, 1973, Two Minute Warning, 1976, Opening Night, 1977, The Brinks Job, 1978, One Summer Night, 1979, Gloria, 1980, Tempest, 1982, Love Streams, 1983, Light of Day, 1987, Another Woman, 1988; TV movies A Question of Love, 1978, Strangers, 1979, Thurday's Child, 1983, Early Frost, 1986, The Betty Ford

Story, 1987; numerous other TV appearances. Recipient Acad. award nomination. Mem. Actors Equity Assn., Screen Actors Guild, AFTRA, Am. Guild Variety Artists. Office: care Internat Creative Mgmt 8899 Beverly Blvd Los Angeles CA 90048

ROWLEY, JANET DAVISON, physician; b. N.Y.C., Apr. 5, 1925; d. Hurford Henry and Ethel Mary (Ballantyne) Davison; m. Donald A. Rowley, Dec. 18, 1948; children: Donald, David, Robert, Roger. B.S., U. Chgo., 1946, M.D., 1948. Intern Marine Hosp., USPHS, Chgo., 1950-51; research fellow Levinson Found., Cook County Hosp., Chgo., 1955-61; clin. instr. neurology U. Ill., 1957-61; research assoc. dept medicine U. Chgo., 1962-71, assoc. prof., 1971-78, prof., 1978—; research cytogenetic analysis of human hematologic malignant diseases; mem. Nat. Cancer Adv. Bd., 1979-84. Contbr. chpts. to books, articles to profl. jours. Trustee Adler Planetarium, 1978—. Served with USPHS, 1950-51. Recipient First Kuwait Cancer prize, 1984. Mem. Nat. Acad. Scis., Inst. Medicine, Am. Soc. Human Genetics, Am. Soc. Hematology, Am. Assn. Cancer Research. Episcopalian. Home: 5310 University Ave Chicago IL 60615 Office: 5841 Maryland Ave Box 420 Chicago IL 60637

ROWSE, PAMELA SUE, nurse; b. Barston, Calif., Jan. 10, 1953; d. Harold Glenn and Gloria Diane (Coyle) Brown; m. William Arthur Rowse Jr., Feb. 24, 1973; children: Amanda Nicole, Casandra Michele, Miranda Erin. Student in pre-nursing, U. Nebr., 1971-72; diploma, Lincoln Gen. Sch. of Nursing, 1974. RN. Operating room staff nurse Lincoln (Nebr.) Gen. Hosp., 1974-76; dir. nursing Syracuse (Nebr.) Community Hosp., 1976-77; field nurse Nuckolls County Home Health, Superior, Nebr., 1978-80; asst. dir. spl. care services Valley Hosp. Med. Ctr., Las Vegas, 1980-84; flight nurse Aeromed. Services Internat., Las Vegas, 1983-84; critical care coordinator Desert Springs Hosp., Las Vegas, 1984-87; pre-hosp. paramedic coordinator Univ. Med. Ctr., Las Vegas, 1987—. Author, creator (ednl. game) Treatment Modalities, 1987. Vol. Frontier Girl Scout council, Las Vegas, 1984-87, assoc. chairperson, 1986—, nat. conv. del., 1986—. Mem. Am. Assn. Critical Care Nurses (cert. critical care nurse, pres. So. Nev. chpt. 1985-86, chairperson publ. pub. relation, 1986-87), Nat. Assn. Female Execs. Democrat. Methodist. Office: Univ Med Ctr 1800 W Charleston Las Vegas NV 89106

ROY, BABETTE CHARLOTTE, artist; b. N.Y.C., Apr. 29, 1922; d. Frederick Christian and Emma Josephine (Sengele) Maasch; m. Francis Albert Roy, May 27, 1944; 1 child, Allan Gregory. Cert., Famous Artists Sch., Westport, Conn., 1971-73; student Traphagen Sch. Design, 1938-40, John Pike Watercolor Sch., 1970-78. Legal sec. Cravath, Swain & Moore, N.Y.C., 1941-44; census taker U.S. Census Bur., Orange County, N.Y., 1950; sec. Supt. Schs., Warwick, N.Y., 1954-65; artist, 1955—. One woman shows in Middletown, N.Y., 1983, Warwick, N.Y., 1965, 72, 80, Florida, N.Y., 1978, Goshen, N.Y., 1983; exhibited in group shows at Goshen, 1963-85, Newburgh, N.Y., 1980-85, N.Y.C., 1968, 70, Old Forge, N.Y., 1982; represented in permanent collections at Orange County Community Coll., Middletown, Pine Island, N.Y., Scottsdale, Ariz. Mem. Warwick Hist. Soc., N.Y., 1985, Warwick Beautification Com., 1985, Hosp. Aux., Warwick, 1985, Humane Soc., 1985. Mem. Salmagundi Club, Hudson Valley Art Assn., Knickerbocker Artists, North East Watercolor Soc. (co-founder, pres. 1975-83), Am. Artists Profl. League, Orange County Art Fedn. (pres. 1976-80, Dedication and Leadership award 1982). Republican. Episcopalian. Clubs: Mathews Garden, Officers (Langley AFB). Lodge: Parrish Mus. Avocations: reading, gardening, sailing, travel. Home: PO Box 916 Pine Hall Mathews VA 23109 Other: Pine Hall Mathews VA 23109

ROY, BERNICE ANITA, real estate agent; b. Los Angeles, Nov. 15, 1941; d. Bernhard and Rosa Lilly (Lieblich) R. Diploma, Trapp Fashion Ctr., Los Angeles, 1964; BS, UCLA, 1968. Cert. fashion designer. Research asst. psychology dept. UCLA, Los Angeles, 1965-67; vocat. counselor Goodwill Industry, Los Angeles, 1977-80; real estate agt. Royal Oaks Realty, Encino, Calif., 1983-86, Real Estate Brokers, Inc., Tarzana, CAlif., 1985-86, Jerry Weislow & Assocs., Tarzana, Calif., 1986—. Mem. San Fernando Valley Bd. Realtors. Republican. Jewish. Office: Jerry Weislow & Assocs 6038 Tampa Ave Tarzana CA 91356

ROY, CATHERINE ELIZABETH, physical therapist; b. Tucson, Jan. 16, 1948; d. Francis Albert and Dorothy Orme (Thomas) R.; m. Richard M. Johnson, Aug. 31, 1968 (div. 1978); children: Kimberly Anne, Troy Michael. BA in Social Sci. magna cum laude, San Diego State U., 1980; MS in Phys. Therapy, U. So. Calif., 1984. Staff therapist Sharp Meml. Hosp., San Diego, 1984—, chairperson patient and family edn. com., 1986-87, chairperson sex edn. and counselling com., 1987—, chairperson adv. bd. for phys. therapy, asst. for edn. program, 1987—; ptnr. C&J Assocs., San Diego, 1987—; lectr. patient edn., family edn., peer edn.; mem. curriculum rev. com. U. So. Calif. Phys. Therapy Dept., 1982; bd. dirs. Ctr. for Edn. in Health; writer, reviewer licensure examination items for phys. therapy Profl. Examination Services.. Researcher: Consumer Education: Physical Therapy, 1984-85. Tennis coach at clinics Rancho Penasquitos Swim and Tennis Club, San Diego, 1980-81; active Polit. Activities Network, 1985. Mem. Am. Phys. Therapy Assn. (research presenter nat. conf. 1985, del. nat. conf. 1986-88, rep. state conf. 1987, 88, Mary McMillan student award 1984, mem. exec. bd. San Diego dist. 1985—), AAUW, Nat. Assn. Female Execs., Am. Coll. Sports Medicine, Am. Congress Rehab. Medicine, Phi Beta Kappa, Phi Kappa Phi, Chi Omega. Home: 13133 Via del Valedor San Diego CA 92129 Office: Sharp Meml Rehab Ctr 7901 Frost St San Diego CA 92123

ROY, DELLA MARTIN, materials science educator, researcher; b. Merrill, Oreg., Nov. 3, 1926; d. Harry L. and Anna (Cacka) Martin; m. Rustum Roy, June 8, 1948; children—Neill R., Ronnen A., Jeremy R. B.S., U. Oreg., 1947; M.S., Pa. State U., 1949, Ph.D., 1952. Various research positions Pa. State U., University Park, part-time 1952-60, sr. research assoc. geochem., 1960-62, sr. research assoc. materials sci. engr., 1962-69, assoc. prof. materials sci. engr., 1969-75, prof. materials sci. engr., 1975—; cons. in field. Editor: Instructional Modules in Cement Science, 1985; editor jour. Cement & Concrete Research, 1971—. Contbr. articles to profl. publs. Chmn. status of cement, concrete Nat. Materials adv. bd., Washington, 1977-80; spl. adv. concrete durability Nat. Research Council, 1985—. Fellow Am. Ceramic Soc. (Jeppson Medal award 1982, Copeland award, 1987), Nat. Acad. of Engring (elected 1987), AAAS, Mineral. Soc. Am., Am. Concrete Inst. (keynote address 1980), Inst. Concrete Tech. (hon.); mem. Materials Research Soc. (chmn. cement symposia 1980, 81, 85, 86, 87), Nat. Acad. Engring. (elected mem. 1987). Democrat. Office: Pa State U 217 MRL University Park PA 16802

ROY, ELSIJANE TRIMBLE, federal judge; b. Lonoke, Ark., Apr. 2, 1916; d. Thomas Clark and Elsie Jane (Walls) Trimble; m. James M. Roy, Nov. 23, 1943; 1 son, James Morrison. J.D., U. Ark., Fayetteville, 1939; LL.D. (hon.), U. Ark., Little Rock, 1978. Bar: Ark. 1939. Atty. Ark. Revenue Dept., Little Rock, 1939-44; mem. firm Reid, Evrard & Roy, Blytheville, Ark., 1945-54, Roy & Roy, Blytheville, 1954-63; law clk. Ark. Supreme Ct., Little Rock, 1963-65; asso. justice Ark. Supreme Ct., 1975-77; U.S. dist. judge for Eastern and Western Dists. Ark., Little Rock, 1977—; judge Pulaski County (Ark.) Circuit Ct., Little Rock, 1966; asst. atty. gen. Ark., Little Rock, 1967; sr. law clk. U.S. Dist. Ct., Little Rock and Ft. Smith, 1967-75; Mem. med. adv. com. U. Ark. Med. Center, 1952-54; Committeewoman Democratic Party 16th Jud. Dist., 1940-42; vice chmn. Ark. Dem. State Com., 1946-48; mem. chmn. com. Ark. Constnl. Commn., 1967-68. Recipient Disting. Alumna citation U. Ark., 1978, Gayle Pettus Pontz award, 1986; named Ark. Woman of Yr. Bus. and Profl. Women's Club, 1969, 76, Outstanding Appellate Judge Ark. Trial Lawyers Assn., 1976-77. Mem. Nat. Assn. Women Lawyers, ABA, Ark. Bar Assn., AAUW, Little Rock Women Lawyers (pres. 1939, 42), Ark. Women Lawyers (pres. 1940-41), Mortar Bd., P.E.O., Delta Theta Phi., Chi Omega. Club: Altrusa. Office: US Dist Ct PO Box 3255 Little Rock AR 72203

ROY, KAREN JAMES, automation analyst; b. Summit, N.J., Aug. 19, 1955; d. Arthur Richard Jr. and Joyce Doyle (Murphy) R. Student, Houston Community Coll., 1977-79, 81-82. Service sec. Palmetto Ford Truck Sales, Miami, Fla., 1974-75; mgr. credit and accounts receivable Isabell Gerhart Co., Houston, 1975-78; mgr. data processing C.J. Thibodeaux & Co., Houston, 1978-84; automation analyst. InteCom Inc., Allen, Tex., 1984—; sec. Hewlett Packard-Greater Houston Regional Users Group, Houston, 1982-84. Mem. Women in Data Processing, Nat. Assn. Female Execs. Democrat. Roman Catholic. Club: Toastmasters (pres. intecommunicators 1981-87, v.p. 1987-88). Avocations: reading, ceramics, crocheting, scuba diving. Home: 6724 Coach House Ln Plano TX 75023 Office: InteCom Inc 601 InteCom Dr Allen TX 75002

ROY, SYLVIA RAY, real estate broker; b. Meridian, Miss., Mar. 19, 1936; d. Charles Adrian and Martha (Singley) Ray; BA, Sophie Newcomb Coll., 1957; MEd, Tulane U., 1968; m. John Overton Roy, Jr., Dec. 26, 1959; children: Charles Overton, John Parker. Tchr. secondary schs., New Orleans, 1957-67; with Trade-Mark Realty, New Orleans, 1968-75; broker, pres. Sylvia Roy Properties, Ltd., New Orleans, 1975-87; asst. prof. Loyola U. of the South, New Orleans, 1979-87; br. mgr. Merrill Lynch Realty, New Orleans, 1987—. Mem. Nat. Assn. Realtors, La. Realtors Assn. (dir.), Real Estate Bd. New Orleans (dir.), Women's Council Realtors (dir.), Grad. Realtors Inst., Certified Comml. Investment Member (pres. La. chpt.). Republican. Clubs: Orleans, D.A.R., World Trade Ctr., Plimsoll. Home: 70 Audubon Blvd New Orleans LA 70118 Office: 7820 Maple St New Orleans LA 70118

ROYER, MARLENE MILDRED, nurse; b. Sun Prairie, Wis., Mar. 21, 1941; d. Floyd Gerald and Sylvia Inga (Halverson) Gallagher; LPN, N.H. Vocat. Tech. Coll., 1975; A in Nursing Stratham Vocat. with honors Tech. Coll., 1987; m. Raymond Arthur Royer, June 4, 1960; children: Daniel R., William Raymond. Seamstress, Jack Winter Garment Co., Columbus, Wis., 1958-60; factoryworker Clarostat Mfg. Co. and United Tanners, Inc., Dover, N.H., 1960-68; nurses aide Riverside Rest Home, Dover, 1969-74; nurse Wentworth Douglass Hosp., Dover, 1975-76; nurse, charge nurse Mapleshade Nursing Home, East Lebanon, Maine, 1976; nurse, charge and med. nurse Riverside Rest Home, Dover, 1976-87, RN, supr., 1987—. Denmother Boy Scouts Am. N.H. nursing grantee, 1974-75; founder Nurse's Support Group for Profls., 1987—. Lutheran. Home: Box 254 County Farm Cross Rd Dover NH 03820

ROYLANCE, LYNN MICHELLE, electrical engineer; b. San Francisco, Nov. 27, 1951; d. Jack Clifton and Alice Helen (Gordh) R.; m. Julian Payne Freret Jr., June 21, 1979. BSEE, BS in Physics, MIT, 1972; MSEE, Stanford U., 1973, PhD in Elec. Engring., 1978. Instr. Stanford U., Stanford, Calif., 1974; mem. tech. staff Hewlett-Packard Labs., Palo Alto, Calif., 1977-81; project mgr. Hewlett-Packard Labs., Calif., 1981-87, project mgr. circuit tech. group research and devel., 1987—; Mem. program com. Internat. Symposium on Very Large Scale Integration Tech., 1982-85. Contbr. articles to profl. jours. NSF fellow, 1972-75. Mem. IEEE, Am. Inst. Mining and Metallurg. Engrs. (mem. program com., No. Calif. Electronic Material Symposium 1981, chmn. 1983-84, treas. No. Calif. section 1985-87), IEEE, Am. Mgmt. Assn., Phi Beta Kappa, Sigma Xi, Tau Beta Pi. Home: 1160 Laureles Dr Los Altos CA 94022 Office: Hewlett-Packard Labs 1501 Page Mill Rd Palo Alto CA 94304

RUARK, THEODORA WILMA, hospital administrator; b. Flandreau, S.D., Jan. 22, 1935; d. Theodore and Louella Lenora (Paul) Lathrop; B.S., U. Houston, Clear Lake, 1986; m. Vernon R. Ruark, May 16, 1976; children—Julie, Dwain, Darrell, Kenneth, Patrick. From credit mgr. to dir. hosp. bus. services U. Nebr. Med. Center, Omaha, 1962-80; mgr. hosp. bus. systems Lifemark Corp., Houston, 1980-84; asst. dir. bus. services St. Mary's Hosp., Galveston, 1985-87; corp. dir. accts. receivable, Sisters of Charity of Incarnate Word, Houston, 1987—. Mem. Internat. Comsumer Credit Soc., Am. Guild Patient Account Mgrs. (treas. elect 1981; award individual achievement, 1979, 80), Hosp. Fin. Mgmt. Assn., Am. Hosp. Assn., Am. Mgmt. Assn., Mensa. Republican. Methodist. Contbr. column to jour., 1979-85. Home: 543 Pompano Dr Hitchock TX 77563 Office: Sisters of Charity of Incarnate Word 6400 Lawndale Houston TX 77023

RUBACH, PEGGY, mayor; b. N.Y.C., July 7, 1947; m. Jon Rubach; children: Kristin, Jon, Matthew. BA in Psychology, SUNY, Buffalo; postgrad., Ariz. State U.; Diploma, Harvard U. Cost analyst, med. claims adminstr. Aetna Life and Casualty; project coordinator Mesa (Ariz.) community Coll.; dist. asst. Congressman John McCain; mayor City of Mesa, 1988—; mcpl. rep. Ariz. Consortium on Edn.; cons. Luth. Healthcare Network. Adv. bd. U. Ariz. Cancer Ctr.; treas. Ariz. Women Mcpl. Govt.; gov's. task force Cactus League Baseball; chmn. math. basic goals com. Ariz. Bd. Edn.; mem. Sister City Assn. of Mesa, East Valley Partnership, policy com. Nat. league of Cities' and Econ. Devel.; bd. dirs. Regional Pub. Transp. Authority; assoc. mem. Urban Land Inst. Home: 2145 E Glencove Mesa AZ 85030 Office: City of Mesa 55 N Center St PO Box 1466 Mesa AZ 85211-1466

RUBACKY, MARJORIE MCLAUGHLIN, career mgmt. co. exec.; d. Francis Michael and Agnes (Whelan) McLaughlin; m. Gerald E. Rubacky. B.A., Catholic U. Am. Product mgr. United Jersey Bank, Hackensack, N.J., 1972-75; sr. assoc. Career Mgmt. Assocs., N.Y.C., 1975-76; pres. Rubacky Assocs., N.Y.C., 1976-80; prin. Gallagher Mgmt. Assocs., 1980-83; corp. dir. Mainstream Access, Inc., N.Y.C. 1983—. Mem. Women's Econ. Round Table, Am. Soc. Personnel Adminstrn., Am. Women's Econ. Devel. Corp. Club: Montclair Golf. Home: 201 Barringer Ct West Orange NJ 07052 Office: 995 3rd Ave New York NY 10022

RUBB, PEGGY-GRACE PLOURD, dancer, artistic director; b. Hartford, Conn., Sept. 27, 1931; d. Launcelot J. and Margaret (Feeney) Plourd; m. Milton Robert Rubb, June 6, 1953; children—Bonnie Leigh, Eric John, Michael Robert. Student Hartt Conservatory of Music, Hartford, 1938-49, Shenandoah Conservatory, Winchester, Va., 1949-51, Froman Profl. Ballet Sch., New London, Conn., 1959-62, Hampton Acad. Ballet, Va., 1962-63, Nat. Ballet, Washington, 1963-66. Tchr., R.H. Lee Elem. Sch., Glen Burnie, Md., 1951-52; dancer Common Glory Jamestown Corp., Williamsburg, Va., 1963; accompanist Annapolis Modern Dance Assn., Md., 1973; ballet mistress dance studio, Crofton, Md., 1974-78; dance instr. gymnastics camp Washington Coll., Chestertown, Md., 1977; dance coach Glen Burnie Artistic Skate Club, 1980-81; artistic dir. Crofton-Bowie Sch. of Ballet and affiliated cos., 1978—; choreographer Tom Thumb Players, Annapolis, 1972; dancer Hampton Roads Civic Ballet, Va., 1962-63. Choreographer; composer; lyricist. Bd. dirs. Annapolis Children's Theatre, 1977-78, choreographer Nat. Assn. for Regional Ballet, Inc. Choreography Conf., 1987. Mem. Md. Council for Dance, Nat. Assn. Female Execs., Profl. Dance Tchrs. Assn., Inc., Internat. Platform Assn., Phi Beta Sigma. Club: U.S. Naval Acad. Class '53 Wives (pres. San Diego 1957-58, pres. New London 1959-60). Avocations: sketching; painting. Home: 1 Pennsylvania Ave Edgewater MD 21037 Office: 2411 Crofton Ln Chelsea House Suite 2 Crofton MD 21114

RUBENFELD, ALISON, human resources executive; b. New Hyde Park, N.Y., Feb. 8, 1958; d. Eugene and Elaine (Dalberg) Bermack; m. Alan A. Rubenfeld, June 21, 1986. BA, Brandeis U., 1980; MS, U. Pa., 1981. Personnel asst. Madison Sq. Garden Corp., N.Y.C., 1982-83; sr. personnel rep. N.Y. State Urban Devel. Corp., N.Y.C., 1983-85, asst. v.p., 1985-86, v.p. human resources, 1986—; rep. Urban Devel. Corp. to N.Y. State Tng. Council. Office: NY State Urban Devel Corp 1515 Broadway New York NY 10036

RUBENS, MONIQUE LIANE, correspondent, communications administrator; b. N.Y.C., May 8, 1951; d. Stanley Maurice and Denise (Blum) R.; m. Douglas Russell Krohn, May 24, 1986. Certificat pratique de la langue francaise, Sarah Lawrence Coll., 1971-72; BA, U. Pa., 1973, MA, 1973; MLitt, Oxford U., Eng., 1978. Editorial asst. Random House, Inc., N.Y.C., 1973-74; asst. to dir. meetings Council on Fgn. Relations, N.Y.C., 1979-80; mgr. Multinat. Strategies Inc., N.Y.C., 1980-82; correspondent Gemini News Service, London, 1983—; mgr. communications Sterling Drug Inc., N.Y.C., 1985—; correspondent West Africa mag., London, 1980-84. Mem. Internat. Assn. Bus. Communicators, UN Correspondents Assn., Fgn. Press Assn. (sec. 1984-85).

RUBENSTEIN, ELIZABETH SUAREZ, cosmetic manufacturing executive; b. Lucena City, P.I., Dec. 28, 1942; d. Inocencio Bolos Suarez and Eufrocina Laceste Quinsaat; came to U.S., 1969, naturalized, 1975; B.S. in Chem. Engring., U. Santo Tomas, Manila, 1964; m. Leslie Ronald Rubenstein, July 2, 1976; 1 dau., Lisa Anne. Chemist, H. Kohnstamm, N.Y.C., 1969; analytical chemist Allied Testing & Research, Hillsdale, N.J., 1970; research dir. Chromex Chem. Corp., Bklyn., 1970-75; tech. dir. Chem. Spray (A.T.I.), Totowa, N.J., 1975, Krueger (Cosmetic) Corp., Bklyn., 1975-78, Paramount Cosmetics, Union City, N.J., 1978—. Mem. Am. Inst. Chem. Engrs., Am. Chem. Soc., Soc. Cosmetic Chemists, Cosmetic Toiletry and Fragrance Assn. Home: 153 Freeman St Brooklyn NY 11222 Office: 3710 Hudson Ave Union City NJ 07087

RUBENSTEIN, NANCY LEE, newspaper editor; b. Fall River, Mass.; d. R. Ralph and Rose (Edelstein) Horne; m. Edwin R. Rubenstein, Sept. 23, 1951; 1 child, David A. BA, Boston U., 1950. With various newspapers, 1951-71; editor Today Newspapers, Butler, N.J., 1972-86; editor Suburban Life, North Caldwell, N.J. Recipient more than 60 journalistic awards. Mem. N.J. Press Assn., N.J. Press Women, PICA Club. Club: North Jersey Press. Home: 33 Meadowbrook Ln Cedar Grove NJ 07009 Office: Today Newspapers 10 Park Pl Butler NJ 07405

RUBIN, ALICE FISHER, civic leader; b. Bklyn., June 8, 1940; d. Harold L. and Betty Fisher; B.A., St. John's U., 1964, M.A. (Ford Found. scholar), 1968, JD Bklyn. Law Sch., 1988; m. Lowell M. Rubin, Dec. 7, 1972; children—David Fisher, Emily Claire. Research asst. N.Y. State Conf. Mayors, Albany, 1966; spl. asst. Nassau County (N.Y.), 1967; research and liaison coordinator N.Y.C. Comptroller's Office, 1970-74; asst. commr. Agy. for Child Devel., N.Y.C., 1974-78; asst. sec. to Gov. N.Y. State for intergovtl. relations Exec. Chamber N.Y. State, N.Y.C., 1978-83; adj. lectr. City U. N.Y., 1971-82, CUNY Tech., 1987—; adj. asst. prof. Grad. Sch. Pub. Adminstrn., L.I. U., 1984. Bd. trustee Bklyn. Pub. Library, 1975—; bd. advisors N.Y.C. Tech. Coll. Para Legal Program 1986; co. chmn. Membership Bklyn. Bar Assn. (chmn. student relations com. 1987-88), bd. dirs. Bklyn. chpt. ARC, 1977—, N.Y.C. Tech. Coll. Found., 1982; founder Jewish Women's Leadership Caucus, Bklyn., 1981. Home: 141 Argyle Rd Brooklyn NY 11218

RUBIN, BARBARA CAROL, psychotherapist, educator; b. N.Y.C., Feb. 20, 1940; d. Charles and Sarah (Heller) Drutman; m. Stanley Joseph Rubin, Dec. 29, 1957 (div. Oct. 1968); children: Gregg, Jennifer Rubin Yates, Michael; m. William Joseph Ruscansky, July 4, 1984. Cert. in English, Northeastern U., Boston, 1970; BA, MA in Psychology, Boston U., 1982; PhD, U. So. Calif., 1987. Cert. tchr., Calif., Mass.; cert. marriage, family and child counselor. Tchr. Hull & Weymouth Schs., Mass., 1981-82; therapist Survival, Inc., Quincy, Mass., 1981-82; pvt. practice psychotherapist Hull, 1981-82; tchr. Los Angeles Unified Sch. Dist., 1982—; pvt. practice psychotherapist West Hollywood, Calif., 1982—; therapist Los Angeles Ctr. for Psychology, 1985-86; tutor U. So. Calif., Los Angeles, 1982—. U. So. Calif. grantee, 1983-85. Mem. Calif. Assn. Therapists, Group Psychotherapy Assn., Psi Chi. Home: 1010 N King's Rd #108 West Hollywood CA 90069

RUBIN, BARBARA JEAN, real estate licensing program director; b. Ashtabula, Ohio, Aug. 30, 1945; d. Marvin Louis and Edith Louise (Stevenson) R. AB, Grove City Coll., 1967; MEd, Temple U., 1971; postgrad., U. Pa., 1978-79. Elem. tchr. Colonial Sch. Dist., Plymouth Meeting, Pa., 1967-79; bus. mgr. Lifespring, Phila., 1979-81; asst. dir. ops. Lifespring, San Rafael, Calif., 1981-82, asst. to v.p., 1982-83; program dir. Assessment Systems, Inc., Phila., 1983—. Trustee Presbyn. Ch. of Chestnut Hill, Phila., 1986—, mem. Christian edn. com. 1986—. Mem. Real Estate Educators Assn., Phi Delta Kappa. Home: 8561 Trumbauer Dr Wyndmoor PA 19118 Office: Assessment Systems Inc 718 Arch St Philadelphia PA 19106

RUBIN, JANICE ANN, lawyer; b. Newark, Nov. 12, 1941; d. Carl and Helen Edith (Baletin) Edelstein; m. Burton Jay Rubin, Feb. 17, 1974; 1 dau., Jennifer Sidell. A.B. cum laude, Smith Coll., 1964; J.D., George Washington U., 1973. Bar: Va. 1974, U.S. Supreme Ct. 1979. Editor McKinsey & Co., Washington, 1971-72; editor Bur. Nat. Affairs, Inc. Patent, Trademark & Copyright Jour., Washington, 1972-74; legis. atty. Am. Law div. Congressional Research Service, Library of Congress, Washington, 1974—; antitrust cons. Contbr. in field. Mem. Fed. Bar Assn. (v.p. D.C. Cir. 1986—, v.p. Capitol Hill chpt. 1983-84, pres.-elect Capitol Hill chpt. 1984-85, pres. Capitol Hill chpt. 1985-86), ABA. Club: Smith Coll. Washington. Office: 101 Independence Ave SE Washington DC 20540

RUBIN, NANCY RUTH ZIMMAN, journalist, author; b. Boston, Nov. 25, 1944; d. Stuart Wendell and Ethel Charlotte (Rabinovitz) Zimman; m. Peter H. Rubin, July 9, 1967; children: Elisabeth Kara, Jessica Ann. BA, Tufts U., 1966; MA in Teaching, Brown U., 1967. English tchr. Brighton High Sch., N.Y., 1967-68, N.Y. Schs., Pittsford, 1969-70; playwright, dir. Equity Library Theatre, Roundabout, Joseph Jefferson and St. Clement's theaters, N.Y.C., 1971-74; writer Westchester-Gannett newspapers and mags., L.I., 1975-77; free-lance reporter N.Y. Times, N.Y.C., 1977—; faculty affiliate Bush Ctr. in Child Devel., Yale U., New Haven, 1981—; mem. Westchester County Women's Adv. Bd., chair, 1988. Author: The New Suburban Women: Beyond Myth and Motherhood, 1982, The Mother Mirror: How A Generation of Women is Changing Motherhood in America, 1984; contbg. editor Parents Mag., 1987—; contbr. articles to nat. jours., mags., newspapers. Time, Inc.-Bread Loaf Writers' Colony scholar, 1979. Fellow McDowell Colony; mem. Author's Guild, Am. Soc. Journalists and Authors, NOW. Democrat. Jewish.

RUBIN, RHEA JOYCE, library consultant; b. Chgo., June 14, 1950; d. Harold and Edith (Botkin) B.; m. Lawrence Berman, June 7, 1975; 1 child, Hannah Rubin. BA, U. Wis., 1972, MA, 1973. Dir. Oreg. Regional Library for The Blind and Handicapped, Salem, 1976-78; librarian Nat. Council on Aging, Inc., Washington, 1978-80; cons. Rubin Cons., Oakland, Calif., 1980—; cons. Ill. Dept. Corrections, Springfield, 1981, Mass. Dept. Corrections, Norfolk, 1985-86, Calif. Dept. Mental Health, Sacramento, 1985-87, Fla. State Library, Tallahassee, 1984, Mo. State Library, Jefferson City, 1985, Oreg. State Library, Salem, 1988, Calif. State Library, Sacramento, 1987-88, N.Y. Dept. Mental Health, Albany, 1987, Tex. State Library, Austin, 1987. Author: Using Bibliotherapy, 1978, Bibliotherapy Sourcebook, 1978; (with others) Challenge of Aging, 1983; contbr. articles to profl. jours., 1973—. Mem. ALA (chair numerous com. 1972—, Shaw award 1980). Home and Office: 5860 Heron Dr Oakland CA 94618

RUBIN, ROCHELLE ELISA, copywriter; b. Bklyn., Feb. 5, 1957; d. Arthur and Madeline (Grossman) Rubin; m. John N. Palumbo, Feb. 23, 1980 (div. 1982). Student Goucher Coll., 1975-76, R.I. Sch. Design, 1975; B.S. in Mktg. Mgmt., NYU, 1979; postgrad. Sch. Visual Arts. Pvt. med. cons., N.Y.C., 1980-82; freelance writer, Dallas, 1982; copywriter Cunningham & Walsh, Dallas, 1983-84, Bozell & Jacobs, Dallas, 1984-86, John Brown & Ptnrs., Seattle, 1986-87; freelance writer, Seattle, 1987—; sr. writer, producer Cole & Weber, Portland, Oreg., 1988—; writer nat. advt. consumer campaign La Quinta Motor Inns. Recipient Cert. of Achievement, Art Dirs. Club Houston, 1983, 1 show cert. merit ADS Mag, 1986. Jewish. Home: 2336 SW Osage St Apt 705 Portland OR 97205 Office: Cole & Weber 55 SW Yamhill Portland OR 97205

RUBIN, SHARON L., film producer, director; b. Chgo., Aug. 6, 1950; d. Joseph and Jewel Rubin. BFA, Drake U., 1971; MFA, UCLA, 1974. Ind. producer Los Angeles, 1981-86; v.p. programming J2 Communications, Los Angeles, 1986-87; ptnr., producer Essanee Prodns., Santa Monica, Calif., 1987—. Producer, dir.: (film) Portrait of a Teenage Drug Abuser, 1987; producer Clio award-winning commls. Mem. Women in Film. Office: Essanee Prodns PO Box 5168 Santa Monica CA 90405

RUBIN, VERA COOPER, research astronomer; b. Phila., July 23, 1928; d. Philip and Rose (Applebaum) Cooper; m. Robert J. Rubin, June 25, 1948; children: David M., Judith S. Young, Karl C., Allan M. B.A., Vassar Coll., 1948, M.A., Cornell U., 1951; Ph.D., Georgetown U., 1954; D.Sc. hon., Creighton U., 1978, Howard U., 1988. Research assoc. to asst. prof. Georgetown U., Washington, 1955-65; physicist U. Calif.-LaJolla, 1963-64; astronomer Carnegie Instns., Washington, 1965—; Chancellor's Disting. prof. U. Calif.-Berkeley, 1981, 87; vis. com. Harvard Coll. Obs., Cambridge, Mass., 1976-82. Assoc. editor: Astrophys. Jour. Letters, 1977-82; editorial bd.: Sci. Mag., 1979—; contbr. numerous articles sci. jours.; assoc. editor: Astron. Jour., 1972-77. Pres.'s Disting. Visitor, Vassar Coll., 1987. Mem. Smithsonian Instn. Council, 1979-85; Phi Beta Kappa scholar, 1982-83. Mem. Am. Astron. Soc. (council 1977-80), Internat. Astron. Union (pres.

Commn. on Galaxies 1982-85), Assn. Univs. Research in Astronomy (dir. 1973-76), Nat. Acad. Scis. (Space Sci. Bd. 1974-77, 81, 87—, com. on human rights), Am. Acad. Arts and Scis., Phi Beta Kappa. Democrat. Jewish.

RUBINI, EILEEN, fashion designer; b. Union City, N.J., June 2, 1948; d. Julius and Mary (Fitzgerald) R. Student, Iona Coll., Fashion Inst. Tech., N.Y.C.; studied design at Parsons Sch., N.Y.C. With pub. relations and advt. depts. Jaeger Co., N.Y.C., 1972-75; merchandiser Arthur Richards Woman, Inc., N.Y.C., 1975-78; v.p., merchandiser Jerry Silverman Sportswear, N.Y.C., 1978-79, Don Sayres Co., N.Y.C., 1979-81; v.p. design Yukiko Hanai, N.Y.C., 1981-83; v.p., designer Signatures Inc., N.Y.C., 1983-86; designer, owner Eileen Rubini Inc., N.Y.C., 1986—; freelance merchandiser, designer Kellwood Cos., N.Y.C., 1986—. Office: 214 W 39th St Suite 902 New York NY 10018

RUBINI, GAIL, education director; b. Washington, Dec. 6, 1950; d. Milton and Frances Kagan; m. Conrad Gleber; children: John Patrick, David Conrad. BA, UCLA, 1972; MFA, R.I. Sch. Design, 1976; MBA, U. Ill., Chgo., 1981. V.p. fin. Artist Prodn. Press, Chgo., N.Y.C., 1976—; adminstr. grants City of Chgo., 1979-80; edn. dean Ctr. for Media Arts, N.Y.C., 1981-86; dir. edn. SCS Bus. and Tech. Inst., N.Y.C., 1986—. Author: Darkroom Dynamics. Recipient grant Polariod Corp., 1979-81, Ill. Arts Council, 1980, Nat. Endowment for Arts, 1982. Home: 158 Franklin St New York NY 10013 Office: Gleber Printing 225 Varick St New York NY 10013

RUBIN PIERCE, HILDA (HILDA HERTA HARMEL), painter; b. Vienna, Austria; came to U.S., 1940; m. S. Thomas Friedman, 1988; 1 child by previous marriage, Diana Rubin Daly. Student, Art Inst. of Chgo.; studied with Oskar Kokoschka, Salzburg, Austria; studied with Dorothy Wood, Eng. Art tchr. Highland Park (Ill.) Art Ctr., YWCA, Highland Park, Sandburg Village Art Workshop, Chgo., Old Town Art Center, Chgo.; owner, operator Hilda Pierce Art Gallery, Laguna Beach, Calif., 1981-85; dir. art workshops on cruise ships; guest lectr. mus. and art tours in France, Switzerland, Austria, Italy. One-woman shows include Fairweather Hardin Gallery, Chgo., Sherman Art Gallery, Chgo., Marshall Field Gallery , Chgo.; exhibited in group shows at Old Orchard Art Festival, Skokie, Ill., Union League Club (awards), North Shore Art League (awards), ARS Gallery of Art Inst. of Chgo.; represented in numerous private and corporate collections; commissioned monoprints, oils and murals for superliner Carnival Cruise Lines; contbr. articles to Chgo. Tribune Mag., American Artist Mag., Southwest Art Mag., SRA publs., others. Mem. Arts Club of Chgo. Office: Hilda Pierce Studio PO Box 7390 Laguna Niguel CA 92677

RUBINSON, LAURNA, social psychologist, educator; b. N.Y.C., Feb. 9, 1945; d. Fred Yale and Sylvia (Newman) Goldberg. BS, L.I. U., 1966; MS, Southern Conn. U., 1969; PhD, U. Ill., Champaign, 1976. Tchr., supr. Branford (Conn.) Pub. Schs., 1966-71; instr. Danville (Ill.) Area Coll., 1971-73; instr. U. Ill., Champaign, 1973-76, prof., 1976—. Author: Health Education: Foundations for the Future, 1984, Research Techniques for the Health Sciences, 1987; mem. editorial bd. Jour. Sch. Health Edn., Jour. Sex Edn. and Therapy, Jour. Sex Research. Fellow Am. Sch. Health Assn. (disting. service award 1986); mem. Am. Pub. Health Assn., Am. Psychological Assn., Assn. for Advancement Health Edn. Office: Univ Ill 1206 S 4th St #114 Champaign IL 61820

RUBINSTEIN, SHIRLEY JOY, nursing service executive; b. Toronto, Ont., Can., Nov. 19, 1927; came to U.S., 1928, naturalized, 1948; d. Harry Hyman and Ida Ruth (Albert) Adel; m. Philip F. Rubinstein, Aug. 17, 1947; children—David Brian, Wendy Sue, Hope Terri. With Jewish Agy. for Palestine, Washington, 1947-49; coordinator Nursing Staff, Inc., 1975-78; co-founder, pres. Nursing Services, Inc., Silver Spring, Md., 1978—; founder, pres. Fantasy Factory Inc., Pegasus Limosine Services. Democrat. Jewish. Club: B'nai Birth. Office: PO Box 4133 Silver Spring MD 20904

RUBLE, ANN, clergywoman; b. Seattle, Oct. 26, 1953; d. Monte Rahe and Stella (Terefinko) Ruble; m. Francis Michael Trotter, Aug. 29, 1984. Cert. sec., Met. Bus. Coll., Seattle, 1972. Ordained to ministry Ch. of Scientology, 1980. Minister Ch. of Scientology, Seattle, 1980—, dir. pub. affairs, 1983; pres. Ch. of Scientology of Wash. State, Seattle, 1984—. Bur. chief Jour. Freedom News, 1984—. Mem. Citizen's Commn. Human Rights, Seattle, 1984—, Com. on Religious Liberties, Seattle, 1985—. Office: Ch of Scientology of Washington State 2004 Westlake Ave Seattle WA 98121

RUBOTTOM, CAROLE MARIE, music educator; b. Seattle, July 28, 1944; d. Virgil Earl and Jessie Margaret (Cress) Cutler; m. Lawrence Lemar Rubottom, July 31, 1965. BA in Music, U. Calif., Santa Barbara, 1966. Cert. tchr., Calif. Music tchr. Pleasant Valley Sch. Dist., Camarillo, Calif., 1967-69; founder, dir., owner Jr. Music Acad., Ventura, Calif., 1967—. Author music instrn. manuals, 1976, 88. Mem. Ventura Arts Council. Mem. Music Tchrs. Assn. Calif., Nat. Assn. Female Execs. Democrat. Home: 697 Via Cielito Ventura CA 93003 Office: Jr Music Acad 2351 E Main St Ventura CA 93003

RUBSCHLAGER, JOAN SNIDER, baking corporation executive; b. Pontiac, Ill., Jan. 16, 1938; d. George W. and Jewel (Underwood) Snider; m. Paul A. Rubschlager, June 29, 1963. B.S. in Elem. Edn., Ill. Wesleyan U., 1960; postgrad. Nat. Coll. Edn., 1971. Tchr. pub. schs., Park Ridge, Ill., 1960-71, tchr. lang. arts, 1971-75, dir. gifted program, 1975-77; sec., treas. Rubschlager Baking Corp., Chgo., 1977—. Mem. Nat. Restaurant Assn., (exhibitors adv. bd. 1980-83, 87-90), Nat. Food Distributors Assn. (mfrs. council 1982—), Ill. and Chgo. Food Mfg. Council, City of Hope (v.p. 1981-84, chmn. bd. dirs. 1984-86), Alpha Lambda Delta, Phi Kappa Phi, Delta Omicron. Office: Rubschlager Baking Corp 3220 W Grand Ave Chicago IL 60651

RUBY, SALLY ANNE, city official; b. Hershey, Pa., Sept. 25, 1944; d. Edward Mark and Sarah Ellen (Tobias) Keeney; B.S., Labanon Valley Coll., Annville, Pa., 1973; M.Ed., Millersville (Pa.) State Coll., 1974. Counselor, Fla. Div. Corrections, 1974-76; compliance coordinator City of Clearwater (Fla.), 1976—. Mem. loan com. Neighborhood Housing Service, Clearwater; mem. bi-racial com. Pinellas County Sch. Bd.; mem. task force Project Self-Sufficency; program chair 3d Ann. State Civil Rights Conf., chairperson fundraising project Family Service Ctr., 1987, mem. devel. com.; sec. adv. bd. Clearwater Adult Eve. Sch.; bd. dirs. Pinellas Opportunity Council. Mem. NAACP (life), Nat. Assn. Human Rights Workers, Internat. Assn. Ofcl. Human Rights Agys., NOW, Fla. Assn. Community Relations Profls., Millersville U. Alumni Assn., Nat. Orgn. on Disability. Home: 416 N Lincoln Ave Clearwater FL 34615 Office: PO Box 4748 Clearwater FL 33618

RUCKER, MARILYN JOANNE, health services administrator; b. Detroit, Sept. 19, 1953; d. Kenneth Joseph and Isabelle Nan (Current) Stanton; m. Laurence Keith Rucker, June 3, 1972; children: Desiree Kristine, Kenneth Laurence. AA in Sociology, Yuba Coll., 1982; BA in Social Psychology, Park Coll., 1982. Enlisted USAF, 1973; clk. nurse research Wilford Hall Med. Ctr, Lackland AFB, Tex., 1973-74; clk. clin. records USAF Clinic, San Vito, Italy, 1974-77; NCOIC personnel and adminstrn. USAF Hosp., Blytheville AFB, Ark., 1977-80; asst. NCOIC resource USAF Hosp., Beale AFB, Calif., 1980-82; chief of adminstrn. USAF Hosp., Wurtsmith AFB, Mich., 1982-84; dir. personnel and adminstrn. USAF Hosp., Reese AFB, Tex., 1984-85, commdr. med. squadron sect., 1984-85, dir. patient affairs, 1985-86; chief tech. plans USAF Sch. Aerospace Medicine, Brooks AFB, Tex., 1986—. Recipient Silver award Girl Scouts Am., 1986. Mem. Am. Coll. Healthcare Execs., Nat. Assn. Female Execs., Air Force Assn., Air Force Sergeants Assn., Nat. Officers Assn., Nat. Assn. Miniature Enthusiasts. Democrat. Methodist. Club: Tuskegee Airmen, Inc. (San Antonio). Office: USAF Sch Aerospace Med TSZ Brooks AFB TX 78235-5301

RUCKER, SUZANNE JUNE, certified financial planner; b. Coral Gables, Fla., June 27, 1945; d. Thomas John, Jr. and June Ethel Agusta (Stones) R.; BBA, Fla. Atlantic U., 1971, MBA, 1975. Cert. fin. planner, lic. real estate agt. Assoc. dir. Am. Soc. Cons. Pharmacists, 1971-73; chpt. specialist Epilepsy Found. Am., 1973-74; assoc. dir. devel. Fairfax Hosp. Assn. Found., Springfield, Va., 1974-81; dir. devel. Arlington Hosp. Found. (Va.), 1982-86; fin. planner Koelz Drake Advisors, Falls Church, Va., 1986—; instr. George Washinton U.; seminar speaker in field. Bd. dirs. Ronald McDonald House Washington, Salvation Army Aux. Washington, Rep. Working Women's Forum. Fellow Nat. Assn. Hosp. Devel. Republican. Lodge: Optimists. Office: 520 N Washington St #401 Falls Church VA 22046-3535

RUCKERT, ANN JOHNS, musician, singer; b. N.Y.C., Mar. 12, 1945; d. G. Wallace and Elizabeth (Johns) R. Student, Julliard Sch., 1961-69, NYU, 1969-70, Royal Acad. Music, London, 1972; studies in composition with Nadia Boulanger, Paris, 1972-73; studies with Helen Hobbs Jordon, N.Y.C., 1973-75; studies with David Sdrin Collyer, 1975-78. Profl. musician over 2, 000 commercially released records, 1960—; owner, pres. Ann Ruckert Music, N.Y.C. and Los Angeles, 1980—; chairperson N.Y. Jazz Mus., N.Y.C. 1977-79; bd. dirs. Jazzmobile, N.Y.C., 1983-87; TV com. Grammy awards, 1985-87; creative staff Lifetime Achievement awards show, 1987; adv. Universal Jazz Coalition, N.Y.C., 1979-87; cons. rec. industry. musician, singer (recs.) Straws, Greatest Hits (Gold Record award, 1975). Commr. Deed, N.Y., 1986—, Schoeberg Collection N.Y.C. Pub. Library; mem. county com. Westside Manhattan, 1980-87. Mem. Nat. Acad. Rec. Arts and Scis. (named Most Valuable Player 1982, trustee, gov., v.p. N.Y. chpt.), Soc. Singers (bd. dirs. N.Y.C. chpt.). Democrat. Episcopalian. Home and Office: 119 W 71st St New York NY 10023

RUCQUOI, GERALAINE KLEIN, genetics educator; b. Beaumont, Tex., Apr. 17, 1939; d. Jack E. and Lurlene (Seale) Klein; m. James Julien Rucquoi, Sept. 8, 1958 (div. Sept. 1981); children: Marc, David. BS with honors, SUNY, Purchase, 1973; MS, Sarah Lawrence Coll., 1976. Cert. family therapist. Cons. N.Y. State Mental Retardation Dept., Queens, 1973-77; genetic counselor Yale U. Sch. Medicine, New Haven, 1977—; clin. instr. genetics Sarah Lawrence Coll., Bronxville, N.Y., 1977—. Contbr. articles to profl. jours. Mem. Conn. Team Theater Sports. Mem. Am. Soc. Human Genetics, Nat. Soc. Genetic Counselors (nominating com. 1987), Alumni Assn. SUNY, Purchase (pres. 1975-76). Club: New Haven Tennis Assn. Office: Yale Sch Medicine Dept Human Genetics 333 Cedar St PO Box 3333 New Haven CT 06510

RUDACILLE, SHARON VICTORIA, medical technologist; b. Ranson, W. Va., Sept. 11, 1950; d. Albert William and Roberta Mae (Anderson) R.; B.S. cum laude, Shepherd Coll., 1972. Med. technologist VA Center, Martinsburg, W. Va., 1972—, instr. Sch. Med. Tech., 1972-76, asso. coordinator edn., 1976-77, edn. coordinator, 1977-78, quality assurance officer clin. chemistry, 1978-80, lab. service quality assurance and edn. officer, 1980-84, clin. chemistry sect. leader, 1984—; adj. faculty mem. Shippensburg (Pa.) State Coll., 1977-78. Mem. Am. Soc. Med. Tech., Am. Soc. Clin. Pathologists, W.Va. Soc. Med. Technologists, Shepherd Coll. Alumni Assn., Sigma Pi Epsilon. Baptist. Home: PO Box 14 Ranson WV 25438

RUDAITIS, LORETTA GLORIA, microbiologist; b. Chgo., Dec. 15, 1956; d. John and Lydia Martha (Marasas) Rudaitis. BS in Biol. Scis., U. Ill., Chgo., 1980. Chem. technician Helen Curtis Industries, Inc., Chgo., 1980-81, microbiologist, 1981-86, sr. microbiologist, 1986—. Mem. Soc. Indsl. Microbiology. Office: Helene Curtis Industries Inc 4401 W North Ave Chicago IL 60639

RUDD, CAROLYN ELAINE, sports management firm executive, consultant; b. Norfolk, Va., Aug. 12, 1949; d. Alvin R. and Margaret E. (McMannenn) R.; m. D.K. Ulrich, Oct. 10, 1978 (div. May 1981); children: Geoffrey Len, Bryan Ray. Student, Queens Coll. Pres. Rudd Racing, Chesapeake, Va., 1975-80; advt. dir. promotions Charlotte Motor Speedway, Harrisburg, N.C., 1980-84; cons. Jefferson Broadcasting, Charlotte, N.C., 1984-85; pres., co-owner Sports Mgmt. Group, Charlotte, 1985—. Fundraiser Multiple Sclerosis, Charlotte, 1984-85. Mem. Nat. Motorsports Press Assn., Nat. Assn. Sportscars, Am. Racing Writers Assn. Home: 4900 Carmel Rd Charlotte NC 28226 Office: Sports Mgmt Group 1901 Roxborough Rd Suite 220 Charlotte NC 28211

RUDDICK, BONNIE LOU KNEEBONE, writer, lecturer; b. Bethlehem, Pa., Aug. 29, 1946; d. George John Gregory Sysko and Shirley (Smith) Kale; children by previous marriage: Kimberly Anne, Mark David; m. Douglas Hampton Ruddick, July 12, 1980; stepchildren: Debbi, Daniel. Student, l'Univ. Laval, Que., Can., summer 1967; BA, East Stroudsburg U., 1977, MA, 1985. Pub. speaker to sales and civic orgns., 1979—; communications specialist Easton Area Sch. Dist., Pa., 1979-80; free-lance writer North Am. Moravian, Bethlehem, 1979—; owner Markim Assocs. Pub. Relations and Writing Cons., Brodheadsville, Pa., 1986—; presenter living history The Moravians-From Herrnhut to Bethlehem, 1980-86; guest speaker City of Bethlehem Advent Breakfast, 1981; guest lectr., 1984—; faculty Am. history dept. Northampton County Area Community Coll., parttime 1985-86; dir. community relations LaBar Village, Pa., 1985; writer, producer children's programs with religious themes; writer, moderator religious book discussion groups Inspirational Exchanges, 1980—. Committeewoman Rep. Party, Bethlehem, 1978-79; co-founder Moravian Hall Sq. Mus. and Gift Shop, Nazareth, Pa., 1980; founder Speakers Bur., 1987, Parents for Students Against Drunk Drivers, 1987; Rep. candidate Pa. House Reps., 1988; bd. dirs. Single Parent Outreach and Housing Devel. Assn., 1987—, Monroe County Com. Housing and Homelessness, 1987—. Mem. Pleasant Valley Citizens' Adv. Com., Monroe County Sesquicentennial Pub. Relations Com. Mem. Moravian Hist. Soc., Pocono Mountains C. of C. Women's Exec. Council, West End Bus. Assn., LWV, Burnley Workshop of the Poconos, Phi Alpha Theta. Club: Faith at Work. Avocations: designer needlepoint canvases, oil painting, sewing, other crafts. Home: RD 2 Box 443-B Saylorsburg PA 18353 Office: Markim Assocs PO Box 756 Broadheadsville PA 18322

RUDELL, FREDRICA, marketing educator, researcher; b. N.Y.C., Nov. 23, 1946; d. Norman J. and Betty M. (Sachs) R.; m. Andrew Alan Beveridge, Apr. 17, 1970; 1 child, Sydney Jocelyn. BA, Vassar Coll., 1968; MBA, Columbia U., 1975, M of Philosophy, 1976, PhD, 1978. Asst. prof. mktg. Baruch Coll. CUNY, 1978-82; asst. prof. mktg. Iona Coll., New Rochelle, N.Y., 1982-85, assoc. prof. mktg., 1985—. Author: Consumer Food Selection and Nutrition Information, 1979. Mem. Am. Mktg. Assn., Assn. for Consumer Research, Beta Gamma Sigma. Office: Iona Coll Hagan Sch Bus 715 North Ave New Rochelle NY 10801

RUDEN, VIOLET HOWARD (MRS. CHARLES VAN KIRK RUDEN), religious educator, practitioner; b. Dallas; d. Millard Fillmore and Henrietta Frederika (Kurth) Howard; B.J., U. Tex., 1931; C.S.B., Mass. Metaphys. Coll., 1946; m. Charles Van Kirk Ruden, Nov. 24, 1932. Radio continuity writer Home Mgmt. Club broadcast Sta. WHO, Des Moines, 1934; joined First Ch. of Christ Scientist, Boston, 1929; C.S. practitioner, Des Moines, 1934—; C.S. minister WAC, Ft. Des Moines, 1942-45; 1st reader 2d Ch. of Christ Scientist, Des Moines, 1952, Sunday sch. tchr., 1934—; instr. primary class in Christian Sci., 1947—. Trustee Asher Student Found. Drake U., Des Moines, 1973. Mem. Women in Communications, Mortar Bd., Orchesis, Cap and Gown, Theta Sigma Phi (pres. 1931). Republican. Club: Des Moines Women's. Home: 5808 Walnut Hill Dr Des Moines IA 50312

RUDERMAN, JEANNE WENDY, pediatrician, neonatologist; b. Los Angeles, June 30, 1953; d. George Lawrence and Ruth (Bornstein) Ruderman. B.S. in Biol. Scis., U. So. Calif., 1974; M.D., UCLA, 1978. Diplomate Am. Bd. Pediatrics. Intern, resident in pediatrics Los Angeles County-U. So. Calif. Med. Ctr., Los Angeles, 1978-81; fellow in neonatology Cedars-Sinai Med. Ctr., Los Angeles, 1981-83, attending staff neonatologist, 1983—; asst. prof. pediatrics UCLA Sch. Medicine, 1984—. Contbr. articles to med. jours. Fellow Am. Acad. Pediatrics; mem. Calif. Perinatal Assn., Phi Beta Kappa. Office: Cedars-Sinai Med Ctr Dept Pediatrics 8700 Beverly Blvd Room 8700 Los Angeles CA 90048

RUDIN, ANNE NOTO, mayor; b. Passaic, N.J., Jan. 27, 1924; m. Edward Rudin, June 6, 1948; 4 children. B.S. in Edn., Temple U., 1945, R.N., 1946; M.P.A., U. Calif., Sacramento, 1983. R.N., Calif. Mem. faculty Temple U. Sch. Nursing, Phila., 1946-48, mem. nursing faculty Mt. Zion Hosp., San Francisco, 1948-49; mem. Sacramento City Council, 1971-83; mayor City of Sacramento, 1983—. Pres., LWV, Riverside, Sacramento, 1957, 61, Calif. Elected Women's Assn., 1973-85; mem. Dem. State Central Com., Calif., 1984-85; bd. dirs. Sacramento Commerce and Trade Orgn., 1984-85. Recipient Woman of Yr. award Soroptimist Club, 1976; Women in Govt. award U.S. Jaycee Women, 1984; Woman of Distinction award Sacramento Area Soroptimist Clubs, 1985; named to Golden Key Honor Soc. Calif. State U., 1985. Mem. U.S. Conf. of Mayors. Office: City of Sacramento 915 I St Sacramento CA 95814

RUDKO, FRANCES HOWELL, lawyer; b. Elgin, Okla., Nov. 25, 1935; d. Paul Basil and Bertie Eleanor (Maggart) Howell; divorced; children—Michael, Stephen Craig, Peter Gregory. B.A., So. Meth. U., 1959; J.D., U. Ark., 1973, M.A. in History, 1983. Bar: Ark. 1973, U.S. Dist. Ct. (we. dist.) Ark. 1973. Tchr. English, Grand Prairie Schs. (Tex.), 1959-60; sole practice law, Fayetteville, 1973—; judge Prairie Grove Mcpl. Ct. (Ark.), 1976. Bd. dirs. Arts Center Ozarks, Springdale, 1976-77, North Ark. Symphony Soc., 1981—, Butterfield Trail Retirement Center, 1981—. Mem. Washington County Bar Assn. (sec. treas. 1977), Ark. Bar Assn (chmn. family law sect. 1975-76), Fayetteville C. of C., ABA, Am. Assn. Women Lawyers, AAUW, Phi Beta Kappa. Methodist. Clubs: Altrusa (treas. 1979-81), Washington County Med. Aux. (pres. 1980-81). Home: 1410 Oakcliff St Fayetteville AR 72701 Office: 3000 Market St Suite B Fayetteville AR 72701

RUDNICK, IRENE KRUGMAN, lawyer, state legislator; b. Columbia, S.C., Dec. 27, 1929; d. Jack and Jean (Getter) Krugman; A.B. cum laude, U. S.C., 1949, JD, 1952; m. Harold Rudnick, Nov. 7, 1954; children—Morris, Helen Gail. Admitted to S.C. bar, 1952; individual practice law, Aiken, S.C., 1952—, now ptnr. Rudnick & Rudnick; instr. bus. law, criminal law U. S.C., Aiken, 1962—; tchr. Warrenville Elem. Sch., 1965-70; supt. edn. Aiken County, 1970-72; mem. S.C. Ho. of Reps., 1972-78, 80-84, 86—.; Active, Aiken County Democratic Party, S.C. Dem. Party. Recipient Citizen of Yr. award, 1976-77, Bus. and Profl. Women's Career Woman of Yr., 1978, Aiken County Friend of Edn. award. Mem. NEA, S.C. Tchrs. Assn., Aiken County Tchrs. Assn., Am. Bar Assn., Aiken County Bar Assn., Nat. Order Women Legislators, AAUW, Alpha Delta Kappa. Jewish. Clubs: Order Eastern Star, Hadassah, Am. Legion Aux., Lioness. Office: PO Box 544 224 Park Ave Aiken SC 29802

RUDNICK, PAULETTE FENTON, educational administrator; b. N.Y.C., May 7, 1947; d. William Nelson and Beatrice June (Lee) Fenton; m. Philip Rudnick, Aug. 28, 1966; children—Danielle Hope, William Alan. B.S., L.I. U., 1974. Adminstrv. asst. Queens Day Prep. Sch., Sunnyside, N.Y., 1964-74; asst. prin. Boro Hall Acad., Bklyn., 1975-82, dir., 1982—. Office: Boro Hall Acad 17 Smith St Brooklyn NY 11201

RUDNIK, SISTER MARY CHRYSANTHA, college administrator; b. Winona, Minn., Dec. 2, 1929; d. Basil John and Sarah (Knopick) Rudnik; student Loyola U., 1951-52, Felician Coll., 1952-54, Cardinal Stritch Coll., 1954-57, Coll. St. Francis, 1957; Ph.B., DePaul U., 1958; postgrad. Mundelein Coll., 1959-60, Northeastern Ill. State U., 1964; M.A., Rosary Coll., 1962. Joined Congregation of Sisters of St. Felix of Cantalice, Roman Cath. Ch., 1948; cert. fund raising exec. Nat. Soc. Fund Raising Execs. Page, clk. Hill Reference Library, St. Paul, 1946-48; tchr. Holy Innocents Sch., Chgo., 1948-49, 50-54, St. Bruno Sch., Chgo., 1954-55, Holy Family Sch., Cudahy, Wis., 1955-57, Good Counsel High Sch., Chgo., 1958-67; instr. Felician Coll., Chgo., 1963-86, head librarian, 1957-82, dir. devel. and public relations, 1975-86. Organizer, coordinator Felician Library Service, 1966-74, Arts and Crafts Festival, 1972-86; coordinator instl. self-study for accreditation North Central Assn.; mem. task force for study of instl. research for Ill. Assn. Community and Jr. Colls., 1968; library cons. St. Clement Sch., 1969. Rev. Andrew Bowhuis meml. scholar Cath. Library Assn., 1960. Cert. fund raising exec. Nat. Soc. Fund Raising Execs. Mem. Council for Advancement and Support of Edn., Cath. Library Assn. (life, chmn. No. Ill. unit 1968-69, exec. bd. 1981-87), Council Support and Advancement Edn., Art Inst. Chgo. (life), Council on Library Tech. (v.p. 1970, pres. 1971). Address: 3800 Peterson Ave Chicago IL 60659

RUDOLPH, BEVERLY ANN, customer relations service and consulting company executive; b. Waukesha, Wis., Dec. 15, 1941; d. George William and Marjorie (Held) Seidl; m. Forest Rudolph, Jr., Nov. 28, 1959 (div. July 1966); children—Ronald George, Rebecca Lynne. Student public schs. Oconomowoc, Wis., 1959. Dancer, entertainer, nightclubs, Milw., 1968-70; exec. sec., agt. Mut. Trust Life Ins. Co., Brookfield, Wis., 1970-73; adminstrv. asst., paraprofl. counselor Counseling Ctr., Milw., 1973-77; dist. sales mgr. Automated Mktg. Systesm, Inc., Detroit, 1979-83; customer relations mgr. Bob Carter Ford Inc., Inver Grove Heights, Minn., 1983-84; pres. Custom Follow-up Inc., South St. Paul, 1984—. Coordinator personnel, sec. bd. dirs. Underground Switchboard crisis line, Milw., 1971-76. Mem. Wilderness Soc., Nat. Assn. Female Execs., Nat. Wildlife Fedn., Sierra Club, St. Paul C. of C., South St. Paul-InverGrove Heights C. of C. Avocations: Hiking; backpacking; horseback riding Office: Custom Follow-up Inc 450 Southview Blvd #250 South Saint Paul MN 55075

RUDOLPH, SONDRA, zoological society executive; b. Phila., Jan. 2, 1934; d. Irving S. and Nettie (Gruman) Bernstein; m. Howard Victor Rudolph, Oct. 3, 1954; children—Steven Paul, Andrew Lawrence. B.S., Temple U., 1955. Vice pres. mktg. U.S. Postal Service Fed. Credit Union, Washington, 1978-83; personnel dir. CMG Telemarketing (formerly Campaign Mktg. Group), Alexandria, Va., 1983-84; dir. dept. human resources Friends of Nat. Zoo, Nat. Zool. Park, Washington, 1985—; mem. Credit Union Promotional Com. Greater D.C., 1981-82. Recipient Golden Mirror award Credit Union Exec. Soc. for newsletter, 1981, for handbook, 1981, for membership brochure, 1982, for splty. advt., 1982. Mem. Am. Mktg. Assn., Am. Soc. for Personnel Adminstrn. Republican. Jewish. Home: PO Box 1107 Bodega Bay CA 94923 Office: Friends of Nat Zoo Washington Zoological Park Washington DC 20008

RUDY, LINDA S(HARON), controller, accountant; b. Newark, Nov. 9, 1957; d. David and Zelda (Cohen) R. BS, Hofstra U., 1979; cert., Inst. Fin. Edn., 1984, Wall St. Tng. Program, 1983. Research mgr. Haley Info. Research, N.Y.C., 1979-82; claims investigator European-Am. Bank, N.Y.C., 1982-84; acctg. supr. Sunrise Savs. and Loan, Boynton Beach, Fla., 1984-85; acctg. mgr. Sunrise Realty and Mgmt., Boynton Beach, Fla., 1985-86; asst. v.p., asst. controller Royal Palm Savs. Assn., West Palm Beach, Fla., 1986—; vol. income tax assistance, Miami, Fla., 1986-87; instr. Inst. Fin. Edn.,Fla., 1985-86; cons. Fla. Atlantic U., Boca Raton, Fla, 1986; acctg. coordinator March of Dimes Walkathon, West Palm Beach, 1987-88. Vol. Project Literacy, Hunger Project. Mem. Fin. Mgrs. Soc., Nat. Assn. Female Execs., Nat. Council Career Women, Mensa. Democrat. Jewish. Office: Royal Palm Savs Assn 100 Australian Ave West Palm Beach FL 33406

RUDY, RUTH CORMAN, state legislator; b. Millheim, Pa., Jan. 3, 1938; d. Orvis E. and Mabel Jan (Stover) Corman; m. C. Guy Rudy, Nov. 21, 1956; children—Douglas G., Donita Rudy Koval, Dianna F. Degree in x-ray tech. Carnegie Inst., 1956; student Pa. State U., 1968-71. Clk. of cts. County of Centre (Pa.), Bellefonte, 1976-82; rep. Pa. Gen. Assembly, Harrisburg, 1982—. Mem. Democratic Nat. Com., 1980—; past pres. Pa. Fedn. Dem. Women, Harrisburg; pres. Nat. Fedn. Dem. Women, 1987—. Named Woman of Yr., Pa. Fedn. Dem. Women, 1982. Methodist. Office: Pa Ho of Reps PO Box 115 Harrisburg PA 17120

RUDY, SHAWN ELIZABETH, advertising executive; b. Chgo., July 13, 1956; d. John Franklin and Nancy (Nern) R. BS in Bus. Adminstrn., Ohio State U., 1978. Brand asst. Procter and Gamble, Cin., 1978-80, asst. brand mgr., 1980-82; asst. account mgr. HBM/Creamer, Boston, 1982-83, account mgr., 1983-85, account supr., 1985-87, v.p., 1987; account supr. Leonard Monahan Saabye Lubars, Providence, 1987—. Office: Leonard Monahan Saabye Lubars 127 Dorrance St Providence RI 02903

RUEBE, BAMBI LYNN, environmental/interior designer; b. Huntington Park, Calif., Nov. 13, 1957; d. Leonard John Ruebe and Vaudis Marie Powell. BS, UCLA. Millwright asst. Kaiser Steel Corp., Fontana, Calif., 1976-79; electrician Fleetwood Enterprises, Riverside, Calif., 1977; fashion model internat., 1977-85; freelance draftsman 1982-83; project coordinator Philip J. Sicola Inc., Culver City, Calif., 1982-83; prin. designer Ruebe Inclusive Design, Highland, Calif., 1983—; cons. mfg. design Burlington Homes New Eng. Inc., Oxford, Maine, 1987—, DeRose Industries, Chambersburg, Pa., 1984, Skyline Corp., Redlands, Calif., 1982-84; cons.

lighting Lightways Corp., Los Angeles, 1984—; mem. design rev. bd. San Bernardino (Calif.) Downtown Main St. Redevel. Co., 1987-88. Mem. World Affairs Council, Inland So. Calif., 1986; co-chmn. civil rights com. AFL-CIO, Fontana, 1978-79. Recipient Cert. Merit Scholastic Art award Scholastic Mags. Inc., Southeastern Calif., 1974. Mem. Nat. Trust for Hist. Preservation. Democrat. Office: Ruebe Inclusive Design 27000 Meines St Highland CA 92346

RUEDY, ELISABETH, mathematician, educator; b. Basel, Switzerland, Feb. 27, 1942; came to U.S., 1968; d. Konstantin and Ruth (Leuenberger) Kaufmann; m. Reto Anton Ruedy, Jan. 11, 1968; children: Lucas, Nicole. Diploma in math., U. Basel, 1965; postgrad. in math. and philosophy, Harvard U., 1968-69; cert. in gestalt synergy, Rubenfeld Synergy Inst., N.Y.C., 1984. Systems engr. IBM Corp., Switzerland, 1965-68; faculty mem. The New Sch., N.Y.C., 1969—; asst. chairperson St. Ann's Sch., Bklyn., 1973-81; pvt. practice as learning therapist N.Y.C., 1980—; dir. Therapy for Post-Traumatic Stress, N.Y.C., 1984—; lectr., seminar leader YWCA, N.Y.C., 1981—; patient advocate rape intervention program St. Luke's Hosp., N.Y.C., 1982—. Mem. Am. Assn. for Counseling and Devel., Gestalt Synergy Assn. Home: 610 W 113th St #4B New York City NY 10025 Office: The New Sch 66 W 12th St New York City NY 10011

RUEGER, SALLY PATRICIA, hotel executive; b. Rockville Ctr., N.Y., Nov. 17, 1959; d. William Frederick and Ann Helen (Arrison) R. BA in cum laude, Middlebury Coll., 1981. Asst. programs office Internat. Ho., N.Y.C., 1981-82; asst. advt., mktg. and sales Club Med Sales, Inc., N.Y.C., 1982-84; mgr. incentive and corp. sales French Nat. Railroads, N.Y.C., 1985-87; mgr. sales USA/ Can. Husa Internat. Hotel, N.Y.C., 1987—. Co-chair recreation com. E. 82d St. Block Assn., N.Y.C., 1984. Mem. Soc. Incentive Travel Execs. (chair N.Y. regional activities, 1987). Democrat. Roman Catholic. Home: 232 E 82d St #5D New York NY 10028 Office: 747 3d Ave New York NY 10017

RUEST, SUE ELLEN, computer specialist; b. Huntington, W.Va., Sept. 19, 1944; d. Ray Shirlon and Edith Abigail (Blood) Colburn; m. Richard G. Ruest, Oct. 3, 1970; children: Christopher Andrew, Peter Michael, Jeffrey Scott. BA, Centre Coll. Ky., 1966. Data analyst market research dept. Procter & Gamble Co., Cin., 1966-68; analyst, programmer Computer Scis. Corp., Glenn Dale, Md., 1968-69; sr. programmer Apollo project UNIVAC, Glenn Dale, Md., 1969-72; programmer customer service Control Data Corp., Rockville, Md., 1980-81; systems mgr. 3-M Corp., Middleway, W.Va., 1981-83; sr. programmer, analyst Mack Trucks, Inc., Hagerstown, Md., 1983—; tchr. adult edn. St. Maria Goretti High Sch., Hagerstown, 1983-85; instr. Hagerstown Jr. Coll., 1986—. Bd. dirs., chmn. water safety, instr. swimming ARC, Martinsburg, W.Va., 1976-79. Democrat. Presbyterian. Home: 304 Greenbriar Rd Martinsburg WV 25401 Office: Mack Trucks Inc 1999 Pennsylvania Ave Hagerstown MD 21740

RUETENIK, SAMMY JEAN, educator; b. Monroe, Mich., June 23, 1929; d. Samuel Jether and Alta Ruth Rubley; B.A., U. Mich., 1950; M.A., Oakland U., 1971; m. David Gibbons Ruetenik, Aug. 25, 1950 (div. 1983); children—Kathryn, Christopher, Heidi, Daniel, Bennett. Tchr., Lansing (Mich.) Schs., 1950-51, Lakewood (Ohio) Schs., 1963-67; tchr. Bloomfield Hills (Mich.) Schs., 1967-78, 79-82, asst. prin., coordinator early entrance program Bloomfield Sch., 1978-79; owner MSSAM, 1979—, Bloomfield Hills Edn. Assn., 1984—. Vice-pres. Lakewood Safety Council, 1959; regional dir., bd. dirs. Mich. Reproductive Freedom Council, 1981-83; elected to Walled Lake, (Mich.) Bd. Edn., 1987, bd. dirs. Mich. Women's Hall of Fame. Cleve. Council Human Relations grantee, 1963. Mem. Mich. Edn. Assn. (women's task force, pres. women's caucus), NEA (regional coordinator, v.p. women's caucus, pres. women's caucus), Mich. Women's Studies Assn., Coalition for Non-Sexist Edn., NOW, Nat. Women's Polit. Caucus, Mich. Women's Polit. Caucus, Mich. Social Studies Council. Democrat. Presbyterian. Author: The Family, 1979. Address: 244 Neptune Walled Lake MI 48088

RUETER, SHARON, artist; b. Childress, Tex., Mar. 21, 1946; d. William Ray and Margaret (Skeels) Woodley; m. Paul Rueter. AA, Kilgore Jr. Coll., 1967; BA in Elem. Edn., Stephen F. Austin State U., 1969, MA in Art, 1970, MEd in Secondary Edn., 1973. Tchr. art Kilgore (Tex.) High Sch., 1970-72; grad. asst. Stephen F. Austin State U., Nacogdoches, Tex., 1972-73; tchr. English, art, speech Kountze (Tex.) High Sch., 1973-76; tchr. art Am. Sch. Guatemala, 1976-78, Am. Sch. Quito, Ecuador, 1979-80; tchr. Am. Sch. Maracaibo, Venequela, 1980-81. One woman shows in Tex. and Venezuela; group shows in Quatemala, Ecuador, Uruguay, Tex.; exhibited in British Inst. of Montevideo, Uruguay, 1985. Mayoral candidate City of Kountze, 1976. Home and Studio: 3604 Branigan Ln Austin TX 78759

RUFFALO, MARIA THERESE, engineer; b. Seattle, Feb. 26, 1963; d. Patrick and Helen (Eckhardt) R.; m. Joseph Patrick Otterbine, May 5, 1987. BS in Mech. Engring., U. Rochester, 1985. Proj. engr. Polycast Tech. Corp., Hackensack, N.J., 1985-86, sr. project engr., 1986-87; cons. Polycast Tech. Corp., Hackensack, 1987; project engr. ink div. J.M. Huber Corp., Edison, N.J., 1987—. Mem. ASME, Nat. Assn. Female Execs. Democrat. Roman Catholic. Home: S-11 Sutton Dr Matawan NJ 07747 Office: JM Huber Corp Printing Ink Div 333 Thornall St Edison NJ 08818

RUGGLES, JANET KAY, strategic planner; b. Paris, Ky., Sept. 13, 1955; d. Alois H. and Mildred (Stone) R. BA in Urban Studies, U. N.C., 1977; MA in City and Regional Planning, Ohio State U., 1979; MBA in Policy Analysis, U. Ky., 1983, postgrad. in internat. diplomacy and commerce, 1983-84; student, Seikei U., Tokyo, 1984. Researcher Battelle Meml. Inst., Columbus, Ohio, 1979-81; project planner Booker Assn., Lexington, Ky., 1981-82; researcher U. Ky. Inst. for Mining and Minerals Research, Lexington, 1982-84; sr. internat. mfg. planner Data Gen., Westboro, Mass., 1984-87, pres.; sr. corp. strategic planner Sencorp, Cin., 1987—. Mem. Nat. Assn. Female Execs. Club: Toastmasters (pres. Westboro chpt. 1986-87). Office: Sencorp 8485 Broadwell Rd Cincinnati OH 45244

RUIZ, AMELIA ESTELLE, bilingual education educator; b. E. Chgo., Ind., Aug. 5, 1931; d. Jose and Juanita (Avaloz) Martinez; m. Rudy Garcia Ruiz, Oct. 12, 1957; children: Rudy, Margie. BS, Purdue U., 1971, MEd, 1973; cert. Bilingual Bicultural Proficiency, Ind. U., 1981. Cert. elem., bilingual tchr. Tchr. English to speakers of other langs. Block Jr. High Sch., E. Chgo., 1971-72, B. Harrison Elem. Sch., E. Chgo., 1972—; pre-sch. tchr. E. Chgo. City Sch., 1986—. Author: Computer Endorsement, 1987. Den mother Boy Scouts Am., Hammond, Ind., 1965. Mem. Ind. Nat. Assn. Bilingual Edn. (sec. 1984-85, treas., 1985—), Ind. Nat. Assn. Edn. (treas. 1984—, cert. 1986), Bilingual Tchrs. E. Chgo. Democrat. Roman Catholic. Office: Benjamin Harrison Elem 4406 Indianapolis Blvd East Chicago IN 46312

RUIZDELUZURIAGA, LAURA LEE, housing grant administrator; b. Melrose, Mass., May 12, 1959; d. Leo Patrick and Pearl Ann Bates Smart; m. Luis Ernest RuizdeLuzuriaga, May 10, 1980 (div. 1985); children: Tania Maris, Nicole Erin. BA, Tufts U., 1981; postgrad., SW Tex. State U. Program devel., instr. Adult Edn./Cen. Tex. Coll., Killeen, 1982-85; program facilitator Greater Lawrence (Mass.) Community Action Council, 1985; programs mgr. Adult Edn. div. Lawrence Pub. Schs., 1985-86, curriculum devel. specialist City of Lawrence, 1986; human services dir. Edn. and Tng. div. Lawrence Housing Authority, 1986—. Author: (textbook) Pre-Literacy ESL, 1984, (curriculum) AT&T Mfg. ESL, 1987; author/producer video series ESL on Television, 1986. Mem. S. Barker Sch. PTO, Methuen, 1987-88. Named one of Outstanding Young Women of Am., 1984. Mem. Nat. Assn. Female Execs., Am. Diabetes Assn., ESL Consortium, Dept. Pub. Welfare/ET Task Force, Mass. Assn. for Adult and Continuing Edn., Lower Merrimack VAlley Pvt. Industry Council. Baptist. Home: 7 Ruskin Ave Metuen MA 01844 Office: Lawrence Housing Authority 353 Elm St Lawrence MA 01841

RUIZ-VALERA, PHOEBE LUCILE, librarian; b. Barranquilla, Colombia, Jan. 27, 1950; d. Ramon and Marion (Mehlman) Ruiz-Valera; m. Thomas Patrick Winkler, Mar. 27, 1981. BA cum laude, Westminster Coll., 1971; MLS, Rutgers U., 1974; MA, NYU, 1978. Library trainee Passaic (N.J.) Pub. Library, 1973-74, reference librarian, 1974; library assoc., cataloger NYU Law Library, N.Y.C., 1974-79, asst. curator, cataloger, 1979-81; librarian III, cataloger Rutgers U. Library, New Brunswick, N.J., 1981-82; chief cataloger Assn. Bar City N.Y., 1982-85, head tech. services, 1985—. Mem. ALA, Am. Assn. Law Libraries, Law Library Assn. Greater N.Y., Reforma, Salalm. Democrat. Presbyterian. Office: Assn Bar City NY 42 W 44th St New York NY 10036

RULE, ANN, author; 4 children. Grad. U. Washington with Deg. in English, 1954, postgrad. in police sci. Former policewoman, Seattle; free-lance writer newspapers, True Detective, Cosmopolitan, others; vol. Seattle Crisis Clinic; author non-fiction books: The Stranger Beside Me, 1980, The I-5 Killer, Want-Ad Killer, Lust Killer, Beautiful Seattle, 1984, Small Sacrifices, 1987, novel Possession, 1983; occasional pseudonym, Andy Stack; speaker on subject of serial killers. Address: PO Box 98846 Seattle WA 98198

RULE, BARBARA JEAN, sales executive; b. Wilmington, Del., Mar. 22, 1957; d. Joseph McBath and Jean Elizabeth (Tuckerman) R. BS in Biology, Emory U., 1979; MBA in Mktg., Ga. State U., 1982. Research analyst Majers Corp., Atlanta, 1982-83; mgr. market research Stone Mfg. Co., Greenville, S.C., 1983-85; asst. mgr. sales research L'eggs Products, Inc., Winston-Salem, N.C., 1985-88, mgr. sales forecasting, 1988—; cons. Edwards Baking Co., Atlanta, 1982. Vol. Big Sister Program. Mem. Am. Mktg. Assn., Alpha Mu Alpha, Chi Omega (pres. chpt. 1978-79, sec. 1977-78). Club: Symphony Chorale (Winston-Salem). Avocations: singing, ice skating, swimming, sports. Office: L'eggs Products Inc 5660 University Pkwy Winston-Salem NC 27105

RULE, GERALDINE LEVINGSTON, nurse; b. Houston, Nov. 23, 1924; d. Charles Graham and Clara Theresa (Hebert) Levingston; m. Carl Allen Rule, Mar. 17, 1947 (div. 1968); children—Charles Ernest, Judy Kaye, Peggy Jean. Lic. vocat. nurse St. Francis Sch. Practical Nursing, Carlsbad, N.Mex., 1962; A.S., San Jacinto Jr. Coll., Pasadena, Tex., 1980. R.N., Tex. Staff vocat. nurse Carlsbad Meml. Hosp., 1963-67, Northshore Med. Plaza, Houston, 1967-76, Eastway Gen. Hosp., Houston, 1976-78; staff nurse Jefferson Davis Hosp., Houston, 1980—. Democrat. Baptist. Home: 11900 Barryknoll Ln Houston TX 77024

RUMACK, CAROL M., radiologist; b. Washington, June 10, 1943; m. Barry H. Rumack, June 20, 1964; children: Rebecca, Marc. BS, U. Chgo., 1965; BS, MD, U. Wis., 1969. Diplomate Am. Bd. Diagnostic Radiology. Intern U. Md., 1969-70; resident in radiology U. Colo., Denver, 1971-74; mem. staff St. Anthony Hosp., 1975-76, Denver Gen. Hosp., 1976-80, U. Colo. Health Scis. Ctr., Denver, 1980—; acting chief diagnostic radiology Sch. Medicine U. Colo., Denver, 1987—, instr. radiology, 1976-78, asst. prof. radiology, pediatrics, 1978-81, assoc prof. radiology, pediatrics, 1987—; dir. pediatric radiology Sch. Med. U. Colo., Denver, 1987—. Mem. editorial bd. Pediatric Radiology, Diagnostic Radiology; contbr. articles to profl. jours. Fellow Am. Coll. Radiology, 1984, Am. Inst. Ultrasound Med. 1986; recipient research award U. Colo. Health Scis. Ctr. Dept. Radiology, 1984. Mem. Am. Assn. Women Radiologists (pres. 1981-82), Am. Coll. Radiology (com. pub. info. 1984—, various others coms.), Am. Inst. Ultrasound Med. (bd. govs. 1984—, mem. various coms.), Am. Med. Women's Assn. (regional gov. of reg. XI, 1984-85), Am. Roentgen Ray Soc., Assn. U. Radiologists, Colo. Radiological Soc.(radiation protection com. 1976—, various other coms.), Midwestern Pediatric Radiologist Assn., Radiological Soc. N.Am., Rocky Mt. Radiological Assn., Soc. Pediatric Radiology, Soc. Radiologists Ultrasound, Am. Acad. Pediatrics (nomination com. sect. radiology, 1981-85). Office: U Colo Health Scis Ctr 4200 E Ninth Ave A030 Denver CO 80262

RUMLEY, FRANCINE CASANOVA, realtor; b. Charleston, S.C.; d. Ernest Casanova and Eugenia Rose (Passailaigue) Gibbs; m. Willard Lee Rumley; children: Jeffery Lane, Willard Lee III, Gary Beecher. Secretarial Sci., King's Bus. Sch., 1964; N.C. Real Estate for Brokers, Pitt Community Coll., 1976. Cert. real estate broker, N.C. Reference librarian George H. & Laura Brown Library, Washington, N.C., 1974-83, real estate broker The Rich Co., Washington, N.C., 1978-86, sales mgr., 1986—; cons. career Beaufort Community Coll., Washington, N.C., 1981—, area high schs., Washington, N.C., 1979—; cons. hist. George H. Brown Library, Washington, N.C., 1972-83. Co-chmn. county Heart Fund Dr., 1975; apptd. mem. Hist. Dist. Commn., 1984—, chmn. 1987—; mem. adv. commn. Washington Devel., 1987—; apptd. Community Adv. Cmnn., 1988. Mem. Washington Bd. Realtors (pres. 1982-83, bd. dirs.), N.C. Bd. Realtors, Nat. Bd. Realtors, Washington Jr. Women's Club (Pres.'s award 1974, pres. 1975-76). Democrat. Presbyterian. Home: 212 W 12th St Washington NC 27889 Office: The Rich Co Route 1 Box 17 Washington NC 27889

RUMMEL, SUE ANN, research scientist; b. Nampa, Idaho, Dec. 3, 1949; d. Talma Henry and B. Jeanne (Mitchell) Rummel; B.S. cum laude in biology, So. Nazarene U., 1971; M.S., U. Mo., 1981; PhD. U. Kans. Sch. Medicine, 1988. Med. technologist Bapt. Meml. Hosp. Clin. Lab., Kansas City, Mo., 1972-75, asst. supr. hematology lab., 1975-81; instr. Affiliated Sch. Med. Tech., Kansas City, Mo., 1981-84, dir. Research/Devel. Dept. Clin. Labs., 1982—; teaching asst. U. Kans., 1984—; lectr. in field. Cert. med. technologist, specialist in hematology. Mem. Am. Soc. Clin. Pathologists, Sigma Xi Sci. Research Soc. Office: Neurosci Research (151) VA Med Ctr 4801 Linwood Blvd Kansas City MO 64128

RUMPFF, BARBARA BRYANT, marketing executive, consultant; b. Orlando, Fla., Sept. 25, 1951; d. Allen Leroy Bryant and Trudy (Whittington) McGarity; m. Cornelis J. Rumpff, May 15, 1976. B.S., Fla. State U., 1972, M.B.A., 1974; student U. Valencia, Spain, 1971, U. Belgrade, Yugoslavia, 1973. Research asst. Chevron Petroleum, The Hague, Holland, 1974; field mgr. Procter & Gamble, Cin., 1975-77; sales promotion mgr. Internat. Playtex, Stamford, Conn., 1978; pres. European Am. Mktg. Corp., Atlanta, 1979—. Pres. Assn. Internat. Students in Econs. and Commerce, Tallahassee, Fla., 1970-74. Mem. Am. Mktg. Assn., Orlando C. of C., World Trade Club, Netherlands C. of C. in the U.S. Office: European Am Mktg Corp 7205 Chattahooche Bluff Dr Atlanta GA 30360

RUMSEY, F. M. CLAIRE, painter, sculptor, poet; b. N.Y.C., May 11, 1916; d. David and Frances (Davidge) Rumsey; grad. N.Y. Sch. Applied Design for Women, 1937, Degree in Advanced Window Display, 1939; money mgmt. student SUNY, 1978-79. One-woman shows: Warner Pub. Library, 1974, 75, Greenburgh Pub. Library, 1975, County Ct. House, White Plains, N.Y., 1977; group shows include: Guild Hall, E. Hampton, N.Y., 1960, Expn. Intercontinentale, Monaco, 1965, 66, Katonah (N.Y.) Gallery, 1958-69; represented in pvt. collections; creator painted poems; contbr. poems to numerous mags. Mem. NOW. Home: 467-A Heritage Hills Somers NY 10589

RUNGE, MARY MUNSON, pharmacist; b. Donaldsonville, La., July 25, 1928; d. John Harvey and Mary Leona (Brown) Lowery; m. Wilbert Percy Munson, Dec. 7, 1946 (div.); 1 dau., Katherine Marie; m. Alfred Joseph Runge, Sept. 4, 1976. B.S., Xavier U., 1948; Sc.D. (hon.), Mass. Coll. Pharmacy, 1980; D.Pharmacy, Ohio No. U., 1984. Pharmacist Roddick Pharmacy, Richmond, Calif., 1949-51, Contra Costa County Hosp., Martinez, Calif., 1951-65, Brookside Hosp., San Pablo, Calif., 1965-71; assoc. pharmacist The Apothecary, Oakland, Calif., 1971—; corp. mem. Calif. Blue Shield, San Francisco, 1981—; preceptor-intern advisor U. of Pacific, Stockton, Calif., 1972-75; mem. Am. Council Pharm. Edn., Chgo., 1972-82. Recipient Pharmacist of Yr., 1968; recipient Geigy Pharm. Leadership, 1963. Mem. Am. Pharm. Assn. (pres. 1979, chmn. bd. 1980), Calif. Pharmacist Assn. (pres. 1974-75), Calif. State Bd. Pharmacy (v.p. 1986-88), Calif. Pharmacist Assn. Ednl. Found. (pres. 1978—), Calif. Soc. Hosp. Pharmacist (pres. 1967-68). Home: 1825 Saint Andrews Dr Moraga CA 94556 Office: The Apothecary 10850 MacArthur Blvd Oakland CA 94606

RUNION, ROBERTA LYNN, editor, communications professional; b. Alexandria, Va., May 24, 1957; d. Wayne Godolphin and Gladys Roberta (Whetzel) R. B.A., George Mason U., Fairfax, Va., 1979. Editorial asst. Am. Hist. Assn., Washington, 1981-82; editorial asst. Washingtonian Mag., Washington, 1982-83, also contbr. articles; freelance editor/writer, 1983-85; assoc. editor Soc. Neurosci., 1985-86; mng. editor, pub. relations dir. Empire Press, 1986—. Editorial asst. Writings on Am. History, 1980-81, Recently Pub. Articles, 1981-82; asst. editor: Guide to Departments of History, 1981-82; editor: Neuroscience Training Programs in North America, 1986; assoc. editor: Call for Abstracts; mng. editor WWII, living, mil., biblical and sports history mags. Mem. Washington Edn. Press Assn. Home: Route 1 Box 348 Chantilly VA 22021

RUNIONS, TAMARA L., advertising executive; b. Cornwall, Ont., Can., June 26, 1964; came to U.S., 1971; d. Joan M. (Becksted) Georgi. BS in Pub. Relations and Journalism, Syracuse U., Utica, N.Y., 1985. Advt. graphic artist Gannett Inc., Utica, 1983-85, advt. account exec., 1985-86; advt. account exec. R.T. Blass, Inc., Old Chatham, N.Y., 1986—. Mem. Nat. Assn. Female Execs. Office: RT Blass Inc Pitts Rd Box 74 Old Chatham NY 12136

RUNKEL, JANE ELIZABETH, educator; b. Port Washington, Wis., Aug. 27, 1952; d. Paul David and Jean (Goettmann) R. AB, Ripon Coll., 1974; MEd, U. Wis., Oshkosh, 1979; PhD, Northwestern U., 1987. Admissions counselor Ripon (Wis.) Coll., 1974-77, asst. dean admissions, 1977-80, asst. with office career planning, 1978-79, asst. dir. career planning and placement, 1979-80, asst. dean students, dir. career planning, 1980-82, dir. career planning and placement, affirmative action officer, 1982-84; practicum dir. Northwestern U., Evanston, Ill., 1984-86, teaching assoc., 1986-87, also class rep. Sch. Edn. Alumni Bd.; assoc. dean students Knox Coll., Galesburg, Ill., 1987-88. Mem. Nat. Assn. Women Deans, Adminstrs. and Counselors, Am. Ednl. Research Assn., New Eng. Hist. and Geneal. Soc., Ill. Assn. Counseling Devel., DAR (Wis. Outstanding Jr. 1984), Soc. Colonial Dames, Phi Delta Kappa, Kappa Delta Pi, Alpha Delta Pi. Club: Bowne House Restoration.

RUNKLE, E. MONA, artist; b. Davenport, Iowa, Dec. 4, 1921; d. Louis and Agnes (Jungjohann) Behrens; m. Karl Ehresman Runkle, Jan. 25, 1947; children: Carol Ann, Richard Louis. Grad., Shimer Coll., Mt. Carroll, Ill., 1942; student, St. Ambrose Coll., Davenport, Iowa, 1943, Chgo. Art Inst., 1945; Degree, N.Y. Sch. Interior Design, 1955. Cert. Nat. Watercolor Soc. Illustrator Rock Island (Ill.) Arsenal, 1942-44; stewardess United Air Lines, Chgo., 1944-46; craft dir. Westbury (N.Y.) Country Club, 1967; owner, operator Polynesian Fashions, Huntington, N.Y., 1967-71, The Woodshed, Escondido, Calif., 1975-77; art dir. Holland-Am. Lines, Seattle, 1986-87; artist San Diego, 1983—; operator Hawaii Condo Rentals, San Diego, 1964—; art demonstrator San Marcos Art Assn., Calif., 1987, Escondido Art Assn., Calif., 1987, La Jolla Art Assn., La Jolla, Calif., 1986. illustration San Diego, 1987; executed mural, 1987; represented in pvt. collections; exhibited in group show of Nat. Watercolor Soc., Los Angeles, 1987. Historian Clipped Wings, San Diego, 1985-86, Lloyd Harbor Hist. Assn., N.Y., 1966-71, Huntington Hist. Soc., N.Y., 1963-71, Soc. Preservation L.I. Antiquities, N.Y., 1967-70. Recipient Pres.'s Citation of Merit, Nat. Soc. Paint Casein & Acrylic, N.Y., 1988, second place award Escondido Art Assn., 1987. Mem. Am. Soc. Marine Artists, Nat. Watercolor Soc. (rep. Alaska and Hawaii, 1987-88), U.S. Coast Guard Art Program, Clairmont Art Guild, San Diego Watercolor Soc. (pres. 1987-88, third place award 1988), La Jolla Art Assn. Republican. Lutheran. Home: 17772 Via Gracia San Diego CA 92128

RUNOWICZ, CAROLYN DILWORTH, physician; b. Willimantic, Conn., May 1, 1951; d. S. Robert and Aline (Bergeron) Dilworth. B.A., U. Conn., 1973; M.D., Jefferson Med. Coll., 1977. Resident ob-gyn Mt. Sinai Hosp., N.Y.C., 1977-81, fellow gynecol. oncology, 1981-83, clin. instr., 1983-85; asst. prof., dir. gynecol. oncology dept. ob-gyn Albert Einstein Coll. Medicine, Montefiore Med. Ctr., N.Y.C., 1985—; dir., gynecol. and oncology div. ob-gyn Our Lady of Mercy, Bronx, N.Y. ; lectr. in field. Diplomate Am. Bd. Ob-gyn., Am. Bd. Gynecol. Oncology. Contbr. articles and chpts. to med. publs. Galloway fellow Sloane-Kettering Meml. Hosp., N.Y.C., 1980. Fellow ACS, Am. Coll. Ob-Gyn.; mem. AMA, Am. Med. Woman's Assn., N.Y. County Med. Soc., Bronx County Ob-gyn Soc., Soc. Gynecologic Oncologist, N.Y. OBS Soc., Phi Beta Kappa, Alpha Omega Alpha, Phi Kappa Phi. Club: Metropolitan (N.Y.C.). Office: 1300 Morris Park Ave Albert Einstein Coll Medicine Dept Ob-Gyn Belfer Bldg Room 501 Bronx NY 10461 also: 2330 Eastchester Rd Bronx NY 10461

RUNTE, ROSEANN, college principal; b. Kingston, N.Y., Jan. 31, 1948; came to Can., 1971, naturalized, 1983; d. Robert B. and Anna Loretta (Schorkopf) O'Reilly; m. Hans-Rainer Runte, Aug. 9, 1969. BA summa cum laude, SUNY-New Paltz, 1968; MA, U. Kans., 1969, PhD, 1974. Lectr. Bethany Coll., W.Va., 1970-71; lectr. adult studies St. Mary's U., Halifax, N.S., Can., 1971-72; from lectr. to assoc. prof. Dalhousie U., Halifax, 1972-83, asst. dean, 1980-82, chmn. dept. French, 1980-83; pres. Universite Sainte-Anne, Pointe-de-l'Eglise, N.S., Can., 1983-88; prin. Glendon Coll., Toronto, 1988—. Author: Brumes bleues, 1982; Faux-Soleils, 1984; editor: Studies in 18th Century Culture, vols. VII, VIII, IX, 1977, 78, 79; co-editor: Man and Nature, 1982, Le Développement régional, 1986, 87; co-translator Local Development, 1987. Bd. dirs. N.S. Gallery Art; mem. edn. com. Victoria Gen. Hosp., adv. bd. Nat. Library; v.p. N.S. Soc. Study Ethnicity, 1984-86, Can. Soc. Study Ethnicity, 1987—; mem. pubs. com. Hannah Found., exec. com. N.S. Writers Fedn., 1985-87, exec. bd. N.S. Cultural Fedns., 1985-86. Regents scholar SUNY-New Paltz, 1965; NDEA Title IV grantee U. Kans., Lawrence, 1968; Acad. Palms, 1986. Mem. Internat. Soc. 18th Century Studies (assoc. treas. 1983-87), Internat. Assn. of Comparative Lit. (treas. 1985—), Can. Fedn. Humanities (pres. 1982-84), Atlantic Soc. 18th Century Studies (pres. 1972-76). Roman Catholic. Home and Office: Glendon College, 2275 Bayview, Toronto, ON Canada M4N 3M6

RUNYAN, REBECCA JANE, computer consultant, educator; b. Boise, Idaho, Aug. 26, 1953; d. Ronald Ralph and Mary Elizabeth (East) R. Student, Inst. de Allende, San Miguel, Mex., 1971-72; BA in Comparative Religion, U. Wash., 1977; postgrad., Wesleyan U. Computer Inst., 1982. Registered in real estate, Mass. Math. tchr. Cape Cod Acad., Osterville, Mass., 1980-82; mgr. of tng. Microsource/Fin., Boston, 1983-85; prin. Boston Computer Lab, Inc., 1985—. Campaign organizer Com. to Elect/Re-Elect William Walsh to Cambridge (Mass.) City Council, 1985-87. Mem. Nat. Assn. Sky Divers. Democrat. Episcopalian. Office: Boston Computer Lab Inc 60 State St Boston MA 02109 Also: Boston Computer Lab Inc 50 Rowes Wharf Boston MA 02110

RUNYON, MARY LUCILLE, banker; b. Mt. Sterling, Ky., Aug. 17, 1927; s. Jess and Mary (Martin) Gilbert; m. Troy H. Runyon, Dec. 23, 1949; children: joy Lynette Ramirez, Pamela Lea Perez, Dreama Carol. Student, U. Ky. Lic. in real estate. V.p. 1st Nat. Bank, Palm Beach, Fla., 1969-85, Bankers Trust of Fla., West Palm Beach, 1987—. Founder, v.p. Adopt-A-Family of Palm Beach, Inc., West Palm Beach, 1984—; bd. dirs. Vol. Ctr. of Palm Beach, 1983—, League of Charities, Palm Beach, 1987—; com. mem. Am. Heart Auction, West Palm Beach, 1985—; v.p. Good Samaritan Hosp. Aux., West Palm Beach, 1987—. Recipient Congrl. award for volunteerism Pres. Reagan, 1984, Jefferson award Channel 12, 1985-86. Fellow Nat. Am. Bank Women. Republican. Baptist. Lodge: Shriners. Home: Seven Springs Blvd Suite 6312 B Lake Worth FL 33463

RUPER, JERAY MARIAN, accountant; b. Painesville, Ohio, May 10, 1952; d. Richard Lewis and Nancy Jean (Few) Bunnell; children—Heather Lynn, Heidi Marie; m. Ronald Thomas Ruper, June 6, 1981. B.A. in Acctg., Thiel Coll., 1974; postgrad. W.Va. U., 1985—. C.P.A., Pa., Ohio, W.Va. Acct., Rex Walker & Assocs., Grove City, Pa., 1976-78; mgr. fin. acctg. Harris Wholesale Co., Solon, Ohio, 1978-83; spl. asst. to chief fin. officer W.Va. U., Morgantown, 1983-84, mgr. mgmt. analysis, 1984-86; coordinator fin. ops. and analysis Dept. Publs., Printing & News Service, Office of Instl. Advancement, W.Va. U., 1986—; cons. fin. systems Human Interface, Morgantown, 1983—. Mem. Am. Inst. C.P.A.s, Am. Women's Soc. CPA's, W.Va. Soc. C.P.A.s, Ohio Soc. C.P.A.s. Republican. Roman Catholic. Avocation: travel. Office: West Va U #117 Communications Bldg Morgantown WV 26505

RUPERT, CAROLA G., museum director; b. Washington, Jan. 2, 1954; d. Jack Burns and Shirley Ann (Orcutt) Rupert. B.A. in history cum laude, Bryn Mawr Coll., 1976; M.A., U. Del., 1978, Cert. in Mus. Studies, 1978. Personnel mgmt. trainee Naval Material Command, Arlington, Va., 1972-76; teaching asst. dept. history, U. Del., Newark, 1976-77; asst. curator/exhibit specialist Hist. Soc. Del., Wilmington, 1977-78; dir. Macon County Mus. Complex, Decatur, Ill., 1978-81; dir. Kern County Mus., Bakersfield, Calif.,

1981—; tchr. mus. studies course U. Calif.-Santa Barbara Extension, 1982; advisor Kern County Heritage Commn.; chmn. Historic Records Commn., 1988; sec.-treas. Arts Council of Kern, 1984-86, pres. 1986—; county co-chmn. United Way, 1981, 82; chmn. steering com. Calif. State Bakersfield Co-op Program, 1982-83; mem. Community Adv. Bd. Calif. State Bakersfield, Anthro; Soc. 1986—; bd. dirs. Mgmt. Council, 1983-86, v.p. 1987, pres. 1988; bd. dirs. Calif. Council for Promotion of History, 1984-86, v.p. 1987-88; Community Adv. Bd. mem. Calif. State U.-Bakersfield Sociology Dept., 1986-88. Hagley fellow Eleutherian Mills-Hagley Found., 1977-78; Bryn Mawr alumnae regional scholar, 1972-76. Mem. Nat. Trust for Hist. Preservation, Am. Assn. Mus., Am. Assn. for State and Local History. Unitarian Universalist. Office: Kern County Mus 3801 Chester Ave Bakersfield CA 93301

RUPP, GERALDLYNN SUE, public relations executive; b. Denver, Apr. 13, 1946; d. Gerald Monroe and Grace Isabel (Evans) R.; m. William S. Yurong, 1967 (div. 1983); children: Tamara Jene, William Anthony. BA, Calif. State U., Sacramento, 1978; postgrad., Calif. State U., 1980—. Asst. for alumni pub. relations McGeorge Sch. Law/U. of the Pacific, Stockton, Calif., 1979-81, dir. alumni pub. relations, 1981-83; asst. devel. dir. Sacramento Symphony, 1983-85; dir. communications and community relations Sacramento Bd. Realtors, 1985—; cons., lectr. in field. Dir. communications Sacramento Realtor mag., 1985 (several awards). Bd. dirs. EnCorps/Symphony Assn., Sacramento, 1985-86, Am. Lung Assn., Sacramento, 1986—; div. chmn. United Way Campaign, 1985; mem. Calif. steering com. Christmas CanTree, steering com. Sacramento Chamber Music Soc., 1987; friend Sta. KVIE-Channel 6 Pub. TV; panel mem. Weekend of the Stars Cerebral Palsy Telethon, 1985. Mem. Am. Soc. Assn. Execs. (Gold Circle trophy 1985), Sacramento Soc. Assn. Execs. (communications-publs. sect. chmn. 1987-88), Internat. Assn. Bus. Communicators (Creativity award 1986), Sacramento Pub. Relations Assn. Club: Toastmasters. Home: 4520 Ulysses Dr Sacramento CA 95864

RUPPEL, BARBARA WIEDEMANN, social welfare administrator; b. Elgin, Ill., July 3, 1943; d. Joseph J. and Margaret T. (Goggin) Wiedemann; m. Howard J. Ruppel Jr., June 3, 1967. BA, St. Dominic Coll., 1967; MSW, U. Iowa, 1978. Lic. social worker, cert. adoption investigator, Iowa. Social worker Iowa Dept. Social Services, Cedar Rapids, 1969-78; adminstrv. coordinator, family therapist Families, Inc., West Branch, Iowa, 1978-85, exec. dir., 1985—; counselor sex and marriage Ctr. Sexual Growth and Devel., Mt. Vernon, Iowa, 1980—. Author: (with others) Child Care Handbook, 1976. Mem. LWV (state bd. dirs. 1976-78), Soc. Sci. Study of Sex (chmn. membership, exhibits, sec. Midcontinent region 1985-87), Nat. Assn. Social Workers, Am. Assn. Marriage and Family Therapists (clin.), Acad. Cert. Social Workers. Office: Families Inc 101 W Main St West Branch IA 52358

RUPPRECHT, CAROL SCHREIER, comparative literature educator, researcher in dreams; b. Stafford Springs, Conn., June 30, 1939; d. William Joseph and Caroline Brown (Comstock) Schreier; m. Glenn Francis Rupprecht, June 10, 1960 (div. 1978); children—Jody Francine, Whitney Glenn; m. Richard P. Stuttmeier, May 8, 1987. B.S., U. Va., 1962; M.A., Yale U., 1963, M.Philosophy, 1973, Ph.D., 1977. Teaching fellow Yale U., 1973; asst. prof. Kirkland Coll., Clinton, N.Y., 1974-78; asst. prof. Hamilton, Coll., Clinton, 1978-81, assoc. dean, 1981-82, assoc. prof. comparative lit., 1982—, chmn. dept., 1984—; lectr. Switzerland, Israel, The Netherlands, Ireland, People's Rep. China. Co-editor and author: Feminist Archetypal Theory, 1985. Contbr. articles to profl. jours., chpts. to books. NEH fellow Dartmouth Dante Inst., 1986. Founding mem. Assn. for Study Dreams, 1983, Conn. Assn. Jungian Psychology, 1981. Merrill fellow Bunting Inst., 1970-72. Mem. MLA, Am. Comparative Lit. Assn., Shakespeare Soc., Assn. Study of Dreams (v.p. bd. dirs., mem. editorial bd.), Conn. Assn. for Jungian Psychology (bd. dirs.). Avocations: sports; wilderness activities. Office: Hamilton Coll Clinton NY 13323

RUPRECHT, MARY MARGARET WYANT, office automation mgmt. cons.; b. O'Neill, Neb., Oct. 20, 1934; d. Charles Ellsworth and Mary Loretto (Cuddy) Wyant; m. Gregory Earl Ruprecht, Sept. 24, 1955; children: Mary Debra, Sharie Marie. Student Coll. St. Benedict, 1952-54; cert. Am. Inst. Banking, 1970. Cert. mgmt. cons. Dist. clk. U.S. Soil Conservation, Aitkin, Minn., 1956-68; comml. loan sec. No. City Nat. Bank, Duluth, Minn., 1965-71; office mgr. Fryberger, Buchanan Law Firm, Duluth, 1971-72; pvt. practice word processing and mgmt. cons., Duluth, 1972-76; v.p., prin. Altman & Weil, Inc., mgmt. cons., 1976-79; pres. Mary M. Ruprecht & Assos., 1979—; tchr. Am. Inst. Banking; internat. lectr. Author: (with others) Managing Office Automation, Office Automation: Concepts and Principles, Office Automation: A Management Approach, Integrated Office Systems, 1987, Integrated Office Systems a management Approach and Office Automation Technologies, 1988, Integrated Office Systems Automation Dictionary, 1987; contbr. editor Office Systems mag. 1986-88; also articles. Mem. adv. council Minn. State Bd. Edn., Duluth Office Edn. Assn., Coll. Applied Scis. at Miami U., Oxford, Ohio, Ball State U., Muncie, treas. Senator Sam Solon 1964—, Ind. Fin. dir. 8th Congressional Dist. Dem.-Farm Labor Party, 1972-73. Mem. Assn. Info. Systems Profl. (former internat. pres.), Internat. Word Processing Assn. (internat. pres. 1974-75), Am. Inst. Banking (nat. chmn. women's com. 1970-71), Adminstrv. Mgmt. Soc., Am. Mgmt. Assn., Office Systems Research Assn. (conf. chmn. 1985, 86), Bus. and Profl. Women's Assn., Internat. Platform Assn. Home: 140 W Myrtle St Duluth MN 55811

RUSCH, BETHALYNN ANN ARNASON, small business owner; b. Foam Lake, Can., July 23, 1957; d. Kristjan Marvin and Dorothy Lillian (Bray) Arnason; m. Edward Grant Rusch, July 20, 1974; 1 child, Krista Raillé. Grad. high sch., Foam Lake. Salesperson Hudson Bay Co., Flin Flon, Man., 1976; realtor Century 21, Calgary, 1977; mgr. Sterling Shoes, Saskatoon, 1978; salesperson Bricker's, Saskatoon, 1979-82; owner Sashay, Foam Lake, 1982—. Mem. Can. Fedn. Ind. Bus., Curling Club, Foam Lake C. of C. (sec. 1983—). Protestant. Lodge: Order Eastern Star, Lioness (officer, pres. 1985-87). Home and Office: Sashay, 316 Main St, Foam Lake CAN S0A 1A0

RUSH, CATHERINE PATRICIA, corporate professional; b. Montclair, N.J., May 29, 1944; d. Thomas Patrick and Helen (Howard) R. Corp. sec., office mgr. Beck's Montclair Moving & Storage, Inc., 1962-68; corp. sec., gen. mgr. Rimback Storage Co., Millburn, N.J., 1968—. Contbr. article to pubs. Mem. Friends of N.J. Opera. Mem. Internat. Health Network for Women and Children (bd. dirs.), N.J. Fedn. Bus. & Profl. Women (chair nominating com. 1987—), Montclair Bus. and Profl. Women (Young Career Woman 1966), Bus. and Profl. Women Millburn-Short Hills, Millburn-Short Hills C. of C. (bd. dirs., chmn. art fair 1986-87). Republican. Office: Rimback Storage Co 161 Spring St Millburn NJ 07041

RUSH, JULIA ANN HALLORAN (MRS. RICHARD HENRY RUSH), artist, writer; b. St. Louis, Oct. 25, 1927; d. Edward Roosevelt and Flavia Hadley (Griffin) Halloran; m. Richard Henry Rush, Aug. 15, 1956; 1 child, Sallie Haywood. Student Washington U., St. Louis, 1945-47; B.A., George Washington U., 1949. One-woman shows: Fort Amador Officers Club, Panama Canal Zone, El Panama Hotel, Panama, George Washington U., Statler Hotel, Roosevelt Hotel, Washington, Newspaper Women's Club, Washington, Waukegan Library, Ill., Epworth Heights Hotel, Ludington, Mich.; exhibited in group shows: Panama Art League, Corcoran Gallery; represented in permanent collections: U. Panama; also pvt. collections; model John Robert Powers Agy., 1950; sec.-treas., dir. N.Am. Acceptance Corp., 1956-58; v.p. Rush and Halloran, Inc., 1957-58, ptnr., 1954-57; research asst. to husband's bi-weekly newsletter Art/Antiques Investment Report, 1973—. Illustrator: Antiques As An Investment (author Richard H. Rush), 1968; research asst.: Investments You Can Live With and Enjoy (author: Richard H. Rush), 1974, 2d, edit., 1975, 3d edit., 1976; Photographer: Automobiles as an Investment, 1982; Investing in Classic Cars, 1984. Recipient 1st prize (Panama) Newspaper Women's Club, 1953; First Prize Panama Art League, 1953. Mem. DAR, Nat. League Am. Penwomen, Florence Crittenton Circle (rec. sec. 1968-69), Kappa Kappa Gamma. Club: Washington.

RUSH, SARAH MAY, federal government financial official; b. Kokomo, Ind., Nov. 23, 1953; d. Lawrence Wayne and Eva Lenor (Burns) R. Tech. degree Ind. Vocat. Tech. Coll., 1979; B.S., Ind. U.-Kokomo, 1982. Owner, operator farm, Windfall, Ind., 1974—; instr. logistics U.S. Army Res., Indpls., 1984—; personnel clk. Dept. of Army, Indpls., 1984-85, operating acct., 1985—. Chmn. mil. units Seed Sity Jamboree Com., Windfall, 1982—. Serve with U.S. Army Res., 1975—. Mem. DAV (life), Nat. Assn. Female Execs., Fraternal Order Police (assoc.), Am. Soc. Mil. Comptrollers, Am. Legion (1st vice comdr. 1983-85, comdr. 1985-87). Republican. Lodge: Tecumseh (life). Avocation: metaphysics study. Home: Route 1 Box 47 Windfall IN 46076 Office: US Army Fin and Acctg Ctr Bldg 1 FINCO-CB Indianapolis IN 46249

RUSKELL, VIRGINIA ANN, librarian, educator; b. Nashville, June 4, 1948; d. George Channing Ruskell and Douglass (McFerrin) Rudkoff. AA, Reinhardt Coll., 1967; BA in history, Emory U., 1969; MLS, George Peabody Coll., 1970; MA in English, West Ga. U., 1975. Library asst. George Peabody Coll. Library Sch., 1969-70; interlibrary loan librarian West Ga. Coll., Carrollton, 1970-76, bibliog. instrn. librarian, 1977-80, reference coordinator, 1980—, assoc. prof., 1980—. Treas. LWV, Carrollton, 1975-77; chmn., bd. dirs. Wesley Found., 1985; chmn. social concerns St. Andrew United Meth. Ch., Carrollton, 1981-82, fin. sec., 1980-81, chmn. fin. com., 1982. Council Library Resources Library Services Enhancement grantee, 1976-77. Mem. Southeastern Library Assn., AAUP (sec. 1974-75, v.p. 1975-76), AAUW (v.p. programs 1982—, v.p. membership 1986-87), Beta Phi Mu, Phi Kappa Phi (pres. elect 1986-87). Democrat. Home: PO Box 844 Carrollton GA 30117 Office: West Ga Coll Library Carrollton GA 30118

RUSS, JOANNA, writer, English language educator; b. N.Y.C., Feb. 22, 1937; d. Evarett and Bertha (Zinner) R. B.A. in English with high honors, Cornell, U., 1957; M.F.A. in Playwriting and Dramatic Lit, Yale U., 1960. Lectr. in English Cornell U., 1967-70, asst. prof., 1970-72; asst. prof. English, Harpur Coll., State U. N.Y. at Binghamton, 1972-75, U. Colo., 1975-77; asso. prof. English, U. Wash., 1977—, prof., 1984—. Author: Picnic on Paradise, 1968, And Chaos Died, 1970, The Female Man, 1975, We Who Are About To, 1977, Kittatinny: A Tale of Magic, 1978, The Two of Them, 1978, On Strike Against God, 1980, The Adventures of Alyx, 1983, The Zanzibar Cat, 1983, How To Suppress Women's Writing, 1983, Extra (Ordinary) People, 1984, Magic Mommas, Trembling Sisters, Puritans and Perverts: Feminist Essays, 1985, The Hidden Side of the Moon, 1987; also numerous short stories. Mem. Modern Lang. Assn., Sci. Fiction Writers Am. (Nebula award for best short story 1972, Hugo award for best novella 1983). Address: U Washington Dept English GN-30 Seattle WA 98195

RUSSELL, DIANE HADDOCK, pharmacology educator; b. Boise, Idaho, Sept. 9, 1935; d. Grove Marden and Eileen Flora (Gridley) H.; m. Kenneth S. Russell, May 27, 1953 (div. Apr. 1975); children: Shauna, Keri. AA, Boise Jr. Coll., 1961; BS summa cum laude, Coll. Idaho, 1963; PhD, Wash. State U., 1967; postdoctoral student, Johns Hopkins U., 1969. Research chemist Balt. Cancer Research Ctr., 1969-73; assoc. prof. pharmacology dept. pharmacology U. Ariz., Tucson, 1973-76, research assoc. dept. internal medicine, 1973-76, prof. dept. pharmacology, 1976-87, prof. dept. pharmacology, molecular cell biology, 1984-87; prof., head dept. pharmacology and therapeutics U. S. Fla. Coll. Medicine, Tampa, 1988—; mem. Nat. Cancer Inst. Manpower Rev. Com., 1977-81. Mem. editorial bd. Life Scis., N.Y.C.; contbr. numerous articles to profl. jours. Fellow Am. Chem. Soc., Endocrine Soc., Am. Soc. Clin. Pharmacology and Exptl. Therapeutics, Soc. Toxicology; mem. AAAS, Am. Soc. Biol. Chemists, Am. Physiol. Soc., Am. Assn. Cancer Research (bd. dirs. 1979-82), Am. Soc. Cell Biology, Soc. Devel. Biology, Sigma Xi. Office: Univ S Fla Dept Pharmacology Tampa FL 33612

RUSSELL, DOLORES JEANNE, nurse; b. Huttonsville, W. Va., June 13, 1931; d. Ray Henry and Ora Mae (Swecker) Tacy; m. Russell Bosworth Updike, Mar. 30, 1956 (div.); children: Marcia, Alan, Kirk (dec.); m. Aubrey Alvin Russell, Sept. 18, 1965 (div.). Diploma, C&O Nursing Sch., 1952. Staff nurse Arlington (Va.) Community Hosp., 1952-53, Mayo Clinic, Meth. Hosp., Rochester, Minn., 1953-55, Golden Clinic, Elkins, W.Va., 1955-56, Morton F. Plant Hosp., Clearwater, Fla., 1956-60, Bay Pines (Fla.) VA, 1960-63, Martinsburg (W.Va.) VA, 1963-66, U.S. Embassy, Cairo, Egypt, 1966, Ft. Belvoir (Va.) Army Hosp., 1967-83; staff nurse VA Hosp., Martinsburg, W.Va., Balt., 1983-87, Lebanon, Pa., 1987—. Pub. Response, 1988—. Methodist. Home: 22 E Cumberland St Lebanon PA 17042

RUSSELL, DORA LEE, seafood industry executive; b. Sanford, Fla., Nov. 11, 1935. Lobbyist Organized Fishermen of Fla., Tallahassee, 1970-77, bd. dirs., 1969—; asst. to dir. research and policy Office of Gov., State of Fla., 1977-78; pres., owner Russell Seafood, Inc., Sanford, Fla., 1968—, Russell Seafood Shoppes, Inc., Sanford, 1985—. Mem. Gulf and South Atlantic Fisheries Devel. Found., 1984—; Central Fla. Comm. Status of Women, 1978-79; bd. dirs. Ballet Guild of Sanford-Seminole, 1965—, Kissimmee Bd. Adjustments, 1983—; chmn. dist. bd. trustees Seminole Community Coll., 1981—. Mem. Southeastern Fisheries Assn., Beta Sigma Phi. Democrat. Baptist. Avocations: reading; flying; travel. Office: Russell Seafood Inc 3801 E State Rd 46 Sanford FL 32772-1634

RUSSELL, ELIZABETH G., military sciences researcher; b. Chgo., Apr. 15, 1958; d. Charles Wilbur and Patricia Ann (Lincoln) R. BA in Internat. Relations, Mount Holyoke Coll., 1980; postgrad., Dartmouth U., 1980-81, Harvard U., 1983-85, U. Md., 1987—. Aide Sen. Charles H. Percy, Washington, 1979-80; legal historian Nat. Vets. Law Ctr., Washington, 1980-83; researcher Resource Policy Ctr., Hanover, N.H., 1980-81; exec. interviewer Temple, Barker & Sloane, Lexington, Mass., 1987; MacArthur fellow Ctr. for Internat. Security Studies, U. Md., College Park, 1987—. Fundraiser Mass. Abortion Coalition, Boston, 1986; legal aide Nat. Vets. Task Force on Agt. Orange, Washington, 1979-83. Thayer Sch. Engring fellow Dartmouth Coll., 1980-81. Democrat. Club: Yankee Rescue (Andover, Mass.). Home: 45 Harrington St Newton MA 02160

RUSSELL, FREDA JEAN, music educator; b. Marion, Ind., Jan. 5, 1953; d. Frederick H. and Mary W. (Thomas) R. BS, Ball State U., Muncie, Ind., 1975, MA, 1978. Cert. music tchr., Ind. Tchr. music Kokomo(Ind.)-Ctr. Twp. Consol. Schs., 1975—; tchr. music Kokomo Migrant Sch., 1980-83; instr. career edn. Kokomo Migrant Sch., 1984-87; adj. faculty Ind. U., Kokomo, 1987—. Choir dir. First Friends Meeting, Kokomo, 1982-88; bd. dirs. Kokomo Community Concerts, 1985-88; musician Kokomo Symphony, 1975-78. Mem. Am.-Orff Schoolwork Assn., Ind.-Orff Schoolwork Assn., Ind. Elem. Music Assn. (treas. 1983-86), Ind. State Tchrs. Assn. (polit. action chairperson 1984-85), Phi Delta Kappa, Sigma Eta Fine Arts Sorority (pres. 1986-87), Delta Kappa Gamma. Republican. Home: 1605 S Courtland Kokomo IN 46902

RUSSELL, HARRIET SHAW, social worker; b. Detroit, Apr. 12, 1952; d. Louis Thomas and Lureleen (Hughes) Shaw; m. Donald Edward Russell, June 25, 1980; children: Lachante Tyree, Krystal Lanae. AB, Detroit Bus. Inst., 1976; BS, Mich. State U., 1974; postgrad. in pub. adminstrn., Mercy Coll. Detroit, 1986—. Cert. notary pub. Factory employee Gen. Motors Corp., Lansing, Mich., 1973; student supr. tour guides State of Mich., Lansing, 1974; mgr. Ky. Fried Chicken, Detroit, 1974-75; unemployment claims examiner State of Mich. Dept. Labor, Detroit, 1975-77, asst. payment worker, 1977-84, social services specialist, 1984—; moderator Michigan Opportunity Skills and Tng. Program, 1985-86. Vol. Mich. Cancer Soc., East Lansing, 1970-72, Big Sisters/Big Bros., Lansing, 1972-73; speaker Triumphant Bapt. Ch., Detroit, 1976-80; chief union steward Mich. Employees Assn., Lincoln Park, 1982-83; leader Girl Scouts U.S.A.; area capt. Life Worker Protect Program. Recipient Outstanding Work Performance Merit award Mich. Dept. Social Services, 1979. Mem. Nat. Assn. for Female Execs., Am. Soc. Profl. and Exec. Women, Assn. Internat. Platform Speakers, Mich. Council Social Services Workers, Delta Sigma Theta. Democrat. Baptist. Office: PO Box 361 Lincoln Park MI 48146

RUSSELL, KATHARINE ANNE, public relations executive; b. Schenectady, N.Y., Mar. 20, 1948; d. Joseph Solomon and Jane (Welsh) R. BA in History, Northwestern U., 1970, MBA in Mktg., 1980; MS in Journalism, Boston U., 1971. Assoc. producer Scientificom, Chgo., 1971-74, v.p., 1974-77; asst. market service mgr. Baxter-Travenol, Deerfield, Ill., 1977-80, mgr. corp. communications, 1980-81, group mgr. corp. communications, 1981-83; dir. pub. relations and investor communications Cetus Corp., Emeryville, Calif., 1983-86, v.p. pub. relations and investor communications, 1986—. Mem. Pub. Relations Soc. Am. Republican. Episcopalian. Club: Press San Francisco. Home: 150 Arbor St San Francisco CA 94131 Office: Cetus Corp 1400 53rd St Emeryville CA 94608

RUSSELL, LIANE BRAUCH, geneticist; b. Vienna, Austria, Aug. 27, 1923; came to U.S., 1941; d. Arthur and Clara (Starer) B.; m. William Lawson Russell, Sept. 23, 1947; children: David Lawson, Evelyn Ruth. AB, Hunter Coll., 1945; PhD, U. Chgo., 1949. Fellow U. Chgo., 1945-46, teaching asst., 1946-47; research asst. Jackson Lab., Bar Harbor, Maine, 1945, 46; research staff mem. Oak Ridge (Tenn.) Nat. Lab., 1947-75, sect. head., 1975—, disting. research staff mem., 1983—; sci. advisor U.S. Del. at 1st Atoms for Peace Conf., Geneva, Switzerland, 1955; mem. numerous sci. bds. including Research Council com. on energy and environment, 1975-77, com. on biol. effects of ionizing radiation, 1977-80, bd. on environ. studies and toxicology, 1981, Nat. Council on Radiation Protection and Measurement Task Group, Washington, NRC, 1975-77, Genetox Program EPA, Washington, 1979—, Internat. Com. for Protection Against Environ. Mutagens and Carcinogens, Lausanne, Switzerland, 1977-83; mem. task group Internat. Agy. for Research on Cancer, Hanover, Fed. Republic of Germany, 1979, com. on energy and environ., 1975-77, com. on biol. effects of ionizing radiation, 1977-80, environ studies and toxicology bd., 1981—. Assoc. editor: Mutation Research, 1976—, Environ. Mutagenesis, 1980-83; editor: TCWP Newsletter, 1966—; editor: (book) Genetic Mosaics and Chimeras, 1979; contbr. over 90 articles in field to profl. jours. Founder Tenn. Citizens for Wilderness Planning, Oak Ridge, 1966, pres. 1967-70, 86—; active numerous environ. groups. Corp. fellow Union Carbide, 1983; corp. fellow Martin Marietta, 1985, sr. corp. fellow, 1988; recipient Merit award Mademoiselle, 1955, Roentgen medal City of Remscheid-Lennep, 1973, Disting. Assoc. award U.S. Dept. Energy, 1987; named to Hall of Fame Hunter Coll., 1979. Fellow AAAS, Environ. Health Inst.; mem. Nat. Acad. Scis. (elected 1986), Environ. Mutagen Soc. (pres. 1984-85), Genetics Soc. Am. (presdl. nominee 1979). Office: Oak Ridge Natl Lab Biol Div Oak Ridge TN 37831

RUSSELL, LOUISE BENNETT, economist; b. Exeter, N.H., May 12, 1942; d. Frederick Dewey and Esther (Smith) B.; m. Robert Hardy Cosgriff, May 3, 1987. BA, U. Mich., 1964; PhD, Harvard U., 1971. Economist Social Security Adminstrn., Washington, 1968-71, Nat. Commn. on State Workmen's Compensation Laws, Washington, 1971-72, Dept. Labor, Washington, 1972-73; sr. economist Nat. Planning Assn., Washington, 1973-75; sr. fellow Brookings Instn., Washington, 1975-87; research prof. Inst. for Health, Health Care Policy, and Aging Research, Rutgers U., New Brunswick, N.J., 1987—; prof. econs. Rutgers U., New Brunswick, N.J., 1987—; mem. U.S. Preventive Services Task Force, Washington, 1984-88. Author: Technology in Hospitals, 1979, The Baby Boom Generation and the Economy, 1982, Is Prevention Better Than Cure, 1986, Evaluating Preventive Care: Report on a Workshop, 1987; also numerous articles. Mem. Inst. of Medicine of Nat. Acad. Scis. (mem. com. to study future pub. health 1986-87). Office: Rutgers U Inst for Health Health Care Policy and Aging Research 30 College Ave New Brunswick NJ 08903

RUSSELL, VIRGINIA DEGANAHL, public relations exec., consultant; b. N.Y.C., Apr. 2, 1931; d. Joe and Josephine (Coombs) deGanahl; m. Thomas Hale Russell, June 21, 1952; children: George, Sarah, Edward, Josephine, Charles, Michael, Kenneth. Student Mt. Vernon Sem. and Coll., 1949-52, U. Calif. extension, George Washington U., 1951. Mem. bd. Vt. Symphony Orch., Burlington, 1970-81; pres. Dvorak Internat., Brandon, Vt., 1976-79, pres., 1981-87, Classic Concepts, Inc., Brandon, 1987—; art historian on Jacob van Ruisdael and 17th century Holland. Mem. Otter Valley (Vt.) Sch. Bd., 1976-77; bd. dirs. Girl Scouts U.S.A., 1967-69, Sterling Coll., Brandon chpt. Am. Cancer Soc., 1967-70. Mem. Am. Nat. Standards Inst., Assn. Computer Mfrs. Democrat. Episcopalian. Clubs: Arts (Washington); Dutch-Am. Acad. Soc. (Boston). Home: 11 Pearl St Brandon VT 05733

RUSSO, CHARLINE SMITH, management educator; b. Queens, N.Y., Mar. 30, 1950; d. Wallace Donald Smith and Filomena Eilse (Calicchio) Boyle; m. Robert Allen Russo, June 15, 1975; children: Jonathan Francis, Alexander Daniel. BA, Rutgers U., 1972, MBA, 1974; MA, Columbia U., 1986, EdD, 1988. Asst. prof., program dir. Rutgers U. Inst. Mgmt. and Labor Relations, New Brunswick, N.J., 1974—; cons. pvt. bus., 1974—; dir. tng. Rutgers Small Bus. Devel. Ctr., 1977-79; asst. prof. Coll. St. Elizabeth Weekend Coll., 1976-82, Douglas Coll., 1977-82. Mem. editorial bd., The Personnel Administrator, 1980—; contbr. articles to profl. jours. Gubernatorial nominee, N.J. div. Civil Rights, 1988. Recipient Tng. and Devel. award Small Bus. Assn., 1978. Mem. Am. Soc. Personnel Adminstrs. (faculty advisor 1978—), Acad. Mgmt., Am. Assn. Adult and Continuing Edn., Am. Ednl. Research Assn., Am. Soc. Tng. and Devel., Indsl. Relations Research Assn., Small Bus. Inst. Dirs. Assn. Office: Rutgers Univ Inst Mgmt & Labor Relations Cook Campus New Brunswick NJ 08903

RUSSO, IRMA HAYDEE ALVAREZ DE, pathologist; b. San Rafael, Mendoza, Argentina, Feb. 28, 1942; came to U. S., 1972; d. José Maria and Maria Carmen (Martinez) de Alvarez; BA, Escuela Normal M.T.S.M. de Balcarce, 1959; MD, U. Nat. of Cuyo, Mendoza, 1970; m. Jose Russo, Feb. 8, 1969; 1 child, Patricia Alexandra. Intern, Sch. of Medicine Hosps., Argentina, 1969-70; resident in pathology Wayne State U. Sch. Medicine, Detroit, 1976-80; research asst. and instr. Inst. of Histology and Embryology Sch. Medicine U. Nat. of Cuyo, 1963-71, asso. prof. histology Faculty of Phys., Chem. and Math. Scis., 1970-72; research asso. Inst. for Molecular and Cellular Evolution, U. Miami, Fla., 1972-73; research asso. exptl. pathology lab. div. biol. scis., Mich. Cancer Found., Detroit, 1973-75, research scientist, 1975-76, vis. research scientist, 1976-82, asst. mem., pathologist, 1982—, co-dir. pathology reference lab., 1982-86; co-dir. Mich. Cancer Found. Lab. Services, 1986—; chief resident physician dept. pathology Wayne State U. Sch. Medicine, 1978-80, asst. prof., 1980-82; mem. staff Harper-Grace Hosps., Detroit, 1980-82; Rockefeller grantee, 1972-73; Nat. Cancer Inst. grantee, 1978-81, 84-87; Am. Cancer Soc. grantee 1988-89; guest lectr. dept. obstetrics Sch. Medicine U. Nat. of Cuyo, 1965-71. Diplomate Am. Bd. Pathology. Mem. AAAS, Coll. Am. Pathologists, Am. Soc. Clin. Pathologists, Am. Assn. for Cancer Research, Mich. Soc. Pathologists, Am. Assn. Clin. Chemistry, Electron Microscopy Soc. Am., Mich. Electron Microscopy Forum, Sigma Xi. Roman Catholic. Contbr. numerous articles on pathology to profl. jours. Office: 110 E Warren Ave Detroit MI 48201

RUSSO, NANCY MARGARET, lawyer; b. Cleve., Oct. 6, 1956; d. Humbert and Maureen Helen (McCaffery) R.; A.B. in Polit. Sci., W. Liberty State Coll., 1977; J.D., Cleveland-Marshall Law Sch., 1981. Bar: Ohio 1982, U.S. Dist. Ct. (northeastern dist.) Ohio 1982. Investigator Lake County Narcotics, Painesville, Ohio, 1977-78; with Marriott Inn, Cleve., 1978-79; legal sec. Bartunek, Garofoli, Cleve., 1979-81; paralegal/litigation asst. Calfee, Halter & Griswold, Cleve., 1981-84; atty., fin. and fraud investigator Blue Cross/Blue Shield of Ohio, 1984—, media rep. 1987—; part-time pvt. practice law. Contbg. author ref. book: Ohio Family Law, 1984. Vol. atty. Cleve. Attys. Seeking Equity, 1983—; participant legal clinic staff Law Day, Cleve., 1980-86; mem. Med.-Legal Commn., bd. dirs. Justinian Forum, Grievance Com. Mem. ABA, Am. Trial Lawyers Assn., Greater Cleve. Bar Assn., Ohio Bar Assn., Nat. Health Lawyers Assn., Met. Crime Bur., Health Law Council , Fraud Investigators Assn., W. Liberty State Coll. Alumni Assn., Chi Omega. Roman Catholic. Avocations: theatre, lit., skiing. Office: Blue Cross/Blue Shield of No Ohio 2060 E 9th St Cleveland OH 44115

RUSSO, VIVIAN ALFONSINA, cosmetic company executive, creative consultant; b. Bklyn., Apr. 21, 1949; d. Louis Anthony and Iole Primetta (Barbaglia) R.; m. Robert Ferro, May 26, 1968 (div. 1975). Student Bernard Baruch Coll., 1966, Brooklyn Coll., 1967, Fashion Inst. Tech., 1971-77. Assoc. advt. mgr. Kayser-Roth Corp., N.Y.C., 1968-77; advt. and sales promotion mgr. GAF Corp., N.Y.C., 1977-80; sales promotion and merchandising mgr. Revlon, N.Y.C., 1980-82; dir. creative services Del Labs., Farmingdale, N.Y., 1982—; lectr. Briarcliff Bus. Coll., Hicksville, N.Y., 1985. Creative dir. (coop. program) Co-op Advt. Credit Card Program (Sales and Mktg. Mgmt. Mag. award), 1976, (sampling program) Excello Shirts-Fabric Swatch (Sales and Mktg. Mgmt. Mag. award), 1977, (product catalogue) View-Master Catalogue (Nat. Endowment Arts award), 1978, GAF Star-Vinyl Floors Catalogue (Nat. Endowment Arts award), 1980. Friend of Bd. Nat. Found. Ileitis and Colitis, Inc., N.Y.C., 1981. Recipient Mgmt. award Am. Mgmt. Assn., 1979. Mem. Cosmetic Exec. Women, Advt.

Women N.Y., Inc., The Fashion Group, Theatre Guild Assn. Republican. Roman Catholic. Avocations: Tennis; painting; photography; fishing. Office: Del Labs 565 Broadhollow Rd Farmingdale NY 11735

RUST, LIBBY KAREN, fund raising counsel; b. York, Maine, Feb. 8, 1951; d. Myron Davis and Meta Mildred (Libby) R.; B.A., Wheaton Coll., 1973; M.S., Columbia U., 1977. Day care field asst. Childhood Ednl. Enrichment Program, Waterville, Maine, 1974-75; cons. Center for Community Planning and Cons., N.Y.C., 1975-76; intern Morgan Guaranty Trust Co., N.Y.C., 1976; staff asst. subcom. on mental health Task Force on N.Y.C. Fiscal Crisis, 1976-77; auditor AT&T, N.Y.C., 1977; budget examiner Legis. Office of Budget Rev., N.Y.C., 1977-78; exec. dir. Strafford County Human Services, Dover, N.H., 1978-79; dir. allocations and agy. relations United Way, Inc., Portland, Maine, 1979-82, planning and allocations div. dir., 1982-84; exec. dir. Seacoast United Way, Portsmouth, N.H., 1984-87; dir. Devel. Am. Cancer Soc., Los Angeles, 1987—. Mem. budget com. Town of York, 1979-80. Mem. Jr. League Portland, Jr. League Los Angeles, Kents Hill Sch. Alumni Assn. (bd. dirs.). Republican. Clubs: Portland Wheaton; Rolling Hills Racquet. Home: Mitchell Rd York ME 03909

RUST, RACHEL LOUISE, family therapist; b. Wharton, Tex., Oct. 18, 1955; d. Lloyd Gates and Rose Marie (Dominy) R. B.Social Work, U. Tex.-Austin, 1978; M.S., U. Tex.-Dallas, 1981; M.S. in Social Work, U. Tex.-Arlington, 1983. Cert. social worker, Assn. Cert. Social Workers. Group counselor Salesmanship Club Youth Camps, Palestine, Tex., 1978-80; case mgr. Juliette Fowler Home, Inc., Dallas, 1981-82; family therapist Salesmanship Club Ctr., Dallas, 1983—. Mem. Nat. Assn. Social Workers, Mental Health Assn., Tex. Corrections Assn. Presbyterian. Club: 500 Inc (Dallas). Home: 6249 Belmont St Dallas TX 75214 Office: Salesmanship Club Dallas Ctr 110 E 10th St Dallas TX 75203

RUSZKOWSKI, LESLEY GAY, television promotion executive; b. Cleve., Aug. 2, 1952; d. Eugene Medard and Elsie Lillian (Chinnock) R. BA, Wittenberg U., 1974; MA, Ohio U., 1976. Various positions Sta. WOUB-TV, Athens, Ohio, 1974-76, Sta. WMPO-AM-FM, Middleport, Ohio, 1977; asst. ops. mgr., promotion dir. Sta. WCHS-TV, Charleston, W. Va., 1977-82; promotion dir. Sta. WTAJ-TV, Altoona, Pa., 1982-85, Sta. WOAC-TV, Canton, Ohio, 1985—; speaker Ohio U. Communications Week, Athens, 1986. Pres. Y-Teens, Strongsville, Ohio, 1974. Mem. Broadcast Promotion and Mktg. Execs. (vis., Silver award 1984), Charleston/Huntington Advt. Club (Addy awards), Sigma Kappa. Office: WOAC-TV 4867 Fulton Dr Canton OH 44718

RUTENBERG-ROSENBERG, SHARON LESLIE, journalist; b. Chgo., May 23, 1951; d. Arthur and Bernice (Berman) R.; m. Michael J. Rosenberg, Feb. 3, 1980; children—David Kaifel and Jonathan Reuben (twins). Student, Harvard U., 1972; B.A., Northwestern U., 1973, M.S.J., 1975; cert. student pilot. Reporter-photographer Lerner Home Newspapers, Chgo., 1973-74; corr. Medill News Service, Washington, 1975; reporter-newsperson, sci. writer UPI, Chgo., 1975—. Interviewer: exclusives White House chief of staff, nation's only mother and son on death row; others. Vol. Chgo.-Read Mental Health Ctr. Recipient Peter Lisagor award for exemplary journalism in features category, 1980, 81; Golden Key Nat. Adv. Bd. of Children's Oncology Service Inc., 1981; Media awards for wire service feature stories, 1983, 84, wire service news stories, 1983, 84, all from Chgo. Hosp. Pub. Relations Soc. Mem. Profl. Assn. Diving Instrs., Nat. Assn. Underwater Instrs., Hon. Order Ky. Cols., Hadassah, Sigma Delta Chi, Sigma Delta Tau. Home: 745 Marion Ave Highland Park IL 60035

RUTH, JOAN LOUISE, health care product manager; b. Sellersville, Pa., Jan. 30, 1951; d. Marvin L. and Lizzie H. (Haldeman) R. Student, Shippensburg (Pa.) State U., 1970-72; BBA, Ga. State U., 1983; postgrad., Pepperdine U., 1987—. Anesthesia technician Grady Meml. Hosp., Atlanta, 1972-76, Crawford Long Meml. Hosp., Atlanta, 1976-77; service rep. Ohio Med. Products, Madison, Wis., 1977-83; gen. sales rep. Ohio Med. Products, Madison, 1983-85; critical care sales rep. Ohmeda, Madison, 1985-86, western region sales specialist, 1986-87, product mgr. U.S. infant care div., 1987—. Foster parent Foster Parent Plan, Warwick, R.I., 1985—; active The Hunger Project, Make-A-Wish Found. Mem. NOW, Nat. Assn. Female Execs. Home: 6027-5 Majors Ln Columbia MD 21045 fffice: Ohmeda 9065 Guilford Rd Columbia MD 21046

RUTHVEN, BECKY, cable company executive; b. Detroit, Mar. 21, 1947; d. Bryant W. and Beatrice (Nesbitt) R. BA, Albion (Mich.) Coll., 1968; MA, U. Mich., 1969. Secondary tchr. Atlanta Pub. Schs., 1970-71, Glenbrook Pub. Sch., Glenview, Ill., 1970-80; mfrs. rep. Thomas Balend & Co., Chgo., 1980-82; pres. Cassidy & Ruthven, Phila., 1980-82; dir. cen. region The Entertainment Channel, Chgo., 1982-83; dir. nat. accounts Rainbow Programming, Woodbury, N.Y., 1983-84; v.p. eastern region The Disney Channel, N.Y.C., 1984-88; v.p. The Weather Channel, Atlanta, 1988—. Mem. Women in Cable, N.Y. Cable Club, Cable TV Am.

RUTLEDGE, JENNIFER MERDITTE, management consultant; b. White Plains, N.Y., Sept. 12, 1951; d. James and Elizabeth (Chesson) R. BS in Indsl. Psychology, Mich. State U., 1973; MBA, Pace U., 1982. Personnel asst. Allstate Ins. Co., White Plains, 1973-76; personnel dir. NAACP Legal Def. Fund, N.Y.C., 1976-79; nat. coordinator work experience program Nat. Council of Negro Women, N.Y.C., 1979-80; dir. NE Service Ctr. Girls Clubs of Am., Inc., N.Y.C., 1984-86, cons., 1986—; ptnr. Delphi Cons. Group, Inc., White Plains, 1986—. Editor (newsletter) The Westsider, 1978. Bd. dirs. Afro-Am. Cultural Found., White Plains, 1975, Westchester Urban League, 1976, Afro-Am. Civic Assn., Yonkers, N.Y., 1978. Named Businesswoman of Yr. Afro-Am. Civic Assn., 1987. Mem. Nat. Assn. Female Execs., Nat. Assn. MBA's, Am. Mgmt. Assn. (assoc.), Meeting Planners Internat. Office: Delphi Cons Group Inc 5 Corporate Park Dr Suite 311 White Plains NY 10604

RUTLEDGE, PATSY LEITH, educational specialist; b. Longview, Tex., Mar. 3, 1951; d. George Edgar and Vivian Laverne (O'Keefe) Leith; m. Thomas Wendell Rutledge, Jan. 26, 1985; 1 child, Erin. BSEd summa cum laude, Abilene Christian U., 1973; MEd, Stephen F. Austin State U., 1977. Tchr. spl. edn., learning disabilities Longview (Tex.) Ind. Sch. Dist., 1973-76, diagnostic tchr., cons., 1976-78, ednl. diagnostician, 1978—; presenter state conf. Tex. Council for Exceptional Children, San Antonio, 1984; test administr. Stanford Binet Intelligence Scale IV norming study, Longview, 1985—. Mem. NEA (del. nat. conv. 1983), Tex. State Tchr. Assn. (del. state conv.), Tex. Ednl. Diagnostician Assn. (sec. 1982-83, publicity chair state conv. 1987-88), Longview Educators Assn. (sec. 1982-83), Women for Abilene Christian U. Mem. Ch. of Christ.

RUTMAN, JOAN MARGARET, communication executive; b. N.Y.C., Dec. 4, 1934; d. Edward Irving and Lee Elizabeth (Mason) R. BS, Fordham U., 1954. Radio buyer Blow Co., N.Y.C., 1954-58; media buyer Grey Advt., N.Y.C., 1958-64; group supr. Doyle, Dane and Bernbach, Inc., N.Y.C., 1964-68; broadcast dir. Ted Bates & Co., Inc., N.Y.C., 1968-1973; account exec. Field Spot Sales, N.Y.C., Los Angeles, 1973-79, Metro Media TV., N.Y.C., 1979-82, John Blair & Co., N.Y.C., 1982-1985; v.p., research dir. Katz Communications, Inc., N.Y.C., 1985—. Dist. leader Westchester Rep. Club, Yonkers, N.Y., 1959-62. Republican. Roman Catholic. Office: Katz Communications Inc One DagHammarskjold Plaza New York NY 10017

RUTMAN, SUSAN H., visual artist, photographer, entrepreneur; b. Bklyn., Jan. 16, 1948; d. Hyman L. and Judy (Sontag) R. B.F.A., Boston U., 1969. Sculptor, art tchr. Pub. Schs., Watertown, Mass., 1969-72; owner, sculptor The Craft Arcade, St. Johnsbury, Vt., 1972-76; freelance photographer, N.Y.C., 1976—; pres. The Townhouse Collection, N.Y.C., 1981-86. Mem. Nat. Assn. Female Execs., Small Bus. Service Bur., Am. Woman's Econ. Devel. Corp., Am. Craft Council, NOW.

RUTTER, DEBORAH FRANCES, orchestra adminstrator; b. Pottstown, Pa., Sept. 30, 1956; d. Marshall Anthony and Winifred (Hitz) R. BA, Stanford U., 1978; MBA, U. So. Calif., 1985. Orch. mgr. Los Angeles Philharm., 1978-86; exec. dir. Los Angeles Chamber Orch., 1986—. Bd. dirs. AIDS project Los Angeles, 1985—; active Jr. League Los Angeles, 1982—. Mem. Am. Symphony Orch. League, Assn. Calif. Symphony Orchs., Chamber Music Soc. Los Angeles (bd. dirs. 1987—). Democrat. Episcopalian. Office: Los Angeles Chamber Orch 315 W 9th St Suite 300 Los Angeles CA 90015

RUTZ, KAREN ELISABETH, marketing executive; b. Chgo., July 29, 1954; d. Erwin August and Gertrud (Staack) R.; m. Daniel Raymond Porth, Sept. 3, 1977 (div. Mar. 1982). BA in Biology, William Woods Coll., 1975; BA in Nursing, Baylor U., 1977; MBA, U. Dallas, 1984. RN. Staff nurse Children's Med. Ctr., Dallas, 1977-78; operating room staff nurse Baylor Univ. Med. Ctr., Dallas, 1978-84; mktg. dir. Emergicenter Physician Care, Dallas, 1983-84; dir. mktg. Baylor Health Care System, Dallas, 1984-86; pres. MediMax Mgmt. Systems, Dallas, 1986-87; sales rep. Ender Assocs., Inc., Dallas, 1987-88; dir. research and devel. Roll-A-Sheet, Inc., Dallas, 1987—; office mgr. Northlake Family Clinic, Dallas; vol. Alumni Career Assistance Program U. Dallas. Author, programmer (software) Lintrax, 1986. Mem. Nat. Honor and Profl. Mgmt., Am. Mgmt. Assn., Nat. Assn. Female Execs., Dallas Women's Found., Health Services Grad. Assn. (pres. 1984-85), Sigma Iota Epsilon, Alpha Phi. Republican. Lutheran. Club: Evangelism and Singles (Dallas) (advisor 1985—). Home: 6520 Stichter Dallas TX 75230 Office: Roll-A-Sheet Inc 9400 N Central Expressway Suite 1211 Dallas TX 75231

RUWART, MARY JEAN, scientist; b. Detroit, Oct. 16, 1949; d. William Wilder and Jean Mary (Choiniere) R.; m. Friedhelm Schroeder (div. 1975). Del. Libertarian Presdl. Nominating Conv., N.Y., 1983; mem. platform com. Libertarian Party, Denver, 1983; chmn. com. internal edn. Libertarian Nat. Com., Seattle, 1987. Recipient Libertarian Activist award Libertarian Party-Mich., 1983, Fred Kagan Lead Finding award, 1986. Unitarian. Office: The Upjohn Co 301 Henrietta St Kalamazoo MI 49001

RUZICKA, ANNE CULTON, accounting company executive; b. Lexington, Ky., Aug. 17, 1946; d. Eugene and Anne Elizabeth (Vaughan) Culton; m. Anthony J. Ruzicka, Jr., Nov. 30, 1974; children—Carrie Culton, Annette Lynne. B.S. in Acctg., U. Ky.-Lexington, 1968, M.S. in Acctg., 1969. C.P.A., Ill. Audit mgr. Arthur Young & Co., Chgo., 1969-76; ptnr. Ruzicka & Assocs., Chgo., 1976-82, v.p., 1982—; dir., v.p., treas. Chgo. Fin. Exchange, 1982—; dir., v.p. C.P.A.s Pub. Interest, Chgo., 1983—. Contbr. in field. Bd. dirs. Coalition on Non-Profit Acctg., Chgo., 1980-83; tchr. Glencoe Union Ch. (Ill.), 1981-83. Recipient award Ernst & Ernst, 1967; Charlotte Danstron Meml. award, 1984. Mem. Am. Inst. C.P.A.s, Exec. Club Chgo., Chgo. Soc. Women C.P.A.s (pres. 1977), Bus. and Profl. Individuals for the Pub. Interest (bd. dirs.), Am. Women Soc. C.P.A.s, Nat. Assn. Women Bus. Owners, Women in Mgmt. (bd. dirs., pres., treas. 1983—), Beta Gamma Sigma, Beta Alpha Psi. Home: 580 Jackson Ave Glencoe IL 60022 Office: Ruzicka & Assocs Ltd 8 S Michigan Ave Chicago IL 60603

RUZICKA, VICKI, marketing executive; b. Chgo., Apr. 30, 1945; d. Victor Hugo and Ellyn Marie (Do le) Reid, stepdaughter John Reid. B.S., Northeastern Ill. U., Chgo., 1976. Prodn. mgr. Signature Direct Response Mktg., Evanston, Ill., 1981-82, purchasing mgr., 1983-84; credit promotions media mgr. Montgomery Ward, Chgo., 1982-83; fulfillment purchasing mgr. The Signature Group, Schaumburg, Ill., 1984-87; sr. credit analyst CitiCorp DinersClub, Chgo., 1987—. Author: Trips: Head, Bod and Side, 1968, American Poetry Anthology, 1988, Poetry Magazine, 1970; Contbr. articles to profl. jours. Served with USAF, 1979-83. Mem. Women's Direct Response Group, Sierra Club, Wilderness Soc. Roman Catholic. Avocations: sailing; golf; classical piano; baseball. Office: CitiCorp Diners Club 8430 W Bryn Mawr Chicago IL 60631

RYALL, JO-ELLYN M., psychiatrist; b. Newark, May 25, 1949; d. Joseph P. and Tekla (Paraszczuk) R.; B.A. in Chemistry with gen. honors, Douglass Coll., Rutgers U., 1971; M.D., Washington U., St. Louis, 1975. Resident in psychiatry Washington U., 1975-78, psychiatrist Student Health, 1980-84, clin. instr. psychiatry, 1978-83, clin. asst. prof. psychiatry, 1983—; inpatient supr. Malcolm Bliss Mental Health Center, St. Louis, 1978-80, psychiatrist outpatient clinic, 1980-82; pvt. practice medicine specializing in psychiatry, St. Louis, 1980—. Bd. dirs. Women's Self Help Center, St. Louis, 1980-83. Diplomate Am. Bd. Psychiatry and Neurology. Fellow Am. Psychiat. Assn. Soc. (pres. Eastern Mo. Dist. Br. 1983-85, sect. council Am. Med. Assn. 1986—); mem. Am. Med. Women's Assn. (pres. St. Louis Dist. br. 1981-82, regional gov. VIII 1986—), AMA, St. Louis Met. Med. Soc. (del. to state conv. 1981—councilor 1985—), Mo. State Med. Assn. (vice speaker ho. of dels. 1986—), Manic Depressive Assn. St. Louis (chmn. bd. dirs. 1985—). Club: Washington U. Faculty. Office: 9216 Clayton Rd Saint Louis MO 63124

RYAN, ADRIANA FRIDA, accountant; b. Santiago, Chile, Mar. 22, 1949; came to U.S., 1964, naturalized, 1970; d. Hans Wolfgang and Ursula Maria (Zondek) Philippi. B.A. in Acctg., San Francisco State U., 1970. C.P.A., Calif. Staff acct. Richard T. Dwyer & Co., Daly City & Co., Daly City, Calif., 1970-72; staff acct., mgr. Good & Fowler C.P.A.s, San Francisco, 1972-79, ptnr., 1979-86, mng. ptnr., 1982-84; acct. Laventhol & Horwath, San Francisco, 1986—. Chmn. accts. div. Jewish Community Fedn., San Francisco, 1980-83, assoc. chmn. San Francisco div., 1984, bd. dirs., 1986—; bd. dirs. Generation to Generation, San Francisco, 1983—. Mem. Calif. Soc. C.P.A.s, Am. Inst. C.P.A.s, Profl. Women's Network (San Francisco chpt.).

RYAN, ALICE MARY, import company executive; b. Bay Shore, N.Y., June 10, 1942; d. James Vincent and Alice Mary (Ryan) Kavanaugh; m. James Anthony Ryan, July 10, 1965; children: Thomas, James, Christopher, Padraig. Diploma, Queen of the Rosary Acad., 1960. Clk. N.Y. Telephone Co., Patchogue, N.Y., 1960-63; receptionist Cantor Bros., Farmingdale, N.Y., 1963-65; owner J.A. Ryan Imports, Babylon, N.Y., 1981—. Pres. Parent Tchr. Group, Babylon, 1975-78; sec. Cub Scout Com., Babylon, 1974-76; active Babylon Varsity Booster Club, Babylon, 1978—. Mem. Nat. Assn. Female Execs., Am. Celtic Pipe Band, Inc., Scottish Tartan Soc., Clan Montgomery Soc., Scottish Clan Assn., Babylon C. of C. Office: JA Ryan Celtic Imports PO Box #585 Babylon NY 11702

RYAN, DEBRA LYNN, marketing representative; b. Utica, N.Y., May 25, 1963; d. Robert K. and Lillian H. (Huluk) R. AS, Green Mountain Coll., 1981-83; BS, Marist Coll., 1983-85. Project mgr. Certified Reports, Kinderhook, N.Y., 1985-86; mktg. rep. and asst. dir. Catamount Ski Area, Hillsdale, N.Y., 1986—. Mem. Nat. Assn. Female Execs., Consumers Union Assocs., Profl. Ski Instrs. Am. Democrat. Lutheran. Home: 33 Ten Broeck Ave Hudson NY 12534 Office: Catamount Ski Area Rt 23 Hillsdale NY 12127

RYAN, ELEANORE A., clinical psychologist; b. Chgo.; BS with honors in Chemistry, Mundelein Coll.; PhD in Clin. Psychology, Northwestern U., 1978; children: Robert, James, Mark, John, Christopher, Marynel. Staff psychologist Porter-Starke Services, Valparaiso, Ind., 1978-80; psychol. cons. Gary (Ind.) Community Mental Health Center, 1980-81; pvt. practice clin. and cons. psychology, Clarendon Hills, Ill., 1981—; psychologist Hines VA Hosp. (Ill.), 1983—. Cert. psychologist, Ill., Ind. Mem. Am. Psychol. Assn., Ill. Psychol. Assn., Midwest Psychol. Assn., Assn. DuPage Psychologists (sec.), Nat. Register Health Service Providers in Psychology, Soc. for Clin. and Exptl. Hypnosis, Soc. for Traumatic Stress Studies, Health Services Adv. Bd., DuPage Assn. for Children with Learning Disabilities (mem. adv. bd.), Chgo. Psychologists in Addictive Behavior, Consortium Vietnam Vet. Service Providers. Roman Catholic. Home and Office: 215 Coe Rd Clarendon Hills IL 60514

RYAN, EVELYN MARIE, management consultant firm executive; b. Mayaguez, P.R., Sept. 21, 1936; d. Arturo R. Oppenheimer and Georgina Castro; m. Michael John Ryan, Jan. 7, 1956; children—Michael, Terence, Cathy, Darren, Jennifer, Arthur, Karl. Grad. with honors in Secretarial Sci. Havana Bus. U., Cuba, 1955; B.S. in Econs. St. Thomas Vilanova U., Cuba, 1955; cert. in Comml. Edn., U. P.R., 1966. Cert. personnel cons., 1985. Translator, adminstrn. asst. M.W. Kellog Co., N.Y.C., 1957-59; translator, interpreter, Tucson, Ariz., San Diego, Calif., 1959-66; comml. edn. tchr. Manpower Bus. Tng. Inst., San Juan, P.R., 1970-75, admissions officer, 1975-77; sales, mktg. mgmt. cons. Careers Inc., Hatorey, P.R., 1977-87; gen. mgr., v.p. JMA/A Ryan Corp., Hato Rey, P.R., 1987—. Contbr. articles to local newspapers. Recipient SVE top mgmt. service award as #1 exec. recruiter, 1988. Surveyor New Progressive Political Party, San Juan, 1974. Mem. Am. Mktg. Assn. (pres., founding mem. P.R. chpt. 1985-87, bd. dirs. 1984-85, sec. 1983-84), Am. Business Women Assn., Sales and Mktg. Execs., Mfrs. Assn., P.R. Products Assn., San Juan of U.S. C. of C., ASPA. Democrat. Roman Catholic. Clubs: Cafe del Puerto (San Juan), Club Caborrajeño, Entrepeneurs. Avocations: reading, music, camping, beach activities, painting, writing, gardening, continued ednl. sems. Office: JMA/A Ryan Corp PH 1615 Mercantil Plaza Hato Rey PR 00918

RYAN, SISTER JANICE, college administrator, nun. BA in English, Trinity Coll., 1965; MEd in Spl. Edn., Boston U., 1967; postgrad., U. Minn., 1968, U. Lund, Sweden, 1971, Harvard U., 1974-76, 80. Dir. pub. relations Trinity Coll., Burlington, Vt., 1967-71, asst. prof. spl. edn., 1967-74, pres., 1979—; mem. Am. Council on Edn.'s Govtl. Relations Commn. on Nat. Challenges in Higher Edn.; corporator, dir. Bank of Vt., trustee Vt. Law Sch.; task force on econ. devel. infrastructure, edn. and tng. NE-Midwest Leadership Council. Exec. com. Campus Compact, chair fed. initiatives task force; active Vt. Higher Edn. Council. Am. Assn. Higher Edn. (participant Spring Hill Conf. 1987). Office: Trinity Coll Office of Pres 208 Colchester Ave Burlington VT 05401

RYAN, JUDITH ANDRE, association executive, nurse; b. Vermillion, S.D., Sept. 11, 1936; d. Hugo Carl and Nelle Marie (Schultz) Andre; m. Darrell Richard Yates, Sept. 13, 1958 (div. June 1975); m. Gerald Odin Ryan, Dec. 22, 1982; children—Allison Marie, Matthew Andre. B.S. in Nursing, St. Olaf Coll., 1958; Ph.D. in Hosp. and Health Care Adminstrn., U. Minn., 1983. Registered nurse, Minn. Staff nurse Mower County Pub. Health Nursing Services, Family Nursing Service, St. Paul, 1958-62; asst. exec. dir. govtl. and pub. relations Minn. Nurses Assn., Mpls., 1964-68; instr. St. Mary's Jr. Coll., Mpls., 1975-76; dir. nursing edn. Rochester Meth. Hosp., Minn., 1976-80; dep. exec. dir. Am. Nurses' Assn., Kansas City, Mo., 1980-81, exec. dir., 1982—; bd. govs. EcuMed, N.Y.C.; cons. in field. Author: Moving and Lifting Patients, 1970; assoc. editor Minn. Nursing Accent, 1964-68; contbr. articles to profl. jours. Mem. exec. com. Minn. Comprehensive Health Planning Adv. Council, 1968-76. Bush Leadership fellow, 1978-79; recipient Disting. Alumnae award St. Olaf Coll., 1984. Mem. Am. Nurses' Assn., Am. Soc. Assn. Execs., Nat. League for Nursing, Nat. Commn. on Nursing. Republican. Lutheran. Office: Am Nurses' Assn 2420 Pershing Rd Kansas City KS 64108 *

RYAN, LAURIE E., insurance undewriter; b. Summit, N.J., Aug. 4, 1960; d. Richard Frances and Patricia Barbara (Hanas) R. Student, Profl. Sch. Bus., 1986. Manual rater Allstate Ins. Co., Murray Hill, N.J., 1979-81; asst. underwriter AGA Ins. Agy., Union, N.J., 1981-83; personal lines mgr. C&C Ins. Assocs., Berkeley Heights, 1983-85; acct. rep., underwriter M.J. Lieberman & Co., Livingston, N.J., 1985—. Office: MJ Lieberman & Co 354 Eisenhower Pkwy Livingston NJ 07039

RYAN, LAVONNE BLINDERMAN, speech pathologist; b. Southampton, N.Y., Aug. 2, 1932; d. Leo M. and Gwen (Smith) Blinderman; m. F. Paul Ryan, July 4, 1955; children: Kathleen Ryan Goodwin, Laura Marie, Scott Paul. BS, SUNY, Buffalo, 1954; MA, Coll. St. Rose, 1963; postgrad. SUNY, Albany, 1963. Speech therapist Buffalo Pub. Schs., 1954; speech lang. therapist Norfolk (Va.) Cerebral Palsy Ctr., 1955, 56, Bethlehem Cen. Sch. Dist., Delmar, N.Y., 1969-74; supr. clin. practicum, dept. speech pathology and audiology SUNY, Albany, 1975-76; chief ednl. therapist VA Hosp., Albany, N.Y., 1977; speech lang. pathologist South Colonie Sch. Dist., Albany, 1978—; pvt. practice speech pathology, 1958-69. Bd. dirs. YWCA, 1962-70. Mem. 3d Dist. Dental Soc. Aux. (bd. dirs. 1959-69), Am. Speech and Hearing Assn., N.Y. State Speech Lang. Hearing Assn., Kappa Delta Pi. Home: 49 Thorndale Rd Slingerlands NY 12159 Office: 329 Sand Creek Rd Albany NY 12205

RYAN, MARLEIGH GRAYER, college dean, Japanese educator; b. N.Y.C., May 1, 1930; d. Harry and Betty (Hurwick) Grayer; m. Edward Ryan, June 4, 1950; 1 child, David Patrick. B.A., NYU, 1951; M.A., Columbia U., 1956, Ph.D., 1965; Cert., East Asian Inst., 1956; postgrad., Kyoto U., 1958-59. Research assoc. Columbia U., N.Y.C., 1960-61, lectr. Japanese, 1961-65, asst. prof., 1965-70, assoc. prof., 1970-72; vis. asst. prof. Yale U., New Haven, 1966-67; assoc. prof. U. Iowa, Iowa City, 1972-75, prof., 1975-81, chmn. dept., 1972-81; dean liberal arts and scis., prof. Japanese SUNY-New Paltz, 1981—; vice chair seminar on modern Japan, Columbia U., 1984-85, chair, 1985-86; co-chmn. N.Y. State Conf. on Asian Studies, 1986. Co-author: (with Herschel Webb) Research in Japanese Sources, 1965; author: Japan's First Modern Novel, 1967, The Development of Realism in the Fiction of Tsubouchi Shoyo, 1975; assoc. editor: Jour. Assn. Tchrs. Japanese, 1962-71, editor, 1971-75. East Asian Inst. fellow Columbia U., 1955; Ford Found. fellow, 1958-60; Japan Found. fellow, 1973, Woodrow Wilson Ctr. Internat. Scholars fellow, 1988-89; recipient Van. Am. Disting. Book award Columbia, 1968. Mem. MLA (sec. com. on teaching Japanese Lang. 1962-68, mem. del. assembly 1979-87, mem. exec. com. div. Asian lit. 1981-86), Assn. Tchrs. Japanese (exec. com. 1969-72, 74-77), Assn. Asian Studies (bd. dirs. 1975-78), Midwest Conf. Asian Studies (pres. 1980-81). Office: SUNY Coll New Paltz FT 614 New Paltz NY 12561

RYAN, MARY A., diplomat; b. New York, N.Y., Oct. 1, 1940. B.A., St. John's Univ., 1963, M.A., 1965. With Foreign Service, Dept. of State 1966—; consular and adminstrv. officer Naples, Italy, 1966-69; personnel officer Am. Embassy, Tegucigalpa, Honduras, 1970-71; consular officer Am. Consulate Gen., Monterrey, Mexico, 1971-73; adminstrv. officer Bur. of African Affairs, Dept. of State, Washington, 1973-75, post mgmt. officer, 1975-77; career devel. officer Bur. of Personnel, Dept. of State, 1977-80; adminstrv. counselor Abidjan, Ivory Coast, 1980-81, Khartoum, Sudan, 1981-82; inspector, Office of Insp. Gen. Dept. of State, Washington, 1982-83, exec. dir. Bur. of European and Can. Affairs, 1983-85, exec. asst. to Under Sec. of State for Mgmt., 1985-88; ambassador to Swaziland 1988—. Address: US Ambassador to Swaziland care Dept of State Washington DC 20520 *

RYAN, MARY PATRICIA, college administrator; b. Ottawa, Ont., Can., Feb. 10, 1949; d. Ward Sanford and Margaret M. (Heckle) R. BA, Duquesne U., 1970, MA, 1972; PhD, Am. U., Washington, 1978. Counselor Cochise Coll., Sierra Vista, Ariz., 1972-73; counselor No. Va. Comunity Coll., Annandale, 1973-78, dir. student activities, 1978-79; dean of students Mt. Vernon Coll., Washington, 1979-84; dir. of interns Washington Ctr., 1985-87, v.p. acad. programs, 1987—; cons. Am. U., 1982-87, Children's Hosp., Richmond, Va., 1984. Mem. Nat. Assn. for Coll. Deans, Adminstrs., and Counselors, Am. Coll. Personnel Assn. Roman Catholic. Office: The Washington Ctr 514 10th St NW Washington DC 20004

RYAN, NANCY JEAN, hotel sales executive; b. Chgo., Nov. 25, 1952; d. Edward Charles Ryan and Mary (Simpson) Ryan Townsend; student John Carroll U., 1970-72, Rome Center of Loyola U. of Chgo., 1972-73; B.S. in Mktg./Bus. Adminstrn., Bradley U., 1974. Reservations mgr. Ambassador West Hotel, Chgo., 1975-78, asst. exec. mgr., 1978-79; front office mgr. Tremont Hotel, Chgo., 1979-80; front office mgr. Mayfair Regent Hotel, Chgo., 1980-81, sales rep./corp. accounts, 1981-82; sales mgr. Grand Met. and Forum hotels, 1982-84; nat. sales mgr. Howard Johnson Co., 1984-86; dir. nat. sales, 1986—. Active Stritch Sch. Medicine Jr. Service League, 1969—, Presentation Ball Jr. Aux., Chgo., 1970, Northwestern Meml. Hosp. Service Bd., 1978-81, Presbyterian-St. Luke's Hosp. Vol. Services, Chgo., 1981-82; mem. Landmarks Preservation Council Ill., 1982-83; mem. Gov. James R. Thompson Re-election Com., 1979, 82. Named to Outstanding Young Women Am., 1982. Mem. Hotel Front Office Execs. Assn. (sec.-treas. 1979-80), Ill. Opera Guild, Chgo. Drama League, Meeting Planners Internat., Nat. Passenger Traffic Assn., Midwest Bus. Travel Assn. Clubs: Jr. League Chgo., Chgo. Travel Women's. Home: 1550 N Lake Shore Dr Chicago IL 60610

RYAN, SHEENA ROSS, museum director; b. Perth, Scotland, Aug. 1, 1944; came to U.S., 1972; d. Douglas George Haig and Johanna Adams (Brown) Ross; m. Raymond John Ryan, Dec. 17, 1978 (div. Feb. 1985); 1 child, Ross McCarthy. Assoc., Inst. Bankers, Glasgow, Scotland, 1964; B. Profl. Studies, Pace U., 1985. Banker, Clydesdale Bank, Glasgow, 1962-65; acct. Newmont Pty. Ltd., Melbourne, Australia, 1965-72; acctg. mgr. Hertz Internat., N.Y.C., 1972-73; asst. controller M&M Internat., N.Y.C., 1974-76;

v.p. human resource planning Marsh & McLennan, N.Y.C., 1976-80; dir. data processing, Town of Ridgefield, Conn., 1986-87, Rotondo Real Estate, Katonah, N.Y., 1981-87; v.p., trustee Hammond Mus., N. Salem, N.Y., 1988—. founder, dir. New Eng. Sch. of Needle Art, Wilton, Conn., 1985-86; dir. Rotondo Real Estate, Katonah, N.Y. Editor: Human Resource Planning newsletter, 1979. Mem. Embroiderers Guild Am., Mensa. Avocation: reading.

RYAN, TULA FLESHMAN, health service consultant and nursing facility administrator; b. Rich Creek, Va., Feb. 5, 1927; d. John Elijah and Ophelia Kline (Cooper) Fleshman; m. James Joseph Ryan, May 1, 1948 (div. June 1973); children: John Keith, James Kenneth. Diploma in gen. nursing, Passaic (N.J.) Gen. Hosp., 1947; BS in Nursing, Ariz. State U., 1963; MA in Nursing Adminstrn., Columbia U., 1970. Pub. health nurse City Health Dept, Newark, 1947-53; supr. nursing Vincent Pallotti Hosp., Morgantown, W.Va., 1953-55; instr. nursing Lewis-Gale Hosp., Roanoke, Va., 1955-60, Good Samaritan Hosp., Phoenix, 1963-67; asst. adminstr., dir. nursing services John C. Lincoln Hosp., Phoenix, 1970-76; adminstr. nursing Whittaker Corp. and Hosp. Corp. Internat., Al-Mutagighani Health Service, Jeddah, Tabuk and Riyadh (Saudi Arabia), Al-Ain Abu Dhabi, United Arab Emirates, 1976-83; cons. Al-Mutabighani Health Service, Jubail Industrial City, Saudi Arabia, 1984—; adminstr. Portamedic, Phoenix, 1985; adminstr. nursing Thunderbird Health Care Ctr., Phoenix, 1986; dir. nursing services Jewish Care Ctr., Phoenix, 1987—; cons. Manzanita Manor, Payson, Ariz., 1986, Hinduja Nat. Hosp., Bombay, 1987—; patient services and nursing adminstrn., 1987—. USPHS scholar, 1963. Mem. Am. Nurses Assn. (del. 1965), Ariz. Nurses Assn. (sec. 1963-64), Gerontol. Nursing Services (edn. coordinator). Republican. Lodge: Soroptimists (sec. Camelback chpt. 1974, v.p. 1975). Home: 518 E Boca Raton Rd Phoenix AZ 85022 Office: Washington Health Care Internat Corp 2009 Massachusetts Ave NW Washington DC 20036

RYCHECK, JAYNE BOGUS (MRS. ROY RICHARD RYCHECK), retired educational administrator; b. Schenectady; d. Peter and Sylvia (Cywinski) Bogus; M.A., N.Y. U., 1953; B.S., State U. N.Y., Albany, 1941; postgrad. Syracuse U., 1957-66; m. R. Richard Rycheck, July 26, 1942. Tchr. various schs., 1935-43; elementary sch. tchr. Schenectady (N.Y.) City Schs., 1943-51, leadership intern, 1951-52, elementary sch. prin., 1952-61, dir. spl. edn., 1961-72. Instr. Russell Sage Coll., 1955-58, State U. N.Y., Oneonta, 1956; cons. bur. handicapped children N.Y. Edn. Dept., 1966-76, mem. commrs. and hoc coms., 1964-72, State Planning Com. Insts. for In-Service Edn., 1964-67; rep. to Community Welfare Council Schenectady County, 1961-62; adv. council N.Y. State Joint Legislative Com. Mental and Phys. Handicapped, 1970-72; mem. adv. com. Schenectady County Office for Aging, 1976-81, vice chmn., 1977-78, chmn., 1978-81; advisory com. Older Ams. Act program N.Y. State Office of Aging, 1977-80. Trustee, chmn. edn. Schenectady Mus., 1974-77; mem. human services adv. com. Schenectady County Community Coll., 1977—. Recipient Humanitarian service awards United Cerebral Palsy Schenectady County, 1966, 67, Capital dist. Assn. for Brain-Injured Children, 1967, Today's Woman award Schenectady YWCA, 1987, various citations from N.Y. State Sen. and Assembly, Am. Assn. Rct. People, AAUW, Schenectady County Legis., N.Y. State Legis., 1986, and others; named Sr. Citizen of Yr. SOFA, 1986; Meritorious Alumni award State U. N.Y. Coll. at Oneonta, 1972; Capitol Dist. Speech and Hearing award, 1972; Distinguished Service award N.Y. Fedn. chpts. Council for Exceptional Children, 1972; Joseph P. Kennedy, Jr. Found. award for outstanding activity for the mentally retarded, 1972, achievement award for contbns. to quality of life for sr. citizens N.Y. State Legislature, 1979; Disting. Service award Council Adminstrs. Spl. Edn., 1980. Mem. N.Y. State (sec. 1967-68), Nat. councils adminstrs. spl. edn., Assn. Childhood Edn. (state sec. 1952-55, state exec. bd. 1951-59), Council Exceptional Children (mem. chpt. regional and state bds. 1966-78, state regional dir. 1966-68, state adv. bd. 1966-72, v.p. 1968-69, state pres. 1970), Schenectady County Assn. Childhood Edn. (treas. and v.p. 1952), N.Y. State Assn. Childhood Edn. Internat. (sec., v.p. 1962-65), Am. Assn. Mental Deficiency, N.Y. State Assn. Brain-Injured Children (state adv. bd. 1963-67, dist. adv. bd. 1966-72), Nat. Soc. Autistic Children, Assn. Retarded Children (adv. bd.), Gifted Children Soc. (adv. com.), Schenectady C. of C. (edn. com.), Schenectady County Ret. Tchrs. Assn. (v.p. 1973, pres. 1974-76), Am. Assn. Ret. People (program com. chpt. 1973-76, legis. chmn., dir. 1981-84), AAUW (topic chmn. 1977-79, chpt. Name Grant honoree 1981), N.Y. Assn. Elementary Prins. (hon. life), N.Y. State Ret. Tchrs. Assn. (county dir. Eastern zone, del. state conv. 1974-76), Schenectady County Hist. Soc. (rec. sec., dir. 1982-84, 1st v.p. 1986-87), Delta Kappa Gamma (chmn. chpt. profl. affairs com. 1972-76, del. state legis. forum 1974-79, mem. state com. profl. affairs 1974-75). Contbr. articles to publs. Home: 1537 Kingston Ave Schenectady NY 12308

RYCZEK, JUDITH GALE, controller; b. Buffalo, Dec. 13, 1942; d. Harlow and Dorothy (Rzoska) Hanes; m. Ronald Gordon Critoph, Oct. 13, 1962 (div. Sept. 1972); children: Ronise, Todd, Jason Lee; m. Norman Joseph Ryczek, Dec. 27, 1972. AAS in Acctg., Bryant & Stratton Bus. Inst., 1978; BS in Mgmt., D'Youville Coll., 1984. Controller Watson Bowman Assocs., Amherst, N.Y., 1972-84, Smith Metal Arts Co. Inc., Buffalo, 1985-87; auditor U.S. Dept. Def., 1987—. Vol. Allentown Assn., Buffalo, 1975, West Seneca (N.Y.) Sch. for Retarded Children, 1975-77. Mem. Nat. Accts. Assn. Home: 54 Tracy St Buffalo NY 14201

RYDALCH, ANN, state senator; m. Vernal Rydalch. Mem. Idaho Senate, 1985—. Past mem. Idaho Bicentennial Commn.; former vice chmn. Idaho Republican Com. Office: Office of the State Senate State Capitol Boise ID 83720 Address: 3824 E 17th St Idaho Falls ID 83401 *

RYDER, GEORGIA ATKINS, educator, university dean; b. Newport News, Va., Jan. 30, 1924; d. Benjamin Franklin and Mary Lou (Carter) Atkins; B.S., Hampton (Va.) Inst., 1944; Mus.M., U. Mich., 1946; Ph.D., N.Y. U., 1970; m. Noah Francis Ryder, Sept. 16, 1947; children—Olive Diana, Malcolm Eliot, Aleta Renee. Resource music tchr., Alexandria, Va., 1945-48; faculty music dept. Norfolk State U., 1948—, prof., 1970—, head dept., 1969-79, dean Sch. Arts and Letters, 1979-86. Bd. dirs. Va. Symphony, ctr. Black Music Research, Columbia Coll., Chgo., Nat. Consortium Arts and Letters for Hist. Black Colls. and Univs., Norfolk Commn. Arts and Humanities, Southeastern Va. Arts Assn.; mem. advisory com. Norfolk chpt. Young Audiences. Grantee So. Fellowship Fund, 1967-69, Consortium Research Tng., 1973; recipient award Norfolk Com. Improvement Edn., 1974. Mem. Music Educators Nat. Conf., Coll. Music Soc., Intercoll. Music Assn., Va. Music Educators Assn., Delta Sigma Theta. Contbr. articles to profl. jours.

RYDER, SANDRA SMITH, communications specialist, publicist; b. Great Lakes, Ill., July 6, 1949; d. Dennis Murrey and Olga (Grosheff) Smith. B.S., Northwestern U., 1971; M.A., Annenberg Sch. Communications at U. So. Calif., 1986. Columnist Camarillo Daily News (Calif.), 1971-76; editor Fillmore Herald (Calif.), 1976-78; pub. info. officer Oxnard Union High Sch. Dist. (Calif.), 1980-82; pub. info. officer Ventura County Community Coll. Dist., 1982-83; pub. relations dir. Murphy Orgn., Oxnard, Calif., 1983-84; pub. affairs rep. Gen. Telephone Calif., Thousand Oaks, 1984—. Co-chmn. Ventura County Commn. for Women, 1981—. Mem. Women in Communications, Soc. Profl. Journalists, life mem. Pub. Info. and Communications Assn. Home: 177 W Green Vale Dr Camarillo CA 93010 Office: GTE Calif One GTE Place Thousand Oaks CA 91362

RYERSON, MARGERY AUSTIN, painter; b. Morristown, N.J., Sept. 15, 1886; d. David Austen and Mary McIlvaine (Brown) R. A.B., Vassar Coll., 1909; studied, Art Students League, N.Y.C.; studied under Robert Henri and Charles W. Hawthorne. Painter, etcher and lithographer. Represented prints in permanent collections, Smithsonian Instn., other mus., U.S. and abroad; exhibited paintings in collections, N.J. Hist. Soc., painting in collections, Norfolk Mus. Arts and Scis., Va., prints in collections, Abbott Labs., painting in collections, NAD, paintings in collections, Vassar Coll., Philbrook Art Ctr., Tulsa, Frye Mus., Seattle, Va. State Coll., Union Theol. Sem.; contbr.: Art in Am., The Am. Scholar, Am. Artist, The Artist, N.Y. Herald Tribune, N.Y. Times Book Rev.; compiler: The Art Spirit, by Robert Henri; co-editor: Hawthorne on Painting; illustrator: Winkle Boo. Recipient 1st prize (oil) Hudson Valley Art Assn., 1956, 57, 58; recipient Gold medal for oil portrait Nat. Arts Club, 1957, 62, 69, Silver medal Nat. Arts Club, 1971, Maynard portrait prize NAD, 1959, 1st prize Balt. Water Color Club, 1960; portrait prize (oil) Silvermine Guild, 1960; recipient Hook Meml. Am. Watercolor Soc., Talens N.J. Watercolor Soc., 1963, Winsor and Newton N.J. Watercolor Soc., 1968, Stevenson prize (oil) Nat. Arts Club, 1967, Grumbacher Nat. Arts Club, 1972, Clinedinst medal Artist Fellowship, 1971, Holton Meml. Watercolor prize Knickerbocker Artists, 1974, prize for graphics Knickerbocker Artists, 1978, Dole prize Am. Artists Profl. Leauge, 1973, prize for graphics Am. Artists Profl. League, 1974, Albany Print Club prize, 1973, N.A., 1959; painter mem. Grand Central Art Galleries. Mem. Am. Watercolor Soc., Balt. Water Color Club, Knickerbocker Artists, Soc. Am. Graphic Artists, Allied Artists Am. (v.p. 1952-53), Audubon Artists (corr. sec. 1958-59), N.J. Watercolor Soc., Print Club Albany, Pen and Brush. Address: care Condon 3 Dingleton Rd Greenwich CT 06830

RYG, KATHLEEN SCHULTZ, mental health center administrator; b. Evanston, Ill., Aug. 6, 1952; d. Robert Coyne and Sheila (Hogan) Schultz ; m. Martin Lee Ryg, Sept. 21, 1974 (div. Apr. 1986). BS, No. Ill. U., 1974; MA, Roosevelt U., 1979. Tng. counselor Clearbrook Ctr., Elk Grove Village, Ill., 1974-77; dir. residential services Clearbrook Ctr., Arlington Heights, Ill., 1977-79; employment supr. Condell Hosp., Libertyville, Ill., 1979-80; dir. residential program NW Mental Health Ctr., Arlington Heights, Ill., 1985—, asst. dir., 1985—. V.p. Career Guidance Ctr., Grayslake, Ill., 1980-82, v.p. summer celebration com., Vernon Hills, Ill., 1986—, bd. dirs., 1986; co-chmn. Programs for Alternative Living, Chgo. area, 1984-86. Mem. Nat. Assn. Female Execs., Am. Mgmt. Assn., Jaycees. Roman Catholic. Home: 728 N Lakeside Dr Vernon Hills IL 60061 Office: NW Mental Health Ctr 1616 N Arlington Heights Rd Arlington Heights IL 60004

RYMER, PAMELA ANN, federal judge; b. Knoxville, Tenn., Jan. 6, 1941. A.B., Vassar Coll., 1961; LL.B., Stanford U., 1964. Bar: Calif. 1966, U.S. Ct. Appeals (9th cir.) 1966, U.S. Ct. Appeals (10th cir.), U.S. Supreme Ct. Assoc. Lillick McHose & Charles, Los Angeles, 1966-72, ptnr., 1973-75; ptnr. Toy and Rymer, Los Angeles, 1975-83; judge U.S. Dist. Ct. (cen. dist.) Calif., Los Angeles, 1983—; faculty The Nat. Jud. Coll., 1986. Mem. Calif. Postsecondary Edn. Commn., 1974—, chmn., 1980-84; mem. Los Angeles Olympic Citizens Adv. Commn.; bd. visitors Stanford U. Law Sch., 1986—, Pepperdine U. Law Sch., 1987; mem. Edn. Commn. of States Task Force on State Policy and Ind. Higher Edn., 1987; bd. dirs. Constl. Rights Found., 1985—. Mem. ABA, Los Angeles County Bar Assn. (chmn. antitrust sect. 1981-82), Assn. of Bus. Trial Lawyers. Office: US Dist Ct 312 N Spring St Los Angeles CA 90012

RYNNING, LORRAINE SCOTT, chiropractor; b. Glendale, Calif., Sept. 17, 1957; d. Maurice Leo and Thela Grace (Reardon) Scott; m. Knut Morten Rynning, June 13, 1981 (div. Sept. 1983). AA, Young Harris Coll., 1977; student, U. Ga., 1977-78; D Chiropractic Medicine, Life Chiropractic Coll., Marietta, Ga., 1981; Cert. in Chiropractic Orthopedics, Los Angeles Coll. Chiropractic Med., 1987. Examiner Khalaf Clinic Chiropractic Medicine, Atlanta, 1981-82; pvt. practice chiropractic medicine Stone Mountain, Ga., 1983—; instr. Profl. Success Mgmt., Atlanta, 1984. Mem. Am. Coll. Chiropractic Orthopedics, Ga. Chiropractic Assn. Republican. Roman Catholic. Office: 870 Main St Stone Mountain GA 30083

RYPCZYK, CANDICE LEIGH, employee relations manager; b. Norman, Okla., Apr. 24, 1949; d. John Anthony and Lee (Brunswick) Wirth; m. Peter Charles Rypczyk, Nov. 27, 1976. BA, Kalamazoo Coll., 1971; cert. labor studies extension program, Cornell U., N.Y. Sch. Indsl., Labor Relations, Middletown, 1985. Personnel asst. PFW div. Hercules Inc., Middletown, N.Y., 1973-77, asst. personnel mgr., 1977-79, mgr. employee relations, 1979—. Mem. Am. Soc. for Personnel Adminstrn. (v.p. Mid-Hudson Valley chpt. 1985, pres. 1986, treas. N.Y. State council 1986, dist. dir. 1988—, cert., dist. dir. 1988), Orange County (N.Y.) Pvt. Industry Council, Orange County C. of C. (Vol. of Yr. 1986, program com., treas., mem. exec. com.), Sierra Club. Office: PFW Div Hercules Inc 33 Sprague Ave Middletown NY 10940

RZEWNICKI, JANET C., state official; b. Akron, Ohio, May 21, 1953; d. Robert Myers; m. Victor Rzewnicki, June 3, 1972. B.S. in acctg. and fin. with distinction, U. Del. CPA. Sr. acct. Peat, Marwick Mitchell, Wilmington, Del., 1978-80; corp. acct. internat. sect. Hercules Inc., Wilmington, 1980-81; acctg. instr. U. Del., Newark, 1980-82; pvt. practice acctg., Wilmington, 1981-82; state treas. State of Del., Dover, 1983—; mem. Del. Econ. Adv. Council. Leader People to People Del., People's Republic of China, 1985; v.p. Del. Children's Fire Safety Found.; treas., bd. dirs. March of Dimes, Newark, 1979—; bd. dirs. United Way of Del., Wilmington, 1980-82; active Gov.'s Council on Devel. Fin., 1982—. Mem. Nat. Assn. State Treas., Am. Inst. C.P.A.s, Del. Soc. C.P.A.s, Pa. Inst. C.P.A.s, Am. Soc. Women Accts. (dir. 1981), Beta Gamma Sigma. Republican. Office: Office of State Treas Thomas Collins Bldg PO Box 1401 Dover DE 19903

SAADAT, MARY, health organization executive; b. Tehran, Iran, Apr. 17, 1956; came to U.S. 1978; d. Ebrahim and Afsar (Seddigh) S.; m. John Davis Comegys, Dec. 7, 1985. GCE in French, U. London, 1977; BA in Communicative Disorders, Calif. State U., Fresno, 1980; MA in Counseling Psychology, U. Santa Clara, 1985. Fgn. student mktg. advisor Mahad, Inc. div. Internat. Bus. Inst., Fresno, 1979-80, dir. ops., mktg., 1980-82; bus. devel. cons. Stone Assocs. Inc., Cupertino, Calif., 1982-84; dir. mktg. Charter Hosp. Long Beach, Calif., 1984-86; dir. bus. devel. Comprehensive Care Corp., Irvine, 1986-87; pres., chief exec. officer Nat. Alternative Care Inc., Seal Beach, Calif., 1987—. Home: 20435 Via Don Juan Yorba Linda CA 92686 Office: Nat Alternative Care Inc 3020 Old Ranch Pkwy Suite 300 G Seal Beach CA 90740

SAAL, MARY VIRGINIA THOMAS, food service brokerage executive; b. Nashville, July 8, 1956; d. George Edwin and Mary Virginia (Haley) Thomas; m. Theodore Michael Saal, Oct. 10, 1979 (div. 1988); 1 child, Mary Virginia. Grad. high sch., Woodbury, Tenn. Office mgr. Penn Mut. Life Ins. Co., Nashville, 1976-77; asst. mgr. Elizabeth Arden, Inc., Nashville, 1977-79, Nashville Trunk and Bag, Nashville, 1979-80; sec. to v.p. Thweatt & Heldman Brokerage Co., Nashville, 1981; sec. to pres. Douglas Food Service Brokerage Co., Nashville, 1982—. Mem. Nat. Assn. Female Execs. Lutheran. Office: Douglas Food Service Brokerage Co 120 Donelson Pike Suite 102 Nashville TN 37214

SABAT, NANCY JANE, electrical engineer; b. Hartford, Conn., July 25, 1952. BS in Biochemistry, U. Mass., 1977; MS in Aerospace/Ocean Engring., U. So. Calif., 1980; postgrad., U. Ariz., 1983; postgrad. in electrical engring., Dartmouth Coll., 1984. Mem. tech. staff Amicon Labs., Lexington, Mass., 1974-75; mem. research staff Mass. Gen. Hosp., Boston, 1977-78; mech. engr. NASA/Jet Propulsion Lab., Pasadena, Calif., 1980-81; power engr. Stone & Webster Engring. Corp., Boston, 1981-82; sr. electrical systems engr. Avco Systems-Textron, Wilmington, Mass., 1985-86; avionics engr. McDonnel Douglas Helicopter Co., Mesa, Ariz., 1986—. Mem. IEEE, AIAA, ASME. Office: McDonnell Douglas Helicopter Co 5000 E McDowell Mesa AZ 85205

SABATELLA, ELIZABETH MARIA, educator, writer; b. Mineola, N.Y., Nov. 9, 1940; d. D. F. and Blanche M. (Schmetzle) S; 1 child, Kevin Woog. BS, SUNY, Brockport, 1961; MA, SUNY, Stony Brook, 1971, MSW, 1983. Lic. social worker, N.Y.; cert. tchr., N.Y. Tchr. physical edn. Comseqogue Sch. Dist., Port Jefferson, N.Y., 1968-73, 84-87, 88—; therapist adolescents, 1973-84; mem. family systems Network for Continuing Edn., Calif. and Colo., 1978-80; with biofeedback, meditation com. McLean Hosp. Tng., Boston, 1978, therapeutic touch team East and West Ctr., N.Y.C., 1980—. Author poetry. Mem. Writers Assn. Democrat. Home: 202 Foxhill Dr Baiting Hollow NY 11933

SABAU, CARMEN SYBILE, chemist; b. Cluj, Romania, Apr. 24, 1933; naturalized U.S. citizen; d. George and Antoinette Marie (Chiriac) Grigorescu; m. Mircea Nicolae Sabau, July 11, 1956; 1 dau., Isabelle Carmen. M.S. in Inorganic and Analytical Chemistry, U. C.I. Parhon, Bucharest, Romania, 1955; Ph.D. in Radiochemistry, U. Fridericiana, Karlsruhe, W.Ger., 1972. Chemist, Argonne (Ill.) Nat. Lab., 1976—. Internat. Atomic Energy Agy. fellow, 1967-68; Humboldt fellow, 1970-72. Mem. Am. Chem. Soc., Am. Nuclear Soc., Am. Romanian Acad. Arts and Sci., Assn. for Women in Sci., N.Y. Acad. Sci., Sigma Xi. Author: Ion-exchange Theory and Applications in Analytical Chemistry, 1967; contbr. articles to profl. jours. Home: 6902 Martin Dr Woodridge IL 60517 Office: Argonne Nat Lab 9700 S Cass Ave Bldg 205 Argonne IL 60439

SABBERT-MUCK, JUDITH KAY, health science association administrator; b. St. Joseph, Mo., Sept. 18, 1952; d. Marvin Lester and Bertha May (Legler) Sabbert; m. Lawrence Richard Muck, Jan. 31, 1981; 1 child, Ryan O'Donnell Muck. BS in Psychology and Human Devel., U. Kans., 1974, MA in Human Devel., 1976; MS in Adminstrn., Cen. Mich. U., 1987. Field cons. Found. for Creative Edn., Lawrence, Kans., 1974-76; asst. coordinator child devel. Interfaith Community Services, St. Joseph, 1976-78, acting coordinator child devel., 1978, asst. coordinator children and youth services, 1979, coordinator children and youth services, 1980; dir. child care services Heartland Health System, Inc., St. Joseph, 1981-86; mgr. grants Heartland Health Found., St. Joseph, 1986—; adv. mem. early childhood services program St. Joseph Sch. Dist., 1985—; mem. permanency planning rev. team Div. Family Services, St. Joseph; lectr. in field. Participant Leadership St. Joseph, 1984; mem. kids in safety seats subcom. St. Joseph Safety Council, 1985—; bd. dirs. Midland Empire Council, Girl Scouts U.S., St. Joseph, 1985—, also chair nominating com., funds devel. com.; mem. Mo. State Rev. Bd. on Daycare Licensing, Jefferson City, 1986—; v.p., bd. dirs., chair personnel com., mem. exec. com. YWCA; active Greater St. Joseph United Way. Recipient Gold award Greater St. Joseph United Way, 1980. Mem. Am. Mgmt. Assn., St. Joseph Jr. League (chair community research, bd. dirs.), Greater Kansas City Council Philanthropy. Republican. Methodist. Home: 1012 Ashland Ct Saint Joseph MO 64506 Office: Heartland Health Found 416 N 7th Saint Joseph MO 64501

SABENA, PATRICIA PIEPER, psychologist; b. Apr. 25, 1942; d. Vincent Francis and Marion (Pohly) Pieper; m. Robert Paul Sabena, Aug. 1, 1964 (div. 1980); children: Matthew, Nicole, Kristin, Ingrid. BSBA, Duquesne U., 1963; MA in Psychology, CUNY, 1978. Research analyst, project dir. Foote, Cone & Belding, N.Y.C., 1963-65; specialist consumer psychology Patricia Sabena Qualitative Research Services, Westport, Conn., 1965—; speaker in field. Author: (with others) Group, 1977. Faculty scholar, Hunter Coll., 1976. Roman Catholic. Home and Office: 12 Pequot Trail Westport CT 06880

SABLAN, SUZANNE BARBARA, banker; b. Plainview, N.Y., Aug. 25, 1962; d. Anthony and Elaine Florence (Freeth) Pellegrino; m. Joseph Andrew Sablan, Aug. 26, 1982. Student, NYU, 1981; AA, Valencia Community Coll., 1985; BA, Rollins Coll., 1987. Night auditor Days Inns Am., Orlando, Fla., 1981-82, Sheraton World Resort, Orlando, 1982-84; dividend processor Sun Banks, Inc., Orlando, 1984, supr., 1984-88; secondary edn. tchr. 1988—. Mem. Nat. Assn. Female Execs., Nat. Writers Club, Phi Theta Kappa. Democrat. Episcopalian. Office: Sun Banks Inc 225 E Robinson St Orlando CA 32802

SABLE, BARBARA KINSEY, educator; b. Astoria, L.I., N.Y., Oct. 6, 1927; d. Albert and Verna Rowe Kinsey; B.A., Coll. Wooster, 1949; M.A., Tchrs. Coll. Columbia U., N.Y.C., 1950; D.Mus., U. Ind., 1966; m. Arthur J. Sable, Nov. 3, 1973. Office mgr., music dir. sta. WCAX, Burlington, Vt., 1954; instr. Cottey Coll., 1959-60; asst. prof. N.E. Mo. State U., Kirksville, 1962-64; asst. prof. U. Calif., Santa Barbara, 1964-69; prof. music U. Colo., Boulder, 1969—. Author: The Vocal Sound, 1982. Mem. Nat. Assn. Tchrs. Singing (past state gov., asso. editor bull.), AAUP, Colo. State Music Tchrs. Assn. Democrat. Avocation: poetry. Home: 3430 Ash Ave Boulder CO 80303 Office: U Colo Coll Music Campus Box 301 Boulder CO 80309

SABLE, PATRICIA, sociologist, filmmaker, writer; b. Syracuse, N.Y., Aug. 4, 1954; d. Charles and Mary (Fisher) S. B, Boston Coll., 1976, M, 1976. Pres. Michaelangelo Prodns., Inc., Rocky Hill, Conn., 1979—, 1985—; leader workshops. Author: (screenplay) Checkmate, 1987; contbr. articles to profl. jours.; inventor sound process for insomnia. Facilitator Native Am. Prison Project, Hartford, Conn., 1983. Mem. Am. Film Inst. Office: Michaelangelo Prodns Inc 34 Kent Ln Rocky Hill CT 06067

SABO, RUTH LECHTER, state government associate, psychologist; b. Newark, N.J., May 13, 1943; d. David Sampson and Ida (Siegal) Lechter; m. Alvin Owen Sabo, Aug. 30, 1964; children: Joshua, Karen, Beth. BA, Rutgers U., 1965; MA, U. Mich., 1968, PhD, 1970. Asst. prof. SUNY, Albany, 1970-76; psychologist N.Y. State Dept. Mental Health & Devel. Disabilities, Albany, 1977-80; legis. assoc. N.Y. State Assembly, Albany, 1980—. Contbr. articles to jours. and mags. Bd. dirs., sec. Cong. Berith Sholom, Troy, N.Y., 1980—; bd. dirs. Upper Hudson Planned Parenthood, 1987—. Mem. AAAS, LWV, Feingold Assn. of U.S. (founder 1975, cons., lectr., v.p. 1975-78), Phi Beta Kappa, Psi Chi. Democrat. Jewish. Home: 40 Buckbee Rd Troy NY 12180 Office: NY State Assembly Room 513 The Capitol Albany NY 12248

SABOTTKE, HELEN LOUISE AHLBERG, educator; b. Middletown, Conn., Dec. 7, 1926; B.S. in Bus. Edn., Central Conn., State Coll., New Britain, 1949; M.S. in Elementary Edn., So. Conn. State Coll., New Haven, 1967, diploma in reading, 1971; certificate in adminstrn., U. Bridgeport, Conn., 1974; children—Craig, Mark. Tchr., Trumbull (Conn.) Bd. Edn.; 1963-70, cons. reading, 1970-74, coordinator, reading and lang. arts, 1974-86, reading program leader, 1986—; owner Craigmark Creations. Cert. elem. edn., reading cons. Title IV grantee. Mem. Internat. Reading Assn., New Eng. Reading Assn., NEA, Conn. Edn. Assn., Nat. Assn. Tchrs. English, Jenny Lind Doll Club, United Fedn. Doll Clubs, Doll Club N.Y., Doll Artisan Guild, Kappa Delta Pi, Delta Kappa Gamma (pres. Beta chpt. 1978-80). Home: 17 Old Orchard Ln Trumbull CT 06611 Office: Long Hill Adminstrn Bldg 6254 Main St Trumbull CT 06611

SABOYA, MARIA ELENA, banker; b. Palma Soriano-Oriente, Cuba, May 27, 1951; came to U.S., 1960, naturalized, 1970; d. Casimiro and Irma (Gross) S.; student in data processing mgmt. Automated Bus. Coll., Harvard U., 1971-72; A.A. in Acctg., Miami Dade Jr. Coll., 1981; M.B.A., Barry U. Computer clk. Sears Roebuck, Chgo., 1972-74; tax clk. Met. Dade County (Fla.), 1974; with Capital Bank, 1974-85, v.p. North Miami Beach office, 1980-81, v.p., br. mgr. North Bay Village office, 1981—; v.p. Miami office Bayshore Bank, 1985-86; v.p.-lending officer Banco Pedroso N.A., 1986—; notary public; mem. faculty Am. Inst. Banking 1982. Mem. North Dade C. of C., North Miami Beach C. of C., Latin C of C. Democrat. Roman Catholic. Home: 1329 71 St Miami Beach FL 33141 Office: Banco Pedroso 5200 SW 8th St Coral Gables FL 33134 also: PO Box 149004 Coral Gables FL 33114-0004

SACCA, HARRIET WANDS, music educator; b. Pittsfield, Mass, July 21, 1919; d. Harry J. and Anna F. (Mara) Wands; B.S., Coll. St. Rose, 1939, M.A., 1962; student SUNY, Albany, Oneonta. Tchr. pub. schs., Albany, N.Y., 1942-66; instr. Coll. St. Rose, 1962-63; dir. music edn. Albany (N.Y.) Bd. Edn., 1966—; bur. assoc. examiner personnel N.Y. State Dept. Edn. Past pres. Soroptimist Internat., 1969-70, City Club Albany, Inc., 1974-75; active Albany County Democratic Com., 1962—; jud. del. 19, 3d Jud. area N.Y. State, 1975-87; mem. Albany Local Devel. Corp.; bd. dirs. St. Joseph's Housing Corp., Albany Tulip Festival; adv. bd. mem. capital Region Ctr. Arts in Edn., 1983—; mem. adv. bd. Albany County Alteratives to Incarceration, 1985-86, chair sub com., 1985—; bd. dirs. Coop. Extension Community Resources Devel., bd. dirs. 7 County Youth Symphony Orch., 1970-84; project dir. N.Y. Council on Arts; chair festival N.Y. Sch. Music, 1988. Recipient Citizen of Yr. award Ford Motor Co., 1971; Women Helping Women award Soroptimist, 1975; Disting. Service award N.Y. State PTA, 1985. Fellow Harry Truman Library; mem. Music Educators Nat. Conf., N.Y. State Sch. Music Assn., Capitol Hill Choral Soc. (dir.), N.Y. St. Council Arts Award Childrens Opera (dir. project), Albany Adminstrs. Assn., Albany Civic Auditorium (dir.), Delta Kappa Gamma, Delta Epsilon. Democrat. Roman Catholic. Clubs: Bus. and Profl. Women's, Soroptimist, Club of Albany, Cath. Women's Service League, Coll. St. Rose Alumni, Pres.'s Soc. Home: 226 Morris St Albany NY 12208 Office: Albany Bd Edn Acad Park Albany NY 12207

SACCOMAN, PATRICIA LINDEN, Arabian horse breeder, writer; b. Chgo., Mar. 27, 1933; d. John Wendell and Ruth (Blanchard) Linden; m.

William John Saccoman, June 11, 1964; children—Melinda, Joseph, John, Mark. Student San Diego State U., U. Ariz. Founder, pres. Pied Pier Tours for Children, San Diego, 1967-71; owner, mgr. Lazy Diamond Ranch, Jerome, Idaho, 1971-82; owner, mgr., pres. Stallion Oaks Arabians, El Cajon, Calif., 1975—, Stallion Oaks Enterprises, El Cajon, 1980—; chmn. bd. The Adventures of Studley, El Cajon, 1984—. Author: Studley Sets his Goal, 1984; The Runaways, 1985. Bd. dirs. Salvation Army, El Cajon, 1982—, YMCA HDD Dept., San Diego, 1970-73, 87. Recipient cert. of appreciation Salvation Army, 1983, YMCA, 1976, Purple Rag award. Mem. Internat. Arabian Horse Assn. (youth com.), Arabian Horse Registry, Arabian Horse Trust (regent 1975—), Arabian Riders and Breeders (del., bd. dirs. 1981—), Desert Arabian Horse Assn., Star World of Arabians, San Diego Med. Aux., Delta Gamma. Republican. Avocations: swimming; tennis; aerobics; music. Home: 5816 Stallion Oaks Rd El Cajon CA 92021 Office: Stallion Oaks Enterprises 505 N Mollison El Cajon CA 92021

SACHS, MARTHA ANN, media specialist; b. Canton, Ohio, Dec. 5, 1951; d. Karl David and Elaine Helen (Robb) S.; divorced; 1 child, Adam Jeffrey. Student, Ohio State U., 1969-70, Ithaca Coll., 1970-71, Tobe-Coburn Sch., 1971-72. Sales assoc. Dunes Mktg. Group, Inc., Hilton Head, S.C., 1979-83; dir. media Smelkinson, Cerrati & Co., Hilton Head, S.C., 1983—; media buyer William R. Biggs/Gilmore Assoc., Hilton Head, S.C., 1985—. Mem. S.C. Real Estate Assn., Hilton Head Advt. Club, Hilton Head C. of C. Democrat. Jewish. Home: 29 Pineland Rd Hilton Head Island SC 29928

SACHSE, BARBARA KAY, home economist; b. Milw., May 18, 1961; d. Thomas Edward and Joyce (Heck) S. B.S., U. Wis.-Stout, 1983. Unit mgr. Szabo Foodservice, Columbus, Ohio, 1983; food service mgr. Saga Corp., Racine, Wis., 1984; research and devel. home economist Croissant Etc. Corp., Milw., 1984-86; field support mgr. Alto-Shaam, Inc., Menomonee Falls, Wis., 1986—. Leader Lutheran Rangerettes, Milw., 1985-87; vol. Milw. Pub. Mus. Recipient chancellor's award U. Wis., Stout, 1983; named One of Outstanding Young Women of Am., 1986. Mem. Nat. Assn. Female Execs., Home Econs. Profl. Improvement Council, Home Economist in Bus. (chmn., chmn. profl. devel. coll. and univ. relations, chmn.-elect membership com.), Wisc. Chpt. Am. Home Econs. Assn. Avocations: aerobics; outdoor activities; reading; sports. Office: Alto-Shaam Inc W164 N9221 Water St Meno Falls WI 53051

SACHSE, ELINOR YUDIN, economist; b. N.Y.C., Sept. 10, 1940; d. Lazarus Simon and Genevive (Goldberg) Yudin; B.A. with honors in Econs., Barnard Coll., 1962; M.A., Columbia U., 1964, Ph.D., 1968; m. Harry R. Sachse, Nov. 30, 1975; children—Michael Judah, Marianna Victoria. Mem. faculty dept. econs. N.Y. U., N.Y.C., 1966-69; various positions World Bank, Washington, 1969-79, chief internat. economy div., 1974-78; sr. staff economist internat. trade Council Econ. Advs., White House, 1980-82; cons. EYS Assocs., Washington, 1982—. Ford Found. fellow, 1965-66; Internat. Econs. Workshop fellow, 1963-64, 64-65; Francis M. Dibblee scholar, 1962-63. Author: Human Capital Migration, Direct Investment and the Transfer of Technology, 1976; also articles. Mem. Am. Econs. Assn. Jewish. Home: 2934 Newark St NW Washington DC 20008

SACHTLEBEN, BETTY JUNE, social services administrator; b. Centralia, Ill., Oct. 29, 1929; d. William Charles and Nellie Josephine (Winstead) Sissom; B.S., Washington U., 1962, M.S.W., 1966; m. Roland Sachtleben, Feb. 9, 1951; children—Stewart Gary, Cynthia Barbara, Sherwood Roland, Sanford Stanley, Kristin Charles. Psychiat. social worker Malcolm Bliss Mental Health Center, St. Louis, 1966-67; with div. pupil personnel St. Louis Public Schs., 1967-68; supr. social service dept. Parkway Sch. Dist., Chesterfield, Mo., 1969-72; social worker Family and Children's Service, St. Louis, 1972-73; pvt. practice psychiat. social work, St. Louis, 1973-75; exec. dir. Mo. Counseling Service, Bridgeton, Mo., 1975-81, REACH Internat. Communications Horizons, Creve Coeur, Mo., 1981—; adj. asst. prof. St. Louis U.; instr. Washington U. Bd. dirs. New Hope Found. for Retarded Children, 1972-73; dir., sec. Sunshine Found., 1973-79; dir. Parents Without Partners, 1975-79. Mem. Nat. Assn. Social Workers, Am. Assn. Marriage and Family Therapists. Lutheran. Home: 12669 Northwinds Dr Creve Coeur MO 63146 Office: Creve Coeur MO 63146

SACINO, SHERRY WHEATLEY, public relations executive; b. Wilmington, Del., July 14, 1959; d. Lawrence McClusky and Carolyn Aria (Alexander) W.; m. Ronald Anthony Sacino, Dec. 29, 1984. BA, Ariz. State U., 1980. Pub. relations exec. Phoenix Pro Soccer, 1980-81; owner, pres. Wheatley Advt. and Pub. Relations, Phoenix, 1981-83; owner, pres. Sherry Wheatley Sacino, Inc., 1983—; acct. supr. Wood, Cohen, Leonard & Bush Advt. and Pub. Relations, Tampa, Fla., 1983-84; founder, exec. dir. Tampa Bay Council for Internat. Visitors, Inc., 1984-87; exec. dir. Internat. Culinary Festival, Tampa, 1984; owner Ariz. Coaching Acad., Phoenix, 1981-83; pub. relations dir. Richard Simmons Concert, Phoenix, 1982, Phoenix Clean Community System, 1982-83, Larry's Ice Cream Exchange, USSR, 1987; nat. spokesperson McDonald's Restaurant, 1977. Creator Ruby Slippers Kit, 1983. Vol. pub. relations coordinator Muscular Dystrophy Assn., Ariz. and Fla., 1974-84, Arthritis Assn., Ariz. and Fla., 1980-84; dir. pub. relations Dan Fogelbert Concert for Ariz. Gov. Babbitt, Phoenix, 1982; mem. Ariz. Gov.'s Council on Health and Fitness, 1983; mem. Global Family Citizens Moscow Summit, 1988, Handshake Exchange Moscow Summit, 1988; bd. dirs. Pinellas County March of Dimes; mem. Tampa Bay Internat. Trade Council. Recipient award Phoenix Clean Community System, 1982. Mem. Phoenix AD2 Club (v.p. 1983), Sigma Delta Chi (sec. 1978-80). Republican. Roman Catholic. Avocations: developing cultural awareness, aviation. Home: 2507 Pass-A-Grille Way Pass-A-Grille Beach FL 33706 Office: 214 First Ave N Saint Petersburg FL 33701

SACKETT, DONNA GURDISON, financial services executive; b. Bklyn., Nov. 26, 1947; d. Benjamin R. and Florence M. (Bender) Gurdison; A.A. with high honors, Brookdale Community Coll., 1975; B.A. with high honors, Douglass Coll., 1977; M.S., Rutgers U., 1981. Staff sec. Bell Telephone Labs., Holmdel, N.J., 1965-75; student intern employee devel. dept. Johnson & Johnson, Skillman, N.J., 1977; tng. and personnel cons. Prudential Property & Casualty Ins. Co., Holmdel, 1977-84, editor The Prudential, 1985-86, assoc. mgr. personnel policies 1986-87; mgr. Prudential Realty Group, 1988—; cons. U.S. Army Res., 1981; instr. Brookdale Community Coll., Lincroft, N.J., 1978—. Mem. adv. bd. Women's Ctr., Brookdale Community Coll. Mem. Indsl. Relations Alumni Assn. (treas.), Network Working Women. Home: 7 E Wilson Circle Red Bank NJ 07701 Office: 4 Prudential Plaza Newark NJ 07101

SACKETT, SUSAN DEANNA, film and television production associate, writer; b. N.Y.C., Dec. 18, 1943; d. Maxwell and Gertrude Selma (Kugel) S. B.A. in Edn., U. Fla., 1964, M.Ed., 1965. Tchr. Dade County Schs., Miami, Fla., 1966-68, Los Angeles City Schs., 1968-69; asst. publicist, comml. coordinator NBC-TV, Burbank, Calif., 1970-73; prodn. assoc. STAR TREK: The Next Generation TV series, asst. to creator Gene Roddenberry, Hollywood, Calif., 1987—; lectr. and guest speaker STAR TREK convs. in U.S., Eng., Australia, 1974—. Author and editor: Letters to Star Trek, 1977; co-author: Star Trek Speaks, 1979; The Making of Star Trek-The Motion Picture, 1979; You Can Be a Game Show Contestant and Win, 1982; Say Good/Night Gracie, 1986. Mem. Acad. Sci. Fiction, Fantasy and Horror Films, ACLU, Mensa, Sierra Club. Democrat. Office: Paramount Pictures 5555 Melrose Ave Hollywood CA 90038

SACKETT-BLACK, MARY LOU, chiropractor; b. Ann Arbor, Mich., May 12, 1949; d. Lester Walter and Helen Beeken (Miller) S.; m. Wayne Edward Black, Dec. 17, 1983; children: Samantha Lou Smith, Terry Lee Knoll; stepchildren: Rose Nicole, Chad Edward Black, Lou Smith. A.S., Monroe County Community Coll., 1975; D in Chiropractic, Palmer Coll. Chiropractic, Davenport, Iowa, 1979. Chiropractor, Hillsdale (Mich.) Family Chiropractic Life Center, 1980—. Diplomate Am. Bd. Chiropractic Examiners. Mem. Planetary Soc. Home and Office: 2806 Carleton Rd Hillsdale MI 49242

SACKLOW, HARRIETTE LYNN, advertising agency executive; b. Bklyn., Apr. 12, 1944; d. Sidney and Mildred (Myers) Cooperman; m. Stewart Irwin, July 2, 1967; 1 son, Ian Marc. BA, SUNY-Albany, 1965, postgrad., 1967-69; postgrad. Union Coll., 1969-70, Telmar Media Sch., N.Y.C., 1981. Tchr. math. Guilderland Cen. Schs. (N.Y.), 1967-76; v.p. Wolkcas Advt., Inc., Albany, N.Y., 1975—; supr. internship programs Coll. St. Rose, Albany, N.Y., 1981; lectr. to area colls., Albany, 1981-83. Vice pres. Sisterhood Congregation Ohav Sholom, Albany, 1983-84; mem. bd. Congregation Ohav Sholom, Albany, 1983—, bd. dirs. northeastern N.Y. chpt. Arthritis Found.; advisor Ronald McDonald House. Mem. Nat. Assn. Female Execs., Am. Women in Radio and TV (pres. 1982-84, chmn. task force for new mem. acquisition, v.p. Northeast area 1987—, chmn. area conf. 1987, pres. 1982-84, speaker, dist. dir.). Club: Advt. of the Capital Dist., Albany (N.Y.) Yacht. Office: Wolkcas Advt Inc 435 New Karner Rd Albany NY 12205

SACRE, MARY ALICE, employee benefits executive; b. St. Louis, Apr. 8, 1933; d. Homer E. and Alice E. (Cameron) Klipstine; m. Byron Lee Sacre, Nov. 21, 1959. A.A., Harris Tchrs. Coll., 1953. Night supr. Mercantile Trust Co., St. Louis, 1952-53; asst. to sales mgr. Shampaine Co., St. Louis, 1953; policy writer Pearl Assurance Co., Los Angeles, 1953-54; personnel specialist, editor Honeywell, Inc., Gardena Calif., 1954-67; indsl. relations mgr. Interform Inc., 1967-73; pension adminstr. So. Calif. Rapid Transit, Los Angeles, 1973-78; corp. benefits mgr. Denny's Inc., La Mirada Calif., 1978-86; exec. dir. Wash. Counties Ins. Fund, Olympia, 1986—. Mem. Self Ins. Inst. Am. (dir. 1984-86), Am. Soc. Personnel Adminstrs. Office: Wash Counties Ins Fund 206 10th Ave SE Olympia WA 98501

SADDLEMYER, (ELEANOR) ANN, critic, theater historian, educator; b. Prince Albert, Sask., Can., Nov. 28, 1932; d. Orrin Angus and Elsie Sarah (Ellis) S. BA, U. Sask., 1953; MA, Queen's U., 1956, LLD, 1977; PhD, U. London, 1961; Master's, Massey Coll., 1988. Lectr. Victoria (B.C.) Coll., 1956-57, instr., 1960-62, asst. prof., 1962-65; assoc. prof. U. Victoria, 1965-68, prof. English, 1968-71; prof. English Victoria Coll., U. Toronto, 1971—, dir. Grad. Centre for Study of Drama, 1972-77, 85-86; sr. fellow Massey Coll., 1975—; Berg prof. N.Y. U., 1975. Dir., Theatre Plus, 1972-84; dir. Colin Smythe Pubs.; Author: The World of W.B. Yeats, 1965, In Defence of Lady Gregory, Playwright, 1966, Synge and Modern Comedy, 1968, J.M. Synge Plays Books One and Two, 1968, Lady Gregory Plays, 4 vols, 1970, Letters to Molly: Synge to Maire O'Neill, 1971, Letters from Synge to W.B. Yeats and Lady Gregory, 1971, Collected Letters of John Millington Synge, Vol. 1, 1983, vol. II, 1984, Theatre Business, The Correspondence of the First Abbey Theatre Director, 1982, (with Colin Smythe) Lady Gregory Fifty Years After, 1987; co-editor: Theatre History in Canada, 1980-86; editorial bds.: Modern Drama, 1972-82, English Studies in Can., 1973-83, Themes in Drama, 1974, Shaw Rev, 1977, Research in the Humanities, 1976, Irish Univ. Rev, 1970, Yeats Ann., 1982-86, Studies in Contemporary Irish Lit., 1986—, McGill Studies in Drama, 1988—; contbr. articles to profl. jours. Can. Council scholar, 1958-59; fellow, 1968; Guggenheim fellow, 1968, 77, sr. research fellow Connaught, 1985; recipient Brit. Acad. Rose Mary Crawshay award, 1986, Disting. Service award Province of Ont., 1985. Fellow Royal Soc. Can., Royal Soc. Arts; mem. Internat. Assn. Study Anglo-Irish Lit. (chmn. 1973-76), Assn. Can. Theatre History (pres. 1976-77), Can. Assn. Irish Studies, Assn. Can. Univ. Tchrs. English, Can. Assn. Univ. Tchrs., Assn. Can. and Que. Lit. Home: 100 Lakeshore Rd E Oakville, ON Canada L6J 6M9 Office: U Toronto Dept English, Victoria Coll, Toronto, ON Canada M5S 1K7

SADER, CAROL HOPE, state representative, legal editor; b. Bklyn., July 19, 1935; d. Nathan and Mollie (Farkas) Shimkin; m. Harold M. Sader, June 9, 1957; children: Neil, Randi Sader Friedlander, Elisa. BA, Barnard Coll., Columbia U., 1957. Sch. tchr. Bd. Edn., Morris, Conn., 1957-58; legal editor W. H. Anderson Co., Cin., 1974-78; freelance legal editor Shawnee Mission, Kans., 1978—; mem. Ho. of Reps. 22d Kans. Dist., 1987—; bd. dirs. CASA Project County, Shawnee Mission. Contbr. articles to profl. jours. Chmn. bd. Johnson County Community Coll., Overland Park, Kans., 1984-86, bd. trustees 1981-86; pres. LWV of Johnson County, Shawnee Mission, 1983-85, mem. state bd., Topeka, 1986-87; treas. United Community Services of Johnson County, Shawnee Mission, 1984-87; v.p. Jewish Vocat. Service Bd., Shawnee Mission, 1983-87. Recipient Trustee award Assn. of Women in Jr. and Community Colls., 1985. Mem. Women Council Women Legislators, Phi Delta Kappa. Democrat. Clubs: Women Resource Ctr., Friends of the Library (Johnson County). Home: 8612 Linden Dr Prarie Village KS 66207 Office: Kans Ho of Reps State Capitol Room 272-W Topeka KS 66612

SADICK, BARBARA ANN, publishing production manager; b. Bklyn., July 31, 1952; d. Richard L. and Marion (Weiss) S. B.A. cum laude, NYU, 1974. Asst. editor Bus. Research Pubs., N.Y.C., 1977-80; prodn. mgr., editor MacRae's Blue Book, 1980-84; prodn. mgr. Bus. Research Publs., N.Y.C., 1982-84, Media Horizons, N.Y.C., 1985-87, Aperture, N.Y.C., 1987; prodn. coordinator Am. Pizzi Offset Corp., N.Y.C., 1987—. Mem. Women in Prodn., NOW. Office: Am Pizzi Offset Corp 141 E 44th St New York NY 10017

SADLE, AMY ANN, watercolorist, printmaker; b. Council Bluffs, Iowa, Aug. 3, 1940; Student State U. Iowa, U. R.I.; studied with Fritz Eichenberg, Claude Croney, Virginia Cobb, Ed Whitney, Naoko Matsubra, and others. One woman shows U. N.D., 1986, San Diego Print Club, 1985, others; exhibited Barcelona, Spain, U. Kans., Dartmouth Coll., N.H., St. Johns, Nfld., Midwest Watercolor, and others; represented in permanent collections Statue of Liberty, Tulsa Library, Des Moines Art Ctr., Nebr. Hist. Commn., Nebr. Indian Commn.; corp. dir. (book and tour) Impact: The Art of Nebraska Women; author: Home of Wooden Men and Iron Men. Recipient Best of Show award San Diego Print Club, 1984, Daniel Smith grant for research art materials, 1987. Mem. Artists Equity, Phila. Print Club, N.J. Internat. Print Club, Midwest Watercolor.

SADOCK, POPSY (EILEEN), journalist; b. Greensburg, Pa., Sept. 26, 1927; d. Samuel and Rhoda (Abramson) Friedlander; m. Martin Theodore Sadock, May 2, 1949; children—Jamie, Seth, Jonathan. Student Sch. Journalism, Pa. State U., 1945-48. Soc. editor, women's editor Tribune Rev., Greensburg, Pa., 1948-50, freelance columnist, writer, 1956-73; talk show hostess Sta. WHJB, Greensburg, 1966; editor Focus mag. Tribune Rev., 1973-80, feature writer, consumer editor, 1980—. Co-chmn. Greensburg Open Tennis Tournament, 1969-79; pres. Nat. Council Jewish Women, Greensburg, 1959-61. Recipient journalistic award Am. Cancer Soc., 1983; Mem. Pa. Women's Press Assn. (award 1982, 83, 84, 86, 87), Pa. Newspaper Pubs. Assn. (Keystone Press award 1976, 77, 82), Women's Press Club, Sigma Delta Chi (exec. com. 1984—, Golden Quill 1986), Pitts. Press Club. Republican. Home: 127 Underwood Ave Greensburg PA 15601 Office: Tribune Review Cabin Hill Dr Greensburg PA 15601

SADOFSKY, STELLA, social worker; b. Vienna, Austria, June 9, 1927; came to U.S., 1940; d. Max and Nellie (Benedek) Streit; m. Harold Irving Sadofsky, Sept. 1, 1947; 1 dau., Melanie. B.A., Bklyn. Coll., 1949; M.S.W., Case Western Res. U., 1951. Case worker, supr. Travelers Aid Soc., N.Y.C., 1951-61; sr. caseworker Mass. Soc. for Prevention of Cruelty to Children, Salem, 1961-63; adoption counselor N.J. Home Soc., Camden, 1964-66; clin. social worker Mt. Laurel Schs. (N.J.), 1966—; adj. prof. Glassboro State Coll., Camden County Community Coll., 1974-76; adolescent and adult group therapist, Haddonfield, N.J., 1984—. Mem. adv. com. Planned Parenthood of So. N.J., Camden, 1981—. Mem. Nat. Assn. Social Workers (diplomate clin. social work), Acad. Cert. Social Workers, Acad. Clin. Social Workers, N.J. Assn. Sch. Social Workers, Jewish Profl. Womens Coalition, Alpha Kappa Delta. Home: 421 Covered Bridge Rd Cherry Hill NJ 08034 Office: Mt Laurel Sch System 330 Mount Laurel Rd Mount Laurel NJ 08054

SADOYAMA, NANCY ARTIS, administrative operations analyst; b. Oakland, Calif., June 12, 1947; d. Robert Lee and Norma Lee (Dyches) Artis; m. Edward T. Sadoyama, June 18, 1978. BA, Calif. State U., Hayward, 1974, M in Pub. Adminstrn. with highest deptl. honors, 1987. Personnel rep. Mack Western, Hayward, 1970-73; with Calif. State U., Hayward, 1974-87, adminstrv. ops. analyst, 1987—; microcomputer cons. Meiklejohn Hall, Calif. State U., Hayward, 1984—. Recipient Vivian Cunniffe Outstanding Staff award Calif. State U., Hayward, 1986. Mem. Calif. Women in Higher Edn., Am. Soc. Pub. Adminstrn., Data Processing Mgmt. Assn., Nat. Assn. Female Execs., Women's Council of the State U. Club: Commonwealth of San Francisco. Office: Calif State U Liberal Studies Hayward CA 94542

SAENZ, NANCY ELIZABETH KING (MRS. MICHAEL SAENZ), civic worker; b. Greenville, Tex., Jan. 28, 1930; d. Henry M. and Vallie (Wheatley) King; m. Michael Saenz, July 28, 1950; children—Michael King, Cynthia Elizabeth. Saenz Ward. A.B. with honors, Tex. Christian U., 1950, B.S. magna cum laude, 1952; postgrad. Hartford Sem. Found., 1952-53, Escuela de Idiomas, 1953, Lexington Theol. Sem., 1953. Missionary, United Christian Missionary Soc., Indpls., serving in P.R., 1954-65; bd. dirs. Adminstrv. Bd. Christian Chs., P.R., 1950-65; chmn. dept. Christian edn. Christian Chs., P.R., 1962-64, sec., 1959-61, state dir., 1963; dept. Christian edn. P.R. Council Chs., 1959-64, sec., 1959-60; sec. and counsellor State Christian Women Fellowship of Christian Chs., P.R., 1955-57, 59-63, dist. chmn. Ind. and Tex., 1968-75, adminstrv. com. Tex., 1971-74; mem. Internat. Christian Women's Fellowship Quadrennial Coms., 1974-82; mem. gen. bd. Christian Ch. in U.S. and Can., 1974-78, 80; pres. Christian Ch. in S.W., 1976-78. Sec., Disciples of Christ Acad. PTA, Bayamon, P.R., 1962-63; mem. state com. Home for Aged, United Ch. Women, P.R., 1963; women's com. Ind. State Symphony Soc., 1967—; women's com. Internat. Christian U. Japan, 1962-64, 65-72, pres. Indpls. chpt. 1967-68; mem. vocational-tech. adv. council Laredo Ind. Sch. Dist., 1971—; vol. coordinator Am. Bible Soc., 1971—dir. Vol. Center Met. Tarrant County. Bd. dirs. Greater Indpls. Fedn. Chs., 1970-71; bd. dirs. Planned Parenthood Assn. Webb County, 1972-74, pres.-elect, 1974-75; bd. dirs. Civic Ballet Laredo, 1972-75; mem. adv. com. Tarrant County Vol. Center, 1976-81, chmn., 1980; mem. Mercy Hosp. Aux., 1973-75, pres.-elect, 1974-75; interim dir. Ft. Worth Council Chs., 1979, pres., 1981; pres. Ch. Women United, Fort Worth, 1980; bd. dirs. ch. fin. council Christian Ch. (Disciples of Christ) U.S. and Can., 1979-83. Mem. Irvington Union of Clubs (exec. bd. 1966—, 2d v.p. 1968-70), Young Mothers Club Irvington (v.p. 1965, pres. 1967), Marion County Guardian Home Guild (pres. 1968-70), Art Assn. Indpls., Art League, Civic Music Laredo, Irvington, AAUW, Laredo and Fort Worth Pan Am. Roundtable, Thistle Hill, Docent Guild, Alpha Chi, Phi Sigma Iota. Mem. Christian Ch. Clubs: Rotary Anns, Women's College (R.P.); Irvington Women's Laredo Tuesday Music and Lit. (pres. 1973-74), Women's City. Author: Winds of Change, 1968; Step by Step, 1984. Home: 4427 Tamworth Rd Fort Worth TX 76116-8127 Office: 210 E 9th St Fort Worth TX 76102

SAENZ, STELLA ISABEL, management consultant; b. Bogota, Colombia, May 3, 1949; came to U.S., 1965; d. Pedro A. and Isabel (Ariza) S.; m. Miguel A. Arce, Nov. 28, 1964 (div. 1981); children: Ricardo, Mauricio, Claudia. Student. U. S.C., 1974, La. State U., 1974-78; BA, Tech. Coll., 1980. Asst. dir. ops. Pressco Engring., Greenville, S.C., 1980-82; mgr. personnel Moseley Assocs., Houston, 1982-84; owner Mgmt. Cons., Houston, 1984—; cons. in field. Com. mem. Am. Heart Assn., Houston, 1986-87, Houston Grand Opera, Houston, 1984-85. Named Honorary Mayor Pres. of Baton Rouge, 1976. Democrat. Roman Catholic. Home: 2901 Briarhurst #403 Houston TX 77057

SAFARS, BERTA See FISZER-SZAFARZ, BERTA

SAFERITE, LINDA LEE, library director; b. Santa Barbara, Calif., Mar. 25, 1947; d. Elwyn C. and Polly (Frazer) S.; m. Andre Doyon, July 16, 1985. BA, Calif. State U., Chico, 1969; MS in Library Sci., U. So. Calif., 1970; cert. in Indsl. Relations, UCLA, 1976; MBA, Pepperdine U., 1979. Librarian-in-charge, reference librarian Los Angeles County Pub. Library System, 1970-73, regional reference librarian, 1973-75, sr. librarian-in-charge, 1975-78, regional adminstr., 1978-80; library dir. Scottsdale (Ariz.) Pub. Library System, 1980—. Bd. dirs. Scottsdale-Paradise Valley YMCA, 1981-86. Recipient Cert. Recognition for efforts in civil rights Ariz. Atty. Gen.'s Office, 1985. Mem. ALA, Ariz. State Library Assn. (pres. 1987-88), Mountain Plains Library Assn. Republican. Clubs: Metropolitan Bus. and Profl. Women (Scottsdale) (pres. 1986-87). Lodge: Soroptimist (pres. 1981-83). Office: Scottsdale Public Library 3839 Civic Ctr Plaza Scottsdale AZ 85251

SAFFORD, EUNICE AGNES, elementary educator; b. Berlin, Wis., Jan. 17, 1928; d. Vernon Michael and Julianna (Czaja) S. BSE, Mt. Mary Coll., 1958; M of Profl. Devel. in Edn., Cardinal Stritch Coll., 1988. Cert. tchr. Grade sch. tchr. Archdiocese of Chgo., 1947-50, Archdiocese of Milw., 1951-76, West Bend (Wis.) Joint Sch. Dist., 1977—; fellow mem. Dist. Reading Com., West Bend, 1976—, Dist. Gifted and Talented Com., West Bend, 1985-87, Dist. Lang. Arts. Com. Mem. NEA, Internat. Reading Assn., Wis. Reading Assn., West Bend Edn. Assn., Barton Sch. Parent Tchr. Assn. Republican. Roman Catholic. Club: Collie (editor newsletter).

SAFFY, EDNA LOUISE, educator; b. Jacksonville, Fla., Mar. 8, 1935; d. Habib Solomon and Sadie Daumit Saffy; m. Grady Earl Johnson, Aug. 9, 1969. B.A., U. Fla., 1966, M.A., 1968, Ph.D., 1976. Asst., then instr. English, U. Fla., 1967, speech, 1972-75; prof. rhetoric Fla. Jr. Coll., Jacksonville, 1968-72, 75—; speaker, guest lectr., cons., polit. activist. Mem. Duval County Hosp. Authority, 1987—, Democratic exec. com. Duval County; del. to Dem. Nat. Conv., 1979; exec. bd. dirs. Jacksonville Citizens for a Nuclear Freeze, 1982-83; mem. State of Fla. Dem. Com. Affirmative Action Com., 1983; mem. Jacksonville Planning Commn., 1979, Duval County Hosp. Authority, 1979, Leadership Jacksonville, 1987. Named Marjorie Kinnan Rawlings Scholar; recipient various recognition awards. Mem. S. Atlantic MLA, Speech Communication Assn., So. Speech Communication Assn., Fla. Speech Communication Assn., Fla. Coll. English Assn., U. Fla. Grad. Speech Assn. (pres. 1975), Fla. Women's Network (dir.), Jacksonville Women's Network (founder), U. Fla. Alumni Assn., NOW (dir., co-convenor Jacksonville chpt. 1970, dir. convenor Gainesville U. of Fla. chpt. 1973, Mary Nolan award, 1987), Fla. Women's Polit. Caucus pres. 1978-79, ERA Jacksonville (pres., 1976-77), Alachua County Women's Polit. Caucus (charter mem.), Duval County Women's Polit. Caucus (v.p. 1983), Nat. Women's Polit. Caucus (chmn. So. Dem. Task Force 1983—), Gen. Fedn. Women's Clubs, Alpha Chi Omega. Club: Women's (Jacksonville). Home: 4273 Pt LaVista Rd Jacksonville FL 32207 Office: Fla Jr Coll South Campus Beach Blvd Jacksonville FL 32216

SAFI, DEBORAH CAVAZOS, lawyer; b. Dallas, Feb. 8, 1953; d. Arnaldo Nelson and Ila Mae (Rinn) Cavazos; m. Hazim Jawad Safi, July 28, 1979; children: Jawad Joseph, Aminah Mae. BA, Baylor U., 1975, JD, 1977. Bar: Tex. 1977. Assoc. Andrews & Kurth, Houston, 1977-81; corp. atty. Transco Energy Co., Houston, 1981-83; sole practice Houston, 1983-85; of counsel Harman & Timby P.C. (formerly Anderson, Harrell & Timby P.C.), Houston, 1985—, Harman and Timby PC, Houston, 1988—. Mem. fund raising com. Children's Mus., Houston, 1986; co-leader Blue Bird/Camp Fire Girls, Waco, Tex., 1972-73. Named one of Outstanding Women of 1982, Transco Energy Co. and YWCA, Houston 1982. Fellow Tex. Bar Found., Houston Bar Found.; mem. ABA, Houston Bar Assn., Houston Young Lawyers Assn. (chmn. directory planning 1987-88, com. chair 1980-82, bd. dirs. 1982-84, treas. 1984-86, v.p. 1986-87, named Outstanding Com. Chmn. 1987-88), Tex. Young Lawyers Assn. (bd. dirs. 1986-88, co-editor newsletter 1986-87, com. chmn. 1980-82, 87-88, treas. 1988—), Fed. Energy Bar Assn., Delta Delta Delta, Phi Delta Phi. Office: Harman and Timby 1415 Louisiana Suite 3100 333 Clay St Houston TX 77002

SAFIAN, SHELLEY CAROLE, advertising agency executive; b. Bklyn., May 29, 1954; d. Jack Israel and Harriet Sara (Cohen) S. B.F.A., Parsons Sch. Design/New Sch. for Social Research, 1975. Asst. art dir. Axelrod and Assocs., N.Y.C., 1975-77; art dir. Sta. WDBO-TV-AM/FM, Orlando, Fla., 1978-80; owner, pres. Safian Communications Services, Inc., Orlando, 1981—; mem. adv. com. Career Edn., Orange County, Fla., 1981—, chmn., 1982-83; advt. cons. post-secondary vocat. and community edn. div. Orange County Pub. Schs., 1983-84. Active govs. council on phys. fitness/Sunshine State Games, 1983; exec. producer/dir. March of Dimes Telethon, Orlando, 1984; exec. dir. United Cerebral Palsy Telethon, Orlando, 1982-83; pub. relations Liaison-United Cerebral Palsy, Orlando, 1983-84; founder Career Dir. for the Deaf, Orlando, 1983. Recipient 2 First Place Addy awards Orlando Advt. Fedn., 1981; First Place Addy award, 2 pl. awards (2), merit awards (2), Orlando Advt. Fedn., 1982. Mem. Broadcast Promotion and Mktg. Execs. Assn. (Silver Medallion 1983, nat. finalist 2 Silver Microphone awards 1986), Broadcast Designer's Assn. (bd. dirs. 1980-82), Am. Women in Radio and TV (bd. dirs. 1980-81). Republican. Avocation: horseback riding. Office: Safian Communications Services 2211 Lee Rd Suite 223 Winter Park FL 32789

SAFIRSTEIN, AMANDA, lawyer, researcher, dental nurse; b. Montreal, Que., Can., Apr. 6, 1909; came to U.S., 1914; d. Ephraim Leon and Sophie

Miriam (Lewis) Ackerman; m. Samuel Safirstein, Dec. 19, 1929; children—G. Richard, Jared Jack, Arnold Alan. B.A., Seton Hall U., 1978, J.D., 1981. Bar: N.J. 1982. Asst. editor Fisher Maritime Cons., South Orange, N.J., 1977-79, Inst. Continuing Legal Edn., Newark, 1979-81; Contbr. articles to various publs. Republican County committeewoman, South Orange; v.p., pres. Faith of Israel Synagogue, East Orange. Mem. ABA, N.J. State Bar Assn. (citation for service 1984), Assn. Trial Lawyers Am., Essex County Bar Assn., Nat. Assn. Investment Clubs (dir. No. N.J. region). Lodge: Hadassah. Jewish.

SAFKO, DEBORAH LEE, health care administrator; b. Alliance, Ohio, Sept. 19, 1951; d. Joseph Paul Safko and Doris Marie (Wolf) Sniegocki; m. Samuel John Costa, Jr., Sept. 2, 1972 (div. April 1984); children—Mario Benjamin, Jeremy Michael. B.S. magna cum laude in Human and Social Scis., Drexel U., 1974; M.B.A. in Health Adminstrn., Temple U., 1982. Bus. mgr., mktg. dir. Occupational Health Services, Pennsauken, N.J., 1983-86; patient service mgr. Children's Hosp., Phila., 1986—. Active mem. Phila. Com. on City Policy, 1972—. Recipient Am. Coll. Hosp. Adminstrs. award, 1981; grantee Pub. Health Services Traineeship, 1980, 81. Mem. Nat. Assn. Female Execs., Phi Mu. Democrat. Roman Catholic. Home: 4809 Beaumont Ave Apt #3-F Philadelphia PA 19143

SAGA-MUTRYNOWSKI, LAURIE MAE, finance company administrator; b. Windsor, Ont., Can., Sept. 11, 1950; came to U.S., 1951; d. John and Virginia Marie (Webber) Sagal; m. Alan Joseph Mutrynowski, May 22, 1976. AA, Macomb Community Coll., 1968; BA, Oakland U., 1972, MBA, 1984. Clk. accounts payable Fruehauf Corp., Detroit, 1972-73; with Fruehauf Fin. Co., Detroit, 1973—, fin. mgr. contracts, 1977-84, fin. mgr. acctg., 1984—. Mem. Nat. Assn. for Female Execs. Democrat. Methodist. Lodge: Masons. Home: 32142 Stricker Warren MI 48093 Office: Fruehauf Fin Co 10900 Harper Detroit MI 48232

SAGE, MARY JEAN, management consultant; b. Mich., July 24, 1946; m. Kenneth G. Sage; 1 child, Karma M. AA, Ferris State Coll., 1966; BBA, U. Redlands, Calif., 1985. Cert. med. asst., Calif. Office mgr. various med. field orgns., Mich., Ill. and Calif., 1966-83; sr. cons. Profl. Mgmt. Concepts, Newbury Park, Calif., 1984-85; owner, operator Profl. Mgmt. Concepts, Danville, Calif., 1985—; lectr. in field. Mem. adv. council Area Agy. on Aging, Contra Costa County, Calif., 1987. Mem. Am. Cons. League, Bus. and Profl. Women U.S.A., Women's Network Contra Costa County. Lodge: Soroptimists. Office: Profl Mgmt Concepts 46A Mariposa Ct Danville CA 94526

SAGER, JOYCE TOSHIYE TANIMOTO, medical infosystems specialist; b. Gridley, Calif., Jan. 23, 1950; d. Masashi Mike and Satomi (Ishihara) Tanimoto; m. Richard A. Sager, Sept. 13, 1975. BS in Foods and Nutrition, U. Calif., Davis, 1968; MPH, U. Calif., Berkeley, 1973; postgrad., U. Utah, 1986—. Dietitian St. Alphonsus Regional Med. Ctr., Boise, Idaho, 1974-75; nutrition lectr. Boise State U., 1974; pub. health nutritionist SW Dist. Dept. Health, Caldwell, Idaho, 1975-76; state dir. women, infants and children nutrition program Idaho Dept. Health and Welfare, Boise, 1976-86; research asst. in med. informatics Latter Day Sts. Hosp., Salt Lake City, 1986—. Recipient Sci. and Math. Achievement award Bank Am., 1968, Certificate of Recognition, Gov. Idaho, 1986. Mem. Am. Dietetic Assn., Utah Dietetic Assn., Nat. Assn. Women, Infants and Children Dirs. (western region rep. 1980-81). Democrat. Home: PO Box 8341 Salt Lake City UT 84108

SAGER, RUTH, geneticist; b. Chgo., Feb. 7, 1918; married, 1973. BS, U. Chgo., 1938; MS, Rutgers U., 1944; PhD, Columbia U., 1948. Merck fellow Nat. Research Council, 1949-51; asst. in biochemistry Rockefeller Inst., 1951-55; research assoc. in zoology Columbia U., N.Y.C., 1955-60, sr. research assoc. in zoology, 1961-65; prof. biology Hunter Coll., CUNY, 1966-75; prof. cellular genetics Harvard Med. Sch., 1975-88, prof. emeritus, 1988—; chief genetics div. Sidney Farber Cancer Inst., from 1975. Recipient Gilbert Morgan Smith medal Nat. Acad. Scis., 1988; Guggenheim fellow, 1972-73. Mem. AAAS, Nat. Acad. Scis., Am. Soc. Cell Biologists, Genetics Soc. Am., Sigma Xi. Office: Dana-Farber Cancer Inst 44 Binney St Boston MA 02115 *

SAHATJIAN, MANIK, nurse, psychologist; b. Tabris, Iran, July 24, 1921; came to U.S., 1951; d. Dicran and Shushanig (Der-Galustian) Mnatzaganian; m. George Sahatjian, Jan. 21, 1954; children: Robert, Edwin. Nursing Cert., Am. Mission Hosps.-Boston U., 1954; BA, San Jose State U., 1974, MA, 1979. RN, Calif., Mass. Head nurse Am. Mission Hosp., Tabris, 1945-46; charge nurse Banke-Melli Hosp., Tehran, 1946-51; research asst. Stanford U., 1979-81, Palo Alto (Calif.) Med. Research Found., 1981-84; documentation supr. Bethesda Convalescent Ctr., Los Gatos, Calif., 1985-86; community worker City of Fremont (Calif.) Dept. Human Services, 1987—. Author (with others) psychol. research reports. Fulbright scholar, 1951; Iran Found. scholar, 1953. Mem. Western Psychol. Assn. Democrat. Mem. St. Andrew Apostolic Church. Home: 339 Starlite Way Fremont CA 94539

SAHLI, NANCY A., government agency administrator; b. Beaver Falls, Pa., Jan. 4, 1946; d. John Rankin and Betty Melville (McClane) S. AB, Vassar Coll., 1967; MA, U. Pa., 1971, PhD, 1974. Research asst. Drexel U., Phila., 1969-74; archivist Nat. Hist. Publs. and Records Commn., Washington, 1975-81, 83-84, archives cons., 1981-84, archives specialist, 1984-87, dir. records program, 1987—; cons. Princeton Theol. Sem., N.J., 1981-82, Vassar Coll., Poughkeepsie, N.Y., 1981-82, Smithsonian Instn., Washington, 1983. Author: Elizabeth Blackwell, 1982, Women and Sexuality, 1984, MARC for Archives and Mss., 1985 (Coker prize 1986); editor Directory of Archives and Mss. Repos., 1978. AAUW fellow, 1973-74; Nat. Endowment for Humanities grantee, 1981-83; recipient Commendable Service award Gen. Services Adminstrn., 1978, Citation, Gen. Services Adminstrn., 1979, 81. Fellow Soc. Am. Archivists (cons. 1983-84); mem. Assn. Records Mgrs. and Adminstrs., Assn. for Documentary Editing, Nat. Assn. Govt. Archives and Records Adminstrs., Orgn. Am. Historians (life), Sierra Club, Appalachian Trail Conf. Democrat. Buddhist. Home: 9 Indian Spring Dr Silver Spring MD 20901 Office: Nat Hist Publs & Records Commn Nat Archives Washington DC 20408

SAIBARA, MARJORIE LYNN, accountant; b. Houston; d. Robert and Rola Saibara; BBA in Acctg., U. Houston, 1972. CPA, Tex. Joint venture acct. Union Oil of Calif., Houston, 1973-74; joint interest, revenue accountant Coastal States Gas Corp., Houston, 1974-78; Dept. Energy liaison for controller's dept. revenue crude oil and gas processing supr., spl. projects acct., asst. mgr. revenue acctg., project leader for revenue acctg. software installation Cabot Corp., Houston, 1978—; counselor U. Houston Career Day. Chmn. worship ministry Presbyn. Ch. of Covenant, 1980-82 ; Presbytery del., 1980; ruling elder Presbyn. Ch., mem. pulpit nominating com., 1982-83, mem. worship ministry 1985. Mem. Am. Soc. Women Accts. (dir., membership chmn.), Petroleum Accts. Soc. of Houston (membership com. 1981-82, membership chmn. 1982-83, 83-84, 84-85, 85-86, 87-88, picnic com. and golf tournament 1984-85, 85, 86, 87, telephone com. 1986-87), Am. Inst. CPA's (pres. 1988), Tex. Soc. CPAs (Houston chpt., young CPAs com.), U. Houston Panhellenic Assn. (treas. 1985, pres. 1986, v.p. 1987), Phi Mu (treas., v.p.). Office: 550 West Lake Pk Blvd Suite 900 Houston TX 77079 also: PO Box 4544 Houston TX 04544

SAIKI, PATRICIA (MRS. STANLEY MITSUO SAIKI), congresswoman; b. Hilo, Hawaii, May 28, 1930; d. Kazuo and Shizue (Inoue) Fukuda; m. Stanley Mitsuo Saiki, June 19, 1954; children: Stanley Mitsuo, Sandra Saiki Williams, Margaret C., Stuart K., Laura H. BA, U. Hawaii, 1952. Tchr. U.S. history Punahou Sch., Kaimuki Internat. Sch., Kalani High Sch., Honolulu, 1952-64; sec. Rep. Party Hawaii, Honolulu, 1964-66, vice chmn., 1966-68, 82-83, chmn., 1983-85; research asst. Hawaii State Senate, 1966-68; del. State Constnl. Conv., Honolulu, 1968; mem. Hawaii Ho. of Reps., 1968-74, Hawaii State Senate, 1974-82; mem. 100th Congress from 1st Hawaii dist., Washington, 1987—; mem. Pres.'s Adv. Council on Status of Women, 1969-76. Mem. Nat. Commn. Internat. Women's Yr., 1969-70; commr. Western Interstate Commn. on Higher Edn.; fellow Eagleton Inst., Rutgers U., 1970. Mem. Kapiolani Hosp. Aux. Sec. Hawaii Rep. Com., 1964-66, vice chmn., 1966-68, chmn., 1983-85; del. Hawaii Constl. Conv., 1968; alt. del. Rep. Nat. Conv., 1968, del., 1984; Rep. nominee for lt. gov. Hawaii, 1982; mem. Fedn. Rep. Women.; trustee Hawaii Pacific Coll.; past bd. govs. Boys and Girls Clubs Hawaii; mem. adv. council Am. Nat. Red. Cross; bd. dirs. Nat. Fund for Improvement of Post-Secondary Edn., 1982-85 ; past bd. dirs. Straub Med. Research Found., Honolulu, Hawaii's Visitors Bur., Honolulu, Edn. Commn. of States, Honolulu, Hawaii Visitors Bur., 1983-85; trustee U. Hawaii Found., 1984-86, Hawaii Pacific Coll., Honolulu. Episcopalian. Avocation: golf. Home: 784 Elepaio St Honolulu HI 96816 Office: US Ho of Reps 1407 Longworth HOB Washington DC 20515

SAILORS, CAROL FIRST, managing editor; b. Phila., May 24, 1944; d. Arthur and Ruth (Ellis) First; m. David A. Sailors, Aug. 25, 1985. BA, U. Calif., Berkeley, 1966, Calif. Teaching Credential, 1968. Tchr. Stuyvesant Pvt. Sch., N.Y.C., 1968-69; editing supr. W. A. Benjamin, N.Y.C., 1969-71; editing supr. McGraw-Hill, N.Y.C., 1971-74, subject-area supr., 1974-75, editing mgr., 1975-76, mgr. editing, 1976-80; supr. editing Harper & Row, N.Y.C., 1982-83; freelance editor N.Y.C., 1980-81; mng. editor W. H. Freeman & Co., N.Y.C., 1983—. Bd. dirs. Woman's Sch., N.Y.C., 1975-80. Office: W H Freeman & Co 41 Madison Ave New York NY 10010

ST. AMAND, GLENDA WEAVER, social worker, counselor; b. Akron, Ohio, Apr. 17, 1923; d. Christian and Selma Fridfelt (Johnson) Weaver; m. Leonard M. St. Amand, Mar. 24, 1951; children—Janet G., David G. B.A., Houghton Coll., 1945; M.S.W., Columbia U., 1947; postgrad. Marywood Coll., 1974-81, Pa. State U., 1981. Cert. social worker, N.Y. Social worker Family Service Bur., Bklyn., 1945-49; med. social worker Roosevelt Hosp., N.Y.C., 1949-51; dir. social service People's Hosp., Akron, Ohio, 1951; med. social work cons. State of N.J., Trenton, 1964-67; sch. social worker Joint Bd. for Exceptional Children, Bucks County (Pa.), 1967-72; guidance counselor Neshaminy Sch. Dist., Langhorne, Pa., 1972-86; supr., treas. Presbyn. Counseling Service, Morrisville, Pa., 1976-78. Author: (handbook) Navy Relief Volunteer, 1951. Leader Freedom Valley council Girl Scouts U.S.A., Cub Scouts, Lower Makefield, Pa.; committeeman Lower Makefield Republican Com. Salvation Army fellow, 1946. Mem. Nat. Assn. Social Workers, NEA, Neshaminy Edn. Assn., Pa. Edn. Assn., Am. Personnel and Guidance Assn., Historic Morrisville Soc. Republican. Presbyterian. Clubs: Lower Makefield Women's (welfare dir.); Buck County Women's (welfare dir.). Home: 20 Oakdale Blvd Morrisville PA 19067 Office: Neshaminy Sch Dist 2001 Old Lincoln Hwy Langhorne PA 19047

ST. AUBIN, PHYLLIS ANN, communications executive b. Camden, Mo., Dec. 24, 1938; d. Charles Daniel and Alberta (Archer) Feeney; student (Lion Oil Co. scholar) Memphis State U., 1956-57; m. Forrest Edmund St. Aubin, Nov. 26, 1971; 1 dau., Pamela DeAnn Gooch Schultz; stepchildren—Mark Randall, Leslie Alexandra St. Aubin Brown. Advt. asst. Mobay Chem. Corp., Kansas City, Mo., 1968-80; mgr. video network Farmland Industries, Kansas City, Mo., 1980-86; mgr. video network Commerce Bancsharen Inc., 1987— . Recipient Voice of Democracy award Lion Oil Co., 1955. Mem. Internat. TV Assn. Republican. Baptist. Home: 8715 Sycamore Kansas City MO 64138 Office: Commerce Bancsharen Inc Kansas City MO 64116

ST. CLAIR, JANE CATHERINE, communications consultant; b. N.Y.C., Dec. 30, 1946; d. Louis and Elizabeth (Bantell) Seligman; m. Alexander Daniel St. Clair, Aug. 1, 1985. BA, Hunter Coll., 1969; postgrad., San Francisco State U., 1973-75. Account exec. Performing Arts Mag., San Francisco, 1978-80, Sta. KWUN Radio, Concord, Calif., 1980-81, Stas. KKIS/KDFM Radio, Concord, 1981-83; v.p. sales Contra Costa Mag. Pubs. Inc., Concord, 1983-86; pres., owner St. Clair Profl. Devel., Oakland, Calif., 1986—. Mem. Nat. Speakers Assn., Am. Soc. Tng. Devel., Nat. Assn. Neurolinguistic Programming, Advt. Mktg. Assn. (1st v.p. 1981). Office: St Clair Profl Devel 235 W MacArthur Blvd Suite 701 Oakland CA 94611

ST. CLEMENT, COURTNEY TOLSON, advertising executive; b. Fort Worth, Nov. 8, 1951; d. J.B. and Dorothy Allison (Marshall) Tolson; m. Reginald St. Clement, Sept. 13, 1981. Art dir. Bloom Advt., Dallas, 1973-77, Cunningham & Walsh, N.Y.C., 1977-82; pres., creative dir. St. Clement Group, N.Y.C., 1982—. Bd. dirs. East Meets West. Recipient Mead award Mead Paper, 1976; Silver Microphone award All Star Radio, 1985. Mem. Dutch Reform Ch. Clubs: Snarks (N.Y.C.); Bklyn. Equestrian. Office: St Clement Group 106 E 19th St New York NY 10003

ST. GERMAIN, JEAN MARY, medical physicist; b. N.Y.C.; d. Herbert and Mary J. (Newman) S.; B.S., Marymount Manhattan Coll., 1966; M.S., Rutgers U., 1967. Fellow radiol. health USPHS, Rutgers U., New Brunswick, N.J., 1967; fellow dept. med. physics Meml. Hosp., N.Y.C., Cornell U. Med. Coll., 1967-68, asst. physicist, 1968-71, instr. radiology (physics), 1971-78, clin. asst. prof., 1979—; asst. attending physicist Meml. Sloan-Kettering Cancer Center; cons. in field. Diplomate Am. Bd. Health Physics. Mem. Am. Inst. Physics (gov. bd.), Health Physics Soc. Am. Assn. Physicists in Medicine (sec., dir.), Soc. Nuclear Medicine, Radiol. Soc. N.Am., N.Y. Acad. Scis., Radiol. and Med. Physics Soc. N.Y. (past pres.), Nat. Soc. Arts and Letters (regional dir., pres. N.Y. chpt.). Iota Sigma Pi (treas., pres. V chpt.). Author: The Nurse and Radiotherapy, 1978; contbr. articles, chpts. to med. jours., texts. Office: 1275 York Ave New York NY 10021

ST. JACQUES, JEANNE D'ARC, nursing administrator; b. St. Pascal Bay, Ont., Can., May 2, 1939; d. Albert and Lucienne (Bergeron) Parent; m. Jean St. Jacques, Oct. 22, 1960; children: Luc, Diane, Roch, Hughes, Charles. Student in nursing, U. Ottawa, Ont., 1956-59. Cert. in community nursing. Nurse Ottawa Gen. Hosp., 1960-65, asst dept. head nurse, 1965-67; head nurse Montfort Hosp., Ottawa, 1967-68, hosp. supr., 1968-75; dir. nursing Cen. d'Accueil Roger Seguin, Clarence Creek, Ont., 1975—; Mem. Dist. Health Council, East Ont., 1986—. Chmn. Scouts and Guide of Can., Clarence Creek, 1980-84; sec., v.p. Can. Cancer Soc., Russell Unit, 1973—. Recipient Humanitarian Commendation Optimist Club, 1986, Clarence Creek, 1986, House of Commons, Clarence Creek, 1986. Mem. Registerd Nursing Assn. Ontario, Geriatric Nursing Ont., Can. Soc. (cert. service). Roman Catholic. Club: Auxiliary Cen. d'Accueil. Office: Cen d'Accueil Roger Seguin, CP 160, Clarence Creek, ON Canada

ST. JEAN, CATHERINE AVERY, advertising executive; b. Dubuque, Iowa, Oct. 10, 1950; d. Harvey Dale and Mary Theresa (Heinz) Avery; m. Kenneth R. St. Jean, June 24, 1978 (div. May 1983); m. Paul J. Frahm, Mar. 7, 1987; children: Ian, Christian. BA in Communications, Loyola U., Chgo., 1977. Video editor Needham, Harper & Steers, Chgo., 1978, creative coordinator, 1979-80, presentations services mgr. Needham, Harper & Steers/U.S.A., Chgo., 1980-82, v.p., corp. dir. communications services Needham, HarperWorldwide, Inc., N.Y.C., 1982 v.p., 1982, v.p., asst. dir. creative services, 1985-86; v.p., dir. creative services DDB Needham Worldwide, 1986, sr. v.p., 1987—. Author, art dir. direct mail brochure: How to Keep the Heart in New York for Tri-State United Way (Merit award 1982, bronze medal N.Y. Internat. Film and TV Festival 1984), 1982. Recipient Crystal Prism award Am. Advt. Fedn., 1987. Mem. Advt. Women in N.Y. (chmn. 1984, bd. dirs. 1-yr. dir. 1985, 2-yr. dir. 1986—, 2d v.p. 1987, chmn. U.S. Premier Cannes Film Festival Gala at Lincoln Ctr. 1986, 87). Avocation: photography. Office: DDB Needham Worldwide 437 Madison Ave New York NY 10022

ST. JOHN, MARGARET KAY, research coordinator; b. Clifton Forge, Va., Apr. 20, 1953; d. Clarence Robinson Jr. and Betty Jean (Miller) St.J. BS in Life Scis., Worcester Poly. Inst., 1975. Electron microscopy asst. St. Vincent Hosp., Worcester, Mass., 1974-80, med. and research technologist I, 1980-81; researcher U. Nebr. Med. Ctr., Omaha, 1981-85, research coordinator, 1985—. Contbr. articles to sci. jours. Counselor Personal Crisis Ctr., 1982-83; sec. Citizens Media Adv. Council, Omaha, 1983-85; mem. Episcopal Ch. Women, 1984—; sci. coach in biology, chemistry, physics NAACP-Afro-Am. Cultural Technol. Sci. Olympics Competition, 1985—; mem. Urban League, Omaha, 1987—. Mem. AAAS, New Eng. Soc. for Electron Microscopy, Electron Microscopy Soc. Am., Am. Assn. Profl. and Exec. Women, N.Y. Acad. Scis., Am. Mgmt. Assn. Democrat. Home: 423 N 40th St #3 Omaha NE 68131 Office: U Nebr Med Ctr Dept Pathology 42d and Dewey Ave Omaha NE 68105

ST. JOHN, NANCY MARIE, computer graphics executive; b. Summerside, P.E.I., Can., Nov. 12, 1953; came to U.S., 1984; d. Ernest Patrick and Agnes C. (McKearney) St. J. BA, Carleton U., 1975. Paralegal McClaws & Co. Barristers & Solic., Calgary, Alta., Can., 1977-78; freelance writer 1978-80; dir., v.p., producer Allen Jones Prodn., Vancouver, B.C., Can., 1980-84; producer mgr. Vertigo Computer Imagery, Vancouver, B.C., Can., 1984, Digital Prodns., Los Angeles, 1985; exec. producer, v.p. Robert Abel & Assocs., Los Angeles, 1985-86; mgr. Nat. Ctr. for Supercomputing Applications, Champaign, Ill., 1986—; cons. in field. Office: Nat Ctr Supercomputing Applications 605 E Springfield Ave Champaign IL 61820

ST. JOHN CURRIE, SANDY, marketing professional; b. Borger, Tex., Sept. 15, 1952; d. Henry Doyle and Bobbie E. (White) St. John; m. Hugh Bob Currie, Aug. 10, 1985. BS in Elem. Edn., North Tex. State U., 1974. Tchr. Arlington, Amarillo and El Paso, Tex., Van Cleave, Miss., 1975-82; dir. Am. Cancer Soc., Amarillo, 1982-84, Amarillo Area Adult Literacy Council, 1984-86; mktg. dir. Currie Eye Inst., Amarillo, 1986—; tech. assistance cons. Laubach Literacy Action, 1987—. Chairperson publicity com. Harrington Cancer Ctr., Amarillo, 1985—; sec. Mothers Against Drunk Driving, 1985-87; active Jr. League, Amarillo; bd. dirs. Amarillo Area Adult Lit. Council, Big Bros./Big Sisters, Samaritan Counseling Ctr. Mem. Amarillo C. of C. (edn. com. 1986-87), Amarillo Lone Star Ballet Guild (2d v.p., cast food chmn.), Zeta Tau Alpha Alumnae Assn. (pres. 1984-86). Republican. Club: Ysleta Jr. Women's (El Paso). Office: Currie Eye Inst 20001 Coulter Dr Amarillo TX 79106

ST. LOUIS, EILEEN MARIE, banker; b. Ft. Ord, Calif., July 5, 1957; d. Norman Edward and Barbara June (Benson) St. L. BA in Econs., Coll. William and Mary, 1979. Asst. area br. mgr. V. Nat. Bank, Alexandria, 1980-81; retail banking officer, mgr. Sovran Bank NA, Falls Church, Va., 1981-84; asst. v.p., mgr. Sovran Bank NA, McLean, Va., 1984-85; mktg. and bus. devel. officer Arlington (Va.) Bank, 1985-86, bus. devel. officer, 1986-87; v.p. Arlington Bank, Tysons Corner, Va., 1987—. Fin. advisor Jr. Achievement Am., Falls Church, 1983. Mem. Greater Rosslyn Bus. and Profl. Assn. (bd. dirs. 1987—, treas. 1986—), Seven Corners Mcht. Assn., Mason Dist. Jaycees, Nat. Assn. Bank Women, Nat. Assn. Female Execs., Am. Mgmt. Assn., Ballston Partnership, Arlington County C. of C., Fairfax County C. of C., McLean Bus. and Profl. Assn., Kappa Alpha Theta. Republican. Roman Catholic. Lodge: Jobs Daus. Office: Arlington Bank 8601 Westwood Center Dr Vienna VA 22180

ST. PIERRE, CHARLOTTE EATON, social worker, consultant; b. Cooperstown, N.Y., Apr. 22, 1955; d. Charles William and Katherine Mildred (Pentz) Eaton; m. Ronald Donald St. Pierre, Sept. 5, 1981. BA cum laude, SUNY-Geneseo, 1977; MSW, SUNY-Albany, 1982. Cert./lic. social worker, cert. in secondary edn., N.Y. Med. claims approver Met. Group Health, Utica and Colonie, N.Y., 1978-83; social service dir. Silver Haven Nursing Home, Rotterdam, N.Y., 1983-85; med. social worker, social services dir. James Eddy Geriatric Ctr., Troy, N.Y., 1985—; group leader Alzheimers Disease and Related Disorders, Troy and Albany, 1985—; cons. fin. planning to families of elderly and/or Alzheimers victims. Vol. Utica Psychiat. Ctr., N.Y., 1977-78. Mem. Nat. Assn. Social Workers, Devon Cattle Assn. Democrat. Avocations: ceramics, quilting, collecting antiques. Home: 8 Drake Ct PO Box 438 Waterford NY 12188 Office: Eddy Meml Geriatric Ctr 2256 Burdell Ave Troy NY 12180

ST. ROSE, EDWINA LOSEY, lawyer; b. Charlottesville, Va., Aug. 25, 1952; d. Edward Lee and Emma Jane (Brown) Losey; m. Dennis Anthony St. Rose, Oct. 6, 1979; 1 child, Dennis Anthony II. BA, Barnard Coll., 1973; JD, George Washington U., 1976. Bar: Pa. 1978, U.S. Ct. Appeals (D.C. cir.) 1984. Legal editor Bur. Nat. Affairs, Washington, 1977-80; atty., advisor Social Security Adminstrn., Arlington, Va., 1980-83; employee relations, devel. specialist Naval Intelligence Command, Washington, 1983-85; sole practice Ft. Washington, 1985—; investigator EEO, 1985—. Named One of Outstanding Young Women of America, 1984. Mem. ABA, Pa. Bar Assn., D.C. Bar Assn., Prince Georges County Bd. of Realtors, Md. Bd. Realtors, D.C. Bd. of Realtors. Baptist. Home: 761 Gleneagles Dr Fort Washington MD 20744

ST. TAMARA (TAMARA KOLBA), painter, printmaker; b. Navahradak, Byelorussia; came to U.S., 1950, naturalized, 1956; d. Alexander and Maria (Boris) Stahanovich; m. Alexander Kolba, Feb. 22, 1958. BA, Western Coll., Oxford, Ohio, 1954; MFA, Columbia U., 1956. Free-lance printmaker, artist, 1956—. One-woman shows include: Western Coll., 1955, Aenle Gallery, N.Y.C., 1956, Avanti Galleries, N.Y.C., 1968, Asbury Park (N.J.) Art Mus., 1973, Free Pub. Library of Woodbridge (N.J.), 1975, Guild of Creative Art, Shrewsbury, N.J., 1975, 77, West Long Branch (N.J.) Library, 1979; exhibited in group shows Young Printmakers traveling exhbn., 1967-69, Herron Sch. Art, Indpls., Nat. Print and Drawing Exhbn., DeKalb, Ill., 1968, UNICEF, N.Y.C., 1969, 74, 76, 79, Audubon Artists, N.Y.C., 1971, 79, Davidson (N.C.) Nat. Print and Drawing Competition, 1972, 73, First Miami (Fla.) Graphics Biennial, 1973, G.W.V. Smith Mus., Springfield, Mass., 1973, 74, 76, 77, 3d Hawaii Nat. Print. Exhbn., Honolulu, 1975, 65th Ann. Exhbn., Wadsworth Atheneum, Hartford, Conn., 1975, Va. Highlands Festival, Abington, Va., Salmagundi Club, N.Y.C., 1979, 11th Ann. Biennial Nat. Art Exhbn., Valley City, N.D., 1979, 81, Printmaking Council of N.J., Somerville, 1981, Charlotte (N.C.) Printmakers Soc., 1981, 1st Ann. Juried Show, Southport, N.C., 1981, Nat. Miniature Show, Cuyahoga Falls, Ohio, 1982, 14th Nat. Art Show, La Junta, Colo., 1982, Lever House, N.Y.C., 1982, N.Mex. Art League, Albuquerque, 1987, Audubon Artists, N.Y.C., 1987, 2d Crossing Gallery, Valley City, N.D., 1987, Castle Gallery, Billings, Mont., 1987, Del Bello Gallery, Toronto, 1987. Illustrator: Biography of a Polar Bear, 1972; Come Visit a Prairie Dog Town, 1976; Animal Games, 1976; Save that Raccoon, 1978; author, illustrator: Asian Crafts, 1970; Chickaree—A Red Squirrel, 1980. Mem. Guild Creative Art, Byelorussian Inst. Arts and Scis., Catherine Lorillard Wolfe Art Club, Print Club of Albany. Home: 235 Hockhockson Rd Tinton Falls NJ 07724

SAITER, NORMA JEAN, educator; b. Ft. Morgan, Colo., June 12, 1932; d. Bertel and Edna (Redmann) Wickstrom; divorced 1974; children: Gerald J. Bristow, Larry G. Bristow; m. George J. Saiter, 1975. BA, U. No. Colo., 1969, MA, 1970; cert. in K-12 edn. of handicapped, U. Colo., Colorado Springs, 1979. Cert. tchr., Colo. Primary tchr. Ashton Pub. Sch., Greeley, Colo., 1952-54; primary educator mentally handicapped Greeley Pub. Schs., 1970-74; tchr. educable mentally handicapped Pikes Peak Bd. Coop. Services, Colorado Springs, 1975-78; tchr. educationally handicapped Acad. Sch. Dist., Colorado Springs, 1978-80, tchr. emotionally behavioral disordered, 1980-81, tchr. 1st grade, 1981-87, tchr. grades 1-2, 1987, tchr. grades 1-3, 1988—. Presenter Citizens' Task Force Learning Disabilities, Colorado Springs, 1986. Mem. Internat. Reading Assn. (presenter 1986), Colo. Reading Assn. (presenter 1987, 88), Colo. Language Arts Soc., Nat. Council Tchrs. of English, Phi Delta Kappa. Democrat. Home: 1175 Garlock Ln Colorado Springs CO 80907 Office: Foothills Elem Sch Acad Sch Dist 825 Allegheny Colorado Springs CO 80919

SAIZAN, PAULA THERESA, oil company executive; b. New Orleans, Sept. 12, 1947; d. Paul Morine and Hattie Mae (Hayes) Saizan; BS in Acctg. summa cum laude, Xavier U., 1969; CPA; m. George H. Smith, May 26, 1973 (div. July 1976). Systems engr. IBM, New Orleans, 1969-71; acct., then sr. acct. Shell Oil Co., Houston, Tex., 1971-76, sr. fin. analyst, 1976-77, fin. rep., 1977-79, corp. auditor, 1979-81, treasury rep., 1981-82, sr. treasury rep., 1982-86; asst. treas. Shell Credit Inc., Shell Leasing Co., Shell Fin. Co. 1986-88, sr. pub. affairs rep., 1988—. Mem. Am. Inst. CPA's, Tex. Soc. CPA's, Nat. Assn. Accts., Am. Petroleum Inst. (constituencies resources task force) Inwood Forest Improvement Assn., Houston Area Urban League, LWV of Houston, Xavier U. Alumni Assn. (membership dir.), Phi Gamma Nu. Roman Catholic. Home: 5426 Long Creek Ln Houston TX 77088 Office: Shell Oil Co 1510 One Shell Plaza PO Box 2463 Houston TX 77252

SAKAI, HIROKO, trading company executive; b. Nishiharu, Aichi-ken, Japan, Jan. 9, 1939; came to U.S., 1956; d. Kichiya and Saki (Shiraishi) S. BA, Wellesley Coll., 1963; MA, Columbia U., 1967, PhD, 1972. Journalist Asahi Evening News, Tokyo, 1963-65; escort interpreter Dept. State, Washington, 1967-68; econ. analyst Port Authority N.Y. and N.J., N.Y.C., 1968-69; sr. cons. Harbridge House, Inc., Boston, 1970-84, Quantum Sci. Corp., White Plains, N.Y., 1984-87; corp. planner C. Itoh & Co. (Am.), Inc., N.Y.C., 1988—. Interpreter Govt. Mass., Boston, 1974. Fellow Wellesley Coll., 1960-83, Columbia U., 1965-68; grantee Columbia U., 1969. Mem. Regional Sci. Assn., Japan Soc. Buddhist. Buddhist. Home: 235 E

51st St Apt 5C New York NY 10022 Office: C Itoh & Co (Am) Inc 335 Madison Ave New York NY 10017

SAKS, JUDITH-ANN, artist; b. Anniston, Ala., Dec. 20, 1943; d. Julien David and Lucy-Jane (Watson) S.; student Tex. Acad. Art, 1957-58, Mus. Fine Arts, Houston, 1962, Rice U., 1962; BFA, Tulane U., 1966; postgrad. U. Houston, 1967; m. Haskell Irvin Rosenthal, Dec. 22, 1974; 1 son, Brian Julien. One-man shows include: Alley Gallery, Houston, 1969, 2131 Gallery, Houston, 1969; group shows include: Birmingham (Ala.) Mus., 1967, Meinhard Galleries, Houston, 1977; Galerie Barbizon, Houston, 1980, Park Crest Gallery, Austin, 1981; represented in permanent collections including: L.B. Johnson Manned Space Mus., Clear Lake City, Tex., Harris County Heritage Mus., Windsor Castle, London, Smithsonian Instn., Washington: commns. include: Pin Oak Charity Horse Show Assn., Roberts S.S. Agy., New Orleans; curator student art collection U. Houston, 1968-72; artist Am. Revolution Bicentennial project Port of Houston Authority, 1975-76. Recipient art awards including: 1st prize for water color Art League Houston, 1969, 1st prize for graphics, 1969, 1st prize for sculpture, 1968, 1st place award for original print, DAR, Am. Heritage Com., 1987. Mem. Art League Houston, Houston Mus. Fine Arts, DAR (curator 1983-85, contbr. Tex. sesquicentennial drawing for DAR mag.), Daus. Republic Tex. Home: PO Box 1793 Bellaire TX 77401

SALAFIA, LINDA MARY, municipal government official; b. Norwich, Conn., Oct. 16, 1946; d. James Washington and Albina (Bawza) Frederick; m. Philip Salafia Jr., Sept. 7, 1968 (div. 1984); children: Christopher, Angela. Grad. high sch., Norwich Free Acad., 1964. Legal sec. George Gilman, Atty., Norwich, 1964-72; ct. clk. Norwich Probate Ct., 1974-81, judge of probate, 1981—, region 7 coordinator, 1987; dir. Dime Savs. Bank, Norwich. Mem. editorial bd. Conn. Probate Law Jour., Bridgeport, 1987. Dir. Vol. Action Ctr., Norwich, 1984—, Am. Cancer Soc., Norwich, 1986, Widowed Persons Service, Waterford, Conn., 1985; bd. dirs. Norwich Free Acad., 1981—, Backus Found., 1987—. Named Woman of Yr., Norwich Bus. and Profl. Women's Club, 1985. Mem. Nat. Coll. Probate Judges, Conn. Probate Assembly, Conn. Council Adoption. Democrat. Roman Catholic. Club: Norwich Federated Womens. Lodge: Rotary. Office: Norwich Probate Ct City Hall 100 Broadway Norwich CT 06360

SALAGA, VIVIAN ODELL, architect, educator; b. Lakewood, Ohio, Oct. 7, 1946; d. George Thomas and Dorothy Elizabeth (Uthe) Allender; m. John W. Salaga, Nov. 26, 1969 (div.); m. John Tennison; children: Lisa Tenninson, Eric Tenninson. Diploma in French, U. Lausanne (Switzerland) Ctrs., 1968; BA in French, Cleve. State U., 1969; MArch, Kent (Ohio) State U., 1979. lic. architect, Fla. Architect Dalton. Dalton, Newport, Cleve., 1979-80; archtl. dir. ednl. mktg. Spillis, Candela, Ptnrs., Coral Gables, Fla., 1980-83; prin. Atelier Architects, Ft. Lauderdale, Fla., 1984—; pres. TASC, Inc., Miami, 1986—; vis. prof. architecture Kent State U., 1979-80; asst. prof., dir. archtl. studies Fla. Internat. U., Miami, 1983—; pres. TASC, Inc., Miami, 1986—. Prin. archtl. works include Pembroke Pines Human Resources Ctr., 1984-89, Old Sch. Sq. Hist. Pres., 1988, Fla. Keys Community Coll., 1988-90; contbr. articles to profl. jours. Bd. dirs. Family Service Agy., Ft. Lauderdale, Fla., 1985-86; mem. adv. com. on minority participation in state univ. constrn. program State Bd. Regents, 1984; chmn. bd. Miami Children's Cultural Exchange, 1983—. Recipient award of merit Pembroke Pines Human Resources Ctr., Fla. Assn. Community Edn., 1983. Mem. AIA (bd. dirs. Fla. South chpt. 1982—, state dir. 1985), Nat. Trust for Hist. Preservation, Inst. for Futures Studies and Research, Fla. Assn. for Community Edn., Nat. Assn. Community Edn., Fla. Leadership Forum, Ft. Lauderdale C. of C., AAUW, Nat. Assn. Female Execs. Democratic. Club: Broward Bus. Exchange (Ft. Lauderdale). Office: Atelier Architects 901 Progresso Dr Fort Lauderdale FL 33304

SALAMON, LINDA BRADLEY, university dean, English literature scholar; b. Elmira, N.Y., Nov. 20, 1941; d. Grant Ellsworth and Evelyn E. (Ward) Bradley; divorced; children: Michael Lawrence, Timothy Martin. B.A., Radcliffe Coll., 1963; M.A., Bryn Mawr Coll., 1964, Ph.D., 1971; Advanced Mgmt. Cert., Harvard U. Bus. Sch., 1978. Lectr., adj. asst. prof. Eng. Dartmouth Coll., Hanover, N.H., 1967-72; lectr. English Smith Coll., Northampton, Mass., 1972-73; mem. faculty lit. Bennington Coll., Vt., 1974-75; dean students Wells Coll., Aurora, N.Y., 1975-77; exec. asst. to pres. U. Pa., Phila., 1977-79; assoc. prof. English Washington U., St. Louis, 1979-88, prof., 1988—, dean Coll. Arts and Scis., 1979—; cons. Acad. Ednl. Devel., 1978-80; mem. faculty Bryn Mawr Summer Inst. Women, 1979—. Author, co-editor: Nicholas Hilliard's Art of Limning, 1983; co-author: Integrity in the College Curriculum, 1985; contbr. numerous articles to literary and ednl. jours. Bd. dirs. Assn. Am. Colls., vice chmn., 1985, chmn., 1986; bd. dirs. Greater St. Louis council Girl Scouts U.S.A.; trustee Coll. Bd., St. Louis Coll. Pharmacy, Mary Inst., St. Louis Council World Affairs, Internat. Edn. Consortium of St. Louis; mem. steering com. Friends St. Louis County Library, 1982-83. Fellow Radcliffe Coll. Bunting Inst., 1973-74; Am. Philos. Soc. Penrose grantee, 1974; fellow Folger Shakespeare Library, 1986, NEH Montaigue Inst., 1988. Mem. Renaissance Soc. Am., AAAS, Modern Langs. Assn., Phi Beta Kappa. Office: Washington U Campus Box 1117 Saint Louis MO 63130

SALAMON, RENAY, real estate broker; b. N.Y.C., May 13, 1948; d. Solomon and Mollie (Friedman) Langman; m. Maier Salamon, Aug. 10, 1968; children: Mollie, Jean, Leah, Sharon, Eugene. BA, Hunter Coll., 1969. Licensed real estate borker, N.J. Mgr. office Customode Designs Inc., N.Y.C., 1966-68; co-owner Salamon Dairy Farms, Three Bridges, N.J., 1968-86; assoc. realtor Max. D. Shuman Realty Inc., Flemington, N.J., 1983-85; pres., chief exec. officer Liberty Hill Realty Inc., Flemington, N.J., 1985—; cons. Illva Saronna Inc. (Illva Group), Edison, N.J. 1985—; real estate devel. joint venture with M.R.F.S. Realty Inc. (Illva Group), 1986—. Environ. Commr. Readington Twp. E.C., Whitehouse Sta., N.J. 1978-87; fund-raiser Rutgers Prep. Sch., Somerset, N.J. 1984-87; mem. N.J. Assn. Environ. Commrs., Trenton, N.J. 1978-87. Named N.J. Broker Record, Forbes Inc., N.Y.C. 1987. Mem. Nat. Assn. Realtors, N.J. Assn. Realtors, Hunterdon County Bd. Realtors (mem. chair 1986), Realtor's Land Inst. Republican. Jewish. Office: Liberty Hill Realty Inc 415 Hwy 202 Flemington NJ 08822

SALANT, MINDI, assistant health facility administrator, nurse; b. Newark, N.J., July 12, 1956; d. Albert Aaron and Lenore (Weiner) S. BS in Nursing, Boston U., 1978; postgrad., Fairleigh Dickinson U., 1985—. RN, cert. occupational hearing conservationist, advanced cardiac life support system operator. Staff nurse Newark (N.J.) Beth Israel Med. Ctr., 1978-80; nursing supr. St. Joseph's Hosp. & Med. Ctr., Paterson, N.J., 1980-85; dir. Gen. Med-Care, East Rutherford, N.J., 1985-86; asst. adminstr. family practice, dir. indsl. health services John F. Kennedy Med. Ctr., Edison, N.J., 1986-87; trauma coordinator N.J. State Trauma Ctr. U. Hosp., Newark, 1987—; instr. emergency med. technician Passaic County Coll., Paterson, 1982—; instr. basic cardiac life support, St. Joseph's Hosp. & Med. Ctr., Paterson, 1982—. Bd. dirs., treas., sec. Carolyn Dorfman Dance Co., Summit, N.J., 1985—. Mem. Exec. Females, Emergency Nurses Assn., Aplastic Anemia Found. Am., Am. Trauma Soc. Office: NJ State Trauma Ct UMDNJ U Hosp 150 Bergen St Newark NJ 07103-2425

SALAS, ANGELA M., management consultant; b. Laredo, Tex., Mar. 14, 1942; d. Hipolito Lucio and Encarnacion (Sanchez) S. BS, Marillac Coll., 1969; MSW, Our Lady of the Lake U., 1973; PhD, U. Wis., 1985. Program specialist HEW, Chgo., 1975-78; pres. S.W. Urban Mgmt., San Antonio, 1985—; instr. San Antonio Coll., 1985—, coordinator vocat. tng. program, 1986—; tech./tng. cons. Nat. Assn. Govt. Employees, San Antonio, 1986—; v.p. C&M Human Services, Ltd., Madison, Wis., 1980-82; trainer Wis. Div. Corrections, 1981; coordinator Cuban entrants Madison Area Tech. Coll., Madison, 1981-82. Chmn. Official of Gov., Madison, 1980-82; organizer, coordinator Hispanic elderly Wis. Dept. Aging, Madison, 1982; chmn. Target EEO Coalition, San Antonio, 1984—; v.p., pres. S. San Antonio Ind. Sch. Dist., 1985—; adminstr. Project Job Match, City of San Antonio. Mem. Council on Social Work Edn., Mexican C. of C. Democrat. Roman Catholic. Office: SW Urban Mgmt Unltd 214 Dwyer St San Antonio TX 78204

SALAS, MARILYN SUE, academic director; b. Sabetha, Kans., June 4, 1943; d. Lee R. and Agnes M. (McPeak) Cashman; m. Henry C. Salas, Aug. 1, 1970. Student, Kans. State U., 1961-62, Kans. U., 1962-64; BA in Bus. Adminstrn., Emporia State U., 1966. Cert. secondary bus. edn. and psychology tchr., Kans., Calif. High sch. tchr. Pacifica High Sch., Garden Grove, Calif., 1966-68; word processor Orange County, Calif., 1968-72; ednl. service rep. IBM, Anaheim, Calif., 1969-70; coll. instr. Cerritos Coll., Norwalk, Calif., 1970-74, adult edn. instr. Lincoln Edn. Tng., Garden Grove, 1972-78; coll. instr. Golden West Coll., Huntington Beach, Calif., 1973-80, Orange Coast Coll., Costa Mesa, Calif., 1976-79, Cypress (Calif.) Coll., 1977-79; freelance word processor Burlington Northern, Newport Beach, Calif., 1978-79; cons. in field, Orange County, 1979; coll. instr. Saddleback Coll., Mission Viejo, Calif., 1979; dir. The Word Processing, Anaheim, 1980-87. Mem. Assn. Info. Systems Profls. (mem. ednl. task force), Am. Soc. Tng. and Devel., Calif. Bus. Educators Assn., Anaheim C. of C., Nat. Assn. Trade and Tech. Schs. Accrediting Agy. (accredited). Democrat. Methodist. Home: 41105 Valle Vista Murrieta CA 92362

SALAVERRIA, HELENA CLARA, educator; b. San Francisco, May 19, 1923; d. Blas Saturnino and Eugenia Irene (Loyarte) S.; AB, U. Calif., Berkeley, 1945, secondary teaching cert., 1946; MA, Stanford U., 1962. High sch. tchr., 1946-57; asst. prof. Luther Coll., Decorah, Iowa, 1959-60; prof. Spanish, Bakersfield (Calif.) Coll., 1961-84, chmn. dept., 1973-80. Vol., Hearst Castle; mem. srs. adv. group edn. Cuesta Coll. Community Services. Mem. Calif. (dir. 1976-77), Kern County (pres. 1975-77) fgn. lang. tchrs. assns., NEA, Union Concerned Scientists, Natural Resources Def. Council, Calif. Tchrs. Assn. (chpt. sec. 1951-52), AAUW (edn. com.), Yolo County Council Retarded, LWV of the U.S., RSVP, Amnesty Internat., Common Cause, Sierra Club, Prytanean Alumnae, U. Women of Cambria, U. Calif. Alumni Assn., Stanford U. Alumni Assn. Democrat. Presbyn. Address: PO Box 63 Cambria CA 93428

SALAY, CAROLYN JEANNE, advertising agency executive; b. Birmingham, Ala.; d. Augustus Alexander and Mary Elizabeth (White) S. BA, Birmingham So. Coll., 1966; postgrad., U. Ala., Tuscaloosa, 1966-68. Client liaison Unigrafix, Birmingham, Ala., 1970-71; traffic mgr. Luckie & Forney Advt., Inc., Birmingham, 1972-76; creative dir. Perry Hoyle Advt., Inc., Birmingham, 1976-77; freelance copywriter Birmingham, 1977; copywriter Bentley Huggins Smith & Whittington, Inc., Birmingham, 1977-78, Bear Britton Black Advt., Montgomery, 1978-82; creative dir. Bear Advt., Montgomery, Ala., 1978—. Copywriter Bank Marketing Assn., Best of Print (awards pub.), 1982; contbr. articles to advertising journals. Charter mem. Montgomery Mus.; profl. adv. Auburn U. Advt. Club, Montgomery, 1988; active various local charities; campaign staff Folmar for Gov., Montgomery, 1982. Recipient Class of '86 award Ala. Bus. Rev., Montgomery, 1986, Best of Show award Huntsville (Ala.) Advt. Fedn., 1988, over 150 Gold and Silver Addys from 3 clubs and dist. Mem. Montgomery Advt.Fedn. (pres. 1986-87, chmn. Pres.'s Council 1988—, chmn. bd. 1987-88, Copywriter of the Yr. 1979, 84, 86, Best of Show 1982, 86, 88), Am. Advt. Fedn. (7th dist. vice chmn. Council of Pres. 1986-87, pub. relations coordinator 1987-88, convs. and meetings coordinator 1988-89, named Ad Club Pres. of Yr. 1986-87), Soc. Advancement of Mgmt., Nat. Assn. Female Execs. Episcopalian. Club: Capital City (Montgomery) (mem. bus. com.). Home: 3261 Gatsby Ln Montgomery AL 36106

SALAZAR, NINFA ALICIA REYES, janitorial services company executive; b. Dexter, Mo., May 27, 1959; d. Juan Q. and Eloisa (Rodriguez) Reyes; m. Julian Salazar Sr., Sept. 10, 1979; 1 child, Julian Jr. Ed. Prairie State Coll., Sawyer Coll. Bus., Med. Career Inst. With Davis Temporaries, Chicago Heights, Ill., 1980-82; office mgr. E&B Painting, Harvey, Ill., 1981-82; owner, pres. J&N's Janitorial Services, Chicago Heights, 1982—. Court watcher Cook County Ct. Watcher's Project, Chicago Heights, 1985. Mem. Women in Mgmt., Women's Referral Services, Entrepreneur Assn. Am., Notaries Assn. Am., Am. Cardiology Tech. Assn., Chicago Heights C. of C. Avocations: bicycle riding; skating; dancing. Home: 175 Thelma Ln Chicago Heights IL 60411 Office: J&N's Janitorial Service PO Box 353 Park Forest IL 60466

SALAZAR, RACHEL, writer; b. Paris, Oct. 27, 1954; came to U.S., 1959; d. Leonard and Jeanne Catherine (Kyras) Dritz; m. Jorge Salazar, Oct. 18, 1976 (div. Mar. 1985). BA, Hunter Coll., 1981; MFA, Bklyn. Coll., 1983. Adj. prof. Bklyn. Coll., 1981-83; editor Fiction Collective, Bklyn., 1982-84, co-dir., 1986—; editor Grove Press, Inc., N.Y.C., 1984-86; freelance writer N.Y.C., 1986—. Author: Spectator, 1986. Recipient Fiction award Creative Artists Pub. Service, N.Y.C., 1984, Syndicated Fiction award PEN Am. Ctr., Washington, 1985; fellow N.Y. Found. for the Arts, 1987. Home and Office: PO Box 1812 Canal St Station New York NY 10013

SALAZAR, SUSAN BETTE, hotel executive; b. Bayshore, N.Y., Mar. 11, 1948; d. Alfred M. and Helen (Paserb) S. BA, SUNY, Buffalo, 1970; cert. in hosp. mgmt., NYU, 1984. Staff artist Rich Advt. Agy., Buffalo, 1970-71, Canterbury Arts, Inc., N.Y.C., 1971-73; desk clk., acctg. supr. Marriott's Essex House, N.Y.C., 1973-76; asst. mgr., asst. exec. housekeeper Barbizon Plaza Hotel, N.Y.C., 1976-81; asst. bldg. service mgr. Mus. Natural History, N.Y.C., 1981-83; residence dir. YMCA, N.Y.C., 1983—; network coordinator YMCA, Chgo., 1986—. Vol. Am. Soc. for Prevention Cruelty to Animals, N.Y.C., 1985-86; chmn., organizer 336 W 95th St Tenants' Assn., N.Y.C. Mem. Nat. Assn. Female Execs., NYU Hosp. Mgmt. Alumni Assn. (chmn. bd. 1985-86). Democrat. Episcopalian. Home: 336 W 95th St New York NY 10025 Office: YMCA Greater NY 224 E 47th St New York NY 10017

SALCITO, CAROL ANN, travel management specialist; b. Bklyn., Dec. 7, 1949; d. Albert and Connie (Sergi) Ballenberg; m. Louis C. Salcito, Oct. 30, 1945. AS, Charter Oak Coll., Hartford, Conn., 1987. Exec. sec. Otis Elevator div. United Techs., N.Y.C., 1976-80; supr. corp. adminstrn. Otis Elevator div. United Techs., Farmington, Conn., 1980-84, supr. personnel and adminstrv. services, 1984-86; mgr. travel ops. United Techs. Corp., Hartford, 1986-87, mgr. corp. travel, 1988—. Mem. Nat. Passenger Traffic Assn., Greater Hartford Passenger Traffic Assn. Home: 36 Regency Dr Norwalk CT 06851

SALDAÑA, ELSA ANTONIA, advertising agency executive; b. Brownsville, Tex., Oct. 13, 1950; d. Juan Angel and Blasita (Garza) Saldaña. BS with spl. honors, U. Tex., 1973. Media planner Compton Advt., N.Y.C., 1977-78; sr. media planner Grey Advt., N.Y.C., 1978-79; supr. Young & Rubicam, N.Y.C., 1979-83; assoc. media dir. Young & Rubicam/Dentsu, Los Angeles, 1983-85; assoc. media dir., v.p. McCann-Erickson, Los Angeles, 1985-87; cons. media planning and buying cons., Los Angeles, 1987-88; media planner and buyer GSD&M, Inc., Austin, Tex., 1988—. Mem. Women in Communications, Advt. Club, Nat. Assn. Female Execs. Office: GSD&M Inc 1 Cielo Ctr 1250 Capital of Texas Hwy Suite 400 Austin TX 78746

SALDANHA, RITA LOUIS, physician; b. Bombay, Aug. 13, 1949; d. Louis and Megan Saldanha. MB, BS, Poona U., India, 1973, MD, 1976. Intern in pediatrics St. Lukes Hosp. Ctr., N.Y.C., 1976-77; resident in pediatrics Children's Hosp. Mich., 1977-78, fellow in neonatology, 1978-80; asst. prof. pediatrics East Carolina U. Sch. Medicine, Greenville, 1980-87, assoc. prof. pediatrics, 1987—. Fellow Am. Acad. Pediatrics; mem. N.C. Perinatal Assn. (pres.-elect 1985-87, pres. 1987), N.C. Pediatric Soc. Democrat. Roman Catholic. Home: 213 Woodhaven Rd Greenville NC 27834 Office: East Carolina U Sch Medicine Dept Pediatrics Greenville NC 27834

SALERNO, EVELYN, pharmacist; b. Passaic, N.J., Dec. 14, 1936; d. John C. and Elvira (Infante) S.; B.S., Rutgers U., 1958; D.Pharmacy, Mercer U., 1975. From clk. to part-time registered pharmacist Martini's Pharmacy, Hackensack, N.J., 1956-60; chief pharmacist Pascack Valley Hosp., Westwood, N.J., 1960; pharmacist Prescription Pharmacy, Hialeah, Fla., 1961-63; registered pharmacist, asst. mgr., dir. pharmacy South Fla. State Hosp., Hollywood, 1963-74, dir. profl. services, asst. dir. hosp. pharmacies, 1973—, with RCW Cons., Inc., 1975-82; dir. clin. services Nursing Home Assos., Inc., 1981-82; vis. lectr. U. Miami Sch. Nursing, asso. prof., 1979-87, grad. facutly appointee, 1984-87; assoc. prof. Southeastern Coll. Pharm. Scis., 1987—, adj. prof. Southeastern Coll. Osteopathic Medicine; cons. Hospice S. Fla., Sunrise, community for retarded. Mem. Am. Pharm. Assn., Am. Soc. Hosp. Pharmacists, Am. Inst. History Pharmacy, Southeastern Soc. Hosp. Pharmacists, S. Fla. Soc. Hosp. Pharmacists, Fla. Pharm. Assn., Fla. Soc. Hosp. Pharmacists, Rutgers U. Alumni Assn., Mercer U. Alumni Assn., Am. Pharm. Assn. Acad. Pharmacy Practice, Heart Assn. Greater Miami. Democrat. Roman Catholic. Author papers in field, profl. reviewer; contbr. chpt. to Pharmacology in Nursing, 17th edit.; columnist Fla. Jour. Hosp. Pharmacy. Office: 8768 SW 131st St Miami FL 33176

SALGUEIRO, CARMEN ESCUDÉ, educator, concert pianist, accompanist; b. Santiago-de-Cuba, May 11, 1950; came to U.S., 1962; d. Juan and Maria del Carmen (Ramos) Escude; m. Robert Da Costa Salgueiro, Nov. 18, 1973. MusB, Cath. U., 1971; MusM, Manhattan Sch. Music, 1973; Degree in Theory & Solfege, Conservatory Music, Santiago, Cuba, 1961. Cert. Ednl. Supr. 1988, Tchr. Vocal Music K-12, Bilingual-Bicultural Edn., Elem. Edn., Tchr. ESL, N.J., Ednl. Supr., N.J. Tchr. piano and theory Villa Walsh Acad., Morristown, N.J., 1971; elem. vocal music tchr. Lafayette St. Sch., Newark, 1972-75, Hawkins St. Sch., Newark, 1975-76; elem. bilingual tchr. South St. Sch., Newark, 1980-84; elem. summer sch. tchr. Oliver St. Sch., Newark, 1984; tchr. ESL, Newark, 1984—; concert pianist (solo and orchestra), Cuba, U.S., Italy, 1955—; Organist Our Lady of Mercy Ch., Park Ridge, N.J., 1982; choir dir. Student Community Concerts, Newark, 1984—. Sec. Congress of Portuguese Speaking Peoples, Newark, 1974, Peter Francisco Meml. Commn., Newark, 1976; mem. Portuguese-Am. Scholarship Found., Newark, 1973—, scholarship com., 1984—. Scholar Villa Victoria Acad., 1962-67, Manhattan Sch. Music, 1971, Cath. U., 1967-71, Kean Coll., 1979-82, Seton Hall U., 1979-81; Master Tchr. Status Newark Bd. Edn., 1985. Mem. N.J. Tchrs. English to Speakers of Other Langs.-Bilingula Educators Assn. (ESL Tchr. Yr. 1988), Newark Tchrs. Union, Sigma Alpha Iota. Avocations: traveling, swimming, composing, astronomy, philology.

SALHANICK, BRENDA CRANE, lawyer; b. Keene, N.H., Aug. 2, 1951; d. Clayton Howard and Anita (Barry) Crane; BA cum laude, St. Anselm Coll., 1974; CLU Northeastern U. 1978; JD cum laude Suffolk U. Law Sch. 1987; m. Joel A. Salhanick, Sept. 19, 1978; 1 child, Marc Allan. With Jules Meyers Assocs., Chestnut Hill, Mass. 1975-83, dir. pension dept. 1977-83, v.p. Employee Benefit Plan Services 1979-83; assoc. Jenkens & Gilchrist, P.C., Dallas, 1987—. Instr. first aid ARC 1972-81.

SALINAS, DORA, communications company public relations executive; b. Brownsville, Tex., Apr. 2, 1936; d. Alfonso E. and Virginia (Garza) Alonso; children: Ruth V., Stephen A. Student, San Antonio Jr. Coll., 1957-58. Operator Southwestern Bell Telephone Co., San Antonio, 1954-71, service rep. customer services, 1971-73, supr. bus. office, customer services, 1973-76, mgr. customer services, 1976-79, dist. mgr. customer services, 1979-84, dist. mgr. community relations, 1984—. Chairperson Mcpl. CSC, Multiple Sclerosis Soc.; elected commr. Fiesta Commn.; planning com. San Antonio Women's Hall of Fame; edl. com. and adv. council Upward Bound; bd. dirs. Centro Del Barrio, Inc., San Antonio Livestock Exposition, Inc., Target 90/Goals for San Antonio, Nat. League of United Latin Am. Citizens Edn. Service Ctr.; co-chair Internat. Mex. Day com., collaborative task force, fin. com. Cumberland Presbyn. Ch., also past ruling elder; bd. contbrs. United Way, also chairperson allocation panel; active Alumni Leadership San Antonio-Greater C. of C., Mexican Am. Legal Def. and Edn. Fund; zoning commr. City of San Antonio; fund raising com. San Antonio Symphony. Recipient Sykes award Nat. Multiple Sclerosis Soc.; Award for Volunteerism San Antonio Coalition for Children, Youth and Families (S.A. CARES), Service to Mankind award Sertoma Club; named Gov.'s Yellow Rose of Tex.; honoree Women's Hall of Fame; inductee Hispanic Hall of Fame. Mem. Mexican C. of C. (past pres. San Antonio chpt., vol. of yr. award 2 yrs.). Office: Southwestern Bell Telephone Co 1010 N Saint Mary's Room 1319 San Antonio TX 78215

SALINGER, MARION CASTING, international studies educator, poet; b. Buffalo, May 22, 1917; d. George Alfred and Mary Helen (Knopf) C.; m. Herman Salinger, Nov. 29, 1941; children: Jill Hudson Salinger Winter, Wendy Lang, Jennifer Wilson Salinger Duffy. Student, U. Buffalo, 1936, U. Wis., 1938-40. Journalist Kenmore (N.Y.) Ind. Record, 1934; syndicated journalist Madison, Wis., 1937-39; pvt. sec. library Duke U., Durham, N.C., 1956-60, adminstrv. mgr. Ctr. for internat. Studies, 1966-85, adminstrv. coordinator Can. Studies Ctr., 1986—. Poems published in mags. Kaleidoscope, N.Mex. Quar., Fantasy, Little Treasury of World Poetry, Dimension, Archive, Chronicle of Higher Edn.; editor, co-editor numerous articles and monographs; contbr. articles to profl. jours. Recipient Silver medal Women of Achievement, Durham, 1984. Mem. Assn. Can. Studies in U.S. (Donner award 1985), Soc. Internat. Devel. (pres. local chpt. 1985-86), So. Atlantic States Assn. for Asian and African Studies (exec. dir. 1980-82), Nat. Council Social Studies, PEO Sisterhood (state pres. 1960). Democrat. Episcopalian. Home: 3444 Rugby Rd Durham NC 27707 Office: Duke U Can Studies Ctr 2016 Campus Dr Durham NC 27706

SALISBURY, ALICIA LAING, state senator; b. N.Y.C., Sept. 20, 1939; d. Herbert Farnsworth and Augusta Belle (Marshall) Laing; m. John Eagan Salisbury, June 23, 1962; children—John Eagan Jr., Margaret Laing. Student Sweet Briar Coll., 1957-60; B.A., Kans. U., 1961. Mem. Kans. Senate, 1985—, chmn. adminstrv. rules and regulations com., vice chmn. edn. com., mem. assessment and taxation com., legis. and congl. apportionment com., econ. devel. commn. local govt. com., pub. health and welfare com., ednl. planning com; mem. Kans. Supreme Ct. Task Force on Permanency Planning, 1987—. Elected mem. State Bd. Edn., Topeka, 1981-85; mem. health care task force Council State Govts.; past pres. Jr. League of Topeka; trustee Leadership Kans., 1982—; bd. dirs. Topeka Community Found., 1983—, Topeka Pub. Sch. Found., 1985—, Kans. Council on Employment and Tng., 1985—; mem. adv. commn. Juvenile Offenders Program, Kans., 1985—; mem. adv. bd. Kans. Action for Children, 1982—, Kans. Ins. Edn. Found., 1984—, Youth Center at Topeka, 1987—; mem. Nat. Fedn. Rep. Women; former bd. dirs. Topeka C. of C., United Way Greater Topeka, ARC, Family Service and Guidance, Topeka, Shawnee County Mental Health Assn., Florence Crittenton Services, Topeka, Kans. Action for Children, Topeka City Commn. Govtl. Adv. Com. Mem. Nat. Conf. State Legislators, Nat. Republican Legislators' Assn., Shawnee County Rep. Women, Kappa Kappa Gamma. Episcopalian. Avocations: tennis; downhill skiing; water sports; horseback riding; gardening. Office: Kans State Senate State Capital Bldg Topeka KS 66612

SALISBURY, JENNY OLIVIA, real estate representative; b. Berea, Ohio, May 15, 1959; d. Donald Edward and Dorothy Olivia (Theurer) S. Student, Bowling Green U., 1977-81, Cleve. State U., 1981—. Collection supr., computer operator, sales rep. Preview Subscription TV, Cleve., 1981-83; account exec. US Sprint Communications, Independence, Ohio, 1983-87; real estate agt. Ohio Savs. Realty, North Olmstead, Ohio, 1987—, Hunter Realty, 1987—; pres., owner North Coast Telemarketing, Cleve., 1987—. Fellow Soc. Telecommunication Profls., Cleve. Bd. Realtors, Nat. Assn. Female Execs. Republican. Episcopalian. Club: Sixth Day (pres. 1987—). Home and Office: 1220 W 6th St #604 Cleveland OH 44113

SALISBURY, PATRICIA DIANNE, printing company executive; b. North Kingstown, R.I., Oct. 6, 1951; d. John Edward and Noella Dianne (Choiniere) S.; m. Kenneth Richard Castle, Dec. 20, 1975. Student, R.I. Coll., 1976-81, Community Coll. R.I., 1981-83. Operator New England Telephone Co., Pawtucket, R.I., 1970-71; sales rep. Standard Wire and Cable Co., Attleboro, Mass., 1972-74; exec. sec. Gold Filled Mfrs. Assn., Attleboro, 1974-78; pvt. practice bookkeeping Pawtucket, 1978-80; asst. to owner Nautical Enterprises, Pawtucket, 1980-82; pres. Rapid Printing Inc., N. Providence, R.I., 1982—. Dir. adv. bd. Fund for Community Progress, Providence, 1986-87; mem. R.I. Coll. Graphics Arts Adv. Bd., Providence, 1984—. Mem. Nat. Assn. Quick Printers, Providence Club of Printing House Craftsmen (bd. dirs.), Nat. Assn. Female Execs., North Cen. C. of C. (bd. dirs.). Office: Rapid Printing Inc 1361 Mineral Spring Ave North Providence RI 02904

SALITERMAN, LAURA SHRAGER, pediatrician; b. N.Y.C., June 26, 1946; d. Arthur M. and Ida (Wildman) Shrager; m. Richard Arlen Saliterman, June 15, 1975; 1 child, Robert Warren. AB magna cum laude, Brandeis U., 1967; MD, NYU, 1971. Intern Montefiore Hosp. and Med. Ctr., Bronx, N.Y., 1971-72, resident in pediatrics, 1972-74; pediatrician Morrisania Family Care Ctr., N.Y.C., 1974-75; pediatrician Share Health Plan, St. Paul, 1975-85, dir. pediatrics, 1976-82; pediatrician Aspen Med. Group, St. Paul, 1985—; clin. asst. prof. U. Minn. Med. Sch. Mem. Am. Acad. Pediatrics (chair accident prevention com. Minn. chpt. 1985—), Phi

Beta Kappa. Club: Oak Ridge. Home: 11911 Live Oak Dr Minnetonka MN 55343 Office: 1020 Bandana Blvd W Saint Paul MN 55108

SALKIN, GERALDINE (JERI) FAUBION, dancer, dance therapist, educator; b. Denver, Mar. 18, 1916; d. George Everett and Hanna Viola (Harvey) Faubion; student Lester Horton Dance Theater, Carmelita Maracci, Trudi Schoop, Los Angeles, 1937-47, Doris Humphrey, N.Y.C., 1952-53, Rudolf Von Laban, London, 1956-57, Hanna Fenichel, Ph.D.,Westwood, Calif., 1965-70, UCLA, 1959-60; Ph.D., 1978; m. Leo Salkin, June 29, 1936; 1 dau., Lynn Salkin Sbiroli. Concert dancer Lester Horton Dance Group, Los Angeles, 1937-47, tchr. creative modern dance, 1939-47; tchr. creative modern dance Dance Assos., Hollywood, Calif., 1949-53, Am. Sch. of London (Eng.), 1956-57, Jeri Salkin Studio and Ctr. for Child Study, Hollywood, 1968-73; developer body ego technique Camarillo (Calif.) State Hosp., 1957-64; movement specialist Nat. Endowment Arts grantee, 1973—; dir., body ego technique dept. Cedars-Sinai Thalians Community Mental Health Ctr., Los Angeles, 1965—; dance cons., tchr. Nat. Head Start Program, Calif., 1964; conductor yearly workshops for tchrs., dancers, psychologists, psychiatrists, therapists, Rome, 1979—, mem. aux. faculty Goddard Coll., Antioch Coll., various hosps. and univs. Calif. Dept. Mental Hygiene grantee, 1960-63. Mem. Am. Dance Therapy Assn., AAHPER, Calif. Dance Educators Assn., Calif. Assn. Health, Phys. Edn. Dance and Recreation, Nat. Assn. Edn. Young Children, Assn. Child Devel. Specialists, Com. Research in Dance. Democrat. Author: Body Ego Technique, an Educational and Therapeutic Approach to Body Image and Self-Identity, 1973; author, choreographer film (with Leo Salkin and Trudi Schoop) Body Ego Technique, 1962 (U.S. Golden Eagle Council on Internat. Nontheatrical Events award 1963). Home: 3584 Multiview Dr Hollywood CA 90068 Office: 6305 Yucca St Suite 500 Hollywood CA 90028

SALLIN, SANDRA F., artist, educator; b. Los Angeles, Nov. 13, 1940; d. Simon and Ann (Kibrick) Friedman; m. Robert S. Sallin; children: Susannah Leigh, Matthew David. BFA, UCLA, 1963. Guest lectr. Calif. State U., Los Angeles, 1983, Laguna Beach Mus. Art, 1984, Calif. State U., Los Angeles, 1987; guest lectr. UCLA, 1987, instr., 1982-87; represented by Koplin Gallery, Los Angeles. Exhbns. include Brea (Calif.) Civic Cultural Ctr. Gallery, 1980, 81, Jewish Community Art Gallery, San Diego, 1980, Chatauqua (N.Y.) Art Assn. Galleries, 1981, Butler Inst., Youngstown, Ohio, 1981, Orange County Ctr. Contemporary Art, Santa Ana, Calif., 1981, Conejo Valley Art Mus., Thousand Oaks, Calif., 1982, Calif. State U., Dominguez Hills, 1983, ARCO Ctr. Visual Art, Los Angeles, 1983, Calif. State U., Hayward, 1984, Fairbanks Art Assn. Civic Ctr. Gallery, 1985, Visual Arts Ctr. Alaska, 1985, Design Ctr. Los Angeles, 1986, Soho 20, N.Y.C., 1986, Alaska State Mus., Juneau, 1986, Los Angeles Conv. Ctr., 1986, Koplin Gallery, Los Angeles, 1986, 87, Sun Valley (Idaho) Art Ctr., 1987; represented in numerous pvt. and corp. collections. Address: care Koplin Gallery 8225 1/2 Santa Monica Blvd Los Angeles CA 90046

SALMAN, JENAN AL-YAZDI, pharmacist, small business owner; b. Basrah, Iraq, May 3, 1946; came to U.S., 1973; d. Mahmood M. Al-Yazdi and Sadeeka Sh. Ridha; m. Kadhim N. Salman, July 17, 1968; children: Ayser, Zaid, Lameace. BA in Pharmacy, Bagdad, Iraq, 1969; postgrad., U. Ky., 1988—. Pharmacist pvt. drug store, Bagdad, 1969-73; research technician Ohio State U. Sch. Pharmacy, Columbus, 1974-75; research asst. Ohio State U. Vet. Sci., Columbus, 1975-77; research analyst Coll. Pharmacy U. Ky., Lexington, 1977-78, Agriculture Sta. U. Ky., Lexington, 11978-79; sci. demonstrator Coll. Medicine King Saud U., Saudi Arabia, 1980-85; pres., owner J.J. Gazelle Ltd., Lexington, 1985—. Contbr. articles to profl. jours. Home: 460 Lamont Dr Lexington KY 40503 Office: JJ Gazelle Ltd 410 W Vine St Lexington KY 40507

SALMON, ALICE SULLIVAN, nurse; b. N.Y.C., July 22, 1949; d. James Stephen and Ellen Hanna (Smith) Sullivan; B.S. in Nursing, Molloy Coll., 1971; M.A. in Nurse Edn., N.Y. U., 1975; m. Francis W. Salmon, Oct. 12, 1975. Staff nurse Jack D. Weiler Hosp. Albert Einstein Coll. Medicine, 1971-72, asst. head nurse, 1972-74, asst. dir. II, 1975-80, asst. dir. nursing, 1980-84, assoc. dir. nursing, 1984—. Mem. Am. Nurses Assn., Nat. League Nursing, Sigma Theta Tau. Office: 1825 Eastchester Rd Bronx NY 10461

SALMON, JUDI ANNE, purchasing agent; b. Beverly, Mass., Dec. 17, 1958; d. Richard Howard and Joan Marie (Bossie) Flinn; m. Dale Joseph Salmon, Mar. 14, 1981; 1 child, Kaycee Carolyn. Grad. high sch., Hamilton, Mass., 1976. Inventory control clk. Thermet, Inc., Gloucester, Mass., 1976-77; sec., office mgr. Clouston Foods USA, Inc., Gloucester, 1977-81; asst. export adminstr. Hatch & Kirk, Inc., Seattle, 1981-82; sec. The BDM Corp., North Ft. Lewis, Wash., 1982-84; regional office adminstr. The BDM Corp., Tacoma, 1984-86, secretarial trainer, 1985-86; chief buyer BDM Mgmt. Services Corp., North Ft. Lewis, 1986—. Parish youth rep. St. Paul's Catholic Ch., Hamilton, Mass., 1976. Mem. Nat. Purchasing Assn. of Wash. Roman Catholic. Office: BDM Mgmt Services Corp 10116 36 Ave Ct SW Tacoma WA 98449

SALMON, PHYLLIS WARD, computer company executive; b. Dallas, Aug. 10, 1948; d. Clinton David and Reba (Gilbert) Ward; m. James Y. Barbo, Dec. 12, 1970 (div. Jan. 1975); m. William Wellington Salmon, Jan. 21, 1977. A. in Acctg., Richland Coll., 1977; B.S. in Edn., Stephen F. Austin U., 1971. Cert. tchr. secondary edn., Tex. Cost acct. Jackson-Shaw, Dallas, 1975-79, Dal-Mac Devel., Dallas, 1979-81; store mgr. Shepard & Vick, Dallas, 1983-84; mktg. coordinator Tex. Instruments, Dallas, 1984-85; pres. Computer Expertise, Richardson, Tex., 1985—; pres. TI's Only, 1986—, pres. TechnaServe, 1987— . Mem. Nat. Assn. Female Execs., Tex. Computer Dealers Assn. (organizing mem.), Dallas Needlework and Textile Guild. Republican. Episcopalian. Club: St. Clare's Guild (bd. dirs. 1980-81)(Dallas). Avocations: needlepoint; photography; travel. Office: Computer Expertise Inc 811 Alpha Dr Suite 359 Richardson TX 75081

SALMONS, JOANNA, nursing administrator; b. Smiths Grove, Ky., Nov. 7, 1933; d. Walter Scott and Birdie Wilma (Jackson) Parker; m. William L. Salmons, June 6, 1970; children by previous marriage—Robert B. Morrow, Scott Alan Morrow. R.N., Fla. Hosp. Sch. Nursing, 1954; student So. Missionary Coll., 1979; cert. in health systems mgmt. Harvard U., 1980, Yale U., 1985; B.S.N. SUNY, 1982; postgrad. Trinity Coll. Dir. nursing Larkin Gen. Hosp., Miami, Fla.; adminstr., Fort Walton Beach (Fla.) Hosp., 1974-75; dir. surg. nursing Fla. Hosp., Orlando, 1976-78; v.p. profl. standards Adventist Health Systems/Sunbelt Corp., Orlando, 1978-79, bd. dirs. 1986-87; sr. v.p. Fla Hosp. Med. Ctr., Orlando, 1979—; dir. Health Care Mgmt. Corp.; cons. in field. Mem. A Thousand Plus com. Am. Cancer Soc. Recipient Outstanding Achievement award, Larkin Gen. Hosp., Miami, 1969. Mem. Fla. Nurses Assn. (bd. dirs. 1980-81, 83-84, Nurse of Yr. award dist. 8 1988), Am. Heart Assn., Retarded Children's Assn. Orange County, Fla. Hosp. Assn., Am. Nurses Assn. (cert. nurse adminstr.), Fla. Orgn. Nursing Execs., Am. Orgn. Nursing Execs., Assn. Seventh-Day Adventist Nursing Execs. (bd. dirs.), Adventist Health Care Execs. (bd. dirs. 1986-87), Am. Health Care Execs. Assn. Club: Buena Ventura Lakes Golf and Tennis. Lodge: Rotary. Home: 1212 Waverly Way Longwood FL 32750 Office: 601 Rollins St Orlando FL 32803

SALSMAN, CONNIE JACKSON, controller; b. Ft. Worth, Apr. 5, 1957; d. O.W. and Dorothy S. (Yates) Jackson; m. Richard D. Salsman, June 15, 1975; children: Robin Wayne, Rodger Dale. BBA, North Tex. State U., 1978. Chief acct. Lewisville (Tex.) Meml. Hosp., 1980-82, asst. controller, 1982-85, controller, 1985—. Mem. Nat. Assn. Female Execs., Bus. and Profl. Womens Assn. (treas. 1987—), Healthcare Fin. Mgmt. ASsn. Office: Lewisville Meml Hosp Inc 500 W Main Lewisville TX 75067

SALSTROM, SARA-JANE, medical technologist; b. Youngstown, Ohio, May 19, 1946; d. Martin and Edna Hazel (Theis) Mueller; B.S., Kent State U., 1971; 1 dau., Valerie Jean. Intern in med. tech. Akron (Ohio) City Hosp., 1970-71, staff med. technologist, 1971-74, research med. technologist specializing in infectious disease research, 1974—. Mem. Am. Soc. Clin. Pathologists (cert. med. technologist), Am. Soc. Microbiology, Nat. Rifle Assn. Republican. Lutheran. Club: Zeppelin Rifle. Contbr. articles to profl. jours. Office: Akron City Hosp 75 Arch St Suite 204 Akron OH 44304

SALTER, MAZY WOMPOLE, retired landscape architect, community planner; b. Los Angeles, May 12, 1925; d. Alton Branch and Anna (Buchholz) Wompole; m. Ludwig Les Salter (div. Mar. 1983); children: Frank, Suzan, Ronald. BS in Landscape Architecture, U. Mich., 1948; MBA in Human Relations, Webster Coll., Keflavik, Iceland, 1981. Registered architect, Ark., community planner, Mich. Sr. planner Contra Costa County Plan Dept., Martinez, Calif., 1949-57; plan dir. Placer County Plan Dept., Auburn, Calif., 1957-60; pvt. practice plan cons. Auburn, 1960-65; community planner, landscape architect USN, San Bruno, Calif., 1965-80, 82-86, Keflavik, 1980-82; ret. 10 Acre Farm Devel., Forest Hill, Calif., 1987—; cons., designer City of Vacaville, Calif., 1953, City of Lincoln, Calif., 1961, City of Byron, Calif., 1963, USN and USMCR Tng. Ctrs. Active Rah for Supr. Placer County, Auburn, 1962; active EEO com. Recipient Outstanding Performance Rating award USN, 1966, Beneficial Suggestion awards, 1967, 68. Mem. Am. Inst. Planners, Internat. Fedn. Housing and Planning, Internat. Soc. City and Regional Planners, Sierra Club, U. Mich. Alumni, U. Calif. Alumni, Webster Coll. Alumni. Democrat. Mem. Christian Sci. Ch. Home: 1408 Castillo Ave Burlingame CA 94010

SALTIEL, NATALIE, accountant; b. Chicago, Mar. 19, 1927; d. Henry Carl and Dorothy (Maremont) S.; m. Sidney D. Levin, Oct. 13, 1963; 1 child, Erica Saltiel Levin. BBA with highest distinction, Northwestern U., 1948. CPA, Ill. Staff acct. firm, Chgo., 1948-52; practice acctg., Chgo., 1952—. Bd. dirs., mem. exec. com., com. chmn. United Way Chgo., 1979-85, United Way/Crusade of Mercy, 1980-88; mem. adv. council, chmn. com. Sta. WBEZ Chicagoland Pub. Radio, 1981—. Mem. Am. Inst. CPAs, Ill. CPA Soc., Chgo. Women's Soc. CPAs, Chgo. Fin. Exchange (bd. dirs. 1987—), Beta Gamma Sigma. Office: 105 W Madison St Chicago IL 60602

SALTZMAN, IRENE CAMERON, perfume manufacturer, art gallery owner; b. Cocoa, Fla., Mar. 23, 1927; d. Argyle Bruce and Marie T. (Neel) Cameron; m. Herman Saltzman, Mar. 23, 1946 (dec. May 1986); children: Martin Howard (dec.), Arlene Norma Hanly. Owner Irene Perfume and Cosmetics Lab., Jacksonville, Fla., 1972—, Irene Gallery of Art, Jacksonville, 1973—. Mem. Cummer Gallery of Art, Jacksonville, 1972—; mem. Jacksonville Gallery of Art, 1972—; mem. The Nat. Mus. of Women in the Arts, Washington, 1972—. Mem. Internat. Soc. Fine Arts Appraisers, Nat. Assn. for the Self Employed, Nat. Assn. Female Execs. Democrat. Episcopalian. Club: Ponte Vedra. Home: 2701 Ocean Dr S Jacksonville Beach FL 32250

SALTZMAN, LINDA RENÉE, insurance executive; b. Phila., Dec. 2, 1951; d. Erwin and Mollie (Finkel) S. BBA in Mktg., Temple U., 1973. Pension sales mgr. Phoenix Mutual Life Ins. Agy., Phila., 1973-77; v.p. pension sales Retirement Plans of Am., Phila., 1977-79; assoc. dir. pension sales Ins. Co. of N. Am., Phila., 1979-81; investment mgr. Butcher & Singer, Inc., Phila., 1981; pension sales specialist Provident Mutual Life Ins. Co., Phila., 1981-82; regional pension mgr. CIGNA Corp., Phila., 1982—; nat. leader, regional pension mgr. Life Ins. Co. N.Am. div. CIGNA Co., 1988—. Mem. Nat. Assn. Female Execs., Phila. Assn. Life Underwriters. Democrat. Jewish. Office: CIGNA 1811 Chestnut St 5th Floor Philadelphia PA 19103

SALVANELLI, GLORIA CAROLE, public relations executive; b. Elizabeth, N.J.; d. Renato Hugh and Ethel Dell (Schmelzer) S.; m. Walter Fritsche, June 14, 1975 (div. 1982). BA in Speech Communications and Mktg., Boston Coll., 1983. Coordinator communications Dow Chem. Europe, Zurich, Switzerland, 1976-79; adminstr. fin. Harvard U. Med. Sch., Boston, 1979-84; corp. mgr. pub. relations Ares-Serono, Inc., Boston, 1984-88; cons. pub. relations Barton & Assocs., Inc., Arlington, Mass., 1986—; owner, pres., cons. Salvanelli & Assocs., Beverly, Mass., 1988—; dir. pub. relations Mass. chpt. U.S. Olympic Com., Boston, 1982-84; instr. North Shore Community Coll., Beverly, Mass., 1983; asst. dir. pub. relation Middlesex County Spl. Olympics, Arlington, 1986. Asst. editor: Jour. of Gerontology, 1978. Mem. Pub. Relations Soc. Am., Swiss Soc. Boston, Nat. Assn. Female Execs. Office: 3A Columbus Ave Beverly MA 01915

SALVERSON, CAROL ANN, library administrator, clergywoman; b. Buffalo, June 30, 1944; d. Howard F. and Estella G. (Zelie) Heavener; B.A. in Philosophy, SUNY, Buffalo, 1966; M.S. in Library Sci., Syracuse U., 1968; grad. Sacred Coll. Jamilian Theology and Div. Sch., 1976. Library trainee and research asst. SUNY, Med. Center, Syracuse, 1966-67; asst. editor SUNY Union List of Serials, Syracuse, 1967-68; readers services librarian, asst. prof. Jefferson Community Coll., Watertown, N.Y., 1968-75; ordained to ministry Internat. Community of Christ Ch., 1974; adminstr. public services dept. Internat. Community of Christ, Chancellery, Reno, 1975-84, dir. Jamilian Theol. Research Library, 1975—; mem. faculty Sacred Coll. Jamilian U. of the Ordained, Reno, 1979—, Jamilian Parochial Sch., Internat. Community of Christ, 1978—. Chmn. religious edn. com. All Souls Unitarian-Universalist Ch., Watertown, N.Y., 1970-71, treas., 1974-75; trustee North Country Reference and Research Resources Council, Canton, N.Y., 1974-75; dir. Gene Savoy Heritage Museum and Library, 1984—; violist Symphonietta, Reno, 1983—. Mem. ALA, Nev. Library Assn., Friends of Library Washoe County, Friends of Library U. Nev. Club: Coll. Women's. Contbr. articles on library sci. to profl. jours. Home: 2025 La Fond Dr Reno NV 89509 Office: Internat Community of Christ Chancellory 643 Ralston St Reno NV 89503

SALVESEN, SYLVIA ROSE, educational associate; b. London, Feb. 27, 1932; came to U.S., 1957; d. Arthur Bardsley and Rose Mary (Aley) Withers, m. William Roy Salvesen, Oct. 9, 1955; children: Karen Elizabeth, Steven Paul, Peter. AB, Kingborough Community Coll., 1983; BS, Staten Island Coll., 1989. Ednl. assoc. Bd. Edn., Bklyn., 1984—. Roman Catholic. Home: 577-77 St Brooklyn NY 11209

SALVETTI, SUSAN, lawyer; b. N.Y.C., Feb. 22, 1955; d. Sergio and Emma (Fucini) S.; m. Peter James Palenzona, Apr. 5, 1981; 1 dau., Marisa Danielle. B.A. summa cum laude, Fordham U., 1976, J.D., 1979. Bar: N.Y. 1980. Student asst. U.S. Attys. Office, N.Y.C., 1978, Manhattan Dist. Attys. Office, N.Y.C., 1979; assoc. Newman, Tannenbaum, Helpern & Hirschtritt, N.Y.C., 1980-82, Martin, Clearwater & Bell, N.Y.C., 1982-85, Zwerling, Schachter & Zwerling, N.Y.C., 1985—. Generoso Pope scholar, 1975. Mem. N.Y. State Bar Assn., Parents League N.Y., Phi Beta Kappa.

SALYARDS, DENISE ANN, bank official; b. Providence, Feb. 10, 1954; d. William Bradford and Dorothy Mary (Thibodeau) Smith; student Providence Coll., 1975-79; m. Michael Jeffrey Salyards, Dec. 29, 1979; children—Michael Jeffrey, II, Kristina Alaine. Clk.-typist money market dept. Indsl. Nat. Bank, Providence, 1972, bookkeeper, 1972-75, asst. fin. analyst, 1975-76, market research asst., 1976-78, market research analyst, 1978-79; dir. market research Hamilton Bank, Lancaster, Pa., 1979-82; mgr. market research 1st Nat. Exchange Bank, Roanoke, Va., 1982; asst. v.p., dir. market research Dominion Bankshares Corp., 1982-83; asst. v.p., retail mktg. systems mgr. Barnett Banks Fla., Inc., Jacksonville, 1983-85; v.p., dir. mktg. Barnett Bank of South Fla. N.A., Miami, 1985-87; sr. v.p. mktg., Sun Bank of South Fla. N.A., 1987—; cons. Strategic Planning Task Force, 1981, Hamilton Bank, 1982—. Bd. dirs. ARC, Broward County chpt., 1986—, Jr. Achievement, 1987—; mem. adv. bd. Ptnrs. in Excellence, 1987—. Mem. Am. Mktg. Assn. (chpt. pres. 1981-82, bd. dirs. South Fla. chpt. 1985-86), Bank Mktg. Assn., Nat. Assn. Bank Women, Nat. Assn. Female Execs., Nat. Assn. Women Bus. Owners (corp. sponsor rep. 1987—). Roman Catholic. Home: 2890 SW 139th Way Davie FL 33330

SALZMAN, MARIAN LYNN, business journalist, public relations executive, writer, lecturer; b. N.Y.C., Feb. 15, 1959; d. Norman E. and Ruby V. (Freeman) S. B.A., Brown U., 1980. Editor Mgmt. Review, Am. Mgmt. Assns., N.Y.C., 1984-85; editorial dir. and co-founder Career Insights Inc., Providence, 1980-83; dir. media relations, Kehoe, White, Savage & Co., N.Y.C., 1986—; lectr. coll. campuses and corps. Author: Inside Management Training, 1985; MBA Jobs, 1986, Wanted: :obera; Arts Graduates, 1987; contbr. articles on career and mgmt. topics to profl. jours. and consumer mags. Trustee Brown Univ. Club N.Y., 1984—. Dorot Found. fellow 1980. Office: Kehoe White Savage & Co 685 Fifth Ave New York NY 10028

SAMBOLD, MARGIE LOU, banker; b. McKees Rocks, Pa., Nov. 22, 1935; d. Fred and Anna Louise (Gernandt) Enghardt; student Am. Inst. Banking; m. Albert James Sambold, May 1, 1956; children—Albert James, Sylvia Ann, Angela Janine. Bookkeeper, proof operator Commonwealth Trust, McKees Rocks, Pa., 1952-56; teller First Nat. Bank Topeka, 1956-59, Bank of Bellevue (Nebr.), 1962-66; teller, credit analyst, loan officer, br. mgr., asst. cashier Bank Meridian (formerly Hampton Nat. Bank), 1971—, also fin. services officer, br. adminstr., now asst. v.p. Active Boy Scouts Am., Friends of Library; Hampton Housing Authority, 1977-78. Mem. Am. Inst. Banking (pres. eastern N.H. chpt., treas. eastern dist.), Nat. Assn. Bank Women, Bus. and Profl. Women's Club, (past pres., chmn. state fin. com.), N.H. Bus. and Profl. Women's Club (state 1st v.p., 2d v.p., past state treas.). Republican. Clubs: Catholic Women's, Officers Wives, Band Boosters. Home: 35 Milbern Ave Hampton NH 03842 Office: 100 Winnacunnet Rd Hampton NH 03842

SAMEK, ARLENE ELLEN, clothing company executive; b. N.Y.C., Sept. 10, 1940; d. Herman P. and Eve (Cohen) DuBoff; m. Abe Rosman, Nov. 12, 1961 (div. 1974); children: René, Mark; m. Paul H. Samek, Dec. 22, 1979; 1 stepchild, Benjamin. Student, Los Angeles City Coll., 1960. Asst. controller Sig Isaccs, Inc., Los Angeles, 1973-76; controller Jonathan Martin, Inc., Los Angeles, 1976-77; v.p. fin. Barbara Barbara, Inc., Los Angeles, 1977-87; v.p. fin., gen. ops. mgr. L'Koral, Inc., Los Angeles, 1987—; v.p. fin. & operation Nina Piccalino, Inc., Los Angeles, 1988—; cons. Bd. Edn., Los Angeles, 1968-69. v.p. PTA Carthay Ctr. Sch., Los Angeles, 1968-70, mem. adv. council, 1969-71; pres. council B'nai Brith, Los Angeles, 1957-58; mem. fellowship bd. Temple Emanuel, Beverly Hills, Calif., 1971—. Recipient Star of Deborah, B'nai Brith, 1959, award of merit Carathy Ctr. Sch., 1971-72. Mem. Coalition Apparel Industry Calif. (bd. dirs. 1986—), Profl. City of Hope (award of merit 1985), Calif. Air Shippers Asssn. (chmn. bd. dirs. 1980-82), LWV (group leader 1962-82), Step-Parents Assn. Los Angeles, Foster Parents of Los Angeles. Jewish. Home: 4461 Van Noord Ave Studio City CA 91604

SAMET, RHONDA CLAIRE, social worker; b. Cambridge, Mass., Jan. 24, 1958; d. Charles Merle and Rochelle Renee (Rosenberg) S. BA, Boston U., 1980; MSW, NYU, 1982. Staff social worker Dr. Charles Samet, Manhassett, N.Y., 1982-84, Kings Harbor Care Ctr., Bronx, 1984—. Mem. Acad. Cert. Social Workers, Nat. Assn. Social Workers. Democrat. Jewish. Home: 22 Olive St Great Neck NY 11020 Office: Kings Harbor Care Ctr 2000 E Gunhill Rd Bronx NY 10469

SAMIIAN, BARAZANDEH, corporate executive; b. Tehran, May 13, 1939; came to U.S., 1958. B.A., Woodbury U., Los Angeles, 1961; B.A., Immaculate Heart Coll., Los Angeles, 1979; M.A., Webster U., Geneva, 1981. 1 child, Mina P. Cullimore. Cons., Design & Architecture, Tehran, 1965-72; bus. cons. multinat. corps., Calif., 1970-77; co-owner Samiian and Solomon Assocs., Geneva, 1978-86; owner, B. Samiian Assocs., Jacksonville, Fla., 1987—; dir., Internat. Cons. Found. Bd., 1987—; adj. prof. Webster U., Geneva, 1981—; cons. and lectr. human resources devel.; bd. dirs. Internat. Cons. Found., 1987. Named Woman of Yr., 1983; recipient Gov's. citation State of Md., 1983. Office: B Samiian Assocs PO Box 23825 Jacksonville FL 32241-3825

SAMIOS-ANDRUNAS, CORINNE, fabric and wallpaper design director; b. N.Y.C.; d. John Pythagoras and Ruth Charlotte S.; Student Traphagen Sch. Fashion, N.Y.C., 1955-57; student interior design Art Students League, 1955-60. Colorist Old Deerfield Fabrics, 1957-63, Everfast, 1963-66, Cohama, 1966-69; stylist Cyrust Clark, 1969-74; stylist Brunschwig & Fils, N.Y.C., 1974—, now design dir.; condr. seminars Phila. Coll. Sci. and Textiles; speaker Am. Assn. Textile Colorists and Chemists. Developed fabric/wallpaper collections based on hist. documents of Brighton Pavillion, Eng., 1980, Old Westbury Gardens, N.Y.C., 1981; Cooper-Hewitt Mus., 1982; Musée des Arts Decoratifs, Paris, 1983; work covered in various publs.; develops musical portraits of people. Active West Side Block Assn., N.Y.C.; tchr. art to handicapped Bird S. Coler Hosp., N.Y.C., 1960-63. Mem. Am. Soc. Interior Designers, Nat. Home Fashions League. Office: Brunschwig & Fils 979 3d Ave New York NY 10022

SAMMARTINO, SYLVIA, university co-founder; b. Boston, Dec. 5, 1903; d. Louis J. and Anna E. (Bianchi) Scaramelli; m. Peter Sammartino, Dec. 5, 1933. A.B., Smith Coll., 1925; M.A., Columbia U., 1926; LL.D. (hon.), Kyung Hee U., Korea, 1964; D.H.L. (hon.), Fairleigh Dickinson U., 1966. Tchr. public high sch. N.Y.C., 1927-28, 33-35; treas. Scaramelli & Co., Inc., N.Y.C., 1928-33; ednl. editor Atlantica, 1933-35; circulation mgr. La Voix de France, N.Y.C., 1935-37; registrar Fairleigh Dickinson U., Rutherford, N.J., 1942-50; dir. admissions Fairleigh Dickinson U., 1950-59, dean of admissions, 1959-67. Chmn. N.J. Commn. on Women, 1971; mem. bd. govs. N.Y. Cultural Center, 1968-73; mem. exec. com. Restore Ellis Island Commn., 1974-79; pres. Garden State Ballet Found., 1975-80; trustee Newark Symphony Hall, 1976-79, William Carlos Williams Center for Performing Arts, Rutherford, N.J., 1980—; trustee, chmn. Integrity, Inc., 1980—; trustee, sec.-treas. Williams Inst., 1981—. Decorated knight Order of Merit Italy; comdr. Order Star of Africa Liberia; officer Order Nat. Ivory Coast; recipient Amita award, 1960; Smith Coll. medal, 1967; President's medal Mercy Coll., 1980; named Woman of Yr., Rutherford C. of C. Home and Office: 140 Ridge Rd Rutherford NJ 07070

SAMMET, JEAN E., computer scientist; b. N.Y.C.; d. Harry and Ruth S. B.A., Mount Holyoke Coll., Sc.D. (hon.), 1978; M.A., U. Ill. Group leader programming Sperry Gyroscope, Great Neck, N.Y., 1955-58; sect. head, staff cons. programming Sylvania Electric Products, Needham, Mass., 1958-61; with IBM, 1961—, Boston adv. program mgr., 1961-65, program lang. tech. mgr., 1965-68; programming tech. planning mgr. Fed. Systems div., 1968-74, programming lang. tech. mgr., 1974-79, software tech. mgr., 1979-81, div. software tech. mgr., 1981-82, programming lang. tech. mgr., 1983—; chmn. history of computing com. Am. Fedn. Info. Processing Socs., 1977-79. Author: Programming Languages: History and Fundamentals, 1969; editor-in-chief: Assn. Computing Machinery Computing Revs, 1979-87; contbr. articles to profl. jours. Mem. Assn. Computing Machinery (pres. 1974-76, Disting. Service award 1985), Math. Assn. Am., Nat. Acad. Engring., Upsilon Pi Epsilon. Office: IBM Systems Integration Div 6600 Rockledge Dr Bethesda MD 20817

SAMMS-MOULTRY, EVA DOLORES, educator; b. Quitman, Ga., Mar. 25, 1937; d. Benjamin Franklin and Ruby Lee (Mitchell) Watts; m. Royce Moultry; children—Rory C. Thomas, Enrique S. Samms. B.A., Shaw U., Raleigh, N.C., 1976; M.S., Nova U., Ft. Lauderdale, 1978, Ed.S., 1982, postgrad., 1982—. Cert. vocat. and adult edn. tchr. Fla. Legal sec. Legal Services of Greater Miami, Fla., 1967-70, Storer Broadcasting Co., Balharbour, Fla., 1970-72; sec., bookkeeper Dade County Pub. Schs., Miami, 1973-76, bus. tchr., 1976-84, vocat. and adult edn. tchr., 1984—; curriculum writer Dade County Schs., 1982—, software evaluator, 1986; pres., cons. Triangle Mgmt., Miami, 1985—. Author: (curriculum) Professional Secretary, 1978. Precinct capt. Democratic Party, Miami, 1977-83, com. woman, 1984—; dep. registrar Voter Registration, Miami, 1980—; pres. Minority Women, Miami, 1982, 84. Recipient Outstanding Service Plaque, Miami Lakes Jr. High Sch., 1981, Service award United Tchrs. of Dade County, 1984, 85; Letter of Commendation, Area Supt., North Miami, 1984. Mem. Vocat. Bus. Edn. Assn., Assn. Supervision and Curriculum Devel., Booker T. Washington Alumni (Miami, pres. 1984-85), Phi Delta Kappa, Beta Tau Zeta. Democrat. Am. Baptist. Club: Scruples (Miami). Avocations: gardening; sports; dancing; people. Office: Lindsey Hopkins Vocat and Tech Ctr 750 NW 20 St Miami FL 33127

SAMOKAR, JUDITH ELAINE, savings and loan association executive; b. Norwich, Conn., Oct. 30, 1950; d. John Edward and Mary Irene (Romanowski) S.; m. Anthony S. Corpuz, Oct. 19, 1969 (div. July 1976). AS, Mohegan Community Coll., Norwich, 1978; BS summa cum laude, U. New Haven, 1982. Acctg. clk. New London (Conn.) Fed. Savs. and Loan Assn., 1970-77, asst. treas., 1977-82, treas., 1982-84, sr. v.p., treas., 1984—. Mem. Fin. Mgrs. Soc., Nat. Assn. Female Execs., Southeastern Conn. Women's Network. Office: New London Fed Savs and Loan Assn 15 Masonic St New London CT 06320

SAMPEDRO, HORTENSIA E., banker; b. Havana, Cuba, Sept. 29, 1950; came to U.S., 1960; d. Luciano Manuel and Eulalia (Carreno) S.; m. Robert Hilton Hacker, Jan. 4, 1975; 1 child, Christina Isabel Elizarda. BBA in

Econs., U. Miami, 1973; MBA in Fin., NYU, 1984. Lending officer Chase Manhattan Bank, Venezuela, 1973-75, P.R., 1975-77; 2d v.p., workout officer Chase Manhattan Bank, N.Y.C., 1977-78; v.p., credit officer Chase Manhattan Bank, Miami, 1978-80; v.p. country risk Chase Manhattan Bank, N.Y.C., 1980-84; chief ops. officer Chase Bank Internat., 1984-87, pres. cooperative bd., 1987—; treas. Cintas Found., N.Y.C., 1983—. Mem. Nat. Assn. Female Execs., Nat. Orgn. of Women. Democrat. Roman Catholic. Club: Havana Yacht. Home: 122 E 82d St #2-B New York NY 10028 Office: Chase Manhattan Bank 101 Park Ave New York NY 10081

SAMPLE, CONSTANCE JEANNE, mortgage company executive and land use planner; b. Balt., June 11, 1950; d. Wayne E. and Albert (Maenner) Colburn; m. Richard Eaton Sample, Dec. 6, 1969;children: Barbara Dianne, Bonnie Kathleen. BS, Fla. State U., 1975. Lic. mortgage broker, realtor, Fla. Quality controller Milton Roy Co., St. Petersburg, Fla., 1976-77; social worker Fla. Dept. Health and Rehab., Tampa, 1978-80; ops. mgr. First Southeastern Co., Tampa, 1981-85; adminstr., real estate broker Cape Sands, Inc., St. Petersburg, 1984—; v.p., real estate broker, adminstr. Profl. Devel. Enterprises, St. Petersburg, 1985—; ops. mgr. Cert. Capital Corp., St. Petersburg, 1986-87, Cert. Investments Corp., St. Petersburg, 1987; mortgage loan officer Gt. Western Bank, Tampa, 1987—; v.p. Cert. Mortgage Corp., 1985—. Tchr. mem. fellowship com. and circle club Village Presbyn. Ch., Tampa, 1988; mem. Berkely Prep. Parents Club, Tampa, 1977—, Countryside Parents Club, 1987-88: vol. worker sport competitions. Mem. Leads Club, Inc. (bd. dirs., 1988—), Fla. State U. Alumni Assn. (life). Home: 15813 Sapwood St Tampa FL 33624 Office: Gt Western Bank 14502 N Dale Mabry Suite 101 Tampa FL 33618

SAMPLE, DOROTHY EATON, state representative; m. Richard L. Sample; 3 children. B.A. in Econs., Duke U., J.D. Bar: N.C.; cert. tchr., real estate salesperson, Fla. Sec. to law firms, law clk.; asst. atty. HOLC; sec., dept. mgr. automobile fin. co.; now mem. Fla. Ho. of Reps. Mem. Fla. State Children's Commn.; mem. adv. council on conservation and environ. Fla. Dept. Natural Resources; mem. state adv. com. on coastal zone mgmt. Dept. Environ. Regulations; Founder Alliance for Conservation of Natural Resources; pres. Save Our Bays; pres. PTA, Pasadena Property Owners Assn., Band Boosters (3 schs.); mem. adminstrv. bd. dirs. Pasadena Community Ch.; legis. chmn. LWV; leader Girl Scouts U.S.A.; sponsor Jr. Coll. Service Club; bd. dirs. Gulf Coast and Fla. State Tb Assn.; bd. dirs. CONA (Council of Neighborhood Assn.); v.p. West St. Petersburg Property Owners Assn.; bd. dirs. Community Welfare Council; bd. dirs. March of Dimes, Mothers' March of Dimes VIP chmn., publicity chmn.; legal asst. Soc. for Prevention Cruelty to Animals; bd. dirs. St. Petersburg Hist. Soc.; area chmn. Sci. Ctr., Easter Seal Guild, Toy Shop, Friends of Library, Multiple Sclerosis, United Fund drives; mem., officer Republican Clubs; bd. dirs. Suncoast Active Vols. for Ecology; mem. Citizens Council on Crime, St. Petersburg Bicentenial Com.; mem. adv. bd. dirs. Pinellas Parkway; mem. Blue Ribbon Charter Com.; chmn. Coast Coordinating Council; mem. Pinellas County Edn. Study Commn; trustee Gulf Coast chpt. Nat. Multiple Sclerosis Soc.; assoc. bd. dirs. Mental Health Assn. in Pinellas County; bd. dirs. Nat. Handicapped Freedom Found., Inc., mem. Cons. Council of FACE Learning Ctr., Inc. Recipient Good Govt. award Conservative Union, 1981, Tampa Women for Responsible Legis. Freedom award, 1982, Outstanding Pub. Ofcl. award St. Petersburg Beach Homeowners Assn., 1982, service award March of Dimes, 1984, also others. Mem. Fla. Wildlife Fedn. (v.p., regional dir.; spl. service award 1977), AAUW (legis. chmn.), Pan Hellenic Assn., Duke U. Alumni Assn. (chmn.), Pinellas C. of C. (govt. action com.), Chi Phi, Delta Phi Rho Alpha. Clubs: St. Petersburg Yacht; Sinawik (pres.).

SAMPLE, JUDITH NEUER, utility company official; b. Rochester, N.Y., Dec. 4, 1943; d. Edward George and Elizabeth Grace (Specht) N.; m. Joseph Paul Sample, July 8, 1987. B.S. in Biology, Alfred U., 1965. Research assoc. U. Rochester Med. Sch., 1965-68; computer systems analyst Rochester Inst. Tech., 1968-70, now lectr.; systems cons. Sybron Corp., 1970-72, mgr. order processing, 1973-75, distbn. and customer service mgr., 1975-76, mgr. stores and receiving Xerox Corp., Webster, N.Y., 1976-77, mgr. systems and ops. planning, 1977-79, mgr. mfg. ops., 1980-85; quality specialist Fla. Power and Light, Miami, 1985—. Program cons. women in bus. and career devel. Rochester YMCA; founding mem. steering com., bd. dirs. Women's Career Center of Rochester; bd. mgrs. Lost Mountain Manor Condominium Complex. Mem. Am. Prodn. and Inventory Control Soc., AAUW. Republican. Presbyterian. Home: 3002 Cove Rd Tequesta FL 33469 Office: Fla Power & Light PO Box 14000 Juno Beach FL 33408

SAMPLE, KAREN ANN, secondary educator, administrator; b. Poteau, Okla., July 12, 1949; d. Paul Leroy and Ruby Nell (Nummy) Coggins; m. Alan Lee Sample, Dec. 7, 1970; children: John, Jeffrey. BS, U. Okla., 1975, postgrad., 1987-88; MEd, East Cen. U., 1978. Cert. secondary tchr., Okla. Instr. sci. Ada (Okla.) Sr. High Sch., 1977-81, instr. sci., chmn. sci. dept., 1981—; spl. cons., ind. study cons. U. Okla., Norman, 1983—. Mem. NEA, Nat. Sci. Tchrs. Assn., Okla. Edn. Assn., Okla. Sci. Tchrs. Assn., Noble Assn. Classroom Tchrs. (v.p. 1982-83), Beta Sigma Phi (pres. Ada chpt. 1978-79, sec. Norman chpt. 1981-82). Home: 212 Forest Hills Noble OK 73068 Office: Noble Sr High Sch 48th Ave SE & Etowah Rd Noble OK 73068

SAMPLE, WENDY ELIZABETH, school system administrator; b. Boston, Jan. 17, 1956; d. Wilbur Harry and Joanne Grace (Demaray) S. Student, U. Maine, 1974; BS in Recreation and Park Mgmt., U. Oreg, 1980. Profl. jazz dancer Bob Heath Co., Portland, Oreg., 1975-77; unit leader, counselor YMCA Camp, Otis, Oreg., 1976-77; mgr. VIP's Restaurant Lounge, Portland, 1977-78; dir. new student host program U. Oreg., Eugene, 1979; with front desk ops. Eugene Family YMCA, 1979-80; community sch. coordinator Oregon City (Oreg.) Sch. Dist., 1980-83, Portland Park Bur., 1983—; dir., lectr. fitness workshops, Portland; publicist Bodyworks, Portland, 1986—. State rep. Hershey (Pa.) Nat. Track and Field Program, 1980-82; co-chair Am. Heart Assn., Portland, 1985—; active big sister program S.E. Service Ctr., Portland, 1987—; mem. Portland YMCA (cert. phys. fitness leader). Recipient vol. research award N.W. Community Edn. Ctr., 1982, Outstanding Service award Atkinson Community Mems., Portland, 1986; named Vol. of Yr., Am. Heart Assn., 1986-87. Mem. Nat. Community Edn. Assn. (conv. liason 1984-85), Oreg. Community Edn. Assn. (bd. dirs. 1984-85, pres. 1985-87), Internat. Dance and Exercise Assn., Nat. Assn. Women. Democrat. Club: Trailsend. Office: Atkinson Community Sch 5800 SE Division Portland OR 97206

SAMPSON, ELLANIE SUE, librarian, editor; b. Ft. Monmouth, N.J., July 30, 1953; d. Arnold Ingvold and Edith Louise (Johnston) Sampson; m. Henry Clark Baisdon, Aug. 23, 1987. B.A. in Fine Arts, U. N.Mex., 1974; M.L.S., U. Okla., 1975. Slide librarian Sch. Art, Okla. U., Norman, 1975-78; adminstr. Northeast Mo. Library Service, Kahoka, 1978-79; librarian, dir. Truth or Consequences Pub. Library (N.Mex.), 1979—; cons. depts. history, English, architecture, Norman, 1975-78, Herron Sch. Art, Purdue U., Indpls., 1977. Mng. editor Dry Country News, 1983-85; compiler/calligrapher/editor: Salad Out with Jazzworks, 1983. Bd. dirs., bookkeeper Black Range Food Coop., Truth or Consequences, 1982—; mem. Ret. Sr. Vol. Program Adv. Council, Truth or Consequences, 1983—; founder Womanswork, 1983—; organizer Stephen King Day, Truth or Consequences, 1983. Mem. N. Mex. Library Assn. (treas.) , ALA, U. Okla. Sch. Library Sci. Alumni Assn., Am. Bus. Women's Assn. (rec. sec. chpt. 1977-78), Grand River Library Conf. (v.p. 1979), Wellness N.Mex. Assn. Club: Jazzworks. Home: 409 Grape St Truth or Consequences NM 87901 Office: Truth or Consequences Pub Library 501 McAdoo St PO Box 311 Truth or Consequences NM 87901

SAMPSON, JUNE ELISABETH, historical museum administrator; b. Phila., May 31, 1946; d. William Herbert and Helen Elizabeth (Whitall) Stafford; B.A. in History, Earlham Coll., Richmond, Ind., 1968; M.A. in History Mus. Tng., SUNY, Oneonta, 1972; m. Earl Sampson, Jan. 22, 1972; stepchildren—Earl Brett, Daniel C., Shawn, Indira. Mus. curator S.D. State Hist. Soc., Pierre, 1969-72; asst. dir. W.H. Over Mus., U. S.D., Vermillion, 1972-73, dir., 1973-79; dir. Western Heritage Center, Billings, Mont., 1980-83; grant writer Powell County Mus. and Arts Found., Deer Lodge, Mont., 1983-84; dir. The Danish Immigrant Mus., Elk Horn, Iowa, 1984—; instr. dept. anthropology U. S.D., 1973-79. Mem. Landmarks, Inc., Billings, 1980-84. Mem. Am. Assn. Mus., Iowa Mus. Assn., Am. Assn. for State and Local History. Office: The Danish Immigrant Mus Box 178 Elk Horn IA 51531

SAMPSON, LE ANN MARIE, data communications executive; b. Leadville, Colo., May 23, 1955; d. John Jr. and Cora Helen (McKenna) S. Computer aide U.S. Civil Service, Ft. Huachuca, Ariz., 1976-80; security mgr. U.S. Civil Service, Ft. Carson, Colo., 1982-83; telecommunications test specialist Validity Corp., Clinton, Md., 1980-82, telecommunications ops. analyst, 1983; telecommunications specialist Electronic Data Systems, Springfield, Va., 1983-84; telecommunications supr. Electronic Data Systems, Detroit, 1984-86; tech. services mgr. Electronic Data Systems, Springfield, 1986—. Mgr. Ponytail Softball Team, Sierra Vista, Ariz., 1978-79; mem. Disabled Am. Vets., Denver, Mfg. Automation Protocol Task Force. Served with U.S. Army, 1973-76.

SAMPSON, PATSY HALLOCK, college president; b. Picher, Okla., July 9, 1932; d. Daniel Webster and Mary Gladys (Whitehead) Hallock; children: Catherine, Jacquelyn, Rebecca. B.A. with spl. distinction, U. Okla., 1961; Ph.D. in Psychology, Cornell U., 1966. Asst. prof. SUNY, Binghamton, 1965-66; NIMH postdoctoral fellow Cornell U., 1966-67; asst. prof. Wellesley (Mass.) Coll., 1967-70; prof., chmn. dept. psychology Calif. State Coll., Bakersfield, 1970-73; adminstr. Nat. Inst. Child Health and Human Devel., Bethesda, Md., 1973-75; psychologist Nat. Inst. Alcohol Abuse and Alcoholism, Washington, 1975-77; dean faculty, prof. psychology Pitzer Coll., Claremont, Calif., 1977-80; dean Coll. Liberal Arts, Drake U., Des Moines, 1980-83; pres. Stephens Coll., Columbia, Mo., 1983—. Bd. dirs. Commn. on Women in Higher Edn., 1984-87, Council for Advancement of Experiential Learning, 1986—; mem. Pres.'s Commn. of Nat. Collegiate Athletic Assn., 1984-86; trustee The Fielding Inst., 1986—; mem. nat. adv. bd. Outward Bound U.S.A., 1987—. Mem. Am. Council Edn. (bd. dirs. 1985-88), AAUP, Am. Conf. Acad. Deans (chmn. bd. 1982-83), Phi Beta Kappa, Sigma Xi. Office: Stephens Coll Office of the Pres Columbia MO 65215

SAMPSON-LANDERS, CAROLE, pharmaceutical company executive; b. Detroit, Aug. 10, 1946; d. Charles Harrie and Lucille (Harper) Sampson; m. Theodore Craig Landers Sr., Dec. 31, 1979; children: Theodore C. Jr., Terrence C. AB, Douglass Coll., 1969; M in Med. Sci., Rutgers U., 1972; MD, Temple U., 1976. Research asst. Ortho Diagnostics, Raritan, N.J., 1969-72; resident physician Howard U. Hosp., Washington, 1976-77; with Ortho Pharm. Corp., 1977—; dir. clin. research Ortho Pharm. Corp., Raritan, 1986—. Career counselor Douglass Alumnai Assn., 1982—, YMCA, 1980—. Recipient Tribute to Woman in Industry award YWCA, 1980. Mem. Drug Info. Assn., AAAS, Nat. Med. Assn., Am. Coll. Clin. Pharm., Nat. Council Negro Women, Ortho 1st Aid Squad (pres. 1979-80). Home: 193 B Stanton-Lebanon Rd Lebanon NJ 08833 Office: Ortho Pharm Corp Rt 202 Box 300 Raritan NJ 08869-0602

SAMS, DORIS LAVERNE, college counselor; b. Youngwood, Pa., Apr. 26; d. Benjamin F. and Lucinda (Myers) S.; B.A., Seton Hill Coll., 1950; M.Ed., U. Pitts., 1959. Lic. mental health counselor, Fla., nat. bd. cert. counselor Nat. Acad. Cert. Clin. Mental Health Counselors. Employment interviewer Conn. State Employment Service, Thompsonville, 1950-53; tchr. Hempfield Area Schs., Greensburg, Pa., 1953-58, sch. psychologist, 1958-66; prof., counselor Broward Community Coll., Ft. Lauderdale, Fla., 1966—; human potential seminar leader Rational Behavior Therapy Workshops. Mem. Gov.'s Com. on Handicapped. Frick scholar. Mem. Am. Mental Health Counselors Assn., Am. Psychol. Assn. (assoc.), Nat. Assn. Cert. Clin. Mental Health Counselors, Am. Assn. Counseling and Devel., Humane Soc., Pet Rescue. Republican. Home: 1400 SW 19th St Fort Lauderdale FL 33315 Office: Broward Community Coll Hollywood FL 33024

SAMS, MARY ANN PACELLA, educational administrator, corporate executive; b. Chgo., Sept. 14, 1933; d. Carmen Harold and Helen Frances (Straub) Pacella; A.B. cum laude, Mundelein Coll., 1958; M.Ed., U. Puget Sound, 1970; postgrad. U. San Francisco, 1977—; certificate San Francisco State U., 1973, Central Wash. State Coll., 1969, Am. Montessori Tchr. Tng. Inst., 1966, U. Kans., 1964, Chgo. Tchrs. Coll., 1960; m. Wendell M. Sams, Aug. 12, 1973; 1 son, Derek John. Spl. services tchr. Chgo. Pub. Schs., 1958-61; social and personal adjustment tchr. Vocat. Rehab. Div., Topeka, Kans., 1962-64; tchr. kindergarten, primary grades Chgo. Pub. Schs., 1964-66; master tchr., tchr.-trainer Park Ridge (Ill.) Montessori Sch., 1966-67, Spring Valley Montessori Sch., Federal Way, Wash., 1967-68; tchr. Annie Wright Sem., Tacoma, Wash., 1968-69; instr. U. Puget Sound, Tacoma, 1968-70; early childhood specialist Franklin Pierce Pub. Sch. Dist., Tacoma, 1969-70; project mgr. Project Learn, Behavioral Research Labs., Menlo Park, Calif., 1970-71; dir. Sullivan Presch. and Sullivan Sch. Redwood City, Calif., 1971, exec. dir. curriculum and personnel Sullivan Presch. and Sullivan Elem. Sch., Irving, Calif., 1971-73; coordinator reading and English as second lang. Dept. Def., Mil. Dependents Schs., Japan, 1973-74; program dir. Western Region, Mini-Skools Ltd., Irving, Calif., 1974-75; supr. personnel San Francisco Unified Sch. Dist., 1975-78, program mgr. Children's Centers Dept., 1978-79; dir. Children's Centers Dept., Oakland (Calif.) Unified Sch. Dist., 1979-80, adminstr. child devel. Piedmont Children's Center, 1981-86; prin., Piedmont Ave. Sch. and Child Devel. Ctr., 1986—; grad. instr. early childhood edn. U. San Francisco; cons. in field; lectr. in field. Recipient Cert. of Appreciation, San Francisco Unified Sch. Dist. Bd. Edn., 1978; Tribute, Oakland Unified Sch. Dist. Bd. Edn., 1980; Appreciation award Oakland Dept. Children's Centers, 1980. Mem. Calif. Child Devel. Adminstrs. Assn. (state exec. bd. 1979-81, Cert. of Excellence 1980, Keeper of Dream award 1981), United Adminstrs. of Oakland Schs., Nat. Assn. for Edn. of Young Children, Council for Exceptional Children, Am. Assn. Sch. Personnel Adminstrs., Am. Soc. for Personnel Adminstrs. Bay Area Sch. Personnel Assn., Am. Montessori Soc., Nat. Black Child Devel. Inst., Assn. Montessori Internationale, Assn. Calif. Sch. Adminstrs., Phi Delta Kappa. Roman Catholic. Contbr. articles in field to profl. jours. Office: 4314 Piedmont Ave Oakland CA 94611

SAMUEL, BARBARA JOAN, business administration educator; b. Scranton, Pa., Dec. 31, 1955; d. David Edward and Joan Elizabeth (Evans) S. B.S., Susquehanna U., 1977; M.B.A., U. Scranton, 1982; postgrad. Syracuse U., 1983—. Traffic mgr. Scranton Broadcasters, 1977-78; account exec. AT&T Info. Systems, Kingston, Pa., 1978-83; doctoral teaching asst. Syracuse U., N.Y., 1983-85; lectr. in mktg. U. Scranton, 1986-88, asst. prof., 1988—. Mem. Am. Mktg. Assn. Republican. Home: 1010 Woodland Way Clarks Summit PA 18411

SAMUELS, CYNTHIA KALISH, journalist, television news producer; b. Pitts., May 21, 1946; d. Emerson and Jeanne (Kalish) S.; m. Richard Norman Atkins, Sept. 12, 1971; children: Joshua Whitney Samuels Atkins, Daniel Jonathan Samuels Atkins. BA, Smith Coll., 1968. Press aide McCarthy for Pres. Campaign, Washington, 1968; assoc. producer Newsroom program Sta. KQED, San Francisco, 1972-73; with CBS News, 1973-80, researcher, Washington, 1969-71, documentary researcher, N.Y.C., 1973-74, asst. fgn. editor, 1974-76, asst. N.Y. bur. chief, 1976-80; writer, field producer Today program NBC News, N.Y.C., 1980-84, polit. producer Today program, 1984—, sr. producer Main Street program, 1987—. Author book revs. N.Y. Times Book Rev., Washington Post Book World. Recipient local Emmy award No. Calif. Acad. TV Arts & Scis., 1974, Columbia DuPont citation, 1975. Office: Today NBC News 30 Rockefeller Pl New York NY 10112

SAMUELS, JANET LEE, lawyer; b. Pitts., July 18, 1953; d. Emerson and Jeanne (Kalish) S.; m. David Arthur Kalow, June 18, 1978; children—Margaret Emily Samuels-Kalow, Jacob Richard Samuels-Kalow. B.A. with honors, Beloit Coll., 1974; J.D., NYU, 1977. Bar: N.Y. 1978, D.C. 1980. Staff atty. SCM Corp., N.Y.C., 1977-80, corp. atty., 1980-83, sr. corp. atty., 1983-85, assoc. gen. counsel Allied Paper div., 1983-86, Holtzmann, Wise & Shepard, 1986—. Adviser student adviser program NYU Law Sch., 1982—. Mem. ABA, Assn. Bar City N.Y., Assn. Trial Lawyers Am., N.Y. State Bar Assn., Mortar Board, Phi Beta Kappa. Office: Holtzmann Wise & Shepard 745 Fifth Ave New York NY 10151

SAMUELS, SHIRLEY CHASINS, psychotherapist; b. Bronx, N.Y., Dec. 6, 1930; d. Rubin and Clara (Traub) Chasins; B.S., Syracuse U., 1952, M.S., 1957; Ed.D., Columbia U., 1969; postgrad. Child Psychoanalysis, Center for Preventive Psychiatry, 1974; m. Stanley Samuels, Sept. 9, 1951; children—Jeffrey, Nita, Mark. Tchr., Syracuse (N.Y.) U. Nursery Sch., 1955-57, Maywood Nursery Sch., Hartsdale, N.Y., 1961-63; dir. Mt. Vernon (N.Y.) YM-YWHA Nursery Sch., 1963-65; dir. early childhood program Conservative Synagogue of Riverdale, Bronx, N.Y., 1966-68; adj. asst. prof. Hunter Coll., N.Y.C., 1968-74; asso. prof. edn. Manhattan Coll., Purchase, N.Y., 1969-80; child psychotherapist Center for Preventive Psychiatry, White Plains, N.Y., 1974-80, clin. supr. 1980—; adj. prof. Coll. New Rochelle (N.Y.), 1978—, Pace U., 1986—; pvt. practice psychotherapy, White Plains, 1977—; mem. adv. bd. Tuckahoe Counseling Ctr., N.Y., 1985-86; cons., lectr. in field. Bd. dirs. Union Day Care, Greenburgh, N.Y., 1981—, Westchester Assn. Young Children, White Plains, 1974—, Early Childhood Resource and Info. Center, N.Y.C. Libraries, 1981—; pres. Youth Bd. Westchester County, 1981—; chmn. Westchester County Internat. Youth, 1985; mem. adv. bd. therapeutic activity program Grasslands Hosp., Valhalla, N.Y., 1981—. Recipient award Youth Bd. Westchester County, 1981—, Proclamation Service award, 1981. Mem. Assn. Marriage and Family Therapy (corr. sec. 1983-85); mem. Assn. Child Psychoanalysis, Am. Psychol. Assn., Am. Orthopsychiat. Assn. Democrat. Jewish. Author: Enhancing Self-Concept in Early Childhood, 1977, Disturbed Exceptional Children: An Integrated Approach, 1981, 2d edit., 1986. Mem. editorial bd. Jour. Preventive Psychiatry, 1981—. Home: 10 Crest Dr White Plains NY 10607 Office: 19 Greenridge Ave White Plains NY 10601

SAMUELS, VALERIE BRYANT, nursing administrator; b. N.Y.C., Aug. 20, 1952; d. David and Lucy B. (Hairstone) Bryant; m. Emmanuel M. Samuels, July 1, 1971 (div. June 1986); children: Christopher D., Diantha L. Student, Sch. Performing Arts, 1970; AA, Eugenio Marie de Hostos Coll., 1972; BS, Herbert Lehmann Coll., 1974; postgrad., St. Joseph Coll., 1985. RN. RN Fordham Hosp., N.Y.C., 1972-76; charge RN Albert Einstein Coll. Medicine, N.Y.C., 1976-77, coordinator, 1977-80; coordinator Good Samaritan Hosp., N.Y.C., 1980-83; head nurse Booth Meml. Hosp., N.Y.C., 1983-86, nursing dir. renal services, 1986—, acting dir., 1987—; nurse cons. Harbor Nephrology, Fla., 1979-83, Good Samaritan Hosp., Bayshore, N.Y., 1983-85, South Shore Renal Hosp., Hempstead, N.Y., 1984-86; lectr. in field. Mem. NAACP, Nat. Assn. Patients on Hemodialysis and Transplantation (exec. bd.), Am. Assn. Nephrology Nurses, Texarkana Nat. Dialysis Assn. (exec. bd. patient and staffing issues), Nat. Assn. Female Execs. Republican. Lodge: Lions Internat. (Roosevelt, N.Y.), (sec. 1985-87, pres. 1987—, Lioness of yr. 1986, first female pres. 1987—). Home: 11 Longbeach Ave Roosevelt NY 11575 Office: Booth Meml Hosp 56-45 Main St Flushing NY 11355

SAMWORTH, ELEANOR ARMSTRONG, chemistry educator; b. Wilmington, Del., May 10, 1936; d. Ernest Greenfield and Helen Cranston (Smith) S. AB, Wilson Coll., 1958; MA, The John's Hopkins U., 1960, PhD, 1963. Postdoctoral fellow Harvard U., Cambridge, Mass., 1963-64; asst. prof. Skidmore Coll., Saratoga Springs, N.Y., 1964-70, assoc. prof., 1970-80, prof., 1980—, chair dept. chemistry and physics, 1985—; guest scientist. Brookhaven Nat. Labs., Upton, N.Y., 1971. Mem. adv. bd., past chair Salvation Army-Saratoga Springs Corps., 1967—; founding mem., past pres. Literacy Vols. of Saratoga, Inc., 1977—. Mem. AAUP, AAUW, Am. Phys. Soc., Am. Chem. Soc. (chair elect), N.Y. Acad. Scis., Sigma Xi. Home: 75 Ludlow St Saratoga Springs NY 12866 Office: Skidmore Coll Dept Chemistry and Physics Saratoga Springs NY 12866-1632

SAMZ, JANE DEDE, editor, author; b. Closter, N.J., Jan. 2; d. Benjamin and Ruth (Burstein) S. A.B. in Math., Smith Coll., 1969; postgrad., U. Ky., 1969-70; M.A. in History of Sci., U. Wis.-Madison, 1971. Teaching asst. physics dept. U. Ky., Lexington, 1969-70; editorial asst. Sci. World mag., Scholastic Mags., Inc., N.Y.C., 1972-73, asst. editor, 1973-76, assoc. editor, 1976-79, editor, 1979-87, sr. editor, sci. cons., 1987-88; lectr. communications dept. Stanford U., Calif., 1979; freelance writer Grolier Ency. Yearbook, 1977-79, Funk & Wagnalls Ency. Yearbook, 1981-83, Prentice-Hall, Inc.; also freelance cons. Author: Drugs & Diet, 1988; creator, author: Matter - Science World Visuals 9, 1975; co-author: Voyage to Jupiter, 1980; freelance writer, editor: Curriculum Concepts, Inc., N.Y.C., 1987; contbr. articles to Sci. World, World Book Science Year, 1988, World Book Health and Medical Annual, 1988, Futures, Creative Classroom. Camille and Henry Dreyfus Found. sci. writer's fellow Stanford U., 1978-79. Mem. AAAS, Am. Mus. Natural History, N.Y. Acad. Scis., N.Y. Newspaper Guild. Clubs: Smith-Princeton Chamber Singers; The Planetary Soc. Home: 55-612 River Dr S Jersey City NJ 07310

SANBORN, ANN, import/export company executive; b. Portsmouth, Va., May 28, 1954; d. Richard Wellington and Ruth Ann (Chenoweth) S. BS, Tex. A&M U., 1979. Master U.S. Steam or Motor Vessels. Third officer Exxon Co. USA, Houston, 1979-80; 2d officer U. Wash./Seattle, 1980-81; chief officer Mobil E & P, Dallas, 1982-85; lectr. Tex. A&M U., Galveston, 1985; pres. Sanborn Industries, Inc., Tampa, Fla., 1985—. Mem. Mensa. Democrat. Episcopalian. Avocations: sewing, cooking, history, skiing.

SANBORN, ANNA LUCILLE, pension and ins. cons.; b. Bklyn., Mar. 29, 1924; d. Peter Francis and Matilda M. (Stumpp) Galligen; B.A., Bklyn. Coll., 1945; 1 son, Dean Sanborn. Head dept. benefit and estate planning Union Central Life Ins. Co., N.Y.C., 1949-51; adminstr. employee benefits Seaboard Oil Co., N.Y.C., 1952-56; with Frank J. Walters Assocs., Inc., N.Y.C., 1957—, pres., 1970—. Bd. dirs. Archdiocesan Service Corp. Mem. Am. Acad. Actuaries, Republican. Roman Catholic. Home: 58-11 Seabury St Elmhurst NY 11373 Office: 509 Madison Ave New York NY 10022

SANBORN, DOREEN KAY, computer engineer; b. Sellersville, Pa., Feb. 5, 1948; d. Harold Wilson and Ruth Violet (Moore) Roberts; m. Richard Ronald Wolownik (div. Apr. 1976); m. Stephen Brock Sanborn, Jan. 4, 1986. Student, Am. Univ., 1979. Service rep. Bell Telephone Co. of Pa., Lansdale, 1966-68; statistician ITT Nesbitt, Phila., 1969; research asst. Ctr. for Naval Analyses, Arlington, Va., 1968, 70-74, Mitre Corp., McLean, Va., 1974-77; computer analyst Nat. Coal. Assn., Washington, 1977-79; tech. adv., systems engr. Motorola Computer Systems, Vienna, Va., 1979-87; tech. engr. Sun Microsystems, Vienna, 1987—. Mem. Nat. Assn. Female Execs. Home: 9733 Ashburn Dr Burke VA 22015 Office: Sun Microsystems 8219 Leesburg Pike Suite 700 Vienna VA 22180

SANBORN, DOROTHY CHAPPELL, librarian; b. Nashville, Apr. 26, 1920; d. William S. and Sammie Maude (Drake) Chappell; BA, U. Tex., 1941; MA, George Peabody Coll., 1947; MPA, Golden Gate U., 1982; m. Richard Donald Sanborn, Dec. 1, 1943; children: Richard Donald, William Chappell. Asst. cataloger El Paso (Tex.) Pub. Library, 1947-52, Library of Hawaii, Honolulu, 1953; cataloger Redwood (Calif.) City Pub. Library, 1954-55, 57-59, Stanford Research Inst., Menlo Park, Calif., 1955-57; librarian Auburn (Calif.) Pub. Library, 1959-62; cataloger Sierra Coll., Rocklin, Calif., 1962-64; reference librarian Sacramento City Library, 1964-66; county librarian Placer County (Calif.), Auburn, 1966—; chmn. Mountain Valley Library System, 1970-71, 75-76, 1984-85; cons. county librarian Alpine County Library, Markleeville, Calif., 1973-80. Served with WAVES, 1944-46. Mem. AAUW (pres. chpt. 1982-84), ALA, Calif. Library Assn. Democrat. Mem. United Ch. Christ. Club: Soroptimists. Home: 135 Midway St Auburn CA 95603 Office: Auburn Placer County Library 350 Nevada St Auburn CA 95603

SANBORN, KIMBERLEE RAE, nurse; b. Bangor, Maine, Mar. 29, 1955; d. Robert Newton and Roxanna (Starbuck) Yarrow; m. Gary Sanborn, Aug. 18, 1984. A.S. in Nursing, Quinnipiac Coll., Hamden, Conn., 1980. R.N., Conn. Dietary aide Luth. Home, Middletown, Conn., 1970-72, nurses aide, 1972-78; security dispatcher Quinnipiac Coll., Hamden, Conn., 1976; nurses aide New Britain Gen. Hosp., Conn., 1979, staff nurse, 1980-82, asst. head nurse, 1982-86; hospice on call nurse, Portland (Conn.) Visiting Nurse Assn., 1986—; rape crisis counselor advocate Bridgeport YWCA, 1987. Avocations: skiing; nature; art; macrame; stained glass. Home: 18 Lake St Middletown CT 06457

SANCHEZ, JUANITA LOUISE, staff social worker, therapist; b. Dodge City, Kans., July 10, 1949; d. Manuel and Frances Ysak (Ontiberos) Blea; m. Jerry L. Sanchez, Apr. 14, 1948; children: Aaron J., Stephanie M., Jeremy D. BA in Sociology, St. Mary of the Plains Coll., Dodge City, 1985; MSW, U. Kans., 1987. Dir. Aubrey Creations, Dodge City, 1979-81; asst. Retired

Sr. Vol. program, Dodge City, 1981-82; residential coordinator Omne program Area Mental Health Ctr., Dodge City, 1983-85, social work asst., 1986-87, social worker, 1987—; Advocate Domestic Violence Care Group, Dodge City, 1981-83; bd. dirs. Crisis Ctr. Pres. Dodge City chpt. Am. Heart Assn., 1984-88, League of United Latin Am. Citizens, Dodge City, 1983-84, dir. for youth State of Kans. chpt., 1982-84; active Women's Chamber, Dodge City, 1980—, Dodge City chpt. Am. G.I. Forum, 1981—. Recipient scholarships League of United Latin Am. Citizens, 1983, 84, St. Mary of the Plains Coll., 1985, Nat. Hispanic Scholarship Fund, 1987, Am. G.I. Forum, 1984, 86; Minority fellow U. Kans., 1985, 86. Mem. Nat. Assn. Social Workers, Dodge City Area C. of C. (grad. leadership program). Democrat. Roman Catholic. Home: 1104 Ave A Dodge City KS 67801 Office: Area Mental Health Ctr W Hwy 50 By-Pass Dodge City KS 67801

SANCHEZ, LYDIA MARIA, development corporation executive, accountant; b. Bronx, N.Y., Sept. 23, 1935; d. Blas Candelario and Ana (Rivera) S.; m. Armando Ramos, Jan. 28, 1958 (dec.); 1 child, Rafael C. BA, Pace U., 1982. Bookkeeper Internat. House, N.Y.C., 1965-73; office mgr. Internat. Ctr. Photography, N.Y.C., 1976-77; comptroller Union Theol. Sem., N.Y.C., 1977-80; staff acct. Sotheby Parke Bernet, N.Y.C., 1975-76; dir. fin. and adminstrn. South Bronx 2000 Local Devel. Corp., N.Y.C., 1980-83, Aspira of N.Y., Inc., N.Y.C., 1983—; dir. fin. and adminstrn. Food for Survival N.Y.C. Foodbank, 1987—. Served with USAF, 1956-58. Mem. Network Bronx Woman Orgn. Inc., Nat. Coll. and Univ. Bus. Officers. Home: 1875 Lafayette Ave Bronx NY 10473 Office: Food for Survival PO Box 359 Bronx NY 10473

SANCHEZ, SARA MARIA, librarian, bibliographer, international studies specialist; b. Havana, Cuba; d. Ramiro Jesus and Sara Maria (Rodriguez-Baz) S.; B.A., U. Villanova, 1957; B.L.S., U. Havana, 1960; M.L.S., SUNY-Geneseo, 1974; M.A. U. Miami, 1984. Librarian, Merici Acad., Havana, 1959-61; librarian Cuban Nat. Library, 1960-67; asst. prof. library sci. U. Miami, 1970-83, assoc. prof., 1984—; cons. Cuban database U. Miami, 1986; conductor seminars Acquisition Latin Am. Materials. Mem. ALA, Am. Council Coll. and Research Libraries, Latin Am. Studies Assn., Met. Mus. Miami, Coalition Hispanic Am. Women, Dade County Library Assn. (sec. 1979-81), Fla. Library Assn., Assn. Caribbean Univ. and Research Libraries, Am. Soc. Indexers, Cuban Mus. Arts. Democrat. Roman Catholic. Home: PO Box 24-8435 Coral Gables FL 33124 Office: U Miami Richter Library Coral Gables FL 33124

SANCHEZ, VICTORIA WAGNER, science educator; b. Milw., Apr. 11, 1934; d. Arthur William and Lorraine Marguerite (Kocovsky) Wagner; m. Rozier Edmond Sanchez, June 23, 1956; children: Mary Elizabeth, Carol Anne, Robert Edmond, Catherine Marie, Linda Therese. BS cum laude, Mt. Mary Coll., 1955; MS, Marquette U., 1957; postgrad., U. N.Mex., 1979-86. Cert. secondary tchr., N.Mex. Chemist Nat. Bur. Standards, Washington, 1958-60; tchr., chmn. sci. dept. Albuquerque Pub. Schs., 1979—; chmn. pub. info. area convention Nat. Sci. Tchrs. Assn., 1984, mem. sci. review com. Albuquerque Pub. Schs., 1985-86. Bd. dirs. Encino House, Albuquerque, 1976—, treas., 1977-79; leader Albuquerque troop Girl Scouts U.S., 1966-77. Named Outstanding Sci. Tchr. N.W. Regional Sci. Fair, Albuquerque, 1983, 1988; recipient St. George's award N.Mex. Cath. Scouting com., Albuquerque, 1978, Focus on Excellence award Assn. Supervision and Curriculum Devel., Albuquerque, 1985. Mem. AAUW (Albuquerque br. officer 1976-77, N.Mex. div. officer 1977-78), Nat. Sci. Tchrs. Assn., N.Mex. Sci. Tchrs. Assn. (treas. 1988—), Albuquerque Sci. Tchrs. Assn. (treas. 1984-85, v.p. and pres.-elect, 1986—, pres. 1987-88), N.Mex. Acad. Sci., Albuquerque Rose Soc. (sec. 1962-63). Democrat. Roman Catholic. Home: 7612 Palo Duro NE Albuquerque NM 87110 Office: Van Buren Sch 700 Louisiana SE Albuquerque NM 87108

SANCHO, GLORIA PRECIOUS MANNEH, accountant; b. Monrovia, Liberia, Feb. 12, 1960; d. Theodore Josiah and Annie Roselyn (Burgess) S.; m. J. Napoleon Cassell, Aug. 8, 1981 (div. Jan. 1984); children: Ayofemi Crystal Yvette. BA, Detroit Inst. Tech., 1981; BSc, Dyke Coll., 1984. Bookkeeper Standard Oil Co. of Ohio, Cleve., 1981-84; acct. SDAC Home Care Services, Bklyn., 1984-86; supr., bookkeeper Home Attendant Vendor Agy., Bklyn., 1986—. Mem. Nat. Assn. MBA Execs., Nat. Assn. Female Execs. Episcopalian. Lodge: Order Eastern Star. Home: 38-09 112th St #C9 Corona NY 11368 Office: Home Attendant Vendor Agy 2720 Mermaid Ave Brooklyn NY 11224

SANCHO, ROSEMARIE, educational administrator; b. Weslaco, Tex., Jan. 14, 1949; d. Frank and Carmen (Gonzalez) S. AA, Reedley Jr. Coll., 1970; BA, Calif. State U., Fresno, 1972; MA in Edn. Adminstrn., Supervision with distinction, Calif. State U., 1983. Cert. tchr., adminstr., Calif. Elem. bilingual tchr. Sanger (Calif.) Unified Sch. Dist., 1972-75, tchr. Spanish, phys. edn. ESL, folk dance, 1975-78, dist. coordinator migrant edn., 1978-85; prin. Lincoln Sch., 1985—; coordinator adult sch. for family edn., 1982-85. Named Educator of Yr., Comite Civico Sanger, 1984. Mem. Assn. for Supervision and Curriculum Devel., Nat. Assn. for Edn. Young Children, Calif. Assn. for Edn. Young Children, Assn. Calif. Sch. Adminstrs., Calif. Assn. for Bilingual Edn. Democrat. Roman Catholic. Home: 2133 N Garden St Fresno CA 93703 Office: Lincoln Sch 1700 14th St Sanger CA 93657

SANDAGE, ELIZABETH ANTHEA, advertising educator; b. Larned, Kans., Oct. 13, 1930; d. Curtis Carl and Beulah Pauline (Knupp) Smith; student Okla. State U., 1963-65; B.S., U. Colo., 1967; M.A., 1970; Ph.D. in Communications U. Ill., 1983; m. Charles Harold Sandage, July 18, 1971; children by previous marriage—Diana Louise Danner White, David Alan Danner. Pub. relations rep., editor Martin News, Martin Marietta Corp., Denver, 1960-63, 65-67; retail advt. salesperson Denver Post, 1967-70; instr. advt. U. Ill., 1970-71, vis. lectr. advt., 1977-84; v.p., corp. sec., dir. Farm Research Inst., Urbana, 1984—. Exec. dir. Sandage Charitible Trust, 1986—. Mem. Kappa Tau Alpha. Republican. Presbyterian. Editor: Occasional Papers in Advertising, 1971; The Sandage Family Cookbook, 1976, 2d edit., 1986; The Inkling, Carle Hosp. Aux. Newsletter, 1975-76. Home: 106 The Meadows Urbana IL 61801

SANDAHL, BONNIE BEARDSLEY, pediatric nurse practitioner; b. Washington, Jan. 17, 1939; d. Erwin Leonard and Carol Myrtle (Collis) B.; m. Glen Emil Sandahl, Aug 17, 1963; children: Cara Lynne, Cory Glen. BSN, U. Wash., 1962, MN, 1974, cert. pediatric nurse practitioner, 1972. Dir. Wash. State Joint Practice Commn., Seattle, 1974-76; instr. pediatric nurse practitioner program U. Wash., Seattle, 1976, course coordinator quality assurance, 1977-78; pediatic nurse practitioner/health coordinator Snohomish County Head Start, Everett, Wash., 1975-77; clin. nurse educator (specialist) Harborview Med. Ctr., Seattle, 1978—, dir. child abuse prevention project, 1986—; speaker legis. focus on children, 1987; clin. assoc. Dept. of Pediatrics, U. Wash., 1987. Mem. Task Force on Pharmacotherapeutic Courses, Wash. State Bd. Nursing, 1985-86; Puget Sound Health Systems Agy., 1975—. pres., 1980-82; mem. child devel. project adv. bd. Mukilteo Sch. Dist., 1984-85; mem. parenting adv. com. Edmonds Sch. Dist., 1985—; chmn. hospice-home health task force Snohomish County Hospice Program, Everett, 1984-85, bd. dirs. hospice, 1985-87; mem. Wash. State Health Coordinating, Council, 1977-82, 86—, chmn. nursing home bed projection methodology task force, 1986-87; mem. Nat. Council Health Planning and Devel., HHS, 1980-87; mem. adv. com. on uncompensated care Wash. State Legislature, 1983-84; mem. Joint Select Com., Tech. Adv. Com. on Managed Health Care Systems, 1984-85. Pres., Alderwood Manor Community Council, 1983—; treas. Wash. St. Women's Polit. Caucus, 1983-84; mem. com. to examine changes in Wash. State Criminal Sex Law, 1987. Named Nurse of Yr., King County Nurses Assn., 1985; recipient Golden Acorn award Seattle-King County PTA, 1973, Katherine Rickey Vol. Participation award, 1987. Mem. Am. Nurses Assn. (chmn. pediatric nurse practitioner subcom. Com. Examiners Maternal-Child Nursing Practice, 1986—, chair Com. Examiners Maternal-Child Nursing Practice 1988—), Wash. State Nurses Assn. (hon. leadership award 1981), King County Nurses Assn., Wash. State Soc. Pediatrics, Sigma Theta Tau. Democrat. Methodist. Home: 1814 200th St SW Alderwood Manor WA 98036 Office: Harborview Med Ctr 325 9th Ave MS ZA-53 Seattle WA 98104

SANDBERG, SUSAN MARIE, nurse; b. St. Croix Falls, Wis., Dec. 12, 1960; d. F. Warren and Carol Marie (Paulson) S. BN, Gustavus Adolphus Coll., 1984. RN, Mich., Minn. Staff nurse Grand View Hosp., Ironwood, Mich., 1984-86, dir. edn., 1986—. Mem. Am. Cancer Soc. (pub. educator 1987), Minn. Nurses Assn., Mich. Nurses Assn., Am. Swedish Inst. Democrat. Lutheran. Home: 106 W Francis Ironwood MI 49938 Office: Grand View Hosp N 10561 Grand View Ln Ironwood MI 49938

SANDE, BARBARA, interior decorating consultant; b. Twin Falls, Idaho, May 5, 1939; d. Einar and Pearl M. (Olson) Sande; m. Ernest Reinhardt Hohener, Sept. 3, 1961 (div. Sept. 1971); children: Heidi Catherine, Eric Christian. BA, U. Idaho, 1961. Asst. mgr., buyer Home Yardage Inc., Oakland, Calif., 1972-76; cons. in antiques and antique valuation, Lafayette, Calif., 1977-78; interior designer Neighborhood Antiques and Interiors, Oakland, Calif., 1978-86; owner, Claremont Antiques and Interiors, Berkeley, Calif., 1987—; cons., participant antique and art fair exhibits, Orinda and Piedmont, Calif., 1977—. Decorator Piedmont Christmas House Tour, 1983, Oakland Mus. Table Setting, 1984, 85, 86, Piedmont Showcase Family Room, 1986, Piedmont Showcase Music Room, 1986, Piedmont Kitchen House Tour, 1985, Santa Rosa Symphony Holiday Walk Benefit, 1986, Piedmont Benefit Guild Showcase "Young Persons Room", 1987, Piedmont Showcase Library, 1988. Bd. dirs. San Leandro Coop. Nursery Sch., 1967; health coordinator parent-faculty bd., Miramonte High Sch., Orinda, 1978, Acalanes Sch. Dist., Lafayette, Calif., 1978; bd. dirs. Orinda Community Ctr. Vols., 1979; originator Concerts in the Park, Orinda, 1979. Assoc. Am. Soc. Interior Design, Am. Soc. Appraisers; mem. Am. Decorative Arts Forum, De Young Mus., Nat. Trust Historic Preservation, San Francisco Opera Guild, San Francisco Symphony Guild. Democrat. Avocations: travel; hiking.

SANDELIN, MARGARET HELEN JENKINS GASKILL, lawyer; b. Phila., Sept. 18, 1921; d. Frederick John and Margaret (Swarz) Jenkins; m. Herbert Leo Gaskill, Mar. 1, 1944; children: Margaret Vesta, Herbert Leo; m. D. Scott Sandelin, July 9, 1977. BS in Law, U. Wash., 1946, JD, 1947. Bar: Wash., 1947. Ptnr. Hardy and Gaskill, Seattle, 1952-54, Holland and Gaskill, Seattle, 1954-57; sole practice Seattle, 1958-64, 69-77; ptnr. Weyer, Sterne and Gaskill, Seattle, 1958-64, Weyer, Sandelin, Sterne and Gaskill, Seattle, 1964-66, Weyer, Sterne and Gaskill, Seattle, 1966-69, Sandelin and Sandelin, Seattle, 1977—. Mem. Citizens' Adv. Com. Senate Interim Com. Fin. Instns., 1973-74, Estate Planning Council Seattle, Seattle Art Mus. Mem. ABA, Wash State Bar Assn. (chmn. family law sect. 1980-81, editor newletter), East King County Bar Assn. (sec. 1962), Am. Trial Lawyers Assn., Wash Women Lawyers, U. Wash. Alumni Assn. (bd. dirs. 1981-84), Phi Alpha Delta. Home: 4022 E Mercer Way Mercer Island WA 98040

SANDERLIN, OWENITA HARRAH, author, educator; b. Los Angeles, June 2, 1916; d. Owen Melville and Marigold (Whitford) H.; B.A. summa cum laude, Am. U., 1937; postgrad. U. Maine, U. Calif., San Diego State U.; m. George William Sanderlin, May 30, 1936; children—Frea Elizabeth, Sheila Mary, David George, John Owen. Freelance writer, speaker, 1940—; tchr. English, U. Maine, 1942, 46; head dept. speech and drama Acad. of Our Lady of Peace, San Diego, 1961-68; cons. gifted programs San Diego city schs., 1971-73, 80—; author: Jeanie O'Brien, 1965; Johnny, 1968; Creative Teaching, 1971; Teaching Gifted Children, 1973; Tennis Rebel, 1978; Match Point, 1979; co-author: Gifted Children: How to Identify and Teach Them, 1979. Recipient Poetry award Alpha Chi Omega, 1936; Double Ruby award Nat. Forensic League, 1965. Mem. Nat. Assn. Gifted Children, Assn. San Diego Educators of Gifted, San Diego Natural History Museum, AAUW, Scripps Clinic and Research Found., Mortar Bd. Clubs: San Diego State U. Women's; Singing Hills Tennis. Address: 997 Vista Grande Rd El Cajon CA 92019

SANDERS, ALTHEA DEBORAH, marketing professional, accountant; b. Waterbury, Conn., Apr. 29, 1936; d. Russell LeRoy and Althea Mae (Barker) Frazier; m. Dale G. Hoyt, Sept. 1971 (div. 1978); children: Althea Coleman, Marie Ceriello, William J. Jr. BBA, Western Conn. State U., 1984. Controller's asst. Stone Co., Inc., Danbury, Conn., 1984-85; various temp. positions Div. Rob't Half Accountemps, Stamford, Conn., 1985-86; jr. acct. Kahan, Steiger & Co., Stamford, 1986; mgr. acctg. dept. La Jolla Marketing, Inc., Chula Vista, Calif., 1987—. Mem. Nat. Assn. Accts., Nat. Assn. Female Execs. Democrat. Jewish. Office: La Jolla Mktg Inc 1065 Bay Blvd Chula Vista CA 92011

SANDERS, AUGUSTA SWANN, nurse; b. Alexandria, La., July 22, 1932; d. James and Elizabeth (Thompson) Swann; m. James Robert Sanders, Jan. 12, 1962 (div. 1969). Student, Morgan State U., 1956. Pub. health nurse USPHS, Washington, 1963-64; mental health counselor Los Angeles County Sheriff's Dept., 1972-79; program coordinator Los Angeles County Dept. Mental Health, 1979—. Mem. Assemblyman Mike Roo's Commn. on Women's Issues, 1981—, Senator Diane Watson's Commn. on Health Issues, 1979—; chmn. Commn. Sex. Equity Los Angeles Unified Sch. Dist., 1984—. Mem. Los Angeles County Employees Assn. (v.p. 1971-72), So. Calif. Black Nurses Assn. (founding mem.), Nat. Assn. Female Execs., Internat. Fedn. Bus. and Profl. Women (pres. Los Angeles Sunset dist. 1981-82, dist. officer 1982—), Chi Eta Phi. Democrat. Methodist. Office: Augustus F Hawkins Mental Health Ctr 1720 E 120th St Los Angeles CA 90805

SANDERS, BOBBYE ROSE, electronics industry executive; b. Dallas, July 1, 1948; d. Huverston and Vauline (Chatman) Fisher; m. Willie Sanders Jr., Aug. 10, 1974; children: Camille, Corey, Chadwick. BA in Maths., Oklahoma City, 1969. Trainee IBM, Dallas, 1969-70, assoc. systems engr., 1970-75, systems engr., 1975-79, market support rep., 1979-82, adv. market support rep., 1982-87, sr. market support rep., 1987—; instr. IBM High Sch. program, Dallas. Mem. adv. bd. St. Luke's Ch. community computer project, Dallas, 1983-84; asst. dir. Mount Moriah Bapt. Ch. Youth Council, 1983-85. Named one of Outstanding Young Women Am., 1984. Mem. South Cen. Bus. and Profl. Women's Assn. (parlimentarian 1984-86, sec. 1986—), Nat. Council Negro Women. Baptist. Home: 2214 Elder Oaks Ln Dallas TX 75232 Office: IBM 225 SW Carpenter Freeway Irving TX 75061

SANDERS, CAROLYN ANN, tour company executive; b. McAlester, Okla., Feb. 17, 1949; d. James Bernard and Darlene (Cresto) Powers; m. Johnny Dee Sanders (dec. 1983); children: Johnny Dee, Justin Dan. Student, Northeastern Okla. A&M U., 1969. Pvt. sec. McAlester Police Dept., 1969-72; office mgr. AB&T Archtl. Firm, McAlester, 1973-79; owner, mgr. Sanders Equipment Co., McAlester, 1979—; owner Internat. Tours, McAlester, 1986—. Mem. McAlester Econ. Devel. Bd., 1986—; bd. dirs. Lake Eufaula Assn., 1986—. Mem. Am. Soc. Travel Agts., Internat. Assn. Travel Agts., McAlester C. of C., Beta Iota (pres. 1980-81). Democrat. Roman Catholic. Club: Kiamichi Country (bd. dirs. 1986—). Home: 2716 Highland Terr McAlester OK 74501 Office: Internat Tours 500 E Wyandotte McAlester OK 74501

SANDERS, DOROTHY, educator; b. Ga., Jan. 30, 1935; m. Nathaniel Sanders, Dec. 17, 1960; children: Albert, Starlene, Nathaniel, Patricia Ann, Emmanuel. AS in Edn., Cumberland Coll., 1971; BA, Shaw U., 1973. Notary pub., N.J. Tchr. Bridgeton (N.J.) Bd. Edn., 1971—, dir. reading lab., 1974-81; real estate salesperson Bridgeton. Active Bridgeton PTA; vol. probation counseling. Mem. NEA, N.J. Edn. Assn., Women With Vision, Nat. Assn. Female Execs. Baptist. Home: Rt 7 Box 68 Bridgeton NJ 08302 Office: Bridgeton Middle Sch Board and West Ave Bridgeton NJ 08302

SANDERS, ELLEN DUGAL, senior systems engineer; b. Rockville Centre, N.Y., Dec. 31, 1955; d. Shafton Dale and Ellen (Dragan) Dugal; m. Harold Roberts Sanders, Feb. 14, 1976 (div. 1986); children: Rosetta Yvonne, Paula Chérie. BSEE, U. Ala., Huntsville, 1985. Dancer, instr. Arthur Murray Studio, Huntsville, 1973-81; enumerator U.S. Census, Gurley, Ala., 1980; with coop. dept. Teledyne Brown Engring., Huntsville, 1982-85, engr. II, 1985-86; sr. systems engr. Intergraph, Huntsville, 1986—. Appeared in musical plays Guys and Dolls, A Chorus Line, My Fair Lady, Music Man, Showboat. Mem. Community Ballet Assn. (scholarship 1983-85), Omicron Delta Kappa, Tau Beta Pi, Eta Kappa Nu. Greek Catholic. Home: 2703 Peel St Huntsville AL 35805 Office: Intergraph One Madison Indsl Pk IW 1507 Huntsville AL 35807-4201

SANDERS, ESTHER JEANNETTE, retired aerospace company executive; b. Ogden, Utah, Feb. 19, 1926; d. Warren Lynn and Esther Marguerite (Harris) Garner, B.A., U. Colo., 1948; m. Thomas Wesley Sanders, Jan. 10, 1946. With Calif., Inst., Tech. Coop. Wind Tunnel, Pasadena, 1948; with Sperry Gyroscope Co., Point Mugu, Calif., 1949-55; with Propulsion Research Corp., Santa Monica, Calif., 1955-57; with TRW, Redondo Beach, Calif., 1957-84, head engring. test data analysis sect., retired. Author 1 pub. story, 3 pub. poems. Home: 15405 Callahan Ranch Rd Reno NV 89511

SANDERS, GWENDOLYNN SUE, accountant; b. Roswell, N. Mex., Aug. 19, 1958; d. Albert Lee Sr. and Carolyn A. (Talley) Wagner; m. David Allen Sanders, Aug. 3, 1985. B in Acctg., N.Mex. State U., 1980. CPA, N.M. Staff acct. John Mobbs, PC, Alamagordo, N.M., 1980—. Mem. Am. Inst. CPA's, N.Mex. Soc. CPA's. Democrat. Methodist. Office: John Mobbs PC PO Box 898 Alamogordo NM 88310

SANDERS, JACQUELYN SEEVAK, psychologist, educator; b. Boston, Apr. 26, 1931; d. Edward Ezral and Dora (Zoken) Seevak; 1 son, Seth. B.A., Radcliffe Coll., 1952; M.A., U. Chgo., 1964; Ph.D., UCLA, 1972. Counselor, asst. prin. Orthogenic Sch., Chgo., 1952-65; research assoc. UCLA, 1965-68; cons. Osawatomie State Hosp. (Kans.), 1965-68; asst. prof. Ctr. for Early Edn., Los Angeles, 1969-72; assoc. dir. Sonia Shankman Orthogenic Sch., U. Chgo., 1972-73, dir., 1973—; curriculum cons. day care ctrs. Los Angeles Dept. Social Welfare, 1970-72; instr. Calif. State Coll., Los Angeles, 1972; lectr. dept. edn. U. Chgo., 1972-80, sr. lectr., 1980—; instr. tchr. edn. program Inst. Psychoanalysis, Chgo., 1979-82. Contbr. articles to profl. jours. UCLA Univ. fellow, 1966-68; Radcliffe Coll. Scholar, 1948-52. Mem. Am. Assn. Children's Residential Ctrs. (program chair 1977-79, treas. 1979-81, 87—), Am. Ednl. Research Assn., Am. Orthopsychiat. Soc., Am. Psychol. Assn., Nat. Soc. Study Edn., Am. Assn. Psychitar. Services for Children (sec.). Jewish. Clubs: Quadrangle, Raquet (Hyde Park, Ill.); Radcliffe of Chgo. (sec/treas. 1986-87, pres. 1987—); Harvard of Chgo. (bd. dirs. 1986—). Home: 5842 S Stony Island Ave Apt 2G Chicago IL 60637

SANDERS, JUANITA FRANCIS, television personality; b. Steubenville, Ohio, May 21, 1939; d. Harry Sr. and Dorothy Mae (Richardson) Blackwell; m. Curtis L. McGee, divorced; children: Karnell, Kelly, Kimberly, Keith; m. Herman Sanders Sr., Aug. 27, 1967; 1 child, Herman Sanders Jr. Degree, Columbus (Ohio) Bus. U., 1965; degree in nursing, Columbus Tech. Inst., 1980. Owner, operator janitorial service, Columbus, 1963-65; adminstrv. trainee Diagnostic Ctr., State of Ohio, Columbus, 1964-65; owner, operator San-Car Boutique, Columbus, 1970-72; assoc. buyer, with accounts payable dept. Lazarus Dept. Store, Columbus, 1972-75; dir. cosmetic bus., Columbus, 1976-84; producer, host TV show Be Informed, Columbus, 1984-86; drug and alcohol counselor Columbus, 1986—; owner jewelry bus., Columbus, 1986—. Mem. Black Alcoholism Council, Inc., Columbus, 1985—. Mem. Nat. Assn. Female Execs., Stonybrook Sch. Social Work, Black Alcoholic Alumni Assn. Republican.

SANDERS, KAREN ELAINE, health professional, entrepreneur; b. Bethesda, Md., Aug. 12, 1954; d. Jack Talmadge and Bessie (Radusin) S. BS in Kinesiological Scis., U. Md., 1976; MS in Health Fitness Mgmt., The Am. U., 1986. Cons. in field 1976—; exercise test technologist Georgetown U. Hosp., Washington, 1978-85, mng. dir. preventive and rehab. cardiology exercise program, 1985-87; dir. cardiar and pulmonary rehab. Greater Washington Rehab. Ctr., Silver Spring, Md., 1987—; lectr. in field. Contbr. articles to profl. jours. Mem. Assn. for Fitness in Bus., Am. Coll. Sports Medicine. Home: PO Box 15386 Chevy Chase MD 20815 Office: Greater Washington Rehab Ctr 3801 International Dr Silver Spring MD 20906

SANDERS, KRISTINE HEFFINGTON, construction project manager; b. Sioux City, Iowa, Aug. 18, 1954; d. LeRoy Charles Sanders and Maxine Lee (Blades) Stepina; m. Jake Alan Sanders Heffington, Feb. 25, 1986. A in Applied Sci. in Archtl. Design, U. S.D., Springfield, 1974, BS in Constrn., 1976; MS in Indsl. Systems Engring., Memphis State U., 1987. Asst. instr. U. S.D., Springfield, 1975; constrn. engr. Ebasco Services Inc., Sergeant Bluff, Iowa; Brush, Colo.; Atlanta; Bay City, Tex., 1976-83; field service engr. United Conveyor Corp., Deerfield, Ill., 1983; project mgr. Fed. Express Corp., Memphis, Tenn., 1984—. Mem. Nat. Soc. Profl. Engrs., Soc. Mfg. Engrs., Project Mgmt. Inst., Soc. Packaging and Handling Engrs., Mensa, Intertel. Home: 5706 Fenway Dr Memphis TN 38115 Office: Fed Express Corp PO Box 727 Memphis TN 38194-2620

SANDERS, LILLIE, college administrator; b. Shaw, Miss., July 27, 1943; d. Landon Johnson and Ardelia (Jones) Thorns; m. Obra Sanders, Sept. 14, 1959 (div. 1977); children: Shari L., Christopher. AA in Social Sci., Loop Jr. Coll., Chgo., 1975; BA in Soc., Chgo. State U., 1976, cert. in edn., 1979, MA in Occupational Edn., 1985. Social worker Dept. Children & Family Services, Chgo., 1977-78; edn. recruiter Chgo. Bd. Edn., 1978-79, elem. educator, 1979-81; adult educator M.S.T.A. Bus. Coll., Chgo., 1981-82, dir. word processor trainers, 1982-84, dir. job placement, 1984—, instr. career awareness, 1984—. Mem. Chatham Orgn. com. to Re-elect Mayor, Chgo. Recipient Cert. Achievement Chatham Bus. Assn., Chgo., 1987, Cert. Achievement Assn. Ind. Colls., Washington, 1987. Mem. Assn. Info. System Profls., Ill. Vocat. Assn., Chgo. C. of C. (cert. of achievement 1984—). Roman Catholic. Club: Lelanders, Carribean (v.p. 1985, sec. 1985-87). Home: 8239 S Evans Chicago IL 60619

SANDERS, MADELINE LOIS, auditor; b. Portage, Ind., July 2, 1936; d. Wayne L. and Hazel Mae (Briggs) Bradford; m. Sidney Commons Sanders, Dec. 3, 1955; children: Keith Evan, Scott Bradley, Denise Joy. BS in Bus. Adminstrn. summa cum laude, Franklin U., Columbus, Ohio, 1981. Exec. dir. Am. Cancer Soc., Circleville, Ohio, 1976-78; acct. I bur. workers' compensation State of Ohio, Columbus, 1982, acct. II bur. workers' compensation, 1982-83; auditor City of Circleville, 1983—; auditor Am. Red Cross, 1983, Trinity Luth. Ch., 1984-85, Circleville. Sec. Trinity Luth. Ch. Council, Circleville, 1982-84; active Rep. Cen. Com., 1984—, Pickaway County Rep. Women, 1983—, adv. com. Congressman McEwen, 1987—; bd. dirs. Planned Parenthood Pickaway County, 1979-84. Mem. Am. Assn. Univ. Women, Circleville Bus. and Profl. Women (sec. 1985-86). Clubs: Circleville Women's Investment Group (treas. 1978—), Women's Golf Assn. (treas. 1980-81).

SANDERS, MARLENE, television correspondent; b. Cleve., Jan. 10, 1931; d. Mac Sanders and Evelyn (Menitoff) Fisher; m. Jerome Toobin, May 27, 1958 (dec. Jan. 1984); children: Jeff, Mark. Student, Ohio State U., 1948-49. Writer, producer Sta. WNEW-TV, N.Y.C., 1955-60, P.M. program Westinghouse Broadcasting Co., N.Y.C., 1961-62; asst. dir. news and public affairs Sta. WNEW, N.Y.C., 1962-64; anchor, news program ABC News, N.Y.C., 1964-68, corr., 1968-72, documentary producer, writer, anchor, 1972-76, v.p., dir. TV documentaries, 1976-78; corr. CBS News, N.Y.C., 1978-87; host Currents Sta. WNET-TV, N.Y.C., 1987—. Recipient award N.Y. State Broadcasters Assn., 1976, award Nat. Press Club, 1976, Emmy awards, 1980, 81, others. Mem. Am. Women in Radio and TV (Woman of Yr. award 1975, Silver Satellite award 1977), Women in Communications (past pres.), Women's Forum, Sigma Delta Chi. Office: Sta WNET-TV 340 W 58th St New York NY 10019

SANDERS, NANCY AUVIL, cosmetics company executive; b. Hambleton, W.Va., Oct. 27, 1933; d. Charles William Auvil and Genevieve (Griffith) Fick; widowed; children: Paul Eye, Connie Kreger, Betty Underhill, Christopher Eye, David Eye. Student, Catherman's Bus. Coll., 1953. Dist. mgr. sales Hamilton Mgmt. Corp., Evansville, Ind., 1968-74; exec. asst. to pres. Jene' Corp., Evansville, Ind., 1974-80, sec.-treas. bd. dirs., 1977-80; pres. Lawton, Okla., 1983—, also chmn. bd.; coordinator mktg. and mgmt., cons. CareFree Internat., Inc., Dallas, 1980-83; bd. dirs., sec.-treas. Double C Corp., Evansville, 1973-77. Republican. Mem. Unity Ch. Home: 619 SE 38th St Lawton OK 73501 Office: Jene' Corp PO 1046 Lawton OK 73502

SANDERS, NANCY CAROL, automotive parts company executive; b. Oakland, Calif., July 7, 1950; d. Kenneth W. and Corrine M. McCuaig; divorced; 1 child, Justin Scott. Student, Chabot Jr. Coll., 1970, 71. Br. sec. Mack Trucks, Oakland, 1971-73; from adminstrv. asst., parts mgr. to br. mgr. Beajay Products, Oakland, 1973-78; mem. equipment sales staff Heath Equipment Co., Concord, Calif., 1982-84; with MBI, Concord, 1982-84, owner, pres., 1984—. Roman Catholic. Office: 431 N Buchanan Circle #3 Pacheco CA 94553

SANDERS, PATRICIA ABBISS, brokerage house executive; b. Chelsea, Mass., Dec. 3, 1953; d. Frances Kenneth Abbiss and Patricia Anne (Davidson) Johnson; m. Victor Allan Sanders, Nov. 25, 1985. Student, U. N.H., 1975-76, North Va. Community Coll., 1982, George Washington U., 1986. Lic. real estate broker, Va. Intern mktg. IBM Corp., Newton, Mass., 1976-77; sales assoc. 3M Co., McLean, Va., 1977-79, Norell Inc., Washington, 1979-80, Panafax Corp., Arlington, Va., 1980-82; v.p. Ferris and Co., Washington, 1983—; pres. Nat. Scholarship Assistance Services, Arlington, Va., 1987—. Chmn. United Way Campaign, 1984-86. Mem. Am. Mgmt. Assn., Nat. Assn. Female Execs., Washington Personnel Assn., Internat. Found. Employee Benefit Plans. Republican. Home: 3004 S Columbus St Arlington VA 22206 Office: Ferris and Co Inc 1720 Eye St NW Washington DC 20006

SANDERS, PHYLLIS ADEN, radio and television broadcaster; b. Buenos Aires, Argentina, June 27, 1919; d. Fred and Anna Almeda (Pettit) Aden; B.A., Occidental Coll., 1941; M.A., Scarritt Coll., 1943; m. Olcutt Sanders, Apr. 8, 1947; children—Lynn Edwin, Marta Almeda, Jay Olcutt, Fred Aden, R. Elizabeth. Formerly tchr.; lectr., workshop leader on changing roles of women, 1973-75; producer/host weekly radio interview show Changing World of Women, Sta. WNYC, N.Y.C., 1972-79; TV reporter/host/commentator on women's issues Sta. WNYC-TV, N.Y.C., 1975-78; regular weekly commentator Prime of Your Life, NBC-TV, N.Y.C., 1979-83; reporter Age Whys, AM Phila., Sta. WPVI-TV, 1981-83; producer, host weekly series Growing Older with Style, WCAU-TV, Phila., 1983-84, feature reporter Noonbreak, 1984, seniors reporter, 1987—; producer, host series on aging WHYY-TV, 1984-85; reporter, interviewer Modern Maturity TV series on aging, nat. PBS-TV, 1986, 88—. Community relations dir. Town of New Castle (N.Y.), 1972-73, originator, coordinator Community Day, New Castle, 1971; coordinator N.Y.C. women's adv. com. on meeting with network mgmt., 1976-77. Recipient award N.Y. chpt. NOW, 1973, N.J. Women, 1976; named to Phila. Mayor's Sr. Citizen Honor Roll, 1984. Mem. AFTRA, Nat. Acad. TV Arts and Scis., Women's Inst. for Freedom of Press, ACLU, Friends Com. on Nat. Legis., NOW, Older Women's League, Occidental Coll. Alumni (award 1985). Mem. Soc. of Friends. Home: 135 S 20th St #305 Philadelphia PA 19103

SANDERS, ROBIN RENEE, diplomat; b. Hampton, Va., July 5; d. Robert M. and Geneva (Machoney) Sanders. B.A., Hampton Inst.; M.A., Ohio U., 1979, M.S., 1979. Broadcast lic. FCC 3d class. Editoral assts. Essence Mag., N.Y.C., 1974-76, Fgn. Broadcast Info. Service, Washington, 1976-77; intern account exec. Burson-Marsteller Co., N.Y.C., 1977-78; pub. relations assoc. Seventeen mag., N.Y.C., 1979-80; polit. and counselor officer Am. embassy, Dominican Republic, 1980-83, consular officer Am. consulate, Oporto, Portugal, 1983-86, dep. polit. sect. chief Am. Embassy Khartoum, Sudan, 1986— ; cons. Profl. Women's Seminar, 1983, 84; speaker U. Oporto, 1983; Oporto, lectr. Am. Lang. Inst., Oporto, 1983; researcher dept. internat. relations Ohio U., 1978; TV producer dept. gerontology Hampton Inst., 1976-77. Recipient 1st place award for painting Two Faces, Scholastic Art Bd., 1981; journalism scholar Syracuse U, 1970. Mem. Women in Communications, Pub. Relations Soc. Am., Am. Fgn. Service Assn., Nat. Council Negro Women, Black Caucus, Mus. African Art, Alpha Kappa Alpha, Alpha Kappa Mu. Consular Corps (Oporto); Diplomatic (Santo Domingo), Thursday Luncheon Group, Capital Press (Washington). Home: 110 E Bloomfield St Rome NY 13440

SANDERS, SHARON MICHELLE, sales and marketing executive; b. Sheffield, Ala., Aug. 2, 1955; d. Charles William Sanders and Gloria Belle (Peters) Sanders Blount. BA in Theatre Arts, Calif. State U., Fullerton, 1977. Sales rep. Bonne Bell Cosmetics, Lakewood, Ohio, 1973-79; sr. asst. mgr. Household Fin. Corp., Pasadena, Calif., 1980-82; sales rep. Drackett sub. Bristol-Myers, Cin., 1982-84; sales rep. Kerr Dental, Romulus, Mich., 1984, dist. mgr., 1986—, western endodontic specialist, 1987—. Recipient Miss Duarte award City of Duarte, Calif., 1972-73. Mem. Nat. Assn. Female Execs. Avocations: bicycling, reading, skiing. Home: 5229 Roswell San Diego CA 92114 Office: Kerr Dental Products 28200 Wick Rd Romulus MI 48174

SANDERS, SUZANNE NANNETTE, nurse, health company executive; b. Tacoma, Mar. 17, 1945; d. Thomas Benton and Eleanor Nannette (Vaughan) Wilson; B.S. in Nursing with high honors, U. Tex., 1975; M.S., Tex. Woman's U., Houston, 1982; m. James L. Sanders, Jan. 25, 1974; children—Jeanene Cooper, Charlotte Cooper, Marilyn Cooper, Lindsey Sanders. Research asst. zoology dept. U. Tex., 1969-71, M.D. Anderson Hosp., Tex. Med. Center, Houston, 1971; nurse St. Joseph's Hosp., Houston, 1975; dir. nursing Richmond (Tex.) State Sch., 1979; pres., owner Liftercise Inc., Sugar Land, Tex., 1980—; mem. bd. Office of Early Childhood Devel., 1977, chmn. bd., 1980-81. Vice pres. Mcpl. Utility Dist. No. 13, 1980, bd. mem., 1977-81; mem. Assistance League Houston. Mem. Sigma Theta Tau. Democrat. Club: Sugar Land Lioness (charter mem.). Various radio and TV appearances: author: Liftercise: A Program for Women Using Weights with Exercise, 1980. Office: 339 Southwestern Blvd Sugar Land TX 77478

SANDERSEN, ELAINE, art director, graphic designer; b. Jersey City, Aug. 19, 1941; d. Alfred A. and Elizabeth Pastine; m. Robert Sandersen, May 19, 1963 (div. May 1978); children: Lynda, Eric. Student, Parsons Sch. Design, 1962. Asst. art dir. Silver Burdett & Ginn, Morristown, N.J., 1978—. Mem. Art Dirs. Club N.J. Office: Silver Burdette & Ginn 250 James St Suite CN 1918 Morristown NJ 07960

SANDERSON, CANDICE MERIWETHER, psychologist; b. Paducah, Ky., Dec. 21, 1950; d. Corbin and Eleanore (Austin) Meriwether; m. Phillip Crabtree, July 2, 1969 (div. Dec. 1979); 1 child, Bubba; m. Daryl K. Sanderson, Aug. 21, 1982 (dec. Sept. 1987); 1 child, Cassie Lee. BA, Murray State U., 1973, MS, 1975, postgrad., 1978. Cert. psychologist, Ky. Child psychologist Paducah (Ky.) Mental Health Cen., 1975-77; dir. psychol. services W.Ky. Easter Seal Cen., Paducah, 1977-78; psychologist McCracken County Sch. System, Paducah, 1978—. Vice chmn. Purchase Are Spouse Abuse Bd., Paducah, 1988. Mem. Ky. Assn. Sch. Adminstrs., W. Ky. Spec. Edn. Coordinators (sec. 1985-87), Women Aware (v.p. 1979-88), Preschool Interagy. Planning Council, Purchase Area Masters' Psychologists (v.p. 1988), Bus. and Profl. Women of Achievement, 1985. Democrat. Baptist. Home: 6515 Candlelight Dr Paducah KY 42001 Office: McCracken County Bd Edn 260 Bleich Rd Paducah KY 42001

SANDERSON, SANDY, real estate broker; b. Los Angeles, Nov. 28, 1944; d. Carl Foree and Mildred Anna Bailey; m. Willis Lloyd Pitkin, Jr., June 9, 1965 (div.); children: Joseph Reeves, Sara Love, Mary Faith; m. Howard Sanderson, July 19, 1984. BA, Whittier Coll., 1966, MAT, 1967. Lic. real estate broker, Utah, Idaho, Ariz., Calif.; leadership tng. grad. Sales assoc., assoc. broker Aloma Real Estate, Logan, Utah, 1979-82; founder, ptnr. Gold Key Realty, 1982-83; mgr. Wardly Corp.-Better Homes and Gardens, Salt Lake City, 1983—; broker Coldwell Banker Baugh Assocs., Logan, 1984-85; owner, ptnr. Ginny Hays Realty, Inc., Sedona, Ariz., 1985—; founder, pres. Sanderson Data Systems, Sedona, 1986—. Contbr. articles to profl. jours. Dem. precinct chmn., 1982; sponsor Logan Swim Team. Mem. Cert. Residential Specialists, Nat. Women's Council Realtors (nat. trainer), Logan Women's Council Realtors (pres., founder), Sedona Women's Council Realtors (pres., founder 1985) Internat. Fedn. Realtors, Utah State Farm and Land Inst. (sec.-treas.), Nat. Mktg. Inst., Logan Bd. Realtors (Sales Assoc. of Yr. 1981, Sales Achievement awards, 1980-83), Utah Assn. Realtors, Nat. Assn. Realtors, Ariz. Assn. Realtors, Calif. Assn. Realtors. Home: 440 El Camino Rd Sedona AZ 86336 Office: PO Box HH Sedona AZ 86336

SANDIDGE, KANITA DURICE, communications company executive; b. Cleve., Dec. 2, 1947; d. John Robert Jr. and Virginia Louise (Caldwell) S. AB, Cornell U., 1970; MBA, Case Western Res. U., 1979. Supervisory assignments service ctrs. and installation AT&T, Cleve., 1970-78, chief dept. data processing and acctg., 1979-80; adminstrn. mgr. exec. v.p. staff AT&T, N.Y.C., 1980-83; sales forecasting and analysis mgr. resources planning AT&T, Newark, 1983-86; planning and devel. mgr. material planning and mgmt. AT&T Network Systems, Morristown, N.J., 1986-87; dir. adminstrv. services AT&T Network Systems, Lisle, Ill., 1987—. Mem black exchange program Nat. Urban League, N.Y.C., 1986—. Named Black Achiever in Industry, Harlem YMCA, 1981; recipient Tribute to Women and Industry Achievement award YWCA, 1985. Mem. Nat. Black MBA's, Alliance Black AT&T Mgrs., Am. Mgmt. Assn., Nat. Assn. for Female Execs., NAACP, Beta Alpha Psi. Mem. African Meth. Episcopal Ch. Home: 820 Cardiff Rd Naperville IL 60565 Office: AT&T Network Systems 2600 Warrenville Rd Lisle IL 60532

SANDIN, CAROLINE TOWLEY, county commissioner; b. St. Peter, Minn., Nov. 18, 1915; d. Gabriel Heiberg and Victoria Louise (Almen) Towley; m. Howard Victor Sandin, July 20, 1941; children: Caroline, Howard II, Sarah, Victoria, Catherine, Martha, Elizabeth. Student pub. schs. Comml. instr. S.W. Bell Telephone Co., East St. Louis, Ill., 1941-44; comml. rep. N.W. Bell Telephone Co., Shakopee, Minn., 1939-41; part-time clk. Windmill Art Gallery, Ashland, Wis., 1983—; county commr. Ashland County Bd., 1978—. Pres., founder LWV, Ashland, 1956-60; mem., pres. Bd. Edn., Ashland, 1961-83; mem. bd. regents U. Wis. system, Madison, 1968-77; mem. Ashland Common Council, 1978-86; mem. bd. visitors U. Wis.-Superior, 1978-86, pres., 1983-85; mem. Bay Area Rural Transit Commn., 1978—, v.p., 1978, sec., 1984-88; mem. Family Forum Bd., 1984—, pres. 1986—; chmn. Health and Social Services Com., 1988; mem. Unified Services Bd., 1980—, pres., 1985—; chmn. Luth. Social Services Adv. Council, 1987—. Mem. Bd. Attys. Profl. Responsibility Wis. Supreme Ct. Recipient Disting. Alumni award U. Wis.-Superior, 1977. Named Woman of Yr., C. of C., 1979; Outstanding Citizen of Yr., Chequamegon VFW, 1984. Republican. Lutheran. Home: 703 W 7th St Ashland WI 54806

SANDLER, BERNICE RESNICK, education association executive; b. N.Y.C., Mar. 3, 1928; d. Abraham Hyman and Ivy (Ernst) Resnick; children: Deborah Jo, Emily Maud. BA cum laude, Bklyn. Coll., 1948; MA, CCNY, 1950; EdD, U. Md., 1969; LLD (hon.), Bloomfield Coll., 1973, Hood Coll., 1974, R.I. Coll., 1980, Colby-Sawyer Coll., 1984; LHD (hon.), Grand Valley State Coll., 1974; Dr. Pub. Service (hon.), North Adams State Coll., 1985. Research asst., nursery sch. tchr., employment counselor, adult edn. instr., sec; psychologist HEW, 1970; tchr. psychology Mt. Vernon Coll., 1970; head Action Com. for Fed. Contract Compliance, Women's Equity Action League, 1970-71; edn. specialist U.S. Ho. Reps., Washington, 1970; dep. dir. Womens Action program, HEW, Washington, 1971; dir. project on status and edn. of women Assn. Am. Colls., Washington, 1971—; vis. lectr. U. Md.; adv. bd. Women's Equity Action League Ednl. and Legal Def. Fund, 1980—, trustee, 1974-80, trustee Women's Equity Action League, 1971-78; adv. com. Math/Sci. Network, 1979—, Wider Opportunities for Women, 1978-85, Women's Legal Def. Fund, 1978-84; commn. on women in higher edn. Am. Council Edn., 1981—; adv. bd. N.J. project Inst. for Research on Women Rutgers U., New Brunswick, 1987—, Nat. Council for Alternative Work Patterns Inc., 1978-85, Women's Hdqrs. State Nat. Bank for Women's Appointments, 1977-78, Project on Equal Edn. Rights, 1975-78; mem. continuing com. Internat. Women's Yr. Conf., 1976-78; mem. internat. adv. bd. 2d Internat. Interdisciplinary Congress on Women, 1983-84; mem. steering com. Coalition for Women's Appointments, 1977-78; Md. del. Houston Internat. Women's Yr. Conf., 1976; chairperson Nat. Adv. Council on Women's Ednl. programs, 1975-77, mem., 1977-82; mem. adv. com. econ. role of women Pres.'s Council Econ. Advisors, 1973-76; del. White House Conf. on Families, 1980. Mem. adv. bd. Jour. Reprints Documents Affecting Women, 1976-78, Women's Rights Law Reporter, 1970-80; contbr. articles to profl. jours. Mem. bd. overseers Wellesley Coll. Ctr. for Research on Women, 1975-87; bd. dirs. Ctr. for Women's Policy Studies, 1972—; mem. exec. com. Inst. for Ednl. Leadership, 1982-87, mem. program adv. com., 1987—, chair bd. dirs., 1981, chair adv. com., 1975-81; mem. affirmative action com., task force on family, domestic affairs commn. Am. Jewish Com., 1978—, treas. D.C. chpt., 1971-85; tech. adv. com. Nat. Jewish Family Ctr., 1980—; adv. council Ednl. Devel. Ctr., 1980-85; adv. bd. Urban Inst., 1981-85, Women Employed Inst., 1981-84, Ex-New Yorkers for N.Y., 1978-79; mem. adv. com. Arthur and Elizabeth Schlesinger Library History of Women in Am., 1981-85, Ctr. for Women Scholars, 1979-83; nat. adv. com. Shelter Research Inst., Calif., 1980-82; chair adv. panel project on self-evaluation Am. Insts. for Research, 1980-82; bd. dirs. Equality Ctr., 1983—, Evaluation and Tng. Inst., Calif., 1980—, Inst. for Studies in Equality, 1975-77. Recipient Athena award Intercollegiate Assn. Women Students, 1974, Elizabeth Boyer award Woman's Equity Action League, 1976; co-winner Rockefeller Pub. Service award Princeton U., 1976; named one of 100 Most Powerful Women, Washingtonian Mag., 1982. Mem. Am. Psychol. Assn., Assn. for Women in Sci. Found. (bd. dirs. 1977—), Am. Soc. Profl. and Exec. Women (adv. bd. 1980—). Office: Assn Am Colls 1818 R St NW Washington DC 20009

SANDLES, FAITH MEYER, social worker; b. Albany, N.Y., Apr. 9, 1942; d. Henry Marten and Anita Charlotte (Witte) Meyer; m. Albert Warren Sandles, Oct. 28, 1972; 1 child, Abigail Beth. BA in Psychology, Hartwick Coll., 1964; cert. in gerontology, U. Mich., 1971. Exec. dir. Cohoes (N.Y.) Multi-Serice Sr. Citifzens Ctr., 1967-77; with various offices and depts. State of N.Y., Albany, 1970-84; interior decorator freelance, Albany, 1984—; coordinator sr. companion program OD Heck Devel. Ctr., Schenectady, N.Y., 1986—; bd. dirs., chair various coms. Voluntary Action Ctr., Albany, 1977-83; bd. dirs., officer, chair various com.s Troy-Cohoes YWCA, 1978-84; ofcl. del. White House Conf. Aging. Officer N.Y. Assn. Learning Disabled, Capital Dist. 1976—; co-founder Capital Dist. Parkinsons Support Group, Albany, 1986; bd. dirs., officer, chair various coms. Troy-Cohoes YWCA, 1978-84; vol. Internat. YWCA to Trinidad, Tobago, Barbados and Antigua, 1965. HEW fellow U.S. Dept. Health Edn. and Welfare, 1971. Mem. Nat. Assn. Female Execs. Lutheran. Office: OD Heck Devel Ctr Balltown and Consaul Rds Schenectady NY 12304

SANDORSE-LOVEY, DONNA IRENE, business systems analyst; b. Elizabeth, N.J., Apr. 21, 1957; d. Ronald Patrick and Barbara Irene (Keller) S.; m. Charles J. Lovey, June 14, 1986. BA, Rutger U., 1979; cert. in Teaching, Grad. Sch. of Edn., 1982. Cert. French tchr., N.J. Tchr. French Benedictine Acad., Elizabeth, N.J., 1979-81; supr. escrow dept. Jersey Mortgage Co., Elizabeth, 1982-84; tchr. reading South Plainfield (N.J.) Bd. Edn., 1981-82; asst. v.p. Crestmont Fed. Savs. and Loan, Westfield, N.J., 1984-86, The Ramapo Bank, Wayne, N.J., 1986-87; bus. systems analyst Citicorp, Teaneck, N.J., 1987—. Tchr. sch. Elmora Presbyn. Ch., Elizabeth, 1973-81, youth advisor, 1975-81. Democrat. Office: Citicorp Mortgage Inc Woodcliff Lake NJ 07675

SANDS, BARBARA LEE, golf company executive, outdoor writer; b. N.Y.C., June 28, 1932; d. Jack D. and Hylda A. (Aptheker) Levine; student Hunter Coll., 1949-52; m. Lawrence Sands, Apr. 6, 1968; children—David, Lori, Doria. Mng. editor True Experience Mag., 1968-70; outdoor editor Sporting Guide mag., 1970-71; N.Y. State editor, columnist Outdoor Jour., 1970—; outdoor video news reporter WFMJ-TV; pres. Par-Mate Golf Gloves, 1972—; corp. dir. Jack D. Levine Inc.; freelance writer various nat. outdoor mags. Mem. Outdoor Writers Assn. Am., N.Y. State Outdoor Writers Assn. (Excellence of Craft award for outstanding achievement 1982), Nassau County Outdoor Writers Assn., Mensa. Office: Par-Mate 4 Willow Park Ctr Farmingdale NY 11735

SANDS, KITI, designer, financier, realtor, beauty and health consultant; b. N.J.; d. Frank and Muriel (Kulla) Reiner; m. Jay I. Sands, 1975; children—Nelson Anthony, Tiffany Ivy, Summer Paige. Diploma Wilsey Sch. Design, 1974; student, NYU, 1974. Cert. cosmetologist and esthetician, 1962. Asst. to Monsieur Jacques as dir. of Antoines de Paris; ptnr. Clarendon Capital Group, N.Y., Fla., also dept. mng. dir.; pres. Tiffany Ivy Inc.; pres. Bio Cellular Systems, Inc., 1981; v.p. New Capital Mgmt. Inc.; design and costume cons., N.Y.C., 1974—; propr. Park Ave. Salon, N.Y.C., 1974-81; dir. Bio-Med Acne Ctr., Fla.; commr. of deeds N.Y.C., to 1981; researcher and developer of skin care, coloring processes and formulae, columnist, feature writer and lectr. on Image Creation for the Working Woman, including "Dressing For Your Career". Aquacade swimmer, 1960-62. Recipient Disting. Service citation Indsl. Home for Blind, 1976; Disting. Mem. award City of Hope, 1977, Cert. Achievement for Acad. and Inst. by Clairol; Clairol Certs. of award for Outstanding Color Expertise; Certs. Achievement for Higher Edn. in the Art of Profl. Coloring. Mem. Congress of Colorists, Ind. Cosmetic Mfrs. and Distbrs. Assn.

SANDS, LISA GWYN, sales executive; b. Knoxville, Tenn., Oct. 20, 1961; d. Gerald L. and Mary Gwyn (Stair) S. Student, Vol. State Coll., 1985-88. Lic. real estate broker, Tenn. Store mgr. Chess King/Melville, Knoxville, 1979-81; adminstrv. supr. Command Performance, Knoxville, 1981; with Ect. div. Bruce Alan Assocs., Inc., 1981—; dist. mgr. Ect. div. Bruce Alan Assocs., Inc., Tenn., Ky., Va., Ala., 1985—. Mem. Nat. Assn. Female Execs. Republican. Baptist. Home: 129 3A Cherry Hill Dr Hendersonville TN 37075 Office: Bruce Alan Assocs Inc 21-15 Rosalie St Fair Lawn NJ 07410-3025

SANDSTROM, ALICE WILHELMINA, accountant; b. Seattle, Jan. 6, 1914; d. Andrew William and Agatha Mathilda (Sundius) S. BA, U. Wash., 1934. CPA, Wash. Mgr. office Star Machinery Co., Seattle, 1935-43, Howe & Co., Seattle, 1943-46; pvt. practice acctg., Seattle, 1945—; controller Children's Orthopedic Hosp. and Med. Ctr., Seattle, 1948-75, assoc. adminstr. fin., 1975-81; lectr. U. Wash., Seattle, 1957-72. Mem. Wash. State Title XIX Adv. Com., 1975-82, Wash. State Vendors Rate Adv. Com., 1980-87, Mayor's Task Force for Small Bus., 1981-83; bd. dirs. Seattle YWCA, 1981—, pres., 1986-88; bd. dirs. Sr. Services Seattle/King County, 1985, treas., 1986; bd. dirs. Children's Orthopedic Hosp. Found., 1982—. Fellow Hosp. Fin. Mgmt. Assn. (charter, state pres. 1956-57, nat. treas. 1963-65, Robert H. Reeves Merit award 1970, Frederick T. Muncie award 1985), Wash. State Hosp. Assn. (treas. 1956-70), Am. Soc. Women Accts. (pres. Seattle chpt. 1946-48), Am. Soc. Women CPA's. Club: Women's Univ. (Seattle); City (Seattle). Home and Office: 5725 NE 77th St Seattle WA 98115

SANDSTROM, BODEN C., sound engineer; b. Rochester, N.Y., Sept. 19, 1945; d. Louis Charles and Marion (Gridley) S. BS in English, St. Lawrence U., 1967; AM in Library Sci., U. Mich., 1968; MS in Audio Tech., Am. U., 1984. Librarian San Jose (Calif.) State Coll., 1968-69; head dept. circulation Northeastern U. Library, 1969-72; librarian lit. div. Martin Luther King Library, Washington, 1972-75; owner, operator Woman Sound, Inc., Washington, 1975—; sound engr. Mich. Women's Music Festival, 1977-78, 81-84, Nat. Women's Writers Conf., 1977, Casse Culver tour, 1980, 3d, 4th, 5th and 7th Nat. Women's Music Festivals, West Coast and So. Women's Music and Comedy Festivals, 1981-84, Am. Folk Life Festivals, 1981, 83, Chris Williamson tour, 1982, Lilly Tomlin tour, 1983, Pete Seeger tour; adj. prof. audio-tech. Am. U., Washington; lectr. in field mgr. office Female Liberation, Boston, 1970-72. Asst. rec. engr. for albums by Casse Culver and Sweet Honey in the Rock. N.Y. State Regents scholar, 1963-67. Mem. Audio Engring. Soc., Acoustical Soc. Am., Nat. Assn. Women Bus. Owners, Mortar Bd. Home: 19 Logan Circle A NW Washington DC 20005 Office: PO Box 1932 Washington DC 20013

SANDWEISS, MARTHA A., museum curator, author; b. St. Louis, Mar. 29, 1954; d. Jerome Wesley and Marilyn Joy (Glik) S. BA magna cum laude, Radcliffe Coll., 1975; MA in History, Yale U., 1977, MPhil in History, 1981, PhD, 1985. Smithsonian-Nat. Endowment Humanities fellow, Nat. Portrait Gallery, Washington, 1975-76; curator photographs Amon Carter Mus., Ft. Worth, 1979-86, adj. curator photographs, 1987—. Author: Carlotta Corpron: Designer with Light, 1980, Masterworks of American Photography, 1982, Laura Gilpin: An Enduring Grace, 1986, (catalogue) Pictures from an Expedition: Early Views of the American West, 1979; editor: Historic Texas: A Photographc Portrait, 1986, Contemporary Texas: A Photographc Portrait, 1986, Denizens of the Desert, 1988. Fellow Ctr. for Am. Art and Material Culture, Yale U., 1977-79, Nat. Endowment for the Humanities, 1988. Office: Amon Carter Mus PO Box 2365 Fort Worth TX 76113

SANFORD, BARBARA H., geneticist; b. Brockton, Mass., Oct. 17, 1927; d. Arthur A. and Grace E. (Brennan) Hendrick; div.; children—Arthur, Jane, Brian, Paul. M.A., Brown U., 1960, Ph.D., 1963; D.Sc. (hon.), Bates Coll., 1985. Prin. research assoc. in pathology Med. Sch. Harvard U., Boston, 1963-72, assoc. prof. microbiology Sch. Pub. Health, 1972-73, assoc. prof. pathology, 1978-81; chief br. cancer biology Nat. Cancer Inst., Bethesda, Md., 1973-78; dir. research Dana Farber Cancer Inst., Boston, 1978-81; dir. Jackson Lab., Bar Harbor, Maine, 1981-88, sr. staff scientist emeritus, 1988—. Mem. Genetic Soc. Am., Am. Assn. Immunologists, Am. Assn. Cancer Research. Office: Jackson Lab Bar Harbor ME 04609

SANFORD, ISABEL GWENDOLYN, actress; b. N.Y.C.; d. James Edward and Josephine (Perry) S.; m. William Edward Richmond (dec.); children—Pamela (Mrs. Eddie Ruff), William Eric, Sanford Keith. Ed. pub. schs. Stage appearances in off-Broadway prodns., also in Los Angeles; Broadway appearance in Amen Corner; film appearances include Guess Who's Coming to Dinner, 1968, Pendulum, 1969, Stand Up and Be Counted, 1972, The New Centurions, 1972, Love at First Bite, 1979; appeared in TV film The Great Man's Whiskers, 1973, series All in the Family, numerous guest appearances various series; co-star: TV series The Jeffersons, 1974-85. Mem. Kwanza Found. Address: care MEW Inc 151 N San Vicente Blvd Beverly Hills CA 90211 *

SANFORD, TRACEY ANN, nurse, consultant; b. Bethesda, Md., Oct. 14, 1952; d. Edward Arnold and Beverly (Beals) S. BS in Nursing, U. Oreg., 1975. RN. Staff nurse in gen. surgery and urology Oregon Health Scis. U., Portland, 1975-77, research asst. surg. oncology, 1977-80, asst. head nurse surg. services/operating room, urology/renal transplant, 1980-85; cons. Circon/Am. Cystoscope Makers, Inc., Stamford, Conn., 1985—. Mem. adult support com. Young Life Portland West, 1980-82, 87—. Mem. Am. Urologic Assn. Allied (pres. local chpt. 1984-86), Assn. Operating Room Nurses, Nurse Cons. Assn. Home and Office: 2766 SW Fairview Blvd Portland OR 97201

SANFORD-HARRIS, JUDITH LESLIE, college administrator; b. Boston, Feb. 22, 1953; d. Harvey Franklin and Alice Elizabeth (Taylor) Sanford; m. Joseph Edwin Harris Jr. AB, Brown U., 1974; MEd, Boston Coll., 1976, postgrad. Coordinator community outreach AID program Salem (Mass.) State Coll., 1976-79; counselor Mass. Bay Community Coll., Wellesley, 1979-80; asst. acad. dean Pine Manor Coll., Chestnut Hill, Mass., 1980-84, Bunker Hill Community Coll., Boston, 1984—. Trustee Commonwealth Sch. Alumna, 1983-85; mem. Garrison-Trotter Neighborhood Assn. Named one of Outstanding Young Women Am., 1981, 82, 84, 86. Mem. Nat. Acad. Advising Assn. (jour. editorial bd. 1984—, bd. dirs. 1981-83, 87—), Assn. Black Women in Higher Edn., Nat. Assn. Women Deans, Adminstrs. and Counselors (coll. bd. council on acad. affairs 1986—), Acad. Affairs Adminstrs., Delta Sigma Theta. Club: E. Alice Taylor Community (Boston). Office: Bunker Hill Community Coll New Rutherford Ave Boston MA 02129

SANGER, ELEANOR, television producer, director, writer; b. Hong Kong, Sept. 15, 1929; d. Richard and Lonni (Wernicke) Sanger; m. Robert Nelson Riger, June 10, 1950 (div. July 1981); children—Christopher Robin, Victoria Riger Phillips, Robert Paris, Charlotte Riger Hull; m. Peter Lersch Keys, Feb. 11, 1985. BA magna cum laude, Smith Coll., 1950; postgrad. Russian Inst., Columbia U., 1951-52. Mgr. pub. affairs Sta. WNBC-TV, N.Y.C., 1957-60; writer ABC News, N.Y.C., 1967; mgr. client relations, assoc. producer ABC Sports, N.Y.C., 1966-69, staff producer, writer, dir., 1973—; producer Bobsled and Luge Competition ABC Sports/Winter Olympics, Calgary, Can., 1987-88; producer equestrian events NBC Sports/Summer Olympics, Seoul, Republic of Korea, 1988; freelance producer, writer TV documentaries 1969-70; producer, writer Tomorrow Entertainment, N.Y.C., 1971-73. Producer: Summer Olympic Preview, 1976, Summer Olympics, 1976, 84, Winter Olympics, 1980, Wide World of Sports, 1980, NCAA Football, 1981, The Open Mind, 1958 (Robert E. Sherwood award). Mem. adv. bd. Women's Sports Found. Recipient Emmy award for sports, 1976, for summer Olympics, 1977, 84, for Wide World of Sports, 1980, for winter Olympics, NCAA Football, 1981, cert. Gold Video award Recording Industry Assn. Am., Vira award for best dir. home video, 1985, cert. Gold Video award Rec. Industry Assn. Am., Smith Coll. medal, 1982; named ABC-YWCA Woman Achiever of Yr., 1983. Mem. Acad. TV Arts and Scis., Writers Guild Am. West, Am. Women in Radio and TV, Women in Communication, Dirs. Guild. Am., Phi Beta Kappa. Democrat. Episcopalian.

SANGER, ESTHER REBECCA, social work administrator; b. Lowell, Mass., Nov. 29, 1925; d. George Frederick and Letitia Alethia (Crosby) Hicks; m. H. Leland Sanger, Sept. 25, 1954; children: Donita Evelyn, David Hobart, Heather Jeanne. Cert. in nursing, St. Vincent's Hosp., Bridgeport, Conn., 1948; BA in Social Work, Eastern Nazarene Coll., 1979, MA in Family Counseling, 1982. RN, Conn.; lic. social worker, Mass. Vocat.

trainer South Shore Mental Health Ctr., Quincy, Mass., 1960-62, tutor, instr., 1961-65; instr. spl. needs Northeastern U., Boston, 1960; trainer for group leaders Hyde Park House, Boston, 1970-72; v.p. dir. tng. Christian Weight Control, Inc., Milford, Mass., 1977-78; group leader, counselor ct. adv. DOVE, Inc., Quincy, 1977-78; dir. family services The Salvation Army, Quincy, 1978; exec. dir. Quincy Crisis Ctr., Inc., Quincy, 1979—; pvt. counselor family counseling, Quincy, 1982—. Mem. adv. bd. Familial Alzheimer's Disease Research Found., Tulsa, 1984—, legis. com. Office for Children, 1988—; exec. bd. Quincy Interfaith Sheltering Coalition, Quincy, 1984—; vol. work with elderly Wollaston (Mass.) Neighbors, 1965-70; mem. Quincy Hist. Soc., 1953—; founder, exec. dir. Quincy Crisis Ctr. Hot Line; founder Mary-Martha Learning Ctr., Hingham, Mass., 1987, Food for Families Program, 1980, Street Feeding Program, 1981, Isolated Elder Advocacy Program, 1983, Faith II Shelter, Quincy, 1985. Recipient Outstanding Achievement award, Eastern Nazarene Coll., 1982, Citation of Merit, Gov. Michael Dukakis, 1985, Cert. of Appreciation, Mayor Francis X. McCauley, 1985; named Citizen of Yr. Quincy City Council, 1984 Jewish War Vets. of World War II, 1985, Communicator of Yr. John Graham Pub. Relations, Inc., 1986. Mem. Nat. Assn. Social Workers. Democrat.

SANGSTER, ESTHER VIRGINIA, hospital official, nurse; b. Clermont, Fla., Feb. 2, 1950. B.S. in Nursing, U. North Fla., 1981; M.S. in Nursing, U. South Fla., 1986. Cert. advanced nurse practitioner. Dir. profl. services Upjohn Co., Jacksonville, Fla., 1980-82; dir. organizational devel. Wellness Ctr. Tampa Gen. Hosp., Fla., 1983—. adv. bd. Industry Services, Tampa, Weekend Coll., U. So. Fla.; adv. council Fla. Medicaid Program, Tallahassee; mem. adv. com. Nursing Service Orgn. Mem. Am. Nurses Assn., Fla. Nurses Assn. (chmn. com. continuing edn. 1983—, dir. 1979-82, chmn. legis. com. 1981-83), Am. Soc. Tng. and Devel., Fla. Soc. Health Educators, Am. Mgmt. Assn., LWV, World Futurist Soc., Sigma Theta. Democrat. Avocations: jogging, tennis; scuba diving; skiing. Home: 909 S Fremont Tampa FL 33606 Office: Tampa Gen Hosp Davis Island PO Box 1289 Tampa FL 33601

SAN JUAN, ELAINE JANE, travel executive; b. Manila, Nov. 7, 1954; came to U.S., 1955; d. Eduardo Carrion and Patricia (Parrott) San J. Student, Ariz. State U., U. Guadalajara, Mex. Adviser Gabriel Travel Agy., Campbell, Calif., 1975-77; cons. Alpine Travel/Happi Tours, Saratoga, Calif., 1977-78; sales rep. United Air Lines, San Francisco, 1978-81; gen. mgr. Am. Hawaii Tours, San Francisco, 1984-85; dir., asst. to pres. Am. Hawaii Cruises, San Francisco, 1981-84, 85-86; dir. reservations Royal Viking Lines, San Francisco, 1986—. Mem. Am. Soc. Travel Agts. Democrat. Roman Catholic. Office: Royal Viking Line 750 Battery St San Francisco CA 94111

SANNA, LUCY JEAN, writer; b. Menomonie, Wis., Apr. 20, 1948; d. Charles Albert and Margaret Sheila (McGee) S.; B.A., St. Norbert Coll., 1969; postgrad. U. Wis., Madison, 1970-74; m. Peter Lawrence Frisch, Jan. 2, 1971; 1 dau., Katherine Sanna. Asst. editor Scott Foresman & Co., Glenview, Ill., 1970-73; freelance editor, Palo Alto, Calif., 1973-75; editor FMC Corp., San Jose, Calif., 1975-78; supr. corp. advt. Memorex Corp., Santa Clara, Calif., 1978-79, exec. presentations adminstr., 1979; mgr. communications services Electric Power Research Inst., Palo Alto, 1980-87, exec. speech writer, 1988—. Office: Electric Power Research Inst PO Box 10412 Palo Alto CA 94303

SANNA, MARGARET LAMB, real estate developer; b. Wallingford, Pa., May 22, 1925; d. David and Ethel (Jew) Kilgour; m. Robert Phillip Sanna, May 11, 1946; children: Roberta Lynn, Kimberly Pryde, Douglas David. BA, Pa. State U., 1947; MS, Long Island U., 1965. Chemistry tchr. Great Neck (N.Y.) North Sr. High Sch., 1961-78; sec., treas. RDM Constrn., Inc., Marathon, Fla., 1979-86. Mem. Am. Cancer Soc. James E. Miller scholar, Wallingford, Pa., 1943-47; U.S. Dept. Edn. fellow, 1967-69. Republican. Unitarian. Club: Sombrero Country (Marathon). Home and Office: 118 Mockingbird ln Marathon FL 33050

SANQUIST, NANCY JEAN, computer software specialist, preservationist, architectural historian, educator; b. Muncie, Ind., Aug. 31, 1947; d. Charles Elof and Pauline Lydia (Murphy) S.; m. William Firschein, Aug. 24, 1974 (div. July 1981). BA, UCLA, 1970; MA, Bryn Mawr Coll., 1973; MS, Columbia U., 1978. Instr. Lafayette Coll., Easton, Pa., 1973-74, Muhlenberg Coll., Bethlehem, Pa., 1974-75, Northampton Area Community Coll., Bethlehem, 1974-75; dir. Preservation Office City of Easton, 1977-78; cons. El Pueblo de Los Angeles State Historic Park, 1978-79; dir. restoration Bixby Ranch Co., Long Beach, Calif., 1979-82; mgr. computer applications Cannel-Heumann & Assoc., Los Angeles, 1982-84; dir., specialist Computer-Aided Design Group, Marina del Ray, Calif., 1984—; adj. instr. UCLA, 1979-86, Grad Sch. Calif. State U., Dominguez Hills, 1981. Author numerous tech. manuals. Bd. dirs. Historic Easton, Inc., 1977-78, Simon Rodia's Towers in Watts, Los Angeles, 1979-81, Los Angeles Conservancy, 1982-86, Friends of Schindler House, West Hollywood, Calif., 1978—, pres., 1982-87. Recipient Outstanding Contbn. award Nat. Computer Graphics Assn., 1987. Mem. Internat. Facility Mgmt. Assn. (seminar leader 1987—). Home: 4 Jib St Marina del Rey CA 90292 Office: Computer-Aided Design Group 4215 Glencoe Ave Marina del Rey CA 90292

SANS, JUDITH, cosmetics manufacturing and salon francise executive; b. Hungary, Feb. 13, 1930; came to U.S., 1936; d. Michael Dubosh and Elaina Takache; children—David, Daniel. Ed. Monmouth Coll., 1953. Vice pres. Belmar Motors, from 1951; v.p. sales Magnolia Inn, from 1960; pres. Atlantis Isle of Beauty, Inc., from 1963, Fair Lady, Inc., from 1967; founder, pres. Judith Sans Internationale, Inc., Atlanta, 1968—; dir. skin care Glemby Internat., from 1973; cons. skin care; guest speaker, lectr., worldwide; TV, radio appearances; del. to confer on nutrition, health and diet U.S. Dept. Commerce to Poland and Romania, 1968, to China, 1979, also Egypt and Moscow; dir. tng. seminars Stellenbosch Acad. South Africa, 1980; founder Sans Inst. Internat., Inc., Atlanta, 1982; mem. adv. bd. cosmetologists and aestheticians State of Ga. 1982-83. Columnist Atlanta Women's News, 1984—; author book; featured in newspapers, mags., worldwide; developed products for use in U.S. Winter Olympics, 1980; Pres. Reagan's liaison to pvt. sector for initiative on women bus. owners, 1984; liaison for pvt. sector SBA, 1983; mem. U.S. Commn. on Aging, HHS, 1984—; mem. DeKalb County Communications Com. (Ga.), 1983—; mem. econ. task force com. Ga. Sec. of state 1983-84; mem. bus. adv. com. for mktg. and distributive edn. Ga. State U., Atlanta, 1983-84; chairperson Enterprise Atlanta, 1983—; mem. fundraising com. Atlanta Cancer Soc.; bd. dirs. Women's Bus. Owners Ednl. Council, State of Ga., 1984—. Named Woman Bus. Owner of Yr., 1980, 81; recipient awards various cosmetic cos. Mem. Com. of 200, Atlanta Women Bus. Owners (pres. 1981-82), Committee Internationale de Esthetique et de Cosmetology (founding), Committee Internationale de Esthetique et de Cosmetology pioneer mem. U.S. chpt.), Aestheticians Internat. Assn., South African Inst. Health and Beauty Therapists, KOSMETIK, Internationale de Esthetica Bologna (Italy), Societe les esthetique (Paris), Soc. Aroma Therapy—Herbal Ltd. of Eng., Brit. Confedn. Estheticians, Fashion Group (Atlanta chpt.), Internat. Visitors (Atlanta chpt.), Sigma Pi Epsilon. Clubs: Atlanta Women's Commerce (founder, dir.), One Hundred. Office: Judith Sans Internationale 3853 Oakcliffe Indsl Ct Atlanta GA 30340

SANSBURY, PAMELA ALTMAN, computer supply industry executive; b. Greensboro, N.C., May 1, 1953; d. James Albert and Lila Doris (Farmer) Altman; m. Robert Alan Sansbury, June 5, 1976. BS in Home Econs., Miss. State U.-Starkville, 1974. With buyers tng. program Sanger-Harris, Dallas, 1975-78; saleswoman Sandy Hancock Enterprises, Dallas, 1978-79; dist. mgr. Syncom div. Schwan Sales, Dallas, 1979-82; regional mgr. Wabash DataTech, Inc., Dallas, 1982-85; nat. sales mgr. Perfect Data Corp., 1985-87; regional sales mgr. Philips & DuPont Optical Co., 1988—. Republican. Methodist.

SANSONE, BARBARA LORRAINE, make-up artist; b. Chgo., Apr. 19, 1951; d. John Joseph and Helen (Gaudio) S. BA in Theatre, Loyola U., Chgo., 1973; grad. hair dresser, Pivot Point Sch., Chgo., 1975. Sr. editor Pivot Point Internat. Publications, Chgo., 1975-78; make-up artist Goodman theater, Chgo., 1978-79, Chgo. Lyric Opera, 1979; free-lance make-up artist in Italy, U.K., U.S., 1980-85; free-lance make-up artist Vicki Cole Inc., 1985—; owner make-up dept. Bumble Bumble Hair Salon, 1985—; Beauty cons. various mags.; make-up artist for press models. Mem. Internat. Alliance Theatrical Stage Employees Motion Picture Studio Mechanics Union. Roman Catholic. Home: 31 East 12th St New York NY 10003 Office: Vicki Cole Inc 134 Reade St New York NY 10001

SANSONE, MARLEEN BARBARA, artist, municipal offical; b. Chgo., Nov. 13, 1942; d. Douglas William and Mary (Zaloudek) Hoover; m. John R. Gabriel, Feb. 10, 1963 (div. June 1971); children: David Gabriel, Benjamin Gabriel (dec.), Naomi Gabriel; m. Joseph A. Sansone, Nov. 12, 1974; 1 child, Eva Marie. Student, Sch. Art Inst. Chgo., 1960-62, Albertus Magnus Coll., 1978-80; BA, Charter Oak Coll., 1980; MA, Goddard Coll., 1982; Specialist in Creative Arts, Wesleyan U., 1984. Tchr. arts, crafts Wooster Sq. Creative Arts Workshop, New Haven, Conn., 1970-74; grant-writer United Way of Greater New Haven, 1974-79; exec. dir. Conn. Advs. for the Arts, Hartford, 1979-86, Cultural Arts Council East Haven, 1980—; tchr. art The Hammonasset Sch., Madison, Conn., 1987—. Exhibited in group shows at N.H. Colony Hist. Soc., 1985, Real Artways Artworks Gallery, Hartford, Randolph St. Gallery, Chgo.; executed murals Park City Hosp., Bridgeport, Conn., numerous other locations; contbr. articles to profl. jours. Cons. Arts Council Greater New Haven, 1980-83, New Haven Found., 1980-83. Recipient numerous prizes and awards at juried art shows in Conn. Mem. Women's Caucus for Art (pres. Conn. chpt. 1984-87), East Haven Arts Council (pres. 1977-82), Shoreline Alliance for the Arts (bd. dirs.). Democrat. Roman Catholic. Home: 43 Maltby Ave West Haven CT 06516 Office: Cultural Arts Council East Haven At the Trolley Trolley Sq East Haven CT 06512

SANSONE, RITA MARIA, communications consultant, scriptwriter; b. Hammond, Ind., Mar. 17, 1950; d. Frank Lawrence and Sophie Theresa (Muha) S.; m. Alvin Loehr Beales, Apr. 9, 1988. BS in Music, Radio-TV, Ind. U., 1972. Camera operator, floor mgr. Sta. WTTV-TV, Bloomington, Ind., 1972; audiovisual dir. Amoco Oil Corp., Chgo., 1973-77; pub. relations media ctr. mgr. AT&T Communications, Cin., 1977-84; dir. communications Kettering Med. Ctr., Dayton, Ohio, 1984; sales and mktg. mgr. VideoStar Connections, Inc., Atlanta, 1985; pvt. practice communications cons. Atlanta, 1984—; sales and mktg. dir. 4th Street Prodns., Atlanta, 1985. Sec. South Commons Music Theatre, Chgo., 1973; pres. Ch. council 2d Unitarian Ch., Chgo., 1977; sr. leader Girl Scouts U.S., Cin., 1978; vol. Children's Hosp., Cin., 1982; vol. for Battered Womens Hotline and Speakers Bur. Cobb County YWCA, Marietta, Ga., 1987. Mem. Internat. TV Assn. (local chpt. sec. 1975-77, bd. dirs. 1987-88, nat. sec. 1978-79, v.p. 1980, nat. pres.-elect 1981, seminar speaker 1981—, nat. pres. 1982-83, bd. dirs. 1985), Aircraft Owners And Pilots Assn. Home and Office: 101 Keith Ln Kennesaw GA 30144

SAN SOUCIE, PATRICIA MOLM, artist, educator; b. Mpls., Nov. 4, 1931; d. Ralph Frederick and Evangeline Mary (Nusbaum) Molm; m. Robert Louis San Soucie, Sept. 5, 1953; children: Richard Peter, Marc David, Mary Frances. BS in Applied Arts, U. Wis., 1953. Chmn. juror selection St. Louis Artists Guild, 1968-70; exhibition chmn. Summit (N.J.) Art Ctr., 1973-76, instr. watercolor, 1981—; v.p., bd. dirs. N.J. Watercolor Soc., Neptune, N.J., 1986-88, pres., 1988—; guest lectr. St. Louis Bd. Edn., 1970—; freelance watercolor painter, 1970—. Contbr. paintings Master-Class in Watercolor, 1975. Recipient Watercolor Purchase award Springfield (Mo.) Art Mus. Travel Exhbn., 1974, Taiwan Mus. Fine Arts, 1986, Chateau de Tours, Tours, France, 1987, Butler Inst. Fine Arts Midyear, 1985. Mem. Nat. Assn. Women Artists, Nat. Watercolor Soc., Watercolor USA Honor Soc., N.J. Watercolor Soc. Roman Catholic. Home: 68 Dortmunder Dr Manalpan NJ 07726

SANTA CRUZ, ALEXANDRA ERMELINDA, international sales company executive; b. Buenos Aires, Feb. 26, 1948; came to U.S., 1961.; d. Aquiles and Alejandra Teresa (Salotto) S.C.. AA, Mo. Western Jr. Coll., 1968; BA in Psychology, Mo. Western State Coll., 1973. Export sec. Boehringer Ingelheim Animal Health Inc., St. Joseph, Mo., 1974-76; coordinator export sales Boehringer Ingelheim Animal Health Inc., St. Joseph, 1976-78, mgr. internat. sales, 1978-85, dir. internat. sales, 1985—, coordinator new product devel., 1986—. Mem. nominating com. St. Joseph YWCA, 1983—. Mem. Pres.'s Dist. Export Council, Animal Health Inst. Internat., St. Joseph Women's Career Network (founder, past pres.), Mo. Western State Coll. Alumni Assn. (bd. dirs. 1984—, Disting. Alumni 1984). Republican. Roman Catholic. Office: Boehringer Ingelheim AHI 2621 N Belt Hwy Saint Joseph MO 64502

SANT'AMBROGIO, FRANCA BRAMBILLA, physiologist, educator; b. Milano, Italy, Nov. 8, 1935; d. Bruno and Amelia (Ricci) Brambilla; m. Giuseppe Sant'Ambrogio, Aug. 30, 1958; children: Paolo, Giorgio, Sara. D in Natural Scis. cum laude, Universita' degli Studi di Milano, 1975; PhD, U. Tex., 1981. Instr. research med. br. U. Tex., Galveston, 1983—. Author: (with others) chpt. Techniques in The Life of Science, 1984, Contemporary Sensory Neurobiology, 1985. Jeane B. Kempner fellow, 1984. Mem. Societa' Italiana di Fisiologia, Am. Physiol. Soc. (Travel award 1983), N.Y. Acad. of Scis. Office: U Tex Med Br Dept Physiology and Biophysics Galveston TX 77550

SANTANDREA, MARY FRANCES, lawyer; b. Melrose Park, Ill., Apr. 14, 1952; d. Francis Paul and Agnes Rose (Franch) S. B.A. (James scholar), U. Ill.-Urbana, 1974, M.A., 1976; J.D. cum laude, Santa Barbara Coll. Law, 1982. Bar: Calif. 1982, U.S. Dist. Ct. (cen. dist.) Calif. 1982, U.S. Dist. Ct. (no., so., ea. dists.) Calif., 1985, U.S. Ct. Appeals (9th cir.) 1982. Legal researcher Cavalletto, Webster, Mullen & McCaughey, Santa Barbara, Calif., 1979-80; legal researcher M.J. Treman, Santa Barbara, 1980-81; legal researcher Bargiel & Carlson, Santa Barbara, 1981-82; research atty. Halde, Thomas, Kallman & Hulse, Santa Barbara, 1982-83; litigation atty. Anderson & Geller, Santa Ana, Calif., 1983-85, Ambrosi & Lavoie 1985-86, Smith & Smith, Costa Mesa, Calif., 1986—. Mem. ABA, Calif. Bar Assn., Los Angeles County Bar Assn., Orange County Bar Assn. Democrat. Roman Catholic. Office: Smith & Smith 888 S Figueroa St Los Angeles CA 90017

SANTANIELLO-BURIEL, BONITA JOAN, Romance languages educator; b. Port Washington, N.Y., Mar. 29, 1943; d. C. Theodore and Blanche Rina (De Meo) Santaniello; m. Juan Heriberto Buriel-Lopez, Mar. 18, 1943. BA, Adelphi U., 1964; MA, NYU in Spain, Madrid, 1965; postgrad., NYU, 1965-73. Tchr. Port Washington High Sch., 1963-64; instr. Spanish lit. Ohio Wesleyan U., Dela., 1965-67; assoc. prof. Nassau Community Coll., Garden City, N.Y., 1967—. Mem. Am. Assn. Tchrs. Spanish and Portuguese (sec. L.I. chpt. 1967-72), Am. Assn. Italian Tchrs., Italy Am. Soc. Republican. Roman Catholic. Office: Nassau Community Coll Stewart Ave Garden City NY 11530

SANTAROSSA, LAURETTA MARIA, publishing representative; b. Casarsa, Pordenone, Italy, Feb. 25, 1952; arrived in Can., 1956; d. Odorino Giuseppe and Antonietta (Pippo) S. BA, U. Toronto, 1981. Staff worker Madonna House Apostolate, Combermere, Ont., Can., 1972-80; arts and media editor, bus. mgr. Cath. New Times, Toronto, 1982-87; pub. rep. Novalis Publs., Ottawa and Oakville, Ont., 1987—; treas. Can. Ch. Press, Toronto, 1982—; cons. various religious periodicals, Toronto, 1984—. Contbr. articles, media revs. to mags. Roman Catholic. Office: Novalis, PO Box 998, 1380 Steers Rd Unit 6, Oakville, ON Canada L6J 5E8

SANTELL, ROBERTA, political worker; b. Los Angeles, July 23, 1937; d. Hyman and Sue (Fields) Thompson; m. Richard Alfred Santell, June 17, 1956; children: Mitchell James, Lisa Gaye. Student, Los Angeles City Coll., 1955-56. Sec. criminal div. Office of Los Angeles County Clk., 1955, CBS-TV, Los Angeles, 1956. Exec. bd. Covina Valley Fair Housing Council, 1969-70; co-organizer Police Community Relations Bd., La Puente area, 1970; mem. Los Angeles County Dem. Cen. Com., 1976—, assembly dist. chair, regional vice-chair, 1978—, exec. vice chair, 1987—; mem. Calif. State Cen. Com., 1978—, exec. bd., 1981—, co-chair credentials com., 1984—; del., mem. credentials com. Dem. Nat. Conv., 1980, temp. mem. credentials com., 1988; del. Nat. Midterm Conv., 1982; mem. community relations com. Jewish Fedn. Council of Greater Los Angeles, Eastern Region, 1984—. Recipient Dem. Women of Yr. award, 1971-72, Los Angeles County Cen. Com. Dem. of Yr. award, 1980. Jewish. Home: 336 S Barranca St West Covina CA 91791

SANTELLA, CAROL ANN, public image consultant; b. Pitts., July 26, 1954; d. Amico and Mary (Pronesti) S. BA in Psychology, Spl. Edn., U. Dayton, 1977. Lic. caterer, Pa. Head hostess TGI Fridays, Dayton, Ohio, 1977; asst. mgr. La Cité Restaurant and Lounge, Pitts., 1979-81; owner, operator Broadway Internat. Co., Pitts., 1981-85, Tres Bon Catering, Pitts., 1981-85; mgr. pub. relations and mktg. Gaymar Co., Pitts., 1985-86; owner, operator G&S Prodns., Pitts., 1987—. Mem. Nat. Restaurant Assn., Nat. Assn. Female Execs., Nat. Specialty Merchandisers Assn., Am. Entrepreneurs Assn. Roman Catholic.

SANTIAGO, ELIZABETH ROSARIO, educator; b. San Juan, P.R.; d. Juan Rosario and Paula Cirino; m. Felix Santiago, Aug. 21, 1965; 1 child, Daniel. BS in Edn., Temple U., 1973, MEd, 1974, cert., 1985. Cert. elem. prin. Sec. Sch. Dist. Phila., 1969-70; tchr. Pa. Potter Thomas Sch., Phila., 1970—. Mem. Women in Edn., Nat. Assn. Female Execs., Phila. Alliance Teaching Humanities in Schs. Republican. Pentecostal.

SANTIAGO, ESMERALDA, small business owner; b. San Juan, May 17, 1948; d. Pablo Santiago Diaz and Ramona Santiago; m. Frank Cantor, June 11, 1978; children: Lucas David, Ila. AB, Harvard U., 1976. Bilingual sec. ACCION/AITEC, Cambridge, Mass., 1974-76; producer H/M Multi Media Co., Boston, 1975-76; pres. Cantomedia Corp., Boston, 1977—; advisor Mass. Film Bur., Boston, 1984—, Mass. Cultural Alliance, Boston, 1986—; apptd. mem. Mass. Small Bus. Adv. Council, Boston, 1985—. Author: (film) Beverly Hills Supper Club Fire, 1980 (Silver award 1981), Button, Button, 1982; mem. adv. bd. Radcliffe Quarterly, 1986—; author short stories. Past trustee Thompson Island Edn. Ctr.; bd. dirs. Alianza Hispana, Roxbury, Mass., 1986—; mem. Norfolk County Human Rights Council. Recipient Silver award Internat. Film and TV Festival, N.Y., 1980, Gold award Houston Internat. Film Festival, 1984. Mem. Assn. Latin Ams. in Communications, Nat. Network Hispanic Women, Nat. Conf. Puerto Rican Women, Women in Film and Video, Ea. Region Writer's Guild of Am., New England Minority Purchasing Council, Nat. Hispanic C. of C. Clubs: Harvard, Radcliffe (Boston). Home: 241 North St Hingham MA 02043 Office: Cantomedia Corp 132 Lincoln St Boston MA 02111

SANTIAGO, GLORIA BONILLA, social work educator; b. P.R., Jan. 17, 1954; d. Pedro Bonill and Nuncia Rodriguez; m. Alfredo Santiago, Aug. 13, 1983. BA in Polit. Sci., Glassboro (N.J.) State Coll., 1976; M in Social Work Adminstrn., Rutgers U., 1978; MA in Philosophy, PhD in Sociology, CUNY, 1986. Cert. social worker. Dir. youth services CAmden (N.J.) Adminstrn., 1979-81; asst. dir. ednl. opportunity fund Rutgers U., Camden, 1981-83, dir. Hispanic affairs, adj. social worker, 1983-86, asst. prof. grad. social work, 1986—; cons. Salem (N.J.) Community Coll., 1986-87, Jersey City State U., 1987, Nat. Puerto Rican Coalition, 1987. Author Puerto Rican Migrant Farm Workers: The New Jersey Experience, 1987. Mem. Camden County Commn. on Women, 1983—, Commn. to Study Sex Discrimination in the Statutes, Trenton, N.J., 1985—; chmn. Hispanic Women Task Force N.J., Trenton, 1986—; bd. dirs. Camden Pub. Library, 1985—, Camden County Heritage and Acts Orgn., 1986—, Camden County Cultural and Heritage Commn., 1986—. Recipient Outstanding Women Acheivement award Girl Scouts U.S., 1983, Outstanding Women Leadership award Puerto Rican Congress N.J., 1984, Puerto Rican Cemi award Puerto Rican Congress N.J., 1986, Unity and Spirit award N.J. Div. on Civil Rights, 1986, Women Outstanding Acheivement and Role award Girl Scouts U.S., 1987. Mem. Am. Sociol. Assn., Am. Pub. Welfare Assn., Hispanic Assn. Higher Edn. (Scholarly Acheivement award 1986). Democrat. Home: 401 the Woods Cherry Hill NJ 08034 Office: Rutgers U 327 Cooper St Grad Sch Social Work Camden NJ 08103

SANTIAGO-DAVIE, MELODY, photographer; b. St. Albans, N.Y., July 13, 1953; d. Alfred Juan and Joan Rudy (Parker) S.; m. Hillary McKenzie Davie Jr., June 24, 1977. AS, Nassau Community Coll., 1979; BA in Fine Arts, C.W. Post Coll., 1982. Mgr. Miss Ann's Boutique, Roslyn, N.Y., 1970; sec. Urban Renewal Program, Roslyn, 1971; flight attendent United Air Lines, Chgo., 1973—; sec. Judick Broadcasting Co., N.Y.C., 1974; tchr. East Elmhurst (N.Y.) Day Care Ctr., 1978; tchr. substitute Uniondale (N.Y.) Sch. Dist., 1983. Exhibited in group shows at Nassau Community Coll., 1979, Fredrick Douglas Democratic Club, 1981, C.W. Post Coll., 1981, Wantagh Pub. Library, 1979. Mem. Assn. Flight Attendents, Black Profl. Orgn., Nat. Rainbow Coalition Inc., NAACP. Democrat. Roman Catholic. Home: 20 Fifth Ave Brentwood NY 11717 Office: United Air Lines PO Box 66100 Chicago IL 60666

SANTILLO, JOANN MARIE, controller; b. Inwood, N.Y., Dec. 28, 1953; d. Joseph Francis and Alfredina (DeMichael) S.; m. Stephen I. Piccininni, Aug. 25, 1975. BS, SUNY, Binghamton, 1975. CPA, N.Y. From staff to sr. acct. Ernst & Whinney, N.Y.C., 1975-78; sr. supr. Coopers & Lybrand, N.Y.C., 1978-80; dist. mgr. AT&T, N.Y.C., 1981-85; controller, resident v.p. Citicorp Finanziaria S.P.A., Milan, 1985—. Mem. Am. Inst. CPA's, N.Y. State Soc. CPA's, Am. Women's Soc. CPA's, Nat. Assn. Accts., Nat. Assn. Female Execs. Republican. Roman Catholic.

SANTO, NANCY, bank executive; b. N.Y.C., Sept. 14, 1928; d. Ascenzio and Maria (Amodeo) S. Student, Am. Inst. Banking, N.Y.C., 1984. Typist Mfrs. Hanover Trust Co., N.Y.C., 1946-53, sec., 1953-60, asst. mgr., 1960-68, asst. sec., 1968-77, asst. v.p., 1977-84, v.p., 1984—. Mem. Nat. Assn. Bank Women (pres. 1984-85, adv. bd. 1985—), Mfrs. Hanover Trust Co. Quarter Century Club (pres. 1987—). Roman Catholic. Home: 3B Village Mall Jamesburg NJ 08831 Office: Mfrs Hanover Trust 270 Park Ave New York NY 10017

SANTONA, GLORIA, lawyer; b. Gary, Ind., June 10, 1950; d. Ray and Elvira (Cambeses) S.; m. Douglas Lee Frazier, Apr. 12, 1980. BS in Biochemistry, Mich. State U., 1971; JD, U. Mich., 1977. Bar: Ill. 1977. Atty. McDonald's Corp., Oak Brook, Ill., 1977-82, dir. staff, 1982-86, dir. home office, 1986—, sr. corp. atty., 1982-87, asst. gen. counsel, 1987—. Mem. ABA, Ill. Bar Assn., Chgo. Bar Assn., Am. Corp. Counsel Assn. Office: McDonalds Corp 1 McDonald Plaza Oak Brook IL 60521

SANTORO, KAREN ANN, accounting executive; b. White Plains, N.Y., Nov. 21, 1954; d. Ernest Daniel and Dorothy Joyce (Wilson) S. Grad., Good Counsel Acad., White Plains, N.Y., 1972. Sec. Owens-Corning Fiberglas Corp., Scarsdale, N.Y., 1973-74; acctg. exec. Lawn Masters Inc., Hawthorne, N.Y., 1977-78; adminstrv. asst. to exec. v.p. Star Case Co. Inc., Pleasantville, N.Y., 1978-80; controller Frank Boufford Co. Inc., Bedford, N.Y., 1980-81; owner, pres. Santoro Office Service Inc., White Plains, N.Y., 1981—. Office: S O S Inc 200 Hamilton Ave White Plains NY 10601

SANTORO, PAMELA LYNNE, automobile salesperson; b. Flint, Mich., July 6, 1959; d. Joseph Anthony and Mary Katherine (Phillips) S.; m. Richard Kenneth Haynes, May 9, 1987. BA in Zoology, Bus., Olivet Nazarene Coll., 1983. Sales rep. Ct. St. Ford, Inc., Kankakee, Ill., 1983-84; mgr. rental and lease Ct. St. Ford, Inc., Kankakee, 1984-85; asst. sales mgr. Al Piemonte Ford Sales, Arlington Heights, Ill., 1985—; cons. Women in Bus. Careers, Chgo., 1983—; com. mem. Million Mile Test Drive, Ford Motor Co., Dearborn, Mich., 1984, New Product Devel. Ford Motor Co., Dearborn, 1987—. Mem. Olivet Nazarene Coll. Alumni Assn., Nat. Assn. Female Execs. Republican. Nazarene. Home: 7027 E Wilson Terr Morton Grove IL 60053 Office: Al Piemonte Ford 801 W Dundee Arlington Heights IL 60004

SANTORO, SUSAN ELAINE, hospital executive; b. White Plains, N.Y., Dec. 13, 1952; d. Edward Joseph and Mary Anne (Pennelle) S. BA, Boston Coll., 1974; MBA, Iona Coll., 1978, postgrad., 1981. Asst. to exec. dir. Bellevue Hosp. Ctr. N.Y.C. Health and Hosp. Corp., 1980-84, asst. to chief fin. officer, 1984-87; asst. v.p. Lenox Hill Hosp., N.Y.C., 1987—. Mem. Health Care Fin. Mgmt. Assn., Diagnostic Related Group Assn., Fieri. Roman Catholic. Home: 100 East 77th St New York NY 10594

SANTOSCOY, RONNA ROWLETTE, industrial relations specialist; b. Chickasha, Okla., July 26, 1942; d. Ivan Lee and Mona (Sims-Smith) Rowlette; m. Gilbert S. Santoscoy, Mar. 2, 1962; children: Susan Santoscoy Goldschmidt, Gilbert Gregory, Deirdre. BS, Friends U., Wichita, Kans., 1986; postgrad., Union Grad. Sch., Cin., 1987. Research asst. Sch.

Medicine, Emory U., Atlanta, 1962-63, Rochester (Minn.) Meth. Hosp., 1967-68; program dir. Epilepsy Kans., Inc., Wichita, 1986-87; cons. human resource devel. Wichita, 1987—; intern social policy Nat. Office Psychologists for Social Responsibility, Washington; lectr., cons. community devel. Baha'i Faith, 1977—. Mem. St. Francis Med. Aux., Wichita, 1969—, Mayor's Task Force on Drug Abuse, Wichita, 1976-77, Peace Links, 1985—; mem. adv. bd. Inst. Logopedics, Wichita, 1970-72; mem. aux. bd. Baha'i Faith, Wilmette, Ill., 1977—; bd. dirs. Inter-Faith Ministries, Wichita, 1985—; mem. organizing com. World Inst. Cooperation, Kans., 1986—. Home: 434 N Belmont Wichita KS 67208 Office: Nat Office Psychologists Social Responsibility 1841 Columbia Rd NW Suite 209 Washington DC 20009

SANTRY, BARBARA LEA, securities analyst and investment banker; b. Key West, Fla., Jan. 20, 1948; d. Jere Joseph and Frances Victoria (Appel) S. BS in Nursing, Georgetown U., 1969; MBA, Stanford U., 1978. Enlisted USN, 1969, advanced through grades to lt., 1971, resigned, 1972; program analyst, br. chief U.S. Dept. HEW, Washington, 1973-76; mgr. cons. div. Arthur Andersen and Co., San Francisco, 1978-80; asst. v.p. Am. Med. Internat., Washington, 1980-83; v.p. Alex Brown and Sons, Inc., Balt., 1983-86; ptnr. Wessels, Arnold and Henderson, Mpls., 1986-88; v.p. Dain Bosworth Inc., Mpls., 1988—. Home: 2521 Princeton Ct Saint Louis Park MN 55416

SAO, MARIA DA CONCEICAO, fashion designer; b. Evora, Portugal, Apr. 27, 1946; came to U.S., 1974; d. Manuel Mendes and Diamantina Maria (Sequeira) Ginja; 1 child Andre Gustav Sa. m. Georg Bo Andresen, June 11, 1964 (div. 1976); m. John Patrick Heininger, Aug. 24, 1976 (div. 1987); student, Nairobi, Kenya, 1972-74. Artist/designer, Aarhus, Denmark, 1964-71; owner/designer Sao's Studio, Washington, 1975-84; pres. SAO Ltd., N.Y.C., 1983—; exhibitor/lectr. Corcoran Gallery, Washington, 1980, Smithsonian Inst., Washington, 1975-83, Textile Mus., Washington, 1979, R.I. Sch. Design, Providence, 1981, Am. Ctr. Arts, Paris, 1981. Author: Wearable Art, 1979; also articles and catalogues. Nat. Endowment Arts grantee, 1981; D.C. Commn. Arts fellow, 1981; recipient Design award Woman in Design Internat., 1981. Roman Catholic. Avocations: horseback riding, exercise. Office: SAO Ltd 202 W 40th St Sute 1201 New York NY 10018

SAPINSLEY, LILA MANFIELD, state official; b. Chgo., Sept. 9, 1922; d. Jacob and Doris (Silverman) Manfield; B.A., Wellesley Coll., 1944; D. Pub. Service, U. R.I., 1971; D.Pedagogy, R.I. Coll., 1973; m. John M. Sapinsley, Dec. 23, 1942; children—Jill Sapinsley Mooney, Carol Sapinsley Rubenstein, Joan Sapinsley Lewis, Patricia Sapinsley Levy. Mem. R.I. Senate, 1972-84, minority leader, 1974-84; dir. R.I. Dept. Community Affairs, 1985; chmn. R.I. Housing and Mortgage Fin. Corp., 1985-87; Commr. R.I. Pub. Utilities Commn., 1987—. Mem. R.I. Gov.'s Commn. on Women; commr. Edn. Commn. of States; pres. bd. trustees Butler Hosp., 1978-84; trustee R.I. State Colls., 1965-70, chmn., 1967-70; trustee U. R.I., R.I. Coll. Found.; bd. dirs. Miriam Hosp., Hamilton House, Trinity Repertory Co., Lincoln Sch., Wellesley Center for Research on Women, 1980. Recipient Alumnae Achievement award Wellesley Coll., 1974; Outstanding Legislator of Yr. award Republican Nat. Legislators Assn., 1984. Republican. Jewish. Home: 25 Cooke St Providence RI 02906

SAPON, PAULA JO, school psychologist, consultant; b. Wheeling, W.Va., Apr. 30, 1950; d. John and Helen Elvira (Clemente) S. BA in Psychology magna cum laude, UCLA, 1972, MA in Ednl. Psychology, 1975, PhD in Ednl. Psychology, 1982; MA in Spl. Edn., Calif. State U., Northridge, 1973, MA in Psychology, 1981. Cert. sch. psychologist; cert. community coll. instr.; registered psychol. asst. Remedial tutor Fernald Sch., Los Angeles, 1971-74; pvt. practice ednl. therapy Encino, Calif., 1973—; lectr., instr. Calif. State U., Northridge, 1979-84; psychol. asst. Clin. and Cons. Assocs., Encino, 1985—; sch. psychologist Ednl. Resource and Services Ctr., Culver City, Calif., 1981—; teaching asst. UCLA, 1975-77; psychol. cons. Head Start, Compton, Calif., 1978. Mem. Am. Assn. for Counseling and Devel., Down Syndrome Parents Group, UCLA Masters and Credential Alumni Assn. Democrat. Club: West Valley Bruins. Office: Ednl Resource & Services Ctr 10101 W Jefferson Blvd Culver City CA 90232

SAPP, BARBARA DIANE, data process executive, realtor; b. Wenatchee, Wash., Nov. 27, 1940; d. John Franklin and Dorothy Doris (Kelsay) Cool; m. Leroy Sapp, Dec. 12, 1959 (div. 1975); children: Michael, Patrick, Stephen. BSBA, U. Redlands, 1979. Tape clk. GTE Data Services, Marina del Rey, Calif., 1975-76, IM-programmer, 1976-77, IM-programmer analyst, 1977-79, IM-systems analyst, 1979-80, IM-sr. tech. analyst, 1980-81; IM-supr. data resource mgmt. Gen. Telephone, Marina Del Rey, 1981-87; IM supr. tech. support systems, 1987—; GTE Calif., Thousand Oaks, Calif. Mem., organizer Conejo Valley Community Ctrs., Newbury Park, Calif., 1976 (council rep. 1988-89). Mem. Gen. Telephone Good Govt. Club, C.S.V.C. (pres. 1988—), Beta Sigma Phi (pres. 1974-75, 87-88, council pres. 1988—), Lambda Omega (preceptor, pres. 1987-88, ways and means 1988-89). Republican. Methodist. Avocations: flying, backpacking. Home: 3441 Frankie Dr Newbury Park CA 91320 Office: GTE of Calif 112 Lakeview Canyon Rd Thousand Oaks CA 91362

SAPP, SHARON ANN, analyst, designer; b. Phila., May 26, 1952; d. Roland Robert and Nedra Lorena (Schleig) Cecconi; m. James Alfred Sapp Jr., Aug. 28, 1976. Student, Montgomery County Community Coll., 1970-77. Gen. clk. Bell of Pa., Conshohocken, 1970-71; sr. clk. Bell of Pa., Conshohocken, 1971; service rep., analyst Bell of Pa., Norristown and Phila., 1971-75; dist. sec. Bell of Pa., Norristown, 1975-76; supr. Bell of Pa., King of Prussia, 1976-77; programmer, designer AT&T, Somerset (N.J.) and Phila., 1977-84; analyst, designer AT&T, Somerset, 1984—. Mem. Nat. Assn. Female Execs. Democrat. Roman Catholic. Home: 26 Sunset Rd Limerick PA 19468 Office: AT&T Bell Labs 100 Atrium Dr Somerset NJ 08873

SAPPENFIELD, DIANE HASTINGS, real estate executive, civic worker; b. Marion, Ohio, Apr. 22, 1940; d. Edgar Dean and Marguerite Elizabeth (Alexander) Hastings; B.A. in Sociology and Econs., Mills Coll., 1962; tchr.'s cert. Calif. State U., Los Angeles, 1963; M.S. in Fin. and Real Estate, Am. U., 1986; m. Ronald Eugene Sappenfield, July 6, 1962; children—Derek Ronald, Ann Elizabeth. Tchr. elem. sch., El Segundo, Calif., 1963-66; asst. dir. admissions Mills Coll., 1972-74; v.p., dir. DDA Assos., Inc., McLean, Va., 1978-87; real estate investment cons., Shannon and Luchs, Washington, 1987—; asst. to chmn. bd. Watergate Complex, Washington, 1979-81; dir. corp. mktg. Watergate Devel. Inc., McLean, 1981-82. Vol. tchr. Saugatuck Elem. Sch., Westport, Conn., 1976-79; active benefits for Corcoran Sch. Art, Nat. Symphony Orch., Women's Bd. Am. Heart Assn., Hope Ball, Meridian House, Washington; bd. dirs. Westport-Weston Arts Council, 1973-79, Young Concert Artists, 1984—; mem. Levitt Pavilion Governing Com., 1974-79; pres. Friends of Levitt Pavilion, 1977; trustee Stauffer-Westport Fund, 1976-79; mem. Westport Young Woman's League, 1969-79, pres., 1975-76; bd. dirs. Stamford-Norwalk br. Jr. League, 1977-78. Mem. Washington Bd. Realtors, Mills Coll. Club N.Y., Washington Jr. League. Home: 7612 Georgetown Pike McLean VA 22102

SARAFIAN, SYLVIA ANNETTE, computer systems specialist; b. Newton, Mass., June 16, 1931; d. Antranig Arakel and Elizabeth (Zorian) S.; B.A., Mt. Holyoke Coll., 1953. Chemist, Mass. Meml. Hosps., Boston, 1953-56; programmer, Honeywell Inc., Newton, Mass., 1956-58, System Devel. Corp., Santa Monica, Calif., 1958-61, Bedford, Mass., 1961-64, computer systems specialist, Santa Monica, 1966-71; programmer Bolt, Benarek & Newman, Cambridge, Mass., 1964-66; owner COMPUFARM and The Aurora, Marina Del Rey, Calif., 1971—, Advanced Bus. Microsystems, Marina Del Rey, 1981—; speaker symposium on computers in agr.; participant programs in field. Asso. mem. Calif. Republican State Central Com., 1975-76, 78; bd. dirs. Marina Rep. Club, 1982; mem. Dornan for Congress campaign, 1976, 78, 80; active Calif. Women for Agr., 1977-79. Mem. Armenian Apostolic Church. Club: Appalachian Mountain. Author CompuFARM, computer system for agr., written for time-sharing, 1971, for microcomputers, 1981; author: The Aurora, written for time-sharing, 1977, for microcomputers, 1982; prodn. asst. for TV show Face to Face, 1976. Home: 519 Lantana St #138 Camarillo CA 93010 Office: PO Box 1909 Camarillo CA 93011

SARALEGUI, CRISTINA MARIA, magazine editor; b. Havana, Cuba, Jan. 29, 1948; came to U.S., 1960; d. Francisco and Cristina (Santamarina) S.; m. Marcos Avila, June 9, 1984; children: Cristina Amalia, Jon Marcos. Student mass communications U. Miami. Features editor Vanidades Continental, Miami, Fla., 1970-73; editor Cosmpolitan Spanish, Miami, 1973-76, editor-in-chief, 1979—; dir. entertainment Miami Herald, 1976-77; editor-in-chief Intimidades mag., Miami, 1977-79, TV y Novelas mag., 1986—. Featured in bestseller Latin Beauty, 1982; keynote speaker Union Am. Women, P.R., 1981, Lgendary Women of Miami. Mem. internat. jury Miss Venezuela Pagent, 1982, Miss Columbia Pagent, 1987. Recipient Keys to City Cartagena, Colombia, 1987. Mem. Women in Communications (keynote speaker 1986), Am. Soc. Profl. and Exec. Women, Nat. Assn. Female Execs., Am. Mgmt. Assn., Nat. Network Hispanic Women (Corp. Leader award), Latin Bus. and Profl. Women's Club. Republican. Roman Catholic. Club: Jockey (Miami). Office: Editorial America SA 6355 NW 36th St Virginia Gardens FL 33166

SARANDON, SUSAN ABIGAIL, actress; b. N.Y.C., Oct. 4, 1946; d. Phillip Leslie and Lenora Marie (Criscione) Tomalin; m. Chris Sarandon, Sept. 16, 1967 (div.); 1 child, Eva Maria Livia Amurri. B.A. in Drama and English, Cath. U. Am., 1968. Actress (plays) including A Coupla White Chicks Sittin' Around Talkin', An Evening with Richard Nixon, A Stroll in the Air, Albert's Bridge, Private Ear, Public Eye, Extremities, (films) including Joe, 1970, Lady Liberty, 1971, The Rocky Horror Picture Show, 1974, Lovin' Molly, 1974, The Great Waldo Pepper, 1975, The Front Page, 1976, Dragon Fly, 1976, Walk Away Madden, The Other Side of Midnight, 1977, The Last of the Cowboys, 1977, Pretty Baby, 1978, King of the Gypsies, 1978, Loving Couples, 1980, Atlantic City, 1981, Tempest, 1982, The Hunger, 1983, Buddy System, 1984, Compromising Positions, 1985, The Witches of Eastwick, 1987, Bull Durham, 1988; TV appearances include The Last of the Belles, The Riders of Eldritch, June Moon, The Haunting of Rosalind, The Satan Murders, The Life of Ben Franklin, Owen Marshall, A World Apart, A.D. 1985, Mussolini and I, 1985, (serial) Search For Tomorrow. Mem. AFTRA, Screen Actors Guild, Actors Equity, Acad. Motion Picture Arts and Scis., NOW, MADRE, Amnesty Internat., ACLU. Office: care Martha Luttrell ICM 8899 Beverly Blvd Los Angeles CA 90048 *

SARAVO, ANNE COBBLE, clinical psychologist, mental health administrator; b. Atlanta; d. William Edwin and Iris Benny (Norman) Cobble; m. James Vincent Saravo, June 13, 1958; children: Stacy Anne, Lisa Ames Furmaneck. BA, Tex. Tech. U., 1959; MS, U. Mass., 1964, PhD, 1965; postgrad., Regional Health Authority, London, 1978-79, U. So. Calif., 1980-81. Lic. psychologist, Calif. Asst. prof. psychology Antioch Coll., Yellow Springs, Ohio, 1966-69; cons. Winchester (Eng.) Day Treatment Nursery Sch., 1971-73; sch. psychologist Muroc Unified Sch. Dist., Edwards AFB, Calif., 1974-75; clinical psychologist Antelope Valley Hosp., Lancaster, Calif., 1975-76, Farnborough Hosp., Kent, Eng., 1978-80; clinical psychologist Orange County (Calif.) Mental Health Service, 1981-84, chief adult outpatient services, 1984—; bd. dirs. High Hopes Neurological Recovery Group, Costa Mesa, Calif.; geriatric coordinator Orange County Mental Health Services, 1985—. Contbr. articles to profl. jours. Chairperson Conf. Geriatric Mental Health, Asilomar, Calif., 1986, So. Calif. Geriatric Mental Health Coordinators, 1985—. U.S. Pub. Health fellow Fels Research Inst., 1966-67. Mem. Am. Psychol. Assn., Calif. State Psychol. Assn., Nat. Acad. Nueropsychology, (graduate) Brit. Psychol. Soc. Office: Orange County Mental Health 14180 Beach Blvd Suite 213 Westminster CA 92683

SARGENT, ALICE GOLDSTEIN, author, consultant; b. Cin., Feb. 5, 1939; d. Harold D. and Adele (Linch) Goldstein; m. G. Dann Sargent, June 2, 1963 (dec. 1976); 1 child, Elizabeth. BA in English Lit., Oberlin Coll., 1960; MA, Brandeis U., 1963; MEd in Group Dynamics, Temple U., 1966; EdD, U. Mass., Amherst, 1974. Cons. to various orgns. including E.I. duPont de Nemours, U.S. Dept. Treasury, Treasury Exec. Inst., Fed. Exec. Inst., U.S. Dept. Energy, Nat. Tng. Labs., European Women in Mgmt.; mem. faculty Am. U. Sch. Govt. and Pub. Adminstrn., Washington, U. So. Calif. Sch. Pub. Adminstrn., Los Angeles; project coordinator Nat. Project on Women in Edn., Office of Asst. Sec. Edn., HEW, Washington, 1975-76; dir. MBA program Trinity Coll., Washington, 1976-77; seminar leader Australian Inst. Mgmt. Author: Beyond Sex Roles, 1976, 2d edit., 1985, The Adrogynous Manager, 1981, 4 other fgn. edits., The National Laboratory Training Manager's Handbook, 1984. Mem. Acad. Mgmt., Am. Psychol. Assn., Organizational Devel. Network (bd. dirs.). Home: 4819 Dexter Terr NW Washington DC 20007

SARGENT, DIANA RHEA, bookkeeper; b. Cheyenne, Wyo., Feb. 20, 1939; d. Clarence and Edith (de Castro) Hayes; grad. high sch.; m. Charles Sargent, Apr. 17, 1975; children: Rene A. Coburn, Rochelle A. Riddle, Weldy, Clayton R. Weldy, Christopher J.; stepchildren: Laurie Branch, Leslie E. Sargent. IBM proof operator Bank Am., Stockton, Calif., 1956-58, gen. ledger bookkeeper, Modesto, Calif., 1963-66; office mgr., head bookkeeper Cen. Drug Store, Modesto, 1966-76; pres. Sargent & Sargent Inc., Modesto, 1976—. Mem. Stanislaus Women's Center, Mem. NOW, San Francisco Mus. Soc., Nat. Soc. Public Accts. Office: 915 14th St Modesto CA 95353

SARGENT, MARGARET HOLLAND, portrait artist, actress; b. Hollywood, Calif., Dec. 30, 1927; d. Cecil Claude and Norma Mary Holland; m. Howard L. Sargent, June 22, 1947, children—Christopher Lee, Kenneth Dean. Student UCLA, 1945-47, 54-55; student Herbert Abrams, N.Y., 1958-61. Owner Sargent Portraits, Los Angeles, 1977-85; ann. staff lectr. Nat. Art Seminars, N.Y.C., Chgo., 1980-85; actress-writer Camelot Prodns., Los Angeles, 1983-85. Prin. portraits include Gerald Ford for Time, Inc., Gen. and Mrs. Alexander Haig, Andrea Hollen for U.S. Mil. Acad. Mus., L.G. Kenneth L. Tallman, Hawaii Gov. George R. Ariyoshi, Army Chief Staff Gen. John A. Wickham, founder British Music Mus. Frank Holland, Jules S. Stein and Lew Wasserman for Music Corp. Am., Prince Turki Saud, Princess Areeg Saud, Dorothy Bullitt for King Broadcasting, Elmer Nordstrom for Swedish Hosp. Named painter of Yr., Painter's Club N.Y., 1974; recipient Painting Yr. award Painter's Club N.Y., 1974, 1st place for profl. oils AFL-CIO, 1979. Mem. Salaagundi Art Club (Navy Art Cooperation and Liaison Com. award for oil painting 1976), Screen Actors Guild, AFTRA, Actors Equity Assn., Am. Portrait Soc. (credentials com. 1983-84). Home and Office: Sargent Portraits 2750 Glendower Ave Los Angeles CA 90027

SARGENT, PAMELA, writer; b. Ithaca, N.Y., Mar. 20, 1948. BA, SUNY, Binghamton, N.Y., 1968, MA, 1970. Am. Editor: The Bulletin of the Sci. Fiction Writers Am., Johnson City, N.Y., 1983—, mng. editor, Binghamton, 1970-73, asst. editor, 1973-75; editor (anthology) Women of Wonder, 1975, Bio-Futures, 1976, More Women of Wonder, 1976, The New Women of Wonder, 1978, (with Ian Watson) Afterlives, 1986; author Starshadows, 1977, The Best of Pamela Sargent, 1987, Cloned Lives, 1976, The Sudden Star, 1979, Watchstar, 1980, The Golden Space, 1982, The Alien Upstairs, 1983, Earthseed, 1983, Eye of the Comet, 1984, Homesmind, 1984, Venus of Dreams, 1986, The Shore of Women, 1986, Alien Child, 1988, Venus of Shadows, 1988. Office: care of Joseph Elder Agy 150 W 87th St 6D New York NY 10024

SARGUT, SUSAN H., pharmacist; b. Gardner, Mass., Feb. 19, 1954; d. John J. and Helen T. (Macionis) S.; B.S. in Pharmacy, U. R.I., 1977; postgrad. Northwestern U., 1978—. Pharmacist, Adams Drug Co., North Kingstown, R.I., 1977-78, Brooks Drug Co., Augusta, Maine, 1978-80, Sun Drug Co., North Versailles, Pa., 1980-81, Eckerd Drug, Uniontown, Pa., 1981-82; pharmacist mgr. Revco Drug, Waynesburg, Pa., 1982-87; staff pharmacist Children's Hosp. Pitts., 1987—; ptnr. Rufff's Double S Farm, Prosperity, Pa., 1981—; cons. Pleasant St. House. Mem. Tex. Pharm. Assn., Maine Pharm Assn., Am. Pharm. Assn., Am. Soc. Hosp. Pharmacists. Home and Office: RD 1 Box 236 Waynesburg PA 15370

SARLIN, JANEEN ALETTA, food service executive; b. Goshen, Ind., Apr. 14, 1941; d. J. Troy and Opal Rubye (Broadwater) Schrock; m. Richard Peter Sarlin, Dec. 27, 1964; children: Scott Peter, Paige Heather. BS, U. Minn., 1963. Sales asst. Peter, Griffin, Woodward, N.Y.C., 1963-67, Petry TV, Inc., N.Y.C., 1972-73; cooking instr. Culinary Arts Shoppe, Inc., N.Y.C., 1973-74; owner, pres. Cooking with Class, Inc., N.Y.C., 1974—; cooking instr. Hamilton Madison Settlement House, N.Y.C., 1987. Author: (cookbook) Lunches To Go, 1984; TV and radio spokesperson Holly Farms, 1986, Proctor and Gamble, 1985, Grey Advt., 1985, Greycom/Pet Dairy, 1986. Co-chmn. World Hunger Task Force, N.Y.C., 1986—. Mem. Internat. Assn. Cooking Profls. (cert. caterer, cert. instr., co-chair com. 1984), James Beard Found. (profl. mem.), The Roundtable for Women in Food Service (profl. mem.), Cooking Advancement Research Ednl. Found. (profl. mem.). Presbyterian. Club: Easthampton. Office: Cooking with Class Inc 110 East End Ave New York NY 10028

SARNO, ANGELA MARIE, health care association executive; b. Oak Park, Ill., Aug. 1, 1957; d. James E. and Rosemarie (Amorosi) S. BS, U. Ill., 1979; MS, Nat. Coll. Edn., Evanston, Ill., 1984. Lic. occupational therapist. Occupational therapist Michael Reese Hosp., Chgo., 1979-80; cons., occupational therapist Forest Park, River Forest and North Berwyn Sch. Dists., Ill., 1980-81; dir. occupational therapy Americana Health Care Ctr., Oak Lawn, Ill., 1981-83, Westlake Community Hosp., Melrose Park, Ill., 1983-86; pres. Better Care, Ltd., Melrose Park, 1986—; treas. Chgo. Area Council Occupational Therapy Dirs., 1986. Mem. Am. Occupational Therapy Assn., Ill. Occupational Therapy Assn., Nat. Assn. Female Execs., Nat. Rehab. Assn. Office: Better Care Ltd 1812 N Broadway Melrose Park IL 60160

SARNO, PATRICIA ANN, biology educator; b. Ashland, Pa.; d. John Thomas and Anna (Harvest) S.; B.S., Pa. State U., 1966, M.Ed., 1971; postgrad. Bucknell U., 1967, Bloomsburg U., 1970. Programmer planetarium, tchr. sci. Pottsville (Pa.) High Sch., 1967; tchr. biology Schuylkill Haven (Pa.) Area High Sch., 1967—, sci. chmn., coordinator dist., 1973—; cons. Pa. Edn. Dept., career program Pottsville Hosp. Dow Chem. Co. grantee, 1971. Mem. Pa. Edn. Assn. (exec. bd.), AAAS, Nat. Assn. Biology Tchrs., Nat. Tchrs. Assn., Pa. Tchrs. Assn., NEA, Am. Inst. Biol. Scis., Pa. Acad. Scis., Pa. State U. Alumni Assn., Schuylkill Haven Edn. Assn., Phi Sigma, Delta Kappa Gamma. Contbr. to profl. jours. Discoverer spider species Atypus snetzingeri, 1973. Home: 49 S Balliet St Frackville PA 17931 Office: Schuylkill Haven High Sch Schuylkill Haven PA 17972

SARNOFF, LILI-CHARLOTTE DREYFUS (LOLO SARNOFF), artist, business executive; b. Frankfurt, Germany (Swiss citizen), Jan. 9, 1916; d. Willy and Martha (Koch von Hirsch) Dreyfus; grad. Reimann Art Sch. (Germany), 1934, U. Berlin, 1935; student U. Florence (Italy), 1936-37; m. Stanley Jay Sarnoff, Sept. 11, 1948; children—Daniela Martha, Robert D.L. Came to U.S., 1941, naturalized, 1944. Research asst. Harvard Sch. Public Health, 1948-54; research asso. cardiac physiology Nat. Heart Inst., Bethesda, Md., 1954-59; pres. Rodana Research Corp., Bethesda, 1958-61; v.p. Catrix Corp., Bethesda, 1958-61; inventor FloLite light sculptures under name Lolo Sarnoff, 1968; one-woman shows: Agra Gallery, Washington, 1969, Corning Glass Center Mus., Corning, N.Y., 1970, Gallery Two, Woodstock, Vt., 1970, Gallery Marc, Washington, 1971, Hood Coll., Frederick, Md., 1972, Internat. Art Mart, Basel, Switzerland, 1972, Franz Bader Gallery, Washington, 1976, Art Barn, Washington, 1976, Art Fair, Washington, 1976, Gallery K, Washington, 1978, 81, Washington Project for Arts, 1980, Alwin Gallery, London, 1981, Galerie von Bartha, Basel, Switzerland, 1982, Gallery K, Washington, 1982, 83, 84, 85, La Galerie L'Hotel de Ville, Geneva, Switzerland, 1982, Washington Women's Art Ctr., 1985, Ctr. Internat. d'Art Contemporain, Paris, 1985, Pfalzgalerie, Kaiserlautern, Fed. Republic of Germany, 1985, Gallery K, Washington, 1987, Garden Show McCrillis Gardens, Bethesda, Md., 1987; represented in collections: Fed. Nat. Mortgage Assn., Washington, Corning Glass Center Mus., Nat. Air and Space Museum, Washington, David Lloyd Kreeger Collection, Washington, Kennedy Center, Washington, Nat. Acad. Sci., Chase Manhattan Bank, N.Y.C., Israel Mus., Jerusalem, others. Past trustee Nat. Ballet, Mt. Vernon Coll., Washington, Art Barn; bd. dirs. Fgn. Student Service Council, Washington Performing Arts Soc. Mem. women's com., trustee Corcoran Gallery of Art. Recipient Gold medal Accademia Italia delle Arti e del Lavoro, 1980. Club: City Tavern (Washington). Democrat. Co-inventor electrophrenic respirator; inventor flowmeter. Home: 7507 Hampden Ln Bethesda MD 20814 Other: Barnard VT 05031

SAROS, CARMEN NYDIA, educator; b. N.Y.C., Feb. 14, 1936; d. Ernesto Alejandro and Carmen Alejandra (Silva) Ruperti; m. William John Saros, July 18, 1959; children: Gregory, Lisa, Laura. BA, U. Conn., 1958; MS, Cen. State U., 1968; postgrad., St. Joseph's Coll., 1986-87. Tchr. Meriden (Conn.) Bd. Edn., 1961; chmn. math. dept. Hanover Elem. Sch., Meriden, 1981-83, chair social studies dept., 1983-84. Pres. Council Community Services, Meriden, 1985-86; bd. dirs. United Way Meriden and Wallingford, Conn., 1987-88. Recipient cert. recognition Meriden YWCA, 1986; Meriden Bd. Edn. grantee, 1986, 87. Mem. NEA, Delta Kappa Gamma. Republican. Lutheran. Home: 125 Amity St Meriden CT 06450

SAROSDY, JANE GRAFFEO, lawyer; b. Dallas, June 22, 1953; d. Joseph Victor Graffeo and Margaret Jane (Dunn) Graffeo Uchman; m. Randall Louis Sarosdy, Oct. 29, 1983; children: William Randall, Francis Robert. BA summa cum laude with honors, Newcomb U. of Tulane U., 1975, postgrad., 1977-78; JD, Stanford U., 1980. Bar: D.C. 1981. Law clerk to presiding justice U.S. Ct. Appeals, D.C., Washington, 1980-81; assoc. Covington & Burling, Washington, 1981-84; atty.-adviser Office Internat. Tax Counsel, U.S. Dept. Treasury, Washington, 1984-86, cons., 1986-87; counsel King & Spalding, Washington, 1987—. Sr. articles editor Stanford Law Rev., 1979-80. Active NOW, Washington, 1980—, Women's Legal Def. Fund, Washington, 1980—. Recipient Pierce Butler prize Tulane U., 1975, alumni medal, 1978, Belcher Evidence award Stanford U., 1980. Mem. ABA, Women's Bar Assn. D.C., Fed. Bar Assn., Phi Beta Kappa. Democrat. Home and Office: 2008 Rhode Island Ave McLean VA 22101-4921

SARRAF, ROBERTA JEAN, planning consultant; b. Pitts., Nov. 9, 1945; d. Walter H. and Margaret E. (Ondof) S. BA, U. Pitts., 1967, M in Urban & Regional Planning, 1969. Intern Rep. James G. Fulton, Washington, 1965; planner Pa. Dept. Community Affairs, Pitts., 1970-76; dir. community devel. Twp. of Upper St. Clair, Pitts., 1976-82; cons. planning Pitts., 1982—; instr. Pa. Dept. Community Affairs, 1976—; del. Environ. Planning to People's Republic of China. Creator and performer (musical program), History of Am. Popular Music. Bd. dirs. Chartiers Mental Health Ctr., Bridgeville, Pa., 1986—; vol. U. Pitts. Annual Giving Fund, 1973—; Dem. committewoman, Mt. Lebanon, Pa., 1965-68, 1982—; speaker Civic and Servic Clubs. Mem. Am. Planning Assn. (pres. Pitts. chpt., 1982-83), Nat. Assn. of Housing and Redevel. Officials (v.p. Pitts. chpt., 1980-81), Pa. Planning Assn. (bd. dirs., 1975-76, state conf. chmn., 1981), Women in Community Devel. (charter), Am. Fedn. of Musicians, Grad. Sch. Alumni Assn. (chmn. com. 1987—), Am. Inst. Cert. Planners. Democrat. Presbyterian. Club: Three Rivers Corvette (activities com. 1987). Lodge: Lions (1st woman in Mt. Lebanon, Pa. club). Home and Office: 1316 Bowerhill Rd Pittsburgh PA 15243

SARRIS, SHIRLEY CORNELIA, publishing and marketing company executive, consultant; b. N.Y.C., July 25, 1938; d. Reuben Alexander and Sarah Sonia (Kahan) Kopatz; m. George Sarris, June 27, 1959 (dec. 1960). BA, CCNY, 1966; MA, U. Chgo., 1967. Mgr. rights, contracts Pron Coord Basic books, N.Y.C., 1967-68; mgr. mktg. Swallow Pross, Chgo., 1968-70; dir. mktg. John Wiley and Sons, N.Y.C., 1979-74, Arno Press, N.Y.C., 1974, Franklin Watts, N.Y.C., 1974-75, R.R. Bowker, N.Y.C., 1975-78; founder, pres. Sarris Bookmktg. Service, N.Y.C., 1978—; leader seminar Folio, 1977—. Mem. JACPAC, N.Y.C., 1987—. Woodrow Wilson fellow, 1966; named One of 70 Women Who Made a Difference in the World of Books, Women's Nat. Book Assn., 1987. Mem. ALA, Publs. Mktg. Group, Book Industry Study Group, Am. Booksellers Assn. Democrat. Jewish. Office: Sarris Bookmktg Service 125 E 23d St New York NY 10010

SARSON, PATRICIA ANNE, computer consulting firm executive, author; b. London, June 6, 1946; came to U.S., 1973, naturalized, 1975; d. Francis Charles and Anne Brown (Nisbet) Sarson; m. Christopher Peter Gane, Apr. 1, 1975. B.Sc. in Zoology, U. London, 1969. Systems engr. IBM, London, 1967-72; cons., lectr. Yourdon Inc., N.Y.C., 1973-75; asst. v.p. Mfrs. Hanover Trust Co., N.Y.C., 1976; exec. v.p. Improved System Tech., N.Y.C., 1977-81; ptnr. Gane-Sarson, N.Y.C., 1981—. Co-author: Learning to Program 1975; Structured Systems Analysis, 1977; (ednl. methodology) STRADIS, 1979; (ednl. video tapes) Analysis and Design, 1979. Avocations: sailing; walking; classical music; collecting antiques.

SARTAIN, MARILYN BRASHER, service administrator; b. West Memphis, Ark., Dec. 15, 1955; d. Thomas Edward and Dorothy (Parker) Barnett; m. Lawrence E. Sartain, Aug. 4, 1979; children: John Lawrence, Clayton Thomas. AA in Edn., NW Jr. Coll., Senatobia, Miss., 1975; BS in Bus. Edn., U. Miss., 1977, M in Bus. Edn., 1979. Cert. profl. sec. Tchr. Horn Lake (Miss.) High Sch., 1977-84; adminstrv. sec. Fed. Express, Memphis, 1984-86, adminstrv. asst., 1986, sr. admistrv. asst., 1987—; instr. NW Jr. Coll., 1979—. Fund-raising coordinator Jr. Achievement, Memphis, 1986-87, classroom cons., 1986-87. Mem. Profl. Secs. Internat. (newsletter chairperson 1987-88), Alpha Delta Kappa, Delta Pi Epsilon. Baptist. Office: Fed Express 2930 Airways Blvd 4th fl Memphis TN 38116

SARTON, MAY, author, poet; b. Wondelgem, Belgium, May 3, 1912; brought to U.S., 1916, naturalized, 1924; d. George Alfred Leon and Eleanor Mabel (Elwes) Sarton; student Shady Hill Sch., Cambridge, Mass., Inst. Belge de Culture Francaise, Brussels, 1924-25; grad. Cambridge High and Latin Sch., 1929; Litt.D. (hon.), Russell Sage Coll., 1959, Clark U., 1975, U. N.H., 1976, Bates Coll., 1976, Colby Coll., 1976, Thomas Starr King Sch. Ministry, 1976, U. N.H., 1976, U. Maine, 1981, Bowdoin Coll., 1983, Bucknell U., 1985. Lectr. poetry U. Chgo., Harvard U., U. Iowa, Colo. Coll., Wellesley Coll., Beloit Coll., U. Kans., Denison U., others; Briggs-Copeland instr. composition Harvard U., 1950-52. Awarded Golden Rose for poetry, 1945; Edward Bland Meml. prize Poetry Mag., 1945; Alexandrine medal Coll. St. Catherine, 1975; Avon/COCOA Pioneer Woman award, 1983; Fund for Human Dignity award, 1984; Am. Book award, 1985, Maryann Hartman award U. Maine, 1986; Bryn Mawr fellow in poetry, 1953-54; Guggenheim Found. fellow, 1954-55; Nat. Found. Arts and Humanities grantee, 1967. Fellow Am. Acad. Arts and Scis.; mem. N.E. Poetry Soc., Poetry Soc. Am. (Reynolds lyric award 1953). Author: Encounter in April, 1937; The Single Hound, 1938; Inner Landscape (poems), 1939; The Bridge of Years, 1946, The Lion and The Rose (poems), 1948; Shadow of a Man, 1950; The Leaves of the Tree (poems), 1950; A Shower of Summer Days, 1952; The Land of Silence (poems), 1953; Faithful Are the Wounds, 1955; The Birth of a Grandfather, 1957; In Time Like Air, 1957; The Fur Person (fiction), 1957; I Knew a Phoenix, 1959; The Small Room, 1961; Cloud, Stone, Sun, Vine, 1961; Joanna and Ulysses, 1963; Mrs. Stevens Hears the Mermaids Singing, 1965; A Private Mythology (poems), 1966; Miss Pickthorn and Mr. Hare, 1966; As Does New Hampshire (poems), 1967; Plant Dreaming Deep (autobiography), 1968; The Poet and the Donkey, 1969, Kinds of Love, 1970; A Grain of Mustard Seed (poems), 1971; A Durable Fire (poems), 1972; Journal of a Solitude, 1973; As We Are Now, 1973; Collected Poems, 1974; Punch's Secret, 1974; Crucial Converstaions (novel), 1975; A World of Light (autobiography), 1976; A Walk Through the Woods, 1976; The House by the Sea (a journal), 1977; A Reckoning (novel), 1978; Selected Poems of May Sarton, 1978; Halfway to Silence (poems), 1980; Recovering (a journal), 1980; Writings on Writing (essays), 1981; A Winter Garland (poems), 1982; Anger, 1982; At Seventy, A Journal, 1984; (poems) Letters from Maine, 1984; The Magnificent Spinster, 1985; May Sarton: a Self Portrait, 1986; assoc. editor: Letter to May, 1986, After the Stroke (jour.), 1988, The Phoenix Again (poems), 1988.

SASEK, GLORIA BURNS, English language and literature educator; b. Springfield, Mass., Jan. 20, 1926; d. Frederick Charles and Minnie Delia (White) Burns; B.A., Mary Washington Coll. of U. Va., 1947; Ed.M., Springfield Coll., 1955; postgrad. Sorbonne, summer 1953; M.A., Radcliffe Coll., 1954; postgrad. Universita per Stranieri, Perugia, Italy, summer 1955; m. Lawrence Anton Sasek, Sept. 5, 1960. Tchr., head dept. jr. and sr. high sch. English, Somers, Conn., 1947-51, 52-59; tchr. English, Winchester (Mass.) pub. schs., 1959-60; faculty La. State U., Baton Rouge, 1961—, asst. prof. English, 1971—, chmn. freshman English, 1969-70. Recipient George H. Deer Disting. Tchr. award La. State U., 1977. Mem. MLA, South Central Modern Lang. Assn., South Central Renaissance Soc., AAUP (chpt. v.p. 1981-84). Address: 1458 Kenilworth Pkwy Baton Rouge LA 70808

SASSO, ELEANOR CATHERINE, state senator; b. Fall River, Mass., Dec. 9, 1934; d. Robert Charles and Ellen (O'Hare) Ashworth; m. Louis Anthony Sasso, 1957; children—Ellen Marie, Ann Marie, Robert. B.S., Immaculata Coll., Pa., 1957. Mem. R.I. State Senate, 1979—; researcher Bur. Nat. Affairs, from 1978. Chmn. Cranston Recycling Commn., 1972-73; mem. Cranston Transvan Com., from 1973; mem. Spl. Gov.'s Commn. To Study Entire Election Process, 1977-78. Mem. LWV, Met. Nursing and Health Assn. (bd.), Common Cause, Save the Bay. Democrat. Roman Catholic. Office: RI Senate State Capitol Providence RI 02903 *

SATCHELL, LISA BOLING, health care executive; b. Panama City, Fla., Sept. 18, 1960; d. William Wallace and Juanita Lee Ruth (Hannah) Boling; m. Richard John Satchell, Oct. 26, 1985. B.A., Belmont Coll., 1982. Dir. ops. Envoy Corp., Nashville, 1983-85; mgr. customer service Synercom Computers, Brentwood, Tenn., 1985-86; installation analyst Health America, Nashville, 1986—. Mem. Nat. Republican Com., 1985, 86, MADD (Mothers' Against Drunk Drivers), 1982—; participant Dance for Heart, Am. Heart Assn., Nashville, 1986. Mem. Nat. Assn. Female Execs., Sigma Tau Delta. Avocations: photography; aerobics; travel. Office: Health Am 3310 West End Ave Nashville TN 37203

SATELL, MARGARET COX, speech pathologist; b. Bklyn., Jan. 28, 1947; d. Jere Coleman Cox and Jane Dunseath (O'Neill) C.; m. Edward M. Satell, July 7, 1985; 1 child, Matthew Jackson. Student Chatham Coll., 1965-67; B.A. cum laude and with distinction, Mt. Holyoke Coll., 1969; M.A., Northwestern U., 1971. Speech pathologist Berkshire Rehab. Center, Pittsfield, Mass., 1972-78, clin. supr., 1978; speech pathologist Hosp. U. Pa., Phila., 1979-86, chief speech pathology, 1985-86; instr. dept. otorhinolaryngology Med. Sch. U. Pa., 1979-86; cons. Ashmere Manor Nursing Home, Hinsdale, Mass., 1975-78, Bennington (Vt.) Convalescent Center, 1975-77. Rehab. Services Adminstrn. trainee, 1969-71. Vol. Meals-on-Wheels; bd. dirs. Tri-County Concert Assn. Recipient award for continuing edn., 1983, 86. Mem. Am. Speech Lang. and Hearing Assn. (cert. clin. competence 1973), Pa. Speech-Lang.-Hearing Assn., Southeastern Pa. Speech and Hearing Assn. Republican. Presbyterian. Clubs: Mendelssohn, Women's Faculty U. Pa., Mt. Holyoke Alumnae. Home: 1158 West Valley Rd Wayne PA 19087

SATLOW, MARCIA FAITH E., neurologist, educator; b. Jamaica, May 1, 1949; d. Godfrey C. and Monica (Nicholson) Lawrence; m. Stephen J. Satlow, Apr. 2, 1974 (div.); 1 son, Aaron James; m. Philip Wyman Danforth, 1985. MB, BS U. W.I., 1973. Diplomate Am. Bd. Psychiatry and Neurology. Intern Univ. Hosp. of the W.I., Jamaica, 1973-74; resident in Neurology Ottawa (Ont., Can.) Civic Hosp., 1975-77, Nassau (N.Y.) County Med. Ctr., 1977-79; asst. instr. dept. neurology SUNY-Stony Brook, N.Y., 1978-79, instr., fellow, 1979-81; vis. fellow Electromyography Neurol. Inst. of N.Y., N.Y.C., 1979-80, asst. prof., 1981-85; cons. neurologist Southbury (Conn.) Tng. Sch., 1985—, Conn. Bur. Disability Determination, Hartford, 1985—; mem. exec. bd. Muscular Dystrophy Assn., Long Island, N.Y., 1981-85. Mem. AMA, N.Y. Acad. Scis, Am. Acad. Neurology, Am. Assn. Electromyography and Electrodiagnosis. Anglican. Office: Southbury Tng Sch Southbury CT 06488

SATO, EUNICE NODA, city administrator; b. Livingston, Calif., June 8, 1921; d. Bunsaku and Sawa (Maeda) Noda; m. Thomas Takashi Sato, Dec. 9, 1950; children—Charlotte Patricia, Daniel Ryuichi, and Douglas Ryuji (twins). AA, Modesto Jr. Coll., 1941; BA, U. No. Colo., 1944; MA, Columbia U., 1948. Public sch. tchr. Mastodon Twp. Schs., Alpha, Mich., 1944-47; ednl. missionary Reformed Ch. Am., Yokohama, Japan, 1948-51; council mem. City of Long Beach, Calif., 1975-86; mayor 1980-82; sec. corp. bd. Los Angeles County Health Systems Agy., 1978-79. Monthly contbr. articles to 2 neighborhood papers, 1975-86. Bd. dirs. Long Beach chpt. ARC, 1975—, mem. exec. com., 1978-81, past v.p., pres. Long Beach chpt.; bd. dirs. Goodwill Industries, 1978-82 ; trustee St. Mary's Bauer Med. Center, 1977—; pres. Industry Edn. Council, Long Beach, 1984-86; bd. dirs. Industry Edn. Council of Calif.; mem. State Adv. Group on Juvenile Delinquency Prevention 1983—; mem. Calif. Council Criminal Justice, 1983—; mem. legis. com. Girl Scout Council Calif., 1986—; bd. dirs. Long Beach council Girl Scouts U.S., Region III United Way, 1974—; mem. Asian Pacific adv. com. Calif. Dept. Rehab., 1985-87; recreation commn. City of Long Beach 1985-86; mem. pub. safety policy com. League Calif. Cities, 1981-86; mem. community econ. and housing devel. com. So. Calif. Assn. Govts.: mem. Calif. Task Force to Promote Self Esteem and Personal and Social Responsibility, 1987—; Long Beach chpt. pres. NCCJ, 1987; pres. Internat. Community Council, 1986-87. Recipient Outstanding Service award Long Beach Coordinating Council, 1969, Mother of Yr. award Silverado United Meth. Ch., 1973, Hon. Service award Calif. PTA, 1963, Continuing Service award, 1974, hon. life membership award Nat. PTA, 1974, Outstanding Laywoman of Yr. award Long Beach Area Council Chs., 1976, Woman of Yr. award State Women's Council-C. of C., 1979, Long Beach Internat. Bus. and Profl. Women's Club,; nat. merit award DAR, 1982; Citizen of Yr. award Los Altos YMCA, 1982, Calif. Community Pool for Handicapped, 1982; Outstanding Citizen award Torch Club of Long Beach, 1983. Mem. Nat. League Cities, League Calif. Cities, So. Calif. Assn. Govts., Long Beach Area C. of C., Alpha Iota (hon.). Republican. Methodist. Home: 2895 Easy Ave Long Beach CA 90810

SATTERFIELD, MARY GRACE, interior designer; b. Los Angeles, Aug. 28, 1922; d. Henry Gerard and Lillian M. (Smith) Hagoort; m. Bert Willliam Justus, Nov. 22, 1941 (dec. May 1951); children: Mary, Patrick, Elizabeth; m. Arthur Elwood Satterfield, Apr. 19, 1958; 1 child, Kathryn. Cert. in interior designing, Compton Jr. Coll., 1952. Cert. kitchen designer. Resident designer Cooks Kitchen Ctr., San Pedro, Calif., 1963-79, Kitchens of the Desert, Palm Desert, Calif., 1979—. Tchr. Confraternity of Christian Doctrine, San Pedro, 1950-63. Mem. Nat. Kitchen and Bath Assn., Kitchen and Bath Assn. (v.p., pres. 1973-75, 1st Place Design award 1975), Am. Inst. Kitchen Dealers (sec., treas. 1975-78, chmn. 1978-79), Contractor State Lic. Bd., Palm Desert C. of C. Democrat. Roman Catholic. Office: Kitchens of the Desert 73-405 El Paseo Palm Desert CA 92260

SATTERFIELD, MARY (YARBROUGH) MCADEN, retired educator, civic worker; b. Semora, N.C., Mar. 15, 1911; d. John H. and Ella T. (Yarbrough) McAden; A.B., Meredith Coll., 1931; postgrad. N.C. State U., 1965, U. Va. Extension, 1965, U. N.C., summer, 1963, Appalachian U., summer 1932; m. Lynn Banks Satterfield, Nov. 29, 1933; children—Lynn Banks, John De Berniere. Tchr. Caswell County (N.C.) elem. schs., 1931-34; tchr. sci. Caswell County high schs., 1934-36; postmaster U.S. Post Office, Milton, N.C., 1936-41; tchr. elem. grades Caswell County Pub. Schs., 1962-71. Clk., Town of Milton, 1959-61, sec. bd. of elections, 1976, registrar bd. of elections, 1979-81, registrar Town Bd. of Elections, 1987—; mem. Caswell County Transp. Efficiency Council, 1981-83. Named Caswell County Mother of Yr., 1980. Mem. N.C., Caswell County (pres. 1962-64, sec. 1977-86) hist. assns., N.C. Assn. Educators, Nat. Ret. Tchrs. Assn., Semora Homemakers Extension, Mus. Assos. of N.C., UDC. Democrat. Baptist. Clubs: Milton Woman's (pres. 1961-62, v.p. 1962-64, sec. 1965—), Milton Community (sec. 1937-44, pres. 1965-67), Order Eastern Star.

SATTERFIELD, ROCHELLE KRILL, psychologist, clinical social worker; b. Cleve., Dec. 22, 1938; d. Harold J. and Hilda (Davis) Krill; B.A., U. Calif., San Diego, 1964; M.S.W., Calif. State U., San Diego, 1969; Ph.D., U. Tex.-Austin, 1984; m. Ben Satterfield, June 22, 1958 (div.); 1 son, Jeffrey Mark. Psychiat. social worker Brown Schs., Oaks Treatment Center, Austin, Tex., 1969-79; pvt. practice psychology, Austin, 1974—; cons. Transitional Treatment Center, Austin, 1978-81. Mem. Austin Group Therapy Assn. (pres., exec. com.), Am. Psychol. Assn., Tex. Psychol. Assn. (chair com. group therapy), Southwestern Group Psychotherapy Assn. (exec. com., sec.), Am. Group Psychotherapy Assn. Home: 5500 Windward Dr Austin TX 78723 Office: 1500 W 6th St Austin TX 78703

SATTERWHITE, AUDREY ANNE, art director; b. N.Y.C., Nov. 30, 1954; d. Norman Keith Shachnow and Lorraine (Lubart) Becker; m. Steven Walter Satterwhite, Jan. 15, 1983; 1 child, Daniel Lars. Student, Washington U., St. Louis, 1972-76. Art dir. CBS Records, N.Y.C., 1982-84, Atlantic Records, N.Y.C., 1984-85; dep. art dir. N.Y. Times Sunday Mag., N.Y.C., 1986; pres., art dir. White Ink, Inc. Graphic Design, N.Y.C., 1985—; tchr., staff Parsons Sch. of Design, N.Y.C., 1984-85, lectr. 1985-86. Dir., producer, Expectations, 1985. Recipient Merit award The Art Dirs. Club, 1984, 85, 86, 87, Award of Excellence Soc. Newspaper Design, 1986-87, N.Y. Times. Mem. Nat. Assn. of Recording Arts and Scis., Nat. Assn. Investment Clubs. Democrat. Jewish. Club: Lysistrata II (presiding officer 1986—).

SATTERWHITE, SANDRA ANNE, advertising sales executive; b. Cambridge, Mass., Aug. 1, 1946; d. Robert H. and Laura E. (Gadecki) Johnston; m. Francis G. Satterwhite, Nov. 25, 1964 (div. Apr. 1976); children: Greg, Lisa. Sales rep. Franklin Pub. Co., Rockland, Mass., 1976-79; devel. mgr. Prudential Ins. Co., Boston, 1979-82; sales mgr. MPG Communications, Plymouth, Mass., 1982-83; account mgr. Washington Dossier, 1984-85; Mid-Atlantic regional mgr. Halsey Pub. Co., Washington, 1985-86; assoc. publisher Mus. and Arts Washington mag., 1986-87; owner The Satterwhite Group, Inc., Washington, 1987—. Mem. Whitman (Mass.) Fin. Com., 1975-76; bd. dirs. Unity Ctr., 1988. Mem. Nat. Assn. Women Bus. Owners, Women in Advt. and Mktg., Women of Boston (bd. dirs. 1977-79), Nat. Assn. for Profl. Saleswomen, Women in Communications Inc., Mensa. Democrat. Club: Washington Ad. Office: 3915 Massachusetts Ave NW Washington DC 20016

SATTLER, JANIECE DONNA, sales executive; b. Avon, S.D., Jan. 28, 1932; d. Fred James and Fannie Grace (Burma) S.; student Colo. State U., 1965-66, City Coll., Seattle, 1979-80. Bookkeeper, King Lumber Co., Loveland, Colo., 1950-53; legal stenographer Seaman & Ball, Attys. at Law, Loveland, 1953-54; statis. clk. U.S. Bur. Reclamation, Loveland, 1955-64; sec. dept. radiology and radiation biology Colo. State U., Ft. Collins, 1964-67; asst. dir. Continuing Edn. Lab. Personnel, Wash./Alaska Regional Med. Program, Seattle, 1967-71; adminstrv. coordinator dept. pathology Providence Med. Center, Seattle, 1971-80, purchasing mgr., 1980-82; supr. sales Advanced Tech. Labs., Inc., Bellevue, Wash., 1983-84, sales div. Hewlett Packard, 1984—. Mem. Nat. Writers Club. Republican. Author: A Practical Guide to Financial Management of the Clinical Laboratory, 1980, 2d edit., 1986; contbr. articles to various publs. Home: 1035 156th Ave NE #8 Bellevue WA 98007 Office: 15815 SE 37th Bellevue WA 98006

SATULA, KIRSTEN REGINA, accountant; b. Milw., Mar. 29, 1960; d. Manfred Erwin and Hanna Ingaberg (Gottschalk) Neumann; m. Keith Otto Satula, June 16, 1979; children: Kevin Matthew, Kyle Jacob. BBA in Acctg., U. Wis., Milw., 1983. CPA, Wis. Jr. acct. Blue Cross & Blue Shield, Omaha, 1980-81; inventory acct. U. Nebr., Omaha, 1981-82; auditor Heritage Bank, Milw., 1983-84; budget analyst Waukesha (Wis.) engine div., Dresser Industries, 1984-85, project acct., 1985-87, mkt. research coordinator, 1988—; cons. CPA Progressive Systems, Waukesha, 1986—. Vol. Roseville Manor Nursing Home, Milw., 1979; mgmt. cons. Wis. Bell Partnership Day, Waukesha, 1987. Mem. Nat. Acctg. Assn. (assoc. dir 1984-85). Office: Dresser Industries Waukesha engine div 1000 W Saint Paul Ave Waukesha WI 53188

SAUER, ELISABETH RUTH, lawyer; b. Charleston, W.Va., July 27, 1948; d. Gordon Chenoweth and Mary Louise (Steinhilbur) S. B.A., Northwestern U., 1970; J.D., U. Mo., 1975. Bar: Mo. 1975. Assoc. firm Campbell, Erickson, Cottingham, Morgan & Gibson, Kansas City, Mo., 1975-80, ptnr., 1980—. Bd. dirs. Planned Parenthood Western Mo. and Kans., 1978—, v.p., 1983-84; bd. dirs. Kansas City Met. Regional Com. on Status of Women, 1976-78. Mem. ABA, Mo. Bar Assn., Kansas City Bar Assn., Assn. Women Lawyers of Greater Kansas City. Club: Rockhill Tennis-Kenwood. Office: Cambell Morgan & Gibson PC 4505 Madison Kansas City MO 64112

SAUER, MARY JULIA, special education specialist; b. Pitts., Oct. 10, 1949; d. Edward Henry and Julia Ann (Polkabla) S.; 1 child, Jason Michael Sauer. BS in Art Edn., Edinboro State Coll., 1971; MS in Spl. Edn., Clarion State Coll., 1980; postgrad, U. Pitts., 1988—. Cert. art tchr., spl. edn. tchr. for mentally retarded. Tchr. Polk (Pa.) State Sch. & Hosp., 1971-72; vol. VISTA, Bath, N.Y., 1972-73; tchr. Polk Ctr., 1973-80, program specialist, 1980—; lectr., speaker, video on local TV on history of Polk Ctr., 1987. Patentee beer bottle shaped cake pan, 1987; cakes displayed in various mags.; creator local history video. Mem. Internat. Cake Expn. Soc., Council for Exceptional Children. Democrat. Roman Catholic. Home: PO Box 98 Stoneboro PA 16153

SAUER, SUSAN MARIE, manufacturing company official; b. Geneva, Ill., Nov. 21, 1952; d. Walter Francis and Margaret Marie Sauer. BS, Ill. State U., 1974; postgrad. in bus. adminstrn., No. Ill. U. With Container Corp. Am., Chgo., 1974-87, casualty mgr., 1979-80, mgr. workers compensation and regional claims coordinator, internat. ins. coordinator, 1980-82, mgr. workers' compensation, 1983-87; mgr. property ins. Navistar Internat. Transp. Corp., Chgo., 1987—; mem. bd. Ill. Insolvency Fund. Mem. Risk Ins. Mgmt. Soc. Lutheran. Office: 401 N Michigan Ave Chicago IL 60611

SAUERBREY, ELLEN ELAINE RICHMOND, state legislator; b. Balt., Sept. 9, 1937; d. Edgar Arthur and Ethel Frederika (Landgraf) Richmond, m. Wilmer John Emil Sauerbrey, June 27, 1959. AB summa cum laude in Biology and English, Western Md. Coll., 1959. Biology instr., chmn. sci. dept. Baltimore County Sch. System, 1959-64; dist. mgr. Baltimore County U.S. Census, 1970; mem. from 10th legis. dist. Md. Ho. of Dels., Annopolis, 1978—, minority leader, 1986—. Del. Rep. nat. convs., 1968, 76, 84, mem. credentials com., 1984: vice chmn. Rep. State Cen. Com. of Balt. County, 1966-71; trustee Md. Council Econ. Edn., Franklyn Sq. Hosp. Named Legislator of Yr. Md. Assn. Builders and Contractors, 1982; recipient Pvt. Property award Greater Balt. Bd. Realtors, 1984. Mem. Md. Fedn. Rep. Women, Am. Legis. Exchange Council (nat. treas.), Nat. Taxpayers Union, Md. Farm Bur., Women Legislators of Md., So. Legis. Conf. (econ. devel., trade, and commerce com., agr. and rural affairs com.), Md. Conservative Union, Nat. Tax Limitation Com., DAR, Beta Beta Beta. Presbyterian. Office: Md Gen Assembly Lowe House Office Bldg Annapolis MD 21401

SAUERESSIG-RIEGEL, SUZANNE, veterinarian, newspaper columnist; b. Nuremberg, Germany, Feb. 4, 1925; came to U.S., 1955; d. Josef and Elizabeth (Walsch) Saueressig; m. Richard T. Riegel, Dec. 26, 1955. D.V.M., Munich U., 1953, Dr. Med. Vet., 1954. Nurse, U.S. 6th Army, W.Ger., 1946-49; staff veterinarian Humane Soc. of Mo., St. Louis, 1955-65, chief of staff, 1965—. Author weekly column Ask the Pet Doctor, St. Louis Globe Democrat, 1980-85; author (booklet) Salmonella in Shellfish, 1954; co-author collaboration research papers St. Louis U. Med. Sch. 1959-61; contbr. article to mag. Served as nurse German Army, 1943-46. Recipient spl. leadership award profl. category YWCA, St. Louis, 1983, 25 yrs. service award Humane Soc. Mo., 1980. Mem. AVMA, Am. Animal Hosp. Assn., Assn. Woman Veterinarians (Woman Vet. of Yr. 1972), Assn. Feline Practitioners, Mo. Acad. Vet. Medicine, Am. Assn. Lab. Animal Sci., Vet. Oncology Soc., Am. Vet. Cardiology Soc., Mo. Control Officers Assn., Mo. Vet. Med. Assn. Roman Catholic. Office: Humane Soc of Mo 1210 Macklind Ave Saint Louis MO 63110

SAUL, SHURA, gerontologist; b. N.Y.C., July 8, 1920; d. Froim Camenir and Rose (Lisenco) Rudin; B.A., Hunter Coll., 1940; M.S.W., Columbia U., 1963, Ed.D., 1972; m. Sidney R. Saul, Dec. 14, 1941; children—Mark, Jonathan, Jennifer, Tchr. kindergarten N.Y.C. Bd. Edn., 1943-48; dir. Bronx River Child Care Center, 1948-49; group worker Jewish Guild for Blind, N.Y.C., 1954-61; cons. social worker United Hosp. Fund, N.Y.C., 1964-67; mem. faculty Sch. Social Work, N.Y.U., N.Y.C., 1967-69; mem. faculty Brookdale gerontology program Adelphi U., Garden City, N.Y., 1975-83, Wurzweiler Sch., N.Y.C., 1981—; dir. student unit Self Help Community Services, N.Y.C., 1969-71; coordinator profl. services Kingsbridge Heights Nursing Home, Bronx, 1971-78, ednl. coordinator, 1978—; cons. psychogeriatrics and edn. Borders Health Bd., others, Scotland, 1974—, Chaim Sheba Med. Ctr., Israel, 1982—. Chmn. bd. dirs. Bronx-North Manhattan Coalition for Elderly and Long Term Care, 1981-84, chmn. edn. com., 1984—; observer, del. White House Conf. on Aging, 1981. Recipient Woman of Yr. award Jewish Welfare Bd., Bronx, 1954. Mem. Goldens Bridge Community Assn. (history com. 1978—), Nat. Assn. Social Workers, Nat. Council on Aging, Am. Group Psychotherapy Assn. Author: The Right To Be Different, 1962, Aging: An Album of People Growing Old, 1974, 2d edit., 1983 Sophia Moses Robison, Woman of the Twentieth Century, 1981; co-author (docudrama) Somewhere A Door Blew Shut; editor: Social Group Work for Frail Elderly, 1982; (with B. MacLennan and M. B. Werner) Group Psychotherapies for the Elderly, 1988; producer, editor: (videotape series) Enhancing the Quality of Life for Institutionalized Elderly, Scotland, 1980, other videotapes on aging, 1976, 82; contbr. articles to profl. publs. Home: Box 431 Goldens Bridge NY 10526

SAULNESS, FIONA, real estate executive; b. Manchester, Eng., Jan. 15, 1956; came to U.S., 1956; d. Douglas Munro Masters and Joan Elina (Gerrard) Hall; m. Robert Paul Saulness, July 11, 1981. Grad. high sch., Seattle. Legal sec. Foster, Pepper and Riviera, Seattle, 1974-78; salesperson, mgr. West Coast Homes Real Estate Co., Seattle, 1978-84; salesperson, trainer Home Realty, Inc., Seattle, 1984—. Episcopalian. Office: Home Realty Inc 12055 15 NE Seattle WA 98125

SAULOVICH, CATHERINE MARY, transportation executive; b. San Francisco, May 24, 1960; d. B. Peter and Carol Ann (Druhan) S. BA, U. Calif., Berkeley, 1981. Mktg. coordinator Royal Cruise Line, San Francisco, 1981-82, mktg. supr., 1982-83, advt. supr., 1983-86, purchasing agent, 1986—. Mem. Nat. Assn. Female Execs., Marine Hotel Catering and Duty Free Assn. Democrat. Home: 2641 College Ave Berkeley CA 94704 Office: Royal Cruise Line One Maritime Pl #660 San Francisco CA 94111

SAULTER-HEMMER, JANET LYNN, computer programmer; b. Glen Ridge, N.J., Nov. 25, 1954; d. Lajoie Alvin and Nancy Harriet (Leatherberry) Saulter; m. Benjamin Joseph Singerline, Dec. 11, 1976 (div. 1981); 1 son, Scott Benjamin; m. Thomas Paul Hemmer, Oct. 7, 1984. AA, Thomas A. Edison Coll., Trenton, N.J., 1977, BA, 1983; grad. Chubb Inst. Computer Tech., Parsippany, N.J. Sec. to v.p. Rapidata Co., Fairfield, N.J., 1974-76; office mgr. Scottish Pedlar Co., South Orange, N.J., 1976-77; contract adminstr. McGraw-Edison Service, Fairfield, 1979-84; computer programmer Dun's Mktg. Services div. Dun & Bradstreet, 1984-87; tech. cons., Tiffany Computer Systems, 1987—; Recycling co-ordinator Presbyn. Ch., West Caldwell, N.J.; organizer, N.J. state pres. Orgn. Enforcement Child Support, past pres., West Caldwell; former mem. Essex County Adv. Commn. on Status of Women; chmn. Foster Grandparents Program, West Caldwell; former dir. Camp Fatima N.J., Livingston; youth adv. del. Presbytery of Newark; elder Presbyn. Ch. of West Caldwell; mem. Cub Scout Pack 177 and Boy Scout Troop 177 (com. chmn.); mem. Morris County Family Ct. Child Placement Rev. Bd., 1987-88. Mem. Jaycee-ettes (state dir. 1979-80, officer yr. 1980). Democrat. Club: Jr. Woman's (West Essex, N.J.). Lodge: Order Easter Star. Home: 8 Maple Ln Lake Hiawatha NJ 07034-1125 Office: Tiffany Computer Systems 170 Changeloridge Rd Suite A2 Montville NJ 07054

SAUNDERS, ALMA ANNETTE, educator; b. Brunswick, Ga., Sept. 24, 1930; d. William Van and Cora Mae (Young) Gunter; B.Bus.Edn., Ga. State U., 1971, M.Bus. Edn., 1978; m. William J. Saunders, Dec. 11, 1948 (dec. 1977); children—Amanda Lou Robertson, Michael William. Sec., United Electric Co., Jacksonville, Fla., 1957-58; bookkeeper Blue Marlin Co., Key West, Fla., 1959-60; billing clk. Hoffmann-La Roche, Inc., Decatur, Ga., 1965-66; statis. asst. Tb program Center for Disease Control, Atlanta, 1966-68; tchr. Blayton Bus. Coll., Atlanta, 1971-72; tchr. bus. edn. Fulton County Sch. System, Atlanta, 1972—; cons., lectr. in field. Mem. exec. bd. North Springs United Methodist Ch., Atlanta, 1979, adult Sunday sch. tchr., 1979. Recipient Educator of Yr. award 5th congl. dist. Ga. Vocat. Assn., 1977, 81; Outstanding Service award Ga. Dept. Edn., Bus. and Office Edn., 1979, 81. Mem. Internat. Soc. Bus. Edn., Nat. Bus. Ednl. Assn., Ga. Bus. Edn. Assn., Am. Vocat. Assn., Ga. Vocat. Assn., Am. Soc. for Tng. and Devel., North Fulton C. of C., Am. Council on Consumer Interests, Delta Pi Epsilon. Home: 6987 J Roswell Rd Atlanta GA 30328 Office: 1131 Alpharetta St Roswell GA 30075

SAUNDERS, BEATRICE NAIR (MRS. DERO AMES SAUNDERS), editor, association executive; b. New Britain, Conn., Dec. 26, 1915; d. Frank and Sophie (Adler) Nair; B.A., Smith Coll., 1936; m. Dero Ames Saunders, May 23, 1936; children—David Nair, Richard Ames. Tchr. pub. schs., New Britain, 1936; editorial asst. Cordon Co., N.Y.C., 1937-39, Family Welfare Assn. Am., N.Y.C., 1939-42; supr. editorial div. publs. div. ARC, Washington, 1943-46; free-lance editor various publs. N.Y.C., 1946-50; editor-in-chief, publs. dept. Girl Scouts U.S.A., N.Y.C., 1950-55; dir. publs. dept., editor Social Work, Nat. Assn. Social Workers, N.Y.C., 1955-82, publs. cons., 1982—; mem. adj. faculty, editor-in-residence Grad. Sch. Social Services, Fordham U., Lincoln Center, N.Y.C., 1982—; cons. Sch. of Social Work, Rutgers U., New Brunswick, N.J., 1985—. Founding editor Affilia, Jour. Women and Social Work, 1986—. Vol., ARC, Freeport, L.I., 1946-47, Child Care Center, Freeport, 1946-47; chmn. parents assn. Downtown Community Sch., 1948-50; chmn. 22d-21st St. Community Council, 1954-58, 62-63; chmn. com. on existing housing Chelsea Community Council, 1957-60; vice chmn. Chelsea Com. for Neighborhood Devel., 1960-63, chmn., 1963-65. Clubs: Smith Coll., Heights Casino. Home: 446 W 22d St New York NY 10011 Office: Fordham Univ Lincoln Ctr New York NY 10023-7479

SAUNDERS, BETH PENN, advertising executive; b. Asher, Okla., Dec. 9, 1932; d. Floyd Glenn and Florence E. (Seckinger) Embry' B.F.A., Art Center, 1952; m. Robert D. Saunders, Dec. 13, 1975; children from previous marriage—Kathryn Elizabeth, Wesley Alan, David Embry. Art dir. Gottschalks, Fresno, Calif., 1952, Scope Advt., 1965-67; advt. dir. BuildMart Corp., 1967-75; head AD-Vantage Advt., Chino, Calif., 1975—; pres. Embryline Inc., Mut. Advt. Corp. Mem. Republican Women of Long Beach (Calif.). Mem. Bus. and Profl. Women, Cooperative Office Products Assn. (exec. dir. 1987—). Home: 8441 Wilson Ct Alta Loma CA 91701 Office: 13364 Central Ave Chino CA 91710

SAUNDERS, DOROTHY ANN, insurance company executive, sales management; b. Roxbury, N.C., Nov. 29, 1932; d. James William and Anna Bell (Wesley) Rice; m. Bernard L. Lewis, June 10, 1950 (dec. Jan. 1957); m. J.R. Saunders, Nov. 26, 1976 (dec. May 1981). Student, Md. U., 1950-53. Bookeeper, office mgr. ANT Cosmetics, Bethesda, Md., 1958; owner, mgr. Donnel's Hall of Gifts, Washington, 1959-63, Gifts, Inc., Washington, 1959-63; with U.S. Govt. Health, Edn., Welfare, Bethesda, 1965-73; owner, mgmt. in sales Dorothy Saunders Ins. Agy., Forest, Va., 1973—; vis. spkr. Bus. & Profl. Woman's Assn., Brookneal, Va., 1986-87. Democrat. Baptist. Home: Rt 1 Huddleston VA 24104 Office: Dorothy Saunders Ins Agy 100 Old Forge Rd Forest VA 24551

SAUNDERS, IVY SIMONE, real estate company official; b. Bklyn., Dec. 31, 1958; d. Gerard Maurice and Norma Sidell (Fischler) S. AS in Bus., Mt. San Antonio Coll., 1979; BA in Fin., Calif. State U., Fullerton, 1982. Mgr. dept. acctg., fin. Pacific Comics Co., San Diego, 1982-84; mgr. fin. and collections City Office Furniture Co., San Diego, 1984-85; sales cons. B&B Sales, Honolulu, 1985-86, Weinstock's, Stockton, Calif., 1986-88; realtor Century 21 Northcutt Realty, San Diego, 1988—; freelance photographer, 1984 . Mem. Alpha Gamma Sigma, Rho Epsilon. Democrat. Jewish. Home: 3550 Lebon Dr Apt 6122 San Diego CA 92122 Office: Century 21 Northcutt Realty 5350 Balboa Ave San Diego CA 92117

SAUNDERS, JACQUELYN RAE, exterior designer; b. Youngstown, Ohio, Mar. 10, 1938; d. Thomas Gilbert Madden and Hazel Elizabeth (Ward) Anderson; divorced; 1 child, Heidi Lee Graber. Student, Kent State U., 1956-57. From sales person to mgmt. Index Pubs., Chgo., 1966-67, owner, 1975-80; owner Lockman Printing, Blue Island, Ill., 1973-80, Colortone, Inc., Blue Island, 1976-80, Sheldon Offset, Blue Island, 1978-80; mgr. classified advt. Houston Post, 1980-81; from mktg. mgmt. to gen. mgr., v.p. ops. Trim Home Design, Inc., Houston, 1983—. Illustrator, cons. Test Yourself Book, 1980. Mem. Ill. Presswomens Assn. Republican. Unitarian. Office: Trim Home Design Inc 9900 Westpark #210 Houston TX 77063

SAUNDERS, JEANNE DOUGHERTY, development and fund raising executive; b. Kansas City, Mo., Nov. 14, 1924; d. Lewis Bissell and Nancy (Moore) Dougherty; m. Louis Alexander Saunders, Jan. 1, 1952; children—Susan, John Stephen, James. Student William Jewell Coll., 1942-43; B.A., U. Mo., 1946; M.A., Columbia U. and Union Theol. Seminary, 1952. Cert. fundraiser. Short term missionary to Philippines, Presbyn. Bd. Fgn. Missions, N.Y.C., 1946-50; instr. religion dept. Tex. Christian U., Ft. Worth, 1958-64, dir. religious activities, 1961-64; dir. pub. info. Vis. Nurse Assn., Dallas, 1973-82; dir. capital campaign Christian Ch., Ft. Worth, from 1982, now v.p. charitable devel. Vis. Nurse Assn. chmn. bd. dirs. Juliette Fowler Homes, Inc., Dallas, 1981-82; active Tex. Bible Chair Found., 1985—, Women's Council Greater Dallas, 1988. Mem. exec. com. Nat. Benevolent Assn., St. Louis, 1981-82; sec., bd. dirs. Fowler Christian Apts., Ind., Dallas, 1978-82; mem. sr. services com. Community Council Greater Dallas, 1979-82; mem. com. on aging Greater Dallas Community Chs., 1980-82. Mem. Mortar Bd., Kappa Kappa Gamma. Democrat. Mem. Christian Ch. Home: 10207 Best Dr Dallas TX 75229 Office: Vis Nurse Assn 8200 Brook River Dr Suite 200N Dallas TX 75247

SAUNDERS, KAREN ESTELLE, educator; b. San Carlos, Ariz., June 13, 1941; d. Walter Carl and Irma Marie (Gallmeyer) Sorgatz; m. John Richard Saunders, Dec. 27, 1962 (div. Nov. 1981). BA, Ariz. State U., 1964, MA, 1968, postgrad., 1982—. Tchr., chair art dept. Corona del Sol High Sch., Tempe, Ariz., 1977—, chair fine arts dept., 1987—; tchr., chair art dept. McClintock High Sch., Tempe, 1965-77; coordinator artists-in-schs. program Tempe Union High Sch., 1975-80, program adminstr. travel/study program, 1976-78, 80; program chair Four Corners Art Educators Conf., Scottsdale, Ariz., 1982; co-chair S.W. Indian Art Collectibles Exhbn., Carefree, Ariz., 1982, also editor and designer catalogue. Mem. State Art Guide Com., Tempe, 1975-77; mem. planning com. Sheldon Lab. Systems Facilities, 1980-83; chair City of Tempe Sculpture Competition, Fine Arts Ctr. Tempe, 1982; bd. dirs. Ariz. Scholastic Art Adv. Bd., Phoenix, 1983-87. Recipient Vincent Van Gogh award Colo. Alliance for Arts Edn., 1978, Ariz. Art Educator of Yr. award Ariz. Art Edn. Assn., 1979, award Four Corners Art Educators Conf., 1982, Lehrer Mel. award Ariz. State U. Sch. Art, 1986; Ariz. State U. fellow, 1967-68. Mem. NEA, Nat. Art Edn. Assn. (v.p., bd. dirs. 1980-82, editorial bd. 1982-85, Secondary Art Educator of Yr. Pacific region 1985), Ariz. Alliance for Arts Edn. (bd. dirs. 1976-81, co-chair western regional confl. 1978), Tempe Secondary Edn. Assn., Ariz. Art Edn. Assn. (pres. 1976-78), Mortar Bd., Phi Delta Kappa, Alpha Phi. Club: Women's Image Now (Tempe). Home: 930 S Dobson Rd #22 Mesa AZ 85202 Office: Corona del Sol High Sch 1001 E Knox Rd Tempe AZ 85284

SAUNDERS, LAUREL BARNES, librarian; b. Ainsworth, Nebr., Aug. 17, 1926; d. Howard Enos and Flossie Agnes (Marr) Barnes; married; 1 child, Kelvin Edwin Saunders. BA, U. S.D., 1948; MA, U. Mich., 1950. Librarian pub. schs. Howell, Mich., 1950-51; asst. librarian, U.S. Army post Ft. Bliss, Tex., 1951-53; librarian, USAF base Biggs AFB, Tex., 1953-62; supervisory librarian U.S. Air Def. Sch., Ft. Bliss, 1962-64; chief cataloguing and acquistions U.S. Army Tech. Library, White Sands Missile Range, N.Mex., 1964-74, chief librarian, 1975—. Pres. Quaestors Sunday Sch. class, Trinity First Meth. Ch., 1985-88, adminstrv. bd., 1986-87. Mem. Fed. Mgrs. Assn. (2d v.p. 1982-83, pres. 1984-87, bd. dirs., Mgr. of Yr. award 1985), N.Mex. Library Assn. (vice-chmn. Documents Roundtable 1984-85, chmn. 1985-86), Border Regional Library Assn., U.S. Army Library Inst. (active procurement working group 1980-84). Republican. Club: Past Matrons (Anthony, N.Mex.). Lodge: Order of Eastern Star (Worthy Matron 1970, treas. 1982-87).

SAUNDERS, PHYLLIS S., financial and business consultant; b. N.Y.C., May 2, 1932; d. Jack and Bella (Bader) Bloom; widowed; children—Todd B., Dean B. Student, U. Miami. Pres. P.S. Export Co., buying service, bus. cons., fin. cons., money mgmt. for Cen. and S.Am., Bahamas, Caribbean; cons., investor since 1961. Mem. Am. Bus. Women's Assn., Nat. Assn. Women Bus. Owners, Am. Liver Found., Am. Jewish Com., Nat. Home Asthmatic Children, Hope Ctr. Mentally Retarded, U. Miami Booster Club, U. Miami Ctr. for Liver Diseases, U. Miami AIDS Research Ctr., Fla. Feminist Bank. Republican. Avocations: golf, tennis, aerobics, fishing, boating. Home: 2 Grove Isle Apt #205 Coconut Grove FL 33133

SAUNDERS, RUTH LYNCH, psychoanalyst, psychotherapist; b. Longview, Wash., Nov. 4, 1927; d. Harry Hudson and Marion Lucille (Gibson) Lynch; BS, UCLA, 1949; MSW, Columbia U., 1976; cert. Psychoanalytic Tng., Inst. for Contemporary Psychotherapy, 1979; m. Frank A. Saunders, May 24, 1958; 1 son, Anthony David. Projects editor The Sat. Rev. of Lit., N.Y.C., 1960-65; asst. med. editor McCall's, N.Y.C., 1965-67; editor Warner Bros., N.Y.C., 1967-69, Roche Med. Image, 1969-73; tng. analyst, supr., Inst. for Contemporary Psychotherapy, N.Y.C., 1976—; supr. staff Ctr. for the Study of Anorexia and Bulimia, N.Y.C., N.Y., 1979—; pvt. practice, N.Y.C. Mem. Manhattan adv. bd. N.Y. Urban League, 1962-74, pres. Lucy Stone League, 1972-74. Mem. Nat. Assn. Social Workers (cert.), Phi Beta Kappa, Alpha Mu Gammaa. Clubs: The Century Assn., Sankaty Head Golf, Siasconset Casino (Nantucket, Mass.). Home: 680 West End Ave 9B New York NY 10025 Other: Box 248 Slasconset MA 02564 Office: 940 Park Ave New York NY 10028

SAUNDERS, SANDRA JEAN, lawyer; b. Cleve., Jan. 1, 1944; d. Alexander V. and Rosemary (Sunyog) Toth. BA, Brown U., 1964; MA, Fordham U., 1965; JD, Lewis and Clark Law Sch., 1978. Bar: Oreg. 1979. Securities analyst various cos., N.Y.C., Boston, Chgo., 1964-73; econ. cons., Portland, 1973-76; pvt. practice law, Portland, 1979—. V.p. bd. dirs. Pittock Mansion Soc., Portland, 1981—; trustee Leukemia Assn. Oreg., 1984—; area rep. Nat. Alumni Schs. Program, Brown U., 1981—; mem. Portland Met. Citizens Cable TV Com., 1973-74; pres. Women's Assn., Oreg. Mus. Sci. and Industry, Portland, 1974, mem. council, 1984—, mem. auction bd., 1987—; mem. women's council Portland Art Assn., 1973—; bd. dirs. Vol. Braille Services, Inc., Portland, 1985—. Law rev. staff Environ. Law, 1977. Recipient Am. Jurisprudence award, 1978. Mem. Oreg. State Bar, Multnomah County Bar Assn., Oreg. Trial Lawyers Assn., Oreg. Young Attys. Assn. (dir. 1981-83), ABA, Phi Alpha Delta. Clubs: Portland City, Multnomah Athletic, International. Office: 700 Morgan Bldg 720 SW Washington St Portland OR 97205

SAUNDERS, TONI LYNNE, construction company executive; b. Columbus, Ohio, Aug. 19, 1949; d. Larry Brook Wells and Mildred Carole (Talbott) Cozart; m. William Kenneth Riley, May 13, 1969 (div. Mar. 1971); m. Albert Eugene Saunders, Sept. 28, 1971; 1 child, Randy Lee Saunders. Grad. high sch., Xenia, Ohio, 1967. Corp. sec. Ind. Horizontal Boring, Inc., Indpls., 1981-82; pres., chmn. bd. Ind. Horizontal Boring, Inc., New Palestine, Ind., 1982—; also bd. dirs. Ind. Horizontal Boring, Inc., Indpls.; founder Pride Cons., New Palestine, Ind., 1986—. Mem. Nat. Assn. Women in Constrn. (fund raiser 1984, 85, 86, chmn. Women's Bus. Enterprise com. 1984-86), Nat. Assn. Female Execs., Nat. Assn. Self-Employed. Office: Ind Horizontal Boring Inc PO Box 197 New Palestine IN 46163

SAUNTRY, SUSAN SCHAEFER, lawyer; b. Bangor, Maine, May 7, 1943; d. William Joseph and Emily Joan (Guenter) Schaefer; m. John Philip Sauntry, Jr., Aug. 18, 1968; 1 child, Mary Katherine. BS in Foreign Service, Georgetown U., 1965, JD, 1975. Bar: D.C. 1975, U.S. Dist. Ct. D.C. 1975, U.S. Ct. Appeals (D.C. cir.) 1975, (4th cir.) 1977, (6th cir.) 1978, (10th cir.) 1983, U.S. Supreme Ct. 1983. Congl. relations asst. OEO, Washington, 1966-68; program analyst EEO Com., Washington, 1968-70, U.S. Dept. Army, Okinawa, 1970-72; assoc. Morgan, Lewis & Bockius, Washington, 1975-83, ptnr., 1983—. Co-author: Employee Dismissal Law: Forms and Procedures, 1986; contbr. articles to profl. jours. Mem. ABA, D.C. Bar Assn., D.C. Women's Bar Assn., Am. Assn. Univ. Women, USA, Phi Beta Kappa, Pi Sigma Alpha. Democrat. Office: Morgan Lewis & Bockius 1800 M St NW Washington DC 20036

SAUSEDO, ANN ELIZABETH, newspaper librarian; b. Douglas, Ariz., Nov. 19, 1929; d. Eugene Ephraim and Bertha Evelyn (Kimpton) Bertram; m. Richard Edward Sausedo, July 22, 1952 (div. 1966); 1 dau., Robin Marie. Student Calif. schs. Asst. librarian Stockton Record (Calif.), 1948-51, head librarian, 1955-67; stewardess Calif. Central Airlines, 1951; library dir. Washington Star, 1967-76; free-lance organizer file systems, Palo Alto, Calif., 1976-78; library dir. Los Angeles Herald Examiner, 1978—. Contbr. chpt. to book in field. Mem. Spl. Libraries Assn., Nat. Assn. Female Execs., Calif. Bus. Women's Network. Office: Los Angeles Herald Examiner 1111 S Broadway Los Angeles CA 90015

SAUVÉ, JEANNE, governor-general of Canada; b. Prud'homme, Sask., Can., Apr. 26, 1922; d. Charles Albert and Anna (Vaillant) Benoit; m. Maurice Sauvé, Sept. 24, 1948; 1 son, Jean-François. Grad., U. Ottawa, D (hon.); diploma in French Civilization, U. Paris, 1952; DSc (hon.), N.B. U., 1974; LHD (hon.), Mt. St. Vincent U., St. Lawrence U.; LLD (hon.), U. Calgary, 1982, Queen's U., McGill U., Carleton U., U. Toronto, Laurentian U.; D (hon.), Laval U., U. Montreal; PhD in Polit. Sci. (hon.), Chulalongkorn U., Bangkok. Nat. pres. Jeuness Etudiante Catholique, Montreal, 1942-47; tchr. French London County Council, 1948-50; asst. to dir. youth sect. UNESCO, Paris, 1951; journalist, broadcaster 1952-72; bd. dirs. Union des Artistes, Montreal, 1961, v.p., 1968-70; v.p. Canadian Inst. on Pub. Affairs, 1962-64, pres., 1964; mem. Can. Centennial Commn., 1967; gen. sec. Fedn. des Auteurs et des Artistes du Can., 1966-72; mem. Parliament for Ahuntsic (Montreal), 1972-79, for Laval-des-Rapides, 1979-84; gov. gen. Canada, 1984—; minister of state in charge of sci. and tech., 1972-74, minister of environment, 1974-75, minister of communications, 1975-79; advisor for external affairs Sec. of State, 1978; speaker House of Commons, 1980-84. Decorated Commander of the Order Mil. Merit, Can. Forces Decoration; named Privy Councillor. Hon. fellow Royal Archtl. Inst. Can.; founding mem. Inst. Polit. Research. Mem. Liberal Party of Can. Roman Catholic. Office: Rideau Hall, 1 Sussex Dr, Ottawa, ON Canada K1A 0A1

SAUVÉ, KAY LYNN, sales professional; b. Portland, Oreg., Nov. 12, 1961; d. David Lawrence and Juanita Joy (Oates) S. BS, Portland State U., 1984. Research analyst City of Portland, 1980-84; retail sales rep. ARCO Petroleum Products Co., Los Angeles, 1984—; pvt. practice business analyst, San Francisco, 1984—. Vol. Spl. Olympics, Walnut Creek, Calif., 1984; gov. Walnut Park Assn.; mem. San Francisco Mus. Soc. Mem. Nat. Assn. Female Execs., Cocha Assn. Republican. Roman Catholic. Club: Pacific, Commonwealth. Office: ARCO Petroleum Products Co PO Box 5811 San Mateo CA 94402

SAVAGE, VANDOLYN JOYCE, librarian; b. Truscott, Tex., Aug. 7, 1929; d. Van Wyck and Mabel Lee (Craig) Browning; m. Vernon Howard Savage, Sept. 8, 1951 (div. 1978); children—Van Howard, Lynn Monroe, Jan Lee. B.A., North Tex. State Coll., 1950; M.L.S., North Tex. State U., 1968. Asst. music librarian North Tex. State Coll. Library, Denton, 1950-52; catalog librarian U. Tex. Library, Austin, 1952-54, sr. cataloger, 1968-70, asst. chief, catalog dept., 1970-73, head librarian end process sect., 1973-74, head librarian, automated bibliographic processing unit, 1974-76, head librarian acquisitions and processing dept., 1976-78; jr. high sch. librarian Quanah (Tex.) Pub. Schs., 1954-55; reference librarian Tarleton State Coll. Library, Stephenville, Tex., 1959-61, cataloger, 1962-67; asst. documents librarian North Tex. State U. Library, Denton, 1968; asst. dir. tech. services U. Houston Univ. Park Libraries, Houston, 1978-85; assoc. dir. Bibliographic Resource Ctr., AMIGOS Bibliographic Council, Inc., Dallas, 1985—; chmn. tech. services com. Houston Area Research Libraries Consortium, 1979-80. Mem. ALA, Assn. Coll. and Research Libraries (sec. chpts. council 1982), Library Adminstrn. and Mgmt. Assn., Tex. Library Assn. (chmn. coll. and univ. libraries div. 1980-82), Tex. Assn. Coll. Tchrs. (vice chmn. U. Houston chpt. 1980-81), Beta Phi Mu, Phi Kappa Phi. Democrat. Mem. Disciples of Christ. Home: 12484 Abrams Rd 1702 Dallas TX 75243 Office: AMIGOS Bibliographic Council Inc 11300 N Central Expre ssway Suite 321 Dallas TX 75243

SAVAGE, XYLA RUTH, government official; b. Norman, Okla., Dec. 17, 1937; d. Joel Frederick and Thelma Gladys (Burgess) Church; B.A., U. Okla., 1969; postgrad. U.S. Dept. Agr., 1971; m. John W. Savage, Jr., Jan. 18, 1955 (dec. Oct. 1982); children—Mark Wayne, John Christian. Interior designer Sears, Roebuck and Co., Petersburg, Va., 1966-67; head tech. illustration dept. ITT, Bladensburg, Md., 1967-69; supr. publs. dept. NASA, Greenbelt, Md., 1969-71; supr. illustration dept. VA, Washington, 1971-72; mgr. forms design and visual communications dept. Bur. Labor Stats., Washington, 1972—; instr. design U.S. Dept. Agr. Grad. Sch., evenings 1972—. Mem. Presidential sub-com. Questionnaire Design, 1987; chmn. publicity Band Parents; officer, parents orgn. Mem. Bus. Forms Mgmt. Assn., Printing Industries Am. Mem. Christian Ch. Author: Forms Design, 1975. Home: 12901 Chalfont Ave Fort Washington MD 20744 Office: 441 G St NW Room 2862 Washington DC 20212

SAVARESE, FRITZI JOLENE, nurse; b. Wheeling, W.Va., Mar. 2, 1926; d. Herman Richard and Della Carolyn (Ward) Hobbs; m. Charles Richard Farley, Sept. 1946 (dec.); children: Charles Richard Jr., Rebecca Lee, Thomas Jackson; m. Charles Joseph Savarese, Aug. 26, 1978. Student, W.Va. U., 1944-46, Marshall U., 1947; diploma, Ohio Valley Med. Ctr. Sch. Nursing, 1973. Library asst. W.Va. Library Commn., Morgantown, 1948-51, U. Md. Med. Sch., Balt., 1951-55; staff nurse Ocean View Meml. Hosp., Myrtle Beach, S.C., 1973-74; orgnl. dir. nursing Hilton Head Hosp., Hilton Head Island, S.C., 1974-76; adminstrv. assoc. Charles Savarsee, M.D., Shallotte, N.C., 1976—; nurse cons. project U.S.A., AMA, Tchula, Miss., 1976-77, Maclenny, Fla., 1977-78. Editor nursing procedures manual, 1975. Vol. Ohio Valley Med. Ctr., Wheeling, W.Va., 1960-69, Rep. Party, Wheeling, 1968; fitness cons. Myrtle Beach Athletic Club, 1984-86. Mem. Internat. Order of Kings Daus. and Sons, Emergency Dept. Nurses Assn., Chi Omega. Republican. Presbyterian. Office: Charles Savarese MD 12 Resort Plaza Shallotte NC 28459

SAVARIEGO, BERTA KOZOLCHYK, foreign language educator; b. Havana, Cuba, Nov. 1, 1946; d. Mane and Flora (Kirstein) Kozolchyk; m. Alberto Savariego, Sept. 5, 1965; 1 dau., Donna. B.A. in Spanish with minor in English, Tex. Woman's U., Denton, 1967, M.A. in Spanish, 1968; Ph.D. in Spanish, Tex. Tech. U., 1974. Instr. Spanish, San Antonio Coll., Dallas, 1968-70; instr. Spanish and English, Richland Coll., Dallas, 1973-76, El Centro Coll., Dallas, 1973-76; translator Rimco, Inc., Dallas, 1976-77; instr. Spanish So. Meth. Univ., Dallas, 1977-79, Miami (Fla.) Dade Community Coll., 1979—. Recipient Matrix award Women in Communications, Inc., 1981; Golden Reel of Merit award Internat. TV Assn., 1981; Bronze award Internat. Film and Festival N.Y., 1981. Mem. Am. Assn. Tchrs. Spanish and Portuguese, MLA, Am. Translators Assn., Am. Lit. Translators Assn., Phi Kappa Phi, Phi Sigma Iota, Pi Delta Phi, other orgns. Author: fiction and textbooks. Home: 1300 Biscaya Dr Surfside FL 33154 Office: Dade County Pub Schs 1450 NE 2d Ave Miami FL 33132

SAVASO, JEANNIE MARIE, mortgage company executive; b. Freeport, Tex., Mar. 19, 1955; d. John C. and Adele M. (Hennig) S. BBA in Acctg. with highest honors, U. Tex., 1979. CPA, Tex. Internal auditor City of Prescott, Ariz., 1980; auditor Peat, Marwick, Mithcell & Co., Houston, 1981-82; sr. acct. Moss, McClure & Krenzke, Inc., Lake Jackson, Tex., 1982-84; controller, asst. v.p. Ameriway Mortgage Corp., Houston, 1984—. Mem. Am. Inst. CPA's, Tex. Soc. CPA's, Tex. Ex Alumni Assn., Beta Alpha Psi, Beta Gamma Sigma, Phi Kappa Phi. Home: 8760 Westheimer #126 Houston TX 77063 Office: Ameriway Mortgage Corp 6363 Woodway Suite 600 Houston TX 77057

SAVIANO, BERNADETTE, clergywoman, graphic arts specialist; b. Fall River, Mass., May 10, 1948; d. Jesse Medeiros and Rosaline (Aguiar) Tavares. BA in Theology, Philosophy, Greensboro (N.C.) Coll., 1988. Lic. minister, 1984. Account exec. Co-Art Ad Agy., Providence, 1973-75; account exec., ptnr. Argentieri Assocs. Advt. Providence, 1975-77; mktg. cons. Christian's, Providence, 1977-78; mgr. graphics dept. Purvis Systems (Computer Systems Engring. Co.), Middletown, R.I., 1978-86; minister adult edn., outreach and evangelism Lawndale Bapt. Ch., Greensboro, N.C., 1986; jr. chaplain Greensboro Coll., 1986—. Author: (poems) Desert Songs, 1982; exhibited photographs Newport Art Mus., 1983. Woodruff fellow Emory U., 1988-89, N.Am. Ministerial fellow, 1988-89; recipient Young Am. Poets award, 1975. Mem. Nat. Contract Mgmt. Assn., Nat. Assn. Female Execs. Home: 1901G Ashwood Ct Suite 116 Greensboro NC 27408

SAVICH, RENÉ, broadway theater executive, producer; b. Chgo., Nov. 14, 1947; d. Nicholas and Elizabeth (Szakurski) S. BS, Northwestern U., 1969. Asst. house mgr. Minskoff Theatre, N.Y.C., 1973; mem. mgmt. staff The Shubert Orgn. Inc., N.Y.C., 1975-77, mgr. dept. maintenance, 1977-80; asst. house mgr. The Shubert Theatre, N.Y.C., 1975-77, Plymouth Theatre, N.Y.C., 1978; house mgr. Barrymore Theatre, N.Y.C., 1978-79; mgr. co. The Elephant Man, N.Y.C., 1980; house mgr. Playhouse Theatre, N.Y.C., 1980-81, Cort Theatre, N.Y.C., 1981-85, Golden Theatre, N.Y.C., 1985-86, Booth Theatre, N.Y.C., 1987—. Producer off-Broadway plays including Wine Untouched, 1979, Lou, 1981, Punchy, 1983. Mem. Assn. of Theatrical Press Agts. and Mgrs., Actors Equity Assn., Treas. and Ticket Sellers Union. Office: The Shubert Orgn Inc 234 W 44th St New York NY 10036

SAVOIE, JOANNE, financial planning company executive; b. ElPaso, Tex., Aug. 27, 1947; d. Joseph James and Mary Catherine (Glosque) Phillip; m. Michael Edward Savoie, Feb. 14, 1968 (div. 1979); children Michael Edward Jr., David Joshua. Student, N. Mex. State U., 1967-68. Mgr., broker Fidelity Capital Service Agy., Brick, N.J., 1981-86; broker, pres. J&L Fin. Concepts., Brick, N.J., 1986—; pres. Lady J. Enterprises, Inc., Brick, N.J., 1987—; owner Body Alive Ctrs. and Tone It All Toning Salons, Brick, 1987—; Bd. adv. N.J. Ins. Commn., Trenton, N.J., 1985. Mem. Internat. Assn. Fin. Planners, Internat. Dance Exercise Assn., Exec. Woman of Am., Ins. Women of Am. Republican. Office: Lady J. Enterprises Inc 580 Brick Rd Brick NJ 08723

SAVOLT, LOUANN SUE, retailer; b. Ft. Wayne, Ind., Sept. 28, 1942; d. Harold Edwin and Norma Esther (Mertz) Hartman; m. Larry Gene Savolt, Sept. 6, 1980; children by previous marriage: Neil Reith, Sheila Reith. AD in Nursing, Garden City Community Coll., 1977. RN, Kans. Health nurse Garden City Community Coll., Kans., 1977-80; staff nurse St. Catherine Hosp., Garden City, 1983; owner, mgr. Personally Yours Lingerie, Garden City, 1984—. Hot line vol. Family Crisis Services, Finney County, Kans., 1982-84; pub. edn. chmn. Am. Cancer Soc., Finney County, 1978-84; co-chmn. Coalition for Prevention of Child Abuse and Neglect, Finney County, 1978-79, chmn., 1979-80. Recipient Service award Finney County Am. Cancer Soc., 1981, Family Crisis Services, 1984. Mem. Women's C. of C., Nat. Retail Mchts. Assn., Nat. Assn. Female Execs. Lutheran. Avocations: reading, snowmobiling, traveling. Home: Route 2 Box 51 Holcomb KS 67851 Office: Personally Yours Lingerie 503 N Main Garden City KS 67846

SAVOY, JACQUELINE SANDRA, investment broker; b. Phila., Aug. 19, 1951; d. Maurice M. and Beatrice (Medoff) S. BS in Health Edn. magna cum laude, Temple U., 1973, postgrad. in bus., 1980, 85; MA in Secondary Sch. Counseling with honors, Villanova (Pa.) U., 1977; JD (hon.), Del. Law Sch. of Widener U., 1986. Cert. in health edn. and secondary sch. counseling; registered rep. N.Y. Stock Exchange. Tchr. health edn. Phila. Sch. System, 1974-75; advisor curriculum and bus. programs Temple U., Phila., 1975-76, advisor acad. and prelaw programs, 1976-83; rep. Roth & Co., Bala Cynwyd, Pa., 1981-83; investment broker Butcher & Singer, Inc., Phila., 1983—. Mem. Am. Coll. Personnel Assn., Am. Personnel and Guidance Assn., Stockbrokers Soc., Phila. Women's Network, Phila. C. of C. (ambassador), Sweet Adelines (Valley Forge chpt.), Kappa Delta Pi. Republican. Jewish. Clubs: Pres.'s, Butcher & Singer Inc. Office: Butcher & Singer Inc 1500 Walnut St Philadelphia PA 19102

SAVRIN, JANET ALANE, lawyer; b. N.Y.C., Oct. 3, 1957; d. Sydney and Isabelle (Tilin) S. BA, U. Buffalo, 1979, JD, 1982. Ptnr. Magier & Savrin, N.Y.C., 1983—. Mem. ABA, N.Y. Bar Assn., N.Y.C. Bar Assn.

SAWYER, BLANCHE MELTON, real estate owner; b. Waynesboro, Tenn., May 23, 1932; d. James Clarence and Edna (Hampton) Melton; m. David W. Sawyer Sr., Nov. 24, 1956; children: David W. Jr., Kerri S. Norman. BS, Union U., 1953; postgrad., Tenn. Tech., 1954, Southwestern U., 1955. Acct. Jackson-Madison County (Tenn.) Gen. Hosp., 1953-54; tchr. Hamburg (Ark.) High Sch., 1954-55, Caney (Kans.) High Sch., 1955-56; realtor Fleming Realty, Ft. Smith, Ark., 1972-74, Phillips-Foltz, Ft. Smith, 1974-76; owner Sawyer Realty, Ft. Smith, 1976—. Inventor patent "Splatter-Platter", 1973. Pres. Jr. Civic League, Ft. Smith, 1977; co-chmn. Ft. Smith United Way, 1978; bd. dirs. ARC, Ft. Smith. Named Realtor of Yr., Ft. Smith Bd. Realtors, 1983. Mem. Ft. Smith Bd. Realtors (sec. 1979, bd. dirs. 1980-83, Realtor of Yr. 1983), Ark. Chpt. Cert. Residential Specialists (charter), Ft. Smith C. of C. (bd. dirs. 1981—), Realtors Nat. Mktg. Inst. Democrat. Baptist. Clubs: Town, Hardscrabble Country (Ft. Smith). Home: 9711 Kingsley Pl Fort Smith AR 72903 Office: Sawyer Realty 3801 Rogers Ave Fort Smith AR 72903

SAWYER, (L.) DIANE, journalist; b. Glasgow, Ky., Dec. 22, 1945; d. E.P. and Jean W. (Dunagan) S.; m. Mike Nichols, Apr. 29, 1988. B.A., Wellesley Coll., 1967. Reporter sta. WLKY-TV, Louisville, 1967-70; adminstr. press office White House, 1970-74; researcher Richard Nixon's memoirs 1974-78; gen. assignment reporter, then Dept. State corr. CBS News, 1978-81; co-anchor CBS Morning News, from 1981; now corr. 60 Minutes, CBS-TV.

Mem. Council Fgn. Relations. Office: CBS News 51 W 52d St New York NY 10019 *

SAWYER, GENE, retired journalist; b. Danvers, Mass., Sept. 9, 1910; d. Morse Leon and Harriet Elizabeth (Adams) Lewis; grad. Cushing Acad., Ashburnham, Mass., 1928; student Syracuse U., 1928-30; m. W.P. Sawyer, Sept. 9, 1930. Radio announcer, writer, producer, Honolulu, N.Y.C., China, 1937-49; officer U.S. Fgn. Service, Burma, Cambodia, Indonesia, Washington, 1950-65; corr. in Honolulu, Voice of Am., Washington, 1966-71; student interviewer manuscripts Hawaii Pacific Coll. and East West Center, Honolulu, 1972-79; editor original material on Burma and Cambodia, U. Hawaii, 1980-81. Vice-pres., Hawaii div. U.N. Assn., 1971-73, bd. dirs., 1975—. Recipient cert. of Merit, Sr. Achievement, 1980, First Lady's award for Outstanding Vol. of Yr., East West Ctr., 1985. Mem. Women in Communications (Headliner award Hawaii chpt. 1986), Honolulu Acad. Arts, Fgn. Service Assocs., Friends of East-West Ctr. (life), Theta Sigma Phi. Author: Celebrations, Asia and the Pacific, 1978. Home: 1465 Aala St Apt 802 Honolulu HI 96817

SAWYER, HELEN ALTON, painter; b. Washington; d. Wells Moses and Kathleen Alton (Bailey) S.; m. Jerry Farnsworth, Aug. 26, 1925. Student at Master's School, Dobbs Ferry, 1914-18; studied art with, Johansen and Hawthorne. Painter, artist in oil and water color, lithographer, exhibited at principal galleries and museums of, U.S.; Represented permanent collections numerous museums including, Whitney Mus. Am. Art, Pa. Acad., Toledo Mus., Syracuse U. Mus., John Herron Mus., Indpls., Atlanta Mus., Amherst Coll. Mus., Williams Coll. Mus. Art, Chrysler Mus., others, IBM collection, Library of Congress, C. & O. R.R. collections; oil painting Clown Still Life owned, Norfolk Mus.; Contbr. articles and verse to jours.; Has painted in, U.S., Spain, France, Mexico. Recipient numerous awards, honors. Mem. N.A.D., Nat. Arts Club, Provincetown, Yonkers, Sarasota art assns., Audubon Artists, Nat. Assn. Women Artists. Home: 3482 Flamingo Sarasota FL 34242

SAWYER, JANICE LYNN, sales executive; b. Memphis, Oct. 21, 1953; d. Maynard Lewis and Rosa Bernice (Berry) Farris; m. James Vernon Sawyer, Aug. 23, 1974 (div. June 1977); 1 child, Jason Allen. Student, U. Tenn., Martin, 1971-72, U. Miss., 1983-85, Memphis State U., 1978—. Sales rep. Signode Corp., Glenview, Ill., 1978-85, territory mgr., 1986—. Mem. Soc. Profl. Materials Handling Engrs., Pi Sigma Epsilon. Republican. Presbyterian. Home: 8096 Canterbury Southaven MS 38671

SAWYER, KATHERINE H. (MRS. CHARLES BALDWIN SAWYER), librarian; b. Cleve., July 11, 1908; d. Willard and Martha (Beaumont) Hirsh; AB, Smith Coll., 1930; MS in Library Sci., Western Res. U., 1956; m. Charles Baldwin Sawyer, Aug. 19, 1933; children: Samuel Prentiss, Charles Brush, William Beaumont. With Cleve. Pub. Library, profl. librarian hosps., instns. dept., 1956-61; med. librarian St. Luke's Hosp., Pittsfield, Mass., 1965-66; library cons. Ministry of Health, Guyana, S. Am., 1966-68; curator Sophia Smith Collection; counselor Friends of Smith Coll. Library, chmn. exec. com., 1959-65; chmn. Friends of Western Res. Hist. Library, 1973-78, hon. trustee, 1980—; dir., trustee Friends of Pima-Green Valley Library; trustee Episcopal Ch. Home, 1965— ; bd. govs. Western Res. U., 1957-66, bd. visitors Sch. Library Sci., 1958-68, 69-72; trustee Friends of Cleve. Pub. Library, 1962-67, Christian Residences Found., 1976-82, WRHS, 1979—; counselor Friends of Smith Coll. Library, 1962-68. Mem. Ariz. State Library Assn., Western Res. Hist. Soc., Archeol. Inst., Spl. Libraries Assn., Nat. League Am. Pen Women. Episcopalian (vestryman 1974-77). Clubs: Union, Allience Française; Green Valley Country; Intown. Co-author (talking books for blind) Gardening for Blind Persons, 1962; Beauty, Glamour and Style, 1963. Home: 525 Paseo del Mundo Green Valley AZ 85614

SAWYER, SANDRA MCCOMMAS, lawyer, former judge; b. Tulsa, Sept. 1, 1937; d. Franklin Delmar and Irene (Adams) McCommas; student Tex. Tech. Coll., Draughon Bus. Sch., LL.B., Oklahoma City U., 1967; m. L.L. Sawyer, Mar. 6, 1981; children—Lise Dyann, Richard Owen, Whitney Michelle. Legal sec., 1956-64; admitted to Okla. bar, 1967, Oreg. bar, 1983; legal asst. to U.S. Ct. Appeals judge, 1964-67, law clk., 1967-68; bill drafter Okla. Legislature, 1969-70; chief traffic ct. project Okla. Supreme Ct., 1970-75; individual practice law, Oklahoma City, from 1967; partner firm Moran & Johnson, Oklahoma City; referee juvenile div. Okla. County Dist. Ct., 1977-78, spl. dist. judge, 1978-80; assoc. Grant, Ferguson & Carter, P.C.; adj. prof. So. Oreg. State Coll.; lectr. Okla. Center Continuing Legal Edn., 1969-75, Okla. Bar Found. Legal Secs. Ednl. Series, 1974; mem. Okla. Legislature Interim. Com. Municipal Cts. Revision, 1973-74. Sunday Sch. tchr., supt. Resurrection Episcopal Ch., Oklahoma City; pres. regional adv. com. So. Oreg. State Coll.; mem. So. Oreg. Drug Awareness Com. Recipient Outstanding Civic Contbn. award Modern Woodmen Am., 1977. Mem. Am. (nat. v.p. law student div. 1966; Gold Key award 1965, 66), Okla. (Outstanding Grad. Law Student award 1967, grievance com. 1977-78), Okla. County, Oreg. bar assns., Oklahoma City U. Law Sch. Alumni Assn. (sec. 1971), Iota Tau Tau, Zeta Tau Alpha. Author, editor in field; spl. cts. reporter Am. Judicature Soc., 1974-78. Home: 585 Thornton Way Ashland OR 97520

SAWYER, SHARON KAY, retail executive; b. Durham, N.C., Nov. 19, 1959; d. Floyd Daniel Sr. and Marion Florence (Buttry) S. BS in Bus. Adminstrn., Meredith Coll., 1982; cert., Rollins Coll., 1986. Sales hostess Walt Disney World, Orlando, Fla., 1983-84, merchandise lead, 1984-86, merchandise supr., buyer, 1986—; leadership devel. Walt Disney World, Orlando, 1986. Mem. edn. com., youth counselor First Meth. Ch., Orlando, 1985—; vol. Shelter for the Homeless, Orlando, 1986-87; chmn. carnival Spl. Olympics, Orlando, 1985. Mem. Nat. Assn. Female Execs., Smithsonian Inst., Audubon Soc. Methodist. Home: 501 Lillian Dr Fern Park FL 32830 Office: Walt Disney World PO Box 10000 Lake Buena Vista FL 32830-1000

SAWYERS, ELIZABETH JOAN, librarian, administrator; b. San Diego, Dec. 2, 1936; d. William Henry and Elizabeth Georgiana (Price) S. A.A., Glendale Jr. Coll., 1957; B.A. in Bacteriology, UCLA, 1959, M.L.S., 1961. Asst. head acquisition sect. Nat. Library Medicine, Bethesda, Md., 1962-63, head acquisition sect., 1963-66, spl. asst. to chief tech. services div., 1966-69, spl. asst. to assoc. dir. for library ops., 1969-73; asst. dir. libraries for tech. services SUNY-Stony Brook, 1973-75; dir. Health Scis. Library Ohio State U., Columbus, 1975—. Mem. Assn. Acad. Health Scis. Library Dirs. (sec./treas. 1981-83, pres. 1983-84), Med. Library Assn., Am. Soc. for Info. Sci., Spl. Libraries Assn., ALA. Office: Ohio State U Health Scis Library 376 W 10th Ave Columbus OH 43210

SAX, MARY RANDOLPH, speech pathologist; b. Pontiac, Mich., July 13, 1925; d. Bernard Angus and Ada Lucile (Thurman) TePoorten; B.A. magna cum laude, Mich. State U., 1947; M.A., U. Mich., 1949; m. William Martin Sax, Feb. 7, 1948. Supr. speech correction dept. Waterford Twp. Schs., Pontiac, 1949-69; lectr. Marygrove Coll., Detroit, 1971-72; pvt. practice speech and lang. rehab., Wayne, Oakland Counties, Mich., 1973—; adj. speech pathologist Southfield, Mich., Farmington, Mich.; mem. sci. council stroke Am. Heart Assn. Grantee Inst. Articulation and Learning, 1969, others. Mem. Am. Speech-Lang.-Hearing Assn., Mich. Speech Pathologists in Clin. Practice, Mich. Speech-Lang.-Hearing Assn. (com. community and hosp. services), Am. Heart Assn. of Mich., Stroke Com. of Am., AAUW, Internat. Assn. Logopedics and Phoniatrics (Switzerland), Founders Soc. of Detroit Inst. Arts, Mich. Humane Soc., Theta Alpha Phi, Phi Kappa Phi, Kappa Delta Pi. Contbr. articles to profl. jours. Home and Office: 31320 Woodside Franklin MI 48025

SAXION, SANDRA LEE, communications executive; b. Cleve., Sept. 6, 1947; d. Robert and Louise A. (Schotsch) Dangel; B.A. in Social Sci. and Edn., Heidelberg Coll., Tiffin, Ohio, 1969; m. Barry Dean Saxion, May 10, 1980. Sales rep. N.J., Gillette Co., 1973-76; mktg. mgr. Warner-Amex Cable Co., N.Y.C., 1977-79; dir. mktg. Teleprompter Manhattan Cable TV, N.Y.C., 1979-80; dir. mktg. UTV Cable Network, Fair Lawn, N.J., 1981-83; pres. Saxion, Inc., 1983—; speaker in field. Mem. Women in Cable, LWV, Bus. and Profl. Women (1st v.p. 1984-85). Republican. Methodist. Home: 137 Rockaway Valley Rd Boonton NJ 07005

SAXON, BRENDA OLIVIA, pharmacist; b. Washington, July 1, 1941; d. Horace Sidney and Theresa Pierre (Spriggs) Kenner; m. Aubrey Gerald Saxon, Oct. 19, 1963; children: Donna Felice, Aubrey Gerald II. BS, Howard U., 1963; postgrad., U. Miami. Retail store owner Garfield Pharmacy, Washington, 1964-66; retail pharmacist Peoples Drugs, Washington, 1966-70; staff pharmacist Providence Hosp., Washington, 1970-79, hosp. pharmacist, 1982—, asst. dir. pharmacy, 1985—; staff pharmacist Jackson Meml. Hosp., Miami, Fla., 1979-80; geriatric cons. Fed. Health Service, Washington, 1980-82. Vol. Met. Police Boys' Clubs, Washington, 1975; fund raiser C. Cooper Scholarship Fund Raising Com., Washington, 1981, 82; philanthropist D.C. Pub. Schs., Washington, 1987. Burroughs Wellcome Drug Co. scholar, Triangle Park, N.C., 1979, 85. Mem. Assn. Black Hosp. Pharmacists (sec. 1979), Am. Soc. Hosp. Pharmacists (moderator mgmt. case study 1984, 85), D.C. Soc. Hosp. Pharmacists (sec. 1986—). Democrat.

SAXON, FRANCES SHIVER, women's center administrator ans counselor; b. Walhalla, q.C., Jan. 12, 1928; d. Noble Calhoun and Caroline (Ansel) Shiver; m. James Hendricks Saxon, Sept. 3, 1949; children: James Hendricks, Frank, Scott, Suzanne, Carol, Andrew, Dorothy, David. Student, U. N.C., Greensboro, 1946-49; BA in Psychology with honors, U. N.C., Charlotte, 1975, MEd, 1981. Commuter life coordinator U. N.C., Charlotte, 1974-77; founder, exec. dir. WomanReach Inc., Charlotte, 1977—; cons. Handicapped Organized Women, Charlotte, 1983-84, Women's Concerns program Mecklenburg Presbytery, Charlotte, 1985. Recipient Outstanding Service award U. N.C., Charlotte, 1975. Mem. Nat. Assn. Counseling and Devel., N.C. Assn. Counseling and Devel., Southeastern Women's Studies Assn., Charlotte Bus. and Profl. Women, Nat. Assn. Group Work, Nat. Assn. Female Execs., Nat. Assn. Women's Centers. Home: 3120 Libeth St Charlotte NC 28205 Office: WomanReach Inc 605 The Gallery Midtown Outlet Square Charlotte NC 28205

SAXON, LAURA LOUISE, banker; b. Ft. Worth, June 26, 1948; d. Reginald Elzey Jones and Marjorie (Roberts) Richardson; m. Cleve H. Saxon Jr., June 28, 1965; children: Cleve H. III, Angela Grace. Student, N.E. La. U., 1967-69. Correspondent banking officer Ouachita Nat. Bank, Monroe, La., 1974-80, mgr. automated clearinghouse, 1980-84; mgr., officer First Nat. Bank of Commerce, New Orleans, 1984-86; ops. dir. GulfNet, Inc., New Orleans, 1986—. Mem. Nat. Assn. Bank Women, Nat. Assn. Female Execs., Am. Bankers Assn. Republican. Methodist. Office: First Nat Bank of Commerce PO Box 60279 New Orleans LA 70160

SAY, MARLYS MORTENSEN (MRS. JOHN THEODORE SAY), superintendent; b. Yankton, S.D., Mar. 11, 1924; d. Melvin A. and Edith L. (Fargo) Mortensen; B.A., U. Colo., 1949, M.Ed., 1953; adminstrv. specialist U. Nebr., 1973; m. John Theodore Say, June 21, 1951; children—Mary Louise, James Kenneth, John Melvin, Margaret Ann. Tchr. Huron (S.D.) Jr. High Sch., 1944-48, Lamar (Colo.) Jr. High Sch., 1950-52, Norfolk Pub. Sch., 1962-63; Madison County supt., Madison, Nebr., 1963—. Mem. N.E.A. (life), Am. Assn. Sch. Adminstrs., Dept. Rural Edn., Nebr. Assn. County Supts. (pres.), Nebr. Elementary Prins. Assn., AAUW (pres. Norfolk br.), N.E. Nebr. County Supts. Assn. (pres.), Assn. Sch. Bus. Ofcls., Nat. Orgn. Legal Problems in Edn., Assn. Supervision and Curriculum Devel., Nebr. Edn. Assn., Nebr. Sch. Adminstrs. Assn. Republican. Methodist. Home: 4805 S 13th St Norfolk NE 68701 Office: Courthouse Madison NE 68748

SAYAD, PAMELA MIRIAM, lawyer; b. San Francisco, Apr. 13, 1949; d. Samuel Daniel and Charlotte (Yonan) S.; A.B. in Polit. Sci., U. Calif.-Berkeley, 1970; J.D., U. Notre Dame Sch. Law, 1973; Bar: D.C. 1974, U.S. Dist. Ct. D.C. 1974, Mass. 1980, U.S. Dist Ct. (no. dist.) Calif. 1981, Calif. 1982, U.S. Dist. Ct. (no. dist.) Calif., 1981, U.S. Ct. Appeals (9th cir.) 1981, U.S. Dist. Ct. D.C. 1974, U.S. Ct. Appeals (D.C. cir.) 1974, U.S. Dist. Ct. Mass. 1980, U.S. Dist. Ct. (ea. dist.) Calif. 1986. Atty. U.S. HEW, Washington, 1973-74; atty. solicitor's office Div. Indian Affairs, U.S. Dept. Interior, Washington, 1974-77; asst. U.S. atty. for D.C., Washington, 1977-80; assoc. Swartz & Swartz, Boston, 1980-81; assoc. Archer, Rosenak & Hanson, San Francisco, 1981-82, Bourhis, Lawless & Harvey, San Francisco, 1982-83; ptnr. Sayad & Trigero, San Francisco, 1983—; bd. of trustees Calif. Indian Legal Services, 1984—; bd. dirs. Found. Study Electorial Reform. Author: (with others) Criminal Practice Inst. Manual, 1980; Litigating for Profit, 1983; also articles. Mem. Jr. League San Francisco, 1981—. Mem. ABA, Assn. Trial Lawyers Am., Calif. Trial Lawyers Assn., Bar Assn. San Francisco, Calif. Women Lawyers, Gamma Phi Beta. Democrat. Presbyterian. Office: Sayad & Trigero 444 Market St Suite 930 San Francisco CA 94111

SAYAH, DOROTHY MAE, corporate professional; b. Williamsport, Pa., July 1, 1938; d. Edmund George and Eunice Alberta (Saeman) Merk; m. Joseph Beck Sayah, July 18, 1959. Grad. high sch., Williamsport. Billing clk. Avco Mfg. Co., Williamsport, 1956-57, sec. to traffic mgr., 1957-58; analyst Jones & Laughlin Steel Co., Muncy, Pa., 1958-59, adminstrv. sec. to traffic mgr., 1959-60; acctg. asst. Sweet's Steel Co., Williamsport, 1960-61; sec. engring. dept. Morse Chain and Cable Co., Ithaca, N.Y., 1961; adminstrv. sec. to dir. of budget Cornell U., Ithaca, 1962-65; sec. to regional mgr. Mason & Dixon Truck Lines, York, Pa., 1966-67; pvt. sec. to adminstrv. v.p. McCrory Variety Stores, York, 1967-69, adminstrv. asst. to v.p. restaurant div., 1969-72; adminstrv. asst. to pres. Sayah Carpet and Wallpaper Outlet, York, 1972-76; sec., treas. Yorktowne Wallpaper Outlet, York, 1976—. Mem. York County Home Builders Assn., Cen. Pa. Floor Covering Assn., York Area Outlet Assn. (treas. 1986-87). Democrat. Roman Catholic. Club: Yorktown Tennis. Home: 775-B Hardwick Pl York PA 17402 Office: Yorktowne Wallpaper Outlet 2445 S Queen St York PA 17402

SAYER, KIMBERLY DAWN MARY, beauty products company executive; b. Bristol, Avon, Eng., Apr. 4, 1959; d. Raymond Graham and Mary Gwendolyne Beryl (Niblet) S.; m. Robert Frank Nuzzo, Nov. 13, 1980 (div. 1985). Ed. pub. schs., Eng. Asst. Tony Chase, Inc., N.Y.C., 1979-80; model (Barbizon Agy.) N.Y.C., 1979-80; beautician, make-up artist Something Different Beauty Salon, N.Y.C., 1980-81; pres. Kimberly Sayer Beauty Care Inc., N.Y.C., 1981—; cons. in field. Contbr. articles to profl. jours. Active World Vision, 1983—, Beauty Without Cruelty, People for the Humane Treatment of Animals. Mem. Nat. Assn. Female Execs., Sigma Pi Epsilon. Mem. Christian Church (Disciples of Christ). Home: 61 W 82d St Suite 5-A New York NY 10024

SAYLOR, MARSHA MEARNS, lawyer, labor arbitrator; b. Bryn Mawr, Pa., July 3, 1952; d. H. Durston and May (Marsh) S. BA, U. Pa., 1974; postgrad., Brown U., 1974; JD, U. Puget Sound, 1976. Bar: Wash. 1977, U.S. Supreme Ct. 1983, Mass. 1988. Prosecutor Pierce County Prosecutor's Office, Tacoma, 1976; staff counsel Internat. Fedn. Profl. and Tech. Engrs., Seattle, 1977-79, Wash. State Council County and City Employees, Seattle, 1979-82; adminstrv. judge U.S. Merit Systems Protection Bd., Boston, 1982-85; sole practice, labor arbitrator Boston, Seattle, 1985—; judge pro tem City of Seattle, 1981-82; mem. com. Boston U. Labor Law Conf. Mem. council, gala com. Mus. Fine arts, 1987—. Mem. Mass. Bar Assn., Seattle Bar Assn. (trustee labor law sect. 1980-82), Boston Bar Assn. (co-chmn. labor arbitration sect.), Women's Bar Assn. (appointments com.), Soc. Fed. Labor Relations Profls. (v.p. 1988), Internat. Wine and Food Soc. (Boston chpt. 1986—).

SAYLOR, NANCY LEE, physical education educator; b. Tucson, May 11, 1941; d. Ellmont Meredith and Margaret Ann (Simmons) Saylor. BS in Health, Phys. Edn., Recreation and Dance , Tex. Woman's U., 1962. Cert. tchr. secondary edn., phys. edn. and recreation, driver edn., elem. edn., computer literacy, Tex. Tchr. elem. and phys. edn. Dallas Ind. Sch. Dist., 1963-76, tchr. phys. edn. and gymnastics, 1976—, girls coach, 1976-86, tchr. drive edn., 1983—; asst. dir. recreation Denton (Tex.) State Sch., 1962-63. Life mem. Tex. PTA, 1969; mem. project 1000, Tex. Educators Polit. Action Com., Austin, 1983—. Recipient Favorite Tchr. award Positive Parents of Dallas, 1983. Mem. NEA, Tex. Tchrs. Assn., Classroom Tchrs. of Dallas Assn. (dist. bd. dirs. 1983-85), AAHPER and Dance, Tex. Assn. for Health, Phys. Edn., Recreation and Dance (regional rep. 1984-87), Dallas Assn. for Health, Phys. Edn. and Recreation (pres. 1981-83). Home: 1415 Matagorda Dallas TX 75232 Office: WE Greiner Mid Sch 625 S Edgefield Dallas TX 75208

SAYLOR, TERRI AMMERMAN, media consultant; b. Altoona, Pa., Nov. 18, 1953; d. Dan Sheridan and Mary Theresa (Graca) Ammerman; m. Alvin Norman Saylor, Jr., Aug. 27, 1983; children: Sheridan Joy, Trace. Student U. Houston, 1972-74, Houston Bapt. U., 1981-84. Model, radio and TV talent, Dallas and Houston, 1976-79; personnel cons. Talent Tree Personnel, Houston, 1979-81; asst. gen. mgr., media trainer Ammerman Enterprises, Houston, 1981—; TV hostess Houston Monthly Mag., 1983. Mem. Am. Women in Radio and TV, Nat. Orgn. Female Execs. Republican. Baptist. Club: Toastmasters (ednl. v.p. 1983). Home: 11715 Dorrance St Stafford TX 77477 Office: Ammerman Enterprises Inc 4800 Sugar Grove Blvd Suite 400 Stafford TX 77477

SCAIA, MARY JULIE, special education educator; b. Torrington, Conn., May 7, 1953; d. Geno William and Mollie Rose (Silano) S. BS, So. Conn. State U., 1975; MEd, Northeastern U., 1985. Cert. elem., secondary spl. edn. tchr., Conn. Spl. edn. resource room tchr. Ledyard Pub. Sch. System, Gales Ferry Sch., Gales Ferry, Conn., 1975-76; spl. edn. tchr., team coordinator Torrington Pub. Sch. System, Vogel Jr. High Sch., Torrington, Conn., 1976—; area coordinator Northwestern Conn. Spl. Olympics, Torrington, 1979-80; mem. sch. adv. panel Conn. Pub. TV, Hartford, 1978-79, Litchfield County Hike for the Handicapped Campaign, Torrington, 1981—, Handicapped Task Force on Learning Disabilities, Boston, 1984-85; mem. profl. sign lang., dance and mime troupe Cridders. Contbr. to Conn. Pub. TV newsletter, 1978. bd. dirs. Litchfield County Assn. for Retarded Citizens, Torrington, 1980-82, Friendship Plus! - An Ind. Citizen Advocacy Network, Torrington, 1987—; master of ceremonies Telethons for local cable, Torrington, 1985-86. Recipient Teacher of the Yr. award Probus Club of Torrington, 1987. Mem. NEA, Conn. Edn. Assn. (del. to Washington NEA program), Torrington Edn. Assn. (v.p. 1980-82), Conn. Registry of Interpreters for the Deaf, Assn. for Children and Adults with Learning Disabilities, Zeta Delta Epsilon, Alpha Delta Kappa (v.p. 1982-84). Democrat. Roman Catholic.

SCANLAN, ESTHER MEADER, psychiatric social worker; b. Providence, Jan. 21, 1932; d. Robert Osmond and Mary Lillian (Arnold) Meader; m. William Arthur Scanlan, Sept. 26, 1954 (div. June 1964); children: James Matthew, William Dustin, Julie Beth. BA, Bennington (Vt.) Coll., 1959; MSW, Simmons Sch. Social Work, Boston, 1965; postgrad., Harvard U., 1987—. Lic. social worker. Psychiat. social worker Boston City Hosp., 1965-68, Putnam Centre for Children, Roxbury, Mass., 1968-69, Children's Hosp., Boston, 1967-70, Somerville (Mass.) Mental Health Ctr., 1970-74; social worker Cath. Charities, Somerville, 1974-75; pvt. practice psychiat. social work Cambridge, Mass., 1975—; mem. adv. council theological opprtunities program Harvard U., 1985—. One-woman and group art shows include: Simmons Coll., 1979, Hirshberg Gallery, 1979, Cambridge Pub. Library, 1981; writer poetry. NIMH fellow, 1963-65; Harvard Div. Sch. scholar, 1987. Mem. Cambridge Poets (leader 1983-87). Democrat. Episcopalian. Home and Office: 51 Walker St Cambridge MA 02138

SCANLAN, SHARON ANN, retail executive; b. Madison, Wis., Feb. 1, 1948; d. William Emmett and Mary Jane (Murrish) Brewer; m. Stephen Robert Scanlan, Oct. 22, 1974; children: Karen Lynn, Christopher Robert. Student Hamline U., St. Paul, 1966-67; BS, U. Wis., 1970. Store mdse. mgr. Sears, Roebuck and Co., Glendale, Calif., 1977-78, group mdse. mgr., Alhambra, Calif., 1978-80, territorial mdse. mgr., 1980, store mgr., San Luis Obispo, Calif., 1981-84, group operating mgr., Phoenix, 1984-87, regional gen. mdse. mgr., Honolulu, 1987—. Bd. dirs. Pvt. Industry Council, San Luis Obispo, 1981-84, San Luis Obispo County Symphony, 1981-84, Crossroads Meth. Ch., Phoenix, 1986-87; pres. San Luis Obispo C. of C., 1984. Republican. Club: Toastmistress. Lodge: Soroptomists. Avocations: golf, sewing. Office: Sears Roebuck & Co Hawaii Region Office 1450 Ala Moana Blvd 1000 Honolulu HI 96814

SCANLON, DOROTHY THERESE, history educator; b. Bridgeport, Conn., Oct. 7, 1928; d. George F. and Mazie (Reardon) S.; A.B., U. Pa., 1948, M.A., 1949; M.A., Boston Coll., 1953; Ph.D., Boston U., 1956; postdoctoral scholar Harvard U., 1962-64, 72. Tchr. history and Latin Marycliff Acad., Winchester, Mass., 1950-52; tchr. history Girls Latin Sch., Boston, 1952-57; prof. Boston State Coll., 1957-82, Mass. Coll. Art, 1982—. Recipient Disting. Service award Boston State Coll., 1979, Faculty Award of Excellence, Mass. Coll. Art, 1985, Faculty Disting. Service award, Mass. Coll. Art, 1987. Mem. Pan-Am. Soc., Latin Am. Studies Assn., Am. Hist. Assn., Orgn. Am. Historians, Am. Studies Assn., Am. Assn. History of Medicine, History of Sci. Soc., AAUP, AAUW, Phi Alpha Theta, Delta Kappa Gamma. Author: Instructor's Manual to Accompany Lewis Hanke, Latin America: A Historical Reader, 1974; contbr. Biographical Dictionary of Social Welfare, 1986. Home: 140 Thornton Rd Chestnut Hill MA 02167 Office: Mass Coll Art Dept History 621 Huntington Ave Boston MA 02115

SCANLON, NANCY MCLAUGHLIN, personnel director; b. Pitts., Jan. 22, 1958; d. John Neil and Jean (Schnars) McL.; m. Thomas John Scanlon, June 23, 1959. BA in Polit. Sci., Bethany Coll., 1979; MBA, Syracuse U., 1982. Recruiter Search, Inc., Woburn, Mass., 1982-83; personnel adminstr. Inframetrics, Inc., Bedford, Mass., 1983-86, personnel mgr., 1986-87, personnel dir., 1987—. Mem. Am. Soc. Personnel Adminstrs. Republican. Office: Inframetrics Inc 37 Hickory Rd Hampstead NH 03841

SCARBROUGH, DAPHNE, designer, fabricator; b. Long Beach, Calif., June 24, 1954; d. DeLayne Myers and Marjory Alice (Nunnery) S. B.A., U. Tex., 1978. Sales rep. Sakowitz, Houston, 1979-80; designer, gen. mgr. George Allens Brass Works, Houston, 1980-82; pres., designer, fabricator The Brass Maiden, Houston, 1982—. Bd. dirs., chmn. membership com. Houston Ctr. for Photography; mem. guild, corp. fin. com. Children's Mus., Houston, Art League of Houston, Mus. Fine Arts, Houston. Mem. Nat. Fedn. Ind. Bus., Cultural Arts Council Houston, Houston Ctr. for Photography (chmn. membership com., bd. dirs., exec. bd., Rice Design Alliance), Nat. Trust for Hist. Preservation, Rice Design Alliance, Art League Houston. Methodist. Club: Houston Livestock Show. Avocations: horse training; antiques. Office: The Brass Maiden 2035 Portsmouth St Houston TX 77098

SCARFF, DEBORAH SUSAN, medical photographer; b. Troy, N.Y., Apr. 5, 1948; d. Donald Raymond and Estelle Hildreth (Boyer) L.; m. Lawrence Alan Scarff, Aug. 18, 1979. Cert. in X-ray tech., Waltham Hosp., 1968; BS, Rochester Inst. Tech., 1981. Radiol. tech. Waltham (Mass.) Hosp., 1968-70, 72-74, Lahey Clinic, Boston, 1970-72, Kaiser Med. Found., Honolulu, 1974-78; med. photographer Mass. Eye and Ear Infirmary, Boston, 1981-83; med., sci. photographic cons. The Better Light, Burlington, Mass., 1984—. Contbr. articles to profl. jours. Recipient 12th place Nikon Small World Contest, 1980. Mem. Biol. Photog. Assn. (v.p. Boston chpt. 1987—), Am. Registry of Radiologic Technologists (cert.). Episcopalian. Home and Office: 9 Luther Rd Burlington MA 01803

SCARITO, KATHRYN VERONICA, director interns; b. Bayonne, N.J., Aug. 11, 1945; d. James Francis and Mary Elizabeth (Drennan) Savard; m. Robert Joseph Scarito, Apr. 25, 1964; children: Robert, Patricia, Michael. AS, Empire State Coll., 1984; student, Suffolk County Community Coll., 1983-85. Licensed realtor, N.Y. With real estate sales Century 21, LindenHurst, N.J., DeSimone Realty; specialist labor Dept. Labor Suffolk County, Hauppauge, N.J., 1977-83; dir. interns Suffolk County Community Coll., Selden, N.Y., 1983—. Editor: Internships Newsletters, 1983—. Councilwoman Town of Smithtown (N.Y.) 1985-86; com. woman Rep. Suffolk County, 1976—. Fed. Gov. educational grantee Suffolk County Community Coll., 1984. Mem. Profl. Women Govt. (chmn. 1982—), Western Suffolk Counselors Assn., Women's Network Smithtown, Hauppauge Indsl. Assn. (presenter 1983—), Bd. Coop. Ednl. Services (mem. adv. bd.), LWV (treas. 1976-78),. Home: 4 Windmill Ct Smithtown NY 11787 Office: Suffolk County Dept. Labor 655 Deer Park Ave North Babylon NY 11702

SCARNE, STEFFI NORMA, English educator, games company executive; b. Englewood, N.J., Jan. 18, 1925; d. Leo Patrick and Marie Elizabeth (Duffy) Kearney; m. John Scarne, 1956 (dec. 1985); 1 child, John Teeko. B.S.

magna cum laude, Seton Hall U., 1971, M.A., 1973; Ph.D., Pacific Western U., 1986. Vice pres., editor, cons. John Scarne Games Inc., North Bergen, N.J., 1950—; exec. sales rep. Hamilton Shoe Co., N.Y.C., 1954-68, Grove Co., N.Y.C., 1968-71; English tchr. North Bergen High Sch., 1971-88. Recipient Dean's Gold Medal for Acad. Excellence, Seton Hall U., 1971. Mem. NEA, Am. Fedn. Tchrs., Nat. Assn. Female Execs. Office: John Scarne Games Inc 4319 Meadowview Ave North Bergen NJ 07047

SCARROW, PAMELA KAY, health care manager; b. Washington, Nov. 4, 1949; d. Edward Charles and Elsie Lorine (Kay) Scarrow; m. Antonio Joseph Franz, Sept. 4, 1979; 1 child, Vanessa Motil Franz. AA, Navarro Coll., Tex., 1981; BS, Golden Gate U., 1983. Cert. med. staff coordinator, 1986. Adminstrv. asst. Trust Ter. of the Pacific Islands, Saipan, Mariana Islands, 1976-79; adminstrv. asst. Navarro Coll., Corsicana, Tex., 1979-81; staff asst. San Francisco Symphony, 1981-82; med. staff liaison Calif. Med. Assn., San Francisco, 1982-87; community outreach coordinator Calif. Med. Rev., Inc., San Francisco, 1987—. Editor: Contracting Resource and Assistance Dept., Inc., Economic Resource Guide, 1986, Medical Staff Resources manual, 1987. Mem. Nat. Assn. Med. Staff Services. Democrat. Roman Catholic. Office: Calif Med Rev Inc 1388 Sutter St Suite 1100 San Francisco CA 94109

SCATES, ALICE YEOMANS, former government official, consultant; b. Pitts., Jan. 21, 1915; d. William E. and Georgiana L. (Lloyd) Yeomans; B.S., State Tchrs. Coll., Glassboro, N.J., 1936; M.Ed., Duke U., 1949; Ed.D., George Washington U., 1963. Tchr. elem. sch., Haddon Heights, N.J., 1937-43; civilian personnel officer Sedalia Army Airfield, Mo., Greenville Army Air Field, S.C., 1944-46; tng. officer VA Center, Dayton, Ohio, 1947-48; research asso., dir. Am. Council on Edn. Staff for Office Naval Research Projects, 1949-53; asst. dir. Nat. Home Study Council, 1954; editor, research asst. Office of Edn., HEW, 1955, research analyst and coordinator coop. research program, 1956-64, program planning officer occupational research program, 1965-66, dir. basic research br. secondary edn., 1967-69, program planning and eval. officer Nat. Center Ednl. Research and Devel., 1969-71, eval. specialist Office Program Eval., 1971-80; eval. officer Office of Mgmt., U.S. Dept. Edn., 1980-82; cons., 1982—. Served to capt. U.S. Army, 1943-46. Fellow AAAS; mem. Am. Sociol. Assn., Am. Anthrop. Assn., Am. Acad. Polit. and Social Sci., Am. Ednl. Research Assn. Adult Edn. Assn., Kappa Delta Pi, Phi Delta Gamma. Author research reports, articles in field. Home: 560 N St SW Washington DC 20024 Office: Box N-501 560 N St SW Washington DC 20024

SCECINA, M. LYNN, chiropractic physician; b. Gary, Ind., Sept. 21, 1953; d. Thomas Joseph and Alice Isabel (Fujko) S. Student, Ind. U., 1971-73; D of Chiropractic, Palmer Coll. of Chiropractic, 1975. Assoc. Chiropractic Life Ctr., Goshen, Ind., 1976-77; assoc., illustrator B.R. Pettibon and Assocs., Tacoma, 1977; assoc. dir. Mendenhall Chiropractic Clinic, Riverside, Calif., 1977-79; prin. Woodcrest chiropractic Offices, Riverside, 1980—. Mem. Am. Chiropractic Assn., Calif. Chiropractic Assn., Riverside Chiropractic Soc. (sec. 1982-83, pres. 1983-84), Riverside C. of C. (v.p., pres. 1981-83, pres., v.p. Woodcrest div., 1981-83, chmn. bus. action com, 1987—). Club: Le Tip of Riverside (pres. 1986). Office: Woodcrest Chiropractic 16801 Van Buren Blvd Riverside CA 92504

SCERBO, FRANCES CAROLYN GARROTT, architectural technician; b. Bowling Green, Ky., Mar. 10, 1932; d. Irby Reid and Carrie Mae (Stahl) Cameron; m. Leslie Othello Garrott, Oct. 12, 1951 (dec. Feb. 1978); children—Dennis Leslie, Alan Reid; adopted children—Carolyn Maria, Karen Roxana; m. Raymond William Scerbo, May 31, 1978. Student Fla. State U., 1951, St. Petersburg Jr. Coll., 1962-74; grad. Pinellas Vocat. Tech. Inst., 1975. With Sears, Roebuck and Co., Rapid City, S.D., 1951-52, St. Petersburg, Fla., 1961-62; bookkeeper Ohio Nat. Bank, Columbus, 1953-54, Sunbeam Bakery, Lakeland, Fla., 1955-56; with Christies Toy Sales, Pennsauken, N.J., 1958-60; exec. sec. Gulf Coast Automotive Warehouse, Inc., Tampa, Fla., 1970-73, office mgr., 1975-78; sec., treas., chief pilot, co-owner Tech. Devel. Corp., St. Petersburg, Fla., 1970-78; freelance archtl. draftsman and designer, archtl. cons., constrn. materials estimator, 1975—, Fla. state judge Vocat. Indsl. Clubs of Am. Skills Olympics, 1986. Nat. Assn. Women in Constrn. scholar, 1974. Mem. Nat. Assn. Women in Constrn., Alpha Chi Omega. Democrat. Home and Office: 11298 53d Ave N Saint Petersburg FL 33708

SCHAAF, BARBARA CAROL, writer, consultant, educator; b. Chgo., Dec. 17, 1940; d. William and Mary (Krutilla) S. B in Gen. Studies cum laude, Roosevelt U., 1971; MBA, U. Chgo. Exec. Program, 1976. Free-lance writer, Harvey, Ill., 1977—; cons. health care delivery systems, transp., housing, taxation, labor and econs., including to Continental Air Transport, 1979-80, Cook County treas., 1980—, Chgo. Health Maintenance Orgn., 1983-85; lectr. urban, labor, mil. and ethnic history, English medieval history; lectr. on urban and ethnic history USIA, 1978; mem. adv. com. Artists in Residence Program, Chgo. Council Fine Arts, 1979-83; bd. dirs. Chgo. Ctr. Hosp., 1982-87 ; treas., bd. dirs. Chgo. Ctr. Health System, 1985-87 . Author: Mr. Dooley's Chicago, 1977 (Carl Sandburg award 1978, also nominee Am. Hist. Assn. Gershoy award and Pulitzer prize), Mr. Dooley, We Need Him Now, 1988; contbr. articles to newspapers, mags. Press sec. Eleanor McGovern, 1971-72, Richard M. Daley campaign, Chgo., 1979-80; treas. Harvey Pub. Library Bd. Trustees, 1977—, J. F. Kennedy presdl. campaigns and other polit. campaigns. Nat. Found. for Humanities fellow Writing in Chgo. Program, 1978. Mem. ALA, Nat. Book Critics Circle, PEN, Soc. Midland Authors, Ill. Library Assn., Richard III Soc. Democrat. Roman Catholic. Ind. scholarship in urban history, English medieval history, and mil. history. Home and Office: 400 Streamside Dr Harvey IL 60426

SCHAAF, LINDA ANN, nurse, educator; b. Balt., Feb. 15, 1944; d. Wilbert Frederick and Rosina Catherine (Lutz) S. Diploma, St. Agnes Hosp. Sch. Nursing, 1967; BSN, U. Md., 1971; MSN, Cath. U. Am., 1973. RN. Staff nurse, charge nurse St. Agnes Hosp., Balt., 1967-71; staff nurse Provident Hosp., Washington, 1972-73; pvt. duty nurse Med. Personnel Pool, Washington, 1973; practitioner, tchr. Rush-Presbyn. St. Luke's Med. Ctr., Chgo., 1973-80; staff nurse Critical Care Services, Inc., Chgo., 1980-82; assoc. prof. Ill. Benedictine Coll., Lisle, 1980—; clin. educator, cons. Glendale Heights (Ill.) Community Hosp., 1983—; cons. curriculum Trinity Coll., Washington Hosp. Ctr., Washington, 1976. Bd. dirs. Woodridge (Ill.) Unit Am Cancer Soc., 1984—; mem. Chgo. Heart Assn., 1973—. Mem. Am. Nurses Assn. (cert.), Ill. Nurses Assn., Am. Assn. Critical Care Nurses (cert. critical care RN), Nat. League for Nursing, Ill. League for Nursing (program developer 1976), Am. Heart Assn. (council on cardiovascular nursing 1970—), Sigma Theta Tau, Internat. Honor Soc. Nursing. Democrat. Roman Catholic. Office: Ill Benedictine Coll 5700 College Rd Lisle IL 60532

SCHACHTER, ESTHER RODITTI, lawyer, author, publisher; b. Los Angeles, Feb. 7, 1933; d. David and Lucy Roditti; m. Oscar H. Schachter, Aug. 8, 1957; children—Charles David, Susan Dayana. B.A., UCLA, 1954; J.D., Harvard U., 1957. Bar: N.Y. 1959. Assoc. Stickles, Hayden and Kennedy, N.Y.C., 1957-62; asst. dir. Legis. Drafting Fund Columbia U., N.Y.C., 1962-65, cons., 1965-67; cons. N.Y.C. Air Pollution Control Dept., 1965-67; instr. and cons. New Sch. for Social Research, N.Y.C., 1968-70; cons. Internat. League for Rights of Man, N.Y.C., 1969, Rand Inst., N.Y.C., 1969, U.S.-Societ Environ. Studies Program, UN Assn., N.Y.C., 1969; sr. research assoc. Ctr. for Policy Research Columbia U., 1970-73; sr. program officer Ford Found., N.Y.C., 1972-78; pres. Esther Roditti Schachter, P.C., N.Y.C., 1978-83; ptnr. Schachter & Froling, N.Y.C., 1983-85, Schachter, Courter, Purcell & Kobert, N.Y.C., 1985—; speaker, lectr., panelist profl. assn. confs., forums, workshops, U.S., Can., Tokyo, London. Author: N.Y.C. Air Pollution Control Code Annotated, 1965; Enforcing Air Pollution Controls, 1979; Financial Support of Women's Programs in the 1970's, 1979; Computer Contracts Reference Directory, 1979-83; co-author: Charities and Charitable Foundations, 1974; author, co-author articles in field; legal editor: Computer Economics, 1983—; editor Computer Law & Tax Report, 1984-86, pub., editor, 1986—. Nat. governing bd. Common Cause, 1979-82, mem. state governing bd., N.Y., 1982-84; mem. com. on urban environ. Citizens Union, N.Y.C., 1969-73; mem. West Side Democratic Club, 1958-63. Ford Found. grantee, 1970; NSF grantee, 1971; recipient Award for Outstanding Service Brandeis U., Nat. Women's Com., 1973. Mem. ABA (lectr. 1987), Assn. Bar City N.Y. (founder, chmn. com. on computer law 1980—), N.Y. State Bar Assn., Computer Law Assn. (lectr. 1985), Am. Arbitration Assn. (chair com. for computer disputes 1985—), Phi Beta Kappa. Club: Panther (Alamuchy, N.J.).

SCHADLER, MARGARET HORSFALL, biologist, educator; b. Geneva, N.Y., Aug. 31, 1931; d. James G. and Sue Belle (Overton) Horsfall; m. Harvey Walter Schadler, Aug. 28, 1954; children: Janet, Edward, Linda Sue. AB, Cornell U., 1953; MS, Union Coll., 1971, PhD, 1977. Research asst. Sloan-Kettering Inst., N.Y.C., 1953-54, Purdue U., West Lafayette, Ind., 1954-57; vis. instr. Union Coll., Schenectady, N.Y., 1969-77; vis. asst. prof. Union Coll., Schenectady, 1977-81, research asst. prof., 1981—; dir. Affirmative Action Union Coll., 1981—. Editor: The Lake George Ecosystem, 1982; contbr. articles to jours. Trustee Ea. N.Y. Chpt. Nature Conservancy, 1970-79; pres. Jr. League, Schenectady, 1971-72; bd. dirs. Environ. Clearinghouse Schenectady, 1971-75; bd. dirs. Orgn. for Action on the Riverfront, Schenectady, 1978—; v.p. Lake George (N.Y.) Assn., 1980-82. Recipient grant N.Y. State Sci. and Tech. Found., 1980, Nat. Sci. Found., 1981-82, 86—. Mem. AAAS, Am. Soc. Mammalogists (com. chair 1986—), Soc. Study of Reprodn., Sigma Xi. Home: 1333 Lowell Rd Schenectady NY 12308 Office: Union Coll Dept Biol Scis Schenectady NY 12308

SCHAEFER, KATHLEEN NORMA, accountant; b. St. Louis, Oct. 9, 1941; d. Walter Frederick and Lulu Emma (Sides) Kelpe; m. Ruston R. Schaefer, June 9, 1962; children: Teresa Jo, Melinda Joy. AA, St. Louis Community Coll., 1984; BSBA, St. Louis U., 1987. Bookkeeper SE Mo. Hosp., Cape Girardeau, 1961-62; sales clk. J.C. Penney Co., St. Louis, 1972; grader acctg. dept. St. Louis U., 1986; accounts payable clk. City Photo Stockhouse, St. Louis, 1986—; accounts acct. Grace and Co., St. Louis, 1987—. Tchr. sunday sch. Resurrection Luth. Ch., 1970-79; mem. solicitation com. Luth. High Sch. Assn. Auction, St. Louis, 1981-84. Mem. Beta Alpha Psi (v.p. 1986). Home: 4874 Arevalo Dr Saint Louis MO 63128

SCHAEFER, LEE ASTRID, counseling hypnotherapist; b. Chgo., Apr. 1, 1927; d. Paul N. Hagstrom and Hedvina R. (Anderson) Blom; m. Raymond L. Schaefer, Aug. 12, 1950; children—Karen, Anita, Sonja. Student U. Chgo., 1945; diploma Art Inst. Chgo., 1950; student Amundsen-Mayfair, Chgo., 1969-70; B.A. in Psychology with honors, Northeastern U., Chgo., 1974, M.A. in Social Sci., 1983. Dress designer, fashion model, Chgo., 1944-58; counselor Omni House, Youth Services Bur., Arlington Heights, Ill., 1976; pvt. practice counseling hypnotherapist, Arlington Heights, 1973—; tchr. self-hypnosis Northeastern Ill. U., 1975—, faculty asst., 1975-77, pres. Autohypnotic Behavioral Conditioning, Arlington Heights, 1980—, chmn. program Midwest Hypnosis Conv., Elmwood Park, Ill., 1975-80, chmn., 1977. Contbr. articles to profl. jours. Mem. Assn. to Advance Ethical Hypnosis (sec. 1976-77, pres. local chpt. 1978, v.p. local chpt. 1987, sec. 1988), Assn. Humanistic Psychology, Psi Chi (sec., treas. Northeastern U. chpt. 1973-76). Unity. Home: 404 N Windsor Dr Arlington Heights IL 60004 Office: ABC Inc 404 N Windsor Dr Arlington Heights IL 60004

SCHAEFER, PATRICIA, librarian; b. Ft. Wayne, Ind., Apr. 23, 1930; d. Edward John and Hildegarde Hartman (Hormel) S.; MusB, Northwestern U., 1951; MusM, U. Ill., 1958; MA in LS, U. Mich., 1963. With U.S. Rubber Co., Ft. Wayne, Ind., 1951-52; sec. to promotion mgr. Sta. WOWO, Ft. Wayne, Ind., 1952, sec. to program mgr., 1953-55; coordinator publicity and promotion Home Telephone Co., Ft. Wayne, 1955-56; sec. Fine Arts Found., Ft. Wayne, 1956-57; library asst. Columbus (Ohio) Pub. Library, 1958-59; audio-visual librarian Muncie (Ind.) Pub. Library, 1959-86, asst. library dir., 1981-86; library dir., 1986—; chmn. Ind. Library Film Circuit, 1962-63; treas. Ind. Library Film Service 1969-70, 83-85; mem. trustees adv. council Milton S. Eisenhower Library, Johns Hopkins U.; cons. in field. Weekly columnist Library Lines, Muncie Evening Press, 1981-83; contbr. articles to profl. jours. Dir. Franklin Electric Co., Inc. Bd. dirs. Muncie Symphony Assn., 1964-74, 85—; bd. trustees Masterworks Chorale, Muncie Mcpl. Band; bd. dirs. Cen. City Bus. Assn. Mem. adv. com., bookshop dir. Midwest Writers Workshop, 1976-77; sec. Del. County Council for the Arts, 1978-79, pres., 1979-81, bd. dirs., 1985-86; mem. pres.'s council Berea Coll.; bd. dirs. Muncie YWCA, 1977-82, 85-86, treas., 1981-82, 88—; gen. chmn. Ind. Renaissance Fair, 1978-79; pres. Muncie Matinee Musicale, 1965-67; past pres. Ind. Film and Video Council; mem. community adv. com. Minnetrista Cultural Ctr. Mem. Ind. Library Assn. (pres. 1987-88), ALA, Nat. League Am. Pen Women (pres. Muncie br. 1974-78), Am. Recorder Soc., Northeastern Ind. Recorder Soc., Delta Zeta, Mu Phi Epsilon. Republican. Roman Catholic. Clubs: Riley-Jones, Altrusa (Muncie) (pres. 1986-87). Home: 405 S Tara Ln Muncie IN 47304 Office: 301 E Jackson St Muncie IN 47305

SCHAEFER, PATRICIA ANN, librarian; b. Lebanon, Ohio, Jan. 22, 1933; d. Riley Ray and Louise Collette (Fraher) Freeze; B.S., Miami U., Oxford, Ohio, 1954; m. William H. Schaefer, Aug. 11, 1956; children—Susan P., Nancy A., William H. III (dec.). Med. technologist Mercy Hosp., Hamilton, Ohio, 1954-58, Middletown (Ohio) Hosp., 1958-62; librarian Middletown City Schs., 1979—, intermediate librarian McKinley Sch., 1982—. Active, YMCA, pres., 1977-79; bd. dirs. Middletown Symphony, 1974-78, Arts in Middletown, 1983—; hon. bd. dirs. Am. Cancer Soc., 1961—; chmn. legis. City Charter Rev. Com., 1970; residential chmn. United Way, 1976; chmn. Sch. Tax Levy, 1978; mem. Middletown City Commn., 1983—; mem. exec. com. Ohio-Ky.-Ind. Regional Council, 1986. Recipient Stuart Ives Service to Youth award, 1980. Mem. Am. Soc. Clin. Pathologists, Registry Med. Technologists, Am. Bus. Women's Assn. (pres. 1961-62), Middletown C. of C., LWV (pres. 1962-63), PEO, Sigma Sigma Sigma. Methodist. Club: Browns Run Country. Home: 1909 Antrim Ct Middletown OH 45042

SCHAEFER, SUSAN MARIE, psychologist; b. New Ulm, Minn., Jan. 31, 1952; d. Henry Roland and Marjorie Lillian (Gilbertson) S. BA in Psychology summa cum laude, U. Minn., 1974, MA in Psychology, 1978. Lic. psychologist, Minn.; cert. chem. dependency counselor. Counselor, program mgr. Chrysalis Ctr. Women, Mpls., 1975-80; instr. U. Minn., Mpls., 1975-78; counselor Relate Counseling Ctr., Minnetonka, Minn., 1981-83; pvt. practice psychology Mpls., 1983—; adj. prof. St. Mary's Coll., Mpls., 1984-86; co-chmn. tng. insts. com. State Task Force Sexual Exploitation by Counselors and Therapists, 1985-86; bd. dirs. Sojourner Shelter, Hokins, Minn., 1982-85; trainer, cons. Program in Human Sexuality, U. Minn. Med. Sch., 1979-85. Contbr. articles to profl. jours. and books. Mem. Minn. Women Psychologists, Minn. Chem. Dependency Assn., Minn. Psychol. Assn. Democrat. Roman Catholic. Office: 2400 Blaisdell Ave S Minneapolis MN 55404

SCHAEFFER, BARBARA HAMILTON, transportation company executive; travel consultant; b. Newton, Mass., Apr. 26, 1926; d. Peter Davidson Gunn and Harriet Bennett (Thompson) Hamilton; m. John Schaeffer, Sept. 7, 1946; children—Laurie, John, Peter. Student, Skidmore Coll., 1943-46; AB in English, Bucknell U., 1948; postgrad. Montclair State U., 1950-51, Bank St. Coll. Edn., 1959-61, Yeshiva U., 1961-62; student Daytona Beach Coll., 1984. Cert. primary, secondary tchr., N.J. Dir. Pompton Plains Sch., N.J., 1959-62; adviser Episcopal Sch., Towaco, N.J., 1968-70; v.p. Deltona-DeLand Trolley, Orange City, Fla., 1980-81; pres. Monroe Heavy Equipment Rentals, Inc., Orange City, 1981—, also Magic Carpet Travel subs., 1986—; cons. TLC Travel Club, Orange City, 1981—; lectr. on children's art, 1959-70. Contbr. articles to profl. publs. Mem. Internat. Platform Assn., Am. Soc. Travel Agts., Deltona C. of C., Orange City C. of C., Small Bus. Devel. Regional Ctr. (Stetson U. chpt.), DeLand Area C. of C. (transp. com. 1981-85). Episcopalian. Avocations: restoring old homes, oil painting, piano. Home: 400 Foothill Farms Rd Orange City FL 32763 Office: Magic Carpet Travel 2425 Enterprise Rd Orange City FL 32763

SCHAEFFER, KAREN PATRICIA, financial planner; b. Wyandotte, Mich., Aug. 23, 1954; d. John Joseph and Lucie Marie (Donnelly) Kelly; m. Richard Wayne Schaeffer, Aug. 20, 1978; children: Kaitlin Kelly, Megan Anne. BS, Grand Valley State. U., Allendale, Mich., 1976; CFP, Coll. for Fin. Planning, Denver, 1982. Cert. Fin. Planner, Md. V.p., mgr. asst. to pres. Am. Fin. Cons., Silver Spring, Md., 1980-87; pres. Schaeffer Fin., Greenbelt, Md., 1987—; mem. adv. bd. Coll. for Fin. Planning, 1985—; adj. faculty George Washington U., Washington, Washington, 1986—; cons. World Bank, Washington, 1986—. Contbr. articles to profl. jours. Mem. Internat. Assn. Fin. Planning (officer), Inst. Cert. Fin. Planners. Republican. Roman Catholic. Office: Schaeffer Fin 7855 Walker Dr #620 Greenbelt MD 20770

SCHAEFFER, LINDA JOAN, accountant, real estate developer; b. Elizabeth, N.J., Aug. 13, 1952; d. William E. and Dolores (Gorski) Wlazlowski; m. William D. Schaeffer, Apr. 24,, 1976; 1 child, Matthew. BBA in Acctg., Seton Hall U., 1974; postgrad., Pace U., 1979-82. CPA, N.J., Pa. Agt. IRS, New Brunswick, N.J., 1972-74; tax acct. Deloitte, Haskins and Sells, Newark, N.J., 1974-75; tax supr. Laventhol and Horwath, East Brunswick, N.J., 1975-79; pvt. practice CPA Princeton, N.J., 1979-85; ptnr. R.D. Hunter & Co., Princeton, 1985—. Pres. Montgomery Knoll Office Condominium Assn., Skillman, N.J., 1987, Village House Reigme, Hilton Head, S.C., 1987. Fellow Am. Inst. CPA's, N.J. Soc. CPA's (com. chmn. continuing profl. edn., 1987, Mid-Yr. Mems. Conf. 1987—). Office: RD Hunter & Co 156 Montgomery Knoll Skillman NJ 08558

SCHAEFFER, SUSAN FROMBERG, author, educator; b. Bklyn., Mar. 25, 1941; d. Irving and Edith (Levine) Fromberg; B.A., U. Chgo., 1961, M.A. with honors, 1963, Ph.D. with honors, 1966; m. Neil J. Schaeffer, Oct. 11, 1970; children—Benjamin Adam, May Anna. Instr. English, Wright Jr. Coll., Chgo., 1964-65; asst. prof. Ill. Inst. Tech., Chgo., 1965-67; successively asst. prof., asso. prof., prof. Bklyn. Coll., 1967—, now Broeklundian prof. English; guest lectr. U. Chgo., Cornell U., U. Ariz., U. Maine, Yale U., U. Tex., U. Mass. John Simon Guggenheim fellow; recipient E.L. Wallant award, Friends of Lit. award.; Prairie Schooner's Lawrence award; O. Henry award; Poetry award Centennial Rev. Mem. PEN, Authors Guild, Poetry Soc. Am. Democrat. Jewish. Author novels: Falling, 1973; Anya, 1974; Time In Its Flight, 1978; Love, 1981; The Madness of a Seduced Woman, 1983; Mainland, 1984, The Injured Party, 1986, Buffalo Afternoon, 1988; poetry: The Witch and the Weather Report, 1972; Alphabet For the Lost Years, 1976; Granite Lady (nominee Nat. Book award), 1974; Rhymes and Runes of the Toad, 1975; The Bible of the Beasts of the Little Field, 1980; short stories: The Queen of Egypt and Other Stories, 1980; children's novel: The Dragons of North Chittendon, 1986, The Four Hoods and Great Dog, 1988. Address: 783 E 21st St Brooklyn NY 11210

SCHAFF, PAULA KAY, industrial company executive; b. Cape Girardeau, Mo., Oct. 10, 1945; d. Charles Henry Sr. and Elnora Pauline (Ridge) Canine; m. Thomas Casad; 1 child, Thomas; m. Fred Jon Schaff; 1 child, Kevin Jon. Student, Washtenaw Community Coll., U. Ill., Dana U. Successively records clk. PTO div., accounts payable clk., sec., sales specialist, exec. sec., plant mgr., customer service specialist Dana Corp., Chelsea, Mich., 1967-78, supr. customer service, 1978-79, supr. customer service, shipping and assembly PTO div., 1979-81; distbn. mgr. Dana Corp., Athens, Ga., 1981-85, Maumee, Ohio, 1985—. Mem. Nat. Assn. Female Execs., Toledo Women in Industry. Republican. Methodist. Office: Dana Corp Warehouse Ops PO Box 455 Toledo OH 43692

SCHAIBLE, GRACE BERG, state attorney general. BA in History and Polit. Sci., U. Alaska; MA in History, George Washington U.; LLB, Yale U., 1959. Mem. Alaska Legis. Council, 1953-56, acting dir., 1956; assoc. McNealy and Merdes, 1959-66, ptnr. Schaible, Staley, DeLisio and Cook (formerly Merdes, Schaible, Staley and DeLisio), from 1966; also past gen. counsel U. Alaska; past city atty. Cities of Fairbanks, Barrow, Kotzebue and North Pole; past gen. corp. counsel Arctic Slope Regional Corp.; now atty. gen. State of Alaska, 1987—. Mem. Fairbanks Estate Planning Council; bd. dirs. United Way of Tanana Valley; past bd. dirs., treas. Fairbanks Devel. Authority; mem. bd. regents U. Alaska, 1985-87. Mem. U. Alaska Found. (trustee), ABA, Alaska Bar Assn., Juneau Bar Assn., Fairbanks C. of C. (past bd. dirs.), U. Alaska Alumni Assn., (past bd. dirs., officer). Office: Office of Atty Gen PO Box K State Capitol Juneau AK 99811

SCHAIVONE, KATHRYN ANGELA, health care administrator; b. Bridgeport, Conn., Oct. 3, 1959; d. Augustine F. and Angelina R. (Morando) S.; m. Jeffrey F. Bork, July 30 ,1982. BS, NYU, 1981; postgrad., U. So. Calif., 1986—. Vocat. dir. South St. Seaport Mus., N.Y.C., 1981-82; dir. research Nat. Bd. YWCA, N.Y.C., 1982-83; program dir. Am. Diabetes Assn., Los Angeles, 1983-85; pres., chief exec. officer KASEP, Inc., Los Angeles, 1984—, also bd. dirs., 1984—. Mem. NOW, Am. Coll. Health Care Execs., Nat. Assn., Fund Raising Execs., Nat. Assn. Female Execs. Democrat. Office: KASEP Inc PO Box 2415 Pasadena CA 91102

SCHAJER, JULIA ALEXANDER, stockbroker; b. Washington, Mar. 16, 1943; d. Peter Warren and Emma Frieda (Welter) Pedrotti; m. Morris Schajer, July 9, 1981; children: Robert, David. BA, U. Calif., Berkeley, 1971; MBA, Columbia U., 1976. Liaison Salomon Bros., N.Y.C., 1976-77; v.p. Muller & Co., N.Y.C., 1977-82; ltd. ptnr. Mabon Nugent & Co., N.Y.C., 1982—. Leader, advisor Girl Scouts Am., Tenn., Calif., 1964-66; coach Citadel Fencing Team, Charleston, S.C., 1966-68; v.p. Protestant Women of the Chapel, Ft. Knox, Ky., 1969-70; pres. Ecumenical Youth Council, Ft. Knox, 1969-70. Named No. Calif. Intercollegiate Fencing champion, 1965. Republican. Jewish. Clubs: Regency Whist, Fairbanks Family in Am. Home: 875 West End Ave New York NY 10025 Office: Mabon Nugent & Co 115 Broadway New York NY 10006

SCHALK, BEVERLY VANDYKE, nurse, educator; b. Hillsboro, Oreg., Aug. 13, 1959; d. Ervin Aloysius and Jane Margaret (Bernards) Van Dyke; m. David Charles Schalk, Aug. 20, 1983; children: Laura Beverly, Christopher David (dec.). B.S., Oreg. State U., 1982, MEd in Adult Edn., 1988; A.S. in Nursing, Chemeketa Community Coll., 1984. Coordinator vols. escape field studies program U. Oreg., Eugene, 1979-80; fetal alcohol syndrome directory coordinator Benton-Linn Council on Alcohol, Corvallis, Oreg., 1982; early pregnancy instr. March of Dimes, Salem, Oreg., 1982-84; staff nurse Salem Hosp., 1983-84, nurse perinatal educator, 1984-88; edn. coordinator Adult Health Resource Ctr. St. Vincent and Med. Ctr., Portland, Oreg., 1987—; stress mgmt. workshop designer/facilitator U. Oreg., 1982, Salem Sr. Ctr., 1983, Village Retirement Ctr., Dallas, Oreg., 1986; early pregnancy instr. March of Dimes, Salem, 1982-84, pub. health edn. com., 1982-84. Mem. Nurses Assn. of Am. Coll. Obstetricians and Gynecologists, Oreg. Council Healthcare Educators, Oreg. Gerontol. Assn., Salem Childbirth Edn. Assn., Eta Sigma Gamma (pres. chpt. 1980-82). Democrat. Roman Catholic. Home: 5080 Fir Dell Ct SE Salem OR 97306 Office: Adult Health Resource Ctr St Vincent Hosp & Med Ctr 9205 SW Barres Rd Portland OR 97225

SCHALK, PAMELA ANN, insurance company executive; b. Tacoma, Wash., Jan. 20, 1952; d. Dallas Patrick Schalk and Rhea Leigh (Wochnick) Fitzgerald; m. Timothy D. Chanter, Oct. 19, 1986. Attended Portland State U. With Aetna Casualty & Surety, Portland, Oreg., 1970-76, bond rep., 1976-81; bond mgr. Aetna Casualty & Surety, Sacramento, Calif., 1981—; bd. dirs. Exec. Publs., Inc. Editor: The Building of the Oregon Country, 1980; regular contbr. to California Constructor mag. Literacy service tutor Sacramento Pub. Library, 1987—. Mem. Assn. Calif. Gen. Contractors (bd. dirs. 1984—, various coms., affiliate com. chair 1986-88). Republican. Roman Catholic. Club: ENCORPS (Sacramento). Lodge: Soroptimists (sec. Sacramento 1983—). Home: 6517 Rio Oso Dr Rancho Murieta CA 95683 Office: Aetna Casualty & Surety 10971 Sun Center Dr Rancho Cordova CA 95870

SCHAMBER, SHARON BINGHAM, accountant; b. Jackson, Miss., May 9, 1958; d. Morgan Everett Sr. and Madeline Mae (Stickney) Bingham; m. Albert Edward Schamber, July 18, 1981. BSBA, U. So. Miss., 1979, M in Profl. Accountancy, 1980. CPA, Miss. Instr. acctg., bus. law Nicholls State U., Thibodaux, La., 1980-83; staff acct. Arthur F. Kersh CPA, Hattiesburg, Miss., 1983-86; ptnr. Kersh & Schamber, CPA's, Hattiesburg, 1986—; faculty advisor Nicholls State Acctg. Club, 1980-83. Mem. exec. task force Hattiesburg's City Council's, 1988. Named one of Outstanding Young Women, 1986. Mem. Am. Inst. CPA's, Miss. Soc. CPA's, Nat. Assn. Female Execs., Delta Sigma Pi. Methodist. Lodge: Order Eastern Star (worthy matron 1987-88, grand matron dep. dist. No. 26). Office: Kersh & Schamber CPAs 1316 Hardy St Hattiesburg MS 39401

SCHANDER, MARY LEA, police official; b. Bakersfield, Calif., June 11, 1947; d. Gerald John Lea and Marian Lea Coffman; B.A. (Augustana fellow) Calif. Luth. Coll., 1969; M.A., U. Calif., Los Angeles, 1970; m. Edwin Schander, July 3, 1971. Staff aide City of Anaheim (Calif.) Police Dept., 1970-72, staff asst., 1972-78, sr. staff asst., 1978-80; with Resource Mgmt. Dept., City of Anaheim, 1980-82; asst. to dir. Pub. Safety Agy., City of Pasadena Police Dept., 1982-85, spl. asst. to police chief, 1985-88, adminstrv.

comdr., 1988—; freelance musician, publisher Australian Traditional Songs, 1985; lectr. Calif. Luth. Coll. Bd. dirs. Community Dispute Resolution Ctr. Pasadena. Producer (cable TV program) Traditional Music Showcase. Contbr. articles in field to profl. jours. Mem. Am. Mgmt. Assn., LWV. Club: Los Angeles Athletic. Home: 430-C Orange Grove Circle Pasadena CA 91105 Office: Pasadena Police Dept 142 N Arroyo Pkwy Pasadena CA 91103

SCHANSTRA, CARLA ROSS, technical writer; b. Berwyn, Ill., Sept. 4, 1954; d. Caroles Schanstra and Heather Millar (Thomson) Alonso. BA, Western Ill. U., 1976; postgrad., U. Ill. Circle, Chgo., 1980-81. Assoc. editor Hitchock Pub., Wheaton, Ill., 1976-80; assoc. product mgr. Advanced Systems, Inc., Elk Grove Village, Ill., 1980-81; tech. writer Profl. Computer Resources, Oak Brook, Ill., 1982; sr. tech. writer AT&T Bell Labs., Naperville, Ill., 1982—; freelance writer, 1980-85. Author: (stage plays) A Little Bit of Both, The Reversible Play, Survivors, Snakes and Apple Pie, It Should Be Obvious; contbr. articles to profl. jours. Violist Du Page Symphony, Glen Ellyn, Ill., 1984-87, Elgin Symphonette, Elgin, Ill., 1985-87. Mem. So. Tech. Communication (Award of Excellence 1985), Dramatists Guild, Feminist Writers Western Suburbs (founder), Internat. Soc. Dramatists, Feminist Writer's Guild, Ill. Theatre Assn. Club: Writers Workshop (Warrenville, Ill.) (co-founder 1980—). Office: AT&T Bell Labs IHP 1B-531 200 Park Plaza Naperville IL 60566

SCHAPIRO, RUTH GOLDMAN, lawyer; b. N.Y.C., Oct. 31, 1926; d. Louis Albert and Sarah (Shapiro) Goldman; m. Donald Schapiro, June 29, 1952; children: Jane Goldman, Robert Andrew. A.B., Wellesley Coll., 1947; LL.B., Columbia U., 1950. Bar: N.Y. 1950, D.C. 1978. Asst. to reporters Am. Law Inst. Fed. Income Tax Statute, N.Y.C., 1950-51; assoc., then ptnr. Proskauer Rose Goetz & Mendelsohn, N.Y.C., 1955—; mem. nominating commn. U.S. Tax Ct., 1978-81. Notes editor: Columbia Law Rev., 1949-50; editor: Tax Shelters, Practising Law Inst., 1983; contbr. articles to legal jours. Vice-chmn. adv. com. NYU Inst. Fed. Taxation, 1979-85; mem. adv. com. NYU-IRS Continuing Legal Edn. Project. Fellow Am. Bar Found., N.Y. Bar Found.; mem. ABA, N.Y. State Bar Assn. (chmn. tax sect. 1981-82, exec. com. 1982-84, ho. of dels. 1981-84, chmn. fin. com. 1984-87, chmn. spl. com. on Women in the Cts. 1986—), Assn. Bar City N.Y. (taxation com. 1972-75, 78-79), N.Y. County Lawyers Assn., Am. Judicature Soc. Jewish. Club: N.Y. Wellesley (N.Y.C.). Home: 1035 Fifth Ave New York NY 10028 Office: Proskauer Rose Goetz & Mendelsohn 300 Park Ave New York NY 10022

SCHARETT, ANN ELIZABETH, rehabilitation center executive; b. Corning, N.Y., Aug. 17, 1941; d. Theodore LeRoy Reed and Elizabeth Almira (Guernsey) Schoonover; m. David Leonard Scharett, Aug. 10, 1962; children: Donna Leigh, David Thomas. BS, St. Joseph's Coll., North Windham, Maine, 1984. From staff nurse to organizer alcoholic treatment program Willard (N.Y.) Psychiatric Ctr. (formerly Willard State Hosp.), 1962-81; nurse adminstr., alcoholism rehab. coordinator Dick Van Dyke Clinic, Willard, 1981-86; asst. dir. John L. Norris Treatment Ctr., Rochester, N.Y., 1986—; guest lectr. Tompkins-Cortland Community Coll., Ithaca, N.Y., 1984-86; chairperson Region 2 Alcoholism Service Providers Group, Rochester, 1980; bd. dirs. Finger Lakes Alcoholism Counsel and Referral Agy., Clifton Springs, N.Y., 1975-77. Vol. United Way, Willard, 1983-85, ARC Seneca County, 1983-87; bd. dirs. Interlaken (N.Y.) Christian Sch., 1977-78, 84-87; youth advisor First Bapt. Ch. Interlaken, 1985-86, Sunday sch. tchr., 1962—. Recipient Cert. for 20 Yrs. Service N.Y. State Div. Alcoholism, 1985. Mem. Nat. Soc. RN's, N.Y. Fedn. Alcoholism Counselors, Nat. Assn. Female Execs. Republican. Baptist. Office: John L Norris Treatment Ctr 1600 South Ave Rochester NY 14620

SCHAROLD, MARY LOUISE, psychoanalyst, educator; b. Wichita Falls, Tex., Mar. 3, 1943; d. Walter John and Louise Helen (Hartman) Baumgartner; m. William Ballew McCollum, Aug. 23, 1964 (div. 1981); m. Harry Karl Scharold, June 19, 1982; children: Margaret Louise, Walter Ballew. BA with highest distinction, U. Kans., 1964; MD, Baylor Coll. Med., 1968; postgrad. Topeka Inst. for Psychoanalysis, 1981. Diplomate Am. Bd. Psychiatry and Neurology. Intern Meml. Baptist. Hosp., Houston, 1968-69; resident in psychiatry Baylor Coll. Med., Houston, 1969-72, chief resident, 1971-72; practice of medicine specializing in psychoanalysis, Houston, 1972—; asst. prof. Baylor Coll. Med., Houston, 1973-76, asst. clin. prof., 1981-84, assoc. clin. prof., 1984—; dir. Baylor Psychiat. Clinic, Houston, 1973-76; co-dir. Rice U. Psychiat. Service, Houston, 1981-82; asst. clin. prof. U. Kans. Sch. Medicine, Kansas City, 1977-81; teaching assoc. Topeka Inst. Psychoanalysis, 1980-81; instr. Houston-Galveston Psychoanalytic Inst., 1984-86, teaching analyst, 1986—; Adv. bd. Leavenworth Mental Health Assn., Kans., 1977-81. Watkins scholar U. Kans., 1961-64. Fellow Am. Psychiatric Assn. (chmn. Tex. peer review 1984-88); mem. Am. Psychoanalytic Assn. (cert. 1982, peer rev. com. 1986—, prof. ins. commn. 1987—), Am. Group Psychotherapy Assn., Houston Psychiatric Soc. (v.p. 1984-85, pres. elect 1985-86, pres. 1988—), Houston-Galveston Psychoanalytic Soc. (sec.-treas. 1984-86, pres.-elect 1986-88, pres. 1988—), Am. Psychiat. Assn. (quality assurance com. 1986-87), Houston Group Psychotherapy Soc. (adv. bd. 1984-85), Mortar Bd., Phi Beta Kappa, Delta Phi Alpha, Alpha Omega Alpha, Hilltopper, Pi Beta Phi Alumni Assn. Republican. Lutheran. Office: 4101 Greenbriar Dr Suite 240 Houston TX 77098

SCHARRER, BERTA VOGEL, anatomy and neuroscience educator; b. Munich, Fed. Republic Germany, Dec. 1, 1906; d. Karl and Johanna V.; widowed. PhD in Zoology, U. Munich, 1930; MD (hon.), U. Giessen, Fed. Republic Germany, 1976; DSc (hon.), Northwestern U., 1977, U. N.C., 1978, Smith Coll., 1980, Harvard U., 1982, Yeshiva U., 1983, Mt. Holyoke Coll., 1984, SUNY, 1985; LLD, U. Calgary, Alta., Can., 1982. Research assoc. Research Inst. for Psychiatry, Munich, 1931-34, Neurol. Inst., Frankfurt-am-Main, 1934-37, U. Chgo. Dept. Anatomy, 1937-38, Rockefeller Inst., N.Y.C., 1938-40; instr., fellow Western Res. U. Dept. Anatomy, Cleve., 1940-46; John Guggenheim fellow U. Colo. Dept. Anatomy, Denver, 1947-48, spl. USPHS research fellow, 1948-50; asst. prof. (research) dept. anatomy U. Colo. Sch. Medicine, Denver, 1950-55; prof. anatomy Albert Einstein Coll. Medicine, 1955-77, acting chmn., 1965-67, 76-77, prof. emeritus anatomy and neurosci., 1978—. Recipient Kraepelin Gold medal, 1978, F.C. Koch award Endocrine Soc., 1980, Nat. Medal Sci., 1983. Mem. Nat. Acad. Scis., Am. Acad. Arts & Scis., Deutsche Acad. Naturforscher Leopoldina (Schleiden medal 1983), Am. Assn. Anatomists (pres. 1978-79, Henry Gray award 1982), Am. Soc. Zoologists, Soc. Neurosci., Endocrine Soc. (F.C. Koch award 1980, Nat. Medal of Sci. 1983), Internat. Brain Research Orgn., Com. on Brain Scis. of NRC, Acad. Ind. Scholars. Home: 1240 Neill Ave Bronx NY 10461 Office: Albert Einstein Coll of Medicine Dept of Anatomy 1300 Morris Park Ave Bronx NY 10461

SCHATTINGER, JOAN MYERS, history writer; b. Cleve., Sept. 6, 1936; d. Walter Edward Myers and Janet Louise (Shelhart) Myers-Clayton; m. James Henry Schattinger, July 28, 1961; children: Elisabeth Myers, James Douglas. BA, Wellesley Coll., 1957; postgrad., Harvard U., 1958; MA, Case Western Res. U., 1965. Cer. tchr., Mass., Ohio. Editorial asst. Harvard Law Sch., Cambridge, Mass., 1957-58; tchr. English Orange Bd. Edn., Cleve., 1958-61, Brookline (Mass.) bd. Edn., 1961-63; free-lance writer, editor Cleve., 1963-79; ptnr. History Assocs., Cleve., 1979—; vis. artist We Clevelanders Program, Cleve., 1984-86; cons. in field, Cleve., 1979—. Author: Cleveland's Flats: The Incredible City Under the Hill, 1979, Cleveland's Flats on Tour, 1987; author study guides. Bd. dirs. Cleve. Wellesley, 1978—, Shaker Lakes Regional Nature Ctr. Women's Bd., Cleve., 1986-87. Mem. Internat. Soc. British Genealogy and Family History (trustee), Cotillion Soc. Club: Cleve. Skating.

SCHATZ, MARY LILLIAN PULLIG, clinical and anatomical pathologist, yoga instructor; b. Ruston, La., Dec. 6, 1944; d. Richard Murphy and Rachael Virginia (Jones) Pullig; m. Fred Schultz, June 7, 1967 (div. 1980); m. Walter Frederick Schatz, Nov. 10, 1983; 1 child, David Douglass. BS, La. State U., Baton Rouge, 1966; MD, Vanderbilt U., 1969. Diplomate Am. Bd. Pathology; cert. Iyengar yoga instr. From intern to chief resident Vanderbilt U. Med. Sch., Nashville, 1969-73; pathologist Associated Pathologists, Nashville, 1973—; dir. med. lab. Westside Hosp., Nashville, 1987—; pvt. practice therapeutic yoga and rehabilitative medicine, Nashville, 1980—. Contbr. articles to profl. jours. Mem. Coll. Am. Pathologists (cert.), Am. Soc. Clin. Pathologists (cert.), Am. Coll. Rehab. Medicine, Am. Coll. Sports Medicine, Iyengar Yoga Soc. North Calif., Iyengar Yoga Soc. South Calif. Office: Associated Pathologists 3401 West End Suite 662 Nashville TN 37203

SCHATZ, PAULINE, dietitian; b. Sioux City, Iowa, Sept. 25, 1923; d. Isaac and Haya (Kaplan) Epstein; B.S., UCLA, 1945, M.S., 1950, M.S. in Public Health, 1963; Ed.D., U. So. Calif., 1984; m. Hyman Schatz, Sept. 2, 1951; children—Barbara, Larry. Head dietitian VA, 1946-54; asso. prof. Los Angeles City Coll., 1958-68; prof. home econs. Calif. State U., Los Angeles, 1968-83, prof. emeritus, 1983—, dir. center dietetic edn., 1979—. Grantee VA, Kellogg Found., HEW. Mem. Am. Dietetic Assn. (Disting. Service award 1986), Am. Home Econs. Assn., Calif. Dietetic Assn. (Disting. Service award 1986), Los Angeles Dietetic Assn., Omicron Nu. Author: Manual for Clinical Dietetics, 1978, 3d edit., 1983; also articles to profl. jours. Office: Calif State U Dept Home Econs Los Angeles CA 90032

SCHAUB, MARILYN MCNAMARA, religious educator; b. Chgo., Mar. 24, 1928; d. Bernard Francis and Helen Katherine (Skehan) McNamara; m. R. Thomas Schaub, Oct. 25, 1969; 1 dau., Helen Ann. B.A., Rosary Coll., 1953; Ph.D., U. Fribourg, Switzerland, 1957; diploma, Ecole Biblique, Jerusalem, 1967. Asst. prof. classics and Bibl. studies Rosary Coll., River Forest, Ill., 1957-69; prof. Bibl. studies Duquesne U., Pitts., 1969-70, 73—; participant 8 archeol. excavations, Middle East.; Hon. asso. Am. Schs. Oriental Research, 1966-67; Danforth asso., 1972-80. Author: Friends and Friendship for St. Augustine, 1964; translator: (with H. Richter) Agape in the New Testament, 3 vols, 1963-65. Mem. Soc. Bibl. Lit., Catholic Bibl. Assn., Am. Acad. Religion. Democrat. Home: 25 McKelvey Ave Pittsburgh PA 15218 Office: Duquesne U Theology Dept Pittsburgh PA 15282

SCHAUBERT, LAUREL VIRGINIA, medical illustrator; b. Portland Oreg., Aug. 3, 1923; d. John and Mildred (Hall) Karg; student Reed Coll., 1940-43, U. Calif., 1947-49, Art League San Francisco, 1950-53, U. Calif. San Francisco Med. Center, 1953-55; m. Arvid D. Schaubert, Nov. 10, 1962; children—Gay Lee Schaubert Giannini, Leslie May (dec.). Med. illustrator Ft. Miley VA Hosp., 1955; sr. illustrator dept. surgery U. Calif., San Francisco, 1955-69; prin. illustrator Lange Med. Publs., Los Altos, Calif., 1961-88; now also co-owner, pres. Biomed Arts Assocs., Inc., San Francisco; instr. U. Calif., San Francisco, 1959-61, 74-78. Recipient cert. of commendation Calif. Dist. Attys. Assn., 1977; Merit award Fedn. Biocommunication Socs., 1979. Fellow Assn. Med. Illustrators (Outstanding Service award 1972; chmn. bd. govs. 1971-72, v.p. 1975-76, pres. 1976-77); mem. Graphic Artists Guild. Co-author: Scientific Illustration: Standards for Publication; contbr. med. illustrations and articles to textbooks, profl. jours. Office: 350 Parnassus Ave Suite 905 San Francisco CA 94117

SCHAUER, CATHARINE GUBERMAN, public affairs specialist; b. Woodbury, N.J., Sept. 24, 1945; d. Jack and Anna Ruth (Felipe) Guberman; m. Irwin Jay Schauer, July 4, 1968; children—Cheryl Anne, Marc Cawin. A.B., Miami-Dade Jr. Coll., 1965; B.Ed., U. Miami, 1967; postgrad. Mercer U., 1968. Writer, Miami (Fla.) News, 1962-63; tchr. Dade County Schs., Miami, Fla., 1967-68; coordinator pub. info. Macon Jr. Coll. (Ga.), 1968-69; writer Atlanta Jour., 1969-72; editor Ridgerunner newspaper, Woodbridge, Va., 1973-75; pub. info. specialist Dept. Interior, Washington, 1980-82; writer Dept. Army, Ft. Belvoir, Va., 1982-84, chief prodn., design and editorial, publs. div., 1984-85; head writer-editor SE region U.S. Naval Audit Service, Virginia Beach, Va., 1986; pub. affairs specialist, tech. rep. for contracting officer for vis. ctr. ops. NASA Langley Research Ctr., Hampton, Va., 1987—; columnist, writer Potomac News, Woodbridge, 1972-85. Contbr. articles to profl. jours. Historian, publicity chmn. PTO, Woodbridge, 1974; publicity chmn. Boy Scouts Am., Woodbridge, 1974-83, Girl Scouts U.S.A., Woodbridge, 1974-79; bd. dirs. Congregation Ner Tamid, Woodbridge, 1984-85. Recipient Outstanding Tng. Devel. Support award U.S. Army, 1983; 1st place news writing award and 1st place for advt. design Fla. Jr. Coll. Press Assn., 1964, 1st place feature writing award, 1964, 1st place news writing award Sigma Delta Chi, 1965, 70th anniversary team NASA, 1988. Mem. Va. Press Women, Women in Communications Nat. Fedn. Press Women. Democrat. Jewish. Home: 120 Tide's Run Yorktown VA 23692-4333 Office: NASA Langley Research Ctr Mail Code 154 Hampton VA 23665-5225

SCHAUMBURG, JANET LEE, mining engineer; b. Rupert, Idaho, Mar. 17, 1953; d. Ronald K. and Florence Arlene (Roselius) Kofoed; m. Robert Clyde Miller, June 23, 1984; m. Gary Lee Schaumburg, Oct. 7, 1974 (div. Mar. 1980). Shift supr. Anaconda Copper Co., Butte, Mont., 1977-79; surface mining engr. Exxon Minerals Co., Douglas, Wyo., 1979-81, planning analyst, N.Y.C., 1981-83, sr. staff mining engr., Houston, 1983-84; sr. community rep. LaBarge Project, Exxon Co. U.S.A., Frontier, Wyo., 1984-86; permits supr. Southwestern Div. Exxon Co., USA, Midland, Tex., 1986-87, sr. human resources specialist, 1988—. Adviser, U. Idaho, Moscow, 1981—. Bd. dirs. United Way, Sweetwater County, Wyo., 1986, Midland-Odessa Symphony and Chorale, 1987—. Newmont Mining Co. scholar, 1973-76; Womens Aux. Soc. Mining Engrs. scholar, 1975. Mem. Soc. Mining Engrs. (nat. tech. papers com. 1982-85), Nat. Soc. Profl. Engrs. (v.p. Butte 1979), Soc. Women Engrs. (nat. long range planning com. 1981-82), Bus. and Profl. Womens Club (pres. chpt. 1979), C. of C. Kemmerer (membership chmn. 1986). Republican. Lodge: Eastern Star. Avocations: cross country skiing, playing piano, reading, racquetball, tapdancing. Office: Exxon Co USA PO Box 1600 Midland TX 79702

SCHAUWECKER, MARGARET LIDDIE, construction executive; b. Louisa, Ky., July 28, 1934; d. Mitchell and Mary Lou (Thompson) McKinster; m. Norman Walter Schauwecker, Aug. 30, 1953 (div. Oct. 1968); children: Johanna L., Mitchell Walter, Shawna Ann. Student, Bliss Coll., 1952-54, El Segundo Coll., 1957-59. Sec. N. Am. Aviation, Columbus, Ohio, 1952-1955, Gilfillan Electronics, Los Angeles, 1956-62; adminstrv. asst. Columbus Wood Preserving Co., 1970-78; pres. Ohio State Tie and Timber Inc., Louisa, Ky., 1978—. Named to Honorable Order Ky. Cols. Commonwealth Ky., 1984; recipient Outstanding Achievement in Sales Vol. award Ohio Dept. Econ. Devel., 1980, 81, 82; recipient Top 100 Small Bus's. in Ohio award Ohio House Reps., 1983. Mem. Am. Wood Preservers Assn., Railway Tie Assn., Bus. and Profl. Women in Constrn. Baptist. Club: Louisa Woman's. Lodges: Order Eastern Star, Rebekah. Home: Rt 1 Box 2360 Louisa KY 41230 Office: Ohio State Tie and Timber Rt 1 Box 2360 Louisa KY 41230

SCHEER, JANET KATHY, mathematics educator; b. Bklyn., Apr. 22, 1947; d. Seymour and Hilda (Shoer) S. BA, Bklyn. Coll., 1968; MS, Syracuse (N.Y.) U., 1969; PhD, Ariz. State U., 1977. Cert. tchr., N.Y., Ariz.; cert. prin., Ariz. Math. tchr. Jamesville (N.Y.) DeWitt Middle Sch., 1969-72; math. tchr., middle sch. coordinator Am. Internat. Sch., Kfar Shmaryahu, Israel, 1972-74; from asst. prof. to assoc. prof. S. Ill. U., Carbondale, 1977-88; cons. in field, 1977—; sr. nat. math. cons. Holt, Rinehart & Winston, N.Y.C., 1986—. Editor Ill. Math. Tchr. jour., 1980-83; author: Manipulatives in Mathematics Unlimited, 1987; contbr. to textbooks and profl. jours. Named one of Outstanding Young Women Am., 1978, 81-85, Outstanding Tchr. Yr. So. Ill. U., 1978-79; recipient numerous grants. Mem. Nat. Council Tchrs. Math., Research Council for Diagnostic and Prescriptive Math. (charter mem., v.p. 1984-86), Ill. Council Tchrs. Math. (various offices), Phi Delta Kappa, Kappa Delta Pi. Office: Holt Rinehart & Winston 577 Airport Blvd Suite 185 Burlingame CA 94010

SCHEETZ, SISTER MARY JOELLEN, college president; b. Lafayette, Ind., May 20, 1926; d. Joseph Albert and Ellen Isabelle (Fitzgerald) S. A.B., St. Francis Coll., 1956; M.A., U. Notre Dame, 1964; Ph.D., U. Mich., 1970. Tchr. English, Bishop Luers High Sch., Fort Wayne, Ind., 1965-67; acad. dean St. Francis Coll., Fort Wayne, 1967-68; pres. St. Francis Coll., 1970—. Mem. Delta Epsilon Sigma. Address: 2701 Spring St Fort Wayne IN 46808

SCHEFTIC, CAROL, educational computing researcher; b. Richmond, Ind., June 11, 1949; d. Harold E. and Lillian M. (Egli) S. BSin Math., Carnegie Mellon U., 1971; M of Math. Edn., U. Pitts., 1973, PhD in Ednl. Tech., 1985. Cert. secondary math. tchr. Lectr. Boreham Wood (Eng.) Coll. Further Edn., 1973-75; instr. Community Coll. of Allegheny County, Pitts., 1976; project dir. Mgmt. Sci. Assocs., Pitts., 1976-80; program specialist Allegheny Intermediate Unit, Pitts., 1980-81, coordinator instructional tech., 1983-84; teaching asst. U. Pitts., 1981-83; mgr. curriculum devel. Carnegie Group, Pitts., 1984-85; research scientist Carnegie Mellon U., Pitts., 1985—; part-time faculty Pa. State U., College Park, 1981—; coordinator Allegheny County Student Computer Fair, 1983-85; dir. Carnegie Mellon U./Allegheny Intermediate Unit Project on Advanced Ednl. Computing, 1985—, Ctr. for Design of Ednl. Computing Scholarship Program in Ednl. Computing, 1985—; chair com. 3d Internat. Conf. on Artificial Intelligence and Edn., 1987. Instr., developer course Sta. WYEP-FM, Pitts., 1976-78, 88—. Vol. Weald & Downland Open Air Mus., Singleton, Eng., 1975. Mem. Assn. for Ednl. Communications and Tech., Internat. Council on Computers in Edn. Office: Carnegie Mellon U Ctr for Design Ednl Computing Pittsburgh PA 15213-3890

SCHEID, LINDA GERALYN, human resources professional; b. Mauston, Wis., Aug. 22, 1956; d. LeRoy William and LaVerne Frances Davis; m. Bruce Allen Scheid, June 21, 1986. BA in English, Theatre, Secondary Edn., S.W. State U., 1978. Tchr. Ind. Sch. Dist. 332, Mora, Minn., 1978-81; adminstr. compensation/corp. tng. Dain Bosworth Inc., Mpls., 1981-86; EEO officer City of Sioux City, Iowa, 1986—. Mem. Nat. Assn. for Female Execs., Sioux City C. of C. (chairperson city beautification com. 1987-88), Siouxland Personnel Assn. Office: City of Sioux City PO Box 447 Sioux City IA 51102

SCHEIDECKER, JANE MARIE, university administrator; b. Billings, Mont., Sept. 5, 1953; d. Donald Cloyd and Marilyn Kathleen (Ness) S.; m. Duane Arthur Partain, 1979. BA, Ea. Mont. Coll., 1974; MA, cert. in teaching, U. Wash., 1976; M in Internat. Mgmt., Am. Grad. Sch. Internat. Mgmt., 1982. Owner, mgr. Academia Rapididiom, Spain, 1976-77; tchr. Lane Community Coll. and Brookings (Oreg.) High Sch., 1977-80; program coordinator learning resources ctr. U. Oreg., Eugene, 1980-81, co-dir. Univ. Forum, 1983-85, assoc. dean for devel., 1986—; v.p. Tara Mgmt. Group, Eugene, 1983-85. Fellow AAUW (dir. publicity Eugene chpt. 1987); mem. Nat. Soc. Fundraising Execs., Council for Advancement and Support of Edn. (Newcomer scholar 1987). Heller fellow, 1980-81. Office: U Oreg 117 Friendly Hall Eugene OR 97403

SCHEIMER, JANICE SCHAEFER, financial consultant, planner; b. Alva, Okla., Sept. 21, 1948; d. Andrew August and Ruth Ida (Boyce) Schaefer; m. Gary Lee Scheimer, Aug. 10, 1968; children: Scott Allen, Eric Lee. BS, Ariz. State U., 1971, MBA, 1972. Cert. fin. planner. Rate analyst Northwest Pipeline, Salt Lake City, 1976-78; mktg. mgr. Western Fed. Savs., Colorado Springs, 1979-82; fin. cons. Shearson, Lehamn, Hutton/Am. Express, Gimsbach, Fed. Republic Germany, 1982-83, Colorado Springs, Fed. Republic Germany, 1982-83, 1985—; fin. cons. Integrated Resources, Gimsbach, Fed. Republic Germany, 1983-85; v.p., treas. Golden Horizons, Inc., Cheyenne Wells, Colo., Fed. Republic Germany, 1979—; sec., treas. Schaefer Farms, Inc., Cheyenne Wells, Colo., Fed. Republic Germany, 1985—; v.p. S.S. & N., Inc., Cheyenne Wells, Colo., Fed. Republic Germany, 1985—; instr. U. Md., Fed. Republic Germany, 1984-85; lectr. Meml. Hosp. Women's Ctr.; cons. Pro-Trac, 1984; v.p., treas. S.S. & N. Inc., Cheyenne Wells, 1984—; mem. econ. devel. com. City Colorado Springs. Soccer team mother Am. Youth Assn., Ramstein, Fed. Republic Germany, 1982-85; mem. Homebuilders Assn., Colorado Springs, 1985—; mem. econ. devel. com. City of Colorado Springs. Mem. Inst. Cert. Fin. Planners, Nat. Assn. Female Execs., Speakers' Bur. Networking Assn. Republican. Clubs: Officers Wives (Ramstein) (treas. 1984-85). Home: 365 Allegheny Pl Colorado Springs CO 80919 Office: Shearson Am Express 101 N Tejon #401 Colorado Springs CO 80903

SCHEIN, LORRAINE SANDRA, university librarian; b. Bklyn., Jan. 29, 1933; d. Abraham Isaac Charnoff and Belle (Siegel) Herenstein; m. Aaron Meyer Schein, June 5, 1960; children: Adam Michael, Rachel Jennifer. BA, Adelphi U., 1954; postgrad., Bklyn. Coll., 1956-59; MS, NYU, 1959; postgrad., Poly. U., 1984—. Lit. chemist Sci. Design Co., Inc., N.Y.C., 1956-60; patent liaison Leesona-Moos Corp., Great Neck, N.Y., 1960-66; librarian Grumman Aerospace Corp., Bethpage, N.Y., 1966-67; library mgr. Poly. U., L.I. campus, Farmingdale, N.Y., 1970—, sec. Friends of Library, 1987—. Mem. Kadimah chpt. Hadassah, Levittown, N.Y., 1970—. Mem. ALA, Am. Chem. Soc., N.Y. Acad. Sci., Assn. for Computing Machinery, Spl. Libraries Assn., Am. Soc. for Info. Sci., Nassau County Library Assn., Delta Tau Alpha, Delta Phi Alpha, Gamma Sigma Epsilon, Beta Phi Mu, Phi Sigma Sigma. Jewish. Home: 17 Admiral Ln Hicksville NY 11801 Office: Polytechnic U Rt 110 Farmingdale NY 11735

SCHEIN, SALLY JOY, special services-learning consultant, marriage, family counselor; b. Chgo., July 6, 1930; d. Rudolph James and Lillian (Cohen) Good; m. Michael Schein, Apr. 9, 1955; children—Jack Edward, David Lee. B.A., U. Chgo., 1950, Columbia U., 1952; M.S., CCNY, 1953; Ed.S., Seton Hall U., 1982, also postgrad.; EdD. Nova U., 1986. Occupational therapist Monmouth Meml. Hosp., Longbranch, N.J., 1953-54; tchr. nursery kindergarten N.Y. Dept. Welfare, N.Y.C., 1954-55; tchr. kindergarten Yonkers Pub. Sch., N.Y., 1955, Dumont Pub. Sch., N.J., 1955-56; learning disabilities teaching cons. Haworth, N.J., 1968-72, Caldwell, N.J., 1972-79, Cranford Pub. Sch., N.J., 1979—; psychologist extern North Caldwell, Closter, N.J., 1976-77; counselor Community Mental Health Ctr., Dumont, 1981-82. Author: Welcome to Danish International Studies, 1979; (with E. Riley et al) Sparking Divergent Ability, 1985. Founding mem. bd. Community Mental Health Ctr., Dumont, 1958-60. Mem. Am. Assn. Marriage and Family Therapists, Bergen County Assn. Sch. Psychologists, Assn. Learning Cons., Council Exceptional Children, Orton Soc. Avocations: Sculpting; art; jogging; travel. Home: 4 Harding Ave Dumont NJ 07628

SCHEIN, VIRGINIA ELLEN, psychologist; b. Rahway, N.J., June 23, 1943; d. Jacob Charles and Anne S.; BA cum laude, Cornell U., 1965; PhD, N.Y.U., 1969; 1 child, Alexander Nikos. Sr. research assoc. Am. Mgmt. Assn., N.Y.C., 1969-70; mgr. personnel research Life Office Mgmt. Assn., N.Y.C., 1970-72; dir. personnel research Met. Life Ins. Co. N.Y.C., 1972-75; asso. prof. Sch. Mgmt. Case Western Res. U., Cleve., 1975-76; vis. asso. prof. Sch. Orgn. and Mgmt., Yale U., New Haven, 1976-77; asso. prof. mgmt. Wharton Sch. U. Pa., Phila., 1977-80; mgmt. cons. Virginia E. Schein, Ph.D., P.C., 1975—; assoc. prof. psychology Bernard M. Baruch Coll., City U. N.Y., 1982-85; prof. mgmt. Gettysburg Coll., Pa., 1986—. Author: (with others) Power and Organization Development, 1988; contbr. articles to profl. jours. Bd. dirs. Gettysburg Planning and Health Ctr. Mem. Am. Psychol. Assn. (council reps. 1978-80, com. on women 1980-83), Met. Assn. Applied Psychology (pres. 1973-74), Acad. Mgmt., (rep. orgn. devel. div. 1979-81), Internat. Assn. Applied Psychology, Gettysburg YWCA (bd. dirs. 1987-90), Psi Chi. Office: Gettysburg Coll Dept Mgmt Gettysburg PA 17325

SCHEIWE, PAULA MARIA GRAVELLE, financial executive, consultant; b. Harvey, Ill., Apr. 14, 1948. BS in Mgmt., No. Ill. U., 1971; MS in Acctg., Roosevelt U., 1975. Auditor Deloitte Haskins Sells, Chgo., 1975-76; chief fin. officer Delta Communications, Inc., Chgo., 1976-87. Badge leader Girl Scouts U.S., Homewood, Ill., 1986-87; mem. PTA, Homewood; active Homewood Hist. Soc., 1986-87; softball coach. Mem. Nat. Assn. Accts., Am. Legion Aux. Home and Office: 1520 186th Pl Homewood IL 60430

SCHELBY, ERIKA KATE, international business consultant; b. Berlin, Oct. 31, 1935; came to U.S., 1970; d. Kurt H. and Edith (Winkler) Mueller; m. Frederick Schelby, June 6, 1982; children by previous marriage—Ulrike, Susanne. B.A., Kans. State U., 1977; M.S., U. Ill., 1978. Asst. to dir. Georg Jensen Silver, Dusseldorf, W.Ger., 1959-60; v.p. Nordlys Ohg., Dusseldorf, 1960-64, pres., 1964-70; bus. research mgr. Goodyear Tire & Rubber Co., Akron, Ohio, 1978-80; mktg. mgr. Mo. Research Labs., Albuquerque, 1980-82; pres. Interteam Assocs., Albuquerque, 1982—. Mem. Am. Mktg. Assn., Phi Beta Kappa, Phi Kappa Phi, Gamma Theta Upsilon. Office: Interteam Assocs 1214 Jackson SE Albuquerque NM 87108

SCHELLING, JOYCE ELAINE, computer software salesperson; b. Fort Wayne, Ind., Oct. 14, 1937; d. George Martin and Lucille Alice (Schuckel) Schmeling. BA, St. Francis Coll., 1962; MA, Catholic U., 1968; PhD, NYU, 1987. Lic. tchr., Ind., N.J. Dir. drama St. Francis Coll., Ft. Wayne, 1966-70; instr. South Plainfield (N.J.) High Sch., 1970-80, NYU, N.Y.C., 1980-82; sales rep. On-Line Software, Fort Lee, N.J., 1982-85, SDI, Hackensack, N.J., 1986-88. Mem. N.J. Network Bus. and Profl. Women, Nat. Assn. Female Execs. Democrat. Home: 2100 Linwood Ave 15R Fort Lee NJ 07024

SCHELZEL, SHARON SULLIVAN, child care consultant; b. Rochester, N.H., June 18, 1949; d. Arthur and Eleanor (Raab) Sullivan; m. Curtis B. Schelzel, Aug. 22, 1970; 1 child, Katie. RN, Sacred Heart Hosp., 1970; AA, Notre Dame Coll., Manchester, N.H., 1987, BA in Behavioral Sci., 1988. Asst. surp. Manchester Pediatric Group, 1975-81; co-dir., co-owner Butterflies are Free Infant/Toddler Ctr., Manchester, 1981-83; asst. dir. Greater Manchester Child Care Assn., 1984-87; cons. Work/Family Directions, Boston, 1987-88; cons., owner New England Child Care Cons. Service, Manchester, 1987—; exec. dir. St. Francis of Assisi Child Care Ctr., Manchester, 1987—; bd. dirs. Child Care Craft Skill Ctr., Manchester, 1987—. Mem. Nat. Assn. for Edn. Young Children, Coalition of Early Childhood Profls., Alpha Sigma Lambda. Roman Catholic. Lodge: Zonta. Office: New England Child Care Cons Service 299 Stark Ln Manchester NH 03102

SCHEMMEL, EVELYN ANN, college administrator; b. Albany, N.Y., Dec. 18, 1940; d. Raymond and Helen Edith (Brockley) Nickel; m. Gerald Bernard Schemmel, Aug. 24, 1963. BS in Bus. Edn., SUNY, Albany, 1963. Instr., dept. head Mary Immaculate High Sch., Key West, Fla., 1965-67; dean of instrn. Kelsey-Jenney Coll., San Diego, 1970-72, dir., 1972-73; dir. acad. affairs Cannon's Bus. Coll., Honolulu, 1974—; pres., dir. colls. Cannon's Bus. Coll. and Educators of the Pacific, 1974—. Recipient Cert. of Recognition, State of Hawaii, Commn. on Manpower and Full Employment, 1980. Mem. Western Bus. Edn. Assn. (pres. 1985—, Disting. Service award 1988), Assn. Pacific Postsecondary Pvt. Schs. (pres. 1986-88), Hawaii Bus. Edn. Assn. (pres. 1978-79, Dist. Service award 1980), Nat. Bus. Edn. Assn. (exec. bd. 1985-86, 87—), Hawaii C. of C. (small bus. council 1986—). Club: Pilot of Downtown Honolulu (pres. 1984-85). Home: 1430 Laukahi St Honolulu HI 96821 Office: Cannon's Bus Coll 1500 Kapiolani Blvd Honolulu HI 96814

SCHENCK, SUSAN JANE, special education educator; b. Providence, July 20, 1949; d. Donald Elwood and Geraldine Frances (Dansereau) S. AA, R.I. Jr. Coll., Providence, 1969; BS, R.I. Coll., 1972, MEd, 1975; cert. advanced grad. study, U. Conn., 1977, PhD, 1979. Cert. elem. and spl. edn. tchr., cert. adminstr. Tchr., title I Coventry, R.I. Pub. Schs., 1972; tchr. mentally handicapped North Kingston, R.I. Pub. Schs., 1972-76; research asst. U. Conn., Storrs, 1976-78; asst. prof. SUNY, Plattsburgh, 1978-79; asst. prof. Coll. of Charleston (S.C), 1979-84, assoc. prof., 1985—, coordinator LD services, 1984—, dir. tchr. cert. and student teaching, 1985-87; curriculum cons. Bristol, Conn. schs. 1976-77; field reader U.S. Office Edn. (Spl. Edn.), Washington, 1983—. Author: Math That Pays Off, 1978; (monograph with others) IEP's: State of the Art; contbr. articles to periodicals. Bd. dirs. Ronald McDonald House, Charleston, 1985—, Exchange Club Prevention Child Abuse, Charleston, 1986—, Friends of Children, Med. Univ. S.C., Charleston, 1988—; mem. sch. bd. Christ Our King Ch., Mt. Pleasant, S.C., 1986-87. Spl. Edn. fellow, U. Conn., 1976-78; U.S. Dept. Edn. grantee, Office Spl. Edn., 1983-86, Project Omni grantee, S.C. Office the Handicapped, 1981. Mem. Am. Edn. Research Assn. (treas. 1980-84, chmn. 1984-87, chair spl. edn. research), Council Exceptional Children, S.C. Tchr. Recruitment Ctr. (policy bd.), Council Learning Disabilities. Office: Coll Charleston 9 College Way Charleston SC 29424

SCHENKEL, BARBARA ANN, minister, counselor; b. Albuquerque, Mar. 17, 1951; d. Richard Henry and Mildred (Voth) S. BSN, U. N.Mex., 1972; MDiv, Iliff Sch. Theology, 1978; MSW, Ariz. State U., 1988. RN, N.Mex.; ordained to ministry Meth. Ch., 1979. Minister intern Christ Ch. U. Meth. Ch., Denver, 1975-77; parish minister Herman (Nebr.) Federated and Riverside Bapt. Ch., 1978-82, Cambridge (Nebr.) Bartley U. Meth. Ch., 1982-85; family minister Red Mountain U.M.C., Mesa, Ariz., 1986-87; Christ Ch. Caring Community Coordinator, Denver, 1975-77; advisor alcohol treatment program Immanuel Hosp., Washington County, Nebr., 1980-82; mem. task group to study Ministry Effectiveness in Nebr., 1981; vis. del. to World Meth. Conf., Honolulu, 1981; registrar for candidacy Bd. or Ordained Ministry, 1980-84, strategy com., 1984-85; drug and alcohol cons. Salvation Army Adult Rehab. Ctr., Phoenix, 1987—. Chaplain Jackson-Peck Am. Legion Post, Herman, 1980-82. Served to 1st lt. USAF Nurse Corps, 1973-75. Mem. Nebr. Ann. Conf. U. Meth. Chs., Mesa Ministerial Assn., Cambridge Ministerial Assn. (pres. 1984), Tekamah-Herman Ministerial Assn. (pres. 1981), Southwest Dist. Council Ministries (past com. memberships), Common Cause, Sierra Club, Amnesty Internat., Nat. Assn. Social Workers, Phi Kappa Phi.

SCHENK-ZIEBELMAN, CYNTHIA MARIAN, import executive; b. Fort Worth, Jan. 18, 1954; d. Eugene F. and Florence (Klein) S.; m. Peter H. Ziebelman, Sept. 1, 1985. BS, Tex. Christian U., 1976. Asst. mgr. Foxmoor Casuals, Livingston, N.J., 1972-75; mgr. Klein Signs, Fort Worth, 1975-76; asst. mdse. mgr. Pier 1 Imports, Fort Worth, 1976-77, mdse. mgr., 1977-81; v.p. Intercontinental Art, Inc., Gardena, Calif., 1981-85; pres. Designer Ideas Inc., Palo Alto, Calif., 1985—. Mem. Nat. Assn. Female Execs.

SCHEPPS, VICTORIA HAYWARD, lawyer; b. Brockton, Mass., June 11, 1956; d. William George and Lucy Victoria (Mitcheroney) Hayward; m. Frank Schepps, Sept. 18, 1982; 1 child, Frank Schepps IV. BA, Suffolk U., 1977; JD, U. San Diego, 1981. Instr., Northeastern U., Boston, 1981-83; assoc. Hoffman & Hoffman, Boston, 1983-85, Mark J. Gladstone, P.C., 1985-87; Doktor, Hirschberg & Schepps, 1987—. Mem. Mass. Bar Assn., ABA, Mass. Conveyancing Assn., Forum Com. Entertainment and Sports Law, Gen. Fedn. Women's Clubs, Jr. Ladies Library Assn. (v.p. 1987). Democrat. Roman Catholic. Home: 11 Overlook Rd Randolph MA 02368 Office: Doktor Hirschberg & Scheppes 402 N Main St PO Box 788 Randolph MA 02368

SCHER, MARLENE DIANA, financial consultant; b. Bklyn.; d. Herman and Rose (Brenner) S.; children: David Lee, Lisa Gail Gottlieb, Pamela Joy Kozak. Attended Skidmore Coll., Bklyn. Coll., attended Poh's Inst. Real Estate. Exec. dir. Video Mate, N.Y.C., 1975-77; account exec. Prudential Bache, N.Y.C., 1980-82; asst. v.p. Advest, Inc., N.Y.C., 1982-86; v.p. Smith Barney, Harris Upham & Co., N.Y.C., 1986-88, Merrill Lynch, Pierce, Fenner & Smith, Inc., N.Y.C., 1988—; exec. dir. Singles Expn., N.Y.C., 1976; weekly TV host Manhattan Cable TV, N.Y.C., 1975-76; lectr. seminars, N.Y.C., 1982; radio and TV guest, 1986—;. Author: Love in N.Y.C. Anthology, 1977; contbg. editor, author Singles World Mag., 1975-76. Past mem. Deborah, N.Y.C.; bd. govs. The Night Owls, N.Y.C. Mem. Art Students League of N.Y. (life), Skidmore Coll. Alumni Assn., Nat. Assn. Female Execs. Republican. Lodges: B'nai Brith (bd. govs. N.Y.C. chpt.), Order Ea. Star. Home: 12 E 86 St Apt 432 New York NY 10028 Office: Smith Barney Harris Upham 717 Fifth Ave 6th Floor New York NY 10019

SCHER, NANCY SLIFKIN, physician; b. N.Y.C., Nov. 18, 1946; d. Meyer and Dorothy Alma (Reiff) Slifkin; m. Kenneth S. Scher, June 23, 1968 (div. 1985); children: Rachel, Alan, Michael. BA, Brown U., 1967; MD, U. Pa., 1971. Diplomate Am. Bd. Internal Medicine, Am. Bd. Hematology, Am. Bd. Med. Oncology. Intern, resident Bellevue Hosp., NYU, 1971-74; fellow in hematology N.Y.U., 1974-76; fellow in medical oncology Hosp. of U. Pa., Phila., 1976-77; asst. prof. Dept. Medicine, Marshall U., Huntington, W.Va., 1978-82, assoc. prof., 1982—. Contbr. articles to profl. jours. Mem. Am. Soc. Clin. Oncology, Am. Soc. Hematology, Am. Coll. Physicians. Office: Marshall U Med Sch Dept Medicine Huntington WV 25701

SCHERBA, ELAINE LOUISE, investment banker, financial analyst; b. Milw., Mar. 24, 1949; d. Raymond Arthur and Isabelle (Benson) Podolske; m. Stephen Scherba Jr., June 19, 1971. BA, Carroll Coll., 1971; MBA, U. Wash., 1977. Fin. analyst Rainier Nat. Bank, Seattle, 1977-78; officer fin. analysis Seattle-1st Nat. Bank, 1978-79, asst. v.p., mgr. capital investment analysis, 1979-80, v.p., mgr. fin. analysis and cons., 1980-81, v.p., mgr. asset-liability div., 1982-83, sr. v.p., mgr. fin. planning and reporting div., 1983-84, sr. v.p., mgr. retail delivery systems div., 1985-86, sr. v.p., mgr. fin. adv. services, 1986—. Pres. bd. trustees Univ. Prep. Acad., Seattle, 1987-88; bd. dirs. Friends of Youth, Seattle, 1987-88. Republican. Episcopalian. Clubs: Rainier, Wash. Athletic (Seattle). Home: 509 Crockett St Seattle WA 98109 Office: Seattle-1st Nat Bank 1110 3d Ave 10th Floor Seattle WA 98101

SCHERER, ANITA (STOCK), advertising agency executive; b. Cleve., Sept. 20, 1938; d. William John Stock and Gertrud Clara (Kaufmann) Bacher; m. Richard Phillip Scherer, Nov. 25, 1961; children—William Richard, Christopher Howard. Student U. Cin., 1956-57; Assoc.Bus., Jones Bus. Coll., 1958. Account sec. Northlich, Stolley LaWarre, Inc., Cin., 1978-79, account asst., 1979-80, asst. account mgr., 1980-81, account mgr., 1981-84, mktg. service assoc., 1984—; lectr. local schs., univs., Cin. 1980—. Co-editor: monthly newsletter Badge, 1967-72; designer, created assorted notepads, 1986. Lector, Our Lady of Victory Roman Cath. Ch., Cin., 1972—; pres. Delhi Hills Community Council, Cin., 1974-75; adv. bd. mem. Coll. Mount St. Joseph, Ohio, 1974-80; v.p. adminstrn. Stagecrafters, Cin., 1983-85, publicity chmn., 1984—; mktg. bd. mem. Contemp. Arts Ctr., 1985—, chmn. Advt./Graphic Arts div. Fine Arts Fund Campaign, 1988. Winner nat. competition Am. Assn. Advt. Agys., 1980; recipient Outstanding Performance award Assn. Community Theatres, Cin., 1983, Excellence in Acting award Ohio Community Theatres Assn., 1984. Mem. Nat. Assn. Female Execs., Cin. Direct Mktg. Assn., Am. Mktg. Assn., Acad. Health Services Mktg., Am. Coll. Healthcare Marketers, Cin. C. of C. (lectr. 1984-86). Avocations: travel, reading, medieval/renaissance history, community theater. Office: Northlich Stolley LaWarre Inc 200 W 4th St Cincinnati OH 45202

SCHERER, JEANNE CATHERINE, nurse, author; b. Buffalo, Apr. 8, 1928; d. Albert and Florence Rose (Steinman) Scherer. R.N., Buffalo Gen. Hosp. Sch. Nursing, 1954; B.S. in Nursing, D'Youville Coll., 1966; M.S., Canisius Coll., 1972. Staff nurse various hosps., 1954-66; clin. instr. Sisters Hosp. Sch. Nursing, Buffalo, 1966-68, 78-86, asst. dir., med. surg. nursing coordinator, 1968-78, cons., 1986—. Author: Introductory Clinical Pharmacology, 1975, 3d edit., 1987; Introductory Medical-Surgical Nursing, 1977, 4th edit., 1986; Student Work Manual for Introductory Medical-Surgical Nursing, 1977, 4th edit., 1986; Student Work Manual for Introductory Clinical Pharmacology, 1982, 3d edit., 1987; Lippincott's Nurses' Drug Manual, 1985. Mem. Western N.Y. League for Nursing. Republican. Roman Catholic. Office: PO Box 763 West Seneca NY 14224

SCHERER, PATRICIA ANN, sales representative; b. Balt., Jan. 7, 1948; d. George R. and Leona F. (Kasper) Labuda; m. Donald G. Scherer; 1 child, Monica Lee. Student, Essex (Md.) Community Coll., Catonsville (Md.) Community Coll. Sec. to adminstrv. asst. to adminstrv. officer VA, Washington, 1966-82; adminstrv. asst. Ryan Homes, Glen Burnie, Md., 1982-86, sales rep., 1986—. Democrat. Roman Catholic. Home: 709 Kearneys Ln Severn MD 21144 Office: Ryan Homes 407 Crain Hwy SE Glen Burnie MD 21061

SCHERGER, MOZELLE SPAINHOUR (MRS. GEORGE RICHARD SCHERGER), librarian; b. Forsyth County, N.C., Dec. 17, 1916; d. Earnest Sidney and Mertie Blanche (Hauser) Spainhour; B.S., Appalachian State Tchrs. Coll., Boone, N.C., 1937; B.S. in L.S., U. N.C., 1943; m. George Richard Scherger, Feb. 23, 1946; children—Teresa Ann (Mrs. Richard Martin), George Richard, Joseph John, Daniel M. Tchr. English and French, sch. librarian Cramerton (N.C.) High Sch., 1937-42; librarian Laurinburg-Maxton AFB, 1943, Piedmont Jr. High Sch., 1944, Pope Field AFB, 1945-46, Charlotte (N.C.) Coll., 1957-64; documents and serials librarian U. N.C. at Charlotte, 1965-69, asst. reference librarian, 1969-78, reference librarian, 1979-80. Mem. AAUP. Home: 701 St Julien St Charlotte NC 28205

SCHERMER, KATHY WILSON, lawyer; b. Rome, Ga., Mar. 31, 1956; d. O. Max and Julia N. (Johnson) Wilson; m. Robert Charles Schermer, June 16, 1979. BA, Davidson Coll., 1974; JD, U. Ala., 1981. Bar: Ga. 1981, Fla. 1983. Ptnr. Schermer & Schermer P.C., Atlanta, 1981-83; gen. counsel, corp. sec. Goldome Savs. Bank, 1984-86; assoc. Shea & Gould, Bradenton, Fla., 1986—. 1984—. Mem. ABA, State Bar Ga., Fla. Bar. Presbyterian. Office: Shea & Gould 1301 6th Ave W Bradenton FL 34205

SCHETLIN, ELEANOR M., retired university official; b. N.Y.C., July 15, 1920; d. Henry Frank and Elsie (Chew) Schetlin; B.A., Hunter Coll., 1940; M.A., Tchrs. Coll., Columbia U., 1942, Ed.D., 1967. Playground dir. Dept. of Parks, N.Y.C., 1940-42; librarian Met. Hosp. Sch. Nursing, N.Y.C., 1943-44, dir. recreation, 1944-48, dir. recreation and guidance, 1948-59; coordinator student activities SUNY, Plattsburgh, 1959-63, asst. dean students, 1963-64; asst. prof., coordinator student personnel services CUNY, Hunter Coll., 1967-68; asst. dir. student personnel Columbia U., Coll. Pharm. Scis., N.Y.C., 1968-69, dir. student personnel, 1969-71; assoc. dean for students Health Scis. Center, SUNY, Stony Brook, 1971-73, asst. v.p. for student services, 1973-74, assoc. dean of students, dir. student services, 1974-85. Mem. Nat. Assn. Women Deans, Adminstrs. and Counselors. Contbr. articles to profl. jours. Home: 20 Barberry Ln Sea Cliff NY 11579

SCHETTINO, MARIA CARMEN, early childhood educator; b. N.Y.C., Mar. 12, 1949; d. Aniello and Mary Louise (Bové) S.; m. Albert Zezulinski (div. Apr. 1986); 1 child, Kerri. A in Early Edn., SUNY, Farmingdale, 1969. Interviewer N.Y. State Planning Commn., Farmingdale, N.Y., 1969-70; asst. tchr. Alphabet Pre-Sch., 1971-72; tchr. art Montessori Sch., St. Thomas, V.I., 1975; substitute tchr. Miss Sue's Nursery Sch. and Kindergarten, Plainview, N.Y., 1975-80; asst. tchr. Bethpage (N.Y.) Nursery Sch., 1979-85, tchr., 1985—; tchr., also mem. sch. bd. Kiddie Junction, Inc., 1987; coach Mid Island Gymnastics Sch., Hicksville, N.Y., 1986—; interviewer N.Y. State Planning Commn., Albany, 1970. Fin. sec. Lantern Road Civic Assn., Hicksville, 1976. Mem. Early Childhood Ednl. Counsel. Democrat. Home: 90 Lantern Rd Hicksville NY 11801

SCHETTL, LYNDA KAY, internal auditor; b. Sheboygan, Wis., Oct. 10, 1954; d. Harold John and Loretta Marian (Siradas) S. BS with high honors, Tulsa U., 1979. CPA, Okla., Cert. Internal Auditor. Accountant James Robertson, CPA, Jenks, Okla., 1979-80; internal auditor Sooner Fed. Savs. & Loan, Tulsa, 1980-86, Home Savs. of Am., Irwindale, Calif., 1986—. Served with USAF, 1972-74. Mem. Am. Inst. CPA's, Calif. Soc. CPA's, Inst. Internal Auditors, Nat. Assn. Female Execs. Democrat. Home: 550 W Stocker #228 Glendale CA 91202 Office: Home Savs of Am 1001 Commerce Dr Irwindale CA 91706

SCHEUERMAN, LOIS JOYCE, product implementation manager; b. Buffalo, May 26, 1953; d. Norbert Louis and Jeannette Louise (Grass) S. BS in Indsl. Engring., Bradley U., 1975. Indsl. engr. mgmt. services div. Eastman Kodak Co., Rochester, N.Y., 1975-78, 79-83, quality control engr. motion pictures films div., 1978-79, client coordinator mgmt. services div., 1983-85, unit dir. mgmt. services div., 1985-87, asst. to dir. mgmt. services div., 1987, asst. to dir. biol. diagnostics, 1987—. Cons. Women' Career Ctr., Rochester, 1983—; leader Jr. Achievement, Rochester, 1975-78; chmn. Hugh O'Brien Youth Found. Office: Eastman Kodak Co 460 Buffalo Rd Rochester NY 14611

SCHEUERMANN, JAN, small business owner; b. Pitts., Sept. 18, 1959; d. Edmund James and Maureen Dorothy (Fitz) S.; m. Robert De Lyser, 1987. BA in Writing cum laude, U. Pitts., 1983. Asst. editor Nutrition Revs., Pitts., 1983-84, Stony Brook, N.Y., 1984-85; owner, founder Deadly Affairs, Pitts., 1986—, Lancaster, Calif., 1988—. Asst. editor Present Knowledge In Nutrition, 1984. Mem. Nat. Assn. for the Self-employed, Am. Med. Writers Assn. Club: Golden Triangle Tall (Pitts.) (editor 1983-86, named Miss Tall Pitts. 1982). Home and Office: 2238 West Ave K-10 Lancaster CA 93536

SCHEUERMANN, MONA, educator; b. N.Y.C., June 6, 1946; d. Philip and Irene Rifkin; B.A., Queens Coll., 1967; M.A., Hunter Coll., 1969; Ph.D., SUNY-Stony Brook, 1974; m. Peter Scheuermann, Dec. 28, 1973. Asst. prof. English, York Coll., 1974-75; asst. prof. J.S. Reynolds Community Coll. 1974-76; asst. prof. Oakton Community Coll., Des Plaines, Ill., 1976-79, assoc. prof. 1979-84, prof., 1984; guest prof. U. Hamburg, 1986; vis. prof. U. Utrecht. NDEA fellow. Mem. MLA, Am. Assn. Eighteenth-Century Studies, Keats-Shelley Assn., Wordsworth Soc., Phi Beta Kappa. Author: The Novels of William Godwin, 1980; Social Protest in the Eighteenth-Century English Novel, 1985; contbr. articles to profl. jours. Office: 1600 E Golf Rd Des Plaines IL 60016

SCHEULEN, MARY EDNA, marketing professional; b. Leslie, Ark., Apr. 3, 1943; d. Ulis and Sallie V. (Overstreet) Rains; m. Albertie C. Scheulen, Apr. 25, 1963; 1 child, Sally Ann. Student, Friends U., 1961-62; BS in Math., Wichita (Kans.) State U., 1969, MBA in Mktg., 1977. Weights technician AeroCommander Co., Bethany, Okla., 1969-70; tchr. math Wichita (Kans.) Pub. Schs., 1971-72; weights analyst Cessna Aircraft Co., Wichita, 1972-74, dynamics engr., 1974-77; market analyst Boeing Mil. Airplane Co., Wichita, 1977-86; mgr. market analysis Gen. Electric, Utica, N.Y., 1986—; cons. mktg. Wichita State U., 1985. Mem. Electronics Industries Assn. (chmn. electronics content subcom. 1986-87), Air Force Commn. and Electronics Assn., Assn. Old Crows, Women in Def. Republican. Baptist. Lodge: Toastmasters (pres. 1981-82). Office: Gen Electric French Rd Md 210 Utica NY 13503

SCHIAVI, ROSEMARY FILOMENA, educator; b. Syracuse, N.Y., Feb. 20, 1947; d. Stefano and Rose (Falso) Schiavi; A.A., Maria Regina Coll., 1967; BA, Brescia Coll., 1969; MS, Syracuse U., 1973, cert. advanced studies tchr. edn. and curriculum devel., 1987. Tchr., Syracuse City Sch. Dist., 1969—, tchr. Meachem Sch., 1980-83, acting prin., 1979; asst. office of profl. devel. and field programs Syracuse U., 1984-85; adminstrv. intern West Genesee/Syracuse U. Teaching Ctr., Bus. Ednl. Exchange Com. Mem. exec. bd. Maria Regina Coll., pres. exec. alumni assn. Mem. Assn. for Supervision and Curriculum Devel., Am. Fedn. Tchrs., N.Y. United Tchrs. Assn., Syracuse Tchrs. Assn., N.Y. State Assn. Tchr. Educators, Brescia Coll. Alumni Assn., Syracuse U. Alumni Assn., Am. Edn. Research Assn., Assn. Tchr. Educators, Assoc. Photographers Internat., Nat. Assn. Female Execs., Audubon Soc., Phi Delta Kappa. Home: 542 Spindrift Ln Columbus SC 29209 Office: U SC Coll of Edn Columbia SC 29208

SCHIAVINA, LAURA MARGARET, artist; b. Springfield, Mass., Nov. 27, 1917; d. Joseph A. and Egidia (Bernini) Schiavina; student Traphagen Sch. of Fashion, 1944-46, U. R.I., 1967, Cornell U., 1968, Art Students League, 1973-74. With Eastern States Farmers Exchange, Springfield, 1935-44; with Marsh & McLennan, 1944-75, adminstrv. asst., 1971-75, librarian Wm. M. Mercer, Inc. subs., 1975-80; one-man shows at Little Gallery, Barbizon Hotel, N.Y.C., 1968, Galerie Internat., N.Y.C., 1969; exhibited in group shows at Westfield (Mass.) Coll., 1968, Nat. Acad., N.Y.C., 1969; Lever House, N.Y.C., 1973, 74, 83, 84, 85, 86, 87, Queensboro Community Coll. Gallery, 1984, Cork Gallery, N.Y.C., 1984, Westbeth Gallery, N.Y.C., 1985, 88, Nat. Arts Club, 1986, Isis Gallery, 1986, also various exhbns. with Wall St. Art Assn., Nat. Art. League and Jackson Heights Art Club, Snug Harbor Cultural Ctr., S.I., N.Y., 1984, Audubon Artists, 1969, 86, 88; represented in pvt. collections. Recipient numerous prizes, awards. Mem. Wall St. Art Assn. (v.p. 1972-76), Am. Artist Profl. League, Nat. Art League, Burr Artists Inc., Nat. League Am. Pen Women, Cath. Artists of 80's, West Side Arts Coalition, Eleanor Gay Lee Gallery Found. Inc. Club: Jackson Heights Art (pres. 1970-71), Salmagundi (N.Y.C.). Home: 35-25 78th St Jackson Heights NY 11372

SCHIAVO, FRAN JEANNE, telephone company executive; b. Hamilton, Ohio, Mar. 25, 1952; d. William Francis and Mildred Jeanne (Morris) Doty; m. Michael Dominic Schiavo, Jan. 1, 1982, 1 child, Audrey Lyn. BA magna cum laude, Bowling Green State U., 1974. Tchg. asst. Bowling Green (Ohio) State U., 1974-75; counselor Com. for Services to Youth, Bowling Green, 1975-77, exec. dir., 1977-78; asst. mgr. employee communications Ohio Bell, Cleve., 1978-80, pub. programs mgr., 1980-83, pubs. mgr., 1983-86, dist. advt. mgr., 1986—; instr. Nat. Drug Abuse Ctr., Ohio, 1977-78, Douglis Visual Workshops, Midwest region, 1979-80. Author numerous poems (North award for poetry 1975). Regional v.p. Ohio Assn. Group Homes, 1977; mem. Greater Cleve. Growth Assn., 1987—. Named Pacesetter Cleve. Enterprising Women, 1987. Mem. Internat. Assn. Bus. Communicators (Bronze Quill award of merit 1984, 85), Cleve. Advt. Club. Republican. Club: Mid Day (Cleve.). Home: 2751 Sharon-Copley Rd Medina OH 44256 Office: Ohio Bell 45 Erieview Plaza Cleveland OH 44114

SCHICK, MARY ELIZABETH, controller; b. St. Louis, Jan. 13, 1956; d. Henry Joseph Jablonski and Mary Ann (Auringer) Gallino; m. Terry R. Schick, July 13, 1975 (div. Apr. 1979). Student, Washington U., St. Louis, 1974-75; AA, Phoenix Coll., 1978-81; BA in Acctg., Ariz. State U., 1984, postgrad., 1987—. CPA, Ariz. Asst. mgr. Shakey's Pizza, Phoenix, 1976-77; supr. Sonitrol of Maricopa County, Phoenix, 1977-80, controller, 1980-88, v.p. fin., 1988—; cons. MacPherson and McCarville, Phoenix, 1981-85. Coordinator lit. program Proposition 100 Campaign, Phoenix, 1986. Mem. Am. Inst. CPA's, Nat. Assn. Accts., Ariz. Herpetol. Soc. Republican. Club: Ariz. Balloon (Phoenix). Office: Sonitrol of Maricopa County 545 E Osborn Rd Phoenix AZ 85012

SCHIEMEL, JOAN MARIE, aerospace engineer; b. N.Y.C., June 19, 1936; d. Frank and Florence Marie (MacDowell) S.; AA, Concordia Collegiate Inst., 1955; BA, Queens Coll., 1957; postgrad. Columbia U., 1957-58; MS, L.I. U., 1971; postgrad. Adelphi U., 1973-79. Student social worker Luth. Social Services, N.Y.C., 1957-58; with Fairchild Republic Co. (and predecessor cos.), 1958-87, flight test engr., 1958-63, sci. programmer, 1963-65, sr. sci. programmer/analyst, 1965-69, flight dynamics analyst, 1969-78, flight simulation engr., 1978-85, sr. sect. chief digital flight simulation, sr. mgr. Flight Systems Simulation Lab., Farmingdale, N.Y., 1985-87; engr. air force systems Grumman Aerospace Corp., Bethpage, N.Y., 1987—. Contbr. articles to profl jours. Mem. AIAA (council 1979-85, exec. sec. 1981-83), Math. Assn. Am., IEEE, Assn. Old Crows, Air Force Assn., Am. Def. Preparedness Assn. Office: Route 110 and Conklin St Farmingdale NY 11735

SCHIER, H. TRACY, English language instructor, planning consultant; b. Youngstown, Ohio, Mar. 23, 1940; d. Harold Nels and Grace (Tracy) Johnson; m. Walter A. Schier, Aug. 3, 1963; children: Thomas B., Jeanne E., Joseph E. BA, St. Mary-of-The-Woods (Ind.) Coll., 1962; MS, Ohio U., 1963; MA, Rivier Coll., 1973; PhD, Boston Coll., 1987. Instr. English St. Mary's Coll., Notre Dame, Ind., 1964-65, U. Lowell, Mass., 1969-75; dir. devel. Rivier Coll, Nashua, N.H., 1975-85; co-founder Woods Assocs., St.-Mary-of-The-Woods, Ind., 1985—; evaluation cons. Lilly Endowment, Inc., Indpls. Trustee N.H. Pub. Broadcasting Council, Durham, 1976, St-Mary-of-The-Woods Coll., Ind., 1983—, Council for Support and Advancement of Edn. (CASE) Dist. I, Washington, 1984-85, Nashua Arts and Sci. Ctr., 1984; bd. dirs. So. N.H. Assn. Commerce and Industry, 1979. Mem. Assn. Governing Bds., New Eng. Cath. Health Assn., Assn. for Psych. Type, AAUW (trustee edn. found. 1983—), Nashua Coll. Club. Democrat. Home: 14 Barnsdale Rd Nashua NH 03062 Office: Woods Assocs Saint Mary-of-the-Woods IN 47876

SCHIER, MARY JANE, science writer; b. Houston, Mar. 10, 1939; d. James F. and Jerry Mae (Crisp) McDonald; B.S. in Journalism, Tex. Woman's U., 1961; m. John Christian Schier, Aug. 26, 1961; children—John Christian, II, Mark Edward. Reporter, San Antonio Express and News, 1962-64; med. writer Daily Oklahoman, also Oklahoma City Times, 1965-66; reporter, med. writer Houston Post, 1966-84; sci. writer, univ. editor U. Tex. M.D. Anderson Cancer Ctr., 1984—. Recipient award Tex. Headliners Club, 1969, Tex. Med. Assn., 1972-74, 76, 78, 79, 80, 82 Tex. Hosp. Assn., 1974, 82, Tex. Public Health Assn., 1976, 77, 78, others. Lutheran. Club: Houston Press (pres. 1974-75). Home: 9742 Tappenbeck St Houston TX 77055 Office: 1515 Holcombe Blvd Houston TX 77030

SCHIESS, BETTY BONE, priest; b. Cin., Apr. 2, 1923; d. Evan Paul and Leah (Mitchell) Bone; B.A., U. Cin., 1945; M.A., Syracuse U., 1947; M.Div., Rochester Ctr. for Theol. Studies, 1972; m. William A. Schiess, Aug. 28, 1947; children—William A. (dec.), Richard Corwine, Sarah. Ordained priest Episcopal Ch., 1974; priest assoc. Grace Episc. Ch., Syracuse, N.Y., 1975; mem. Gov.'s Task Force on Life and Law, 1985—. Recipient Gov.'s award Women of Merit in Religion, 1984; U. Cin. Disting. Alumna award, 1981; chaplain Syracuse U., 1976-78, Cornell U., Ithaca, N.Y., 1978-79; rector Grace Episc. Ch., Mexico, N.Y., 1984—; instnl. rev. bds. Crouse-Irving Hosp. and Upstate Med. Ctr., Syracuse, 1986—; cons. Women's Issues Network Episc. Ch. in U.S., 1987—; writer, lectr., cons. religion and feminism, 1979—. Bd. dirs. People for Public TV in N.Y., 1978, Religious Coalition for Abortion Rights; mem. infant care rev. com. Crouse-Meml. Hosp.; trustee Elizabeth Cady Stanton Found., 1979; mem. policy com. Council Adolescent Pregnancy. Recipient Ralph E. Kharas award ACLU Cen. N.Y., 1986, hon. life membership Na'amat U.S., 1987. Mem. NOW (past pres. Syracuse), Internat. Assn. Women Ministers (dir. 1978, pres. 1984-87), Am. Soc. Law and Medicine, Clergy Assn. Diocese of Central

N.Y. (v.p. 1985—), Mortar Bd., Theta Chi Beta. Democrat. Home: 107 Bradford Ln Syracuse NY 13224

SCHIESSWOHL, CYNTHIA RAE SCHLEGEL, lawyer; b. Colorado Springs, July 7, 1955; d. Leslie H. and Maime (Kascak) Schlegel; m. Scott Jay Schiesswohl, Aug. 6, 1977; children: Leslie Michelle, Kristen Elizabeth. BA cum laude, So. Meth. U., 1976; JD, U. Colo., 1978; postgrad U. Denver, 1984. Bar: Colo. 1979, U.S. Dist. Ct. (Colo.) 1979, U.S. Ct. Appeals (10th cir.) 1984, Wyo. 1986, Ind. 1988. Research clk. City Atty.'s Office, Colorado Springs, 1976; investigator Pub. Defender's Office, Colorado Springs, 1976; dep. dist. atty., 4th Jud. Dist. Colo., 1979-81; sole practice law, Grand Junction, Colo., 1981-82, Denver, 1983-84; assoc. Law Offices of John G. Salmon P.C., 1984-85; sole practice, Laramie, Wyo., 1985-88, Indpls., 1988—; guest lectr. Pikes Peak Community Coll., 1980. Staff U. Colo. Law Rev., 1977. Advisor, Explorer Law Post, Boy Scouts Am., 1980-81; ex officio mem. ch. devel. com. Cen. Rocky Mt. region Christian Ch. (Disciples of Christ), 1986-88; hearing officer Wyo. Dept. Edn., 1987-88; vol. Project Motivation, Dallas, 1974; chairperson Wyo. Med. Rev. Panel, 1987. Mem. ABA, Wyo. State Bar, Colo. Bar Assn. (ethics com. 1984-85, long range planning com. 1985-88, chairperson 1986-87), Denver Bar Assn., Ind. State Bar Assn., Pi Sigma Alpha, Alpha Lambda Delta, Alpha Delta Pi. Republican. United Methodist (mem. evangelism commn. 1987-88, mem. fin. com. youth and music depts. 1979-81, lay del. to Rocky Mountain Ann. Conf. 1986-87).

SCHIFF, HELEN DEBORAH, fashion designer; b. Bklyn., May 17, 1947; d. Harry Bale and Esther Genin; m. Stuart B. Schiff, Oct. 22, 1972. student Fashion Inst. Tech., SUNY, 1964-67. Designer infantswear Playmore Knits, 1971-72, Little Topsy, 1972-73, Catton Bros., 1973-76; dir. design Mayfair Infantswear, N.Y.C., 1976-85; fashion merchandiser, China import dir. David Pik Internat., 1985-87; corp. ptnr., v.p. PCL Designs Ltd., N.Y.C., Hong Kong, 1987—. Pres. Par-Troy chpt. Cancer Care, Inc., 1980-82, v.p. regional fundraising, N.J., 1979-80, fundraising co-chmn., vice chmn. chpts. coordinating com., 1985-86, leadership tng. co-chmn., 1986-87, chmn. fundraising, 1983-84. Recipient various awards Cancer Care, Inc. Office: PCL Designs Ltd Suite 2104 264 W 35th St New York NY 10018

SCHIFF, JAYNE NEMEROW, insurance underwriter; b. N.Y.C., Aug. 8, 1945; d. Milton E. Nemerow and Shirley (Kaplan) Wachtel; m. Albert John Schiff, Mar. 7, 1971; children: Matthew Evan, Kara Anne. Student, Fashion Inst. Tech., 1962-63, Am. Coll., 1977, NYU, 1976-77; BS in Bus., Marymount Coll., 1981. Corporate sec., treas. Albert J. Schiff Assocs., Inc., N.Y.C., 1970-78; field underwriter MONY Fin. Services, Greenwich, Conn., 1973—; freelance employee benefit cons. Greenwich, 1979—; regional dir. mktg., MONY Fin. Services, N.Y.C., 1978-79. Bd. dirs. N.Y. League Bus. and Profl. Women, 1976-78, Temple Sinai, Stamford, Conn., 1979-84, N.Y. Ctr. Fin. Studies; leader Webelos Cub Scouts, 1977-78; treas. Annual Mother's Bd. Benefit Greenwich Acad., 1988. Mem. Am. Soc. Chartered Life Underwriters, N.Y. Ctr. Fin. Studies, N.Y.C. Life Underwriters Assn. (bd. dirs. 1977-78), League Women Voters. Jewish. Office: 30 Stanwich Rd Greenwich CT 06830

SCHIFFMAN, NANCY ELIZABETH, consultant; b. Everett, Mass., May 6, 1937; d. Joseph Coelho and Helen (Buchanan) Perry; B.A. cum laude, Boston U., 1973, M.S. in Urban Affairs, 1976; m. Yale M. Schiffman, June 23, 1974; children—David, Steven. Community relations specialist YWCA, Natick, Mass., 1975-76; regional transp. planner Central Mass. Regional Planning Commn., Worcester, 1977-79; Congressional research staff Rockwell Internat., Arlington, Va., 1980-82; v.p. SES, Inc., Springfield, Va., 1982-84, chief exec. officer, 1984-86; pres., 1982-86; cons., 1986—. Mem. women's and minority com. Area Manpower Planning Bd., Marlboro, Mass., 1976; mem. subcom. Sudbury Housing Authority, 1977; pres., Conf. Connection, Inc., 1987—; chairperson bd. dirs. Offender Aid and Restoration of Arlington, Va., 1980; pres. Orange Hunt Sq. Homeowners Assn., 1987—; chmn. Springfield Council Civic Assns., 1986—. mem. Republican County Com., Fairfax, Va., 1982-86, chmn. Springfield dist. Coryell for 8th Congl. Dist. and Kemp for Pres., 1986; mem. exec. com. Fairfax Rep. Com.; candidate for Va. Senate, 1983; vice chmn. Springfield Council Civic Assns., 1985; pres. Orange Hunt Sq. Homeowners Assn., 1986; mem. Citizens' Adv. Council on Pub. Safety, Fairfax County, 1986. Mem. Am. Pub. Transit Assn. (council on preserving urban motility), Am. Meteorol. Soc. (editor publs.), Am. Assn. Geographers (editor publs.), Nat. Fedn. Rep. Women (patron). Editor profl. publs. for NASA, NOAA, 1982—; contbr. articles to profl. jours. Home: 7406 Forest Hunt Ct Springfield VA 22153

SCHIFFMAN, PENNY CLAIR, manufacturing company executive; b. Chgo., Jan. 4, 1960; d. Merrill Clifford and Susan Leslie (Stein) S. BS, Ariz. State U., 1982; MBA, Loyola U., Chgo., 1985. V.p., mktg. dir. Global Container Equipment Ltd., Chgo., 1982—; owner, cons. Price Computer Co., 1985—. Mem. exec. com. Jewish United Fund Young Communicators, Chicago, 1986—; advisor Shalom El Amee B'nai B'rith girls, Buffalo Grove, Ill. 1982-87. Mem. Ariz. State U. Alumni Assn., Assn. Ind. Corrugated Converters (bd. dirs. 1984—, sec. 1987, v.p. 1988), Delta Sigma Pi Alumni Assn. Democrat. Jewish. Office: Global Container Equip Ltd 1900 W Kinzie St Chicago IL 60622

SCHIFFMAN, SHARON KAY, accountant; b. deRidder, La., Mar. 2, 1958; d. William Wayne and Doris Marie (Brossmann) Schaffer; m. William Phelps Schiffman, Oct. 29, 1982; 1 child, Jamie Marie. A of Acctg., U. Houston, 1980. Acctg. asst. Wanda Petroleum, Houston, 1976-77; computer programmer Warren Automatic Tool, Rosenberg, Tex., 1977-82; accounts payable mgr. Suniland Furniture Co., Houston, 1982-87, accounts payable mgr./traffic mgr., 1987—; cons. Warren Automatic Tool, Rosenberg, 1982-84. Author short story Laura, Come Home, 1976, poems Life's History, 1980. Del. Dem. Dist. Conv., Houston, 1976-77; treas. Needville PTA, 1985-86, chmn. PTA Elem. Carnival, 1985-87. Mem. Nat. Assn. Female Execs., Am. Legion Aux. Democrat. Roman Catholic. Lodge: Lions. Home: 3311 Schroeder PO Box 1019 Needville TX 77461 Office: Suniland Furniture Co 2800 Fondren Houston TX 77063

SCHIFLETT, MARY FLETCHER CAVENDER, researcher, educator; b. El Paso, Tex., Sept. 23, 1925; d. John F. and Mary M. (Humphries) Cavender; 1 son, Joseph Raymond. BA in Econs. with honors, So. Meth. U., 1946, BS in Journalism with honors, 1947; MA in English, U. Houston, 1971. Writer, historian Office Price Adminstrn., Dallas, 1946-47; asst. editor C. of C. Publs., Dallas, 1947-48; bus. writer Houston Oil, 1948-49; market analyst Cravens-Dargan, Ins., Houston, 1949-52; bus. writer Bus. Week and McGraw-Hill Pub. Co., Houston, 1952-56; freelance writer in bus. econs., banking and ins., 1956-68; spl. projects coordinator Center for Human Resources, Houston, 1969-73; dir. publs. Energy Inst., U. Houston, 1974-78; sr. research assoc. Inst. Labor and Indsl. Relations, 1973-80, adj. faculty Coll. Architecture, 1976-85, dir. Ctr. for Health Mgmt., Coll. Bus. Adminstrn., 1980-83; assoc. dir. research and planning Tex. Med. Ctr., Inc., Houston, 1984; dir. pub. affairs Tex. Med. Ctr., 1985—. Bd. dirs. Houston Acad. Motion Pictures, Houston World TRAde Assn., Performing Arts Council for Tex. Med. Ctr. Pres., Houston Ct. Humanities, 1978-80; project dir. Houston Meets Its Authors I-IV, 1980-84; pub. program dir. Houston: Internat. City, 1980-83. Mem. Internat. Council Indsl. Editors, World Future Soc., Tex. Folklore Soc., Friends of the Library, Houston C. of C. (future studies com. 1975-84, small bus. council 1981-83), Nat. Assn. Bus. Economists, AIA (profl. affiliate; profl. devel. com., health com.), Cultural Arts Council Houston, Mortar Bd., Theta Sigma Phi, Alpha Theta Phi, Delta Delta Delta. Methodist. Club: Downtown (pres. 1987—). Lodge: Rotary. Author: (with others) Dynamics of Growth, 1977, Applied Systems and Cybernetics, 1981, The Ethnic Groups of Houston, 1984, Names and Nicknames of Places and Things, 1986. Office: Tex Med Ctr 406 Jesse H Jones Library Bldg Houston TX 77030

SCHILKE, SHIRLEY PLATT, corporate executive; b. Berlin, Pa., July 23, 1925; d. Frank I. and Matilda H. (Baughman) Platt; student Strayers Bus. Coll., Washington, 1943, High Mus. Sch. Art, Atlanta, 1948; m. Carl Richard Schilke, Dec. 3, 1944; children—Kristie Lee, Wendy Lee, Richard Frank. Civilian sec., fin. officer Ft. Belvoir, Va., 1942-46; with Harcar Aluminum Products Co., Sanford, Fla., 1957—, now sec.-treas.; co-owner, v.p. Schilke Enterprises, Inc., Sanford, Fla., 1975-78, pres., 1978—. Past pres. Seminole Meml. Hosp. Aux., Women of First Presbyn. Ch., Sanford; past mem. U.S. Sen. Bus. Adv. Bd.; vice chmn., Greater Sanford Regional Airport Authority Bd; mem. chmn.'s com. U.S. Senatorial Bus. Adv. Bd., 1981, 82; past sec. Seminole County PTA Council, Seminole-DeBary Heart Council; trustee Washington Legal Found.; past bd. dirs. United Fund of Seminole County; bd. dirs., Community Coordinated Care of Cen. Fla.; mem. adv. bd. Salvation Army, Golden Arms, Inc., Am. Pioneer Bank; appointed to Fla. Council on Ednl. Mgmt.; mem. City of Sanford Pub. Employees Relations Commn. Recipient Benefactor award Fla. Community Edn. Found., Inc., award Martin Luther King Brotherhood, Topper award. Mem. Fla. C. of C., Greater Sanford C. of C. (pres., dir., past chmn. bd. dirs., award of merit), Greater Seminole County C. of C., C. of C. U.S., Nat. Fedn. Ind. Bus., Fla. Exec. Women's Club, Internat. Platform Assn., Smithsonian Assocs., U.S. Senatorial Club, Nat. Soc. Lit. and Arts. Club: Women's of Sanford (life). Author: (poetry) The Many Facets of Love, 1976. Home: 107 Country Pl PO Box 2101 Sanford FL 32772-2101 Office: 106 E First St PO Box 1148 Sanford FL 32772-1148

SCHILLER, ARDITH MARLENE, secretarial/bookkeeping consultant; b. Jackson, Minn., Oct. 12, 1939; d. Thomas William and Maxine Dorothy Raine; m. Jerome J. Schiller, Oct. 11, 1968; 1 child, Gretchen Susan. AA in Bus. Adminstrn. and Office Occupations, U. Alaska, 1979, AAS in Bus. Adminstrn., 1980. Cert. profl. sec. Stenographer, Prudential Ins. Co., Winona, Minn., 1957, 1st Nat. Bank, Winona, 1959; sec., stenographer Monarch Marking System Co., Garden Grove, Calif., 1960-62; exec. sec. Acoustica Assocs., Inc., Los Angeles, 1962-65; adminstrv. sec. Fgn. Services, Dept. State, Washington, 1965-67; sec., office mgr. U.S. Army Europe Hdqrs. Polit. Adv.'s Office, Dept. Army, Heidelberg, Fed. Republic Germany, 1968-69, Hamilton Bros. Oil Co., Anchorage, 1971-73; owner, mgr. Bus. Cache, Anchorage, 1974-81; dir., sec. C.C. Hawley and Assos., Inc., 1974; freelance bus. and fin. mgr., 1983—. Roman Catholic. Home: 5320 Shaun Circle Anchorage AK 99516

SCHILLING, CLAIRE ELIZABETH, financial executive; b. Balt., July 24, 1959; d. Edward M. and Anne F. (Zimmermann) Schilling. BA magna cum laude, James Madison U., 1981. Lic. security dealer. Sales rep. Tenneco Corp., Balt., 1981-82, Chesapeake Corp., Winston-Salem, N.C., 1982-86; account exec. Prudential-Bache Securities, McLean, Va., 1986-87; dir. fin. inst. services Packard Press, Washington, 1987—. Cons. Com. to Reelect Del Cox, Bel Air, Md., 1978, 82, 86. Mem. Nat. Assn. Female Execs., McLean Bus. and Profl. Women's Assn., AAUW. Democrat. Presbyterian. Home: 1726 Court Petit McLean VA 22101 Office: Packard Press 1025 Connecticut Ave NW Suite 905 Washington DC 20036

SCHILLING, JANET NAOMI, dietitian; b. North Platte, Neb., Mar. 1, 1939; d. Jens Harold and Naomi Frances (Meyer) Hansen; m. Allan Edward Schilling Jr., June 1, 1969; children: Allan Edward III, Karl Jens. BS, U. Neb., 1961; MS, Ohio State U., 1965. Registered dietitian. Tchr. home econs. Peace Corps., Dimbokro, Ivory Coast, 1962-64; cons. nutrition Wis. Div. Health, La Crosse, 1966-67, 69; dietary cons. Cozad (Neb.) Community Hosp., 1968; instr. Viterbo Coll., La Crosse, 1974-81; lectr. U. Wis., La Crosse, 1982-84; teaching asst. English as second language Sch. Dist. La Crosse, 1984-87; nutrition educator WIC Program, 1988—; nutrition cons. LaCrosse, 1987—. Author: Life in the Nutrition Community, 1980, Life on the Nutrition Cycle II, 1980; co-author: Nutrition Activities, 1984, Recipe Book of Nutritious Snacks, 1985. Mem. La Crosse Sch. Dist. Nutrition Task Force, 1976—; sunday sch. tchr., supr. Our Saviors Luth. Ch., 1976-86, chmn., Mobile Meals, 1982-86; v.p. membership booster club Cen. High Sch., La Crosse, 1985-87, pres. 1987-88; bd. dirs. YMCA, La Crosse, 1982-88. Mem. AAUW (pres. 1978-80, Name Grant scholar 1981), La Crosse Area Dietetic Assn. (1st pres. 1968-69, Outstanding Dietitian Yr. 1985), Wis. Dietetic Assn. (chmn. educators 1983-85), No. Wis. Dietetic Assn. (pres. 1982), Am. Dietetic Assn. (educators practice group 1978—), La Crosse Jaycees (Carol award 1973), French Discussion Group. Democrat. Home: 2120 Orchard Valley Dr LaCrosse WI 54601

SCHILLINGER, ELISABETH HUPP, journalism educator, editor, author, graphic designer; b. Springfield, Ill., Mar. 28, 1943; d. Walter Wayne and Joyce Dayle (Hartwig) Hupp; BS in Journalism, U. Ill., 1965, MS in Mass Communications, Okla. State U., 1985; m. John A. Schillinger, Aug. 28, 1965; children—Liesl Katharine, Justin Hupp, Nathaniel Hartwig. Tech. editor U. Ill. Coll. Engring., 1965-67; writer, editor U. Wis. Office Publs., 1967-70; asst. dir. info. Saginaw (Mich.) Valley State Coll., 1970-73; tech. writing, design cons., 1973-75; engring. editor Purdue U. Schs. Engring., 1975-82; editor Okla. State U. Publs. Office, 1982-84, asst. prof. Okla. State U. Sch. Journalism, 1984—. Co-author: Men and Ideas in Engineering, 1967. Contbr. articles to profl. publns. Home: 2015 N Husband St Stillwater OK 74075 Office: Okla State U 206 Paul Miller Bldg Stillwater OK 74078

SCHILTZ, JANE ANN, lawyer, insurance company executive; b. Denton, Tex., Oct. 20, 1955; d. James Henry and Teresa Loretta (Ungs) S. BBA, St. Mary's Coll., Notre Dame, Ind., 1977; JD, U. Iowa, 1980. CLU, fin. cons. Atty., asst. mgr. advanced mktg., officer Northwestern Mut. Life Ins. Co., Milw., 1980—. Author: The Unfunded Irrevocable Life Insurance Trust, 1984, rev. edit., 1987; contbr. articles to profl. jours. Mem. charitable giving task force Million Dollar Round Table, Chgo., 1985, deferred giving com., trust and estate adv. com. Marquette U., Milw., 1987—, devel. com. Wis. affiliate Am. Heart Assn., 1986-87; chmn. planned giving com. Mem. ABA, Wis. Bar Assn., Am. Soc. CLU, Am. Soc. Chartered Fin. Cons., St. Mary's Coll. Alumnae Assn. (nat. bd. dirs. 1981-86), Phi Delta Phi. Home: 8620 N Port Washington Rd Fox Point WI 53217 Office: Northwestern Mut Life Ins Co 720 E Wisconsin St Milwaukee WI 53202

SCHILZ, YVONNE ELIZABETH, military officer; b. Waco, Tex., Nov. 23, 1958; d. John David and Charleen Kay (Leaverton) Wilhelm; m. Michael Thomas Schilz, May 29, 1981. BS, USAF Acad., 1981; MEd, S.D. State U., 1985. Commd. 2d lt. USAF, 1981, advanced through grades to capt., 1985; chief air traffic control tng. 2148 Communications Squadron, Ellsworth AFB, S.D., 1982-84; chief air traffic control ops. 2148 Info. Systems Squadron, Ellsworth AFB, S.D., 1984, dep. chief air traffic control ops., 1984-85; chief air traffic control ops. officer 390 Info. Systems Ops., Offutt AFB, Nebr., 1985—. Tchr. catechism Cath. Ch., Offutt AFB, 1985-86. Named one of Outstanding Young Women of Am., 1983, 84, 86. Mem. USAF Assn. (life), USAF Acad. Assn., Profl. Women Controllers, Armed Forces Communications Electronics Assn., Air Traffic Control Assn. Republican. Roman Catholic.

SCHIMMEL, NANCY MALVINA REYNOLDS, storyteller, songwriter; b. Omaha, Feb. 21, 1935. BA, U. Calif., Berkeley, 1957, MLS, 1965. Librarian San Francisco Pub. Library, 1965-67, Martin Luther King Sch., Sausalito, Calif., 1967-68, San Mateo County Library, Belmont, Calif., 1969-75; storyteller Berkeley, Calif., 1975—; founder, owner Sister's Choice Press, Berkeley, 1978—; instr. U. Wis., Madison, summer 1977, 81, U. Calif., Berkeley, summer 1979, UCLA, summer 1982-84; mem. cons. com. Nat. Storytelling Jour., Jonesborough, Tenn., 1984—; owner, pub. Schroder Music Co., Berkeley, 1978—. Author: Just Enough to Make a Story, 1978, 82; storyteller album Plum Pudding, 1982; singer, songwriter audiotape Dinosaur, 1986; storyteller videotape Tell Me a Story, 1986. Artist in residence Idaho Arts Commn., spring 1986, 87; com. mem. Bay Area Storytelling Festival, 1982, 84-85; mem. Berkeley Citizen's Action, Berkeley, 1978—, Emergency Response Network, San Francisco, 1986—, Freedom Song Network, San Francisco, 1985—. Mem. ASCAP, Nat. Assn. Preservation and Perpetuation of Storytelling, Calif. Library Assn. (children's services chpt.), Librarians Nuclear Arms Control. Club: Folk Music (San Francisco). Home: 1639 Channing Way Berkeley CA 94703 Office: Sister's Choice Press 1450 6th St Berkeley CA 94710

SCHINDEL, RONNIE SUSAN LEVINE, advertising executive, writer; b. N.Y.C., Oct. 14, 1939; d. Harold and Ada (Simon) Levine; m. Samuel M. Schindel, July 2, 1960; children—Robert Harold, Shari Jill. B.S. magna cum laude, NYU, 1960; M.A., Columbia U., 1962. Tchr. Pub. Sch. 125, Manhattan, N.Y.C., 1960-62, Walker AFB Elem. Sch., Roswell, N.Mex., 1962-64; freelance writer, Huntington, N.Y., 1964—; movie reviewer Radio Sta. WGSM, Huntington, 1977—, Women's Record, Roslyn, N.Y., 1985—; creative dir. Ray Adell Media Enterprises, Inc., Greenlawn, N.Y., 1977—, v.p., 1982—, v.p., sec., 1983—, also bd. dirs. Author: (children's books) I Am Jungle Soup, 1967, Hermit Crab, 1967; also programmed reading instruction materials, radio commls., movie revs. Pres., Woodhull Sch. PTA, Huntington, 1975-76, Kehillath Shalom Synagogue, Cold Spring Harbor, N.Y., 1976-77; vol. Sta. WGSM Call for Action, Huntington, 1975-77. Recipient Founders Day award NYU, 1960; grantee Columbia U., 1960-62. Mem. Nat. Assn. Women Bus. Owners, Delegation L.I. Bus. and Profl. Women (bd. dirs. 1986—, co-chair publicity 1985—), L.I. Ctr. for Bus. and Profl. Women, Nat. Assn. for Female Execs., L.I. Communicators Assn., Advancement for Commerce and Industry, L.I. Assocs., Press Club of L.I., Sigma Delta Chi. Office: Ray Adell Media Enterprises Inc 103 Broadway Greenlawn NY 11740

SCHINDLER, GAYLE ANN, network specialist; b. Bay Village, Ohio, May 4, 1950; d. Clayton Aloysius and Marcella Belle (Stockard) Smith; m. David Stanley Schindler, Feb. 16, 1980. Grad. high sch., Rocky River, Ohio. Keypunch operator Sherwin-Williams Paint Co., Cleve., 1970-74, tape librarian, 1974-77, remote ops. controller, 1977-80; hardware specialist Informatics, Inc., Columbus, Ohio, 1980-81; network specialist BancOhio Nat. Bank, Columbus, 1981-85, sr. network specialist, 1985-88, datacommunications specialist II, 1988—. Democrat. Lutheran. Office: BancOhio Nat Bank PO Box 657 Columbus OH 43216

SCHIRO-GEIST, CHRISANN, rehabilitation counselor; b. Chgo., Dec. 31, 1946; d. Joseph Frank and Ethel (Fortunato) Schiro; m. John J. Conway Sr., Oct. 26, 1985; children: Jennifer, Daniel; stepchildren: Patricia, Nicole, John Jr., Denise, Christine. BS, Loyola U., Chgo., 1967, MEd, 1970; PhD, Northwestern U., 1974. Registered psychologist, Ill.; cert. sex edn. cons. Tchr. sci. Northbrook (Ill.) Jr. High Sch., 1967-70; dir. career counseling and placement Mundelein Coll., Chgo., 1972-74; counselor human devel. Regional Service Agy., Skokie, Ill., 1975-87; assoc. prof. psychology, rehab. counselor Ill. Inst. Tech., Chgo., 1975-87; assoc. prof. rehab. and counseling psychology U. Ill., Champagne-Urbana, 1987—. Co-author: Placement Handbook for Counseling Disabled Persons, 1982. Research grantee Northwestern U., 1974; Region V Short-Term Tng. grantee Rehab. Services Adminstrn., 1978-79, Long-Term Tng. grantee, 1983-86, 86-89. Mem. Am. Psychol. Assn., Am. Assn. Counseling and Development, Nat. Rehab. Assn., Nat. Council Rehab. Edn., Ill. Rehab. Counseling Assn. (pres. 1979-80), Council on Rehab. Edn. (pres. 1982-85, Educator of Yr. 1987), Kappa Beta Gamma Alumni Assn. (nat. officer). Office: U Ill Div Rehab Edn 1207 S Oak Champaign IL 61820

SCHIVEK, ELAINE RONA, legal researcher; b. Boston, Mar. 9, 1930; d. Rueben and Sarah (Berch) Weinberg; m. James Schivek, Oct. 30, 1949 (dec. Feb. 1982); children—Helene Marcia Schivek Demeo, Alan Jay, Howard Richard. B.A. in Edn. cum laude, Suffolk U., 1953, M.Ed. in Adminstrn. and Supervision magna cum laude, 1980; postgrad. Boston U., 1953, 65, 68, Boston State Coll., 1967-69, Simmons Coll., 1968-69, Lesley Grad. Sch., 1976-78, Suffolk Law Sch., 1986—. Lic. tchr., cert. in adminstrn., spl. edn., Mass. Elem. tchr. Boston Sch. Dept., Boston and Roxbury, Mass., 1957-69, Westwood Elem. Sch., Mass., 1969-70, Revere Sch. Dept., Mass., 1970-71; office mgr. Storm/Check Aluminum Co., Hyde Park, Mass., 1971-79; elem. and secondary tchr. Cambridge (Mass.) Schs., 1979-84; legal researcher Registry of Motor Vehicles, Boston, 1984—; pvt. tutor Randolph Sch. Dept., Mass., 1983—. Mem. Randolph Clean Up Com., 1985-86, Dem. Town Com., Randolph, 1986—; candidate for sch. com. Randolph Sch. Dept., 1986, 88; active Mass. Polit. Caucus Women's Group, Boston, 1985-86, Women's Democratic Networking Group, Newton, Mass., 1985-86; fundraiser Senator John Kerry's Campaign, Boston, 1984-86, Gerald D'Amico for lt. gov., Mass., 1986—, Gov. Michael Dukakis for President, 1988, New Hampshire; fundraiser, campaign mgr. state rep. candidate, Mass., 1986—, candidate Boston City Council, 1987; past v.p. and pres. Jewish War Vets. of Milton, Mass.; bd. dirs. Combined Jewish Philanthropies Career Div., 1985—; active Randolph Conservation Commn., 1986—. Five undergrad. scholarships Suffolk U., Boston, 1948-53; teaching fellow Suffolk U. Grad. Sch., 1979-80; named Outstanding Woman Alumni Class of 1953 Suffolk U., 1988; Ednl. Coll. Greater Mass. intern, Brookline, Mass., 1984-85. Mem. Mass. Deans, Counselors and Adminstrs., Suffolk U. Alumnae (fundraiser), Mass. Caucus for Women, Knights of Pythias (bd. dirs., trustee, 1960-75). Club: Brandeis U. (bd. dirs. 1976-80). Avocations: travel; reading; writing. Office: Registry Motor Vehicles 18 Country Club Dr Boston MA 02368

SCHLAEPFER, CYNTHIA JANE, computer operations administrator; b. Ithaca, N.Y., Aug. 12, 1956; d. Walter Woodley and Esther Susan (Youker) S. Student, Principia Coll., 1974-75; BS, Cornell U., 1978. Co-mgr. The Kroger Co., Columbus, Ohio, 1978-81; asst. mgr. Wendy's Internat., Columbus, 1981; computer operator Warner-Amex, Columbus, 1981-84; supr. computer ops. Online Computer Library Ctr., Inc., Dublin, Ohio, 1984—. Umpire Ohio High Sch. Athletics, Columbus, 1986—. Inducted into Athletic Hall of Fame, Cornell U., Ithaca, 1985. Mem. Sierra Club. Democrat. Mem. Christian Sci. Ch. Club: Toastmasters (former sgt.-at-arms). Home: 129 E Beaumont Rd Columbus OH 43214 Office: Online Computer Library Ctr Inc 6565 Frantz Rd Dublin OH 43017

SCHLAFLY, PHYLLIS STEWART, author, lawyer; b. St. Louis, Aug. 15, 1924; d. John Bruce and Odile (Dodge) Stewart; m. Fred Schlafly, Oct. 20, 1949; children: John F., Bruce S., Roger S., Phyllis Liza Forshaw, Andrew L., Anne V. B.A., Washington U., St. Louis, 1944, J.D., 1978; M.A., Harvard U., 1945; LL.D., Niagara U., 1976. Bar: Ill. 1979, D.C. 1984, Mo. 1985, U.S. Supreme Ct. 1987. Syndicated columnist Copley News Service, 1976—; pres. Eagle Forum, 1975—. Author, pub.: Phyllis Schlafly Report, 1967—; broadcaster, Spectrum, CBS Radio Network, 1973-78, commentator, Cable TV News Network, 1980-83, Matters of Opinion, radio sta. WBBM, Chgo., 1973-75; author: A Choice Not an Echo, 1964, The Gravediggers, 1964, Strike From Space, 1965, Safe Not Sorry, 1967, The Betrayers, 1968, Mindszenty The Man, 1972, Kissinger on the Couch, 1975, Ambush at Vladivostok, 1976, The Power of the Positive Woman, 1977, Child Abuse in the Classroom, 1984, Pornography's Victims, 1987; editor: Equal Pay for Unequal Work, 1984. Del. Republican Nat. Conv., 1956, 64, 68, 84, 88, alt., 1960, 80; pres. Ill. Fedn. Rep. Women, 1960-64; 1st v.p. Nat. Fedn. Rep. Women, 1964-67; mem. Ill. Commn. on Status of Women, 1975-85; nat. chmn. Stop ERA, 1972—; mem. Ronald Reagan's Def. Policy Adv. Group, 1980; mem. Commn. on Bicentennial of U.S. Constn., 1985—; mem. Adminstrv. Conf. U.S., 1983-86. Recipient 10 Honor awards Freedoms Found.; Brotherhood award NCCJ, 1975; named Woman of Achievement in Pub. Affairs St. Louis Globe-Democrat, 1963, one of ten most admired woman in world Good Housekeeping poll, 1977—. Mem. DAR (nat. chmn. Am. history 1965-68, nat. chmn. bicentennial com. 1967-70, nat. chmn. nat. def. 1977-80, 83—), ABA, Ill. Bar Assn., Phi Beta Kappa, Pi Sigma Alpha. Office: Eagle Forum Box 618 Alton IL 62002

SCHLAIN, BARBARA ELLEN, lawyer; b. N.Y.C., May 28, 1948; d. William and Evelyn (Youdelman) S.; B.A., Wellesley Coll., 1969; M.A., Columbia U., 1970; J.D., Yale U., 1973. Bar: N.Y. 1974, U.S. Dist. Ct. (so. dist.) N.Y. 1974, U.S. Ct. Appeals (2d cir.) 1975, U.S. Dist. Ct. (ea. dist.) N.Y. 1977. Assoc. firm Donovan Leisure Newton & Irvine, N.Y.C., 1973-76, Graubard Moskovitz McGoldrick Dannett & Horowitz, N.Y.C., 1976-79; atty. McGraw-Hill, Inc., N.Y.C., 1979-80, asst. gen. counsel, 1980-86, v.p., assoc. gen. counsel, asst. sec., 1986—. sec. proprietary rights com. Info. Industry Assn., 1982-83. Author outlines Practicing Law Inst., 1983, 84, 85, 86, 88; contbr. numerous articles to profl. jours. Bd. dirs., v.p., sec. Dance Research Found., N.Y.C., 1983-86, chmn. 1986—. Phi Beta Kappa scholar, Durant scholar Wellesley Coll., 1967-69. Mem. Assn. Am. Pubs. (lawyers com. 1979—), Assn. Bar City N.Y. (communications law com. 1985—), N.Y. State Bar Assn. Office: McGraw-Hill Inc 1221 Ave of the Americas New York NY 10020

SCHLATTER, KATHERINE ANN, banker, accountant; b. Peoria, Ill., Jan. 14, 1956; d. Theodore Jacob and Veronica (Hibser) S. BA, William Woods Coll., 1977. CPA, Ill. Mem. audit staff McGladrey Hendrickson & Co., Rockford, Ill., 1977-83; asst. controller First Nat. Bank, Rockford, 1983-86, asst. v.p., mgr. assets/liability, 1986—. Mem. Am. Inst. CPA's, No. Ill. CPA Soc., Nat. Assn. Accts. Office: First Nat Bank 401 E State St Rockford IL 61110-4900

SCHLEF, AILEEN ROBERTA, corporate communications specialist, writer; b. N.Y.C., July 11, 1945; d. Irwin Martin and Gertrude Lois Schlef. BA, SUNY, Albany, 1968; MEd, Antioch (N.Y.) U., 1973; postgrad., U. So. Calif., 1982—. Adminstr. Antioch U., 1972-74; prof., adminstr. Universidad Boricua, Washington, 1974-76; program specialist U.S. Dept. Edn., Washington, 1976-81, mem. transition team, 1980-81; dir. devel. East Los Angeles (Calif.) Coll., 1981-82; freelance writer, fundraising cons. Los Angeles, 1982—; dir. of communications AltaMed Health Services Corp., Los Angeles, 1985-88; cons. Herndon Enterprises, Hispanic mag., 1988; bd. trainer Kellogg/United Way Tng. Ctr., Los Angeles, 1985—; bd. dirs. Brockman Prodns. Exec. producer: In Recognition of Hispanics in the Entertainment Industry, 1988. mem. spl. events com. Hollywood (Calif.) Heritage, 1985—; student congl. aide Herb Tenzer, 1965, Senator Robert F. Kennedy, 1966-67; fundraiser Congl. Hispanic Caucus, 1973-81; mem. exec. com. Congressman Esteban Torres, Los Angeles, 1981-86; chmn. Latino Media Task Force, Washington, 1972-76; pres. bd. dirs. Spanish Edn. Devel. Ctr., Washington, 1976-81. Mem. Women in Communications. Democrat. Home and Office: 2909 Arizona Ave Santa Monica CA 90403

SCHLEGEL, KIMBERLY BETH, scientific equipment company manager; b. New Castle, Pa., Feb. 25, 1958; d. Joseph James and Betty Lucille (Homer) Mulcahy; m. James Louis Schlegel, July 12, 1980. BS in Behavioral Sci., Rollins Coll., 1981; MBA, U. Cen. Fla., 1986. Service coordinator Coulter Electronics, Inc., Orlando, Fla., 1979-80; quotes rep. Curtin Matheson Scientific, Inc., Orlando, 1980-82, customer service supr., 1982-83, systems analyst, 1983-84, ops. mgr., 1984—. Assoc. mem. Orland Mus. Art, 1986-87. Fellow Nat. Assn. Female Execs.; mem. Key Soc., Beta Gamma Sigma, Phi Mu (alumnae pres. 1981-82), Toastmasters Internat. Democrat. Presbyterian. Clubs: Orlando Area Panhellenic (sorority rep. 1986-87), Rocket City Remote Control (contest dir. 1985-87). Office: Curtin Matheson Scientific 6301 Hazeltine National Dr Suite 100 Orlando FL 32822

SCHLEICHER, ESTELLE ANN, lawyer; b. Buffalo, Sept. 28, 1947; d. Martin Edward and Peggy (Lewin) S. B.A., SUNY-Brockport, 1969; J.D., U. Pacific, 1979. Research asst. SRI Internat., Menlo Park, Calif., 1969-72; clk. Wallace J. Smith Inc., Sacramento 1976-78; assoc., 1980-81; sole practice, Sacramento, 1981—; judge pro tem Sacramento County Claims Ct.; instr., Pacific Coll. Legal Careers, Sacramento, 1982-85. Bd. dirs. Sacramento County Law Library Found. Judge, coach high sch. Law-related Ednl. Conf., Sacramento, 1982—. Soroptimist scholar, 1978; McGeorge scholar, 1977-79. Mem. ABA, Calif. State Bar Assn. (com. on appellate cts. 1986—, sec., adv. com. 1986—), Sacramento County Bar Assn. (dir. small law practice sect. 1986—), Calif. Trial Lawyers Assn. (assoc. editor CTLA Forum), Capitol City Trial Lawyers Assn. (dir. 1986—), McGeorge Sch. Law Alumni Assn. (bd. dirs. 1987—, sec. 1988). Jewish. Office: 2201 21st St Sacramento CA 95818

SCHLEIFER, ALISON PEDICORD, educational consultant; b. Norristown, Pa., Nov. 6, 1942; d. Harry William and Adah (Alison) Pedicord; A.B., Mt. Holyoke Coll., 1964; certs. U. Paris, 1962, 63; M.S., So. Conn. State Coll., 1975; m. James Thomas Schleifer, Aug. 15, 1964; children—Katharine Alison, Margaret Elizabeth. Tchr., Amity Regional Sch. Dist., Woodbridge, Conn., 1964-71, dept. chmn. fgn. langs., 1968-71, tchr. French, part-time, 1976-77; ednl. cons., New Haven, 1976—. Bd. dirs. YWCA, 1971-76, v.p., 1976; bd. dirs. Downtown Cooperative Ministry, 1971—, pres., 1973-75, v.p., 1976-82; del. gen. synod United Ch. of Christ, 1975, 77; bd. dirs. United Way Greater New Haven, 1986—. Mem. Ind. Ednl. Cons. Assn. (bd. dirs. 1987—). Mem. United Ch. of Christ. Club: Mt. Holyoke. Contbr. articles to profl. jours. Address: 220 Alston Ave New Haven CT 06515

SCHLEIMER, SHIRLEY BRASSAW, accountant; b. Saginaw, Mich., Sept. 2, 1926; d. Guy Edward and Helen (Siller) Brassaw; student Walton Sch. Commerce, 1947-51; m. Edward C. Schleimer, Dec. 22, 1951 (dec. 1975); 1 dau., Jane Elizabeth. Pvt. practice acctg. Shirley B. Schleimer, C.P.A., Saginaw, 1954-75; ptnr. Rehmann, Robson, Osburn & Co. (name now Rehmann Robson & Co.), Saginaw, 1976—. Treas., Saginaw YWCA, 1980-82; treas. Salvation Army, 1981-82, chmn., 1984-86, treas. Saginaw Gen. Hosp. Found., 1987— ; mem. Saginaw Community Found. C.P.A., Mich.; trustee YWCA Trust, 1982—. Mem. Am. Inst. C.P.A.s, Am. Women's Soc. C.P.A.s (Nat. Public Service award 1980), Am. Soc. Women Accts. (founder, chpt. pres. 1952-54, 76-78), Mich. Soc. C.P.A.s, Networking (founder, treas. 1979-81). Lutheran. Club: Zonta (state treas. 1980-82, internat. treas. 1982-83, Saginaw Woman of Yr. 1982). Office: PO Box 2025 Saginaw MI 48605

SCHLEIN, CAROL LESLIE, lawyer; b. Oceanside, N.Y., Apr. 8, 1955; d. Richard Spencer and Betty Lee (Goldman) S. BA, U. Rochester, 1977; JD, N.Y. Law Sch., 1980. Bar: N.Y., 1982. Staff atty. Legal Def. & Edn. Fund, N.Y.C., 1980-82; assoc. Glazer & Gottlieb, N.Y.C., 1983-85; mgr. legal systems Future Info. Systems, N.Y.C., 1985-86; cons. Hildebrandt Inc., Somerville, N.J., 1986-87; pres. Law Office Systems, N.Y.C., 1987—. Contbr. articles to profl. jours. Mem. ABA, N.Y. State Bar Assn. (law office econs. and mgmt. com.), N.J. State Bar Assn. (law office adminstrn. mgmt. com.), N.Y. Women's Bar Assn. Democrat. Jewish. Home: 201 E 21st St New York NY 10010 Office: Law Office Systems 201 E 21st St New York NY 10010

SCHLEIN, MIRIAM, author; N.Y.C.; d. William and Sophie (Bigleisen) S.; children—Elizabeth Weiss, John Weiss. B.A. in Psychology, Bklyn. Coll., 1947. Author over 60 books for children, natural sci. books, concept books, story books, picture books, including: Shapes, 1952, It's About Time, 1955, The Way Mothers Are, 1963, I, Tut: The Boy Who Became Pharaoh, 1978, Antarctica, the Great White Continent, 1980, Project Panda Watch, 1984 (Children's Sci. Book award N.Y. Acad. Scis. 1985), Giraffe, The Silent Giant (Children's Book of Yr. Child Study Assn. 1976), What the Elephant Was, 1986; author adult fiction and non-fiction in publs. including Redbook, McCall's, Ladies Home Jour., Good Housekeeping, Univ. Rev., Creative Living, Colorado Quar.; included in anthologies; transl. into Danish, Swedish, Italian, French, Dutch, Norwegian, German, Braille. Awards include: Outstanding Sci. Trade Book for Children, Nat. Sci. Tchrs. Assn./Children's Book Council Joint Com. for: Snake Fights, Rabbit Fights, and More, 1979, Lucky Porcupine, 1980, Billions of Bats, 1982; The Dangerous Life of the Sea Horse, 1986, Virginia Kirkus 100 Best Books and Westchester Library Best Children's Books 1974-75 for What's Wrong with Being a Skunk?, 1974; Children's Book Showcase Title/Children's Book Council for Giraffe, The Silent Giant, 1976; Jr. Lit. Guild selections include: The Four Little Foxes, 1952, Elephant Herd, 1954, City Boy, Country Boy, 1955, The Big Cheese, 1957, The Pile of Junk, 1962; Herald Tribune Honor Book award for Elephant Herd, 1954; Boys' Clubs Am. Jr. Book Award for Fast Is Not a Ladybug, 1953; Children's Books of Yr. award Child Study Assn. for Giraffe, The Silent Giant, 1976; honor book N.Y. Acad. Scis. for Project Panda Watch, 1985. Mem. Authors Guild, PEN Am. Center, Forum of Writers for Young People (pres. 1975-76). Author filmstrip materials Guidance Assocs.; textbook editor Harcourt Brace Jovanovich, 1980; editor Scribner Ednl. Pubs., 1985. Home and Office: 19 E 95th St New York NY 10128

SCHLENVOGT, KAREN ANN, service company executive; b. Milw., Aug. 21, 1957; d. Walter Ervin and Marjorie Ann (Knott) S. Grad., Milw. Tech. Coll., 1988; student, Carroll Coll., 1988—. Bookkeeper, office mgr. Milw. Beverage Co., Wauwatosa, Wis., 1975-77; bookkeeper Willowglen Acad., Inc., Milw., 1977-79; partnership acct. Nat. Devel. & Investment, Brookfield, Wis., 1979-82; chief bookkeeper Milw. Brewers Baseball Club, 1982-86; acctg. mgr. Ace Worldwide Moving and Storage, Cudahy, Wis., 1986—; bd. dirs. Bluemound Automotive Service, Inc., Wauwatosa. Leader Girl Scouts U.S.A., New Berlin, 1980-81. Mem. Nat. Assn. Female Execs. Lutheran. Home: 3953 W College Ave Franklin WI 53221 Office: Ace Worldwide Moving & Storage 1900 E College Ave Cudahy WI 53110

SCHLETTE, SHARON ELIZABETH, utility company executive; b. Bklyn., May 25, 1945; d. Albert Valentine and Dorothy Lee (Jacobs) Kunz; m. Arthur F. Schlette, Oct. 25, 1985. Student, St. Johns U., 1978-82. With Consol. Edison Co., 1963—, dist. office teller, 1967-69, acctg. clk., customer service, 1967-72; asst. supr. Manhattan customer service, 1972-78; unit mgr. Br. III-Westside, Manhattan customer service, 1978-81, Lincoln Center Br., 1981-82; unit mgr. Yorkville Br., 1982-87, with final accounts/collections dept., 1987—. Mem. Consol. Edison Engring. Soc., Nat. Rifle Assn., Nat. Assn. Female Execs., Aircraft Owners and Pilots Assn. (lic. pilot). Republican. Home: 446 Madison Ave Brentwood NY 11717 Office: 708 First Ave New York NY 10017

SCHLICHTING, CATHERINE FLETCHER NICHOLSON, librarian, educator; b. Huntsville, Ala., Nov. 18, 1923; d. William Parsons and Ethel Louise (Breitling) Nicholson; B.S., U. Ala., 1944; M.L.S., U. Chgo., 1950; m. Harry Fredrick Schlichting, July 1, 1950 (dec. Aug. 1964); children—James Dean, Richard Dale, Barbara Lynn. Asst. librarian U. Ala. Edn. Library, Tuscaloosa, summers 1944-45; librarian Sylacauga (Ala.) High Sch., 1944-45, Hinsdale (Ill.) High Sch., 1945-49; asst. librarian Centre for Children's Books, U. Chgo., 1950-52; instr. reference dept. library Ohio Wesleyan U., Delaware, 1965-69, asst. prof., 1969-79, asso. prof., 1979-85, prof., 1985-86, curator Ohio Wesleyan Hist. Collection, 1986—, student personnel librarian, 1966-72, adviser Mortar Bd., 1969-72, mem. exec. com., 1973-79, 85—, sec. com., 1973-74, 76-77. Mem. adminstrv. bd. Methodist Ch., 1963-81, chmn. adminstrv. bd., 1985—, mem. Council on Ministries, 1975-81, chmn., 1975-77. Recipient Algernon Sidney Sullivan award U. Ala., 1944. Ohio Wesleyan U.-Mellon Found. grantee, 1972-73, 84-85; GLCA Teaching fellow, 1976-77. Mem. ALA, Ohio Library Assn., Midwest Acad. Librarian Conf., Acad. Librarians Assn. Ohio (dir. 1984-86), AAUP (chpt. sec. 1967-68, chpt. exec. com. 1973-78), Kappa Delta Pi, Alpha Lambda Delta. Democrat. Clubs: Ohio Wesleyan U. Womans (exec. bd. 1969-72, 77-79, 81-84, pres. 1969-70, sec. 1977-78), History (pres. 1971-72, v.p. 1978-79), Fortnightly (pres. 1975-76), Am. Field Service (pres. Delaware chpt. 1975-76) (Delaware). Author: Introduction to Bibliographic Research: Basic Sources, 4th edit., 1983; Checklist of Biographical Reference Sources, 1977; Audio-Visual Aids in Bibliographic Instruction, 1976; Introduction to Bibliographic Research: Slide Catalog and Script, 1980; also articles. Home: 414 N Liberty St Delaware OH 43015 Office: Ohio Wesleyan U LA Beeghly Library Delaware OH 43015

SCHLICKSUP, BETH EILEEN, publishing administrator; b. Gary, Ind., June 6, 1956; d. Paul Joseph and Willaneta Flourine (Armstrong) Pieroni; m. Harold Allen Schlicksup, July 29, 1957. BS in Edn., Ind. U., 1979. Fulfillment mgr. PJS Publs., Inc., Peoria, Ill., 1985—. Presbyterian. Home: 125 E Glen Ave #206B Peoria IL 61614 Office: PJS Publs Inc News Plaza PO Box 1790 Peoria IL 61656

SCHLOSNAGLE, CAROL ANN, communications executive; b. Carlisle, Pa., Dec. 23, 1950; d. Eugene Stanley and Ethel Mae (Smeltzer) S.; B.A. in English Lit., Hood Coll., 1972; MBA, U. Wash., 1988. Photojournalist, feature writer Carlisle Evening Sentinel, Carlisle, 1968-71, Frederick (Md.) News-Post, 1971-72; v.p. public relations Cole & Weber, Inc., Seattle, 1974-82; v.p. communications Group Health Coop., Seattle, 1982—. Publicity dir., fund raiser Am. Expdn. to K2, Pakistan, 1978; v.p. bd. dirs. Pike Market Community Clinic; mem. recruitment and pub. relations coms. Leadership Tomorrow; bd. dirs. Nat. Coop. Bus. Found. Mem. Seattle Advt. Fedn., Public Relations Soc. Am. (Wash. State chpt. award of Merit, 1978), Am. Hosp. Assn., Mktg. Exec. Communicators Internat. Republican. Presbyterian. Clubs: Washington Athletic, Seattle Press, Seattle Athletic, City. Publicity and travel writer and photographer for consumer and trade mags., newspapers. Home: 2728 Fairview Ave E Seattle WA 98102 Office: 300 Elliott Ave West Seattle WA 98119

SCHLOSS, JO ANN BOCK, entrepreneur; b. Denver, Aug. 9, 1932; d. Samuel and Rose Bock; B.A. in Communications, U. Colo., 1972, M.A. in Orgnl. Behavior and Communications (grad. fellow 1975), 1975; m. Charles M. Schloss, Jr., Dec. 19, 1948; children—Charles M., III, Sindi Jo, Kristy Anne. Community relations cons. Denver Commn. Community Relations, 1972-73, project dir. commn. youth, 1973-75; with Central Bank of Denver, 1976-82, v.p. staff relations and devel., 1979-81, v.p. human resources planning and devel., 1981-82; chief operating officer Schloss & Shubart, Inc., 1983-84; pres., chief exec. officer Profitable Decisions, Inc., Englewood, Colo., 1985—. Chair Arap. County Pvt. Industry Council; chair course devel. task force Denver Lions Club, Rockies Venture Club; bd. dirs. Women's Resource Ctr., Arapahoe Community Coll. Named hon. faculty dept. communication U. Colo. Mem. Am. Soc. Tng. and Devel., Internat. Assn. Bus. Communicators, Human Resources Planning Soc., Internat. Assn. Quality Circles, Am. Soc. Personnel Adminstrs., Leadership Denver, Women's Forum Colo., World Future Soc., Women Bus. Owners Assn., Denver C. of C., (small bus. steering com., mgmt. assistance task force, chair course devel. task force), Phi Beta Kappa.

SCHLOSSER, ANNE GRIFFIN, librarian; b. N.Y.C., Dec. 28, 1939; d. C. Russell and Gertrude (Taylor) Griffin; m. Gary J. Schlosser, Dec. 28, 1965. BA in History, Wheaton Coll., Norton, Mass., 1962; MLS, Simmons Coll., 1964; cert. archives adminstrn. Nat. Archives and Records Service, Am. U., 1970. Head UCLA Theater Arts Library, 1964-69; dir. Louis B. Mayer Library, Am. Film Inst., Los Angeles, 1969-88, dir. film/TV documentation workshop, 1977-87; head cinema-TV library and archives of the performing arts, U. So. Calif., Los Angeles, 1988—. Project dir.: Motion Pictures, Television, Radio: A Union Catalogue of Manuscript and Special Collections in the Western United States, 1977. Active Hollywood Dog Obedience Club, Calif. Numerous grants for script indexing, manuscript cataloging, library automation. Mem. Soc. Am. Archivists, Soc. Calif. Archivists (pres. 1982-83), Theater Library Assn. (exec. bd. 1983-86), Assn. Entertainment Industry Computer Profls. (bd. dirs. 1986—). Democrat. Episcopalian. Avocations: running, swimming, reading, dog obedience training. Office: U So Calif Cinema-TV Library Univ Library Los Angeles CA 90089-0182

SCHLOTFELDT, ROZELLA MAY, educator; b. DeWitt, Iowa, June 29, 1914; d. John W. and Clara C. (Doering) S. B.S., State U. Iowa, 1935; M.S., U. Chgo., 1947, Ph.D., 1956; D.Sc. (hon.), Georgetown U., 1972, Adelphi U., 1979, Wayne State U., 1983, U. Ill.-Chgo., 1985; L.H.D. (hon.), Med. U. S.C., 1976; DSc, Kent State U., 1987. Staff nurse State U. Iowa, VA Hosp., 1935-39; instr., supr. maternity nursing (State U. Iowa), 1939-44; asst. prof. U. Colo. Sch. Nursing, 1947-48; asst., then asso. prof. Wayne State U. Coll. Nursing, 1948-55; prof., asso. dean Wayne State U. Coll. Nursing (Coll. Nursing), 1957-60; dean Frances Payne Bolton Sch. Nursing, Case Western Res. U., 1960-72, prof., 1960-82, prof., dean emeritus, 1982—; Spl. cons. Surgeon Gen.'s Adv. Group on Nursing, 1961-63; mem. nursing research study sect. USPHS, 1962-66; mem. Nat. League for Nursing-USPHS Com. on Nursing Edn. Facilities, 1962-64; mem. com. on health goals Cleve. Health Council, 1961-66; mem. Cleve. Health Planning and Devel. Commn., 1969-72; adv. com. div. nursing W.K. Kellog Found., 1959-67; v.p. Ohio Bd. Nursing Edn. and Nurse Registration, 1970-71, pres., 1971-72; mem. Nat. Health Services Research Tng. Com., 1970-71; mem. supply and edn. panel Health Manpower Com., 1966-67; rev. com. Nurse Tng. Act, 1967-68; bd. visitors Duke U. Med. Center, 1968-70; mem. council, exec. com. Inst. Medicine of Nat. Acad. Scis., 1971-75; mem. nat. adv. health services council Health Services and Mental Health Adminstrn., 1971-75; mem. def. adv. com. on women in services Dept. Def., 1972-75; bd. mem., treas. Nursing Home Adv. and Research Council, 1975—; mem. adv. panel Health Services Research Commn. on Human Resources, Nat. Acad. Sci., 1977-85; cons. Walter Reed Army Inst.; adv. council on nursing, U.S. VA, 1965-69, chmn., 1966-69; mem. Yale U.; Council Com. on Med. Affairs, 1981-86; mem. adv. bd. Scholarly Inquiry for Nursing Practice, 1987—. Mem. editorial bd.: Advances in Nursing Sci, Inquiry, 1982-85, Jour. Nursing Edn., 1982; contbr. numerous articles to profl. jours. Served to 1st lt. Army Nurse Corps, 1944-46. Recipient Distinguished Service award U. Iowa, 1973. Fellow Am. Acad. Nursing (v.p. 1975-77), Nat. League Nursing; mem. Am. Nurses Assn. (chmn. commn. on nurse edn. 1967-70, mem. com. for studying credentialling 1976-79, adv. com. W. K. Kellogg Nat. Fellowship program 1981-85), Sigma Theta Tau (nat. v.p. 1948-50, selection com., disting. lectr. program 1986-87), Pi Lambda Theta. Home: 1111 Carver Rd Cleveland Heights OH 44112 Office: 2121 Abington Rd Cleveland OH 44106

SCHLUTTER, LOIS COCHRANE, psychologist; b. Indpls., Oct. 18, 1953; d. Roy and Mavis (Wolfe) Cochrane; m. Dennis James Schlutter, Oct. 30, 1976; 1 child, Nathan Paul. BS, U. S.D., 1974, MA, 1975, PhD, 1978. Licensed cons. psychologist, Minn. Psychologist, asst. Neurol. Inst. and Pain Ctr., Sioux City, Iowa, 1975-77; staff Mpls. Psychotherapy Inst., St. Louis Park, Minn., 1978-80; pvt. practice psychology St. Louis Park, 1980-81; bd. dirs. Vail Pl.; allied health staff, cons. Meth. Hosp., St. Louis Park., 1978—, mem. hospice adv. com., 1984—, child abuse consortium, 1985—; staff psychologist, Sister Kenny Inst., Mpls., 1980-81; cons. Dept. Vocat. Rehab., St. Paul. 1984—; supr. Pastoral Care/AAPC, St. Louis Park, 1984—; lectr. St. Mary's Hosp. and Coll., Mpls., 1984—; psychologist, dir. Family Dynamics, St. Louis Park., 1980—. Co-author: (play) The Extrapolator, 1968; contbr. articles to profl. jours. Recipient research grant Lederle Pharms., 1979. Mem. Minn. Psychol. Assn., Am. Assn. Pastoral Counselors (profl. affiliate), Brookside Condominium Assn., The Blvd. Condominium Assn., Phi Beta Kappa, Kappa Alpha Theta, Alpha Lambda Delta, Psi Chi. Office: Family Dynamics 4039 Brookside Ave S Saint Louis Park MN 55416

SCHMALTZ, KATHLEEN MARY (KATHLEEN MARY REARDON), television news anchor, writer; b. Detroit, Apr. 7, 1958; d. Donald Edward and Gwendolyn Rita (Strotz) S. BA in Communication Arts, Criminal Justice, Mich. State U., 1980. Promotion asst., coordinator tour guides Sta. WJBK-TV2, Detroit, 1974-76; news, sports, pub. affairs Mich. State Radio Network, East Lansing, Mich., 1976-79; news reporter, announcer Sta. WKAR-AM-FM, East Lansing, 1978-79, Sta. WITL-AM-FM, Lansing, Mich., 1979—; news anchor, writer Sta. WILX-TV, Lansing and Jackson, Mich., 1979—; ascertainment study researcher Mich. State Radio Network, East Lansing, 1978—; host, Easter Seal Telethon, 1984-88; guest speaker various orgns. Mem. Mich. State U. Student Adv. Group, 1977-79. Recipient Recognition award USAF, 1983, Disting. Service award Royal Oak Beaumont Hosp., 1983, Outstanding Community Service award for Crime Prevention in City of Lansing, 1984, Outstanding Mich. Media award Crime Prevention Assn. Mich., 1984, Tri-County Recognition award for Outstanding Vol. Service, 1987, Spl. award for Outstanding Service Big Bros./Big Sisters, 1987. Mem. Women in Communications. Office: WILX-TV 10 PO Box 30380 Lansing MI 48909

SCHMALZ, GRETCHEN MARIE, occupational therapist; b. Mpls., Jan. 22, 1936; d. Walter Ernest and Theresa Henrietta (Naumann) S. BS in Occupational Therapy, U. Minn., 1957; MA in Occupational Therapy, U. So. Calif., 1969; EdD in Allied Health, U. Houston, 1987. Cert. therapist Am. Occupational Therapy Cert. Bd. Staff occupational therapist Cleve. City Hosp., 1957-58; asst. supr. U. Ill. R&E Hosp., Chgo., 1958-61; clin. supr. VA Hosp., Hines, Ill., 1961-68; asst. prof. U. Ala., Birmingham, 1969-73; assoc. prof. U. Tex. Sch. Allied Health Scis., Galveston, 1973-77, prof., 1977—, assoc. chair dept. occupational therapy, 1973—. Mem. East End Hist. Dist., Galveston, Tex., 1976—, Galveston Hospice, 1984—; chair nom. com. Krewe of Hygeia, Galveston, 1987-88. Mem. Am. Occupational Therapy Assn., Am. Soc. Allied Health Professions, Tex. Assn. Coll. Tchrs., Tex. Occupational Therap Assn. Lutheran. Office: U Tex Sch Allied Health Scis Dept Occupational Therapy Galveston TX 77550-2782

SCHMEES, HAZEL KOEHNE, medical technologist; b. Hamilton County, Ohio, June 20, 1934; d. Arthur and Ethel (Poertner) Koehne; B.S., Ohio U., 1956; M.T., Mt. Carmel Hosp. Sch. Med. Tech., 1956; m. William B. Schmees, June 6, 1959; 1 son, Douglas Benard. Lab. technician, Dr. Dab. Osborn, 1956-59, med. technologist Children's Hosp., 1959-60, Jack Kirschner, M.D., Cin., 1961; night supr. EPP Meml. Hosp., 1961-63; dept. head St. Francis Hosp., Cin., 1963-65; lab. supr. Drs. Clin. Lab., Cin., 1965-78; acting lab. dir. Biederman Allergy Clinic, Cin., 1978-83; clin. instr. Ohio Coll. Bus. and Tech., 1983—, dept. head, 1985—. Republican precinct exec., 1966-69; mem. ch. council St. Peter's United Ch. of Christ, 1983—, recorder, 1984-85, 86—. Cert. med. technologist. Mem. Am. Soc. Clin. Pathologists, Ohio Soc. Med. Technologists (membership chmn. dist. 8 1957-61), Am. Assn. Bioanalysis, Internat. Soc. for Lab. Tech., Am. Bd. Bioanalysis, South Central Assn. Microbiologists. Republican. Clubs: Ohio U. Alumni (dir. 1982—), St. Peter's Women's Guild (pres. 1970-78, treas. 1979-84, pres. 1984—. Home: 886 Krupp Dr Fayetteville OH 45118 Office: 415 W Court St Cincinnati OH 45203

SCHMELZER, PATRICIA ANNE, health physicist; b. West Union, Iowa, June 7, 1951; d. William John and Shirley Anne (Coglan) S. BS, U. Iowa, 1976. Lab. asst. U. Iowa, Iowa City, 1974-78, lab. technician, 1978-82, chemist, 1982-84; health physicist Iowa Elec. Light & Power, Cedar Rapids, 1984-87, ALARA coordinator, 1987—. Foster parent Dept. Human Services, Iowa City, 1987-88; vol. Dept. Corrections, Cedar Rapids, 1981-82. Mem. Health Physics Soc. Democrat. Roman Catholic.

SCHMERZLER, BARBARA HARLIB, real estate broker; b. Bklyn., Nov. 23, 1933; d. Abraham S. and Yetta (Goldstein) H.; m. Seymour Barash Schmerzler, Jan. 26, 1958; children—Alan Matthew, Robert Alexander, David Laurence, Daniel Harlib. Prodn. asst. NBC-TV, N.Y.C., 1951-58; writer TV quiz show Walt Framer Prodns., N.Y.C., 1958-59; realtor, assoc. U.S. Homefinders, Inc., Westport, Conn., 1972-77, pres., 1977—. Mem. Westport Weston Bd. Realtors (pres. 1984-86, Realtor of Yr. 1982, 85), Conn. Assn. Realtors (state conv. chmn. 1984, 85, v.p. 1987-88), Nat. Assn. Realtors. Jewish. Avocations: creative writing; singing; tennis.

SCHMIDT, ALTHEA JUNE, oil and gas consulting company executive; b. Washington, Jan. 10, 1941; d. Ernest Russel and Lorene Ellen (Rion) Shifflett; divorced; children: Daniel Karl, Wayne Russel, Michael Wallace. Student, Ohio State U., 1981. Service rep. C & P Telelphone Co., Washington, 1958-62; sec. Harris Furniture Co., Clinton, Md., 1966-76; adminstrv. asst. Brasel & Brasel Oil and Gas Co., Columbus, Ohio, 1981-83; prodn. mgr. Leader Equities, Columbus, 1983-85; pres. A. June Schmidt & Assocs., Columbus, 1985—. Mem. Ohio Oil and Gas Assn. Home and Office: 4781 Smoketalk Ln Galena OH 43021

SCHMIDT, ANDRA I., utility commisioner; b. Billings, Mont., May 6, 1939; d. Claud Andrew and Helen (Muir) Riggs; children: Stephen, Jeffrey. BA in English, U. No. Colo., 1970. cert. tchr., Colo. Hwy. commr. Colo. Dept. Hwys., 1976-83; account exec. Denver Research Group, 1980-83; commr. Pub. Utilities Commn., Denver, 1983—; mem. tech. pipeline safety com. Dept. Transportation, Washington, 1984—, adv. com. Gas Research Inst., 1987—; bd. dirs. Greeley Nat. Bank, 1978-80. Columnist local newspaper, 1977-80. Andra Schmidt Day proclaimed Gov. Colo., 1979. Mem. Nat. Assn. Regulatory Utility Commrs. (gas com. 1983—), Western Conference of Pub. Service Commrs. (pres. 1986-87). Office: Pub Utilities Commn 1580 Logan OL2 Denver CO 80203

SCHMIDT, BETTY J., motel and trailer court executive, accountant; b. Kearney, Nebr., Sept. 3, 1938; d. LaVerne Ivan and Vivian Jane (Johnson) Banks; student U. Wyo., BBA in Acctg. U. San Diego, 1982; m. Aug. 25, 1954; children—LaVerne, Dennis, Linda. Owner, mgr. Blue Ribbon Cafe & Lounge, Meeteetse, Wyo., 1976-78; mgr. Schmidt Ranch and Limousin Cattle Co., Meeteetse, 1965-78, Don Neet Limousin Cattle Co., Meeteetse, 1970-76; head bookkeeper First State Bank, Cody, Wyo., 1968-71; bookkeeper Barling Constrn. Co., Meeteetse, 1971-73; owner, mgr. Sagebrush Motel and Trailer Ct., Wamsutter, Wyo., 1978—; fin. dir., treas. City of Imperial Beach., Calif., 1987-88; chief fiscal officer Legal Aid Soc. San Diego, 1984-87; custodian of the fund, Marine Corps Recreation Depot, San Diego, 1982-84.Mem. Wyo. Limousin Assn., Nat. Assn. Limousin Breeders, Wyo. Stockgrowers Assn., Mcpl. Treas.'s Assn., City Mcpl. Officers Assn., Beta Alpha Psi. Republican. Lutheran. Home and Office: 8110 Stadler La Mesa CA 92042

SCHMIDT, CAROL SUZANNE, hospital administrator; b. River Rouge, Mich., Aug. 8, 1936; d. J. T. Grant Vaden and Virginia Jean (Senker) Vaden Webster; m. Ronald Lee Schmidt, Aug. 18, 1957; children: Karen Suzanne Corsilius, Linda Martin, Ronald Lee. RN diploma Hinsdale Hosp. Sch. Nursing, Ill., 1958; BS in Nursing cum laude, Met. State Coll., Denver, 1981; M.A. cum laude, Webster U.-Denver, 1984. R.N., Colo. Operating room nurse Porter Meml. Hosp., Denver, 1961-69, charge relief nurse, 1975-76, adminstrv. supr., 1976-77, head nurse ortho/neuro unit, 1977-82; disease control nurse Vis. Nurse Assn., Denver, 1961-63; nurse Denver Gen. Hosp., 1966-67; office mgr., bookkeeper Timber Ridge Constrn., Evergreen, Colo., 1967-79; asst. dir. nursing Boulder Meml. Hosp., Colo., 1982-83, dir. nursing, 1983-84, v.p. patient care, 1984—. Tchr. Seventh Day Adventist Ch., Boulder and Denver, 1958-85; vol. Colo. Health Fair, Denver, 1979, 80; tchr. basic life support Am. Heart Assn., Denver, 1980-82. Recipient Dist. Nurse of Yr. award Colo. Nurse Assn., 1975. Mem. Am. Coll. Hosp. Execs. of Am. Hosp. Assn., Am. Orgn. Nurse Execs., Assn. Seventh Day Adventist Nurses (bd. dirs. 1984-86), Colo. Soc. Nurse Execs. (active image of nursing 1985), Bus. and Profl. Women (legis. com. 1985). Avocations: needlework; travel. Office: Boulder Meml Hosp 311 Mapleton Ave Boulder CO 80302

SCHMIDT, LYNN ANNE, accountant; b. Passaic, N.J., July 31, 1958; d. William W. and Barbara M. (Urban) Butler; m. Donald A. Schmidt, June 28, 1980; children: Kristine, Andrea, Steven. BS, N.H. Coll., 1980; cert., NAt. Tax Tng. Sch., 1986. Bookkeeper Cogan-Zeitlin CPA, Paramus, N.J., 1976, United Parcel Service, Manchester, N.H., 1977; acctg. asst. Unified Data Products, Paramus, 1978; comptroller Lamont Labs. Inc, Londonderry, N.H., 1978-79; acct. World Relief Refugee Services, Nyack, N.Y., 1980, Modafferi, Ritter & Furfaro, CPA's, Nanuet, N.Y., 1980-81; pvt. practice acctg. Sloatsburg, N.Y., 1983—; acct., mgr. office Marvin Nyman, CPA, Bardonia, N.Y., 1985—; speaker in field. Mem. Nat. Alliance Homebased Bus. Women, Nanuet, 1968-88. Mem. N.Y. Soc. Pub. Accts., Nat. Soc. Pub. Accts. Episcopalian. Home and Office: Eagle Valley Rd Tuxedo Sloatsburg NY 10974

SCHMIDT, MARIA CERES, educator, lawyer; b. Newark, June 28, 1950; d. Joseph Michael and Edith (Primamore) Ceres; m. Robert Edward Schmidt, Aug. 23, 1970. BA, Montclair State Coll., 1972, MA, 1975; JD, Seton Hall U., 1978. Bar: N.J. 1979. Tchr. Westfield (N.J.) Sr. High Sch., 1972—; sole practice Westfield (N.J.) Sr. High Sch., Livingston, N.J., 1979-80, 81—; ptnr. Gray, Schmidt & Van Pelt, Plainfield, N.J., 1980-81. Committeewoman Essex County Rep. Party, 1981-84; mem. adv. com. on recycling Livingston Twp. Council, 1987-88. Mem. Westfield Edn. Assn., NEA, N.J. Edn. Assn., Eagleton Inst. Politics (tchr. assoc. 1987—).

SCHMIDT, MARILYNN JO, speech pathologist; b. Fostoria, Ohio, July 11, 1931; d. George William and Dorothy (Fry) S.; B.S. in Secondary Edn., Bob Jones U., 1954; M.A. in Speech Pathology, Denver U., 1960, Ph.D. in Speech Pathology, 1972. Tchr., Russellville (Mo.) High Sch., 1954-56, Boonville (Mo.) High Sch., 1956-59; tchr. Denver U., 1960-62; asst. prof. speech pathology Central Mo. State U., Warrensburg, 1962-73, asso. prof., 1973-78, prof., 1978—; cons. in field. Office Vocat. Rehab. fellow, 1959-60; VA grantee, 1971-72. Mem.Am. Speech-Lang.-Hearing Assn., Mo. Speech-Lang.-Hearing Assn., P.E.O., Phi Delta Kappa. Methodist. Home: 409 10th St Warrensburg MO 64093 Office: Mo State U Speech and Hearing Clinic Cen Warrensburg MO 64093

SCHMIDT, MARY MAY, educator, consultant, bookkeeper; b. Batavia, N.Y., June 3, 1949; d. Ralph Ellis and Mary Frances (Watson) Swenson; m. Gary Charles Schmidt, July 3, 1971; children: Daniel Glenn, Christopher Gregory. BS in English, SUNY, Potsdam, 1971; MS in English Edn., SUNY, New Palto, 1983; postgrad., Marist Coll., 1988—. Cert. English tchr., N.Y. Instr. in humanities Sullivan County Community Coll., Loch Sheldrake, N.Y., 1981-85; instr. English Pace U., N.Y.C., 1986—; speech adj. Pace U., Swan Lake, N.Y., 1988—. Author poetry, Emergency First Aid Manual. Vol. Ambulance Corp, 1972-86; multiple offices PTA, Monticello, 1981-84; v.p., bd. dirs. United Way, Sullivan County, Monticello, 1984-86 (chairwoman, 1986-88). Mem. AAUW (com. chmn. 1982-85), Catskill Art Soc. Republican. Methodist. Home: 55 Jefferson St Monticello NY 12701 Office: Pace Univ Swan Lake NY 12783

SCHMIDT, NAOMI, magazine editor; b. Johannesburg, South Africa, Oct. 22, 1954; d. Louie and Patricia (Emden) Trevor: m. Thomas Charles Schmidt, July 15, 1949. Drafter Simon & SImon, Johannesburg, 1973-74; stage mgr. The Company, Johannesburg, 1974-76, Theater Kit, London, 1976-77; community worker Inst. Race Relations, Johannesburg, 1977-79; editor Karma Triyana Dharmarchakra, Woodstock, N.Y., 1980—. Writer play Thine Is, 1973. Buddhist. Office: Karma Triyana Dharmachatra 352 Meads Mountain Rd Woodstock NY 12498

SCHMIDT, PATRICIA ANN, marketing professional; b. Red Bud, Ill., Apr. 6, 1942; d. Justin Joseph and Norma Mary (Burgdorf) Zipfel; m. David Ralph Hoffman, Oct. 24, 1964 (div. Aug. 1973); 1 child, Elizabeth Ruth; m. Robert Edward Schmidt, May 16, 1987. BS, Bradley U., 1964, postgrad. Cert. secondary tchr. Tchr. English, speech Sch. Dist. #150, Peoria, Ill., 1964-72; personnel clk., free-lance reporter Peoria Jour. Star, 1973-75; adminstrv. asst. Southwestern Drug Corp., Dallas, 1975-77; account exec. Taylor Pub. Co., Dallas, 1977; grants officer Lakeview Mus., Peoria, 1977-79; coordinator clerical ops. Foster & Gallagher, Inc., Peoria, 1979-80, mgr. customer service, 1980—; part-time speech instr. Bradley U., 1969-70. Sec. Community Children's Theatre, Peoria, 1981-84, pres. 1985-87. Mem. Internat. Customer Service Assn., Phi Kappa Phi. Methodist. Home: 2 Grand Oaks Estates Pekin IL 61554

SCHMIDT, RUTH ANN, college president; b. Mountain Lake, Minn., Sept. 16, 1930; d. Jacob A. and Anna A. (Ewert) S. B.A., Augsburg Coll., Mpls., 1952; M.A., U. Mo., 1955; Ph.D., U. Ill., 1962; LLD, Gordon Coll., 1987. Asst. prof. Spanish Mary Baldwin Coll., Staunton, Va., 1955-58; asst. prof. Spanish SUNY-Albany, 1962-67, assoc. prof., 1967-78, dean of humanities, 1971-76; provost Wheaton Coll., Norton, Mass., 1978-82; pres. Agnes Scott Coll., Decatur, Ga., 1982—; chair Women's Coll. Coalition, 1986-88. Author: Ortega Munilla y sus novelas, 1973, Cartas entre dos amigos del teatro, 1969. Trustee Gordon Coll., Wenham, Mass., 1980-86; dir. DeKalb C. of C., 1982-85; mem. exec. com. Women's Coll. Coalition, 1983—. Named Disting. Alumna Augsburg Coll., 1973. Mem. Assn. Am. Colls. (dir. 1979-82, treas. 1982-83), Soc. Values in Higher Edn., Am. Council Edn. (commn. on women in higher edn. 1985-88), AAUW. Democrat. Presbyterian. Office: Agnes Scott College Pres's Office Decatur GA 30030

SCHMIDT, RUTH CAROLINE, civic worker; b. Appleton, Wis., Apr. 2, 1922; d. William Gustavus and Gladys (Emily) Richter Gust; m. Robert Walter Schmidt, Nov. 14, 1941; 1 child, David Robert. Student Appleton Bus. Coll., 1940-41. Contbr. articles to ednl. jours. and newspapers. Pres. Elkhart Lake Sch. Bd., Wis., 1964-82; pres. Wis. Assn. Sch. Bds., Madison, 1978; del., mem. steering com. White House Conf. on Libraries, 1978-83; pres. Wis. PTA, Madison, 1983-85; chmn. Council of Library and Network Devel., Madison, 1981—; bd. dirs. Nat. PTA, Chgo., 1983-85; organizer student assistance program Drug and Alcohol Abuse Program, Elkhart Lake, 1983—; founder Am. Field Service Program, Elkhart Lake. Recipient Recognition of Service award Wis. Sch. Library Assn., 1978, Reading for Excellence award Sch. Bd., Elkhart Lake, Wis., 1984, Citation, Wis. Legislature, 1982, Dedicated Service to Edn. award Wis. Assn. Sch. Adminstrs., 1986. Mem. Nat. PTA (hon. life), Wis. PTA (hon. life), Wis. Assn. Sch. Bds. (life). Republican. Mem. United Ch. of Christ. Clubs: Elkhart Lake Study (pres.), Quit Quie Golf (Elkhart Lake) (pres.). Lodge: Order Eastern Star. Avocations: golf; swimming; bridge; reading. Home: 220 Crystal Lake Dr Plymouth WI 53073

SCHMIDT, SANDRA KAY, financial aid coordinator; b. Franklin, Nebr., Nov. 12, 1941; d. Floyd Nelson and Leola Fern (Boyce) Meade; m. Gene LeRoy Schmidt, Nov. 1, 1941. Student, Cen. Comm. Coll., 1976, Kearney State Coll., 1987. Sec., bookkeeper Franklin Pub. Schs., 1963-69; office mgr. George Risk Industries, Columbus, Nebr., 1969-71; VA certifying official Cen. Comm. College-Platte, Columbus, 1971-83; fin. aid officer Cen. Comm. Coll.-Platte, Columbus, 1983-86, fin. aid coordinator, 1986—; ptnr. Images Unlimited Photography. Mem. An. Bus. Women (scholarship chair, Bus. Woman of Yr. 1986), Nat. Assn. Female Execs., Nebr. Assn. Student Fin. Aid Adminstrs., Nat. Assn. Student Fin. Aid Adminstrs., Adult Continuing Edn. Assn. Office: Cen Community Coll-Platte 4500 63d Columbus NE 68601-1027

SCHMIDT, SHERYL A., advertising executive; b. Waukegan, Ill., Jan. 24, 1955; d. Paul Eugene and Hazel Ellen (Williams) Cain; m. Keith William Schmidt, Dec. 22, 1973 (div. 1986). BA in English, San Francisco State U., 1983. Customer service, mktg. rep. numerous cos., Calif., 1973-80; office mgr. Lubricating Specialties, Pico Rivera, Calif., 1980-82; news accounts, customer service rep. Apple Bank, Smithtown, N.Y., 1983, Letts of London, Hauppauge, N.Y., 1983-84; asst. advt. mgr. Handy and Harman, N.Y.C., 1984—. Vol. S.I. chpt. Am. Cancer Soc., N.Y., 1986. Mem. Nat. Assn. Female Execs., Am. Soc. Profl. and Exec. Women. Democrat. Methodist. Club: N.Y. Road Runners (N.Y.C.). Home: 275 E 237th St #1B Bronx NY 10470 Office: Handy and Harman 850 3d Ave 7th fl New York NY 10022

SCHMIDTKE, KELLI LEANNE, construction executive, consultant; b. Canoga Park, Calif., Feb. 17, 1963; d. Jack E. and Karen L. (Lawson) S. Cert. in bus. acctg., Calif. State U., Chico, 1983; cert. in fin., 1984, cert. in bus. mgmt., 1985, cert. in constrn. mgmt., 1986; cert. in interior design, Sheffield Sch., 1988. Mgr. constrn. dept. Bel-Aire Contractors Chico, 1980-87; corp. chief fin. officer 1985—; constrn. coordinator Spectrum Foods, Inc., San Francisco, 1987-88, Fulwiler James, Inc., Moss Beach, Calif., 1988—; pvt. practice notary pub., Calif., 1985—; cons. interior design KEL SCH Design, San Francisco, 1987—. Active Vols. Under 30, Denver, 1988—. Participating mem. Women in Constrn. (No. Calif. chpt.), Nat. Women's Polit. Caucus; mem. Nat. Rotary Assn., Am. Soc. Interior Designers (affiliate), Nat. Assn. Female Execs. Club: Women's Golf Assn. Home: 472 Vallejo St San Francisco CA 94133 Office: Fulwiler James Inc PO Box 886 Moss Beach CA 94038

SCHMIDTMANN, NANCY K., librarian, educator; b. N.Y.C., Apr. 13, 1940; d. Charles Bernard and Anna Mary (Gorman) Koonmen; A.B. cum laude, Chestnut Hill Coll., 1961; M.A., St. John's U., 1962, M.L.S., 1982; m. Otto S. Schmidtmann, Dec. 26, 1962; children—Lucie Ann, Mary Catherine, Peter, Emily Jean, Charles. Research asst. St. John's U., Jamaica, N.Y., 1961-62, 80-81; tchr. English Francis Lewis High Sch., Flushing, N.Y., 1962-63; copywriter Barth-Spencer Corp., Valley Stream, N.Y., 1968-70; editor/copywriter Barron's Ednl. Series, Woodbury, N.Y., 1970-72; sch. media specialist Our Lady of Mercy Sch., Hicksville, N.Y., 1973—; part-time children's librarian Syosset Pub. Library, reference librarian Jericho Pub. Library; panelist Nassau Suffolk Library Inst., 1980; audio-visual reviewer Sch. Library Jours., 1980—; speaker NCEA convention; cons. in field. Mem. exec. bd. PTA, Plainview Old-Bethpage pub. schs., 1967-70; 4-H leader, Nassau County, N.Y., 1970-86; vol. Roman Cath. Diocese of Rockville Centre, 1965—. Recipient Freedoms Found. award, 1957; Ancient Order of Hibernians award, 1956; N.Y. State Coll. Teaching fellow, 1961-62; St. John's U. grad. assistantship, 1961-62, 80-81. Mem. Cath. Library Assn. (chpt. pres., nat. adv. bd.), Nat. Cath. Edn. Assn., Nassau County Library Assn., ALA, Delta Epsilon Sigma, Beta Phi Mu. (v.p.). Contbr. articles to profl. jours. Home: 149 Orchard St Plainview NY 11803 Office: 520 S Oyster Bay Rd Hicksville NY 11801

SCHMIED, SYLVIA, restaurant executive; b. San Salvador, El Salvador, Nov. 11, 1953; came to U.S., 1957; d. Carlos A. Barrera and Leonor Castaneda; m. Stephen douglas Ordway, June 20, 1974 (div. 1979); m. Wayne R. Schmied, Dec. 5, 1982; children: David, Aaron, Joshua, Sylvia Rebecca, Rachel Ann. AS in Nursing, U. Bridgeport, 1974; BA in Psychology, Fairleigh Dickinson U., 1979. Nurse Hackensack (N.J.) Med. Ctr., 1974-77; head nurse Englewood (N.J.) Hosp., 1977-79; nursing coordinator Somerset (N.J.) Med. Ctr., 1980-82; owner, officer The Bagelsmith Food Store & Deli, Hampton, N.J., 1983—; owner, corp. fin. officer Smith and Barrera Assocs., Inc., Pittstown, N.J., 1982—; cons. The Bagelsmith Franchise, 1982—, owner, bd. dirs. Mem. Hunterdon (N.J.) C. of C. (Entrepreneur Small Bus. award 1985). Home: RD 1 Box 195 Annandale NJ 08801

SCHMIEGEL, KAROL ANN, museum registrar; b. Washington, Apr. 10, 1945; d. Garnet Charles and Evelyn Rose (Brown) Grubbs; m. Walter Werner Schmiegel. AB, Smith Coll., 1966; MA, U. Dela., 1975. Asst. registrar Winterthur (Dela.) Mus., 1969-76, assoc. registrar, 1976-83; reviewer Inst. Mus. Services, Washington, 1987—. Contbr. articles to profl. jours. Bd. dirs. The Friends of Rockwood, Wilmington, Dela., 1982—. Mem. Internat. Council Mus., Am. Assn. Mus. (registrars com., reviewer MAP II), Mid-Atlantic Assn. Mus. (treas.). Episcopalian. Club: Smith Coll. (Dela.) (pres. 1978-80). Office: Winterthur Mus Winterthur DE 19735

SCHMITT, ANN B., public relations executive; b. Chgo., May 14, 1945; d. Albert George and Evelyn (Hilgers) S. Student, No. Ill. U., 1963-65. Coordinator post prodn. Sarra Studios UPI, Chgo., 1965-71; west coast rep. Internat. Digisiconics, Hollywood, Calif., 1971-72; sales rep. Imagic (Opticals), Hollywood, 1972-74; producer, prodn. coordinator Creative Film Arts, Hollywood, 1974-83; owner Ann B. Schmitt Pub. Relations, Van Nuys, Calif., 1984—. Mem. Book Publicists of So. Calif., LEADS (coordinator 1985), Inside Edge, San Fernando Valler Pub. Relations Roundtable, The Network. Club: Toastmasters.

SCHMITT, DEBRA LINDA, sales executive, consultant; b. Seminole, Fla., Dec. 12, 1962; d. Charles A. and Walburga (Eringma) S. Student, St. Petersburg Jr. Coll., 1979-81; BS in Polit. Sci., Fla. State U., 1982, BS in Computer Sci, 1984; postgrad., U. South Fla., 1985—. Pvt. practice paralegal St. Petersburg, 1979-83; pres., owner Suncoast Data Processing, St. Petersburg, 1983—; with sales and mktg. dept. Basis, Inc., Dallas, 1982—; mgr. regional sales Parker T. Computers, Dallas, 1985—. Author: How to Select a Computer, 1986. Mem. Young Reps., Fla., 1984—. Named to Lt. Gov. Circle K, 1979. Mem. Am. Assn. Independent Investors, Seminole C. of C., Phi Rho Pi, Phi Theta Kappa. Republican. Methodist. Club: Toastmasters (St. Petersburg). Home: PO Box 3987 Saint Petersburg FL 34642 Office: Suncoast Data Processing PO Box 3987 Saint Petersburg FL 34642

SCHMITT, SUE ANN, academic administrator; b. Caledonia, Minn., Jan. 27, 1946; d. Edward Theodore and O'Delia (Klug) S. BA, Viterbo Coll., 1969; MEd, U. Mo., 1972; EdD, Miss. State U., 1984. Cert. rehab counselor, therapist and sex educator. Counselor Wis. div. Vocat. Rehab., Madison, 1972-76; instr. ctr. rehab. edn. U. Wis., Menomonie, 1976-78, asst. to dir. vocat. rehab. inst., 1978-80, dir. Program Ind. Living, 1980-85, chmn. dept. rehab., 1985-87; adminstrv. assoc. to v.p. for acad. affairs systems adminstrn. U. Wis., Madison, 1988, assoc. vice chancellor, 1988—; peer reviewer Office of Spl. Edn. and Rehab. Services, Washington 1984—, program reviewer Mankato (Minn.) State U., 1986; cons., instr. U. Minn., St. Paul, 1986-88. Author workbook, video tapes, slide series Courtesy Needs of Disabled Customers, 1981; co-author workbook, video tape, tng. manual Steps to Quality, 1987; co-editor tng. manual WRA Accessibility of Hotel Motel and Conference Sites, 1978 (Nat. Rehab. Assn. award 1980); project dir. video tape Alternate Housing in the Rural Area, 1986. Mem. tech. adv. com. Madison Housing Authority, 1974-75, vocat. rehab. adv. council Women's Issues Disabled Women's Project, Madison, 1984-87; mem. exec. com. Govt. Com. Persons with Disabilities, Madison, 1979-80, 84, 86. Fellow Bush Found., 1982; recipient Gold Medallion award Fed. Interagency Com., 1982. Mem. Nat. Rehab. Assn. (mem. bd. dirs., chmn. commn. on rights and access, adv. bd. info. ctr.), Phi Delta Kappa, Phi Kappa Phi. Office: Vice Chancellors Office Adminstrn Bldg Menomonie WI 54751

SCHMITZ, ELLEN MARIE, marketing professional; b. St. Louis, May 5, 1956; d. Richard Louis and Jerry Heloise (Farrar) S. BS, U. N.H., 1978; MBA, NYU, 1983. Sr. research analyst Lorillard Corp., N.Y.C., 1979-80, asst. product mgr., 1980-81, assoc. product mgr., 1981-83, product mgr., 1983; product mgr. Heublein Corp. div. R.J. Reynolds Corp., Farmington, Conn., 1983-84; sr. mktg. mgr. RJR Nabisco Corp., San Francisco, 1984-86; group mktg. mgr. RJR Nabisco Corp., Parsippany, N.J., 1986—. Republican. Office: RJR Nabisco 6 Campus Dr Parsippany NJ 07054-4464

SCHMITZ, EUGENIA EVANGELINE, librarian, educator; b. Grand Rapids, Mich.; d. Joseph A. and Eugenia (Newhouse) S.; A.B., Western Mich. U.; B.S., Coll. St. Catherine; A.M., U. Mich., Ph.D., 1966. Br. librarian Grand Rapids Public Library; librarian, Creston High Sch., Grand Rapids, Sr. High Sch., Benton Harbor, Mich.; lectr. dept. library sci. U. Mich., 1963-67, asst. prof., 1967-68; asst. prof. library sci. U. Wis. at Oshkosh, 1968-70, assoc. prof., 1970-75, prof., 1975—, chmn. dept. library sci., 1968-80. Mem. ALA, Wis. Library Assn., Phi Beta Kappa, Phi Kappa Phi, Beta Phi Mu, Pi Lambda Theta, Sigma Pi Epsilon. Contbr. book revs. to Jour. Acad. Librarianship, others.

SCHMUDE, JUDY GAIL, health care administrator; b. Kenosha, Wis., Mar. 2, 1939; d. Howard D. and Joycelyn V. (Correll) Ohlgart; divorced; children: Frederick E., Randall H. BS, U. Wis., Whitewater, 1962, MS, 1971; MT, Kenosha Mem. Hosp., 1971; PhD, Marquette U., 1983. Cert. tchr. Tchr. gen. sch. Kenosha Unified Schs., 1962-67; instr. sci. Gateway Tech. Inst., Kenosha, 1967-75; edn. coordinator Kenosha Mem. Hosp., 1975-80, dir., 1980-86; v.p., women's care St. Joseph's Hosp. and Med. Ctr., Phoenix, 1986—; adj. faculty U. Phoenix, 1986—; faculty Cardinal Stritch Coll., Milw., 1985-86; cons. Kenosha Mem. Hosp., 1983-86. Author: Quality Assurance Nursing Schools, 1985, Politics in Health Care Administration, 1988; contbr. articles to profl. jours. Pres. Wish. Health Edn., 1986, Am. Cancer Soc., Kenosha, 1985. Elected to Ariz. Women's Town Hall, 1987. Mem. Am. Coll. of Hosp. Execs., Ariz. Hosp. Assn., Phi Delta Kappa. Democrat. Lutheran. Clubs: Squaw Peak Hiking (Phoenix). Office: St Josephs Hosp Med Ctr 350 W Thomas Rd Phoenix AZ 85001

SCHNACK, GAYLE HEMINGWAY JEPSON (MRS. HAROLD CLIFFORD SCHNACK), corporate executive; b. Mpls., Aug. 14, 1926; d. Jasper Jay and Ursula (Hemingway) Jepson; student U. Hawaii, 1946; m. Harold Clifford Schnack, Mar. 22, 1947; children: Jerrald Jay, Georgina, Roberta, Michael Clifford. Skater, Shipstead & Johnson Ice Follies, 1944-46; v.p. Harcliff Corp., Honolulu, 1964—, Schnack Indsl. Corp., Honolulu, 1969—, Nutmeg Corp., Cedar Corp.; ltd. ptnr. Koa Corp. Mem. Internat. Platform Soc., Beta Sigma Phi (chpt. pres. 1955-56, pres. city council 1956-57). Established Ursula Hemingway Jepson art award, Carlton Coll., Ernest Hemingway creative writing award, U. Hawaii. Office: PO Box 3077 Honolulu HI 96802 also: 1200 Riverside Dr Reno NV 89503

SCHNEBLY, DIXIE JEAN, management consulting firm executive; b. Denver, Nov. 10, 1941. Grad. Parks Sch. of Bus., 1960; BSBA, U. Denver, 1959-63; interior designer, Chgo. Sch. Interior Design, 1974. Lic. real estate broker. Exec. sec. various oil cos., Denver, 1961-77; truck driver Mobile Pre Mix Co., Denver, 1977-80; cons. Unique Designs & Interiors, Denver, 1968-77; pres. DHS Trucking, Inc., Wheat Ridge, Colo., 1980-84; pres. Dixie Corp., Wheat Ridge, 1984—. Editor: (newsletter) IWLA Nat. Paper, 1972. Active Witness for Peace, Denver, 1985—. Mem. Nat. Assn. Female Execs. (exec. sec. 1984—), Srs. Rights Advocates, Colo. Organic Growers Assn.. Republican. Avocations: poetry writing, photography, wildlife preservation. Office: Dixie Corp/DHS Trucking Inc 4015 Carr St Box 433 Wheat Ridge CO 80033

SCHNECKENBURGER, KAREN LYNNE, finance executive; b. Peoria, Ill., Sept. 12, 1949; d. Walter Carl and Judith Jane (Grimshaw) S. BS in Acctg., Bradley U., 1971. CPA, Ill. Auditor Ernst & Whinney, Chgo., 1971-76; controller C.A. Roberts Co., Franklin Park, Ill., 1976-78; mgr. fin. and investments Gould Inc., Rolling Meadows, Ill., 1978-86; dir. fin. Fairchild Industries, Inc., Chantilly, Va., 1986—. adviser Jr. Achievement, Chgo., 1979-83. Mem. Am. Inst. CPA's, Ill. CPA Soc., Chgo. Fin. Exchange. Home: 2249 Cedar Cove Ct Reston VA 22091-4108 Office: Fairchild Industries Inc 300 Service Rd Chantilly VA 22021-9998

SCHNEE, AMANDA MERYL MACNAB, physician; b. North Berwick, Scotland, Dec. 3, 1945; came to U.S., 1975; d. Hamish Stuart Duncan and Marjorie Daphne Croal (McDonald) M.; M.B., Ch.B., St. Andrews U., Scotland, 1968; m. Mark Schnee, Oct. 21, 1967; children—Samantha Joanne, Jicky Miranda, Pippa Meryl, Briony Amanda. Intern, Ballochmyle Hosp., Mauchline, Ayrshire, Scotland, 1968-69; resident in family practice Ayrshire Central Hosp., Irvine, Ayrshire, 1969-71; gen. practice medicine, Glasgow, Scotland, 1971-75; physician USAF, Omaha, 1975-77; mem. faculty U. Tex. Med. Sch., Houston, 1977-81. asst. prof. dept. family practice, 1979-81; dir. Student Health Center, Rice U., Houston, 1981—. Diplomate Am. Bd. Family Practice. Mem. Am. Acad. Family Practice, Am. Med. Women's Assn. Home: 2318 Underwood Blvd Houston TX 77030 Office: Rice U Student Health Ctr PO Box 1892 Houston TX 77251

SCHNEEBERG, HELEN BASSEN, retired educator; b. Phila., Apr. 5, 1920; d. Carl and Minnie (Aion) Bassen; m. Norman Grahn Schneeberg, Nov. 3, 1940; children—Susan, Karen. B.A., U. Pa., 1941, Cert. of Advanced Studies, 1984; M.L.S., Drexel U., Phila., 1966. Cert. librarian. Bacteriologist, Mount Sinai Hosp., Phila., 1941-43; librarian West Phila., High Sch., 1966-67, Temple U., Phila., 1967-68; research asst. Franklin Inst. Research Lab., Phila., 1968-69; teaching assoc. Temple U., Phila., 1970-71; dir., listen-read project Sch. Dist., Phila., 1971-76. Contbr. articles to research rports. Bd. dirs. Please Touch Mus., Phila., 1979-81; steering com. Physicians for Social Responsibility, Phila., 1982-84; area legis. coordinator Women's Agenda, Phila., 1984—; mem. Phila. task force for Sch.-age Child Care, 1988. Mem. N.Y. Acad. Scis., Soc. Research in Child Devel., Infant Mental Health of De. Valley. Democrat. Avocations: travel, reading, music, theatre, sailing, swimming. Home: 2010 Rittenhouse Sq Philadelphia PA 19103

SCHNEIDER, ADELE GOLDBERG, librarian, educator; b. N.Y.C., May 13, 1924; d. Abraham and Anna (Levy) Goldberg; B.A., Bklyn. Coll., 1945; M.L.S., Pratt Inst., 1965; M.A., L.I.U., 1971; m. Noel Schneider, Jan. 1, 1950; children—Adam Matthew, Tracy Lynn. Field interviewer Gallup Poll, N.Y.C., 1941-48; social worker N.Y.C. Dept. Social Services, 1949-52; editor Bklyn. Coll. Alumni Quarterly, 1961-65; instr. Kingsborough Community Coll. CUNY, 1965-70, asst. prof. dept. library, 1970-72, assoc. prof., 1972—. Contbr. articles to profl. jours. Mem. ALA, Library Assn. City U. N.Y., N.Y. Tech. Services Librarians, Beta Phi Mu. Home: 124 Oxford St Brooklyn NY 11235 Office: 2001 Oriental Blvd Brooklyn NY 11235

SCHNEIDER, ANNA MARY, postal service arbitration advocate, b. Denver, Feb. 10, 1951; d. Andrew and Anna (Kestel) Wysowatcky; m. Gerald John Schneider, Aug. 12, 1972. BS in Biology, Colo. State U., 1973, postgrad., 1982; postgrad., U. Colo., 1982; MBA, Regis Coll., 1987. Window/distbn. clk. U.S Postal Service, Berthoud, Colo., 1973-79; clk. U.S Postal Service, Longmont, Colo., 1975-76, postmaster, 1979-86; labor relations asst. U.S Postal Service, Denver, 1983—; rev. mem. promotion bd. U.S. Postal Service, 1982, model delivery unit auditor, Denver, 1982, officer-in-charge, Loveland, 1982-83, rep. to Fed. Republic Germany, 1983. Co-chmn. United Way Campaign; mem. Berthoud Town Planning Council, Berthoud Scholarship Com.; adv. mem. solicitation task force McKee Med. Ctr., also chmn. fund raising drive for facility expansion, bd. dirs.; chmn. Berthoud Day com.; ; mem. adv. com. Thompson R2-J Sch. Dist. Bus. and Office Edn., Job Tng. Partnership Act of 1982; sec. Longspeak chpt. Nat. Assn. Postmasters U.S., 2d v.p. Colo. chpt., legis. rep. to Washington, 1983. Named Colo. Angus Queen, 1969. Mem. Colo. Pharm. Wives Assn., Berthoud C. of C. (pres. 1982). Home: 1432 NUS 287 Berthoud CO 80513 Office: US Postal Service 425 3d St Berthoud CO 80513

SCHNEIDER, CLAUDINE CMARADA, congresswoman; b. Clairton, Pa., Mar. 25, 1947. Student, U. Barcelona, Spain, Rosemont Coll., U. R.I. Sch. Community Planning; B.A., Windham Coll., 1969. Exec. adminstr. Concern, Inc., 1969; founder R.I. Com. on Energy, 1973; exec. dir. Conservation Law Found., 1974; fed. coordinator R.I. Coastal Zone Mgmt. Program, 1978; producer, hostess public affairs program Sta. WJAR-TV, Providence, 1978-79; mem. 97th-100th Congresses from 2d R.I.Dist. State chmn. spl. events Am. Cancer Soc., 1979. Named Woman of Year R.I., Women's Polit. Caucus, 1978. Office: Room 1512 Longworth House Office Bldg Washington DC 20515

SCHNEIDER, ELOISE COVELL, legal assistant; b. Casale, Italy, Feb. 1, 1923; came to U.S., 1924; d. Joseph and Rosina (Malchiodi) Malchiodi; m. Robert E. Covell, Oct. 20, 1944 (div. Apr. 1947); 1 child, Margaret Rose Covell; widowed. Grad. high sch., Amityville, N.Y. Legal asst. various attys., L.I. area, N.Y., 1942—, Law Office Joseph Cardino Jr., Copiague, N.Y., 1987—; real estate agt. L.I. area, 1950—; speaker in field. Author numerous poems; contbr. articles to profl. jours. Chmn. Bicentennial for Babylon (N.Y.) Village, 1975-76; worked on various polit. campaigns, 1961-78. Lodge: Sons of Italy (historian 1970-78, past bd. dirs.). Office: Law Office Joseph Cardino Jr 1475 Great Neck Rd Copiague NY 11726

SCHNEIDER, HELEN LILLIAN, advertising and public relations executive; b. Stamford, Conn., July 10, 1947; d. George William and Wilhelminia Helen (Bellmar) Meier; m. Arlin L. Schneider, Nov. 10, 1973; children: Christopher Mitchell, Mark Robert. AA, Brian McMahon Community Coll., 1965-67; student, U. Wash., 1967-69. Asst. personnel mgr. W. H. Brady Co., Milw., 1976-78; mgr. mktg. Cornwell Services, Milw., 1978-80; owner Schneider & Assocs., Waco, Tex., 1981—. Dir. Assn. Locally Involved Vols., Waco, 1980—. Named one of Outstanding Young Women Am., Jr. Woman's Clubs Am., 1984, 85, Outstanding Vol. of Yr., Tex. Jr. Woman's Clubs, 1985. Mem. Advt. Club Am., Pub. Relations Soc. Am., Am. Soc. for Quality Control, Waco Advt. Club (bd. dirs. 1984—), Waco C. of C. (communications com. 1985—). Lutheran. Club: Jr. Woman's (Waco) (pres. 1983-84); Brown Deer Jr. Women's (Milw.) (pres. 1979-80). Home: 208 Woodfall Dr Waco TX 76710 Office: 6801 Sanger Ave #255 Waco TX 76710

SCHNEIDER, INGER MARIE, publishing company executive; b. Gamvik, Norway, Nov. 5, 1932; came to U.S., 1956; d. Halfdan Olai and Marie Grete (Johannsen) Korneliussen; m. Sigvart Wathne, Feb. 23, 1957 (dec. April 1964); children: Roy, Tom, Helen; m. Hans J. Schneider, Oct. 7, 1967; children: Josef, Rose. Counselor, lectr. World Wide Pub. Corp. and World Wide Evangelism, Ashland, Oreg., 1967—; v.p. World Wide Pub. Corp., Ashland, 1980—. Author: From the Polar Night to Eternal Light, 1980; contbr. articles mags. and newspapers. Fund raiser Red Cross, Norway, 1947-55. Republican. Home: PO Box 105 Ashland OR 97520

SCHNEIDER, IRENE MARGARET, sales and marketing executive; b. Balt., Feb. 1, 1951; d. Aruther Watson and Alice (Saures) Watson-Witt-Rayner; m. John O. Altomare, May 6, 1966 (div. April 1972); children: John J., Troy Edward; m. William Gene Schneider, Aug. 4, 1979; 1 child, Stephanie Dawn. Student, Va. Commonwealth U., 1973. Shift supr. J & N Restaurant Corp., College Park, Md., 1970-74; dir. sales Sheraton Corp., Silver Spring, Md., 1974-76; regional mktg. rep. Info. Handling Services, Denver, 1976-84; regional mgr. Piedmont div. Ziff Davis Tico, N.Y.C., 1984-87; area mgr. ILS div. Ryder Systems, Memphis, 1987—; instr. tech. and mktg. info. systems, 1978. Mem. Nat. Assn. Female Execs., Standards Engrng. Soc., Assn. Records Mgmt. Adminstrs., Am. Soc. Naval Engrs., Am. Legion Ladies Aux. Office: Rydes Systems ILS Div 3821 Premier Cove Memphis TN 38181

SCHNEIDER, PHYLLIS LEAH, writer, editor; b. Seattle, Apr. 19, 1947; d. Edward Lee Booth and Harriet Phyllis (Ebbinghaus) Russell; m. Clifford Donald Schneider, June 14, 1969; 1 child, Pearl Brooke. B.A., Pacific Luth. U., 1969; M.A., U. Wash., 1972. Fiction, features editor Seventeen Mag., N.Y.C., 1975-80; mng. editor Weight Watchers Mag., N.Y.C., 1980-81; editor Young Miss Mag., N.Y.C., 1981-86. Contbr. articles and fiction to mags. Mem. Am. Soc. Mag. Editors. Democrat. Episcopalian.

SCHNEIDER, ROBIN HILARY, sales executive; b. N.Y.C., Apr. 17, 1952; d. Morton Seymour and Clara (Buller) S. BA in Urban History, SUNY, Buffalo, 1973; postgrad., NYU, 1973-74. Sales rep. Amtec, Inc., N.Y.C., 1973-75; pres. New Era Fabrics, Ltd., N.Y.C., 1975-87; v.p. Odyssey Fabrics, Ltd., Los Angeles, 1983; nat. sales mgr. Hilary Lynn Designs, N.Y.C., 1987—. Mem. Am. Photographers Internat. Democrat. Office: Hilary Lynn Designs 390 Fifth Ave New York NY 10018

SCHNEIDER, VALERIE LOIS, speech educator; b. Chgo., Feb. 12, 1941; d. Ralph Joseph and Gertrude Blanche (Gaffron) S.; B.A., Carroll Coll., 1963; M.A., U. Wis., 1966; Ph.D., U. Fla., 1969; cert. advanced study Appalachian State U., 1981. Tchr. English and history Montello High Sch. (Wis.), 1963-64; dir. forensics and drama Montello High Sch., 1963-64; instr. speech U. Fla., Gainesville, 1966-68, asst. prof. speech, 1969-70; asst. prof. speech Edinboro (Pa.) State Coll., 1970-71; assoc. prof. speech East Tenn. State U., Johnson City, 1971-76, prof. speech, 1976—; instr. newspaper course Johnson City Press Chronicle, 1979, Elizabethton Star, Erwin Record, Mountain City Tomahawk, Jonesboro Herald and Tribune, 1980. Editor East Tenn. State Univ. evening and off-campus newsletter, 1984—. Chmn. AAUW Mass Media Study Group Com., Johnson City, 1973-74. Recipient Creative Writing award Va. Highlands Arts Festival, 1973; award Kingsport (Tenn.) Times News, 1984, 85, Tri-Cities Met. Advt. Fedn., 1983, 84; Danforth assoc., 1977. Mem. Speech Communication Assn. (Tenn. rep. to states adv. council 1974-75), So., Tenn. (exec. bd. 1974-77, publs. bd. 1974-78, pres. 1977-78), Religious Speech Communication Assn. (Best article award 1976), Tenn. Basic Skills Council (exec. bd. 1979-80, v.p. 1980-81, pres. 1981-82), AAUW (v.p. chpt. 1974-75, pres. 1975-76, corp. rep. for East Tenn. State U. 1974-76), Am. Assn. Continuing Higher Edn., Bus. and Profl. Women's Club (chpt. exec. bd. 1972-73, v.p. 1976-77), Nat. Assn. Remedial Developmental Studies in Post Secondary Edn., Mensa, Delta Sigma Rho-Tau Kappa Alpha, Phi Delta Kappa, Delta Kappa Gamma, Pi Gamma Mu. Presbyterian. Assoc. editor: Homiletic, 1974-76; columnist Video Visions, Kingsport Times-News (Tenn.), 1984-86; book reviewer Pulpit Digest, 1986—; contbr. articles on speech to profl. jours., newspapers. Home: 3201 Buckingham Rd Johnson City TN 37604 Office: East Tenn State U Box 24429 Johnson City TN 37614

SCHNEIDER-CHANCE, JANET SUE, court administrator; b. Seattle, Mar. 22, 1940; d. Herbert Wilbert and Florence Nancy (Edgar) Baier; m. Charles Vern Schneider, Aug. 27, 1960 (div. May 1978); children: Charles Martin, Melinda Sue, Matthew Herbert; m. Neil Jay Chance, June 28, 1986; 1 child, Jay R. Grad. high sch., Seattle. Legal sec. Swett & Crawford, Seattle, 1958-61; tchr. asst., counselor Capt. Wilks Elem. Sch., Bainbridge Island, Wash., 1967-75; asst. to mayor City of Winslow, Bainbridge Island, 1976-81; ct. adminstr. Winslow Mcpl. Ct., Bainbridge Island, 1981—, ct. probation officer, alcohol coordinator, 1985—; bd. dirs. Winslow (Wash.) Wharf Marina, 1982—. Pres. Children's Orthopedics Guild, Bainbridge Island, 1974-82; leader Girl Scouts Am., Bainbridge Island, 1970-79, Boy Scouts Am., Bainbridge Island, 1974-78; coach Girls Softball, Bainbridge Island, 1979-83, Boys Softball, Bainbridge Island, 1980-82; bd. dirs., sec. Bainbridge Island Broadcasting, 1980—; vol. Heart Assn., Bainbridge Island, 1976-81, Bainbridge Island Library, 1977—, Ednl. TV., Bainbridge Island, 1980—, Winslow Beautification Com., 1981—. Mem. Wash. State Assn. Ct. Adminstrs., Smithsonians Assocs., Exec. Female. Republican. Presbyterian. Home: 3223 46th SW Seattle WA 98116 Office: Winslow Mcpl Ct 625 Winslow Way E Winslow WA 98110

SCHNEIDERHAN, ELIZABETH ROSALIN, community services administrator; b. Niagara Falls, Ont., Can., July 4, 1927; d. Joseph Alphonse and Mary Lucy (Pappaianni) Madia; m. Charles William Schneiderhan, Apr. 7, 1956; children—Charles Joseph, John William. B.A., Toronto U., 1948; M.A. candidate Western Conn. State Coll., 1970. Translator, adminstrv. asst. Carborundum Co., Niagara Falls, N.Y., 1949-56; instr. Bruce High Sch., Westernport, Md., 1957, St. Jude Apostle Sch., Atlanta, 1965-66; legal asst. M.E. Zacharias, Atty., Wilton, Conn., 1975; exec. dir. Ridgefield Community Ctr. (Conn.), 1976-80; specialist program devel. YWCA, Fairfax County, Va., 1981-83; founder, dir. Ridgefield Community Ctr. Adult Edn., 1976-80, editor newsletter, 1976-80; founder, coordinator YWCA Women's Network, Fairfax County, Va., 1982, YWCA Artisan's Studio, Fairfax County, 1982; founder, owner Victorian Inn at Harwich, Harwich Center, Mass. Founder, coordinator Ridgefield Community Ctr. Arts Festival, 1979-80, Ridgefield Arts Council Community Arts Calendar, 1979-80, Ridgefield Arts Council, 1979. Mem. Women in Communications, Am. Soc. Tng. and Devel., AAUW, Fairfax County Council Arts, Darien Community Assn. (treas. 1967-69). Roman Catholic. Home: 102 Parallel St PO Box 340 Harwich MA 02645

SCHNEIDER SMITH, CHRISTINE ANN, human resources consultant; b. Bucyrus, Ohio, Aug. 27, 1951; d. Frank Adolf Jr. and Jeannette Ann (Hall) Schneider; m. Mark Joseph Smith, Dec. 28, 1979; stepchildren: Chad William, Ryan Joseph. MA in Teaching Spanish, U. N.Mex., 1977. Cert. tchr., Ohio. County coordinator Wood, Seneca, Ottawa, Sandusky Community Action Commn., Inc., Fremont, Ohio, 1978-81, planner, contract specialist, 1984-86; exec. vol. United Way of Sandusky County, Fremont, 1981-82; office mgr. A. Schulman Inc., Bellevue, Ohio, 1982-84; cons., trainer CASS Enterprises, Fremont, 1986—; coordinator human resource devel., instr. Vanguard-Sentinel Joint Vocat. Sch. Dist., Fremont, 1986—. Vol. United Way Sandusky County, Fremont, 1980, orientation chmn., 1983-87; bd. mem. Econ. Devel. Corp., Fremont, 1987. Rotary scholar, 1973. Mem. C. of C. Democrat. Methodist. Office: CASS Enterprises PO Box 196 Fremont OH 43420

SCHNEIER, CAROL ANN, computer scientist; b. N.Y.C., Aug. 16, 1951; d. Arthur George and Lillian Frances (Novotny) S.;. BS magna cum laude, SUNY, Stony Brook, 1972; MS, Syracuse (N.Y.) U., 1978; PhD, Ga. Inst. Tech., 1987. With IBM, 1972—; computer programmer Systems Devel. div., Poughkeepsie, N.Y., 1972-75; systems engr. World Trade Corp., Hursley, England; operating systems designer Data Systems div., Poughkeepsie, N.Y., 1976-82; usability analyst Info. Systems group, Atlanta, 1982-87; product planner Application Systems div., Atlanta, 1987-88, applications designer, 1988—. Patentee computer interface simulator, 1986; inventor computer application simulator, 1988; contbr. articles to prof. jours. Mem. staff Women in Sci., St. Lawrence U., Canton, N.Y., 1980. Mem. Spl. Interest Group on Human and Computer Interaction, Assn. for Computing Machinery, Soc. Ga. Archeologists, Nature Conservancy, German Wine Soc., Les Amis du Vin., Audubon Soc. (bd. dirs.), Sig Chi.

SCHNEYER, CHARLOTTE ALPER, physiologist, researcher, educator; b. St. Louis, Nov. 21, 1923; d. Nathan and Anna (Schoenfeld) Alper; m. Leon H. Schneyer, June 11, 1945 (dec. Oct. 1976). A.B. with final honors, Washington U., St. Louis, 1945; M.S., NYU, 1947, Ph.D., 1952. Research asst. Marine Biology Lab. Woods Hole, Mass, 1944; grad. teaching fellow NYU, 1945-52; research assoc. U. Ala., Birmingham, 1952-55, asst. prof. dentistry, 1955-59, assoc. prof. dentistry, 1959-64, prof. dentistry, 1964—, asst. prof. physiology, 1962-65, assoc. prof. physiology, 1965-67, prof., 1967—, dir. Lab. Exocrine Physiology, 1977—, sr. scientist Cystic Fibrosis Research Ctr., 1981—; grant reviewer NIH; mem. spl. grants rev. com. Nat. Inst. Dental Research, 1979-82; mem. nat. adv. gen. med. scis. council Nat. Inst. Health and Gen. Med. Scis., 1972-76. Co-editor: Secretory Mechanisms of Salivary Glands, 1967; contbr. chpts. to numerous books; manuscript reviewer Am. Jour. Physiology, Jour. Autonomic Nervous System, Archives Oral Biology, Jour. Oral Pathology, Jour. Dental Research, others. adj. curator art glass Birmingham Mus. Art, 1985—. Nat. Inst. Dental Research research grantee, 1958—. Mem. Am. Physiol. Soc., Soc. for Exptl. Biology and Medicine, N.Y. Acad. Scis., Sigma Xi, Omicron Kappa Upsilon (hon.), Alpha Lambda Delta. Office: U Ala at Birmingham Dept Physiology University Sta Birmingham AL 35294

SCHNITZER, ARLENE DIRECTOR, art dealer; b. Salem, Oreg., Jan. 10, 1929; d. Simon M. and Helen (Holtzman) Director; m. Harold J. Schnitzer, Sept. 11, 1949; 1 son, Jordan. Student U. Wash., 1947-48; BFA (hon.) Pacific NW Coll. Art., 1988. Founder, pres. Fountain Gallery of Art, Portland, Oreg., 1951-86; sr. v.p. Harsch Investment Corp., 1951—. Appointed to Oreg. State Bd. Higher Edn., 1987; former bd. dirs. Oreg. Symphony Assn., v.p. Oreg. Symphony; bd. dirs., exec. com. U.S. Dist. Ct. Hist. Soc.; mem. Gov.'s Expo '86 Commn., Oreg.; mem. exec. com., former bd. dirs. Artquake; mem. adv. bd. New Beginnings; Recipient Aubrey Watzek award Lewis and Clark Coll., 1981; Pioneer award U. Oreg., 1985; Met. Arts Commn. award, 1985; White Rose award March of Dimes, 1987, disting. service award Western Oreg. Coll. 1988, Oreg. Urban League Equal Opportunity award 1988; Gov's. award for Arts, 1987; honored by Portland Art Assn., 1979; Woman of Achievment award YWCA, 1987. Clubs: University, Multnomah Athletic (Portland), Portland Golf. Office: Harsh Investment Corp 1121 SW Salmon St Portland OR 97205

SCHNURR, CONSTANCE BURKE, personnel specialist; b. Lynn, Mass., Feb. 5, 1932; d. John Edmund Jr. and Beatrice Thérese (Feero) Burke; m. William Bernhardt Schnurr, Nov. 28, 1959. BA, Wellesley (Mass.) Coll., 1953; student, Art Students League, 1953, Am. Art Sch., 1955, Columbia U., 1960-62. Sec. Young & Rubicam, Inc., N.Y.C., 1953-55; art sec. Brooke, Smith, French & Dorrance, N.Y.C., 1955-57; adminstrv. asst. The Rockefeller U., N.Y.C., 1970-75; curatorial asst. Essex Inst. Mus., Salem, Mass., 1957-59; personnel specialist FMC Corp., Phila., 1976—. Author, Illustrator: The Crazy Lady, 1969; illustrator, designer in field. Mem. Wellesley in Phila., The Career Group-W-in-P, Burlington County Footlighters. Democrat. Roman Catholic. Home: 124 Boxwood Ln Cinnaminson NJ 08077 Office: FMC Corp Agr-Chem 2000 Market St Philadelphia PA 19103

SCHNYDER, LINDSAY ANNE, broadcasting company executive; b. Bloomington, Ill., July 2, 1952; d. Robert John Schnyder and Constance (Sherbert) Chaplin. Grad. high sch., Huntington Beach, Calif. Gen. mgr. KZZX Radio, Albuquerque, 1978-80; account exec. KRDO TV, Colorado Springs, Colo., 1980-81, KVOR Radio, Colorado Springs, 1981; mktg. dir. Columbus (Ohio) Zoo, 1981-83; pres., gen. mgr. KOTE-KKZZ Radio, Lancaster, Calif.; v.p., gen. mgr. Programming Consultants, Inc., Albuquerque, 1987-88; v.p. Drake-Chenault Radio Cons., Albuquerque, 1987—; bd. dirs. Antelope Valley Health Found., Lancaster. Bd. dirs. C. of C., Lancaster. Named Exec. of Yr., Sunbelt Communications, 1979, Wagontrain Communications, 1986. Home: 2300 Artesanos Albuquerque NM 87107 Office: Programming Cons Inc 2000 Randolph Rd SE Albuquerque NM 87106

SCHOBER, DOROTHY FLORENCE, consultant; b. Green Bay, Wis., Sept. 19, 1910; d. Max William and Addie (Stone) S.; B.A., U. Wis., 1932; M.P.H., Yale U., 1948; m. Ralph E. Hoffmeyer, Sept. 3, 1982. Visitor, dist. supr., dist. dir. Fla. Welfare Bd., Jacksonville, 1932-37; dir. Pub. Welfare Dept., Green Bay, Wis., 1937-42; cons. Div. Pub. Assistance, Wis. Dept. Pub. Welfare, Madison, 1942-44; counselor USPHS, 1944-45; health edn. cons. Council Social Agys., New Haven, 1946-49; heart work cons. State Com. on Tb and Pub. Health, N.Y., 1949-52; program cons., exec. asst. Am. Heart Assn., 1952-64, asst. dir. affiliate relations and services, 1964-65, asst. dir. dept. councils and internat. program, 1965-70, assoc. dir., 1970-73, assoc. dir. dir. sci. affairs, chief sci. councils, 1973-75. Recipient Gold Heart Bracelet in appreciation 10 year service Staff Conf. Heart Assn., 1962. Fellow Am. Pub. Health Assn.; mem. Phi Kappa Phi, Alpha Kappa Delta. Home: 58-B Calle Cadiz Laguna Hills CA 92653 Home: 1114 11th Ave Albany GA 31707

SCHOCH, CLARISSA ANTHONY, singer, educator, executive assistant; b. Redmond, Oreg., Jan. 17, 1935; d. John Henry and Eleanor (Edwards) Berning; m. Jack Williams Anthony, Jr., June 26, 1960 (dec. 1982); m. Albert E. Schoch, Mar. 22, 1986; children: Rebecca Ellen, Julia Kathleen. B.A., U. Oreg., 1957, M.Mus., 1959. Voice instr. William Paterson Coll., Wayne, N.J., 1979-84, Fairleigh Dickinson U., Rutherford, N.J., 1983—; pvt. practice voice and flute tchr., Upper Montclair, N.J., 1971—; exec. sec. Nat. Westminster Bancorp N.J., 1985—; owner garden ctr. Jack and the Preacher's, Holmdel, N.J., 1972-83; profl. singer, 1959—; soprano soloist Montclair State Coll., 1981-85, William Paterson Coll., 1981-82, Temple Emanu-EL, N.Y.C., 1962-79, Union Congl. Ch., Montclair, 1973—. Chmn. youth com. Union Congl. Ch., 1983-87, mem. parish life, 1985—, mem. music com., 1983-85. Winner voice and oratorio N.J. Young Artists, Nat. Fedn. Music Clubs, N.J., 1966. Mem. Nat. Assn. Tchrs. of Singing (treas. N.J. 1984—), N.Y. Singing Tchrs. Assn. (chairperson young artists auditions 1980-86), Internat. Bach Soc. (performing fellow 1969), AAUW, Phi Beta (nat. grad. grantee 1964). Democrat. Clubs: Montclair Music (Young Artists Audition chairperson 1982—), Rehearsal. Home: 8 Waterbury Rd Upper Montclair NJ 07043

SCHOCH, JACQUELINE LOUISE, university official; b. DuBois, Pa., July 17, 1929; d. Horace Gordon and Cora (Wineberg) S.; B.Sc. in Health and Phys. Edn., Pa. State U., 1951, M.Ed. in Counseling and Psychology, 1960, D.Ed. in Counseling and Psychology, 1965; cert. Inst. Ednl. Mgmt., Harvard U., 1979. Tchr. girls' phys. edn. Jr.-Sr. High Sch., Ford City, Pa., 1951-52; tchr. girl's phys. edn., acad. U.S. history DuBois Area Sr. High Sch., 1952-56, girls' guidance counselor, 1956-65; dir. guidance DuBois Area Sch. Dist., 1965-67, dir. instrn., 1967-70; asst. dir. for resident instrn. DuBois campus Pa. State U., 1970-76, asso. dir. acad. affairs, 1976—, dir. DuBois campus, 1978-83, campus exec. officer, 1983—, also mem., chmn. univ. coms., faculty senate. Instr. polit. action courses local C. of C., 1963; instr. adult swimming classes local YMCA, 1953-55; instr. continuing edn. program Pa. State U., 1967-70, also asst. prof. edn., 1970—. Cons. Appalachia project, W.Va., 1967-68; mem. evaluating teams for evaluating secondary schs. Middle States Evaluation Com., 1960-62; chair Penelec Consumer Adv. Com.; mem. Penelec Ednl. Com.; mem. commn. for women Pa. State U.; mem. adv. com. Pa. State U. Alumni Assn. Bd. dirs. DuBois area United Fund, co-chmn. fund raising campaign, 1967-68, 2d v.p., 1970—; bd. dirs. DuBois council Girl Scouts, 1954-56, Family Life Center-Luth. Services, 1972-76; treas. DuBois Ednl. Found., 1981—; bd. dirs. DuBois Area YMCA; v.p. bd. dirs. Clearfield County Area Agy. on Aging; deacon St. Peters United Ch. of Christ. Named Boss of Yr., Internat. Secs. Assn., 1977. Delta Mu Sigma, Delta Psi Omega, Iota Alpha Delta, Delta Kappa Gamma, Pi Lambda Theta, Phi Delta Kappa. Lodge: Rotary (DuBois). Office: DuBois Campus Pa State U DuBois PA 15801

SCHOCKET, ELINOR, accountant; b. N.Y.C., July 29, 1933; d. Benjamin and Minnie (Hamburger) Horowitz; m. Howard Donalds, Mar. 6, 1953 (div. 1968); children: Beth, Bennett; m. Harold Schocket, Nov. 17, 1972. BS, N.Y.U., 1951-55. Pvt. practice acctg. Fair Lawn, N.J., 1970—; controller N.Y. Delicatessen, N.Y.C., 1983—. Pres. B'nai Brith Women, Fair Lawn, N.J., 1968-69; com. mem Fair Lawn Dem. Club, 1965-70. Mem. N.J. Assn. Pub. Accts., Nat. Assn. Pub. Accts. Office: PO Box 218 Fair Lawn NJ 07410

SCHOCKET, EVE, lawyer; b. Chgo., Apr. 18, 1938; d. Theodore and Sophie (Feldman) Kaplan; m. Lee I. Schocket, Oct. 30, 1960; children—Eric Neal, Luanne Elizabeth. B.S., U. Wis., 1958, M.S.W., 1960; J.D. with distinction, U. Ariz., 1977. Bar: Ariz., 1977. Psychiat. social worker, Wis., Colo., Ariz., 1958-65; lawyer State Ariz. Ct. of Appeals, Tucson, 1977-78, Rabinowitz & Dix, P.C., Tucson, 1978-79; ptnr. Kerry, Schocket & Dusenberry, Tucson, 1979-87; prin., 1987—. Bd. dirs. Law Coll. Assocs., U. Ariz., Tucson, 1983—; mem. bd. edn. Catalina Foothills Sch. Dist., Tucson, 1978-84, clk., 1981-82, pres., 1983. Mem. ABA, Ariz. State Bar, Pima County Bar (bd. dirs.), Ariz. Women Lawyers (pres. So. Ariz. chpt. 1985-86), Nat. Assn. Social Workers, Ariz. Women Lawyers State (bd. dirs.), LWV (bd. dirs. 1970-74), Exec. Women's Council. Home: 2815 E Cerrado Los Palitos Tucson AZ 85718 Office: 2949 E Broadway Tucson AZ 85716

SCHOELD, CONSTANCE JERRINE, financial planner, investment broker; b. Wichita, Kans., July 20, 1935; d. Joe Delos and Volna May (Liston) Lumbert; m. Edmund Allan Schoeld, Oct. 4, 1953 (div. Dec. 1974); children: Nancy Ann., Elsa Charlene, Jennie Marie, Brian Shelton, Richard Zweibruck. Student, St. Olaf Coll., 1953-54, Lindenwood Coll., 1960-62, U. Mich., 1967-68, Harper Jr. Coll., 1970. Cert. fin. planner. Mgr. Walden Books, Schaumburg, Ill., 1972-74; owner Books, Etc., Mt. Prospect, Ill., 1974-77; sales rep. Fawcett Books/CBS, N.Y.C., 1977-78, Lawyers Cooperative Pub., Rochester, N.Y., 1978-83; owner Associated Lawyers Service, Palatine, Ill., 1982-86; broker investments A.G. Edwards & Sons, Aurora and Roselle, Ill., 1983—. Sec. Rep. Orgn. Schaumburg Twp., 1970, Northwest Mental Health/Retardation Ctr., Arlington Hts., Ill., 1971, Mental Health Ctr. Elk Grove/Schaumburg Twp., Ill., 1970-72, vice chmn., bd. dirs.; v.p. PTA, St. Charles, Mo., 1964; pres. St. Charles Girl Scouts Am., 1965-66; mem. com. Dist. 54 Bd. Edn., Schaumburg, 1969-72; bd. dirs. Mental Health Ctr. St. Charles, 1963-66, Mental Health Ctr. Schaumburg Twp., chmn. 1969-72. Named one of Outstanding Young Women Am., 1964. Mem. Internat. Bd. Cert. Fin. Planners, League Women Voters (bd. dirs. St. Charles 1964-66, Hoffman Estates/Schaumburg 1969-71), DAR (outstanding mem. award 1964), Greater O'Hare Assn., Nat. Assn. Women in Careers, Nat. Assn. Female Execs., Epsilon Sigma Alpha (outstanding mem. award 1970). Republican. Episcopalian. Office: AG Edwards & Sons 1350 W Lake St Roselle IL 60172

SCHOENBERGER, NANCY JANE, poet, educator, arts administrator; b. Oakland, Calif., Dec. 3, 1950; d. Sigmund Bernard and Betty Ellen (Beydler) S. B.A., La. State U., 1972, M.A., 1974; M.F.A., Columbia U., 1981. Instr. U. Mont., Missoula, 1975-78; editor Columbia, A Mag. of Poetry & Prose, Columbia U., N.Y.C., 1980-81; assoc. producer N.Y. Ctr. for Visual History, N.Y.C., 1981-82; program dir. Acad. Am. Poets, N.Y.C., 1982—; cons. Mont. Com. for Humanities, 1976-78; vis. artist Poetry in the Schs., Missoula, 1978-79; instr. creative writing workshop Acad. Am. Poets, 1983—, assoc. prof., adjunct poetry workshop, Columbia U., 1988—; presenter poetry readings; resident Centrum, Port Townsend, Wash., 1984, Rockefeller Found.'s Bellagio Study and Conf. Ctr., 1985. Author: The Taxidermist's Daughter, 1979; Girl on a White Porch (Devins award), 1987; contbr. poems to various jours. Nat. Endowment for Arts poetry fellow, 1984; recipient N.Y. Found. for the Arts award, 1988. Mem. Poetry Soc. Am. (Mary Carolyn Davies Meml. award 1984). Office: Acad Am Poets 177 E 87th St New York NY 10128

SCHOENEBERG, DEBRA SUE, graphic designer; b. Amory, Miss., Nov. 30, 1953; d. Kenneth Walter and Margaret Christina (Linville) S. Assoc. of tech., Am. Acad. Art, 1974. Artist J & J Publs., Evanston, Ill., 1974-75; dir. art Ken Roush & Assocs., Lincolnwood, Ill., 1975-76, Hahn, Crane Advt., Chgo., 1976-82; owner Schöeneberg Design, Evanston, 1982—. Recipient Chgo. Addy award Am. Advt. Fedn. 6th Dist., 1980, Cert. of Excellence Direct Mktg. Echo, 1980, Cert. of Achievement Chgo. Assn. Direct Mktg., 1984, Desi award Graphic Design USA, 1987; named Ad Woman of Yr. nominee, 1982; named one of Outstanding Young Women in Am., 1987. Mem. Women in Design/Chgo. (designer/coordinator newsletter 1986—, bd. dirs. 1986—, dir. spl. programs 1988—, Cert. Excellence, 1985), Women's Advt. Club Chgo., Chgo. Artists Coalition. Presbyterian. Home and Office: 337 Sherman Ave Evanston IL 60202

SCHOENEMAN, MARCELLE ANN, federal agency administrator; b. Wausau, Wis., June 4, 1921. BA in Applied Behavioral Sci., Nat. Coll. Edn., 1981, MS in Mgmt. and Devel. of Human Resources, 1983. Supr. clerical processing U.S. Govt., Milw., 1956-66, loan asst., 1966-71, loan specialist, 1971-76, chief loan mgmt. br., 1976—. Lay reader St. Thomas of Canterbury Episcopal Ch., Greendale, Wis., 1980—. Mem. Fed. Mgrs. Assn., Nat. League Am. Penwomen, Fed. Execs. Assn., Milwaukee County Geneal. Soc., AAUW. Lodge: Rosicrucians (AMORC). Home: 3174 S 57th St Milwaukee WI 53219 Office: US Dept Housing and Urban Devel 310 W Wisconsin Ave Suite 1380 Milwaukee WI 53203

SCHOENER, LYNN ANN, marketing professional, interior decorator; b. Dayton, Ohio, Aug. 2, 1956; d. Henry Paul and Ann Elizabeth (Lyons) Blaeser; m. John Robert Schoener, Sept. 6, 1980. BS summa cum laude, U. Cin., 1979. Fashion and publicity dir. Saks Fifth Ave., Houston, 1979-81; designer TransDesigns, Houston, 1981-83, design dir., 1983-86; mktg. coordinator TransDesigns, Houston and Atlanta, 1986-88, dir. nat. pub. relations, 1988—; owner Tiger Lilly and Friends, Houston, 1981-86, Post Scripts, Houston, 1981-86; speaker, instr. on decorating various groups, Houston, 1984—. Co-editor (newsletter) Transitions, 1985-86. Recipient Klopman award Klopman Mills, 1979, Litwin Diamond award Litwin Diamond Co., 1979. Democrat. Home: 8823 Cold Lake Dr Houston TX 77088 Office: TransDesigns 1000 Transart Pkwy Woodstock GA 30188

SCHOENIKE, SALLY ANN, agricultural extension agent; b. Hustisford, Wis., Aug. 26, 1956; d. Lester J. and Lucille (Schuett) Schwartz; m. James H. Schoenike, May 23, 1987. BS in Bus. Edn., U. Wis., Whitewater, 1978, MS in Teaching, 1979. Bus. tchr. Hartford (Wis.) Union High Sch., 1978-82; 4-H and youth agt., asst. prof. dept. youth devel. U. Wis. Extension, Juneau, 1982—. Contbr. articles to profl. jours. Named Outstanding Young Alumni U. Wis.-Whitewater, 1982. Mem. Assn. Extension 4-H and Youth Agts. (Wis. treas. 1986), Nat. Assn. Parliamentarians, Wis. Assn. Parliamentarians, Phi Beta Lambda, Delta Pi Epsilon, Kappa Delta Pi. Lutheran. Club: Toastmasters. Home: W1917 Washington Rd Oconomowoc WI 53066 Office: U Wis Extension Courthouse Annex Juneau WI 53036

SCHOENWETTER, JANET LOREE, claims specialist; b. Des Moines, June 30, 1956; d. Wilbur Alfred and Margaret Loree (Audlehelm) Musson; m. Randall Robert Schoenwetter, Aug. 14, 1976. Cert. in Fashion Mdsg., Patricia Stevens Career Coll., Milw. Claims processor Aetna Life and Casualty, Milw., 1977-79, sr. claims processor, 1979-80, claims specialist, 1980-81, auditor, trainer, 1981-82; claims supr. NBP Inc., Milw., 1982-85; claims dir. Primecare Health Plan, Milw., 1985-87; spl. projects coordinator Mgmt. Employee Group Adminstrs. Corp., Milw., 1987-88, claims supr., 1988—; cons. NBP Inc., Milw., 1985—. Mem. Village of Elm Grove Artists, Wis., Wis. Mem. Nat. Assn. Female Execs., Smithsonian Instn. Republican. Home: N 5 W 29156 Venture Hill Rd Waukesha WI 53188 Office: 2 Park Plaza 10850 W Park Pl Milwaukee WI 53224

SCHOESSOW, DONNA KAY, manager of interior design firm; b. Los Angeles, Mar. 25, 1943; d. Theodore Charles and Hildegarde Alice (Albrecht) Schoessow. Student Santa Monica City Coll., 1961-62, Fullerton Jr. Coll., 1963-66, Coll. of San Mateo, 1973-74, Cabrillo Coll., 1977-78. Lic. real estate salesman, Calif.; notary pub. Constrn. coordinator Walter Beeson & Assocs., Fullerton, Calif., 1965-70; coordinator partnership affairs Fox and Carskadon Fin., Menlo Park, Calif., 1972-74; dir. land acquisition and planning McKeon Constrn., San Mateo, Calif., 1975-78; systems coordinator Concordia Devel. Corp., San Bernardino, Calif., 1978-80; sec., gen. mgr. Vesper Corp., Downey, Calif., 1981-86; manager interior design Catherine Wallick Interiors, Newport Beach, Calif., 1987—; corp. officer Elizabeth Gardens Homeowners Assn., Cudahy, Calif., 1982-86; corp. officer Elizabeth Gardens, Cudahy, Calif., 1982-85. Author: To See or Not To See, 1982; editor: How To Become a Developer, 1983. Pres. Fish of Fullerton, 1983-86, v.p., 1986—; bd. dirs. Emergency Med. Info., Inc., Santa Ana, Calif., Good

Shepherd Homes/Value Village Mgmt. Mem. Nat. Assn. Women in Constrn. (corr. sec. 1979-80, pres. 1981-82, 85-86, dir. 1982-83, 86-87, scholarship chmn. 1981-82, 85-86, chmn. profl. edn., 1979-81, chaplain 1982-83, 86-87), Juvenile Diabetes Found. Republican. Lutheran. Home: 4237 E Alderdale Ave Anaheim CA 92807 Office: Catherine Wallick Interiors 666 Baker St # 315 Costa Mesa CA 92626

SCHOETTLER, GAIL SINTON, state treasurer; b. Los Angeles, Oct. 21, 1943; d. James and Norma (McLellan) Sinton; m. John H. Schoettler, Sept. 11, 1965; children: Lee, Thomas, James. BA in Econs., Stanford U., 1965; MA in History, U. Calif., Santa Barbara, 1969, PhD in History, 1975. Businesswoman Denver, 1975-83; exec. dir. Colo. Dept. of Personnel, Denver, 1983-86; treas. State of Colo., Denver, 1987—; bd. dirs. Pub. Employees Retirement Assn., Denver; past bd. dirs. Women's Bank, Denver; Littleton, Colo., Equitable Bankshares of Colo., Denver. Mem. Douglas County Bd. Edn., Colo., 1979-87, pres., 1983-87; trustee U. No. Colo., Greeley, 1981-87; pres. Denver Children's Mus., 1975-85. Mem. Nat. Women's Forum (bd. dirs., pres. 1983-85), Women Execs. in State Govt. (bd. dirs. 1981-87, chmn. 1988), Leadership Denver Assn. (bd. dirs. 1987, named Outstanding Alumna 1985), Nat. Assn. State Treas., Stanford Alumni Assn. Democrat.

SCHOFIELD, ELLEN TINA, marketing executive; b. N.Y.C., Feb. 14, 1959; d. Leonard and Clara (Grubman) Dinner; m. Steven E. Schofield, July 29, 1957. BA, SUNY, Albany, 1980. Entertainment agt. New Line Presentations, N.Y.C., 1980-81; contracts adminstr. Random House, Inc., N.Y.C., 1981; sales adminstr. Sky Courier Network, N.Y.C., 1981-85, sales and mktg. rep., 1986-87; asst. acct. exec. Deutsch, Shea and Evans., N.Y.C., 1985; asst. v.p. Express Courier Network, N.Y.C., 1987—. Sponsor Covenant House 1987, So. Poverty Law Ctr., Montgomery, Ala., 1985—; mem. Raoul Wallenberg New Leadership Soc. of Simon Weisenthal Ctr., N.Y.C., 1984—. Mem. Mail Systems Mgmt. Assn., The Wilderness Soc., People For The Ethical Treatment of Animals. Democrat. Jewish. Club: Sierra. Home: 652 Carroll St Brooklyn NY 11215 Office: Express Courier Network 250 W 57th St New York NY 10007

SCHOLL, DEBORAH SUE, banker; b. South Bend, Ind., Sept. 16, 1953; d. Karl Henry and Elizabeth Anna (Eckel) S.; m. Mark C. Kellberg, Dec. 30, 1981. BA, Mundelein Coll., 1982; postgrad., DePaul U., 1984—. Long distance operator Ill. Bell Telephone Co., Barrington, 1974-76; research asst. Quaker Oats Co., Barrington, 1976-78; various positions Quill Corp., Northbrook, Ill., 1978-79; systems analyst Harris Bank, Chgo., 1979-85; systems officer First Nat. Bank Chgo., 1985—; cons. Fed. Wood Floors, Evanston, Ill., 1986—, Pleasure Travel Unltd., Chgo., 1987. Vol. March of Dimes, Chgo., 1982—, Blind Service Assn., 1985—. Mem. Info. Ctr. Exchange (mktg. and membership dir.). Lutheran. Office: First Nat Bank Chgo Suite 0249 Chicago IL 60670-0249

SCHOLL, DEBRA LYNN, sales executive; b. Myrtle Point, Oreg., Sept. 29, 1956; d. Elsworth Leroy Nelson and Sandra Jean (Roberson) Nelson Elbert; m. Douglas Kent Scholl, Aug. 25, 1984. Student Chapman Coll., 1976-77, Saddleback Coll., 1980; teaching cert. J.R. Powers Trade Sch., 1978. Personnel asst. Chapman Coll., Orange, Calif., 1976-78; personnel asst. Kimstock, Inc., Santa Ana, Calif., 1978-79, sales rep., 1979-84, sales mgr. for So. Calif., 1984-87; owner, founder D & D Sales, Mission Viejo, Calif., 1987—. Active fund raising for City of Hope, Los Angeles, 1983—. Mem. The Exec. Female, NOW, Republican Nat. Com. Avocations: sewing, reading. Home: 24671 Sadaba Mission Viejo CA 92692 Office: D & D Sales 25108 Marguerite Pkwy Suite B-249 Mission Viejo CA 92692

SCHOLL, IDAMAE, bank administration executive; b. St. Paul; d. Louis Gotlieb and Isabelle Mae (Campbell) Reeck; m. Lloyd Leonard Scholl; children: Thomas, Steven, Jerome. BA, U. Mo., Carthage, 1954; postgrad. bus. mgmt., Mgmt. Ctr., 1970; postgrad. mgmt. sci., Mpls. Tech. Inst., 1971; postgrad. telecommunications, Drake U., 1984. Savs. supr. First Nat. Bank, St. Paul, 1963-69; with Norwest Bank, St. Paul, 1969—, adminstrv. services mgr., 1982—. Pres., bd. dirs. Capitol Community Services, St. Paul, 1983—; bd. dirs. Nat. Coll. Bd., St. Paul, 1982—; vol. Battered Women's Shelter, St. Paul, 1983-86; float chmn. St. Paul Winter Carnival Assn., 1983, 85; solicitor St. Paul United Way,1985-86, mem. steering com. 1987—; solicitor ARC, 1983-86, Am. Cancer Soc., 1985-86. Recipient Theme awards, St. Paul Winter Carnival Assn., 1983, 86, 87, YWCA Leadership award, Norwest Corp., 1984, 86. Mem. Internat. Women in Telecommunications (charter), Nat. Fedn. Bus. and Profl. Women (nat. task force, 1985-86, Minn. 2d v.p. 1986-87, Minn. 1st v.p. 1987—, named Bus. Woman of Yr., 1983, Minn. Woman of Achievement award 1987, pres. elect 1988), Nat. Assn. Bank Women, Am. Inst. Banking, Minn. Women's Consortium, Minn. Econ. Devel. Assn., Female Execs. Minn., Minn. Minority Purchasing Council, Northwest Corp. Vol. Council (service award 1987). Home: 6301 Oak Knoll Plaza Woodbury MN 55125

SCHOLL, PRISCILLA IRENE, nursing administrator; b. Amherst, Wis., Mar. 17, 1925; d. Charles Gerald and Lydia Francis (Schrader) Shanklin; grad. Deaconess Hosp. Sch. Nursing, 1946; student Milw. Tech. Coll., 1957-58, U. Wis., Milw., 1958-71; B.S. in Health Arts, Coll. of St. Francis, 1981; m. Robert Philip Scholl, May 22, 1948; children—Judith Ann, Susan. Staff nurse Deaconess Hosp., Milw., 1946-49, staff nurse circulating evenings, 1956-57, asst. clin. instr. and nursing service supr., 1957-64, inservice supr., 1964-67, supr. and instr. of renal program, 1966, ret. Good Samaritan Med. Ctr., 1987, cons. Dialysis Mgmt. and Nephrology Nursing. guest lectr. on renal failure to various nursing orgns. and lay orgns., 1970-78. Bd. dirs. Kidney Found. of Wis., 1973—, mem. med. and sci. com., 1973—, patient services com., 1971-75, chmn., 1974-75. Mem. Am. Nurses Assn., Am. Assn. Nephrology Nurses and Technicians (organizer Wis. chpt. 1978, pres. 1985-86) Am. Nephrology Nurses Assn. (pres. 1987—), Network 13 (sec.-treas. exec. com. 1984-86). Pioneer in nephrology nursing.

SCHOLTZ, ELIZABETH, botanical garden administrator; b. Pretoria, South Africa, Apr. 29, 1921; came to U.S., 1960, naturalized, 1978; d. Tielman Johannes and Vera Vogel (Roux) Roos-Scholtz. B.Sc., Witwatersrand U., 1941; D.H.L., Pace U., 1974; D.Sc., L.I. U., 1982. Technician South African Inst. Med. Research, Johannesburg, 1942-44; technician dept. medicine Johannesburg and Pretoria gen. hosps., 1944-46; with Groote Schuur Hosp., Capetown; as technician charge student labs. Groote Schuur Hosp., 1948-52, technician charge hematology lab., 1952-60; mem. staff Bklyn. Bot. Garden, 1960—, asso. curator instrn., 1964-71, acting dir., 1972-73, dir., 1973-80, v.p., 1980-87, dir. emeritus, 1987—; trustee Independence Savs. Bank. Recipient Arthur Hoyt Scott Garden and Horticulture award, 1981. Mem. Am. Hort. Soc. (Liberty Hyde Bailey medal 1984), Am. Assn. Bot. Gardens and Arboreta (dir. 1976-79). Clubs: Brooklyn Heights Casino, Cosmopolitan. Home: 115 Henry St Brooklyn NY 11201 Office: Bklyn Bot Garden 1000 Washington Ave Brooklyn NY 11225

SCHOLZ, JANE, publisher; b. St. Louis, July 31, 1948; d. Robert Louis and Mildred Virginia (Hudgins) S.; m. Jay W. Johnson, June 1979 (div. Dec. 1981); m. Douglas C. Balz, Jan. 1, 1983. B.A., Mich. State U., 1970; M.B.A., U. Miami, 1981. Reporter Jour.-Gazette, Fort Wayne, Ind., 1970-73; reporter The Miami Herald, Fla., 1973-77, asst. city editor, 1977-80; advanced mgmt. devel. participant Knight-Ridder Inc., Miami, Fla., 1980-85; pres., pub. Post-Tribune, Gary, Ind., 1985—. Bd. dirs. United Way of Lake county, Ind., Gary chpt. Urban League, Ind., NW Ind. Forum, Tradewinds Rehab. Ctr. Mem. Am. Newspaper Pubs. Assn., Ind. C. of C. (bd. dirs.), Inland Press Assn. (bd. dirs.), Sigma Delta Chi. Home: 7118 Forest Ave Hammond IN 46324 Office: Post-Tribune Post-Tribune Pub Inc 1065 Broadway Gary IN 46402

SCHOLZ, PAMELA DELL, artist; b. San Antonio, June 9, 1944; d. Dan Robert and Dell (DuBose) S. BFA, La. State U., 1962, MA, 1971, MFA, 1972. Exhibited in group shows at 10th ann. Piedmont Painting and Sculpture Exhbn., Mint Mus. Art, Charlotte, N.C., 1970, 3d Greater New Orleans Nat. Exhbn. at Internat. Trade Mart, 1973, Mainstreams Exhbn., Grover M. Herman Fine Arts Ctr., Marietta (Ohio) Coll., 1974, 19th ann. Juried Exhbn. Delta Regional Primate Ctr., 1984, Contemporary Art Ctr., La., Tex., New Orleans, 1980, Lawndale Annex U. Houston Cen. Campus, 1980, Cin. Mus. Nat. History, 1982, 84, 85, Faber Birren Color Award show, Stamford, Conn., 1983, Nat. Soc. Painters in Cassin and Acrylic Painting, Nat. Arts Club, N.Y.C., 1984. One woman shows at U. Southwestern La., Lafayette, 1971, Crescent Gallery, 1980, Nahan Galleries, New Orleans, 1976, Reinike Gallery, New Orleans, 1987; creator drawing for mag. cover Arts and Humanities Council of La., 1985, other group and one-woman shows; commd. mural East Baton Rouge City-Parish Govt., 1977. Treas. Baton Rouge Orchid Soc., 1985. Recipient Purchase award Internat. Trade Mart, 1973, Award of Merit Faber Birren Color Award Show, 1983, 2d pl. award Delta Regional Primate Ctr., 1984, hon. mention painting and graphics 8th ann. Contemporary Art Festival, Baton Rouge, 1970, 1st pl. award 23d ann. Regional Juried Exhbn., 1985. Mem. Baton Rouge Orchid Soc. (treas. 1985—). Office: Reinike Gallery 300 Dauphine New Orleans LA 70112

SCHONTHALER, JOAN ANN, psychotherapist; b. Providence, Nov. 7, 1948; d. Kurt William and Mildred Emily (Lutz); m. James Anthony Charles, Aug. 14, 1976; children: Justin Joseph, Lauren Elizabeth. BA in English and Psychology, Mercy Coll., Detroit, 1976; MS in Clin. Psychology, Ea. Mich. U., 1980. Cert. forensic examiner, profl. counselor, Ga.; lic. social worker, Mich. Regional youth coordinator Fla. Drug Abuse Program, West Palm Beach, 1972-74; therapist Boniface Community Action Corp., Detroit, 1974-76; sr. women's therapist Rubicon-Odyssey House, Detroit, 1975-76; chief clinician Ctr. Forensic Psychiatry, Ann Arbor, Mich., 1976-80; dir. adult services Dekalb County Mental Health, Decatur, Ga., 1980-82; profl. devel. cons. So. Co. Services, Atlanta and Birmingham, Ala., 1984-85; pres. The Counseling Coop., Atlanta, 1985—; dir. psychol. services Nat. Med. Systems, Inc., Atlanta, 1987-88; cons. in field. Contbr. articles to profl. jpurs. Bd. dirs. Open City/CREATE, Atlanta, 1985-88. Mem. Ga. Psychol. Assn., Am. Assn. Counseling and Devel. Democrat. Home: 519 Saint Charles Ave NE Atlanta GA 30308 Office: Counseling Coop PO Box 8391 Atlanta GA 30306

SCHOOLEY, DOLORES HARTER, entertainment administrator; b. Nora Springs, Iowa, May 2, 1905; d. Amil A. and Elizabeth (Sefert) Zemke; m. Leslie J. Harter, June 5, 1934 (dec. 1963); m. Charles Earl Schooley, Apr. 1, 1966. B.E., B.A., U. Colo., 1927; M.A., Northwestern U., 1931. Tchr. high sch. Consol. Schs., Johnstown, Colo., 1927-28, Byers, Colo., 1928-29, Clayton, Mo., 1931-34; theatrical makeup, 1937-86; instr. theatrical makeup, dramatic clubs, N.J. Theatre League; lectr., demonstrator theatrical makeup, dramatic and women's clubs, high schs., N.J. and N.Y. area, 1937-53; dir., entertainer mil. posts First Army, 1951-53; dir. mil. project Phi Beta, 1951-61, nat. officer, mem. nat. council, 1956-61, cons. radio broadcast series WNYC, 1962-65; dir. community relations Wingspread Summer Theatre, Colon, Mich., 1955; co-chmn. Valley Shore Community Concerts, Conn., 1958-61; artist mgr., 1959—; chmn. benefit ball Sharon Hosp., 1970; founder, pres. Berkshire Hills Music and Dance Assn., 1970-78; mem. Music Mountain Corp., Falls Village, Conn., 1975-81. Trustee Sharon Creative Arts Found., 1970-73; hon. trustee Bar Harbor Festival, 1968—; founder, pres. Wingspread Found., 1977—. Mem. Alpha Omicron Pi, Phi Beta. Congregationalist. Clubs: Montclair (N.J.) Dramatic (chmn. makeup, instr. makeup); Rehearsal (program chmn.); Women's (dir. plays, chmn. drama dept.) (Glen Ridge, N.J.); Sharon Women's, Sharon Republican Women's (pres. 1982-85), Sharon Country (Conn.). Address: PO Box 633 Winter Haven FL 33882 also: 210 Crooked Creek Rd Hendersonville NC 28739

SCHOOLS, ANNA LOUISE, town official; b. Littleton, Maine, May 17, 1915; d. Thomas Allen and Hannah Teresa (Rugan) Schools. Student public schs. Houlton, Maine. Town mgr. City of Littleton, Maine, 1945—, collector, treas., 1943—, town clk., 1944—. Mem. Maine Town and City Mgrs. Assn. Democrat. Roman Catholic. Clubs: So. Aroostook Campers (past pres.), Sno-Rovers Inc. (sec. treas.). Avocation: Camping. Home: 3 Watson Ave Houlton MA 04730 Office: Town Littleton RFD 1 Box 70 Monticello ME 04760

SCHOON, DORIS VIVIEN, ophthalmologist; b. Luverne, Minn., Dec. 31, 1928; d. Jacob and Esther Viola (Hansen) S. B.A., U. Minn., 1950, M.D., 1954. Intern, Kings County Hosp., Bklyn., 1954-55; physician Embudo Presbyterian Hosp. (N. Mex.), 1955-57; resident in clin. pathology U. Colo. Med. Ctr., Denver, 1957-58; gen. practice medicine, Anaheim, Calif., 1958-61; resident in ophthalmology Los Angeles Eye and Ear Hosp. at Hollywood Presbyn. Hosp., 1961-64; practice medicine specializing in ophthalmology, Anaheim, 1965-75; dir. Electrophysiology Lab. of Ophthalmology Dept. U. Calif., Irvine, 1978—. Research in field of using fast random stimuli to obtain electroretinograms and visually evoked potentials. Diplomat Am. Bd. Ophthalmology. Fellow Am. Acad. Ophthalmology and Otolaryngology; mem. Am. Women's Med. Assn., N.Y. Acad. Scis., Internat. Soc. Clin. Electrophysiology in Vision. Republican. Presbyterian. Lodge: Order Eastern Star. Office: 19732 MacArthur Blvd Irvine CA 92715

SCHOONOVER, JEAN WAY, public relations executive; b. Richfield Springs, N.Y.. AB, Cornell U., 1941. With D-A-Y Pub. Relations, Ogilvy & Mather Co., N.Y.C., 1949—; with D-A-Y Pub. Relations Inc. and predecessor, N.Y.C., 1949—; owner, pres. Dudley-Anderson-Yutzy Pub. Relations Inc. and predecessor, N.Y.C., 1970—; chmn. Dudley-Anderson-Yutzy Pub. Relations Inc. and predecessor, 1984—; merger with Ogilvy & Mather, 1983; sr. v.p. Ogilvy & Mather U.S., 1984—; vice chmn. Ogilvy & Mather Pub. Relations Group, 1986—; mem., historian, Pub. Relations Seminar; mem. U.S. Dept. Agriculture Agribusiness Promotion Council, 1985—. Trustee Cornell U., 1975-80. Named Advt. Woman of Yr. Am. Advt. Fedn., 1972, one of Outstanding Women in Bus. & Labor, Women's Equity Action League, 1985.; recipient Matrix award, 1976, Nat. Headliner award, 1984, N.Y. Women in Communications, 1976, leadership award Internat. Orgn. Women Bus. Owners, 1980, Entreprenurial Woman award Women Bus. Owners N.Y., 1981. Mem. Women Execs. in Pub. Relations N.Y.C. (pres. 1979-80), Advt. Women N.Y., Pub. Relations Soc. Am., Pub. Relations Soc. N.Y. (pres. 1979), Am. Women in Communications (presdl. adv. com. 1982-84), Def. Adv. Com. on Women in The Services. Home: 25 Stuyvesant St New York NY 10003 Office: D-A-Y Pub Relations 40 W 57th St New York NY 10019

SCHOONOVER-CRICHTON, SHARI LYNN, communications company executive; b. Seattle, June 19, 1957; d. Quinton Roy and Virginia Marguerite (Millo) Schoonover; m. Robert Edward Crichton, Aug. 23, 1986; 1 child, Brooke Erin. AA in Bus., Everett Community Coll., 1979; BA in Mktg./Mgmt., U. Puget Sound, 1983. Mgr. non foods Olsons Foods, Lynnwood, Wash., 1977-79; sales rep. Tim Aspinall and Assocs., Bellevue, Wash., 1979-80, Revlon, Inc., N.Y.C., 1980-82; account exec. AT&T Info. Systems, Seattle, 1982-83, Pacific NW Bell, US West, Seattle, 1983-84; sales rep. U.S. West Info Systems, Seattle, 1984-86; account exec. Rho Co., Inc., Redmond, Wash., 1986-87; personnel dir. Bonneville Constrn. Co. Inc., Bellevue, Wash., 1987—. Editor newsletter Dial Tone, 1987. Mem. Wash. Communications Assn. (sec., treas. 1987—), Profl. Bus. Women Assn.

SCHOONOVER-SHOFFNER, KATHRYN LOUISE, nurse; b. Chanute AFB, Ill., Dec. 20, 1957; d. Russell Dean Sr. and Elizabeth Ann (Congdon) Schoonover; m. Richard Wayne Shoffner, July 10, 1982. BS in Nursing, U. Tex., Arlington, 1979; MS in Nursing, Oral Roberts U., 1982. RN, Clin. Nursing Specialist. Staff nurse, relief asst. patient care coordinator Med. Plaza Hosp., Ft. Worth, 1979-80; staff nurse, relief charge nurse, team leader, intensive care areas St. John Med. Ctr., Tulsa, 1980-82; adminstrv dir. cardiac rehab. program St. Francis Regional Med. Ctr., Wichita, Kans., 1982-85; research nurse coordinator Midwest Heart and Vascular Inst., Wichita, 1985—; doctoral student, research asst. U. Kans. Sch. of Nursing, 1987—; adj. clin. instr. Wichita State U., 1986—. Vol., speaker ARC, Wichita, Am. Heart Assn. Mem. Am. Nurses Assn., Kans. State Nurses Assn., Am. Assn. Critical Care Nurses, Greater Wichita Area Assn. Critical Care Nurses, Nat. League of Nursing, Midwest Nursing Research Soc., Sigma Theta Tau, Alpha Phi.

SCHOR, MARY ANN MCCARTHY (MRS. WARREN SCHOR), public relations exec.; b. Washington; d. Jeremiah John and Ann (Horstkamp) McCarthy; grad. George Washington U., 1962, grad. publ. specialist program, 1977; EPS Program, Trinity Coll., 1982; m. Warren Schor, May 2, 1964; 1 dau., Elizabeth Ann. Public relations, various accounts, Washington, 1962-66; dir. public relations program Met. Police Dept., Washington, 1966-69; public relations D.C. Dept. Public Health, Washington, 1979-70, D.C. Police Dept., Washington, 1970-75; public relations cons., 1976—. Mem. public relations com. D.C. Tb and Respiratory Disease Assn., 1969—. Mem. Am. Newspaper Women's Club (bd. dirs 1988), Advt. Club Washington, Zonta. Roman Catholic. Editor: Rambling thru Georgetown, 1978-80; Rambling thru Alexandria, 1978-80. Home: 6206 Wedgewood Rd Bethesda MD 20817

SCHOR, OLGA SEEMANN, mental health counselor, real estate broker; b. Havana, Cuba, Mar. 2, 1951; came to U.S., 1961; d. Olga del Carmen (Hernandez) S.; m. David Michael Schor, Apr. 22, 1979; 1 child, Andrew. A.A., Miami Dade Community Coll., 1971; B.A., U. Fla.-Gainesville, 1973; M.Edn., U. Miami, Fla., 1976; Psy.D., Nova U., 1981; cert. Bert Rodgers Sch. Real Estate, Miami, 1981, Gold Coast Sch. Real Estate, 1988; lic. real estate broker. Teaching asst. U. Fla., Gainesville, 1972-73; counselor U. Miami, Fla., 1974-79; assoc. psychotherapist Linda H. Jamrozy & Assocs., Miami, 1976-78, Interactive Systems, Miami, 1978-79; psychometrist Jackson Meml. Hosp., Miami, 1978-79; assoc. psychotherapist Behavioral Medicine Inst., Miami, 1979-85, Tony Ciminero & Assocs., Miami, 1985-86; lectr. U. Miami, 1976-78, Jackson Meml. Hosp. Sch. Nursing, Miami, 1976; real estate broker The Keyes Co. Realtor, Coral Gables, 1981—; sec./treas. bd. dirs. BODS Inc., Miami. Recipient Assoc. of Quarter award Keyes Co. Realtors, 1986. Mem. Am. Psychol. and Guidance Assn., Keyes Comml. Roundtable, Coral Gables Bd. Realtors, Dade County Mental Health Assn., Million Dollar Sales Club. Club: South Fla. Sailing Assn. (Miami). Avocations: sailing; diving; reading; running; theater; acting; tennis. Office: 357 Miracle Mile Coral Gables FL 33134

SCHORR, BEVERLY HELEN, counselor; b. Phila., Aug. 23, 1934; d. Isadore and Anne (Greber) Rubin; m. David Jay Schorr, Aug. 31, 1952; children—Alan, Michael, Steven, Devra. B.A., Villanova U., 1975, M.A., 1977. Dir. adult programs Villanova U., Pa., 1976-83; treas. D.J.S. Assocs., Inc., Abington, Pa., 1982—; sales assoc. Milton Levy Real Estate. Chmn. Lower Southampton Commn., Trevose, Pa., 1978—; bd. dirs. Beth Sholom Synagogue Sisterhood. Office: 1603 Old York Dr Abington PA 19001

SCHORR, LISBETH BAMBERGER, child and family policy analyst, author, educator; b. Munich, Germany, Jan. 20, 1931; d. Fred S. and Lotte (Krafft) Bamberger; m. Daniel L. Schorr, Jan. 8, 1967; children—Jonathan, Lisa. B.A. with highest honors, U. Calif., Berkeley, 1952. Med. care cons. U.A.W. and Community Health Assn., Detroit, 1956-58; asst. dir. Dept. Social Security AFL-CIO, Washington, 1958-65; acting chief CAP Health Services, 1965-66; chief program planning Office for Health Affairs, OEO, Washington, 1967; cons. Children's Def. Fund, Washington, 1973-79; scholar-in-residence Inst. of Medicine, 1979-80; chmn. Select Panel on Promotion Child Health, 1979-80; adj. prof. maternal and child health U. N.C., Chapel Hill, 1981-85; lectr. social medicine and health policy Harvard U. Med. Sch., 1984—; mem. working group early life and adolescent health policy Harvard U. Div. Health Policy Research and Edn., 1982—; nat. council Alan Gutmacher Inst., 1974-79, 82-85; pub. mem. Am. Bd. Pediatrics, 1978-84; vice chmn. Found. for Child Devel., 1978-84, bd. dirs. 1976-84, 86—,; bd. dirs. Nat. Center Clin. Infant Programs, 1981—; mem. Inst. of Medicine Bd. Mental Health and Behavioral Medicine, 1984—; mem. council Nat. Resource Ctr. for Children in Poverty, 1987—; mem. children's program adv. com. Edna McConnell Clark Found., 1987—; mem. steering com. Nat. Forum on the Future of Children and Their Families, 1988—. Author: Within Our Reach: Breaking the Cycle of Disadvantage, 1988. Mem. Inst. Medicine, Nat. Acad. Scis. (mem. council 1975-78), Phi Beta Kappa. Home: 3113 Woodley Rd NW Washington DC 20008

SCHORR, THELMA M., publishing company executive, nurse; b. New Haven, Dec. 15, 1924; d. Simon and Rebecca (Katz) Mermelstein; m. Norman A. Schorr, Mar 6, 1955; children—Susan, Marjorie, Elizabeth. Diploma, Bellevue Sch. Nursing, 1945; B.S., Columbia U., N.Y.C., 1952; D.Sc. in Nursing (hon.), U. Pa., 1985; D Nursing (hon.), Vt. Coll., Norwich U.; D.Sc. (hon.), Curry Coll., 1988. Head Nurse Bellevue Hosp., N.Y.C., 1945-50; asst. editor Am. Jour. of Nursing, N.Y.C., 1950-53, assoc. editor, 1953-63, sr. editor, 1963-70, editor-in-chief, 1970-81; pres., pub. Am. Jour. of Nursing Co., N.Y.C., 1981—; mem. bd. dirs. Nurses Ednl. Funds, N.Y.C., 1981—. Community Family Planning Council, N.Y.C., 1984—, Palliative Care Project, Calvary Hosp., Bronx, N.Y., 1984—; cons. pub. relations com. Sigma Theta Tau, Indpls., 1984—. Co-author Making Choices, Taking Chances, 1988; contbr. articles to profl. jours. Recipient Disting. Service award Boston U., 1975, Leadership award Tchrs. Coll., 1983; Hon. Recognition award N.Y. County Registered Nurses Assn. Mem. Am. Nurses' Assn., Am Soc. Mag. Editors, Mag. Pubs. Assn., Sigma Theta Tau, Sigma Delta Chi. Democrat. Jewish. Home: 32 East 64th St New York NY 10021 Office: Am Jour of Nursing 555 W 57th St New York NY 10019

SCHOTT, MARGE, professional sports team owner; b. 1928; d. Edward and Charlotte Unnewehr; m. Charles J. Schott, 1952 (dec. 1968). Owner Schottco, Cin.; ltd. ptnr. Cin. Reds, 1981-84, gen. ptnr., 1984-85, owner, pres., 1985—, chief exec. officer. Office: Cin Reds 100 Riverfront Stadium Cincinnati OH 45202 *

SCHOULTHEIS, SUSAN, industrial relations and training specialist; b. Hamilton, Ohio, Feb. 12, 1955; d. Arthur Carl and Marcella Maragret (Roell) S.; m. Anthony Lee Turner, 1977. BS in Edn. cum laude, U. Cin., 1985; postgrad. with honors, Miami U., Oxford, Ohio, 1985—. Graphic communications instr. Butler County Joint Vocat. Sch., Hamilton, 1980-85; plant tng. specialist Deluxe Check Printers, Cin., 1985—; instructional technologist Westinghouse Corp., Fairfield, Ohio, 1987—. Mem. Am. Vocat. Assn., Ohio Vocat. Assn., Nat. Assn. Female Execs., Am. Soc. for Tng., U. Cin. Alumni Assn., The Smithsonian Assocs., Nat. Geog. Soc. Roman Catholic. Home: 2646 S Wynn Rd PO Box 33 Okeana OH 45053

SCHRADE, ROLANDE MAXWELL YOUNG, composer, pianist, educator; b. Washington, Sept. 13; d. Harry Robert and Isabelle Martha (Maxwell) Young; pupil Harold Bauer, N.Y.C., Vittorio Giannini; student Manhattan Sch. Music, Juilliard Sch. Music; m. Robert Warren Schrade, Dec. 21, 1949; children: Robelyn, Rhonda Lee, Rolisa, Randolph, Rorianne. Debut as concert pianist Town Hall, N.Y.C., 1953, Nat. Gallery, Washington, 1954; founder, dir. ann. performances Sevenars Concerts, Inc., Worthington, Mass., 1968—, music dir., 1975—, also broadcasts, 1984, 85; recitalist radio sta. WGMS-FM, Washington; mem. music faculty Allen-Stevenson Sch., N.Y.C., 1968—; v.p., treas. Sevenars Music House, Inc., N.Y.C., 1968—. Concerts include Lincoln Ctr., Alice Tully Hall, 1980, Sevenar's Concerts, Inc., annual music festival, Worthington, Mass., 1968—, tour, N.Z., 1982, 84; appearances PM Mag., TV, 1980, 81. Mem. ASCAP, DAR (Bicentennial award 1972), Mut. Artists Mgmt. Alliance (founder, bd. dirs.). Episcopalian. Composer, pub. and recorded over 100 songs; albums America 76, Original and Traditional Songs for Special Days, 1988; editor: songs of Carrie Jacobs Bond, Boston Music Co. Home and office: 30 E End Ave New York NY 10028 also: Sevenars Worthington MA 01098

SCHRAGER, MINDY RAE, business executive; b. Paterson, N.J., Jan. 18, 1958; d. Julius Maxwell and Miriam (Max) S. Student Middlebury Coll., 1977, Inst. European Studies, Nantes, France, 1977-78; BA, Dickinson Coll., 1979; MBA, Babson Coll., 1981. Cons., Nolan Norton & Co., Lexington, Mass., 1981-86; mgr. sales support Logos Corp., Dedham, Mass., 1986-87; resource ctr. supr. Codex Corp., Canton, Mass., 1987—. Mem. Nat. Assn. Female Execs., Am. Mgmt. Assn. Avocations: reading, travel, music, dance. Home: 80 Walnut St Unit 310 Canton MA 02021

SCHRAM, NORMA CHERYL, management and educational consultant; b. Houston, Apr. 5, 1957; d. Albert Julius and Betty Laverne (Deskin) S. Student, Tex. Tech U., 1978; BSED in Guidance Counseling, North Tex. State U., 1980; MEd in Ednl. Adminstrn., Tex. Christian U., 1985. Admissions counselor Richland Community Coll., Dallas, 1978-80; interim youth dir. Park Cities Bapt. Ch., Dallas, 1980-81, asst. to single adult ministers, 1980-81; admissions counselor Dallas Bapt. U., 1981-83, dir. admissions, dir. student affairs; Youth Program Specialist City of Dallas, 1983; dir. residential living-learning program Tex. Christian U., Ft. Worth, 1983-86; tng. specialist City of Dallas Housing Authority, 1986—; owner, cons. Norma Schram and Assocs., Dallas, 1986—; youth counselor, Dallas, Ft. Worth, 1978—; cons. Pregnancy Lifeline, Ft. Worth, 1985-86; instr. CPR, first aid, ARC, Dallas, instr. defensive driving Greater Dallas Safety Assn., 1987, Dallas County Community Coll., 1986-87; keynote speaker So. Bapt. Conv.,

1980-83. Cons. City of Dallas, Inner City Task Force, 1983. Named one of Notable Women of Tex., 1985, Outstanding Student Devel. Profl., 1981, DHD and Assocs., Admissions Assoc. of Yr., Nat. Assn. Coll. Registrars and Admissions Officers, 1980. Mem. Assoc. Women Entrepreneurs Dallas, Dallas C. of C., Nat. Assn. Female Executives, Am. Soc. Tng. and Devel., Nat. Assn. Housing and Redevel. Officials. Republican. Home and Office: 704 Versailles Mesquite TX 75149

SCHRAMM, VERA MINELLI, mental health center administrator; b. East Chicago, Ind., June 7, 1934; d. Leonard Anthony and Jennie Marie (Crispi) M.; m. Kenneth Eugene Schramm, Oct. 23, 1954; children—Linda, Douglas, Diane, Anita. Sec. to registrar Purdue U., Hammond, Ind., 1952-55; vol. coordinator Riverbend Ctr. for Mental Health, Florence, Ala., 1972-78, coordinator community relations, 1978—, adminstrv. coordinator cardiac rehabs., 1982—, fin. counselor, 1984—; chairperson Ala. Council of Consultation and Edn. Dirs., 1982; mem. adv. com. Midsouth Home Health, Florence, 1983-84. Bd. dirs. council Roman Catholic Parish, Tuscumbia, Ala., 1982-85; agy. mem. United Way of Shoals, Florence, 1983-84; chairperson council Florence Community Services, 1984. Mem. Muscle Shoals Advt. Fedn. (Addy for excellence in advt. 1982, 83, bd. dirs. 1983-84). Republican. Clubs: Allithom Study (pres. 1970-71), Inclusive Study (pres. 1974) (Sheffield, Ala.). Home: 108 Rivermont Dr Sheffield AL 35660 Office: Riverbend Ctr for Mental Health 635 W College St Florence AL 35631

SCHRANDT, MARY MAGDALENE, home economist; b. Coronado, Calif., Mar. 2, 1954; d. Theodore J. and Edna Louise (Schnitzler) S. BS, Iowa State U., 1976; MS, Kans. State U., 1985. Home economist Mitchell County Extension Service, Beloit, Kans., 1976—, extension dir., 1985—; v.p. Andromeda, 1988. Bd. dirs. Am. Cancer Soc. Mitchell County chpt., Beloit, Kans., 1978—. Mem. Bus. and Profl. Women, Nat. Assn. Extension Home Economists (regional dir. 1988—, Dist. Service award 1987), Kans. Assn. Extension Home Economists (pres. 1983-84, Eleanor Anderson scholarship 1984), Kans. Extension Agts. Assn. (sec., treas. 1985-87), Kans. Home Econs. Assn. (dist. pres. 1980). Democrat. Roman Catholic. Club: Andromeda (reporter 1987). Office: Mitchell County Extension Office Box 546 Courthouse Beloit KS 67420

SCHREIBER, ALICE MILDRED, research engineer; b. Havertown, Pa., Nov. 26, 1927; d. Augustus Darnell and Florence Charlotte (Richter) S.; m. Miles Jamison Willard Jr., June 22, 1950 (div. June 1970); children: Nancy E., Janice M., David A.; m. John Campbell Williamson, June 27, 1981. BS in Chem. Engring., Drexel U., 1950; MEd in Guidance and Counseling, U. Idaho, 1975; MS in Chem. Engring., Washington State U., Pullman, 1978. Sales engr. Brown Instrument, Phila., 1950-51; adminstrv. asst. Miles Willard, Food Processing Cons., Idaho Falls, 1964-70; substitute tchr. Latah County and Whitman County Sch. Dists., Idaho and Wash., 1974-76; engr. Rockwell Hanford Ops., Richland, Wash., 1977-80; research engr. Battelle N.W. Lab., Richland, Wash., 1980—. Precinct committeewoman Benton County Dems., Wash., 1980-86; moderator bd. and congregation N.W. United Protestant Ch., Richland, 1988. Mem. Soc. Women Engrs., AAUW, Am. Inst. Chem. Engrs., Am. Nuclear Soc., Nat. Assn. Female Execs., Phi Kappa Phi, Tau Beta Pi, Pi Nu Epsilon. Democrat. Home: 1509 Cimarron Ave Richland WA 99352 Office: Battelle NW Labs PO Box 999 Richland WA 99352

SCHREIBER, EILEEN SHER, artist; b. Denver; d. Michael Herschel and Sarah Deborah (Tannenbaum) Sher; student U. Utah, 1942-45, N.Y.U. extension, 1966-68, Montclair (N.J.) State Coll., 1975-79; also pvt. art study; m. Jonas Schreiber, Mar. 27, 1945; children—Jeffrey, Barbara, Michael. Exhibited Morris Mus. Arts and Scis., Morristown, N.J., 1965-73, N.J. State Mus., 1969, Lever House, N.Y.C., 1971, Paramus (N.J.) Mus., 1973, Newark Mus., 1978, Am. Water Color Soc., Audubon Artists, N.A.D. Gallery, N.Y.C., Pallazzo Vecchio Florence (Italy), Art Expo 1987, 1988; represented in permanent collections Morris Mus., Seton Hall U., Bloomfield (N.J.) Coll., Barclay Bank of Eng., N.J., Somerset Coll., NYU, Morris County State Coll., Broad Nat. Bank, Newark, IBM, Am. Telephone Co., RCA, Johnson & Johnson, Champion Internat. Paper Co., SONY, Mitsubishi, Celanese Co., Squibb Corp., Nabisco, Nat. Bank Phila., NYU, Data Control, Sperry Univac, Ga. Pacific Co., Public Service Co. N.J., others; also pvt. collections. Recipient awards N.J. Watercolor Soc., 1969, 72, Nat. Assn. Women Artists, 1970; 1st award in watercolor Hunterdon Art Center, 1972, Best in Show award Short Hills State Show, 1976, Tri-State Purchase award Somerset Coll., 1977, Art Expo, N.Y.C. 1987, 88; numerous others. Mem. Nat. Assn. Women Artists (chmn. watercolor jury; Collage award 1983), Nat., N.J. artists equity, Nat. Painter and Sculptors Assn., Hunterdon Art Center. Home: 22 Powell Dr West Orange NJ 07052 Office: Reece Galleries 24 W 57th St New York NY 10019 Other: CS Schulte Gallery Broadway NY 10021

SCHREIBER, FLORA RHETA, theatre arts and speech specialist, author, educator; b. N.Y.C., Apr. 24, 1918; d. William and Esther (Aaronson) S. BS, Columbia U., 1938, MA, 1939; cert., U. London, 1937, NYU Radio Workship, 1942. Instr. speech and dramatic art Bklyn. Coll., 1944-46; drama critic Players mag., 1941-46; instr. Exeter Coll., U. S.W., Eng., 1937; asst. prof. Adelphi Coll., Garden City, N.Y., 1947-53; dir. radio-TV div. Center Creative Arts, 1948-51; lectr. New Sch. Social Research, 1952-76; prof. English and speech John Jay Coll. Criminal Justice, City U. N.Y., 1974—, dir. pub. relations, 1965-80, asst. to pres., 1970-83. Creator, producer Bklyn. Coll. Radio Forum, Sta. WYNC, N.Y.C., 1944-46; Author: William Schuman, 1954, Your Child's Speech, 1956, Jobs with a Future in Law Enforcement, 1970, Sybil, 1973, paperback edit., 1974, fgn. edits., 1974-76, The Shoemaker, 1983, paperback edits., 1984, fgn. edit., 1983—; also short stories plays, opera libretti and art songs.; contbr. to nat. mags.; columnist nat. mags. including Sci. Digest, 1966-72, Bell McClure, United Features; feature writer: nat. mags. including N.Y. Times Spl. Features; producer radio forum on Community Theater for NBC, 1949; numerous radio and TV appearances in U.S. and Eng. including Oprah Winfrey Show, ABC News, Morton Downey Jr. Show. Cornelia Otis Skinner scholar, 1937; awards Am. Med. Writers Assn., Family Service Assn. Mem. AAUW, AAUP, Speech, Assn. Am., ANTA, Speech Assn. Eastern States, Am. Soc. Journalists and Authors (past v.p., Author of Yr. 1985), Authors League Am., PEN. Club: Overseas Press. Home: 32 Gramercy Park S New York NY 10003 Office: John Jay Coll of Criminal Justice 444 W 56th St New York NY 10019

SCHREINER, BEVERLY ETHEL, medical transcriptionist; b. Spokane, Wash., Dec. 7, 1931; d. Charlie P. and M. Jerrine (Cannon) Nolasco; m. George J. Schreiner, Feb. 4, 1951 (div. Feb. 1961); children—Michael, David, Judy. Student Franklin Hosp. Sch. Nursing, 1951, San Francisco City Coll., 1953, Am. Inst. Banking, San Francisco. Certified med. transcriptionist. Sec. Darrell Kammer, M.D., Nampa, Idaho, 1967-73; supr. med. records Idaho State Sch. and Hosp., Nampa, 1966-75; self-employed med. transcriptionist, Nampa, 1984—; med. sec. Caldwell Internal Medicine, Idaho, 1976—; supr. evening shift med. records office Mercy Med. Ctr., Nampa, 1967-87. Mem. Nat. Assn. Med. Transcriptionists, Idaho Assn. Med. Transcriptionists. Mem. Coll. Ch. of the Nazarene. Avocations: reading, sewing, sports, ceramics. Home: 320 Nectarine St Nampa ID 83651 Other: Caldwell Internal Medicine 222 E Elm St Caldwell ID 83605

SCHREINER, JOAN MAU, accountant; b. Appleton, Wis., July 12, 1944; d. John F. and Agnes M. (Hartzheim) Mau; m. Edwin A. Schreiner, June 17, 1967; children: Teri Lee, Douglas Edwin, Catherine Anne. BBA, U. Wis., Madison, 1966, MS, 1968. CPA, N.Y. Staff acct. Price Waterhouse & Co., Milw., 1968-69; sr. tax acct. Price Waterhouse & Co., Seattle, 1969-72; pvt. practice acct. Rochester, N.Y., 1973-80; tax analyst GTE Corp., Stamford, Conn., 1981-83; tax mgr. U.S. Tobacco Co., Greenwich, Conn., 1983-84; dir. tax acctg. U.S. Tobacco Co., Greenwich, 1984—. Mem. Am. Inst. CPA's, Tax Execs. Inst. Home: 529 Nod Hill Rd Wilton CT 06897 Office: UST Inc 100 W Putnam Ave Greenwich CT 06830

SCHREUR, SARA ELLEN, real estate manager, marketing executive; b. Kalamazoo, Aug. 10, 1961; d. David Lewis and Sara Ellen (Hazelton)S. BA in Sociology, Labor Relations, Mich. State U., 1984. Rep. First Investors Corp., Grand Rapids, Mich., 1984-85; ins. agt., fin. cons., tech. recruiter, account mgr. Atwood Tech. Services, Troy, Mich., 1985-87; mgr. property Cassard And Mead Mgmt. Corp., Grand Rapids, 1987—; property mgr., mktg. rep. Waters Corp., Grand Rapids, 1987—; realtor assoc. Waters Realty, Grand Rapids, 1987—. Mem. Grand Rapids Real Estate Bd., Bldgs. Owners and Mgrs. Assn. Republican. Episopalian. Home: 4325-7 Timber Ridge Trail SW Grand Rapids MI 49509 Office: Waters Corp 161 Ottawa NW Grand Rapids MI 49503

SCHREYER-THOMSON, CAMELLA JOY, artist, editor, corporate executive; b. Lawrence, Kans., July 17, 1949; d. George Maurice and Camella Inez (Burnette) Schreyer; BA cum laude, Pfeiffer Coll., 1971; MA, East Carolina U., 1974; research studies Europe and Gt. Britain; m. Douglas Arthur Thomson, May 6, 1973. One-woman shows: Allas Art Galleries, Charlotte, N.C., 1971, Pfeiffer Coll. Gallery, 1975, 79; group shows include: Durham (N.C.) Art Guild, Fayetteville (N.C.) Mus. Art, Shooren's, Rockport, Mass., East Carolina U.; represented in permanent collection Pfeiffer Coll., also pvt. collections; editor-in-chief Am. Biog. Inst., Raleigh, N.C., 1973—; class agt. Pfeiffer Coll. Alumni Assn., 1976—. Mem. citizens adv. council Am. Inst. Cancer Research. Cert. tchr. kindergarten through 9th grades, N.C. Mem. Am. Fedn. Arts, Nat. League Am. Pen Women, Stanly County Art Guild, Durham Arts Council, Nat. Wildlife Assn., Raleigh C. of C., Raleigh Bus. and Profl. Women, Soc. Suisse de Phaleristique (hon.), Order Sundial, Phi Delta Sigma. Methodist. Contbr. poems to lit. jours.; art editor The Phoenix of Pfeiffer Coll., also various annuals. Address: 5436 Pine Top Circle Raleigh NC 27612

SCHRIBER, JACQUELYN BUSHNER, management consultant, researcher; b. Milw.; d. John and Jennie Bushner. BA, Lawrence U., 1970; MA, Northwestern U., 1978; MA, Claremont Grad. Sch., 1981, PhD, 1986. Placement asst. Globe-Union Inc., Milw., 1970-72; supr. compensation analysis Container Corp. Am., Chgo., 1972-76; lectr. Calif. State U.-Fullerton, 1981; various positions Claremont Colls., Calif., 1980-83; mgmt. cons., Pomona, 1983-85; dir. research Coldwell Banker Residential Group, Newport Beach, Calif., 1985-86; sr. cons. The Orgn. Devel. Ctr., Los Angeles, 1986-87; mem. core faculty Calif. Sch. Profl. Psychology, Los Angeles, 1986-87; sr. cons. Touche Ross, 1987-88; dir. research Coldwell Banker Residential Group, Newport Beach, 1988—. Claremont Grad. Sch. fellow, 1979-81. Mem. Am. Psychol. Assn. (assoc.), Acad. Mgmt. (student mem.), Am. Soc. Tng. and Devel., Am. Assn. Counseling and Devel., Sigma Xi (assoc.).

SCHRIEBER, LYNN HOUSEL, human resources manager; b. Doylestown, Pa., Oct. 2, 1950; d. Harry C. and Audrey V. (Burroughs) Housel; m. Frederick W. Rehm, June 22, 1968 (div. 1971); m. Robert W. Schrieber, July 7, 1973; children: Jeffrey W., Jennifer L. Student, Rider Coll., 1972-79. Sec. ERC div. AT&T, Princeton, N.J., 1969-70, acct., 1970-71, employee interviewer, statis. analyst, 1971-78, plant facilities disposal analyst, 1978-79, wage practices and personnel specialist, 1979-84, employee and pub. relations supr., 1984-85; salary adminstrv. supr. OSTC Network Systems div. AT&T, Warren, N.J., 1986-87, TPR personnel dept. supr., 1987—. Mem. Princeton Personnel Assn., Nat. Assn. Female Execs., Alpha Sigma Lambda. Republican. Methodist. Home: 11 Pleasant View Way Flemington NJ 08822 Office: AT&T Network Systems 184 Liberty Corner Rd Warren NJ 07060

SCHROCK, JANET MARIE MOREHOUSE, interior designer; b. Carlisle, Pa., June 30, 1942; d. Harley Francis and Helen Elizabeth (Kitzmiller) Morehouse; B.S., Indiana U. of Pa., 1964; M.Ed., Pa. State U., 1971; M.S., Okla. State U., 1973; Ph.D., U. Mo., 1978; m. Jay Rupert Schrock, Aug. 3, 1968. Elem. art tchr., Leighton, Pa., 1964-66; art tchr., Chitose, Japan, 1969-70; instr. interior design. Kans. State U., 1974-76; instr. housing and interior design U. Mo., 1976-78; asst. prof. housing and interior design Tex. Tech. U., Lubbock, 1978-88, assoc. prof., 1986—. Teaching Devel. grantee Tex. Tech. U., 1982. Mem. Am. Assn. Housing Educators (exec. com., rec. sec.), Interior Design Educators Council, Am. Assn. Home Econs., Am. Soc. Interior Designers. Contbr. articles profl. jours. Office: Tex Tech U Merchandising Eviron Design and Consumer Econs Lubbock TX 79509

SCHROCK, ROSALIND, small business owner; b. Toowoomba, Queensland, Australia, May 26, 1937; d. Francis Smedley-Seagrave and Evelyn Mary (Stewart) MacFarlane; m. Lyle Eugene Schrock, Dec. 20, 1975. Diploma, Nat. Inst. Dramatic Art, U. New South Wales, Australia, 1962; ATCL in Speech, Trinity Coll., London/Brisane, Queensland, Australia, 1955; postgrad. in directing, Barat Coll., Lake Forest, Ill., 1983-84. Profl. actress, radio, TV, theatre various theatre companies, radio and TV programs, New Zealand and Australia, 1959-71; internat beauty cons. Dorothy Gray Skin Care House, Sydney, Australia, 1971-73, Coty Cosmetics, New Zealand, 1973-75; ptnr. Radiant Attractions Enterprises, Lake Forest, 1984—; owner English Garden Enterprises, Lake Forest, 1986—. Organizing mem. Touchstone Theatre, Lake Forest, 1985—; mem. Chicago Botanic Garden, Glencoe, Ill., 1977—, Jr. Garden Club of Lake Forest, 1986—. Republican.

SCHRODER, REGINA JABLONSKI, lawyer; b. Riverhead, N.Y., June 15, 1955; d. Zygmont and Jean (Jalbrzykowski) Jablonski; m. Henry Carl Schroder, July 19, 1975. B.A., U. Calif.-Davis, 1979, J.D., 1982; LL.M. in Taxation, McGeorge Sch. Law, Sacramento, 1984. Bar: Calif. 1982. Legal sec. Horan, Lloyd, Dennis Farr, Monterey, Calif., 1974; teller, clk. Security Pacific Bank, Carmel, Calif. and Davis, Calif., 1974-76; clk. Fin. Aids Office, U. Calif.-Davis, 1976-77; researcher, bibliographer Office of Adminstrn. of Criminal Justice, U. Calif.-Davis, 1978-80; law clk. Weintraub, Genshlea, Esqs., Sacramento, Calif., 1981; atty. tax and securities Van Camp & Johnson, Sacramento, Calif., 1983-86, Wilke, Fleury, Hoffelt, Gould & Birney, Sacramento, 1986—. U. Calif. grantee, 1976-78, Calif. Scholarship awardee, 1976-79; Bing Crosby Meml. Fund Scholarship, 1979; recipient Internat. Relations Outstanding Grad. award, 1979. Mem. ABA, Calif. State Bar Assn. (tax sect., adv. com. taxation 1985-86), Women Lawyers of Sacramento, Phi Beta Kappa, Phi Kappa Phi. Office: Wilke Fleury Hoffelt Gould & Birney 300 Capitol Mall 13th Floor Sacramento CA 95814

SCHROEDEL, HUBERTA GOWEN WOLF, non-profit foundation administrator; b. Phila., Oct. 8, 1943; d. Richard O'Shea and Huberta Horan (Gowen) Wolf. BS in Sociology, Daemen Coll., 1967; MS in Counseling, U. Ariz., 1969. Rehab. counselor Fountain House, Inc., Rockland State Hosp., N.Y.C., 1969-72; tchr. of the deaf N.Y.C. BD. of Edn., Hearing Edn. Services, 1974—; exec. dir. N.Y. Ctr. for Law and the Deaf, N.Y.C., 1980—; cons. St. Joseph Sch. for the Deaf, Bronx, N.Y., 1978-82. Exec. producer TV video series, New York Connection, 1980. Chairperson N.Y. Deaf Women, 1981; adv. bd. N.Y.C. Mayor's Office for Handicapped, 1984—. Recipient Durfee award for enhancing human dignity Durfee Found., 1987. Mem. Lexington Mental Health Ctr. for the Deaf (adv. bd.). Democrat. Roman Catholic. Office: NY Ctr for Law and the Deaf 275 7th Ave New York NY 10001

SCHROEDER, BETTY LOUISE, bookkeeper; b. Aldrich, Mo., Apr. 20, 1937; d. Raymond Fenton and Josie Margaret (Redman) Slagle; m. Earl Freddie Schroeder, Mar. 8, 1958 (div. 1981); children—Kathryn, David, Robert. Student pub. schs., Pleasant Hope, Mo. Head sec. Jackson Extension Ctr., Independence, Mo., 1964; typist MWM Colorpress, Aurora, Mo., 1965; income tax preparer, H&R Block, Aurora, 1969-77, preparer, owner, 1977-83, preparer, owner, West Plains, Mo., 1984—; registered rep. Waddell and Reed Fin. Services, 1986. Fund raiser Houn Dawg Band, Aurora, 1975-85. Baptist. Avocation: handcrafts. Office: H&R Block-Schroeder Bookkeeping 1406 Kentucky St West Plains MO 65775

SCHROEDER, ELIZABETH CARSON, corporate training director; b. Havre de Grace, Md., Sept. 21, 1943; d. Omar L. and Catharine (Smith) Carson; m. John W. Schroeder, Jr., Sept. 15, 1984. BA, Gettysburg Coll., 1965; MEd, Loyola Coll., 1971. Cert. rehab. counselor. Counselor to supr. Md. Div. Vocat. Rehab., 1968-79; cons. tng., Balt., 1979-84; corporate trainer MCI, Washington, 1984-85; dir. tng. Nat. Corp. Housing Partnerships-Property Mgmt., Inc., Washington, 1985-86; pres. CCC, Inc., Annapolis, Md., 1986—. Mem. Nat. Assn. for Rehab. Counseling-Mid Atlantic (pres. 1971-72), Am. Assn. Tng. and Devel. Democrat. Lutheran. Avocations: breeding Siberian huskies, sports-volleyball, softball.

SCHROEDER, JANIS LYNN, chemist; b. Grosse Point, Mich., June 22, 1963; d. Francis Joseph and Anne Margaret (Rezak) S. Student, Kalamazoo Coll., 1981-82; BS in Chemistry and German, Lake Forest Coll., 1985. Research chemist Domino Amjet, Inc., Waukegan, Ill., 1985-87; research asst. Baxter Healthcare Corp., Round Lake, Ill., 1987—. Scholar Ruth Boot Found., 1981, Am. Legion, 1981. Mem. Am. Chem. Soc., Phi Sigma Iota. Roman Catholic. Office: Baxter Healthcare Corp Wilson Rd and Rt 120 Round Lake IL 60073

SCHROEDER, MARY ESTHER, wood products executive; b. Dayton, Ohio, July 29, 1947; d. James Walter and Mary Agnes (Danzig) McIver; m. Reinhard Schroeder, Sept. 10, 1966. BS in Forest Industries Mgmt., Ohio State U., 1978. Fiber supply supr. Crown Zellerbach, Inc., Port Townsend, Wash., 1978-83; fiber supply and transp. mgr. Port Townsend Paper Corp., Bainbridge Island, Wash., 1983-87; dir. Pacific Wood Fuels, Redding, Calif., 1987—; bd. dirs. Peninsula Devel. Assn., Port Angeles, Wash., 1985—. Precinct committeeman Kitsap County Reps., Poulsbo, Wash., 1984-86. Mem. Soc. Am. Foresters. Home: 320 Hilltop Dr #216 Redding CA 96003 Office: Pacific Wood Fuel 2659 Balls Ferry Rd Anderson CA 96007

SCHROEDER, MARY MURPHY, judge; b. Boulder, Colo., Dec. 4, 1940; d. Richard and Theresa (Kahn) Murphy; m. Milton R. Schroeder, Oct. 15, 1965; children: Caroline Theresa, Katherine Emily. B.A., Swarthmore Coll., 1962; J.D., U. Chgo., 1965. Bar: Ill. 1966, D.C. 1966, Ariz. 1970. Trial atty. Dept. Justice, Washington, 1965-69; law clk. Hon. Jesse Udall, Ariz. Supreme Ct., 1970; mem. firm Lewis and Roca, Phoenix, 1971-75; judge Ariz. Ct. Appeals, Phoenix, 1975-79, U.S. Ct. Appeals (9th Cir.), Phoenix, 1979—; vis. instr. Ariz. State U. Coll. Law, 1976, 77, 78. Contbr. articles to profl. jours. Mem. Am. Bar Assn., Ariz. Bar Assn., Fed. Bar Assn., Am. Law Inst., Am. Judicature Soc. Democrat. Club: Soroptimists. Office: US Ct of Appeals 6421 US Courthouse & Fed Bldg 230 N 1st Ave Phoenix AZ 85025

SCHROEDER, PATRICIA SCOTT (MRS. JAMES WHITE SCHROEDER), congresswoman; b. Portland, Oreg., July 30, 1940; d. Lee Combs and Bernice (Lemoin) Scott; m. James White Schroeder, Aug. 18, 1962; children: Scott William, Jamie Christine. B.A. magna cum laude, U. Minn., 1961; J.D., Harvard U., 1964. Bar: Colo. 1964. Field atty. NLRB, Denver, 1964-66; practiced in Denver, 1966-72; hearing officer Colo. Dept. Personnel, 1971-72; mem. faculty U. Colo., 1969-72, Community Coll., Denver, 1969-70, Regis Coll., Denver, 1970-72; mem. 93d-100th congresses from 1st Colo. dist., 1973—; co-chmn. Congl. Caucus for Women's Issues, 1976—; mem. Ho. of Reps. armed services com., judiciary com., post office and civil service com.; chair civil service subcom.; mem. select com. on children, youth and families. Congregationalist. Office: 2410 Rayburn House Office Bldg Washington DC 20515

SCHROEDER, RITA MOLTHEN, chiropractor; b. Savanna, Ill., Oct. 25, 1922; d. Frank J. and Ruth J. (McKenzie) Molthen; m. Richard H. Schroeder, Apr. 23, 1948 (div.); children—Richard, Andrew, Barbara, Thomas, Paul, Madeline. Student, Chem. Engring., Immaculate Heart Coll., 1940-41, UCLA, 1941, Palmer Sch. of Chiropractic, 1947-49; D. Chiropractic, Cleve. Coll. of Chiropractic, 1961. Engring.-tooling design data coordinator Douglas Aircraft Co., El Segundo, Santa Monica and Long Beach, Calif., 1941-47; pres. Schroeder Chiropractic, Inc., 1982—; dir. Pacific States Chiropractic Coll., 1978-80, pres. 1980-81. Recipient Palmer Coll. Ambassador award, 1973. Parker Chiropractic Research Found. Ambassador award, 1976, Coll. Ambassador award Life West Chiropractic Coll. Mem. Internat. Chiropractic Assn., Calif. Chiropractic Assn., Internat. Chiropractic Assn. Calif., Assn. Am. Chiropractic Coll. Presidents, Council Chiropractic Edn. (Pacific State Coll. rep.). Home: 9870 N Millbrook Ave Fresno CA 93710 Office: Schroeder Chiropractic Inc 2535 N Fresno Ave Fresno CA 93703

SCHROEDER, TERRI LEA, city manager, educator; b. Elgin, Ill. Mar. 11, 1955; d. Earl and Caroline Louise Christensen. Student William Rainey Harper Coll., summers, 1973-77; BSEd, No. Ill. U., 1977, MA in Pub. Adminstrn., 1979. Lic. pub. water supply operator Ill. EPA Class C; cert. water treatment plant operator Iowa Dept. Environ. Quality Grade I. Tchr., English, Sch. Dist. 202, Plainfield, Ill., 1977-78; adminstrv. asst. to village mgr. Village of Deerfield (Ill.), 1978-79; asst. village mgr. Village of Lincolnshire (Ill.), 1979-81, village mgr., 1981-82; city mgr. City of Iowa Falls (Iowa), 1982—; cons. exec. dir. Lake County Youth Service Bur., Lake Villa, Ill., 1979-80; communications and pub. relations coordinator Univ. Health Ctr., DeKalb, Ill., 1977-78; legal asst. Winnebago County Legal Aid, Rockford, Ill., spring 1979; feature speaker KIFG Radio Sta., fall 1982. Trustee, mem. budget com., bd. dirs. Iowa conf. 1st Congl. Ch., Iowa Falls, 1982—; bd. dirs., mem. leadership com. Com. of 80's Iowa Falls, 1982—; mem. DeKalb Human Relations Commn., 1977-79; lobbyist for Student Assn. on Higher Edn. Appropriations, 79th Gen. Assembly, Washington; chairperson for polit. awareness week, DeKalb, 1977; mem. Gov.'s Com. on Future of Econ. Growth of Iowa, 1984; mem. Gov.'s Ptnrship Econ. Progress, 1985—; mem. Iowa Electric's Indsl. Adv. Panel, 1986; mem. direct dialonge Northwestern Bell Telephone, 1984-86; founder Iowa Falls 2000, 1985, Iowa Falls Area Arts Council, 1985. Named Iowa's Young Career Woman of 1982-83, Iowa Fedn. Bus. Profl. Women, 1983; named Outstanding Young Working Woman, Glamour Mag., 1984; Esper A. Peterson Found. scholar, 1976-79; Gen. Assembly scholar. Mem. Bus. Profl. Women (Young Career Woman, chmn. dist. IV northwest Iowa 1983-84), Internat. City Mgmt. Assn. (assoc.), Iowa City Mgmt. Assn. (newsletter editor 1983-84), North Cen. Iowa City Mgmt. Assn. (founder, exec. bd. dirs.), Mcpl. Fin. Officers Assn., Am. Pub. Works Assn., Am. Econ. Devel. Council. Home: 315 Estes St Iowa Falls IA 50126 Office: City of Iowa Falls 315 Stevens St PO Box 698 Iowa Falls IA 50126

SCHROEDER-DESMOND, MELODIE ANNE, data processing company executive; b. New Haven, Conn., Sept. 1, 1954; d. Rudolf Johann and Annette Schroeder; m. John B. Desmond, Jr., May 16, 1981. Student, Tufts U., Medford, Mass., 1973; BA, U. N.H., Durham, 1976; postgrad., U. Salzburg, Austria, 1977; MBA, Columbia U., 1983. Treas. The Antique Porcelain Co., N.Y.C., 1978-81; analyst Citibank, N.Y.C., 1982; sales rep. Banking Decision Systems, Waltham, Mass., 1983-86; mgr. corp. mktg. Banking Decision Systems, 1987—. Named Million Dollar Salesperson, Internat. Computer Programs, Inc., 1986. Office: Banking Decision Systems 245 Winter St Waltham MA 02154

SCHROPP, MARY LOU, public relations company executive; b. Havre-de-Grace, Md., Aug. 13, 1947; d. Howard James and Maude Elizabeth (Parker) S. Student, George Washington U., 1965-68. Vice pres. Snyder Assoc., Inc., Washington, 1969-76; pres. Health Communications, Inc., Washington, 1976-80; creative services project mgr. U.S. Catholic Conf., Washington, 1980-81; pres., owner MLS Creative Services, Falls Church, Va., 1981—. Editor: Electronic Media, Popular Culture and Family Values, 1985; Rehabilitation Facilities Sourcebook, 1984, 85; periodicals, textbooks. Exec. producer videotapes, 1982. Coordinator World Communications Day, Washington, 1982—; cons. Catholic Communication Campaign, Washington, 1982-84; fund raising cons. Nat. 4-H Council, Chevy Chase, Md., 1985-86, devel. dir. Aviation Research and Edn. Found., Herndon, Va., 1985—. Mem. Pub. Relations Soc. Am., Washington Independent Writers, Religious Pub. Relations Council (v.p. local chpt. 1981-82, DeRose-Hinkhouse Communications award 1981, 82, 80), Nat. Soc. Fund Raising Execs. Democrat. Roman Catholic. Office: MLS Creative Services 7711 Trevino Ln Falls Church VA 22043

SCHROTH, EVELYN MARY, retired language educator; b. Ellington, Wis., Aug. 5, 1919; d. Henry A. and Clara M. (Komp) Schroth. BS, U. Wis., 1940; MS, U. Ill., 1948, AM, 1955; PhD, Pacific Western U., 1979. Tchr. Rhinelander (Wis.) High Sch., 1940-42; chmn. English dept. Waupun (Wis.) High Sch., 1942-44; tchr. Chgo. pub. schs., 1953-63, chmn. dept. English Lindblom High Sch., 1956-62; instr. dept. English U. Ill., Urbana, 1948-50; lectr. Northeastern U., Chgo., 1962-63; assoc. prof., then prof. English, Western Ill. U., Macomb, 1963-87. Program dir. U.S.O., 1946-48. John Hay fellow, 1961. Mem. Linguistic Soc. Am., Nat. Council Tchrs. English, Ill. Tchrs. English, AAUP, Phi Beta, Phi Kappa Phi. Home: 139 Kurlene Dr Macomb IL 61455

SCHRUM, NANCY HOWARD, communications executive; b. Newton, N.C., Apr. 2, 1950; d. Edward Plonk and Edith Virginia (Kiser) S. BA in Elem. Edn., Va. Intermont, 1972; postgrad., N.C. State U., 1980. Cert. tchr., N.C. Tchr. Hickory City (N.C.) Schs., 1972-78; personnel adminstr. Carolina Mills, Inc., Maiden, N.C., 1978-80, mgr. ednl. program, 1980-84, dir. communications, 1984—. Co. advisor Jr. Achievement, 1981-82, dist. adv. council, 1983; mem. Catawba County trust fund adv. com. N.C. Sch. of the Arts, 1981-83, campaign leadership com, 1980; appointed to Gov.'s Oversight Com. for Ofl. Labor Market Info., 1983; trustee Catwba Coll., Salibury, N.C.; bd. dirs. Catawba County Council of the Arts, 1982-84, Catawba County Sci. Ctr., 1984. Mem. Am. Textile Mfrs. Assn. (crafted with pride, communications coms., chair textile week com. 1986), N.C. Textile Mfrs. Assn. (communications com., chair textile week 1983, 84, 85, edn. and tng. com. 1979, econ. edn. com., 1980, sub-com. on community awareness, 1980), N.C. Textile Assn. (Plaque of Appreciation, 1986), Catawba County C. of C. (free enterprise speakers bureau, econ. awareness com. 1980, econ. awareness/pub. schs. com. 1980, Free Enterprise award 1982). Home: 480 17th Ave Dr NE Hickory NC 28601 Office: Carolina Mills Inc PO Box 157 Maiden NC 28650

SCHUBERT, ELIZABETH M(AY), paralegal administrative assistant; b. Hamilton, Ohio, Sept. 10, 1913; d. A(ndreas) Gordon and Grace Symmes (Laxford) S.; B.S. in Edn. cum laude, Miami U., 1933. Sec., Beta Kappa Nat. Frat., Oxford, Ohio, 1931-38; adminstrv. asst. to dir. Ohio State Employment Service, Columbus, 1938-45, supr. procedures, 1945-47; adminstrv. asst. to pres. Schaible Co., Cin., 1948-50; paralegal adminstrv. asst. to Gordon H. Scherer, Atty.-at-Law, mem. U.S. Congress, U.S. del. to UN, U.S. rep. to exec. bd. UNESCO, Paris, 1950—. Mem. Phi Beta Kappa. Republican. Presbyn. Home: 1071 Celestial St Apt 1701 Cincinnati OH 45202 Office: 1071 Celestial St Suite 2103 Cincinnati OH 45202

SCHUBERT, NANCY ELLEN, beauty industry executive, management consultant, franchise director; b. Chgo., June 25, 1945; d. Raymond James and Kathleen Mary (Gibbons) Nugent; m. Emil Joseph Schubert, Jan. 14, 1967; children—James Bryant, Erin Heather, Shannon Kathleen. B.F.A., Mundelein Coll., 1968. Freelance artist, Chgo., 1968; tchr. St. Pius X Sch., Lombard, Ill., 1975-76; pres., treas., dir. Super Style, Inc., Hoffman Estates, Ill., 1981—, Super Six, Inc., Glendale Heights, Ill., 1983—, N.E.S. Mgmt. Inc., Schaumburg, Ill., 1985—, Super Style III, Inc., Berwyn, Ill., 1985—; created and developed Super Style concept and system of operation; created SuperStyle logo and design trademarked in 1983. Mem. Cermak Plaza Mcht. Assn. (bd. dirs.). Republican. Roman Catholic. Avocations: licensed pilot, downhill skiing, horseback riding. Office: Super Style Inc 707 W Golf Rd Hoffman Estates IL 60194

SCHUBERT, RUTH CAROL HICKOK, artist; b. Janesville, Wis., Dec. 24, 1927; d. Fay Andrew and Mildred Willmette (Street) Hickok; m. Robert Francis Schubert, Oct. 20, 1946; children—Stephen Robert, Michelle Carol. Student DeAnza Coll., 1972-73; A.A., Monterey Peninsula Coll., 1974; B.A. with honors, Calif. State U.-San Jose, 1979. Owner, mgr. Casa De Artes Gallery, Monterey, Calif., 1977-86; dir. Monterey Peninsula Mus. Art Council, 1975-76; one-woman shows: Aarhof Gallery, Aarau, Switzerland, 1977, Degli Agostiniani Recolletti, Rome, 1977, Wells Fargo Bank, Monterey, 1975, 78, 79, Seaside (Calif.) City Hall Gallery, 1979, Village Gallery, Lahaina, Hawaii, 1983, 86, Portola Valley Gallery, 1984, 85, Rose Rock Gallery, Carmel, 1984-86; include: Sierra Nev. Mus. Art, Reno, 1980, Bard Hall Gallery, San Diego, 1980, Rahr-West Mus., Manitowoc, Wis., 1980, Rosicrucian Mus., San Jose, 1981, 84, Calif. State Agri-Images, Sacramento, 1984; XVII Watercolor West, Brea Civic Cultural Ctr., 1985, Marjorie Evans Gallery, Carmel, Calif., 1986, Monterey Peninsula Mus. Art, Monterey, Calif., 198687; represented in permanent collections: Monterey Calif. Peninsula Mus. Art, Nat. Biscuit Co. subs. RJR Nabisco, San Jose, Muscular Dystrophy Assn., San Francisco, also numerous pvt. collections. Recipient 1st prize Monterey County Fair, 1979, Nat. Art Appreciation, 1984, Norcal State Art Fair, 1985; numerous other awards for watercolor paintings. Mem. Artists Equity Assn., Am. Watercolor Soc., Nat. Watercolor Soc. (assoc.), Soc. Western Artists, Oreg. Watercolor Soc., LaHaina Arts Soc., Rogue Valley Art Gallery, Monterey Peninsula Watercolor Soc., Watercolor West (assoc.), Cen. Coast Art Assn. (pres. 1977-78), Nat. League Am. Penwomen (pres. 1983-84, 86-87), Art Alumni San Jose State U., Monterey Civic Club. Club: Eastern Star (Milw.). Contbr. to profl. publs. Home: 2462 Senate Way Medford OR 97504

SCHUCH, CYNTHIA SILLECK, nurse; b. Oceanside, N.Y., Oct. 31, 1956. A in Applied Sci., SUNY, Morrisville, 1976; cert. in Cardiovascular Nursing, Meth. Hosp., Houston, 1978; BS in Nursing, U. Ala., 1984, MS in Nursing, 1985. RN, N.Y., Va., Ala., Calif. Staff nurse, relief charge nurse, postoperative surgical nurse Meth. Hosp., Houston, 1976-77, staff nurse maternity ICU, 1977-78, cardiovascular nurse specialist, 1978-79; staff nurse ICU U. Va. Hosp., Charlottesville, 1979; staff nurse, relief charge nurse U. Ala. Hosp., Birmingham, 1979-80, scrub nurse, circulating nurse, 1980-83, staff nurse CICU, 1983-84, charge nurse CICU, 1984-86; staff nurse CICU Sutter Meml. Hosp., Sacramento, 1986—. Vol. instr. cardiac maintenance YMCA Shades Valley Br., Birmingham, 1984; instr. for family night CPR, Sacramento, 1987. Mem. Am. Assn. Critical Care Nurses (Houston-Gulf chpt. 1976-79, Greater Birmingham chpt. 1985-86, Sacramento chpt. 1986—), Phi Theta Kappa, Phi Kappa Phi, Sigma Theta Tau. Office: Sutter Meml Hosp 5275 F St Sacramento CA 95819

SCHUCK, VICTORIA, political science educator; b. Oklahoma City, Mar. 16, 1909; d. Anthony B. and Anna (Priebe) S. A.B. with great distinction, Stanford U., 1930, M.A., 1931, Ph.D., 1937; L.H.D. (hon.), Mt. Vernon Coll., 1980. Univ. fellow Stanford U., 1931-33, teaching asst., 1934-35, acting instr., 1935-36, instr., 1936-37; asst. prof. Fla. State Coll. Women, 1937-40; mem. faculty Mt. Holyoke Coll., 1940-77, prof. polit. sci., 1950-77; pres. Mt. Vernon Coll., Washington, 1977-80; vis. lectr. Smith Coll., 1948-49; vis. prof. Stanford U., summer 1952, resident scholar polit. sci., 1982—; guest scholar Brookings Instn., 1967-68, summers 68, 70, Woodrow Wilson Ctr. Internat. Scholars, 1980; Prin. program analyst, planning for local bds. OPA, 1942-44; rep. Am. Polit. Sci. Assn. UN World Conf. of UN Decade for Women, Nairobi, Kenya, 1985; sponsor. Women's Fgn. Policy Council, N.Y., 1986; cons. Office Temporary Controls, 1945-47; mem. internat. secretariat UN Conf. San Francisco, 1945; mem. Mass. Commn. Interstate Coop., 1957-60, U. Mass. Bldg. Authority, 1960-68; Mass. adv. com. U.S. Commn. Civil Rights, 1962-78; cons. GAO, 1980-82. Regional editor: Ency. Brit., 1958-61; co-editor and contbr.: Women Organizing: An Anthology, 1979, New England Politics, 1981; contbr. articles to profl. jours. Mem. Pres.'s Commn. Registration and Voting Participation, 1963; mem. Berkshire Community Coll. Planning Com., 1964-68, Greenfield Community Coll. Planning Com., 1965-68, Mass. Bd. Higher Edn., 1976-77; mem. Town of South Hadley Planning Bd., 1959-67, chmn., 1961-67; trustee U. Mass., 1958-65; sponsor Women's Fgn. Policy Council, New York, 1986—. Grantee Haynes Found., 1951-52; Grantee Asia Soc., 1971-72. Mem. Am. Polit. Sci. Assn. (sec. 1959-60, v.p. 1970-71, rep. UN World Conf. of Decade for Women 1985, sponsor Women's Fgn. Policy Council, N.Y.C., 1986—), New Eng. Polit. Sci. Assn. (pres. 1950-51), Northeastern Polit. Sci. Assn. (pres. 1972-73), AAUW (pres. Mass. 1946-50, nat. chmn. legis. program com., bd. dirs. 1965-69), Am. Soc. Pub. Adminstrn., AAUP (pres. Mt. Holyoke 1962-64), Internat. Polit. Sci. Assn., Phi Beta Kappa, Chi Omega, Mortar Bd. (hon.). Club: Cosmopolitan (N.Y.C.). Home: 4000 Cathedral Ave NW Washington DC 20016

SCHUCKETT, SANDY, librarian; b. Los Angeles, Aug. 20, 1937; d. Max M. and Bluma (Kreisberg) S. B.A., U. Calif.-Berkeley, 1960; M.A., Calif. State U.-Los Angeles, 1978. Cert. tchr., Calif., 1969. Tchr., Los Angeles pub. schs., 1962-66, librarian, 1966-74, library media specialist, 1974—; sec. White House Conf. Library and Info. Services Task Force, Washington, 1982-86, western regional rep., 1986-88. Editor Focal Points jour., 1980—. Pres. Friends of Children and Lit., 1979-86; active PTA, Los Angeles Sch. Library Assn. Mem., ALA, NEA, Am. Assn. Sch. Librarians, Calif. Library Assn., Calif. Media and Library Educators' Assn., Educare; Kappa Delta Pi. Democrat. Jewish. Office: Los Angeles Unified School Dist 4112 E Olympic Blvd Los Angeles CA 90023

SCHUCKMAN, NANCY LEE, educational adminstrator; b. Bklyn., June 3, 1939; d. Abraham Benjamin and Sophie (Kalefsky) S. B.A., Bklyn. Coll., 1961, M.S., 1964, postgrad., 1965-69; postgrad. Hofstra U., 1970-72, Columbia U., 1979-80. Tchr. N.Y.C. Bd. Edn., 1961-69, adminstr., Bklyn., 1969-77, prin., 1977—; ednl. journalist East New Yorker, East N.Y. Devel. Corp., Bklyn., 1974-76, Starrett City Sun, Bklyn., 1975-76; co-owner Lanah Ednl. Toys, Bklyn., 1975-76. Mem. Thomas Jefferson Democratic Club, Bklyn., 1978—, Kings County Democratic. Com., 1981-87; polit. campaign coordinator John F. Kennedy Democratic Club, Bklyn., 1974-76; mem. exec. bd. John F. Kennedy Democratic Club, Bklyn., 1974-75. Mem. Council Suprs. and Adminstrs. (conv. registration chmn.), Adminstrv. Women in Edn., Am. Assn. Sch. Adminstrs., N.Y.C. Elementary Prins. Assn. (exec. bd. 1984—), Bklyn. Reading Council. Democrat. Jewish. Avocations: edn. law; journalism; oil painting; photography; traveling; sports. Office: PS 202 982 Hegeman Ave Brooklyn NY 11208

SCHUESSLER FIORENZA, ELIZABETH, religion educator; b. Tschanad, Germany, Apr. 17, 1938; came to U.S., 1970; d. Peter and Magdalena Schuessler; m. Francis Fiorenza, Dec. 17, 1967; 1 child, Christina. M of Div., U. Wuerzburg, 1962; ThD, U. Muenster, 1970. Asst. prof. theology U. Notre Dame, South Bend, Ind., 1970-75, assoc. prof., 1975-80, prof., 1980-84; instr. U. Muenster, 1976-77; Talbot prof. New Testament Episcopal Div. Sch., Cambridge, Mass., 1984-88; Krister Stendahl prof. div. in New Testament studies Harvard U., Cambridge, Mass., 1988—; Harry Emerson Fosdick vis. prof. Union Theol. Sem., N.Y.C., 1974-75. Author: Der Vergessene Partner, 1964, Priester fuhr Gott Zum Herrschafts, 1972, The Apocalypse, 1976, Invitation to the Book of Revelation, 1981, In Memory of Her, 1982; also editor other works. Mem. Am. Acad. Religion, Soc. Bibl. Lit. (pres.). Roman Catholic. Office: Harvard Div School 45 Francis St Cambridge MA 02138 *

SCHUK, LINDA LEE, food chain executive; b. Scott Field, Ill., July 19, 1946; d. Frank A. Schuk and Jessie (Bumpass) Stearns, divorced, 1 child, Earl Wade. BBA, U. Tex., El Paso, 1968. Lic. life and health ins. agt., Tex. Acct., traffic mgr. Farah Mfg. Co., El Paso, 1970-71; adminstrv. asst. Horizon Corp., El Paso, 1971-76; adminstrv. asst. in charge office ops. Foster-Scwartz Devel. Corp., El Paso, 1976-78; legal sec. Howell and Fields, El Paso, 1978-80; supr. Southland Corp., San Antonio, 1980-83, sales mgr., 1983-84, dist. mgr., 1984-87; dist. supr. E-Z Mart Conveniance Stores, San Antonio, 1987—; tchr. San Antonio Community Coll., 1988—. Mem. Nat. Assn. Female Execs. Democrat. Baptist. Home: 6418 Gray Ridge San Antonio TX 97233 Office: E-Z Mart Convenience Stores 2368 Austin Hwy San Antonio TX 78218

SCHUK, ROSALIND, small business owner; b. Ellenville, N.Y., Jan. 5, 1949; d. Max and Edith (Rubnitz) Blut; married; 1 child, Dawn. Mgr., buyer Sample Nook Stores, Blkyn., 1968-73; owner Quality and Prestige, Rockville Ctr., N.Y., 1977—; cons. fashion, displays, merchandiser Conspiquous, Rockville Ctr., 1977—. Bd. dirs. City of Long Beach Disasters Com., 1987—, bd. dirs. City of Long Beach St. Fund rebuild com. 1983-85, beautify com. 1983-85. Mem. Nat. Mcht. Assn. (pres. 1982-86). Democrat. Jewish. Office: Conspicuous 313 Sunrise Hwy Rockville Centre NY 11570

SCHULDT, KAREN, human resource consulting executive; b. Schenectady, N.Y., Apr. 14, 1957; d. Robert Reiss Jr. and Laura (Dubaich) S. BA, Dartmouth Coll., 1979. With personnel dept. Dartmouth Coll., Hanover, N.H., 1979-80; compensation analyst Itek Corp., Nashua, N.H., 1980-81; pres. Robert R. Schuldt and Assocs., Fairfax, Va., 1982—. Mem. Am. Compensation Assn., Am. Soc. Personnel Adminstrs., Network of Entrepreneurial Women, Nat. Assn. Women Bus. Owners. Office: Robert R Schuldt & Assocs Ltd 10777 Main St Suite 200 Fairfax VA 22030

SCHULER, ALISON KAY, lawyer; b. West Point, N.Y., Oct. 1, 1948; d. Richard Hamilton and Irma (Sanken) S.; m. Lyman Gage Sandy, Mar. 30, 1974; 1 child, Theodore. A.B. cum laude, Radcliffe Coll., 1969; J.D. Harvard U., 1972. Bar: Va. 1973, D.C. 1974, N.Mex. 1975. Assoc., Hunton & Williams, Richmond, Va., 1972-75; asst. U.S. atty. U.S. Atty's. Office, Albuquerque, 1975-78; adj. prof. law U. N.Mex., 1983-85; ptnr. Sutin, Thayer & Browne, Albuquerque, 1978-85, Montgomery & Andrews, P.A., Albuquerque, 1985-88; sole practice, Albuquerque, 1988—. Bd. dirs. Am. Diabetes Assn., Albuquerque, 1980-85, chmn. bd. dirs., 1984-85, bd. dirs. June Music Festival, 1980—, pres., 1983-85; bd. dirs. Albuquerque Conservation Trust, 1986—; chairperson Albuquerque Com. Fgn. Relations, 1984-85; mem. N.Mex. Internat. Trade and Investment Council, Inc., 1986—, sec., 1987—. Mem. Fed. Bar Assn. (coordinator), ABA, Va. Bar Assn., N.Mex. State Bar Assn. (chmn. corp., banking and bus. law 1982-83, bd. dirs. internat. and immigration law sect. 1987—), Nat. Assn. Women Lawyers, Am. Jud. Soc., Harvard Alumni Assn. (mem. fund campaign, regional dir. 1984-86, v.p. 1986—, chmn. clubs com. 1985—), Radcliffe Coll. Alumnae Assn. Bd. Mgmt. (regional dir. 1984—). Club: Harvard-Radcliffe (pres. 1980-84). Home: 632 Cougar Loop NE Albuquerque NM 87122 Office: 5700 Harper Dr NE Suite #300 PO Box 14721 Albuquerque NM 87109-4721

SCHULMAN, BETTY ANNE, psychologist; b. Newark, Sept. 23, 1950; d. Lawrence J. and Blanche (Weller) Cohen; m. Martin J. Schulman, Feb. 13, 1977 (div. 1984); 1 child, Aryeh. BA, Yeshiva U., 1972; MS in Edn., Queens Coll., 1984; postgrad., Yeshiva U. Cert. sch. psychologist, N.Y. Sch. psychologist dept. of gifted Queens Coll., Flushing, N.Y., 1981-84; research asst. CUNY, 1982-84; sch. psychologist Jamaica (N.Y.) Bd. Edn., 1984—. Mem. Internat. Assn. Applied Psychologists, Nassau County Psychol. Assn., N.Y. State Assn. Sch. Psychologists. Democrat. Jewish. Office: Dist 27 Bd Edn PS 104 2601 Mott Ave Far Rockaway NY 11691

SCHULMAN, EVELINE DOLIN, psychologist, author, consultant; b. N.Y.C.; d. George and Fannie (Simon) Dolin; m. Sol Schulman, June 3, 1941; children: Mark H., Ken S. BS, CCNY, 1939, postgrad., 1940-42; postgrad., State U. Iowa, 1939-40, Am. U., 1947; MEd, U. Md., 1954, EdD, 1957, postgrad., 1979-81. Tchr. Children's Colony, N.Y.C., 1941-42; registrar-tchr. Rockwood Nursery Sch., N.Y.C., 1942-43; asst. dir. Settlement House, Juanita Kauman Nye Council House; dir./tchr. nursery sch., Washington, 1947-48; dir.-tchr. Greenway Co-op. Nursery Sch., Washington, 1947-48, Fairfax Co-op. Nursery Sch., Washington, 1948-50, Community Nursery Sch., Silver Spring, Md., 1952-54; grad. asst. U. Md., 1954-55; psychologist, cons. Prince Georges County Council of Kindergarten and Nursery Schs., 1955-57; psychologist, lectr. Am. U., Washington, 1957; instr. psychology Community Coll. Balt., 1958-62, chmn. dept., 1962-73, prof. psychology, 1964-73, dir. mental health tech. program, 1967-73; lectr. human devel. Inst. for Child Study, U. Md., 1967-68, 69-71; prof. mental health Morgan State Coll., Towson, 1971-77; dir. evaluation and tng. Md. Mental Retardation Adminstrn., Balt., 1974-76, asst. dir. adminstrn., 1976-77; dir., cons. human services Ctr. for Devel. Inter-Personal Skills, Silver Spring, 1977—; cons. Pres.'s Com. on Employment of Handicapped, 1980. Author: Intervention in Human Services—A Guide to Skills and Knowledge, 1974, 3d edit., 1982, Focus on the Retarded Adult, 1980, Retardation of the Mentally Ill—An International Perspective, 1981; contbr. articles in field to profl. jours. Mem. Clifton T. Perkins Adv. Bd., 1972-80, chmn., 1974-80; mem. Mental Health Assn. Montgomery County, 1972, Montgomery County Assn. for Retarded Citizens, 1977; chmn. Montgomery County Council of Disabled Persons Rev. Bds. of Md., 1986—, Wheaton Community Mental Health Adv. Com., 1978—; mem. Montgomery County Com. for Community Edn., about Mentally Ill, 1982-86. Fellow, U. Md., 1954-55. Mem. Am. Psychol. Assn., Ea. Psychol. Assn., Am. Assn. Mental Health Counselors Assn., Am. Counseling and Devel. Assn., Gerontol. Soc., Nat. Council on Aging, Md. Assn. Jr. Colls. (pres. 1967-69). Office: Ctr for Devel Inter-Personal Skills 1103 Caddington Ave Silver Spring MD 20901

SCHULTE, LYNNE NAN, small business owner; b. N.Y.C., Jan. 19, 1958; d. Barney and Florence (Schneiderman) S. AAS, N.Y.C. Fashion Inst., 1976; BBS, Cornell U., 1978. Salesperson, exec. trainer Procter & Gamble, Cranford, N.J., 1978-79; v.p. sales Safian Enterprises Inc., N.Y.C., 1979-84; pres., chief exec. officer The Creative Factor Inc., Hollywood, Fla., 1984—. Mem. Advt. Specialty Inst., Specialty Advt. Assn. Internat., Hollywood C. of C. Office: The Creative Factor Inc 1750 S Young Circle Suite 204 Hollywood FL 33020

SCHULTE, MARY ANN, finance executive; b. Phoenix, Feb. 6, 1953; d. Walter Barry and Norma Gladys (Caffey) S. BSBA, U. So. Calif., 1975. Mgr. acctg. Coldwell Banker, Los Angeles, 1975-78; controller Adams, Ray and Rosenberg, Inc. (now Triad Artists), Century City, Calif., 1978-81; co-owner Marwal, Inc., Los Angeles, 1976-82; controller, chief fin. officer DNA Group, Inc., Pasadena, Calif., 1982-86; chief fin. officer Sukut Constrn., Inc., Santa Ana, Calif., 1986—; cons. Mikeselle DeKorff, Los Angeles, 1981-82, Hollywood (Calif.) High Sch., 1986-87; cons., bd. dirs. Inner Ear Prodns., Los Angeles, 1983-85. Staff leader drop out prevention program Hollywood High Sch., 1986. Mem. Nat. Assn. Accts. (past bd. dirs.), U. So. Calif. Commerce Assocs., Alpha Chi Omega. Republican. Roman Catholic. Office: Sukut Constrn Inc 4010 W Chandler Santa Ana CA 92704

SCHULTZ, DIANE MARIE, food company executive; b. Buffalo, Dec. 23, 1948; d. Richard Frank and Genevieve Mary (Nowak) Buczkowski; m. Clifford Frank Schultz, Jr., July 4, 1975; 1 child, Jennifer Lynn. AS with highest honors in Computer Data Processing, Sumter Area Tech. Coll. Accounts payable clk. Union Carbide Corp., Tarrytown, N.Y., 1969-71; bookkeeper East Aurora Tire Corp., N.Y., 1972-74; sr. account payable clk. Moog, Inc., Hydra-Point Inc., Cheektowaga, N.Y., 1974-75; sr. accounts payable clk. lead purchasing clk., programmer trainee Campbell Soup Co., Sumter, S.C., 1975-85, buyer expediter, 1985—. Mem. welcoming com. St. Ann Cath. Ch., Sumter, 1985; bd. dirs YWCA of Sumter, 1987—, membership com. 1986-87, chmn. fin. devel. com. 1987—. Mem. Purchasing Assn., Nat. Assn. Female Execs. Avocations: organ, cross stitch, sewing. Office: Campbell Soup Co 2050 Hwy 15 S Sumter SC 29150

SCHULTZ, EILEEN HEDY, graphic designer; b. Yonkers, N.Y.; d. Harry Arthur and Hedy Evelyn (Morchel) S. B.F.A., Sch. Visual Arts, 1955. Staff artist C.A. Parshall Studios, N.Y.C., 1955-57; editorial art dir. Paradise of the Pacific, Honolulu, 1957-58; graphic designer Adler Advt. Agy., N.Y.C., 1958-59; art dir. Good Housekeeping Mag., N.Y.C., 1959-82; creative dir. advt. and sales promotion Good Housekeeping Mag., 1982-86; creative dir. Hearst Promo, 1986-87; pres., creative dir. Design Internat., N.Y.C., 1987—. Art dir., editor, designer, 50th Art Directors Club Annual, 1973; columnist: Art Direction, 1969—. Dir. Sch. Visual Arts, N.Y.C., 1978—; trustee Sch. Art League, 1978—; advisor Fashion Inst. Tech., 1979—; mem. adv. commn. N.Y.C. Community Colls., 1979—. Named Yonkers Ambassador of Good Will to Netherlands, 1955; recipient Outstanding Achievement Sch. Visual Arts Alumni Soc., 1976, Sch. Art League Youth award, 1976. Mem. Art Dirs. Club (pres. 1975-77), Joint Ethics Commn. (chmn. 1978-80), Soc. Illustrators (bd. dirs. 1985—), Am. Inst. Graphic Arts, Soc. Publ. Designers, Type Dirs. Club.

SCHULTZ, JANET DARLENE, credit union executive; b. Oakland, Calif., July 22, 1942; d. Charles Emile and Viola Iva (Ogden) Ranvier; m. Orville Carl Schultz Sr., Apr. 7, 1971; children: Carol Marie, Donald Courtland. BSBA, U. Wis., 1978. Cert. credit union mgmt. Loan officer Sierra Schs. Fed. Credit Union, Reno, 1974-79; mgr. Nev. Realtors Credit Union, Reno, 1979-81; pres., chief exec. officer Reno Fed. Credit Union, 1979-85; cons. Union Credit Union, Sparks, Nev., 1986; mgr., chief exec. officer Union Credit Union, Sparks, 1986—; vice chmn. Nev. Cen. Credit Union, Las Vegas, 1980-83; treas. Western Nev. Chpt. Nev. CLU, Reno, 1980-84. Tng. chmn. Boy Scouts Am., 1980, Pow Wow chmn., 1978; treas. Pop Warner Football League, Sparks, 1981, pres. 1987. Recipient Dist. Award of Merit, Boy Scouts Am., 1978. Mem. Nat. Assn. Female Execs., Reno Women Bus. Network, Nat. Notary Assn., Cuna Mktg. Inst., Cuna Fin. Inst., Cuna Alumni Assn., Inc. Democrat. Roman Catholic. Home: 914 Glen Martin Dr Sparks NV 89431 Office: Union Credit Union 1110 Greg St Sparks NV 89431

SCHULTZ, KAREN LEE, fire and water restoration company executive; b. Hempstead, N.Y., June 24, 1953; d. Odd Andre and Irene Mae (Cortez) Solbakken; 1 child, Miakoda Li. Sr. recreation therapist Posada del Sol, Tucson, 1977-81; pres., owner Intimate Luxury, Tucson, 1981-85; gen. mgr. Global Restoration, Tucson, 1985—; pres., owner A&D Restoration, Tucson, 1986—; owner, sec., treas. Ariz. Quality Refinishing, Inc., 1988—. Pres. Activities Dirs. Assn. Tucson, 1979-80; mem. candidate evaluation com. C. of C., Tucson, 1984-86; asst. leader Girl Scouts U.S.A., 1984-85. Mem. Tucson Bus. and Profl. Women, (pres., chmn. Trade Fair 1985-86), Tucson Women's Symposium, So. Ariz. Claims Adjusters, Nat. Assn. Female Execs. Democrat. Office: A&D Restoration Inc 1665 E 18th Suite #108 Tucson AZ 85706

SCHULTZ, LORRAINE HELENE, association executive; b. North Tonawanda, N.Y., Oct. 23, 1930; d. Francis and Michalina Sofia (Jok) Szemraj; student Alma Coll., 1948-50; m. Arthur Henry Schultz, June 18, 1955; children—Brian, Tracey. Stewardess, Eastern Airlines, 1953-55; v.p. Slenderella Internat., 1955-64; pres., owner Detroit Model Bur., 1964-69; dir. Am. Express Travel Club, Mich., 1969-73; pres., owner LHS Assocs., Birmingham, Mich., 1975—; dir. AutoLeather Guild, Birmingham, 1975—. Bd. dirs. Juvenile Diabetes Assn., pres. midwest region, 1988; pres. People Reaching Out, March of Dimes; mem. Republican Leadership Com. of Oakland County. Mem. Nat. Assn. Female Execs., Am. Soc. Profl. and Exec. Women, Nat. Council Career Women, Women's Assn. for Detroit Symphony Orch. (v.p.), Detroit Inst. Arts (treas. Art of Poland Assocs.), Oakland Citizen's League, Birmingham/Bloomington Bd. Realtors, Fashion Group Detroit (regional dir. 1985-86), Am. Lung Assn. (pres. womens com.), Publicity Club N.Y. Roman Catholic. Clubs: Village Players, Rolls Royce Owners (newsletter editor region), Ferrari Owners. Home: 776 Waddington St Birmingham MI 48009 Office: 2501 M St NW Washington DC 20037

SCHULTZ, MARILYN, psychologist; b. Bklyn., Feb. 1, 1936; d. Rubin and Mildred (Cutler) S.; children: Robert, David, Sabrina. MA, Mich. State U., 1966; EdD, U. Houston, 1979. Lic. psychologist, Tex. Clin. psychology intern VA Hosp., Houston, 1979-80; psychologist Clear Lake Ind. Sch. Dist., Houston, 1980-82; instr. Houston Community Coll., 1978-80, 82-83; cons. Harris County Juvenile Probation Program, Houston, 1982-84, Tex. Youth Commn., Houston, 1984-86; pvt. practice psychology Clearlake, Tex., 1980—; instr. U. Houston, 1983—; cons. State Tex. Rehab. Commn., 1985—. Bd. dirs. Ed White Youth Ctr., Seabrook, Tex., 1983—; El Lago Keys Club, Seabrook, 1987. Mem. Am. Psychol. Assn., Tex. Psychol. Assn., Houston Psychol. Assn. Jewish. Office: 17629 El Camino Real Suite 400 Houston TX 77058

SCHULTZ, MARY ELIZABETH, lawyer; b. Seattle, June 12, 1958; d. Peter James and Lillian (Parma) S. BA with honors, U. Tex., 1980; JD, Gonzaga U., 1983. Bar: U.S. Dist. Ct. Wash. 1984, U.S. Dist. Ct. (we. dist., ea. dist.) Wash. 1985, U.S. Ct. Appeals (10th cir.) 1986. From intern to dep. prosecutor City of Spokane Legal Dept., Wash., 1983-84; dep. prosecutor Spokane County Prosecutor's Office, 1984-85; solo practice Spokane, 1985—. Poetry included in Am. Poetry Anthology, 1986. Mem. Assn. Trial Lawyers Am., Wash. State Trial Lawyers Assn., Spokane Bar Assn., Wash. Women Lawyers. Roman Catholic. Office: W101 Indiana Spokane WA 99205

SCHULTZ, PAMELA KAY, real estate broker, supermarket executive; b. Madison, Wis., Oct. 21, 1947; d. Charles Floyd and Delores Marie (Rector) Duane; student Madison Area Tech. Coll., 1975; m. James Mallory Schultz, Jan. 22, 1966; children: Julie Katherine, Jennifer Kay, Karen Elizabeth. Sec. to v.p. Nat. Mut. Benefit Life Ins. Co., Madison, 1965-66; sec., bookkeeper Family Market Enterprises, Inc., DeForest, Wis., 1966—, v.p., sec. 1986—; real estate broker, DeForest; founder Win-Fore Women's Investment Club. Leader, Blackhawk council Girl Scouts U.S.A., 1974, 75, 77, 79-80; founder DeForest Area Hist. Soc., 1975, active membership dr., 1975-79, sec.-treas., 1975-79, bd. dirs., 1975-81; treas. DeForest Moravian Ch., 1977-83, bd. elders, 1986—, mem. Christian edn. com., 1986-88. Recipient Small Bus. award U. Wis., 1986. Mem. DeForest C. of C. (dir. 1984-85, pres. 1986, chmn. retail revitalization com. 1987-88). Home: 305 Meadow Ln DeForest WI 53532 Office: 302 N Main St DeForest WI 53532

SCHULTZ, SANDRA KAY, accountant; b. Fremont, Mich., June 19, 1950; d. Herm Gordon and Cora Grace (Gillette) Nieboer; m. William E. Schultz, Dec. 4, 1971 (div. Apr. 1978); 1 child, Denise Lynn. Student, Davenport Coll., 1968-70. Accounts payable clk. No. Air Service, Grand Rapids, 1969-73; payroll clk. Holwerda-Huizinga, Grand Rapids, 1973; comptroller C&H Moving & Storing Inc, Grand Rapids, 1976—. Mem. Nat. Assn. Female Execs. Republican. Mem. Reformed Christian Ch. Lodge: Altrusa (treas.).

Office: C&H Moving & Storage INc 2740 29th St SE Grand Rapids MI 49508

SCHULTZ, SHELLY L., business entrepreneur; b. Oak Park, IL, June 9, 1953; d. Davis William and Irene Francis (Rock) Shaw; m. Robert V. Schultz, Feb. 12, 1971; children: Robert G., Trina Reneè, Cheriè Anne. Student, Moody Bible Inst., Chgo., 1972-73; artistry master workshops tng., Grand Rapids, Mich., 1978, 80, 82, 84, 86, 88. Exec. sec. H.C. Prange & Co., Rockford, Ill., 1978-80; asst. mgr. Nat. Car Rental, Rockford, 1980-81, Budget Rent-A-Car, Rockford, 1981-82; mgr. Bonanza Restaurant, Rockford, 1982-83; ptnr., owner Diamond Pubs., Inc., Aurora, Ill., 1987—; owner, mgr. TrendSetters, Aurora, 1971—. Vol. Rep. Party, Ill., 1980-84; organizer Awana Youth Club, Polo, Ill., 1977-78; counselor Summit Seekers Kid's Camp, Ala., 1988. Mem. Internat. Diamond Bldrs. (sec. 1980-88), Ambassadors Internat. (award of appreciation 1988). Office: TrendSetters 100 N Lincolnway Suite E Aurora IL 60542

SCHULTZ, THERESA MARIE, systems engineer; b. Spring Valley, Ill., July 9, 1956; d. Raymond E. and Bertha (Golden) S.; m. William J. Krypel, Nov. 15, 1980. BA in Psychology, Rosary Coll., 1977, student; grad. course multiple virtual storage, IBM Corp., 1983; student, Keller Gra. Sch., 1979, 85. Customer service dispatcher Field Engring. div. IBM Corp., OakBrook, Ill., 1978-79; adminstrv. specialist Regional Adminstrv. Support Ctr. IBM Corp., Chgo., 1979-81; sr. adminstrv. specialist Field Engring. div. IBM Corp., Rolling Meadows, Ill., 1981-85; assoc. mktg. support rep. NAD Hdqrs. IBM Corp., Chgo., 1983-86; systems engr. IBM Corp., Northfield, Ill., 1986—; cons. Rosary Coll. Alumni Career Network, River Forest, Ill., 1986. Mem. Art Inst. Chgo.; v.p., sec. Chgo. Metro Bd., Nat. Assn. for Anorexia Nervosa and Associated Disorders, Highland Park, Ill., 1985—; sponsor Grant-A-Wish, Chgo., 1985—; vol. counselor Chgo. North Shore Jr. Achievement Group, 1986; adv. and adv. rep. Northwest Action Against Rape, 1986—. Recipient Alumni Caritas Veritas award Rosary Coll., 1987. Mem. Rosary Coll. Alumni Assn., Nat. Assn. Female Execs., Kappa Gamma Pi. Office: IBM Corp 2 Northfield Pl Northfield IL 60093

SCHULTZE, MARIBETH JANE, psychologist; b. Dayton, Ohio, May 28, 1947; d. Richard Charles and Eileen Rita (Keane) S. BS cum laude, Wright State U., 1969; MA, Clark U., 1973, PhD, 1981. Lic. clin. psychologist, Tex. Resident in clin. psychology Wilford Hall USAF Med. Ctr., San Antonio, 1983; clin. psychologist Sheppard Regional USAF Hosp., Wichita Falls, Tex, , 1983-86; chief psychol. services USAF Hosp., Blytheville, Ark., 1986-87; clin. psychologist Dallas VA Med. Ctr., 1987—; cons. family practice clinic, oral surgery Sheppard Regional Hosp., 1984-86. Contbr. articles to profl. jours. Mem. Am. Psychol. Assn. (div. clin. neuropsychology 1983—), Internat. Neuropsychol. Soc., Soc. Air Force Clin. Psychologists, Assn. Mil. Surgeons of U.S., Tex. Psychol. Assn. (continuing edn. achievement award 1984, 85, 86). Office: Dallas VA Med Ctr 4500 S Lancaster Rd Dallas TX 75115

SCHULTZE, SALVATRICE G., librarian; b. Bklyn., Sept. 3, 1932; d. Salvatore and Carmela (Consolino) Gurissi; m. Edward W. Schultze, Aug. 30, 1952; children: Edward Jr., Paula Kate, Elizabeth Ann, Robert A. BS, Cen. Conn. State U., 1969; MLS, So. Conn. State U., 1974. Children's librarian Hartford (Conn.) Pub. Library, 1975-84, coordinator children's services, 1984—. Pres. Wethersfield (Conn.) Community Theater. Mem. ALA, Conn. Library Assn. Democrat. Office: Hartford Pub Library 500 Main St Hartford CT 06103

SCHULTZ-HOWARD, CRYSTALE MC-CHELLE, service organization administrator; b. Harrisburg, Pa., July 11, 1962; d. Edward Wilson and Lorraine Anna (Long) S; m. Randall Eugene Howard, April 7, 1984 (div. June 1987); 1 child, Jeremy Randy. Student, Mansfield U., 1980-83, Harrisburg Community Coll., 1983-84. Counselor Assn. for Retarded Citizens, Harrisburg, 1977-80, dir., 1981-85; resident asst. Mansfield (Pa.) U., 1980-83; resident advisor Devel. Resources, Harrisburg, 1984, program mgr., 1984—; chairperson Treatment and Ethics, Harrisburg, 1984—; cert. trainer Medication Adminstrn., Selisgrove, Pa., 1986—; mem. Cross Problems, Harrisburg, 1986—. Co-editor People in Partnership, 1987. Bd. dirs. Assn. for Retarded Citizens, 1987; mem. Hist. Soc., 1987—, Mental Retardation Com., 1988. Mem. Nat. Assn. Female Execs., Am. Bus. Women's Assn., Assn. for Retarded Citizens, Alpha Sigma Alpha, Sigma Tau Gamma (White Roses). Home: 268 Church St Millersburg PA 17061 Office: Devel Resources Inc 3554 N Progress Ave Harrisburg PA 17110

SCHULZ, ELSA RUTH, educational administrator; b. Diamante, Argentina, Dec. 25, 1942; came to U.S., 1973; d. Miguel and Emma (Hardy) Esparcia; m. Victor A. Schulz, Jan. 25, 1967; children—Ronald A., Leroy Ed. B.A. in Music Edn., River Plate Coll., Argentina, 1963, B.A. in Edn., 1965; postgrad. Ind. U., 1982, Valparaiso U., 1981; M.A., Andrews U., Mich., 1979. Lic. tchr., Ind. Sch. prin. and tchr., Argentina, 1963-73; acting dir. and bilingual resource tchr. Hobart Sch. Corp., Ind., 1979-82; ESL coordinator Ivy Tech. Coll., Gary, Ind., 1982-85, dept. chair, 1985—. Author: Practical Classroom Suggestions, 1982; Curriculum Guide for Reading Instruction, 4 vols., 1983; numerous film appearances as singer. Mem. Nat. Assn. Female Execs., Nat. Assn. Bilingual Edn., Internat. Conf. Bilingual Edn., Nat. Conf. Bilingual Edn. Avocations: singing; organ and piano. Home: 15808 81st St, Edmonton, AB Canada T5Z 1S5 Office: Ivy Tech Coll 5727 Sohl Ave Hammond IN 46410

SCHULZ, KAREN GAYLE, financial planner; b. Wessington Springs, S.D., Nov. 16, 1959; d. Walter William and Lois Augusta (Thomas) S. BS, S.D. State U., 1982. Asst. mgr. Lerner Shops, Rapid City, S.D., 1982-84, mgr., Denver, 1984-85; fin. planner IDS/Am. Express, Northglenn, Colo., 1985—. Mem. Internat. Assn. for Fin. Planning, Bus. and Profl. Women's Orgn. (treas., chair young careerist com. Colo. chpt. 1987-88). Lutheran. Avocations: skiing, swimming, antique furniture investing. Home: 13467 N Osage St Northglenn CO 80234 Office: IDS/Am Express 11990 Grant St Suite 110 Northglenn CO 80233

SCHUMACHER, SUE BETH, association executive; b. Bklyn.; d. Hyman I. and Gloria (Deutsch) Schoenfeld. BFA, BEd, U. Cin., 1964. Tchr. Elmwood Pl. (Ohio) Sch., 1964-65, Scioto Village High Sch., Delaware, Ohio, 1965-67; program coordinator Nat. Acad. Scis., Washington, 1968-78; sr. analyst Planning Research Corp., McLean, Va., 1978-80; program mgr. Solar Am. Inc., Washington, 1980-85; dir. adminstrn. Am. Fgn. Service Assn., Washington, 1985-87; cons. to community action groups ANC, Washington, 1988—. treas. Adv. Neighborhood Commn., Washington, 1984—; sec. West End Citizens Assn., Washington, 1984—; founder Ward 2 Dems., Washington, 1982; mem. Mayor's Citizen Adv. Bd. on the Budget, Washington, 1983—. Mem. Am. Soc. Assn. Execs., Greater Washington Soc. Assn. Execs. Lodge: Soroptimists (sec. 1987). Office: ANC 1920 G St NW Washington DC 20006

SCHUMACK, JOAN MARIA, poet, journalist; b. Methoni, Greece, Nov. 4, 1953; came to U.S., 1958; d. Eugene John and Lydia Mary (Stellpflug) S. BA, Marquette U., 1976, postgrad. Editor Post Newspapers, West Allis, Wis., 1975-79; with employee communications dept. Allis-Chalmers Corp., 1979; freelance writer Wauwatosa, Wis., 1979-81; info. officer Common Council, Milw., 1981-84; founder, editor, publisher ETHNOS mag., Wauwatosa, 1985—; community programmer Viacom Cablevision, Glendale, Wis., 1983—. Author (poetry) appearing in various jours., assoc. editor Am. Cyclist sect. Bicycling mag., 1980. Active Adoption Info. and Direction, Milw., 1982—; Friend of Milw. Symphony, 1985—, Milw. Art Museum, 1984—; sponsor Cyprus Childrens' Fund, N.Y.C., 1985—; established (with Mrs. Lydia M. Schumack) Eugene J. Schumack Meml. Journalism Fund in the Coll. of Journalism at Marquette U. for grad. study, 1986. Recipient Spl. Award Nat. Council Tchrs. of English, 1972. Mem. Soc. Profl. Jours. (Mark of Excellence award 1975), Milw. Press Club, Women in Communication, Inc., Nat. Assn. Female Execs., Marquette Journalism Alumni Assn. (bd. dirs. 1976-78, 1980-82), Nat. Fedn. Local Cable Programmers, Phil-Hellenic Greek Profl. Soc., Alpha Sigma Nu, Kappa Tau Alpha. Democrat. Eastern Orthodox. Club: Florentine Opera (Milw.). Office: ETHNOS Mag PO Box 25805 Milwaukee WI 53225-0805

SCHUMAN, MARY ELLEN, educational administrator; b. Columbia City, Ind., Jan. 18, 1935; d. Homer Earl and Dorothy Charlotte (Kanable) Schuman; BS, Purdue U., 1957; MS, Colo. State U., 1968. Merchandising trainee Morehouse Fashion Dept. Store, Columbus, Ohio, 1957-58; home demonstration agt. Purdue U., Portland, Ind., 1958-62, New Castle, Ind., 1962-69, area extension agt. youth, 1969-73; extension agt. youth, Marion County (Ind.), Indpls., 1973-81; area adminstr. Coop. Extension Service, 1981-84; dist. dir. Coop. Extension Service for Purdue U., 1984—. Mem. Ind. Youth Council, 1971. Mem. Nat. Assn. Extension Home Economists (Distinguished Service award 1972), Am., Ind. Home Econs. Assns. (Flame award 1987, Honor award 1988), Ind. Extension Agts. Assn. (sec. 1976-77, v.p. 1977-78, pres. 1978-79, Career award 1980), Ind. Extension Home Economists (pres. 1967), Nat. Assn. 4-H Agts. (Distinguished Service award 1972), Ind. Extension Youth Agts. (sec. 1976, pres. 1977), Purdue Alumni Assn., Epsilon Sigma Phi (v.p. 1983-84, pres. 1984-85, Disting. Service award 1987), Gamma Sigma Delta. Club: Altrusa (Indpls.) (rec. sec. 1982-84, pres. 1986-88, Woman of Yr. 1988). Home: 3834 Wilderness Trail Indianapolis IN 46237 Office: 3510 E 96th St Suite 34 Indianapolis IN 46240

SCHUMANN, CLARA (MRS. FREDERICK JOHN SCHUMANN), civic worker; b. Detroit, Dec. 21, 1905; d. Otto Henry and Clara (Schultz) Helm; cert. Detroit Tchrs. Coll., 1926; B.S., Wayne State U., 1932; m. Frederick John Schumann, June 29, 1931; 1 dau., Linda Diane. Bd. dirs. LWV, Grosse Pointe, Mich., 1952-54; v.p. Keep Detroit Beautiful, 1958; Mayor's Com. Keep Grosse Pointe Park Beautiful; bd. dirs. Women's City Club of Detroit, 1941-43; pres. Coll. Women's Club of Detroit, 1936-37; Detroit pres. Women's Nat. Farm and Garden Assn., 1938-40; pres. Federated Garden Clubs of Mich., Inc., 1955-57, bd. dirs., 1970—; bd. dirs. Nat. Council State Garden Clubs, 1955-57; pres. Detroit Garden Center, 1943-44, bd. dirs., 1970—, pres., 1975, 78; sec. Grosse Pointe (Mich.) War Meml. Assn., 1956-58; pres. YWCA of Met. Detroit, 1959, now trustee; mem. world service council of nat. bd. YWCA, 1964; mem. council Internat. Inst. Met. Detroit, v.p., 1970—; pres. Mich. Questers; mem. adv. panel Sta. WTVS, Detroit, 1981—, Sta. WTVS-TV; bd. dirs. Adult Service Centers, 1982—. Mem. Alpha Sigma Tau. Unitarian. Home: 836 Harcourt Rd Grosse Pointe MI 48230

SCHUMER, MIRIAM HERNANDEZ, scientific journal editor; b. Aguas Buenas, P.R., Sept. 11, 1925, came to U.S., 1944, d. Ramon and Mary (Melendez) Hernandez; children—Gerard M. Soto, Leonard, Daniel Anthony, Naomi Nilza Jacobsen; m. William Schumer. Student U. P.R., Rio Piedras, 1942-43, CCNY, 1944-45, Brown's Bus. Coll. and Edison Ediphone Sch., N.Y.C., 1947-48, spl. programs cons. on rehab. tuberculosis and health assn., N.Y.C., 1947, Sacramento Coll., 1965-67. Exec. sec. physics Meml. Cancer Ctr. and Sloan-Kettering Inst., N.Y.C., 1952-53, U.S. Vitamin Corp., N.Y.C., 1953-55; consumer columnist El Diario de Nueva York, N.Y.C., 1955-57; adminstrv. asst. dept. surgery Chgo. Med. Sch., 1960-65, U. Calif.-Davis, 1965-67, U. Ill. and VA West Side Hosp., Chgo., 1967-75; adminstrv. and editorial asst. dept. surgery U. of Health Scis./Chgo. Med. Sch. and VA North Chicago (Ill.) Med. Ctr., 1975-80; asst. exec. editor dept. surgery U. of Health Scis./Chgo. Med. Sch., North Chicago, Ill., 1980—; asst. exec. editor Circulatory Shock jour., N.Y.C., 1979-88, cons. editorial office, N.Y.C., 1988—; counselor equal opportunity employment 1976-79. Founder Beneficent Hispanic Soc. N.Y., 1947; founding mem. Hispanic Theater of N.Y., 1948; mem. Lake County Health Systems Agy., 1980-81. Recipient commendations VA, 1971, 79. Club: Espanol of North Shore. Home: 1995 Shore Acres Rd Lake Bluff IL 60044 Office: U Health Sci/Chgo Med Sch Dept of Surgery 3333 Green Bay Rd North Chicago IL 60064

SCHUNEMAN, DAWN MARIE, marketing professional; b. Mankato, Minn., Feb. 19, 1963; d. Donald Duane and Jacqualine Ann (Olson) S. BS in Speech and Mass Communications, Mankato State U., 1985. Reporter, anchor person Sta. KMSU Nat. Pub. Radio, Mankato, 1981-85; mktg. assoc. Sta. KGAC Minn. Pub. Radio, St. Peter, 1985—; reporter, writer Ultra High Frequency Channel 22, New Ulm, Minn., 1983-84, Sta. KEYC-TV, Mankato, 1985; writer, producer Sta. SAVE-TV, Mankato, 1983-84. Aide Mankato mayoral race, 1986. Lutheran. Lodge: Lions. Home: 111 Parkway Ave Mankato MN 56001 Office: Sta KGAC-FM Minn Pub Radio PO Box 236 Saint Peter MN 56082

SCHUPP, PRISCILLA LISTER, publishing company executive; b. La Jolla, Calif., Oct. 31, 1949; d. Keith F. and Margaret Jean (Boman) L.; m. Robert Olds Schupp, Nov. 18, 1982. B.A. in English, Northwestern U., 1971; student U. Wash., 1973-74, Western Wash. State U., 1974-75. Cert. secondary sch. tchr., Wash. Asst. account exec. Cole & Weber, Inc., Seattle, 1975-77; catalog copy chief Recreational Equipment, Inc., Seattle, 1978-80; editor La Mesa (Calif.) Courier, 1980-84, pub., 1981—; city editor San Diego Daily Transcript, 1984—. co-founder, dir. Seattle Women in Advt.; 1976. Office: San Diego Daily Transcript 2131 3d Ave San Diego CA 92101

SCHUPP, SUSAN WAGNER, data processing executive; b. Norfolk, Va., Apr. 3, 1953; d. Charles Orville and Elizabeth Irene (Hundley) Wagner; m. Donald Lawrence Schupp Jr., Sept. 19, 1981; 1 child, Julie Rebecca. BA, East Carolina U., 1979. Pension processor I. A. M. Nat. Pension Fund, Washington, 1976-79, asst. supr. pension dept., 1979-80, asst. mgr. programming and analysis, 1980-81; systems analyst Am. Automobile Assn., Falls Church, Va., 1981-82, sr. systems analyst, 1982-83, mgr. office info. systems, 1983-86, dir. office info. system, 1986—. Sec. Fairfax (Va.) Audubon Soc., 1981-83. Mem. Assn. Info. Systems Profls., Va. Soc. Ornithology.

SCHUR, SUSAN DORFMAN, state legislator; b. Newark, Feb. 27, 1940; d. Norman and Jeanette (Handelman) Dorfman; B.A., Goucher Coll., 1961; children—Diana Elisabeth, Erica Marlene. Adminstr. fed. housing, fgn. aid, anti-poverty programs, 1961-67; mem. Mass. Housing Appeals Com., 1977-81; mem., v.p. Bd. of Alderman, Newton, Mass., 1974-81; mem. Mass. Ho. of Reps., 1981—; mem. Spl. Commn. on Divorce. Bd. dirs. Mass. chpt. Ams. for Democratic Action. Mem. Newton Democratic City Com., 1970—. Mem. LWV, Boston Network Women in Politics and Govt., Nat. Women's Polit. Caucus, Mass. Caucus Women Legislators. Office: State House Boston MA 02133

SCHUSTER, EULA ELAINE, lawyer; b. Oklahoma City, June 8, 1936; d. John Otto and Eula Delone (Campbell) Schuster; AB, Sweet Briar Coll., 1958; MA, U. Okla., 1961, JD, 1968. Bar: Okla. 1968. Prof. econs. Southeastern State U., Durant, Okla., 1961-65; pvt. practice Whitten & Whitten, Oklahoma City, 1968-71; asst. dist. atty. Oklahoma County, 7th Dist., 1972-78; ptnr. Jones, Schuster & Flaugher, Oklahoma City, 1978-82, E. Elaine Schuster, P.C., 1982—; lectr. in field. Mem. Oklahoma County Bd. Adjustment, 1978—, chmn., 1984-86, citizen mem. profl. liaison com. City of Oklahoma City, 1980—; mem. Bd. Edn., Oklahoma City Area Vocat. Tech. Sch., Dist. 22, 1982—, pres., 1984-85; mem. ch. bd. University Pl. Christian Ch., 1982-86; bd. overseers Sweet Briar Coll., 1986-1990; bd. dirs. Okla. Christian Ch. Found., 1988. Gen. Electric grantee, 1963; named Outstanding Bus. Woman. of Okla., 1986. Mem. ABA, Okla. Trial Lawyers Assn., Fed. Bar Assn., AAUW (br. pres. 1978-80, Okla. div. bd. 1969-75, 81-83, 85-87), Oklahoma County Bar Assn., Okla. Bar Assn., Kappa Beta Pi, Delta Kappa Gamma. Office: Heritage Law Ctr 515 NW 13th Oklahoma City OK 73103

SCHUSTER, SAUNDRA KOHL, academic administrator; b. Springfield, Ohio, Oct. 14, 1948; d. Frederick I. and Opal L. (Salyer) Kohl; m. Russell Eugene Schuster II, Aug. 28, 1971; children: Russell Eugene III, Kristopher Frederick. BS, Miami U., Oxford, Ohio, 1970, MS, 1972; postgrad., Ohio State U., 1984-87. Cert. tchr., Ohio. Asst. to dean of students Western Coll., Oxford, Ohio, 1972-73; dir. head start Preble County Social Services, Eaton, Ohio, 1973-74; asst. coordinator devel. edn. Miami U., 1974-76, coordinator devel. edn., 1976-79, dir. devel. edn., 1979-82; judicial affairs dir. Ohio State U., Columbus, 1983—, coordinator alcohol and drug edn., 1985—, dir. student devel., 1987; instr. Miami U., 1974-82; cons. in field, 1983—. Pres. Children's Hosp. Twig, Columbus, 1984—; v.p. Worthington (Ohio) PTA, 1986-87; bd. dirs. Ctr. for Sci. and Industry, Columbus, 1985-87; active Worthington Welcome Wagon, Columbus, 1983-84. Mem. Am. Assn. Counseling and Devel., Nat. Assn. Student Personnel Adminstrn., Am. Soc. for Tng. and Devel, Nat. Assn. Judicial Affairs. Club: Worthing Women's Reading Circle. Lodge: Order Eastern Star. Home: 1952 Samada Dr Worthington OH 43085 Office: Ohio State U Student Life 1739 N High St Columbus OH 43210

SCHUTTE, PAULA MARION, information systems strategist, consultant; b. St. Paul, Oct. 29, 1941; d. Paul Maurice and Marion (McAllister) S. BA in Chemistry, Rosary Coll., River Forest, Ill., 1963; MBA, NYU, 1985. Med. research chemist Geigy Chem. Corp., Ardsley, N.Y., 1964-70; group leader, sci. systems CIBA-Geigy Corp., Ardsley, N.Y., 1970-77, mgr. sci. info., 1980-83, sr. research fellow, 1985-86, dir. end user services, 1986-87; dir. info. techs. CIBA-Geigy Corp., Ardsley, 1987—; dir. med. systems pharm. div. CIBA-Geigy Corp., Summit, N.J., 1977-80; dir. sci. info. systems pharm. div. CIBA-Geigy Corp., Summit, 1983-85; research coordinator Prism, Cambridge, Mass., 1985—; info. systems cons. St. Jude's, Thornwood, N.Y., 1985-86; adv. Pace U. Computer Sci. and Info. Systems Bd. Patentee in field. Mem. Am. Mgmt. Assn., Assn. Computing Machinery, Chem. Notation Assn. Office: CIBA-Geigy Corp 444 Saw Mill River Rd Ardsley NY 10502

SCHUTZBANK, CAROL LYNNE, public relations and marketing specialist; b. Trenton, N.J., Jan. 5, 1961; d. Merrill and Muriel Mavis (Berger) S. BA cum laude, Temple U., 1982. Asst. dir. Soviet Jewry Council, Phila., 1983-85; asst. dir. mktg. S.I.A.M. Inc., Phila., 1985-87; mktg. and pub. relations assoc. Schutzbank & Banks, Phila., 1987-88; pres. Modern Music & Entertainment, Phila., 1988—; cons. Hard Times Prodns., Phila., 1985—, Raw Entertainment Prodns., Phila., 1986—. Sr. editor B-Side mag., 1986—, San Francisco, dir. advt. and mktg., 1984—; author poetry (Golden Poet award Am. Poetry Assn. 1985, Silver Poet award 1986, 87); contbr. articles to mags. Founder, assoc. dir. Concerned Arts Coalition, Phila., 1985—. Mem. Nat. Writers' Union, NOW, Sonic Options Network, Nat. Council Women in the Arts (co-founder 1985), Naral, Music Network (Phila.) (bd. dirs.), Musicians, Artists, Poets and Performers (bd. dirs. 1988). Office: Schutzbank & Banks PO Box 15921 Philadelphia PA 19103

SCHUYLER, JANE, fine arts educator; b. Flushing, N.Y., Nov. 2, 1943; d. Frank James and Helen (Oberhofer) S.; BA, Queens Coll., 1965; MA, Hunter Coll., 1967; PhD, Columbia U., 1972. Asst. prof. art history Montclair State Coll., Upper Montclair, N.J., 1970; coordinator fine arts, asst. prof. York Coll., CUNY, Jamaica, 1973-77, 78-87, assoc. prof., 1988— , C.W. Post Coll., LIU, Greenvale, N.Y., 1971-73, adj. assoc. prof., 1977-78. Mem. Fine Arts Com. Internat. Women's Arts Festival, 1974-76; pres. United Community Democrats of Jackson Heights, 1987—. N.Y. Columbia U. Summer Travel and Research grantee, 1969. Mem. Coll. Art Assn. Am., Women's Caucus for Art, AAUP, Nat. Trust Hist. Preservation, Renaissance Soc. Am. Roman Catholic. Contbr. articles on occult and art to Cakes and Ale, 1978, Italian Quar., 1982, Secac Jour. on Italian Renaissance art, 1983, 85, Source, 1986, 87, Studies in Iconography, 1987. Author: Florentine Busts: Sculpted Portraiture in the Fifteenth Century, 1976. Home: 35 37 78th St Jackson Heights NY 11372

SCHWAB, CAROL ANN, lawyer; b. Washington, Mo., Mar. 2, 1953; d. Calvin George and Edith Emma (Starke) Schermann; m. Steven Joseph Schwab, May 31, 1975. BA, Southeast Mo. State U., 1975; JD, U. Mo., 1978; LLM, Washington U., St. Louis, 1985. Bar: Mo. 1979, N.C. 1986. Law clk. to presiding justice U.S. Dist. Ct. (we. dist.), Kansas City, Mo., 1979-82; assoc. Bryan, Cave, McPheeters & Roberts, St. Louis, 1982-84, Smith, Anderson, Blount, Dorsett, Mitchell & Jernigan, Raleigh, N.C., 1985-87; asst. prof., resource mgmt. specialist Extension div. N.C. State U., Raleigh, 1988—; instr. legal writing St. Louis U. Sch. Law, 1984. Contbr. articles to profl. jours. Recipient John S. Divilbiss award U. Mo., 1977. Mem. ABA, N.C. Bar Assn., Mo. Bar Assn. Republican. Roman Catholic.

SCHWAGER, ELAINE SUSAN, psychologist; b. Pitts., Aug. 3, 1949; d. Carl and Inge Susi (Weihl) S.; m. Marvin Hurvich, Nov. 1, 1981; children—Carl Harry, Julia Beth. B.A. cum laude in English Lit., CCNY, 1969; M.A. in English Lit., SUNY, Stony Brook, 1971; PhD, in Clin. Psychology, L.I.U., 1977; cert. pschoanalysis, psychotherapy, NYU, 1986—. Intern, then postdoctoral fellow N.Y. Hosp. Cornell U. Med. Center, White Plains, 1975-79; asst. prof. psychology Downstate Med. Center, Bklyn., 1979—; staff psychologist Blueberry Treatment Center, Bklyn, 1980-81; ind. practice psychoanalytic psychotherapy, 1978—. Mem. Am. Psychol. Assn., Soc. Personality Assessment, N.Y. Psychol. Assn. Home and Office: 228 W 22nd St New York NY 10011

SCHWALB, ANN WEISS, editor, writer, photographer, information specialist, consultant; b. Modena, Italy, July 17, 1949; came to U.S., 1951, naturalized, 1959; d. Leo and Athalie (Schaefer) Weiss; m. Allen J. Schwalb, June 27, 1971; children: Julia Emily, Rebecca Lauren. BA magna cum laude, U. Rochester, 1971; MA, Drexel U., 1973. Cert. med. librarian, cert. pub. librarian, cert. sch. librarian. Tchr. English, Bay Trail High Sch., Pittsford, N.Y.; cataloguer Drexel U., Phila., 1971-73; librarian Akiba Lower Sch., Merion, Pa., 1973; head children's dept. Tredyffrin Pub. Library, Strafford, Pa., 1973-79, co-head reference dept., 1979-86; editor chief cons. monographs, articles, freelance photographer, 1974—; cons. Rabbi Zalman Schachter-Shalomi, P'nei Or Fellowship, 1987—; photojournalist in Poland and Czechoslovakia, 1987-88. Chief editorial cons. Puppetry and the Art of Story Creation, 1981, Puppetry in Early Childhood Education, 1982, Puppetry, Language and the Special Child: Discovering Alternative Language, 1984, Humanizing the Enemy... and Ourselves, 1986, Imagination, 1987, Celebrate! Holidays, Puppetry and Creative Dramatics, 1987; co-author, lyricist (musical) Zosia's Story, 1987. Active So. Poverty Law Ctr.; Common Cause; advocacy and fundraising for Ethiopian Jews; active Shalom Ctr., Jewish Resource Ctr. for Nuclear Arms Abolition, Council for Soviet Jews, Internat. Network Children Holocaust Survivors. Photographer Bob Edgar's Campaign U.S. Senate, 1985-86, David Landau's Congl. Campaign, 1986. Mem. ALA, Pa. Library Assn., ACLU, Free Wallenberg Alliance, Union Concerned Scientists, SANE, Physicians for Social Responsibility, Amnesty Internat., Shalom Ctr. Home: 438 Barclay Rd Rosemont PA 19010

SCHWALB, SUSAN AMELIA, artist, educator; b. N.Y.C., Feb. 26, 1944; d. Morris and Evelyn C. Schwalb; m. Martin Boykan, Nov. 6, 1983. B.F.A., Carnegie-Mellon U., 1965. Designer Dell Pub. Co., N.Y.C., 1965-67, asst. art dir. Holt, Rinehart & Winston, N.Y.C., 1967-68; free-lance artist, Watertown, Mass., 1968—; instr. art Kean Coll., Union, N.J., 1978-79; adj. lectr. CUNY, 1979-82; assoc. adj. prof. Mass. Coll. Art, Boston, 1982—; spl. instr. Simmons Coll., 1988; dir. Internat. Festival of Women Artists, Copenhagen, 1979-81. Represented in permanent collections Silverpoint Drawings, Norton Gallery of Art, West Palm Beach, Fla., Fogg Art Mus., Harvard U., Chase Manhattan Bank, N.Y.C., Ark. Arts Ctr. Found., Little Rock, Mus. Modern Art, Belgrade, Yugoslavia, Boston Pub. Library. Del. Internat. Women's Yr. Conv., Houston, 1977, mem. presdl. Continuing Commn. Conf., 1978. Va. Ctr. for Creative Arts fellow, 1973; MacDowell Colony fellow, 1974, 75; Yaddo fellow, 1981. Mem. Coalition Women's Art Orgns. (founding exec. com. 1977-78, v.p. 1985-87, nat. advt. bd. 1987—), Women's Caucus for Art, (co-coordinator Boston chpt. 1982-83). Democrat. Jewish. Home: 10 Winsor Ave Watertown MA 02172 Office: Mass Coll Art Boston MA

SCHWALLER, SHIRLEY FILES, publisher; b. Ft. Worth, Feb. 16, 1946; d. John Thomas and Janette Elizabeth (Hicks) Files; m. Leonard Edward Kowitz, Oct. 6, 1968 (div. Mar. 1979); children: Jeffrey Edward, Kendra Denise; m. Robert Corbett Schwaller, Sept. 17, 1983; children: Mark Files Schwaller. BBA, U. Tex., 1968; BA in Communications, U. Houston, 1979. Reporter The Mirror, Houston, 1977-78; bus. editor Saudi Research and Mktg., Houston, 1978-79; writer Houston Bus. Jour., 1979-81; v.p. Hart & Assocs., Houston, 1981-82; freelance writer Wall St. Jour. and Houston Bar Jour., Houston, 1982-83; editor Dallas-Ft. Worth Bus. Jour., 1983-85, Dallas Times Herald, 1985-87; co-founder, editor SR Dallas, 1987—. Contbr. numerous articles to profl. jours. Mem. Mayor's Task Force on Employing the Handicapped, Dallas, 1985—; adv. bd. Shared Housing, City of Dallas; bd. dirs. Metro Dallas YMCA Communities Service. Finalist Best Healdine Portfolio Tex. Press Assn., 1987. Mem. Nat. Assn. Bus. Editors and Writers, Joint Christian Sci. Adv. Com. (co-chmn. 1987—), Dallas Press Club (Finalist Best Headline Portfolio 1986, Finalist Best Specialty Pub. 1986), Soc. Profl. Jours., Dallas C. of C. (chmn. pub. relations com. 1985—). Democrat. Office: SR Dallas 7557 Rambler Rd Suite 819 Dallas TX 78231

SCHWANER, ANNIE MAE GINN, state legislator; b. Carnesville, Ga., Apr. 24, 1912; d. Charles Holman and Mary Elizabeth (Terrell) Ginn; m. Nelson Marshall Schwaner (dec. 1967); children—Gordon Wesley, Audrey Mae, Susan Anne, Marsha Mae, Nelson Marshall II. Sec., Tubize Corp., Hopewell, Va., 1934-35; former reporter Hopewell News; former columnist Progress Index, Petersburg, Va.; mem. N.H. Ho. of Reps., 1963—, mem. mcpl. and county govt. com., 1963, mem. state constl. conv., 1964, 74-84, resources, recreation, and devel. com.; mem. exec. bd. Rockingham County Legis. Del., 1973—. Mem. State Security Task Force, also Price Stblzn. Bd., 1964—; founder, 1st pres. Plaistow (N.H.) Civic Orgn., 1959-60; chmn. vols. Greater Haverhill (Mass.) chpt. ARC, 1954-57, nat. del., 1955, exec. bd., 1954-57; com. chmn. PTA council, Worcester, 1947-48; exec. bd. Sea Coast Regional Plan, 1965-67; v.p. Seacoast Regional Devel. Assn.; mem. Diocesan Sch. Bd., 1965-71; chmn. various fund-raising drs.; mem. nat. fund raising and adv. bd. Am. Heart Assn.; mem. Rockingham County Selective System Draft Bd.; pres. Plaistow Women's Republican Club, 1964-66; bd. dirs. N.H. Heart Assn., state heart fund chmn., 1973; bd. dirs. Greater Salem Mental Health Clinic, 1976, So. Rockingham Mental Health Assn., 1975—; mem. N.H. Commn. on Status of Women. Recipient Bronze medal N.H. Heart Assn, 1959, cert. of merit Am. Mothers Com., 1960, cert. of honor N.H. DAV, 1965; citation White House, ARC. Mem. Cath. Daus. Am., Cath. Women's Guild (past pres.), Nat. Order Women Legislators (state pres. 1973). Roman Catholic (ch. adv. bd.).

SCHWARTZ, BELLA, artist; b. N.Y.C.; d. Maurice and Rachel (Greenberg) S. BA, George Washington U., 1944, MA, 1951. Commr. Dupont Circle Adv. Neighborhood Commn., 1987-88. Mem. Artists Equity (pres. Washington chpt. 1977-78), Washington Water Color Assn. (pres. 1975). Club: DuPont Circle (Washington) (commr. adv. neighborhood commn. 1987—). Home and Office: 2122 Massachusetts Ave NW Washington DC 20008

SCHWARTZ, CAROL LEVITT, federal agency administrator; b. Greenville, Miss., Jan. 20, 1944; d. Stanley and Hilda (Simmons) Levitt; m. David H. Schwartz; children: Stephanie, Hilary, Douglas. BS in Spl. and Elem. Edn., U. Tex., 1965. Mem. transiton team Office of Pres. Elect, 1980-81; con. office presdl. personnel The White House, Washington, 1981; cons. U.S. Dept. Edn., Washington, 1982; pres. sec. U.S. Ho. Reps., Washington, 1982-83; mem. at large staff Council Dist. Columbia, Washington, 1985—; active Nat. Adv. Council on Edn. Disadvantaged Children, 1974-79, D.C. Bd. Edn., 1974-82, lectr. in field. asst. treas. Metropolitan Police Boys and Girls Clubs, 983, asst. sec., 1984, sec., 1985—, chmn. membership program, 1984—, bd. dirs., 1981—., mem. adv. council Am. Council Young Polit. Leaders, 1982—, active nat. council Friends of Kennedy Ctr., 1984—; active numerous other civic, cultural and ednl. orgns. Republican. Jewish. Office: Council of DC 101 The District Bldg Washington DC 20004

SCHWARTZ, CHERYL ANN, health lecturer, video and television producer, writer, actress; b. Cin., Sept. 4, 1949; d. Denny Lee and Alice Jane (Taylor) S. A.S., U. Cin., 1970, student 1967-72; student West Los Angeles Coll., 1977-79, Calif. State U.-Northridge, 1979-80, Pierce Coll., Woodland Hills, Calif., 1981-83, UCLA, 1986, U. So. Calif., 1986. Publisher, editor The Well Woman, Beverly Hills, Calif., 1980—, The Showhawk Flash, Hawaii Expressions; lectr. Internat. Toxic Shock Syndrome Network, Beverly Hills, 1980—, also founder, dir.; dir. Hawaii Express, Los Angeles, 1982; owner, mgr. C.A. Schwartz & Assocs., Beverly Hill, 1982—; producer, host. The Well Woman, Encino, 1983-84, Cheryl & Co., Santa Monica, Calif., 1984—; pres. Cheryl A. Schwartz Prodns., Beverly Hills, 1983—; cons. Nat. Women's Health Network, Washington, 1981—. Author: In the Gutter Looking at Stars, 1980; editor: The Showhawk Flash, Hawaii Expressions; exec. producer, writer Easy Does It: The Excercise Video for the Rest of Us; editor: The Showhawk Flash, Hawaii Expressions. Mem. commn. on Status of Women, Los Angeles, 1980—; bd. dirs. Womens Equal Rights Legal Def. and Edn. Fund, 1983—; vol. UCLA Med. Center 1976-80; mem. Inter-Agy. Council on Child Abuse and Neglect, Los Angeles, 1983, Wildlife Waystation, Starlight Found., So. Calif. Coalition on Battered Women, United Friends of the Children; media cons. Wild Horse Sanctuary; mem. women's aux. John Wayne Cancer Clinic; co-chmn. Olympic Women's Marathon Celebration, Los Angeles, 1984. Mem. Am. Fedn. TV and Radio Artists, ASTM, Am. Film Inst., Screen Actors Guild, Aircraft Owners and Pilots Assn., Calif. Women's Health Network, Writers Guild Am., Empire State Consumer Assn., Nat. Consumers League, Women in Show Bus., Women in Film, Women Health Internat. (resourcee). Republican. Clubs: Farkus (Beverly Hills); Los Angeles Polo, Show Hawks Flying. Office: PO Box 1248 Beverly Hills CA 90213-1248

SCHWARTZ, DORIS RUHBEL, nursing educator, consultant; b. Bklyn., May 30, 1915; d. Henry and Florence Marie (Shuttleworth) S. B.S., NYU, 1953, M.S., 1955. RN, Mass., N.Y. Staff nurse Methodist Hosp., Bklyn., 1942-43; pub. health nurse Vis. Nurse Assn., Bklyn., 1947-51; pub. health nurse Cornell U. Med. Coll., Cornell-N.Y. Hosp. Sch. Nursing, N.Y.C., 1951-61, tchr. pub. health nursing, geriatric nursing, 1961-80; sr. fellow U. Pa. Sch. Nursing, Phila., 1981—. Contbr. articles to profl. jours. Served to capt., N.C., U.S. Army, 1943-47, PTO. NSF fellow, 1975-76; recipient Diamond Jubilee Nursing award N.Y. County Registered Nurses Assn., 1979. Fellow Am. Pub. Health Assn. (disting. career award nursing sect. 1979) mem. Am. Nurses Assn. (Pearl McIver award 1979), Am. Acad. Nursing (governing council 1973-74), Inst. Medicine, Sigma Theta Tau (recipient founders award 1979). Democrat. Mem. Soc. of Friends. Club: Soroptimist Internat. (N.Y.C.) (v.p. 1974-75). Office: U Pa Sch Nursing Teaching Nursing Home Office 420 Service Dr Philadelphia PA

SCHWARTZ, ELEANOR BRANTLEY, academic administrator; b. Kite, Ga., Jan. 1, 1937; d. Jesse Melvin and Hazel (Hill) Brantley; children—John, Cynthia. Student Mercer U., Ga. So. Coll., 1956-57; B.B.A., Ga. State U., 1961, M.B.A., 1963, D.B.A., 1969. Adminstrv. asst. Fin. Agy., 1954, Fed. Govt., Va., Pa., Ga., 1959-61; asst. dean admissions Ga. State U., Atlanta, 1961-65, asst. prof., 1965-70; assoc. prof. Cleve. State U., 1970-80, assoc. dean, 1975-80; dean, Harzfeld prof. U. Mo., Kansas City, 1980-87, vice chancellor acad. affairs, 1987—; disting. vis. prof. Berry Coll., Rome, Ga., N.Y. State U. Coll., Fredonia, Mons U., Belgium; cons. pvt. industry, U.S., Europe, Can.; dir. Sentinel Consumer Products, Inc., Ameri-Bank, Inc., 1986—, Am. Carriers, Inc. Author: Sex Barriers in Business, 1971, Contemporary Readings in Marketing, 1974; (with Muczyk and Smith) Principles of Supervision, 1984. Chmn., Mayor's Task Force in Govt. Efficiency, Kansas City, Mo., 1984; mem. community planning and research council United Way Kansas City, 1975-78; bd. dirs. Jr. Achievement, 1982—, Greater Kansas City ARC. Recipient Disting. Faculty award Cleve. State U., 1974, Cleve. Community Career Achievement award YMCA, 1980, 60 Women of Achievement Girls Scouts Council Mid Continent, 1983. Mem. Am. Mktg. Assn., Acad. Internat. Bus., Am. Mgmt. Assn., Am. Case Research Assn., Internat. Soc. Study Behavioral Devel., Beta Gamma Sigma (bd. govs.). Office: Univ Mo Sch Acad Affairs Kansas City MO 64110

SCHWARTZ, ILENE, psychotherapist, educator; b. Phila., June 19, 1942; d. Israel Gerson and Jean (Soloway) Schiffman; m. Victor Louis Schwartz, Jan. 6, 1970 (div. 1980); 1 child, Amy Jill. B.S., Temple U., 1970; postgrad. U. Pa., 1981-82. Instr. psychology Pratt Inst., Bklyn., 1969-70; psychotherapist Phila. Mental Health Clinic, 1972-74, Phila. Consultation Ctr., 1974-80, Help, Inc., Phila., 1974-80; pvt. practice psychologist, Phila., 1980—; instr. Community Coll. Phila., 1974-80; cons. in field. Mem.Am. Psychol. Assn.

SCHWARTZ, JOYCE GENSBERG, pathologist; b. San Antonio, July 24, 1950; d. Frank and Sara Gensberg; B.A., U. Tex.-Austin, 1971, M.A., 1972; M.D., U. Tex.-San Antonio, 1980; m. Alan R. Schwartz, July 17, 1977. Speech pathologist Northeast Ind. Sch. Dist., San Antonio, 1971-73; vet. asst., 1973-74; resident in pathology Audie Murphy VA Hosp., San Antonio; pathology Faculty U. Tex. Health Sci. Ctr. at San Antonio, 1984. Mem. AMA, Coll. Am. Pathologists, Bexar County Med. Assn., Women's Faculty Assn. (pres. 1988-89), San Antonio Soc. Pathologists (pres. 1988-89), Phi Kappa Phi. Jewish.

SCHWARTZ, JUDY ELLEN, navy cardiothoracic surgeon; b. Mason City, Iowa, Oct. 5, 1946; d. Walter Carl and Alice Nevada (Moore) Schwartz. B.S., U. Iowa, 1968, M.D., 1971. Diplomate Am. Bd. Surgery, Am. Bd. Thoracic Surgery. Intern, Nat. Naval Med. Center, Bethesda, Md., 1971-72, gen. surgery resident, 1972-76, thoracic surgery resident, 1976-78, staff cardiothoracic surgeon, 1979-82, chief cardiothoracic surgeon, 1982-83; chmn. cardiothoracic surg. dept. Naval Hosp., San Diego, 1983-85, quality assurance program dir., 1985—, exec. officer Rapidly Deployable Med. Facility Four, 1986—; asst. prof. surgery Uniformed Services Univ. Health Scis., Bethesda, 1983—; cardiothoracic speciality cons. to naval med. command U.S. Navy, Washington, 1983-84. Contbr. articles to various publs. Fellow Am. Coll. Cardiology, Am. Coll. Surgeons; mem. Am. Thoracic Soc., Am. Med. Women's Assn., AMA, Uniformed Services Univ. Surg. Assocs., Am. Mgmt. Assn., Am. Acad. of Med. Dirs. Lutheran. Office: Quality Assurance Unit Naval Hosp San Diego CA 92134

SCHWARTZ, KAREN MARCIA, clinical psychologist; b. Bklyn.; d. Bernard Leonard and Irene (Zanderer) S.; m. John Paddock, Sept. 5, 1982. B.S. summa cum laude in Psychology and Fine Arts, Tufts U., 1975; M.A. in Clin. Psychology, Emory U., 1978, Ph.D. in Clin. Psychology, 1980. Intern in psychology Emory U. Med. Sch.-Grady Meml. Hosp., Atlanta, 1979-80, Clayton Mental Health Ctr., Riverdale, Ga., 1980-81; asst. prof. counseling, counselor Counseling Ctr., Ga. State U., Atlanta, 1981—; asst. adj. prof. dept. psychology Emory U., 1987-88; pvt. practice family and couples therapy, individual psychotherapy; cons. in field. Ga. State U. Urban-Life grantee, 1982-83, 83-84. Mem. Am. Psychol. Assn., Ga. Psychol. Assn. (chmn. div. women psychologists), Southeast Psychol. Assn., Phi Beta Kappa. Office: 2905 Piedmont Rd Suite B Atlanta GA 30303

SCHWARTZ, KATHERINE FRANCES, market research executive; b. N.Y.C., Dec. 31, 1946; d. Robert Norman Van Gilder and Muriel Pearl (Roth) Heatley; m. Paul Morton Schwartz, Aug. 21, 1966. BA, CCNY, 1967. Project dir. Russell Mktg. Research, N.Y.C., 1967-72; v.p., research dir. William Knobler Co., Inc., Manhasset, N.Y., 1972-87; group head CRC Info. Systems Inc., N.Y.C., 1988—. Mem. L.I. Ctr. Bus. and Profl. Women. Jewish. Club: Sea Cliff Yacht (N.Y.). Home: 24 Fairview Ave Port Washington NY 11050 Office: CRC Info Systems Inc 435 Hudson St New York NY 10014

SCHWARTZ, LAURIE KOLLER, association executive, development consultant; b. Munich, Germany, Oct. 19, 1947; came to U.S., 1949, naturalized, 1954; d. Felix and Sally (Wiernik) Koller; m. Michael Louis Schwartz, Aug. 20, 1967; children: Jonas David, Adam Avi, Samara Beth. Diploma in radiol. tech. Mercy Hosp., Balt., 1967; BA, U. Balt., 1988. Lic. real estate agt., Md. Radiol. technologist Central Med. Ctr., Balt., 1967-68, Greenstein, Baitch & Friedman, Balt., 1968-70; ptnr. Creme de la Creme, Balt., 1976-78; bd. dirs., coordinator Mid-Atlantic region Internat. Assn. Near Death Studies, U. Conn., Storrs, 1982—; pres. Koller Cons.; cons. Mgmt. Tng. Systems, Inc., Springfield, Va., 1985—. Active various polit. campaigns, Balt.; chmn. study group Hadassah Med. Orgn., Balt., 1975-76. Mem. Am. Soc. Tng. and Devel., Assn. Transpersonal Psychology, Inst. Noetic Scis., Am. Register Radiol. Technologists, Exec. Women's Network, Nat. Alliance Female Execs., Second Generation-Children of Survivors of the Holocaust, Inst. Noetic Scis., Assn. Transpersonal Psychology. Democrat. Jewish. Club: Mercantile (Balt.) Avocations: jazz and aerobic dancing, theatre, reading, French cooking. Home: 7041 Concord Rd Baltimore MD 21208 Office: 800 N Charles St Suite 400 Baltimore MD 21201

SCHWARTZ, LILLIAN FELDMAN, artist, filmmaker, art historian, author; b. Cin., July 13, 1927; d. Jacob and Katie (Green) Feldman; m. Jack James Schwartz, Dec. 22, 1946; children: Jeffrey Hugh, Laurens Robert. RN, U. Cin., 1947; LHD (hon.), Kean Coll., 1988. Nurse Cin. Gen. Hosp., 1947; head supr. premature nursery St. Louis Maternity Hosp., 1947-48; cons. AT&T Bell Labs., Murray Hill, N.J., 1968—; pres. Lilyan Prodns., Inc., Watchung, N.J., 1972—; cons. Bell Communications Research, Morristown, N.J., 1984—; artist-in-residence Sta. WNET, N.Y.C., 1972-74; cons. T.J. Watson Research Lab. IBM Corp., Yorktown, N.Y., 1975, 82-84; vis. mem. computer sci. dept. U. Md., College Park, 1974-80; adj. prof. fine arts Kean Coll., New Brunswick, N.J., 1980-82, Rutgers U., New Brunswick, N.J., 1982-83; adj. prof. dept. psychology NYU, N.Y.C., 1985-86; guest lectr. Princeton U., Columbia U., Yale U., Rockefeller U. Co-author: Computer Art Handbook; contbr. chpts. to books, also Trans. Am. Philos. Soc., Vol. 75, Part 6, 1985; one-woman shows of sculpture and paintings include Columbia U., 1967, 68, Rabin and Krueger Gallery, Newark, 1968; films shown at Met. Mus., N.Y.C., Franklin Inst., Phila., 1972, U. Toronto, 1972, Am. Embassy, London, 1972, Los Angeles County Mus., Corcoran Gallery, Washington, 1972, Whitney Mus., N.Y.C., 1973, Grand Palais, Paris, Musée National d'Art Moderne, Paris, IBM, Zurich, 1973, Sydney, Australia, 1974, retrospective exhbn., Cinémateque Française, 1980; numerous group shows in U.S., Sweden, Eng., Amsterdam, Brazil, Can., Scotland, Australia, Germany, France, Switzerland; represented in permanent collections at Mus. Modern Art, N.Y.C., Moderna Mus., Stockholm, Newark Mus., Smithsonian Instn., Washington, Stedelik Mus., Amsterdam, Columbia U., IBM, AT&T, numerous others, also pvt. collections. Recipient numerous art and film awards, Emmy award Mus. Modern Art, 1984; named Outstanding Alumnus, U. Cin., 1987; grantee Nat. Endowment for Arts, 1977, 81, Corp. Pub. Broadcasting, 1979, Nat. Endowment Composers/Librettists, 1981. Mem. Nat. Acad. TV Arts and Scis., Am. Film Inst., Info. Film Producers Am., Soc. Motion Picture and TV Engrs., Internat. Sculptors Assn.

SCHWARTZ, LINDA EVELYN, insurance executive; b. Chgo., Mar. 9, 1951; d. Robert John Hogan and Evelyn Anna (Redel) Heidke; m. Steven Mark Schwartz, July 22, 1972. BA in English with honors, U. Ill., 1972. Lic. All Lines Producers, Ill. Editorial proofreader Commerce Clearing House, Chgo., 1972-73; direct response copywriter Combined Ins. Co. of Am., Chgo., 1973-77, Nat. Ben Franklin Life Ins. Co., Chgo., 1977-78; mktg. communications supr. Am. Res. Corp., Chgo., 1978-79; v.p. mktg. James Group Service, Inc., Chgo., 1979—. Recipient Award for Excellence in Mass Mktg. Profl. Ind. Mass-Mktg. Adminstrs., 1980, 86, 87. Fellow Life Office Mgmt. Assn.; mem. Chgo. Assn. Direct Mktg. (judge creative awards competition, 1982, awards com. 1983). Club: River (Chgo.). Office: James Group Service Inc 230 W Monroe St Chicago IL 60606

SCHWARTZ, LINDA S., training specialist, consultant; b. N.Y.C., July 25, 1936; d. Samuel and Beatrice (Blumenthal) Cohen; m. Sydney E. Schwartz, Sept. 8, 1957; children: Barbara, Pamela. BA in Social Psychology, Queens Coll., 1958; MS in Edn. Guidance, Bank Street Coll., 1972. Cert. guidance counselor, N.Y. Social investigator Dept. Welfare in N.Y.C., 1958-61; tchr., dir. Rochdale Village Nursery Sch., Queens, N.Y., 1968-72; sr. counselor Methodone Maintenance Treatment Progam City N.Y., 1972-77, admissions coordinator, 1977-82; training and safety coordinator Bd. Edn. Office Pupil Transp. City N.Y., 1982—. Bd. dirs., pres., Rochdale Village Nursary Sch., 1965-66. Mem. Orgn. Staff Analysts, Women's Am. Orgn. Rehab. through Tng. (sec. 1961-66). Democrat. Jewish. Home: 102-10 66 Rd 24F Forest Hills NY 11375 Office: NYC Bd Edn Dept Pupil Trans 28-11 Queens Plaza N Long Island City NY 11101

SCHWARTZ, MONA, toy company sales executive; b. N.Y.C., Jan. 30, 1953; d. Harry and Annette (Ressler) S. BA, Bklyn. Coll., 1974. High sch. tchr. biology N.Y.C. Sch. System, 1974-76; sales inventory person Eden Toys Inc., N.Y.C., 1976-77, salesperson, 1977-80, sales mgr., 1980-87; nat. sales coordinator, 1988—. Mem. Nat. Assn. Female Execs., Childrenswear Mfrs. Assn. Democrat. Jewish. Avocations: racquetball, boating, reading. Home: 1123 Sussex Rd Teaneck NJ 07666

SCHWARTZ, RHEA S., lawyer; b. Miami Beach, Fla., Sept. 27, 1950; d. Walter and Linda (Rosenthal) S.; B.A., Pa. State U., 1971; student U. Strasbourg, France, 1970; J.D., Georgetown U., 1974; m. Paul Martin Wolff, Oct. 9, 1976. Admitted to Ill. bar, 1974, D.C. bar, 1976; asso. firm Schiff, Hardin & Waite, Chgo., 1974-75; atty. Office of Solicitor, Dept. Labor, Washington, 1975-77; labor counsel U.S. Air, Inc., Washington, 1977-79; spl. asst. to Sec. Edn., Washington, 1979-80, asst. gen. counsel Dept. Edn., Washington, 1980-86; atty. FDIC, real estate devel.; lectr. continuing legal edn. program Georgetown U. Law Ctr.; adj. prof. law U. So. Calif. Grad. Sch. Pub. Adminstrn. Bd. dirs. HALT, Inc., Am. Jewish Com. (exec. bd.); gov.'s com. Girl Scouts of Am. Recipient Spl. Achievement award U.S. Govt., 1980-86. Mem. ABA, Ill. Bar Assn., D.C. Bar Assn., U.S. Figure Skating Assn. (del., governing council), Phi Beta Kappa. Author: Women and Credit, 1974. Office: 550 17th St NW Washington DC 20429

SCHWARTZ, RUTH, physician; b. New London, Wis.; d. Louis M. and Kathryn Ann (Schwall) W.; m. Seymour I. Schwartz, June 18, 1949; children: Richard, Kenneth, David. BS, U. Wis., 1947, MD, 1950. Diplomate Am. Bd. Ob-Gyn. Intern Genesee Meml. Hosp., Rochester, N.Y., 1950; resident Strong Meml. Hosp., Rochester, N.Y., 1951-54; pvt. practice ob-gyn. Rochester, 1954—; dir. colposcopy, dysplasia and DES Clinic, colposcopy and laser tutor, The Genesee Hosp.; clin. prof. of Ob/Gyn, U. Rochester Sch. Medicine and Dentistry; pres. The Genesee Hosp. med. staff, 1986-87; acting chief Dept. Ob/Gyn, The Genesee Hosp., 1972-74; bd. dirs. The Genesee Health Service, 1972-75, ARC (med. adv. com.), bd. trustees Rochester Acad. Medicine, 1975-78.; vis. prof. U. Kuwait Med. Sch., 1984, U. Toledo Sch. Medicine, 1985. Contbr. numerous articles to med. jours. and chpts. to med. textbooks; cons. editor and contbr. to The Merck Manual, 15th edit, 1983, 16th edit., 1987. Mem. med. adv. bd. N.Y. State Task Force on Child Abuse. Named one of Best Women Doctors in Am., Harper's Bazaar mag., Nov., 1985. Mem. Am. Coll. Surgeons, Am. Coll. Obstetricians and Gynecologists (health care commn., Women in Ob/Gyn task force, patient edn. com. 1879-83, task force on hysterectomy 1987-89, adv. bd. Dist. II 1982), Am. Soc. of Colposcopy and Colpomicroscopy, Gynecologic Laser Soc. (bd. dirs., Am. Fertility Soc., AMA (accreditation council on continuing med. edn. 1987-91), N.Y. State Med. Assn., Monroe County Med. Soc. (maternal mortality com., pub. health com.), Am. Bd. Med. Specialties (fin. com.). Home: 18 Lake Lacoma Dr Pittsford NY 14534

SCHWARTZ, RUTH A., sociologist, consultant; b. Bklyn., July 7, 1946; d. Morris Schwartz and Evelyn Huber. BA in Sociology, Bklyn. Coll. of CUNY, 1969, MA in Sociology, 1976; postgrad., NYU, 1973-79. Sociology instr. Bklyn. Coll. of CUNY, 1973; research assoc. Sociol. Cons., Inc., Bklyn., 1974—. Head alternative birth task force NOW, N.Y. State, 1987. Mem. Am. Soc. Profl. and Exec. Women, Nat. Assn. Female Execs., Bklyn. Writers Network (dir., founder 1986—), Bklyn. Coll. Alumni Assn. (pres. social sci. affiliate0. Democrat. Home: 2509 Ave K Brooklyn NY 11210

SCHWARTZ, (ELLEN) SHIRLEY ECKWALL, chemist; b. Detroit, Aug. 26, 1935; d. Emil Victor and Jessie Grace (Galbraith) Eckwall; m. Ronald Elmer Schwartz, Aug. 25, 1957; children: Steven Dennis, Bradley Allen, George Byron. B.S., U. Mich., 1957; M.S., Wayne State U., 1962, Ph.D., 1970; B.S., Detroit Inst. Tech., 1978. Asst. prof. Detroit Inst. Tech., 1973-78, head div. math. sci., 1976-78; research staff mem. BASF Wyandotte Corp., Wyandotte, Mich., 1978-81, head sect. functional fluids, 1981; staff research scientist Gen. Motors Corp., Warren, Mich., 1981—. Contbr. articles to profl. jours.; patentee in field. Corr. sec. Childbirth Without Pain Edn. Assn., 1962; corr. sec. Warren-Centerline Human Relations Council, 1968. Mem. Am. Soc. Lubrication Engrs. (treas. Detroit sect. 1981, pres. sect. 1982-83, dir. 1985—), Am. Chem. Soc., Tissue Culture Assn., Soc. Automotive Engrs., Mensa, Sigma Xi. Lutheran. Club: Classic Guitar Soc. Mich. Office: Gen Motors Research Labs Warren MI 48090

SCHWARTZ, TILLIE, pediatrician; b. Winnipeg, Man., Can.; d. Leon and Sophie (Idell) Schwartz. B.A., U. Man., 1936, M.D., 1950. Rotating intern St. Boniface Hosp., Winnipeg, 1949-50; resident in medicine Gouverneur Hosp., N.Y.C., 1950-51; resident in pediatrics Met. Hosp., N.Y.C., 1951-52; Univ. Hosp., N.Y.C., 1952-53; practice medicine specializing in pediatrics, Kew Garden, N.Y., 1953—; asst. in clin. pediatrics N.Y. U., 1953-74, asst. prof. clin. pediatrics, 1974—; head pediatric allergy clinic Booth Meml. Hosp. Med. Center, Flushing, N.Y., 1958—. Fellow Am. Acad. Pediatrics, Am. Acad. Allergy; mem. AMA, N.Y. State Med. Assn., Queens County Med. Assn., Am. Med. Women Assn., N.Y. State Med. Women, N.Y.C. Med. Women, N.Y.C. Allergy Soc., Queens Pediatrics Soc. Home: 1620 Boathouse Circle Sarasota FL 33581

SCHWARTZ, VALERIE BREUER, interior designer; b. Senica, Czechoslovakia, May 13, 1912; came to U.S., 1928, naturalized, 1928; d. Jacob and Ethel (Weiss) Breuer; m. Leo Schwartz, Feb. 5, 1939; children—Catherine, Robert, William. Student States Real Gymnazium, Prague, 1925-28; Parsons N.Y. Sch. of Fine and Applied Arts, 1930-32. Cert. Am. Soc. Interior Designers. Self-employed interior designer, N.J., 1932—. Contbr. to various mags. including N.Y. Times, House & Garden, Cue Mag., Confort, Argentina; guest radio talk shows. Mem. Hadassah (life). Designed Holocaust Room, Kean Coll., N.J.

SCHWARTZBERG, JOANNE GILBERT, physician; b. Boston, Nov. 30, 1933; d. Richard Vincent and Emma (Cohen) Gilbert; m. Hugh Joel Schwartzberg, July 7, 1956; children: Steven Jonathan, Susan Jennifer. BA magna cum laude, Radcliffe Coll., 1955; MD, Northwestern U., 1960. Diplomate Am. Bd. Quality Assurance and Utilization Rev. Physicians. Founder, bd. dirs., sec., med. dir. Home Health Service Chgo., No., 1972—; founder, bd. dirs., v.p., med. dir. Suburban Home Health Service, Chgo. area, 1975-87; clin. asst. prof. preventive medicine and community health U. Ill. Coll. Medicine, 1985—. Mem. Health Planning Commn. Chgo., 1961-63; mem. Community Adv. Bd. Joint Youth Devel. Commn. Chgo., 1963-67; pres. Near North Montessori Sch., Chgo., 1972-75, bd. dirs., 1970—. Recipient Mayor's citation City of Chgo., 1963. Fellow Inst. Medicine, Am. Coll. Utilization Rev. Physicians; mem. AMA, Ill. Med. Soc., Chgo. Med. Soc., Am. Acad. Med. Dirs., Am. Geriatrics Soc., Chgo. Geriatrics Soc. (founding dir. 1984, sec.-treas. 1986—), Am. Med. Women's Assn., Am. Pub. Health Assn., Ill. Pub. Health Assn., Alexander Graham Bell Assn. for Deaf (dir. 1984—; 1st vice-chmn. internat. parents orgn. 1984—, gen. chmn. internat. conv. 1986). Jewish. Contbr. articles to profl. jours. Home: 853 W Fullerton Pkwy Chicago IL 60614 Office: 33 W Grand Ave Chicago IL 60610

SCHWARTZKOPF, DENISE LESLIE, health association executive, educator; b. Denver, July 9, 1963; d. Walter Lee and Kathleen Angela (Hyland) S. Student, Metro State Coll., Denver, 1981-83; AA, Colo. Coll. Med. Careers, Denver, 1986. Commn. salesperson Montgomery Ward, Denver, 1984-85; mktg. coordinator Doubletree Hotel, Aurora, Colo., 1985-86; diabetes educator, program dir, cons. Am. Diabetes Assn., Denver, 1986—. Grantee Colo. Coll. Med. Careers, 1985. Mem. Nat. Assn. Female Execs., Am. Assn. Diabetes Educators, Dirs. of Vols. in Agys. Democrat. Methodist. Office: Am Diabetes Assn 2450 S Downing Denver CO 80210

SCHWARTZMAN, LOIS PAULA, psychologist; b. N.Y.C., Feb. 6, 1937; d. Solomon and Sadie (Goldstein) Shapiro; m. Allan Jules Schwartzman, Sept. 15, 1957; children: Linda, Charles (dec.), Eric. BA, CUNY, 1958, MS, 1972; PhD with distinction, Yeshiva U., 1982. Tchr. N.Y.C. Bd. Edn., 1958-60, 67-69, guidance counselor, 1972-76; tchr. Tappan (N.Y.) Bd. Edn., 1969-70; dir., founder Options Unltd. Women's Counseling Service, Mt. Vernon, N.Y., 1976-78; pvt. practice psychology New Canaan, Conn., 1982—; cons. Cooperative Ednl. Services, Norwalk, Conn., 1987. Active Ft. Hill Players Club, White Plains. Mem. Am. Psychol. Assn., Council for Nat. Register Health Service Providers. Office: 166 Cherry St New Canaan CT 06840

SCHWARTZTOL, HOLLY WECHSLER, psychologist; b. Washington, Dec. 20, 1946; d. James Arthur and Nancy (Fraenkel) Wechsler; B.A., Finch Coll., 1968; M.A., C. W. Post Coll., 1971; Ph.D., U. Miami, 1981; m. Robert Ira Schwartztol, Nov. 16, 1975; children—Laurence, Andrew. Instr. psychology C. W. Post Coll., Greenvale, N.Y., 1971; tchr. Yorktown High Sch., Yorktown Heights, N.Y., 1971-73; sch. psychologist Dade County Schs., Miami, Fla., 1973-84; pvt. practice psychology, Miami, 1983—; adj. asst. prof. counseling psychology U. Miami, 1984-85; co-founder, co-dir. Miami Inst. Clin. Hypnosos, 1986—. Mem. Dade County Psychol. Assn. (pres. 1988—), Fla. Psychol. Assn., Am. Psychol. Assn., Am. Mental Health Assn. Dade County, Citizens for Advancement of Mentally Ill. Democrat. Author: (with James A. and Nancy F. Wechsler) In a Darkness, 1972, 2d rev. edit., 1988. Office: 9485 Sunset Dr Miami FL 33173

SCHWARZ, BARB (BARBARA ANN BOHRER), professional speaker, author; b. Emporia, Kans., Jan. 9, 1944; d. Max Moore and Merle L. Jones; m. Theodore S. Schwarz, Sept. 12, 1965 (div. Apr. 1982); 1 child, Andrea Louise; m. Richard Kirk Bohrer, July 29, 1983. B Edn., U. Wash., 1966. Tchr. Bellevue (Wash.) Pub. Schs., 1966-69, Renton (Wash.) Pub. Schs., 1969-70; interior designer Barb Schwarz Interiors, Bellevue, 1971-75; employment counselor Adams and Assocs., Bellevue, 1975-77; real estate sales agt. Coldwell Banker, Harper bond, The Heller Co., Windermere Real Estate, Bellevue, 1977-86; profl. speaker, author Barb Schwarz & Assocs., Inc.,

Bellevue, 1986—. Author: Career Book, 1977, Marketing Portfolio, 1979, Let Me Tell You How I Work, 1987, Selling Power, 1988, Turning the job search into a treasurer hunt, 1988; speaker (audio cassette program) How to List Residential Real Estate Successfully, 1985; speaker, author (10 Tape training set) How to Prepare Your Home For Sale...So It Sells, 1987; author, speaker (book, videotape) How to List Residential Real Estate Successfully, 1987. Mem. Nat. Speakers Assn., Pacific N.W. Speakers Assn. Office: Barb Schwarz & Assocs Inc 150 Bellevue Way SE Suite 106 Bellevue WA 98004

SCHWARZ, KAREN ANNE, psychotherapist; b. San Francisco, Mar. 15, 1957; d. George Joseph and Bernice Annette (Matulich) S. BA in Psychology, BA in Religious Studies magna cum laude, Mt. St. Mary's Coll., Los Angeles, 1980; MA in Counseling Psychology, U. Notre Dame, Ind., 1981; postgrad., U. Calif., Berkeley, 1986—. Cert. psychol. asst., Calif. Clin. intern Cath. Social Services, Van Nuys, Calif., 1978-79; campus minister El Camino Coll., Los Angeles, 1979-80; clin. intern Family Counseling Services, Elkhart, Ind., 1980-81; staff psychotherapist Ctr. for the Whole Person, San Carlos, Calif., 1981—. Mem. NOW, Am. Psychol. Assn., Am. Assn. Counseling and Devel. (various divs.), Calif. Assn. Counseling and Devel., Am. Mental Health Counselors Assn., Calif. Mental Health Counselors Assn. (bd. dirs. 1986-88, various assns.). Democrat. Office: Ctr for the Whole Person 1350 Cherry St San Carlos CA 94070

SCHWARZ, SHIRLEE, library consultant; b. Bound Brook, N.J., June 30, 1934; d. E. Walter and Esther (Wahl) Citrenbaum; m. Edward W. Schwarz; children: Thomas Michael, Carolyn Jane. BS, Syracuse U., 1956; MLS, Wayne State U., Detroit, 1971. Design cons. Shirlee Schwarz Assocs., Bloomfield Hills, Mich., 1967-70; librarian adult services Bloomfield Township Pub. Library, Bloomfield Hills, 1972-78; pres. Library Cons. Services, Westport, Conn., 1980—; dir. New Vistas for Libraries, Bloomfield Township, 1977; mem. faculty Norwalk Community Coll., 1985—. Contbr. articles to profl. jours. Vol. Jewish Home for Elderly, Fairfield, Conn., United Way, Bloomfield Hills, Allied Jewish Campaign, Detroit. Mem. Am. Library Assn., SW Library Council (bd. dirs. 1987—), Women in Mgmt. Assn., Spl. Libraries Assn. (bd. dirs. Fairfield chpt. 1980—). Democrat. Home and Office: Library Cons Services 240 N Ave Westport CT 06880

SCHWARZBACH, KAREN ROSE, personnel director; b. Santa Monica, Calif., Apr. 9, 1961; d. Alvin Leon and Denise Dora (Damenstein) S. BA, U. Calif., Santa Barbara, 1984; postgrad., U. Calif., Berkeley, 1986—. Personnel asst. Fairmont Hotel, San Francisco, 1985-86; asst. personnel mgr., staff planner I. Magnin, San Francisco, 1986-88. Mem. No. Calif. Human Resource Council. Jewish. Home: 43 Castillejo Dr Daly City CA 94015

SCHWARZENTRAUB, SARA ANN, real estate appraisal executive; b. Bloomington, Ill., July 15, 1950; d. Franklin James and Jean Lucille (Van Dolah) Finks; m. Milton Glenn Schwarzentraub Jr., July 15, 1972; children: David Lee, Kristen Ann. BS, U. Ill., 1972. Escrow sec. Minn. Title Co., Phoenix, 1973-74; appraiser Morton (Ill.) Community Service Corp., 1974-79; proprietor, appraiser Schwarzentraub Appraisals, Morton, 1980-84; pres., gen. mgr. Inter-State Appraisal Service, La Mesa, Calif., 1984—. Lay reader All Saint's Episc. Ch., Morton, 1975-84, St. Andrews Episc. Ch., La Mesa, 1984—; area rep. intercultural program Am. Field Service Internat., N.Y.C, 1981-84. Mem. Soc. Real Estate Appraisers (cert., treas., v.p. Peoria Ill. chpt., 1977-78, pres. 1978-79, bd. dirs. San Diego chpt. 1986—, treas. San Diego chpt. 1987—, mem. Young Adv. Council 1987—), East San Diego County Bd. Realtors (assoc.). Office: Inter-State Appraisal Service 4215 Spring St Suite 123 La Mesa CA 92041

SCHWARZROCK, SHIRLEY PRATT, author, lecturer, educator; b. Mpls., Feb. 27, 1914; d. Theodore Ray and Myrtle Pearl (Westphal) Pratt; B.S., U. Minn., 1935, M.A., 1942, Ph.D., 1974; m. Loren H. Schwarzrock, Oct. 19, 1945 (dec. 1966); children: Kay Linda, Ted Kenneth, Lorraine V. Sec. to chmn. speech dept., U. Minn., Mpls., 1935, instr. in speech, 1946, team tchr. in creative arts workshops for tchrs., 1955-56, guest lectr. Dental Sch., 1967-72, asst. prof. (part-time) of practice adminstrn. Sch. Dentistry, 1972-80; tchr. speech, drama and English, Preston (Minn.) High Sch., 1935-37; tchr. speech, drama and English, Owatonna (Minn.) High Sch., 1937-39, also dir. dramatics, 1937-39; tchr. creative dramatics and English, tchr.-counselor Webster Groves (Mo.) Jr. High Sch., 1939-40; dir. dramatics and tchr.-counselor Webster Groves Sr. High Sch., 1940-43; exec. sec. bus. and profl. dept. YWCA, Mpls., 1943-45; tchr. speech and drama Covent of the Visitation, St. Paul, 1958; editor pro-tem Am. Acad. Dental Practice Adminstrn., 1966-68; guest tchr. Coll. St. Catherine, St. Paul, 1969; vol. mgr. Gift Shop, Eitel Hosp., Mpls., 1981-83; cons. for dental med. programs Normandale Community Coll., Bloomington, Minn., 1968; cons. on pub. relations to dentists, 1954—; guest lectr. to various dental groups, 1966—; lectr. Internat. Congress on Arts and Communication, 1980, Am. Inst. Banking, 1981; condr. tutorials in speaking and profl. office mgmt., 1985—. Author books (series): Coping with Personal Identity, Coping with Human Relationships, Coping with Facts and Fantasies, Coping with Teenage Problems, 1984; individual book titles include: Do I Know the "Me" Others See?, My Life-What Shall I Do With It?, Living with Loneliness, Learning to Make Better Decisions, Grades, What's So Important About Them, Anyway?, Facts and Fantasies About Alcohol, Facts and Fantasies About Smoking, Food as a Crutch, Facts and Fantasies About the Roles of Men and Women, You Always Communicate Something, Appreciating People-Their Likenesses and Differences, Fitting In, To Like and Be Liked, Can You Talk With Someone Else? Coping with Emotional Pain, Some Common Crutches, Parents Can Be a Problem, Coping with Cliques, Crises Youth Face Today; Effective Dental Assisting, 1954, (with J.R. Jensen) 6th edit., 82; (with Lorraine Schwarzrock) Workbook for Effective Dental Assisting, 1979, 6th edit., 1982, Manual for Effective Dental Assisting, 1978, 6th edit., 1982; (with Donovan F. Ward) Effective Medical Assisting, 1969, 1976; Workbook for Effective Medical Assisting, 1969, 76; Manual for Effective Med. Assisting, 1969, 2d edit., 1976; author: (with C.G. Wrenn) The Coping With series of books for high sch. students, 1970, 73, The Coping With Series Manual, 1973, 2d edit., 1984, Contemporary Concerns of Youth, 1980. Pres. University Elem. Sch. PTA, 1955-56. Fellow Internat. Biog. Assn.; mem. Minn. Acad. Dental Practice Adminstrn. (hon.), Internat. Platform Assn., Zeta Phi Eta (pres. 1948-49), Eta Sigma Upsilon.

SCHWEBEL, BERNICE LOIS, educator, corporate executive; b. Hartford, Conn., Sept. 27, 1916; d. Joseph and Sara (Brewer) Davison; B.A., Russell Sage Coll., 1938; teaching cert. SUNY, 1949; M.A., NYU, 1963; m. Milton Schwebel, Sept. 3, 1939; children—Andrew, Robert. Co-founder, dir. Counseling and Placement Services for Refugees, Jewish Community Center, Troy, N.Y., 1936; social case worker Troy Orphan Asylum, 1938-39; cottage mother Pleasantville (N.Y.) Cottage Sch., 1939-40; head tchr. Birnby Nursery Sch., N.Y.C., 1945-46; tchr. kindergarten, primary grades, Valley Stream, N.Y., 1950-67; supr. student tchrs. edn. dept. Douglass Coll., Rutgers U., New Brunswick, N.J., 1973-76; v.p. ednl. programs and materials Univ. Assocs., Columbus, Ohio, 1976—; treas. Continental Land Holding, New Brunswick, 1984—. Trustee, Rutgers-Livingston Day Care Ctr., 1977-80; chmn. Rutgers-Old Queens Visitation Com., New Brunswick Tercentenary, 1979-80. Mem. Authors Guild, LWV, NOW, Women's League of Voters, Russell Sage Alumnae Assn., N.Y.U. Alumni Assn. Co-author film script Resistance to Learning, 1962; author: Student Teachers Handbook, 1979; contbr. articles to various publs. Home: 1050 George St New Brunswick NJ 08901 Office: Univ Assocs 4123 Kendra Ct S Columbus OH 43220

SCHWEINHART, BELINDA JANE, plastics engineer; b. Edwards, Calif., July 6, 1957; d. Russell Edgar Jr. and Phyllis Eileen (Lansing) Rosell; m. Mark Allen Schweinhart, Aug. 1, 1981. BS in Mech. Engring., U. Dayton, 1980, postgrad. Co-op Delco Moraine, Div. GM, Dayton, Ohio, 1975-80; with process tech. program-plastics Gen. Electric Co., Louisville, 1980-82, engr. mfg., 1982-83, engr. advance product quality, 1983-84; engr. quality Torrington Co., Cairo, Ga., 1984-85; engr. service Delco Moraine, Div. GM, Dayton, Ohio, 1985-86; engr. plastics Bluegrass Plastics Engring. Inc., Louisville, 1986—; proprietor Brass Pig Gift Shop and Tea Room, Springboro, Ohio, 1986—. Mem. Soc. Plastics Engrs. Republican. Baptist. Clubs: Porsche Am., Olde Springsboro Village Merchants. Home: 225 S Main St Springboro OH 45066

SCHWEINHAUT, MARGARET COLLINS, state senator; b. Washington; ed. George Washington U., Nat. U. Law Sch.; LL.D., St. Joseph Coll. Mem. Md. Ho. of Dels., 1955-61; mem. Md. Senate, 1961-63, 67—. Chmn. Md. Commn. on Aging, 1959-82. Bd. dirs. Nat. Council of Aging. Recipient Certificate of Merit, Nat. Council of Sr. Citizens; Margaret Schweinhaut Sr. Ctr. named in her honor, 1982. Mem. Internat. Gerontological Soc., Montgomery Retarded Children's Assn. Office: Md Senate State Capitol Bldg Annapolis MD 21401

SCHWEITZER, MARY-ELIOT SMITH (MRS. ROBERT SCHWEITZER, JR.), civic worker, electronics company executive; b. San Jose, Calif., July 7, 1927; d. Julius Avery and Elise (Peyton) Smith; A.A., Marymount Coll., 1948; Engring. Tech. degree Normandale Community Coll., 1981 m. Robert Schweitzer, Jr., Sept. 18, 1952; children—Mary-Eliot, James-Peyton, Mary-Neale. Sec., Teen-age Jr's, Stanford Convalescent Home, Palo Alto, Calif., 1944-45; receptionist, driver A.R.C., Palo Alto, 1947-51; mem. Jr. League, San Francisco, 1950-54; mem. Jr. League, N.Y.C., 1956-58; mem. Jr. League, Mpls., 1963—, bd. dirs., 1966-67. Leader, Girl Scouts U.S.A., Mpls., 1966-69; mem. Citizens Com. for Pub. Edn., Mpls., 1968-76, Citizens League, Mpls., 1968-80; docent Mpls. Inst. Arts, 1965-66, Hennepin County Hist. Soc., 1965-66; pres. Douglas Elementary Sch. P.T.A., 1968-70; v.p. West High Sch. P.T.A., 1970-71, pres., 1971-73; bd. dirs. Womens UN Rally, 1966-72; bd. dirs. Assos. James Ford Bell Library, 1968—, pres., 1972-75; bd. dirs. Friends Mpls. Inst. Arts, 1968-73; bd. dirs. Mpls. Council P.T.A.'s, 1969-76, treas., 1974-76; bd. dirs. Minn. World Affairs Ctr., 1969-76, UN Assn. of Minn., 1970-76; adv. bd. Childrens Theatre Co., Mpls., 1969-72, house mgr., 1971-72; vice chmn. Hennepin Lowry Council, 1972-74; chmn. bd. Jr. League Thrift Shop, 1966-67; mem. citywide adv. com. for ednl. facilities and plant planning Mpls. Pub. Schs., 1975-76; unit test mgr. Control Data Corp., Magnetic Peripherals, Inc., 1981—. Named Beautiful Activist, 1973. Mem. DAR, Mpls. Soc. Fine Arts, Womens Assn., Mpls. League Cath. Women (dir. 1974-80), West Dist. Schs. Assn. (vice-chmn. 1972-73, chmn. 1974-75), Peyton Soc. Va. Republican. Home: 5140 W 102d St Bloomington MN 55437

SCHWEITZER, N. TINA, writer, photojournalist, counselor in public relations, media relations, government relations; b. Hartford, Conn., Apr. 7, 1941; d. Abraham Aaron Morris and Ruth Blanche (Shifreen) S.; B.S., Emerson Coll., 1964. Free-lance writer, Boston and Washington, 1965-67; editor, chief prodn. maj. feature publ., mem. press-info. staff Embassy of Republic of Indonesia, Washington, 1967-68; researcher, writer Congl. Quar., Inc., Washington, 1969-70; owner Schweitzer Assocs., Hartford, Conn. and Washington, 1970-78, 79—; dir. community and govtl. relations Advocacy Services for the Deaf, West Hartford, Conn., 1978-79; del. White House Conf. Small Bus., 1986; profl. model, Mem. State-wide Health Coordinating Council, a U.S. Govt./Conn. Health Dept. project, 1978-80; adviser Conn. Office Advocacy to Handicapped; mem. legis. task force State of Conn.; del. first Conn. Gov.'s Conf. on Library and Info. Services, 1978. Candidate Conn. Ho. of Reps., 1982; aux. police officer Hartford Police Dept., 1976-77; acting chmn. communications com. Unitarian Meeting House, West Hartford; dir. pub. relations Greater Hartford Com. UNICEF, 1984; affiliated Republican Town Com., Hartford. Corr. The Farmington (Conn.) Valley Herald, 1984; contbr. articles to numerous govtl. and comml. publs.; author nat. Media Kit, 1978, Women's Job Hunting Guide, 1983, You Can Do It! A Practical Guide for Job Hunting and Career-Changing, 1987; writer, designer, producer series of TV videotape pub. service announcements on employment deaf or hard-of-hearing, 1983-84; contbr. to TV Stas. WFSB, 1977, 84, 87, WVIT, 1983; writer, ind. producer Sta. WVIT-TV, 1987-88. Mem. Nat. Press Photographers Assn., Community Council of the Capital Region, Mensa (Achievement award 1982), Sigma Delta Chi. Office: Schweitzer Associates 30 Woodland St Suite 9P Hartford CT 06105

SCHWENZER, KRISTINE ANN, writer; b. Springfield, Pa., Dec. 4, 1957; d. Christian Jon and Dorothy Susan (Kropf) S. BA in English and Communications, Millersville (Pa.) U., 1979; postgrad., Franklin and Marshall U., 1978-79, Phila. Coll. Art, 1984-85, Temple U., 1983-85. Copy dir. Packer, Oesterling & Smith, Harrisburg, Pa., 1984—. Author: (screenplay) The Wedding, Open Season; recorded comedy album Not Playing With Full Deck, 1982. Mem. Common Cause, Washington, 1984, Sta. WITF Radio/TV, Harrisburg, 1984—; bd. dirs., publicity chair Harrisburg Theatre, 1986—. Recipient Addy award 1985, 86, 87, 88, Citation of Excellence Am. Advt. Fedn., 1987. Mem. Cen. Pa. Advt. Fedn. (publicity chair 1984-85, Appreciation award 1985), Am. Women in Radio and TV, Nat. Assn. Female Execs. Democrat. Office: Packer Oesterling & Smith 124 State St PO Box 968 Harrisburg PA 17108

SCHWERIN, MARY ETTA, state agency administrator; b. Rhodes, Mich., Apr. 18, 1935; d. Henry and Myrtle (Bennett) S; 1 child, Scott. Student, Lansing Community Coll., 1979, 87, Mott Community Coll., 1985. Claims worker State of Mich., Flint, 1961-65, claims examiner, 1970, supr., 1971-76; br. mgr. State of Mich., Lapeer and Bay City, 1976—. Mem. Internat. Assn. of Personnel in Employment Security, Pvt. Industry Council. Lutheran. Home: 6332 Rio Mesa Flint MI 48506

SCHWIER, PRISCILLA LAMB GUYTON, television broadcasting company executive; b. Toledo, Ohio, May 8, 1939; d. Edward Oliver and Prudence (Hutchinson) L.; m. Robert T. Guyton, June 21, 1963 (dec. Sept. 1976); children—Melissa, Margaret, Robert; m. Frederick W. Schwier, May 11, 1984. B.A., Smith Coll., 1961; M.A., U. Toledo, 1972. Pres. Gt. Lakes Communications, Inc., 1982—; vice chmn. Seilon, Inc., Toledo, 1981-83, also dir.; pres. Lamb Enterprises, Inc., Toledo, 1983—; dir. Lamb Enterprises, Inc., Toledo, 1976—. Contbr. articles to profl. jours. Trustee Wilberforce U., Ohio, 1983—, Planned Parenthood, Toledo, 1979-83; trustee Maumee Valley Country Day Sch., Toledo. Episcopal Ch., Maumee, Ohio, 1983—; bd. trustees Toledo Hosp. Democrat. Episcopalian. Home: 345 E Front St Perrysburg OH 43551 Office: 1630 Ohio Citizens Bank Toledo OH 43604

SCHWOPE, MARY KATHRYN, state legislator; b. Rock Springs, Wyo., July 21, 1917; d. Charles Alfred and Mary Frances (Moriarty) Viox; student public schs., Green River, Wyo., 1923-35; m. Eldridge Lawson Schwope, July 15, 1940; children—Michael Lawson, Fachon J. Schwope Wilson, Patricia K. Schwope Murphy, Madalaine M. Schwope Connolly. With Union Pacific R.R., 1936-46; mem. Wyo. Ho. of Reps., 1975-76, 79—. Mem. Democratic Precinct Com., Cheyenne, 1957-67; vice chmn., dist. capt. County Dem. Com.; sec. City-County CD Council, 1962-63, Laramie County Fair Bd., 1966-76; mem. State Adv. Council Vocat. Edn., 1976-81; mem. Silver-Haired Legis. Adv. Com., 1982-83, Wyo. Gov.'s Task Force for Employment Older Ams., 1981-86. Recipient nat. merit cert. Am. Revolutionary Bicentennial Adminstrn., 1976, cert. Nat. Disabled Am. Vets. Orgn. for Legis. Action, 1987; Four Chaplains Legion of Honor, 1979. Mem. Am. Legion Aux. (state pres. 1968-69, nat. exec. com. 1969-70), Am. Assn. Ret. Persons, Wyo. Hist. Soc., Wyo. Wildlife Fedn., Cheyenne Sr. Citizens. Roman Catholic. Clubs: Zonta, Cheyenne Women's.

SCIACCA, PATRICIA FREDRICA, systems analyst, consultant; b. Buckhannon, W.Va., Jan. 1, 1943; d. Frank Arthur Sammarco and Genevieve Gene (Westfall) Morgan; m. Frank A. Sciacca, Apr. 1, 1967; 1 child, Richard Alan; step-children: Frank A. II, Antony. BS in Computer Info. with honors, DeVry Inst. Tech., Columbus, 1985. Pres. Capitol Diversified Services, Columbus, 1967-70; owner Angelina's Italian Pizza, Columbus, 1970-76; pres. Coney King Inc., Columbus, 1976-83; owner Systematic Solutions, Columbus, 1985—; sr. tech. assoc. AT&T Bell Labs, Columbus, 1986—; exec. dir. Entrepreneur Devel. Inst. Tng., Columbus, 1985—. Grad. Columbus Area Leadership Program. Mem. Reynoldsburg Area C. of C. (sec. 1978, trustee 1979-83). Methodist. Home: 6172 Roselawn Ave Columbus OH 43232

SCIBAL, BARBARA ANN, insurance executive; b. Somers Point, N.J., Oct. 12, 1943; d. Stephen and Barbara Alice (Balsley) S.; m. Henry Nunn Sweeney, Jan. 4, 1970 (div. 1978). AA, Cazenovia Coll., 1963; postgrad., Glassboro (N.J.) State Coll., 1967. Tchr. Somers Point Bd. Edn., 1968-72; sales assoc. James T. O'Brien Realty, Mt. Laurel, N.J., 1972-74; agt. Phoenix Mut. Life Ins. Co., Phila. and Atlanta, 1974-81; owner, officer Scibal Ins. Group, N.J. and Pa., 1981-87; pres. Atlantic Third Party Adminstrs., Somers Pt., 1987—. Treas. bd. trustees Zion United Meth. Ch., Bargaintown, N.J., 1985; bd. dirs. United Cerebral Palsy N.J., Trenton, 1986, pres. bd. Atlantic County, Somers Point, 1986. Mem. Pa. Claims Assn., Phila. Workers' Compensation Claim Assn., Ins. Soc. Phila., Nat. Audubon Soc. Republican. Club: Jr. League. Office: Atlantic Third Party Adminstrs 91 Mays Landing Rd Somers Pt Rd Somers Point NJ 08244

SCIBECK, MAE LORRAINE, medical administrator; b. Colonie, N.Y., Sept. 23, 1942; d. James Joseph and Mae Lorraine (Manley) Wheeler; m. Phillip Paul Vermette, June 21, 1958 (div. 1962); children: Mark, Barbara; m. Joseph Charles Scibeck, Mar. 2, 1968 (div.); children: Douglas, Derek. A in Med. Sci., Laboure Jr. Collage, 1981. Technologist VA Hosp., Boston, 1981-82, registered technologist, 1982; registered technologist St. Joseph's Hosp., Tampa, Fla., 1982-84, instr. sch. of electroencephalography, 1982—, supr., 1984—; cons. in field. Mem. New. Eng. Soc. Electrencephologic Technologists, Fla. Soc. of Electroencephalis Technologists (pres. 1988—), Nat. Assn. Female Execs. (vice dir. Tampa Bay chpt. 1987—), Beta Sigma Phi. Home: 2112 Two Lakes Rd T-1 Tampa FL 33604

SCIMONE, PATRICIA LYNN, marketing executive; b. Amityville, N.Y., May 28, 1955; d. Thomas Mathew and Josephine (Galante) S. Student Fashion Inst., N.Y.C., 1974, Hunter Coll., 1975-76. Mdse. mgr. Diamond Co. Am., N.Y.C., 1976-79; buyer Service Mdse. Co., Nashville, 1979-81; new product mgr. Harlyn Products, Los Angeles, 1981-83; pres. Marriage Mktg., Encino, Calif., 1983—; mfg. cons. Harlyn Products, 1983; media and mktg. cons. Santa Monica C. of C. 1983. Mem. Am. Mgmt. Assn., Calif. Bus. Womens Assn., Nat. Assn. Female Execs., Sales and Mktg. Execs. Internat. Office: European Am Realty 1201 W Jericho Turnpike Huntington NY 11743

SCITOVSKY, ANNE AICKELIN, economist; b. Ludwigshafen, Germany, Apr. 17, 1915; came to U.S., 1931, naturalized, 1938; d. Hans W. and Gertrude Margarete Aickelin; 1 dau., Catherine Margaret. Student, Smith Coll., 1933-35; B.A., Barnard Coll., 1937; postgrad., London Sch. Econs., 1937-39; M.A. in Econs., Columbia U., 1941. Mem. staff legis. reference service Library of Congress, 1941-44; mem. staff Social Security Bd., 1944-46; with Palo Alto (Calif.) Med. Research Found., 1963—, chief health econs. div., 1973—; Lectr. Inst. Health Policy Studies, U. Calif., San Francisco, 1975—; mem. Inst. Medicine, Nat. Acad. Scis., Pres.'s Commn. for Study of Ethical Problems in Medicine and Biomed. and Behavioral Research, U.S. Nat. Com. on Vital and Health Stats., 1975-78; cons. U.S. Dept. Health and Human Services, Inst. Medicine Council on Health Care Tech. Assessment. Mem. Am. Econ. Assn., Am. Public Health Assn. Home: 161 Erica Way Menlo Park CA 94025 Office: Palo Alto Med Found/Research Inst 860 Bryant St Palo Alto CA 94301

SCLAFANI, FRANCES ANN, state commissioner; b. N.Y.C., Aug. 25, 1949; d. Joseph John and Clementina Theresa (Polite) S. BA (hon.), St. John's U., 1971, JD, 1974. Bar: N.Y. 1975, U.S. Dist. Ct. (ea. and so. dists.) N.Y., 1975, U.S. Ct. Appeals (2d cir.) 1975, U.S. Supreme Ct. 1978. Spl. congl. asst. U.S. Congress, Washington, 1971; asst. dist. atty. County of Suffolk (N.Y.), Riverhead, 1974-76; assoc. dir. U.S Office Personnel Mgmt., Washington, 1986—; head of Office Fed. Investigations, Washington, 1986—; bd. fgn. service Dept. State, Washington, 1986—; bd. dirs. Fed. Law Enforcement Tng. Ctr., Glynco, Ga., 1986—; dep. chief Felony Trial Bur., 1981-82, Major Offense Bur., 1982-83. Rep. candidate for N.Y. state atty. gen., 1982; commr. President's Commn. on Organized Crime, Washington, 1983—, mem. com. on narcotics control and interdiction, 1984—; rep. to Western Hemisphere Conf. on Narcotics Control, Washington, 1985—; faculty U.S. Dept. of Justice Ann. Internat. Drug Traffickers Prosecution Conf., 1983. Recipient award for service to victims rights Decision for Women in Commerce and Professions, 1984. Mem. Nat. Dist. Attys. Assn. (assoc. dir. 1980-86), ABA (asst. sec. criminal justice sect. 1980-82), D.C Bar Assn., N.Y. Bar Assn. Roman Catholic.

SCLAFANI, IRENE MARIE, accountant, financial director; b. Fall River, Mass., Nov. 6, 1956; d. Lazaro Nunes and Alice A. (Nascimento) Bastos; m. Joseph A. Sclafani. AS in Secretarial Sci., Bristol Community Coll., Fall River, 1976; BS in Mgmt., Southeastern Mass. U., 1982. Exec. sec. Fisher Jr. Coll., North Dartmouth, Mass., 1975-78; exec. sec. Family Service Assn., Greater Fall River, Mass., 1978-81, mgr. office, 1981-83, adminstrv. asst., 1986—; bd. dirs. Office for Children, Fall River, 1984-88. Mem. Am. Mgmt. Assn., Nat. Assn. for Female Execs. Club: Altrusa (Fall River). Home: 593 Palmer St Fall River MA 02721 Office: Family Service Assn 151 Rock St Fall River MA 02720

SCOFIELD, SANDRA KAY, state legislator; b. Chadron, Nebr., June 16, 1947; d. Maurice William and Mildred Elizabeth (Connell) S. BS, U. Nebr., 1969, MA, 1974. Tchr. Westside High Sch., Omaha, 1969-71; tech. writer, coordinator Kentron Hawaii, Honolulu, 1971-73; script writer Nebr. Dept. Edn., Lincoln, 1974-75, U. Mid-Am., Lincoln, 1975, Nebr. Ednl. TV Consortium for Higher Edn., Lincoln, 1975-79, Nebr. Ednl. TV, Lincoln, 1975-79; dir. planning Chadron State Coll., 1979-81, career counselor, 1979, 82-83, dir. career devel. ctr., 1983; mem. Nebr. Legislature, Lincoln, 1983—; vice chair com. on agriculture, food policy and rural devel. Nat. Conf. State Legislators; chmn. Nebr. Legislature Select Com. on Children and Families. Bd. dirs. Nebr. Preservation Council, Nebr. Groundwater Found., Nebr. Tourism Council, Nebr. 4-H Devel. Found.; mem. Environmental Control Council, Lincoln, 1983; pres. Dawes County Hist. Soc., Chadron, 1981-83. Mem. Bus. and Profl. Women, AAUW, Delta Kappa Gamma. Democrat. Lodge: Eagles. Office: Nebr State Legislature State Capitol Bldg Lincoln NE 68509

SCOFIELD, TERTTU S. (TERRI), security officer; b. Viipuri, Karjala, Finland, Dec. 4, 1936; came to U.S., 1949; d. Arne and Anna (Kilappa) Seely; m. Albert H. Scofield, May 1, 1959; children: Jeffrey A., Kim A. G-rad., Katharine Gibbs Sch., 1957. Cert. tng. Def. Indsl. Security Inst. Sec. to v.p. Dunlap and Assocs., Inc., Stamford, Conn., 1957-71; security officer Dunlap and Assocs., Inc., Darien, Conn., 1971-78, Norden Systems, Inc., Norwalk, Conn., 1978-80, Perkin-Elmer Corp., Danbury, Conn., 1980—. Donating mem. Pres. Reagan's Rep. Com., 1987—. Mem. Am. Soc. for Indsl. Security (chmn. So. Conn. chpt. 1986, 87, editor newsletter 1986, sec. 1976, 84, cert. appreciation awardee 1986), Nat. Classification Mgmt. Soc., White German Shepherd Dog Club Internat. (v.p. 1987—, editor nat. newspaper 1973-80, nat. pres. 1974-78, chpt. pres.). Lutheran. Club: Breed (Wilton, Conn.) (pres. 1974-78). Home: 102 St John's Rd Wilton CT 06897 Office: Perkin-Elmer Corp 100 Wooster Heights Rd Danbury CT 06810

SCOLLON, BONNIE LEW, computer analyst; b. Geneva, Ohio, Jan. 5, 1942; d. Lewis DeForrest and Aletha Genevieve (Klinger) Cone; m. Francis L. Scollon, Jr., Aug. 28, 1965; children: Erik Lee, Wendy Kathleen. BS, Ohio State U., Columbus, 1964; MA, Oakland U., Rochester, Mich., 1971. Producer/dir. WOSU-TV, Columbus, Ohio, 1963-64; adminstrv. asst. Ohio State Rep. Com., Columbus, 1964; recreation dir. Dept. of the Army, Schwaebisch Hall, Fed. Republic Germany, 1965; tchr. Owosso (Mich.) Pub. Schs., 1965-67, Houghton (Mich.) High Sch., 1967-69, Romeo (Mich.) Community Schs., 1969-72; product support staff Tex. Instruments, Farmington, Mich., 1982; tng. analyst Henry Ford Hosp., Troy, Mich., 1982-86; computer analyst Henry Ford Hosp., Detroit, 1986—. Contbr. articles to profl. jours. Mem. Mich. Assn. Computer Use in Learning, Detroit Area Trainers Assn. (sec. 1986). Office: Henry Ford Hosp 2799 W Grand Blvd Detroit MI 48202

SCOPINICH, JILL LORIE, editor, writer; b. Seattle, Dec. 7, 1945; d. Oscar John and Marcella Jane (Hearing) Younce; 1 child, Lori Jill. AA in Gen. Edn., Am. River Coll., 1969; BA in Journalism with honors, Sacramento State U., 1973. Reporter Carmichael (Calif.) Courier, 1968-70; mng. editor Quarter Horse of the Pacific Coast, Sacramento, 1970-75, editor, 1975-84; editor Golden State Program Jour., 1978, NRCNA News, Sacramento, 1983—, Pacific Coast Jour., Sacramento, 1984—, Nat. Snaffle Bit Assn. News, Sacramento, 1988—; mag. cons., 1975—. Bd. dirs. Carmichael, Winding Way, Pasadena Homeowners Assn., Carmichael, 1985-87. Recipient 1st pl. feature award, 1970, 1st pl. editorial award Jour. Assn. Jr. Colls., 1971, 1st pl. design award WCHB Yuba-Sutter Counties, Marysville, Calif., 1985. Mem. Am. River Jaycees (recipient speaking award 1982), Am. Horse Publs. (recipient 1st pl. editorial award 1983), MENSA (bd. dirs., asst. local sec., activities dir. 1987-88, membership chair 1988—). Republican. Roman Catholic. Club: 5th Wheel Touring Soc. (Sacramento) (v.p. 1970).

Home: 1307 Santa Ynez Wy Sacramento CA 95816 Office: Pacific Coast Jour Gate 12 Cal-Expo Sacramento CA 95815

SCOPINICH, JUNE TOWNSEND, physical education educator, educational administrator; b. Freeport, N.Y., Dec. 28, 1942; d. Anthony A. and Sylvia R. (Townsend) S. BS, SUNY, New Paltz, 1964; MS, Smith Coll., 1971; EdD, U. San Diego, 1987. Tchr. art Freeport (N.Y.) Unified Sch. System, 1964-69; physical edn. tchr., coach Wilson Coll., Chambersburg, Pa., 1971-72, Hampshire Regional High Sch., Westhampton, Mass., 1972-74, U. Calif., Berkeley, 1974-75; from physical edn. educator to asst. dean dept. physical edn. and athletics Southwestern Coll., Chula Vista, Calif., 1975—. Mem. Am. Assn. Physical Edn. and Recreation and Dance, Am. Assn. Women in Jr. Coll., Maritime History Soc. Episcopalian. Office: Southwestern Coll 900 Otay Lakes Rd Chula Vista CA 92010

SCOTT, ALEXANDRA SOLAZZO, executive education company executive; b. N.Y.C., Dec. 12, 1948; d. Gennaro and Mary (Salata) de Ruvo; m. John R. Simak, Sept. 23, 1967 (div. Mar. 1981); children: Graham David, Craig Alexander; m. Alfonso J. Solazzo, Nov. 12, 1983. Student, Adelphi U. Mgr., assoc. M. Rosen Assocs., Garden City, N.Y., 1975-81; asst. to pres. Gallard-Schlesinger Corp., Carle Place, N.Y., 1981-84; dir. mktg. Exec. Solutions, Locust Valley, N.Y., 1984-85; exec. v.p. Inst. for Internat. Research, N.Y.C., 1985—. Vol. Kings County Hosp., Queens, N.Y., 1967. Recipient Community Service award City of N.Y., Bklyn. 1959, Best Brochure award Strategic Mktg. Conf., N.Y.C., 1985. Mem. Nat. Assn. Female Execs. Home: 40 Sycamore Ln Levittown NY 11756 Office: Inst Internat Research 310 Madison Ave New York NY 10017

SCOTT, ALICE HOLLY, library administrator; b. Jefferson, Ga.; d. Frank David and Annie (Colbert) Holly; m. Alphonso Scott, Mar. 1, 1959; children—Christopher, Alison. A.B., Spelman Coll., 1957; M.L.S., Atlanta U., 1958; Ph.D., U. Chgo., 1983. Librarian, Bklyn. Pub. Library, 1958-59; librarian Woodlawn br. Chgo. Pub. Library, 1955-60, br. head, 1961-72, dir. Woodson regional library, 1974-77, dir. community relations, 1978-81, dep. commr., 1982-88, asst. commr., 1988—. Com. Instl. Cooperation fellow, 1973. Mem. ALA (councillor 1982-86), Ill. Library Assn., Chgo. Library Club, Beta Phi Mu. Democrat. Baptist. Office: Chgo Pub Library 1224 W Van Buren Chicago IL 60607

SCOTT, ANN BESSER, musicologist, educator; b. Newark, June 8, 1933; d. Hyman and Fannie (Bear) Besser; A.B., Radcliffe Coll., 1955; M.F.A., Brandeis U., 1957; Ph.D., U. Chgo., 1969; m. Gordon H.S. Scott, May 3, 1958; children—Ellen, Melinda. Instr., then asst. prof. music U. Chgo., 1968-73; mem. faculty Bates Coll., Auburn, Maine, 1973—, prof. music, 1979—, chmn. dept., 1974—, chmn. div. humanities, 1976-80; mem. music panel Maine Commn. Arts and Humanities, 1975-81; mem. Maine Humanities Council, 1981—, vice chmn., 1985-87, chmn., 1987—. Editor book review; editor: College Music Symposium, 1986—. Fellow Nat. Endowment Humanities, 1981. Mem. Am. Musicol. Soc. (sec. council 1974-79, editorial bd. jour. 1975-80, bd. dirs. 1985-87), Coll. Music Soc., Phi Beta Kappa. Jewish. Author articles in field. Office: Box 1218 RFD 3 Winthrop ME 04364

SCOTT, ANNE BYRD FIROR, history educator; b. Montezuma, Ga., Apr. 24, 1921; d. John William and Mary Valentine (Moss) Firor; m. Andrew Mackay Scott, June 2, 1947; children: Rebecca, David MacKay, Donald MacKay. A.B., U. Ga., 1940; M.A., Northwestern U., 1944; Ph.D., Radcliffe Coll., 1958; L.H.D., Lindenwood Coll., 1968, Queens Coll., 1985. Congressional rep., editor LWV of U.S., 1944-53; lectr. history Haverford Coll., 1957-58, U. N.C., Chapel Hill, 1959-60; asst. prof. history Duke U., Durham, N.C., 1961-67; assoc. prof. Duke U., 1968-70, prof., 1971-80, W.K. Boyd prof., 1980—, chmn. dept., 1981-85; vis. prof. Johns Hopkins U., 1972-73, Stanford U., 1974, Harvard U., 1984; bd. dirs. Carnegie Corp. N.Y., 1977-85, Woodrow Wilson Internat. Ctr., 1980-85, Nat. Humanities Ctr., 1987; adv. com. Schlesinger Library. Author: The Southern Lady, 1970, (with Andrew MacKay Scott) One Half the People, 1974, Making the Invisible Woman Visible, 1984; editor: Jane Addams, Democracy and Social Ethics, 1964, The American Woman, 1970, Women in American Life, 1970, Women and Men in American Life, 1976; editorial bd.: Revs. in Am. History, 1976-81, Am. Quar., 1974-78, Jour. So. History, 1978-84; contbr. articles to profl. jours. Chmn. Gov.'s Commn. on Status of Women, 1963-64; mem. Citizens Adv. Council on Status of Women U.S., 1964-68. AAUW fellow, 1956-57; grantee Nat. Endowment for Humanities, 1967-68, 76-77; grantee Nat. Humanities Center, 1980-81; fellow Ctr. Advanced Study in Behavioral Sci., 1986-87. Mem. Am. Antiquarian Soc., Orgn. Am. Historians (exec. bd. 1973-76, pres. 1983), So. Hist. Assn. (exec bd. 1976-79, v.p. 1987). Democrat. Office: Duke Univ Dept History Durham NC 27706

SCOTT, AUDREY EBBA, federal agency administrator; b. Boston, Nov. 25, 1935; d. Carl Arthur and Vera (Bisbee) Hallberg; m. John Joseph Scott, May 5, 1962; children: Lawrence, Bryan, Kenneth, Edward. BA, Tufts U., 1957; postgrad., So. Conn. U., 1957-58, Harvard U., 1958. Tchr. North Haven (Conn.) Sch. System, 1957-59; tchr. U.S. Dept. Def.-Overseas Sch. System, LaRochelle, France, 1959-61, Zama, Japan, 1961-63; councilwoman City of Bowie, Md., 1974-76, mayor, 1976-82; dir. community relations Prince George's Hosp. and Med. Ctr., Cheverly, Md., 1980-81; spl. asst. HUD, Washington, 1981-84, assoc. dep. asst. sec., 1984-86, dep. asst. sec., 1986—; past bd. dirs. Council of Govts., Washington. Pres. Bowie Health Ctr., 1971-75, 82—, Md. Mcpl. League, 1979-80; bd. dirs. Multiple Sclerosis Soc., Washington, 1975—; del. Rep. Nat. Conv., Detroit, 1980; candidate for U.S. Congress from 5th dist. Md., 1981; elder, commr. Nat. Presbytery. Recipient Women Helping Women award Soroptimists, 1982; named Outstanding Mcpl. Ofcl. Mcpl. Assn., 1977, Outstanding Mayor VFW, 1979. Mem. AAUW (program chmn. 1985-87), Rep. Women Capitol Hill. Club: Bus. and Profl. Women's (Bowie) (chmn. status of women com. 1983-84, Woman of Yr. 1984). Home: 12109 Long Ridge Ln Bowie MD 20715 Office: HUD Legis and Congl Relations 451 7th St SW Room 10148 Washington DC 20410

SCOTT, BARBARA JEAN, civil engineer; b. Lamar, Colo., Nov. 11, 1932; d. Merrill Lockler and Ruth Elizabeth (Brown) S. BSCE, U. Wyo., 1959, MSCE, 1973. Registered profl. engr., Wyo., Colo., Tex. Materials engr. Wyo. State Hwy. Dept., Cheyenne, 1959-67, landscape engr., 1967-69, cons. engr. environ. services, 1981—; planning engr. City of Cheyenne, 1969-70; environ. engr. Tex. State Hwy. Dept., Houston, 1970; mem. faculty U. Wyo., Laramie, 1970-74; cons. engr., owner S&R Land Co., Cheyenne, 1976—; mem. part-time faculty Chapman Coll. Warren AFB, Cheyenne, 1984—; owner Rocky Mountain Computer Inst., Cheyenne, 1982—. Del. Wyo. First Internat. Conf. Women Engrs. and Scientists, N.Y.C., 1962; vol. mus. Cheyenne, 1981; mem. Nat. Trust Hist. Preservation, Am. Mus. Natural History. Mem. ASCE (state treas. 1967-69), Wyo. Engring. Soc., Pi Beta Phi Alumna Club, Tau Beta Pi. Republican. Presbyterian. Home: 7006 Willshire Blvd Cheyenne WY 82009

SCOTT, BEVERLY ANN, distribution company official; b. Scottsbluff, Nebr., Dec. 27, 1941; d. Henry Clay and Illma Elizabeth (Moody) S.; m. Alan S. Davenport, Aug. 29, 1964 (div., 1980); 1 child, Darby Layne. BA with honors in Sociology, U. Puget Sound, 1963; MA in Sociology, State U. Iowa, 1966; postgrad. U. Mich., 1976-79; M in Human Resources Devel., Univ. Assocs., 1980. Instr. Cornell Coll., Mt. Vernon, Iowa, 1965-66, Coe Coll., Cedar Rapids, Iowa, 1966-67; program developer Linn Econ. Action Project, Cedar Rapids, 1967-68; exec. dir. Hawkeye Area Community Action Program, Cedar Rapids, 1968-70; program developer YWCA, Detroit, 1972; social planning and devel. analyst City of Detroit, 1972-75; cons. and edn. specialist Wayne County Community Coll., Detroit, 1975-76; sr. ptnr. Change HRD, Detroit, 1976-79; sr. assoc. Cons. Assocs., Detroit, 1979-81; corp. cons. Bendix Corp., Detroit, 1981; mgr. orgn. and mgmt. devel. McKesson Corp., San Francisco, 1982—; speaker HRD Conf., 1987. Author: (with Ronald Kregoski) Quality Circles: How to Create Them, How To Manage Them, How to Profit from Them, 1982. Mem. adv. bd. North End Concerned Citizens Community Council, 1973, dist. adv. com., 1975-76; chair YWCA, 1972-73, mem., 1971-81; fin. chair Montessorri Sch., 1972-73; chair social awareness group Faculty Women's Group U. Mich., 1972-73; pres. Women's Justice Ctr., 1979-80; co-chair Women's Equality Day Planning Com., 1980; steering com. UCS Met. Camp Council, 1977-81; chair program com. Detroit Women's Forum, 1977-80; mem. tng. team People Acting for Change Together, 1972-75. Named Mgr. of Yr., McKesson Foods Group, 1983. Mem. NOW, Am. Soc. Tng. and Devel., The Women's Found. (devel. com. 1986—), Am. Sociol. Assn., Nat. Council Family Relations, Midwest Sociol. Assn., Youth Employment Service, Iowa Community Action Dirs., United Community Service Execs., Mich. Episcopal Tng. Network, Univ. Assocs., Women Decision Makers of Detroit, Women in Orgn. Devel., Orgn. Devel. Network (co-chmn. program com. conf. 1985, devel. com. Equal Rights Advocates 1987-88), Am. Camping Assn. (camping unlimited com. 1976-77, editor Vision/Action Jour. 1987-88). Home: 166 Castro St San Francisco CA 94114 Office: McKesson Corp 1 Post St San Francisco CA 94104

SCOTT, BRENDA F., sales executive; b. Brighton, Tenn., Nov. 18, 1949; d. Carl Edward and Sadie Lee (Cullum) S. BA, Memphis State U., 1973; postgrad., Skyline Coll., 1979-81. Asst. adminstrv. Colonial Baking Co., Memphis, 1968-78; exec. sales account Kilpatrick's Inc., San Francisco, 1978-87; with Chancellor's Office U. Tenn., Memphis, 1988—. Photographer, editor: (film) We've Got the Best Right Here, 1984. Mem. exec. bd. Spl. Olympics, San Francisco, 1981-84; bd. dirs. Com. to Save High Sch. Sports, San Francisco, 1980-82. Democrat. Episcopalan. Home: PO Box 251 Munford TN 38058

SCOTT, CATHERINE DOROTHY, librarian, consultant; b. Washington, June 21, 1927; d. Leroy Stearns Scott and Agnes Frances (Meade) Scott Schellenberg. AB in English, Cath. U. Am., 1950, MS in Library Sci., 1955. Asst. Librarian Export-Import Bank U.S.A., Washington, 1951-55; asst. librarian Nat. Assn. Home Builders, 1955-62, reference librarian, 1956-62; chief tech. librarian, Bellcomm, Inc., subs. AT&T, Washington, 1962-72; chief librarian Nat. Air and Space Mus., Smithsonian Instn., Washington, 1972-82, chief librarian Mus. Reference Ctr., 1982—; bd. visitors Cath. U. Am. Library Sci. Sch. and Libraries, 1984—; mem. Nat. Commn. Libraries and Info. Sci., 1971-76. Editor International Handbook of Aerospace Awards and Trophies, 1980, 81, Directory of Aerospace Resources, 1984; guest editor Spl. Collections in Aeronautics and Space Flight Collections, 1985. Vice-chmn. D.C. Rep. Com., 1960-68; mem. platform com. Rep. Nat. Com., 1964, sec., 1968; del. Rep. Nat. Conv., San Francisco, 1964, Miami, Fla., 1968. Recipient Sec.'s Disting. Service award Smithsonian Instn., 1976, Alumni Achievement award Cath. U. Am., 1977. Mem. Spl. Libraries Assn. (pres. Washington chpt. 1973-74, cons. 1976—, chmn. aerospace div. 1980-81, Disting. Service award 1982, nat. dir. 1986—), Am. Soc. Info. Scis. (com. chmn.), Internat. Fedn. Library Assns. (del. 1976, 83, 85, 88), Friends of Cath. U. Libraries (pres. 1984—), Nat. Fedn. Rep. Women, Rep. Women's Fed. Forum. Roman Catholic. Club: Capital Yacht (assoc. mem.) (Washington). Office: Smithsonian Instn A & I Bldg Room 2235 900 Jefferson Dr SW Washington DC 20560

SCOTT, COLLEN MARIE, health care executive, accountant; b. Waterbury, Conn., Sept. 17, 1957; d. Walter M. Sr. and Virginia R. (Post) S. BS in Acctg., Cen. State U., New Britain, Conn., 1979; MBA, U. New Haven, 1987. CPA, Conn. Acct. J.S. Monagan, CPA, Waterbury, 1978-80, Kelly & Fitzgerald, CPA's, P.C., Waterbury, 198-82, Waterbury Hosp., 1982-83; acctg. mgr. Griffin Hosp., Derby, Conn., 1983-84, asst. controller, 1984-85; assoc. controller Griffin Health Services, Derby, 1985-86, acting v.p. fin., controller, 1987-88; fin. planner Waterbury Hosp. Health Ctr., 1988—. Mem. Am. Inst. CPA's, Conn. Soc. CPA's, Health Care Fin. Mgmt. Assn., Am. Guild Patient Account Mgrs., Conn. Assn. Patient Account Mgrs., Alpha Beta Sigma. Office: Waterbury Hosp Health Ctr 64 Robbins St Waterbury CT 06721

SCOTT, DARLA JEAN, real estate executive; b. Butler, Pa., Jan. 2, 1944; d. Earl Charles and Ida Edith (Nagy) Ausel; m. Thomas L. Scott (div. 1987). Cert. real estate broker. Officer mgr. Kaiser Engrs., Pitts., 1968-74; owner Blue Diamond Frozen Foods, Plymouth Meeting, Pa., 1975-77; regional v.p. Fox and Lazo, Inc., Cherry Hill, N.J., 1977-87. Mem. Nat. Assn. Realtors, Camden County Bd. Realtors (grievance com. 1986—), Cherry Hill C. of C., N.J. Assn. of Woman Bus. Owners. Republican. Presbyterian. Home: 38 Borton Rd Medford NJ 08055 Office: Fox and Lazo Inc 575 Swedesford Rd Wayne PA 19087

SCOTT, DEIRDRE ANN, curator; b. Newark, Dec. 31, 1961; d. Dudley Fairfax and Marion (James) S. Student, N.Y. Inst. Tech., 1980, 81; BA, NYU, 1987. Asst. librarian Temple U. Library, Phila., 1982; rep. gallery Greengrass Art Gallery, Garden City, N.Y., 1983-84; asst. curator Studio Mus. in Harlem, N.Y.C., 1985—; curator Adam Clayton Powell State Bldg. State Gallery, N.Y.C., 1985—; project adminstr. Studio Mus. in Harlem for the Ford Found., N.Y.C., 1986—; curatorial researcher Met. Mus. Art, N.Y.C., 1987-88; dir., curator Cinque Gallery, Soho, N.Y., 1988—; creative cons. Graph/X Inc., Hempstead, N.Y., 1984-85. Vol. The Sculpture Ctr., N.Y.C., 1984-85. Mem. NOW, Am. Assn. Mus., Smithsonian Instn., Visions Found., Nat. Assn. Female Execs., Am. Craft Council. Republican. Roman Catholic. Office: The Cinque Gallery 560 Broadway New York NY 10012

SCOTT, ELEANOR MEYER, educator; b. Houston, Mar. 10, 1933; d. Gustav Jackson and Lillian Elizabeth (Piehl) M.; m. Henry Lee Scott, June 2, 1956 (dec. June 1967); children: Stephen Lee, Stuart Henry. BS in Home Economics, U. Tex., 1956; MEd, U. Houston-Park, 1976. Cert. elem. tchr., Tex. With Clear Creek Schs., 1958—; elem. tchr. Clear Creek Schs., League City, Tex., 1958-64, tchr. gifted/talented program, 1985—; elem. tchr. Stewart Elem., Kemah, Tex., 1964-66, White Elem. Sch., Seabrook, Tex., 1969-72, Clear Lake City Sch., Houston, 1976-85. Author: (with others) Math Manipulatives in Elem., 1986. Pres. Seabrook (Tex.) Civic Club, 1975-76, Seascape Property Owners Assn., Seabrook Tex. 1973-74; mem. Bi-Centennial Com., Seabrook, 1976; chmn. Lunar Rendezvous Festival Children's Fair, Houston, 1977. Mem. Clear Creek Educators Assn. (conv. del. 1961-62, sec. 1962-63, scholar 1988), Tex. State Tchrs. Assn. (scholar 1986-87), Nat. Edn. Assn., Tex. Classroom Tchrs. Assn., Tex. Assn. Gifted and Talented, Bay Area Panhellenic Assn. (Most Outstanding Mem. award 1975-76, Golden Egg award 1972, 73, 74), Delta Kappa Gamma Soc. Internat., Theta Zeta (pres.). Republican. Methodist. Home: 625 Bay Club Dr Seabrook TX 77586 Office: Clear Creek Schs Gifted Programs 1506 Anders St Seabrook TX 77586

SCOTT, ELIZABETH LEONARD, statistics educator; b. Ft. Sill, Okla., Nov. 23, 1917; d. Richard C. and Elizabeth (Waterman) S. B.A., U. Calif., Berkeley, 1939, Ph.D., 1949. Research fellow U. Calif., Berkeley, 1939-49; mem. faculty U. Calif., 1949—, assoc. prof., 1957-62, prof. stats., 1962—, now emeritus; chmn. dept. stats., 1968-73; asst. dean U. Calif. (Coll. Letters and Sci.), 1965-67, co-chmn. group in biostats., 1972—; mem. Commn. on Nat. Stats., Nat. Acad. Scis., 1971-77, Commn. on Women in Sci., 1977-82, Commn. on Applied and Theoretical Stats., 1981-84, Oversight Com. on Radioepidemiol. Tables, 1983-85. Research and articles in math. stats. and applications. Fellow Royal Statis. Soc. (hon.), Inst. Math. Stats. (pres. 1977-78, mem. council 1971-74, 76-79); mem. Biometric Soc. (council 1978-81), Am. Astron. Soc., Internat. Astron. Union, Internat. Stats. Inst. (v.p. 1981-83), Internat. Assn. Stats. in Phys. Sci. (sci. sec. 1960-72), Bernoulli Soc. (mem. council 1978-81, pres.-elect 1981-83, pres. 1983-85), Astron. Soc. Pacific, AAAS (chmn. sect. U 1970-71, mem. council 1971-76). Home: 34 Tunnel Rd Berkeley CA 94705 Office: U Calif Dept Stats Berkeley CA 94720 *

SCOTT, GERTRUDE ROSE, metal processing executive; b. Pitts., Oct. 12, 1932; d. Leroy Lewis and Dorothea Margaret King; m. William B. Ward, 1984. B.A. magna cum laude, U. Pitts., 1969, M.A., 1971. Public relations supr. Allegheny Gen. Hosp., Pitts., 1971-73; mgr. communications Jones & Laughlin Steel Corp., Pitts., 1973-76; v.p. corp. communication Meldrum & Fewsmith, Cleve., 1976-81; v.p. Steel Service Center Inst., Cleve., 1981—. Mem. Public Relations Soc. Am. (chpt. pres. 1982-83). Office: Steel Service Center Inst 1600 Terminal Tower Cleveland OH 44113

SCOTT, IRENE FEAGIN, federal judge; b. Union Springs, Ala., Oct. 6, 1912; d. Arthur H. and Irene (Peach) Feagin; m. Thomas Jefferson Scott, Dec. 27, 1939; children: Thomas Jefferson, Irene Scott Carroll. A.B., U. Ala., 1932, LL.B., 1936, LL.D., 1978; LL.M., Catholic U. Am., 1939. Bar: Ala. 1936. Law librarian U. Ala. Law Sch., 1932-34; atty. Office Chief Counsel, IRS, 1937-50, mem. excess profits tax council, 1950-52, spl. asst. to head appeals div., 1952-59, staff asst. to chief counsel, 1959-60; judge U.S. Tax Ct., 1960-82, sr. judge serving on recall, 1982—. Mem. Ala. Bar Assn., Fed. Bar Assn., D.C. Bar Assn. (hon.), ABA (sect. taxation), Nat. Assn. Women Lawyers, Nat. Assn. Women Judges, Nat. Lawyers Club, Kappa Delta, Kappa Beta Pi. Office: US Tax Ct 400 2nd St NW Washington DC 20217

SCOTT, JANICE MARIE, insurance executive; b. Loreauville, La., Mar. 29, 1955; d. Hurley Davis and Lovenia (Willis) Williams; m. Johnny Lee Scott, Nov. 17, 1979 (div. 1981). BS in Criminal Justice, Sam Houston State U., 1976. Adjuster Allstate Ins. Co., Houston, 1977-83, supr., 1983-84, mgr., 1984—. Mem. Job Plus, Houston, 1986—, Houston Proud, 1987—, Urban League. Recipient Vol. Recognition Houston Proud, 1987. Mem. NAACP, Nat. Assn. Female Execs., Delta Sigma Theta (Civic award 1988). Club: Ski Jammers. Home: 15902 Jersey Dr Houston TX 77040

SCOTT, JENNIFER ANN, accountant; b. Springfield, Ohio, Feb. 11, 1953; d. Donald Smith and Thelma (Davis) Spriggs; m. Steven Andrew Scott, Jan. 19, 1949; children: Sarah Ann, Jacob Andrew, Jonah Andrew, Rebecca Ann. A, Stevens Henager Coll., 1973; student, Wright State U., 1976, Urbana U., 1977. Acct. Phillips 66, Salt Lake City, 1973-74, Parent-Infant Ctr., Springfield, Ohio, 1984—; treas. Ridgewood Pvt. Sch., Springfield, 1984-86, sec. 1983-84. Vol. Right to Life, Springfield, Ohio, 1974—; pres. Young Women, Fairborn, Ohio, 1978-80, stake counselor, Dayton, Ohio, 1980-81; sec., treas. Relief Soc., Springfield, 1985—. Named Treas. of Yr. Jr. Achievement, 1971; recipient Young Womenhood Recognition award Relief Soc., 1980. Mem. Tri-County Trained Childbirth Assn. (treas. 1982—, Vol. of Yr. award 1982). Republican. Mormon. Home: 139 Miramar Dr Enon OH 45323

SCOTT, JOAN WALLACH, historian; b. Bklyn., Dec. 18, 1941; d. Samuel and Lottie (Tanenbaum) Wallach; m. Donald M. Scott, Jan. 30, 1965; children: Anthony Oliver, Elizabeth Rose. BA, Brandeis U., 1962; MA, U. Wis., 1964, PhD, 1969. Asst. prof. history U. Ill., Chgo., 1970-72; asst. prof. Northwestern U., 1972-74; assoc. prof. U. N.C., Chapel Hill, 1974-77, prof., 1977-80; Nancy Duke Lewis prof., prof. history Brown U., Providence, 1980-85, now adj. prof.; dir. Pembroke Ctr. for Teaching and Research on Women, 1981-85; now prof. Sch. Social Sci., Inst. for Advanced Study, Princeton, N.J.; dir. Summer Seminar for Coll. Tchrs., NEH, 1977, dir. Seminar for Coll. Tchrs., 1980-81; mem. Inst. for Advanced Study, Princeton, 1978-79. Social Sci. Research Council research tng. fellow, 1966-68, NEH fellow, 1975-76; Am. Council Learned Socs. grantee, 1978. Mem. Am. Hist. Assn. (chmn. com. on women historians 1978-80), Social Sci. History Assn., Soc. French Hist. Studies. Author: The Glassworkers of Carmaux, 1974 (Am. Hist. Assn. Herbert Baxter Adams prize 1974), (with Louise Tilly) Women Work and Family, 1978, Gender and the Politics of History, 1988. Office: Inst for Advanced Study Olden Ln Princeton NJ 08540

SCOTT, KAREN ANN, dentist; b. Gary, Ind., Jan. 7, 1957; d. Jay R. and Bernadette (Hogan) S. BS, U. Notre Dame, 1979; BSD, U. Ill., Chgo., 1983, DDS, 1985. Pvt. practice dentistry Chgo., 1985—. Active Grant Park Concert Soc. Notre Dame scholar, 1975-79. Mem. ADA, Ill. Dental Soc. (sci. presenter 1987), Chgo. Dental Soc., Internat. Vis. Ctr., Alpha Epsilon Delta, Omicron Kappa Upsilon. Clubs: Young Variety (Chgo.), Young Internat. Home: 1400 N State Pkwy Chicago IL 60610 Office: 55 E Washington St Suite 3102 Chicago IL 60602

SCOTT, KAREN WEST, archeologist; b. San Antonio, July 4, 1945; d. Klinker Heller and Gladys Irene (Bryant) West; m. Robert Forbes Scott IV; children: Lisa, Karen. BA in Anthropology, U. Tex., San Antonio, 1980; MS in Forestry, Stephen F. Austin State U., 1984. Archeologist State Archeologist's Office U. Wyoming, Laramie, 1980-82; personnel officer Amon Carter Mus., Ft. Worth, 1982-83; park supt. archeologist Tex. Parks & Wildlife Dept., Alto, 1983-85; supervisory archeologist U.S. Army C.E., Ft. Worth, 1985—. Mem. Council Tex. Archeologists, Tex. Archeol. Soc., Soc. For Am. Archeologists, Assn. Interpretive Naturalists. Home: 2605 Poplar Spring Rd Fort Worth TX 76123 Office: US Army CE SWFPL-R PO Box 17300 Fort Worth TX 76102

SCOTT, LYNDA LEIGH, plastics company executive, communications consultant; b. Berlin, N.J., Oct. 22, 1961; d. Robert Edward and Elizabeth (Robertson) Honeywell S. BA, Westminster Coll., 1983. Staff asst. Ams. for the Competitive Enterprise System, Erie, Pa., 1983-84, cons., 1983—; employee relations mgr. Westminster Mfg. Corp., Girard, Pa., 1984—. Author: Nifty Publishing Company, 1987; editor Changing Tools, 1984-86. Inventor stencil art overlays, 1986. Mem. Internat. Assn. Bus. Communicators (sec. 1984-85, treas., publicity 1985-86), Personnel Assn. N.W. Pa., Soc. Craft Designers, NOW. Republican. Presbyterian. Avocations: racquetball, skiing, reading. Office: Westminister Mfg Corp 227 Hathaway St Girard PA 16417

SCOTT, MALORA COURTNEY, construction company executive; b. Cin., Mar. 1, 1949; d. Court and Mildred Catherine (Neeley) C. Student So. Ohio Coll. Computer operator, invoice supr. Parke Davis div. Warner Lambert, Blue Ash, Ohio, 1967-83; mgr. data processing Micro Med, Inc., Fairfield, Ohio, 1983-85; credit mgr. Bobcat of Atlanta, Conley, Ga., 1985-86, Ogden Materials, Handling Systems, Inc., Atlanta, 1986-87; March Constrn., Inc., Atlanta, 1987—. Leader Campfire Girls Southwestern Ohio, Cin., 1972-1974; vol. Muscular Dystrophy Assn., Cin., 1972-74, ARC, Cin., 1968-70; sponsor GOP Victory Fund, 1984-86. Mem. Nat. Rifle Assn., Nat. Assn. Female Execs (N. Atlanta treas.), Internat. Platform Assn. Republican. Avocations: camping, music, needlework, swimming. Home: 2641 Arbor Glen Pl Marietta GA 30066

SCOTT, MARGARET LOUISE, aerospace company executive; b. Santa Monica, Calif., June 21, 1925; d. Earl Joseph and Stella May (Miller) Scott; student Los Angeles City Coll., 1947-51, El Camino Coll., 1973. Flight test analyst N.Am. Aviation, Los Angeles, 1943-51; graphics artist N.Am. Rockwell, Los Angeles, 1951-74; illustrations project coordinator Rockwell Internat., Los Angeles, 1974-75, dept. head graphics art dept., Los Angeles div., El Segundo, Calif., 1975—. Mem trade advisory com. El Camino Coll., Glendale Community Coll., West Los Angeles Coll., 1975—. Home: 1601 Sunset Plaza Dr Los Angeles CA 90069 Office: 100 N Sepulveda Blvd El Segundo CA 90245

SCOTT, MARIANNE FLORENCE, librarian, educator; b. Toronto, Ont., Can., Dec. 4, 1928; d. Merle Redvers and Florence Ethel (Hutton) S. BA, McGill U., Montreal, Que., Can., 1949, BLS, 1952; LLD, York U., 1985. Asst. librarian Bank of Montreal, 1952-55; law librarian McGill U., 1955-73, law area librarian, 1973-75, dir. libraries, 1975-84, lectr. legal bibliography faculty of law, 1964-75; nat. librarian Nat. Library of Can., Ottawa, Ont., 1984—. Co-founder, editor: Index to Can. Legal Periodical Lit, 1963—; contbr. articles to profl. jours. Mem. Internat. Assn. Law Libraries (dir. 1974-77), Am. Assn. Law Libraries, Can. Assn. Law Libraries (pres. 1963-69, exec. bd. 1973-75, honored mem. 1980—), Can. Library Assn. (council and dir. 1980-82, 1st v.p. 1980-81, pres. 1981-82), Corp. Profl. Librarians of Que. (v.p. 1975-76), Can. Assn. Research Libraries (pres. 1978-79, past pres. 1979-80, exec. com. 1980-81, sec.-treas. 1983-84), Ctr. for Research Libraries (dir. 1980-83), Internat. Fedn. Library Assns. (honors com. for 1982 conf. 1979-82). Home: 2084 Chalmers Rd, Ottawa, ON Canada K1H 6K6 Office: Nat Library of Can, 395 Wellington St, Ottawa, ON Canada K1A 0N4

SCOTT, MARILYN KAY WRIGHT-SCHULZ, advertising agency executive, marketing consultant, public relations specialist; b. Bath, N.Y., Dec. 1, 1944; d. Elmer Edward Wright and Louise Emma (Buckley) Hastings; m. Elton Schulz, Sept. 30, 1967 (div. 1982); children—Steven Edward, Christina Louise; m. George Scott, June 22, 1985 (div. 1988). A.A., Alfred Tech. U., 1964; B.A., Syracuse U., 1966. Coordinator mktg. and advt. Eastman Kodak Co., Rochester, N.Y., 1966-70; freelance writer, Rochester, 1975-83, tech. writer, 1977—; program producer, host Radio and Cable TV, Rochester, 1980-83; dir. pub. relations WGMC Radio, Greece, N.Y., 1980-83; pres., owner Pilgrim Assocs. Rochester, 1982-87; with Windsor Advt., Rochester, 1987—; editor Rochester Sesquicentennial Book, 1984. Bd. dirs. YMCA, Downtown Promotion Council ; v.p. Community Ednl. Adv. Council, Greece, 1979-81; bd. dirs. Nat. Tech. Inst. for Deaf; advisor Monroe County

Reps. Recipient Cert. of Merit, County Sch. Bd., Rochester, 1981, Disting. Am. award for Creative Achievement, 1985. Mem. Am. Women in Radio and TV, Women in Communications, Inc., Rochester C. of C., Rochester Women's Council. Republican. Home: 49 Cloverland Dr Rochester NY 14610 Office: Windsor Advt 3000 Winton Rd S Rochester NY 14623-2854

SCOTT, MARJO ANN, nurse; b. Chgo., Dec. 27, 1937; d. Thomas and Josephine (Bandola) Hodgson; m. Duane L. Scott, Aug. 29, 1959; children: Todd, Lori Scott Kelley, Cheri Scott Simmons, Brent. Student, Kans. State Tchrs. Coll., 1955-57; BS in Nursing cum laude, U. Kans., 1959. RN, Kans. Pediatric staff nurse Kans. U. Med. Ctr., Kansas City, Kans., 1959-60, Menorrah Hosp., Kansas City, 1960; orthopedic staff nurse Wesley Hosp., Wichita, Kans., 1960-61; psychiatric staff nurse St. Joseph Hosp., Concordia, Kans., 1978—; nurse profl. resource Kans. Families for Mental Health, Concordia, 1985-87. Fund raiser, officer Rep. County Assn. for Retared Citizens, Belleville, Kans., 1974-79; fund raiser Rep. County Hist. Soc., Belleville, 1976-78. Mem. Am. Nurse's Assn., Kans. State Nurse's Assn., Delphian Federated Women, PEO. Republican. Roman Catholic.

SCOTT, MARY ANNE HALL, engineering administrator; b. Shelbyville, Tenn., Nov. 6, 1943; d. Leo Frank and Mary June (Hickerson) Hall; m. Terry Allen Scott, Apr. 15, 1965 (div. June 1972): children: Bretton Allen, Barton Ayers. BSEE, Tenn. Technol. U., 1965; MSEE, U. Tenn., 1970, PhD in Engring. Sci., 1976. Research engr. ARO, Inc., Arnold Air Force Sta., Tenn., 1965-70; grad. research asst. U. Tenn. Space Inst., Tullahoma, Tenn., 1970-76, mgr. gasdynamics sect. energy conversion programs, 1976-86, adj. asst. prof. elec. engring., 1977-86; fusion program mgr. Chgo. Ops. Office U.S. Dept. Energy, Argonne, Ill., 1986—; mem. organizing com. symposium for instrumentation and control for fossil energy processes, Argonne, 1979-81; bd. dirs. symposium on engring. aspects of MHO, Washington, 1979-83, chmn. bd., 1982. Contbr. articles to profl. jours. Recipient Young Career Woman Tenn. Bus. and Profl. Women, 1967. Mem. IEEE, Sigma Xi, Tau Beta Phi. Lutheran. Home: 242 Northridge Bolingbrook IL 60439 Office: Dept of Energy Chgo Ops Office 9800 S Cass Ave Argonne IL 60439

SCOTT, MARY CELINE, pharmacologist; b. Los Angeles, July 14, 1957; d. Walter Edward and Shirley Jean (Elvin) S. BS in Biological Scis., U. Calif., Irvine, 1978; MS in Biology, Calif. St. U., 1980; PhD in Pharmacology, Purdue U., 1985. Teaching asst. Calif. St. U., Long Beach, 1979-80; teaching asst. Purdue U., West Lafayette, Ind., 1980-81; teaching asst. Purdue U., West Lafayette, 1981-82, grad. instr., 1982-83, research fellow, 1983-85; research fellow Mayo Found., Rochester, Minn., 1985-87, Purdue U., W. Lafayette, Ind., 1987—. Contbr. articles to profl. jours. Active Girl Scouts U.S., now service unit chmn. River Trails council. Mem. AAAS, Am. Soc. Pharm. and Experimental Therapeutics, Assn. Women Sci., N.Y. Acad. Sci., Soc. Electroanalytical Chemistry, Soc. Neuroscience, Women Neuroscience, Sigma Xi. Democrat. Office: Purdue U Lynn Hall West Lafayette IN 47906

SCOTT, MELLOUISE JACQUELINE, media specialist; b. Sanford, Fla., Mar. 1, 1943; d. Herbert and Mattye (Williams) Cherry; m. Robert Edward Scott, Jr., July 1, 1972. B.A., Talladega Coll., 1965; M.L.S., Rutgers U., 1974, Ed.M., 1976, Ed.S., 1982. Media specialist Seminole County Bd. Edn., Sanford, 1965-72, Edison Bd. Edn. (N.J.), 1972—. Mem. ALA, N.J. Edn. Assn., NEA, Ednl. Media Assn. N.J. Baptist. Home: PO Box 8 Fords NJ 08863 Office: Edison Bd Edn Mcpl Complex Edison NJ 08817

SCOTT, NANCY, psychological counselor; b. El Paso, Tex., Nov. 1, 1960; d. Robert Churchill and Annie Jo (Schmidt) S. BS, U. Tex., 1982; MS, Springfield Coll., 1985; MA, Columbia U., 1987. Cert. tchr., Tex. Assoc. Occupational Health Consulting Inc., W. Nyack, N.Y., 1985-88; psychiat. rehab. counselor Met. Hosp., N.Y.C., 1988—. Contbr. articles to profl. jours. Mem. Am. Psychol. Assn. (affiliate), Western Social Sci. Assn., Internat. Assn. Conflict Mgmt. Home: 1230 Amsterdam Ave Apt 923 New York NY 10027 Office: Metropolitan Hosp Ctr 1901 2d Ave at 97th St New York NY 10029

SCOTT, PATRICIA JEAN, telecommunications educational administrator; b. Tacoma, Wash., Oct. 30, 1946; d. Donald Matthew and Gladys Myrtle (Olson) Gregurich; m. George Larkham Scott IV, Aug. 1, 1969; 1 child, Matthew Larkham. BA, Wash. State U., 1968; MA in Instrl. TV, Gonzaga U., 1975; postgrad., U. Oreg. Ednl. Policy and Mgmt. Div., 1988—. Cert. secondary tchr., Wash. Tchr. secondary Moses Lake (Wash.) Schs., 1968-70; project dir. Wash. Commn. for Humanities, Spokane, 1975-77; adminstrv. asst. for telecourses Spokane Falls Community Coll., 1977; adminstrv. asst. Oreg. Community Coll. Telecommunications Consortium, Portland, 1983—; grant writer Riggs Inst., Beaverton, Oreg., 1986—; tchr. adult literacy, Portland, 1986—. Fundraiser St. Mary of the Valley Cath. Sch., Beaverton, 1982-83; precinct com. person Spokane County, 1976-80; mem. Catlin Gabel Sch. Auction com., Portland, 1983—. Mem. Women in Communications Internat., Nat. Assn. Female Execs. Home: 11445 SW Lanewood Portland OR 97225 Office: Oreg Community Coll Telecomunications Consortium PO Box 19707 Portland OR 97219

SCOTT, RITA MOROSKY, general property executive; b. Erie, Pa., Oct. 24, 1946; d. Peter and Inez (Tootle) Morosky; m. Kenneth Edward Scott, Mar. 31, 1979; 1 child, Tera. Diploma in cosmetology, Ga. Tech. Coll., 1967; student, U. Ga., 1986, U. Mich., 1986. Mgr. Contempo Ltd., Vidalia, Ga., 1977-79; with sales and mktg. div. Ferguson Jewelry, Homestead, Fla., 1979-80; floor supr. J.C. Penney, Statesboro, Ga., 1983-85; mgr. mktg. Statesboro (Ga.) Mall, 1983-85, Normandale Mall, Montgomery, Ala., 1986—. Mem. PTA, Montgomery, 1986—; room mother Brewbaker Sch., Montgomery, 1986—. Recipient Cert. of Appreciation, Am. Heart Assn., 1985. Mem. Nat. Assn. Female Execs., Internat. Council Shopping Ctrs. Baptist. Home: 6037 Arbor Glen Dr Montgomery AL 36117 Office: Mark Devel Co 111 Normandale Arcade Montgomery AL 36111

SCOTT, SUSAN IVY, purchasing professional; b. Brockton, Mass., Oct. 29, 1952; d. Donald Francis and Barbara Louise (Aird) S. BA, U. Mass., 1974. Cert. purchasing mgr. Purchasing agt. Morton's Shoe Stores, Inc., Boston, 1976-82; buyer New Balance Athletic Shoes, Allston, Mass., 1982-84; sr. buyer Stride Rite Corp., Cambridge, Mass., 1984—; bd. dirs. Purchasing Mgmt. Assn. of Boston, Concord, Mass., 1986—. Mem. Nat. Assn. Female Execs., Women in Mgmt. Office: Stride Rite Corp 5 Cambridge Ctr Cambridge MA 02142

SCOTT, WILLODENE ALEXANDER, library administrator; b. Ethridge, Tenn., Sept. 4, 1922; d. Jesse Cary and Maud (Goff) Alexander; B.A., George Peabody Coll. for Tchrs., 1946, B.S. in L.S., 1947, M.A., 1949, Ed.S., 1972, Ph.D., 1986; m. Ray Donald Scott, Nov. 27, 1959; 1 dau., Pamela Dean. Librarian, Sylvan Park Elem. Sch., Nashville, 1947-51, Waverly Belmont Jr. High Sch., Nashville, 1951-54, Howard High Sch., Nashville, 1954-62, Peabody Demonstration Sch., Nashville, 1962-63; librarian McCann Elem. Sch., Nashville, 1963-66; supr. instructional materials, library div. Metro Nashville-Davidson County Schs., Nashville, 1966-73, dir. instructional materials and library services, 1973-87; dir. libraries Watkins Inst., Nashville, 1987—; lectr. Peabody Coll. Library Sch., Nashville, summers, 1950-66, 71, 72, 76, U. Tenn., Nashville Center, 1970; Tenn. rep. White House Conf., 1970. Chmn. nat. alumni fund-raising George Peabody Coll. for Tchrs., 1975-76, nat. alumni pres., 1977-78, trustee, 1976-78; bd. dirs. Friends of Music, 1977-79; mem. vis. com. bd. trustees Vanderbilt U., 1979-85. Recipient Disting. Alumni award Peabody Library Sch., 1987. Mem. ALA, Southeastern Library Assn. (scholarship com. 1968-70), Tenn. Library Assn. (membership chmn. 1955, 64, treas. 1977-78, honor award 1986), Tenn. Edn. Assn. (library sect. pres. 1954), Met. Nashville Edn. Assn., NEA (life), Children's Internat. Edn. Center of Nashville (charter mem. at large), AAUW, Woman's Nat. Book Assn. (charter mem.), DAR (organizing treas. Buffalo River chpt. 1967-69), Delta Kappa Gamma (v.p. 1984-86). Baptist. Club: Nashville Library (pres. 1952-53). Lodge: Order Eastern Star. Home: 525 Clematis Dr Nashville TN 37205 Office: Watkins Inst 601 Church St Nashville TN 37219-2309

SCOTT-COHOON, JANICE LEE, health care executive; b. Oakland, Calif., Jan. 30, 1950; d. Royal M. and Betty Jean (Flynn) Scott; m. Stephen Michael Cohoon; 1 child, Caroline Scott. B.B.A., U. Tex., 1972. Auditor, Werner & Arendale, CPAs, Houston, 1972-73, Allstate Ins. Co., Menlo Park, Calif., 1973-74; acct. Santa Cruz County (Calif.), 1975-77; dir. acctg. San Jose Hosp. (Calif.), 1977-78; budget office mgr. North Colo. Med. Center, Greeley, Colo., 1978-79; asst. fin. mgr. Humana Hosp.-Garland (Tex.), 1979-80; asst. controller Methodist Hosps. of Dallas, 1980-81, dir. data processing, 1981-82, fin. analyst, 1982-83, v.p. data processing, 1983-84; mktg. dir. Infostat, Inc., Dallas, 1984-85; mktg. rep. Keane, Dallas, 1985-86; gen. acctg. product mgr. product planning div. Electronic Data Systems Corp., Plano, Tex., 1986—. Mem. Data Processing Mgmt. Assn., Tex. Hosp. Info. Systems Soc., Healthcare Fin. Mgmt. Assn. Home: PO Box 795063 Dallas TX 75379-5063

SCOTT-COOPER, NEDRA DENISE, judicial administrator; b. Detroit, May 5, 1953; d. William Eldredge and Jeri (Weaver) Cooper; m. Benny Lee Scott, Feb. 10, 1973 (div. May 1982); children: Morenike Renee, Moneer Abdullah. BA in Psychology, Internat. Coll., 1977; BSW, U. Las Vegas, 1982; MBA, MA in Mgmt., Nat. U., 1986. Youth counselor aide Clark County Juvenile Cts., Las Vegas, 1974, youth counselor I, 1974-76, youth counselor II, 1976-77, supr. Child Haven, 1977-86, supr. intake, 1986—; coordinator parenting project Clark County Juvenile Ct. System. Appointed to gov. commn. on King Holiday, Las Vegas, 1987; consul to Haiti, Martin Luther King Commn., Washington, 1987; mem. Barbara Jordan Dem. Caucus, Las Vegas, 1987. Mem. NAACP (life), AAUW, Nat. Assn. Female Execs., Delta Sigma Theta (1st v.p., treas. Las Vegas chpt.). Club: Am. Topical (Milw.). Office: Clark County Juvenile Cts 3401 E Bonanza Rd Las Vegas NV 89101

SCOTTI, AUDREY JANICE, youth services administrator; b. Middletown, Conn., Apr. 8, 1939; d. John Louis and Constance Agatha (DiGiandomenico) S.; divorced; children: Joanne, Jonathan, Richard. BS in Human Services, N.H. Coll., 1987. Acting dir., head tchr. Portland (Conn.) Child Devel. Ctr., 1971-72; dist. mgr. MacMillan Pubs., N.Y.C., 1972-73; exec. dir. Locational Motor Math, Inc., Middletown, 1973-74; supr. children's services Henry D. Altobello Children and Youth Ctr., Meriden, Conn., 1974—; tutor, cons. Spl. Edn. Placement, Conn., 1970—; chair, bd. dirs. Conn. Task Force for Children. Counselor div. hdqrs. travelers aid soc. ARC, Hartford, Conn., 1980—; crisis counselor New Horizon's Battered Women's Shelter, Middletown, 1984—; coordinator women's issues Mondale-Ferraro Conn. Campaign, 1984; bd. dirs. Middletown Community Concert Assn., Interagy. Council on Legislation; pres. bd. mgmt. Nutmeg Big Brothers/Big Sisters, Hartford. Mem. Assn. Adminstrs. of Vol. Service. Democrat. Episcopalian. Home: 357 Main St Apt 3 Cromwell CT 06416

SCOTT-MARTIN, LAURIE BETH, festival producer; b. Syracuse, N.Y., Apr. 29, 1958; d. John Lawrence and Phyllis Marguerite (Sanderson) Scott; m. Stephen Andrew Martin, July 16, 1983. B.Mus. in Music Edn., U. Hartford, 1980. Mgr. Conn. Valley Youth Wind Ensemble, Hartford, Conn., 1980-81; mktg. dir. Nashville Symphony Assn., 1982-84; devel. dir. Buffalo Philharm. Orch., 1984-86, Goodspeed Opera House, 1986-87; festival producer Greater Buffalo C. of C., 1988—. Mem. steering com. Met. Arts Commn. Summer Lights Arts Festival, Nashville, 1983-84; resource com. mem. YWCA Try Angle House, Nashville, 1983-84. Agy. recipient Diamond award Nashville Advt. Fedn., 1982. Mem. Am. Symphony Orch. League (mgmt. fellow N.Y. Philharmonic, Nashville Symphony, Cleve. Orch. 1981-82), Nashville Area Jr. C. of C. (com. mem.). Presbyterian.

SCOTT-SACCONE, MARY ANNE, computer programmer and analyst; b. Sioux City, Iowa, June 18, 1958; d. Gene Paxton and Joyce Annette (Roadman) Scott; m. Richard Joseph Saccone, Aug. 23, 1982; children: Dustin Ryan, Tyson John. AS, Aurora (Colo.) Community Coll., 1985. Assoc. in real estate The West Co., San Diego, 1977; reservationist Vic Braden's Tennis Coll., Trabuco Canyon, Calif., 1978; with retail dept. Wolfes Sporting Goods, Park City, Utah, 1979; sec. Office Overload, Denver, 1979-81, Mission Viejo Co., Englewood, Colo., 1981-82; computer programmer Applied Data Systems, Aurora, Colo., 1982-1987; computer programmer/analyst Pace Membership Warehouse, Aurora, 1987—. Methodist. Home: 1125 Macon St Aurora CO 80010 Office: Pace Membership Warehouse 3350 Peoria St Aurora CO 80011

SCOVILL, RUTH ALATHEA, television facility executive; b. Hudson, N.Y., Nov. 26, 1950; d. Robert Barnard and Janet Patricia (Goodman) S.; B.F.A., San Francisco Art Inst., 1972; M.A., Calif. State U., 1976. Scheduler, One Pass Video, San Francisco, 1977-78, ops. supr., 1978-79; prodn. supr. Reeves Teletape, N.Y.C., 1979-80, mgr. studio facilities, 1980-82, gen. mgr. studio facilities, 1982-83; gen. mgr. remote facilities, 1983-85; dir. ops. One Pass Film and Video, 1985-86, v.p., gen. mgr., 1986—. Mem. Profl. Women's Network, Bay Area Career Women, Am. Women in Radio and TV, Soc. Motion Picture & TV Execs., Bay Area Film/Tape Council (bd. dirs.). Home: 1936 McAllister St San Francisco CA 94115 Office: One China Basin Bldg San Francisco CA 94107

SCRENCI, ELYSE PUMA, construction company executive, owner, operator; b. Bklyn., Apr. 23, 1955; d. Albert Joseph and Eleanor (Fiore) Puma; m. Fiore Anthony Screnci, Apr. 11, 1987. AS, Kingsboro Community Coll., 1975; BS, C.W. Post, 1979. Pres., owner, operator Epic Contracting Corp., Bklyn., 1979—. Mem. Nat. Assn. Women Bus. Owners, Women in Family Owned Bus. Office: Epic Contracting Corp 1228 60th St Brooklyn NY 11219-4992

SCRIBNER, BEVERLY KINNEAR, lawyer; b. Chandler, Okla., Mar. 8, 1941; d. Howard James and Helen Vista (Smith) Kinnear; m. Edward L. Scribner, Aug. 26, 1961 (div. 1970); 1 child, John Edward; m. Don M. Claunch, July 9, 1983. BS with distinction in Math., U. Okla., 1963, JD, 1977. Bar: Okla. 1977. Office mgr. McAfee & Taft, Attys. at Law, Oklahoma City, 1970-72; adminstrv. asst. GHK Cos., Oklahoma City, 1972; legal asst. Hines & Smith, Oklahoma City, 1972-74; dir. legal assts. program U. Okla. Sch. Law, Norman, 1974-77; assoc. Kerr, Davis, Irvine, Krasnow, Rhodes & Semtner, Oklahoma City, 1977-79; ptnr. Claunch, Bryant & Scribner, Oklahoma City, 1979—. Mem. ABA, Okla. Bar Assn., Okla. County Bar Assn., Okla. City Title Attys. Assn. (pres. 1987), Mineral Lawyers Soc. Okla. City (pres. 1986-87), Okla. City Mgmt. and Profl. Women (pres. 1982), Phi Beta Kappa. Republican. Presbyterian. Office: Claunch Bryant & Scribner 3030 NW Expressway Suite 710 Oklahoma City OK 73112

SCRIVNER, BARBARA E., piano educator; b. Oreg., May 25, 1931; student (piano student of Lawrence Morton), Bob Jones U., 1962-66; corr. student Inst. Children's Lit., Redding Ridge, Conn., 1974-76; children—R. Dick, Lawrence C., Barbara Ann, Betty Jo. Part time sec., Oreg., 1948-50, 60-62, 74-76, 80-82, 86—, Census Bur., S.C., 1974-76, 80-82; piano tchr., Greenville, S.C., 1963—; instr. more than 80 student/tchr. recitals; freelance pianist, local chs. and restaurants. Active Republican Nat. Com., Nat. Rep. Senatorial Com., Nat. Rep. Congressional Com., S.C. Rep. Party. Mem. S.C. Music Assn., Music Tchrs. Nat. Assn., Liberty Found. Contbr. articles, letters to newspapers and columns; editor, pub. Golden Nuggets of Truth, 1982—.

SCRIVNER, JOYCE KAY, design automation engineer; b. Denver, June 12, 1950; d. Mansil Wayne and Harriet Lorraine (Webster) S. SSTP, Colo. Sch. Mines, 1967; student U. Colo., 1968-72, Mich. State U., 1974, Clarion (Pa.) State Coll., 1974; BSCS, Purdue U., 1976. Clk. U.S. Book Exchange, Washington, 1972-73, Govt. Printing Office, Washington, 1973-74; programmer SCADA group Leeds & Northrup Corp., North Wales, Pa., 1976-78; programmer/analyst Energy Mgmt. Systems div. Control Data Corp., Mpls., 1979-84; sr. design automation engr. Mercury div. Unisys Corp. (formerly Sperry Corp.), Mpls., 1984—, adminstr. Down Under Fan Fund, 1981-83; chmn. Plergbcon, Mpls., 1982, Notanokon, 1986; mem. staff SIGGRAPH, 1985, SIGPLAN, 1987. Editor: (mags.) Gypsy, 1979—, Of Such are Legends Made, 1978—. Mem. World Sci. Fiction Conv. Staff, 1977-78, 80-81, 83-85; chairperson art show Minicon, Mpls., 1980-81, 83, 86. Down Under Fan Fund grantee, 1981. Mem. Assn. Women in Computing (program v.p. 1982-83), Assn. for Computing Machinery, Minn. Sci. Fiction Assn., IEEE Computer Assn.

SCRUGGS, MOLLIE SUE, transportation executive; b. Tampa, Fla., Aug. 4, 1957; d. Paul Beckley Scruggs and Lucy Margarite Proctor. BS in Psychology, U. South Fla., 1976. Asst. mgr. Hotel Mutiny, Miami, Fla., 1978-82; mgr. Dolo Corp., Miami, 1983-85; ops. mgr. Hampton Hackney, Ltd., East Hampton, N.Y., 1985—; owner Leisure Limousine, Sag Harbor, N.Y., 1987—; co-ptnr. Clause Limousine, Southampton, N.Y., 1988—. Mem. East Hampton C. of C. (cons. 1986—). Democrat. Club: Fleet (Miami) (pres. 1982-83). Home: 21 Conklin Terr East Hampton NY 11937 Office: Clause Limo Ltd 801 Montauk Hwy Clause Commons Southampton NY 11968

SCUDIERI, LORRAINE ALBERTO, educator; b. Montclair, N.J., Apr. 25, 1940; d. Harry and Evelyn C. (Palmerie) Alberto; B.A., Montclair State Coll., 1962; M.A., Rutgers U., 1966, M.S. in Statistics, 1987. m. Bart Scudieri, Aug. 14, 1965; children—Laura, Matt, Chris, Tim, Patrick. Tchr., Pascack Valley High Sch., Hillsdale, N.J., 1962-65, Pascack Hills High Sch., Montvale, N.J., 1976-77, Montclair State Coll., Upper Montclair, N.J., 1966-68, 69-70, 71, 74, 79-83, 85-87; stat. studies analyst bus. research div., Bell Atlantic Corp., Newark, 1987—; instr. Fairleigh Dickinson U., 1969-72, 79-81, William Paterson Coll., Wayne, N.J., 1974-76, 82-83, Wyckoff (N.J.) Community Learning Center, 1979, Upsala Coll., East Orange, N.J., 1979-81; instr. decision scis. Rider Coll., Lawrenceville, N.J., 1983-85. Den mother Boy Scouts Am. NSF grantee, 1962-66. Mem. Ops. Research Soc. Am., Soc. Indsl. and Applied Math.

SCULLY, CELIA G., writer; m. Thomas J. Scully, B.A., Trinity Coll., Washington, 1954; M.A., U. Nev., Reno, 1980, postgrad., 1981—. Writer, co-author: (with Thomas J. Scully) How to Make Money Writing about Fitness and Health, 1986; contbr. articles to mags.; contbg. editor Travel Agt. mag., N.Y.C., 1976-79; instr. non-fiction mag. writing Western Nev. Community Coll., Reno, 1977-78. Author: Playing God: The New World of Medical Choices, 1988. Mem. Authors Guild, Am. Soc. Journalists and Authors, Inc., Am. Med. Writers Assn., Kappa Tau Alpha.

SCULLY, JULIA S., magazine editor; b. Seattle, Feb. 9, 1929; d. Julius and Rose (Hohenstein) Silverman. BA, Stanford U., 1951; MA, NYU, 1970. Asst. editor Argosy Mag., N.Y.C., 1952-53; assoc. editor U.S. Camera, N.Y.C., 1956-61; editor Camera 35 Mag., N.Y.C., 1961-66; editor Modern Photography, N.Y.C., 1966-87, contbg. editor, 1987—. Author, editor: Disfarmer: The Heber Springs Portraits, 1976; author: Sutter Street Reverie; editor: The Family of Women, 1978. Office: Modern Photography Mag 825 7th Ave New York NY 10019 *

SCULLYWEST, ELIZABETH MARY, geologist; b. Bklyn., Dec. 10, 1953; d. Michael R. and Mary L. (McQueeney) Scully; m. Edward Stember Scullywest, May 19, 1979; 1 child, Michael Charles. B.A. with honors, Skidmore Coll., 1976; M.S., U. Kans., 1978. Geologist, ArCo Exploration Co., Denver, 1978-80, sr. geologist, Lafayette, La., 1980-84, Midland, Tex., 1984-85; geologist U.S. Army C.E., Seattle, 1985-86. Vol., Weicker for Senator, Conn., 1970. Mem. Geol. Soc. Am., Am. Assn. Petroleum Geologists, Sierra Club, Nat. Assn. Female Execs., Sigma Gamma Epsilon. Home: 19529 2d Dr SE Bothell WA 98012

SEABLOOM, PATRICIA ANN, banking administrator; b. Moline, Ill., Apr. 3, 1945; d. Richard William and Avenell (Banfield) Bos; m. Harold Robert Seabloom, Sept. 3, 1965; 1 child, Jeremy Carl. AA, Blackhawk Jr. Coll., Moline, Ill., 1965; cert., Inst. Fin. Edn., Chgo., 1985. Clk. Dr. Heil & Dr. May, Rock Island, Ill., 1967, Mills Chevrolet, Moline, Ill., 1967, Sword's Veneer & Lumber Co., Rock Island, 1967; personnel clk. Container Corp. Am., Rock Island, 1967-68; firm loan clk. Modern Am. Mortgage Co., Rock Island, Ill., 1968-71; mgr., pres. Homestead Mortgage Co., Davenport, Ia., 1971-77; loan officer, asst. mgr. N.W. Fed. Banking and Savs., Fin. and Acctg., FA, New Richmond, Wis., 1978—. Treas. Redeemer Luth. Ch., Amery, Wis., 1982-86. Mem. Nat. Assn. Female Execs., Western Wis. Bd. Realtors (assoc.). Republican. Home: Rural Rt #3 Box 129 Amery WI 54001 Office: NW Fed Banking and Savs Fin and Acctg 532 S Knowles New Richmond WI 54017

SEABOLT, ZOE JOHNSON, accounting executive; b. Madison, Wis., Oct. 26, 1960; d. Gordon Heldt and Betty Ann (Rynders) J.; m. John Paul Seabolt, May 18, 1985. BBA with distinction, U. Wis., 1982. CPA, Wis., Tex. Sr. auditor Arthur Andersen & Co., Dallas, 1982-85; controller Lyn Zanville, Inc., Dallas, 1985-86; mgr. gen. acctg. Meth. Hosps. of Dallas, 1986—. Mem. Beta Alpha Psi. Republican. Presbyterian. Office: Meth Hosps of Dallas 301 W Colorado Dallas TX 75208

SEABORNE, LINDA LEE, real estate broker; b. Durand, Mich., June 2, 1948; d. Ira R. and Betty Jean (Ray) Merrill; m. Arthur Roy Seaborne, July 15, 1978. Degree in real estate, U. Mich., 1982. Supr. several state agys., Mich., 1968-78; broker, owner Re/Max Properties Inc., Petoskey, Mich., 1978-83; broker Exec. Real Estate Service Inc., Sarasota, Fla., 1984-87, Schlott Realtors inc., Sarasota, 1987—. Mem. Realtor's Nat. Mktg. Inst. (cert.), Nat. Assn. Realtors, Sarasota Bd. Realtors, Women's Council Realtors (chair 1986, pres. Emmet County chpt. 1982-83, Million Dollar Club 1986-87), Am. Bus. Women's Assn. (chair 1985-87, Woman of Yr. 1987), Women's Owners Network (pres. elect 1987), Grad. Realtors Inst. (cert.), Bus. and Profl. Women (pres. 1982-84). Republican. Roman Catholic. Club: Women's Resource Ctr. Home: 1768 Pine Harrier Circle Sarasota FL 34231

SEABRA-VEIGA, LISA RUTH, dentist, convalescent home dental consultant; b. Waterbury, Conn., Sept. 25, 1956; d. Adriano and Rita Seabra-Veiga; m. Jack Zazzaro. BA, Vassar Coll., 1978; DMD, U. Conn., Farmington, 1984. Gen. practice dental resident Waterbury (Conn.) Hosp., 1984-85; gen. practice dentistry Waterbury, 1985—; assoc. dir. Security Savs. and Loan Bank, Waterbury, 1987—. Bd. dirs. Waterbury Symphony Orch., Am. Cancer Soc. Mem. ADA, Conn. State Dental Assn., Acad. Gen. Dentistry, Dental Soc. Greater Waterbury, Acad. Cosmetic Dentistry, U. Conn. Health Ctr. Alumni Assn. (exec. com.). Democrat. Roman Catholic. Office: 1389 W Main St Suite 202 Waterbury CT 06708

SEABROOK, BONNIE MERCIER, risk and insurance executive; b. Atlanta, Oct. 13, 1947; d. D.B. and Louise (McCurry) Mercier; divorced; 1 son, Robert Hunter Seabrook. B.A., Clemson U., 1969; M.Ed., Clemson U., 1971. Tchr., Pickens County (S.C.) Sch. System, 1969-73; adult instr. Tri-County Tech, 1973-74; adminstrv. officer, personnel dir. W.B. Johnson Properties, Atlanta, 1976-77; mgr. of ins. McBurney Corp., Atlanta, 1978-85; owner, risk mgr. Indsl. Risk Mgmt. Services, Atlanta, 1985—, AIG Ins. Co., 1985-86, SunTrust Banks, Inc., 1986—; ins. cons. Panhellenic House Corp. Assn., Emory U. Bd. dirs. Scholarship Atlanta Found., 1984—, v.p. pub. relations, 1986 . Named Miss Summerville (S.C.), 1967, 68; participant Miss S.C. Pageant, 1967, 68. Mem. Risk and Ins. Mgmt. Soc., Jaycees (hon.), Assoc. Builders and Contractors of Ga. (chmn. safety com., 1984, 85; bd. dirs. 1985; Nat. award of excellence 1985), Angel Flight, Jr. League, Chi Omega (personnel advisor Emory U. chpt., nat. chmn. ins. 1982—, del. nat. conv. 1982-88 leader Firesides House Corp. 1983 del. 1985), Kappa Delta Pi. Republican. Presbyterian. Home: 6830 Sunny Brook Ln Atlanta GA 30328

SEALS, LINDA, graphic designer; b. Dallas, May 26, 1951; d. Fred Clifford and Dorothy (Hardy) S. BA, Colo. State U., Ft. Collins, 1973. Co-founder B. Vader Phototypesetting, Ft. Collins, ptnr., 1975-77, pres., gen. mgr., 1977-84, designer, owner, 1985—; mng. ptnr. The CLS Co., Ft. Collins, 1980-87; co-founder Salt Cedar mag., art. dir., 1977-80; judge bus. graphics competition Colo. Future Bus. Leaders Am., 1984; bd. dirs. Crossroads Safehouse, 1988. Designer poster in permanent collection Auschwitz Mus., Poland, 1985; group shows include: Auschwitz Mus., 1985. Sponsor Ft. Collins Parks and Recreation teams, 1979-80; mem. Task Force on Alt. Trolley Routes, 1984-85, Pkwy. Preservation Soc., 1983—. Recipient Design award Rocky Mountain Book Pubs. Assn., 1986. Mem. Typographers Internat. Assn. (typographic excellence awards), Nat. Composition Assn. (awards), U.S. Tennis Assn., Ft. Collins Tennis Assn., Rocky Mountain Book Pub. Assn. Democrat. Avocations: tennis, gardening, reading. Office: B Vader Design Prodn 1331 W Mountain Ave Fort Collins CO 80521

SEALY-HARDESTY, ADRIENNE VERMELLE, psychologist, writer; b. Bklyn., Sept. 8, 1958; d. Thomas Augustus and Ruby (Martin) S.; m. Larry L. Hardesty, Spet. 8, 1984; 1 child, Lawrence Thomas Shomari

Hardesty. BA, CUNY, N.Y.C., 1980; MS, CUNY, 1981; postgrad., New Sch. for Social Research. Writer N.Y. Amsterdam Newspaper, Bklyn., 1979-82, Assn. Study of Family Living, Bklyn., 1977—; psychologist Bklyn. Bd. Edn., 1982—; founder, dir. The Adrienne Sealy Pubs., Bklyn., 1977—; cons. N.Y.C. Bd. Edn., 1986—. Author No Hill is too High, 1979, Color Your Way Into Black History, 1980, The Skin I'm In, 1984, Women We Be, 1987. Mem. People United to Save Humanity, Chgo., 1980—; fundraiser COncord Baptist Ch., Bklyn., 1958—. Recipient various awards for literary and humanitarian achievements. Mem. Bus. and Profl. Women, Am. Librarians' Assn., Assn. for Study of Family (pres. 1977—), Bklyn. Athletic Assn., Psi Chi Soc. Democrat. Home and Office: PO Box 130 Brooklyn NY 11208

SEAPKER, JANET KAY, museum director; b. Pitts., Nov. 2, 1947; d. Charles Henry and Kathryn Elizabeth (Dany) S.; m. Edward F. Turberg, May 24, 1975. BA, U. Pitts., 1969; MA, SUNY, Cooperstown, 1975. Park ranger Nat. Pk. Service, summers 1967-79; archtl. historian N.C. Archives and History, Raleigh, 1971-76, hist. preservation adminstr., 1976-77, grant-in-aid adminstr., 1977-78; dir. New Hanover County Mus., Wilmington, N.C., 1978—; bd. dirs. Bellamy Mansion Found., Inc., Wilmington, Lower Cape Fear Hist. Soc., Wilmington; N.C. state rep. Southeast Mus. Conf., 1986—; field reviewer Inst. of Mus. Services, 1982—. Contbr. articles to profl. jours. Bd. dirs. Downtown Area Revitalization Effort, Wilmington, 1979-81, Hist. Wilmington Found., 1979-84, pres., 1980-81; mem. Community Appearance Commn., Wilmington, 1984-88, 250 Ann. Commn., Wilmington, 1986—. Grad. program fellow SUNY, Cooperstown, 1969-70. Mem. N.C. Mus. Council (sec.-treas. 1978-84, pres. 1984-86), Am. Assn. Mus. (mem. accreditation vis. com. 1983—, mus. assessment program reviewer 1982—), Nat. Trust Hist. Preservation, Hist. Preservation Found. of N.C. (sec. 1976-78). Democrat. Presbyterian. Home: 307 N 15th St Wilmington NC 28401 Office: New Hanover County Mus 814 Market St Wilmington NC 28401

SEARIGHT, PATRICIA ADELAIDE, retired radio and television executive; b. Rochester, N.Y.; d. William Hammond and Irma (Winters) S. BA, Ohio State U. Program dir. Radio Sta. WTOP, Washington, 1952-63, gen. mgr. info., 1964; radio and TV cons., 1964-84; ret., 1984; producer, dir. many radio and TV programs; spl. fgn. news corr. French Govt., 1956; v.p. Micro Beads, Inc., 1955-59; sec., dir. Dennis-Inches, Corp., 1955-59; exec. dir. Am. Women in Radio and TV, 1969-74; fgn. service officer U.S. Dept. State, AEC, ret. Mem. pres.'s council Toledo Mus. Art. Recipient Kappa Kappa Gamma Alumna achievement award. Mem. Am. Women in Radio and TV (program chmn.; corrs. sec.; dir. Washington chpt.; pres. 1958-60, nat. membership chmn. 1962-63, nat. chmn. Industry Info. Digest 1963-64, Mid-Eastern v.p. 1964-66), Soc. Am. Travel Writers (treas. 1957-58, v.p. 1958-59), Nat. Acad. TV Arts and Scis., Kappa Kappa Gamma. Episcopalian. Clubs: Women's Advt. (Washington) (pres. 1959-60), Nat. Press. Lodge: Soroptimits. Home: 10549 E Desert Cove Ave Scottsdale AZ 85259

SEARL, JACALYN JOY, special education teacher; b. Sioux Falls, S.D., Mar. 16, 1953; d. Robert Edwin and Myrna Mae (Groeneveld) D. BS in Spl. and Elem. Edn., U. S.D., 1976, MA in Spl. and Early Childhood Edn., 1986. Tchr. spl. edn. Emerson Sch., Sioux Falls, 1976-84; tchr. early childhood Hawthorne Elem. Sch., Sioux Falls, 1985-86; cons. early childhood for handicapped Region 18 Edn. Service Ctr., Midland, Tex., 1986—. Sec. Emerson Sch. PTA, 1976-83; chaperone S.D. Spl. Oympics, 1976-84; chaperone/coach Internat. Spl. Olympics, Baton Rouge, summer 1983; mem. pub. relations staff Sioux Falls Republican. Com. 1983. Mem. Council Exceptional Children, Assn. Sch. and Community Devel., Nat. Assn. Female Execs., Am. Legion Aux., Phi Delta Kappa, Phi Beta Pi. Lutheran. Home: 4100 E 50th St Apt 510 Odessa TX 79762 Office: Region 18 Edn Service Ctr PO Box 6020 Midland TX 79711

SEARLE-KUBBY, JAN L., sculptor; b. Ellensburg, Wash., Aug. 27, 1938; d. Kenneth Gifford and Lillian (Storey) B.; m. Sheldon Walter Searle, Dec. 5, 1969 (div. Nov. 1982); m. Dan Kubby July 24, 1983; children: Scott William, LoyAnne. Student in art and edn., Cen. Wash. State U., 1957-59, U. Colo., 1962-63. Supr., art dir. Yakima (Wash.) Herald, 1963-69; owner, art dir. Ad Mauk, Denver, 1970-72, Nat. Western Mktg., Ft. Worth, 1972-74, Jan Dihel & Assoc., Denver, 1975-81; sculptor Denver, 1976—. Works include permanent exhibits at State Capitol, Bismark, N.D., 1981, Buffalo Bill Cody Mus., 1978-82, Cowboy Hall of Fame, 1978-80, Profl. Rodeo Cowboys Mus., 1978-84, Tex. Tech. U. Western Heritage Art Mus., 1983-84 (1st and 2d in sculpture 1979-80, 82), Omni Banks one man show, Denver, 1982 and encore, 1983, life size statue founder Nat. Jewish Hosp., Colo., 1987, commn. Colo. Ballet, 1987; sculpture shown on 6 month European tour sponsored by TWA, 1986-87, 6 month exhibit World's Fair, 1982; contbr. articles to profl. jours. Recipient Florence Nightengale award Colo. Nurses Assn. Mem. Internat. Sculptor Soc., Woman Artists Am. West (v.p., Best of Show and 1st in sculpture 1979-83), Nat. Western Artists (1st in sculpture Nat. Western Art Show 1980, 82), Profl. Artists of Colo., Am. Artists Profl. League. Home: 8 Cherrymoor Dr Englewood CO 80110

SEARLES, ANNA MAE HOWARD, educator, civic worker; b. Osage Nation Indian Terr., Okla., Nov. 22, 1906; d. Frank David and Clara (Bowman) Howard; A.A., Odessa (Tex.) Coll., 1961; B.A., U. Ark., 1964; M.Ed., 1970; postgrad. (Herman L. Donovan fellow), U. Ky., 1972—; m. Isaac Adams Searles, May 26, 1933; 1 dau., Mary Ann Rogers (Mrs. Herman Lloyd Hoppe). Compiler news, broadcaster sta. KJBC, 1950-60; corr. Tulsa Daily World, 1961-64; tchr. Rogers (Ark.) High Sch., 1964-72; tchr. adult class rapid reading, 1965, 80; tchr. adult edn. Learning Center Benton County (Ark.), Bentonville, 1973-77, supr. adult edn., 1977-79; tchr. North Ark. Community Coll., Rogers, 1979—, CETA, Bentonville, 1979-82; tchr. Joint Tng. Partnership Act, 1984-85; coordinator adult edn. Rogers C. of C. and Rogers Sch. System, 1984—. Sec. Tulsa Safety Council, 1935-37; leader, bd. dirs. Girl Scouts U.S.A., Kilgore, Tex., 1941-44, leader, Midland, Tex., 1944-52, counselor, 1950-61; exec. sec. Midland Community Chest, 1955-60; gray lady Midland A.R.C., 1958-59; organizer Midland YMCA, Salvation Army; dir. women's div. Savings Bond Program, Midland; mem. citizens com. Rogers Hough Meml. Library, women's aux. Rogers Meml. Hosp.; vol. tutor Laubach literacy orgn., 1973—; sec. Beaver Lake Literacy Council, Rogers, 1973-83, Little Flock Planning Commn., 1975-77, Benton County Hist. Soc., 1981—; pub. relations chmn. South Central region Nat. Affiliation for Literacy Advance, 1977-79; bd. dirs. Globe Theatre, Odessa, Tex., Midland Community Theatre, Tri-County Foster Home, Guadalupe, Midland youth centers, DeZavala Day Nursery, PTA, Adult Devel. Center, Rogers CETA, 1979-81; vol. recorder Ark. Hist. Preservation Program, 1984—. Recipient Nice People award Rogers C. of C., 1987, Thanks badge Midland Girl Scout Assn., 1948; Cert. of recognition, Rogers Pub. Schs., 1986; Instr. of Yr. award North Ark. Community Coll. West Campus Mem. NEA (del. conv. 1965), Ark. Assn. Public Continuing and Adult Edn. (pres. 1979-80), South Central Assn. for Lifelong Learning (sec. 1980-84), PTA (life), Future Homemakers Am. (life; sec. 1980—), Delta Kappa Gamma. Episcopalian. Clubs: Altrusa (pres. 1979—), Apple Spur Community (Rogers). Home: Route 2 Rogers AR 72756

SEARLES, PATRICIA J. CARTER, small business owner; b. Stamford, Conn., Jan. 16, 1942; d. Edward L. and Jean E. (Briscoe) Carter. Student, U. Conn., 1959-61. Owner, bookkeeper Pat's Bookkeeping and Tax Service, Weber City, Va., 1982—. Home and Office: Pat's Bookkeeping and Tax Service 386 Hwy 23 Weber City VA 24251

SEARLS, EILEEN HAUGHEY, lawyer, librarian, educator; b. Madison, Wis., Apr. 27, 1925; d. Edward M. and Anna Mary (Haughey) S.; B.A., U. Wis., 1948, J.D., 1950, M.S. in L.S., 1951. Admitted to Wis. bar, 1950; cataloger Yale U., 1951-52; instr. law St. Louis U., 1952-52, asst. prof., 1953-56, asso. prof., 1956-64, prof., 1964—, law librarian, 1952—. Mem. Wis. Bar Assn., Bar Assn. Met. St. Louis, Am. Assn. Law Librarians, Mid-Am. Assn. Law Libraries, Council Law Library Consortium (chmn.), Southwestern Assn. Law Libraries. Club: Altrusa. Office: 3700 Lindell Blvd Saint Louis MO 63108

SEARS, ALICE HART, company executive, consultant; b. Baden, Austria, Apr. 13, 1923 (parents Am. citizens); d. Benjamin and Augusta (Naswich) Hart; m. William R. Sears, Apr. 24, 1942; children—Richard C., Beth S., Catherine. Student NYU, 1941-43. Communications specialist UN Info. Ctr., N.Y.C., 1943-45; v.p. W.R. Sears, Inc., San Mateo, Calif., 1969—. Mem. IEEE. Republican. Club: Metropolitan (San Francisco).

SEATON, CLARRUTH ANNE, computer analyst; b. Madison, Wis., Jan. 11, 1956; d. Clarence Allen and Merruth Joanne (Potgieter) S. BA, Stephens Coll., 1978; MA, U. Mo., Columbia, 1981. Profl. singer Ad Hoc Singers, Columbia, 1979-81; supr. library Amoco Prodn., Houston, 1981-85, computer analyst, 1985-86, 86—, supr. learning ctr., 1988; piano tchr. Houston, 1984-86; cons. Library Houston Photography, 1984-85; cons. educator Chgo., 1986. Contbr. articles to profl. jours; Author/editor newsletter Dynasoft User's Group, 1935. Sunday sch. tchr. Meth. Ch., Columbia, 1979-81. Stephens Coll. acad. scholar, 1974-78. Mem. Spl. Libraries Assn. (sec. 1980), Dynasoft Users, Geosci. Info. Soc., Smithsonian Instn., Dataset, Jr. C. of C. Republican. Clubs: Amoco Baroque Music (dir. 1984-88). Lodges: Rainbow Girls, DAR. Home: 12403 Wedgehill Houston TX 77077 Office: Amoco Prodn Co 501 Westlake Park Blvd Houston TX 77077

SEATON, EVA MARIE, insurance company executive; b. Sacramento, Calif., Sept. 14, 1961; d. Samuel Lee Jr. and Lani (Moulton) Thomas; m. Jerome Charles Seaton Jr., Oct. 25, 1987. Student, Sierra Community Coll., 1980-81; diploma in bus. II, Life Underwriters' Tng. Council, 1986, diploma in disability, 1987. Office mgr. Stranco, Newcastle, Calif., 1979-81; sales rep. Florence Filter co., Compton, Calif., 1981-84; ins. agt. Transamerica Life Cos., Sacramento, 1984—. Mem. Nat. Assn. Life Underwriters, Sacramento Assn. Life Underwriters. Republican. Office: Transamerica Life Cos 1750 Howe Ave Suite 100 Sacramento CA 95825

SEATON, ROXANN T., financial consultant; b. Owensboro, Ky., Sept. 12, 1957; d. George Eugene and Shirley E. (Simmons) Twiggs; m. Samuel G. Seaton, June 16, 1979. BA in Journalism, U. Fla., 1975-79. Lic. Security and Exchange, Health and Life Ins. agt. In-house advt. coordinator Sun 'n Lake Estates/Land Devel., Sebring, Fla., 1981-82; heartland area rep. Tampa (Fla.) Tribune, 1982-83; sales rep./spl. sections coordinator Sebring (Fla.) News, 1983-85; fin. cons. Merrill Lynch, Sebring, Fla., 1985—. Fund raiser Ridge Area Assn. for the Retarded, Avon Park, Fla., 1986. Recipient ADDY award, 1983, Co-op Advt. award for best use of co-op advt. in pring, 1984. Mem. Bus. and Profl. Women (sec. 1986-87), Am. Assn. Bus. Women. Republican. Roman Catholic. Club: Toastmasters (treas. 1985-86). Home: 3421 Austin St Sebring FL 33870 Office: Merrill Lynch 2420 SE Lakeview Dr Sebring FL 33870

SEAY, VALERIE KAYE, educational adminstrator; b. Detroit, Nov. 8, 1963; d. Walter M. and Ruth M. (Austin) S. BS, Ferris State Coll., 1985; BA, Spring Arbor Coll., 1987. Placement coordinator Ross Learning Inc., Oak Park, Mich., 1985-87; edn. and placement coordinator Detroit Bus. Inst., Southfield, Mich., 1987-88; English teaching asst. Japan Exchange and Teaching Program, Hyogo, Japan, 1988—. Youth care worker Counterpoint Runaway Shelter, Inster, Mich., 1985-86. Fellow Internat. Personnel Mgmt. Assn., Nat. Assn. Female Execs., Japan Assn. Lang. Tchrs. Democrat. Home: 19551 Hazelhurst Southfield MI 48075

SEBASTIANI, SUSAN MARIE, title insurance company executive; b. Trenton, N.J., Jan. 16, 1954; d. Louis Peter and Emma (Rendemonti) Carlucci; m. Anthony E. Sebastiani, Sept. 17, 1977. Student, Mercer County Community Coll., 1972. Sec. Eastern Abstract Co., Trenton, 1973-75; sec., title examiner Commonwealth Land Co., Trenton, 1975-77; asst. v.p. Continental Title Ins. Co., Trenton, 1977-84; pres. Mercer Title Services Agy., Inc., Trenton, 1984—. Mem. Mercer County Bd. Realtors, Mercer County Bar Assn. (affiliate), U.S. C. of C., N.J. Land Title Assn., Am. Land Title Assn. Home: 820 Fairmount Ave Trenton NJ 08629 Office: Mercer Title Services Agy Inc 5 Stults Ave PO Box 3710 Trenton NJ 08629

SEBASTIANI-CUNEO, MARY ANN, property manager; b. Sonoma, Calif., July 1, 1947; d. August David and Sylvia Emily (Scarafoni) Sebastiani; m. Richard Angelo Cuneo, Feb. 1, 1940; children: Angelo, Marc, Josef. BA, U. Santa Clara (Calif.), 1969; student, U. Calif., Davis, 1970, Anthony Schs., 1985. Elem. tchr. West Davis Elem., Davis, Calif., 1971-72; tchr. Northwood Elem., Napa, Calif., 1972-74; pub. relations person Sebastiani Vineyards, Sonoma, Calif., 1974—; founder, chief exec. officer, pres. Plaza Properties, Inc., Sonoma, 1980-84; real property mgr. Triple C Investments, Sonoma, 1978—; v.p. Sebastiani Vineyards-Real Estate, Sonoma, 1987—. Chairperson Sonoma County Boy Scouts Am., 1987. Mem. Sonoma County Winegrowers. Republican. Roman Catholic. Office: PO Box 4 Vineburg CA 95487

SEBESTYEN, OUIDA, author; b. Vernon, Tex., Feb. 13, 1924; d. James Ethridge and Byrd (Lantrip) Dockery; m. Adam Sebestyen, Dec. 21, 1960 (div. 1966); 1 child, Corbin. Student, U. Colo. speaker, leader workshops at pub. schs. and ednl. orgns. Author: Words by Heart, 1979 (Internat. Reading Assn. award 1979, Am. Book award 1982), Far from Home, 1980 (Silver Pencil award 1984), IOU's, 1982 (Tex. Inst. Letters award 1983), On Fire, 1985. Home and Office: 115 S 36th St Boulder CO 80303

SEBRING, MARJORIE MARIE ALLISON, home furnishings company executive; Burnsville, N.C., Oct. 8, 1924; d. James William and Mary Will (Ramsey) Allison Shockey; student Mars Hill Coll., 1943, Home Decorators Sch. Design, N.Y.C., 1948, Wayne State U., 1953; cert. home furnishings rep. U. Va., 1982; 1 dau., Patricia Louise Banner Krohn. Dir. decorating div. Robinson Furniture, Detroit, 1949-57; head buyer Tyner Hi-Way House, Ypsilanti, Mich., 1957-63; head buyer Town and Country, Dearborn, Mich., 1963-66; instr. Nat. Carpet Inst., 1963-65; owner Adams House, Inc., Plymouth, Mich., 1966-72; exec. v.p. mktg. and sales, regional sales and mktg. mgr. Triangle Industries, Los Angeles, 1972—; co-owner Markham-Sebring, Inc., St. Petersburg, Fla., 1983—; dir. contract div. Kane Furniture, 1978-85; co-owner Accessories, Etc., 1985—; rep. at large Heritage Lakes, U.S. Home. Mem. Presdl. Task Force. Recipient nat. sales awards, recognition for work with youth and aged. Mem. Internat. Home Furnishings Assn., Fla. Home Furnishings Rep. Assn. (officer), Am. Security Council, Williamsburg Found., USCG Aux., Nat. Audubon Soc., Internat. Platform Assn. Republican. Contbr. creative display to Better Homes and Gardens, 1957-64. Home: 2601-3 Grist Mill Circle New Port Richey FL 34655-1311

SECCOMBE, VIRGINIA ZIU, school administrator; b. Southbridge, Mass., Oct. 19, 1947; d. Themistocli and Katherine (Christo) Ziu; m. Donald Alton Seccombe Jr., Dec. 27, 1970; 1 child, Sarah Elizabeth. BA, U. Bridgeport, 1969; MA, Wesleyan U., 1973; MEd, Lehigh U., 1977, EdD, 1987. Tchr. math. Darien (Conn.) Pub. Schs., 1969-75; math. coordinator East Penn Sch. Dist., Emmaus, Pa., 1975-79, asst. prin., 1979-82; coordinator curriculum Northwestern Lehigh Sch. Dist., New Tripoli, Pa., 1982-84; asst. supt. Cheshire (Conn.) Pub. Schs., 1984—. Mem. Am. Assn. Sch. Adminstrs., Am. Mgmt. Assn., Conn. Assn. for Supervision and Curriculum Devel. (Ednl. Leader of Yr. semi-finalist 1987), New Haven Area Supts. Assn., Delta Kappa Gamma, Phi Delta Kappa. Office: Cheshire Dept Edn 29 Main St Cheshire CT 06710

SEDAR, BARI BIERN, playwright, actress; b. Cin., Aug. 26, 1949; d. Harvey A. and Natalie A. (Smith) Biern; m. Scott Randall Sedar, Apr. 9, 1983. B.A., Stephens Coll., Columbia, Mo., 1970; M.F.A., Emerson Coll., 1973. Dir. sales Prodn. Media, Inc., Cin., 1974-75; account rep. J. Walter Thompson Co., Washington, 1975-78, copywriter, 1978-80, v.p., sr. copywriter, 1982-85; v.p., sr. copywriter Brouillard Communications, Washington, 1980-81; ptnr. Two Writers ... No Waiting; actress, singer, 1983—. Author, lyricist TV-print campaign for Am. Cancer Soc.: Draggin' Lady (Creative Excellence in Black Advt. award 1983), 1983; playwright, lyricist A Dance Against Darkness: Living with AIDS, 1987. Mem. pub. relations com. Nat. Hospice Orgn., Washington, 1982-83; mem. internat. adv. council Children's Hospice Internat., Washington, 1983-84; vol. Washington Home Hospice, 1983-87.

SEDDON, JOANNA M., opthalmologist; b. Pitts., June 13, 1948. BS, U. Pitts., 1970, MD, 1974; MS, Harvard U., 1976. Diplomate Am. Bd. Ophthalmology, Mass. Intern Framingham (Ma.) Union Hosp., 1974-75; resident Tufts New Eng. Med. Ctr., Boston, 1976-80; fellow research ophthalmic path. Mass. Eye and Ear Infirmary, Boston, 1980-81; clin. fellow viteoretinal Retina Service Mass. Eye and Ear Infirmary, Boston, 1981-82; instr. clin. ophthalmology Harvard Med. Sch., Boston, 1982-84, asst. prof., asst. surgeon ophthalmolgy, 1984; dir. ultrasound service Mass. Eye and Ear Infirmary, Boston, 1982—, mem. orgn. epidemiology research unit, 1984-85, dir. epidemiology unit, 1985—; mem. com. vision Commn. Behavioral and Social Scis. and Edn., Nat. Research Council, Washington, 1984—. Contbr. articles to profl. jours. Grantee Nat. Eye Inst., 1984, Nat. Cancer Inst., 1986; recipient senatorial scholarship, 1970-74, Henry H. Clark Med. Edn. Found., 1973, awards NIH Nat. Service Research, 1975, 80-81, Nat. Eye Inst. Contract, 1985. Mem. Am. Acad. Ophthalmology, AMA, Am. Med. Women's Assn., Assn. Research Vision and Ophthalmology, Soc. Epidemiologic Research, Am. Pub. Health Assn., New Eng. Ophthalmological Soc., Am. Coll. Epidemiology. Home: 117 Myrtle St Boston MA 02114

SEDERGREN, MURIEL DWYER, bank executive; b. Barnet, Vt., July 14, 1942; d. Dale Stuessel and Elizabeth Julia (Champany) Dwyer; m. Rodney Doane Sedergren, Aug. 6, 1960; 1 child, Anita Marie Hughes. AA, Williams Coll., 1976; cert., Am. Inst. of Banking, 1986; MS in Banking with honors, Fairfield U., 1982; student, N.Eng. Sch. Banking. Asst. treas., br. mgr. Proctor (Vt.) Bank, 1962-79; v.p. ops. Marble Bank, Rutland, Vt., 1979-84; v.p., sr. loan officer Woodstock (Vt.) Nat. Bank, 1984—. Trustee Ottauquechee Health Ctr., 1987; dir. ARC, Rutland, 1980-84; mem. Pentangle Council of the Arts., 1987; v.p., fundraiser Vt. and N.H. Easter Seals. Mem. Vt. chpt. Am. Inst. Banking (v.p., edn. chair 1973-75, Woman of Yr. award 1975), Vt. Bankers Assn. (ednl. chair mortgage com. 1987), Vt. chpt. Bank Admistrn. Inst. (pres., state dir. 1979-80), Ottauquechee Bus. and Profl. Women (pres. 1985-86), Nat. Assn. Banking Women, Nat. Assn. Female Execs., Woodstock Area C. of C. (dir., mem. chair), Woodstock Hist. Soc., Billings Farm and Mus. Republican. Episcopalian. Office: Woodstock Nat Bank 21 Elm St Woodstock VT 05091

SEDGWICK, RAE, psychologist, lawyer; b. Kansas City, Kans., Apr. 7, 1944; d. Charles and Helen (Timmons) Sedgwick. R.N., Bethany Sch. Nursing, 1965; B.S., U. Iowa, 1967; M.A., U. Kans., 1970, Ph.D., 1972, JD, 1986. Cert. psychologist, Kans.; bar: Kans. 1986. Med./surg., orthopedic and obstet. nurse, Iowa City, Iowa, 1965-67; with Community Mental Health Nursing, Kansas City, Kans., 1967-68; specialist Lab. Edn., Washington, 1971-72; adj. clin. staff community psychiatry, 1975-76; coordinator Health C.A.R.E. Clinic, Pa. State U., 1974-76; head grad. program in community mental health nursing and family therapy, Pa. State U., 1974-76, asst. prof., 1972-76; pvt. practice psychology, Bonner Springs, Kans., 1976—; cons. in field.; staff Bethany Med. Ctr., Kansas City, Kans., Cushing's Meml. Hosp., Leavenworth, Kans., St. John's Hosp., Leavenworth; del. Internat. Council Nurses, Frankfurt, Germany, People for People, People's Republic of China, 1982. Active Am. Heart Assn.; city councilwoman Bonner Springs, 1981—, pres. pro tem, 1983-87; mem. Kans. Internat. Women's Yr. Commn. Recipient Outstanding Young Woman award, U. Kans., Bus. and Profl. Women's Club scholar; elected to Kans. U. Women's Hall of Fame, 1987. Fellow Am. Orthopsychiat. Assn.; mem. AAAS, ABA, Kansas Bar Assn., Am. Assn. Psychiatric Services for Children, Am. Group Psychotherapy Assn. (dir.), Am. Nurses Assn., Am. Psychol. Assn., Anthrop. Assn. for Study of Play, Council of Advanced Practitioners in Psychiat. Mental Health Nursing, Kans. Psychol. Assn., Council Nurse Researchers, Sigma Theta Tau. Republican. Methodist. Club: Pilot. Author: Family Mental Health, 1980; The White Frame House, 1980; contbr. articles to profl. jours.

SEDGWICK-HIRSCH, CAROL ELIZABETH, corporate executive; b. Cin., Apr. 16, 1922; d. Howard Malcolm Sedgwick and Lucile Alleen (Willard) Sedgwick-Schenk; m. Donald Sebastian Freewan, Nov. 25, 1944 (div. July 1968); children: Elizabeth P. Freewan Nord, Lucy S. Freewan Kyle; m. William Christian Hirsch, June 16, 1983. BS, U. Cin., 1944, postgrad., 1972; student, Art Acad. of Cin., 1953-56; MEd, Xavier U., 1966. Head dir. and tchr. Sacred Heart Acad. PreSch., Cin., 1952-53; caseworker dependent children Hamilton County Welfare Dept., Cin., 1959-62; instr. ednl. psychology and child devel. Wright State U., Fairborn, Ohio, 1970-71, 71-72; pres., chief exec. officer Joseph England Hutton Enterprises, Cin., 1979—; vol. with Office of Prosecuting Atty Emmet County, Petoskey, Mich.; ptnr. Feldhaus Home Improvement, Inc., Cin. Mem. Dayton St. Neighborhood Assn., Cin. Womans Club (philanthropic com. 1985-87). Club: Coll. of Cin. Home: 605 E Epworth Ave Cincinnati OH 45225 Home: PO Box 72 Conway MI 49722-0072 Office: Joseph England Hutton Enterprises 605 E Epworth Ave Cincinnati OH 45223

SEDLAK, VALERIE FRANCES, educator; b. Balt., Mar. 11, 1934; d. Julian Joseph and Eleanor Eva (Pilot) Sedlak; 1 child, Barry. AB in English, Coll. Notre Dame, Balt., 1955; MA, U. Hawaii, 1962; postgrad., U. Pa., 1982. Tchr. Sacred Heart Sch., Pensacola, Fla., 1955-56; grad. teaching fellow East-West Cultural Ctr., U. Hawaii, 1959-60; adminstrv. asst. Korean Consul Gen., Honolulu, 1959-60; tchr. Boyertown (Pa.) Sr. High Sch., 1961-63; asst. prof. English, U. Balt., 1963-69; asst. prof. Morgan State U., Balt., 1970—, sec. to faculty, 1981-83, faculty research scholar, 1982-83. Author poetry and lit. criticism. Coordinator Young Reps., Berks County, Pa., 1962-63; chmn. Md. Young Reps., 1964; election judge Baltimore County, Md., 1964-66; regional capt. Am. Cancer Soc., 1978-79; adv. bd. Our Md. Anniversary, 1984, The Living Constitution: Bicentennial of the Fed. Constitution, 1987. Fellow Morgan-Penn Faculty, 1977-79, Nat. Endowment Humanities, 1984; named Outstanding Teaching Prof., U. Balt. Coll. Liberal Arts, 1965, Outstanding Teaching Prof. English, Morgan State U., 1987. Mem. MLA, South Atlantic MLA, Coll. Lang. Assn., Coll. English Assn. (v.p. Mid.-Atlantic Group, 1987—), Women's Caucus for Modern Langs., Md. Council Tchrs. English, Md. Poetry and Literary Soc., Mid. Atlantic Writers' Assn. (founding 1981), AAUW. Roman Catholic. Club: U. Auburn. Home: 102 Gorsuch Rd Lutherville-Timonium MD 21093 Office: Morgan State U Dept English Baltimore MD 21239

SEDLIS, MARGARET JOAN, architect; b. Boston, Dec. 6, 1950; d. Edward Gabriel and Cynthia Joy (Miller) S. B.F.A. in Environ. Design, Parsons Sch. Design, New Sch. for Social Research, 1972; M.Arch., Washington U., St. Louis, 1975. Jr. project mgr. Hoffman Partnership, St. Louis, 1976-77, John Cohen & Assocs., St. Louis, 1977-78; dir. space planning Planned Expansion Group/Architects, White Plains, N.Y., 1978-83; assoc./project dir. interiors Hellmuth, Obata & Kassabaum/Architects, N.Y.C., 1983-86, dePolo Dunbar, 1986—. Mem. AIA, Alliance of Women in Architecture. Home: 85 East End Ave New York NY 10028 Office: dePolo/Dunbar 330 W 42d St New York NY 10011

SEDLOCK, JOY, psychiatric social worker; b. Memphis, Jan. 23, 1958; d. George Rudolph Sedlock and Mary Robson; m. Thomas Robert Jones, Aug. 8, 1983. AA, Ventura (Calif.) Jr. Coll., 1978; BS in Psychology, Calif. Luth. U., 1980; MS in Counseling and Psychology, U. LaVerne, 1983; MSW, Calif. State U., Sacramento, 1986. Research asst. Camarillo (Calif.) State Hosp., 1981, tchr.'s aide, 1982; sub. tchr. asst. Vertura County Sch. Dist., 1981; teaching asst. Ventura Jr. Coll., 1980-82, tchr. adult edn., 1980-84; psychiatric social worker Yolo County Day Treatment Ctr., Broderick, Calif., 1986, Napa (Calif.) State Hosp., 1986—. Mem. Nat. Assn. Social Workers, NOW (campaign 1984 presdl. election). Mem. Humanist Orgn. Ch. Home: 17 Griggs Ln Napa CA 94558 Office: Napa State Hosp Napa/Vallejo Hgwy Napa CA 49558

SEE, KAREN MASON, judge; b. Springfield, Mo., Jan. 31, 1952; d. Robert Wayne and Mildred Lucille (Stockstill) Mason; m. Andrew B. See, Nov. 24, 1979. BS in Edn., SW Mo. State U., 1973; JD, U. Mo., 1978. Tchr. Springfield (Mo.) Dist., 1973-75; law clk. Judge William E. Turnage, Mo. Ct. of Appeals, Kansas City, 1978-79; assoc. atty. Slagle & Bernard, Kansas City, 1979-84, ptnr., 1984-86; judge U.S. Bankruptcy Ct., Kansas City, 1986—. Vol. instr. Kansas City Law Sch., U. Mo., Kansas City, 1985—; mem. Mo. Bicentennial Commn., Jefferson City, Mo., 1987—, Kansas City Bicentennial Commn., 1987—. Mem. ABA, Mo. Bar Assn., Kansas City Met. Bar Assn., Kansas City Lawyers Assn., Nat. Conf. of Bankruptcy Judges, Am. Judicature Soc. Office: US Bankruptcy Ct 811 Grand Ave Room 905 Kansas City MO 64106

SEE, PATRICIA ANN, finance manager; b. Chadron, Nebr., Nov. 23, 1950; d. Chappell William and Violet Ann (Grant) Moore; m. Allen Bruce See, May, 1974. Student, Chadron State Tchrs. Coll., 1970-72. Lic. ins. agt., Calif. Fin. mgr. Rosen-Novak Ford, Denver, 1974-80; sales and fin. mgr. Victory Toyota, Seaside, Calif., 1980-85; fin. mgr. Stevens Creek BMW,

Santa Clara, Calif., 1985—. Loan exec. Monterey Peninsula United Way, 1985. Republican. Methodist. Lodge: Soroptomists.

SEEGER, MELINDA WAYNE, realtor; b. Albert Lea, Minn., Dec. 31, 1940; d. Oscar Earnest and Evelyn Josephine (Pihl) Wayne; B.S., U. Minn., 1963; m. Robert Charles Seeger, Mar. 16, 1964; 1 son, Jeffrey Wayne. Chief occupational therapy Rehab. Inst. Oreg., Portland, 1964-66; supr. phys. disabilities and gen. medicine and surgery occupational therapy Mpls. VA Hosp., 1966-68; supr. phys. disabilities occupational therapy Nat. Naval Med. Center, Bethesda, Md., 1968-71; assoc. chief rehab. services, dir. occupational therapy UCLA Med. Center, 1974-85, cons., prin. investigator rheumatology div. dept. medicine, 1985-86; realtor Merrill Lynch Realty, Los Angeles, 1987—. Mem. utilization rev. com. Vis. Nurse Assn. Los Angeles, 1975-85, mem. profl. adv. com., 1979-80; mem. exec. com. Allied Health Professions sect. Arthritis Found., 1980-85, chmn. edn. com., 1982-85, mem. profl. edn. com.; bd. dirs. Calif. Occupational Therapy Found., 1984-85, Westwood-Holmby Hills Homeowners Assn., Los Angeles. Recipient Spl. Achievement award Nat. Naval Med. Center, 1971, Outstanding Performance award, 1971; Spl. Performance award UCLA, 1980, 84; Addie Thomas Service award for outstanding service to rheumatology community Arthritis Found., 1986; mem. Million Dollar Club. Mem. Am. Occupational Therapy Assn., Occupational Therapy Assn. Calif., Allied Health Professions Assn. (chmn. edn. com. 1982—), Los Angeles Bd. Realtors, San Fernando Valley Bd. Realtors, West Los Angeles C. of C., Blue Diamond Club. Author, editor articles in field. Office: 1401 Westwood Blvd Los Angeles CA 90024

SEEKINGS, SARA MARGARET, industrial chemist; b. Mt. Vernon, N.Y., Jan. 22, 1953; d. John Kenneth and Irene Clare (Conner) Seekings. BS, Framingham State Coll., 1974; MBA, Simmons Coll., 1987. Research asst. Worcester Found. of Exptl. Biology, Shrewsbury, Mass., 1974-76; research technician GTE Labs., Waltham, Mass., 1976-77; research chemist Barnstead Co., W. Roxbury, Mass., 1977-78; assoc. scientist Polaroid Corp., Waltham, Mass., 1978-85, scientist, 1985—, vice chmn. affirmative action com. Chem. Ops. div., 1978-80, 85—. Patentee in field. Mem. Am. Chem. Soc., AAAS, Nat. Assn. Female Execs., Support Women in Mgmt. Roman Catholic. Avocations: reading; music; guitar; tennis. Home: 39 Walcott Valley Dr Hopkinton MA 01748 Office: Polaroid Corp 1265 Main St W6 Waltham MA 02154

SEEKINS, ANNA MARIE, manufacturing executive; b. Lexington, Nebr., Oct. 22, 1948; d. Frederick Reo and Doris Louise (Hollibaugh) Green; m. James Lee Seekins, Jan. 3, 1969; children: Heidi Anne, Amy Marie. Grad. Westminster High Sch., Colo., 1966. With Forsythe & Dowis Carnival, 1950-64, Green's Amusements, 1964-68; collator, Joppesen Time-Mirror, Denver, 1967-73; typesetter AAA Marking, Colorado Springs, Colo., 1975-78; seamstress Camp 7, Longmont, Colo., 1978-80; co-owner AMS Products, Inc., Longmont, 1980—; order clk. Staydynamics, Longmont, 1982-84. Vol., Army Community Service Ctr., Colorado Springs. Republican. Baptist. Home: 2242 Sherman St Longmont CO 80501 Office: AMS Products 824 S Lincoln PO Box 1842 Longmont CO 80502

SEELEY, KIMBERLEY ANN, police officer; b. Urbana, Ill., Oct. 21, 1960; d. William Edward and Patricia Ann (Philbeck) Tarte; m. Ronald Eugene Seeley, Jan. 21, 1985. AS, Parkland Coll., 1981; BS, U. Ill., 1982. Sec., bookkeeper Tarte's TV and Marine, Rantoul, Ill., 1972-78; police dispatcher City of Champaign, Ill., 1978-82, police officer, 1982—, mem. tactical unit, 1985-86; realtor, Coldwell Banker Hallmark Realtor, Inc., 1987—. Recipient Merit award Champaign Police Dept., 1984, 86. Mem. Police Protective and Benevolent Assn., Nat. Assn. Female Execs., Fraternal Order of Police, Ill. Police Assn., Nat. Assn. Realtors, Ill. Assn. Realtors, Champaign County Bd. Realtors. Republican. Lutheran. Lodge: Fraternal Order Police. Avocations: downhill snow skiing, target shooting. Office: Champaign Police Dept 82 E University Champaign IL 61820

SEELEY, MARYANN DEL VISCO, communications and marketing executive; b. Newark, Oct. 14, 1948; d. James and Vincenzina (Cimirro) Del Visco; m. Timothy Allen Seeley, May 30, 1981; children—Vanessa Christina, Timothy Allen Jr. BA in English, Rutgers U., 1970; MA in Communications Arts, William Paterson Coll., 1974; postgrad., SUNY, 1987—. Mgr. communications, asst. cashier Midlantic Nat. Bank div. Midlantic Banks, Inc., Newark, 1970-74; supr. info. N.J. Bell Telephone Co., Newark, 1974-75; exec. printing sales Newark Printing Co., 1975-76; sales rep. Xerox Corp., 1976-78, mgr. shareholder relations, 1978-81; co-owner T.A. Seeley Office Systems Co., Glens Falls, N.Y., 1981—. Assoc. editor N.J. Bell and Communication Mags., 1974-75; innovator in design of magapaper publs. Active communications group N.J. Bicentennial Celebrations Com. Recipient awards Publ. Design Writing, Soc. Publ. Designers, 1974, Financial World, 1974, N.Y. Bus. Communicators, 1974. Mem. Communicators Assn. N.J. (pres. 1973-75, dir. 1976-78, Publ. Design Writing award 1974), Internat. Assn. Bus. Communicators (Pub. Design Writing award 1974, speaker creative supervision ann. conf.), Art Dirs. Club N.J., Lake George Bus. and Profl. Women's Club (co-chair pub. relations 1985-87). Office: Rural Rt Box 3023 Lake George NY 12845

SEELY, ANNE LOFGREN, investment executive, consultant; b. Corning, N.Y., Aug. 6, 1947; d. Harry Gustav and Marie Arlene (Ford) Lofgren; m. H. Marvin Hosier Jr., Dec. 10, 1966 (div. July 1973); m. John Conor Seely, Feb. 24, 1983. BS, Elmira Coll., 1975. Asst. instr. media specialist Corning Community Coll., 1974-76; retail buyer B. Forman Co., Rochester, N.Y., 1976-79; v.p. ops. Real Equity Diversification, Inc., Denver, 1979-80; v.p., sec. Resort Accomodations, Inc., 1980-84; exec. v.p. Real Equity Investment, Inc., 1984-85, v.p., sec., 1985—; cons. Real Equity Diversification, Inc., Denver, 1980—; bd. dirs. Resort Accomodations, Inc., Real Equity Investment Fund Inc. Republican. Office: The Seely Group 5680 Greenwood Plaza Blvd Suite 300 Denver CO 80111

SEELY, NANCY DIANE, financial planner; b. New London, Conn., Jan. 22, 1950; d. Warren Donald Hollandersky and Bernice (Shapiro) Stern; m. Ronald B. Seely, Aug. 22, 1965 (div. 1981); children: Tammie Lynn, Heather Lyn. Lic. in real estate, Lee Inst., Brookline, Mass., 1979; student, U. New Haven, 1982, U. Conn., 1983, Stone Sch., New Haven, 1985; cert. in fin. planning, Coll. of Fin. Planning, Denver, 1987. Property mgr. Conn. Westridge Assn., Bridgeport, 1973-75; rental mgr. Investment Property Assn., Westport, Conn., 1975-81; fin. planner Investors Diversified Services, New London, 1981-82; fin. planner, field trainer Investors Diversified Services, Groton, Conn., 1982-83, fin. planner, dist. mgr., 1983—. Active Easter Seals TV Telethon, Norwich, Conn., 1982-83; bd. dirs. Lakeside Assn., Ledyard, 1983-85. Mem. Inst. Cert. Fin. Planners, Internat. Assn. Registered Fin. Planners, Internat. Assn. Fin. Planners, Southeast Conn. C. of C., Better Bus. Bur. of S.E Conn., Women's Network, Gold. Star Hwy Office Park Assn. (treas. 1987, 88). Club: Lakeside (Ledyard) (bd. dirs. 1983-85). Lodge: Soroptomists (v.p. 1988—). Home: 2 M Lakeside Dr Ledyard CT 06339 Office: IDS Fin Services Inc 489 Gold Star Hwy Office Park Groton CT 06340

SEELYE, BARBARA JANE, small business executive, lecturer, consultant; b. Manito, Ill., Nov. 29, 1930; d. John Arvil and Mayme (Dwyer) S. B.S., Eureka Coll., 1952; M.A., U. Denver, 1955, Ph.D., 1967. Instr. Washington U., St. Louis, 1957-59; from instr. to assoc. prof. speech St. Louis U., 1959-68, assoc. prof., chmn. dept. communication disorders, 1968-72, asst. to pres., ACE fellow, 1973-74; dean Coll. Profl. Studies, prof. communication disorders No. Ill. U., DeKalb, 1974-80; pres. Keene State Coll., N.H., 1980-86, Highland Hill Enterprises, 1986—; cons., lectr. Nat. Higher Edn. Com., 1986-87; mem. Pres.'s Commn. Nat. Collegiate Athletic Assn., 1984-86; dir. Am. Inst. Fgn. Study, 1985-87, Am. Council Edn. Commn. Leadership Devel., 1986-87. Voting mem. N.H. Postsecondary Edn. Commn., Concord, 1980-86; trustee Univ. System of N.H., Durham, 1980-86; nat. panelist Am. Council Edn.-Women's Forum, Washington, 1982—; incorporator Harrisville Ct. for Conservation, 1981—; bd. dirs. N.H. Council on World Affairs, 1981-86; advisor Greater Monadnock Arts Council, 1981—, Colony House Mus., 1981-86. Mem. Am. Speech and Hearing Assn., Am. Council Edn., Am. Assn. Higher Edn, Am. Assn. Colls. for Tchr. Edn., Am. Assn. State Colls. and Univs., Keene C. of C. (dir. 1983-86). Club: College (Boston). Home and Office: Rt 1 Box 192 Walpole NH 03608

SEEMAN, CAROL MISCH, furniture sales and manufacturing company executive; b. Chgo., June 2, 1927; d. Charles E. and Selma (Herschman) Misch; m. Manfred Seeman, May 6, 1951; Children—Clarles Alan, William Henry. B.A., Goucher Coll., 1948. Sec., treas. Helikon Furniture Co., Inc., Taftville, Conn., 1959-86; corporator Norwich Savs. Soc., Conn., 1978-86. Bd. dirs. Sr. Citizens Job Bank, Norwich, 1983-85; hon. consul Republic of Haiti, Conn., 1979—; budget and fin., com., United Community Services, Norwich, Conn., 1987—; bd. dirs. Literacy Vols., Norwich, 1987—. Democrat. Jewish. Home: 211 Harland Rd Norwich CT 06360 Office: Helikon Furniture Co Inc 607 Norwich Ave Taftville CT 06360

SEEWALD, CAROL SANDRA, foundation administrator; b. Bklyn., Feb. 9, 1947; d. Jack and Irene (Lippman) Gross; m. Jeffrey Seewald, Oct. 9, 1965; 1 child, Jay. Student, Coll. of S.I., 1972-74; BS, Barry U., 1986; MBA, Nova U., 1988. Exec. sec. Michael G. Cohen, Inc., N.Y.C., 1964-65, Level Export Corp., N.Y.C., 1965-67; adminstrv. asst. YWCA, S.I., N.Y., 1969-72; adminstrv. sec. Superior Confections, Inc., S.I., 1973, Pompano Fence Co., Pompano Beach, Fla., 1974; adminstrv. asst. YMCA, Boca Raton, Fla., 1974-77, ops. dir., 1977-80, exec. dir., 1980—, mem. cluster steering com., 1984-85, also bd. dirs., mktg. cons., 1986—. Bd. dirs. Boca Del Mar Improvement Assn., Boca Raton, 1985-86. Mem. NOW, YMCA Assn. Profl. Dirs. (bd. dirs. 1985-87), Nat. Soc. Fund Raising Execs. (charter), Council Human Service Execs. (treas. 1984-85), West Boca C. of C., Women's Forum, Alpha Chi. Democrat. Jewish. Lodge: Soroptimists (treas. Boca Raton 1983-84, v.p. 1984-85, pres. 1985-86), Kiwanis. Home: 22860 Ponderosa Dr Boca Raton FL 33428 Office: YMCA of Boca Raton 6631 Palmetto Circle S Boca Raton FL 33433

SEFFER, YVONNE KATHRYN, financial consultant, import-export company executive; b. Chgo.; d. Urosh Lazar and Helen (Musulin) S.; B.A., Ohio U., 1972. Pres., Ivanka Internat. Imports, Chgo., 1973—; realtor asso. Coldwell Banker Co., Oak Brook, Ill., 1979—; internat. fin. cons., 1980—. Mem. Nat. Assn. Exec. Women, Nat. Assn. Realtors, Ill. Assn. Realtors, DuPage Bd. Realtors, La Grange Bd. Realtors, Internat. Sports Core, Internat. Order St. John of Jerusalem Hospitallers-Knights of Malta, Augustan Soc. Office: 1225 W 22d St Suite 110 Oak Brook IL 60521

SEGAL, ALETHEA BIGHAM, retired medical technologist; b. Rock Hill, S.C., Oct. 2, 1921; d. Boyce Hyatt and Sarah Dorcas (Whiteside) Bigham; B.S. in Chemistry and Zoology, Winthrop Coll., Rock Hill, 1942; M.T., Duke U., 1944; m. William Segal, July 28, 1950; children—Janet Cheryl Segal Fixel, Alethea Gail. Med. technician, office mgr. Dr. Louie Limbaugh and Dr. Karl Hanson, Jacksonville, Fla., 1944-60; med. technician The Clinic for Digestive Diseases, Jacksonville, Fla., 1960-62, clinic mgr., 1963-75, dir. patients accts., 1976-86. Mem. Am. Soc. Clin. Pathologists, Fla. Soc. Med. Technologists, Credit Women Internat., Winthrop Coll. Alumni Assn., AAUW. Democrat. Baptist. Club: Ponte Vedra. Home: 5138 Rosebay Terr Jacksonville FL 32207

SEGAL, ARLENE ESTA, radiologist; b. N.Y.C., Nov. 12, 1937; d. Moe and Fanny (Schlussel) S.; m. Richard Thomas Logan, Aug. 14, 1969. BA, Duke U., 1958; MD, Albert Einstein Coll. Medicine, 1962. Diplomate Am. Bd. Radiology, Am. Bd. Nuclear Medicine. Intern Bronx Mcpl. Hosp. Ctr., N.Y.C., 1962-63, resident in radiology, 1963-66; instr. radiology Albert Einstein Coll. Medicine, N.Y.C., 1966-68, asst. prof., 1968-71; practice medicine specializing in gen. diagnostic radiology Rye, Nanuet and Hornell, N.Y., 1971-82; assoc. prof. U. Mo. Sch. Medicine, Kansas City, 1982—; staff radiologist Children's Mercy Hosp., Kansas City, 1982-83, radiologist-in-chief, 1983—. Mem. Soc. for Pediatric Radiology, Radiol. Soc. N.Am., Am. Coll. Radiology. Office: Children's Mercy Hosp 24th & Gillham Kansas City MO 64108

SEGAL, GERALDINE ROSENBAUM, sociologist; b. Phila., Aug. 26, 1908; d. Harry and Mena (Hamburg) Rosenbaum; m. Bernard Gerard Segal, Oct. 22, 1933; children: Loretta Joan, Richard Murry. BS in Edn., U. Pa., 1930, MA in Human Relations, 1963, PhD in Sociology, 1978; MSLS, Drexel U., 1968. Social worker County Relief Bd., Phila., 1931-35; sociologist, Phila., 1935—; cons. and lectr. in field. Author: In Any Fight Some Fall, 1975; Blacks in the Law, 1983. Bd. dirs. NCCJ, 1937-47, 82—, sec., 1983—; bd. overseers U. Pa. Sch. Social Work, 1983—; bd. dirs., Juvenile Law Ctr., 1984—; chair Phila. Tutorial Project, 1966-68. Co-recipient Nat. Neighbors Disting. Leadership in Civil Rights award. Democrat. Jewish. Home: 2401 Pennsylvania Ave Apt 19-C-44 Philadelphia PA 19130

SEGAL, KATHLEEN RITA, advertising executive; b. Chgo., May 26, 1952; d. Harry L. and Margaret (Casey) Segal; m. Craig S. Baron, Oct. 16, 1982. BA in English, No. Ill. U., 1974. Broadcast buyer Lee King & Ptnrs., Inc., Chgo., 1974-77; media/research supr. Campbell Mithun, Inc., Chgo., 1977-79; dir. media planning, v.p. BBDO Chgo., 1979—. Mem. NOW, Women's Advt. Club Chgo, Broadcast Advt. Club. Office: BBDO Chgo 410 N Michigan Ave Chicago IL 60611

SEGAL, LINDA GALE, insurance executive; b. Panama City, Fla., Dec. 14, 1947; d. Homer Ford Jr. and Mary Virginia (Phillmon) F. m. Howard Arthur Segal, Dec. 29, 1970; 1 child, David Samuel. Student, Orlando (Fla.) Jr. Coll., 1966-69, Rollins Coll., 1972. Sales asst. Sta. WESH-TV, Orlando, Fla., 1973-76; mktg. coordinator Sta. WFBC-TV, Grenneville, S.C., 1976-77; traffic mgr. STa. WRDW-TV, Augusta, Ga., 1978-80; field underwriter Liberty Life Ins. Co., Greenville, 1980-81; agt. benefits dept. J. Rolfe Davis Ins. Agy., Orlando, 1981-84; sr. market sales rep. Humana, Inc., Orlando, 1984-86; dir. mktg. Nat. Med. Mgmt., Orlando, 1986-87; sr. account exec. Physicians Health Plan Fla., Inc., Tampa, 1987-88, N.E. Fin. Services, Orlando, 1988—; ins. cons., Tampa, Orlando, 1986—. Mem. Am. Bus. Women's Assn., Nat. Assn. Profl. Saleswomen, Nat. Assn. Health Underwriters, Cen. Fla. Assn. Life Underwriters, Women Life Underwriters Confedn., Nat. Assn. Securities Dealers (registered rep. Orlando, Tampa, 1986—). Republican. Methodist. Club: Horizon.

SEGAL, NORMA JULIA, human resources executive; b. Lebanon, Pa., Apr. 15, 1949; d. Henry and Elaine Patricia (Burros) Breitstein; divorced. BS in Edn., Temple U., 1971; MBA, SUNY, Buffalo, 1978. Assoc. buyer Lane Bryant, N.Y.C., 1973-75; mgr. nat. sales tng. Parklane Hosiery Co., New Hyde Park, N.Y., 1975-77; specialist internat. personnel The Carborundum Co., Niagara Falls, N.Y., 1978-80; analyst internat. compensation Philip Morris Internat., N.Y.C., 1980-83; sr. analyst compensation PHH Group, Inc., Hunt Valley, Md., 1983-87; mgr. compensation Peterson, Howell & Heather, Inc., Hunt Valley, 1987—. Mem. Bklyn. Philharm. Chorus, 1980-83, Balt. Symphony Chorus, 1983-85; vol. Big Bros./Big Sisters, Balt., 1985-87. Mem. Human Resource Systems Profls. (dir. 1984-87, Mem. of Yr. Mid-Atlantic chpt. 1986), Am. Compensation Assn., Am. Soc. Personnel Adminstrs. Home: 1408 Eutaw Pl Baltimore MD 21217 Office: PHH Group Inc 11333 McCormick Rd Hunt Valley MD 21031

SEGALL, THRESA HOPE, publishing executive; b. Balt., Oct. 15, 1958; d. Gilbert Irvin and Shirley (Gertz) S. BA, Am. U., 1980; postgrad., Fordham U., 1985-89. Audio-visual specialist U.S. Dept. Labor, Washington, 1980-81; news aide Washington Post, 1981-83; assoc. producer, mktg. coordinator Newsweek Mag., N.Y.C., 1983-84, promotion mgr., 1984—. Contbr. articles and photographs to various newspapers. Recipient acad. scholarship Am. U., 1976-80. Mem. Nat. Orgn. for Female Execs. Democrat. Home: 33-52 Crescent St Apt 9-C Long Island City NY 11106 Office: Newsweek Mag 444 Madison Ave New York NY 10022

SEGER-OLMSTEAD, GERALDINE, television hostess, nurse, realtor; b. Merrill, Mich., Dec. 18, 1938; d. Joseph Rudolph and Rose Marie (Prikasky) Lednicky; m. Dean W. Seger, Nov. 29, 1958 (dec. Jan. 1973); children—Mary, Brad, Craig, Clark, Wayne; m. Glen Olmstead, Sept. 28, 1983. Diploma Mercy Sch. Practical Nursing, 1958; student Mid-Mich. Coll., 1980, Kirkland Community Coll., 1981. Cert. realtor, Mich. L.P.N., Mich. Sec. Blair Transit, Saginaw, Mich., 1956-57; nurse Mercy Hosp., Cadillac, Mich., 1975-78, Pub. Health Home Care, Lake City Mich., 1978-80; pvt. nurse, Cadillac, 1981-83; hostess Cable TV-3-GRK Prodns., Cadillac, 1985—. Active Scenic Trails council Boy Scouts Am., Lake City, 1967-80; past pres Med. Aux., Cadillac, 1958-83; fund raiser Mercy Hosp., Missaukee County Mich., 1965, various congressional candidates, 1962, 74, 83; hospice trained vol., instr. ARC Teaching programs. Recipient Silver Beaver award Scenic Trails council Boy Scouts Am., 1977, Den Mother of Yr. award, 1976; Letter of Appreciation, USN, 1985, ARC, 1985; named Queen of Centennial, City of Lake City, 1968. Roman Catholic. Avocations: sailing; canoeing; water and snow skiing; cross country skiing; ceramics; wood refinishing; biking; walking. Home: 107 West Lake St PO Box N Lake City MI 49651

SEGERSON, JOAN ELIZABETH, financial manager; b. Rochester, N.Y., Feb. 26, 1951; d. James Edward and Margaret Isabelle (Crowley) S. B.A. in Art History, Newton Coll., 1972; M.B.A. in Fin., Boston Coll., 1977. Sec. Inst. of Open Edn., Cambridge, Mass., 1972-73, adminstrv. asst., 1973-74, dir. fin., 1974-76, dir. fin., adminstrn., 1976-78; mgmt. analyst SEC, Washington, 1978-81; budget examiner Office Mgmt. and Budget, Washington, 1981-82; sr. cons. Price Waterhouse, Washington, 1982-83; exec. dir. Nat. Women's Polit. Caucus, Washington, 1983-85; dir. grad. programs Boston Coll. Grad. Sch. Mgmt., 1985-87; fin. programs specialist Dept. Treasury, Washington, 1987-88; sr. budget analyst Agy. Internat. Devel., Washington, 1988—. Dir. pub. relations No. Va. Spl. Olympics, 1987—. Recipient Wall St. Jour. award Boston Coll., 1977; named Outstanding Young Woman of 1981, Outstanding MBA Alumnus, Boston Coll., 1986. Roman Catholic. Office: Agy Internat Devel Bur Program and Policy Coordination Office Planning and Budget SA-1 Washington DC 20523

SEGIL, LARRAINE DIANE, materials company executive; b. Johannesburg, South Africa, July 15, 1948; came to U.S., 1974; d. Jack and Norma Estelle (Cohen) Wolfowitz; m. Clive Melwyn Segil, Mar. 9, 1969; 1 child, James Harris. BA, U. Witwatersrand, South Africa, 1967, BA with honours, 1969; JD, Southwestern U., Los Angeles, 1979; MBA, Pepperdine U., 1985. Bar: Calif. 1979, U.S. Supreme Ct. 1982. Cons. in internat. transactions, Los Angeles, 1976-79; atty. Long & Levit, Los Angeles, 1979-81; chmn., pres. Marina Credit Corp., Los Angeles, 1981-85; pres., chief exec. officer Electronic Space Products Internat., Los Angeles, 1985-87; mng. ptnr. The Lared Group, Los Angeles, 1985-87, pres., 1987—. Bd. govs. Cedars Sinai Med. Ctr., Los Angeles, 1984—; bd. dirs. So. Calif. Tech. Execs. Network. Mem. ABA (chmn. internat. law com. young lawyers div. 1980-84), Internat. Assn. Young Lawyers (exec. council 1979—, council internat. law and practice 1983-84), Word Tech. Execs. Network (chmn.). Club: Regency (Los Angeles) (house com.). Avocations: piano, horseriding. Office: 1901 Avenue of the Stars Suite 280 Los Angeles CA 90067

SEGOVIS, ELIZABETH WILSON, lawyer; b. Pasadena, Calif., Aug. 10, 1948; d. Frank Stedman and Jeannette Frances (MacKenzie) Wilson; m. James Courtney Segovis, Dec. 22, 1971; children—Colin Michael, Ian Patrick, Courtney Michelle. B.A., Cornell U., 1970; M.A., SUNY-Albany, 1973; J.D., So. Meth. U., 1978. Bar: Tex. 1978, U.S. Dist. Ct. (no. dist.1979, ea. dist. 1987) Tex. 1979. Social worker George Jr. Republic, Freeville, N.Y., 1970-72; felony probation officer Supreme Ct. N.Y., Bklyn., 1973-74; family ct. counselor Dallas County Juvenile Dept., Dallas, 1974-75; assoc. Johanes Robertson & Wilkinson, Dallas, 1976-79; asst. county atty. County Atty.'s Office, Sherman, Tex., 1979-84; assoc. Thompson, Green, Shaffer, Redwine, Denison, Tex., 1984-85; staff atty. North Tex. Central Legal Services Found., McKinney, Tex., 1985—; bd. dirs. Legal Services Found., Dallas, 1978-79, Women's Crisis Line of Grayson County, 1984—. Adv. bd. Grayson County Guidance Clinic, Sherman, Tex., 1984; trustee Grace United Meth. Ch. 1982-83. Mem. Grayson County Bar Assn. (v.p. 1980-81, 84-85), State Bar Tex., Collin County Bar Assn., ABA, Dallas County Bar Assn. Home: 707 Concord Ln Allen TX 75002 Office: N Central Tex Legal Services Found 114 W Louisiana St McKinney TX 75069

SEGURA, NAIDA SYLVIA, school counselor; b. Kingsville, Tex., May 31, 1943; d. Edmundo Leyva and Guadalupe (Gonzalez) Garcia; m. Luis Mendias Segura (dec. Dec. 1983); children—Elvia T., Orlando R. B.A. in English, Incarnate Word Coll., 1965; tchr. certification, St. Mary's U., 1968, M.A., 1980. Lic. profl. sch. counselor Tex. Tchr. English, Southwest Middle Sch., San Antonio, 1965-68; tchr. English and Spanish, Lakeside High Sch., Atlanta, 1968-69; English tchr. Southwest High Sch., San Antonio, 1970-78, Pease Middle Sch., San Antonio, 1978-80; elem. sch. counselor Northside Ind. Sch. Dist., San Antonio, 1980—; state advisor Future Tchrs. Am., San Antonio, 1974-75; counselor, cons. Sunshine Cottage Sch. Hearing Impaired, 1984-86; sch. counselor Dolores B. Linton Elem. Sch., 1980—; mem. Hispanic Task Force Widowed Persons Service, Chgo., Phila, 1987, presenter conf. workshop on Hispanic grief, Washington, 1987; speaker Hispanic Women's Conf., San Antonio, 1984, Fed. Program Parents, San Antonio, 1982; judge U. Tex. Prose Reading, San Antonio, 1985, Harlandale Ind. Sch. Dist. Festival Cultural Prose Reading, San Antonio, 1985; 1st v.p. Linton Elem. Sch. PTA, 1985-86; mem. Hispanic Widowed Persons Task Force, Washington, 1987—; sec., bd. dirs. Barrio Comprehensive Health Care Clinic, 1986—; state del. Hispanic Women's Network of Tex., Dallas, 1987. Named Tchr. of Yr., Southwest Educators Assn., 1975, Outstanding Educator, Tex. Tchrs. Assn. 1976; Outstanding Educator Pease Middle Sch. 1979, Tchr. of Yr., 1979; recipient Outstanding Achievement award Northside Ind. Sch. Dist., 1984, Tex. New Traditional award and S.W. regional winner, 1987; Inst. Coop. Ibero-Am. scholar, Madrid, 1984. Mem. Southwest Personnel and Guidance Assn., Tex. Personnel and Guidance Assn., S.W. Educators Assn. (pres. 1974-75), Am. Assn. Counseling and Devel., Career Counselors Tex., Northside Counselors, Assn., United Teaching Profession, NEA, Tex. State Tchrs. Assn., San Antonio Area Women Deans, Adminstrs. and Counselors, Hispanic Women of Tex. (San Antonio rep., founder). Democrat. Roman Catholic. Home: 1422 E Sunshine Dr San Antonio TX 78228 Office: Dolores B Linton Elem Sch 2103 Oakhill Rd San Antonio TX 78238

SEIBERT, JOY HART, communications reasearcher, educator; b. Mt. Sterling, Ky., Dec. 9, 1959; d. Charles Henry and Florene (Long) Hart; m. Kenneth L. Seibert, Dec. 29, 1984. BA in English, U. Ky., 1982, BA in Edn., 1982, MA in Communication, 1984. Cert. tchr., Ky. Pool mgr. Bath County Swimming Pool, Owingsville, Ky., 1982-84; teaching asst. U. Ky., Lexington, 1983—, research asst., 1984—; research assoc. Council State Govts., Lexington, 1987—; faculty Lexington Community Coll., 1985-87; instr. mgmt. devel. Arthur Andersen & Co., St. Charles, Ill., 1987—. Mem. Internat. Assn. Bus. Communicators, Internat. Communication Assn. (Outstanding Grad. Student Tchr. award 1986), Speech Communication Assn., So. Speech Communication Assn., Ky. Assn. Communication Arts (co-chair organizational communicational interest group 1987). Democrat. Home: 1345 Sequoia Dr Lexington KY 40502

SEIBERT, SHARON LEE, banker; b. Herrin, Ill., Feb. 2, 1945; d. William Alfred and Geneva Ester (Miles) Futrell; m. Roland Lee Seibert, Apr. 6, 1963; 1 child, Tracy Lee Seibert. Studied Bank Mgmt. Skills & Theory, Founds. of Banking, Am. Bankers Assn., St. Louis, 1985; A in Banking and Fin., Belleville Area Coll., 1986; postgrad., Ill. Bankers Sch., Carbondale, 1988—. Bookkeeping Belleville Nat. Savs. Bank, Belleville, Ill., 1962-64; claims clk. Home Ins., St. Louis, 1964; asst. v.p. Magna Bank of Belleville, 1964—; trainer Bank of Belleville, 1983—; liaison Magna Data & Bank of Belleville, 1986—. Coordinating advisor Jr. Achievement, Belleville, Ill., 1981-87. Mem. Am. Inst. of Banking (assoc. bd. govs., assoc. v.p. 1985-86, chairperson 1985-86, instr. 1986—), Am. Soc. of Tng. & Devel., Nat. Assn. of Bank Women. Lodges: Order of Eastern Star, Elks (ladies div. pres. 1981-82). Home: 9903 Old Lincoln Trail Fairview Heights IL 62208 Office: Magna Bank of Belleville 4800 W Main St Belleville IL 62223

SEIBOLD, SHERI LEE, home economist; b. Warsaw, N.Y., Oct. 30, 1955; d. Harry Julian and Patricia (Frey) S. BA in Home Econs. Edn., Iowa Wesleyan Coll., 1977; MS in Home Econs. Edn., No. Ill. U., 1981. Tchr. home econs. Dist. 116, Round Lake, Ill., 1977-78; home econs. extension adviser U. Ill. Coop. Extension Service, Lake County, 1978-81, Grundy, 1981-88; 4-H youth adviser McHenry County Extension Service, Woodstock, Ill., 1988—. Mem. flower show com. Grundy County Corn Festival, Morris, 1982-88; v.p., bd. dirs. No. Ill. 4-H Camping Assn., Manteno, 1984-88; bd. dirs. United Fund Grundy County, Morris, 1987-88. Mem. Nat. Assn. Extension Home Economists, Ill. Assn. Extension Home Economists (chmn. profl. improvement 1986-87), Am. Home Econs. Assn. (cert.), Ill. Home Econs. Assn., Lakeshore Home Econs. Assn., Alpha Xi Delta (adviser Kappa chpt. 1987-88), Omicron Nu (Beta Gamma chpt.), Gamma Sigma

Delta. Mem. United Ch. of Christ. Office: McHenry County Extension Service 789 McHenry Ave Box 431 Woodstock IL 60098

SEIDEL, DIANNE MARIE, finance executive; b. Reading, Pa., Feb. 1, 1959; d. Frederick Jacob and Claire Marie (Paskey). ASBA, Pa. State U., 1986; BA, Alvernia Coll., Reading, Oa., 1988. Office asst. Berks-Lehigh Valley Farm Credit Service, Fogelsville, Pa., 1977-80, sr. office asst., 1980, office supr., 1980-83, office mgr., 1983-86; v.p. fin. and adminstrv. services, chief fin. officer Berks-Lehigh Valley Farm Credit Service, Fogelsville, 1986—. Mem. Nat. Assn. Female Execs., Pa. State U. Alumni Assn. Home: 720 Girard Ave Hamburg PA 19526

SEIDEL, GLENDA LEE, newspaper publisher; b. Pitts., Feb. 21, 1936; d. Howard Arthur and Elizabeth Jean (Peters) Jackson; m. Frederick Rex Seidel, Jan. 19, 1963; children: Paula Jean, Carol Ann. Grad. high sch., Ft. Myers, Fla., 1976. Editorial asst. Success Unltd. Mag., Chgo., 1953-54; sec. various cos., Chgo. and Skokie, Ill., 1955-68; editorial asst. Popular Sci. mag., Chgo., 1959-68; reporter, columnist, photographer weekly Suburban Reporter, Ft. Myers, 1975-76; editor Lehigh (Fla.) News, 1977-78, mng. editor, 1979-84, publisher, 1984—, also columnist, 1977—; v.p. Lehigh Corp., Lehigh Pub. Co., 1985—. Past sec. Lehigh Players; past mem. Lehigh Acres Community Council. Named Best Actress of Yr. Lehigh Players, 1970, Best Supporting Actress, 1975. Mem. Nat. League Am. Pen Women, Fla. Press Assn., Nat. Newspaper Assn., Lehigh C. of C. (Community Service award). Republican. Office: Lehigh News PO Box 908 Lehigh Acres FL 33970-0908

SEIDELMAN, SUSAN, film director. Attended Drexel Inst., NYU. Dir. films Smithereens, 1982, Desperately Seeking Susan, 1985, Making Mr. Right, 1987; dir. debut with short film and You Act Like One, Too (Student film award Acad. Motion Picture Arts and Scis.). Address: care Sanford/Beckett 1015 N Gayley Suite 301 Los Angeles CA 90024 *

SEIDEMAN, RUTH EVELYN YOUNG, nurse educator; b. Okeene, Okla., July 7, 1934; d. Ewald Julius and Alma Alexander (Smith) Kramer; m. Jack Lee Young, Nov. 27, 1954 (div. Mar. 1986); children: Stanley Daryl, Steven Glenn, Roger Neil; m. Walter Elmer Seideman, May 21, 1988. BS, Tex. Woman's U., 1958; MA, U. Okla., 1970, MS, 1975, PhD, 1987. RN, Okla. Staff nurse, supr. U. Hosp., Oklahoma City, Okla., 1955-57; sch. nurse Dallas Pub. Schs., 1958-60; staff nurse St. Francis Hosp., Tulsa, 1963-65, Cen. State Hosp., Norman, Okla., 1966-68; supr. Cen. State Hosp., Norman, 1970-71; instr. Oklahoma City U., 1971-72, Sch. Nursing St. Anthony Hosp., Oklahoma City, 1972-75; asst. prof. Coll. Nursing U. Okla., 1975-82, assoc. prof., 1982—. Author: Community Nursing Workbook:Family as Client, 1983; contbr. articles to profl. jours. Mem. Am. Nurses Assn. (del. 1985—), Midwest Nursing Research Soc., Sigma Theta Tau, Sigma Xi. Home: 10812 Quail Cir Oklahoma City OK 73120 Office: Coll Nursing PO Box 26901 Oklahoma City OK 73190

SEIDEN, GELLA MARCIA, real estate broker; b. N.Y.C., Jan. 29, 1938; d. Robert and Ethel (Staub) Kaplan; m. R. Matthiew Seiden, June 25, 1961; children: Douglas Yale, Diana Lynn. BA, U. Conn., 1959, MA, 1960. Cert. real estate appraiser, residential broker, N.J. Tchr. Stanton Sch., Norwich, Conn., 1959, Clark Ln. Sch., Waterford, Conn., 1960-61, North Arlington (N.J.) Jr. High Sch., 1961; real estate salesman Livingston, N.J., 1970-72; real estate broker, pres. ERA Kaden Realty Inc., Livingston, 1972—. Pres. Amos Harrison Elem. Sch., Livingston, 1973; trustee Sr. Service Corp. Essex County, Orange, N.J., 1987—; bd. dirs. Nat. Council Jewish Women, Essex County, N.J., 1986—. Mem. Bd. Realtors Orange and Maplewood (trustee 1979, sec. 1982, treas. 1983, pres. 1984), N.J. Assn. Realtors (bd. dirs. 1982—), AAUW (sec. 1977), Livingston Area C. of C. (pres. 1987-88), Grad. Realtors Inst. (cert. residential broker), Orgn. for Rehab. Tng., League of Women Voters. Club: Womens Am. ORT (Livingston). Home: 14 Ridgewood Dr Livingston NJ 07039 Office: ERA Kaden Realty Ave 175 S Livingston Ave Livingston NJ 07039

SEIDEN, JEAN TRAGER, interior designer; b. Cin., July 21, 1941; d. Newton Junior and Louise (Goldsmith) Trager; student U. Miami (Ohio), 1959-60, U. Cin., 1960-63, Internat. Inst. Interior Design, 1974-76; m. Louis W. Seiden, Mar. 10, 1962; children—Ellen Louise, Richard Neal, Steven Alva. Owner, mgr. Jean T. Seiden Interior Design, Rockville, Md., 1975—; owner, v.p. Spectra Design Group, Ltd., 1985—; assoc. Potomac Designs, Rockville, 1973-77; v.p. Capitol Homes, Inc.; renovator hist. property, Washington, 1974-78. Bd. dirs. Civic Assn., 1965-66, Elem. Sch. PTA, 1966-69, Citizens Com. for Reading, 1972-74. Mem. Nat. Urban League, Nat. Home Fashion League, Nat. Hist. Soc., Nat. Women's Polit. Caucus, Bethesda-Chevy Chase Bus. and Profl. Women's Club, Mothers Against Drunk Driving, Nat. Trust Historic Preservation, Nat. LWV, NOW. Office: 1160 Rockville Pike Suite 211 Rockville MD 20852

SEIDERMAN, SUSAN LEVIN, publisher; b. Phila., Nov. 6, 1938; d. Leon and Ann (Vitz) Levin; m. Arthur Stanley Seiderman, Aug. 19, 1965; children—David, Leeann, E. Scott. Chief exec. officer Comp-Art, Phila., Welcomat, Phila., Review/Chronicle, Phila., 1979-86, pub., limited ptnr., 1986—. Bd. dirs. NCCJ, Phila., 1981-83; mem. com. on aging United Way, Phila., 1981-83; bd. dirs. YM-YWHA, Phila., 1982, Greentree Sch. Mem. Fedn. Bus. and Profl. Women (steering com. 1980-83). Democrat. Jewish. Office: Welcomat 1816 Ludlow St Philadelphia PA 19103

SEIDMAN, AMY PEREGO, real estate developer; b. Ft. Lauderdale, Fla., Sept. 9, 1955; d. Thomas John Perego Sr. and Carole (Meyer) Lokker; m. Harry Arthur Seidman, Dec. 31, 1985. Student, Daytona Beach (Fla.) Community Coll., 1972-73; AA, Broward Community Coll., Ft. Lauderdale, Fla., 1973; student, Nova U., 1973-74. Mgr. restaurant Holiday House Corp., Deland, Fla., 1977-78; office mgr., with drafting dept. R. Wm. Clayton Architect, Ft. Lauderdale, Fla., 1979-82; ptnr. Triple A Devel., Delray Beach, Fla., 1983—. Mem. Exec. Suite Network, Nat. Assn. Secretarial Services, Nat. Bus. Women Network. Republican. Office: Triple A Devel 1050 S Federal Hwy Delray Beach FL 33444

SEIDMAN, FRANCES LEVENSON, clinical psychologist; b. N.Y.C., Mar. 25, 1917; d. Jacob B. and Elizabeth (Carlin) Levenson; m. Morris Seidman, Oct. 15, 1939; children: Vivian Wang Lee, Beth Estill. BS, Glassboro (N.J.) State U., 1939; MS, U. Pa., 1944, MA, 1950, EdD, 1953. Elem. sch. tchr. State N.J., 1936-40; tchr. sight conservation Phila., 1943-44; assoc. in psychology U. Pa., Phila., 1944-53; chief psychologist Child Guidance Ctr. Mercer County, Trenton, N.J., 1953-73; dir. Community Guidance Ctr., Trenton, N.J., 1973-77; pvt. practice in clin. psychology Lawrenceville, N.J., 1977—. Named Citizen of Yr. Glassboro State U., 1977. Fellow Am. Orthopsychiat. Assn.; mem. Internat. Transactional Analyses Assn., Am. Psychol. Assn. (life), Am. Group Therapy Assn. (life), N.J. Psychol. Assn. (mem. emeritus), Practioner-Neurolinguistic Programming. Home: 4507 Newportville Rd Newportville PA 19056 Office: 183 Franklin Corner Rd Lawrenceville NJ 08648

SEIDNER-EDELSON, SUELLEN, data processing executive; b. Bklyn., Dec. 26, 1952; d. Morris Irwin and Joan Hariett (Salit) Naham; m. Mark Seth Edelson, Dec. 8, 1985. AAS, Kingsborough Coll., Bklyn., 1971; student, Bklyn. Coll., 1971-73. Assoc. analyst City of N.Y., 1972-82; sr. systems analyst First Jersey Nat. Bank, Jersey City, 1982-84; data processing cons. NYSE/AMEX, N.Y.C., 1984-86; ind. data processing cons. N.Y.C., 1986-87; v.p. Bear Stearns & Co. Inc., N.Y.C., 1987-88; dir. mktg. Comprehensive Computer Solutions, Inc., N.Y.C., 1988—. Campaigner mayoral election, N.Y.C., 1977, coordinator, 1981; campaigner Congl. election, N.Y.C., 1980. Recipient award for community service Kingsborough Coll., Bklyn., 1971. Mem. Am. Mgmt. Assn., Am. Assn. Systems Mgmt.

SEIFER, JUDITH HUFFMAN, psychology educator; b. Springfield, Ill., Jan. 18, 1945; d. Clark Lewis and Catherine Mary (Fisher) Huffman; married; children: Christopher, Patrick, Andrea. RN, St. John's Hosp./Quincy Coll., 1965; MHS, Inst. Advanced Study Human Sexuality, 1981, PhD, 1986. Charge nurse Grandview Hosp., Dayton, Ohio, 1967-70; v.p. Sego, Inc., Dayton, 1970-84, pres., 1984—; marital and sex therapist Grandview Ob-Gyn., Inc., Dayton, 1975-87; asst. clin. prof. psychiatry and ob-gyn Wright State U. Sch. Medicine, Dayton, 1985—; prof. dept. psychology U. Dayton, 1985—; cons. in field. Author, screenwriter film script: Mercari Communications, 1988; editor: The D.O., 1985; contbr. articles to profl. jours. Pres. Dayton Osteopathic Aux., 1974-75, Aux. Ohio jOsteopathic Assn., Columbus, 1981-82, Sister City Assn., Oakwood, Ohio, 1985-86. Dayton Found. grantee, 1980-82. Fellow Internat. Council Sec. Educators and Parenthood of Am. U., Masters & Johnson Inst.; mem. Am. Assn. Sex Educators, Counselors and Therapists (cert., rec. sec. 1986—), Am. Coll. Sexologists. Roman Catholic. Office: U Dayton 2400 College Park Dr Dayton OH 45469

SEIFERT, NANCY SHARON, accountant, association executive; b. Wausau, Wis., Nov. 3, 1952; m. Michael E. Seifert, April 30, 1977. BBA, U. Wis., 1974, MBA, 1978. CPA, Wis. Tax auditor Wis. Dept. Revenue, Madison, 1974-75; systems acct. Wis. Dept. Adminstrn., Madison, 1975-76, budget, mgmt. analyst, 1976-77; asst. budget dir. U. Wis. Extension, Madison, 1977-82, budget dir., 1982-83; dir. fin., adminstrn. World Council of Credit Unions, Madison, 1983—; fin. cons. African Cooperatives & Credit Union Assn., Nairobi, Kenya, 1986. Vol. Sta. WHA-Radio and TV, Madison, 1980—, Am. Cancer Soc., Madison, 1986. Mem. Am. Soc. Assn. Execs., Wis. Inst. CPA's, Pvt. Voluntary Fin. Officers Assn. Club: One Percent Investment (pres. 1987—). Office: World Council of Credit Unions 5810 Mineral Point Rd Madison WI 53711

SEILER, CHARLOTTE WOODY, retired educator; b. Thorntown, Ind., Jan. 20, 1915; d. Clark and Lois Merle (Long) Woody; A.A., Ind. State U., 1933; A.B., U. Mich., 1941; M.A., Central Mich. U., 1968; m. Wallace Urban Seiler, Oct. 10, 1942; children—Patricia Anne Bootzin, Janet Alice Seiler Sawyer. Tchr. elem. schs., Whitestown, Ind., 1933-34, Thorntown, Ind., 1934-37, Kokomo, Ind., 1937-40, Ann Arbor, Mich., 1941-44, Willow Run, Mich., 1944-46; instr. English div. Delta Coll., University Center, Mich., 1964-69, asst. prof., 1969-77, ret., 1977; organizer, dir. Delta Coll. Puppeteers, 1972-77. Mem. Friends of Grace A. Dow Meml. Library, 1974—, treas. 1974-75, 77-79, corr. sec., 1975-77; mem. Midland Art Assn.; adv. bd. Salvation Army, 1980—, sec., 1984-87; leader Sr. Ctr. Humanities program Midland Sr. Ctr., 1978—. Mem. Am., Mich. Library Assn., AAUW (fellowship honoree 1979), Midland Symphony League, Pi Lambda Theta, Chi Omega. Presbyterian. Clubs: Tuesday Review (pres. 1979-80), Seed and Sod Garden (v.p. 1986-87, pres. 1987-88). Home: 5002 Sturgeon Creek Pkwy Midland MI 48640

SEILER, MARIPAT SMITH, veterinary care facility administrator; b. Oklahoma City, May 28, 1945; d. Clarence Carnahan and Helen Louise (Fenity) Smith; m. William George Seiler, June 10, 1967; 1 child, Kathleen Louise. BA, Lebanon Valley Coll., Annville, Pa., 1967. Registered animal technician, Ohio, vet. technician, Md. Research asst. Retina Found., Boston, 1967-69; lab. supr. Rockland Labs., Gilbertsville, Pa., 1970-71; vet. technician David H. Taylor Animal Hosp., Mattydale, N.Y., 1971-74; animal technician West Toledo (Ohio) Animal Hosp., 1975-79; sr. technician Westview Animal Hosp., Balt., 1979-83; asst. dir. Animal Med. Hosp. of Belair Rd, Balt., 1983—. Mem. North Am. Vet. Technician Assn., Inc. (recording sec. 1981-82, chair nominating and election com. 1982-83), Ohio Assn. Animal Technicians (pres. 1976-78), Giant Schnauzer Club Am. (chair health and hereditary disease com.). Lutheran. Office: Animal Med Hosp of Belair Rd 7688 Belair Rd Baltimore MD 21236

SEITNER, RITA A., researcher, consultant; b. Milw., July 11, 1940; d. Robert and Esther (Steren) Seitner; m. Alfred F. Huete, Nov. 3, 1973 (div.). B.A., Beaver Coll., 1962; M.S., U. Wis.-Milw., 1977. Mktg. asst. Advanced Learning, Milw., 1972-75; adminstv. asst. J. Walter Thompson, N.Y.C., 1962-67; assoc. planner David M. Walker, Phila., 1967-68; urban analyst HUD, Phila., 1968-70; market analyst Gen. Electric, Milw., 1977-82; mgr. research Hoffman, York & Compton, Milw., 1982-84, pres. RS Research Cons., Inc., Milw., 1984—. Fellow Am. Mktg. Assn., Am. Mgmt. Assn., Direct Mktg. Club. Jewish. Office: 1219 N Jackson St Milwaukee WI 53202

SEITZ, JUDY CAROLE, physical education educator; b. Meadville, Pa., Sept. 29, 1945; d. Joe Bernard and Gloria Irene (McMahon) S.; adopted children: Christine, Stephanie, Elizabeth. BS, Pan Am. U., Edingburg, Tex., 1967; MA, Tex. Women's U., 1972, postgrad., 1977, 87; postgrad., Our Lady of the Lake, San Antonio, 1973. Cert. tchr. Tchr., coach Point Isabel Ind. Sch. Dist., Port Isabel, Tex., 1967-68; tchr., coach N.E. Ind. Sch. Dist., San Antonio, 1968-70, 73—, adaptive specialist phys. edn., 1983—, coordinator spl. olympics, 1984—; tchr., coach Pilot Point (Tex.) Ind. Sch. Dist., 1970-71, Mansfield (Tex.) Ind. Sch. Dist., 1971-72, Samuel Clemens Sch., Schertz, Tex., 1972-73. Life mem. PTA, San Antonio, 1967—; trainer, dir. games Area 20 Spl. Olympics, San Antonio, 1986—. Named Tchr. of Yr., Woodstone Elem. Sch., San Antonio, 1982. Mem. NEA, Tex. State Tchrs. Assn., N.E. Tchrs. Assn. (rep. faculty 1980), Tex. Assn. for Health, Phys. Edn., Recreation and Dance (chair registration 1977), Alpha Chi. Home: 12818 Independence San Antonio TX 78233

SEKULSKI, BARBARA LOUISE, operations/credit manager; b. Torrington, Conn., Apr. 18, 1952; d. Julian Bernard and Geneva (Scruggs) S.; m. Allen David Smith, Sept. 1, 1973 (div. May 1980). With internat. credit The Torrington (Conn.) Co., 1972-79; advt. mgr. asst. The Hartford (Conn.) Courant, 1979-82; with ops. Kero-Sun, Inc., Kent, Conn., 1982-83; credit, account receivable mgr. Multimate Internat., East Hartford, Conn., 1983-85; credit mgr. Rykoff/Sexton, Hartford, 1985-87; mgr. ops./credit Microtech Internat., Branford, Conn., 1987—. Mem. Rep. Town Com., Torrington, 1976-78, Goshen, Conn., 1978; publicity coordintor 6th Dist. Lewis Rome for Gov., Torrington area, 1976. Mem. Nat. Assn. Credit Mgmt., Nat. Assn. Female Execs., Nat. Microcomputer Credit Orgn., Restaurant Industry Credit Mgrs. (Conn. chpt.). Roman Catholic. Home: 56-58 Atwood St Unit B-2 Hartford CT 06105 Office: Microtech Internat 29 Business Park Dr Branford CT 06405

SELBY, CECILY CANNAN, educator, scientist; b. London, Feb. 4, 1927; d. Keith and Catherine Anne Cannan; m. Henry M. Selby, Aug. 11, 1951 (div. 1979); children: Norman, William, Russell; m. James Stacy Coles, Feb. 21, 1981. A.B. cum laude, Radcliffe Coll., 1946; Ph.D. in Phys. Biology, MIT, 1950. Teaching asst. in biology MIT, 1948-49; adminstrv. head virus study sect. Sloan-Kettering Inst., N.Y.C., 1949-50; asst. mem. inst. Sloan-Kettering Inst., 1950-55; research assoc. Sloan-Kettering div. Cornell U. Med. Coll., N.Y.C., 1953-55; instr. microscopic anatomy Cornell U. Med. Coll., 1955-57; tchr. sci. Lenox Sch., N.Y.C., 1957-58; headmistress Lenox Sch., 1959-72; nat. exec. dir. Girl Scouts U.S.A., N.Y.C., 1972-75; mem. speakers program Edison Electric Inst., 1976-78; adv. com. Simmons Coll. Grad. Mgmt. Program, 1977-78; mem. Com. Corp. Support of Pvt. Univs., 1977-83; spl. asst. acad. planning N.C. Sch. Sci. and Math., 1979-80, dean acad. affairs, 1980-81, chmn. bd. advisors, 1981-84; cons. U.S. Dept. Commerce, 1976-77; dir. Avon Products Inc., RCA, NBC, Loehmanns Inc., Nat. Edn. Corp. pres. Am. Energy Ind., 1976; co-chmn. commn. pre-coll. math and sci. Nat. Sci. Bd., 1982-83; adj. prof. NYU, 1984-86, prof. sci. edn., 1986—. Contbr. articles to profl. jours., chpt. to book. Founder, chmn. N.Y. Ind. Schs. Opportunity Project, 1968-72; mem. invitational workshops Aspen Inst., 1973, 75, 77, 79; Trustee Mass. Inst. Tech., Bklyn. Law Sch., Radcliffe Coll., Woods Hole Oceanographic Instn., Women's Forum N.Y., N.Y. Hall of Sci., 1982—; mem. Yale U. Peabody Mus. Adv. Council, 1981—. Mem. Headmistresses of East (hon. mem.; pres. 1970-72), Nominating Com. N.Y. Stock Exchange, Cum Laude Soc. (past chpt. pres., dist. regent), Sigma Xi. Clubs: Cosmopolitan (N.Y.C.); Women's Forum N.Y. Home: 45 Sutton Pl S New York NY 10022 Office: 933 Shimkin Hall 50 W 4th St New York NY 10003

SELBY, NANCY CHIZEK, educator; b. South Bend, Ind., Sept. 15, 1935; d. Cletus and Mildred (Mauck) Chizek; m. David K. Selby, June 22, 1957; children—Pamela, Katherine, Susan, Elizabeth. B.S., Miami U., Oxford, Ohio, 1957. Instr., v.p. Verbal Communications, Dallas, 1972-79; founder, dir. Spine Edn. Ctr., Dallas, 1979—; mem. adv. bd. Dallas Safety Council, 1985—. Author: Care for Your Back, 1983; Back Injury Prevention Resource Handbook, 1984. Author videotape: Backache Blues, 1983. Telephone recruiter Republican Party, Dallas, 1976—, Friends of the Library; pres. elect S.W. chpt., chmn. safety council Greater Dallas Citizens Safety adv. com. Mem. Am. Soc. Tng. and Devel., Tex. Safety Assn. (dir.), Am. Soc. Safety Engrs., Dallas County Med. Aux., Pi Beta Phi. Avocations: sailing; running; reading. Office: Spine Edn Ctr 6161 Harry Hines Blvd Dallas TX 75225

SELDNER, BETTY JANE, environmental engineer, aerospace company executive; b. Balt., Dec. 11, 1925; d. David D. and Miriam M. (Mendes) Miller; m. Warren E. Gray, June 20, 1945 (div. 1965); children: Patricia, Deborah; m. Alvin Seldner, Nov. 15, 1965; children: Jack, Barbara. BA in Journalism, Calif. State U., Northridge, 1975, MA in Communications, 1977. Dir. pub. info. United Way, Van Nuys, Calif., 1958-63; dir. edn. United Way, Los Angeles, 1963-68; dir. pub. relations, fin. SFV Girl Scout Council, Reseda, Calif., 1968-73; asst. dir. pub. info. Calif. State U., Northridge, 1973-75; dir. environ. mgmt. HR Textron Corp., Valencia, Calif., 1975-87; environ. engr. Northrop Aircraft, Hawthorne, Calif., 1987—. Author nonfiction. Mem. Santa Clarita Valley Energy Mgrs. Soc. (bd. dirs. 1978—), Santa Clarita Valley Environ. Mgrs. Soc. (bd. dirs. 1984), Santa Clarita Valley Energy Soc. (chmn. 1978-80), San Fernando Valley Round Table (pres. 1971-72). Republican. Jewish. Club: San Fernando Valley Press. Lodge: Soroptimists. Office: Northrop Aircraft One Northrop Ave Hawthorne CA 91205

SELEY, JEAN ROXANNE, training specialist, administrative consultant; b. Oakland, Calif., Dec. 18, 1927; d. Charles Russell and Florence Gertrude (MacAfee) Cartmel; m. Russell C. Seley, June 11, 1949 (div. 1970); children: Debra Joan, Russell David. BA, Coll. of Pacific, 1950; postgrad., U.S. Internat. U., 1973-74, 80. Staff asst., tng. specialist Pacific Telephone Co., San Diego, 1968-70; educator Abraxas Alternative Sch., San Diego, 1971-72; edn. specialist Neighborhood Youth Corps, San Diego, 1972-74; asst. dir. Youth Service Ctr. Neighborhood House Assn., San Diego, 1974-76, coordinator client-support services, 1976-83; coordinator Harmonium, Inc., San Diego, 1983-85; dir. resource devel. Domestic Workers Home Care Ctr., National City, Calif., 1985-87, exec. dir., 1987—; resource devel. cons., San Diego and Los Angeles, 1985—; mem. employment task force San Diego Urban Coalition, 1969-70; mediation counselor San Diego Community Mediation Ctr., 1984—; program dir. labor/mgmt. cooperation project United Domestic Workers and Remedy Home and Health Care Inc, 1986—. Co-author: Self Development for Writers, 1987. Chmn. bd. dirs. House of Metamorphsis (cert. appreciation 1981), San. Diego, 1981-82; campaign worker numerous elected mcpl. ofcls., San Diego, 1970—; co-founder Citizens for Racial Equality, San Diego, 1967; bd. dirs. Women's Econ. Agenda Project. Recipient Employee Recognition award Neighborhood House, 1982, Community Service award Commuinty Mediation Ctr., 1986. Mem. Founding Mother, Womanquest. Democrat. Home and Office: 4722 33rd St Apt 5 San Diego CA 92116

SELF, MARY OLDERSHAW, computer professional; b. Ancon, CZ, Republic of Panama, Oct. 19, 1950; came to U.S., 1952; d. Arthur Salvin and Darlene Rosetta (Henning) Oldershaw; m. Edward Ronald Self, May 26, 1979 (div. Dec. 1984); 1 child, Darlene. Student, High Point Coll., 1968-70; BS in Mgmt. Info. System, Christopher Newport Coll., 1974; postgrad., George Washington U., 1975-79. Applications programmer George Washington U., Hampton, Va., 1975-80; analyst/designer OAO Corp., Hampton, 1980-82; scientist Systems and Applied Scis. Corp. Techs., Hampton, 1982-85; project program analyst Systems Devel. Corp., Newport News, Va., 1985-86; sr. systems analyst Bell Tech. Ops. Corp., Sierra Vista, Ariz., 1986—. Instr. computer post Explorer's Boy Scouts Am., Hampton, 1982-86. Mem. Am. Bus. Women's Assn. (chmn. 1977-85), Assn. for Computing Machinery, Nat. Rifle Assn. (life), U.S. Practical Shooters Assn. (life), Peninsula Indoor Pistol League (statistician 1982-86), Lafayette Gun Club (range officer 1978—), Combat Pistol Team (treas. 1981-85). Baptist. Office: Bell Tech Ops PO Box 850 Sierra Vista AZ 85636

SELF, PEGGY JOYCE, accountant; b. Jones County, Tex., Oct. 3, 1938; d. Charles Ernest and Ollie Bea (Morton) Glazner; m. Jerry M. Self, June 11, 1960 (div. Apr. 1986); children: Jay Mark, Angela B.; m. Harry Newcombe Hollis, Nov. 21, 1987. BS, Hardin-Simmons U., 1960; postgrad., SW Baptist Theol. Sem., 1962-63; MB in Edn., Stephen F. Austin State U., 1974. Acctg. instr. Stephen F. Austin State U., Nacogdoches, Tex., 1972-78; mgr. acctg. dept. Bapt. Sunday Sch. Bd., Nashville, Tenn., 1979-84; mgr. compensation and benefits Bapt. Sunday Sch. Bd., Nashville, 1984-87, bd. dirs. retirement trust fund, 1985—; v.p. controller UPI, Brentwood, Tenn., 1984; mgr. pension and benefits analysis No. Telecom, Inc., Nashville, 1987—; cons. State Funded Day Care Ctr., Nacogdoches, 1972-74. Contbr. articles to profl. jours. Treas. YWCA, Nashville, 1982-87. Mem. Am. Soc. Personnel Administrs, Mid. Tenn. Employee Benefits Council, Tex. Bapt. Ministers Wives (sec. 1973), Beta Alpha Psi, Phi Chi Theta (hon.). Club: Newcomers (pres. 1970). Home: 1223 Parker Pl Brentwood TN 37027 Office: No Telecom Inc 200 Athens Way Nashville TN 39228

SELIGMAN, LINDA HELEN, psychology educator, counselor; b. Hartford, Conn., Feb. 17, 1944; s. Irving and Florence (Scolnick) Goldberg; m. Eugene Barry Seligman, June 3, 1972 (div. 1978). AB Brandeis U., 1966; MA Columbia U., N.Y.C., 1968, PhD, 1974. Psychology intern VA Hosp., N.Y.C. and Newark, 1969-73; lectr. Bklyn. Coll., 1973-74; asst. prof. counselor edn. CUNY, S.I., 1974-77; prof. counselor edn. George Mason U., Fairfax, Va., 1977—, Disting. prof., 1986, assoc. chmn., 1981-85; cons. psychologist Montgomery County Dept. Corrections, Rockville, Md., 1984-88, dir. Ctr. Counseling and Consultation, Springfield, Va., 1985—, South Md. Hosp., Clinton, 1979-82, Salvation Army, N.Y.C., 1975-77; pvt. practice psychology, Laurel, Md., also Alexandria and Springfield, Va., 1979—. Author: Assessment in Developmental Career Counseling, 1980; Diagnosis and Treatment Planning in Counseling, 1986. Editor Jour. Am. Mental Health Counseling Assn., 1983-87 . Contbr. articles to profl. jours. Mem. Am. Psychol. Assn., Am. Assn. Counseling and Devel., Va. Mental Health Counseling Assn.(pres. 1982-83). Home: 6114 Lynley Terr Alexandria VA 22310 Office: George Mason U Dept Ednl Leadership and Human Devel 4400 University Dr Fairfax VA 22030

SELIKOFF, RACHEL ANDISMAN, marketing executive. BS in English, Boston U., 1973; postgrad., U. Balt., 1976-79; MBA, Boston Coll., 1984. Tchr. English, Journalism Balt. County Sch. System, 1973-75; chair English dept. Balt. City Sch. System, 1976-81; market planning mgr. Digital Equipment Corp., Chelmsford, Mass., 1983-84; market program mgr. Selikoff, P.C., Boston, 1984-85; market acct. mgr. Prime Nat. Corp., Weston, Mass., 1984-85; mgr. sales Prime Nat. Corp., Weston, 1985-86, mgr. nat. sales, 1986-87; columnist Developing Profl. Priorities, Weston, Mass., 1988—.

SELIN, CAROLE LOUISE, psychologist; b. Los Angeles, Aug. 30, 1948; d. Robert Russell and Sophie S. BA, Mount Holyoke Coll., 1970; PhD in Clin. Psychol., SUNY, Albany, 1976. Lic. psychologist, Calif. Asst. prof. SUNY, Albany, 1973-74; intern psychology Fairfield Hills Hosp., Danbury, Conn., 1974-75; asst. prof. in psychology Pomona Coll., Claremont, Calif., 1976-78; psychologist Orange County Dept. Mental Health, Westminster, Calif., 1977-78, Capistrano by the Sea Hosp., Dana Point, Calif., 1978-79; pvt. practice psychology Newport Beach, Calif., 1979—; mem. med. staff Hoag Meml. Presbyn. Hosp., Newport Beach, 1985—, Newport Harbor Psychiat. Inst., Newport Beach, 1986—. Author: How to Manage the Schizophrenic: A Manual for Parents, 1987. Mem. Internat. Neuropsychol. Assn., Calif. State Psychol. Assn., Orange County Psychol. Assn., Orange County Soc. Clin. Hypnosis (program chair 1984-85). Office: 200 Newport Ctr Dr Suite 205 Newport Beach CA 92660

SELK, ELEANOR HUTTON, artist; b. Duboise, Nebr., Oct. 21, 1918; d. Anderson Henry and Florence (Young) Hutton; R.N., St. Elizabeth Hosp., Lincoln, Nebr., 1938; m. Harold Frederick Selk, Aug. 3, 1940; children—Honey Lou, Katherine Florence. Nurse, Lincoln, 1938-40, Denver, 1940-50; with Colo. Bd. Realtors, 1956-66; owner, mgr. The Pen Point, graphic art studio, Colorado Springs, 1974—; one-woman shows: Colo. Coll., 1970, 72, Nazarene Bible Coll., 1973, 1st Meth. Ch., 1971 (all Colorado Springs); exhibited in group shows: U. So. Colo., 1969, 70, 71, 72, Colorado Springs Art Guild, 1969-72, Pike's Peak Artists Assn., 1969-73, Mozart Art Festival, Pueblo, Colo., 1969-74, numerous others; represented in permanent collection U.S. Postal Service, Pen-Arts Bldg., Washington, Medic Alert Found. Internat. Hdqrs., Turlock, Calif. Rec. sec. Colo. chpt. Medic Alert Found. Internat., 1980—, chairperson El Paso County and Colorado Springs chpt., 1980—, Colo. bd. dirs., 1980—, rec. sec., 1980—. Recipient 3d pl. award Nat. Tb and Respiratory Disease and Christmas Seal Art Competition, 1969, finalist award Benedictine Art competition Hanover Trust Bank, N.Y.C., 1970; numerous awards and certs. for pub. service and art. Mem. Nat. League Am. Pen Women (rec. sec. 1972-74; travelling art slide collection 1974—, awards for book cover art, numerous Gold Bangle awards). Contbr. med. articles, short stories, poetry to newspapers. Home: 518 Warren Ave Colorado Springs CO 80906 Office: 333 N Tejon St Agora Mall Colorado Springs CO 80903

SELKE, ELOISE WILDENTHAL, language educator; b. Cotulla, Tex., Feb. 18, 1924; d. John and Lois (Pearce) Wildenthal; m. Harold E. Selke, Sept. 1, 1946 (Div. July 1966); children—Harold Edward, Kenneth Wayne. B.S. in Edn., U. Tex., Austin, 1945; M.Elem. Edn., Tex. A&M U., 1974. Trust dept. clk.-typist Frost Bank, San Antonio, 1945-46; clk.-typist R.R. Commn., Austin, 1946-47, Exxon Co., Corpus Christi, 1947-49; elem. tchr. Spanish and English, Houston Ind. Sch. Dist., 1966-84; tchr. Spanish, Richmond Plaza Bapt. Sch., Houston, 1986-88. Mem. Congress Houston Tchrs. (life), Tex. State Tchrs. Assn. (life), Sigma Delta Pi, Pi Lambda Theta. Democrat. Methodist. Home: 5010 Carew St Houston TX 77096

SELKE-KERN, BARBARA ELLEN, academic administrator, writer; b. Houston, Dec. 14, 1950; d. Oscar Otto Jr. and Edith Hicks (Hardey) Selke; m. Homer Dale Kern, May 31, 1985. BS, U. Colo., 1973; MA, U. Tex., 1981, PhD, 1986. Cert. elem. and secondary tchr., Tex. Co-owner Colo. Sound, Denver, 1972-76; tchr. Jefferson County Schs., Lakewood, Colo., 1974-76; dir. Harvest Time Day Care Ctr., Austin, 1976-77; mgr. TourService, Inc., Austin, 1977-82; curriculum specialist U. Tex., Austin, 1982-87, materials devel. coordinator, 1987—. Author (books): Retail Travel Marketing, 1983. Communication Skills, 1984, Orientation to Cosmetology Instructor Training, 1984, Resumes and Interviews, 1984, Competency in Teaching, 1985, Guidelines for the Texas Cosmetology Commission Instructor Licensing Examination, 1985, Effective Communication, 1986, Effective Teaching, 1986, Balancing the Curriculum for Marketing Education, 1987, Bulletin Board Designs for Marketing Education, 1987, Marketing Education I, 1988; author (computer software): Emergency Aid, 1986, Measuring Employee Productivity, 1986, Retail Pricing in Action, 1987; editor: Training Plans for Marketing Education, 1987, Correspondence, 1988, Instructional Planning, 1988, Financial Records and Reports, 1988, Student Records and Reports, 1988; contbr. articles to profl. jours. Recipient scholarship Am. Bus. Women's Ass., 1985. Mem. Am. Assn. Adult and Continuing Edn., Phi Delta Kappa, Kappa Delta Pi, Phi Kappa Phi. Home: 6518-B Hart Ln Austin TX 78731 Office: U Tex PO Box 7218 Austin TX 78713-7218

SELKOWITZ, JUDITH, art specialist; b. Pittsfield, Mass., Dec. 21, 1944; d. Milton M. Selkowitz and Molly L. Levitt. BA, Skidmore Coll., 1966. Pres. Art Adv. Services Inc., N.Y.C.; lectr. in field. Author: Art in Interiors, 1981. Fulbright scholar, 1967. Mem. Art Table, Am. Soc. Appraisers. Office: Art Advisory Services 530 Park Ave New York NY 10021

SELKREGG, LIDIA LIPPI, geologist; b. Florence, Italy, July 24, 1920; came to U.S., 1947, naturalized, 1951; d. Otello and Ida (Chiasserini) Lippi; B.S., Sci. Licee, Tunis, Tunisia, 1938; Dr. Natural Sci., U. Florence, 1942; m. Frederick Mills Selkregg, Sept. 15, 1945; children—Alicia L. (Mrs. R.E. Iden), Sheila (Mrs. J.E. O'Malley), Leif L. Geologist, Ill. State Geol. Survey, Urbana, 1952-58; geologist, engr. U.S. Army C.E., Anchorage, 1959-61; capital improvement coordinator City of Anchorage, 1968-70; planning officer Fed. Field Com. Devel. and Planning, Alaska, 1970-71; sr. scientist Arctic Environ. Info. and Data Center, U. Alaska, 1970-77, prof. resource econs. and planning, 1977-85, prof. emeritus, 1985—, founder, dir. Alaska Home Fed. Loan Assn. Mem. Greater Anchorage Area Borough Planning and Zoning Commn., 1965-75; mem. Alaska Growth Policy Council, Office of Gov., 1975-80; sci. com. Outer Continental Shelf adv. bd. Dept. Interior, 1979-81; mem. Alaska Coastal Zone Mgmt. Council, 1977-83; mem. Anchorage Mcpl. Assembly, 1975-83; prin. investigator Seismic Hazards Mitigation Planning and Policy Implementation: The Alaska Case NSF, 1984; adv. com. White House Conf. Balanced Nat. Growth and Econ. Devel., 1977-78; mem. Anchorage Geotech. Commn., 1984-87; adv. Com. Alaska Land Use Council, 1984—. Recipient Spl. Achievement award for superior performance Dept. Commerce, 1970; lic. geologist, Alaska; cert. profl. geologist Am. Inst. Profl. Geologists. Mem. Alaska Planning Assn. (pres. 1974), Geol. Soc. Am., Alaska Press Club, AAAS, Sigma Xi, Nat. Fedn. Bus. and Profl. Women's Clubs, NAACP. Democrat. Unitarian. Club: Anchorage Dem. Author: (with others) Urban Planning and the Reconstruction-Human Ecology vol. The Great Alaska Earthquake of 1964, 1972; Alaska Regional Profiles, 6 vols., 1974-77; editor: Environmental Atlas of Greater Anchorage Area Borough, 1972. Lodge: Soroptimist (Women Helping Women award Alaska and Western region 1986). Home: 5811 Radcliffe Dr Anchorage AK 99504 Office: U Alaska 3210 Providence Dr Anchorage AK 99508

SELL, ELLA LUCILLE, nurse; b. Kenosha, Wis., Oct. 19, 1950; d. Franklin Keller and Castella May (Petersen) S.; m. James Ralph Stemmer., May 15, 1969 (div. 1972). BS in Nursing, U. Ill., Chgo., 1977. Cert. emergency nurse. Staff nurse U. Ill., Chgo., 1975-83, asst head nurse, 1983—. Mem. Emergency Nurses Assn., South Side All Breed Dog Tng. Club (bd. dirs. 1981-87). Home: 2506 Braddock Dr Naperville IL 60565 Office: U Ill 1740 W Taylor Chicago IL 60612

SELLERS, REGINA TERESA, educator; b. Pitts., Oct. 15, 1934; d. Herman Anthony and Gertrude Anne (Engel) Schwartz; A.A., San Antonio Jr. Coll., 1970; B.A., Incarnate Word Coll., 1973; postgrad. Our Lady of the Lake U., 1976, U. Sci. and Philosophy, 1976; children—John, Larry, Jerry, Joni, Jesse. Staff, Alcoholic Rehab. Center, San Antonio, 1972-73, San Antonio Children's Center, 1978; tchr. adutl edn. San Antonio Jr. Coll., 1976—; cons. to nursing homes, San Antonio, 1976—; pvt. practice clin. social work and hypnosis, San Antonio, 1976—; family therapist HCA Hill Country Hosp., 1976—; developer workshops/teaching in substance abuse, 1960—. Served with USN, 1953-54. Recipient Better Life award in Edn., Tex. Nursing Home Assn., 1976; Public Welfare Dept. grantee, 1974-76. Mem. Acad. Cert. Social Workers, Nat. Assn. Social Workers, Tex. Psychotherapy Assn. Contbr. articles to profl. jours. Address: 7888 Caribou Dr Spring Branch TX 78070-9999

SELLMAN, DONNA DUVALL, educational administrator; b. Balt., Jan. 13, 1925; d. George Wilmer and Marion Mercedes (Brown) DuVall; m. Russell Armstrong Sellman, June 15, 1948; children—Maura Mercedes Sellman Sheridan, R. Thomas. B.A., Western Md. Coll., 1945; M.A., Columbia U., 1950. Cert. tchr., prin., Md. Tchr. Carroll County Bd. Edn., Westminster, Md., 1945-69, asst. prin., 1969-80; dir. alumni affairs Western Md. Coll., Westminster, 1980—; dir. Union Nat. Bank, Westminster. Mem. Council Advancement and Support Edn., Nat. Retired Tchrs. Am., Carroll County Retired Tchrs. Assn. (pres. 1985-87), AAUW (pres. Carroll County br. 1954-55), Phi Delta Kappa (pres. Towson State U. chpt. 1979-80), Phi Delta Gamma (pres. Psi chpt. 1978-80). Republican. Avocations: social dancing, travel, theater. Home: 59 Ridge Rd Westminster MD 21157 Office: Western Md Coll College Hill Westminster MD 21157

SELTZER, DEVORA S., automobile dealer, attorney; b. Louisville, Feb. 3, 1927; d. Joseph Schiff and Birdie (Rosenberg) Liebling; m. Harold Seltzer, Oct. 19, 1946 (dec. Mar. 1973); children: Norton, Sidney Ann, Maggi, Ira. BS, Ill. State U., 1962; JD, John Marshall Law Sch., 1978. Bar: Ill. 1978, Fla. 1979. Part-time tchr. Leroy and Normal, Ill., 1962-75; ptnr. Seltzer Motors, Bloomington, Ill., 1962-75; assoc. Harfred Auto, Gainesville, Fla., 1970—; sole practice law, Chgo., 1978-80. Bd. dirs. LWV, Bloomington, 1948-73; sec. Normal (Ill.) Police Pension Fund, 1970-73; chmn. Constn. Conv. com. McLean County (Ill.); bd. dirs., pres. Mose Montefiore Temple Sisterhood, Bloomington, 1946-73. Mem. Ill. Bar Assn., Fla. Bar Assn., Nat. Auto Dealers Assn., Gainesville New Auto Dealer Assn. (pres.). Office: Harfred Auto 506 E University Gainesville FL 32601

SELTZER, VICKI LYNN, physician; b. N.Y.C., June 2, 1949; d. Herbert Melvin and Marian Elaine (Willinger) S.; m. Richard Stephen Brach, Sept. 2, 1973; children: Jessica Lillian, Eric Robert. BS, Rensselaer Poly. Inst., 1969; MD, NYU, 1973. Diplomate Am. Bd. Ob-Gyn, Intern, Bellevue Hosp., N.Y.C., 1973-74, resident in Ob-Gyn, 1974-77; fellow gynecol. cancer Am. Cancer Soc., N.Y.C., 1977-78, Meml. Sloan Kettering Cancer Ctr., N.Y.C., 1978-79; assoc. dir. gynecol. cancer Albert Einstein Coll. Medicine, N.Y.C., 1979-83; assoc. prof. Ob-Gyn, SUNY, Stony Brook, N.Y.C., 1983—; dir. Ob-Gyn, Queens Hosp. Ctr., Jamaica, N.Y., 1983—, pres. med. bd., 1986—. Author: Every Woman's Guide to Breast Cancer, 1987; mem. editorial bd. Women's Life mag., 1980-82; contbr. articles to profl. jours. Chmn. health com. Nat. Council Women, N.Y.C., 1979—; mem. Mayor Beame's Task Force on Rape, N.Y.C., 1974-76; bd. govs. Regional Council Women in Medicine, 1985—; chmn. Council on Resident Edn. in Ob-Gyn, 1987—. Galloway Fund fellow 1975; recipient citation Am. Med. Women's Assn., 1973, Nat. Safety Council, 1978, Achiever award Nat. council Women, 1985, Achiever award L.I. Ctr. Bus. and Profl. Women, 1987. Fellow N.Y. Obstet. Soc., Am. Coll. Ob-Gyn (gynecol. practice com. 1981); mem. Women's Med. Assn. (v.p. N.Y. 1974-79, editorial bd. jour. 1985—), Am. Med. Women's Assn. (com. chmn. 1975-77, 78-79, editorial bd. jour. 1986—), N.Y. Cancer Soc., NYU Med. Alumni Assn. (bd. govs. 1979—, v.p. 1987—), Alpha Omega Alpha. Office: OB Gyn Queens Hosp Ctr 82-68 164th St Jamaica NY 11432

SEMPLE, JANE FRANCES, marketing professional; b. Lakewood, Ohio, Feb. 14, 1951; d. Frank Joseph and Margaret Eleanor (Carpenter) S.; m. Nick N. Morana, June 24, 1977 (div. Sept. 1981). A.A.B., Cuyahoga Community Coll., Cleve., 1977; B.A., Baldwin-Wallace Coll., Berea, Ohio, 1980; M.B.A., Case Western Res. U., 1984. Adminstrv. asst. DeVilbiss Co., Cleve., 1969-77; project dir. Nat. Survey Research Ctr., Cleve., 1977-80; market research mgr. Sherwin-Williams Co., Cleve., 1980-85; cons. Resource, Careers, Cleve., 1983. Mem. S.B. Anthony Soc. Womenspace, Cleve., 1980-88. Mem. Am. Mktg. Assn., Nat. Assn. Female Execs., NOW. Democrat. Club: Sherwin-Williams Women's. Home: 26969 Greenbrooke Olmsted Twp OH 44138 Office: Sherwin-Williams Co 101 Prospect Ave Cleveland OH 44114

SEMPLE, MARLENE COCKER, journalist; b. Sarasota, Fla., Feb. 10, 1932; d. Oswald McKellar and May (Branch) Cocker; student U. Miami, Fla., 1950-53; B.A., George Washington U., 1958; M.Ed., Loyola U., Chgo., 1983; m. William R. Cotton, Sept. 4, 1954; children—William R., David M., Lynn C.; m. 2d, Dale D. Semple, May 19, 1973. Reporter, Washington Post, 1964-67; editor Croft Ednl. Services, New London, Conn., 1967-69; sr. editor Follett Ednl. Corp., Chgo., 1969-70; ptnr. Other Words Writing and Editing Service, Chgo., 1971-75; editor Sci. Research Assocs., Chgo., 1975-78, test mktg. coordinator, 1979-81, project editor test devel., 1981-82, project adminstr., 1982-83; planner info. devel. IBM, 1983—. Mem. Soc. Tech. Communication, Chgo. Women in Pub. (pres. 1976). Author: Introductory Guide to Midwest Antiques, 1976. Office: IBM PO Box 1328 Boca Raton FL 33432

SEMPLE, MURIEL V., retired educator, civic worker; b. Bklyn., Aug. 22, 1915; d. Michael James and Jennie Anne (Maguire) Campion; m. Robert L. Semple, Apr. 19, 1944 (dec. 1977); children—Edmund Campion, Susan Jane, Robert Louis, Michael James Semple. B.A., St. Joseph's Coll., Bklyn., 1937; M.D.H., Columbia U., 1939; M.S. in Edn., New Paltz State Coll., N.Y., 1961. Cert. tchr. N.Y., dental hygienist N.Y., cert. tchr. Fla. Dental hygienist Raymond M. Bristol, DDS, N.Y.C., 1939-42; tchr. dental hygiene Elwood Schs., N.Y., 1957; elem. tchr. Huntington, Port Jefferson, Copiague Schs., N.Y., 1957-80; vol. Citizen Crime Watch, Boca Raton, Fla., 1983-88, Covenant House, Fort Lauderdale, Fla., 1985-88; vol., resource person in field. Sec., Maidstone Park Springs Civic Assn., East Hampton, N.Y., 1970-72, Boca Towne Centre Owners Assn., 1982-83; mem. St. Joan of Arc Ch., St. Joan of Arc Guild, 1984-88. Mem. Columbia U. Sch. Dentistry Alumni Assn., NEA, N.Y. State Tchrs. Assn.; mem. AAUW, S. Huntington PTA (Tchr. of Yr. 1980). Republican. Roman Catholic. Clubs: Royale Woman's (corresponding sec. 1988, editor newsletter 1985, rec. sec. 1986—, chmn. Irish sweepstakes Irish Country Fair, 1988) (Boca Raton), Boca Raton Garden, Boca Raton Hist. Soc.

SEMRAU, JEANNINE ARAGON, librarian; b. Pueblo, Calif., Apr. 7, 1941; d. James and Carmen Caroline (Salinas) Aragon; m. Terry Semrau, Mar. 16, 1962 (div.); children—Milton, Becka, Stanley; m. 2d, Robert Clyde Parmeter, Mar. 1972; stepchildren—Diana, Susan, Tom, David. Student Fresno State U., 1974; B.S. in Sociology, Calif. State U., 1975, M.S. in L.S., 1977. Social worker aide Fresno Social Services (Calif.), 1967-68; library asst. Fresno County Free Library, 1968-74, librarian I, 1977-78, young adult coordinator, head. cen. children's library, 1979-82, prin. librarian community libraries, 1982-87, county librarian for Madera County, 1988 . Parent adv. bd. bilingual program Jefferson Sch., Fresno, 1977; pres. Fresno Area Library Council, 1986-88. Recipient Innovative Teaching award Chancellors Office, Calif., 1976; Mex.-Am. Librarians scholarship Calif. State, 1976; Minority Intern Librarian award Pomona Pub. Library, 1976; Minority Mgmt. Seminar scholarship Calif. State Library, 1982; LSCA grantee, 1985. Mem. Calif. Library Assn., ALA. Democrat. Unitarian. Home: 242 N Yosemite Fresno CA 93701 Office: Madera County Library 121 North G St Madera CA 93637

SENDRA-ANAGNOST, TERESA AMOR, nurse, writer; b. Mt. Pleasant, N.Y., Nov. 20, 1936; d. Fernando Miralles Sendra and Hazel Ellene (Rice) Estruch; div. Oct. 1985; children: James Christopher, Karen Ellen, Andrew John. AA, Los Angeles Valley Coll., 1971; BS, Calif. State U., Northridge, 1979. Registered nurse practitioner, Calif. Nurse So. Calif. Permanente Med. Group, Panorama City, 1971-75, nurse practitioner adult medicine, 1975—. Active Am. Cancer Soc. Project Outreach, Los Angeles, 1986—. Mem. United Nurses Assn. Calif., Am. Nurses Assn. Democrat. Home: 5630 Ranchito Ave Van Nuys CA 91401 Office: So Calif Permanente Med Group 13652 Cantara St Panorama City CA 91402

SENG, MINNIE ANNA, librarian, editor; b. Muskegon, Mich., Nov. 30, 1909; d. Edward and Ella Barbara (Pattie) S.; student Muskegon Community Coll., 1927-29; A.B., U. Mich., 1932, A.B. in Library Sci., 1935, M.A. in Library Sci., 1943. Asst. med. librarian U. Iowa, 1935-39; cataloger Bay City (Mich.) Pub. Library, 1939-40; order librarian Mich. Technol. U., Houghton, 1940-42; continuations cataloger U. Ark., 1943-44; head cataloger Calif. State U., Fresno, 1944-59; editor Edn. Index, H.W. Wilson Co., Pubs., Bronx, N.Y., 1959-66; head cataloger St. Ambrose Coll., Davenport, Iowa, 1967-72; periodicals librarian Frostburg (Md.) State Coll., 1972-74; ret., 1974. Mem. Am. Hort. Soc., AAUW. Democrat. Mem. Christian Ch. Home: 110 S Broadway Townhouse Q Frostburg MD 21532

SENGSTOCK, MARY CATHERINE, educator; b. Detroit, Mar. 24, 1936; d. John A. and Ida (Tobie) Walsh; m. Frank S. Sengstock, Feb. 3, 1962 (dec. 1975); m. Kathleen, Frank, David; m. Frederick Charles Rosenberry, June 4, 1988. PhB, U. Detroit, 1958; MA, U. Mich., 1960; PhD, Washington U., 1967. Cert. clin. sociology, 1985. Instr. to prof. sociology Wayne State U., Detroit, 1966—, dept. chmn., 1984—. Author: Chaldean-Americans, 1982 (U. Bd. Govs. award 1984). Contbr. articles to profl. jours. Bd. dirs. United Community Services, Detroit, 1986—, Holy Cross Hosp. Detroit, 1978—, Help the Elderly Maintain Independence and Dignity, Detroit, 1986—, Social Program Evaluators and Cons. Assocs., Detroit, 1984—. Office: Wayne State U Sociology Dept Detroit MI 48202

SENIOR, FAITH ARDELLE, publisher; b. Springfield, Vt., July 31, 1906; d. Fred Andrew and Nellie (Simpson) Richardson; m. Herbert Frank Senior, Nov. 18, 1926 (dec. Oct. 1959); 1 child, Joanne. Student, Hesser Bus. Coll., 1926. With U.S. Govt. Service, various locations, 1926-45, ret., 1945; operator ABC Secretarial Service, Fla., thrift shop, Fla. Editor, publisher The Pet Gazette, 1984—. Office: The Pet Gazette 1309 N Halifax Daytona Beach FL 32018 Home: 1309 N Halifax Ave Daytona Beach FL 32018

SENISI, ANN MCNULTY, nursing and community health educator; b. Bklyn., May 10, 1938; d. Michael and Teresa (Carron) McNulty; m. Daniel A. Senisi, July 2, 1960; children—Vincent, Margaret, Carolyn, Daniel, Michael, Kenneth. B.S., St. Josephs Coll., 1978; R.N., Prospect Heights Hosp., 1959; teaching cert. CUNY, 1976; M.A., Adelphi U., 1982. Head nurse Prospect Heights Hosp., Bklyn., 1959-63, Daleview Nursing Home, Farmingdale, N.Y., 1972-73, Lydia Hall Hosp., Freeport, N.Y., 1973-75; tchr. Nassau Tech-BOCES, Westbury, N.Y., 1975-87, coordinator nursing/health occupations, 1987—; community health educator Am. Diabetic Assn., Melville, N.Y., 1982—; advisor nat. and local com. Health Occupation Students Am., N.Y., 1982-86; curriculum writer Futuring Project Health Occupations, N.Y. State Dept. Edn. Mem. sch. bd. Our Lady of Lourdes Sch., Massapequa Park, N.Y., 1983, mem. adult folk choir. Mem. Am. Vocational Assn., N.Y. State Health Occuaptions Educators Assn. (pres.), Eta Sigma Gamma. Home: 226 Cypress St Massapequa Park NY 11762 Office: Nassau Tech-BOCES 1196 Prospect Ave Westbury NY 11590

SENK, MARCYANNE ROSE, telecommunications analyst; b. New Britain, Conn., July 17, 1941; d. Stanley S. and Mildred (Koscieniak) S.; divorced; children: William, Todd, Christopher, Kerilee, Alyssa, Derrick. BA in Math., St. Joseph Coll., West Hartford, Conn., 1963; MS in Computer Sci., Rensselaer Poly. Inst. Tchr. math. St. Paul High Sch., Bristol, Conn., 1980-81; analyst telecommunications Hartford (Conn.) Ins. Group, 1981—. V.p. PTO, Burlington, Conn., 1975. Republican. Roman Catholic. Home: 3 Summit Dr Burlington CT 06013 Office: Hartford Ins Group Hartford Plaza NP-5 Hartford CT 06105

SENN, GLENDA EDNA NICHOLS, small business owner; b. Montgomery, Ala., Mar. 9, 1950; d. Glenn Thomas and Louise Anna (Powers) Nichols; m. Frank James Senn, Apr. 14, 1979; children: Jonathan Ashley, Christopher Patrick, Frank James II. Cert. in gen. bus., So. Nazarene U., 1971. Legal sec. Piel & Lynn, Attys. at Law, Montgomery, 1979-80; dept. sec. social work services Bapt. Med. Ctr., Montgomery, 1981-86; co-owner, corp. sec. All Pest Exterminators, Inc., Montgomery, 1980—; co-owner All Lawn, Landscape & Tree Service, Montgomery. Mem. Frazer Meml. United Meth. Ch., Montgomery, 1980—. Mem. Ala. Pest Control Assn., Montgomery Apt. Assn. (assoc.), Montgomery Area Bd. Realtors (affiliate), Nat. Alliance for the Mentally Ill. Home: 616 Fieldbrook Ct Montgomery AL 36117 Office: All Pest Exterminators Inc 1813 W Third St Montgomery AL 36106

SENSABAUGH, MARY ELIZABETH, financial consultant; b. Eastland, Tex., Aug. 15, 1939; d. Johnnie and L.G. (Tucker) Roberts; m. Dwight Lee Sensabaugh, Dec. 22, 1956; children: Robert Lee, Mark Jay. Student, Odessa Jr. Coll., 1959-63, North Tex. State U., 1963-67. Sr. acct. Braniff Internat. Airlines, Dallas, 1967-68; acct. Computer Bus. Services, Dallas, 1972-76; sec.-treas. Robert D. Carpenter, Inc., Dallas, 1972-76; controller Broadway Warehouses, Dallas, 1976-78; asst. controller S.W. Offset, Dallas, 1978-79; sec.-treas., cons. Carpenter, Carruth & Hover, Inc., Dallas, 1979—. Mem. Nat. Assn. Women in Constrn. (bd. dirs. Dallas chpt. 1983-84), Beta Sigma (pres. Irving, Tex. chpt. 1973-74). Home: 702 Hughes Irving TX 75062 Office: Carpenter Carruth & Hover Inc 1210 River Bend Dr Suite 200 Dallas TX 75247

SENSENICH, ILA JEANNE, lawyer, magistrate; b. Pitts., Mar. 6, 1939; d. Louis E. and Evelyn Margaret (Harbourt) S.; B.A., Westminster Coll., 1961; J.D., Dickinson Sch. Law, 1964. Asso. firm Stewart, Belden, Sensenich and Herrington, Greensburg, Pa., 1964-70; asst. public defender Westmoreland (Pa.) County, 1970-71; U.S. magistrate for Western Dist. Pa., Pitts., 1971—; adj. prof. law Duquesne U., 1982-87; mem. magistrate's com. Judicial Conf. of U.S.; liason 3d Cir. Judicial Council. Mem. Nat. Council U.S. Magistrates (sec. 1979-88, rec. sec. 1981-82), Am. Bar Assn., Pa. Bar Assn., Allegheny County Bar Assn., Nat. Assn. Women Judges. Author: Compendium of the Law of Prisoner's Rights, 1979. Contbr. in field. Office: 1026 US PO & Courthouse Pittsburgh PA 15219

SENSOR, MARY DELORES, hospital official, consultant; b. Erie, Pa., July 20, 1930; d. Sergie Pavl Malinowski and Leocadia Mary Francis (Machalinski) Harner; m. Robert Louis Charles Sensor, Apr. 21, 1945; children—Robert Louis Paul, Stephen Maxmillian Augustus, Therese Blaze, Katryn Anne. Student in Pre-Medicine, Gannon U., 1968-72, M.S. in Health Care Adminstrn., 1986; B.S. in Hosp. Adminstrn., Daemon Coll., 1972. Intern in hosp. adminstrn. Harvard U., Boston, 1972; dir. med. records St. Mary Hosp., Langhorne, Pa., 1972-74, Moses Taylor Hosp., Scranton, Pa., 1975-77, Erie County Geriatric Ctr., Fairview, Pa., 1977-82; dir. utilization rev. Millcreek Community Hosp., Erie, Pa., 1983—; bd. dirs. Christian Health Care Ctr., Erie, 1983-84; cons. prof. in-hosp. adminstrn. and med. records U. Pitts. and Temple U., 1972-74; contbr. paper 6th World Congress Automated Med. Data, Washington; presenter paper, Computer Adaption of SNOMed to DRG Assignment, to 12th Annual Symposium on Computer Application in Med. Care, Washington., Bd. dirs St. John Kanty Prep. Sch., Erie, 1970-71, pres. Ladies Aux., 1970-71. Mem. Am. Med. Rec. Assn., Pa. Med. Record Assn., NW Pa. Med. Record Assn. (sec. treas. 1982-84), Nat. Assn. Quality Assurance Profls., Pa. Assn. Quality Assurance Profls. Roman Catholic. Club: Siebenburger Singing Soc. Avocations: Profl. classical dancing; researcher early man's migration patterns; gourmet cooking; collecting jazz. Home: 3203 Regis Dr Erie PA 16510

SENTENNE, JUSTINE, association administrator; b. Montreal, Que., Can., Mar. 22, 1936; d. Paul Emile and Irene Genevieve (Laliberte) S. Student, McGill U., U. de Que. a Montreal. Fin. analyst, assoc. mgr. portfolio Bush Assocs., Montreal, 1970-82; city councillor, mem. exec. com. City of Montreal and Montreal Urban Com., 1978-82; adminstrv. asst. Palais des Congres, Montreal Conv. Ctr., 1983; dir. sponsorship Cen. Com. for Montreal Papal Visit, 1984; dir. pub. relations Coopers & Lybrand, Montreal, 1985-87; exec. dir. Quebec Heart Found., 1987—; v.p., bd. dirs. Armand Frappier Found., Laval, Can.; chmn. bd. Wilfrid Pelletier Found., Montreal, 1986-87 ; mem. jury John Labatt Ltd., London, Ont., 1982-86. Adminstr. Caisse Populaire Desjardins Notre Dame de Grace, Montreal, 1980—; mem. bd. govs. Youth and Music Can., Montreal, 1981-86; chmn. bd. The Women's Ctr., Montreal, 1986-88, Vol. Bus. Montreal, 1986-87; bd. dirs. Palais des Congres de Montreal, 1981; mem. St. Joseph's Oratory, 1979—, Can. Ctr. for Ecumenism, Montreal, 1968-85, Villa Notre-Dame de Grace, Montreal, 1979-87, Chateau Dufresne Mus. Decorative Arts, Montreal, 1985—. Named Career Woman of Yr., Sullivan Bus. Coll., 1979; recipient Silver medal Ville de Paris, 1981, Women's Kansas City Assn. for Internat. Relations and Trade medal, 1982. Fellow Fin. Analysts Fedn. N.Y., Inst. Fin. Analysts, Montreal Soc. Investment Analysts; mem. Cercle Fin. et Placement. Roman Catholic.

SENTER, MICHELLE FAYE, nutritionist; b. Emporia, Kans., Aug. 5, 1959; d. James J. and Laurretta Faye (Howard) Williams; m. Bill Scott Senter, Aug. 27, 1983; 1 child, Brandon Shay. BS Dietetics Mgmt., Abilene Christian U., 1981, BEd in Phys. Edn., Health, 1982; student, Cisco Jr. Coll., Abilene, Tex., 1984. Registered dietetic technician. Dietetic technician W. Tex. Med. Ctr. Humana, Abilene, 1981-83; asst. mgr., nutritionist The Fitness Racquet, Inc. & Health Ctr., Abilene, 1983-85; nutritionist Abilene Independent Sch. Dist., 1985—; menu planner Serenity House, Abilene, 1985-88; task force mem. Am. Heart Assn., Abilene, 1986—, Project Comply. Active Leadership Abilene Class, Taylor County Young Reps., Abilene Philharmonic Guild, Patron 200, Friends Abilene Pub. Library, Abilene Preservation League, Abilene Fine Arts Mus., Abilene Zool. Soc. Mem. Abilene Sch. Food Service Assn., Tex. Sch. Food Service Assn., Am. Sch. Food Service Assn., Tex. Dietetics Assn., Am. Dietitcs Assn., Abilene Bd. Realtors, Tex. Assn. Realtors, Nat. Assn. Realtors, Jaycee (assoc. 1985—, numerous coms. 1983-84, Miss Taylor County 1981), Sigma Theta Chi, Sigma Tau Alpha. Mem. Church of Christ. Home: 2901 S 1st Abilene TX 79605

SENTER, SYLVIA, psychologist; b. N.J., Mar. 3, 1921; d. Samuel and Gertrude (Raphael) Kapralik; B.A., 1975, M.A., 1976; Ph.D. in Child Psychology, Goddard Coll., 1978; m. Jonas Senter, Sept. 30, 1941; children—Leigh Senter Saul, Jill. Intern, Temple U.; staff psychologist, lectr. behavior therapy unit dept. psychiatry Inst. of Phila.; dir. Behavioral Assos., Greenwich, Conn.; former mem. staff Bellevue Hosp., Univ. Hosp. Author: Women at Work, 1982. Office: 27 Alden Rd Greenwich CT also: 910 Fifth Ave New York NY 10021

SEPA, LISA JOAN, information specialist; b. N.Y.C., Jan. 20, 1960; d. Frank Raymond and Joan Nella (Pike) S. AB, Sarah Lawrence Coll., 1980; MS, Pratt Inst., N.Y.C., 1985; MA, NYU, 1988. Librarian Kelley Drye & Warren, N.Y.C., 1984; Info. specialist Touche Ross/FSC, N.Y.C., 1985, N.Y.U., N.Y.C., 1986—. Mem. Am. Libraries Assn., Special Libraries Assn. Office: NYU 11 W 42d St New York NY 10036

SEPAHPUR, HAYEDEH C(HRISTINA), investment banker; b. Lincoln, Nebr., Dec. 8, 1958; d. Bahman and Marylin Lou (Duffy) S. BS, Lehigh U.,

1983. Assoc. Drexel Burnham Lambert Inc., N.Y.C., 1982—. Sponsor Jr. Statesmen of Am. Found., Washington, 1976—; charter mem. Nat. Mus. Women in the Arts, Washington, 1985—; active Friends of Library, French Inst.; literacy vol. Film Soc. Lincoln Ctr. Mem. Am. Film Inst., Mensa, Nat. Trust Hist. Preservation, The Asia Soc., N.Y. Hist. Soc., Japan Soc., Mcpl. Art Soc., Gamma Phi Beta. Club: Downtown Athletic (N.Y.C.). Home: 417 Park Ave New York City NY 10022 Office: Drexel Burnham Lambert Inc 55 Broad St 2d Floor New York City NY 10004

SEPPALA, KATHERINE SEAMAN (MRS. LESLIE W. SEPPALA), business executive, clubwoman, b. Detroit, Aug. 22, 1919; d. Willard D. and Elizabeth (Miller) Seaman; B.A., Wayne State U., 1941; m. Leslie W. Seppala, Aug. 15, 1941; children—Sandra Kay, William Leslie. Mgr. women's bldg. and student activities adviser Wayne State U., 1941-43; pres. Harper Sports Shops, Inc., 1947-85, chmn. bd., treas., sec., v.p. 1985—; ptnr. Seppala Bldg. Co., 1971—. Mich. service chmn. women grads. Wayne State U., 1962—, 1st v.p., fund bd., Girl and Cub Scouts; mem. Citizen's adv. com. on sch. needs Detroit Bd. Edn., 1957—, mem. high sch. study com., 1966—; chmn., mem. loan fund bd. Denby High Sch. Parents Scholarship; bd. dirs., v.p. Wayne State U. Fund; precinct del. Rep. Party, 14th dist., 1956—, del. convs.; mem. com. Myasthenia Gravis Support Assn. Recipient Ann. Women's Service award Wayne State U., 1963. Recipient Disting. Alumni award Wayne State U., 1971. Mem. Intercollegiate Assn. Women Students (regional rep. 1941-45), Women Wayne State U. Alumni (past pres.), Wayne State U. Alumni Assn. (dir., past v.p.), AAUW (dir. past officer), Council Women as Public Policy Makers (editor High lights) Denby Community Ednl. Orgn. (sec.), Met. Detroit Program Planning Inst. (pres.), Internat. Platform Assn., Detroit Met. Book and Author Soc. (treas.), Mortar Bd. (past pres.), Karyatides (past pres.), Anthony Wayne Soc., Alpha Chi Alpha, Alpha Kappa Delta, Delta Gamma Chi, Kappa Delta (chmn. chpt. alumnae adv. bd.). Baptist. Clubs: Zonta (v.p., dir.); Les Cheneaux. Home: 22771 Worthington Saint Clair Shores MI 48081 Office: 17157 Harper Detroit MI 48224

SERBEN, ROBERTA IRIS, educator, graphic artist; b. N.Y.C., Feb. 10, 1948; d. Reuben and Sylvia (Hyman) S. BEd, U. Fla., 1969; MS, U. So. Calif., 1984. Bilingual tchr. Dade County Edn. System, Miami, Fla., 1967-70; tchr. sci. N.Y.C. Bd. Edn., 1970-77; graphics designer Citation-Langley, Los Angeles, 1977-84; tchr. computer lab. Los Angeles County Office Edn., Downey, Calif., 1984—; cons. computer art Pepperdine U., Los Angeles, 1984—; graphic artist cons. Sch. Visual Arts, N.Y.C., 1987—. Author: Cooking for Keeps, 1983, Ascendants Delights, 1985; editor computer software Can You Be Swayed?, 1984. Mem. NEA, Calif. Tchrs. Assn., Los Angeles Edn. Assn., Writers Guild Am., Screen Actors Guild, Artists Anonymous (vice chancellor), Astrologers Club (treas.). Democrat. Jewish. Home: 8033 Sunset Blvd Suite 4033 Los Angeles CA 90046 Office: 7285 E Quill Dr Downey CA 90242

SERGEANT, HILDEGARDE, minister; b. N.Y.C., Jan. 17, 1941; d. Otto Ernest and Gertrude (Schurmann) Lehmann; m. Bruce Herbert Sergeant, Dec. 21, 1984; 1 child, William Scott Tonsfeldt. Diploma, Rhema Bible Tng. Ctr., Broken Arrow, Okla., 1982-84, Sch. of the Psalmist, Ft. Worth, 1986; cert., Christian Family Inst., Tulsa, 1987. Ordained to ministry, 1988. Evangelist/psalmist Love of God Ministries, Broken Arrow, U.S., Jamaica, 1984—; marriage counselor Victory Christian Ctr., Tulsa, 1985—, tchr., 1987—; dir., founder Women Alive in Christ Internat., Broken Arrow, 1986—. Author: The Listening Heart, 1960. Tchr. Sunday Sch., marriage class, Victory Christian Ctr., communication skills workshop, Broken Arrow, 1988; dir. Cherub Choir, 1978-79. Republican. Home and Office: Love of God Ministries 1604 W Knoxville Broken Arrow OK 74012

SEROVY, ANITA MORIN, academic administrator, corporate-university relations consultant; b. Damar, Kans., Feb. 12, 1945; d. William Edward and Irene Delphine (Roberts) Morin; m. George K. Serovy, Apr. 17, 1971; children: David, Dana. BS, Iowa State U, 1969, MA, 1975. Info. specialist Iowa State U., Ames, 1979-80, project devel. specialist, 1980-82, corp. relations officer, 1982-88; indsl. liasion officer Inst. for Phys. Research and Tech., Ames, 1988—; pres. Morin & Assocs., Inc., Ames, 1988—. Adv. Assn. for Children and Adults with Learning Disabilities, Ames, 1984—; bd. dirs. Ames Economic Devel. Commn., 1985-86, 88—, Area XI Regional Coordinating Council, Iowa, 1986-87; mem. exec. com. Ames 2000, 1986-87. Mem. Soc. Research Adminstrs., Assn. Univ. Affiliated Research Parks, Am. Electronics Assn., Phi Kappa Phi. Episcopalian.

SERRANO, TERI ANN, real estate broker; b. San Jose, Calif., Aug. 19, 1960; d. William Wilson and Raelene (Fanizzi) S. BS in Agrl. Econs., U. Calif., Davis, 1982. Analyst ROLM Corp., Santa Clara, Calif., 1982-84; assoc. Eastdil Realty, N.Y.C. and San Francisco, 1984—. All-Am. Athlete, NCAA, 1982. Mem. Women in Real Estate, AAUW (historian 1983). Democrat. Roman Catholic. Home: 1568 Edgewood Dr Palo Alto CA 94303

SERRATORE, PATRICIA ANN, communications executive; b. Norristown, Pa., July 5, 1961; d. John Joseph and Rita Joanne (Cimino) S. BA in English, LaSalle U., 1983. Bus. editor Motor Age Mag., Chilton Co., Radnor, Pa., 1983-87; acct. exec. Target Communications, Inc., Plymouth Meeting, Pa., 1987—. Bus. editor Motor/Age mag., Radnor and Chilton, Colo., 1983-87. Mem. Internat. Motor Press Assn., Del. Valley Press Club. Republican. Roman Catholic.

SERSTOCK, DORIS SHAY, microbiologist, educator; civic worker; b. Mitchell, S.D., June 13, 1926; d. Elmer Howard and Hattie (Christopher) Shay; B.A., Augustana Coll., 1947; postgrad. U. Minn., 1966-67, Duke U., summer 1969, Communicable Disease Center, Atlanta, 1972; m. Ellsworth I. Serstock, Aug. 30, 1952; children—Barbara Anne, Robert Ellsworth, Mark Douglas. Bacteriologist, Civil Service, S.D., Colo., Mo., 1947-52; research bacteriologist U. Minn., 1952-53; clin. bacteriologist Dr. Lufkin's Lab., 1954-55; chief technologist St. Paul Blood Bank of ARC, 1959-65; microbiologist in charge mycology lab. VA Hosp., Mpls., 1968—; instr. Coll. Med. Scis., U. Minn., 1970-79, asst. prof. Coll. Lab. Medicine and Pathology, 1979—. Mem. Richfield Planning Commn., 1965-71, sec., 1968-71. Fellow Augusta Coll.; named to Exec. and Profl. Hall of Fame; recipient Alumni Achievement award Augustana Coll., 1977; Superior Performance award VA Hosp., 1978, 82; Golden Spore award Mycology Observer, 1985, 87. Mem. Am. Soc. Microbiology, N.Y. Acad. Scis., Minn. Planning Assn. Republican. Lutheran. Clubs: Richfield Women's Garden (pres. 1959), Wild Flower Garden (chmn. 1961). Author articles in field. Home: 7201 Portland Ave Richfield MN 55423 Office: VA Hosp Minneapolis MN 55417

SESSA, BEVERLEY EVANS, social services administrator; b. Downey, Calif., Mar. 14, 1937; d. John Wesley and Edna (Hickernel) Evans; m. William James Sessa, May 5, 1961; children: Chris Anthony, Curtis Lee. AA in Human Services, Long Beach (Calif.) City Coll., 1976; BA in Social Work, Calif. State U., Long Beach, 1980; MSW, U. So. Calif., 1982. Lic. clin. social worker. Med. social worker Inter-Community Hosp., Covina, Calif., 1982-83; clin. social worker FHP, Inc., Long Beach, 1983-84, sr. clinician, 1984-85, dir. clin. social services, 1985—, also bd. dirs.; pvt. practice psychotherapy Long Beach, 1987—. Mem. Nat. Assn. Social Workers, Soc. Clin. Social Workers, Am. Hosp. Assn., Assn. Women in Social Work, Nat. Assn. Exec. Women, Am. Mgmt. Assn. Democrat. Baptist. Office: FHP Inc 1000 Studebaker Rd Long Beach CA 90815

SESSION, WILLIE MAE, nurse, clinical instructor; b. Daytona Beach, Fla., Jan. 1, 1943; d. Willie Lee and Mamie (Jones) Edwards; m. Johnny Van Session, Jan. 27, 1975; children: Tyrone, Theressa, Vanessa. AA, Volusia County Community Coll., Daytona Beach, 1962, Advanced degree in nursing, 1975; BS, Bethune-Cookman Coll., 1983; MS in Nursing, U. Fla., 1987. Nurse Am. Heart Assn., Daytona Beach, 1984-86; with Halifax Med. Ctr., Daytona Beach, 1975—, clin. instr. ednl. services dept., 1987—; CPR instr. ARC, Daytona Beach, 1985—. Mem. Fla. Nurses Assn., Fla. Assn. Health and Social Services, Sigma Theta Tau. Democrat. Baptist. Home: 1108 Lakewood Park Dr Daytona Beach FL 32017

SESSLER, JERI DECARLO, technical and corporate researcher, consultant; b. Oak Park, Ill., Oct. 6, 1953; d. Michael A. and Esther (Galucci) DeCarlo; m. Nicholas Eugene Sessler, Dec. 3, 1977; children—Michael Joseph, Nicole Christina. Student Loyola U., 1972-75; B.A. in Anthropology, No. Ill. U., 1976; cert. emergency med. technician, Kishwaukee Coll., 1976; postgrad., Lake Forest Sch. Mgmt. Instr., fellow in anthropology No. Ill. U., 1973-76; emergency med. technician, paramedic Berz Ambulance Service, Chgo., 1976-77; trade fair coordinator Schenkers Internat., Schiller Park, Ill., 1977-79; research assoc. Staub Warmbold Co, Chgo., 1979-81; dir. research A.T. Kearney Inc. Chgo., 1981-85, dir. research services div., 1985—; adult edn. instr. Moraine Valley Community Coll., Orland Park, Ill., 1982. Mem. Am. Network of Exec. Women (pres. 1980-83), Am. Chem. Soc., Planning Forum, Am. Soc. Tng. and Devel. Democrat. Roman Catholic. Home: 5167 Winona Ln Gurnee IL 60031 Office: A T Kearney Inc 222 S Riverside Plaza Chicago IL 60606

SESTILE, CYNTHIA JEANNE, financial analyst, management consultant; b. Ambridge, Pa., May 24, 1956; d. Joseph John and Elise May (Blackford) S. AA, U. South Fla., 1977, BA in Polit. Sci., 1979; postgrad., So. Meth. U., 1980-81; MBA, U. Tex., Arlington, 1987. Acct. NDC, Dallas, 1984-87; cons. fin. and acctg. Dallas, 1987-88; mgr. fin. services Cathey Hutton & Assocs., Dallas, 1988—. Mem. Nat. Assn. Female Execs., MBA Assn., Beta Gamma Sigma, Pi Sigma Alpha. Republican. Methodist.

SETTLE, MARY LEE, author; b. Charleston, W.Va., July 29, 1918; d. Joseph Edward and Rachel (Tompkins) S.; student Sweet Briar Coll., 1936-38; m. William Littleton Tazewell, Sept. 2, 1978; 1 son, Christopher Weathersbee. Asso. prof. Bard Coll., Annandale-on-Hudson, N.Y., 1965-76; vis. lectr. U. Va., 1978, U. Iowa, 1976. Served with Womens Aux., RAF, 1942-43. Recipient Merrill Found. award, 1974, Nat. Book award, 1978, Janet Heidinger Kafka Prize for fiction, 1983. John Simon Guggenheim fellow, 1958, 60. Democrat. Author: The Love Eaters, 1954; The Kiss of Kin, 1955; O Beulah Land, 1956; Know Nothing, 1960; Fight Night on a Sweet Saturday, 1964; All The Brave Promises, 1966; The Clam Shell, 1971; Prisons, 1973; Blood Tie, 1977; The Scapegoat, 1981; The Killing Ground, 1982; Celebration, 1986. Office: care Farrar Straus & Giroux 19 Union Sq W New York NY 10003

SETTLEMIRE, BEVERLY MAY, nursing home administrator; b. Allen County, Ohio, Jan. 3, 1933; d. Harry Franklin and Margurite (Brothers) Holden; R.N., Lima (Ohio) Meml. Hosp., 1954; B.S. in Nursing Arts, Findlay (Ohio) Coll., 1969; m. Robert Eugene Settlemire, June 11, 1955; children—Edward Eugene, Larry Franklin. Part-time staff nurse Defiance (Ohio) City Hosp., 1958-64, Blanchard Valley Hosp., Findlay, 1964-69; dir. nurses Manley Manor, Findlay, 1972-75; adminstr. Fox Run Nursing Home, Findlay, 1976; dir. nursing Heritage Manor, Findlay, 1978-79; adminstr. Blakely Care Center, North Baltimore, Ohio, 1979-83; dir. nurses Hilton Nursing Home, Phoenix, 1985; dir. nurses Desert-Valley Rehab. Med. Ctr., 1986-87; RN, suprv. Life Care of Paradise Valley, 1987—. Pres. Defiance and Hancock Counties Soc. Crippled Children and Adults, 1960-82; bd. dirs. Ohio Soc. Crippled Children and Adults, 1978-84. Mem. Phi Beta Lambda, Beta Sigma Phi. Episcopalian. Club: Findlay Country. Home: 5912 E Aire Libre Scottsdale AZ 85254

SETZMAN, EILEEN JUDITH, psychoanalyst; b. Phila., Nov. 26, 1942; d. Bernard and Eleanor (Cohen) S.; B.A., U. Pa., 1964; M.A., Temple U., 1967; Ph.D., NYU, 1973, cert. in psychoanalysis, 1979; m. Gary Wankoff. Lic. psychologist, N.J. NIMH grantee Phila. State Hosp., 1965-66; staff psychologist, therapist, ward adminstr. Bronx (N.Y.) Psychiat. Center, 1967-73; counselor in field; pvt. practice individual and group psychotherapy, psychoanalysis and supervision, 1974—; asst. prof. Bloomfield Coll., 1975-77; adj. prof. Marymount-Manhattan Coll., 1973-75; faculty L.I. Inst. for Mental Health, 1977-79, Met. Inst. for Tng. in Psychoanalytic Psychotherapy, 1979—; faculty continuing edn. postdoctoral program psychoanalysis NYU, 1981—, Faculty Nat. Inst. for the Psychotherapies, 1986; cons. women's counseling project Barnard Coll., 1980-81; supr., presenter workshops on sex role stereotypes, peer supervision, use of group modalities with coll. students and love to psychol. convs., 1972—. Mem. Nassau County Psychol. Assn., Am. Psychol. Assn., Psychoanalytic Soc. N.Y.U.

SEUFER, SHARON LYNN, human resource specialist; b. Tucson, 1953; d. Edward George and Marjorie Mary (Robbs) S. BA in Sociology, Calif. State U., Fullerton, 1977; MBA, U. Calif., Irvine, 1987. Personnel mgr. Newport Electronics, Inc., Santa Ana, Calif., 1979—. Mem. Am. Soc. Personnel Adminstrs., Am. Compensation Assn. Republican. Methodist. Office: Newport Electronics Inc 630 E Young St Santa Ana CA 92705

SEVAYEGA, DINA MARÍA, education specialist, administrator; b. Rio Hondo, Tex.; d. Manuel B. and Sara (Flores) Garza; children: Reginald Brandon, Mario Antonio. BS, Ohio State U., 1964; postgrad., Miami U., Oxford, Ohio, 1975-76; MS, Youngstown (Ohio) State U., 1976; DEd, Ind. U., 1983. Tchr. Columbus (Ohio) Bd. Edn., 1964-67, Youngstown Bd. Edn., 1967-76; asst. dir. devel. edn. Miami U., Oxford, 1976-79; research assoc. Ind. U., Bloomington, 1979-82; dir. ednl. opportunity program Ithaca (N.Y.) Coll., 1982-86; assoc. Dept. Edn. State N.Y., Albany, 1986-88, assoc. profl. edn. acad. program review, 1988—. Home: 21 Feiden Ln Latham NY 12110 Office: State NY Dept Edn Cultural Edn Ctr #5A47 Albany NY 12230

SEVERINO, ELIZABETH FORREST, consulting company executive; b. Bryn Mawr, Pa., Dec. 29, 1945; d. John Joseph and Elizabeth (Patton) Girard-diCarlo; m. Joseph Domenic Severino, Oct. 20, 1973 (div. Oct. 1983); 1 child, Nicole Marie. AB, Vassar Coll., 1967; MS in Computer Sci., Syracuse U., 1969. Systems programmer IBM Corp., Poughkeepsie, N.Y., 1967-71; competitive analyst IBM Corp., Phila., 1977-79; systems analyst Fidelity Bank, Phila., 1971-72; mng. editor Auerbach Pubs., Phila., 1972-77; v.p. editorial and technology McGraw-Hill Pubs., Delran, N.J., 1979-81; v.p. Symcro Systems, Pennsauken, N.J., 1981-82; pres. The PC Group, Inc., Cherry Hill, N.J., 1982—, also bd. dirs.; bd. dirs. CompCar Leasing, Cherry Hill. Author over 125 articles on computers. Mem. Assn. of Personal Computers Cons. (bd. dirs. Phila. chpt., pres. 1987-88), Nat. Assn. Female Execs., Phila. Area Computer Soc. Republican. Episcopalian. Office: The PC Group Inc 1020 N Kings Hwy Suite 114 Cherry Hill NJ 08034

SEVERNS, PENNY L., state legislator; b. Decatur, Ill., Jan. 21, 1952. BS in Polit. Sci. and Internat. Relations, So. Ill. U., 1974. Spl. asst. to adminstr. AID, Washington, 1977-79; city councilwoman Decatur, from 1983; Ill. Dem. state senator 1987—. Address: Office State Senate Ill State Capitol Springfield IL 62706 *

SEVERO, LEANNE, social services administrator; b. Meadville, Pa., July 10, 1959; d. Richard Joseph and Katherine Ann (Piccirillo) S.; m. Timothy Wynn Hunter, Sept. 27, 1986. BS, Edinboro U., 1983. Residential program aide United Cerebral Palsy, Meadville, Pa., 1984, dir. ind. living rehab. program for Crawford, Venengo and Clarion Counties, 1984-87, asst. administr., 1987—; camp counselor Easter Seals, Conneact Lake, Pa., summers 1975, 76, 77, 81, Assn. Retarded Citizens, Meadville, summer 1984. Active Meadville Community Council, 1986-87. Mem. Nat. Assn. Female Execs., Speech and Hearing Soc. (bd. dirs. Meadville 1986—). Roman Catholic. Home: RD #6 Stauffer Rd Meadville PA 16335 Office: United Cerebral Palsy 405 Finley Ave Meadville PA 16335

SEVERS, DIANA LYNNE, health care executive; b. Springfield, Ohio, Oct. 2, 1959; d. Donald Fremont and Estel Faye (Niswonger) S. BS in Health Systems Engring., Ga. Inst. Tech., 1981. Mgmt. engr. Geisinger System Services, Danville, Pa., 1981-82, Health East, Inc., Roanoke, Va., 1982-83; sr. mgmt. engr. Good Samaritan Hosp. and Health Ctr., Dayton, Ohio, 1983-85; sr. cons. Price Waterhouse, Columbus, Ohio, 1986—. Author: (with others) Management of Rehabilitation Medicine, 1983. Am. Soc. Women Engrs. scholar, 1981. Mem. Hosp. Mgmt. Systems Soc., Tau Beta Pi, Alpha Pi (sec. 1984). Republican. Home: 1642 Worthington Club Dr Westerville OH 43081 Office: Price Waterhouse 41 S High St Columbus OH 43215

SEVERY, JANAKI GAYLE (JANICE), special education educator; b. Portland, Oreg., Aug. 17, 1948; d. Malcolm Moore and Ada Clare (McCall) S.; m. Anastassios Ioannis Bountalis, Aug. 16, 1980; children: Eleni Ashling, Alexandra Clare. BA in Drama and Edn., U. Wash., 1970, postgrad. in spl. edn., 1973-74; postgrad. in spl. edn. U. Ariz., 1977-79, EdM in Counseling and Guidance, 1985. Cert. tchr., counselor. Supr. detention King County Juvenile Ct., Seattle, 1968-70; educator, program designer Juvenile Parole Services Sch., Seattle, 1970-73; dir., trainer Youth Services Bur. Sch., Seattle, 1974-75; spl. end. tchr. Seattle Pub. Schs., 1975-76, Tucson Pub. Schs., 1975-81, 84—; mgr., coordinator The Tng., Tucson, weekends 1979-80; instr. continuing edn. program U. Ariz., Tucson, 1979-81; wellness cons. various local businesses, Tucson, 1984—; cons. in field; speaker, facilitator Corondelet Health Services, Tucson, 1985—; condr. seminars, stress mgmt. workshops; cons. for hosps., physician relations, stress mgmt. for nurses, conflict resolution, team bldg., assertiveness tng.; workshops Open U., Tucson, 1985—; nat. cons. Hosps. in Human Resource Devel., owner, co-founder Career Path ventures, 1985—. Author: Women, The Inner Journey, workshop manual, 1985, Self-Marketing for Nurses, 1987. Cons. Performax Systems Internat., Inc.; co-founder Career Path Ventures, 1986; assoc. Prepaid Legal Services. Mem. Nat. Speakers Assn. (com. mem. Ariz.), Ariz. Counselors Assn., Nat. Assn. Female Execs., Action Linkage. Avocations: scuba diving, traveling, writing, reading, metaphysics. Home: 2701 N Desert Ave Tucson AZ 85712

SEVILLE, MARY ALICE, accountant, educator; b. Sandwich, Ill., July 25, 1942; d. Harold Thornton and Margaret Raed (Miller) S. BA, So. Meth. U., 1964; BBA, U. Alaska, 1975; MA, U. Ill., 1968, PhD in Accountancy, 1983. CPA, Alaska. Tchr. Byron (Ill.) Community Schs., 1964-65; asst. dir. Head Start Rural Alaska Community Action, Anchorage, 1968-70; tchr. Quality Edn. Devel., Anchorage, 1970-71; child devel. specialist State Operated Schs., Anchorage, 1971-73; staff acct. Va. Cutshall, CPAs, Anchorage, 1973-75, Johnson and Morgan, CPAs, Anchorage, 1975-77; asst. prof. U. Alaska, Anchorage, 1977-79; controller Alaska Legal Services, Anchorage, 1979-80; asst. prof. Oreg. State U., Corvallis, 1983—. Contbr. articles to profl. jours. U. Ill. fellow, 1980-82. Mem. Oreg. Soc. CPAs (discussion leader 1986), Alaska Soc. CPAs (discussion leader 1987), Am. Soc. Women Accts. (chpt. pres. 1984-87), Nat. Assn. Female Execs., Am. Acctg. Assn., Am. Inst. CPAs, Am. Women's Soc. CPAs, Assn. Gov. Accts. Office: Oreg State U Coll of Bus Corvallis OR 97331

SEWALL, CHARLOTTE Z., state senator; b. Damariscotta, Maine, Nov. 28, 1947; d. Bernard Tucker and Anna (Bartlett) Zahn; m. Loyall F. Sewall, 1977. Ed. New Eng. Coll., U. Maine. With William L. Buyers, Inc., 1968-75, security ptnr., 1973-75; v.p. Electronic Countermeasures Maine, 1971-75; mem. Maine Ho. of Reps., 1974-80, Maine Senate, 1980—; pres. Keene Narrows Lobster, Inc. Trustee New Eng. Coll., Miles Health Care Found. Republican. Office: Maine Senate State Capitol Augusta ME 04333 Other Address: Keene Narrows Medomak ME 04551

SEWARD, DORIS KLUGE, service executive, consultant; b. Washington, Dec. 12, 1920; d. Russell O. and Edna Ashford Kluge; m. Robert F. Seward, June 18, 1947. BA, Tex. U., 1943; MS in Edn., U. So. Calif., 1968, M in Pub. Adminstrn., 1972, D in Pub. Adminstrn., 1974. Mgmt. analyst U.S. Dept. Air Force, Columbus AFB, Miss., 1959-62; tng. asst. Los Angeles City Schs., 1963-66; tng. officer Los Angeles County, 1967-79, personnel mgmt. specialist, 1979-84; pres. Pub. Adminstrn. Research and Edn., Whittier, Calif., 1981—, Temporary Tng. Skills, Whittier, 1984—; instr. UCLA extension, Los Angeles, 1973—, Calif. State U., Long Beach, 1975—, Northrop Corp., Hawthorne, Calif., 1984—; lectr. Calif. State Poly. U., Pomona, 1987—; cons. Exec. Service Corps So. Calif., 1984—. Mem. Los Angeles County Grand Jury, 1986-87; chmn. Editorial, Continuity Com., Govt. Ops. and Audit Com.; mem. Los Angeles County Economy and Efficiency Commn., 1987—. Recipient Research award Western Govt. Research Assn., 1974, Henry Reining Jr. award U. So. Calif., 1975. Mem. Am. Soc. Pub. Adminstrn. (exec. council mem. Los Angeles Met. chpt., 1974-76, membership chmn. 1974-76), Women's Equity Action League (nat. pres. 1974-75), Am. Soc. Tng. and Devel. (exec. council mem., dir. programming Los Angeles chpt., 1976), Internat. Personnel Mgmt. Assn., So. Calif. Personnel Mgmt. Assn. (life, hon.), Los Angeles County Mgmt. Council (chmn. mgmt. devel. com.,1972, editor jour. 1972-75, chmn. program com. for mgmt. conf., 1976, mem. edn. and tng. com. 1980-84). Republican. Methodist. Club: Whittier Women's, Soroptimist.

SEWARD, KATHRYN ELLEN, county official; b. Flint, Mich., May 2, 1926; d. Benjamin Franklin Sharp and Edna Vigor (Davis) Sharp Smith; m. Orville Herbert Seward, June 28, 1947; children—Duane Orville, Keith Brian, Gayle Rene Seward Gibbs. Student Owosso Bus. Coll., 1943-44, Lansing Community Coll., 1973-77, Mich. State U., 1980, U. Mich. 1981. Clk. planning dept. Redmond Co., Mich., 1943-44, sec. methods dept., 1944-48, with operation and routing dept., 1948-52; assignment clk., clk. of ct. Shiawassee County, Mich., 1966-76, register of deeds, 1976—; cabinet officer preservation com. Shiawassee County Courthouse, 1986—. Cubscout denmother, 1956-65; bd dirs. United Way, Owosso (Mich.), 1985—; v.p. Shiawassee County Republicans, 1979-80, Shiawassee County coordinator of Mich. 150 First Lady award, 1987. Mem. Internat. Assn. Clks., Recorders, Election Ofcls. and Treasurers, Mich. Assn. Registers of Deeds (liaison chmn. chmn. legal forms and fees), United County Officers Assn., Shiawassee County Geneology Assn., Shiawassee County Hist. Soc. Methodist. Lodge: Zonta (sec. 1982-83) Avocation: genealogy and history of the county. Home: 4601 Simpson Rd Owosso MI 48867 Office: Shiawassee County Register Deeds 208 N Shiawassee St Corunna MI 48817

SEWELL, PHYLLIS SHAPIRO, retail chain executive; b. Cin., Dec. 26, 1930; d. Louis and Mollye (Mark) Shapiro; m. Martin Sewell, Apr. 5, 1959; 1 child, Charles Steven. B.S. in Econs. with honors, Wellesley Coll., 1952. With Federated Dept. Stores, Inc., Cin., research dir. store ops., 1961-65, sr. research dir., 1965-70, operating v.p., research, 1970-75, corp. v.p., 1975-79, sr. v.p., research and planning, 1979—; dir., mem. exec. compensation com. and audit com. Lee Enterprises, Inc., Davenport, Iowa; dir., mem. nominating and exec. compensation coms. Huffy, Inc., Dayton, Ohio; bd. dirs. Pitney and Bowes Inc. Bd. dirs. Nat. Cystic Fibrosis Found., Cin., 1963—; chmn. div. United Appeal, Cin., 1982; mem. bus. adv. council Sch. Bus. Adminstrn., Miami U., Oxford, Ohio, 1982-84. Named One of 100 Top Corp. Women Bus. Week mag., 1976; named Career Woman of Achievement YWCA, 1983; recipient Alumnae Achievement award Wellesley Coll., 1979, Disting. Cin. Bus. and Profl. Woman award, 1981; named to Ohio Women's Hall of Fame, 1982. Office: Federated Dept Stores Inc 7 W 7th St Cincinnati OH 45202

SEWELL, POLLY MCGINNIS, marketing executive; b. El Dorado, Kans., Mar. 5, 1935; d. Walter Fletcher and Wannah Alice (Mosier) McGinnis; m. Philip M. Sewell, Aug. 4, 1956 (div. 1986); children—Jeffrey Philip, Jennifer Sewell Fountain. Student U. Kans., 1953-56; B.A., Washburn U., 1957. Office mgr. James D. Watters, Dallas, 1975-79; mktg. rep. Ticor Title Ins., Dallas, 1979-82, mktg. mgr., 1983—, now v.p., sr. mktg. mgr. Bd. dirs. Jr. League, Topeka and Dallas, 1962—; bd. dirs. Salvation Army, 1967-70; sec., treas. Topeka Arts Council, 1966-70; precinct committeewoman Republican Party, Topeka, 1967-70; com. chmn. Guild, Wadley Inst., Dallas, 1976—; mem. adv. bd. Dallas Econ. Devel., 1987—; sec. bd. dirs. Dallas Small Bus. Corp., 1987—; chmn. polit. involvement com. Greater Dallas Bd. Realtors. Mem. Women's Council Realtors (mem. coms. 1979—), Nat. Assn. Corp. Real Estate Execs. (mem. steering com. regional meeting 1983, sec.-treas. 1984-86, chmn. regional conf. 1987), Comml. Real Estate Women (chmn. vol. com. 1988), Nat. Assn. Indsl. and Office Parks, The Exec. Women's Forum (bd. dirs. 1983—), Chi Omega Alumni. Republican, Episcopalian. Office: Ticor Title Ins 350 N St Paul Suite 2500 Dallas TX 75201

SEXTON, JAN BLUE, employment manager, nurse; b. Amarillo, Tex., Nov. 8, 1953; d. N.D. and Juanita (Salmon) Blue. RN diploma, NW Tex. Hosp Sch. Nursing, 1977; BSN, West Tex. State U., 1981. RN, team leader NW Tex. Hosp., Amarillo, 1977-78; RN, team leader High Plains Bapt. Hosp., Amarillo, 1978-79, coordinator nurse recruitment, 1983-86; occupational health nurse Am. Cotton Growers, Littlefield, Tex., 1979-80; head nurse Meth. Hosp., Lubbock, Tex., 1980-81; pub. health nurse Lubbock City Health Dept., 1981-83; recruiting specialist, RN Irving (Tex.) Community Hosp., 1986-87; healthcare recruiter Presbyn. Hosp. of Dallas, 1987-88, employment mgr., 1988—; recruitment cons., seminar speaker Dallas/Ft. Worth Hosp. Council, 1986—. Vice chair March of Dimes Phonathon, Dallas, 1987. Mem. Nat. Assn. Health Care Recruitment, Tex. Assn. Health Care

Recruitment (dist. rep. 1984-85, v.p. 1985-86), Dallas Personnel Assn., Dallas-Ft. Worth Hosps. Personnel Assn., Dallas-Ft. Worth Health Care Recruiters. Office: Presbyn Hosp of Dallas 8200 Walnut Hill Ln Dallas TX 75231

SEYBERT, JANET ROSE, lawyer, military officer; b. Cin., Feb. 7, 1944; d. Peter Robert and Helen Rose (Young) S. BA in Classics, BS in Edn., U. Cin., 1966; MA in Classics, U. Iowa, 1968; JD, Chase Coll. Law, 1975; ML, Army JAG Sch., 1984. Bar: Ohio 1975, U.S. Ct. Mil. Appeals 1975, Colo. 1981, U.S. Ct. Claims 1985. Instr. Latin, ancient history Salem Coll., Winston-Salem, N.C., 1968-70; instr. N.C. Gov.'s Sch., Winston-Salem, N.C., 1969; instr. phys. edn., Latin Kemper Hall, Kenosha, Wis., 1970-71; instr. in Latin Carthage Coll., Kenosha, Wis., 1970-71; commd. 2d lt. USMC, 1972; completed interservice transfer to USAF, 1978, advanced through grades to maj., 1982; lawyer USAF Acad. USAF, Colorado Springs, Colo., 1978-81; chief civil law Sheppard AFB, Tex., 1981-84; dep. staff judge adv., chief mil. justice Homestead AFB, Fla., 1984-88; chief civil law Lowry AFB, Colo., 1988—; legal advisor Armed Forces Disciplinary Control Bd., Child and Family Advocacy Council USAF, Homestead AFB, 1984-88. Vol. Muscular Dystrophy Assn., Colorado Springs, 1978-81; contbr. Ellis Island Restoration Program, Homestead AFB, 1985-88. Mem. ABA, Judge Adv. Assn., Edn. Profl. Assn., Ohio Bar Assn., Colo. Bar Assn., Am. Bus. Women's Assn. (chairperson audit com. Homestead charter chpt., hist. com. 1987, Top 10 Bus. Women 1987, Woman of Yr. 1987), Phi Beta Kappa, Kappa Delta Pi. Home: 378 Florence Aurora CO 80010 Office: USAF LTTC/JA Lowry AFB CO 80230-5000

SEYBOLD, ADELE NEELY, former Democratic nat. committeewoman, civic worker; b. Comanche, Tex., Nov. 11, 1919; d. Eugene Gentry and Nell (Orand) Neely; B.A., U. Tex., 1940; tchrs. certificate U. Tex., 1940; m. Eugene Murphy Locke, Oct. 27, 1941; children—Aimee Locke Jacoble, John, Tom; m. 2d, William Dempsey Seybold, 1977. State chmn. women's activities Tex. gov.'s primary campaign, 1964; mem. Democratic Nat. Com., 1964-66, exec. com., 1964-66. Mem. hospitality bd. Met. Opera, Dallas, 1962-66, 69-70; mem. exec. com. Greater Dallas Council Chs., 1964-66; area chmn. Dallas Mental Health Assn., 1964; bd. dirs. women's group Dallas Council of World Affairs, 1970—, Bishop Mason Retreat and Conf. Center; hon. chmn. pub. edn. Tex. div. Am. Cancer Soc., also bd. dirs.; bd. dirs., sec. to bd. visitors U. Tex. System Cancer Center, M.D. Anderson Hosp. and Tumor Inst.; mem. found. adv. council Coll. Liberal Arts, U. Tex., Austin, mem. exec. com. chancellor's council U. Tex. Timberlawn Found., mem. Fine Arts Commn., U.S. Dept. State. Mem. Daus. Republic Tex. (asso.), Ashbel Lit. Soc., Jr. League, Mus. Fine Arts, Young Women of the Arts, Dallas County Heritage Soc. (dir.), Dallas Jr. Assembly (dir. 1961-64). Soc. for Abandoned and Neglected Children, Mortar Bd., Phi Beta Kappa, Alpha Lambda Delta, Sigma Delta Pi, Phi Eta Sigma, Pi Lambda Theta, Pi Beta Phi. Episcopalian (edn. guild leader). Clubs: Dallas Country, Dallas Woman's; River Oaks Country; Houston, Houston City. Home: 3805 McFarlin Blvd Dallas TX 75205

SEYMOUR, ELLEN KATHLEEN, nursing educator; b. East St. Louis, Ill., Sept. 20, 1951; d. Edward Herman and Vivian Geraldine (Eisele) Schmitt; m. Harlan Francis Seymour, Aug. 17, 1973; children—Melissa Ann, Harlan Francis. R.N., DePaul Hosp., 1971; B.S. in Nursing, St. Louis U., 1977; M.S. in Nursing, U. Ill., 1981. Staff nurse Cardinal Glennon Children's Hosp., St. Louis, 1971-72; dist. nurse Vis. Nurse Assn., St. Louis, 1972-73, liaison nurse, 1973-77; liaison nurse Community Nursing Service, Lombard, Ill., 1977-78, spl. projects coordinator, 1980-81; instr. clin. nursing Ga. Baptist Hosp., Atlanta, 1982—. Mem. Sigma Theta Tau. Roman Catholic. Home: 1662 Barn Swallow Pl Marietta GA 30062

SEYMOUR, MARY FRANCES, lawyer; b. Durand, Wis., Oct. 20, 1948; d. Marshall Willard and Alice Roberta (Smith) Thompson; m. Marshall Warren Seymour, June 6, 1970; 1 foster child, Nghia Pham. BS, U. Wis., LaCrosse, 1970; JD, William Mitchell Coll., 1979. Bar: Minn. 1979, U.S. Dist. Ct. Minn. 1979, U.S. Ct. Appeals (8th cir.) 1979, U.S. Supreme Ct. 1986. With Cochrane and Bresnahan, P.A., St. Paul, 1979—. Mem. Fed. Bar Assn. (bd. dirs. Minn. chpt.), Assn. Trial Lawyers Am., Minn. Bar Assn., Ramsey County Bar Assn., Minn. Trial Lawyers Assn. Office: Cochrane and Bresnahan PA 24 E Fourth St Saint Paul MN 55101

SEYMOUR, MARY POWELL, state senator; b. Raleigh, N.C., Apr. 12, 1922; d. Robert C. and Annie (Seymour) Powell; m. Hubert Elmo Seymour, Feb. 3, 1945; children: Hubert Seymour III, Robert John. AA, Peace Coll., Raleigh, 1941; postgrad., Harvard U., 1946-47, U. Mich., 1949-50. Lic. real estate broker. Legal sec., ct. reporte; sec. to dean Harvard U. Grad. Sch. Bus.; adminstr. med. supply ORD, Greensboro; sec., claims adjustor Social Security; rep. N.C. Gen. Assembly, 1976-84, senator, 1987—; govtl. cons., lobbyist N.C. R.R. Assn., N.C. Bankers Assn., 1985-86; mayor pro tempore City of Greensboro, N.C., 1973-75; mem. Greensboro City Council, 1967-75. Active Tar Heel Triad Girls Scout Council Inc., Hayes Taylor YMCA, N.C. Arts Council, N.C. Parks and Recreation Council, United Arts Council; bd. visitors Peace Coll.; mem. N.C. Inst. Medicine, N.C. Task Force Pub Radio Interconnection, N.C. Bd. Nat. Conf. Ins. Legis., Nat. Conf. State Legis. Telecommunications Com., transp. adv. council, N.C. law-related edn. bd., women and econ. devel. bd. Named Disting. Alumna, Peace Coll., Woman of Yr., Quota Club; recipient Disting. Service award YWCA, Legis. award N.C. Bar Assn., Disting. Service award N.C. Pub. Health, Good Sam award for Legislation for Hearing Impaired, Community Service award Bennett Coll., Legis. award N.C. Recreation and Parks, 1984, Eleanor Roosevelt award, Bryant Citizenship award, Dolley Madison award. Mem. Carolina Soc. Assn. Execs., Women's Profl. Forum, Nat. Order Women Legislators, U.S. Power Squadron. Clubs: O. Henry Womans, Greensboro Council of Garden, Dem. Women, Belews Creek Sailing. Address: 1105 Pender Ln Greensboro NC 27408

SEYMOUR, PATTI FOX, stencil artist; b. N.Y.C., Mar. 14, 1953; d. Arthur T. Fox and Helen Fried; student Pratt Inst., 1970-72; B.F.A., Tufts U. and Sch. Mus. Fine Arts, 1974; m. Terry L. Seymour, Dec. 16, 1979; children—Terence Patrick, Ryan Samuel. Personnel dir. Internat. Weekends, Boston, 1974-76, Career Devel. Team, N.Y.C., 1976-78; asst. to pres., corp. adminstrv. mgr. Interglobal, N.Y.C., 1979-83; membership services dir. Direct Mktg. Assn., N.Y.C., 1983-86; founder Rye Brook Country Stenciling, 1986— . Contbg. author: Guerilla Tactics, 1978.

SEYMOUR, STEPHANIE KULP, federal judge; b. Battle Creek, Mich., Oct. 16, 1940; d. Francis Bruce and Frances Cecelia (Bria) Kulp; m. R. Thomas Seymour, June 10, 1972; children: Bart, Bria, Sara, Anna. B.A. magna cum laude, Smith Coll., 1962; J.D., Harvard U., 1965. Bar: Okla. 1965. Practiced in Boston 1965-66, practiced in Tulsa, 1966-67, 71-79, practiced in Houston, 1968-69; assoc. firm Doerner, Stuart, Saunders, Daniel & Anderson, Tulsa, 1971-75; ptnr. firm Doerner, Stuart, Saunders, Daniel & Anderson, 1975-79; judge U.S. Ct. Appeals 10th Circuit, Tulsa, 1979—; assoc. bar examiner Okla. Bar Assn., 1973-79; trustee Tulsa County Law Library, 1977-78; mem. legal adv. panel Tulsa Task Force on Battered Women, 1971-77. Mem. various task forces Tulsa Human Rights Commn., 1972-76. Mem. Am. Bar Assn., Okla. Bar Assn., Tulsa County Bar Assn., Phi Beta Kappa. Office: US Ct Appeals 4562 US Courthouse 333 W 4th St Tulsa OK 74103 *

SHABAREKH, THERESA EVERS, retail management executive; b. St. Joseph, Tenn., Nov. 18, 1951; d. William Thomas and Cecilia Wilhemina (Halter) Evers; m. Robert Allen Shabarekh, July 3, 1976. Staff acct. Service Mdse. Co. Inc., Nashville, 1973-75, sr. acct., 1975-79, mgr. coop. advt., 1979-81, mgr. mdse. control, 1981-84, dir. mdse. control, 1984-86, dir. mdse. support, 1986-88, dir. special projects, 1988—. Mem. Am. Soc. Women Accts. (nat. bd. dirs. 1984-86, chpt. pres. 1980), Nat. Assn. Accts. (chpt. bd. dirs. 1987—), Nat. Assn. Female Execs. Office: Service Merchandise Co Inc PO Box 24600 Nashville TN 37202

SHABAZZ, AIYSHA MUSLIMAH, social work administrator; b. Columbia, S.C., Aug. 9, 1942; d. Jerry James Gadson and Edna Louise (Bellinger) Gadson Smalls; m. Abdullah Muslim Shabazz, July 28, 1959; children: Ain, Wali. BA, Fed. City Coll., Washington, 1973; postgrad., Howard U., 1973, U. S.C., 1979-80. Cert. child protective services investigator, S.C. Sec., asst. social worker Family Service Ctr., Washington, 1966-68; admission counselor Washington Tech. Inst., Washington, 1968-70; program dir. Park Motor Community Ctr., Washington, 1970-75; adminstrv. asst. Neighborhood Planning Council, Washington, 1974-75; substitue tchr. D.C. Pub. Sch. System, Washington, 1974-75; substitute tchr. Dist. I Pub. Schs., Columbia, 1977; home sch. coordinator Community Care, Inc., Columbia, 1977-81; monitor summer program U. S.C., Columbia, 1982; with Dept. Social Services, Columbia, 1984—, case auditor, 1987-88, social worker supr., 1988—. Sec. Travel Audit Com., Columbia, 1987-88, Dept. Youth Services, Columbia, 1988—; bd. dirs. Frederick Douglas Inst., Washington, 1968-69; pres. Park Motor Resident council, Washington, 1972-75; expert witness Family Ct. Fellow State Dept. health; mem. S.C. Child Abuse Neglect Task Force, AIDS Task Force (chmn. 1987—). Democrat. Muslim. Home: 119 Butternut Ln Columbia SC 29210 Office: Dept Social Services 2020 Hampton St Columbia SC 29204

SHABBIR, MAHNAZ MEHDI, healthcare marketing manager; b. Phila., Apr. 6, 1959; d. M.I. and Meher (Mehdi) Ali Khan; m. S. Farrukh Shabbir, June 29,1979; children: S. Ali, S. Adil. BBA, U. Mo., 1982, MBA, 1984. Resident adminstrv. Bapt. Med. Ctr., Kansas City, 1983-84; with gerontology practicum Mid-Am. Regional Council, Kansas City, 1984; mkt. research analyst St. Joseph Health Ctr., Kansas City, 1984-87; dir. mktg. and planning support services Carondelet Health Corp., Kansas City, 1987—; mentor U. Mo., 1987. Fund raiser United Way, 1986-87. Mem. Am. Coll. Health Execs. (adv. council 1986—), Kansas City Regional Soc. Healthcare Planning and Mktg. (pres. 1986-87), Am. Mktg. Assn., Soc. Healthcare Planning and Mktg. Home: 13009 St Andrew Dr Kansas City MO 64145 Office: Carondelet Health Corp 1310 Carondelet St Suite 230 Kansas City MO 64114

SHABEL, KAREN LIND, printing company executive; b. East Chicago, Ind., Oct. 3, 1948; d. Earl R. Lind; m. Dennis Shabel. A.B., Ind. U., 1970. Tchr. Gen. Edn. Devel. program OEO, 1970-72; dir. consumer div. Better Bus. Bur., Chgo., 1972-77; pres. Communicate, Inc., Westchester, Ill., 1977—; mem. faculty adult continuing edn. dept. Moraine Valley Community Coll., 1974-76; speaker various colls. and univs., civic and community orgns.; arbitrator constrn. panel Am. Arbitration Assn. Past bd. dirs., past sec. to bd. N.Am. Family and Ednl. Resources Found.; v.p. Oakwood Homeowners Assn.; past trustee Ill. Council on Econ. Edn.; v.p. Oakwood Homeowners Assn.; consumer div., adv. council Better Bus. Bur., Chgo.; past bd. dirs., v.p. local PTO Manning Sch. Dist. 201; bd. dirs.local Luth. ch. women, DAR, La Grange, Ill.; past bd. dirs. Family Fin. Counseling Service Greater Chgo.; past mem. nursing and health programs com. Mid-West chpt. ARC. Mem. AAUW (sec. Oak Brook, Ill. chpt.), Soc. Consumer Affairs Profls. (founding and charter mem.), DAR (corr. sec. La Grange, Ill. chpt.). Office: Communicate Inc 10407 W Cermak Rd Westchester IL 60153

SHACKELFORD, JUDITH A., toy company executive; b. 1941. BS, So. Ill. U., 1963. Product mgr. Marvin Glass & Assocs., 1975-76; mgr. pre-sch. toys div. Mattel, Inc., Hawthorne, Calif., 1976-78, dir. mktg., 1978-79, v.p. dolls and pre-sch. toys div., 1979-82, sr. v.p., 1982-85, exec. v.p., 1985—. Office: Mattel Inc 5150 Rosecrans Ave Hawthorne CA 90250 *

SHACKELFORD, LAUREL, editor, writer; b. New Brunswick, N.J., Nov. 19, 1946; d. James Murdoch and Laura (Stevens) S.; m. Donald R. Anderson, June 18, 1971. Student Rutgers U., 1964, Upsala Coll., 1964-66; A.B., U. N.C., 1968. Writer Civil Rights Digest, Washington, 1968-69; reporter Louisville Times, 1969-73, 76-79, city editor, 1982-86; editorial writer Courier Jour., 1986—; editor Appalachian Oral History, Pippa Passes, Ky., 1973-75; asst. city editor Courier Jour., Louisville, 1979-82. Contbr. articles to various publs.; editor: Our Appalachia: An Oral History (Weatherford award 1972), 1971. Nieman fellow Harvard U., 1981. Office: Louisville Courier-Jour 525 W Broadway Louisville KY 40202

SHACKELFORD, LOTTIE, mayor. BBA, Philander Smith Coll., Little Rock; Hon. Human Letters, Philander Smith Coll., 1988; student, Harvard U., Hendrix Coll., U. Ark., Little Rock. City dir. City of Little Rock, 1978-87, mayor, 1987—; del. Italian Econ. Trade Mission, 1987, U.S.-Soviet Women's Wilderness Dialogue, USSR, 1987; panelist Harvard U. Inst. Polits. Pub. Affairs Forum, 1987; bd. dirs. Little Rock Advt. and Promotion, Econ. Opportunity Agy., Little Rock Job Corps, Elizabeth Mitchell's Children Ctr., Links, Inc.; adv. com. Ark. Vocat. and Tech. Edn., Sta. KARK-TV; speaker in field. Del., platform com. mem. Dem. Nat. Conv., San Francisco, 1984; active Dem. Policy Commn.; bd. dirs. Nat. League Cities', So. Regional Council, Atlanta, Ark. Mcpl. League, Ark. Women's Polit. Council, Urban League, ARC, Ark. State PTA, YWCA; regional dir. Nat. Black Caucus of Local Elected Ofcls., 1979—; youth dir. St. Peter's Bapt. Ch., 1969-73; pres. Little Rock PTA Council, 1973; coordinator human and civil rights workshops, 1975-77; co-chair Little Rock Sch. Dist. Bi-Racial Com., 1968, Com. for Better Gov., 1976; project chmn. United Way, 1974, others. Recipient Women of Style award Pulaski County Council, 1987. Mem. Nat. Assn. State Dem. Chairs (sec.), Delta Sigma Theta, Gamma Phi Delta, Alpha Kappa Mu. Office: Office of the Mayor 500 W Markham St Little Rock AR 72201

SHACKELFORD, MARY JO, personnel executive; b. Zanesville, Ohio, Mar. 7, 1949; d. Moneer and Nellie Rita Hatem; m. Douglas A. Shackelford, Dec. 14, 1968; 1 child, Joseph. BA, Ohio Dominican Coll., 1977. Sales coordinator Roach, Inc., Columbus, Ohio, 1977-78; instr. Milw. Stratten Coll., 1978-81; franchise owner Norrell Corp., Atlanta, 1981-84, dist. mgr., 1984-87; regional mgr. Word Processors Personnel Inc., Palo Alto, Calif., 1987—; mem. franchise adv. bd. Norrell Services, Inc., Atlanta, 1983-84, ops. task force, 1984—, mem. Pres.'s Club, 1985-86. Bd. dirs women's aux. St. Francis CAAC, Milw., 1978-81, v.p. 1980-81; bd. dirs. St. Vincent's Children's Ctr., Columbus, Ohio, 1976-78; vol. Spl. Olympics, West Chester, Pa.; mem. adv. bd. Lima Tech. Ohio State U., 1982-84. Mem. Bus. and Profl. Women, Nat. Assn. Female Execs., Nat. Mgmt. Assn. (chair arrangements 1981-84). Democrat. Roman Catholic. Home: 886 Westtown Rd West Chester PA 19382 Office: Word Processors Personnel 490 S California Ave Palo Alto CA 94306

SHACKLETT, MARY E., infosystems specialist; b. Milw., Nov. 20, 1952. Mgr. infosystems FSI Internat., Chaska, Minn. Home: 5738 Holiday Ct Minnetonka MN 55345 Office: FSI Internat 322 Lake Hazeltine Dr Chaska MN 55318

SHADLE, SUSAN BETH, security company executive; b. Pottsville, Pa., July 6, 1957; d. Irvin Elias and Louise Hilman (Reise) S. B.S., Pa. State U.-Middletown, 1979. Security supr. Marriott Hotel, Harrisburg, Pa., 1980-81; officer Paxtang Police Dept., Harrisburg, 1980-81; press attendant AMP Inc., Tower City, Pa., 1981; officer U.S. Secret Service, Washington, 1981-82; ops. supr. MVM Inc, Washington, 1982-86; mgr. in charge Boston br., Guardsmark, Inc., Memphis, 1987—; resident mgr. mass dept. pub. safety, 1984—. Mem. Nat. Assn. Female Execs., Am. Soc. Indsl. Security. Republican. Home: 26 Chestnut W Randolph MA 02368 Office: Guardsmark Inc 31 Milk St Boston MA 02109

SHAFER, ETTA BEESLEY, insurance agent; b. Vevay, Ind., May 31, 1950; d. Chester Glen and Irma Elaine (Browning) Fivecoat; m. Daniel R. Beesley, May 1970 (div. June 1980); children: Shaun, Vanessa, Lance; m. Robert Z. Shafer, July 4, 1980; stepchildren: Jack Shafer, Jill Shafer. Gen. lines, surety, life and health agt. Friendly Ins. Co., Kissimmee, Fla., 1981-87, Preferred Ins. Agy., Kissimmee, 1987—. Active Young Reps., St. Cloud, Fla. Mem. Am. Soc. Notaries, Nat. Assn. Ins. Women, Profl. Ins. Agts. Soc., Fla. Surety Agts. Assn. (cert.). Methodist. Lodges: Order Eastern Star (past matron asst. mother advisor Rainbow Girls), Odd Fellows (Deborah Rebecca lodge). Home: 206 Vermont Ave Saint Cloud FL 32769 Office: Preferred Ins Agy 10 E Monument Ave Kissimmee FL 32741

SHAFER, SHERRY R(AE), marketing and communication research company executive; b. Nebraska City, Nebr., June 27, 1941; d. Ken E. and Harriet V. (Johnson) Norris; children—Brent, Brad, Romy. B.A., Drake U., 1980, M.A. candidate, 1986. Paralegal staff mem. Leff, Leff, Leff, Iowa City, 1961-65; office mgr., physician's office, Los Angeles, 1971-75; account exec., pub. relations PFC, Des Moines, 1978; researcher IPBN, Des Moines, 1979; communication asst. City of Des Moines, 1979-80; asst. dir. pub. relations Iowa Methodist Med. Ctr., Des Moines, 1981-84; pres. K&S Assocs., West Des Moines, 1985—. Mem. Pub. Relations Soc. Am., (accredited, Iowa bd. dirs.), Women in Communication, Inc. (Iowa bd. dirs.), C. of C. (small bus. com.), Friday Forum, Round table, Theta Alumni Assn.

SHAFFER, ANITA MOHRLAND, educator, counselor; b. Racine, Wis., Apr. 5, 1939; d. Milton Arthur and Gudrun Amanda (Sundvoll) Stoffel; m. Ronald Dean Williams, June 24, 1987. BS magna cum laude, U. Wis.-Madison, 1961; MEd, U. Wash., 1966; postgrad. Ariz. State U., 1971-76. Cert. in elem. edn., social sci. secondary edn., spl edn., Tex., Ariz.; lic. profl. counselor, Tex.; diplomate Internat. Acad. Behavioral Medicine, Counseling and Psychotherapy. Tchr. Racine Unified Dist. 1, 1961-63, Edmonds Sch. Dist. 15, Alderwood Manor, Wash., 1963-70; tchr. Ariz. Dept. Corrections, Phoenix, 1971-77; tchr. spl. edn. Pasadena Ind. Sch. Dist. (Tex.); 1977-78, spl. edn. counselor, 1978—. Mem. Am. Assn. Counseling and Devel., Am. Mental Health Counselors Assn., Am. Sch. Counselor Assn., Tex. Assn. Counseling and Devel., AAUW, Nat. Assn. Female Execs., Mus. Fine Arts Houston (patron), Beta Sigma Phi, Pi Lambda Theta. Home: 260 El Dorado Blvd Apt 801 Webster TX 77598 Office: Pasadena Ind Sch Dist Spl Services 3010 Bayshore Dr Pasadena TX 77502

SHAFFER, AUDREY JEANNE, medical records administrator, educator; b. Hutchinson, Minn., Nov. 24, 1929; d. Floyd R. and Edna C. (Seppman) Kleiman; m. Frank L. Shaffer, July 15, 1948; 1 child, Cynthia Louise Shaffer Wilkinson. B.S., Loma Linda U., 1973; M.A., Central Mich. U., 1982. Registered records adminstr. Med. records clk. San Bernardino County Hosp., Calif., 1948-50; radiology receptionist White Meml. Med. Ctr., Los Angeles, 1950-52; med. records clk. Portland Adventist Hosp., Oreg., 1952-53; med. record mgr. Tempe Community Hosp., Ariz., 1953-54; clin. faculty Loma Linda U., Calif., 1975—; dir. med. info. services Corona Community Hosp., Calif., 1973—; med. records cons. Calif., Utah and Philippines Pilot, med. asst. Liga Internat., Mex., 1964-68; chmn. Corona Blood Bank, 1957-68; chmn. vols. Corona Community Hosp. Aux., 1965-68; archaeology supr. Caesarea Expdn., Am. Schs. Oriental Research, Israel, summers 1974—. Recipient Vol. Service award Corona Community Hosp., 1968; Congeniality award Caesarea Archeol. Expdn., 1975. Mem. Loma Linda U. Med. Record Alumni (pres. 1979-81), Am. Med. Record Assn., Calif. Med. Record Assn. (quality assurance com. 1980-81), Nat. Assn. Quality Assurance Profls., Archeol. Inst. Am., Inland Quality Assurance Network (pres. 1988). Clubs: Women's Improvement (program chmn. 1960-61), Corona Flying (sec. 1960-68) (Corona). Home: 880 Encanto Dr Corona CA 91719 Office: Corona Community Hosp 800 S Main St Corona CA 91720

SHAFFER, CAROLYN (CARI) LEE, temporary staffing service executive; b. Denver, June 3, 1944; d. Richard Michael, Sr. and Joyce Adele (Carnahan) Knoll; m. Charles Larry Shaffer, Dec. 11, 1965; 1 child, Kelly Michael. Student, So. Oreg. Coll., 1962-64, U. Nev., 1964-78. Free lance sec. Colorado Springs, Colo., 1977-80; mgr. Accel Temporaries Colorado Springs, 1980-82, MG Temps div. Marshall Group, Colorado Springs, 1982-84; owner, mgr. Add Staff, Inc., Colorado Springs, 1984—; bd. dirs. Tech. Research Assocs., Colorado Springs, 1971-73. Spl. events chmn. London county unit Am. Cancer Soc., Sterling, Va., 1975-77; speaker for Goodwill, Colorado Springs, 1980—, Wagon Wheel council Girl Scouts U.S., Colorado Springs, 1980—, Jr. Achievement, Colorado Springs, 1980—, U. Colo., 1984, Pikes Peak Community Coll., 1984, Blair Jr. Coll., 1984, Pikes Peak Inst., 1984. Mem. Internat. Assn. Personnel Women (v.p. 1982-83), Colorado Springs Personnel Women (pres. 1983—), Adminstrv. Mgmt. Soc. (salary survey chmn. 1984—), Am. Soc. For Tng. and Devel., Amigos de Ser, Colorado Springs C. of C. (life mem., chmn. ambassador club, chamber vice chmn. exec. com. 1985-86, Ambassador of Yr. award 1984, exec. com. 1986), Woman of the Year award 1988. Republican. Roman Catholic. Club: Little People of Am. (Colorado Springs). Office: Add Staff Inc 6155 Lehman Dr Suite 205 Colorado Springs CO 80918

SHAFFER, DOROTHY BROWNE, educator, mathematician; b. Vienna, Austria, Feb. 12, 1923; d. Hermann and Steffy (Hermann) Browne; arrived U.S., 1940; naturalized, 1944; m. Lloyd Hamilton Shaffer, July 25, 1943 (dec. 1978); children—Deborah Lee, Diana Louise, Dorothy Leslie. A.B., Bryn Mawr Coll., 1943; M.A., Harvard U., 1945, Ph.D., 1962. Mathematician, MIT, Cambridge, 1945-47; tchg. fellow, research asso., Harvard U., Cambridge, 1947-48; asso. mathematician Cornell Aeronautical Lab, Buffalo, N.Y., 1952-56; mathematician Dunlap & Assoc., Stamford, Conn., 1958-60, lectr. grad. engrng. U. of Conn. at Stamford, 1962; prof. math Fairfield (Conn.) U., 1963—; vis. prof. Imperial Coll. Sci. and Tech., London, fall 1978, U. Md., College Park, spring 1981; vis. prof. U. Calif.-San Diego, summer 1981; vis. scholar, 1986; NSF faculty fellow IBM-T.J. Watson Research Center, Yorktown Heights, N.Y., 1979. Contbr. numerous papers in math. analysis. Mem. Am. Math. Soc., Math. Assn. of Am., Assn. for Women in Math., London Math. Soc. Home: 156 Intervale Rd Stamford CT 06905 Office: Fairfield U Dept of Math & Computer Sci Fairfield CT 06430

SHAFFER, GAIL S., state government official; b. Kingston, N.Y., Aug. 1, 1948; d. Robert E. and Marion (Gallagher) S. BA summa cum laude, Elmira Coll., 1970; student, U. Paris, 1968-69. Editor Sam Har Press, 1972-76; legal asst. Rahmas Law Firm, 1973-76; spl. asst. to commr. N.Y. State Environ. Conservation, 1977-79; exec. dir. N.Y. State Rural Affairs Council, 1979-80; mem. NY. State Assembly, 1981-83; sec. state State of N.Y., Albany, 1983—. Mem. N.Y. State Democratic Com., 1976—. Mem. Phi Beta Kappa. Presbyterian. Office: Office of Sec of State State of New York 162 Washington Ave Albany NY 12231

SHAFFER, JUDY ANN, educator, data processing professional; b. Boone, Iowa, Dec. 24, 1942; d. Vernon Sherwood and Josephine (Bean) Peterson; m. James Nelson Shaffer, Jr., Feb. 28, 1970. B.S., Morningside Coll., 1965; M.S., Iowa State U., 1969. Cert. tchr., Va. Tchr. math. Plaza Jr. High Sch., Virginia Beach, 1971; instr. Ivy Ind. Vocat. Tech. Coll., Ft. Wayne, Ind., 1973-74, Ind. Purdue U., Fort Wayne, 1974-76; programmer Bowmar, Fort Wayne, 1976-77; programmer analyst GTE Data Service, Fort Wayne, 1977-79, sr. programmer analyst, supr. ops. Med. Mgmt. Systems Inc., Fort Wayne, 1979-87, instr. Dept. Math. Scis., Ind., Purdue, Ft. Wayne, 1987—; mem. assoc. faculty IPFW, Fort Wayne, 1984-85. Charter mem. Ft. Wayne Area Community Band, 1979—, personnel mgr., 1979-84; mem. Ft. Wayne Women's Bur., 1977—, Career Planners, Ft. Wayne, 1985—. Mem. PEO (treas. 1973-75), Kappa Mu Epsilon. Avocations: music; model railroading; gardening.

SHAFFER, KAREN ALICE, lawyer, educator; b. Dayton, Ohio, Oct. 12, 1947; d. John Richard and Helen Maxine (Baker) S. BA, The Am. U., 1969, JD, 1972. Bar: D.C. 1973, Va. 1987. Dir. placement and alumni office The Am. U. Law Sch., Washington, 1972-73; atty., advisor Interstate Commerce Commn., Washington, 1974, U.S. Dept. of Interior, Washington, 1974-78; sole practice Washington, 1978-81, 85—; counsel interior U.S. Ho. Reps., Washington, 1981-85; mem. com. on disposal excess spoil Nat. Acad. Scis., Washington, 1980-81; cons. Nat. Coal Council, Arlington, Va., 1986; guest speaker First Am. Violin Congress, U. Md., 1987. Author: Maud Powell, Pioneer American Violinist, 1988; contbr. articles to profl. jours. Chair The Maud Powell Found., Arlington, 1986—; sec. Washington Bach Consort, Washington, 1986-88; bd. dirs. Gary Karr Doublebass Found., Conn., 1984—. Mem. ABA, Washington Area Lawyers for Arts. Republican. Methodist. Home and Office: 5333 N 26th St Arlington VA 22207

SHAFFER, SUSAN E., insurance company administrator; b. Nashville, Apr. 14, 1947; d. James G. and Esther W. Shaffer; m. Robert Gallinari, June 30, 1982. B.A. in English, Elmhurst (Ill.) Coll., 1969; postgrad. Rutgers U., 1987—. Mem. claim dept. Allstate Ins. Co., 1971-76, unit mgr., Springfield, Pa., 1976-77, regional life claim mgr., Basking Ridge, N.J., 1977-79, dist. claim mgr., Latham, N.Y., 1979-87. Mem. Albany Claim Mgrs. Council, Colonie C. of C., Life Office Mgmt. Assn., Ins. Inst. Am. (asso. in mgmt.). Office: 700 Troy Schenectady Rd Latham NY 12110

SHAFFNER, CLAIRE RUSSELL, broadcast executive; b. Durham, N.C., Sept. 19, 1932; d. Charles Phillips and Caro Mae (Green) Russell; m. Henry William Cheney, Sept. 5, 1955; children: Jeffrey Phillips, Caroline Elizabeth, Robert Walton, Elinor Avery; m. Fries Shaffner, Sept. 26, 1969 (div. 1975); children: Josephine Walker, Amalie Fries. AB, U. N.C., 1955. Cert. Nat. Assn. Broadcasters. Gen. mgr. Sta. WAYS/WROQ, Charlotte, N.C., 1978-

80, Sta. WTMA/WSSX, Charleston, S.C., 1980-81; v.p., gen. mgr. Sta. WRAL-FM, Raleigh, N.C., 1981-83, Sta. WRNC/WRXL, Richmond, Va., 1983—. Pres. Better Bus. Bur., Charlotte, 1979-80; sec. Advt. Club, Charlotte, 1978-79; bd. dirs. Goodwill Industries, Richmond, 1987—, Family & Children's Service, 1988—. Mem. Richmond Broadcasters Assn. (pres. 1986-87). Democrat. Episcopalian. Club: Richmond Ad. Home: 2510 Stuart Ave Richmond VA 23220 Office: Sta WRNL/WRXL 3245 Basie Rd Richmond VA 23228

SHAFIR, GRACE CHASTAIN, sales and marketing executive; b. Anderson, S.C., May 5, 1948; d. David Ramsey and Margaret Caroline (Littlejohn) Chastain; m. Jere Adam Shafir, Dec. 15, 1972 (dec.); children: Nicole, Melody, Jereann, Georgeanna; m. Robert Sidney Reiss, Apr. 30, 1988. BA in journalism, U. S.C., 1970. Treas. Kingshead Corp., Hackensack, N.J., 1972-84; v.p. sales and advt. Kingshead Corp., Hackensack, 1979-81, pres., 1981—. Mem. Com. of 200, Nat. Assn. Chain Drug Stores, Nat. Mass Retailing Inst., Nat. Sch. Supply & Equipment Assn., Nat. Assn. Service Merchandisers, Mortar Board, Phi Beta Kappa, Kappa Tau Alpha. Republican. Presbyterian. Clubs: Coral Ridge Country, Ft. Lauderale, Englewood Field. Office: Kingshead Corp 165 Chubb Ave Lyndhurst NJ 07071

SHAFTON, GAIL ANN, health care executive; b. Fond Du Lac, Wis., May 8, 1948; d. Harold John and Willie Belle (Hathaway) Rautenberg; m. Joel Roger Shafton (div.); children: Alan, Aaron, Jacob. BA in Edn., U. Mo., 1971; BS in Nursing, U. Kans., 1983. Cancer nurse Menorah Med. Ctr., Kansas City, Mo., 1983-84; case mgr. Care Options, Inc., Kansas City, 1984-86; pres., chief exec. officer Managed Healthcare Resources, Prairie Village, Kans., 1986—; mng. ptnr. Quality Healthcare Resources, Kansas City, 1986—; cons. Blue Cross & Blue Shield of Kansas City, 1986—. Mem. Am. Med. Care and Rev. Assn., Am. Assn. for Continuity of Care, Group HEalth Assn., Nat. Assn. Female Execs., Nurse Cons. Assn., Sigma Theta Tau. Office: Managed Healthcare Resources 7930 State Line Suite 214 Prairie Village KS 66208

SHAHINIAN, SIROON PASHALIAN, psychologist; b. N.Y.C., June 28, 1926; d. Leon and Margaret (Mardirosian) Pashalian; m. Zareh Shahinian, Dec. 5, 1960 (dec. Aug. 1987); 1 child, John Zareh. BA in Math., CUNY, 1946; MA in Indsl. Psychology, NYU, 1949, PhD in Indsl. Psychology, 1957. Lic. psychologist, N.Y. Research assoc. in psychology Fordham U., Bronx, N.Y., 1951-53; researcher Aging Community Service Soc., N.Y.C., 1955-58; asst. personnel mgr. N.W. Moody Corp., Flushing, N.Y., 1958-59; staff assoc. Herrold Assocs., N.Y.C., 1959-60; field interviewer Lea, Inc., Ambler, Pa., 1960-72; research psychologist N.Y. State Dept. Mental Hygiene, Queens Village, N.Y., 1961-68; research assoc. Hillside Hosp., Glen Oaks, N.Y., 1965-69; placement counselor Alpha Employment Agy., Great Neck, N.Y., 1971-72; adminstrv. asst. N.Y. State Psychol. Assn., N.Y.C., 1972; instr. and placement counselor York Coll. CUNY, Jamaica, N.Y., 1972-76; asst. prof. St. John's U., Jamaica, 1977-78; adminstrv. asst. City Hosp. at Elmhurst, N.Y., 1981—; vis. lectr. in human devel. Empire State Coll. L.I. Regional Ctr., 1979-80. Contbr. articles to profl. jours. sec., trustee Student Fund of the Union of Marash Armenians, N.Y.C., 1982—; past sec. Career Adv. Council Great Neck Pub. Schs., chmn., 1980-85; past bd. dirs. Hye Bardez Nursery Sch., Bayside, N.Y.; past exec. sec. N.Y. Armenian Home for the Aged, Flushing; former chmn. scholarship com. Armenian Relief Soc. NIMH grantee, 1965. Mem. Am. Psychol. Assn., Nassau County Psychol. Assn. (employment com.), Eastern Psychol. Assn., Met. N.Y. Assn. Applied Psychology, Psi Chi. Mem. Armenian Apostolic Ch. Lodge: Daus. of Vartan. Home: 1 Sussex Rd Great Neck NY 11020-1828

SHAILER, SUZANNE CAMP, bank operations officer; b. Waterbury, Conn., July 21, 1952; d. Harold Read and Nance (Camp) S. BA in English, Skidmore Coll., 1974; postgrad., U. Phoenix. Various clerical positions United Bank of Denver, 1974-77, systems analyst, 1979-80, float mgmt. analyst, 1980-85, float administr., 1985-88; writer, analyst United Banks Service Co. subs. United Banks Co., Denver, 1977-79; float adminstr. Barnett Ops. Co. (subs. United Bank Denver), Jacksonville, Fla., 1988—. Bd. dirs. Denver chpt. Young Audiences. Office: Barnett Ops Co 7898 Baymeadowsway Suite 200 Jacksonville FL 32216

SHAKER, SALLAMA M., diplomat; b. Cairo, Egypt, Dec. 25, 1948; came to U.S., 1983; d. Mahmoud and Fullah (Ahmad) S.; m. Ghaleb Abdul-Rahman, Apr. 11, 1987. B in Politics, Royal U. of Malta, 1967; M in Econs., London Sch. Econs., 1977. Attaché Embassy of Egypt, Malta, 1973-77; second sec. Embassy of Egypt, Turkey, 1978-82; third sec. Office of Asst. to Foreign Minister, Cairo, 1977-78, first sec., 1982-83; counselor, consul gen. Consulate of Egypt, Washington, 1985—. Rockefeller scholar Rockefeller Found, 1983-85, MIIP scholar Johns Hopkins, 1984-87. Home: 4200 Cathedral Ave #507 Washington DC 20016 Office: Consulate of Egypt 2300 Decatur Pl Washington DC 20008

SHALALA, DONNA EDNA, political scientist, educator; b. Cleve., Feb. 14, 1941; d. James Abraham and Edna (Smith) S. AB, Western Coll., 1962; MSSC, Syracuse U., 1968, PhD, 1970; 12 hon. degrees, 1981-88. Vol. Peace Corps, Iran, 1962-64; asst. to dir. met. studies program Syracuse U., 1965-69; instr. asst. to dean Syracuse U. (Maxwell Grad. Sch.), 1969-70; asst. prof. polit. sci. Bernard M. Baruch Coll., U. City N.Y., 1970-72; assoc. prof. politics and edn. Tchrs. Coll. Columbia U., 1972-79; asst. sec. for policy devel. and research HUD, Washington, 1977-80; prof. polit. sci., pres. Hunter Coll., CUNY, 1980-88; prof. polit. sci., chancellor U. Wis., Madison, 1988—. Author: Neighborhood Governance, 1971, The City and the Constitution, 1972, The Property Tax and the Voters, 1973, The Decentralization Approach, 1974. Gov. Am. Stock Exchange, 1981-87; trustee TIAA, 1985—, Com. Econ. Devel., 1982—; bd. dirs. Inst. Internat. Econs., 1981—, Children's Def. Fund, 1980—, Am. Ditchley Found., 1982—. Ohio Newspaper Women's scholar, 1958; Western Coll. Trustees scholar, 1958-62; Carnegie fellow, 1966-68; Nat. Acad. Edn. Spencer fellow, 1972-73; Guggenheim fellow, 1975-76. Mem. Am. Polit. Sci. Assn., Am. Soc. Public Adminstrn., Nat. Acad. Public Adminstrn., Council Fgn. Relations, Nat. Acad. Edn. Office: U Wis-Madison 158 Bascom Hall 500 Lincoln Dr Madison WI 53706

SHALLAHAMER, PATRICIA ANN, pharmaceutical representative; b. Akron, Aug. 13, 1959; d. Russell Freeman and Marilyn Lois (Gsellman) Doty; m. John J. Shallahamer, Nov. 29, 1986. BS in Nursing, Akron U., 1981; postgrad., Kent State U. Cert. R.N., Ohio. R.N. Akron Gen. Med. Ctr., 1981-83; ctr. coordinator Medaccess, Inc., Akron, 1983-86; sales rep. Smith-Kline & French, Canton, Ohio, 1986-87; mgr. hosp. based health care facility St. Thomas Med. Ctr., Hudson, Ohio, 1987—. Mem. Sigma Theta Tau.

SHANAHAN, TERRY FREY, auditor; b. Chgo., Oct. 10, 1958; d. Donald W. and Theresa Marie (Rippel) Frey; m. Cornelius Matthew Shanahan, July 11, 1981; 1 child, Bryan Matthew Frey. BA, Northeastern Bus. Coll., Chgo., 1982. CPA, Ill. With Citizens Bank & Trust Co., Park Ridge, Ill., 1978-87, acctg. officer, 1981-83, experienced staff auditor, 1983-85, asst. auditor, 1985-87; audit officer, mgr. NBD High Park (Ill.) Bank, N.A., 1987—. Mem. Assn. Chgo. Bank Women, Nat. Assn. Female Execs. Office: Citizens Bank & Trust Co 1 S Northwest Hwy Park Ridge IL 60068

SHANAS, ETHEL, sociology educator; b. Chgo., Sept. 6, 1914; d. Alex and Rebecca (Rich) S.; m. Lester J. Perlman, May 17, 1940; 1 child, Michael Stephen. A.B., U. Chgo., 1935, A.M., 1937, Ph.D., 1949; L.H.D. (hon.), Hunter Coll., N.Y.C., 1985. Instr. human devel. U. Chgo., 1947-52, research assoc. prof., 1961-65; sr. research analyst City of Chgo., 1952-53; sr. study dir. Nat. Opinion Research Ctr., Chgo., 1956-61; prof. sociology U. Ill.-Chgo., 1965-82, prof. emerita, 1982—; vice chmn. expert com. on aging UN, 1974; mem. com. on aging NRC, Washington, 1978-82, panel on statistics for an aging population, 1984-86; mem. U.S. Com. on Vital and Health Stats., Washington, 1976-79. Author: The Health of Older People, 1962; (with others) Old People in Three Industrial Societies, 1968; editor: (with others) Handbook of Aging and the Social Sciences, 1976, 2d edit., 1985. Bd. govs. Chgo. Heart Assn., 1972-80; mem. adv. council on aging City of Chgo., 1972-78. Keston lectr. U. So. Calif., 1975; recipient Burgess award Nat. Council on Family Relations, 1978. Fellow Gerontol. Soc. Am. (pres. 1974-75, Kleemeier award 1977, Brookdale award 1981), Am. Sociol. Assn. (chmn. sect. on aging 1985-86 Disting. Scholar award, 1987); mem. Midwest Sociol. Soc. (pres. 1980-81), Inst. Medicine of Nat. Acad. Scis. (sr. mem.). Home: 222 Main St Evanston IL 60202 Office: U Ill-Chgo Dept Sociology PO Box 4348 Chicago IL 60680

SHANE, DEBORAH LYNNE, broadcasting executive; b. Chgo., Mar. 24, 1950; d. Raymond and Francine Shane; student Bradley U., 1967-68; B.A., U. Miami, 1971, Ph.D., 1977. Performer, Theatre on the Lake, Chgo., summer 1967; asst. programming dir., disk jockey, audio engr. WRBU-AM, Peoria, Ill., 1967-68; asst. sta. mgr., audio engr. WTVP-TV, Peoria, 1967-68; performer, tech. adviser Ring Theatre Childrens Theatre Touring Co., Miami, Fla., 1968; asst. producer, dir. pub. affairs and childrens programming Learning Ladder, WPLG-TV, Miami, 1969-70; asst. programming dir. WINZ-AM, Miami, 1970-71; Midwest office mgr., dir. pub. relations and communications Gulf Leasing Corp., Chgo., 1971-72; comedy scriptwriter, guest performer Bozo's Circus, WGN-TV, Chgo., 1973-75; freelance writer, producer, dir. and performer for radio, television, films and theatre, Chgo., 1975-77; co-hostess, writer-producer television show Self Discovery from A to Z, WLRN-TV, Miami, 1977; v.p. broadcast and communications div. Asso. Leasing Internat. Corp., Ft. Lauderdale, Fla., 1977—; cons. Miami and S.E. Fla. area U.S. Inst. Theatre Tech.; guest author Lighting Dimensions mag.; guest author Backstage Mag.; asst. instr. U. Wis. Summer Speech Inst. Press coordinator Gov. Askew's Sunshine Amendment Day, Miami, 1976. Recipient B'nai B'rith Woman of Year award for pub. service to Greater Chgo. Met. Community, 1974; judge 17th Ann. Chgo. Emmy awards, 1975, 11th ann. Fla. Hosp. Pub. Relations awards, 1978; awarded Key to City of Miami Beach, 1979. Mem. Am. Women in Radio and TV (membership chmn., dir., 1976, pres. chpt. 1977-80, mem Speakers Bur. 1971—), AFTRA, Soc. Motion Picture and TV Engrs., Fla. Motion Picture and TV Assn. (rec. sec., dir., com. chmn. state bd.), Nat. Acad. TV Arts and Sci. (bd. govs.), Women in Communications, Playwrights Center (charter), Chgo. Women in Broadcasting (Spl. award for promoting better children's programming 1973, Radio and TV appreciation award 1978, 79), Panhellenic Assn. Ft. Lauderdale, Women's Fla. Assn. Broadcasters (pres. 1978-83), U. Miami Young Alumni Assn., Nat. Thespians Troupe 113 (life), Am. Soc. Notaries, Ft. Lauderdale/Broward County C. of C., Delta Zeta (Outstanding Alumni Recognition award 1977), Sigma Phi Epsilon (pres. Little Sisters Orgn.). Jewish. Clubs: B'nai B'rith Women (Chaverim chpt.); Cricket of Miami; Woodlands Country. Writer, hostess 24 episodes Self Discovery television talk show, 1976-77; writer, star 20 shows Debbie and Friends, 1973-74; screenplay collaborator The Eddie Faye Story. Office: Associated Leasing Internat Corp Trafalgar Plaza I Suite 219 5300 NW 33d Ave Fort Lauderdale FL 33309

SHANE, JO ANN, insurance company representative; b. Burbank, Calif., Feb. 14, 1949; d. Hugo Eugene and Hanna Lore (Stein) S.; m. D. E. Parmer II, July 5, 1975 (div. 1978). Student, Coll. San Mateo, 1967-69, San Jose State Coll., 1970-72. Program mgr. DCA Reliability Labs., Mountain View, Calif., 1974-76; adminstr. mktg. Wine World, Inc., St. Helena, Calif., 1976-78; internat. product mktg. staff Monolithic Memories, Sunnyvale, Calif., 1978-80; pres. Shane & Assocs., Pleasanton, Calif., 1980-85; distbr., sales mgr. mil. products Signetics Corp., Sunnyvale, 1984-85; sales rep. Lincoln Nat. Life Ins. Co., Pleasanton, 1985—. Mem. Employee Benefits Council No. Calif., Met. Houseman's Assn. (pres. Oakland chpt., 1985-87), Internat. Apple Core (sec. 1983-85). Office: Lincoln Nat Pension Co 3875 Hopyard Suite 301 Pleasanton CA 94566

SHANHOUSE, LINDA FILLINGHAM, savings and loan executive; b. Niagara Falls, N.Y., June 25, 1941; d. Kenneth Edward and Marian Georgina (Cooper) F.; m. Bill Shanhouse, Dec. 29, 1980. Asst. to v.p. Riggs Nat. Bank, Washington, 1965-73; exec. v.p., chief operating officer, dir. Friendship Savs. & Loan Assn., Chevy Chase, Md., 1973-84; sr. v.p. Ind. Am. Savs. Assn., Irving, Tex., 1984—. Trustee Studio Theatre (Washington). Mem. Mortgage Bankers Assn., U.S. League Savs. Assns., Md. Savs. and Loan League, Fin. Instns. Mktg. Assn., Bank Mktg. Assn., Women's Econ. Roundtable, Washington Women's Network, Women in Housing and Fin., Fin. Mktg. Council of Greater Washington. Republican. Home: 502 San Juan Dr Southlake TX 76092 Office: 300 E Carpenter Irving TX 75062

SHANK, CLARE BROWN WILLIAMS, political worker; b. Syracuse, N.Y., Sept. 19, 1909; d. Curtiss Crofoot and Clara Irene (Shoudy) Brown; m. Frank E. Williams, Feb. 18, 1940 (dec. Feb. 1957); m. Seth Carl Shank, Dec. 28, 1963 (dec. Jan. 1977). B.Oral English, Syracuse U., 1931. Tchr. 1931-33, merchandising exec., 1933-42; Pinellas County mem. Rep. State Com., 1954-58; life mem. Pinellas County Rep. Exec. Com.; exec. com. Fla. Rep. Com., 1954-64; Fla. committeewoman Rep. Nat. Com., 1956-64, mem. exec. com., 1956-64, asst. chmn. and dir. women's activities, 1958-64; alt., mem. exec. arrangements com., major speaker Rep. Nat. Conv., Chgo., 1960; alt., program and arrangement coms. Rep. Nat. Conv., 1964. Pres. St. Petersburg Women's Rep. Club, 1955-57; Mem. Def. Adv. Com. on Women in Services, 1959-65; trustee St. Petersburg Housing Authority, 1976-81. Recipient George Arents medal Syracuse U., 1959; citation for patriotic civilian service 5th U.S. Army and Dept. Def. Mem. AAUW, Gen. Fedn. Women's Clubs, DAR, Colonial Dames 17th Century, Fla. Fedn. Women's Clubs (dist. pres. 1976-78), Zeta Phi Eta, Pi Beta Phi (nat. officer 1945-48). Methodist. Clubs: Woman's (St. Petersburg) (pres. 1974-76), Yacht (St. Petersburg). Home: 1120 North Shore Dr NE Apt 901 Saint Petersburg FL 33701

SHANK, MARY LOU, human resources director; b. Wilkes-Barre, Pa., May 1, 1954; d. Walter P. and Celestine C. (Pienta) Gottlieb; m. John C. Shank, Aug. 8, 1987. BA in Psychology cum laude, Wilkes Coll., 1976; postgrad., U. Scranton, 1988—. Cert. profl. in human resources. Dept. mgr. Pomeroy's Dept. Store, Wilkes-Barre, 1979-81, personnel mgr., 1981-85; dir. human resources Penn Security Bank & Trust Co., Scranton, Pa., 1985—. Active Scranton Job Service Employer Adv. Council. Mem. Tri-County Personnel assn. (v.p. 1988—, sec. 1987-88, chairperson membership com. 1987-88, chmn. by-laws com. 1984-85), Am. Soc. for Personnnel Adminstrn., Am. Inst. Banking (Lackawana chpt.). Home: 134 Spruce St Merrywood Hills Mountaintop PA 18707 Office: Penn Security Bank & Trust N Washington and Spruce St Scranton PA 18503

SHANKS, JUDITH WEIL, editorial administrator; b. Montgomery, Ala., Nov. 2, 1941; d. Roman Lee and Charlotte (Alexander) Weil; m. Hershel Shanks, Feb. 20, 1966; children: Elizabeth Jeannette, Julia Emily. BA in Econs., Wellesley Coll., 1963; MBA, Trinity Coll., 1980. Econs. asst. Export-Import Bank, Washington, 1963-68; cons. econs. and social sci. 1968-76; researcher Time-Life Books, Alexandria, Va., 1976-80, prin. researcher, 1980-83, illustrations editor, 1983, editorial adminstr., 1984—. Mem. Garden Writers Am., Internat. Alliance, Washington Wellesley Club (career caucus). Democrat. Jewish. Home: 5208 38th St NW Washington DC 20015

SHANKS, KATHRYN MARY, health care administrator; b. Glens Falls, N.Y., Aug. 4, 1950; d. John Anthony and Lenita (Combs) S. B.S. summa cum laude, Spring Hill Coll., 1972; M.P.A., Auburn U., 1976. Program evaluator Mobile Mental Health, Ala., 1972-73; dir. spl. projects Ala. Dept. Mental Health, Montgomery, 1973-76; dir. adminstrn. S.W. Ala. Mental Health/Mental Retardation, Andulusia, Ala., 1976-78; adminstr. Mobile County Health Dept., 1978-82; exec. dir. Coastal Family Health Ctr., Biloxi, Miss., 1982—; ptnr. Shanks & Allen, Mobile, 1979—; cons. S.W. Health Agy., Tylertown, Miss., 1984-86; preceptor Sch. Nursing, U. So. Miss., Hattiesburg, 1983, 84; advisor Headstart Program, Gulfport, Miss., 1984—, LPN Program, Gulf Coast Community Coll., 1984—; lectr. Auburn U., Montgomery, 1977-78. Bd. dirs. Mobile Community Action Agy., 1979-81; mem. S.W. Ala. Regional Goals Forum, Mobile, 1971-72, Cardiac Rehab. Study Com., Biloxi, Miss., 1983-84, Mothers and Babies Coalition, Jackson, Miss., 1983—, Gulf Coast Coalition Human Services, Biloxi, Miss., 1983—. Spring Hill Coll. Pres.'s scholar, 1972. Mem. Miss. Primary Health Care Assn. (pres.), Med. Group Mgmt. Assn., Biloxi C. of C., ACLU, Soc. for Advancement of Ambulatory Care, Spring Hills Alumni Assn. Avocations: tennis; home restoration. Office: Coastal Family Health Ctr PO Box 475 300 E Division St Biloxi MS 39530

SHANNON, CAROLYN JEAN, interior designer, career counselor; b. Vincennes, Ind., Nov. 22, 1943; d. Melvin Eugene and Melita Harriet (Bair) Powell; children: Timothy Carl, Heather Caroline. BA in Telecommunications and Interior Design, Ind. U., 1985. Interior designer Buchanan & Sons Furniture, also Kitchen and Bath Ctr., also free-lance, Bloomington, Ind., 1975-81; sales mgr. Kittle's Ethan Allen, Bloomington and Indpls., 1981-82; owner, cons. The Profl. Woman, career enhancement seminars, Bloomington, 1982—; interior designer Interiors, Bloomington, 1984-87; prin.Carolyn Shannon Interiors, Bloomington, 1984-87; owner Carolyn Shannon Interiors, 1987—. Rep. Local Council of Women, owners Bloomington Hosp., 1985-86. Mem. Nat. Assn. Female Execs., Golden Key, Psi Iota Xi, Phi Beta Kappa (scholarship 1984), Phi Delta Kappa. Methodist. Avocations: bridge, travel, tennis. Home: 2715 Bluff Ct Bloomington IN 47401 Office: Carolyn Shannon Interiors Bloomington IN 47401

SHANNON, IRIS REED, educational administrator; b. Chgo.; d. Ira Paul and Iola Sophia (Williams) S.; m. Robert Alwood Shannon, Aug. 21, 1953. B.S. in Nursing, Fisk U.-Meharry Med. Coll., 1948; M.A., U. Chgo., 1954; Ph.D., U. Ill., Chgo., 1987. Staff nurse Chgo. Bd. Health, 1948-50; instr. pub. health nursing Meharry Med. Coll., Nashville, 1951-56; tchr.-nurse, health coordinator child devel. Head Start, Chgo. Bd. Edn., 1957-66; dir. community nursing Mile Sq. Neighborhood Health Center, Presbyn.-St. Luke's Hosp., Chgo., 1966-69; co-dir. nurse assoc. programs Rush Presbyn.-St. Luke's Hosp., 1971-76; chairperson community nursing Rush U., Chgo., 1972-77; asst. prof. pub. health nursing U. Ill., 1971-74; assoc. prof. community nursing Rush U., 1974—; adj. faculty Sch. Public Health, U. N.C., 1977-85; mem. profl. adv. bd. Vis. Nurse Assn. Chgo., 1973-75; cons. Video Nursing, Inc.; mem. profl. adv. com. Mile Sq. Home Health Unit, Chgo., 1975-77; mem. Nat. Adv. Council on Nurse Tng., HEW, 1978-81; Mem. Nat. Task Force on Credentialing in Nursing, 1979-82; mem. Chgo. regional com. Ill. White House Conf. on Children, 1979-80. Recipient award of merit Ill. Public Health Assn., 1979; Rockefeller fellow, 1953-54. Fellow Am. Pub. Health Assn. (chmn. pub. health nursing sect. 1977-79, governing council 1980-82, exec. bd. 1985-87, pres.-elect 1987), Am. Acad. Nursing; mem. Am. Nurses Assn., Am. Sch. Health Assn., Inst. Medicine of Nat. Acad. Scis., Delta Sigma Theta., Sigma Theta Tau.

SHANNON, LORIS KAY, association executive; b. Butte, Mont., Sept. 27, 1941; d. George Robert and Loris Marguerite (Brown) Powe; m. James Norman Bertelson, Aug. 8, 1964 (div. 1973); children—Christopher James, Bonnie Kay; m. Donald Sutherlin Shannon, Dec. 30, 1977; stepchildren—Stacey Eileen, Gail Alison, Michael Corbett. B.A. in English, Carleton Coll., 1963; M.A. in Teaching., Coll. St. Thomas, St. Paul, 1964; M.B.A., U. Ky., 1982. Tchr., Central Jr. High Sch., St. Louis Park, Minn., 1964-67; lab. technician U. Ky., Lexington, 1973-80, grad. research asst., 1980-81; assoc. editor Am. Assn. Individual Investors, Chgo., 1982-84, dir. communications, 1984—. Mem. Pub. Relations Soc. Am. Home: 1624 Elmwood Ave Wilmette IL 60091 Office: Am Assn Individual Investors 625 N Michigan Ave Chicago IL 60611

SHANNON, MARGARET RITA, retired education educator, retired college dean; b. Cambridge, Mass.; d. James J. and Catherine M. (McDonough) S. BS, U. Lowell, 1936; MEd, Harvard U., 1947, Ed.D., 1959. Tchr. pub. schs. Cambridge, 1936-51; from asst. prof. to prof. Mass. State Coll., Lowell, 1951-79, chmn. dept. edn., 1969-74, dean Coll. Edn., 1974-79, prof. emeritus, dean emeritus, 1979—; lectr. in field. Author textbooks; contbr. articles to profl. jours. Mem. Internat. Reading Assn. (cons. nat. conf.), Am. Ednl. Research Assn., Nat. Council Tchrs. English (com. on linguistics and reading), Delta Kappa Gamma, Pi Lambda Theta (chpt. pres. 1958-61). Home: 374 Park Ave Arlington MA 02174 Office: U Lowell Coll Edn S Campus Lowell MA 01854

SHANNON, MARGARET SHERRY, personnel executive; b. Buffalo, N.Y., Oct. 24, 1954; d. John Patrick and Elizabeth Amelia (Kieffer) S. BS, SUNY, Buffalo, 1976; BA, SUNY, 1979. Acct. Mobil Oil Corp., Buffalo, 1976-78; acct. personnel dept. Pyramid Constrn. Co., Syracuse, N.Y., 1980-81; benefits adminstr. HBH Co., Arlington, VA., 1981-83, Nat. Railway Labor Conf., Washington, 1983—. Advisor Jr. Achievment, Buffalo, 1978; career counselor Displaced Homemakers, Buffalo, 1979. Mem. SUNY Alumni Assn. (steering com. 1986-87). Roman Catholic. Office: Nat Railway Labor Conf 1901 L St NW Suite 500 Washington DC 20036

SHANNON, MARTHA ALBERTER, portfolio manager; b. Johnstown, Pa., Oct. 9, 1958; d. Rodman Russell and Eleanor Ruth (Christner) S. BA in Econs., U. Pitts., Johnstown, Pa., 1980; MBA magna cum laude, U. Alaska, 1987. Area mgr. Fed. Gold Exchange, Inc., Denver, 1980-81; dept. mgr. Time Service, Inc., Aurora, Colo., 1981-82; security analyst John E. Randall II, Investments, Anchorage, 1982-85; portfolio mgr. M.B.A. Co., Anchorage, 1986-87; v.p. portfolio mgmt., corp. sec./treas. Security Portfolio Mgrs., Inc., Anchorage, 1987-88, also bd. dirs.; agt. N.Y. Life Ins. Co., Anchorage, 1988—. Mem. Am. Mktg. Assn., Fin. Analysts Fedn., Internat. Chartered Fin. Analysts Fedn., Women Life Underwriters Confederation, Nat. Assn. Life Underwriters. Office: NY Life Ins Co 1400 W Benson Blvd Suite 200 Anchorage AK 99503

SHANTZ, INA CLAIRE, insurance agent; b. Rochester, N.Y., Nov. 11, 1945; d. Edson Boman and Marion (Kelly) S. Student, Boston U., 1963-64; BA, Syracuse (N.Y.) U., 1967. CLU. Agt. Prudential Ins. Co. Am., Syracuse, 1975-78, sales mgr., 1978-85; agt., registered rep. Prudential Ins. Co. Am., Hollywood, Fla., 1985—. Mem. Am. Soc. CLU's, Nat. Assn. Securities Dealers. Republican. Office: Prudential Ins Co Am 9050 Pines Blvd Suite 155 Pembroke Pines FL 33024

SHAPIRO, AMY ROSEMARIE, film studio executive; b. Stamford, Conn., Dec. 13, 1949; d. Salem Seeley and Edith Geraldine (Herwitz) S. BA, Goucher Coll., Towson, Md., 1971. Asst. to dir. Manpower Adminstrn. U.S. Dept. Labor, Washington, 1971-73; editorial asst. Distbn. Codes, Inc., Washington, 1973-75; asst. to v.p. Pay-TV dept. Universal Pictures, Inc., N.Y.C., 1976-80; adminstr. Pay-TV div. Universal Pictures, Inc., Los Angeles, 1980-82; dir. sales Pay-TV div. Universal Pictures Inc., Los Angeles, 1983-84; v.p. sales Pay-TV div. MCA Home Entertainment Group, Los Angeles, 1985-87, v.p. adminstrn. and new mktg. devel., 1988—. Coordinator Udall Presdl. Campaign, Weston, Conn., 1976; mem. Dem. Town Com., Weston, Conn., 1976-77; vol. coordinator Gary Hart Presdl. Campaign, Los Angeles, 1984. Recipient Case Study award Cable TV Adminstrn. and Mktg. Soc., 1988. Democrat. Jewish. Home: 4717 Willis Ave Sherman Oaks CA 91403 Office: Universal Pay TV 70 Universal City Plaza Universal City CA 91608

SHAPIRO, ANN R., English language educator; b. Bklyn., Feb. 28, 1937; d. Murray and Jeanette Rabinowitz; children: Rona Gail, Wendy Lynn, Edward Ira. AB cum laude, Radcliff Coll., 1958; MA in Teaching, Harvard U., 1960; PhD, NYU, 1985. Instr. English Rider Coll., New Brunswick, N.J., 1962-65, Suffolk County (N.Y.) Community Coll., 1966-67; prof. SUNY, Farmingdale, 1974—; speaker in field. Author: Unlikely Heroines: Nineteenth-Century American Women Writers and the Woman Question; Introduction (with Joy Gould Boyum), A Country Doctor (Sarah Orne Jewett); contbg. author: Smashing the Idols; contbr. articles to profl. jours. Fellow Nat. Inst. for Leadership Devel., 1987, Salzburg seminars, 1988. Mem. MLA, Women's Caucus in the Modern Langs., Nat. Council Tchrs. Club: Harvard (N.Y.C.). Home: 1148 Fifth Ave New York NY 10128 Office: SUNY Dept English Farmingdale NY 11735

SHAPIRO, BARBARA PHYLLIS, financial executive; b. Bklyn., May 31, 1947; d. Marvin and Marcia Seena (Colodner) Shapiro; m. Howard A. Kogut, Feb. 14, 1972 (dec. 1973). BA in Anthropology, SUNY, New Paltz, 1970. Computer programmer analyst Blue Cross/Blue Shield of Greater N.Y., N.Y.C., 1978-81, Sterling Drug Inc., N.Y.C., 1981-82, Continental Grain Co., N.Y.C., 1982-83; computer cons. Staten Island, N.Y., 1983-85; sr. projects analyst Chrysler Capital Corp., Greenwich, Conn., 1985—. Author health study, 1974. Founding bd. dirs. Dutchess County Health Planning Council, Poughkeepsie, N.Y., Hudson Valley HSA; bd. mgrs. Mental Health Com., Hudson Valley; psychodrama dir. Columbus Psychodrama Inst., N.Y.C.; cons. Creative Artists Trust, New Rochelle, N.Y., 1980-86; bd. dirs. disaster svcs. ARC, Poughkeepsie, 1975. Mem. NOW. Democrat. Jewish. Office: Chrysler Capital Corp Greenwich Office Park I Greenwich CT 08636

SHAPIRO, DENISE LAURA, sales and marketing executive; b. Oceanside, N.Y., Apr. 24, 1954; d. Arthur G. and Sylvia (Wieder) Cohen; m. Larence Lang Shapiro, Sept. 4, 1977. BA, Syracuse U., 1975; MA in Mgmt., N.Y. U., 1977. Asst. Halston Enterprises, N.Y.C., 1976-77; asst. designer Malcolm Starr, N.Y.C., 1977; designer Salerno Handbag, N.Y.C., 1977; mdse. mgr. Honeybunch Handbag, N.Y.C., 1978-79; dir. ABC Inc., N.Y.C., 1979-82; pres. Preferred Lics. Ltd., N.Y.C., 1982-84, cons., 1982-87; v.p., gen. mgr. for licensing ops. ITT, 1984; v.p. mktg., sales Daily Bus. Satellite div. Potomac Communications, Inc., Washington, 1987-88; v.p. sales, mktg. Newslink, Inc., 1988—; developed retailing techniques for licensed product, nationwide, consumer advt. program for Statue of Liberty fund; instr. UN, N.Y.C., 1977-78; cons. in field. History guide Met. Museum Art, N.Y.C., 1978-79; bd. dirs. San Remo Tenants Corp., N.Y.C., 1980-83; active Pat Murphy for Judge Campaign, N.Y.C., 1983. Mem. Licensing Industry Assn., Am. Women in Radio and TV. Clubs: Sandanona Hare Hounds (Millbrook, N.Y.); Greenwich Polo Players. Home: 146 Central Park W New York NY 10023 Office: Newslink Inc 1251 Avenue of the Americas New York NY 10020

SHAPIRO, ELLEN LOUISE, environmental health program director; b. Boston, Oct. 25, 1950; d. Thelma (Novick) S. BS in Math. cum laude, U. Mass., 1972; MS in Chem. Engring., N.C. State U., 1978. Lab. technician dept. microbiology U. Colo., Boulder, 1972-73; research asst. Appalachian Research and Def. Fund, Inc., Charleston, W.Va., 1973-75; programmer Union Carbide Corp., South Charleston, W.Va., 1976; engr. W.Va. Air Pollution Control Commn., Charleston, 1978-83; policy analyst Jellinek, Schwartz, Connolly and Freshman, Inc., Washington, 1983-85; program dir. Pub. Health Found., Washington, 1985—. Author, editor: Resource Guide for Environmental Health Risk Assessment, 1986; (newsletter) Environ. Health Bull., 1985—. Bd. dirs. W.Va. chpt. Nat. Abortion Rights Action League, Charleston, 1982-83. Mem. Amnesty Internat., World Affairs Council, Am. Pub. Health Assn., Air Pollution Control Assn., Nat. Environ. Health Assn., Soc. Risk Analysis, Met. Washington Environ. Profls. (bd. dirs., v.p. 1987—), Folklore Soc. of Greater Washington, Alpha Lambda Delta. Democrat. Jewish. Office: Pub Health Found 1220 L St NW Suite 350 Washington DC 20005

SHAPIRO, ELLEN LOUISE, music educator; b. Oil City, Pa., Nov. 19, 1942; d. Harry Gene and Dorothy (Gordon) Goldberg; m. Samuel Wolf Shapiro, Aug. 8, 1971; children: Jeremy Aaron, Jessica Leigh. Student, Eastman Sch. Music, 1960-61; BA, Northwestern U., 1965; M of Music, Boston U., 1970. Tchr. music Scituate (Mass.) Pub. Schs., 1970-71; tchr. piano South Shore Conservatory Music, Hingham, Mass., 1970-75; tchr. music Willingboro (N.J.) Pub. Schs., 1977-79, Cinnaminson (N.J.) Pub. Schs., 1979-81; dir., tchr. Shapiro Sch. Music, Marlton, N.J., 1981—; lectr. Phila. Music Tchrs. Assn., 1987. Contbr. articles to profl. mags. and jours. Chairperson publicity com. PTA, Marlton, N.J., 1986; mem. advt. com. Womens Am. Orgn. for Rehab. through Tng., Marlton and Medford, N.J., 1983-85; active Hadassah, Natick, Mass., bull. editor, 1973-75; mem. N.J. Symphony Orch. Mem. Nat. Guild Piano Tchrs. (faculty, adjudicator 1985-87, chairperson 1981—), South Jersey Music Tchrs. Assn. (pres. 1987-89), Music Tchrs. Nat. Assn. (rep. N.J. state conv. 1988). Home: 136 Five Crown Royale Marlton NJ 08053

SHAPIRO, ESTHER JUNE, television producer, writer; b. Bklyn., June 6, 1934; d. Jack and Flora (Salmoni) Mayesh; m. Richard Allen Shapiro, Dec. 4, 1960; children—Florie Sonya, Eden Jacqueline. B.A., U. So. Calif., 1952; postgrad., UCLA, 1955-56. Secondary teaching credential, Calif. Free-lance writer-producer 1959—; exec. story cons. Paramount Pictures Corp., 1973; v.p. mini-series and novels ABC TV, 1977-79; prin. Richard and Esther Shapiro Prodns., Los Angeles, 1979—; sr. v.p. creative and corp. affairs Aaron Spelling Prodns., 1986—. Episodic writer various TV series, 1959-68; head writer TV series Love of Life, 1969; exec. story cons.-writer TV series Love Story, 1973; creator-writer TV films Sarah T.: Portrait of a Teenage Alcoholic, 1974, Minstrel Man, 1977 (Christopher award 1977, Internat. Cath. Assn. for Radio and TV award 1977, World Assn. Christian Communicators award 1977, prix Italia 1978); creator-writer-producer TV film Intimate Strangers, 1977; creator, writer-exec. producer TV series Dynasty, 1980 (Golden Globe award Hollywood Fgn. Press Assn. 1983, numerous other awards), Emerald Point, N.A.S., 1982, Dynasty II: The Colbys, 1985. Mem. steering com. Hollywood Women's Coalition, 1984; bd. dirs. Los Angeles Actors Theatre, 1984, World Interdependence Fund, 1984. Recipient Disting. Community Service award Maple Ctr., Beverly Hills, Calif., 1984, GENII award So. Calif. chpt. Am. Women in Radio and TV, 1985, Bullock's Wilshire Portfolio award for exec. women, 1985 Leadership award Am. Woman's Econ. Devel. Corp.; honored as writer and producer of award-winning TV prodns. Brandeis U. Nat. Women's Com., 1985;. Mem. Writers Guild Am. West, Am. Film Inst., Acad. TV Arts and Scis., Caucus for Producers Writers and Dirs., Trusteeship (com. of 200). Club: Regency.

SHAPIRO, JOAN ISABELLE, laboratory administrator, nurse; b. Fulton, Ill., Aug. 26, 1943; d. Macy James and Frieda Lockhart; m. Ivan Lee Shapiro, Dec. 28, 1968; children—Audrey, Michael. R.N., Peoria Methodist Sch. Nursing, Ill., 1964. Nurse, Grant Hosp., Columbus, Ohio, 1975-76; nurse Cardiac Thoracic and Vascular Surgeons Ltd., Geneva, Ill., 1977—, mgr. non-invasive lab., 1979—; owner, operator Shapiro's Mastiff's 1976-82; sec.-treas. Sounds Services, 1976—, Mainstream Sounds Inc., 1980-84; co-founder Cardio-Phone Inc., 1982—; co-founder Edgewater Vascular Inst., 1987—; v.p., dir. Computer Specialists Inc., 1986—. Mem. Soc. Non-invasive Technologists, Soc. Peripheral Vascular Nursing (community awareness com. 1984—), Kane County Med. Soc. Aux. (pres. 1983-84, adviser, 1984-85). Lutheran. Office: Cardiac Thoracic and Vascular Surgeons Ltd PO Box 564 Geneva IL 60134

SHAPIRO, JUDITH R., anthropology educator, university official; b. N.Y.C., Jan. 24, 1942. B.A., Brandeis U., 1963; postgrad. Ecole des Haute Etudes Institut d'Etudes Politiques, Paris, 1961-62; Ph.D., Columbia U., 1972. Asst. prof. U. Chgo., 1970-75; postdoctoral fellow U. Calif.-Berkeley, 1974-75; Rosalyn R. Schwartz lectr., asst. prof. anthropology Bryn Mawr Coll., Pa., 1975-78, assoc. prof., 1978-85, prof., 1985—, chmn. dept., 1982-85, acting dean undergrad coll., 1985-86, acad. dep. to pres., 1986—; contbr. articles to profl. jours., chpts. to books. Fellow Woodrow Wilson Found., 1963-64, Columbia U., 1964-65, NEH Younger Humanist, 1974-75, Am. Council Learned Socs., 1981-82; grantee NSF summer field tng., 1965, Ford Found. 1966, NIMH, 1974-75, Social Sci. Research Council, 1974-75; Mem. Phila. Anthrop. Soc. (pres. 1983), Am. Ethnol. Soc. (nominations com . 1983-84, pres. elect 1984-85, pres. 1985-86), Am. Anthrop. Assn. (ethics com. 1976-79, bd. dirs. 1984-86, exec. com. 1985-86), Social Sci. Research Council (com. social sci personnel 1977-80), Royal Anthrop. Inst., Phi Beta Kappa, Sigma Xi. Office: Bryn Mawr Coll Dept of Anthropology Bryn Mawr PA 19010

SHAPIRO, NORMA SONDRA LEVY, judge; b. Phila., July 27, 1928; d. Bert and Jane (Kotkin) Levy; m. Bernard Shapiro, Aug. 21, 1949; children: Finley, Neil, Aaron. B.A. in Polit. Theory with honors, U. Mich., 1948; J.D. magna cum laude, U. Pa., 1951. Bar: Pa. 1952, U.S. Supreme Ct. 1978. Law clk. to justice Pa. Supreme Ct., 1951-52; instr. U. Pa. Law Sch., 1951-52, 55-56; assoc. Dechert Price & Rhoads, Phila., 1956-58, 67-73; ptnr. Dechert Price & Rhoads, 1973-78; judge U.S. Dist. Ct. Eastern Dist. Pa., 1978—; assso. trustee U. Pa. Law Sch., 1978—; trustee Women's Law Project, 1978—, Albert Einstein Med. Center, 1979—, Fedn. Jewish Agys., 1980—, Jewish Publ. Soc., 1980—; mem. lawyer's adv. panel Pa. Gov.'s Commn. on Status of Women, 1974; legal adv. Regional Council Child Psychiatry. Guest editor: Shingle, 1972. Mem. Lower Merion County (Pa.) Bd. Sch. Dirs., 1968-77, pres., 1977, v.p., 1976; v.p. Jewish Community Relations Council of Greater Phila., 1975-77; chmn. legal affairs com., 1978; pres. Belmont Hills Home and Sch. Assn., Lower Merion Twp.; legis. chmn. Lower Merion Sch. Dist. Intersch. Council; mem. Task Force on Mental Health of Children and Youth of Pa.; treas., chmn. edn. com. Human Relations Council, Lower Merion; v.p., parliamentarian Nes Ami Penn Valley Congregation, Lower Merion Twp. Named Woman of Yr., Oxford Circle Jewish Community Center, 1979, Woman of Distinction, Golden Slipper Club, 1979; Gowen fellow, 1954-55. Mem. Am. Law Inst., Am. Bar Found., ABA (vice chmn. com. law and mental health sect. family law), Pa. Bar Assn. (ho. of dels. 1979—), Phila. Bar Assn. (chmn. com. women's rights 1972, 74-75, chmn. bd. govs. 1977—, chmn. public relations com. 1978), Fed. Bar Assn., Nat. Assn. Women Lawyers, Phila. Trial Lawyers Assn., Am. Judicature Soc., Phila. Fellowship Commn., Order of Coif (chpt. pres. 1973-75), Tau Epsilon Rho. Office: US Dist Courthouse 10614 US Courthouse Independence Mall West Philadelphia PA 19106 *

SHAPIRO, ROSE TURBOW, educational psychologist; b. Kiev, USSR, Apr. 11, 1917; d. Mair and Myrel (Biniamoff) Turbow; m. Nathan Shapiro, Jan. 10, 1943; children: Matthew, Joel, David, Elaine. AB, U. Chgo., 1939; student, Northwestern U., 1939-41; MA in Edn., Cal State U., Northridge, 1965; postgraduate, U. South Calif., 1967-69. Plan reviewer U.S. Social Security Bd., Washington, 1941-43; probation officer D.C. Juvenile Ct., Washington, 1943-44; occupational analyst U.S. Dept. of Labor, Washington, 1944-47; tchr. Los Angeles Unified Sch. Dist., 1958-65, counselor, psychologist, 1965-73; pvt. practice ednl. psychologist, marriage, family, child counselor Pacific Palisades, Calif., 1974—; vol. UCLA Neuropsychiatric Inst., Los Angeles, 1974—; vol. counselor Santa Monica (Calif.) Sr. Health and Peer Counseling Ctr., 1980-85. Mem. Calif. Assn. of Sch. Psychologists, Los Angeles Assn. of Sch. Psychologists, Calif. State Psychol. Assn., Calif. Assn. of Lic. Ednl. Psychologists, Group Psychotherapy Assn. of So. Calif. Lodge: Hadassah. Home and Office: 1407 Chautauqua Blvd Pacific Palisades CA 90272

SHAPIRO, RUTH ANNE, nurse, jewelry designer; b. Newark, Nov. 21, 1947; d. Alvin Grant and Eleanore (Kohn) Mayer; m. Carl W. Shapiro, Aug. 27, 1972 (div.); children: Benjamin, Lauren. BSN, U. Mich., 1970. Staff nurse Mass. Gen. Hosp., Boston, 1970-72; clin. research nurse Beth Israel Hosp., Brookline, Mass., 1972-76; staff nurse maternity ward Centinela Hosp., Inglewood, Calif., 1976-80; cons. in med. legal field Los Angeles, 1983—, Judaic artist, jewelry designer, 1984—. Work exhibited in juried shows Richmond Jewish Community Ctr. (Blue Ribbon 1985), Morristown (N.J.) Jewish Community Ctr., 1985, Congregation Solel, Highland Park, Ill., 1986, 87, Bay Cities Jewish Community Ctr., Santa Monica, Calif., 1987, Temple Isaiah Festival Jewish Artisans, Los Angeles, 1985, 86, 87; commissioned work includes The Wagner Found. U. Judaism, Los Angeles, 1986, 87.; featured in Am. Jewish Artists show Mizel Mus. Judaica, Denver, 1987; contbr. articles to profl. jours. Troop leader Girl Scouts U.S., Los Angeles, 1987. Mem. Child Passenger Safety Assn., Am. Friends of Tel Aviv U., Pomegranate Guild, Sigma Theta Tau, Phi Kappa Phi. Lodge: B'nai Brith. Home: 3541 St Susan Pl Los Angeles CA 90066

SHAPLEY, MARIAN JEFFRIES, farmer, investor; b. Amarillo, Tex., Feb. 25, 1947; d. Warren and Colleen (Rafferty) Jeffries; widowed; children: Bart, Dala, Tara, Chuck Morgan; m. Rex Gruver Shapley, Nov. 8, 1985. Grad. high sch., Gruver, Tex., 1965. Ptnr. Shapley Farms, Gruver, 1970—; bd. dirs. Amarillo Investment Inc., 1985—, Gruver Inc., 1978—. Mem. Rep. Task Force, Washington, 1980—; bd. dirs., fundraiser Gruver Swimming Pool, 1984. Mem. Greyhound Mothers (pres. 1986—), Beta Sigma Phi, Alpha Mu Psi, Xi Psi Kappa. Methodist. Club: Hansford Golf (Spearman, Tex.) (bd. dirs. 1979-83).

SHARFMAN, CAROLINE SHARP, commercial paper credit analyst; b. Ann Arbor, Mich., Aug. 27, 1942; d. Mahlon Samuel and Mary Patricia (Potter) Sharp; m. William Lee Sharfman, Sept. 5, 1964 (div. 1985). B.A. with distinction, U. Mich., 1964; M.B.A., Columbia U., 1975. Assoc. Goldman, Sachs & Co., N.Y.C., 1975-80, v.p., 1980-83; v.p. Goldman Sachs Money Markets Inc., N.Y.C., 1983—. Chmn. fin. com., vestry mem. Christ & St. Stephens Ch. Mem. Phi Beta Kappa, Beta Sigma Iota, Beta Gamma Sigma. Episcopalian. Office: Goldman Sachs Money Markets Inc 85 Broad St New York NY 10004

SHARIAT-PANAHI, JALEH, physician; b. Mashad, Iran, May 24, 1945; came to U.S., 1972; d. Askari and Narjes Movahed S.-P.; m. Ali Madani, Nov. 21, 1975; children—Leila, Mina, Susanne, Cyrus. M.D., Pahlavi U. Sch. Medicine (Iran), 1971. Resident in internal medicine U. Ala., Birmingham, 1973-75, fellow in infectious diseases, 1975-76; practice medicine, specializing in internal medicine and infectious diseases, Kingston, N.Y., 1978—; attending physician Kingston Hosp., 1978—, Benedictine Hosp., Kingston, 1978—. Office: 51 Hurley Ave Kingston NY 12401

SHARKE, INGRID, librarian; b. Troy, N.Y., July 21, 1951; d. Karl G.E. and Ann (Swensson) Sharke. B.A., The Western Coll.-Oxford, Ohio, 1973; M.L.S., SUNY-Geneseo, 1974. Librarian, Samaritan Hosp. Sch. Nursing, Troy, N.Y., 1976; asst. librarian The Times Record/The Sun. Record, Troy, N.Y., 1977-80; librarian The Times Record/Sunday Record, 1980-87, librarian and Adminstrv. asst., Bruno Machinery Corp., 1987—. Mem. ALA, Spl. Library Assn. Republican. United Ch. of Christ. Office: Bruno Machinery Corp 1 Madison St PO Box 898 Troy NY 12181

SHARLAT, SANDE DIANE, metapsychologist, musician; b. Queens, N.Y., Nov. 23, 1958; d. Stanley and Arlene (Goldsmith) S.; m. Thomas Frederic Streit, July 9, 1988. Student, New Coll., Sarasota, Fla., 1976-78; summa cum laude, Berklee Coll. Music, 1982. Freelance musician 1979-86; pvt. practice, seminar leader, producer metapsychology, Boston, 1985—; tchr. Theosophical Soc., Boston, 1987—. Mem. Healer's Resource Ctr. Home and Office: 74 Hinckley St Boston MA 02145

SHARP, ANNE CATHERINE, artist; b. Red Bank, N.J., Nov. 1, 1943; d. Elmer Eugene and Ethel Violet (Hunter) S. B.F.A., Pratt Inst., 1965; M.F.A. (teaching fellow 1972), Bklyn. Coll., 1973. tchr. art Sch. Visual Arts, 1978—, NYU, 1978, SUNY-Purchase, 1983, Pratt Manhattan Ctr., N.Y.C., 1982-84, Parson's Sch. Design, N.Y.C., 1984—. One-person shows Pace Editions, N.Y.C., Ten/Downtown, N.Y.C., Katonah (N.Y.) Gallery, 1974, Contemporary Gallery, Dallas, 1975, Art in a Public Space, N.Y.C., 1979, Eatontown Hist. Mus., N.J., 1980, N.Y. Pub. Library Lepiphany Br., N.Y.C., 1988, N.Y. Pub. Library Epiphany Br., 1988; group shows include Arnot Art Mus., Elmira, N.Y., 1975, Bronx Mus., 1975, Mus. Modern Art, N.Y.C., 1975-76, Nat. Arts Club, N.Y.C., 1979, Calif. Mus. Photography, Riverside, 1983, 85, 86, 87, Jack Tilton Gallery, N.Y.C., 1983, Lincoln Center, N.Y.C., 1983, Cabo Frio Print Biennale, Brazil, 1983, Pratt Graphic Ctr., N.Y.C., 1984, State Mus. N.Y., Albany, 1984, Mus. Modern Art, Weddel, West Germany, 1985, Kenkeleba Gallery, N.Y.C., 1985, Hempstead Harbor Art Assn., Glen Cove, N.Y., 1985, Mus. Modern Art, Weddel, Fed. Republic of Germany, 1985, Kenkeleba Gallery, N.Y.C., 1985, Paper Art Exhbn. Internat. Mus. Contemporary Art, Bahia, Brazil, 1986, Mus. Salon-de-Provence, France, 1987, Mus. Contemporary Art, Sao Paulo, Brazil, 1985-86, Salon de Provence, France, 1987, Adirondack Lakes Ctr. for Arts, Blue Mountain Lake, N.Y., 1987, Self-Portrait Kent Parks Dept., Wash.; represented in permanent collections Smithsonian Instn., Nat. Air and Space Mus., Washington, Albright Knox Gallery, Buffalo, St. Vincent's Hosp, N.Y.C., City Art Collection, Kent, others; Public demonstration of painting in progress, Moon Shot series to commemorate moon landing, 1970-76, Cloud Structures of the Universe Painting series, 1980-86, Thoughtline, fall 1986, Swimming in the Mainstream with Her, U. Va., Charlottesville. Artist-in-residence grantee Va. Center for Creative Arts, 1974; Artist-in-residence grantee Artpark, Lewiston, N.Y., 1980; recipient Pippin award "Our Town" N.Y.C., 1984. Mem. Coll. Art Assn. Am., Nat. Space Soc., Found. for Community Artists, Pratt Alumni Assn., L-5 Soc., Artists Equity. Address: 20 Waterside Plaza Apt 11H New York NY 10010

SHARP, BEVERLY ANNE, correctional treatment specialist; b. Charleston, W. Va., Sept. 30, 1958; d. Cornelius Merton and Betty Anne (Hammack) S. BS, Marshall U., 1980. Supr. security Advance Indsl. Security, Charleston, 1980-81; correctional officer Fed. Bur. Prisons, Ashland, Ky., 1981-82; correctional treatment specialist Fed. Bur. Prisons, Ashland, 1982—; EEO counselor Fed. Bur. Prisons, Ashland, 1982—; teaching asst. Marshall U., Huntington, W. Va., 1983. Trainer Martin Luther King Ctr. for Nonviolent Social Change, Atlanta, 1986. Recipient Environ. Protection award Pres. Nixon, 1973. Mem. Am. Correctional Assn., Fraternal Order of Police (assoc.), Nat. Assn. Female Execs. Democrat. Baptist. Home: PO Box 1831 Ashland KY 41105-1831 Office: Fed Bur Prisons PO Box 888 Ashland KY 41101

SHARP, JANE ELLYN, protocol director; b. Chgo., Jan. 5, 1934; d. Truman V. and Mildred L. (Sweitzer) Lasswell; m. David H. Sharp, July 24, 1965 (div. Aug. 1979); children: Michelle Lynn, Lisa Elizabeth. BBA, Coll. Santa Fe, 1985, MBA, 1988. Adminstrv. asst. San Diego State U., 1956-58; dir. classified personnel Grossmont (Calif.) Union High Sch. and Jr. Coll. Dist., 1959-62; legal asst. Stockly & Boone, Attys., Los Alamos, N.Mex., 1974-75; adminstrv. asst. Los Alamos Nat. Lab., 1976-78, pub. relations specialist, 1978-81, asst. group leader, 1981-82, dep. group leader, 1982-83, asst. div. leader, 1983-84, office dir. protocol, 1984—. Mem. adv. bd. Youth Working for Youth, Los Alamos, 1985—; mem. Adults Working for Youth, Los Alamos, Bingaman Circle. Recipient Woman at Work award Council on Working Women, 1984. Mem. Tri Area Assn. for Econ. Devel., Los Alamos Nat. Lab. Community Council (rep. exec. bd. 1986—). Democrat. Office: Los Alamos Nat Lab PO Box 1663 MS P368 Los Alamos NM 87544

SHARP, LINDA LOUISE, insurance company executive; b. St. Louis, May 8, 1948; d. Rodney B. and Mary Louise (Zook) S. AA, Prairie State Coll., 1968; BA, Purdue U., 1972; MS in Edn., Ind. U., Gary, 1981. Tchr. English Sch. City of East Chicago, Ind., 1972-74; unit mgr. St. Catherine Hosp., East Chicago, 1974-83, unit mgr., coordinator, 1979-83, unit service coordinator, 1983-85; sales rep. Met. Life and Affiliated Cos., Munster, Ind., 1985-87; br. mgr. sales Met. Life and Affiliated Cos., Indpls., 1987—; instr. med. terminology Ind. Coll. of Commerce, Hammond, 1981-84. Active Leaders Club, Leaders Conf., 1987. Fellow Nat. Assn. Life Underwriters. Home: 8423 N Pennsylvania Indianapolis IN 46240 Office: Met Life and Affiliated Cos 9202 N Meridian #233 Indianapolis IN 46260

SHARP, MARY BRAY, interior designer, consultant; b. Oshkosh, Wis., June 19, 1945; d. Charles Paige and Marion (Diehl) Bray; m. G. Kendall Sharp, May 27, 1976; children: Kendall, Julia. AA, Stephens Coll., 1965; BFA, U. Colo., 1967. Comml. interior designer, space planner Aiello, Inc., Denver, 1967-70, Seal Furniture, Denver, 1970-72; residential interior designer Davis and Shaw Furniture, Denver, 1972-73; mgr., interior designer Lodge Furnishings, Vero Beach, Fla., 1973-74; prin. Interior Design of Vero Beach, Inc., 1974-84; asst. prodn. mgr. Jack Cox Prodns., Los Angeles and Vero Beach, 1982; interior designer, cons. Ideas and Concepts, Orlando, Fla., 1983-87; archtl. design specialist FLM Bldg. Products, Orlando, 1988—; lectr. interior decorating State of Fla. Jud. Conf., 1978-83; instr. Indian River Sch. System, Vero Beach, 1977-81, Indian River Community Coll., Vero Beach, Ft. Pierce, 1978-82; speaker, lectr. Indian River Area Clubs, Treasure Coast of Fla., 1976-83. Editor: Decorating Can be Fun, 1975-80. Chmn. Indian River County for Paula Hawkins for Senator, 1979; sec., treas., v.p., pres., dir. United Way of Indian River County, Vero Beach, 1974-83; exec. officer, bd. dirs. United Way of Cen. Fla., Orlando, 1983—; sec., treas., v.p., pres., dir. United Way of Fla., 1979—; mem., dir. Govs. Council on Humanities, Stae of Fla., 1981-84. Recipient Indian River County Woman of the Yr., 1979, Disting. Service award United Way of Indian River County, 1981-84, Disting. Service award United Way of Fla., 1985. Mem. Stephens Coll. Alumni of Cen. Fla. (chmn. laison). Presbyterian. Home and Office: 351 Agnes St Orlando FL 32801

SHARPE, KATHLEEN CONKLIN, probation and parole officer, tax accountant; b. Suffern, N.Y., Sept. 29, 1955; d. Robert Charles and Shirley Ann (Oakley) Conklin; m. Joseph Darius Causey, Nov. 17, 1976 (div. 1981); 1 child, Angela Diane; m. Leland J. Sharpe Jr., Sept. 26, 1986; 1 child, Leland J. Sharpe, III. BS in Acctg., U. S.C., 1986. Asst. to merchandise mgr. Western Big Wheel, North Bergen, N.J., 1974-75; telecom supr. Dept. of Army, Fort Jackson, S.C., 1977-82; tax acct., Columbia, S.C., 1977—; asst. to dir. S.C. Sentencing Guidelines Commn., Columbia, 1982-86; probation and parole pub. service employment coordinator Parole and Community Corrections, Columbia, 1986—; data analysis staff S.C. Jail Commn., 1982-83, Gov.'s JJ Council, 1982-83, Sentencing Guidelines, 1982-83. Guardian-ad Litem Guardian-Ad-Litem Project, 1983—; choir dir. children's choir Incarnation Lutheran Ch., 1984-86; parents' adv. council Richland Sch. Dist. 1, 1984-85. Served with U.S. Army, 1975-77. Recipient Sustained Superior Performance award Dept. Army, 1981. Mem. Am. Correctional Assn., S.C. Correctional Assn., S.C. Victim Assistance Network, Nat. Assn. Female Execs., Am. Soc. Notaries, Am. Philatelic Soc., Golden Key. Republican. Avocation: professional singer. Home: 9 Upton Ct Columbia SC 29209 Office: SC Parole and Community Corrections 2221 Devine St Box 50666 Columbia SC 29250

SHARPE, VERMON RENEE, systems analyst; b. Jackson, Tenn., Oct. 24, 1953; d. Marvin J. and Vermon (Huddleston) Cathey; m. Tommy Lee Sharpe, July 28, 1979. BBA, Memphis State U., 1974, MBA, 1979. Systems analyst NCR, Memphis, 1977-79; sr. analyst Transam. Ins. Co., Los Angeles, 1979-81; programmer Fed. Express, Memphis, 1981-82, sr. programmer, 1982-83, programmer analyst, 1983-85, sr. devel. analyst, 1985-86, sr. systems analyst, 1986—. cons. Adopt-a-Sch., Memphis, 1982-85; tutor Neighborhood Christian Ctr., Memphis, 1983-87. Mem. Nat. Assn. MBA Execs., Nat. Assn. Female Execs., Black Data Processing Assocs. (corr. sec. 1987—). Democrat. Home: 3144 Mackham Memphis TN 38118 Office: Fed Express 3171 Directors Row Memphis TN 38118

SHARPLES, VIRGINIA MITCHELL, engineering writing consultant; b. Indpls., July 3, 1942; d. James S. and Ruth K. Mitchell; BA (Operation Outstanding award 1974), Butler U., Indpls., 1964, MS, 1970; m. Richard J. Sharples, Dec. 24, 1973; children: Allison Virginia, Scott Brydson, Gregory Mitchell, Glen Ryan. High sch. tchr., Phoenix, 1971-74, Tucson, 1974-75, Houston, 1977-78, Rockwall, Tex., 1987; customer services rep. Advanced Computer Techniques, Tucson, 1976-77; tech. services engr. SWACO div. Dresser Industries, 1978-81, engring. writer Atlas div., Houston, 1981-82; copywriter Ogilvy & Mather, 1982-83; nat. editor U.S. Woman Engr. Mag. seminar leader, engring. writing cons. Mem. Soc. Women Engrs. Dallas (v.p. 1987-88, producer slide show 1985, mem. nat. editorial bd. 1986-88), Soc. Petroleum Engrs. Episcopalian. Club: Dresser Toastmasters (pres. 1981, area gov. 1983-84). Author papers in field. Home and Office: 321 Yacht Club Dr Rockwall TX 75087

SHARRAR, VICTORIA ANNE, publishing company executive; b. San Jose, Calif., June 2, 1958; d. Hans Christian Gunnar and Dolores Valerie (Barton) Sorensen; m. Kenneth Andrew Sharrar, Aug. 6, 1983. BS, U. So. Calif., 1981. Office adminstv. mgr. nat. radio div. CBS, Inc., Los Angeles, 1982-84; account exec. Orange (Calif.) Broadcasting Corp., 1984-85; account exec. Dun and Bradstreet/Donnelley Info. Pub., Garden Grove, Calif., 1985-86, gen. tng. mgr., 1986, dist. sales mgr., 1986—. Mem. Nat. Assn. Female Execs., Broadcast Music Inc. (writer), Long Beach C. of C. Republican. Office: Donnelley Info Pub 300 Plaza Alicante Garden Grove CA 92640

SHARROW, MARILYN JANE, library administrator; bd. Oakland, Calif.; d. Charles L. and H. Evelyn S.; m. Lawrence J. Davis. BS in Design, U. Mich., 1967, MALS, 1969. Librarian Detroit Pub. Library, 1968-70; head fine arts dept. Syracuse (N.Y.) U. Libraries, 1970-73; dir. library Roseville (Mich.) Pub. Library, 1973-75; asst. dir. libraries U. Wash., 1975-77, assoc. dir. libraries, 1978-79; dir. libraries U. Man., Winnipeg, Can., 1979-82; chief librarian U. Toronto, Can., 1982-85; univ. librarian U. Calif., Davis, 1985—. Mem. program com. Ctr. for Research Libraries. Recipient Woman of Yr. in Mgmt. award Winnipeg YWCA, 1982; named Woman of Distinction, U. Calif. Faculty Women's Research Group, 1985. Mem. ALA, Research Libraries Group (bd. dirs.), Assn. Research Libraries (bd. dirs.), Internat. Fedn. Library Assns. (univ. libraries sect.). Office: U Calif-Davis 108 Shields Library Davis CA 95616

SHATAN, NORMA ALTSTEDTER, painter; b. N.Y.C., July 18, 1932; d. Irving Charles and Renee Rose (Green) Altstedter; student Academie de la Grande Chaumiere, Ecole du Louvre and Sorbonne, 1950-51; B.A., Goucher Coll., 1952; M.A., Columbia U., 1983; m. Chaim F. Shatan, May 29, 1955; children—Gregory, Gabrielle, Jessica, Jeremy. One-person exhbns. include: Prince St. Gallery, 1970, 72, 73, 76, 77, 82, 84, 87, Paddlewicker Gallery, Lenox, Mass., 1977, 79, Silvermine Guild Galleries, 1987, Chautauqua Assn. Art Galleries, 1987; group shows include: Prince St. Gallery, Bklyn. Mus., Berkshire Mus, Salon des Comparaisons, Paris, Loch Haven Art Ctr., Orlando, Fla.; treas. Prince St. Gallery, 1970-80. Millay Colony for Arts fellow. Mem. Women in the Arts, Women's Caucus for Art. Translator: (with Alice Muehsam) The Sense of Form in Art (Heinrich Wolfflin), 1958. Home and Office: 415 Central Park W New York NY 10025

SHATTO, GLORIA MCDERMITH, college president, economist; b. Houston, Oct. 11, 1931; d. Ken E. and Gertrude (Osborne) McDermith; m.

Robert J. Shatto, Mar. 19, 1953; children: David Paul, Donald Patrick. B.A. with honors in Econs., Rice U., 1954, Ph.D. (fellow), 1966. Market research Humble Oil & Refining Co., Houston, 1954-55; tchr. pub. sch. C.Z., 1955-56; tchr. Houston Independent Sch. Dist., 1956-60; asst. prof. econs. U. Houston, 1965-69, asso. prof., 1969-72; prof. econs., asso. dean Coll. Indsl. Mgmt., Ga. Inst. Tech., Atlanta, 1973-77; George R. Brown prof. bus. Trinity U., San Antonio, 1977-79; pres. Berry Coll., Mount Berry, Ga., 1980—; small bus. adv. com. U.S. Treasury, 1977-81; trustee Joint Council Econ. Edn., 1985—; dir. Ga. Power Co., K-Mart Corp., So. Co., Becton Dickinson and Co., Citizens and So. Ga. Corp., The Citizens and So. Nat. Bank. Contbr. articles to profl. jours.; Editor: Employment of the Middle-Aged, 1972; mem. editorial bd.: Ednl. Record, 1980-82. Mem. Tex. Gov.'s Commn. on Status of Women, 1970-72; trustee Ga. Tech. Research Inst., 1975-77, Berry Coll., Ga., 1975-79, Ga. Forestry Commn., 1987—; mem. Ga. Gov.'s Commn. on Status of Women, 1975; mem. commn. on women in higher edn. Am. Council on Edn., 1980-82, chmn., 1982; mem. Ga. Study Com. on Public Higher Edn. Fin., 1981-82; v.p. Ga. Fund Ind. Colls., 1981, pres., 1982; mem. adv. bd. to Sch. Bus. Adminstrn., Temple U., Phila., 1981-83; mem. Study Com. on Ednl. Processes, So. Assn. Colls. and Schs., 1981-82, Ga. United Meth. Commn. on Higher Edn. and Campus Ministry, 1981—; bd. trustees Redmond Park Hosp., Rome, Ga., 1981-87. Recipient Disting. Alumni award Rice Univ., 1987; OAS fellow, summer 1968. Mem. Royal Econ. Assn., Am. Econ. Assn., So. Econ. Assn., Southwestern Econ. Assn. (pres. 1976-77), Am. Fin. Assn. (nominating com. 1976), Southwestern Social Scis. Assn., Fin. Execs. Inst. (chmn. Atlanta edn. com. 1976-77, mem. com. on profl. devel. 1981), AAUW (area rep. 1967-68, Tex. chmn. legis. program 1970-71, mem. internat. fellowships and awards com. 1970-76, chmn. 1974-76), Phi Beta Kappa, Phi Kappa Phi, Omicron Delta Epsilon. Office: Berry Coll Mount Berry Sta Rome GA 30149

SHATTUCK, BARBARA ZACCHEO, investment banking firm executive; b. New Rochelle, N.Y., Dec. 25, 1950; d. John Nicholas and Mary-Jane (Haller) Zaccheo; m. John Garrett Shattuck (div.); m. Arthur M. Dubow. AB, Conn. Coll., 1972; postgrad. NYU Sch. Bus., 1974-75. Bond analyst Standard & Poor's, N.Y.C., 1972-76; assoc. Blyth, Eastman Dillon & Co., N.Y.C., 1976; v.p. Goldman, Sachs, N.Y.C., 1976-82; ptnr. Cain Bros, Shattuck & Co., N.Y.C., 1982—; speaker Practicing Law Inst., Am. Hosp. Assn. Fundraiser Mondale for Pres., N.Y.C., 1983-84, mem. nat. fin. com. Dukakis for Pres.; bd. dirs. Seltzer Found.; mem. friends of collection com. Parrish Art Mus., Southampton, N.Y. Mem. Women's Econ. Round Table. Democrat. Episcopalian. Club: India House (N.Y.C.).

SHATTUCK, CATHIE ANN, lawyer, government official; b. Salt Lake City, July 18, 1945; d. Robert Ashley S. and Lillian Culp (Shattuck). B.A., U. Nebr., 1967, J.D., 1970. Bar: Nebr. 1970, Colo. 1971, U.S. Supreme Ct. 1974, U.S. Dist. Ct. Nebr. 1970, U.S. Dist. Ct. Colo. 1971, U.S. Ct. Appeals (10th cir.) 1977, U.S. Dist. Ct. D.C. 1984, U.S. Ct. Appeals (D.C. cir.) 1984. Vice pres., gen. mgr. Shattuck Farms, Hastings, Nebr., 1967-70; asst. project dir. atty. Colo. Civil Rights Commn., Denver, 1970-72; trial atty. Equal Employment Opportunity Commn., Denver, 1973-77; vice chmn. Equal Employment Opportunity Commn., Washington, 1982-84; sole practice Denver, 1977-81; mem. Fgn. Service Bd., Washington, 1982-84, Presdl. Personnel Task Force, Washington, 1982-84; ptnr. Epstein, Becker & Green, Los Angeles and Washington, 1984—; lectr. Colo. Continuing Legal Edn. Mem. Met. Opera Guild, N.Y.C.; bd. dirs. KGNU Pub. Radio, Boulder, Colo., 1979, Denver Exchange, 1980-81, YWCA Met. Denver, 1979-81. Recipient Nebr. Young Career Woman Bus. and Profl. Women, 1967; recipient Outstanding Nebraskan Daily Nebraskan, Lincoln, 1967. Mem. ABA (mgmt. chair employment law sect. com. on immigration, labor and employment law sect. com. on immigration law), Nebr. Bar Assn., Colo. Bar Assn., Colo. Women's Bar Assn., D.C. Bar Assn., Nat. Womens Coalition, Delta Sigma Rho, Tau Kappa Alpha, Pi Sigma Alpha, Alpha Xi Delta. Club: Denver.

SHAUGHNESSY, AMY ELISABETH, association administrator; b. N.Y.C., Dec. 6, 1942; d. John Arthur and Alice (Miller) S.; m. David T. Humes, June, 14, 1984; 1 stepchild, Elizabeth. BS in Linguistics, Georgetown U., 1964, MS in Linguistics, 1970. Editorial assoc. Ctr. Applied Linguistics, Washington, 1964-70; asst. mng. editor Am. Jour. Psychiatry, Am. Psychiat. Assn., Washington, 1970-74; mng. editor, bus. mgr. Ctr. Personalized Instrn. Georgetown U., Washington, 1974-76; sr. editor Transp. Research Bd. Nat. Acad. Scis., Washington, 1976-81; free-lance editor, writer Washington, 1982-83; dir. pubs. Am. Ednl. Research Assn., Washington, 1983—; Judge typographic excellence competition Nat. Composition Assn., Washington, 1972-75. Mem. Soc. Nat. Assn. Pubs., Washington Edn. Press., Greater Washington Soc. Assn. Execs., Nat. Assn. Female Execs., AAUW, MENSA (nat. gov. com. 1981—, 1st vice chmn. 1983-85, chmn. 1985—, internat. bd. dirs. 1985—). Home: 369 O Street SW Washington DC 20024 Office: Am Ednl Research Assn 1230 17th St NW Washington DC 20036

SHAUGHNESSY, MARIE KANEKO, broker-distributor warehouse company executive, artist; b. Detroit, Sept. 14, 1924; d. Eishiro and Kiyo (Yoshida) Kaneko; m. John Thomas Shaughnessy, Sept. 23, 1959. Assocs. in Liberal Arts, Keisen Women's Coll., Tokyo, 1944. Ops. mgr. Webco Alaska, Inc., Anchorage, 1970-88; ptnr. Webco Partnership, Anchorage, 1983—, also bd. dirs. Paintings include Lilacs, 1984, Blooms, 1985, The Fence, 1986 (Purchase award 1986). Bd. dirs. Alaska Artists Guild, 1971-87; commr. Mcpl. Anchorage Fine Arts Commn., 1983-87; organizing com. Japanese Soc. Alaska, 1987. Recipient Arts Affiliates award, Anchorage Community Coll., 1975, 1978, 1984; named Univ. Artist, Alaska Pacific U., 1986. Mem. Potomac Valley Watercolorists, Va. Watercolor Soc., Art League, Sumi-e Soc. Am. (Washington chpt.), San Diego Watercolor Soc., Alaska Watercolor Soc. (life). Republican. Episcopalian. Home: 1200 Allendale Rd McLean VA 22101

SHAUGHNESSY, MARY ELLEN, educator; b. Buffalo, Oct. 21, 1938; d. John L. and Mary Ellen (McCarthy) S. BA in English Edn., Medaille Coll., 1964; MA in English, Niagara U., 1967; PhD in Lit. and Psychology, SUNY, Buffalo, 1977. Adminstr., instr. Trocaire Coll., 1970-72; instr. program coordinator SUNY, Buffalo, 1972-81; personnel mgr., tng. coordinator Del. North Cos., 1981-85; allocations mgr., dir. community problem solving United Way of Buffalo and Erie County, Buffalo, 1985-87; mentor/instr. Empire State Coll., Buffalo, 1988—; cons. in fiedl; mem. adv. council dept. bus. studies Buffalo State Coll.; mem. adj. faculty bus. writing and career planning Cornell U.; tutor writing Empire State Coll. Bd. dirs. Ctr. Women in Mgmt., 1981—; assoc. dir. leadership tng. family life dept. Diocese of Bubbalo, 1969-72; vol. telephone counselor Suicide Prevention and Crisis Services, 1973-75; vol. mediator Better Bus. Bur., 1984—. Mem. Mid. States Assn. (accrediting team 1969), AAUW (bd. dirs., dir. publicity), Indsl. Relations Assn. (bd. dirs., chmn. program com.), Buffalo Investors Group (bd. dirs.). Home: PO Box 243 Buffalo NY 14216 Office: Empire State Coll 564 Franklin St Buffalo NY 14209

SHAUGHNESSY, NANCY BACZENAS, finance company executive; b. St. Louis, May 28, 1953; d. Carl Peter and Shirley Mary (Fischer) Baczenas; m. Thomas Joseph Shaughnessy, Aug. 24, 1986. BS in Acctg. cum laude, U. Mo., St. Louis, 1983; MBA in Fin., Western New Eng. Coll., 1986. Mgmt. trainee Smith & Wesson, Springfield, Mass., 1984-85, supr. accounts payable, 1985-86, supr. gen. acctg., 1986-87; mgr. acctg., fin. Century Fin. Services Group, Chesterfield, Mo., 1987, v.p. fin., chief fin. officer, 1987—. Democrat. Roman Catholic. Office: Century Fin Services Group Ltd 15400 S Outer 40 Rd Chesterfield MO 63017

SHAVER, PATRICIA ANN, corporate professional, public information officer; b. Harrisburg, Pa., Sept. 19, 1943; d. James J. and Rose L. (Fleck) Faley; m. John R. Shaver, Dec. 9, 1961; children: Richard J., Sharian E. Student, Harrisburg (Pa.) Area Community Coll., 1986—. Adminstrv. asst. Foremost Ins. Co., Harrisburg, 1975-78; recorder Mohrbach & Marshall, Harrisburg, 1978-82; asst. sec., asst. treas. Hist. Times, Inc., Harrisburg, 1982—, exec. adminstrv. asst., 1988—; sec. Profl. Pict, Harrisburg, 1972-79; chief proctor Pa. Dept. of State, Harrisburg, 1981—; asst. sec., asst. treas. Early Am. Soc., Harrisburg, 1983-87. Mem. Am. Soc. of Notaries, Nat. Assn. of Female Execs., Pa. Notaries Assn., Am. Soc. Profl. and Exec. Women. Republican. Home: 5008 Colorado Ave Harrisburg PA 17109 Office: Hist Times Inc 2245 Kohn Rd Harrisburg PA 17110

SHAVER, PAULA RUTH, small business owner; b. Wynnewood, Okla., Apr. 5, 1955; d. George William and Frances Jeanette (VanHooser) Allison; m. David Ray Shaver, Dec. 25, 1973; children: Robert Ray, Richard Ray. Student, Crowley's Ridge Coll., 1973-74. Sec., v.p. Mountaire Poultry, Little Rock, 1974-75; sec. legal McDaniel and Gott, Jonesboro, Ark., 1978; owner, mgr. Diamonds Plus Inc., Jonesboro and Paragould, Ark., 1980—. Tchr. Sunday Sch. Mem. Ark. Jewelers Assn., Indian Mall Merchants Assn. (bd. dirs. 1987—, pres. 1988), Sales and Mktg. Exec. Republican. Mem. Ch. Christ. Club: N.E. Ark. Striders, Jonesboro. office: Diamonds Plus Indian Mall Jonesboro AR 72401

SHAVERS, DONNA JEAN, association executive; b. Springfield, Ill., Mar. 23; d. Frank and Ethel (Nance) Higgins; m. Conrad Shavers, Sept. 22, 1956 (div. 1986); children: Vance N., Karla J. BS, Roosevelt U., 1974; postgrad., Nat. Coll. of Edn., Chgo., 1987—. V.p. Planned Parenthood Assn., Chgo., 1958-78; patient health coordinator Chgo. Urban League, 1979-82; travel cons. Joy Travel Service, Chgo., 1979—; coordinator of pediatrics sickle cell program Michael Reese Hosp., Chgo., 1982-85; supr. Chgo. Youth Ctrs., 1985—; coordinator partnership-in-health program Cook County Hosp., Chgo., 1986—; youth instr. Northwood River Dist. Assn., 1986; instr. Ill. State Bapt. Conv. of Chgo., 1983-85. Mem. Civic Aux., Chgo., 1974-78; organizer Concerned Parents Com., Chgo., 1982—; mem. bd. dirs. O'Keefe PTA, Chgo., 1970-73, pres. St. Anselms PTA, Chgo., 1968-70; pres., fin. sec. Phila. Bible Ch., 1980—, instr., 1983-86, banquet chmn. 1980—; mem. Chgo. Urban League, Sr. Missionary Club, Sr. Women's Missionary Circle. Democrat. Home and Office: Fox Travel Inc 2941 S Michigan #517 Chicago IL 60616

SHAW, ARACELIS GOBERNA, educator; b. Pinar del Rio, Cuba, June 22, 1922; came to U.S., 1948, naturalized, 1955; d. Jose B. and Eloisa (Santiuste) Goberna; B.S., B.L., Inst. Pinar del Rio, 1941; Ph.D. and Letters, U. Havana, 1948; M.A., U. Fla., 1957; m. Steven J. Shaw, June 8, 1952. Instr., Berlitz Sch. Langs., Miami, Fla., 1949-52, N.Y.C., 1952-54; research asst. U. Fla., 1955-57; mem. faculty Columbia (S.C.) Coll., 1957—, prof. Spanish, 1963-88, chmn. dept. fgn. langs., 1962—, head Intercultural and Lang. Center, 1977-87; dir. lang. workshops, cons. in field. Pres. S.C. chpt. Partners of Americas, 1975-78, 81-87 exec. dir. 1987—. Recipient Cervantes award, 1976, S.C. Bicentennial award, 1976; Am. Express award for excellence in internat. volunteerism, 1983. Mem. Am. Assn. Tchrs. Spanish and Portuguese (pres. S.C. chpt. 1973-74), Southeastern Conf. Latin Am. Studies, Sigma Delta Pi. Roman Catholic. Club: Columbia Coll. Internat. Author: (for TV) El Espanol Paso a Paso, 1969; also workbooks, lab. manuals. Home: 4832 Forest Ridge Ln Columbia SC 29206 Office: Columbia Coll Ptnrs of the Americas Columbia SC 29203

SHAW, CAROL JEAN, insurance company executive; b. Joliet, Ill., July 27, 1952; d. Henry and Ethel Virginia (Klipfel) S.; m. Daniel Wilson Hopkins, Aug. 17, 1974 (div. Sept. 1978). BA cum laude, No. Ill. U., 1974. CPCU. Collection dept. Sears, Roebuck & Co., Schaumburg, Ill., 1974-76; sec. City of Bloomington, Ill., 1976-79; supr. State Farm Ins. Co., Bloomington, 1979-81, tng. analyst, 1981-84. Panel mem. McLean County (Ill.) United Way, McLean County, 1985—; fundraiser McLean County Humane Soc., 1988. Mem. Soc. CPCU's (new desingee rep. 1986-87, chmn. candidate devel. 1988—). Democrat. Methodist. Office: State Farm Ins Co 1 State Farm Plaza Bloomington IL 61710

SHAW, CAROLE, editor; b. Bklyn., Jan. 22, 1936; d. Sam and Betty (Neckin) Bergenthal; m. Ray Shaw, Dec. 27, 1957; children: Lori Eve Cohen, Victoria Lynn. BA, Hunter Coll., 1962. Owner The People's Choice, Los Angeles, 1975-79; founder, editor-in-chief BBW Mag., Tarzana, Calif., 1979—; creator BBW label clothing line. Author: Come Out, Come Out Wherever You Are, 1982; singer: Capitol Records, Hilton Records, Rama Records, Verve Records, 1952-65; TV appearance: Ed Sullivan, Steve Allen, Jack Paar, Colgate Comedy Hour, George Gobel Show, 1957. Office: BBW: Big Beautiful Woman 9171 Wilshire Blvd #300 Beverly Hills CA 90210

SHAW, DIANE HUGHES, health science association administrator; b. Lawrenceville, Ga., Oct. 17, 1940; d. William Henry and Bertha Irene (Thompson) Hughes; m. James Michael Shaw, July 10, 1971. BS, U. Ga., 1963. Dispensing optician Golden S. Hinton, Athens, Ga., 1963-67, Med. Ctr. Clinic, Pensacola, Fla., 1967-69, Ophthalmology Clinic, Ft. Smith, Ark., 1969-71; sales mgr. World Wide Travel, Little Rock, 1984-87; area dir. Am. Cancer Soc., Little Rock, 1980—; cons. Jr. League, Ft. Smith, 1975-82. Bd. dirs. Sparks Med. Ctr., Ft. Smith, 1971, Art Ctr., Ft. Smith, 1972-76, Jr. League of Ft. Smith, 1974—, Gregory Kistler Found., Ft. Smith, 1976-80. Recipient Award of Excellence, Ga. Soc. of Opticians, 1967. Mem. Am. Bd. of Opticianry, Southeastern Soc. of Opticians, Nat. Acad. of Opticianry. Republican. Episcopalian. Home: 4615 Free Ferry Rd Fort Smith AK 72903

SHAW, ELEANOR JANE, newspaper editor; b. Columbus, Ohio, Mar. 23, 1949; d. Joseph Cannon and Wanda Jane (Campbell) S. BA, U. Del., 1971. With News-Jour. newspapers, Wilmington, Del., 1970-82, acting bus. editor, 1976-77, editor HEW desk, asst. met. editor, 1977-80, bus. editor, 1980-82; topics editor USA Today, 1982-83; asst. city editor The Miami Herald, 1983-85; projects editor The Sacramento Bee, 1985-87, news editor, 1987—. Bd. dirs. Del. 4-H Found., 1978-83. Mem. Soc. Profl. Journalists. Office: The Sacramento Bee PO Box 15779 Sacramento CA 95852

SHAW, ESTHER WEFALD, communications executive; b. Hawley, Minn., July 10; d. Peder and Matilda Wefald; m. Howard Bernard Shaw, Dec. 15, 1961. Grad. high sch., Chgo. Key distributor Amway Corp., Ada, Mich., 1957—; chmn. bd. Shaw Communications Cons., Miami, Fla., 1975—. Active Sunny Isles Civic Assn., Miami, 1974-80. Mem. Am. Contract Bridge Assn. Republican. Lutheran. Home and Office: 20341 NE 30th Ave Miami FL 33180

SHAW, GRACE GOODFRIEND (MRS. HERBERT FRANKLIN SHAW), editor; b. N.Y.C.; d. Henry Bernheim and Jane Elizabeth (Stone) Goodfriend; m. Herbert Franklin Shaw; 1 son, Brandon Hibbs. Student, Bennington Coll.; B.A. magna cum laude, Fordham U., 1976. Reporter Port Chester (N.Y.) Daily Item; editorial coordinator World Scope Ency., N.Y.C.; assoc. editor Clarence L. Barnhart, Inc., Bronxville, N.Y.; free-lance writer for reference book; editing supr. World Pub. Co., N.Y.C., 1965-68; mng. editor World Pub. Co., 1968-69, sr. editor, 1969; mng. editor Peter H. Wyden Co., N.Y.C., 1969-70; assoc. editor Dial Press, N.Y.C., 1971-72; sr. editor Dial Press, 1972, David McKay Co., N.Y.C., 1972-75, Grosset & Dunlap, 1975-77; chief editor Today Press, 1977-79; sr. editor, coll. dept. Bobbs-Merrill, N.Y.C.; mng. editor Bobbs-Merrill, exec. editor trade div., 1979-80, pub., 1980-84; mng. editor Rawson Assocs. div. MacMillan Pub., 1985—. Club: Overseas Press (bd. dirs. 1984—, chmn. fgn. policy book awards 1983-87). Home: 85 Lee Rd Scarsdale NY 10583 Office: 115 Fifth Ave New York NY 10017

SHAW, JERRY G., publisher; b. Marlin, Tex., July 15, 1927; d. Eugene C. and Gladys (Moore) Pool; m. Charles E. Stailey, May 30, 1946 (dec. July 1958); children: Sherry, Judy; m. Richard L. Shaw, Jan. 7, 1963. Student, Tex. Tech. U., 1944-46, 1958-62. Writer Roswell Daily Record, Ruidoso, N.Mex., 1965-67; inventory control mgr. Montgomery Ward, Amarillo, Tex., 1967-70, Orlando, Fla., 1970-73; real estate sales agt. Wimberley, Tex., 1975-76; writer Ruidoso News, N.Mex., 1976-77; owner, optician Looking Glass Optical Shop, Ruidoso, N.Mex., 1978-88; owner, founder, pub. Best Bet Magazine, Ruidoso, 1978—. First woman councillor, mayor pro tem, Village Ruidoso, 1984-88; Dem. precinct chmn. Lincoln County, 1987-88; bd. dirs. FLincoln County Humane Soc., Ruidoso, 1985—, Ruidoso Transp. Commn., 1985—; chmn. Econ. Devel. Commn., Ruidoso, 1985—; dist. dir. N.Mex. Mcpl. League, Santa Fe, 1986. Named Todays Woman in Govt., Ruidoso Womens Club, 1985. Mem. Beta Sigma Phi. Methodist. Club: Pilot (Ruidoso) (sec. 1983). Home: PO Box 2077 Ruidoso NM 88345

SHAW, KAREN, artist, curator; b. Bronx, N.Y., Oct. 25, 1941; d. Emanuel and Jeanne (MIller) Tobias; m. Ronald Jay; children: David, Stephan. BFA, Hunter Coll., 1965. Curator Islip (N.Y.) Art Mus., 1981—; artist-in-residence U. Tenn., Knoxville, 1986; adj. prof. drawing and 2D design CUNY, 1987-88. Exhibited in one person and group shows throughout the U.S. and Europe; author: Market Research, 1978; contbr. short stories to popular mags. Nat. Endowment for the Arts grantee, 1978; named N.Y. Found. for the Arts Artist-in-Residence, 1985; recipient N.Y. Times Short Story contest award, 1976. Home: 712 Lakeside Dr Baldwin NY 11510 Office: 10-27 46th Ave Long Island NY 11101

SHAW, KATHLEEN KAY MARTIN, management consultant; b. Freeport, Ill., June 3, 1950; d. Burnham Nelson Martin and June Beatrice (Moore) Drake; m. Walter Richard Shaw Jr., Aug. 26, 1972 (div. June 1977). BA in French, Lawrence U., 1972; MBA, U. Va., 1984. Sec. NCR, Providence, R.I., 1972-74; sec. Lenox Candles, Inc., Oshkosh, Wis., 1974-76, product coordinator, 1976-78, product mgr., 1978-81; sr. assoc. APM, Inc., N.Y.C., 1984-85; dep. dir. Ethics Resource Ctr., Inc., Washington, 1985-87, dir. adv. services, 1987—. Republican. Presbyterian. Office: Ethics Resource Ctr Inc 1025 Connecticut Ave NW Washington DC 20036

SHAW, MADELINE READ, machine tool company executive; b. Saginaw, Ala., July 16, 1910; d. Thomas H. and Eleanor (Satterwhite) Read; student U. Ala., 1919-22; m. Ralph M. Shaw Jr., June 15, 1927. 1 child Mary Eleanor Shaw Carretta (dec.). Tchr., Stafford Sch., Tuscaloosa, Ala., 1922-24; pvt. tchr. music, Gorgas, Ala., 1924-25; organist Paramount Publix Co., Miami, Fla. and N.Y.C., 1925-27; with Pedrick Tool & Machine Co., Riverton, N.J., 1939—, v.p. fin., 1940-79, pres., 1979—. Republican. Episcopalian. Club: Cosmopolitan (Phila). Home: Shawnee Hall Beverly NJ 08010 Office: 1518 Bannard St Riverton NJ 08077

SHAW, MARJORIE BETTS, magazine editor; b. Des Moines, Dec. 17, 1938; d. Jerry Waltz and Dorothy Jane (Coy) Betts; m. Albert Michael Shaw, July 19, 1973. B.A. in Journalism, San Diego State U., 1961. Prodn. asst. KFMB-TV, San Diego, 1961-62; sec. San Diego Zoo, 1962-65, librarian, 1966-78, editor, 1979—; cons. Quality Prodns., Inc., San Diego, 1985. Editor: (with others) Wild in the City, 1985; contbr. articles to profl. jours. Recipient Graphics award Am. Assn. Zool. Parks-Aquariums, 1979, Best Continuing Publ., Pub. Relations Club of San Diego, 1980, 82, 83, 85, 87; Champion award Internat. Corp., 1985, Champion award for high standards in graphic arts, 1986, Best in the West award Assn. Pubs., 1987. Mem. Am. Assn. Travel Editors, Soc. History of Natural History. Office: Zoonooz PO Box 551 San Diego CA 92112

SHAW, MARY ANN, psychologist; b. Dallas, July 5, 1937; d. Leon V. and Mabel (Bartlett) S.; B.S., U. Tex., 1959; M.Ed., U. Houston, 1966, Ed.D., 1973. Tchr. educable mentally retarded Spring Branch, Tex., 1959-64; vocat. counselor, Houston, 1964-66; psychometrist pvt. psychol. clinic, Houston, 1966-70; coordinator research Tex. Edn. Agency grant project, 1970-72; dir. psychol. services Tex. Scottish Rite Hosp. for Crippled Children, Dallas, 1972-82; dir. Dean Evaluation Ctr., Dallas, 1982-84; mem. clin. staff U. Tex. Health Sci. Center; cons. pvt. and public schs. Mem. Am. Psychol. Assn., Dallas Psychol. Assn., Assn. Pediatric Psychologists. Author: What Do I Do When; contbr. article to profl. jour.; research in field.

SHAW, MARY LEE, health care educator, consultant; b. Kokomo, Ind., Oct. 11, 1933; d. John Frederick and Mary Elizabeth (Bola) Maher; m. Thomas Arthur Shaw, Feb. 18, 1956 (div. 1975); children—Tracy Elizabeth, Susan Margaret, Kathryn Lee. A.A., William Woods Coll., 1952; A.B. in French, Ind. U., Bloomington, 1954, M.S., 1961. Instr. modern lang. dept. Purdue U.-Calumet, Hammond, Ind., 1961-70; tchr., cons. Burnham Pub. Schs., Hammond Pub. Schs., 1970-74; tng. specialist nursing edn. U. Tex., M.D. Anderson Hosp. and Tumor Inst., Houston, 1975-78; nurse recruiter, 1978-80, group supr., dept. tng. and devel., 1980—, supr. personnel tng. programs, 1986-87, trainer, cons., 1988—; speaker in field. Mem. Alliance Française, Literacy Vols. Am., Phi Theta Kappa (pres. Fulton, Mo. chpt. 1951-52), Alpha Chi Omega (pres. Hammond chpt. alumni 1966-67). Home: 3000 Greenridge #1202 Houston TX 77057 Office: MD Anderson Hosp & Tumor Inst 6723 Bertner Houston TX 77030

SHAW, RENATA VITZTHUM, library administrator; b. Mantta, Hame, Finland, July 21, 1926; came to U.S., 1947, naturalized, 1957; d. Burghard and Helle (Sirén) Vitzthum von Eckstadt; m. Russell Ramon Shaw, Aug. 14, 1954; children—Rembert B.V., Lori R.H. M.A. in Art History, U. Chgo., 1949; Magister Philosophiae, U. Helsinki (Finland), 1951; Diploma in Museology, Ecole de Louvre, Paris, 1952; M.S. in L.S., Catholic U., 1962. With Library of Congress, Washington, 1962—, supervisory librarian, 1967-71, bibliog. specialist, 1971-82, asst. chief prints and photographs div., 1982-83, acting chief, 1983-84, asst. chief, 1984—, mem. Pennell purchasing com., 1983-84, mem. acquisitions com. 1985-86. Compiler: (bibliography) Picture Searching, 1973; (essays) Graphic Sampler, 1978, Century of Photographs, 1980; chmn. editorial com. Art Serials (D.C.), 1981, Washingtoniana, a guide to photog. resources in Prints and Photos Div., 1984-86. Recipient Meritorious Service award Library of Congress, 1975. Mem. ALA, Art Libraries Soc. N.Am., Washington Art Library Resources Com. (founder 1974), Spl. Libraries Assn. (dir. 1976-78), Huguenot Soc. S.C., Beta Phi Mu. Republican. Episcopalian. Home: 4850 Langdrum Ln Chevy Chase MD 20815 Office: Prints and Photographs Div Library of Congress 10 1st St SE Washington DC 20540

SHAW, SHARRILYN WHITING, personal products company executive; b. Mobile, Ala., Oct. 6, 1946; d. James Allen and Virginia G. (Hearn) Whiting; student U. Ala., 1965-67, U. South Ala., 1968-70, Sterling Inst., 1979, Tex. Tech. Profl. Devel. Center, 1981; 1 son, Ivey. Writer, Nashville Tennessean, 1970, Mobile (Ala.) Press Register, 1968-69; account exec. The Pitluk Group, San Antonio, 1976-77; advt./promotion mgr. Sta. KSAT-TV, San Antonio, 1977-79; advt. mgr. Lone Star Brewing Co., San Antonio, 1979-80, mgr. mktg., 1980-82; v.p. mktg. Swiss Watch Distbn. Center, Inc., San Antonio, 1982; pres., chief exec. officer Dans Un Jardin Tex., Inc., Dallas, 1982-86; chmn. Bella Madonna, Inc., 1986—. Chmn., ABC-TV Network Promotion Adv. Bd., 1978-79, San Antonio Women's Edn. and Employment, Inc., 1981-82; commr. San Antonio Conv. and Visitors Bur., 1981-82; mem. steering com. Leadership San Antonio, 1981—; v.p. bd. dirs. Children's Hosp. Found., 1979—; bd. dirs. Monte Vista Hist. Assn., Tex. Women's Employment and Edn., Inc., others; mem. Leadership Tex., 1986-87; gala chair Am. Heart Assn., 1988; vol. breast screening project Am. Cancer Soc., 1988. Recipient Pro-Liner awards Women in Communications, 1980, award AP Ala., 1969, Addy awards, 1977, 78, 79, Internat. Assn. Bus. Communicators - Dallas award, 1981, Community Service award City of San Antonio, 1985. Mem. Am. Mktg. Assn., Tex. Public Relations Assn., Women in Communications, (v.p. 1979-80), Alpha Chi Omega. Clubs: Bright Shawl, St. Anthony, Mills County Hunting & Fishing, First Wednesday Breakfast, San Antonio 100 (v.p. 1987—), Oakes (pres. 1988—). Home: 7887 Broadway #405 San Antonio TX 78209

SHAW, UNEVA REAGAN, respiratory therapist; b. Chattanooga, Tenn., Sept. 21, 1956; d. Radford Burket and Susie Bernice (Flowers) Reagan; m. Charles Lee Shaw, June 19, 1986. A.S. in Respiratory Care, Cleveland Community Coll., Tenn., 1976; B.S. in Mgmt., U. Tenn.-Chattanooga, 1987. Registered respiratory therapist. Staff therapist East Ridge Hosp., Chattanooga, 1976, Diagnostic Hosp., Chattanooga, 1976-79; mgr. respiratory therapy Hutcheson Med. Ctr., Ft. Oglethorpe, Ga., 1978-85, adminstrv. dir. respiratory care, cardiology, neurology, pulmonology, 1987—; mgr. respiratory therapy and hosp. quality assurance NME-Metro Hosp., Chattanooga, 1985-87; instr. Am. Heart Assn., 1981—, Chattanooga Tech. Coll., 1980-85. Mem. Am. Assn. Respiratory Therapy. Republican. Mem. Ch. of Christ. Avocations: skiing, photography, hiking. Home: PO Box 22576 Chattanooga TN 37422 Office: Hutcheson Med Ctr 100 Gross Crescent Fort Oglethorpe GA 30742

SHAW-ALVAREZ, KIMBERLY CAROL, tax accountant; b. Las Vegas, Nev., Mar. 5, 1955; 1 child, Deema Evelyn Marie. BA, U. Tex., El Paso, 1975; postgrad., Am. Grad. Sch. of Internat. Mgmt., 1975-76; A in Computer Sci., City Colls. Chgo., 1985; postgrad., U. Tex., 1987—. Proprietor Kimbe's, El Paso, Tex., 1976-78; gen. acctg. various salons, schs., El Paso, 1978-81; ptnr., tax specialist Individualized Systems, Acctg. & Tax Services, El Paso, 1987, owner, tax specialist, 1988; cons. Moulin Gouge Dinner Theatre, 1983—, Robert Wales Atty. at Law, 1986—, Sound Performance, 1986—, Gladys R. Shaw CPA, 1987—. Author, editor Budgeting Standard Operations, 1985. Vol. Community Theatres, Europe, Ga., Tex., 1974—, Battered Women's Shelter, Europe, 1983-85, Foster Home for Abused Children, Europe, 1983-85, Army Community Services, Army Emergency Relief, Columbus, 1982-83. Mem. Assn. MBA Execs., Nat. Assn. Female Execs., Am. Soc. Women Accts., Am. Grad. Sch. Internat. Mgmt. Alumni Assn., La Leche League Internat. (leader 1983-85), Nat. Hair Dresser and Cosmetologist Assn. (sec. 1979-80). Republican. Roman Catholic. Office: Individualized Systems 1435 Fewel El Paso TX 79902

SHAY, SHIRLEY, fashion designer; b. Phila., Oct. 11, 1951; d. Arnold Leo and Bala (Saionz) S. Student, U. Pa., 1972; BFA, Moore Coll. Art, 1973. Designer Villager div. Jonathan Logan, N.Y.C., 1973-75, Puritan Fashions Corp., N.Y.C., 1975-77, Ellen Hart Inc., N.Y.C., 1977-81, Smoler Bros. Inc., N.Y.C., 1981-82; owner, designer S. Shay Designs, N.Y.C., 1982-85; designer, merchandiser Kenly Mfg. Co., N.Y.C., 1985-88; cons. Patricia Magali, N.Y.C. 1987—. Mem. NOW, Murray Hill Com., Second Generation Children Holocaust Survivors, Fashion Apparel Assn., Nat. Assn. Female Exec. Democrat. Jewish. Office: 530 Second Ave #3G New York NY 10016

SHEA, CHARLENE RIOPELLE, personal motivation speaker, consultant; b. Lawrence, Mass., Sept. 3, 1934; d. George Andrew and Ruth Knowlton (Pickard) Riopelle; B.S., U. Maine, 1957; m. Thomas Everett, Mar. 30, 1956; children—Valerie Ruth, Thomas Leon, Gwendolyn Beryl. Tchr. 1st grade, Okinawa, Japan, 1958-60, El Paso, Tex., 1961-65, Highland, N.J., 1965-68, Frankfurt, Germany, 1969-72; dir. sales tng. Mary Kay Cosmetics, Inc., Manchester, N.H., 1972-80; pres. Charlene Shea., Inc., motivational speaking and cons. firm, Manchester, 1980—; instr. U. N.H., Manchester, 1979—. Mem. fin. com. YWCA, 1981, bd. dirs., 1982-84; bd. dirs. WON, 1981. Recipient N.H. Woman in Bus. adv. award SBA, 1982; Cert. Speaking Profl. award, 1986. Mem. Internat. Platform Assn., Manchester C. of C., Nat. Speakers Assn., New England Speakers Assn. (pres.), Meeting Planner Internat. Home and Office: 121 Allied St Manchester NH 03103

SHEA, CYNTHIA POLLOCK, researcher, writer; b. Nurenberg, Fed. Republic of Germany, Jan. 12, 1959; d. Lindsay and Eleanor (Babb) P. BA in Econs., Environ. Studies, Internat. Relations, U. Wis., 1982. Research assoc. Resource Dynamics Corp., McLean, Va., 1983; sr. researcher Worldwatch Inst., Washington, 1984—; assoc. mem. Global Tomorrow Coalition, Washington, 1983—; cons. U.S. Congress, 1986—, World Bank, Washington, 1987; workshop chmn. Soc. Internat. Devel., Washington, 1986—. Author: (with others) State of the World series, 1985, 86, 87, 88; contbr. articles to profl. jours. Active Sierra Club, Washington, 1983—, Virginians for Recycling, Richmond, 1986—, Natural Resources Def. Council, Washington, 1984—, Environ. Def. Fund, Washington, 1984—. Office: Worldwatch Inst 1776 Massachusetts Ave NW Washington DC 20036

SHEA, DEBORAH HEATHER GUBNER, marketing executive; b. N.Y.C., Jan. 30, 1955; d. Richard Sigmund and Yvonne Lucille (Luke) Gubner; m. Bill Shea, Apr. 21, 1984 (div. 1986). B.A., U. South Fla., 1977; postgrad. in mktg. Northwestern U., 1979-81. First scholar First Nat. Bank Chgo., 1977-78, mgr. comml. mktg. communications, 1978-80, dir. internat. mktg., 1980-81; dir. mktg. planning and communications Arthur Andersen & Co., Chgo., 1981-83, dir. mktg. Rocky Mountain region, 1983-84; dir. Shea Cons. Group, 1981-86; dir. mktg. Cigna Healthplan, Tampa, 1986-88; mgr. industry mktg. GTE Data SERvices, 1988—; profl. theatre actress, dir. Actors Studio, Circle in Square, N.Y.C., 1969-77. Bd. dirs. Goodman Theatre's Inner Circle, Chgo., 1979-81, Colo. Contemporary Dance, 1983-84; mem. jr. governing bd. Chgo Symphony Recipient Eagle award for top fin. advt., Chgo Advt. Club, 1980, 81. Contbr. articles to profl. jours. Home: 2905 Mill Stream Ct Clearwater FL 33519

SHEA, ELAINE EVANS, civic association executive; b. Ithaca, N.Y., Aug. 1, 1935; d. William Arthur and Genevieve (Covert) Evans; m. Michael Henry Shea, June 28, 1956; children: Elizabeth Ann, Linda Evans, William Michael. AA, Stephens Coll., 1955. Writer, film previewer Sta. KWTV, Oklahoma City, 1955-56; exec. dir. Save the Tallgrass Prairie, Inc., Shawnee Mission, Kans., 1974-84. Bd. dirs. Kans. Natural Resource Council, 1982-83; registered lobbyist, 1980-82; pres. Porter Sch. PTA, 1969; leader Girl Scouts; tchr. Sunday Sch., Shepherd deacon Village United Presbyn. Ch.; tract chmn. Am. Cancer Soc., 1982; exec. dir. Grassland Heritage Found., 1982-85, bd. dirs., 1985—; mem. Kans. Gov.'s Adv. Commn. on Environ., 1983-86 . Recipient Environ. Quality award EPA, 1978. Clubs: Stephens Coll. Dinner (pres. 1966), Prairie Planters Garden (pres. 1972), Kansas City Country. Editor: Tallgrass Prairie News, 1974-84. Home: 6025 Cherokee Dr Shawnee Mission KS 66205 Office: 5450 Buena Vista Shawnee Mission KS 66205

SHEA, PAMELA JANE, lawyer; b. Concord, N.H., Aug. 14, 1948; d. Ernest Francis and Cynthia Pamela (Horwood) Gaudreau; m. Dennis James Shea, Aug. 21, 1971; children—Kelly, Tracey. BA cum laude, Smith Coll., 1970; JD, U. Mich., 1973. Bar: Mich. 1974. Law clk. organized crime, racketeering sect. U.S. Dept. Justice, Detroit, 1971; assoc. Beier, Howlett, Ternan, Jones, Shea and Hafeli, Bloomfield Hills, Mich., 1973-79, ptnr., 1979—; lectr. I.C.L.E. Trial Advocacy Workshops, 1983—. Mem. Oakland County Bar Assn., State Bar Assn. Mich. (Tort Law Rev. Com. 1983—, Circuit Ct. com. Bloomfield Hills 1983—, Mediation Com. 1986—), ABA, Women's Bar Assn., Assn. Def. Trial Counsel, Sigma Xi. Republican. Episcopalian. Club: Smith (Birmingham-Bloomfield Hills). Home: 420 Dunston Rd Bloomfield Hills MI 48013 Office: Beier Howlett Ternan 74 W Long Lake Rd Suite 1 Bloomfield Hills MI 48013

SHEAHAN, CLAIRE MATHER, insurance company executive; b. Bridgeport, Conn., May 9, 1942; d. Robert Elston and Ruth Evelyn (Allen) S.; B.A., Vassar Coll., 1964. Copy editor Yale U. Press, New Haven, 1964-65; advt. press relations Tchrs. Ins. & Annuity Assn.-Coll. Retirement Equities Fund, N.Y.C., 1965-70, editor employee communications, 1970-72, communications specialist, 1972-78, corp. communications adminstr., 1978-80, asst. publs. officer, 1980-84, pub. info. officer, 1984-86, asst. v.p., pub. info. officer, 1986-88, mgr. pub. relations div., asst. v.p. and pub. info. officer, 1988—. Mem. Fin. Communications Soc., Pub. Relations Soc. Am., N.Y. Fin. Writers Assn., Internat. Assn. Bus. Communicators, N.Y. Assn. Bus. Communicators, Nat. Investor Relations Inst., Am. Mgmt. Assn. Episcopalian. Clubs: Vassar (pres. emeritus), Women's City (N.Y.C.). Office: TIAA-CREF 730 3d Ave New York NY 10017

SHEAHAN, MELODY ANN, transportation executive; b. Cin., Aug. 5, 1959; d. Earl Sterling and Willie Catherine (Stonestreet) McCoy. AA in Mech. Engring. Tech., U. Cin., 1979; student, Marshall U., 1980-86, U. N. Fla., 1987—, Fla. Community Coll., 1988—. Engring. tech. Chessie System R.R., Huntington, W.Va., 1979-81, asst. supr. motor vehicles, 1981-86; staff asst. CSX Transp., Jacksonville, Fla., 1986, engr. system material, 1986—. Named Outstanding Young Women Am., 1985. Mem. Am. Council R.R. Women, (sec. 1984-86, 1st v.p. 1986—, pres. 1988—), Nat. Assn. Female Exec., Engrs. Club Huntington, Am. R.R. Engring. Assn., U. Cin. Alumni Assn. Lodge: Order of Eastern Star. Home: 5321 Buggy Whip Dr Jacksonville FL 32223 Office: CSX Transp 500 Water St Jacksonville FL 32202

SHEAR, IONE MYLONAS, archaeologist; b. St. Louis, Feb. 19, 1936; d. George Emmanuel and Lella (Papazoglou) Mylonas; B.A., Wellesley Coll., 1958; M.A., Bryn Mawr Coll., 1960, Ph.D., 1968; m. Theodore Leslie Shear, June 24, 1959; children—Julia Louise, Alexandra. Research asst. Inst. for Advanced Study, Princeton, N.J., 1963-65; mem. Agora Excavation, Athens, 1972—; lectr. art and archaeology Princeton U., 1983-84; also excavator various other sites in Greece and Italy. Mem. Archaeol. Inst. Am. Author: The Panagia Houses at Mycenae, 1987; contbr. articles to profl. jours. Address: 87 Library Pl Princeton NJ 08540

SHEAR, NANCY L., broadcaster; b. Phila., July 1, 1946; d. Leonard and Mildred (Goldstein) S. MusB, Temple U., 1972. Orchestra librarian Phila. Orchestra, 1964-69, Curtis Inst. Music, Phila., 1972-78, Internat. Festival Youth Orchestras, Eng., Scotland, Wales, summers 1974-76; broadcaster, producer Sta. WHYY-FM, Phila., 1978-80, Sta. MNYC-FM, N.Y.C., 1980—; free-lance writer, 1978—; speaker in field. Bd. dirs. Eleanor Roosevelt Ctr. at Val-Kill, Hyde Park, N.Y., 1986—; mem. exec. com. Eleanor Roosevelt Meml. Fund, N.Y.C., 1987—; coordinator pub. relations Musicians Against Nuclear Arms, N.Y.C., 1985—. Mem. Am. Women in Radio and TV, Classical Music Assn., Am. Symph. Orchestra League, NAPAMA. Home: 180 West End Ave New York NY 10023

SHEARER, DARLENE B., business executive, researcher; b. Albany, N.Y., Nov. 7, 1956; d. Carl Michael Baggetta and Joyce Evelyn (Ward) Forscy. B.A. in Mgmt. and Bus. cum laude, Barat Coll., 1985. Customer service specialist Pyle Nat. Co., Chgo., 1977-78, product specialist, 1978-79, systms analyst, 1979-80, systems support supr., 1980, supr. customer service, 1981-83, mgr. customer service, 1983-84; v.p. ops. Tektac, Inc., 1984—; pres. Gina and Assocs., Riverside, Ill., 1980—. Mem. Republican Nat. Com., Washington, 1981—; vol. '84 Presdl. campaign, Riverside, 1984. Mem. Delta Epsilon Sigma. Home: 116 Northgate Rd Riverside IL 60546

SHEARER, JOY BRAMPTON, lawyer; b. Bryn Mawr, Pa., Nov. 27, 1953; d. Andrew Willard Shearer and Joy Lorraine (Riley) McLeieer; m. John Robert Angstadt, Aug. 28, 1977; 1 son, John Robert. BA, Fla. Atlantic U., 1973; JD, U. Fla., Gainesville, 1975. Bar: Fla. 1976, U.S. Dist. Ct. (so. dist.) Fla. 1976, U.S. Ct. Appeals (11th cir.) 1981, U.S. Supreme Ct. 1981. Atty. Legal Aid Soc. Palm Beach County Inc., 1976-77; asst. atty. gen. Fla. Dept. Legal Affairs, West Palm Beach, 1977-83; bur. chief, 1983—. Contbr. chpt. to book. Mem. ABA, Fla. Assn. Women Lawyers (pres. Palm Beach County chpt. 1983-84), Fla. Bar Assn. (appellate rules com. 1982—), Palm Beach County Bar Assn. (vice chmn. law week com. 1983), Phi Alpha Delta. Office: Dept Legal Affairs 111 Georgia Ave Suite 204 West Palm Beach FL 33401

SHEDD, REBECCA LYNN, wholesale distribution company manager, literacy trainer; b. Toledo, Nov. 24, 1954; d. Richard George and Marjorie Ann (Lunn) S. B.A. in Edn., Depauw U., 1976; postgrad. U. Minn. Purchasing agt. Water Products Co., Eden Prairie, Minn., 1977—, mgr. data processing, 1984—; tutor, trainer Laubach Literacy, Mpls., 1979—. Tutor, trainer, bd. dirs. Minn. Literacy Council, Roseville, 1979—; lead trainer Mpls. Literacy Project, 1979—; block capt. Mpls. Crime Prevention program, Mpls. Recycling program. Recipient Gold award Minn. Literacy Council, 1984 Mem. Laubach Literacy Action, Minn. Literacy Action, Assn. Women in Computing, DePauw U. Alumni Assn., Am. Soc. Tng. and Devel. Methodist. Avocations: skiing. biking, swimming, reading, traveling. Home: 4554 Wentworth Ave S Minneapolis MN 55409 Office: Water Products Co 15801 W 78th St Eden Prairie MN 55344

SHEDRICK, MARY BERNICE, state legislator; b. Chickasha, Okla., Aug. 9, 1940; m. R. Mike Shedrick, 1957; children: Crystal Dawn, Michael Scott (dec.), Steven Link. BS, Okla. State U., 1969, MS, 1972; JD, Okla. City U. Law Sch., 1983. Educator 1969-80, atty., mem. Okla. State Senate. Mem. Stillwater Okla. C. of C., Stillwater Arts and Humanities Council, Okla. State U. Alumni Found., Delta Kappa Gamma, Kappa Kappa Iota. Democrat. Baptist. Address: PO Box 843 Stillwater OK 74076 *

SHEEDY, KATHLEEN CROWLEY, medical technologist; b. Bridgeport, Conn., Mar. 23, 1950; d. Edward V. and Jeanne (Duhamel) Crowley; B.S., Western Conn. State U., 1972; student Danbury (Conn.) Hosp. Sch. Med. Technology, 1971-72, SUNY Upstate Med Center, Syracuse, 1973-74; m. Mark E. Sheedy; children: Paul C., John E., James D. Lab. technologist, Danbury Hosp., 1972-73; instr. med. technology SUNY Upstate Med. Center, 1975-81, supr. blood bank, 1974-81; blood bank supr. Vassar Brothers Hosp., Poughkeepsie, N.Y., 1982—. Barlow House Council scholar, 1968. Mem. Am. Soc. Clin. Pathologists, Am. Assn. Blood Banks. Roman Catholic. Contbr. articles to profl. jours. Home: 24 Horseshoe Dr Hyde Park NY 12538 Office: Hosp Shared Services 191 Delafield St Poughkeepsie NY 12601

SHEEHAN, DEBORAH ANN, radio station and theater executive; b. Paterson, N.J., Mar. 29, 1953; d. John J. and Ruth (Badertschier) S.; m. Emidio S. Quattrocchi, Mar. 15, 1985. B.A., William Patterson Coll., 1975. With radio Sta. WWDJ, Hackensack, N.J., 1980-83, Shadow Traffic, N.Y.C., 1981-83; dir. news, community affairs WPAT-AM/FM, N.Y.C., 1979—. Actress-tchr. Paterson Arts Ctr., 1975-79; host radio show Bus. Jour. N.J., 1984; host, producer radio show Debbie Sheehan mag., 1983; host FDU Focus, Cable Network N.J.; writer plays. Exec. dir., actress Learning Theater Co., Paterson, 1975—; sec. bd. dirs. YMCA Passaic Valley, Paterson, 1983—; mem. N.J. Legal Bd., Montclair, N.J., 1984—; mem. Paterson Edn. Found., 1984—; bd. dirs. United Way Passaic Valley, Conn., 1985. Recipient Edward R. Murrow Gold medal B'nai B'rith, 1983, finalist 1984-85; Gold medal Internat. Radio Festival, 1983; Best Reporter award Sigma Delta Chi, 1985-87, Personality Profile award local chpt., 1987, Best Pub. Service award, 1987; Best Feature award AP, 1985, 87; Angel Excellence award, Los Angeles, 1985, 87; Internat. Press Assn. fellow, Japan, 1985. Club: Zonta. Avocations: weaving; travel; acting. Office: WPAT-AM/FM 1396 Broad St Clifton NJ 07013

SHEEHAN, LINDA SUZANNE, educational administrator; b. Dayton, Ohio, Aug. 1, 1950; d. Paul J. and Betty L. (Fowler) King; m. J. Scott Sheehan, Dec. 18, 1971. 1 child Amy Elizabeth. BS in Edn. with honors, Ohio State U., 1971; MEd, U. Tex., 1974; adminstrn. cert. Houston Bapt. U., 1983. Cert. tchr., Tex. Tchr. Upper Arlington Schs., Columbus, Ohio, 1971-72, Brown Sch., San Marcos, Tex., 1972-73, Comal Ind. Sch. Dist., New Braunfels, Tex., 1973-75, Alief Ind. Sch. Dist., Houston, 1975-79; asst. prin. Killough Mid. Sch., Houston, 1979-84; prin. Olle Mid. Sch., Houston, 1984—. Named Tchr. of Yr., Olle Mid. Sch., Houston, 1978. Mem. NEA, Nat. Mid. Sch. Assn., Nat. Assn. Secondary Sch. Prins., Tex. Assn. Secondary Sch. Prins., Tex. Mid. Sch. Assn. (dir. 1979—), Houston Council Social Studies, Kappa Delta Pi (pres. 1984-85), Phi Delta Kappa. Roman Catholic. Home: 11615 Shady Grove Ln Houston TX 77024 Office: Olle Mid Sch 9200 Boone Rd Houston TX 77099

SHEEHAN, SUSAN, writer; b. Vienna, Austria, Aug. 24, 1937; came to U.S., 1941, naturalized, 1946; d. Charles and Kitty C. (Herrmann) Sachsel; m. Neil Sheehan, Mar. 30, 1965; children—Maria Gregory, Catherine Fair. B.A. (Durant scholar), Wellesley Coll., 1958. Editorial researcher Esquire-Coronet, N.Y.C., 1959-60; free-lance writer N.Y.C., 1960-62; staff writer New Yorker mag., N.Y.C., 1962—. Author: Ten Vietnamese, 1967, A Welfare Mother, 1976, A Prison and a Prisoner, 1978, Is There No Place on Earth for Me?, 1982, Kate Quinton's Days, 1984, A Missing Plane, 1986; contbr. articles to various mags., including N.Y. Times Sunday Mag., The Washington Post Sunday Mag., Harper's, Atlantic, New Republic, McCall's, Holiday. Judge Robert F. Kennedy Journalism Awards, 1980, 84; mem. lit. panel D.C. Commn. on Arts and Humanities, 1979-84; mem. pub. info. and edn. com. Nat. Mental Health Assn., 1982-83; mem. adv. com. on employment and crime Vera Inst. Justice, 1978-86; chair Pulitzer Prize nominating jury in gen. non-fiction for 1988. Recipient Sidney Hillman Found. award, 1976, Gavel award ABA, 1978, Individual Reporting award Nat. Mental Health Assn., 1981, Pulitzer prize for gen. non-fiction, 1983, feature writing award N.Y. Press Club, 1984, Alumnae Assn. Achievement award Wellesley Coll., 1984; Guggenheim fellow, 1975-76; Woodrow Wilson Ctr. for Internat. Scholars fellow, 1981. Mem. Phi Beta Kappa. Home: 4505 Klingle St NW Washington DC 20016 Office: New Yorker Mag 25 W 43rd St New York NY 10036

SHEEHEY, SHEILA CELESTE, manufacturing company executive; b. Boston, May 13, 1924; d. Thommas Joseph and Charlotte Mary (Cronin) S.; B.A., N.Y.U., 1975. Asst. to social editor Newark News, 1947-56; asst. to advt. mgr. Handy & Harman, precious metal fabricator and refiner, N.Y.C., 1957-76, adv. mgr., 1976—. Mem. Bus. and Profl. Advt. Assn. Office: 850 3d Ave New York NY 10022

SHEEHY, MARYANN C., English educator; b. Greenwich, Conn., June 7 1954; d. Joseph William and Mary Carol (Modugno) Gagon; m. Joseph John Sheehy, July 25, 1981. BS in English Edn., Western Conn. State U., 1976, MS, 1983. Cert tchr., Conn. Tchr. English, New Milford High Sch., Conn., 1978—. Mem. Nat. Council Tchrs. English, Conn. Edn. Assn., NEA. Democrat. Roman Catholic. Avocations: writing, music, guitar, historic restoration.

SHEETS, JANET ELIZABETH, librarian; b. Winston-Salem, N.C., Jan. 25, 1943; d. John McKaughan and Madge Elizabeth (Burton) S. BA, Coll. William and Mary, 1965; MLS, U. N.C., 1967. Adult librarian Free Library Phila., 1967-68; reference librarian Duke U., Durham, N.C., 1968-72, Joint Univs. Library System, Nashville, Tenn., 1973-75; coordinator pub. services Northeast La. Univ. Library, Monroe, 1975-77; reference librarian Baylor U., Waco, Tex., 1977-83, head reference services, 1983—. Contbr. chpts. to book: Reference Sources for Small and Medium-Sized Libraries, 1984. Active Hist. Waco, 1984—. Mem. ALA (sec. coll. research libraries sect. 1984-85), Tex. Library Assn., Beta Phi Mu, Phi Beta Kappa. Baptist. Office: Baylor U Libraries Waco TX 76706

SHEETS, PEGGY DAWN, health science facility administrator; b. Harrisonburg, Va., July 2, 1952; d. Richard Lee and Eva (Houff) Botkin; m. Thomas G. Sheets, Jul. 8, 1972; 1 child Heather. Student, Elizabeth Brant Sch. bus., 1970-71. Clk. stenographer Woodrow Wilson Rehabilitation Ctr., Fishersville, Va., 1972-77, tchr. rehabilitation vocation, 1977-86, supr. rehabilitation, 1986—; dir., supr. rehabilitation Woodrow Wilson Ctr. Independent Living Program, Fishersville, Va., 1986—. Named Outstanding Young Women Am., 1984. Mem. Va. Council Independent Living, Staunton Bus. Profl. Women's Orgn., Staunton Mayor's Com. Handicapped Persons, Handicapped Unlimited Va., Nat. Female Exec. Group. Methodist. Home: Rt 5 Box 78 Staunton VA 24401

SHEETS, SUE LAURA, newspaper editor; b. Dayton, Ohio, Nov. 15, 1929; d. Charles LeRoy and Dorothy Ethel (Leis) Schaaf; student Ohio State U., 1947-48, hon. degree Nat. Cash Register Posting Sch., Denver, 1952; student YMCA Coll. of Commerce, Newark, Ohio, 1968; grad. Inst. Children's Lit., Redding Ridge, Conn., 1982; m. R.E. Walters; children—Steven Mitchell, Douglas Charles, Gregg Joseph; m. 2d, Ralph D. Sheets, June 21, 1969. Sec. with Ohio Fin. Co., Dayton, 1948-50, Goulds Pumps, Seneca Falls, N.Y., 1950-52, 53-54; poster, Colo. Nat. Bank, Denver, 1952-53; reporter Ace News, Heath, Ohio, 1966-68; founding dir. LEADS, Buckeye Lake, Ohio, 1968-72; sec. with Garwood Industries, Heath, 1973-74; columnist, editor, editor bus. and farm page, The Advocate, Newark, Ohio, 1978-82, entertainment and TV editor, 1982—; tchr. painting oils and acrylics, owner, operator arts and crafts shop, Hebron, Ohio, 1986-77. Organizer sr. citizens group, Buckeye Lake, 1968. Mem. Licking County Art Assn., Friends of Daweswood, NRA. Democrat. Methodist. Clubs: Order Eastern Star (Hebron)., Land of Legend Rifle and Pistol. Home: 180 S 5th St Newark OH 43055 Office: 25 W Main St Newark OH 43055

SHEETZ, CHRISTINE NINFA, food service director; b. Hilongos, Leyte, Phillipines, Nov. 10, 1940; d. Heracleo and Elena (Urgel) Suarez; m. Donald Lester Sheetz, May 9, 1981. BS in Home Econs. magna cum laude, U. San Carlos, Cebu City, Phillipines, 1962; MA in Edn. with high honors, U. San Carlos, 1974; postgrad., Lebanon Valley Coll., Annville, Pa., 1979. Cert. tchr. Pa. Elem. sch. tchr. Phillipine Pub. Schs., 1962-65; high sch. tchr. Franciscan Coll., Phillipines, 1965-70, instr., 1970-73; secondary prin. Santo Nino Acad., Phillipines, 1973-76, St. Christopher Acad., Phillipines, 1976-79; resident advisor Threshold Rehab. Services, Reading, Pa., 1981-82; food services supr. Fleetwood (Pa.) Area Sch. Dist., 1983-86, Exeter Twp. Sch. Dist., Reading, 1986—. Mem. Pa. Sch. Food Service Assn. (pres. ea. chpt. 1986-87). Democrat. Roman Catholic. Home: Rte 4 Box 4355A Fleetwood PA 19522 Office: Exeter Twp Sch Dist 3650 Perkiomen Ave Reading PA 19606

SHEFF, HONEY A., clinical psychologist, educator; b. Bklyn., Nov. 24, 1954; d. Herbert Jack and Helene Ida (Sussman) Mendelson; m. Michael Robert Sheff, May 30, 1976; BA summa cum laude, Queens Coll., CUNY, 1975; MA, SUNY-Stony Brook, 1978, PhD, 1981. Lic. clin. psychologist. Clin. psychologist Callier Ctr. for Communication Disorders, U. Tex., Dallas, 1981-83; pvt. practice clin. psychology cons., Dallas, 1983—, TV and radio appearances, Dallas, 1983—; lectr. U. Tex., Dallas, 1982—, clin. instr. psychology, dept. psychiatry U. Tex. Health Sci. Ctr. Southwestern Med. Sch., Dallas, 1983-86; clin. asst. prof. in psychology, 1986—; mem. Allied Health Profls. Staff, Green Oaks Hosp., Dallas, 1988—; guest lectr. dept. emergency med. services U. Tex. Health Sci., Southwestern Med. Sch., Dallas, 1985—, also cons. research project dept. psychiatry; cons. psychologist McKinney Job Corps Ctr., Tex., 1984-86; presenter, workshop leader, tng. on family violence, Tex., N.Y. and N.H., 1977—; liaison com. Mental Health Assn. Dallas County and Mental Health Assn. Collin County; mem. profl. adv. bd. Dallas Ind. Sch. Dist. Psychol. Services, 1988—. Chmn. Dallas County Mental Health-Mental Retardation Ctr. task force to rev. services to children and adolescents, 1985; chmn. Profl. Adv. Com. on Child and Adolescent Services, Dallas County Mental Health-Mental Retardation Ctr., 1986—; founding mem. Parents Helping Parents Task Force, 1982-85; project designer Adolescent Mental Health Needs Dallas County, 1984; coauthor jour. article, paper for profl. conf. (now chpt. in book). Charter mem. Parker Vol. Fire Dept., Tex., 1982—, sec.-treas., 1983-85. Recipient Robert S. Woodworth medal for excellence in psychology, Queens Coll., CUNY, 1975; commendation dept. psychology SUNY-Stony Brook, 1977, spl. recognition and award Dallas County Rape Crisis and Child Sexual Abuse Ctr. for Service to Community, 1985; . Mem. Am. Psychol. Assn., Tex. Psychol. Assn., Dallas Psychol. Assn. (pub. forum 1984), Nat. Register of Health Service Providers in Psychology, Mental Health Assn. Dallas County (mem., chmn. coms., award 1985, elected to bd. dirs.), Nat. Council Family Relations, Tex. Council Family Violence, Internat. Soc. Prevention Child Abuse and Neglect, Phi Beta Kappa. Democrat. Jewish. Avocations: Horseback riding; knitting and needlepoint; reading. Office: Stone Tower 13760 Noel Rd Suite 805 Dallas TX 75240

SHEFFERT, BONNIE KAY, postmaster; b. Strawberry POint, Iowa, June 3, 1947; d. Floyd Peter and Winifred Jean (Brooks) Schmidt; m. Edward Lester Ohl, June 19, 1965 (div. Feb. 1980); children: Douglas Floyd, Robert William. Student, Upper Iowa U., 1987—. Clk., carrier U.S. Postal Service, Strawberry Point, 1967-82; postmaster Earlville, Iowa, 1982-84, Sumner, Iowa, 1984-87, Knoxville, Iowa, 1987—. Treas., pub. relations Athletic Booster Orgn., Strawberry Point, 1978-80; sec. Campbell Park Bd., Strawberry Point, 1978-80; pager coordinator Sumner Emergency Med. Services, 1985—; v.p. Del. County Heart Assn., 1983-84, pres., 1984; vol. ct. appointed spl. advocate, 1988. Mem. Nat. Assn. Postmasters, League Postmasters, Nat. Assn. Female Execs., Ben Franklin Stamp Club (coordinator 1983-84); Knoxville C. of C. Republican. Club: Women's (Earlville). Home: RR 2 Hickory Ridge PO Box 484 Knoxville IA 50138-0484 Office: US Postal Service 201 E Marion St Knoxville IA 50138-9998

SHEFFIELD, BENITA CARROLL, bank officer; b. Lexington, Mo., June 5, 1950; d. Bruce Byron and Willie Otella (Lorren) Carroll; m. James Wilbur Sheffield, Jr., May 8, 1982. Student, Jacksonville (Fla.) U., 1968-69; AA, Fla. Jr. Coll., 1980; BBA cum laude, U. North Fla., 1987, postgrad., 1988—. Authorization and control clk. First Union Nat. Bank of Fla., Jacksonville, 1970-74, supr. ops. and control, 1974-78, bankcard acctg. mgr., 1978-80, loss prevention officer, 1980-87, asst. v.p., 1987—. Presdl. scholar Jacksonville U., 1968-69. Mem. Bank Security Assn. of NE Fla. (pres. Jacksonville chpt. 1986-87), Phi Kappa Phi, Beta Gamma Sigma. Democrat. Presbyterian. Home: 2331 Herschel St Jacksonville FL 32204 Office: First Union Nat Bank of Fla 200 W Forsyth St Jacksonville FL 32202

SHEFFIELD, JANE ELIZABETH, financial editor; b. Wichita, Kans., Mar. 25, 1952; d. John Thomas and Sarah Elizabeth (Nusbaum) S. BA, Kans. U., 1974; MA, Cambridge U., Eng., 1976. Assoc. editor Janeway Pub. and Research Corp., N.Y.C., 1977-78, mng. editor, 1978-80; sr. editor Dean Witter Reynolds Inc., N.Y.C., 1980—; v.p. Oppenheimer & Co., Inc., N.Y.C., 1980—. Home: 129 Barrow St Apt 2A New York NY 10014 Office: Oppenheimer & Co Inc Oppenheimer Tower World Financial Ctr New York NY 10281

SHEFFIELD, SIMONE, film company executive; b. Englewood, N.J., Mar. 19; d. Richard Lee and Dolores Ann (Faison) S. Attended So. Fla. Coll. Asst. dist. mgr. United Artists, N.Y.C., 1971-77; v.p. Motown Industries, Los Angeles, 1977-81; mgr. Canyon Entertainment Complex, Los Angeles, 1981—; cons. Ad Week, Los Angeles, 1985-87, Fox and Friends Advt., Inc., Los Angeles, 1980-87; personal mgr. various entertainers. Active Dem. campaign, Los Angeles, 1967—. Mem. Am. Film Inst., Women of the Motion Pictures Industries. Roman Catholic.

SHEININ, ROSE, biochemist, educator; b. Toronto, Ont., Can., May 18, 1930; d. Harry and Anne (Szyber) Shuber; B.A., U. Toronto, 1951, M.A.

(scholar), 1953, Ph.D. in Biochemistry, 1956, L.H.D., 1985; D.H.L. (hon.), Mt. St. Vincent U., 1985; DSc (hon.) Acadia U., 1987; m. Joseph Sheinin, July 15, 1951; children—David Matthew Khazanov, Lisa Basya Judith, Rachel Sarah Rebecca. Demonstrator in biochemistry U. Toronto (Ont., Can.), 1951-53, asst. prof. microbiology, 1964-75, asst. prof. med. biophysics, 1967-75, prof. microbiology, 1975—, prof. med. biophysics, 1978—, assoc. prof. med. biophysics, 1975-78, chmn. microbiology and parasitology, 1975-82, vice dean Sch. Grad. Studies, 1984—; mem. Health Scis. Com.; vis. research assoc. chem. microbiology, Cambridge U., 1956-57, Nat. Inst. Med. Research, London, 1957-58; research assoc. fellow div. biol. research Ont. Cancer Inst., 1958-67; sci. officer cancer grants panel Med. Research Council Can.; mem. Can. Sci. Del. to People's Republic of China, 1973; mem. adv. com. Provincial Lottery Health Research Awards; mem. adv. com. on biotech. NRC Can., 1984-87; mem. Sci. Council Can., 1984-87; adv. com. on sci. and tech. CBC, 1980-85; vis. prof. biochemistry U. Alta., 1971. Nat. Cancer Inst. Can. fellow, 1953-56, 58-61; Brit. Empire Cancer Campaign fellow, 1956-58; recipient Queen's Silver Jubilee medal, 1978; Josiah Macy Jr. Faculty scholar, 1981-82; fellow Ligue Contre le Cancer, France, 1981-82. Fellow Am. Acad. Microbiology, Royal Soc. Can.; mem. Can. Biochem. Soc. (pres. 1974-75), Can. Soc. Cell Biology (pres. 1975-76), Am. Soc. Virology, Am. Soc. Microbiologists, Assn. Canadian Women in Sci., Scitech, Soc. Complex Carbohydrates, Toronto Biochem. and Biophys. Soc. (pres. 1960-70, council 1970-74). Assoc. editor Can. Jour. Biochemistry, 1968-71, Virology, 1969-72, Intervirology, 1974-85; editorial bd. Microbiol. Revs., 1977-80; author, co-author various publs. Office: U Toronto Dept Microbiology, 150 College St, Toronto, ON Canada M5S 1A8

SHEIRR, OLGA, artist; b. N.Y.C., June 7, 1931; d. Edward E. and Lillian (Tobias) S.; m. Maurice Krolik, Jan. 28, 1973. BA, Bklyn. Coll., 1953; postgrad., Art Students League, 1953, Pratt Graphic Ctr., 1953, NYU, 1953, N.Y. Inst. Fine Arts, 1953. guest lectr. Fla. Gulf Coast Art Ctr., Belleair, 1988. One-woman exhbns. include: Internat. Art Exchange, N.Y.C., 1962-63, Noho Gallery, N.Y.C., 1975-76, 78-80, 82, 83, Cicchinelli Gallery, N.Y.C., 1982, New Sch. Social Research, N.Y.C., 1984, Barbizon Gallery, Greenwich, Conn., 1984, Fairleigh Dickinson U., 1985, Noho Gallery, 1987, The Kendall Gallery, 1986; group shows Ken Keleba Gallery, 1985, Kipp Gallery, others; bd. dirs. Noho Gallery, 1975—, treas., 1982-83; exhbn. organizer Noho for the Arts, 1975-78; v.p., sec. Assn. Artists Run Galleries, N.Y.C., 1976-80, reviewer Artists View Art, 1976-80; group exhbns. include: A.A.A. Gallery, N.Y.C., 1965, 71, Silvermine Guild Artists, New Canaan, Conn., 1966, 76, Landmark Gallery, N.Y.C., 1976, The Arsenal, N.Y.C., 1978, Community Gallery, N.Y.C., 1980-81, 83, Springville (Utah) Mus. Art, 1981, 83, Riyadh, Saudi Arabia, 1982, Fairleigh Dickinson U., N.J., 1983, N.Y. Soc. Women Artists, 1984; represented in permanent collections: Mus. City of N.Y., St. Vincent's Hosp., N.Y.C., Greenville County (S.C.) Mus., NYU Hosp., others. Mem. Women's Caucus for Art, N.Y. Artists Equity (bd. dirs. 1985—, sec. 1988—), Women in the Arts, N.Y. Soc. Women Artists (rec. sec., asst. v.p., bd. dirs. 1984—). Home: 360 1st Ave 11 G New York NY 10010

SHELBY, CAROLYN JUNE, writer; b. Long Beach, Calif., June 17, 1949; d. Eugene Forrest and Barbara May (Magruder) S.; m. Christopher Ames, Feb. 11, 1973; 1 child, Samantha Shelby. BA in Theatre Arts, UCLA, 1972. Writer feature MGM, 1980-81, CBS Theatrical, 1980-81; feature writer Paramount Pictures, Los Angeles, 1982-83, Disney Pictures, Burbank, Calif., 1983-84, Tristar, 1984; writer cable TV Paramount Pictures, Los Angeles, 1985, Showtime Entertainment, Westwood, Calif., 1985-86; writer feature Vista Films, Los Angeles, 1986-87, Interscope Communications, Westwood, Calif., 1985-88; writer Growing Pains Warner Bros. TV, Burbank, 1986-88; story editor, writer The Charmings Embassy Communications, Hollywood, 1987; exec. story cons., writer Once A Hero New World TV, Los Angeles, 1987. Mem. Women's Com. Writers Guild Am., Women in Film. Unitarian.

SHELDEN, MIRIAM FEELY, physical education educator; b. Poughkeepsie, N.Y., Oct. 21, 1938; d. Edgar Vail and Mary Catherine (Hart) S. BA, U. Iowa, 1960; MS, U. Oreg., 1963; PhD, U. So. Calif., 1974. Tchr. Lakeview (Oreg.) Pub. Schs., 1960-62; instrn. Northwest Mo. State Coll., Maryville, 1963-66; jr. supr. U. Calif., Berkeley, 1966-67; instr. U. So. Calif., Los Angeles, 1967-68; asst. prof. phys. edn. Cen. Mich. U., Mt. Pleasant, 1971-75; prof. U. S.C., Spartanburg, 1975—. Chairperson safety com. ARC, Spartanburg, 1983-86. Mem. N.Am. Soc. For Sport History, Am. Alliance fo Health, Phys. Edn., Recreation and Dance (life), Am. Assn. Univ. Profs., S.C. Assn. for Health, Phys. Edn., Recreation and Dance, Kappa Delta Pi (treas. 1980—).

SHELDON, BEATRICE EVERETT, political worker; b. Gunn, Miss., May 16, 1915; d. John Broadus and Pency Ann (Wooley) Everett; R.N., Dr. Willis Walley Sch. Nursing, Jackson, Miss., 1937; m. Anson H. Sheldon, Feb. 5, 1939; children: Patricia Ann Sheldon Strauss Ekstrum, Anson H., Lawson. Nurse Kings Daus. Hosp., Canton, Miss., 1937, Greenville, Miss., 1937, Helena (Ark.) Hosp., 1938-39; sec.-treas. Machinery Inc., 1966—. Mem. Miss. Rep. county com., 1944-60; alt. del. to Rep. State Conv., 1948, 52, 56, 60. Trustee South Washington County Hosp., Hollandle, Miss., 1985—, chmn. bd. dirs., 1985-86. Mem. Miss. Registered Nurse Assn. Episcopalian. Clubs: Longwood Community Culture (pres. 1975-78), Federated Women's. Home: Keystone Plantation Avon MS 38723

SHELDON, BROOKE EARLE, librarian, educator; b. Lawrence, Mass., Aug. 29, 1931; d. Leonard Hadley and Elsie Ann (Southerl) Earle; m. George Duffield Sheldon, Mar. 28, 1955 (dec.); children: L. Scott, G. Stephen. B.A., Acadia U., 1952, D.C.L. (hon.), 1985; M.L.S., Simmons Coll., 1954; Ph.D., U. Pitts., 1977. Youth librarian Detroit Public Library, 1954-55; base librarian Ent AFB, Colorado Springs, Colo., 1955-57, U.S. Army, Germany, 1956-57; br. librarian Albuquerque Public Library, 1959-61; coordinator adult services Santa Fe Public Library, 1965-67; head library devel. N.Mex. State Library, Santa Fe, 1967-72; asst. dir. leadership tng. inst. U.S. Office Edn., Washington, 1971-73; head tech. services and tng. Alaska State Library, Juneau, 1973-75; dean Sch. Library Info. Studies, Tex. Woman's U., Denton, 1977—, provost, 1979-80. Recipient Alumni Achievement award Simmons Coll., 1983; Disting. Alumni award Sch. Library Info. Sci., U. Pitts., 1986. Mem. ALA (pres. 1983-84), Tex. Library Assn., S.W. Library Assn., Beta Phi Mu. Democrat. Episcopalian. Office: Tex Woman's U Sch Library & Info Studies Denton TX 76204

SHELDON, ELEANOR HARRIET BERNERT, sociologist; b. Hartford, Conn., Mar. 19, 1920; d. M.G. and Fannie (Myers) Bernert; m. James Sheldon, Mar. 19, 1950 (div. 1960); children: James, John Anthony. A.A., Colby Jr. Coll., 1940; A.B., U. N.C., 1942; Ph.D., U. Chgo., 1949. Asst. demographer Office Population Research, Washington, 1942-43; social scientist U.S. Dept Agr., Washington, 1943-45; asso. dir. Chgo. Community Inventory, U. Chgo., 1947-50; social scientist Social Sci. Research Council, N.Y.C., 1950-51; research grantee Social Sci. Research Council, 1953-55, pres., 1972-79; research asso. Bur. Applied Social Research, Columbia, 1950-51; social scientist UN, N.Y.C., 1951-52; lectr. sociology Columbia U., 1951-52, vis. prof., 1969-71; research assoc., lectr. sociology UCLA, 1955-61; assoc. research sociologist, lectr. Sch. Nursing U. Calif., 1957-61; sociologist, exec. assoc. Russell Sage Found., N.Y.C., 1961-72; vis. prof. U. Calif. at Santa Barbara, 1971; dir. Equitable Life Assurance Soc., Mobil Corp., H.J. Heinz Co. Author: (with L. Wirth) Chicago Community Fact Book, 1949, America's Children, 1958, (with R.A. Glazier) Pupils and Schools in N.Y.C, 1965; Editor: (with W.E. Moore) Indicators of Social Change; Concepts and Measurements, 1968, Family Economic Behavior, 1973; Contbr. (with W.E. Moore) articles to profl. jours. Bd. dirs. Colby-Sawyer Coll., UN Research Inst. for Social Devel., 1973-79; trustee Rockefeller Found., 1978-85, Nat. Opinion Research Ctr., Inst. East-West Security Studies, 1984-88. William Rainey Harper fellow U. Chgo., 1945-47. Fellow Am. Acad. Arts and Scis., Am. Sociol. Assn., Am. Statis. Assn.; mem. U. Chgo. Alumni Assn. (Profl. Achievement award), Sociol. Research Assn. (pres. 1971-72), Council on Fgn. Relations, AAAS, Am. Assn. Pub. Opinion Research, Eastern Sociol. Soc., Internat. Sociol. Assn., Internat. Union Sci. Study of Population, Population Assn. Am. (2d v.p. 1970-71), Inst. of Medicine (chmn. program com. 1976-77). Club: Cosmopolitan. Home: 630 Park Ave New York NY 10021 Office: Mobil Corp 150 E 42nd St New York NY 10017

SHELDON, FRANCES DOROTHY GIGANTE, retail executive; b. Bronx, Mar. 9, 1949; d. John C. and Frances T. Gigante; m. Thomas Hewey Sheldon, Aug. 22, 1970 (div. Mar. 1978); children: Thomas Hewey Jr., John Edward. Student, Brevard Community Coll., 1967, Cornell U., 1969. Various positions Publix Supermarkets, Inc., Jacksonville, Fla., 1967-81; asst. store mgr. Publix Supermarkets, Inc., Lakeland, Fla., 1981-85, store mgr., 1985—. cons. adv. bd. for coop. edn. students Titusville High Sch., 1986—; mem. St. Theresa's PTA, Titusville, Fla., 1978—; active St. Teresa's Catholic Womens Club, Titusville, 1980—. Mem. Am. Bus. Women's Assn., Nat. Assn. Female Execs., Nat. Police Res. Officers, Am. Nat. Red. Cross. Home: PO Box 1035 Titusville FL 32780 Office: Publix Supermarkets Inc PO Box 407 Lakeland FL 33802

SHELDON, GEORGIANA HORTENSE, consultant; b. Lawrenceville, Pa., Dec. 2, 1923; d. William Franklin and Georgiana (Root) S.; m. James R. Sharp, May 18, 1979. B.A., Keuka Coll., 1945; M.S., Cornell U., 1949. Dir. admissions Stetson U. Coll. Law, 1954-56; exec. asst. Republican Nat. Com., 1956-61; exec. sec. Hon. Rogers Morton (rep., Md.), 1962-69; dep. dir. Def. Civil Preparedness Agy., Washington, 1969-75; dir. Office Fgn. Disaster Assistance, dep. dir. internat. disaster assistance AID, 1975-76; vice chmn. CSC, 1976-77; mem. Fed. Power Commn., 1977—; mem. Fed. Energy Regulatory Commn., 1977-85. Recipient Alumni award for profl. advancement Keuka Coll., 1966. Republican. Presbyn. Home: 1200 N Nash St Arlington VA 22209

SHELDON, NANCY WAY, management consultant; b. Bryn Mawr, Pa., Nov. 10, 1944; d. John Harold and Elizabeth Semple (Hoff) W.; m. Robert Charles Sheldon, June 15, 1968. BA, Wellesley Coll., 1966; MA, Columbia U., 1968, M in Philosophy, 1972. Registered pvt. investigator, Calif. Mgmt. cons. ABT Assocs., Cambridge, Mass., 1969-70; mgmt. cons. Harbridge House, Inc., 1970-79, Los Angeles, 1977-79, v.p., 1977-79; mgmt. cons., pres. Resource Assessment, Inc., 1979—; ptnr., real estate developer Resource Devel. Assocs., 1980—; ptnr. Anubis Group, Ltd., 1980—. Author: Social and Economic Benefits of Public Transit, 1973. Contbr. articles to profl. jours. Columbia U. fellow, 1966-68; recipient Nat. Achievement award Nat. Assn. Women Geographers, 1966. Mem. Am. Mining Congress, Am. Inst. Mining, Metall. and Petroleum Engrs., Nat. Wildlife Fedn., Nat. Audubon Soc., Nature Conservancy, World Wildlife Fund (charter mem.), Nat. Assn. of Chiefs of Police, Grad. Faculties Alumni Assn. Columbia U., DAR, Am. Wildlife Soc., Air Pollution Control Assn., East African Wildlife Soc. Club: Wellesley (Los Angeles). Office: Resource Assessment Inc 1431 Washington Blvd Suite 2811 Detroit MI 48226

SHELDON, SUSAN FRANCES, data administrator; b. Portland, Oreg., Dec. 3, 1948; d. Arthur John and Mary Frances (Blake) Tonsing; m. Donald L. Sheldon, July 4, 1976 (div. 1984); 1 child, Stephanie Koren. BS in Edn. with honors, U. Oreg., 1970; postgrad., Portland Community Coll., 1973-75, 74-76. Bus. analyst Fred Meyer Inc., Portland, 1970-76; supr. payroll services Am. Data Services, Portland, 1976-77; systems analyst Meier & Frank subs. May Co., Portland, 1977-79; systems analyst Nike Inc., Beaverton, Oreg., 1979-83, data adminstr., 1983—. Group leader and sponsor Beaverton Alcoholics Anonymous programs, 1985-87. Mem. Data Adminstrn. Mgmt. Assn. (founder, sec. Portland chpt. 1984-86), Nat. Assn. Female Execs. Republican. Episcopalian. Home: 8345 SW 133d St Beaverton OR 97005 Office: Nike Inc 3900 SW Murray Rd Beaverton OR 97005

SHELL, CHERYL S., real estate broker, owner; b. Columbus, Ohio, Jan. 31, 1964; d. Joseph Lawrence and Sue Shell. BS in Computer Engring., Ohio State U., 1985; student, Ashland Coll., 1987; postgrad. in law, Capital U., 1987—. Pvt. practice instr. clarinet Pickerington, Ohio, 1978-82; programmer II IRCC, Columbus, 1982-83; treas. Shell Enterprises, Inc., Pickerington, 1985—; treas., broker Priority Realty, 1985—; real estate investor. Mem. ABA, Nat. Assn. Realtors, Columbus Bd. Realtors, Ohio Bd. Realtors, Bldg. Industry Assn., Nat. Assn. Female Execs., Donnelly Club (bd. dirs.), Grad. Realtors Inst. (Order of Engr.), CBR Million Dollar Club.

SHELL, SANDRA MOORE, accountant, consultant; b. Bourne, Mass., June 25, 1954; d. Lamoin and Rose Teresa (Maloof) Moore; m. Terry Lynn Shell, June 27, 1975 (div. Apr. 1986). BA in Acctg., U. So. Fla., 1982. CPA, Fla. Student apprentice Lovelace, Roby CPAs, St. Petersburg, Fla., 1982; staff CPA Ladell, Downs, Hicks and Frankenberg CPAs, Clearwater, Fla., 1982-84; exec. v.p., dir. Cambridge Fin. Corp., St. Petersburg, 1984-86; exec. v.p. Christi Harris, Inc., Dallas, 1986-87; acctg. cons. Am. Capital Cons., Deerfield Beach, Fla., 1987; cons. The Alexander Group, N.Y.C., 1987—, United Capital Group, Inc., Bellemead, N.J., 1987; comptroller Gen. Med. Service Corp., Deerfield Beach, Fla., 1988—; cons. Hugh York & Assocs., Beverley Hills, Calif., 1986-87, Note Brokers Assn. U.S., Dallas, 1986-87, Cambridge Fin. Corp., St. Petersburg, 1986—. Mem. Am. Inst. CPA's, Nat. Assn. Female Execs., Fla. Inst. CPA's, Phi Kappa Phi, Beta Gamma Sigma, Phi Theta Kappa. Democrat. Club: Suncoast Cocker Spaniel (Clearwater, Fla.) (treas. 1985-86). Office: Gen Med Services Corp 1287 E Newport Ctr Dr #208 Deerfield Beach FL 33442

SHELLEY, CAROLE AUGUSTA, actress; b. London, Aug. 16, 1939; came to U.S., 1964; d. Curtis and Deborah (Bloomstein) S.; m. Albert G. Woods, July 26, 1967 (dec.). Student, Arts Ednl. Sch., 1943-56, Prepatory Acad. Royal Acad. Dramatic Art, 1956-57; studies with Iris Warren. Trustee Am. Shakespeare Theatre., 1974-82. Appeared in revues, films, West End comedies, including Mary Mary at the Globe Theatre; appeared as Gwendolyn Pigeon in stage, film and TV versions of The Odd Couple; The Norman Conquests (Los Angeles Drama Critics Circle award 1975); appeared as Rosalind in As You Like It, as Regan in King Lear, as Neville in She Stoops to Conquer, Stratford, Ont., Can., 1972, as Mrs. Margery Pinchwife in The Country Wife, Am. Shakespeare Festival, Stratford, Conn., 1973, as Nora in A Doll's House, Goodman Theatre, Chgo., as Ann in Man and Superman, as Lena in Misalliance, Zita in Grand Hunt; appeared at Shaw Festival, 1977, 80, Steppin Out, 1986, Broadway Bound, 1987; appeared in: The Play's the Thing, Bklyn. Acad. Music, 1978; played Eleanore in stage prodn. Lion in Winter, 1987; other stage appearances include Nat. Co. of The Royal Family (Los Angeles Drama Citics Circle award 1977), The Elephant Man (Outer Critics Circle award 1978-79 season, Tony award for best actress 1978-79 season); appeared inaugural season, Robin Phillips Grand Theatre Co. (Tony award nomination 1986-87), London, Ont., Can., 1983-84, Broadway and Nat. Co. of Noises Off, 1985, Waltz of the Toreadors, 1986, Oh Coward, 1986-87; co-dir. Lion in Winter, 1987; appeared as Kate in Broadway Bound by Nat. Co.; appeared in films The Boston Strangler, The Odd Couple, Three Men and a Baby, 1987; created: voice characters in Walt Disney films Robin Hood, The Aristocats. Recipient Obie Award for Twelve Dreams N.Y. Shakespeare Festival, 1982. Jewish. Office: care Lionel Larner 850 7th Ave New York NY 10019

SHELLEY, LOUISE ISOBEL, sociology educator; b. N.Y.C., Mar. 13, 1952; d. Bertram J. and Ricca (Brody) S.; m. Donald E. Graves, June 26, 1975; children: Hester, Richard. BA cum laude, Cornell U., 1972; MA, U. Pa., 1973, PhD, 1977. Asst. prof. justice, dept. of justice, law and soc., Sch. Internat. Service Am. U., Washington, 1977-81, assoc. prof., 1981-86, prof., 1986—; mem. adv. council Coll. Arts & Scis. Cornell U., Ithaca, N.Y., 1977-84. Author: Crime and Modernization, 1981, Lawyers in Soviet Work Life, 1984; editor: Readings in Comparative Criminology, 1981; editor Crime and Devel., 1986. NEH grantee, 1984; Fulbright-Hays fellow, 1974-75, Guggenheim fellow, 1984-85. Mem. Internat. Sociol. Assn. (1st v.p. crime and social control com. 1986—), Am. Criminology Soc., Am. Assn. for Advancement of Slavic Studes (bd. dirs. 1987—), Law and Soc., Ea. Sociol. Soc. (sec. 1986—). Democrat. Jewish. Home: 4538 Cathedral Ave NW Washington DC 20016 Office: Am U Dept Justice Law and Soc Washington DC 20016

SHELLEY, MICHAELENE CHELLY, pharmaceutical sales professional; b. Wilmington, Del., Sept. 16, 1959; d. Irvan Vincent Paul and Angelene LaVerne (Redman) C.; m. Michael Ronald Shelley, May 9, 1987. BA in Psychology, U. Del., 1980. Sales mgr. The GAP, Wilmington, Del., 1980-83, Maceys, Wilmington, 1983-84; claims adjustor Allstate Ins., Chaddsford, Pa., 1984-86; sales-retail agt. Allstate Ins., Media, Pa., 1986-88; pharm. sales rep. Rorer Pharm. Corp., Ft. Washington, Pa., 1988—. Vol. Am. Cancer Soc., Chaddsford, 1986. Mem. Nat. Assn. Female Execs. Roman Catholic. Club: Toastmasters Internat. (pres. local club 1985-86). Home: 1614 Painters Crossing Chaddsford PA 19317 Office: Rorer Pharm Corp 500 Virginia Dr Fort Washington PA 19034

SHELLEY, PAULA DIANE, choreographer, theatre historian; b. Oakland, Calif., Sept. 8, 1953; d. Robert Richard and Sherma (Neusihin) S. BA summa cum laude, U. Calif., Davis, 1975; MA, U. Calif., Los Angeles, 1979, PhD, 1985. Tching. assoc. Dept. Theater Arts, U. Calif., Los Angeles, 1980-82; choreographer, asst. prof. Calif. State U., Los Angeles, 1986-88; vis. lectr. U. Calif. Santa Cruz, 1983; fgn. expert Shanghai U. Tech., 1988-89. Choreographer Calif. State U., NEH, Bakersfield, 1983, Robert Wilson's King Lear, U. Calif. Los Angeles Ext., 1985, The Latest Stage, Los Angeles, 1985; movement cons. West Coast Ensemble, Los Angeles, 1987. Recipient fellowship U. Birmingham, Eng., 1981. Mem. Internat. Shakespeare Soc., Congress Research Dance, Phi Kappa Phi.

SHELLY-SUMAN, SANDRA MARIE, social worker, human services coordinator; b. Ashland, Ohio, June 5, 1948; d. Stanley Marshall and Margaret Jeanette (Plank) Shelly; m. Harold David Suman, Nov. 23, 1967 (div. July 1983); children: Philip David, Mikel James (dec.), Brett Lee. B in Social Work, St. Mary of the Woods Coll., 1981; postgrad., U. Minn., 1987, Ind. U., Indpls., 1987—. Social worker Community and Family Services, Portland, Ind., 1976-81; employment counselor Council on Rural Services, Greenville, Ohio, 1981-82; rehab. therapist Richmond (Ind.) State Hosp., 1982-83; shelter dir. YWCA Friends of Battered, Richmond, 1983-86; human services coordinator City of Richmond, 1986—; instr. Ind. Vocat. Tech. Coll., Richmond, 1985—; mem. Human Services Adv. Bd. Ind. U. East, 1985—, minority concerns adv. bd. Ind. Vocat. Tech. Coll., policy council Headstart Community Action East Cen. Ind., 1985—. Bd. dirs., pres. Community Services Council, 1986—; bd. dirs., sec. Richmond Jr. Players, 1985—; bd. dirs., grantwriter Wayne Opportunities Industrialization Ctr., 1986—; mem. League Women Voters; candidate Wayne County (Ind.) Trustee (Democrat), 1986. Mem. NASW, NAFE. Democrat. Home: 104 Henley Rd Richmond IN 47374 Office: Human Services Coordinator 50 N 5th St Richmond IN 47374

SHELTON, BETSY CAMPBELL, financial executive; b. Redlands, Calif., May 1, 1949; d. Richard Bailey and Priscilla Alden (Simonds) Cook; student U. Calif., Santa Barbara, 1967-69; B.A. in Econs., U. Redlands, 1971; m. Robert Maurice Shelton, Feb. 8, 1975; 1 stepson, Scott Maurice. Adminstrv. asst. trust dept. Bank of Am., Los Angeles, 1971-72; sales asst./money market desk Goldman Sachs & Co., Los Angeles, 1972-74; sales liaison Bateman Eichles, Los Angeles, 1974-77; investment officer trust investment dept. Security Pacific Nat. Bank, Los Angeles, 1977-80; v.p., mcpl. bond trader Bateman Eichler, Los Angeles, 1980-82, v.p. instnl. sales, 1982-84; v.p. instnl. sales First Boston, Los Angeles, 1984—; outside instr. for securities test passing firm, 1981—. Bd. dirs. Sierra Madre Council Girl Scouts U.S.A. Mem. Los Angeles Mcpl. Bond Club, Los Angeles Assn. Investment Women. Office: 333 S Grand Los Angeles CA 90071

SHELTON, GLORIA DEAN, finance executive; b. Union City, Tenn., Nov. 19, 1946; d. Ellis Grey and Mary Louise (Ping) Cochran; m. Jerry Shelton. BS, Ariz. State U., 1984. Asst. cashier Ariz. Bank, Phoenix, 1969-80; loan servicing mgr. Great Western Bank, Phoenix, 1980-83; assumption mgr. Century Bank, Phoenix, 1986-87; asst. v.p., loan servicing mgr. Combined Mortgage, Phoenix, 1987—. Mem. Nat. Assn. Bank Women (treas. 1979-80). Republican. Lodge: Eastern Star. Office: Combined Mortgage 3225 N Central #1200 Phoenix AZ 85012

SHELTON, JACQUELYNE SMITH, accountant; b. Paris, Tex., Aug. 9, 1958; d. John A. and Carol (Rattan) Smith; m. Michael B. Shelton, July 15, 1978; children: Carolyn Blair, Jared Wishard. AA in Sci. summa cum laude, Paris Jr. Coll., 1978; B in Bus. Adminstrn., E. Tex. State U., 1980. CPA, Tex. With McClanahan & Holmes CPA's, Paris, 1980—, staff acct., then sr. acct., then mgr., now ptnr., 1986—. Past pres., bd. dirs., vice chmn. campaign drive YWCA of Paris and Lamar County, Tex., 1982—; bd. dirs. Family Haven Battered Wives' Shelter, Paris, 1984-85, United Way of Lamar County; mem. interim adv. com. Paris Main Street Project, 1984-85; vol. Arthritis Found., Salvation Army, Am. Cancer Soc.; treas. Interfaith Disaster Services of Paris and Lamar County, 1982. Named one of Outstanding Young Women Am., 1982, 85, 86, Outstanding Young Woman of Lamar County, Paris Jaycee Women, 1985. Mem. Exec. Women of Paris (orgnizational steering com.), Paris Bus. and Profl. Women's Club (pres. 1984-85, 2d v.p. 1982-83, Young Careerist 1983, 84, dist. conf. chair 1986), Tex. Soc. CPA's, Am. Inst. CPA's, C. of C. Mem. Ch. of Christ. Office: McClanahan & Holmes CPA's 228 Sixth St SE Paris TX 75460

SHELTON, JUDY MCLELLAND, wildlife ranch executive administrator; b. Ft. Worth, July 31, 1958; d. Charles Edward and Phillip Irene (Van Dyke) McLelland; m. Dennis Dean Ross, Feb. 19, 1977 (div. 1981); m. William H. Shelton, Aug. 22, 1987. Student, Tarrant County Jr. Coll., 1977-81. Adminstrv. coordinator Fox and Jacobs, Inc., Ft. Worth, 1977-79; sec. Rotan Mosle, Inc., Ft. Worth, 1979-80; adminstrv. asst. Am. Quasar Petroleum Co., Ft. Worth, 1980-82; exec. adminstr. Fossil Rim Wildlife Ranch, Inc., Ft. Worth, 1982—; wardrobe and fashion cons., Ft. Worth, 1986—. Vol. Big Bro.-Big Sisters Ft. Worth. Mem. Nat. Assn. Female Execs., Ft. Worth Civic Leaders Assn. Republican. Baptist. Home: 5540 Jewell Ave Fort Worth TX 76112 Office: Fossil Rim Wildlife Ranch Rural Rt 1 Box 210 Glen Rose TX 76043

SHELTON, LUCY, soprano; B.A., Pomona Coll.; Mus. M. in Voice, New Eng. Conservatory Music, 1968. Asst. prof. voice Eastman Sch. Music, U. Rochester, 1979; vis. prof. Cleve. Inst. Music, 1986; appeared at Chamber Music N.W., Bethlehem Bach and Aspen music festivals, Casals Festival with Baroque ensemble; appeared as soloist with orchs., including Chgo., Boston, Denver, Houston, Balt., St. Louis symphonies, Los Angeles Chamber Orch., St. Paul Chamber Orch., Minn. Orch., BBC Proms in London, performance world premiere of Schwantner work with St. Louis Symphony, and nationwide tour as soloist with Helmuth Rilling and Los Angeles Chamber Orch.; also recitals, guest appearances with various groups, including Calliope and Twentieth Century Consort; recs. with Nonesuch Records, Vox, Vanguard, Grenadilla, Sonory, and Smithsonian Instn.; winner Walter W. Naumburg prize, 1977 (with Jubal trio) and 1980 (solo). Office: care Sheldon Softer Mgmt Inc 130 W 56th St New York NY 10019

SHELTON, SANDRA ANNE, management consultant; b. Ardmore, Tex., Jan. 26, 1947; d. Dale Earnest and Mary Ellen (Morrison) S.; m. Lester J. Little, Dec. 20, 1975 (div. July 1980). BA, Tex. Tech. U., 1979; MEd, Sam Houston State U., 1980. Tchr. Spring (Tex.) Independent Sch. Dist., 1975-77, Cypress-Fairbanks Independent Sch. Dist., Houston, 1977-81; rep. nat. account sales Standard Meat Co., Ft. Worth, 1981-84; cons. Shelton & Co., Bedford, Tex., 1984—; independent contractor Lou Smith Realtors, Bedford, 1984-87; assoc. realtor Henry S. Miller Realtors, 1987—; pres. Telemktg. by Design, 1987—; speaker CareerTrack, 1987—. Named Outstanding Young Women Am., 1982. Mem. Assn. Tng. and Devel., Nat Speakers Assn., Nat. Assn. Realtors, NE Tarrant County Bd. Realtors, Internat. Assn. Quality Circles, Alliance Profl Telemktg., Performax Internat. Office: Shelton and Co PO Box 993 Euless TX 76039-0993 Office: Telemktg by Design PO Box 824 Bedford TX 76095-0824

SHELTON, SARA VALENA, state representative, retired educator; b. Union County, S.C., July 29, 1919; d. Jeremiah Morgan and Mary Lucile (Sims) Beatty; m. LeRoy Anthony Shelton, May 5, 1944; 1 child, Sara Valena Shelton Boggs. BS, Benedict Coll., 1940; postgrad., Atlanta U., 1944, Columbia U., 1951; MEd, Furman U., 1968. Cert. elem. tchr. specialist, 1973. Mem. S.C. Ho. of Reps., 1985—; mem. Joint Legis. Com. to Study Problems of Drug and Alcohol Abuse, 1983—, Adv. Com. on Intergovernmental Relations, 1984—, Joint Legis. Com. on Cultural Affairs, 1985. Sec. Greenville County Dem. Com., 1984—. Mem. Nat. Council State Legislatures (Health and Human Resources com.).

SHELTON-COLBY, SALLY, banker, foreign policy analyst, former ambassador; b. San Antonio, Aug. 29, 1944; d. Harlan Bryan and Edith Angela (Pratka) S.; m. William E. Colby. B.A., U. Mo., 1966; M.A. (Univ. fellow), Johns Hopkins U., 1968; postgrad. (Fulbright scholar) Institut de

Sciences Politiques, Paris, 1968, Georgetown U., 1969. Research asst. Brookings Instn., 1969; prof. internat. relations Iberomerican U. and Nat. Autonomous U. Mex., Mexico City, 1969-71; legis. asst. for fgn. policy to Sen. Lloyd Bentsen, 1971-77; dep. asst. sec. state for Latin Am., Washington, 1977-78; ambassador to Barbados, Grenada, Dominica, St. Lucia, and St. Vincent, 1979-81; spl. rep. to Antigua, St. Kitts-Nevis, Montserrat and Brit. V.I., 1979-81; v.p. Internat. Bus.-Govt. Counsellors, Inc., Washington, 1982-84; v.p. Bankers Trust Co., N.Y.C., 1984-86 ; fellow Center Internat. Affairs, Harvard U., 1981-82; cons. to internat. banks and investors; adj. prof. Georgetown U. Bd. dirs. U.S. Com. of UN Fund for Women; trustee Mt. St. Mary's Coll.; vice chair Nat. Endowment for Democracy; bd. dirs., treas. Council Am. Ambassadors. Co-editor: (jour.) Global assessment. NDEA fellow. Fellow Italian Fgn. Ministry; mem. Assn. Polit. Risk Analysts (bd. dirs.), NOW, Nat. Women's Polit. Caucus, Council Fgn. Relations, Fulbright Alumni Assn., Phi Beta Kappa. Democrat. Home: 3028 Dent Pl NW Washington DC 20007

SHEMER, MARTHA EVVARD, investment company executive; b. Ames, Iowa, Apr. 19, 1919; d. John Marcus and Martha (Cooper) Evvard; m. Jack Corvin Shemer, June 24, 1937 (dec. 1967); m. Andrew Bobby, July 11, 1987; children: Jack Evvard, William Barry. Pioneer of properties, Phoenix, Scottsdale, Ariz., LaJolla, Calif. and Del Mar, Calif., 1941-75; pres. Shemer Enterprises, Phoenix, 1975-83, Shemer Investment Co., Phoenix, 1975—. History columnist Paradise Valley Ind. newspaper, 1987. Benefactor Shemer Art Ctr. and Mus. to City of Phoenix, 1984. Recipient Quill and Scroll nat. contest award, 1936. Republican. Avocations: helping humanity, bridge, poker, spite malice card games, reading, writing, travel, horses, inventing, needlepoint.

SHEMESH, LORRAINE R., artist; b. Jersey City, Mar. 27, 1949; d. Murray and Mildred Behar (Nissim) S. BFA in Painting magna cum laude, Boston U., 1971; postgrad., Tyler Sch. Art, Rome, 1971-72, MFA in Painting, Tyler Sch. Art, Elkins Park, Pa., 1973. Asst. prof. drawing R.I. Sch. Design, Providence, 1973-80; asst. prof. painting and drawing Amherst (Mass.) Coll., 1980-81. One-woman shows include R.I. Sch. Design, 1976, Alpha Gallery, Boston, 1978, Allan Stone Gallery, N.Y.C., 1983, 85, 88; exhibited in group shows at Smith Coll., Northhampton, Mass., 1973, Bell Gallery, Brown U., Providence, 1976, Inst. Contemporary Art, Boston, 1977, DeCordova Mus., Lincoln, Mass., 1979, Mead Art Mus., Amherst Coll., 1981, A.I.R. Gallery, N.Y.C., 1981, Staempfli Gallery, N.Y.C., 1981, Mus. City of N.Y., 1983-84, San Francisco Mus. Modern Art, 1985-86, Duke U. Mus. Art, Durham, N.C., 1987, Akron (Ohio) Art Mus., 1987, Bronx River Mus., N.Y.C., 1988; represented in pub. collections Mus. City of N.Y., DeCordova Mus., Mus. R.I. Sch. Design, AT&T, Chgo., Boise (Idaho) Art Mus. Grantee R.I. State Council for the Arts, Providence, 1979; fellow Tyler Sch. Art, 1972-73, Corp. Yaddo, Saratoga Springs, N.Y., 1981. Home and Office: 548 E 82d St #2A New York NY 10028

SHEMORRY, CORINNE JOYNES, marketng executive; b. Rolla, N.D., Jan. 24, 1920; d. William H. and Edna Ruth (Conn) Joynes; children: Gay, Jan. Publisher, Williston (N.D.) Plains Reporter, 1953-78; mktg. dir. Williston Credit Union, 1979—; journalist, lectr., cons., author, reporter. Recipient numerous awards in journalism on state and nat. level, including being named Outstanding Woman in Journalism in N.D., 1975, 1st Place Golden Mirror award Credit Union Nat. Assn. Mem. N.D. Press Assn., N.D. Press Women (past pres.), Nat. Press Women, Williston C. of C., Nat. Assn. Female Execs., Fin. Mktg. Assn. (charter), Sigma Delta Chi. Mem. United Ch. Club: Bus. and Profl. Women's (past pres.). Home: 210 E 14th St PO Box 1030 Williston ND 58801

SHENHOUSE, BERNICE, research economist; b. N.Y.C., Dec. 20, 1934; d. Solomon and Bella (Moseman) Cohen; m. Marin Shenhouse, Apr. 4, 1954; children: Joni B. Fox, Michael David. BA, Bklyn. Coll., 1975. Temporary office asst. Met. Life, N.Y.C., 1969-73, jr. econ. research asst., 1976-77, jr. econ. analyst, 1977-79, econ. analyst, 1979-82, research economist, 1983-85, sr. research economist, 1986—. Office: Bus Econ Met Life 1 Madison Ave New York NY 10010

SHENK, DENA, educator; b. N.Y.C., Feb. 22, 1952; d. Jerome and Rose (Weber) S.; m. Kenneth Quilty, June 18, 1977; children: Adam , Shayna. BA, SUNY, Stony Brook, 1973; MA, U. Mass., 1976, PhD, 1979. Asst. prof. St. Cloud (Minn.) State U., 1979-85, assoc. prof., 1985-88, chair dept. interdisciplinary studies, 1987—, prof., 1988—; dir. gerontology program, St. Cloud (Minn.) State U., 1980—. Contbr. articles & papers to profl. jours. Bd. advs., Foster Grandparents Program, 1983-86, Retired Sr. Vol. Program, 1979-84; mem. Sr. Citizens adv. com., St. Cloud, 1984—, nominations com., Central Minn. Group Health Plan, St. Cloud, 1985-86; convener St. Cloud Area Gray Panthers, 1981-82. Recipient Research award Minn. Chpt. of Am. Coll. of Health Care Adminstrs., 1985-86, Curriculum Improvement grant BUSH Found., 1985-86, research & curriculum improvement grants St. Cloud State U., 1983-84, 86-87; Cen. Minn. Arts Council grantee, 1987. Mem. Assn. for Anthropology & Gerontology (pres. 1985-86, newsletter editor 1983-85), Minn. Gerontological Soc. (program com. chair, 1983-84), Am. Anthropological Assn., Gerontology Soc. of Am., Nat. Council on the Aging, Nat. Women's Studies Assn., Central Minn. Council on Aging, Internat. Commn. on the Study of Aging & the Aged (charter), Biennial Review of Anthropology & Gerontology (editorial bd. 1987), Jour. of Cross-Cultural Aging (editorial bd. 1985-87). Office: St Cloud State Univ Stewart Hall Saint Cloud MN 56301

SHENK, PATRICIA WOOTEN, adult care facility administrator; b. Chapmansville, W.Va., Apr. 17, 1935; d. Jasper W. and Hatha (Bays) Wooten; m. Raymond R. Shenk, May 23, 1959; children—Roanne Shenk Mazzucco, Ellen Shenk Perrotto, Mark Greenlee, Raymond Shenk, Timothy Shenk, Zachary Shenk. Rec. clk., mailroom supr. FBI, Washington, 1953-55; registration clk. Santa Clara Jr. Coll., part-time 1966; inventory control clk. Preiser Sci., Charleston, W.Va., 1967-69; owner, adminstr. Summit House, Alton, N.Y., 1973-84; owner, adminstr. Glen House, Eldercare, Moravia, N.Y., 1988— ; pres. Shenk Properties, Inc., sec. bd. dirs. Grape Hill Gardens, Inc. Mem. Nat. Assn. Female Execs., Nat. Fedn. Ind. Bus., U.S. C. of C., Moravia C. of C., Empire State Assn. Adult Care Homes, Internat. Platform Assn. Republican. Methodist. Office: PO Box 194 Alton NY 14413

SHEPANEK, HELENE ANNA, educator; b. Regensburg, Germany, July 26, 1929; came to U.S., 1948, naturalized, 1950; d. Alfons and Alicia (Heidecker) Heiss; diploma Prinzessin von Arnheim Sch., Munich, 1947; B.A. summa cum laude, Am. U., 1972, M.A. with distinction, 1973; children—Marc Allen, Bruce Albert. Instr. German and French, C.I.A., Washington, 1965-66; teaching asst. Am. U., Washington, 1971-72, instr. German, 1972-78, professorial lectr., lang. specialist German studies, 1978—. Mem. AAUP, Am. Assn. Tchrs. of German, Am. Goethe Soc., Delta Phi Alpha, Phi Kappa Phi. Roman Catholic. Home: 850 Whann Ave McLean VA 22101 Office: Am U Dept Langs and Fgn Studies Washington DC 20016

SHEPARD, LINDA MARY, real estate management company executive; b. Rochester, N.Y., Feb. 23, 1949; d. Angelo Anthony and Mary M. (Steiner) Costanza; m. Theodore L. Shepard, Jr., July 8, 1972; 1 son, Theodore James. A.A., Green Mountain Coll., 1969; B.A., U. Rochester, 1971. Vice pres. Glenbrook Manor Assocs., Rochester, 1972-83; pres. Shepard Signal, Inc., Canandaigua, N.Y., 1980-83, Costanza Enterprises, Rochester, 1983—; bd. dirs. Costanza Constrn. Co., Rochester, Shepard Bros., Inc., Canandaigua. Mem. Inst. Real Estate Mgmt., Bldg. Owners and Mgrs. Assn., Phi Theta Kappa. Office: Costanza Enterprises 14 Franklin St Rochester NY 14604

SHEPARD, MIKKI MAUREEN ALLISON, real estate broker; b. Queens, N.Y., May 12, 1951; d. George William and June Rita (Ferrary) S.; m. Tom C. Blankenheim, July 2, 1983. BA, U. Colo., 1982. Cert. real estate brokerage mgr. Employment counselor Centennial Personnel, Colorado Springs, Colo., 1977-78; ins. auditor Associated Ins. Utah, Colorado Springs, 1978-79; broker, co-owner TCB Realty and Investment Co., Inc., Colorado Springs, 1979—; speaker Nat. Assn. Realtors, Chgo., 1985—. Contbr. articles to Real Estate Today, Colo. Realtor News Communiqué, Gazette Telegraph. Pres. Christmas Unlimited Found., Colorado Springs, 1988; campaign worker El Paso County Reps., Colorado Springs, 1977-78; mem. Realtors Polit. Action Com., Chgo., 1979—; mem. Profl. Women's Rep. Club, Colorado Springs, 1987. Served with USAF, 1970-74. Mem. Colo. Assn. Realtors (dir. 1986—), Colorado Springs Bd. Realtors (bd. dirs. 1981, 84, treas. 1985-86, sec. 1987-88), Realtors Nat. Mktg. Inst., Womens Council Realtors (Colo. chpt. pres. elect 1988, Pikes Peak chpt. treas. 1984-85, pres. 1986-87, Woman of Yr. Pikes Peak chpt. 1986), Nat. Women's Council Realtors (leadership tng. grad. 1987, edn. chmn. 1987-88). Methodist. Office: TCB Realty and Investment Co Inc 819 N Nevada Ave Colorado Springs CO 80903

SHEPARD-TAGGART, GLORIA HARVEY, communications company executive; b. Ridgeland, S.C., June 20, 1932; d. Leroy Everett and Addie Gertrude (Gray) Harvey; m. Ray Lester Shepard (dec.); children: Michael Ray, Glenn Eric; m. Eugene Sheppard Taggart, June 1, 1986. Student Armstrong Coll., 1950-52. Head bookkeeper Liberty Nat. Bank, Savannah, Ga., 1952-55; v.p. Hargray Telephone Co., Inc., Hilton Head Island, S.C., 1953-82, pres., 1982—; bd. dirs. Citizen & So. Nat. Bank of S.C. Bd. dirs. Better Bus. Bur., Hilton Head Heart Assn., Cultural Council Hilton Head Island. Mem. U.S. Telephone Assn., S.C. C. of C., S.C. Indsl. Developers Assn., Nat. Assn. Female Execs., Am. Mgmt. Assn., Ind. Telephone Pioneers, Profl. Women's Club, Beta Kappa. Baptist. Club: Christian Women's. Avocations: biking, cards. Office: Hargray Telephone Co Inc PO Box 5519 Hilton Head Island SC 29938

SHEPHERD, BARBARA KITTERMAN, editor, publisher; b. Glenridge, N.J., Mar. 21, 1947; d. Douglas Barrett Kitterman and Doris (Muriel) Dunster; m. James A. Shepherd II, July 24, 1971; children: James A. III, Douglas Barrett. Grad. high sch., Buenos Aires, Argentina; student, U. Iowa, 1968-70. Clk. Naples (Fla.) Hosp., 1971-73, Naples (Fla.) Police Dept., 1973-76; owner, publisher, editor Clockworks Events Mag., Solon, Iowa, 1984—. Named Poet of the Yr. Poets Guild, 1970. Republican. Presbyterian. Home and Office: Rt 4 Box 81 Solon IA 52333

SHEPHERD, ELSBETH WEICHSEL, operations engineer; b. Youngstown, Ohio, Dec. 5, 1952; d. Richard Henry and Lesley Frances (Lynn) Weichsel; BS in Math., Carnegie-Mellon U., 1974; MBA, U. Cin., 1978; m. Gordon Ray Shepherd, Aug. 28, 1976. Asst. indsl. engr. Armco, Inc., Middletown, Ohio, 1974-76, asso. indsl. engr., 1976-78, indsl. engr., 1978-82, sr. ops. engr., 1982-86, supr. process planning, 1986-88; project mgr. Integrated Mfg., 1988—. Mem. news mag. staff Jr. League Cin., 1980-81; vol. Miami Purchase Assn. Am. Iron and Steel Inst. fellow, 1978-81 Mem. Soc. Women Engrs. (pres. sect. 1981-82, provisional regional dir. 1983-84), Assn. Computing Machinery, Am. Inst. Indsl. Engrs. (v.p. services, pres. 1985-86), Tech. Socs. Council of Cin. (pres. 1986-87, 1st v.p. 1985-86, 2d v.p. 1984-85, treas. 1983-84), Engrs. and Scientists of Cin. (sec. 1986—, pres. elect 1987-88). Home: 6255 Howe Rd Middletown OH 45042 Office: 1801 Crawford St Middletown OH 45043

SHEPHERD, GRETA D(ANDRIDGE), educational administrator; b. Washington, Aug. 15, 1930; d. Philip J. and Bertha (Johnson) Dandridge; m. Clifton Murchison (div.); 1 dau., Michele M.; m. 2 Gilbert Shepherd (dec. Dec. 1983). B.S., Miner Tchr. Coll., Washington, 1951; M.A., D.C. Tchrs. Coll., 1961. Tchr. D.C. Pub. Schs., 1951-65, guidance counselor, 1965-66, asst. prin., 1966-69, prin., 1969-72; dir. East Orange Pub. Schs. (N.J.), 1972-80, acting supt., 1980-82; supt. Plainfield Pub. Schs. (N.J.), 1982-84; Mercer County supt. N.J. Dept. Edn., Trenton, 1984—; mem. Tchr. Corps, NEA, Jamaica, W.I. 1967; profl. field reader Office Civil Rights Title IV, Washington, 1978-79. Bd. dirs. YWCA of Essex and West Hudson, Orange, N.J., 1973-76, East Orange Pub. Library, 1980-82. Named Woman of Yr., Gamma Omicron chpt. Zeta Phi Beta, 1983. Mem. Am. Assn. Sch. Adminstrs., Nat. Assn. Fed. Program Adminstrs. (sec. 1981-83), Assn. Supervision and Curriculum Devel., N.J. Assn. Sch. Adminstrs., N.J. Coalition Ednl. Leaders. Baptist. Office: Mercer County Office Edn 2300 Hamilton Ave Trenton NJ 08619

SHEPHERD, JUDY CARLILE, retired government and communication official; b. Kansas City, Mo.; d. John Mercer and Mary Almeda (Chapin) Ellis; student Okla. State U., Tulsa U.; B.A., Am. U., Washington, 1960; m. Joseph Elbert Shepherd; 1 son from previous marriage, John Philip Carlile. Chief probation officer Tulsa County Ct., 1947-50; real estate broker United Farm Agy., 1952-58; bldg. fund campaign mgr. AAUW, Washington, 1958-59; govt. and public relations ofcl. Nat. Counsel Assos., Washington, 1959-61; congressional liaison Dept. Agr., Washington, 1961-65; public info. officer OEO, 1965-70, spl. asst. to dep. dir. ops. Head Start, elderly, Indian and migrant programs, 1970-73; dir. public relations Nat. Assn. Social Workers, Washington, 1973-74; social sci. analyst Congressional Research Service, Library Congress, Washington, 1976-85. Author: The Statutory History of the United States Capitol Police Force, 6 vols., 1985. Pres. bd. govs. Agr. Symphony Orch., 1961-64; bd. dirs. ARC, Boy Scouts Am., 1948-50; bd. dirs. Little Theatre, 1956-57. Recipient 1st place Fed. Editors Blue Pencil award, 1967; cert. humanist counselor. Mem. Nat. Press Club, Public Relations Soc. Am., Nat. Assn. Govt. Communicators, Am. Humanist Assn., Assn. Humanistic Psychology, Am. U. Alumni Assn., Okla. State Soc., Mo. State Soc., Ark. State Soc., Library Congress Profl. Assn., Humanist Assn. Nat. Capital Area (pres. 1977-78), Nat. Congress Am. Indians, DAR, Am. Soc. Access Profls. (charter). Club: Woman's Nat Democratic. Coordinator, Am. Discovers Indian Art exhibit, Smithsonian Instn., 1967. Home: 2365 N Oakland St Arlington VA 22207

SHEPHERD, KIKUKO, artist; b. Nagano, Japan, Jan. 28, 1934; d. Kataro and Hana Takemura; m. James B. Shepherd, Jr., Dec. 27, 1959; children: Kenneth S., Scott L., Craig S. Translator Japan Pub. Trading Co., Tokyo, 1952-55, U.S. Air Force, Yokota, Japan, 1957-59; lectr. pvt. practice Dayton, Ohio, 1960-65; interpreter, pvt. practice Okinawa, Japan, 1966-71; artist Annandale, Va., 1987—. Mem. Sumi-e Soc. Am. Home: 3724 Linda Ln Annandale VA 22003

SHEPHERD, MARY ANNE, educator; b. Washinhgton, Jan. 26, 1950; d. Edwin Joseph and Louise Therese (McKay) Zabel; m. John Russell Caulk, June 5, 1971 (div. Feb. 1985); 1 child, Heidi; m. Robert A. Shepherd, June 25, 1988. BS, U. Md., 1972; MEd, George Mason U., 1976. Tchr. elem. schs. Montgomery County Public Schs., Rockville, Md., 1971-74, Fauquier County Pub. Schs., Warrenton, Va., 1974-76, Wooster (Ohio) Pub. Schs., 1976—. Advisor 4-H Club, Apple Creek, Ohio, 1982-87; vestrywoman St. James Episcopal Ch., Wooster, 1984-88, 88—. Mem. Wooster Edn. Assn. (treas. 1984—). Republican. Home: 6137 Ely Rd Wooster OH 44691 Office: Wooster City Schs 144 N Market St Wooster OH 44691

SHEPHERD, MARY JANE, nursing educator, consultant; b. Indpls., Sept. 16, 1935; d. Donald Raymond, Sr., and Rose Ellen (Doll) Fargo; m. Vernon Lee Shepherd, May 30, 1953; children—Matthew Lee, Mark William, Lois Rose Shepherd Farley. A.A. in Nursing, Ind. U.-Indpls., 1970, B.S. in Nursing, 1976, M.S. in Nursing, 1981; postgrad. Ind. U., Bloomington, 1983—. R.N., Ind. Nursing attendant Muscatatuck State Hosp., Butlerville, Ind., 1962-68; camp nurse Camp James Whitcomb Riley, Martinsville, Ind., 1970-78; staff nurse Riley Hosp. for Children, Indpls., 1970-75; home service nurse United Cerebral Palsy Central Ind., Indpls., 1979-81, cons., 1981—; lectr. nursing Ind. U., Indpls., 1976-81, asst. prof., 1981—. Author articles video rec., computer programs; created Nursing Computer Interest Group, 1986. Bd. dirs. United Cerebral Palsy Central Ind. Recipient Exceptional Achievement award United Cerebral Palsy Ind., 1978, Spl. Individual award, 1982; Outstanding Tchr. award Ind. U. nursing students, 1981. Mem. Am. Nursing Assn., Nat. League Nursing, Century Club Am. Nurses Found., Assn. Ind. Media Educators, Assn. Ednl. Communications Tech., Sigma Theta Tau. Republican. Episcopalian. Home: 5380 N 901 E Brownsburg IN 46112 Office: Ind U Sch Nursing 610 Barnhill Dr NU 333 Indianapolis IN 46223

SHEPHERD, MICKI JO, commercial lending officer; b. Wheeling, W.Va., June 28, 1957; d. Paul Clayton and Bonnie (Dorsch) S. B.A., Ohio State U., 1977. Loan adminstr. Union Bank, San Diego, 1980-82, credit trainee, Los Angeles, 1982, credit mgr., 1982-83, loan analyst, 1984, sr. analyst, 1984, loan officer, Bakersfield, Calif., 1985-87, asst. v.p., San Diego, 1988. Bd. dirs. Mid-state Devel. Corp. Active United Republican Women of Calif., 1985, United Reps. of Calif., 1985. Mem. Nat. Assn. Accts., Nat. Assn. Female Execs. Methodist. Home: 4801 Mt Barnard Ave San Diego CA 92111

SHEPHERD, NANCY KAY, financial planner; b. Belleville, Ill., Aug. 11, 1948; d. Richard George and Martha Lou (Cheek) Hamann; m. Michael David Shepherd, Oct. 20, 1973; children—Monika Michelle, Niklas David. B.A., Ill. State U., 1970; M.Ed. in Counseling, Boston U., 1977. Instr. North Greene High Sch., White Hall, Ill., 1970-73; bookkeeper Army and Air Force Exchange Service, Ft. Lewis, Wash., 1973-75; instr. Dept. Defense, Overseas Schs., Mannheim, W.Ger., 1975-80; instr. Trinidad High Sch., Colo., 1980-82; fin. planner IDS/Am. Express, Durango, Colo., 1982-86; fin. planner Shepherd, Shepherd & Limback Fin. Cons., Farmington, N.Mex., 1986—; instr. San Juan Coll., Farmington, 1985-88, Women at Work Conf., Farmington, 1986-87. Fund raiser Civitan, Durango, Colo., 1984-85; organizer The Network, profl. women's org., Farmington; dir. Better Bus. Bur., Farmington, 1985-88; instr. Gov.'s Conf. for Women, Farmington, 1985, also co-chair 1986-87. Div. Fin. Planner of Yr., IDS/Am. Express, Colorado Springs, 1983, 84. Mem. Inst. Fin. Planners, P.E.O. (chaplain 1985-86). Club: Civitan (Durango, Colo.). (sec. 1985-86). Avocations: racquetball, crocheting, reading. Home: 1729 E 21st Farmington NM 87401 Office: Shepherd Shepherd & Limback 2110 N Sullivan St Farmington NM 87401

SHEPPARD, POSY (MRS. JOHN WADE SHEPPARD), social worker; b. New Haven, Aug. 23, 1916; d. John Day and Rose Marie (Herrick) Jackson; m. John W. Sheppard, May 16, 1936; children—Sandra S. (Mrs. Allan Gray Rodgers), Gail G. (Mrs. S. Stinor Gimbel), Lynn S. (Mrs. William Muir Manger), John W. Student, Vassar Coll., 1938. Vol. field cons. Conn. A.R.C., 1955-60; vice chmn. bd. govs. Am. Nat. Red Cross, 1962-66; rep. League Red Cross Socs. to UN, 1957-80, Am. Nat. Red Cross to com. internat. social welfare Nat. Social Welfare Assembly, 1957-61; chmn. Non-Govtl. Orgn. Com. for UNICEF, 1963-64, 71-73; chmn. Non-Govtl. Orgn. Com. exec. com. for Office Pub. Information, UN, 1964-66; pres. conf. non-govtl. orgns. in consultative status with UN Econ. and Social Council, 1966-69. Nat. Inst. Social Scis., Am. Soc. Polit. and Social Sci., Soc. Internat. Devel., Nat. Soc. Colonial Dames, Descs. Signers of Declaration Independence. Clubs: Cosmopolitan, Field of Greenwich, Round Hill. Home: 535 Lake Ave Greenwich CT 06830

SHEPPARD, TERRY JEAN, accountant; b. Great Falls, Mont., Feb. 4, 1954; d. John A. Rubens and Berta m. (Stuker) Robinson; m. Robert M. Sheppard, Dec. 27, 1977; 1 child, Ryan N. BBA, U. Mont., 1977. CPA, Mont. Bookkeeper Oggs Shoes, Missoula, Mont., 1977; staff acct. Kindred, Holland & Lindberg CPAs, Helena, Mont., 1978-79; pvt. practice acctg. Ovando, Mont., 1980—; sec., treas. Center Ridge Industries Inc., Ovando, 1987. Mem. Am. Soc. CPAs, Mont. Soc. CPAs. Office: PO Box 132 Ovando MT 59854

SHER, ILONA, systems manager; b. Montreal, Can., May 20, 1955; d. Benjamin and Olga (Korec) Sher. BA, McGill U., 1977; MBA, U. Pa., 1981. Systems programmer, analyst Can. Pacific Ltd., Montreal, 1977-79; cons. Grant Thornton, N.Y.C., 1981-85; systems mgr., Macmillan, Inc., N.Y.C., 1985-87; mgr. fin. ops. Merrill Lynch, 1987—. Office: Merrill Lynch 30 Montgomery St Jersey City NJ 07302

SHER, JOANN GIFFUNI, lawyer, insurance executive; b. N.Y.C., May 30, 1942; d. Joseph and Flora (Baldini) Giffuni; B.A., Jackson Coll., Tufts U., 1963; LL.B., Fordham U., 1966; postgrad. U. Va., 1977; m. Michael L. Sher, Feb. 2, 1970 (div. 1977). Bar: N.Y. 1968. With Mfrs. Hanover Trust Co., N.Y.C., 1966-71; atty. Tchrs. Ins. and Annuity Assn., Coll. Retirement Edn. Fund., N.Y.C., 1972-73, asst. counsel, 1973-74, assoc. counsel, 1974-76, counsel, 1976-78, v.p., 1978—; lectr. in field. Mem. Family Edn. Com., Community Service Soc., 1970-72, mem. com. on edn., 1972-77, bd. dirs., 1985—; bd. dirs. Women's Prison Assn., 1972-74, Turtle Bay Music Sch., 1982—, Pastel Soc. Am., 1977—. Mem. ABA, Assn. Bar City N.Y., Nat. Assn. Coll. and Univ. Attys. Club: Cosmopolitan. Office: 730 3d Ave New York NY 10017

SHER, JOANNA RUTH, physician; b. Winnipeg, Man., Can., May 23, 1933; came to U.S., 1949, naturalized, 1958; d. Joseph and Dorothy Hollenberg; A.B., U. Chgo., 1952, B.S., 1956, M.D., 1956; m. Norman Sher, Dec. 28, 1955; children—Jonathan Aaron, Katherine Amy. Rotating intern Kings County Hosp., Bklyn., 1956-57, resident pathology, 1957-58; fellow pathology Kings County Hosp., SUNY Downstate Med. Center, Bklyn., 1960-62; Nat. Inst. Neurol. Diseases spl. fellow in neuropath. SUNY Downstate Med. Center, 1962-64; asst. neuropathologist Kings County Hosp., Bklyn., 1964-70, dir. neuropath. lab., 1970—; prof. clin. pathology, SUNY Health Sci. Ctr., Bklyn., 1977-87, asst. dean, 1977-83, disting. service prof., 1987—; cons. depts. pathology Brookdale Hosp. and Med. Center, Bklyn., Maimonides Hosp. and Med. Center, Bklyn., Bklyn. Hosp., L.I. Coll. Hosp. Diplomate Am. Bd. Pathology. Fellow Am. Soc. Clin. Pathologists; mem. Internat. Acad. Pathology, Am. Acad. Neurology, Am. Assn. Neuropathologists, Phi Beta Kappa, Sigma Xi, Alpha Omega Alpha. Editor: (with D. Ford) Primary Intracranial Neoplasms, 1979; contbr. articles in field to profl. jours. Home: 2347 E 63d St Brooklyn NY 11234 Office: SUNY Health Sci Ctr Box 25 450 Clarkson Ave Brooklyn NY 11203

SHERBELL, RHODA, painter, sculptor; b. Bklyn.; d. Alexander and Syd (Steinberg) S.; m. Mervin Honig, Apr. 28, 1956; 1 dau., Susan. Student, Art Students League, 1950-53, Bklyn. Mus. Art Sch., 1959-61; also; pvt. study art, Italy, France, Eng., 1956. Cons., council mem. Emily Lowe Gallery, Hofstra U., Hempstead, N.Y., 1978, pres., 1980-81, life mem. bd. friends, pres. bd. trustees; tchr. Mus. Modern Art, Nat. Acad. Design, Art Students League, N.Y.C.; instr. Mus. Modern Art, N.Y.C., 1956, Art Students League, N.Y.C., 1988, Nat. Acad. Design Art Sch., N.Y.C., 1988. Exhibited one-woman shows Country Art Gallery, Locust Valley, N.Y., Bklyn. Mus. Art Sch., 1961, Adelphi Coll., A.C.A. Galleries, N.Y.C., 1967, Capricorn Galleries, Rehn Gallery, Washington, 1968, Gallery Modern Art, N.Y.C., 1969, Morris (N.J.) Mus. Arts and Scis., 1980, Bergen Mus. Arts and Scis., N.J., 1984, William Benton Mus., Conn., 1985, Palace Theatre of the Arts, Stamford, Conn., Bronx Mus. Arts, 1986; one-woman retrospective at N.Y. Cultural Ctr., 1970, Nat. Arts Collection, Washington, 1970, Montclair Mus. of Art, 1976, Nat. Art Mus. of Sport, 1977, Jewish Mus. of N.Y.C., 1980, Black History Mus., 1981, Queens Mus., 1981, 82, Nat. Portrait Gallery, Washington, 1981, 82, Bronx Mus., N.Y., Bklyn. Mus., Mus. Modern Art, N.Y.C., Country Art Gallery, Port Washington Library, Nat. Mus. Am. Art, The Smithsonian Instn., 1982, Nat. Acad. Design, N.Y.C., 1984, Castle Gallery Mus., N.Y.C., 1987, Emily Lowe Mus., N.Y.C., 1987; exhibited group shows downtown Gallery, N.Y.C., Maynard Walker Gallery, N.Y.C., F.A.R. Gallery, N.Y.C., Provincetown Art Assn., Detroit Inst. Art, Pa. Acad. Fine Arts, Bklyn. and L.I. Artists Show, Old Westbury Gardens Small Sculpture Show, Audubon Artists, NAD, Allied Artists, Heckscher Mus., Nat. Art Mus. Sports, Mus. Arts and Scis., Los Angeles, Am. Mus. Natural History, Post of History Mus., 1987, Caslte Gallery Mus., N.Y.C., 1987, Emiloy Lowe Mus., N.Y., 1987, Bronx Mus. Arts, 1987, Chgo. Hist. Soc., NAD, others; represented permanent collections, Stony Brook Hall of Fame, William Benton Mus. Art, Colby Coll. Mus., Oklahoma City Mus., Montclair (N.J.) Mus., Schonberg Library Black Studies, N.Y.C., Albany State Mus., Hofstra U., Bklyn. Mus., Colby Coll. Mus., Nat. Arts Collection, Nat. Portrait Gallery, Smithsonian Instn., Baseball Hall of Fame Cooperstown, N.Y., Nassau Community Coll., Hofstra U. Emily Lowe Gallery, Art Students League, Jewish Mus., Queens Mus., Black History Mus., Nassau County Mus., Stamford Mus. Art and Nature Ctr., Jericho Pub. Library, N.Y., African-Am. Mus., Hempstead, N.Y., 1988; also pvt. collections, TV shows, ABC, 1968, 81; ednl. TV spl. Rhoda Sherbell-Woman in Bronze, 1977; important works include Seated Ballerina, portraits of Aaron Copland, Eleanor Roosevelt, Variations on a Theme (30 works of collaged sculpture), 1982-86; appeared several TV shows; guest various radio programs; contbr. articles to newspapers, popular mags. and art jours. Council mem. Nassau County Mus., 1978, trustee, 1st v.p. council; asso. trustee Nat. Art Mus. of Sports, Inc., 1975—; cons., community liaison WNET Channel 13, cultural coordinator, 1975-83; host radio show Not for Artists Only, 1978-79; trustee Women's Boxing Fedn., 1978. Recipient Am. Acad. Arts, Letters and Nat. Inst. Arts and Letters grant, 1960; Louis Comfort Tiffany Found. grant, 1962; Alfred G. B. Steel Meml. award Pa. Acad. Fine Arts, 1963-64; Helen F. Barnett prize NAD, 1965; Jersey City Mus. prize for sculpture, 1961; 1st prize sculpture Locust Valley Art Show, 1966, 67; Ann. Sculpture prize Jersey City Mus.; Bank for Savs. 1st prize in sculpture, 1950; Ford Found. purchase award, 1964; MacDowell Colony fellow, 1976; 2 top sculpture awards Mainstreams 77; Cert. of Merit Salmagundi Club, 1978; prize for sculpture, 1980, 81; award for sculpture Knickerbocker Artists, 1980, 81; top prize for sculpture Hudson Valley Art Assn., 1981; Sawyer award NAD, 1985; Gold medal of honor AudubonArtists, 1985; Ford Found. grantee, 1964. Fellow Nat. Sculpture Soc.; mem. Nat. Arts Club, Sculpture Guild (dir.), Nat. Assn. Women Artists (Jeffery Childs Willis Meml. prize 1978), Allied Artists Soc. (dir.), Audubon Artists (Greta Kempton Walker prize 1965, Chaim Gross award, award for disting. contbr. to orgn. 1979, 80, Louis Weskeem award; dir.), Woman's Caucus for Art, Coll. Art Assn., Am. Inst. Conservation Historic and Artistic Works, N.Y. Soc. Women Artists, Artists Equity Assn. N.Y., Nat. Sculpture Soc., Internat. Platform Assn., Profl. Artists Guild L.I., Painters and Sculptors Soc. N.J. (Bertrum R. Hulmes Meml. award), Am. Watercolor Soc. (award for disting. contbn. to orgn.), Catharine Lorillard Wolfe Club (hon. mention 1968). Home: 64 Jane Ct Westbury NY 11590

SHERBIN, JAN, television and radio news broadcaster; b. Hartford, Conn. BS in Journalism, Boston U., MS in Journalism. Mgr., TV and radio dept. Henry Ford Mus., Greenfield Village, Detroit, 1980-82; reporter Sta. WPTA-TV, Ft. Wayne, Ind., 1982-84; news dir. Sta. WAJI, Ft. Wayne, 1984-86, host and producer TV Bus. News Program, 1984—; corr. AP, UPI, RKO networks and Network Ind. Freelance writer. Tchr. Jr. Achievement; speaker, contest judge numerous civic and charity groups. Recipient Best Radio News Series award AP, Ind., 1985, Best TV Investigative Report AP, Ind., 1984, Best TV Investigative Report UPI, Ind., 1984, Health Journalism award Am. Chiropractic Assn., 1985, Golden Mike award Am. Legion Aux., 1985, 86, Internat. Assn. Bus. Communicators award, 1987, Editor's Assn. awards, 1987, Freedom Found. award. Mem. Am. Women in Radio and TV (pres. Detroit chpt. 1982), New England Women's Press Assn. (pres. 1977-79). Office: Procter & Gamble Pub Affairs Cincinnati OH 45230

SHERF, SANDEE CROFT, real estate corporation executive; b. Okmulgee, Okla., Feb. 24, 1950; d. C. Don and Joyce Marie (Harris) Croft; m. Paul P. DeGeronimo, Nov. 4, 1970 (div. 1980); children: Shawn Dale, Aimee Vanessa; m. E.W. Sherf, May 15, 1983; 1 child, Summer Ashley. Student Maryville Coll., 1969. Flight attendant Piedmont Airlines, Salem, N.C., 1969-70; credit card mgr. Blount Nat. Bank, Maryville, Tenn., 1970-72; travel agt. AAA of Va., Lynchburg, 1972-76; real estate agt. Century 21, Houston, 1979-81; real estate developer E.W. Sherf Interests, Humble, Tex., 1981-84; comml. property mgr. SCS Mgmt. Co., Inc., Spring, 1984—; pres. Reid Rd. Mcpl. Utility Dist., Houston, 1983—. Leader, San Jacinto council Girl Scouts U.S., 1983; mem. Champion Forest Civic Club, Houston, 1983, Mus. Fine Arts, Houston, Smithsonian Inst., Washington. Recipient Managerial Acctg. and Fin. Concepts award Bldg. Owners and Mgrs. Inst., 1983. Mem. Tex. Assn. Realtors, Nat. Assn. Realtors, Houston Bd. Realtors, Real Estate Securities and Syndications, Realtors Nat. Mktg. Inst., Inst. Real Estate Mgmt., Houston Apt. Assn., Internat. Council Shopping Ctrs., Writer's Guild. Republican. Baptist. Avocations: skiing, swimming, race car driving, dancing, writing. Office: SCS Mgmt Co Inc 7623 Louetta Dr Suite 109 Spring TX 77379

SHERFEY, GERALDINE RICHARDS, educational administrator; b. Pontiac, Mich., Dec. 11, 1929; d. William and Ethel (Spurr) Richards; m. William E. Sherfey, Aug. 4, 1950 (div.); children—Emily J., Laura A., Susan E., William E. B.S., Ind. State U., 1963, M.S., 1965; Ed.S., U. Ga., 1973, Ed.D., 1978. Biology and gen. sci. instr. Hammond (Ind.) Tech.-Vocat. High Sch., 1963-65; advanced biology instr. Griffith (Ind.) Sr. High Sch., 1965-70, dept. chmn. grades K-12, acting sci. cons., 1968-70; mgr. sch. programs (asst. supt. for curriculum and instrn.) Greenville (S.C.) Pub. Schs., 1972-73; instr. edn. Purdue U., Calumet Campus, Hammond, Ind., 1973-75; guest lectr. Purdue U. Calumet Campus and Ind. U. N.W., Gary, 1975-78; sci. instr. grades 7 and 8, Spohn Middle Sch., Hammond, 1975-78, prin. A.L. Spohn Elem./Middle Sch., 1978-80, adminstrv. asst. for curriculum and instruction Hammond Schs., 1980-82, coordinator vocat. program devel. and extended programs 1982-85, dir. curriculum/operation, area career ctr., 1985—; dir. Curriculum and Plant Mgmt., 1985—. Ind. State U. teaching fellow, 1964-65; U. Ga. grad. asst., 1970-72. Co-editor, Ind. State newsletter for adult and continuing edn., 1985; contbr. articles to profl. jours. Mem. World Council for Curriculum and Instruction, Assn. for Supervision and Curriculum Devel., Nat. Sci. Tchrs. Assn., Nat. Middle Schs. Assn., Ind. Middle Schs. Assn., Ind. Assn. Adult and Continuing Edn. (recipient Outstanding Contbn. award 1986. Democrat. Roman Catholic. Contbr. articles to profl. jours. Home: 540 W 56th Ave Merrillville IN 46410 Office: 5727 Sohl Ave Hammond IN 46320

SHERIDAN, EMILY JEAN O'NEIL, banker; b. Jamaica, N.Y., Jan. 8, 1948; d. James Coyle and Emily (Olff) O'Neil; m. Paul Sheridan, Nov. 20, 1982; 1 child, Sarah Elizabeth. A.A., Suffolk County Community Coll., 1968; B.S., SUNY, Stony Brook, 1970; M.A., Adelphi U., 1975, cert. mgmt., 1977, M.B.A., 1980. Sales-person/cashier Rainbow Shops, Port Jefferson Station, N.Y., 1966-70; tchr. Sachem Sch. Dist., Holbrook, N.Y., 1970-72; tax examiner IRS, Holtsville, N.Y., 1973-77; adminstrv. systems analyst Nat. West USA, N.Y.C., 1977-80, unit mgr. planning and control, systems officer, 1980-84, group controller, asst. v.p., 1984—. Committee person Suffolk County Democratic Party, 1972-73; treas. Com. of People for Lutz, Brookhaven Twp., N.Y., 1978—; mem. com. Citizens Adv. Com., Brookhaven Twp., 1975-76; mem. Brookhaven Town Adv. Com. on Youth, 1976-77; mem. Brookhaven Town Youth Bur. Bd., 1977-82. Mem. Nat. Assn. Bank Women, Nat. Assn. Female Execs., AAUW. Roman Catholic. Home: 2 Essex Ln Hicksville NY 11801

SHERIDAN, HELEN MARIE, homecare manager; b. Providence, Apr. 4, 1953; d. Edward William and Edith Alice (Ryan) S.; m. Thomas Peter Marsden, July 11, 1987. Diploma in respiratory therapy, R.I. Hosp., 1973; student in bus. adminstrn., We. Conn. State U., 1982—. Cert. respiratory therapy technician. Staff respiratory therapist R.I. Hosp., Providence, 1973-75; respiratory therapist Pulmonary Assocs., Providence, 1975-79; contract respiratory therapist Linde Homecare Med. Systems, Inc., Warwick, R.I., 1979-80, sales mgr., 1980-81; sales mgr. Linde Homecare Med. Systems, Inc., Wilton, Conn., 1981-83, dist. mgr., 1983-85; region mgr. Linde Homecare Med. Systems, Inc., Brookfield, Conn., 1985—; vice chmn. pub. affairs com. Union Carbide Corp., 1986-87. Mem. Nat. Assn. Female Execs., Am. Assn. Respiratory Care, Am. Lung Assn. of Conn., Conn. Thoracic Soc., Conn. Assn. Med. Equipment Dealers (bd. dirs. 1986—), Danbury Area Women's Network. Office: Linde Homecare Systems Inc 61 Commerce Dr Brookfield CT 06805

SHERIFF, MARSHA ANN, insurance agency executive; b. Columbus, Ohio, Oct. 2, 1949; d. Willis Robert and Ruth Ann (Eastwood) Daniels; divorced; children: Suzanne Elaine, Brian Kelly. BA, Fairleigh Dickinson U., 1983. Cert. ins. profl. Tech. support underwriter Continental Ins. Co., Columbus, 1967-77; tng. coordinator Aetna Ins. Co., Livingston, N.J., 1977-79; office services mgr. Continental Ins. Co., Livingston, N.J., 1979-81, mgr., 1981-82; mgr. mktg. Continental Ins. Co., Piscataway, N.J., 1982-85; mgr. mktg. devel. Fred S. James & Co., Short Hills, N.J., 1985-86; v.p. Beneficial Ins. Group, Peapack, N.J., 1986—, ISU-Griffith-Prideaux Insurors, Morristown, N.J., 1987—. Contbr. articles to profl. jours. Vol. Leana Brown for Senate campaign, Parsippany, N.J., 1977-78; mem. Boonton Sr. Citizens Commn., 1983-86. Mem. Nat. Assn. Ins. Women (regional officer 1986-87, named Ins. Women of Yr. 1983, chmn. state council 1982-84, pres. NW N.J. chpt. 1981-82), Nat. Assn. Female Execs., AAUW (pres. NW N.J. chpt. 1981-82), Delta Mu Delta, Phi Epsilon Omega. Republican. Lutheran. Home: 457 Rockaway St Boonton NJ 07005 Office: ISU Griffith Prideaux Insurors 225 Madison Ave Morristown NJ 07960

SHERLOCK, VALERIE JUNE, public relations executive; b. Berwyn, Ill., Feb. 18, 1945; d. Gordon William and June Elaine (Allen) S. BA in Journalsim, U. Wis., 1967. Asst. editor World Book Ency., Chgo., 1967-68; with community relations Sta. WBBM-TV, Chgo., 1968-69; co-ordinator advt. Ronnie Boyd & Assocs., Houston, 1969-70; asst. fin. relations. Internat. Systems & Controls, Houston, 1970-75; dir. relations Houston Pub. Library, 1975-80; owner, mgr. Valerie Sherlock Pub. Relations, 1972-86; dir. communications Houstonian Hotel & Club, 1982-84, v.p. pub. relations, 1984-85; v.p. corp. pub. relations Living Well Inc., 1985-86; pres., mng. dir. Criterion Pub. Relations & Advt., Houston, 1986-88; dir. community relations Conoco Inc. (div. DuPont Co.), Houston, 1988—; v.p., ptnr. B.R.G. Enterprises, Houston, 1983-85, Cavalier Group Inc., 1986—. Author: (newspaper column) Pet Set, 1973-80. Precinct capt. Houston Republican Com., 1974; mem. mktg. adv. Arts for Everyone, 1985. Recipient 1st place award John Cotton Dana Library Pub. Relations contest, 1979. Mem. Houston Advt. Fedn. (bd. dirs. 1988—), Inst. Art Edn. (bd. dirs. 1988—), Houston Mus. Fine Arts (bd. dirs., 19886, corp. ptnrs.), Houston C. of C. (civic affairs com. 1977-82, edn. com. 1988—), Pub. Relations Soc. Am., Women Communications, Tex. Press Women (pres. 1982, 1st place award 1981), Publicity Club N.Y., Am. Mktg. Assn., Delta Delta Delta (project com. 1985). Republican. Christian Scientist. Club: River Oaks Tennis. Home: 2701 Westheimer Houston TX 77098 Office: Conoco Inc 600 N Dairy-Ashford Dr Houston TX 77079

SHERMAN, BEATRICE ETTINGER, business executive; b. N.Y.C., May 29, 1919; d. Max and Stella (Schrager) Ettinger; m. Herbert Jacob Howard, Feb. 15, 1942 (dec. 1971); children—Robert David Howard, Carolyn Howard Smith; m. Ernest John Sherman, Dec. 29, 1974. Student, Shimer Jr. Coll., Mt. Carroll, Ill., 1936-38; B.A., U. Miami, Fla., 1940; postgrad. Harvard U., 1940, Paris-Am. Acad., Paris, 1972, Alliance Française, Paris, 1973. Corp. sec., dir. Save Electric Corp., Toledo, 1940-67, Verd-A-Ray Corp., Toledo, 1944-67, Penetray Corp., Toledo, 1962-67; ptnr. Stella Assocs., Newark, 1960-80; pres. Besman Inc., Coral Gables, Fla., 1975—, All Am. Mobile Telephone Co., Coral Gables, 1986. Vol. worker Jewish Welfare Fedn., Toledo, 1942-69; nat. speaker United Jewish Appeal; mem. womens div. Greater Miami Jewish Fedn., 1969—, trustee, 1986; active Miami advertiser adv. bd. Bell South Pub. Recipient Lion of Judah award. Mem. Assn. Telemessaging Services Internat., Telocator Network Am., Nat. Council Jewish Women (edn. v.p. 1962-63, bull. editor 1961-62), League City Mothers (v.p. 1953), Hadassah (chpt. v.p. 1963-64). Home: 5108 SW 72d Ave Miami FL 33155 Office: Besman Inc 141 Aragon Ave Coral Gables FL 33134

SHERMAN, BERNICE MAE, educator; b. Brockton, Mass., Oct. 7, 1930; d. John Alfred and Gladys Josephine (Boyd) Swan; B.S. in Edn., Bridgewater State Coll., 1970, M.Ed. in Reading, 1975, postgrad. 1984; m. James Owen Pritchard, Feb. 12, 1955 (dec. 1963); 1 dau., Rhonda Mae; m. 2d Robert A. Sherman, Dec. 27, 1980 (dec. Feb. 1987). Tchr. Carver (Mass.) Pub. Schs., 1968-70; reading, learning disabilities specialist, 1970-76, dir. visual motor tng. program, 1973-76, coordinator in-service programs, 1973-76; reading, learning disabilities coordinator Plymouth (Mass.) Sch. System, 1976-82; coordinator programs for children with learning disabilities Fed. Furnace Sch., Plymouth, 1976-79; reading and learning disabilities coordinator Hedge Sch., Plymouth, 1979-83; cons. tchr. reading Mt. Pleasant Sch., Plymouth, 1983-86, Hedge Sch., 1983—. Mem. Plymouth-Carver Edn. Assn., Plymouth-County Edn. Assn., Mass. Reading Assn., Mass. Tchrs. Assn., NEA, Internat. Reading Assn. Methodist. Club: Mem. Order Eastern Star. Home: 220 Bedford St Apt D8 Bridgewater MA 02324

SHERMAN, ELAINE C., educator, business owner; b. Chgo., Aug. 1, 1938; d. Arthur E. and Sylvia (Miller) Friedman; (divorced); children: Steven J., David P., Jaime A. Student, Northwestern U., 1956-58; diploma in cake decorating, Wilton Sch. Profl. Cake Decorating, 1973; diploma, Dumas Pere, L'école de la Cuisine Française. Tchr. cooking and adult edn. Maine, Oakton, Niles Adult and Continuing Edn. Program, Park Ridge, Ill., 1972-82; corp. officer The Complete Cook, Glenview, Ill., 1976-82, Madame Chocolate, Glenview, 1983-87; food columnist Chgo. Sun Times, 1985-87; dir. mktg. Sue Ling Gin, Chgo., 1987-88; co-owner Critical Eye, Chgo., 1988—. Author: Madame Chocolate's Book of Divine Indulgences, 1984 (nominated Tastemaker award 1984). Mem. Les Dames D'Escoffier, Women's Foodservice Network, Confrerie de la Chaine Des Rotisseurs, Am. Inst. Food and Wine. Home and Office: 1728 D Wildberry Dr Glenview IL 60025

SHERMAN, FRANCES BUCK, artist, photographer; b. Barahona, Santo Domingo; d. Harry Catlett and Elizabeth F. Buck (parents Am. citizens); student Sophie Newcomb Coll., New Orleans, 1936-37, St. Mary's Jr. Coll., Raleigh N.C., 1937, New Orleans Acad. Art, 1947-48, Atlanta Sch. Art., 1967-68, Jacksonville Mus. Art, 1976, N.Y. Inst. Photography, 1981, Writer's Digest Sch. of Writing, 1981-82; m. Walter Scott Sherman, Jr., Nov. 9, 1950; children—G. Scott, F. Carolyn; children by previous marriage—Thomas M. Frasier, Harry B. Frasier. Pvt. art tchr., New Orleans, 1947; pvt. practice modeling, New Orleans, 1947-48; staff fashion model Burdines Dept. Store, Miami, 1949-50, asst. fashion coordinator, 1951-52; fashion cons. Coronet Sch. Modeling, Miami, 1953-54; instr. art Tampa Realistic Artists Gallery (Fla.), 1969-70; one-woman shows: Tampa Realistic Art Gallery, 1970, St. Marys Episcopal Ch., Tampa, 1971, Britton Theatre Corp., Tampa, 1970, Royal Trust Bank, Jacksonville, Fla., 1980, 81; group shows include: Va. Mus. Fine Arts, Richmond, Mint Mus. Art, Charlotte, N.C., Isaac Delgado Mus. Art, New Orleans, Swan Coach House Gallery, Atlanta, Jacksonville Art Mus. (Fla.), 1979, St. Augustine Art Assn. (Fla.), 1979, St. Augustine Art Assn., 1982-87; represented in permanent collections: Jacksonville Shipyards Corp., Robinson-Humphrey Investors, Atlanta, Jacksonville (Fla.) U.; hostess Jacksonville Art Assembly Art Festival, 1977. Active fund raising Pub. Broadcasting TV Sta., Tampa, 1970-71, Jacksonville, 1972-78; active Republican Campaign Hdqrs., Jacksonville, 1976; bd. mem. Nat. Adv. Com. Restore Sch. Prayer; mem. Nat. Rep. Congl. Com., Duval County Rep. Women's Club. Recipient Certificate of Recognition, The Bicentennial Commn. Jacksonville, 1976; named Outstanding Patriot, Patriots of Am. Bicentennial, 1976. Mem. Am. Artists Profl. League, Inc., Nat. League Am. Pen Women, Inc. (pres. Jacksonville br. 1974-76; Fla. v.p. 1974-76), St. Augustine Art Assn., Fla. Poetry Soc., Arts Assembly Jacksonville, Jacksonville Art Mus., Jacksonville Coalition Visual Artists, Nat. Writers Club. Episcopalian. Contbr. poetry to books and mags. Home: 4331 San Jose Ln Jacksonville FL 32207

SHERMAN, LENORE, hospital administrator; b. Phila., Sept. 4, 1939; d. Oscar and Yetta Arost; m. Bernard Sherman, Mar. 21, 1965; children: Meredith, David. BS, Temple U., 1961, MBA, 1979. Cert. mental health adminstr. Social worker Youth House, Welfare Island, N.Y., 1961-63; probation officer Bklyn. Juvenile Term Ct., 1963-68; dir. Phoenix House, Bryn Mawr, Pa., 1975-77; grad. asst. Temple U., Phila., 1978-79; adminstr. Catchement Area Community Health Ctr., Phila., 1979-81; assoc. hosp. adminstr. Med. Coll. Pa., Phila., 1981-88, v.p. for ops., 1988—. Com. mem. Lower Merion (Pa.) Dem. Assn., 1972-80; bd. dirs. Lower Merion Crew Assn., Phila. Internat. Program, 1981—; pres. Temple U. Health Adminstrn. Alumni Assn., 1986—. Mem. Hosp. Assn. Pa., Mental Health Assn. Southeastern Pa., Forum Del. Valley Hosp. Council, Am. Coll. Health Care Execs. Jewish. Home: 115 Merion Ave Narbeth PA 19072 Office: Med Coll Pa 3200 Henry Ave Philadelphia PA 19129

SHERMAN, MELINDA ANNE, advertising executive; b. Chgo., Sept. 17, 1946; d. Gerald Wilfred and Dorothy Anne S.; m. Nathan Butler Swift, Nov. 17, 1984. B.A., U. Colo., 1968; M.S.J., Northwestern U., 1973. High Sch. tchr. English, journalism and drama, Albion and Reading, Mich., 1968-70; account rep. Equitable Life Assurance Soc., Chgo., 1970-72, Young & Rubicam N.Y. Advt., 1973-76; v.p., account dir. Leo Burnett USA Advt., Chgo., 1976—; mem. faculty Keller Grad. Sch. Mgmt., Chgo., 1984, 85. Bd. dirs. Chgo. Opera Theater, Chgo. Opera Theater, Chgo. Drama League. Recipient Spl. Performance award Young & Rubicam Advt., 1975, 76. Mem. Chgo. Advt. Club. English Speaking Union, Gamma Phi Beta. Clubs: Women's Athletic, Plaza (Chgo.). Home: 1560 N Sandburg Terr Chicago IL 60610 Office: Prudential Plaza Chicago IL 60601

SHERMAN, PATRICIA ANN, hospital medical records administrator; b. St. Louis, June 11, 1952; d. Robert L. and Ola M. (Jackson) S.; married (div.); children: Francesca Bynes, Frenchye Diane Bynes. BS in Med. Records Adminstrn., St. Louis U., 1977; MS in Health Care Adminstrn., New Sch. Social Research, N.Y.C., 1982. Registered Records Adminstr. Adminstr. Northside Gen. Hosp., St. Louis, 1977, Doctors' Hosp. of Staten Island (N.Y.), 1978-85, St. Louis Regional Med. Ctr., 1985—; cons. State of Ill. Dept. of Corrections. Contbr. articles to profl. jours. Named Mother of Yr. Staten Island PTA-Salvation Army Pre-sch. Mem. Am. Med. Record Assn. (Journal Club), Nat. Assn. Female Execs., Female Execs., Inc., Found. for the Preservation of Health, Inc., Active Awareness for Today's Woman (Springield, Ill. chpt.), Women's Power Council (v.p., St. Louis Chpt.), Readers of Am. Methodist. Home: 5321 Savoy Ct Apt 101 Saint Louis MO 63112 Office: Saint Louis Regional Med Ctr 5535 Delmar Blvd Saint Louis MO 63112

SHERMAN, RITA MITTRA, systems engineer; b. Detroit, Mar. 2, 1963; d. Sid and Bani (Sarkar) M. BS in Mech. and Systems Engring., Oakland U., 1984; MSEE, U. Rochester, 1988. Sec., acct. Meadowbrook Montessori Ctr., Rochester, Mich., 1977-83; systems engr. Xerox Corp., Rochester, N.Y., 1984—. Mem. Nat. Assn. Female Execs., Assn. Minority Engrs., Indian Assn. Rochester, Tau Beta Pi, Golden Key Nat. Honor Soc. Hindu. Office: Xerox Corp 800 Phillips Rd Bldg 207-01B Webster NY 14580

SHERMAN, SUSAN ELAINE, extension home economist; b. Lawton, Okla., Jan. 10, 1952; d. Frank S. and B. Joyce (DeWolf) Miller; m. Joey Lynn Sherman, June 3, 1977 (div. 1982); children: David Justin, Christopher Joe, Susanne Angela. BS in Home Econs., Southwestern Okla State U., 1978. Home economist Coop. Extension Service, Cheyenne, Okla., 1982—. Norma Brumbaugh scholar Southwestern Okla. State U., 1988. Mem. Am. Home Econs. Assn., Okla. Assoc. Extension Home Economists, Cheyenne C. of C. Democrat. Methodist. Club: UMW (Cheyenne). Office: Okla State U Coop Extension Service PO Box 9 Cheyenne OK 73628

SHERN, STEPHANIE MARIE, accountant; b. Taylor, Pa., Jan. 7, 1948; d. Joseph and Stephanie (Malodovitch) Andrews; m. George Emil Shern, Sept. 25, 1971. A.A., Keystone Jr. Coll., 1967; B.S., Pa. State U., 1969. C.P.A., N.Y. Staff accountant to ptnr. Arthur Young & Co., N.Y.C., 1969—; dir. Met. Retail Fin. Execs., N.Y.C. Contbr. articles to profl. jours. Named Keystonian of Yr., Keystone Jr. Coll., 1984. Mem. N.Y. State Soc. C.P.A.s (bd. dirs. 1985—), Am. Inst. C.P.A.s, Women's Econ. Round Table, Beta Alpha Psi (mem. adv. forum 1984—). Republican. Ukrainian Orthodox. Club: Panther Valley Golf (Allamuchy, N.J.). Home: 113 Prospect St Little Falls NJ 07424 Office: Arthur Young & Co 277 Park Ave New York NY 10172

SHERREN, ANNE TERRY, chemistry educator; b. Atlanta, July 1, 1936; d. Edward Allison and Annie Ayres (Lewis) Terry; m. William Samuel Sherren, Aug. 13, 1966. B.A., Agnes Scott Coll., 1957; Ph.D., U. Fla.-Gainesville, 1961. Grad. teaching asst. U. Fla., Gainesville, 1957-61; instr. Tex. Woman's U., Denton, 1961-63, asst. prof., 1963-66; research participant Argonne Nat. Lab., 1973-80; assoc. prof. chemistry N. Central Coll., Naperville, Ill., 1966-76, prof., 1976—. Clk. of session Knox Presbyn. Ch., 1976—, ruling elder, 1971—. Mem. Am. Chem. Soc., Am. Inst. Chemists, AAAS, AAUP, Ill. Acad. Sci., Sigma Xi, Delta Kappa Gamma, Iota Sigma Pi (nat. pres. 1978-81, nat. dir. 1972 78). Presbyterian. Contbr. articles to field to profl. jours. Office: N Central Coll Naperville IL 60566

SHERRILL-EDWARDS, IVA, communications company executive, professional development consultant, columnist; b. Little Rock, Aug. 18, 1937; d. Leroy and Beulah (Wardlow) Sherrill; m. John Moses Edwards, May 19, 1956 (div. Jan. 1979); children—Delmonte, Dennis, Tina Marie. B.A., The Union, Cin., 1985. Service rep. Cin. Bell, 1968-79, customer advisor, 1979-81, facilities coordinator, 1981—; instr. Discovery Learning Ctr., Cin., 1985—; image cons. Iva S. Edwards Cons., Cin., 1984—; producer cable TV show and talk show host. Com. mem. allocations Community Chest, Cin., 1986. Mem. Nat. Assn. Female Execs. (network dir. 1985), Am. Bus. Women Assn. (com. mem. 1985). Republican. Mem. African Methodist Episcopal Ch. Avocations: tennis; swimming; reading; traveling. Office: Iva Sherrill-Edwards & Assocs PO Box 37555 Cincinnati OH 45222

SHERRY, MARILYN MORIN, psychiatric social worker; b. Worcester, Mass., Mar. 25, 1935; d. Jacob and Gertrude (Greenberg) Morin; A.B., Clark U., 1956; M.S., Simmons Coll., 1958; m. Gerald B. Sherry, Jan. 3, 1960; children—Samuel, Trudy. Diplomate Am. Bd. Clin. Social Work. Social worker Child and Family Services of Conn., Manchester, 1958-61, Hartford, Conn., 1966-71, Dept. Human Services, New Britain, Conn., 1977-79, social worker palliative care and geriatrics Mt. Sinai Hosp., Hartford, 1979-81; psychiat. social worker U. Conn. Health Center, Farmington, 1981-86 ; pvt. practice social work, 1981—; instr. Ea. Conn. State Coll., 1986-87; social work fellow McClean Hosp., Belmont, Mass., 1987—; adv. bd. Encore, YWCA Post-mastectomy Program, 1980-81; cons. in field. Mem. Registry of Clin. Social Workers, Acad. Cert. Social Workers, Nat. Soc. Clin. Social Workers, Coalition Social Work Orgns. Conn. (founding mem., sec.-treas. 1981-85), Am. Group Psychotherapy Assn., Nat. Registry Health Care Providers in Clin. Social Work, Am. Assn. for Marriage and Family Therapy. Office: 682 Prospect Ave Hartford CT 06106

SHERRY, PRISCILLA MAE, music educator; b. Hagerstown, Ind.; d. Ray C. and Ruth P. (Cromer) S. BS, Ball State U., 1952, MA, 1964. Cert. elem. and music tchr. Tchr. vocals,instruments Richmond (Ind.) Community Schs., 1953—; instr. pvt. music lessons, 1950-62; organist 1st United Meth. Ch., 1948-68, pianist 1st Ch. Christ Scientist, Hagerstown, Ind., 1958-68. Mem. Profl. Educators Assn., Ind. State Music Assn. Methodist. Clubs: Hartley Hills Country, Hartley Hills Ladies' Golf Assn., Eastern Ind. Ladies' Golf Assn., Ind. Women's Golf Assn. Home: 11 ES Market Hagerstown IN 47346 Office: Richmond Community Schs 300 Whitewater Blvd Richmond IN 47374

SHERRY, SUZANNA, law educator; b. N.Y.C., Mar. 29, 1954; d. Leonard Isaac and Bernice (Cohen) S. AB cum laude, Middlebury Coll., 1976; JD cum laude, U. Chgo., 1979. Bar: D.C. 1980. Law clk. to presiding judge U.S. Ct. Appeals (5th cir.), Montgomery, Ala., 1979-80; assoc. Miller, Cassidy, Larroca & Lewin, Washington, 1980-82; assoc. prof. U. Minn. Law Sch., Mpls., 1982-88, prof., 1988—. Author (with others): A History of the American Constitution, 1988; contbr. numerous articles to law revs. Mem. ABA, D.C. Bar Assn., Am. Lawyers Inst. Office: Univ Minn Law Sch 229 19th Ave S Minneapolis MN 55455

SHERWIN, ROBERTA MAE, physician; b. Phila., May 10, 1930; d. Robert S. and Matilda C. (Schweers) Sherwin; m. Raymond Sidney Jones, Jan. 27, 1962. B.S., Wheaton Coll. (Ill.), 1951; M.D., Med. Coll. Pa., 1955; M.S. in Medicine, Temple U., 1958. Intern, Episcopal Hosp., Phila., 1955-56; resident Temple U. Hosp., Phila., 1956-59; instr. medicine Temple U. Med. Ctr., Phila., 1960-66; practice medicine specializing in internal medicine and cardiology, Cheltenham, Pa., 1960-76; physician Exxon Co. U.S.A., Houston, 1977-78, asst. med. dir., 1978-80, med. dir. refinery, Baytown, Tex., 1980-83; asst. med. dir. Exxon Chems. Am., Houston, 1983-87; practice internal medicine, Houston, 1987—; cons. Friends Hosp., Phila., 1970-77; staff physician Frankford Hosp., Phila., 1962-77, Jeanes Hosp., Phila., 1970-77; bd. dirs. Christian Med. Soc., Chgo., 1976-77. Mem. AMA, ACP, Am. Coll. Cardiology, Tex. State Med. Assn., Pa. State Med. Soc., Harris County Med. Soc., Philadelphia County Med. Soc., Bus. and Profl. Women. Club: Doctor's (Houston). Office: 9219 Katy Freeway Suite 260 Houston TX 77024

SHERWOOD, CANDACE ANN, infosystems specialist; b. Vestal, N.Y., May 11, 1957; d. Willett Benjamin and Ellen Ingasbord (Delfs) S. BA in Biology, Hamilton Coll., 1979; MBA, U. Puget Sound, 1985. Retirement plans analyst No. Life Ins., Seattle, 1980-81, methods analyst trainee, 1981-82, methods analyst, 1982-84, programmer analyst, 1984-85; assoc. systems analyst Xerox Corp., Tukwila, Wash., 1985-86, systems analyst, 1986—; adv. bd. dirs. systems tech. conference Xerox Corp., 1987-88. Mem. Eastside Coalition for Homeless, Bellevue, Wash., 1987—, social justice com., Bellevue, 1987. Democrat. Unitarian. Clubs: Mountaineers, Nastar Ski Team. Office: Xerox Corp 6400 Southcenter Blvd Tukwila WA 98188

SHERWOOD, GRETCHEN WIETING, financial consultant, cosmetics company executive; b. Birmingham, Mich., May 13, 1953; d. Harry Nye II and Jean Kathryn (Wyckoff) Wieting; m. Roderick Mackenzie Sherwood III, Aug. 21, 1983; 1 child, Roderick MacKenzie IV. Student, U. Ariz., 1971-73, Oakland U., Rochester, Mich, 1974-76; BA, U. Mich., 1977, MA in Communication, 1977. Fin. cons. Merrill Lynch, Ann Arbor, Mich., 1978-83, sr. fin. cons., 1984—; pres. Trimetiques, Inc., Ann Arbor, 1986—; instr. Mich. Inst. Tech., Ann Arbor, 1979-80, Washtenaw Community Coll., Ann Arbor, 1982-83. Pres. Huron Residential Services for Youth, Ann Arbor, 1984—; founder, past pres. Ronald McDonald House, Ann Arbor, 1982-86; past pres., active mem. Jr. Service League of Ann Arbor, 1983—, Lucille B.

Congor Alumnae Group, Ann Arbor, 1984—. Recipient Vol. Commendation award William Beaumont Hosp., 1969. Mem. Internat. Assn. Registered Reps., Nat. Assn. Bank Women, Sigma Gamma (leadership 1971). Republican. Episcopalian. Clubs: Ann Arbor Women's City; Orchard Lake (Mich.) Country. Office: Merrill Lynch 201 S Main St Suite 200 Ann Arbor MI 48104

SHERWOOD, LEONA, artist; b. N.Y.C., May 20, 1914; d. William and Caroline (Maile) Herrmann; m. Joseph S. Kliper, Aug. 11, 1940 (div. 1948); m. William C. Sherwood, Sept. 17, 1961 (dec. 1978). Pvt. studies with John Chetcuti, N.Y.C.; pvt. studies with Robert Gelinas, U. South Fla.; pvt. studies with Philip Hicken, Nantucket, Mass.; student workshop, Mint Mus., Charlotte, N.C. Exec. sec. fund raising and sales Nat. Council Episcopal Ch., N.Y.C., 1940-48; asst. to religious dir. Crusade for Freedom, N.Y.C., 1951-53; exec. sec. collegiate sch. liaison West End Collegiate Ch., N.Y.C., 1954-61; instr. painting, drawing Longboat Key (Fla.) Art Ctr., 1969—, Manatee Art League, Bradenton, Fla., 1974—; exhibit chmn. Longboat Key Art Ctr., 1969-73. One-man shows include S.W. Fla. Art Council, Ft. Myers (Fla.) Art League, 1966, Venice (Fla.) Art League, 1969, S. Fla. Mus., Bradenton, 1971, Nat. League Am. Penwomen State, Tampa, Fla., 1972, Mus. Fine Art, Hickory, N.C., 1979, Edison Coll., Ft. Myers, 1982, Fla. Watercolor Soc., Boca Raton, 1984, 85, Fla. Artist Group, Tampa, 1985, numerous others with various awards and placings. Mem. Longboat Key Art Ctr. Mem. Fla. Artist Group, Fla. Watercolor Soc., Nat. League of Am. Penwomen, Suncoast Watercolor Soc., Artists Fellowship. Democrat. Episcopalian. Home: 615 Buttonwood Dr Longboat Key FL 33548 Office: Lake Manatee Art Groups Longboat Key FL 33548

SHERWOOD, SUE H., real estate investor; b. Manhattan, Kans., Dec. 2, 1941; d. Alvin Albert and Ruth (Helstrom) Hostetler; m. Richard G. Siever, June 11, 1962 (div. 1977); children: Elizabeth Sue Siever Baska, Bryan Travis Siever; m. Ormand Kier Sherwood, Jan. 15, 1979. BS, Kans. State U., 1958-62; postgrad., Colo. State U., 1966. Salesperson OK Sherwood and Assocs., Ft. Collins., Colo., 1977-79, Jack McIntosh and Assocs., Bellevue, Wash., 1979-84; co-owner NW Investors Services, Inc., Bellevue, 1984—. Chmn. Tiny Tots Concert Devel., 1974, Barton Elem. Sch. PTO, Youth Ministry Team Holy Trinity Luth. Ch., 1983-86, Mercer Island, Wash. 1983-86, Mercer Island Arts Council, 1986—, organizing bd. dirs. Mercer Island Community Fund, 1985—, Ft. Collins Symphony Soc., 1975-79, pres. 1978—; bd. dirs. Colo. Commn. on Status of Women, Denver, 1974-76, Fort Collins Lincoln Ctr. For the Performing Arts, Fort Collins Symphony Soc., 1975-79, pres., 1978, Mercer Island Community Gallery, 1987—; pres. Colo. State U. Women's Assn., 1973. Recipient Doroty Mullen Arts and Humanities award, Nat. Parks and Recreation Assn., 1987. Mem. Nat. Assn. Realtors, C. of C., Kappa Kappa Gamma (chpt. advisor 1973, pres. alumnae 1974, v.p. 1983-86). Home: 7444 W Mercer Way Mercer Island WA 98040 Office: NW Investors Services Inc 1800 112th Ave NE Suite 304 E Bellevue WA 98004

SHESS, PHYLLIS ADKISSON, lawyer; b. Ft. Sill, Okla., Nov. 28, 1948; d. Glenn W. and Phyllis Victoria (Trax) A.; m. Thomas Shess Jr., Sept. 1, 1985; 1 child, T. Michael III. BA in Journalism, CUNY, 1976; JD, Loyola U., 1984. Bar: Calif. 1985. Corp. communications mgr. Continental Corp., N.Y.C., 1972-76; v.p. Stoorza Co., San Diego, 1976-79; pres. Meadows Co., Los Angeles, 1979-84; enforcement atty. U.S. SEC, Los Angeles, 1984-85; litigation atty. Miller & Gibbs, San Diego, 1985-86; v.p., gen. counsel CEI, Inc., Santa Ana, Calif., 1986-87; assoc. Weissburg & Aronson, San Diego, 1987—. Recipient award Loyola Law Alumni Assn., 1984. Mem. San Diego County Bar Assn., Assn. Trial Lawyers Am., San Diego Trial Lawyers Assn. Home: 3845 Camino Lindo San Diego CA 92122 Office: Weissburg & Aronson 101 W Broadway San Diego CA 92101

SHETTEL, PATRICIA FRANCES, research facility administrator; b. McKees Rock, Pa., Nov. 11, 1934; d. John William and Marcella (Sacklowski) Rogansky; m. Anthony Vitale, Feb. 16, 1954 (div. 1974); children: Deborah Jean, Craig Douglas; m. Harris Harlan Shettel, Mar. 20, 1984. Student, U. Pitts., 1964-65, Montgomery Coll., Rockville, Md., 1975-82, George Washington U., 1987. Clk./sec. Alocoa Co., Pitts., 1952-54, Equitable Life Assurance Soc., Denver, 1954-55; exec. sec. W. Craig Chambers Advt., Pitts., 1958-60, Sta. WQED-TV, Pitts., 1961-64, U. Pitts., 1964-65, Miller-Thomas-Gyekis, Inc., Pitts., 1965-71; adminstrv. assoc. Am. Inst. for Research, Pitts., 1971-80; adminstrv. officer Washington, 1980-88, dir. research support service, 1988—; bd. dirs. Exhibit Communications Research, Inc. Author: Serialized Bibliography, 2 vols., 1979, Sponsor Index, 1980, Serialized Bibliography, 3 vols., 1987, Sponsor Index, 1988. Active Nat. Mus. for Women in Arts, Washington, 1987, Rockville Little Theatre, 1988. Democrat. Roman Catholic. Office: Am Inst for Research 3333 K St Washington DC 20007

SHEVLAND, JEAN ELLEN, underwriter; b. St. Paul, July 15, 1922; d. William and Matilda Helen (Herning) Suiter; m. Charles William Shevland, June 23, 1945; children—Susan Jean, William Charles. Student, Globe Bus. Coll., 1941. Sec., F.M. Raver, Tacoma, Wash., 1942-45; sec., underwriter Rathbone King & Seeley, Portland, Oreg., 1951-54; accounts sec. Alfred J. Davis Co., Portland, 1954-57; underwriter United Pacific Ins. Co., Portland, 1957-61; underwriter, asst. comml. sec. Fire JBL&K Corp., Portland, 1962-70; sec. Saling Dodd Ins., Portland, 1971-85. Named Women of Yr., Portland Rose chpt. Am. Bus. Women's Assn., 1981. Mem. Ins. Women Mt. Hood (corr. sec. 1980-81, v.p. 1981-82), Am. Bus. Women's Assn. (chpt. pres. 1977-78, rec. sec. 1983-84). Democrat. Methodist. Address: 6114 NE Alameda Portland OR 97213

SHEW, LINDA, insurance and securities salesperson; b. Fresno, Calif., Apr. 5, 1949; d. Ah Bun and Lily (Lum) S. BA in English, Fresno State Coll., 1971; cert. CLU, Am. Coll., 1980. Mgmt. trainee Bank of Am., Fresno, 1971-72; salesperson Equitable of Iowa Ins. Co., Des Moines, 1972—. Pres. Val-Pac-Fresno Rental Assn. Served to capt. USAR. Mem. Nat. Econ. Devel. Assn., Fresno Estate Planning Council (bd. dirs.), Fresno State Coll. Alumni Assn., Women's Leader Round Table, Jr. League. Club: Midstate Arabian. Home and Office: 2110 N Winery Fresno CA 93703

SHIELDS, ADDIE LAWRENCE, county historian; b. Beekmantown, N.Y., June 24, 1916; d. Howard Clifton and Agnes Elizabeth (Dupee) Lawrence; m. Francis Matthew Shields, Nov. 21, 1940 Ddec. 1964); children—Charlotte Frances, Charles Howard. Lic. Plattsburgh State Normal Sch., 1937; BS in Early Childhood, SUNY-Plattsburgh, 1973. Tchr. Dist. 3 Beekmantown, 1937-41; with family farm, 1940-65, farm operator, 1964-73; asst. dir. Migrant Mexican Day Care Ctr., 1973; historian Clinton County, Plattsburgh, 1978—; chmn. women's com. Farm Bur., mem. State Women's Com.; pres. Clinton County Farm Bur.; sec., treas. NE Local Dairymen's League; chmn. Clinton County's Bicentennial Celebration, 1988. Editor: Landmark in a Passageway-Beekmantown, 1976. Compiler and editor: The Diary of John Jersey McFadden in year 1872, 1982; The John Townsend Addoms Homestead-Underground RR Station, 1981. Compiler: Account Book for the Farmer-1876-Amos Barber (1828-89), 1984. Author preface for M. Benoit Pontbriands Comte Clinton-Marriages a Repertory 1830-80. Dedication by author Morris Glenn-Glenn's History of Adirondacks (Essex County), 1980. Addie Shields Day named in her honor No. N.Y. Am.-Can. Geneal. Soc., 1985. Mem. Clinton County Hist. Assn., N.Y. State Assn. County Historians (sec.), North County Local Historians Assn. (assoc. mem.). Republican. Presbyterian. Home: Point au Roche Plattsburgh NY 12901 Office: County Govt Ctr 137 Margaret St Plattsburgh NY 12901

SHIELDS, LAURA AULL, public relations counselor; b. Taylorville, Ill., Oct. 24; d. Frank and Gladys (Montgomery) Aull; m. Roger V. Shields, Nov. 20, 1940 (div.); children—Deborah, Beth, Roger, Clark, Constance. Student Ill. State U., 1935-37. Feature writer San Gabriel Valley Tribune, Covina, Calif., 1960; Owner Shields Communications, Santa Monica, Calif., 1974—; speaker in field. Mem. Pub. Relations Soc. Am. and Counselors Acad., Women in Communications, Women in Bus., Santa Monica Bay Area C. of C. Office: 214 Main St Venice CA 90291

SHIELDS, MARY, service executive; b. Pitts., May 20, 1955; d. Robert Gerard and Helen Marie (Stein) S.; m. Scott A. Leibold, May 7, 1977. BS, U. Pitts., 1977, MEd, 1979. Clk. U.S. Postal Service, Pitts., 1974-81, customer service rep., 1981-86, sr. account rep., 1986—. Mem. NOW (treas. East Hills chpt. 1987-88), Womens Traffic Club Pitts. (pres. 1986-87, v.p. 1985-86, chmn. 1987-88, chmn. nominating com. Ea. States Conf. 1987-88), Nat. Assn. Female Exec., Nat. Assn. Postal Suprs. Roman Catholic. Home: 4755 Nob Hill Dr Murrysville PA 15668 Office: US Postal Service 1001 California Ave Pittsburgh PA 15290

SHIELDS, MARY LYNN, educator, librarian; b. Yakima, Wash., Apr. 20, 1940; d. Frederick Samuel and Hazel Grace (Meiners) S. BA in Ednl. Psychology, Whitman Coll., Walla Walla, Wash., 1962; MA in Edn. Communication, U. Wash., 1979. Cert. elem. tchr., Wash. Tchr. Edmonds (Wash.) Sch. Dist., 1962-64; tchr. U.S. Dept. Defense Schs., Ipswich, Eng., 1964-65, Fuchu, Japan, 1966; tchr. Shoreline Sch. Dist., Seattle, 1967-78, remedial reading librarian, 1979, librarian, 1980—; mem. curriculum coms. Shoreline Sch. Dist., Seattle, 1980—; speaker U. Wash., 1987. Recipient Golden Acorn award Shoreling PTA, 1985; State of Wash. grantee, 1983, 1986-87. Mem. Internat. Reading Assn., Wash. Library Media Assn. (regional co-chmn 1986-87), Wash. Edn. Assn., Shoreline Edn. Assn. (rep. 1968-75, sec. 1972-73, chmn. bargaining com. 1974-75, grievance com.), Puget Sound Ednl. Consortium (tchr. leadership strand 1987-88), Alpha Delta Kappa. Office: 8813 Bowdoin Way Edmonds WA 98020 Office: Shoreline Sch Dist 18500 37th NE Seattle WA 98155

SHIELDS, NANCY B., chamber of commerce executive; b. Daytona Beach, Fla., June 14, 1943; d. Levi Lloyd and Willie Melba (Groover) Brannam; m. David Scott Shields, Apr. 9, 1965; children: Gregory Scott, Matther Ryan. BEd, U. Fla., 1964. Elem. tchr. Fairfax County Pub. Schs., Oakton, Va., 1968-69; asst. mgr. Bonny Children's Shop, Vienna, Va., 1969-75; consumer affairs intern Giant Food, Landover, Md., 1981; cons. Courtesy Counts, Potomac, Md., 1982; adminstrv. asst. Greater Vienna C. of C., 1983-85, excec. dir., 1985—; mem. consumer affairs bd. Giant Food., 1975-82. Editor newsletter Vienna Voice, 1983—. Bd. dirs., Va. Conservative Forum, McLean, 1986—; mem. exec. com., Town of Vienna Centennial Found., 1986—; mem., Republican Women's Club. Recipient Chmn.'s award Viva Vienna!, 1985, 86, 87. Mem. Nat. Assn. Female Execs., Va. Assn. Female Execs., Va. Assn. C. of C. Execs. (inst. scholar 1984). Republican. Episcopalian. Club: NOEL. Home: 515 Creek Crossing Rd NE Vienna VA 22180 Office: Greater Vienna C of C 402 Maple Ave W Vienna VA 22180

SHIELDS, TAMARA WEST-O'KELLEY, accountant; b. Lewiston, Idaho, Oct. 23, 1948; d. Brooks E. and Dona I. (Rogers) O'Kelley; BBA cum laude, North Tex. State U., 1976; 1 son, Stewart Alan. Staff acct. James C. Beach CPA, Carrollton, Tex., 1972-76, Deloitte, Haskins & Sells, CPA, 1976-77; chief fin. officer Communications Systems, Inc. (name changed to Scott Cable Communications 1983), Irving, Tex., 1977-84; pvt. practice acctg., Dallas, 1984—. lectr. in field. Pres. local sch. charity. Mem. Am. Inst. CPAs, Tex. Soc. CPAs (Dallas chpt. vice chmn. ethics com.), Beta Alpha Psi. Mem. Unity Ch.

SHIERY, JULIE ANN, engine parts and supplies shop owner, trainer and owner thoroughbreds; b. Scottdale, Pa., July 31, 1963; d. George Edward and Toni Lee (Helmick) S.; 1 child, Clarissa Renee. Grad. with honors, Bus. Career Inst., Greensburg, Pa., 1982. Mgr. HY SY Stable, Connellsville, Pa., 1976-78, mgr., trainer Black Creek Stable, Connellsville, 1978-80; sec., machinist Bill's Performance Shop, New Alexandria, Pa., 1982-83, owner, 1983—; owner J.A.S. Stables, New Alexandria, 1984—; cons. to several auto racing orgns., 1983—. Teen leader Ripple Ridge 4-H Club, Scottdale, 1978-81. Named Grand Nat. Champion, Madison Sq. Gardens, N.Y.C., 1978, Grand Nat. Champion, All Am. Quarter Horse Congress, Ohio, 1979, Grand Champion, Ky. Horse Trails, 1979, Grand Champion, Pa. State 4-H Show, 1977. Democrat. Avocations: stock car racing, drag racing, tractor/truck pulling, equestrian events. Home: RD 1 New Alexandria PA 15670 Office: Bill's Performance Shop RD 1 Box 61HX New Alexandria PA 15670

SHIGEOKA, AUDREY JUNKO, marketing professional; b. Hilo, Hawaii, June 23, 1947; d. Mitsuho and Fusae (Tanaka) Takaki; divorced; children: Reid, Neil, Dean. BS, U. Hawaii, 1969. Buyers asst. J.C. Penney Co., Honolulu, 1970; sales rep. G. Von Homm Textiles, Honolulu, 1970-75; tchr. Hilo Community Sch., 1974-75; sales rep. You & Me Naturally, Hilo, 1976-78; mgr. Kuhio Garden Restaurant, Hilo, 1983-84; sales rep. Superior Coffee, McNeil Lab. and S.E. Johnson, Hilo, 1984—; prin. AJG Enterprises, Hilo. Bd. dirs. United Way Hawaii. Mem. Hawaii Chefs and Purveyors Assn. (pres. 1985, v.p. 1986), Hilo Hawaii Visitors Industry Assn., Japanese C. of C. (bd. dirs.), Hawaii Island C. of C. Home: 250 Naniakea Hilo HI 96720

SHIH, JOAN FAI, artist, educator; b. Kwang Tong, China, Sept. 4, 1932; came to U.S., 1953; d. Henry Ken-Wai and Laura Suk-Wee (Chen) S. Student, Art Students' League, N.Y.C., 1953; BFA, Kansas City Art Inst., 1956, MFA, 1961; postgrad., Pa. Acad. Fine Arts, 1957-59, 61-63. Instr. art Kansas City (Mo.) Art Inst., 1959-61, Converse Coll., Spartanburg, S.C., 1966-67; lectr. painting Rosemont (Pa.) Coll., 1969—. One man shows include Brit. Council, Gloucer Bldg., Hong Kong, 1956, Cedar Crest Coll., Allentown, Pa., 1969, Danville (Va.) Mus. Fine Arts, 1986; exhibited in group shows including Nelson and Atkins Mus. Art, Kansas City, Mo., 1954, Pa. Acad. Fine Arts, 1963, 69-70, 72, 74, 76, 81, 83, Phila. Civic Ctr. Mus., 1970, 74, 79-80, 82, Woodmere Art Mus., Phila., 1987, Art Inst. Phila., 1987, John Geiszel All Transparency Watercolor Show., Phila, 1988, Plastic Club Ann. Art Exhbn., Phila., 1988; traveling exhbn. Nat. Assn. Women Artists, 1978-80, 80-82, 83-85, 85-87, Huntington Mus., N.Y.C., 1981, Bergen Mus., Paramus, N.J., 1983; represented in permanent collections including D.W. Newcomer's Sons Gallery, Kansas City, Mo. (Ann. Show award 1960), Meth. Hosp., Phila. Kansas City Art Inst. scholar, 1953-56; Kansas City Art Inst. grantee, 1959-61. Mem. Nat. Assn. Women Artists (Elizabeth Erlanger Meml. prize 1980), Fellowship of Pa. Acad. Fine Arts, Coalition of Women's Art Orgns., Phila. Watercolor Club, Hong Kong Art Club. Episcopalian. Home: 2013 Locust St Philadelphia PA 19103 Office: Rosemont Coll Rosemont PA 19010

SHILDNECK, BARBARA JEAN, accounting magazine editor; b. Waynesboro, Pa., Apr. 1, 1937; d. Barry Price and Helen Matilda (Armstrong) S. B.A. in English Lit., Wilson Coll., Chambersburg, Pa., 1959. With Am. Inst. C.P.A.s, N.Y.C., 1959—, jr. prodn. asst., 1959-62, sr. prodn. asst., 1962-66, editor The CPA, 1969-73, asst. editor to manuscript editor Jour. of Accountancy, 1966-79, from mng. editor to exec. editor, 1979—; panelist edn. program video tapes Dunwoody & Co., Chartered Accountants, Toronto, Can., 1977, Am. Inst. CPA's, 1980; lectr. in field. Contbr. articles to profl. jours. Mem. Am. Soc. Bus. Press Editors, Nat. Assn. Female Execs. Democrat. Office: Am Inst CPAs 1211 Ave of the Americas New York NY 10036

SHILLER, DORIS BARKER, lawyer; b. N.Y.C., May 9, 1933; d. Chester and Fay (Chasnoff) Barker; m. Jack Shiller, July 18, 1954 (div. 1981). AB, Barnard Coll., 1954; JD, Yale U., 1979. Bar: Conn. 1979, U.S. Dist. Ct. 1979, U.S. Ct. Appeals (2d cir.) 1982. Assoc., ptnr. Marsh, Day & Calhoun, Bridgeport, Conn., 1979-85; ptnr. Berkowitz & Balbirer, P.C., Westport, Conn., 1985—. Contbr. article to jour. Mem. Westport Bd. Edn. (Conn.), 1971-78; bd. dirs., pres. Coop. Ednl. Services Fairfield County, Darien Conn., 1972-76; bd. dirs. Child Care Council Westport, 1981-85, Westport Ctr. Arts Ctr., 1984-88. Recipient Provost Econs. prize Barnard Coll., 1954. Mem. ABA, Conn. Bar Assn. Democrat. Home: 10 Cypress Pond Rd Westport CT 06880 Office: Berkowitz Balbirer 253 Post Rd W Westport CT 06881

SHILLING, ESTHER, nurse, pacemaker clinician; b. Summit, N.J., Feb. 11, 1931; d. Charles and Mildred (Wright) Engel; m. Allan B. Shilling, Sept. 11, 1955; children—Jeffrey, Larry, Michael. R.N., Newark Beth Israel Hosp. Sch. Nursing, 1951; student Rutgers U., 1953-55. R.N., N.J. Operating room staff nurse Newark Beth Israel Hosp., Newark, N.J., 1951-53, asst. operating room supr., 1953-57; operating room scrub nurse Irvington Gen. Hosp., Irvington, N.J., 1958-59; sch. nurse New Providence High Sch., 1963-65; adminstr. pacemaker team Newark Beth Israel Med. Ctr., Newark, N.J., 1968-74, pacemaker clinician, 1974—; nurse adminstr. N.J. Regional Medico Program for Eval. Pacemakers, 1969-72; trustee Pacemaker Found. Inc., 1969-80; cons. ESB/Medcor Corp., Yardly, Pa., 1974-77; courtesy instr. Mountainside Hosp. Sch. Nursing, Montclair, N.J., 1973—. Editor: Heartbeat newsletter, 1972, 73, 74; editor Pacemaker Clinic Brochure, 1974—; contbr. articles to profl. jours; chpt. to book. Pres. sisterhood Jewish Community Ctr., Summit, N.J., 1965, 66, 67. Mem. N.Am. Soc. Pacing and Electrophysiology, Am. Assn. Critical Care Nurses, Am. Heart Assn., Newark Beth Israel Hosp. Alumni Assn. Democrat. Jewish. Home: 4 Lavina Ct Summit NJ 07901 Office: Newark Beth Israel Med Ctr Pacemaker Ctr 201 Lyons Ave Newark NJ 07112

SHILLING, KAY MARLENE, psychiatrist; b. Scottsbluff, Nebr., July 1, 1952; d. Harrison Gene and Rose Marie (Allen) Herber; m. Mark Randall Shilling, July 2, 1977. B.S., U. Nebr.-Lincoln, 1976; M.D., U. Nebr.-Omaha, 1980. Diplomate Nat. Bd. Med. Examiners. Resident in psychiatry Nebr. Psychiat. Inst., Omaha, 1981-84; practice medicine specializing in psychiatry, Omaha, 1984—; cons. Meth. Childrens Hosp. Family Life Ctr., Omaha, 1985—; bd. dirs. Indian-Chicano Health Ctr., Omaha. Mem. Am. Med. Women's Assn. (pres. Omaha br. 1986-88, dir. Nebr. State chpt. 1988—), Am. Psychiat. Assn., AMA, Met. Omaha Med. Soc., Nebr. Med. Assn., Alpha Xi Delta. Avocations: gourmet cooking, interior decorating, house renovation. Home: 1103 S 80th St Omaha NE 68124 Office: 7602 Pacific St Suite 302 Omaha NE 68114

SHILLINGSBURG, MIRIAM JONES, educator; b. Balt., Oct. 5, 1943; d. W. Elvin and Miriam (Reeves) Jones; BA, Mars Hill Coll., 1964; MA, U. S.C., 1966, PhD, 1969; m. Peter L. Shillingsburg, Nov. 21, 1967; children: Robert, George, John, Alice, Anne Carol. Asst. prof. Limestone Coll., Gaffney, S.C., 1969; asst. prof. Mississippi State (Miss.) U., 1970-75, assoc. prof., 1975-80, prof., 1980—, asst. to provost, 1987-88, assoc. v.p. for acad. affairs, 1988—; Fulbright lectr. U. New South Wales, Duntroon, Australia, 1984-85. Nat. Endowment Humanities fellow in residence, Columbia U., 1976-77. Mem. MLA, Soc. Study So. Lit., Am. Studies Assn., Southeastern Soc. Eighteenth Century Studies. Author: Mark Twain in Australasia, 1988; editor: Conquest of Granada, 1988; mem. editorial bd. Works of W.M. Thackeray; contbr. articles to profl. jours. and mags.

SHIM, KATHYLEEN SHERROD, public relations executive; b. Uniontown, Ala., Feb. 14, 1948; d. Benjamin Herndon and Kathyleen S. BS cum laude, U. Fla., 1975; MA, George Washington U., 1980. Film prodn. asst. Barton Film Co., Jacksonville, Fla., 1969-70; writer Sta. WTLV-TV, NBC affiliate, Jacksonville, 1970-71; studio prodn. crew Sta. WUFT-TV, PBS affiliate, Gainesville, Fla., 1973-75; reporter, photographer Vero Beach (Fla.) Press Jour., 1975-78; writer press dept. U.S. Senator Bill Roth, 1978-80; press sec. U.S. Rep. Larry J. Hopkins, Washington, 1981-84; freelance newspaper columnist, 1983; communications and mktg. cons., 1984—; pub. affairs specialist Peace Corps, Washington, 1984-86; dir. communications Indsl. Biotech. Assn., 1986—; v.p. C&C Food Service, Inc., Washington, Key Jobs, Inc., Lakeland, Fla. Recipient 2d place awards Nat. Better Newspaper Contest, 1977, 78; 1st place award Fla. Press Assn., 1979, 2d place award, 1977, 78, 79, Claudia Ross Meml. award, 1977; 1st place award Journalism in Agriculture Agribus. Inst. Fla., 1978, 1st place award Fla. Farm Bur. Fedn.; outstanding performance award Peace Corps, 1985. Mem. Republican Communications Assn., Senate Press Secs. Assn., Nat. Leadership Coalition on AIDS, Womens Polit. Caucus Capitol Hill. Home: 6591 Cypress Point Rd Alexandria VA 22312

SHIMADA, LINDA MICHI, financial consultant; b. Honolulu, Oct. 22, 1963; d. Glenn Atsuo Shimada and Amy Ayako (Takeda) Shimada Wong. BBA, U. Hawaii, 1985. Lic. life ins. solicitor, registered issuer of securities, Hawaii. Salesperson McInerny, Honolulu, 1982-83; clk. U. Hawaii Bd. Regents, Honolulu, 1982-84; sales rep. A.L. Williams, Honolulu, 1984, sales mgr., 1984-85, dist. mgr., 1985, div. mgr., 1986; traffic prodn. mgr., account exec. DiCarlo Advt. Agy., Honolulu, 1986-87; asst. account exec. Pearlman/Wohl/Olshever/Marchese, Los Angeles, 1987-88; fin. cons. Merrill Lynch, Pierce, Fenner & Smith, Inc., Long Beach, Calif., 1988—. Mem. Am. Entrepreneurs Assn., Nat. Assn. Securities Dealers (cert.), Nat. Assn. Female Execs., Advt. Club Los Angeles, Alpha Beta Chi (chpt. sec. 1983-84, chpt. pres. 1984-85). Democrat. Office: Merrill Lynch Pierce Fenner Smith Inc 211 E Ocean Blvd #680 Long Beach CA 90802

SHIMBERG, ELAINE FANTLE, writer; b. Yankton, S.D., Feb. 26, 1937; d. Karl S. and Alfreda (Edelson) Fantle; B.S., Northwestern U., 1958; m. Mandell Shimberg, Oct. 1, 1961; children—Karen, Scott, Betsy, Andrew, Michael. Continuity dir. WALT Radio, Tampa, Fla., 1959-60, WFLA Radio, 1960-61; freelance writer, 1961—; co-hostess WFLA-TV talk show Women's Point of View, Tampa, Fla., 1976-81; tchr. Writing for Publication and Profit, Hillsborough Community Coll., Tampa 1980-82. Mem. public info. com. Fla. div. Am. Cancer Soc., 1974—, mem. childhood cancer com. 1975-79; bd. devel. council St. Joseph Hosp., 1982—; bd. dirs. United Way, 1986—. Mem. Am. Soc. Journalists and Authors, Authors Guild, Women in Communication, Am. Med. Writers Assn., Athena Soc. Author: How to be A Successful Housewife/Writer, 1979; Two for the Money: A Woman's Guide to a Double Career Marriage, 1981; contbg. author: The Complete Guide to Writing Non-Fiction, 1983; Teenage Drinking and Driving: A Deadly Duo, 1984; Coping with Kids and Vacation, 1986; Relief From Irritable Bowel Syndrome, 1988. Contbr. articles to various mags.

SHIMMIN, KATHLEEN GRACE, environmental agency executive; b. Santa Rosa, Calif., Mar. 7, 1939; d. Melvin Raleigh and Helen Marguerite (Grace) S.; m. Louis John Lenertz, Feb. 14, 1973 (div. 1980); m. Donald Phillip Harvey, June 27, 1980. BS in Sanitary Sci., U. Calif., Berkeley, 1960, MA in Bacteriology, 1963, postgrad. in environ. health scis., 1963-69; postgrad. in counseling psychology, U. San Francisco, 1986—. Research, tchr. Sch. Pub. Health U. Calif., Berkeley, 1963-64, 66-69; chief microbiology sect. EPA, Alameda, Calif., 1969-73, co-chair women's com., 1972-74, chief regional lab., 1974-78; chief water enforcement EPA, San Francisco, 1978-81, chief compliance and response, 1981-83, chief field ops. br., 1983-86, chief Office of Health and Emergency Planning, 1986—; instr. John F. Kennedy U., Martinez, Calif., 1969. Vol. counselor alcoholism outpatient clinic VA Hosp., Martinez, 1987—. Republican. Club: Women's Faculty (Berkeley), Presidio Officers (San Francisco). Office: EPA 215 Fremont St San Francisco CA 94105

SHIMOKOCHI, DENISE DAWLET, engineer; b. Detroit, Oct. 23, 1954; d. Albert Abdullah and Julia Margaret (Megyesi) Darian; m. David Kiyoshi Shimokochi, Sept. 10, 1983; children: Nicholas Albert, Daniel Nobuyuki. BS in Zoology, U. Mich., 1976, MS in Biomedical Engring., 1983; postgrad., Bowman Gray Sch. of Med., 1976-79. Research asst. Dept. Computer Engring. U. Mich., Ann Arbor, 1982-83; field clin. engr. Medtronic, Inc., Mpls., 1983-88; sr. regulatory/clin. coordinator Sarns 3M Health Care Group, 1988—. Mem. IEEE, Nat. Assn. Female Execs.

SHIMOMURA, TERRI NOBUKO, banker; b. Honolulu, Apr. 3, 1957; d. Allen Yasunobu Shimomura and Alice Miyuki Nishimura; m. Francisco Javier de la Hoz Ulloa, June 18, 1982. B.A. magna cum laude, Princeton U., 1979. Credit trainee Chase Manhattan Bank, N.Y.C., 1979-80, credit auditor, 1980-81, relationship mgr. Chase Manhattan's Instnl. Portfolio in Mexico, Mexico City, 1982-83, 2d credit officer Chase Manhattan Bank in Mexico, Mexico City, 1983-84, relationship mgr. Chase Manhattan's Corp. Portfolio in Mex., 1984-86, acting credit officer, credit support unit officer, Mexico, 1986-87, tng. instr., team mgr. Chase Rea Pacific Tng. Ctr. Recipient Lt. John A. Larkin Jr. Meml. prize for Polit. Economy Woodrow Wilson for Pub. and Internat. Affairs of Princeton U., 1979. Mem. Phi Beta Kappa. Club: Princeton of N.Y., World Trade Centre Club. Home: PO Box 521 C/O Chase-Hong Kong Bowling Green Station New York NY 10004

SHINAGEL, VICTORIA STUART, sales executive; b. Cambridge, Mass., July 4, 1961; d. Michael Shinagel and Ann (Mitchell) Seemann. BS, U. Vt., 1982; postgrad., Harvard U., 1983, 87. Mgr. store Guy Laroche, Boston, 1982-83; dist. mgr. Fanny Farmer Candies, Boston, 1983-85; sales mgr. Weatherend Furniture, Rockland, Maine, 1985-86; dir. sales DLP Internat. Inc., Wakefield, Mass., 1986—; cons. in field. Mem. Nat. Orgn. for Female Execs., Reebok Instrs. Alliance. Home: 676 Tremont St #6 Boston MA 02118 Office: DLP Internat Inc 333 North Ave Wakefield MA 01880

SHINBERG, ROSITA CUAN, jewelry executive; b. Habana, Cuba, July 19, 1949; came to U.S., 1962; d. Enrique and Matilde (Perez) Cuan; m. Aaron Marvin Ian Shinberg, Dec. 6, 1968; 1 child, Natasha Gabriella. Student, San Francisco de Sales, Habana, 1960, Baldor Bus. Coll., Habana, 1962.

Researcher Mass. Ho. of Reps., Boston, 1965-68; mktg. Eve Roma, Boston, 1969-72, The Gillette Co., Boston, 1972-74; v.p. Oriental Trading Corp., Boston, 1975—; real estate broker Sterling Properties, Boston, 1972—. Elected Dem. State committeewoman Mass., 1975-79; founder, dir. Spanish Flamenco Ballet, Boston. Roman Catholic. Home: 893 W Roxbury Pkwy Chestnut Hill MA 02167 Office: Oriental Trading Corp 387 Washington St Boston MA 02108

SHINEHOUSE, ELFREDA JANE, biologist, educator; b. Chestnut Hill, Pa., Apr. 13, 1931; d. Arthur Dewey and Elfreda Frances (Ross) Perreten; B.S., Ursinus Coll., 1952; postgrad. U. Pa., 1953; m. Robert R. Shinehouse, Apr. 5, 1952; children—Linda Anne, Patricia G., James P., Lisa Susan. Phys. therapist Montgomery County Hosp., Norristown, Pa., part time 1953, Phoenixville (Pa.) Hosp., part time 1958-60; instr. biology Ursinus Coll., Collegeville, Pa., part time 1960-77, asst. prof., 1977-83, assoc. prof., 1984—, asst. premed. adviser, 1981—. Sec., Home and Sch. Assn., 1961-62; tchr. aide Oaks Elem. Sch., 1977-78; Sunday Sch. tchr. St. James Episcopal Ch., 1978-79, chmn. Christian Women in Soc., 1979-80. Recipient Lindback award for disting. teaching Ursinus Coll., 1981; March of Dimes Found. grantee, 1952. Mem. Registry Am. Phys. Therapists, Pa. Acad. Sci., Nat. Assn. Biology Tchrs., Sigma Xi (assoc.), Beta Beta Beta, Pi Nu Epsilon. Republican. Home: 1747 S Collegeville Rd Collegeville PA 19426 Office: 209 LSB Ursinus Coll Collegeville PA 19426

SHINER, JOSETTE SHEERAN, editor; b. Orange, N.J., June 12, 1954; d. James Joseph and Sarah Ann (Gallagher) Sheeran; m. Whitney Taylor Shiner, Nov. 10, 1984; 1 child, Nicole Munier. BA, U. Colo., 1976. Nat. desk editor N.Y. News World, 1976-77; Washington bur. chief N.Y. News World, 1977-80, corr. The White House, 1980-82; Capital Life and mag. editor Washington Times, 1982-84, asst. mng. editor, 1984-85, dep. mng. editor, 1985—. Mem. Leadership Washington, 1987-88. Recipient Atrium award U. Ga., 1984. Mem. Nat. Press Club (newsmaker chmn. 1980-82; Meritorious Service award 1981, Vivian award 1981), Am. Soc. Newspaper Editors, Sigma Delta Chi. Office: Washington Times 3600 New York Ave NE Washington DC 20002

SHINN, LINDA J., nurse, association executive; b. Ft. Wayne, Ind., Jan. 10, 1948; d. Richard Kenneth and Dorothy Elaine (Carrier) S. Nursing degree, Meml. Hosp., South Bend, Ind., 1965-68; B, Ind. U., Indpls., 1977; M, Ind. Cen. U., 1983. Staff nurse Meml. Hosp., South Bend, 1968, Robert Long Hosp, Indpls., 1969-70; dir. legisl. and labor relations program Ind. State Nurses Assn., Indpls., 1969-71, asst. exec. dir., 1971-73, assoc. exec. dir., 1973-80, exec. dir., 1980-83; div. dir. Am. Nurses' Assn., Kansas City, Mo., 1983-87, dep. exec. dir., 1987—; adj. lectr. Ind. U., 1980-83; adj. instr. U. Kans., Kansas City, 1986—. Contbg. author Networking for Nurses, 1983. Mem. Gov.'s Commn. on Status of Women, Indpls., 1975, Gov.'s Council on Sports Medicine, Indpls., 1980-82; mentor Purdue U., Lafayette, Ind., 1974-83, Avila Coll., Kansas City, Mo., 1986; 2d v.p. Spay-Neuter Services, Inc., Indpls.; mem. adv. group Nat. Disaster Med. System, Washington, 1985. Mem. Am. Nurses' Assn., Am. Soc. Assn. Execs., Sigma Theta Tau, Epsilon Sigma Alpha. Office: Am Nurses' Assn 2420 Pershing Rd Kansas City MO 64108

SHIPLEY, LILLIAN LOREEN, psychologist; b. Cleve., July 7, 1943; d. William and Dorothy A. (Haeberle) Fox; divorced; children: Trent Carter, Traci Christine. BS, Grand Canyon Coll., 1964; MA, No. Ariz. U., 1967; PhD, Ariz. State U., 1978. Lic. psychologist, Ariz. Exec. dir. Glenhaven, Glendale, Ariz., 1973-78, United Cerebral Palsy Assn. of Cen. Ariz., Phoenix, 1978-81; pvt. practice psychology Valley West Counseling Assocs., Phoenix, 1981—. Pres. Glendale Community Council, 1981, 82, bd. dirs. 1983; chairperson policy com. Maricopa Council for children, Youth and Families, 1983-84, mem. 1982-84; mem. Greenlee County Task Force for Prevention of Family Violence, 1982-84, adv. com. Ariz. Ctr. for Law in Pub. Interest, 1984—; bd. dirs. Westside Mental Health Services, 1980-83; ex-officio mem. Community Council Bd., 1983-84, Gov.'s Council for Children, Youth and Families, 1983-84. Mem. Am. Psychol. Assn. Democrat. Mennonite. Office: Valley West Counseling Assocs 10000 N 31st Ave Suite A-111 Phoenix AZ 85051

SHIPLEY, NANCY LOUISE, health science association executive; b. Wilkinsburg, Pa., June 26, 1950; d. Oran G. and Catherine P. (Soisson) S. BS, Slippery Rock (Pa.) State Coll., 1972, MEd, 1974. Tchr. phys. edn. Monroeville (Pa.) Jr. High Sch., 1972-77; rep. sales Knoll Pharms., Whippany, N.J., 1978-80; regional rep. med. sales Surgidev Corp., Morristown, N.J., 1980-82, Ioptex, Morristown, 1982-84; pres. surg. custom trays Surg. Services and Supplies, Inc., Montvale, N.J., 1984-85; sales med. instruments Allergan Humphrey Corp., New Eng., 1985-87; exec. adminstr. Eye Inst. Essex, Belleville, N.J., 1987—; cons. for pvt. outpatient eye surg. ctrs., 1980-87. Contbr. articles to profl. jours. Mem. Lake Hopatcong Boaters Assn. Republican. Home: PO Box 484 Fanwood NJ 07023 Office: Eye Inst Essex 5 Franklin Ave Suite 209 Belleville NJ 07109

SHIPLEY, SHIRLEY DAHL, oil company executive; b. Orange, N.J., Oct. 17, 1932; d. Conrad George and Sylvia Marion (Gronquist) D.; B.S., Cedar Crest Coll. Allentown, Pa., 1954; m. William Stewart Shipley II, July 2, 1955; children—William Stewart III, Linda Ann, Elizabeth Marion. Tchr., Radnor Twp. (Pa.) Schs., 1954-55, Sarasota County (Fla.) Schs., 1955-56; adminstrv. v.p. Shipley Oil Co., Inc., York, Pa., 1977—. Pres., York Suburban Sch. Dist. Bd., 1973-79; bd. dirs., co-chmn. York Country Day Sch., York County Library System, York County Mental Health Center, Greater York, Inc., United Community Services, York County Literacy Council, ARC, Women's Assn. York Symphony Orch.; 1st v.p. Childrens Home; trustee, mem. exec. com. York Coll. of Pa., 1972—; mem. York, Franklin and Adams County Intermediate Unit Sch. Bd. pres. Jr. League York, 1967-69; nat. bd. dirs. Assn. Jr. Leagues, 1970-72; mem. Pa. adv. council U.S. Commn. Civil Rights; trustee York Coll. Pa. Mem. Pa. Petroleum Assn., Petroleum Marketers Assn. Am. Republican. Presbyterian. Home: 1000 Clubhouse Rd York PA 17403 Office: 550 E King St PO Box 946 York PA 17405

SHIPLEY, V. FERN WILSON, personnel recruiting company executive; b. Manchester, Okla., Sept. 29, 1921; d. Charles C. and Oma (Ready) Wilson; m. David McNalley Shipley, Jan. 21, 1943 (div. Nov. 1968); children—Davon David, Sondra Fern Busch. Student U. Colo., 1961-62. Cons., Cartwright Employment Agy., Boulder, 1969-71, head cons., 1973-77; mgr. Western Permanent Services, Boulder, 1972; owner, mgr. Shipley Personnel Recruiting, Boulder, 1978—. Currently doing exec. recruiting book research. Fund raiser Mountain View Methodist Ch., 1960; tchr. Sunday Sch., Meth. Ch., 1954-56, chmn. Bible Sch., 1954; leader, Colo. Muscular Dystrophy Research Fund Drive, 1955; mgr. telethon drive, Boulder, 1955. Republican. Avocations: Travel; sewing; oil painting; interior design; swimming. Home: 2820 Dover Dr Boulder CO 80303 Office: 1300 Canyon Blvd Suite 1 Boulder CO 80302

SHIPP, MAURINE SARAH HARSTON (MRS. LEVI ARNOLD SHIPP), realtor; b. Holiday, Mo., Mar. 6, 1913; d. Paul Edward and Sarah Isabel (Mitchell) Harston; grad. Ill. Bus. Coll., 1945; student real estate Springfield Jr. Coll., 1962; student law LaSalle Extension U., 1959-62; m. Levi Arnold Shipp, Jan. 30, 1941; children—Jerome Reynolds, Patricia (Mrs. Rodney W. England). With Ill. Dept. Agr., Springfield, 1941-65, supr. livestock industry Brucellosis sect.; saleswoman Morgan-Hamilton Real Estate Co., Springfield, 1962-64; owner, mgr. Shipp Real Estate Agy., Springfield, 1965—. Prin. appraiser urban renewal HUD, 1971-72; mem. Public Bldg. Commn. Springfield. Bd. dirs. Springfield Travelers Aid, 1971—. Mem. NAACP, Urban League, Iota Phi Lambda. Episcopalian. Mem. Order Eastern Star. Club: Bridge. Home: 31 Bellerive Rd Springfield IL 62704

SHIPPE, MARY LOU, instructional designer and developer; b. Kansas City, Mo., Nov. 25, 1942; d. Hiram Arthur and Clio (Robinson) Cooley; m. Donald Louis Shippe, Aug. 13, 1966; children—Kenneth Louis, Angela Lou. B.A., Kans. U., 1964; M.P.A., Okla. U., 1979; D.P.A. candidate Nova U., 1983—. Research technician Dept. Def., Md., 1964-66, analyst, 1970-71; substitute tchr. Howard County Schs., Md., 1972-76; instr. Los Angeles Community Coll. Overseas, Japan, 1976-79; asst. Pub. Today News Service, Washington, 1979; village mgr. Town Ctr. Community Assn., Md., 1980-83; instructional designer, developer computer based tng. Ford Aerospace and Communications Corp., Hanover, Md., 1983—; test specialist People to People technology del. to Australia and New ZEaland, 1988. Mem. Columbia Forum, Md., 1980—, Housing and Human Services Task Force, Columbia, 1980-82. Mem. Am. Soc. Pub. Adminstrn., Am. Bus. Womens Assn. (v.p. 1985-86, pres. 1986-88, named Woman of the Year 1987, 88), Assn. Ednl. Communications and Tech., LWV Howard County, 1982-83. Club: Zonta (v.p. 1986—, dir. 1982-86). Avocations: travel, theatre, boating. Home: 9573 Long Look Ln Columbia MD 21045 Office: Ford Aerospace & Communications Corp 7100 Standard Dr Hanover MD 21076

SHIRK, AUDREY HOPE, artist, painter; b. Rochester, N.Y., Sept. 18, 1921; d. David Daniel and Ethel Edith (Sachs) Salisch; m. Mortimer I. Metzger, June 22, 1941 (div. Oct. 1964); children—Jane Metzger Laffend, Warren Stanley; m. Stanley E. Shirk, Nov. 23, 1965. Assoc., Parsons Sch. Fine and Applied Art, 1941. Instr., Parsons Sch. Fine and Applied Art, N.Y.C., 1943-44; centennial chmn. Nat. Assn. Women Artists, Inc., N.Y.C., 1983-85, exec. producer cable TV documentaries and videotapes, 1984, 85; bd. dirs. East/West Fusion Theatre, Sharon, Conn., Kings and Couriers Theatre Co., 1987, 88. Recipient Samuel Gelband award 1976, Woman Art award 1977, Medal Honor Nat. Assn. award 1983; Solveig Stromsoe Palmer Meml. award, 1988. Mem. Nat. Assn. Women Artists Inc. (chmn. traveling painting exhibitions 1978-82, bd. dirs. 1978—), Sharon Creative Arts Found. (gallery dir. 1980-83, exec. com., bd. dirs. 1980-83, mem. exec. com. 1981-83). Office: Box 151 Cornwall CT 06796

SHIRK, EVELYN URBAN, philosophy educator; b. Flushing, N.Y., Sept. 12, 1918; d. Amos Urban and Mary Jane (Welchans) S.; m. Justus Buchler, Feb. 20, 1943; 1 child, Katherine Urban. B.A., Wilson Coll., 1940; M.A., Columbia U., 1942, Ph.D., 1949. Instr. Bklyn Coll., 1942-48; asst. prof. Hofstra Coll., Hempstead, N.Y., 1949-53, assoc. prof., 1953-63; prof. Hofstra U. (formerly Hofstra Coll.), 1963—, dept. chmn., 1980—. Editor: (with others) Readings in Philosophy, 1946; Adventurous Idealism: The Philosophy of Alfred Lloyd, 1952; The Ethical Dimension, 1965; In Pursuit of Awareness, 1967. Mem. Am. Philos. Assn., Soc. Advancement Am. Philosophy (program chmn. 1976, exec. com 1977-79), L.I. Philos. Soc. (exec. com.), AAUP, Phi Beta Kappa. Home: 3 Homestead Ave Garden City NY 11530 Office: Hofstra U Dept Philosophy 1000 Fulton Ave Hempstead NY 11550

SHIRK, MARIANNE EILEEN, veterinarian; b. Detroit, Aug. 11, 1944; d. Wesley Emerson and Eleanor Jane (Grossman) Lickfeldt. Student U. Mich., 1962-64; D.V.M., Mich. State U., 1968, M.S. in Vet. Pathology, 1969. Diplomate Am. Bd. Vet. Practitioners. Grad. asst. Mich. State U., East Lansing, 1968-69; veterinarian Dandy Acres Vet. Clinic, Hartland, Mich., 1969-71, Quartz Mountain Animal Hosp., Scottsdale, Ariz., 1972—; speaker at various profl. meetings; host of twice monthly call-in talk show Pet-Vet, Sta. KTAR, Phoenix, 1982—. Author article in profl. jour. Recipient Disting. Alumnus award Mich. State U., 1985. Mem. Am. Acad. Vet. Dermatology, AVMA, Am. Animal Hosp. Assn., Ariz. Vet. Med. Assn. (pres.-elect 1982-83, pres. 1983-84, chmn. ann. state meeting 1979—, dir. 1980-81), Central Ariz. Vet. Med. Assn. (pres.-elect 1980-81, pres. 1981-82, dir. 1978-80), Ariz. Acad. Vet. Practice (Outstanding Continuing Edn. record 1983), Am. Assn. Equine Practitioners. Republican. Home: 6900 E Gold Dust Ave Scottsdale AZ 85254 Office: Sundown Animal Clinic 10616 N 71st Pl Scottsdale AZ 85254 *

SHIRLEY, ELEANOR, social service agency executive; b. Adams, Mass., May 9, 1937; d. Joseph Lucian and Elsie (Barschdorf) Freeman; m. Edward Salmond Shirley, Aug. 10, 1963; 1 child, Rebecca Salmond. BA, Wheaton Coll., Mass., 1959; MA, Hartford (Conn.) Sem. Found., 1961; MBA, Tulane U., 1985. Dir. edn. St. Peter's Ch., Beverly, Mass., 1961-63; dir. coll. work Mt. Holyoke Coll., South Hadley, Mass., 1965-68; staff La. State U. Episcopal Chapel, Baton Rouge, 1969; dir. Women and Employment Program, Baton Rouge, 1977-80; dir. program devel. Office of Women's Services, Baton Rouge, 1980—. Pres. LWV, Baton Rouge, 1972-75; mem. alumni admissions com. Tulane U., Baton Rouge, 1987-88. Named Outstanding Woman, Links Inc. of Baton Rouge, 1975. Mem. Nat. Assn. Female Execs., Baton Rouge C. of C. (pres. alpha adv. bd. to Northdale Magnet Sch. 1987-88, mem. edn. com. 1987-88, mem. Leadership program 1987-88). Democrat. Club: Episcopalian Ch. Women (Baton Rouge) (pres. 1985-86). Home: 10203 Winterhue Dr Baton Rouge LA 70810 Office: Women's Services 150 Riverside Mall Baton Rouge LA 70802

SHIRLEY, JULIA LINN, editor; b. San Pedro, Calif., June 27, 1956; d. Johannes Harrison and Barbara Ann (Barton) Shirley. B.A., Calif. State U.-Long Beach, 1979. Asst news editor Anaheim Bull. (Calif.), 1979-81, tempo editor, 1981-86, mng. editor, 1986—. Mem. Orange County Press Club, Sigma Delta Chi. Office: Anaheim Bull 1771 S Lewis St Anaheim CA 92805

SHIRLEY, NORMA, librarian, bibliographer; b. Chatham, N.Y., Mar. 22, 1935; d. George and Bertha (Shattuck) Shirley. B.A., Russell Sage Coll., 1962; M.L.S., SUNY-Albany, 1963, M.S. in Ednl. Adminstrn., 1980. Asst. reference librarian Jr. Coll. Albany, 1963-65; librarian Hudson Area Library (N.Y.), 1966-67; reference librarian Russell Sage Coll., Troy, N.Y., 1967-69; librarian Poughkeepsie High Sch. (N.Y.), 1970-71; library media specialist Spl. Edn. Ctr., Dutchess County BOCES, Poughkeepsie, 1971—. Co-author: Checklist of Serials in Psychology and Allied Fields, 1969; Serials in Psychology and Allied Fields, 1976. Mem. Dutchess County Library Assn. (past pres.), Sch. Library Media Specialists Southeastern N.Y. (past pres.), ALA, N.Y. Library Assn., NEA, Dutchess County Mental Health Assn., N.Y. State Tchrs. Handicapped. Home: PO Box 2401 Poughkeepsie NY 12603

SHISHKOFF, MURIEL MENDELSOHN, educational administrator; b. Chgo., Mar. 5, 1917; d. Henry Robert and Anita (Arnow) Mendelsohn; B.A., U. Chgo., 1936; M.A., Northwestern U., 1940; m. Nicholas Shishkoff, Aug. 26, 1946; children—Andrew, Debra. Elem. tchr., Fond du Lac, Wis., 1936-41; personnel mgr. Twentieth Century Glove Co., 1946; tchr. Newport-Mesa (Calif.) Unified Sch. Dist., 1963-69; founding dir. Women's Opportunities Center, U. Extension, U. Calif., Irvine, 1970-72, asst. dir. Office Relations with Schs. and Colls., 1974-82. Vice pres. LWV, Palos Verdes Peninsula, Calif., 1963. Served to lt. USNR (W-VS), 1942-45. Recipient grant award Reachout, Dept. Mental Hygiene, Sacramento, 1972. Mem. Nat. Assn. Women Deans, Adminstrs. and Counselors, NOW, Women For. Home: 19542 Sandcastle Ln Huntington Beach CA 92648

SHISLER, ALICE HAFLING, dancer; b. Richmond, Va., Nov. 23, 1923; d. Jacob Mathew and Elise (Atkinson) Hafling; children by previous marriage: Elise Amory Miller, Otis Taylor Amory III, Marcie Tuck Amory; m. James Douglas Shisler, Apr. 17, 1965. BA in French with distinction, U. Va., 1972, postgrad., 1972-75. Student, asst. Elinor Frye Dance Sch., Richmond, 1940-44; editorial sec. Commonwealth mag., 1944-46; owner Acad. Dance Arts, Charlottesville, Va., 1947—; dir., choreographer Charlottesville Dance Co., 1973—; cons. in field. Active Docent Bayly Mus. of U. Va., 1984—. Recipient Appreciation award Charlottesville Lions Club Minstrel Shows, 1981. Mem. Dance Masters Am. Republican. Episcopalian. Club: Farmington Country. Address: 901 Rugby Rd Charlottesville VA 22903

SHIVER, MOLLY TYUS, personnel director; b. Milner, Ga., Oct. 27, 1939; d. James Drewery and Wynona Alice (Bevil) Tyus; m. James Thomas Shiver, July 1, 1958; children—Wanda Lea, Patricia Ann. Student Gordon Coll., 1976-78. Regional sales mgr. Sarah Coventry, Newark, N.Y., 1972-79; senate staff State of Ga., Atlanta, 1980; v.p. sales Jennifer Lynn Ltd., Atlanta, 1980-81; dir. personnel A.L. Williams, Atlanta, 1981-85; v.p. adminstrn. Classique Creations, Dallas, 1984-85; ptnr. Royalty Mgmts. & Assocs., Tallahassee, 1986—. Treas., bd. dirs. Assn. Retarded Citizens, Barnesville, Ga., 1975-78. Democrat. Baptist. Clubs: Barnesville Bus. and Profl. Women's (pres. 1976), Barnesville Womens (pres. 1977). Home: Route 1 Milner GA 30257

SHKURKIN, EKATERINA (KATIA) VLADIMIROVNA, social worker; b. Berkeley, Calif., Nov. 20, 1955; d. Vladimir Vladimirovich and Olga Ivanovna (Lisenko) S. Student, U. San Francisco, 1972-73; BA, U. Calif., Berkeley, 1974-77; MSW, Columbia U., 1977-79; postgrad., Union Grad. Sch., 1986. Cert. police instr. domestic violence, Alaska. Social worker Tolstoy Found., N.Y.C., 1978-79, adminstr., 1979-80; program supr. Rehab. Mental Health Ctr., San Jose, Calif., 1980-81; dir. service counselor Kodiak (Alaska) Crisis Ctr., 1981-82; domestic violence counselor Abused Women's Aid in Crisis, Anchorage, 1982-85; pvt. practice social work specializing in feminist therapy Susitna Therapy Ctr., Anchorage, 1985—; field instr. Abused Women's Aid in Crisis, Anchorage, 1983—; expert witness Anchorage Mcpl. Cts., 1982—; interim faculty U. Alaska, Anchorage, summer 1985, LaVerne U., Anchorage, spring 1986, fall, 1987. Coordinator Orthodox Christian Fellowship, San Francisco, 1972-76; pub. speaker Abused Women's Aid in Crisis, Anchorage, 1982—; active nat. and local election campaigns, 1968—. Mem. Nat. Assn. Social Workers (cert.). Democrat. Russian Orthodox. Home: 3605 Arctic Blvd #768 Anchorage AK 99503-5704

SHNEIER, LESLEY ANN, management consultant; b. Johannesburg, South Africa, Apr. 24, 1949; came to U.S., 1985; d. Lionel Bernard and Naomi (Heller) Shneier. BA with honors in Social Work, U. Witwatersrand, Johannesburg, 1970, MS in Personnel Mgmt., 1975. Social worker Dept. of Social Welfare, Johannesburg, South Africa, 1971-72, Queen Victoria Maternity Hosp., Johannesburg, 1972-75; sr. social worker Hammersmith Hosp., London, 1976-77; personnel mgr. Motorola, Inc., Johannesburg, 1977-78; gen. mgr. human resources Dun & Bradstreet, Johannesburg, 1978-81, Australia, 1981-84; mgmt. cons. World Bank, Washington, 1985—; career counselor scholastic program Am. C. of C., Australia, 1981-84. Mem. Am. Mgmt. Assn. Club: World Bank Theater (Washington). Office: World Bank 1818 H St NW Washington DC 20433

SHOAFF, PAMELA LESLIE, health marketing executive; b. Washington, Dec. 13, 1959; d. Clark Stuart and Marilyn Jeanette (Wadsworth) S. BS, James Madison U., 1981. Project sec., then coordinator Group Health Assn. Am., Washington, 1982-83; adminstr. CIGNA Health Plan, Tampa, Fla., 1983-84; mktg. adminstr. Capitol Care, Inc., Arlington, Va., 1984-85; account exec. George Washington Univ. Health Plan, Washington, 1985-87, sales dir., 1987—. Office: George Washington U Health Plan 1901 Pennsylvania Ave NW Washington DC 20006

SHOCK, KATHY BETH, data processing professional; b. Ponca City, Okla., July 10, 1956; d. D'Arcy Adriance and Barbara Beth (Lounsbury) S. BA, Okla. State U., Stillwater, 1978. Programmer Cities Service Oil and Gas Corp., Tulsa, 1978-79, programmer/ analyst, 1979-81, systems analyst, 1981-82, 1982-83; programmer/analyst Hilti Inc., Tulsa, 1982; systems analyst, project leader Citgo Petroleum Corp., Tulsa, 1983—. Vol. Reagan Presdl. Campaign, Tulsa, 1980. Mem. Nat. Assn. Female Execs. Republican. Club: Swing Dance.

SHOCKLEY, NANCY ELEANOR, survey researcher; b. Balt., July 23, 1954; d. Marion Kent Shockley and Elizabeth Eleanor (Scharf) Sitzman. BA, U. No. Colo., 1976; postgrad., U. Md. Co-dir. Colo. Pub. Interest Research Group, Greeley, 1976; asst. spl. events, dir. edn. Metro Denver March of Dimes, 1977-78; media print buyer Tracy-Locke Advt., Englewood, Colo., 1978-79; jr. cons. Consumer Costs Cons., Mt. Rainier, Md., 1979-80; survey researcher The Arbitron Ratings Co., Laurel, Md., 1980-88; tng. specialist Quantum Computer Services, Inc., Vienna, Va., 1988—; cons. COPIRG manuals, Denver, 1977. Author consumer protection manuals. Campus campaign mgr. Hart for Senate, Greeley, Colo., 1974; tutor Literacy Assn. Mem. Nat. Assn. Female Execs., Am. Soc. for Tng. and Devel., Internat. Listening Assn. Democrat. Episcopalian. Home: 204 Marrin Rd Silver Spring CO 20901 Office: Quantum Computer Services Inc 8619 Westwood Ctr Dr Vienna VA 22180

SHOEMAKER, ELEANOR BOGGS, small business owner, beef producer; b. Gulfport, Miss., Jan. 20, 1935; d. William Robertson and Bessie Eleanor (Ware) Boggs; m. D. Shoemaker, April 9, 1955 (div. 1987); children: Daniel W., William Boggs. Student in protocol, Southeastern U., 1952-53; student, George Washington U., Washington, 1953-56; BA in Communications and Polit. Sci. with honrs, Goucher Coll., 1981. Feature writer Washington Times Herald, 1951-54; dir. Patricia Stevens Modeling Agy., Washington, 1955-56; free-lance model Julius Garfinkel, Woodward & Lothrop, Washington, 1951-56; research analyst Balt. County Council, Towson, Md., 1980-81; feature news reporter WGCB-TV, Red Lion, Pa., 1980—; pub. speaker, protocol The Reliable Corp., Columbia, Md., 1982-86; media cons. The Enterprise Found., Columbia, Md., 1985-86; faculty, TV prodn. and communication St. Francis Prep Sch., Spring Grove, Pa., 1985—; mem. conservation bd. Pa. Parks and Recreation Soc., 1984—. Producer: The Pa. County TV prodn., 1981. Bd. dirs. York (Pa.) County Parks and Recreation, 1972-87; exec. com. York County Republicans, 1972-82; bd. dirs. YWCA, York, 1957-82; accreditation adv. com. York Coll. of Pa., instr. YWCA Women in politics; founder, mem. Child Abuse Taskforce, York, 1983—; founder Women in Politics, York, 1985—; mem. select com. Pa. Agrl. Zoning, 1988. Recipient pro bono child legal representation grant Pa. Bar Assn., 1983; named Pa. Lay Person of Yr. Pa. Recreation and Parks Soc. and Gov. Thornburg, 1982. Mem. York Area C. of C., Masters of Foxhounds Assn., The Weybright Hounds. Episcopalian. Home and Office: PO Box 167 Felton PA 17322

SHOEMAKER, MARY CAROLYN, nursing educator; b. Pekin, Ill., July 9, 1945; d. Honor K. and Millie L. (Gosnell) Little; m. Edward A. Shoemaker, June 14, 1964; 1 son, Mark E. R.N., Graham Hosp. Sch. Nursing, 1967; B.S., Bradley U., 1971; M.S., Tex. Woman's U., 1976; Ph.D. in Ednl. Adminstrn. and Founds., Ill. State U., 1985. Staff charge nurse Peoria State Hosp. (Ill.), 1967-71; instr. Graham Hosp. Sch. Nursing, Canton, Ill., 1971-73; instr. St. Francis Hosp. Sch. Nursing, Peoria, 1973-77, instr., dept. chmn., 1977-85; level 1 coordinator Saint Francis Med. Ctr. Coll. Nursing, Peoria, 1986-88, assoc. prof., 1988—; chairperson Forward Peoria! Action I Group subcom. on health care services, 1986-88. Grantee Helene Fuld Found., 1987, 88. Mem. Nat. League Nursing, Nat. Nurses Assn., Ill. League Nursing (planning com. Area 12-F 1987—), Ill. Nurses Assn. (v.p. 7th dist. 1986-87, pres., 1987—, various other offices), Tex. Woman's U. Alumni Assn., Ill. State Univ. Adminstrs. Club, Kappa Delta Pi. Methodist. Office: St Francis Med Ctr Coll Nursing 211 Greenleaf Peoria IL 61603

SHOEMAKER, PAMELA JEAN, educator; b. Chillicothe, Ohio, Oct. 25, 1950; d. Paul E. and Nettie K. (Steed) S.; m. John H. Parrish, Mar. 10, 1979. BS in Journalism, MS in Communications, Ohio U., 1972; PhD in Mass Communication, U. Wis., 1982. Editorial, advt. asst. Ohio Contractor Mag., Columbus, Ohio, 1972-74; advt. mgr. Uni-Tool Attachments, Inc., Columbus, 1974-76; mng. editor Ohio Dental Assn., Columbus, 1976-77; sec. to Council on Journalism, Am. Dental Assn., 1977-79; lectr., teaching asst. U. Wis. Dept. Journalism and Mass Communication, Madison, 1980-82; asst. prof. journalism U. Tex., Austin, 1982-87, assoc. prof., 1987—; editorial bd. Journalism Quarterly, 1984—; dir. Office of Survey Research, U. Tex., Coll. of Communication. Author: monograph Building a Theory of News Content, 1987; contbr. articles to profl. jours and chpts. to books. Mem. Univ. United Meth. Ch. choir, Austin, Tex., 1983—. Grantee AT&T Communications, 1984, Gannett Found., 1983, Am. Student Dental Assn., 1984; recipient research fellow Coll. of Communications U. Tex. at Austin, 1986-87. Mem. Assn. for Edn. in Journalism and Mass Communication (head theory and methodology div. 1987—), Internat. Communication Assn. (chair membership com. 1985-86, sec. mass communications div. 1988—), Am. Assn. for Pub. Opinion Research, Speech Communication Assn. Democrat. Methodist. Office: Coll Communication U Tex Austin TX 78712

SHOEN, JUDITH ANNE, marketing company executive; b. Rockford, Ill., Dec. 25, 1940; d. Abe J. and Bertha Deborah (Polinsky) S. B.S., U. Wis., 1962. Editorial asst. Mademoiselle Mag., N.Y.C., 1962-63; food editor Restaurants & Instns. mag., Chgo., 1963-64, merchandising editor, 1964-66, sr. editor, 1971-74; Eastern editor, internat. editor Service World Internat. mag., N.Y.C., 1966-71, editor-in-chief, N.Y.C., 1967-71, Chgo., 1971-74; dir. pub. relations Dispenser Juice Distbrs./Consol. Foods, San Francisco, 1974-75; pres. Judith Shoen Assocs., San Francisco, 1975-78; v.p. Foote, Cone & Belding, San Francisco, 1978-81, also dir. FCB Foodservice; dir. mktg. Telstar Corp., San Francisco, 1981-82; pres. Foodservice Promotions, Inc., Mill Valley, Calif., 1982-85, Washington, 1985—. Mem. Internat. Foodservice Mfrs. Assn., Internat. Foodservice Editors Council, Les Dames d'Escoffier, Alpha Epsilon Phi, Theta Sigma Phi. Office: 5020 Lowell St NW Washington DC 20016

SHOENFELT, CATHERINE RUTH, marketing executive; b. Dallas, Dec. 9, 1954; d. Marion Justus and Nell (Harden) S. B of Music Edn., U. Tex., San Antonio, 1980. Tchr. music Viva Musica, San Antonio, 1980-81, Northside Ind. Sch. Dist., San Antonio, 1981-84; mktg. mgr. Austin Pathology Assocs., Tex., 1984-86; dir. mktg. Nat. Lab. Services, Inc., Austin, 1987; clin. sales rep. Roche Biomed. Labs., Inc., 1987—. Singer Chamber Choralet Symphony, San Antonio, 1982; vol. Symphony Designer Showplace, Austin, 1986-87, Healthfest-Pathology Booth, Austin, 1986. Mem. Nat. Assn. Female Execs. Republican. Lutheran. Club: Blair County Genealogy Soc. (Altoona, Pa.). Avocations: music, tennis, reading, needlework, swimming. Home: 114 Weld St Roslindale MA 02131 Office: Roche Biomedical Labs Inc 1 Roche Dr Raritan NJ 08869

SHOENIGHT, PAULINE ALOISE SOUERS (ALOISE TRACY), author; b. Bridgeport, Ill., Nov. 20, 1914; d. William Fitch and Carrie (Milhouse) Souers; B.Ed., Eastern Ill. U., 1937; m. James Richard Tracy, Sept. 18, 1946 (dec. Aug. 1972); m. 2d, Hurley F. Shoenight, June 25, 1976. Mem. hon. bd. advs. Am. Biog. Inst. Mem. Nat. Ret. Tchrs. Assn., Eastern Ill. Alumni Assn. (life), PEO Sisterhood, Performing Arts Assn., Am. Poets Fellowship Soc. (hon. life mem.), The Pensters, Pleasure Island Sr. Citizens Club (charter), Am. Poetry League, Ill. Poetry Soc. (charter), Book Club for Poetry, Ala. State Poetry Soc., Acad. Am. Poets, Baldwin Heritage Mus. Assn. (charter life), Friends of U. Mo. Libraries (life), Friends of Foley Library. Republican. Baptist. Club: Baldwin Sr. Travelers. Author: His Handiwork, 1954; Memory is a Poet, 1964; The Silken Web, 1965; A Merry Heart, 1966; In Two or Three Tomorrows, 1968; All Flesh Is Grass, 1971; Beyond The Edge, 1973. Address: 7425 Riverwood Dr Foley AL 36535

SHOHEN, SAUNDRA ANNE, health care communications and public relations executive; b. Washington, Aug. 22, 1934; d. Aaron Kohn and Malvina (Kleiman) Kohn Blinder; children: Susan, Brian. BS, Columbia Pacific U., 1979, MS in Health Services Adminstrn., 1981. Adminstr. in social work Roosevelt Hosp., N.Y.C., 1978-79; adminstr. emergency dept. St. Luke's-Roosevelt Hosp. Ctr., N.Y.C., 1979-83, assoc. dir. pub. relations, 1983-87; pres. Saundra Shohen Assocs., Ltd., N.Y.C., 1987—; v.p. PRISM Internat., N.Y.C., 1988—; cons. Tureck Bach Inst., N.Y.C., 1985—, also dir.; panelist ann. Emmy awards Nat. Acad. TV Arts and Scis., N.Y.C., 1983, 84; v.p. program devel. and media relations Pub. Relations in Sci. and Medicine Internat., 1988—. Author: (with others) AIDS: A Health Care Management Response; (health scripts for radio) Voice of America, 1983 (Presdl. Recognition award 1984). Mem. Internat. Hosp. Fedn., Am. Soc. Hosp. Mktg. and Pub. Relations, Nat. Acad. TV Arts and Scis, Vols. in Tech. Assistance. Democrat. Jewish. Home: 240 Central Park South New York NY 10019 Office: 488 Madison Ave New York NY 10022

SHOLLENBERGER, SYDNI (SYDNEY) ANN CRAWFORD, author, publicist; b. Cleve., June 23, 1940; d. Charles Burger and Carolyn Louise (Hull) Crawford; B.A., Allegheny Coll., 1962; m. Lewis W. Shollenberger, Jr., Aug. 18, 1962. Public info. officer and editor Space News Roundup, NASA, Houston, 1970-72. mng., editor Travel Publs., Am. Automobile Assn., Washington, 1972-74; free lance journalist, publicist, 1974-84; adminstrv. asst. for community relations Walnut Creek (Calif.) Sch. Dist., 1984-87; public relations cons., 1988—; Publicity dir. Falls Church Bicentennial Commn., 1976-81; bd. dirs. Falls Church Village Preservation and Improvement Soc.; publicity co-chmn. Falls Church Citizens for a Better City, 1978, fin. chmn., 1982 docent Cherry Hill Farm; pres. Broadmont Citizens Assn., 1978-79; press cons. Fisher for Congress campaign, 1978, 80; chmn. Falls Church Adv. Bd. on Parks and Recreation 1979-83; community relations coordinator Fairfax County Reentry Women's Employment Center; sec. Welcome to Washington Internat. Club, 1978-80. Mem. Pub. Relations Soc. Am., Nat. Fedn. Press Women, Capital Press Women (v.p. 1976-78), Nat. Sch. Pub. Relations Assn., Washington Edn. Press Assn., Calif. Sch. Pub. Relations Assn. Club: Capital Speakers (class pres. 1977, chpt. 3 pres. 1980-81); Commonwealth (San Francisco). Home: 3221 Sugarberry Ln Walnut Creek CA 94598

SHOLTZ, KATHERINE LOUISE, librarian, chemist; b. Waukegan, Ill., July 14, 1931; d. E. Albin and Helmi Rachel (Salmi) Junnila; m. Paul N. Sholtz, Aug. 30, 1952; children—Karen, Peter. B.S., U. Ill., 1952, M.S., 1953; M.L.S., SUNY-Albany, 1967. Research assoc. Harvard U., Boston, 1953-55, Iowa State U., Ames, 1955-57; librarian IBM, Rochester, Minn., 1966-67; computer applications librarian Mayo Clinic, Rochester, 1967-72, assoc. dir. library, 1972-80; dir. library services Western Conn. State U., Danbury, 1980—. Contbr. articles to profl. jours. Chmn., Rochester Housing and Redevel. Agy., 1974-77; chmn. adv. bd. Council of Govt. Housing, Rochester, 1977-80; pres. LWV, Rochester, 1969-71; mem. Conn. State Library adv. bd., 1984-87. Recipient award for promotion of sci. research Sigma Xi, New Haven, 1983. Mem. ALA, Med. Library Assn., Conn. Library Assn. Lutheran. Home: Milltown Rd RD 5 Brewster NY 10509 Office: Ruth A Haas Library Western Conn State U 181 White St Danbury CT 06810

SHONTZ, MARILYN LOUISE, library science educator; b. Cleve., Nov. 5, 1943; d. William Painter and Marie Rita (Kessler) S. B.A., Heidelberg Coll., 1965; M.L.S., Case Western Res. U., 1967; A.M.L.S., Fla. State U., 1982, PhD, 1986. Children's librarian Cleve. Pub. Library, 1965-67; sch. librarian Cleve. Pub. Schs., 1967-70; sch. library media specialist Marion County Schs., Ocala, Fla., 1970-80; assoc. prof. library sci. Shippensburg (Pa.) U., 1982-88, chmn. dept. library sci., 1983-86, asst. dean Coll. Edn. and Human Services, 1986-88; asst. prof. U. N.C., Greensboro, 1988—. Teaching fellow Fla. State U., Tallahassee, 1981. Mem. ALA, Am. Assn. Sch. Librarians, Am. Assn. Teacher Educators, Pa. Sch. Librarians Assn., Beta Phi Mu. Home: RD 1 Box 441 Newburg PA 17240

SHONTZ, PATRICIA JANE, restauranteur; b. Mercer, Pa., Mar. 29, 1933; d. Thomas Cloyd and Glaydes Evelyn (Pease) Buckley; student pub. schools, Grove City, Pa.; m. George Edward Shontz, July 22, 1962; 1 dau. by previous marriage, Sandra Lee McCandless. Clerical asst. Am. News Co., Washington, 1950-51; acct., office mgr. Mundt Motors Chevrolet & Buick, Grove City, 1953-62; sec.-treas. Cajun Corp., Madeira Beach, Fla., 1972—; pres. John's Pass Seafood Festival Corp., 1981—. Madeira Beach City commr., 1973-79, vice mayor, 1977-79, co-chmn. planning bd., 1979-82, city commr., 1983-87; chmn. Bicentennial Com., Madeira Beach, 1975-76; mem. John's Pass Village Assn., 1970—, Pinellas County Tourist Devel. Council, 1978-79, Madeira Beach Taxpayers Assn., 1964—; mem. Republican Nat. Com. Named Madeira Beach Citizen of Yr., 1974, 79. Mem. Nat. Restaurant Assn., Fla. Restaurant Assn., Madeira Beach C. of C. (dir. 1965, 81-82, 87, 88, pres. 1967-69, 83). Presbyterian. Clubs: Bus. and Profl. Women, Soroptimist, Order Eastern Star, Order White Shrine. Office: 100 Medeira Way Medeira Beach FL 33708

SHOPIRO, ELEANOR MARCHIGIANI, insurance company executive; b. Mount Kisco, N.Y., Jan. 21, 1929; d. Angelo and Frances (Scerrati) Marchigiani; m. Carl D. Jolivette, Jr., Feb. 1956 (dec. Mar. 1963); m. Donald E. Shopiro, Aug. 27, 1966; 1 child, Suzanne L. B.S., Cornell U., 1950. Buyer, mgr. Day Bros. & Co., Syracuse, N.Y., 1952-56; owner, mgr. Suburban Hardware Co., Syracuse, N.Y., 1956-68; dir. devel Syracuse Symphony Orch., 1977-79, gen. mgr., 1979-83, cons., 1983-84; v.p. D.E. Shopiro & Co., Inc., ins. and retirement planning, Syracuse, 1984—. V.p. Better Bus. Bur., Syracuse, 1977-83, bd. dirs., 1979—; pres. Syracuse Symphony Orch. Guild, 1973-74; v.p., dir. Syracuse Symphony, 1975; charter pres. Landmark Theatre, 1975; pres. LeMoyne Coll. Pres.'s Assocs., 1978—, regent, 1978—; bd. dirs. Citizen's League, Corinthian Found.; community advisor Jr. League Syracuse; pres. Onondaga Citizens League. Named Woman of Achievement for Cultural Devel., 1984. Mem. Thursday Morning Round Table, Nat. Assn. Life Underwriters, Syracuse Assn. Life Underwriters. Office: D E Shopiro & Co Inc 224 Harrison St Suite 802 Syracuse NY 13202

SHORE, CLARE, composer; b. Winston-Salem, N.C., Dec. 18, 1954; d. James Clarence and Helena (Weir) S. BA, Wake Forest U., 1976; MusM, U. Colo., 1977; DMus Arts, Juilliard Sch., 1984. Instr. Manhattan Sch. Music, N.Y.C., 1981-83, Fordham U., Bronx, N.Y., 1983-84, U. Va., Charlottesville, 1984-85, George Mason U., Fairfax, Va., 1985. Recipient award ASCAP, 1981—, also grantee, 1983; Am. Music Ctr. grantee 1984, 86; Irving Berlin fellow, 1981; recipient Alexander Gretchaninov award Juilliard Sch., 84. Mem. ASCAP, Am. Music Ctr., Coll. Music Soc., Am. Women Composers, Internat. League Women Composers. Home: 12329 Cliveden St Herndon VA 22070

SHORES, JANIE LEDLOW, state justice; b. Georgiana., Ala., Apr. 30, 1932; d. John Wesley and Willie (Scott) Ledlow; m. James L. Shores, Jr., May 12, 1962; 1 dau., Laura Scott. J.D., U. Ala., Tuscaloosa, 1959. Bar: Ala. 1959. Pvt. practice Selma, 1959; mem. legal dept. Liberty Nat. Life Ins. Co., Birmingham, Ala., 1962-66; asso. prof. law Cumberland Sch. Law, Samford U., Birmingham, 1)66-74; asso. justice Supreme Ct. Ala., 1974—; legal adviser Ala. Constn. Revision Commn., 1973; mem. Nat. Adv. Council State Ct. Planning, 1976—. Contbr. articles to legal jours. Mem. Am. Bar Assn., Am. Judicature Soc., Farrah Order Jurisprudence. Democrat. Episcopalian. Office: Ala Supreme Court PO Box 157 Montgomery AL 36101 *

SHORES, PEARL MARIE, health care company executive; b. Warsaw, N.Y., Aug. 29, 1946; d. Lawrence Dean and Mary Ellen (Sly) Arnold; m. Bruce Reid Dedrick, May 9, 1964 (div. 1966); 1 child, Dawn Aileen; m. James Lee Shores, Sept. 13, 1981. BBA cum laude, Nat. U., San Diego, 1979; MBA, Nat. U., 1981. Chief lab. technician Schoenfield Clin. Lab., Alburquerque, 1970-76, Allergy Med. Group, San Diego, 1976-78; chemstrip specialist BioDynamics/BMC, San Diego, 1978-80; sr. ter. mgr. Hollister, Inc., San Diego, 1980-84; dist. mgr. Hollister, Inc., New Eng. dist., 1984-86; sales rep. E.R. Squibb/CONVATEC, San Diego, 1986-87; br. mgr. Nat. Med. Homecare, San Diego, 1987—. Office: Nat Med Homecare 7525 Mission Gorge Rd Suite H San Diego CA 92120

SHORES, TONI, personnel executive; b. Pasadena, Calif., Dec. 28, 1949; d. Leonardo and MArianne (Aloisi) Lampasona; m. Ronald Eugene Robbins, Jan 27, 1970 (div. Sept. 1974); m. Robert David Shores, Apr. 19, 1975; children: Melissa Lorraine, Sarah Marie, Robert David Jr., Michael Franklin. Student, Pasadena City Coll., 1968-70. Cons. Lynn Carrol EMployment Agy., Pasadena, 1970-71; mgr., cons. Alosta Enterprises, Covina, Calif., 1972-81; pres. Prestige Personnel Services Inc, Rowland Heights, Calif., 1981—; Mem. adv. bd. Whittier (Calif.) Hosp. Med. Ctr., 1985-86; ambassador Industry (Calif.) Mfrs. Council, 1986-87. V.p. Killian Sch. Community Assn., Rowland Heights, 1986-87. Mem. Calif. Assn. Personnel Cons. (pres. San Gabriel Valley chpt. 1986-87, chair mktg. 1987, 3d v.p. state exec. bd. 1987, State Mktg. award 1987), Nat. Assn. Personnel Cons., Nat. Assn. Female Execs., La Puente C. of C., Walnut (Calif.) C. of C. Democrat. Roman Catholic. Office: Prestige Personnel Services 19069 Colima Rd Rowland Heights CA 91748

SHORR, MIRIAM KRONFELDT, artist; b. N.Y.C.; student Hunter Coll.; m. Eli Yale Shorr, 1931. Exhibited in ann. shows Audubon Artists, City Center Gallery, Bklyn. Mus., Nat. Soc. Painters in Casein, Norfolk Mus., Riverside Mus.; one man shows Brandeis U., Bklyn. Coll., U. Maine, Rutgers U., So. Ill. U., LaSalle Coll., Hillsdale U., Gettysburg Coll., others; group shows U. Houston, N.D. State U., Colo. Mountain Coll., Ottawa (Kans.) U., Washington and Jefferson Coll., others; traveling one-man shows throughout U.S. Recipient 1st prize for drawing Nat. Assn. Women Artists, 1962; Lena Newcastle award, 1961, 65; Aileen O. Webb prize, 1974; 1st prize Fibers and Fabrics Exhbn., Longboat Key Art Assn., 1979; 1st prize enamels Venice (Fla.) Art League, 1982; 2d prize Sarasota Art Assn., 1983; Longboat Key Art Center West Coast Parade of Prize Winners, 1982-88; 1st prize Venice Art League, 1985; One-man showing of tapestries Cen. Library, St. Petersburg, Fla., 1982, Cen. Library, Bradenton, Fla., 1987. Mem. Artists Equity Assn. (dir. 1958-64), Nat. Assn. Women Artists (dir. 1970-72), Sarasota Art Assn. (chmn. exhbns. 1976-78, editor The Bull. 1979-81), Art League Manatee County, Fla. Artists Group. Home: 7252 Broughton St Sarasota FL 34243

SHORS, SUSAN DEBRA, lawyer; b. Detroit, Nov. 23, 1954; d. Clayton Marion and Arlene Lois (Towle) S.; m. Brian F. Connors. B.A., Pitzer Coll., 1976; J.D., Golden Gate U., 1984. Bar: Calif. Extern, Calif. Supreme Ct., San Francisco, 1983; research atty. Calif. Ct. Appeal, San Francisco, 1984-85; appellate atty., San Francisco, 1985—; cons. Nob Hill Neighbors, San Francisco, 1982-86. Sr. editor Golden Gate Law Rev. Notes and Comments, 1985; mem. editorial bd. Barrister's Club Mag., 1986—. Atty. Lawyers Com. for Urban Affairs/Asylum Project, San Francisco, 1986. Mem. ABA, Calif. Bar Assn., Calif. Women Lawyers, Bar Assn. San Francisco (mem. appellate com. 1986—), ACLU, Nat. Assn. Criminal Def. Lawyers. Democrat. Office: Law Offices 2500 Clay St San Francisco CA 94115

SHORT, KAREN JO, information systems administrator; b. Oklahoma City, Dec. 6, 1938; d. Walter Scott and Jessie Faye (Childers) Thornton; m. Jodie F. Short, Feb. 5, 1957 (div. 1964); children: Jodie Jr., Scott, Thomas, Michael (dec.). BS, Oklahoma City U., 1966. Ptnr. Orbach's Varsity Shop, Tulsa, 1958-64; acct. Tinker AFB, Oklahoma City, 1966-67, programmer, analyst, 1968-79, project mgr., 1979-86; system analyst McClellan AFB, Sacramento, 1986, adminstr. data base, 1986—; Chmn. bd. dirs. Scuba World Tampa, Fla., 1987—; mem. Share, Inc., Chgo., 1987—. Mem. Friends of the Zoo, Oklahoma City, 1968-78. Named Nat. Miss Future Bus. Exec. Phi Beta Lambda, 1966; named one of Outstanding Young Women Am., 1970. Republican. Methodist. Home: 6690 Riverside Blvd Sacramento CA 95831 Office: SM-ALC/SCJD McClellan AFB Sacramento CA 95652

SHORT, PAULA MYRICK, educational administration educator; b. Pinehurst, N.C., Feb. 25, 1945; d. John Howard and Ruby Pauline (Fields) Myrick; m. Rick Jay Short, Feb. 2, 1980; children—Jeffrey Brent, John Ryan, Rick Jay Jr. B.A., U. N.C.-Greensboro, 1967, M.Ed., 1970; Ph.D., U. N.C., Chapel Hill, 1983. Tchr., Greensboro City Schs., N.C., 1967-68, Orange County Schs., Hillsborough, N.C., 1968-69; media coordinator Alamance County Schs., Mebane, N.C., 1970-71; tchr. Neal Jr. High Sch., Durham, N.C., 1971-74, Chewing Jr. High Sch., Durham, 1977-79; system level media supr. Chapel Hill-Carboro City Schs., 1979-80, vice-prin.; ednl. cons. div. ednl. N.C. Dept. Pub. Instrn., Raleigh, 1980-82; asst. prof. ednl. adminstrn. Coll.Edn., Tex. Woman's U., Denton, 1984-85, Centenary Coll., Shreveport, La., 1985-86, U. Nebr. at Omaha, 1986-87, Auburn (Ala.) U., 1987—. Mem. editorial bd. Rural Educator. Chmn. day care com. Chapel Hill Service League, 1977-78; mem. Danforth Found. Program for Profs. of Ednl. Adminstrn., 1986—. Delta Kappa Gamma state scholar 1982; Danforth Found. fellow, 1986—. Mem. Editoral Bd. jour. Teh Rural Educator, S.W. Ednl. Research Assn., La. Assn. Sch. Execs., Tex. Assn. Supervision and Curriculum Devel., Nebr. Assn. Sch. Adminstrs., Nebr. Assn. for Supervision and Curriculum Devel., Nebr. Assn. Student Councils (asst. exec. dir.), Soc. Sch. Librarians Internat. (bd. dirs. 1985-86), Assn. Supervision and Curriculum Devel., N.C. Media Council (pres. 1982), Delta Kappa Gamma, Phi Delta Kappa (pres.), Pi Lambda Theta. Methodist. Home: 926 Vickers Dr Richmond KY 40475 Office: Auburn U 314 Kayser Hall Auburn AL 36849

SHORT, SUSAN GAIL, educator; b. Binghamton, N.Y., Nov. 16, 1949; d. Paul Theodore and Mildred (Robords) Benjamin; m. James Edward Short Jr., Dec. 18, 1976; 1 child, Amanda Rei. BS in Spl. Edn., Ind.State U., Terre Haute, 1976; MS in Elem. Edn. Tchr. N.E. Sch. Corp., Dugger, Ind., 1971-83; dir. Apple Tree Learning Ctr., Linton, Ind., 1983—. Learning Disabilities leader Girl Scouts U.S., Linton, 1986—. Club: TRAID (Linton) (pres. 1988—). Home and Office: Rural Rt 3 PO Box 446 Linton IN 47441

SHOTZ, LINDA FLEISCHMAN, marriage and family therapist, artist; b. Asbury Park, N.J., Aug. 16, 1949; d. Erwin Lewis and Ruth (Koegel) Fleischman; m. Frederick A. Shotz, Sept. 18, 1973. AA Miami Dade Jr. Coll., 1969; BA cum laude U. Fla., 1971; MS summa cum laude Nova U., 1975; Ph.D. Calif. Coast U., 1985; licensed marriage and family therapist, lic. mental health counselor. Social worker Div. Family Services, Miami, Fla., 1971-73; clin. psychotherapist Counseling Assocs., Davie, Fla., 1974—; exec. dir. Intimacy Disorders Found., Inc., Davie, 1983—; registered art therapist, 1975—, fellow in sex therapy, fellow in med. psychotherapy; artist, sculptor Bakehouse Art Complex, Inc., Miami. Author: (with others) Training Crisis Counselors; (book of erotic art & poetry) Breathmarks in the Wind, 1988. Fellow Menninger Found., 1983, Am. Bd. Med. Psychotherapists, Am. U., Washington, 1985. Fellow Internat. Council Sex Edn. and Counseling; mem. Am. Assn. Sex Educators, Counselors, and Therapists, Soc. for Sci. Study of Sex, Am. Assn. Counseling and Devel., Am. Assn. of Artists-Therapists, Am. Art Therapy Assn. Avocations: reading, video art, travel. Office: Counseling Assocs 4801 S University Dr Davie FL 33328

SHOWALTER-KEEFE, JEAN, data processing executive; b. Louisville, Mar. 11, 1938; d. William Joseph and Phyllis Rose (Reis) Showalter; m. James Washburn Keefe, Dec. 6, 1980. BA, Spalding U., 1963, MS in Edn. Adminstrn., 1969. Cert. tchr., Ky. Tchr., asst. prin. Louisville Cath. Schs., 1958-71; cons. and various editorial positions Harcourt Brace Jovanovich Co., Chgo. and N.Y.C., 1972-82; dir. editorial Ednl. Challenges, Alexandria, Va., 1982-83; mgr. project to cons. Xerox Corp., Leesburg, Va., 1983-88, mgr. systems edn., 1988—; instr. Sales Exec. Club N.Y., 1974-79; cons. Houston, 1980-83. Moderator Jr. Achievement, Louisville, 1968-70; cons. Future Bus. Leaders Am., Dade County, Fla. 1983. Named Outstanding Young Educator Louisville Jaycees, 1968. Mem. Nat. Assn. Female Execs., Am. Soc. Tng. and Devel., Am. Mgmt. Assn. Home: 12766 Flat Meadow Ln Herndon VA 22071 Office: Xerox Corp PO Box 2000 Leesburg VA 22075

SHPERLING, IRENA, internist; b. Tallin, USSR, Sept. 20, 1938; came to U.S., 1976; d. Ber Epstein and Maria Minkov; m. Betsalel R. Shperling, June 16, 1960; 1 child, Elena. MD, First Pavlov's Med. Inst., Leningrad, USSR, 1961. Diplomate Am. Bd. Internal Medicine. Med. dr. City Hosp., Leningrad, USSR, 1961-75; resident in internal medicine Winthrop U. Hosp. SUNY, 1977-80; gen. practice medicine Mineola, N.Y., 1980—. Mem. Am. Soc. Internal Medicine, N.Y. State Soc. Internal Medicine, Nassau County Soc. Internal Medicine, Am. Coll. Physicians, Am. Coll. Physicians, Nat. Assn. Female Execs. Office: 134 Mineola Blvd Mineola NY 11501

SHRAGER, BARBARA E. BERNSTEIN, corporate and marketing communications consultant; b. N.Y.C., Mar. 25, 1952; d. Marvin and Muriel (Blonstein) Bernstein; m. Samuel Abraham Shrager, Jan. 12, 1986. BA, Mt. Holyoke Coll., 1972; MA, U. Pa., 1974, PhD, 1979; MBA, NYU, 1983. Instr. U. Pa., Phila., 1972-76, LaSalle Coll., Phila., 1976-78, U. Del., Newark, 1978-79; assoc. product mgr. Nabisco Brands, N.Y.C., 1979-81; mktg. mgr. Avon Products, Inc., N.Y.C., 1981-84; mgmt. supr. Lefkowith Inc., N.Y.C., 1984-87, prin., 1987—, also bd. dirs. Mem. Met. Mus. Art, N.Y.C., Mus. Modern Art, N.Y.C., Whitney Mus., N.Y.C., Guggenheim Mus., N.Y.C. U. Pa. teaching fellow, 1972-76; NEH grantee, 1978. Mem. Am. Mktg. Assn., Am. Mgmt. Assn., Am. Women Econ. Devel. Office: Lefkowith Inc 845 Third Ave New York NY 10022

SHRAUNER, BARBARA WAYNE, electrical engineer, educator; b. Morristown, N.J., June 21, 1934; d. Leonard Gladstone and Ruth Elizabeth (Thrasher) Abraham; m. James Ely Shrauner, Oct. 30, 1965; children: Elizabeth Ann, Jay Arthur. BA, U. Colo., 1956; MA, Harvard U., 1957, PhD, 1962. Postdoctoral fellow U. Brussels, 1962-64; resident research assoc. NASA Ames Research Ctr., Moffett Field, Calif., 1964-65; asst. prof. elec. engring. Washington U., St. Louis, 1966-69, assoc. prof., 1969-77, prof., 1977—; vis. researcher Los Alamos (N. Mex.) Lab., 1975-76, Lawrence Berkeley, (Calif.) Lab., 1985; cons. in field. Assoc. editor Jour. Geophysics Research and Space Physics, 1987—; contbr. articles to profl. jours. Mem. Am. Phys. Soc., AAUP, Am. Geophys. Union. Office: Washington U Dept Engring 1 Brookings Dr Saint Louis MO 63130

SHREDNICK, ANDREA MERRYL, human sexuality and infertility counselor; b. N.Y.C., Dec. 18, 1950; d. Harold Lester Goodman and Judith (Hoffman) Hayflick; children: Bryan, Marni. BA in Edn., Hofstra U., 1972; MS, Long Island U., 1982; PhD, Columbia Pacific U., 1984; postgrad., UCLA, 1985. Pvt. practice fertility counseling 1970—; fertility counselor Fertility Med. Group, Tarzana, Calif., 1984—; clin. instr. U. So. Calif., Los Angeles, 1986—; bd. dirs. United Infertility Orgn., Scarsdale, N.Y., 1974-82; founder Infertility Network, Danbury, Conn., 1978-84; leader Hudson Valley Infertility, Manopac, N.Y., 1980-84. Author: (with others) Common Gynecology Problems, 1987, Successful Adoption, 1987; contbr. articles to profl. jours. Mem. Am. Assn. Marriage and Family Therapy, Am. Fertility Soc., Am. Assn. Sex Educators Counselors and Therapists, Pacific Coast Fertility Soc. Office: 1344 Wilshire Blvd Los Angeles CA 90017

SHREVE, SUSAN RICHARDS, author, English literature educator; b. Toledo, May 2, 1939; d. Robert Kenneth and Helen (Greene) Richards; m. Timothy Seldes, Feb. 7, 1987; children—Porter, Elizabeth, Caleb, Kate. B.A., U. Pa., 1961; M.A., U. Va., 1969. Prof. English lit. George Mason U., Fairfax, Va., 1976—; vis. prof. Columbia U., N.Y.C., 1982—; Author: (novels) A Fortunate Madness, 1974, A Woman Like That, 1977, Children of Power, 1979, Miracle Play, 1981, Dreaming of Heroes, 1984, Queen of the Heart, 1986; (children's books) The Nightmares of Geranium Street, 1977, Family Secrets, 1979, Loveletters, 1979, The Masquerade, 1980, The Bad Dreams of a Good Girl, 1981, The Revolution of Mary Leary, 1982, The Flunking of Joshua T. Bates, 1984, How I Saved the World on Purpose, 1985, Lucy Forever and Miss Rosetree, Shrinks, Inc., 1985. Recipient Jenny Moore award George Washington U., 1978; John Simon Guggenheim award in fiction, 1980; Nat. Endowment Arts fiction award, 1982. Mem. Phi Beta Kappa.

SHRIVER, EUNICE MARY KENNEDY (MRS. ROBERT SARGENT SHRIVER, JR.), civic worker; b. Brookline, Mass.; m. Robert Sargent Shriver, Jr., May 23, 1953; children: Robert Sargent III, Maria Owings, Timothy Perry, Mark Kennedy, Anthony Paul Kennedy. B.S. in Sociology, Stanford U., 1943; student, Manhattanville Coll. of Sacred Heart, L.H. D., 1963; Litt.D., U. Santa Clara, 1962; L.H.D., D'Youville Coll., 1962; LL.D., Regis Coll., 1963; L.H.D., Newton Coll., 1973, Brescia Coll., 1974, Holy Cross Coll., 1979, Princeton U., 1979; also hon. degrees, U. Vt., Albertus Magnus Coll., St. Mary's Coll. With spl. war problems div. State Dept. Washington, 1943-45; sec. Nat. Conf. on Prevention and Control juvenile Delinquency, Dept. of Justice, Washington, 1947-48; social worker Fed. Penitentiary for Women, Alderson, W.Va., 1950; exec. v.p. Joseph P. Kennedy, Jr. Found., 1950—; founder (1968), since chmn. Spl. Olympics Internat.; social worker House of Good Shepherd, Chgo., also Juvenile Ct., Chgo., 1951-54; regional chmn. women's div. Community Fund-Red Cross Joint Appeal, Chgo., 1958; mem. Chgo. Commn. on Youth Welfare, 1959-62; cons. to Pres. John F. Kennedy's Panel on Mental Retardation, 1961. Editor: A Community of Caring, 1982. Active worker in congl. and presdl. campaigns of John F. Kennedy, 1948-60; co-chmn. women's com. Democratic Nat. Conv., Chgo., 1956. Decorated Legion of Honor; recipient Lasker award, Humanitarian award A.A.M.D., 1973, Nat. Vol. Service award, 1973, Phila. Civic Ballet award, 1973, Prix de la Couronne Française, 1974, Presdl. Medal of Freedom, 1974, others. Address: care Joseph P Kennedy Jr Found 1350 New York Ave Suite 500 Washington DC 20005 *

SHROKA, JOYCE ANN, steel company manager; b. Gary, Ind., Mar. 8, 1955; d. Albert Andrew and Patricia Ann (Kennedy) Krieter; m. Steven Paul Shroka, May 24, 1980; children: Adrienne Lea, Gregory Charles. AAS, Purdue U., 1976, AAS in Computer Programming, BS in Computer Sci., 1977. Programmer Standard Oil of Ind., Chgo., 1977-79; cons. WD Farlow & Assoc., South Holland, Ill., 1979-82, account mgr., 1982-86; supr. systems payroll maintenance Inland Steel, East Chicago, Ind., 1983-87, supr., 1986—, supr. order processing systems, 1987—. Mem. Nat. Assn. Female Execs. Roman Catholic. Home: 13521 Schneider Court Cedar Lake IN 46303 Office: Inland Steel 3210 Watling St East Chicago IN 46312

SHROUT, CYNTHIA LOUISE, hospital management; b. Princeton, W.Va., Aug. 22, 1958; d. Edgar Allen and Dorothy (Harris) S. A in Applied Scis., Fairmount State Coll., 1978. Registered respiratory therapist, W.Va. Staff respiratory therapist United Hosp. Ctr., Clarksburg, W.Va., 1978-79, Va. Univ. Med. Ctr., Morgantown, W.Va., 1979; lead respiratory therapist Cabell-Huntington Hosp., W.Va., 1979-84; supr. respiratory therapy Cabell-Huntington Hosp., 1984—. Mem. Nat. Assn. Female Execs., Nat. Bd. Respiratory Care, Am. Assn. Respiratory care, W.Va. Soc. Respiratory Care. Home: 2959 Shepard Dr Huntington WV 25705 Office: Cabell-Huntington Hosp 1340 Hal Greer Blvd Huntington WV 25701

SHUGRUE, ELIZABETH ESTELLE, government administrator; b. Chgo., Aug. 20, 1953; d. Thomas Frederick and Dolores Estelle (Buchter) S. Student, U. Colo., Denver, 1971-73. Receptionist Benham's Photography, Arvada, Colo., 1970-73; billing clk. South Park Motor Lines,

Denver, 1972-73; mem. sales staff Montgomery Ward Co., McAllen, Tex., 1973-74; copy girl The Monitor, McAllen, 1974-75; cashier Railroad Restaurant, Golden, Colo., 1975; procurement clk. then procurement agent U.S. Geol. Survey, Denver, 1975-81, contract specialist, 1981—; Mem. Info. Systems Council Dept. Interior, Denver, 1983—. Vol. leader Ch. Youth Activities Program, Arvada, 1976-86; instr. religious edn., 1970-76. Mem. Nat. Contract Mgmt. Assn. (cert.). Office: US Geol Survey Box 25046 MS 204B DFC Denver CO 80225

SHULER, SALLY ANN SMITH, telecommunications company executive; b. Mt. Olive, N.C., June 11, 1934; d. Leon Joseph and Ludia Irene (Montague) Simmons; m. Henry Ralph Smith Jr., Mar. 1, 1957 (div. Jan. 1976); children: Molly Montague, Barbara Ellen, Sara Ann, Mary Kathryn; m. Harold Robert Shuler, Aug. 2, 1987. BA in Math., Duke U., 1956; spl. studies, U. Liège, Belgium, 1956-57; postgrad. in bus. econs., Claremont Grad Sch., 1970-72. Mgr. fed. systems Gen. Electric Info. Services Co., Washington, 1976-78; mgr. mktg. support Gen. Electric Info. Services Co., Rockville, Md., 1978-81; dir. bus. devel. info. tech. group div. Electronic Data Systems, Bethesda, Md., 1981-82; v.p. mktg. optimum systems div. Electronic Data Systems, Rockville, 1982-83; v.p. planning and communications Electronic Data Systems, Dallas, 1983-84; exec. dir. comml. devel. U.S. West Inc., Englewood, Colo., 1984—. Recipient Gen. Electric Centennial award, Rockville, 1978. Fellow Rotary Internat. Found.; mem. Phi Beta Kappa, Tau Psi Omega, Pi Mu Epsilon. Democrat. Presbyterian. Home: 1626 S Syracuse St Denver CO 80231 Office: U S West 7800 E Orchard Rd Englewood CO 80111

SHULKO, PATSY LEE, nutrition consultant, realtor; b. Indpls., Sept. 24, 1934; B.S., Mich. State U., 1956, M.A., 1970; m. Richard M. Shulko, Aug. 4, 1973; 1 son, Gregory. Asst. prof. Med. Coll. Ga., Augusta, 1972-82; nutrition cons., 1982—; assoc. Meybohm Realty, Inc., Augusta, 1987—. Mem. Am. Dietetic Assn., Ga. Dietetic Assn., Augusta Dietetic Assn., Am. Home Econ. Assn., Ga. Heart Assn., Ga. Nutrition Council, Soc. Nutrition Edn., Nutrition Today Soc. (charter), Nutritionists in Nursing Edn. (nat. chmn. 1983-84), AAUP, AAUW, Omicron Nu, Pi Beta Phi. Clubs: Houndslake Country, Racquet. Home: 425 Waverly Dr Augusta GA 30909

SHULMAN, TAMARA, psychologist; b. N.Y.C., Apr. 8, 1953; d. Bernard and Miriam S.; m. Barry J. Bendes, 1984. B.A. magna cum laude, Bklyn. Coll., 1973; M.A., Hofstra U., 1974, Ph.D., 1977; cert. in psychotherapy and psychoanalysis NYU, 1987 . Diplomate in clin. psychology Am. Bd. Profl. Psychology; lic. psychologist, N.J., N.Y. Staff psychologist Mental Health Clinic of Passaic (N.J.), 1977-78; staff psychologist Elizabeth Gen. Hosp. Community Mental Health Clinic (N.J.), 1978-79, chief childrens services, 1979-81; pvt. practice psychology, Clifton, N.J., 1979—; consulting psychologist N.J. Div. Narcotics, 1978-84, Clifton Pub. Sch. System, 1981-87 ; mem. allied clin. staff St. Mary's Hosp., Passaic, 1982—; adj. prof. C.W. Post Coll., Greenvale, N.Y., 1977, Nassau Community Coll., Garden City, N.Y., 1975; assoc. clin. prof. Pace U., N.Y.C., 1986—; Contbr. articles to profl. jours. Mem. Am. Psychol. Assn., N.J. Psychol. Assn., The Psychoanalytic Soc., Phi Beta Kappa. Home: 340 E 64th St Apt 25A New York NY 10021 Office: 66 Mt Prospect Ave PO Box 754 Clifton NJ 07015 also: 340 E 64th St New York NY 10021

SHULTZ, SUSAN KENT FRIED, executive search and international business consultant; b. N.Y.C., Mar. 25, 1943; d. L. Richard and Jane (Kent) Fried; B.A. in Govt. and Econs., U. Ariz., 1964; postgrad. in internat. affairs George Washington U., 1967. Congl. legis. asst., 1964-68; campaign and press dir. various polit. campaigns, 1968-78; public relations cons., 1974-81; contbr. editor Phoenix mag., 1973—; pres. Susan Shultz and Assos., exec. search cons., Paradise Valley, Ariz., 1981—, Assoc. Exec. Search Cons.; assoc. Morgan & Ptnrs. Exec. Search, Europe, Lamay Assoc. Recruiters Conn.; writer Beverly Hills Diet and sequel, 1981-82. Republic Nat. Conv., 1964, 68, 80; charter mem. Charter 100, 1980; charter class mem. Valley Leadership, 1980; membership chmn. Village 5 Phoenix Planning Com., 1980; del. White House Conf. Small Bus., 1986. Mem. Phoenix Com. Fgn. Relations (exec. com.), Nat. Assn. Corporate Dirs., Ariz. Dist. Export Council Jr. League of Phoenix. Episcopalian. Address: 6001 E Cactus Wren Rd Paradise Valley AZ 85253

SHUMAKER-MACKEY, SUSAN LEE, transportation executive; b. New Castle, Ind., June 6, 1955; d. Daniel Ray Oakes and Susan Jean (Brown) Stewart; m. C. Michael Shumaker, May 25, 1974 (div. 1979); 1 child, Sean Elliot; m. Christopher J. Mackey, Nov. 7, 1986; 1 child, Leslie Elizabeth. Student, Ball State U., 1973-75, Ind. U., Ft. Wayne, 1979-80. Credit clk. N.Am. Van Lines, Ft. Wayne, 1978-79, asst. credit mgr., 1979-80, internat. credit mgr., 1980-82, sales mgr. S.Am., 1982-84; internat. sales mgr. Chipman Mayflower, San Leandro, Calif., 1984-85; v.p., gen. mgr. Shepard's, Inc. Calif., San Leandro, 1985—. Mem. Pacific Traffic Assn., Calif. Moving and Storage Assn., Overseas Moving Network, Inc., Household Goods Forwarding Assn., Female Execs. Republican. Methodist. Office: Shepard's Inc Calif 1955 Davis St San Leandro CA 94577

SHUMATE, DOROTHY LEE, pharmacist; b. Oak Hill, W.Va., Feb. 4, 1956; d. Garland Lee and Betty Alice (Perry) Pugh; m. David Keith Shumate, Mar. 14, 1981; 1 child, John David. Student Concord Coll., 1974-76; B.S. in Pharmacy, W.Va. U., 1979. Registered pharmacist. Pharmacist, Rural Acres Pharmacy, Beckley, W.Va., 1979-81, Beckley Hosp., 1979, Fairway Drug, Addison, Ill., 1981-82, Martin Ave. Pharmacy, Naperville, Ill., 1982-85, Pulaski (Va.) Drugs, 1985-87, SuperX Drugs, Pulaski, 1987—; Mem. Am. Pharm. Assn., Va. Pharm. Assn., AAUW, Rho Chi, Gamma Beta Phi, Alpha Chi, Lambda Kappa Sigma. Republican. Mem. Ch. of the Brethren. Avocations: ping pong, piano, organ, racquetball. Home: Rt 2 Box 8 1747 Newbern Rd Pulaski VA 24301

SHUMATE, GLORIA JONES, educational administrator; b. Meridian, Miss., Jan. 8, 1927; d. Thomas Marvin and Flora E. (Suggs) Jones; m. Jack B. Shumate, Nov. 19, 1946; children: Jack B. Jr., Thomas Edward. BS, Miss. State U., 1960; MA, U. South Fla., 1969, postgrad. in vocat. edn., 1970-72. Cert. guidance counselor, psychology and social studies specialist, Fla. High sch. tchr. Lauderdale County Schs., Meridian, 1952-56; tchr. vocat. edn. Manpower Devel. and Tng., St. Petersburg, Fla., 1964-69; counselor City Ctr. for Learning St. Petersburg Vocat.-Tech. Inst., 1969-70, registrar, 1970-72, asst. dir., 1972-80, exec. dir., 1980-85; dir. vocat.-tech., adult edn. ops. Pinellas County Schs., Largo, Fla., 1985—; chmn. Fla. Equity Council, 1980-81; mem. Fla. Adv. Council on Vocat. Edn., 1980-85, Fla. Job Tng. Coordinating Council, 1983-84. Named Outstanding Educator Pinellas Suncoast C. of C., 1980. Mem. Nat. Council Local Adminstrs., Am. Vocat. Assn., Fla. Vocat. Assn., So. Assn. Colls. and Schs. (standards com. 1975-81), Phi Delta Kappa, Kappa Delta Pi. Democrat. Baptist. Home: 900 63d St S Saint Petersburg FL 33707 Office: Pinellas County Schs Curriculum and Instrn Ctr 205 4th St SW Largo FL 34640

SHURBERG, BARBARA JEAN, administrative associate; b. Houston, Nov. 9, 1944; d. Otto and Eva Lee (Evans) S. Student, Arizona State U., 1962-63; BBA, U. Houston, 1966. Sec., then asst. buyer Foley's Dept. Store, Houston, 1967-71; sec. Washington Post, 1971-72, Neuhaus & Taylor Architects, Houston, 1972-74; adminstrv. assoc. Baylor Coll. Medicine, Houston, 1974—. Vol. Am. Cancer Soc. "Reach to Recovery" Program, Houston, 1985—; bd. dirs. Live Oak Hills Courthomes, Houston, 1984—; pub. relations council St. Joseph's Hosp., 1981-82, 85-88; community relations council Met. Issues Committee Jewish Fedn. Greater Houston. Mem. Am. Pathology Found., Hadassah (pres. Houston chpt. 1981-83, v.p. Greater Tex. Region 1983—), Med. Adminstrs. Tex. (pathology mgmt. assembly), Med. Group Mgmt. Assn. Jewish. Home: PO Box 1043 Bellaire TX 77401 Office: Baylor Coll Med Dept Pathology One Baylor Plaza Houston TX 77030

SHURE, MYRNA BETH, psychologist, educator; b. Chgo., Sept. 11, 1937; d. Sidney Natkin and Frances (Laufman) S.; student U. Colo., 1955; BS, U. Ill., 1959; MS, Cornell U., 1961, PhD, 1966. Asst. prof. U. R.I., head tchr. Nursery Sch., Kingston, 1961-62; asst. prof. Temple U., Phila., 1966-67, assoc. prof., 1967-68; instr. Hahneman Med. Coll., Phila., 1968-69, sr. instr. psychology, 1969-70, asst. prof., 1970-73, assoc. prof., 1973-80, prof., 1980—. NIMH research grantee, 1971-75, 77-79, 82-85, 87, 88—. Recipient Lela Rowland Prevention award Nat. Mental Health Assn., 1982; . lic. psychologist, Pa. Fellow Am. Psychol. Assn. (Disting. Contbn. award div. community psychology 1984); mem. Am. Psychol. Assn. (mem. Task Force on Prevention award 1987), Eastern Psychol. Assn., Soc. Research in Child Devel., Phila. Soc. Clin. Psychologists. Author: (with George Spivack) Social Adjustment of Young Children, 1974; (with George Spivack and Jerome Platt) The Problem Solving Approach to Adjustment, 1976; (with George Spivack) Problem Solving Techniques in Childrearing, 1978. Editorial bd. Jour. Applied Developmental Psychology. Office: 1505 Race St Philadelphia PA 19102

SHUSTERMAN, LISA, finance company executive; b. Phila., Feb. 22, 1959; d. Philip and Freda Helen (Keces) S. BA, U. N.C., Chapel Hill, 1981. Cert. fin. planner. Asst. fin. planner Am. Fin. Cons., Silver Spring, Md., 1983-84; assoc. fin. planner Am. Fin. Cons., Silver Spring, 1984-85; v.p. Dolan Fin. Corp., Silver Spring, 1985—. Mem. Internat. Assn. Fin. Planners (cert.), Nat. Assn. Female Execs., Women Bus. Owners. Republican. Jewish. Home: 9039 Sligo Creek Pkwy #1515 Silver Spring MD 20901 Office: Dolan Fin Corp 1100 Wayne Ave Suite 1225 Silver Spring MD 20910

SHUTLER, BETTY A(NN), career placement executive; b. Toledo, Ohio, Jan. 28, 1940; d. Carl Edward and Mildred (Rupley) Roemmele; m. Robert E. Shutler, Sept. 2, 1972. Student, Davenport Coll., Grand Rapids, Mich., 1972, Tulsa Jr. Coll., 1986—. Adminstrv. asst. Foremost Ins., Grand Rapids, 1968-77; personnel cons. Virginia Webb Personnel, Tulsa, 1977-82; pres. Shutler Personnel, Tulsa, 1982—. Bd. dirs. Burning Tree Homeowners Assn., Tulsa, 1985—. Mem. Exec. Women's Forum (program chmn. 1980—), Am. Bus. Women's Assn. (newsletter editor 1977-80), Tulsa Bus. Club (pres. 1983). Republican. Roman Catholic.

SHUTT, CONSTANCE, air traffic control specialist; b. Lexington, Ky., Mar. 16, 1955; d. Charles Noble and Jane Ruth (Markarian) S.; m. David Allan Wilson, Feb. 9, 1987. Student, Thomas Edison State Coll., 1986—. Cert. control tower operator, comml. pilot. Air traffic asst. FAA, Morrisville, N.C., 1981-83; air traffic controller FAA, Morrisville, 1983—. Mem. adv. com. Boy Scouts Am., Durham, N.C., 1986—. Mem. Profl. Women Controllers.

SHYMANSKI, CATHERINE MARY, psychiatric clinical nurse specialist; b. Omaha, Jan. 23, 1954; d. Leo Michael and Mildred Mary (Swank) Shymanski. A.A.S. in Nursing, Iowa Western Community Coll., 1977; B.S.N., Buena Vista Coll., 1978; B.F.A., Drake U., 1980; M.S.N., Columbia Pacific U., 1984. Staff nurse Menninger Found., Topeka, 1978-79; staff devel. instr., clin. coordinator Stormont Vail Regional Med. Ctr., Topeka, 1979-80; charge nurse Allen County Hosp., Iola, Kans., 1980-81; asst. dir. nursing Arkhaven at Erie, Kans., 1980; dir. shift ops. Truman Med. Ctr., Kans. City, Mo., 1983; nursing supr. Osawatomie State Hosp., Kans., 1981—. Mem. River City Players, Osawatomie, Kans., 1984—. Mem. Osawatomie Bus. & Profl. Women (pres. 1985-86, dist. dir.-elect 1986-87, dist. dir. 1987-88, Young Career Woman award 1982, 84, Woman of Year, 1982-83), AAUW. Democrat. Roman Catholic. Avocations: raise and show cats; gardening; reading. Office: Osawatomie State Hosp Osawatomie KS 66064

SIBLESZ, ISABEL MARIA, word processing supervisor; b. Miami, Fla., May 17, 1962; d. Rodolfo Maximo and Isabel Elvira (Fernandez) S. AA, Miami-Dade Community Coll., 1981; BS, Fla. Internat. U., 1983, MS, 1986. Sec. Miami Beach Sr. High Sch., Fla., 1979-81; bus. edn. instr. Miami-Dade Community Coll., Miami, Fla., 1982-83; instr. Charron Williams Coll., Miami, Fla., 1983, Miami-Dade Community Col., Miami, 1983-85; supr. word processing Miami Herald Pub. Co., 1983—; office tech. chairperson, instr. CompuTech Inst., Miami, 1986—; researcher for Fla. Internat. U. on word processing equipment and its ednl. value, 1986. Mem. Corona Coll of Edn. Alumni chpt. Fla. Internat. U., Fla. Vocat. Assn., Dade Vocat. Assn., U.S. Assn. for Supervision and Curriculum Devel., Fla. Assn. for Supervision and Curriculum Devel., Am. Soc. Notaries, Nat. Assn. Female Execs. Inc., Nat. Bus. Edn. Assn., Fla. Bus. Edn. Assn. Republican. Roman Catholic. Office: The Miami Herald Pub Co 1 Herald Plaza Miami FL 33132

SIBLEY, CAROL MORSE, medical communications consultant; b. San Antonio, Jan. 11, 1944; d. Edison Spencer and Cecile (Bernard) Morse; student U. Del., 1962-64; B.S., Hahnemann Med. Coll., 1966; m. Frederick Drake Sibley, Mar. 15, 1975; 1 child, Janet Bernard. Med. writer internat. div. Bristol-Myers, N.Y.C., 1968-72; assoc. biomed. communications Turner Assocs., Greenwich, Conn., 1972-73; clin. research assoc. Pfizer Pharms., N.Y.C., 1974-76, mgr. sci. communications, 1976; cons. pharm. industry, Montclair, N.J., 1976—; assoc. biomed. communications J.L. Shapiro Assocs., Metuchen, N.J., 1979-82; dir. sci. affairs Audio Visual Med. Mktg., N.Y.C., 1982-83. Committeeman, Republican party, Phila., 1965-66. Mem. Am. Soc. Microbiology, N.Y. Acad. Scis., Am. Soc. Clin. Pathologists. Republican. Episcopalian. Home and Office: 196 Christopher St Montclair NJ 07042

SIBLEY, CHARLOTTE ELAINE, pharmaceutical industry executive; b. Holliston, Mass., June 11, 1946; s. C. Edward and Jane Forbes (Kelly) S. A.B., Middlebury Coll., 1968, M.B.A., U. Chgo., 1970. Market research mgr. Pfizer Inc., N.Y.C., 1970-73; security analyst Donaldson, Lufkin & Jenrette, N.Y.C., 1973-76; cons., N.Y.C., 1976-78; mktg. research mgr. Lipton Co., Englewood Cliffs, N.J., 1978-80; market research mgr. Johnson & Johnson Products Inc., New Brunswick, N.J., 1980-84; research dir. Med. Econs. Co., Inc., Oradell, N.J., 1984-87; dir. worldwide mktg. research Squibb Corp., Princeton, N.J., 1987—. Cons., Vol. Urban Cons. Group, N.Y.C., 1974-78. V.p., treas. St. Cecilia Chorus, N.Y.C., 1974—. Mem. Med. Surg. Market Research Group, N.Y. Soc. Security Analysts. Republican. Home: 15 Eggert Ave Metuchen NJ 08840 Office: Squibb Corp PO Box 4000 Princeton NJ 08543-4000

SIBLEY, REBECCA LEIGH CARDWELL, dietitian; b. Starkville, Miss., Dec. 29, 1955; d. Joe Thomas and Leota (Patterson) Cardwell; m. Daniel Paul Sibley, May 22, 1976; children: John Paul, Jennifer Leigh. BS, Miss. State U., 1977, MS, 1978. Dietary supr. Oktibbeha County Hosp., Starkville, Miss., 1975-76; nutrition instr. Miss. State Dept. Pub. Welfare, Starkville, 1978-80; univ. food service mgr. Miss. U. for Women, Columbus, 1978, instr. foods, nutrition, 1979; dietary cons. Martha Coker Convalescent Home, Yazoo City, Miss., 1981-86, Yazoo Community Action, 1984—; dietary cons. King's Daughters Hosp., Yazoo City, 1981-82, 88—, dir. dietary div., 1982-88; dietary cons. various civic orgns., lectr. in field. Active Yazoo County Extension Gen. Service Adv. Bd., 1984—; pres. chmn. Yazoo Extension Home Econs. Adv., 1984—; food chmn. Miss. State U. Alumni, Yazoo City, 1985-86. Named One of Outstanding Young Women of Am., 1987; Agriculture and Home Econs. scholar Miss. State U., 1974-77; Miss. Home Econ. Assn. scholar, 1974. Mem. Am. Dietetic Assn., Phi Kappa Phi, Phi Tau Sigma, Gamma Sigma Delta, Kappa Omicron Phi, Alpha Zeta, Alpha Lambda Delta. Republican. Methodist. Home: 2230 Wildwood Terr Extension Yazoo City MS 39194 Office: 823 Grand Ave Yazoo City MS 39194

SICHENZE, CELESTE MARIE, business educator; b. Bklyn., Aug. 28, 1937; d. Louis R. and Carmela M. (Esposito) Costagliola; m. John Anthony Sichenze, July 4, 1959; children: John A. II, Louis D., Andrea C. BS in Gen. Bus. cum laude, L.I. U., 1959, MS in Bus. Adminstrn. cum laude, 1965; PhD, George Washington U., 1988. Adminstrv. asst. to v.p., provost L.I. U., 1959-61; tchr. adult edn. Manchester (Mass.) Schs., 1965-68; tchr. Pingree Sch., Hamilton, Mass., 1968-71; substitute tchr. Fairfax City (Va.) Pub. Schs., 1972-74; from lectr. to prof. bus. mgmt. No. Va. Community Coll., Annandale, 1974—. Contbr. articles to profl. jours. Mem. Fairfax County Fedn. Citizens Assn., bus. mgmt. curriculum adv. com. No. Va. Community Coll.; pres. Carriage Hill Civic Assn., Vienna, Va., 1975-76, 88—, v.p. 1985-86, Oakton High Sch. PTA, Vienna, 1977-79; chmn. ways and means com. Oakton High Sch. Band Boosters, Vienna, 1980-83. Named an Outstanding Young Woman of Am., Chgo., 1969. Mem. Am. Mgmt. Assn., Indsl. Relations Research Assn., Va. Community Coll. Assn. (chmn. research and publs. commn. 1984-86). Roman Catholic. Home: 2020 Post Rd Vienna VA 22180 Office: No Va Community Coll 8333 Little River Turnpike Annandale VA 22180

SICILIANO, ANN P., cytologist; b. Neptune, N.J., Dec. 20, 1930; d. Gavino and Theresa Siciliano; asso. degree in med. tech. Wilson Jr. Coll., 1948; cert. in cytology Parkway Hosp., 1949; B.S., Northwestern U., 1962. With Parkway Hosp., Brookline, Mass., 1949-53; supr. cytology and isotopes labs. Highland Park (Ill.) Hosp., 1954-60; cytologist U. Ill. Med. Sch., Chgo., 1960-61; cytologist supr. Edgewater Hosp., Chgo., 1961-68, North Suburban Clinic, Skokie, Ill., 1964—. Mem. Internat. Acad. Cytology, Am. Soc. Cytotechnologists, Am. Soc. Clin. Pathology (assoc.), Am. Soc. Cytology (assoc.), Ill. Soc. Cytology (treas.). Roman Catholic. Office: PO Box 206 Kenilworth IL 60043

SICKLESMITH, DONNA LOU, art director; b. Uniontown, Pa., Oct. 13, 1953; d. James V. Sicklesmith and Mary E. (Kriner) Honsaker. Student, Georgetown U., 1972-74; BA in Polit. Sci., Purdue U., 1975; cert. publ. specialist, George Washington U., 1981. Designer Ice House Graphics, Washington, 1981-82; art. dir., owner Donna Sicklesmith Graphic Design, Washington, 1982-83; designer Wickham & Assocs., Washington, 1983-84; art dir., ptnr. Sicklesmith & Egly, Washington, 1984-86; art dir., owner Sicklesmith Design, Washington, 1986—; instr. in publ. specialist program continuing edn. George Washington U., 1982-83. Mem. Art Dirs. Club Met. Washington (5 Certs. Merit 1985, 86, 87, sec. 1985-86, 2d v.p. 1986-87). Unitarian. Home and Office: 1737 17th St NW Washington DC 20009

SICKON, ANN CATHERINE, health care business administrator; b. Wyandotte, Mich., Dec. 29, 1955; d. Thomas Stanley Sickon and Josephine (Dame) Rawlings; m. Kenneth Robert Gordon, May 31, 1981 (dec. 1985). Diploma in nursing, Henry Ford Hosp. Sch. Nursing, 1976; BS in Health Care Adminstrn., U. Mich., 1983. RN. Staff nurse Henry Ford Hosp., Detroit, 1976-78, Vis. Nurse Assn., Flint, Mich., 1979-81; nursing supr. Kelley Home Care, Flint, 1981-82; sales rep. Travenol Home Respiratory Therapy, Flint, 1983-84, br. mgr., 1984; area mgr. Travenol Home Respiratory Therapy, Mich., Minn., Mo., 1985; mgr. tng. devel. Travenol Labs., Travacare Div., Deerfield, Ill., 1985-86; dir. reimbursement Travenol Labs., Travacare Div., Deerfield, 1986. Mem. Republican Nat. Com., 1986—. Mem. Nat. Health Lawyers Assn., Am. Mgmt. Assn., Nat. Assn. Female Execs., U. Mich. Alumni Assn., Quota. Republican. Clubs: Flushing Golf and Country, University. Home: PO Box 7219 Deerfield IL 60015 Office: Travenol Labs Inc 1415 Lake Cook Rd Deerfield IL 60015

SIDELL, PAMELA JOAN, health care administrator; b. Brookline, Mass., Mar. 7, 1953. BA, Brandeis U., 1974; MCRP, Harvard U., 1980. Asst. br. mgr. U.S. Trust Co., Boston, 1975-77; research analyst Mass. Dept. Mental Health, Danvers, 1977-78; cons. Mass. Dept. Mental Health, Beverly, 1978-80; dir. program ops. Mass. Medicaid, Boston, 1980-82; v.p. planning and devel. Am. Internat. Health Services, Woburn, Mass., 1982—. Mem. Newton-Well-Weston-Needham Mental Health Area Bd., Mass., 1980-82, Com. for Community Edn., 1980-82; sponsor Parents Anonymous, Mass., 1981-82; mem. steering com. Care, Inc., 1986—. Mem. Am. Pub. Health Assn., Nat. Assn. Female Execs. Home: 50-56 Broadlawn Park #319 Chestnut Hill MA 02167 Office: Am Internat Health Services 36 Commerce Way Woburn MA 01801

SIDELL, SUE ANN FRY, quality engineer; b. Harrisburg, Pa., Jan. 31, 1953; d. William Lyman and Martha Luvara (Swenson) F.; m. Charles Maynard Sidell, Aug. 30, 1984. Student, Cen. Coll. Ky., 1970-72; BBA, U. Cen. Fla., 1985. Cert. quality engr. Supr. incoming inspection Invenex Labs., Orlando, Fla., 1979-82; quality mgr. Calibron Corp., LakeMary, Fla., 1982-85; quality engr. Martin Marietta Electronics & Missiles Group, 1985—, mem. rotational tng. program, 1986-87. Pres. Quota Club Orlando, Fla., Inc., 1983. Mem. Am. Soc. for Quality Control (publicity chmn. 1984, program chmn. 1987-88, Henry deZwart award 1988), Nat. Assn. Female Execs., Phi Kappa Phi. Clubs: Quota (Orlando) (pres. local chpt.); Martin Marietta Mgmt. Office: Martin Marietta Electronics & Missiles Group ESC PO Box 628007 MP 1202 Orlando FL 32862-8007

SIDERMAN, SHEILA JILL, educational publishing consultant; b. N.Y.C., Nov. 1, 1943; d. Max and Ray (Cooperstein) S.; m. Jerry Palin, June 4, 1978. BS, CCNY, 1964; student, NYU, 1976-78; MA, Harvard U., 1965. Tchr. Gorton High Sch., Yonkers, N.Y., 1965-67; thcr. White Plains (N.Y.) High Sch., 1967-70; instr. Urban Systems Staff Devel. Ctr., White Plains, 1968-70; editor Appleton, Century, Crofts Pubs., N.Y.C., 1970-71, Harcourt Brace Jovanovich, N.Y.C., 1971-75; supervising editor Scholastic, Inc., N.Y.C., 1976-79; pres. Contemporary Ednl. Services, Princeton, N.J., 1979—; instr. Upward Bound, Fla. A&M U., Tallahassee, 1965, Upward Bound, Sarah Lawrence Coll., Bronxville, N.Y., 1966; cons. Scholastic Math Mags., N.Y.C., 1979-83. Author: (textbooks) Measuring in Metric, 1976, Calendar Math, 1980. Mem. Assn. Am. Pubs., Nat. Council Tchrs. Math., Music Educators Nat. Conf., A.S.C.D. Jewish. Club: Harvard (N.Y.C. and Princeton). Home and Office: 85 Bouvant Dr Princeton NJ 08540

SIEBELS, CELESTE MARIE, health and fitness executive; b. Buffalo, May 30, 1955; d. Stan Vincent and Felicia (Carducci) Georger; m. Mark Allan Siebles, May 27, 1953; children: Erica Kristin, Mark Henry. BS in Hotel and Restaurant Mgmt., Fla. Internat. U., 1977. Fitness coordinator The Sporting Clubs of Am., San Diego, 1984-85, asst. dir., 1985-87; owner East Bay's Pulse, San Ramon, Calif., 1987—; mgr. Orinda Sports Fitness Ctr., San Ramon, 1987—; mgmt. cons., fitness tng. specialist, 1980—; wine cons. 1979-82. Wine Editor Diplomat Internat., 1981-82; editor The Sports Page, 1986-87. Recipient Arthur S. Packard Meml. award 1974, Charles Fitzsimmons award Fitzsimmons Found. 1976-77; Hilton scholar 1974, Statler Found. scholar 1974, Nat. Airlines scholar 1976-77. Mem. Internat. Dance Exercise Assn., Am. Alliance Health Recreation Phys. Edn. and Dance, Bus. and Profl. Women. Republican. Roman Catholic. Office: East Bay's Pulse 4081 Greenwich Dr San Ramon CA 94583

SIEBERT, JOSEPHINE JOAN CONSTANCE, editor; b. Bronxville, N.Y., Sept. 30, 1944; d. Leo Paul and Josephine Evelyn (Arno) S. AB in English summa cum laude, NYU, 1966; postgrad., U. Fla., 1967. Mgr. promotions, editor MBA News Dell Pub., N.Y.C., 1972-75; dir. media and communications Berkey Tech. Co., Woodside, N.Y., 1975-78; mgr. advt., pub. relations Harmers Internat., N.Y.C., 1978-80; editor, publisher, founder Clipboard Art Newsletter, N.Y.C., 1980—; lectr. in field. Organizer Bicentennial Celebration Internat. Ctr. N.Y., 1975. Mem. AAUW, Phi Beta Kappa. Office: Clipboard Art Newsletter Po Box 389 Bronx NY 10471

SIEBERT, MURIEL, business executive, former state official; b. Cleve.; d. Irwin J. and Margaret Eunice (Roseman) Siebert; student Western Res. U., 1949-52; D.C.S. (hon.), St. John's U., St. Bonaventure U., Molloy Coll., Adelfi St. Francis Coll., Mercy Coll. Security analyst Bache & Co., 1954-57; analyst Utilities & Industries Mgmt. Corp., 1958, Shields & Co., 1959-60; partner Stearns & Co., 1961, Finkle & Co., 1962-65, Brimberg & Co., N.Y.C., 1965-67; individual mem. (first woman mem.) N.Y. Stock Exchange, 1967; chmn., pres. Muriel Siebert & Co., Inc., 1969-77; trustee Manhattan Savs. Bank, 1975-77; supt. banks, dept. banking State of N.Y., 1977-82; dir. Urban Devel. Corp., N.Y.C., 1977-82, Job Devel. Authority, N.Y.C., 1977-82, State of N.Y. Mortgage Agy., 1977-82; chmn., pres. Muriel Siebert & Co., Inc., 1983—; assoc. in mgmt. Simmons Coll.; mem. adv. com. Fin. Acctg. Standards Bd., 1981; guest lectr. numerous colls. Mem. women's adv. com. Econ. Devel. Adminstrn., N.Y.C.; trustee Manhattan Coll.; v.p., mem. exec. com. Greater N.Y. Area council Boy Scouts Am.; mem. N.Y. State Econ. Devel. Bd., N.Y. Council Economy; bd. overseers NYU Sch. Bus., 1984; bd. dirs. United Way of N.Y.C.; trustee Citizens Budget Commn.; mem. bus. com. Met. Mus. Recipient Spirit of Achievement award Albert Einstein Coll. Medicine, 1977; Women's Equity Action League award, 1978; Outstanding Contbns. to Equal Opportunity for Women award Bus. Council of UN Decade for Women, 1979; Silver Beaver award Boy Scouts Am., 1981; Elizabeth Cutter Morrow award YWCA, 1983; Emily Roebling award Nat. Women's Hall of Fame, 1984; NOW Legal Def. and Edn. Fund award, 1981. Clubs: River, Doubles, Nat. Arts, Economic (N.Y.C.). Home: 435 E 52d St New York NY 10022 Office: Muriel Siebert & Co Inc 444 Madison Ave New York NY 10022

SIEGAL, RITA GORAN, engineering company executive; b. Chgo., July 16, 1934; d. Leonard and Anabelle (Soloway) Goran; m. Burton L. Siegal, Apr. 11, 1954; children: Norman, Laurence Scott. Student, U. Ill., 1951-53; BA, DePaul U., 1956. Cert. elem. tchr., Ill. Tchr. elem. schs. Chgo. Public Schs.,

1956-58; v.p., founder Easy Living Products Co., Chgo., 1960-62, pres., founder, 1980—; freelance interior designer, Chgo., 1968-73; dist. sales mgr. Super Girls, Chgo., 1976; v.p. and founder Budd Engring., Skokie, Ill., 1974—; founder Profit Plus Investment Club, Skokie, 1970; lectr. on product devel. and nutrition, Chgo., 1979—; guest speaker bus. on various nat. radio and TV programs, 1979—; lectr. Northwestern U., Evanston, Ill., 1983. Contbr. articles to profl. jours. Mem. adv. council Skokie High Schs., 1975-79; advisor Cub Scouts Skokie Council Boy Scouts Am., 1975; bus. mgr. Nutrition for Optimal Health Assn., 1980-82, pres., 1982-84, v.p., med./profl. liaison, 1985—; leader Great Books Found., 1972. Recipient Cub Scout awards Boy Scouts Am., 1971-72; Sales award Super Girls, 1976, Women of Corp. Achievement award, 1988. Mem. Women in Mgmt. (bd. dirs. 1986-87, pres. 1987—), Nat. Assn. Female Execs., North Shore Women in Mgmt. Inc. (pres. 1987-88, Charlotte Danstrom Women of Achievement Nat. award 1988), No. Ill. Indsl. Assn., Ill. Mfrs. Assn., Inventors Council, North Shore Art League. Club: Profit Plus Investment (founder 1970). Office: Budd Engring Corp 8707 Skokie Blvd Skokie IL 60077

SIEGEL, BARBARA Z(ENZ), research biology educator; b. Detroit, July 22, 1931; d. Joseph and Barbara (Justh) Zenz; m. Sanford Marvin Siegel, June 24, 1950; children: Stephanie Siegel Morgan, Andrea, Peter Marc, David Nathaniel. AB in Philosophy, U. Chgo., 1960; MA in Zoology, Columbia U., 1963; PhD in Biology, Yale U., 1966. Postdoctoral fellow Yale U., New Haven, 1966-67; dir. biology program U. Hawaii, Honolulu, 1967-72, sr. researcher Pacific Biomed. Research Ctr., 1975-87, interim dir. research adminstrn., dean grad. sch., 1979-82, dir. pesticide hazard assessment project, 1983-87, prof. microbiology and botany grad. dept. pub. health, 1986—; co-chmn. radiation sub-com. Com. Space Research Hdqrs., Paris, 1975-82; vis. prof. Heidelberg (Fed. Republic of Germany), 1973, Weizmann Inst., Rehovot, Israel, 1986, vis. prof. Geology, Botany, U. Brit. Columbia, 1982; vis. scholar People's Republic of China, 1985; vis. colleague Nat. Research Council of Italy, Pisa. Editor: Hawaii Energy Resource Overviews: Geothermal Development, 1980; contbr. numerous articles to profl. jours. Chmn. Govs. Panel on Pesticides, Honolulu, 1985; nominated by gov. to Commn. on Pesticides, Honolulu, 1986—; exec. council, chmn. research com. U. Hawaii Peace Inst., Honolulu, 1985, univ. commn. status of women Hawaii Assn. Women in Sci. and Faculty Women's Caucus, 1986. Fulbright Research fellow U.S. Info. Services, Yugoslavia and Fed. Republic of Germany, 1972-73, scholar to Finland, 1988—. Mem. Am. Chem. Soc., Internat. Chem. Ecology Assn., Sigma Xi. Home: 3119 Beaumont Woods Pl Honolulu HI 96822 Office: U Hawaii Sch Pub Health Biomed D104M Honolulu HI 96822

SIEGEL, BETTY LENTZ, college president; b. Cumberland, Ky., Jan. 24, 1931; d. Carl N. and Vera (Hogg) Lentz; m. Joel H. Siegel, June 6; children: David Jonathan, Michael Jeremy. B.A., Wake Forest Coll., 1952; M.Ed., U. N.C., 1953; Ph.D., Fla. State U., 1961; postgrad., Ind. U., 1964-66; hon. doctorate, Miami U., 1985, Cumberland Coll., 1985. Asst. prof. Lenoir Rhyne Coll., Hickory, N.C., 1956-59; assoc. prof. 1961-64; asst. prof. U. Fla., Gainesville, 1967-70; assoc. prof. U. Fla., 1970-72, prof., 1973-76, dean acad. affairs for continuing edn., 1972-76; dean Sch. Edn. and Psychology Western Carolina U., Cullowhee, N.C., 1976-81; pres. Kennesaw Coll., Marietta, Ga., 1981—; bd. dirs. Atlanta Gas Light Co., Equifax Inc., Nat. Services Industries; cons. numerous sch. systems. Author: Problem Situations in Teaching, 1971; contbr. articles to profl. jours. Mem. Gov.'s Commn. on Growth Strategies, 1987. Recipient Outstanding Tchr. award U. Fla., 1969; Mortar Bd. Woman of Yr. award U. Fla., 1973, Mortar Bd. Educator of Yr., Ga. State U., 1983, CASE award, 1986. Mem. Am. Psychol. Assn., Am. Ednl. Research Assn., Assn. Supervision and Curriculum Devel., Am. Assn. Colls. Tchr. Edn., Nat. Univ. Extension Assn., Adult Edn. Assn., Nat. Assn. of Intercollegiate Athletics (nat. exec. com.), Nat. Assn. State Univs. and Land Grant Colls., Am. Assn. State Colls. (bd. dirs.), Am. Council on Edn. (bd. dirs.), Atlanta C. of C. (bd. dirs.) Phi Alpha Theta, Pi Kappa Delta, Alpha Psi Omega, Kappa Delta Pi, Pi Lambda Theta, Phi Delta Kappa, Delta Kappa Gamma. Baptist. Office: PO Box 444 Marietta GA 30061

SIEGEL, DEBORAH RACHEL, personnel director; b. Forest Hills, N.Y., June 11, 1952; d. Aaron and Helen (Balish) S. BS, L.I. U., 1974; MS, Adelphi U., 1980. Sr. counselor Eastgate Med. and Surg., Mineola, N.Y., 1978-80; project coordinator Ctr. Health Edn., Mineola, 1980; dir. long range planning Med. Soc. State of N.Y., Lake Success, 1980-86, personnel dir., spl. projects coordinator, 1986—; staff dir. Medicine/Bus. Coalition, Lake Success, 1980—. Contbr. articles to profl. jours. Mem. Nat. Assn. Female Execs. Republican. Jewish. Office: Med Soc State NY 420 Lakeville Rd Lake Success NY 11042

SIEGEL, JUDITH S., foundation administrator; b. Richmond, Va., June 27, 1940; d. Meyer Harry and Mildred (Meyers) Salsbury; m. Murray Siegel, June 18, 1960; children: Lisa Siegel Machlin, Sheri, Harry. Student in Liberal Arts, U. N.C., Greensboro, 1958-60; student, Smithdeal-Massey Coll., Richmond, 1960-61; student in Music Edn., U. Richmond, 1968-79; student, Columbia U. Tchrs. Coll., 1970. Exec. dir. The Pianoforte Studio, Richmond, 1965-80; mgr., ptnr. Fashion Post Ltd., Richmond, 1965-80; dir. spl. events The Washington Opera, 1983-86; pres. Spl. Events Unltd., Gaithersburg, Md., 1985—; nat. dir. ops. and devel. Jewish War Vets. of U.S.A., Washington, 1986-88; cons., chief exec. officer The Right Source, Washington, 1988—. Author: At Thy Feet, 1974, Mission from Ischl, 1977, Family Traditions, 1986; contbr. over 50 articles to profl. jours.; composer of music and poetry. Sunday sch. and choir tchr. Beth El Synagogue, Richmond, 1956-58, short play and song writer, 1965-75, v.p., 1970-74; editor monthly newsletter Richmond Music Tchrs. Assn., 1973-80, sec., 1970-72, v.p., 1972-76, pres., 1976-80; v.p. Va. Music Tchrs. Assn., 1974-76, editor quar. newsletter, 1974-78; event coordinator Richmond Symphony Orch., 1973-76; Sunday sch. tchr. Beth Israel Synagogue, Richmond, 1975-80; dir. spl. events, fundraiser Washington Opera, 1982-85; choir dir. Gaithersburg Hebrew Congregation, 1985-86; originator Strategic Devel. Plan, Inc. for Jewish War Vets. of U.S.A., 1986-88, mgr. ops., 1986-88. Mem. Nat. Soc. Fund Raising Execs., Nat. Assn. Female Execs., Direct Mktg. Assn. of Washington. Home and Office: 9302 Sparrow Valley Dr Gaithersburg MD 20879

SIEGEL, LYNNE ELISE MOORE, lawyer; b. Sterling, Colo., Sept. 28, 1957; d. James Hamilton and Mabel Louise (White) Moore. B.A. in Liberal Arts, Colo. Coll., 1979; J.D., U. Denver, 1983. Bar: Colo. 1983. Law clk. Dailey, Goodwin et al, Aurora, Colo., 1980-81; asst. to prof. U. Denver, 1981; law clk. Gorsuch, Kirgis et al, Denver, 1982; summer assoc. Kirkland & Ellis, Denver, 1982; intern to presiding justice Denver Dist. Ct., 1983; assoc. Montgomery, Little, Young, Campbell & McGrew, Denver, 1983-88; law clk. to presiding judge, Colo. Ct. Appeals, 1988—. Past bd. dirs. Colo. Women's Employment and Edn., Inc.; bd. dirs. Colo. Spl. Olympics, Jr. League of Denver, Inc. Contbr. articles to profl. jours, chpts. to book. Denver Panhellenic scholar, 1977. Mem. ABA, Colo. Bar Assn., Kappa Alpha Theta (Founders' Meml. scholar). Home: 765 Lafayette St Denver CO 80218

SIEGERT, BARBARA MARIE, health care administrator; b. Boston, May 22, 1935; d. Salvatore Mario and Mary Kathleen (Wagner) Tartaglia; m. Herbert C. Siegert (dec. Apr. 1974); children: Carolyn Marie, Herbert Christian Jr. Diploma, Newton-Wellesley (Mass.) Hosp. Sch. Nursing, 1956; MEd, Antioch U., 1980. RN, Diplomate Am. Bd. Med. Psychotherapists. Supr. nursing Hogan Regional Ctr., Hathorne, Mass., 1974-78; community mental health nursing advisor Cape Ann area office Dept. Mental Health, Beverly, Mass., 1978-79, dir. case mgmt., 1979—; nursing edn. adv. com. North Shore Community Coll., Beverly, Mass., 1983—; tng. staff Balter Inst., Ipswich, Mass., 1987—. Recipient Spl. Recognition award Lexington (Mass.) Pub. Schs., 1973, Peter Torci award Lexington Friends of Children in Spl. Edn., 1974. Mem. Mass. Nurses Assn. Home: 63 B Willow Rd Boxford MA 01921 Office: Dept Mental Health Greater North Shore Office 180 Cabot St 2d Floor Beverly MA 01915

SIEGFRIED, JUDITH ANN, travel agency executive; b. Bethlehem, Pa., Jan. 20, 1943; d. Elmer John and Helen (Buich) Lopert; m. John W. Siegfried, Nov. 27, 1965 (div. 1976); children: Devon, Scott, Corey. Student, Bethlehem Bus. Coll., 1960-62. Sec. exec. offices Bethlehem Steel Corp., 1962-66; exec. sec., adminstrv. asst. Pearl Burns, eastern area mgr. Home Interiors & Gifts, Inc., Bethlehem, 1969-84; exec. dir. Westgate Travel, Bethlehem, 1984—. Mem. Am. Soc. Travel Agts., Cruise Lines Internat. Assn., Bethlehem Area C. of C. Democrat. Roman Catholic. Office: Westgate Travel 2640 Schoenersville Rd Bethlehem PA 18017

SIEH, MAURINE KAY, nurse; b. Leon, Iowa, Sept. 28, 1950; d. Vernon Charles and Dorothy Maxine (Akes) Dobson; B.S. in Nursing, N.E. Mo. State U., 1972; M.S. in Nursing, U. Miss.; m. Robert Hans Sieh, Nov. 18, 1972; children—Robert Carter, Jennifer Clarissa. Charge nurse psychiat. unit St. John's Hosp., Springfield, Mo., 1972-74; public health nurse Will County Health Dept., Joliet, Ill., 1974-75; unit nurse Mental Health Inst. (Elizabeth Ludeman Ctr.) Mentally Retarded Children, Park Forest, Ill., 1977-79; instr. Lamaze method childbirth, Park Forest, 1977-81; psychiat. nurse, chmn. nurse practice and standards com. Menninger Found., Topeka, 1981; nurse neuro-neurosurg. unit Univ. Med. Center, Jackson, Miss., 1981-82; prenatal nurse ob/gyn clinic U. Miss. Med. Ctr., 1982-86; with nursing faculty U. So. Miss., 1986—; instr. Lamaze method. Mem. Nat. League Nursing, Am. Soc. Psychoprophylaxis in Obstetrics, Internat. Childbirth Edn. Assn., Audubon Soc. and Nature Conservancy, Smithsonian Inst., Hastings Ctr., Sigma Theta Tau. Mem. Brethren Ch. Home: 4953 Oak Leaf Dr Jackson MS 39212

SIEKIERSKI, KAMILLA MALGORZATA, dental laboratory technician; b. Warsaw, Poland, Aug. 4, 1938; came to U.S., 1963, naturalized, 1970; d. Tomasz and Janina W. (Sendzimir) Piotrowski; cert. dental technician Sch. Dental Technicians, Krakow, Poland, 1957; m. Kazimierz Siekierski, Nov. 25, 1959; children—Marzanna, Eva. Owner, operator Kama's Dental Lab., Krakow, 1963; dental technician Dan's Dental Lab., Waterbury, Conn., 1963-65, Wilcox Dental Lab., Wethersfield, Conn., 1965-68; pres. Dentek, Inc., Milford, Conn., 1980—. Mem. Conn. Dental Lab. Assn. (pres. 1977-79), Nat. Assn. Dental Labs., Conf. Dental Labs. Home: 350 Gulf St Milford CT 06460 Office: 158 Cherry St Milford CT 06460

SIETMAN, ANNETTE MARIE, enrolled tax agent; b. Akron, Ohio, Mar. 13, 1944; d. Orville George and Ann Marie (Kloskowski) Seaver; B.S.Ed., Ohio State U., 1966; m. William Howard Ashcraft, Nov. 4, 1966 (dec. Dec. 1972); children—Julie, Joel; m. 2d, J. David Sietman, Mar. 22, 1974. Music tchr. Atherton Community Schs., Flint, Mich., 1966-67; music and math. tchr. Field Schs., Brimfield, Ohio, 1967-68; adminstrv. asst. H & R Block, Akron, 1970-72; bookkeeper Town & Country Interiors, Tallmadge, Ohio, 1972-75; owner Ashcraft Sietman Tax & Acctg. Service, Kent, Ohio, 1976—; income tax instr., 1971-72. Treas., St. Patrick Home and Sch. Assn., 80; mem. Kent City Income Tax Rev. Bd., 1982—. Mem. Ohio Soc. Enrolled Agts. (pres. 1977-78, 78-79, dir. 1979-85), Nat. Assn. Enrolled Agts. (sec. 1979-80, dir. 1980-82, v.p. 1982-83). Democrat. Roman Catholic. Home: 724 Grove Ave Kent OH 44240

SIEVERS, ARLENE MOORE, librarian; b. Evansville, Ind., Dec. 15, 1951; d. Fred Nunnelly and Billie Virginia (Moore) S. AB, Ind. U., 1972, MLS, 1973; postgrad., Butler U., 1977-80. Cataloger Willard Library, Evansville, 1973-76; librarian Indpls.-Marion County Pub. Library, 1976-80; acct. exec. Swets Subscription Service, Lisse, The Netherlands, 1980-84; sales rep. Ebsco Subscription Services, Birmingham, Ala., 1985; head serials dept. Ind.-Purdue U., Ft. Wayne, 1986—; del. Ind. Statewide Conf. on Libraries, Indpls., 1980, ann. conf. United Kingdom Serials Group, Oxford, Eng., 1987; N.Am. corr. United Kingdom Serials Group Jour., Serials. rep. Evansville Arts Council, 1975-76. Mem. ALA, Ind. Library Assn., N.Am. Serials Interest Group, United Kingdom Serials Group. Home: 7023 Lake Forest Village Circle Fort Wayne IN 46815 Office: Ind-Purdue U 2101 Coliseum Blvd E Fort Wayne IN 46805

SIEVERS, JUDY LOUISE, lumber company executive, controller, treasurer; b. Everett, Wash., May 27, 1942; d. Ralph Clarence and Peggy Joyce (Martin) Hershaw; m. John Henry Sievers, Aug. 31, 1972; children: Larry W. Jr., Lon Gregory, Lena Marie, Lee Edgar. Grad. high sch., Everett. Harvest truck driver Twin City Foods, Stanwood, Wash., 1957-60; pvt. practice in comml. art Arlington and Everett, Wash., 1960-69; florist staff mem. Peg's Floral Shop, Arlington, 1961-68; receptionist Reinell Boat Co., Marysville, Wash., 1969; with acctg., log control dept. Buse Timber & Sales, Inc., Marysville, 1969-84; store owner Clearwood Community Assn., Yelm, Wash., 1984-86; controller Brazier Forest Products, Inc., Tacoma, 1984-86, controller, corp. treas., 1986—. Tchr. Trinity Episcopal Ch., Everett, 1978; mem. Bald Hill Fire Dept., Yelm, 1984-86. Office: Arlington Forest Products Inc PO Box 3189 Arlington WA 98223

SIEWERT, ROBIN NOELLE, chemical engineer; b. Heidelberg, Fed. Republic Germany, Dec. 14, 1956; (parents Am. citizens); d. Orville Ray and Norma Idella (Sprink) S. BS in Chem. Enging., U. Tex., 1979. Registered profl. engr. Start-up engr. Cen. Power and Light Co., Fannin, Tex., 1979-81; chem. engr. Cen. Power and Light Co., Corpus Christi, Tex., 1981-85, performance analysis engr., 1985-87, performance analysis supr., 1987—. Mem. NSPE, Am. Inst. Chem. Engrs., Soc. Women Engrs., Alpha Chi Sigma (pres. 1975). Republican. Baptist. Home: 4005 C Acushnet Corpus Christi TX 78413 Office: Cen Power and Light Co PO Box 2121 Corpus Christi TX 78403

SIFF, MARLENE IDA, artist; b. N.Y.C., Sept. 20, 1936; d. Irving Louis and Dorothy Gertrude (Lahn) Marmer; m. Elliott Justin Siff, July 11, 1959; children: Bradford Evan, Brian Douglas. BA, Hunter Coll., 1957. Cert. elem. tchr., N.Y., N.J. Tchr. Stewart Manor (N.Y.) Sch. System, 1957-59, Teaneck (N.J.) Sch. System, 1959-60; free-lance interior designer Westport, Conn., 1966-70; designer indsl. plant design sect. Varo Inertial Products, Trumbull, Conn., 1970; corp. sec., treas. Belmar Corp., Westport, 1972—, also bd. dirs.; chmn. bd. Marlene Designs Inc., Westport, 1973-77; owner Marlene Siff Design Studio, Westport, 1978—; designer Signature Collections J.P. Stevens & Co., Inc., 1974-78, J.C. Penney Co., N.Y.C., 1978, C.R. Gibson Co., Norwalk, Conn., 1980; aesthetic cons. ALCIDE Corp., Norwalk, 1980—. One-woman shows include David Segal Gallery, N.Y.C., 1987, Conn. Pub. TV Gallery 24, Hartford, 1987. Mem. Westport Weston Arts Council, 1975-88; decorator ann. charity ball Easter Seal Home Service, 1976; mem. women's bd. dirs. United Jewish Appeal, Westport, 1982-86; mem. com. Levitt Pavillion Performing Arts, Westport, 1982-86. Recipient award Lower Conn. Mfrs. Assn., 1970. Mem. Kappa Pi. Jewish. Home: 15 Broadview Rd Westport CT 06880

SIFFORD, MARILYN OAKLEY, human resources director; b. Roxboro, N.C., May 18, 1948; d. Osborne Hanley Jr. and Remell (Tingen) Oakley; m. C. Darrell Sifford, June 16, 1977; stepchildren: Jay, Grant. Student, Mars Hill Coll., 1966-67; BA In Psychol., E. Carolina U., 1970; MS, Am. U., 1983. Truant officer Raleigh City Schs., 1970-72; analyst test research and devel. N.C. Employment Security Commn., Raleigh, 1972-74; personnel generalist Charlotte Observer and News, 1974-75, mgr. mkt. promotion, 1975-76; specialist tng. Colonial Penn. Ins. Co., Phila., 1976-77, supr. tng., 1977-80; cons. mgmt. Sun Co. Inc., Radnor, Pa., 1980-84; dir. human resource devel. Hosp. U. Penn., Phila., 1984-87; v.p., cons. CoreStates Fin. Corp., Phila. 1897—. Bd. dirs. Acad. House Condominium Council, Phila. 1985—. Mem. Human Resources Planning Group (sr. practitioner planning com. 1987-88), Orgn. Devel. Network (co-chair program com. 1987-88). Home: 1420 Locust St 37-K Philadelphia PA 19102 Office: CoreSts Fin Corp Broad and Chestnut Sts PO Box 7618 Philadelphia PA 19101

SIGAL, MARJORIE ANN, sales representative; b. Cin., May 12, 1956; d. Martin Richard and Paula E. (Schiff) Holstein; m. Marvin David Sigal. BS in Mktg., Ind. U., 1978. Asst. buyer women's sportswear Macy's Dept. Stores, Kansas City, Mo., 1978-79; sales mgr. jr. dept. Macy's Dept. Stores, Kansas City, 1979-80, supr. Elder Beerman, Dayton, Ohio, 1980-81; asst. buyer Elder Beerman, Dayton, 1981; buyer jr. activewear F&R Lazarus Co., Columbus and Cin., Ohio, 1981-86; mfrs. sales rep. Expression Wear Inc., Columbus, 1986—. Mem. Nat. Assn. Female Execs. Home: 752 S Roosevelt Columbus OH 43209

SIGERSON, MARJORIE LORRAINE, librarian; b. Pitts., June 11, 1923; d. Roy Allen and Myrtle Mae (Bering) Parke; student Carnegie Inst. Tech., 1941-42, U. Pitts., 1942-43; m. David Kinley Sigerson, Apr. 9, 1943 (div. Dec. 1985); children—Diane Parke, David Kinley. Librarian, Mus. Arts and Scis., Daytona Beach, Fla., 1963—, trustee, 1978—, pres. Guild, 1978-79. Mem. com. Halifax Art Festival, 1963—; mem. council Garden Clubs of Halifax Dist., 1965-67; charter mem. Ormond Beach (Fla.) Meml. Hosp. Aux., 1967-76; pres. Street Sch. P.T.A., New City, N.Y., 1958-59; leader Girl Scouts U.S.A., 1956-58. Recipient award for disting. service, Mus. Arts and Scis., 1977, 79, 80, 81, 82. Presbyterian. Clubs: Harvard Dames (sec. 1946-47), Cherry Laurel Garden (pres. 1966-67), Oceanside Country (v.p. 9-Hole Golf Group). Home: 410 John Anderson Dr Ormond Beach FL 32074 Office: Mus Arts and Scis 1040 Museum Blvd Daytona Beach FL 32014

SIGMAN, DEBORAH ELAINE, cosmetics and skin-care products company research executive. B.S.B.A., Loyola Coll., Balt., 1983. Market research analyst dept. market research Noxell Corp., Hunt Valley, Md., 1984, research guidance supr., 1984—, also mem. corp. packaging com., 1984—. Mem. ASTM. Office: Noxell Corp 11050 York Rd Hunt Valley MD 21030-2098

SIGMAN, HELENE HANNAH, public rlations executive; b. Chgo., Dec. 22, 1946; d. Edward Sigman and Helen Amanda (Hebert) Sigman Weil. AAS, Monticello Coll., 1967; BFA, U. Denver, 1969. Graphic designer Morgen Press, Hastings-on Hudson, N.Y., 1972, Murphey Printing Co., White Plains, N.Y., 1972-73; art dir. Cliggott Pub. Co., Greenwich, Conn., 1973-86; pub. relation supr. Ameritech, Chgo., 1987—. Recipient award Soc. Illustrators, 1986; Silver and Gold awards Advt. Club of Westchester, 1985. Jewish. Office: Ameritech 30 S Wacker Chicago IL 60606

SIGMON, ANNE ELIZABETH, marketing professional; b. Roanoke, Va., May 12, 1953; d. William E. and Betty (Hale) S.; m. John David Sutton, Feb. 14, 1987. ABJ magna cum laude, U. Ga., 1974; MBA, Golden Gate U., 1984. Writer Publs. South, Atlanta, 1973-74, Univ. System Ga., Atlanta, 1974-75; with pub. relations dept. Bechtel Group, Inc., San Francisco, 1975-79, editor, 1979-81, mgr. employee communications, 1981-84, mgr. communications, 1985-87; mgr. pub. relations Bechtel Petroleum, Inc., Houston, 1984-85; mgr. mktg. Bechtel Nat., Inc., San Francisco, 1987—; instr. profl. seminars, 1980—. Recipient profl. achievement awards Internat. Assn. Bus. Communicators, profl. achievement awards Film and TV Festival N.Y.C. Mem. Am. Mktg. Assn., Pub. Relations Soc. Am. (accredited), Phi Beta Kappa, Kappa Tau Alpha. Office: Bechtel Nat Inc PO Box 3965 San Francisco CA 94119

SIGNER, GLORIA JOYCE, automobile and truck dealer; b. Portland, Oreg., Apr. 23, 1925; d. Wilfred and Hazel Lucille (Pretty) Watson; m. Richard Ernest Signer, Sept. 6, 1947 (dec. 1970); children—Donald Richard, Janet Signer Muller, Jeanine Signer Garrett. B.S., Oreg. State U., Corvallis, 1947. Tchr. pub. schs., Portland, Oreg., 1948-50; automobile and truck dealer Signer Motors, Inc., Corvallis, 1970—; corp. treas. Wheels Life Ins. Co. Ltd., Grand Cayman, W.I., 1985—. Mem. Corvallis City Budget Rev. Commn., 1978—; mem. adv. council Coll. Bus, Oreg. State U., Corvallis, 1985—; mem. alumni bd. Oreg. State U., 1986—. Named Retailer of Yr., Corvallis C. of C., 1979; Time Quality Dealer (Oreg.), Time mag., 1983. Mem. Nat. Automobile Dealers Assn., Oreg. Automobile Dealers Assn. (dir. 1974-77), Corvallis Automobile Dealers Assn. (pres. 1975-78), Women Entrepreneurs of Oreg. (sec. 1984-85). Lodge: Rotary. Office: Signer Motors Inc 705 NW Buchanan St Corvallis OR 97330

SILACCI, HELEN BERNADETTE, nurse; b. Hanford, Calif., Apr. 19, 1943; d. Antone P. and Mary P. (Portugal) Silveira; m. Gary E. Silacci, Dec. 2, 1966; children: Gary Jr., Nicole, Brent. BS in Nursing, Calif. State U., Fresno, 1966; postgrad., San Jose (Calif.) State U., 1971, U. San Francisco, 1976, U. Santa Cruz, 1986—. Cert. sch. nurse, Calif.; cert. fin. planner, Calif. Pub. health nurse Santa Clara County Health Dept., San Jose, 1967-69; sch. nurse Morgan Hill (Calif.) Unified Sch. Dist., 1969—; model Merchants Assn. Morgan Hill, 1980—; fin. planner Silacci Enterprises, Morgan Hill, 1986—; trainer health edn. Editor Nutrition Edn. Newsletter for Community, 1979-83. Officer Alice In Wonderland chpt. Children's Home Soc., Morgan Hill, 1970—; instr. first-aid ARC, San Jose, 1970-78; writer Project Self, 1971-73; commr. health City of Morgan Hill, 1974-78; coordinator Berkeley Health Edn. Project for Schs., 1977-82; mem. Citizens Against Drug Abuse, Morgan Hill, 1980—; chairperson fin. com. St. Catherine's Parish, Morgan Hill, 1983-86. Recipient Health Edn. award Santa Clara County, 1978; Calif. State Dept. Edn. grantee, 1980-83. Mem. Internat. Assn. for Fin. Planning, Nat. Assn. Sch. Nursing, Nat. Comml. Fin. Assn., Calif. Sch. Nurses Orgn. (chairperson research com. 1981-83, chairperson membership com. 1983-86, treas. 1987—, Outstanding Leadership award 1983-85, Sch. Nurse of Yr. award 1986-87), Morgan Hill C. of C., Delta Gamma. Republican. Office: Silacci Enterprises PO Box 68 Morgan Hill CA 95037

SILBERSTEIN, MARY ELIZABETH, retail executive; b. India, Tex., Sept. 12, 1936; d. Willie Lee and Essie (Hall) Witherspoon; m. Ross Lyman Silberstein, aug. 11, 1962 (dec. 1987); children: William Brett, Elizabeth Kate Wallace. Grad. high sch., Ferris, Tex. Pres. MS Ladies Shoe Boutique Inc., Ennis, Tex., 1987—. Treas. Glenwood Park Little League Assn., Decatur, Ga., 1973-75; vol. Home Meals Delivery, Richmond, Ky., 1983-87; tchr. Girl's Aux., 1970-78; dir. Sunday Sch. grades 1 & 2, 1976-80, grades 5 & 6, 1980-85, divisional dir. grades 1-6, 1985-86; active Ch. Women's Missionary Soc., 1964-87, children and youth choirs, 1970-81; treas. Pattie A. Clay Hosp. Aux. 1985-87, bd. dirs., Pink Lady, 1985-87, vol. gift shop, 1984-87, mem. com. for annual charity ball, 1984-86. Mem. U.S. C. of C., Ennis C. of C., Ennis Downtown Merchants Assn. Republican. Baptist. Office: MS Ladies Shoe Boutique 113 N Dallas Rd Ennis TX 75119

SILBERT, JACQUELINE, service company executive, accountant; b. Bklyn., Dec. 15, 1921; d. Leon and Mary Gittell; children—Laurence, Amy Silbert Block. B.A. in Edn. with honors, Hunter Coll., 1942. Co-founder MacClean Service Co. Inc., Bellerose, N.Y., 1953, pres., chief exec. officer, 1982—; dir. Liberty Nat. Bank, Conn. Editor: Hunter Coll. Alumni Newspaper, 1970-72. Contbr. articles to real estate publications. Mem. R.I. State Bd. Edn., 1950-52; bd. dirs., v.p. The Lighthouse, Queens, N.Y., 1970-74, chmn. fund raising, 1971-72; pres., bd. dirs. St. John's U. Aux., 1970—, co-chmn. fund raising, 1976—; bd. dirs. Walter Kaner's Childrens Fund, 1982—, Forest Hills Jewish Ctr. Aux., 1972-74. Named Woman of Yr., Nat. Conf. Christians & Jews, 1975; Pres. medal St. John's U., 1978. Mem. Bldg. Service Contractor's Assn., Internat. Sanitary Supply Assn., Service Employer's Assn. Club: Old Westbury Hebrew Congregation Bridge. Avocation: growing trees. Office: MacClean Service Co Inc PO Box 78 Bellerose NY 11426

SILBURN, ELAINE GWENDOLYN, banker; b. Denver, June 3, 1937; d. Russell Edwin and Genevieve (Johnson) Seay; m. David L. Silburn, June 16, 1957; children: Carla Anne, James Russell. A in Bus. Adminstrn., U. Denver, 1957; student Northwestern U., 1960, U. Okla., 1981. Trust officer United Bank of Denver, 1957-65; personal banker, personal banking officer, asst. v.p., v.p. United Bank of Skyline, Denver, 1978-83, sr. v.p., 1983—, dir., 1984—; treas. Historic Denver, Inc., bd. dirs., 1988 . Vol. Denver Pub. Schs., alumni fund campaign U. Denver, Channel 6 Pub. TV Auction, 1983, Am. Cancer Soc., mem. major gifts fund com. Denver Symphony Orch., 1984—; adv. bd. Mile High United Way, 1985; del. Rep. county and state assemblies; vol. Hist. Denver, Inc. Recipient Women of Achievement award YWCA, 1985, 87. Mem. Nat. Assn. Bank Women, Mental Health Assn. Colo. (fin. devel. com.), Leadership Denver Assn., Denver C. of C., Cultural Affairs Task Force, Gamma Phi Beta. Episcopalian. Club: Sweet Adelines, (High Country chpt.) (pres. 1977). Home: 3119 S Akron Ct Denver CO 80231 Office: United Bank of Skyline NA 1055 16th St Denver CO 80202

SILER, INA CATHY, trainer, educator; b. Washington, July 10, 1951; d. Floyd Howard and Helen (Gill) Siler. Student Fisk U., 1969-71; B.A. magna cum laude, Howard U., 1973, M.A., 1975; postgrad., Purdue U., 1976-77; Ph.D., U. Okla., 1980. Instr. Bowie (Md.) State Coll., 1975-76, U. D.C., 1975-76; communications specialist Nat. Park Service, Washington, 1975-77; asst. prof. No. Ill. U., DeKalb, 1980-83; account exec. trainer Home Box Office, Inc., Atlanta, 1983—; cons. Nat. Capitol Parks, Washington, 1976-77, Ill. Bd. Edn., Springfield, 1980-83; recruiter grad. sch. U. Okla., Norman, 1979-80. Vol. Stateville Correctional Ctr., Joliet, Ill., 1982, Dwight (Ill.) Correctional Ctr., 1983; com. mem. NAACP, Atlanta, 1983—. Recipient awards United Way, 1986, 87; named outstanding tchr. dept. communications, U. Okla., 1979; Nat. Fellowships Fund fellow, 1983—. Mem. Am. Soc.

Tng. and Devel., Internat. Listening Assn., Ill. Speech and Theatre Assn., Women in Cable, Atlanta Women's Network. Mem. United Ch. of Christ. Office: Home Box Office Inc 3475 Lenox Rd NE Suite 1000 Atlanta GA 30319

SILFEN, NINA PAMELA, lawyer; b. N.Y.C., July 14, 1956; d. Milton and Mae (Cosiver) S. BA, Cornell U., 1978; JD, Boston U., 1981. Bar: N.Y. 1982. Assoc. Howard I. Brenner, P.C., N.Y.C., 1982-83; estate adminstr. Chase Manhattan Bank, N.A., N.Y.C., 1983-85; assoc. Brauner Baron Rosenzweig Kligler Sparber Bauman & Klein, N.Y.C., 1985—. Topics editor Am. Jour. Law and Medicine, 1980-81; contbr. articles to profl. jours. Mem. N.Y. State Bar Assn., Assn. of Bar of City of N.Y. Office: Brauner Baron Rosenzweig et al 61 Broadway New York NY 10006

SILHAN, GAILYA S(UE), radio station executive; b. Salzburg, Austria, July 31, 1955; came to U.S., 1956; d. Ronald Thomas and Linda Gaye (Richards) Williams; m. Jerry Daniel Silhan, Dec. 3, 1982. Student pub. schs., Ft. Worth. Sec. Stewart Title Co., Ft. Worth, 1971-74, Tex. Title Co., Ft. Worth, 1974-75; sec./closer 1st Land Title, Ft. Worth, 1975-78; sales and account exec. Sta.-KPLX, Ft. Worth/Dallas, 1978-83, sales promotion dir. Stas.-KPLX/KLIF, Ft. Worth/Dallas, 1983-85, account exec., 1985-86; local sales mgr. Sta. KTXQ, CBS Radio, Dallas, 1986-87; gen. sales mgr. KTKS/KOAI, 1987-88; v.p., gen. mgr. KOAI, 1988—. Named Top Salesperson, Susquehanna Broadcasting Co., 1981-83; named to Million Dollar Sales Club, 1983. Mem. Am. Women in Radio and TV (bd. dirs. Ft. Worth chpt. 1980-81), Assn. Broadcasting Execs. (pres. Tex. chpt.), Radio Mktg. Assn. Home: 7017 Meadow Lake Dallas TX 75214 Office: 8235 Douglas Suite 700 Dallas TX 75225

SILKOTCH, CHERYL MAE, financial executive, consultant; b. Sioux City, Iowa, Oct. 15, 1948; d. Leland Leroy and Frances Elaine (Beaubien) Masters White; m. Stephen Paul Silkotch, June 1, 1973; children—Stephen Paul IV, Sheri Lynn. Student U. Alaska, 1969-70, Los Angeles Harbor Coll., 1983-84. Lobby desk clk. Polaris Hotel, Fairbanks, Alaska, 1968-69; sec. security Loomis Armored Car, Fairbanks, 1969; sec., asst. mgr. R & M Engring., Fairbanks, 1969-71; sec. acctg. E.W. Hahn, Inc., El Segundo, Calif., 1971-73; sales rep. Tri-Chem Inc., Newark, 1977-81; acctg. cons. Silkotch Enterprises, Anza, Calfi., 1979—; bookkeeper, payroll clk., sec., various bus.; v.p. PTA, Harbor City, Calif., 1981-82, 83-84 (Outstanding Achievement award Los Angeles 10th Dist. 1983); modeling coordinator Miss Anza Queen Com., 1980-82. Recipient Outstanding Service awards Lions Club Am., Anza, Calif., 1980. 1981. Mem. Nat. Assn. Female Execs., Terwilliger Assn., North Shore Animal League (Gold Club 1980-84), Anza C. of C. (bookkeeper new memberships 1981-83, Outstanding Service award 1981). Clubs: DeAnza Heritage (Anza); Postal Commemorative Soc. (Norwalk, Conn.). Home and office: 60710 Coyote Canyon Rd Star Route 1 Box 239 Anza CA 92306

SILLIMAN, ELAINE JOYCE RUBENSTEIN, speech and language pathologist, educator; b. Buffalo, June 16, 1938; d. Joseph and Dorothy Fineberg Rubenstein; B.S., Syracuse U., 1960; Ph.D. (NDEA fellow), CUNY, 1976; m. Paul Harris Silliman, Jan. 28, 1961; children—Scott L., Dawn R. Speech-lang. clinician Bronx Mcpl. Hosp. Center, 1960-62; supr. speech-lang. services USPHS community health project Albert Einstein Coll. Medicine, Bronx, 1966-68; clin. supr. Center for Communication Disorders, Hunter Coll., CUNY, 1973-76, prof. Sch. Health Scis., 1976-87, dir. communication scis. program, 1981-84, 85-87, acting dean, 1984-85; doctoral faculty CUNY program speech and hearing scis., 1984-87; prof., chair Dept. Communicology U. South Fla., 1987—.Fellow Am. Speech-Lang.-Hearing Assn. (cert. clin. competence); mem. N.Y. Acad. Scis., N.Y. State Speech-Lang.-Hearing Assn. (pres. 1982-84), Fla. Speech-Lang.-Hearing Assn., Soc. Research in Child Devel. Contbr. articles to profl. jours.; editorial bd. Lang., Speech & Hearing Services in Schools, 1983—. Office: U South Fla Dept Communicology CBA255 Tampa FL 33620

SILLMAN, EDLYNNE MINA, caseworker, consultant; b. Bklyn., July 25, 1943; d. Israel and Frances L. (Katz) S. BS, N.Y.U., 1965; MA, Bklyn. Coll., 1968; certificate Mediation, Ill. Psychol. Inst., 1985. Licensed realtor, Ill. Tchr. art Lefferts Jr. High Sch., Bklyn., 1965-69, Ridge High Sch., Basking Ridge, N.J., 1969-72; tchr. art history Middlesex City Jr. Coll., Edison, N.J., 1973; owner, mgr. Edlynne and Friends Inc., New Brunswick, N.J., 1972-73; instr. travel and sales Wal-Mar Hobby Distbr., Boston, 1973-74; mgr. sales Halperin Galleries, Chgo., 1975; instr., salesperson Lanier Bus. Systems, Chgo., 1974-76; with real estate sales Kaplan Real Estate, Chgo., 1977-79; caseworker Dept. Supportive Services Cook County, Chgo., 1979—; owner Sillman Advt. Design, Chgo., 1985—; loan originator Attys. Nat. Mortgage Network Inc., Chgo., 1987—; playbill designer Victory Gardens Benefit, Chgo. 1986—. Asst. pub. Key Line and Design Mag., 1985-86. Vol. Chgo. Symphony Marathon, 1987. Mem. HAKAFA, Women's Advt. Chgo. (edu. com. 1985—, pub. service com. 1985—), Nat. Assn. Female Exec., Bklyn. Coll. Alumni Assn. Chgo. chpt. (pres. 1981-84). Democrat. Jewish. Home: 5415 N Sheridan Rd #2209 Chicago IL 60640 Office: Cook County Dept Supportive Services 118 N Clark St Room 618 Chicago IL 60602

SILLS, BEVERLY (MRS. PETER B. GREENOUGH), opera company director, coloratura soprano; b. Bklyn., May 25, 1929; d. Morris and Sonia (Bahn) Silverman; m. Peter B. Greenough, 1956; stepchildren: Lindley, Nancy, Diana; children: Meredith, Peter B. Grad. pub. schs.; student voice, Estelle Leibling; student piano, Paolo Gallico; student stagecraft, Desire Defrere; hon. doctorates, Harvard U., NYU, New Eng. Conservatory, Temple U. Gen. dir. N.Y.C. Opera, 1979-88; radio debut as Bubbles Silverman on Uncle Bob'sRainbow House, 1932; appeared on Major Bowes Capitol Family Hour, 1934-41, on Our Gal Sunday; toured with Shubert Tours, Charles Wagner Opera Co., 1950, 51; operatic debut Phila. Civic Opera, 1947; debut, N.Y.C. Opera Co. as Rosalinda in Die Fledermaus, 1955; debut San Francisco Opera, 1953; debut La Scala, Milan as Pamira in Siege of Corinth, 1969, Royal Opera, Covent Garden in Lucia di Lammermoor, London, 1971, Met. Opera, N.Y.C., 1975, Vienna State Opera, 1967, Teatro Fenice in La Traviata, Venice; appeared Teatro Colon, Buenos Aires; recital debut Paris, 1971, London Symphony Orch., 1971; appeared throughout U.S., Europe, S. Am. including Boston Symphony, Tanglewood Festival, 1968, 69, Robin Hood Dell, Phila., 1969; title roles in: Don Pasquale, Norma, Manon, Louise, Tales of Hoffmann, Daughter of the Regiment, The Magic Flute; ret. from opera and concert stage, 1980; numerous TV spls; author: Bubbles-A Self-Portrait, 1976, autobiography Beverly, 1987. Nat. chmn. March of Dimes' Mothers' March on Birth Defects; chmn. bd. Nat. Opera Inst.; cons. to council Nat. Endowment for the Arts; bd. dirs. N.Y.C. Opera. Recipient Handel medallion, 1973, Pearl S. Buck Women's award, 1979, Emmy award for Profiles in Music, 1976, Emmy award for Lifestyles with Beverly Sills, 1978, Medal of Freedom, 1980. Office: NYC Opera NY State Theater Lincoln Ctr New York NY 10023 •

SILSBY, LUCILLE LINDA, systems analyst; b. Saco, Maine, Aug. 22, 1953; d. Joseph Ronald and Doris Yvonne (Geoffroy) Boucher; m. Michael Joseph Silsby, Mar. 18, 1972; 1 child, Joseph Michael. Rater, coder Liberty Mut. Ins., Co., Portsmouth, N.H., 1972-73, tech. asst., 1973-80, programmer, 1980-85, systems analyst, 1985—; real estate assoc. CB Meadowbrook, York, Maine, 1986-88. Com. mem. Boy Scouts Am.; mem. choir St. Christopher's Ch., York. Mem. Million Dollar Club. Democrat. Roman Catholic. also: CB Meadowbrook Rt 1 York ME 03909

SILVA, JAYNE LANDIS, trade commission executive; b. Dover, Ohio, Nov. 26, 1925; d. Merle Dewey and Orpha (MutschelKnaus) Landis; m. Daniel Joseph Silva, Mar. 30, 1946; children: Elena Silva Cunningham, Karen Silva Morales, Janiel Silva Gammon, David Mark. Student, Prince George's Coll., 1970-74, U. Md., 1974-76. Columnist Prince George's Post, Hyattsville, Md., 1949-51; writer Am. Hort. Soc., Bladensburg, Md., 1954-58; sec. Fed. Prison Industries, Inc., Washington, 1958-62; asst. to atty. gen. Washington, 1962-63; adminstrv. asst. Goddard Space Flight Ctr., Greenbelt, Md., 1963-72; staff asst. U.S. Trade Commn., Washington, 1972-84, asst. to sec., 1980-84; treas., co-editor Scop Publs. Inc., College Park, Md., 1979—, also bd. dirs. Contbr. poetry to mags., anthologies. V.p. Glenn Dale (Md.) PTA, 1965-66; bd. dirs. Hammond Village Citizens Assn. Mem. Md. Poetry Soc. (v.p. 1977-78, bd. dirs. 1979-80, 1st place award 1977). Republican. Seventh Day Adventist. Home: 10479 Graeloch Rd Laurel MD 20707

SILVA, LADON GAY, dietitian; b. Ft. Campbell, Ky., Oct. 22, 1954; d. Smiles Manning and Martha Jane (Porter) S. BS, Calif. Poly. State U., 1977. Dir. food services Cottonwood (Calif.) Union Sch. Dist., 1977-78; dietetic intern U. Calif. Hosps. and Clinics, San Francisco, 1978-79; clin. dietician Bakersfield (Calif.) Meml. Hosp., 1979—; cons. Centre for Neuroskills, Bakersfield, 1980-85, Dr. Shivinder Deol, Bakersfield, 1985-86, Bakersfield Community Hosp., 1984—, Kern Valley Hosp., Colonial Hosp., Hilltop Convalescent Hosp., 1985—, Charter Hosp. Bakersfield, 1988—. Mem. Bakersfield Rep. Assembly, 1987—. Mem. Calif. Sch. Food Service Assn. (v.p. Shasta Cascade chpt. 1978), Calif. Dietetic Assn. (rep. legisl. info and pub. policy com. 1986-87), Diabetic Educators Assn., Cons. Nutritionists Assn., Kern County Nutrition Council. Methodist. Office: Bakersfield Meml Hosp 420 34th St Bakersfield CA 93301

SILVA, MARIANNE ALTER, health science facility administrator; b. Santa Monica, Calif., Aug. 28, 1952; d. Marvin Scribner Alter and Ellen May (Scott) Wursten; m. Jan Corwyn McHenry, Nov. 22, 1975 (div. 1980); m. Michael Dean Silva, Apr. 20, 1985; children: Michael Leonard, Mary Katharine. BA in Biology, Calif. State U., Northridge, 1975; MS in Med. Tech., Calif. State U., Dominguez Hills, 1980. Cert. med. technologist, specialist in blood banking. Intern med. tech. St. John's Hosp. and Health Ctr., Santa Monica, Calif., 1976; bench technologist Meml. Hosp. Long Beach, Calif., 1976-78, sr. technologist, 1978-80; supr. reference lab. U. Calif. Irvine Med. Ctr., Orange, 1981-82; supr. blood bank Northridge Hosp. Med. Ctr., 1982-86; cons., lectr. Encino, Calif., 1986-87; assoc. prof. Calif. State U. Dept. Microbiology, Los Angeles, 1987—. Mem. Am. Assn. Blood Banks (insp.), Am. Soc. Clin. Pathologists, Serum Cell Soc. (bd. dirs. 1981-82, chair 1982-84). Republican. Baptist. Office: PO Box 192 Encino CA 91316

SILVA, PAULINE MARIE, product technology analyst; b. Arlington, Mass., Aug. 18, 1959. BA in Polit. Sci., Dickinson Coll., 1982; MA in Telecommunications Policy, George Washington U., 1987. Data collector Met. Radio Telephone Systems, Kensington, Md., 1982-83; market analyst Radiotel of Am., Rockville, Md., 1983-85; product tech. analyst Arlington (Va.) County Govt., 1985-87, telecommunications project mgr., 1987—. Internat. Communications Assn. scholar, 1986, 85. Mem. Nat. Assn. Telecommunications Officers and Advisors (conf. speaker 1987), Alumnet. Office: Arlington County Govt 2100 N 14th St G-3 Arlington VA 22201

SILVA, PHYLLIS C., state official; b. Woonsocket, R.I., May 6, 1928; d. Reuben Ballou and Alice (Carr) Cook; m. J. Camille Peloquin, Sept. 5, 1949 (div. 1973); children—J. Camille, Linda Peloquin Clayton, Ronald, Theodore; m. 2d John L. Silva, June 26, 1977. Student U. R.I., Catholic Tchrs. Coll. Reg. genealogist. Spinner Black Cotton Mill, Blackstone, Mass., 1944-49; lacquer sprayer Brier Mfg. Co., Providence, 1949-56; tchr. Woonsocket Sch. System (R.I.), 1956-67; asst. sec. of state in charge of archives Office of R.I. Sec. of State, Providence, 1967—; coordinator Hist. Records Adv. Bd. R.I., 1976—; lectr. on state archives, 1980—; coordinator Nat. Hist. Publs. and Records, 1976—. Bd. dirs. New Eng. Conservation Ctr., 1978-82. Named Brevet col. Newport Arty. (R.I.), 1976. Mem. R.I. Geneal. Soc. (1st v.p.), Soc. Am. Archivists, Bristol Hist. Soc. Roman Catholic. Office: Sec of State's Office State House Rm 43 Providence RI 02903

SILVA, RUTH CARIDAD, political scientist; b. Lincoln, Nebr.; d. Ignatius Dominic and Beatrice (Davis) S. BA, U. Mich., 1943, MA, 1943, PhD, 1948. Instr. Wheaton Coll., Norton, Mass., 1946-48; faculty Pa. State U., University Park, 1948—, prof. polit. sci., 1959—; Fulbright prof. polit. sci. Cairo U., 1952-53; vis. prof. Hunter Coll., N.Y.C., 1948, John Hopkins U., 1965; spl. cons. U.S. Dept. Justice, 1957, N.Y. State Constn. Commn., 1959-60, Pa. State Constn. Commn., 1967-68; mem. Pres.'s Commn. Post Secondary Edn., 1972-73. Author: Presidential Succession, 1951, Legislative Apportionment in New York, 1960; Rum, Religion and Votes: 1928 Re-examined, 1962; co-author: American Government, Democracy and Liberty in Balance, 1976; contbr. articles in field to profl. jours. Mem. Am. Polit. Sci. Assn. (past sec., chmn. com. status of women in profession 1972-73, v.p. 1972-73), Acad. Polit. Sci., AAUP (chmn. com. relation of govt. to higher edn. 1964-68), Nat. Municipal League, Phi Kappa Phi, Chi Omega. Republican. Roman Catholic. Clubs: University; U. Mich. Pres.'s (Ann Arbor). Home: 801 Southgate D Apt B-4 State College PA 16801

SILVER, ADELE ZEIDMAN, museum editor; b. Birmingham, Ala., Feb. 16, 1932; d. Eugene Morris and Ida L. (Fisher) Zeidman; m. Daniel Jeremy Silver, July 19, 1956; children: Jonathan M., Michael L., Sarah V. BA, Goucher Coll., 1953. Editorial asst. Sunday dept. N.Y. Times, 1954-56; freelance editor, book reviewer N.Y.C., 1963-70; columnist editorial pages The Plain Dealer, Cleve., 1968-74, book reviewer, 1968—; dep. project dir., editor Council on Museums and Edn. in the Visual Arts, N.Y.C., Cleve., 1972-76; arts editor, critic Sta. WKYC-TV, Cleve., 1975-79; editor edn. publs. Cleve. Mus. Art, 1971-82, head pub. info. dept., 1982—; mem. Artable, N.Y.C., 1980; cons. Albright-Knox Art Gallery, Buffalo, 1978-79, Mpls. Inst. Arts, 1981. Co-editor: The Art Museum As An Educator, 1978. Trustee Cleve. Opera, 1974-86, Cleve. Internat. Film Festival, 1975—. Democrat. Jewish. Office: Cleveland Mus Art 11150 East Blvd Cleveland OH 44106

SILVER, BELLA WOLFSON, day care center executive; b. N.Y.C., Mar. 10, 1937; d. David Michael and Edith (Bienenstock) Wolfson; B.S., Adelphi U., 1958; postgrad. Bank St. Coll., 1958-59; m. Kenneth A. Silver, Oct. 19, 1958; children—James, Daniel. Kindergarten tchr., N.Y.C., 1958, Madison (Wis.) Public Schs., 1959-61, White Fish Bay (Wis.) Public Schs., 1961-65; nursery sch. tchr., Deerfield, Ill., 1975-77; substitute tchr. Deerfield Public Schs., 1975-77; founder., dir., pres. Deerfield Day Care Center, 1978—; corp. cons. Day Care/Child Care Services, 1983—; pub. speaker on child care to North Shore high schs., 1984. Mem. Deerfield Caucus; active Cub Scouts, Deerfield, Outstanding Service award 1973-77; mem. exec. bd. Jewish United Fund; sec. Parents-Tchrs. Orgn. Recipient award Bahais of Deerfield, 1981; teaching cert., Wis., Ill.; lic. tchr., N.Y.C. Mem. AAUW, Assn. Childhood Edn. Internat., Nat. Assn. Edn. Young Children, Chgo. Assn. Edn. Young Children, Nat. Assn. Female Execs., Deerfield C. of C., Phi Sigma Sigma (Pyramid award 1965). Jewish. Home: 309 Willow Ave Deerfield IL 60015 Office: 445 Pine St Deerfield IL 60015

SILVER, FERN RENÉE, small business owner; b. Chgo., Jan. 24, 1943; d. Milton and Ida (Glickman) Simon; divorced; children: Stacey, Lisa, Judd. BE, U. Ill., 1963; student, U. Ill. Chgo. Tchrs. Coll., 1964. Tchr. Chgo. Bd. Edn., 1964-66; adminstr. civil rights div. State of Ohio, Columbus, 1975-76; with sales dept. Xerox Corp., Toledo, 1976-78; sales cons. recognition div. Jostens, Toledo, 1978-80; prin. Fern Silver & Assocs., Toledo, 1980—; cons., speaker New Eng. Life Ins., Boston, 1983—; speaker Nat. Assn. Life Underwriters, Kansas City, Mo., 1984, Tex. Assn. Life Underwriters, Dallas, 1985, Shelby Williams, Morristown, Tenn., 1986. Contbr. Nalu mag., 1984; creator, designer commemorative mugs, 1981 (P.M. Mag. award 1983), 1983. Pres. Steps Toward Ending Personal Prejudice, Chgo., 1958-60; chmn. polit. action No. Communities Operation Breadbasket, Chgo., 1969-70; bd. dirs. Make A Wish Found., Toledo, 1983-86; active Entertainment Action Team, Chgo., 1986-87. Named Woman of Month Lerner Newspapers, 1970. Mem. Nat. Assn. Female Execs., Specialty Advt. Assn., Advt. Specialty Inst., Specialty Advt. Chgo. Jewish. Home and Office: 5453 N Kenmore Chicago IL 60640

SILVER, HELENE MARCIA, health educator; b. Oakland, Calif., Apr. 2, 1947; d. Sam and Shirley Betty (Kerns) Silver. BA, UCLA, 1968; postgrad., San Francisco State Coll., 1970-72, Holistic Life U., 1978-79, Antioch U., 1979-80. Tchr. pub. schs., Oakland, 1968-76; nutritional counselor, Mill Valley, Calif., 1976-79; creator Women's Health Intensive, Mill Valley, 1977-79; project dir. nutrition edn. project Calif. Dept. Edn., San Rafael, 1979-80; founder, dir. Inst. Colon Hygiene, Inner Beauty Inst., San Rafael, 1980—; health edn. cons. 1976—; founder Inner Beauty Mountain Retreat, 1987—; mem. Health Task Force in Marin County, 1978—. Author: Inner Beauty/Outer Beauty. Mem. Soc. Nutrition Edn., AAUW, Prison Reform Assn. Office: 3A Gate 5 Rd Sausalito CA 94965

SILVER, JEAN, state legislator, accountant; b. Spokane, Wash., July 25, 1926; d. Harlow Eugene and Helen Grace (Merten) Merrill; m. Charles Wesley Silver; children: Douglas W., Mitchell C., Kipp E. BBA, Eastern Wash. U., 1975; postgrad., U. Wash., 1980-87. CPA, Wash. Prin. Jean Silver Acctg. Service, Spokane, 1950—; acct. Coopers & Lybrand, Spokane, 1976-80; state legislator State of Wash., Olympia, 1983—; cons. econ. devel. financing City and County of Spokane, 1980-86; bd. dirs. Washington Water Power Co. Bd. dirs. Greater Spokane Bus. Devel. Assn., 1980—, Med. Service Corp. of Eastern Wash., Spokane, 1984—, Holy Names Ft. George Wright, Spokane, 1984—, Displaced Homemakers, Spokane, 1985—; trustee Holy Family Hosp., Spokane, 1986—, Jr. League, 1987—; mem. adv. bd. Spokane Incubator Assn., 1987—. Named Legislator of Yr. Assn. Builders and Contractors, 1985, Outstanding Govt. Woman of Yr. YWCA, 1988. Mem. CPAs Soc., Econ. Devel. Execs. of Wash. Republican. Office: Washington State Legislature HOB #413 Olympia WA 98504

SILVER, JOYCE ALAINE, business executive, banker, former pharmaceutical manufacturing company executive; b. N.Y.C., Dec. 2, 1942; d. Leo and Ida Vera Silver; B.A., Simmons Coll., Adelphi U., 1962; M.S., L.I. U., 1973; Ph.D. candidate Cornell U. Med. Center, N.Y. U. Med. Center, 1973-76; div.; children—Edward Erik, Lisa Sheryl. Research fellow Cornell U.-N.Y. U. Med. Center, 1973-76; supervising engr., plant trouble shooter Ford Motor Co., Dearborn, Mich., 1976-79; with Pfizer, Inc., Bklyn., 1979-82, sr. mfg. supr. diagnostics and sterile products, 1981-82, mgr. materials resource planning, mgr. pharm. warehousing, distbn. ops., 1981-82; v.p. customer service Bankers Trust Co., N.Y.C., 1982-84, pres. and owner Artistic Floors Inc., L.I., N.Y., 1984—. Lobbyist, Continuation of NSF Funds, 1974; mem. Com. to Re-Elect Carol Berman, Senator, 1979. NIH Fellowship, 1973-76; L.I. U. Teaching Fellowship and Scholarship award, 1971-73. Mem. AAAS, Fedn. Am. Scientists, Engring. Soc. Detroit, N.Y. Acad. Sci., Women's Economic Club Detroit, N.Y. Women's Bus. and Profl. Group, N.Y. Networking.

SILVER, JOYCE RUTH, psychotherapist; b. Cambridge, Mass., Sept. 4, 1933; d. Irving and Iris (Alpert) S.; m. Ralph Goldberg, July 2, 1970 (div. Mar. 1985); 1 child, Shoshana. Cert., Cooper Union Coll., N.Y.C., 1954; BFA, U. N.Mex., 1957. Pvt. practice specializing in psychotherapy N.Y.C., 1970—. Contbr. articles to profl. jours. Mem. Assn. for Psychoanalytic Self Psychology, Internat. Inst. Bioenergetic Analysts (trainer), Boston Bioenergetic Soc. (trainer), Phila. Bioenergetic Soc. (trainer), Chgo. Bioenergetic Soc. (trainer), N.Y. Soc. Bioenergetic Analysis (bd. dirs. 1979-84), Conn. Soc. Bioenergetic Analysis (assoc. trainer 1984—). Home and Office: 127 Greene St New York NY 10012

SILVER, RUGENIA, lawyer, accountant; b. Hollister, N.C., Oct. 26, 1950; d. Blake and Geneva (Lynch) S. BA, Temple U., 1975; JD, George Washington U., 1980. Bar: D.C. 1980. Atty. Fed. Res. Bd., Washington, 1980-85; auditor U.S. GAO, Washington, 1976-77; sr. assoc. Weiner, McCaffrey, Brodsky & Kaplan, Washington, 1985-88; assoc. gen. counsel The Prudential Home Mortgage Co., Md., 1988—. Vol. D.C. Vols., Washington, 1979. Pres.'s scholar Temple U., 1975; named one of Outstanding Young Women in Am., 1982. Mem. Women in Housing and Fin., Mortgage Bankers Assn. (cons. truth in lending 1986—), ABA. Office: The Prudential Home Mortgage Co 900 Clopper Rd Gaithersburg MD 20878

SILVERHART, SONDRA (GOLDMAN), real estate executive; b. Bklyn., Dec. 13, 1932; d. Sol and Mae (Terry) Goldman; m. David Silverhart, Apr. 4, 1954; children: Todd, Peter (dec.). Cert. residential specialist, Realtors Mktg. Inst., 1979. Pres. Silverhart Assocs., Saratoga Springs, N.Y., 1969-82, Saratoga Ctr. for Real Estate, Inc., Saratoga Springs, 1982—; mem. adv. bd. Norstar Bank Upstate N.Y., Saratoga Springs, 1981—, Transitional Services, Saratoga Springs, 1986—; sec., treas. Real Estate Appraisal Ctr, Inc., 1987. Bd. dirs. Saratoga County Arts Council, Saratoga Springs, 1986-87; mem. adv. bd. Empire State Coll. Found., Saratoga Springs, 1986—. Named Realtor of Yr., Saratoga County Bd. Realtors, 1977. Mem. N.Y. State Assn. Realtors (regional v.p. 1972-73, 1979-81). Lodge: Soroptimists (pres. Saratoga County chpt. 1979-81). Office: Saratoga Ctr for Real Estate Inc 398 Broadway Saratoga Springs NY 12866

SILVERMAN, ANNA MAE, nurse; b. Phila., July 5, 1928; d. Charles Girth and Maude Yoast; m. Edward Silverman, Sept. 1, 1955 (div. Oct. 1978); children: Gail, Debra, Jeffrey. Diploma, Meth. Hosp., 1953. RN; cert. psychiatric nurse. Mem. RN staff Meth. Hosp., Phila., 1953-55, Wernesville (Pa.) State Hosp., 1968-70, St. Joseph Hosp., Reading, Pa., 1974—. Contbr. article to Nursing World Jour., 1986. Home: RD3 Box 3786 Mohnton PA 19540-9231

SILVERMAN, BERNICE GRACE ABEL, steel products executive; b. Chgo., Apr. 19, 1932; d. Jacob Israel and Celia (Surkin) Abel; student U. Ill., U. Chgo., De Paul U., m. William J. Silverman, Mar. 14, 1959; children—Robin Lee Silverman Sturman, Jaci Lynn Friedlander. Owner, operator Best Locker Service, Washington, 1968—; pres., chief operating officer, dir. Best Steel Products, Inc., Washington, 1975—. Active Multiple Sclerosis Soc., Am. Cancer Soc. Mem. Nat. Automatic Merchandising Assn., Internat. Assn. Amusement Parks and Attractions, Internat. Council Shopping Centers, NOW, Nat. Fedn. Bus. and Profl. Women, Nat. Ski Area Assn., Am. Waterpark Assn. Clubs: Hadassah (life), B'nai B'rith (life). Home: 4606 Kenmore Dr NW Washington DC 20007 Office: 5402 Connecticut Ave NW Washington DC 20015

SILVERMAN, DONNA LEE, personnel director; b. Lynn, Mass., June 20, 1960; d. Norman and Beatrice (Cohen) S. BA in Psychology, Mgmt., Eckerd Coll., 1982; MS in Human Resource Mgmt., Nova U., 1987. Recruiter Office Specialists, Plantation, Fla., 1983-84; exec. recruiter R.K. Exec. Search, Coral Springs, Fla., 1984; dir. recruiting Mass. Mut. Life Ins. Co., Ft. Lauderdale, Fla., 1984—; adj. faculty human resources Nova U., 1987—; leader seminars South Fla. Skills Exchange, Tamarac, 1986-87. Author poetry. Vol. Spl. Olympics, 1985-87; mem. curriculum planning com. Youth Leadership Broward, chmn. Bus. and Industry Day, 1987; bd. dirs. Multiple Sclerosis Soc., Broward County, Fla., 1987—. Plantation Women's Club scholar, 1985, 86. Mem. Am. Soc. Personnel Adminstrs., Personnel Assn. Broward County, Bus. and Profl. Women (chmn. young careerist com. 1985-86, scholarship 1985), Nat. Assn. Female Execs., Mus. of Art, Plantation C. of C. (speakers' bur. 1985—, mgr. membership growth task force 1987, mgr. speakers' bur. task force 1988—, Expo com. 1988, chmn. Expo seminar com. 1988, bd. dirs. 1988—, chmn. trade show, 1989). Republican. Jewish. Home: 7027 W Sunrise Blvd Plantation FL 33313 Office: Mass Mut Life Ins Co 2101 N Federal Hwy Fort Lauderdale FL 33305

SILVERMAN, ELAINE ROSLYN, educator; b. Washington, Aug. 28, 1941; d. Mark and Rebecca (Leopold) S. B.S. in Edn., Temple U., 1963; Ed.M., George Mason U., 1977. Cert. tchr., Va. Group leader Dixon House, Phila., 1962; tchr. Hammond High Sch., Alexandria, Va., 1963-65, T.C. Williams High Sch., Alexandria, 1965—. Participant Alexandria City Democratic Mass Meeting for Presdl. Nomination, 1984. Mem. Va. Edn. Assn., Alexandria Edn. Assn., NEA, Nat. Council for Social Studies, Va. Council for Social Studies. Jewish. Avocation: reading in area of history of English monarchy. Office: TC Williams High Sch 3330 King St Alexandria VA 22311

SILVERMAN, GAIL ANN, nurse, consultant; b. Los Angeles, Mar. 19, 1955; d. Stanley Irwin and Rita B. (Alexander) Silverman. A.A. in Liberal Arts, Los Angeles Valley Coll., 1974; A.A. in Nursing, 1976. Sales, asst. mgr. Bullock's, Sherman Oaks, Calif., 1972-75; nurse aide Los Angeles New Hosp., 1975-76; critical care nurse Motion Picture and TV Fund Hosp., Calabassas, Calif., 1982-84; critical care nurse Cedars-Sinai Med. Ctr., Los Angeles, 1976—; critical care cons. Motion Picture and TV Fund Hosp., Calabasses, 1982-84, critical care cons., 1982-84; ednl. cons. ARC, 1985—; legis. spl. cons. Am. Fedn. Nurses, Los Angeles, 1983-87; critical care cons. Am. Fedn. Nurses, Los Angeles, 1983-87; ednl. cons. critical care Save a Heart Found., Los Angeles, 1984-86. Instr., Am. Heart Assn., Los Angeles, 1976—; vol. ARC, Los Angeles, 1976—, relief diaster supv., 1986—, health activities specialist, 1987—; mem. Jewish Labor Com., Los Angeles, 1983-85; Calif. state bd. mem. Nurses Alliance Calif., 1983-86; relief disater coordinator Multi-AID, 1986-87; emergency aid coordinator Calif. Spl. Olympics Summer Games, 1986—; cons. health and edn. services Am. Red Cross Spl. Projects, 1986—. Mem. Am. Assn. Critical Care Nurses, San Fernando Valley Assn. Critical Care Nurses (exec. bd. 1987-88), Am. Heart Assn. Democrat. Jewish. Home: 4424 Woodman Ave #103 Sherman Oaks CA

91423 Office: Cedars Sinai Med Ctr 8700 Beverly Blvd Los Angeles CA 90048

SILVERMAN, JUDITH, human resources administrator, author, consultant; b. Bklyn., Aug. 26, 1933; d. David and Shirley Beatrice (Maltz) Marks; m. Myron Bernard Silverman, July 3, 1955; 1 son, Brian Scott. B.A. cum laude, Bklyn. Coll., 1960; M.L.S., Pratt Inst., 1963; P.D., L.I.U. 1985. Sec. Fairchild Publs., N.Y.C., 1954-56; tchr., librarian N.Y.C. Bd. Edn., Bklyn., 1956-62; sr. librarian Bklyn. Pub. Library, 1964-68, Queens Borough Pub. Library, Queens, N.Y., 1973-76; asst. dir. personnel Baldwin (N.Y.) Pub. Library, 1976-80; exec. adminstr. for personnel Bd. Cooperative Ednl. Services Nassau County, Westbury, N.Y., 1980—; cons. books R. R. Bowker Co., N.Y.C., 1971—. Author: Index to Collective Biographies for Young Readers, 1970, 3rd edit., 1979. Mem. N.Y. State/Sch. Personnel Adminstrs., L.I. Assn. Sch. Personnel Adminstrs., Nat. Assn. Ednl. Negotiators, N.Y. Library Assn. (mem. com.), Nassau County Library Assn. (mem. com.), Beta Phi Mu. Office: Bd Coop Ednl Services Nassau County Valentines and The Plain Rds Westbury NY 11590

SILVERSTEIN, ETHEL BOLD, finance educator; b. Bklyn., Sept. 27, 1924; d. Samuel and Yechevah (Belson) Bold; m. Benjamin Silverstein; children: Stephen, Harriet. BA, Bklyn. Coll., 1944; MBA, NYU, 1947; MS, St. John's U., 1971; PhD, NYU, 1971. Statistician Bache & Co., N.Y.C., ASCAP, N.Y.C.; asst. prof. fin. N.Y. Inst. Tech., Old Westbury, N.Y.; adj. assoc. prof. fin. Hofstra U., Hempstead, N.Y. Mem. Am. Econ. Assn., Fin. Mgmt. Assn., Nat. Assn. Bus. Economists, N.Y. State Economics Assn., Hadassah, United Jewish Appeal. Democrat. Jewish.

SILVERSTON, BESS ELLESBERG, educator; b. N.Y.C., Feb. 15, 1947; d. Harold and Rose Leah (Kleban) Ellesberg; m. Randall A. Silverston, May 24, 1970; children: Hallie Alana, Matt Emanual. BA, Calif. State U., Northridge, 1968; MA, U. Mich., 1970; postgrad., So. Ill. U., 1973; PhD, Claremont Grad. Sch., 1984. Cert. handicapped and severely handicapped tchr., cert. English tchr., cert. preliminary adminstr., cert. community coll. instr., Calif. Tchr. pub. schs. Ypsilanti and Romulus, Mich., and Marion, Ill., 1970-74; psychometrician Dean Meml. Learning Ctr., Shelton Sch., Dallas, 1974-76; tchr., counselor Poseidon Sch., Los Angeles, 1976-80; adminstrv. staff assoc. tchr. edn. program Claremont (Calif.) Grad. Sch., 1981-84, placement facilitator, 1985; asst. prof. elem. edn. Calif. State U., Los Angeles, 1984-85; asst. dir., master tchr. Erikson High Sch., Tarzana, Calif., 1985—; resource program specialist Wilson Elem Sch., San Gabriel, Calif., 1984. Mem. Am. Ednl. Research Assn., Council for Exceptional Children, Calif. Council Edn. Tchrs., Alliance for Survival, Greenpeace, Assn. for Curriculum and Supervision, Kappa Delta Pi, Pi Lambda Theta. Home: 17147 Gunther St Granada Hills CA 91344

SILVESTRIS, ELAINE JOY, employee relations administrator; b. Worcester, Mass., Jan. 8, 1943; d. Roland Joseph and Margaret Ann (Arnieri) Gustafson; m. Maurice Richard Silvestris, Nov. 6, 1965. Cert. in human resources, Moravian Coll., Bethlehem, Pa., 1985. Legal sec. Mirick, O'Connell, DeMallie and Lougee, Worcester, 1961-65, Edward J. Brady, Camden, N.J., 1966-69; legal sec. to ptnr. Sigmon, Briody, Littner and Ross, Bethlehem, 1969-70; legal sec. to sr. ptnr. Weaver, Weaver and Weaver, Catasauqua, Pa., 1970-76; adminstrv. sec. to pres. and v.p. sales Lehigh Sales and Products, Allentown, Pa., 1976-78; sr. stenographer U.S. Postal Service, Lehigh Valley, Pa., 1978-82, injury compensation supr., 1982-85, employee relations mgr., 1985—; account rep. DialAmerica Mktg., Inc., 1988. Recipient Cert. Appreciation for Outstanding Efforts in Hiring Visually Disabled People, Commonwealth Pa., 1987. Mem. Nat. Assn. Profl. Saleswomen (Lehigh Valley chpt.), Pa. Assn. Notaries, Pa. Soc. Profl. Engrs. (aux. group chmn. 1983-84, sec. 1978-80, v.p. 1978-79, 2nd v.p. and Pa. del. 1976-77), Nat. Assn. for Female Execs. Inc. Republican. Methodist. Office: US Postal Service 1000 Postal Rd Lehigh Valley PA 18001-4024

SILVEY, ANITA LYNNE, editor; b. Bridgeport, Conn., Sept. 3, 1947; d. John Oscar and Juanita Lucille (McKitrick) S. BS in Edn., Ind. U., 1965-69; MA in Communication Arts, U. Wis., 1970. Editorial asst. children's book dept. Little Brown and Co., Boston, 1970-71; asst. editor Horn Book Mag., Boston, 1971-75; mng. editor, founder New Boston Rev., 1975-76; mktg. mgr. children's books, library services mgr. trade div. Houghton Mifflin, Boston, 1976-84; editor in chief Horn Book Mag., Boston, 1985—. Contbr. articles to profl. jours. Named one of Seventy Women Who Have Made A Difference Women's Nat. Book Assn., 1987. Mem. ALA (chmn. children's librarians, Laura Ingalls Wilder award 1987-89), Internat. Reading Assn. (IRA Book award com. 1985-87), Assn. Am. Pubs. (lib. com.), New Eng. Round Table (chmn. 1978-79). Office: Horn Book 31 St James Ave Boston MA 02116

SILVIA, KATHLEEN FORD, insurance executive; b. Bronxville, N.Y., Dec. 29, 1954; d. James William and Evelyn (Gates) Moriarty; m. Ronald Joseph Silvia, May 1, 1982; children: Ronald Ford, Jennifer Ann. Cert. Ins. Inst. Am., 1976. CPCU, lic. ins. advisor. Claim service rep. Allstate Ins. Co., Weston, Mass., 1973; claim service rep. Fair & Yeager Agy., Inc., Natick, Mass., 1974, claim mgr., 1974-78, personal lines mgr., 1979-80, edn. mgr., 1978-82, comml. account exec., 1980-82; br. mgr. Centerville, Mass., 1982-87; owner, ptnr. The Fair Ins. Agy., Centerville, 1987—. Contbr. articles to newspapers. Mem. pastor parish relations com. United Meth. Ch., Osterville, Mass., 1982—, choir mem., 1982-84, chair worship com., 1986—. Mem.. Nat. Assn. Ins. Women Internat. (recipient awards), Mass. Assn. Ins. Women (Ins. Woman Yr. 1984, v.p. 1982-83, pres. 1985, past pres. 1985-86, chair various coms., bd. dirs. 1987-88), Soc. CPCUs, Profl. Ins. Agts., Ind. Ins. Agts. Mass., Profl. Ins. Agts. N.E. (bd. dirs. 1987). Lodge: Rotary. Home: 190 Great Marsh Rd Centerville MA 02632 Office: The Fair Ins Agy Inc 619 Main St Centerville MA 02632

SIMER, CHERYL, marketing professional; b. Greenbay, Wis., Dec. 5, 1948; d. Harold Leslie Albert and Helen June Augusta (Delzer) Black; m. Harvey Josef Simer. BA in Math., Beloit Coll., 1971. Research asst. Nat. Consumer Fin. Assn., Washington, 1971; project dir. Pillsbury Co., Mpls., 1972-74, research analyst, 1975-77, research mgr., 1978-79; dir. mktg. research Munsingwear, Inc., Mpls., 1980-82; v.p., dir. mktg. research BBDO, Mpls., 1983—. Mem. Am. Mktg. Assn.

SIMKUS, BARBARA ANN, limousine service executive; b. Oak Park, Ill., Oct. 9, 1938; d. Oldrich and Libuse Sylvia (Kocian) Skaryd; m. Robert Peter Simkus, May 24, 1958; children—Karen, Sharyl, Laura, Robert Peter, Scott. Grad. high sch., Cicero, Ill. Sec., Martin Fan & Blower Co., Cicero, 1955-59; home-typist Monarch Printing Co., Chgo., 1967-79; reservationist West Suburban Limousine Service, Carol Stream, Ill., 1975-80, bus. mgr., 1980—. Editor Carol Stream News, 1967-79 (Village award 1979). Co-chmn., sec. Carol Stream 25th Anniversary Commn., 1983-84. Named Citizen of Yr., Community Improvement, Carol Stream, 1972, Spl. Citizen of Yr., Community Improvement, 1981. Mem. Ill. Limousine Assn. (sec.), Carol Stream Hist. Soc. (sec. 1974—), Carol Stream Bus. and Industry (v.p. 1983—). Republican. Roman Catholic. Club: Carol Stream Woman's (pres. 1980-84). Avocations: bowling; reading; stitchery; cross-country skiing. Home: 841 Papoose Ct Carol Stream IL 60188

SIMMONS, ADELE SMITH, college president; b. Lake Forest, Ill., June 21, 1941; d. Hermon Dunlap and Ellen T. (Thorne) Smith; m. John L. Simmons; children—Ian, Erica, Kevin. B.A., Radcliffe Coll., 1963; Ph.D., Oxford U., Eng., 1969; L.H.D. (hon.), Lake Forest Coll., 1976, Amherst Coll., 1977, Franklin Pierce Coll., 1978, U. Mass., 1982, Alverno Coll., 1986, Marlboro Coll., 1987. Dean Jackson Coll., Tufts U., Medford, Mass., 1970-72; asst. prof. history, dean student affairs Princeton U., N.J., 1972-77; pres. Hampshire Coll., Amherst, Mass., 1977—; dir. Affil. Publs., Boston, Marsh & McLennan, N.Y.C., Boston Globe, Zayre Corp., Framingham, Mass. Author: Modern Mauritius, 1980. Contbr. articles to profl. jours. Commr. Pres.'s Commn. on World Hunger, Washington, 1978-80; trustee, chmn. bd. Carnegie Found. for Advancement Teaching; trustee Union Concerned Scientists, World Policy Inst. Mem. World Policy Inst., Council on Fgn. Relations, Am. Assn. Higher Edn. (pres.), Phi Beta Kappa. Clubs: Cosmopolitan (N.Y.C.); Princeton. Office: Hampshire Coll Amherst MA 01002

SIMMONS, ANN ELMIRA, business management and international communication company executive; b. Havre de Grace, Md., Nov. 21, 1940; d. C. Russell and Myrtle Spencer (Munnikhuysen) Denbow; m. Larry Kenneth Simmons, Sept. 12, 1964; children: David Spencer, Teressa Elmira. AA, Hartford Jr. Coll., Bel Air, Md., 1963; postgrad., Oxford U., Eng., 1964; BBA, Calif. Poly. U., 1985, MBA, 1987. Instr., receptionist Hanover Sch. Modeling, New Haven, 1959-60; with TECOM div. U.S. Army, Aberdeen, Md., 1963; tchr. Emmanuel Luth. Ach., Balt., 1974-75; instr. Gifted & Talented Program State of Md., 1983-85, 87-88; pres. Ann Simmons & Assocs. Ltd., Ellicott City, Md., 1984—; cons. in field; adj. prof. Catonsville Community Coll., Balt., 1981—; lectr., cons. Duquesne U., Johns Hopkins U., others, 1984—, diplomatic, fgn. service, govtl. agys.; advisor, cons. Essex Community Coll., Balt., 1986—; lectr. in field, worldwide, 1983—; condr. seminars in field. Contbr. articles to profl. jours. Mem. Balt. Council Fgn. Affairs, 1987; del. White House Briefing on Women in Bus., 1984; adv. bd. Internat. Edn. Bd., Catonsville Community Coll., 1985—; adv. bd. on internat. bus. grant Essex Community Coll., 1986-87; mem. Mus. of Women in the Arts. Mem. Md. Internat. Trade Assn., Middle East Inst., Arab Am. Cultural Council, Internat. Soc. for Intercultural Edn., Tng. & Research, Nat. Assn. Female Execs., Am. Soc. Tng. & Devel., Lit. Soc., Epsilon Sigma Omicron. Clubs: Gateway, Federated Women's (Catonsville). Office: Ann Simmons & Assocs Ltd PO Box 735 Ellicott City MD 21043

SIMMONS, BARBARA J., human resources director; b. Detroit, Oct. 28, 1938; d. Jessie Stanley and Bernice Olivia (Abrams) Stanley; m. William Clark Estes, Dec. 26, 1959 (div. 1977); children: Brian Keith, Brenda Kay; m. David Louis Simmons, Dec. 6, 1980. BS, Wayne State U., 1969, MS in Bus., 1971. Tchr., coordinator Detroit Pub. Schs., 1969-72; project coordinator Wayne State U., Detroit, 1972-73; with indsl. relations dept. Ford Motor Credit Co., Rouge, Mich., 1973-74; personnel officer Mfgrs. Nat. Bank, Detroit, 1974-75; dir. employee relations The Bendix Corp., South Bend, Ind., Utica, N.Y., Troy, Mich., 1975-81; v.p., dir. personnel Advance Mortgage Corp., Southfield, Mich., 1981-83; dir. employment Fed. Nat. Mortgage Co., Washington, 1983-85; 1st v.p. human resources Mich. Nat. Corp., Farmington Hills, 1985—; bd. dirs. Am. Inst. Banking, Detroit, 1985—, Blue Cross/Blue Shield, Detroit, 1985—. Mem. Detroit Urban League, Detroit, 1985—, NAACP, Detroit, 1985—. Mem. Am. Soc. Personnel Adminstrs., Internat. Assn. Personnel Women, Am. Inst. Banking (bd. regents, bd. dirs. 1985—), Am. Banking Assn. (mem. adv. council), Blue Cross/Blue Shield (bd. dirs. 1985—). Episcopalian. Home: 38694 Northfarm Dr Northville MI 48167 Office: Mich Nat Bank Corp 30665 Northwestern Hwy Farmington Hills MI 48333-9065

SIMMONS, CAROL, oil company official; b. N.Y.C., Jan. 30, 1943; d. Gennaro Robert and Rose Immaculate (Migliore) Scrimo; m. Robert Eugene Cavallo, July 27, 1968 (div. 1983); m. Allan Lee Simmons, June 14, 1986. BS, Marymount Coll., 1983. With Texaco Inc., White Plains, N.Y., 1961—, staff asst. mktg., 1975-77, sr. personnel asst. ops., 1977-78, supr. employment services, 1978-80, supr. employment and adminstrn., 1980-82, coordinator planning and research, 1982-84, Western region employee relations rep., tng. coordinator, 1984—. Loaned exec. United Way of Westchester, White Plains, 1981; adv. bd. Office for Women, Westchester County, 1982-84, YWCA, White Plains, 1983-84. Mem. Westchester Personnel Mgmt. Assn. (pres. 1983, 84), Personnel Council White Plains C. of C. (co-chmn. 1981-82). Democrat. Roman Catholic. Office: Texaco Inc 10 Universal City Plaza North Hollywood CA 91608

SIMMONS, CAROLINE THOMPSON, civic worker; b. Denver, Aug. 22, 1910; d. Huston and Caroline Margaret (Cordes) Thompson; A.B., Bryn Mawr Coll., 1931; m. John Farr Simmons, Nov. 11, 1936; children—John Farr (dec.), Huston T., Malcolm M. Chmn. women's com. Corcoran Gallery Art, 1965-66; vice chmn. women's com. Smithsonian Assos., 1969-71; pres. Decatur House Council, 1963-71; mem. bd. Nat. Theatre, 1979-80; trustee Washington Opera, 1955-65, bd. dirs. Fgn. Student Service Council, 1956-79; mem. Washington Home Bd., 1955-60; bd. dirs. Smithsonian Friends of Music, 1977-79; commr. Nat. Mus. Am. Art, 1979—; mem. Folger com. Folger Shakespeare Library, 1979-86, trustee emeritus, 1986— (recipient award for eminent service, 1986); mem. Washington bd. Am. Mus. in Britain, 1970—; bd. dirs. Found. Preservation of Historic Georgetown, 1975—; trustee Marpat Found., 1987—, Amherst Coll., 1979-81, Dacor-Bacon House Found.; v.p. internat. council Mus. Modern Art, N.Y.C., 1978—; mem. council Phillips Collection, 1982—; bd. dirs. Alliance Française. Mem. Soc. Women Geographers. Presbyterian. Clubs: Sulgrave, Chevy Chase. Address: 1508 Dumbarton Rock Ct Washington DC 20007

SIMMONS, CORLIS TAYLOR, design engineer; b. Houston, Oct. 17, 1956; d. William Hamilton and Betty J. (Williams) Taylor; m. Ferness Craig Simmons, Oct. 11, 1980; 1 child, Dustin Keith. BS, U. Houston, 1979; postgrad., Roosevelt U., Chgo. Equipment engr. Southwestern Bell Telephone Co., Houston, 1979-83; staff mgr. AT&T, Houston, 1984, design engr., 1984—; subject matter expert Regional Engring. Ctr., Chgo., 1986—, tng. coordinator, 1987—. Press release coordinator City-Wide Festivals, Chgo., 1986. Mem. Nat. Assn. Female Execs. Democrat. Roman Catholic. Club: St. Francis Adult (Houston) (treas. 1981-84). Home: PO Box 3917 Chicago IL 60654

SIMMONS, DIANE EILEEN, corporate executive; b. New Smyrna Beach, Fla., Jan. 28, 1950; d. George Andrew and Carolyn Margaret (Cross) Naser; A.A., Daytona Beach Community Coll., 1971; student U. N.C., 1978, U. South Fla., 1980; m. Paul L. Simmons, June 2, 1973; children—Thomas David (dec.), Paula Kay. Pres., Fla. Trade Publ., Daytona Beach, Fla., 1971-74; project engr. Pollak & Skan Inc., Rosemont, Ill., 1977-78; mgr. S.E. region, 1978-79; exec. dir. Internat. Soc. Pharm. Engrs., Tampa, Fla., 1979-81; exec. dir. Seminars, Inc., Tampa, Fla., 1978-84; exec. sec., treas. ROST Inc., 1977—; pres. Regulatory Info. Systems, Inc., 1983-84; sec.-treas. Tam-Rock Devel., Inc.; exec. dir. Internat. Ctr. for Tech. Transfer, Inc. (ICT-2), Tampa, 1985—. Mem. Parenteral Drug Assn., ASME, Nat. Assn. Female Execs. Republican. So. Baptist. Pub., FACT mag., 1971-74; editor Pharm. Engring. Jour., 1979-81, Bio Process Engring., 1984-85. Office: Internat Ctr Tech Transfer 13014 N Dale Mabry Suite 140 Tampa FL 33618

SIMMONS, DONNA MARIE, histotechnologist, neurobiology researcher; b. Hartford, Conn., Oct. 13, 1943; d. John Henry and Ellen Louise (Meehl) Strayer; m. Corvin Gale Simmons, Sept. 17, 1964. Student U. Wash., Western Wash. State U., Tacoma Gen. Hosp. Sch. Med. Tech. Lab. technician U. Wash. Med. Sch., 1964; histologic technician Northgate Med. Lab., Seattle, 1964-67; research technologist in neuroanatomy Regional Primate Research Ctr., U. Wash., 1967-82; research asst. Devel. Neurobiology Lab. Salk Inst., La Jolla, Calif., 1982-85; sr. technician, lab. mgr. Neural Systems Lab. Howard Hughes Med. Inst. at Salk Inst., 1985—; cons., lectr. in field.; judge Greater San Diego Sci. and Engring. Fair, 1987, 88. Author tech. articles, revs. in field; mem. editorial bd. Jour. Histotech.; lead sci. del. to People's Rep. of China, 1986; chair China Scientist Exchange Fund, 1986-87. Recipient various service awards; best non-clin. pub. in field, 1985. Mem. AAAS, Am. Soc. Clin. Pathologists (affiliate), Wash. State Histology Soc. (past pres., histology liaison Am. Soc. Med. Tech.), Nat. Soc. Histotech. (charter mem., regional dir. 1980-82, jud. chair 1983-86), Calif. Soc. Histotech. (San Diego dir. protem 1985-86), Assn. Women in Sci. (San Diego charter mem., dir. 1985-88), Soc. for Neurosci., Swiss Soc. for Histotech., N.Y. Acad. Sci., NOW. Club: Am. Alpine. Office: 10010 N Torrey Pines Rd La Jolla CA 92037

SIMMONS, GAIL LINDSAY, lawyer; b. N.Y.C., June 15, 1949; d. James Lambert Simmons and Jacqueline (Chambers) Cook; m. Allen Howard Feldman, Jan. 5, 1980; children—Andrew Thomas Alexandra. Student U. London, 1968, Harvard U., 1970; B.A., Carnegie-Tech., Pitts., 1971; J.D., Case Western Res. U., Cleve., 1974. Bar: D.C. 1975, Ohio 1974, others. Law clk. Thurlow Smoot, Cleve., 1972-74; atty. U.S. Customs, Washington, 1974-75, U.S. Dept. Labor, Washington, 1975-79; asst. corp. counsel D.C. Govt., Washington, 1979-81; ptnr. Cotten, Day & Doyle, Washington, 1981-87, Doyle & Savit, Washington, 1987—. Active Jr. League Washington, Don't Tear It Down, Washington, Preservation of Assateague Nat. Seashore (Va.). Mem. ABA, Fed. Bar Assn., D.C. Bar Assn., Trial Lawyers Assn. Am. Republican. Presbyterian. Home: 3708 Morrison St NW Washington DC 20015 Office: Doyle & Savit 919 18th St NW Suite 1000 Washington DC 20006

SIMMONS, GLENDA BROCK, academic administrator; b. Dallas, Aug. 4, 1936; d. Choyce Glen and Allie L. (Bransom) B.; m. Gerald L. Simmons, May 26, 1954; 1 child, G. Kirk. BS, Tex. Woman's U., 1960, MA, 1961; PhD, No. Tex. State U., 1983. Cert. tchr., Tex. Instr. assoc. prof. Tex. Woman's U., 1961—, v.p., 1982—; lectr., speaker, resource person various women's, adminstrv. groups, Tex., 1961—. Officer Denton Area Tchrs. Credit Union, Denton, 1974-80; bd. dirs., officer of bd. United Way, Denton, 1980—. Recipient Women Helping Women award, Soroptimists, Denton, 1988; named Outstanding Bus. Tchr. Tex. Bus. Edn. Assn., 1974, Top Prof. Bapt. Student Union, 1960s. Mem. Council Student Services, Tex. Assn. Coll. and Univ. Student Personnel Adminstrs., Nat. Assn. Student Personnel Adminstrs., Nat. Orientation Dirs. Assn., SW Assn. Student Personnel Adminstrs., Nat. Assn. Female Execs., Leadership Tex.,Delta Kappa Gamma Internat. (treas., pres. state coms.). Home: Rt 2 Box 35 Argyle TX 76226 Office: Tex Womans U Sta Denton TX 76204

SIMMONS, JEAN, actress; b. London, Eng., Jan. 31, 1929; d. Charles and Winifred Ada (Lovel) S.; m. Stewart Granger, Dec. 20, 1950 (div. June 1960); 1 dau., Tracy; m. Richard Brooks, Nov. 1, 1960; 1 dau., Kate. Ed., Orange Hill Sch., Burnt Oak, London. Motion picture actress, appearing in English and Am. films including Great Expectations, 1946, Black Narcissus, 1947, Hamlet, 1948 (Acad. award nomination), Adam and Evelyn, 1949, The Actress, 1953, Young Bess, 1953, Guys and Dolls, 1956, The Big Country, 1958, Home Before Dark, 1958, Spartacus, 1960, Elmer Gantry, 1960, The Grass Is Greener, 1960, All the Way Home, 1963, Rough Night in Jericho, 1967, Divorce American Style, 1967, The Happy Ending, 1969 (Acad. award nomination); also theatre appearance A Little Night Music, Phila. and on tour, 1974; appeared in: TV mini-series The Dain Curse, 1978, A Small Killing, 1981, Valley of the Dolls, 1981, The Thornbirds, 1983, North and South Book II, 1986. Office: care Geoffrey Barr 9400 Readcrest Dr Beverly Hills CA 90210 *

SIMMONS, JOAN, federal agency administrator; b. Portland, Maine, Sept. 13, 1942; d. Edward and Louise (Thorndike) Hoglund; m. Paul Barrett Simmons, June 12, 1965; 1 child, Charles Barrett. BA, St. Joseph's Coll., N. Windham, Maine, 1964. Music, dance critic Albany (N.Y.) Times Union, 1965-69; legs. asst.l N.Y. State Senate, Albany, 1970-73; program assoc. N.Y. State Gov.'s Office, Albany, 1973-74; freelance writer, cons. Washington, 1974-77; program assoc. Nat. Govs. Assn., Washington, 1977-79; exec. asst. to chmn. Ill. Commerce Commn., Springfield, 1979-81; dir. intergovtl. affairs Fedl. Energy Regulatory Commn., Washington, 1981-87; dir. research Presdl. Commn. on Privatization, Washington, 1987—. Author several books and articles on arts and edn. Recipient various awards for music criticism. Mem. Exec. Women in Govt. Republican. Home: 17 2d St NE Washington DC 20002

SIMMONS, LAURA LEE, airline executive; b. Chgo., May 7, 1930; d. Clark Washington and Muriel Florence (Spiegel) S. BA in Anthropology and Psychology, CUNY, 1977. Sec. Mpls. Honeywell Regulator Co., Chgo., 1947-50, E.I. DuPont DeNemours and Co., Chgo., 1950-52; adminstrv. asst. Burlington Industries, N.Y.C., 1952-55; exec. sec., coordinator, mgr. tech. purchasing and forwarding Scandinavian Airlines System, Jamaica, N.Y., 1955—. Mem. DAR, Purchasing Mgmt. Assn. N.Y., Nat. Assn. Female Exec. Democrat. Presbyterian. Office: Scandanavian Airlines System 138-02 Queens Blvd Jamaica NY 11435

SIMMONS, MARGUERITA DENISE, mortgage company executive; b. Memphis, June 24, 1951; d. Greene William and Precious Loyal (Jackson) Flowers; m. Calvin Lee Simmons Jr., Aug. 19, 1980 (div. June 1985); children: Calvin Lee III, Ira Demetrius. BBA, Fla. State Christian Coll., 1976. Fundraising coordinator, research ops. coordinator Operation PUSH, Los Angeles, 1974-77; asst. mgr. personal lines Empire Ins., Upland, Calif., 1977-79; corp. sec. Jackie Flowers Investment Corp., La Verne, Calif., 1979—; v.p., br. mgr. All Cities Mortgage Co., Riverside, Calif., 1983—; co-owner Unique Nails, San Bernardino, Calif., 1987—; cons. in field. Active Parents Against Drugs, Parents Against Gangs, San Bernardino, 1988—. Mem. Black Profl. Women. Democrat. Islam. Office: All Cities Mortgage Co 3600 Lime St Suite 117 Riverside CA 92501

SIMMONS, SYLVIA, advertising agency executive, author; b. N.Y.C.; B.A., Bklyn. Coll.; M.A. in English Lit., Columbia U.; m. Hans H. Neumann, 1962. Dir. sales promotion and direct mail div. McCann Erickson, Inc., N.Y.C., 1958-62; v.p., asst. to pres. Young & Rubicam, Inc., N.Y.C., 1962-73; sr. v.p., dir. spl. projects Kenyon & Eckhardt, Inc., N.Y.C., 1975-86; cons. Bozell, Jacobs, Kenyon & Eckhardt, 1986-88; free-lance advt. cons., 1987—. Recipient Medal of Freedom, 1946, award for best radio comml. N.Y. Radio Broadcasters Assn., 1976-77, award for contbns. in direct mail promotions Sales Promotion Execs. Assn. Mem. Direct Mail Advt. Assn., Authors Guild, Propylaea, Sigma Tau Delta. Clubs: Sales Promotion Execs., Advt. Women of N.Y., Copy (N.Y.C.). Author: New Speakers Handbook, 1972; The Great Garage Sale Book, 1982; How To Be The Life of the Podium, 1982; (with Hans H. Neumann) The Straight Story on VD, 1974; Dr. Neumann's Guide to the New Sexually Transmitted Diseases, 1983; co-author (with Thomas D. Rees) More Than Just a Pretty Face, 1987; also articles.

SIMMONS, SYLVIA JEANNE QUARLES (MRS. HERBERT G. SIMMONS, JR.), educator; b. Boston, May 8, 1935; d. Lorenzo Christopher and Margaret Mary (Thomas) Quarles; B.A., Manhattanville Coll., 1957; M.Ed., Boston Coll., 1962; m. Herbert G. Simmons, Jr., Oct. 26, 1957; children—Stephen, Alison, Lisa. Montessori tchr. Charles River Park Nursery Sch., Boston, 1965-66; registrar Boston Coll. Sch. Mgmt., Chestnut Hill, Mass., 1966-70; dir. fin. aid Radcliffe Coll., Cambridge, Mass., 1970-75, asso. dean admissions and fin. aid, 1972-75, asso. dean admissions, fin. aid and women's edn., 1975; asso. dean admissions and fin. aid Harvard and Radcliffe, from 1975; assoc. v.p. for acad. affairs, central adminstrn. U. Mass., Boston, 1976—, spl. asst. to chancellor, 1979—; v.p. field services Mass. Higher Edn. Assistance Corp., 1982-84, sr. v.p., 1984—; mem. faculty Harvard U.; cons. Mass. Bd. Higher Edn., 1973-77. Bd. dirs. Rivers Country Day Sch., Weston, Mass., Simon's Rock Coll., Great Barrington, Mass., Wayland (Mass.) Fair Housing, Cambridge Mental Health Assn., Family Service Greater Boston, Concerts in Black and White, Mass. Higher Edn. Assistance Corp.; chmn. bd. dirs. North Shore Community Coll., 1986—; trustee and alumnae bd. dirs. Manhattanville Coll. Mem. adv. com. Upward Bound, Chestnut Hill Boston Coll., 1972-74; Camp Chimvey Corners, Becket, Mass., 1971-77. Named One of Ten Outstanding Young Leaders, Boston Jr. C. of C., 1971; recipient Bicentennial medal Boston Coll., 1976; Achievement award Greater Boston YMCA, 1977. Mem. Women in Politics, Nat. (exec. council 1973-75), Eastern (1st v.p. 1973) assns. financial aid officers, Coll. Scholarship Service Council, Links, (pres. local chpt. 1967-69), Nat. Inst. Fin. Aid Adminstrs. (dir. 1975-77), Jack and Jill Am. (pres. Newton chpt. 1972-74, Mass. Am. Cancer Soc. (bd. dirs. 1987—), Delta Sigma Theta, Delta Kappa Gamma. Club: Manhattanville (pres. Boston 1966-68). Home: 3 Dean Rd Wayland MA 01778 Office: 330 Stuart St Boston MA 02116

SIMMONS-SIXTO, CAMILLE ANN, transportation company administrator; b. Newtown Kitty, Guyana, Sept. 12, 1953; came to U.S., 1973; d. Cardwell Joseph Simmons and Lucille Norma Hinds; m. Alfredo Sixto. AA, Queensborough Community Coll., 1979; BBA, Bernard M. Baruch Coll., 1982. Sec. C.I.T. Fin. Corp., N.Y.C., 1973-77; adminstrv. asst. Community Service Soc., N.Y.C., 1977-84; asst. to chief exec. officer Bramson Ort Tech. Inst., N.Y.C., 1984-85; instr. data processing Comml. Programming Unltd., N.Y.C., 1985; mgr. adminstrn. Metro-North Commuter R.R., N.Y.C., 1985—. Mem. NAACP, Nat. Assn. Female Execs., Bernard M. Baruch Coll. Alumni Assn. Home: 6 Cohill Rd Valley Stream Long Island NY 11580

SIMMS, PRISCILLA CLAYTON, human resources consultant; b. San Francisco, Apr. 26, 1933; d. George and Genevieve (Dale) S. BS, U. Calif., Santa Barbara, 1955; MS, NYU, 1956. Job methods analyst Walker Scott Co., San Diego, 1956-59, supt. ops. systems dept., 1960-63, store mgr., 1963-65, asst. dir. personnel, 1966-87, v.p. personnel, 1968-87; pres. Personnel/HUman Resources Cons. Services, San Diego, 1987—; bd. dirs. Walker-Scott Corp., San Diego, 1972-74. Chair Greater San Diego Industry Edn. Council, 1971-77, San Diego County Employee Relations Council, 1976-80, San

Diego Employers Health Cost Coalition, 1980—; pres., trustee Sr. Adult Services, San Diego, 1980—. Mem. Am. Soc. for Personnel Adminstrn. (chair dist. 1972-73), Personnel Mgmt. Assn. of San Diego (pres. 1971-72), Greater San Diego C. of C. (leader seminars 1987—), Sigma Kappa (dir. alumnae 1974—). Republican. Episcopalian. Home: 4196 Falcon St San Diego CA 92103 Office: Personnel Human Resources Cons Services 701 B St Suite 1300 San Diego CA 92101

SIMON, CARLY, singer, composer; b. N.Y.C., June 25, 1945; d. Richard S.; m. James Taylor, 1972 (div. 1983); children: Sarah Maria, Benjamin Simon; m. James Hart, Dec. 23, 1987. Studied with Pete Seeger. Singer, composer, rec. artist 1971—. Appeared in film No Nukes, 1980; albums include Carly Simon, 1971, Anticipation, 1972, No Secrets, 1973, Hotcakes, 1974, Playing Possum, 1975, The Best of Carly Simon, 1975, Another Passenger, 1976, Boys in the Trees, 1978, Spy, 1979, Come Upstairs, 1980, Torch, 1981, Hello Big Man, 1983, Spoiled Girl, 1985, Coming Around Again, 1987; single record Nobody Does It Better, 1977; recipient Grammy award as best new artist 1971. Office: care Champion Entertainment 130 W 57th St New York NY 10019

SIMON, CAROLINE K(LEIN), lawyer; b. N.Y.C.; d. Julia (Feist) and David Klein; m. Leopold King Simon (dec. 1952); children—Lee, Cathy Simon Silver; m. Irving W. Halpern, 1953 (dec.). Student Columbia U.; LL.B., NYU; L.H.D. (hon.), Jewish Inst. Religion, Hebrew Union Coll., 1966. Bar: N.Y., U.S. Dist. Ct. (so. dist.) N.Y., U.S. Supreme Ct. Gen. practice, N.Y.C.; of counsel Kaplan Kilsheimer & Foley; sec. of state State of N.Y., 1959-63; judge N.Y. State Ct. Claims, 1963-71. Mem. spl. legis. com. on ct. reorgn. N.Y. State Senate; formerly chmn. subcom. on the jury N.Y. Appellate Divs. 1st and 2d Depts.; mem. com. on discrimination in employment N.Y. State War Council, 1943-45; commr. State Workmen's Compensation Bd., 1944-45, State Commn. Against Discrimination, 1945-55, State Youth Commn., 1956-59; legal adviser U.S. del. UN Human Rights Commn., 1958; mem. White House Confs. on Children, 1950, 60; bd. dirs., exec. com. Com. on Modern Cts., Fund for Modern Cts.; mem. med. malpractice mediation panel 1st Jud. Dept.; adv. council Nat. Ctr. for State Cts.; past chmn. bd. trustees, past mem. exec. com. Nat. Council on Crime and Delinquency, also mem. nat. adv. council; hon. bd. trustees, past chmn. com. on social affairs and pub. responsibility Jewish Bd. Family and Children's Services; life mem. exec. bd., mem. adminstrv. com. and bd. govs. Am. Jewish Com.; mem. Nat. Jewish Welfare Bd.; pres., chmn., trustee Fedn. Employment and Guidance Service; bd. dirs., former v.p. Willkie House; bd. dirs. USO of N.Y.; former bd. dirs., asst. treas. Freedom House, also exec. com. and counsel to bd.; trustee N.Y. County Lawyers Found.; hon. bd. dirs. Manhattan chpt. Brandeis U. Nat. Women's Com.; hon. v.p. Nat. Assn. Women Artists, Inc., 19—; trustee, exec. com. Fedn. Jewish Philanthropies; former chmn. Legacy com. Temple Emanu-El; candidate of Republican Party for pres. City Council of N.Y., 1957; Contbr. to books; contbr. articles on govt., law, social problems to publs. including N.Y. Times Mag., Jour. of Living, legal jours. Recipient Presdl. citation NYU, 1962. Outstanding Citizenship award Am. Heritage Found., 1961, citation and testimonial, Mass. Com. on Caths. Protestants and Jews, 1960. Bond Between Us Award for outstanding service to Israel, 1960, citation and testimonial dinner Assn. for Help of Retarded Children, 1960, Ann. Brotherhood award Temple Emanu-El, N.Y.C. 1961, Woman of Achievement award Fedn. Jewish Women's Orgns., Salute to Women award, 1962; named Woman of Achievement, Women's Internat. Exposition, 1957, Woman of Yr., Beth Israel Hosp. Sch. Nursing, 1960, Woman of History N.Y. State, 1980; named to Hall of Fame Mt. Vernon High Sch. (N.Y.), 1981. Mem. ABA (sect. jud. adminstrn., alt. del. to Internat. Bar Assn. 1966), N.Y. State Bar Assn. (sec. jud. administrn., former chmn. adminstrv. law com., currently mem. cts. and community com., com. on profl. issues and standards, com. on election law), N.Y. County Lawyers Assn. (coms. judiciary, forum, spl. com. profl. ethics, former mem. bd. dirs.), Assn. Bar City N.Y. (com. on profl. responsibility, joint com. on fee concilliation, sr. vol. lawyers com.), World Habeus Corpus (exec. com.), Nat. Assn. Spl. Ct. Judges, Nat. Ctr. for State Cts. (adv. council), Am. Arbitration Assn. (law com. comml. sect.), Delta Kappa Gamma (internat. hon.). Home: 200 E 66th St New York NY 10021 Office: 122 E 42nd St 40th Floor New York NY 10168

SIMON, CHARLOTTE TULCHIN, psychology educator; b. N.Y.C., Dec. 10, 1925; d. Sam and Celia (Kamin) Tulchin; m. Ralph Simon, Sept. 5, 1947; children: Ellen, Lisa, Russell. BA, Bklyn. Coll., 1945; PhD, Syracuse U., 1953. Instr. psychology Syracuse (N.Y.) U., 1947-50; social psychologist VA Hosp., Perry Point, Md., 1958-59; asst. prof. psychology U. Md., College Park, 1959-60; cons. NIMH, Rockville, Md., 1964, Montgomery County Dept. Health, Rockville, 1966-69; prof. Montgomery Coll., Rockville, 1969—. Mem. Am. Psychol. Assn., Psychology of Women div. Am. Psychol. Assn. Home: 6213 Hollins Dr Bethesda MD 20817 Office: Montgomery Coll Dept Psychology Rockville MD 20850

SIMON, DEBRA KAY, account manager, consultant; b. Hinsdale, Ill., Dec. 19, 1957; d. Howard Thomas and Marie (Stauber) S. BA, N.Y. Sch. Interior Design, 1983; postgrad., Mo. So. U., 1977-79. Prin. Debi & Assocs., Wichita, Kans., 1983-85; acct. rep. Goldsmiths, Wichita, 1985-86, Facilitec Interiors for Bus., Tempe, Ariz., 1986—; cons. designer Show Case Homes, 1985. Coordinator Leukemia Soc., Wichita, 1985, Leukemia Soc., Scottsdale, 1987. Mem. Nat. Assn. Female Execs., Interior Design Soc. (million dollar sales award 1985), Nat. Assn. Women Bus. Owners. Republican. Roman Catholic. Club: Bicycle of Wichita. Home: 9275 E Mission Ln #111 Scottsdale AZ 85258 Office: Facilitec 1860 W University Tempe AZ 85281

SIMON, DEBRA WAGNER, accountant; b. Phila., July 24, 1959; d. Joseph and Annette (Schmerling) Wagner; m. Paul Stephen Simon, Sept. 5, 1982. BSBA, Drexel U., 1982. CPA, Pa. Jr. acct. Mann Judd Landau, Phila., 1983-84, staff acct., 1984, sr. acct., 1985—. Mem. Surrey Pl. Civic Assn., Cherry Hill, N.J., 1985-86. Mem. Am. Inst. CPA's, Pa.Inst. CPA's, Am. Women's Soc. CPA's, Am. Soc. Women Accts., Beta Alpha Psi. Avocations: tennis, computers. Office: Mann Judd Landau 1401 Walnut St Philadelphia PA 19102

SIMON, DORIS MARIE, nurse; b. Akron, Ohio, Jan. 24, 1932; d. Gabriel James and Nannie Eliza (Harris) Tyler; m. Matthew Hamilton Simon, Apr. 20, 1952; children: Matthew Derek, Denise Nanette, Gayle Machele, Doris Elizabeth. AA, El Paso (Tex.) Community Coll., 1976; student, St. Joseph's Coll., North Windham, Maine, 1985—. Med. asst. Dr. Melvin Farris, Akron, 1962-63, Dr. Samuel Watt, Akron, 1967-68, Drs. May, Fox and Buchwald, El Paso, 1972-76; nurse Providence Meml. Hosp., El Paso, 1976-77, head nurse transplant coordinator, 1987—; head nurse dialysis and transplant Hotel Dieu Med. Ctr., El Paso, 1977-87; med. asst. instr. Bryman Sch. Med. Assts., El Paso, 1970-72. Leader children's choirs, Ft. Sill, Okla., 1964-67; choir dir. Ft. Sill area and Ft. Bliss, Tex., area, 1964-74; instr. piano and music theory, Ft. Sill, 1974—; leader Ft. Sill council Girl Scouts Am., 1965-67; instr. Sch. for Handicapped, Lawton, Okla., 1965-67; del. to Peoples Republic China citizen ambassador program People to People Internat., 1988. Recipient Molly Pitcher award U.S. Army, 1966-67. Mem. Am. Nurses Assn., Am. Med. Assts. Assn., Am. Nephrology Nurses Assn. Baptist. Clubs: Les Charmantes (Akron) (pres./sec. 1950-52), Links. Home: 8909 Parkland Dr El Paso TX 79925 Office: Providence Meml Hosp 2001 N Oregon St El Paso TX 79902

SIMON, DOROTHY ELAINE, educator; b. Madison, Wis., Nov. 17, 1931; d. William Rees and Beatrice Helena (Reque) Beckett; m. William Henry Simon, Oct. 1, 1955; children—Stephen Eric, William Edward. BS, So. Conn. State U., 1954. Cert. elem. tchr., Conn. Tchr. grade 1 Ctr. St. Sch., North Haven, Conn., 1954-57; tchr. grades 3-4 Clover St. Sch., Windsor, Conn., 1968-87; cooperating tchr. Internship Program, U. Hartford and Cen. Conn. State U., 1973-85; unit leader Multi Unit Sch., Windsor, 1972-87. Corr. sec. Women's Aux. of Hartford Symphony, 1966-70; v.p. PTO, Windsor, 1965-68; co-chmn. Windsor ARC Drive, 1969. Recipient honorarium So. New Eng. Telephone. Mem. NEA, Conn. Edn. Assn., Windsor Edn. Assn., Nat. Assn. Individually Guided Edn. Episcopalian. Clubs: Green Mountain (Vt.); Millbrook Golf (Windsor). Avocations: sketching, writing, hiking, camping, bicycling. Home: 17 Priscilla Rd Windsor CT 06095 Office: Clover St Sch 57 Clover St Windsor CT 06095

SIMON, DOROTHY MARTIN, chemist, business executive; b. Harwood, Mo., Sept. 18, 1919; d. Robert William and Laudell (Flynn) Martin; m. Sidney L. Simon, Dec. 6, 1946 (dec. Nov. 26, 1975). A.B., S.W. Mo. State U., 1940; Ph.D., U. Ill., 1945; postdoctoral work, Cambridge (Eng.) U., 1953-54; Sc.D. (hon.), Worcester Poly. Inst., 1971; D.Eng. (hon.), Lehigh U., 1978. Grad. teaching asst. U. Ill., 1941-45; research chemist rayon div. E. I. Du Pont de Nemours & Co., Inc., Buffalo, 1945-47; chemist Oak Ridge Nat. Lab., 1947; asso. chemist Argonne (Ill.) Nat. Lab., 1948-49; aero. research scientist, group leader NACA, Cleve., 1949-53; asst. br. chief chemistry NACA, 1954-55; group leader combustion fundamentals Magnolia Petroleum Co. subs. Mobil Corp., Dallas, 1955-56; prin. scientist, tech. asst. to pres. research and advanced devel. div. Avco Corp., Greenwich, Conn., 1956-62; dir. corp. research def. and indsl. products group Avco Corp., 1962-64, group v.p., 1964-68, corp. v.p. research, 1968-84; pres. Simon Assocs., 1984—; Marie Curie lectr. State U. Pa., 1962; exec. lectr. U. Ill., 1981; bd. dirs. Crown Zellerbach Corp., Warner Lambert Corp.; corp. mem. Drape Lab.; mem. Pres.'s Com. on Nat. Medal Sci., 1979-81; mem. space systems and tech. adv. com. NASA; mem. NSF panel sci. and tech., 1973-84; mem. statutory com. Nat. Bur. Standards, Dept. Commerce, 1979-84; chmn. nat. materials adv. bd. NRC; vis. com. aeros. and astronautics M.I.T., 1980-83; mem. def. policy adv. com. on trade Dept. Def., 1982-84. Contbr. articles to profl. jours. and collected symposia books. Trustee Worcester Poly. Inst., Northeastern U.; mem. vis. com. sponsored research Mass. Inst. Tech., 1972-78; mem. overseers' com. for applied research Harvard U.; mem. Daniel Guggenheim Bd. Awards, 1978-82, chmn., 1982. Recipient Rockefeller Pub. Service award, 1953, Outstanding Alumnus award S.W. Mo. State U., 1957, Outstanding Profl. Woman award Bus., Profl. Women's Club N.Y., 1966; Engring. Achievement award U. Mo., 1980; Illini Achievement award U. Ill., 1983. Fellow Am. Inst. Chemists, AIAA (chmn. sect. 1977-79, nat. dir. 1979-81); mem. Am. Chem. Soc., Internat. Combustion Inst., Soc. Woman Engrs. (Achievement award 1966), Sigma Xi. Home and Office: 222 Stagecoach Rd Chapel Hill NC 27514

SIMON, EVELYN, lawyer; b. N.Y.C., May 13, 1943; d. Joseph and Adele (Holzschlag) Berkman; m. Frederick Simon, Aug. 18, 1963; children: Amy Jocelyn, Marcie Ann. AB in Physics, Barnard Coll., 1963; MS in Physics, U. Pitts., 1964; JD, Wayne State U., 1978; LLB, Monash U., Melbourne, Australia, 1980. Bar: Mich. 1980, Victoria (Australia) 1981. Supr. engring. Chrysler Corp., Detroit, 1964-72; edn. and profl. mgr. Engring. Soc. Detroit, 1972-78; solicitor Arthur Robinson & Co., Melbourne, 1980-81; sr. atty. Ford Motor Co., Detroit, 1981—. Mem. Mich. Bar Assn., Law Assn. Victoria, Engring. Soc. Detroit. Office: Ford Motor Co 300 Renaissance Ctr Detroit MI 48243

SIMON, JACQUELINE ALBERT, political scientist, journalist; b. N.Y.C.; d. Louis and Rose (Axelroad) Albert; B.A. cum laude, NYU, M.A., 1972, Ph.D., 1977; m. Pierre Simon; children—Lisette, Orville. Adj. asst. prof. Southampton Coll., 1977, 79—; mng. editor Point of Contact, N.Y.C., 1975-76; assoc. editor, U.S. bur. chief Politique Internationale, Paris, 1979—; research assoc. Inst. French Studies, N.Y. U., N.Y.C., 1980—, asst. prof. govt., 1982-83; cons., 1977—; assoc. Inst. on the Media for War and Peace; frequent appearances French TV and radio. Contbg. editor Harper's, 1984—. Bd. dirs. Fresh Air Fund. 1974. Mem. Ams. for Democratic Action, Nat. Acad. Sci., Am. Polit. Sci. Assn., French-Am. Soc., Phi Beta Kappa. Contbr. articles to profl. jours. Home: 988 Fifth Ave New York NY 10021

SIMON, JOAN M., academic administrator; b. Chgo., Feb. 27, 1934; d. William E. and Marie (Doherty) Cochrane; m. James William Simon;children: James William, Gary William, Christy Lee. BA, Nat. Coll. Edn., 1985, postgrad., 1985—. Dir. adult edn. Community Cen. Found., Palos Park, Ill., 1973-79; v.p. spl. mktg. AMS Life Ins. Co., Oakbrook Terrace, Ill., 1979-84; dir. community edn. St. Xavier Coll., Chgo., 1984—, mem. adv. bd. tchr. profl. devel., 1987—; mem. evaluation team North Cen. Accreditation, Chgo., 1986-87; dir. special programs and extended services Prarie State Coll., Chicago Heights, Ill. Columnist Suburbanite Economist, 1971-75, Midwest Nursing News, 1983. Sec. Bridgeview (Ill.) Park Dist., 1965-73; mem. dist. com. Boy Scouts Am., LaGrange, 1987—; elected Bridgeview Village Bd., 1984-88; bd. dirs. Bridgeview Library Bd., 1965-84, Community Ctr., Palos Park, 1979-86. Mem. Women In Mgmt. (pres. Oakbrook Chpt. 1987, Woman of Achievement award 1985, 88), Learning Resources Network, Ill. Women Govt., The Exec. Female, Chgo. C. of C. Lodge: Women of the Moose (chair 1970-72). Home: 7712 S Ferdinand Ave Bridgeview IL 60455

SIMON, JOANNA THEODORA, telecommunications manager, technical writer; b. N.Y.C., Apr. 13, 1943; d. Joachim N. and Henrietta (Hirsch) S.; m. Gilmer L. Blankespoor, Jan. 28, 1967 (div. 1980); children: Juliet, Kevin, Jill. BA, NYU, 1965. Dir. press relations Nat. Planning Assn., Washington, 1968-70; dir. publicity, sr. editor Acropolis Books, Washington, 1970-73; proposal prodn. mgr. Computer Scis. Corp., Herndon, Va., 1979-84; sr. proposal coordinator Contel, Fairfax, Va., 1984-85; mgr. proposal support U.S. West, Rockville, Md., 1985-87; proposal engr. Telex Computer Products, 1987-88; dir. corp. proposal div. CRC Systems, Inc., Fairfax, 1988—. Contbr. articles to mags.; editor articles in profl. jours., software reference books. Mem. Soc. for Tech. Communications. Home: 2047 Durand Reston VA 22091

SIMON, LINDA ANN, airline captain; b. Lubbock, Tex., July 13, 1948; d. Levi Jackson and Lenora Irene (Lueck) Coble; m. Paul N. Simon, Apr. 9, 1975; children: Randi, Eric, Garrett. BS, Tex. Christian U., 1970, MEd, 1972; PhD, Pacific Western U., 1985. Tchr., coach Dept. Def. Overseas Dependent Sch., Goose Bay, Labrador, 1972-73, Zama, Japan, 1973-74, Machinato, Okinawa, 1974-75; grad. studies coordinator Pepperdine U., Ft. Gordon, Ga., 1976-78; flight instr. Ft. Gordon (Ga.) Flying Club, 1978-80; flight instr., charter pilot Augusta (Ga.) Aviation Inc, 1980-83; chief pilot R.W. Allen & Assocs., Augusta, 1983-84, constrn. safety inspr., 1983-84; pilot Atlantic Southeast Airlines, Atlanta, 1984—, chair safety com., 1984—. Instr. ARC, Augusta, 1976-80. Mem. Nat. Assn. of Flight Instrs., Airplane Owners and Pilots Assn., Civil Air Patrol (safety officer 1976-80). Lutheran. Club: Officers Wives. Home: 3303 Cockatoo Rd Augusta GA 30907 Office: Atlantic SE Airlines 1688 Phoenix Blvd College Park GA 30490

SIMON, LIZ A., social worker; b. Kaplan, La., Mar. 21, 1949; d. Luke and Lucy (Marceaux) S.; B.A., St. Mary's Dominican Coll., 1971; M.S.W., Tulane U., 1972. Coordinator Satellite Clinics, Charters Mental Health Center, New Orleans, 1973-74, clin. social worker, 1974-77; field instr. Tulane U. Sch. Social Work, New Orleans, 1975-76; clin. cons., community edn. facilitator Family & Child Services, New Orleans, 1977-79; pvt. practice psychotherapy, New Orleans, 1977—; mem. La. State Bd. Cert. Social Workers; cons. YWCA Battered Women's Program, New Orleans, 1978-79, bd. dirs., 1979-80. Clin. fellow Tulane U., 1973. Mem. New Orleans Feminist Counseling Collective (founding mem. 1976), Women Against Violence Against Women (chmn. interium com. 1978-79, dir. 1981), La. Soc. Clin. Social Work, Assn. Women in Social Work, Acad. Cert. Social Workers, Nat. Assn. Social Workers (La. state bd. dirs. 1983-86, 87—, v.p. La. state pvt. practice SIG 1987-88, chairperson La. state Lesbian and Gay Issues SIG 1985-88, mem. La. state task force on AIDS 1987-88, state nat. com. mem., nat. com. on lesbian and gay rights 1983-86), La. com. Social Work Vendershop (steering com. mem. 1985, regional rep. 1987-88), ACLU, NOW. La. Gay Polit. Action Caucus (bd. dirs. 1981-82), Nat. Gay Task Force, Gay Rights Nat. Lobby, Council for Devel. of French in La. Feminist Writers Guild. Home: 220 S Gayoso New Orleans LA 70119 Office: 3500 St Charles Ave New Orleans LA 70115

SIMON, LORENA COTTS, music educator, composer, poet; b. Sherman, Tex., Jan. 16, 1897; d. George Godfrey and Willie (Jones) Cotts; student Am. Conservatory, summer 1938, Juilliard Music Sch., summer 1939; diploma Sherwood Music Sch., 1941; LittD (hon.), Internat. Acad. Leadership, Quezon City, Philippines; LHD (hon.), No. Pontificial Acad., Malmo, Sweden, 1969; MusD (hon.), St. Olav's Acad., Sweden, 1969; m. Samuel C. Simon, Nov. 6, 1918 (dec.). Tchr. violin, piano, theory and harmony, Port Arthur, Tex., 1919—. Organizer, dir. Schubert's Violin Choir, Port Arthur, 1919-55. Named Poet Laureate of Tex. 1961; Poet Laureate of Magnolia Dist., 1962-64; Poet Laureate of Port Arthur, 1962—; recipient gold plaque Tex. Fedn. Women's Club, 1962, spl. award 1st place in poetry and music Tex. heritage dept., 1963; medal of merit and diploma of merit Centro Studi Scambi Internat., Rome, Italy, 1965; Gold medal award, and hon. poet laureate-musician United Poets Laureate Internat., 1966, named Cath. Lady of Humanity, 1977; decorated Equestrian Order of Holy Sepulchre, 1981; inducted into Knights and Ladies of the Holy Sepulchre, Pope John II, 1982, Nat. Guild of Piano Tchrs.' Hall of Fame, 1986, Southeast Tex. Women's Hall of Fame, 1987; recipient Greatness and Leadership award U. Manila, 1967; Silver medal, Gold medal, Diploma Centro Studi E Scambi—Internazionali, 1967; Gold Laurel Wreath, Gold medal, Karte of Award, 1966; named to International Poets' Hall of Fame, 1969, named most outstanding woman internationally Congress of Doctors, Quezon City, Philippines, 1969; named Cath. Poet Laureate of World, 1967. Mem. Nat., Tex. press women's assns., Nat. Council Cath. Women, Nat. Guild Piano Tchrs. (charter mem.; adjudicator), Am. Coll. Musicians (adjudicator), Internat. Guild Library, Am. Poetry League, Poets Soc. Tex. (critic judge), Am. Poets Fellowship Soc. Corp., UN Assn. U.S.A., Alpha Delta Kappa. Clubs: Writers' (pres. 1963-64), Symphony. Author: The Golden Keys, 1958; From My Heart (1st place award Ann. Poetry Writers Contest of Tex. Press Women's Assn. 1961), 1959; Children's Story Hour (1st place award Nat. Fedn. Press Women's Ann. Writers' Contest 1962), 1960. Songs pub. include: Live Expectantly, 1962, In Search for Growth, 1963, Freedom's Light, 1963, What Can I Do for Jesus, 1963, I Was a Star, I Was a Lamb, I Was a Donkey; organ piece Mediation, 1967. Chmn. spl. editorial com. World Poets Laureate Anthology, 1969-70. Donor funds for constrn. of 9 churches in Africa. Home: 411 5th Ave Port Arthur TX 77642

SIMON, MELANIE VASS, management executive; b. N.Y.C., Dec. 8, 1952; d. Kamala (Shrinagesh) Vass; m. John S. Simon, Aug. 14, 1981. BA cum laude, U. So. Calif., 1974; postgrad., Harvard U., 1978-79. Research asst. Fed. R.R. Adminstrn., Washington, 1974-75; ops. analyst, mgr. U.S. Ry. Assn., Washington, 1975-76; sr. cons. Peat, Marwick Mitchell & Co., Washington, 1976-78; cons. AT&T Long Lines, Bedminster, N.J., 1979, Input Output Computer Services, Bethesda, Md., 1979-80; various positions WED Enterprises div. Disney Studios, Glendale, Calif., 1980-84; treas. WET Enterprises, Burbank, Calif., 1984-85; pvt. practice cons. Los Angeles, 1985-86; mgr. Walt Disney Imagineering, Glendale, Calif., 1986—. Treas. T.H.E. Clinic, Los Angeles. Home: 1048 W Ave 37 Los Angeles CA 90065

SIMON, NANCY WYNN, academic administrator; b. Needham, Mass., Apr. 2, 1942; d. Stearns Hibbard and Helen Charlotte (Binner) Smalley; m. Frank J. Simon, Jr., Dec. 21, 1963 (div. Mar. 1985); 1 child, Gregory Robert. BA, U. Pa., 1964; MA, Dominican Coll., 1971. Tchr. Latin Robinson Sch., West Hartford, Conn., 1966-68; tchr. English Renbrook Sch., West Hartford, Conn., 1968-69, acad. dean, camp dir., 1976-80; asst. dean students Dominican Coll., San Rafael, Calif., 1970-71; tchr., dorm master Ethel Walker Sch., Simsbury, Conn., 1971-76; founder, headmaster San Francisco Day Sch., 1981—. Mem. Bay Area Minority Affairs Coalition, San Francisco, 1982—. Mem. Nat. Assn. Prins. Schs. for Girls, Nat. Assn. Ind. Schs. (devel. com., staff mem. New Heads Workshop 1986—), Elem. Sch. Heads Assn., Calif. Assn. Ind. Schs., Headmistresses' Assn. East. Episcopalian. Office: San Francisco Day Sch 350 Masonic Ave San Francisco CA 94118

SIMON, PHEBE EUPHEMIA, marketing professional; b. Abbeville, Ga., Jan. 16, 1945; d. Ernest and Sallie Mae (Fortson) Lewis; m. Ira Lee, Sept. 5, 1962 (div. Aug. 1974); 1 child Ira Dennis; m. Thomas H. Simon, Dec. 23, 1979. Student, Greenwood Tech., 1963-64; BA in Mgmt., Furman U.; postgrad., Cains House Talent. With mgmt., lab tech. Bigelow and Sanford, Abbeville, S.C., 1964-74; specialist special accounts First Nat. Bank, Atlanta, 1974-76; mgr. cash control Sid and Morty Kroft, Atlanta, 1975-77; mgr. sales City Beverage Co., Atlanta, 1977-80; dir. sales, mktg. Premium Beverage Inc., Atlanta, 1980—. Producer: Miss Black U.S.A. Scholarship Pageant, Miss Black Atlanta Scholarship Pageant. Producer Miss Black Atlanta Pageant, 1986. Mem. Atlanta Assn. Female Exec., (dir. 1985—), Womens Connection Protection, (pres. 1984), League Women Voters, Fulton County, Womens Commerce, Atlanta Womens Networ, Nat. Assn. Female Exec., (pres. 1985—), NAACP. Democrat. Baptist. Home: 2369 Dodson Dr East Point GA 30344

SIMONE, GAIL ELISABETH, military affairs administrator; b. Boston, Dec. 3, 1944; d. Hugh Nelson and Louise Amelia (Shedrick) Saunders; m. Edburnne R. Hare, Sept. 7, 1968 (div. 1974); m. Joseph R. Simone, June 27, 1987. BA, The King's Coll., 1966; postgrad., Harvard U., 1976-77. Placement dir. Boston Bar Assn., 1966-67; pub. relations Emerson Coll., Boston, 1967-69; asst. to v.p. Vance, Sanders, Inc., Boston, 1969-70; office mgr. Trans. DIsplays, Inc., Boston, 1970-71; seminar coordinator Assn. Trial Lawyers Am., Cambridge, Mass., 1971-74; writer, researcher Ednl. Expeditions Internat., Belmont, Mass., 1975-76; analyst United Brands Co., N.Y.C., 1976-80; analyst Mil. Sealift Commd., USN, Washington, 1980-84, legis. affairs officer, 1984—; free-lance writer, editor, Boston, 1970-73. Vol. McCarthy Presdl. Campaign, Boston, 1968, Mass. Pax, Boston; foster parent Warwick, R.I., 1986—; mem. Amnesty Internat., N.Y.C., 1987—, various other orgns. Mem. Nat. Assn. Female Execs., Women's Trans. Seminar. Office: Mil Sealift Commd Washington Navy Yard Washington DC 20398-5100

SIMONE, M. SUZAN, sales administrator; b. Honolulu. BA in Social Ecology, U. Calif., Irvine, 1982. Co-founder, pres. U. Calif. Radio Network, Irvine, 1982-83; dir. corp. communications Capital Tech. Group, Inc., Costa Mesa, Calif., 1986; mgr. sales Laser Video, Inc., Anaheim, Calif., 1983—; mgmt. cons., Costa Mesa, 1983-85; licensing rep. Discovision Assocs., Costa Mesa, 1984—. Mem. Nat. Assn. Ind. Record Distbrs., Nat. Assn. Record Merchandisers, Nat. Assn. for Female Execs., Friends of KUCI. Office: Disctronics Inc 3500 W Olive Ave Suite 1020 Burbank CA 91505

SIMONETTI, JOAN ESTHER, consumer goods and health products company executive; b. San Antonio, Aug. 17, 1952; d. Lino D. and Florence (Arida) S. BS in Biology, Bethany (W.Va.) Coll., 1974; postgrad. in indsl. relations, Rutgers U., 1977—. Ptnr. Lyons & Assocs., New Brunswick, N.J., 1975-79; mgr. suture mfg. Ethicon, Inc., Somerville, N.J., 1979-82, dept. mgr. fibre finishing, Johnson & Johnson Products, Sherman, Tex., 1982-86, dept. mgr. sterilization and receiving Patient Care div., 1986—; bus. cons. to local high schs. Participant Women in N.J. bus. com. Kean for Gov. campaign, 1981; bd. dirs. YWCA Cen. Jersey, 1976-78, Jr. Achievement, Groyson County, 1988 (cons. bus. program 1985-86); bd. dirs., publicity chmn. House of Hope, 1984-87; chair Sherman Chamber Youth Devel. Com., 1986—. Recipient cert. Women in Bus. and Industry, 1981; Bethany Coll. scholar, 1974. Mem. Nat. Assn. Female Execs., Am. Bus. Women's Assn. (v.p. chpt. 1985-86, Woman of Month 1985), Am. Soc. Personnel Adminstrs., Indsl. Relations Research Assn., Sherman C. of C. (active Leadership Sherman program 1987). Republican. Roman Catholic. Home: 2212 Ridgewood Rd Sherman TX 75090

SIMONS, ELIZABETH R., biochemist, educator; b. Vienna, Austria, Sept. 1, 1929; came to U.S., 1941, naturalized, 1948; d. William and Erna Engle (Weisselberg) Reiman; B.Ch.E., Cooper Union, N.Y.C., 1950; M.S., Yale U., 1951, Ph.D., 1954; m. Harold Lee Simons, Aug. 12, 1951; children—Leslie Ann Mulert, Robert David. Research chemist Tech. Operations, Arlington, Mass., 1953-54; instr. chemistry Wellesley (Mass.) Coll., 1954-57; research asst. Children's Hosp. Med. Center and Cancer Research Found., Boston, 1957-59, research asso. pathology, 1959-62; research asso. Harvard Med. Sch., 1962-66, lectr. biol. chemistry, 1966-72; tutor biochemical scis. Harvard Coll., 1971—; asso. prof. biochemistry Boston U., 1972-78, prof., 1978—. Grantee in field. Mem. AAAS, Am. Chem. Soc., Am. Heart Assn., Am. Soc. Biol. Chemists, Am. Soc. Cell Biology, Am. Soc. Hematology, Am. Fedn. Clin. Research, Assn. Women in Sci., Biophys. Soc., Internat. Soc. Thrombosis and Hemostasis, N.Y. Acad. Sci., Sigma Xi. Contbr. in field. Office: Boston U Sch Medicine 80 E Concord St Boston MA 02118

SIMONS, HELEN, school psychologist; b. Chgo., Feb. 13, 1930; d. Leo and Sarah (Shrayer) Pomper; m. Broudy Simons, May 20, 1956 (May 1972); children: Larry, Sheri. BA in Biol., Lake Forest Coll., 1951; MA in Clin. Psychology, Roosevelt U., 1972; D of Psychology, Ill. Sch. Profl. Psychology, 1980. Intern Cook County Hosp., Chgo., 1979-80; pvt. practice psychotherapist Chgo., 1980—; sch. psychologist Chgo. Bd. Educators, 1974-79, 80—. Mem. Am. Psychol. Assn., Ill. Psychol. Assn., Nat. Sch. Psychologist's Assn., Ill. Sch. Psychologist's Assn., Chgo. Sch. Psychologist's

Assn., Chgo. Psychol. Assn. Home: 6145 N Sheridan Rd 29D Chicago IL 60660 Office: Dist 2 6110 N California Chicago IL 60659

SIMONS, LYNN OSBORN, state education official; b. Havre, Mont., June 1, 1934; d. Robert Blair and Dorothy (Briggs) Osborn; B.A., U. Colo., 1956; postgrad. U. Wyo., 1958-60; m. John Powell Simons, Jan. 19, 1957; children—Clayton Osborn, William Blair. Tchr., Midvale (Utah) Jr. High Sch., 1956-57, Sweetwater County Sch. Dist. 1, Rock Springs, Wyo., 1957-58, U. Wyo., Laramie, 1959-61, Natrona County Sch. Dist. 1, Casper, Wyo., 1963-64; credit mgr. Gallery 323, Casper, 1972-77; Wyo. state supt. public instrn., Cheyenne, 1979—; mem. State Bds. Charities and Reform, Land Commrs., Farm Loan, 1979—; mem. State Commns. Capitol Bldg., Liquor, 1979—; Ex-officio mem. bd. trustees U. Wyo.; ex-officio mem. Wyo. Community Coll. Commn.; mem., treas. steering com. Edn. Commn. of the States; adv. State Bd. Edn., 1971-77, chmn., 1976-77; bd. dirs. Council Chief State Sch. Officers. Mem. LWV (pres. 1970-71), Am. Assn. Sch. Adminstrs., Council Chief State Sch. Officers, Wyo. Assn. Sch. Adminstrs. Democrat. Episcopalian. Home: Box 185 Cheyenne WY 82002 Office: Hathaway Bldg Cheyenne WY 82001

SIMONSON, DONNA MARIE, social services administrator; b. Decatur, Ill., Jan. 25, 1948; d. Howard Joseph and Geneva Darlene Gleespen. Student, Alverno Coll., 1966-68; BA, U. Ill., 1971, MSW, 1975. Specialist Ill. Dept. Mental Health, Danville, 1971-74; student assoc. Com. on Women in Social Welfare, Nat. Assn. Social Workers, Washington, 1974; children's cons. Ill. Commn. Children, Springfield, 1975, exec. dir., 1977-85; social service planner Ill. Dept. Children and Family Services, Springfield, 1985—; mem. faculty Sch. of Health and Human Services, Sangamon State U., Springfield, 1986-87. Editor various reports in field. Mem. Juvenile Justice Del., Citizen ambassador, People to People, USSR and Western Europe, 1982. Mem. Nat. Assn. Social Workers (various offices), U. Ill. Sch. Social Work Alumni Assn. (pres. program bd. 1986-87). Club: Altrusa of Springfield (pres. 1986-88). Office: Dept Children and Family Services 406 E Monroe Springfield IL 62701

SIMONSON, SUSAN KAY, hospital administrator; b. LaPorte, Ind., Dec. 5, 1946; d. George Randolph and Myrtle Lucille (Opfel) Menkes; m. Richard Bruce Simonson, Aug. 25, 1973. BA with honors, Ind. U., 1969; MA, Washington U., St. Louis, 1972. Perinatal social worker Yakima Valley Meml. Hosp., Yakima, Wash., 1979-81, dir. social service, 1982—, dir. patient support and hospice program, 1981—; Spanish instr. Yakima Valley Coll., Yakima, Wash., 1981—; pres. Yakima Child Abuse Council, 1983-85; developer nat. patient support program, 1981. Contbr. articles to profl. jours. Mem. Jr. League, Yakima; mem. adv. council Robert Wood Johnson Found. Rural Infant Health Care Project, Yakima, 1980, Pregnancy Loss and Compassionate Friends Support Groups, Yakima, 1982—, Teen Outreach Program, Yakima, 1984—. Recipient NSF award, 1967, discharge planning program of yr. regional award Nat. Glassrock Home Health Care Discharge Planning Program, 1987; research grantee Ind. U., 1968, Fulbright grantee U.S. Dept. State, 1969-70; Nat. Def. Edn. Act fellowship, 1970-73. Mem. AAUW, Soc. Med. Anthropology, Soc. Hosp. Social Work Dirs. of Am. Hosp. Assn., Nat. Assn. Perinatal Social Workers, Nat. Assn. Social Workers, Phi Beta Kappa. Office: Yakima Valley Meml Hosp 2811 Tieton Dr Yakima WA 98902

SIMPSON, ADELE, costume designer; b. N.Y.C., Dec. 8, 1908; d. Jacob and Ella (Bloch) Smithline; m. Wesley William Simpson, Oct. 8, 1930; children: Jeffrey R., Joan Ellen. Grad., Pratt Inst., Bklyn. With Ben Gershel, N.Y.C., 1922-23; head dress designer Ben Gershel, 1923; chief designer William Bass, N.Y.C., 1927-28; designer (own label) Mary Lee Fashions (named changed to Adele Simpson, Inc. 1949), N.Y.C., 1928-49, pres., dir., from 1949, now chmn. bd. Work displayed in Met. Costume Inst., Bklyn. Mus., Dallas Library. Recipient Neiman-Marcus Fashion award, 1946, Coty Fashion award, 1947, First Nat. Cotton Council award, 1953. Mem. Fashion Group, N.Y. Couture Group. Office: Adele Simpson Inc 530 7th Ave New York NY 10018 •

SIMPSON, ANDREA LYNN, energy company communications executive; b. Altadena, Calif., Feb. 10, 1948; d. Kenneth James and Barbara Faries Simpson; m. John R. Myrdal, Dec. 13, 1986. B.A., U. So. Calif., 1969, M.S., 1983; postgrad. U. Colo., Boulder, 1977. Asst. cashier United Calif. Bank, Los Angeles, 1969-73; asst. v.p. mktg. 1st Hawaiian Bank, Honolulu, 1973-78; v.p. corp. communications Pacific Resources, Inc., Honolulu, 1978—. Bd. dirs. Hawaii Heart Assn., 1978-83, Child and Family Services, 1984-86, Council of Pacific, Girl Scouts U.S.A., 1982-85, Arts Council Hawaii, 1977-81; trustee Hawaii Loa Coll., 1984-86; commr Hawaii State Commn. on Status of Women, 1985-87. Bd. dirs. Honolulu Symphony Soc., 1986—; active Jr. League of Honolulu. Named Outstanding Young Person of Hawaii, Hawaii Jaycees, 1978; Panhellenic Woman of Yr., Hawaii, 1979; Outstanding Woman in Bus., Hawaii YWCA, 1980; Outstanding Young Woman of Hawaii, Hawaii Legislature, 1980. Mem. Am. Mktg. Assn., Pub. Relations Soc. Am. (bd. dirs. Honolulu chpt. 1984-865, Silver Anvil award 1984), Pub. Utilities Communicators Assn. (Communicator of Yr. 1984), Honolulu Advt. Fedn. (Advt. Woman of Yr. 1984), U. So. Calif. Alumni Assn. (bd. dirs. Hawaii 1981-83), Alpha Phi (dir. Hawaii). Clubs: Outrigger Canoe, Pacific, Jr. League. Office: Pacific Resources Inc PO Box 3379 Honolulu HI 96842

SIMPSON, BARBARA L., educational administrator; b. Cleve., Apr. 6, 1947; d. Curley and Cora (Chambliss) Brown; children—Michelle, Crystal, Twilla. BE, Ohio State U., 1967; M.S. in Edn. Media, Kent State U. (Ohio), 1971, MLS, 1971. Adminstrv. supr. Cleve. pub. schs., 1968-72; librarian Cuyahoga Community Coll., Cleve., 1972-75, coordinator, 1975-77, interim dir., 1977-78, asst. dean, 1978-80, dir., 1980-84; dir. library Kean Coll., Union, N.J., 1984—; cons. Dembsy Assocs., Boston, 1967-81; editorial cons. Max Pub. Co., N.Y.C., 1967-81; cons. reader U.S. Office Edn., Washington, 1979-80; editorial cons. Jossey-Bass Pub. Co., 1979. Cons. editor Probe, 1975, Sch. Media Ctr., 1968, Booklist, 1969; contbr. articles to profl. jours. Bd. dirs. N.J. Adv. Bd. on the Status of Women, 1988, Africana Studies, 1988, N.J. Library Adv. Bd., 1987. Recipient Phillips award Kent State U., 1970. Mem. ALA, Higher Edn. Reps., N.J. Acad. Library Network (chmn. 1987), Council N.J. Coll. Libraries (pres. 1987—), N.J. Library Assn., Oral History Soc., N.J. Hist. Soc., Jr. League (Cleve. vice chmn. 1981, 83) Clubs: Concerned Parents (pres. 1984) (Beachwood, Ohio), Women's City . Avocations: music, reading. Office: Kean Coll Library Morris Ave Union NJ 07083

SIMPSON, CATHY ANN, land title company executive, real estate broker; b. Ripley, Miss., Aug. 6, 1953; d. Booth Obed and Annette Grace (Tapp) Simpson. m. Thomas Earl Jones, July 21, 1973 (div. Dec. 1981). B.A. with honors, Harding U., 1975. Real estate broker Houston Bd. Realtors, 1976—; mktg. broker cons. Capital Title Co., Houston, 1979-81; founder, owner The Settlers, 1979—, asst. v.p. Commerce Title Co., Houston, 1981-85; mktg. broker Capital Title Co., 1985—; faculty The Real Estate Sch. Mem. Tex. Real Estate Polit. Action Com. Mem. Nat. Assn. Realtors, Houston Bd. Realtors. Democrat. Mem. Ch. of Christ. Home: 11710 Bowlan Ln Houston TX 77035 Office: Capital Title Co 2929 Allen Pkwy Suite 200 Houston TX 77019

SIMPSON, CONSTANCE ANN, academic administrator; b. Hydaburg, Alaska, May 4, 1936; d. Arthur Andrew Helgesen and Florence Lois (Lee) Johnson; m. Jerry Dixon Simpson, June 1, 1957; children: Darren Arthur, Lynelle Grace. Student, Western Wash. Coll., 1953-55; AA, Sheldon Jackson Coll., 1974; student, U. Alaska, 1974—. Edn. counselor Sheldon Jackson Coll., Sitka, Alaska, 1972-74, dir. student services, 1974-76, coordinator instn. devel., 1976-78, asst. dir. advancement, 1978-79; career resource specialist Sitka Community Assn., 1979-80, higher edn. adminstr., 1980—. V.p. Statewide Alaska Native Sisterhood, 1973-75; mem. Alaska Health Council, Juneau, 1977-80; bd. dirs. Sitka Teen Resource, 1986 Mem. Alaska Vocat. Assn., Western Assn. Fin. Aid Adminstrs., Bus. and Profl. Women. Republican. Presbyterian. Home: 1101 Edgecumbe Dr Sitka AK 99835 Office: Sitka Community Assn PO Box 1450 Sitka AK 99835

SIMPSON, HARRIETT STONER, personnel executive; b. Abbeville, S.C., Nov. 18, 1945; d. Guy Lafayette and Ethel (Brownlee) Stoner; 1 son, Christopher. Student, Ga. Coll., 1964-65, Lander Coll., 1976-80. With Flexible Tubing, Abbeville, S.C., 1965—, personnel asst., 1971-79, employment mgr., 1979-84, personnel mgr., 1984—. Co-chmn. Abbeville County Spring Festival, 1984; mem. Abbeville County Devel. Bd. Recipient Work award Abbeville County Devel. Bd., 1984. Mem. Am. Soc. Personnel Adminstrn., Piedmont Area Personnel Assn., Nat. Assn. Female Execs. Republican. Baptist. Office: Flexible Techs Box 888 Abbeville SC 29620

SIMPSON, JUDITH KAY, development company executive; b. Shelbyville, Tenn., Mar. 5, 1944; d. Albert Donald and Jessie Ruth (Casteil) Snell. B.S. in Office Mgmt., Middle Tenn. State U., 1966. Prin. stenographer Tenn. Dept. Edn., Nashville, 1967-73; asst. office mgr. Lee Co., Nashville, 1977-81; controller Sharondale Constrn. Co., Brentwood, Tenn., 1981-87, dir. fin., 1987-88; controller Cross Properties, Brentwood, 1988—. Vice pres. United Methodist Women, South End United Methodist Ch., Nashville, 1974, chmn. Council on Ministries, 1976-77; dir. prison ministry Ch. Women United, Nashville, 1975-76. Mem. Am. Mgmt. Assn., Constrn. Fin. Mgmt. Assn. (bd. dirs. Middle Tenn chpt., sec.). Republican. Presbyterian. Avocations: music; reading; interior decorating. Office: Cross POrperties 1749 Mallory Ln Suite 100 Brentwood TN 37027

SIMPSON, KATHRYN JACQUIN, retired publishing company executive; b. Peoria, Ill., June 22, 1924; d. Wentworth Cory and Kathryn Mathilda (Niehaus) Jacquin; m. Howard M. Simpson, Nov. 25, 1948; children—John N., Cory Simpson Christian, Michael H., David M., Dana Simpson Lyddon. AB with honors, Bradley U., 1946. With Charles A. Bennett Co. (name changed to Bennett Publ. Co. 1975-76), 1946-83, also dir.; sec. Cabco, Inc., 1970-76. Bd. dirs. Heart of Ill. United Fund, 1961-66, sec. 1962-66; bd. dirs. YWCA, Peoria, 1966-86, treas. 1970-71, vice pres. 1974-79, 83-85, chmn. planned giving 1984-86, chmn. fin. development 1980-83, mem. adv. bd. 1986—; mem. ch. council St. Philomena Catholic Ch., 1981-85, sec. parish council, 1983. Mem. Nat. Council Boy Scouts Am., East Central Region Com. Boy Scouts Am., East Central Region Fin. Com. Boy Scouts Am., mem. W.D. Boyce council Boy Scouts Am., 1970—, exec. bd. W.D. Boyce Council, 1972—, v.p., 1974-79; mem. Diocese of Peoria Cath. Com. Scouting, 1974—. Co-author: The United Way and the Local Council, 1979, rev. 1981. Recipient Silver Beaver award W.D. Boyce Council Boy Scouts Am., 1971, St. George Emblem award Nat. Council Boy Scouts Am., 1974. Mem. Jr. League Peoria, Women's Civic Fedn., Lakeview Ctr. for Arts and Scis., Crystal Lakeshore Assn. (Benzie County bd. dirs. 1986—, treas. 1986—, exec. com. 1986—), Theta Alpha Phi, Pi Beta Phi. Republican. Clubs: Willow Knolls Country, Crystal Lakeshore Assn. (Frankfort, Mich.)..

SIMPSON, LAURA EVELYN, accountant; b. Herrin, Ill., July 19, 1917; d. Roy and Mary (Trout) Wilson; student public schs., Ill.; diploma acctg., income tax and C.P.A. coaching LaSalle Extension U., 1952; m. Levi C. Simpson, Oct. 16, 1936; children—Doris I. Simpson Hill, Suzanne Simpson Barnett, Troy E., Joy. Bookkeeper, Atlas Powder Co., 1932-48; self-employed, 1934-41; with acctg. div. Sherwin Williams Def. Corp., 1942-45, Roy Barger Acctg. Service, Marion, Ill., 1945-52; propr. acctg. service, Marion and Harrisburg, Ill., 1953-79; part-time practice acctg., New Port Richey, Fla., 1980—. Treas., Sunday sch. tchr. Cedar Grove United Meth. Ch., Marion, 1946-79; pres. women's div. Holiday United Meth. Ch., New Port Richey, Fla., until 1984, chmn. missions commn., 1984—, also ch. treas., nominating com. United Meth. Women; leader 4-H Club, 1951, 52; treas. United Meth. Ch. of Holiday; mem. nominating com. United Meth. Ch., St. Petersburg Dist. Card holder IRS. Mem. Nat. Fedn. Ind. Bus. (chmn. Saline and Williamson County 1966, nat. adv. council 1971), Nat. Soc. Public Accts., Internat. Platform Assn. Republican. Home: 3634 Claremont New Port Richey FL 34652

SIMPSON, LESSYE MARY, government agency executive; b. Dundee, Miss., Dec. 14, 1938; d. William Tell and Gemmie Alma (Davis) Godfrey; m. Oldell Hawkins, Feb. 14, 1958 (div. June 1978); children: Linda Fields, Jeffrey Hawkins, Cathy Awad, Cynthia Hawkins, Carolyn Anderson. Student, U. Mo., 1974-75, Florissant Valley Community Coll., 1979. Figure clk. Libson Shope, St. Louis, 1967-68; ins. adminstr. Gen. Am. Life Ins., St. Louis, 1968-79; bus. mgr. Mo. Dept. Corrections, St. Louise, 1980—. Chair United Way Campaign, St. Louis, 1981-86. Mem. NOW, Am. Mgmt. Assn., Nat. Assn. Female Execs., Mo. Assn. Pub. Purchasers. Democrat. Lutheran. Office: Mo Dept of Corrections 1548 Papin St Saint Louis MO 63103

SIMPSON, MADELINE LOUISA, psychologist; b. Norfolk, Va., June 22, 1923; d. David Edward and Zenobia Eleanor (Ross) S. BA, Fisk U., 1944; MS, Boston U., 1951; MA, The New Sch., 1967; PhD, U. Md., 1981; MS in Pub. Adminstrn., Va. Commonwealth U., 1985. Social work practitionar, supr. Child Welfate Agy. and Hosps., N.Y.C. and Norfolk County, Va., 1946-69; founder, dir. Centre d'Etudes Sociales, Port-au-Prince, Haiti, 1959-61; asst. prof. psycyhol. Del. State Coll., Dover, 1969-72; assoc. prof. psychol. Cheyney (Pa.) State Coll., 1972-75, 78; asst. prof. phsychol. Longwood Coll., Farmville, Va., 1979-85; assoc prof. St. Paul's Coll., Lawrenceville, Va., 1985—. Mem. local human rights com. Dept. Mental Health and Mental Retardation Commonwealth Va., Piedmont Geriatric Hosp., Burkeville, 19846. Mem. Am. Psychol. Assn., Delta Sigma Theta. Democrat. Baptist.

SIMPSON, MARILYN JEAN, artist; b. Birmingham, Ala., Aug. 24, 1929; d. Homer Kyle and Ellen (Allan) Parker; student U. Ala., Art Students League N.Y., San Miguel, Mex., Robert Brackman Sch., Conn., Am. U., Avignon, France, Rome and Florence, Italy; children—Carol Leann, Charles Boyd. Dir., Acad. Fine Arts, Ft. Walton Beach, Fla., 1974-77; Marilyn Simpson Sch. Fine Art, Ft. Walton Beach, 1962-73, Artists Workshop, Ft. Walton Beach, 1982—; exhbns. include: Kotter Gallery, Nat. Arts Club, Lever House, Paula Insel Gallery (all N.Y.C.), Destin (Fla.) Gallery Fine Art. Recipient award Am. Artist Profl. League, 1975, Golden Egg Gallery award, Golden Centaur award, 1982. Mem. Am. Artists Profl. League, Pastel Soc. of Southwest (recipient Dick Blick award), Acad. Italia. (recipient Gold medal, hon. degree, 1979). Address: Route 1 Box 43C Mary Esther FL 32569

SIMPSON, MARY ELIZABETH, personnel and benefits administrator; b. Newport News, Va., Dec. 13, 1946; d. Carl Edward and Edith Marie (Johnston) Routten; m. William Hugh Simpson Jr., Nov. 26, 1966; 1 child, William Charles. Student, Columbia (S.C.) Coll., 1985—. Clk. Allied Corp., Columbia, 1965-70, sec., 1970-78, adminstr. benefits, 1978—, asst. adminstr. personnel, 1979—; emergency med. technician Allied Corp., 1977—. cons. Jr. Achievement, Columbia, 1985-86; instr. ARC, 1980—; mem. Irmo Mid. Sch. Adv. council, 1986-87. Mem. Midlands Employer Health Council (sec. 1984-85). Republican. Methodist. Home: 2015 Cedarbrook Ct Columbia SC 29212 Office: Allied Corp 4402 St Andrews Rd Columbia SC 29210

SIMPSON, MARY MICHAEL, priest, psychotherapist; b. Evansville, Ind., Dec. 1; d. Link Wilson and Mary Garrett (Price) S.; B.A., B.S., Tex. Women's U., 1946; grad. N.Y. Tng. Sch. for Deaconesses, 1949; grad. Westchester Inst. Tng. in Psychoanalysis and Psychotherapy, 1976; S.T.M., Gen. Theol. Sem., 1982. Missionary, Holy Cross Mission, Bolahun, Liberia, 1950-52; acad. head Margaret Hall Sch., Versailles, Ky., 1958-61; pastoral counselor on staff Cathedral St. John the Divine, N.Y.C., 1974-87, canon residentiary, canon counselor, 1977-87, hon. canon, 1988—; ordained priest Episcopal Ch., 1977; cons. psychotherapist Union Theol. Sem., 1980-83; dir. Cathedral Counseling Service, 1975-87; priest-in-charge St. John's Ch. Wilmot, New Rochelle, N.Y., 1987—; pvt. practice psycholanalyst, 1974—; Bd. dirs. Westchester Inst. Tng. in Psychoanalysis and Psychotherapy, 1982-84; trustee Council on Internat. and Pub. Affairs, 1983-87. Mem. Nat. Assn. Advancement of Psychoanalysis, N.Y. State Assn. Practicing Psychotherapists, N.Y. Soc. Clin. Psychologists. Author: The Ordination of Women in the American Episcopal Church: the Present Situation, 1981; contbg. author: Yes to Women Priests, 1978. Home and Office: 225 E 95th St #3B New York NY 10128

SIMPSON, RUTH MARYANN RASEY, English teacher; b. Rupert, Vt., Jan. 21, 1902; d. Henry Lee and Hattie (Harwood) Rasey; m. E. Wilbur Simpson, Sept. 22, 1968. BS in Edn., N.Y. State Coll., 1932; postgrad. Cornell U., 1936, U. N.H., 1946, U. Buffalo, 1946-58. Tchr. rural sch. Salem, N.Y., 1921-24, Jackson, N.Y., 1924-25; tchr. Village Sch., Valley Falls, N.Y., 1925-27, Felton Jr. High Sch., North Tonawanda, N.Y., 1929-57. Author: Out of the Salt Box, Savour of Old Vertmont, 1962 (Pen Womens award 1964), Hand-Hewn in Old Vermont, 1979; (poetry) Mountain Fortitude, 1969 (Pen Woman's award 1970); contbr. non-fiction articles to mags. chair festival Bicentennial of Revolution City of North Tonawanda, 1975-76; mem. Friends of the LIbrary, North Tonawanda, 1970, Hist. Soc. of Tonawanda, 1976, Womens Hosp. Aux., Tonawanda, 1956—. Mem. Retired Tchrs. Assn., Nat. League of Am. Pen Women (pres. 1958-60, sec. 1952-54, 66-68, regional editor 1970-72), Alpha Delta Kappa. Ecumenical. Club: Fortnightly Literary (pres. 1973-75). Home: 286 Goundry St North Tonawanda NY 14120

SIMPSON, VI, state senator; b. Los Angeles, Mar. 18, 1946; d. Lloyd M. and Helen (Chacon) Sentman; m. Kenneth N. Simpson; children—Jason, Kristina. B.A. in Bus., Calif. State U.-Hayward, 1968. Asst. to chmn. Com. on Status of Women, Calif., 1974-75; dir. pub. affairs Calif. Parks and Recreation Soc., Sacramento, 1975-77; county auditor Monroe County, Ind., 1980-84; mem. Ind. Senate, 1984—; pres. Vi Simpson and Co., Inc., Bloomington, Ind., 1983—. Editor: Equal Rights Monitor mag., 1974-76. Syndicated newspaper columnist Know Your Rights, 1975-76. Named Freshman Democrat Senator of Yr., Ind. broadcasters Assn., 1985, Legis. of Yr., Ind. State Employees Assn., 1985. Bd. dirs. Ind. Am. Lung Assn. Mem. Ind. Constructo Inc., NAACP, AAUW. Methodist. Avocations: jogging; skiing; camping; hiking. Office: Vi Simpson and Co Inc 5185 W State Rd 46 Bloomington IN 47401

SIMS, ELIZABETH BALLARD SIMS, court reporter; b. Gastonia, N.C., Aug. 17, 1944; d. Fred Wilson and Mabel Elizabeth (Allen) Ballard; m. Robert Vincent Sims, Sept. 4, 1964; 1 dau., Candace Elizabeth Barkley. Student Gaston Meml. Hosp. Sch. Nursing, 1962-63, Gaston Coll. Dep. registrar deeds Gaston County, 1964-69; ofcl. ct. reporter, N.C., 1969-74; free-lance reporter, Dallas, N.C., 1974-86; ofcl. ct. reporter 26th Jud. Dist., State of N.C., 1986—; ofcl. ct. reporter U.S. Bankruptcy Ct. Western dist. N.C., Charlotte div., 1983-84; jud. div. 26th Jud. Dist. Superior Ct., State N.C., 1986—. Mem. com. Adminstrv. Office of Cts., 1977-78, N.C. Gov.'s Council on Status of Women, 1978—. Active Gaston County Democratic Women; Dem. precinct judge, 1973, youth rep. to area precinct meeting; chmn. Gaston County Mother's March of Dimes campaign, 1980-81. Mem. Nat. Shorthand Reporters Assn., N.C. Shorthand Reporters Assn. (legis. com., treas. 1987-88). Methodist. Home: 402 Sunset Circle Dallas NC 28034

SIMS, LINDA ANN, microelectronics program administrator; b. South Bend, Ind., Dec. 9, 1955; d. Roman S. Sims and Greta H. (Grall) Beard. BSEE, Purdue U., 1978. Sales engr. microelectronics div. CTS Corp., West Layfayette, Ind., 1979-80, med. sales engr., 1981-82, med. program mgr., 1982-86, med. and indsl. program mgr., 1987-88; program mgr. Tektron Micro Electronics, Inc., Hanover, Md., 1988—. Campaign chmn. CTS United Way Dr., 1986, mem. planning com., 1986—; exec. advisor Jr. Achievement, Layfayette, 1982—, bd. dirs. 1984—. Mem. Internat. Soc. for Hybrid Microelectronics (sec. 1982—), Nat. Assn. Female Execs., Purdue Alumni Assn., Eta Kappa Nu. Club: CTS Golf League. Home: 7917 Red Barn Way Elkridge MD 21227 Office: Tektron Micro Electronics Inc 7483A Candlewood Rd Hanover MD 21076

SIMS, LORETTA JAMES, employment counselor; b. Holly Springs, Miss., Feb. 7, 1948; d. Sylvester and Elmer (Greer) James; 1 dau., Chyreese Tawana. BS in Bus. Edn. cum laude, Miss. Indsl. Coll., Holly Springs, 1971. Personnel mgmt. specialist, then personnel staffing specialist U.S. CSC, Jackson, Miss., 1971-78; equal opportunity specialist Office Fed. Contract Compliance Programs, Kansas City, Mo., 1978-87; supervisory equal opportunity specialist, Birmingham, Ala., 1987—. Mem. ACLU, Common Cause, Urban League, NAACP. Baptist. Home: 1720-A 14th Ave South Birmingham AL 35205 Office: DOL/OFCCP 2015 2nd Ave North Suite 202 Birmingham AL 35203

SIMSON, JO ANNE, anatomy and biology educator; b. Chgo., Nov. 19, 1936; d. Kenneth Brown and Helen Marjorie (Pascoe) Valentine; m. Arnold Simson, June 1961 (div.); 1 child, Maria; m. Michael Smith, Nov. 10, 1971 (div.); children: Elizabeth Smith, Briana Smith. BA, Kalamazoo Coll., 1959; MS, U. Mich., 1961; PhD, SUNY, Syracuse, 1969. Postdoctoral fellow Temple U. Health Sci. Ctr., Phila., 1968-70; asst. prof. Med. U. S. C., Charleston, 1970-76, assoc. prof., 1976-83, prof. anatomy and cell biology, 1983—. Author short stories and poems; contbr. articles to profl. jours.; mem. editorial bd. Anat. Record, 1974-85. Active adult edn. Unitarian Ch., Charleston, 1973-75; chmn. Town Meeting Organizing Com., Charleston, 1976; mem. standing com. Circular Congl. Ch., Charleston, 1983-85. Grantee NSF, 1959-60, NIH, 1966-67, 72-87; postdoctoral fellow NIH, 1968-70. Mem. Am. Assn. Anatomists, Am. Soc. Cell Biology, Histochemical Soc. (sec. 1979-82, exec. council 1985—), Amnesty Internat. (newsletter editor Group 168 1982-86). Home: 1760 Pittsford Circle Charleston SC 29412 Office: Med U SC Anatomy 171 Ashley Ave Charleston SC 29425

SIMUNICH, MARY ELIZABETH HEDRICK (MRS. WILLIAM A. SIMUNICH), public relations executive; b. Chgo.; d. Tubman Keene and Mary (McCamish) Hedrick; student Phoenix Coll., 1967-69, Met. Bus. Coll., 1938-40; m. William A. Simunich, Dec. 6, 1941. Exec. sec. sales mgr. KPHO radio, 1950-53; exec. sec. mgr. KPHO-TV, 1953-54; account exec. Tom Rippey & Assos., 1955-56; pub. relations dir. Phoenix Symphony, 1956-62; co-founder, v.p. Paul J. Hughes Pub. Relations, Inc., 1960-65; owner Mary Simunich Pub. Relations, Phoenix, 1966-77. Pub. relations dir. Walter O. Boswell Meml. Hosp., Sun City, Ariz., 1969-85; instr. pub. relations Phoenix Coll. Evening Sch., 1973-78. Bd. dirs. Anytown, Ariz., 1969-72; founder, sec. Friends Am. Geriatrics, 1977-86. Named Phoenix Advt. Woman of Year, Phoenix Jr. Advt. Club, 1962; recipient award Blue Cross, 1963; 1st Pl. award Ariz. Press Women, 1966. Mem. Internat. Assn. Bus. Communicators (pres. Ariz. chpt. 1970-71, dir.), Pub. Relations Soc. Am. (sec., dir. 1976-78), Am. Soc. Hosp. Pub. Relations (dir. Ariz. chpt. 1976-78), Nat., Ariz. press women. Club: Phoenix Press. Home: 4133 N 34th Pl Phoenix AZ 85018

SINANOGLU, PAULA ARMBRUSTER, social work educator, director; b. N.Y.C., June 30, 1935; d. William and Anna Bertha Armbruster; B.A., U. Conn., 1956, M.S.W., 1974; M.A., Yale U., 1964; children—K. Levni, Elif-Lale A., Murat H. Intelligence analyst Nat. Security Agy., Washington, 1956-62; clin. instr. social work Yale Child Study Center, Sch. Medicine, Yale U., New Haven, Conn., 1974-80, clin. asst. prof., 1980—, dir. social work tng., 1984—, dir. outpatient services, 1985—; fellow Pierson Coll., Yale Coll., 1976—; assoc. project dir. HEW tng. grant, asst. prof. residence U. Conn. Sch. Social Work, West Hartford, 1979-80; Johnson Wax fellow, vis. prof. U. Surrey (Eng.), 1984. Chmn. regional adv. council Conn. Dept. Children and Youth Services, also chmn. chmns. regional adv. councils. Mem. Nat. Acad. Social Work (sec. Conn. chpt.), Conn. Soc. Clin. Social Work, Nat. Assn. Social Workers, Acad. Cert. Social Workers, Council Social Work Edn., Mory's Assn., AAUP. Club: Yale (N.Y.C.). Author, editor works in field. Clubs: Yale (N.Y.) (New Haven).. Office: Yale Child Study Ctr 230 S Frontage Rd New Haven CT 06510

SINCAVAGE, BEVERLY ANN, communications executive; b. Hartford, Conn., Jan. 4, 1945; d. Anthony Joseph and Mary Elizabeth (Dapkus) S. BSE, Cen. Conn. U., 1966; postgrad. in Spanish, Stanford U., 1968-69; MBA in Bus. and Govt., George Washignton U., 1979. Adminstrv. asst. ITT Corp., Washington, 1969-73; tariff adminstr. TRT Telecommunications Corp., Washington, 1973-76; mgr. regulatory affairs Telenet Communications Corp., Washington, 1976-81, mgr. mktg. programs, 1981-84, sr. product mgr., 1984-86; dir. telecommunications standards and practices Telenet Communications Corp., Reston, Va., 1986—; mem. Women in Govt. Relations, 1980-84. Bd. dirs. Downtown Jaycees, Washington, 1978-80, external v.p., 1980. Stanford U. PhD fellow, 1968. Mem. Nat. Assn. Female Execs. Avocations: ballroom dancing, photography, travel. Office: Telenet Communications Corp 12490 Sunrise Valley Dr Reston VA 22096

SINCLAIR, BEVERLEY ANN, broadcast journalist; b. Saskatoon, Sask., Can., Jan. 22, 1955; d. Don Smith and Betty Elena S. Student B.C. Inst. Tech., 1973-75. Reporter, editor CBC Radio, Vancouver, 1973-75; reporter, editor Sta. CKIQ, Kelowna, B.C., 1975-77, pub. affairs, news dir. Sta. CJOV-FM, Kelowna, 1977-78; pub. affairs dir. Sta. C-FAX, Victoria, B.C., Can., 1978-86, talk show host, 1978-86; host Mixed Co., CHEK-TV,

Victoria, 1985-86, host Daily Edition, 1986-87; v.p. Focus Prodns. Ltd, 1987—; guest lectr. B.C. Inst. Tech., dir. Assn. for Responsible Communication. Recipient Edward R. Murrow award for radio documentary of social significance, 1979. Office: 982-W 21st Ave, Vancouver, BC Canada V52 121

SINCLAIR, CAROLE, publisher, editor; b. Haddonfield, N.J., May 13, 1942; d. Earl Walter and Ruth (Sinclair) Dunham; 1 child, Wendy Sinclair Gross. Student, U. Florence, Italy, 1963; BA in Polit. Sci., Bucknell U, 1964. Advt. copywriter BBD&O Advertising, N.Y.C., 1966-67; sales promotion mgr. Macmillan Pub. Co., N.Y.C., 1967-71; mktg. mgr. Doubleday & Co., Inc., N.Y.C., 1972-74, promotion dir., 1974-76, advt. mgr., sales and promotion, chmn. mktg. com., 1976-80; v.p. mktg., editorial dir. Davis Pubs., N.Y.C., 1980-83; founder, pub., editorial dir., sr. v.p. Sylvia Porter's Personal Fin. Mag., N.Y.C., 1983—; mktg. dir. Denver Pub. Inst., summers 1975-78; lectr. Columbia U. Bus. Sch. and Sch. of Journalism, 1976; host nationally syndicated TV show, Sylvia Porter's Money Tips, syndicated daily radio show, Sylvia Porter's Personal Fin. Report, audio cassette series on fin. topics. contbg. editor Pushcart Prize, 1977; contbr. The Business of Publishing, 1980. Renaissance Art Program fellow, Florence, Italy, 1963; White House intern, 1962. Mem. Women's Forum, Intercorp. Communications Group, Mag. Pubs.' Assn., Advt. Women in N.Y., Spence Sch. Parent's League. Presbyterian. Club: Pubs. Lunch. Office: Sylvia Porter's Personal Fin Mag 380 Lexington Ave New York NY 10017

SINDAB, TONJA LEATRIC, retail executive; b. Newark, Jan. 22, 1962; d. David Augustus and Willie Mae (Reese) S. BS in Mktg., Fairleigh Dickinson U., 1984. Jr. exec. mgr. Bambergers, East Brunswick, N.J., 1984-86; jr. exec. mgr. Stern Bros., Willowbrook and Wayne, N.J., 1987-88, South Plainfield, N.J., 1988—. Home: 111 Royal Dr Apt 474 Piscataway NJ 08854

SINDT, CYNTHIA LOU, traffic coordinator; b. Dubuque, Iowa, Mar. 8, 1961; d. Richard Carl and Sandra Jeanne (Schumacher) Saul; m. David Lee Sindt, Oct. 15, 1983. Computer sec. Loras Coll., Dubuque, 1981-82; traffic coordinator Empak, Inc., Deer Park, Tex., 1982—. Mem. Houston Traffic Clks. Assn. (sec. 1987-88). Republican. Roman Catholic. Home: 3902 Country Rd Pasadena TX 77505 Office: Empak Inc 2759 Battleground Rd PO Box 897 Deer Park TX 77536

SINER, JUDY LOUISE, marketing director; b. San Jose, Calif., Feb. 9, 1951; d. Bernard Benjamin and Barbara (Minowitz) S. BA in Internal Relations, U. Calif., Berkeley, 1973. Sales rep. Sta. KSJO-FM, San Jose, 1974-80, Sta. KNTV-ABC-TV, San Jose, 1980-83; adv. coordinator Activision Internat., Palo Alto, Calif., 1983-84; western rep. Hotel and Motel Mgmt., San Jose, 1984-85; western mktg. dir. Hotel and Motel Mgmt., Chgo., 1985—. Recipient Dale Carnegie Sales award, 1979. Mem. San Jose Women in Advt. (sec. 1980-84). Office: HBJ Publs 111 E Wacker Dr Chicago IL 60601

SINGER, BETTY JOAN, publisher, editor; b. Hackensack, N.J., Oct. 29, 1949; d. Maurice Leonard and Louise M. (Bitterman) S. AB, Clark U., 1971. Editor, pub. Options Pub. Co., Wayne, N.J., 1974—. Author: Friends of the Jews, 1976, Conversations with my Soul, 1977. Mem. Coalition for Advancement of Jewish Edn., Jewish War Vets. Lodge: B'nai B'rith Women (Service award 1978). Office: Options Pub Co PO Box 311 Wayne NJ 07474

SINGER, GLADYS MONTGOMERY, writer; b. Natick, Mass.; d. Charles Norton and Myrtle (Cates) Taylor; B.A., Wellesley Coll.; m. Alexander John Montgomery (dec. 1955); m. 2d, Russell E. Singer, 1975 (dec. 1975). Sci. and semi-tech. writer McGraw-Hill mags. in Washington office, 1942-61, Washington reporter editor Textile World, 1943-46, Washington reporter Electronics, 1943-44, Washington editor, 1944-57, Washington rep., Nucleonics, 1947-48, co-editor, 1949-52; Washington reporter Bus. Week, 1952-61; feature writer Sci. Illustrated, 1957-61; then freelance, now ret. Mem. Pres.'s Adv. Com. on Arts, Kennedy Center, 1970-76; bd. dirs. D.C. League Republican Women 1983-85; adv. com. Former Senator Margaret Chase Smith Library, 1984—. Recipient citation Armed Forces Communications and Electronics Assn., 1970. Mem. AAAS, Nat. Assn. Sci. Writers, Women's Nat. Press Club (pres. 1957-58), Nat. Press Club, Am. News Women's Club. Clubs: Sulgrave, Chevy Chase, Wellesley College (Washington). Home: 2725 29th St NW Apt 605 Washington DC 20008

SINGER, JANICE GAIL, psychotherapist, consultant; b. Chgo., Aug. 14, 1947; d. Harold and Dorothy (Kagen) S.; 1 child, Rachael Jacqueline. BA, U. Toledo, 1969; MSW, U. Wis., Milw., 1977; postgrad., Gestalt Inst., Cleve., 1982, Dreikers Relationship Ctr., Boulder, Colo., 1985; Reiki II, Nancy Retzlaff R.M., Milw., 1986. Program evaluator, project cons. Mental health Planning Council of Milw., 1976-78; counselor abortion WomanCare-West, Milw., 1978, treatment foster care worker Children's Service Soc. of Wis., Milw., 1978-81; mental health coordinator, primary psychotherapist Bread and Roses Women's Health Ctr., Inc., Milw., 1981-84; originator Friends' Psychotherapy Collective, Milw., 1984—; group facilitator People to People, Waukesha, Wis., 1976-80; mem. taskforce on sexual misconduct by psychotherapists, Wis., 1984-87; cons. Woman to Woman, Inc., Milw., 1981—. Co-author: (consumer guide) Making Therapy Work for You, 1986; creator therapy mode Action Oriented Therapy, 1983; co-creator: (workshops) Celebration in Living, 1984, Living Beyond AIDS, 1987, Transforming Body Image, 1987. Workshop leader Milw. AIDS Project, 1987; co-creator workshops Celebration in Living, 1984, Living Beyond AIDS, 1987, Transforming Body Image, 1987; active Maple Dale Sch. Human Sexuality, Milw., 1983-86; cirriculum com. Nicolet High Sch. Human Sexuality, 1987. Mem. Feminist Therapy Network (pres. 1981—), Nat. Assn. Social Workers, Assn. for Human Animal Bonding, Wis. Assn. Outpatient Mental Health Facilities. Democrat. Home: 8428 N Regent Rd Milwaukee WI 53217 Office: Friends Psychotherapy Collective 777 W Glencoe Pl #200 Milwaukee WI 53217

SINGER, JEANNE (WALSH), composer, concert pianist; b. N.Y.C., Aug. 4, 1924; d. Harold Vandervoort and Helen (Loucks) Walsh; B.A. magna cum laude, Barnard Coll., 1944; artist diploma Nat. Guild Piano Tchrs., 1954; student in piano Nadia Reisenberg, 1945-60, composition, Douglas Moore, 1942-44, Ph.D. (hon.) in Music World U., 1984; m. Richard G. Singer, Feb. 24, 1945, dec.; 1 son, Richard V. Composer, concert pianist solo chamber ensembles N.Y., 1947—; tchr. piano Manhasset, N.Y., 1960—; lectr. in field. Recipient spl. award merit Nat. Fedn. Music Clubs, 1st prize in nat. competition Composers Guild, 1979, Grand prize Composers Guild, 1982, 1st prize Composers and Songwriters Internat., 1985, also various nat. awards; honored at all-Singer concert, Bogotá, Colombia, 1980; N.Y. Council Arts grantee. Fellow Internat. Biog. Assn.; mem. ASCAP (awards 1978-88), Am. Music Center, Internat. League Women Composers, Nat. League Am. Pen Women (nat. music chmn.), Composers, Authors and Artists Am. (v.p. N.Y.C., music mag. editor 1972-80, nat. award 1981), Am. Women Composers, Phi Beta Kappa. Clubs: Barnard Coll. of L.I., Tuesday Morning Music Douglaston; Bohemians (N.Y.C.). Composed numerous instrumental, vocal works including: Summons (baritone), 1975, A Cycle of Love (4 songs with piano), 1976, Suite in Harpsichord Style, 1976, From The Green Mountains (trio), 1977, (choral work) Composers' Prayer, Nocturne for Clarinet, 1980, Suite for Horn and Harp, 1980, From Petrarch (voice, horn, piano), 1981, Quartet for Flute, Oboe, Violin, Cello, 1982, Trio for Viola, Oboe, Piano, 1984, Come Greet the Spring (choral), 1981, An American Vision (song cycle), 1985, Wry Rimes (voice and Bassoon), 1986; performed Lincoln Center, radio, TV. Home and Office: 64 Stuart Place Manhasset NY 11030

SINGER, MARTHA HOUX, marketing professional; b. Warrensburg, Mo., Feb. 7, 1942; d. James Robert and Doris Lorraine (Smith) Houx; m. Lawrence Alan Singer, July 22, 1967; children—Robert Alan, Michael Stuart. B.J., U. Mo., 1963; M.B.A., U. So. Calif., 1980. Advt. copywriter Sears, Roebuck & Co., Chgo., 1963-66; asst. to exec. dir. Chgo. Maternity Ctr., 1966-67; staff writer, spl. edit. editor Santa Monica (Calif.) Evening Outlook, 1969-75; pub. relations dir. West Los Angeles-Beverly Hills YWCA, 1975-77, mem. adminstrn. com., 1988; cons. to various Los Angeles businesses, 1978-80; promotion mgr. Shepherd Machinery/POWER SYSTEMS, Los Angeles, 1980-83; dir. research Kessler & Assocs., Los Angeles, 1983—. Mem. Women in Communications (dir. 1976-6, chpt. recognition 1976), Am. Mktg. Assn. Lodge: P.E.O. Office: Kessler & Assocs 11661 San Vincente Blvd Los Angeles CA 90049

SINGER, MAXINE FRANK, biochemist; b. N.Y.C., Feb. 15, 1931; d. Hyman S. and Henrietta (Perlowitz) Frank; m. Daniel Morris Singer, June 15, 1952; children: Amy Elizabeth, Ellen Ruth, David Byrd, Stephanie Frank. A.B., Swarthmore Coll., 1952, D.Sc. (hon.), 1978; Ph.D., Yale U., 1957; D.Sc., Wesleyan U., 1977, U.Md.-Baltimore County, 1985, Cedar Crest Coll., 1986, CUNY, 1988, Brandeis U., 1988. USPHS postdoctoral fellow NIH, Bethesda, Md., 1956-58; research chemist (biochemistry) NIH, 1958-74; head sect. on nucleic acid enzymology Nat. Cancer Inst., 1974-79; chief Lab. of Biochemistry, Nat. Cancer Inst., 1979-87, research chemist, 1987-88; pres. Carnegie Inst. Washington, 1988—; Regents vis. lectr. U. Calif., Berkeley, 1981; bd. dirs. Found. for Advanced Edn. in Scis., 1972-78, 85-86; mem. sci. council Internat. Inst. Genetics and Biophysics, Naples, Italy, 1982-86. Mem. editorial bd. Jour. Biol. Chemistry, 1968-74, Sci. mag, 1972-82; chmn. editorial bd. Procs. of Nat. Acad. Scis., 1985-88; contbr. articles to scholarly jours. Trustee Wesleyan U., Middletown, Conn., 1972-75; trustee Yale Corp., New Haven, 1975—; bd. govs. Weizmann Inst. Sci., Rehovot, Israel, 1978—; bd. dirs. Whitehead Inst, 1985—. Recipient award for achievement in biol. scis. Washington Acad. Scis., 1969, award for research in biol. scis. Yale Sci. and Engring. Assn., 1974, Superior Service Honor award HEW, 1975, Dirs. award NIH, 1977, Disting. Service medal HHS, 1983, Presdl. Disting. Exec. Rank award, 1987, U.S. Disting. Exec. Rank award, 1987. Fellow Am. Acad. Arts and Scis.; mem. AAAS (Sci. Freedom and Responsibility award 1982), Am. Soc. Biol. Chemists, Am. Soc. Microbiologists, Am. Chem. Soc., Inst. Medicine (Nat. Acad. Scis.), Nat. Acad. Scis. (council 1982-85), Pontifical Acad. of Scis. Home: 5410 39th St NW Washington DC 20015 Office: Carnegie Instn Washington 1530 P St NW Washington DC 20015

SINGER, NIECEE, genetic counselor; b. N.Y.C.; d. A. Nathan and Doris (Tenzer) Levy; children: Mark, Patricia, Nancy. BA magna cum laude, Wheaton Coll., 1950; MS, Sarah Lawrence Coll., 1976. Cert. in genetic counseling Am. Bd. Med. Genetics. Supr. genetics unit Westchester County Med. Ctr., Valhalla, N.Y., 1976-82; supr. Genetics and Birth Defects Ctr. Morristown (N.J.) Meml. Hosp., 1982—. Contbr articles to profl. jours. Sec., bd. dirs. Foxwood II Condominium Assn., Morris Plains, N.J., 1985—; mem. Gov.'s Council on Prevention of Mental Retardation, 1988—. Mem. Am. Soc. Human Genetics, Human Genetics Assn. N.J. (pres. 1985-87, chairperson edn. com. 1984-85, co-chairperson legis. com. 1987—), Nat. Soc. Genetic Counselors (founding, treas. 1978-81), Mid-Atlantic Regional Human Genetics Network (steering com. 1985—), Phi Beta Kappa. Democrat. Office: Morristown Meml Hosp Genetics Birth Defects Ctr 100 Madison Ave PO Box 53 Morristown NJ 07960

SINGER, SUSAN ARNETT, research specialist; b. Phila., June 1, 1929; d. James Francis and Hazel Milne (Shennan) McMullan; m. Robert E. Singer, Oct. 17, 1953 (div. Mar. 1979); children: Judith H. Singer Polen, Cynthia C. Singer Marcille, Ronald P. AB, U. Rochester, N.Y., 1951; MLS, Rutgers U., 1967; postgrad., U. Ariz., 1976-78. Librarian VA Hosp., Lyons, N.J., 1966-68; head reference dept. Morris County Free Library, Whippany, N.J., 1968-75; br. mgr. Tucson Pub. Library, 1975-79; info. broker Info Assocs., Ltd., Tucson, 1979-81; real estate salesperson Century 21, Piscataway, N.J., 1982-85; research specialist AT&T, Morristown, N.J., 1985—; adj. instr. library sci. U. Ariz. Grad. Sch., 1978. Mem. Ariz. State Library Assn. (chmn. standards com. 1976-79, chmn. conf. 1978), Spl. Libraries Assn. Republican. Presbyterian. Home: 6 Brandywine Rise Green Brook NJ 08812 Office: AT&T 412 Mount Kemble Ave Suite 190-26 Morristown NJ 07060 *Dec. Mar. 29, 1988.*

SINGER, SUZANNE FRIED, editor; b. N.Y.C., July 9, 1935; d. Maurice Aaron and Augusta G. (Ginsberg) Fried; m. Max Singer, Feb. 12, 1959; children: Saul, Alexander, Daniel, Benjamin. BA with honors, Swarthmore Coll., 1956; MA, Columbia U., 1958. Program asst. NSF, Washington, 1958-60; assoc. editor Bibl. Archaeology Rev., Washington, 1979-84, mng. editor, 1984—; mng. editor Bibl. Rev., Washington, 1985—; exec. editor Moment, Washington, 1987—. Mem. Am. Schs. Oriental Research. Jewish. Office: Bibl Archaeology Soc 3000 Connecticut Ave NW Suite 300 Washington DC 20008

SINGER-GOLDBERG, GRETA ELIZABETH, guidance counselor; b. Bklyn., June 6, 1939; d. Daniel and Esther (Perler) Malament; m. Daniel Goldberg; children: Emily Singer, Juliet Singer, Ethan Singer. BA, Bklyn. Coll., 1959, MA, 1969; CAS, Hofstra U., 1983. Cert. tchr., N.Y. English tchr. N.Y.C. Bd. of Edn., 1971-84, counselor, 1984—. Mem. Women Strike for Peace, Queens, N.Y., 1965-71; leader Girl Scouts Am., Monterey, Calif., 1971-72. Fellow N.Y.C. Guidance Counselor Assn. Office: Morris High Sch Bronx NY 10456

SINGH, JOYCE HIDEKO, educator; b. Stockton, Calif., July 21, 1942; d. Ichiro and Mitsue (Nakai) Nakahara; BA, San Jose State Coll., 1965, MA, 1968; MA, San Jose State U., 1976; m. Gurnam Singh, Aug. 22, 1970. Substitute tchr. Alumn Rock Sch. Dist., San Jose, Calif., 1965; tchr. Northwood Elem. Sch., Berryessa Union Sch. Dist., San Jose, 1965—. Mem. Soc. Baptist Conv., 1960-67; chmn., coordinator dist. kindergarten com., 1982-86; mem. report card and math. coms., early childhood gesell steering com., presch. caucus, sch. level. Sch. Improvement Program Council and Booster Club, scholarship com. Mem. Santa Clara County Service Ctr. Council, 1984-86, mem. polit. action com., selection com., chair consitution com., 1987-88, others; alt. rep. State Council Edn., 1984-87; chmn. fringe benefit com. Berryessa Coalition for Pub. Edn. and County Wide Coalition Pub. Edn.; mem. dist. election and constitution coms.; assembly rep. NEA, Washington, 1985; mem. Mt. Hamilton Council, 1985-86; co-contact coordinator legislature and Calif. Tchrs. Assn.; tchr. summer sch. Suzumeno Gakko, 1984. PTA. Milpitas Metalcraft scholar, 1960; recipient grants in field, 1982-83, (3) 1984; cert. kindergarten-primary tchr., cert. adminstr., Calif. Mem. Calif. Tchrs. Assn. (women's caucus, Asian-Am. caucus, sec. Berryessa chpt. 1983-84, exec. bd. 1983-86, v.p. 1984-85), NEA (Asian Pacific Islanders caucus), Asian Am. Edn. Assn. Assn. Supervision and Curriculum Devel.

SINGH, SUSHILA, artist; b. Fatehgarh, India, Aug. 29, 1940; came to U.S., 1969; d. Ramlal and Ramkumari Katiyar; m. Ramchandra Sitaram Singh, Dec. 12, 1964; children—Rajiv, Sanjay. B.A., Agra U., 1964, M.A., 1968; diploma advt. and illustrating art Art Instrn. Schs., Mpls., 1977, diploma in painting, 1978. One-woman shows include Dharam Samaj Coll., Aligarh, India, 1968, Indian Inst. Tech., Kanpur, India, 1968, U. Ill. Art Gallery, Urbana, 1969, 70, Zigler Mus., Jennings, La., 1977; represented in permanent collection: Spindletop Mus., Beaumont, Tex., Art Instrn. Schs., Mpls.; portrait of Prince Charles, accepted by same as gift; commd. to paint Dr. Denton Cooley, Houston. Lectr. art classes in community ctrs., 1977—; tchr. painting leisure learning program McNeese State U., 1979—. Recipient 3 Gold medals Agra U., 1st prize for painting Rhythm, Art Instrn. Schs., 1972. Mem. Art Assocs. Lake Charles. Address: 4801 Orleans St Lake Charles LA 70605

SINGLETARY, ADELLE, mail order company executive; b. Newark; d. John and Eva (Green) S. BA in English, St. Peter's Coll., Jersey City, 1978; postgrad., U. London, 1979. Propr. Anmis House, Vauxhall, N.J., 1983—, Pinsar Pub. Co., Vauxhall, 1987—. Author: Lieutenant Pearse, 1976. Mem. Nat. Assn. Female Execs., Am. Entrepreneurs Assn. Home: 59 1/2 Hayes St Newark NJ 07103 Office: Anmis House PO Box 296 Vauxhall NJ 07088

SINGLETARY, ELOISE, educator; b. Lake City, S.C., Aug. 21, 1942; d. Otto and Lillie (Barr) S. BS, Fayetteville U., 1969; student, Winthrop Coll., 1973, U. Va., 1974; EdM, U. S.C., 1978, EdM in Sch. Adminstrn., 1982. Bus. tchr. Lake View (S.C.) High Sch., 1969-76, Hemingway (S.C.) High Sch., 1976-83, Florence (S.C.) Area Vocat. Ctr., 1983—. advisor Hemingway High Sch. Newspaper, 1976-83, Future Bus. Leaders Am., Hemingway, 1976-79. Pres. Dem. Caucus, Lake City, 1984-85, Dem. precinct 2, Lake City, 1984—; del. State and Local Convs., Columbia and Florence, S.C., 1984-85. Mem. Nat. Bus. Edn. Assn. (Merit award 1969), So. Bus. Edn. Assn., S.C. Bus. Edn. Assn., Nat. Edn. Assn., Nat. Assn. Femal Execs., Assn. Supervision and Curriculum Devel., NAACP, Fayetteville State U. Alumni Assn., U. S.C. Alumni Assn., Alpha Kappa Alpha. Baptist. Lodge: Joint Stock #151 (sec. 1972—). Home: Rt 3 Box 202-A Lake City SC 29560 Offfice: Florence Area Vocat Ctr 126 E Howe Springs Rd Florence SC 29501

SINGLETON, JOAN VIETOR, publishing executive, writer; b. Los Angeles, Nov. 8, 1951; d. Carl William and Elizabeth Anne (Caulfield) Vietor; m. W. Alexander Shaefe, Apr. 23, 1977 (div. 1981); m. Ralph Stuart Singleton, Dec. 21, 1984, 1 child, Katherine Elizabeth. Premiere degre, Universite de Paris, 1971; BA, Hollins Coll., 1972. Asst. pres. Calif. Fed. Savs., Los Angeles, 1972-73, dir. promotion, publicity, 1973-74; publicist Dave Mirisch Enterprises, Beverly Hills, Calif., 1974-75; owner, pres. Joan Vietor Enterprises, Los Angeles, 1975-79; dir. devel., bus. affairs Warner Bros., Inc., Burbank, Calif., 1979-80; pres. Lone Eagle Pub. Co., Los Angeles, 1981—. Assoc. producer film First Blood, 1980-81. Mem. Pubs. Mktg. Assn. (bd. dirs. 1984—). Republican. Presbyterian. Office: Lone Eagle Pub Co 9903 Santa Monica Blvd Beverly Hills CA 90212

SINGLETON, LISHA D'NEILLE, child development specialist, small business owner; b. Duarte, Calif., Aug. 17, 1960; d. Doris Ann (Massey) S. BA in Criminal Justice, Calif. State U., Fullerton, 1983. Placement counselor Parks-Sniderman Assoc., Los Angeles, 1984-87; child devel. specialist Pacific Clinics, Pasadena, Calif., 1987—; journeyman clk. Vons, Arcadia, Calif., 1977-84; small group counselor Youth Tng. Sch., Chino, Calif., 1980-81; counselor Family Ctr., Coving, Calif., 1985—; pres. 210 West Records, Monrovia, Calif., 1987—.

SINGLETON, SARA, banker; b. Reading, Pa., Feb. 19, 1940; d. Walter S. and Sarah (Hain) Shearer; m. John H. Singleton, Nov. 9, 1957; children: Joanne Reagan, Suzanne Oliver. Student, Ursinus Coll., Collegeville, Pa., 1979-86. Teller, customer service rep. Southeast Nat. Bank, Phoenixville, Pa., 1972-81; mgmt. trainee Red Hill (Pa.) Savs. and Loan Assn., 1981, asst. mgr. ops., 1982-84; mgr. deposit acctg. Pa. Savs. Bank, Wyomissing, 1984, asst. v.p. deposit services, 1984-86, v.p. deposit services, 1987—; mem. check product adv. group Phila. Res. Bank, 1988—. Pres. Mont Clare (Pa.) Home and Sch. Assn., 1973-75; officer, bd. dirs. Holy Ghost Ch., Phoenixville, 1974-84; cons. Greater Valley Council Girls Scouts U.S.A., Reading, 1988—. Mem. Nat. Assn. Banking Women(treas. Reading 1988—), Berks County C. of C. (ambassador com. 1986-88). Home: 310 Woodlyn Dr Collegeville PA 19426 Office: Penn Savs Bank 1130 Berkshire Blvd Wyomissing PA 19610

SINIARD, SHEILA COSTNER, interior designer; b. Columbia, S.C., Sept. 8, 1954; d. Dennis Dale and Anita Louise (Whitener) Costner; 1 child, Robert Adam. B.S., Western Carolina U., Cullowhee, N.C., 1976. Asst. resident mgr. pub. relations/mktg. Club Regency/Governors Club, Myrtle Beach, S.C., 1976-78; designer, sales rep. S.S. Interiors, Myrtle Beach, 1978-83; comml. designer John Gore & Assocs., Myrtle Beach, 1983-84; designer, owner Design Dimension, Myrtle Beach, 1984-85; dir. contract sales div., buyer, display coordinator Stuckey Furniture, Charlotte, 1985—. Mem. Am. Soc. Interior Designers, Inst. Bus. Designers, Nat. Assn. Female Execs. Avocations: art; golf; flying. Office: Stuckey Furniture 6600 N Tryon St Charlotte NC 28213

SINK, ALVA GORDON (MRS. CHARLES A. SINK), clubwoman; b. Rose Twp., Mich.; d. Nathaniel J. and Ella M. (Highfield) Gordon; student Eastern Mich. U., summers 1914, 18; A.B., U. Mich., 1923; m. Charles A. Sink, June 18, 1923 (dec.). Tchr. pub. schs., Rose Center, Mich., 1914-17, Hickory Ridge, Mich., 1917-18, Holly, Mich., 1918-19, Canfield Pvt. Sch., Ann Arbor, Mich., 1919-22. Mem. Women's Republican Club, Ann Arbor. Dir. Washtenaw County chpt. ARC, 1943-48, 53-59, in charge First Aid and Accident Prevention, 1941-61; pres. Mich. House and Senate Club, 1929-30, U. Mich. Alumnae Club, 1931-33, Sara Browne Smith Group Alumnae Club, 1957-59, Women's Soc. Congl. Ch., 1946-48; regent Sarah Caswell Angell chpt. DAR, 1955-57. Recipient Red Cross citation, 1959, Alumnae Council award U. Mich., 1971, Disting. Alumni Service award U. Mich., 1978; Alva Gordon Sink Group of U. Mich. Alumnae named in her honor. Mem. Hist. Soc. Mich., Alumni Assn. U. Mich., French Huguenots, AAUW, Ann Arbor Art Assn., Henry P. Tappan Soc., P.E.O. Clubs: Art Study, Garden, Faculty Women, Presidents of U. Mich. (pres. emeritus 1975-76), Ann Arbor Women's City. Home: 1325 Olivia Ave Ann Arbor MI 48104

SINKFORD, JEANNE CRAIG, dentist, educator; b. Washington, Jan. 30, 1933; d. Richard E. and Geneva (Jefferson) Craig; m. Stanley M. Sinkford, Dec. 8, 1951; children: Dianne Sylvia, Janet Lynn, Stanley M. III. B.S., Howard U., 1953, M.S., 1962, D.D.S., 1958, Ph.D., 1963, D.Sc. (hon.), Georgetown U., 1978. Instr. prosthodontics Howard U. Sch. Dentistry, Washington, 1958-60; mem. faculty dentistry Howard U. Sch. Dentistry, 1964—, assoc. dean research coordinator, co-chmn. dept. restorative dentistry, 1968-75, dean Coll. Dentistry, 1975—, prof. prosthodontics Grad. Sch., 1977—; instr. research and crown and bridge Northwestern U. Sch. Dentistry, 1963-64; cons. prosthodontics and research VA Hosp., Washington, 1965—; resident Children's Hosp. Nat. Med. Ctr., 1974-75; cons. St. Elizabeth's Hosp.; mem. attending staff Freedman's Hosp., Washington, 1964—; adv. bd. D.C. Gen. Hosp., 1975—; mem. Nat. Adv. Dental Research Council, Nat. Bd. Dental Examiners; mem. ad hoc adv. panel Tuskegee Syphilis Study for HEW; sponsor D.C. Pub. Health Apprentice Program; mem. adv. council to dir. NIH; adv. com. NIH/NIDR/NIA Aging Research Council; mem. dental devices classification panel FDA; mem. select panel for promotion child health, 1979-80; mem. spl. med. adv. group VA; bd. overseers U. Pa. Dental Sch., Boston U. Dental Sch.; bd. advs. U. Pitts. Dental Sch. Contbr. Nat. Symphony Orch.; adv. bd. United Negro Coll. Fund, Robert Wood Johnson Health Policy Fellowships; mem. Mayor's Block Grant Adv. Com., 1982; mem. parents council Sidwell Friends, 1983. Louise C. Ball fellow grad. tng., 1960-63. Fellow Internat., Am. colls. dentists; mem. Internat. Assn. Dental Research, Dist. Dental Soc., Am. Inst. Oral Biology, North Portal Civic League, ADA (chmn. appeal bd. council on dental edn. 1975-82), Inst. Grad. Dentists (trustee), Wash. Council Adminstrv. Women, Assn. Am. Women Dentists, Am. Assn. Dental Schs., Am. Pedodontic Soc., Inst. Medicine (council), Am. Soc. Dentistry for Children, N.Y. Acad. Scis., Golden Key Honor Soc., Sigma Xi, Phi Beta Kappa, Omicron Kappa Upsilon, Psi Chi, Beta Kappa Chi. Address: 1765 Verbena St NW Washington DC 20012

SINKHORN, MARY JEAN, real estate executive; b. Athens, Ga., May 19, 1941; d. Howard J. and Helen (Fields) Pickelsimer; m. Michael J. Gordon, Aug. 21, 1965 (div. 1985); children: Michael J. Jr., Mitzi J.; m. Walt P. Sinkhorn, Mar. 28, 1986. Degree, Lakeland Bus. Coll., 1960. Lic. realtor, Pa., Fla. Legal sec. C.A. Boswell, Sr., et al., Attys., Bartow, Fla., 1960-69; owner, operator Gordon and Whitaker Interiors, Phila., 1977-1978; assoc. realtor Fox and Lazo, Haverford, Pa., 1979-83; dir.real estate services Mario Polo Realty Inc., Tampa, Fla., 1984—. V.p. Tampa Jr. Woman's Club, 1971; treas. Bartow Jr. Woman's Club, 1966; sec. Bartow Jayceettes, 1967; vol. Fla. Soc. for Prevention of Blindness, 1971. Mem. Women's Council Realtors (civic project chmn. 1986), Tampa Bd. Realtors, Edn. and Realtor Assn. (com. main line bd. realtors 1979-83). Office: Mario Polo Realty Inc 12966 N Dale Mabry Tampa FL 33618

SINNARD, ELAINE JANICE, painter, sculptor; b. Fort Collins, Colo., Feb. 14, 1926; d. Elven Orestes and Catherine (Bennet) S.; student Art Students League, 1948, N.Y. U., 1953, Sculpture Center, N.Y.C., 1954, Academie de la Grande Chaumiere, Paris, 1956. Painter, sculptor; works exhibited Riverside Mus., N.Y.C., 1955, City Center, N.Y.C., 1954-56, Nat. Arts Club, N.Y.C., 1959-88, Lord & Taylor, N.Y.C., 1963-78, Bergdorf Goodman, N.Y.C., 1980-88, Zantman Art Galleries, Carmel-by-the-Sea, Calif., 1970-73, Chevy Chase Gallery, Washington, 1981-88; one woman shows and group exhbns. include: Bergdorf Goodman Nena's Choice Gallery, Chevy Chase Gallery, Bjorn Lindgren Gallery, Sinnard Art Studios; tchr. open workshop for artists. Mem. Nat. Arts Club N.Y.C. Home and Studio: Box 304 New Hampton NY 10958

SINNEMAKI, ULLA ULPUKKA, nurse, educator; b. Antrea, Finland, Sept. 11, 1928; d. Otto William and Kaisa Viola (Jappinen) Spjut; m. Maunu Matti J. Sinnemaki, June 12, 1949 (div. Feb. 1968); children—Markku Taneli, Sirkka Astrid. B.A., NYU, 1972; B.S., SUNY-Stony Brook, 1976; M.Ed., McNeese State U., 1978, Ed.S., 1979, M.Ed., 1981. R.N., N.Y., La., Tex. Field interviewer Bur. Census, N.Y.C., 1973-75; Operating room asst. St. Charles Meml. Hosp., N.Y.C., 1965-72; staff nurse Lake Charles Meml.

Hosp., La., 1976-77; head nurse South Cameron Hosp., Cameron, La., 1977-80, dir. nursing, 1983-84; staff nurse Humana Hosp., Oakdale, La., 1984, Lake Charles, La., 1987—. Translator books, articles from English to Finnish, 1961—; designer rya rugs. Mem. Com. 1000 Baton Rouge, 1983. Mem. Nat. League Nursing, Am. Nurses Assn., Assn. Ednl. Communictions and Tech., Assn. Supervision and Curriculum Devel., Nat. Assn. Female Execs. Democrat. Lutheran. Avocations: gardening; music; photography. Address: 332 W State St Lake Charles LA 70605

SINNREICH, NAOMI WENDY BRAININ, lawyer; b. Bronx, N.Y., Jan. 18, 1953; d. William David and Beatrice Roslyn (Horowitz) Brainin; m. Abraham Isaac Sinnreich, Aug. 10, 1975; 1 child, Elizabeth Rachel. B.A., SUNY-Stony Brook, 1974; J.D. cum laude, Benjamin N. Cardozo Sch. Law, 1981. Bar: N.Y. 1982. Legal adminstrv. asst. Garbarini, Scher & DeCicco, N.Y.C., 1974-75; law clk., legal asst. Mandel & Resnik, N.Y.C., 1975-80; assoc. firm Graubard Moskovitz McGoldrick Dannett & Horowitz, N.Y.C., 1981-83; corp. atty.-assoc. Lowenthal, Landau, Fischer & Ziegler, N.Y.C., 1983—. Editor moot ct. bd., 1980-81. Mem. ABA, N.Y. State Bar Assn., Assn. Bar City N.Y. Democrat. Jewish. Office: Lowenthal Landau Fischer & Ziegler 250 Park Ave New York NY 10177

SIPE, ILENE GOLDBAUM, lawyer; b. Tucson, Mar. 8, 1954; d. Arthur and Miriam (Saltzman) Goldbaum; m. Dean Allen Sipe, Mar. 26, 1978; 1 child, Allen Christopher. B.S. in Speech and Hearing Scis. with high distinctions and honors, U. Ariz., 1975, J.D., 1978. Bar: Ariz. 1978, U.S. Dist. Ct. Ariz. 1978. Assoc., Kenneth Allen, Tucson, 1979-81, Waterfall, Economidis, Tucson, 1981-83; sole practice, Tucson, 1983—; founder, dir. Pima County PrivaCourt, Inc., Tucson, 1983-86; legal counsel, bd. dirs., Boys and Girls Clubs of Tucson, 1987—; speaker before profl. groups. Mem. ABA, Ariz. Bar Assn., Pima County Bar Assn., Ariz. Trial Lawyers Assn., Ariz. Women Lawyers Assn., Phi Kappa Phi. Democrat. Office: 310 S Williams Blvd Suite 222 Tucson AZ 85711

SIPE, JANE MARIE, jewelry designer, manufacturing executive; b. Piqua, Ohio, Nov. 12, 1947; d. Roy Sipe and Iris May (Smith) Ellis. BA, Calif. State U., Fullerton, 1969. Dep. probation officer Orange (Calif.) County Probation, 1969-75; jeweler Classic Jewelers, Jacksonville, Fla., 1976; jewelry repair person R.P. Lewis & Co., Santa Rosa, Calif., 1977-81; owner Jane Sipe Jeweler, Graton, Calif., 1982—; cons. The Mulberry Co., Oakland, Calif., 1982—, N.J. Searcy, Inc., Albuquerque, 1985—. Mem. staff, writer Runes Womens News, 1977-78; contbr. articles to profl. jours. Coordinator Womens Craft Fairs, Sonoma County, Calif., 1982-83. Mem. Nat. Assn. Female Execs., Sonoma County Womens Craft Guild. (treas. 1983-84). Office: PO Box 608 Graton CA 95444

SIPOS, CHIQUITA AGNES, community services consultant; b. Chgo., Apr. 21, 1939; d. Joaquin Angeles and Margaret Ross Arcala; m. Raymond E. Sipos, 1962 (divorced 1971); children: Sandra Rene, Stephanie Susan, Sheri Annette. AA, Pasadena City Coll., 1962; BA, Calif. State U., Los Angeles, 1967; BS in Law, Glendale U., 1978, JD, 1980. Bar: Calif. 1988. Playground dir. Melvindale (Mich.) Recreation Dept., 1958-59; probation attendant Los Angeles County Probation Dept., Commerce, Calif., 1961-62; group supr. Los Angeles County Probation Dept., El Monte, Calif., 1963-68; dir. Friendship Nursery Sch., El Monte, 1967-68; parole agent I Dept. Youth Authority, East Los Angeles, Calif., 1968-72; Parole Agent Specialist Dept. Youth Authority, Los Angeles, 1972-75, asst. supr., 1975-77; parole agent specialist Dept. Youth Authority, El Monte, 1977-78; cons. Dept. Youth Authority, Glendale, Calif., 1978—; instr. Dept. Youth Authority, Calif., 1975-87; cons. youth and criminal justice agys., Los Angeles County, 1980-87; panel mem. Am. Probation Parole Assn., Boston, 1985; mem. Health and Welfare Agy. Filipino Advisory Comm., 1976-78, Los Angeles County Commn. comm. on Law, Soc. & Children's Rights, 1979. Tech. advisor: (film and video) Victim to Victimizer: Breaking the Cycle of Male Sexual Abuse, 1986. Campaign mgr. Calif. Youth Authority, So. Calif., 1981-82; Commn. on Status Women Adv. Com., Sacramento, 1978-79. Recipient Women's Achievement award The East Los Angeles Community Union, 1976, Resolution award Calif. Legislature, Sacramento, 1976, Los Angeles County Bd. Suprs., 1982, commendation Californians Against Crime, Los Angeles, 1982. Mem. Los Angeles County Bar Assn. Juvenile Justice Commn., Calif. Probation Parole Correctional Assn. (pres. 1981-82), Am. Correctional Assn. (bd. govs. 1984-86). Democrat. Roman Catholic. Office: Dept of Youth Authority 143 S Glendale Ave Suite 305 Glendale CA 91030

SIRED, DONNA MAUREEN, health records administrator; b. Edmonton, Can., Sept. 10, 1959; d. Donald Frederick and Doreen Ruth (Bayliss) Hart; m. Robert Roy Sired, Aug. 3, 1985. Diploma, No. Alberta Inst. Tech., 1979; student, U. Alb., Edmonton, 1984-87. Supr. med. record dept. Misericordia Hosp., Edmonton, 1979; supr. med. record dept. U. Alb. Hosps., Edmonton, 1979-83, asst. dir. med. record dept., 1983—; preceptor health record technician program Can. Hosp. Assn.,1983-85, cons. adv. bd. health scis. facility No. Alberta Inst. Tech., 1985-87. Mem. Alb. Health Records Assn. (by laws com. 1981-82, pub. relations com. 1986-87, conv. com. 1986—, chmn. pub. relations com. 1988—), Can. Coll. Health Records Adminstrs. (cert. 1979), Coll. Health Record Adminstrs. (cert. 1979). Office: Univ Alberta Hosps, 8440 -112 St, Edmonton CAN T6G 2B7

SIROCHMAN, BRIDGET MARDINE, financial executive; b. St. Petersburg, Fla., Jan. 3, 1959; d. Michael Joseph Sirochman and Mardine Ellen (Huske) Kovach. B in Fin., St. Petersburg Coll., 1978; MBA, U. Sydney, 1985. Owner operator Matey Yacht Sales, St. Petersburg, 1976-79, Naples (Fla.) Service Co., 1979-85; chief fin. officer, dir. Kanga Ltd., Sydney, Australia, 1985—, Manly (Australia) Beach Developers, Ltd., 1985—; chief fin. officer, pres. S.B. Funding Services, Inc., Monrovia, Calif., 1987—; chief fin. officer, treas. C.G. Investments, Inc., Monrovia, 1988—. Republican. Roman Catholic.

SIROF, HARRIET TOBY, writer, educator; b. N.Y.C., Oct. 18, 1930; d. Herman and Lillian (Miller) Hockman; m. Sidney M. Sirof, June 18, 1949; children—Laurie, David, Amy. B.A., New Sch. Social Research, 1962. Pvt. tutor Bklyn., 1962-76; instr. L.I. U., Bklyn., 1978-79, South Shore Adult Center, Bklyn., 1977-83, Bklyn. Coll., 1980-81, 1984—; instr. writing St. John's U., Jamaica, N.Y., 1978-87. Author: The If Machine, 1978; A New Fashioned Love Story, 1977; Junior Encyclopedia of Israel, 1980; Save the Dam, 1981; That Certain Smile, 1982; The Real World, 1985 (Jr. Lit. Guild selection); Anything You Can Do, 1986. Recipient Louis Weiss award New Sch. Social Research, 1962. Mem. Authors Guild, Internat. Womens Writing Guild, Soc. Children's Book Writers. Democrat. Jewish. Home: 792 E 21st St Brooklyn NY 11210

SIROIS, BARBARA THERESA MAZZADRA, management executive; b. Stratford, Conn., Nov. 7, 1941; d. William N. and Helen E. (DeBiase) Mazzadra; m. Howard Frederick Sirois, May 7, 1966. Grad. high sch., Stratford. Exec. asst. to asst. v.p. sales and contracts ops. Avco Lycoming div. Textron Corp., Stratford, 1962-69; asst. to v.p. merchandising Caldor, Inc., Norwalk, Conn., 1969-71; v.p. ops. and devel. Am. Shakespeare Theatre, Stratford, 1973-86; pres. The Devel. Workshop, Huntington, Conn., 1982—; mgr. bus. and prodn. Libby TV Prodns., Ltd., Westport, Conn., 1987—; U.S. rep. Young Shakespeare Co. of London, 1987—; mem. adv. bd. Sta. WSHU-FM, Sacred Heart U., Fairfield, Conn., 1983—; mgmt. cons., Huntington, 1986—. Author, developer numerous fundraising, mktg. and tourism publs. Commr. Stratford Tourism Commn., 1984—, chmn., 1985-86; chmn. Hill and Harbor Conv. and Visitors Dist., Stratford, Milford, Trumbull and West Haven, Conn., 1985-86, Stratford Bus. Edn. Support Team, 1988—. Mem. Nat. Soc. Fund Raising Execs., Devel. Assn. So. Conn., Nat. Assn. Female Execs., Women in Mgmt., Women in Communications, Stratford C. of C. (bd. dirs. 1983—), Am. Orchid Soc., Cymbidium Soc. Am., Conn. Orchid Soc., Westchester Orchid Round Table.

SIROWER, BONNIE FOX, fundraising executive; b. Bklyn., Jan. 9, 1949; d. Stanley S. and Harriet (Fischer) Fox; m. Martin Alan Sirower, Sept. 20, 1970; children—Kenneth, Daniel. A.B., Barnard Coll., 1970; M.A., Tchrs. Coll., Columbia U., 1971. Tchr., United Cerebral Palsy, N.Y.C., 1970-73, Bergen County Bd. Spl. Services, Paramus, N.J., 1973-76; spl. events coordinator Am. Heart Assn., Glen Ridge, 1979-81; dir. devel. Goodwill Industries, Astoria, N.Y., 1981-83; pres. Access Unltd., 1984-85; dir. devel. Cheshire Home, Inc., 1986—; cons. New Concepts for Living, Hillsdale, N.J., 1983. Pres. Sisterhood Temple Beth Haverim, Mahwah, 1976-77; co-chmn. Glen Rock Independence Day Assn., 1983. Mem. N.J. Soc. Fund Raising Execs. (chair soc. and registration, Women in Fin. Devel., Assn. Fund Raisers for Disabled (pres. 1981-83), N.J. Puzzlers' League (pres.), Phi Beta Kappa. Jewish. Home: 69 Godfrey Terr Glen Rock NJ 07452

SISCO, MARY ELIZABETH, lawyer, consultant; b. Fort Worth, Nov. 16, 1937; d. Daniel Louis and Mary Elizabeth (Blanton) Creson; m. William Theodore Sisco, Aug. 7, 1959; children—Christopher Theodore, Gregory Samuel, Lois Danine. B.A., Tex. Christian U., 1959; J.D., Tex. Tech U., 1979. Bar: Tex. 1979. Provisional secondary teaching cert., Tex. Tchr., Fort Worth Ind. Sch. Dist., 1959-61, Memphis Ind. Sch. Dist., 1961-65; ind. market researcher, Rochester, Minn., 1968-72; solo practice, Lubbock, Tex., 1979—; treas., bd. dirs. Y-Not Better Papers, Dallas, 1975-86. Trustee, Lubbock Ind. Sch. Dist., 1980-86; bd. dirs. Caprock council Girl Scouts U.S.A., Lubbock, 1980-88; chmn. Tex. Legis. Cabinet, Girl Scouts U.S.A., Dallas, 1981-87, chmn., 1988—; bd. dirs. Lubbock Civic Ballet, 1983-85; mem. West Tex. Mus. Assn., Tex. Tech. U., 1974—; co-chmn. Lubbock Assn. Concerned with Teenage Sexuality, 1984, pres., 1985; mem. adv. bd. Tex. Assn. Sch. Age Parents, 1987—, State Council of Vols., March of Dimes, 1987—; bd. dirs. Lubbock div. March of Dimes; bd. dirs. Found. for Excellence, Lubbock, 1987—; mem. Vol. Lawyers and Accts. for the Arts; life mem. Lubbock PTA, Tex. PTA. Mem. ABA, Order of Coif, Alpha Chi, Delta Delta Delta. Methodist. Clubs: Lubbock Women's, Classic Toastmasters. Office: 3607 22d St Lubbock TX 79410

SISKO, MARIE FERRARIS, fund raising executive; b. N.Y.C., Feb. 3, 1938; d. Joseph and Jean (Boaro) F.; B.A., Queens Coll., 1975; postgrad. Adelphi U., 1976; m. Joseph Edward Sisko, Dec. 26, 1948; children—Warren Joseph, Robert Edward. Asst. acct. N.Y.C. Bd. Edn., 1968-69; dir. personnel Daypac Inc., 1969-70; exec. asst. Ponder & Best, 1971-73; sales adminstr. Ampacet Corp., 1973-75; mktg. rep. Better Bus. Bur., 1975-77; asst. exec. dir. Leukemia Soc. Am., 1978-82; pub. relations assoc., campaign dir. Ketchum, Inc., 1982-85; dir. maj. gifts Seton Hall U., South Orange, N.J., 1985—; v.p. Sisko Enterprises, N.Y. World's Fair, 1964-65; editor, salesperson Malba (N.Y.) News & Views Newspaper, 1969-80. Del. White House Conf. on Small Bus., N.Y.C., 1978. Mem. N.Y. Assn. Women Bus. Owners (founding 1976, edn. com.), Queens Coll. Alumni Assn. (trustee 1976—, pres. Ace chpt. 1977-79), Nat. Soc. Fund Raising Execs., AAUW. Lutheran. Home: 32 Center Dr Malba NY 11357 Office: Seton Hall U South Orange NJ

SISSELSKY, SHARON LEE, educator; b. Rochester, N.Y., July 13, 1957; d. Julian and Carol (Fritt) Lee; m. Lee Sisselsky, Dec. 21, 1985; 1 child, Carla Beth. Student, Endicott Coll., Beverly, Mass., 1975-76; BS, Ithaca (N.Y.) Coll., 1979; MS, Nazareth Coll. Rochester, 1985. Cert. in physical edn. and driver edn., N.Y., cert. math tchr. Driver edn. tchr. Rush-Henrietta (N.Y.) Cen. Sch., 1979-80, Hilton (N.Y.) Cen. Sch., 1980-81, Herkimer (N.Y.) Cen. Sch., 1981—; curriculum cons. N.Y. State Edn. Dept., Albany, 1987; advisor student council Herkimer High Sch., 1984—, students against drunk driving orgn., 1985—, pep club, 1985—. Vol. N.Y. State United Tchrs. vote cope program Mario Cuomo campaign, Utica, 1982; advisor Temple Emanu-el youth group, 1987—; chmn. publicity Hadassah, 1987—. Mem. Am. Driver and Traffic Safety Educators Assn., N.Y. State United Tchrs., Driver Educators of N.Y. State (sec.-treas. Mohawk Valley chpt. 1985—), Herkimer Faculty Assn. (sec. 1984-87). Democrat. Jewish. Club: Hadassah (Utica). Home: 12 Woodland Village Utica NY 13501

SISSON, BETTY, real estate broker; b. Burbank, Calif., Apr. 21, 1934; d. Harvey Orville and Isabel Marion (Melville) Angermeir; student public schs., Burbank; children—James Harvey, William Frank. Sales asso. Rich Port Realtors, Oak Brook, Ill., 1971-76, sales mgr., 1976-78, v.p., 1978-83; exec. v.p. Am. Growth Real Estate Corp., Oak Brook, 1979-80, The Midwest Club, Oak Brook, 1980-83, Selected Properties, Inc., Oak Brook, 1983-85, Pringley & Booth, Inc., Chgo., 1985—, Ambriance! Inc., Burr Ridge, Ill., 1987—. Mem. Nat. Assn. Realtors, Realtors Nat. Mktg. Inst., DuPage Bd. Realtors, Oak Brook Assn. Commerce and Industry. Republican. Club: Internat. Chgo. Home: 1405 Burr Ridge Club Burr Ridge IL 60521 Office: Ambriance Inc One Ambriance Dr Burr Ridge IL 60521

SISTERSON, JANET MARGOT, physicist; b. Edinburgh, Scotland, July 7, 1940; came to U.S. 1968, naturalized, 1985; d. Thomas James and Lucy Margaret (Smith) Brownlee; BS, U. Durham, 1961; PhD, Imperial Coll. Sci. and Tech., U. London, 1965; m. L. Keith Sisterson, Oct. 23, 1965; children: James, Mark. Basic grade physicist London Hosp., 1964-66; sr. physicist Chelsea Hosp. for Women, London, 1966-68; research fellow Cambridge (Mass.) Electron Accelerator, 1968-73; research assoc. Harvard Cyclotron Lab., 1973—. Mem. exec. bd. Harrington Sch. PTA 1977-83. Mem. Am. Phys. Soc., Am. Assn. Physicists in Medicine, Am. Nuclear Soc., Am. Women in Sci. Contbr. articles to profl. jours. Office: 44 Oxford St Cambridge MA 02138

SITTER, CLARA MARIE LOEWEN, librarian, media specialist; b. Watonga, Okla., June 28, 1941; d. Arthur Harold and Virginia Mae (Wood) Loewen; m. Lester Dewey Sitter, Aug. 19, 1962; children—Susan Elizabeth, Scott Douglas. B.A., U. Okla., 1962; M.L.S., U. Tex., 1966; cert. advanced study Denver U., 1981; Ph.D., U. Colo.-Boulder, 1982. Cert. tchr., Colo. With U. Tex. Libraries, Austin, 1962-66; cataloger West Tex. State U., Canyon, 1967; librarian, assoc. dir. Amarillo (Tex.) Coll., 1968-71; library media specialist St. Mary's High Sch., Colorado Springs, Colo., 1971-73, Harrison High Sch., Colorado Springs, 1973-84, Sierra High Sch., Colorado Springs, 1984—; part-time faculty U. Colo., Denver, 1987— . Contbr. articles profl. jours. Mem. ALA, Assn. Ednl. Communications and Tech., Colo. Library Assn., Colo. Ednl. Media Assn., Am. Assn. Sch. Librarians, AAUW, NEA, Colo. Edn. Assn., Harrison Edn. Assn., Alaska Library Assn., Colo. Council of Internat. Reading Assn., Kappa Delta Pi, Chi Omega, Phi Delta Kappa. Methodist. Home: PO Box 19 Anchorage AK 99510 Office: Sierra High Sch 2250 Jetwing Dr Colorado Springs CO 80916

SIVERSON, JUDITH BUNT, clinical psychologist; b. Phila., June 27, 1935; d. Michael and Katherine (Lemon) Bunt; A.B. magna cum laude, Temple U., Phila., 1968; M.A., 1969, Ph.D. in Clin. Psychology, 1974; 1 dau., Michele Lyn. Staff psychologist rehab. medicine dept. Temple U. Hosp., 1971-72; staff psychologist alcoholism unit Diagnostic and Rehab. Center, Phila., 1972-73; staff psychologist Community Mental Health Center Gloucester County, Woodbury, N.J., 1973-75; chief psychologist rehab. medicine dept. Rolling Hill Hosp., Elkins Park, Pa., 1975-77; chief psychol. services rehab. medicine dept. Temple U. Hosp., 1977-80; pvt. practice psychology, cons., Glassboro, N.J., and Phila., 1980—; coordinator head injury rehab. program St. Lawrence Rehab. Center, Lawrenceville, N.J., 1983. Served with WAC, U.S. Army, 1955-57. Lic. psychologist Pa., N.J. Mem. Nat. Acad. Neuropsychologists, Am. Psychol. Assn., Pa. Psychol. Assn., N.J. Psychol. Assn., Phila. Soc. Clin. Psychologists. Address: 22 Dickinson Rd Glassboro NJ 08028

SIWAKOWSKY, EVELYN, computer specialist; b. Brussels, July 30, 1943; came to U.S., 1950; d. Philip and Rachael Singer; m. Andrew Siwakowski; children: Michele Alpern, Debbie Alpern. BA, Rutgers U., 1965; MA, Georgian Ct. Coll., 1980; student in computer sci., Brookdale Community Coll., Lincroft, N.J., 1980-82. Elem. sch. tchr. Freehold, N.J., 1965-67; math tchr. Freehold Intermediate Sch., 1977-82; Unix instr. Concurrent Computer Corp., Oceanport, N.J., 1982—; tchr. for the mathematically gifted Freehold Intermediate Sch. Contbr. articles to profl. jours. Mem. Women for Math. Edn., MENSA. Office: Concurrent Computer Corp 2 Crescent Pl Oceanport NJ 07757

SIZEMORE, DEBORAH LIGHTFOOT, writer, editor; b. Lamesa, Tex., Mar. 18, 1956; d. Glenn Billy and Francis Earlene (Cable) Lightfoot; m. O.E. Gene Sizemore, June 19, 1981. B.S. in Agrl. Journalism summa cum laude, Tex. A&M U., 1977. Writer, Tex. Agrl. Extension, College Station, 1976-77; copy editor Abilene Reporter-News (Tex.), 1978; customer service rep. Motheral Printing Co., Ft. Worth, 1978-79; prodn. coordinator Graphic Arts, Inc., Ft. Worth, 1980-81; writer, editor, Crowley, Tex., 1981—; agrl. writer, editor Boy Scouts Am., Irving, Tex., 1981—; contbg. editor Dairymen's Digest, Arlington, Tex., 1981—. Longhorn Scene, Ft. Worth, 1982-84; writer, photographer Harvest Times, Dallas, 1983-84; Simbrah World, Ft. Worth, 1985-87; contbg. editor Lone Star Horse Report, Ft. Worth, 1985—; contbr. photographs to mags.; contbr. articles mags. Women's issues chmn., v.p. membership, pub. info. officer, newsletter editor AAUW of Tarrant County, 1981-86; organizer nat. security pub. debate, Ft. Worth, 1983. Recipient Sr. Merit award in Agrl. Journalism, Tex. A&M U., 1978, Thomas S. Gathright Acad. Excellence award, 1976, Cert. of Merit, Livestock Publs Council, 1984, 86, @d place Nonfiction Book award Tex.-Wide Writers' Competition, 1988. Mem. Nat. Writers Club, Western Writers Am., Am. Agrl. Editors Assn., Am. Agri-Women, Phi Kappa Phi, Gamma Sigma Delta. Club: Ft. Worth A&M. Office: 19 Frazier Ln Crowley TX 76036

SJOGREN, DEBORAH MARY, accountant; b. Ely, Minn., Aug. 1, 1953; d. Stanley Joseph and Justine Pauline (Korent) Boldine; m. Mark Robert Sjogren, Aug. 21, 1976. A.A., Vermillion Community Coll., 1973; B.S., St. Cloud State U., Minn., 1975. Br. acct. Montgomery Ward, St. Paul, 1975-77; fin. processing cons. region III Mgmt. Info. Service/Elem., Secondary, Vocat., St. Cloud, Minn., 1977-78; acctg. supr. Vision Ease Corp., St. Cloud, 1978-83; controller Franciscan Sisters of Little Falls, Little Falls, Minn., 1983—. Yugoslav Nat. Home scholar, 1971. Mem. Profl. Women's Orgn. (founder), CORT (vice chair Region XI), Nat. Assn. Female Execs., Cen. Minn. Nat. Assn. Accts., Phi Chi Theta (charter). Avocations: horseback riding, needlecrafts, reading. Office: Franciscan Sisters Little Falls 116 8th Ave SE Little Falls MN 56345

SKAGGS, BECKY SUE, computer programmer; b. Ft. Worth, Apr. 26, 1956; d. Don Royce and Ruth (Pax) Adams; m. Earl Lee Skaggs, May 7, 1983. BA in Math, U. Tex., Arlington, 1977. Cert. tchr., Tex. Tchr. Everman (Tex.) High Sch., 1978-81; programmer/analyst Tandy Corp., Ft. Worth, 1981-85; mgr. interface systems Transfirst Corp., Dallas, 1985-87; software project mgr. Verifone Inc., Dallas, 1987—. Home: 401 Fairhaven Dr Hurst TX 76054 Office: Verifone Inc 14881 Quorum Dr Dallas TX 75240

SKALL, TERRY ROBERTSON, newspaper editor; b. Chgo., May 3, 1943; d. Robert Irving and Beatrice Hannah (Winter) Robertson; m. Richard A. Skall, May 23, 1963; children—Barbara, Jeffrey, David. Student Northwestern U., 1961-63; B.S., Western Res. U., 1966. News editor Chagrin Valley Pub. Co., Chagrin Falls, Ohio, 1974-80; editor-in-chief Chagrin Valley-Solon Times Currents, Chagrin Falls, 1980—; freelance travel writer, 1983—. Mem. Sigma Delta Chi (award for editorial writing 1980, award for news reporting 1981). Office: Chagrin Valley/Solon Times Box 150 34 S Main St Chagrin Falls OH 44022

SKALSKY, CHERYL COLLEEN, social welfare administrator; b. Kenmare, N.D., Apr. 1, 1944; d. Charles William and Charlotte (Haggerty) Doran; m. Duane Adam Skalsky, Aug. 24, 1963; children: Todd Wendelin, Wade Jonathan. Student, U. N.D., 1963, Minot (N.D.) State Coll., 1977, 82, Pima Community Coll., 1986, 87,; BA in Bus. Adminstrn., U. Phoenix, 1988. Lic. social worker, N.D. Reporter, columnist Beulah (N.D.) Beacon, 1977-79; exec. dir. Mercer County Women's Action and Resource Ctr., Beulah, 1979-86, Pima Council on Devel. Disabilities, Tucson, 1986—; exec. officer VanCleve and Doran, Tucson, 1987-88; chiar transp. com. Tuscon Commn. on Handicapped, 1987-88, chair, 1988—; mem. human rights and ethics com. div. developmental disabilities Ariz. Dept. Econ. Security, Tucson, 1987—; chair transp. com. Tucson Commn. on the Handicapped, 1987—. Pres. Eagles Aux. #3728, Beulah, 1980-81; exec. mem. Gov.'s Council Driving Under the Influence Task Force, 1984-86; chair St. Joseph's Ch., Beulah, 1985-86; v.p. N.D. Council on Abused Women, 1986; mem. Oro Valley (Ariz.) Town Council, 1988—. Home: 9110 N Shadow Mountain Dr Oro Valley AZ 85737 Office: Pima Council Devel Disabilities 2160 N 6th St Tucson AZ 85705

SKEANS, CAROLOU, education educator; b. Dayton, Ohio, Nov. 26, 1932; d. Ledford and Sue Ann (Brown) Smith; children: Max Howard, Mark Timothy. BA, Georgetown Coll., 1964; MEd, U. Cin., 1969, EdD, 1980. Cert. tchr. bus. and music; cert. supr. bus. office edn. Tchr. Johnsonville New Lebanon (Ohio) High Sch., 1964-65; coordinator bus. Trotwood (Ohio)-Madison High Sch., 1965-75; assoc. prof. Miami U., Middletown, Ohio, 1975—; cons. Nat. Adv. Council, Columbus, Ohio, 1967, Armco Steel Corp., Middletown, 1977-78, Fifth Third Bank, Cin., 1979-80; U.S. del. to Helsinki, Finland for Internat. Bus. Edn. Soc., 1985. Co-author: Advanced Information Processing, 1980; editor (book) Office Procedures, 1984. Choir dir. Triumphant Luth. Ch., Trotwood, 1964-66, Ft. McKinley Meth. Ch., Dayton, 1967-75. Scholar Georgetown Coll., 1961, U. Cin., 1977. Mem. Adminstrv . Mgmt. Soc. (coll. advisor), Internat. Soc. Bus. Educators' Congress (U.S. del. to Finland 1984), Beta Gamma Sigma, Delta Omicron (scholarship coordinator 1981-83), Delta Pi Epsilon. Republican. Baptist. Office: Miami U 4200 E University Blvd Middletown OH 45042

SKEEN, PATSY LOUISE, child and family development educator, author, consultant; b. Norton, Va., Oct. 14, 1946; d. James Rucker and Georgia (Bevins) S. BS, Radford (Va.) Coll., 1968; MS, U. Tenn., 1969; EdD, U. Ga., 1976. Instr., head tchr. lab sch. U. Ga., Athens, 1969-74, instr. child and family devel., 1974-77, asst. prof. of child and family devel., 1977-84, assoc. prof. of child and family devel., 1984—; cons. Ga. Extension Service, Athens, 1973-74, Head Start, North Ga. area, 1975, Gwinnett County Schs., Lawrenceville, Ga., 1976-78; bd. dirs. Community Coordinated Child Care, Athens, 1976-80; mem. adv. bd. Athens Vocat. Tech. Sch., 1975-81. Author: (with others) Child Development and Relationships, 1983, Woodworking for Young Children: A Curriculum Guide for Teachers, Parents, and Workshop Leaders, 1984; contbr. numerous articles to profl. jours. Presentor, interviewer TV, radio, and print media, 1974—; bd. dirs. Athens Communtiy Coordinated Child Care, Athens, 1976-80. Bascom Slemp Scholarship award for Academic Excellence, 1964-65, 65-66, 66-67, 67-68; named one of Outstanding Young Women in Am., 1978. Mem. Assn. for Childhood Edn. Internat. (research reviewer 1979—), So. Assn. on Children Under Six (editorial bd. 1983—), Ga. Assn. on Young Children (program chair 1983-84, chair scholarship com. 1985—), Southeastern Council on Family Relations (program com. 1977-78), Groves Conf. on Marriage and Family, Soc. for Research in Child Devel., Nat. Assn. for the Edn. of Young Children, Am. Assn. of Marriage and Family Therapists (assoc. 1978-80), Assn. for Childhood Edn. Internat., Nat. Assn. for Edn. of Young Children, Nat. Council on Family Relations, Soc. for Research in Child Devel., Ga. Early Childhood Edn./Child Devel. Higher Edn. Assn., Chi Beta Phi, Gamma Sigma Delta, Phi Kappa Pi. Office: U Ga Dawson Hall CLG HEC Athens GA 30602

SKELTON, DOROTHY GENEVA SIMMONS (MRS. JOHN WILLIAM SKELTON), educator; b. Woodland, Calif.; d. Jack Elijah and Helen Anna (Siebe) Simmons; B.A., U. Calif., 1940, M.A., 1943; m. John William Skelton, July 16, 1941. Sr. research analyst War Dept., Gen. Staff, M.I. Div. G-2, Pentagon, Washington, 1944-45; vol. researcher, monuments, fine arts and archives sect. Restitution Br., Office Mil. Govt. for Hesse, Wiesbaden, German, 1947-48; vol. art tchr. German children in Bad Nauheim, Germany, 1947-48; art educator, lectr. Dayton (Ohio) Art Inst., 1955; art educator Lincoln Sch., Dayton, 1956-60; instr. art and art edn. U. Va. Sch. Continuing Edn., Charlottesville, 1962-75; researcher genealogy, exhibited in group shows, Calif., Colo., Ohio, Washington and Va.; represented in permanent collections Madison Hall, Charlottesville, Madison (Va.) Center. Mem. Nat. League Am. Pen Women, AAUW, Am. Assn. Museums, Coll. Art Assn. Am., Inst. for Study of Art in Edn., Dayton Soc. Painters and Sculptors, Nat. Soc. Arts and Letters (life), Va. Mus. Fine Arts, Cal. Alumni Assn., Air Force Officers Wives Club. Republican. Methodist. Clubs: Army Navy Country, Lake of the Woods (Va.) Golf and Country. Chief collaborator: John Skelton of Georgia, 1969; author: The Squire Simmons Family, 1746-1986, 1986. Address: Lotos Lakes Brightwood VA 22715

SKENDER, LAVERNE JANET, electric motor services co. exec.; b. Berwyn, Ill., Aug. 28, 1935; d. Edward Louis and Philamina Tillie (Baumruk) Stedron; A.A., Morton Jr. Coll., 1955; m. George Joseph Skender, June 9, 1956 (dec.); children—Jeffrey Scott, Patricia Diane, Edward George, Jacalyn Louise, Amy Lynn. Sec., Sears Roebuck, 1952-58; asst. purchasing agt. Prater Industries, 1967-69; sec. Dykema & Dykema, 1970-71; outside salesman DeBar Electric Motors, Chgo., 1971-83; pres. City Suburban Electric Motors, Inc., 1983—; dir. Stedcor Corp. Pres. U.S. Navy

League, Forest Park, 1976, 77, 79, 81, 82; active NOW; bd. dirs. Fillmore Family Services. Named to scroll of honor U.S. Navy League. Mem. Elec. Apparatus Service Assn. (mem. mgmt.), Elec. Motor Distbrs., Elec. Assn., Cicero Assn. Bus. and Industry, Greater O'Hare C of C., Northwest Suburban Assn. Commerce and Industry, Women in Elec. Trades, Women in Bus., Nat. Assn. Women Bus. Owners, Am. Soc. Profl. and Exec. Women, Nat. Assn. Female Execs. Clubs: West Suburban Exec., West Suburban Breakfast (dir. 1980-82), Bus. and Profl. Women (legis. chmn. Cicero, 1976-77, 80-81, pres. 1974-75, 79-71, Nike award, dist. dir. 1976, state expansion chmn., 1980-81). First woman in outside motor sales, first woman shop foreman, first woman pres. of motor shop, first woman pres. U.S. Navy League Council. Home: 2211 W Clifton Pl Hoffman Estates IL 60195 Office: 2740 N Pulaski Rd Chicago IL 60639

SKERRITT, ELIZABETH, information scientist, consultant; b. N.Y.C., 1932; d. James Lewis and Grace M. Skerritt. Student (under auspices of Smith Coll.), U. Geneva, 1952-53; BA, Smith Coll., 1954; MA, Columbia U., 1965, MS, 1973. Cert. profl. librarian, N.Y. Instr. Douglass Coll., Rutgers U., New Brunswick, N.J., 1968-69; slide curator, librarian Sch. Visual Arts, N.Y.C., 1969-71; registrar, librarian E.V. Thaw Gallery, N.Y.C., 1972-73; head librarian, mgr. microfilm-index sales Am. Banker, N.Y.C., 1973-75; researcher Devel. Office Columbia U., N.Y.C., 1976; corp. librarian info. ctr. Internat. Paper Co., N.Y.C., 1977-85; cons., researcher Gossage Regan, N.Y.C., 1985-86; asst. librarian Bolling Library, St. Luke's Hosp., N.Y.C., 1986—. Author, editor: Subject Guide to Sources in the American Revolutionary Period in New York City and Environs, 1976; editor, researcher: TAPPI Bibliography of Papermaking Terminology (12 langs.), 1982; editor Am. Banker Index Ann., 1974; creator tng. videotape info. sci. applications in med. field, 1988. Mem. Spl. Libraries Assn. (nat. officer div. advt.-mktg. 1984-85, chmn. N.Y.C. chpt., newspaper group 1974-75, Bicentennial com. 1976, Mus. Arts Humanities group 1977-78, advt.-mktg. group 1983-84), TAPPI (chmn. info. mgmt. com. 1983-85, vice-chmn. 1980-82), Med. Archives Soc. (bd. dirs. 1976—), Columbia U. Grad. Faculties Alumnae Assn. (bd. dirs. 1976-78).

SKIBA, DIANE JEAN, medical educator; b. Danbury, Conn., Dec. 2, 1952; d. Thaddeus and Josephine (Osiecki) S. BA, So. Conn. U., 1974; MEd, U. Va., 1975, PhD, 1979. Research assoc. U. Va., Charlottesville, 1975-77; asst. prof. Boston U. Sch. Nursing, 1977-86; assoc. prof. U. Mass. Med. Ctr., Worcester, 1986—; ednl. cons. Pinpoint Pub., Inc., Emeryville, Calif., 1988—; mem. adv. bd. MediOSims Corp., Kansas City, Mo., 1984-85, At-Work Corp., Raleigh, N.C., 1986—. Research editor: Computers in Nursing, 1986—; contbr. articles to profl. publs. Mem. Boston Computer Soc., Am. Psychol. Assn., Am. Ednl. Research Assn., Assn. Computing Machinery, Nat. League Nursing (mem. exec. bd. dirs. 1985—, bd. dirs. 1987—), Sigma Theta Tau (hon.). Home: 23 Holmes St Dedham MA 02026 Office: Univ Mass Med Ctr 55 Lake Ave North Worcester MA 01655

SKIBA-JONES, CHERYL LYNN, health educator; b. Mpls., Apr. 23, 1955; d. Jerome Martin and Corrine Elsie (Neurauter) S.; m. Donald Paul Jones. BS in Home Econs., U. Minn., 1977; MA in Communications, U. Dayton, 1983. Research asst. Edn. Psychol. Dept. U. Minn., Mpls., Ind., 1978-79; rep. community services March Dimes, Dayton, Ohio, 1981-83; exec. dir. March Dimes, Muncie, Ind., 1983-84; free lance writer Muncie, Ind., 1984-85; office mgr. Mkt. Share Inc., Indpls., 1985-86; fund raiser Leukemia Soc., Indpls., 1985-86; health educator So. Seven Health Dept., Ullin, Ill., 1986—; bd. dirs. Appeals Bd. Coll. Home Econs., St. Paul, So. Community Health Ctr., Kettering, Ohio; counselor Unitarian Universalist Ch., Kettering, 1982-83. Named Outstanding Young Woman Am., 1983. Mem. Women Communications, Nat. Assn. Future Women (pub. relations rep. 1982-83), Am. Assn. Home Econs. (pres. 1976-77); fellow AAUW, Phi Upsilon Omicron, Eta Sigma Gamma. Home: 706 N James Carbondale IL 62901 Office: S-7 Health Dept Rt 2 Ullin IL 62992

SKIDMORE, NELL BURDEN, educational specialist; b. Ala., Dec. 15, 1931; d. John Gurley and Velma Elizabeth (Hyatt) Burden; m. Wade Elmer Skidmore, Sept. 10, 1953; children: Elizabeth, David W. BS, Ala. Polytech. Inst. now Auburn U., 1953; MA, Vanderbilt U., 1960, PhD, 1981. Cert. instr., supr. and adminstr., Ala. Library asst. Tech. Library Redstone Arsenal, Huntsville, Ala., 1953; social worker Marshall County Dept. Pub. Welfare, Guntersville, Ala., 1953-54; tchr. city schs., Albuquerque, 1954-56, county schs., Cullman, Ala., 1956-65, Morgan County Schs., Decatur, Ala., 1966; tchr. Huntsville City Schs., 1966-86, curriculum specialist, 1986—; vis. instr. U. Ala.; seminar, workshop leader/coordinator Huntsville City Schs., 1980—. Presenter weekly radio broadcast Children's Minute, 1967-84. Mem. Marshall-Jackson Mental Health Bd., Guntersville, 1978—, pres., 1987—; Republican candidate Dist. 9, Ala. Senate, 1987; state-at-large candidate Rep. Nat. Conv., 1988. Recipient (with husband) Disting. Service award Ala. Poultry and Egg Assn., 1984, Outstanding Farm Couple award Marshall County Poultry Producers, 1985. Mem. Huntsville Orgn. Profl. Educators, Huntsville Assn. Sch. Adminstrs., Nat. Assn. Educators of Young Children, Assn. Supervision and Curriculum Devel., Ala. Reading Assn., So. Assn. for Children Under Six, Arab C. of C., Wesley Found., Sphinx (now Mortar Bd.), Alpha Delta Kappa (com. chair 1982—, Outstanding Educator award 1987), Kappa Delta Pi, Pi Tau Chi., Phi Delta Kappa. United Methodist. HOme: Route 1 Box 274 Union Grove AL 35175 Office: Hutsville City Schs PO Box 1256 Huntsville AL 35807-4801

SKIMMONS, JOAN DOROTHEA, data processing professional; b. Elizabeth, N.J., Oct. 11, 1948; d. Joseph Bernard and Dorothea Olga (Stutzke) S.; m. Henry Hugh Loscher, July 21, 1981; 1 child, Kelly Dorothea. Student, Union Coll., 1967-72. Sales rep. Bur. Nat. Affairs Inc., N.Y.C., 1974-77; mktg. rep. Service Bur. Co. div. Control Data Corp., N.Y.C., 1977-80; mgr. mktg. services Citicorp Info. Resources, Greenwich, Conn., 1980-81, dir. communications and tng., 1981-82, product mgr., 1982-83, mgr. offering planning, 1983-85, mgr. mktg. communications, 1985—. Home: 427 Belden Hill Rd Wilton CT 06897

SKINDZIER, FRAN TERESA, telecommunications company executive; b. Pitts., Apr. 9, 1938; d. Francis Joseph and Mary Margaret (McDonough) Figura; m. Melvin Francis Skindzier, Jan. 28, 1961; children: Melanie A., Christopher E., Susan E. BSBA, Duquesne U., Pitts., 1962. Gen. mgr. Ea. Signal Control Co., Pitts., 1978-82; cons. CPS Assocs., Schaumburg, Ill., 1983-85; contract adminstr. IBM/ROLM Systems Div., Schaumberg, 1985-86; contract adminstrn. mgr. IBM/ROLM Systems Div., Pitts., 1986-87, br. mgr. fin. and adminstrn., 1987—. Mem. Nat. Assn. Female Execs., Western Pa. Geneal. Soc., Beta Gamma Sigma. Republican. Office: IBM Corp ROLM Systems Div Penn Center W II 4th Floor Pittsburgh PA 15276

SKINNER, MARY JUST, state legislator; b. South Bend, Ind., July 7, 1946; m. Scott Skinner, 2 children. A.B. cum laude, Barnard Coll., 1968; J.D., Columbia U., 1971. Bar: Vt., N.Y., Pa. Mem. Vt. State Senate, 1979—, asst. minority leader, 1983-84. Mem. Vt. and Washington County Bar Assns. Democrat. Office: Vt Senate State Capitol Montpelier VT 05602 Address: PO Box 412 Montpelier VT 05602 *

SKINNER, NANCY JO, recreation executive; b. Ogallala, Nebr., Nov. 5, 1956; d. Dale Warren Skinner and Beverly Jane (Fister) Berry. AA, Platte Community Coll., 1977; BS, U. Ariz., 1981; postgrad. in Mgmt., U. Phoenix, Tuscon, 1985—; postgrad., U. Phoenix, Tucson, 1987-88. Sports specialist YWCA, Tucson, 1981, asst. dir. summer day camp, 1981, dir. health, phys. edn. and recreation, 1981-82; sr. recreation specialist Pima County Parks and Recreation Dept., Tucson, 1983, coordinator recreation program, 1983—; labor mgmt. quality of work life rep. Pima County Govt., 1987; dist. coordinator Atlantic Richfield Co. Jesse Owens Games, Tucson, 1986-88; adv. Pima County Health Dept. Better Health Through Self Awareness, 1982-83. Dir. tournament Sportsman Fund-Send a Kid to Camp, Tucson, 1984, 85, 86; dir. Labor Mgmt. Quality of Working Life com. Pima County govt., 1987; dist. coordinator Nat. Health Screening Council, Tucson, 1982-83, 84-85; event coordinator Tucson Women's Commn. Saguaro Classic, Tucson, 1984; mem. com. United Way, Tucson, 1982-83. Mem. Ariz. Parks and Recreation Assn. (treas. 1987, v.p. 1988, pres.-elect 1989, recipient Tenderfoot award, 1984, cert.), Nat. Assn. Female Execs., Delta Psi Kappa (pres. U. Ariz. chpt. 1980-81). Democrat. Methodist. Office: Pima County Parks & Recreation Dept 1204 W Silverlake Rd Tucson AZ 85713

SKINNER, PATRICIA MORAG, state legislator; b. Glasgow, Scotland, Dec. 3, 1932; d. John Stuart and Frances Charlotte (Swann) Robertson; m. Robert A. Skinner, Dec. 28, 1957; children—Robin Ann, Pamela. BA, NYU, 1953; Mdse. trainee Lord & Taylor, N.Y.C., 1955-59; adminstrv. asst. Atlantic Products, N.Y.C., 1954-59; newspaper corr. Salem Observer, N.H., 1964-84; mem. N.H. Ho. of Reps., 1973—, chmn. labor, human resources and rehab. com., 1975-86, Health Edn. Com., 1987, exec. com. Nat. Conf. State Legislatures, 1987—; chmn. N.H. Adv. Council Unemployment Compensation. Bd. dirs. Castle Jr. Coll., 1975, Swift Water council Girl Scouts U.S., v.p. 1987—; mem. adv. council N.H. Voc-Tech. Coll., Nashua, 1978-83; trustee Nesmith Library, Windham, N.H., 1982—. Mem. N.H. Fedn. Women's Clubs (parliamentarian, legis chmn. 1984—), N.H. Fedn. Republican Women's Clubs (pres. 1979-82). Christian Scientist. Club: Windham Woman's (pres. 1981-83). Lodge: Order Eastern Star. Office: 204 Legislative Office Bldg Concord NH 03301

SKINNER, RUTH YODER, travel consultant; b. Los Angeles, June 15, 1912; d. Earl Henry and Rosalia (Hoegerman) Yoder; m. John L. Young (dec. 1950); children: Philip, Tom; m. Roger Ashford Skinner; 1 child, Brenda. Grad. high sch., Los Angeles. Cons. for deaf Ask Mr. Foster Travel Service, Encino, Calif., 1972—. Founder, pres. So. Calif. Women's Club of Deaf, Inc., 1965-71. Home: 17301 Citronia St Northridge CA 91325 Office: Ask Mr Foster 16660 Ventura Blvd Encino CA 91436

SKIPTON, MARY SULLIVAN, municipal administrator; b. Chgo., Nov. 15, 1947; d. Michael James and Helen (D'Arcy) Sullivan. BA, Loyola U., 1969. Supervising personnel officer HUD, Chgo., 1969-83; dep. commr. fin. adminstrn. City of Chgo. Dept. Housing, 1983-85; purchasing agt. City of Chgo. Dept. Purchases, Contracts and Supplies, 1985—. Mem. Nat. Inst. Govtl. Purchasing (bd. dirs.), Nat. Assn. Purchasing Mgrs., Am. Contract Compliance Assn. Democrat. Roman Catholic. Home: 6215 N Lenox Ave Chicago IL 60646 Office: City Chgo Dept Purchases Contracts & Supplies 121 N LaSalle St Room 403 Chicago IL 60602

SKLAR, KATHRYN KISH, historian, educator; b. Columbus, Ohio, Dec. 26, 1939; d. William Edward and Elizabeth Sue (Rhodes) Kish; children—Leonard Scott, Susan Rebecca. B.A. magna cum laude, Radcliffe Coll., Harvard U., 1965; Ph.D., U. Mich., 1969. Lectr., asst. prof. U. Mich., Ann Arbor, 1969-74; assoc. prof. history UCLA, 1974-81, prof., 1981-88, chmn. com. to administer program in women's studies Coll. Letters and Sci., 1974-81; prof. history SUNY, Binghamton, 1988—; mem. adv. bd. So. Calif. Inst. Hist. Research and Services, 1981—; mem. Calif. Council for Humanities, 1981-85; Pulitzer juror in history, 1976; fellow Newberry Library Family and Community History Seminar, 1973; NEH cons. in women's studies U. Utah, 1977-79, Santa Clara U., 1978-80, Roosevelt U., 1980-82; hist. cons. AAUW. Author: Catharine Beecher, A Study in American Domesticity (Berkshire prize 1974), 1973; editor: Catharine Beecher: A Treatise on Domestic Economy, 1977, Harriet Beecher Stowe: Uncle Tom's Cabin, or Life among the Lowly: The Minister's Wooing; Oldtown Folks, 1981, Notes of Sixty Years: The Autobiography of Florence Kelley, 1849-1926, 1984; mem. editorial bd. Am. Quar., 1976-79, Jour. Am. History, 1978-81. guest editor Feminist Studies, 1976; mem. scholarly adv. bd. Ms., 1980-84; contbr. articles to profl. jours. Fellow Woodrow Wilson Found., 1965-67, Danforth Found., 1967-69, Radcliffe Inst., 1973-74, Nat. Humanities Inst., 1975-76, Daniels fellow Am. Antiquarian Soc., 1976, Rockefeller Found. humanities, 1981-82, Woodrow Wilson Internat. Ctr., 1982, NEH fellow Newberry Library, 1982-83, Guggenheim Found., 1984, Ctr. Advanced Study Behavioral and Social Scis., Stanford U., 1987-88; grantee NEH, 1976-78, UCLA Council for Internat. and Comparative Studies, 1983, Ford Found. faculty research grantee, 1973-74. Mem. Am. Hist. Assn. (program com. Pacific Coast br. 1982, chmn. com. on women historians 1980-83, v.p. Pacific Coast br. 1986-87, pres. 1987-88), Orgn. Am. Historians (exec. bd. 1983-86, Merle Curti award com. 1978-79, lectr. 1982—), Am. Studies Assn. (council mem.-at-large 1978-80), Berkshire Conf. Women Historians, Am. Antiquarian Soc., Phi Beta Kappa. Office: SUNY Dept History Binghamton NY 13901

SKLAREK, NORMA MERRICK, architect; b. N.Y.C., Apr. 15, 1928; d. Walter and Amy (Willoughby) Merrick; m. Rolf Sklarek, Feb. 14, 1967 (dec. Feb. 1984); children: Gregory Ransom, David Fairweather; m. Cornelius Welch, Oct. 12, 1985. B.Arch., Columbia U., 1950. Architect Skidmore, Owings, Merrill, N.Y.C., 1955-60; dir. architecture Gruen Assocs., Los Angeles, 1960-80; project dir. Welton Becket Assocs., Santa Monica, from 1980; ptnr. Siegel-Sklarek-Diamond Architects, 1985—; mem. faculty N.Y.C. Community Coll., 1957-60, UCLA, 1972-78. Prin. works include Am. embassy, Tokyo, Pacific Design Center, Los Angeles, Courthouse Center, Columbus, Ind., Fox Plaza, San Francisco, City Hall, San Bernardino, Calif., Los Angeles Airport Terminal. Fellow AIA (v.p. Calif. chpt.). Office: 2501 Colorado Ave Santa Monica CA 90404 also: Siegel Sklarek Diamond AIA 10780 Santa Monica Blvd Suite 260 Los Angeles CA 90025

SKLARZ, ELLEN, television and film producer; b. N.Y.C., Oct. 30, 1953; d. Robert Bernard and Florence Anne (Bromet) S.; m. Michael Joel Shapiro, Sept. 9, 1984. BA in Speech Communications summa cum laude, SUNY, Buffalo, 1974; MA in Speech Communications, U. N.Mex., 1976. Cert. coll. tchr. in English and lit., Calif. Univ. instr. U. N.Mex., Albuquerque, 1975-76; writer, editor New West Mag., Los Angeles, 1977-78; columnist, editor Los Angeles Times, 1978-82; research developer Alan Landsburg Prodns., Inc., Los Angeles, 1982; free-lance ghost writer, author, editor Simon & Schuster, Los Angeles, 1982-85; founding assoc. editor, columnist L.A. Style mag., Los Angeles, 1985—; sr. v.p., TV and film producer Threshold Prodns., Inc., Los Angeles, 1986—; investigative reporter CBS News, 1978. Author: How to Meet Men, 1984; producer (film) The Morris Dees Story, 1988. Active in philanthropic work Hope U., UNICO Coll., Anaheim, Calif., 1987—. Mem. Phi Beta Kappa.

SKLOOT, BETSY A(NN), health care administrator; b. Batesville, Ind., Mar. 29, 1942; d. James Robert and Cynthia Hahn (Stocker) Lee; m. Floyd Steven Skloot, Aug. 10, 1970; children—Matthew Lee, Rebecca Lee. B.A. with high honors, So. Ill. U., 1966, M.A., 1970. Instr. in English, Carbondale High Sch. and So. Ill. U., 1966-72; budget analyst and mgr. State of Ill., Springfield, 1973-76, assoc. Medicaid adminstr., 1978-81, Medicaid adminstr., 1981-84; budget analyst and mgr. State of Wash., Olympia, 1976-78; dir. Multnomah County Dept. Human Services, Portland, Oreg., 1984-87; planning and mktg. adminstr. Providence Med. Ctr., Portland, 1988—. Mem. State Medicaid Dirs.' Assn. (sec. 1982-84), Am. Pub. Health Assn., Am. Pub. Welfare Assn., Ill. Pub. Welfare Assn. Office: Providence Med Ctr Portland OR

SKLUZACEK, GAYLE MARIE, fine art and wine appraiser, consultant; b. Lonsdale, Minn., Mar. 29, 1953; d. Edward P. and Lucille E. (Hartmann) S.; m. Alan M. Grupp, May 16, 1987. BA in Art History, Barat Coll., 1975; postgrad. in architecture history U. Minn., 1973-77, in art history U. Chgo., 1977-80; cooking and wine studies, France, Ger., Italy, 1979. Cert. tchr., N.Y.C. Assoc. curatorial asst. Carnegie Instn., Pitts., 1980-81; staff tng. dir.-wine cons. Sardi's, N.Y.C., 1981-86; dining room service and wine tasting tchr. N.Y.C. Bd. Edn., 1982—; dir. fine arts dept. Jason Rahm & Assocs., N.Y.C., 1983-85; research dir. Lawrence Gallery, N.Y.C., 1985-87; pres., dir. fine arts div. Abigail Hartmann Assocs., N.Y.C., 1985—. Author newsletter Art Investment Strategies, 1985-87; author tng. manuals. Bd. dirs. Adv. Council Occupational Edn., 1982—; leader Girl Scouts U.S., 1980; active Mondale Presdl. Campaign, 1984. Docent Oriental Inst., U. Chgo., 1980-81. Mem. Internat. Soc. Appraisers, Am. Assn. Appraisers, Les Amis du Vin, Mus. Modern Art, Met. Mus. Art, Am. Mus. Women in the Arts (charter). Democrat. Roman Catholic. Avocations: art, computers, gourmet cooking, wine, tennis. Office: 200 W 93d St #6L New York NY 10025

SKOGLUND, ELIZABETH RUTH, marriage, child and family counselor; b. Chgo., June 17, 1937; d. Ragnar Emmanuel and Elizabeth Alvera (Benson) S. BA, UCLA, 1959; MA, Pasadena Coll., 1969. Cert. tchr., Calif.; cert. marriage, family and child counselor, Calif. Tchr. Marlborough Sch., Los Angeles, 1959-61; tchr., counselor Glendale (Calif.) High Sch., 1961-72; pvt. practice counseling Burbank, Calif., 1972—. Author: Beyond Loneliness, 1980, Growing Through Rejection, 1983, More than Coping, 1987, Safety Zones, 1987, It's OK to Be a Woman Again, 1988, A Divine Blessing, 1988, 10 other books. Mem. Simon Wiesenthal Ctr., UCLA Alumni Assn. Republican.

SKOLER, CELIA REBECCA, art gallery director; b. Sioux City, Iowa, Apr. 7, 1931; d. Jacob and Flora (Gorchow) Stern; m. Louis Skoler, Aug. 24, 1952; children: Elisa Anne, Harry Jay. BFA in Art and Music magna cum laude, Syracuse U., 1976. Fin. planner Architects' Partnership, Syracuse, N.Y., 1969-71; bus. mgr. Skoler & Lee Architects P.C., Syracuse, 1971—; owner, dir. New Acquisitions Gallery, Syracuse, 1981—; art cons. IBM, Syracuse, Rochester, Albany, 1983-86, Costello, Cooney & Fearon, Syracuse, 1984-86, Menter, Rudin & Trivelpiece, Syracuse, 1987-88; supr. community internship program Syracuse U., 1981-87, commn. of mayoral portrait City of Syracuse,1983, Gelling Meml. Portrait U. Coll., 1984, Levine Meml. Commn. Temple. Concord; TV producer Syracuse U. Friends of Art, 1979-80; curated 40 exhibits, 1981-88. One-man shows include Camillus Plaza, 1972, The Associated Artists Gallery, Syracuse, 1973, Pub. Library of Fayetteville, N.Y., 1974; exhibited in group show at N.Y. State Fair (1st prize 1974), U. Coll, 1967, 69, 71, Rochester Meml. Gallery, 1969, 70, 71, 72, 74, The Associated Artists, 1971, 72, Cen. N.Y. Art Open, 1970, 71, (Purchase prize 1970, 71), Munson Williams Protor Inst, Utica, N.Y., 1971, 72, Cayuga Mus., Auburn, N.Y., 1972, Oneida (N.Y.) Art Festival, 1969, (1st prize), Jewish Community Ctr., Syracuse, 1968, 69, St. David's Invitational, Dewitt, N.Y., 1970, 71, 72, 73, 74, 75, Cooperstown Art Inst., Nat. Show, 1973, 74, Arena Nat. Show, Binghamton, N.Y., 1975 (Purchase prize 1975). Counselor Univ. Coll., Syracuse, 1980-85; art auctioneer pub. broadcasting sta. WCNY, Liverpool, N.Y., 1982; mem. steering and implementation com. Gelling Meml. Lounge U. Coll., 1984-85; exec. bd. Syracuse U. Friends of Art, 1977-80; fine art juror N.Y. State Fair, Syracuse, 1982, Downtown Com., Syracuse, 1982, Oswego (N.Y.) Art Guild, 1984. Recipient Purchase prize Marine Midland Bank, 1974, Crouse-Irving Hosp., 1974. Fellow Everson Mus. Art (corp. support program); Mem. Phi Kappa Phi, Alpha Sigma Lambda (pres. 1980-81). Home: 213 Scottholm Terr Syracuse NY 13224 Office: New Acquisitions Gallery 120 E Washington St Suite 207 Syracuse NY 13202

SKOLNICK, SARA HATCHER, association executive; b. Washington, May 22, 1933; d. Robert Stetinius and Heloise (Young) Hatcher; m. Alfred Skolnick, June 8, 1957; children: David Harold, Susan Alyn. Student, Immaculata Coll., Washington, 1950-51, Am. U., 1955-56; AS, No. Va. Community Coll., 1979; BBA, Marymount Coll., Arlington, Va., 1980. Asst. to exec. dir. Am. Soc. Naval Engrs., Washington, 1981-82; asst. sec.-treas. Am. Soc. Naval Engrs., Alexandria, Va., 1982—. Bd. dirs. Alexandria Hosp. Employees Assistance Program for Assns., 1986—; v.p. Duke Street Metro Assn., Alexandria, 1986-88. Mem. Am. Soc. Assn. Execs., Nat. Assn. Female Execs. Republican. Home: 5432 N Carlin Springs Rd Arlington VA 22203 Office: Am Soc Naval Engrs 1452 Duke St Alexandria VA 22314

SKONBERG, MADELON BAENZIGER (MRS. JOSEPH E. SKONBERG), educator; b. Chgo., Sept. 8, 1906; d. Rudolph Solomon and Olga Mathilde (Schiska) Baenziger; m. Joseph Emil Skonberg, Apr. 20, 1935; children: Kristin, Karen. Student, Bush Consevatory, 1927-28, Ill. State Norman U., 1932, Chgo. Mus. Coll., 1935-37, North Park Coll., 1940-42, Tchrs. Coll., 1957-58; MusB in Piano, MusB in Theory, Cosmopolitan Sch Music; postgrad., Northwestern Sch. Music Grad. Sch., 1963—. Music reviewer Music Leader, Chgo., 1950-67; adjudicator Nat. Guild Piano Tchrs., Austin, Tex., 1955—; tchr. piano organ Cosmopolitan Sch. Music, Chgo., 1956-62. Mem. Art Inst. Chgo., Soc. Am. Mjsicians, Nat. League Am. Pen Women, Nat. Music Tchrs. Assn., Ill. State Music Tchrs. Assn., Nat. Fedn. Music Clubs, Nat. Soc. Sci. Study Edn., Nat. Fedn. Women Clubs, Mu Phi Epsilon. Club: Women's Literary. Home: 226 Dogwood Trail Battle Creek MI 49017

SKONEY, SOPHIE ESSA, educational administrator; b. Detroit, Jan. 29, 1929; d. George Essa and Helena (Dihmes) Cokalay; Ph.B., U. Detroit, 1951; M.Ed., Wayne State U., 1960, Ed.D., 1975; postgrad. Ednl. Inst. Harvard Grad. Sch. Edn., 1986, 87; m. Daniel J. Skoney, Dec. 28, 1957; children—Joseph Anthony, James Francis, Carol Anne. Tchr. elem. sch. Detroit Bd. Edn., 1952-69, remedial reading specialist, 1969-70, curriculum coordinator, 1970-71, region 6 article 3 title I coordinator, 1971-83, area achievement specialist, 1984—; cons. in field. Mem. Wayne State U. Edn. Alumni Assn. (pres. bd. govs. 1979-80, newsletter editor 1975-77, 80—), Macomb Dental Aux. (pres. 1969-70), Mich. Dental Aux. (pres. 1980-81), Am.-Assn. Sch. Adminstrs., Wayne State U. Alumni Assn. (dir., v.p. 1985-86), Internat. Reading Assn., Mich. Reading Assn., Mich. Assn. State and Fed. Program Specialists, Profl. Women's Network (newsletter editor 1981-83, pres. 1985-87), Assn. for Supervision and Curriculum Devel., Delta Kappa Gamma, Beta Sigma Phi, Phi Delta Kappa. Roman Catholic. Home: 20813 Lakeland St St Clair Shores MI 48081 Office: Detroit Pub Schs 1121 E McNichols Detroit MI 48203

SKOOG, JOYCE EILEEN, communications specialist; b. Chgo., Feb. 21, 1940; d. Albert Anthony and Florence (Kubicki) Anicich; m. Roy Allen Skoog, May 2, 1959; children: Cheryl, Linda, Bradley, Melissa. BA, DePaul U., 1977; MEd, U. Ill., Urbana, 1982. Coordinator program Coll. DuPage Extension Div., Glen Ellyn, Ill., 1978-79; coordinator women's program Coll. DuPage, Glen Ellyn, 1979-82, dep. dir. arts ctr. capital campaign, 1983-84; coordinator spl. projects Inst. Study Devel. Disabilities U. Ill., Chgo., 1984-87; dir. communications United Way of Suburban Chgo., Hinsdale, Ill., 1987—; bd. dirs., chair pub. awareness com. Nat. Assn. Down Syndrome, Oak Brook, Ill., 1984—; cert. vol. trainer of bd. devel. United Way Suburban Chgo., Hinsdale, 1985—; trustee Hinsdale Hosp. Found., 1987—. Author, editor, pub.: This is Your Community Hinsdale, Oak Brook, Clarendon Hills, 1977. Fin. chair LWV, Hinsdale, 1975—; planning commr. Village of Hinsdale, 1977-83, trustee, 1983-87; fire and police commr., 1987—. Recipient grant Gov.'s Planning Council, 1986. Mem. Ill. Women in Govt. (treas. 1986—), Ill. Tng. and Devel. Assn. Republican. Roman Catholic. Club: Chicago Publicity. Home: 133 Princeton Rd Hinsdale IL 60521 Office: United Way Suburban Chgo 15 Spinning Wheel Rd #26 Hinsdale IL 60521

SKOPP, ROBERTA JOYCE, publicity executive; b. N.Y.C., Apr. 20, 1947; d. Sara (Perlman) S. BA, Queens Coll., 1967. Asst. editor Record World Mag., N.Y.C., 1972-75; dir. publicity and artist devel. Kirshner Entertainment, N.Y.C., 1975-77; v.p. publicity Casablanca Record and FilmWorks, Los Angeles, 1977-80, Boardwalk Entertainment, Beverly Hills, Calif., 1980-82, Zagoren Group, Manhasset, N.Y., 1983—. Recipient BOLI award L.I. Ad Club, 1985, 86. Club: N.Y. Ad. Office: Zagoren Group 19 Orchard St New York NY 11030

SKOV, ANDRÉA RIIS, computer executive; b. Zurich, Switzerland, Sept. 10, 1952; d. Niels Aage and Camille Emery (Burleigh) Skov; B.S. in Physics, Northeastern U., 1973, M.S. in Physics, 1974; m. Michael Franklin Gordon, Aug. 30, 1980. Project engr. aerospace div. Gen. Electric Co., Hanscom AFB, Bedford, Mass., 1975-77; N.E. dist. salesman Ramtek Corp., Lexington, Mass., 1977-78, product mktg. mgr. color graphic terminals, Santa Clara, Calif., 1978-81; dir. product mgmt. Logical Bus. Machines, Sunnyvale, Calif., 1981-82, v.p. mktg. and ops. 1982-83; v.p. Indian Ridge Enterprises Inc., Oakland, Calif., 1983—. Mem. Soc. Women Engrs., Tech. Mktg. Soc. Am., NOW, Nat. Dance Tchrs. Assn. Republican. Unitarian. Home: 14970 Sobey Rd Saratoga CA 95070 Office: Indian Ridge Enterprises 508 2d St Oakland CA 94607

SKOWRONSKI, JOYCE A., sales and marketing representative; b. Pittston, Pa., Aug. 24, 1951; d. Thomas Francis and Florence Bernadette (Wascavage) S. BA in English, Wilkes Coll., 1973, MS in Edn., 1976. Clk. Leslie Fay, Inc., Wilkes-Barre, Pa., 1973-78; dist. mgr. Airborne Freight Corp., Avoca, Pa., 1978-82; export mgr. Schott Optical Glass, Duryea, Pa., 1982-83; traffic rep. Overnite Transp., Dunmore, Pa., 1983-84; account rep. Roadway Package System, Scranton, Pa., 1984-88; membership dir. Greater Wilkes-Barre Partnership, Inc., 1988—; pres. World Trade Club of Northeastern Pa., Wilkes-Barre, 1986-87. Mem. Am. Bus. Women (v.p. 1985), Nat. Assn. Female Execs., World Trade Club (pres. 1986-88), Wyo. Valley Traffic Club, Delta Nu Alpha (pres. 1986-88). Democrat. Roman Catholic. Home: 262 Main St Duryea PA 18642

SKRABA, DIANE MARY, hospital administrator; b. DuBois, Pa., May 18, 1952; d. Steve Charles and Lillian Jean (Zaffuto) Skraba; children—Michael Joseph Blakley (dec.), Benjamin Spencer Blakley IV. B.A., Mansfield U., 1974. Mem. placement staff Duquesne U. Sch. Law, Pitts., 1977-78; mem.

advt. staff DuBois Courier-Express, 1978-79; dir. pub. relations DuBois Hosp., Pa., 1981-85; pub. relations mgr. DuBois Regional Med. Ctr., 1985—; pres. DuBois Hosp. Aux., 1984-85; adminstrv. liaison DuBois Regional Med. Ctr. Aux., 1985-87; bd. dirs. DuBois Hosp., 1984-85; bd. dirs. Clearfield County unit Am. Cancer Soc., 1981-84, chmn. pub. relations Gateway unit, 1984; publicity chmn. DuBois Area Prepared Childbirth Assn., 1978-81. Mem. Am. Soc. for Hosp. Mktg. and Pub. Relations, Nat. Assn. Hosp. Devel., Hosp. Council Western Pa. (pub. affairs adv. com.), Hosp. Assn. of Pa. Pub. Relations and Mktg. Soc., AAUW. Democrat. Roman Catholic. Avocations: writing; gourmet cooking; physical fitness activities; photography; the arts. Home: 939 Treasure Lake DuBois PA 15801 Office: DuBois Regional Med Ctr PO Box 447 DuBois PA 15801

SKRATEK, SYLVIA PAULETTE, labor relations executive; b. Detroit, Dec. 23, 1950; d. William Joseph and Helen (Meskauskas) S.; m. John Wayne Gullion, Dec. 21,1984. BS, Wayne State U., 1971; MLS, Western Mich. U., 1976; PhD, U. Mich., 1985. Media specialist Jackson (Mich.) Pub. Schs., 1971-79; contract specialist Jackson County Edn. Assn., 1976-79; field rep. Mich. Edn. Assn., E.Lansing, 1979-81; contract adminstr. Wash. Edn. Assn., Federal Way, 1981-85, regional coordinator, 1985—; dir. mediation services Conflict Mgmt. Inst., Lake Oswego, Ore., 1986-87; exec. dir. N.W. Ctr. for Conciliation, 1987—; tng. cons. City of Seattle, Wash., 1986—; trustee Group Health Cooperative of Puget Sound, Wash., 1984-87. Contbr. articles to legal jours. Vol. Brock Adams Senatorial campaign, Seattle, 1986. Mem. Soc. for Profls. in Dispute Resolution, Indsl. Relations Research Assn., Mediation Consortium of Wash. Office: Wash Edn Assn 33434 8th Ave S Federal Way WA 98003

SKROBELA, KATHERINE CREELMAN, data processor; b. N.Y.C., Jan. 18, 1941; d. George Douglas and Marjorie Ethel (Broer) Creelman; A.B., Vassar Coll., 1962; M.L.S., Columbia U., 1964; m. Paul John Skrobela, May 23, 1970. Music cataloger Bklyn. Coll., 1964-71; music librarian Middlebury (Vt.) Coll., 1971-80; programmer ADT Co., N.Y.C., 1981-83; sr. cons. Marathon Software & Services, Inc., 1983—. Treas., bd. dirs. Middlebury Farmers Market, 1979; dir. St. Stephen's Motet Choir, Middlebury, 1975-78. Mem. ALA, Music Library Assn. (chmn. com. on cataloging, rep. to ALA catalog code revision com.), Music OCLC Users Group, Vol. Staff, Participate on the Source, UFO Users Group (bd. dirs. Northeast region). Country Dance and Song Soc. Am. Editor Music Cataloging Bull., 1970-75. Home: 234 Lincoln Rd Brooklyn NY 11225 Office: 145 Porter Ave Bergenfield NJ 07621

SKUBINNA, TAMELYN KAY, association agent; b. Walla Walla, Wash., Nov. 9, 1951; d. Everett Kenneth Skubinna and Marvel Joye (End) Pettet. BA in Social Welfare, Pacific Lutheran U., 1974; vol. mgmt. cert., Tacoma Community Coll., 1979; MA in Social Scis., Pacific Lutheran U., 1981. Recreation leader Spokane (Wash.) Parks Dept., 1970-73; student office worker Pacific Lutheran U., Tacoma, 1970-74; tennis instr. Clover Park Sch. Dist., Tacoma, 1975; tchr.'s aide Sunset Elem. Sch., Tacoma, 1974-75; extension aide, 4-H Wash. State U. Extension, Tacoma, 1975-83; extension agt., 4-H Oreg. State U. Extension, Corvallis, Oreg., 1983—. Vol. Food Bank, High Sch. coach, Tacoma, 1982-83; bd. dirs., mem. Benton County Council Social Agys., Corvallis, Oreg., 1984-86; mem. Benton for Youth, Corvallis, 1985—. Mem. Assn. Vol. Adminstrn., Nat. 4-H Agts. Assn. (western regional contact-elect profl. improvement com. 1988), Oreg. 4-H Agts. Assn. (sec. 1984-85, chmn. profl. improvement com. 1986). Democrat. Lutheran. Lodge: Altrusa. Office: OSU Extension Benton County 2720 NW Polk Corvallis OR 97330

SKURDENIS, JULIANN VERONICA, librarian, educator, writer; b. Bklyn., July 13, 1942; d. Julius J. and Anna M. (Zilys) S.; A.B. with honors, Coll. New Rochelle, 1964; M.S., Columbia U., 1966; M.A., Hunter Coll., 1974; m. Lawrence J. Smircich, Aug. 21, 1965 (div. July 1978); m. 2d, Paul J. Lalli, Oct. 1, 1978; 1 adopted dau., Kathryn Leila Skurdenis-Lalli. Young adult librarian Bklyn. Pub. Library, 1964-66; periodicals librarian, instr. Kingsborough Community Coll., Bklyn., 1966-67; acquisitions librarian Pratt Inst., Bklyn., 1967-68; acquisitions librarian, asst. prof. Bronx (N.Y.) Community Coll., 1968-75, head tech. services, assoc. prof., 1975—. N.Y. State fellow, 1960-66, Columbia U. fellow, 1964-66, Pratt Inst. fellow, 1965. Mem. AAUP, NOW, Library Assn. CUNY (chairwoman numerous coms.), Archaeol. Inst. Am., CUNY Women's Coalition. Author: Walk Straight Through the Square, 1976; More Walk Straight Through the Square, 1977; also numerous travel, hist., and archaeol. pieces; travel editor Archaeology mag., Voyager Internat. Avocations: archaeology, travel, travel writing. Office: CUNY Bronx Community Coll University Ave Bronx NY 10453

SKYE, SUSAN MERYL, personal development consultant, lecturer; b. Phila., Apr. 11, 1941; d. Harry Fox and Frances (Belsky) Lazar. BA, Bryn Mawr Coll., 1962; MA, Yale U., 1967. Tchr. Alpha Acad., Kingston, Jamaica, 1968-70; lectr. UCLA, 1972-76, dir., asst. dean Women's Resource Ctr., 1973-76; owner, dir. Skye Assoc., Venice, Calif., 1976—; speaker various Calif. groups and orgns., 1976-86. Author tape The Money Seminar, 1978; contbr. articles to profl. jours. Co-founder Westside Women's Commn., Westwood, Calif., 1972, Nat. Women's Polit. Caucus, Los Angeles, 1974. NDEA fellow Yale U., 1965-67. Mem. Santa Monica C. of C. Democrat. Home and Office: 1377 Appleton Way Venice CA 90291

SKYLER, DENISE COURSHON, image consultant; b. Miami Beach, Fla., Nov. 23, 1948; d. Jack Robert and Dolores Mae (Bloom) Courshon; m. Ronald Keith Lavan, Apr. 1, 1969 (div. 1981); children: Melissa Jane, Heather Anne; m. Jay Samuel Skyler, July 19, 1987; 1 child, Jennifer Ann. Student, U. Wis., 1966-69, U. Miami, Coral Gables, Fla., 1970-71. Design coordinator RKL Properties, Inc., Miami, 1976-77; prin. Denise Boutique, Miami, 1977-88; mgr. pub. relations Berenaka Boutique, Miami, 1977-88; mgr. Artspace-Virginia Miller, Coral Gables, 1982-83; pub. relations assoc. Carole Korn Interiors, Miami, 1983-87; pres., owner Best Image, Inc., Miami, 1988—; pub. relations cons., 1987—; instr. Fla. Internat. U., 1987-88. Bd. dirs. Bass Mus., Miami Beach, 1986-88; mem. com. Sister Cities Project, Miami, 1987. Mem. Greater Miami C. of C., Young Patronesses of Opera, Entrepreneurial Women (founding mem.), Women's Forum U. Miami (founding mem.). Democrat. Jewish. Club: Grove Isle (Coconut Grove, Fla.). Home: 1 Grove Isle Dr Coconut Grove FL 33133 Office: Best Image Inc 1111 Crandon Blvd Suite C 301 Key Biscayne FL 33149

SLAATEN, DORIS ADELE, educator; b. Charlson, N.D., Oct. 5, 1920; d. Alfred O. and Maude L. (Dukette) S.; B.S., Minot State Coll., 1949; M.A., Northwestern U., 1957; Ph.D., Colo. State U., 1975. Tchr. public schs., N.D., Mont., 1942-57; faculty Minot (N.D.) State Coll. Div. Bus., 1957-84, prof. bus., 1976-84, now prof. emeritus N.D. rep. to bd. dirs. Mountain Plains Bus. Edn. Assn., 1977-84; mem. Minot State Coll. Devel. Bd., 1977—, chmn. bd. 1988—, bd. regents, 1979—; bd. dirs. Minot Chamber Chorale, 1979-85, Metigoshe Ministries, 1987—, Minot Commn. on Aging, 1984—, N.D. Luth. Social Services (bd. trustees 1988—)ran . Recipient Sigma Sigma Sigma Outstanding Alumni Recognition award, 1970; Alumni Golden award Minot State Coll., 1979; Nat. Bus. Edn. Meritorious Service award, 1979; 25-Yr. Profl. award Minot C. of C., 1979. Mem. N.D. Office Edn. Assn. (pres. 1969-70), Nat. Alumni Minot St. U. (co-chmn. Jubilee '88, 75th anniversary), Nat. Bus. Edn. Assn., N.D. Bus. Edn. Assn., NEA, Am. Vocat. Assn., Bus. and Profl. Women (Woman of Yr. 1979), Phi Beta Lambda (state adv. com. 1985—), Pi Omega Pi, Pi Lambda Theta, Phi Delta Kappa, Delta Pi Epsilon, Delta Kappa Gamma. Lutheran. Club: M1000. Author: Office Education for Tomorrow's World, 1972; manual for N.D. office edn. coordinators, 1980. Address: 1000 20th Ave NW Apt B4 Minot ND 58701

SLACK, BEVERLY JEAN, cable television executive; b. North Manchester, Ind., Sept. 18, 1936; d. Raymond B. and Imogene B. (Vickery) Schroll; m. Max E. Slack, Sept. 19, 1954; children—Jennifer L., Andrew E. Cert. GTE Secretarial Sch., 1965; Ameri-Comm CATV Tng., 1983. With Gen. Telephone-Ind., North Manchester and Wabash, 1956-79, central office supervisory asst., 1975-79; with Omega Communications, North Manchester, 1979-84, Three Rivers, Mich., 1984—, regional mgr., 1984-85, ops. mgr., 1985—. Mem. Women In Cable (bd. dirs. Ind.-Ill. unit 1982, v.p. Ind.-Ill. 1986—), North Manchester C. of C., Epsilon Sigma Alpha. Republican. Lutheran. Lodge: Order Eastern Star. Avocations: reading; snowmobiling; camping. Home: 1404 Villa Ct North Manchester IN 46962 Office: Omega of Mich Cable Co 414 W Hoffman PO Box 128 Three Rivers MI 49093

SLACK, FRANCES TAYLOR, computer software company executive; b. Princeton, N.J., July 28, 1954; d. Charles William Slack and Josephine Bliss (Ives) Mahaffy. BA in Psychology, U. Calif., Berkeley, 1983; BA in English Lit., Conn. Coll., 1976. Regional sales mgr. UniSoft Corp., Emeryville, Calif., 1984-87; dir. sales MBP Software and Systems Tech., Inc. div. Hoesch AG, Alameda, Calif., 1987-88, v.p., 1988—; co-founder, editor Free Agts. Internat., Oakland, Calif., 1987—. Editor, pub. Beatitude Press, 1979—, Sequoia Press, 1983—. Mem. Sierra Club (wilderness leader 1984—, inner-city youth leadership trainer 1984—), Phi Beta Kappa. Democrat. Mem. Christian Scientist Ch. Clubs: Commonwealth, World Affairs Council (San Francisco). Home: 1731-B Tenth St Berkeley CA 94710 Office: MBP Software & Systems Tech Inc 1131 Harbor Bay Pkwy Suite 260 Alameda CA 94501-6540

SLACKE, SALLY ANN, contracting company executive; b. S.I., N.Y., Apr. 16, 1933; d. Patrick and Mary G. (Granito) Magdalen; student Drake Bus. Sch., 1951, Adelphi U., 1968, Suffolk County (N.Y.) Community Coll., 1969; m. Felix P. Slacke, Oct. 8, 1955 (dec. 1975); children—Barbara, Diane, Carole Lynn Burch. Sec., Netherland Trading Soc., N.Y.C., 1951-58; v.p. Slacke Drilling Co., Kings Park, N.Y., 1963-73; pres. Slacke Test Boring, Inc., Smithtown, N.Y., 1973—; dir. Allstate Life Ins. Co.; del. White House Conf. Small Bus., Washington. Coordinator sr. citizen activities Town of Smithtown, 1968-69; trustee L.I. Loves Bus., Inc., Suffolk County Community Coll.; chmn. L.I. Project Pride, 1981, Small Bus. Council of L.I., 1985—, L.I. Regional Econ. Devel. Council, 1985—. Recipient L.I. Bus. Leadership award, 1980, Big Brother/Big Sister award, 1987.; Clara Barton Humanitarian award Suffolk County chpt. ARC, 1981; B'nai B'rith Youth Services award, 1982; AAUW Woman of Year award, 1982; Woman in Bus. Adv. of Year SBA, 1982; L.I. Achievers award, 1982. Mem. Nat. Assn. Female Execs. Inc., 110 Center for Bus. and Profl. Women, L.I. Assn. Commerce and Industry, Nat. Assn. Women Bus. Owners (chmn. 1986—), Women Econ. Developers of L.I. Republican. Roman Catholic. Club: Zonta Internat. Office: One Village Plaza Kings Park NY 11754

SLADE, JOANN KAYE, secondary teacher; b. Billings, Mont., Dec. 10, 1933; d. Joseph Frank and Erma Mae (Giltner) S. BA, St. Mary Coll., Xavier, Kas., 1956; MA, Ariz. State U., 1968; postgrad., U. Nev., Las Vegas, 1965—, U. Va. in Washington, 1980. Cert. art specialist. Tchr. art Lewiston (Mont.) Jr. High Sch., 1957-58, McCormic Jr. High Sch., Cheyenne, Wyo., 1958-62; camp dir., counselor Cen. Mont. Girl Scouts USA, Lewistown, 1958-63; tchr. art, English Wheelus High Sch. USAF Base, Tripoli, Libya, 1962-63, Toul-Rosier (France) USAF Base, 1963-64, Western High Sch., Las Vegas, 1964—; past pres. Clark County Art. Edn., Las Vegas, (Publicity chmn. 1980-87). Work exhibited Portfolio Inc. Art Gallery, 1985-88, Clark County Library Dist. Show, 1986. Active Cen. Com. Rep. Party, Las Vegas; del. Edinburgh Soc., 1985. Recipient Gov.'s Art award Nev. Council Arts, 1988, Experience Tchr. Scholarship Ariz. State U., 1968, Fed. Forum fellowship Fed. Forum, 1980. Mem. Nat. Art Edn. Assn. Clark County Classroom Tchrs. Assn., Nev. State Edn. Assn. Democrat. Home: 6655 W Edna Las Vegas NV 89102 Office: Western High Sch 4601 W Bonanza Rd Las Vegas NV 89107

SLADE, PATTI ANN, computer systems operations analyst; b. Stamford, Conn., Aug. 31, 1953; d. Charles Arthur Slade and Barbara Rose (Scribner) Keeler; m. Mark D. Barrett, Mar. 27, 1975 (div. Apr. 1982). BS in Edn., Western Conn. State U., 1975. Stock clk. Pitney Bowes, Inc., Newtown, Conn., 1975-77, ordering specialist, 1977-81, ops. control specialist, 1981-85, 86-87, ops. analyst, 1987—; inventory control specialist Pitney Bowes, Inc., Los Angeles, 1985-86, supr. ops. control, 1987—. Mem. Nat. Assn. Female Execs. Democrat. Presbyterian. Office: Pitney Bowes Inc Edmond Rd Newtown CT 06470

SLADEK, MARTHA J., public relations executive; b. Columbus, Ohio, Sept. 24, 1946; d. Keith Lloyd and Phyllis Elaine (Clayton) McClatchie; m. Don Sladek, Nov. 6, 1970. BS in Edn., Kent State U., 1968; MA in Journalism, Ohio State U., 1969. News and talk show producer 1969-75; dir. pub. relations Ill. State Office Tourism, Chgo., 1975-79; pub. relations supr. AT&T, Chgo., 1979-86; dir. univ. relations Northeastern Ill. U., Chgo., 1986—; writer, cons. in field, 1973—; cons. Kraft Co., Glenview, Northbrook, Ill., 1986, AT&T, Chgo., 1986; mktg. dir. TAG-A-PET Co., Downers Grove, Ill.; pub. relations dir. Spiritual Pathways Inst., Downers Grove. Author: Two Weeks With the Psychic Surgeons, 1976. Active various political campaigns DuPage and Cook Counties, Ill.; bd. dirs. Ill. Coll. Relations Council, 1988—; cons. DuPage Environmental Awareness Ctr., 1988—, Ill. Nature Conservancy, 1988—. Mem. Nat. Wildlife Fedn., Soc. for Prevention to Cruelty to Animals, Wilderness Soc., Smithsonian Found., Sierra Club. Presbyterian.

SLAGLE, PAULA MARIE, marketing executive; b. N.J., May 26, 1953; d. John Francis and Gladys Rose Krausche; m. Vernon Lee Slagle, Jr., Oct. 6, 1974. AAS, Bergen Community Coll., 1974; BA, Ramapo Coll. N.J., 1984; MBA, L.I. Univ., Greenvale, N.Y., 1986; postgrad., Iona Coll. Corr. U.S. Steel Corp., Saddlebrook, N.J., 1974-84; mktg. mgr. Alloy Technology Internat., Inc., West Wyack, N.Y., 1984—; mktg. cons. CDS Mktg. Cons., Harrington Park, N.J., 1987—. Pres. Woman's Guild, Fair Lawn, 1975-76. Mem. Bus. and Profl. Advt. Assn. Republican. Presbyterian. Home: 23 Names Ct Harrington Park NJ 07640

SLAPPEY, MARY MCGOWAN, writer, artist; b. Kitrell, N.C., Nov. 22, 1914; d. Walter Gordon and Mary Jouvette (McGowan) S. BA, George Washington U., Washington, D.C., 1947; JD, George Mason U., 1977; DLitt, World U., Benson, Ariz., 1981. Tchr. Nat. Bus. Sch., Washington, 1950-59; editor, exec. sec. Nat. Newman Apostolate, Washington, 1960-87; freelance writer Washington, 1987—. Author: Miracle of Believing, 1985, Glory of Wooden Walls, 1986, Exploring Military Opportunities, 1986. Counsel for new Americans becoming citizens. Served to lt. comdr. USNR, 1942-46. Mem. Res. Officers Assn., Fed. Poets (pres. 1976-78), Columbian Women (historian 1981-83), Nat. League Am. Pen Women. Republican. Roman Catholic. Home and Office: 4500 Chesapeake St NW Washington DC 20016

SLATER, ANDREA, biomechanical engineer; b. Troy, N.Y., Nov. 10, 1958; d. Andrew Albert and Theresa Mary (Giuliano) Inco; m. Jeffrey Clark Slater, Sept. 26, 1982; 1 child, Mark Andrew. BSME, Union Coll., 1981, BS in Biology, 1981. Mech. engr. Instrumentation Lab., Inc., Lexington, Mass., 1981-82; product devel. engr. U.S. Catheters and Instruments div. C.R. Bard, Inc., Billerica, Mass., 1982-83; project engr. div. C.R. Bard, Inc., Billerica, Mass., 1983-85; sr. project engr. United Satellite Communications, Inc. div. C.R. Bard, Inc., Billerica, Mass., 1985-87, engrng. section head, 1987—. Mem. Nat. Assn. Female Execs., AAAS. Roman Catholic. Office: USCI div CR Bard Inc 129 Concord Rd Billerica MA 01821

SLATER, BARBARA RUTH, psychologist, educator; b. Potsdam, N.Y., Feb. 18, 1934; d. Gilson M. and Eleanor (Robinson) S.; B.A., St. Lawrence U., Canton, N.Y., 1955, M.Ed., 1959; Ph.D. in Sch. Psychology, Tchrs. Coll., Columbia U., 1966. Secondary sch. tchr. Port Dickinson (N.Y.) Schs., 1956-62; sch. psychologist, Pelham, N.Y., 1966-68; asst. prof. psychology Hofstra U., Hempstead, N.Y. 1968-71; prof. psychology, coordinator sch. psychology Towson (Md.) State U., 1971—; ind. practice psychology, 1967—. Diplomate in sch. psychology Am. Bd. Profl. Psychology. Fellow Am. Psychol. Assn., Nat. Assn. Sch. Psychologists, Eastern Psychol. Assn. Co-author: Cognitive Skills Assessment Battery; Psychodiagnostic Evaluation of Children. Home: 322 Jodyway Timonium MD 21093 Office: Towson State U Dept Psychology Towson MD 21204

SLATER, FRANCES MARIE, hospital manager; b. Galveston, Tex., Oct. 22, 1947; children—Julie, Denise, John. B.S., Domnican Coll., Houston, 1969; postgrad. Houston Bapt. U., 1985—. Head nurse St. Joseph Hosp., Houston, 1969-74, shift dir., 1974-75, infection control coordinator, 1975-81; asst. mgr. Methodist Hosp., Houston, 1981—. Mem. Kingwood Republican Women's Orgn., 1980—. Mem. Assn. Practitioners Infection Control (chpt. pres. 1978-80, chpt. treas. 1976-78). Republican. Roman Catholic.

SLATER, GAIL POUST, investment broker, counselor; b. Evanston, Ill., Feb. 23, 1950; d. John Gordon and Patricia (Moore) Poust; m. A. David Slater, Aug. 14, 1971; 1 child, William David. BA with honors, Vanderbilt U., 1972. Math. tchr. Father Ryan High Sch., Nashville, 1972-75; investment broker Paine Webber, Ann Arbor, Mich., 1975-83; account v.p. Paine Webber, New Orleans, 1983-84; v.p. investments Paine Webber, Clearwater, Fla., 1984-85; asst. br. mgr. Paine Webber, Louisville, 1985—. Mem., provisional treas. Jr. League, Clearwater, 1984-85; mem. Louisville Jr. League, 1985—. Mem. Ann Arbor Profl. Women, Bus. and Profl. Womens' Assn. New Orleans. Republican. Presbyterian. Office: Paine Webber Inc Meidinger Tower Louisville KY 40202

SLATER, SUSAN BUYER, health care agency program executive; b. Paterson, N.J., Nov. 8, 1949; d. Edward Michael and Marilyn Patterson (Stier) Buyer; m. Eugene A. Slater, Feb. 9, 1980; children: Laura Patterson, Thomas Michael. Student Wellesley Coll., 1967-69; BA in Polit. Sci., George Washington U., 1971, MA in Health Care Adminstrn., 1975. Mgmt. intern. NIH, Bethesda, Md., 1971-72; sr. program analyst planning office, Nat. Library Medicine, Bethesda, 1972-85, chief planning br., 1985-87, dep. asst. dir. planning and evaluation, 1987— . Recipient Sustained High Quality Work Performance award Nat. Library Medicine, 1980, 86, 87, 88, Spl. Achievement award, 1987. Mem. Am. Pub. Health Assn., NOW, Nat. Assn. Female Execs., Am. Soc. Pub. Adminstrn., Nat. Abortion Rights Action League. Office: 8600 Rockville Pike Bethesda MD 20209

SLATON, BRENDA DALE, mechanical engineer; b. Anderson, S.C., Sept. 28, 1962; d. Thomas Jerry and Brenda Joyce (Charping) S. BSME, Clemson U., 1984. Project engr. Celanese Fibers Op., Charlotte, N.C., 1984-85; drafting cons. Nat. Council Engring. Examiners, Seneca, S.C., 1985-86; quotations analyst I.T.E. Elec. Products div. Siemens Energy and Automation, Tucker, Ga., 1986—; sales control specialist Siemens Energy and Automation Inc., Charlotte. Mem. ASME, NSPE, Nat. Assn. Investment Clubs, High Mus. Assn. Young Careers Club. Republican. Baptist. Home: 7300 Apt 207 Creekwood Quorum Dr Charlotte NC 28212 Office: Siemens Energy and Automation 7512 E Independence Blvd Suite 114 Charlotte NC 28212

SLAUGHTER, DIANA TERESA, educator; b. Chgo., Oct. 28, 1941; d. John Ison and Gwendolyn Malva (Armstead) S.; B.A., U. Chgo., 1962, M.A., 1964, Ph.D., 1968. Instr. dept. psychiatry Howard U., Washington, 1967-68; research asso., asst. prof. Yale U. Child Study Center, New Haven, 1968-70; asst. prof. dept. behavioral scis. and edn. U. Chgo., 1970-77; asso. prof. edn. and African Am. studies Northwestern U., Evanston, Ill., 1977—; mem. nat. adv. bd. Fed. Center for Child Abuse and Neglect, 1979-82, Ednl. Research and Devel. Center, U. Tex., Austin; chmn., dir. public policy program com. Chgo. Black Child Devel. Inst., 1982-84; dir. Ill. Infant Mental Health Com., 1982-83; mem. res. adv. bd. Chgo. Urban League, 1986—. Mem. Am. Psychol. Assn. (bd. ethnic and minority affairs), Soc. for Research in Child Devel. (governing council 1981-87), Am. Ednl. Research Assn., Assn. Black Psychologists, Groves Conf. Family, Nat. Acad. Scis. (com. on child devel. and publ. policy, 1987—), Delta Sigma Theta. Contbr. articles to profl. jours. Home: 835 Ridge Ave Evanston IL 60202 Office: 2003 Sheridan Rd Evanston IL 60201

SLAUGHTER, JANE MUNDY, author; b. Buchanan, Va., Oct. 2, 1905; d. Luther Thomas and Pearl Carnce (Karnes) Mundy; R.N., Jefferson Hosp., Roanoke, Va., 1926; m. Frank G. Slaughter, June 10, 1933; children—Frank G., Randolph M. Operating Room supr. Jefferson Hosp., 1923-24; pvt. duty nurse, 1924-33; freelance author, 1970—; author: Espy and the Catnappers, 1975; also 1st history of Fla. Med. Assn. Aux. Bd. dirs. Jacksonville (Fla.) YWCA, 1960-65. Mem. Fla. Hist. Soc., Jacksonville Hist. Soc., Fla. Fedn. Garden Clubs (life mem. Jacksonville), Fla. Med. Assn. Aux. (historian 1950). Democrat. Presbyterian. Club: Timuquana Country. Address: 5051 Yacht Club Rd Jacksonville FL 32210

SLAUGHTER, LOUISE MCINTOSH, congresswoman; b. Harlan County, Ky., Aug. 14, 1930; d. Oscar Lewis and Grace (Byers) McIntosh; m. Robert Slaughter, 1956; children: Megan Rae, Amy Louise, Emily Robin. BS, U. Ky., 1951, MS, 1953. Bacteriologist Ky. Dept. Health, Louisville, 1951-52, U. Ky., 1952-53; market researcher Procter & Gamble, Cin., 1953-56; mem. staff Office of the Lt. Gov. N.Y., Albany, 1978-82; state rep. N.Y. Gen. Assembly, Albany, 1983-86; U.S. congresswoman 100th Congress from 30th Dist. N.Y., Washington, 1987—; co-chair Monroe County Citizens for McGovern, 1972; del. Dem. Nat. Conv., 1972, 76, 80. Mem. Monroe County Pure Water Adminstrn. Bd., Common Cause, League of Women Voters, Nat. Women's Polit. Caucus. Office: US House of Reps Office of House Mems 1313 Longworth Washington DC 20515

SLAUGHTER, LURLINE EDDY, artist; b. Heidelberg, Miss., June 19, 1919; d. Gilbert Emmings and Lurline Elizabeth (Heidelberg) Eddy; B.S., Miss. U. for Women, 1939; m. James Fant Slaughter, Jan. 27, 1946; children—Beverly Lowery, Anne Towles. Tchr. high sch., Silver City, Miss., 1939-41; clk. VA, Washington, 1941-42; one-woman shows Ahda Artzt Gallery, N.Y.C., 1967, Nat. Design Center, N.Y.C., 1967, 68, Delta State U., Cleveland, Miss., 1973, 84, Gulf States Gallery, Greenville, Miss., 1973, 76, 80, 84, Southeastern La. U., Hammond, 1977, Cheekwood Fine Arts Center, Nashville, 1978, Byars Gallery, Little Rock, 1984, San Pedro Theatre, San Antonio, 1981, Cottonlandia Mus., Greenwood, Miss., 1984 exhibited in group shows U. Fla., 1969, Brooks Art Mus., Memphis, 1970, Miss. State U., 1970, 85, Delta State U., 1971, 84; represented in permanent collection Miss. U. for Women, Miss. State U., Delta State U., Pine Bluff (Ark.) Art Ctr., Southeastern La. U., U. of South, Sewanee, Tenn., Eudora Welty Mepl. Library, Jackson, Miss.; represented in pvt. collections, Acapulco, Guadalajara, Mex., San Francisco, N.Y.C., so. states. Recipient Best in Show award Acapulco Ann., Hilton Hotel, 1979, Best in Show award Cottonlandia Mus., Greenwood, Miss., 1987. Tchr. Sunday Sch., Meth. Ch., 1953-67; pres. PTA; bd. dirs. Miss. Art Colony, 1965-85. Served as lt. (j.g.) USNR, 1942-45. Mem. Miss. Art Mus. and Mepl. Gallery, Nat. Mus. for Women in the Arts (charter). Republican. Club: Humphreys Country. Address: Seldom Seen Plantation Silver City MS 39166

SLAUGHTER, SUSAN LEE BRUNDIGE, graphic designer, lecturer; b. Cin., Feb. 24, 1947; d. Jerry A. and Betty L. (Thorp) Brundige; B.F.A., Ohio State U., 1969; postgrad. U. Cin., evenings 1971-72; m. James L. Slaughter III, Sept. 16, 1972. Instr. painting Cin. Art Mus., part-time 1969-76; graphic designer Cin. Time Recorder Co., 1969-71, Hank Marowitz Advt. Agy., Cin., 1971-72; pres., graphic designer, cons. Slaughter & Slaughter, Inc., Cin., 1972—; lectr. graphics Xavier U., 1982—; painter. Chmn. spl. advt. project, designer posters, folder Radio Reading Services, 1981-82, Appreciation cert., 1981; designer posters, folder Arthritis Found. campaign, 1980—, Appreciation cert., 1979, Disting. Public Service award, 1981; designer Christmas card for fundraising Cancer Family Care, 1981; designer, dir. interior mus., permanent exhbn. African, Latin Am., S.Am. art, curator Comboni Mus. African, South Am. and Latin Am. Art and Artifacts, 1984—; co-designer program book on Nutcracker ballet for Cin. Ballet, 1985; trustee, corr. sec. in charge pub. relations, curator art gallery Unity Ctr. Cin., 1983—; treas., 1985, v.p., 1986; trustee Appalachian Community Council, Appalachian Festival, 1986—. Bd. govs. Arthritis Found. Southwestern Ohio, chmn. mktg. com., bd. govs. Recipient awards Art Dirs. Club Cin., 1972-82, Am. Advt. Fedn., 1974, 80, Internat. Typographic Composition award, 1980, Bus. and Profl. Advt. Assn., 1981. Mem. Women in Communications (spl. project v.p., dir. 1981-82, recognition cert. 1981), Cin. Indsl. Advertisers (dir. 1979-81, Person of Distinction 1980, 81), Cin. Women's Network, Internat. Assn. Profl. Artists, Alliance Profl. Artists Ohio, Ky. and Ind., Women Entrepreneur's Conf. (roundtable speaker and program com. 1986). Office: Slaughter & Slaughter Inc 4307 Erie Ave Cincinnati OH 45227

SLAVIN, ROSANNE SINGER, textile converter; b. N.Y.C., Mar. 24, 1930; d. Lee H. and Rose (Winkler) Singer; student U. Ill.; divorced; children—Laurie Jo, Sharon Lee. Prodn. converter Doucet Fabrics, silk prints, N.Y.C., 1953-57; sales mgr., mdse. mgr. print div. Crown Fabrics, N.Y.C., 1957-65; owner Matisse Fabrics Inc., printed fabrics, N.Y.C., 1965—. Recipient Tommy award, 1978; designated ofcl. printed fabric supplier for U.S. Olympic swimteam, 1984. Office: 1457 Broadway New York NY 10036

SLAWSON, LAURIE VIVIAN, archaeologist; b. Detroit, Nov. 19, 1952; d. Luman Reed and Muriel (Robertson) S. BA, U. Mich., 1974; MA, U. Cin., 1977; PhD, Ariz. State U., 1988. Lab dir., asst. field dir. dept. anthropology U. Cin., 1974-76, lab. dir. field sch., 1977; contract archaeologist dept. anthropology Ariz. State U., Tempe, 1977-80; coordinator U. Ariz., Tucson, 1980-82, contract archaeologist Ariz. State Mus., 1982-83; project dir. TerraMar Internat. Services, Inc., Tucson, 1983-84; prin. investigator, co-owner Cultural & Environ. Systems, Inc., Tucson, 1984—; lectr. in field. Author: The StarPass Archaeological Project, 1986, The Early Classic Period Hohokam, 1988; (with others) The Cortaro Site, 1986, Archaeological Investigations at the Classic Period Continental Site, 1987, The San Xavier Archaeological Project, 1987, Archaic and Hohokan Land Use in the Santa Catalina Mountains, 1987, The Espinosa Site: An Example of Prehistoric and Historic Utilization of the Santa Cruz River, 1987; contbr. articles to profl. jours. Election asst. Stop ERA, Rep. Party, Livonia, Mich., 1967-76. U. Cin. scholar, 1974-76; Ariz. State U. scholar, 1976-77. Mem. Soc. Am. Archaeology, Am. Archaeol. Inst., Soc. Profl. Archeologists (cert. com. 1987—), Ariz. Archaeol. Council, Ariz. Archaeol. and Hist. Soc., Ariz. Hist. Soc., Cen. States Anthropol. Assn., Southwestern Anthrop. Assn., Am. Anthrop. Assn. Republican. Club: So. Ariz. Mustang (Tucson) (pres.1984-85). Avocations: restoring classic Mustangs, figure skating, middle ea. dancing. Home: 7561 E Dos Mujeres Tucson AZ 85715 Office: Cultural & Environ Systems Inc 459 S Convent Tucson AZ 85701

SLAYDON, KATHLEEN AMELIA, lawyer; b. Ft. Worth, June 1, 1951; d. A. Glynn and E. Jeanne (Miller) S.; m. John Mayer. B.A., Rice U., 1973; J.D., U. Tex., 1976. Bar: Tex. 1977, U.S. Dist. Ct. (so. dist.) Tex. 1978, U.S. Ct. Appeals (5th cir.) 1978, U.S. Ct. Appeals (11th cir.) 1981, U.S. Dist. Ct. (we. dist.) Tex. 1984. Assoc. Reynolds, Allen Cook, Houston, 1977-78; assoc. Ross, Banks, May Cron & Cavin, Houston, 1978-83, ptnr., 1983—; speaker continuing legal edn. State Bar Tex., 1983-88. Chairperson Rice Alumni 1973 Fund Dr., Houston, 1978. Mem. Tex. Assn. Bank Counsel, State Bar Tex., Houston Bar Assn., Rice Alumni Assn. Home: 725 E Creekside Dr Houston TX 77024 Office: Ross Banks May Cron & Cavin 9 Greenway Plaza 20th Floor Houston TX 77046

SLAYMAKER, (CAROLYN) JANE HOYT, occupational therapist, educator; b. Detroit, Nov. 25, 1930; d. Douglas Granger and Elizabeth Carola (Wyker) Hoyt; B.A. in Art History, Wellesley Coll., 1953; cert. in interior decoration N.Y. Sch. Interior Design, 1954; cert. in occupational therapy (N.Y. State Dept. Mental Health and Hygiene scholar) N.Y.U., 1962, M.A. in Edn. (Am. Occupation Therapy Assn. scholar), 1966; postgrad. in guidance and counseling U. Ill., Urbana, 1969-70, in social change Walden U. West, 1980-83; also various seminars, workshops, insts., short courses. Recreational therapist Montefiore Hosp., Bronx, N.Y., 1958-60; staff occupational therapist Manhattan State Hosp., N.Y.C., 1962-65, Manhattan VA Hosp., N.Y.C., 1965-66; asst. prof. occupational therapy U. Fla., 1966-68, assoc. prof., 1970—, assoc. chmn., 1985—; activity therapist IV, Ill. Dept. Mental Health and Hygiene, Champaign, 1968-70; cons. gerontology, mental health; bd. dirs. North Central Fla. Community Mental Health Center, Inc., Gainesville, 1979-83, sec., 1981-82; bd. dirs. Mental Health Assn. Alachua County (Fla.), 1975-81, 85—, treas., 1976, 79, 80, 81, pres., 1978, 86-87. Bd. dirs. United Way Alachua County, 1976-80, Alachua County Council Child Abuse, 1978-81. Recipient Cert. of Appreciation, Mental Health Assn. Alachua County, 1975, Cert. of Commendation, 1977; Gold award United Way, 1978; Faculty Devel. award Coll. Health Related Professions, summer 1980; assoc. Center Gerontol. Studies and Programs, 1977—. Fellow Am. Occupational Therapy Assn.; mem. World Fedn. Occupational Therapy, Fla. Occupational Therapy Assn. (pres. 1971-73, rep. to Occupational Therapy Council, Bd. Med. Examiners State of Fla., 1975-83, assn. alt. rep. 1973-75, 79-82, Award of Excellence 1977, award of recognition 1983), Am. Gerontol. Soc., So. Gerontol. Assn., Pi Lambda Theta, Eta Rho Pi. Episcopalian. Contbr. articles to profl. jours. Office: Box J-164 JH Miller Health Center Gainesville FL 32610

SLAYMAN, CAROLYN WALCH, geneticist, educator; b. Portland, Maine, Mar. 11, 1937; d. John Weston and Ruth Dyer (Sanborn) Walch; m. Clifford L. Slayman; children—Andrew, Rachel. B.A. with highest honors, Swarthmore Coll., 1958; Ph.D., Rockefeller U., 1963; D.Sc. (hon.), Bowdoin Coll., 1985. Instr., then asst. prof. Case Western Res. U., Cleve., 1967; from asst. prof. to prof. human genetics Yale U. Sch. Medicine, New Haven, 1967—, chmn. dept. human genetics, 1984—; chmn. genetic basis of disease rev. commn. NIH, 1981-85; dir. J. Weston Walch Pub., Portland, Maine. Contbr. articles to sci. jours. Trustee Foote Sch., New Haven, Conn., 1983—; bd. overseers Bowdoin Coll., Brunswick, Maine, 1976—. Recipient Deborah Morton award Westbrook Coll., 1986. Mem. Am. Soc. Biol. Chemists, Genetics Soc. Am., Soc. Gen. Physiologists, Am. Soc. Microbiology, Phi Beta Kappa. Office: Yale U Sch Medicine Dept Human Genetics 333 Cedar St New Haven CT 06510

SLEEMAN, JANEANN CHAMNESS KING, personnel executive; b. Charleston, W.Va., July 7, 1945; d. W.E. and Maxine (Broyles) Chamness Walsh. B.S., Radford Coll., 1967. Personnel analyst, div. dir. W.Va. Civil Service System, Charleston, 1967-73; personnel officer Fin. and Adminstrn., Charleston, 1973-75; asst. dir. W.Va. Civil Service System, Charleston, 1975-78, dir., 1978-84; dir. human resources McDonough Caperton Ins. Group, 1984-86; dir. human resource devel. Lockheed Kennedy Space Ctr., Fla., 1987—; mem. Pay Equity Task Force, Charleston, 1984; ex-officio mem. W.Va. Women's Commn., Charleston, 1978—; mem. adv. curriculum com. Salem Coll., 1980—. Bd. trustees YWCA, Charleston, 1984, W.Va. Indsl. Relations Research Assn., 1984. Mem. Nat. Assn. State Personnel Execs., Internat. Personnel Mgmt. Assn. (pres. W.Va. chpt. 1977-78, bd. dirs. 1975-77), Mid-Atlantic Personnel Assessment Consortium, Am. Soc. Personnel Adminstrs., AMA. Baptist.

SLEEMAN, MARY (MRS. JOHN PAUL SLEEMAN), librarian; b. Cleve., June 28, 1928; d. John and Mary Lillian (Jakub) Gerba; B.S., Kent State U., 1965, also M.L.S.; m. John Paul Sleeman, Apr. 27, 1946; children—Sandra Sleeman Swyrydenko, Robert, Gary, Linda. Supervising librarian elementary schs. Nordonia Hills Bd. Edn., Northfield, Ohio, 1965-—; children's librarian Twinsburg (Ohio) Pub. Library, 1965-66. Mem. ALA, Ohio Sch. Librarians Assn., NEA, Summit County Librarians Assn., Storytellers Assn., North Eastern Ohio Tchrs. Assn. Methodist. Home: 18171 Logan Dr Walton Hills OH 44146 Office: 115 Rushwood Ln Northfield OH 44067

SLEIGHT, JEANETTE MARIE, sculptor, dental technician; b. Toledo, Ohio, Aug. 27, 1956; d. Richard Franklin and Myrtle Marie (Haynes) S. AA in dental lab. tech., Durham Tech. Inst., 1977. Lab. technician Jeannetta Lab., Durham, N.C., 1977-78, Forsyth Dental Lab., Winston-Salem, N.C., 1978-79. Exhibited drawing, painting and sculpture in Mass. and Ohio.

SLEITH, BARBARA ANN BALKO, educator; b. Elizabeth Twp., Pa., Jan. 29, 1946; d. Andrew and Elizabeth (Kurutz) Balko; A.A., Robert Morris Jr. Coll., 1966; B.S., California U. (Pa.), 1968, M.Ed., 1970; postgrad. U. Pitts., 1976, U. Indiana (Pa.); m. Melvin R. Sleith, Dec. 18, 1971; 1 dau., Melynda Sue. Tchr., Elizabeth (Pa.) Forward Sch. Dist., 1968-70; learning disabilities tchr. Allegheny Intermediate Unit 3, 1970-77, I.E.P. specialist, 1977-80; tchr. socially, emotionally maladjusted students, 1980—; distbr. Royal Am. Foods; cons. in field. Developer Math Pass game. Neighborhood chmn. Girl Scouts U.S.A., 1978-80, asst. leader, 1986; adult cons. ch. youth group, 1975-78; program rep., mem. liaison bd. Allegheny Intermediate Unit Edn. Assn., 1970-74; active PTA, William Penn Sch. Mem. Assn. Children with Learning Disabilities, Three Rivers Reading Council, Phi Delta Gamma (chpt. exec. officer). Democrat. Roman Catholic. Club: Confraternity of Christian Mothers (various offices) Address: RD 2 Box 115 West Newton PA 15089

SLESAR, PAULA JEAN, communications company official; b. Milw., Feb. 8, 1955; d. Daniel L. and Louise J. (Moresco) S. BA, Marquette U., 1977. Claims rep. Social Security Adminstrn., HEW, Waukegan, Ill., 1978-79; market adminstr. Wis. Telephone Co., Milw., 1979-80, account exec., 1980-84; sr. account exec. Wis. Bell Communications, Milw., 1984—. Vol., Italian Community Ctr. Festa Italiana, Milw., 1978-84; participant Lake Front Festival, 1986-87. Mem. Am. Mktg. Assn. (chpt. sec. 1983-85), Internat. Orgn. Women in Telecommunications, Telecommunications Profls. of Wis., Marquette U. Coll. Speech Alumni Assn. (pres. 1984, bd. dirs. 1979-85), Marquette U. Alumni Assn. (bd. dirs. 1985—). Roman Catholic. Home: 1603 S Carriage Ln New Berlin WI 53151 Office: Wis Bell Communications 200 S Executive Dr Brookfield WI 53005

SLEWITZKE, CONNIE LEE, retired chief army nurse corps, academic director; b. Mosinee, Wis., Apr. 15, 1931; d. Leo Thomas and Amelia Marie (Hoffman) S. B.S.N., U. Md., Balt., 1971; M.A. in Counseling and Guidance, St. Mary's U., San Antonio, 1976. Staff nurse Sacred Heart Hosp., Eau Claire, Wis., 1952-53; staff nurse Los Angeles County Hosp., 1953-54, U. Ill. Research Hosp., Chicago, 1954-56, George Washington Hosp., Washington, 1956-57; enlisted U.S. Army, Fort Sam Houston., Tex., 1957; staff nurse Brooke Army Med. Ctr., Fort Sam Houston, Tex., 1957-59, Tripler Army Med. Ctr., Honolulu, Hawaii, 1959-61; asst. head nurse Kimbrough Army Hosp., Fort George G. Meade, Md., 1962-63, head nurse, 1963-64; med., surg. nurse 44th Surg. Hosp., Korea, 1964-65; asst. chief nurse U.S. Army Hosp., Albuquerque, 1965-67, 36th Evacuation Hosp., Vietnam, 1967-68; chief nurse 6th Convalescent Ctr., Vietnam, 1968; nurse supr. Walk-In Clinic, Fort Myer, Va., 1968-69; with Nursing Adminstrn. Br., 7th MEDCOMEUR, 1971-73; nurse, officer Hdqrs. Health Services Command, Fort Sam Houston, Tex., 1974-75, nursing cons., 1975-76; chief nurse U.S. Army Hosp., Seoul, Korea, 1977-78; chief dept. nursing Letterman Army Med. Ctr., Presidio of San Francisco, Calif., 1978-80; asst. chief Army nurse corps Office Surgeon Gen., Washington, 1980-83, chief Army nurse corps, 1983-87; ret. U.S. Army, 1987; dir. devel. Sch. Nursing, U. Md., Balt., 1988—. Contbr. articles to profl. jours. Decorated D.S.M., Legion of Merit, Bronze Star medal, Meritorious Service Medal with 1 oak leaf cluster, Joint Services Commendation medal, Army Commendation Medal, Nat. Def. Service medal, Vietnam Service medal with 4 devices, Overseas Service ribbon with 4 devices, Republic of Vietnam Campaign medal. Mem. Am. Nurses Assn., Va. State Nurses Assn., Alumni Assn. U.S.A. War Coll., Nat. Orgn. Nurse Execs., Assn. U.S. Army, Sigma Theta Tau. Office: U Md Sch Nursing Baltimore MD

SLEZAK, KAREN PATRICIA, credit company executive; b. Paterson, N.J., July 20, 1950; d. Stephen and Florence (Scarmazzo) Messineo; m. Norman M. Slezak, May 29, 1971; 1 child, Kimberly Ann. Student, William Paterson Coll., 1979-82. Bookkeeper J.L. Prescott Co., Passaic, N.J., 1969-70; accounting clk. Drakes Bakeries, Wayne, N.J., 1970-72; mgr. Retailers Comml. Agy., Paterson, N.J., 1972-81; salesperson Equifax Services, Lyndhurst, N.J., 1982-83; pres. Credit Resources, Inc., West Paterson, N.J., 1983—. V.p. Park West Meadows Condominium Assn., 1986—. Mem. Nat. Assn. Female Execs., Women Entrepreneurs of N.J., Internat. Internat. Credit Assn., Mortgage Bankers Assn. of N.J. (YMBC membership chmn. 1982), Mortgage Bankers Assn. of N.Y. Republican. Roman Catholic. Office: Credit Resources Inc 999 McBride Ave PO Box 540 West Paterson NJ 07424

SLINGSBY, ANN MARY, art director; b. Bronx, N.Y., Aug. 10, 1930; d. Charles Angelo and Sarah (Smeraldi) Cimitile; m. Harry Stafford Slingsby, June 7, 1953; children—Robert, Keith, Tara. Degree in Art, Indsl. Arts Coll., N.Y.C., 1948; student Hunter Coll., N.Y.C., 1952-54. Head file dept. South African Govt., N.Y.C., 1950; salesperson, model Lord & Taylor, N.Y.C., 1950-53; art tchr. Bklyn. Archdiocese Schs., 1953-55, Archdiocese of N.Y. Schs., 1955-71; art dir. Clarkstown Recreation, New City, N.Y., 1973—; writer, producer, dir. sr. citizen annual show Town of Clarkstown, 1976—. Author: Arts and Crafts Teaching Experiences, 1975. Den mother Rockland County council Boy Scouts Am., 1962-63; vol. dir. Clarkstown Sr. Citizen Show, 1984; mem. Elmwood Playhouse, 1983—; assoc. Hudson Valley Leisure Services, 1980—. Recipient Cert. Appreciation Summit Park Hosp. Vol. Services, 1984, N.Y. State Achievement award, 1984. Roman Catholic. Avocations: Sculpture; painting; crafts; drama; dance. Home: 46 Briarwood Dr New City NY 10956

SLOAN, A. ELIZABETH, publishing executive, food scientist; b. Hackensack, N.J., Sept. 1, 1951; d. Kenneth Thomas Spencer and Anna Sember (Kundrat) Sloan Velebir; m. Theodore Peter Labuza, Jan. 22, 1976 (div. Jan. 1980). B.S., Rutgers State U., 1973; Ph.D., U. Minn., 1976. Communications specialist nutrition Gen. Mills, Inc., Mpls., 1976-77, mgr. nutrition edn. and communications services, 1977-79, mgr. nutrition communiction and tech. services, 1979-80; dir. sci. services Am. Assn. Cereal Chemists, St. Paul, 1980-81, also editor-in-chief Cereal foods World, Cereal Chemistry; dir. Good Housekeeping Inst., N.Y.C., 1981-85, also asst. to editor-in-chief Good Housekeeping mag., 1981-85; editor-in-chief McCall's mag., 1985—. Judge Mrs. America/Mrs. N.J. Pageant, 1984; mem. food update bd. govs. Food and Drug Law Inst., 1982-85; trustee Internat Life Scis. Inst., 1982—. Author: (with T.P. Labuza) Food for Thought, 1977; Contemporary Nutrition Controversies, 1979; coordinating editor Good Housekeeping American Family Christmas Book, 1985; mem. editorial adv. bd. Rutgers U. Contbr. articles to profl. jours. Tenneco Found. scholar, 1969-73; George H. Cook scholar, Rutgers U., 1973; Ralston Purina fellow, 1975; recipietn Women Achiever award YMCA, 1986. Mem. Inst. Food Technologists (nat. chmn. nutrition div. 1981-82), Am. Assn. Cereal Chemists, Am. Dietetic Assn., Am. Coll. Nutrition, Assn. Ofcl. Analytical Chemists, Am. Film Inst., Am. Home Econs. Assn., Home Economists in Bus., Smithsonian Instn., AAAS, Am. Soc. Prevention Cruelty to Animals, Soc. Nutrition Edn., Am. Mgmt. Assn., Soc. Consumer Affairs Profls. in Bus., Defenders of Wildlife, Am. Soc. Mag. Editors, Whitney Mus. Am. Art, Fashion Group, Womens City Club N.Y., Nat. Assn. Female Execs., N.Y. Acad. Scis., Am. Chem. Soc., Alpha Zeta, Phi Epsilon Omicron, Gamma Sigma Delta, Phi Tau Sigma, Sigma Delta Epsilon. Club: Rutgers (N.Y.C.). Avocation: golf. Office: McCall's 230 Park Ave Room 721 New York NY 10169 *

SLOAN, BESSIE BERNICE, accountant; b. Middletown, Ohio, Apr. 17, 1949; d. Jessie and Pearlie Mae (Riley) Jemison; m. Ronald E. Sloan, Sr., Aug. 27, 1966; children—Ronald E., Natasha L. Student acctg., Miami U., Oxford, Ohio, 1978-82. Operator, Ohio Bell Telephone, Dayton, 1968-76; receptionist City of Middletown, 1976-77, account clk. I, 1977-78, account clk. II, 1978-81, city acct., 1981—. Sec. Middletown City Employees Assn., 1977—; com. chair Middfest, 1980—, Elk Creek Festival, 1983—. Mem. Nat. Assn. Female Execs., Nat. Assn. Accts., Profls. in Action (sec.-treas. 1984—), Am. Payroll Assn., NAACP. Democrat. Mem. African Methodist Episcopal Ch. Club: Ebone Inc (officer 1972—) (Middletown). Avocations: golfing; reading; gardening; reupholstering furniture. Office: City of Middletown One City Ctr Plaza Middletown OH 45042

SLOAN, CAROLYN JUNE, cosmetic company executive; b. Conroe, Tex., June 30, 1937; d. Hulon Jesse and Bessie Adeline (Stewart) White; m. Howard Sinclair Sloan, June 17, 1955 (div.); children—Sharon Sloan Kincannon, Kathryn Sloan Thomas, Christine D.; m. Gregory P. Kohler, July 22, 1987. Student Conroe pub. schs. Receivables clk. Germalene Chem. Co., Houston, 1960-61; sec. Kelly Girl Services, Houston, 1961-62; receptionist Watson Oil Co., Houston, 1962-63, Letbetter Clinic, Houston, 1963-67; sec. Parker Methodist Ch., Houston, 1967-69; owner, operator Merle Norman Cosmetic Studio, Magnolia, Tex., 1969-80, Navasota, Tex., 1976-81, Houston, 1978—. Mem. Conroe Montgomery County C. of C., Cy-Fair C. of C. (bd. dirs.). Baptist. Home: 11830 Westlock Tomball TX 77375 Office: Merle Norman Cosmetics 1554 Willowbrook Mall Houston TX 77070

SLOAN, ELAINE FRANK, librarian; b. Pitts., May 20, 1938; d. Maurice and Sarah (Blecher) Frank; m. Howard R. Sloan, Aug. 30, 1959; children: Michael, Stephen, Eric. B.A., Chatham Coll., Pitts., 1959; M.A., U. Pitts., 1962; M.L.S. (Smithsonian Instn. fellow 1970-72, Outstanding Grad. award), U. Md., 1972, Ph.D., 1974. Research asst. Johns Hopkins U., 1962-66; asst. to dir. for planning and research, asst. dir. mgmt. and devel. Smithsonian Instn. Libraries, 1974-76; asso. univ. librarian public services, lectr. Sch. Librarianship, U. Calif., Berkeley, 1977-78; dean univ. librarians Ind. U., Bloomington, 1978—. Mem. Assn. Research Libraries (pres. 1987—), ALA (chmn. pub. com. 1980-81), Beta Phi Mu (pres. 1987—). Home: 4901 E Ridgewood Dr Bloomington IN 47401 Office: Ind Univ at Bloomington Univ Libraries 10th and Jordan Sts Bloomington IN 47405

SLOAN, JODY BETH, real estate executive; b. Atlanta, July 16, 1953; d. Myer and Beryl (Cowan) S.; Student, U. Tenn., 1970-71; B.A., Ga. State U., 1976; M. in City Planning, Ga. Inst. Tech., 1979. Office mgr. Exec. Chairs, Atlanta, 1972-76; researcher Ga. Inst. Tech., Atlanta, 1977-79; planning cons. CMCA Cons., Atlanta, 1976-78; urban planner Jefferson County, Ala. 1978-79; transp. planner, rep. U.S. Dept. Transp.-Urban Mass. Transp. Adminstrn., Ft. Worth and Atlanta, 1979-85; cons. The Real Estate Consortium Atlanta, 1985-86 ; real estate specialist U.S. Postal Service, Atlanta, 1986—; co-owner The Bare Walls, Atlanta, 1981—; owner Say CHEESE-cake, 1987—. Contbr. articles to profl. jours.; contbr. restaurant reviews. Mem. conservation com. Sierra Club, Atlanta, 1977—; mem. fundraising com. City of Hope Hosp. and Med. Ctr., Atlanta, 1983—; v.p., bd. dirs. Westover Plantation, 1984-86. Mem. Arthritis Found., Am. Planning Assn., Women in Transp., Nat. Assn. Female Execs. (assoc. 1982—), Nat. Assn. Corp. Real Estate Execs., Corp. Real Estate Women, High Mus. Art. Democrat. Home: 8 Newport Pl NW Atlanta GA 30318 Office: US Postal Service 4000 DeKalb Tech Pkwy Bldg 500 Suite 550 Atlanta GA 30340

SLOAN, SUZANNE BARKIN, director of marketing and sales; b. N.Y.C., Aug. 20, 1959; d. Stephen Samuel and Nanette Ruth (Barkin) Sloan; m. Gary Gittelsohn. B.A., U. Rochester, 1981; M.S., Columbia U., 1983; Cert. Sign Lang., Nat. Tech. Inst. for Deaf, 1980. Cert. social worker, N.Y. Dir. mktg. Anchorage Yacht Club, Lindenhurst, N.Y., 1983—; rep. alumni affairs Horace Mann-Barnard Sch., Bronx, 1985—;mem. Assoc. Humane Soc., 1980—, Am. Soc. Prevention of Cruelty to Animals, 1979—. Mem. Nat. Assn. Social Workers, Nat. Marine Mfrs. Assn., Nat. Maritime Assn. Home: 44 W 62d St New York NY 10023 Office: Anchorage Yacht Club 401 E Shore Rd Lindenhurst NY 11757

SLOANE, BEVERLY LEBOV, writer, consultant; b. N.Y.C., May 26, 1936; d. Benjamin S. and Anne (Weinberg) LeBov; AB, Vassar Coll., 1958; MA, Claremont Grad. Sch., 1975, postgrad., 1975-76; grad. exec. program. Sch. Mgmt., UCLA, 1982, 87; grad. pub. course Stanford U., 1982; postgrad. bioethics Kennedy Inst. Ethics, Georgetown U., 1987, 88; m. Robert Malcolm Sloane, Sept. 27, 1959; 1 dau., Alison Lori. Circulation librarian Harvard Med. Library, Boston, 1958-59; social worker Conn. State Welfare, New Haven, 1960-61; tchr. English, Hebrew Day Sch., New Haven, 1961-64; instr. creative writing and English lit. Monmouth Coll., West Long Branch, N.J., 1967-69; freelance writer, Arcadia, Calif., 1970—. Mem. public relations bd. Monmouth County Mental Health Assn., 1968-69; adv. council tech. and profl. writing dept. English, Calif. State U., Long Beach, 1980-82; v.p. Council of Grad. Students, Claremont Grad. Sch., 1971-72, mem. Foothill Health Dist. (adv. council), County of Los Angeles, 1987—, task force edn. and cultural activities, City of Duarte, 1987-88; trustee Ctr. for Improvement of Child Caring, 1981-83; mem. League Crippled Children, 1982—; bd. dirs. Los Angeles Commn. on Assaults Against Women, 1983-84; v.p. Temple Beth David, 1983-86; mem. community relations com. Jewish Fedn. Council Greater Los Angeles, 1985-87; bd. dirs. Los Angeles Commn. Assaults Against Women, 1983-84; del. Task Force on Minorities in Newspaper Bus., 1987— Coro Found. fellow, 1979. Fellow Am. Med. Writers Assn. (dir. 1980—, Pacific S.W. del. to nat. bd. 1980-87, chmn. various conv. coms., chmn. nat. book awards trade category 1982-83, chmn. Nat. Conv. Networking Luncheon 1983, 84, chmn. freelance and pub. relations coms. Nat. Midyr. Conf. 1983-84, workshop leader ann. conf. 1984, 85, 86, 87, nat. chmn. freelance sect. 1984-85, gen. chmn. 1985 Asilomar Western Regional Conf., speaker 1985, 88, program co-chmn., 1986-87, nat. exec. bd. dirs. 1985-86, nat. adminstr. sects. 1985-86, pres.-elect Pacific Southwest chpt. 1985-87, moderator gen. session nat. conf. 1987, chairperson general session nat. conf., 1986-87, chairperson Walter C. Alvarez Meml. Found. award 1986-87); mem. Women in Communications (dir. 1980—, v.p. community affairs 1981-82, N.E. area rep. 1980-81, chmn. awards banquet 1982, sem. leader ann. nat. profl. conf., 1985, program adv. com. Los Angeles chpt. 1987, chmn. Los Angeles chpt. 1st ann. Agnes Underwood Freedom of Info. Awards Banquet 1982, recognition award 1983, nominating com. 1982, 83, com. Women of the Press Awards luncheon 1988), Am. Assn. for Higher Edn., AAUW (legis. chmn. Arcadia br. 1976-77, books and plays chmn. Arcadia br. 1973-74, creative writing chmn. 1969-70, 1st v.p. 1975-76, networking chmn. 1981-82, chmn. task force promoting individual liberties 1987—, Woman of Achievement award 1986, cert. of appreciation 1987), Coll. English Assn., Am. Pub. Health Assn., Calif. Press Women (v.p. programs Los Angeles chpt. 1982-85, pres. 1985-87, state pres. 1987—), AAUP, Internat. Communication Assn., N.Y. Acad. Scis., Ind. Writers So. Calif., Hastings Inst., AAAS, Am. Med. Writers Assn. (pres.-elect Pacific S.W. chpt. 1985-87, pres. 1987—, nat. adminstr. sects. 1985-86, exec. bd. dirs. 1985-86, chmn. nominating com. 1987—, workshop leader annual conf. 1984-87, steering com. Seminar on Med. Writing 1988), bd. dirs. Nat. Fedn. Press Women, Inc. 1987— (nat. co-chmn. task force recruitment of minorities 1987—, delegate 1987—), chmn. state women of achievement com. 1986—), AAUW (chpt. Woman of Achievement award 1986, chmn. task force promoting individual liberties 1987—, speaker 1987, recipient cert. of appreciation 1987), Soc. for Tech. Communication (workshop leader, 1985, 86), Kennedy Inst. Ethics, Soc. Health and Human Values, Assoc. Writing Programs. Clubs: Rotary of Duarte, Women's City (Pasadena), Vassar of So. Calif., Claremont Colls. Faculty House, Pasadena Athletic, Stock Exchange of Los Angeles, Town Hall of Calif. (vice chmn. cs sect. 1982—, speaker, 1986, instr. Exec. Breakfast Inst., 1985-86, mem. study sect. council, 1986—). Author: From Vassar to Kitchen, 1967; A Guide to Health Facilities: Personnel and Management, 2d rev. edit., 1977; mem. adv. bd. Calif. Health Rev., 1982-83. Home and Office: 1301 N Santa Anita Ave Arcadia CA 91006

SLOANE, MARILYN AUSTERN, lawyer; b. N.Y.C., June 29, 1944; d. Leo Ellis and Betty (Schlanger) Austern; m. Judd Sloane, May 7, 1966 (div. 1981); 1 child, Craig. BA, U. Vt., 1965; LLB, Columbia U., 1968. Bar: N.Y. 1969; cert. CLU. Lawyer L.I. (N.Y.) Lighting Co., 1968-70, Community Legal Assistance Corp. and Nassau County Community Devel. Corp., Long Island, 1970-74, Mutual of Am., N.Y.C., 1974—; v.p. Nat. Health Welfare Retirement Assn., N.Y.C.; sr. v.p. devel. fin. services corp. Mut. Am., N.Y.C., sr. v.p., assoc. gen. counsel. Fellow Life Mgmt. Inst.; mem. CLU (N.Y. Chpt. v.p. 1988—). Republican. Jewish. Home: 8 Shawnee Trail Harrison NY 10528 Office: Mutual of Am 666 5th Ave New York City NY 10103

SLOAT, JANE ROBERTS DEGRAFF, government official; b. N.Y.C., Dec. 31, 1939; d. John Wynne and Agnes (Murton) Roberts; m. Elliott Dodd DeGraff, June 28, 1959 (div.); children: Pamela DeGraff Porter, Jill Katherine; m. Jonathan Welsh Sloat, June 19, 1983. Active Hospitality and Info. Service, Washington, 1964-70, sec. bd., 1971-73; spl. asst. to ambassador-at-large for cultural affairs Dept. State, Washington, 1981, now spl. asst. to ambassador at large for refugee affairs; spl. asst. to U.S. coordinator refugee affairs, Washington, 1982-85, coordinator conf. on Ethical Issues and Moral Principles in U.S. Refugee Policy, 1983. Tour lectr. Corcoran Gallery Art, Washington, 1965-70; vice chmn. UN Concert, Washington, 1971, 50th Jubilee Nat. English Speaking Union, 1971; spl. asst. to chmn. United Givers Fund, Washington, 1971-72; chmn. ball Opera Soc. Washington, 1972; bd. dirs. Jr. League, 1970-71, Nat. Ballet Soc., 1972-74, Washington Performing Arts Soc., 1972-75; mem. D.C. Mayor's Com. on Internat. Visitors, 1972-77; trustee Hosp. for Sick Children, Washington, 1973-76; editor Washington Antiques Show Catalogue, 1972-75; mem. D.C. Rep. Fin. Com., 1972-75; trustee Meridian House Internat. Ctr., Washington, 1964-82, sec. 1974-75, vice chmn. bd., 1976-82; mem. bd. advisers D.C. Lung Assn., 1975—; active fund-raising drive for Washington Cathedral, 1976; bd. dirs. Washington Home for Incurables, 1976-88, Nat. Eye Found., 1976-78, Children's Hosp. Nat. Research Found., 1978-81, D.C. chpt. ARC, 1976-84, Travelers Aid Soc., 1976-88; chmn. Washington Antiques Show, 1976-78, Washington Cathedral Flower Mart; dir. fin. devel. YWCA of Nat. Capital Area, 1979; vice chmn. Reagan Bush Inaugural, Washington, 1981; mem. transition team for Reagan Bush for NEA, 1981; bd. dirs. Family Stress Services, 1981-84; founder, chmn. Entertaining People, 1982-88; bd. dirs. All Hallows Guild, Washington br. English Speaking Union, 1988. Episcopalian. Clubs: Sulgrave, Chevy Chase (Washington).

SLONE, SANDI, artist; b. Boston, Oct. 1, 1939; d. Louis and Ida (Spindiak) Sudikoff; children—Eric Solomon, Jon Solomon. Student Wheaton Coll., 1957-59, Boston Mus. Fine Arts Sch., 1970-73; B.A., Wellesley Coll., 1974. Instr. painting Boston Mus. Fine Arts Sch., 1970—, Brandeis U., Waltham, Mass., 1976, Harvard U., Cambridge, Mass., 1982. One person shows include: Harcus Krakow Gallery, Boston, 1978, 79, 80, 82, 84, Acquavella Contemporary Art, N.Y., 1977, 79, 80, 82, 84; group shows include Mus. Fine Arts, Boston, 1977, Corcoran Gallery of Art, Washington, 1977, Hayden Gallery, MIT, 1978, New Generation Andre Emmerich Gallery,

N.Y., 1980-81, Am. Ctr., Paris, 1980-81, Amerika Haus, Berlin, 1980-81, Carpenter Ctr., Harvard U., 1983, Edmonton Art Gallery, 1977, 85, Gallery One, Toronto, Ont., Can., 1981; represented in permanent collections including Mus. Modern Art, N.Y.C., Albright-Knox, Buffalo, Mus. Fine Arts, Boston, Hirshhorn Mus., Washington, Mus. Fine Arts Boston fellow, 1977, 81; Ford Found. grantee, 1979. *

SLOSHBERG, LEAH PHYFER, museum director; b. New Albany, Miss., Feb. 21, 1937; d. Sisco Knox and Mary Rachel (Sandlin) Phyfer; m. Willard Sloshberg, Dec. 8, 1961; 1 son, Simeon. B.F.A., Miss. State Coll., 1959; M.A. (Woodrow Wilson fellow), Tulane U., 1961. Arts curator N.J. State Mus., Trenton, 1968-69, asst. dir., 1969-71, dir., 1971—. Home: Box 190 RD #2 Stockton NJ 08559 Office: New Jersey State Mus 205 W State St CN 530 Trenton NJ 08625

SLOSS, CAROLANNE BURKE, education administrator; b. Phila., May 24, 1945; d. Richard Francis and Kathryn M. (Wellner) Burke; children: Frank A. Jr., Eric Christopher. BS, Newmann Coll.; postgrad, Widener Coll., Chester, Pa., 1986—. Program adminstr. Office of Employment & Tng., Media, Pa., 1979-81; founding dir. of job placement services & coop. edn. Delaware County Community Coll., Media, 1981—. Author: (poetry) Dawn, 1974. Bd. dirs. Mental Health/Mental Retardation Council of Delco, Media, 1984—; counselor Domestic Abuse Project, Media, 1973-76; campaign organizer Curt Weldon for congress, 1983-87. Mem. Am. Assn. Women in Jr. Colls., Nat. Coll. Placement Council, Nat. Assn. Female Execs., Pa. Coll. Personnel Assn. (bd. dirs. 1985—); Mid-Atlantic Placement Assn. (com mem. 1981—), Eastern Regional Placement Assn., Delco C. of C., Media. Republican. Roman Catholic. Home: 3045 Surrey Ln Aston Township PA 19014 Office: Delaware County Community Coll RR 252 Media PA 19063

SLOSS, MERLE, shoe company executive; b. Atlantic City, N.J., Feb. 26, 1948; d. Ralph and Annette (Nemirosky) S.; m. Matthew Barry Smith, June 10, 1973. BA in Chemistry, U. Pa., 1970; MBA, Boston U., 1972. Asst. product mgr. Gen. Foods Corp., White Plains, N.Y., 1972-73, assoc. product mgr., 1974-75, product mgr., 1976-78, group product mgr., 1979-82; dir. mktg. Bally of Switzerland, New Rochelle, N.Y., 1982-83, v.p. mktg., 1984, exec. v.p., gen. mgr., 1985—, also bd. dirs. Mem. Women in Mgmt., Phi Lamda Upsilon, Beta Gamma Sigma. Democrat. Jewish. Office: Bally of Switzerland One Bally Pl New Rochelle NY 10801

SLOVER, GAIL PENNIMAN TURNER, biologist; b. Bradford, Pa., Mar. 14, 1938; d. Prescott Kingsbury Turner and Priscilla (Clark) Baker; m. William P. Slover, June 18, 1960 (div. July 1984); children: Cheryl Nordbeck, Gregory Lincoln, David William. BA, Conn. Coll., 1960; MEd, U. Hartford, 1978. Trainee med. technologist Harbor Gen. Hosp., Torrance, Calif., 1960-61; research asst. biochemistry Inst. of Living, Hartford, Conn., 1961-64; pvt. practice parent effectiveness tng. Glastonbury, Conn., 1978-80; tchr., researcher Talcott Mountain Sci. Ctr., Avon, Conn., 1983—; dir. chronobiology, cons. Body Time Tech., Glastonbury, 1986-87; cons. Newington (Conn.) VA Hosp., 1987—, United Techs. Corp., Hartford, 1987—. Bd. dirs. Montessori Sch. Hartford, West Hartford, Conn., 1968-69; pres., v.p. Hebron Ave Sch. PTO, Glastonbury, 1971-74; rep. task force for gifted/talented, Conn., 1977-78; diaconate Covenant Ch., 1985-86. Mem. Internat. Soc. for Chronobiology, European Soc. for Chronobiology, DAR. Club: Toastmasters. Home and Office: 20-C Esquire Dr Manchester CT 06040

SLOVITER, DOLORES KORMAN, federal judge; b. Phila., Sept. 5, 1932; d. David and Tillie Korman; m. Henry A. Sloviter, Apr. 3, 1969; 1 dau., Vikki Amanda. A.B. in Econs. with distinction, Temple U., Phila., 1953, L.H.D. (hon.), 1986; LL.B. magna cum laude, U. Pa., 1956; LL.D. (hon.), The Dickinson Sch. Law, 1984. Bar: Pa. 1957. Assoc., then partner Dilworth, Paxson, Kalish, Kohn & Levy, Phila., 1956-69; mem. firm Harold E. Kohn (P.A.), Phila., 1969-72; assoc. prof. then prof. law Temple U. Law Sch., 1972-79; judge U.S. Ct. Appeals 3d Circuit, Phila., 1979—; mem. Disciplinary Bd. Supreme Ct. Pa., 1978-79. Mem. S.E. region Gov. Pa. Council Aging, 1976-79; mem. Com. of 70, 1976-79; trustee Jewish Publ. Soc. Am., 1983—. Mem. ABA, Am. Law Inst., Fed. Bar Assn., Fed. Judges Assn., Phila. Bar Assn. (gov. 1976-78), Phi Beta Kappa, Order of Coif (pres. U. Pa. chpt. 1975-77). Office: US Ct of Appeals 18614 US Courthouse Independence Mall W 601 Market St Philadelphia PA 19106

SLUDER, CHERYL LYNN, military officer; b. Maberzell, Hessen, Fed. Republic of Germany, July 17, 1960; came to U.S., 1961; d. Olen Vance and Irmtraud (Zittlau) S. BS in Animal Sci., Tarleton State U., 1981. Commd. 2d lt. U.S. Army, 1981, advanced through grades to capt., 1985; platoon leader 2d Ops. Bn. USAFSA, Augsburg, Fed. Republic of Germany, 1982-83; tng. standards officer U.S. Army Field Station, Augsburg, Fed. Republic of Germany, 1983-84; adj. Support Bn. USAFSA, Augsburg, Fed. Republic of Germany, 1984-85; chief collection mgmt. G2 101st Abn div. Air Assault, Ft. Campbell, Ky., 1986-87; chief all source prodn. section G2 101st Abn div. U.S. Army, Ft. Campbell, Ky., 1987—. Mem. Assn. U.S. Army, Nat. Assn. Female Execs., Assn. Old Crows, Tarleton Alumni Assn., Alpha Zeta. Lutheran. Club: Officer's (Ft. Campbell). Office: AFZB-GS-ASP 101st Abn Div Air Assault Fort Campbell KY 42230

SLUNECKA, KAREN LYNN, home economist; b. Gettysburg, S.D., Aug. 20, 1959; d. Lorren Earl and Carletta Mary (Vail) Kilian; m. James Wyatt Slunecka, Sept. 30, 1958; 1 child, Colin. BS in Home Econs., S.D. State U., 1981. Home economist S.D. Coop. Extension Service, Timberlake, 1981-82; home economist Highmore, 1983-87, Faulkton, 1987—. Mem. S.D. Assn. Extension Home Econs. (bd. dirs. 1982-83), S.D. Home Econs. Assn. Republican. Methodist. Home: Box 222 Faulkton SD 57438 Office: SD Coop Extension Service Courthouse Box 39 Faulkton SD 57438

SMAISTRLA, JEAN ANN, family therapist; b. South Gate, Calif., Oct. 12, 1936; d. Benjamin J. and Janet (Pollock) Craig; m. Charles J. Smaistrla, July 12, 1958; children—Amy Jean, Ben, John. B.B.A. in Mktg., Lamar U., 1958; elec. edn. cert. Tex. Wesleyan Coll., 1963; M.Ed. in Counseling, Tex. Christian U., 1975. Tchr. Houston Ind. Schs., 1958-61, Arlington Ind. Schs., Tex., 1961-72; counselor, therapist Arlington Counseling and Cons. Ctr., 1983-85; family therapist Willow Creek Adolescent Ctr., Arlington, 1985-86, dir. edn., 1986—; therapist, Bob Caprenter PhD and Assoc., 1987—; owner, founder Adolescent Services Arlington, 1981—; cons. Charles J. Smaistrla, D.D.S., Arlington, 1978-85. Vice chmn. bd. Arlington Community Hosp., 1981-85; life mem. PTA; bd. dirs. Arlington Art Assn., 1981-85, bd. S. Arlington Med. Ctr., 1987, Ctr. for Well-Being, 1985. Mem. Am. Assn. Marriage and Family Therapy, Tarrant County Assn. Marriage and Family Therapy, North Central Tex. Assn. Counseling and Devel., Am. Assn. Counseling and Devel., Alpha Delta Pi. Republican. Roman Catholic. Clubs: Jr. League Arlington, Arlington Women's. Avocations: Sailing; sewing; doll collecting.

SMALBACH, BARBARA SCHILLER, foreign language educator; b. N.Y.C., Feb. 18, 1942; d. Sylvan Bertram and Frances (Siegel) Schiller; m. Mervyn Stockman, Nov. 21, 1962 (div. Jan. 1966); m. David H. Smalbach, Aug. 29, 1969. BA Adelphi U., 1963, MA 1968. Tchr. fgn. langs. Long Beach Pub. Sch. System, N.Y., 1963-64; teaching fellow dept. fgn. langs. Queens Coll., Flushing, N.Y., 1964-65; tchr. fgn. langs. Farmingdale Pub. Sch. System, N.Y., 1966—. Mem. Rockville Centre BiCentennial Festival Com., 1975-76; founder, pres. Friends of Rockville Centre Pub. Library, 1980-82; founder, co-chmn. Hist. Homes Tour, 1980-84; co-chmn. Rockville Centre Anniversary Celebration, 1983; pres. Mus. of The Village of Rockville Centre, 1985-87, Rockville Centre Village historian, 1986—; treas. Assn. of Nassau County Hist. Orgns., 1984—. Mem. NE Conf. on Teaching Fgn. Langs., AAUW (N.Y. state div. br. council rep. 1987, Div. Com. on Pub. Support for Pub. Ed., Dist. VI, 1984-87; Div. Com. Br. Council, Dist. VI, 1982-84; Nassau County Br. Pres., 1980-82; co-founder and chair L.I. AAUW Rep. 1982-86; Area Coordinator Project WIPE, 1984—, co-creator and co-developer of anti-censorship workshops); Delta Kappa Gamma, Sigma Delta Pi. Republican. Jewish. Club: Tam O'Shanter (Brookville, N.Y.); Gleneagles (Delray Beach, Fla.). Avocations: travel, golf, reading. Home: 10 Allen Rd Rockville Centre NY 11570

SMALL, ELISABETH CHAN, physician, educator; b. Beijing, July 11, 1934; came to U.S., 1937; d. Stanley Hong and Lily Luella (Lum) Chan; m. Donald M. Small, July 8, 1957 (div. 1980); children Geoffrey Brooks, Philip Willard Stanley. Student, Immaculate Heart Coll., Los Angeles, 1951-52; BA in Polit. Sci., UCLA, 1955, MD, 1960. Intern Newton-Wellesley Hosp., Mass., 1960-61; asst. dir. for venereal diseases Mass. Dept. Pub. Health, 1961-63; resident in psychiatry Boston State Hosp., Mattapan, Mass., 1965-66; resident in psychiatry Tufts New Eng. Med. Ctr. Hosps., 1966-69, psychiat. cons. dept. gynecology, 1973-75; asst. clin. prof. psychiatry Sch. Medicine Tufts U., 1973-75, assoc. clin. prof., 1975-82, asst. clin. prof. ob-gyn, 1977-80, assoc. clin. prof. ob-gyn, 1980-82; assoc. prof. psychiatry, ob-gyn U. Nev. Sch. Med., Reno, 1982-85; practice psychiatry specializing in psychological effects of bodily changes on women 1969—; clin. prof. psychiatry U. Nev. Sch. Medicine, Reno, 1985-86, prof. psychiatry, 1986—, clin. assoc. prof. ob-gyn, 1985—; mem. staff Tufts New Eng. Med. Ctr. Hosps., 1977-82, St. Margaret's Hosps., Boston, 1977-82, Washoe Med. Ctr., Reno, Sparks (Nev.) Family Hosp., Truckee Meadows Hosp., Reno, St. Mary's Hosp., Reno; lectr. various univs., 1961—; cons. in psychiatry; mem. psychiatry adv. panel Hosp. Satellite Network; mem. office external peer rev. NIMH, HEW; psychiat. cons. to Boston Redevelopment Authority on Relocation of Chinese Families of South Cove Area, 1968-70; mem. New Eng. Med. Ctr. Hosps. Cancer Ctr. Com., 1979-80, Pain Control Com., 1981-82, Tufts Univ. Sch. Medicine Reproductive System Curriculum Com., 1975-82. Mem. editorial bd. Psychiat. Update Am. (Psychiat. Assn. ann. rev.), 1983-85; reviewer Psychosomatics and Hosp. Community Psychiatry, New Eng. Jour. of Medicine, Am. Jour. of Psychiatry Psychosomatic Medicine; contbr. articles to profl. jours. Immaculate Heart Coll. scholar, 1951-52; Mira Hershey scholar UCLA, 1955; fellow Radcliffe Inst., 1967-70. Mem. AMA, Am. Psychiat. Assn. (rep. to sect. com. AAAS, chmn. ad hoc com. Asian-Am. Psychiatrists 1975, task force 1975-77, task force cost effectiveness in consultation 1984—, caucus chmn. 1981-82, sci. program com. 1982—, courses subcom. chmn. sci. program com., 1986-88), Mass. Med. Soc., Am. Coll. Sports Medicine, Am. Geriatrics Soc., Am. Soc. Psychomatic Ob-Gyn (mem.-at-large 1982-83, curriculum com. 1981-82), New Eng. Soc. Clin. Hypnosis, Assn. Acad. Psychiatry (fellowship com. 1982—), Am. Pain Soc., Nev. Psychiat. Assn., Washoe County Med. Assn., Nev. Med. Soc., Am. Soc. Clin. Hypnosis, Am. Coll. Psychiatrists, Eastern Profl. Ski Instrs. Assn. Home: 2105 Chicory Way Reno NV 89509 Office: 1000 Locust St Reno NV 89520

SMALL, JANET LOUISE, nursing administrator; b. Durand, Mich., Oct. 20, 1943; d. Earl F. and Eva C. (Krueger) Routson; m. Lennie D. Small, Dec. 31, 1985; children: Andrew, Anthony, Chris. BSN, Mich. State U., 1978; MS, U. Mich., 1982. Staff nurse Owosso (Mich.) Meml. Hosp., 1972-77; supr. Saginaw (Mich.) Osteo. Hosp.D, 1977-78, Genesee Meml. Hosp., Flint, Mich., 1978-82; asst. dir. McLaren Gen. Hosp., Flint, 1982-88, dir. critical care, 1988—; cons. in field. Lutheran. Office: McLaren Gen Hosp 401 S Ballenger Hwy Flint MI 48502-2256

SMALLEY, EDITH RENEE, restaurant professional; b. West Union, Ohio, Sept. 13, 1960; d. Donald Eugene and Mabel Mildred (Gustin) S. BBA, Morehead State U., 1984. Youth counselor Adams County Youth Services, West Union, Ohio, 1984; clk. front desk Breckenridge (Colo.) Inn, 1984-85; asst. mgr. trainee Red Lobster Inns Am., Cin., 1985; asst. mgr. Red Lobster Inns Am., Huntington, W.Va., 1986, Lexington, Ky., 1986-87; asst. mgr. Red Lobster Can., Kitchner, Ont., 1987, St. Catherine, Ont., 1987; asst. mgr. Red Lobster Inns Am., Lexington, 1987; assoc. mgr. Red Lobster Inns Am., Owensboro, Ky., 1987—. Mem. Nat. Assn. Female Execs., Grange (fellow). Republican. Presbyterian. Home: 155 Glen Gustin Rd Peebles OH 45660 Office: Red Lobster Inns Am 3410 Fredrica St Qwensboro KY 42301

SMALLWOOD, CAROL ANN, librarian, educator. BS, Ea. Mich. u., 1961; M in History, Ea. Mich. U., 1963; MLS, We. Mich. U., 1976. Tchr. Redford Union High Sch., Livonia, Mich., 1961-62, Flat Rock (Mich.) Jr. High Sch., 1963-64; grad. asst. We. Mich. U., Kalamazoo, 1975-76; librarian Kalamazoo Valley Community Coll., 1976, Grand Traverse (Mich.), Northland (Mich.) Library Systems, 1976-77, Pellston (Mich.) Pub. Schs., 1977—; asst. dir. Northland Library System, Alpena, Mich., 1977, developer, operator ednl. materials clearinghouse, 1981-83; columnist Detroit News, 1983-85; adult edn. tchr. Cheboygan Area Schs., 1985-86. Author: Free Mich. Materials for Educators, 1980, Exceptional Free Library Resource Materials, 1984, Librarians' and Teachers' Free Resource Builder, 1985, A Guide to Selected Federal Agency Programs and Publications for Librarians and Teachers, 1986, An Educational Guide to the National Park System, 1988, Health Resource Builder, 1988; contbr. articles to mags, profl. jours.; author software. Charter bd. mem. Cheboygan Arts Council, publicity chmn.; founder Cheboygan County Humane Soc.; active Hist. Soc., Band Boosters, others. Mem. ALA, NEA, NOW (humane edn. com.), Humane Soc. U.S., Pellston Edn. Assn., Internat. Soc. Animal Rights, Mich. Edn. Assn., Nat. Women Studies Assn., Cheboygan County Humane Soc. Home: 1359 Michigami Dr Cheboygan MI 49721 Office: Pellston High Sch Library 172 N Park Ave Pellston MI 49769

SMARIGA, LILLIAN ALLEN, accountant; b. Waco, Tex., Sept. 2, 1927; d. Homer Eugene and Lillian Louise (Smith) Allen; student U. Houston, 1964-65; m. Stanley Edward Smariga, Apr. 21, 1950; children—Robert, Melanie, Mary Hope, Russell. Bookkeeper, sec. Houston Carbide Corp., 1951-55; div. sec., bookkeeper, office mgr. Houston Carbide div. Firth Sterling, Inc., 1955-68; asst. to acctg. mgr. F. W. Gartner Co., Houston, 1968-70, asst. to acctg. mgr., office mgr., 1970-75, acctg. mgr., asst. sec.-treas., 1975—, controller, asst. sec.-treas., 1977—. Mem. Nat. Assn. Accts., Am. Soc. Women Accts. Republican. Episopalian. Home: 1605 Alabama St Pasadena TX 77503 Office: 3805 Lamar St Houston TX 77001

SMART, DIANE GREER, public relations executive; b. Cambridge, Mass., May 31, 1934; d. Don Swint and Charlotte Wedgwood (Mason) G.; m. Edward Prescott Williams, Sept. 5, 1956 (div. Aug. 1975); children: Charlene, Lauren, John; m. Paul William Smart, Feb. 17, 1979. BA, Smith Coll., Northampton, Mass., 1956. Asst. to dir. Taft Mus., Cin., 1964-66; dir. community affairs Contemporary Arts Ctr., Cin., 1970-72; dir. devel. and spl. projects Cin. Symphony Orch., 1975-80; cons. pub. events Smart Williams Assocs., Cin., 1980-84; dir. vol. services Boston Symphony Orch., 1984-86; assoc. dir. pub. relations Nat. Assn. Retired Fed. Employees, Washington, 1987—; cons. Ohio Arts Council, Columbus, 1979-84, Cin. Recreation Commn., 1980-84; commr. Georgetown Waterfront Arts Commn., Washington, 1987—; v.p. Customer Satisfaction, Inc., Washington, 1987—. editor/author Gift Catalogue, 1983. Co-founder, bd. dirs. Urban Appalachian Council, Cin., 1968-69; co-founder, chmn. Appalachian Festival, Cin., 1970-72; pres. Jr. League, Cin., 1973-75; bd. dirs. Taft Mus., Cin., 1982-84. Mem. Pub. Relations Soc. Am. Office: Nat Assn Retired Fed Employees 1533 New Hampshire Ave Washington DC 20036

SMART, DOROTHY CAROLINE, retired social worker; b. Osborn, Mo.; d. Allen A. and Caroline (Totzke) Smart; student U. Mo., 1929-30; A.B., U. Kans., 1937, M.S.W., 1950; postgrad. U. Chgo., 1963, 65. Advt. copy writer Emery Bird Thayer, Kansas City, Mo., 1937-38; case worker Dept. Pub. Welfare, Kansas City, 1938-44, Jackson County chpt. ARC, Kansas City, 1944-49; disaster rep. Am. Nat. Red Cross, St. Louis, 1950-59, home service rep. area office, 1959-65, regional dir. service mil. families, 1965-70, asst. area dir. service to mil. families, 1970-76. Mem. Group Action Council; bd. dirs. Barnes Hosp. Aux. Mem. Nat. Assn. Social Workers, Nat. Conf. Social Welfare, Women in Communications (pres. Kansas City alumni chpt. 1943), Am. Assn. Ret. Persons (pres.-elect 1988). Club: Pilot (St. Louis) (pres. 1975-77). Home: 4475 W Pine Blvd Apt 905 Saint Louis MO 63108

SMART, MARRIOTT WIECKHOFF, geologist, information specialist; b. Memphis, Aug. 26, 1935; d. Gerhard Emil and Beatrice (Flanegan) Wieckhoff; m. John A. Smart, May 9, 1959; children: Denise, Holly. BS in Geology, U. Tex.-Austin, 1957; M.L.S., U. Pitts., 1976. Geophysicist Mobil Corp., New Orleans, 1957-59; geologist Hanson Oil Co., Roswell, N.Mex., 1959-62; info. specialist Gulf Corp., Pitts., 1977-79, library mgr., Denver, 1979-84, library cons. team, Pitts., 1984; supr. Library-Info. Ctr., Amoco Minerals Co., Englewood, Colo., 1984; dir. Library-Info. Ctr., Cyprus Minerals Co., 1985—. Dist. chmn. Am. Cancer Soc., Arapahoe County, Colo., 1981-84; mem. choir Grace Presbyn. Ch., Littleton, Colo., 1979—; block worker Republican party, Arapahoe County, 1981—. Mem. Spl. Libraries Assn. (bull. bus. mgr. 1982, treas. petroleum and energy div. 1984-86, chmn. petroleum and energy div. 1987-88), Rocky Mountain Online Users Group, Geosci. Info. Soc., Engring. Info. Network, Women in Mining, Geosci. Energy Minerals Info. Specialists, Women in Mining, Alpha Chi Omega (career network coordinator 1984). Home: 3337 E Easter Pl Littleton CO 80122 Office: Cyprus Minerals Co 7200 S Alton Way Englewood CO 80112

SMART, MARY-LEIGH CALL (MRS. J. SCOTT SMART), farm operator, civic worker; b. Springfield, Ill., Feb. 27, 1917; d. S(amuel) Leigh and Mary (Bradish) Call; jr. coll. diploma Monticello Coll., 1934; student Oxford U., 1935; B.A., Wellesley Coll., 1937; M.A., Columbia U., 1939, postgrad., 1940-41; postgrad. N.Y. U., 1940-41; painting student with Bernard Karfiol, 1937-38; m. J. Scott Smart, Sept. 11, 1951 (dec. 1960). Dir. mgmt. Central Ill. Grain Farms, Logan County, 1939—; art collector, patron, publicist, 1954—; cons., 1970—; program dir., sec. bd. Barn Gallery Assos., Inc., 1958-69, pres., 1969-70, 82-87, asst. treas., 1987—, hon. dir., 1970-78; curator Hamilton Easter Field Art Found. Collection, 1978-79, curator exhbns., 1979-86; owner Lowtrek Kennel, 1957-73, Cove Studio Art Gallery, 1961-68 (all Ogunquit, Maine). Mem. acquisition com. DeCordova Mus., Lincoln, Mass., 1966-78; mem. chancellor's council U. Tex., 1972—, U. N.H., 1978—; bd. dirs. Ogunquit C. of C., 1966, treas. 1966-67, hon. life mem., 1968—; bd. overseers Strawbery Banke, Inc., Portsmouth, N.H., 1972-75, 3d vice chmn., 1973, 2d vice chmn., 1974; bd. advisors Univ. Art Galleries, U. N.H., 1973—, v.p., bd. overseers, 1974-81, pres., 1981—; bd. dirs. Old York Hist. and Improvement Soc., York, Maine, 1979-81, v.p., 1981-82; mem. adv. com. Bowdoin Coll. Mus. Art Invitational Exhibit, 1975, '76 Maine Artists Invitational Exhbn., Maine State Mus., Maine Coast Artists, Rockport, 1975-78, All Maine Biennial '79, Bowdoin Coll. Mus. Art juried exhbn.; mem. jury for scholarship awards Maine Com. for the Skowhegan Sch. Painting and Sculpture, 1982-84; mem. nat. com. Wellesley Coll. Friends of Art, 1983—; adv. trustee Portland Mus. Art, 1983-85, fellow, 1985—; mem. mus. panel Maine State Commn. on Arts and Humanities, 1983-86; mem. adv. com. Maine Biennial, Colby Coll. Mus. Art, 1983; mem. council advisors Farnsworth Library and Art Mus., Rockland, Maine, 1986—. Served to lt. jg. WAVES, 1942-45. Mem. Am. Fedn. Arts, Am. Assn. Museums, Mus. Modern Art, Springfield Art Assn., Boston Mus. Fine Arts, Solomon R. Guggenheim Mus., Whitney Mus. Am. Art., Jr. League of Springfield, Inst. Contemporary Art Boston (corporator 1965-73). Republican. Episcopalian. Club: Western Maine Wellesley. Editor: Hamilton Easter Field Art Found. Collection Catalog, 1966; originator, dir. show, compiler of catalog Art: Ogunquit, 1967; Peggy Bacon-A Celebration, Barn Gallery, Ogunquit, 1979. Address: Rural Rt 2 Box 381 York ME 03909

SMART, MELISSA BEDOR, environmental consultant company executive; b. St. Johnsbury, Vt., Mar. 5, 1953; d. Leslie Oscar and Helen Catherine (Kenney) Bedor; m. Glenn Robin Smart, Oct. 1, 1983; children: Catherine Jean, Jenny Laura. BS in Ecology and Environ. Conservation, U. N.H., 1975; MS in Water and Land Use Planning, SUNY, Syracuse, 1981. Environ. instr. NSF, Hooksett, N.H., 1975; environ. scientist, planner Parsons Brinckerhoff Quade & Douglas, Inc., Boston, 1976-78, sr. environ. scientist, planner, 1981-82; research asst. SUNY Coll. Environ. Sci. and Forestry, Syracuse, 1978-79; environ. planner St. Lawrence Eastern Ontario Commn., Watertown, N.Y., 1979; sr. environ. scientist, mktg. dir. VTN Consolidated, Inc., Boston, 1982-83; pres. The Smart Assocs., Inc., Contoocook, N.H., 1984—; water resource cons. Soc. Protection N.H. Forests, Concord, 1984—; water resource lectr. Harris Ctr. Conservation Edn., Hancock, N.H., 1985; mem. steering com. N.H. Rivers Campaign, Concord, 1986. Author: Directory of Water Testing Expertise in New Hampshire, 1985. Vol. Hopkinton (N.H.) Master Plan Com., 1986—; chair New Mem. Ministry, St. Paul's Ch., Concord, 1987. Am. Field Service scholar, Australia, 1970. Mem. Am. Water Resources Assn., Assn. State Wetland Mgrs. Democrat. Episcopalian. Clubs: St. Paul's Book, Fellowship. Home: Route 2 Box 7 Contoocook NH 03229 Office: The Smart Assocs Inc Route 2 Box 14 Contoocook NH 03229

SMATHERS, BARBARA, educational program director; b. Bridgeton, N.J., May 6, 1956; d. Elvira B. (Killian) Dixey. AS in Bus. Adminstrn., Salem Community Coll., Carneys Point, N.J., 1976; BBA, Glassboro State Coll., 1978. Prin. coordinator computer service Salem Community Coll., Carneys Point, N.J., 1978—, dir. MIS, System Adminstrn., 1986—; macrobiotic cons., reflexology practitioner, Swedish massager B&D Naturals, Pennsville, N.J.; coordinator, instr. Salem Community Coll. Computer Inst., adj. faculty staff. Mem. Internat. Acad. of Massage Sci., N.J. Coll. and U. Computer Ctr. Mgmt. Assn., Nat. Nutritional Foods Assn., Glassboro State Coll. Alumni Assn., Salem Community Coll. Alumni Assn. Baptist. Home: 68 E Pittsfield St Pennsville NJ 08070 Office: Salem Community Coll 460 Hollywood Ave Carneys Point NJ 08070

SMEAL, ELEANOR CUTRI, organization executive; b. Ashtabula, Ohio, July 30, 1939; d. Peter Anthony and Josephine E. (Agresti) Cutri; m. Charles R. Smeal, Apr. 27, 1963; children: Tod, Lori. B.A., Duke U., 1961; M.A., U. Fla., 1963. Mem. bd. Upper St. Clair (Pa.) chpt. LWV, 1968-72, sec.-treas. Allegheny County Council, 1971-72; mem. NOW, 1971—; convenor, 1st pres. S. Hills (Pa.) chpt. NOW, 1971-73, 1st pres., state coordinator, 1972-75; nat. bd. dirs. NOW, 1973-75, chairwoman bd., 1975-77, pres., 1977-82, 85-87, mem. bd. Legal Def. and Edn. Fund, 1975—, chairwoman ERA Strike Force, 1977—; mem. 1st nominating com., founding conf. Nat. Women's Polit. Caucus, 1971; bd. dirs. Allegheny County Women's Polit. Caucus, 1971-72; co-founder, bd. dirs. S. Hills NOW Day Nursery Sch., 1972—; mem. Nat. Commn., Observance of Internat. Women's Year, 1977; mem. exec. com. Leadership Conf. on Civil Rights, 1979—; mem. Nat. Adv. Com. on Women, 1978. Named One of 25 Most Influential Women in U.S. World Almanac, 1978. Office: Fund for Feminists Majority 8105 W 3rd St Los Angeles CA 90048 *

SMEDLEY, DELORIS KING, publishing executive; b. Tallulah, La., Aug. 17, 1949; d. Edward Moses and Ceal Jane (Goffner) King; m. Joseph William Smedley, June 30, 1984. BS, So. Ill. U., 1972; postgrad., Chgo. State U., 1975-76. Instr. math Chgo. Bd. Edn., 1972-77; software sales rep. Burrough Corp., Chgo., 1977-78; ednl. cons. Holt Rinehart and Winston, Chgo., 1978-82, sr. ednl. cons., 1982-86, regional mktg. mgr., 1986—. Mem. Chgo. Urban League, Nat. Assn. Female Execs., Profl. Women's Network (pres. 1986—). Democrat. Baptist. Home: 5471 S Hyde Park Blvd #10B Chicago IL 60615

SMEDRESMAN, INGEBORG FREUNDLICH, artist; b. Germany; came to U.S., 1937, naturalized, 1943; d. Paul and Erna Betty (Simon) Freundlich; B.S., U. Frankfurt, Germany, 1934; postgrad. in chemistry U. Zurich, Switzerland, 1934-37, art edn. Nat. Acad. Art Students League, Queens Coll; m. Sidney Smedresman, Aug. 10, 1937; children—Ingrid Braslow, Leonard C., Paulette Mehta, Suzanne van Oers. Art lectr. Forest Hills Jewish Center, 1966-68, Guggenheim Mus., 1973-76; art tchr. Queensboro Art Soc., 1969; art dir. Temple Beth El, Great Neck, L.I., 1969-75, YM-YWHA, Little Neck, 1975. One woman shows at Fine Arts Gallery, N.Y.C., 1970, Queens Coll., N.Y.C., summer 1975, 78, 81, 85, Harrison (N.Y.) Library, 1979, 80, Vleigh Place Library, 1984, Alley Pond Gallery, 1986, Alley Pond Eviron. Ctr., 1986; exhibited in group shows at ACA Gallery, 1959, Contemporary Art Gallery, 1965-66, Raymond Duncan Gallery, Paris, France, 1965-66, Ahda Arzt Gallery, N.Y.C., 1970, Ten Voorde Gallery, Amsterdam, 1973, Carrol Condit Gallery, White Plains N.Y., 1973, Westchester Art Soc., 1970-75; represented in permanent collections Godwin-Ternbach Mus. of Queens Coll., Pfizer Inc. Internat. Hdqrs., N.Y.C., City Hall, Moncton, N.B., Can., Israel Mus., Jerusalem; art instr. YM-YWHA, Flushing; lectr. Cooper-Hewitt Mus. Recipient art awards Paris Water Colors, 1965, 66, Suffolk County Artists, 1966, Queensboro Art Soc., 1975, 1st prize Westchester Art Soc., 1975. Mem. Art Students League N.Y. (life), Artists Equity Assn., Am. Chem. Soc. Home: 117-10 77th Rd Kew Garden Hills NY 11367

SMEENGE, LORI HASHIMOTO, nurse; b. San Francisco, Aug. 31, 1958; m. Jim Smeenge, Sept. 4, 1983. BS in Nursing, Loma Linda U., 1982. Nursing asst. Stanford U. Med. Ctr., Palo Alto, Calif., 1980-82; primary care staff nurse Loma Linda (Calif.) U. Med. Ctr., 1982-84; nursing dir. Quality Care Nursing Service, San Jose, Calif., 1984-85; pub. health nurse II Santa Clara County Health Dept., San Jose, 1985—, mem. various coms., 1986—; Counselor Health Promotion Program, San Jose, 1987; AIDS Lead Pub. Health Nurse Advisor, San Jose, 1987—. Mem. Am. Pub. Health Assn., Adventist Women's Assn., TZ Assocs. Democrat. Seventh-Day Adventist.

Home: 442 Sobrato Dr Campbell CA 95008 Office: Narvaez Pub Health Nursing 614 Tully Rd San Jose CA 95111

SMELKINSON, LYNN MARIE, lawyer; b. Washington, May 4, 1955; d. Reuben and Kay (Rosenthal) S. BS, George Washington U., 1978; JD, U. San Francisco, 1981. Bar: Calif. 1982, N.Y. 1983, D.C. 1985, U.S. Supreme Ct. 1985. Research assoc. EPA, Washington, 1979; law clk. U.S. Atty's Office, San Francisco, 1980, Santa Rosa (Calif.) Mcpl. Ct., 1981; assoc. Roth & Ishida, Oakland, Calif., 1982; atty. Legal Facilities Mgmt., N.Y.C., 1983—; sr. counsel U.S. C. of C., Washington; legis. analyst Queen's Bench, San Francisco, 1982; legal advisor Washington Counsel for Progressive Radio, 1983. Mediator community bds., San Francisco, 1982; arbitrator Better Bus. Bur., San Francisco, 1982; publicist Bay Area Lawyers for Arts, San Francisco, 1982; vol. Washington Humane Soc. Mem. ABA, N.Y. State Bar Assn., Calif. Bar Assn., D.C. Bar Assn. (co-chmn. computer contract com.), Am. Corp. Counsel Assn. (co-chmn. intellectual property com.). Club: Toastmasters (adminstrv. v.p., Washington br.). Home: 3239 N St NW Washington DC 20007

SMELKINSON, MARSHA ELLEN, marketing executive; b. Balt., Dec. 29, 1948; d. Isadore I. and Florence L. (Ruben) S. BS magna cum laude, Syracuse U., 1970. Copywriter The Rouse Co., Columbia, Md., 1970-71; assoc. publicist, dir. pubs. AAU, Indpls., 1971-73; dir. pub. relations, advt. Palmetto Dunes Resort, Hilton Head, S.C., 1974-78; pres. Smelkinson, Cerrati and Co., Hilton Head, 1978-85; mng. dir. William R. Biggs/Gilmore Assocs., Hilton Head, 1986; v.p. mktg. Seinsheimer Cos., Hilton Head, 1987-88, CAT Sports, Inc., Encinitas, Calif., 1988—; pres. MS, Inc., Hilton Head, 1968—. Editor: AAU News, AAU Yearbook, 1971-73. Democrat. Jewish. Club: Long Cove (Hilton Head), Melrose (Hilton Head).

SMELSER, BONNIE JEAN, biochemical engineer, consultant; b. Niagara Falls, N.Y., Jan. 19, 1953; d. William Henry and Betty J. (Procter) Williams; m. David Paul Smelser, Apr. 10, 1976 (div. 1987); 1 child, David William. BS in Chemistry, U. Del., Newark, 1976, BS in Chem. Engring., 1976; MBA, Ind. State U., 1981. Process supr. Pfizer, Inc., Terre Haute, Ind., 1975-77; prodn. supr. Pfizer, Inc., 1977-80, sr. devel. supr., 1981; sr. control systems engr. Fluor, Inc., Irvine, Calif., 1981-85; sr. biochem. engr. Fluor, Inc., Irvine, 1985-86; prin. biochem. engr. Fluor, Inc., 1986—; acct. Zettleband Printing, Santa Ana, Calif., 1983-85; owner Zettleband Printing, 1985-86. Mem. Am. Inst. Chem. Engrs., Nat. Assn. Female Execs., Marinita Town Home Assn. (sec. 1983, 84), Beta Gamma Sigma. Club: Summit (Irvine). Home: 144 E Yale Loop Irvine CA 92714 Office: Flour Daniel Inc 3333 Michelson Irvine CA 92730

SMELTZER, MARY SUSAN, pianist, composer; b. Sapulpa, Okla., Sept. 13, 1941; d. Frank Cecil and Mary Margaret (Robertson) S.; MusB (scholar), Oklahoma City U., 1964, MusM magna cum laude, U. So. Calif., 1969; postgrad. (Fulbright scholar) Akademie fur Musik, Vienna, 1969-70; master class with Gregor Piatigorsky, Los Angeles, Rosina Lhevinne, Los Angeles; m. Philip S. Snyder, June 14, 1973. Pvt. tchr. music, Sapulpa, Okla., 1956-62, Los Angeles, 1964-72; instr. piano Oklahoma City U., 1961-64, Holy Name Convent, Los Angeles, 1964-65, Valley Conservatory Music, Studio City, Calif., 1965-66, First Congl. Ch., Los Angeles, 1966-67, Mt. St. Mary's Coll., Los Angeles, 1966-69, 70-72; vis. piano faculty mem. Rice U., Houston, 1972-73; profl. accompanist U. Houston, 1972-73; artist-in-residence, instr. humanities Coll. of Mainland, Texas City, Tex., 1972-79; organist various chs., Okla., Calif., 1957-71; profl. accompanist throughout midwest, 1961-64, Los Angeles area, 1964-72, Houston, 1972—; performed with chamber groups, Los Angeles area, 1964-69, 70-72; Carnegie Recital Hall debut, 1975, European debut Brahmssaal, Vienna; numerous orchestral appearances; composer: Reverie, 1962, Kaleidescope, 1968, Twelve Mood Pictures (variations for piano on theme of Yankee Doodle and the interval sets 1-9-7-6:1-7-7-6), 1975, The Bald Eagle March, 1979, Psalm 121 (for choir and orch.), 1979, An American Tribue For A Royal Marriage, 1982; author: Selected Orchestrations of Poetic Expressions, 1981. Recipient numerous awards including Bloch Young Artist award Ladies Music Club, 1962, award Nat. Fedn. Music Clubs, 1962, Okla. Music Tchrs. Assn., 1962. Fellow Internat. Biog. Assn., Internat. Acad. Poets, Sigma Alpha Iota; mem. Internat. League Women Composers, Am. Women Composers, Nat. Guild Piano Tchrs. (judging staff), Chamber Music Am., Broadcast Music Inc., Pi Kappa Lambda. Democrat. Baptist. Club: Tuesday Musica. Avocations: art, poetry, geneology, medicine. Home: 8102 Tavenor St Houston TX 77075

SMETANA, E. BETH SEIDMAN, consulting company manager; b. Chgo., Nov. 23, 1941; d. Lawrence J. and Ann (Masin) Seidman; m. Gerard C. Smetana, Apr. 17, 1966; children—Susannah, Frederick. Student L'Institut des Etudes Politiques, Paris, 1961-62; B.A., Sarah Lawrence Coll., 1963; M.S. in Journalism, Northwestern U., 1965; postgrad. Loyola U., Chgo., 1974-78. C.P.A., Ill. Reporter, copy editor Hollister Publs., Wilmette, Ill., 1966-68; asst. editor The Trib, Chgo. Tribune, 1965-66; staff acct. Arthur Young & Co., Chgo., 1978-80; cash mgr. Electrographic Corp., Chgo., 1980-81; treasury mgr. A.T. Kearney, Inc., Chgo., 1981—. Rep. for Sarah Lawrence Coll., Coll. Bd. of Chgo., 1972-75; mem. alumni bd. Francis W. Parker Sch., Chgo., 1973—. Mem. Am. Inst. C.P.A.s, Ill. Soc. C.P.A.s, Women in Communications, Alliance Francaise, Beta Alpha Psi. Clubs: Chgo. Press, River, Casino. Office: A T Kearney Inc 222 S Riverside Plaza Chicago IL 60606

SMILEY, CLEERETTA HENDERSON, educator, home economist; b. Whatley, Ala., June 20, 1930; d. Edward and Rebecca Ann (Odom) Henderson; B.S., Miles Coll., 1954; M.S., U. Md., 1971, postgrad., 1972-73; diploma esoteric sci. and psychology Am. U., 1976; children—Consuela Angelia, Robert Edward, Lisa Kay, Joan Alyssa. Correctional officer Fed. Reformatory for Women, Alderson, W.Va., 1954-55, culinary officer, 1955-56, tchr. home econs., 1956-61, asst. vocat. ednl. dir., 1959-61; tchr. gen. home econs. edn. D.C. Public Schs., 1963-80, asst. supervising dir. home econs., 1980-84, dir. Model HERO Youth Employment Tng. Program, Coolidge Sr. High Sch., 1975-80; state adv. for D.C., Future Homemakers Am./HERO, 1980-84; dir. Network of Light, Lorton Transformation Project; condr. fashion shows, model; tchr. coordinator Show Prodns. Tng. Program, 1967-80; mem. Home Econs. Adv. Council, D.C. Public Schs. and Logan Community Sch. Adv. Council; practitioner esoteric sci. Minority affairs adv. to bd. dirs. Social Services Agy., Eastern region Ch. Jesus Christ of Latter-day Saints, 1979-82, stake missionary, edn. counselor Relief Soc., ward missionary, gospel essentials tchr., ward activities com.; mem. hosting com. Public Communications Council, Kensington, Md., 1979-81; co-chairperson Health Commn., D.C. PUSH, 1979-80; bd. dirs. Aum Spiritual Sci. Ctr., Washington, 1980-82; mem. First Spiritual Leadership Conf. Network Leaders, McLean, Va., 1981; mem. family and futures bd. dirs. of FHA; mem. Worldwide Peace Found, Washingon Peace Movement, Friends Kennedy Ctr.; sr. fellow John F. Kennedy Library Found. Named Mrs. D.C., Mrs. America Pageant, 1968, Mrs. D.C. Savs. Bonds, 1968; Harambee Mother of Yr., Sta. WDVM-TV, 1969. Mem. Am. Vocat. Edn. Assn., D.C. Vocat. Edn. Assn., Future Homemakers Am. Home Econs. Related Occupations Youth Orgn., Nat. Assn. Black Am. Vocat. Educators (life), Am. Assn. Retired Persons, Nat. Collaboration of Youth Orgns., Nat. Assn. Female Execs., World Modeling Assn., Afro Am. Jubilee Commn., Am. Meta-Phys. Inst. Network Soc., Nat. Assn. Single Persons, Inst. Noetic Sci., Internat. Platform Assn., Nat. Hist. Preservation Soc., Brigham Young U. Mgmt. Soc., Iota Phi Lambda. Democrat. Club: Circle I Am. Lodges: Order Eastern Star, Majestic Eagles Inc. (internat. program devel.). Home: 2209 Ross Rd Silver Spring MD 20910

SMILEY, KAREN JANE, computer software engineer; b. New Kensington, Pa., Jan. 25, 1961; d. Paul Cornelius and Maureen Frances (Gross) S. BS in Indsl. Engring. and Ops. Research summa cum laude, U. Pitts., 1982; MS in Computer Sci., Stevens Inst. Tech., 1987. Engring. intern Armco Inc., Butler, Pa., 1980; research asst. Health Ops. Research Group, U. Pitts., 1981-82; computer software engr. Singer Kearfott, Little Falls, N.J., 1982—. Richard King Mellon Found. scholar, 1979-82, Armco, Inc. scholar, 1979-82. Mem. Nat. Assn. Female Execs., Tau Beta Pi (pres. chpt. 1982). Avocations: reading, knitting, photography, cooking, bicycling. Office: Singer Kearfott Mail Code 1DA73 1150 McBride Ave Little Falls NJ 07424

SMILIE, MOLLIE KAY WILLIAMS, accountant, educator; b. Bradford, Pa., Aug. 11, 1949; d. Albert Franklin and Martha Rae (Moore) Williams; m. Christopher Stephen Arthur, Sept. 11, 1969 (div. Apr. 1976); 1 child, Erik Ian; m. Michael Steven Smilie, May 9, 1980. B.S., Colo. State U., 1979. C.P.A., Colo. Staff acct. Cady & Co., Fort Collins, Colo., 1979-80, Colo. State U., Fort Collins, 1980-81, asst. to controller, 1981-83, controller, 1983—; lectr. in field; mgmt. cons. Research Inst. of Colo., Fort Collins, 1985—; bd. dirs. Open Stage Inc., Ft. Collins. Dem. Precinct Chmn. Larimer County, Fort Collins, 1978; bd. dirs. Larimer County Boy Scouts Am., Fort Collins, 1979; bd. dirs. Colo. Com. on Acctg. Standards for Higher Edn., Denver, 1983—. Mem. Am. Inst. C.P.A.s, Colo. Soc. C.P.A.s, Nat. Assn. Coll. and Univ. Bus. Officers, Council on Govtl. Relations, Beta Alpha Psi. Republican. Unitarian. Avocations: acting; writing; horseback riding; skiing; travel. Home: 3509 N County Rd 23E LaPorte CO 80535 Office: Colo State U 202E Johnson Hall Fort Collins CO 80523

SMIRNOW, DIANE ELAINE, graphic designer; b. Nashville, Sept. 7, 1947; d. Edwin Harold and Bettye Anne (Hersh) S. BFA, Columbus Coll. Art and Design, 1970. Art dir. The Creative Dept., Inc., Atlanta, 1970-74; graphic designer/art dir. Silver Spring, Md., 1975—; co-dir. Aquarian Ankh Tour Groups, Brewster, N.Y., 1982—; owner, designer The Light Hearted Press, Silver Spring, 1982—. Recipient award for Excellence, Nat. Paper Box Packaging Assn., 1986, 87.

SMITH, ALICE ELIZABETH SWILLEY, hospital services executive, consultant, clinical educator; b. Coral Gables, Fla., Sept. 24, 1948; d. Thomas and Alva (Zebendon) Swilley; m. Philip Edward Smith, June 26, 1971, 1 child, Eve Elizabeth. Cert. elementaire Le Cordon Bleu, Paris, 1969; B.A. in Home Econs., The Western Coll., 1970; postgrad. U. Dayton, 1972-73; dietetic intern Miami Valley Hosp., Dayton, Ohio, 1973-74; M.S. in Nutrition, No. Ill. U., 1978. Tchr. Miami Dade Jr. High, Opa Locka, Fla., 1970-71; food service coordinator Mercy Med. Ctr., Springfield, Ohio 1972-73; pub. health nutritionist Chgo. Bd. Health, 1974-78; assoc. dir. clin. dietetics Children's Meml. Hosp., Chgo., 1980-84, asst. clin. prof. U. Ill., Chgo., 1983—; dir. clin. dietetics Children's Meml. Hosp., Chgo., 1985—; liaison rep. Am. Acad. Pediatrics Com. on Nutrition, Am. Dietetic Assn., Chgo., 1981—. Contbr. articles to profl. jours. Vol. 8th Day Ctr. for Justice, Chgo., 1976-77. Grantee Mead Johnson Nutritional Co., 1983-88, Ross Labs, 1987-88. Mem. Am. Dietetic Assn., AAAS, Clin. Nutrition Mgmt. Practice Group (newsletter editor, 1983-84), Chgo. Dietetic Assn., Am. Soc. Parenteral and Enteral Nutrition, Dietitians in Pediatric Practice. Avocations: Creative cookery, indoor gardening. Office: Children's Meml Hosp 2300 Children's Plaza Chicago IL 60614

SMITH, ALISON J(ANN) DOCOS, management and marketing consultant; b. Syracuse, N.Y., Apr. 27, 1950; d. Andre S. Docos and Aurise P. (Coté) Fey. BA, Skidmore Coll., 1972; MBA, Coll. William and Mary, 1978. Corp. banking account mgr. Swiss Bank Corp., N.Y.C., 1979-81; asst. product mgr. Colgate-Palmolive Co., N.Y.C., 1981-83; mktg. dir. Schwab and Twitty Architects, Palm Beach, Fla., 1984-85; founder, pres. AJS Cons., Inc., Palm Beach, 1986—. Pub. William and Mary Bus. Rev., 1978. Mem. Nat. Trust for Hist. Preservation; trustee Hist. Palm Beach County Preservation Bd., Boca Raton, Fla., 1984—. Mem. Exec. Women of the Palm Beaches, Jr. League, French-Am. C. of C., English Speaking Union. Republican. Roman Catholic. Office: AJS Consulting Inc PO Box 1056 Palm Beach FL 33480

SMITH, ALISON VERONICA, sales executive; b. Wyandotte, Mich., Aug. 15, 1959; d. Stewart Gene and Veronica Lucille (Latta) S. BBA, U. Mich., 1981. Sales rep. Procter & Gamble, Cleve., 1981-83; dist. field rep. Procter & Gamble, St. Louis, 1983-84; unit mgr. Procter & Gamble, Mpls., 1984-87; dist. mgr. Richardson-Vicks subs. Procter & Gamble, Dallas, 1987—. Mem. Nat. Assn. Female Execs. Republican. Roman Catholic. Avocation: golf. Home and Office: 2024 Carillon Ln Carrollton TX 75007

SMITH, ALLISON BARBARA, medical education administrator; b. Natick, Mass., Feb. 9, 1962; d. Donald and Patricia Ann (Hatje) Shapiro; m. Blake DeVor Smith, Feb. 3, 1963. BA in Psychology, U. Mich., 1984; postgrad., Katharine Gibbs, 1984. Research sec. III U. Mich. Hosp., Ann Arbor, Mich., 1984-87, asst. dir., 1987—. Contbr. articles to profl. jours. Mem. Am. Med. Assn., Nat. Assn. Anorexia Nervosa and Associated Disorders, Ctr. for Eating Disorders lectr. speakers bur., counselor 1986—). Club: Living Well (Ann Arbor) (instr.). Office: U Mich Hosp 3100 Taubman Ctr Box 0368 1500 E Med Ctr Dr Ann Arbor MI 48109

SMITH, ANN MARIE, brokerage house executive; b. Phila., Nov. 3, 1960; d. Fred Nelson and Anna Marie (Garson) S. Student, Gettysburg Coll., 1978-79, Eastern Coll., 1981-83, W. Chester U., 1983-85. Registered rep. Shearson, Lehman and Hutton, Strafford, Pa., 1987—. Mem. Nat. Assn. Female Execs. Democrat.

SMITH, ARLETTE THÉRÈSE, social worker; b. Nashville, May 24, 1958; d. Robert Peter and Arlette Marie (Carlton) S. BA in Psychology cum laude, Boston U., 1979, MSW and MA in Afro-Am. Studies, 1982. Lic. social worker, Mass. Milieu counselor Kennedy Meml. Hosp. Children, Boston, 1979-82; social worker protective service Roxbury Children's Service, Boston, 1982-83; high sch. guidance counselor McKinley Vocat. High Sch., Boston, 1983-86; social worker foster care Children's Home Soc., San Francisco, 1986—. Mem. Nat. Assn. Social Workers. Roman Catholic. Office: Children's Home Soc 3000 California St San Francisco CA 94115

SMITH, AUDREY STEELE, realtor; b. Manassas, Va., Dec. 8, 1908; d. Jacob Harvey and Elizabeth (Barrett) Steele; m. Holmes Harden Smith, June 1, 1934 (dec. Nov. 1977), Holmes Steele, Patricia Marshall Juliano. BS in Edn., Mary Washington Coll., 1931; MA in Bus. Edn., NYU, 1935; postgrad., Va. Poly. Inst., 1979-82. Lic. realtor, Va. Prin. Front Royal (Va.) Bus. Coll., 1932-36; head bus. machines dept. Smithdeal Bus. Coll., Richmond, Va., 1936-38; sec., treas. Holmes H. Smith, Inc., Richmond, Va., 1952—; owner, pres. Harden Realty Co., Richmond, 1950—; sec., treas. Steele Properties, Manassas, Va., 1979—. Mem. Manassas Mus., 1984, Manassas Mus., 1984—; mem. visitation com. Annaburg Manor Nursing Home, 1985—. Mem. Prince William Bd. Realtors (mem. com. 1978—, comml., indsl., land exchange com. 1978—), Am. Assn. Univ. Women, Greater MAnassas C. of C. Republican. Mehtodist. Lodge: United Daughters of Confederacy. Home and Office: 9708 Main St Manassas VA 22110

SMITH, BARBARA ANN, accountant, tax consultant; b. Dallas, May 6, 1935; d. George Jefferson and Ina Pearl (Nowlin) Gardner; Asso. Mid. Mgmt., Mountain View Jr. Coll., 1975; 1 dau., Cynthia Marie Dixon. Asst. cashier U.S. Rubber Co., Dallas, 1954-57; sec.-treas. Am. Graphics Co., Dallas, 1974-79; pres. Am. Way Credit Union, Dallas, 1974-76; sec.-treas. Am. Legal Printing Co., Dallas, 1964-79, Abco Inc., Dallas, 1964-79, Am. Poster & Printing Co., Dallas, 1964-79; asst. sec.-treas. Am. Equity Press Inc., Dallas, 1974-79; prin. MS Services, Dallas, 1979—v.p. Brainstorm, Inc., Dallas, 1984-86; pres. Body Telesis, Inc., 1987, v.p. Staffelback Designs Inc., 1988—. Republican. Home: 3515 Brown St Apt 109 Dallas TX 75219 Office: 2525 Carlisle Dallas TX 75201

SMITH, BARBARA ANNE, corporate administrator; b. N.Y.C., Oct. 10, 1936; d. John Allen and Lelia Maria (De Silva) Santoro; m. Joseph Newton Smith, Feb. 5, 1956 (div. Sept. 1984); children: J. Michael, Robert Lawrence. BS, Oceanside/Carlsbad Coll., 1956. Real estate agt. Routh Robbins, Inc., Washington, 1973-75; gen. mgr. Mall Shops, Inc., Kansas City, Kans., 1975-80; regional mgr. FAO Schwarz, N.Y.C., 1980-84; clin. adminstr. North Denver Med. Ctr., Thornton, Colo., 1984—; bd. dirs. Franz Carl Weber Internat., Geneva, 1982-84. Pres. Am. Women Chile, 1968; v.p. Oak Park Assn., Kansas City, 1977-78, pres., 1978-79. Mem. Nat. Assn. Female Execs., Network Colo., Profl. Bus. Women Assn. Home: 1551 Larimer St Denver CO 80202

SMITH, BARBARA GAIL, economist; b. Phoenix, June 6, 1957; d. Loren Leonard Smith and Geneva May (Gabbert) Hewlett. BS in Environ. Sci., Grand Canyon Coll., 1979; postgrad., Ariz. State U. Power supply analyst Ariz. Pub. Service, Phoenix, 1981-84, rate devel. analyst, 1984-86, regulatory economist, 1986—; team supr. RGIS Inventory Services, 1981-83, Phoenix, tng. cons., 1982-85; profl. pianist, Phoenix, 1976—; free lance arranger, Phoenix, 1981—. Vol. Nat. Cancer Soc., Nat. Red Cross. Named Girl of the Yr. Ariz. Red Cross, 1974, one of Outstanding Young Women Am., 1979. Mem. Nat. Assn. Female Execs., Ariz. Bus. Women's Assn., Alpha Chi. Republican. Baptist. Home: 501 W Pontiac #7 Phoenix AZ 85027 Office: 411 N Central Ave Phoenix AZ 85003

SMITH, BARBARA JEANNE, library administrator; b. Jersey Shore, Pa., Apr. 14, 1939; d. Moyer Emerson and Mary Kathryn (Ebner) S. BS, Pa. State U., 1961; MS, SUNY, Oswego, 1967; MLS, U. Pitts., 1970; DEd, Pa. State U., 1981. Cert. secondary sch. tchr. Tchr. Binghamton (N.Y.) Sch. Dist., 1961-62, North Syracuse (N.Y.) Cen. Schs., 1962-69; reference librarian Pa. State Libraries, University Park, 1970-75, dept. head, 1975-82, asst. dean., 1982—; grad. faculty, prof. edn. Pa. State U., University Park, 1984—; regional dir. U.S. Newspaper Project/NEH, University Park, 1985-87. Contbr. articles to profl. jours. Life mem. Centre County Hist. Soc., State Coll., Pa., 1975—; mem. Friends of the Mus., State Coll., 1975—; bd. dirs. Georgetown Homeowners Assn., State Coll., 1975-82; trustee Pitts. Regional Library Center, 1978—. UCLA sr. fellow, 1982. Mem. ALA (councilperson 1988—), Assn. Coll. and Research Libraries (chair com. on standards and accreditation 1984-86), Pa. Library Assn. (various offices 1976—), AAUW, Phi Delta Kappa. Republican. Office: Pa State Libraries E 505 Pattee Library University Park PA 16802

SMITH, BARBARA JOYCE, quality assurance manager, consultant; b. Pasadena, Calif., Feb. 25, 1954; d. Philip L. and Barbar J. (Douglass) S. BS in Med. Records Adminstrn., York Coll. of Pa., 1977. Cert. profl. in quality assurance. Quality assurance mgr. The Consortium, Phila., 1980-86; pres. Quality Assurance Resources, Phila., 1984—. Mem. Nat. Assn. Female Execs., Nat. Assn. Quality Assurance Profls., Southeastern Pa. Assn. Quality Assurance Profls. Office: Quality Assurance Resources Ltd 1530 Locust St Suite 161 Philadelphia PA 19102

SMITH, BARBARA JOYCE, restaurant executive, entrepreneur; b. Hahira, Ga., May 23, 1947; d. Silas E. Reaves and Lovelle C. (Coppage) Reaves; children: Jon, Jennifer; m. A. Robert Vetrone, Feb. 8, 1987. Student, Valdosta (Ga.) State Coll., 1965-67; BS in Edn., U. Guam, 1971. From sales rep. to gen. mgr. Griswold Vending, Mpls., 1974-80; owner, pres. Vending Services, Inc., Eau Claire, Wis., 1980-85; pres. Vending Services Rochester, Inc., Minn., 1981-83; owner Exec. Services, Inc., Mpls., 1984-85; owner, pres. B. J. Tweed's, Eau Claire, 1985—; Presenter, chairperson workshops. Bd. dirs. YMCA, Eau Claire, 1987—, Kinship, Eau Claire, 1987—, United Way, Eau Claire, 1987—. Named SBA Women In Bus. Advocate, Wis., 1986. Mem. Wis. Women's Bus. Coalition, Eau Claire Women's Network, Eau Claire C. of C. Republican. Baptist. Home: 120 Country Club Ln Altoona WI 54720 Office: B J Tweed's Inc 2903 Hendrickson Dr Eau Claire WI 54701

SMITH, BARBARA LYNN, nurse; b. Highland Park, Ill., Feb. 27, 1953; d. Alan Roderick and Elisabeth (Knauer) S.; m. William F. Bolte, July 16, 1977 (div. Jan. 1983). AA, Kendall Coll., Evanston, Ill., 1973; BS in Nursing, Rush U., Chgo., 1976; MSN, U. San Diego, 1988. RN, family practitioner; cert. pub. health nurse. Nurse Rush Presbyn. St. Lukes Med. Ctr., Chgo., 1976-81; clin. specialist Alvarado Community Hosp., San Diego, 1981-83; unit supr. Scripps Meml. Hosp., La Jolla, Calif., 1983-85, staff nurse, 1985—. Mem. San Diego Nurse Practitioners, Calif. Coalitian Nurse Practitioners, Oncology Nursing Soc., Am. Assn. Critical Care Nurses, Nat. Assn. Female Execs., Sigma Theta Tau. Republican. Methodist. Clubs: Golden Retriever of Am., Golden Retriever of San Diego. Office: Scripps Meml Hosp 9888 Genesee Ave La Jolla CA 92038

SMITH, BETTE BELLE, banker, civic worker; b. Modesto, Calif., Jan. 17, 1921; d. James Alfred and Maysel Elizabeth (Hughes) Anderson; A.A., Modesto Jr. Coll., 1939; B.A., UCLA, 1941; m. Jean T. Smith, May 4, 1945; children—Talbott Anderson, Timothy Melton and Mary Margaret (twins). Vice pres., bank relations officer, asst. corp. sec. Modesto Banking Co., 1979—. Mem. Modesto Culture Commn., 1979-85, bd. dirs.; mem. Greater Modesto Found.; former mem. Muir Trail council Girl Scouts U.S.A.; former v.p. Stanislaus County Drug Abuse Coordinating Council; bd. dirs. United Crusade, 1969-72; organizing bd., v.p. McHenry Mus. Soc.; organizing bd. pres. McHenry Mus. Guild, 1979; mem. Calif. Republican Central Com., 1970-74; v.p. Modesto Rep. Women; pres. Modesto Jr. Coll. Alumni Found., 1977-80; organizing bd. Gt. Valley Mus.; mem. Stanislaus County Hist. Soc.; past pres. PTAs, hon. service award; former leader Cub Scouts, Brownies, Jr. Girl Scouts U.S.A.; grand pres. Omega Nu, 1954; pres. 50 Plus Club of Stanislaus County; bd. dirs. Downtown Modesto Assn., Modesto Symphony Orch., Friends of Music, Modesto Arts Adv. Council; chairperson Stanislaus County Fair Bd., 1984—; mem. Modesto City Beautification Com.; chmn. May Clean Up Month; mem. Charter Rev. Com., 1970; chmn. sr. citizen sect. Progress Greater Modesto Com.; parade chmn. All Am. City Com.; dist. rep. Stanislaus County internat. intercultural scholarship program Am. Field Service, 1961—; mem. sponsor com. Stanislaus County 4-H Club. Named Woman of Yr., Soroptimist Internat., 1958, One of 10 Outstanding Women of Yr., Stanislaus County Commn. on Women; recipient Loyalty Day award VFW, 1979, Liberty Bell award Stanislaus County Bar Assn., 1980, Calif. Parks and Recreation Soc. award, 1986. Club: Soroptimist (hon.). Home: 415 Sycamore St Modesto CA 95354 Office: 1120 11th St Modesto CA 95354

SMITH, BETTY DENNY, county official, civic worker, fashion exec.; Centralia, Ill., Nov. 12, 1932; d. Otto and Ferne Elizabeth (Beier) Hasenfuss; student U. Ill., 1950-52, Los Angeles City Coll., 1953-57, UCLA, 1965, U. San Francisco, 1982-84; m. Peter S. Smith, Dec. 5, 1964; children—Carla Kip, Bruce Kimball. Free-lance fashion coordinator, Los Angeles and N.Y.C., 1953-58; instr. fashion Rita LeRoy Internat. Studios, 1959-60; mgr. Mo Nadler Fashions, Los Angeles, 1961-64; showroom dir. Jean of Calif. Fashions, Los Angeles, 1966—; staff writer Valley Citizen News, 1963; free-lance polit. book reviewer community newspapers, 1961-62. Bd. dirs. Pet Assistance Found., 1969-76; founder, pres., dir. Vol. Services to Animals of Los Angeles, 1972-76; mem. County Com. to Discuss Animals in Research, 1973-74; mem. blue ribbon com. on animal control Los Angeles County, 1973-74; dir. Los Angeles County Animal Care and Control, 1976-82, ind. legis. advocate for humane causes, 1969—; mem. State of Calif. Animal Health Technician Exam. Com., 1975—, chmn., 1979; chief fin. officer Coalition for Pet Population Control, 1987-88; dir. West Coast regional office Am. Humane Assn., 1988—; bd. dirs. Am. Soc. for Prevention of Cruelty to Animals, 1984—. Mem. exec. com. Rep. State Cen. Com., 1971-72; mem. Calif. Rep. Cen. Com., 1964-72; mem. Rep. Los Angeles County Cen. Com., 1964-70, mem. exec. com., 1966-70; chmn. 29th Congl. Central Com., 1969-70; sec. 28th Senatorial Central Com., 1967-68, 45th Assembly Dist. Central Com., 1965-66; mem. speakers bur. George Murphy for U.S. Senate, 1970; campaign mgr. Los Angeles County for Spencer Williams for Atty. Gen., 1966. Mem. Lawyers Wives San Gabriel Valley (dir. 1971-74, pres. 1972-73), Mannequins Assn. (dir. 1967-68), Internat. Platform Assn., Delta Gamma, Pi Phi Theta. Clubs: Los Angeles Athletic, Town Hall. Home: 1766 Bluffhill Dr Monterey Park CA 91754

SMITH, BETTY LEE, international conference planner, consultant; b. Mt. Airy, N.C., Oct. 26, 1938; d. Robert Otis and Edna Onedia (Harman) Smith. BA in English, Longwood Coll., 1959; MRE, So. Bapt. Theol. Sem., 1962. Dir. religious activities Va. Intermont Coll., Bristol, 1961-66; asst. sec. for conf. and youth work, 1st woman exec. Bapt. World Alliance, Washington, 1966-81; dir. confs. Am. Soc. for Tng. and Devel., Washington, 1981-82, dir. conf. services, 1986—; corp. meeting planner Mars, Inc., McLean, Va., 1983-86. Vol. Bristol Community Hosp., 1964-66, Alexandria (Va.) Hosp., 1967, 86—. Mem. Prost-Profl. Women in Travel (treas. 1979), Am. Soc. for Assn. Execs., Pacific Area Travel Assn., Washington Soc. Assn. Execs., Meeting Planners Internat. Avocations: music, oil painting, reading, travel, swimming. Home: 5055 Seminary Rd Apt 333 Alexandria VA 22311 Office: ASTD 1630 Duke St Alexandria VA 22313

SMITH, BETTY LORETTA, artist; b. Tulare, Calif., Feb. 2, 1937; d. Arthur L. and Mary Alice (Etier) Thweatt; m. Harry T. Webb (div. 1968); 1 child, Margo V. Moon; widowed; 1 child, Betty Josephine Alexandra. Pink lady Fallbrook (Calif.) Hosp. Auxiliary, 1980—; leader Girl Scouts, Fallbrook, 1985—; trustee, dir. M.J. Smith Trust, San Diego, 1980—; vol. Presdl.

Task Force, Washington, 1983-86. Charter mem. Nat. Orgn. Female Execs. Republican.

SMITH, BETTY LOUISE, financial group executive; b. Coplay, Pa., May 15, 1940; d. Henry Fuhlburg and Marian Alta (Ward) Schaadt; m. Robert W. Perry, Nov. 14, 1966 (div. 1971). Student Stevens Finishing Sch., Indpls., 1960-62. Asst. to pres. Snelling & Snelling, Indpls., 1966-71; adminstrv. asst. R. E. Siss & Assocs., Indpls., 1971-72; exec. officer, v.p. Yegen Holdings Corp.-Integrity Fin. Group, Paramus, N.J., 1972—; pres. Synetics, Inc., Paramus, N.J., 1968. . Bd. dirs. Mid-Bergen Community Mental Health Ctr., Paramus, N.J. Mem. Am. Mgmt. Assn., Nat. Assn. Female Execs., Am. Soc. Personnel Adminstrs., Bergen County C. of C. Republican. Presbyterian. Office: Yegen Holdings Corp-Integrity Fin Group Mack Centre Dr Paramus NJ 07652

SMITH, BILLIE NELL BRYSON, nurse; b. Linden, Tenn., May 29, 1933; d. Barney Lee and Julia Mae (Hufstedler) Bryson; grad. St. Thomas Sch. Nursing, Nashville, 1955; m. Lee Garry Smith, Aug. 20, 1960; children—Lee Garry. Office nurse for Drs. G.H. Turner and B.L. Holladay, Linden, Tenn., 1955-56; dir. nursing Perry County Hosp., Linden, 1956-80, inservice dir., 1956-80; staff nurse, charge nurse Perry Meml. Hosp., Linden, Tenn., 1980—. Vol. nurse for mass polio vaccination Pub. Health Dept., 1963, 64; vol. nurse Am. Nat. Red Cross, 1955—. Licensed Tenn. Bd. Nursing. Mem. Tenn. Hosp. Assn., Tenn. Assn. Nursing Service Dirs., St. Thomas Sch. of Nursing Alumni Assn. Home: Route 4 Box 232 Linden TN 37096 Office: Perry Meml Hosp Squirrel Hollow Dr Linden TN 37096

SMITH, BONNIE JEAN, educator; b. Long Branch, N.J., Aug. 15, 1944; d. Louis W. and Bonnie (Jones) Letsche; m. Kingsley Richard Smith II, June 10, 1965; children: Christine, Kingsley. BS, W.Va. U., 1970; MA, Hampton (Va.) U., 1983; postgrad., Coll. of William and Mary, Williamsburg, Va., 1984—, Va. Commonwealth U., 1985-86. Cert. in spl. edn. Operator N.J. Bell, Asbury Park, 1961-64; librarian Occidental Life Ins., Los Angeles, 1965-66; collector Credit Bur. of Morgantown, W.Va., 1970; layreader Hampton City Schs., 1979-81; tchr. Assn. for Retarded Citizens, Hampton, 1982-84, Williamsburg-James City Schs., 1984—. Pres. Sanford PTA, 1980-81. Mem. NEA, Council for Exceptional Children, Assn. for Severely Handicapped, Kappa Delta Pi. Republican. Club: Jr. Woman's of Newport News (v.p. 1973-83, Most Valuable Mem. 1976).

SMITH, CAROL ANN, lawyer; b. Birmingham, Ala., Apr. 23, 1949; d. James William and Mildred Viola (Ferguson) S. B.A., Birmingham So. Coll., 1971; J.D., U. Ala. Tuscaloosa, 1975; LL.M., NYU, 1977. Bar. Ala. 1975, U.S. Dist. Ct. (no. dist.) Ala. 1977, U.S. Dist. Ct. (mid. dist.) Ala. 1976, U.S. Ct. Appeals (11th cir.) 1981, U.S. Ct. Appeals (5th cir.) 1979. Law clk. Ala. Supreme Ct., Montgomery, 1975-76; assoc. Lange, Simpson, Robinson & Somerville, Birmingham, 1977-81; assoc. Starnes & Atchison, Birmingham, 1981-83, ptnr., 1983—. Editorial bd. Ala. Law Rev., 1973-75. Mem. bd. mgmt. Downtown YMCA, Birmingham, 1984—, mem. exec. com., 1985—. Mem. Birmingham Bar Assn. (pres. young lawyers sect. 1984), Ala. Bar Inst. for Continuing Legal Edn. (exec. com. 1979—), Ala. Bar Assn. (editorial bd. The Ala. Lawyer 1979—, assoc. editor 1984—, exec. com. young lawyers sect. 1983-84, chmn. continuing legal edn. com. of young lawyers sect. 1984, mem. pres.'s adv. task foce 1984-85), Eleventh Cir. Jud. Conf. (alt. del. 1985—), Phi Beta Kappa. Methodist. Club: Birmingham Jr. Music Bd. Home: 1511 Ridge Rd Homewood AL 35209 Office: Starnes & Atchison One Daniel Plaza Daniel Bldg Birmingham AL 35233

SMITH, CAROL ANN, music therapist, psychologist; b. Montgomery County, Tenn., Apr. 19, 1951; d. Carl and Ruth (Gettinger) S.; B.M.E. in Music Therapy, U. Kans., 1974; M.A. in Clin. Psychology, Middle Tenn. State U., 1977; Ed.S. in Human Service Mgmt.; Vanderbilt U., 1979. Gen. therapeutic recreation specialist VA Med. Ctr., Murfreesboro, Tenn., 1973-79; music therapist VA Med. Ctr., Marion, Ind., 1979; chief, recreation therapy service VA Med. Ctr., Tucson, 1979-84; chief recreation therapy VA Med. Ctr., Northport, N.Y., 1984-87 ; Health Systems Specialist, Dir.'s Office, VA Med. Ctr., Cleve., 1987-88, adminstrv. asst. to assoc. dir., 1988—; adj. instr. Middle Tenn. State U., part-time 1978—; guest speaker, 1975—; Mem. Am. Psychol. Assn. (asso.), Nat. Assn. Music Therapy (cert.), Nat. Assn. Female Execs., Am. Mgmt. Assn., Pi Lambda Theta. Democrat. Methodist. Contbr. articles to profl. jours. Home: 5800 Laurent Dr Suite 712 Parma OH 44129 Office: VA Med Ctr 10701 E Blvd Cleveland OH 44106

SMITH, CAROLE JEAN, banker; b. Russellville, Ark., Aug. 23, 1949; d. Garland Dee and Elmo (Williamson) Nichols. BSBA in Mktg., U. Ark., 1971, MBA, 1972; cert., Am. Inst. Banking, 1976; M in Banking, So. Meth. U., 1980. Mgmt. auditor U.S. GAO, St. Louis, 1972-73; asst. v.p. First Nat. Bank, Little Rock, 1973-80; v.p. Republic Bank and Trust, Tulsa, 1980-83; sr. v.p. Worthen Bank and Trust Co., Little Rock, 1983—; instr. banking Systematics, Inc., Little Rock, 1980—; mng. dir. Worthen Profl. Women's Adv. Bd., Little Rock, 1986—; dir., gen. mgr. Worthen Fin. and Investment, Inc., Little Rock, 1986—; bd. dirs. mid-south chpt., cen. Ark. chpt. Robert Morris Assocs., 1986—; mem. edn. standards com. Ark. State Bd. Accountancy,, 1986—. Bd. dirs. Ballet of Ark., 1986—, Leadership Inst., 1986, Multiple Schlerosis, 1987; mem. com. Fair and Rep. Govt., Little Rock, 1987. Recipient Pres.'s award Civitan Internat., 1977; named Ark. Outstanding Young Career Women, 1977, one of Outstanding Young Women Am., 1979. Mem. Assn. Female Execs., Little Rock C. of C. (com. chair 1987), Kappa Kappa Gamma Alumni Assn. Democrat. Methodist. Club: Pleasant Valley Country. Home: 4712 Kavanaugh Blvd Little Rock AR 72207 Office: Worthen Bank & Trust Co 200 W Capitol Little Rock AR 72201

SMITH, CAROLYN SUE, oil company executive; b. Doeran, Ga., Feb. 17, 1944; d. James Washington and Corrie Irene (Hufstetler) Gunn; m. Jack Samuel Smith Sr., Apr. 3, 1942; children: Jack, Jill, Jody, John. Grad., Worth County High Sch., 1962. Lic. real estate. Program asst. USDA-ASCS Office, Moultrie, Ga., 1973-76; exec. Lubrico, Inc., Albany, Ga., 1977-83; owner, chief exec. officer S.E. Oil & Grease Co., Inc., Albany, 1983—. Mem. Women Bus. Owners, Nat. Lubricating Grease Inst., Am. Soc. Lubrication Engrs., Women In Constrn. Republican. Baptist. Lodge: Elks. Home: PO Box 4340 Albany GA 31706 Office: SE Oil & Grease Co Inc PO Box 4897 Albany GA 31706

SMITH, CHARLOTTE DUNCAN, insurance holding company executive; b. Bogalusa, La., July 31, 1938; d. Prather Wesley Duncan and Cleo Louise (Scroggs) Sticker; m. Melvin Ray Smith, Apr. 23, 1956 (div. 1960); children: Wanda Louise Kelly, Melvin Wade. Student, Elizabeth Sullivan Meml., 1959-61, La. State U., 1964. Office mgr. Cutrer Ins. Agy., Bogalusa, La., 1958-63; office mgr. R.M. Cochran Co., Ltd., Baton Rouge, 1964-79, also bd. dirs.; casualty underwriter Hearin-Collins Ins. Agy., Baton Rouge, 1963-64; exec. v.p. Protective Holding Corp., Baton Rouge, 1979—, Protective Casualty Ins. Co., Baton Rouge, 1979—; sr. exec. v.p. Protective Mgmt. Corp., Baton Rouge, 1979—, Protective Adjustment Co., Baton Rouge, 1979—; bd. dirs. Protective Holding Corp. and all subs. Author ins. policies and fidelity bonds to profl. jours. Mem. fin. com. Richard Baker for Congress, Baton Rouge, 1986-87. Named Boss of Yr., Denham Springs Coop. Office Edn., 1978. Mem. La. Assn. Fire and Casualty Cos. (bd. dirs. 1984—), Nat. Council on Compensation Ins. (LA rating and classification com.), Nat. Risk Retention Assn. (founding dir., treas.). Democrat. Baptist. Home: 13011 Dorset Ave Baton Rouge LA 70818 Office: Protective Casualty Ins Co PO Box 80293 Baton Rouge LA 70898

SMITH, CHARLOTTE REED, educator; b. Eubank, Ky., Sept. 15, 1921; d. Joseph Lumpkin and Cornelia Elizabeth (Spenser) Reed; m. Walter Lindsay Smith, Aug. 24, 1949; children—Walter Lindsay IV, Elizabeth Reed. B.A. in Music, Tift Coll., 1941; M.A. in Mus. Theory, Eastman Sch. of Music, 1946; postgrad. Juilliard Sch., 1949. Asst. prof. theory Okla. Bapt. U., 1944-45, Washburn U., 1946-48; prof. music Furman U., Greenville, S.C., 1948—; chmn. dept. music, 1987—; evaluator compositions Jr. Music Clubs of S.C., Nat. Fedn. Music Clubs, 1970-74. Editor: Seven Penitential Psalms with Two Laudate Psalms, 1983; author: Manual of Sixteenth-Century Contrapuntal Style, 1988. Mem. Am. Musicol. Soc., Soc. for Music Theory, AAUP (sec.-treas. Furman chpt. 1984-85), Nat. Fedn. Music Clubs, Pi Kappa Lambda. Republican. Baptist. Office: Furman U Poinsett Hwy Greenville SC 29613

SMITH, CHARLOTTE THERESE WERTZ, manager legal resources; b. Springfield, Ill., July 11, 1959. B.S. in Music Edn., Duquesne U., 1980. Cert. paralegal. Paralegal Dickie, McCamey & Chilcote, Pitts., 1981—; advisor to bd. dirs. Pitts. Paralegal Assn., 1986—; rep. Triangle Corner Ltd., Pitts., 1985-88; mgr. legal resources Assn. Trial Lawyers Am., Washington, 1988—. Author So You Want to be a Paralegal pamphlet, 1983. Editor Nat. Paralegal Reporter, 1984-85. Contbr. articles to newsletter. Mem. Pitts. Paralegal Assn. (pres. 1985-86, treas. 1983-85), Y-Net/YWCA (v.p. 1986—), Nat. Assn. Female Execs.

SMITH, CHERYL LYNN, copy editor, writer, reporter; b. Newark, June 20, 1958; d. Joseph and Earline Elizabeth (Gadson) S. BS in Journalism, Fla. A&M U., 1980; MS in Human Relations and Bus., Amber U., 1986, postgrad. 1987-88. Exec. editor Capital Outlook News, Tallahassee, 1980-81; nat. prodn. coordinator TV Watch of Scripps Howard, Dallas, 1981-82; mktg. compliance assoc. J.C. Penney Ins. Co., Dallas, 1983-84; prodn. asst. Am. Equity Press, Dallas, 1984-86; copy editor Jaggars Chiles Stovall, Dallas, 1986-88; sr. writer Dallas Weekly, 1988—. Author play: Sizzlin Red and the Seven Dudes, 1981. Editor newsletter Dallas Pan Hellenic Council, 1986—. Mem. Nat. Council Negro Women, Dallas, 1982; active, sec. Just Friends: Pregnant Teenagers Support Group; rep. Dallas chpt. Nat. Pan Hellenic Council, 1985—, sec. 1986-88. Named one of Outstanding Young Women in Am., 1983-87. Mem. NAACP, Dallas/Ft. Worth Assn. Black Journalists, Dallas Metroplex Council of Black Alumni Assns., Fla. Black Pubs. (rep. 1980-81), Fla. A&M U. Alumni Assn. (pres. local chpt. 1985—), Soc. Profl. Journalists, Nat. Assn. Female Execs., Delta Sigma Theta (rep. local chpt. 1981—, Service award 1981, 85, one of Outstanding Young Women 1987-88), Dallas Metroplex Council Black Alumni Assns. (media specialist 1987—), Nat. Polit. Congress Black Women. Democrat. Baptist. Avocations: reading, working with children, writing, dancing. Home: Box 45331 Dallas TX 75245

SMITH, CHRISTIE LISA, radio announcer; b. San Antonio, Dec. 17, 1954; d. Walter Joseph and Barbara Alice (Bell) Smith. Student Tulane U., 1972-74, Fla. State U., 1976-77. Announcer Sta. WHBQ, Memphis, 1977-78; program dir. Sta. WICE, Providence, 1978-79; announcer Sta. WROR, Boston, 1979-80; program dir. Sta. WBGM, Tallahassee, Fla., 1981; morning announcer Sta. WOWD, Tallahassee, 1981-82; announcer Sta. WQXI, Atlanta, 1982—. Author poetry: Seaside Serendipity, 1974. Vol. March of Dimes, Memphis, 1977, Leukemia Soc., Providence, 1980, Tallahassee Jaycees, 1981, Am. Cancer Soc. Atlanta, 1982. Recipient Best D.J. of Yr. award Tulane U., 1972; Pres.'s award Forward Communications, Wausau, Wis., 1981. Mem. Nat. Assn. Female Execs. Democrat. Episcopalian. Office: 302 DeFoor Landing NW Atlanta GA 30318

SMITH, CHRYSA MAE, advertising executive, free-lance writer; b. Bklyn., May 17, 1960; d. Walter John Sandewicz and Dorothy Helen (Oshmialowski) Osmialowski; m. Mark Irwin Smith, Oct. 20, 1985. BS in Mgmt., St. John's U., Jamaica, N.Y., 1982. Mgr. sales adminstrn. Nat. Screen Service, N.Y.C., 1982-84; editor, mgr. mktg. services Harcourt, Brace, Jovanovich Am. Salon Mag. Co., N.Y.C., 1985-86; mgr. sales promotion Mettler Instrument Corp., Hightstown, N.J., 1986-88; freelance copywriter Chrysa M. Smith Mktg. Communications, Jamison, Pa., 1988—; freelance writer Harcourt, Brace, Jovanovich, 1986, Xetron Corp., Cedar Knolls, N.J., 1985—, Windsor Advt., Princeton Junction, N.J., 1986—. Vol. tchr. St. Nicholas of Tolentine Sch., Jamaica., N.Y., 1979-82. Mem. Nat. Assn. for Female Execs. Republican. Roman Catholic. Home: 1340 Brook Ln Jamison PA 18929 Office: Chrysa M Smith Mktg Communications 1340 Brook Ln Jamison PA 18929

SMITH, CINDY A., social worker; b. Canton, N.Y., Dec. 12, 1957. BA in Sociology, Social Work, Coll. of St. Rose, 1979. Rape crisis counselor Albany County Rape Crisis Ctr., N.Y., 1979-81; dir. Rape Crisis Program Rensselaer County, Troy, N.Y., 1981-84; child welfare specialist I N.Y. State Dept. Social Services, Albany, 1986-87; dir. Schenectady (N.Y.) YWCA Services to Families in Violence, 1987—. Adv. bd. Rape Crisis Program for Rensselaer County, 1984—; vol. N.Y. State Nat. Abortion Rights Action League, 1984—; mem. Rensselaer County Task Force on Child Abuse and Neglect Troy, 1981—, Schenectady County Coalition Against Child Sexual Abuse, 1987—, Schenectady County Violence Against Women Com., 1987—; founder, co-chmn. com. on Child Sexual Abuse, Rensselaer County Task Force on Child Abuse/Neglect, 1984, co-chmn. polit. adv. com., 1983. Mem. Nat. Assn. Social Workers.

SMITH, CLARA JEAN, retired nursing home administrator; b. Berwick, Pa., Aug. 31, 1932; d. Barton Fredrick and Evelyn Miriam (Bomboy) Hough; R.N., Williamsport (Pa.) Hosp., 1953; B.S. in Nursing Edn., Wilkes Coll., Wilkes-Barre, Pa., 1960; M.S. in Edn., Temple U., Phila., 1969; m. Robert W. Smith, June 7, 1958. From staff nurse to dir. nursing Retreat State Hosp., Hunlock Creek, Pa., 1953-80; dir. long term care facility Danville (Pa.) State Hosp., 1980-82; ret., 1982; dir. accrediatation coordination and quality assurance Nursing Home Adminstrs., 1980—; speaker, instr. in field. Mem. Lake Pinecrest Sportsmen's Assn. (dir., sec.), Pa. State Employees Retirement Assn., Williamsport Hosp. Sch. Nursing Alumni. Methodist. Clubs: Sunshine; Town Hill Hobby Group, Town Hill Over 50 Group. Author tng. and ednl. programs. Home: Lake Pinecrest PO Box 5 Huntington Mills PA 18622

SMITH, CLAUDETTE HELMS, municipal official; b. Monroe, N.C., Oct. 16, 1937; d. James Lee and Maud Lee (Smith) Helms; m. Homer Letcher Smith, July 28, 1956; 1 child, Olin Letcher. Cert., Cen. Piedmont Community Coll., Charlotte, N.C., 1975, U. N.C., Charlotte, 1976. Asst. tax collector City of Monroe, 1955-57, asst. clk., 1957-73, clk., 1973—, asst. mgr., 1981—. Mem. Profl. Secs. Internat. (various offices and coms.), N.C. Mcpl. Clks. Assn., N.C. Personnel Dirs. Assn. Democrat. Baptist.

SMITH, CONNIE MAE, travel industry manager; b. Oxford, Wis., May 17, 1938; d. Wendell Ried and Irene Louise (Stone) Ingraham; m. Omer Lee Smith, June 8, 1963; 1 child, Wendell Russell. Student, Stout State Coll., 1966-68, Inst. Cert. Trave Agts., Wellesley, Mass., 1986. Stewardess United Airlines, Chgo., 1958-63; file clk. McDonald Aircraft, St. Louis, 1963-65; travel agt. Fishburn World Travel, Ogden, Utah, 1972-75; sr. travel counselor Regency Travel, Spokane, Wash., 1975-80; mgr. travel Seven Sea Travel, Santa Barbara, Calif., 1980-82; pres. Come Travel Corp., San Luis Obispo, Calif., 1983-86; cons. mgr. ops. Rice Travel Service, Santa Barbara, 1986—. Home: 642 Daniel Dr Santa Maria CA 93454

SMITH, CORINNE ROTH, psychologist; b. Reading, Pa., May 22, 1945; d. Zoltan and Elizabeth (Foldes) Roth; m. Lynn Helden Smith, June 9, 1968; children: Juliette Sarah, Rachael Eliza. BA in Psychology cum laude, Syracuse U., 1967, PhD, 1973; MA, Temple U., Phila., 1969. Lic. sch. psychologist, N.Y. Psychologist reading clinic Syracuse (N.Y.) U., 1969-70, coordinator lab. sch. and clinic, 1971-72, founder, dir. psychoednl. teaching lab., 1972—, founder, dir. comprehensive assessment ctr., 1981-83; psychologist experimental presch. program Syracuse City Schs., 1970-71; assoc. prof. Syracuse U., 1988—; mem. Council for Exceptional Children; reviewer Aspen, Ablex, Little, Brown & Co., N.Y., 1985—, Allyn & Bacon, Boston, 1985—; apptd. mem. Gov. N.Y. Council for Youth, Albany, 1984—; speaker in field. Author: Learning Disabilities: The Interaction of Learner, Task and Setting, 1983; contbr. articles to profl. jours. and chpts. to books. Bd. dirs. Cen. N.Y. United Way, 1987—; pres. Jewish Community Ctr., Syracuse, 1978-81; bd. dirs., chairperson career women's network Syracuse Jewish Fedn., 1985-87, women's campaign chairperson, 1987—. Recipient Disting. Service award Jewish Community Ctr., 1976, Community Leadership award Syracuse Jewish Fedn., 1986, N.Y. State Office Mental Retardation and Devel. Disabilities grantee, 1985-88. Mem. Am. Psych. Assn., Nat. Assn. Sch. Psychologists, Assn. for Children and Adults with Learning Disabilities, N.Y. State Assn. for Children and Adults with Learning Disabilities, and others. Office: Syracuse U 805 S Grouse Ave Syracuse NY 13244-2280

SMITH, COZEE LYNN, marketing executive; b. Tampa, Fla., June 14, 1949; d. Albert Preston and Anne (Hensley) S. BA in English Edn., U. South Fla., 1972. Office mgr. Apple Industries, N.Y.C., 1973-74, Am. Phonetronics, N.Y.C., 1974-75; mgr. advt. and mktg. Solar Energy Products, Inc., Gainesville, Fla., 1976-81; dir. newcomers Barnett Bank of Pinellas Co., Clearwater, Fla., 1981, mktg. officer, 1982, v.p. mktg., 1983-87; v.p. community affairs Barnett Bank of Pinellas Co., St. Petersburg, Fla., 1987—. Bd. dirs. YWCA (chmn. Tribute to Women and Industry 1987-88) and Pinellas County Arts Council, Clearwater, 1986-87; chairperson Dreams Come True Hospice Care Found., Pinellas Park, Fla., 1987-88. Mem. Bank Mktg. Assn., Pinellas Suncoast C. of C. (chairperson super auction 1986-87), Clearwater C. of C. (bd. dirs. 1984—, chairperson jazz holiday 1985-86, chmn. events com.), Pinellas Suncoast C. of C. (vice chmn. mktg. and communications). Republican. Methodist. Office: Barnett Bank of Pinellas County PO Box 5128 Clearwater FL 33702

SMITH, CYNTHIA JOY, management analyst, computer programmer; b. Glen Ridge, N.J., Dec. 25, 1951; d. Herbert James and Frances Jane (Van Ness) S. BA, Springfield Coll., 1973; MSW, U. Hawaii, 1976; MBA, Pepperdine U., 1982. Coordinator, Pacific Allied Health Project, Honolulu, 1977-78; programmer analyst Computab, Inc., Honolulu, 1980-82; exec. dir. Hale Ho'Ola Hou, Honolulu, 1977-80; med. cons. Microsystems U.S.A. Inc., Honolulu, 1982-84; med. social worker Upjohn's Home Health Agy., Honolulu, 1976-86, Kokua Nurses Home Health Agy., 1986—; analyst, programmer The Queen's Med. Ctr., Honolulu, 1982-83; mgmt. analyst Straub Clinic and Hosp., Inc., Honolulu, 1983—; instr. U. Hawaii Sch. Social Work, 1977-83. Contbr. articles to profl. jours. Mem. Women in Small Bus. Com., SBA, 1983; chmn. pub. affairs, bd. dirs. Hawaii Planned Parenthood Assn., 1981-87, pres. 1983-84; bd. dirs. Craigside Condominium, 1987—; elected ofcl. Nuuanu Neighborhood Bd., 1987—; active friends and alumni U. Hawaii Sch. Social Work. Mem. Hawaii Soc. Hosp. Social Work Dirs. (sec. 1983-85), Hosp. Mgmt. Systems Soc. (sec.-treas. 1985—), Assn. Women Entrepreneurs, Am. Bus. Women's Assn. (pres. 1983-84, Woman of Yr. award 1984-85), Nat. Assn. Social Workers (cert.), Am. Assn. Med. Systems and Info., Computer Profls. for Social Responsibility. Democrat. Office: Straub Clinic and Hosp Inc 888 S King St Honolulu HI 96813

SMITH, DEB URSULA, lawyer; b. Miami, Fla., May 18, 1957; d. Bernard Leland and Ursula Marie (Wojtasiak) S. BA, U. N.C., 1979; JD, U. Tenn., Knoxville, 1982. Bar: Tenn. 1983. Clk., assoc. Ridenour & Ridenour, Clinton, Tenn., 1981-83; assoc. Gamble & Stevens Law Firm, Crossville, Tenn., 1983-84, York & York Attys., Crossville, 1984-85; sole practice Crossville, 1985-88; city atty. City of Crossville, 1987-88; asst. dist. atty. gen. State of Tenn., Smithville, 1988—. Mem. Tenn. Bar Assn., Cumberland County Bar Assn. (sec. 1984-85), Assn. Tenn. Trial Lawyers, Crossville Jaycees, Crossville C. of C., Soc. of Hellenas (del. 1978), Phi Alpha Theta. Democrat. Episcopalian. Office: Dekalb County Courthouse Room 305 Smithville TN 37166 Office (also): 39 Fleming Ave Cookeville TN 38501

SMITH, DEBORAH DEMOSS, television producer; b. Plain Dealing, La., Jan. 12, 1949; d. C.C. and Alma Jean (O'Daniel) DeMoss; m. Barry Richard Smith, Aug. 25, 1979; 1 child, Austin Rebecca. BA cum laude, La. Tech. U., 1970; MEd magna cum laude, U. New Orleans, 1976. Tchr. English East Feliciana Parish Sch. Bd., Jackson, La., 1971-72, St. Charles Parish Sch. Bd., St. Rose, La., 1976-82; writer, producer Sta. WWL-TV News, New Orleans, 1982—. Vol. news anchor Sta. WRBH (Radio for Blind/Print Handicapped), New Orleans, 1986—; mem. Audubon Zool. Garden and Park, New Orleans, 1983—, Preservation Resource Ctr., New Orleans, 1985—. Recipient 1st place documentary award for Beating the Odds, AP, 1987, 1st place documentary award for It's All in the Family: The Genetics Connection, Women in Communication, 1988, also 3d place documentary award New Orleans Press Club, 1988, 1st place documentary award AP, UPI, 1988; Edward R. Murrow award Radio-TV News Dirs. Assn., 1988. Mem. Phi Kappa Phi. Democrat. Home: 829 Washington Ave New Orleans LA 70130 Office: WWL-TV 1024 N Rampart St New Orleans LA 70116

SMITH, DEBORAH LEE, hospital management engineer, nurse; b. Richmond, Va., Feb. 1, 1952. Staff nurse Petersburg Gen. Hosp., Va., 1973-76, 77-78; head nurse, part-time supr. Psychiat. Med. Surg. Hiram Davis Med. Ctr., Petersburg, 1976-77; staff nurse Leigh Meml. Hosp., Norfolk, Va., 1977-78; instr., part-time supr. Norfolk Gen. Hosp Sch. Profl. Nursing, 1980-82; head nurse ear, nose and throat, otolaryngology Norfolk Gen. Hosp., 1984, research coordinator, project developer, 1984-86, mem. nursing mgmt. engring. com., 1984-86, chair 1986; mem. quality rev. for home health care, 1983—, mem. mktg. red team, 1983-86; cons. Wren IV Therapy Ctr., Alliance Health Systems, Norfolk, 1984-85; mem. standardization com. Med. Ctr. Hosp., 1982—; mem. mgmt. cert. task force Alliance Health System, 1985; presenter seminars in field. Basic cardiac life support instr. Am. Heart Assn., 19—, advanced cardiac life support instr., 1981—; loaned exec. United Way, 1984. Mem. Am. Assn. Critical Care Nurses, Am. Nurses Assn., Va. Nurses Assn. (program com. chmn. local dist. 1981-85, del. 1983-85, sec. 1985—). Home: 41 King George Quay Chesapeake VA 23325

SMITH, DEBORAH LYNN, songwriter, public relations specialist; b. Akron, Ohio, July 18, 1951; d. Leo and Selma B. (Cohen) S. Musician Audio Rec. Co., Cleve. Rec. Co., Suma, Criteria Rec. Studios, Bushflow Studios, 1964—; pres. Shemusic, BMI Pub., Akron, Ohio, 1978—; cons. in field; pres. booking agy. Moxie Music; mem. Harry Fox Agy. Recipient Gold record for album Freedom of Choice, 1980. Mem. Am. Fedn. Musicians, Broadcast Music Inc. Club: Kovetas (Detroit). Office: Shemusic 456 Sandhurst Rd Akron OH 44313

SMITH, DENISE BREWER, financial analyst; b. Chgo., May 28, 1959; d. Carl Rouzie and Janet Rosa (Brewer) Smith. BS magna cum laude, Purdue U., 1981; MBA, Harvard U., 1985. CPA, Ill. Auditor Ernst & Whinney, Chgo., 1981-83; sr. fin. analyst Amoco Corp., Chgo., 1985-86; pres. Brewer-Smith, Ltd. CPA's, Chgo., 1986—; instr. Loop Coll., Chgo., 1986-87. Creator (bd. game) Entrepreneurs and Raiders, 1987. Vol. tutor Ill. Literacy Council, Chgo., 1986—. Mem. Am. Inst. CPA's, Cosmopolitan C. of C. Home: 1212 S Michigan Ave #1110 Chicago IL 60605 Office: Brewer-Smith Ltd 180 N Michigan Ave #407 Chicago IL 60601

SMITH, DENISE GROLEAU, information analyst; b. Worcester, Mass., Feb. 7, 1951; d. Edmond Laurence and Audrey Mildred (Paquin) Groleau; m. Wayne Marshall Smith, Apr. 17, 1976; 1 child, Andrew. BSBA, Fitchburg State U., 1983. Bindery worker Atlantic Bus. Forms, Hudson, Mass., 1969-73; proofreader New Eng. Bus., Townsend, Mass., 1974-75; computer operator New Eng. Bus., Groton, Mass., 1975-80, adminstrv. asst. bus. systems, 1980-82, adminstrv. asst. info. ctr., 1982-85; info. ctr. analyst Wright Line Inc., Worcester, 1985—; cons. personal computer Buckingham Transp., Groton, 1987. Mem. Nat. Assn. Female Execs. Home: 14 Cedar Circle Townsend MA 01469 Office: Wight Line Inc 160 Gold Star Blvd Worcester MA 01606

SMITH, DORIS HELEN, college president; b. Cleve., June 1, 1930; d. Harold Peter and Ellen Mary (Keane) S. B.S., Coll. of Mt. St. Vincent, 1952; M.A., NYU, 1957; postgrad. Fordham U., 1960-65; L.H.D., (hon.), Manhattan Coll., 1979. Joined Sisters of Charity (N.Y.), 1952. Mem. faculty Coll. of Mount St. Vincent, Bronx, N.Y., 1955-71, adminstrv. asst. to pres., 1971-72, exec. v.p., 1972-73, pres., 1973—; spl. asst. to pres. Chatham Coll., Pitts., 1970-71; dir. Hudson River Fund of Equitable Variable Life Ins., N.Y.C.; trustee Higher Edn. Service Corp., Albany, N.Y., 1980-85, Com. on Independent Colls. and Univs., Albany, 1980-83. Recipient Higher Edn. Leadership award Com. on Independent Colls. and Corning Glass Works, 1983, several interfaith and brotherhood awards; named Riverdalian of Yr. Riverdale Community Council, 1978; Am. Council Edn. fellow, 1970-71. Mem. Bronx C. of C. Roman Catholic. Home and Office: Coll Mt St Vincent Riverdale Ave Bronx NY 10471

SMITH, DORIS JANE, nutritional consultant, retail store owner; b. Detroit, Jan. 9, 1933; d. George James and Martha (Milinski) Miller; m. Ted Carlyle Smith, Aug. 31, 1954 (div. 1987); children—Holly, Cathy Smith Gray, Randall. B.A., U. Ark., 1977. Pres. Consol. Security Corp., Inc., Memphis, 1973-80, Sun Tree Health Foods, Inc., Fayetteville, Ark., 1977—, Sunshine Investments, Inc., Fayetteville, 1983—; nutritional cons. Hulvey Metabolic Service, Searcy, Ark., 1983-87. Founder and dir. Memphis chpt. Huxley Inst. Biosocial Research, Memphis, 1975. Mem. Am. Assn. Nutritional Cons., Nat. Nutritional Foods Assn. (mem. legal/legis. com., dir.

regional health orgn., chair legis. advocacy com. of Ark. chpt. Nat. Health Fedn.). Republican. Baptist. Avocations: water skiing, snow skiing, golf. Home: PO Box 456 Johnson AR 72741 Office: Sun Tree Health Foods Inc 1242 N College St Fayetteville AR 72703

SMITH, ELIZABETH ADAMS, producer; b. Long Beach, Calif., May 21, 1944; d. Francis H. and Virginia R. (Wells) Adams; m. Richard Yeadon Smith, III, Sept. 27, 1969; children—Jason Colyer, Amanda Wells. B.S. in Broadcast Journalism, Boston U., 1966; postgrad., NYU, Sch. Visual Arts, New Sch. Copywriter Batten, Barton Durstine and Osborn, N.Y.C., 1966-71; mgr. software div. Adwell Audio-Visual Co., Bellerose, N.Y., 1971-72; freelance writer, producer, N.Y.C., 1972-76; pres. Adams-Smith Prodns. Ltd., 1976—; dir., v.p., Granlyn Farm Products, Schaticoke N.Y., 1980-84. Contbr. numerous articles to popular and profl. jours.; producer TV, audio-visual materials videos, short films. Mem. Westchester Nuclear Freeze Com.; v.p. fundraising Rye High Sch. Parents' Assn. Mem. NOW, Westchester County C. of C., Westchester Assn. Women Bus. Owners, Women in Communications (v.p. membership), Small Bus. Council (community com.), Ind. Feature Project, Assn. Ind. Video and Film Makers, Assn. Visual Communicators. Club: Apawamis (Rye). Home: 127 Evergreen Ave Rye NY 10580 Office: Adams-Smith Productions Ltd Box 52 Rye NY 10580

SMITH, ELIZABETH BLOXOM, real estate broker; b. Newport News, Va., Aug. 9; d. Dennis Joseph and Elizabeth Veronica (Carter) Antinori; student Golden Gate U., 1973-74; m. Blair Eldred Smith, Aug. 30, 1968; children: Robert E., Dennis L. Salesman, half owner Bloxom Realty Co., Newport News, Va., 1962-66, broker, 1963—; owner, pres. Libby Bloxom, Inc., Newport News, 1966—. Mem. Nat. Assn. Realtors, Realtor's Nat. Mktg. Inst. (cert. residential broker), Nat. Assn. Parliamentarians (local treas. 1978, 79, pres. local unit 1981-83, pres. Va. Peninsula 1986-87), Va. Assn. Realtors (past regional v.p., Cert. of Appreciation 1979), Cert. Resdl. Brokerage Mgrs. (pres. 1986), Peninsula Retail Merchants Assn. (dir.), Newport News-Hampton Bd. Realtors (pres. 1975, plaque of appreciation 1975, Realtor of Yr. 1976), Pioneer Internat. Tng. and Communication Club (rec. sec. 1985-86). Republican. Presbyterian. Clubs: Soroptimists (corr. sec. Va. Peninsula 1985-86). Home: 924 Etna Dr Newport News VA 23602 Office: 14801 Warwick Blvd Newport News VA 23602

SMITH, ELIZABETH MACKEY, financial planner, consultant; b. Phila., Mar. 23, 1941; d. William Norman Mackey and Celeste Parvin Barley; m. George Van Riper Smith, Aug. 15, 1964; children: Douglas George, Todd Mackey. BA, Gettysburg Coll., 1963; MA in Teaching, Ga. State U., 1978. Tchr. fgn. lang. Haverford (Pa.) High Sch., 1963-65; registered rep. IDS Fin. Services, Inc., Macon and Savannah, Ga., 1979—. Reader Atlanta Services for the Blind, 1968; hostess Atlanta Council for Internat. Visitors, 1972-74; pres. Forest Hills Elem. Sch. PTA, Decatur, Ga., 1975. Mem. Phi Sigma Iota, Delta Phi Alpha, Delta Gamma. Home: 59 Fiddler's Ct Savannah GA 31419 Office: IDS Fin Services Inc Abercorn Profl Bldg Suite 205 6606 Abercorn St Savannah GA 31405

SMITH, ELOUISE BEARD, restaurant owner; b. Richmond, Tex., Jan. 8, 1920; s. Lee Roy and Ruby Myrtle (Foy) Beard; m. Omar Smith, Nov. 27, 1940 (dec. July 1981); children: Mary Jean Smith Cherry, Terry Omar, Don Alan. Student, Tex. Womens U., 1937-39. Sec. First Nat. Bank, Rosenberg, Tex., 1939-41; owner Smith Dairy Queens, Bryan, Tex., 1947—. Author: The Haunted House, 1986; editor The College Widow, 1986. Omar and Elouise Beard Smith chair named in her honor Tex. A&M U., College Station, 1983, Elouise Beard Smith Human Performance Labs. named in her honor Tex. A&M U., 1984. Mem. AAUW. Republican. Baptist. Home: 411 Crescent Dr Bryan TX 77801 Office: Metro Ctr 3833 S Texas Ave Bryan TX 77802

SMITH, ESTHER THOMAS, editor, writer; b. Jesup, Ga., Mar. 13, 1939; d. Joseph H. and Leslie (McCarthy) Thomas; B.A., Agnes Scott Coll., 1962; m. James D. Smith, June 2, 1962; children—Leslie, Amy, James Thomas. Staff writer, Sunday women's editor Atlanta Jour.-Constn., 1961-62; mng. editor Bull. of U. Miami Sch. Medicine, 1965-66; corr. Atlanta Jour.-Constn. and Fla. Times-Union, 1964, 67-68; founding editor Bus. Rev. of Washington, 1978-81; ind. bus. writer, communications cons. Peat, Marwick, Mitchell & Co., Washington, 1981-82; editor Scripps-Howard Washington Bus. Jour., 1982; corp. officer, contbg. editor Washington Woman Mag., Inc., 1983-85; pres. Tech News, Inc., pub. Washington Tech., 1986—; lectr. Pres., Episcopal Young Churchmen, Diocese of Ga., 1955-57; dir. pub. relations Army Community Service, Ft. Bragg, N.C., 1969-71; co-founder Army Family Symposium, 1979-80; adv. bd. bus. edn. Fairfax County Pub. Schs., 1981-82; bd. dirs. MIT Enterprise Forum of Washington/Balt., 1981-82; mem. Women's Forum, Washington, 1981—, Nat. Mil. Family Assn., 1986-87, Fla. Tech. Republican. Episcopalian. Home: 1335 Timberly Ln McLean VA 22102 Office: 1953 Gallows Rd Suite 130 Vienna VA 22180

SMITH, EUGENIA SEWELL, funeral home executive; b. Albany, Ky., Oct. 24, 1922; d. Leo Matheny and Marjorie (Warinner) Sewell; m. James Frederick Smith, June 25, 1948; 1 child, Bryson Sewell. Student Berea Coll., 1937-41, Bowling Green Coll. Commerce, 1944-45. Owner, operator Sewell Funeral Home, Albany, 1977—. Sec. Albany Woman's Club, 1950-54; den mother Cub Scouts, Boy Scouts Am., 1958-62; pres. Clinton County Homemakers, Albany, 1968-70; mission action chmn. Missionary Baptist Ch., 1965-82. Democrat. Lodge: Demolay Mother's (Albany club 1966-67), der Eastern Star (former assoc. conductress). Home: Rural Route 4 Burkesville Rd Albany KY 42602 Office: Sewell Funeral Home 115 Cross St Albany KY 42602

SMITH, EVELYN, association executive; b. Statesboro, Ga., Jan. 13, 1949; d. Ollie and Ruthie Mae (Williams) S. BS in Biology, Chemistry, Albany (Ga.) State Coll., 1971, cert. in teaching, 1975. Cert. tchr., Ga. Mgr. domestics Zayres, Decatur, Ga., 1971-72, area mgr. trainee, 1972; instr. Candler County Sch. System, Metter, Ga., 1972-77; dir. UniServ S.E. region Ga. Assn. Educators, Metter, 1977-84; dir. field services Decatur, 1984-86, Atlanta, 1986-87; dir. membership organ., field services Decatur, 1987—. Mem. textbook adoption com. first dist. Ga. Dept. Edn., Metter, 1980; vol. Nat. Council Negro Women Inc., 1987; radio ministry announcer, Fairfield Bapt. Ch., Redan, Ga. Mem. NAACP (edn. com. 1987—), NEA (UniServ coordinators s.e. regional), Nat. Assn. Female Execs. Democrat. Club: Jackpot Birthday (Atlanta) (pres. 1986—). Office: Ga Assn Educators 3951 Snapfinger Pkwy Decatur GA 30035

SMITH, FAITH, educational administrator; b. Chgo. B.S., Purdue U., 1979; M.A., U. Chgo., 1982. Counselor, Clyde Warrior Inst. Am. Indians, Boulder, Colo., 1969; coordinator Am. Indian Fesitval, Field Mus. Natural History, 1968; exec. asst. Nat. Congress Am. Indians, 1966; caseworker Am. Indian Ctr., Chgo., 1966-69, exec. asst., 1968-71; coordinator Am. Indian Health Project, Am. Med. Student Assn., Rolling Meadows, Ill., 1971-76; mem. faculty Antioch U., Yellow Springs, Ohio, 1974-84; Coordinator Native Am. Ednl. Services Coll., Chgo., 1974-75, dir., 1975-78, pres., 1978—. co-chair Indian Treaty Rights Task Force, 1987—; mem. Nat. Governing bd. Common Cause, Washington; bd. dirs. Assn. Community Based Edn., Washington. Bd. dirs. Uptown Community Health Assn., Chgo., 1969-70, United Scholarship Service, Denver, 1969-70, Adv. Council to FTC, 1969-70, Uptown Community Health Ctr., Chgo., 1971-74, Native Am. Com., Chgo., 1971-77, Comprehensive Health Council Chgo., 1974-75, Seven Nations Indian Opportunity Program, Central YMCA Community Coll., 1974-77. trustee Robert W. Rietz Am. Indian Scholarship Fund, Chgo., 1971-78; mem. exec. com. Edgewater-Uptown Community Mental Health Ctr., Chgo., 1974-75; cons. Health Manpower Devel. Corp., Washington, 1975, numerous Ill. pub. schs., 1978-82; chmn. Ill. Adv. Council in Indian Edn., 1978-79; mem. adv. council D; Arcy McNickle Ctr. for History of Am. Indian, Newberry Library, 1978-86; mem. commn. on women's affairs Office of Mayor, Chgo., 1984-85, mem. hunger task force, 1983-84; mem., presenter Gov.'s Conf. on Human Rights, Ill., 1983; bd. dirs. Crossroads Fund, 1985—, Chgo. Access Corp., 1986—; mem. venture grants com. United Way of Met. Chgo., 1984—, mem. agy. services com., 1983—. Fellow Leadership Greater Chgo.; mem. Regional Networking for Minority Women, Am. Indian Bus. Assn. (cons., bd. dirs. tng. and devel. program 1977-78). Home: 4880 N Hermitage St Chicago IL 60640 Office: Native Am Ednl Service Coll 2838 W Peterson Chicago IL 60659

SMITH, FERN MEYERSON, judge; b. San Francisco, Nov. 7, 1933; d. Samuel and Sophie (Blank) Meyerson; m. Don Avery Smith, Oct. 20, 1955 (div. 1977); children—Susan Elizabeth, Julie Ann; m. F. Robert Burrows, Feb. 25, 1984. A.A., Foothill Coll., 1970; B.A., Stanford U., 1972, J.D., 1975. Bar: Calif. 1975. Assoc. firm Bronson, Bronson & McKinnon, San Francisco, 1975-82, ptnr., 1982-86; judge San Francisco County Superior Ct., 1986—; mem. hiring, mgmt. and personnel coms., active recruiting various law schs. Co-author article in legal publ. Mem. ABA, Queen's Bench, Nat. Assn. Women Judges, Calif. Women Lawyers, Downtown Women Lawyers, Phi Beta Kappa.

SMITH, FRANCES CHERRY, funeral director; b. Williamston, N.C., June 21; d. Leo and Omenella (Riddick) Cherry; m. Alfred J. Smith, Nov. 24, 1949; children—Randy A., Trent L. Grad. McAllister Sch. Embalming, N.Y.C., 1952. Lic. funeral dir., N.J. With David D. Woody Funeral Home, Newark, 1945-49; owner, operator Smith Funeral Home, Elizabeth, N.J., 1952—. Mem. Elizabeth Bd. Edn.; mem. Elizabeth Devel. Corp.; mem. Egenolf Nursery Adv. Bd.; Recipient Key to City of Elizabeth, 1976, Appreciation and Service award Northeast region Nat. Caucus Black Sch. Bd. Mems., 1985. Mem. Union County Negro Bus. and Profl. Women (Bus. Woman award 1980), N.J. Bd. Mortuary Sci., North Jersey Negro Bus. and Profl. Women's Clubs (Profl. Woman of Yr. 1959), Women's Scholarship Club (Recognition award 1980, Service award 1980), Nat. Assn. Negro Bus. and Profl. Women (treas. com. for UN). Democrat. Lodge: Soroptimists. Office: Smith Funeral Home 45 Cherry St Elizabeth NJ 07202

SMITH, FRANCES PAULINE, medical librarian; b. Long Beach, Calif., Aug. 20, 1934; d. Walter Paul Philip Goodnough and Juanita (Deskin) Goodnough Downing. A.A., Leeward Community Coll., 1972, A.S. in Library Sci., 1973; B.A. in Liberal Arts, Hawaii Pacific Coll., 1979; M.L.S., U. Hawaii Grad. Sch., 1985. Med. librarian Straub Clinic, Honolulu, 1974—; online search analyst Medline, Dialog, BRS, AMA/Net; designer Straub Clinic Library, 1984. Den mother Boy Scouts Am., Big Bear Lake, Calif., 1965-70; organizer Little League, Big Bear Lake, 1967-70. Mem. Hawaii Library Assn., Med. Library Assocs., Med. Group of Hawaii (pres. 1986), MLA, Pacific Area Community Tech., Spl. Libraries Assn. Office: Straub Clinic and Hosp Inc Arnold Library 888 S King St Honolulu HI 96813

SMITH, GAIL ELAINE GREWELL, oil company executive; b. Dover, Ohio, Oct. 10, 1955; d. Floyd Madison and Mary Catherine (Sica) G.; m. Larry Alan Fagley, Jan. 22, 1986 (div.); children from previous marriage—John Paul Marino, Vanessa Marie Marino; m. Albert J. Smith, Feb. 10, 1988; 1 stepson, Michael Alex. Student Am. Inst. Banking, 1974, Kent State U., 1980-82, cert. Am. Inst. Paralegal Studies, 1987-88. Land mgr. Penn-Ohio Energy Corp., New Philadelphia, Ohio, 1980-83; pres., Citi-Energy Ops. Inc., Dover and Vancouver, B.C., Can., 1983—; ptnr. Citisystems Mgmt. Co., Dover, 1987—. cons. Atwood Resources Inc., Dover, Environ. Exploration Co., Canton, Ohio, 1987; mktg. dir. Aleve Profl. Mgmt. Services, Inc.; participant first ann. bus. symposium Kent State U. Tuscampus, 1986. Mem. Sacred Heart Sch. Bd., New Philadelphia, 1985—; bd. dirs. Muskingum Lakes chpt. ARC, 1986-89. Mem. Eastern Mineral Law Found., Ohio and Gas Assn. (vice chmn. 1986—, participant sem. 1984, 6th ann. inst. 1985), Internat. Mgmt. Council (conflict mgmt. sem. 1984, youth and bus. chmn. 1985, one day seminar chmn. 1986), North East Ohio Paralegal Assn., Ohio Petroleum Producers Assn., U.S. C. of C., Am. Assn. Petroleum Landmen. Democrat. Roman Catholic. Avocations: water skiing, cooking, horses. Home: 34751 Johnson Hills Rd Cadiz OH 43907 Office: PO Box 2247 Dover OH 44622

SMITH, GAIL HUNTER, artist; b. Nashville, Mar. 18, 1948; d. Walter Gray Smith and Eleanor Theresa (Cregar) Egan. Student, Memphis State U., 1966-67; BFA in Advt. Design, Memphis Acad. Arts, 1971. Prodn. asst. Visual Studios, Phila., 1970; asst. art dir. Eric Ericson and Assocs. and Ken White Design, Inc., Nashville, 1971-72; art dir. Contemporary Mktg., Inc., Ivan Stiles Advt., Bala Cynwyd (Pa.), Phila., 1972-74; specialist publs. design Temple U., Phila., 1974-75; represented by Mystic (Conn.) Maritime Gallery, Capricorn Gallery, Bethesda, Md., Alice Bingham Gallery, Memphis, Julie Fletcher & Assocs., Park Ridge, N.J., GWS Galleries, Southport, Conn.; judge Haddonfield (N.J.) Artists Exhbn., 1976; tchr. in field. Editor: Artists USA, 7th edit., Yacht Portraits, 1987; one-woman show Dow Jones & Co., Inc., Princeton, N.J., 1987; exhibited in group shows at 17th Tenn. All-State Artist Exhbn., Nashville, 1977, Arnold Art Gallery, Newport, R.I., 1986, Wildfowl Festival, Easton, Md., 1987. Recipient award Nashville Ad Fedn., 1973. Mem. Am. Inst. Graphic Arts, Am. Soc. Marine Artists, Artists Equity Assn., Nat. Mus. of Women in the Arts, Soc. Illustrators, Soc. of Scribes, Nat. Assn. for Female Execs., Am. Council for the Arts, Nat. Audubon Soc., Wilderness Soc., World Wildlife Fund, Sierra Club. Office: PO Box 217 Barnegat Light NJ 08006

SMITH, GERALDINE WRIGHT, gas company supervisor; b. Birmingham, Ala., May 16, 1945; d. William Joe and Lucinda (McMillan) Peeples; 1 child, Lisa Dyonne; m. Emmanuel Smith, June 11, 1980. Grad., Booker Washington Bus. Coll., 1965; student, Met. State Coll., 1968-72; cert. Legal Sec., Los Angeles City Coll., 1972; BA, U. Ala., 1987. Sec. State of Calif. Dept. of Rehab., Los Angeles, 1965-67; personnel clk. Warner Bros. Studios, Burbank, Calif., 1968-71; legal sec. Harry E. Weiss Law Firm, Los Angeles, 1971-72; legal sec. So. Natural Gas Co., Birmingham, 1972-77, supr. records, 1977—. Author: Prayer: The Key to Success. Tutor Adopt-a-Sch., Birmingham, 1985—. Mem. Nat. Assn. Female Execs., Assn. Records Mgrs. and Adminstrs. (bd. dirs. 1984-86, editor newsletter 1983-85). Home: 2317 9th St NW Birmingham AL 35215 Office: So Natural Gas Co PO Box 2563 Birmingham AL 35215

SMITH, GRACE DONALDSON, social science educator; b. Statesboro, Ga., Oct. 11, 1930; d. George and Gussie (Lanier) Donaldson; m. Willie Albert Smith, Sr., June 5, 1951; children: Willie Albert Jr., Eric George. BA, Paine Coll., 1951; MEd, Ga. So. Coll., 1976. Social sci. tchr. Statesboro (Ga.) High Sch., 1969—, dept. head, 1973—. Sec. Ga. Fedn. of Dem. Women, Statesboro, 1976-78; chairperson Ga. Council for Social Studies, Statesboro, 1976; mem. adv. bd. Ogeeche Home Health Agy., Statesboro, 1980—; treas. Bulloch County Bi-centennial Commn., 1987—. Named Sch.'s Tchr. Yr. Bullock County Bd. Edn., Statesboro, 1982. Mem. AAUW (Stateboro chpt. v.p., chmn. program 1984-86, chmn. individual liberties), NEA, Ga. Assn. Educators, Bullock County Assn. Edn. (treas. 1975, sec. 1987), Negro Bus. and Profl. Women, Kappa Delta Pi (treas. Eta Gamma Pi chpt. 1987). Democrat. Methodist. Club: Stabucettes (Statesboro) (pres. 1976-78). Home: 18 James St Statesboro GA 30458

SMITH, GRACIE BERNON, dress designer, tailor; b. Hyden, Ky., Aug. 1, 1932; d. Joe and Eva Lee (Howard) Maggard; m. William Robert Smith, June 10, 1972; children by previous marriage—Donald Eugene Turpin, Jr., Daniel Edwin Turpin; stepchildren: Steven Carson Smith, Vicki Lynn Booth. Student Nat. Sch. Dress Design-Chgo., 1955-58; student in real estate Purdue U., 1973. Tailor Sovern Tailors, Lafayette, Ind., 1965-68; mgr. Millers Sportswear, Lafayette, 1968-70; with Benker Realty, Lafayette, 1973-75; service contract dept. head Montgomery Ward, Lafayette, 1975-77; alteration dept. head Montgomery Ward, 1977-80; owner, operator Bernon Custom Fashions, Lafayette, 1955—; cons. local 4-H Clubs, 1983—; local sales rep. Leiters Designer Fabrics, Kansas City, Mo., 1982-87; local sales mgr. House of Laird Fabrics, Lexington, Ky., 1985—. Com. mem. Tippecanoe County Fair, Lafayette, 1983-85. Fellow The Custom Tailors and Designers Assn. Am., Am. Bus. Womens Assn., mem. Nat. Assn. Female Execs. Baptist. Avocations: bowling; gardening; knitting; cooking; crocheting. Home and Office: 2350 N 23d St Lafayette IN 47904

SMITH, HELEN CATHARINE, author; b. Chgo., June 7, 1903; d. J. A.; B.A., U. Calif. at Los Angeles, 1926; postgrad. U. Wis., 1954-56; M.Sc., Christian Coll., 1962, Ph.D., 1965, Psy.D., 1966; Ph.D. (hon.) Free U., hon. doctorate Gt. China Arts Coll., 1969, St. Olav's Acad., Sweden, 1969, Internat. Acad. Soverign Order Alfred Gt., Eng., 1969; J.D., Ohio Christian Coll., 1969; Ph.D., U. Reno (Nigeria), 1975; m. H. C. Smith, June 7, 1932 (dec. 1972); children—Glen Dean, DeEtta Ellen (Mrs. Gerald L. Amdahl), George Dale. Tchr. 2d grade Maple Lawn Sch., Clinton, Wis.; legal sec., Janesville, Wis., Office of City Atty., Evansville, Wis., 1933—; dir. Blue Moon poetry mag., 1952-57. Recipient 1st pl. award for article Herdman Meml. Competition Brit. Press, 1957; John Francis Sims Meml. award for poetry, 1955; award of honor UN Day, Philippines, 1967; laurel wreath, gold medal Pres. Philippines, 1967; certificate recognition Nat. Poetry Day Com., 1972; Distinguished Service award Wis. Jaycees, 1975, certificate Am. Bicentennial Research Inst., 1975, Hall of Honor award U. Wis., 1988, named Hon. Poet Laureate (Am.-Visayan), 1967; Internat. Woman of 1975 with laureate honors by Imelda R. Marcos. Fellow Intercontinental Biog. Assn.; mem. AAUW (awards poetry, short stories 1972), Wis. Regional Writers Assn. (sec. 1949-55, 61—, hon. life dir., leadership citation 1956, Jade Ring winner for short story 1957), Nat. League Am. Pen Women, Am. Poetry League, Wis. Fellowship Poets, Wis. Acad. Scis. Arts and Letters, Brit. Press Assn., United Poets Laureate Internat. (Karta award), Wis. Council for Writers (life, 2d pl. award for short story 1980), Centro Studie Scambi Internazionali Roma (medal of honor 1966-67, internat. exec. bd.), Wis. Edn. Assn., Wis. Regional Artists, State Hist. Soc. Wis., Accademia Internazionale Leonardo Da Vinci (Rome; Gold medallion 1972), Accademia Internazionale Di Pontzen, Am. Lit. Assn. (life), World Poetry Soc. (hon. life), UN Assn., Phi Beta Kappa (sustaining), Alpha Psi Omega, Sigma Iota XI. Author: Laughing Child, books I, II, III, 1945, 46, 47; Off the Record, 1949; From the Countryside, 1952; Stars in My Eyes, 1954; Wind-Falls, 1955; Chiaroscura, 1964; But Not Yet, 1973; You Can't Cry All the Time, 1975. Editor: Evansville Anthology of Verse, 1952, No. Spring, anthology, 1956; Chiaroscura, 1964; Helen's Sketch Book, 1978; contbr. articles, stories to numerous mags., newspapers, anthologies. Home: 455 S 1st St Apt 19 Evansville WI 53536

SMITH, IRIS FRANCINE, health maintenance organization director; b. N.Y.C., July 6, 1945; d. Peter and Belle (Nitzberg) S. BS, U. Bridgeport, 1967; teaching credential, San Francisco State U., 1972. Cert. tchr., Calif. Supr. computer room Pacific Telephone Co., San Francisco, 1970-71; personnel adminstr., intake social worker City and County of San Francisco, 1971-73; fin. coordinator, admitting dept. supr. Presbyn. Hosp., San Francisco, 1973-77; regional quality assurance dir. Quality Care Nursing Services, San Francisco, 1977-80; mktg. rep. Heals Health Plan, Emeryville, Calif., 1981-83; regional sales mgr. Health Plan of Am., Emeryville, 1983-85; dir. mktg. Westworld Community Health Plans, El Toro, Calif., 1985; dir. provider services Health Plan of America, Orange, Calif., 1985—. Fellow Nat. Assn. Female Execs. Democrat. Jewish. Club: 20/30 (Orange) (1st v.p. 1986-88). Home: 57 Laurel Creek Ln Laguna Hills CA 92653 Office: Health Plan of Am 505 S Main St Suite300 Orange CA 92668

SMITH, JACKLYN, state legislator; b. Campbell, Nebr., Nov. 12, 1934; m. Ramon G. Smith, 1952; children: Robb, Jeff, Kurt, Jon. BA, Kearney (Nebr.) State Coll. Asst. dir. Midland Area Agy. on Aging; mem. Nebr. State Legislature. Mem. Nebr. Bicentennial Commn.; bd. dirs. Adams County 4-H. Republican. Office: Office State Legislature State Capitol Lincoln NE 68509 also: Rt 3 Box 21 Hastings NE 68901 *

SMITH, JAMIE C., education educator; b. N.Y.C., June 11, 1948; d. Harry Frank and Dorothea M (Rankin(S. BA in Math, Northeastern U., 1971; MA in Elem. Edn. Teaching, William Paterson Coll., 1974; EdD in Early Childhood Edn., U. Ga., 1977. Cert. tchr., N.C. Tchr. Philmon Baptist Day Care Ctr., Paterson, N.J., 1972, Guidance Guild Day Care and Nursery Sch., Passaic, N.J., 1973, Wayne (N.J.) Country Day Sch., 1973-74; from asst. to assoc. prof. Appalachian State U., Boone, N.C., 1976-86; prof. Gov.'s State U., University Park, Ill., 1986-87; instr. Great Books Found., Chgo., 1987—; instr. Children's World, 1987; adv. Bethel (N.C.) Elem. Sch., 1985-86; ednl. cons., 1976—;. Author: Beginning Early: Adult Responsibility to Gifted Young Children, 1986, What Color is Newton's Apple, 1987. Mem. adv. bd. CAISS, Flossmoor, 1986-87. Mem. Nat. Assn. for Gifted Children (steering com.), Nat. Assn. for Edn. of Young Children, World Council for the Gifted, Ill. Assn. for the Edn. of Young Children, Arabian Horse Assn., Phi Delta Kappa. Office: Great Books Found 40 E Huron Chicago IL 60611

SMITH, JANE ANN, engineering administrator; b. Bloomington, Ill., Aug. 29, 1956; d. Donald Duane and M. Jean (Costigan) S. BS in Gen. Engring., U. Ill., 1978; MSME, U. Cin., 1984. Test engr. aircraft engine div. Gen. Electric Co., Evendale, Ohio, 1978-81, design engr., 1981-85, engring. mgr., 1985—.

SMITH, JANE ELLEN, electrical engineer; b. Amherst, Ohio, Oct. 26, 1958; d. Franklyn Allen and Kathleen Jane (Wilhelm) Nesbit; m. Robert Alan Smith, July 10, 1982; 1 child, Robert William. BEE, U. Dayton, 1981. Registered profl. engr., Ohio. Elec. engr. Bailey Controls Co., Wickliffe, Ohio, 1981—. Co-inventor control system for an electro-pneumatic converter, variable speed resistive network for a pneumatic servo assembly of an electo-pneumatic converter, on-line replacement sensor assembly for a vortex shedding flowmeter. Mem. NSPE, IEEE. Roman Catholic. Office: Bailey Controls Co 29801 Euclid Ave Wickliffe OH 44092

SMITH, JANE KNOBLOCH, food products company executive; b. Terre Haute, Ind., Aug. 31, 1959; d. Richard F. Knobloch and Joan Margaret (Trimble) Minnick; m. Gordon Mark Smith, Oct. 4, 1986. BS in Indsl. Tech., Purdue U., 1981. Div. mgr. prodn. dept. Home and Automotive div. Union Carbide, Rogers, Ark. and Atlanta, 1981-86; regional mgr. Dole Food Co., Memphis, 1986—.

SMITH, JANE SCHNEBERGER, city clerk; b. Chgo., Aug. 9, 1928; d. Frank R. and Marion (Durante) Schneberger; m. Z. Erol Smith, Jr., Oct. 28, 1950 (div. 1974); children—Suzan McCue Kuester, Tracy Smith Cawley, Cameron Farley, Z. Erol III, Kimberly, Scott. B.A. in Chemistry, U. Colo., 1950; M.A. in Communication, Mich. State U., 1978, PhD in ednl. adminstrn. Mich. State U., 1987. Chemist, Kellogg Switchboard, Chgo., 1950-51; tchr. Crab Orchard Sch., Palos Heights, Ill., 1969-70; staff advisor South Cook County Girl Scouts, Harvey, Ill., 1970-72; program and tng. dir. Mich. Capitol council Girl Scouts U.S., Lansing, 1972-75; dir. service learning ctr. Mich. State U., East Lansing, 1975-81; city clk. City of Ashland, Wis., 1981—; cons. vol. adminstrn., Mich., Wis., 1975—. Co-editor Looking Backward Moving Forward; Contbr. articles to profl. jours. Vice pres. South Cook County Girl Scout Council, Harvey, Ill., 1967-69 (Thanks badge 1972), Mich. Capitol Girl Scout Council, Lansing, 1976-78 (cert. appreciation 1975); bd. dirs. Lansing RSVP, 1976-81, Ashland Mus., 1985-87, Ptnrs. in Recovery, 1985-87, New Horizons, 1985—. Mem. Internat. Assn. Municipal Clks., Wis. Municipal Clks. Assn. (dist. dir. 1984-86). Roman Catholic. Club: Am. Bus. Women's Assn. (scholarship chmn. 1985) (Ashland). Lodge: Zonta (pres. 1979-81). Avocations: stained glass, gardening. Home: 700 MacArthur St Ashland WI 54806 Office: City Ashland 601 W 2nd St Ashland WI 54806

SMITH, JANET ERLENE, sales and marketing executive; b. Athens, Ga., Apr. 7, 1956; d. Phyletus Robert and Erlene (Hendricks) S. BS, Ga. So. U., 1978. Staff asst. The White House Press Office, Washington, 1978-81; exec. asst. USA Today, Washington, 1981-82, nat. salesperson, 1982-85, dir. nat. sales, 1985—. Democrat. Office: USA Today PO Box 500 Washington DC 20044

SMITH, JANET SUE, systems specialist; b. Chgo., Jan. 15, 1945; d. Curtis Edwin and Margaret Louise (Yost) Smith; B.A., Ind. U., 1967. Sales mgr. Marshall Field & Co., Chgo., 1968-70, programmer, 1970-72; sr. programmer, analyst Trailer Train Co., Chgo., 1972-75; mgr. data base and systems devel. RAILINC-Assn. Am. R.R., Washington, 1975-85, asst. v.p. bus. services, 1985—. Nat. student v.p. YWCA, 1966-67; bd. dirs., v.p. planning and fin. Guide Internat., Friends of the Nat. Zoo; advisor Jr. Achievement. Mem. Am. Council R.R. Women, Ind. U. Alumni Assn. (life), Women's Transp. Seminar. Home: 2000 N St NW Washington DC 20036 Office: 50 F St NW Washington DC 20001

SMITH, JANICE FAYE (JAN), software engineer; b. Oneonta, Ala., July 11, 1945; d. Robert Conrad and Jeanette (Bailey) Hays; m. Fred Almon Smith, Oct. 19, 1974 (div. Dec. 1984); 1 child, Lance Almon. BS in Math., Jacksonville State U., 1967. Assoc. engr. Boeing, Huntsville, Ala., 1967-69; mem. tech. staff Computer Sci. Corp., Huntsville, 1969-77, 79; engr. McDonnell-Douglas Automation Co., St. Louis, 1977-79; dir. computer services and software applications divs. Nichols Research Corp., Huntsville, 1979—. Rep. for industry State of Ala. Super Computer com., Huntsville,

1985-86. Republican. Methodist. Office: Nichols Research Corp 4040 S Memorial Pkwy Huntsville AL 35802

SMITH, JANIE WILKINS, chemical company information educator; b. Columbia, La., Apr. 5, 1930; d. James Climent and Hester (Bibb) Wilkins; B.A., La. Tech. U., 1951; postgrad. Fla. State U., 1962-70, U. Fla., 1962-63, U. South Fla., 1963-64; m. Thomas L. Smith, Nov. 3, 1950 (div.); children—Linda Karen, Thomas, Jr., Eric Andrew. English librarian Morehouse Parish Sch. Bd., Bastrop, La., 1951-52, Union Parish Sch. Bd., Farmerville, La., 1952-56, East Carroll Parish Sch. Bd., Lake Providence, La., 1957-60, Union Parish Schs., Farmerville, 1970-75, Ouachita Parish Schs., Monroe, La., 1976-79; ref. librarian Ouachita Parish Public Library, 1960-62; librarian lang. arts Brevard County Bd. Public Instrn., Titusville, Fla., 1962-70; info. specialist Columbian Chems. Co., Swartz, La., 1980—. Mem. AAUW (membership com.), Spl. Library Assn., Nat. Library Assn. Methodist. Office: 1001 Cherry Ridge Rd Bastrop LA 71220

SMITH, JEAN WEBB (MRS. WILLIAM FRENCH SMITH), civic worker; b. Los Angeles; d. James Ellwood and Violet (Hughes) Webb; B.A. summa cum laude, Stanford U., 1940; m. George William Vaughan, Mar. 14, 1942 (dec. Sept. 1963); children—George William, Merry; m. 2d, William French Smith, Nov. 6, 1964. Mem. Nat. Vol. Service Adv. Council (ACTION), 1973-76, vice chmn., 1974-76; dir. Beneficial Standard Corp., 1976-85. Vol., Nat Center, 1977—; Community TV So. Calif. (KCET); mem. Calif. Arts Commn., 1971-74, vice chmn., 1973-74; bd. dirs. The Founders, Music Center, Los Angeles, 1971-74; bd. dirs. costume council Los Angeles County Mus. Art, 1971-73; bd. dirs. United Way, Inc., 1973-80; bd. fellows Claremont Univ. Ctr. and Grad. Sch., 1987—; trustee Calif. Hist. Soc., 1970-71; bd. dirs. Hosp. Good Samaritan, 1973-80; mem. exec. com., 1975-80; mem. nat. bd. dirs. Boys' Clubs Am., 1977-80; bd. dirs. Los Angeles chpt. NCCJ, 1977-80, Nat. Symphony Orch., 1980-85; mem. adv. bd. Salvation Army, 1979—; mem. President's Commn. on White House Fellowships, 1980—, Nat. Council on the Humanities, 1987—. Named Woman of Yr. for community service Los Angeles Times, 1958; recipient Citizens of Yr. award Boys Clubs Greater Los Angeles, 1982, Life Achievement award Boy Scouts Am., Los Angeles council, 1985. Mem. Jr. League of Los Angeles (pres. 1954-55), Assn. Jr. Leagues of Am. (dir. Region XII, 1956-58, pres. 1958-60), Phi Beta Kappa, Kappa Kappa Gamma. Home: 1256 Oak Grove Ave San Marino CA 91108

SMITH, JEANNE, marketing research and telemarketing company executive, consultant; b. Richmond, Va., May 2, 1955; d. John Herman and Joyce (Divers) Crostic; m. Donald Wayne Smith, July 11, 1976. Nurse Richmond Pub. Schs., 1973; freelance field service worker, Richmond, 1974-80; field service worker N.Am. Mktg., Richmond, 1981-82, field service supr., 1982-83, dir. field services, 1983; owner, operator Smith Research Ctr., Richmond, 1983—. Served with U.S. Army, 1973-76. Mem. Am. Mktg. Assn., Mktg. Research Assn. Republican. Baptist. Clubs: Va. Bass'n Gals (sec., treas.), Lady Bass. Lodge: Women of Moose. Avocation: professional bass fisherwoman. Office: Smith Research Ctr PO Box 13676 Richmond VA 23225

SMITH, JO ANNE, journalist, educator; b. Mpls., Mar. 18, 1930; d. Robert Bradburn and Virginia Mae S. B.A., U. Minn., 1951, M.A., 1957. Wire and sports editor Rhinelander (Wis.) Daily News, 1951-52; staff corr., night mgr. UP, Mpls., 1952-56; interim instr. U. N.C., Chapel Hill, 1957-58; instr. U. Fla., Gainesville, 1959-65; asst. prof. journalism, communications U. Fla., 1965-68, assoc. prof., 1968-76, prof., 1976—, Disting. lectr., 1977. Author: JM409 Casebook and Study Guide, 1976, Mass Communications Law Casebook, 1979, 3d edit., 1985. Active, Friends of Library, Alachua County Humane Soc. Named Tchr. of Yr., U. Fla. Coll. Journalism, 1973, 74, 75, 76, 81, 86, Outstanding Tchr., Journalism Dept. of U. Fla., 1973, 74, 75, 76; recipient outstanding Prof. award Fla. Blue Key, 1976; Danforth assoc., 1976-85. Mem. Women in Communications, Soc. Profl. Journalists, Assn. Edn. in Journalism, Phi Beta Kappa, Kappa Tau Alpha. Democrat. Unitarian. Home: 208 NW 21 Terr Gainesville FL 32603 Office: U Fla 3044 Weimer Hall Gainesville FL 32611

SMITH, JOAN LEITA, school media specialist; b. Syracuse, N.Y., Sept. 17, 1938; d. James and Lucille (Fiske) Wilcox; m. Robert David Smith, July 22, 1961; children—Kenneth, Karen, B.S. in Elem. Edn., SUNY-Cortand, 1960; M.A. in Library Sci., Ind. U., 1964. Tchr., Bay Shore (N.Y.) Sch. Dist. 1960-61, Mad River Twp., Dayton, Ohio, 1962, 64; bookmobile children's librarian Dayton and Montgomery County, Ohio, 1962-63; sch. library media specialist Rome (N.Y.) Sch. Dist., 1979—; ch. librarian Bowie United Meth. Ch., Md., 1970-72. Active PTA, Rome, 1976-82; leader Girl Scouts U.S.A., Rome, 1974-81. Mem. ALA, Central N.Y. Library Assn., N.Y. Library Assn., AAUW, Beta Phi Mu, Pi Lambda Theta. Clubs: Air Force Officers Wives. Address: 18 Pleasant Dr Rome NY 13440

SMITH, JOSEPHINE WOOLLEY, advertising agency executive; b. Findlay, Ohio, Mar. 15, 1934; d. Walton Douglas and Charlotte Josephine (Bente) Woolley; m. Lawrence Sophian, June 22, 1954; children—Celia, Catherine. B.A., Sarah Lawrence Coll., 1954. Advt. copywriter Batten, Barton, Durstine & Osborn, 1954-62; copy supr. Ogilvy & Mather, N.Y.C., 1962-70; v.p. Ogilvy & Mather, 1970-73, creative dir., 1973, sr. v.p., 1974—. Office: Ogilvy & Mather 2 E 48th St New York NY 10017

SMITH, JUANITA RANKIN, accountant; b. Bridgeton, N.J., Nov. 1, 1949; d. Andrew Jackson and Jessie Lee (Bryant) Rankin; m. Ronald Delaneo Smith, Mar. 23, 1968 (div. Nov. 1978); 1 child, LaJuana. BS, Glassboro State Coll., 1982. Operating acct. Communications-Electronics Command U.S. Army, Ft. Monmouth, N.J., 1984—. Bd. dirs. Bridgeton Housing Devel. Corp., 1984-85; pres. Bridgeton High Sch. PTA, 1982; trustee Macedonia Bapt. Ch., Neptune, N.J., 1986. Mem. Am. Soc. Mil. Comptrollers, Nat. Assn. Negro Bus. and Profl. Women. (fin. sec. N.J. chpt. 1988—), Assn. Govt. Accts. Democrat. Baptist. Home: 2130 Aldrin Rd Apt #6-A Ocean NJ 07712 Office: US Army Communications and Electronics Command AMSEL-CP-FA-GAB Fort Monmouth NJ 07703-5009

SMITH, JUDITH BROOKS, marketing executive; b. Shreveport, La., Sept. 10, 1947; d. Louis Andrew and Hazel Lula (Veuleman) Brooks; m. Ronald Edward Smith, Aug. 30, 1968 (div. 1976). B.Bus. magna cum laude, Baylor U., 1969. Sales promotion asst. Success Motivation, Waco, Tex., 1969; advt. asst. Shell Chem. Co., Houston, 1970-71; bus. devel. asst. Golemon & Rolfe Architects, Houston, 1973; mktg. dir. Drawing Bd., Dallas, 1976-80, Parker-Garrick, Dallas, 1980-82; mgr. planning Heublein, Chgo., 1982-84, mktg. mgr., Hartford, Conn., 1984-88, dir. mktg.. Thermo-Serv, Dallas, 1988— . Mem. Am. Mktg. Assn. (pres. Dallas chpt. 1982, treas. Chgo. chpt. 1984, Marketer of Yr. candidate 1980), Bus. and Profl. Women, Women's Assn. Allied Beverge Industries. Theta Chi. Office: Thermo-Serv 2777 Stemmons Freeway Suite 1225 Dallas TX 75207

SMITH, JUDITH PELHAM, hospital administrator; b. Bristol, Conn., July 23, 1945; d. Marvin Curtis and Muriel (Chodos) Pelham; m. Hubert Lipscomb Smith, Jan. 27, 1968; children: Rachel, Molly. BA, Smith Coll., 1967; MPA, Harvard U., 1975. Various govt. postions 1968-72; prin. analyst Urban Systems, Cambridge, Mass., 1972-73; dir. devel. and planning Roxbury Dental and Med. Group, Boston, 1975-76; asst. to dir. for gen. medicine and ambulatory care Peter B. Brigham Hosp., Boston, 1976-77, asst. dir. ambulatory care, 1977-79; asst. v.p. Brigham and Women's Hosp., Boston, 1980-81; dir. planning and mktg. Seton Med. Ctr., Austin, Tex., 1980-82, pres., 1982—, chief exec. officer, 1987—; pres., chief exec. officer Daughters of Charity Health Services, Austin, 1987—; cons. Robert W. Johnson Found., Princeton, N.J., 1980-81. Author: Financial Management of Ambulatory Care, 1985; contbr. articles to profl. jours. Trustee A. Shivers Radiation Therapy Ctr., Austin, 1982—, Marywood Maternity and Adoption Agy., 1982-86; bd. dirs. Quality of Life Found., Austin, 1985, Austin Rape Crisis Ctr., adv. bd., 1986-88; bd. dirs., trustee League House, 1982—, Seton Fund, 1982—; mem. Gov's Job Tng. Coordinating Council, 1983-85; adv. council U. Tex. Social Work Found., 1983-85; charter mem. Leadership Tex., Austin, 1983—. Recipient Leadership award YWCA, Austin, 1986. Mem. Am. Coll. Healthcare Execs., Am. Hosp. Assn., Tex. Hosp. Assn. (mem. various council 1982-87), Austin Area Research Orgn., Cath. Health Assn. (bd. dirs. 1987—, com. on govt. relations 1984—), Tex. Conf. Cath. Health Facilities (bd. dirs. 1985—, pres. 1988). Office: Seton Med Ctr 1201 W 38th St Austin TX 78705

SMITH, JULIANN JOCELYN, lawyer; b. Hazleton, Pa., Nov. 30, 1953, d. Stanley John and Elsie Antoinette (Matusick) S.; married. B.S. in Community Devel., Pa. State U.-University Park, 1975; postgrad. Boston U., 1978-79; J.D., U. Denver, 1981. Bar: Colo. Supreme Ct. 1983, U.S. Dist. Ct. (Colo.) 1983. Assoc. Kutak Rock & Campbell, Denver, 1981-85, Gorsuch, Kirgis, Campbell, Walker and Grover, 1985-87; lawyer Colo. Housing and Fin. Authority, 1987—. Articles editor: Denver Law Jour., 1980-81; contbr. articles to profl. jours. Recipient scholarships, 1972-74. Mem. ABA, Colo. Bar Assn., Denver Bar Assn.

SMITH, KAREN LEE, telephone company executive; b. Cin., May 11, 1946; d. Marshall Dale and Doris Lee (Slaughter) S. AA with honors, Brevard Jr. Coll., 1966; BBA, Mundelein Coll., 1986. Service rep. Ill. Bell, 1967-70, service observer, 1970-71, bus. office supr., 1971-75, staff supr., 1975-76; asst. mgr. corp. edn. Ill. Bell, Chgo., 1976-81, asst. mgr. info. systems, 1981—; active Ill. Bell Speakers Bur., Chgo., 1975-78. Advisor Jr. Achievement, Evanston, Ill., 1976-77. Mem. Nat. Soc. for Performance Instrn. (v.p. 1978-79, program com. 1977-78), Women in Mgmt. (membership com. Chgo. Loop chpt. 1983-84, hospitality com. 1984-85), Phi Theta Kappa, Psi Tau Omega. Republican. Clubs: Corinthian Yacht (mdse. chmn. 1987—), Catalina Fleet 21 (Chgo.) (sec. 1983-86). Office: Ill Bell 225 W Randolph HQ 17-D Chicago IL 60601

SMITH, KAREN PHYLLIS, education service company executive; b. New Brunswick, N.J., Mar. 15, 1953; d. George and Gladys (Czap) S. BA in Edn., Fairleigh Dickinson U., 1975; postgrad., Montclair (N.J.) State Coll., 1978-80. Cert. tchr. elem., social studies, N.J., Ohio. Tchr. Leonia (N.J.) Pub. Schs., 1975-81; asst. mgr. Gift Bazaar, Pompano Beach, Fla., 1981-82; gen. mgr. Touch of Class Restaurant, Carlstadt, N.J., 1982-83; dir. Huntington Learning Ctrs., River Edge, N.J., 1983-85; coordinator tng. Oradell, N.J., 1985-86, gen. mgr. franchise ops., 1986—. Mem. Am. Soc. for Tng. Devel. Republican. Office: Huntington Learning Ctrs 660 Kinderkamack Rd Oradell NJ 07649

SMITH, KATHLEEN ANN, medical technologist; b. Buffalo, Mar. 13, 1935; d. Joseph John and Rose Ann (Starke) S.; B.A., Mercyhurst Coll., 1956. From chemist to supr. hemostasis lab. Hamot Hosp., Erie, Pa., 1956-69; with Warner Lambert Co., 1969-85, supr. hemostasis ednl. services, 1972-85; system specialist Hemostasis Organon Teknika Co., 1985-87, mgr. quality control release and inspection, 1987—; adv. bd. Morris County Coll., 1980-86; presentor seminars in field. Named Med. Technologist of Yr. in N.J., 1982. Mem. Am. Soc. Med. Tech. (chmn. hemotology-hemostasis sect. 1982-84), N.C. Soc. Med. Tech., Am. Soc. Quality Control, Am. Soc. Clin. Pathology, N.J. Soc. Med. Tech. (pres. 1975), Alpha Mu Tau. Republican. Roman Catholic. Club: Morristown (N.J.) Woman's. Co-author Hemostasis Manual. Assoc. editor Clotters Corner, 1980-87. Office: 8300 Redmill Rd Durham NC 27704

SMITH, KATHLEEN KEER MCGOWAN, artist; b. Newark, Mar. 8, 1918; d. Theodore F. and Florence (MacRae) Keer; B.A., Smith Coll., 1940; postgrad. Columbia U., 1943, N.J. Tchrs. Coll., 1946-49; m. B.C. Breeden, June 29, 1940 (div. 1943); 1 dau., Kathy; m. Harold F. Allenby, July 28, 1949 (div. 1977); m. John Francis McGowan, Apr. 24, 1981. (dec. Apr. 28, 1986); m. Bev Smith, Sept. 4, 1987. Kindergarten tchr. Kimberly Sch., Montclair, N.J., 1946-49; tchr. art to handicapped Kessler Inst. Rehab., West Orange, N.J., 1961-77. Exhibited one-man shows Woman's Club Montclair, 1st Savs. & Loan Bank, Cedar Grove, N.J., Music Sch., Cedar Grove, Piggins Art Gallery, Montclair, N.J., all 1972; 2-man show 1st Nat. Bank of Palm Beach, 1978; exhibited in group shows N.J. State Fedn. Women's Clubs, Art Center of Oranges. Leader, Girl Scouts U.S.A., Little Falls, N.J., 1955-56, social dir. PTA, Great Notch, N.J., 1955-56. Recipient art awards Upper Montclair Women's Club; cert. of merit in art N.J. Fedn. Women's Clubs, 1st place essay award, 1973; 2 awards for oil paintings Lighthouse Art Gallery, Tequesta, Fla. Recipient Golden Poet award, 1987, numerous hon. mentions. Mem. Art Center Oranges, West Essex Art Assn., N.J. State Fedn. Women's Clubs (7th dist. art chmn. 1973-74), West Palm Beach Coin Club (sec. 1978-81). Clubs: Glen Ridge Country (N.J., handicap chmn. 1970, past publicity chmn. women's golf group); Upper Montclair Women's (dir. art dept. 1971-72, garden chmn. 1976-77); Little Falls Women's (treas. 1959-61); Quill (sec. 1985-87), Beach (Palm Beach); Smith of the Palm Beaches (treas. 1976-77); Jonathan's Landing Golf. Home: 583 North Lake Way Palm Beach FL 33408

SMITH, KATHRYN ANN, advertising executive; b. Harvey, Ill., Mar. 30, 1955; d. Kenneth Charles and Barbara Joan (Wise) S.; m. Donald Eugene Stonerock, Jr., Oct. 27, 1973 (div. Apr. 1977); m. Charles David Okoren, Oct. 31, 1980; 1 stepchild, Gwynne Marie. Student Art Inst. Chgo., 1973. Advt. salesperson Calumet Index, Inc., Riverdale, Ill., 1974-77, Towne & Country Ind., Hammond, 1977-78; owner, sales person Ad-Com, Merrillville, Ind., 1978—; pres. Ad-Com, Crown Point, Ind., 1978—. Dir., producer cable TV comml., 1982; dir., producer TV comml., 1987-88. Mem. Advt. Agy. Owners Assn. (chair 1985-88). Avocations: painting, flying, outdoor activities.

SMITH, KATHRYN BAKER, educational administrator, economist; b. Atlanta, Feb. 8, 1946; d. William Martin Ross and Mildred (Walker) Ross Eatmon; m. William Hugh Baker, III, June 10, 1965 (div.); 1 child, William Hugh IV; m. R.C. Smith, Nov. 23, 1979. Student, Lubbock Christian Coll., 1963-64, U. N.Mex., 1964-65, Fla. State U., 1968; BA, U. Tex., Austin, 1974, MA, 1978. Research assoc. Ctr. for Study of Human Resources, Austin, 1975-76; field researcher MDC, Inc., Chapel Hill, N.C., 1976-78; research assoc. Nat. Rural Ctr., Austin, 1976-79; statewide coordinator policy, planning, and programs N.C. Dept. Nat. Resources and Community Devel., Employment and Tng., 1979-82; asst. to state pres. for policy Dept. of Community Colls., Raleigh, N.C., 1982-86, dir. planning, 1986—; adv. bd. Small Bus. and Tech. Devel. Ctr., 1985—, U. N.C. Govt. Execs. Inst., 1983, N.C. Edn. Policy Seminars, 1984-85, Rural Edn. for Action Learning, 1985—; mem. steering com. N.C. Higher Edn., 1982—; cons. on employment and tng. Co-author: Rural Jobs from Rural Public Works, 1979; contbr. articles to profl. jours. Bd. dirs. N.C. Women's Forum, 1984-87; bd. dirs., sec. Tex. Housing Devel. Corp., 1977-79; affirmative action com. Dem. Party of Tex., 1974; exec. sec. Young Dems. of Tex., 1973-75. Office: Dept of Community Colls 200 W Jones St Raleigh NC 27603

SMITH, KATHY ANN, educator, senator; b. Muncie, Ind., Apr. 10, 1944; d. John Francis and H. Emily (Walter) Wallace; m. George Frederick Smith, June 22, 1979; 1 child, Alison Marie Smith. BS in Edn., Ind. U., 1966; postgrad., Ball State U., 1973. Cert. secondary lang. arts tchr., Ind. English tchr. New Albany (Ind.) Floyd Co. Sch. Corp., 1966—; adj. faculty Ind. U. Southeast, New Albany, 1977-84. Ind. State senator Ind. Gen. Assembly, Indpls., 1986—; del. Dem. Nat. Conv., N.Y., 1976-80, San Francisco, 1988, Ind. Dem. State Conv., Indpls., 1980, 82, 84, 86, 88; mem., del. Dem. Nat. Platform Com., Washington, 1984. Mem. New Albany Floyd County Edn. Assn. (legis. chair 1977-86, exec. com. 1979-86), Ind. State Tchrs. Assn. (chair polit. action com. 1978-81, 83-86), Nat. Edn. Assn. (NEA polit. action com. 1978-81, 83-84), Nat. Council Tchrs. of English, Pi Lambda Theta (hon., pres. 1986—), Psi Iota Xi. Democrat. Home: 1214 Beechwood Ave New Albany IN 47150 Office: Ind State Senate Ind Capitol Bldg Indianapolis IN 46204

SMITH, KRALEEN STANFIELD, information specialist, librarian; b. Swindon, Eng., June 5, 1958; came to U.S. 1958; d. James Krahe and Marjorie Janette (King) Stanfield; m. Tolby Lynn Smith, Jan. 5, 1985. B.A. cum laude, Tex. Woman's U., 1980, M.L.S., 1981. Info. specialist Price Waterhouse, Dallas, 1981—. Mem. Spl. Libraries Assn., Dallas Soc. Acctg. Librarians (pres. 1983-85), Dallas Assn. Law Librarians (2d v.p. 1985), Beta Phi Mu. Baptist. Home: 10336 Chelmsford Dallas TX 75217 Office: Price Waterhouse 1400 First City Center Dallas TX 75201

SMITH, LAURIE KATHRYN, judge; b. Eugene, Oreg., Aug. 1, 1938; d. Laurence Edwin and Georgia Ruth (Staton) Fischer; m. Peter Evan Smith, July 27, 1962 (div. June 1969); m. 2d, William Frye, Jan. 10, 1977 (div. Apr. 1987). B.A. in English, U. Oreg., 1961, J.D., 1973. Bar: 1973. Tchr. Sisters Sch. Dist. (Oreg.), 1962-63, Bend Sch. Dist. (Oreg.), 1963-69; ptnr. firm Frye & Smith, Eugene, 1973-81; judge Lane County Dist. Ct., Eugene, 1981—, presiding judge, 1986—; mem. Oreg. Jud. Fitness Commn., 1983-84. Chmn. bd. trustees Pub. Defender Services Lane County, 1980-81; bd. visitors U. Oreg. Law Sch., Eugene, 1980-84; pres. bd. dirs. Eugene Opera, 1982-84. Mem. Lane County Bar Assn. (pres. 1981-82), Profl. Women's Network Oreg., Nat. Assn. Women Judges; Oreg. Dist. Judges Assn. (pres. 1985-86). Office: Lane County Dist Ct 125 E 8th Ave Eugene OR 97401

SMITH, LEAH JOHNSON, economist, college official; b. Ft. Worth, Feb. 1, 1943; d. Francis Bonneau and Leah Townsend (Zeigler) Johnson; m. Woollcott Keston Smith; children: Amelia, Keston. BA, Stanford U., 1964; PhD, Johns Hopkins U., 1972. Instr. econs. N.C. State U., 1969-72; economist 1st Nat. Bank Boston, 1972-73; with Woods Hole Oceanographic Instn., 1973-82, assoc. marine policy and ocean mgmt., 1982; asst. prof. Haverford (Pa.) Coll., 1981-82; asst. prof. Swarthmore (Pa.) Coll., 1982-85, asst. to pres., dir. instl. research, 1985—; mem. sci. and statis. com. New Eng. Fishery Mgmt. Council; mem. adv. bd. Dept Interior; cons. in field. Contbr. articles to profl. jours. Trustee Woods Hole Library, 1976-81, pres., 1978-80; mem. vestry Trintiy Episcopal Ch., Swarthmore, 1987—. Research grantee Nat. Marine Fisheries Service. Mem. Am. Econ. Assn., AAAS, Assn. Instl. Research. Episcopalian. Office: Swarthmore Coll Office of Pres Swarthmore PA 19081

SMITH, LINDA LEA, university counselor; b. Wichita, Kans., June 18, 1958; d. Clifford Allen and Myrtle Elizabeth (Hoyne) S. B.S., Ball State U., 1981; M.S., N.W. Mo. State U., 1984. Counselor Julia Jameson Health Camp for Children, Inc., Indpls., 1979, program dir., 1980; mem. student staff Ball State U., Muncie, Ind., 1979-81; hall dir. N.W. Mo. State U., Maryville, 1981-84; student life counselor Ark. State U., Jonesboro, 1984—, asst. advisor Panhellenic Council. Mem. adminstrv. bd., conf. and edn. commn., coordinator singles 1st United Meth. Ch.; coordinator young adults United Meth. Ch. Jonesboro Dist. Council on Ministry; bd. dirs., self-help group co-facilitator N.E. Ark. Council on Family Violence (bd. dirs. 1988). Mem. Ark. Coll. and Personnel Assn. Democrat. Club: Jonesboro Women of Today (chmn. bd. dirs.), Ark. Women of Today (adminstrv. v.p. 1987-88, Outstanding Local Pres. award 1987). Avocations: swimming, weight lifting. Office: Ark State U Student Affairs PO Box 119 Jonesboro AR 72403

SMITH, LISA ELAINE, food products executive; b. Cleve., Aug. 18, 1959; d. Richard Lee and Patricia Jean (Grace) S. BSBA, Ohio State U., 1981. Travel coordinator Ohio State U., Columbus, 1979-81; store mgr. Cole Nat. Corp., Cleve., 1981-82; adminstrv. asst. Fabri-Centers Am., Cleve., 1982-83; support staff supr. Touche Ross & Co., Cleve., 1983-84; office mgr. McDonald's Corp., Cleve., 1984-86, regional adminstrv. mgr., 1986—. Corp. liaison Ronald McDonald House. Named Internat. Office Mgr. of Yr., McDonald's Corp., 1987. Mem. Adminstrv. Mgmt. Soc., Nat. Assn for Female Execs., Young Profls. of Cleve., Ohio State U. Alumni Assn. Republican. Methodist. Home: 1182 Cook Lakewood OH 44107 Office: McDonalds Corp 28253 Lorain Rd North Olmsted OH 44070

SMITH, LOIS MARIE (JO), publishing company executive, welcome service executive; b. Wickenburg, Ariz., Aug. 17, 1929; d. Wilbur R. and Vivian Beulah (Jenkins) McCarter; m. John Alan Smith, Nov. 4, 1950; children: Laura Brooke, Holly Marquette. Student Ariz. State Tchrs. Coll., 1948-50; BA in Nutrition, Mainz U., Ger., 1969. Various positions USAF Officer Wives Clubs, U.S. and Europe, 1952-69; v.p. High Valley Enterprises, Inc., Ft. Collins, Colo., 1972-75; co-owner, editor HollyBrooke House Press, Foster City, Calif., 1978—; pres. and chief exec. officer HollyBrooke House Pub., Las Vegas, 1981—; owner City Welcome Service, Las Vegas, 1984—, personal mgr., pub. relations cons. to entertainment field. Author: Crocked, 1975; author, editor-in-chief: Las Vegas Celebrity Cookbook, 1982, The Entertainers Cookbook, 1983. Mem. Las Vegas C. of C. (mem. Women's Council), Ariz. Authors Club. Republican. Episcopalian. Avocations: running, gourmet cooking, horticulture, music, art. Home: 5150 E Sahara Ave #183 Las Vegas NV 89122 Office: HollyBrooke House 1674 Elaine Dr Las Vegas NV 89122

SMITH, LYNDA MARIE, insurance company administrator; b. Ft. Wayne, Ind., Dec. 16, 1946; d. Fred Richard and Betty Jane (Shaneyfelt) Williams; m. Kenneth Lynn Smith, June 23, 1946; children—Bryan David, Brandon Daniel, Brady Dane. B.A. in Religious Edn., Central Bible Coll., Springfield, Mo., 1970; cert. CLU, Am. Coll., 1987. Music tchr. Jennings Music Studio, Ft. Wayne, 1972-74; office adminstr. First Assembly God, Evansville, Ind., 1974-76; music dir. Calvary Assembly, West Palm Beach, Fla., 1976-77; tchr. Ft. Wayne Christian Sch., 1977-79; ins. agt. Guarantee Mut. Ins. Co., Ft. Wayne, 1979-80; ins. agt., gen. agt., dir. mktg. and devel., asst. supt. agys. Mut. Security Life Ins. Co., Ft. Wayne, 1980-82, Houston, 1982-84, Atlanta, 1984-86; pres. Covenant Holding Group, Inc., Ins. Mktg. Co., Atlanta, 1985-86; regional mgr. sales Pyramimd Life Ins. Co., Atlanta, 1986—. Pres., Ft. Wayne Christian Sch. Aux., 1979-81. Recipient Blue Vase award Guarantee Mut. Ins. Co., 1979; Most Progressive Salesperson award Am. Heritage Co., Ft. Wayne, 1978. Mem. Nat. Assn. Life Underwriters, Atlanta Assn. Life Underwriters, North Fulton/Cherokee County Assn. Life Underwriters (chairperson health com.), Nat. Assn. Health Underwriters, Atlanta Assn. Health Underwriters (chairperson scholarship and edn. com.), Gen. Agts. and Mgrs. Assn., Houston Assn. Life Underwriters. Republican. Mem. Calvary Assembly. Home: PO Box 1565 Roswell GA 30077-1565

SMITH, MARCIA RAE, social services administrator; b. Indpls., Aug. 27, 1949; d. John George and Lydia Louise (Hancock) S. BA, U. Conn., 1971; MS, U. Bridgeport, 1973; PhD, U. Ill., 1980. Registered psychologist, Ariz., Ill. Instr., asst. project dir. dept. family practice Sch. Medicine, So. Ill. U., Springfield, 1979-82; coordinator edn. U. Okla. Gerontology Ctr., Oklahoma City, 1982-83; exec. dir. Intergenerational Care Adult Day Care Ctr., Oklahoma City, 1983-84; planning specialist Aging Services div. Dept. Human Services, State Okla., Oklahoma City, 1984-87; psychologist Cleve. County Health Dept., 1987—; chair membership com. Alzheimers Disease and Related Disorders, Oklahoma City, 1987—; bd. dirs. Daily Living Ctrs., Inc., Oklahoma City. Author: Primary Care Geriatrics, 1983; contbr. articles to profl. jours. Mem. Gerontology Soc. Am. (grantee 1981), Okla. Psychol. Assn., S.W. Soc. Aging (bd. dirs. 1986—), Phi Beta Kappa. Democrat. Mem. Reformed Ch. Am. Home: 2632 Lynn Ln Oklahoma City OK 73120

SMITH, MARCIA SUE, government official; b. Greenfield, Mass., Feb. 22, 1951; d. Sherman Kenneth and Shirley Fay (Schafer) S. B.A., Syracuse U., 1972. Adminstrv. asst., corr. AIAA, Washington, 1973-75; analyst in aerospace and energy tech. Sci. Policy Research div. Congressional Research Service, Library of Congress, Washington, 1975-80, specialist in aerospace and telecommunications systems, 1980-85; exec. dir. Nat. Commn. on Space, Washington, 1985-86; specialist in aerospace policy, Congl. Research Service, Washington, 1986—. Mem. editorial bd. Space Policy jour.; author reports and articles. Fellow Brit. Interplanetary Soc., AIAA (assoc., disting. lectr. 1983—, pub. policy, internat. activities and space systems tech. coms.); mem. AAAS, Am. Astronautical Soc. (dir. 1982-86, pres. 1985-86), Women in Aerospace (founder, pres. 1987), Internat. Acad. Astronautics, Internat. Inst. Space Law, N.Y. Acad. Scis. (life), Washington Acad. Sci., Sigma Xi. Office: CRS/SPRD Library of Cong Washington DC 20540

SMITH, MARGARET, state legislator; b. Chgo.; m. Fred J. Smith; 2 sons, (dec.). Student, Tenn. Stae U. Mem. Ill. Ho. of Reps., 1981-83; mem. Ill. Senate, dist. 12, 1983—. Trustee Chgo. Bapt. Inst. Democrat. Office: State Capitol Springfield IL 62706 also: 130 E Garfield Blvd Chicago IL 60615 *

SMITH, MARGARET CHANDLER, accountant, educator; b. Chattanooga, July 10, 1944; d. Daniel Brooks and Miriam Virginia (Lamoreaux) Chandler; m. Lanty Lloyd Smith, June 11, 1966; children: Abigail, Margaret, Amanda. BS, Duke U., 1966, PhD, 1986, MBA, Case Western Res. U., 1978. CPA, N.C., Ohio. Fin. analyst Cleve. Trust Co., 1967-68; instr. U. N.C., Greensboro, 1978-80; asst. prof. Guilford Coll., Greensboro, 1986-88, U. N.C.-Greensboro, 1988—. Contbr. articles to profl. jours. Deloitte, Haskins & Sells fellow, 1981-82, 1985-88. Mem. Am. Inst. CPA's, Am. Acctg. Assn. (fellowship 1981-82), N.C. Assn. CPA's. Episcopalian. Office: Sch Bus and Econs U NC Greensboro NC 27412

SMITH, MARGARET HELEN HUGHES, accountant, educator; b. Mineola, N.Y., Apr. 6, 1941; d. D. Wendell Lochead and Sarah Arwilda (Rupp) Hughes; m. Roy B. Smith; children: Deborah A., Roy A., Barrett H. AS summa cum laude, Nassau Community Coll., Garden City, N.Y., 1976; BBA summa cum laude, Hofstra U., 1978; MBA summa cum laude, C.W. Post U., 1987. CPA, N.Y. Tutor Nassau Community Coll., Garden City, 1976-78; auditor Seidman & Seidman CPA's, N.Y.C., 1978-80; sr. acct. Boyce, Hughes & Farrell CPA's, Roslyn, N.Y., 1980-81; asst. prof. Nassau Community Coll., Garden City, 1981—. Mem. Nat. Assn. Accts. (dir. 1978—), Am. Inst. CPA's, N.Y. Soc. CPA's (sec. 1984-85, var. bd. dirs.). Office: Nassau Community Coll Dept Acctg and Bus Garden City NY 11530

SMITH, MARILYN NOELTNER, science educator, consultant; b. Los Angeles, Feb. 14, 1933; d. Clarence Frederick and Gertrude Bertha (Smith) Noeltner; m. Edward Christopher Smith, Sept. 11, 1971. BA, Marymount Coll., 1957; MA, U. Notre Dame, 1966; MS, Boston Coll., 1969. Cert. tchr.; cert. community coll. tchr., Calif.; cert. adminstr., Calif. Tchr., chmn. sci. dept. Marymount High Sch., Santa Barbara, Calif., 1954-57, Los Angeles, 1957-58, 69-79; tchr., chmn. sci. and math. depts. Marymount High Sch., Palos Verdes, Calif., 1959-69; tchr., chmn. math. dept. Corvallis High Sch., Studio City, Calif., 1958-59; instr. tchr. tng. Marymount-Loyola U., Los Angeles, 1965-71, instr. freshman interdisciplinary program, 1970-71; tchr. math. Santa Monica (Calif.) High Sch., 1971-72; instr. math., chemistry, physics Santa Monica Coll., 1971—; tchr. sci. Beverly Vista Sch., Beverly Hills, Calif., 1972—; cons. Calif. State Sci. Framework Revision Com., Los Angeles, 1975; chmn. NASA Youth Sci. Congress, Pasadena, Calif., 1968-69, Hawaii, 1969-70; participant NASA Educators Conf. Jupiter Mission, Ames Research, San Francisco, 1973, NASA Educators Conf. Viking-Mars Ames Project, San Francisco, 1976-77, NASA Landsat Conf., Edward's AFB, Calif., 1978, NASA Uranus Mission, Pasadena, Calif., 1986. Author articles, books and computer programs on space and physics. Sponsor Social Service Club, Palos Verdes, 1959-69, moderator, sponsor ARC Youth Service Chmn., Beverly Hills, 1974-77, judge Los Angeles County Sci. Fair, 1969, mem. blue ribbon com. Nat. Acad. TV Arts and Scis., 1971—. Recipient Commendation in Teaching cert. Am. Soc. Microbiology, 1962, Salute to Edn. award So. Calif. Industry Edn. Council, 1962, Outstanding Teaching citationCons. Engrs. Assn. Calif., 1967, Cert. Honor, Silver Plaque Westinghouse Sci. Talent Search, 1963-68, Tchr. award Ford-Future Scientists of Am., 1968, Biomed. award Com. Advance Sci. Tng., 1971, Outstanding Tchr. award Los Angeles County Sci. Fair Com., 1975-76, Contbns. to Youth Service citation ARC, 1976-77, Outstanding Tchr. award Kiwanis Club Beverly Hills, 1987. Mem. We. Assn. Schs. and Colls. (vis. com. 1968, writing com. 1969—), Assn. Advancement Biomed. Edn. (pres. 1970-71), 1st Internat. Sci. Tchrs. Conf. (presider, evaluator 1977), Nat. Sci. Tchrs. Assn. (presider, evaluator 1976, chmn. contributed papers com. 1977-78), Beverly Hills Edn. Assn. Faculty Council (pres. 1980-81, 85-86), Chemist's Club, Calif. Statewide Math. Adv. Com., So. Calif. Industry Edn. Council, Calif. Assn. Chemistry Tchrs. (program chmn. 1960), Calif. Sci. Tchrs. Assn., Am. Chem. Soc., AAAS, South Bay Math. League (sec. 1967-68, pres. 1968-69, 72, 1969-70), Calif. Math. Council, Nat. Assn. Biology Tchrs. Republican. Roman Catholic. Home: 3934 Sapphire Dr Encino CA 91436 Office: Beverly Vista Sch 200 S Elm Dr Beverly Hills CA 91202

SMITH, MARILYN RUEDEANE, microbiologist; b. Americus, Ga., Jan. 12, 1950; d. Eddie Frank and Charlie Bell (Small) S. BS, Fla. A&M U., 1972; MS, Long Island U., 1988; cert., Women's Mgmt. Tng. Initiative, 1985. Microbiologist FDA, Bklyn., 1976-85; supervisory microbiologist FDA, Los Angeles, 1985—; mgr. womens's program FDA, Bklyn., 1984-85. Conbr. articles to profl. jours. Trainer Literacy Volunteers of Am., N.Y.C., 1978-79; Sarah Gorham Masai missionary. Mem. Am. Soc. Microbiology, So. Calif. Am. Soc. Microbiology, Nat. Orgn. Black Chemists and Chem. Engrs., Nat. Assn. Female Execs., Black Women's Network, Internat. Training in Communication Assn. (sec. 1985, v.p., 1986), NAACP, NAACP (Pasadena, Calif. br.), Federally Employed Women, Nat. Council of Negro Women, Am. Chem. Soc., Delta Sigma Theta. Democrat. Mem. African Methodist Episcopalian Ch. Home: 833 S Plymouth Blvd Los Angeles CA 90005

SMITH, MARION C., educator, former health care administator; b. Catskill, N.Y., Oct. 23, 1922; d. Nathaniel and Agatha Marie (Delanoy) Smith; B.A., Coll. of St. Rose, 1952; M.A., Siena Coll., 1964. Entered Order of Sisters of Mercy, Roman Catholic Ch., 1940; tchr. elem. and high schs., Albany, Troy, Cuhoes and Oneonta, N.Y., 1943-65; chmn. journalism dept. Cath. Central High Sch., Troy, 1961-65; prin. St. Mary's Sch., Oneonta, 1965-67; asso. dir. Oneonta Newman Found., 1967-76; adminstrv. asst. Stephen Smith Geriatric Center, Phila., 1977-82; faculty SUNY, Oneonta, 1976. Co-founder, chmn. Campus Ministry Com. of Oneonta, 1968-70, 74-75; co-founder, cons., counselor City Drug Crisis Center, "85", Oneonta, 1971-75; active Human Relations Task Force, 1974-75, Family Service Com. of Oneonta, 1972-76; counselor Planned Parenthood Clinic of Otsego County, 1972-75; campus ministry com. Oneonta, 1968-76, Mayor's Commn. Services to Aging; project counselor Srs. in Community Service Program; asst. to dir. Pvt. Sector Initiative Program; active Urban League. Fellow Am. Coll. Nursing Home Adminstrs.; mem. Nat. Council for Basic Edn., Nat. Cath. Campus Ministry Assn., Nat. Inst. Campus Ministry, Religious Edn. Assn., Am. Acad. Religion, Hastings Center Inst. Soc., Ethics and Life Scis., Fellowship of Reconciliation, AAUW, Siena Coll. Alumni Assn., Nat. Assn. Female Execs., Nat. Assn. Profl. and Exec. Women. Lit. editor profl. papers and book reviews for non-English speaking profs. in higher edn.; asst. to editor Asian Thought and Soc., 1976. Home: 6119 Ellsworth St Philadelphia PA 19143

SMITH, MARJORIE ANN, college registrar; b. Seattle, May 21, 1942; d. Harold Lloyd and Irene Lucille (Lynch) Elliss; m. Forbes Denny Nichols, June 22, 1963 (div. 1970); m. 2d David DeWitt, June 9, 1975. B.S. in Bus. Adminstrn., U. Maine, 1980. Adminstrv. asst. Holy Rosary Hosp., Ontario, Oreg., 1970-72; placement service dir. Multnomah County Med. Soc., Portland, Oreg., 1972-75; asst. dir. admissions U. Tex. Med. Br., Galveston, 1981-82; registrar Galveston Coll. (Tex.), 1982-85; bus. mgr. Heritage Med. Group, 1987—. Mem. Tex. Assn. Collegiate Registrars and Admissions Officers, Jr. Coll. Student Personnel Assn. Tex., Nat. Assn. Fgn. Student Affairs, Tex. Jr. Coll. Tchrs. Assn., Galveston Bus. and Profl. Women, Exec. Career Women. Republican. Home: 3 Bandera Ct Pueblo CO 81005

SMITH, MARJORIE HAGANS, librarian; b. Atlanta, Nov. 24, 1936; d. Simon Peter and Erma Ruth (Miller) Hagans; m. Jimmie L. Smith, Dec. 26, 1959; children: Jimmie Marquette, Jocelyn Marcella, Jevon Marcel. BA, Clark Coll., 1959; MLS, Atlanta U., 1969. Cataloger Livingstone Coll., Salisbury, N.C., 1961-62; tchr., librarian Berean Jr. Acad., Atlanta, 1965-68; media specialist, librarian Atlanta Bd. Edn., 1968—. Co-author: Ethnic Book Bibliography. Sec. West Manor PTA, Atlanta, 1976-77, corr. sec., 1977-78; sec. SW High Sch. Band Parents Club. Mem. Am. Library Assn., Ga. Library Assn., Metro Atlanta Library Assn., Atlanta Assn. Educators. Seventh-Day Adventist (leader hostess com., tchr. Cradle Roll Dept.). Home: 3176 Kingsdale Dr SW Atlanta GA 30311 Office: 1550 Boulevard Dr NE Atlanta GA 30317

SMITH, MARSHA ANN, government financial executive; b. Greenville, Tex., Aug. 29, 1951; d. Wilson Marshall and Henrietta Charlotte (Fritz) S. B.B.A., U. Tex., 1973. Petroleum acct. Superior Oil Co., Houston, 1974-75; mgr. fund acctg. Prudential Group, Inc., Houston, 1975-78; systems analyst AID, Washington, 1978-80, fin. analyst regional office, Abidjan, Ivory Coast, 1980-83, dep. controller regional office, Abidjan, 1983-84, controller AID Mission, Yaounde, Cameroon, 1985-87, Niamey, Niger, 1987—; commd. fgn. service officer Dept. State, 1984. Named to Outstanding Young Women Am., U.S. Jaycees, 1973; recipient Superior Honor award AID, 1984. Mem. Nat. Assn. Female Execs., Nat. Mus. Women in Arts. Democrat. Presbyterian. Avocations: reading about and travelling to various cultures; flying small planes.

SMITH, MARSHA ELAINE, accountant, educator, consultant; b. Portsmouth, Ohio, Apr. 21, 1949; d. A. Mac and A. Mary (Delabar) Wamsley; B.B.A. in Acctg. cum laude, Ohio U., Athens, 1974; children—David Alan, Trisha Jabrina. CPA, Ohio, Tenn. Asst. ops. mgr. Chase Manhattan Bank, N.A., Agana, Guam, 1971-73; dorm and dining acct. Ohio U., 1974; organized research acct. U. Akron (Ohio), 1975; owner, operator public acctg. firm, McConnelsville, Ohio, 1976, staff acct. Dorsey L. Arnold, C.P.A., Bath, Ohio, 1977; supr., office mgr. Dwite A. Polos, C.P.A., Cuyahoga Falls, Ohio, 1978; pres. Smith & Assocs., C.P.A.s, 1978—; chief Fin. officer Quest Cons., Inc., 1982-86; adminstr. Prima Care Home Health, Bowling Green, Ky., 1986-88; instr. acctg. Washington Tech. Coll., 1976, U. Akron, 1982-84. Treas. ladies aux. Bath Fire Dept., 1979-83; mem. Ky. Medicaid Appeals Panel. Mem. Am. Women's Soc. CPA's, Assn. MBA Execs., Nat. Assn. Accts., Am. Inst. CPA's, Ohio Soc. CPA's, Ky. Home Health Assn. (govt. affairs com.). Home: 1040 Shive Ln #E6 Bowling Green KY 42101

SMITH, MARVETTE THOMAS, college administrator; b. Montgomery, Ala., Jan. 27, 1953; d. Robert Marvin and Bernice Johnetta (Morgan) Thomas; m. Richard E. Cobb, May 7, 1971 (div. 1982); 1 child, Janel Bernice; m. Charlie M. Smith, Mar. 27, 1982. BS, Austin Peay State U., 1978; MS, Murray State U., 1980; EdD, Vanderbilt U., 1984. Grad. asst. Vanderbilt U., Nashville, 1981; spl. edn. instr. N.W. High Sch., Clarksville, Tenn., 1979-83; counselor La. State U. Eunice, 1984, acting dir. spl. services and devel., 1984-85, dir. student support services, 1985—. La. Leadership Tng. Project, Project WINC 1986—; bd. dirs. Bayou council Girl Scouts U.S.; mem. bd. commrs. Hosp. Dist. 1, St. Landry Parish, La.; active La. State Folklife Festival, also chmn. Black Cultural program Mem. Am. Assn. Counseling and Devel., S.W. Assn. Student Assistance Programs, Nat.Council of Ednl. Opportunity Assns. (mem. President's Council), Nat. Assn. Female Execs., AAUW, Nat. Council Negro Women, La. Assn. Student Assistance Programs (congl. team 1985, pres.), La. Assn. Devel. Edn. (exec. council 1985-88), La. Black Festivals Network, Eunice C. of C. (bd. dirs.), Chi Sigma Iota, Phi Delta Kappa, Delta Sigma Theta (pres. 1982-83). Democrat. Clubs: Nat. Commodore-Vanderbilt (New Orleand), Socialite (Eunice). Avocations: travel, tennis, reading. Office: La State U Eunice PO Box 1129 Eunice LA 70535

SMITH, MARY ALBERTA HAMPTON, physician assistant; b. Hopkinsville, Ky., July 18, 1950; d. Richard H. and Bessie M. (Clardy) Hampton; B.S., Austin Peay State U., 1972; B.S., physician asst. cert., Baylor U. Coll. Medicine, 1977; cert. in CPR, Am. Heart Assn.; cert. adult reading tutor; m. Tommy R. Smith, July 19, 1981. Nursing asst. Gen. Care Convalescent Center, Clarksville, Tenn., 1971; substitute tchr. Clarksville-Montgomery County Sch. System, 1972-74; dir. nursery St. John Missionary Bapt. Ch., Clarksville, 1972-74; nursing asst. cardiovascular/ICU units St. Luke Episcopal Hosp., Houston, 1975; child care attendant for autistic children First Presbyn. Ch., Houston, 1976-77; emergency room clk. Med. Center Del Oro Hosp., Houston, 1977-81; cert. physician asst. C. R. Higgins Jr., M.D. and Assocs., Houston, 1977-81; with Iowa Vets. Home, Marshalltown, 1982-85, L'Abri Health Care, Montclair, Calif., 1986-87, Kaiser Permanente So. Calif., Woodland Hills, 1987—. Former resource person Concord Elem. Sch., Houston Ind. Sch. Dist., 1979-81. Mem. Am. Acad. Physician Assts., Calif. Acad. Physician Assts., AAUW . Baptist. Home: 2017 East Ave R-12 Palmdale CA 93550

SMITH, MARY LOUISE, politics and public affairs consultant; b. Eddyville, Iowa, Oct. 6, 1914; d. Frank and Louise Anna (Jager) Epperson; BA, U. Iowa, 1935; LHD (hon.), Drake U., 1980, Grinnell Coll., 1984; m. Elmer Milton Smith, Oct. 7, 1934; children:Robert C., Margaret L., James E. Mem. Eagle Grove (Iowa) Bd. Edn., 1955-60; Republican precinct committeewoman, Eagle Grove, 1960-62, vice-chairwoman, Wright County, Iowa, 1962-63; mem. Rep. Nat. Com., 1964-84, mem. exec. com., 1969-84, mem. conv. reforms com., 1966, vice-chairwoman Steiger com. on conv. reform, 1973, co-chmn. nat. com., 1974, chmn. Com., 1974-77; vice-chairwoman U.S. Commn. on Civil Rights, 1982-83; vice-chairwoman Midwest region Rep. Conf., 1969-71; del. Rep. Nat. Conv., 1968, 72, 76, 80, 84, alt. del., 1964, organized and called to order, 1976; vice-chairwoman Iowa Presdl. campaign, 1964; nat. co-chmn. Physicians Com. for Presdl. Campaign, 1972; co-chairwoman Iowa Com. to Reelect the Pres., 1972; mem. Nat. Commn. on Observance Internat. Women's Year, 1975-77; vis. fellow Woodrow Wilson Fellowship Found., 1979. Mem. U.S. del. to Extraordinary Session of UNESCO Gen. Conf., Paris, 1973; mem. U.S. del. 15th session population commn. UN Econ. and Social Council, Geneva, 1969; mem. Pres.'s Commn. for Observance of 25th Anniversary of UN, 1970-71; mem. Iowa Commn. for Blind, 1961-63, chairwoman, 1963; mem. Iowa Gov.'s Commn. on Aging, 1962; trustee Robert A. Taft Inst. Govt., 1974-84, Herbert Hoover Presdl. Library Assn., Inc., 1979—. Pres. Eagle Grove Community Chest; bd. dirs. Mental Health Center North Iowa, 1962-63, YWCA of Greater Des Moines, 1983—, Orchard Place Resdl. Facility for Emotionally Disturbed Children, 1983-88, Learning Channel, cable TV, 1984-87, Planned Parenthood of Mid-Iowa, 1986—, Iowa Peace Inst., 1985—, U. Iowa Found., 1987—; mem. adv. council U. Iowa Hawkeye Fund Women's Program, 1982-87. Named hon. col., mil. staff Gov. Iowa, 1973; Iowa Women's Hall of Fame, 1977; recipient Disting. Alumni award U. Iowa, 1984; Cristine Wilson medal for equality and justice Iowa Commn. on Status of Women, 1984. Mem. Women's Aux. AMA, UN Assn., Nat. Women's Polit. Caucus (adv. bd. 1978—), PEO, Kappa Alpha Theta. Address: 654 59th St Des Moines IA 50312

SMITH, MARY LOUISE, real estate broker/salesperson; b. Eldorado, Ill., May 29, 1935; d. Joseph Henry and Opal Marie (Shelton) S.; m. David Lee Smith, June 18, 1961; children: Ricky Eugene, Brenda Sue. Student, So. Ill. U., 1954-56, 57-58. Cert. tchr., Mo.; cert. real estate broker/salesperson, Mo. With acctg. dept. Cen. Hardware Co., St. Louis, 1958-61; mgr. income tax office Tax Teller Inc., St. Louis, 1967-69, H&R Block Co., St. Louis, 1970-76; with acctg. dept. Weis Neumann Co., St. Louis, 1976-79; sales assoc. Century 21 Neubauer Realty, Inc., St. Louis, 1981-83, John R. Green Realtor, Inc., St. Louis, 1983-85; sales assoc. Century 21 Action Properties, St. Louis, 1985-86, real estate broker/salesperson, 1986—; substitute tchr., St. Louis Bd. Edn., 1967—. Children's dir. Lafayette Park Bapt. Ch., St. Louis, 1981—. Mem. St. Louis Metro Realtors Assn., Real Estate Bd. Met. St. Louis, Nat. Assn. Realtors, Mo. Assn. Realtors. Home: 2627 Nebraska Saint Louis MO 63118

SMITH, NANCY HOHENDORF, sales and marketing executive; b. Detroit, Jan. 30, 1943; d. Donald Gerald and Lucille Marie (Kopp) Hohendorf; m. Richard Harold Smith, Aug. 21, 1978 (div. Jan. 1984). BA, U. Detroit, 1965; MA, Wayne State U., 1969. Customer rep. Xerox Corp., Detroit, 1965-67; major account mktg. exec. Xerox Corp., Hartford, Conn., 1978-79, New Haven, Conn., 1979-80; state of N.Y. account exec. Xerox Corp., N.Y.C., 1981, N.Y. region mgr. customer support, 1982; N.Y. region sales ops. mgr. Xerox Corp., Greenwich, Conn., 1982; Ohio account exec. Xerox Corp., Columbus, 1983; new bus. sales mgr. Xerox Corp., Dayton, Ohio, 1983, major accounts sales mgr., 1984; info. systems sales and support mgr., quality specialist Xerox Corp., Detroit, 1985—; mktg. rep. Univ. Microfilms subs. Xerox Corp., Ann Arbor, Mich., 1967-73, mktg. coordinator, 1973-74, mgr. dir. mktg., 1975-76; mgr. mktg. Univ. Microfilms subs. Xerox Corp., Can., 1976-77; ops. new product launch mgr., ops. quality mgr. Univ. Microfilms subs. Xerox Corp., 1988—. Named to Outstanding Young Women of Am., 1968, Outstanding Bus. Woman, Dayton C. of C., 1984. Mem. Nat. Assn. Female Execs. Republican. Roman Catholic. Club: Women's Economic (Detroit). Home: 23308 Reynard Dr Southfield MI 48034 Office: Xerox Corp Systems Sales 27710 Northwestern Hwy Suite 500 Southfield MI 48034

SMITH, NANCY HOWES, educator; b. Hyannis, Mass., Mar. 27, 1945; d. Harold Dudley and Dorothy (Canning) Howes; B.A., Bridgewater State Coll., 1967; M.Ed., Rivier Coll., 1981; children—Eric R., David E. English tchr. Hanover (Mass.) High Sch., 1967-68; English tchr., dept. chmn. Hudson (N.H.) Meml. Sch., 1969-71, 74-85; English tchr., chmn. dept. Windham Center Sch., N.H., 1985—; tchr. history and English, Alvirne High Sch., Hudson, N.H., 1974. Bd. dirs. Kendallwood Condominium Assn., 1977-79; troop leader Cub Scouts Am., Girl Scouts U.S.A.; unit commr. Boy Scouts Am., 1987—, ch. youth adv. Cert. prin., N.H., Mass. Mem. Nat. Council Tchrs. English, Assn. for Supervision and Curriculum Devel., Smithsonian Nat. Assocs., Nat. Assn. Female Execs., Rivier Coll. Alumni Assn. (bd. dirs. 1987-89, 88-89). Republican. Home: Bowers Rd Derry NH 03038 Office: Windham Mid Sch Lowell Rd Windham NH 03087

SMITH, NANCY LYNNE, journalist; b. San Antonio, July 31, 1947; d. Tillman Louis and Enid Maxine (Woolverton) Brown; m. Allan Roy Jones, Nov. 28, 1969 (div. 1975); 1 dau., Christina Elizabeth Woolverton Jones. B.A., So. Meth. U., 1968; postgrad. So. Meth. U., 1969-70, Vanderbilt U., 1964, Ecole Nouvelle de la Suisse Romande, Lausanne, Switzerland, 1962. Tchr. spl. edn. Hot Springs Sch. Dist. (Ark.), 1970-72; reporter, soc. editor Dallas Morning News, 1974-82; soc./celebrity columnist Dallas Times Herald, 1982—; stringer Washington Post, 1978; contbg. editor Ultra mag., Houston, 1981-82, Tex. Woman mag., Dallas, 1979-80, Profl. Woman mag., Dallas, 1979-80; mem. bd. advisors Ultra Mag., 1985—; appeared on TV series Jocelyn's Weekend, Sta. KDFI-TV, 1985. Bd. dirs. TACA arts support orgn., Dallas, 1980—, asst. chmn. custom auction, 1978-83; judge Miss Tex. USA Contest, 1984; mem. adv. bd. Cattle Baron's Ball Com., Dallas Symphony Debutante presentations; hon. mem. Dallas Opera Women's Bd., Northwood Inst. Women's Bd., Dallas Symphony League; mem. Friends of Winston Churchill Meml. and Library, Dallas Theatre Ctr. Women's Guild, Childrens' Med. Ctr. Auxiliary; mem. Community Council Greater Dallas Community Awareness Goals Com. Impact '88, 1985—. Mem. Soc. Profl. Journalists (v.p. communications 1978-79), Nat. Press Club, Dallas Press Club, DAR, Daus. of Republic of Tex. (registrar 1972), Dallas So. Memorial Assn., Dallas County Heritage Soc., Dallas Mus. Art League, Dallas Opera Guild. Club: Argyle (sec. 1983-84), The 500 (Dallas). Home: 5105 Mill Run Rd Dallas TX 75234 Office: Dallas Times Herald 1101 Pacific Ave Dallas TX 75202

SMITH, NANCY WEITMAN, advertising executive; b. Bklyn., Feb. 4, 1950; d. Warren Pershing Weitman and Esther (Lichterman) Sahn; m. Sidney James Smith, July 25, 1970 (div. July 1979); m. William Jackson Green, Mar. 21, 1987. BA in English, U. Pa., 1970. Purchase service asst. Young, Rubicam N.Y., N.Y.C., 1970-71, media planner, 1971-74, media supr., 1974-78, media group supr., 1978-79, v.p., 1979-84, sr. v.p., 1984-87, media dir., 1987—. Mem. Assn. U.S. Army. Office: Young & Rubicam Army Group 285 Madison Ave New York NY 10022

SMITH, NELDA ANDERSON, banker; b. Dallas, Jan. 3, 1948; d. James Quincy and Brunette (Tyler) Anderson; m. Larry Wayne Smith, Oct. 8, 1974; children: Tonya Leanne, Tricia Ann. Diploma in Retail Banking, U. Okla., 1985. With collection/exchange 1st Republic Bank, Garland, Tex., 1972-75; past due loan collector, auditor 1st Citizens Bank, Dallas, 1975-79; loan and credit ops. mgr. Century Bank, Garland, 1979-82; adminstrv. asst., loan officer, compliance officer Plaza Nat. Bank, Dallas, 1982—. Mem. Am. Inst. Banking. Democrat. Baptist. Office: Plaza Nat Bank 9090 Skillman Suite 100 Dallas TX 75243

SMITH, NELL WHITLEY, state senator; b. Washington, N.C., Nov. 12, 1929; d. Arthur H. and Alice (Whitley) S.; m. Harris Page Smith, Apr. 18, 1952 (dec.); children—Sam, Susan, Hugh, Phyllis. Student Salem Coll., 1947-48; B.S., U. N.C., 1951. Owner, mgr. The House Antiques and Gifts; tchr. sci. Easley Pub. Schs., 6 yrs.; mem. S.C. Senate, 1981—. Mem. Pickens County Art Com. Bd., 1976-80, bd. dirs. Pickens County Library, 1975-78, Home Health Care, 1977-79; pres. Palmetto Cabinet, 1977-78. Democrat. Presbyterian. Club: Easley Book. Office: 512 Gressette Bldg Columbia SC 29202 *

SMITH, NORA LEE, national accounts manager; b. Governors Island, N.Y., Oct. 11, 1959; d. Allen T. and Gertrude Maria (Spitta) S. AA, Manatee Jr. Coll., 1979; BS in Communications for Bus., Fla. State U., 1982. Sales rep. food service and lodging Procter and Gamble Corp., Orlando, Fla., 1982-84; field mktg. mgr. E.& J. Gallo Winery, Orlando, 1984-85, nat. accts. mgr. hotels and restaurants, 1985-86; nat. accounts mgr. S.E. div. hotels and restaurants Hiram Walker, Inc., Orlando, 1986—. Mem. Nat. Assn. Female Execs. Republican. Roman Catholic. Home and Office: 6801 Wayside Ct Tampa FL 33634

SMITH, OLIVE IRENE PERRY, realty company executive; b. nr. Shelbyville, Ill., Dec. 13; d. Joseph Luther and Pearl (Bushart) Perry; grad. Sparks Coll., 1928; student Milligan U., 1929, Northwestern U., 1934-36, UCLA, 1959-60; m. William Smith, May 11, 1942. Hosp. librarian, registrar Chgo. State Hosp., Cook County, 1929-40; dep. assessor San Diego County, Calif., 1951-52; real estate broker O.I. Smith, Hemet, Calif., 1953—; real estate investment and loan counselor. Local rep. Nat. Inst. Real Estate Bds. Active Southland Water Com., 1960-68. Mem. adv. bd. San Jacinto (Calif.) Jr. Coll., 1967-68. Mem. Nat. Inst. Real Estate Brokers, Nat. Traders, Comml., and Investment Brokers Div. (pres. 1961), Hemet-San Jacinto Bd. Realtors (sec. 1960), Calif. Real Estate Assn. (regional v.p. 1964-65), Riverside Art Assn. Republican. Club: Soroptimist (San Jacinto-Hemet, Calif.). Home: 3701 Fillmore St #180 Rancho Riverside Park Riverside CA 92505

SMITH, PAMELA BARRINGER, internal auditor; b. Rocky Mount, N.C., Apr. 17, 1956; d. Rufus and Nanette Darden (Fletcher) Barringer; m. Ronald Wayne Smith, Feb. 3, 1979; 1 child, David Barringer. BSBA in Acctg., Appalachain State U., 1976. CPA. Staff auditor Peoples Bank & Trust Co., Rocky Mount, 1977-80; dir. audit services Pioneer Savs. Bank, Rocky Mount, 1980—. Mem. Fin. Mgr.'s Soc. (N.C. internal auditors div.), Inst. Internal Auditors, Am. Inst. CPA's, Nat. Assn. Female Execs. Club: Pilot of Rocky Mt. (pres. 1983-84).

SMITH, PAT PITTMAN, home economist, consultant; b. Mabank, Tex., Nov. 25, 1940; d. Jeff Burr and Edna Lee (Odom) Teet; m. Joel P. Pittman, Dec. 26, 1961 (div. 1975); m. 2d, William C. Smith, Jr., Nov. 21, 1976. B.S., East Tex. State U., 1962; postgrad. Cordon Bleu Cooking Sch., London, 1978, Leith's Sch. Food and Wine, London, 1979. Home economist Dallas Power & Light, 1962-69; freelance home economist, Dallas, 1969-75; home economist So. Living mag., Birmingham, Ala., 1975—, asst. dir. Cooking Schs., 1977—; freelance home economist, Houston, 1976—. Mem. Am. Home Econs. Assn., Home Economists in Bus. (nat.-internat. relations chmn. 1984-86), Houston Home Economists in Bus. (chmn. 1983-84), Home Economists in Homemaking (chmn. 1974), Chi Omega. Republican. Episcopalian. Home: PO Box 814 Bellville TX 77418

SMITH, PATRICIA, Canadian provincial official. Mem. Province of Sask. Legis. Assembly; former minister of edn., now minister of energy and mines. Office: Sask Legis Assembly, Legis Bldg, Regina Can S4S 0B3

SMITH, PATRICIA GRACE, government official; b. Tuskegee Institute, Ala., Nov. 10, 1947; d. Douglas and Wilhelmina (Griffin) Jones; m. J. Clay Smith, Jr., June 25, 1983; children—Eugene Douglas, Stager Clay, Michelle L., Michael L. B.A. in English, Tuskegee Inst., 1968; postgrad. Auburn U., 1969-71, Harvard U., 1974, George Washington U., 1983; cert. sr. exec. service 1987; exec. mgmt. tng. devel. assignments Dept. Def., 1986, U.S. Senate Commerce Com., 1987. Instr. Tuskegee Institute, Ala., 1969-71; program mgr. Curber Assocs., Washington, 1971-73; dir. placement Nat. Assn. Broadcasters, Washington, 1973-74, dir. pub. affairs, 1974-77; assoc. producer Group W Broadcasting, Balt., 1977, producer, 1977-78; dir. affiliate relations and programming Sheridan Broadcasting Network, Crystal City, Va., 1978-80; chief consumer assistance and small bus. Office Pub. Affairs, FCC, Washington, 1980—; vice chmn. Nat. Conf. Black Lawyers Task Force on Communications, Washington, 1975-87. Mem. D.C. Donor Project, Nat. Kidney Found., Washington, 1984—; trustee, mem. exec. com., nominating com., youth adv. com. Nat. Urban League, 1976-81; mem. communications com. Cancer Coordinating Council, 1977-84; mem. Braintrust Subcom. on Children's Programming, Congl. Black Caucus, 1976—; mem. adv. bd. Black Arts Celebration, 1978-83; mem. journalism and communications adv. council Auburn U., 1976-78; mem. Washington Urban League, 1985—, Ala. State Soc., Washington, 1984—; mem D.C. Commn. on Human Rights, 1986-88, chmn. 1988. Named Outstanding Young Woman of Yr., Washington, 1975, 78; recipient Sustained Superior Performance award FCC, Washington, 1982, 83, 84, 85, 86, 87. Mem. Women in Communications, Inc. (mem. nat. adv. com.), NAACP, Lambda Iota Tau. Club: Broadcasters (bd. dirs. 1976-77). Democrat. Baptist. Avocations: writing, swimming. Home: 4010 16th St NW Washington DC 20011 Office: FCC 1919 M St NW Suite 254 Washington DC 20554

SMITH, PATRICIA JACQULINE, marketing executive; b. Orange, N.J., June 13, 1944; d. Michael Joseph and Helen Francis (Costello) S. BS, U. Md., 1967. Field dir. Colgate Palmolive Co., N.Y.C., 1967-71; account exec. Foote Cone & Belding, N.Y.C., 1971-72; dir. regional sales ARA Services, Inc., Phila., 1973-76; dir. funded programs Ogden Food Service, Boston,

1976-79; v.p. Smith Tool Co., Manesquan, N.J., 1979-84; chmn., chief exec. officer Hygolet Metro, Inc., New Canaan, Conn., 1984-87; mktg. cons. Smith Mktg. Services, LaJolla, Calif., 1987—; bd. dirs. Smith Tool Co., Manesquan, N.J., Shore Precision, Inc., Manesquan, P.J. Smith Interiors, N.Y.C. Mem. Women in Sales, Nat. Assn. Profl. Saleswomen, Bus. and Profl. Women's Club N.Y. State. Republican. Home: 425 E 63d St New York NY 10021

SMITH, PATRICIA K., educator; b. East Stroudsburg, Pa., Mar. 8, 1934; d. Joseph George and Mabel Lorraine (Repsher) Kuchinski; m. Edwin Raymond Smith, Aug. 18, 1956; children: Timothy E., Steven M., Marianne F. BS in Edn., East Stroudsburg State Coll., 1955; MA, W.Va. U., 1969, DEdn, 1975. Elem. tchr. Pleasantdale Elem. Sch., West Orange, N.J., 1955-56, Tuscarora Sch. Dist., Mercersburg, Pa., 1956-59; reading specialist Robert F. Kennedy Ctr., Morgantown, W.Va., 1970-72; asst. prof. W.Va. U., Morgantown, 1975-79, assoc. prof. reading and lang. arts, 1979-86, prof., 1986—; mem. rev. bd. Prentice-Hall, Inc., Englewood Cliffs, N.J., 1979—; cons. Chpt. 1, Monongalia Pub. Schs., Morgantown, W.Va., 1983-84. Co-author: Keeping Yourself Out of Federal Court, 1980, 2d revision, 1986; mem. editorial bd. Reading Improvement, Chula Vista, Calif., 1983—. Postdoctoral teaching fellow Lilly Endowment, Inc., 1975-76; recipient Outstanding Tchr. award Coll. Human Resources and Edn., Morgantown, W.Va., 1978. Mem. W.Va. State Reading Council (pres. 1979-80), Human Resources and Edn. Alumni Assn. (pres. 1979-80, exec. dir. 1981-85), Kappa Delta Pi, Phi Delta Kappa. Democrat. Roman Catholic. Avocations: traveling, reading. Home: 1456 Dogwood Ave Morgantown WV 26505 Office: W Va U 607 Allen Hall Morgantown WV 26506

SMITH, PEGGY MARIE, government official; b. Balt., Nov. 21, 1940; d. John Weldon and Cecelia Agnes (Goddard) S. Student U. Md., 1978-79, Catonsville Community Coll., 1979-80. Various secretarial positions, until 1973; adminstrv. officer Health Care Financing Adminstrn., Balt., 1973-80; adminstrv. specialist Social Security Adminstrn., Balt., 1980-85, mgmt. analyst, 1985-87; social ins. claims examiner, 1987—. Vol. Mercy Hosp., Balt., 1960-62, Baltimore County Gen. Hosp., Balt., 1971; hotline counselor Lighthouse, Inc., Balt., 1975-77; tchr. Salem Lutheran Ch. Sch., Balt., 1962-67. Mem. Nat. Assn. Female Execs., Sierra Club, Cousteau Soc., Nat. Aquarium, Smithsonian Inst., Nat. Guild Hypnotists. Avocations: writing, mainly poetry; reading; psychology; parapsychology; gardening. Office: Social Security Adminstrn 6401 Security Blvd Baltimore MD 21235

SMITH, PHOEBE, state agency official; b. Irwin County, Ga., Oct. 11, 1939; d. James Cleve and Winnie Eva (Thompson) S. Student pub. schs., Atlanta. Asst. office mgr. Rich's Dept. Store, Atlanta, 1959-69; statistical analyst assoc. State of Ga., Atlanta, 1970—. Author: Phoebe, 1979; Editor: Transsexual Voice Newsletter, 1981—. Mem. Friendship Force Exchange Program. Avocation: Self-help. Home: 764 North Ave Hapeville GA 30354 Office: PO Box 16314 Atlanta GA 30321

SMITH, PHYLLIS JOY, music educator; b. Kingston, Pa., June 22, 1944; d. Willard Joseph and Hazel (Forbes) Dreistadt; m. James Donald Smith, July 3, 1963; children: Steven, Sheri, Scott. Student, Met. State Coll., 1962-65, Cerritos (Calif.) Jr. Coll., 1964-66, Fullerton (Calif.) Coll., 1967-69. Owner, tchr. music Sunstyle Music Studio, Anaheim, Calif., 1963-75; office mgmt. Whittier (Calif.) Christian High Sch., 1979-85, mem. faculty, 1979-85; adminstr. Leffingwell Christian High Sch., Norwalk, Calif., 1985-87; prin. Sunstyle Gifts and Decorator Items, Mfr. and Sales, 1984—. Author poetry; composer gospel music. Dir. music Grace Bretheren Ch., Anaheim, 1973-75; organist Anaheim Community Ch., 1975-79. Republican. Baptist. Office: Sunstyle 16309 Landmark Dr Whittier CA 90604

SMITH, PHYLLIS MAE, health care consultant; educator; b. Couer d'Alene, Idaho, May 2, 1935; d. Elmer Lee Smith and Kathryn Alice (Newell) Wilson. Diploma, Lutheran Bible Inst., Seattle, 1956, Emanuel Hosp. Sch. Nursing, Portland, Oreg., 1959; student Coll. San Mateo, Calif., 1971. Staff nurse in surgery Emanuel Hosp., Portland, 1959-61, St. Vincent's Hosp., Portland, 1962-63; head nurse central service Sacred Heart Hosp., Eugene, Oreg., 1964-69; dir. central services Peninsula Hosp., Burlingame, Calif., 1969-74; pres. Phyllis Smith Assocs., Inc., Lewiston, Idaho, 1975-88; sr. tech. advisor, dir. edn. programs, Parkside Material Mgmt. Services, Park Ridge, Ill., 1988—; lectr., cons. in field in over 8 countries. Contbr. to manuals, profl. jours. Mem. Internat. Assn. Hosp. Central Service Mgmt. (dir. edn. 1973-88, chmn. technician edn. and affairs com. 1978-88, John Perkins award, 1977, Chesire award 1977), Assn. for Advancement Med. Instrumentation, Nat. Assn. Female Execs. Episcopalian. Lodge: Eagles Aux. Avocations: fishing, walking, photography, chess, reading. Home and Office: 3730 11th St Lewiston ID 83501

SMITH, PHYLLIS MCQUEEN, writer, artist; b. Kaslo, B.C., Can., Jan. 22, 1912; came to U.S., 1929; d. Alfred and Eleanor Margaret (McCallum) McQueen; m. Albert Glenn Smith, June 25, 1934; children—Glenn McQueen, Shelley Louise, Craig Warren. B.A., Wash. State U., 1934. Sec. to publicist Farm Credit Adminstrn., Spokane, Wash., 1934-35; publicist Boeing Aircraft Co., Seattle, 1937-39; co-pub. Whidbey Press, Oak Harbor, Wash., 1939-65; freelance writer, artist. Author, editor: The McQueen Story, 1983-84. Pres. Seattle Co-Arts; (recipient best watercolor award 1976). Recipient Cert. of award OPA, 1946; Excellence in Feature Writing award Whidbey Island Record, 1948; 1st prizes for Best Column in State Weeklies, 1961, 66. Mem. Theta Sigma Phi (Women in Communications, Inc.). Republican. Congregationalist. Home: 2314 Rosemont Pl Seattle WA 98199

SMITH, RAE NADINE, communications executive; b. Dunkirk, N.Y., Sept. 17, 1937; d. Lloyd Burton and Shirley (Harris) S. BSN, U. Mich., 1961, MS, 1965. Staff nurse neurosurgery dept. U. Mich. Hosp., Ann Arbor, 1961-62; staff nurse UCLA, 1963, 65; clinical specialist, head nurse U. Mich. Hosp., Ann Arbor, 1965-67; research assoc. Bur. Hosp. Adminstrn. U. Mich., Ann Arbor, Mich., 1967-68; clinical nurse specialist II U. Md., Balt., 1968-71; clinical nurse specialist Med. Coll. Va., Richmond, 1971-73. Contbr. articles to profl. jours. Mem. Am. Assn. Critical Care Nurses, Soc. Critical Care Med., Assn. Advancement Med. Instrumentation, Sigma Theta Tau. Republican. Presbyterian. Office: Med Communicators & Assocs Inc 3760 S Highland Dr Suite 252 Salt Lake City UT 84106

SMITH, RAMONA LOUISE, word processing service executive; b. Dayton, Ohio, Oct. 11, 1954; d. Frank Ray and Patricia (Mattingly) S.; m. Hardy Lee Jones, July 2, 1983. BS, U. Mo., Columbia, 1976. Sales rep. St. Louis Mktg. Surveys, 1976-77; retail salesman Sears Roebuck & Co., Chesterfield, Mo., 1977-78; word processing composition specialist Harris Data Communication, Dallas, 1978-79; v.p. W.P. Services, Plano, Tex., 1979-81; pres., owner, Words Plus, Dallas, 1981—. Mem. state bd. Women's Polit. Caucus, 1975-76; Mo. chmn. 18-year-old voter registration drive, Parkway West High, 1972; exec. mem. The 500 Inc., Dallas; precinct chmn. 1986—; election judge 1985—, del. to state polit. conv., 1986. Mem. Women in Exec. Leadership (publicity dir. 1986-87, 1st v.p. programs 1985-86, 2d v.p. membership 1984-85), Sales and Mktg. Execs. Dallas (Rookie Mem. of Yr. 1981, bd. dirs. 1982-83), North Dallas Network of Career Women (pres. 1985, treas., 1984, 83), Dallas Women's Found., Dallas Geneal. Soc., Data Processing Mgmt. Assn. (Dallas chpt.), Daughters of the Republic of Tex., Dallas C. of C. Democrat. Club: Toastmasters (chpt. sec. 1981, treas. 1982. Home: 13352 Maham Rd Apt 174 Dallas TX 75240

SMITH, RÄNDI SIGMUND, industrial psychologist, consultant; b. Washington, Mar. 18, 1942; d. Frederick William and Marie Rändi (Ensrud) Sigmund; m. Richard Peter Smith, Feb. 13, 1965; children—Robin Lynne, Rändi Marie. B.A. in Sociology, Coll. William and Mary, 1963; M.A. in Indsl. Psychology, Norwich U., 1985; postgrad. in adult edn. Columbia U., 1985—. Info. ctr. staff mem. Nat. Assn. Food Chains, Washington, 1963-65; asst. corp. librarian Combustion Engring., Windsor, Conn., 1965-66; telephone usage counselor So. New Eng. Telephone, Hartford, Conn., 1966; quality assurance/systems analyst Aetna Life & Casualty, Hartford, 1966-67; pres. Smith and Assocs. Inc., West Hartford, Conn., 1968—; cons. interpersonal skills, corp. edn. Aetna Life & Casualty, Hartford, 1969-84, IBM Corp., White Plains, N.Y., 1975—, Xerox Corp., Webster, N.Y., 1975-85. Author: Written Communication for Data Processing, 1976-81; also profl. articles, children's story. Active Jr. League Hartford, 1976—, Lupus Found. Am.; pres. parent council, trustee Kingswood-Oxford Sch., West Hartford, 1985-86; eucharistic minister Roman Catholic Archdiocese of Hartford, 1972. Mem. Am. Soc. Tng. and Devel., Am. Mgmt. Assn., Internat. Assn. Airline Passengers, Nat. Assn. Female Execs. Club: Hartford Golf. Avocations: scuba diving; bridge. Office: Smith & Assocs Inc 87 Westmont Hartford CT 06117

SMITH, REBECCA MCCULLOCH, educator; b. Greensboro, N.C., Feb. 29, 1928; d. David Martin and Virginia Pearl (Woodburn) McCulloch; m. George Clarence Smith Jr., Mar. 30, 1945; 1 child, John Randolph. BS, Woman's Coll., U. N.C., 1947, MS, 1952; PhD, U. N.C., Greensboro, 1967. Tchr. pub. schs., N.C. and S.C., 1947-57; instr. U. N.C., Greensboro, 1958-66, asst. prof. to prof. child devel. and family relations, 1967—, dir. grad. program, 1975-82; ednl. cons. depts. edn. N.C., S.C., Ind., Ont., Man.; vis. prof. N.W. La. State U., 1965, 67, U. Wash., 1970, Hood Coll., 1976, 86. Named Outstanding Alumna Sch. Home Econs., 1976; recipient Sperry award for service to families N.C. Family Life Council, 1979. Mem. Am. Home Econs. Assn., Nat. Council Family Relations (exec. com. 1974-76, treas. 1987-89, Osborne award 1973), Omicron Nu. Author: Teaching About Family Relationships, 1975, Klemer's Marriage and Family Relationships, 2d edit., 1975, Resources for Teaching About Family Life Education, 1976, Family Matters: Concepts in Marriage and Personal Relationships, 1982, assoc. editor Family Relations (Jour. Applied Family and Child Studies), 1980—; ednl. cons. Current Life Studies, 1977-84. Home: 1212 E Ritters Lake Rd Greensboro NC 27406 Office: U NC Dept Child Devel Sch Human Environ Scis Greensboro NC 27412

SMITH, REBECCA VIRTUE, state agency administrator; b. Oklahoma City, July 9, 1953; d. Richard Linn Cowan and Suzanne (Starr) Virtue; m. Dale R. Smith, Dec. 30, 1983. BS in Elem. Edn. magna cum laude, Lewis and Clark Coll., 1976; MA in Secondary Edn., U. Colo., Colorado Springs, 1983; postgrad., U. Colo., Denver, 1987. Cert. tchr., Colo. Tchr. kindergarten Fossil (Oreg.) Sch. Dist., 1976-78; tchr. remedial reading Cripple Creek (Colo.)-Victor Sch. Dist., 1978-80; coordinator newspaper in edn. Gazette Telegraph, Colorado Springs, 1980-83, Denver Post, 1983-85; coordinator pub. edn. Colo. Jud. Dept., Denver, 1985—, coordinator info., 1986—; mem. task force social studies Colo. State Bd. Edn., Denver, 1983—, chairperson state-wide newspaper in edn. task force. Author, creator, editor Colorado Kids' Corner. Mem. Bicentennial of U.S. Constn. com. Colo. Bar Assn., 1986. Recipient award Mesa County Valley Sch. Dist. Bd. Edn., 1986; named a Dynamite Denverite Denver Mag., 1987. Mem. Am. Judicature Soc., Nat. Council for the Social Studies, Colo. Council for the Social Studies, Colo. Assn. Trial Ct. Adminstrs., Colo. State Mgrs. Assn., Colo. Council Govtl. Communicators, Colo. Press Assn. (assoc.), Nat. Assn. Female Execs., Women Communications. Home: 1026 Steele St Denver CO 80206

SMITH, ROBIN GRIGG, physical therapist; b. Los Angeles, Jan. 7, 1934; d. Richard Wyman and Virginia Elizabeth (Gardner) Grigg. BA, cert. in phys. therapy, Stanford U., 1956. Staff phys. therapist Childrens Hosp., San Diego, 1956-57, Stanford Convalescent Ctr., Palo Alto, Calif., 1958-59; sr. phys. therapist Leahi Hosp., Honolulu, 1961-63, chief phys. therapist, 1964—; sr. phys. therapist Orthopaedic Hosp., Los Angeles, 1963-64; pres., owner Honolulu Sports Phys. Therapy, Inc., 1980—. Columnist Body Mechanics mag. Head med. tent Honolulu Marathon Assn., 1980—; vol. Ironman Triathlon, Kona, Hawaii, 1982-86. Mem. Am. Phys. Therapy Assn. (head numerous coms. 1961—, pres., v.p. Hawaii chpt. 1964, 70, 81, chief del.). Club: Outrigger Canoe (Waikiki, Hawaii) (chair athletic com.). Office: Honolulu Sports Med Clinic 932 Ward Ave Honolulu HI 96814

SMITH, ROBYNE MARIA, legal assistant; b. Gary, Ind., Aug. 26, 1959; d. Sylvia Maria Hill. BA, DePaul U., 1981; cert. paralegal U. So. Calif., 1982. Paralegal asst. Fields & Fields, Chgo., 1978-80; legal clk. Walzer & Gabrielson, Los Angeles, 1981-82; legal asst. Northrop Corp., Los Angeles, 1982-85; legal asst. Shea & Gould, Los Angeles, 1985-87, McKenna, Conner & Cuneo, Los Angeles, 1987—. Sec., Provisions, Inc., Los Angeles, 1984-86; legal cons. Telview Communications Group, Los Angeles, 1982-86; legal cons., exec. asst. Seventh St. Prodns., 1988—. Mem. NAACP, Los Angeles Paralegal Assn., Nat. Fedn. Legal Assts., Am. Film Inst., Nat. Assn. Female Execs. Democrat. Roman Catholic. Avocations: piano, reading. Office: McKenna Conner & Cuneo 444 S Flower Los Angeles CA 90071

SMITH, ROSE MEISNER, public relations officer, business executive; b. Deggendorf, Germany, July 7, 1947; came to U.S., 1951; d. Joseph and Bertha (Posikow) Meisner; m. Carl Michael Smith, Apr. 13, 1969; 1 child, Joel Michael. BS, Temple U., 1969, MA, 1972; MBA, Manhattan Coll., 1983. Pub. info. trainee N.J. Dept. Community Affairs, Trenton, 1969-70, pub. info. asst., 1970-72, prin. pub. info. asst., 1972-75; pub. affairs officer N.J. Housing Fin. Agy., Trenton, 1975-82; pub. affairs adminstr. N.J. Econ. Devel. Authority, Trenton, 1982-88; sec.-treas. Hillary's Gourmet Ice Cream, King of Prussia, Pa., 1987—. Recipient Communications award Temple U., 1969, award for ann. report N.J. Econ. Devel. Authority, 1984. Mem. Internat. Assn. Bus. Communicators. Office: NJ Econ Devel Authority 200 S Warren St Trenton NJ 08625

SMITH, RUBY LUCILLE, librarian; b. Nobob, Ky., Sept. 19, 1917; d. James Ira and Myrtie Olive (Crabtree) Jones; A.B., Western Ky. State Tchrs. Coll., 1943, M.A., 1966; m. Kenneth Cornelius Smith, Dec. 25, 1946; children—Kenneth Cornelius, Corma Ann. Tchr. rural schs., Barren County, Ky., 1941-42; tchr. secondary sch. English, librarian Temple Hill Consol. Sch., Glasgow, Ky., 1943-49, 49-51, 53-56, sch. librarian, 1956-83. Sec. Barren County Cancer Soc., 1968-70, Barren County Fair Bd., 1969-70; leader 4-H Club, 1957-72, mem. council Barren County; coordinator AARP tax-aide program, 1985—. Trustee Mary Wood Weldon Meml. Library, 1964—; trustee Barren County Pub. Library, 1969—, sec., 1969—. Mem. NEA (life), Ky. Edn. Assn., Ky. Assn. Sch. Librarians (sec. 1970-71), 3d Dist. Library Assn. (pres. 1944, 66), Barren County Edn. Assn. (pres. 1960-62, treas. 1979-80), Ky. Audio Visual Assn., Ret. Tchrs. Assn. (pres. 1984-86), Ky. Library Trustee Assn. (bd. dirs. 1985—, pres. 1986—, dir. Barren River region 1985—), Barren County Republican Women's Club, Monroe Assn. Woman's Missionary Union (dir. 1968-72, 79-83 Monroe Assn. Baptists (library dir. 1972—), Ky. Library Assn.Delta Kappa Gamma. Home: 54 E Nobob Rd Summer Shade KY 42166

SMITH, RUTH HODGES, city clerk; b. Roanoke, Va., Jan. 15, 1931; d. James Elpherson and Ruth Elizabeth (Morgan) Hodges; m. Leon Menaclus Smith, June 18, 1978; children—Dorothy Ruth Smith Swift, Marvis Frances Smith Mills. Student Potomac State Coll., 1949-51. Cert. mcpl. clk., Va. Legal sec. Commonwealth Atty., Woodstock, Va., 1952-54; adminstrv. asst. Nelson Oil Corp., Mt. Jackson, Va., 1954-56; exec. sec., office mgr. Tidewater Va. Devel. Co., Norfolk, Va., 1956-72; personnel mgr. Nepratex Industries, Virginia Beach, Va., 1972-77; realtor, life agt. Real Estate/Ins., 1976-78; city clk. City of Virginia Beach, 1978—. Sec.-treas. Hospice Virginia Beach, 1981—. Mem. IIMC Acad. Advanced Edn., 1984-87, 87—; founder Z House shelter for battered spouses. Mem. Internat. Mcpl. Clks., Va. Mcpl. Clks. (pres. 1982-84), Club: Pilot (officer 1960-72). Lodges: Zonta Internat. (dir. 1983—), Order Eastern Star, Daus. of Nile, Shriners. Avocations: crafts; bicycling; skating; traveling. Home: 1153 Belvoir Ln Lake James Virginia Beach VA 23464 Office: City of Virginia Beach Room 281 City Hall Mcpl Ctr Virginia Beach VA 23456

SMITH, RUTHANN ADELIA, senior buyer; b. Columbus, Ohio, Dec. 1, 1954; d. Wendell Benton and Naomi Emma (Lash) S. BA, Bowling Green State U., 1976. Nat. mgmt. trainee Eaton Corp., various locations, 1976-77; buyer Eaton Corp., Humboldt, Tenn., 1977-79, Cleve., 1979; sr. buyer Chgo. Pneumatic Tool Co., Utica, N.Y., 1979-81, cert. purchasing mgr., 1981—. Mem. N.Y. and Pa. Nat. Assn. Purchasing Mgmt. (vice chairperson program com. 1981-83), Utica Purchasing Mgmt. Assn. (profl. devel. chairperson 1981-82, 2d v.p. 1982-83), Chgo. Pneumatic Mgmt. Club (treas. Utica area 1986-87, sec. 1987-88). Republican. Presbyterian. Office: Chgo Pneumatic Tool Co 2200 Bleecker St Utica NY 13501

SMITH, SALLY JO, health care administrator; b. Peoria, Ill., June 10, 1936; d. Clement Henry and Ina Maude (McPike) Siepker; m. Laurence Redmond Smith, Sept. 7, 1957; children: Nanette, Cindy, Larry, Caroline, Julie. BS in Nursing, U. Iowa, 1958; postgrad., Western Ill. U., 1985-87. RN instr. St. Mary Hosp., Quincy, Ill., 1958-62; RN St. Mary Hosp., Quincy, 1975-76, inservice instr., 1976-78, assoc. dir. nursing, 1978-81; instr. John Wood Community Coll., Quincy, 1981-85; clin. supr. Upjohn Health Care Services, Quincy, 1985-86, adminstr., 1986—. Chairperson Family Planning Bd., Quincy, 1986-87, profl. edn. Ill. Cancer Soc., 1979—; mem. Am. Cancer Soc.; CPR instr. AHA. State of Ill. Nursing Assn. (chmn. membership 1981—), Ill. Council Home Health, Mo. Assn. of Home Care, Mo. Council Homemakers. Republican. Roman Catholic. Home: 2315 Mary Ln Quincy IL 62301 Office: Upjohn Health Care Services 1415 Vermont Quincy IL 62301

SMITH, SANDRA LOUISE, small business owner; b. Clarksburg, W.Va., July 24, 1950; d. Raymond Junior and Dicie Chloe (Simmons) Hoover; m. Clayton Edwin Snider, July 24, 1970 (div. Dec. 1978); m. Joe W. Smith, July 20, 1984; 1 child, Amanda RaeSnider. Student, Three Rivers Tree Community Coll., 1972-73; cert., Dale Carnegie Course, Polar Bluff, Mo., 1975, Britt Corp. Sales Seminar, 1985. Endorsement underwriter GEICO, Bethesda, Md., 1969-71; collections mgr. Snider's IGA Foods, Poplar Bluff, 1971-82; owner, operator Tower Restaurant, Poplar Bluff, 1979-82, Brandy's Restaurant, Cabot, Ark., 1984-86; owner, sec. S & J Enterprises Inc., Cabot, 1984—; owner, pres. Cabot Conoco #2 Inc., 1984—; owner Smith's Feed Store, 1987—, Popcorn, Etc., 1986—. Mem. Mo. Restaurant Assn., Am. Barhman Assn., Jaycees Wives (Poplar Bluf) (pres. 1975-76), Cabot C. of C. Democrat. Methodist. Home: PO Box 133 Cabot AR 72023 Office: PO Box 133 Cabot AR 72023

SMITH, SARA ELIZABETH, accountant; b. Detroit, Aug. 2, 1951; d. Harold Hawkins and Shirley Jane (Morgan) S. BBA, Western Mich. U., 1973. CPA, Mich. Intern Price Waterhouse, Battle Creek, Mich., 1973; acct. Seidman & Seidman, Kalamazoo, 1974, Sugarloaf Mt. Ski Resort, Cedar, Mich., 1974-75, Dennis & Gartland, Traverse City, Mich., 1975-76, Smith, Fought & Bunker, Petoskey, Mich., 1976-78; pvt. practice acct. Harbor Springs, Mich., 1978—. Mem. Harbor Springs Hist. Commn., 1986—. Mem. Am. Inst. CPA's, Mich. Assn. CPA's, Am. Women's Soc. CPA's. Office: 373 E Main St Harbor Springs MI 49740

SMITH, SARAH JANE (SALLY), state official; b. Pekin, Ill., Jan. 23, 1945; d. Claude P. and Jane (Prettyman) S.; B.S. in Music Edn., U. Ill.; postgrad. U. Alaska. Tchr. jr. high sch. Los Angels City Schs., 1966-69; adminstrv. asst. Office of Gov. of Alaska, 1971-74; project field rep Alaska Dept. Community and Regional Affairs, 1974-76; expeditor H.W. Blackstock, Inc., 1979-82; mem. Alaska Ho. of Reps. from 20th Dist., 1977-83, majority whip, 1977-79, mem. fin. com., 1979-81, chmn. rules chmn., 1981; exec. dir. Fairbanks Pvt. Industry Council, 1983-84; dir. div. pub. services Alaska Dept. Revenue, 1984—. Dir. choir Juneau Meth. and Presbyn. chs., 1972-74, 86—, Fairbanks Presbyn. Ch., 1974-75; historian Fairbanks Drama Assn., 1974-76; adv. bd. Assn. Children with Learning Disabilities, 1978-80; commr. Fairbanks Historic Preservation Commn., 1982-84; bd. dirs. Friends of U. Alaska Mus., 1983-84. Named Outstanding Freshman Legislator, 1976. Mem. Fairbanks Assn. Arts. Democrat. Club: PEO. Office: 1111 W 8th St Room 108 Juneau AK 99801

SMITH, SHARON BARBER, management consultant; b. Balt., Mar. 25, 1952; d. Samuel Franklin and Ruth (Ward) Barber; m. Charles Timothy Smith, Sept. 20, 1970 (div. Dec. 1979). BS, Towson State U., 1973, U. Md., 1974; M in Adminstrv. Scis., Johns Hopkins U., 1979. Prodn. supr. Vectra Corp., Odenton, Md., 1974-76; supr. grocery products div. McCormick and Co., Balt., 1976-79, prodn. control mgr. grocery products div., 1979-80; prodn. and inventory control mgr. EMC Controls, Inc., Cockeysville, Md., 1980-84; dir. prodn. and inventory control Rexnord Automation Inc. Electronic Ops. Group, Cockeysville, 1984-85, dir. cost acctg., 1985-86; mgmt. cons. Coopers and Lybrand, Washington, 1986—. Mem. Am. Prodn. and Inventory Control Soc. Club: Balt. Canoe. Office: Coopers and Lybrand 1525 Wilson Blvd Arlington VA 22209

SMITH, SHARON LEE CHESNUTT, advertising executive; b. Corpus Christi, Tex., Aug. 18, 1947; d. James Horace and Harriet Leona (McCune) Chesnutt; m. Roger John Barry, Sept. 20, 1970 (div. 1975); m. Jerry Clark Smith, Oct. 14, 1975; 1 child, Wesley Chesnutt. Student Western Wash. State U., 1965-69, Bklyn. Mus. Art Sch., 1971, Pratt Inst., 1972, Sch. Visual Arts, N.Y.C., 1973. Reservation agt. United Air Lines, N.Y.C., 1969-70; art dir. Folwell Assocs., N.Y.C., 1970-71; ptnr. Folwell & Barry Advt., N.Y.C., 1971-73; freelance graphic artist, advt. cons. Cornwallville, N.Y., 1973-75; ptnr. Hudson River Graphics, Catskill, N.Y., 1976-77; ptnr. Chesnutt & Smith, Catskill, 1977—; instr. advt. Coxsackie Corr Inst., N.Y., 1974-75. Pres., Fedn. Block Assns., Bklyn., 1972. Mem. Catskill Mountain Kennel Club (pres. 1986-87), Albany Schenectady Golden Retriever Club (pres. 1980-82), Bernese Mountain Dog Club Am., Golden Retreiver Club Am. (Outstanding DAM award 1979, Dog Show Hall of Fame 1979, Best in Show 1988), Mohawk Kennel Club, Mid-Hudson Kennel Club. Republican. Lutheran. Office: Chesnutt & Smith 22 Spring St Catskill NY 12414

SMITH, SUE IRBY, insurance company executive; b. Dorchester, Tex., July 22, 1932; d. Titus Ardell and Daisy Mae (Adams) Irby; m. Charley William Smith, Nov. 5, 1948; 1 child, Linda S. Smith Cumming. Student math. and mgmt. Tex. Christian U., 1960-64. From clk. to mgr. World Service Life Ins. Co., Ft. Worth, 1957-80; v.p. Savers Annuity Ins. Co., Ft. Worth, 1981—. Democrat. Baptist. Home: 7224 Monterrey Dr Ft Worth TX 76112 Office: Savers Annuity Ins Co 235 NE Loop 820 Suite 500 Hurst TX 76053

SMITH, SUELLEN FANDT, marketing professional; b. Newton, N.J., June 9, 1943; d. Edward Lloyd and Mary (Boitano) Fandt; B.Mus., Westminster Coll., New Wilmington, Pa., 1965; postgrad. Trenton (N.J.) State Coll., Pace U.; m. Gary Thomas Smith, Aug. 3, 1968 (div. Sept. 1983). Tchr. elem. sch. music and reading, N.J., 1965-81; with E-Systems Co., Tampa, Fla., 1981; ops. clk. RAC Ctr. and Dart Ctr., GTE Co., Tampa, 1982—, Bus. Phone Systems div., 1984—, GTE Communications Corp., 1985—, system ops. instr., communications service advisor, 1986—; lectr., Workshop presenter; cons. in field. Vol. counselor Hillsborough County Suicide and Crisis Center, 1984-86. Recipient John Phillip Sousa award, 1961. Mem. NEA, Music Educators Nat. Conf., N.J. Edn. Assn., Mu Phi Epsilon. Author curriculum materials. Office: GTE Communications Corp 1907 US Hwy 301 North Tampa FL 33619

SMITH, SUSAN ANN, printing company executive; b. Chgo., Apr. 15, 1952; d. Charles Kenneth and Emily Ann (Jankowski) S. BS in Communications, U. Wis., Lacrosse, 1970-74; postgrad., Aurora U. Prodn. coordinator Chicago Tribune, Hinsdale, Ill., 1979-81; prodn. mgr. Campbell, Scholl & Johnson, Hinsdale, 1981-82; customer service rep. Solar Press, Inc., Naperville, Ill., 1982-85, plant supt., 1985—; on-site supr. Naperville Cen. High Sch. Speaker Alcoholics Anonymous, 1979—. Mem. Quality Circle Inst. (cert. leader). Office: Solar Press Inc 1120 Frontenac Rd Naperville IL 60566

SMITH, SUSAN ELLEN, marketing professional; b. Lynchburg, Va., May 13, 1960; d. Thomas Edward and Betty Anne (Wright) S. Diploma with highest hons., Pan-Am. Sch., 1979; student, Va. Western Community Coll., 1987—. Sec. State Farm Ins., Lynchburg, 1979; sec. job placement Lynchburg Pub. Schs., 1979-81; clk. Limitorque Corp., Lynchburg, 1981-84; coordinator mktg. services Optical Cable Corp., Salem, Va., 1984—. Republican. Roman Catholic. Home: 5321 Century Dr NW Roanoke VA 24019 Office: Optical Cable Corp 870 Harrison Ave Salem VA 24153

SMITH, SUSAN KIMSEY, lawyer; b. Phoenix, Jan. 15, 1947; d. William Lewis and Margaret (Bowes) Kimsey; m. Alfred Jon Olsen, Apr. 16, 1973. Student U. Ariz., 1965-66; B.A., Principia Coll., 1969; M.A., U. Va., 1970; J.D., Ariz. State U., 1975. Bar: Ariz. Atty. trust dept. Valley Nat. Bank Ariz., Phoenix, 1976-77; assoc. Lane & Smith, Ltd., Phoenix, 1977-78; mem. Olsen-Smith, Ltd., Phoenix, 1979—, pres., 1979—; mem. Phoenix Tax Workshop, 1976—, Tax Study Group, 1979—, 401 - II Com., 1982—; chmn. taxation sect. State Bar Ariz., 1985-86; lectr. profl. confs. and univs., 1977, 80—. Author: Estate Planning Practice Manual, 1984; editorial adv. bd. Practical Tax Lawyer, 1985—; contbr. writings to profl. publs. Recipient J.P. Walker Am. History award, Principia Coll., 1969, Ethics award, State Bar Ariz., 1974. Fellow Am. Coll. Probate Counsel; mem. ABA (chmn. com. econs. of tax practice 1983-84 , chmn. com. liaison with other ABA sects.

and coms., sect. econs. of law practice 1983—, sect. corp., banking and bus law 1976—, com. mem. sect. taxation 1976—, com. mem. sect. real property probate and trust law 1982—, editorial bd. Practical Tax Lawyer), State Bar Ariz. (chmn. taxation sect. 1985—), Maricopa County Bar Assn., Fed. Bar Assn. (vice chmn. estate and gift taxation com., taxation council 1979-80), Valley Estate Planners (pres.), Central Ariz. Estate Planning Council (bd. dirs. 1986—), The Group, Alpha Lambda Delta, Phi Alpha Eta. Republican. Office: Olsen-Smith Ltd 301 E Virginia Ave Suite 3300 Phoenix AZ 85004

SMITH, SUSAN SCHUYLER, interior designer, space planner; b. Newburgh, N.Y., Mar. 28, 1945; d. Robert Warren and Edith May (Thomas) S.; student Wheaton Coll., Norton, Mass., 1963-64; B. Design with honors, U. Fla., 1970. Interior designer Hasco, West Palm Beach, Fla., 1970-72, Robert Shaw & Assos., Palm Beach, Fla., 1972-74; partner Interior Assocs., West Palm Beach and Chgo., 1974-76, Michalaros & Smith, Palm Beach and Chgo., 1976-78; pres., owner Spectrum, Interior Design, West Palm Beach, 1978—. Mem. West Palm Beach Downtown Devel. Authority, 1981-85, sec.-treas., 1981-84; bd. dirs. West Palm Beach Downtown Assn., 1980—, pres., 1981—; bd. dirs. Palm Beach County Jr. Achievement, 1981—, Palm Beach County Devel. Bd., 1982—, Palm Beach County Expressway Authority, 1985—; bd. dirs. Big Bros./Big Sisters of Palm Beach County, 1979—, pres. 1980-81, nat. bd. dirs. 1982—; bd. dirs. United Way Palm Beach County, 1982-85; mem. Palm Beach County Econ. Council, 1983—. Mem. Am. Soc. Interior Designers, Inst. Bus. Design, AIA (affiliate), West Palm Beach C. of C. (dir. 1981—, v.p. 1981-83). Palm Beach C. of C., C. of C. of Palm Beach County (dir. 1981-84, v.p. 1981-82, pres.-elect 1983, pres. 1985). Presbyterian. Home: 3701 S Flagler Dr West Palm Beach FL 33401 Office: 325 S Olive Ave West Palm Beach FL 33401 also: 6000 No AIA Vero Beach FL 32963

SMITH, SUSAN VERNON, author; b. Harrow, Eng., June 6, 1950; came to U.S., 1957; d. Vernon and Phyllis (Hunt) S.; children: Trina Mendonca, Cory Mendonca. BA in Communications, Adult Edn., U. Calif., Berkeley, 1980. instr. Learning Annex, N.Y.C., 1986. Author: (under pseudonym Susan Mendonca) Tough Choices, 1980, Broken Dreams, 1983, Once Upon A Kiss, 1985; (under pseudonym Rosemary Vernon) The Popularity Plan, 1981, The Problem With Love, 1982, The Popularity Summer, 1982, Dear Amanda, 1983, Love In The Fast Lane, 1984, Language of Love, 1984, Question of Love, 1985, First Comes Love, 1985, With All My Heart, 1985; (under pseudonym Carrie Enfield) Songbird, 1981, Secret Admirer, 1983, Picture Perfect, 1983; Changing Places; (series) Samantha Slade, 1987; Monster Sitter, Confessions of a Teenage Frog, Our Friend: Public Nuisance No.1, Terrors of Rock & Roll, 1988; (under pseudonym Sonya Begonia series, 1988), The 11th Birthday Blues, Angela & TheKing-Siza Crusade; developer Best Friends; contbr. articles to Parents Inc., Guideposts, others 1975-80. Mem. Soc. Children's Book Writers, Pen Am. Ctr. Home: 537 E Fourth St Brooklyn NY 11218

SMITH, SUSIE IRENE, histotechnologist; b. Columbus, Ohio, Oct. 10, 1942; d. Taft and Evelyn (Samuels) Woodford; student Boston State Coll., 1975-80; m. Eugene Smith, Dec. 2, 1960; children—Regina Marie, Kimberly Denise, Teresa Yvette, Stacia Ann. Med. worker Boston City Hosp., 1970; lab. asst. Boston City Hosp., 1970-75, lab. technician hematopathology lab. Mallory Inst. Pathology, 1975-80, chief med. technologist, 1982—; lectr. and cons. in field. Sec., Com. to Elect Jesse L. Corbin for State Rep., 1981-82; Mem. Whittier St. Tenants Assn. (treas. 1985-86, pres. 1987—), Tenants United for Pub. Housing Progress 1985-87, Com. for Boston Pub.Housing 1987. Mem. Am. Soc. Clin. Pathologists. Roman Catholic. Office: 784 Massachusetts Ave Boston MA 02118

SMITH, TARA LYNN, marketing manager; b. Pensacola, Fla., May 8, 1957; d. Randolph and Betty Ann (Smithfield) S. BS in communications, U. Tenn., 1979. Staff writer The Neighbor newspapers, Marietta, Ga., 1979; account asst. McCann-Erickson Inc., Atlanta, 1980-81; mktg. coordinator Cooper Carry & Assocs., Atlanta, 1981-83; bus. developer Heery & Heery, Atlanta, 1983-84; mktg. mgr. Jova, Daniels, Busby, Atlanta, 1985-87, W.L. Thompson Consulting Engrs., Inc., Atlanta, 1987—. Mem. High Mus., Atlanta, 1987; mem. Leadership Buckhead, 1988—. Mem. Soc. for Mktg. Profl. Services (bd. dirs. 1982-85). Episcopalian. Club: Atlanta Yacht (bd. dirs. 1984-87). Office: W L Thompson Consulting Engrs 3475 Lenox Rd NE Suite 300 Atlanta GA 30326

SMITH, THELMA TINA HARRIETTE, artist, gallery owner; b. Folkston, Ga., May 5, 1938; d. Harry Charles and Malinda Estelle (Kennison) Causey; m. Billy Wayne Smith, July 23, 1955; children: Sherry Yvonne, Susan Marie, Dennis Wayne, Chris Michael. Student, U. Tex., Arlington, 1968-70; studies with various art instrs. Gen. office worker Superior Ins. Corp., Dallas, 1956-57, Zanes-Ewalt Warehouse, Dallas, 1957-67; bookkeeper Atlas Match Co., Arlington, 1967-68; sr. acct. Automated Refrigerated Air Conditioner Mfg. Corp., Arlington, 1968-70; acct. Conn. Gen. Life Ins. Corp., Dallas, 1972-74; freelance artist Denton, Tex., 1974—; gallery owner, custom framer Tina Smith Studio-Gallery, Mabank, Tex., 1983—. Editor Cedar Creek Art Soc. Yearbook, 1983—. Treas. Cedar Creek Art Soc., 1987-88. Recipient numerous watercolor and pastel awards Henderson County Art League, Cedar Creek Art Soc. Mem. Southwestern Watercolor Soc., Pastel Soc. of the S.W., Cedar Creek Art Soc. (v.p. 1983-86, treas.). Baptist. Office: Tina Smith Studio-Gallery 701 S 3d St Mabank TX 75147

SMITH, TONI LYNN, educator, small business manager; b. Denver, Aug. 15, 1948; d. Doral E. and Irene M. (Stade) S. BS, Colo. State U., 1970; MA, U. Colo., 1977. Cert. home econs. tchr. Tchr. home econs. Jefferson County R-1 Dist., Lakewood, Colo., 1970-86; mgr. 1st String Sporting Goods, Camarillo, Calif., 1987—. Named Colo. Tchr. Yr., Colo. Dept. Edn., Denver, 1986. Mem. NEA, Colo. Edn. Assn., Jefferson County Edn. Assn. (treas. 1984-86, negotiator 1982-86). Republican. Home: 225 Erbes Rd #111 Thousand Oaks CA 91362 Office: 1st String Sporting Goods 606 N Las Posas Rd Camarillo CA 93010

SMITH, VANGY EDITH, accountant, consultant, writer, artist; b. Saskatoon, Sask., Can., Dec. 17, 1937; d. Wilhelm and Anne Ellen (Hartshorne) Gogel: m. Clifford Wilson, May 12, 1958 (de. Dec. 1978); children: Kenneth, Koral, Kevin, Korey, Kyle; m. Terrence Raymond Smith, Dec. 14, 1979. Student, Saskatoon Tech. Collegiate Inst., 1956, BBA, 1958, MBA, 1987, PhD in English with honors, 1988. Accounts payable clk. Maxwell Labs., Inc., San Diego, 1978; invoice clk. Davies Electric, Saskatoon, 1980-81; office mgr. Ladee Bug Ceramics, Saskatoon, 1981-87, Lazars Investments Corp., Eugene, Oreg., 1987; bookkeeper accounts payable Pop Geer, Eugene, Oreg., 1987; office mgr., bookkeeper Willamette Sprts Ctr. Inc., Eugene, Oreg., 1987—. Contbr. articles to scholarly jours. (recipient doctoral award 1987). Counselor Drug and Rehab. Ctr., Eugene, 1970-88. Recipient 3d and 4th place artists' awards Lane County Fair, 1987, 1st and 2d place awards Nat. Writing 1987, 88. Mem. Women's Christian Temperance Union (life, pres., state dir. projection methods 1987—, Appreciation award 1982, Presdl. award 1985), Found. for Christian Living, Lane County Council Orgns. (3d v.p. 1988—), Am. Soc. Writers, Beta Sigma Phi. Democrat. Home and Office: 1199 N Terry St Space 371 Eugene OR 97402

SMITH, VERNA GREEN, editor; b. Oklee, Minn., Aug. 23, 1919; d. Roy Alva and Sarah Mathilda (Lindberg) Green; m. Alfred Nelson Smith, II, July 8, 1942 (dec.); children—Philip Roger, Alfred Nelson III, Stuart Thomas. BA in Journalism, U. Mont., 1940; MA in Edn., Washington U., St. Louis, 1961; PhD in Edn. St. Louis U., 1970. Advt. mgr., columnist Glasgow (Mont.) Courier, 1940-41; reporter Gt. Falls (Mont.) Tribune, 1941-42; editor staff communication U.S. C.E., Ft. Peck, Mont., 1942; news editor Community News of Overland (Mo.), 1953-56; dir. pub. relations, tchr. English, Ritenour Sch. Dist., St. Louis County, Mo., 1956-66, adv. com. vocat. edn., 1979-80; tchr. sch. pub. relations St. Louis U., 1969; dir. communication services, editor CEMREL Reports, CEMREL, Inc., St. Louis, 1966-82; dir. publs. Midcontinent Regional Ednl. Lab., St. Louis, 1983-86; cons., 1986—; asst. dir., editor, OASIS, 1986—. Pres. PTA, 1953-54; adminstrv. bd. Stephan Meml. Meth. Ch.; bd. dirs. The Learning Ctr., 1978-83. NDEA fellow St. Louis U., 1965; U. Mont. scholar, 1940; recipient ann. awards for publs. Mo. Press Women, 1967-80, 1st prize award (2), Nat. Fedn. Press Women, 1969, 2d prize, 1970, Disting. Alumnus award U. Mont. Alumni Assn., 1982. Mem. Nat. Sch. Pub. Relations Assn. (pres., founder Greater St. Louis chpt. 1965-66, citation of appreciation, 1973), Conf. Edn. St. Louis (charter), Met. St. Louis Press Club, Nat. Fedn. Press Women, Mo. Press Women, Ednl. Press Assn. Am., Ednl. Writers Assn., Women in Communications (pres. St. Louis chpt. 1951-52, 56-57; Regional Disting. Service award 1983) Council Ednl. Devel. and Research (exec. com. communications group 1969-73, chmn. 1981-82), Hist. Soc. Mont., Overland Hist. Soc., Women's Soc., Washington U., U. Mont. Alumni Assn. (life), Mortar Bd., Kappa Delta Pi (chpt. pres. 1965-66), Delta Kappa Gamma, Pi Lambda Theta. Alpha Chi Omega. Home: 10311 Pineview Ct Saint Louis MO 63114

SMITH, VIRGINIA DODD (MRS. HAVEN SMITH), congresswoman; b. Randolph, Iowa, June 30, 1911; d. Clifton Clark and Erville (Reeves) Dodd; m. Haven N. Smith, Aug. 27, 1931. A.B., U. Nebr., 1936; hon. degree, Nebr. U., 1987. Nat. pres. Am. Country Life Assn., 1951-54; nat. chmn. Am. Farm Bur. Women, 1954-74; dir. Am. Farm Bur. Fedn., 1954-74, Country Women's Council; world dep. pres. Asso. Country Women of World, 1962-68; mem. Dept. Agr. Nat. Home Econs. Research Adv. Com., 1960-65. Mem. Crusade for Freedom European inspection tour, 1958; del. Republican Nat. Conv., 1956, 72; bd. govs. Agrl. Hall of Fame, 1959—; mem. Nat. Livestock and Meat Bd., 1955-58, Nat. Commn. Community Health Services, 1963-66; adv. mem. Nebr. Sch. Bds. Assns., 1949; mem. Nebr. Territorial Centennial Commn., 1953, Gov.'s Commn. Status of Women, 1964-66; chmn. Presdl. Task Force on Rural Devel., 1969-70; mem. 94th-100th Congresses from 3d Dist. Nebr.; mem. appropriations com., ranking minority mem. agrl. appropriations subcom., appropriations subcom. on energy and water devel. 94th-100th Congresses from 3d dist. Nebr.; v.p. Farm Film Found., 1964-74, Good Will ambassador to Switzerland, 1950. Apptd. adm. Nebr. Navy. Recipient award of Merit, DAR, 1956; Disting. Service award U. Nebr., 1956, 60; award for best pub. address on freedom Freedom Found., 1966; Eyes on Nebr. award Nebr. Optometric Assn., 1970; Internat. Service award Midwest Conf. World Affairs, 1970; Woman of Achievement award Nebr. Bus. and Profl. Women, 1971; selected as 1 of 6 U.S. women Govt. France for 3 week goodwill mission to France, 1969; Outstanding 4H Alumni award Iowa State U., 1973, 74; Watchdog of Treasury award, 1976, 78, 80, 82, 83, 84, 86, 88; Guardian of Small Bus. award, 1976, 78, 80, 82, 84, 86, 88; Nebr. Ak-Sar-Ben award, 1983, Agrl. Achievement, Nebr. U., 1987. Mem. AAUW, Delta Kappa Gamma (state hon. mem.), Beta Sigma Phi (internat. hon. mem.), Chi Omega, PEO (past pres.), Eastern Star. Methodist. Club: Business and Professional Women. Office: US House of Reps 2202 Rayburn Washington DC 20515

SMITH, VIRGINIA ROWAN, advertising executive; b. Newton, Mass., May 20, 1946; d. Henry Madison and Betty (Long) Rowan; m. Manning J. Smith III, June 17, 1978; children: Rowan Lynn, Manning J. IV. AB, Cornell U., 1968; MBA, U. Calif., Berkeley, 1978. Account exec. Foote Cone and Belding, San Francisco, 1978-80, McCann-Erickson, San Francisco, 1980-82; mgr. advt. and publs. Inductotherm Corp., Rancocas, N.J., 1984—; bd. dirs. Inductotherm Industries, 1983—. Republican. Office: Inductotherm Corp 10 Indel Ave Rancocas NJ 08073

SMITH, VIRGINIA WARE, psychotherapist, consultant; b. Chattanooga; d. Josh H. and Elizabeth (Johnson) Ware; m. Arthur B. Smith, May 30, 1959 (div. Dec. 1969); children: April Liza, Cindy Gaye. BA, Fisk U., 1951; MSW, Howard U., 1955; PhD, St. Louis U., 1980. Lic. clin. social worker, Calif. Social worker, supr. dept. social work Homer Phillips Hosp., St. Louis, 1955-64; instr., asst. prof. St. Louis U., 1965-74; supr. Children's Services, St. Louis, 1974-75; assoc. prof. La. State U., Baton Rouge, 1979-82; psychotherapist, acting social work cons. King Drew Community Health Plan, Los Angeles, 1983-87; psychotherapist family practice ctr. King/Drew Med. Ctr., Los Angeles, 1987—; cons. Golden Key Stroke Program, Los Angeles, 1984—; research study coordinator King Drew Med. Sch., 1985-86; workshop leader Los Angeles County Dept. Health Services, 1986. Staff writer King Drew Hosp. newsletter, 1983—; contbr. articles to profl. jours. Mem. Crenshaw Christian Ctr. Fellow Polio Found., 1954-55, Ford Found., 1975-79. Mem. Nat. Assn. Soc. Workers (sec., treas. 1959-61), Acad. Cert. Soc. Workers, Alpha Kappa Alpha. Democrat. Office: King Drew Community Health Plan 12021 S Wilmingon Ave Los Angeles CA 90059

SMITH, WANDA JEAN, insurance professional; b. Atmore, Ala., July 25, 1949; d. Lloyd and Edith (DuBois) Scott; m. James A. Smith, Jr., May 29, 1970; children—Joyce A., Jeffrey A. B.A., St. Mary's U., 1970. Registered securities rep. Sec., So. Regional Edn. Bd., Atlanta, 1976-78; adminstrv. asst. Discovery Learning, Atlanta, 1978-79; sales sec. Mobay Chems., Atlanta, 1979-80; sales assoc. Lincoln Nat. Ins. Co., Atlanta, 1980-81, Am. Nat. Ins. Co., Atlanta, 1981-87 , Century 21 Grand South, College Park, Ga., 1984—, N.Y. Life Ins. Co., 1987—. Pub. relations vol. East Point Track Club, 1985; mem. parents orgn. Clayton County Athletic Assn., 1986. Mem. Nat. Assn. Female Execs., Nat. Assn. Life Underwriters. Avocations: bowling; crafts. Office: WJ Smith & Assocs 1868-G W Washington Ave East Point GA 30344

SMITH, WILMA JANICE, writer, columnist; b. Pryor, Okla., Aug. 15, 1926; d. William Henry and Mary Jo (Buffington) Bell; m. Merle Thomas Smith, Apr. 30, 1948. Student Okla. A&M Coll., 1946, Okla. Sch. Bus., 1947; continuing edn. in law, history and theology. Clk. U.S. Postal Service, Tulsa, 1945; clk.-typist Social Security Office, Tulsa, 1947-50; rec. sec. Acad. Country Music, Hollywood, Calif., 1975-78; contbg. editor Nashville Star Reporter, 1977-78; freelance writer on country music field, 1973-85; publicist U. Ill. Press, Urbana, 1975-76; profl. talent booker, Hollywood, 1975-80; record and book reviewer various pubs.; biographer, cons. to Country and Western music performers; photographer for Country and Western publs., frequent TV and Radio guest; contbr. to Am. Poetry Anthology, 1989. Rep. precinct worker, No. Ill. area, 1960, So. Calif. area, 1964-85; speaker in field. Mem. Acad. Country Music (sec. 1975-77), Calif. Country Music Assn. Mem. Ch. of Nazarene, Smithsonian Instn. (assoc.). Lodge: Rainbow Girls. Avocations: collecting celebrity and presidential autographed photos, raising and showing Boston Terriers, Indian affairs, travel, gardening. Home and Office: 503 N Platina Dr Diamond Bar CA 91765

SMITH, YVONNE ELSIE, public relations specialist; b. Lincoln, Nebr., July 12, 1939; d. Rudolph Ernest and Elsie Lillian (Rockenbach) Umland; m. Daniel Freeman Jaffe, Aug. 6, 1960 (div. 1967); children: Michael Adam, Sara Ann; m. Linister Gordon Smith II, Mar. 21, 1970. BA in Polit. Sci., U. Nebr., 1960. Dir. pub. info. parks and recreation dept. City of Kansas City, Mo., 1966-68; editor The Sun Newspapers, Shawnee Mission, Kans., 1968-69; copywriter Quastler Advt., Kansas City, 1969-72; v.p., copy dir. The Ibis Co., Kansas City, 1973-84; owner, writer Concept Devel., Kansas City, 1984-87; mktg. asst. H&R Block, Inc., Kansas City, 1987—; instr. Penn Valley Community Coll., Kans. City, 1976-78, 1981-82. Contbr. articles to Mags. Pres. adv. council Westport-Roanoke Community Ctr., Kansas City, 1974-77. Mem. Pub. Relations Soc. Am. Democrat. Presbyterian. Home: 3202 Karnes Blvd Kansas City MO 64111 Office: H&R Block Inc 4410 Main St Kansas City MO 64111

SMITH-DORNAN, MAGGIE JO, marketing educator, academic administrator; b. Ft. Worth, Apr. 6, 1945; d. John Walter and Maggie Thelma (French) Williams; m. Paul Joseph Smith, Nov. 28, 1963 (div. Sept. 1974); 1 child, Stephen Christopher Smith; m. Randall Everett Dornan, July 10, 1982. BS in Bus., Northeastern U., Boston, 1976; MBA, U. Miami, 1977; PhD in Bus., U. Okla., 1980. Lic. real estate broker. Research asst. dept. mktg. U. Miami, Coral Gables, Fla., 1976-77; instr. mktg. U. Okla., Norman, 1977-80; asst. prof. Northeastern U., 1980-83; lectr. dept. mktg. Coll. Bus. Adminstrn. U. Fla., Gainesville, 1985—, assoc. dir. Ctr. for Retail Research and Edn., 1986—, mem. undergrad. program com., 1986; cons. retail, Fla., 1985—. Contbr. articles to profl. jours. Named Mktg. Tchr. of Yr., Coll. Bus. Adminstrn., U. Fla., 1985-87; Mass. State scholar, 1973-76. Mem. Am. Mktg. Assn. (advisor 1982-83), Jacksonville Bd. Realtors, Sigma Epsilon Rho, Delta Sigma Pi (advisor 1985—). Republican. Home: 8112 Sarcee Trail Jacksonville FL 32244 Office: U Fla Dept Mktg 205 Matherly Hall Gainesville FL 32611

SMITHEIMER, LUELLA SUDE, speech and language pathologist; b. N.Y.C., Nov. 19, 1928; d. William and Stella (Meltzer) Sude; m. Aaron Charles Smitheimer, Oct. 19, 1952; children: Roy Jeffrey, Don Lawrence, Eileen Terry. BA, Adelphi Coll., 1950; MS, Adelphi U., 1967; PhD, NYU, 1980. Speech pathologist Adelphi U., Garden City, N.Y., 1965-66, BOCES, Nassau County, Wantagh, N.Y., 1966-70; lectr. St. John's U., Jamaica, N.Y., 1971; pvt. practice pathologist Port Washington, N.Y., 1971—; adj. assoc. prof. Hofstra U., Hempstead, N.Y., 1971-83, NYU, 1984—. Contbr. articles to profl jours. Co-pres. AFS Port Washington Chpt., 1983 ; bd. dirs. Port Children's Ctr., Day Care, 1985—. Mem. Am. Speech, Lang., Hearing Assn., N.Y. State Speech, Lang., Hearing Assn., Assn. for Children with Learning Disabilities. Office: Port Washington Speech Lang 191 Main St Port Washington NY 11050

SMITHERS, JANE BRAITMAYER, manufacturing company executive; b. Washington, May 25, 1915; d. Otto Ernest and Kathleen (Ketcham) Braitmayer; B.A., Vassar Coll., 1937; m. William Henry Howell, Aug. 7, 1937 (dec. 1961); children—Kathleen, William David, Marian Braitmayer; m. 2d, John Abram Smithers, June 13, 1964; stepchildren—Margaret Smithers Koeniger, John A., Eleanor Smithers Blahnik, James P. Rec. sec. Children's Home, Inc., Poughkeepsie, N.Y., 1942, Dutchess County Planned Parenthood, 1941; corp. sec., dir. Smithers Tools and Machine Products, Inc., Rhinebeck, N.Y., 1965—; former dir. Bankers Trust Hudson Valley, N.A. Chmn. com. on detention Dutchess County Social Planning Council, 1949; pres. Dutchess County Soc. Mental Health, 1958-59; mem. Dutchess County Youth Bd., 1968-70; founder, pres. No. Dutchess Community Services, 1969; founder, pres. No. Dutchess Day Care Center, Inc., 1971-73, now mem. adv. bd.; bd. dirs. No. Dutchess Hosp. Republican. Episcopalian. Clubs: Sippican Tennis, Beverly Yacht (Marion, Mass.); Jr. League of Poughkeepsie-Vassar. Home: RD 2 Box 116 Red Hook NY 12571

SMITH-HOWARD, D. STEPHANIE, insurance company executive; b. Chgo., Jan. 17, 1950; d. Donald Harold and Dorothy Patricia (Shelton) Smith; m. Daniel J. Howard, July 25, 1981; stepchildren: Kelly, Brigid, Ryan. AA, Triton Coll., River Grove, Ill., 1972. Lic. ins. broker, Ill. Successively sec., adminstrv. asst., service rep., sales rep. Blue Cross/Blue Shield, Chgo., 1969-81; mgr. Cranwill Assocs., Inc., Chgo., 1981-86; pres. Design Ins. Brokers, Mundelein, Ill., 1986—. 2d. lt. Civil Air Patrol, Chgo., 1976—. Mem. Nat. Assn. Female Execs., Nat. Assn. Health Underwriters, Nat. Assn. Life Underwriters, Women in Mgmt., Grayslake C. of C., Northbrook C. of C., Lake Zurich C. of C., Libertyville/Mundelein/Vernon Hills C. of C. Home: 245 N Garfield St Mundelein IL 60060 Office: Design Ins Brokers PO Box 416 Mundelein IL 60060

SMITH-PALINKAS, BARBARA ANNE, English language educator; b. Sparta, Wis., Feb. 2, 1950; d. Dale William and M. Patricia (Lieser) Smith; m. Klaus Guenter Palinkas, June 16, 1979. BA, U. Wis., 1975, MA, 1977. Instr. ESL Nat. Coll. Edn., Evanston, Ill., 1978-79, Coll. Lake County, Waukegan, Ill., 1978-82; tng. coordinator SER/Jobs for Progress, Inc., Waukegan, 1982-85; Instr. Eng. as second lang. Coll. Lake County Naval Tng. Sch., Great Lakes, Ill., 1985—; coordinator, instr. Adult Continuing Edn., Highland Park, Ill., 1979—. Mem. Ill. Tesol/Be Assn., Nat. Assn. Female Execs., Mensa, Tesol Nat. Home: 689 Homewood Ave Highland Park IL 60035

SMITHSON, SUSAN MARY, sales executive; b. Evanston, Ill., Apr. 18, 1952; d. Paul Busby and Janet Clara (Baker) S.; m. William Joseph Cherf, Aug. 29, 1987. BBA in Fin., U. Denver, 1976, MBA in Fin., 1977. Acct. AccounTemps, Denver, 1977; fleet mgr. Carol Buick Co., Evanston, 1977-81; dist. sales mgr. Buick Motor div. Gen. Motors Corp., Flint, Mich., 1981-87, dist. mgr.-sales and service, 1987—.

SMITH-YOUNG, ANNE VICTORIA, health science services administrator; b. Long Beach, Calif., Aug. 25, 1947; d. James Warren and Jeanne Anne (Cooney) Wright; m. Lynn Walker Smith, Aug. 11, 1968 (div. Feb. 1980); children: Amy Lyanne and Caroline Walker (twins); m. Stephen Nicholas Young, May 29, 1982. AS, Long Beach City Coll., 1967; BS, Marymount Coll., 1984. Diplomate Am. Bd. Urologic Allied Profls. Mgr. office Williams-Brinton Med. Corp., Huntington Beach, Calif., 1975-80; adminstr. Westchester Urol. Assocs., White Plains, N.Y., 1980-82; adminstr. Pediatric Urol. Assocs. Westchester County Med. Ctr., Valhalla, N.Y., 1982-86, clin. coordinator urodynamics lab. dept. urology, 1986—; cons. Office Career Services, Marymount (N.Y.) Coll., 1984—, Am. Bd. Urol. Allied Health Profls., Inc., Stamford, Conn., 1984—; co-dir., pres. Continence Restored, Inc., N.Y.C., 1985—; participant People to People Med. Delegation to China, 1986; lectr. in field. Contbr. articles to profl. jours. Bd. dirs. Help for Incontinent People, Spartanburg, S.C., 1985—; participant IAET Incontinence Task Force for HCFA, 1987, Nat. Agenda to Promote Urinary Continence, 1984, Pub. Hearings for Health and Human Services, Nat. Kidney and Urologic Diseases Adv. Bd., 1988. Mem. Am. Urol. Assn. Allied (nat. fundraiser 1980-86, bd. dirs. N.Y. chpt. 1988—, Recognition award 1985), Am. Assn. Med. Assts., Nat. Assn. Female Execs., Nat. Hist. Preservation Trust. Democrat. Club: Mothers of Twins (Long Beach) (pres. 1974-75). Home: 407 Strawberry Hill Ave Stamford CT 06902 Office: Westchester County Med Ctr Dept Urology Valhalla NY 10595

SMITT, JULIANN, author, photographer; b. Spokane, Wash., Apr. 19, 1955; d. John William and Gloria Elizabeth (Stauffer) S. AA, Spokane Falls Community Coll., 1975; BA, Wash. State U., 1977. Writer, photographer Grant County Jour., Ephrata, Wash., 1977—. Recipient 2d place news features award Wash. Newspaper Pubs. Assn., 1983, 1st pl. Comprehensive News Coverage Wash. Newspaper Pubs. Assn., 1985, 2d pl. features Wash. Newspaper Pubs. Assn., 1985, 3d pl. spot news Wash. Newspaper Pubs. Assn., 1985, 1st and 2d place feature photos awards Wash. Newspaper Pubs. Assn., 1986, 2d place gen. news award Wash. Newspaper Pubs. Assn., 1986, 2d place features award Wash. Newspaper Pubs. Assn., 1986. Mem. Soc. Profl. Journalists, Ephrata Bus. and Profl. Women's Club (pres. 1980-81, 82-83, Young Career Woman award 1979), Soap Lake C. of C. (dir. 1980-81, sec. 1982), AAUW. Club: Ephrata Bus. and Profl. Women's. Lodge: Ephrata Kiwanis (hon. mem.).

SMITTKAMP, JANET MARIE, pharmaceutical executive; b. Ft. Gordon, Ga., June 28, 1954; d. James Ralph and Joyce Amanda (Broxton) Wengler; m. Keith E. Smittkamp, Nov. 6, 1976. AS, Danville Jr. Coll., 1972-74; BS in Zoology, Eastern Ill. U., 1974-76; postgrad., Sangamon State U., 1984—. Cert. quality engr. Animal technician Indsl. Biotest Inc., Decatur, Ill., 1976-77; quality assurance specialist I Indsl. Biotest, Inc., Decatur, 1978-79; quality control technician ConAgra, Inc., Sherman, Tex., 1977-78; quality assurance specialist II ToxiGenics, Inc., Decatur, 1979-81; quality assurance assoc. Wallace Laboratories, Decatur, 1982—. Mem. Am. Soc. Quality Control (sec. 1982-83, treas. 1983-84, v. chmn. 1983-84, chmn. 1984-85, Berg award 1985), Nat. Assn. Female Execs. Home: 1150 Nottingham Ct Mount Zion IL 62549 Office: Wallace Laboratories 434 N Morgan St Decatur IL 62525

SMOLKO, OWNIE (MARY) MCBRIDE, media and public affairs deputy assistant secretary; b. Louisville, June 18, 1954; d. Thomas Owen and Mary Virgina (Constance) McBride; m. John Francis Smolko, Jr., Nov. 29, 1986. Student, Ind. U., 1972-74. Spl. asst. to press sec., dir. pub. affairs U.S. Dept. of Interior, Washington, 1983-85; dep. asst. sec. for pub. affairs U.S. Dept. of Transp., Washington, 1985—; fin. dir. Hopkins for Congress, Lexington, Ky., 1978; asst. fin. dir. Rep. Party of Ky., Frankfort, 1979; asst. dir. Rep. Senate House Dinner, Washington, 1980; campaign mgr., fin. dir. Hultman for Congress, Red Oak, Iowa, 1980; fin. asst. Presdl. Inaugural Com., Washington, 1980-81; dir. Rep. senatorial i circle and bus. adv. bd. Nat. Rep. Senatorial Com., Washington, 1981-83. Mem. Jr. League, Washington, 1985—, Am. Assn. Polit. Cons., Washington, 1982; founding men., chmn., Taste of th South Charity Event, Washington, 1983-86. Mem. Nat. Press Club. Roman Catholic. Home: 2810 Summerfield Rd Falls Church VA 22042

SMOOK, BARBARA BEATRICE LIPSCOMB, insurance executive, marketing consultant; b. Houston, Sept. 29, 1942; d. Nathan Wyott and Violet A. (Payne) Lipscomb; m. S.L. Quinn, Dec. 14, 1957 (div. 1970); children: Sherwood P., Bruce C., Bradford L., September Quinn Roth; m. John Thomas Smook, Feb. 2, 1984. AA in Bus. Adminstrn., Smithdeal Massey Coll., 1972. V.p. Kosmo Corp., Glen Allen, Va., 1975—; underwriting mgr. Atlas Underwriters, Ltd., Richmond, 1977-81; v.p., founder, dir. Mid-Atlantic Inc., Richmond, 1981—; sec., dir. Internat. Security Vault Systems, Inc., Glen Allen, 1982—. Mem. Women's Resource Ctr., Richmond, 1982—; mem. Republican Nat. Com., 1983. Mem. Profl. Ins.

Agts., Ind. Ins. Agts. of Va., Nat. Assn. Female Execs., Hanover County Bus. Assn., Va. His.t Soc., Va. Geneal. Soc. Republican. Mormon. Office: Mid Atlantic Inc 3121 W Marshall St Richmond VA 23230

SMOOT, MYRNA L., art association executive; b. Los Angeles, June 3, 1945. BA in Economics, U. Calif., Berkeley, 1966, MA in Economics, 1967, postgrad. art history UCLA, 1976. Econ. analyst Prudential Ins., Los Angeles, 1967; project leader Transam. Research, San Francisco, 1967-70; teaching asst. UCLA, Los Angeles, 1972-74; exhibit assoc. Los Angeles Museum of Art, 1977-78, special asst. 1978, exhibit coordinator, 1978-81, asst. dir., 1981-86; exec. dir. Art Mus. Assn. Am., San Francisco, 1986-87; dir. The Am. Fedn. of Arts, N.Y.C., San Franciso, 1987—. Contbr. articles to profl. jours. Co-producer Com. Olympic Arts Festival, Los Angeles, 1983-84; mem. Arts Adv. Com., Los Angeles Bicentennial, 1979-80. Edward A. Dickson Art History grantee, 1975-76; fellow NDEA; U. Calif. Regent scholar, 1963-66. Mem. Art Table, Am. Assn. Museums, Women in Bus., Phi Beta Kappa. Office: Am Fedn of Arts West 270 Sutter St San Francisco CA 94108 Office: AFA 41 E 65th St New York NY 10021

SMOOT, SUE ANN, photographer; b. Lakewood, Ohio, Oct. 3, 1955; d. Edwin T. and Peggy Ann (Winningham) Syvertsen; m. Michael Dwayne Smoot, Jan. 16, 1950; children: Michael D., Linzi Anne. Grad. high sch., Cin. Free-lance photographer Color Cen., Wichita, Kans., 1974-76, Cleve., 1977—, Clayton, Brelo, Att & Assocs., Cleve.; studio photographer Painesville, Ohio, 1985-86. Mem. Profl. Photographers Inst., PTO. Home and Office: Crystal Image Photography 9905 Crestwood Dr Twinsburg OH 44087

SMULLIN, PATRICIA CLARA, broadcasting and cable television executive; b. Eureka, Calif., Dec. 20, 1949; d. William Brothers and Patricia (Duell) S. BS in Communications and Psychology, Oreg. State U.; postgrad. Stanford U., So. Oreg. State U. Office mgr. So. Oreg. Cable TV, Medford, 1973-74, dir. consumer relations, 1974-76, v.p., 1976-82; pres. Calif. Oreg. Inc., Medford, 1982—; pres., bd. dirs. Pacific N.W. Cable Communications; mem. adv. council Rogue Community Coll. Mem. bd. dirs. YMCA, Medford, Rogue Valley Med. Ctr.; apptd. by Gov. to Oreg. Commn. Pub. Broadcasting. Recipient Oreg. Cable TV award. Mem. Oreg. Cable Communications Assn. (past pres., bd. dirs.), Nat. Assn. Broadcasters (bd. dirs., mem. 100-plus TV market com., congrl. relations com.), Oreg. Assn. Broadcasters (bd. dirs. and past pres.), Medford-Jackson C. of C. (bd. dirs.), Women in Cable TV (charter), Nat. Cable TV Assn., Stanford U. Alumni Assn., Rogue Valley Med. Ctr. (bd. dirs.), Rogue Valley Health Found., Medford-Jackson County C. of C. (bd. dirs.). Office: Calif Oreg Broadcasting Inc 125 S Fir St Medford OR 97501

SMYLY, CHARLENE R., banker; b. Enid, Okla., Jan. 22, 1946; d. Ralph F. and LaVerne (Moser) Crawford; m. Gary L. Smyly, May 20, 1946; children: Christopher James, Brian Todd. BS, Northwestern State U., 1968. From auditor to acct. corp. services San Diego Fed. Savs. and Loan, 1968-75; cash mgr. corp. hdqrts. Fleming Cos., Oklahoma City, 1975-80, Champlin Petroleum Co., Enid, 1980-82; v.p. customer service Cen. Nat. Bank. and Trust, Enid, 1982—; instr. Am. Bankers Sch., 1985—, Cen. Nat. Bank, 1985—. Mem. Okla. Cash Mgmt. Assn. (pres. 1984-85), Okla. Bankers Assn., Pilot Club Internat., Enid C. of C. (New Membership Achievement award 1984). Republican. Mem. Christian Ch. Club: Oakwood Country. Office: Cen Nat Bank and Trust Co 324 W Broadway Enid OK 73701

SMYTH, DIANE ELIZABETH, writer; b. N.Y.C., May 18, 1952; d. Edward David Duane and Elizabeth Kathryn Burke; m. Robert Peter Smyth, Feb. 15, 1987. Student, Dowling Coll.; RN, Pilgrim State Hosp. Sch. Nursing, West Brentwood, N.Y., 1974. Staff nurse Payne Whitney Psychiat. Clinic div. N.Y. Hosp., N.Y.C., 1974-76; writer's asst. Northridge, Calif., 1976-78; free-lance writer Phila., 1978—; staff writer Filmation Studios, 1983-84; story editor Dinosaucers TV series DIC Enterprises, Encino, Calif., 1986-87; story editor Commander Video TV series Marvel Prodns., Sherman Oaks, Calif., 1987—; leader Boskone Writer's Workshop, Boston, 1985—. Author: The Door Into Fire, 1979, So You Want To Be A Wizard?, 1983, The Wounded Sky, 1983, The Door Into Shadow, 1984, My Enemy, My Ally, 1984, Deep Wizardly, 1985, The Romulan Way, 1987; author short stories, screenplays, computer game. Mem. Writers' Guild Am. (East chpt.). Office: c/o Donald Maass Lit Agy 64 W 84th St New York NY 10024

SMYTH, FRAN(CES) DALE, insurance company executive; b. N.Y.C., Sept. 6, 1941; d. Max and Aida (Heimerdinger) Goldfarb; B.S., Poly. Inst. N.Y., 1963; M.B.A., Baruch Coll. CUNY, 1973; 1 son, Kevin Jeffrey. Programmer, CIT Fin., N.Y.C., 1965-66; programmer analyst Saks Fifth Ave., N.Y.C., 1966-67; sr. programmer Sealtest Co., N.Y.C., 1967-68; mgr. Kennecott Copper Corp., N.Y.C., 1968-74; asst. v.p. Met. Life Co., N.Y.C., 1974—; mem. exec. com. 14th St Local Devel. Corp.; lectr. Council N.Y. City Cooperatives . Chmn. bd. dirs. CSC Repertory; chmn. 15th St. Block Assn. Home: 40 W 15th St Apt 1C New York NY 10011 Office: Met Life Ins Co 1 Madison Ave New York NY 10010

SMYTHE, MARSHA SUSAN HALLER, nurse practitioner, consultant; b. Joliet, Ill., Nov. 6, 1949; d. Eugene Keith and Margaret Evelyn (Hrebenyak) Haller; m. Bryan Edward Smythe, Nov. 15, 1969; children—Christopher, Jason. A.Arts and Scis. in Nursing, Joliet Jr. Coll., 1973; B.S. in Nursing with honors, Purdue U., 1983; postgrad., Med. U. of S.C., 1986—. R.N., cert. family nurse practitioner, Ill., S.C. Operating room nurse Silver Cross Hosp., Joliet, 1973-79; ob-gyn nurse practitioner Michael Reese Health Plan, Chgo., 1983, Joliet Med. Group, 1984-85; gynecol./pediatric nurse practitioner Kankakeeland Community Action Agy. (Ill.), 1983-84; nursing cons., Joliet, 1982-85, Charleston, 1985—; labor and delivery staff Trident Regional Med. Ctr., Charleston, S.C., 1985—. Mem. Am. Nurses Assn., Nurses Assn. of Am. Coll. Obstetricians and Gynecologists, Council Primary Care Nurse Practitioners, S.C. Nurses Assn., Trident Nurses Assn. Republican. Roman Catholic. Home: 103 Runnymeade Ln Summerville SC 29483

SMYTHE-GREEN, SHERRY, video cassette publishing company executive; b. Alameda, Calif., May 16, 1936; d. Lester Andrew and Alma (Farek) S.; student Brigham Young U., Atlanta Baptist Coll., Dekalb Coll., m. Wayne S. Green II; children—Abra Michelle Smith Pofelski, Roger Sunday Smith, Matthew Clinton Smith; m. 2d, Wayne Green, 1979. Exec. sec. Dairypak, Fort Worth, Tex., 1954-55; mgr. Child Care Registry, Atlanta, 1963-71; chief exec. officer Contract Carpets, Orem, Utah, 1971-73; asst. to controller Cayman Devel. Co., Rolling Hills Estates, Calif., 1973-76; exec. v.p. Wayne Green, Inc., Peterborough, N.H., 1976-83, Instant Software, Inc., 73, Inc., 1976-83; pres. Flambouyant Ltd., 1983—; pub. Butterfly Video, 1986—; producer 22 videos for Kathy Blake Let's Learn How to Dance Series, 9 videos David Nicholas Make-Up Techniques Series; pres. XL Systems; Republican. Mormon. Columnist, Kiloband Microcomputing mag., Desktop computing mag., 80 Microcomputing mag. Home: PO Box 60 Hancock NH 03449 Office: PO Box 184 Antrim NH 03440

SNAPP, ELIZABETH, librarian, educator; b. Lubbock, Tex., Mar. 31, 1937; d. William James and Louise (Lanham) Mitchell; BA magna cum laude, North Tex. State U., Denton, 1968, MLS, 1969, MA, 1977; m. Harry Franklin Snapp, June 1, 1956. Asst. to archivist Archive of New Orleans Jazz, Tulane U., 1960-63; catalog librarian Tex. Woman's U., Denton, 1969-71, head acquisitions dept., 1971-74, coordinator readers services, 1974-77, asst. to dean Grad. Sch., 1977-79, instr. library sci., 1977—, acting Univ. librarian, 1979-82, dir. libraries, 1982—, mem. adv. com. on library formula Coordinating Bd. Tex. Coll. and Univ. System, 1981—; del. OCLC Nat. Users Council, 1985-87, mem. by-laws com., 1985-86, com. on less-than-full-services networks, 1986-87; project dir. Nat. Endowment for Humanities consultancy grant on devel. core curriculum for women's studies, 1981-82; chmn. Blue Ribbon com. 1986 Gov.'s Commn. for Women to select 150 outstanding women in Tex. history; project dir. math./sci. anthology project Tex. Found. Women's Resources. Co-sponsor Irish Lecture Series, Denton, 1968, 70, 73, 78. Sec. Denton County Democratic Caucus, 1970. Recipient Ann. Pioneer award Tex. Women's U., 1986. Mem. ALA (standards com. 1983-85) Southwestern, Tex. (program com. 1978, Dist. VII chmn. 1985-86) library assns., Women's Collecting Group (chmn. ad hoc com. 1984—), AAUW (legis. br. chmn. 1973-74, br. v.p. 1975-76, br. pres. 1979-80, state historian 1986—), So. Conf. Brit. Studies, AAUP, Tex. Assn. Coll. Tchrs. (pres. Tex. Woman's U. chpt. 1976-77), Woman's Shakespeare Club (pres. 1967-69), Beta Phi Mu (pres. chpt. 1976-78; sec. nat. adv. assembly 1978-79, pres. 1979-80, nat. dir. 1981—), Alpha Chi, Alpha Lambda Sigma (pres. 1970-71), Pi Delta Phi. Episcopalian (directress altar guild 1966-68, 73-76). Club: Soroptimist Internat. (Denton) (pres. 1986-88). Asst. editor Tex. Academe, 1973-76; contbg. author: Women in Special Collections, 1984, Special Collections, 1986; book reviewer Library Resources and Tech. Services, 1973—. Contbr. articles to profl. jours. Home: 1904 N Lake Trail Denton TX 76201 Office: TWU Sta PO Box 24093 Denton TX 76204

SNEAD, LINDA JEAN, speech-language pathologist, educator; b. Orange, N.J., July 16, 1951; d. Frank and Minnie (Horton) S. BA, Rutgers U., 1973; MA, Montclair State Coll., 1978. Speech-lang. pathologist Matawan (N.J.)-Aberdeen Bd. Edn., 1974-79; lang.-learning specialist Montclair (N.J.) Pub. Schs., 1979-81; speech-lang. pathologist Glen Ridge (N.J.) Bd. Edn., 1981—; adj. instr. Field of Communication Scis. and Disorders Montclair State Coll., 1987—; N.J. State Commnr. Edn.'s adv. council for the handicapped, 1987—; v.p. L.S. Enterprises: Resources for Personal Communication. Mem. N.J. Parent-Profl. Task Force. Named one of Outstanding Young Women of Am., 1985. Mem. Am. Speech-Lang.-Hearing Assn. (supervision com. 1985-87), N.J. Speech-Lang.-Hearing Assn. (advisor, newspaper supplement 1987, exec. bd. 1979-82, conv. chmn. 1985, honors 1987). Office: Glen Ridge Bd Edn 235 Ridgewood Ave Glen Ridge NJ 07028

SNEARLY, SANDRA JO, accountant; b. East Chicago, Ind., May 13, 1954; d. Eugene John and Josephine Ann (Thomas) Smith; m. Dennis Dale Snearly, Oct. 2, 1976. BS, Ball State U., 1976. CPA Ind. Cost reviewer Prudential Ins., Merrillville, Ind., 1976-78; acct. St. Pierre and Krafft, Merrillville, 1978-80; sr. acct. Krafft and Co., Merrillville, 1980-85, ptnr., 1985—. Chmn. panel Lake Area United Way, Griffith, Ind. 1984-86. Mem. Am. Inst. CPA's, Ind. CPA Soc., Ind. St. Bd. Pub. Accountancy, Duneland Bus. and Profl. Women (founder, pres. 1986—), Lakeshore Bus. and Profl. Women (v.p. 1983-85, treas. 1981-83), Merrillville C. of C. (treas. 1988—, Athena award 1986). Republican. Roman Catholic. Home: 3289 Rustic Ln LOFS Crown Point IN 46307 Office: Krafft and Co 398 W 80th Place Merrillville IN 46410

SNEATH, JUDITH MARIE, personnel executive; b. Houston, Nov. 23, 1943; d. Leonard F. and Flora Delfina (Gigliotti) Tritico; 1 dau., Alison Lea. BS in Elem. Edn., Tex. Tech U., 1965. Tchr., Kermit pub. schs. (Tex.), 1965-66, Garland Ind. Sch. Dist. (Tex.), 1966-67; with Crum & Forster Ins., Dallas, 1968-69, 71-73; adminstrv. mgr. Am. Internat. Group, Dallas, 1973-76; word processing mgr. Am. Internat. Group, N.Y.C., 1976-78; asst. v.p. personnel/adminstr. Constellation Reins. Co., N.Y.C., 1978-85; 2d v.p. human resources, adminstr. N.Am. Co. Property & Casualty Ins., Greenwich, Conn., 1985—. Mem. Adminstrv. Mgmt. Soc. (past pres.), Ins. Human Resources Assn. Democrat. Unitarian. Office: N Am Co Property & Casualty Ins One Greenwich Plaza Greenwich CT 06836-2568

SNEDAKER, CATHERINE RAUPAGH (KIT), editor; b. Fargo, N.D., Apr. 2; d. Paul and Charity (Primmer) Raupagh; B.A., Duke U., 1943; m. William Brooks, 1943; children—Eleanor, Peter William; m. 2d, Weldon Snedaker, Sept. 17, 1950. Pub. relations exec. United Seamen's Service, 1950-57; promotion mgr. sta. WINR-TV and WNBF-TV, Binghamton, N.Y., 1957-60; TV editor, feature writer Binghamton Sun, 1960-68; mem. staff Los Angeles Herald Examiner, 1968—, food editor, 1978—, restaurant critic, 1978-80, food and travel editor, 1980-86; editor The Food Package; columnist Copley News Service; instr. food/travel writing UCLA Extension. Author: The Great Convertibles; contbr. numerous articles on food and travel to nat. mags. and newspapers; guest editor Mademoiselle mag., 1942. Recipient 3 awards Los Angeles Press Club, VISTA award, 1979. Mem. Am. Travel Editors Assn., Soc. Am. Travel Writers. Democrat. Home: 140 San Vicente Blvd Apt C Santa Monica CA 90402

SNEDDEN, MARY JANE HEFFNER (MRS. HOMER GRANGER SNEDDEN), city official; b. McKeesport, Pa., Mar. 14, 1917; d. Samuel Harrison and Meda (Calhoun) Heffner; m. Homer Granger Snedden, Nov. 6, 1943. Secretarial student Douglas Bus. Coll., McKeesport, Pa., 1936-37; student Duquesne U., 1942. Sec. legal dept. Westinghouse Air Brake Co., Wilmerding, Pa., 1940-44. Leader Brownie Scouts, Fayetteville, N.C., 1947-48; pres. East McKeesport Recreation Bd., 1968-76; majority inspector, dist. 1, East McKeesport Election Bd., 1966-69; councilwoman Borough of East McKeesport, 1972-81, 84-87, chmn. fin., 1972-78, mem. fin. com., 1978-81, chmn. st. com., 1978-80, v.p. council, 1976-80, chmn. fire and water com., 1980-81, chmn. light and ordinance com., 1984-85, pres. Council 10, 1985, chmn. fin. com., 1986-87, mem. police and property and recreation coms., 1986-87; mem. Rep. Com., Dist. 1, East McKeesport, 1971-76, mem. Rep. County Com.; Rep. com. woman Dist. 1, 1982—; chmn. Rep. Party, Borough of East McKeesport, 1984-86; bd. dirs. Pre-Sch. for Exceptional Children Greater McKeesport Area, 1966—, pres. bd., 1985-87; trustee Allegheny Acad., 1969-74; mem. citizens adv. com. Gov.'s Traffic Safety Council, 1978—; W. Pa. rep. Pa. Assn. Women Hwy. Safety Leaders, 1980-81; exec. bd. CAC/GTSC, 1979-87, sec. exec. bd., 1981-84. Recipient Gov.'s award for outstanding contbn. to traffic safety Commonwealth of Pa., 1968-85, 1st place individual award Women's div. Nat. Safety Council, 1985, Community Leader of Am. award and Commemorative medal of honor Am. Biographical Inst., 1987. Mem. Pa. Huguenot Soc., DAR (chpt. regent 1966-68, state vice chmn. U.S.A. Bicentennial com. 1971-74, state chmn. Am. history month 1974-75, state vice chmn. student loan and scholarship com. 1977-80, mem. state student loan and scholarship com. 1980-83, chpt. rec. sec. 1982-84, chmn. Americanism com., chmn. transp. and safety com. 1982—, mem. program com. 1982-84, mem. state Jr. Am. Citizen com. 1983-86, state Am. Heritage com., 1986-88, chpt. librarian 1984-86, corr. sec. 1986-88, chpt. chmn. various coms.). Presbyterian. Lodge: Order Eastern Star (past matron, pres. McKeesport Past Matrons Club 1975-76). Home: 722 Broadway East McKeesport PA 15035

SNEED, EMOGENE MILDRED, nurse; b. Kingsport, Tenn., Nov. 11, 1929; d. O.H. and Ida Theresa (King) Cox; m. John H. Sneed, Jan. 11, 1956; children: Jerry Lee, Rex Ronald, Scott Donald. R.N., Knoxville Gen. Hosp., 1953; student U. Tenn., 1952, East Tenn. State U., 1955, postgrad. Margaret Hague Maternity Hosp., 1953. Staff nurse Holston Vally Hosp. Med. Ctr., Kingsport, Tenn., 1953—. Den mother Kingsport council Cub Scouts Am., 1965-66. Mem. ARC, Tenn. Nursing Assn., Am. Heart Assn., Tenn. Mental Health Assn., Am. Operating Nurses Assn. Baptist. Home: 2041 Sherwood Rd Kingsport TN 37664

SNEED, GENEVA BELL, union official; b. nr. Knoxville, Tenn., Oct. 10, 1920; d. Westly W. and Louie V. (Stallings) Fox; student U. Tenn., 1952-53; m. Luther J. Sneed, May 15, 1936; children—Mackie A., Larry K., Linda K. Sneed Helton, Martha Lou Sneed Mashburn. Officer mgr. Western Union, Sevierville, Tenn., 1936-45; operator Pub. Shirt Corp., Knoxville, 1946-49; head grievance ofcl. Local 90, AFL-CIO, Knoxville, 1948-50; pres. Knoxville CIO Council, 1951-53; dir. Women's Activities div. AFL-CIO Area Council, 1953-55; staff rep. Amalgamated Clothing Workers Am., Knoxville, 1952-69, asst. mgr. Southeastern clothing regional bd., 1969-82, mgr., 1982—; sec.-treas. Southeastern Clothing Bd. Realty Corp., 1969-82, pres., 1982—; v.p. Tenn. State Labor Council, 1959—. Co-chmn. women's div. Estes Kefauver campaign, 1956; v.p. Tenn. AFL-CIO Com. on Polit. Edn., 1959—; exec. 2d v.p. Tenn. State Labor Council AFL-CIO, 1971-81. Alderwoman, Sevierville, Tenn., 1982-86. Democrat. Office: 1124 N Broadway Knoxville TN 37917

SNEED, MARIE ELEANOR WILKEY, retired educator; b. Dahlgren, Ill., June 12, 1915; d. Charles N. and Hazel (Miller) Wilkey; student U. Ill., 1933-35; B.S., Northwestern U., 1937; postgrad. Wayne State U., 1954-60, U. Mich., 1967; m. John Sneed, Jr., Sept. 18, 1937; children—Suzanne (Mrs. Geoffrey B. Newton), John Corwin. Tchr. English, drama, creative writing Berkley (Mich.) Sch. Dist., 1952-76. Mem. Mich. Statewide Tchr. Edn. Preparation, 1968-72, regional sec. 1969-70; mem. Pleasant Ridge Arts Council, 1982—, Pleasant Ridge Parks and Recreation Commn., 1982-88. Mem. NEA, Mich., Berkley (pres. 1961-62, 82-87) edn. assns., Oakland Tchr. Edn. Council (exec. bd. 1973-76), Student Tchr. Planning Com. Berkley (chmn. 1971-72), Phi Alpha Chi, Pi Lambda Theta, Alpha Delta Kappa, Alpha Omicron Pi. Club: Pleasant Ridge Woman's (pres. 1980-83). Home: 21 Norwich Rd Pleasant Ridge MI 48069

SNEED, PAULA ANN, food products executive; b. Everett, Mass., Nov. 10, 1947; d. Thomas Edwin and F. Mary (Turner) S.; m. Lawrence Paul Bass, Sept. 2, 1978; children: Courtney Jameson. BA, Simmons Coll., 1969; MBA, Harvard U., 1977. Dir. plans, program devel. and evaluations Ecumenical Ctr. in Roxbury, Mass., 1971-72; program coordinator Boston Sickle Cell Ctr., 1972-75; with Gen. Foods Corp., White Plains, N.Y., 1977—, category mgr., 1983-86, asst. product mgr. to v.p. consumer affairs, 1987—; bd. dirs. Crispus Attucks Scholarship Fund, Ridgewood, N.J., 1982. Bd. dirs. Crispus Attucks Scholarship Fund, Ridgewood, N.J., 1982—. Recipient Benevolent Heart award Graham-Windham, 1987, Black Achiever award Harlem YWCA, 1982; named MBA of Yr. Harvard Bus. Sch. Black Alumni Orgn., 1987. Mem. AAUW, Nat. Assn. Negro Bus. and Profl. Women, Coalition of 100 Black Women, Soc. Consumer Affairs Profls. Home: 303 Pershing Ave Ridgewood NJ 07450 Office: Gen Foods Corp USA 250 North St White Plains NY 10625

SNELL, MARIE LETTY, artist; b. Detroit, May 15, 1924; d. Samuel Harris and Sylvia Doris (Cohen) Glucksman; m. John Richard Snell, Apr. 1, 1948; children: Jane Hannah Fonfara Snell, Florence Ann Davis Snell. Student, Wayne State U., 1941-43, 56, 75; B of Design, U. Mich., 1947; postgrad., Soc. Arts and Crafts, 1947-53. art therapist Pontiac Gen. Hosp., 1986; lectr. in field; juror various exhibits, 1985-86. One woman shows include Oak Park (Mich.) Pub. Library, 1980, Clerestory Gallery Pontiac Art Ctr., 1982, Southfield Civic Ctr., 1983, 86, COMERICA Hdqrs., 1983, State Capitol Bldg., 1986, Mich. Tech. U., 1987; group shows include Pontiac Art Ctr., 1981, 82, Marygrove Coll., 1981, Mill Gallery, 1982, Oakland County Galleria, 1983, 87, Paint Creek Ctr. for the Arts, 1983, 87, Port con Toronto, 1982-83, Oak Park Pub. Library, 1983-87, La Galerie du Vitrail, Chartres, France, 1985, Artsource Gallery, 1986, Detroit Artists Market, 1987, Corning (N.Y.) Mus. of Glass, 1987, Watertower Art Assn., Louisville, 1987; work exhibited in permanent collections The Art of Crafts Gallery, Royal Oak, La Galerie du Vitrail, Chartres; designed stained glass windows for Temple Bapt. Ch., Windsor, Ontario, Can., 1988; contbr. articles to art mags. Commr. Arts and Cultural Commn., Oak Park, 1982—; bd. dirs. Com. for Mich. Glass Month, 1981-85. Served with USMC, 1944-46. Grantee Ohio Arts Council, Arts Council of Greater Toledo, 1985, Mich. Council for the Arts, 1981-82, 86. Mem. Stained Glass Assn. Am. (assoc., sec. 1980-84, exhibitor various group shows, Best of Show award 1981-83, 1st prize 1982-83, Best Use of Opalescent Glass 1986), Mich. Glass Guild, Centre Internat. du Vitrail, Women's Caucus for Art. Democrat. Home: 14201 Hart Oak Park MI 48237

SNELL, THECKLA HELIDES, health agent, nurse; b. Taunton, Mass., Oct. 26, 1924; d. Ernest Michael and Alexandra (Evans) Helides; m. Charles R. Snell Jr., June 15, 1946. Degree in nursing, Mt. Sinai Hosp., 1945. RN, N.Y., Ohio, Mass.; cert. health officer; real estate broker. Head nurse health services Mt. Sinai Hosp., N.Y.C., 1945-46; pub. health nurse Cin. Health Dept., 1947-49; head nurse Taunton State Hosp., 1950-51; pub. health nurse Taunton Bd. of Health, 1951-66, health agt., 1966—; pres. Community Health Improvement Com., Taunton, 1984; trustee Foxboro (Mass.) State Hosp. Sec. Am. Cancer Soc., Taunton, 1984—. Mem. Am. Pub. Health Assn., Mass. Pub. Health Assn., New Eng. Pub. Health Assn. (past pres., Pres. award 1982), Mass. Health Officers Assn. Republican. Greek Orthodox. Club: Quota (Taunton) (past pres.). Home: 68 Davis St Taunton MA 02780

SNELLING, MURRIEL INEZ, small business owner; b. Moretown, Vt., Aug. 20, 1934; d. Harris Kitchener and Grace Ione (Sawyer) Conrad; m. Carroll Frederick Snelling, Nov. 1, 1952; 1 child, Timothy Forrest. Grad. high sch., Windsor, Vt. Bookkeeper Snelling Lumber Co., Thetford, Vt., 1956-72; ptnr. Snelling Equipment Co., Bath, N.H., 1974-75; office mgr. Kenison Lumber Co., Lancaster, N.H., 1975-79; stitcher Woodsville Industries, Haverhill, N.H., 1980-82, insp., supr., 1982-83; mgr. Activewear, Inc., Littleton, N.H., 1983-87; owner MS Sampleworks, Littleton, 1987—. Mem. Nat. Assn. Female Execs. Home: 185T Union St Littleton NH 03561

SNIBBE, PATRICIA MISCALL, advertising agency executive; b. Hackensack, N.J., June 1, 1932; d. Jack and Margaret Lois (Drake) Miscall; m. Richard Wilson Snibbe, Sept. 8, 1962; stepchildren: John Robinson, Paul Clor. BFA, R.I. Sch. Design, 1954; postgrad., New Sch. for Social Research, 1975-80. Dir. art, film producer Peckham Productions, N.Y.C., 1960-64; dir. art, ptnr. Stallman and Snibbe, N.Y.C., 1964-66; dir. art Shevlo Advt., N.Y.C., 1966-72, Bernard Hodes Advt., N.Y.C., 1972-77; owner, creative dir. Designstuff, N.Y.C., 1978—; v.p., creative dir. Archtl. Film Library, N.Y.C., 1980—; pres. Crommelin and Bliss, Parfumier, 1988—. Author, artist: Feminist Funnies, 1981—. Recipient Golden Circle award Affiliated Advt. Agys. Internat., 1975-77, Creativity award Affiliated Advt. Agys. Internat., 1978. Mem. NOW (bd. dirs. N.Y.C. 1983-84), Graphic Artists Guild (steering com. Cartoonists Guild div. 1984-85), Nat. Acad TV and Scis. Home: 139 E 18th St New York NY 10003

SNIDE, CYNTHIA MARIE, chapter developmentdirector; b. Columbus, Ohio, Aug. 15, 1962; d. Richard Edward and Marilyn Jane (Morris) S.; m. Stuart Edwin Volker. BA, Ohio State U., 1985; postgrad., U. S.C., 1987-88. Nat. chpt. cons. Alpha Xi Delta Nat. Fraternity, Indpls., 1985-86; residence hall dir. Baldwin Wallace Coll., Berea, Ohio, 1986-87; dir. chpt. devel. div. student affairs U. S.C., Columbia, 1987—; cons. Piedmont Airlines, Cleve., 1985—, Alpha Xi Delta Fraternity, Indpls., 1985—. Bd. dirs. Maple Grove United Meth. Ch., Columbus, 1983-86. Named one of Outstanding Young Women Am. Republican. Methodist. Home: 3121 Duncan St Columbia SC 29205

SNIDER, PATRICIA ANN, college counselor; b. Fremont, Ohio, Sept. 7, 1937; d. Millard Alfred and Mary (Danchisen) Snider. B.S. in Edn., Bowling Green State U., 1959; M.Ed., Ohio U., 1963. Instr. St. Joseph Coll., Emmitsburg, Md., 1959-61; grad. asst. tchr. Ohio U. Athens, 1961-63; head resident advisor Western Ill. U., Macomb, Ill., 1963-67; counselor Morton Coll., Cicero, Ill., 1967—. Author: (with others) Community College Career Alternatives Handbook, 1979; Women on their Way-A Guide for Women Returning to School, 1984. Contbr. articles to profl. jours. Bd. dirs. Cicero chpt. Am. Cancer Soc.; flotilla vice comdr. U.S. Coast Guard Aux., 1969-82. Recipient Faculty Mem. of Yr. award Morton Coll. Endowment Found., 1982. Mem. Am. Assn. for Counseling and Devel., Nat. Acad. Advisors Assn., Nat. Assn. for Women Deans, Adminstrs. and Counselors, Ill. Assn. for Counseling and Devel., Nat. Coll. Personnel Assn., Ill. Coll. Personnel Assn. Roman Catholic. Avocations: Reading; fishing. Home: 1540 S 59th Ct Cicero IL 60650 Office: Morton Coll 3801 S Central Ave Cicero IL 60650

SNIDER-ORTH, ARLENE MARGARET, quality assurance consultant; b. Trenton, N.J., Apr. 18, 1952; d. Darrell Luther and Anne (Brophy) Snider; m. William H. Orth, Nov. 1, 1980; children: Ashley Anne E., Derek W. AA in Edn., Wesley Coll., 1972; BS in Biology, Fairleigh Dickinson U., 1974. Tech. service technician Johnson & Johnson Baby Products Co., Skillman, N.J., 1976-77, primary and finishing supr., 1977-79, regulatory affairs assoc., 1979-82, quality assurance sci., 1982-85; pres., cons. Specifications Unltd., Hazleton, Pa., 1985—. Mem. League Women Voters (bd. dirs. Hazleton chpt. 1986), Am. Soc. Quality Control, Am. Bus. Women's Assn.

SNODGRASS, GRETA, real estate representative; b. Seattle, Dec. 21, 1957; d. Robert Carl and Margaretta (Hickey) Osterlund; m. Dwight Merlin Snodgrass III, Nov. 21, 1984; 1 child, Aaron Matthew. Student, Bellevue Community Coll., 1978, Lake Washington Vo-Tec, 1979. Lic. real estate agt. Adminstr. The Koll Co., Bellevue, Wash., 1976-78, Broadmoor Investments, Bellevue, 1978-79; sec. Skipper's, Inc., Bellevue, 1979-81, devel. coordinator, 1981-84, real estate rep., 1984—. Republican. Home: 12333 SE41st Ln Bellevue WA 98007 Office: Skipper's Inc 14450 NE 29th Pl Bellevue WA 98007

SNOW, ALANA LEA, military officer; b. Leesville, La., Sept. 23, 1962; d. William Ward and Elmer Hazel (Kemp) Carrington. BS, U. So. Miss., 1984; MBA, U. West Fla., 1987. Coll. sales mgr. Ashcraft Corp., Birmingham, Ala., 1981-82; bookkeeper Fleming Foods, Inc., Brandon, Miss., 1982-84; commd. 2d lt. USAF, 1984, advanced through grades to capt., 1988; base level auditor USAF, Eglin AFB, Fla., 1984-88, analyst air-to-surface guided weapons program, 1988—. Mem. Am. Soc. Mil. Comptrollers, Nat. Assn.

Female Execs., USAF Assn. Club: Eglin AFB (v.p. 1986-87, pres. 1987-88). Office: Hdqrs Armament Div AD/ACP-YGG Eglin AFB FL 32542-5000

SNOW, CINDY (CYNTHIA DAWN), manufacturing executive; b. Carlsbad, N.M, Apr. 24, 1957; d. Amos Austen Snow; m. Steven W. Hallock, Jan. 19, 1984. Student, Pitzer Coll., Claremont, Calif., 1975, U. Calif., Berkeley, 1977, U. Calif., Santa Cruz, 1980. Export affairs advisor Taifung Flexible Tubing, Taipei, Rep. of China, 1980-82; v.p. Airmax Inc., Gilmer, Tex., 1983-87. Organizer YWCA Big Sisters of Am., Monrovia, Calif., 1977; counselor YMCA, Los Angeles, 1977. Mem. Nat. Assn. Female Execs, Air conditioning and Refrigeration Inst., Air conditioning and Refrigeration Wholesalers Assn. Home: PO Box 495 Gilmer TX 75644 Office: Airmax Inc PO Box 159 400 Dean St Gilmer TX 75644

SNOW, JUDITH ROHLETTER, jewelry store executive, gemologist, jeweler; b. Miami, Fla., May 6, 1948; d. Guy Eugene and Mary Evelyn (York) Rohletter; student Miami-Dade Community Coll., 1966-67; cert. in diamond evaluation Gemological Inst. Am., 1979, cert. in colored stones and gem indentification, 1980; grad. Berlitz Sch. Langs., Coral Gables, Fla., 1987; m. Edward Hugh Snow, May 11, 1974; children: Judith Diane, Kelly Michelle, Mary Alice. Office mgr. Ross Printing Corp., Miami, 1965-74; corp. exec., gemologist Snow's Jewelers, Inc., Coral Gables, 1974—, also dir. Active Scott Kelly for Gov. of Fla. Campaign, 1965. Mem. Retail Jewelers Am., Jewelers Security Alliance, Coral Gables C. of C., Miracle Mile Mchts. Assn., Exec. Women Internat., Coral Bay Property Owner's Assn., Ferrari Club Am., Ferrari Owners Club, Zonta, Mus. Patrons. Democrat. Clubs: Ocean Reef, Coral Bay Yacht, Coral Reef Yacht, Fla. Philharm. Prelude, Noteworthy, Progress, Bimini (Bahamas) Big Game, Beach Colony. Office: 219 Miracle Mile Coral Gables FL 33134

SNOW, ROSLYN, English language educator; b. Chgo., July 28, 1936; d. David and Regina (Kohn) S. BA, U. Ill., 1958, MA, 1959. Cert. tchr. English and philosophy, Calif. Instr. Orange Coast Coll., Costa Mesa, Calif., 1962-66, 1968—, Golden West Coll., Huntington Beach, Calif., 1967-68. Author: (with others) Man: Alternatives of Experience, 1967, Spelling, 1980. Bd. dirs. Orange County br. Orton Dyslexia Soc., Irvine, Calif., 1984—. Recipient Appreciation in English award Nat. Tchrs. Hall of Fame, 1976. Democrat. Jewish. Home: 260 Cagney Ln #117 Newport Beach CA 92663 Office: Orange Coast Coll 2701 Fairview Rd Costa Mesa CA 92626

SNOW, SARAH TURNBULL, telecommunications company executive; b. Winter Haven, Fla., June 2, 1952; d. James Phineas and Margaret Ann (Lawhon) Turnbull; m. Thomas A. Hunter, June 15, 1974 (div. Aug. 1980); children: Thomas, Catharine; m. Claude Henry Snow, Sept. 26, 1981. BA, Wesleyan Coll., Macon, Ga., 1974; cert. in teaching, U. N.C., Charlotte, 1975; cert. in info. systems, MIT, 1983. Communication cons. So. Bell Telephone Co., Atlanta, 1976-79; communications satellite relay systems designer So. Bell Telephone Co., Charlotte, 1979-83; staff mgr. policy adminstrn. AT&T Info. Systems, Atlanta, 1983, sr. tech. cons., 1983-85; div. mgr. tech. support MCI Telecommunications, Atlanta, 1985—; chmn. program com. Women Info. Processing, Atlanta, 1983-85. Mem. Women's C. of C., Atlanta, Henrietta Egleston Aux. (chmn. advanced sales com. 1984—), Nat. Assn. Female Execs. Democrat. Episcopalian. Club: U. N.C. Chancellor's (Chapel Hill). Home: PO Box 88351 Atlanta GA 30356 Office: MCI Telecommunications 400 Perimeter Ctr Terr Atlanta GA 30346

SNOWDEN, BERNICE RIVES, former construction company executive; b. Houston, Mar. 21, 1923; d. Charles Samuel and Annie Pearl (Rorex) Rives; grad. Smalley Comml. Coll., 1941; student U. Houston, 1965; m. Walter G. Snowden; 1 dau., Bernice Ann Ogden. With Houston Pipe Line Co., 1944-45; clk.-typist Charles G. Heyne & Co., Inc., Houston, 1951-53, payroll asst., 1953-56, sec. to pres., also office mgr., 1956-62, sec. to pres., also controller, 1962-70, sec.-treas., 1970-77, chief fin. officer, also dir. Mem. Women in Constrn., Nat. Assn. Women in Constrn. (past pres.), San Leon C. of C. Methodist. Club: Lord and Ladies Dance. Home: 1638 Walton St Houston TX 77009

SNOWE, OLYMPIA J., congresswoman; b. Augusta, Maine, Feb. 21, 1947. B.A., U. Maine, 1969. Businesswoma; mem. Maine Ho. of Reps., 1973-76, Maine Senate, 1976-78; mem. 96th-100th Congresses from 2d Maine Dist. 1979—, mem. fgn. affairs com., joint econ. com., select com. on aging; co-chair Congl. Caucus for Women's Issues; dep. Republican whip; corporator Mechanics Savs. Bank. Republican. Greek Orthodox. Club: Philoptochos Soc. Office: 2464 Rayburn House Office Bldg Washington DC 20515

SNUTTJER, ANN MARIE CHAMBERS, nurse, educator; Harlan, Iowa, Sept. 11, 1941; d. Floyd V. and Phyllis Maureen (Carstensen) Chambers; R.N., Jennie Edmundson Hosp., Council Bluffs, Iowa, 1962; B.S. in Nursing, U. Nebr. Omaha, 1970; M.S. in Nursing, Creighton U.; m. Norman Snuttjer, June 8, 1963; children—Deborah, Thomas, Michael. Mem. nursing staff Jennie Edmundson Hosp., 1964-65, staff devel. instr., 1977-80, dir. community and personnel edn., 1980-82, mem. faculty Sch. Nursing, 1965-70; tchr. adult health edn. Iowa Western Community Coll., 1974-77; mem. faculty div. nursing Coll. of St. Mary, Omaha, 1982—; bd. dirs. Pottawattamie County chpt. Am. Cancer Soc., 1974-83, pres., 1976-79, mem. Iowa edn. com., 1976-77; bd. dirs. Vis. Nurses Assn. Council Bluffs, 1981-83. Mem. S.W. Iowa Health Educators (pres. 1981), Iowa Soc. Health Manpower, Edn. and Tng. Home: 3 Nall Rd Council Bluffs IA 51501 Office: Coll St Mary Div Nursing Omaha NE

SNYDER, ALLEGRA FULLER, dance educator; b. Chgo., Aug. 28, 1927; d. R. Buckminster and Anne (Hewlett) Fuller; m. Robert Snyder, June 30, 1951 (div. Apr. 1975, remarried Sept. 1980); children: Alexandra, Jaime. BA in Dance, Bennington Coll., 1951; MA in Dance, UCLA, 1967. Asst. to curator, dance archives Mus. Modern Art, N.Y.C., 1945-47; dancer Ballet Soc. of N.Y.C. Ballet Co., 1945-47; mem. office and prodn. staff Internat. Film Found., N.Y.C., 1950-52; editor, dance films Film News mag., N.Y.C., 1966-72; lectr. dance and film adv., dept. dance UCLA, 1967-73, chmn. dept. dance, 1974-80, acting chair, spring 1985, prof. dance and dance ethnology, 1973—; vis. lectr. Calif. Inst. of Arts, Valencia, 1972; co-dir. dance and TV workshop Am. Dance Fest., Conn. Coll., New London, 1973; dir. NEH summer seminar for coll. tchrs. Asian Performing Arts, 1978, 81; coord. Ethnic Arts Intercoll. Interdisciplinary program, 1974-83, acting chmn., 1986; vis. prof. performance studies NYU, 1982-83; hon. vis. prof. U. Surrey, Guildford, Eng., 1983-84; bd. dirs. Buckminster Fuller Inst.; cons. Thyodia Found., Salt Lake City, 1973-74; mem. dance adv. panel Nat. Endowment Arts, 1968-72, Calif. Arts Commn., 1974; mem. adv. screening com. Council Internat. Exchange of Scholars, 1979-82; mem. various panels NEH, 1979-85; mem. adv. bd. Los Angeles Dance Alliance, 1978-84; cons. dance film series Am. Film Inst, 1974-75. Dir. film Baroque Dance 1625-1725, in 1977; co-dir. film Gods of Bali, 1952; dir. and wrote film Bayanihan, 1962 (named Best Folkloric Documentary at Bilboa Film Festival, winner Golden Eagle award); asst. dir. and asst. editor film The Bennington Story, 1952; created films Gestures of Sand, 1968, Reflections on Choreography, 1973, When the Fire Dances Between Two Poles, 1982; created film, video loop and text Celebration: A World of Art and Ritual, 1982-83; supr. post-prodn. film Erick Hawkins, 1964, in 1973. Also contbr. articles to profl. jours. and mags. Adv. com. Pacific Asia Mus., 1980-84, Festival of the Mask, Craft and Folk Art Mus., 1979-84; adv. panel Los Angeles Dance Currents II, Mus. Ctr. Dance Assn., 1974-75; bd. dirs. Council Grove Sch. III, Compton, Calif., 1976-81; apptd. mem. Adv. Dance Com., Pasadena (Calif.) Art Mus., 1970-71, Los Angeles Festival of Performing Arts com., Studio Watts, 1970; mem. Technology and Cultural Transformation com., UNESCO, 1977. Fulbright research fellow, 1983-84; grantee Nat. Endowment Arts, 1981, Nat. Endowment Humanities, 1977, 79, 81, UCLA, 1968, 77, 80, 82, 85. Mem. Am. Dance Therapy Assn., Congress on Research in Dance (bd. dirs. 1970-76, chairperson 1975-77, nat. conf. chair 1972), Council Dance Adminstrs., Am. Dance Guild (chairperson com. awards, 1972), Soc. for Ethnomusicology, Am. Anthropol. Assn., Am. Folklore Soc., Soc. Anthropology of Visual Communication, Soc. Anthropol. Study of Play, Soc. Humanistic Anthropology, Calif. Dance Educators Assn. (conf. chair 1972), Los Angeles Area Dance Alliance (adv. bd. 1978-84, selection com. Dance Kaleidoscope project 1979-81), Fulbright Alumni Assn. Home: 15313 Whitfield Ave Pacific Palisades CA 90272 Office: UCLA Dept Dance 124 Dance Bldg Los Angeles CA 90024

SNYDER, ANN MCNELIS, educator, b. Hazleton, Pa., Sept. 21, 1940; d. Paul Dominic and Mildred Ann (DeCosmo) McNelis; m. Alvin Daniel Snyder III, Aug. 7, 1965; children: Anthony O'Malia, Rory McNelis. BA, Manhattanville Coll., 1962; MS, Marywood Coll., 1967. Cert. tchr., Pa. Tchr. reading Hazleton Area Sch. Dist., 1962-66; elem. tchr. Belmont Sch., Phila., 1970—; realtor Century 21 Cochran Real Estate, Springfield, Pa., 1981—; guest lectr. various cruise lines, 1977—. Publicity chair Students for Kennedy and Johnson, Manhattanville Coll., Purchase, N.Y., 1959; alternate del. Dem. Nat. Conv., Miami, Fla., 1972; mem. Lansdowne (Pa.) Dem. Com., 1976—; campaign worker and coordinator Delaware County, Pa., 1976—; v.p. Hazleton chpt. Internat. Fedn. Catholic Alumnae, 1964-65, pres., 1965-66. Named fellow James Finnegan Com., 1960; recipient Popular Tchr. award Sta. WAZL Radio, 1964, Frances Perkins award U.S. Dept. Labor, 1980. Mem. U.S. Assn. Realtors, Pa. State Realtors, Del. County Assn. Realtors, Phila. Fedn. Tchrs. (labor relations rep. 1972-82). Roman Catholic. Club: Villager Jesuit Guild. Home: 277 Wayne Ave Lansdowne PA 19050 Office: Belmont Sch 41st & Brown Sts Philadelphia PA 19104

SNYDER, BARBARA IRENE, free-lance art director; b. Pittsburg, Kans., Dec. 22, 1937; d. Ian and Vera Tomasene (Jones) Pierce; m. Herman Dale Snyder, July 5, 1959 (dec. May 1967). B.F.A., Kansas City Art Inst., 1959. Visual merchandising mgr. Coach House Stores, Kansas City, Mo., 1957-59; designer Hallmark Cards, Kansas City, Mo., 1959-61; advt. mgr. Kaufman's, Colorado Springs, Colo., 1961-65, 66-67, Bain's, Colorado Springs, 1965-66; advt. mgr. Regenstein's, Atlanta, 1967-69, visual merchandising dir., 1974-76; art dir. Davison's, Atlanta, 1970-72; instr. Atlanta Sch. Fashion and Design, 1972; art dir. Case/Hout, Atlanta, 1973-74, Richway Inc., Atlanta, 1976-78, Hahne's, 1978-79, direct mail advt. mgr., Newark, 1979-83; free-lance retail catalogue art dir., South Orange, N.J., 1983—. Designer Bicentennial Exhbn. at Southeastern State Fair, Atlanta, 1979. Democrat. Avocations: fine art; painting. Home and Office: 367 Vose Ave South Orange NJ 07079

SNYDER, DEBRA JEANNE, music industry executive; b. Rahway, N.J., July 15, 1956; d. James Willard and Joan Elizabeth (Thorn) S. BA in Music Edn., Kean Coll., 1978. Box office mgr. N.J. Symphony, Newark, 1978-80; program annotator Columbia Artists Mgmt., Inc., N.Y.C., 1980-83; cons. Schuzan Enterprises, N.Y.C., 1983-84; sec. BMI, N.Y.C., 1984-86, coordinator concert music, 1986—; cons. Cooper Court Studios, N.Y.C., 1980—; performing arts dir. Medieval Festival Guild, N.Y.C., 1985-87. Mem. Am. Symphony Orch. League, Am. Music Ctr., Nat. Mus. Women in Arts, Nat. Music Council, Nat. Orgn. Women, Sigma Alpha Iota (Sgt.-at-arms 1974-78). Office: BMI 320 W 57th St New York NY 10019

SNYDER, ELAYNE PHYLLIS, speech consultant; b. Atlantic City, Mar. 2, 1931; d. Samuel and Bella Diana (Lewis) S. BA, U. Miami, 1952. Broadcaster Sta. WOND, Pleasantville, N.J., 1952-54; asst. account exec. Kenyon & Eckhardt, N.Y.C., 1954-59; asst. mktg. v.p. Colgate-Palmolive, N.Y.C., 1959-69; dir. mktg. rep. The Young Group, N.Y.C., 1969-74; customer account rep. Bankers Trust, N.Y.C., 1975-83; pres. NOW, N.Y.C., 1974, Elayne Snyder Speech Cons., N.Y.C., 1974—. Author: Speak for Yourself-With Confidence, 1983; author/voice (audio tape) The Persuasive Speaker; contbr. articles to profl. jours. Mem. NOW, Nat. Speakers Assn., Am. Soc. Tng. and Devel., Wednesday Writer's Club (founder, mem.). Home and Office: 333 E 49th St 8J New York NY 10017

SNYDER, GAY HARRIET, lawyer; b. Bklyn., Aug. 1, 1956; d. Ben and Ruth (Donnenfeld) S. BA summa cum laude, SUNY, Albany, 1977; JD, Georgetown U., 1980. Bar: N.Y., D.C. 1981, U.S. Ct. Appeals (1st, 2d, 3d, fed. cirs.) 1982, U.S. Dist. Ct. (Ea.) N.Y. 1981 (we. , no. dists.) N.Y. 1985. Tchr. Capitol Page High Sch., Washington, 1978-79; intern Am. Assn. Ret. Persons, Washington, 1979-80; atty. advisor Office of Adminstrv. Law Judges U.S. Dept. Labor, Washington, 1980-81; staff atty. Am. Fedn. of Govt. Employees, N.Y.C., New Brunswick, N.J., 1981-85; sole practice Bklyn., 1985-86; atty. Sheft, Wright & Sweeney, N.Y.C., 1986-87, Speyer & Perlberg, N.Y.C., 1987—. Mem. Phi Beta Kappa, Phi Alpha Theta. Democrat. Jewish. Office: Speyer & Perlberg 26 Broadway New York NY 10004

SNYDER, JANE LOIS, retired educator; b. Greensburg, Pa., Dec. 19, 1916; d. Harry John and Alice (Keech) S.; B.Ed., Frick Tng. Sch., U. Pitts., 1937, M.Ed., U. Pitts., 1948, postgrad., 1957-58; postgrad. (scholar) Pa. State Coll., summers 1946-47; postgrad. in communications (scholar) U. Wis., summer 1955; postgrad. in communications U. Mich., summer 1948. Elem. tchr. Avonworth, Pa., 1937-47; specialist speech and lang. therapy, Pitts. Schs., 1947-79, ret., 1979. Chmn. programs for Better Films and TV Guild, 1964; speaker Kindergarten Inst., 1964; judge Optimist Oratorical Contest, 1969; mem. Allegheny County LWV, 1980-87, 2d v.p., 1987-88; mem. Vets. Hosp. Radio and TV Guild, 1960-82, program dir., 1977-87; mem. YWCA; founding mem. Ft. Pitt Mus. Assocs.; dir. pet therapy programs in retirement and children's homes Animal Friends Shelter, 1984—. Recipient several awards for pub. service and volunteerism, 1983-84. Cert. supr. spl. edn. Mem. Am. Speech and Hearing Assn. (life, award, 1981), Pa. Speech and Hearing Assn. (life, co-founder), Nat. Ret. Tchrs. Assn., Frick Scholarship Alumnae Assn. (bd., 1970), Am. Assn. Ret. Persons (editor monthly newsletter, pres. 1983-84), Smithsonian Assocs., Carnegie Inst., Pitts. Poetry Club (2d v.p. 1988—), AAUW (sec. 1963-64, chmn. ednl. funding 1979-80). Republican. Episcopalian. Clubs: Swiss-Am. Soc. of Pitts., Welsh Women's, St. David's Soc. for Welsh Ams. (sec. 1983-86), Gen. Fedn. Women's Clubs of Swissvale (Pa.) (chmn. edn. com. 1985-86, 2d v.p. 1988—). Condr. first survey on Non-English speaking students, 1969; author, participant 36 ednl. TV programs, questionnaire in ednl. field; contbr. poems to anthology. Home: 1713 Tonette St Pittsburgh PA 15218

SNYDER, JANE PETERS, public relations executive; b. Manassas, Va., July 23, 1925; d. James Walker and Alma Dorothy (Cross) Peters; student George Washington U., 1943-45, Columbia U. Sch. Public Health, 1962; div.; children—Susan Leland, James Peters. Reporter, Montgomery County (Md.) Sentinel, 1952-54, Chatham (N.J.) Courier, 1956-59, Morris County (N.J.) Daily Record, 1959-61; pub. relations asst. East Orange (N.J.) Gen. Hosp., 1962-64, United Hosp., Newark, 1964-65; dir. community relations Georgetown U. Hosp., Washington, 1966-68; dir. public relations Hosp. Council and Met. Regional Med. Program, Washington, 1968-70, Washington Hosp. Ctr., Washington, 1970-82; v.p. pub. relations The Pathfinder Corp., Washington, 1982—; v.p. pub. relations and edn. Delaware Valley Hosp. Council, Phila., 1984—; appointed to adv. bd. Nat. Insts. of Health's Nat. Kidney and Urological Diseases, 1987—; lectr. George Washington U. Sch. Health Care Adminstrn., 1973, 78, 79, 80, 82. Recipient Excellence award Assn. Am. Med. Colls., 1981. Mem. Am. Soc. Hosp. Public Relations (dir. 1973-75), Acad. Hosp. Public Relations (treas. 1973, dir. 1973-78, MacEachern awards 1963, 72-81). Home: 5 Reaney Ct Philadelphia PA 19103 Office: 1315 Walnut St Philadelphia PA 19107

SNYDER, JANET RUTH, violinist, music educator; b. Berkeley, Calif., Nov. 29, 1932; d. Harry Birge and Marion Virginia (Biggerstaff) O'Brien; m. John Valentine Snyder, Nov. 28, 1952; children—Carol Jeanne, Jeffrey William, Michael William. A.A. in Bus., Armstrong Coll., 1951. Exec. sec. Kaiser Steel Corp., Oakland, Calif., 1951-57; pvt. violin tchr., Idaho Falls, Idaho, 1955—; affiliate violin and viola instr. Idaho State U., Pocatello, Idaho, 1987—; tchr. strings Dist. 91, Idaho Falls, 1980-82; prin. violist Idaho Falls Symphony, 1980—; concert mistress Idaho State Civic Symphony, Pocatello, 1981—; concertmistress Idaho Falls Opera Assn., 1980—; violist Teton Music Festival Seminar, Jackson, Wyo., 1982. Mem. Idaho Music Educators Assn., Pocatello Music Club, Idaho Falls Music Club. Republican. Presbyterian. Home: 1675 Shasta St Idaho Falls ID 83402

SNYDER, JOAN, painter; b. Highland Park, N.J., Apr. 16, 1940; d. Leon D. and Edythe A. (Cohen) S.; 1 child, Molly Fink. A.B. in Sociology, Douglass Coll., 1962; M.F.A., Rutgers U., 1966. mem. faculty SUNY, Stony Brook, 1967-69, Yale U., 1974, U. Calif., Irvine, 1975, San Francisco Art Inst., 1976, Princeton U., 1975-77. One-women exhbns. include, Paley and Lowe, New Brunswick, N.J., 1971, 73, Michael Walls Gallery, San Francisco, 1971, Parker 470, Boston, 1972, Los Angeles Inst. Contempory Art, 1976, Portland (Oreg.) Center Visual Arts, 1976, Carl Solway Gallery, N.Y.C., 1976, Neuberger Mus., Purchase, N.Y., 1978, Hamilton Gallery Contemporary Art, 1978, 79, 82, 83, Nielson Gallery, Boston, 1983, Hirshl & Adler Modern, N.Y.C., 1985-87, Nielson Gallery, 1986, Hirshl and Adler Modern Art Mus., 1988; travelling one-woman show, San Francisco Art Inst., Grand Rapids Art Mus., Renaissance Soc., U. Chgo., Anderson Gallery, Va. Commonwealth U., Richmond, 1979-80, group exhbns. include, Whitney Ann., 1972, Whitney Bienniel, 1974, 80, Corcoran Bienniel, 1975, 87, Mus. Modern Art, N.Y.C. Grantee Nat. Endowment Art, 1974; Guggenheim fellow, 1981-82. Address: PO Box 375 Eastport NY 11941

SNYDER, JOY ISENBERG, real estate broker; b. Huntingdon, Pa., Oct. 14, 1948; d. Roy Miles and Dorothy (Goodman) Isenberg; m. David R. Powell, May 21, 1971 (div. Sept. 1979); 1 child, Heather Shay Snyder. Lic. real estate broker, W.Va., Md. Artistic dir. Kinetic Dance Soc., Huntington, 1971-76; exec. dir. Raystown Devel. Co., Huntingdon, 1976-79; v.p. Lee Industries, Philipsburg, Pa., 1979-80; project mgr. Youngstoun Apts., Hagerstown, Md., 1980-81; assoc. Coldwell Banker, Hagerstown, 1981-83, Realty World, Hagerstown, 1983-84; assoc., owner Omni Bus. and Realty Brokerage, Hagerstown, 1984-85; broker, owner RE/MAX omni, Hagerstown, 1985—; instr. pre-licensing courses, Hagerstown, 1986—; speaker civic and social orgns., Hagerstown, 1986—; expert witness Cir. Ct. Washington County, Hagerstown, 1986—. Bd. dirs. Washington County Student Trade Found., Hagerstown, 1986-87; mem. Washington County Children's Council, Hagerstown, 1986-87; mem. City of Hagerstown Taskforce, 1987; mem. Hagerstown Comml. and Indsl. Commn., 1987. Mem. Exec. Council (Million Dollar award 1986), Sales Counselor (Residential Specialist award 1986), Bus. and Profl. Women Club. Democrat. Home: 28 Mealey Pkwy Hagerstown MD 21740 Office: RE/MAX Omni 1200 Dual Hwy Hagerstown MD 21740

SNYDER, JULIA ANN, international trade and coffee company executive; b. Springfield, Mo., May 17, 1950; d. Arthur Jennings and Catheryn Laverna (Gallion) Swain; m. Orville Edward Kelley, Dec. 29, 1968 (div. 1972); 1 child, Adam Wayne; m. Ronald Warren Synder, May 29, 1982. Cert. Graff Vocat. Tech. Ctr., 1974. Sales sec. Paul Mueller Co., Springfield, 1971-73; surg. technician Cox Med. Ctr., Springfield, 1974-76; corp. sec., dir. OR&D, Inc., Springfield, 1979—; v.p., dir. Hey Mon Coffee Ltd., Everton, Mo., 1984—. Active Nat. Republican Com., 1980, Rep. Presdl. Task Force, 1981. Recipient Medal of Merit, Rep. Presdl. Task Force, 1982; named One of Outstanding Young Women of Am., 1984. Mem. Nat. Assn. Female Execs., Am. Notary Assn., Am. Film Inst. Mem. Assembly of God Ch. Avocations: latch hooking, stitchery, collecting depression era glassware, writing poetry, walking. Office: Hey Mon Coffee Ltd 294A Coffee Ln Everton MO 65646

SNYDER, KARIN RINGDAHL, electronics executive, technologist; b. Pensacola, Fla., June 22, 1945; d. Eskil Berg and Adelaide Mary Ann (Glow) Ringdahl; m. Jeffrey Snyder, Jan. 1967 (div. June 1977); children: Frederick, Dennis, Stacey. BS in Med. Tech., U. Vt., 1967, postgrad., 1979-83. Med. tech. Med. Ctr. Hosp. Vt., Burlington, 1967-69, 77-82; med. technician ARC, 1969-70; tech. specialist Coulter Electronics, Inc., Hialeah, Fla., 1982-85, capital instrument specialist, 1985—. Mem. Am. Field Service Mgrs., Clin. Lab. Mgrs. (assoc.). Republican. Episcopalian. Club: Shelburne (Vt.) Garden. Home: 22 Saratoga Ct Piscataway NJ 08854 Office: Coulter Electronics Inc 98 Mayfield Ave Edison NJ 08818-4060

SNYDER, MELANIE GAYE, infosystems specialist; b. Phila., June 5, 1961; d. Melvin Guy Snyder and Karen Elaine (Green) Snyder Powell; m. Bruce Gordon Synder, Nov. 12, 1983. BS, Elizabethtown Coll., 1982; MBA, SUNY, Binghamton, 1985. Mktg. rep. Lourdes Hosp. Profl. Services, Binghamton, N.Y., 1985; engring. analyst Link Flight Simulation Div. Singer Co., Binghamton, 1985-88, systems analyst, computer coordinator, 1988, corp. PC specialsit, 1988—. Mem. Nat. Assn. Female Execs., Assn. for Computing Machinery, Women's Network So. Tier. Republican. Presbyterian. Home: 37 Lathrop Ave Binghamton NY 13905

SNYDER, RUTH COZEN, painter, sculptor; b. Montreal, Can.; d. Harry and Rachel Cozen; student UCLA, Otis Art Inst.; children—Harry M., Robert Lewis, Douglas M., Nancy J. One-woman shows include: Coos Art Mus., Coos Bay, Oreg., Riverside (Calif.) Art Center and Mus., Galerie Arcadia, Paris, Brigham Young U., Provo, Utah, HHS, Washington, Braithwaite Fine Arts Gallery, So. Utah State Coll., Cedar City, Bridge Gallery, Los Angeles City Hall, Edge Gallery, Fullerton, Calif., Merging One Gallery, Santa Monica, Calif.; group exhbns. include: Mussavi Gallery, N.Y.C., 1985, Flow Ace Gallery, Los Angeles, UN Conf., Nairobi, Mussavi Gallery, N.Y.C., Santa Barbara Contempory Arts Forum, Calif.; represented in permanent collections: Smithsonian Instn., Frederick S. Wight Gallery of UCLA, Textron Corp., Washington, Clorox Corp., San Francisco, Intercontinental, Singapore, Hyatt-Watertower, Chgo., U.S. Embassy Lisbon, Coos Art Mus., Laguna Mus. Art, Laguna Beach, Calif., Washington, So. Utah U., Cedar City, Cedars-Sinai Med. Ctr., Los Angeles, Betty Ford Ctr., Eisenhower Hosp., Palm Springs, Calif., U.S. Embassy, Riyadh, Saudi Arabia; juror art exhibits San Diego, Long Beach and Los Angeles, Calif.; lectr., demonstrator. Recipient 6 awards Nat. Watercolor Soc.; award Scottsdale Watercolor Biennial, 1978, San Bernardino Mus. Art. Mem. Nat. Watercolor Soc., Artists Equity, Watercolor West, Women Painters West, Santa Monica C. of C. Studio: 2200 Main St Santa Monica CA 90405

SNYDER, SONYA RUTH MCGINNIS, hospital personnel administrator; b. Ft. Leavenworth, Kans., Jan. 30, 1936; d. Velmer Wayne and Ruth Maxine (Babbitt) McGinnis; B.A., Northwestern U., 1957; M.S. in Indsl. Relations, Loyola U., Chgo., 1967; M. Health Sci. Adminstrn., Govs. State U., 1984; m. Daniel W. Snyder, Jr., Nov. 29, 1968. Personnel dir. Luth. Deaconess Hosp., Chgo., 1961-68; dir. personnel policies and procedures Rush Presbyn.-St. Lukes Med. Center, Chgo., 1968-71; personnel dir. Schwab Rehab. Hosp., Chgo., 1971-73, Copley Meml. Hosp., Aurora, Ill., 1973-79, Palos Community Hosp., Palos Heights, Ill., 1979—. Elder Palos Park (Ill.) Presbyterian Community Ch., 1985-87; mem. Palos Park Bicentennial Com., 1975-76. Mem. Am. Soc. Personnel Adminstrs. (accredited exec. in personnel), Am. Soc. Hosp. Personnel Adminstrs., Chgo. Hosp. Personnel Mgmt. Assn. (pres. 1975-76), Chgo. Hosp. Council. Office: Palos Community Hosp 80th Ave and McCarthy Rd Palos Heights IL 60463

SNYDER, SUSAN BROOKE, English literature educator; b. Yonkers, N.Y., July 12, 1934; d. John Warren and Virginia Grace (Hartung) S. B.A., Hunter Coll., CUNY, 1955; M.A., Columbia U., 1958, Ph.D., 1963. Lectr. Queens Coll., CUNY, N.Y.C., 1961-63; instr. Swarthmore Coll., Pa., 1963-66, asst. prof. English lit., 1966-70, assoc. prof., 1970-75, prof., 1975—, Eugene M. Lang research prof., 1982-86. Author: The Comic Matrix of Shakespeare's Tragedies, 1979; editor: Divine Weeks and Works of DuBartas, 1979; editorial bd.: Shakespeare Quar., 1972—. Folger Library sr. fellow, 1972-73; Nat. Endowment for Humanities fellow, 1967-68; Guggenheim Found. fellow, 1980-81; Huntington Library summer grantee, 1966, 71; Folger Library grantee, 1969; Nat. Endowment for Humanities grantee, 1970; Nat. Endowment for Humanities summer grantee, 1976. Mem. Renaissance Soc. Am. (council 1979-81), Shakespeare Assn. Am. (trustee 1980-83), MLA, Spenser Soc. Office: Swarthmore Coll Dept English Swarthmore PA 19081

SOBEL, BERNESE PANZER, investment financial planner; b. Newark, June 4, 1920; d. Murray Alfred and Tess (Levy) Panzer; divorced May, 1976; children: Charles S., Jeffrey G., Maxine L. Student, CUNY. V.p. Assn. for the Help Retarded Children, Bklyn., 1954-70; rep. IDS Fin. Services, Inc. subs. Am. Express Co., Melville, N.Y., 1976-84, fin. planner, mem. pres.' adv. council, 1986—. Mem. Nat. Assn. Life Underwriters, Women Life Underwriters Council. Club: Diamond Ring. Office: IDS Fin Services Inc 225 Broad Hollow Rd Suite 116W Melville NY 11747

SOBERON, PRESENTACION ZABLAN, legal association administrator; b. Cabambangan, Bacolor, Pampanga, Philippines, Feb. 23, 1935; came to U.S., 1977, naturalized, 1984; d. Pioquinto Yalung and Lourdes (David) Zablan; m. Damaso Reyes Soberon, Apr. 2, 1961; children—Shirley, Sherman, Sidney, Sedwin. Office mgmt., stenography, typing cert. East Central Colls., Philippines, 1953; profl. sec. diploma, Internat. Corr. Schs., 1971; student Skyline Coll., 1979, LaSalle Extension U., 1980-82, Diablo Valley Coll., 1983—. Various clerical and secretarial positions U.S. Naval Base, Subic Bay, Philippines, 1955-73, adminstrv. asst., 1973-77; secretarial positions Mt. Zion Hosp. and Med. Center, San Francisco, 1977, Oakland City Hall (Calif.), 1978; secretarial positions gen. counsel div. State Bar of Calif.,

San Francisco, 1978, state bar ct. div., 1978-79, adminstrv. asst. fin. and ops. div., 1979-81, office mgr. sects. and coms. dept., profl. and pub. services div., 1981-83, adminstr. non-disciplinary standing coms. and appointment process of state bar entities, office of bar relations, 1983-86; adminstr. state bar sections bus. law section, estate planning, trust and probate law section, labor and employment law section, office of bar relations, 1986—; disc jockey, announcer Philippine radio stas. DZYZ, DZOR and DWHL, 1966-77. Organizer Neighborhood Alert Program, South Catamaran Circle, Pittsburg, Calif., 1979-80. Recipient numerous certs. and awards U.S. Fed. Service with USN, 1964-75, 20 Yr. pin and cert., 1975; Nat. 1st prize for community projects Inner Wheel Clubs Philippines, 1975; several plaques and award certs. for community and sch. activities, Olongapo City, Philippines. Mem. Nat. Assn. Female Execs., Subic Bay-Olongapo City Assn. No. Calif. (Pittsburg rep. 1982-87, bus. mgr. 1988—), Castillejos Assn. of No. Calif. Roman Catholic. Home: 207 S Catamaran Circle Pittsburg CA 94565 Office: State Bar of Calif 555 Franklin St San Francisco CA 94102

SOBOLEWSKI, CAROLINE, transportation administrator; b. Buffalo, Dec. 1, 1938; d. Otto Wieben and Charlotte (Mendrykowski) Gomolski; m. John James Sobolewski Sr., Nov. 8, 1958; children: John James Jr., Daniel Wayne. Grad. high sch., Buffalo, 1956. Bookkeeper Goodyear Tire and Rubber Co., Medina, Ohio, 1968-70; supr. transp. Medina City Schs., 1970-79, Berea (Ohio) City Schs., 1979—. Mem. Ohio Assn. Sch. Bus. Officials, Ohio Assn. Pupil Transp. Democrat. Roman Catholic. Home: 4620 Foote Rd Medina OH 44256 Office: Berea City Schs 235 Riveredge Pkwy Berea OH 44017

SOBOTA, LOIS ANN, designer, senior project manager; b. Newark, May 5, 1958; d. Edward Stanley and Sophie Barbara S. Student, Fashion Inst. Tech., 1976-77; BA, Kean Coll., Union, N.J., 1981; postgrad., Rutgers U., 1983-86. Cert. interior designer. Jr. draftsman F.J. Stine Group, Ft. Lee, N.J., 1981-82; interior designer Drexel Burnham Lambert, N.Y.C., 1982-83, Bellemead Devel. Corp., Roseland, N.J., 1983-85; project architect Chase Manhattan Bank, N.Y.C., 1985-86; project mgr. Shearson Lehman Bros., N.Y.C., 1986—. Mem. Am. Soc. Interior Designers, Inst. Bus. Designers (various offices 1984—). Democrat. Roman Catholic. Club: New Jersey Bicycle Touring. Home: 146B Vanderburgh Ave Rutherford NJ 07070 Office: Shearson Lehman Bros 2 World Trade Ctr New York NY 10048

SOBRALSKE, BARBARA NILA, educator; b. Wild Rose, Wis., May 10, 1949; d. Kenneth John and Beverly Janice (Rasmussen) Graydon; m. Michael John Sobralske Jr., Oct. 17, 1970; 1 child, Mark Michael. Cert., Waushara County (Wis.) Tchrs. Coll., 1969; BS, U. Wis., Oshkosh, 1974. Cert. elem. tchr., Wis. Tchr. elem. schs. Waupun (Wis.) Sch. Dist., 1969-72; title I aide Wild Rose Sch. Dist., 1975, tchr. elem. schs., 1975—. Mem. NEA, Wis. Edn. Assn., Wis. Assn. Environ. Edn., Internat. Reading Assn., Wis. State Reading Assn., Cen. Wis. Reading Council. Home: Rt 1 Box 88 Wild Rose WI 54984 Office: Wild Rose Sch Dist PO Box 276 Wild Rose WI 54984

SOCHEN, JUNE, historian; b. Chgo., Nov. 26, 1937; d. Sam and Ruth (Finkelstein) S. B.A., U. Chgo., 1958; M.A., Northwestern U., 1960, Ph.D., 1967. Project editor Chgo. Superior and Talented Student Project, 1959-60; high sch. tchr. English and history North Shore Country Day Sch., Winnetka, Ill., 1961-64; instr. history Northeastern Ill. U., 1964-67, asst. prof., 1967-69, assoc. prof., 1969-72, prof., 1972—. Author: books including The New Woman, 1971, Movers and Shakers, 1973, Herstory: A Womans View of American History, 1975, 2d edit., 1981, Consecrate Every Day: The Public Lives of Jewish American Women, 1981, Enduring Values: Women in Popular Culture, 1987, Cafeteria America: New Identities in Contemporary Life, 1988; contbr. articles to profl. jours. Nat. Endowment for Humanities grantee, 1971-72. Mem. Am. Studies Assn. Office: Northeastern Ill U 5500 N Saint Louis St Chicago IL 60625

SOCOLOFSKY, IRIS KAY, lawyer; b. Davenport, Iowa, May 3, 1952; d. Forest Wesley and Josephine Jeanette (Barnett) Shaffer; 1 son, Eric Scott. BS, Mich. State U., 1976; JD, U. Mich., 1980. Bar: Mich. 1980, U.S. Dist. Ct. (we. and ea. dists.) Mich. 1980. Atty. Fraser, Trebilcock, Davis & Foster, P.C., Lansing., Mich., 1980—. Co-author: Michigan Usury Manual, 1982. Bd. dirs. Capitol Area council Girl Scouts U.S., 1986—; mem. planning bd. Ingham County Office for Young Children, 1986-87. Recipient Book award U. Mich. Law Sch., 1980. Mem. Ingham County Bar Assn., State Bar Assn. Mich., ABA, Lansing Regional C. of C. (bus. women's council 1984—, bd. dirs. 1987—), Lansing Assn. Career Women. (bd. dirs. 1983-85), Nat. Assn. Career Women (bd. dirs. 1985-87), Athena Found (bd. dirs. 1986-87). Home: 2000 Wembley Way East Lansing MI 48823 Office: Fraser Trebilcock Davis & Foster 1000 Michigan Nat Tower Lansing MI 48933

SODAWALLA, ANITA B., nurse, training and development consultant; b. Quezon City, Philippines, Dec. 5, 1942; came to U.S., 1972; d. Jose Canete Bustamante and Esperanza Manzano Carino; m. Badruddin Hussain Sodawalla, Dec. 26, 1975; 1 child, Ibrahim Badruddin. Diploma in Nursing, U. Philippines, 1968, MS in Nursing, 1971; BS in Nursing, Philippine Women's U., 1970; postgrad. Wayne State U., 1977-80. Charge nurse neonatal and pediatric ICU, Henry Ford Hosp., Detroit, 1972-73; instr., coordinator critical care Grace Hosp., Detroit, 1973-76; sr. instr. Harper Hosp. div. Harper-Grace Hosps., 1976-79, asst. dir. nursing Grace Hosp. div., 1980; pres., exec. dir. Critical Care Unltd., Inc., Southfield, Mich., 1979-84; dir. nursing services and continuing edn. Critical Care Profl. Services, 1980-84; pres., exec. dir. Profl. Success Systems, Inc., 1982-85, dir. human resources tng. and devel., 1986—; program coordinator, cons. Critical Care Edn. Ctr., 1984—; instr. Am. Heart Assn. Mich., Detroit, 1974—, bd. dirs. Macomb County Chpt., 1981-84; mem. First Presbyn. Ch. Detroit. Mem. Am. Assn. Critical Care Nurses, Nat. Assn. Female Execs., Nat. Assn. Nurse Cons. and Entrepreneurs. (founder, pres.), Philippine Nurses Assn. Mich. (life, pres., cons. 1975-78). Avocations: swimming, singing, reading.

SODER, DONNA GLICK, food products company administrator; b. Phila., Apr. 29, 1953; d. Bernard Glick and Lenora Danan; m. Scott Soder, Aug. 16, 1975; 1 child, Jordan Michael. BS, Cornell U., 1975; postgrad., Boston Coll., 1984. Clin. adminstr. Spl. Children's Ctr., Ithaca, N.Y., 1976-77; program asst. Spl. Olympics, Inc., Washington, 1977-78, program coordinator, 1978-83; office mgr. McDonald's Corp., Westwood, Mass., 1984-85, mgr. adminstr., 1985-86, mgr. facilities and systems, 1986-87; mgr. facilities and systems San Diego, 1987—; mem. com. Ronald McDonald Children's Charities, Westwood, 1987. Editor: McDonald's Boston area newsletter. Vol. Mass. Spl. Olympics, Mass. 4-H Found. Jewish. Office: McDonald's Corp 8840 Complex Dr Suite 300 San Diego CA 92123

SODERBERG, JANET MARIE, insurance company executive, lawyer; b. Evanston, Ill., Dec. 10, 1955; d. John William and Georgina Marie (Navigator) S. B.A., U. Denver, 1977; J.D., John Marshall Law Sch., Chgo., 1982. Bar: Ill. 1982. Exec. v.p. Constitutional Casualty Co., Chgo., 1979—; instr. Robert Morris Coll., Chgo., 1982. Mem. Chgo. Bar Assn., Ill. Bar Assn., ABA. Republican. Episcopalian. Office: Constl Casualty Co 5618 N Milwaukee Ave Chicago IL 60646

SODERQUIST, INGEBORG MARTA MARGARETH, business consultant, diversified companies executive; b. Sjalevad, Sweden, Feb. 23, 1948; d. Stig Samuel and Rakel Magdalena Kristina (Westman) Sodersquist; m. Barry Evan Clayton, May 5, 1966 (div. Apr. 1973); children: Christopher Adam, Scoti Melissa, Swane Saxon Dean; m. Richard Anthony Taddonio, Nov. 26, 1977 (div. 1986); 1 child, Tanja Rakel. Student, Oakland U., Rochester, Mich., 1967-69, Oakland Community Coll., Farmington Hills, Mich., 1973-74. Agt. Am. Realty, Southfield, Mich., 1974-77; owner Mrs. T.'s Automotive Products, Detroit, 1983—; coordinator sales Mich. area Vast Corp., Boston, 1984—; project mgr. Park Place Salon, West Bloomfield, Mich., 1986-87; founder, exec. dir. The Exec. Exchange, Detroit, 1986—; pres. Son Mar Corp., Detroit, 1986—. Fashion model Mademoiselle Agy., Southfield, 1974-77. Mem. Nat. Assn. Female Execs. (bd. dirs. 1986—, cert. of merit 1986), Am. Entrepreneurs' Assn., Am. Poolplayers' Assn., Alano Clubs Pool League (officer, bd. dirs. 1986—). Republican. Home: 8260 Honeytree Blvd E Canton MI 48187-4111 Office: Son Mar Corp 9335 Winston Detroit MI 48239

SOECHTIG, JACQUELINE ELIZABETH, telecommunications executive; b. Manhasset, N.Y., Aug. 12, 1949; d. Alvin Hermann and Regina Mary (Murphy) Venzke; m. James Decatur Miller, June 28, 1976 (div. Oct. 1982); M. Clifford Jon Soechtig, Oct. 19, 1983. B.A. cum laude, Coll. of New Rochelle (N.Y.), 1974; M.A. summa cum laude, U. So. Calif., 1978. Computer operator IBM, White Plains, N.Y., 1970-72, ops. job scheduler, 1972-74, various spl. assignments, 1974-75, mktg. rep., Bethesda, Md., 1975-76, Charleston, W. Va., 1979-81, adv. regional mktg. rep. Dallas, 1981-82; dist. mgr. Am. Speedy Printing Co., Dallas, 1982-83, nat. sales devel. mgr., Detroit, 1984; regional mgr. major and nat. accounts MCI Telecommunications, Southfield, Mich., 1984-85; dir. nat. accounts, 1985—; v.p. nat. accounts, 1987—; interviewer, Sergio Segre, Bolonga, Italy, 1977, Radio Free Europe, Brussels, 1978, World Health Program, Rome, 1978, ITT, Brussels, 1977, Franz Josef Strauss, 1978. Recipient Golden Circle Achievement award IBM, 1980, Quar. Recognition award, 1980, 81; named New Bus. Pacesetter, 1980, 81. Republican. Club: German Am. Women's (v.p. Stuttgart, W.Ger. 1977-78). Office: MCI Telecommunications Corp 400 Perimeter Ctr Terrace Atlanta GA 30346

SOFFER, REBA N., history educator; b. Nashville, Dec. 22, 1934; d. Phillip and Ida (Finesilver) Nusbaum; m. Bernard Harold Soffer, Jan. 28, 1956; 1 child, Roger Phillip. BA magna cum laude, Bklyn. Coll., 1955; MA in History with honors, Wellesley (Mass.) Coll., 1957; PhD, Harvard U., 1962. Asst. prof. history Calif. State U., Northridge, 1962-67, assoc. prof. history, 1967-71, prof. history, 1971—; vis. prof. history U. Calif., Los Angeles, 1980; Christiansen vis. fellow St. Catherine's Coll., Oxford, Eng., 1987—; sr. panelist NEH; chmn. adv. screening com. in history Council for Internat. Exchange Scholars, 1980-83. Author: Ethics and Society in England, 1978; contbr. articles to profl. jours. Bd. dirs. environmentalist group Pacific Palisades (Calif.) Resident's Assn., 1977—, Los Angeles Theater Works, Los Angeles, 1984—. NEH fellow, 1981-82, 88; recipient Outstanding Prof. award for 19 campuses of the Calif. State System, 1985. Fellow Royal Hist. Soc.; mem. Am. Hist. Assn. (Anglo-Am. Hist. com., Best Book award Pacific Coast br. 1978), Pacific Coast Conf. in Brit. Studies (pres. 1976-78), N.A. Conf. in Brit. Studies (assoc. exec. sec. 1978-83), Pacific Coast Am. Hist. Assn. (council 1980-83, chair program com. 1988-89), Calif. Women in Higher Edn., Calif. State U. Alumni Assn. (pres. Northridge chpt. 1986-8). Home: 665 Bienveneda Ave Pacific Palisades CA 90272 Office: Calif State U Dept of History Northridge CA 91338

SOFFERMAN, DEBORAH ANN BLECHER, syndicated radio show host; b. N.Y.C., June 20, 1951; d. Jerome and Shirley (Stein) Blecher; m. Bruce Robert Sofferman, Dec. 19, 1982; 1 child. AS, Dean Jr. Coll., 1971; BS cum laude, Ithaca Coll., 1973. Model, Raphael Soyer, Painter, N.Y.C., 1975-87; freelance photographer, N.Y.C., 1975-80; writer Intermezzo, Carnegie Hall and Town Hall program publs., 1975-78; freelance prodn. coordinator and prodn. asst. for TV commls. and feature films, 1977-81; producer, coproducer various original video tapes, N.Y.C., 1977-81; prodn. supr. TV series OMNI: The New Frontier, 1981; pres. Southport Bags, Inc., Conn., 1982-85; mktg. dir. Smile Dental Ctr., Derby, Conn., 1982—; host radio show In Your Prime WADS-AM and syndicated radio, 1985—. Vol. Tng., Edn. and Manpower Team, Inc., 1987, Lower Naugatuck Valley, 1984-85; co-chmn. Valley Food Bank, food collection, 1985, Toys 4 Tots, Team Inc., 1985. Named Co-Vol. of Yr., Team Inc., 1985. Avocations: writing, photography, singing, dancing, acting. Office: In Your Prime c/o 61 Elizabeth St Derby CT 06418

SOJA, CLAIRE ELAINE, banker, portfolio manager; b. Fall River, Mass., May 2, 1946; d. Harold and Florence Molly (Popkin) Shapiro; m. Donald Thomas Soja, Dec. 6, 1970 (div. Dec. 1985). Student, Northeastern U., 1964-66; BA, Boston U., 1968. Registered rep. Kidder Peabody & Co., Boston, 1971-73; investment officer, asst. mgr. investments Brown Bros. Harriman & Co., Boston, 1974—; career cons. Boston U., 1983—. Jewish. Office: Brown Bros Harriman & Co 40 Water St Boston MA 02109

SOKOL, SUSAN, apparel company executive. Pres., Calvin Klein Ltd., N.Y.C. Office: Calvin Klein Ltd 205 W 39th St New York NY 10018 *

SOKOLOWSKI, GAIL EVELYN, journalist; b. Trenton, N.J., Dec. 18, 1956; d. Stanley C. and Evelyn (Kovacs) S. BA in Journalism, Rider Coll., 1978. Asst. internat. pub. affairs Squibb Corp., Princeton, N.J., 1978-82, assoc. editor, SQUIBBLINE, 1982-84, editor SQUIBBLINE, 1984-85, mgr. publications, 1985-87; mgr. corp. editorial services Squibb Corp., 1987—. Contbr. articles to profl. jours. Mem. Internat. Assn. Bus. Communicators (Award of Excellence N.J. chpt. 1986, Award of Merit N.J. chpt. 1987), Women in Communications, Inc. (Sarah award Phila. chpt. 1986, 87), Am. Med. Writers Assn., Pub. Relations Soc. Am. (various editorial/graphic awards 1984—). Roman Catholic. Office: Squibb Corp Rt 206 Province Line Rd Princeton NJ 08543-4000

SOLA, DEBRA ANN, personnel company executive; b. Phila., Dec. 13, 1959; d. Charles Edward and Mary Jane (Hampson) S. BA in Psychology, Am. U., 1981. Investigator div. mental health Pub. Defender Service, Washington, 1982-83; mgr. adminstrn. Maxcell Telecom Plus, Washington, 1983-86; pres. ExecuCell Inc., Maitland, Fla., 1986—; bd. dirs. Execucell Inc., Maitland, 1986-87. Asst. Mondale-Ferraro presidential campaign, Washington, 1984. Mem. Nat. Assn. Personnel Cons., Am. Soc. Personnel Adminstrs. Democrat. Roman Catholic. Office: ExecuCell Inc 900 Winderley Pl Suite 140 Maitland FL 32751

SOLBERG, ELIZABETH TRANSOU, public relations executive; b. Dallas, Aug. 10, 1939; d. Ross W. and Josephine V. (Perkins) Transou; m. Frederick M. Solberg, Mar. 8, 1969; 1 son, Frederick W. B.J., U. Mo., 1961. Reporter, Kansas City (Mo.) Star, 1963-70, asst. city editor, 1970-73; reporter spl. events, documentaries Sta. WDAF-TV, Kansas City, Mo., 1973-74; prof. dept. journalism Park Coll., Kansas City, Mo., 1975-76, advisor, 1976-79; mng. ptnr. Fleishman-Hillard, Inc., Kansas City, Mo., from 1979, now exec. v.p., sr. ptnr., gen. mgr. Kansas City br. Mem. Kansas City Commn. Planned Indsl. Expansion Authority, 1974—; mem. long-range planning com. Heart of Am. council Boy Scouts Am., 1980-82, bd. dirs., 1986—; mem. Clay County (Mo.) Devel. Commn., 1979—; bd. govs. Citizens Assn., 1975—. Recipient award for contbn. to mental health Mo. Psychiat. Assn., 1973. Mem. Pub. Relations Soc. Am. (nat. honors and awards com., co-chmn. Silver Anvil Com. 1983; Silver Anvil award 1979-82), Mo. C. of C. Pub. Relations Council, Kansas City C. of C., Pi Beta Phi. Clubs: Jr. League, Kansas City, Carriage, Central Exchange. Office: Fleishman Hillard Inc One Crown Ctr Kansas City MO 64108

SOLBERG, LISA MARGARET, communications executive; b. Missoula, Mont., Apr. 8, 1959; d. Gerald Francis and Helen Eloise (Pilcher) Raunig; m. John Robert Solberg, Dec. 4, 1982. BS in Bus. Mgmt., Mont. State U., 1981; MBA, Seattle Pacific U., 1987. Legal asst. Scribner and Huss Law Firm, Helena, Mont., 1975-77; office mgr. H&H Secretarial Service, Helena, 1977-78; adminstrv. mgr. John Graham Co., Seattle, 1981-85; bus. mgr. Cornerstone Investment Corp., Seattle, 1985-86; dir. legal adminstrn. U.S. West, Inc., Englewood, Colo., 1986—. Mem. Am. Mgmt. Assn., Assn. Legal Adminstrs., ABA (law office adminstrv. assoc.), Inst. Law Office Mgmt. Office: US West 7800 E Orchard Rd Suite 480 Englewood CO 80111

SOLEM, MAIZIE ROGNESS, educator; b. Hendricks, Minn., Nov. 8, 1920; d. John A. and Nora Adeline (Engelstad) Rogness; B.A., Augustana Coll., 1942; postgrad. George Washington U., 1955-57, Wright State U., 1970-71; M.Ed., Miami U., Oxford, Ohio, 1970-71; Ed.D., U. S.D., 1976; postgrad. U. Calif., 1978. Tchr., LeMars, Iowa, 1942-43, Internat. Children's Centre, Bangkok, Thailand, 1952-53, George Washington U., Washington, 1957, Fairfax (Va.) schs., 1956-58, Maxwell AFB Sch., Montgomery, Ala., 1963-66; tchr., librarian Central High Sch., Madison, S.D., 1943; dir., tchr., supr. remedial reading tchrs. City schs., Fairborn, Ohio, 1966-71; Title I resource tchr. L.B. Anderson Elem. Sch., Sioux Falls, S.D., 1971-73; primary coordinator Instructional Planning Ctr., Sioux Falls, 1973-77; curriculum coordinator Sioux Falls public schs., 1973—. Mem. adv. bd. Ret. Sr. Vol. Program, 1974-78, publicity chmn., 1975-78; mem. adv. bd. Vol. Action Ctr., 1976-78, mem. service com., 1974-78; chmn. exec. bd. Augustana Fellows, 1979-81; scholarship chmn. LaSertoma, 1979-80; active various drives including Heart Fund, Muscular Dystrophy, Cancer Fund; bd. regents Augustana Coll., 1984—. Recipient Vol. Yr. in Edn. awardGov. S.D, 1984, Leader Luncheon award YWCA, 1984, Alumni Achievement award Augustana Coll., 1986, IRA Literacy award, 1987; named S.D. Adminstr. of Yr., 1987. Mem. AAUW, DAR (bd. dirs. found. 1986-87, chmn. publicity com. 1986-87, chmn. grants com. 1986-87), Sch. Adminsrs. S.D. (v.p. 1977-78), Assn. Supervision Curriculum Devel. (pres. 1976-78, nat. exec. council 1979-82), Nat. Assn. Supervision Curriculum Devel. (bd. dirs. 1977-79; mem. nat. selection com. 1977-78), Assn. Childhood Edn. Internat., S.D. Assn. Elem. Prins., Elem., Kindergarten, Nursery Sch. Edn., Nat. Assn. Edn. Young Children, Sioux Land Assn. for Edn. Young Children, NEA, S.D. Edn. Assn., Nat. Council Social Studies, Internat. Reading Assn., S.D. Tchrs. Maths. Orgn., S.D. Assn. Supervision and Curriculum Devel., Orton Soc. Republican. Lutheran. Home: 1600 North Dr Box 911 Sioux Falls SD 57101 Office: 201 E 38th St Sioux Falls SD 57102

SOLER, DONA KATHERINE, civic worker; b. Grand Rapids, Mich., Mar. 7, 1921; d. Melbourne and Katherine Anne (Herbst) Welch; 1 child, Suzette Maria. Student pvt. and pub. schs., Grand Rapids, Mich. Artist-instr., metaphys. councilor, researcher, editor, pub. Psychic Exchange, 1979—. Author: What God Hath Put Together, 1979, Our Heritage From the Angels, 1981, Expose the Dirty Devil, 1984, Contemporary Poets of America (anthology), 1984, For Love of Henry, 1985, Greyball, 1986, House of Evil Secrets, 1986. Founder, 1st pres. South Coast Art Assn., San Clement, Calif., 1963-65, Orange Coast Cath. Christian Singles, 1970-73, Psychic Exchange, Orange County, 1979; founder, chief Lake Riverside Estates Communicators, Riverside, 1974-79. Mem. Rep. Nat. Com., Nat. Tax Limitation and Balanced Budget Com., Calif. Tax Reduction Movement, Halt Legal Reform, Internat. Platform Assn., Animal Assistance League of Orange County, Animal Protection Inst. Am., Greenpeace, People for the Ethical Treatment of Animals, Internat. Fund for Animal Welfare, World Wildlife Fund-U.S., Humane Soc. U.S., Am. Soc. Prevention Cruelty Toward Animals, In Def. of Animals, others.

SOLER, TERRELL DIANE, dramatic soprano, real estate and marketing executive; b. South Bend, Ind., Apr. 26; d. Harold J. Metzler and Margaret Terrell (Whiteman) Fogarty. BA, Ithaca Coll., 1960; diploma, Brown's Bus. Coll., Decatur, Ill., 1960; postgrad. in real estate sales, NYU, 1984. Lic. securities dealer, real estate salesperson. Exec. legal asst. Carb Luria Glassner Cook & Kufeld, N.Y.C., 1962-64, Graubard Moskovitz McGoldrick Dannett & Horowitz, N.Y.C., 1964-79; opera and concert singer, N.Y.C., 1979—; real estate salesperson Rosemary Edwards Realty, N.Y.C., 1985-87, Kenneth D. Laub & Co., Inc., N.Y.C., 1987—; pres. Terrell Internat., Whiteman and Stewart Prodns., TS Assocs., TS Enterprises; corr. sec., bd. dirs. Community Opera, Inc., N.Y.C., 1984—. Mem. internat. affairs com. and other coms. Women's Nat. Rep. Club, N.Y.C., 1968—; active Rep. County Vols., N.Y.C., 1976—; mem. nominating com. Ivy Rep. Club, N.Y.C., 1983—; bd. dirs. Am. Landmark Festivals, 1986—. Named Female Singer of Yr., Internat. Beaux Arts, Inc., 1978-79, Princess Nightingale, Allied Indian Tribes N.Am. Continent-Cherokee Nation, 1985. Mem. Nat. Arts Club (music com. 1983—), Wagner Internat. Instn. (dir. pub. relations 1982-84), N.Y. Opera Club, Navy League U.S. (life, mem. N.Y. council), World Ship Soc., Assn. Former Intelligence Officers (assoc.), Friends of Spanish Opera (bd. dirs. 1982—). Avocations: tennis, swimming, dancing, travel, antiques. Home: 2 Tudor City Pl Apt 4-J South New York NY 10017

SOLES, ADA LEIGH, state legislator; b. Jacksonville, Fla., May 19, 1937; d. Albert Thomas and Dorothy (Winter) Wall; B.A., Fla. State U., 1959; m. James Ralph Soles, 1959; children—Nancy Beth, Catherine. Mem. New Castle County Library Adv. Bd., 1975-80, chmn., 1975-77; chmn. Del. State Library Adv. Bd., 1975-78; mem. Del. State Ho. Reps., 1980—. Adminstrv. asst. U. Del. Commn. on Status of Women, 1976-77; acad. advisor U. Del. Coll. Arts and Scis., 1977—. Mem. LWV (state pres. 1978-80), Phi Beta Kappa, Phi Kappa Phi, Mortar Bd., Alpha Chi Omega. Episcopalian. Office: Del Ho of Reps State Capitol Dover DE 19901

SOLFISBURG, BETSY ANN, public relations counselor; b. Aurora, Ill., Feb. 5, 1957; d. John Knell and Betty (Kelley) S. Student, DePauw U., 1975-77; BJ, U. Mo., 1979. Account exec. Margie Korshak Assocs., Chgo., 1979-80; account exec. Golin-Harris Communications, Chgo., 1980-85, sr. account exec., 1982, supr., 1983; supr. The Bohle Co., Los Angeles, 1985; v.p. Ketchum-Bohle Pub. Relations, Los Angeles, 1986-87; v.p., group mgr. Ketchum Pub. Relations, Los Angeles, 1988—. Recipient Golden Trumpet awards Publicity Club of Chgo. and Internat. Assn. Bus. Communicators, 1981-83, award Los Angeles Advtg. Women, 1985, awards Publicity Club of Los Angeles, 1988. Mem. Pub. Relations Soc. Am. (mem. counselors acad., bd. dirs. Los Angeles chpt., Prism award Los Angeles chpt. 1986), Pi Beta Phi, Kappa Tau Alpha. Republican. Office: Ketchum Pub Relations 55 Union St San Francisco CA 94111

SOLLAMI, ROSEANN, educator, administrator, politician; b. Trenton, N.J., Dec. 30, 1935; d. Joseph Thomas and Anne Esther (Lipani) Bruno; m. Paul J. Sollami, May 4, 1963; children—Paula, Maryann. B.A., Douglass Coll., 1957; student Trenton State Coll., 1964, Rutgers U. Grad. Sch. Edn., 1959-61. Tchr. history, econs. Ewing Township, Trenton, 1957-59; asst. dir. admissions Rutgers U., New Brunswick, N.J., 1959-63; ascertainment coordinator Sta. NJP-TV Channel 52, N.J., 1975-81; tchr. English Ewing Twp. High Sch., 1985—. Committeewoman Democratic Party, Trenton, 1969—; polit. fundraiser Merlino for Gov., 1982; chairwoman fundraising dinner Mercer County Dems., 1978. Mem. Douglass Coll. Alumni Assn., Ravine Club, Trenton Coll. Club, N.J. Fedn. Dem. Women. Avocations: drama; swimming; politics; photography. Home and Office: 11 Seven Oaks Ln Trenton NJ 08628

SOLLENBERGER, DONNA FITZPATRICK, educational administrator; b. Tuscola, Ill., Jan. 13, 1949; d. Vincent Norman and Marian Louise (Mumbower) Fitzpatrick; student U. Kans., 1968-70; B.A., Sangamon State U., 1971, M.A., 1974; children: Shannon, Blake, Bradley. Tchr., Springfield (Ill.) S.E. High Sch., 1971-74; public info. officer Ill. Dept. Transp., Springfield, 1974-75; exec. asst. to dir. Ill. Dept. Conservation, Springfield, 1975-76; adminstrv. asst. to chmn. dept. surgery So. Ill. U. Sch. Medicine, Springfield, 1976-80, asst. to chmn. dept. surgery, 1984—; instr. communications Lincoln Land Community Coll., Springfield, part-time, 1976-77, instr. English, 1980-84. Mem. Springfield area Arts Council. Recipient Conservation Merit award Ill. Dept. Conservation, 1976. Mem. Med. Group Mgmt. Assn., Springfield Art Assn., Delta Gamma Alumnae Assn. Morman. Home: 2107 Lindsay Rd Springfield IL 62704 Office: 801 N Rutledge St Springfield IL 62702

SOLLEY, MARY-SUE PASTORELLO, home entertainment products distributing executive; b. Chgo., Aug. 4, 1955; d. Daniel and Angela (Gatsos) Pastorello; m. Richard James Solley, Oct. 8, 1977; children—Daniel, Stephanie, Jennifer. Student Eastern Ill. U., 1973-76, Roosevelt U., 1980-82. Acct., office mgr. Burton's Shoes, Inc., Northbrook, Ill., 1976-80; asst. controller Sound Video Unltd., Inc., Niles, Ill., 1980-82, controller, 1982-86, chief fin. officer, 1986-87, also dir.; v.p., gen. mgr. Speedy Messenger Service, Inc., Arlington Heights, Ill., 1987—; treas., dir. JLT Films, Inc., Niles, 1983-87. Mem. exec. council St. John's Parish, Des Plaines. Mem. Nat. Assn. Accts., Bus. Planning Bd., Nat. Assn. for Female Execs., Controllers Council. Republican. Greek Orthodox. Club: St. John's Philoptochos (Des Plaines, Ill.). Avocations: piano, theatre, horseback riding, boating, swimming. Home: 811 E Appletree Ln Arlington Heights IL 60004 Office: Speedy Messenger Service 8 S Dunton Arlington Heights IL 60005

SOLLITT, BETTYE HERB, civic worker; b. Alton, Ill., June 4, 1911; d. Harrison Blaine Herb and Elizabeth (Green) Reticker; m. Harry Gale Nye, Jr., Dec. 4, 1935 (div. 1949); children—Julia Gale, Nancy Pogue, Sally Barbara; m. Sumner Shannon Sollitt, Nov. 30, 1949 (dec. 1964); 1 child, Bettye Martin. Student Northwestern U., 1929-31, U. Chgo., 1969-70. Acct. and circulation mgr. Barks Publs., Chgo., 1970-75; profl. fund raiser U. Mich. Coll. Engring. and Occidental Coll. Los Angeles, 1975-78. Mem. women's bd. dirs., officer Arthritis Found., Chgo., 1951—, U. Chgo. Cancer Research Found., 1958—, Henrotin Hosp., Chgo., 1964—; officer of bd. trustees Latin Sch. of Chgo., 1964-68; mem. Guild of Chgo. Hist. Soc., 1961—; past mem., officer Chgo. council Girl Scouts U.S.A., 1952-68, Parents Council Latin Sch., 1959-61, 64-68; bd. dirs. English Speaking

Union, Chgo., 1981—. Republican. Episcopalian. Clubs: University, Chgo. Yacht (Chgo.). Avocation: sailing.

SOLLOD, ELLEN, arts administrator, artist; b. Rockville Center, N.Y., Apr. 16, 1951; d. Norman and Phyllis Laurel (Freed) S.; m. Barry Michael Pierce, May 20, 1973 (div. June 1981). BA, U. N.C., 1972; MA, U. Md., 1975. Fellow Aspen Inst. for Humanistics Studies, 1985, Artist Residency Fellow, Ucross Found., 1987. One woman shows: Antioch Coll., 1980, Columbia Ctr. for Visual Arts (Md.), Gensler and Assocs., 1985; group shows include: Arvada Ctr. for Arts and Humanities (Colo.), 1983, Boulder Ctr. for Visual Arts (Colo.), 1984, Colo. Artists and Craftsmen, Arvada Ctr. for Arts and Humanities, 1985, Colo. Graphic Arts Ctr., 1985, Foothills Art Ctr., Golden, Colo., 1986, Joan Robey Gallery, Denver, 1987, Evelyn Siegel Gallery, Ft. Worth, 1987, 1999 Broadway Gallery, Denver, 1987, Power Plant Visual Art Ctr., Ft. Collins, Colo., 1988, Alpha Gallery, Denver, 1988; asst. art dir. Md.-Nat. Capital Park and Planning Commn., Riverdale, Md., 1975-78; mem. adj. faculty U. Md., College Park, 1978; policy specialist Nat. Endowment for the Arts, Washington, 1978-79, asst. dir. dance program, 1979-81; exec. dir. Colo. Council on Arts and Humanities, Denver, 1981-87; dir. research and develop. The Dance Project, Sta. WNET-TV, N.Y.C., 1987—; mem. adv. coms. Denver Partnership, 1983; mem. adv. council Colo. Tourism Adv. Council, Denver, 1983-84. Aspen Inst. for Humanistic Studies fellow, 1985. Mem. Western States Art Found. (chmn. bd. 1985), Am. Crafts Council, Nat. Assembly State Arts Agys.

SOLOMON, A. MALAMA, state legislator; b. Honolulu, Mar. 3, 1961; d. Randolph Folau Solomon and Flora Beamer. B.Ed., U. Hawaii-Manoa, 1972, M.A., 1973; B.A., U. Hawaii-Hilo, 1974; Ph.D., Oreg. State U., 1980. Market and sales mgr. beef cattle Kohala Farms, from 1972; lectr. U. Hawaii-Hilo, 1973-75; program coordinator Aloha Week Festivals Inc., 1977-87. Trustee, Office Hawaiian Affairs, 1980-82; mem. Hawaii Senate, Dist. 3, 1983—. Native Am. Ford fellow, 1976-80; recipient Outstanding Community Service award Hilo Coll., 1973-75; Outstanding Leadership award Council Hawaiian Civic Clubs, 1982; named Outstanding Woman of Yr., Hawaii Nat. Women's Week, 1982. Mem. Kohala Community Assn., Dist. Council Hawaiian Civic Clubs. Congregationalist. Office: Office State Senate State Capitol Honolulu HI 96813 Address: PO Box 219 Kapaau HI 96755

SOLOMON, DEBORAH ANTOINNETTE, volunteer; b. N.Y.C., Oct. 25, 1938; d. Robert Benjamin and Helene Catherine (Skaluba) Gross; m. Arthur Paul Solomon, Dec. 20, 1958; children: Melanie Elizabeth, Denise Carol, Russell David, Lauren Jodi. BA, Queens Coll., 1958, MEd, 1960. Profl. TV dancer June Taylor Dancers, Jackie Gleason Show, N.Y.C., 1955-59; high sch. tchr. William H. Maxwell Vocat. High Sch., Bklyn., 1959-61. Vol. Woman's Am. Orgn. for Rehab. Through Training, 1970—, dir. ORT Strolling Players, 1977—, co-convener Women's Pleas for Soviet Jewry through ORT, L.I., N.Y., 1986-87, chmn. exec. com. ORT, pres. North Shore Nassau Region, 1988—; choreographer fund-raising shows Temple Israel Great Neck, 1978-82. Named Woman of Yr. ORT, 1987. Democrat. Jewish. Home: 10 Somerset Dr S Great Neck NY 11020 Office: Women's Am ORT 275 Warner Ave Roslyn Heights NY 11517

SOLOMON, ELAINE DEBORAH, elementary school administrator; b. N.Y.C., Dec. 8, 1938; d. Abraham and Mimi (Moskowitz) S. BS in Edn., CCNY, 1959; MA in Edn., NYU, 1962, MA in Guidance, 1966. Cert. tchr., guidance counselor, prin., guidance dir. Tchr. Pub. Sch. 119, Bronx, N.Y., 1959-64, tchr. of gifted, 1964-65; guidance counselor Pub. Sch. 100, Bronx, 1965-69; asst. prin. Pub. Sch. 64, Bronx, 1969-71, prin., 1971-74; prin. Midland Sch., Paramus, N.J., 1974-79; curriculum coordinator Paramus Pub. Schs., 1974-79; prin. Demarest (N.J.) Pub. Schs., 1979-81; prin., dir. elem. edn. Pequannock Pub. Schs., Pompton Plains, N.J., 1981—; adminstr. Community Progress Ctrs., Bronx, 1969; dir. headstart N.Y.C. Bd. Edn., Bronx, 1970-71; evening guidance counselor title I N.Y.C. Bd. Edn., 1971-75; adj. prof. dept. edn. Kean Coll., Union, N.J., 1987-88. Merck Pharm. Inst. for Research fellow, 1986—. Mem. Internat. Reading Assn., Assn. Adminstrs. and Suprs., Prins. Suprs. Assn. N.J., Pequannock Adminstrs. and Suprs. Assn. Club: Bergen County Recorder.

SOLOMON, ELLEN JOAN, management consultant; b. Orange, N.J., Aug. 26, 1943; d. Abram Shrier and Mildred Elizabeth (Berger) S. B.A. in Psychology, U. N.C., Chapel Hill, 1965; M.S. in human resource devel. Am. U., 1985. Contract writer Conn. Gen. Life Ins. Co., Bloomfield, 1965-66; mgmt. trainee, asst. buyer G. Fox & Co., Hartford, Conn., 1966-68; account exec. WLAE-FM, Hartford, 1968; sr. analyst Travelers Ins. Co., Hartford, 1968-70; job analyst Conn. Blue Cross, New Haven, 1970-71; sr. ops. auditor Govt. Employees Ins. Co., Washington, 1972-75; employee devel. specialist Employment Standards Adminstrn., U.S. Dept. Labor, Washington, 1975-81, mgmt. analyst, 1981-82, supervisory mgmt. analyst, 1982-87; program designer, cons. Eastman Kodak Co., Rochester, N.Y., 1987—; conf. speaker; workshop leader; cons. Recipient spl. achievement award U.S. Dept. Labor, 1977, 78, 83, 85. Mem. Am. Soc. Tng. and Devel., OD Network, Gestalt Inst. Cleve., NOW, Rochester Women's Network, Alpha Gamma Delta. Democrat. Jewish. Club: U. N.C. Alumni. Home: 67 Cornhill Pl Rochester NY 14608 Office: Eastman Kodak Co 343 State St Rochester NY 14650

SOLOMON, ILENE JUDITH SINSKY, educator; b. Washington, May 24, 1944; d. Herbert Brown Sinsky and Martha Bass (Sinsky) Glukenhous; m. Marvin M. Solomon, Sept. 11, 1966; children—Jonathan Jacques, Evan Derek. B.A., U. Md., 1966; M.A., George Washington U., 1969; M.A. in Internat. Service, Am. U., 1975. Tchr. Rock Terrace High Sch. and Westland Jr. High Sch., Montgomery County Pub. Schs., Rockville, Md., 1966-69, system tchr. speech-drama, spl. edn., 1980—; with Montgomery County Day Care Assn., 1984-86; tchr. nursery sch. Adas Israel Congregation Preschool, 1985. Active Columbian Women of George Washington U., Washington, 1975—, pres., 1981-83, Quinn Casting, Silver Spring, Md., 1985—; bd. dirs. summer activity ctr. Montgomery County Md. Recreation Dept., 19877; actress Cedar Lane Stage, 1985, dir. play Cedar Lane Stage, 1987. Kennedy Ctr., De La Croix Prodns., 1985; appeared in several motion pictures; tchr. Washington Hebrew Congregation, 1986; council del. Montgomery County, 1986; 20th Century Fox movie actress Broadcast News, 1987; mem. Corcoran (Washington) Gallery. Recipient award for leadership and accomplishments D.C. Bus. and Profl. Womens' Club, 1981. Mem. Council Exceptional Children, English Speaking Union, U. Md. Alumni Assn. Internat. (life), Am. U. Sch. Internat. Service Alumni Assn., Gavel Speakers Bur., Gen. Alumni Assn. George Washington U. (del. 1981-83), Pi Sigma Alpha.

SOLOMON, LISA ANN, financial planner; b. Ft. Smith, Ark., May 13, 1957; d. Robert and Rosalyn Myrna (Ross) Shapiro; m. Shimon Josef Solomon, Oct. 31, 1982. BA, George Washington U., 1979; student, Montclair State Coll., 1981, Coll. for Fin. Planning, 1986-88. Cert. elem. tchr., N.J., spl. educator, N.J. Spl. educator Alpine (N.J.) Pub. Sch., 1979-80, South Orange (N.J.) Middle Sch., 1980-82; asst. equity coordinator Mutual Benefit Fin. Service Co., Roseland, N.J., 1982-83, regional equity coordinator, 1983; stock broker Security Pacific Brokers, Inc., Florham Park, N.J., 1983-86; fin. planner/casewriter The Fin. Network, Mt. Lakes, N.J., 1986—; assn. rep. South Orange Maplewood Edn. Assn., 1981-82; mem. com. Bergen County Region III Spl. Edn. Curriculum, Closter, N.J., 1979-80. Author (with others) Bergen County Region III Special Education Curriculum Guide, 1980. Instr. phys. devel. Council for Exceptional Children, Potomac, Md., 1978-79. Mem. Nat. Assn. Female Execs., Internat. Assn. for Fin. Planning. Office: The Fin Network 57 Old Bloomfield Ave Mountain Lakes NJ 07046

SOLOMON, MARLENE G., publisher; b. Scranton, Pa., Nov. 11, 1935; d. R. Harold and Mildred (Greenfield) Stein; widowed; children: Susan A. Turner, Diana Herzan, Wendy Jablow. Pub. Magna Corp., Cabin John, Md., also bd. dirs.; bd. dirs. Publ. Mgmt. Group Inc., Bethesda, Md. Democrat. Jewish. Office: Magna Corp/Publ Mgmt Group Inc PO Box 286 Cabin John MD 20818

SOLOMON, PENNY SUE, association executive; b. Monahans, Tex., Dec. 28, 1952; d. Jean Cope S. Student U. So. Miss., 1982-85, Baylor U., 1972-73, Mid Am. Nazarene Coll., 1971-72. Mgr., Career Girl Shops, Inc., Waco, Tex., 1973-75; pvt. sec. 1st Bapt. Ch., Waco, 1975-81; exec. asst., Chattanooga, 1981-82; adminstrv. asst. 1st Bapt. Ch., Hattiesburg, Miss., 1982-85; exec. v.p. Colorado City Area C. of C., Tex., 1985-87, v.p. Azle (Tex.) C. of C., 1987—. Mem. West Tex. Travel Council and Tex. Tourist Council, 1985—; bd. dirs. Wallace Community Edn. Council, 1985—; actress Colorado City Playhouse, best actress award, 1985, chmn. publicity 1987. Mem. Permian Basin Chamber Mgrs. Assn. (sec. 1986, pres. 1986-87), Nat. Assn. Female Execs., C. of C. Execs. Assn. West Tex. (bd. dirs. 1986—), Tex. C. of C. Execs. Baptist. Avocations: Reading, writing, physical fitness, theater.

SOLOMON, PHYLLIS, personnel firm executive; b. N.Y.C., May 9, 1935; d. Herman Aaron and Sylvia (Haymes) Kanarick; m. Harvey Charles Solomon, Feb. 5, 1955 (div. Oct. 1976); children—Deborah, William, David. Sec. Scovill Mfg., Montclair, N.J., 1955-56; co-owner, officer mgr. Bloomfield Glass Co., N.J., 1962-75; office mgr. Am. Service, Inc., Bronx, N.Y., 1975-76, PDI, Englewood Cliffs, N.J., 1976-77; pres., owner V.I.P. Exec. Personnel, Englewood Cliffs, 1977—; founder, chief exec. officer Park Ave. Faces, Inc., 1981—, Phyllis Temps, Inc., Englewood Cliffs, N.J., 1983—; pres., owner V.I.P. Temps II, Ramsey, N.J., 1987—; pres. V.I.P. Temps III, Nanuet, N.Y., 1988—. Pres. Women's Am. Orgn. Rehab. Tng., Verona, N.J., 1960-61. Fellow Healthcare Businesswomen's Assn.; mem. N.J. Assn. Personnel Counsellors (bd. dirs.), Pharm. Advt. Council, Nat. Assn. Female Execs., Englewood Cliffs C. of C., Fort Lee (N.J.) C. of C. Jewish. Rotary (pres., sec. 1987). Avocations: golf; tennis; music; reading. Office: VIP Exec Personnel 701 Palisade Ave Englewood Cliffs NJ 07632

SOLOMON, TERRI MARCIA, lawyer; b. Passaic, N.J., July 22, 1955; d. Sol and Arlene (Stiskin) S.; m. Howard Michael Topaz, July 4, 1982; 1 child, Richard Harris Topaz. B.A. summa cum laude, U. Mass., 1976; J.D., U. Pa., 1979. Bar: N.Y. 1980, N.J. 1979, U.S. Dist. Ct. (so. dist.) N.Y., 1980, U.S. Dist. Ct. (ea. dist.) N.Y., 1980, U.S. Dist. Ct. N.J., 1979, U.S. Ct. Appeals (2d cir.) 1981, U.S. Ct. Appeals (3d cir.) 1981. Assoc., Simpson, Thacher & Bartlett, N.Y.C., 1979-87, sr. atty., 1988—. Mem. ABA, N.Y. State Bar Assn., Assn. Bar City N.Y. Democrat. Jewish. Office: Simpson Thacher & Bartlett 1 Battery Park Plaza New York NY 10004

SOLTIS, MARTHA A.C., industrial engineer; b. Lansing, Mich., Dec. 9, 1957; d. Leland B. and Beverly J. (Langham) Christiansen; m. David J. Soltis, Aug. 7, 1982. BSIE, Gen. Motors Inc.; Ma in Hosp. Adminstrn., Webster U. Engr. indsl. Gen. Motors, Detroit, 1981-82; engr. mgmt. Bapt. Med. System, Little Rock, 1982-84, sr. engr. mgmt., 1984-85; dir. VHAE Cons. Service, Tampa, 1985—. Mem. Am. Inst. Indsl. Engrs. (pres. Ark. 1985-86, Outstanding Mem. 1982), Hosp. Mgmt. Systems Soc. (editor newsletter 1985-86), NOW. Democrat. Roman Catholic. Home: 1346 Whitacre Dr Clearwater FL 34624 Office: VHAE Cons Service 4919 Memorial Hwy Wuite 200 Tampa FL 33634

SOLTYSIAK, SANDRA KANTNER, automotive company executive; b. Dearborn, Mich., Aug. 19, 1948; d. John Henry and Ileine Lucille (Merz) Kantner; m. Gregory Peter Soltysiak, June 20, 1970; 1 son, John. B.A., Mich. State U., 1971, M.Labor and Indsl. Relations, 1978. Dissertation sec. U. Mich., Ann Arbor, 1970-72, research asst. Survey Research Ctr., 1972-73; placement rep., compensation rep. and labor relations rep. Ford Motor Co., Dearborn, Mich., 1973-76; compensation adminstr., mgr. compensation, dir. compensation, benefits and services Mich. Consol. Gas Co., Detroit, 1976-78; dir. compensation and benefits Mich. Nat. Bank, Lansing, 1979; supr. salaried personnel Oldsmobile div. Gen. Motors Corp., Lansing, 1979-80, adminstrv. coordinator, 1981-85; supt. material prodn. control Buick-Oldsmobile-Cadillac group, 1985-86; supt. materials, quality, 1986-87; instr. Lansing Community Coll, 1980-81; seminar leader Mich. State U. Bus. Sch., 1980-81. Vol. Capital Area United Way, Lansing, 1981-82, team capt., 1983; chmn. personnel and adminstrv. com., 1985. Maj. firms div., bd. dirs., 1985—, Lansing Health Found., 1986—; chmn. vocations com. St. Mary's Cathedral, Lansing, 1982-87; adv. bd. Sch. Labor and Indsl. Relations Mich. State U., 1983—. Recipient Chmn.'s Excellence in Community Activities award GM, 1987. Roman Catholic. Office: Buick-Oldsmobile-Cadillac Group 920 Townsend Lansing MI 48921

SOLVANG, PAMELA JEAN, broadcast marketing executive, marketing consultant; b. Bellingham, Wash., Nov. 14, 1956; d. Merlin Nils and Phyllis Ann (Wynne) S. Student Clark Coll., Vancouver, Wash., 1975-77, Seattle U., 1977; B.A. in Communications, U. Portland, 1979. Copywriter Sugden-Freeman Advt., Portland, Oreg., 1979; writer, producer Ryan Advt., Portland, 1979-83; mktg. dir. KGON-KSGO Radio, Portland, 1983-85; corp. broadcast mktg. dir. Ackerley Communications, 1985—; video writer/producer Nat. Salon Edn. Tapes, KMS Shampoos and Research Labs., Bella Vista, Calif., 1985; writer, producer TV spl. Rose City Rock Awards, 1984, 85. Recipient Nat. Telly award Nat. Assn. TV Commls., 1982, 83, 86, 87, 88. Mem. Broadcast Promotion/Mktg. Execs. (outdoor advt. gold medallion awards 1985, 86, 87; Audience Promotion gold medallion award 1987, 88; Print Advt. Gold medallion award 1988), Portland Advt. Fedn. Excellence award, Sales brochure, 1986. Avocations: traveling; snow skiing; scuba diving, golf. Home: 19212 15th Ave NW Seattle WA 98177 Office: 190 Queen Anne Ave N Seattle WA 98109

SOMA, ROSE SMERALDI, broadcaster, writer, women's rights activist, television and radio producer; b. Bronx, N.Y., Feb. 17, 1940) d. Albert and Jeanette (DiCostanzo) Smeraldi; attended NYC public schs. until 1955; m. Fraser Soma, Sept. 13, 1967; children—Michael, Carl, Paul, Steven, Nancy, Errol. Producer, interviewer, reporter WALK radio, L.I., N.Y., 1976—, producer weekly feminist radio program, 1976—; lectr., condr. workshops on women's rights; media public relations cons. feminist issues for radio and TV, 1978. Chmn. reprodn./abortion rights task force Suffolk (N.Y.) chpt. NOW, 1975—, chmn. media task force, 1975—; producer/host Women Speak Out and People Speak Out, Brookhaven Cable TV, Port Jefferson Sta., N.Y., 1979—, Women Speak Out, Sta. WYFA, Medford, N.Y., 1979—, Suffolk Cablevision, 1979—, Sta. WBLI-FM, 1980—; media coordinator, personal mgr. entertainment acts, 1981—; bd. dirs. Planned Parenthood of East Suffolk, 1977—; coordinator L.I. chpt. Nat. Coalition to Defend the Bill of Rights, 1978—; coordinator public relations and media for L.I. chpt. Internat. Women's Yr. Meeting for N.Y. State, 1977; exec. dir., co-founder Americans United to Save Legal Abortion, 1977—; founder Women Speak Out Internat., 1978; adv. bd. Women's Health Alliance L.I., 1978; chmn. abortion rights task force N.Y. State orgn. NOW, 1978; coordinator L.I. Coalition for Reproductive Rights; asso. Women's Inst. for Freedom of Press, 1976—. Mem. Am. Women in Radio and TV, Nat. Fedn. Press Women. Author: Women Speak Out About Abortion, 1978; contbr. numerous articles to profl. jours.; author monthly column for NOW newsletter, 1974—; editorial asst. and AdViews mag.; editorial asst. AdViews mag.; video editor, features editor Good Times mag. Home: PO Box AW Miller Place NY 11764 Office: UACC Brookhaven Cable TV Industrial Rd Port Jefferson Station NY 11776 also: Sta WBLI 106 FM Long Island NY 11763 also: AdViews Mag PO Box 268 Greenville NY 11548

SOMERS, CARIN ALMA, retired librarian; b. Frankfurt/Main, Ger., Mar. 18, 1934; d. Josef and Helen Josephine (Badham) Stein; m. Frank George Somers, Aug. 23, 1958. B.A., Newton (Mass.) Coll. Sacred Heart, 1955; M.A., Dalhousie U., Halifax, N.S., Can., 1956; B.L.S., U. Toronto, 1961. Registrar, then lectr. French, St. Mary's U., Halifax, 1956-60; with Halifax City Regional Library, 1958-64, librarian tech. services, 1961-64; asst. librarian, then chief librarian Halifax County Regional Library, 1964-73; supr. pub. libraries N.S. Provincial Library, Halifax, 1973-74; dir. N.S. Provincial Library, 1974-87; occasional lectr. Dalhousie U. Sch. Library Service. Contbr. articles to profl. jours. Decorated Gov. Gen.'s medal, Can. (Queen Elizabeth II) Silver Jubilee medal; grantee Province N.S., 1960-61; grantee French Govt., 1956. Mem. Can. Library Assn. (2d v.p. 1974-75), Atlantic Provinces Library Assn. (past pres.), N.S. Library Assn., N.S. Bird Soc., Can. Nature Fedn. Roman Catholic. Club: Royal N.S. Yacht Squadron. Home: Box 772, Armdale PO, Halifax, NS Canada B3L 4K5

SOMMER, MARY MARGARET ST. JOHN, accountant; b. Long Beach, Calif., Jan. 5, 1940; d. James Stewart and Zenie Elizabeth (Walker) St. John; m. Errol Dey Sommer, June 1959 (div. 1964); 1 child, Robert Stewart. Grad. high sch., Los Angeles. Lic. Realtor. Acct. Robinson & Rootenberg CPA's, Los Angeles, 1956-59, Rootenberg & Getz CPA's, Beverly Hills, 1959-69, Rootenberg Rosenthal & Getz CPA's, Beverly Hills, 1969-79, Rootenberg & Rosenthal CPA's, Beverly Hills, 1979-87, Anderson Bros. Engring., Culver City, Calif., 1969-72, Inland Pacific Co., Rolling Hills, Calif., 1972-76, Edward C. Ellis Co., Los Angeles, 1976-78, Asphalt Service Co., Oceanside, Calif., 1978-80, Stegeman & Scott, Stegeman & Scott Services (now Stegeman & Kastner, Inc.), 1980—; pvt. practice acctg. Calif., 1982—; acct. Music Distbrs., Carson, Calif., 1985-86, Bus. Mgmt. Co., Redondo Beach, Calif., 1986-88, Quail Meadows Ltd., Santa Maria, Calif., 1988—. Democrat. Presbyterian. Office: Quail Meadows Ltd 2102 N Railroad Ave Santa Maria CA 93454

SOMMERS, ESTELLE JOAN, retail executive; b. Balt.; d. David Isaac and Mary Agnes (Curland) Goldstein; grad. high sch.; m. Ben Sommers, Dec. 2, 1962 (dec. Apr. 30, 1985); children: Gayle Joan, Cathy Harriet, Debbie Jane. Stylist, owner Loshins, Cin., 1948-62; mgr., owner Capezio Fashion Shop., N.Y.C., 1964-79; stylist, owner Estar Ltd., N.Y.C., 1969-79; head adminstr., joint owner Capezio Dance-Theatre Shops, N.Y.C., Boston, Chgo., Hollywood, 1970—. U.S. chmn. Dance Library of Israel, 1979—; bd. dirs. Dance Notation Bd., 1980—; bd. dirs. Am.-Israel Cultural Found., 1979-82, The Ctr. for Dance Medicine, 1983—; co-chmn. nat. adv. com. Internat Ballet Competition U.S.A., 1979—; acting pres. Internat. Dance Alliance, 1985—; bd. dirs. New Dance Group, 1985-86, New Dance Studios, 1985—, The Yard, 1986—; mem. Jacob's Pillow Bd. Overseers, 1988—, mem. artistic adv. com. Internat. Conf. Jews and Judaism in Dance, 1986. Recipient Peridance Annual award Peridance Dance Co., 1987. Office: 755 7th Ave New York NY 10019

SOMMERS, MARILYN PETERSON, law enforcement supervisor; b. Phila., Nov. 12, 1946; d. William Edmund and Grace (Whipple) Birchall; m. Mark Arthur Peterson, Aug. 26, 1967 (div. Aug. 1979) 1 child, Jon Fredrik; m. Paul David Sommers Jr., Aug. 23, 1985. Student, Temple U., 1964-68. Writer, pub. relations cons. Phila., 1976-79; research cons. Pa. Ho. of Reps., Harrisburg, 1979-80; asst. communications mgr. Pa. Crime Commn., Phila., 1980-81; mgr. MAGLOCLEN, Malvern, Pa., 1981-87; tng. coordinator N.J. Statewide Narcotics Task Force Dept. Law and Pub. Safety, Trenton, 1987-88, analytical supr., 1988—; lectr. various police agencies, 1984—. Author: (with others) Decade of Organized Crime, 1980; contbr. articles to profl. jours. Pres. Chestnut Hill Community Assn., Phila., 1980-82; mem. Spring Garden Coll. Pres. Council, Phila., 1981. Mem. Police Mgmt. Assn., Nat. Criminal Justice Assn. (regional rep. to adv. bd. 1988), Internat. Narcotics Enforcement Officers Assn., N.J. Narcotics Enforcement Officers Assn., Internat. Assn. Law Enforcement Intelligence Analysts (bd. dirs. 1985-86, editor Intelscope 1985-87, Spl. award for most significant written contbn. to lit. Law Enforcement Analysis 1987), Fraternal Order Police (Most Significant Contbn. to Lit. Law Enforcement Analysis award 1987). Home: 178 Benezet St Philadelphia PA 19118 Office: NJ Narcotics Task Force Hughes Justice Complex 25 Market St Trenton NJ 08625

SOMMERVILLE-O'BRIEN, EDITH LYNN, aerospace electrical engineer; b. Beverly Hills, Calif., Apr. 18, 1958; d. Harry Eugene and Mary Edith (Landman) Sommerville; m. William R. O'Brien Jr., June 23, 1984. BSEE, Pacific Coll., 1981. Jr. elec. specialist Grumman Aerospace, Point Mugu Nas, Calif., 1979-80, sr. elec. specialist, 1980-81; tech. writer, editor quality assurance Stanwick Corp., Ventura, Calif., 1980; test ops. engr. Martin Marietta Corp., Vanderberg AFB, Calif., 1981-83, integrated flight safety ops. engr., 1984-85; group leader software safety engrs. Rockwell Internat., Vanderberg AFB, 1983; flight test engr. Gen. Dynamics/Convair, San Diego, 1983-84; night supr. field engring. Eaton Corp., Edwards AFB, Calif., 1985—. Served with USAF, 1977-79. Fellow AAAS; mem. Nat. Assn. for Female Execs., Air Force Sgts. Assn. (life). Republican. Methodist. Home: 641 W Ave J Suite 342 Lancaster CA 93534

SOMMER-YEAGER, LINDA DIANNE, health science facility executive; b. Bklyn., Aug. 24, 1951; d. David and Blossom (Furman) Eskenazi; m. Marc Dennis Sommer, June 3, 1973 (div. 1974); m. Joseph Cornelius Yeager, Sept. 1, 1983; children: Joseph Benjamin, Rachel Leigh. BA in Edn. magna cum laude, Queens Coll., 1972; MS in Edn., Bklyn. Coll., 1976. Cert. neurolinguistic programmer trainer. Tchr. N.Y.C Pub. Schs., Bklyn., 1973-82; pres. Eastern NLP Inst., Newtown, Pa., 1982—, also bd. dirs.; bd. dirs. Reflections Unltd., N.Y.C., S. Am. Inst. of NLP, Buenos Aires. Author: (with others) Power of Persuasion, Teen Power, 1987. Trainer teenage scholarship program, Princeton, N.J., 1985—; vol. neurolinguistic programming trainer PTA, Bucks County, Pa., 1985—, Big Sisters Am., Bucks County, 1986. Fellow Soc. Neurolinguistic Programming (bd. dirs.); mem. Am. Soc. Tng. and Devel., Nat. Assn. Women Execs. Office: Eastern NLP Inst PO Box 697 Newtown PA 18940

SONCHIK, SUSAN MARIE, analytical chemist; b. Maple Heights, Ohio, Mar. 10, 1954; d. Stephen Robert and Gloria Ann (Hach) S. BS in Chemistry magna cum laude, John Carroll U., 1975; MS in Analytical Chemistry, Case Western Res. U., 1978, PhD in Phys. Chemistry, 1980. Asst. chemist Horizons Research Inc., Beachwood, Ohio, 1974-75; chemist specialist Standard Oil of Ohio, Warrensville Heights, Ohio, 1975-79; organic chemistry br. mgr. Versar, Inc., Springfield, Va., 1980-83; mgr. gas chromatography program IBM Instruments Inc., Danbury, Conn., 1983-87, radiation safety officer, 1985-87; expert witness, cons. Martin, Craig, Chester & Sonnenschein, Chgo., 1981-83; adv. engr. in advanced lithography IBM Corp., Essex Junction, Vt., 1987—; mem. exec. com. Am. Standard for Testing and Materials E-19, Phila., 1985-89; speaker in field. Author: African Walking Safari, 1985; editorial adv. bd. Jour. Chromatographic Sci., 1977—, guest editor, 1987. Troop leader Lake Erie council Girl Scouts Am., 1972-80, Southeastern Conn. council, 1983-87; leader Explorer Post, Greater Cleve. council Boy Scouts Am., 1977-78; managerial adviser Jr. Achievement, Warrensville Heights, Ohio, 1977-78; sci. fair judge Electrochem. Soc., 1977, 80, 81; asst. leader Internat. Folk Dancers, Newtown, Conn., 1985-87. Recipient Overall Best Paper award Eastern Analytical Symposium, 1984, First Gas Chromatograph award IBM Instruments Inc., 1985, contbn. award (tech. paper) 10th Internat. Congress of Essential Oils, Flavors, Fragrances, Washington, 1986. Mem. Am. Chem. Soc., ASTM (E-19 exec. com. 1985-89, subcom. chmn. 1986-87), Internat. Union for Pure and Applied Chemistry, Danbury Conservation Commn. (religion tchr. 1981-82, 83-84, 87-88), Nat. Assn. Female Execs., Iota Sigma Pi (pres. Northeast Ohio, 1978-79). Roman Catholic. Club: Green Mountain Hiking; Wilderness Soc.; No. Vt. Canoe Cruisers; Civilian Corp of Brigade of Am. Revolution. Avocations: camping, racquetball, dancing, travel, mountain climbing. Home: 14 Forest Rd Essex Junction VT 05452-3818 Office: IBM Corp Gen Tech Div Dept G40 Bldg 966-2 Essex Junction VT 05452

SONDOCK, RUBY KLESS, judge; b. Houston, Apr. 26, 1926; d. Herman Lewis and Celia (Juran) Kless; m. Melvin Adolph Sondock, Apr. 22, 1944; children—Marcia Cohen, Sandra Marcus. A.A., Cottey Coll., Nevada, Mo., 1944; B.S., U. Houston, 1959, LL.B., 1961. Sole practice, Houston, 1961-73; judge Harris County Ct. Domestic Relations, 1973-77, 234th Jud. Dist. Ct., Houston, 1977-82, 83—; justice Tex. Supreme Ct., Austin, 1982. Mem. ABA, Tex. Bar Assn., Houston Bar Assn., Nat. Assn. Women Lawyers, Houston Assn. Women Lawyers, Order of Barons, Phi Theta Phi, Kappa Beta Pi, Phi Kappa Phi, Alpha Epsilon Pi. Jewish. Office: 234th Dist Ct 301 Fannin St Houston TX 77002

SONGER, FRANCES VIRGINIA, marketing and motivational consultant; b. Atlanta, Feb. 13, 1957; d. Francis Harold and Lois Irene (Stringer) S.; m. Christopher Lee Clinkenbeard, Sept. 1, 1979 (div. 1980). B.A. in Exptl. Psychology magna cum laude, Ga. State U., 1982. Mgr., stores asst. Pepperidge Farm, Atlanta, 1976-82; mgr. S&A Corp., Atlanta, 1982-83; food and beverage asst. mgr., dir. meetings and banquets dir., sales dir. dir. mktg. Guest Quarters, Atlanta/Charlotte, 1983-87; hypnotherapist Hypnosis Motivation Inst., Atlanta, 1984-86; handwriting analyst, Atlanta, 1985-86; mktg. and image cons., public speaker, Total Mind Cons., Charlotte, N.C., 1987—; v.p. P.K.G.'s-Charlotte, N.C., 1988—. Mem. Nat. Assn. Female Execs., Blue Key, Psi Chi, Phi Kappa Phi. Republican. Avocations: photography, racquetball, gardening. Home: 6120 Old Providence Ln Charlotte NC 28226 Office: Total Mind Cons PO Box 220184 Charlotte NC 28222-0184

SONIES, BARBARA CAROL, speech and language pathologist; b. Gloversville, N.Y., Aug. 25, 1939; d. George and Eleanor S. (Kall) Myzal; B.S. with distinction, U. Minn., 1961; M.A., Stanford U., 1963; Ph.D., U. Md., 1981; m. Harvey J. Kupferberg, Jan. 5, 1975; 1 son, Mitchel H. Sonies. Speech therapist Alhambra (Calif.) Schs., 1963-65; speech pathologist U.

Minn. Hosps., Mpls., 1965-67; coordinator speech diagnostic clinic Mpls. Public Schs., 1967-68; supr. speech pathology U. Minn. Health Scis. Center, Mpls., 1968-72; instr. communication disorders U. Minn., 1969-72; coordinator speech program Robbinsdale (Minn.) Public Schs., summer 1970; project mgr. sch. programs Am. Speech, Lang. and Hearing Assn., 1972-73; instr., clinic supr. dept. hearing and speech sci. U. Md., College Park, 1974-77; chief Speech-Lang. Pathology Clin. Center, NIH, Bethesda, Md., 1977—; instr. continuing edn. U. Va., Falls Church, 1975-82; research assoc. prof. U. Md., College Park, 1981—; assoc prof. Loyola Coll., Balt.; guest prof. George Washington U.; cons. Montgomery County Health Dept., Rockville, Md., 1974-79; lectr. in field. Hunt scholar, 1957-61; Rehab. Services Adminstrn. grantee, 1961-63. Mem. Am. Speech-Lang.-Hearing Assn. (chmn. augmentative communic com. 1985—, mem. ad hoc com. on dysphagia, editor rehab. reports, 1st place award for sci. and tech. merit 1985, Joseph H. Holmes award excellence in ultrasound research 1985), Md. Speech-Lang.-Hearing Assn. (sec. 1977-79, editor jour. 1981-83), Internat. Neuropsychol. Soc., Mortar Bd., Phi Beta Kappa, Order of Ski-U-Mah. Contbr. articles to profl. jours. Home: 8826 Tuckerman Ln Potomac MD 20854 Office: NIH Clin Center Speech Pathology Rm 6N226 Bethesda MD 20892

SONKIN, MICHELLE ANNE EISEMANN, publisher; b. N.Y.C., Aug. 12, 1952; d. Ralph and Beatrice (Sichel) Eisemann; m. Richard Sonkin, May 30, 1976; 1 child, Lauren Sydney. BA in Psychology, Journalism, Syracuse U., 1974. Corp. dir. recruitment advt. Crain Communications, N.Y.C., 1974-75; pres. Eisemann & Assocs., N.Y.C., 1975-76; advt. dir. Fairchild Publs., N.Y.C., 1976-83; pub. Ave. Mag. Inc., N.Y.C., 1983—. Office: Ave Mag Inc 145 E 57 St New York NY 10022

SONNENFELD, GRACIELA DIANA, bank manager; b. Buenos Aires, Argentina, Oct. 31, 1949; came to U.S., 1978; d. Egon Manfredo and Beatriz (Kamil) Horn; B.S., St. Catherine's Inst., 1967, London Cultural Inst., 1973. Asst. to pres. OKS KNOS Y CIA, S.A., Buenos Aires, 1970-75; asst. to pres. Aurora S.A., Buenos Aires, 1975-78; asst. v.p. Chgo. br. Banco de la Nacion Argentina, 1979—. Pres., Gradia S.R.L., Buenos Aires; partner Regente S.R.L. Argentina. Mem. Women in Internat. Trade, Soc. Personnel Adminstrs. Jewish. Club: Italian Circle Buenos Aires. Home: 333 E Ontario St Apt 2301B Chicago IL 60611 Office: 135 S LaSalle Room 2240 Chicago IL 60603

SONNENSCHEIN, SUSAN MARION, psychologist, educator; b. N.Y.C., Oct. 18, 1951; d. Isidor and Elfriede (Ball) S.; m. Garry Sheldon Grossman, July 20, 1980; children: Elyse, Julie. BA, NYU, 1972; MS, Pa. State U., 1975; PhD, SUNY, Stonybrook, 1979. Research assoc. Pa. State U., University Park, 1972-73, instr. ednl. psychology, 1974-75; supr. undergrad. teaching personnel Toscanini Infant Day Care Ctr., Stony Brook, N.Y., 1976; instr. Leeway Sch., 1976; instr. psychology SUNY, 1977-78; psychol. cons. West Islip (N.Y.) Sch. Dist., 1977; research asst. SUNY, 1975-78, research coordinator, 1978-79; asst. prof. psychology U. Md. Balt. County, Stony Brook, 1979-84; child devel. cons. BioTech. Assocs., 1983-84; assoc. prof. psychology U. Md. Balt. County, 1984—, acting head, 1985; reviewer Southeastern Conf. Human Devel., 1980; adv. bd. Child Specialist Cert. program, Washington; chmn. Paper Session Southeastern Conf. Human Devel., 1982; mem. com. Montgomery County Juvenile Court, 1983—. Contbr. articles to profl. jours. N.Y. State Regents scholar, 1969-72; Sigma Xi grantee, 1978; U. Md. Balt. County fellow, 1980, 82, 85. Mem. Am. Psychol. Assn., Soc. for Research in Child Devel., Ea. Psychol. Assn. Home: 995 Farm Haven Dr Rockville MD 20852 Office: U Md Balt County Dept Psychology Catonsville MD 21228

SONSKI, JANICE ANNE, television director, marketing consultant; b. Bklyn., Mar. 22, 1955; d. Sherman and Bernice (Menchel) Weinstein; m. Roman Blaufarb, Jan. 1, 1979 (div. Mar. 1983); m. Paul Michael Sonski, June 22, 1986. BS, Syracuse U., 1977. Sales account exec. Swank Motion Pictures, Boston, 1978-79; dir. pub. relations Allied Advt., Boston, 1979-82; sr. field publicist MGM/United Artists Entertainment, Boston, 1982; mktg. mgr. 20th Century Fox Film Corp., Los Angeles, 1982-84; publicity cons. CBS Records, Los Angeles Internat. Film Festival, 1985; mgr. print advt. NBC Inc., Los Angeles, 1985-87; dir. children's programming NBC-TV, Inc., Los Angeles, 1987—. Author press publicity kits. Mem. Women in Communications, Acad. TV Arts & Scis., Publicists Guild. Office: NBC Inc 3000 W Alameda Ave Los Angeles CA 91523

SONTAG, SUSAN, author, film director. Author: (novels) The Benefactor, 1963, Death Kit, 1967, (stories) I, etcetera, 1978, (essays) Against Interpretation, 1966, Styles of Radical Will, 1969, On Photography, 1977, Illness as Metaphor, 1978, Under the Sign of Saturn, 1980, (anthology) A Susan Sontag Reader, 1982, (film scripts) Duet for Cannibals, 1970, Brother Carl, 1974; editor, author introduction Antonin Artaud: Selected Writings, 1976, A Barthes Reader, 1982; dir.: (films) Duet for Cannibals, 1969, Brother Carl, 1971, Promised Lands, 1974, Unguided Tour, 1983. Guggenheim fellow, 1966, 75; Rockefeller Found. fellow, 1965, 74; recipient Ingram Merrill Found. award in lit. in field of Am. Letters, 1976; Creative Arts award Brandeis U., 1976; prize Nat. Book Critics Circle, 1978; named Officier de l'Ordre des Arts et des Lettres, France, 1984. Mem. Am. Acad. Inst. Arts and Letters (recipient Arts and Letters award 1976), PEN (pres. Am. Ctr. 1987—). Address: care Farrar Straus & Giroux Inc 19 Union Sq W New York NY 10003

SOOHOO, ELENA, health administrator; b. N.Y.C., Apr. 13, 1955; d. Jim Gung and Louise Sue Wah (Louie) S.; m. Paul Man Ong, Aug. 28, 1981. Student, U. Calif., Berkeley, 1975-79; BS in Nursing, U. Calif., San Francisco, 1981; MS, Harvard U., 1987. RN. Research asst. Div. Ambulatory and Community Med. U. Calif., San Francisco, 1976-77; bibliographer Inst. Health Policy Studies U. Calif., San Francisco, 1978; nurse Moffitt Hosp. U. Calif., San Francisco, 1981-82, On Lok Sr. Health Services, San Francisco, 1982-83; intern health policy Office Sen. Rosenthal, Los Angeles, 1984; specialist health scis. VA, Los Angeles, 1985-86; asst. to chief fin. officer E. Boston Health Cen., 1986-87; bd. dirs. Bay Area Asian Health Alliance, San Francisco, 1980-84. Mem. planning com. KRON-TV Health Fair, San Francisco 1979-82; co-chmn. Hop Jok/Chinatown Health Fair, San Francisco 1975-81; mem. Chicanos Health Edn., Berkeley 1977-79; vol. Northbeach Chinatown Family Planning, San Francisco 1974-76, Chinatown Health Fair, N.Y.C. 1971-72. Mem. Am. Pub. Health Assn., Health Fin. Mgmt. Assn., Com. Status Women, Harvard (affirmative action com. 1987), U. Calif. San Francisco (affirmative action com. 1980-81). Home: 827 Levering Ave #601 Los Angeles CA 90024 Office: Los Angeles County Dept Health Services Suite 831 313 N Figueroa St Los Angeles CA 90031

SORELL, CAROLE SUZANNE, public relations agency executive; b. N.Y.C., Oct. 6, 1940; d. Joseph and Lillian (Zeitlin) Spector; children: Melissa Bushell, Craig Bushell. BA with honors, Hunter Coll., 1961; MS, Central Conn. State Coll., 1966. Dir. pub. relations Children's Mus. and Planetarium, Hartford, Conn., 1972-73; dir. media United Jewish Appeal, N.Y.C., 1973-75; sr. v.p. Ruder & Finn Fine Arts, N.Y.C., 1975-79; v.p. Adams & Rinehart, N.Y.C., 1979-80; pres. Carole Sorell Inc., N.Y.C., 1980—; author, moderator book revs. Hartford Times, 1970; writer, producer Sta. WNEW-TV, 1974; media coordinator openings world hdqrs. insts. Chem. Bank, Philip Morris Cos. Inc., Nat. Bldg. Mus., Portland Mus. Art, Nat. Mus. Women in the Arts, Palazzo Grassi, Venice, Italy, others. Fund raiser, publicity dir. Conn. Valley Regional Ballet, Hartford, 1971-72; mem. Mayor's All Am. Festival, Hartford, 1972; publicist South Bronx Community Action Theatre and Bronx Mus. Arts, 1978-79. Mem. Pub. Relations Soc. Am., Am. Assn. Mus., Nat. Assn. Womens Bus. Owners, ArtTable. Home and Office: 345 E 56th St New York NY 10022

SORENSEN, CAMEY, writer; b. Boston, May 31, 1933; d. John Alabiso and Rose DiFrancesco; m. Charles F.; 1 child, Richard. Student, Northeastern U. Sec. Alford Mfg. Co., Woburn, Mass., 1984—; owner, author, songwriter Camey's Freelance Service, Woburn, 1986—. Author: It Could Happen to You, 1981; songwriter: Brown Eyes, How Could I Know, Your Guardian Angel, My Heart Went Bing-Bong and numerous other songs; hostess Job Search (Sta. WLHE), Burlington, Mass.; contbr. articles to many newspapers and mags. Office: Camey's Freelance Service care Frank Paul Enterprises PO Box 113 Woburn MA 01801

SORENSEN, ELIZABETH JULIA, cultural administrator; b. Kenora, Ont., Can., Nov. 24, 1934; d. John Frederick and Irene Margaret (Dowd) MacKellar; m. O. Leo P. Sorensen, July 7, 1956 (div. 1963); children: Lianne Kim Sorensen Kruger. BA, Lakehead U., 1970; MA, Brigham Young U., 1972; Assoc. Royal Conservatory, U. Toronto, 1978; Assoc., Mt. Royal Coll., Calgary, AB, 1978. Sec. Canadian Med. Assn. Manitoba div., Winnipeg, 1956-59; legal sec. Filmore, Riley & Co., Winnipeg, 1961-63; tchr. Fort Frances (Ont.) High Sch., 1963-70; instr. drama, speech, English Lethbridge (Alta.) Community Coll., 1972-77; tchr. bus. edn. Henderson Coll. Bus., Lethbridge, 1978-80; coordinator community services cultural programs City Medicine Hat, Alta., 1980—. Mem. Alta. Recreation and Parks Assn. (programmers seminar com. 1987-88), Alta. Mcpl. Assn. for Culture (sec, treas. 1982—). Mormon. Office: City of Medicine Hat, 580 1 St SE, Medicine Hat, AB Canada T1A 8E6

SORENSEN, JACKI FAYE, aerobic dance company executive, choreographer; b. Oakland, Calif., Dec. 10, 1942; d. Roy C. and Juanita F. (Bullon) Mills; m. Neil A. Sorensen, Jan. 3, 1965. B.A., U. Calif., 1964. Cert. tchr., Calif. Ptnr., Big Spring Sch. Dance, 1965; tchr. Pasadena Ave. Sch., Sacramento, 1968; founder, chmn. bd. dirs., choreographer Aerobic Dancing, Inc., Northridge, Calif., 1969—; cons., lectr. on phys. fitness. Author: Aerobic Dancing, 1979, Jacki Sorensen's Aerobic Lifestyle Book, 1983; choreographer numerous dance exercises for records and videocassettes. Trustee Women's Sports Found. Recipient Diamond Pin award Am. Heart Assn., 1979; Individual Contbn. award Am. Assn. Fitness Dirs. in Bus. and Industry, 1981; Spl. Olympics Contbn. award, 1982; Contbn. to Women's Fitness award Pres.'s Council Phys. Fitness and Sports, 1982; Healthy Am. Fitness Leader award U.S. Jaycees, 1984; Lifetime Achievement award Internat. Dance Exercise Assn., 1985; New Horizons award Caldwell (N.J.) Coll., 1985; Legend of Aerobics award City Sports mag., 1985; Pres. Council award Calif. Womens' Leadership Conf., 1986; Hall of Fame award Club Industry mag., 1986. Mem. Am. Coll. Sports Medicine, AAHPERD, Nat. Intramural and Recreation Assn., AFTRA. Office: Aerobic Dancing Inc 19420 Business Center Dr Northridge CA 91324

SORENSON, LORNA JEAN, public relations executive, writer; b. Marshfield, Wis., July 8, 1944; d. Harry Paul and Florence O. (Charboneau) Bassuener; m. Carl John Sorenson, Feb. 20, 1965; children: Harry Paul, Robert DeLong. Student, Milw. Downer Coll., 1962-64; BA, U. Wis., 1975. Columnist The Milw. Sentinel, 1975-83; spokeswoman Wis. Bell Inc., Milw., 1983-86, editor trend sect., 1987—. Author features Milw. Journ., 1975. Bd. dirs. United Cerebral Palsy, S.E. Wis., Milw., 1986—. Mem. Profl. Womens Club, Internat. Assn. Bus. Communicators. Lutheran. Clubs: Pioneers of Am. Telephone (Milw.), Milw. Press. Office: Wis Bell Inc 722 N Broadway Milwaukee WI 52302

SORENSON, SANDRA LOUISE, computer systems educator; b. Santa Monica, Calif., Nov. 30, 1948; d. Edward John and Gordon Dudley (Pollock) S. BA in Telecommunications, BS in Mktg., U. So. Calif., 1970. Merchandiser Montgomery Ward Inc., Los Angeles, 1970-82; sr. fin. planner Plums Co., Los Angeles, 1982-84; mgr. merchandising systems devel. and tng. Millers Outpost, Ontario, Calif., 1984—. Active Shakespeare Festival Guild, Garden Grove, Calif., 1985—; chairperson membership com. Gem Theatre Guild, Garden Grove, 1986—. Recipient Achievement award Bicentennial Com. Norwalk, Calif., 1976. Mem. Am. Soc. Tng. and Devel. (v.p.), Commerce Assocs., Assn. Retail Mgmt. Info. Systems, Mensa. Republican. Mem. Reformed Ch. Am. Club: Players of Orange. Home: 76 Carriage Way Phillips Ranch CA 91766 Office: Millers Outpost 2501 E Guasti Rd Ontario CA 91761

SORIANO, DORIS JEAN, library administrator; b. Cedar Rapids, Iowa, Feb. 23, 1941; d. Hughie J. and Helen Doris (Daniels) N.; m. Ernest Soriano, Apr. 20, 1979. BA, Coe Coll., 1962; MLS, Columbia U., 1963; MPA, Calif. State U., Long Beach, 1986. Librarian Cedar Rapids Pub. Library, 1963-66; assoc. dir. Clinton (Iowa) Pub. Library, 1966-69; librarian Long Beach Pub. Library, 1969-70, dept. librarian, 1970-81, assoc. dir., 1981—. Lydia Roberts fellow Columbia U., 1963. Mem. ALA, Calif. Library Assn., Beta Phi Mu, Pi Alpha Alpha. Home: 5575 Westminster Ave Westminster CA 92683 Office: Long Beach Pub Library 101 Pacific Ave Long Beach CA 90802

SOROOS, CAROL STERN, management consultant. BA cum laude, Carleton Coll., 1967; PhD, Northwestern U., Evanston, Ill., 1975; MBA, Duke U., 1982. Intern U.S. Dept. State, Washington, 1967; adj. faculty N.C. State U., Raleigh, 1970-80; mktg. rep. N.C. State Port Authority, Raleigh, 1981; mgr. mktg. Aerotron Inc., Raleigh, 1982-83; sr. market analyst No. Telecom, Inc., Research Triangle Park, N.C., 1983-85, mgr. market info., 1985-86, mgr. market forecast, 1986-87; pres. The Competitive Advantage, Raleigh, 1987—. Chair internat. students host family program N.C. State U., 1984; pres. Friends of Scandinavia, Raleigh, 1986-87. Carnegie Endowment for Internat. Peace grantee, 1970. Mem. Am. Mktg. Assn. (registration hospitality com. Triangle chpt. 1983-84, sec. 1984-85, treas. 1985-86, bd. dirs. 1986-87, v.p. 1987-88), N.C. World Trade Assn. (bd. dirs. Triangle chpt. 1988—), Council for Entrepreneurial Devel., Greater Raleigh C. of C. Office: The Competitive Advantage PO Box 30651 Raleigh NC 27622

SORRIER, ISABEL LANE, librarian; b. Statesboro, Ga., Aug. 13, 1917; d. Brooks Blitch and Caroline Viola (Moore) Sorrier; B.S., Ga. So. Coll., 1938; postgrad. U. Ga., 1940; B.S., George Peabody Coll., 1942. Intern, Warder Pub. Library, Springfield, Ohio, 1942; librarian Homerville (Ga.) High Sch., 1939-41; head librarian Waycross (Ga.) Pub. Library, 1942; librarian Newnan (Ga.) High Sch., 1943; dir. Statesboro (Ga.) Regional Library, 1944—; mem. library adv. com. bldg. constrn. Ga. Dept. Edn., mem. book selection com. Sec. chpt. ARC, 1945-48; mem. library services and constrn. Act Adv. Council, 1976—. Named Boss of Yr., Am. Bus. Women's Assn., 1980. Mem. ALA, S.E., Ga. (exec. bd. 1960, chmn. sect. 1960-62) library assns., Ga. Edn. Assn., Bus. and Profl. Women's Club (treas. 1950-52). Presbyterian. Home: 112 Park Ave Statesboro GA 30485 Office: 124 S Main St Statesboro GA 30458

SOSNOWSKI, DONNA LEE, human resource director; b. Flushing, NY, Mar. 8, 1954; d. Murray and Gertrude (Wasserman) Pozner; m. Michael Felix Sosnowski, Aug. 8, 1976. BS in Spanish Edn. cum laude, SUNY, New Paltz, 1974, MS in Adminstrv. Edn. summa cum laude, 1976. Cert. tchr., N.Y., R.I. Program dir. Cen. Falls (R.I.) Sch. Dept., 1976-80; benefits coordinator to mgr. tng. and employment Monet Jewelers div. Gen. Mills, Providence, 1981-86; dir. compensation and benefits The Provident Instn. for Savs., Boston, 1986-87, asst. v.p., 1987—; cons. State of R.I. Dept. Edn., Providence, 1977-78, Jr. Achievement, Providence, 1984-85, dir. Human Resources Groundwater Tech., Inc., Norwood, Mass., 1988. Mem. Internat. Assn. Personnel Women (bd. dirs. 1987—), Am. Compensation Assn., Am. Soc. Tng. and Devel., Am. Soc. Personnel Adminstrn., Northeast Human Resource Assn. Office: Groundwater Tech Inc 220 Norwood Park South Norwood MA 02062

SOTO, LEONA ENDRICA, sales manager; b. Honolulu, Jan. 6, 1949; d. Saturnino Flores and Sybil H.L. (Lee) Rellin; m. Edward Soto, Aug. 21, 1969; Dean Douglas, Ward Lee. Cert. real estate sales, pre-licensing course, Real Estate Sch. of St. Michael, 1978; cert. real estate brokerage, Mary Shern Sch., 1981. Cert. real estate salesperson and broker, residential specialist. Sec. Allied Aviation Service Co. of Hawaii, Honolulu, 1973-80; realtor assoc. Liberty Homes, Inc., Mililani, Hawaii, 1978-81, realtor, broker, 1981-85; sales mgr. Century 21 Liberty Homes, Inc., Mililani, 1985-87; Mem. Aloha Cert. Residential Specialist chpt., Honolulu, 1985—, treas., 1988; chmn. Hawaii Cert. Residential Broker, Honolulu, 1986-87, chmn. Scrapbook of Yr., 1987, ambassador, 1987—; dir. Honolulu Bd. Realtors, 1986-87, mem. audit com. 1987—, chmn. audit com., 1988. Dir. Mililani Shopping Ctr. Assn. 1984—; Sustaining Mem. Enrollment, chmn. Boy Scouts Am., Mililani, 1987. Mem. Hawaii Assn. Realtors (conv. com. 1988), Cert. Residential Specialists (treas. Aloha Hawaii chpt. 1988), Honolulu Bd. Realtors (bd. dirs. 1986-87, audit com. 1987-89, convention com. 1988). Roman Catholic. Lodge: Soroptimists (sec. 1986—).

SOTO, THERESA JOSEPHINE (TERRY), banking and financial executive; b. St. Petersburg, Fla., May 29, 1942; d. Phillip Evan and Virginia Mary (Draa) Anderson; m. Henry Dominquez Soto, Aug. 14, 1960; children—Kimberly, Patrick, Noel, Nathan, Andrew. Student Pima Community Coll., 1972-75. Cert. personnel cons. Exec. recuiter Mgmt. Recruiters, Tucson, 1976-80; corp. sr. v.p., mgr. real estate/fin. div. Kingston & Assocs., Tucson, 1981—. Leadership tng., mem. steering com. OEO, Tucson, 1964-66; mem. community relations bd. Tucson Job Corps., 1977-79; treas. Tucson Loan Chest, 1983-86; bd. dirs. Saharo Girl Scout Council, Inc., 1988—. Named Outstanding Fraternalist, Ariz. Frat. Congress, 1985. Mem. Nat. Assn. Personnel Cons., Am. Mktg. Assn. (co-chairperson spl. programs 1982-83, program chairperson 1981-82, sec. chpt. 1979-80, pres. Greater Tucson chpt. 1984-85). Republican. Roman Catholic. Club: Parkwest Women's (chairperson program 1967-68, pres. 1968-69) (Tucson). Lodges: Columbiettes (K.C. aux., pres. 1982-83), Ind. Order of Foresters (chief ranger 1980-81, pub. relations officer Tucson 1983—, Ariz., N.Mex. and Nev. 1986—). Home: 2832 W Calle Carapan Tucson AZ 85745 Office: Kingston & Assocs 101 N Wilmot Suite 210 Tucson AZ 85711

SOUCY, PATRICIA CALLISON, personal property appraiser, educator; b. Lafayette, Ind., Apr. 11, 1950; d. Charles F. and Eileen P. (Neville) Callison; m. John C. Soucy Jr., July 10, 1965; children: Maureen, John. BS in Nursing, Loretto Heights Coll., 1962; MA in Valuation Sci., Lindenwood Coll., 1982, MA in Art History, 1986—. Antique dealer Country Rd. Antiques, Centralia, Mo., 1975-86; antique and decorative arts appraiser Mid-Mo. Appraiser Services, Centralia, 1977—; core faculty Lindenwood Coll., St. Charles, Mo., 1983—; co-chair Internat. Bd. Examiners for Antiques and Decorative Arts, 1987—. Mem. Am. Soc. Appraisers (sr., chpt. sec. 1985, treas. 1986, v.p. 1987, chmn. valuation scis. program, 1985-87, personal property com. 1985, chmn. designation in antiques, decorating arts, splty. designation furniture, Valuation Scis. medal 1982), Am. Arbitration Assn. Home and Office: Rt 1 Box 178 Centralia MO 65240

SOUKUP, NANCY JEAN, aircraft company executive; b. Klamath Falls, Oreg., Nov. 13, 1943; d. Louis William and Mildred Dorothy (Osborn) S.; m. Dieter Seebold, Feb. 25, 1976 (div. 1980). Student, U. Oreg., U. Calif., San Mateo Coll., Portland State U. Flight attendant Hughes Airwest, Seattle, San Francisco, 1965-77; realtor Dolphin Real Estate, San Carlos, Calif., 1979; investment counselor Behling Montross Assn., San Mateo, Calif., 1979-80; ptnr. Four Seasons Unltd., Vancouver, Wash., 1985-87; gen. mgr. Turbotech, Inc., Vancouver, 1980—; ski instr. Night Owl Ski Sch., Seattle, 1970-75; union officer Flight Attendants. Union, Seattle, 1966-77. Pres. Cen. Homeowners Assn., Belmont, Calif., 1979-80; mem. state bd. Master Gardeners of Wash., Vanouver, 1985-86; bd. dirs. YWCA, Clark, Co., 1987—; pres. state bd. Master Gardener Found., Washington, 1987-88. Named Woman of Achievement, Clark Coll. and YWCA, 1987. Mem. Nat. Assn. Female Execs., Ind. Bus. Assn., Aircraft Modification Orgn. (organizer 1984), Pearson Airpark Hist. Soc. (treas. 1986-87), Mensa. Republican. club: Ft. Vancouver Rose (pres. 1986-87). Office: Turbotech Inc PO Box 61586 Vancouver WA 98666

SOULAKIAN, SANDRA CAROL, industrial association executive; b. Chgo., Oct. 22, 1955; d. Nick Haig and Josephine (Alexanoff) Ohanjanian; m. Assadour Agop Soulakian, Sept. 23, 1985. BA in Philosophy, Roosevelt U., Chgo., 1978. Dir. bus. ops. Diamond Toymakers Ltd., Skokie, Ill., 1976-79; v.p. purchasing Precision Welding, Inc., Chgo., 1979-87; pres. Ohan Enterprises, Inc., Chgo., 1979-83; indsl. field rep. North Bus. and Indsl. Council, Chgo., 1987-88; asst. purchasing agt. Hodag Corp., Skokie, Ill., 1988—. Lodge: Order Eastern Star.

SOULE, SALLIE THOMPSON, retired state official; b. Detroit, May 13, 1928; d. Hayward Stone and Elizabeth Robinson Thompson; A.B., Smith Coll., 1950; M.A., U. Vt., Burlington, 1952; m. Gardner Northup Soule, July 26, 1958; stepchildren—Gardner Northup, Nancy Soule Brown; children—Sarah Goodwin, Trumbull Dickson. Sec. trade sales dept. Macmillan Pub. Co., N.Y.C., 1952-57; tech. writer sales service div. Eastman Kodak Co., Rochester, N.Y., 1957-58; feature writer Brighton-Pittsford Post, Pittsford, N.Y., 1958-68; v.p., gen. mgr. F. H. Horsford Nursery, Inc., Charlotte, Vt., 1968-76; ptnr., v.p. Bygone Books, Inc., Burlington, Vt., 1978—; mem. Vt. Ho. of Reps., 1976-80, mem. ways and means com., 1976-80; mem. Vt. Senate, 1980-84, mem. appropriation com., energy and natural resources com. 1980-84; commr. Vt. Dept. Employment and Tng., Montpelier, 1985-88; chmn. Vt. Employment Security Bd., 1985-88. mem. governing bd. Vt. ETV; bd. dirs. Vt. Community Found., Inc., Preservation Trust. Lodge: Rotary.

SOUMOFF, CYNTHIA, biologist, educator; b. Bklyn., Dec. 21, 1950. BA, U. Conn., 1972; PhD, UCLA, 1979. Postdoc. investigator Oak Ridge Nat. Lab. U. Tenn., 1980-83, asst. prof. Oak Ridge Biomed. Grad. Sch. Biology, 1983—. Contbr. articles to profl. jours. Mem. AAAS, Assn. Women Sci. Office: U Tenn Oak Ridge Biomed Grad Sch Biology div PO Box Y Oak Ridge Nat Lab Oak Ridge TN 37831

SOUSA, PATRICIA LOUISE, television network associate director; b. Chincoteague, Va.; d. Joseph Michael and Frances Irene (McDermont) S.; m. Lawrence Herbert Shapiro, Jan. 13, 1977. Student U. Fla., 1966-68; B.A., NYU, 1971. With Young & Rubicam, N.Y.C., 1969-70; adminstrv. asst. Home Mag., N.Y.C., 1971-74, Hughes TV Network, N.Y.C., 1974-76; adminstrv. asst., researcher, assoc. producer WNBC-TV, N.Y.C., 1976-78; assoc. dir. NBC Television Network, N.Y.C., 1979—. Vol., Jr. Army Navy Guild Orgn., Jacksonville, Fla., 1964-65. Mem. Dirs. Guild Am. (council 1984-86). Democrat. Roman Catholic. Avocation: travel. Home: 25 W 15th St New York NY 10011 Office: NBC Television Network 30 Rockefeller Plaza New York NY 10020

SOUSA, THERESA ELLEN MALONE, former govt. ofcl.; b. Frederick County, Va., Mar. 17, 1927; d. Joseph Harrison and Lillie May (Lehigh) Malone; student Strayer Bus. Coll., Columbia Tech. Inst., Washington, Oceanside-Carlsbad (Calif.) Jr. Coll., Am. U.; m. Joseph Earl Sousa, III, Oct. 20, 1946. Various adminstrv./community relations positions, 1945-50; with U.S. Geol. Survey, 1952-82, visual info. officer, Reston, Va., 1975-80, exhibits and visual info. officer, 1980-82; ret., 1982; pres. TMS Assocs., conv. and meeting planning, McLean, Va., 1982—. Served with USMCR, 1949-62. Recipient various achievement and service awards. Mem. Nat. Mus. Women in the Arts, Meeting Planners Internat., McLean Citizens Assn., Am. News Women's Club, Women Marines Assn. (nat. pres. 1974-76). Presbyterian. Home: 1415 Springvale Ave McLean VA 22101

SOUTH, GRACE DEVITA, photograph and graphic display designer; b. Boston, Jan. 9, 1957; d. Robert Allen and Sylvia Marcia (Roazen) Berman; m. James Alan Devita, Aug. 23, 1978 (div. Apr. 1980); 1 child, Jacob Elijah; m. Richard William South, June 30, 1985. Student, U. Md., 1974-75. Mgr. plant Color King, Hollywood, Fla., 1983; cons. Color Corp. Am., Tampa, 1984; sales rep. Berkey K&L, N.Y.C., 1984-85; owner Graphics reSource, Woodstock, Ga., 1985—. Mem. Photo Mktg. Assn., Soc. Photofinishing Engrs., Art Dirs. Atlanta. Home and Office: 1760 Old Country Pl Woodstock GA 30188

SOUTH, MOLLY MADSEN, real estate investment principal; b. Shreveport, La., June 18, 1949; d. Lawrence Edwards and Margaret Marion (Murray) Madsen; m. J. Gregory South, May 6, 1972; children—J. Madsen, J. Taylor. B.A. in Journalism, U. Tex., 1971. Head copywriter Continental Advt., Dallas, 1973-74; v.p. mktg., cons. and pub. affairs, Homart Devel. Co. Chgo., 1974-80; gen. ptnr. Moor & South, Highland Park, Ill., 1980—; ptnr. RMB Realty Co., Inc. (formerly Ameribass Realty Co.), Highland Park and Phila., 1980—; prin., gen. ptnr. Pier 39, San Francisco, Century City Ctr., Chgo., Ocean One, Atlantic City, numerous other comml. properties, dir. Alexanders Dept. Stores, N.Y.C., 1984-86; lectr. in field. Author column Chain Store Age Mag., 1980-86. Editorial bd. Shopping Ctr. World Mag., 1978-81. Contbr. articles to profl. jours. Bd. dirs. Highland Park Hosp. Jr. Bd., 1985—, also edn. chmn. Mem. Internat. Council Shopping Ctrs. (profl. standards com. 1983—, publs. com., 1984—, cert. shopping ctr. mktg. dir., bd. trustees 1986—, chmn. fall conv. 1987), Urban Land Inst. Republican. Roman Catholic. Office: Moor & South 525 Elm Pl Highland Park IL 60035

SOUTHER, JULIA JOANN, quality control engineer; b. Statesville, N.C., Apr. 3, 1961; d. Luther Morris and June (Ha) S.; m. Donald Douglas Doggett, June 30, 1984. A, Wingate (N.C.) Coll., 1981; B, U.N.C., 1983.

Product devel. technician Rexham Corp., Matthews, N.C., 1984-85, product devel. assoc. chemist, 1985, product devel. chemist, 1986-87, quality control engr., 1987—. Chair com. Sweet Adelines, Inc., Charlotte, N.C., 1984—. Mem. Am. Inst. Chemists, Nat. Assn. for Female Execs., Smithsonian Assocs. Baptist. Home: 10301 Crestwood Dr Charlotte NC 28226 Office: Rexham Corp Indls Films Div PO Box 368 Matthews NC 28106

SOUTHERLAND, MAXINE AYCOCK, museum director, educator; b. Alexandria, La., Mar. 21, 1922; d. Frank Aycock; m. Thomas Paul Southerland, Apr. 2, 1943; children: Judith A. Southerland Kessler, Lisa Louise Southerland Allen. BS, La. Normal Coll., Natchitoches, 1942; MS, Northwestern State U., Natchitoches, 1957. Cert. home econs. tchr., dietician. Tchr. Bossier (La.) City High Sch., 1945-46; dietician La. Charity Hosp., Pineville, 1946-47; tchr. home econs. Oak Hill High Sch., Elmer, La., 1947-49; dietician VA Hosp., Pineville, 1949-50; tchr. home econs. Boyce (La.) High Sch., 1950-54, Bolton High Sch., Alexandria, 1955-65; assoc. prof. Northwestern State U., Natchitoches, 1966-78; dir. La. State Mus. for Edn. at Northwestern State U., 1979—. Pres. Preservation Hist. Natchitoches, 1985—, Natchitoches Northwestern Symphony Soc., 1982-83; bd. dirs. Council on Aging. Named Woman of Yr., Natchitoches C. of C., 1985; Ctr. History La. Edn. grantee, 1983, 84, 87. Mem. Alpha Delta Kappa (pres. 1954), Kappa Iota (pres. 1955), Phi Kappa Phi (pres. 1980), Delta Kappa Gamma (pres.). Democrat. Methodist. Clubs: Fleur de Lis Book, St. Denis Garden (Natchitoches). Office: Northwestern State U Ctr History La Edn Natchitoches LA 71457

SOUTHERN, EILEEN (MRS. JOSEPH SOUTHERN), music educator; b. Mpls., Feb. 19, 1920; d. Walter Wade and Lilla (Gibson) Jackson; m. Joseph Southern, Aug. 22, 1942; children: April, Edward. A.B., U. Chgo., 1940, M.A., 1941; Ph.D., NYU, 1961; M.A. (hon.), Harvard U., 1976; D.A. (hon.), Columbia Coll., Chgo., 1985. Instr. Prairie View U., Hempstead, Tex., 1941-42; asst. prof. So. U., Baton Rouge, 1943-45, 49-51; tchr. N.Y.C. Bd. Edn., 1954-60; instr. Bklyn. Coll., CUNY, 1960-64, asst. prof., 1964-69; assoc. prof. York Coll., CUNY, 1969-71, prof., 1972-75; prof. music Harvard U., Cambridge, Mass., 1976-87, chmn. dept. Afro-Am. studies, 1976-79, prof. emeritus, 1987—. Concert pianist, 1940-55; Author: The Buxheim Organ Book, 1963, The Music of Black Americans: A History, 1971, 2d edit., 1983, Readings in Black American Music, 1971, 2d edit., 1983, Anonymous Chansons in MS El Escorial Biblioteca del Monasterio, IV a 24, 1981, Biographical Dictionary of Afro-American and African Musicians, 1982; editor, pub.: The Black Perspective in Music, 1973—; contbr. articles to profl. jours., encys. Active Girl Scouts U.S.A., 1954-63; chmn. mgmt. com. Queens Area YWCA, 1970-73. Recipient Alumni Achievement award U. Chgo., 1970; Deems Taylor award ASCAP, 1973; NEH grantee, 1979-83. Mem. Internat. Musicol. Soc., Am. Musicol. Soc. (dir. 1974-76), Sonneck Am. Music Soc. (bd. dirs. 1986-88), Renaissance Soc., NAACP, Phi Beta Kappa (hon. Radcliffe Coll.), Alpha Kappa Alpha. Home: 115-05 179th St Saint Albans NY 11434 Office: Harvard U Cambridge MA 02138

SOUTHWORTH, LOIS GILL, educator, psychologist; b. Atoka, Okla., July 21, 1915; d. James Hugh and Lois Elizabeth (McCuiston) Gill; B.S., NE Okla. State U., 1934; Ed.S., U. Tenn., 1973; m. James Larry Southworth, Feb. 29, 1936 (dec.); children—John Scott, Bruce Alan. Tchr., Strayer Coll., Washington, 1938-39, Ballard Sch., N.Y.C., 1939-45; pvt. practice psychology, Knoxville, Tenn., 1964-68; asst. prof. dept. child and family studies, U. Tenn., Knoxville, 1967-83, ret., researcher Appalachian Children and Families. Active Knoxville Symphony Assn., Dulin Art Gallery Assn., Women's Center of Knoxville, Children's Internat. Village, Common Cause. Lic. psychol. examiner, Tenn. Mem. AAUP, AAUW, Am. Psychol. Assn., Nat. Assn. Psychology in the Schs., Nat. Assn. of Disability Examiners, Nat. Assn. of Children with Learning Disabilities, LWV, NOW, Pi Lambda Theta, Phi Delta Kappa. Democrat. Unitarian. Club: Women's Aux. of Knoxville Acad. Medicine. Author: Screening and Evaluating the Young Child—A Handbook of Instruments to Use from Infancy to Six Years, 1980; contbr. articles in field to profl. jours. Home: 921 Kenesaw Ave Knoxville TN 37919

SOUTHWORTH, MARY ANN, accountant; b. Denver, Aug. 27, 1957; d. Charles Henry and Helen Mercedes (Blakeslee) Mitchell; m. Dale Lee Southworth, May 12, 1984. BS, Colo. State U., 1979. CPA, Colo. Staff acct. Joe Heard CPA, P.C., Englewood, Colo., 1979-80; staff acct. Ben May CPA, Englewood, 1980-83, CPA, 1983—; cons. Variety Rocky Mountain Heart Fund for Children, Englewood, 1985—. Treas. bd. dirs. South Slope Homeowners Assn., Englewood, 1983-86. Mem. Am. Inst. CPA's, Colo. Soc. CPA's. Presbyterian. Club: Denver Womens' Bowling Assn. (sec., treas. various leagues 1982—). Home: 6127 S Windermere Way Littleton CO 80120

SOUZA, JUDI ANN, insurance company executive; b. Hutchinson, Kans., Aug. 2, 1946; d. Ernest William and Ila May (Woodward) Shelanskey; m. David Joe Almgren (div. 1976); 1 child, Matthew Joseph; m. William J. Sourza Jr. (div. 1985). AA in Banking and Fin., San Jose City Coll., 1970. Cert. sr. escrow officer, Calif., Oreg., Mich. Credit mgr. Paul's Jewelers, San Jose, 1963-64; vault teller The Bank of Am., Santa Clara, Calif., 1964-66; ops. officer The Bank of Calif., San Jose, 1966-70; mgr. escrow/title Transamerica Title Inc., Holland, Mich., 1970-74; escrow mgr. Transamerica Title Ins. Co., San Jose, 1980-83; asst. mgr. patient svcs. O'Connor Hosp., San Jose, 1974-77; asst. v.p. Deschutes Co. Title, Bend, Oreg., 1977-80; mgr. Am. Title Ins. Co., Campbell, Calif., 1983—; instr. Oreg. Community Coll., Bend; lectr. in field; conductor seminars in field. Mem. Calif. Escrow Assn. (edn. chmn. 1988), Oreg. Escrow Assn. (pres. 1979), Am. Escrow Assn. (dir./del. 1979), Nat. Notary Assn., Cen. Oreg. Multiple Listing Service (sec. 1979), C. of C. Republican. Baptist. Office: Am Title Ins Co of Miami 950 E Campbell Ave Campbell CA 95008

SOUZA, MAURENE GLORIA, toy company executive; b. Providence, July 31, 1949; d. Joseph Antonio and Georgina Irene (Matta) S. B.A. in English, U. R.I., 1973. Copywriter, Outlet Dept. Stores, Providence, 1971-73; copywriter Hasbro Industries, Pawtucket, R.I., 1973-78, product mgr., 1978-81, mktg. dir., 1981-84, assoc. v.p. mktg., 1984—. Bd. dirs. Children's Mus. of R.I. Recipient Merrill Hassenfeld award Hasbro Inc., 1986; named One of top 50 corp. women to watch, 1987. Office: Hasbro Industries 1027 Newport Ave Pawtucket RI 02861

SOVIE, MARGARET DOE, nursing administrator, college dean; b. Ogdensburg, N.Y., July 7, 1934; d. William Gordon and Mary Rose (Bruyere) Doe; m. Alfred L. Sovie, May 8, 1954; 1 child, Scot Marc. Student, U. Rochester, 1950-51; diploma in nursing, St. Lawrence State Hosp. Sch. Nursing, Ogdensburg, 1954; postgrad., St. Lawrence U., 1956-60; BS in Nursing summa cum laude, Syracuse U., 1964, MS in Edn., 1968, PhD in Edn., 1972. Staff nurse, clin. instr. St. Lawrence State Hosp., Odgensburg, 1954-55, instr. nursing, 1955-62; staff nurse Good Shepherd Hosp., Syracuse, 1962; nursing supr. SUNY Upstate Med. Ctr., Syracuse, 1963-65, inservice instr., 1965-66, edn. dir. and coordinator nursing service, 1966-71, asst. dean Coll. Health Related Professions, 1972-84, assoc. prof. nursing, 1973-76, dir. continuing edn. in nursing, 1974-76, assoc. dean and dir. div. continuing edn. Coll. Health Related Professions, 1974-76; spl. assignment in pres.'s office SUNY Upstate Med. Ctr. and Syracuse U., 1972-73; assoc. dean for nursing U. Rochester, N.Y., 1976-88, assoc. prof. nursing, 1976-85, prof., 1985-88; assoc. dir. for nursing Strong Meml. Hosp., U. Rochester Med. Ctr., 1976-88; dir. nursing, assoc. exec. dir. Hosp. U. Pa., Phila., 1988—, assoc. dean for nursing practice, Jane Delano prof. nursing adminstrn. Sch. Nursing, 1988—; nursing coordinator and project dir. Cen. N.Y. Regional Med. Program, Syracuse, 1968-71; mem. edn. dept. State Bd. Nursing, Albany, N.Y., 1974-84, chmn., 1981-83, chmn. practice com., 1975-80, mem. joint practice com., 1975-80, vice chmn., 1980-81; mem. adv. com. to clin. nurse scholars program Robert Wood Johnson Found., Princeton, N.J., 1982—; adj. assoc. prof. Syracuse U. Sch. Nursing, 1973-76; mem. Gov.'s Health Adv. Panel N.Y. State Health Planning Commn., 1976-82, task force on health manpower policy, 1978, informal support networks sect. steering com., 1980; mem. health manpower tng. and utilization task force State N.Y. Commn. on Health Edn. and Illness Prevention, 1979; mem. task force on nursing personnel N.Y. State Health Adv. Council, 1980; mem. adv. panel on nursing services U.S. Pharm. Conv. Inc., Washington, 1985—; cons. Nat. Ctr. for Services Research and Health Care Tech. Assessment, Rockville, Md., 1987—; mem. various other adv. coms.; lectr. in field. Mem. editorial bd. Health Care Supr., 1982-87; mem. editorial bd., manuscrpit rev. panel Nursing Econs., 1983—; manuscript rev. panel Nursing Outlook, 1987—; contbr. articles to profl. jours., chpts. to books. Mem. bd. visitors Sch. Nursing U. Md., Balt., 1984—; mem. bd. mgrs. Strong Meml. Hosp., Rochester, 1983-88; bd. dirs. Monroe County Assn. for Hearing, Rochester, 1979-82, Vis. Nurse Service Rochester and Monroe County, 1978. Spl. nurse research fellow NIH, 1971-72; grantee various orgns.;. Fellow Am. Acad. Nursing (program com. 1980-81, task force on hosp. nursing 1981-83); mem. Inst. Medicine, Am. Nurses Assn. (nat. rev. com. for expanded role programs 1975-78, site visitor to programs requesting accreditation 1976-78, cabinet on nursing services 1986-88, cert. bd. nursing adminstrn. 1983-86), Am. Orgn. Nurse Execs. (standards task force 1987), N.Y. State Nurses Assn. (med. surg. nursing group, chmn. edn. com. dist. 4 1974-76, chmn. community planning group for nursing dist. 4 1974-76, council on regional planning in nursing 1974-76, del. to conv. 1978, Nursing Service Adminstrn. award 1985), Sigma Theta Tau, Pi Lambda Theta. Republican. Roman Catholic. Club: Locust Hill Country (Rochester). Office: Hosp U Pa 3400 Spruce St Philadelphia PA 19104-4283

SOWELL, VIRGINIA MURRAY, educator; b. Presidio, Tex., Mar. 23, 1931; d. Marshall Bishop and Mary Alice (Daniel) Murray; BA, Sam Houston State U., 1951; MA, Trinity U., 1957; PhD, U. Tex., 1975; children—John Houston, III, Paul Orin. Tchr. San Antonio (Tex.) Ind. Sch. Dist., 1951-52, 1955-58; asst. prof. San Antonio Coll., 1969-75, assoc. prof., 1976—; assoc. prof. spl. edn. Tex. Tech. U., Lubbock, 1976-85, asst. v.p. acad. affairs, 1984—. Bd. govs. Tex. Sch. for Blind, v.p., 1983-86, pres., 1986-89; adv. com. Iowa Braille and Sight Saving Sch.; dir. vols. Witte Mus.; mem. research adv. com. Tex. Tech. U., 1981-82, pres. faculty senate, 1982-83; bd. dirs. Developmental Edn., Birth through Two, 1977—, SW Lighthouse for the Blind, 1984—, v.p., 1987, chmn. bd., 1988; pres. elect Visually Handicapped, 1986-87, pres, 1987-88. HEW grantee, 1977—; recipient Sammie K. Rankin award Tex. Assn. for Edn. and Rehab. of Blind and Visually Handicapped. Mem. Council for Exceptional Children (bd. govs. 1982-85, pres. div. visually handicapped 1987-88), Tex. Council Exceptional Children (treas. 1981-85), Tex. Div. Children with Learning Disabilities, Internat. Reading Assn., Assn. for Edn. and Rehab. of Blind (pres. S. Central region 1984-86, bd. dirs. 1988—), Am. Ednl. Research Assn., Assn. Edn. of Visually Handicapped (pres. South Central region 1984-86), Tex. Assn. Coll. Tchrs., AAUP, Phi Delta Kappa, Delta Kappa Gamma, Zeta Tau Alpha. Republican. Episcopalian. Home: 4610 28th St Lubbock TX 79410 Office: Tex Tech U Office Acad Affairs Box 4609 Lubbock TX 79409

SOWERS, KAY LINDAMOOD, realtor; b. Eureka, Kans., Feb. 23, 1941; d. John Lewis and Hazel Ruth (Gilbert) Lindamood; m. Lloyd Wayne Sowers, Aug. 4, 1965; children: Derek Wayne, Jilinda Kay. BS in Home Econs., Kans. State U., 1963. Home service advisor Kans. Gas & Electric Co., Ft. Scott, 1963-66; home econs. tchr. Bartlesville (Okla.) Pub. Schs., 1967-68; realtor assoc. Hopper Realty Co., Bartlesville, 1976-81; realtor, co-owner Wilkins & Sowers Realtors, Bartlesville, 1981—; Mem. community adv. council First Nat. Bank Bartlesville, 1987—. Guild chair United Meth. Women, Bartlesville, 1974. Mem. Nat. Assn. Realtors, Okla. Assn. Realtors, Women's Council Realtors, Bus. and Profl. Women (sec. Ft. Scott 1963-66), Bartlesville Bd. Realtors (pres. 1987), Kappa Alpha Theta, Omicron Nu, Phi Upsilon Omicron. Republican. Methodist. Home: 5901 Martin Pl Bartlesville OK 74006

SPACEK, SISSY (MARY ELIZABETH), actress; b. Quitman, Tex., Dec. 25, 1949; d. Edwin S. and Virginia S.; m. Jack Fisk, 1974; 1 child, Schuyler Elizabeth. Student, Lee Strasberg Theatrical Inst. Actress: (films) Prime Cut, 1972, Ginger in the Morning, 1972, Badlands, 1974, Carrie, 1976 (Acad. award nomination for best actress 1976), Three Women, 1977, Welcome to L.A., 1977, Heartbeat, 1980, Coal Miner's Daughter, 1980 (Acad. award for best actress 1980), Raggedy Man, 1981, Missing, 1982, The River, 1984, Marie, 1985, 'Night Mother, 1986, Crimes of the Heart, 1986, Violets Are Blue, 1986, (TV movies) The Girls of Huntington House, 1973, The Migrants, 1973, Katherine, 1975, Verna: USO Girl, 1978; guest host: Saturday Night Live, 1977. Named Best Actress for Carrie, Nat. Soc. Film Critics, 1976, Best Supporting Actress, N.Y. Film Critics, 1977. Office: care Creative Artists 1888 Century Park East Suit 1400 Los Angeles CA 90067 *

SPADA, NANCY ELLEN, research director; b. Huntington, N.Y.; d. Peter John and Eleanor Dorothy (Ward) S. AAS, SUNY, Farmingdale, 1972; BSBA, Ohio State U., 1981, MBA, 1983. Security analyst State Tchrs. Retirement System, Columbus, Ohio, 1981-82, E.I. DuPont de Nemours, Wilmington, Del., 1983-86; dir. research Valley Forge (Pa.) Asset Mgmt., 1986—. Mem. Fin. Analysts Assn. Office: Valley Forge Asset Mgmt 120 S Warner Rd Box 837 Valley Forge PA 19482

SPADARO, CHARLOTTE, lawyer, mayor; b. N.Y.C., June 29, 1941; d. Sol and Eva (Malach) Rubinfeld; student UCLA, 1958-60; BA, Calif. State U., 1962; JD, U. So. Calif., 1969; m. George Spadaro, Apr. 8, 1960; children: Michele, Jonathan. Tchr. English, Portola Jr. High Sch., Orange, Calif., 1962-63; substitute tchr. English and French, Santa Ana (Calif.) Unified and Orange (Calif.) Unified Sch. Dists., 1963-64; admitted to Calif. bar, 1970; law clk. Dist. Ct. of Appeals, Los Angeles, 1969; mem. firm Eliot B. Feldman, Los Angeles, 1970—; vice mayor City of Beverly Hills, Calif., 1986, mayor, 1986-87. Beverly Hills Gen. Plan Update Study, 1979-80; mem. Nat. Com. for Citizens in Edn.; safety chmn. Beverly Hills PTA Council, 1978-79; mem. early childhood edn. adv. com., sch. improvement site council Beverly Vista Sch.; mem. Beverly Hills Unified Sch. Dist. Bd. Edn., 1979-83, pres., 1983; mem. Beverly Hills City Council, 1984. Mem. Women Lawyers Assn., Ephebian Soc., LWV (fin. chmn. Santa Ana 1965), U. So. Calif. Alumni Assn., World Affairs Council. Home: 221 S El Camino Dr Beverly Hills CA 90212 Office: 9465 Wilshire Blvd Beverly Hills CA 90212

SPADAVECCHIA, CHARMAINE T., marketing professional; b. Kingston, Jamaica, West Indies; came to U.S., 1970; d. Albert and Veronica Berril (Hofatt) Chin; m. Francesco Spadavecchia; 1 child, Nicolé. Student, U. West Indies, Kingston, Fashion Inst. Tech., N.Y.C., 1980-81, NYU, 1987-88. Coordinator TRG Communications, Inc., N.Y.C., 1982-83, project mgr., 1983-88; account exec. TRG Communications, Inc., 1988—. Mem. Astoria Civic Assn. Mem. Japan Soc., Research Inst., PMA Advisor, Mktg. Communications. Club: Salle Social (Astoria, N.Y.). Home: 25-47 14th St Astoria NY 11102 Office: TRG Communications Inc 10 E 34th St New York NY 10016

SPADY, CALLIE JEANETTA, social worker, human resource administrator; b. Townsend, Va., Aug. 24, 1938; d. Willie Lee and Rosie Mae (Reid) S. Student Kittrell Jr. Coll., 1956-58; B.A., Allen U., 1961. Cert. civil service investigator. Tchr. English, Marion County Sch. Bd., Ocala, Fla., 1961-62; children's counselor Human Resources Adminstrn. Bur. Child Welfare, N.Y.C., 1962-76, civil service investigator, 1976—, asst. to IRS coordinator, 1980-84; asst. tchr. Sunshine Nursery Schs., Bronx, N.Y., 1968-76. Active Met. Opera Guild, Friends of Carnegie Hall, 55th St. Dance Theater Found., Transit Riders in Pursuits, 1983—, ACLU, Archdiocese of N.Y. Cardinal's Ann. Appeal, N.Y. State Tenant and Neighborhood Coalition, 1983-84; vol. sr. citizen program St. Patrick Cathedral, N.Y.C., 1983-84; mem. Concerned Democratic Coalition No. Manhattan, Audubon Reform Dem. Club, N.Y.C., 1982—; mem. payroll deduction com. Combined Mcpl. Campaign, N.Y.C., 1982—; mem. lobby corp. LWV City N.Y., 1981—; mem. legis. com. N.Y.C. Opera Guild-Lincoln Ctr., 1983—; mem. N.Y.C. Edn. and Environ. Coms., Exec. Community Bd. No. 12, N.Y.C., 1984; charter mem. Statue of Liberty, 1985—, Ronald Reagan Trust, 1985—; mem. Rep. Nat. Com., 1985—; mem. Dem. Nat. Com., 1985—; dep. gov., nat. advisor Am. Biog. Inst., 1985—; dep. gen. dir. Internat. Biog. Centre, 1987— ; Recipient Twenty Years Dedicated Service award Human Resources Adminstrn., 1983. Mem. Nat. Assn. Social Workers, Nat. Assn. Black Social Workers, Assn. for Study of Afro-Am. Life and History, Nat. Assn. Female Execs., AAUW, Internat. Fedn. Bus. and Profl. Women (treas. local chpt. 1981-82), NAACP (participant legal def. and ednl. fund 1983), AFL-CIO Am. Fedn. State, County and Mcpl. Employees, N.Y.C. Civil Service Ret. Employees Assn., N.Y. Urban League, Coalition of 100 Black Women, Nat. Council Negro Women, Internat. Platform Assn., Nat. Trust for Hist. Preservation, Am. Inst. for Cancer Research, Internat. Biog. Assn., N.Y. State Bus. and Profl. Women, Am. Assn. Ret. Persons (Andrus Found.), Assn. for Childhood Edn. Internat., Am. Biog., Inc., World Inst. Achievement. Roman Catholic. Club: Womens (com. on status of women 1984) (N.Y.C.). Home: Washbridge Station PO Box 211 New York NY 10033 Office: Human Resources Adminstrn Bur Child Support - Central Office 6th Floor 66 Leonard St New York NY 10013

SPAGNOLI, NANCY ANN, trust administrator; b. Springfield, Mass., Apr. 27, 1942; d. Albert and Florence (Tuber) S. AB in Bus. Adminstrn., Holyoke Community Coll., 1983. Bookkeeper, credit mgr. Bart Jewelers, Springfield, Mass., 1963-73; credit investigator Shawmut First Bank and Trust, Springfield, 1973, collector, adjuster, 1973-77, estate operations clk., 1977-81, adminstrv. asst., 1981-83, asst. account adminstr., 1983-85, trust adminstr., 1985—. Advisor Jr. Achievement, Springfield, 1977-78, 79-80; vol. channel 57 Action Auction, Springfield, 1977-85, Read Aloud Sch. Vol. Program, Springfield, 1986, 87, Easter Seal Telethon, Springfield, 1987; mem. adv. bd. Spl. Council Elderly Victim's Crime, Springfield, Mass.; exec. officer, treas. Community Care Mental Health, Springfield. Mem. Holyoke Community Coll. Alumni. Democrat. Office: Shawmut First Bank and Trust Co 127 State St Springfield MA 01103

SPAHR, CAROLE, school system administrator; b. Harrisburg, Pa., Mar. 26, 1938; d. Percy N. and Catherine E. Dorwart; m. William Spahr, Nov. 10, 1956; children: Pamela Spahr Fuller, Jill Spahr Siegfried, Angela, Brian. AS in Edn., Harrisburg (Pa.) Area Community Coll., 1971; BS in Elem. Edn., York Coll. Pa., 1973; MEd, Millersville U., 1976; EdD, U. Pa., 1982. Cert. elem. tchr., reading specialist, elem. prin., supt., Pa. Tchr. West Shore Sch. Dist., Lemoyne, Pa., 1973-75, reading specialist, 1975-80; prin., asst. supt. Columbia (Pa.) Borough Sch. Dist., 1980-85; supt. schs. Annville (Pa.)-Cleona Sch. Dist., 1985—; mem. dist. task force Gov. of Pa. Bd. dirs. Mental Health/Mental Retardation Ctr., Lebanon, Pa., 1985—, local task force on mental retardation, East Petersnburg, Pa., 1985—; mem. exec. com. Women's Caucus, Harrisburg, 1986—, Lebanon County extension 4-H, 1986—. Recipient Fellows award Nat. Assn. Elem. Sch. Prins., 1983; mem. to Cen. Pa. Sports Hall of Fame, 1987. Mem. Am. Assn. Sch. Adminstrs., Pa. Assn. Sch. Adminstrs. (exec. com.), Pa. Sch. Bds. Assn., Female Exec. Educators, Bus. and Profl. Women, Delta Kappa Gamma. Home: 315 Reigerts Ln Annville PA 17003 Office: Annville-Cleona Sch Dist S White Oak St Annville PA 17003

SPAIN, JAYNE BAKER, corporate executive, educator; b. San Francisco; d. Lawrence Ian and Marguerite (Buchanan) Baker; student U. Calif. at Berkeley, 1944-47, Music U. Cin., 1947-50; LL.D., Edgecliff Coll., Cin., 1969; Dr. Pub. Service, George Washington U., 1970; LL.D., U. Cin., 1971, Dumbarton Coll., 1972, Springfield (Mass.) Coll., 1973, Gallaudet Coll., Washington, 1973; L.H.D. Bryant Coll., 1972, Russell Sage Coll., Troy, N.Y., 1973, Loyola Coll., Balt., 1975; m. John A. Spain, July 14, 1952; children—Jeffry Alan, Jon Kimberly. Pres., Alvey-Ferguson Co., Cin., 1952-66, pres. Alvey-Ferguson Operations div. Litton Industries, Inc., 1966-70, also dir. parent co., 1970—; vice chmn. CSC, 1971—; sr. v.p. Gulf Oil Corp., Pitts., from 1975; Disting. vis. prof. and exec.-in-residence George Washington U., Washington, 1979—; dir. Beatrice Foods, Chgo., Ohio Nat. Life Ins., Cin. Vice chmn. Pres.'s Com. on Employment Handicapped, 1966—; participant internat. trade fairs U.S. Depts. State, Commerce, Europe, North Africa, 1961-66, mem. trade and investment mission, India, 1965; mem. U.S. com. Internat. Council Social Welfare; mem. Pres.'s Adv. Com. on Productivity; dir. Pvt. Sector Council, Washington, Dean's Adv. com. Coll. of Bus. U. Cin.; mem. Internat. Soc. Rehab. Disabled; mem. adv. com. sheltered workshops U.S. sec. labor; mem. Ohio Gov.'s Commn. on Status of Women; mem. bldg. com. Children's Med. Center, Cin. Bd. dirs., past pres. Convalescent Hosp. Children, Cin., Greater Cin. Hosp. Council, Children's Neuromuscular Diagnostic Center, Cin., Cin. Sci. Center; bd. dirs. President's Commn. on Personnel Interchange; chmn. bd. trustees Fed. Women's Award; mem. dean's adv. council Coll. Bus. Adminstrn. U. Cin.; chmn. Found. of Ams. for the Handicapped; bd. dirs. Recs. for the Blind. Recipient Distinguished Service award for work overseas blind People Com., Washington, 1965; Migel medal Am. Found. Blind, N.Y., 1966; Golden Plate award industry Acad. Achievement, Dallas, 1967; Top Hat award Bus. and Profl. Women's Clubs. Am., N.Y., 1967. Mem. Conveyor Equipment Mfrs. Assn. (sec., treas., dir. 1960-63), Machinery and Allied Products Inst., Am. Mgmt. Assn. (dir.) Internat. Platform Assn. Episcopalian. Contbr. articles to profl. jours. Home: 700 New Hampshire Ave NW Washington DC 20037 Office: George Washington U Sch Govt and Bus Washington DC 20052

SPALDING, AMY JANETTE, accountant; b. Ann Arbor, Mich., Nov. 9, 1963; d. Martin John and Ruth Elaine (Wolter) S. BBA, Western Mich. U., 1985; postgrad., Walsh Coll., 1988—. Asst. br. mgr. Nat. Bank Detroit, 1985-86; mktg. cons. Promark Innovations, Southfield, Mich., 1986; staff acct. Molly Maid, Inc., Ann Arbor, 1986—. Vol. Friends of Mich. Parade Assn., Detroit, 1986, U. Mich. Hosp., Ann Arbor, 1987. Mem. Am. Mktg. Assn., Western Mich. U. Alumni Assn., Detroit Inst. Arts (founding). Home: 46121 Willage Green Dr Belleville MI 48111

SPALDING, DIANA J(ESUROGA), computer systems company executive; b. Miami, Fla., July 22, 1960; d. Richard Steven and Cleah June (Finley) S.; m. Richard Thomas Jesuroga, Feb. 16, 1982 (div. Feb. 1986). BA, U. Colo., 1983. Cert. paraprofl. counselor. Computer coder Dun & Bradstreet, N.Y.C., 1978, Parsippany, N.J., 1978-79; computer scientist NOAA/Program Regional Observing and Forecasting Services, Boulder, Colo., 1981-84; engr. NBI, Inc., Boulder, 1984-87; engr. Bell Labs, 1988—. Vol., counselor and pub. speaker Boulder County Safehouse, 1985—; peace activist, contbr. Women's Internat. League for Peace and Freedom, Boulder, 1985—, action chair, 1987; affiliate Friendship City Project, 1985—; founding mem. Word Processors for Peace, 1986—; suporting mem. N.Am. Congress on Latin Am., 1986—, Am. Civil Liberties Union, 1986, Greenpeace, 1986—, Amnesty Internat., 1984—, Found. Nat. Progress, 1985—, Rocky Mountain Peace Ctr., 1985—. Mem. Oxfam Am., The Nature Conservancy, Nat. Pub. Radio (KGNU), The Nation Assocs., Am. Peace Test, Nat. Hon. Soc. Clubs: Colo. Mountain. Avocations: hiking, bicycling, cross-country skiing. Office: Bell Labs PO Box 13242 Boulder CO 80308

SPALDING, ELAINE R., sales executive; b. Elmhurst, N.Y., June 26, 1940; d. John Arpod and Thelma (Smith) Rado; student Coll. Wooster, 1958-60; m. Larry Spalding, Dec. 24, 1966; children—Timothy A., Linda L., Med. sec. Duke U. Med. Center, Durham, N.C., 1967-70; adminstrv. sec. Tampa Heights Hosp., Tampa, Fla., 1973-74; nat. distbr. Seyforth Labs., Inc., Dallas, 1975-79; nat. distbr. Futuron Industries, Inc., Dallas, 1979-83, dir. Futuron Distbr. Orgn., 1979—, nat. distbr. Slendernow Internat., 1984—. Aide to Pinellas County Commr. Barbara Sheen Todd, 1980—; v.p. Peninsula Republican. Club, 1982—. Recipient Distbr. of Year award, 1980, Spirit of Futuron award, 1981. Mem. Women in Mgmt. Address: 1211 Brookside Dr Clearwater FL 34624

SPALDING, JUDY ANN, computer programmer, analyst; b. Bardstown, Ky., Apr. 17, 1960; d. Joseph Leo and Shirley Marie (Culver) S. Cert. acct. and bus. mgmt., Sullivan Jr. Coll., 1979; student, U. Louisville, 1981—. Computer operator, account clk. Modern Industries, Louisville, 1979-80; computer programmer Druthers, Inc., Louisville, 1980-82; computer programmer, analyst Meidinger, Inc., Louisville, 1982-85, Commonwealth Land Title Co., Louisville, 1985-87; cons. analyst Meidinger, Inc., Louisville, 1987—. Vol. John Y. Brown for Gov. campaign, Louisville, 1987. Mem. Nat. Assn. Female Execs. Democrat. Roman Catholic. Home: 8616 Longborough Way Louisville KY 40299 Office: Mercer Meidinger Hanson 1500 Meidinger Tower Louisville KY 40202

SPALDING, MARY BRANCH, psychologist, psychotherapist; b. Roanoke, Va., Oct. 27, 1938; d. Branch and Mary (Hancock) S.; m. John H. Land, June 13, 1964 (div. 1974); m. Hugh C. Welborn, May 25, 1985; 1 child, Catherine. BA in Art History, Vassar Coll., 1964; MA in Psychology in Edn., Columbia U., 1972, MEd in Counseling Psychology, 1974; EdD in Counseling and Applied Human Devel., Columbia U. Tchrs. Coll., 1979. Counselor, research asst. Ruth M. Knight Counseling Service, Manhattan Sch. Music, N.Y.C., 1971-76; psychologist Rockland County Community Mental Health Ctr., Pomona, N.Y., 1975—; pvt. practice psychotherapy Nyack, N.Y., 1978—; psychotherapist Eating Disorders Team Approach, Rockland C unty, N.Y., 1987. Mem. Rockland Ctr. for The Arts, Nyack, Met. Mus. Art, N.Y.C., Nat. Mus. Women in Arts, Washington. Fellow

Am. Orthopsychiat. Assn.; mem. Am. Assn. for Counseling and Devel., Am. Psychol. Assn., Rockland County Psychol. Soc., Sierra Club. Democrat. Office: 53 S Broadway Nyack NY 10960

SPALE, CAROL ANNE, real estate appraiser, broker; b. Pitts., Dec. 10, 1938; d. James Joseph and Margaret Rose (Dugan) Klaus; m. Pasquale James DeFusco (div. 1966); m. Robert Louis Spale; children: Ana, William, Christina, Nancy, Charles. BA, Calif. State U., Northridge, 1975. Real estate broker Coldwell Banker, Simi Valley, Calif., 1966-85; ind. appraiser Simi Valley, Calif., 1980-85, Newhall, Calif., 1985-87. Bd. dirs. Vista del Monte Assn., Simi Valley, 1968-70, Friendly Valley Villas Homeowners, Newhall, 1985-87. Named Realtor of the Yr. Simi Valley Bd. Realtors, 1979. Mem. AAUW.

SPALLA, ANNE BUCK, interior designer; b. Chgo., June 16; d. W. Gerald and Rita Bernadine (Maher) Buck; 1 child, Frank Gerald. BEd, Chgo. State U., 1959, postgrad, 1965; postgrad, Roosevelt U., 1960-61; cert. in interior design with honors, Seminole Coll., 1986. Cert. tchr., Chgo. Tchr. Chgo. Pub. Schs., 1959-63, 64-71, Huntsville (Ala.) Pub. Schs., 1961-62, Dallas Pub. Schs., 1971-72; artist Woodstock (Ill.) Gallery, 1975-77; interior designer Joan Carron Interiors, Lake Forest, Ill., 1977-79; pres. Anne Spalla Interiors, Inc., Longwood, Fla., 1980—; lectr. interior design Seminole Coll., Sanford, Fla., 1986; interior designer Orlando (Fla.) Opera Showhouse, 1985-86, March of Dimes Gourmet Gala, 1987-88; soloist Orlando Opera Edn. Program, 1979-82; mem. Orlando Opera Co., 1979—. Contbr. articles to various publs. Vol. Birth Edn. Tng. Acceptance, Orlando, 1979-82. Mundelein Coll. scholar., 1955-56. Mem. Am. Soc. Interior Design (assoc., chmn. fund-raising com. Orlando chpt.), Nat. Assn. Female Execs., Nat. Trust for Hist. Preservation. Republican. Roman Catholic. Clubs: Horizon (Orlando) (founder); Sweetwater Country (Longwood) (founder). Office: 150 W Jessup Ave Longwood FL 32750

SPANDORFER, MERLE SUE, artist, educator; b. Balt., Sept. 4, 1934; d. Simon Louis and Bernice P. (Jacobson) S.; m. Lester M. Spandorfer, June 17, 1956; children: Cathy, John. Student, Syracuse U., 1952-54; B.S., U. Md., 1956. Mem. faculty Cheltenham (Pa.) Sch. Fine Arts, 1969-88, dir. edn., 1970-88; instr. printmaking Tyler Sch. Art Temple U., Phila., 1980-84; faculty Pratt Graphics Ctr., N.Y.C., 1985-86. One woman shows Richard Feigen Gallery, N.Y.C., 1970, U. Pa., 1974, Phila. Coll. Textiles and Sci., 1977, Ericson Gallery, N.Y.C., 1978, 79, R.I. Sch. Design, 1980, Syracuse U., 1981, Marian Locks Gallery, Phila., 1973, 78, 82, Temple U., 1984, Tyler Sch. Art, 1985, University City Sci. Ctr., 1987, Gov.'s Residence, 1988; group shows Bklyn. Mus. Art, 1973, San Francisco Mus. Art, 1973, Balt. Mus. Art, 1970, 71, 74, Phila. Mus. Art, 1972, 77, Fundacio Joan Miro, Barcelona, Spain, 1977, Del. Mus. Art, Wilmington, 1978, Carlsberg Glyptotek Mus., Copenhagen, 1980, Moore Coll. Art, Phila., 1982, Tyler Sch. Art, 1983; represented in permanent collections Met. Mus. Art, N.Y.C., Whitney Mus. Am. Art, N.Y.C., Mus. Modern Art, N.Y.C., The Israel Mus., Balt. Mus. (gov's prize and purchase award 1970), Phila. Mus. Art (purchase award 1977), Toyoh Bijutsu Gakko, Tokyo, Library of Congress, Temple U. Recipient Md. Inst. Art Balt. Mus., 1971; recipient Graphics Joan Mondale, Wallingford (Pa.) Art Ctr., 1978. Mem. Artist Equity, Am. Color Print Soc. (graphics 1980), Pa. Art Edn. Assn. (Outstanding Art Educator 1981-82), Coll. Art Assn. Jewish. Office: 307 E Gowen Ave Philadelphia PA 19119

SPANGLER, DAISY KIRCHOFF, educational consultant; b. Lancaster, Pa., Jan. 27, 1913; d. Frank Augustus and Lida Flaharty (Forewood) Kirchoff; BS, Millersville State Coll., 1963; MEd, Pa. State U., 1966, EdD, 1972; PhD, Stanton U., 1974; m. Francis R. Cosgrove Spangler, June 3, 1939 (dec.); children: Stephen Russell, Michael Denis. Tchr. rural sch., Providence, Pa., 1933-35, Rapho Twp., Pa., 1935-42, Mastersonville, Pa., 1942-51; elem. sch. prin. Manheim Central, Pa., 1952-66; tchr., Manheim, Pa., 1967-68; assoc. prof. elem. edn. Millersville U., Pa., 1968-78, prof. emeritus, 1978—, advisor Kappa Delta Phi, 1968-88; ednl. cons., 1978—. Dist. chmn. ARC, 1965-66; mem. Hempfield PTA, 1966-67. Mem. Pa. Edn. Assn., Pa. Elem. Prins. Assn., Assn. Pa. State Coll. and Univ. Profs., Nat., Lancaster (pres. 1963-64) prins. assns., Pa. Assn. Ret. State Employees, Pa. Assn. State Retirees, Lancaster Area Ret. Pub. Sch. Employees Assn., Am. Ednl. Research Assn., Manheim Tchrs. Assn. (pres. 1964-65), Hempfield Profl. Women, Am. Assn. Ret. Persons (chpt. pres. 1983-85, 88-89), Pi Lambda Theta (nat. com. 1980—, advisor Millersville U. 1968—, named outstanding advisor 1988—), Delta Kappa Gamma (pres. 1976-78). Lutheran (pres. Luth. Women 1966-67, 79-81). Club: Order Eastern Star. Home and Office: Route 7 Box 510 Manheim PA 17545

SPANGLER, NANCY LEE, school psychologist; b. Peoria, Ill., Apr. 4, 1949; d. Robert L. and Lerose (Hejda) S.; student Fla. So. Coll., Lakeland, 1967-68, We. Ill. U., Macomb, 1968-71; B.S. in Psychology, Bradley U., Peoria, Ill., 1972, M.A. in Psychology, 1974. Sch. psychology intern Spl. Edn. Coop. South Cook County, Chicago Heights, Ill., 1974-75; sch. psychologist Joliet (Ill.) Pub. Schs. Dist. 86, 1975—; supr. sch. psychology interns Joliet Pub. Schs., also coordinator diagnostic and related services. Named Exceptional Educator of Yr., Joliet Pub. Schs., 1983; cert. sch. psychologist, Ill. Mem. Ill. Sch. Psychology Assn., Nat. Assn. Sch. Psychologists, Delta Kappa Gamma. Methodist. Office: 420 N Raynor St Joliet IL 60435

SPANN, MARCIA MYERS, small business owner; b. Kokomo, Ind., Dec. 12, 1937; d. Lloyd Chester and Lillie Inez (Bennett) M.; m. Robert Allan Spann, Sept. 2, 1960 (div. Nov. 1978); children: Karen Alyn, Kimberly Jean. Student, U. Ariz., 1957-59. Lic. real estate broker, Calif. Coordinator fringe benefits Placentia (Calif.) Sch. Dist., 1973-74; counselor career edn. Scottsdale (Ariz.) Pub. Schs., 1975-77; asst. stock broker Shearson Am. Express, Phoenix, 1978-80; exec. v.p. Metro Home Loans, Scottsdale, 1980-85; acting gen. mgr. Marathon Home Loans, Santa Barbara, Calif., 1985-86; sr. account exec. San Diego, 1986-87; owner Sundance Mortgage, Inc., San Diego, 1987—. Contbr. articles to profl. jours. Vol. Animal Welfare Friends of County Animal Shelters, La Jolla, Calif., 1986-87. Mem. S. Coast Bus. Network, Nat. Assn. of Female Execs., Humane soc. of U.S., Am. Bus. Women's Assn. Democrat. Mem. First Christian Ch. Office: Sundance Mortgage 7220 Trade St Suite 101 San Diego CA 92121

SPANN, MARGARET ANN, banker; b. Mt. Pleasant, Tex., Feb. 16, 1930; d. Frank Minor and Clara (Arnold) C.; m. Alvin Loyd Spann, June 13, 1947; children: Karen Kay Spann Hall, Roger Caldwell, Stephen Bruce. Cert. Am. Inst. Banking; grad. Southwestern Grad. Sch. Banking-So. Meth. U., 1980. Clk.-typist Am. Liberty Oil Co., Mt. Pleasant, 1947-62, USDA-Soil Conservation, Mt. Pleasant, 1962-64; note teller credit First Nat. Bank, Mt. Pleasant, 1964-66, sec., 1966-77, asst. trust officer, 1977-80, trust officer (name changed to Inter First Bank Mt. Pleasant, N.A.), 1980—; mem. E. Tex. Estate Planning Council, Tyler, 1980—. Mem. Nat. Assn. Bank Women, Mt. Pleasant C. of C., Am. Inst. Banking (bd. dirs. E. Tex. chpt. 1978-80). Democrat. Presbyterian. Club: Pilot (Mt. Pleasant). Avocation: fishing. Office: First Republic Bank N Am PO Box 71 Mt Pleasant TX 75455

SPANN-BYRD, KAY, editor, writer; b. Sumter, S.C., Jan. 16; d. Willie and Susan (Mickens) Spann; m. Ulysses C. Byrd, Nov. 12, 1983. AA, Midlands Tech. Coll., 1978, U. S.C., 1980; BS, U. S.C., 1982. Dirs. asst. S.C. Gov.'s Physical Fitness Council, Columbia; adminstrv. support specialist, editor div. employment and tng. S.C. Gov.'s Office, Columbia, 1979-83; calendar, desk clk. S.C. Ho. Reps., Columbia, 1985; program monitor, editor pub. service employment monitoring Fifth Cir. Solicitors Office, Columbia, 1985-86; writer, mgr. Profl. Resume and Writing Service, Columbia, 1986; pubs. editor William S. Hall Psychiat. Inst., S.C. Dept. Mental Health, Columbia, 1987—; pres. Kconcepts, Columbia, 1986. Author: Twas the Night Before Halloween, 1980, The Legend of the Bunny, 1985; work published in New Voices in Am. Poetry, 1975, A Vision, A Verse, 1976. Home: PO Box 9847 Columbia SC 29209 Office: William S Hall Psychiat Inst PO Box 202 Columbia SC 29202

SPARAGO, DIANE KATHERINE, personnel executive; b. Bklyn., Aug. 26, 1946; d. Joseph William and Pauline Amon (Mandell) S. BA in Am. History, William Smith Coll., 1967. Portfolio analyst Walston & Co., N.Y.C., 1968-70; adminstrv. asst. N.Y.C. Dept. Hwys., 1970-73; office mgr. Cotter, Atkinson, Campbell, Kelsey & Hanna, Albuquerque, 1973; personnel dir. Lovelace-Bataan Med. Ctr., Albuquerque, 1974-77; personnel dir. Six Sandoval Indian Pueblos, Bernalillo, N.Mex., 1977-78, Automatic Data Processing, Dallas, 1982-85; personnel mgr. Sunbelt Corp., Albuquerque, 1978-79, Pertec Computer Corp., N.Mex. and N.J., 1979-81, Sutin, Thayer & Browne, Albuquerque, 1985—. Vol. N.Y.C. Reformed Dem. Com., 1969-73. Mem. Am. Soc. Personnel Adminstrn. (state dir. 1978-80, dist. dir. 1985-86, nat. employment practices com. 1981-85, practices com. 1987), N.Mex. Personnel Assn. (v.p. 1976, pres. 1977). Home: 9721 Snow Heights NE Albuquerque NM 87112 Office: Sutin Thayer & Browne PO Box 1945 Albuquerque NM 87103

SPARKIA, ALISA A., lawyer; b. Grand Rapids, Mich., Oct. 1, 1955; d. Roy B. and Renee Anne (Nemerov) Sparkia; m. John T. Moore, 1985. B.A., Mich. State U., 1977; J.D., U. Mich., 1981; cert. Nat. Inst. Trial Advocacy, 1983. Bar: N.Mex. 1981, U.S. Dist. Ct. N.Mex. 1982, U.S. Ct. Appeals (10th cir.) 1981. Assoc., Civerolo, Hansen & Wolf, Albuquerque, 1981-82, Faurot & Titus, P.A., Farmington, N.Mex., 1982-83, Ferguson & Lind, P.C., Albuquerque, 1983-84; sole practice, Albuquerque, 1984—. Active polit. campaigns and orgns. Mem. ABA, Assn. Trial Lawyers Am., N.Mex. Trial Lawyers Assn., Albuquerque Bar Assn., N.Mex. Bar Assn., Solo Practitioners Assn., Greater Albuquerque C. of C. Club: Civitan. Office: 500 Marquette NW Suite 301 Albuquerque NM 87102

SPARKMAN, MARY BARNWELL RHETT, abstractor; b. Boston, Oct. 18, 1956; d. Edward Heriot and Merle Helen (Hodges) S.; m. Keating L. Simons III, Aug. 12, 1978 (div. 1986); 1 child, Keating. BS, Coll. Charleston, 1980. Salesperson Hist. Charleston (S.C.) Reprodns., 1977-80; sec. John H. Bennett, Jr., Atty., Charleston, 1981-84; propr. M.R. Simons, Abstractor, Charleston, 1984—. Treas. Episcopal Ch. Women St. Michael's, Charleston, 1984—. Mem. Nat. Assn. Female Execs., Jr. League Charleston, Order St. Elegius.

SPARKMAN, MYRA DUKE, advertising agency executive; b. Cooperton, Okla., Nov. 13, 1926; d. Samuel Church Scott and Mamie Hardegree; m. Joe Neal Sparkman, May 14, 1944; (div. 1964); children—Susan Melissa Sparkman Cox, Gregory Scott. Student UCLA, 1967-68. Vice pres. Elgin Davis Advt. Agy., Los Angeles, 1970-73, Graham & Sparkman, Torrance, Calif., 1973-81; pres. Sparkman Advt. Co., Palos Verdes, Calif., 1981—. Recipient numerous awards in advt. Democrat. Mem. Ch. of Religious Sci. Avocations: writing; decorating; traveling. Home: 27902 Ridgebrook Ct Rancho Palos Verdes CA 90274 Office: Sparkman Advt Inc 655 Deep Valley Dr Suite 200 Palos Verdes CA 90274

SPARKS, KATHRYN WIMBERLY, administrative assistant; b. Augusta, Ga., Oct. 31, 1952; d. Francis Linton and Violet (Blanchard) S. Student, Middle Ga. Coll., 1970-71, Augusta Coll., 1971, 77. Sec. Meco, Inc. of Augusta, 1972-73; stenographer Ga. Dept. of Vets. Services, Augusta, Ga., 1973-77; sec. One Way Bapt. Ch., Augusta, 1977-81, Fulcher Law Firm, Augusta, 1981-84; adminstrv. asst. Lily-Tulip, Inc., Augusta, 1984-86, First R.R. & Banking Co., Augusta, 1986, GOSL Acquisition Corp., Hilton Head Island, S.C., 1986-87; sec. to former U.S. Rep. Elliott H. Levitas Kilpatrick & Cody, Atlanta, 1987—. Mem. Nat. Assn. Female Execs. Home: 937 Wood Hollow Dr Marietta GA 30067 Office: Kilpatrick & Cody 100 Peachtree St Suite 3100 Atlanta GA 30043

SPARKS, MARY BELLE, teacher; b. Bedford County, Tenn., Feb. 14, 1936; s. Frank and Lenice Irene (Bible) Hutchings; m. Herbert Blackman Sparks Sr., Apr. 18, 1958; children: Herbert Blackman Jr., Harold Christopher. BS, George Peabody Coll. for Tchrs., Nashville, 1957; MEd summa cum laude, Middle Tenn. State U., 1971. Cert. elem. tchr. Tchr. 6th grade Bedford County Schs., Wartrace, 1957-58, 59-60; tchr. 3d and 4th grade Tullahoma (Tenn.) City Schs., 1964-73; tchr. title I/chpt. I Bedford County Schs., Shelbyville, 1973—. Treas., asst. chairperson adminstrv. bd. Normandy (Tenn.) United Meth. Ch. Mem. NEA, Tenn. Edn. Assn., Tullahoma Edn. Assn. (v.p., pres. 1969-70, chmn. pub. relations and publicity com.), Bedford County Edn. Assn. (del. to legis. assembly 1985), Internat. Reading Assn. (recording sec.), Nat. Geographic Soc., Smithsonian Assocs., Delta Kappa Gamma (research com. Beta Nu chpt. 1986-87, leadership devel. com. 1987-88). Home: 410 Cortner Rd Normandy TN 37360 Office: Harris Mid Sch 400 Elm St Shelbyville TN 37160

SPARLING, REBECCA HALL, materials engineer, energy consultant; b. Memphis, June 7, 1910; d. Robert Meredith and Kate Wallace (Sampson) Hall; m. Edwin Kinmonth Smith, Oct. 30, 1935 (div. 1947); 1 child, Douglas Kinmonth; m. Joseph Sparling, July 10, 1948; B.A., Vanderbilt U., 1930, M.S., 1931. Registered profl. engr., Calif. Design specialist Gen. Dynamics, Pomona, Calif., 1951-68, Northrop Aircraft, Hawthorne, Calif., 1944-51; cons. engr., Detroit, 1936-44; tech. writer William H. Baldwin, N.Y.C., 1934-35; metallurgist Lakeside Malleable, Racine, Wis., 1933-34, Am. Cast Iron Pipe, Birmingham, Ala., 1931-32; energy cons., Laguna Hills, Calif., 1973-85. Author; contbr. articles to profl. jours. Officer, leader Fgn. Policy Assn. of Leisure World, Laguna Hills, 1980-84; bd. dirs. AAUW, 1974-84; mem. Air Pollution Control Bd., San Bernardino County, 1973; cons., intervenor Calif. Energy Commn., 1975-82. Recipient Engring. Merit award Orange County Council Engrs. Soc., 1978; named Outstanding Engr. Inst. Advancement of Engring., 1978, Los Angeles Engrs. Week, 1965. Fellow Soc. Woman Engrs., Inst. Advancement Engring.; Fellow Am. Soc. Metals; mem. Am. Soc. Nondestructive Testing, Delta Delta Delta. Republican. Religious Sci. Ch. Address: 650 W Harrison Ave Claremont CA 91711

SPARROW, BARBARA JANE, Canadian legislator; b. Toronto, Ont., Can., July 11, 1935; d. Thomas Henry and Alice (Rusgrove) O'C.; m. Robert Eugene Sparrow, Oct. 19, 1956 (dec.); children: Thomas, Jane, James, John. Student, Wellesley Hosp. Sch. Nursing. RN. Mem. from Calgary South Ho. of Commons, Can., 1984—. Mem. Progressive Conservative Party. Anglican. Address: 68 Baycrest Pl SW, No 9, Calgary, AB Canada T2V 0K6 *

SPARROW, DOROTHY TALMADGE, casualty adjuster, editor; b. Balt., Mar. 7, 1943; d. Charles Edward and Margaret Elizabeth (Willis) Sparrow Jr. A.B. in Sociology, U. Balt., 1965. Social worker Dept. of Welfare, White Plains, N.Y., 1965-66; mil. dance hostess dir. YWCA West Point, White Plains, 1967-72; asst. women's editor Reporter Dispatch, White Plains, 1967-73; news bur. dir. Meth. Coll., Fayetteville, N.C., 1973-74; casualty adjuster Crawford & Co., Fayetteville, 1974-76, outside casualty, life & health adj., Newport News, Va., 1976—. Contbr. articles to profl. jours. Vol. coordinator, hostess dir. USO, Hampton, Va., 1985—; area rep. Youth for Understanding Fgn. Exchange, Hampton, 1979-83; bd. dirs. Fayetteville Arts Council, 1974-76, Jr. Woman's Clubs of Fayetteville and Hampton, 1973-84. Recipient cert. appreciation Yorktown Bicentennial Commn., 1981, Marjorie Branch award Va. Fedn. Women's Club, 1984, award Vol. Action Ctr., 1988, others. Mem. Nat. Assn. Female Execs., Peninsula Claims Assn. (pres. 1983, 88, sec. 1986, Adjuster of Yr. award 1984), Am. Bus. Women's Assn. (Woman of Yr. award 1982), Alpha Xi Delta. Republican. Episcopalian. Clubs: Woman's of Hampton; Ft. Eustis Officers. Avocations: bridge; needlework; travelling; reading; literacy counseling; crafts; sports; cooking; friends. Office: Crawford & Co 11101 Warwick Blvd Newport News VA 23601

SPARROW, JANET CRUZ, aircraft company official; b. Los Angeles, May 4, 1934; d. Eulogio Emilio and Inez Juanita (Bragg) Cruz; m. Edward Akers Sparrow, July 23, 1957 (div. July 1977); children: Douglas, Jacqueline, David. AA, Los Angeles City Coll., 1961; BA, Calif. State U., Los Angeles, 1963; MEd, Loyola Marymount U., 1973; JD, U. West Los Angeles, 1979. Tchr. Los Angeles Unified Sch. Dist., 1963-74; dir. Inglewood (Calif.) Unified Sch. Dist., 1974-75, prin., 1975-76; subcontract adminstr. Hughes Aircraft Co., El Segundo, Calif., 1981-85, subcontract specialist, 1985-87, mgr. procurement, 1987—. Speaker Youth Motivation Task Force, Los Angeles/Inglewood, 1981—. Recipient Outstanding Achievement award YWCA, 1985. Republican. Home: 2151 Rosecrans Ave El Segundo CA 90245

SPARROW, MARY MANNING, publishing executive; b. Smithfield, N.C., Feb. 16, 1949; d. Wheeler Martin and Evelyn (Hinnant) Manning; m. Ronald Wilford Sparrow, Dec. 3, 1966 (div. Jan. 1987); children: Mary, John. BA, U. Richmond, 1971. Tchr. Richmond Pub. Schs., Va., 1971-73; sales mgr. Allyn and Bacon Pub., Newton, Mass., 1973-86; sales rep. Scholastic, Inc., N.Y.C., 1973-83, sales mgr., 1986-88, nat. field mktg. mgr., 1988—. Mem. N.C. Ednl. Pub. Assn. (pres., Bookman of Yr. award 1979), S.C. Bookmans Assn. Republican. Episcopalian. Home: 112 Lee St Wilmington NC 27892

SPAS, SHIRLEY ANNE, computer systems engineer; b. Woonsocket, R.I.; d. Stanley D. and Dorothea Aileen (Ambler) S. AB in Chemistry, Boston U., 1960. Instr. chemistry Boston U., Boston, 1960-66; research chemist Kendall Co., Cambridge, Mass., 1964-66; assoc. scientist Avco Missiles Div., Wilmington, Mass., 1966-69; systems engr. IBM, Waltham, Mass., 1969—, sr. systems engr., 1985—.

SPATAFORE-SYMANSKI, LAUREN ANN, systems manager; b. Pitts., July 4, 1962; d. Robert Louis and Lois Frances (Schwerer) S. AS, Pa. State U., 1982; student, U. Pitts., 1983-85. Sales person Kinney Shoe Corp., Pitts., 1979-85; aide day care Olde Schoolhouse Day Care, Gibsonia, Pa., 1983; clk. data entry Hartz Mountain Corp., Leetsdale, Pa., 1983-85; mgr. field office system Hartz Mountain Corp., Harrison, N.J., 1985—. Mem. Nat. Assn. Female Execs., PRO PC Users' Group Pitts. Democrat. Roman Catholic. Club: Western PA Wheelmen (Pitts.). Office: Hartz Mountain Corp Buncher Indsl Dist Leetsdale PA 15056

SPATARO, JANIE DEMPSEY WATTS, writer; b. Chattanooga, May 17, 1951; d. Ray Dean and Anne America (Dempsey) Watts; m. Stephen Anthony Spataro, June 18, 1977; children—Anthony Dempsey, Stephen Jackson. B.S. in Journalism, U. Calif.-Berkeley, 1974; M.A. in Broadcast Journalism, U. So. Calif., 1982. Writer, editor McGiffin Newspapers, South Gate, Calif., 1976; news bur. mgr. Loyola Marymount U., Westchester, Calif., 1976; asst. dir. pub. relations Hawthorne (Calif.) Community Hosp. 1977-78; writer, with pub. relations dept. Moneywise, Los Angeles, 1980-81; pub. relations cons. Security Pacific Bank, Los Angeles, 1978-82; writer Cable Card, Inc., Marina del Rey, Calif., 1983; writer Reality Prodns., Huntington Beach, Calif., 1983-86. Writer, producer, editor TV documentary: Who's Minding the Children?, 1983; contbr. articles to mags. and newspapers. Speaker on child care on TV, 1983-84. Beatrice E. Rice scholar U. Calif., 1973-74; Calif. State fellow, 1981-83. Mem. Women in Film, Women in Communications, DAR. Home and Office: 2629 Arizona Ave Santa Monica CA 90404

SPAUDE, DORIS ANITA SCHROEDER, educator, freelance artist, interior decorator; b. Reedsburg, Wis., Sept. 7, 1942; d. Gilbert Edward and Anita (Mueller) Schroeder; m. Alfred Jimmie Spaude, Mar. 29, 1964 (div. Jan. 1988); children: Michelle Renee, Chantelle Kareen. BS in Elem. Edn., Wis. State U., Oshkosh, 1965; BS in Computer Graphics, Marycrest Coll., Davenport, Iowa, 1986; postgrad., Marycrest Coll., 1988—. Lic. tchr., Iowa. Tchr. various schs., various locations, 1964-74, Pleasant Valley (Iowa) Community Schs., 1974—; freelance artist Wis., Oreg., Ill., Iowa, and France, 1960—; freelance interior decorator and stenciler, Moline, Ill., 1979—. Copyright 7 computer graphic images. Mem. Computer Image Assn. Mary Crest Coll., Davenport, Iowa, 1983-86, bldg. com. Prince of Peace Luth. Ch., Davenport, 1976-77, edn. chmn. ch. council; alt. sponsor Am.-Soviet Youth Exchange Initiative for Understanding, 1988. Mem. Nat. Assn. Female Execs., NEA, Iowa State Edn. Assn., Pleasant Valley Edn. Assn., Nat. Mus. Women in Arts (charter). Home: 1923 13th St Moline IL 61265

SPAULDER, JOAN ROISTACHER, publishing executive; b. N.Y.C., Jan. 5, 1939; d. Charles and Ina (Zirinsky) Roistacher; B.A., Brandeis U., 1959; M.S., Queens Coll., 1963; children—Debra Val, Mara Jill. Tchr., N.Y.C., Westfield, N.J., Scotch Plains, N.J., 1959-69; account exec. Consumer Mktg. Research Services, Inc., Hackensack, N.J., 1969-70; dir. research and edn. Allen Levis Orgn., Inc., Northfield, Ill., 1971-73; dir. mktg. research Food Fair, Inc., Phila., 1974-78; dir. mktg. W. B. Saunders div. CBS, Phila., 1978—. Pres., Women's Am. ORT, Westfield, N.J., 1968; v.p. PTA, Scotch Plains, N.J., 1969; mem. Brandeis U. Alumni Admissions Council, 1975—; mem. mktg. com. Balch Inst., 1984-86; bd. dirs. Rittenhouse Plaza, 1984-85. Mem. Forum Exec. Women (dir. 1978-80, chairperson membership 1982-85), Am. Mktg. Assn. (dir. 1977-79), Assn. Am. Pubs. (mktg. com. 1981-87, chmn. mktg. com. 1986-87), Direct Mktg. Assn., Phila. Direct Mktg. Club (chair Benny Awards 1986), Phila. Postal Customers Council (chmn. 1981-82), Brandeis U. Alumni Assn. (steering com. Greater Phila. chpt. 1980-85). Home: Rittenhouse Plaza Philadelphia PA 19103 Office: WB Saunders Co W Washington Sq Philadelphia PA 19105

SPAULDING, LORA JEAN, university administrator; b. South Bend, Ind., Aug. 29, 1951; d. Leo Alfred and Lois Mae (Myers) S. BA, Ind. U., Bloomington, 1973; M of Pub. Adminstrn., Ind. U., South Bend, 1978. Asst. mgr. Pier I Imports, Mishawaka, Ind., 1973-74; account mgr. Sta. WNIT-TV, Mishawaka and South Bend, 1974-76; clk. St. Joseph County Police Dept., South Bend, 1976-79, police officer, 1980-86; asst. to registrar U. Notre Dame (Ind.) Du Lac, 1986-87, asst. registrar, 1987—. V.P. Southhold Restorations, Inc., South Bend, 1983, treas., 1984-87, pres., 1987. Mem. Am. Assn. Collegiate Registrars and Admissions Officers, Ind. Assn. Collegiate Registrars and Admissions Officers. Roman Catholic. Home: 1135 N Kaley St South Bend IN 46628 Office: U Notre Dame Du Lac 215 Administration Bldg Notre Dame IN 46556

SPEAR, JACQUELINE DAWN, communications executive; b. Balt., Dec. 5, 1949; d. Gruver Howard and Lillian J. (Jackson) Martin; m. Matthew J. Krimski, Sept. 5, 1969 (div. Apr. 1979); m. Kenneth B. Spear, Nov. 17, 1979; children: Melody S., Kelly M., Michael C. BS cum laude, U. Balt., 1986. Communications rep. C&P Telephone Co. Md., Balt., Wheaton, 1971-75, phone power rep., 1975-77; sr. mktg. analyst Am. Bank Stationery, Balt., 1977-80; mgr. telecommunications Alexander & Alexander, Inc., Balt., 1980-84; pres. Integrated Systems Planning, Inc., Balt., 1984—; coordinator spl. program telecommunication mgmt. Goucher Coll., Balt., 1986—. Mem. Nat. Assn. Female Execs., Exec. Women's Network, Delta Mu Delta. Republican. Presbyterian.

SPEAR, JEAN EVELYN HINSON, nurse; b. Quincy, Fla., Oct. 7, 1944; d. Wash Sr. and Emma Ree (Harris) Hinson; m. Thomas Robert Smith, Oct. 26, 1962 (div. 1983); children: Theophilus Rodney, Roderick O'Brien; m. Joshua Spear, July 26, 1986. BS, Fla. A&M U., 1976, postgrad., 1979; postgrad., Fla. State U., 1978, 79, 83, U. Fla., 1983. RN Fla. RN supr. Goodwood Manor, Tallahassee, Fla., 1978-79; crisis intervention counselor Apalachee Community Mental Health, Inc., Quincy, Fla., 1978-79; RN III, team leader Apalachee Community Mental Health, Inc., Quincy, 1977-79; sr. RN supr. State of Fla., Fla. State Hosp., Chattahoochee, Fla., 1979-87; instr. Gadsden County Vocat. Sch., Quincy, Fla., 1987—; chmn. forensic nursing com., Chattahoochee, 1986-87; mem. Nursing Policy and Procedure Commn., Chattahoochee, 1981-82; substitute tchr. Gadsden County Bd. Edn., Quincy, 1978—. Recipient Gov.'s Cert. Merit State of Fla., 1983. Mem. Am. Nurses Assn., Fla. Nurses Assn., Nat. Assn. Female Execs., Am. Bus. Women's Assn. Silver Dome chpt. Democrat. Missionary Baptist. Home: 119 E Washington St #3 Chattahoochee FL 32324 Office: Fla State Hosp PO Box 1000 Chattahoochee FL 32324

SPEAR, MARY PATRICIA, sales and marketing executive; b. Sheridan, Wyo., May 4, 1954; d. Bradford Johnson and Patricia Ann (Brooder) S.; m. Kenneth Ray Gleason, June 3, 1972 (div. June 1982); children: Seth Kendy, Susan Michele. Grad. high sch., Dayton, Wyo. Bookkeeper Padlock Ranch, Ranchester, Wyo., 1972; ranch ptnr. Eagle Point Ranch, Busby, Mont., 1972-82; purchasing agt. Top Office Products, Inc., Sheridan, 1982-86, sales rep., 1985-87; nat. sales and mktg. dir. GeoLearning Corp., Sheridan, 1988—; ski instr. Antelope Butte Corp., Sheridan, 1987—. Del., alt. Big Horn County Farm Bur., Hardin, Mont., 1981; bd. dirs. Sch. Dist. 17K Big Horn County, Kirby, Mont., 1980-82. Recipient Outstanding Skiing award Sheridan C. of C., 1970; named 1st Runner-up Mother of Yr. Big Horn County, 1980. Fellow Nat. Assn. Female Execs.; mem. Profl. Ski Instrs. of Am. Republican. Episcopalian. Lodge: Kiwanis. Home: 355 Smith St Sheridan WY 82801 Office: Geolearning Corp 555 Absaraka Sheridan WY 82801

SPEARIN, ROSEMARY, publisher; b. Salem, Mass., Mar. 29, 1954; d. Theophanis Hadji and Sophia George (Ravanis) Manolakis; m. Edward W. Spearin, Nov. 11, 1984. A in Fashion Merchandising, Bryant & Stratton, 1974. Asst. buyer Deerskin Trading Post, Peabody, Mass., 1975-77, Charles Sumner Inc., Boston, 1978; catalogue coordinator Noymer Mfg., Boston, 1979-81; product designer/retailer Eleni Designs, Peabody, Mass., 1981-83; retailer, importer The Aegean, Provincetown, Mass., 1983; asst. to pres. Kieran Gray Advt., Boston, 1984-85; pres. The Catalog Co., Bradford, Mass., 1986—. Home and Office: 19 Rainbow Dr Bradford MA 01830

SPEARS, ELNA ROSE, home economics educator; b. Gainesboro, Tenn., Feb. 11, 1936; d. Frank Fussell and Fannie Lawrence (Spivy) Gaw; m. Charles Edward Spears, Mar. 14, 1959; children: Timothy, Vicki, Eddie. BS, Tenn. Tech. U., 1957; MEd, Mid. Tenn. State U., 1975. Clk. Bursar Office Tenn. Tech. U., Cookeville, 1959-60, J.O. Parrish Law Office, Cookeville, 1960-61; secondary home econ. tchr. Putnam County Bd. Edn., Baxter, Tenn., 1961-62; secondary English, sci. tchr. Lincoln County Bd. Edn., Fayetteville, Tenn., 1962-66; tchr. Franklin County Bd. Edn., Winchester, Tenn., 1966-67; Franklin County agrl. extension agt. Univ. Tenn. Agr. Extension Service, Winchester, 1967—. Mem. Resource Devel. Assn., Winchester, 1967—; mem. Farm Bur., Winchester, 1967—; mem. community council Mid-South Bank and Trust, Winchester, 1984—; fund raising com. mem. U. Tenn. Agr. Extension, Knoxville, 1985-86; planning com. Homecoming 1986, Winchester, 1986. Mem. Tenn. Extension Homemakers Council (agt. advisor 1985—), Tenn. Assn. Extension Home Economists (dist. co-dir.), Nat. Home Econ. Assn. (cert. 1986), Nat. Assn. Extension Home Economists (dist. service award 1976), Tenn. Home Econs. Assn. (disting. service com., research and studies com., profl. improvement com.), Epsilon Sigma Phi. Mem. Ch. of Christ. Home: Rt 4 Box 263 Winchester TN 37398 Office: Agr Extension Service County Courthouse Winchester TN 37398

SPEARS, JAE, state legislator; b. Latonia, Ky.; d. James and Sylvia (Fox) Marshall; m. Lawrence E. Spears; children: Katherine Spears Cooper, Marsha Spears-Duncan, Lawrence M., James W. Student, U. Ky. Reporter Cin. Post, Cin. Enquirer newspapers; research Stas. WLW-WSAI, Cin.; tchr. Jiya Gakuen Sch., Japan; lectr. U.S. Mil. installations East Anglia, Eng.; del. State of W.Va., Charleston, 1974-80, state senator, 1980—; mem. adv. bd. W.Va. Women's Commn., Charleston, 1976—; mem. state visitors com. W.Va. Extension and Pub. Service Com., Morgantown, 1977—. Council mem. W.Va. Autism Task Force, Huntington, 1981—; mem. W.Va. exec. bd. Literacy Vols. of Am., 1985—; bd. dirs. Found. Ind. Colls. of W.Va., 1986—. Recipient Susan B. Anthony award NOW, 1982, nat. award Mil. Order Purple Heart, 1984, Edn. award Profl. Educators Assn. W.Va., 1986, Ann. award W.Va. Assn. Ret. Sch. Employees, 1985, Meritorious Service award W.Va. State Vets. Commn., 1984, Vets. Employment and Tng. Service award U.S. Dept. Labor, 1984, award W.Va. Vets. Council, 1984; named Admiral in N.C. Navy, Gov. of N.C., 1982, Hon. Brigadier W.Va. N.G., 1984. Mem. Bus. and Profl. Women (woman of yr. award 1978), Nat. League Am. Pen Women (pen woman of yr. 1984), Nat. Order Women Legislators, DAR, VFW Aux., Am. Legion Aux., Delta Kappa Gamma. Democrat. Home and Office: PO Box 2088 Elkins WV 26288

SPEARS, JANET E., educator; b. Chambersburg, Ill., Sept. 5, 1933; d. Enoch E. and Marguerite Irene (Riley) Downey; A.A., Black Hawk Coll., 1978; B.S. (Chris Hoerr scholar), Bradley U., 1980; postgrad., St. Ambrose Coll., 1981-84; postgrad., Nova U., 1987; m. Keith A. Spears, July 6, 1952; children—Bruce, Roger, Darci, Paul. Secretarial positions Kewanee Machinery Conveyor (Ill.), 1951-52, William E. Trinke, atty., Lake Geneva, Wis., 1952-53, Walworth Co., Kewanee, 1968-72; adminstrv. asst. Kewanee Pub. Hosp., 1972-75; asst. personnel dir. Davenport (Iowa) Osteo. Hosp., 1980-81; bus. mgr. Franciscan Med. Center, Rock Island, Ill., 1981; bus. prof. Black Hawk Coll., Kewanee, 1981—, Henry County Rep. Women; liturgist, Sunday sch. tchr., mem. adminstrv. council). Mem. Am. Mgmt. Assn., AAUW, Nat. Assn. for Female Execs., Kewanee Pub. Hosp. Assn., Kewanee Art League, Phi Chi Theta. Republican. Clubs: Annawan Jr. Women's (pres. 1964-65), United Fairview Women. Home: Rural Route 1 Sheffield IL 61361 Office: Black Hawk Coll East Campus PO Box 489 Kewanee IL 61443

SPEARS, JOYCE ANN, financial executive; b. St. Louis, Mar. 2, 1939; d. Roy Edward and Theada Irene (Stanley) Nunn; m. James Arnold Spears, May 13, 1972; children: Juliana Palmer, J.J. AA, Westark Community Coll., 1988; BS cum laude, U. Ozarks, 1988. Bookkeeper/sec. Graham Paper Co., Oklahoma City, 1959-66; legal asst. trainee/mgr. Wiliam M. Stocks, Atty., Ft. Smith, Ark., 1967-70; supr. lab. office Sparks Regional Med. Ctr., Ft. Smith, 1970-71, adminstrv. asst. dietary dept., 1971-74, payroll clerk, 1974-75, mgr. acct. dept., 1975-80, asst. controller fin., 1980—; fina. aid adminstr. Sparks Sch. Med. Tech., Ft. Smith, 1980—, Sparks Sch. Radiol. Tech., Ft. Smith, 1980—; Sparks Sch. Respiratory Service, Ft. Smith, 1980—, Ark. Assn. FAA, 1980—. Treas., vol., St. Jude Children's Research Hosp., Memphis, 1977-86; mem., tutor, The Ft. Smith Literacy Council, 1984—; mem., vol., The Ft. Smith Pub. Library, 1984—. Mem. Ark. Fedn. Bus. and Profl. Women (dist. dir. 1985-86, pres.-elect 1988—, Best Conf. award 1985), Ft. Smith Bus. and Profl Women (1st v.p. 1980-81, pres. 1982-83, Outstanding Bus. Woman 1982, Woman of Yr. 1983, best speaker competition). Republican. Baptist. Lodge: Altrusa (pres., award). Home: 3034 S 58 St Fort Smith AR 72903 Office: Sparks Regional Med Ctr 1311 S I St Fort Smith AR 72901

SPECHT, BARBARA MAE, community service organization director; b. Lynwood, Calif., May 9, 1951; d. William James and Dorothy Mae (Orton) S. AA in Liberal Arts, Rancho Santiago Community Coll., Santa Ana, Calif., 1980; BS Organizational Behavior, U. San Francisco, 1987. Clk. Orange County Marshal, Santa Ana, 1972-79; investigative asst. Orange County Dist. Atty., Santa Ana, 1979-81; legal sec. Guerini-Bolt & Verdon, Newport Beach, Calif., 1981-83, Halkides & Morgan, Redding, Calif., 1984; exec. dir. Crisis Pregnancy Ctr. No. Calif., Redding, 1984-87, Crisis Pregnancy Ctr. San Francisco, 1988—; cons. Ind. Search Consultants, Costa Mesa, Calif., 1980-84. assoc. field staff Falls Church, Va. Christian Action Council, 1985—; mem. Calif. Women's Lobby, 1986. Mem. Concerned Women for Am. Republican.

SPECHT, MARY NANETTE, sales executive; b. Redlands, Calif., Apr. 6, 1949; d. William Hugh Johnson Jr. and Dorothy (Robbins) Rule; m. Clifford J. Specht, Dec. 13, 1986. Grad. high sch., Redlands, Calif. Bookkeeper Citrus Packers, Redlands, 1970-72; from bookkeeper to office mgr. to div. acct. Blue Goose Groners, Redlands, 1972-82; with export sales Sun World Internat., Indio, Calif., 1982-86; sales ops. mgr. Dole Citrus, Ontario, Calif., 1986-87, dir. export mktg., 1988—. Mem. Fresh Produce Council, Calif. Women for Agr. Republican. Home: 10646 Independence Ct Redlands CA 92374 Office: PO Box 9269 Ontario CA 91762-9269

SPECIAN, ROSEMARIE THERESE, pharmaceutical company executive; b. Somerville, N.J., Nov. 4, 1944; d. William Michael and Maryann (Dudek) Specian; m. Edward J. Sinusas, Jr. Dec. 28, 1985. B.S. in Home Econs. (Ella Mae Shellshy Holmes award), Albright Coll., Reading, Pa., 1966; M.S. in Human Behavior and Devel., Drexel U., Phila., 1971; M.B.A., Loyola-Marymount U., Los Angeles, 1980. Sales rep. Atlas Crown Brokerage, Los Angeles, 1973-75; regional rep. Reynolds Metals Co., Los Angeles, 1975-77; mktg. mgr. nat. accounts Glass Containers Corp., Anaheim, Calif., 1977-79; sr. package developer Lederle Labs., Pearl River, N.Y., 1980—. Recipient various sales awards. Mem. Am. Mktg. Assn., Packaging Inst., N.J. Mktg. Assn., N.J. Packaging Assn, AAUW. Home: 85 New Holland Village Nanuet NY 10954 Office: Lederle Labs N Middletown Rd Pearl River NY 10965

SPECK, HILDA, social worker; b. Stalybridge, Cheshire, England, Mar. 2, 1916; came to U.S., 1923; d. John Robert and Rose Ethel (Tymns) Smith; m. Willmot Hilton Speck, Sept. 4, 1937 (dec. Jan 1968); foster children: Barbara Ann Beranek Renfrow, Winifred June Beranak Aguilar. Grad. high sch., Flint, Mich. Lic. social worker, Mich. Dir. social services The Salvation Army, Flint, 1945—; estab. 4C Child Care Agy. Assisted in establishing Safe House for Victims of Domestic Violence, Flint, 1976-80; mem. Churchwomen United Convalescence Home; appt. clothing distbn. adminstr., Flint Civil Def.; mem. Red Feather Million Dollar Disaster Fund com. United Way, 1953, administered Salvation Army Rehab. Program, 1953; mem. Day Care co,m., Genesee County; mem. origional planning com. Planned Parent Orgn. Recipient Hands of Mercy award The Salvation Army, 1967, Centennial Youth award The Salvation Army, 1965, 20 Year Service award Big Brothers of Genesee County; named Woman of Week Stoney Brook Radio Sta., 1987. Mem. Council of Social Agys., Genesee County Commn. on Aging (v.p. 1971—), GLS Counties Health Planning Council Bd., Genesee County Emergency Task Force. Lodge: Zonta. Home: 2015 Stoney Brook Ct Flint MI 48507

SPECTOR, ELEANOR RUTH, government executive; b. N.Y.C., Dec. 2, 1943; d. Sidney and Helen (Kirschenbaum) Lebost; m. Mel Alan Spector, Dec. 10, 1966; children: Nancy, Kenneth. BA, Barnard Coll., 1964; postgrad. sch. pub. adminstrn., George Washington U., 1965-67; postgrad sch. edn., Nazareth Coll., 1974. Indsl. investigator N.Y. State Dept. Labor, White Plains, 1964-65; mgmt. intern Navy Dept., Washington, 1965, contract negotiator, 1965-68, contract specialist, 1975-78, contracting officer/br. head, 1978-82, dir. div. cost estimating, 1982-84; dep. asst. sec. def. for procurement Dept. Def., Washington, 1984—; advisor Nat. Contract Mgmt. Assn., 1984—. Office: Dept Def Procurement The Pentagon Room 3E144 Washington DC 20301-8000

SPECTOR, JOHANNA LICHTENBERG, emeritus ethnomusicology educator; b. Libau, Latvia; came to U.S., 1947, naturalized, 1954; d. Jacob C. and Anna (Meyer) Lichtenberg; m. Robert Spector, Nov. 20, 1939 (dec. Dec. 1941). D.H.S., Hebrew Union Coll., 1950; M.A., Columbia U., 1960. Research fellow Hebrew U., Jerusalem, 1951-53; faculty Jewish Theol. Sem. Am., 1954—, dir., founder dept. ethnomusicology, 1962-85, assoc. prof. musicology, 1966-70, Sem. prof., 1970-85, prof. emeritus, 1985—. Author: Ghetto-und Kzlieder, 1947, Samaritan Chant, 1965, Musical Tradition and Innovation in Central Asia, 1966, Bridal Songs from Sana Yemen, 1960; documentary film The Samaritans, 1971, Middle Eastern Music, 1973, About the Jews of India: Cochin, 1976 (Cine Golden Eagle 1979), The Shanwar Telis or Bene Israel of India, 1978 (Cine Golden Eagle 1979), About the Jews of Yemen, A Vanishing Culture, 1986 (Cine Golden Eagle 1986, Blue Ribbon, Am. Film Festival 1986); contbr. articles to encys., various jours.; editorial bd. Asian Music. Fellow Am. Anthrop. Assn.; mem. Am. Ethnol. Soc., Am. Musicol. Soc., Internat. Folk Music Council, World Assn. Jewish Studies, Yivo, Asian Mus. Soc. (v.p. 1964—, pres. 1974-78), African Mus. Soc., Soc. Ethnomusicology (sec.-treas N.Y.C. chapt. 1960-64), Soc. Preservation of Samaritan Culture (founder). Home: 400 W 119th St New York NY 10027

SPECTOR, SHELLEY JOY ZUCKERMAN, public relations company executive; b. Bklyn., Dec. 28, 1953; d. Max and Zelda (Steck) Zuckerman; m. Barry Spector, July 6, 1986; 1 child, Zoewy Dorian. B.A. in Journalism, U. R.I., 1974; M.S. in TV and Radio, Syracuse U., 1975. Account exec. Hill & Knowlton, N.Y.C., 1978-80; asst. dir., press relations Am. Stock Exchange, N.Y.C., 1980-82; exec. v.p. Lobsenz-Stevens Pub. Relations, N.Y.C., 1982-88; sr. v.p. Ruder, Finn & Rotman, N.Y.C., 1988—. Mem. Internat. Assn. Bus. Communications (mem. com.), Women Execs. in Pub. Relations. Democrat. Jewish. Avocations: skiing; scuba diving; tennis. Home: 20 Campbell Rd Short Hills NJ 07078 Office: Ruder Finn & Rotman 301 E 57th St New York NY 10022

SPEED, MARGARET ANN, school administrator; b. Burlington, Iowa, Nov. 17, 1949; d. Francis Xavier and Mary Kathleen (Riffel) Prior. AA, Southeastern Community Coll., 1970; BA in English, U. No. Iowa, 1972. Copywriter Nat. Research Bur., Burlington, 1968-70; adminstrv. asst. Miracle Recreation Equipment Co., Grinnell, Iowa, 1973-74; grant writer, planner LaSalle County, Ottawa, Ill., 1975-79; dir. info. Burlington Schs., 1980—; crwkshop leader Area 16 Supt.'s Assn., Burlington, 1982, Assn. Iowa Ednl. Adminstrs., Des Moines, 1983-84. Contbr. articles to profl. mags. Chmn. regional campaign Des Moines County Heart Assn., Burlington, 1981; chmn. newspaper publicity City Sesquicentennial, Burlington, 1982-84; bd. dirs. YWCA, Burlington, 1981-82. Mem. Nat. Sch. Pub. Relations Assn. (Seminar scholar 1981, workshop leader 1983-84, 2 Golden Achievement awards 1985, regional v.p. 1987—), Iowa Sch. Pub. Relations Assn. (pres. 1984-85), Burlington C. of C. (pub. relations com., community attitude survey com.). Office: Burlington Schs 1429 West Ave Burlington IA 52601

SPEED, SHIRLEY ADAMS, data processing executive, consultant; b. Spokane, Wash., June 9, 1937; d. Claude M. and Berneice D. (Weiseger) Adams; m. Marvin E. Speed, July 9, 1958; children: Marva Jeanne Speed-Copeland, Marvin Ernest II. BA in Math., U. Wash., 1958; MBA, Calif. Coast U., 1985; postgrad., The Hartford Grad. Ctr. Tchr. math. U.S. Govt. HEW Schs., P.R., 1961-64, Upper Heyford, England, 1974-75; programmer, sr. analyst Aetna Life & Casualty, Hartford, Conn., 1976-79; data processing HE coordinator Aetna Life & Casualty, Hartford, 1979-81, data processing HE cons., 1981-82, data processing HE adminstr., 1982-83, data processing HR adminstr., 1983-85; pvt. practice software cons. Del. and Conn., 1985-86; sr. software project specialist Digital Equipment Corp., Meriden, Conn., 1986-87; sr. software specialist with tech. sales support Digital Equipment Corp., West Hartford, Conn., 1987-88, project mgr., 1988—; keynote speaker UN Internat. Womens' Day in Eng., 1975; speaker at various univs. and colls., 1980-85, Impact, Hartford, 1984; mem., curriculum advisor Windsor (Conn.) Bd. Edn., 1984-85. Producer, co-editor, camera operator: (TV show) Graduation Days, 1986. Initiator, pres. Concerned Parents for Better Edn., Plattsburgh, N.Y., 1972; v.p. Plattsburgh Officers Wives Club, 1973, pres., 1974-75; organizer Windsor Edn. Perserve Arts, 1980-82; village rep. USAF Strategic Air Command, Plattsburgh and San Antonio, 1975. Mem. Am. Mgmt. Assn., Assn. Systems Mgrs., Data Processing Mgmt. Assn., Black Data Processing Assn., Am. Women in Computing (exec. bd. 1985-86, conv. speaker 1985). Home: 55 Windbrook Dr Windsor CT 06095 Office: Digital Equipment Corp 433 S Main St West Hartford CT 06110

SPEETH, KATHLEEN TRELAIRE, psychologist, educator; b. N.Y.C., Feb. 12, 1937; d. John Francis and Mavis (McIntosh) Riordan; children: Deborah, Lauren. BA cum laude, Barnard Coll., 1959; MA, Columbia U., 1963, PhD, 1967. Lic. psychologist, N.Y., Calif. Asst. in psychology Columbia U., N.Y.C., 1959-64; assoc. mem. tech. staff Bell Labs., Murray Hill, N.J., 1961; psychologist Basic Systems, Inc., N.Y.C., 1963-66, Xerox Corp., N.Y.C., 1966-68; cons. OEO, Responsive Environments, Inc., Ludi Edn., Ednl. Design, Inc., New Century., 1968-70; v.p. Individual Learning Systems, San Rafael, Calif., 1970-72; faculty Coll. Marin and Indian Valley Colls., Kentfield, Calif., 1972; psychologist SAT Inst., Kensington, Calif., 1972-77; faculty Nyingma Inst., Berkeley, Calif., 1974-78; core faculty Calif. Inst. Transpersonal Psychology, Menlo Park, 1978-81; psychologist pvt. practice Berkeley, 1978-81, Nat. Inst. for the Psychotherapies, N.Y.C., Amagansett, N.Y., and El Cerrito, Calif., 1984—; mem. faculty Calif. Inst. Transpersonal Psychology, Menlo Park, Calif., 1978-81, John F. Kennedy U., Orinda, Calif., 1980-81. Barnard Fellow, 1959. Mem. Am. Psychol. Assn., Assn. for Transpersonal Psychology, Sigma Xi. also: 85 Mill Hill Ln East Hampton NY 11937

SPEICHER, JACQUELYN LOU, educator; b. Holdrege, Nebr., May 18, 1946; d. Jack Louis and Norma Fern (Corder) McKenzie; m. David Ross Speicher, Oct. 7, 1972; children—Jill Marie, Tracey Ann, Stepanie Jane. B.S., U. Nebr., 1969. Tchr. pub. schs., Holdrege, 1969-70; urban services worker United Meth. Ch. Bd. Global Ministries, N.Y.C., 1970-74; tchr. John F. Kennedy Sch., Berlin, 1974-77; trainer Inst. Cultural Affairs Internat., Chgo., 1977-79; instr. Central YMCA Community Coll., Chgo., 1979-80; dir., program set-up Inst. Cultural Affairs, Indpls., 1980-81; program dir. Ind. U.-Purdue U./Tng., Inc., Indpls., 1981-83; program dir. Ind. Vocat.-Tech. Coll./Tng. Inc., Indpls., 1983—. Chmn. Women's programs com. YWCA, Indpls., 1985-86, bd. dirs., 1984-86; trustee, treas. Mobile Homes Trust, 1984-88; v.p. Knowledge Systems, Inc., 1986—. Mem. Am. Soc. Personnel Adminstrs., Am. Soc. Tng. and Devel., Am. Vocat. Assn., Ind. Vocat. Assn., Community Service Council, Ind. Employment and Tng. Assn. (sec. 1985-86, v.p. membership 1986—), Profl. Secs. Internat. (exec. adv. bd. 500 chpt. 1985-88), Tng. Inc. Nat. Assn. (sec.-treas. 1987-88). Republican. Methodist. Office: Training Inc 47 S Pennsylvania St Suite 801 Indianapolis IN 46204

SPEIER, KAREN RINARDO, psychologist; b. New Orleans, Aug. 19, 1947; d. William Joseph Rinardo and Shirley Eva (Spreen) Christensen; m. Joe Max Sobotka, Nov. 27, 1970 (div. 1972); m. Anthony Herman Speier, May 29, 1982; children: Anthony Herman III, Austin Clay. Student, Vanderbilt U., 1965-67; BA, La. State U., New Orleans, 1969; MS, U. New Orleans, 1974; PhD, La. State U., 1985. Lic. psychologist, La. Tchr. spl. edn. Huntsville (Ala.) Achievement Sch., 1970-72; instr. neurology La. State U. Med. Ctr., New Orleans, 1972-78; clin. assoc. Dawson Psychol. Assocs., Baton Rouge, 1979-81; tchr. asst. dept. psychology La. State U., Baton Rouge, 1979-81; psychol. examiner La. Sch. for Deaf, Baton Rouge, 1979-80; psychology intern VA Med. Ctr., Martinez, Calif., 1981-82; psychology extern East La. State Hosp., Jackson, 1982-83; clin. assoc. Baton Rouge Psychol. Assocs., 1983-86, pvt. practice clin. psychology, 1986—; sec. bd. dirs. Baton Rouge Employment Devel. Services, 1987—; mem. cons. com. meadow Wood Hosp., Baton Rouge, 1987—; mem. adult adv. com. Parkland Hosp., Baton Rouge, 1987—. Contbr. articles to profl. publs. Mem. steering com. Baton Rouge Stepfamily Support Group, 1983—; tchr. St. James Episcopal Sunday Sch., Baton Rouge, 1984-86. Mem. Orton Dyslexia Soc., Nat. Head Injury Found., Agenda for Children, Baton Rouge Area Soc. Psychologists, La. Psychol. Assn., Am. Psychology Assn., Internat. Soc. Child Abuse and Neglect, Mental Health Assn. La. Clubs: Baton Rouge, YWCA Connections. Office: Ctr Psychol Resources 7942A Goodwood Blvd Baton Rouge LA 70806

SPEIGHT, VELMA RUTH, counselor, educator; b. Snow Hill, N.C., Nov. 18, 1932; d. John Thomas and Mable Lee (Edwards) S.; m. Howard H. Kennedy, 1953 (div. 1961); 1 child, Chinéta K. Bowen. BS, N.C. A&T U., 1953; MEd, U. Md., 1965, PhD, 1976. Cert. counselor, tchr. Md. Tchr. Math., French Kinnard High Sch., Centreville, Md., 1954-60; counselor Kennard High Sch., Centreville, Md., 1960-66; coordinator guidance dept. Queene Anne's County High Sch., Centreville, 1966-69; adv. specialist in civil rights Md. State Dept. Edn., Balt., 1969-72, supr. guidance, 1972-76, dep. asst. state supt., 1976-82, asst. state supt., 1982-86; dir. EEO recruitment U. Md., College Park, 1972; coordinator guidance and counseling U. Md. Ea. Shore, Princess Anne, 1986-87; assoc. prof. counselor edn. East Carolina U., Greenville, 1987—; adj. prof. Loyola U., Balt., 1976-80, Johns Hopkins U., Balt., 1980; cons. 25 states, 1987—; speaker numerous seminars. Mem. Nat. Coalition for Chpt. 1 Parents, Washington, 1980-87, Human Rights Commn., Howard County, Md., 1987—; chmn. Gov.'s com. Studying Sentencing Alternatives for Women, Annapolis, Md., 1987; founder, chmn. Mothers to Prevent Dropouts, Centreville. Recipient Early Childhood Edn. award Japanese Govt., 1984. Mem. Am. Assn. Sch. Adminstrs., Am. Assn. Counseling and Devel., Nat. Alliance Black Educators, Assn. for Supervision and Curriculum Devel., N.C. Assn. for Counseling and Devel., N.C. A&T U. Alumni Assn. (nat. pres. 1979-83, Excellence award 1983). Democrat. Presbyterian. Club: Community Action (Centreville). Home: Rt 1 Box 106 Snow Hill NC 28580 Office: East Carolina U Greenville NC 27834

SPEIR, BETTY SMITH, foundation administrator; b. Bethel, N.C., Mar. 3, 1928; d. William Jasper and Carolyn (Pollock) Smith; A.B., Duke U., 1949; M.A., East Carolina U., 1963; m. David Ordway Speir, June 10, 1950; children—Carolyn G. Speir Brown, Christine St. Clair Speir Price. Tchr. English, Farmville (N.C.) High Sch., 1949-50, Bain High Sch., Charlotte, N.C., 1950-51, Bethel High Sch., 1961-70; cotton buyer Bethel Mfg. Co. (N.C.), 1958-60; guidance counselor North Pitt High Sch., Bethel, 1970-86; exec. dir. Pitt Edn. Found, 1986—. Sec., N.C. Commn. on Edn. and Employment of Women, 1970-74; mem. N.C. State Bd. Edn., 1982—, N.C. Gov.'s Crime Commn., 1977-82, N.C. Commn. on Length of Sentencing, 1981-82; mem. Blue Ribbon Commn. to Study Needs of Tng. Schs.; mem. N.C. Commn. Edn. for Econ. Growth; vice chmn. N.C. Democratic Com., 1978-80, 81-84, chmn., 1980; mem. Dem. Nat. Com., 1978—; del. Dem. Nat. Conv., 1980, 84, 88, mem. site selection com., 1984, mem. credentials com., 1988; mem. N.C. State Bd. Edn., 1982-87, N.C. Women's Forum. Named one of Winning Dem. Women of Decade, Nat. Fedn. Dem. Women, 1980. Mem. NEA, N.C. Assn. Educators, Delta Kappa Gamma. Methodist. Home: PO Box 340 Bethel NC 27812 Office: 1717 W 5th St Greenville NC 27834

SPEIRS, CAROL LUCILLE, nurse, naval officer; b. Plainfield, N.J., Apr. 20, 1942; d. Alexander Walker and Catherine Lucille (McGovern) S.; diploma St. Peters Med. Center Sch. Nursing, New Brunswick, N.J., 1963; student Seton Hall U., 1966-72, Pacific Lutheran U., Tacoma, Wash., 1987-88; B.A., San Diego State U., 1976; M.A., Webster Coll., 1980. Staff nurse Muhlenberg Hosp., Plainfield, N.J., 1963-64, Burdette Tomlin Meml. Hosp., Cape May Court House, N.J., 1964, 65, Georgetown U. Hosp., Washington, 1964-65; pvt. duty nurse, North Plainfield, N.J., 1965-66; staff nurse, charge nurse Raritan Valley Hosp., Greenbrook, N.J., 1966-72; commd. lt. (j.g.) U.S. Navy, 1973, advanced through grades to comdr., 1985; charge nurse Naval Regional Med. Center, San Diego, 1973-76, Iwakuni, Japan, 1977-78, Long Beach, Calif., 1978-83, Naval Hosp.; charge nurse, Bremerton, Wash., 1983-86, patient care coordinator, 1986. Mem. Founders Ball Com., City of Cypress (Calif.), 1981. Recipient Outstanding Cath. Young Adult award Diocese of Trenton, 1970. Mem. Nat. League Nursing, Emergency Dept. Nurses Assn., Nat. Assn. Female Execs., Quality Assurance Profls., Sigma Theta Tau, Crocker Art Mus. Assn., Nat. Mus. Women in Arts. Republican. Roman Catholic. Home: 3737 NW Highland Ct Silverdale WA 98383 Office: U Wash Naval ROTC Unit Seattle WA 98195

SPELKE, LAURA SONNINO, marketing professional; b. N.Y.C., Apr. 24, 1945; d. Mario and Silvana (Fubini) Sonnino; children: Jonathan Eric, Jessica Ann. BS, Simmons Coll., 1967; MS, U. Bridgeport, Conn., 1980. Programmer AT&T, White Plains, N.Y., 1967-69; systems programmer Nash Engring., Norwalk, Conn., 1969-70; social service coordinator Head Start, Stamford, Conn., 1979-80; dir. youth services Stamford Jewish Ctr., 1980-83; project dir. Leferman Assocs., Stamford, Conn., 1983-85; mng. dir. Greenwich Opinion Ctr., Old Greenwich, Conn., 1985-88, Clinton Cos., Inc., Stamford, 1988—. Leader Girl Scouts, Stamford, 1979-81; counselor, bd. dirs. Jewish Family Services, Stamford, 1984-85; adv., supr. Safe Rides, Stamford, 1985-87; travel coordinator New Cannan (Conn.) YMCA. Mem. Am. Mktg. Assn., Mktg. Research Assn., Low Heywood Alumnae (fundraiser 1967—). Democrat. Jewish. Clubs: Long Ridge Swim (Stamford) (bd. dirs., swim chairperson 1981-86). Home: 22 McIntosh Ct Stamford CT 06903 Office: Clinton Cos 1177 Summer St Stamford CT 06905

SPELL, JANYCE JOHNSON, human ecology educator; b. Atlanta, July 27, 1953; d. William Nelson and Norma-Jane (Rader) Johnson; m. B. Eldred Spell, Dec. 21, 1974. BA, Furman U., 1975; MA, Mich. State U., 1982, PhD, 1986. Cert. tchr., Mich., S.C. Tchr. pub. schs. N.C. and S.C., 1975-79; pub., editor, pres. The Flute Network, Little Wizard Enterprises, East Lansing, Mich., 1984—; asst. prof. Coll. Human Ecology, Mich. State U., East Lansing, 1986—; bd. dirs. Flute Industries Council, 1986—. Mem. Nat. Council Family Relations, Omicron Nu, Phi Kappa Phi. Democrat. Methodist. Office: Little Wizard Enterprises PO Box 6441 East Lansing MI 48826

SPELLMIRE, SANDRA MARIE, systems analyst, programmer; b. San Francisco, Feb. 20, 1950; d. Robert Joseph and Catherine Louise (Sockett) S. BS, Calif. State U., Los Angeles, 1977. Project controls analyst Ralph M. Parsons Co., Pasadena, Calif., 1978-81, C.F. Braun & Co., Alhambra, Calif., 1981-84; configuration mgr. software systems Burroughs Corp., Santa Ana, Calif., 1984-85; sr. scientific analyst, programmer Electronic Data Systems, Los Angeles, 1985, Denver, 1985-87, Mpls., 1987—. Mem. AAAS, IEEE (affiliate), Nat. Assn. Female Execs., Assn. for Computing Machinery (assoc.).

SPENCE, BARBARA HARRINGTON EARNSHAW (MRS. KENNETH M. SPENCE, JR.), publishing company executive; b. Bryn Mawr, Pa., July 8, 1921; d. Geoffrey Strange and Mary (Harrington) Earnshaw; m. Kenneth M. Spence Jr., June 29, 1944; children: Kenneth M. III, Christopher E., Hilary B. Grad. high sch. Movie, radio editor Parade Mag., N.Y.C., 1941-45; with Merchandising Group, N.Y.C., 1946-47; exec. dir. Greenfield Hill Congl. Ch., Fairfield, Conn., 1958-74, dir. religious edn., 1968-74; personnel dir. William Morrow & Co., Inc., N.Y.C., 1976—. Chmn. pub. relations, bd. dirs. ARC, 1951-56, Family Service Soc., Fairfield, 1956-57, 61-63; chmn. pub. relations Citizens-for-Eisenhower, 1952, Fairfield Teens Players, 1968-71; bd. dirs. Fairfield Teens, Inc., 1965-70, Planned Parenthood, Greater Bridgeport, 1969-75, chmn. pub. affairs, 1971-72, chmn. personnel, 1972-73, chpt. vice chmn., 1973-75; pres. steering com. Am. Playwrights Festival Theatre, Inc., Fairfield, 1969-70, v.p., bd. dirs., 1971—; bd. govs. Unquowa

Sch., Fairfield, 1963-69; bd. dirs. Fairfield U. Playhouse, 1971-73, Downtown Cabaret Theatre, Bridgeport, 1975-76. mgr., assoc. Ten Eyck-Emerich Antiques, 1974-76; mem. compensation survey com. A.A.P. Home: 101 Twin Brooks Ln Fairfield CT 06430 Office: William Morrow & Co Inc 105 Madison Ave New York NY 10016

SPENCE, EVELYN BATTEN, insurance company executive; b. Huntington, W.Va., May 19, 1934; d. Lacy A. and Mary Frances (Wilhoit) B.; m. Charles I. Spence, May 28, 1954; 1 child, Larry S. Grad. high school, Huntington, 1952. CLU. V.p. Orange State Life Ins. Co., Largo, Fla., 1975-81; state regional mgr. Ministries Life Ins. Co., Lake Worth, Fla., 1981-83; asst. v.p. Am. Pioneer Life, Orlando, Fla., 1983-85; v.p., chief adminstrv. officer Fin. Benefit Life Ins. Co., Boca Raton, Fla., 1985-87, also bd. dirs.; v.p., chief underwriter Kanawha Ins. Co., Lancaster, S.C., 1987—. Editor company newsletter, 1980; free-lance photographer. Campaigner United Way, Orlando, 1984. Mem. Am. Coll. CLU's, Assoc. Photographers Internat. Club: Toastmasters. Office: Kanawha Ins Co 210 S White St Lancaster SC 29720

SPENCE, JANET BLAKE CONLEY (MRS. ALEXANDER PYOTT SPENCE), civic worker; b. Upper Montclair, N.J., Aug. 17, 1915; d. Walter Abbott and Ethel Maud (Blake) Conley; student Vassar Coll., 1933-35; certificate Katharine Gibbs Sch., 1936; m. Alexander Pyott Spence, June 10, 1939; children—Janet Blake Spence Kerr, Robert Moray, Richard Taylor. Formerly active Jr. League, Neighborhood House, ARC, Girl Scouts U.S.A.; active various community drives; chmn. Darien (Conn.) Assembly, 1955-56; sec., chmn. Wilton Jr. Assembly, 1961-63; subscription chmn. Candlelight Concerts Wilton, Conn., 1963-65; rec. sec. Pub. Health Nursing Assn. Wilton Bd., 1964-67; corr., rec. sec. Royle Sch. Bd., Darien, 1952-55; fund raiser Vassar Class of 1937; mem. Washington Valley Community Assn.; mem. N.J. Symphony Orch. League (treas. Morris County br. 1978-83, corr. sec. 1982-83, pres. 1985-88, state council mem. 1985-89). Mem. Vassar Alumni Assn., Dobbs Alumni Assn. Congregationalist. Clubs: Jersey Hills Vassar, Wilton Garden, Washington Valley Home Econs. (life, corr. sec. 1977-82, pres. 1982-84, v.p. 1984-85, co-pres. 1985-86, chmn. membership com. 1987—). Home: Hilltop Washington Valley Rd Morristown NJ 07960 also: 8 Evergreen Ave Kennebunk ME 04043

SPENCE, VALORIE ANNETTE, watersports company executive; b. Annapolis, Md., Oct. 21, 1954; d. Roy Douglas and Annette Vohn (Whetstone) Woods; m. Stephen Ragsdale Spence, Sept. 21, 1982. Student, Santa Monica Coll., 1972-74, Highline Community Coll., Wash., 1975. Instr., mgr. Fason Marine Service, Olympia, Wash., 1974-80; instr. Cen. Pacific Divers, Lahaina, Hawaii, 1981-82; prin. Blue Chip Charters, Lahaina, Hawaii, 1982—; instr. ocean adventures, Scuba Sch. Internat. Mem. Profl. Assn. Diving Instrs. (cert., 1975, master scuba instr., 1986—, course dir., medic., 1987—), Nat. Assn. Diving Instrs., Nat. Assn. Female Execs, Lahaina C. of C. Republican. Episcopalian. Club: Hood Canal Seals (pres. 1979). Office: Blue Chip Charters Ltd 888 Wainee St #130 Lahaina HI 96761

SPENCER, BILLIE JANE, lawyer; b. Caro, Mich., Sept. 16, 1949; d. William Norman and Jane Isabel (Putnam) S. AB in Econs., U. Miami, Coral Gables, Fla., 1971, LLM in Tax, 1980; JD, U. Fla., Gainesville, 1973; course cert. St. Catherine's Coll., Oxford U., 1973; grad., Naval War Coll., Washington, 1985-88; student, Nat. Def. U., Washington, 1986—. Bar: Fla., Calif. Assoc. Frates Floyd, et. al., Miami, Fla., 1973-74; commd. lt. (j.g.) USNR, 1974, advanced through grades to commdr., 1988; judge advocate USNR, Subic Bay, Pensacola, 1975-78; sole practice San Francisco, and Stuart, Fla., 1978-85; asst. staff judge advocate USNR, Lemoore, Calif., 1982-83; DOD liaison USNR, Washington, 1985-88; instr. econs. Fla. Inst. Tech., Jensen Beach, 1984-85; litigation cons. Castle & Cooke, Inc., San Francisco, 1979-83; clk. Ehrlichmann Watergate Trial team, Washington, 1974; del. state conf. on small bus., 1982. Mem. U.S. Naval Inst., Res. Officers Assn., The Navy League, Am. Mgmt. Assn. Republican. Unitarian. Home: 3224 S Stafford St Arlington VA 22206

SPENCER, DIANE BROWN, marketing specialist; b. Montclair, N.J.; d. Isaac Washington and Nellie (Bratton) Brown; m. Clint Spencer; children: Derrick, Donna. BS in Mktg., Rutgers U., 1976; MBA, Fairleigh Dickinson U., 1983. Supr. mktg. Schering-Plough Pharmacy, Kenilworth, N.J., 1975-78; mgr. mkt. analysis Squibb Pharm., Princeton, N.J., 1978-80; mgr. product research Squibb Pharm., Princeton, 1980-84, sr. mgr. mkt. research, 1984-87, mgr. strategic planning, 1987—; cons. Transworld Enterprises, Newark, N.J., 1970—, Venture & Venture, New Brunswick, N.J., 1986—; pres. Connections Network, Montclair, N.J., 1984-86, Sidelines Network, 1987—. Recipient Achiever in Industry, YMCA, 1980. Mem. Nat. Assn. Female Execs. Democrat. Methodist. Home: 32 Stephen St Montclair NJ 07042 Office: Squibb Pharm PO Box 4000 Princeton NJ 08540

SPENCER, ELEANOR ANN, foundation executive; b. Pace, Fla., Mar. 19, 1941; d. William Dexter and Eunice Love (Pitts) Gallops; m. William Clifton Spencer, Feb. 4, 1966 (div. 1980); children: Suzanne C. Spencer Collard, Kathleen L. SPencer Cole. Student, North Fla. Jr. Coll., 1959-60, Pensacola Jr. Coll., 1980. Dental asst. Dr. James Watson, Milton, Fla., 1963-66; community vol. Telcare, Inc., Milton, 1969-74; exec. dir. Santa Rosa County Council on Aging, Milton, 1975—; bd. dirs. Santa Rosa Mental Health Assn., Milton, 1972, Santa Rosa Guidance Clinic, Milton, 1973-74; mem. council Ctr. on Aging, Pensacola, 1982—; bd. dirs. Fla. Council on Aging, Tallahassee, 1983—. Chair bd. mem. SSS, Local Bd. I, 1983—; mem. govt. affairs com. Santa Rosa C. of C., Milton, 1986—. Mem. Nat. Council on Aging, Nat. Inst. of Sr. Ctrs., Fla. Assn. Sr. Ctrs. (sec. 1984-86), Fla. Transit Assn., So. Gerontology Soc. Club: Tanglewood Country (Milton). Home: 1795 Anderson Ln Milton FL 32570 Office: Santa Rosa County Council on Aging 609 Alabama St Milton FL 32570

SPENCER, ELIZABETH, author; b. Carrollton, Miss., 1921; d. James Luther and Mary James (McCain) S.; m. John Arthur Blackwood Rusher, Sept. 29, 1956. BA, Belhaven Coll., 1942; MA, Vanderbilt U., 1943; LittD (hon.), Southwestern U. at Memphis, 1968. Instr. N.W. Miss. Jr. Coll., 1943-44; reporter The Nashville Tennessean, 1945-46; instr. U. Miss., Oxford, 1948-51, 52-53; adj. prof. Concordia U., Montreal, Que., Can., 1981—. Writer-in-residence, U. N.C., 1969, Hollins Coll., 1973, Concordia U., 1977-78; Author: Fire in the Morning, 1948, This Crooked Way, 1952, The Voice at the Back Door, 1956, The Light in the Piazza, 1960, Knights and Dragons, 1965, No Place for an Angel, 1967, Ship Island and Other Stories, 1968, The Snare, 1972, The Stories of Elizabeth Spencer, 1981, Marilee, 1981, The Salt Line, 1984; contbr. short stories to mags. and collections. Recipient Women's Democratic Com. award, 1949; recognition award Nat. Inst. Arts and letters, 1952; Guggenheim Found. fellow, 1953; Richard and Hinda Rosenthal Found. award Am. Acad. Arts and Letters, 1957; Award of Merit medal for the short story Am. Acad. Arts and Letters, 1983; Kenyon Rev. fellow in fiction, 1957; 1st McGraw-Hill Fiction award, 1960; Bryn Mawr Col. Donnelly fellow, 1962; Henry Bellamann award for creative writing, 1968; Nat. Endowment for Arts grantee in lit., 1983. Mem. Am. Inst. Arts and Letters. Home: 2300 Saint Mathieu, Apt 610, Montreal, PQ Canada H3H 2J8 *

SPENCER, GERALDINE BRAILO, newspaper editor, journalist; b. Panama City, Panama, Nov. 8, 1943; came to U.S., 1948; d. Chester Vernon and Virginia (Dell) Sullins; m. David George Brailo, June 6, 1964 (div. June 1980); children—Christopher, Stephen; m. Riley John Spencer Jr., Sept. 16, 1980. AA, Los Angeles Pierce Coll., 1979. Adminstrv. asst. City of Los Angeles, 1963-67; supr. Dept. Water and Power, Los Angeles, 1967-71; reporter, bus. editor Simi Valley Enterprise, Calif., 1979; editor-in-chief The Tolucan newspaper, Toluca Lake, Calif., 1979-81; freelance journalist, Moorpark, Calif., 1981-83; editor-in-chief The Mirror, Simi Valley, Calif., 1983; stringer Los Angeles Times, 1984-86; radio broadcaster KWNK, Simi Valley, 1986. Editor: 1982-83 Ventura County Grand Jury Report, 1983, The Moorpark Mirror, 1987—; contbg. writer Excellence in College Journalism, 1983. Pub. relations vol. St. Jude Children's Research Hosp., Los Angeles, 1975-78; mem. Ventura County Grand Jury, Ventura, Calif., 1982-83; commr. Area Housing Authority, Ventura, 1983-86; v.p., found. mem. Moorpark Coll., Calif., 1983-87; chmn. bd. trustee Los Robles Regional Med. Ctr., Thousand Oaks, Calif., 1985-89, pres. Moorpark Beautiful, 1987. Recipient 1st place award Journalism Assn. Community Colls., 1979; 1st place award San Fernando Valley Press Club, 1983, 84. Mem. Women in Communications. Republican. Roman Catholic. Home: PO Box 92 Moorpark CA 93020

SPENCER, JAN LOUISE ROTENBERRY, artist; b. St. Paul, May 30, 1957; d. Everett Garland and Nancy Mae (Reitz) Rotenberry; m. John Hennessy Walsh, Aug. 3, 1985. Student art and music, U. Minn., 1974-81, 83; BA magna cum laude, Macalester Coll., St. Paul, 1979; postgrad. in edn., Coll. St. Thomas, St. Paul, 1984; MA, Calif. State U., Chico, 1987. Cert. kindergarten and elem. tchr., Minn. Tchr. tech. theatre and acting, artist-in-residence St. Paul Pub. Schs., 1978-79; tchr. arts and crafts, program dir. and designer Vols. in Mission, United Presbyn. Ch., Klukwan and Haines, Alaska, 1979; tchr. art, acting and tech. theatre, coordinator music and dance Wilson Jr. High Sch., St. Paul, 1979-80; tchr. English Harding and Johnson Sr. High Schs., St. Paul, 1980-81; tchr. art awareness Minn. Mus. Art, St. Paul, 1981; tchr. elem. Skagway (Alaska) City Schs., 1982-83; dir., tchr. Paradise (Calif.) Montessori Children's House, 1984-85; asst. to dir. Art Gallery, Calif. State U., Chico, 1985—; designer lighting, master electrician Martin Luther King Ctr., St. Paul, 1980; co-dir. 1078 Gallery, Chico, 1987—, also bd. dirs.; assessment officer Butte Coll., Calif., 1988—. Works exhibited in Minn. Mus. Art, St. Paul, 1979, Fairfield-Suisun Arts Council Juried Show, Vacaville, Calif., 1984-85 (1st place award 1984), AAO Gallery, Buffalo, 1985, Redding (Calif.) Mus., 1985-86, 1078 Gallery, 1986-87, U. Hawaii, Hilo, 1986, Southern Exposure Gallery, San Francisco, 1987, Cherry St. Gallery, Chico, 1987, Auburn (Calif.) Arts Mus., 1987, Calif. State U., Chico, 1987, Coll. Siskiyous, Weed, Calif., 1987, Studio 13 for Fine Arts, Mpls., 1987, Roche Bobois, San Francisco, 1988; represented by Art Works, Santa Barbara, Calif., 1988. Recipient Lt. Robert Merton Rawlins Merit award Calif. State U., 1986; Calif. State U. Mary Ahlquist scholar, 1986, Arrowmont Sch. Arts and Crafts Isable Mulholland Cramer scholar Arrowmont Sch. Arts and Crafts, Gatlinburg, Tex., 1987. Presbyterian. Home: 1290 Salem St Chico CA 95928

SPENCER, MARY EILEEN, biochemist, educator; b. Regina, Sask., Can., Oct. 4, 1923; d. John J. and Etta Christina (Hamren) Stapleton; m. Henry Anderson Spencer, July 3, 1946; 1 dau., Susan Mary. A.A., Regina Coll., 1942; B.A. with high honors in Chemistry, U. Sask., 1945; M.A. in Chemistry, Bryn Mawr Coll., 1946; Ph.D. in Agrl. Chemistry, U. Calif.-Berkeley, 1951. Chemist, Ayerst, McKenna and Harrison Ltd., Montreal, Que., Can., summer 1945, full time, 1946-47, Nat. Canners Assn., San Francisco, 1948; teaching fellow U. Calif.-Berkeley, 1949, instr. food chemistry, 1951; faculty U. Alta., Edmonton, Can., 1953—, instr., asst. prof., asso. prof., acting head biochem. dept., 1960-61, plant sci. dept., 1962, prof. plant sci., 1964-83 , McCalla research prof., 1983-84, univ. prof., 1984—; sec.-treas. Spencer-Lemaire Industries Ltd.; mem. NRC Can., 1970, 70-73, 73-76, Task Force on Post-Secondary Edn., Alta. Govt. Commn. on Ednl. Planning, 1970-72; chmn. Nat. Adv. Com. on Biology, Nat. Research Council; adv. bd. Prairie Regional Lab.; bd. govs. U. Alta., 1976-79; chmn. ad hoc vis. com. in forestry research NRC, 1975-76; mem. Agr. Can. Cons. Com. IBT Pesticides, 1981-82; bd. dirs. Natural Scis. and Engring. Research Council Can., 1986—. Recipient Queen Elizabeth II Silver Jubilee medal. Fellow Chem. Inst. Can., Royal Soc. Can.; Mem. Can. Soc. Plant Physiologists (pres. 1971-72), Scandinavian Soc. Plant Physiology, Plant Growth Regulator Soc. Am., Am. Soc. Plant Physiologists, Can. Assn. Univ. Tchrs., Japanese Soc. Plant Physiologists, Internat. Plant Growth Regulator Soc. Office: Univ Alberta Dept Plant Sci, Faculty Agr and Forestry, Edmonton, AB Canada T6G 2E3

SPENCER, MARY MILLER, civic worker; b. Comanche, Tex., May 25, 1924; d. Aaron Gaynor and Alma (Grissom) Miller; 1 child, Mara Lynn. BS, North Tex. State U., 1943. Cafeteria dir. Mercedes (Tex.) Pub. Schs., 1943-46; home economist coordinator All-Orange Dessert Contest, Fla. Citrus Commn., Lakeland, 1959-62, 64; tchr. purchasing sch. lunch dept. Fla. Dept. Edn., 1960. Clothing judge Polk County (Fla.) Youth Fair, 1951-68, Polk County Federated Women's Clubs, 1964-66; pres. Dixieland Elem. Sch. PTA, 1955-57, Polk County Council PTA's, 1958-60; chmn. public edn. com. Polk County unit Am. Cancer Soc., 1959-60, bd. dirs., 1962-70; charter mem., bd. dirs. Lakeland YMCA, 1962-72; sec. Greater Lakeland Community Nursing Council, 1965-72; trustee, vice chmn. Polk County Eye Clinic, Inc., 1962-64, pres., 1964-82; bd. dirs. Polk County Scholarship and Loan Fund, 1962-70; mem. exec. com. West Polk County (Fla.) Community Welfare Council, 1960-62, 65-68; mem. budget and audit com. Greater Lakeland United Fund, 1960-62, bd. dirs., 1967-70, residential chmn. fund drive, 1968; mem. adv. bd. Polk County Juvenile and Domestic Relations Ct., 1960-69; worker children's services div. family services Dept. Health and Rehab. Services, State of Fla., 1969-70, social worker, 1970-72, 74-82, social worker OFR unit, 1977-81, pub. assistance specialist IV, 1984-88. Mem. exec. com. Suncoast Health Council, 1968-71; mem. Polk County Home Econs. Adv. Com., 1965-71; sec. bd. dirs. Fla. West Coast Ednl. TV, 1960-81; bd. dirs. Lake Region United Way, Winter Haven, 1976-81; mem. Polk County Community Services Council, 1978—. Mem. Nat. Welfare Fraud Assn., Fla. Congress Parents and Tchrs. (hon. life; pres. dist. 7 1961-63, chmn. pub. relations 1962-66), AAUW (pres. Lakeland br. 1960-61), Polk County Mental Health Assn., Fla. Health and Welfare Council, Fla. Health and Social Service Council, North Tex. State U. Alumni Assn. Democrat. Methodist. Lodge: Order of Eastern Star. Home: 535 W Beacon Rd Lakeland FL 33803 Mailing Address: PO Box 2161 Lakeland FL 33806

SPENCER, PATRICIA ANN, advertising agency director; b. San Angelo, Tex., July 5, 1950; d. Francis Milton and Phyllis Mae (McPherson) S. BFA, U. Tex., 1972. Asst. personnel dir. pub. relations Hyatt Regency Hotel, Houston, 1972-78; copywriter Farnam Cos. Inc., Phoenix, 1978-79, product mgr., 1979-82, dir. advt. horse product div., 1982-84, creative dir. The Charles Duff Agy., 1984—, editorPet Care Publs. div. The Charles Duff Agy., 1986—; free-lance copywriter, Phoenix, 1979—. Contbr. articles to profl. jours. Recipient Bronze award Internat. Film and TV Festival, 1984, OMA Bronze award Point of Purchase Inst., 1984, Popai Gold award Point of Purchase Inst., 1985. Mem. Am. Advt. Assn. (Excellence award 1985), Am. Advt. Fedn. (Best in the West award 1985, 86), Bus. Profl. Advt. Assn., Nat. Agrl. Mktg. Assn. Democrat. Presbyterian. Office: Farnam Cos Inc 301 W Osborn Rd Phoenix AZ 85013

SPENCER, SUSAN LYNN CRANE, controller; b. Hartford, Conn., Mar. 20, 1947; d. Allen Edward and Wilma Darlene (Bachmann) Crane; m. William Albert Spencer, Nov. 6, 1965 (div. 1970); 1 child, Sharon Lynn; m. Lawrence Newton Spencer, Dec.7, 1970; children: Lawrence Scott, Angela Lee. AS, Mohegan Community Coll., 1979; student, Cen. Wash. State U., 1980-85. Bookkeeper, acct. eastern div. NAPA, Middletown, Conn., 1970-71; acct. Oswalt and DeWitt, Kennewick, Wash., 1979; mgr. acctg. office Flight, Inc., Richland, Wash., 1980; auditor cost acctg. Bechtel Constrn. Co., Richland, 1981-85; controller All-Time Mfg. Co., Inc., Montville, Conn., 1985—. Mem. Nat. Assn. Female Execs., Beta Sigma Phi (pres. 1980-81, chmn. program and service coms. 1985—). Republican. Congregationalist. Home: 662 Raymond Hill Rd Oakdale CT 06370 Office: All-Time Mfg Co Inc Bridge St Montville CT 06353

SPENCER, TRICIA JANE, limousine company executive; b. Springfield, Ill., Dec. 8, 1952; d. Frank Edward and LaWanda (Edwards) Bell; m. Mark Edward Spencer, Aug. 21, 1982. Student pub. schs. Instr., Falcons Drum & Bugle Corps, Springfield, 1969-72; concert, stage, TV, film performer, 1970-82, part-time 1982—; guest dir. Sing out Salem, Ohio, 1973; contbg. writer Saddle Tramps Wild West Revue, 1977—; legal sec. to pvt. atty., Tustin, Calif., 1980-82; owner Am. Dream Balloons & Services, Orange, Calif., 1982—; founder, corp. pres. Am. Dream Limousine Service, Inc., Orange, 1983—. Songwriter; designer greeting cards, one-of-a-kind automobile producer, dir. mus. stage shows, 1974-82, author: TIPS - The Server's Guide to Bringing Home the Bacon, 1987. Performer, Up With People, 1972-73; organizer Bicentennial Com. Springfield, 1976; mediator Limousine and Chauffeur Council, Orange County, 1984—; vol. Orange County Performing Arts Soc., 1985—. Recipient Appreciation, Achievement awards Muscular Dystrophy Assn., 1977-79. Mem. Am. Entrepreneurs Assn., Internat. Platform Assn., Nat. Limousine Assn., So. Calif. Limousine Owners Assn., Nat. Assn. Female Execs., Orange County C. of C. Republican. Avocations: guitar, piano, writing. Office: Am Dream Limousine Service Inc 795 N Tustin Orange CA 92667

SPENCER-STARK, CHERRY ELLERBEE, nursing administrator, consultant; b. Atlanta, Apr. 29, 1948; d. Gerald Brooks and Kathryn Eloise (Lester) Ellerbee; m. James Thomas Spencer, Sept. 7, 1968 (div. Apr. 1977); children—G. Todd, G. Christian; m. 2d, James Edwin Stark, Apr. 5, 1981; stepchildren—David E., Thomas C. B.S. in Nursing, U. Fla., 1971; M.N., Emory U., 1982; postgrad. Kennesaw Coll. R.N., Ga. Staff nurse Emory U. Hosp., Atlanta, 1976-77; adolescent asst. head nurse Peachtree-Parkwood, Atlanta, 1977-79, adult asst. head nurse, 1979-80; adminstrv. head nurse Ga. Bapt. Med. Ctr., Atlanta, 1980-81, nursing supr., 1981-83; dir. patient services So. Christian Home, Atlanta, 1983-85; assoc. administr. Brawner Psychiat. Inst., Smyma, Ga., 1985—, Psychiat. Inst. Atlanta, Smyma, 1985—, Laurel Heights Hosp., Smyma, 1985—; guest lectr. Nell Hodgson Woodruff Sch. Nursing, Emory U., 1982—. Co-pres. aux. Northside Youth Orgn., Atlanta, 1983-84. Mem. Am. Nurses Assn., Ga. Nurses Assn. (treas. 1986—), Emory U. Alumni Assn. (founding mem. bd. gov. 1988—) Sigma Theta Tau. Unitarian.

SPERO, DAWN LOUISE, association executive; b. Carlisle, Pa., Aug. 18, 1957; m. Mitchell E. Spero, June 27, 1981. BA, U. Pitts., 1979; cert., Inst. for Paralegal Tng., Phila., 1979; MBA, U. Miami, 1986. Paralegal Mershon, Sawyer et al, Miami, Fla., 1979-80, Fowler, White et al, Miami, 1980-84; mgr. King Motor Ctr., Ft. Lauderdale, Fla., 1984-86, Fabri Ctrs. of Am., Pompano, Fla., 1986; exec. dir. Sunrise (Fla.) C. of C., 1987—. Vol. Ft. Lauderdale Winterfest and Boat Parade, 1987. Chancellor U. Undergrad. teaching fellow, Pitts., 1979. Mem. Assn. for MBA Execs., Nat. Assn. Female Execs., Mental Health Assn. Broward County. Club: Bus. and Profl. Women (Plantation, Fla.) (bd. dirs.). Office: C of C 3591 N University Dr Sunrise FL 33351

SPERRY, JEAN ELIZABETH, educator; b. Des Moines, July 30, 1951; d. Herbert J. and Helen (Anderson) S.; B.S., Drake U., 1972; M.A., Coll. St. Thomas, 1980. Tchr. spl. edn. West St. Paul Ind. Sch. Dist. 197, 1973—; mgr. concessionary St. Paul Civic Center, 1976-84; seminar leader Coll. St. Thomas, 1980-83; owner, cons. Sperry & Assocs., 1983-85. Mem. task force United Handicapped Fedn. Mem. Am. Bus. Women Assn., Minn. Fedn. Tchrs. (ednl. policies com., MFT state spl. edn. com., dist. spl. edn. steering com.), Minn. Assn. For Adults and Children with Learning Disabilities, CEC, Assn. Retarded Citizens, Bus. and Profl. Women, Nat. Assn. Female Execs., Nat. Found. Ileitis and Colitis. Democrat. Presbyterian. Office: 181 W Butler Ave West Saint Paul MN 55118

SPETZ, KATHRYN FRANCES, costume design firm executive, interior decorator, landscape consultant; b. Mpls., Oct. 22, 1949; d. Glen Rudolph and Charlotte Ellen (Perks) S. B.S., Fla. State U., 1971. Corporate designer 6 Flags Over Ga., Atlanta, 1974-78; owner Spetz Prodns., Atlanta, 1978—. Publicity co-chmn. Lung Run, Am. Lung Assn. Atlanta, 1982, 83, High Mus. Art, Atlanta, Colonial Williamsburg Found. Mem. Sales and Mktg. Execs. Internat., Nat. Assn. Female Execs., Ga. Assn. Image and Fashion Cons., Alpha Xi Delta (v.p. Atlanta 1984-86, pres. 1986—, pres. Atlanta area council, 1987—, province nominating com., 1987—). Republican. Presbyterian. Club: Atlanta Women's Rugby Football (v.p., union rep., match sec., selector 1974-81). Avocations: scuba diving, sailing, show jumping (horses), rugby. Address: 4087 Admiral Dr Atlanta GA 30341

SPICAK, DORIS ELIZABETH, health services company executive; b. Balt., Sept. 6, 1943; d. Elwood Lee and Georgianna E. (Thomas) Fletcher; m. Marvin Ray Spicak, May 18, 1968; children: Charles Frank, Lisa Marie. Student, Towson State Coll., 1961-62, Balt. Jr. Coll., 1962-64; diploma in nursing, Sinai Sch. Nursing, Balt., 1965; AS, Bee County Coll., Beeville, Tex., 1976. RN. Inservice dir. Meml. Hosp., Beeville, 1975-76, dir. nurses, 1980-81; dir. nurses Hillside Nursing Ctr., Beeville, 1978-80; dir. br. agy. Coastal Bend Home Health, Victoria, Tex., 1981-85; adminstr. Crossroads Home Health, Victoria, 1985—, pres. bd. dirs., 1985—; pres. bd. dirs. Crossroads Nursing Service, Victoria, 1986—. Active John F. Kennedy Presdl. campaign, Balt., 1960. Served to 1st lt. U.S. Army, 1965-68, Vietnam. Mem. Tex. Assn. Home Health Agys. (medicare com. 1986—), Nat. Assn. for Home Care, Victoria C. of C. Democrat. Roman Catholic. Club: Coastal Plains Continuity of Care (Victoria) (treas. 1983-84). Office: Crossroads Home Health 1501 E Mockingbird #403A Victoria TX 77904

SPICER, CAROLYN MARIE, banker; b. Durand, Mich., July 31, 1947; d. Clarence Edward and Joyce Magdeline (McCarthy) Ackerman; m. Neal J. Spicer, Oct. 8, 1966 (div. Feb. 1978); children: Anthony J., Bethany L. Honors student, Bank Adminstrn. Inst., 1987. Bookkeeper Genesee Mchts. Bank, Vernon, Mich., 1966-67; teller Citizens Comml. and Savs. Bank, Durand, 1967-69, Flint, Mich., 1976; teller State Savs. Bank, Fenton, Mich., 1976-78, asst. br. mgr., 1979, main br. mgr., 1980, adminstrv. asst. ops., 1981-82, ops. officer, 1983-86, v.p. ops., 1986—. Contbr. articles to profl. jours. Treas. Cliffview Assn., Fenton, 1980, pres., 1981. Named Profl. Banker of Yr., 1987. Mem. Am. Inst. Banking. Republican. Roman Catholic. Office: State Savs Bank of Fenton 1 Fenton Sq Drawer E Fenton MI 48430-0725

SPICHER, BONNIE GOLDSTROHM, training director; b. Kittanning, Pa., Mar. 16, 1945; d. Harry L. and Christina (Dodds) Goldstrohm; m. D. Keith Spicher, Aug. 1, 1963; children: Brian Keith, Kevin Todd. Grad. high sch., Kittanning, Pa. Cert. real estate broker. Sales, assoc., asst. mgr. Real Estate One, Inc., Brighton, Mich., 1979-84; assoc. broker, asst. mgr. The Mich. Group, Inc., Brighton, 1984-86, dir. tng., 1986—; relocation coordinator Merrill-Lynch Relocation, Southfield, Mich., 1985—. Active Realtors Polit. Action Com., 1986. Recipient Speaking award Toastmasters of Am., 1983. Mem. Nat. Assn. Realtors, Mich. Assn. Realtors, Western Wayne, Oakland Counties Bd. of Realtors, Livingston County Bd. Realtors (bd. dirs. 1984-86, equal opportunity trainer, 1984—). Republican.

SPICKNALL, SANDRA FULLER, systems analyst; b. Charlottesville, Va., July 14, 1955; d. Melvin Eugene and Dorothy Lee (Mitchell) Fuller; m. Robert Hale Spicknall, Sept. 6, 1980. BA, Coll. William and Mary, 1977, MBA, 1980. Budget coordinator A.H. Robins Co., Inc., Richmond, Va., 1982-86; info. ctr. analyst A.H. Robins Co., Inc., Richmond, 1986—. Mem. The Planning Forum (v.p. membership 1986—), Va. Info Ctr. Exchange, Beta Gamma Sigma, William and Mary Alumni Chpt. (bd. dirs. 1985-87, pres. 1987-88). Republican. Baptist. Office: AH Robins Co Inc 1407 Cummings Dr Richmond VA 23220

SPIEGEL, JEANNE S., economist; b. Merion, Pa., Oct. 23, 1926; d. Stanley R. and Julia (Nusbaum) Sundheim; B.A., Wellesley Coll., 1948; postgrad. U. Pa., 1976-78; m. Walter F. Spiegel, Oct. 8, 1950; children—Walter D., Karen J., James R. Economist, Dept. Labor, Washington, 1949-50; with Walter F. Spiegel, Inc., Cons. Engrs., Jenkintown, Pa., 1963—, office mgr., 1965-78, contract adminstr., 1965-75, energy analyst, chief economist, 1975—, corp. sec., 1967—. Mem. Nat. Assn. Women in Constrn. (chpt. pres.). Home: 434 Copper Beach Circle Elkins Park PA 19117 Office: 309 York Rd Jenkintown PA 19446

SPIEGEL, KATHLEEN MARIE, health care manager, registered nurse; b. Erie, Pa., May 15, 1948; d. Julius B. and Helen K. (Schiller) S.; m. John Stuart Coffey, Nov. 14, 1970 (div. 1975). BS in Nursing, Villa Maria Coll., 1970; postgrad., Edinboro U., 1980. Diplomate Am. Bd. Quality Assurance and Utilization Rev. Staff nurse U. Hosps. of Cleve., 1970-71, Citizens Gen. Hosp., New Kensington, Pa., 1971-72; referral coordinator, staff nurse Kiski Valley Vis. Nurse Assn., Apollo, Pa., 1972-74; patient coordinator Medicenter Of Erie, 1974-75; coordinator, instr. St. Vincent Health Ctr. Sch. Nursing, Erie, 1975-82; asst. dir., hospice program dir. Vis. Nurse Assn. of Erie County, Erie, 1982-85, mgr. discharge planning and ops. Equicor The Equitable HCA Corp., Pitts., 1986-87; dir. quality assessment and utilization rev. U. Health Services, Inc., Pitts., 1987—; bd. dirs. Pa. Hospice Network, 1983-87. Served to maj. U.S. Army Res., 1978—. Mem. Am. Bd. Quality Assurance UR, Nat. Assn. Female Execs., Am. Mgmt. Assn., Assn. Quality Assurance Profls. Western Pa., Sigma Theta Tau. Democrat. Roman Catholic. Club: Erie 80. Home: 6 Oakville Dr Pittsburgh PA 15220 Office: Univ Health Services 3520 Fifth Ave Suite 402 Pittsburgh PA 15213

SPIEGEL, LINDA ELLEN, diversified energy company manager; b. Phila., Aug. 6, 1953; d. Louis and Laura Widman; m. Barry S. Spiegel, Jan. 25,

1983; children: Jill A., David L. B.S. with highest honors, Phila. Coll. Textiles and Sci., 1975; M.B.A. with highest honors, Drexel U., 1982. Pvt. practice public acctg., Pa., 1975-78; acctg. specialist Sun Petroleum Product Co., Phila., 1978-79; mgr. internal control and adminstrn. Sun Co., Inc., Radnor, Pa., 1979-83, mgr. auditing., Phila., 1983-88; cons., 1988—; speaker in field. C.P.A., Pa.; recipient Achievement award YWCA, 1983. Member Am. Inst. C.P.A.s, Pa. Inst. C.P.A.s (chmn. industry com., mem. exec. com., Scholastic award 1975), N.J. Soc. CPA's. Office: 17 Orchard Ln Marlton NJ 08053

SPIEGEL, MARILYN HARRIET, real estate executive; b. Bklyn., Apr. 3, 1935; d. Harry and Sadie (Oscher) Unger; m. Murray Spiegel, June 12, 1954; children: Eric Lawrence, Dana Cheryl, Jay Barry. Grad. high sch., Bklyn. Exec. sec. S & W Paper Co., N.Y.C., 1953-54, Japan Paper Co., N.Y.C., 1954-58; salesperson Red Carpet Realtors, Los Alamitos, Calif., 1974-75, Coll. Park Realtors, Garden Grove, Calif., 1975-79; owner, broker S & S Properties, Garden Grove, 1979—. Mem. Calif. Assn. Realtors (bd. dirs. 1984—), West Orange County Bd. Realtors (bd. dirs. 1984—, 1st v.p. 1987, pres. 1988), Million Dollar Sales Club, Long Beach C. of C., Seal Beach C. of C., Orange County C. of C., Summit Orgn. Home: 4765 Candleberry St Seal Beach CA 90740 Office: S & S Properties 5250 Lampson St Garden Grove CA 92645

SPIEGEL, SUSAN LYNN, manufacturing company executive; b. N.Y.C.; d. Irving and Beatrice (Albert) Jaffe; m. Maurice Spiegel, Aug. 31, 1975; children by previous marriage: Robert Wayne, Stephen Mark. BS, Boston U., 1964; postgrad., Hofstra U., C.W. Post U. Elem. sch. tchr. Long Beach, N.Y., 1964-67; pres. Fashions by Appointment, Glen Cove, N.Y., 1967-71; adminstrv. asst. Peerless Sales Corp., Elmont, N.Y., 1967-71; sales mgr., then mktg. dir. United Utensils Co., Inc., Port Washington, N.Y., 1973-78; v.p. ops. and control United Molded Products, 1978—. Past fund raiser Glen Cove Community Hosp., Geln Cove Library. Home: 249 12th Ave Sea Cliff NY 11579 Office: United Utensils Co Inc Yennicock Ave Port Washington NY 11050

SPIEGELBERG, EMMA JO, educator; b. Mt. View, Wyo., Nov. 22, 1936; d. Joseph Clyde and Dorcas (Reese) Hatch; B.A. with honors, U. Wyo., 1958, MEd, 1985; m. James Walter Spiegelberg, June 22, 1957; children: William L., Emory Walter, Joseph John. Tchr. bus. edn. Laramie (Wyo.) High Sch., 1960-61, 65—, chmn. Bus. Edn. Dept., mgr. computer system, 1974—; chmn. Gov.'s and State Supt.'s Task Force on Vocat. Edn., 1982-83. Bd. dirs. Cathedral Home for Children, Laramie, 1967-70, 72—, pres., 1985-88; bd. dirs. Laramie Plains Mus., 1970-79. Author: Branigan's Accounting Simulation, 1986. Named Wyo. Bus. Tchr. of Yr., 1982. Mem. Am. Vocat. Assn. (policy com. region V 1984-87, region V Tchr. of Yr. 1986), Wyo. Vocat. Assn. (exec. bd. 1978-80, pres. 1981-82, Outstanding Contbns. to Vocat. Edn. award 1983, Tchr. of Yr. 1985, exec. sec. 1986—), Nat. Bus. Edn. Assn.(bd. dirs. 1987-88), Mt. Plains Bus. Edn. Assn. (Wyo. rep. to bd. dirs. 1982-85, rep. to Internat. Soc. Bus. Edn. 1985-86, pres. 1987-88), Wyo. Bus. Edn. Assn. (pres. 1979-80), NEA, Wyo. Edn. Assn., Albany County Edn. Assn. (sec. 1970-71), Laramie C. of C. (bd. dirs. 1985-88), U. Wyo. Alumni Assn. (bd. dirs. 1985-90, v.p. 1986-87, pres.-elect 1987-88, pres. 1988-89), Kappa Delta Pi, Phi Delta Kappa, Alpha Delta Kappa (state pres. 1978-82), Chi Omega. Mem. United Ch. of Christ. Club: Zonta. Home: 3301 Grays Gables Laramie WY 82070 Office: Laramie High Sch 1275 N 11th St Laramie WY 82070

SPIEGELBERG, HELEN KAZOLIAS, nursing educator; b. Mt. Kisco, N.Y., Sept. 30, 1931; d. C. LeRoy and Helen C. (Rodgers) Hancock; m. Frederick Spiegelberg, Aug. 13, 1979; children by previous marriage—George S., Michael A., A. Peter. B.S., Russell Sage Coll., 1968; M.Ed., Tchrs. Coll., Columbia U., 1971, Ed.D., 1979. Instr., Columbia Meml. Hosp., Hudson, N.Y., 1964-71; asst. prof. nursing Pace U., N.Y.C., 1971-74, SUNY-Downstate Med. Ctr., 1974-79; assoc. prof. U. Tulsa, 1979-81; cons. nursing edn., Tulsa, 1981-83; asst. dean, assoc. prof. Coll. Nursing, U. Southwestern La., Lafayette, 1983-85; pvt. practice nursing, 1986—; cons. sex edn. N.Y.C. Bd. Edn., 1974-79; cons. nursing edn. Margaret Sanger Inst., N.Y.C., 1978; cons. elderly health care Heights Hills Community Council, Bklyn., 1974-79; asst. project coordinator HEW Pilot Program on Migrant Worker Health Care, Columbia County (N.Y.), 1969-70. Researcher: (audio-visual program and booklet) The Nursing Process, 1983; contbr. articles to profl. jours. Instructional programs chmn. ARC, Tulsa, 1982-83; bd. dirs. Margaret Hudson Program, Tulsa, 1980-83, Nursing Service, Inc., Tulsa, 1980-83, Children's Service adv. bd. Dept. Human Services, Tulsa, 1980-83. Recipient Hon. Recognition for Disting. Service, Dist. 13 N.Y. State Nurses Assn., 1979; Mead Johnson fellow, 1968; Am. Nurses Assn. fellow, 1968. Mem. Am. Nurses Assn., Nat. League Nursing, AAUP, Childbirth and Family Life, Sigma Theta Tau. Home: 1701 Hermann Dr Apt 3503 Houston TX 77004

SPIERING, NANCY JEAN, accounting manager; b. Park Ridge, Ill., Apr. 15, 1958; d. Richard Arthur and Helen Mary (Henry) S. BS, De Paul U., 1982. CPA, Ill. Staff acct. Ruzicka & Assocs., Inc., Chgo., 1980-84; supr. acctg. Cargill, Inc., Carpentersville, Ill., 1984-87, regional asst. acctg. mgr., 1988—; mgr. maintenance crew Twin Pines Janitorial Service, Elgin, Ill., 1980—; pvt. practice tax service, Elgin, 1984—. Official Michael Bakalis campaign, Chgo., 1980; vol. Disabled Am. Vets., Cin., 1987. Mem. Am. Soc. CPA's, Ill. Soc. CPA's, Chgo. Soc. Women CPA's, Cargill Women's Council, Nat. Assn. Female Execs. Roman Catholic. Club: Dundee Dart (Ill). Home: 875 Mohawk Dr Elgin IL 60120 Office: Cargill Inc Cottage Ave Carpentersville IL 60110

SPIES, ANNETTE JOAN, mortgage company executive; b. Alhambra, Calif., Feb. 26, 1945; d. Hubert Otho Hicks and Sara Margaret (Wiley) Vincent; m. Charles William Chappell, Sept. 19, 1963 (div. 1981); 1 child, Elizabeth Ann; m. Arthur Thomas Spies, Dec. 18, 1982. BS, So. Ill. U., 1985. Adminstr. Croddy Corp., Santa Ana, Calif., 1974-76; br. mgr. Calif. Nat. Mortgage, Riverside, 1976-78; adminstr. Pacific Mortgage and Loan Co., Riverside, 1978-79; br. mgr. Internat. Mortgage Co., Anaheim, Calif., 1982-83; adminstr. Marina Mortgage, Inc., Riverside, 1983-84; exec. v.p. Eagle Am. Mortgage Corp., San Diego, 1985-86; sr. v.p. Equity Mortgage Corp., Corona, Calif., 1986—; prin., cons. Annie Can, Riverside, 1984—. Author: Loan Speaking, 1985. Mem. Mortgage Bankers Assn., Assn. Profl. Mortgage Women (pres. Raincross chpt. 1987—), Garden Grove (Calif.) Bus. and Profl. Women (pres. 1972-73). Republican. Office: Equity Mortgage Corp 268 N Lincoln Suite 10 Corona CA 91720

SPIGAI, FRANCES GAGE, electronic publishing consultant; b. Salina, Kans., Sept. 29, 1938; d. Frances Dana and Mina Lola (Jackson) Gage; m. Edwin B. Parker, Dec. 28, 1976. B.S., CCNY, 1960. Asst. prof. library and computer ctr. Oreg. State U., Corvallis, 1967-70; staff engr. Intrex, Cambridge, Mass., 1970-71; editor Becker & Hayes, Los Angeles, 1971-73; asst. to dir. Osshe Library Council Ashland, Oreg., 1974-76; mktg. dir. Dialog, Palo Alto, Calif., 1976-79; pres. Database Services, Los Altos, Calif., 1979—; editor, pub. Microcomputer Index, 1984—; instr. computer appreciation Linn-Benton Community Coll., Albany, Oreg., 1973. Author: (with P. Sommer) Guide to Electronic Publishing, 1982; editor series Database Search Aids, 1980-82; contbr. articles to profl. jours. Recipient disting. service cert. Nat. Micrographics Assn., 1976; cert. of appreciation Am. Soc. Info. Sci., 1976. Mem. Info. Industry Assn. (bd. dirs. 1986—). Address: Database Services 2685 Marine Way Suite 1305 Mountain View CA 94043

SPIKE, MICHELE KAHN, lawyer; b. Paterson, N.J., Oct. 1, 1951; d. Nathan and Clara (Spinella) Kahn; m. John Thomas Spike, May 26, 1973; 1 child, Nicholas Nathan. BA summa cum laude, Conn. Coll., 1973; JD cum laude, Boston U., 1976. Bar: N.Y. 1977, U.S. Dist. Ct. (so. and ea. dists.) N.Y. 1977. Assoc. Hale, Russell & Gray, N.Y.C., 1976-82; sole practice, N.Y.C., 1982-86; ptnr. Dolgenos, Newman & Cronin, N.Y.C., 1986—. Editor: (exhbn. catalogue) Italian Still Life Paintings, 1983, Baroque Portraiture in Italy, 1984. Mem. ABA, Bar Assn. City N.Y., Phi Beta Kappa. Home: 85 East End Ave New York NY 10028 Office: Dolgenos Newman & Cronin 101 Wooster St New York NY 10012

SPILLANE, MARY CATHERINE, television news producer; b. S.I., N.Y., Nov. 30, 1956; d. Joseph Bernard and Mary Catherine (Minoque) Spillane. B.A., U. Hartford, 1978. Exec. sec. CBS Evening News, N.Y.C., 1978-80, asst. to producer, 1980; weekend producer/E.N.G. coordinator KTVI-TV, St. Louis, 1981-82, spl. projects producer, 1982-83, asst. news dir., 1983-86; assoc. producer CBS News, Detroit, 1986 , N.Y.C. 1986-87, sr. producer, 1987—. Avocations: reading; travel. Office: 524 W 57th St New York NY 10019

SPILLER, MIRIAM BRITTON, fine arts appraiser; b. Reading, Pa., Sept. 4, 1926; d. William Wainwright and Katie Irene (Miller) Britton; student ceramics and sculpture Fleisher Art Meml., Phila., 1958, interior design Phila. Coll. Art, 1961; m. Raymond M. Spiller, Nov. 17, 1956. Practice interior design, 1958—; antiques cons., 1958—; officer R.M. Spiller & Assos., appraisal, conservation and restoration fine arts, Phila., 1960—; mem. Strawberry Mansion, historic preservation; slide lectr. in field. Certified fine arts appraiser, Pa. Mem. Appraisers of Fine Arts Soc. (dir., sec., treas. 1975—), Phila. Mus. Art. Republican. Address: 1025 Westview St Philadelphia PA 19119

SPINDLER, BECKY JEANE, tax specialist; b. Los Angeles, Nov. 29, 1957; d. Fred Marcus and Jeane (Mooney) S. BSBA, Calif. State U., Dominguez Hills, 1978; M in Bus. Taxation, U. So. Calif., 1987. With audit, tax staff Alexander Grant & Co., Los Angeles, 1979-81, tax supr., 1982-83; tax supr. McGladrey, Hendrickson & Pullen, San Diego, 1984; tax supr., tax mgr. Wickes Cos., Inc., Santa Monica, Calif., 1985—. Mem. Am. Inst. CPA's, Calif. Soc. CPA's, Beta Gamma Sigma. Home: 3761 Berry Dr Studio City CA 91604 Office: Wickes Companies Inc 3340 Ocean Park Blvd Suite 2000 Santa Monica CA 90405

SPININGER, CLAIRE MARIE, physician; b. Bklyn.; d. Charles John and Clara Elizabeth (Faeth) S. BS, Fordham U., 1964; MD, Albert Einstein Coll. Medicine, 1973. Intern Lenox Hill (N.Y.) Hosp., 1973-74; resident in internal medicine New Rochelle (N.Y.) Hosp. Med. Ctr., 1974-76, chief resident, 1976-77; assoc. med. dir. Equitable Life, N.Y.C., 1977-81; gen. practice medicine, New Rochelle and Bronx, N.Y., 1981—; mem. staff New Rochelle Hosp. Med. Ctr., Pelham Bay Gen. Hosp. Mem. Am. Soc. Internal Medicine, Am. Geriatrics Soc. Westchester County Med. Soc., New Rochelle Med. Soc. Office: 421 Huguenot St New Rochelle NY 10801 also: 3857 E Tremont Ave Bronx NY 10465

SPINKS, NELDA HUGHES, educator; b. Ruston, La., Sept. 3, 1928; d. Willie B. and Elizabeth Hughes; m. Wyman Allison Spinks, June 12, 1948; 1 son, Hugh Allison. BA, La. Tech. U.; MEd, U. Southwestern La.; Ed.D., La. State U. Cert. tchr., La. Instr. Acadia Baptist Acad., Eunice, La., 1954-63, Lafayette Parish Sch. Bd., 1963-67; asst. prof. U. Southwestern La., Lafayette, 1967-73, 75-87, assoc. prof., 1987—. Author: A Study of the Educational Needs of Potential Office Managers, 1974, (with others) Organizational Communication: A Practical Approach, 1987; guest editorial panelist Baptist Message newspaper, 1988—; contbr. articles to mags. Dir. Elizabeth Hughes Meml. Library, Bethel Bapt. Ch., Lafayette, 1987—. Recipient Postsecondary award Nat. Fed. Ind. Bus. Principles and Econs., 1987, career achievement award Connections, 1987; nominee Outstand Prof. award Amoco Found., 1987. Mem. Am. Bus. Communication Assn., Assn. Bus. Communication, S.W. Assn. Adminstrv. Services, Am. Mgmt. Assn. Nat. Collegiate Assn. for Secs. (sponsor), La. Assn. Bus. Educators (v.p. 1987—, pres.-elect 1988—), Nat. Fedn. Ind. Bus. (Outstanding Contributor award 1987), Lafayette C. of C. (edn. com. 1977), Kappa Delta Pi, Omicron Delta Epsilon, Delta Pi Epsilon (historian, editor newsletter 1987-88), Phi Delta Kappa, Phi Kappa Phi. Avocations: needlework, sports, reading. Home: 218 Brentwood Blvd Lafayette LA 70503 Office: U Southwestern La PO Box 41503 Lafayette LA 70504

SPINKS, RUTHANN, municipal corrections director; b. Terre Haute, Ind., Sept. 4, 1959; d. Earl and Leota Ethel (Jantz) S. BS, Wichita (Kans.) State U., 1984; postgrad., U. Kans., 1986—. Cert. law enforcement officer, Kans. Paramedic Leavenworth (Kans.) Emergency Med. Service, 1980-81; dep. sheriff Leavenworth Sheriff's Dept., 1981-86; dir. Saline (Kans.) County Community Corrections, 1986—. Author: Suicide Intervention for Law Enforcement Officers, 1983. Com. mem. Kans. Women's Task Force on Crime and Delinquency, Topeka, 1986—; instr. ARC, Kans., 1980. Mem. Nat. Assn. Female Execs., Kans. Community Corrections Assn. (bd. dirs.), Kans. Correctional Assn., Kans. Women in Criminal Justice, Domestic Violence Assn. of Kans. (bd. dirs. 1987), LWV, Am. Canoe Assn. (chpt. pres. 1984—). Office: Saline County Community Corrections 300 W Ash Room 306 Salina KS 67401

SPINNEY, VIVIEN BEATON, hospital executive; b. Winchester, Mass.; d. Ernest G. and Minnie C. (Cantwell) Beaton; m. Russell G. Spinney, June 21, 1953 (dec.); children: Debra Jeanne Spinney Morrison, Russell G. Lic. in opticianry; lic. real estate broker. Asst. office mgr. Winchester Hosp., 1953-54; med. asst. to gen. surgeon Arlington, Mass., 1965-68; asst. to owner NE Rehab. Hosp., Woburn, Mass., 1968—, also bd. dirs., now exec. v.p. Mem. Am. Bd. Opticianry, Soc. Notary Pubs., Am. Mgmt. Assn. Roman Catholic. Home: 14 Chestnut St Woburn MA 01801

SPINOSA, PATRICIA ANN, small business owner; b. Detroit, June 23, 1943; d. Clinton Cornelius Henson and Alma Lee (Perry) Stilwell; m. Lloyd Jacob Krein, Jan. 25, 1962 (div. 1963); 1 child, Lloyd Charles; m. Vincent Anthony Spinosa, June 12, 1965; 1 child, Valerie Lynn. Student, Goldenwest Jr. Coll., 1974; cert. in real estate, Lunblean Real Estate Sch., 1975; cert. in brokerage, Anthony Real Estate Sch., 1979. Office mgr. Pepsi-Cola Mgmt. Inst., San Pedro, Calif., 1964-70; adminstrv. sec. Westminster (Calif.) Sch. Dist., 1972-75; salesman Red Carpet Real Estate, Garden Grove, Calif., 1975-76, College Park Realtors, Garden Grove, 1976-79; owner, pres. S&S Properties, Garden Grove, 1979—. Mem. West Orange County Bd. of Realtors, Long Beach Bd. of Realtors. Democrat. Methodist. Lodge: Toastmasters (pres. 1987—). Office: S&S Properties 5250 Lampson Garden Grove CA 92645

SPIRER, JUNE DALE, marketing executive, psychologist; b. N.Y.C., May 14, 1943; d. Leon and Gloria (Wagner) Spirer; BA, Adelphi U., 1965; MS, Yeshiva U., 1980, Psy.D., 1984. TV/radio buyer BBD&O, 1965-66, SSC&B, 1966-68; sr. media planner Norman, Craig & Kummel, N.Y.C., 1968-71; assoc. media dir. Ted Bates Co., 1971-72; v.p., account supt. C.T. Clyne Co., N.Y.C., 1972-74; dir. advt. Am. Express, 1974-75; corporate dir. advt. Del Labs., Farmingdale, N.Y., 1975-79; pres. J. Spirer & Assocs., Inc., N.Y.C., 1978—; pres., chief exec. officer Media Placement Services, Inc., 1985-87; pres. Tactics, Inc., 1985—, chief exec. officer, 1988—. Mem. Am. Psychol. Assn., Nassau County Psychol. Assn., N.Y. State Psychol. Assn., Soc. Personality Assessment (assoc.). Office: Tactics Inc 2 Horatio St New York NY 10014 also: MPSI Inc 317 W 13th St New York NY 10014

SPISAK-GAMBLE, ANTONINA STANISLAWA, recording company executive; b. Krakow, Poland, Feb. 22, 1946; came to U.S., 1974; d. Mieczyslaw Roman and Zofia Helena (Tworzydlo) Spisak; divorced; 1 child, Dominik M. M in Math., Yagellonian U., Krakow, 1968, PhD in Math., 1974. Asst. prof. math. Yagellonian U., 1968-74; lectr, Grinnell (Iowa) Coll., 1975-80, Tufts U., Medford, Mass., 1980-86; pres. Cathedral Prodns. Inc., Toronto, Can., 1987—; bd. dirs. Dorian Digital Recordings, Toronto, Can.; pres. Assn. of Friends of Papal Organ, Vienna, Austria, 1983—. Author, editor, translator numerous articles in profl. jours. Republican. Roman Catholic. Office: Cathedral Prodns Inc, 9 Humewood Dr Suite 26, Toronto, ON Canada M6C 1C9

SPITZ, BARBARA SALOMON, artist; b. Chgo., Jan. 8, 1926; d. Fred B. and Sadie (Lorch) Salomon; m. Lawrence S. Spitz, Mar. 19, 1949; children—Thomas R., Linda J., Joanne L. A.B., Brown U., 1947; student, Art Inst. Chgo., 1942-43, R.I. Sch. Design, 1945. One-woman exhbns. include Benjamin Galleries, Chgo., 1971, 73, Kunsthaus Buhler, Stuttgart, Fed. Republic Germany, 1973, Van Straaten Gallery, Chgo., 1976, 80, Elca London Studio, Montreal, Que., Can., 1977, Loyola U. Chgo., 1988; group exhibitions include Am. Acad. Arts and Letters, Library of Congress traveling print exhbn., Tokyo Cen. Mus. Arts, Nat. Acad. Design, N.Y.C., Pratt Graphic Ctr., Honolulu Acad. Arts, Wadsworth Atheneum, Nat. Aperture, 1986—, others; represented in permanent collections, Phila. Mus. Art, DeCordova Mus., Okla. Art Ctr., Milw. Art Ctr., Los Angeles County Mus. Art, Art Inst. Chgo. Vice-chmn. Chgo. area Brown U. Bicentennial Drive; treas. Hearing and Speech Rehab. Center, Michael Reese Hosp., 1960. Mem. Artists Equity, Print Club Phila., Boston Printmakers, Arts Club of Chgo., Soc. Am. Graphic Artists. Address: 1106 Somerset Ln Newport Beach CA 92660

SPITZER, DOREEN CANADAY, archaeological institution executive; b. New Castle, Ind., Dec. 5, 1914; d. Ward Murphey and Mariam Louise (Coffin) Canaday; m. Lyman Spitzer Jr., June 29, 1949; children: Nicholas C., Dionis C., Sarah L., Lydia S. BA, Bryn Mawr Coll., 1936; HHD (hon.), U. Toledo, 1987. Instr. archaeology U. Toledo, 1940; mem. Am. Sch. Classical Studies Athens, Greece, 1936-38, trustee, v.p., pres. bd.; docent Princeton U. Art Mus.; spl. rep. bd. trustees Bryn Mawr Coll. Author: Leaders' Guide, 1954, By One and One, 1983. Mem. Am. Hellenic Edn. Progressive Assn. (Disting. Service award 1979), Archeol. Inst. Am. Home: 659 Lake Dr Princeton NJ 08540 Office: Am Sch Classical Studies Athens 41 E 72d St New York NY 10021

SPITZER, SHIRLEY CARLYNE, commercial and industrial real estate executive; b. Bklyn., Dec. 28, 1934; d. Benjamin Willian and Betty (Kesselman) Mermelstein; m. Leo Spitzer, Feb. 24, 1962 (dec. Dec. 1979); 1 child, Marc Adam. Ed., Bklyn. Coll.; student, Town Coll., Adelphia U. Troubleshooter in bookkeeping and acctg. 1959-73; controller Eleanor Brenner Inc., N.Y.C., 1973-79; self-employed in acctg. 1979-85; v.p. Ea. Modular Inc., 1986—. Mem. Nat. Assn. Female Execs., Orgn. Rehab. Through Tng. (program dir. 1984). Home: 20 Spinning Wheel Rd Massapequa NY 11758

SPITZNAGEL, ANNE MOULTON SIRCH, psychologist; b. N.Y.C., Mar. 14, 1923; d. Thor Rheudy and Helen Trowbridge (Dutton) Sirch; m. John Keith Spitznagel, Feb. 2, 1947; children: John Jr., Jean, Margaret, Elizabeth, Paul. BA, Barnard Coll., 1944; BS in Nursing, Columbia U., 1947; MA, George Washington U., 1949; PhD, Duke U., 1981. lic. psychologist, Ga., 1982, marriage and family therapist, 1984. Rehab. counselor Tuberculosis Assn., Washington, 1948; RN in personnel dept. George Washington U. Hosp., Washington, 1947-48; RN Johns Hopkins Hosp., Balt., 1947, Barnes Hosp., St. Louis, 1950; research assoc. U. N.C. Child Study Project, Chapel Hill, 1962-65; psychometrist, chief research asst. Edn. Improvement Program Duke U., Durham, N.C., 1965-67; staff psychologist, research asst., instr. dept. psychiatry U. N.C., Chapel Hill, 1969-76; grad. asst. sch. psychologist Durham (N.C.) County Schs., 1977-79; psychologist Atlanta Pediatric Psychol. Assocs., Tucker, Ga., 1982-83; pvt. practice child psychology and family therapy Decatur, Ga., 1982—; marriage and family therapist Cath. Social Services, Atlanta, 1984—; cons. Village of St. Joseph Residential Sch., Atlanta, 1985—; psychologist and marriage and family therapist Cath. Social Services, Atlanta, 1984—; mem. com. exceptional child Council for Children, Atlanta, 1983-85. Author: I'll See You in the Morning, 1974. Past leader, den mother Girl Scout U.S., Boy Scouts Am., Chapel Hill. Mem. LWV, Am. Psychol. Assn., Am. Assn. Marriage and Family Therapy (clin. mem. 1987), Ga. Psychol Assn., Assn. Children Learning Disabilities (past local pres., N.C. bd. dirs.). Democrat. Episcopalian. Office: Cath Social Services 680 W Peachtree NW Atlanta GA 30308

SPIVAK, JACQUE R., bank executive; b. San Francisco, Nov. 5, 1929; d. Robert Morris and Sadonia Clardine Breitstein; m. Herbert Spivak, Aug. 26, 1960; children—Susan, Donald, Joel, Sheri. B.S., U. So. Calif., 1949, M.S., 1950, M.B.A., 1959. Mgr. Internat. Escrow, Inc., Los Angeles, 1960-65, Greater Los Angeles Investment Co., 1965-75; mgr. escrow Transam. Title Ins. Co., Los Angeles, 1975-78; mgr. escrow, asst. v.p. Wells Fargo Bank, Beverly Hills, Calif., 1979-80; adminstr. escrow, v.p. 1st Pacific Bank, Beverly Hills, 1980-85; escrow adminstr. Century City Savs. & Loan Assn., Los Angeles, 1986-87; pres. Producers Escrow Corp., Beverly Hills., 1987—. Recipient awards PTA, Girl Scouts U.S.A., Jewish Fedn. Los Angeles, Hadassah. Mem. Calif. Escrow Assn., Nat. Assn. Bank Women, Inst. Trustees Sales officers. Republican. Jewish. Office: Producers Escrow Corp 9328 Civic Ctr Dr Beverly Hills CA 90210

SPIVAK, K. RENÉ, psychologist; b. Hollywood, Fla., June 2, 1953; d. Noreen B. (MacIntosh). AA, Briarcliff Coll., 1973; BA, NYU, 1975; MS, U. Fla., 1983, PhD, 1986. Clin. intern Duke U., Durham, N.C., 1985-86; psychiat. asst. Grasslands Inst. Autistic Children, White Plains, N.Y., Coral Ridge Hosp., Ft. Lauderdale, Fla.; therapist VA Med. Ctr., Gainsville, Fla., Psychol. Vocat. Counseling Ctr., Gainsville; care team assoc. Alachua County Suicide and Crisis Ctr., Gainsville; counselor specialist CREST Services, Inc., Gainsville; therapist, cons. Robert Lee & Assocs., Inc., Gainsville; psychol. cons. NorthRidge Hosp., Ft. Lauderdale; pvt. practice therapist, cons. Ft. Lauderdale; mem. adv. bd. Parents Anonymous, Ft. Lauderdale, 1986-87; cons., trainer, ct. cert. guardian Guardian Ad Litem Program, Ft. Lauderdale; cons. Sexual and Phys. Abuse Resource Ctr., Gainsville;. Mem. Performing Arts Ctr., Broward Art Guild, Ft. Lauderdale, 1987; chmn. Mental Health Com. Am. Cancer Soc., chmn. I Can Cope, profl. edn. com. mem.; adv. bd. mem. Nat. Sr. Citizens Assn. Mem. Am. Psychol. Assn., Southeastern Psychol. Assn., Mental Health Assn. Presbyterian. Address: The Adams Bldg 2601 E Oakland Park Blvd Suite 602 Fort Lauderdale FL 33306

SPLITT, CODY, lawyer; b. Wausau, Wis., Aug. 13, 1919; d. Anne Monahan Wendt; m. Harley B. Splitt, Apr. 17, 1948; 1 child, Leigh Rogers. B.A., U. Wis.-Madison, 1947, LL.B., 1949. Bar: Wis. 1949, U.S. Dist. Ct. (we. dist.) Wis. 1949. Sole practice, Appleton, Wis., 1949—; asst. dir. U.S. Agr. Census, 1955; dist. dir. U.S. Census, 1960; lectr., moderator Law for Laymen, Appleton, 1975-80; dir. Legal Service Northeastern Wis., Inc., 1984-85. Mem. Equal Rights Council, Wis., 1966-73, Equal Opportunities, Appleton, 1973-81; vice chmn. Outagamie County Republican Club, 1965; pres. Outagamie County Rep. Women's Club, 1951; co-pres. Appleton PTA, 1971; v.p. Appleton Big Sisters, 1974. Served with WAVES, 1942-45. Named Woman of Yr. Outagamie County, NOW, 1974. Mem. State Bar Wis. (sect. sec. 1974), Outagamie County Bar Assn. (exec. com. 1978-85, sec. 1985-86, pres. 1986-87), Fed. Bus. and Profl. Women (v.p. 1978), Fedn. Rep. Women. Home: 1611 W Glendale Ave Appleton WI 54914 Office: 103 W College Ave #1204 Appleton WI 54911-5706

SPOEHEL, JERRI HOSKINS, volunteer agency executive; b. Oak Park, Ill., Mar. 13, 1932; d. George Alex and Myrtle Jean (McBean) Hoskins; B.A. in English cum laude, Coll. Wooster; m. Edwin H. Spoehel, Apr. 16, 1955; children—Ronald Ross, Jacqueline Jean. Instr., Success-Plus, 1974; columnist Daily News, San Fernando Valley, Van Nuys, Calif., 1970-85; community relations dir. Sta. KCSN-FM, Nat. Pub. Radio, Northridge, Calif., 1975-85; exec. dir. Vol. Ctr. of San Fernando Valley, 1985—; sec. Vol. Ctrs. of So. Calif.; mem. Pres. Assocs. Calif. State U., Northridge; panelist/seminar instr. Nat. Devel. Conf., Corp. Pub. Broadcasting. Recipient Nat. Abe Lincoln Merit award So. Baptist Radio and TV Commn.; named Disting. Citizen of Northridge; other awards. Mem. AAUW (pres.), Pub. Relations Roundtable, Dirs. Vols. in Agys. Club: Soroptimists (pres.), Northridge Cultural Arts. Mem. Unity Ch. Home: 9615 Shoshone Ave Northridge CA 91325 Office: 6931 Van Nuys Blvd Suite 309 Van Nuys CA 91405

SPOERR, WENDY SUE, educator; b. Sandusky, Ohio, Aug. 15, 1950; d. Everett J. and Shirley J. (Benton) S. BS in Early Childhood, Kent State U., 1975, MEd, 1979. Tchr. Badger Local Schs., Kinsman, Ohio, 1975—; cons. Trumbull County Schs., Warren, Ohio, 1984-88; co-chmn. Hartford (Ohio) Library Constrn., 1987-88; presenter arts grant Trumbull County Inservice, Champion, Ohio, 1985, presenter NASA grant, 1987. Fundraiser Badger Levy Team, Kinsman, 1987-88. Psychomotor Skills grantee Trumbull County Schs., 1980, Sci./Health/Social Studies grantee Martha Holden Jennings, 1987; recipient Action award N.E. Ohio Tchrs. Assn., 1981-82; candidate tchr. in space NASA, 1986. Mem. Badger Edn. Assn. (pres. 1988-89), Phi Delta Kappa, Delta Kappa Gamma. Democrat. Home: 1128 Niles Cortland Rd NE Warren OH 44484

SPONTAK, BARBARA ANN, nurse; b. Pottstown, Pa., Nov. 10, 1943; d. Wellington Farel and Mary Eleanor (Hampton) Davidheiser; A.S., Coll. DuPage (Ill.), 1974; B.S. in Nursing, U. Ill., 1978, MS, 1987; m. Stephen John Spontak, Aug. 18, 1962; children—Stephen F., Gregory A., Mark T., Michael A. Charge nurse burn unit, then staff nurse emergency dept. Loyola U. Med. Center, 1974-77; nursing supr., asst. dir. nursing Good Samaritan Hosp., Downers Grove, Ill., 1978; asst. dir. nursing medicine U. Ill. Med.

Center, 1979-81, asst. dir. nursing, coordinator nursing resources, 1981-85; div. dir. critical care I Cook County Hosp., 1985-87; instr. nursing Coll. of DuPage, 1981-83, 87—, U. Ill.-Chgo., 1984-85. Sec., Park View Sch. PTA, 1975. Mem. Ill. Nurses Assn., Lombard Nurses Club. Lutheran. Club: Rams Gymnastics (pres. 1980-82). Home: 332 W Sunset Ave Lombard IL 60148

SPOONER, ELAINE MARGARET, information services director; b. Woodsville, N.H., Mar. 22, 1952; d. Parker Jonas and Marilyn Blanche (Foss) S. BA, Boston U., 1978. Project leader John Hancock Life Ins., Boston, 1971-77; project mgr. Union Bank, L.A., 1977-78; systems analyst Warner Bros, Burbank, Calif., 1978-80; dir. mgmt. info. systems, facilities div. 20th Century Fox, Beverly Hills, Calif., 1980-83; sr. cons., prodn. automation mgr. MCA, Inc., Universal City, Calif., 1983-87; dir. info. services MCA TV Group, Universal City, 1988—. Mem. Assn. Entertainment Industry Computer Profls. (bd. dirs. 1984-88), Nat. Assn. Female Execs., Women in Film. Office: MCA Inc 100 Universal City Plaza Universal City CA 91608

SPOONER, SARA ANN, advertising agency executive; b. Indpls., Jan. 31, 1955; d. Robert Fulton and Margery (Ralph) S. BA in Econs., U. Chgo., 1976, MBA, 1978. Trainee Leo Burnett, Chgo., 1978-79, asst. account exec., 1979-80, account exec., 1981-84; v.p., account supr. N.W. Ayer, Chgo., 1984-87, v.p., mgmt. supr., 1987—. Office: N W Ayer Inc 111 E Wacker Dr Chicago IL 60601

SPORTSMAN, SALLY JEAN, teacher; b. St. Louis, Oct. 26, 1948; d. Irwin and Mae Ann (Hyatt) Walpert; m. Michel Allain Sportsman, Feb. 21, 1970; children: Elise M., Gregory D. BS in Edn., U. Mo., 1970, MA in English, 1983. Cert. tchr., Mo. Tchr. J.C. Nichols Sch., Kansas City, 1972-73, Grandview (Mo.) Pub. Schs., 1973-75, Peculiar (Mo.) Elementary Sch., 1979-81; tchr. gifted program and French Raymore-Peculiar Middle Sch., 1981-85; tchr. secondary English and French Raymore-Peculiar High Sch., 1985—; mem. faculty Mo. Scholars Acad., U. Mo., Columbia, 1987—; pvt. tutor, Kansas City, 1980-86; sponsor Nat. Writing Project U. Calif., Berkeley, 1983—. Contbr. articles to profl. jours. Liason Kansas City Regional Council for Higher Edn., Leawood, Kans., 1986—. U. Mo. scholar, 1966-70, 1983. Mem. Phi Kappa Phi, Pi Lambda Theta, Delta Kappa Gamma (v.p. Mu chapt., 1987—). Home: 509 N Washington St Raymore MO 64083 Office: Raymore-Peculiar High Sch 211 & School Rd Box 366 Peculiar MO 64078

SPOTTSVILLE, DEBORAH DENISE, contract analyst; b. Los Angeles, Apr. 26, 1955; d. Mitchell and Marilyn (Strickland) S. BBA, U. Redlands, 1981. Sr. contract analyst Northrop Corp., Hawthorne, Calif., 1981-84, 87—; actress, movie extra, Los Angeles, 1976-78, 84-87; co-host cable TV program, Compton, Calif., 1986. Mem. Nat. Contract Mgmt. Assn., Nat. Assn. Female Execs., NAACP, Nat. Council Negro Women, Urban League, Black Women's Forum, Compton Alumni Assn. Democrat. Baptist. Home: 2030 W El Segundo Blvd Gardena CA 90249 Office: Northrop Corp Aircraft Div 1 Northrop Ave Hawthorne CA 90250

SPRABERRY, MARY NELL, infosystems specialist; b. Calhoun City, Miss., Apr. 8, 1931; d. Thomas Dee and Mary Sam (Magness) Wall; m. Charles E. Spraberry, June 22, 1952; 1 child, Charles Brian. BS, Miss. U. for Women, 1952; MPH, U. Ala., 1981, DrPH, 1987. Med. technologist U. Tenn. Med. Ctr., Memphis, 1952-53, Houston (Miss.) Hosp., 1953-54, Simon Williamson Clinic, Birmingham, 1954-56; adminstrv. technologist U. Ala. Hosps., Birmingham, 1956-76, dir. infosystems, 1976-85, asst. adminstr., 1977—; asst. v.p. health affairs, infosystems U. Ala. Med. Ctr., Birmingham, 1985—; asst. prof. sch. pub. health U. Ala., Birmingham, 1986—; cons. AT&T Bell Labs., Holmdel, N.J., 1984-86; bd. dirs. Electronic Computing Health Oriented, Bethesda, 1985-87, v.p. 1987—. Mem. Am. Pub. Health Assn., Ala. Assn. Coll. Adminstrs. (Exemplary Service award 1987), Am. Soc. Med. Technologists (Profl. Achievement award 1974). Home: 3424 Stoneridge Dr Birmingham AL 35243 Office: U Ala at Birmingham University Sta Birmingham AL 35294

SPRADLIN, CAROLYN SHARLENE, nursing administrator; b. Opportunity, Nebr., June 26, 1939; d. Charles Edwin and Marjorie Ethel (Siders) Russell; m. Donald Dean Bruning, Jan. 20, 1955 (div.); children: Gwendolyn Whitten, Rochelle Bastura, Karl, Otto, Greta Ready; m. John William Spradlin, April 1, 1984. AS in Nursing, State Fair Community Coll., 1978; BS, SUNY, Albany, 1979; BS in Nursing, Southwest Mo. State U., 1981. RN; lic. nursing home adminstr. Dir. nursing Chastain's of Buffalo (Mo.), 1979-82; assoc. dir. nursing San Diego Physician's and Surgeon's Hosp., 1982-84; dir. nursing Barstow (Calif.) Community Hosp., 1984-86; adminstr., dir. nursing Pilgrim Place Health Services Ctr., Claremont, Calif., 1987-88; owner, nurse cons., mgmt. cons. Challenge Enterprises, San Bernadino, Calif., 1988—; sec. Long Term Care Dirs. Nursing, San Diego County, 1983. Mem. Am. Nursing Assn., Sigma Theta Tau (Theta Lambda chpt.) Phi Kappa Phi, SW Mo. State U. Nursing Honor Soc., Mensa. Office: Challenge Enterprises Box 3358 San Bernardino CA 92413

SPRAGUE, AMARIS JEANNE, real estate broker; b. Jackson, Mich., Feb. 18, 1935; d. Leslie Markham and Blanche Lorraine (Basnaw) Reed; student Mich. State U., 1952-53; B.S., Colo. State U., 1965; m. John M. Vetterling, Oct. 1985; children by previous marriage—Anthony John, James Stuart. Real estate sales Seibel and Benedict Realty, Ft. Collins, Colo., 1968-69; salesman Realty Brokers Exchange, Ft. Collins, 1969-72; broker, pres. Sprague and Assos., Inc., Realtors, Ft. Collins, 1972-80; broker assoc. Van Schaack & Co., Ft. Collins, 1980-86; broker ptnr. The Group, Inc., 1986—; dir. Univ. Nat. Bank. Mem. bus. adv. council Colo. State U., 1976-84, chmn. 1979-80, mem. adv. council Coll. of Engring., 1981. Cert. real estate broker. Mem. Nat. Assn. Realtors, Colo. Assn. Realtors, Ft. Collins Bd. Realtors, Ft. Collins C. of C. (dir. 1975-78, 80-83, pres. 1982-83). Republican. Episcopalian. Home: PO Box 475 Fort Collins CO 80522 Office: 2120 S College Ave Fort Collins CO 80525

SPRAGUE, DAWN, lawyer; b. New Haven, Feb. 8, 1956; d. Seth and Anne (Hauser) S.; m. Stephen Mark Foley, children: Anne Elizabeth, Stephen, Catherine. B.A. summa cum laude, Providence Coll., 1978; J.D. cum laude, Suffolk Law Sch., 1981. Bar: Mass. 1981, R.I. 1981. Assoc., McMahon & McMahon, Providence, 1981-82; Ptnr. Foley & Sprague, Boston, 1982—; cons. atty. Client Trust Fund Project, Dept. Mental Health, Boston, 1983-84. Recipient Am. Jurisprudence award for estate planning, 1981. Mem. ABA, R.I. Bar Assn., Mass. Bar Assn. Office: Foley and Sprague Attys at Law 726 E 8th St South Boston MA 02127

SPRAGUE, LISA MARI, personnel director; b. Berea, Ohio, Aug. 6, 1954; d. William and Carle (Ruhe) S.; m. Jerome Bernard Kernan, Nov. 29, 1986. AB in English, Wellesley (Mass.) Coll., 1976; MBA, U. Cin., 1981. Program and mgmt. analyst Office of Child Support Enforcement div. Dept. HHS, Washington, 1976-79; asst. to v.p. investor relations Great Am. Broadcasting Co., Cin., 1981, mgr. human resources, 1981—; unit producer news dept. Sta. WKRC-TV subs. Taft Broadcasting Co., Cin., 1980; research analyst Strategic Mkt. Planning and Research, Cin., 1980-81. Active Family Services Allocation com., Community Chest and Council of the United Way of Cin., 1982-85; bd. dirs. Cin. Scholarship Found., 1986—. Mem. Internat. Assn. Personnel Women. Republican. Episcopalian. Club: Cin. Wellesley (v.p. 1986-87, pres. 1987-88). Office: Great Am Broadcasting Co 1718 Young St Cincinnati OH 45210

SPRAGUE, ROBERTA JANE, accountant; b. Riverside, N.J., May 28, 1947; d. Robert L. Sprague and Doris Mae (Wiley) Dobry. AAS, Burlington County Coll., 1982; cert., Harris Sch. Bus., 1986. Bookkeeper Bob White Flower Shop, Mt. Holly, N.J., 1968-72; office mgr. U.S. Supply Corp., Bristol, Penn., 1972-79; acct. Accountemps, Phila., 1980; controller, acct. H.A. Perotti, Inc., Bristol, 1981-85; acct. Winter Fruit, Inc., Phila., 1985-86; acct., adminstr. Paramount Fruit, Inc., Phila., 1987-88; gen. acct. Union Camp Corp., Trenton, N.J., 1988—. Fellow Nat. Notary Assn., Nat. Assn. Female Execs., Am. Soc. Profl. and Exec. Women; mem. Nat. Assn. Accts. (dir. mem. relations 1987—), Phi Theta Kappa (treas. 1981-82). Baptist. Home: 45 Edgely Ln Willingboro NJ 08046 Office: Union Camp Corp 1400 E State St PO Box 2040 Trenton NJ 08609

SPRATT, CHERYL LEE, advertising executive; b. Someville, N.J., Oct. 30, 1954; d. Robert Warren and Frances Mary (Jaas) S. BS, Trenton State U., 1976, MS in Edn., 1980. Dir. publications U.S. Tennis Assn., Princeton, N.J., 1978-82; mgr. communications Doane Mktg. Research, Princeton, N.J., 1982-84; asst. account exec. Benton and Bowles, N.Y.C., 1984, Richardson, Myers and Donofrio, Phila., 1985-86; asst. communications mgr. Rhone Poulenc, Monmouth Junction, N.J., 1986-87; account exec. Bergelt Litchfield Inc., N.Y.C., 1987—. Editor: (booklets) Tennis for the Handicapped, 1982, Tennis for Seniors, 1982. Coach Twp. Softball League Children, Hillsborough, N.J. 1976-78. Mem. Nat. Assn. AgriMarketers (awards nominations com. 1987—), Nat. Assn. Exec. Females, Delta Psi Kappa. Home: Rt 29 Box 613 Titusville NJ 08860

SPRATT, LINDA DIANE, human resources director; b. Los Angeles, Oct. 3, 1942; d. Jesse Erwin and Mildred (Lazich) S. BA in Sociology, U. Calif., Riverside, 1965. Personnel mgr. employee relations, tng. supr. Broadway Dept. Stores, Los Angeles, 1965-71, mgr. coll. relations and placement, spl. projects supr., exec. recruiter, 1972-80; dir. Liberty House of Hawaii, Honolulu, 1980—. Mem. employment opportunities com. Retail Mchts. Hawaii, 1980—; tng. chmn. Goodwill Projects with Industry, Honolulu, 1981—; vocat. adv. bd. McKinley High Sch., Honolulu, 1987—. Mem. Am. Soc. Personnel Adminstrs., Am. Arbitration Assn. Office: Liberty House of Hawaii Box 2690 Honolulu HI 96845

SPRECHMAN, EVELYN TERRY, nurse, consultant; b. N.Y.C., Feb. 25, 1930; d. Robert and Emma (Tewes) Redfield; m. Harry Sprechman, Dec. 3, 1950; children: Susan, David. Assoc. Degree in Nursing, State U. at Farmingdale, 1972. Asst. head nurse North Shore U. Hosp, Manhasset, N.Y., 1972-75; dir. in-service edn. Woodbury (N.Y.) Health Related Facility, 1975-81; supr. operating room endoscopy unit Dr's Howard J Eddy & Jian Chu Yu, Garden City, N.Y., 1982—; cons. in field, 1986—. Mem. Soc. Gastrointestinal Assts. Hebrew. Office: Drs Howard J Eddy & Jian Chu Yu 520 Franklin Ave Garden City NY 11530

SPREIER, LOIS JOANNE, librarian; b. Burley, Idaho, July 27, 1932; d. Blair Howard and Gladys Lenore (Rudolph) Gochnour; m. Clifford Herman Spreier, Dec. 27, 1953; children—Annette Louise, Douglas Mark (dec.), Janet Lynne. B.A., Idaho State U., 1967. Cert. tchr., media specialist, Idaho. Sixth grade tchr. pub. schs., Buhl, Idaho, 1954-55, Filer, Idaho, 1960-61, Twin Falls, Idaho, 1962-67; Am. lit. tchr. Buhl High Sch., 1967-82, media specialist, 1982—. Mem. NEA, Idaho Edn. Assn., Buhl Edn. Assn. (sec. 1978-79, bldg. rep. several terms), Idaho Ednl. Media Assn., ALA, Idaho Library Assn., Am. Assn. Sch. Librarians; Nat. Council Tchrs. English, Alpha Delta Kappa (treas. Twin Falls 1980-82, v.p. 1982-84, pres. 1984-86). Home: 1097 Pinewood Circle Twin Falls ID 83301 Office: Buhl High Sch Buhl Sch Dist 412 Rt 5 Sawtooth Blvd Buhl ID 83316

SPREITZER, CYNTHIA ANN, computer programming professional; b. Chgo., July 16, 1953; d. John Herbert and Patricia Virginia (Ticman) S. BS in Math., Loyola U., Chgo., 1975. Cert. data processor, 1986. Sr. Arthur Andersen and Co., Chgo., 1975-80; lead analyst Larimer County, Ft. Collins, Colo., 1980—. Mem. Assn. Inst. Cert. Computer Profls., Computer Security Inst., Data Processing Mgmt. Assn., Nat. Assn. Female Execs. Roman Catholic. Home: 610 Grove Ct Loveland CO 80537 Office: Larimer County PO Box 1190 Fort Collins CO 80522

SPRINGER, ANN MURPHY, management consultant; b. Boston, Apr. 13, 1935; d. William James, Jr. and Katherine Mary (Danehy) Murphy; m. David Alan Springer, Nov. 27, 1971. B.S., Simmons Coll., Boston, 1956; M.S. (teaching asst.), Purdue U., 1958. Home economist, 1956-59; program developer U.S. Spl. Services, W.Ger., 1959-62; with Ford Found. project, Oakland, Calif., 1962-65; mem. staff War on Poverty, 1965-67; tng. cons. Western Community Action Tng., Oakland, 1967-69; dir. tng. Internat. Tng. Cons., Berkeley, Calif., 1969-71; ind. mgmt. cons., Bodega, Calif., 1971—; prof. mgmt. studies Sonoma (Calif.) State U., 1979—; resident, adj. faculty Nat. Fire Acad., Md., 1978—; chief Bodega Vol. Fire Dept., 1979-84; adv. com. re-entry and women's studies Santa Rosa Jr. Coll., 1977-84, mem. fire tech. adv. com., 1982-85. Co-author: The Organizational Operations Process, 1972; Management for the Fire Officer, 1981. Contbr. articles to profl. publs. First chairperson Sonoma County Commn. Status Women, 1975-76. Grantee Indian Valley Colls., Novato, Calif., 1977, 79. Mem. Internat. Assn. Fire Chiefs, Internat. Assn. Fire Service Instrs., Calif. Fire Chiefs Assn., Calif. Tng. Officers Assn., Sonoma County Fire Chiefs Assn. (past pres.), Bodega Bay Allied Arts Assn. Address: 1931 Joy Rd PO Box 139 Bodega CA 94922

SPRINGER, PENNY ANN, broadcasting executive; b. Queens, N.Y., Apr. 9, 1952; d. Benjamin Herman and Florence (Goldman) Seltzman; m. Herbert J. Springer, Nov. 24, 1973 (dec. May 1985). BA, SUNY, Cortland, 1974. Resident mgr. Chelsea Townhouses, Cortland, 1974-75; pub. relations asst. Am. Land Title Assn., Washington, 1976-78; promotions coordinator Sta. WMAL-FM, Washington, 1978-81; dir. sta. relations Washington Broadcast News, 1982-84; pres., treas. RGR Broadcasting Co., Gouverneur, N.Y., 1984—, also bd. dirs., 1984-87; pres. AIRWAVES Ltd., San Francisco, 1988—. Democrat. Jewish.

SPRINGER, WILMA MARIE, elementary educator; b. Goshen, Ind., Jan. 13, 1933; d. Noah A. and Laura D. (Miller) Kaufman; m. Walter Frederick Springer, May 25, 1957; children: Anita Daniel, Timothy, Mark. BA, Goshen Coll., 1956; MS, Bradley U., 1960. Tchr. Topeka (Ind.) Elem. Sch., 1956-57, Metamora (Ill.) Grade Sch., 1957-59, Bellflower (Calif.) Unified Sch. Dist., 1960—; chairperson gifted and Talented Edn. Lindstrom Elem. Sch., Lakewood, Calif., 1986-88, Regional Ednl. TV Adv. Council, Lakewood, 1985-87; stage mgr. Hour of Power T.V., Crystal Cathedral, 1983. Contbr. articles in field. Campaigner Sch. Bd. Mem., 1984, Bellflower City Council, 1988, State Senator and Assemblymen, 1986-87; petition circulator, State Initiatives, 1987-88; mem. Women's Ministries of Crystal Cathedral, Garden Grove, Calif. (bd. dirs. 1978-88, recipient Cathedral Star 1985). Classroom Tchrs. Instructional Improvement Program grantee, State of Calif., 1986-87; recipient Recognition award Regional Ednl. TV Adv. Council, 1986. mem. Bellflower Edn. Assn. (elem. dir. 1986-88), Calif. Tchrs. Assn. (del. 1986-87), Nat. Edn. Assn. (del. nat. conv. 1986, 87), AAUW. Republican. Mem. Reformed Churches of Am. Office: Lindstrom Elem School 5900 N Canehill Lakewood CA 90713

SPRINGFIELD, MARY SUSAN (PANCOAST), construction management, school bond services company executive; b. Okmulgee, Okla., Feb. 25, 1944; d. Ardo Lee and Lula Mary (Matheney) Pancoast; m. Ronald Dean Springfield, Aug. 6, 1966; 1 child, Julie Lynn. B.F.A., U. Okla., 1966; M.A., Central Okla. State U., Edmond, 1974. Cert. tchr., Okla. Secondary tchr. Mid-Del Pub. Schs., Midwest City, Okla., 1966-78; gen. mgr. Redland Constrn. & Supply, Norman, Okla., 1978-80; pres. Williams-Springfield Sch. Services, Inc., Moore, Okla., 1980—. Mem. Statue of Liberty-Ellis Island Centennial Commn., N.Y., 1984. Mem. Nat. Wildlife Fedn., U. Okla. Alumni Assn. (life), DAR (chpt. sec.), Okla. Wildlife Fedn., Gamma Phi Beta (Psi chpt.). Democrat. Methodist. Avocations: flying (pvt. pilot). Home: 3636 Rolling Ln Circle Midwest City OK 73110 Office: Williams-Springfield Sch Services Inc 2522 N Moore Ave PO Box 7008 Moore OK 73153

SPROUSE, SHERRI LOCKWOOD, food broker; b. Poplar Bluff, Mo., June 24, 1953; d. Lewis Dale and Eudora (McGruder) Lockwood; m. Danny Eugene Sprouse, Dec. 4, 1970; 1 child, Heather. Acct. exec. Exec. Food Sales, Inc., Dallas, 1976-83, exec. v.p., 1983—. Mem. Nat. Food Brokers Assn., N. Tex. Food Service Broker Assn., Nat. Ogrn. of Women Bus. Owners. Home: 3902 Merriman Plano TX 75074 Office: Exec Food Sales 13659 Jupiter #200 Dallas TX 75238

SPRUNK, TRUDY POST, therapist; b. Warren, Ohio, Feb. 24, 1945; d. Merle Ensign and Thelma Geraldine (Campbell) Post; m. David Frederick Sprunk, June 2, 1967; 1 child, Toby David. BS, Bowling Green U., 1967; MEd, Wright State U., Dayton, Ohio, 1970; cert. Sch. Psychology, Wright State U., 1972; postgrad., Ga. State U., 1972, 85. Lic. marriage and family therapist, tchr., counselor, sch. psychometrist. Staff psychologist Montgomery Retarded Children's Program, Dayton, Ohio, 1971-72; specific learning disabilities staff psychologist DeKalb Schs., Atlanta, 1972-85; marriage and family therapist Tucker (Ga.) Counseling Group, 1985-87; mem. adv. bd. Montessori Child Devel., Atlanta, 1978-79, Parent to Parent, 1985—. Author: (booklet) Catch 'Em Being Good Coupons, 1980; contbr. articles to profl. jours. Mem. Am. Assn. Marriage and Family Therapists (clin.), Assn. Children Learning Disabilities (bd. dirs. 1980-82). Republican. Mem. Christian Ch. Office: Tucker Ctr Personal Growth 4893 La Vista Rd Tucker GA 30084

SPUNG, CATHERINE ANN, bank executive; b. San Lois Obispo, Calif., Oct. 9, 1963; d. Richard Allen and Jennie Antionnette (Foulk) Roller; m. Peter Link Spung. Grad. high sch., Paris, Ill. Salesperson Sycamore Store, Paris, Ill., 1981-82; asst. mgr. Paragraphs, Paris, 1981-85; profl. travel agt. McMullen Travel Agy., Paris, 1981-85; mgr. The Cage, Paris, 1985, Fashion Crossroads, Paris, 1985; asst. mgr. Brooks Fashions, Terre Haute, Ind., 1985-86; teller The Citizen's Nat. Bank, Paris, 1986—. Asst. dir. Edgar County Fair Beauty Pageant, Paris, Ill., 1982—; chmn. fundraising com. Young Republicans, Edgar County, 1987. Recipient Scholastic Art award Eastern Ill. U., 1980-81, Achievement award Beta Sigma Phi, 1987; named one of Outstanding Young Women in Am., 1987, Women of Yr. Phi Epsilon Gamma, 1987. Mem. Paris Bus. and Profl. Women's Club, Phi Epsilon Gamma (pres. local chpt. 1986-87), Beta Sigma Phi (pres. local chpt. 1988-89). Republican. Presbyterian. Home: 703 Marshall Paris IL 61944 Office: The Citizens Nat Bank 110-114 East Ct Paris IL 61944

SPURGEON, ZELMA PEARL, educator, school administrator; b. Alexandria, Mo., Nov. 15, 1936; d. James Albert and Marguerite Louise (Jones) Rennaker; m. Mirl Eigene Spurgeon, Aug. 30, 1959; children—Vicki Lynn, James Dale, Joseph Eugene. A.A., Hannibal-LaGrange Jr. Coll., 1959; B.S., Culver-Stockton Coll., 1969, postgrad., 1985—. Cert. elem. tchr., Mo. Tchr. Ballard Sch., Kahoka, Mo., 1960-63, Hermann Sch., Mo., 1963-66, Wells Carey Sch., Keokuk, Iowa, 1967-70; co-owner, bookkeeper Gene's Graphics Signs, Alexandria, 1970-79; founder, prin., tchr. Kara Baptist Acad., Alexandria, 1979—; assn. youth leader Wyaconda Bapt. Ch., LaBelle, Mo., 1970-72; vol. phys. edn. tchr. Calvary Bapt. Ch., Keokuk, 1973-75; lectr. in field. Active mem. Right to Life, Keokuk, 1980-83, Moral Majority, Lynchburg, Va., 1979—, PTO, Herman and Keokuk, 1963-70, Booster Club Kara Bapt. Acad., 1979—, Womens Missionary Assn., Wayland, 1970-80, Civic Music Assn. Mem. NEA, Assn. of Christian Edn. Democrat. Avocations: bowling, golf, reading, music, church work. Home: PO Box 68 Alexandria MO 63430 Office: Kara Bapt Acad PO Box 68 Alexandria MO 63430

SPURLING, JUDITH H. DEIST, veterinarian; b. Ketchikan, Alaska, June 25, 1941; d. William Moyer and Mildred Louisa (Willard) Hemsing; m. Gary Spurling, Sept. 1961 (div.); children—Jody, Jay; m. 2d, Harold R. Deist, Mar. 11, 1971. B.S., Colo. State U., 1962, D.V.M., 1966. Veterinarian Belleview Animal Hosp., Englewood, Colo., 1966-69; pvt. practice Centennial Vet. Clinic, Littleton, Colo., 1969—. Mem. Assn. Women Vets. (pres. elect 1982-84, pres. 1984-86, sec. 1976-82), Denver Area Vet. Med. Soc. (treas. 1980-81), Am. Soc. Vet. Clin. Pathology, Colo. Vet. Med. Assn., Vet. Cancer Soc., AVMA Am. Animal Hosp. Assn. (dir.), Am. Morgan Horse Assn. (youth leader), Beta Beta Beta. Club: Mysterious Morgan Youth (leader 1979—), Leads. Office: 2731 W Belleview Ave Littleton CO 80123

SPURLOCK, RACHEL YVONNE, banker; b. Princeton, Ark., Sept. 16, 1937; d. Willie Roscoe and Croma Lee (Gresham) Hughes; cert. Am. Inst. Banking, 1979; grad. Southwestern Grad. of Banking, 1982; m. Burk Hobson Spurlock, Oct. 7, 1956; children—William Marcus, Gregory Morgan. Officer mgr. Salling Wiping Cloth Co., Shreveport, La., 1960-63, So. Towel, Shreveport, 1963-64; clerk Comml. Nat. Bank, Shreveport, 1964-73, mgr. ops. consumer loans, 1973—, asst. cashier, 1978-82, asst. v.p., 1982—. Mem. Am. Bus. Women's Assn., Nat. Assn. Bank Women. Democrat. Baptist. Home: 4280 Pruett Rd Shreveport LA 71107 Office: 333 Texas St Shreveport LA 71101

SPYCHE, AGNES MAGDELENE (PITTNER), health association executive, nurse; b. Buffalo, Oct. 27, 1936; d. Peter John and Agnes Rose (Kolasz) Pittner; diploma Sisters of Charity Hosp. Sch. Nursing, Buffalo, 1954-57; B.S. in Nursing, SUNY, Buffalo, 1961, M.S. in Health Care Planning and Mgmt., 1981; m. Gerald John Spyche, Feb. 23, 1963; children—Gerald John, Peter J., Mary A. With Sisters Hosp., Buffalo, 1957-64, 65-66, in-service coordinator, 1960-61, supr. spl. dept. emergency room, urology, out-patient dept. and ICU, 1961-64, staff nurse, 1965-66; night supr. St. Joseph's Intercommunity Hosp., Cheektowaga, N.Y., 1961-64; with Emergency Hosp., Buffalo, 1964-65; 67-78, asst. dir. nursing service, 1969-71, dir. nursing service, 1971-78; asst. dir. nursing service DeGraff Meml. Hosp., North Tonawanda, N.Y., 1979, dir. nursing service, 1979-80; dir. blood service nursing ARC, Buffalo, 1981-85; instr. obstet. nursing, acute care Sisters Hosp. Sch. Nursing, 1985—; bd. dirs. Western N.Y. High Blood Pressure Screening; cons. for developing ICUs. Mem. Erie County (N.Y.) CD Com.; mem. Erie County Disaster Com. Recipient Med. award Sisters Hosp., 1957; Hill Burton Act of 1956 trainee, 1957—. Mem. Alumni Sisters of Charity Hosp. Sch. Nursing, Alumni Sch. Nursing SUNY Buffalo, Am. Assn. Blood Banks. Roman Catholic. Home: 124 Cresthaven Dr West Seneca NY 14224 Office: 2157 Main St Buffalo NY 14214

SQUAIR, JEAN MARIE, educational administrator; b. Vancouver, B.C., Can., Jan. 19, 1925; came to U.S., 1943; d. Alfred Ernest and Bertha Edith (Bailey) Hall; student Stanford U., 1943-47, Boston U., 1964-65, U. Calif., Berkeley, 1965-68; m. Stuart Davidson Squair, Feb. 14, 1948; children—Roslyn Marie, Elizabeth Ann. Mgr., Oakland (Calif.) Symphony Chorus, 1963-70; dir. vol. services Goodwill Industries, Oakland, 1970-80; sr. adj. prof., Golden Gate U., San Francisco, 1976—, dir. Grad. Sch. Arts Adminstrn., 1976—. Bd. govs. San Francisco Symphony, 1976-81; bd. dirs. San Francisco Opera Western Opera Theater, 1970-78; trustee Calif. Hist. Soc., 1970-76; co-chmn. Piedmont Arts Festival, 1970-78; pres. San Francisco Symphony League, 1973-76. Recipient Disting. Service award Oakland Symphony, 1966; award Nat. Aux. to Goodwill Industries, 1978, Disting. Work and Achievement award City and County of San Francisco Arts Commn., 1986, Cert. Honor, Bd. Suprs. San Francisco, 1986. Mem. Assn. Arts Adminstrn. Educators (dir.), Assn. Calif. Symphony Orchs. (founding pres.), Am. Symphony Orch. League (mem. vol. council bd.). Home: 6001 Acacia Ave Oakland CA 94618 Office: Golden Gate 536 Mission St San Francisco CA 94105

SQUAZZO, MILDRED KATHERINE (OETTING), corp. exec.; b. Bklyn., Dec. 22; d. William John and Marie M. (Fromm) Oetting; student L.I. U. Sec.-treas., Stanley Engring., Inc. and v.p. Stanley Chems., Inc., 1960-68; founder, pres. Chem-Dynamics Corp., Scotch Plains, N.J., 1964-68; gen. adminstr., purchasing dir., Richardson Chem. Co., Metuchen, N.J., 1968-69; owner Berkeley Employment Agy. and Berkeley Temp. Help Service, Berkeley Heights, N.J., 1969—, Berkeley Employment Agy., Morristown, N.J., 1982, Bridgewater, N.J., 1987—; pres. M.K.S. Bus. Group, Inc., Berkeley Heights, 1980—; mgmt. cons.; personnel fin.; lectr. Served with Nurse Corps, U.S. Army, 1946-47. Mem. Nat. Bus. and Profl. Women's Club. Office: 312 Springfield Ave Berkeley Heights NJ 07922

SQUILLANTE, JUDITH ANN, human resources executive; b. Providence, Jan. 29, 1942; d. David Joseph and Hilda Theresa (Jamiel) Ferris; m. John Emilio Squillante, Sept. 4, 1961 (div.); children: Mark David, Jason Richard. BS, Bryant Coll., 1960; mgmt. cert. program, U. R.I., 1965-67. Asst. to town treas. Town of Bristol, R.I., 1960-64; ops. coordinator Speidel div. Textron, Providence, 1964-71; asst. v.p. CE Maguire, Inc., Providence, 1971-78; mgr. customer affairs Deltona Corp., Miami, Fla., 1978-79; dir. human resources, sr. assoc. Post, Buckley, Schuh & Jernigan, Miami, Fla., 1979—; bd. dirs. Tradcom Internat., Miami; cons. Modern Bus. Applications, Miami, 1986-88. Chmn. Pack 22 Cub Scouts, Miami, 1985; mem. com. Miller-Sunset Homeowner's Assn., Miami, 1986, Beacon Council Liaison, Miami, 1986. Named one of Outstanding Women in Bus. and Industry YWCA, Miami, 1983. Mem. Am. Soc. Personnel Adminstrn., Personnel Assn. Greater Miami (Outstanding Company Achievement in Human Resources award 1987), Women's C. of C., Nat. Assn. Female Execs., YWCA Women's Network, Greater Miami C. of C. (mem. first nationally established labor and personnel mgmt. com. 1987—). Democrat. Roman Catholic. Club: South Fla. Democrat. Home: 9725 SW 64th St Miami FL 33173 Office: Post Buckley Schuh & Jernigan Inc 8600 NW 36th St Miami FL 33166

SQUIRE, MATTIE LUE, educator; b. Goshen, Ala., Jan. 1, 1925; d. Brunie and Bertha M. (Smith) Sconions; m. Robert L. Squire, July 31, 1940; children—Barbara L., Madelyn C., Linda A., Robert L. A.A., Miami Dade Coll., 1970; B.S., Fla. Internat. U., 1973, M.S., 1974. Sch. lunch cashier, maid Dade County Pub. Schs., Miami, Fla., 1957-64, tchr.'s aide, 1964-69, tchr. asst., 1969-73, tchr., 1973—; mgr. New Century Reading Lab., 1975-76, mgr. Title I Reading Lab., 1976-79. Chmn. Miami Women's Com. of 100, 1980; bd. dirs. Brownsville Neighborhood Civic Assn., Miami, 1975; founder Back to Coll. Brunch, Miami, 1960; founder Israel Bethel P.B. Ch. Scholarship Fund, Miami, 1980, also Sunday Sch. tchr., 1942—. Recipient Cert. of Achievement, Fla. Internat. U., Miami, 1974. Mem. Nat. Assn. Female Execs., AAUW, Fla. Fedn. Bus. and Prof. Women's Clubs, Dade Fedn. Bus. and Profl. Women's Clubs (Woman of Yr. 1981), Fla. State Reading Council, Epsilon Tau Lambda.

SQUIRES, PATRICIA EILEEN COLEMAN, freelance journalist; b. Beaver Falls, Pa., Jan. 28, 1927; d. John Wiley and Helen Marie (Barstow) Purtell; B.A. in Journalism, Ind. U., 1949; m. Mark B. Squires, Sr., June 30, 1951; children—Sally Regan, Mark B., Susan Barstow. Staff reporter LaPorte (Ind.) Herald-Argus, 1949-51, daily columnist, 1950-51, sect. editor, 1949-51; women's news and feature writer Muskegon (Mich.) bur. Grand Rapids Herald, 1956-57; editor suburban sect. North Shore Line, Chicagoland Mag., Chgo., 1967-69; staff writer Fairpress, Westport, Conn., 1972-73; regular contbr. New Canaan (Conn.) Advertiser, 1975-78, Bridgeport (Conn.) Sunday Post, 1976-78, Soundings, Essex, Conn., 1977-78, N.Y. Times, N.Y.C., 1976—; tchr. English, journalism, social studies jr. and sr. public high schs., Jackson, Mich., 1966-67, Niles Twp., Skokie, Ill., 1967-68; vol. tutor Social Cultural Ednl. Enrichment Program, Protestant Community Center, 1979—. Public relations, promotion dir. Ella Sharp Mus., Jackson, 1964-66; publicity chmn. New Canaan Soc. for Arts, 1977-78; bd. dirs. Centennial Celebration Com., Winnetka, Ill., 1968-69; Community Council New Canaan, 1972-75; New Canaan Bicentennial Com., 1975-76; publicity chmn. parent-tchr. council Frost Jr. High Sch., Jackson, 1963-64; active Girl Scouts Am. Mem. Women in Communications, N.J. Press Women, Nat. Fedn. Press Women, AAUW, Ind. U. Alumni Assn. Presbyterian. Clubs: Cedar Point Yacht (Westport, Conn.); Lake Mohawk Golf (Sparta, N.J.). Home and Office: 688 West Shore Trail Sparta NJ 07871

SREENAN, BARBARA THOMAS, psychotherapist; b. Rockford, Ill., May 18, 1932; d. Charles Alexander and Irene (Freeman) Thomas; m. H.P. Sreenan, June 20, 1953 (div. Apr. 1970); children: Gregory, Melaney, Charene, Ronald, Patrick, Kevin, Casey, Daniel, Mary Kate. BS, U. Wis., 1954; MS, No. Ill. U., 1972; PhD, Fla. State U., 1977. Prof. criminal justice, chmn. dept. Fla. Southern Coll., Lakeland, 1976-87; founder, exec. dir., psychotherapist Sreenan Human Resource Assocs., Lakeland, 1976—; adj. prof. Fla. State U., 1982, Tallahassee Community Coll., 1973-76, Harlaxton Coll., Grantham, Eng., 1981; internat. guest lectr.; police psychologist Lakeland Police Dept., 1988—; stress mgmt. cons. Inst. for Personality Assessment and Testing, Lakeland, 1986—. Bd. dirs. Transition House, Winter Haven, 1977-82, Polk County Mental Health Assn., 1988—; chmn. Citizens' Adv. Com. for Probation and Restitution Ctr., Lakeland, 1977-87. Recipient Mental Health award, 1981, Certs. of Appreciation, Fla. State Dept. Corrections, 1985, Fla. United Way, 1985. Fellow Am. Orthopsychiat. Assn.; mem. Am. Assn. Marriage and Family Therapists, Fla. Assn. Marriage and Family Therapists (sec.-treas., pres.-elect 1981-84), Nat. Assn. Social Workers, Am. Psychol. Assn., Fla. Psycho-Logical Assn., Lakeland C. of C. Democrat. Roman Catholic. Home: 5520 Driftwood Dr Lakeland FL 33809 Office: Sreenan Human Resources Assocs 217 Hillcrest St Lakeland FL 33801

SROCK, MARTHA D., police officer; b. Arlington, Tex., Nov. 30, 1959; d. Homer C. and Grace R. DeWolfe; m. Jerry D. Srock, 1986; stepchildren: Jeff, Debbie. Student, N. Tex. State U., 1978-79, Larimer County Vocat.-Tech., Ft. Collins, Colo., 1983; cert. peace officer, Tarrant County Jr. Coll., Euless, Tex., 1984. Police officer Grand Prairie (Tex.) Police Dept., 1984—. Sec. Grand Prarie Police Assn., 1985-86. Mem. Internat. Assn. Women Police, Tex. Assn. Women Police, Fraternal Order Police, Mensa, SW Karate Assn. (achieved 9th degree orange belt). Club: Leo (sec. 1977-78). Office: Grand Prairie Police Dept 801 Conover Grand Prairie TX 75051

SROGE, MARIAN, association executive, consultant; b. N.Y.C., Jan. 12, 1941; d. Eli and Charlotte (Radlauer) Stern; m. Marshall I. Sroge, Jan. 14, 1962; children: Rebecca, Joshua, Deborah. BA, Queens Coll., 1962. Community resource coordinator Mut. Aid Project, N.Y.C., 1977-79; dir. info. ref. and advocacy Aging in Am., Bronx, N.Y., 1979-81; dir. Empire region B'nai B'rith Women, N.Y.C., 1981-86; nat. dir. Orgn. dept., Women's Am. ORT, N.Y.C., 1986-88; nat. dir. Sect. Services, Nat. Council of Jewish Women, N.Y.C., 1988—. Mem. N.Y. Soc. Assn. Execs., Am. Soc. Assn. Execs.

STAAS, GRETCHEN LEE, librarian; b. Dallas, Oct. 1, 1938; d. Fred Raike and Martha (Garten) Hyde; B.S., Tex. Christian U., 1961; M.S. in Library Sci., East Texas State U., 1974; PhDNorth Tex. State U., 1987; m. Gene L. Staas, Aug. 29, 1959; 1 dau., Gayla Lynn. Classroom tchr. Garland (Tex.) Ind. Sch. Dist., 1967-74, librarian, 1974-78, cons. library and media services, 1978—. Mem. ALA, Tex. Library Assn. (pres. 1988—), Tex. Assn. Sch. Library Adminstrs. (pres. 1982-83), Tex. Assn. Sch. Librarians, North Cen. Tex. Assn. for Supervision and Curriculum Devel., Tex. Assn. Ednl. Tech., North Central Tex. IRA, Phi Delta Kappa, Kappa Delta Pi. Office: 221 S 9th St Garland TX 75040

STABENOW, DEBORAH ANN, state legislator; b. Gladwin, Mich., Apr. 29, 1950; d. Robert Lee and Anna Merle (Hallmark) Greer; m. Dennis Richard Stabenow, June 12, 1971; children: Todd Dennis, Michelle Deborah. BS magna cum laude, Mich. State U., 1972, MSW magna cum laude, 1975. With spl. services Lansing (Mich.) Sch. Dist., 1972-73; county commr. Ingham County, Mason, Mich., 1975-78; state rep. State Mich., Lansing, 1979—. Founder Ingham County Women's Commn.; co-founder Council Against Domestic Assault; mem. Dem. Bus. and Profl. Club, Mich. Dem. Women's Polit. Caucus, Grance United Meth. Ch. (past lay leader, chair Social Concerns Task Force, Sunday Sch. music tchr., Lansing Boys' Club, profl. adv. com. Lansing Parents Without Ptnrs., adv. com. Ctr. Handicapped Affairs, Mich. Council Family and Divorce Mediation Adv. Bd., Nat. Council Children's Rights, Big Bros./Big Sisters Greater Lansing Adv. Bd., Mich. Child Study Assn. Bd. Advisors, Mich. Women's Campaign Fund. Recipient Service to Children award Council for Prevention of Child Abuse and Neglect, 1983, Disting. Service to Mich. Families award Mich. Council Family Relations, 1983, Outstanding Leadership award Nat. Council Community Mental Health Ctrs., 1983, Snyder-Kok award Mental Health Assn. Mich., Awareness Leader of Yr. award Awareness Communications Team Developmentally Disabled, 1984, Communicator of Yr. award Woman in Communications, 1984, Lawmaker of Yr. award Nat. Child Support Enforcement Assn., 1985, Disting. Service award Lansing Jaycees, 1985, Disting. Service in Govt. award Retarded Citizens of Mich., 1986; named One of Ten Outstanding Young Ams. Jaycees, 1986. Mem. NAACP, Lansing Regional C. of C., Delta Kappa Gamma. Home: 2709 S Deerfield Lansing MI 48911 Office: Ho Reps PO Box 30014 Lansing MI 48909

STABILE, CAROL, banker; b. Bklyn., Mar. 1, 1951; d. Charles Joseph and Marion Theresa (Iovino) Corsentino. A.A.S., Fashion Inst. Tech., 1970; B.B.A., Pace U., 1981. Notary pub., N.Y. Supr. check processing Anchor Savs. Bank, N.Y.C., 1973-78; asst. br. mgr. Am. Saving Bank, N.Y.C., 1978-79; group leader customer liaison Phila. Internat. Bank, N.Y.C., 1979-81, adminstrv. asst. internat. div. Tokyo desk, Phila., 1981-83, asst. treas., mgr. Asia, N.Y.C., 1983-85, v.p., mgr. internat. customer service, 1986—; v.p., gen. mgr. ops. Phila. Internat. Fin. Co. Ltd., Hong Kong, 1988—. Active Pineapple Tenants Assn., Bklyn., 1984; asst. treas. bd. dirs. Pineapple Owners' Corp. Mem. Nat. Assn. Female Execs. (mem. adv. bd. Tng. Program Service Fund). Democrat. Roman Catholic. Avocations: collectors' plates, Asian art, fgn. films. Office: Phila Internat Bank 55 Broad St New York NY 10004

STABILE, ROSE TOWNE (MRS. FRED STABILE), bldg. and mgmt., public relations cons.; b. Sunderland, Eng.; d. Stephen and Amelia Bergman; student English schs., Tchrs. Coll., Columbia; m. Wilfred Kermode (dec. Feb. 1934); m. 2d, Arthur Whittlesey Towne, May 29, 1936 (dec. 1954); m. 3d, Norbert Le Veille, June 10, 1961 (div. Feb. 1969); m. 4th, Fred Stabile, May 30, 1970. Formerly auditor Brit. Govt., Whitehall, London; activities and membership dir. N.Y. League of Girls Clubs, N.Y.C.; real estate exec., now semi-ret. bldg. mgr. State Tower Bldg., Syracuse, N.Y.; cons. public relations, office designer and decorator; lectr. real estate dept. Syracuse U. An initiator Syracuse Peace Council; mem. area sponsoring com. Assn. for Crippled Children and Adults. Mem. Syracuse Real Estate Bd., English Speaking Union (membership com.), Nat. N.Y. assns. real estate bds., Nat. Assn. Bldg. Owners and Mgrs., N.Y. Soc. Real Estate Appraisers, Syracuse C. of C., League Women Voters, Assn. UN, Women of Rotary, Bus. and Profl. Women's Clubs, Everson Mus. Art Friends of Reading, Mus. Modern Art (N.Y.C.), Internat. Center of Syracuse. Unitarian (chmn. service com. 1956-57.). Club: Corinthian. Home: 304 Malverne Dr Syracuse NY 13208 Office: State Tower Bldg Syracuse NY 13202

STABLES, JEAN BARBARA, data processing executive; b. Burlington, Vt., May 31, 1946; d. George Richard and Marian Alice (Blaine) S.; m. William Milton Rieken Jr., Sept. 8, 1983. BA, U. Vt., 1968; MS in Computer Sch., U. R.I., 1974. Programmer analyst Pratt and Whitney, E. Hartford, Conn., 1970-72; statistician Bur. Census, Suitland, Md., 1972-73; sr. programmer analyst R.I. Health Services Research, Providence, 1973-76; sr. info. scientist Hoffmann-LaRoche, Nutley, N.J., 1976-88; sr. software engr. Schlumberger Graphics, Montain View, Calif., 1988—. Mem. Assn. Computer Machinery (mem. chair 1983-84), Am. Statistical Assn., N.E. Autocad Users Group (v.p., pres. 1987-88). Home: 3355 Brookdale Dr Santa Clara CA 95051 Office: Schlumberger Graphics 385 Ravendale Dr Montain View CA 94039-7169

STACE-NAUGHTON, DENISE KAY, records adminstrator; b. Madison, Wis., July 21, 1960; d. Ralph Wayne and Nellie Mae (Wilke) Stace; m. Patrick John Naughton, Aug. 16, 1980. BS, U. Wis., Milw., 1983. Head med. records Pavilion Nursing Home, Milw., 1981-82; med. record analyst County Gen. Hosp., Milw., 1982-83, shift supr. med. records, 1983-84, supr. med. records cen. files, 1984-85; med. record dir., transcription dir. DePaul Rehab. Hosp., Milw., 1985-87; mem. faculty Concordia Coll., Milw., 1987—; clin. instr. U. Wis., Milw., 1985-87; cons. in field. Recipient the coveted Oscar Mayer Nat. Scholarship, 1978. Mem. Am. Med. Record Assn., Wis. Med. Record Assn. (cons. com. 1986—), Southeastern Wis. Med. Record Assn., Nat. Assn. Female Execs. Lutheran. Home: 5712 N Argyle Ave Glendale WI 53209

STACEY, PAMELA, editor, writer; b. Salt Lake City; Mar. 29, 1945; d. Jack Nordvall Freeze and Peggy (Whelan) Sherman; m. Richard C. Murphy, Feb. 22, 1981; stepchildren—Greg, Jeanne. B.A. in English, UCLA, 1968, teaching credential, 1970; M.A. in English, Calif. State U.-Long Beach, 1985. Researcher, Drew Pearson-Journalist, Washington, 1964, 66; adminstr. UNESCO, Paris, 1968-69; Rand Corp., Santa Monica, Calif., 1972-76; editor, writer Cousteau Soc., Los Angeles, 1976—. Editor, creator (mag. for children) Dolphin Log for Cousteau Soc., 1981. Avocations: scuba diving; sailing; skiing. Office: Cousteau Soc 8440 Santa Monica Blvd Los Angeles CA 90069

STACK, PATRICIA ELIZABETH, hospital professional; b. Freeport, N.Y., July 10, 1947; d. Thomas Joseph Nolan and Marilyn Louise (Koelpin) Nolan Klein; m. Stephen Paul Stack, Aug. 17, 1968; children: Leanne Marie, Jeanne Elizabeth. Diploma, Mercy Hosp. Sch. Nursing, 1968; postgrad., St. Joseph's Coll., North Windham, Maine, 1983-85, 87—. RN night charge Mercy Hosp., Portland, Maine, 1968-69, RN, head nurse, 1969-70, RN evening charge, 1970-80, coordinator utilization, 1980-81, mgr. utilization, 1981-87; RN med. reviewer Blue Cross/Blue Shield, Portland, 1987—. Leader Girl Scouts U.S., Standish, Maine, 1984-87, troop cons., 1985-87; vol 4H, 1987—, also chaperone dairy projects; mem. women's aux. ctr. Meml. Clinic, Standish. Mem. Am. Bd. Quality Assurance and Utilization Rev. (cert.), Nat. Assn. for Female Execs. Club: So. Maine Holstein (Gorham) (sec. 1983—). Home: Box 193 Sebago Lake ME 04075

STACKELL, ESTHER ILANA, lawyer; b. Lvov, USSR, May 31, 1954; came to U.S. 1965, naturalized 1974; d. Joseph and Rose (Zilber) Goldstein; m. Isaac Barry Stackell, Jan. 8, 1977; 1 child, Zachary Alexander. BA, Lehigh U., 1974; JD, Hofstra U., 1979. Bar: N.Y. 1980. In-house counsel Jewish Hosp and Med. Ctr., Bklyn., 1979-81; assoc. gen. counsel Fedn. Jewish Philanthropies, N.Y.C., 1981; assoc. Bergner, Bergner, Blum & Ruditz, N.Y.C., 1981-84; sole practice, Bklyn., 1984-86 asst. corp. counsel spl. services for children div. Family Ct. City of N.Y.; cons. in field. Chair 9425-9437 Shore Rd. Tenants Assn.; mem. Union Women's Ctr., Bklyn., 1985. Mem. N.Y. County Lawyers (medicine and mental health com.), N.Y. State Bar Assn., Suffolk County Women's Bar Assn., Greater N.Y. Hosp. Assn., Med. Malpractice Com., Nat. Assn. Female Execs. Republican. Club: Lehigh Alumni Greater N.Y. Lodge: B'nai B'rith Women. Avocation: stained glass design.

STACY, ESTHER MADELINE, real estate broker; b. Phila., Oct. 27, 1941; d. Bernard Frances and Elizabeth Anne (Fitzpatrick) Murphy; divorced, 1983); children: Jennifer, John. Student, Phila. Coll. Art, 1964, Framingham State Coll. Realtor Century 21/Harvest Real Estate, Sudbury, Mass., 1978-81, Coldwell Banker/Foster & Foster Realtors, Wayland, Mass., 1981—. Mem. Mass. Assn. Realtors, Greater Boston Real Estate Bd. Republican. Roman Catholic. Office: Coldwell Banker/ Foster & Foster Realtors 311 Boston Post Rd Wayland MA 01778

STADLER, KATHERINE LOY, advertising sales executive; b. N.Y.C., Mar. 26, 1930; d. William L. and Catherine (Schmidhauser) Stadler; student St. John's U., 1948-49, Hunter Coll., 1957-59, NYU Mgmt. Inst., 1963-69. Br. mgr. Hull Travel Service, Inc., N.Y.C., 1959-63; with Loire Imports, Inc., N.Y.C., 1963-69; dist. mgr. McGraw-Hill Info. Systems Co., Sweet's Div., N.Y.C., 1969-74; nat. sales mgr. Floor Covering Weekly, N.Y.C., 1974-76; account exec. Ziff-Davis Pub. Co., Hotel & Travel Index, Los Angeles, 1976-81; founder Katherine Stadler & Assocs., 1981—; regional mgr. Modern Salon, 1984—. Mem. Med. Mission Sisters, Roman Catholic Ch., 1949-57. Named Sweet's Eastern Region Salesman of Yr., 1972. Mem. Nat. Assn. Profl. Saleswomen, Early Music Ensemble Los Angeles, 1985—. Clubs: Los Angeles Ad, Toastmasters. Home: 427 S Curson Ave Los Angeles CA 90036

STADLER, SUZANNE MARCY, marketing executive; b. Queens, N.Y., May 12, 1962; d. Max Joel and Sydelle (Scholom) S. AS in Merchandising, Johnson & Wales Coll., 1982, BS in Mktg., Fashion Mgmt., 1984. Asst. mktg. dir. Josephson Kluwer Legal Ednl. Ctr., N.Y.C., 1984-86; product mgr. Stanley Kaplan Ednl. Ctrs. Ltd., div. Washington Post, N.Y.C., 1986—. Mem. Nat. Assn. Female Execs. Office: Stanley Kaplan Ednl Ctrs Ltd 810 7th Ave New York NY 10019

STADTMAN, THRESSA CAMPBELL, biochemist; b. Sterling, N.Y., Feb. 12, 1920; d. Earl and Bessie (Waldron) Campbell; m. Earl Reece Stadtman, Oct. 19, 1943. B.S., Cornell U., 1940, M.S., 1942; Ph.D., U. Calif.-Berkeley, 1949. Research assoc. U. Calif.-Berkeley, 1942-47; research Harvard U. Med. Sch., Boston, 1949-50; biochemist Nat. Heart, Lung and Blood Inst., NIH, USPHS, HHS, Bethesda, Md., 1950—. Editor Jour. Biol. Chemistry, Archives Biochemistry and Biophysics, Molecular and Cellular Biochemistry; editor-in-chief Bio Factors; contbr. articles on amino acid metabolism, methane biosynthesis, vitamin B12 biochemistry, selenium biochemistry to profl. jours. Helen Haye Whitney fellow Oxford U., Eng., 1954-55; Rockefeller Found. grantee U. Munich, Fed. Republic Germany, 1959-60; recipient Rose award, 1987. Mem. Am. Soc. Microbiology, Biochem. Soc., Soc. Am. Biochemists, Am. Chem. Soc., Nat. Acad. Scis., Am. Acad. Arts and Scis., Sigma Delta Epsilon (hon.). Home: 16907 Redland Rd Derwood MD 20855 Office: Nat Heart Lung and Blood Inst HHS Bethesda MD 20892

STAFFORD, BARBARA PRESTON, public relations specialist; b. Phila., Sept. 20, 1929; d. James Alexander and Elizabeth Marcy (Conover) Preston; m. Linley Montell Stafford, July 17, 1954 (div. June 1971); children—Preston Conover, Mary Clay. Student Wilson Coll., 1946-48; A.B., U. Ky., 1950; postgrad. in edn., Hunter Coll., 1960-62. Copywriter, Boone Advt. Agy., Louisville, 1950-51, Commonwealth Life Ins., Louisville, 1951-52; publicity asst. Rosemary Sheehan, N.Y.C., 1953-54, 55-57; pub. relations account exec. Aubrbach Agy., N.Y.C., 1957-60; elem. tchr. N.Y.C. Bd. Edn., 1962-66, copy editor Reader's Digest, Chappaqua, N.Y., 1969-74, press coordinator, 1974-85, employee communications mgr., 1985-87, publ. info. officer Children's Village, Dobbs Ferry, N.Y., 1987—. Bd. dirs., v.p. Child Care Council Westchester, Inc., 1980-84; sec. Hastings (N.Y.) Towne House Coop. Bd., 1983-84; treas. Grace Episc. Ch., Hastings, 1987—. Mem. Women in Communications (v.p. Westchester chpt.). Home: 445 Broadway Hastings on Hudson NY 10706 Office: Children's Village Dobbs Ferry NY 10522

STAFFORD, DOT MELBA, banker; b. Brownwood, Tex., Feb. 27, 1928; d. A.R. and Julia M. (Sherrod) Elliott; m. Joe M. Stafford, June 11, 1946; children: Ray M., Bobby G.; Cindy Stafford Ward, Michelle Stafford Acker. Grad. high sch., Pecos, Tex. Sec. Community Pub. Service, Pecos, 1946-53, Sta. KJBC, Midland, Tex., 1953-60, Estes Enterprises, Pecos, 1960-63; v.p. publ. relations First Nat. Bank, Pecos, 1963—. Mem. city council Town of Pecos City, 1986—; bd. dirs. Pecos chpt. Am. Heart Assn., 1986—, Pecos Rodeo Com. Mem. Nat. Assn. Banking Women, Bus. and Profl. Women, Pecos C. of C. (bd. dirs. 1983—), Beta Sigma Phi. Republican. Mem. Ch. Christ. Home: 2220 Wyoming St Pecos TX 79772

STAFFORD, HELEN ELIZABETH THOMSON, management consultant; b. Port Chester, N.Y., Mar. 1, 1926; d. James Ramage and Helen Cunningham (McGill) Thomson; B.S. in Psychology, Coll. William and Mary, 1948; m. Paul Tutt Stafford, Dec. 14, 1951; children—Paul Tutt, Timothy Alden, Mark Thornton, Todd Lawton. Exec. asst. commn. on worship Nat. Council Chs., N.Y.C., 1950-51; co-founder, dir., treas., sr. v.p. Paul Stafford Assos., Ltd., Mgmt. Cons., N.Y.C., 1959-82. Bd. dirs. Princeton Area YWCA, 1985—; active Commn. on the Tercentenary Observances of The Coll. of William and Mary. Mem. Assn. Exec. Recruiting Cons. (dir. 1968-70), Soc. Alumni Coll. William and Mary (dir. 1984—), Mortar Board, Phi Beta Kappa, Kappa Kappa Gamma. Republican. Presbyterian. Clubs: Bedens Brook, Nassau (Princeton, N.J.); Hillsboro (bd. dirs. 1986—) (Pompano Beach, Fla.).

STAFFORD, REBECCA, college president, sociologist; b. Topeka, July 9, 1936; d. Frank C. and Anne Elizabeth (Larrick) S.; m. Willard VanHazel, Apr. 12, 1973. A.B. magna cum laude, Radcliffe Coll., 1958, M.A., 1961; Ph.D., Harvard U., 1964. Lectr. dept. sociology Sch. Edn., Harvard U., Cambridge, Mass., 1964-70, mem. vis. com. bd. overseers, 1973, 79; assoc. prof. sociology U. Nev., Reno, 1970-73, prof., 1973-80, chmn. dept. sociology, 1974-77, dean Coll. Arts and Scis., 1977-80; pres. Bemidji (Minn.) State U., 1980-82; exec. v.p. Colo. State U., Ft. Collins, 1982-83; pres. Chatham Coll., Pitts., 1983—; bd. dirs. Union Nat. Bank. Bd. dirs. Univ. Presbyn. Hosp., Pitts. Symphony, Winchester-Thurston Sch.; chmn. Harvard U. Grad. Soc. Council, 1987—. Recipient McCurdy-Rinkle prize for research Eastern Psychiat. Assn., 1970; grantee Am. Council Edn. Inst. Acad. Deans, 1979, Inst. Ednl. Mgmt., Harvard U., 1984; named Man of Yr. in Edn. City of Pitts., 1986. Mem. Harvard U. Alumni Assn. (bd. dirs. 1985-87), Phi Beta Kappa, Phi Kappa Phi.

STAFFORD, VIRGINIA FRANCES, sorority administrator; b. Burlington, Iowa, Feb. 21, 1927; d. Neils Alfred and Florence Cecelia (Johansen) Rosenberg; B.A., U. Iowa, 1948; postgrad. U. Maine, 1950-51; m. Robert William Stafford, Aug. 29, 1948; children—Marcia Stafford Jorgensen, Craig William, Brian James, Maren Stafford Smith. Sub. tchr., tchr. speech Des Moines Public Schs., 1948-50; chmn. Iowa state membership Alpha Delta Pi, Ames, 1955-58, nat. chmn. membership selection, 1958-67, nat. chmn. pledge edn., 1967-73, grand sec., 1973-77, v.p. collegiate chpts., 1977-79, grand pres., 1977-83; chmn. collegiate expansion, 1983-85; 2nd del., Nat. Panhellenic Conf.,, 1983—; chmn. Alumnae Panhellenics com., 1983—. Bd. dirs. Ames Internat. Festival Assn., sec., 1972-78; chmn. Ames Bicentennial Commn., 1974-76; bd. dirs. Ames Found., 1976—; bd. dirs. Mamie Eisenhower Birthplace Found., 1979-85; pres. bd. dirs. Ames Community Art Council; bd. dirs. Ames Found. Mem. Assn. of Frat. Advs. (asso.), LWV, U. Iowa Alumni Assn. (com. to provide A. Craig Baird Endowment, speech dept. 1977—), Phi Beta Kappa, Delta Sigma Rho, Zeta Phi Eta. Republican. Presbyterian. Club: P.E.O. Home: 2044 Pinehurst Dr Ames IA 50010 Office: Alpha Delta Pi 1386 Ponce de Leon Ave NE Atlanta GA 30306

STAGG, EVELYN WHEELER, educator, state legislator; b. Waterbury, Vt., Sept. 30, 1916; d. Aiton Grover and Edythe (Boyce) Wheeler; m. David Stagg, May 15, 1942; children: Christie Stagg Austin, Bonnie Stagg-Michlein, Carol Stagg Kevan. BA, Middlebury Coll., 1939; MA, U. Vt., 1971. Assoc. prof. Castleton State Coll., Vt., 1966-82; mem. Vt. Ho. of Reps., 1982-88, chmn. house edn. com., 1982-88, vice chmn. health and welfare com., 1985-86, chair edn. com., 1987-88; commr. Edn. Commn. of the States, 1987-88; cons. communications projects, Bomoseen, Vt., 1982—. Contbr. articles to profl. jours. Chmn. Women's Legis. Caucus; pres., mem. Rutland Area Vis. Nurse Assn., 1969-75; bd. dirs. Rutland Mental Health Assn.; trustee pub. funds Townof Castleton. Mem. Women's Caucus, Vt. Women's Polit. Caucus, Nat. Women's Polit. Caucus, AAUW, Inst. for Gen. Semantics, Internat. Soc. for Gen. Semantics, Am. Philatelic Soc., Castleton Hist. Soc. Democrat. Clubs: Women's, Rutland County Stamp. Avocations: stamp and coin collecting, dolls, sailing, skiing, traveling. Home: Mason's Point Bomoseen VT 05732 Office: State House Montpelier VT 05602

STAHL, ELAINE HANNA, food consultant; b. Halifax, Yorkshire, Eng., May 11, 1931; came to U.S., 1955; d. Herbert Oliver and Eveline (Ainley) Falshaw; m. Kenneth William Stahl, Nov. 23, 1974; 1 child, Carolyn. Diploma in Instnl. Mgmt., Gloucester (Eng.) Coll., 1952; BS in Nutrition and Dietetics, Leeds (Eng.) Poly. U., 1954. Registered dietician, U.K. Food editor Ladies Home Jour., N.Y.C., 1958-64; author cookbooks Doubleday Co. Inc., N.Y.C., 1966-72, 82—; mgr. sales promotions Lehn & Fink Co. Inc., Montvale, N.J., 1972-82; free-lance food cons. 1982—; cons. Reader's Digest, N.Y.C., 1983. Co-author: The Doubleday Cookbook, 1975 (award 1975), The New Doubleday Cookbook, 1985; cons. to Quick, Thrifty Cooking, 1985; contbr. to Ladies' Home Jour., Cosmopolitan, Family Circle. Home and Office: 55 Anona Dr Upper Saddle River NJ 07458

STAHL, LESLEY R., journalist; b. Lynn, Mass., Dec. 16, 1941; d. Louis and Dorothy J. (Tishler) S.; m. Aaron Latham; 1 dau. B.A. cum laude, Wheaton Coll., Norton, Mass., 1963. Asst. to speechwriter Mayor Lindsay's Office, N.Y.C., 1966-67; researcher N.Y. Election unit London-Huntley Brinkley Report, NBC News, 1967-69; producer, reporter WHDH-TV, Boston, 1970-72; news corr. CBS News, Washington, from 1972; moderator Face the Nation, 1983—. Trustee Wheaton Coll. Recipient Tex. Headliners award, 1973. Office: CBS News 51 W 52nd St New York NY 10019 *

STAHL, MARILYN BROWN, interior designer; b. Boston, Dec. 11, 1929; d. Benjamin M. and Nettie D. (Glazer) Brown; B.S. in Art Edn., Mass. Coll. Art, 1951; m. Alvan L. Stahl, July 1, 1951; children—Robert, Barry, Kim. Instr. painting, Newton, Mass.; free-lance fabric designer, 1960-63; owner gallery, Newton, 1963-66, M.B. Stahl Interiors, Chestnut Hill, Mass., 1966; founder, pres. Maab Inc., mfrs. French furniture, 1979; pres. Decorators' Clearing House, Newton Upper Falls, Mass. Mem. Nat. Home Fashions League, Am. Soc. Interior Designers Industry Found., Nat. Home Fashions League Industry. Found. Home: 15 Manet Circle Chestnut Hill MA 02167 Office: Decorators' Clearing House 1029 Chestnut St Newton Upper Falls MA 02164

STAHL, RUTHANNE, legal administrator; b. Albuquerque, Dec. 3, 1939; d. Benjamin Byron and Newel Harriett (Webb) Crego; m. David Dale Stahl, Nov. 7, 1980; children: Ginger Le'Ann Davidson Wells, Lindsey Trey Davidson. Student, Colo. Woman's Coll., Denver, 1957-58, U. Denver, 1976-77, Ga. State U., 1979-80. Several mgmt. positions Pub. Service Co. N.Mex., 1965-74; mgr. regional credit and collection tng., field support JCPenney Co., Denver, 1975-80; dir. personnel and regional credit ops. JCPenney Co., Atlanta; project mgr. tng. and devel. corp. staff JCPenney Co., Dallas; corp. tng. dir. Peoples Gas System Inc., Tampa, Fla., 1980-81; dir. adminstrn. Schwall Ruff and Goodman Atty., Atlanta, 1982—; guest NBC TV Not For Women Only, 1979. Author: (tng. manual) Effective Collection, 1978. Mem. Assn. Legal Adminstrs., Legal Assts. Mgmt. Assn., Assn. Personnel Adminstrn., Atlanta Consumer Credit Assn., Nat. Assn. Female Execs., Pilot Club (dir. fin. 1972-74). Republican. Presbyterian.

Lodge: Daus. of Nile. Office: Schwall Ruff and Goodman Atty 1615 Peachtree St NE Atlanta GA 30367

STAHLKA, WENDY TOBIN, radio executive; b. Quincy, Mass., Nov. 11, 1950; d. Joseph Henry and Eileen (Bell) Tobin; m. Clayton A. Stahlka, Sept. 18, 1975; stepchildren: Clay W., Krisann, Rachel. Diploma with honors, U. Caen (France), 1971; BA, Newton Coll. of Sacred Heart, 1972. Asst. to editor Laser Focus Mag., Newton, Mass., 1972-73; account exec. Stahlka/Faller Advt., Buffalo, 1973-74; asst. to program dir. Sta. WBEN-AM & FM, Buffalo, 1979-83, dir. sales promotion, 1983-85; dir. mktg. and promotion Algonquin Broadcasting Corp., 1985-87, v.p. mktg., 1987—; freelance announcer radio and TV commls. Mem. women's bd. Millard Fillmore Hosp., Buffalo, 1977-79; bd. dirs. United Way. Recipient award for excellence Profl. Communicators Western N.Y., 1984. Mem. Women in Communications, Profl. Communicators of Western N.Y., Broadcast Promotion and Mktg. Execs. Home: 60 Westchester Rd Buffalo NY 14221 Office: Sta WBEN/WMJQ 2077 Elmwood Ave Buffalo NY 14207

STAIGER, BONNIE LARSON, commercial printing executive; b. Bismarck, N.D., Sept. 23, 1947; d. Harvey C. and Jean (Burman) Larson; m. Raymond J. Staiger, June 7, 1980; 1 child, Stacy. BS, Valley City State U., 1970. Tchr. Anoka Isanti Sch. Dist., Minn., 1970-72; owner, prin. Secs. Unltd., Bismarck, 1980-83; dir. pub. relations Hart Agy., Bismarck, 1983-85; pres., chief exec. officer Comml. Printing, Bismarck, 1985—. Pres. Ch. of the Cross council, 1987. Mem. Bismarck C. of C. (bd. dirs. 1987—), Bus. and Profl. Women Assn. (Named Woman of Yr. 1987, chmn. pub. relations 1988), Young Printing Pres.'s Orgn., Printing Industries Am., N.D. Printing Industries Assn., Bismarck Symphony League (charter mem.). Republican. Lutheran. Club: Working Women's Network. Lodges: Rotary (1st woman inducted 1987), Order of Eastern Star. Office: Comml Printing 112 N 2nd St Bismarck ND 58501

STAIGH, DIANE, health care publisher; b. Ottawa, Ont., Can., Oct. 4, 1949; d. Alexis Edouard and Marie-Anna (Demers) Bisson; m. Ronald Edward Staigh, Sept. 3, 1976; 1 child, Christian Adam. BA with honors, Carleton U., Ottawa, 1972. Editor Nat. Def., Ottawa, 1972-73; info. officer Nat. Research Council, Ottawa, 1973-81; v.p. info. services Can. Hosp. Assn., Ottawa, 1981—; owner Word Age, Ottawa, 1985—. Contbr. articles to profl. jours. Mem. Can. Direct Mktg. Assn., Internat. Assn. Bus. Communicators. Office: Can Hosp Assn, 17 York St, Ottawa, ON Canada K1N 9J6

STAIMER, CAROLE G., learning disabilities educator, management consultant; b. N.Y.C.; d. Murray and Esther (Roth) Green; m. George G. Staimer, Dec. 21, 1952; children: Marcia, Marc. BA, Queens Coll., 1953; MA in Spl. Edn., Kean Coll., 1977, MA in Counseling, 1981; postgrad., Rutgers U., 1984. Elem. sch. tchr. N.Y.C. Pub. Schs., 1953-55; tchr., lectr. Bank St. Sch. Edn., N.Y.C., 1955-57; free-lance cons. Westfield, N.J., 1957-67; elem. sch. tchr. Scotch Plains (N.J.) Bd. Edn., 1967-71, learning disabilities educator, 1971—; v.p. Staimer & Co., Scotch Plains, 1979—; vice-chmn. S.P.F. Discipline Com., 1974-76; chmn. Mid. Sch. Resource Room, Scotch Plains, 1977-78; co-chmn. Basic Skills Testing, Scotch Plains, 1982-84; trainer Staff Devel. Learning Strategies, Scotch Plains, 1985-87; cons. Scotchwood Property Assn., Scotch Plains, 1984. Author computer programs. Trustee Temple Emanu-El, Westfield, 1977. Mem. NEA, N.J. Edn. Assn., Council for Exceptional Children, Computer Using Educators, Computer Adv. Council, Learning Disabilities Assn. (sec. 1980), Guidance and Counselor Assn., N.J. Suprs. Assn., Phi Beta Kappa. Jewish. Clubs: Beaver Brook Country (Clinton, N.J.) (v.p. for ladies golf 1982-85), Duplicate Bridge Group (Westfield) (co-chmn. 1983—). Office: Park Mid Sch Park Ave Scotch Plains NJ 07076

STALEY, ELAINE MARY, administrative assistant and grants manager; b. Wisconsin Rapids, Wis., Sept. 26, 1943; d. Maurice Philip and Mary Ann (Menke) S. B.S. in Communication Arts, U. Wis.-Madison, 1965. Registered profl. parliamentarian. Program specialist U. Wis. Extension, Madison, 1966-69; specialist, exec. sec. U. Wis. System-Faculty Council and Assembly, Madison, 1969-73; adminstrv. asst., exec. sec. Exec. Office, Wis. Council on Criminal Justice, Madison, 1973-75; asst. to chmn. dept. communication arts U. Wis.-Madison, 1975-80, adminstrv. asst., grants mgr. Sch. Social Work, 1980—; parliamentary cons. Nat. Assn. Parliamentarians, Kansas City, Mo., 1976—. Contbr. articles to profl. jours. Mem. Women's Polit. Caucus, Madison, 1973-77; mem. steering com. Dane County's Citizen Orgn., Madison, 1980-81; staff asst. Gov's Commn. on Edn., Wis., 1970-71; mem. Big Bros./Sisters Dane County, 1979—, bd. dirs., 1985—; chmn. Dane County Bowl for Kids Sake, 1987-88; bd. dirs. Madison Theatre Guild, 1974-76, treas., 1974-76, cert. of merit awards 1971-72, 72-73; chmn. Dane County Bowl for Kids Sake, 1987-88; treas., bd. dirs. Madison Packer Backers, Inc., 1984-88; mem. Gov.'s Inaugural Ball Arrangements Com., Madison, 1979; mem. Madison Civic Opera Guild, 1977—, Madison Civic Ctr. Friends, 1983-86, Friends of WHA-TV, 1977-85, Friends of the Waisman Ctr., Madison, 1980—, pres., 1984-85. Recipient Exceptional Performance awards U. Wis.-State Wis., Madison, 1983, 84, 87. Mem. Commn. on Am. Parliamentary Practice of Speech Communication Assn. (chmn. 1978-80), Am. Inst. Parliamentarians, Nat. Assn. Parliamentarians (profl. registered parliamentarian 1976—, state bd. dirs. 1977—, co-chmn. publicity and newsletter coms. 1983-85, unit treas. 1985-87), Assn. Univ. Faculty Women and Univ. Extension League, 1968-74. Democrat. Roman Catholic. Avocations: downhill and cross-country skiing; golf; swimming; crafts; reading; sailing. Home: 933 Magnolia Ln Madison WI 53713 Office: U Wis-Madison Sch Social Work 425 Henry Mall Madison WI 53706

STALKER, JACQUELINE D'AOUST, academic administrator; b. Penetang, Ont., Can., Oct. 16, 1933; d. Phillip and Rose (Eaton) D'Aoust; m. Robert Stalker; children: Patricia, Lynn, Roberta. Teaching cert., U. Ottawa, 1952; tchr. music, Royal Toronto Conservatory Music, 1952; teaching cert., Lakeshore Tchrs. Coll., 1958; BEd with honors, U. Manitoba, 1977, MEd, 1979; EdD, Nova U., 1985. Cert. tchr. Ont., Man., Can. Adminstr., tchr., prin. various schs., Ont. and Que., 1952-65; area commr. Girl Guides of Can., throughout Europe, 1965-69; administr., tchr. Algonquin community Coll., Ottawa, Ont., 1970-74; tchr., program devel. Frontenac County Bd. Edn., Kingston, Ont., 1974-75; lctr., faculty advisor Dept. Curriculum, Edn. U. Man., Ont., Can., 1977-79, U. Winnipeg, Man., Can., 1977-79; cons. Colls. Div. Man. Dept. Edn., Can., 1980-81; sr. cons. Programming Br. Man. Dept. Edn., 1981-84, Post-Secondary, Adult and Continuing Edn. Div. Man. Dept. Edn., 1985—; cons. lectures, seminars, workshops throughout Can. Contbr. articles to profl. jours. Mem. U. Man. Senate, 1976-81, 86—, bd. govs., 1979-82; ; Can. rep. Internat. Youth Conf., Garmisch, Fed. Rep. Germany 1968; vol. Cancer Soc. Mem. Am. Assn. Adult and Continuing Edn., Can. Cong. Learning Opportunities Women, Can. Soc. Study Higher Edn., Higher and Postsecondary Edn. N. Am. Network, Manitoba Action Com. Status Women, Manitoba Tchrs. Soc., Teaching English Second Language Assn., Teachers English Speakers Other Language Internat. Assn., Alumni Assn. U. Manitoba, Can. Club. Roman Catholic. Home: 261 Baltimore Rd, Winnipeg Can R3L 1H7 Office: Post Secondary Adult Edn, Continuing Edn Div, 418-185 Carlton St, Winnipeg Can R3C 3J1

STALKER, SUZY WOOSTER, human resources executive; b. Atlanta, Oct. 12, 1948; d. George Edward Wooster and Mary Evelyn (Dayton) Schmidt; m. James Marion Stalker, Nov. 11, 1966; children: Marian Paige, Jason Alexander. Student, Ga. State U., 1981—. Tng. rep. Rich's, Atlanta, 1980-81, tng. supr., 1981-82, regional tng. coordinator, 1982-84, employee communications specialist, 1983-84; dir. human resources Home Fed. Savs. & Loan, Atlanta, 1984-85, v.p. human resources, 1985—, 1985—. Editor Richbits, 1983-84. Leader Girl Scouts U.S., Austell, Ga., 1972-74; pres. Clarkdale Elem. PTA, Austell, 1975-76. Mem. Nat. Assn. for Female Execs., Inc., Ga. Exec. Women's Network. Avocations: sailing, cross-stitching, watercolors. Home: 4820 Glore Rd Mableton GA 30059

STALLING, ETHEL B., chiropractor; b. Wellington, Mo., Apr. 1, 1921; d. George Henry and Edith Sophia (Kruetz) S. D of Chiropractic, Cleve. Chiropractic Coll., 1941. Pvt. practice chiropractor Kansas City, Mo., 1941-46, Pleasant Hill, Mo., 1946-49. Leader and dist. rep. Girl Scouts U.S., 1951-59; trustee Cleve. Chiropractic Coll., Kansas City, 1975—, v.p. bd. trustees 1978—, Service award 1960, Cleve. Chiropractic Coll., Los Angeles, 1977—. Recipient Service award Mo. State Chiropractors Assn., 1970. Fellow Internat. Chiropractors Assn. (pres. 1975-78, Service award 1964, Presdl. award 1985); mem. Acad. Mo. Chiropractors (pres. 1971-79, exec. sec. 1974—, Service award 1983), Cleve. Chiropractic Coll. Alumni Assn. (pres. 1961-65, Alumnus of Yr. award 1985). Office: 1001 Cedar Pleasant Hill MO 64080

STALSBERG, GERALDINE MCEWEN, accountant, systems analyst consultant, computer programmer, tax consultant; b. Springfield, Mo., May 10, 1936; d. Gerald Earl McEwen and Marie LaVerne (Pennington) Plautz; m. Bill Eugene Bottolfson, Mar. 10, 1956 (div. 1978); children: Bill Earl, Robert Edward, Brian Everett, Michelle Marie; m. Arvid Ray Stalsberg, Sept. 21, 1979; stepchildren: Angelite Renae, Neil Ray, Terry Jay. Diploma Hastings Beauty Acad., 1955; cert. in interior design, Central Tech. Community Coll., 1975; student Doane Coll., 1982; cert. computer programmer Lincoln Sch. Commerce, Nebr., 1984. Cosmetologist, Marinello Beauty Shop, Hastings, 1955-57; owner Nursery Sch. for Toddlers, 1958-67; acct. grain dept. Morrison-Quirk Elevator, Hastings, Nebr., 1968-69; acct., exec. sec., interior decorator Uerling's Home Furnishings, Hastings, 1970-79; acct., computer programmer, Lincoln Transp., Nebr., 1980-86, systems analyst, 1984-86; tax cons. H&R Block, Lincoln, 1983-86; pvt. practice acctg. and tax cons., 1987—; acct., systems analyst, computer programmer, tax cons. EBKO Industries, Hastings, 1988—. Emergency radio dispatcher Adams County Civil Def., Hastings, 1973-78; active YWCA, Girl Scouts USA, PTA, 4-H Clubs Am. Recipient Civic Achievement award City of Hastings, 1974. Mem. Nat. Assn. Govt. Employees, Bus. Profl. Women, Library Assn., Nat. Assn. Female Execs., Soroptimists Internat., Beta Sigma Phi (Woman of Yr. 1978, Order of Rose). Republican. Lutheran. Avocations: reading; bowling; fishing; swimming; jogging. Home: 414 W 14th St Hastings NE 68901 Office: PO Box 1123 Hastings NE 68902

STAMAS, LAURIE ANNE, sales professional; b. Kalamazoo, Nov. 7, 1962; d. Andrew Rodney Lenderink and Barbara Joyce (Lyons) Tallman; m. James Peter Stamas, Aug. 30, 1986. BA in Mktg., Mich. State U., 1984. Sales rep. Procter and Gamble, Lansing, Mich., 1984-85; dist. field rep. Procter and Gamble, Chgo., 1985, unit sales mgr., 1985-87; unit sales mgr. Procter and Gamble, Phoenix, 1987—. Mem. Nat. Assn. Female Execs., Mich. State U. Alumni Assn. (v.p. 1983-84). Greek Orthodox. Office: Procter and Gamble PO Box 440004 Aurora CO 80044

STAMETS, LILLIAN CAROL, retail executive; b. New Brighton, Pa., June 16, 1947; d. William Kerr and Patricia Ann (North) S. BS, The Ohio State U., 1969. Buyer, budget mgr. Emporium-Capwell, San Francisco, 1970-81; planning mgr. Levi Strauss & Co., San Francisco, 1981-82; pres., chief operating officer The Franciscan Shops Inc., San Francisco, 1982—; bd. dirs. The Fashion Group, Inc., N.Y.C, San Francisco, 1974—. Mem. Sales and Mktg. Exec., Nat. Assn. Coll. Stores (fin. com. 1982—), Calif. Acad. Scis. (acad. store com. 1986—), Am. Management Assn. (Pres.'s Assn. 1984—). Republican. Home: 16 Underhill Rd Mill Valley CA 94941 Office: The Franciscan Shops Inc 1650 Holloway Ave San Francisco CA 94132

STAMPER, SHERI LYNN, advertising specialist; b. Kansas City, Mo., Aug. 16, 1954; d. James Wiley Stamper and Mary Ann (Orendorff) Smith. BS, U. Mo., 1976. Graphic artist Hank Jankus & Assocs., Kansas City, Kans., 1977-80; creative dir. Fred Pryor Seminars, Shawnee Mission, Kans., 1980-82; artist The Graphic Designer, Kansas City, Mo., 1982-85; advt. mgr. Nat. Seminars, Inc., Shawnee Mission, 1985-87, v.p. advt., 1987—. Mem. Direct Mktg. Assn. Republican. Lutheran. Lodge: Soroptimists. Office: Nat Seminars Inc 6901 W 63d St Shawnee Mission KS 66202

STAN, PATRICIA, savings consultant, real estate executive; b. Chgo., Oct. 10, 1952; d. Paul and Olga (Zyluk) S.; m. Donald Ross Crabtree, Feb. 27, 1982 (div.). Student Monmouth Coll., 1964-66; B.F.A., Drake U., 1969; postgrad. U. Houston, 1974-76, Houston Coll., 1977-78. Cert. tchr., Tex.; cert. real estate broker, Tex. Tchr., Spring Branch Meml. Ind. Sch. Dist., Houston, 1976-78; cons. Sam Feldt Co., Houston, 1978-80; counselor Doyle Stuckey Homes, Houston, 1980-82; pres. Stan Internat., Houston, 1981—; counselor Am. Classic Homes, Houston, 1982-83; cons. Savs. of America, Houston, 1983—. Patron Houston Mus. Fine Arts. Mem. Mensa, Tex. Edn. Assn., Nat. Women's Council Realtors, Houston Bd. Realtors, Tex. Real Estate Commn., Archaeol. Soc. Houston, Sierra Club, Kappa Kappa Gamma.

STANCILL, DOROTHY POLEK, mining company executive; b. Balt., Jan. 8, 1943; d. John Walter and Dallas Elizabeth (Baker) Polek; m. Joseph S. Zuramski, Apr. 1965 (div. 1975); children: Joseph S., Janet Alyssa; m. Larry Godfrey Stancill, Sept. 12, 1976; children: Dobson L., Kelly L. Student, Bucknell U., 1961-63, Goucher Coll., 1982. Sales mgr. Imperial Marine, Inc., White Marsh, Md., 1963-65; pub. relations asst. Head Ski Co., Timonium, Md., 1965-66; adminstrv. asst. The Rouse Co., Balt., 1966-68; exec. v.p. Harford Indsl. Minerals, Inc., Joppa, Md., 1975—; lectr. in field. Mem. U.S. Service Acad. Rev. Bd., 1986, 87; moderator confs. on small bus., Md. and Washington, 1985, alt. del., 1986; vice chmn. adv. bd. Sec. Dept. Natural Resources, 1980—; chmn. Harford County Commn. for Women, 1980-81; small bus. rep. Congl. Action Com.; bd. dirs. Jr. Achievement of Harford County, Susquehanna Symphony Assn., mem. adv. group Helen Bentley Congl. campaign, 1984, numerous others. Mem. Nat. Fedn. Ind. Bus. (guardian mem.), Md. Mfrs. Assn. (bd. dirs.), Md. SUrface Mining Assn. (pres.), U.S. C. of C., Md. C. of C. (chmn. small bus. council 1987—), Harford County C. of C., Mid-Atlantic Golf Course Supts. Assn., Pi Beta Phi. Republican. Home: 1209 Whitaker Mill Rd Joppa MD 21085 Office: Harford Indsl Mineral Inc PO Box 210 40 Fort Hoyle Joppa MD 21085

STANCLIFFE, ELAINE RORABACK, rehabilitation center executive; b. Hartford, Conn., Aug. 28, 1949; d. Frederick L. and Claire (Werre) Roraback; divorced; children: Scott, Jason. B of Social Work, St. Joseph Coll., West Hartford, Conn., 1982. Exec. dir. Genesis Center, Inc., Manchester, Conn., 1982—. Contbr. articles on homelessness and mental illness to newspapers. Mem. bd. religious edn. Colchester (Conn.) Federated Ch., 1982-84; pres. Manchester Community Services Council. Mem. Nat. Assn. Social Workers. Democrat. Office: Genesis Center 105 Main St Manchester CT 06040

STANDARD, MARY RUSSELL, computer software company executive, consultant; b. Orange, Tex., Mar. 8, 1926; d. Junius Brownrigg and Lily Amanda (McIlroy) Russell; m. Richard Clinton Armstrong, Jan., 1952 (div.); m. Jack Standard, Nov. 1955 (dec.). B.A., Baylor U., Waco, Tex., 1947; postgrad. U. So. Calif., 1948-49, NYU, 1964-66. Sr. computer systems analyst Continental Group, Stamford, Conn., 1959-82; pvt. practice consulting, N.Y.C., 1982—; v.p. software engring. Signature Software & Services, Princeton, N.J., 1984-87. Mem. Data Processing Mgmt. Assn. Democrat. Office: 232 W 16th St New York NY 10011

STANDFAST, SUSAN J(ANE), health department administrator; b. Callicoon, N.Y., July 2, 1935; children: Henry S., Margaret S., Catherine B. AB in Biology and Chemistry, Wells Coll., 1957; MD, Columbia U., 1961; MPH In Epidemiology, U. Calif., Berkeley, 1965. Cert. Am. Bd. Preventive Medicine. Intern King County Hosp., Swedish Hosp, Seattle, 1961-62; pediatric resident U. Wash., Seattle, 1963, research assoc., part-time clinician adolescent program div. child health, 1964; sr. resident in epidemiology N.Y., 1965-67; instr. dept. community health Albany (N.Y.) Med. Coll., 1965-67, asst. prof. dept. preventive and community medicine, 1968-72, cons. in epidemiology, 1968-72, adj. asst. prof. preventive and community medicine, 1975-80, adj. assoc. prof., 1980—, cons. preventive medicine dept. family practice, 1983—; research physician bur. cancer control, div. epidemiology N.Y. State Dept. Health, Albany, 1975-83, dir. cancer surveillance unit cancer control sect. bur. chronic disease prevention, 1985, asst. to dir. div. epidemiology, 1985-86, dir. injury control program div. epidemiology, 1986—; physician pub. health Albany, 1983—; research assoc. epidemiology Sch. Pub. Health U. Calif. Berkeley, 1967; vis. lectr. G.S. Med. Coll., Bombay, 1969-70, cons. in epidemiology Bombay Cancer Registry Tata Meml. Hosp., Albany, 1968-72, cons. infectious disease sect. VA Med. Ctr., Albany, 1979; mem. ad hoc task force on data resource devel. for dir. epidemiology and biometry research program Nat. Inst. Child Health and Human Devel., Bethesda, Md., 1979-80; adj. prof. preventive medicine clin. campus SUNY, Binghamton. 1985, Upstate Med. Coll., Syracuse, 1985—, assoc. prof., 1987—; lectr. in field. Contbr. numerous articles to profl. jours. Mem. med. adv. bd. Hudson-Mohawk chpt. Nat. Founs. SIDS, 1976-84; mem. med. adv. bd. council on human sexuality Planned Parenthood, Albany, 1971—; mem. Physicians for Social Responsibility, 1984—, Doctors Ought to Care, 1984—, also numerous pub. health task forces and coms. Fellow Am. Coll. Preventive Medicine, Am. Coll. Epidemiology; mem. Soc. Epideiologic Research, Am. Pub. Health Assn. Home: 27 Vandenburg Ln Latham NY 12110

STANEK, RHONDA MARIE, sales executive; b. Washington, Pa., Oct. 18, 1963; d. Bernard Walter and Alma Rose (Dietrich) S. BA, Washington and Jefferson Coll., 1985. Tech. sales rep. J.T. Baker Inc., Phillipsburg, N.J., 1985—. Mem. Nat. Assn. Profl. Sales Women (mem. program com. 1986—). Republican. Roman Catholic. Home: 1600 Lehigh Pkwy E Apt 11-G Allentown PA 18103 Office: JT Baker Inc 222 Red School Ln Phillipsburg NJ 08865

STANFIELD, ELIZABETH POPLIN, spanish educator, translator; b. Jacksonville, Fla., Aug. 9, 1930; d. Thomas William and Mattie Olene (Padgett) Poplin; B.A. summa cum laude, U. N.C., Greensboro, 1952; M.A., Emory U., 1966; m. William Thomas Stanfield, June 30, 1956; children—C. Freeman, William Thomas. Tchr., fgn. langs. Atlanta City Schs., 1952-57, Fulton County (Ga.) High Sch., 1963-69; instr. Spanish, Ga. State U., Atlanta, 1968-78, asst. prof., 1978—, lectr. Learning Resources Ctr., 1975—, Speakers Bur., 1979—; cons. Internat. Bus. Council Inst. Internat. Cons. Directory, 1984; coll. supr. student tchrs. Ga. State Dept. Edn. Author: From Plantation to Peachtree: A Century and a Half of Atlanta Classic Homes, 1987; poems. Contbg. editor So. Homes Mag., 1983—; contbr. articles to profl. jours. AAUW fellow, 1964-65. Mem. Am. Assn. Tchrs. Spanish and Portuguese (pres. Ga. 1979-81), MLA, So. Conf. Lang. Teaching, Fgn. Lang. Assn. Ga., 19th Century Studies Assn., Atlanta Assn. Interpreters and Translators (bd. dirs. 1985—), Am. Translators Assn. (assoc.), AAUP, Acad. Alliances in Ga. (convenor), Daus. of Am. Revolution, United Daus. of Confederacy, Phi Beta Kappa, Omicron Delta Kappa, Sigma Delta Pi, Phi Sigma Iota, Lambda Iota Tau. Mem. Ch. of Christ. Office: Ga State U Dept Fgn Langs Atlanta GA 30303

STANFIELD BROWN, ANNETTE KAY, lawyer; b. Hamtramack, Mich., Dec. 19, 1952; d. Willis Alfred and Lucille Carolyn (Caver) Stanfield; m. Terrance L. Brown, Dec. 28, 1974. BA cum laude, U. Mich., 1974, JD, 1977. Bar: Mich. 1977. Intern U.S. Atty.'s Office, Detroit, 1976; asst. gen. counsel Southeastern Mich. Transit Authority, Detroit, 1977-81; sole practice Southfield and Detroit, Mich., 1981-87; magistrate 46th Dist. Ct. Mich., Southfield, 1987—; ptnr. Sims & Stanfield, Attys. at Law, Detroit and Southfield, 1988—; mgmt. cons. Ross and Co. CPA's, Southfield, 1985-86; instr. Am. Inst. for Paralegal Studies, 1987. Bd. dirs. Unity of Hands, Detroit, 1987. Mem. ABA, Mich. Bar Assn., Women's Bar Assn. Mich., Oakland County Bar Assn., Southfield Bar Assn., Wolverine Bar Assn., NAACP, U. Mich Alumni Assn., Assn. Black Judges Mich. Lodge: Optimists. Office: 400 Internat Ctr 400 Monroe St Detroit MI 48226 Office: 24400 Northwestern Hwy Suite 204 Southfield MI 48075

STANFORD, KAREN BEAZLEY, insurance supervisor; b. Richmond, Va., July 19, 1956; d. Arthur Webb and Mary Frances (Smith) Beazley; m. James Arthur Stanford, Oct. 3, 1976; 1 child, Jason Scott. Student in criminal justice, J. Sargeant Reynolds Community Coll., 1985—. Lic. pvt. investigator, Va. Supr. Aetna Life Ins. Co., Richmond, 1977—. Bd. dirs. Am. Heart Assn., Richmond, 1984—, ARC, 1988—; mem. Rep. Nat. Com., Richmond, 1987. Mem. Nat. Assn. Female Execs. Methodist. Home: 8325 Emerald Ln Richmond VA 23236 Office: Aetna Life Ins Co 2809 Emerywood Pkwy Richmond VA 23236

STANFORD, KIMBERLEY ALICE, health science facility administrator; b. Concordia, Kans., Nov. 17, 1954; d. Cheslie Carl and Enola Evelyn (Steier) Boylan; m. Charles Stephen Stanford, Dec. 27, 1986. BS, U. Tex., 1976; MS, U. Houston, 1980. Occupational therapist Angels, Inc., Dallas, 1976-77, U. Tex. Med. Br., Galveston, 1977-79, Galveston Ind. Sch. Dist., 1980; supr. occupational therapy Bexar County Hosp. Dist., San Antonio, 1980-82; dir. occupational therapy Bexar County Hosp. Dist., 1982-83, adminstrv. dir. physical medicine and rehab., 1983—. Mem. Inst. Profl. Health Service Adminstrs., Am. Occupational Therapy Assn., Tex. Occupational Therapy Assn., Tex. Hosp. Assn., Nat. Assn. Female Execs. Baptist. Home: 6807 Forest Crest N San Antonio TX 78240

STANFORD, PATRICIA ANN, medical technologist; b. Poplarville, Miss., Oct. 24, 1937; d. Herman Thomas and Anna M. (Lee) Holden; A.A., Pearl River Jr. Coll., 1957; B.A., U. So. Miss., 1959; cert. med. tech., Miss. Bapt. Hosp. Sch. Med. Tech., 1959; m. Hiram B. Stanford, July 3, 1962; children—Herman Curtis, Lawanna Lee. Med. technologist Pearl River County Hosp., Poplarville, Miss., 1959—, chief lab. and x-ray technologist, 1959—; vol. local sch. sci. dept. Active PTA; mem. Pearl River County Hosp. and Extended Care Facility Aux. Mem. Am. Soc. Clin. Pathologists (assoc. mem., cert. med. technologist), Nat. Certification Agy. for Med. Lab. Personnel (clin. lab. scientist), Miss. State Soc. for Med. Tech., Am. Soc. Med. Tech., U. So. Miss. Alumni Assn. Beta Beta Beta, Alpha Epsilon Delta. Baptist. Home: Rt 3 Box 94 Poplarville MS 39470 Office: PO Box 392 Poplarville MS 39470

STANFORD, ROSE MARY, criminology educator, researcher; b. Portsmouth, Va., May 12, 1942; d. Robert Marion and Ruth (Watson) S.; children: Dion C. Greenwell, Cheryl L. Greenwell. BA magna cum laude, U. So. Fla., 1976, MA in Criminal Justice, 1979; PhD, Fla. State U., 1984. Interviewer U. South Fla., Tampa, 1975, researcher, interviewer, 1976; adj. instr. dept. criminal justice U. South Fla., St. Petersburg, 1977; parole and probation officer Fla. Dept. Corrections, Tampa, 1977-79; researcher Arthur Young and Co., Tallahassee, 1979-80; researcher, coder Office of State Cts. Adminstrs., Fla. Supreme Ct., Tallahassee, 1980; tutor dept. athletics Fla. State U., Tallahassee, 1981, teaching asst. Sch. Criminology, 1981; planner and evaluator planning and devel. Fla. Dept. Health and Rehab. Services, Tallahassee, 1980-81; asst. prof., intern coordinator dept. criminal justice Pan Am. U., Edinburg, Tex., 1982-85; asst. prof. dept. criminology U. South Fla., Ft. Myers, 1985—; cons. in field; chair 20th Jud. Cir. Task Force on Spouse Abuse; presenter Gernder Bias Study Commn., 1988; chmn. Twentieth Jud. Cir. Task Force on Spouse Abuse . Contbr. articles to profl. jours., chpts. to books. Book reviewer Criminal Justice, Rev., 1985. Mem. community rev. bd. Rio Grande State Ctr., Harlingen, Tex., 1985, Community Adv. Council, McAllen Halfway House and Parole, Tex., 1984-85, Inter-Agy. Council for Youth Services, Hidalgo County, Tex., 1983-85; mem. oral bd. for sgt. promotion, Mission Police Dept., Tex., 1982; mem. Tex. Council on Crime and Delinquency, 1982-85; active in media on child abuse. Grantee in field. Mem. Am. Soc. Criminology, Acad. Criminal Justice Scis. (program com. 1985-86, chmn. student affairs com. 1987-88), Fla. Council on Crime and Delinquency (pres. chpt. 1, 1978-79, sec. chpt. 19, 1985-86, state bd. dirs. 1978-79, Criminal Justice plaque), Alpha Phi Sigma, Phi Kappa Phi (pres. elect), Phi Theta Phi. Democrat. Roman Catholic. Avocations: dancing; movies; reading. Office: U South Fla 8111 College Pkwy SW Fort Myers FL 33919

STANFORD-JONES, KATHLEEN LOUISE, computer systems consultant; b. Aiea, Hawaii, Feb. 13, 1948; d. Harold Revis and Dorothy Louise (Swedling) S.; m. Charles Edward Jones, Jr., Apr. 27, 1985; children: Sterling Colin, Lindsey Kara. B.A., U. Tulsa. Computer programmer Kaiser Permanente, Los Angeles, 1975-81; project leader Lockheed Corp., Burbank, Calif., 1981-83; pres. K.L. Stanford, Inc., Century City, Calif., 1983—; cons. in field; condr. seminars in field, 1982—. Co-author; ADF Workbook, 1984; publisher: Documentation Resources Quarterly. Mem. Ind. Computer Cons. Assn. Republican. Office: 4444 Aukland Toluca Lake CA 90602

STANKEY, SUZANNE M., editor; b. Grand Rapids, Mich., Apr. 4, 1951; d. Robert Michael and Elizabeth (Rogers) Stankey. B.A., Ohio U., Athens, 1973; B.J., U. Mo., Columbia, 1977. Editor Living Today, The Blade, Toledo, 1980-82; editor Toledo Magazine, The Blade, Toledo, 1982—. Mem. Toledo Jazz Soc. (bd. dirs.), Press Club. Home: 2508 Kenwood Blvd Toledo OH 43606 Office: The Blade 541 Superior St Toledo OH 43660

STANKIEWICZ, JOYCE ELAINE, educational administrator; b. Stratford, Ont., Can., Jan. 4, 1935; d. Elver Theron and Ada Evalyn (Polzin) Sauder; m. William Patrick Stankiewicz, Dec. 26, 1951; children: James, Richard, William Kimberly, Thomas. BA, Wilfrid Laurier U., Waterloo, Ont., 1987. Cert. profl. sec. V.p., mgr. Towne & Country Driver Tng. Ctr.; agt. opera and concert singers, 1969-75; sec. St. Aloysius Parish, Kitchener, Ont., 1970-75; exec. sec. to dir. edn. Waterloo Region Separate Sch. Bd., Ont., 1975-80; exec. asst. to dir. edn. Waterloo Region Separate Sch. Bd., 1980-87, equal opportunity advisor, 1987—; Coordinator Can. Dist. Conf. PSI, 1985; speaker various schs. and profl. groups; mem. adv. com. Can. Sch. Mgmt., Toronto, 1986-87. Mem. Networking for Women, Can. Fedn. Univ. Women, Employment Equity Practitioners Assn., Profl. Secs. Internat. (chpt. pres. 1977-79), Waterloo Region Edn. and Employment Equity Network, Women in Ednl. Adminstrn. Ont. Liberal. Roman Catholic. Office: Waterloo Region Separate Sch Bd, 91 Moore Ave Box 1116, Kitchener, ON Canada N2G 4G2

STANLEY, JEAN AGATHA FULLER, chemistry educator; b. White Hall, St. Thomas, Jamaica, Sept. 17, 1951; came to U.S., 1978; d. Clifford Alexander and Lovina Rebecca (Wilson) Fuller; m. Ernie Stanley, Oct. 4, 1976; children—Sofia, Nadia. B.Sc. with honors, U. London, 1976; M.S. in Chemistry, U. Nebr., 1980, Ph.D. in Organic Chemistry, 1984. Teaching asst. U. Nebr., Lincoln, 1978-84; asst. prof. chemistry Wellesley Coll., Mass., 1984—. Contbr. articles in organic chemistry to profl. jours. Mem. Am. Chem. Soc., Royal Soc. Chemistry, Am. Inst. Chemistry, Phi Lambda Upsilon, Sigma Xi. Avocations: sports; music; dancing; reading; sewing. Office: Wellesley Coll Sci Ctr Wellesley MA 02181

STANLEY, JEAN COOPER, accountant, food products executive; b. Atlanta, Sept. 7, 1953; d. Fleet R. and Evelyn (Parris) Cooper; m. Methen Ann Stanley, June 22, 1984. BS in Acctg., Berry Coll., 1975, MBA, 1984. CPA, Ga. Acct. Coosa Baking Co., Rome, Ga., 1975-77, asst. officer mgr., 1977-78, mgr. office, 1978-79; sec.-treas. Skipco, Inc., Rome, 1979-85; controller Mondo Baking Co. (formerly S.E.M. Baking Co.), Rome, 1985-87, v.p. fin., 1987—; acct., 411 Mfg. Co., Rome, 1978—; cons. various small bus., Rome, 1982—; tax preparer, bus. and individuals, 1982—. With allocations and solications United Way, Rome, 1986-87. Mem. Am. Mgmt. Assn., Am. Assn. Accts., Am. Inst. CPA's, Ga. Soc. CPA's, Rome C. of C. (chmn. Women in Mgmt. 1985). Baptist.

STANLEY, LANETT LORRAINE, state legislator; b. Atlanta, Nov. 5, 1962; d. Archie and Ethel Francis (Dixon) S. BS, U. Tenn., 1985. Children's reporter Sta. WXIA-TV, Atlanta, 1979-80; model, sales clk. Rich's Dept. Store, Atlanta, 1979-83; copy clk. Knoxville (Tenn.) Jour., 1984-85; reporter Atlanta Daily World, 1986; intern Sta. WTBS-TV, Atlanta, 1986; adminstrv. aide Bd. Commrs. Fulton County, Atlanta, 1986-87; mem. Ga. Ho. of Reps., Atlanta, 1987—; mem. Nat. and Ga. Legis. Black Caucus, 1987. Bd. dirs. Atlanta Southside Community Council, 1987. Democrat. Baptist. Office: Ga Gen Assembly Ga State Capitol Atlanta GA 30318

STANLEY, MARGARET KING, performing arts administrator; b. San Antonio, Tex., Dec. 11, 1929; d. Creston Alexander and Margaret (Haymore) King; children—Torrey Margaret, Jean Cullen. Student Mary Baldwin Coll., 1948-50; BA, U. Tex., Austin, 1952; MA, Incarnate Word Coll., 1959. Tchg. cert. 1953. Elem. tchr. San Antonio Ind. Sch. Dist., 1953-54, 55-56, Arlington County Schs., Va., 1954-55, Ft. Sam Houston Schs., San Antonio, 1955-57; art, art history tchr. St. Pius X Sch., San Antonio, 1959-60; designer-mfr., owner CrisStan Clothes, Inc., San Antonio, 1967-73; founder, exec. dir. San Antonio Performing Arts Assn., 1976—, founder Arts Council of San Antonio, 1962; founding chmn. Joffrey Workshop, San Antonio, 1979; originator, first chairwoman Student Music Fair, San Antonio, 1963; radio program host On Stage, San Antonio, 1983—. Originator of the idea for a new ballet created for the City of San Antonio, "Jamboree", commnd. from the Joffrey Ballet, world premiere in San Antonio, 1984. Pres. San Antonio Symphony League, 1971-74; v.p. Arts Council of San Antonio, 1975; bd. govs. Artists Alliance of San Antonio, 1982. Recipient Outstanding Tchr. award Arlington County Sch. Dist., 1954, Today's Woman award San Antonio Light Newspaper, 1980, Woman of Yr. in Arts award San Antonio Express News, 1983, 84, Emily Smith award for outstanding alumni Mary Baldwin Coll., 1973, Headliner award Women in Communications Inc., 1982; named to Women's Hall of Fame, San Antonio, 1984; teaching fellow Trinity U., San Antonio, 1964-66. Mem. Internat. Soc. Performing Arts Adminstrs. (regional rep. 1982-85), Met. Opera Nat. Council, Women in Communications, Inc., Texas Arts Alliance (bd. govs. 1983—), San Antonio Opera Guild (vice pres. 1974-76), Women in Communications (San Antonio chapter), Jr. League of San Antonio, Battle of Flowers Assn.; clubs: San Antonio Symphony League (pres. 1971-74), San Antonio Opera Guild (v.p. 1974-76); avocations: traveling, reading. Office: San Antonio Performing Arts Assn 110 Broadway Suite 230 San Antonio TX 78205

STANLEY, MARY CAROLYN, vocational rehabilitation counselor; b. Carthage, Mo., Nov. 15, 1948; d. Ralph Eugene and Marian Jean (Van Buren) Reynolds; B.A., Marymount Coll., Salina, Kans., 1970; postgrad. Ariz. State U., Tempe, S.W. Mo. State U., Springfield. Supr. work adjustment Goodwill Industries, Phoenix, 1971-75; vocat. counselor Ariz. Found. Handicapped Maryvale, Phoenix, 1975-76, Kans. Vocat. Rehab. Center, Salina, 1977, Yuma WORC Center (Ariz.), 1977-78; project aide U. Mo. Extension Services, Springfield, 1978; case mgr. Lakes County Rehab. Center, Springfield, 1979-81; field counselor Mo. Vocat. Rehab., Springfield, 1981-83; probation and parole officer Mo. State Bd. Probation, 1983—; mem. council Region VI Adv. Council Devel. Disabilities, Springfield, 1979-81; citizen mem. Youth Services Group, Mo. State Penitentiary. Vice chmn. Ozarks Area Community Action-Family Planning Program, Springfield, 1980-81. Cert. Nat. Commn. Rehab. Counselors. Mem. Nat. Rehab. Assn. (cert.). Office: 2413 Fairlawn Dr PO Box 676 Carthage MO 64836

STANLEY, PEGGY DEVER, hospital administrator; b. Gaylord, N.Mex., Jan. 15, 1953; d. Virgil Kenneth and Joanne (Scanlon) Streich; m. William Dever Jr., Oct. 20, 1973 (div. 1984); children: Eryn Jo, Matthew Steven; m. Rik Stanley, Aug. 10, 1985. AA, Santa Fe Community Coll., Gainesville, Fla., 1976. Sec. FBI, Washington, 1972-74; sec. dept. criminal justice U. Fla., Gainesville, 1974-76; legal sec. Wear and Wear Attys., Springfield, Mo., 1976-77; admin. asst. Fairchild Space and Electronics, Lompoc, Calif., 1977-78; dir. spl. projects Bowling Proprietors Assn. Am., Arlington, Tex., 1981-86; mgr. sales Embassy Suites Hotel, Irving, Tex., 1986-87; mgr. office Voluntary Hosps. Am., Irving, 1987—; cons. Royal Conf. Ctr., Dallas, 1986-87. Mem. PTA, Euless, Tex., 1984-87. Mem. Nat. Assn. Female Execs., Women's Internat. Bowling Assn. Roman Catholic.

STANLEY, REBECCA ANN, banker; b. South Bend, Ind., Apr. 8, 1947; d. Edward Clinton and DaMaeis Ellen (Troyer) S. B in Bus. Fin., Ind. U., 1976; grad. degree in banking, U. Del., 1987. Office mgr. Western Union Telegraph Co., Cleve., 1965-71; supr. St. Joseph Bank & Trust Co., South Bend, 1971-75, trust ops. officer, 1975-78; trust ops. officer Union Bank & Trust Co., Bethlehem, Pa., 1978-84; group exec. Lehigh Valley Bank, Bethlehem, 1984—. Mem. Hist. Bethlehem Inc., 1987; bd. dirs. Musikfest Internat., Bethlehem, 1986—, Cedar Crest Coll. Mem. Nat. Assn. Female Execs., Nat. Assn. Bank Women (exec. council). Office: Lehigh Valley Bank 65 E Elizabeth Ave Bethlehem PA 18018

STANLEY, SANDRA ORNECIA, educational researcher; b. Jersey City, July 6, 1950; d. McKinley and Thelma Louise (Newberry) S.; BA, Ottawa (Kans.) U., 1972; MS in Edn., U. Kans., 1975, PhD (fellow), 1980; postgrad. St. George's U. Sch. Medicine, Grenada, W.I., 1984—. Dir., head tchr. Salem Bapt. Nursery Sch., Jersey City, 1972-73; spl. ednl. instr. Joan Davis Sch. Spl. Edn., Kansas City, Mo., 1975-76; instructional media/materials trainee, then research asst. U. Kans. Med. Center, 1976-79; research asst. U. Kans., Lawrence, 1979; dir., coordinator tng. and observation Juniper Gardens Children's project Bur. Child Research, U. Kans., Kansas City, 1979-82, research assoc., 1980; lectr., speaker, cons. edn. and med. sci. Coll. Women Inc. scholar, 1977; Easter Seal grantee, 1975; recipient various certs. of recognition. Mem. Christian Med. Soc., Women's Ednl. Network, Coll. Women Inc., Nat. Assn. Female Execs. Democrat. Author papers and manuals in field. Home: 70 Madison Ave Jersey City NJ 07304

STANLEY, SUSAN TATE, marketing consultant; b. Burlington, Iowa, Aug. 21, 1957; d. Marvin Mize and Violet (Wendhausen) Tate; m. Craig Allen Stanley, Oct. 10, 1955. BA, Knox Coll., 1979; MS, Drake U., 1986. Dir. housing rehab. City of Burlington, 1979-83; community organizer Sen. Alan Cranston Presdl. Campaign, Des Moines, 1983-84; community relations coordinator Horizon Health Mgmt., Oak Brook, Ill., 1984-86, mktg. cons., 1986—. mem. Dem. Cen. Com., Burlington, 1984; commr. Burlington Civil Service Commn., 1981-84; chmn. Burlington Human Rights Commn., 1982-83, commr., 1980-84. Mem. Am. Mktg. Assn., Acad. for Health Care Mktg., Delta Delta Delta. Office: Horizon Health Mgmt 1100 Jorie St 330 Oak Brook IL 60521

STANMYRE, KAREN PHYLLIS, food products company executive; b. Detroit, Dec. 30, 1940; d. Arthur Daniel and Margaret Elinore (Thomson) Knapp; m. Frederick William Stanmyre, Jan. 20, 1962 (div. 1974); children: Richard William, Carla Elizabeth. AS, SUNY, Albany, 1977. Adminstrv. asst. to v.p. Manhattanville Coll., Purchase, N.Y., 1972-78; sec. to v.p. Lone Star Industries, Inc., Greenwich, Conn., 1978-81; adminstrv. asst. to pres. The Nestlé Co., Inc., White Plains, N.Y., 1981-84; mgr. consumer panels The Nestlé Co., Inc., White Plains, 1984-85; mgr. consumer affairs Nestlé Foods Corp., Purchase, 1985—. Founder, bd. dirs. New Orch. of Westchester, Hartsdale, N.Y., 1982—, mem. exec. com., 1984—, chmn. budget com., 1984-86, chmn. nominating com., 1985-86, chmn. found. fund raising, 1986—. Mem. Soc. Consumer Affairs Profls. in Bus., Grocery Manufacturers Assn. (mem. consumer affairs com.). Home: 80 Round Hill Rd Armonk NY 10504 Office: Nestlé Foods Corp 100 Manhattanville Rd Purchase NY 10577

STANTON, ELIZABETH MCCOOL, lawyer; b. Lansdale, Pa., Apr. 12, 1947; d. Leo J. and Helen M. (Gillooly) McCool; m. Robert J. Stanton, June 13, 1970; children: Jonathan R., James Alfred. BBA, Drexel U., 1969; JD magna cum laude, U. Houston, 1979. Bar: Tex. 1979, U.S. Dist. Ct. (so. dist.) Tex. 1980, Ohio 1982, U.S. Dist. Ct. (so. dist.) Ohio 1983. Assoc. Friedman & Chaffin, Houston, 1979-80, Law Offices of Elaine Brady, Houston, 1980-81, Moots, Cope & Weinberger Co., L.P.A., Columbus, Ohio, 1981-86, Moots, Cope and Kizer Co. L.P.A., Columbus, 1986—. Campaign worker Susan Walker for Judge Campaign, Columbus, 1983; mem. legal com. Met. Womens Ctr., Columbus, 1983-84. Drexel Bd. Trustees scholar, 1965-67, Internat. Ladies Garment Workers Union scholar, 1965-69. Mem. ABA, Ohio Bar Assn., Columbus Bar Assn., Nat. Assn. Women Lawyers, Plantiff Employment Lawyers Assn., Women's Lawyers Franklin County, St. Thomas Moore Soc., Phi Kappa Phi, Beta Gamma Sigma. Democrat. Roman Catholic. Office: Moots Cope & Kizer Co LPA 3600 Olentangy River Rd Columbus OH 43214

STANTON, JANE GRAHAM, advertising executive, trade association executive; b. Rice, Tex., Mar. 4, 1922; d. William Edward and Kathryn Ruth (McKay) Tidwell; student Tex. State Coll. Women, 1938-39, Abilene Christian Coll., 1939-40, N. Tex. State Coll., 1941; m. Joseph Wesley Graham, Jan. 5, 1946 (div. Aug. 1974); 1 dau., Kathryn Ann; m. 2d, Hinds Victor Thomas, Dec. 18, 1975 (div. 1977); m. 3d, Hank Stanton, June 10, 1980. Profl. singer on radio, 1941-49; producer, writer radio-TV drama, N.Y.C., 1948-56; v.p. United Nat. Films, Dallas, 1957-59; with Tracy-Locke Advt., Dallas, 1964-66; owner Jane Graham Advt., 1967—; exec. dir. S.W. Apparel Mfrs. Assn., Dallas. Active United Fund. Recipient numerous awards Dallas Advt. League. Mem. Fashion Group. Editor Dallas Fashion Update, 1988—, Am. Fashion mag., 1974—; contbr. articles to profl. jours.; columnist Dallas Times Herald. Home: 4727 N Central Expy Dallas TX 75205

STANTON, JEANNE FRANCES, retired lawyer; b. Vicksburg, Miss., Jan. 22, 1920; d. John Francis and Hazel (Mitchell) S.; student George Washington U., 1938-39; B.A., U. Cin., 1940; J.D., Salmon P. Chase Coll. Law, 1954. Admitted to Ohio bar, 1954; chief clk. Selective Service Bd., Cin., 1940-43; instr. USAAF Tech. Schs., Biloxi, Miss., 1943-44; with Procter & Gamble, Cin., 1945-84, legal asst., 1952-54, head advt. services sect. legal div., trade practices dept., 1954-73, mgr. advt. services, legal div., 1973-84, ret., 1984. Team capt. Community Chest Cin., 1953; mem. ann. meeting com. Archaeol. Inst. Am., 1983. Mem. AAAS, ABA (chmn. subcom. #4 of com. #7 patent and copyright sect. 1988), Ohio Bar Assn. (chmn. uniform state laws com. 1968-70), Cin. Bar Assn. (sec. law day com. 1965-66, chmn. com. on preservation hist. documents 1968-71), Vicksburg and Warren County, Cin. hist. socs., Internat. Oceanographic Found., Otago Early Settlers Assn. (asso.), Intercontinental Biog. Assn., Cin. Lawyers (pres. 1983, exec. com. 1978—), Cin. Women Lawyers (treas. 1958-59, nominating com. 1976). Clubs: Terrace Park Country, Cin. Club; Cincinnati. Home: 2302 Easthill Ave Cincinnati OH 45208

STANTON, JUDITH ELAINE, public relations executive; b. N.Y.C., May 13, 1949; d. Irving and Florence Ruth (Warren) Spiro; m. John Cooper Stanton, Nov. 27, 1971; children: Karlie, Sara. BA, U. Fla., 1970, MEd, 1971. Tchr. Bryan Sr. High Sch., Dallas, 1971-72; info. officer Jackson Meml. Hosp., Miami, Fla., 1973-76; editorial asst. Mt. Sinai Med. Ctr., Miami Beach, Fla., 1972-73, dir. pub. relations, 1976-87; pres. Judy Stanton Pub. Relations, Miami Beach, 1987—; vis. prof. Fla. Internat. U. Recipient MacEachern Cert. of Merit Acad. Hosp. Pub. Relations, 1982. Mem. Pub. Relations Soc. Am. (past pres. Greater Miami chpt. 1985-86), South Fla. Hosp. Pub. Relations Assn. (past pres. 1976-77), Fla. Hosp. Assn. Pub. Relations and Mktg. Council (pres. 1980-81). Club: Michael Ann Russell Jewish Community Ctr. Office: PO Box 600053 North Miami Beach FL 33180

STANWYCK, BARBARA (RUBY STEVENS), actress; b. Bklyn., July 16, 1907; d. Byron and Catherine (McGee) Stevens; m. Frank Fay, Aug. 26, 1928 (div. 1935); m. Robert Taylor, May 14, 1939 (div. 1951); 1 son. Ed. pub. schs., Bklyn. Began as chorus girl; later scored success in Burlesque, prod. by Arthur Hopkins; motion picture appearances include Meet John Doe, 1941, The Great Man's Lady, The Gay Sisters, 1942, Double Indemnity, 1944, My Reputations, 1945, Christmas in Connecticut, Two Mrs. Carrolls, 1946, The Bride Wore Boots, Strange Love of Martha Ivars, 1947, Cry Wolf, The Other Love, B.F.'s Daughter, 1948, Sorry Wrong Number, File on Thelma Jordon, The Lady Gambles, The Lie, East-Side, West-Side, The Furies, 1949, To Please a Lady, 1950, The Man in the Cloak, 1951, Clash by Night, 1951, Jeopardy, 1952, Titanic, 1952, Executive Suite, Witness to Murder, Escape to Burma, 1955, Cattle Queen of Montana, There's Always Tomorrow, 1956, Maverick Queen, 1956, These Wilder Years, 1956, Crime of Passion, 1957, Trooper Hook, 1957, Walk on the Wild Side, 1962, Roustabout, 1964, The Night Walker, 1965; TV shows The Barbara Stanwyck Theater, NBC-TV, 1960-61, The Big Valley, ABC-TV, The Colbys, 1985-87; appeared in: TV movie The Letters, 1973; TV mini-series The Thorn Birds (Emmy award 1983); guest star numerous TV shows. Recipient Emmy award, 1960-61, 66, hon. Acad. award, 1982, Am. Film Inst. award, 1987. Office: care A Morgan Maree & Assoc Inc 6363 Wilshire Blvd Los Angeles CA 90048 *

STAPLES, JUDITH LINWOOD, social welfare administrator; b. Bklyn., Sept. 13, 1947; d. Sheldon Linwood and Gladys (Anthon) S.; m. Alan L. Smith, (div. Feb. 1979). AA in Fine Arts, Coll. of San Mateo, 1967; BFA, San Jose (Calif.) State U., 1970. Prodn. artist Beeline Specialty Printers, South San Francisco, 1972-73; advt. artist Transcontinental Music Corp., Burlingame, Calif., 1974; prodn. artist Schwabacher Frey, Inc., San Francisco, 1975-77; account exec. Schwabacher Frey, Inc., Emeryville, Calif., 1977-82; indsl. liaison Comprehensive Care Corp., Hayward, Calif., 1982-83; drug and alcohol services coordinator Comprehensive Care Corp., San Francisco, 1983-84, 1983-84; program mgr. St. Catherine's Care Unit for Women, San Francisco, 1984-86; program dir. Parkside Recovery Ctrs., Inc., San Jose, 1986—. Producer numerous seminars on drug abuse. Fundraising chair Chem. Awareness and Treatment Services, San Francisco, 1984—; chairperson exec. bd. Problems of Alcoholism in Labor and Mgmt., San Jose, 1986—. Recipient Fine Art award Bank of Am., 1965. Democrat. Office: Phoenix/Good Samaritan Hosp 2425 Samaritan Dr San Jose CA 95124

STAPLES, MARY DECKER, health care facility administrator; b. Highland Park, Mich., Apr. 15, 1950; d. John Robert and Helen Louise (Banko) Decker; m. John Grant Staples, May 1, 1971 (div. Oct. 1, 1986); 1 child, Kathryn Mary. BA in Soc. Work, U. Mich., 1972; MBA, Eastern Mich. U., 1976. Staff asst. Mt. Carmel Mercy Hosp. and Med. Ctr., Detroit, 1975-78; v.p. Samaritan Health Ctr., Detroit, 1978-86; assoc. hosp. adminstr. U Mich. Hosp., Ann Arbor, Mich., 1987—; Pres. women in mgmt. orgn., chair programs com., chair nominating com. Sisters of Mercy Health Corp. Treas. St. John's Episc. Ch., Plymouth, Mich., 1985-87; mem. Ann Arbor (Mich.) PTO, 1987-88. Mem. Am. Coll. Health Care Execs. Office: U Mich Hosps D4207/0718 1500 E Med Ctr Dr Ann Arbor MI 48109-0800

STAPLES, VICKIE LEE, data processing executive; b. Portland, Oreg., Oct. 21, 1955; d. Doyle DeWaine and Grace O. (Lunsford) S. AS in Computer Programming Tech., Umpqua Community Coll., 1977; student, Portland State U., 1978-80. Programmer analyst Poorman Douglas Corp., Portland, 1980-81; mgr. data processing Presnell, Gage & Co., CPA's, Lewiston, Idaho, 1981-82; mgr. in-house systems Prodata Systems, Seattle, 1982-83; mgr. micro systems Safeguard Bus. Systems, Fairbanks, Alaska, 1985; systems analyst Frontier Cos. Alaska, Anchorage, 1985-86; mgr. data processing MarkAir Airlines, Anchorage, 1986—; instr. COBOL Lewis-Clark State Coll., Lewiston, Idaho, 1982; cons. in field. Author computer user manuals, 1980-81; contbr. articles to profl. jours. Campaign mgr. Haas-James for City Council, Lewiston, 1981; mem. Econ. Devel. Com., Lewiston, 1981-82; firefighter, bd. dirs., editor newsletter Steese Area Vol. Fire Dept., Fairbanks, 1984-85; founding mem., sec./treas., bd. dirs., co-chmn. David Boyles heart transplant com. Alaska Heart Transplant Found. Inc., 1988—. Mem. Data Processing Mgmt. Assn., Nat. Assn. for Female Execs., Phi Beta Lambda (Oreg. ambassador 1978, state pres. 1978-79, awards). Office: MarkAir 4100 W Internat Airport Rd Anchorage AK 99502

STAPLETON, JEAN (JEANNE MURRAY), actress; b. N.Y.C., Jan. 19, 1923; d. Joseph E. and Marie (Stapleton) Murray; m. William H. Putch, Oct. 26, 1957 (dec.); 2 children. Student, Hunter Coll., N.Y.C., Am. Apprentice Theatre, Am. Actors Co., Am. Theatre Wing; student with, Harold Clurman; LHD (hon.), Emerson Coll.; hon. degree, Hood Coll., Monmouth Coll. Opera debut in Candide with Balt. Opera Co.; appeared in The Italian Lesson with Balt. Opera; first N.Y. stage role in The Corn is Green, Equity Library Theatre; starred as mother in Am. Gothic, Circle-in-the-Sq.; Broadway debut with Judith Anderson In The Summer House; also appeared on Broadway in Damn Yankees, Bells Are Ringing, Juno, Rhinoceros and Funny Girl; first major break in comic ingenue role as Myrtle Mae with Frank Fay in Harvey; played with nat. tour of Come Back, Little Sheba starring Shirley Booth; starred in tour of Morning's at Seven; appeared in motion pictures including Damn Yankees, 1958, Bells Are Ringin, 1960, Up the Down Staircase, 1967, Cold Turkey, 1971, The Buddy System, 1984; appeared in numerous TV shows including Studio One, Naked City, Armstrong Circle Theater, The Defenders, Jackie Gleason Show, with guest appearances on Laugh-In, Sonny and Cher, Mike Douglas, Dinah, The Carol Burnett Show; starred in the title role of Aunt Mary on Hallmark Hall of Fame, 1979; most famous TV role as Edith Bunker on All In The Family, 1971-79; TV films include Dead Man's Folly, Tail Gunner Joe, 1977, Isabel's Choice, 1981, Angel Dusted, 1981, Eleanor: First Lady of the World, 1982, A Matter of Sex; appeared the Totem Pole Playhouse, Fayetteville, Pa., starred at Kennedy Ctr. in Daisy Mayme, 1978, The Late Christopher Bean, 1982; appeared on Broadway in Arsenic and Old Lace, 1986, also nat. tour. U.S. commr. to Internat. Woman's Yr. Commn. and Nat. Conf. Women, Houston, 1977; bd. dirs. Women's Edn. and Research Inst., Eleanor Roosevelt's Val-Kill. Recipient Emmy award for best performance in comedy series 1970-71, 71-72, 78, Golden Globe awards Hollywood Fgn. Press Assn. 1972, 73. Mem. Actors Equity Assn. (council 1958-63), Screen Actors Guild, AFTRA. Office: care Bauman Hiller & Strain 9220 Sunset Blvd Los Angeles CA 90069 *

STAPLETON, KATHARINE HALL (KATIE), food broadcaster, author; b. Kansas City, Mo., Oct. 29, 1919; d. William Mabin and Katharine (Hall) Foster; B.A., Vassar Coll., 1941; m. Benjamin Franklin Stapleton, June 20, 1942; children—Benjamin Franklin, III, Craig Roberts, Katharine Hall. Cookbook reviewer Denver Post, 1974-84; producer, writer, host On the Front Burner, daily radio program Sta. KOA-CBS, Denver, 1976-79, Sta. WGN, Portland, Maine, 1979-81, Cooking with Katie, live one-hour weekly, Sta. KOA, 1979-88; guest broadcaster Geneva Radio, 1974, London Broadcasting Corp., 1981, 82; tour leader culinarys to Britain, France and Switzerland, 1978-85. Eng., 1978. Chmn. women's div. United Fund, 1955-56; founder, chmn. Denver Debutante Ball, 1956, 57; regional v.p. Nat. Travelers Aid Assn., 1952-56; commr. Denver Centennial Authority, 1958-60; trustee Washington Cathedral, regional v.p., 1967-73; mem. world service council YWCA, 1961-87; trustee, Colo. Women's Coll., 1975-80, Harmes C. Fishback Found. Decorated Chevalier de L'Etoile Noire (France); recipient People-to-People citation, 1960, 66, Beautiful Activist award Altrusa Club, 1972, Gran Skillet award Colo./Wyo. Restaurant Assn., 1981. Mem. Alliance Française (hon., pres. 1968-70). Democrat. Episcopalian. Clubs: Denver Country, Denver. Author: Denver Delicious: 150 Past and Present Recipes from the Queen City, 1980, 3d. edit., 1983; High Notes: Favorite Recipies of KOA, 1984. Home: 8 Village Rd Englewood CO 80110

STAPLETON, MAUREEN, actress; b. Troy, N.Y., June 21, 1925; d. John P. and Irene (Walsh) S.; m. Max Allentuck, July 1949 (div. Feb. 1959); children: Daniel, Katharine; m. David Rayfiel, July, 1963 (div.). Student, Siena Coll, 1943. Debut in Playboy of the Western World, 1946; toured with Barretts of Wimpole Street, 1947; other plays include Anthony and Cleopatra, 1947, Detective Story, The Bird Cage, Rose Tattoo, 1950-51, The Sea Gull, Orpheus Descending, The Cold Wind and the Warm, 1959, Toys in the Attic, 1960-61, Plaza Suite, 1969, The Gingerbread Lady, 1970, Country Girl, 1972, Secret Affairs of Mildred Wild, 1972, The Gin Game, 1977-78, The Little Foxes, 1981; motion pictures include Lonely Hearts, 1959, The Fugitive Kind, 1960, A View from the Bridge, 1962, Bye Bye Birdie, 1963, Trilogy, 1969, Airport, 1970, Plaza Suite, 1971, Interiors, 1978, The Runner Stumbles, 1979, Reds, 1981 (Oscar award as best supporting actress), The Fan, 1981, On the Right Track, 1981, The Electric Grandmother, 1982, Mother's Day, 1984, Johnny Dangerously, 1984, Cocoon, 1985, The Money Pit, 1986, Nuts, 1987, Made in Heaven; TV films include Tell Me Where It Hurts, 1974, Cat On a Hot Tin Roof, 1976, All the King's Men, 1958, For Whom the Bell Tolls, 1959, Save Me a Place at Forest Lawn, 1966, Mirror, Mirror, Off the Wall, 1969, Queen of the Stardust Ballroom, 1975, The Gathering, 1977, Part II, 1979, Letters From Frank, 1979, Little Gloria ... Happy at Last, 1982, Sentimental Journey, 1984, Private Sessions, 1985. Tony award for the Gingerbread Lady, 1970; Recipient Nat. Inst. Arts and Letters award, 1969. Office: care Internat Creative Mgmt 8899 Beverly Blvd Los Angeles CA 90048 *

STARAN, KATHLEEN ANNE, marketing professional, consultant; b. Detroit, Mar. 6, 1959; d. Terrence Joseph and Dorothy Joy (Johnson) McKernan; m. Michael Edward Staran, July 12, 1986. Student, Walsh Coll., Troy, Mich., 1987. Legal asst. Orlowski & Assocs., Sterling Heights, Mich., 1981-84; sales coordinator Johnson Controls, Inc., Madison Heights, Mich., 1984-86, sales and mktg. rep., 1986-87; cons. sales and mktg., office services KMS Assocs., Bloomfield Hills, Mich., 1987—; cons. dir. Johnson Controls Body System, Madison Heights, 1984—. Mem. Am. Soc. Body Engrs. Republican. Roman Catholic.

STARFIELD, BARBARA HELEN, physician, educator; b. Bklyn., Dec. 18, 1932; d. Martin and Eva (Illions) S.; m. Neil A. Holtzman, June 12, 1955; children—Robert, Jon, Steven, Deborah. A.B., Swarthmore Coll., 1954; M.D., SUNY, 1959; M.P.H., Johns Hopkins U., 1963. Teaching asst. in anatomy Downstate Med. Center, N.Y.C., 1955-57; intern in pediatrics Johns Hopkins U., 1959-60, resident, 1960-62, dir. pediatric med. care clinic, 1963-66, dir. community staff comprehensive child care project, 1966-67, dir. pediatric clin. scholars program, 1971-76, prof. health policy, head Health Policy div., joint appointment in pediatrics, 1975—; cons. DHHS. Contbr. articles to profl. jours.; Mem. editorial bd.: Med. Care, 1977-79, Pediatrics, 1977-82, Internat. Jour. Health Services, 1978—, Med. Care Rev, 1980-84, Pediatrician, 1985—. Recipient Dave Luckman Meml. award, 1958; HEW Career Devel. award, 1970-75. Mem. Nat. Acad. Sci. Inst. Medicine (governing council 1981-83), Am. Pediatric Soc., Soc. Pediatric Research, Internat. Epidemiologic Assn., Ambulatory Pediatric Assn. (pres. 1980), Am. Public Health Assn., Sigma Xi, Alpha Omega Alpha. Office: 624 N Broadway Baltimore MD 21205

STARK, AMY LOUISE, clinical psychologist; b. St. Paul, May 13, 1954; d. Douglas Arvid and Irene Eleanor (Frokjer) S. BA, Gustavus Adolphus Coll., 1976; MA, Calif. Sch. Profl. Psychology, 1979, PhD, 1981. Lic. psychologist, Calif. Psychology intern Juarez-Lincoln Sch., Chula Vista, Calif., 1978-79, Cath. Family Services, San Diego, 1979-80, Southwood Mental Health Ctr., San Diego, 1980-81; clin. psychologist Orange County Children and Youth Services, 1982-84; clin. coordinator Western Youth Services, Tustin, Calif., 1986-88; indsl. psychologist Frederick Capaldi & Assocs., Tustin, 1982—; psychologist Tustin Psychology Ctr., 1985—; cons., presenter in field. Contbr. articles to profl. jours. Mem. Am. Psychol. Assn., Orange County Psychol. Assn., Newport Beach C. of C. Office: 131 N Tustin #210 Tustin CA 92680

STARK, JEANNE, educator, dean of college; b. Scranton, Pa., Feb. 4, 1927; d. Samuel and Evelyn (Pink) Tiney; m. Clarence Stark, Apr. 6, 1947; children: Jeffrey, Sherri Holsman, Randy. BSN, St. John U., 1967; MSN, Tchr's. Coll. of Columbia, 1969; EdD, Nova U., 1977. Coordinator, instr. Roosevelt Hosp. Sch. Nursing, N.Y.C., 1967-73; assoc. prof. MCH Miami-Dade Community Coll., Fla., 1973-75, adminstrv. asst. curriculum and faculty devel., 1975-78, dean, prof. nursing, 1978—; chmn. Fla. State Bd. of Nursing, Jacksonville, 1985—; mem. adv. com. FIU, Barry U. F.A.U. Mem. Am. Nurses Assn., Nat. League for Nursing, Assn. Instructional Adminstrs., Fla. Acad. Affairs Council, Assn. for Advancement of ADN. Office: Miami-Dade Community Coll Med Ctr Campus 950 NW 20th St Miami FL 33127

STARK, JILL DIANE, chemical company professional; b. Bowman, N.D., Feb. 11, 1957; d. William David and Priscilla (Hadler) S.; m. Fredrick Lainhart, Apr. 11, 1980 (div. 1985); children: William Warren, Michael David. BA, St. Olaf Coll., 1978. Sales rep. Hoffmann La Roche, Nutley, N.J., 1979-82; pharma. sales rep. USV Labs.; Revlon, Detroit, 1982-84; sales rep. food service Kraft Food, Kansas City, Mo., 1984-85; sales rep. mfg. Monsanto Agrl. Co., St. Louis, 1985—. Mem. Home Econs. Assn., Iowa Corn Growers Assn., Nat. Soybean Assn. Republican. Lutheran. Home and Office: RR 1 PO Box 55 Aurora IA 50607

STARK, JOAN SCISM, educator; b. Hudson, N.Y., Jan. 6, 1937; d. Ormonde F. and Myrtle Margaret (Kirkey) S.; m. William L. Stark, June 28, 1958 (dec.); children: Eugene William, Susan Elizabeth, Linda Anne, Ellen Scism; m. Malcolm A. Lowther, Jan. 31, 1981. B.S., Syracuse U., 1957; M.A. (Hoadly fellow), Columbia U., 1960; Ed.D., SUNY, Albany, 1971. Tchr. Ossining (N.Y.) High Sch., 1957-59; free-lance editor Holt, Rinehart & Winston, Harcourt, Brace & World, 1960-70; lectr. Ulster County Community Coll., Stone Ridge, N.Y., 1968-70; asst. dean Goucher Coll., Balt., 1970-73; asso. dean Goucher Coll., 1973-74; assoc. prof., chmn. dept. higher postsecondary edn. Syracuse (N.Y.) U., 1974-78; dean Sch. Edn., U. Mich., Ann Arbor, 1978-83, prof., 1983—; dir. Nat. Ctr. for Improving Postsecondary Teaching and Learning, 1986—. Contbr. numerous articles to various pubs. Leader Girl Scouts U.S.A., Cub Scouts Am.; coach girls Little League; dist. officer PTA, intermittently, 1968-80; mem. adv. com. Gerald R. Ford Library, U. Mich., 1980-83; trustee Kalamazoo Coll., 1979-85; mem. exec. com. Inst. Social Research, U. Mich., 1979-81; bd. dirs. Mich. Assn. Colls. Tchr. Edn., 1979-81. Mem. Assn. Study Higher Edn. (dir. 1977-79, v.p. 1983, pres. 1984), Assn. Innovation Higher Edn. (nat. chmn. 1974-75), Am. Assn. for Higher Edn., Am. Ednl. Research Assn., Assn. Instnl. Research, Assn. Colls. and Schs. Edn. State Univs. and L and Grant Colls. (dir. 1981-83), Phi Beta Kappa, Phi Kappa Phi, Sigma Pi Sigma, Eta Pi Upsilon, Lambda Sigma Sigma, Phi Delta Kappa, Pi Lambda Theta. Office: U Mich 2002 Sch of Edn Ann Arbor MI 48109

STARK, MARY BARBARA, retired educator; b. Boston, Jan. 1, 1920; d. Charles Rathbone and Dorothea Brenton (Burge) S. BA, Whitworth Coll., 1965, MEd, 1968; EdS, U. of the Pacific, 1975; PhD, Southeastern U., New Orleans, 1981. Cert. elem. tchr., jr. high tchr., spl. edn. tchr. Play dir. Spokane (Wash.) Park Dept., 1937-41; tchr. Lanham Act Nursery Sch., Spokane, 1941-45; owner, mgr. Children's Play Room, Spokane, 1945-63; supr. Guild's Sch for Mentally Retarded, Spokane, 1962-66; tchr. primary educable mentally retarded Sacramento City Unified Sch. Dist., 1966-68, tchr. educable kindergarten mentally retarded, 1968-70; kindergarten educator Sacramento (Calif.) City Unified S.D., 1970-87. Mem. Sacramento Bus. and Profl. Women's Club (pres. 1973-74), Assn. Childhood Edn. Internat. (pres. 1983-85, state treas. 1984-86), Delta Kappa Gamma (pres. 1984-86), Phi Delta Kappa. Mem. United Ch. of Christ. Home: 5989 Lake Crest Way #1 Sacramento CA 95822

STARK, PATRICIA ANN, psychologist; b. Ames, Iowa, Apr. 21, 1937; d. Keith C. and Mary L. (Johnston) Moore. B.S., So. Ill. U., Edwardsville, 1970, M.S., 1972; Ph.D., St. Louis U., 1976. Counselor to alcoholics Bapt. Rescue Mission, East St. Louis, 1969; researcher alcoholics Gateway Rehab. Center, East St. Louis, 1972; psychologist intern Henry-Stark Counties Spl. Edn. Dist. and Galesburg State Research Hosp., Ill., 1972-73; instr. Lewis and Clark Community Coll., Godfrey, Ill., 1973-76, asst. prof., 1976-84, assoc. prof., 1984—, coordinator child care services, 1974-84; mem. staff dept. psychiatry Meml. Hosp., St. Elizabeth's Hosp., 1979—; supr. various workshops in field, 1974—; dir. child and family services Collinsville Counseling Center, 1978-82; clin. dir., owner Empas-Complete Family Psychol. and Hypnosis Services, Collinsville, 1982—; cons. community agys., 1974—; mem. adv. bd. Madison County Council on Alcoholism and Drug Dependency, 1977-80. Mem. Am. Psychol. Assn., Ill. Psychol. Assn., Midwestern Psychol. Assn., Nat. Assn. Sch. Psychologists, Am. Soc. Clin. Hypnosis, Internat. Soc. Hypnosis. Office: 2802 Maryville Rd Collinsville IL 62234

STARK, ROBIN CARYL, psychotherapist; b. Yonkers, N.Y., Apr. 16, 1953; d. Louis and Bernice (Cooper) S. BA cum laude Psychology, CUNY, 1979; MSW, NYU, 1982; cert. in psychoanalytic psychotherapy, Psychoanalytic Inst., 1985. Pvt. practice psychotherapy N.Y.C., 1983—; social work supr./coordinator services for handicapped Plaza Head Start, N.Y.C., 1983-85; client coordinator Young Adult Inst., N.Y.C., 1985-88; mem. adj. field faculty Grad. Sch. Social Service, Fordham U., N.Y.C., 1986-87, Sch. Social Work, Hunter Coll., N.Y.C., 1987-88; patent care coordinator Achievement and Guidance Ctrs. Am. Inc., N.Y.C., 1988—. Recipient Service award Young Adult Inst., 1987; N.Y.C. Youth Bur. grantee, 1983-85. Mem. Nat. Assn. Social Workers, N.Y. State Soc. Clin. Social Work Psychotherapists (fellow), Acad. Cert. Social Workers (fellow). Office: 110 East End Ave SUite 19 New York NY 10028

STARKEY, JANET VOIGT, nutritionist; b. Bklyn., July 6, 1953; d. Clinton Joseph and Rose Marie (Drusotis) Voigt; m. James Edward Starkey, Aug. 7, 1976. AA in Liberal Arts summa cum laude, Nassau Community Coll., 1973; BS in Clin. Dietetics/Food Sci. summa cum laude, SUNY, Buffalo, 1976. Registered dietitian. Therapeutic dietitian Sister's of Charity Hosp., Buffalo, 1976-78; asst. nutritionist Med. Coll. Va., Richmond, 1978-79, chief clin. out-patient nutritionist, mgr. ops., 1979—; cons. nutrition Gov. and Mrs. Chuck Robb, Richmond, 1982, Ctr. for Behavioral Medicine, Richmond, 1983—; prin. Comprehensive Nutritional Services, Richmond, 1986—; liaison pub. relations speaker's bur. Va. Commonwealth U., Richmond, 1986—. Mem. adv. bd. Weighty Matters, 1985-86; contbr. articles to profl. jours. Mem. Am. Dietetic Assn. (Young Dietitian of Yr. 1983), Va. Dietetic Assn., Richmond Dietetic Assn. Home: 14007 Copper Hill Rd Midlothian VA 23112 Office: Med Coll of Va Nutrition Clinic Box 46 Richmond VA 23298

STARLING, BARBARA JOYCE, human resources consulting firm executive, consultant; b. Nashville, Jan. 4, 1935; d. William Louis and Edna Earl (Francis) Watson; m. Donal J. Starling, Sept. 21, 1957; 1 child, Karen Marie Starling Dallas. Student Kent State U., 1961, U. Tenn.-Nashville, 1965-67. In sales and promotion, various rec. cos., Nashville, 1965-74; forms [illegible] H.W. Black & Assocs. Inc., Nashville, 1974-76; plan adminstrn. unit supr. William M. Mercer, Inc., Nashville, 1976-81, programmer, 1981-83; plan adminstrn. unit supr. Mercer-Meidinger Hansen, Inc., Nashville, 1983-85, mng. cons., 1985—. Bible tchr. Tenn. Prison for Women, Nashville, 1983-87, Met. Criminal Justice Ctr., Nashville, 1983-85. Mem. Middle Tenn. Employee Benefits Council, Tennessee Valley Employee Benefits Council; rehab counsellor Tenn. Prison for Women, 1983—. Mem. Church of Christ. Avocations: computing; photography; walking; reading. Home: 623 Hickory Glade Ct Antioch TN 37013 Office: Mercer-Meidinger Hansen Inc 424 Church St Suite 1300 Nashville TN 37219

STARR, MIRIAM CAROLYN, communications company excutive; b. Pitts., Apr. 13, 1951; d. Donald Curtis and Virginia Ruth (Weise) S. BS in Math., Bucknell U., 1973; MBA in Fin., Drexel U., 1984. Mgmt. trainee Bell Pa., Allentown, 1973-75; equipment engr. Bell Pa., Phila., 1975-76, short range planner, 1976-77; chief switchman Bell Pa., Langhorne, 1977-78; long range planner Bell Pa., Phila., 1978-80, cost analyst, 1980-81, forecaster, 1981-83; inventory analyst AT&T, Parsippany, N.J., 1983-85, budget analyst, 1985-87, expense analyst, 1987-88, asst. controller gen. bus. systems, 1988—. Mem., treas. Stone Run II Neighborhood Assn., 1987—. Mem. Nat. Assn. for Female Execs., Am. Soc. Profl. and Exec. Women, Delta Zeta. Home: 16 Cambridge Rd Bedminster NJ 07921 Office: AT&T 5 Wood Hollow Rd Parsippany NJ 07054

STARRATT, PATRICIA ELIZABETH, writer, actress, composer; b. Boston, Nov. 7, 1943; d. Alfred Byron and Anna (Mazur) S.; A.B., Smith Coll., 1965; grad. prep. dept. Peabody Conservatory Music, 1961. Teaching asst. Harvard U. Grad. Sch. Bus. Aminstrn., 1965-67; mng. dir. INS Assocs., Washington, 1967-68; adminstrv. asst. George Washington U. Hosp., 1970-71; legal asst. Morgan, Lewis & Bockius, Washington, 1971-72; profl. staff energy analyst Nat. Fuels and Energy Policy Study, U.S. Senate Interior Com., 1972-74; cons., exec. asst. energy resource devel. Fed. Energy Adminstrn., Washington, 1974-75; sr. cons. energy policy Atlantic Richfield Co., 1975-76; energy cons., Alaska, 1977-78; govt. affairs assoc. Sohio Alaska Petroleum Co., Anchorage, 1978-85; pres. Starratt Monarch Prodns., 1986—; Econ. Devel. Commn., Municipality of Anchorage, 1981; actress/asst. dir. Brattle St. Players, Boston, 1966-67, Washington Theater Club 1967-68, Gene Frankel, Broadway 1968-69; actress Aspen Resident Theater, Colo. 1985-86; entertainer The Crazy Horse, Anchorage, 1987—; writer and assoc. producer Then One Night I Hit Her, 1983; appeared Off-Broadway in To Be Young, Gifted and Black; performed as Mary in Tennessee, Blanche in A Streetcar Named Desire, Stephanie Dickinson in Cactus Flower, Angela in Papa's Wine, Elizabeth Procter in The Crucible, Candida in Candida, Zeuss in J.B., Martha in Who's Afraid of Virginia Woolf, Amy in Dinny and The Witches, as Columbina in Servant of Two Masters, as Singer in Death of Morris Biederman, as Joan in Joan of Lorraine, as Mado in Amadee, as Mrs. Rowlands in Before Breakfast, as the girl in Hello Out There, as Angela in Bedtime Story, as Hannah in Night of the Iguana, as Lavinia in Androcles and the Lion, as Catherine in Great Catherine, as Julie in Lilliom, as First Nurse in Death of Bessie Smith, as Laura in Tea and Sympathy, as Amelia Earheart in Chamber Music; appeared at Detroit Summer Theatre in Oklahoma, Guys and Dolls, Carousel, Brigadoon, Kiss Me Kate, Finnian's Rainbow; asst. to dir. Broadway plays A Cry Of Players, A Way Of Life, Off-Broadway play To Be Young, Gifted, and Black; screenwriter Challenge in Alaska, 1986, Martin Poll Films; asst. dir. Dustin Hoffman, 1974. Bd. dirs. Anchorage Community Theatre; industry rep. Alaska Eskimo Whaling Commn.; mem. Alaska New Music Forum. Mem. Actors' Equity. Episcopalian. Author Among the Stars, The Adventures of a Multi-Talented Women, 1988; contbr. articles on natural gas and Alaska econ. policy to profl. jours. Avocations: skiing, horseback riding, biking, hiking. Home: 1054 W 20th Ave #2 Anchorage AK 99503

STARRS, ELIZABETH ANNE, lawyer; b. Detroit, Jan. 1, 1954; d. John Richard and Mabel Angeline (Gilchrist) S. BA, U. Mich., 1975; JD, Suffolk U., 1980. Bar: Mass. 1980, U.S. Dist. Ct. Mass. 1980, U.S. Ct. Appeals (1st. cir.) 1980, Colo. 1983, U.S. Dist. Ct. Colo. 1983, U.S. Ct. Appeals (10th cir.) 1983. Assoc. Denner & Benjoya P.C., Boston, 1980-83; assoc. Cooper & Kelley P.C., Denver, 1983-86, ptnr., 1986—; instr. bus. law Bay State Community Coll., Boston, 1981-82. Leader Girl Scouts U.S., Denver, 1984-85; mem. Denver Young Dems., 1983; sec., adv. council Colo. Taxpayers for Choice, Denver, 1985—. Mem. Mass. Bar Assn., Colo. Bar Assn., Denver Bar Assn., Mass. Assn. Women Lawyers, Colo. Women's Bar Assn. (bd. dirs. 1984, v.p. 1988-89), Colo. Def. Lawyers Assn. Roman Catholic. Home: 115 S Clarkson Denver CO 80209 Office: Cooper & Kelley PC 1660 Wynkoop #900 Denver CO 80202-1197

STASCO, DAPHNE JO, financial executive; b. Bronx, N.Y., Oct. 1, 1942; d. Paul Joseph and Joan Marie (Grimaldi) Ott; 1 child, Vanessa. Assoc. Applied Sci., SUNY, Farmingdale, 1962; BBA, Hofstra U., 1964. CPA, N.Y. Sr. acct. Peat, Marwick, Mitchell and Co., N.Y.C., 1962-68; controller Grolier, Inc., N.Y.C., 1968-73; pvt. practice acctg. Manhasset, N.Y., 1973-78; controller N.Y.C. Offtrack Betting Corp., 1978-82, v.p. real estate and facilities, 1982-84; chief fin. officer, asst. sec. Sunnydale Farms, Inc., Bklyn., 1984—. Mem. NOW (bd. dirs. Nassau chpt.), Am. Soc. Women Accts. (bd. dirs.). Office: 400 Stanley Ave Brooklyn NY 11207

STASI, LINDA, author, producer, editor; b. N.Y.C., Apr. 14, 1947; d. Anthony John and Florence (Barbera) Stasi; m. John Rovello, Nov. 22, 1970 (div.); 1 child, Jessica Stasi Rovello. BFA, N.Y. Inst. Tech., 1970; postgrad., Hofstra U., 1971. Editor edn. Seventeen mag., N.Y.C., 1970-74; freelance writer, N.Y.C., 1974-79; producer, creator, host Good Looks Line, 1979-81; pres. Linda Stasi & Assocs., Inc., 1978-84; editor beauty and health New Woman mag., 1984-86; editor-in-chief Beauty Digest mag., 1986-88; editor health and beauty Elle mag., 1988—. Author: Simply Beautiful, 1983, Looking Good is the Best Revenge, 1984, A Fieldguide to Impossible Men, 1987; syndicated newspaper writer: N.Y. Daily News and Tribune Syndicate, 1984, Times of London Syndicate; feature writer: Redbook, Mademoiselle, Cosmopolitan, Elle; on-camera host, producer: 5-part health series Disney Channel, 1983; freelance feature writer: Washington Post. Mem. Writer's Guild. Home: 20 Waterside Plaza New York NY 10010 Office: Elle Mag 551 5th Ave New York NY 10016

STASKO BARREIRA, LINDA, software sales professional; b. Danbury, Conn., June 7, 1959; d. Vincent Emil and Elizabeth Ann (Catuogno) S.; m. James Michael Barreira, Oct. 5, 1985. BS, Rutgers U., 1980; MBA, N.H. Coll., 1987. Software engr. Western Electric Co., North Andover, Mass., 1980-84; sales rep. Hewlett-Packard Co., Burlington, Mass., 1984—. Home: 15 Spring Rd Londonderry NH 03053 Office: Hewlett Packard Co 29 Mall Rd Burlington MA 01803

STATHAM, POLLY JANE, accountant; b. Woodville, Okla., July 12, 1926; d. James Monroe and Mary Ellen (Formby) Bostick; m. Francis Edward Burks Sr., Sept. 11, 1946 (div. 1952); 1 child, Francis Edward Jr.; m. William Eugene Statham, Dec. 6, 1975. Student, Austin Coll., 1958. CPA, Tex., Okla. With George L. DeArmond, CPA, Denison, Tex., 1954-73; ptnr. DeArmond, Burks & Co., CPA, Denison, Tex., 1973-76; pvt. practice acctg. Sherman, Tex., 1976—. Mem. Am. Inst. CPA's, Tex. Soc. CPA's, Am. Women's Soc. CPA's, DAR (regent 1988), United Daughters Confederacy (pres. 1986), Nat. Geneal. Soc., Grayson County Geneal. Soc., Huguenot Soc. Democrat. Methodist. Club: Story League. Office: 622 E Lamar PO Box 844 Sherman TX 75090

STATON, DONNA ELLEN, interior designer; b. Newman, Ga., Feb. 26, 1955; d. Ezra Eugene Whittle and Jackie Ruth (Dukes) Jones; m. William Russell Staton, Sept. 22, 1973 (div. Feb. 1977). AA, Art Inst. Atlanta, 1984. Legal sec. Schwall and Huett, Atlanta, 1975-76; word processor Sears, Roebuck and Co., Atlanta, 1976-79; legal sec. Garland Nuuckolls and Kadish, Atlanta, 1979-80; legal word processor Dennis Corry Webb and Carlock, Atlanta, 1980-84; contract sales rep. Seabrook Wallcoverings, Inc., Atlanta, 1984-86; interior designer BAker Interiors, Chamblee, Ga., 1986-87; prin. interior designer Design II and Assocs., Inc., Atlanta, 1987—. Interpreter for the Deaf Marietta First United Meth. Ch., Cobb County, 1986-87; vol. safeway house Safe Night Rest, Marietta, 1987, 88. Mem. Nat. Assn. for Female Execs., Internat. Soc. Internat. Designers, Cobb C. of C. Methodist. Office: Design II and Assocs Inc 200 Sandy Springs Pl Suite 301 Atlanta GA 30328

STAUB, ANITA (KILPATRICK), management analyst, educator; b. Oakland, Calif., Dec. 24, 1947; d. Homer Lenel and Martha Bernice Kilpatrick; m. Jay Palmer Eickenhorst, Dec. 9, 1983. BA with honors, U. Calif., Berkeley, 1971, teaching cert., 1974; postgrad., Calif. State U., Hayward, 1972, Calif. Pacific U., 1986—. Cert. secondary tchr., Calif. Substitute tchr. Marin County Schs., San Francisco, 1974—; civil engring. tech. U.S. Army C. E., Sausalito, Calif., 1974-76; substitute tchr. Hendersonville (N.C.) City Schs., 1976-78, Henderson County (N.C.) Schs., 1976-79; park technician Nat. Park Service, Flat Rock, N.C., 1978-81; park technician Nat. Park Service, San Francisco, 1981-83, voucher examiner, 1983-85; mgmt. analyst intern Headquarters 6th U.S. Army, San Francisco, 1985-86; mgmt. analyst Hdqrs. 6th U.S. Army, San Francisco, 1986—; cons. for interpretive prospectus Golden Gate Nat. Recreation Area, Nat. Park Service, San Francisco, 1981, recording sec. EEO com., 1984-85. Author: Temporary Duty Travel Handbook, 1984, Payroll Handbook, 1985; co-designer: Alcatraz Island interpretive display, 1981. Mem. Am. Mgmt. Assn., Am. Soc. Mil. Comptrollers, Nat. Assn. Female Execs., Calif. Nature Conservancy, Nat. Audubon Soc., Mus. Soc., San Francisco Opera Guild, Stinson Beach Allied Arts Guild, Marin Conservation League. Home: PO Box 913 Stinson Beach CA 94970 Office: Hdqrs 6th US Army Presidio of San Fransisco San Francisco CA 94129-7000

STAUBER, ROSEMARY JANE, social service director, psychotherapist; b. Bristow, Okla., Mar. 13, 1931; d. Sanford Glen Starry and Opal Mary (Campbell) Schmitz; m. Robert Andrew Stauber, Aug. 4, 1951 (div. Dec. 1975); children: Beverly Elaine, Carol Sue, Linda Ash, Patricia Canela. BA, Oklahoma City U., 1952; postgrad., Trinity U., 1972-74; MSW, Our Lady Lake U., 1980; postgrad., The Fielding Inst., Santa Barbara, Calif., 1981—. Cert. social worker, Tex., advanced clin. practitioner, Tex. With seismograph computer dept. Shell Oil Co., Oklahoma City, 1951-56; founder, exec. dir. Bexar City Women's Ctr., San Antonio, 1977-88; pvt. practice psychotherapy San Antonio, 1988—; developer self-sufficiency tng. programs. Founder The Happening, Crystal City, Tex., 1967; bd. dirs. Network Power Tex., San Antonio, 1982-85; regional leader Wider Opportunities for Women, Washington, 1985-88. Named Woman of Yr., San Antonio Light, 1980, Am. Muslim Ctr., 1985, Ind. Order Foresters, 1985; charter mem. San Antonio Women's Hall of Fame, 1984. Mem. Nat. Assn. Social Workers, Acad. Cert. Social Workers. Democrat. Clubs: SA 100, Tex. Women's Forum. Home: 6718 Callaghan #501 San Antonio TX 78229 Office: Behavioral Sci Assocs 359 E Hildebrand San Antonio TX 78212

STAUBLIN, JUDITH ANN, financial executive; b. Anderson, Ind., Jan. 17, 1936; d. Leslie Fred and Esta Virginia (Ringo) Wiley; student Ball State U., 1954-55, 69-70, Savs. and Loan Inst., 1962-67, U. Ga., 1974, Wright State U., 1975; children—Juli Jackson, Scott Jackson. Teller, Anderson Fed. Savs. and Loan Assn., Anderson, 1962-64, data processing mgr., 1965-70, loan officer, 1970-72, v.p. systems, 1972-74, fin. systems mktg., 1974-76; fin. dist. mgr. data centers div. NCR Corp., Atlanta, 1977-81, nat. sales mgr. EFT services Data Center Div., Dayton, Ohio, 1982-83; fin. dist. mgr. EFT and data services So. Thrift, Atlanta, 1983—. Active United Way. Mem. Am. Savs. and Loan Inst., Fin. Mgrs. Soc., Ga. Exec. Women's Network, Am. Soc. Profl. and Exec. Women, Anderson C. of C. Home: 6115 Woodmont Blvd Norcross GA 30092 Office: 5 Executive Dr NE Atlanta GA 30329

STAUROVSKY, LINDA GOLDIE, nursing educator; b. Bridgeport, Conn., Mar. 1, 1942; d. Charles and Goldie (Kochan) S. BS, U. Conn., 1963; M in Nursing, Emory U., 1967; cert. nurse midwife, N.Y. Med. Coll., 1968. Staff nurse Grace New Haven Hosp., 1963-64; asst. instr. U. Conn., Storrs, 1964-66; asst. prof. Sch. Nursing Univ. N.C., Chapel Hill, 1968-71, instr. Sch. Medicine, 1971-78; asst. prof. Sch. Nursing U. Tex. Health Sci. Ctr., San Antonio, 1978—; cons. African Health Tng. Instn. Project, Chapel Hill, 1975-78. Author: (with others) Maternity Nursing Theory to Practice, 1983. Speaker March of Dimes, San Antonio, 1985—. Mem. Am. Coll. Nurse Midwives, Nurses Assn. Am. Coll. Obstetricians and Gynecologists (faculty continuing edn. 1975—, contbr. vols. 1, 4 update series 1983, 86, mem. editorial bd. 1985-86, coordinator local chpt. 1985-86), Sigma Theta Tau, Kappa Delta Pi. Home: Rt 1 Box 1691 Boerne TX 78006 Office: U Tex Health Sci Ctr Sch Nursing 7703 Floyd Curl Dr San Antonio TX 78284-7948

STAUTBERG, SUSAN SCHIFFER, communications executive; b. Bryn Mawr, Pa., Nov. 9, 1945; d. Herbert F. and Margaret (Berwind) Schiffer; B.A., Wheaton Coll., 1967; M.A., George Washington U., 1970; m. T. Aubrey Stautberg, Jr., Dec. 10, 1979. Nat. TV corr., Washington, 1970-74; White House fellow, 1974-75; dir. communications U.S. Consumer Products Safety Commn., Washington, 1976-78, McNeil Consumer Products Co., 1978-80; v.p. Fraser/Assos., Washington, 1980; exec. asst. to pres. Morgan Stanley & Co., N.Y.C., 1980-82; dir. communications Touche Ross & Co., N.Y.C., 1982— pres. MasterMedia Ltd., 1986—; Author: Making It in Less Than an Hour, 1976, Pregnancy Nine to Five: The Career Woman's Guide to Pregnancy and Motherhood, 1985, The Pregnancy and Motherhood Diary: Planning the First Year of your Second Career, 1987. Mem., nat. chmn. adv. council Ctr.for Study of the Presidency, 1976—; mem. Phila. Regional Panel for Selection White House Fellows; bd. dirs. Schiffer Pub., The Berwind Found.; mem. Reagan-Bush Presdl. Transition Team; mem. Commn. Presdl. Scholars; State Dept. speaker various countries. Selected as one of Wheaton's 10 Most Outstanding Grads., Alumnae Assn., Wheaton Coll., 1982. Mem. Pub. Relations Soc. Am. (dir.), Pub. Affairs Profls., Nat. Soc. Colonial Dames. Clubs: Acorn, City Tavern, Cosmopolitan, Colony, Radnor Hunt. Home: 17 E 89th St New York NY 10128 Office: Touche Ross & Co 1633 Broadway New York NY 10019

STAY, BARBARA, zoologist, educator; b. Cleve., Aug. 31, 1926; d. Theron David and Florence (Finley) S. A.B., Vassar Coll., 1947; M.A., Radcliffe Coll., 1949, Ph.D., 1953. Entomologist Army Research Center, Natick, Mass., 1954-60; vis. asst. prof. Pomona Coll., 1960; asst. prof. biology U. Pa., 1961-67; asso. prof. zoology U. Iowa, Iowa City, 1967-77; prof. U. Iowa, 1977—. Fulbright fellow to Australia, 1953; Lalor fellow Harvard U., 1960. Mem. Am. Soc. Zoologists, Am. Inst. Biol. Scis., Am. Soc. Cell Biology, Entomol. Soc. Am., Iowa Acad. Scis., Sigma Xi. Office: U Iowa Dept Biology Iowa City IA 52242

STEAD, BETTE ANN, marketing educator; b. San Antonio, May 22, 1935; d. Charles Albert Jr. and Mildred Mary (Behrman) S. BBA, Lamar U., 1957; MBA, U. Tex., 1961; EdD, U. Houston, 1967. Tchr. Beaumont (Tex.) High Sch., 1957-62; asst. prof. Lamar U., Beaumont, 1962-67; prof. mktg. U. Houston, 1968—; cons. Sun Oil Co., Houston and Dallas, 1971-72, Shell Oil Co., Houston, 1973, Pullman Kellogg Constrn. Co., Houston, 1973-80, Gulf Oil Co., Houston, 1975. Author: Women in Management, 1978, 2d edit., 1985; contbr. articles to profl. jours. Mem. Acad. Mgmt. (chmn. com. on status of women 1974-76), Southwest Fedn. Adminstrv. Disciplines (bd. dirs. 1974-75), River Oaks Bus. Women's Exchange (v.p. 1985, 87), Phi Kappa Phi, Alpha Chi Omega (alumnae pres. Beaumont 1960). Episcopalian. Lodge: Rotary. Home: 2828 Bammel Ln Apt 1211 Houston TX 77098 Office: U Houston 4800 Calhoun St Houston TX 77204-6283

STEAD, FRANCESCA MANUELA LEWENSTEIN, health care consultant, massage therapist; b. Bklyn., May 2, 1949; d. Robert Gottschalk Lewenstein and Shirley Winifred (Goodman) Lewenstein Ozgen; m. Thomas David Stead, May 28, 1975; children: Chandra Dharani, Thomas Robert. Student, Case Western Res. U., 1967-69; BA in Govt. cum laude, Ohio U., 1973; cert. in Massage Therapy, Cen. Ohio Sch. Massage, Columbus, 1978. Lic. massage therapist. Youth service coordinator Adams-Brown Community Action Agy., Decatur, Ohio, 1973; child welfare worker Scioto Children's Services, Portsmouth, Ohio, 1975-77; project dir. youth services Scioto County Community Action Agy., Portsmouth, Ohio, 1978-79; co-owner Stead Enterprises, Otway, Ohio, 1978—; self-employed massage therapist Stead Enterprises, Portsmouth, Ohio, 1979—; drug and alcohol counselor Council on Alcoholism, West Union, Ohio, 1982; instr. Yoga Shawnee State U., Portsmouth, 1985—; staff mem. Massage Therapy Assoc., Area Psychiat. and Psychotherapy Group, Huntington W.Va., 1986—; instr. summer [illegible] edn. program Shawnee State U., 1986—; reimbursement officer Ohio Dept. Mental Health, Columbus, 1982-85; cons. Portsmouth Police Dept., 1977, Total Health Care Cons., Portsmouth, 1985—; cons. drug abuse Aberdeen Sch., Ohio, 1982; Yoga instr. YMCA, Portsmouth, 1979-80, 85—. Dem. campaign worker, Ohio, 1968—; mem., organizer So. Ohio Taskforce on Domestic Violence, 1976—; organizer campus ministry Shawnee State Coll., Portsmouth, 1976-77; organizer Portsmouth Food Coop., 1975. Flora Stone Mather scholar Case Western Res. U., 1967. Mem. So. Ohio Mental Health Assn., Portsmouth Area Women's Network (adv. bd. 1988), Nat. Assn. Female Execs., Am. Massage Therapy Assn., Pi Gamma Mu. Democrat. Kagyupa Buddhist. Club: Poetry Circle (Portsmouth). Home: 4140 Mt Unger Rd Otway OH 45657 Office: 1025 1/2 9th St Portsmouth OH 45662

STEARLEY, MILDRED SUTCLIFFE VOLANDT, foundation executive; b. Ft. Myer, Va., Aug. 3, 1905; d. William Frederick and Mabel Emma (Sutcliffe) Volandt; student George Washington U., 1923-24, 25-28; m. Ralph F. Stearley, Sept. 19, 1931. Elementary tchr. Brent Sch., Baguio, Philippines, 1929-30; staff aide vol. services ARC, also acting chmn., Charlotte, N.C., 1943, staff asst., Washington, 1943-47, Gray Lady vol., Okinawa, 1950-53, Brazil, Ind., 1954; trustee Air Force Village Found., San Antonio, 1975-78, sec. bd., 1975-77; sustaining mem. Tex. Gov.'s Com.; mem. 300 com. Bexar County Republican Com.; mem. decoration com. St. Andrew's Epis. Ch., San Antonio. Recipient commendation ARC, Washington, 1943. Mem. Army Daus., Am. Legion Aux., Army-Navy Club Aux., P.E.O. (life), Am. Security Council (nat. adv. bd.), San Antonio Mus. Assn., Smithsonian Inst., Pi Beta Phi. Episcopalian. Clubs: Ladies Reading (hon. mem.) (Brazil, Ind.); Lackland Officers Wives, Bright Shawl (San Antonio). Home: 4917 Ravenswood Dr Apt 311 San Antonio TX 78227

STEARMAN, GAIL WEHRMANN, nurse; b. Charlotte, N.C., Nov. 22, 1953; d. Robert Henry and Anna Lee (Prather) Wehrmann; m. Gordon Kim Stearman, Aug. 27, 1976; children: Robert Shannon, Taylor Lee. BS, U. Ariz., 1976; MS in Pub. Health, U. Mo., 1981; MS in Nursing, U. Tenn., 1986. RN, family nurse practitioner. Vol. Peace Corps, Jalapa, Nicaragua, 1976-79; rural health educator Mo. Extension Service, Columbia, 1980-81; health educator Colo. Migrant Health, Denver, 1981, V.I. Dept. Edn., St. Thomas, 1981-84; family nurse practitioner Rural Community Health Services, Parrottsville, Tenn., 1986—; health cons. Tenn. Opportunity Program, Newport, 1987—; migrant health coordinator Rural Community Health Services, Parrottsville, 1987—. U. Ariz. Faculty scholar, 1974-76, U. Mo. scholar, 1979-81; Hilton A. Smith fellow, 1986. Mem. Am. Nurses' Assn., Tenn. Nurses' Assn., Am. Pub. Health Assn., Amnesty Internat., East Tenn. Pledge of Resistance, Phi Kappa Phi, Sigma Theta Tau. Office: Rural Community Health Services PO Box 99 Parrottsville TN 37843

STEARNS, BETTY JANE, public relations executive; b. St. Paul. Ph.B., U. Chgo., 1945, M.A., 1948; cert. advt. studies, U. London, 1949. Editor Chgo. Stagebill, 1948-49; sec. U. Chgo. Cancer Research Found., 1949; writer Chas. A. Stevens & Co., 1949-50; account exec. The Pub. Relations Bd., Chgo., 1950-53, v.p., 1953-63, sr. v.p., 1963-78, mng. ptnr., 1978-85; vice chmn. PRB/Needham Porter Novelli, Chgo., 1985-86; exec. v.p. Porter Novelli (formerly Pub. Relations Bd.), Chgo., 1986—; chmn. bd. dirs. Sta. WBEZ, Chgo., 1980-84, now dir.; dir. Chgo. Apparel Industry Bd. Author, editor: Careers in Music, 1976, Winning The Money Game, 1979; editor-writer, producer: book, radio series Instrumental Odyssey, 1970. Bd. dirs. Bus. Vols. for Arts, Friends of Libraries USA. Recipient Golden Trumpet award Publicity Club of Chgo., 1959, 64, 68-70, 72-73, 76-79, 84, 85. Mem. Pub. Relations Soc. Am. (Silver Anvil award 1972, 76, 82), Home Fashions League, The Fashion Group of Chgo. (pres. 1967-68), Com. of 200, Chgo. Network (dir. 1982-85), Chgo. Assn. Commerce and Industry (bd. dirs.). Club: Arts Chgo. Office: Porter Novelli 303 E Wacker Dr Chicago IL 60601

STEARNS, E(LIZABETH) CAROLYN, medical administrative officer; b. Mooresville, Ind., Aug. 16, 1928; d. Gale Able and Ercie Louise (Smith) Rose; grad. Mooresville public schs.; m. William Joseph Sawyers, Sept. 6, 1946, (div. May 1951); children—William Joseph, Sherry Lou; m. John Pershing Stearns, Oct. 4, 1954 (div. Mar. 1980); 1 son, Dennis Gale. Sec., Lab. Equipment Corp., Mooresville, 1946-49; sec. to chief surg. service VA Hosp., Indpls., 1950-57, sec. radiology service, 1963-64, sec. to chief med. service, 1964-66, adminstrv. asst. to chief med. service, 1966-70, adminstrv. officer med. service, 1970-72; staff asst. med. service VA Hosp., Tampa, Fla., 1972-80, adminstrv. officer, med. service, 1981—; adminstrv. officer dept. internal medicine U. So. Fla. Coll. Medicine, Tampa, 1972—. Mem. bus. edn. adv. com. J. Everett Light Career Center, Indpls., 1969-72. Mem. Adminstrs. of Internal Medicine Assn., Med. Group Mgmt. Assn., Nat. Notary Assn., Nat. Assn. Female Execs. Inc., Am. Soc. Profl. and Exec. Women, Hillsborough County Med. Assts. Assn., Fla. Med. Group Mgmt. Assn., Acad. Practice Assembly. Office: Dept Internal Medicine 12901 Bruce B Downs Blvd Box 19 Tampa FL 33612

STEARS, SHARON LYNN, educator; b. Butte, Mont., May 21, 1957; d. Charles Fred and Virginia (Aleksich) S. BA, Mont. State U., 1979. Cert. tchr. Tchr., head coach Service High Sch., Anchorage, 1980-88, head gymnastics coach, 1980-88; head gymnastics coach Hanshew Jr. High Sch., Anchorage, 1980-88; trustee, adminstr. Hillside Gymnastics, Anchorage 1984-88. Mem. Nat. Fedn. High Sch. Coaches. Democrat. Roman Catholic. Home: 7548 Foxridge Way #F Anchorage AK 99518 Office: Robert Service High Sch 5577 Abbott Rd Anchorage AK 99507

STEBBINS, SHERYL BETH, retail company executive; b. Erie, Pa., May 23, 1953; d. Roger Harold and Helen Virginia (Shirley) S. BS in Communications Edn., Calif. U. of Pa., 1975. Store mgr. Waldenbooks, Erie, 1977-80; field trainer Waldenbooks, Stamford, Conn., 1980-81, asst. buyer, 1981-82, buyer books, 1982-85, mdse. mgr., 1985-87, dir. mdse. buying, 1987—. Republican. Methodist. Home: 208 Flax Hill Rd Apt 42 Norwalk CT 06854 Office: Waldenbooks 201 High Ridge Rd Stamford CT 06904

STEBER, ELEANOR, soprano; b. Wheeling, W.Va., July 17, 1914; d. William Charles and Ida A. (Nolte) S. MusB, New Eng. Conservatory Music, 1938; MusD (hon.), Bethany Coll., U. W.Va., Fla. So. Coll., Temple U., Ithaca Coll., Marshall Coll.; L.H.D. (hon.), Wheaton Coll., 1966; DFA, U. Oklahoma City.; DFA (hon.), U. Charleston. Head vocal dept. Cleve. Inst. Music, 1963-73; voice faculty Juilliard Sch. Music, 1971—, New Eng. Conservatory Music, 1971—, Phila. Music Acad., 1975; Bd. dirs. Bklyn. Opera Co., Opera Soc., Washington; founder, pres. Eleanor Steber Music Found., 1975—. Singer (1935); won: Met. Auditions of Air, spring 1940, with Met. Opera Co., 1940-66, San Francisco Opera Co., 1945, Central City Opera Festival, 1946, Cin. Summer Opera, 5 summers; appeared with Met., all maj. Am. opera cos., and, all maj. European festivals including, Glynbourne, 1948, Bayreuth, 1953, Florence, Italy, 1954, Salzburg, 1959, sang with, 7 opera cos. in, Yugoslavia, 1955, Vienna Staats Oper, 1956; soloist with, N.Y. Philharmonic, NBC, Boston, Mpls., Chgo., Cin., Kansas City, Denver, Montreal, Phila. Symphony orchs., others, makes radio, TV appearances; star of: TV's Voice of Firestone, 10 yrs; pres., Concert tours throughout, U.S., Can., Europe, Orient. Mem. Delta Omicron, Pi Kappa Lambda. Lutheran. Home: Box 342 Port Jefferson NY 11777 Office: 2109 Broadway New York NY 10023

STECKER, BONNIE YANKY, public relations executive; b. Balt., Dec. 1, 1958; d. Arthur Emil and Bette Emma (Muhl) Yanky; m. Richard George Stecker, Sept. 29, 1984; 1 child, Julie Marie. B.A., Salisbury State Coll., 1979. Pub. relations specialist Md. Nat. Bank, Balt., 1980-83; employee communications specialist Martin Marietta Aerospace, Balt., 1983-87, pub. relations officer Family and Children's Services of Cen. Md., 1987—. Mem. Internat. Assn. Bus. Communicators (treas. Balt. 1984), Phi Kappa Phi. Office: Family and Children Services of Cen Md 204 W Lanvale St Baltimore MD 21217

STECKLER, PATRICIA, clinical psychologist; b. Mt. Vernon, N.Y., Dec. 4, 1951; d. Seymour Sidney Steckler and Jane Faggen; m. Phiroz Maneck Bhagat, Oct. 13, 1979; children: Kay Hannah, Sarah Maneck. BA, Brandeis U., 1973; MA, Case Western Res. U., 1976, PhD, 1980. Lic. clin. psychologist, N.Y., N.J. Intern Cleve. VA Hosp., 1976-77; intern Albert Einstein Coll. Medicine, Bronx, N.Y., 1977-78, faculty psychologist, 1980-81; pvt. practice Westfield, N.J., 1984—. Mem. Am. Psychol. Assn., N.J. Assn. Women Therapists (v.p. 1986—, pres. 1988—), N.J. Psychol. Assn. (program chairperson 1987—). Office: 134 S Euclid Ave Westfield NJ 07090

STECKLER, PHYLLIS B., publishing company executive; b. N.Y.C.; d. Irwin H. and Bertha (Fellner) Schwartzbard; m. Stuart J. Steckler, June 3, 1956; children: Randall, SharonSteckler Slotky. BA, Hunter Coll., 1954; MA, NYU, 1957. Editorial dir. R.R. Bowker Co., N.Y.C., 1954-69, Crowell Collier Macmillan Info. Pub. Co., N.Y.C., 1969-71, Holt Rinehart & Winston Info. Systems, N.Y.C., 1971-73; pres., chief exec. officer Oryx Press, Scottsdale, Ariz., 1973-76, Phoenix, 1976—. Elected to Hunter Coll. Hall of Fame, 1985. Mem. ALA, Spl. Library Assn., Ariz. Library Assn., Calif. Library Assn., Am. Soc. for Info. Sci. Club: Univ. (Phoenix). Home: 5024 N 45th Pl Phoenix AZ 85018 Office: Oryx Press 2214 N Central at Encanto Phoenix AZ 85004

STECKMAN, MAUREEN JEANETTE, service company executive; b. Elyria, Ohio, May 22, 1951; d. Alfred W. and Geraldine (Leonard) Gerhart; m. Ralph Arthur Steckman; children: Randall James, Ryan Paul, Justus Erin, Aaron Kristopher. Student, Baldwin-Wallace Coll., Berea, Ohio, 1969-70, Alverno Coll., Milw., 1970-71. Mgr. fine jewelry MayCo Dept. Stores, North Olmsted, Ohio, 1969; asst. mgr. Trust House Forte Hotels, N.Y.C., 1970-72; sales mgr. Hotel Roosevelt, N.Y.C., 1972-75; owner, seminar instr. Creative Natural Foods, throughout N.E. Ohio, 1975-83; regional sales mgr. Hotel Systems Internat., Los Angeles, 1983-84; sales mgr. Gateway Plaza Holiday Inn, La Mirada, Calif., 1984-85; pres., owner Am. Semco, Belgrade, Mont., 1986—; dir. sales and mktg. Am. Semco, Sheraton, Missoula, Mont., 1988—. Council City of Belgrade, 1987—; program chmn., mem. precinct com. Rep. Women of Ballatin County. Mem. Nat. Assn. Female Execs. Office: Am Semco Inc 108 N Weaver St Belgrade MT 59714

STEED, DIANE K., government official; b. Hutchinson, Kans., Nov. 29, 1945. B.S., U. Kans., 1967. Mgmt. analyst Contract Adminstrn. Services, Def. Supply Agy. Dept. Def., Washington, 1968-72; sr. budget analyst ACTION, Washington, 1972-73; mgmt. assoc. Office of Mgmt. & Budget, 1973-78, chief regulatory policy br., 1978-81; dep. adminstr. Nat. Hwy. Traffic Safety Adminstrn., Washington, 1981-83, adminstr., 1983—. Office: Nat Hwy Traffic Safety Adminstrn Dept Transp 400 7th St Sw Washington DC 20590 *

STEEL, CLAUDIA WILLIAMSON, artist; b. Van Nuys, Calif., Mar. 19, 1918; d. James Gordon and Ella (Livingston) Williamson; B.A. in Art, U. Calif., Berkeley, 1939, secondary credential, 1940; M.F.A., Mills Coll., 1978; m. Lowell F. Steel, Aug. 15, 1941; children—Claudia Steel Rosen, Dogulas Lowell, Roger Conant. Tchr. art Greenville Jr./Sr. High Sch., Calif., 1940-42; faculty Calif. State U., Chico, 1967-69; pvt. tchr. art, Chico; one-woman shows include: Laboudt Gallery, San Francisco, 1958, Witherspoon Bldg., Phila., 1959, traveling show with Old Bergen Guild to nat. galleries, 1971-84, Redding (Calif.) Mus., 1973, Central Wyo. Mus. Art, Casper, 1976, U. Portland 1976, U. Wis., LaCrosse, 1978, Purdue U., West Lafayette, Ind., 1979, Pratt Inst., Manhatten Gallery, N.Y.C., 1980, Creative Arts Ctr., Chico, Calif., 1980, 84; exhibited in group shows at: Santa Barbara Art Mus., 1951, San Francisco Arts Festival (award), 1953, Oakland Art Mus., 1954, San Francisco Women Artists juried shows, 1958, 68 (award), 72, 73, 75, 76, Crocker Mus., Sacramento, 1958, 59, 60, 65, 67 (award), 73, Richmond Mus. (Calif.), 1960, DeYoung Mus. Art, San Francisco, 1960, San Francisco Mus. Art, 1959, 61 (award), Legion of Honor Mus., San Francisco, 1960, Mills Coll. Gallery, 1962, 67, 78, Berkeley Art Ctr. Gallery, 1969, San Francisco Art Commn. Gallery, 1972, Brandeis U., Mass., 1973, Ohio State U., Columbus, 1973, Brandt Gallery, Glendale, Calif., 1978, 1987, Chico State U., 1979, 1987, Fisher Gallery, Chico, Walnut Creek Art Gallery and Sonoma State U., 1979, Pratt Inst., Manhattan Gallery, N.Y.C., 1980, 1980, Calif. Soc. Printmakers traveling show, 1981, juried show, Singapore and Switzerland, 1984, Purdue U., 1982, U. Wis.-Eau Claire, 1982, Nat. Gallery, Bangkok, Malmo, Sweden, 1984-86, gallery show, Tokyo, 1985, Pacific Art League Gallery, Palo Alto, Calif., 1986, others. Bd. dirs. Creative Art Ctr., Chico, 1977-81, Omni Arts, Chico, 1979-82. Recipient San Francisco Mus. of Art Serigraphy award, 1961; trustees' scholar Mills Coll., 1935, others. Mem. Calif. Soc. Printmakers (v.p., dir. 1973-77), Los Angeles Printmakers Soc., others. Republican.

STEEL, DANIELLE FERNANDE, author; b. N.Y.C., Aug. 14, 1947; d. John and Norma (Stone) Schuelein-Steel. Student, Parsons Sch. Design, 1963, NYU, 1963-67. Vice pres. pub. relations and new bus. Supergirls Ltd., N.Y.C., 1968-71; copywriter Grey Advt., San Francisco, 1973-74. Author novels Going Home, 1973, Passion's Promise, 1977, Now and Forever, 1978, The Promise, 1978, Season of Passion, 1979, Summers End, 1979, To Love Again, 1980, The Ring, 1981, Loving, 1980, Love, 1981, Remembrance, 1981, Palomino, 1981, Once in a Lifetime, 1982, Crossings, 1982, A Perfect Stranger, 1982, Thurston House, 1983, Changes, 1983, Full Circle, 1984, Family Album, 1985, Secrets, 1985, Wanderlust, 1986, Fine Things, 1987, Kaleidoscope, 1987, Zoya, 1988; (non-fiction) Having a Baby, 1984; contbr. poetry to mags., including Cosmopolitan, McCall's, Ladies Home Jour., Good Housekeeping. Office: care Dell Pubs Dell Pub Co Inc One Dag Hammarskjold Plaza New York NY 10017

STEEL, DAWN, movie production company executive; b. N.Y.C., Aug. 19, 1946; m. Charles Roven; 1 child, Rebecca. Student in mktg., Boston U., 1964-65; student in mktg., NYU, 1966-67. Sportswriter Major League Baseball Digest and NFL, N.Y.C., 1968-69; editor Penthouse Mag., N.Y.C., 1969-74; pres. O'Dawn, Inc., N.Y.C., 1975-78; merchandising cons. Playboy mag., N.Y.C., 1978-79; v.p. merchandising Paramount Pictures, N.Y.C., 1979-80; sr. v.p. prodn. Paramount Pictures, Los Angeles, 1980-85, pres. prodn., 1985-87; pres. Columbia Pictures Internat., New York, 1987—; mem. bd. trustees Am. Film Inst. Served as prodn. co. pres. for numerous feature films including, Flashdance, Footloose, Top Gun, Star Trek IV, Beverly Hills Cop II, The Untouchables, Fatal Attraction, 1985-87. Active Neil Bogart Cancer Found., Calif. Abortion Rights Action League, Los Angeles, AIDS Project Los Angeles. Mem. Acad. Motion Picture Arts and Scis. Office: Columbia Pictures Office of the Pres Columbia Plaza Burbank CA 91505

STEEL, ROBIN PATRICIA, software engineer; b. South Bend, Ind., Mar. 8, 1953; d. Munro Hubbard and Gloria Robbins (Crawford) S.; m. John Michael Corliss, June 18, 1976 (div. Feb. 1985); m. James Edward O'Bryant, Nov. 14, 1985: 1 stepchild, Erin Louise. BS in Engring., Purdue U., 1974; MS in Engring. Mechanics, Ga. Inst. Tech., 1976. Mktg. engr. Linde div. Union Carbide Corp., Tarryton, N.Y., 1976-77; region engr. Merrillville, Ind., 1977-78; project engr. environ. activities staff Gen. Motors Corp., Warren, Mich., 1978-80; engr. Vitro Corp. (formerly Vitro Labs.), Silver Spring, Md., 1980-81, project supr., 1981-82, asst. group supr. div. Automated Industries, 1982-84, project head, 1984-87, group supr., 1987—. Mem. NSPE (bd. govs. 1982-86), Md. Soc. Profl. Engrs. (div. chmn. 1982-86, treas. Potomac chpt. 1982-83, sec. 1987—). Home: 18708 Willow Grove Rd Olney MD 20832 Office: Vitro Corp 14000 Georgia Ave Silver Spring MD 20906-2972

STEELE, ANA MERCEDES, government official; b. Niagara Falls, N.Y., Jan. 18, 1939; d. Sydney and Mercedes (Hernandez) S.; m. John Hunter Clark, June 2, 1979. A.B. magna cum laude, Marywood Coll., 1958. Actress, 1959-64; sec. Nat. Endowment for Arts, Washington, 1965-67, dir. budget and research, 1968-75, dir. planning, 1976-78, dir. program coordination, sr. exec. service, 1979-81, assoc. dep. chmn. for programs, dir. program coordination, sr. exec. service, 1982—; guest lectr. George Washington U., 1987. Author, editor report: History of the National Council on the Arts and National Endowment for the Arts During the Johnson Administration, 1968; editor: Museums USA (Fed. Design Council award of Excellence 1975), 1974; National Endowment Arts 1965-1985; A Brief Chronology of Federal Involvement in the Arts, 1985. Former reader Rec. for the Blind, N.Y.C.; former tutor Future for Jimmy, Washington. Named Disting. Grad. in Field of Arts, Marywood Coll., 1976; recipient Sustained Superior Performance award Nat. Endowment for Arts, Washington, 1980, Disting. Service award, 1983, 84, 85. Mem. Actors' Equity Assn., Screen Actors Guild, Delta Epsilon Sigma, Kappa Gamma Pi. Office: Nat Endowment for Arts Nancy Hanks Ctr 1100 Pennsylvania Ave NW Washington DC 20506

STEELE, ANDREA WHITE, personnel director; b. Washington, June 1, 1955; d. Raymond Benjamin and Elizabeth Mae (Koons) White; m. Michael William Steele, Apr. 26, 1980 (div. 1984). B.A. in Behavioral Sci., U. Md., 1977; M.Bus., Central Mich. U., 1982; postgrad. in law U. Balt. Employment rep. Dart Drug Corp., Landover, Md., 1977-79; employment supr. Duron Paints and Wallcoverings, Beltsville, Md., 1979-81, dir. personnel, 1981—; guest speaker profl. assns. Editor: Law Forum, U. Balt. Bd. dirs. Laurel/Beltsville unit Am. Cancer Soc. Mem. Am. Soc. Personnel Adminstrn., Washington Personnel Assn., Washington Retail Bd. Trade, Sigma Iota Epsilon, Kappa Kappa Gamma. Republican. Methodist. Office: Duron Paints and Wallcoverings 10406 Tucker St Beltsville MD 20705

STEELE, ANITA (MARGARET ANNE MARTIN), law librarian, legal educator; b. Haines City, Fla., Dec. 30, 1927; d. Emmett Edward and Esther Majulia (Phifer) Martin; m. Thomas Dinsmore Steele, June 10, 1947 (div. 1969); children—Linda Frances, Roger Dinsmore, Thomas Garrick, Carolyn Anne; m. James E. Beaver, Mar. 1980. B.A., Radcliffe Coll., 1948; J.D., U. Va., 1971; M.Law Librarianship, U. Wash., 1972. Asst. prof. law U. Puget Sound, Tacoma, 1972-74, assoc. prof. law, 1974-79, prof. law, 1979—, dir. law library, 1972—. Contbr. articles to profl. jours.; mem. editorial adv. bds. various law book pubs., 1980—. Treas., Congl. Campaign Orgn., Tacoma, 1978, 80; mem. adv. bd. Clover Park Vocat.-Tech. Sch., Tacoma, 1980-82. Mem. Am. Assn. Law Libraries, Internat. Assn. Law Libraries, Am. Soc. Info. Sci. Republican. Home: 1502 Fernside Dr S Tacoma WA 98465 Office: U Puget Sound Sch of Law 950 Broadway Tacoma WA 98402

STEELE, ELIZABETH ANN, civic counselor-advocate, community organizer; b. Indpls., Oct. 27, 1942; d. Richard Monticue and Betty (Kalleen) S. B.A., Butler U., 1965; M.Counseling, Ariz. State U., 1979. VISTA vol. OEO, Winnebago Indian Reservation, Nebr., 1966-67; community organizer-developer Bd. Global Ministries, United Meth. Ch., Cheyenne-Arapaho Tribe, Okla., 1968-70, Cherokee Tribe, N.C., 1970-73, Buffalo Creek, W.Va., 1973-76; counselor/adv. New Directions for Young Women, Tucson, 1980—; mem. Okla. Gov.'s Council on Children and Youth, 1969-70, Watonga City Planning Council, 1969-70, Buffalo Creek Citizen's Adv. Council, 1974-76, Second 40 Survival, Tucson, 1983-84, City of Tucson Rape Task Force, 1984—. Support person Take Back the Night, Tucson, 1983—, Surging Wave Womyn, Tucson, 1984. Recipient Extraordinary/Ordinary Woman award, 1984; Eli Lilly Found. scholar, 1963. Mem. Affirmation (charter), Possible Human Soc., Tucson Women's Network (co-founder 1981), NOW, Tucson Networking Task Force, Am. Cetacean Soc., Pi Lambda Theta, Kappa Kappa Gamma. Democrat. Methodist. Avocations: camping; snorkeling; tidepooling; travel; writing. Home: 7335 E 28th St Tucson AZ 85710 Office: New Dirs for Young Women 209 S Tucson Blvd Suite F Tucson AZ 85716

STEELE, ELLEN LIVELY, business development executive, publishing executive; b. Fayette County, W.Va., Jan. 22, 1936; d. Alfred French and Sarah Ellen (Pritchard) L.; student N.Mex. State U., 1962-74; m. Henry Gilmer Steele, July 20, 1981; children—Gregory Benjamin Pake, Seana Ellen Pake. Civilian adminstrv. officer Dept. Army, White Sands Missile Range, N.Mex., 1962-67; mgr. Kelly Services Inc., Las Cruces, N.Mex., 1967-85; pres. Lively Enterprises, Inc., Las Cruces, 1967-76; sec., treas. Adam II, Ltd., Las Cruces, 1973-77; pres. Symposium Internat. Inc., Las Cruces, 1977-78, Asset & Resource Mgmt. Corp., Organ, N.Mex., 1978-83; lit. agt., prin. Ellen Lively Steele & Assos., 1979—; mng. partner AVVA III, Las Cruces, 1981-82, Internat. Alliance Sports Ofcls., Las Cruces, 1982—; mng. ptnr. Steele Lehnert, 1986—; ptnr., exec. producer Triple L Prodns., 1986—; dir. mktg. Los Cruces Conv.and Visitors Bur., 1984-85; dir. Santa Rosa Resources Corp., Denver; exec. GASCO Internat. Inc., Las Cruces, 1981-82; mem. N.Mex. State Senate, 1985—, co-chmn. higher edn. reform com., 1985, 86, mem. interim coms., jud. com., edn. com., criminal justice com., Human Needs & Aids com.; mem. nat. conf. state legislatures; N.Mex. Federated Rep. Women, Am. Legis. Exchange Commn.; mem. task force El Paso Electric Co. Rate Moderation; mem. firearms preemtion statute rev. Served with USAF, 1954-57. Mem. Internat. Assn. Fin. Planners, Sales and Mktg. Execs. Internat., Am. Mgmt. Assn., DAR. Episcopalian. Clubs: Order Eastern Star; Picacho Hills Country (Co-chmn. bd. dirs. 1980-84) (Las Cruces). Home: PO Drawer 447 Organ NM 88052

STEELE, EVELYN JANE, public relations and advt. agy. exec.; b. Berkeley, Calif., Feb. 14, 1911; d. Carlos Louis and Jane Catherine (Jensen) de Clairmont; grad. Munson Bus. Coll., San Francisco, 1929-30; m. Donald Dickinson Steele, May 8, 1932; 1 son, Donald de Clairmont. Pvt. sec., 1930-32; engaged in public relations, publicity and advt., 1940—; v.p., dir. Steele Group, San Francisco, 1977—; sec.-treas. Internat. Pub. Relations Co., Ltd., San Francisco; sec.-treas. Internat. Bus. Interface, Inc., Don Steele Advt. Pres. Ladies Aid Retarded Children, San Francisco, 1977-78, bd. dirs., 1978-88. Mem. Fashion Group (regional dir. 1965-67). Republican. Unitarian. Clubs: Metropolitan (dir. 1961-68), Order Rainbow Girls. Office: 703 Market St San Francisco CA 94103

STEELE, HILDA HODGSON, retired home economist, consultant; b. Wilmington, Ohio, Mar. 24, 1911; d. George and Mary Jane (Rolston) Hodgson; AA, Wilmington Coll., 1931, BS, 1935; MA in Home Econs. Edn., Ohio State U., 1941; postgrad. Ohio U., 1954, Miami U., 1959; m. John C. Steele (dec. Jan. 1973). Tchr., Brookville (Ohio) Elementary Sch., 1932-37; tchr. home econs. Lincoln Jr. High Sch., Dayton (Ohio) Pub. Schs., 1937-40, coordinator home econs. dept., traveling exptl. home econs. tchr., 1940-45, supr. home econs., 1945-81, cons., 1981—; program dir. Family Life Adult Disadvantaged Program, 1969-81. Mem. Ohio Farm Electrification Com., 1964-66. Mem. town and country br. career com. Miami Valley br. YMCA, 1948-59. Adv. bd. Dayton Sch. Practical Nursing, 1951—; adv. com. Dayton Miami Valley Hosp. Sch. Nursing, 1951-63; jr. adv. com. Montgomery County chpt. ARC, 1940-80; mem. com. United Appeal, 1970—; bd. dirs. (Ohio) FHA-HERO, 1979-81. Recipient Outstanding Service recognition Dayton Met. Girl Scouts U.S., 1987. Mem. Dayton area Nutrition Council, Am. Home Econs. Assn. (del. 1961), Ohio Home Econs. Assn. (chmn. elem. and secondary edn. com. 1947-51, co-chmn. ann. conv. 1961-77, mem. housing and equipment coms. 1965-68, chmn. found. com. 1979-81), Dayton Met. Home Econs. Assn. (pres. 1949-50, 60-61); Nat., Ohio edn. assns., Ohio Council Local Adminstrs., Dayton Sch. Adminstrs. Assn., Elec. Women's Round Table, Dayton City Sch. Mgmt. Assn. (charter), Ohio Vocat. Assn. (Disting. Service award 1981), Am. Vocat. Edn. Assn., Ohio Vocat. Edn. Assn., Phi Upsilon Omicron (hon.). Mem. Ch. of Christ. Mem. Order Eastern Star. Club: Zonta (pres. Dayton 1950-52). Research in pub. sch. food habits, 1957. Home: 1443 State Route 380 Xenia OH 45385

STEELE, KATHLEEN PATRICIA, science educator; b. Staten Island, N.Y., Sept. 18, 1950; d. Thomas Leo and Patricia Marguerite (Hinman) S. BA, Caldwell Coll., 1972; PhD, W.Va. U., 1977. Postdoctoral trainee Inst. for Cancer Research, Phila., 1977-79; asst. prof. biology Moravian Coll., Bethlehem, Pa., 1979-86; sci. tchr. Pius X High Sch., Bangor, Pa., 1986—; book reviewer coll. textbook pubs., 1983-86; health prof. adv. com. Lehigh Valley March of Dimes, Allentown, Pa., 1986-88. Mem. Audubon Soc., Nat. Wildlife Fedn., Hawk Mt. Wildlife Sanctuary, Lehigh Valley Conservancy. Mem. AAAS, Am. Soc. Microbiology, Am. Genetics Assn., Genetics Soc. Am., Nat. Assn. Advisors for Health Professions, Nat. Assn. Biology Tchrs., Nat. Sci. Tchrs. Assn., Am. Assn. Physics Tchrs., Am. Chem. Soc., Sigma Xi. Republican. Roman Catholic. Club: Great Books (co-leader 1980—). Office: Pius X High Sch 3d Ave and Division Sts Bangor PA 18013

STEELE, L. MARIKA, development and public relations executive; b. Honolulu, Feb. 22, 1963; d. William Alexander and Leila Meeri (Saavalainen) S. BA, Washington U., 1984; postgrad., Columbia U., 1987—. Programming dir. Sta. KWLLR Radio, St. Louis, 1983-84; media exec. Young and Rubicam, N.Y.C., 1984-86; devel. officer Double Discovery Ctr. Columbia U., N.Y.C., 1987—; cons. Body Know How, The Knitting Factory, N.Y., 1987—. Vol., cons. Planned Parenthood, N.Y., 1997—. Mem. Nat. Assn. Female Execs., Washington U. Alumni Club, Omicron Delta Kappa. Office: Columbia U Double Day Discovery Ctr 401 Ferris Booth Hall New York NY 10027

STEELE, LINDA DAIGLE, accountant; b. Haskell, Tex., Nov. 1, 1978; d. Elbert D. and Nadine (Booher) S.; m. Wayne E. Daigle, Dec. 23, 1973 (div. Feb. 1986); children: Forrest Daigle, Cami Daigle. BBA in Acctg. with highest honors, S.W. Tex. State U., 1973. Staff acct., office mgr. Baldridge & Co., CPA's, San Marcos, Tex., 1968-73; dir. tax R.A. Werner, Acct. Firm, Huntsville, Tex., 1974-79, Briedenthal & Reynolds CPA's, Huntsville, 1980-83; tax supr. Touche Ross & Co., Lincoln, Nebr., 1983-87, sr. mgr., 1987&. Loaned exec. United Way, Lincoln, 1985-86; bd. dirs. Nebr. Human Resources Found., Lincoln, 1986-87. Mem. Lincoln C. of C., Bus. and Profl. Women Club, Jr. Service League, Updowntowners, Beta Sigma Phi. Republican. Office: Touche Ross & Co 1040 NBC Ctr Suite 1040 Lincoln NE 68508

STEELE, MARIAN WILLIAMS, artist; b. Trenton, N.J., Jan. 4, 1916; d. Daniel and Mary (Phillips) Williams; m. Chauncey Depew Steele, Jr., Jan. 30, 1942 (div. 1965); children: Chum, Pam. Student, Sch. Indsl. Arts, 1930-33, Pa. Acad. Fine Arts, 1933-37, Albert Barnes Found., 1937-39. One woman shows include New Hope Gallery, Pa., 1940, Laguna Beach (Calif.) Art Galleries, 1943, Doll and Richard's Gallery,Boston, 1966, 68, 70, Rockport (Mass.) Art Assn., 1975-81, Arvest Galleries, Boston, 1975-76, Robinson Gallery, Miami, Fla., 1963, Babson Coll., Wellesley, Mass., 1980, Guild of Boston Artists, 1976-78, 80, 84, 86, Hudson Valley Art Assn., White Plains, N.Y., 1986; exhibited in numerous group shows including Allied Artists Am., N.Y.C., Springfield (Mass.) Mus., 1969, 72, 75, Springville (Utah) Mus., 1960-61, Am. Watercolor Soc., N.Y.C., 1975, 84, 86, Butler Mus. Am. Art, Youngstown, Ohio, 1981-83; represented in permanent collections including Oakland (Calif.) Mus., Andrew Mellon Collection, Pitts., John Hancock Mut. Life Ins. Co., Boston, Prudential of Boston, Brookline (Mass.) Hosp., State House, Trenton, 1st Nat. Bank Boston, The Presbyn. Hosp., N.Y.C., Rider Coll., Laurence, N.J., C. Brewer Collection, Honolulu, Lowal (Mass.) City Hall, Mary Bryan Meml. Gallerie, Jefferson Ville (Vt.) Art Ctr. Recipient numerous awards including 5 gold medals. Mem. Guild Boston Artists (bd. govs. 1979—), Am. Watercolor Soc., Acad. Art Assn., Springfield, Mass., No. Shore Art Assn., Rockport Art Assn., Knickerbocker Artists, N.Y.C., New Eng. Watercolor Soc., Salmagundi Club, N.Y.C., Hudson Valley Art Assn., Am. Artists Profl. League, N.Y.C. Home and Studio: 11 Salt Island Rd Gloucester MA 01930

STEELE, SHIRLEY MAY, nurse, educator; b. Waterbury, Conn., Nov. 26, 1932; d. Frank Steele and Edna (Clark) Geigle. BS, Columbia U., 1961, MA, 1963; PhD, Ohio State U., 1973. Assoc. prof. nursing SUNY, Buffalo, 1964-75; asst. dean, prof. nursing Tex. Woman's U., Houston, 1975-77; prof. nursing, assoc. dean U. Tex. at Galveston, 1978-84; dir. nursing div. Sparks Ctr. for Develop. and Learning Disorders, Birmingham, Ala., 1984—; co-dir. Heshi Computing Co., Hitchcock, Tex., 1981—. Author (with others): Values Clarification in Nursing, 1979 (Book of Yr. award 1980), Creativity in Nursing, 1981; author, editor: Health Promotion Child with Long Term Illness, 1983. Bd. dirs. St. Vincent's House, Galveston, 1980-84, Hospice, Galveston, 1981-84, Interfaith Hospitality House for Homeless Families, Birmingham, 1986—; mem. exec. com. United Way of Galveston, 1983. Mem. Am. Nurses Assn., Am. Assn. Mental Deficiency, Nat. League for Nursing (baccalaureate reviewer and higher degree accreditation bd. 1979-81), Creative Edn. Found. Episcopalian. Office: Sparks Ctr Devel Learning Disorders PO Box 313 University Sta Birmingham AL 35294

STEELEYSMITH, DEBORAH LYGIA, artist, human resources specialist and administrator; b. N.Y.C., Oct. 6, 1951; d. Ellis Robert and Deressa Doris (Moultrie) Steeley; m. Allan David Smith, Oct. 14, 1978; 1 child, DeMarisa Nona. B.A. in Psychology, Coll. Mt. St. Vincent, 1974; M.S.Ed., Fordham U., 1981. Cert. trainer group and Orgnl. Devel. Mental health counselor Harlem Hosp., N.Y.C., 1973-74, Project Create, N.Y.C., 1974-77; tng. specialist N.Y. State Bur. Tng. and Resource Devel., N.Y.C., 1978-82; dir. tng. and staff devel. Kirby Psychiat. Ctr., 1985, Manhattan Psychiat. Ctr., N.Y. State Office Mental Health, 1982-87; free-lance artist, tng. cons., N.Y.C., 1988—; trainer Gov.'s Office Employee Relations, State of N.Y. Cons. Nat. Inst. Drug Abuse, Adelphi U. Nat. Tng. Inst., Native N.Am. Drug and Alcohol Program, Yellowknife, N.W.T., Can., Native N.Am. Tng. and Support System, Winnipeg, Alta., Can., 1984, 85, others, 1977—; active PBS-Channel 13, N.Y.C., 1971—. Cert. trainer Nat. Drug Abuse Tng. Center. Mem. N.Y. Zool. Soc. Democrat. Home and Office: 430 W 125th St New York NY 10027

STEENBERG, MARIE TERESA (TERI), municipal offical; b. Portsmouth, Va., Sept. 26, 1954; d. Frank Joseph and Mary Jane (Radel) Miller; m. Clayton Wallace Steenberg Jr., Nov. 2, 1974. Grad. high sch., Magna, Utah. Sec., bookkeeper Utah Idaho Sch. Supply, Salt Lake City, 1972-73; sec., police matron Keokuk (Iowa) Police Dept., 1973-78; clk. City Assessors Office, Keokuk, 1978-79, chief dep. assessor, 1979—. Mem. Nat. Assn. Master Appraisers, Iowa State Assn. Assessors, Internat. Assn. Assessing Officers, Southeast Dist. Assessors (sec.-treas. 1986—). Roman Catholic. Office: City Assessor's Office 425 Blondeau PO Box 966 Keokuk IA 52632

STEENBURGEN, MARY, actress; b. Newport, Ariz., 1953; m. Malcolm McDowell, 1980; children: Lilly, Charlie. Student, Neighborhood Playhouse. Films: Goin' South, 1978, Ragtime, 1981, A Midsummer Night's Sex Comedy, 1982, Time After Time, 1979, Romantic Comedy, 1983, Cross Creek, 1983, Melvin and Howard (Oscar for best supporting actress), 1980, One Magic Christmas, 1985, Dead of Winter, 1987, End of the Line, 1987, also exec. producer, The Whales of August, 1987; appeared in Showtime TV's Faerie Tale Theatre prodn. of Little Red Riding Hood and (miniseries) Tender Is the Night, 1985; TV films: The Attic: The Hiding of Anne Frank, 1988; theater appearance Holiday, Old Vic, London, 1987. Office: care Internat Creative Mgmt 8899 Beverly Blvd Los Angeles CA 90048 *

STEFAN, PEGGY SEHLIN, marketing communications executive; b. Mpls., Feb. 19, 1960; d. Arthur Andrew and Zana (Windahl) Sehlin; m. Scott L. Stefan, July 23, 1983. B.S. in Bus. Fin., Mont. State U., 1981. Lic. stockbroker. Registered rep. Investors Diversified Services, Mpls., 1981-83; mktg. rep., tng. cons. Golle & Holmes Fin. Learning, Mpls. and N.Y.C., 1983-84; dir. mktg. communications Integrated Resources Equity Corp., N.Y.C., 1984-88, v.p. regional br. office Integrated Resources Equity Corp., 1988— ; owner Equinox, Inc., East Rutherford, N.J., 1985—. Recipient sales achievement awards Investors Diversified Services, 1982. Mem. Internat. Assn. Fin. Planners, Nat. Assn. Female Execs., Mont. State U. Alumni Assn., Pi Beta Phi. Avocations: skiing; travel. Office: Integrated Resources Equity Corp 733 3d Ave New York NY 10017

STEFANATOS, JOANNE, veterinarian; b. N.Y.C., Aug. 26, 1945; d. Fotios and Adele (Zaferatos) Stefanatos; m. David Ross Hetzel, June 26, 1983. B.S. in Zoology, U. Nev., 1967; D.V.M., U. Mo., 1972; postgrad. (fellow) St. Louis U., 1967-68. Vet. surgeon Paradise Pet Clinic, Las Vegas, 1972-73; vet. surgeon, bird specialist Angel Nev. Pet Clinic, Las Vegas, 1973-74; owner, veterinarian, hosp. dir. Animal Kingdom Vet. Hosp., Las Vegas, 1974—; Nev. wildlife veterinarian, 1972—; Nev. commr. of fish and game, 1977-80; co-owner Animal Emergency Clinic, Las Vegas, 1978-80, Animal Birth Control Clinic; Patentee in field; contbr. articles to profl. jours. Bd. dirs. Animal Rescue Found., 1979-83; chmn. CCVMA Ethics Com., 1975-77. Mem. Am. Animal Hosp. Assn., Holistic Vet. Med. Soc., Am. Assn. Zoo Veterinarians, Soc. Ultramolecular Medicine (bd. dirs.), Am. Radiologists Soc., Clark County Vet. Assn., Tri Penta, Phi Zeta. Democrat. Greek Orthodox. Home: 379 Desert Palm Dr Las Vegas NV 89124 Office: Animal Kingdom Vet Hosp 1325 Vegas Valley Dr Las Vegas NV 89109

STEFANICK, PATTI ANN, surgeon; b. Elizabeth, N.J., Sept. 25, 1957; d. John Joseph and Johanna (Breza) S. BA in Biol. Scis., Rutgers U., 1979; DO, U. New England, Biddeford, Maine, 1983. Intern Kennedy Meml. Hosps., Stratford, N.J., 1983-84; resident in gen. surgery, chief resident Met. Hosp., Phila., 1984-88; breas cancer fellow Meml. Sloan-Kettering Cancer Ctr., N.Y.C., 1988—. Mem. AMA, Am. Osteopathic Assn., N.J. Assn. Osteopathic Physicians and Surgeons (alumni com. 1988), Pa. Osteopathic Med. Assn., Rutgers Alumni Assn. Democrat. Roman Catholic. Club: Rutger's Scarlet R (new Brunswick, N.J.). Home and Office: 1708 Linden Hill Apts Lindenwold NJ 08021

STEFANIK, JEAN MARIANNE, educator; b. Springfield, Mass., June 10, 1949; d. Edward Carl and Suzanne Florence (Chelkonas) S. BS in Elem. Edn., Am. Internat. Coll.; MEd, Norwich U.; then postgrad. studies; postgrad., U. Vt., Merrimack Valley Coll., Franklin Pierce Coll., U. Mass. Reading specialist Easthampton (Mass.) Schs., 1973-74; dir. curriculum Barre (Vt.) Town Sch. Dist., 1974-80; attended edn. tchr., Amherst, N.H., 1980—; part-time educator Radio Shack Computer Center, Tandy Corp., Manchester, N.H., 1981-82; part-time instr. Notre Dame Coll., Manchester, 1981-83, Merrimack Valley Coll., 1981-86, U. N.H. Sch. for Lifelong Learning, 1982-87. Mem. Assn. Supervision and Curriculum Devel. (bd. dirs. 1979-80, 82-87), Vt. Assn. Supervision and Curriculum Devel. (pres. 1979-80, treas. 1977-79), N.H. Assn. Supervision and Curriculum Devel. (pres. 1982-84, 86-87), Phi Delta Kappa, Alpha Chi. Home: PO Box 6464 Nashua NH 03063 Office: Wilkins Sch Boston Post Rd Amherst NH 03031

STEFANKO, LEONA EVANS, religious educator, administrator; b. Chgo., Jan. 25, 1945; d. Hyman and Sophie Shapiro; m. George Stefanko. BA in Religion, Ottawa U., 1985; MA in Religion, Park Coll., 1988. Ordained to ministry, Unity Ch., 1986. Instr. Unity Sch. Christianity, Unity Village, Mo., 1985-86, dept. chmn., 1986—. Active theatre, U.S., Can., South Am., Asia, 1963-76. Office: Unity Sch of Christianity Unity Village MO 64065

STEFCHAK, LINDA FAITH, banker; b. Harrisburg, Pa., May 9, 1959; d. Martha Jean (Neiman) Zidick; m. Harry Joseph Stefchak Jr., Sept. 3, 1981. BA in History, Dickinson Coll., 1981. Realtor Adler Better Homes and Gardens, Camp Hill, Pa., 1981-84, Hoopes Better Homes and Gardens, Media, Pa., 1984; v.p. lending Sharon Sav. Bank, Darby, Pa., 1984—. Sec. Marcus Hook Mary P. Campbell Library Bd., 1986; bd. dirs. Marcus Hook Community Devel. Corp., 1986, Chichester (Pa.) Sch. Dist., 1987. Republican. Home: 27 W Third St Marcus Hook PA 19023 Office: Sharon Sav Bank 9 Chester Pike Darby PA 19061

STEFFEY, LELA, state legislator, banker; b. Idaho Falls, Idaho, Aug. 8, 1928; d. Orawell and Mary Ethel (Owen) Gardner; m. Carl A. Hendershott, Jr., Apr. 16, 1949 (div. 1961); children: Barry G., Bradley Carl, Barton P.; m. 2d Warren D. Steffey, July 13, 1973; children: Dean, Wayne, Luann, Scott, Susan. Grad. Am. Inst. Banking, 1972. With Pacific Tel. & Tel., San Diego, 1948-49, Bank of Am., San Diego, 1949-52, Gen. Dynamics/Astro, San Diego, 1960-61; escrow officer, mgr. consumer loans Bank of Am., San Diego, 1961-73; real estate agt. Steffey Realty, Mesa, Ariz., 1978—; mem. Ariz. Ho. of Reps, Phoenix, 1982-86, vice chmn. banking and ins. com., 1982-86, mem. house appropriations, judiciary, counties and municipalities coms., 1982—, chmn. counties and municpalities com., 1987—, chmn. appropriations sub-com. Founder, Citizens Com. Against Domestic Abuse; precinct com. Legis. Dist. 29, 1978—, dep. registrar, 1978—; pres. Mesa Rep. Women, 1980; chmn. Mesa Mus. Adv. bd., 1981-83; del. to conv. Nat. Fedn. Rep. Women, Colo., 1981, del. to Rep. Nat. Conv., Dallas, 1984. Bd. dirs. Mesa Community Council, 1985-88. Mem. Nat. Order Women Legislators (v.p. 1987-88, sec.), Am. Mothers Assn., Nat. Fedn. Rep. Women, Ariz. Fedn. Rep. Women (dir.), Ariz. Assn. of Women (dir.), Am. Legis. Exchange Council, Pi Beta Phi. Mem. Ch. of Jesus Christ of Latter-Day Saints. Home: 1439 E Ivyglen St Mesa AZ 85203 Office: Ariz Ho Reps 1700 W Washington Phoenix AZ 85007

STEGEMOELLER, SUSAN WARNER, loan specialist; b. Rochester, N.Y., July 20, 1956; d. Harold J. and Jeannette (Nichols) Warner; m. James Fred Stegemoeller, July 28, 1979; 1 child, Jennifer Lynn. BA, Miami U., Oxford, Ohio, 1978; postgrad. Xavier U. Loan specialist HUD, Columbus, Ohio, 1978-79, Cin., 1979-83; fin. planner IDS Fin. Services, Inc., Cin., 1983-86, Manufacturer's Hanover Mortgage Corp., 1986, Shawmut Mortgage Corp., 1986-87, U.S. Dept. HUD, St. Louis, 1987—; housing cons., Cin., 1985—. Author: Community Land Coop. Residents' Handbook, 1986. Adv., Cin. Tech. Coll., 1984—; mem. fin. com. Community Land Coop., Cin., 1985—; exhibits chair Conf. Cin. Women, 1985, corp. patrons chair, 1986, conf. coordinator, 1987—; vol. Am. Cancer Soc., 1981-84. Recipient profl. awards; Mercury awards IDS, Cin., 1984. Mem. Nat. Assn. Female Execs. Republican. Roman Catholic. Avocations: reading, gardening, making teddy bears, softball, theater. Home: 771 Seven Hills Ln Saint Charles MO 63303 Office: US Dept HUD 210 N Tucker Blvd Saint Louis MO 63101

STEIDLEY, WILMA LOUISE, gas transmission company administrative analyst; b. Carlinville, Ill., Oct. 19, 1935; d. Charles Oliver and Mary Ann (Greenwalt) Uder; m. Walter Ray Steidley, Sept. 17, 1955; children: Kevin Ray, Cindy Louise, Cheryl Lynne. Student, Blackburn U., 1953-55; BA in Mgmt., Sangamon State U., 1981. Bank teller Wemple State Bank, Waverly, Ill., 1964-70; sec. Panhandle Ea. Pipe Line Co., Waverly, 1970-76, Glenarm, Ill., 1976-80, Springfield, Ill., 1980-83; adminstrv. analyst Panhandle Ea. Pipe Line Co., Indpls., 1983—. Tutor ESL, Indpls., 1987. Mem. Nat. Assn. for Female Execs. Office: Panhandle Ea Pipe Line Co 5980 W 71st Indianapolis IN 46278

STEIGER, JANET DEMPSEY, government official; b. Oshkosh, Wis., June 10, 1939; 1 son, William Raymond. B.A., Lawrence Coll., 1961; postgrad. U. Reading (Eng.), 1961-62, U. Wis., 1962-63. Legis. corr. Office of Gov. Wis., 1965; v.p. The Work Place, 1975-80; commr. Postal Rate Commn., Washington, 1980—, acting chmn., 1981-82, chmn., 1982—. Chmn. Commn. on Vets. Edn. Policy, 1987—. Author: Law Enforcement and Juvenile Justice in Wisconsin, 1965; co-author: To Light One Candle, a Handbook on Organizing, Funding and Maintaining Public Service Projects, 1978, 2d edit., 1980. Woodrow Wilson scholar; Fulbright scholar, 1961. Mem. Phi Beta Kappa. Office: Postal Rate Commn Office of the Chmn 1333 H St NW Suite 300 Washington DC 20268 *

STEIN, ADLYN ROBINSON (MRS. HERBERT ALFRED STEIN), jewelry company executive; b. Pitts., May 8, 1908; d. Robert Stewart and Pearl (Geiger) Robinson; Mus.B., Pitts. Mus. Inst., U. Pitts., 1928; m. F. J. Hollearn, Nov. 14, 1929 (dec.); children—Adlyn (Mrs. Brandon J. Hickey), Frances (Mrs. Ralph A. Gleim); m. Allen Burnett Williams, Dec. 5, 1955 (dec.); m. Herbert Alfred Stein, Nov. 28, 1963 (dec. Oct. 1980); 1 dau., Rachel Lynn (Mrs. Stephen M. Kampfer). Treas., R. S. Robinson, Inc., Pitts., 1947—. Mem. Tuesday Musical Club, Pitts.; former mem. women's com. Cleve. Orch. Mem. DAR. Republican. Anglican. Clubs: Duquesne, University, South Hills Country (Pitts.); Lakewood Country, Clifton (Cleve.). Home: 22200 Lake Rd Rocky River OH 44116

STEIN, BARBARA LAMBERT, marriage and family therapist; b. Detroit, Feb. 10, 1945; d. Joseph J. and Sylvia (Siegel) Lambert; m. David Joel Stein, Jan. 1, 1967; children—Craig Andrew, Todd Alexander. Student psychology Mich. State U., 1962-64; B.A. in Sociology, Wayne State U., 1966, postgrad. in psychiat. social work, 1972-74; M.S. in Counseling Psychology, Nova U., 1980; student, Art Inst. Ft. Lauderdale, 1985. Vol. abuse and neglect dept. Wayne County Juvenile Ct., Detroit, 1964-65; vol. D.J. Healy Shelter for Children, 1965-67; med. social worker Hutzel Hosp., Detroit, 1967-68; developer neighborhood teen drug program City of West Bloomfield (Mich.), 1970-71; med. social worker Extended Care Facilities, Inc., Birmingham, Mich., 1972-73; vol. group and occupational therapist Henderson Psychiat. Clinic Day Treatment Ctr., Ft. Lauderdale, Fla., 1977-78; pvt. practice family and marital therapy, Deerfield Beach, Coral Springs, and Boca Raton, Fla., 1980-85. Mem. Boca Raton Museum of Art (exec. chmn. antique show, sale and gala dinner fundraiser, 1988), The Friends of Photography, San Francisco, Mothers Against Drunk Driving, Sch. Edn. Bd. Temple Beth El of Boca Raton, until 1985; founding mem. Levis Jewish Community Ctr., Boca Raton. Recipient cert. of Meritorious Achievement, Henderson Psychiat. Clinic Day Treatment Ctr. Mem. Am. Assn. Marriage and Family Therapy (assoc.), Am. Psychol. Assn. (assoc.), Wayne State U. Alumni Assn., Nova U. Alumni Assn., Photogroup Miami, Camera Club of Boca Raton, Friends of Photography of San Francisco, Nat. Trust Historic Preservation, Opera Soc. Ft. Lauderdale, Zool. Soc. Fla., Orton Dyslexia Soc., Assn. Children and Adults with Learning Disabilities, South County Jewish Fedn. (bd. dirs. until 1986, chmn. community relations council 1984-85, chmn. speakers bur. 1985-86).

STEIN, DOROTHY ESTELLE, marketing professional, researcher; b. Chelsea, Mass.; d. David Israel Bloomberg and Lillian Sophia (Stolpher) Cheses; m. Marvin N. Stein, Jan. 23, 1944; children: Paul Michael, Deborah Susan Blair, Dale Ilene. Student, Northeastern U., Boston, 1941, Monmouth Coll., 1956-57, Am. U., 1966-67. V.p., sales mgr. Sibs Assocs., Red Bank, N.J., 1960-63; product mgr. The Arbitron Ratings Co., Beltsville, Md., 1963-77; dir. research Sta. WDCA-TV, Bethesda, Md., 1977-85; pres. The Market and Audience Research Group, Inc., Germantown, Md., 1985—; chair INTV Research Adv. Com., N.Y.C. and Washington, 1983-86; mem. Coltam com., Nat. Broadcasters Assn., Washington, 1986; bd. dirs. Market Research Assocs., Mid-Atlantic chpt., Washington. Democrat. Jewish. Office: The Market and Audience Research Group Inc 13260 Country Ridge Dr Germantown MD 20874

STEIN, ELEANOR BANKOFF, judge; b. N.Y.C., Jan. 24, 1923; d. Jacob and Sarah (Rashkin) Bankoff; m. Frank S. Stein, May 27, 1947; children—Robert B., Joan Jenkins, William M. Student, Barnard Coll., 1940-42; B.S. in Econs., Columbia U., 1944; LL.B., NYU, 1949; grad. Ind. Jud. Coll., 1986. Bar: N.Y. 1950, Ind. 1976, U.S. Supreme Ct. 1980. Atty. Hillis & Button, Kokomo, Ind., 1975-76, Paul Hillis, Kokomo, 1976-78, Bayliff, Harrigan, Kokomo, 1978-80; judge Howard County Ct., Kokomo, 1980—; co-juvenile referee Howard County Juvenile Ct., 1976-78. Mem. Republicans Women's Assn. Kokomo, 1980—; bd. dirs. Howard County Legal Aid Soc., 1976-80; dir. Howard County Ct. Alcohol and Drug Services Program, 1982—; bd. advisors St. Joseph Hosp., Kokomo, 1979—; commn. mem. Kokomo Bd. Human Relations, 1967-70. Mem. law rev. bd. NYU Law Rev., 1947-48. Mem. Am. Judicature Soc., Ind. Jud. Assn., Nat. Assn. Women Judges, ABA, Ind. Bar Assn., Howard County Bar Assn. Jewish. Clubs: Kokomo Country, Altrusa. Home: 3204 Tally Ho Dr Kokomo IN 49602 Office: Howard County Ct Howard County Courthouse Kokomo IN 46901

STEIN, ELLEN GAIL, urban planner; b. N.Y.C., May 19, 1951; d. Manuel W. and Bella (Skutel) Stein; B.A., SUNY-Stony Brook, 1972; M.U.P., Hunter Coll., 1976. Sr. research assoc. Nassau Suffolk (N.Y.) Regional Med. Program, 1976-77; sr. planner N.Y.C. Dept. Correction, 1977-79; group leader criminal justice Mayor's Office Ops., N.Y.C., 1979-81, dep. asst. dir. citywide spl. projects, 1981, dir. citywide audit implementaion, 1981-84; adminstr. Bur. Supplies, N.Y.C. Bd. Edn., 1984—. Mem. Assn. Sch. Bus. Ofcls., Nat. Inst. Govt. Purchasing Agts., Am. Soc. for Pub. Adminstrn., Am. Planning Assn. Home: 67 Park Terr E New York NY 10034 Office: 44-36 Vernon Blvd Long Island NY 11101

STEIN, GERTRUDE EMILIE, educator, pianist, soprano; b. Ironton, Ohio; d. Samuel A. and Emilie M. (Pollach) S.; Mus.B., Capitol Coll. Oratory and Music, 1927; B.A., Wittenberg Coll., 1929, M.A., 1931, B.S. in Edn., 1945; Ph.D., U. Mich., 1948; piano and voice student Cin. Coll. Conservatory Music; cert. in piano Cin. Coll. Music, 1939. Music supr. Centralized County Schs. Ohio, Williamsburg, 1932-37; dir. jr. high sch. music, 1937-68, elem. music, 1968-71; mem. faculty Adult Evening Sch. Springfield (Ohio) Public Schs., 1951-68; head dept. music, asso. prof. piano and music edn. Tex. Lutheran Coll., Seguin, 1948-49. Donor, founder Rev. Dr. and Mrs. Samuel A. Stein Meml. Funds, 1955—. Mem. Am. Assn. Univ. Women, Am. Symphony Orch. League, NEA, Ohio Edn. Assn., Ohio Assn. Supervision and Curriculum Devel., Council for Exceptional Children, Assn. Tchr. Educators, Ohio Assn. Adult Educators, Associated Council Arts, Met. Opera Guild, Soc. Educators and Scholars, Am. Film Inst., Ohio Music Tchrs. Assn., Nat. Story League, Clark County Hist. Soc., Music Tchrs. Nat. Assn., Music Educators Nat. Conf., Nat. Assn. Schs. Music, Nat. Fedn. Music Clubs (spl. mem. Ohio), Fortnightly Musical Club, Amateur Chamber Music Players, Women's Assn. Springfield Symphony Orch., Springfield Authors Guild, Zonta Internat., Nat. Fedn. Bus. and Profl. Women, Phi Kappa Phi (hon.), Pi Lambda Theta (hon.). Lutheran. Contbr. articles to profl. jours.; research in field. Home: 133 N Lowry Ave Springfield OH 45504

STEIN, PEGGY LOUISE, professional writing service executive; b. Shreveport, La., Dec. 3, 1934; d. Paul David and Edna Louise (Alexander) Pugh; children: Michael Lee Hanson, Patricia Suzanne Hanson Moynihan. Student, Trinity U., San Antonio, 1953-54. Keypunch instr. Calif. Coll. Bus. Edn., Los Angeles, 1964-66; procedure writer, dir. EDP tng., asst. mgr. EDP Pacific Architects & Engrs., Saigon, Vietnam, 1966-68; asst. to advt. mgr. Volvo Southwest, Houston, 1972; owner, operator profl. writing service Writer's Ink, Austin, Tex., 1977—; designer computerized record-keeping system McDonnell Couglas Astronatics, Houston, 1986. Author: Keypunching, 1966, Operating Data Entry Systems, 1976, Moving to America: A Guide for Foreign Nationals, 1980. Office: Writer's Ink PO Box 2686 Lubbock TX 79408

STEINBACH, ALICE, journalist; b. Balt.. Student, U. London. Feature writer Balt. Sun, 1981—; formerly dir. pub. info. Balt. Mus. Art. Recip. Pulitzer Prize for feature writing, 1985. Office: Balt Sun Calvert at Centre St Baltimore MD 21278 *

STEINBAUER, MARTHA JUNE, nurse; b. Niles, Mich., Aug. 21, 1955; d. Robert Andrus and June Louise (Young) S. Student Kans. State U., 1973-75; B.S.N., U. Kans., 1977. Cert. in advanced cardiac life support. Staff nurse ICU, Presbyn. Hosp., Dallas, 1977-79, head nurse ICU, 1979—, chmn. incident report com., 1982—, resource person nursing seminars, unit dir. thoracic ICU, 1985—, dir. nursing quality assurance for critical care, 1987—. Mem. Am. Assn. Critical Care Nurses (sec. 1980-81), Music Service Guild Kans. State U., U. Kans. Alumni Assn., Sigma Theta Tau, Kappa Alpha Theta. Presbyterian. Office: Presbyn Hosp Dallas 8200 Walnut Hill Ln Dallas TX 75231

STEINBECK, BARBARA ALBRIGHT, infosystems specialist; b. Colfax, Wash., Apr. 19, 1932; d. Alvin Milton and jeanette Emily (Gilbert) Rubin; m. Darrell Lee Albright, Aug. 24, 1952 (div. 1976); children: Jan Lee, L. Ben., Barry Wayne; m. Ted Carl Steinbeck Jr., Aug. 24, 1979. Cert. med. asst. Psychiat. sec. Menningers Sch. Psychiatry, Topeka, Kans., 1952-54; owner, mgr. Med. Word Processing Ctr., Inc., Portland, 1976-82; computer cons. Info. Processing Ctr., Portland, 1974—; seminar leader Oreg. State U., Corvallis, 1980-83. Contbr. articles to profl. jours. Mem. Ctr. Community Mental Health, Portland, 1978-81; mem. computer evaluation com. Portland Pub. Schs., 1983—, chmn., 1984; mem. adv. com. Portland Community Coll., 1983—. Mem. Adminstrn. Mgmt. Soc. (pres. 1981-82), Assn. Info. Profls. (program chair 1985-86). Republican. Baptist. Club: Hookey. Home and Office: 645 Rose Dhu Rd Savannah GA 31419

STEINBERG, BEATRICE DUBIN, educational board administrator; b. N.Y.C., May 23, 1923; d. Louis and Jennie (Jaffee) Dubin; m. Samuel I. Steinberg, Oct. 19, 1941; children: Lawrence, Paul, Richard. BA in Polit. Sci., CUNY, 1967, MA in Urban Studies, 1972; JD, Bklyn. Law Sch., 1987. Bar: N.Y., 1988. Researcher Mayor's Adv. Panel, N.Y.C., 1966-67, CUNY, Columbia U., N.Y.C., 1966-67; spl. asst. in research and edn. N.Y.C. Bd. Edn., 1967-79, asst. sec., 1979—; adj. instr. Queens Coll., N.Y.C., 1971-78, lectr. internship program, 1978; lectr. Tng. Inst. Baruch Coll., N.Y.C., 1978, lectr. tng. program Bd. Edn., N.Y.C., 1979. Bd. dirs. Met. N.Y. Project Equality, 1975—; hon. bd. mem. Queens Child Guidance Ctr. (pres. 1977-80); mem. planning commn. N.Y. Network, N.Y.C., 1982—; advisor, planner Women in Govt. N.Y.C. Bd. Edn., 1984—; friend of commn. Mayor's Commn. on Status of Women, N.Y.C., 1985—. Mem. AAUW, Adminstrv. Women in Edn., Women's City Club, Com. Pub. Higher Edn., Queens Coll. Alumni Assn., Am. Jewish Com. (exec. bd. dirs. 1975-83), Am. Jewish Congress. Office: NYC Bd Edn 110 Livingston St Brooklyn NY 11201

STEINBERG, HARRIET BARBARA, writer, feline care consultant; b. N.Y.C., Feb. 12, 1954; d. Charles Side and Hortense (Rosenson) S.; m. Thomas Edward Zafan, June 12, 1983. BA, NYU, 1975; MS, Columbia U., 1976. adj. instr. journalism Hunter Coll., N.Y.C., 1977-81; cons. in field. Storywriter TV No Place to Hide, 1980-81; screenwriter TV, The Most Beautiful Girl in the World, 1983, A Personal Choice, 1985; author: Wish You Were Here, 1987. Dir. The Cat Ctr., N.Y.C., 1988—. Mem. Internat. Radio and TV Soc., Am. Acad. TV, Arts & Scis., Writers Guild Am. Democrat. Jewish.

STEINBERG, JANET DEBERRY, optometrist, educator, researcher; b. Phila., July 28, 1940; d. Bill and Florence (Kurtz) DeBerry; 1 child, J. Douglas Milner. Student Rider Coll., 1975-77; BS, Pa. Coll. Optometry, 1978, OD, 1981. Cons. Ophthalmic Eye Assocs., Levittown, Pa., 1982—; dir. Hopewell Valley Eye Assocs., Hopewell, N.J., 1982—; chief Low Vision Ctr., Scheie Eye Inst. dept. ophthalmology U. Pa., Phila., 1984—, also clin. assoc., 1985—; assoc. ophthalmology Pa. Hosp., Phila., 1988—; assoc. Louis A. Karp MD Dept. of Ophthalmology, Pa. Hosp., Phila., 1987—; asst. adj. prof. Pa. Coll. Optometry, Phila., 1983-85, mem. adj. faculty, 1986—; mem. N.J. Low Vision Panel, 1981—; cons. healthcare industry, 1985—; assoc. Louis A. Karp, M.D., Phila., 1987—; cons. to Healthcare Industry, 1985—. Fellow Am. Acad. Optometry; mem. Am. Optometric Assn. (Optometric Recognition award 1983-87), N.J. Optometric Assn., Central N.J. Optometric Assn., Assn. Research in Vision and Ophthalmology, Beta Beta Beta. Avocations: sailing, snorkeling, scuba. Office: Hopewell Valley Eye Assocs 84 E Broad St Hopewell NJ 08525 also: Scheie Eye Inst Low Vision Ctr 51 N 39th St Philadelphia PA 19104 also: Pa Hosp 7th and Spruce Sts Suite 100 Philadelphia PA 19106

STEINBERG, JANET ECKSTEIN, journalist; b. Cin.; d. Charles and Adele (Ehrenfeld) Eckstein; m. Marvin B. Steinberg, June 24, 1951 (dec.); children—Susan Carole Steinberg Somerstein, Jody Lynn Steinberg Lazarow. B.S., U. Cin., 1964. Free-lance writer; guest appearances Braun and Co., Sta.-WLW-TV. Contbr. numerous articles to newspapers, mags. and books, U.S., Can., Singapore, Australia, N.Z.; weekly travel columnist Cin. Post, 1978-86, Ky. Post, 1978-86; contbr. Singles Scene and Cin. Mag., 1980—; contbg. editor Travel Agt., 1986-88, Birnbaum Travel Guides, 1988-89, The Writer, 1988 , Entree, 1986—; travel columnist Northeast mag., 1986—, South Fla. Single Living, 1984—. Recipient Lowell Thomas travel journalism award, 1985, 86, Henry E. Bradshaw Travel Journalism award, 1st place, best of show, 1988. Mem. Am. Soc. Journalists and Authors, Soc. Am. Travel Writers (1st place award for best newspaper story 1981, 3d place award for best mag. story 1981, 1st place award for best newspaper article award 1984, best mag. article 1985, 2d place award best pathos article, 1984, 88), Midwest Travel Writers Assn. (Best Mag. Story award 1981, Best Series award 1981, 84 Cipriani award 1981 2d place award for best article 1982, 83, 84), Pacific Area Travel Assn., Internat. Food, Wine, and Travel Writers Assn. Club: Losantiville Country. Home: 2676 Fair Oaks Ln Cincinnati OH 45237

STEINBERG, JILL ENID, computer sales executive; b. Jersey City, Oct. 27, 1955; d. Edwin Jay and Renee Ruth (Kaufman) S. B.A., U. Miami (Fla.), 1979. Salesperson luggage Burdine's, Miami, Fla., 1979-80, asst. mgr. area, 1980-81, commn. sales advanced consumer electronics, 1981-83, asst. mgr. computer sales, 1983-87, mgr. Computerbanc booth, 1987—; participant Apple seminar, 1983. Named outstanding salesperson So. Region, Hartmann Luggage, 1980; mem. Burdine's B Club. Mem. AAUW (com.), Nat. Assn. Female Execs., Alpha Kappa Delta, Phi Beta Phi Epsilon. Lodge: Hadassah (life). Home: 15725 SW 88th Ct Miami FL 33157 Office: Computerbanc at Burdine's 7303 N Kendall Dr Miami FL 33156

STEINBERG, MARGERY S., marketing educator, consultant; b. N.Y.C., Oct. 11, 1948; d. Noah and Janet (Horowitz) Greenstein; m. Lewis J. Steinberg, Aug. 20, 1978. B.A., Boston U., 1970; M.A., U. Conn., 1972, M.B.A., 1979, Ph.D., 1984. Tchr. Manchester pub. schs. (Conn.), 1970-71, Regional Sch. Dist. 13, Durham, Conn., 1971-74; book club editor Xerox Edn. Publs., Middletown, Conn., 1974-77; lectr. Asnuntuck Community Coll., Enfield, Conn., 1976-79; asst. prof. Post Coll., Waterbury, Conn., 1979-80; asst. prof. mktg. U. Hartford, West Hartford, Conn., 1980—, seminar leader Div. Adult Ednl. Services, 1982—; cons. Coleco Industries Inc., West Hartford, 1983—, Soc. for Savs., Hartford, 1978; cons. trainer Westfarms Mall Mgmt., Farmington, Conn., 1983—. Author: Animalympics Guide to the Olympics, 1980; Christopher Reeve Scrapbook, 1980; 1987: Opportunities in Marketing Careers; author series of children's books. Mem. Bd. Edn., Cromwell, Conn., 1971-74; mem. Dem. Town Com., Cromwell, 1970-75; bd. dirs. Greater Hartford Chamber Orch., 1983-85. Inst. Ednl. Leadership edn. policy fellow, 1976. Mem. Am. Mktg. Assn. (pres. Conn. 1984-85, internat. v.p. collegiate div. 1986-88), Coll. and Univ. Bus. Instrs. Conn. (bd. dirs. 1976-82). Home: Terry Rd Hartford CT 06105 Office: U Hartford 200 Bloomfield Ave West Hartford CT 06117

STEINBUCHEL, CARLA FAYE, nurse, foundation administrator; b. Wichita, Kans., Aug. 6, 1949; d. Conrad Vernon Sr. and Dolores Mae (Jacobs) Jansson; m. Mark Joseph Steinbuchel, June 5, 1969; children: Carla Lara, Cara Nicole. BS in Nursing, Wichita State U., 1978, M of Nursing, 1985. Nurse supr. Osteopathic Hosp., Wichita, 1978-85; nurse Wesley Med. Ctr., Wichita, 1982-85, Huntsville (Ala.) Hosp., 1985-86; neonatal outreach coordinator North Ala. Perinatal Outreach Ctr., Huntsville, 1986—; manuscript reviewer Neonatal Network, Petaluma, Calif., 1987-88. Mem. Am. Assn. Critical Care Nurses (past sec., pres.), Nat. Assn. Neonatal Nurses (charter), Ala. Perinatal Assn. (mem. program com. 1987-88). Democrat. Methodist. Home: 2511 Galahad Dr SE Huntsville AL 35803-1809 Office: North Ala Perinatal Outreach Huntsville Hosp 101 Sivley Huntsville AL 35803

STEINECKE, MAUREEN KANE, assn. exec.; b. Boston, Dec. 18, 1932; d. Martin and Helen (Leonard) Kane; A.B. in Am. Lit., Middlebury Coll., 1954; M.S. in L.S., Pratt Inst., 1956; m. Charles Steinecke, July 7, 1956; children—John, Ann, Patricia. Asst. to coordinator children's services D.C. Pub. Library, Washington, 1956-59; free-lance indexer, 1959-65; exec. dir. Md. Assn. Bds. of Edn., Annapolis, 1978—. Vice pres. LWV of Prince George's County, 1971-73; mem. Prince George's County Bd. Edn., 1973-78; bd. mgmt. Prince George's County YMCA, 1979-82. Named Prince Georgian of yr., Sentinel Newspapers, 1977. Mem. Am. Soc. Assn. Execs., Md. Govt. Relations Assn., Greater Wash. Soc. Assn. Execs., Md. Congress Parents and Tchrs. (hon. life). Democrat. Episcopalian. Office: 130 Holiday Ct Suite 105 Annapolis MD 21401

STEINEM, GLORIA, writer, editor, lecturer; b. Toledo, Mar. 25, 1934; d. Leo and Ruth (Nuneviller) S. B.A., Smith Coll., 1956; postgrad. (Chester Bowles Asian fellow), India, 1957-58; D. Human Justice, Simmons Coll., 1973. Co-dir., dir., ednl. found. Ind. Research Service, Cambridge, Mass. and N.Y.C., 1959-60; editorial asst., editorial cons., contbg. editor, free-lance writer various nat. and N.Y.C. publs., 1960—; co-founder, contbg. editor New York mag., 1968—; feminist lectr. 1969—; co-founder, editor Ms. mag., 1971-87, columnist, 1980—, cons. editor, 1988—; Active various civil rights and peace campaigns including United Farmworkers, Vietnam War Tax Protest, Com. for the Legal Def. of Angela Davis (treas., 1971-72); active polit. campaigns of Adlai Stevenson, Robert Kennedy, Eugene McCarthy, Shirley Chisholm, George McGovern; Co-founder, bd. dirs. Women's Action Alliance, 1970—; convenor, mem. nat. adv. com. Nat. Women's Polit. Caucus, 1971—; co-founder, pres. bd. dirs. Ms. Found. for Women, 1972—; founding mem. Coalition of Labor Union Women, 1974; mem. Internat. Women's Year Commn., 1977. Author: The Thousand Indias, 1957, The Beach Book, 1963, Outrageous Acts and Everyday Rebellions, 1983, Marilyn: Norma Jeane, 1986; contbg. corr. NBC Today Show, 1987-88; contbr. to various anthologies. Bd. dirs. Voters for Choice, 1979—. Recipient Penney-Missouri Journalism award, 1970; Ohio Gov.'s award for Journalism, 1972; Bill of Rights award A.C.L.U. of So. Calif., 1975; named Woman of the Year McCall's mag., 1972; Woodrow Wilson Internat. Center for Scholars fellow, 1977. Mem. Nat. Orgn. for Women, AFTRA, Nat. Press Club, Soc. Mag. Writers, Authors' Guild, P.E.N., Phi Beta Kappa. Address: care Ms Magazine 119 W 40th St New York NY 10018

STEINER, FRANCES JOSEPHINE, conductor, cellist, educator; b. Portland, Oreg., Feb. 25, 1937; d. Ferenz Joseph and Elizabeth (Levy) S.; m. Mervin Israel Tarlow, June 8, 1965; 1 child, Sarah Leah Tarlow. Studied with Nadia Boulanger, France, 1957; BE with honors, Temple U., 1956; MusB, Curtis Inst. Music, 1956; MA, Radcliffe Coll., 1958; DMus.Arts, U. So. Calif., 1969; Hans Beer, others, 1972-82. Tchr., orch. dir. Roosevelt Jr. High Sch., Phila., 1956, Brown Jr. High Sch., Malden, Mass., 1957-58; mem. faculty Newton Jr. and Sr. high schs., Mass., 1958-62; instr. Bklyn. Coll., 1962-65; mem. faculty Fullerton Jr. Coll., Calif., 1966-67; mem. faculty Calif. State U.-Dominguez Hills, 1967—, prof., 1975—, chairperson music dept., 1978-84; condr., music dir. Carson-Dominguez Hills Symphony Orch., 1977—, Baroque Consortium Chamber Orch. (now named Chamber Orch. of the South Bay), 1974—; guest condr. Glendale Symphony Orch., 1977, asst. condr., 1984-85; guest condr. MIT Orch., Cambridge, 1980, Maracaibo Symphony, Venezuela, 1984, others, Nat. Symphony Orch. of Dominican Republic, Brevard (County) Symphony Orch., 1986, Bay Area Women's Philharm., 1986, Billings (Mont.) Symphony, 1987; prin. cellist Glendale Symphony Orch., 1975-85, Calif. Chamber Symphony, 1970-76; asst. prin. cellist Los Angeles Chamber Orch., 1970-73, Pasadena Symphony, 1970-71; also soloist. Author: (with Max Kaplan) Musicianship for the Classroom, 1966. Co-editor: Introduction to Music, 1964. Arranger: Six Menuets in Two Celli (Haydn), 1967; rec. artist. Russell Kingman scholar, 1957; Thomas Dana fellow, 1956-57; Temple U. scholar, 1952-56; Curtis Inst. Music scholar, 1945-56; recipient citation Nat. Fedn. Music Clubs, 1975, 76; Faculty Disting. Pub. Service award Calif. State U.-Dominguez Hills; Status of Women award Palos Verdes chpt. AAUW. Mem. Condrs. Guild, Am. Symphony Orch. League, AAUW, Mu Phi Epsilon. Democrat. Jewish. Avocations: gourmet cooking, wines. Office: Calif State U Dominquez Hills Carson CA 90747

STEINER, JANET ELAINE, library director; b. Racine, Wis., Sept. 21, 1947; d. Ralph John and Virginia Alice (Powers) S.; m. Edward C. Kokkelenberg, June 19, 1977; 1 child, Katherine. BA, Dominican Coll., 1969; MLS, U. Wis., 1971; MA, Marquette U., 1974. Head adult services Elk Grove Village (Ill.) Pub. Library, 1974-75, head librarian, 1975-80; exec. dir. South Cen. Research Library Council, Ithaca, N.Y., 1980—. Mem. ALA (library adminstrn. and mgmt. program com. 1978-83), N.Y. Library Assn. (council-at-large 1983-85, pres. academic and social libraries sect. 1987), 3 R's Orgn., Beta Phi Mu. Unitarian. Home: 101 Raiford Rd Vestal NY 13850 Office: SCRLC 215 N Cayuga St Ithaca NY 14850

STEINER, SABINA, epidemiologist; b. N.Y.C., Dec. 8, 1943; d. Sidney Isidore and Adelaide Rose (Weber) Davidson; married; children: Felicia Anne, Andrew Joseph. AAS, Queensborough Coll., 1981; BS in Nursing, Lehman Coll., 1983; MPH and MS in Nursing, Columbia U., 1985. RN, N.Y. Office mgr. Gen. Ophthalmology, Bklyn., 1973-79; staff nurse St. Vincents Hosp., N.Y.C., 1981-84, Montefiore Hosp., Bronx, 1984-85; coordinator Huntington (N.Y.) Surgery Ctr., 1985-86; project coordinator SUNY, Stony Brook, 1986-87, asst. instr. sch. medicine, 1987—. Mary Neil White scholar, Lehman Coll., 1983, Gertrude B. Wertenbaker scholar, Lehman Coll., 1983, Presdl. scholar, Lehman Coll., 1983. Mem. APHA, Assn. of Women in Sci., Am. Nurses Assn., Sigma Theta Tau. Democrat. Jewish. Office: SUNY Sch of Medicine Health Science Center 3L 099 Stony Brook NY 11794-8036

STEINFELD, NAOMI ROSE, writer, book developer, educator; b. N.Y.C., Nov. 12, 1945; d. Max and Lillian (Makofsky) Berton; m. Richard George Steinfeld, Dec. 14, 1968; 1 son, Gabriel. Student Hunter Coll., 1962-63; B.A. Cum laude, City Coll., CUNY, 1966; M.A., U. Conn., 1970; postgrad. John F. Kennedy U., 1983-85. Writing instr., 1982-84. Author: The Chaos of Something Extraordinary, Shaman's Drum, 1986; author, editor: The New Holistic Health Handbook, 1985. Editor The Human Element (Will Schutz), 1984; Writing, 2d edit., 1986; High Level Wellness, 2d edit., 1986. Mem. Assn. for Transpersonal Psychology. Avocations: storytelling, speaker, healer on spiritual emergence. Home: 21 Sunset Ct Kensington CA 94707

STEINFELS, MARGARET O'BRIEN, editor. m. Peter Steinfels, Aug. 31, 1963; 2 children: Gabrielle, John Melville. Founding editor, Church mag; social sci. editor Basic Books; bus. mgr., later exec. editor Christianity and Crisis; dir. publications Nat. Pastoral Life Ctr.; editor Commonweal mag., 1987—. Office: Commonweal 15 Dutch St New York NY 10038 *

STEINHARDT, DORIS EDITH, state official; b. N.Y.C., Mar. 7, 1949; d. Herbert Harold and Blanche Edith (Gormann) S. B.S., SUNY-Albany, 1971, M.S.W., 1976; J.D., Albany Law Sch., 1979; LL.M. in Taxation, NYU, 1986. Bar: N.Y. 1980, U.S. Dist. Ct. (no. dist.) N.Y. 1980, U.S. Tax Ct. 1983. Social worker, community organizer SUNY, Albany, 1975-76; student atty. Prisoners' Legal Services, Albany, 1977-79; atty. Mental Health Info. Service, Valhalla, N.Y., 1979-80; adminstrv. law judge N.Y. State Tax Commn., Albany, 1980-85; asst. sec. N.Y. State Tax Commn., 1985-87, chief tax law judge, N.Y.S. Div. of Tax Appeals, 1987—; mem. N.Y. Dept. Taxation and Finance Affirmative Action Subcom. for Women, 1980-83, statewide activities dir., 1983-85, counsel, 1985-87. Sec., Albany County chpt. Liberal party, 1983-87. ACLU, N.Y. State Bar Assn., N.Y. Women's Bar Assn. Home: 101 Grove Ave Albany NY 12208 Office: NY State Div Tax Appeals Harriman Campus Albany NY 12227

STEINHOFF, WENDY MAYER, computer data base administrator; b. N.Y.C., Mar. 14, 1947; d. Victor and Marilyn (Marksville) Mayer; divorced; children: Jeffrey, Carrie. BA, Pa. State U., 1967. Programmer N.Y. Telephone Co., N.Y.C., 1969-71; tng. supr. Integrated Bus. Systems, Inc., Cedar Grove, N.J., 1980-83; database adminstr. The Children's Place, Pine Brook, N.J. Mem. CADRE Nat. User Group (chmn. infra-structure products com. 1987).

STEINMAN, JOAN ELLEN, lawyer, educator; b. Bklyn., June 19, 1947; d. Jack and Edith Ruth (Shapiro) S.; m. Douglass Watts Cassel, Jr., June 1, 1974 (div. July 1986); children—Jennifer Lynn, Amanda Hilary. Student U. Birmingham, Eng., 1968; A.B. with high distinction, U. Rochester, 1969; J.D. cum laude, Harvard U., 1973. Bar: Ill. 1973. Assoc., Schiff, Hardin & Waite, Chgo., 1973-77; asst. prof. Ill. Inst. Tech. Chgo.-Kent. Coll. Law, 1977-82, assoc. prof., 1982-86, prof., 1986—; cons. in atty. promotions Met. San. Dist. Greater Chgo., 1981, 85. Contbr. articles to law jours. Coop. atty. ACLU Ill., Chgo., 1974, Leadership Council for Met. Open Communities, Chgo., 1975, Better Govt. Assn., 1975; arbitrator Better Bus. Bur. Met. Chgo., 1987; appointed to Ill. Gov.'s Grievance Panel, 1987. Mem. ABA, Soc. Am. Law Tchrs., Chgo. Council Lawyers, Phi Beta Kappa. Democrat. Jewish. Office: IIT Chgo Kent Coll Law 77 S Wacker Dr Chicago IL 60606

STEINMAN, LYNNE ANN, psychologist; b. N.Y.C., June 15, 1953; d. Alfred Maurice and Roslyn (Bennett) S. BS, U. Ill., Champaign, 1974; MA, U. So. Calif., 1978, PhD, 1982; postdoctoral, UCLA, 1986-88. lic. clin. psychologist, Calif. Pvt. practice psychology Los Angeles, 1980—; staff psychologist VA, Los Angeles, 1984—; cons. in field. Vol. various community orgns. on aging. Mem. Am. Psychol. Assn., Gerontological Soc. of Am., Phi Kappa Phi. Office: Ingleside Hosp 7500 E Hellman Rosemead CA 91770

STEINMAN, SHIRLEY MARY, civic worker; b. Ecorse, Mich., Oct. 21, 1930; d. John Nathaniel and Edna Irene (Paige) Wright; m. George Albert Steinman, May 22, 1954; children: Jan W., Lauda M. Nagel, Kurt J., Karl G., Gretchen Steinman Turner. BS, Mich. State Normal Coll., 1956; MA, Eastern Mich. U., 1962. Elem. tchr. Monroe County (Mich.) Pub. Schs., 1950-86. Contbr. The Writer's Block, Monroe. Active Safe Energy Coalition Mich., Detroit, Monroe, Ann Arbor, 1981—, Shut it Down, Monroe, 1987—, Friends of the Earth, 1983—, Amnesty Internat. U.S.A., 1982—, So. Poverty Law Ctr., 1983—, Pax Christi, Monroe, Interfaith Justice and Peace Ctr., Sylvania, Ohio. Mem. Mich. Assn. Retired Sch. Personnel, Sierra Club. Roman Catholic. Home: 3011 Vivian Rd Monroe MI 48161

STEINMEYER, ELISABETH, hotel chain executive; b. Brattleboro, Vt., Apr. 29, 1956; d. Georg Frederick and Johanna Eleanor (Heckel) S. BS in Hotel, Restaurant and Travel Adminstrn., U. Mass., 1978. Asst. dir. agy. and tour sales Capital Hilton Hotel, Washington, 1978-79, dir. agy. and tour sales, 1979-80, dir. conv. services, 1980-82; dir. sales nat. accounts Hilton Hotels Corp., Los Angeles, 1983-84; dir. sales Los Angeles Airport Hilton and Towers, 1984-85, Los Angeles Hilton and Towers, 1985-88; mng. dir. sales Hilton Hotels Corp., Los Angeles, 1988—. Vol. interpreter summer games 1984 Olympics, Los Angeles. Mem. Meeting Planners Internat., Travel and Transp. Council Los Angeles, Los Angeles Downtowners Assn., Iota Gamma Upsilon. Office: Hilton Hotels Corp 900 Wilshire Blvd Los Angeles CA 90017

STEINMILLER, ANITA MARY, nurse; b. Pitts., Feb. 4, 1951; d. Henry James and Ann Frances Steinmiller; diploma Ohio Valley Gen. Hosp. Sch. Nursing, 1972; B.S.N. magna cum laude LaRoche Coll., 1981, B.A., 1979; M.Nursing Adminstrn., U. Pitts., 1984. Cert. in nursing adminstrn. Am. Nurses Assn. Staff nurse Ohio Valley Gen. Hosp., McKees Rocks, Pa., 1972-75, patient care coordinator infection control, audit inservice edn., 1975-81, asst. dir. nursing, 1981-87; case mgr. Univ. Health Network, Oakland, Pa., 1987—; vol. instr. nursing service ARC; vol. lectr. Am. Cancer Soc. Mem. Ohio Valley Nurses Alumni Assn., Sigma Theta Tau. Roman Catholic. Home: 334 Bascom Ave Pittsburgh PA 15214 Office: Univ Health Network Oakland PA 15213

STEINSKY, VERONICA HAYES, computer company executive; b. Rochester, N.H., Dec. 12, 1947; d. William Francis and Rita Claudia (Roux) Hayes; m. Rudolph Stanley Steinsky, Nov. 4, 1978. BA, St. Joseph's Coll., 1969. Mgr. ops. M. Hoffman and Co., Boston, 1969-74; dir. computer system software TMS, Waltham, Mass., 1974-86; pres., owner Communications Support Systems, Inc., Waltham, 1981—; v.p. OEM Systems Design, Watlham, 1986—; trustee Steinsky Real Estate Trust, Waltham, 1986—, trust #2, 1987—, V&S Real Estate Trust, 1988—. Fund raiser Robert Kennedy Election Com., Portland, Maine, 1968; mem. election com. Stanley for Mayor, Waltham, 1986. Democrat. Roman Catholic. Office: 123 Felton St Waltham MA 02154

STEITZ, JOAN ARGETSINGER, biophysics educator; b. Mpls., Jan. 26, 1941; d. Glenn D. and Elaine (Magnusson) Argetsinger; m. Thomas A. Steitz, Aug. 20, 1966; 1 child, Jonathan Glenn. B.S., Antioch Coll., 1963; Ph.D., Harvard U., 1967; D.Sc. (hon.), Lawrence U., Appleton, Wis., 1982, Rochester U. Sch. Medicine, 1984. Postdoctoral fellow MRC Lab. Molecular Biology, Cambridge, Eng., 1967-70; asst. prof. molecular biophysics and biochemistry Yale U., New Haven, 1970-74; assoc. prof. Yale U., 1974-78, prof. molecular biophysics and biochemistry, 1978—. Recipient Young Scientist award Passano Found., 1975, Eli Lilly award in biol. chemistry, 1976, U.S. Steel Found. award in molecular biology, 1982, Lee Hawley, Sr. award for arthritis research, 1984, Nat. Medal of Sci., 1986. Fellow AAAS; mem. Am. Acad. Arts and Sci., Nat. Acad. Arts and Sci. Home: 45 Prospect Hill Rd Stony Creek Branford CT 06405 Office: Yale Univ Sch Medicine 333 Cedar St PO Box 3333 New Haven CT 06510

STELLATO, SUSAN ANN, publishing professional; b. Bklyn., Nov. 12, 1957; d. Fred and Rose (Nespoli) S. From asst. circulation mgr. to circulation supr. McGraw Hill Inc., N.Y.C., 1981-83; supr. customer service, credit and collection Hightstown, N.J., 1983-86, purchasing agt., 1986—. Mem. Nat. Assn. Puchasing Mgrs., Dir. Mktg. Credit Assn. (sec. 1986), Internat. Assn. Quality Circles. Office: McGraw Hill Inc Corp Purchase Princeton Rd Hightstown NJ 08520

STELLMAN, L. MANDY, lawyer; b. Toronto, Ont., Aug. 22, 1922; came to U.S., 1946, naturalized, 1948; d. Abraham and Rose (Rubinoff) Mandlsohn; m. Samuel David Stellman, July 11, 1943; children—Steven D., Leslie Robert. B.Sc. summa cum laude, Ohio State U., Columbus, 1966; J.D., Marquette U., 1970. Bar: Wis. 1971. Tchr., Toronto Pub. Schs., 1943-46; recreation specialist, Toronto, 1942-46; educator, social worker Columbus (Ohio) Jewish Ctr., 1951-64; instr. U. Wis. Extension, Milw., 1970-76; sole practice, Milw., 1971—. Bd. dirs. Women's Crisis Line, Women's Coalition, Milw. Jewish Home for Aged. Recipient Disting. Alumni award Ohio State U., 1976; Hannah G. Solomon award Nat. Council Jewish Women, 1984. Mem. Assn. Trial Lawyers Am., Lawyers Assn. for Women, ABA, Milw. Bar Assn., Wis. Assn. Trial Lawyers, Nat. Council Jewish Women (life), Women's Polit. Caucus, Common Cause, NOW (Milw. Woman of Yr. 1977). Jewish. Home: 1545 W Fairfield Ct Glendale WI 53209 Office: 606 W Wisconsin Ave Suite 308 Milwaukee WI 53203

STELTZLEN, JANELLE HICKS, lawyer; b. Atlanta, Sept. 18, 1937; d. William Duard and Mary Evelyn (Embrey) Hicks; divorced; children: Gerald William III, Christa Diane. BS, Okla. State U., 1958; MS, Kans. State U., 1961; JD, U. Tulsa, 1981. Bar: Okla. 1981, U.S. Dist. Ct. (no., ea. and we. dists.) Okla. 1981, U.S. Tax Ct. 1981, U.S. Ct. Claims 1981, U.S. Ct. Appeals (10th and Fed. cirs.) 1981, U.S. Supreme Ct. 1981; lic. real estate broker. Sole practice Tulsa, 1981—; lectr. Coll. of DuPage, Glen Ellyn, Ill., 1976, Tulsa Jr. Coll., 1981—; dietitian, Tulsa. Bd. dirs. Youth for Christ, Christian Living Ctr. Tulsa; Christian counselor 1st United Meth. Ch., Tulsa, 1986—, lay pastor, 1987—. Mem. Okla. Bar Assn., Tulsa County Bar Assn., Vol. Lawyers Assn. (bd. dirs.), Am. Dietetic Assn., Delta Zeta. Republican. Methodist. Home: 6636 S Jamestown Place Tulsa OK 74136 Office: 1150 E 61st St Tulsa OK 74136

STELZER, KELLY COOPER, anthropologist, educator, herb farmer, anthropologist; b. Washington, June 9, 1942; d. Donald Hamilton and Elise Marvel (Wallace) Cooper; m. Michael William Giorgio, Oct. 10, 1965 (div. 1972); 1 child, Michael Angelo; m. John H. Stelzer, May 25, 1982. BA in Anthropology, George Washington U., 1973, MA in Anthropology, 1975. Owner, ptnr. Elderflower Farm, Roseburg, Oreg., 1975—; asst. prof. anthropology Umpqua Community Coll., Roseburg, 1978—. Author: Raised Bed Gardening, 1985, Cooking With Culinary Herbs, 1985, Growing Culinary Herbs, 1986. Office: Umpgua Community Coll PO Box 967 Roseburg OR 97470

STENBORG, CAROL ANN, computer educator; b. Columbus, Ohio, Oct. 22, 1956; d. Frank Batista and Caroline (Fata) Decaminada; m. Frederic J. Stenborg, June 24, 1978; children—Eric John, Karl Joseph. BA in Journalism, Ohio State U., 1977; postgrad. U. Wis., 1977-78; MA in Tech. Communication, U. Minn., 1986. Reporter, wire editor Ohio State Daily Lantern, Columbus, 1977; grad. asst. U. Wis., Madison, 1977-78; freelance writing cons., St. Paul, 1980—; adminstrv. asst. ACM-SIGGRAPH, St. Paul, 1984; mem. faculty Mpls. Coll. Art and Design, 1984—, dir. computer ctr. Membership chmn. Minn. Women's Polit. Caucus, St. Paul, 1982, newsletter editor, 1981; neighborhood rep. Neighborhood Press Assn., St. Paul, 1983. Mem. Nat. Computer Graphics Assn., Women in Communications, (pres. Ohio State U. chpt. 1976-77, v.p. for membership Twin Cities St. Paul 1981-82, scholar 1974, 77), Soc. for Tech. Communicators, Minne'Apples Computer User Group. Democrat. Roman Catholic.

STENBORG, MARGARET ANN, music educator; b. Bellville, Tex., Sept. 28, 1940; d. Lawrence Jerome and Arminda Pascual (Gomez) Schwender; m. Rodney Eugene Stenborg, Dec. 19, 1967; children—Jeanne Alicia, Derek Vincent, Julia Christine. Student Juilliard Sch. Music, 1965-66; B.A. in Music Edn., Sacred Heart Dominican Coll., 1962. Music tchr. Alcott Sch., 1962-65, St. Peter's Sch., Houston, 1974-75, St. Christopher Sch., Houston, 1973, 75-78, Mahanay Sch., Alief, Tex., 1980-82, Cornelius Sci. and Math. Acad., Houston, 1982—, Gregg Elem. Sch., Houston, 1982-86, Cornelius Math and Sci. Acad., Houston, 1986—; profl. chorister Amor Artists Chorale, N.Y.C., Camerata Singers, N.Y.C., 1966-68, Robert Shaw Chorale, N.Y.C., 1965-66; opera chorister Oberhausen City Theater (W. Ger.), 1970-73, Houston Grand Opera, 1959-65, 76—. Choir dir. St. Christopher's Cath. Ch., Houston, 1975-81, 83—. Named 2d Place Finalist Met. Opera Southwest Auditions, San Antonio, 1964, one of Outstanding Young Women of Am., 1965, Tchr. of Yr., Gregg Elem. Sch., 1984; study grantee Tuesday Music Club, 1964, Phi Beta, 1965. Mem. Am. Guild Mus. Artists (bd. govs. Tex. 1982-85), Houston Fedn. Tchrs., Tex. Music Educators' Assn., Gulfcoast Orff Assn., Houston Music Educators Assn., Orgn. Am. Kodaly Educators. Roman Catholic. Home: 5403 Oriole St Houston TX 77017 Office: Cornelius Math & Sci Acad 7475 Westover Houston TX 77087

STENBUCK, JO ANNE, special education educator; b. Fairbury, Ill., June 25, 1952; d. Paul Frederick and Doris Mae (Kelly) Salzman; m. Jonathan Frederick Stenbuck, Aug. 20, 1983. BS in Edn., Ill. State U., 1974; postgrad., No. Ill. U., 1978-80, Ea. Ill. U., 1978, Kaskaskia Coll., Centralia, Ill., 1980-83, Bridgewater (Mass.) State Coll., 1986, Fitchburg (Mass.) State Coll., 1987; cert., Northeastern U., 1988. Cert. tchr. visually impaired, Ill., Mass., elem. tchr., Ill. Tchr. Kaskaskia Spl. Edn. Dist., Centralia, 1974-83, Weymouth (Mass.) Pub. Schs., 1983-86; presch. tchr. visually impaired North River Collaborative, Rockland, Mass., 1986—; ednl. advisor Central City Child Care Ctr., Centralia, 1982-86; cons. in field. Mem. Assn. Educators Visually Impaired, Alpha Delta Kappa (chaplain 1982-83). Baptist. Home: 23 East St Apt 4 Mansfield MA 02048 Office: North River Collaborative 394 Union St Rockland MA 02370

STEORTS, NANCY HARVEY, management consultant; b. Syracuse, N.Y., Nov. 28, 1936; d. Frederick William and Josephine Elizabeth (Jones) Harvey; 1 dau., Deborah Joan. B.S., Syracuse U., 1959. Asst. buyer, public relations coordinator Woodward & Lothrop, Washington, 1958-61; home economist Washington Gas Light Co., 1961-64; sales assoc. real estate Summit, N.J., 1967-68; survey specialist Dept. Agr., Washington, 1968-69; chmn. Consumer Product Safety Commn., Washington, D.C., 1981-85; pres. Nancy Harvey Steorts & Assocs., Dallas, 1985—; cons. Exec. Reorgn. Govt., Washington, 1971; nat. dir. women's speakers' bur. Com. Re-elect Pres., Washington, 1971-72; dir. candlelight dinners Presdl. Inaugural Commn., 1972-73, 81; expns. dir. Dept. Commerce, Washington, 1973; spl. asst. for consumer affairs to sec. agr., 1973-77; pres. N.H. Steorts & Assocs., 1977-81; disting. lectr., Strom Thurmond Inst. Govt. and Pub. Affairs, Clemson U.; mem. advisory council to bd. dirs., Adolph Coors Co.; mem. U.S. Dept. of Commerce Export Council for Texas; dir. People to People Trade Mission to Spain, 1987. Trustee Food Safety Council Conf. Consumer Orgn.; bd. dirs. Women's Inst. Am. U.; bd. advisers Coll. Human Devel. Syracuse U.; commr. Montgomery County Commn. Women; pres. Welcome Wagon Clubs from 1986, Dallas Citizens Council, 1986-87, Council of Better Bus. Burs.;

bd. adv. Am. U. Women's Inst.; bd. dirs. Med. Coll. Pa., Tex. Women's Alliance; bd. dirs., vice-chmn. regional devel. Nat. Assn. Women Bus. Owners; mem. internat. com. Com. 2000; bd. dirs. Jr. Achievement, United Way, Dallas, Goals of Dallas, Internat. Mayor's Ball; internat. del. 1st Women's Internat. Trade Mission to Europe for Women Entrepeneurs; mem. advisory council to So. Meth. U. Dept. Economics; co-chmn. fundraising, Dallas Symphony. Recipient George P. Arents Pioneer medal Syracuse U., 1979, spl. award for consumer concern Nat. Diet Workshop, named one of five outstanding pub. servants Gallagher Report, 1984. Mem. Nat. Bd. Dirs., Am. Home Econs. Assn., AAUW, Nat. Consumers League, Am. Women in Radio and TV, Exec. Women in Govt. (chmn.), Nat. Conf. Consumer Orgns. Office: NH Steorts & Assocs 4689 S Versailles Dallas TX 75209

STEPHAN, INEZ VALLS, secretarial service company executive; b. Columbus, Ohio, Nov. 22, 1911; d. Rafael W. and Euphemia (Lloyd) Valls; 2 children. Student pub. schs., Cleveland Heights. Sec. Harlow Co., Coral Gables, Fla., 1959-63, U. Miami, Coral Gables, 1963-75; pres., owner Stephan Secretarial Coral Gables, 1975—; real estate salesperson Wirth Realty, Coral Gables, 1975—. Mem. Nat. Assn. Female Execs., Notary Pub. Assn., Coral Gables Bd. Realtors, Coral Gables C. of C. Republican. Roman Catholic. Avocations: swimming; playing bridge. Home: 8690 SW 74th Terr Miami FL 33143 Office: Stephan Secretarial Service 3132-B Ponce de Leon Blvd Coral Gables FL 33134

STEPHENS, ALISON AMY, cosmetics executive; b. Brainerd, Minn., May 29, 1949; d. Clark Merton and Amanda Elizabeth (Tufteland) Amy; m. Robert Gregory Stephens, Aug. 12, 1972 (div. Jul. 1983); m. B. Michael Stuppy, May 29, 1988. AA, Brainerd Coll., 1969; BS, U. Minn., 1971, postgrad. Cert. Lowthian Fashion Coll. Instr. Lowthian Fashion Coll., Mpls., 1969-79; tchr. English Hopkins (Minn.) Sch. Systems, 1971-79; profl. beauty cons. Mary Kay Cosmetics, Edina, Minn., 1977—, exec. sr. dir., 1985—. Mem. Nat. Assn. Female Exec., Nat. Assn. Women Bus. Owners, Edina C. of C., Mpls. C. of C. Republican. Clubs: U. Minn. Alumni Assn., Am. Legion. Office: Mary Kay Cosmetics 5125 Duggan Pl Edina MN 55435

STEPHENS, JOYCE LAVERNE, professional parliamentarian; b. Valdosta, Ga., July 25, 1936; m. Sankey Frederick Stephens, Jr., 1960; 1 child, Juliet Suzanne. Student, St. Petersburg Coll., 1980-82, Eckerd Coll., 1985—. Ptnr. SEBCO, Inc., Tampa, Fla., 1962-85; pvt. practice profl. parliamentarian Clearwater, Fla., 1980—. Author: Basic Parliamentary Procedure, 1984; editor Humanitas jour.; contbr. articles to profl. jours. Pres. council Girl Scouts U.S., Suncoast Tampa, 1979-81; bd. parliamentarian United Way, Pinellas County, Fla., 1980-87; mem. Dem. exec. com. Pinellas County, 1985, Fla. Orch. Guild (v.p.), Sunrise Homewowners Guild (past pres.); mem. Pinellas County Adv. Com. 4-H. Mem. Acad. Parliamentary Procedure and Law (nat. pres. 1986—, parliamentary specialist, cert. tchr.), Nat. Assn. Parliamentarians (profl. registered parliamentarian), Fla. State Assn. Parliamentarians (1st v.p. 1987—), Fla. Alpha Parliamentarians (pres. 1978-80), Fla. Registered Sect. (chair 1987—), Mental Health Assn. (exec. com. Pinellas County). Democrat. Home and Office: 1846 Sunrise Blvd Clearwater FL 34620

STEPHENS, LISA ANN, real estate appraiser; b. Brady, Tex., Aug. 21, 1959; d. Harold L. and Peggy (Shuffield) S. BS in Agrl. Econs., Tex. A&M U., 1982. Mgr., bookkeeper The Stephens Co., Stephens Wool & Mohair & Grain Elevators, Eden, Tex., 1982-83, Stephens Real Estate, San Angelo, Tex., 1983-86; residential appraiser Robert A. Elliott Real Estate, San Angelo, Tex., 1986-87; ptnr. H&L Ranch Co., Eden, 1986—; property mgr. City of San Angelo, 1987, div. asst. supt., 1985-87; right of way appraiser Dallas County, Tex., 1987—. Named one of Notable Womem of Tex. Emerson Pub., 1984-85. Mem. Nat. Assn. Realtors, Tex. Bd. Realtors, Southwestern Cattle Raiser's Assn., Tex. Cattle Raiser's Assn., Tex. Sheep & Goat Raisers Assn., San Angelo Stock Show and Rodeo Assn. (div. asst. supt. 1985—). Methodist. Home: 8650 Southwestern #3918 Dallas TX 75206 Office: Dallas County Dept Pub Works 411 Elm Dallas TX 75202

STEPHENS-BASSI, KAREN ANITA, manufacturing executive; b. Pasadena, Tex., Apr. 4, 1945; d. Patrick Kitchener and Francena (Ryan) McPearson; m. Phillip Von Stephens, Dec. 28, 1968 (div. Apr. 1981); m. Marco Vinicio Bassi, Dec. 3, 1984. BS, West Tex. State U., 1969, MFA, 1970. Cert. comml. investment mem. Tchr. Houston Ind. Sch. Dist., 1969-73, North Harris County Jr. Coll., Spring, Tex., 1973-76; instr. Market of Tex. Inc., Houston, 1976-79; v.p. Tecnomatic, Inc., Houston, 1979-81, chmn. bd., 1981-85; v.p., sec. bd. dirs. Mfrs. Group, Inc., Houston, 1981—; pres. Kaki Inc., San Leon, Tex. 1987—. Bd. dirs. Cultural Art Council of Houston, 1978-83. Mem. Instrument Soc. Am. Home: 3217 Iola Houston TX 77017 Office: Kaki Inc 1562 Railroad St San Leon TX 77539

STEPHENSON, BETTE M., Canadian provincial official, physician; b. Aurora, Ont., Can., July 31, 1924; d. Carl Melvin and Clara Mildred (Draper) S.; grad. Earl Haig Coll. Inst.; M.D., U. Toronto, 1946; m. Gordon Allan Pengelly, 1948; children—J. Stephen A., Elizabeth Anne A., C. Christopher A., J. Michael A., P. Timothy A., Mary Katharine A. Mem. med. staff Women's Coll. Hosp., 1950—, chief dept. gen. practice, dir. outpatient dept., 1956-64; mem. med. staff N.Y. Gen. Hosp., 1967—; elected Ont. Legislature for York Mills, 1975, 77, 81, 85; minister labor, 1975-78; minister edn., minister colls. and univs., 1978-85, treas. and dep. premier, 1985. Fellow Coll. Family Physicians Can. (chmn. nat. coordinating com. on edn. 1961-64, chmn. confs. on edn. for gen. practice 1961, 63), Acad. Med. Toronto; mem. Ont. Med. Assn. (dir. 1964-72, pres. 1970-71), Can. Med. Assn. (dir. 1968-75, pres. 1974-75), Art Gallery Ont., Royal Ont. Mus. Office: Parliament Bldgs, Toronto, ON Canada M7A 1A1

STEPHENSON, DONNA GILBERT, communications executive; b. Indpls., June 24, 1955; d. Alvin Duvall and Jo Ann (Cowles) Gilbert; m. Robert Gary Stephenson, May 12, 1973 (div. Aug. 1984). BA in Fine Arts and Design, Spalding Coll., 1978; cert. in computer sci., Bellarmine Coll., 1983, MBA, 1986. Freelance artist 1978-79; interior designer Brownsboro Design, Louisville, 1979-80; sales mgr. Bentley Bros., Louisville, 1980-82, gen. mgr., 1982-84; mgr. creative devel. Courier Communications Corp., Louisville, 1984-86, mgr. mktg. and creative services, 1986—; instr. Webster Univ., 1987—. Bd. dirs. Suicide Prevention and Edn. Ctr., Louisville. Mem. Videotex Designers Group. Club: Advt. of Louisville. Home: 1048 Cherokee Rd Louisville KY 40204-1231

STEPHENSON, DOROTHY GRIFFITH See GRIFFITH, DOTTY

STEPHENSON, HELEN ROSE, writer; b. Pitts.; d. Charles E. and Ruth L. (Bowers) Gibson; B.A., U. Pitts.; m. George M. Stephenson, June 10, 1961; children—Rosalind, Karen. Account supr. Ketchum, MacLeod & Grove, Inc., Pitts., 1955-61; editor-supr. printed materials Gen. Foods Corp., White Plains, N.Y., 1964-73; free-lance writer, 1973—, contbr. articles to various publs., including N.Y. Times, Wall St. Jour., Ladies Home Jour., Town & Country. Recipient Golden Quill award Sigma Delta Chi, 1960. Mem. Conn. Press Club, Nat. League Am. PEN. Editor, author various cookbooks Gen. Foods Corp., 1964-73. Home and Office: 190 Chestnut Ridge Rd Bethel CT 06801

STEPHENSON, IRENE HAMLEN, biorhythm analyst, consultant, editor, teacher; b. Chgo., Oct. 7, 1923; d. Charles Martin and Carolyn Hilda (Hilgers) Hamlin; m. Edgar B. Stephenson, Sr., Aug. 16, 1941 (div. 1946); 1 child, Edgar B. Author biorhythm compatibilities column Nat. Singles Register, Norwalk, Calif., 1979-81; instr. biorhythm Learning Tree Open U., Canoga Park, Calif., 1982-83; instr. biorhythm character analysis 1980—; instr. biorhythm compatibility, 1982—; owner, pres. matchmaking service Pen Pals Using Biorhythm, Chatsworth, Calif., 1979—; editor newsletter The Truth, 1979-85, Mini Examiner, Chatsworth, 1985—; researcher biorhythm character and compatibility, 1974—, selecting a mate, 1985—. Author: Learn Biorhythm Character Analysis, 1980; Do-It-Yourself Biorhythm Compatibilities, 1982; contbr. numerous articles to mags; frequent guests clubs, radio, TV. Office: Irene Hamlen Stephenson PO Box 3893 Chatsworth CA 91313

STEPHENSON, JAN LYNN, professional golfer; b. Sydney, Australia, Dec. 22, 1951; d. Francis John and Barbara (Green) S.; m. Eddie Vossler, 1982. Student, Australian schs. Profl. golfer 1972—; mem. Australian Ladies Profl. Golf Assn. tour, 1972-73, U.S. Ladies Profl. Golf Assn. tour, 1974—. Winner New South Wales (Australia) Jr. Championship, 1963-69; winner Australian Jr. Championship, 1968-71, Australian Title, 1973, Sarah Coventry Championship, 1976, Birmingham Championship Ala., 1976, Women's Internat., 1978, Sun City Classic, 1980, Peter Jackson Classic, 1981, Mary Kay Classic, 1981, United Va. Bank Classic, 1981, Ladies Profl. Golf Assn. Championship, 1982, Women's Tucson Open, 1983, Women's U.S. Open, 1983, Lady Keystone Open, GNA Tournament, 1985, French Open, 1985, Santa Barbara Open, 1987, Safeco Seattle Classsic, 1987, Konica San Jose Classic, 1987; named Rookie of Yr., U.S. Profl. Golfers Assn., 1974; Sportsman of Yr., Sportswriters Assn., Australia, 1976. Office: 6300 Ridglea Pl Suite 1118 Fort Worth TX 76116

STEPHENSON, LINDA SUE, cosmetic company executive; b. Monroeville, Ind., June 30, 1939; d. LeRoy Lloyd and Edith Lillian (Marquardt) Koehlinger; m. Jack Lynn Stephenson, Dec. 31, 1961. Student modeling Ft. Wayne Finishing Sch., 1959, instr. cert., 1961. Bus. mgr. Ft. Wayne Finishing Sch., Ind., 1960-64; dir., tchr. Cameo Finishing Sch., Ft. Wayne, 1964-65; assoc. dir. Fashion Two Twenty, Decatur, Ind., 1969-71; dir. Marjo Cosmetics, Ft. Wayne, 1971-81; founder, dir. Cozme Cosmetics. Ft. Wayne, 1981—; founder, tchr. Image Projection Workshops, Ft. Wayne, 1981—; dir. Your Total Look, Ft. Wayne. Author: New Dimensions, 1982; Eyes on Ft. Wayne, 1983, also articles. 4-H leader 4-H Horse and Pony Club, Monroeville, Ind., 1962-75; foster parent Adams County Welfare, Decatur, Ind., 1969-73, Indian Program, Ft. Wayne, 1970-72; choral dir. Community Youth Choir, Monroeville, 1967-80, Methodist Men's Chorus, 1980—. Named Equity Queen, Nat. Farmers Equity, 1960. Mem. Ft. Wayne Better Bus. Bur., Ft. Wayne Women's Bur., Women Bus. Owner's Assn., Nat. Hairdressers and Cosmetologists Assn., Ft. Wayne C. of C., Nat. Assn. Female Execs. Avocations: physical fitness; music; bird watching; flower gardening. Home: Rural Route 2 Monroeville IN 46773 Office: Cozme Cosmetics 5821 Decatur Rd Fort Wayne IN 46816

STEPHENSON, MARY RITA, association executive; b. Toronto, Ont., Can., Mar. 27, 1917; d. John Alexander and Marie Josephine (Kennedy) Pickett; m. Harald Jon Stephenson, June 19, 1945 (div. 1969); children—Helga Maria, Fridrik Jon, Helen Veronica, Donald Joseph. Student, U. Toronto, 1933-36. Advt., sales promotion mgr. Assos. Textiles, Montreal, Que., Can., 1941-45; head pub. relations dept. Cardon Rose Ltd., Montreal, 1968-73; exec. dir., founder Fashion Designers Assn. of Can. Ltd., Montreal, 1974—; pres. Mary Stephenson & Assocs. Inc., Toronto, 1979—; v.p. Fashion/Canada; bd. dirs. Can. Colour Service. Mem. Fashion Group Internat., Inst. Assn. Execs. Roman Catholic. Home: 675 Roselawn Ave, Toronto, ON Canada M5N 1L2 Office: 2084 Danforth, Toronto, ON Canada M5V 2J1

STEPHENSON, TONI EDWARDS, publisher, investment management executive; b. Bastrop, La., July 23, 1945; d. Sidney Crawford and Grace Erleene (Shipman) Little; BS, La. State U., 1967; enrolled owner/pres. mgmt. program Harvard Bus. Sch.; m. Arthur Emmet Stephenson, Jr., June 17, 1967; 1 dau., Tessa Lyn. Computer programmer Employers Group Ins., Boston, 1967-68; systems analyst Computer Tech., Inc., Cambridge, Mass., 1968-69; sr. v.p., founder E. Stephenson & Co., Inc., Denver, 1971—, Stephenson Mcht. Banking, 1980—; gen. ptnr. Viking Fund; ptnr. Stephenson Properties, Stephenson Ventures, Stephenson Mgmt. Co.; pres., dir. Gen. Communications, Inc., Globescope Corp.; underwriting mem. Lloyd's of London; founder, dir. Charter Bank & Trust. Co-pub. Denver Bus. Mag., 1978—, Denver Mag., 1982—, Vail Mag., 1980—, Development Sales Catalog, 1980—, Colorado Book, 1986—; former dir. The Children's Hosp. Past pres. Children's Hosp. Assn. Vols. Mem. DAR, Delta Gamma. Clubs: Annabel's of London, Thunderbird Country, Petroleum. Office: E Stephenson & Co Inc 100 Garfield St Denver CO 80206

STEPHENSON-BAILEY, SHARON ANN, custom press shop owner, business educator, consultant; b. Pitts., Feb. 8, 1958; d. Samuel B. and Amy Bell (Humphries) Stephenson. BBA, Temple U., 1979. Clk. The Peoples Natural Gas Co., Pitts., 1979-81, tax analyst, 1981-82; sr. tax acct. Consol. Natural Gas, N.Y.C., 1982-84; sr. acct. Consol. Natural Gas, Pitts., 1984-86; tax mgr. The Union Corp., Norwalk, Conn., 1986; controller Am. Bus. Products Inc., 1987—; auditor Abarta, Inc., Pitts., 1988; owner Amy's, Pitts., 1986—; ptnr. Amy's Fashions; instr. Community Coll. Allegheny, Pitts., 1986—, U. Pitts., 1986—; cons. SAS Services, Pitts., 1979—, Hill House Assn., Pitts., 1986; mem. Vol. Income Tax Assistance, Pitts., 1980. Vol. Big Brothers/Big Sisters, Pitts., 1981; mem. Dem. Com., Pitts., 1986; fin. sec. Met. Baptist Ch., Pitts., 1985—. Mem. Nat. Assn. Black Accts. (sec. 1980-81). Home: 102 E Jefferson St Pittsburgh PA 15212

STEPLER, HILDE, nurse; b. Campbellsville, Ky., Nov. 26, 1948; d. Edwin Garnett and Irma (Weissthanner) Ford; m. Richard Murray Stepler, May 16, 1970; children: Laura, Erica, Gregory. BS in Nursing cum laude, Spalding Coll., 1970; MS in Nursing, U. Ky., 1986. RN. Staff nurse Dewitt Army Hosp., Ft. Belvoir, Va., 1970-71; temporary nurse Med. Personnel Pool, Arlington, Va., 1973; staff nurse Arlington Hosp., Arlington, 1973, nursing supr., 1973-76; primary nurse Mt. Vernon Hosp., Alexandria, Va., 1978-83; dir. nursing Miller's Nursing Home, Lexington, Ky., 1984; clin. nurse specialist, coordinator spl. nursing documentation project Univ. Hosp., Lexington, Ky., 1986—. Mem. Ky. Nurses Assn. (membership com. 1986—), Am. Nurses Assn., Nat. Gerontologic Nurses Assn., Sigma Theta Tau. Home: 3265 Yellowstone Pkwy Lexington KY 40502 Office: Albert B Chandler Med Ctr Rose St Lexington KY 40536-0084

STEPNER, LARAINE E. ADLER, public relations executive; b. Boston, Sept. 25, 1943; d. Neil and Sadie Adelman (Adler). BA in English, Wellesley Coll., 1978; MA in Econs., Internat. Studies, Johns Hopkins U., 1980; Cert., Washington Sch. Protocol, 1979. Airline rep. Can. Pacific Airlines, San Francisco, 1968-70; tour escort AAA, others, 1970-76; travel rep. Trans Nat. Travel, Boston, 1973-76; chief exec. officer Internat. Photography Soc., Washington, 1981-83; also bd. dirs. Internat. Photography Soc.; prin. Laraine Stepner & Assocs., Boston, 1983-85; pres. Stepner & Sayre PR Ltd., Natick, Mass., 1985—; Owner mag. The Social Calendar, 1986—. Cable TV Host Women on the Move, 1987—; contbr. articles to profl. jours. Fundraiser Presdl. campaign, Washington, 1980-81, Boston Ballet, 1984, Vietnam VA, Boston, 1985, Fulbright U. Alumni Assn., 1988—; com. mem. Fair Housing Panel, Natick, 1987, Affordable Housing Com.; chosen to C. of C. Leadership Acad., 1987. Mem. Bus. and Profl. Women, New Women's Network, Soc. Female Execs., Women's Mus. Art., Mass. Women's Polit. Caucus. Office: Stepner & Sayre Ltd 5 Summer St PO Box 882 Natick MA 01760

STEPP, MARY JAN, corporate executive; b. Atlanta, Nov. 21, 1957; d. Roy A. and M. Frances (Harbin) S.; 1 adopted child, Ashley. Grad. high sch., Mableton, Ga., 1975. Acctg. clk. Atlanta News Agy., 1975-77; bookkeeper Vicrtex Sales Div., Atlanta, 1977-79; sales rep. Life of Ga. Ins. Co., Atlanta, 1979-82, Nat. Life Ins. Co., Marietta, Ga., 1982-83; office mgr. Gunold & Stickma of Am., Inc., Marietta, 1983-86, v.p. adminstrn., 1986—. Mem. Nat. Assn. Exec. Females. Office: Gunold & Stickma of Am Inc 2140 Newmarket Pkwy Suite #112 Marietta GA 30067

STERBENZ, JOANNE RUTH, accountant; b. New Orleans, June 16, 1947; d. Joseph Roch and Merlin (Prieto) S.; B.S., U. Southwestern La., 1969; M.B.A., Tulane U., 1971. With Arthur Young & Co., Los Angeles, 1971-83, mgr., 1976-80, coordinator computer auditing, 1976-79, prin., 1980-83, office dir. edn., 1979; controller Met. Theatres, Los Angeles, 1985—. Assoc. v.p. for ticketing Los Angeles Olympic Organizing Com., 1984. C.P.A., Calif.; Tulane U. fellow, 1969-71. Mem. Am. Inst. C.P.A.s, Nat. Assn. Female Execs., Am. Women's Soc. C.P.A.s, EDP Auditors Assn., NOW, Tulane Assn. Bus. Alumni, Greater Los Angeles Zoo Assn., Smithsonian Assn. Democrat. Roman Catholic. Home: 222 7th St Apt 107 Santa Monica CA 90402 Office: Met Theatres Corp 8727 W 3d St Los Angeles CA 90048

STERLING, A. MARY FACKLER, lawyer; b. Pioneer, Ohio, Sept. 4, 1955. AB cum laude, Harvard U., 1976; MA, Ohio State U., 1977; JD, NYU, 1980. Bar: Mo. 1980, U.S. Dist. Ct. (we. dist.) Mo. 1980, U.S. Ct. Appeals (8th cir.) 1983, U.S. Ct. Appeals (10th cir.) 1985. Assoc. Watson, Ess, Marshall & Enggas, Kansas City, Mo., 1980-82; asst. U.S. atty. we. dist. Mo. U.S. Dept. Justice, Kansas City, 1982-85, fed. prosecutor organized crime and racketeering strike force, 1985-86; White House Fellow and spl. asst. to U.S. Atty. Gen. U.S. Dept. Justice, Washington, 1987—; instr. U.S. Atty. Gen.'s Advocacy Inst., Washington, 1986, 88; guest lectr. NYU Sch. Law, 1986. Sec. 8th cir. Root-Tilden Scholarship program, NYU, 1982—; mem. Urban Crime Prevention Authority, Kansas City, 1980-81, Friends of Art, Kansas City, Friends of Symphony, Kansas City. Root-Tilden scholar NYU, 1977-80; named One of Top Ten Coll. Women in U.S., 1975, one of ten Outstanding Young Working Women in Am., 1987, Kansas City Career Woman of Yr., 1988; recipient Thompson award Ohio State U., 1988; Ohio State U. fellow, 1976-77. Mem. ABA (assembly del. 1986—, house of dels. 1986—, assembly resolutions com. 1986—, com. on govt. litigation counsel litigation sect., com. complex crimes litigation), Mo. Bar Assn. (bd. govs. 1986—, chmn. pro bono task force 1984-86, young lawyers council, Outstanding Service award 1984, Pro Bono Publico award 1986), Kansas City Met. Bar Assn. (fed. cts. and bench bar coms.), Nat. Assn. Women Lawyers (chmn. torts and litigation sect. 1982-83, 85-87, state del. 1981-83, 85, rec. sec. 1986-87, exec. com. 1986-87, nominating com. 1988), Greater Kansas City Assn. Women Lawyers, Am. Soc. Pub. Adminstrn. Club: Harvard (Kansas City).

STERLING, JANET LEIGH, social worker; b. Morgantown, W.Va., Feb. 5, 1950; d. Frederick Lee and Margaret Elizabeth (McWhirter) Wotring; m. Donald Eugene Sterling, Apr. 23, 1983. AB in Sociology and Anthropology, W.Va. U., 1977, MSW, 1979. Asst. dir. Florence Crittenton Home, Wheeling, W.Va., 1979-81; exec. dir. Charleston (W.Va.) Dist. Outreach Ministries, 1981-86; project mgr. adult services network Community Council Kanawha Valley, Charleston, 1986—; field instr. W.Va. State Coll., 1985—. Mem. W.Va. United Meth. Ann. Conf. Bd. Ch. and Soc., 1984-88; pres. Charleston Covenant House, 1987; pres., bd. dirs. Charleston Interdenominational Council Social Concerns, 1987. Mem. Nat. Assn. Social Workers, W.Va. Human Resources Assn. Home: 821 Scenic Dr Charleston WV 25311 Office: Community Council Kanawha Valley 702 1/2 Lee St Box 2711 Charleston WV 25330

STERMER, NANCY LOUISE, human resources executive; b. Canandaigua, N.Y., Dec. 19, 1952; d. Gordon Ernest and Elaine Louise (Jones) S. B.A., Mich. State U., 1975; M.A., U. Mich., 1979. Cert. tchr. continuing edn., Mich. Teaching asst. Mich. State U., East Lansing, 1974-75; tchr. adult edn. Flint Community Schs., Mich., 1976; tchr. elem. edn., jr. high sch. Waterford Sch. Dist., Pontiac, Mich., 1976-80; tng. specialist Fed.-Mogul Corp., Southfield, Mich., 1981-83, office systems analyst and tng. specialist, 1983-86, info. systems coordinator, 1986; lead systems designer, trainer Comerica, Inc., Detroit, 1986-87, sr. tng. project mgr., 1987-88, human resources officer, sr. tng. project mgr., 1988—. Bd. dirs. Mich. chpt. Am. Lupus Soc., 1985-87. Named Outstanding Sr., Class of '75, Mich. State U., 1975. Mem. Nat. Assn. Female Execs., Assn. for the Devel. of Computer-Based Instrn., Nat. Tng. & Computers Network, Am. Soc. for Tng. & Devel., Soc. for Applied Learning Tech., Detroit Area Trainers Assn., Office Automation Mgmt. Assn., NOW, U. Mich. Alumnae, Kappa Delta Pi. Office: Comerica Inc 211 W Fort St Detroit MI 48275-2455

STERN, ARLENE HELEN, human resources administrator; b. Bklyn., Nov. 7, 1950; d. Irving and Shirley Judith (Koretz) Stern. BS in Labor Relations, U. Bridgeport, 1971; postgrad. Pace U., 1972-75. Personnel asst. Pathmark, Woodbridge, N.J., 1971-72, regional personnel mgr., 1972-75, dir. human resource planning, 1975-77, dir. personnel and labor relations, Phila., 1977-81; v.p. human resources Howland-Steinbach-Hochschild's, White Plains, N.Y., 1981-85; sr. v.p. human resources P.A. Bergner & Co., Milw., 1985—; mem. Frederick Atkins Personnel Adv. Bd., N.Y.C., 1981-86, chmn., 1984. Bd. dirs. Clavis Theatre, 1986—, women's div. Milw. Jewish Fedn., 1987—, Milw. Jewish Council, 1987—, Wis. State of Israel Bonds, 1988—. Mem. Am. Soc. Personnel Adminstrs., Am. Soc. Tng. and Devel. Home: 4800 N Lake Drive Whitefish Bay WI 53217

STERN, BARBARA ELLEN, librarian; b. N.Y.C., June 9, 1954; d. Hugo Gale and Shirley Rosalind (Levy) Geller; m. James Max Stern, Mar. 28, 1982. BA, Calif. State U., Northridge, 1978; postgrad., UCLA, 1986—. Library asst. UCLA, 1979-87. Mem. ALA. Democrat. Jewish.

STERN, BERNICE G., national director of fundraising; b. Chgo., June 17, 1928; d. Samuel and Cecelia (Weise) Goldblatt; m. Myron H. Stern, May 20, 1951; children: Steven D., H. Thomas, Beth I. LittB, Douglas Coll., 1950; postgrad., Rutgers Coll., 1946-50. Fundraiser Jewish Fedn. Metro West, N.J.; dir. women's div. pub. relations United Jewish Community, Bergen County, N.J.; nat. dir. fundraising Women's Am. ORT, N.Y.C., 1979—. Pres. UOTS Hosp., East Orange, N.J, 1959-61, Fidelity-Hulda, PTA, Maplewood. Mem. Am. Jewish Pub. Relations Soc., Am. Jewish Community Profls., N.J. Conf. Jewish Communal Profls., Nat. Assn. Female Execs., N.J. Women's Network, Nat. Women's Devel. Fund. Office: Women's Am ORT 315 Park Ave S New York NY 10010

STERN, GRACE MARY, state representative; b. Holyoke, Mass., July 10, 1925; d. Frank McLellan and Marguerite M. (Nason) Dain; m. Charles H. Suber, June 21, 1947 (div. 1959); children: Ann, Peter, Thomas, John; m. Herbert L. Stern, May 13, 1962; stepchildren: Gwen, Herbert III, Robert. Student, Wellesley Coll., 1942-45; LLD (hon.), Shimer Coll., 1984. Asst. supr. Deerfield Twp., Lake County, Ill., 1967-70; county clk. Lake County, Ill., 1970-82; mem. Ill. Ho. of Reps., 1984—; candidate for lt. gov. Ill., 1982. Author: With a Stern Eye, 1967, Still Stern, 1969. Democrat. Presbyterian. Home: 291 Marshman St Highland Park IL 60035 Office: 559 Roger Williams Ave Highland Park IL 60035

STERN, JOANNE SUE, television station executive; b. Cleve., June 17, 1953; d. Sterling and Shirley Minette (Scragg) S. B.A., Ohio State U., 1975. Continuity clerk Sta. WJKW-TV (now WJW-TV), Cleve., 1976, continuity writer, 1976-77, publicity dir., 1977-79, on-air promotion dir., 1979-80, asst. dir. creative services, 1980-81, dir. creative services, 1981—; mem. CBS promotion mgrs. caucus CBS Network, N.Y.C., 1984-85. Exec. producer commls.: B-Movie (Distinctive Merit award 1982), 1981, Bootcamp: The New Secret Weapon (Monitor award 1983), 1982; producer commls.: You Sure Look Like a Winner (Twyla M. Conway award 1983), 1983, Managers Tape (Graphic Excellence award 1984), 1983. Vol. Easter Seal Soc. Greater Cleve., 1983. Recipient 3 Bronze/3 Silver awards Internat. Film and TV Festival N.Y., 1980-84; Cleve. Communicators awards Women in Communications, Inc., 1982 through 85; Broadcast Media award San Francisco State U., 1983; Bronze Telly awards Local/Regional TV Commls. Festival, Cin., 1983, 84, 85; Spl. Recog. award Cleve. Advt. Club, 1983; 2 Fifth Dist. Addy awards Am. Advt. Fedn., 1982-83, Nat. Addy award, 1983; Finalist award Clio Awards, 1983; Finalist award Internat. Radio Festival N.Y., 1984. Mem. Nat. Acad. TV Arts and Scis. (bd. govs. 1981-85, 2d v.p. 1985, 5 Emmys 1980-81-82-83), Broadcast Promotion and Mktg. Execs. Assn. (Gold Medallion finalist-2), Am. Women in Radio and TV. Office: Sta WJW-TV 5800 S Marginal Rd Cleveland OH 44103 *

STERN, MARIANNE, advertising agency executive; b. Elizabeth, N.J., July 17, 1950; d. Arthur Leo and Anne (De Paola) Monaghan; m. Manfred Joseph Stern, July 11, 1970 (div.); children: Kathryn Anne, Manfred Joseph III. Student, Montclair (N.J.) State Coll., 1970; BA in English summa cum laude, Kean Coll. of N.J., 1978. Copywriter Patrick J. Gallagher Advt., Westfield, N.J., 1978-79; media dir. Rapp Advt., Springfield, N.J., 1979-85; account exec. Spectrum advt., Springfield, 1985; pres., account exec. Whitney A. Morgan Advt., Montclair, 1985—; cons. Monadel, Inc., Rahway, N.J., 1985—; bd. dirs. Delatush Systems, Inc., Montclair. Mem. publicity com. 200 Club of Union County, N.J., 1978; pub. chmn. Boy Scouts Am. Union County chpt., 1987. Mem. Nat. Assn. Female Execs., Phi Kappa Phi, Lambda Alpha Sigma, Alpha Sigma Lambda. Office: Whitney A. Morgan Advt 37 N Fullerton Ave Montclair NJ 07042

STERN, ROSLYNE PAIGE, magazine publisher; b. Chgo., May 26, 1926; d. Benjamin Gross and Clara (Sniderman) Roer; m. William E. Weber, May 3, 1944 (div. Mar. 1956); m. Richard S. Paige, June 28, 1958 (div. Apr. 1978); children: Sandra Weber Porr, Barbara Weber Taylor Sharp, Elizabeth; m. Robert D. Stern, June 5, 1978. Cert., U. Chgo., 1945. Profl. model, singer 1947-53; account exec. Interstate United, Chgo., 1953-58; sales mgr. Getting To Know You Internat., Great Neck, N.Y., 1963-71, exec. v.p., 1971-78; pub. After Dark Mag., N.Y.C., 1978-82; assoc. pub. Dance Mag., N.Y.C., 1978-85, pub., 1985—; bd. dirs. Rudor Consol. Industries, Inc.,

N.Y.C. Founding pres. Dance Mag. Found., N.Y.C., 1984—; mem. nat. women's com. Brandeis U., Waltham, Mass., 1958—. Mem. Pub. Relations Soc. Am., LWV, Am. Theatre Wing. Democrat. Jewish. Home: 2 Imperial Landing Westport CT 06880 Office: Dance Mag Inc 33 W 60th St New York NY 10023

STERN, SHIRLEY, lawyer, author; b. Bklyn., Aug. 16, 1929; d. Bernard and Bessie (Tasgal) Gartenstein; m. Leonard W. Stern, Dec. 24, 1949; children—Erwin Samuel, Elana Debra, Gil Avram. B.A., CUNY, 1950, M.A., 1956; J.D., St. John's U., 1982. Bar: N.Y. 1983. Freelance writer, New Hyde Park, N.Y., 1972—; sole practice, New Hyde Park, 1983—. Author: Exploring Jewish History, 1979; Exploring Jewish Wisdom, 1980; Exploring Jewish Holidays, 1981; Exploring the Prayerbook, 1982; Exploring the Torah, 1984. Mem. Nat. Assn. Temple Educators, ABA, N.Y. Bar Assn., Nassau County Bar Assn., Nassau/Suffolk Women's Bar Assn. Democrat. Jewish. Office: 26 Birchwood Dr New Hyde Park NY 11040

STERN, SONIA WYNTREE, writer, retired editorial services executive; b. N.Y.C.; d. Mark Efimovitch and Rose (Goldenberg) Weinbaum; m. Charles Stern, Nov. 3, 1955 (div. 1981); 1 son, Adam Richard. Student Columbia U., Art Students League; cert. Winona Sch. Photography, 1959. Mgr., Louelle Photographers, Inc., N.Y.C., 1960-73; contbg. editor PTN Publs., L.I., N.Y., 1972-75; pub. relations account exec. Gilbert, Felix & Sharf, Inc., N.Y.C., 1975-78; sr. product publicist GAF Corp., N.Y.C., 1978-81; pres. Prism Internat. Co., N.Y.C., 1981-84, ret. 1984. Contbr. articles on photography to profl. jours. Recipient Bronze medal Profl. Photographers N.Y. State; fellow Am. Photographic Hist. Soc. (pres. 1977-78); mem. Photographic Adminstrs., Inc., Photographic Adminstrs., Inc., Am. Photographic Hist. Soc.

STERNBERG, DONNA UDIN, lawyer; b. Phila., May 3, 1951; d. Jack and Frances (Osner) Udin; m. Harvey J. Sternberg; 1 child, Zachary Samuel. Student Tel Aviv U., 1971; BA, Northwestern U., 1973; JD, Loyola U., Chgo., 1976. Bar: Ill. 1976, Pa. 1979. Profl. actress, dancer, model, 1961-76; dancer Boishoi Ballet Co., 1965, 66, 67, Leningrad Kirov Ballet Co., 1966; actress Broadway prodn., 1966; appeared stage plays, TV and film roles, 1961-77; model nat. fashion mags. and publs., 1961-77; assoc. firm Ronald H. Balson & Assocs., Chgo., 1976-79, Mesirov, Gelman, Jaffe, Cramer & Jamieson, Phila., 1979-81; mem. firm Blank, Rome, Comisky & McCauley, Phila., 1981—. Active young leadership council Fedn. Allied Jewish Appeal, 1982-84; mem. Israel Bonds New Leadership Cabinet, 1982-87. Mem. ABA, Pa. Bar Assn., Phila. Bar Assn., Chgo. Bar Assn. Jewish. Club: Locust (Phila.). Office: Blank Rome Comisky & McCauley Four Penn Ctr Plaza Philadelphia PA 19103

STERNER, JULIE ANN, accounting educator; b. Carbondale, Ill., July 17, 1953; d. Joe H. and Lilah P. (Notman) S. BBA in Acctg., U. Miami, 1974; MBA in Acctg., So. Ill. U., 1975; PhD in Acctg., St. Louis U., 1982. CPA. Instr. acctg. U. Wis., Platteville, 1975-76; instr. acctg. So. Ill. U., Carbondale, 1976-78, asst. prof. acctg., 1985—; instr. acctg. St. Louis U., 1978-82; asst. prof. acctg. Marquette U., Milw., 1982-85; bd. advisors Midwest Bus. Adminstrn. Assn., Chgo., 1983—. Contbr. articles to profl. jours. Grantee Marquette U., 1983, 84, So. Ill. U. Coll. Bus. and Adminstrn., 1986-87. Mem. Am. Inst. CPA's, Am. Acctg. Assn., Midwest Acctg. Soc. (sec.-treas. 1986—), Beta Gamma Sigma, Beta Alpha Psi. Democrat. Baptist. Office: So Ill U Sch of Accountancy Carbondale IL 62901

STERRANTINO, CYNTHIA ELLEN, accountant; b. Dallas, May 18, 1950; d. Jesse Ray Houston and Martha Louise (Williams) Stewart; m. Adolphus Taylor Rohlman, Dec. 23, 1969 (div. Nov. 1976); 1 child, Kimberly; m. John Charles Sterrantino, June 25, 1988. BBA in Acctg. and Info Systems, U. Tex., 1981. Tax acct. Main Hurdman, Dallas, 1981-82; asst. controller Women's and Children's Hosp., Odessa, Tex., 1983-84; dir. acctg. Med. Plaza Hosp., Ft. Worth, 1984—. Mem. 500 Inc. Benefitting Performing Arts. Named one of 10 Most Outstanding Young Women in Am., 1981. Mem. Nat. Assn. Accts., Healthcare Fin. Mgmt. Assn., Tex. Hosp. Assn., Tex. Hosp. Info. Systems Soc., Nat. Controllers Council, Nat. Assn. Female Execs. Home: 1612 Shirley Way Bedford TX 76022

STETS, DEBRA KAY, distribution company executive; b. Painesville, Ohio, Jan. 7, 1958; d. David L. and Phyllis J. (Lockard) Rosenbaum; m. Mark A. Stets, June 25, 1983; children: Courtney M., Joshua D. A in Bus., Lakeland Community Coll., Mentor, Ohio, 1986. Sec. to dir. sales Bowman Distbn./Barnes Group Inc., Cleve., 1977-79, sec. to dir. mktg., 1979-81, sec. to gen. mgr., 1981, asst. sales adminstr., 1981-87, sales adminstr., 1987—. Mem. Nat. Assn. for Female Execs., Inst. Cert. Profl. Mgrs. Roman Catholic. Office: Bowman Distbn Inc 850 E 72nd St Cleveland OH 44103

STEVENS, ANNE HAWLEY, executive search firm principal, consultant; b. Altoona, Pa., May 30, 1956; d. John King McLanahan and Carol (Bradford) S. BA, Boston U., 1978, MEd, 1981. Workshop/residential coordinator Task Oriented Communities, Waltham, Mass., 1978-80; clin. intern Counseling Services, Inc., Boston, 1980-81; dir. human resources, assoc. dir. Fee Mail Couriers, Boston, 1981-84; prin. A. H. Stevens Assocs., Boston, 1984—; housing renovator. Mem. Mass. Assn. Personnel Cons. (regional bd. dirs. 1984-87), Assn. Women in Psychology, New England Women in Real Estate, Associated Builders and Contractors, Thespian Soc., Nat Mus. of Women in Arts (charter), Nat. Assn. Female Execs. Democrat. Episcopalian. Avocations: water skiing, cooking. Home and Office: 284 K St South Boston MA 02127

STEVENS, BEVERLY D., college administrator; b. Melrose, Mass., Jan. 28, 1943; d. Wilmot H. and Glena (Bruce) Decker; children: Rebecca, Jeffrey, Jennifer. BA, Wheaton Coll., Norton, Mass., 1964. Mgr. admissions office Williams Coll., Williamstown, Mass., 1981-83, dir. alumni devel. info. systems, 1983-87, dir. devel. ops., 1987—; cons. in field. Mem. sch. com. Williamstown Pub. Schs., 1970-75, chmn. 1975-77; deacon First Congl. Ch. Mem. Council for Advancement and Support of Edn. Office: Williams Coll PO Box 231 Williamstown MA 01267

STEVENS, BOBBIE RAY, management consultant; b. Cooksprings, Ala., May 1, 1935; d. Talley Bert and Clurcy Augusta (Masters) S.; m. Billy Ray Watson, June 6, 1953 (div. 1957); m. Dean Richard Portinga, Sept. 1, 1979. Student, U. Ala., Brimingham, 1957-59; PhD in Psychology Bus. Mgmt., Columbia Pacific U., 1981. Exec. secretary Hayes Aircraft Corp., Birmingham, 1955-60; model, tchr. Margo George Modeling Agy., Birmingham, 1959-60; flight attendant Northwest Orient Airlines, St. Paul, 1960—; office mgr. Minn. Twins, Bloomington, 1960-61; acct. Rochlin & Lurie CPA's, Mpls., 1962-64; pub. relations agt. Breezy Point Estates, Piquot Lakes, Minn., 1964; sales rep. Success Motivation Inc., 1965-66; pub. relations rep. Employers Overload Inc., Mpls., 1966-67; cons. Dolphin Employment Agy., Mpls., 1968; real estate agt. Relocation Realty, Bloomington, 1971; assoc. townhouse developer Wakely Investment Co., Bloomington, 1971-74; assoc. broker Century 21, Red Carpet Realty, Bloomington, 1974-76; broker, fin. planner Bobbie Stevens Real Estate & Fin. Planning, Bloomington, 1976-82; pvt. practice counseling 1982-86; pres., chmn. bd. dirs. Exec. Futures Inc., Excelsior, 1984. Bd. dirs. Continuum Minn., Mpls., 1983—. Home and Office: 400 Hwy 7 Excelsior MN 55331

STEVENS, CAROLE BASKIN, civic leader; b. San Francisco, Sept. 29, 1934; d. Leo M. and Ida (Sommers) Baskin; m. Norman E. Stevens, Sept. 23, 1956; children: Jeffrey, Curt, Suzanne L. Student, Northwestern U., 1952-53; AA, U. Calif., Berkeley, 1954; AB, UCLA, 1956, M of Journalism, 1971. Editorial asst. Los Angeles mag., 1971; with Equal Opportunity Forum mag., Los Angeles, 1971-81; free-lance writer New West, PSA Flightime, Continental Flightime mags., Los Angeles; dir. pub. affairs Econ. Literacy Council of Calif., Los Angeles, 1986—. Bd. dirs. Santa Monica Mountains Conservancy, 1983—; pres., chmn. bd. dirs. Fedn. of Hillside and Canyon Assns., Inc., Los Angeles, 1981-85; mem. Mountains Recreation and Conservation Authority, Ventura, Calif., 1985—; parliamentarian Los Angeles Women's Campaign Fund, 1982; mem. editorial bd. Town Hall Ballot Measures, 1984, 86, 88, steering com. Wilshire Blvd. Temple Bus. and Profl. Women, 1986-87; mem. community relations com., law and legis. com., govtl. outreach subcom. Jewish Fedn. Council of Los Angeles, 1986-87; v.p. polit. action com. Nat. Women's Polit. Caucus, Los Angeles, 1982-83, chairperson legis. com. San Fernando Valley, 1984-86. Republican. Home: 16611 Park Ln Circle Los Angeles CA 90049

STEVENS, CHRIS ANNE, food products company executive; b. Detroit, June 6, 1939; d. Frank and Angeline Malinowski; m. Walter S. Stevens (div. 1980); children: Linda Sue Stevens Fry, Laurie Ann, Lois Marie. Diploma in Nursing, Mercy Coll., Detroit, 1960; BA in Health Scis., Stephens Coll., 1975; postgrad., U. No. Colo., 1978-79. Coordinator Allied Health Program El Paso (Tex.) Community Coll., 1974-76; corp. mgr. health services Stanley Structures, Inc., Denver, 1976-80; pres. Chris Stevens Cons. Service, Sacramento, 1980-81; internat. cons. to mgmt. cons. Upjohn Health Care, Kalamazoo, Mich., 1981-87; pres. Crissy's Cheesecake Co., Ontario, Calif., 1986—. Contbr. articles to women's pubs. Mem. Bus. Women's Network, Nat. Assn. Female Execs., Am. Entrepreneurs Assn., Stephens Alumni Assn., Am. Soc. Profl. Cons. Roman Catholic. Office: PO Box 1340 Alta Loma CA 91701

STEVENS, CHRISTINA LEA, film director, writer; b. Sydney, N.S.W., Australia, Apr. 9, 1948; came to U.S., 1971; d. William James and Margaret Diana (Young) Stevens. writer Young & Rubicam, Inc., N.Y.C., Sydney, Hong Kong, Paris, 1971-76; cons. N.Y.C., 1979-81; sr. writer Wells Rich Green, Los Angeles, 1977-79; sr. v.p. creative dir. Ogilvy & Mather, Los Angeles, 1981-84; pres. Blue Sky Prodns., Inc., Santa Paula, Calif., 1984—; creative dir., cons. Ogilvy & Mather, Inc., 1984—. Author: Vic the Viking, 1968; Illuminations, 1984. Founder, pres. Angel Found., Los Angeles, 1983. Recipient Gold Lion, Cannes Film Festival 1975; Lulu award Los Angeles Advt. Women, 1977, 80; Clio awards, 1978, 79; IBA awards Internat. Advt. Bur., 1978, 81, 82. Mem. Dirs. Guild Am. (mem. spl. projects com., bd. dirs.), Screen Actors Guild Am. Home: 16812 S Mountain Rd Santa Paula CA 93060

STEVENS, ELISABETH GOSS (MRS. ROBERT SCHLEUSSNER, JR.), author, journalist; b. Rome, N.Y., Aug. 11, 1929; d. George May and Elisabeth (Stryker) Stevens; m. Robert Schleussner, Jr., Mar. 12, 1966 (dec. 1977); 1 child, Laura Stevens. B.A., Wellesley Coll., 1951; M.A. with high honors, Columbia U., 1956. Editorial assoc. Art News Mag., 1964-65; art critic and reporter Washington Post, Washington, 1965-66; free-lance art critic and reporter Balt., 1966—; contbg. art critic Wall Street Jour., N.Y.C., 1969-72; art critic Trenton Times, N.J., 1974-77; art and architecture critic Balt. Sun, 1978-87. Author: Elisabeth Stevens' Guide to Baltimore's Inner Harbor, 1981, Fire and Water: Six Short Stories, 1982, Children of Dust: Portraits and Preludes, 1985; contbr. articles, poetry and short stories to jours., nat. newspapers and popular mags. Recipient A.D. Emmart award for Journalism, 1980, citation for critical writing Balt.-Washington Newspaper Guild, 1980; art critics' fellow Nat. Endowment Arts, 1973-74; fellow MacDowell Colony, 1981, Va. Ctr. for Creative Arts, 1982, 83, 84, 85, Ragdale Found., 1984; Work in Progress grantee for poetry Md. State Arts Council, 1986; Creative Devel. grantee for short fiction collection Mayor's Com. on Art and Culture, Balt., 1986. Mem. Coll. Art Assn., Am. Internat. Assn. Art Critics, Md. Writers Council, Balt. Writers Alliance, Balt. Bibliophiles, MLA., Popular Culture Assn., Authors Guild, Am. Studies Assn., Soc. Archtl. Historians. Home: 6604 Walnutwood Circle Baltimore MD 21212

STEVENS, FLORALINE INGRAM, city agency administrator; b. Los Angeles, Apr. 17, 1934; d. Leo and Charline (Hoag) Ingram; m. Melvin Maurice Stevens: 1 child, Melva Charline. BS, U. So. Calif., 1955; MEd, UCLA, 1965, EdD, 1973. Resident psychologist Cen. City Community Health, Los Angeles, 1974-75; tchr. Los Angeles Unified Schs., 1955-56, evaluation cons., 1966-69, testing coordinator, 1974-75, asst. dir., 1975-79, dir. research and evaluation, 1979—; mem. nat. adv. bd. UCLA, 1979-81; chair research com. Council Gt. City Schs., Los Angeles, 1979—; mem. electronics panel McGraw-Hill, Monterey, Calif., 1986—; mem. Mayor's Small Bus. Adv. Bd., Los Angeles, 1986—. Pres. Lullaby Guild, Children's Home Soc., Los Angeles, 1971—; v.p. Ebony Guild, 1984-87; sec., v.p. Crittenton Ctr. Bd. Dirs., Los Angeles, 1979-87;. Vol. award Los Angeles City Human Relations Commn., 1985. Mem. Am. Edn. Research Assn. (v.p. div.-H 1987-89, pres. dir. research 1984-85), Women in Leadership, Delta Sigma Theta. Democrat. Methodist. Club: Links. Office: Los Angeles Unified Sch Dist 450 N Grand Ave G-265 Los Angeles CA 90012

STEVENS, JILL WINIFRED, control systems technologist; b. Southampton, Eng.; came to U.S., 1964; d. William Horace Routledge and Winifred Mabel (Richards) S. Student, Houston Community Coll. System, 1987—. Asst. to producer BBC, London, 1961-64; governess pvt. home, Hillsboro, Calif., 1964-65; adminstrv. asst. Cambridge U. (Eng.), 1965-66; expediter, buyer, technician Bechtel Petroleum Inc., San Francisco, 1966-77, control systems technologist, Houston, 1978-83; control systems technologist Bechtel Power Corp., Houston, 1983—. Recipient awards in English lang. and English lit. with honors, Royal Soc. Arts and Scis., City of London, 1956. Mem. Instrument Soc. Am., Soc. Women Engrs. (assoc.). Roman Catholic. Home: 2121 Fountainview Condo E81 Houston TX 77057

STEVENS, LYDIA GREENE, home economics educator; b. Sumter, S.C., Mar. 19, 1947; d. Julius Sr. and Angeline (Major) G.; m. Edmund B. Stevens, June 24, 1972. BS, S.C. State Coll., 1968; MEd, Western Md. Coll., 1978. Sci. tchr. Greenwood (S.C.) Sch. Dist., 1968-72; home econ. tchr. Montgomery County Pub. Schs., Rockville, Md., 1972—; chmn. home econs. dept. Takoma Park Intermediate Sch., Silver Springs, Md., 1974—; tchr. Takoma Park Intermediate Sch. Basic Skills, Silver Springs, 1986-87; cons. in field. Mem. NEA, Am. Home Econ. Assn., Md. State Tchrs. Assn., Montgomery County Edn. Assn., S.C. State Alumni Club (fin. sec. 1978-79), Alpha Kappa Alpha. Democrat. Methodist. Home: 4601 N Park Ave #121 Chevy Chase MD 20815

STEVENS, LYDIA HASTINGS, civic worker; b. Highland Park, Ill., Aug. 2, 1918; d. Rolland T.R. and Ruth Shotwell (Beebe) Hastings; m. George Cooke Stevens, Nov. 2, 1940; children: Lydia Stevens Gustin, Priscilla Stevens Goldfarb, Frederick S., Elizabeth Stevens MacLeod, George H., Ruth Stevens Stellard. BA, Vassar Coll., 1939. Pres. Greenwih YMCA, Conn., 1971-74; v.p. planning Greenwich United Way, 1973-76; pres. Greenwich Housing Coalition, 1982-86; warden Greenwich Christ Episcopal Ch., 1981-86; chmn. Diosecian Rev. Commn. Episcopal Diocese Conn., 1985-87; bd. dirs. Greenwich LIbrary, 1985—, Greenwich Hosp. Nursing Home Corp., 1987—; chmn. Greenwich Commn. Aging, 1987—; pres., bd. mem. Greenwich Broadcasting Corp., 1977-79; cons. Nat. Exec. Service Corps, N.Y.C., 1985. Protestant. Episcopal.

STEVENS, MARILYN RUTH, publishing company executive; b. Wooster, Ohio, May 30, 1943; d. Glenn Willard and Gretchen Elizabeth (Ihrig) Amstutz; B.A., Coll. Wooster (Ohio), 1965; M.A.T., Harvard U., 1966; J.D., Suffolk U., 1975; m. Bryan J. Stevens, Oct. 11, 1969; children—Jennifer Marie, Gretchen Anna. Tchr., Lexington (Mass.) Public Schs., 1966-69; in various editorial positions Houghton Mifflin Co., Boston, 1969—, editorial dir. sch. depts., 1978-81, editorial dir. math. and scis. Sch. Div., 1981-84, mng. editor, 1984—; admitted to Mass. bar, 1975. Mem. Mass. Bar Assn., Am. Bar Assn.

STEVENS, MARY, librarian; b. Grand Forks, B.C., Can., Sept. 9, 1943; d. Philip and Pauline (Stooshinoff) Popow; m. Lawrence Raymond Stevens, Dec. 20, 1970; children: Sarah, Andrew. BA, U. B.C., Vancouver, 1965; B in Library Sci., U. B.C., 1967. Librarian III, Slavic book selector Robarts Library U. Toronto, 1967—. Asst. editor jour. Can. Slavonic Papers, 1980-85. Mem. Can. Assn. Slavists, Am. Assn. Advancement Slavic Studies. Anglican. Office: U Toronto Library, 130 St George St, Toronto, ON Canada M5S 1A5

STEVENS, NANCY MARIA, real estate executive; b. Milford, Mass.; d. Vincent Steven and Yvonne (Currier) Fiori; m. John Henry Stevens; children: John Vincent, Theresa Maria. BS, Northeastern U., Boston. V.p. Gateway Realty, Inc., Silver Spring, Md., 1961-74; gen. mgr. Berman Enterprises, Laurel, Md., 1974-80; v.p. Charles E. Smith Mgmt., Inc., Arlington, Va., 1980—; cons. on book Guide to Comml. Mgmt., 1981. Commr. Landlord-Tenant Commn., Prince Georges Co., 1973-81; chmn. Eviction Task Force, Prince Georges Co., 1986-87; pres. Bond Mill Woods Civic Assn., Laurel, Md., 1970, W. Laurel Civic Assn. Recipient Bus and Civic award Prince Georges Co., 1977. Mem. Inst. Real Estate Mgmt., Soc. Real Property Adminstrs., No. Va. Bd. Realtors, Apt. and Office Bldg. Assn., Property Mgrs. Assn., Washington Bd. Trade, Am. Women Overseas, Balt.-Washington C. of C. (chmn. legis. com. 1971-77). Lodge: Soroptimists (pres. Laurel chpt. 1974-76). Home: 16006 Kent Rd Laurel MD 20707 Office: Charles E Smith Mgmt Inc 1735 Jefferson Davis Hwy Arlington VA 22202

STEVENS, PATRICIA CAROL, university administrator; b. St. Louis, Jan. 11, 1946; d. Carroll and Juanita Donohue; AB, Duke U., 1966; MA, U. Mo.-Kansas City, 1974, PhD, 1982; m. James H. Stevens, Jr., Aug. 27, 1966 (div. Mar. 1984); children: James H. III, Carol Janet. Tchr. math, secondary schs., Balt., St. Louis, Shawnee Mission, Kans., 1966-71; lectr. U. Mo., Kansas City, 1975-76, research asst. affirmative action, 1976-79, coordinator affirmative action, 1979-82, instl. research assoc., 1982-84, acting dir. affirmative action and acad. personnel, 1984; dir. institutional research Lakeland Community Coll., 1984-86; asst. dean acad. affairs, math., engring. and tech. dept. Harrisburg Area Community Coll., 1986—. Bd. dirs., v.p. Am. Cancer Soc. Jackson County, 75-84; council leader Hemlock Girl Scout U.S.A. bd. dirs., 1986—, PTA, 1975-77. Recipient Outstanding Service and Achievement award U. Mo. Kansas City, 1976; Jack C. Coffey grantee, 1978. Mem. Nat. Council Tchrs. Math., Mat. Assn. Am., Women in Leadership Inst., Am. Assn. Women in Community and Jr. Colls. (Pa. state coordinator 1988), Soc. Mfg. Engrs. (chmn.-elect 1988), Assn. Supervision and Curriculum Devel., Women's Equity Project, Nat. Assn. Student Personnel Adminstrs., Women's Network, Assn. Inst. Research, Phi Delta Kappa, (pres.), Phi Kappa Phi, Pi Lambda Theta, Delta Gamma (v.p., del. nat. conv. 1988, Cream Rose Outstanding Service award 1970). Home: 925 Pennsylvania Ave Harrisburg PA 17112 Office: Harrisburg Area Community Coll MET Dept 3300 Cameron Street Rd Harrisburg PA 17110

STEVENS, ROSEMARY ANNE, public health educator; b. Bourne, Eng.; came to U.S., 1961, naturalized, 1968; d. William Edward and Mary Agnes (Tricks) Wallace; m. Robert B. Stevens, Jan. 28, 1961 (div. 1983); children: Carey Thomasine, Richard Nathaniel. B.A., Oxford (Eng.) U., 1957; Diploma in Social Adminstrn., Manchester (Eng.) U., 1959; M.P.H., Yale U., 1963, Ph.D., 1968. Various hosp. adminstrv. positions Eng., 1959-61; research asso. Yale Med. Sch., 1962-68, asst. prof., 1968-71, asso. prof., 1971-74, prof. pub. health, 1974-76; master Jonathan Edwards Coll., 1974-75; prof. dept. health systems mgmt. and polit. sci. Tulane U., New Orleans, 1976-78; chmn. dept. health systems mgmt. Tulane U., 1977-78; prof. history and sociology of sci. U. Pa., 1979—, chmn. dept., 1980-83, 86—; vis. lectr. Johns Hopkins U., 1967-68; guest scholar Brookings Instn., Washington, 1967-68; acad. visitor London Sch. Econs., 1962-64, 1973-74; mem. health program adv. com. Office Tech. Assessment, U.S. Congress. Author: Medical Practice in Modern England: The Impact of Specialization and State Medicine, 1966, American Medicine and the Public Interest, 1971, Sweet Charity: American Hospitals in the Twentieth Century, 1988; (with others) Foreign Trained Physicians and American Medicine, 1972, Welfare Medicine in America, 1974, Alien-Doctors: Foreign Medical Graduates in American Hospitals, 1978. Bd. mgrs. Presbyn./Univ. Pa. Med. Ctr.; bd. overseers Dartmouth Med. Sch. Mem. Inst. Medicine of Nat. Acad. Sci., History of Sci. Soc., Am. Assn. for History of Medicine, Am. Bd. Pediatrics (pub.). Club: Cosmopolitan (Phila.). Home: 319 S Hicks St Philadelphia PA 19102 Office: U Pa 215 S 34th St Philadelphia PA 19104

STEVENS, ROSLYN NÉNETTE, educator, minister; b. Bronx, N.Y., Jan. 14, 1947; d. Junius Lee and Roslyn (Cummings) Coleman; m. John Stevens Jr. Sept. 10, 1964; children: John III, Nenette, Hasan. BA, York Coll., 1973; MA, Columbia U., 1979; MA of Divinity, New Brunswick Sem., 1987. Asst. tchr. Queens Coll. Parents Head Start, Jamaica, N.Y., 1966-69; dir. edn. Afro-Am. Day Care Ctr., Jamaica, 1973-74; tchr. Bd. Edn. of N.Y.C., 1974—; asst. pastor, exec. dir. programs Mt. Moriah AME Ch., Hollis, N.Y., 1988—; radio co-host Zoc Tabanadl. Mem. poll watcher Com. Elect Floyd Flake Congress, Rochdale Village, 1986; assoc. minister, dir. Christian edn. Allen A.M.E. Ch., Jamaica, 1986-87. Democrat. Home: 172-30 133rd Ave Jamaica NY 11434 Office: Mt Moriah AME Ch 93-24 197th St Hollis NY 11423

STEVENS, SERITA DEBORAH, writer; b. Chgo., Jan. 20, 1949; d. Albert Stanley and Frances Zipporah (Rosenberg) Mendelson; m. Raymond Glassenberg, Aug. 29, 1971 (div. 1980). BSN, U. Ill., Chgo., 1971; MA in Lit. with honors, Antioch U., London, 1979. Staff nurse Dept. of Psychiatry; instr. U.S. Calif., Los Angeles, Loyola U., Santa Monica Calif. City Coll.; investigative reporter CBS. Author: This Bitter Ecstasy, 1981, Tame the Wild Heart, 1983, The Shriekings Shadows of Penporth Island, 1983, A Dream Forever, 1984, Cagney and Lacey, 1985, Bloodstone Inheritance, 1985, A Gathering Storm, 1986, Secrets At Seventeen, 1986, Days of Our Lives, 1986, Lighting and Fire, 1987, Daughters of Desire, 1987, Deceptive Desires, 1987, Lilac Dreams, 1986, numerous short stories; contbr. articles to writer's mags. and jours. Recipient Cape Cod Writer's scholarship, Best Synopsis award Dell Publishing. Mem. Soc. Children's Books Writers, Mystery Writers Am. (bd. dirs. S. Calif. chpt. 1987-88), Romance Writers Am. (regional bd. dirs.), HUNA Soc. Democrat. Jewish. Office: 2265 Westwood #271 Los Angeles CA 90064

STEVENS, TRESA B(OGGUS), insurance company executive; b. Kilgore, Tex., Feb. 1, 1954; d. Clarence Leo Boggus and Lillian LaVerne Montgomery; m. Buddy Marshall Stevens. Student, Am. Coll., Huebner, Pa., 1985—. Cert. Nat. Assn. Securities Dealers Registered rep. Sales rep. IVACO, Inc. of Montreal, Can., Tonawanda, N.Y., 1980-83; pvt. practice sales cons. Niagara Falls, N.Y., 1982-84; sales agt. Met. Life Ins. Co., Niagara Falls, 1984-86; regional brokerage mgr., pension and annuity div. Met. Life Ins. Co., Houston, 1987—; pvt. practice fin. services cons. Baytown, Tex., 1986-87. Active Life Underwriter Polit. Action Com., Niagara Falls, 1984-86; youth dir. St. Mark's Ch., Tonawanda, 1981-84. Mem. Profl. Ins. Agts., Life Underwriters Assn. (bd. dirs., sec. 1984-86, mem. chmn. 1985-86), Student Soc. of CLUs., Houston Assn. Life Underwriters, Southwestern Pension Conf. Office: Met Life Ins Co 5 Post Oak Park Suite 2460 Houston TX 77027

STEVENSON, BARBARA JEAN, sales executive; b. Tucson, Apr. 3, 1955; d. Carl Glenn and Barbara Patricia (Fritz) Stevenson; student U. Ariz., 1972-74; B.S. in Animal Sci., Wash. State U., 1976. Area sales rep. Syntex Animal Health, Inc., Wash., Oreg., Idaho, 1977-78; office mgr. Red Rock (Ariz.) Feeding Co., 1978-79; area sales cons. for Tex. Panhandle and N.Mex., 1980-84, nat. accounts coordinator, 1982-84, mgr. advt. and sales promotion, 1984-85, mgr. advt. and pub. relations, 1985-86, western region sales mgr., 1986-87; pres. Turnkey Promotions Inc., 1987—. Mem. Pres.'s Council, 1981, 82, 83, 84. Quotamaster, Syntex, 1980. Mem. Am Nat. Cattlewomen, Ariz. Cattle Feeders' Assn. Republican. Home: PO Box 324 Tucson AZ 85702 Office: Turnkey Promotions Inc 292 N Ash Alley Tucson AZ 85701

STEVENSON, DENISE L., business executive, banking consultant; b. Washington, Sept. 18, 1946; d. Pierre and Alice (Mardrus) D'Auga; m. Walter Henry Stevenson, Oct. 17, 1970. AA, Montgomery Coll., 1967; BA in Econs./Bus. Mgmt., N.C. State U., 1983. Lic. ins. agt. Savs. counselor Perpetual Bldg. Assn. (now Perpetual Savs. Bank), Washington, 1968-70; regional asst. v.p. 1st Fed. Savs., Raleigh, N.C., 1971-83; pres., owner Diversified Learning Services, Raleigh, 1983—; instr. Inst. Fin. Edn., Raleigh, 1983—, Am. Inst. Banking, 1986; cert. leader Nat. Assn. Bank Women, 1987. Mem. Inst. Fin. Edn. (2d v.p. 1982-83), Am. Bus. Women's Assn. (woman of yr. award 1982), Nat. Assn. Female Execs., Nat. Assn. Bank Women (cert. leader 1987), Assn. Bank Trainers and Cons., Am. Soc. Tng. and Devel., Omicron Delta Epsilon. Clubs: Laurel Hills Women's (pres. 1974-75) (Raleigh). Avocation: fishing. Office: Diversified Learning Services PO Box 33231 Raleigh NC 27636

STEVENSON, ELIZABETH CHESTON, psychoanalyst; b. Phila., Sept. 11, 1935; d. Robert Stuart and Suzanne Essex (Parsons) Newhall; m. Samuel Christopher Stevenson, Dec. 27, 1962 (div. Nov. 1974); children: Peter Wistar, William Worth. BA, Vassar Coll., 1957; MTS, Harvard Div. Sch., 1976. Pvt. practice psychology Cambridge, Mass., 1976—; mem. faculty, com. C.G. Jung Inst., Boston, 1985—. Mem. Nat. Assn. for Advancement of Psychoanalysis, Internat. Assn. Analytical Psychology. Democrat. Episcopalian. Home: 18 Royal Circus, Edinburgh Scotland EH3 655 Office: 44 Winslow St Cambridge MA 02138

STEVENSON, MAYBELLE IDA, nurse; b. Clinton, Mass., July 31, 1933; d. John Franklin and Doris Ardella (Hinsman) Sleeper; m. Alexander Stevenson, Aug. 27, 1960; 1 child, Scott. RN, Newton-Wellesley Hosp., 1951-54; BS in Profl. Arts, St. Joseph's Coll., 1980; MA in Health Care Adminstrn., Framingham State Coll., 1984. Asst. clin. instr., head nurse med. surg. Newton (Mass.) Wellesley Hosp., 1954-56; head nurse ICU Newton (Mass.)-Wellesley Hosp., 1959-62; office nurse Dr. William Taggart, Wellesley, Mass., 1963-65; staff nurse nursing home, Needham, Mass., 1965-66; staff nurse float Newton-Wellesley Hosp., 1966-68, supr. nursing, 1968-80, staff edn. instr., 1980-84; assoc. dir. edn. ARC, Dedham, Mass., 1984—. Fellow Am. Nurses Assn., Nat. Assn. Female Execs., Am. Assn. Blood Banks, Mass. Nurses Assn., Mass. Assn. Blood Banks. Republican. Home: 7-D Hawthorne Village Franklin MA 02038

STEVENSON, RENÉE DEAN, marketing mgr.; b. Ann Arbor, Mich., Jan. 8, 1955; d. Dean Ornell and Virginia Caroline S. AS, Washtenaw Community Coll., 1976. Adminstrv. asst., fin. analyst Sanger Harris Federated Dept. Stores, Dallas, 1978-79; fin. staff asst., mgmt. devel. asst. Frito Lay, Inc., Dallas, 1979-80; assoc. editor, typesetter, graphic artist Dallas Observer, 1980-82; sales support specialist Compugraphic Corp., Wilmington, Mass., 1982-83; sales and support trainer Linotype Co. USA, Hauppauge, N.Y., 1983-84; internat. product planning mgr. laser printers and raster image processors Linotype AG, Eschborn, Fed. Republic Germany, 1984-86; product marketing mgr. Gradco Systems, Inc., Irvine, Calif., 1986; product line mgr. A.S.T. Research, Inc., Irvine, 1986-88; product mgr. Epson Am., Inc., Torrance, Calif., 1988, mgr. sales and dealer tng. dept., 1988—; cons. Mac Type Net Desktop Pub. Solutions, Livonia, Mich., 1986, John Deubert Cons. Services, La Jolla, Calif., 1985-86. Vol. Catholic Social Services Recreation Program, Ann Arbor, Mich., 1967-70, Right to Life Com., Ann Arbor, 1972-75, Glenmary Home Missioners, Vanceburg, Ky., 1973-74, St. Patrick's Parish Lector, Ann Arbor, 1972-76. Mem. Nat. Assn. Desktop Pubs., Am. Soc. Tng and Devel. Roman Catholic. Office: Epson Am Inc 2780 Lomita Blvd Torrance CA 90505

STEVENSON, RUTH CARTER, art patron; b. Ft. Worth, Oct. 19, 1923; d. Amon Giles and Nenetta (Wiess) Carter; m. J. Lee Johnson III, June 8, 1946 (div. Feb. 1978); children—Sheila Broderick Johnson, J. Lee, Karen Carter Johnson Hixon, Catherine Johnson Tekstar, Mark Lehane; m. John R. Stevenson, May 21, 1983. B.A., Sarah Lawrence Coll., 1945. Pres. Ft. Worth Jr. League, 1954-55; chmn. bd. Amon Carter Mus. Western Art, Ft. Worth, 1961—; pres. Amon G. Carter Found., 1982—, Arts Council Greater Ft. Worth, 1963-64; bd. regents U. Tex. at Austin, 1963-69; v.p. internat. council Mus. Modern Art, 1965-72; bd. dirs. Nat. Trust Historic Preservation, 1968-74, Nat. Coll. Fine Arts, Smithsonian Instn., Washington, 1966-70, U. Dallas, 1971-74; trustee Tex. Christian U., 1974-86, Nat. Gallery Art, Washington, 1979—; pres. Ft. Worth City Art Commn., 1960-80; nat. chmn. collector's com. Nat. Gallery Art, Washington, 1975—; mem. vis. com. Fogg Mus., Cambridge, Mass., 1978-83. Roman Catholic. Home: 1200 Broad Ave Fort Worth TX 76107

STEVENSON, SANDRA JEAN, retail executive; b. Butler, Pa., Oct. 5, 1949; d. William Ross and Shirley Elizabeth (Pfaff) Stevenson. BA, Carlow Coll., 1975. Gen. mgr. Pa. Liquor Control Bd. Store, Harrisburg, Pa., 1980-82, 87—; trainer Pa. Liquor Control Bd., Harrisburg, Pa., 1982—. Author dramatizations and prototype for conf. on stigma and mental illness 1980. Office coordinator, bd. dirs. Lifeline of Southwestern Pa. (Crisis Pregnancy Ctr.), Butler, Pa., 1985-88; sec. Mental Health Assn. Pa., Harrisburg, 1981-83, regional v.p. 1979-81. Mem. Nat. Assn. Female Execs., NAACP, Mensa. Democrat. Roman Catholic. Club: Condor Aero. Office: Pa State Liquor Store #1007 Cranberry Mall 20 111 Route 19 Mars PA 16046-9269

STEVENSON-BRADSHAW, LINDA LORINE, nurse; b. Cleve., Apr. 1, 1951; d. James H. Bailiff and Betty L. (Keeble) Woods; m. Kenneth Michael Stevenson, Nov. 9, 1973 (div. May 1983); children: Amanda, Lindsey; m. Bruce Lee Bradshaw, Sept. 24, 1986. Student, St. John Coll., Cleve., 1971-72; grad., St. Alexis Sch. Nursing, 1974. RN. Charge nurse Pioneer Valley Hosp., Salt Lake City, 1974-83; med. dir. Western Med. Tempories, Salt Lake City, 1975-76; house supr. Doxey-Hatch Med. Ctr., Salt Lake City, 1977; supr. utilization rev. and quality assurance FHP-Utah, Salt Lake City, 1983-84; dir. utilization rev. and quality assurance Maxicare-Utah, Salt Lake City, 1984-85; charge nurse Univ. Med. Ctr., Salt Lake City, 1986-87; nurse, installation specialist Intermountain Health Care, Salt Lake City, 1987—; dir. quality assurance and utilization rev., medical record and case mix software devel. and installation, Salt Lake City, 1981-85. Mem. Utah Heart Assn. (cert. 1987), Advanced Cardiac Life Support (cert. 1986), Nat. Assn. Female Execs. Home: 3506 Royalwood Circle Salt Lake City UT 84118 Office: Intermountain Health Care/ASI 36 S State Salt Lake City UT 84102

STEVER, MARGO TAFT, poet; b. Cin., Mar. 4, 1950; d. David Gibson and Katharine Longworth (Whittaker) Taft; m. Donald Winfred Stever Jr., July 31, 1976; children: David Whittaker, James Taft. A.B., Radcliffe Coll., 1972; Ed.M., Harvard U., 1974; MFA, Sarah Lawrence Coll., 1988. Asst. dir. N.H. Civil Liberties Union, Concord, 1976-77, dir. women's rights project, 1976-77; classroom tchr. learning disabled children The Krebs Sch., Lexington, Mass., 1975-76; staff asst. Senator Ted Stevens, U.S. Senate, Washington, 1974-75; dir. Sleepy Hollow Poetry Series, Warner Library, Tarrytown, N.Y., 1983-88. Author: (teacher's manual) Behavior Influence and Personality, 1973; A Psychological Approach to Abnormal Behavior, 1975. Poetry published in mags. Bd. dirs., sec. N.H. Pro Bono Referral System, N.H. Bar Assn., Concord, 1977-78; bd. dirs. Tarrytown Coop. Nursery Sch., N.Y., 1983-86, Sleepy Hollow Nursery Sch., Scarborough, N.Y., 1984-85, 1987-88. Mem. Poets and Writers, Acad. Am. Poets, Poetry Soc. Am. Democrat. Episcopalian. Clubs: Adirondack League; Abenakee (Biddeford Pool, Maine). Avocations: riding; tennis. Home: 157 Millard Ave North Tarrytown NY 10591

STEVICH, ALISON JOY, office management executive; b. Chicago, Feb. 12, 1952; d. Chrisalogo Mendoza and Ruby Marie (Johnson) Aguirre; m. David Charles Wiegel, Feb. 14, 1969 (div. 1972); 1 child, Yuri Christian. AA, Kendall Coll., 1971. Shipping processor Gen. Products Corp., Chgo., 1972-73; med. biller Mason-Barron Labs. Inc., Chgo., 1973-74, Rheumatology Assocs., Chgo., 1974-76; sec. Tala Engel, Atty. at Law, Chgo., 1976-78; office mgr. Imrich A. Weiss, M.D., Chgo., 1978-84; med. biller Strauss Surg. Group, Chgo., 1984-85; office mgr. Lakeview Imaging & X-Ray Ltd., Chgo., 1985-86, Ibbotson Assocs. Inc., Chgo., 1986-87; office mgr. comml. loan dept. Columbia Nat. Bank Chgo., 1987—; cons. A&M Services, Chgo., 1985-87. Prodn. mgr.: Stocks, Bonds, Bills and Inflation, 1987. Mem. Nat. Assn. Female Execs. Club: Ice Skating Inst. Am. (Wilmette, Ill.). Home: 640 S York Rd Apt 313 Bensenville IL 60106 Office: Columbia Nat Bank Chgo Comml Loan Dept 5250 N Harlem Ave Chicago IL 60656

STEWARD, BARBARA MARKHAM, occupational therapy educator, clinical coordinator; b. Istanbul, Turkey, Aug. 14, 1925; d. Rual Finney and Evangeline (McNaughton) Markham; m. George Erwin Steward, June 1, 1957 (div. 1981); children: Pamela Steward Harding, Richard M., Scott R. BS, Va. Commonwealth U., 1952; MS, So. Conn. State Coll., 1974. Occupational therapist Upshur St. Hosp., Washington, 1952-55, NIH, Bethesda, Md., 1955-57, New Haven Rehab. Ctr., 1958-60, VA Hosp., West Haven, Conn., 1960-66, Yale-New Haven Hosp., 1966-67, Hosp. of St. Raphael, New Haven, 1970-72; asst. prof. occupational therapy Quinnipiac Coll., Hamden, Conn., 1972-84, clin. coordinator, 1984—; cons. Hamden Health Care Facility, 1984-87. Med. advisor Easter Seal Rehab. Ctr., New Haven, 1981—, bd. dirs., 1981-84. Mem. Am. Occupational Therapy Assn., World Occupational Therapy Fedn., Conn. Occupational Therapy Assn. Democrat. Congregationalist. Club: Clowns of Am. Internat. (Stratford, Conn.). Home: 24 Nash St New Haven CT 06511 Office: Quinnipiac Coll Mount Carmel Ave Hamden CT 06518

STEWARD, JANE ALLISON, human resources director; b. Fresno, Calif., Mar. 6, 1957; d. Allison Herbert and Dorothy Louise (Boyer) S. BA, U. Calif., Santa Barbara, 1979. With personnel VisiCorp, San Jose, Calif., 1981-84; mgr. human resources United Resources, Inc., Santa Ana, Calif., 1984-86; employment mgr. Maxicare, Los Angeles, 1986; dir. human resources planning Downey Savs. & Loan, Costa Mesa, Calif., 1986—. Sponsor Children's Hosp. Orange County, Calif., 1987-88, South County Cancer League, Laguna, Calif., 1987-88, March of Dimes, Orange County, 1987-88; mem. policy and procedure com. Bur. Nat. Affairs, Washington, 1987-88.. Mem. Personnel Indsl. Relations Assn., Am. Soc. Personnel Adminstrs., Nat. Assn. Female Execs., Internat. Assn. Personnel Women, Newport Area Preferred Profls. Republican. Episcopalian. Home: 53 W Yale Loop Irvine CA 92714 Office: Downey Savs & Loan 3501 Jamboree Rd Newport Beach CA 92660

STEWARD, PATRICIA ANN RUPERT, real estate consultant; b. Panama City, Panama, Apr. 20, 1945 (parents Am. citizens); d. Paul S. and Ernestina M. (Ward) Rupert; grad. Sch. of Mortgage Banking, Grad. Sch. of Mgmt., Northwestern U., 1979; m. Robert M. Levine, Oct. 28, 1978; children by previous marriage—Donald F. Steward, Christine Marie Steward. Vice pres. Asso. Mortgage & Investment Co., Phoenix, 1969-71; v.p., br. mgr. Sun Country Funding Corp., Phoenix, 1971-72, Freese Mortgage Co., Phoenix, 1972-74, Utah Mortgage Loan Corp., Phoenix, 1974-81; pres. Elles Corp., 1982—; condr. numerous seminars on mortgage fin. State chmn. Ariz. Leukemia Dr., 1977-78, mem. exec. com., 1979-80; troop leader Cactus Pine council Girl Scouts U.S.A., 1979-80; bd. dirs. Nat. Mental Health Assn., 1986-87, Ariz. Mental Health Assn., pres., 1986-87, bd. dirs., treas. Maricopa Mental Health Assn., 1984-85, v.p., 1985-86, pres., 1986-87; apptd. by state supreme ct. to Ariz. Foster Care Rev. Bd., 1984—, chairperson Bd. 8, 1986-87. Recipient cert. of appreciation Multiple Listing Service, Phoenix Bd. Realtors, 1975, Multiple Listing Service, Glendale Bd. Realtors, 1977. Lic. mortgage broker, Ariz. Mem. Ariz. Mortgage Bankers Assn. (dir. 1981-82, chmn. edn. com. 1981-82, founder continuing edn. seminar series 1981), Young Mortgage Bankers Assn. (chmn. exec. com. 1980-81), Cen. Ariz. Homebuilders Assn. Republican. Author: A Realtors Guide to Mortgage Lending, 1972. Office: Elles Corp 320 E McDowell Rd Suite 100 Phoenix AZ 85004

STEWART, AMY, safety engineer; b. Syracuse, N.Y., Nov. 19, 1956; d. Carroll Robin and Gertrude Helen (Schuder) S. AA, SUNY, Morrisville, 1976; BA, SUNY, Oswego, 1978; MS, Cen. Mo. State U., 1984. Driver educator Jamesville Dewitt (N.Y.) High Sch., 1979, Onondaga-Madison Boces High Sch., Syracuse, N.Y., 1979-83, Liverpool (N.Y.) High Sch., 1981-83; safety specialist Mo. Div. Hwy. Safety, Jefferson City, 1984-87; sr. defensive driving safety engr. Doron Precision Systems, Inc., Binghamton, N.Y., 1987—; driver educator Onondaga Council on Alcoholism, Syracuse, 1981-83; project graduation coordinator Mo. Div. Hwy. Safety, 1984-87. Com. chmn. Madison County Traffic Safety Bd., Wampsville, N.Y., 1980-83; singer Jefferson City Cantorum, Mo. Music Makers (pres.), J.C. Symphony, 1984—. Mem. Am. Driver and Safety Edn. Assn., Driver and Safety Educators of N.Y. State (v.p. 1982-83), Am. Soc. Safety Engrs. Methodist. Office: Doron Prescision Systems Inc 174 Court St Binghamton NY 13902

STEWART, ANN HARLEMAN, English language educator. BA in English, Douglass Coll., 1967; PhD in Linguistics, Princeton U., 1972. Asst. prof. dept. English Rutgers U., New Brunswick, N.J., 1973-74; asst. prof. dept. English U. Wash., Seattle, 1974-79, assoc. prof. dept. English, 1979-84; vis. assoc. prof., research affiliate Writing Program MIT, Cambridge, 1984-86; vis. scholar Program in Am. Civilization Brown U., Providence, 1986—. Author: Graphic Representation of Models in Linguistic Theory, 1976, (with Bruce A. Rosenberg) Ian Fleming: A Critical Biography; contbr. poems and short stories to lit. mags. Guggenheim fellow, 1976-77, Huntington Library fellow, 1979-80, MacDowell Colonyfellow, 1988, Fulbright-Hays Lectr., 1980-81; ACLS/IROX sr. scholar, 1976-77; recipient grant Rockefeller Found., 1989, Raymond Carver prize, 1986, Nelson Algren runner-up award Chgo. Tribune, 1987, 3d prize Judith Siegal Pearson award, 1988. Mem. Modern Lang. Assn. (chair exec. com. Gen Linguistics), Linguistic Soc. Am., Poets and Writers, Inc. Home: 55 Summit Ave Providence RI 02906 Office: Brown U Dept English Providence RI 02912

STEWART, ARLENE JEAN GOLDEN, designer, stylist; b. Chgo., Nov. 26, 1943; d. Alexander Emerald and Nettie (Rosen) Golden; B.F.A. (Ill. state scholar), Sch. of Art Inst. Chgo., 1966; postgrad. Ox Bow Summer Sch. Painting, Saugatuck, Mich., 1966; m. Randall Edward Stewart, Nov. 6, 1970; 1 child, Alexis Anne. Designer, stylist Formica Corp., Cin., 1966-68; with Armstrong World Industries, Lancaster, Pa., 1968—, interior furnishings analyst, 1974-76, internat. staff project stylist, 1976-78, sr. stylist Corlon flooring, 1979-80, sr. exptl. project stylist, 1980—; exhibited textiles Art Inst. Chgo., 1966, Ox-Bow Gallery, Saugatuck, Mich., 1966. Home: 114 E Vine St Lancaster PA 17602 Office: Armstrong Tech Ctr 2500 Columbia Ave Lancaster PA 17604

STEWART, BARBARA DEAN, writer, musician, educational consultant; b. Rochester, N.Y., Sept. 17, 1941; d. George Adgate and Louise (Griswold) Dean; children: Allison, Whitney. AB, Cornell U., 1962; MS, Simmons Coll., 1964; diploma with honors in flute, prep. dept. Eastman Sch. Music, 1958. Asst. law librarian Cornell U., 1963-64; writer/performer Kazoophony, Rochester, N.Y., 1972—; pres. Stewart Assocs. Ednl. Systems Group, Rochester, 1979-85; pres. SmartWriters, Inc., 1985—; flutist La Jolla Civic Orch., 1966-68. Dir. jr. devel. U.S. Squash Racquets Assn.; pres. bd. dirs. Rochester Chamber Orch.; bd. dirs. Rochester chpt. English Speaking Union, 1982-85. Author: How to Kazoo. Winner 11 nat. championships in 10 different masters track and field events; holder one Am. record. Mem. Am. Fedn. Musicians, ASCAP. Home and Office: 292 Wintergreen Way Rochester NY 14618

STEWART, BONNIE L., state legislator; b. West Warwick, R.I., Nov. 19, 1947; m. William J. Stewart. Grad. high sch., West Warwick, 1965. Mem. R.I. State Senate, 1985—; mem. West Warwick Rep. Womans Club. Republican. Office: State Senate Office State Capitol Providence RI 02903 *

STEWART, CHERIE ANITA, painter/neo-impressionist; b. Gadsden, Ala., Sept. 20, 1945; d. Earl Donald Williams and Frances Morgan Bellenger; m. Walter Hurd Stewart, Apr. 2, 1966; children: Don Paul, Virginia Elizabeth. BS, U. Ala., Tuscaloosa, 1968; BA, U. Ala.-Birmingham, 1983. One-man shows include Barker Gallery, Palm Beach, Fla., 1984, St.Vincent's Gallery, Birmingham, Ala., 1987; exhibited in group shows at Birmingham Frame and Art Gallery, 1984-86, Maralyn Wilson Gallery, Birmingham, 1985—; Abstein Gallery, Atlanta, 1985—, Gateway Ctr., Newark, 1987, Ariel Gallery, N.Y.C., 1988; contbr. advt. layouts The Stewart Orgn., Birmingham, 1983-84; painter Shippee Gallery, N.Y.C., 1985—, Art South Inc., Washington, 1987—, Archtl. Arts Co., Dallas, 1988. Recipient numerous awards. Mem. Birmingham Mus. Art, Birmingham Art Assn., Nat. Mus. Women in the Arts, Knickerbocker Artists N.Y. (assoc.), Allied Artists Am. (assoc.).

STEWART, CHERYL MAURINE, social worker; b. Phoenix, Jan. 20, 1944; d. William Frank Wayne and Stella Maurine (Boyd) Edel; m. Richard Alan Stewart, June 7, 1966 (div. July 1982); children: Scott Edel, Michael Boyd. AA, Phoenix Jr. Coll., 1964; BA, Ariz. State U., 1966, MSW, 1972. Diplomate Nat. Register Clin. Soc. Workers. Social worker Maricopa County Gen. Hosp., Phoenix, 1970-73, Ariz. State Dept. Child Protective Services, Phoenix, 1974, West Yavapai Guidance Clinic, Prescott, Ariz., 1974-81; pvt. practice social work Yavapai Big Bros./Sisters, Prescott, 1981-83; pvt. practice psychotherapy Prescott, 1981—; expert witness child sexual abuse Yavapai County Superior Ct., Prescott, 1981—; coordinator sexual assault vols. Prescott Police Dept., 1982—; cons. Turning Point, 1988—; mediator, conciliator Yavapai County Superior Ct., 1985—; therapist Prescott Child Devel. Ctrs., 1981-87; contracted therapist Huddleston House, 1984—, Ariz. State Dept. Econ. Security, 1984—; mem. faculty Prescott Coll., 1986—. Mem. Prescott Town Hall, 1981—; den mother Boy Scouts Am., Prescott, 1981-85; vol. educator Prescott Pub. Schs. Faith House, 1981—; cons. Turning Point, 1988. Recipient Women Helping Women award Soroptomists, Prescott, 1986. Mem. Nat. Assn. Social Workers (cert.), Alpha Kappa Delta, Kappa Kappa Gamma (scholarship chmn. 1965-66), Phi Theta Kappa. Democrat. Home: 1205 Country Club Dr Prescott AZ 86301

STEWART, CLARA WOODARD, advertising executive; b. Mineola, N.Y., May 1, 1952; d. Samuel Woodard and Irene (Colm) S.; BA in Broadcasting and Psychology, Mich. State U., 1974; MA in Journalism and Communications, U. Fla., 1975. Sales rep. Sta. WSBR, Boca Raton, 1976-77; media dir. Fred Wagenvoord Assoc., Inc., Boca Raton, Fla., 1977-81; v.p., sr. account exec., media dir. Birkenes & Foreman Advt., Boca Raton, 1981—, v.p. sr. account exec., media dir. Bd. dirs. Boca Raton Community Theater, 1977-78, publicity chmn., 1977-78; bd. dirs. United Way Greater Boca Raton, 1979—; pres. Friends of Boca Raton Public Library, 1981-83; mem. adv. bd. Boca Raton Symphony Orch., 1983-85; mem. Young Pres.'s Council Norton Gallery; treas. Friends of Caldwell Playhouse, 1984—. Mem. B/PAA (treas. Southeast Fla. chpt. 1984—), Women in Communications, Advt. Fedn. Greater Ft. Lauderdale (bd. dirs. 1986—, sec. 1987—), Am. Mktg. Assn. (sr. v.p. spl. programs, Gold Coast chpt., 1987-88) Mensa (SE regional public relations asst. 1978-80, treas. Palm Beach County 1981-83), Palm Beach County Hist. Soc. (newsletter editor 1980-82), Palm Beach County Geneal. Soc., Am. Film Inst., Nat. Trust Historic Preservation, BMW Car Club of Am., DAR, Phi Kappa Phi. Home: 6443 Parkview Dr Boca Raton FL 33433 Office: 2900 N Military Trail Suite 200 Boca Raton FL 33431

STEWART, DOROTHY ANNE, research physicist; b. Beach Grove, Ind., June 2, 1937; d. Thomas Edward and Dorothy Anne (Browne) S.; B.S., U. Tampa, 1958; M.S., Fla. State U., 1961, Ph.D., 1966. Tchr. math, sci., high sch., Live Oak, Fla., 1958-59; research physicist U.S. Army Missile Command, Redstone Arsenal, Ala., 1966—. Mem. Am. Meteorol. Soc., Am. Geophys. Union, AAAS, Ala. Acad. Scis., Sigma Xi. Contbr. articles to profl. jours. Home: 5204 Whitesburg Dr Huntsville AL 35802 Office: US Army Missile Command Attn AMSMI-RD-RE-AP Redstone Arsenal AL 35898-5248

STEWART, ELAINE LAURA, mail order company owner; b. Kingston, N.Y., Oct. 18, 1946; d. Bert Francis and Pauline Lulu (Garrison) Stokes; m. Russell Conwell Stewart, June 24, 1967; 1 child, Bryan Keith. Student, Ulster County Community Coll., 1982-84. Sec., bookkeeper Johnson Ford, Inc., Kingston, 1964-67, Island Dock Lumber Co., Kingston, 1968-69; account exec. Colonial Advt., Kingston, 1976-78; sec., salesman Fla. Girl Service/George Washington Life Ins., Clearwater, 1978; office mgr. Combined Protection Systems, Clearwater, 1978-79; bookkeeper Miron Lumber Co., Kingston, 1979-80; sec., sales asst. NPC Temporary Service, Kingston, N.Y., 1980; personnel mgr., accts. receivable supr., pub. relations, purchasing agent Rylance, Inc., Kingston, 1981—; owner E.L. Stewart, Ltd., Boiceville, N.Y., 1987—. Supporter Boy Scouts Am., 1977—. Mem. Nat. Assn. Female Execs. United Methodist. Lodge: Zonta (pres. 1988—, bd. dirs. 1986-88, 2d v.p.). Home: HCR 2 Box 44 Upper Boiceville Rd Boiceville NY 12412 Office: Rylance Inc PO Box 3336 Kingston NY 12401

STEWART, ELIZABETH JASON, lawyer; b. Boston, Sept. 3, 1936; d. Richard Eliot and Elizabeth Harding (McClure) Jason; m. Robert B. Stewart, July 2, 1960 (div.); children—Eleanor Anne, Robert Jason, Lee Bamford. B.A. in History, U. Mass., 1958; M.Ed., U. Hartford, 1969; J.D., Western New Eng. Coll., Springfield, Mass., 1977. Bar: Mass. 1977, U.S. Dist. Ct. Mass. 1978, Va. 1981, U.S. Dist. Ct. (ea. dist.) Va. 1981, U.S. Dist. Ct. D.C. 1981, U.S. Dist. Ct. (we. dist.) Va. 1982, U.S. Ct. Appeals (4th cir.) 1982, U.S. Supreme Ct. 1984. Ptnr. firm Thompson & Stewart, Ludlow, Mass., 1977-80; adminstr. Office Atty. Gen., Commonwealth of Va., Richmond, 1980-82, asst. atty. gen., 1982-84; dep. Commr. Indsl. Commn. Va., 1984—. Trustee Ludlow Hosp., 1979-80. Mem. ABA, Richmond Bar Assn., Va. Bar Assn., Ludlow C. of C. (pres. 1980). Episcopalian. Home: 5606 Matoaka Rd Richmond VA 23226 Office: Indsl Commn Va PO Box 1794 Richmond VA 23214

STEWART, ELLEN BARNETT, publishing executive; b. Atlanta, Nov. 2, 1962; d. Herbert Ledyard and Mary Ellen (Luttrell) S. Student, U. Paris, 1983; BA, U. of the South, 1984. Intern Atlanta Art Papers Inc., summer 1984, mng. editor, 1984-86; free-lance cons. 1986-87; gen. mgr. Southline Press Inc., Atlanta, 1987—. Mem. The Nature Conservancy, The Arts Exchange (bd. dirs. 1985-86), Atlanta Art Papers Inc. (bd. dirs. 1984-87). Episcopalian. Home: 1140 Springdale Rd NE Atlanta GA 30306 Office: Southline Press Inc 761 Peachtree St Atlanta GA 30309

STEWART, JEANNIE CALDER, psychologist; b. Aberdeen, Scotland, Nov. 29, 1913; d. Jonathan and Isabella Jane (Calder) S. AB magna cum laude, Brown U., 1945; MA, U. Calif., 1945; postgrad., Stanford U., 1948-49, 50-51. Tchg. asst. U. Calif., Berkeley, 1944-45; research asst. Jackson Lab., Bar Harbor, Maine, 1946; research asst. to instr. Vassar Coll., Poughkeepsie, N.Y., 1946-48, 49-50; student house dir. Pembroke Coll. Brown U., Providence, 1954-61; sec. to physician Fitchburg, Mass., 1961-64; adv. Garland Jr. Coll., Boston, 1965-66, 70-71; sec. residence program Boston U., 1967-70; house dir. House in the Pines Sch., Norton, Mass., 1971-72; sec. Manpower Program, Boston, 1972-73; clerical worker Stone and Webster Engring. Corp., Boston, 1973-84; part time clerical worker Skill Bur., Boston, 1984-88, Jr. League of Boston, 1986—; del. 19th Internat. Congress of Psychology, London, 1969. Author: Ancient and Cherished Treasures of Scotland, 1982. Mem. Nat. Trust for Hist. Preservation, Washington, 1986—, Nat. Trust for Scotland, Edinburgh, Scottish Heritage U.S.A, 1977—. Margaret Floy Washburn fellow Vassar Coll., 1950, Miss Abbott's Sch. Alumnae fellow Brown U. Mem. Am. Psychol. Assn. (life), Eastern Psychol. Assn., AAAS (emeritus), Daus. of the British Empire, Royal Overseas League, English Speaking Union (del. world mems. conf. 1977, 86), The British Psychol. So., Internat. Biog. Assn. Conf. on Arts and Communications (del. 1979, 80), Psi Chi, Sigma Xi. Republican. Presbyterian. Club: Brown U. (Boston). Home: 3 Concord Ave Apt B-3 Cambridge MA 02138

STEWART, JENNIFER, advertising executive; b. Sutton Coldfield, Eng., May 30, 1940; d. Eric Laughlan and Rita Joan (Taylor) S.; B.A. with honors in Philosophy and Econs., Univ. Coll., U. London, 1961. With Cement Mktg. Co., London, 1961-63, ICI Fibres Ltd., London, 1963-65, Research Services Ltd., London, 1965-68, Batton, Barton, Durstine & Osborne, Inc., N.Y.C., 1968-69; with Ogilvy & Mather Inc., N.Y.C., 1969—, exec. v.p., dir. branding and strategic services, Ogilvy and Mather Worldwide. Mem. Am. Mktg. Assn. (past dir. N.Y., past chmn. Effie awards com.), Am. Assn. Advt. Agencies (research com.), Market Research Council, Communication Research Council (past pres.), Copy Research Council (past pres.), Conf. Board (trustee). Home: 130 W 67th St New York NY 10023 Office: 2 E 48th St New York NY 10017

STEWART, JENNIFER LYNN, natural gas company executive; b. Williamsport, Pa., July 11, 1960; d. Joseph Grafius and Margretta (Furst) S. Student, Richmond Coll., London, 1978-79; BS, U. Bridgeport, 1982, MBA, 1983; postgrad. Econ. Devel. Inst., U. Okla., 1987. Mktg. research analyst Pitney Bowes, Stamford, Conn., 1980; price analyst trainee U.S. Dept. Defense, Stratford, Conn., 1980, contract negotiations trainee, 1981; asst. housing dir. U. Bridgeport (Conn.), 1981-83, grad. asst., 1982-83; commerce devel. rep. Commonwealth of Pa., Harrisburg, 1984-85; dir. econ. devel. City of Petersburg (Va.), 1985-87; mgr. econ. devel. Commonwealth Gas Services, Inc. and Columbia Gas of Va., Richmond, Va., 1987—. Author: Chocolate Milk, 1974 (2d place award 1974), Oasis House, 1987. Dir. community services Quota Club Petersburg, 1985, Jr. League of Richmond, 1985, Scottish Soc. Richmond, 1985; vol. Maymount Park, Richmond, 1986; v.p. Council for Urban Econ. Devel., 1987—; pres. Council for Urban Econ. Devel., 1988; mem. Petersburg Econ. Action Corp. Recipient Cert. of Recognition award Heritage Savs. and Loan, 1986, Jr. Achievement of Richmond, 1986, Kiwanis Club of Petersburg, 1986, Lions Club of Petersburg, 1987. Named one of Outstanding Young Woman of Am., Outstanding Americans, 1986, Young Outstanding Leader in Econ. Devel., 1988. Mem. Nat. Assn. Female Execs., So. Indsl. Devel. Council, So. Indsl. Devel. Council, Am. Econ. Devel. Council, Va. Econ. Devel. Assn., Va. C. of C. (legis. chmn. for ind. devel. com.). Republican. Presbyterian. Home: 1 Surry Lane Petersburg VA 23803 Office: Commonwealth Gas Services Inc 800 Moorefield Park PO Box 35800 Richmond VA 23235-0800

STEWART, JUDITH UNDERWOOD, securities analyst; b. Auburn, N.Y., Aug. 5, 1955; d. Martha (Davenport) Heard; m. Gordon Bennett Stewart III, June 13, 1981; 1 child, Gordon Bennett IV. BA, Wellesley Coll., 1977; student, MIT, 1975-77; MBA, Wharton Grad. Sch. Bus., 1979. Corp. fin. assoc. Shearson Loeb Rhoades Inc., N.Y.C., 1979-80; asst. treas. Chase Manhattan Bank, N.Y.C., 1980-83; mgr. Citicorp, N.Y.C., 1983-85; rating officer Standard & Poor's Corp., N.Y.C., 1985—. Contbr. writer: Standard & Poor's Structured Finance Criteria, 1988. Mem. Wharton Grad. Bus. Sch.

Club N.Y., Jr. League City of N.Y. (chmn. provisional com. winter ball 1984, vice-chmn. and treas. career awareness com. 1985-87), Am. Cancer Soc. N.Y. Div. (jr. com. 1982), French Library (jr. com. 1978), Soc. Mayflower Descendants, Nat. Soc. Colonial Dames, DAR Mary Washington Coll. chpt., New Eng. Soc. City of N.Y., Princeton Club N.Y., Wellesley Coll. Club N.Y., U. Pa. Club N.Y.C.

STEWART, KATHLEEN MARIE, business educator; b. Blue Island, Ill., Sept. 7, 1951; d. Thomas John and Rita Dorina (Ouimet) S. BS in Edn., So. Ill. U., 1972, MS in Edn., 1975; MBA, Loyola U., Chgo., 1984. Tchr. Downers Grove South High Sch., Downers Grove, Ill., 1972-76; assoc. prof. bus., chmn. dept. Moraine Valley Community Coll., Palos Hills, Ill., 1976—; corp. trainer Norrell Services, Chgo., 1985—. Author (software) tng. materials. Mem. Nat. Bus. Edn. Assn., Office Automation Soc. Internat., Phi Kappa Delta, Beta Gamma Sigma. Office: Moraine Valley Coll Dept Bus 10900 S 88th Ave Palos Hills IL 60465

STEWART, KIM KRISTINE, protective services official; b. Lynwood, Calif., Nov. 11, 1952; d. Harry David and Marilyn Mathilda (Olson) S. BA in History, U. Calif., Irvine, 1974. Cert. peace officer, Calif. Exec. dir. Girls' Club of Laguna, Inc., Laguna Beach, Calif., 1973-75, Girls' Club of Santa Ana (Calif.), Inc., 1975-77; exec. v.p. Nat. Programmed Learning Inst., Newport Beach, Calif., 1978; loan adjustor Security Pacific Nat. Bank, Santa Ana, 1979-81; police officer Cypress (Calif.) Police Dept., 1981-83; sheriff's dep. Santa Barbara (Calif.) County Sheriff's Dept., 1983—; speaker Neighborhood Watch Programs, Santa Barbara, 1984—. Fundraiser Shelter Services for Women, Inc., Santa Barbara, 1985-86, Santa Barbara Youth Charity Relay, 1986. Mem. Calif. Orgn. Police and Sheriffs, Santa Barbara Law Enforcement Assn. Democrat. Office: Santa Barbara County Sheriff's Dept 4434 Calle Real Santa Barbara CA 93110

STEWART, MARGARET JENSEN, chemist; b. Miami, Fla., Nov. 15, 1950; d. Arden Edward Jensen Sr. and Elizabeth Emma (Stevenson) Galliher; m. Lawrence Simpson Stewart, June 2, 1969; 1 child, Lawrence Simpson Jr. BS in Chemistry, Auburn U., 1972; postgrad., U. So. Miss., 1986—. Chemist Am. So. Dyeing and Finishing Corp., Opa Locka, Fla., 1972-74; sr. chemist Morton Thiokol Corp., Moss Point, Miss., 1976—; treas. Dog River Fed. Credit Union, Moss Point, 1981-83. Mem. city and county taxation com. Miss. Econ. Council, Jackson, 1985-86. Mem. AAUW (br. v.p. 1980-82, br. pres. 1984-87, Miss. state ednl. found. chmn. 1984-86, Miss. state equity action vote chmn. 1986-87, crisis in higher edn. forum chmn. 1986). Episcopalian. Clubs: Gulf Coast Orchid Soc.; Ocean Springs Yacht. Home: 43 Pittman Rd Ocean Springs MS 39564 Office: Morton Thiokol Corp PO Box 666 Moss Point MS 39563

STEWART, MARLENE JEAN, costume designer; b. Boston, Aug. 25, 1949; d. William Edward and Germaine (Cormier) S. AA, Fashion Inst. Tech., N.Y.C., 1975, Fashion Inst. Design and Mdsing., Los Angeles, 1976; BA, MA, U. Calif., Berkeley, 1972. Fashion designer, owner Covers Inc., Calif., 1978-84. Costume designer (movies) Body Rock, The Apprentice, (commercials) Toyota, Honda, 1984, (videos) Material Girl, Dress You Up, Would I Lie, 1985, (commercials) Chrysler, Levi Strauss, 1985, Madonna's Virgin Tour, 1985, (movies) Siesta, The Women's Club, Feel The Heat, 1986, (movie) Back to the Beach, 1987, Madonna World Tour, 1987. Cons. wardrobe Duran Duran, Earth Wind and Fire, Eurythmics, Pointer Sisters, Madonna, Janet Jackson, Grace Jones, Sylvie Vartan, Isabella Rosellini, Michael Pare. Redipient award design, Designer Bob Mackie, 1977, best costume designer Am. Video awards, 1985. Mem. Nat. Acad. Video Arts and Scics., Nat. Orgn. Female Exec., Costume Designers Guild, Am. Film Inst. (Women Film award, 1987), Mus. Contemporary Art. Home: 1416 N Havenhurst Dr #1C Los Angeles CA 90046

STEWART, MARY AGNES, music critic, journalist; b. Battle Creek, Mich., Feb. 25, 1899; d. William Ray and Mary Ann (Hays) Simpson; ed. Pacific Union Coll., U. Wash., U. Md., Am. U., Southeastern U., Washington, San Diego State U.; m. William Robert Stewart, May 4, 1918; children—William Robert, Ray Simpson, Stanley Hays. Asso. editor Calif. Hawaii Hotel-Life and Ocean Travel, 1925-36; impresario L. E. Behymer, Honolulu, 1926-29, La Jolla, Calif., 1941-44; San Diego rep. Pacific Coast Musician, 1945-54; La Jolla corr. Los Angeles Times, 1952-60; interior decorator Mary Stewart Interiors, La Jolla, 1942-88; researcher books The Spanish West, 1976, San Diego County Pioneer Families, 1976; free-lance writer, La Jolla, 1982—; contbr. Opera News, San Diego Union, San Francisco Chronicle. Historian, San Diego Opera Guild; chmn. San Diego Woman's Philharm. Com., La Jolla, Los Angeles Philharm. Orch., 1975-78; life mem. Scripps Meml. Hosp. Aux. Recipient Letter of Commendation, USN, 1972; Agnes Ave. (North Hollywood) named in her honor. Mem. Nat. League Am. Pen Women (br. pres. 1960-62), DAR (chpt. registrar 1966-67), Women in Communications, Nat. Geneal. Soc., Nat. Soc. Colonial Dames Am., First Families Va., San Diego Geneal. Soc., Social Service League La Jolla (life), Library Assn. La Jolla (life), Scottish Record Soc., Friends of Glasgow Cathedral (life), Magna Charta Soc., Owsley Family Hist. Sigma Alpha Iota. Clubs: Woman's (La Jolla); Clan Hay (life). Home: 7118 Olivetas Ave La Jolla CA 92037

STEWART, MARY CATHERINE, psychologist; b. Sault Ste. Marie, Mich.; d. Alexander Pringle and Marguerite Louise (Mc Carron) S.; A.B., U. Miami, 1941, M.S., 1960; m. Charles William Marker, Nov. 14, 1942 (div.); 1 son, Kevin Charles Stewart Marker. Human engring. analyst Boeing Co., Seattle, 1960-69; cons., Seattle, 1969-71, MITRE Corp., McLean, Va., 1971-74; research contract mgr. U.S. Dept. Transp., Washington, 1974-76; supervisory auditor psychologist GAO, Washington, 1976-78; established human factors group Idaho Nat. Engring. Lab. EG&G Idaho, Inc., Idaho Falls, 1978, mgr., 1978-82; profl. staff TRW Def. Systems Group, Norton AFB, Calif., 1982—. Mem. Human Factors Soc. (founder, 1st pres. Idaho chpt.). Office: TRW Def Systems Group Norton AFB CA 92409

STEWART, MYRNA LOUISE, educator; b. San Angelo, Tex., June 11, 1939; d. Grady Cleo Huckaby and Anna Florene (Shawn) Gibson; m. Jerry Ray Stewart, Dec. 27, 1957; children—Deborah Anne, Jerry Ray II, Randy Scott. B.S., East Tex. State U., 1980, M.S., 1983. Life cert. tchr., Tex. Dir., Nat. Child Care, Dallas, 1974-78; tchr. Dallas Ind. Sch. Dist., 1980-81, 84—, Allen (Tex.) Ind. Sch. Dist., 1981-84. Mem. Assn. Tex. Profl. Educators, Kappa Delta Pi, Alpha Chi. Republican. Mem. Ch. of Christ. Home: 10403 Robindale Dr Dallas TX 75238

STEWART, ORO ROZELLA, retail executive; b. Pendleton, Oreg., July 8, 1917; d. Joseph Allen and Oro Rozella (Overholtzer) Holaday; m. Ivan Stewart, Apr. 4, 1943 (dec.). BE, Oreg. State Coll., 1940; postgrad., Wash. State Coll., 1940-42. Owner, mgr. Stewart's Photo Shop, Anchorage, 1943—; owner Stewart's Jewel Jade Mine, 1970—; instr. TV Sch. Photograhpy; lectr. on Alaskan movies. Writer Alaskan directory on rockhound and internat. locations. Mem. Anchorage Centennial Com., 1967, organizer time capsule to be buried in Juneau; mem. Anchorage Downtown Assn., Fairview Homowners Assn. Recipient various awards at gem and mineral shows. Mem. Alaska Geol. Soc., Alaska Miners Assn., Chugach Gem and Mineral Soc. (chair field trips 1965-78, 81-84, pres. 1967, internat. chair 1967—), Am. Fedn. Lapidary Socs. (internat. relations com. 1977-80), N.W. Fedn. Mineral Socs., Nat. Businessmens Assn., Anchorage C. of C., Rifleman's Assn., Master Photo Dealers Assn., Profl. Photographers Alaska, Pioneers of Alaska. Democrat. Mem. Soc. of Friends. Clubs: Scottish, Tropical Fish. Lodge: Zonta (v.p. 1971). Home: 840 W 10th Anchorage AK 99501 Office: 531 4th Ave Anchorage AK 99501

STEWART, PAMELA LOUISE, aerospace engineering administrator; b. Hawthorne, Calif., May 21, 1950; d. Paul F. and Drusilla Ione (Bidwell) S.; m. Daniel Addington, Aug. 3, 1968 (div. 1973) 1 child, Dawn Marie Addington. Student, Mira Costa Jr. Coll., 1968-70, San Diego State U., 1969-70, Long Beach (Calif.) State U., 1970-71; BS in Physics, East Carolina U., 1977. Elem. level substitute tchr. Twenty-nine Palms, Calif., 1971-73; advanced tech. product line mgr. TRW Corp., Redondo Beach, Calif., 1983-86; program mgr. Aerospace Systems div. Ball Corp., Boulder, Colo., 1986—; tchr. math. City Coll. of Chgo. extension campus Hahn AFB, Fed. Republic Germany, 1981; ptnr., architect PGPS, Los Angeles, 1986-87. Served to capt. USAF, 1977-83, reserve. Republican. Office: Aerospace Systems div Ball Corp Arapahoe Blvd Boulder CO 80303

STEWART, PATRICIA ANN, bank executive; b. Phoenix, Nov. 3, 1953; d. Travis Delano and Ann Helen (Lopez) Hill; B.S., Ariz. State U., 1975. Programmer, analyst Victor Comptometer Corp., Phoenix, 1975-77, Lewis & Roca, Attys., Phoenix, 1977-79; data processing mgr. Central Mgmt. Corp., Phoenix, 1979-80; corp. systems cons. S.W. Forest Industries, Phoenix, 1981-87; human resources system mgr. Western Savs. and Loan, Phoenix, 1987—; ptnr. Abacus Group, 1981-83. Mem. Data Processing Mgmt. Assn. (pres. Phoenix chpt. 1982), Ariz. HP Users Group (mem. dir. 1987). Home: 15849 N 20th Pl Phoenix AZ 85022 Office: Western Savs 3200 E Camelback Suite 349 Phoenix AZ 85011

STEWART, PATRICIA CARRY, foundation administrator; b. Bklyn., May 19, 1928; d. William J. and Eleanor (Murphy) Carry; m. Charles Thorp Stewart, May 30, 1976. Student U. Paris, 1948-49; BA, Cornell U., 1950. Fgn. corr. Irving Trust Co., N.Y.C., 1950-51; with Janeway Research Co., N.Y.C., 1951-60, sec., treas., 1955-60; dir. Galt Malleable Iron Ltd., 1958-60; with Buckner & Co., N.Y.C., 1961-71, ptnr., 1962-71; pres., treas. Knight, Carry, Bliss & Co., Inc., N.Y.C., 1971-73; pres., treas. G. Tsai & Co., Inc., 1973; v.p. Edna McConnell Clark Found. Inc., 1974—; dir. TW Services Inc., Borden Inc., Continental Corp., Bankers Trust Co.; allied mem. N.Y. Stock Exchange, 1962-73; past mem. nominating com. Am. Stock Exchange, N.Y. Stock Exchange; past chmn., dir. Investor Responsibility Research Ctr. Trustee Cornell U., bd. overseers Med. Coll.; vis. com. Grad. Sch. Bus., Harvard U., 1974-80; bd. dirs. Women in Founds./Corp. Philanthropy 1980-86; vice chmn. CUNY, 1976-80; bd. dirs. United Way of Tri-State, 1977-81, Inst. for Edn. and Research on Women and Work; voting mem. Blue Cross and Blue Shield Greater N.Y., 1975-82; trustee N.Y. State 4-H Found., 1970-76, Internat. Inst. Rural Reconstruction, 1974-79; mem. N.Y.C. panel White House Fellows, 1976-78. Recipient Elizabeth Cutter Morrow award, 1977, Catalyst award, 1978, Wings Club N.Y. award, 1984. Mem. NOW (bd. dirs., treas. legal def. and edn. fund 1988—), Council Fgn. Relations, Pi Beta Phi. Clubs: University (N.Y.C.); Gullane Golf (Scotland). Home: 135 E 71st St New York NY 10021 Office: 250 Park Ave New York NY 10017

STEWART, RUTH SCHAEFER, educator; b. Cisco, Tex., Jan. 11, 1945; d. Henry A. and Thelma (Whatley) Schaefer; m. Tommy Dale Stewart, Aug. 27, 1982. AA, Cisco Jr. Coll., 1965; BS in Edn., Tarleton State Coll., 1967, MEd, 1982. Cert. elem. tchr. Tchr. Calhoun County Ind. Sch. Dist., Port Lavaca, Tex., 1967-71; sci. and English tchr. Weslaco (Tex.) Ind. Sch. Dist., 1974-77; resource tchr. Lakeview (Tex.) Ind. Sch. Dist., 1977-81, Cisco Ind. Sch. Dist., 1981—; distbr. Shaklee; art agt. Stewart Bronze. Sunday sch. tchr., pianist, soloist various ch. schs.; mem. Cisco Civic League. Mem. Assn. Tex. Prof. Educators (organizer, pres. Cisco unit, 1987-88), Delta Kappa Gamma, Kappa Delta Pi. Clubs: Microplex Photography, Cisco Writers (treas. 1986-87).

STEWART, SHARON DIANE, writer; b. Cleveland, Miss., June 16, 1951; d. Elton Stewart and Mary Ruth (Speights) Boyland. BS in Mktg., San Diego State U., 1974; MBA, U. San Diego, 1977; AA in Tech. Writing, Mesa Coll., 1985. Sr. acctg. specialist Motorola Corp., San Diego, 1977-79; supr. acctg. Security Pacific Fin., San Diego, 1979-84; sr. acctg. specialist Sun Savs. and Loan, San Diego, 1984-85; publs. specialist Sundstrand Turbomach, San Diego, 1985—; owner SDS Prodns., San Diego, 1981—. Contbr. articles to profl. jours. Vol. COMBO 1982-83, Sta. KPBS Pub. Radio 1984-87; bd. dirs. Community Coll. Tech. Writing Council, 1985—. Copley Assoc. scholar, 1983, Grocery Industry scholar, 1974. Mem. Naval Res. Assn. (v.p. 1987—), Res. Officers Assn., Soc. Tech. Communicators, San Diego Writers Guild, Nat. Acad. TV Arts (acting chair 1984, cert. 1985). Republican. Baptist. Clubs: San Diego Evening Coll. Bowling League, Toastmasters (Toastmaster Yr. 1983). Home: 3441 Ruffin Rd #1B San Diego CA 92123 Office: Sundstrand Turbomach 4400 Ruffin Rd San Diego CA 92123

STEWART, SUE STERN, lawyer; b. Casper, Wyo., Oct. 9, 1942; d. Fraizer McVale and Carolyn Eliabeth (Hunt) Stewart; B.A., Wellesley Coll., 1964; postgrad. Harvard U. Law Sch., 1964-65; J.D., Georgetown U., 1967; m. Arthur L. Stern, III, July 31, 1965 (div.); children—Anne Stewart, Mark Alan; m. John A. Ciampa, Sept. 1, 1985. Admitted to N.Y. bar, 1968; clk. to Judges Juvenile Ct., Washington, 1967-68; mem. firm Nixon, Hargrave, Devans & Doyle, Rochester, N.Y., 1968-74, partner, 1975—; lectr. in field; trustee Found. of Monroe County (N.Y.) Bar, 1976-78. Sec., dir. United Community Chest of Greater Rochester, 1973-87; trustee, sec. Internat. Museum Photography at George Eastman House, Rochester, 1974—, Genesee Country Mus., Mumford, N.Y., 1976—; bd. dirs. Ctr. for Govtal. Research. Mem. Am. (chmn. task force on charitable giving, exempt orgns. com. tax sect. 1981—), N.Y. State (exec. com. tax sect., 1974-76, chmn. com. exempt orgns. 1975-76), Monroe County Bar Assn. (trustee 1974-75), BNA Portfolio, Pvt. Found. Distbns. Author: Charitable Giving and Solicitation. Office: Nixon Hargrave Devans & Doyle Lincoln First Tower Rochester NY 14603

STEWART, SUZANNE, pension consultong firm executive; b. Schenectady, June 3, 1948; d. George Curtis and Janet (Gurney) S.; B.A., U. Pa., 1970, M.S. in Cardiovascular Physiology (teaching fellow), 1978. Plan adminstr. Todd Service Corp., Greenwich, Conn., 1978-80; spl. agt. Northwestern Mut. Life Ins. Co., Milw., 1980-82; sec.-treas. John O. Todd Orgn., Stamford, Conn., 1980-82; service co. exec., ins. agt. Servestate Corp., Stamford, 1980-82; Todd Service Corp., Stamford, 1980-82; sr. assoc. John O. Todd Orgn., 1980-82; pension cons., sr. v.p. Future Planning Assocs., Inc., South Burlington, Vt., 1983-88, pres., 1988—, also bd. dirs.

STEWART, VLENAETHA, psychologist; b. Ala., Feb. 28, 1957. BA, U. Mich., 1978; MA, Adelphi U., Garden City, N.Y., 1980, PhD, 1983. Psychology extern Westbury (N.Y.) Sch. System, 1978-79, Nassau County (N.Y.) Med. Ctr., 1979-80; psychotherapist Psychol. Services, Garden City, 1980-81; psychology intern Lafayette Clinic, Detroit, 1981-82; staff psychologist Greater Flint (Mich.) Health Maintenance Orgn., 1983-87, Mott Childrens Health Ctr., Flint, 1987—; mem. Headstart Health Adv. Bd., Flint, 1984—, Nat. Urban League Task Force, 1987. Mem. Am. Psychol. Assn., Orthopsychiat. Assn., Assn. Black Psychologists. Office: Mott Childrens Health Ctr 806 Turri Place Flint MI 48503

STICKLE, MARGARET ALICE, controller; b. Russell, Ky., Oct. 3, 1934; d. Russell De Atley and Lorah Ellen (Ferrell) Kegley; B.A., Marshall Coll., 1956; postgrad. UCLA 1973-75; 1 child, David Brent. Asst. controller R & B Devel., Los Angeles, 1973-78; pres. Evergreen Realty Corp., and Evergreen Realty Corp., Tex., Los Angeles, 1978-80; v.p., controller Consol. First Nat. Corp., Los Angeles, 1980-83; treas., controller Western Cons. Group, Inc., real estate syndicators, 1983—; controller western div. Niagara Cyclo Massage, 1968-70; sec. various corps. Treas., Boy Scouts Am., 1965-68; mem. election bd. Republican Party, 1968-71. Mem. Nat. Acctg. Assn., Nat. Notary Assn. Presbyterian. Club: Northridge Woman's (sec. 1967). Home: 8338 Woodley Pl Unit #41 Sepulveda CA 91343 Office: 8718 Woodley Ave Sepulveda CA 91343

STICKLES, BONNIE JEAN, nurse; b. Waukesha, Wis., Nov. 24, 1944; d. Donald William and Betty Jane S.; B.S. in Nursing, U. Wis., 1967; M.S. in Nursing, Midwifery, Columbia U., 1974. Mem. nursing staff Grace Hosp., Detroit, 1970-73; mem. faculty and staff U. Minn. Sch. Nursing and Nurse-Midwifery Service, Mpls., 1974-76; chief nurse-midwife, clin. instr. St. Paul-Ramsey Med. Center, 1976-84; midwifery supr. IHS/PHS Chinle Hosp., 1984-85; program mgr. maternal health sect. N.Mex. Dept. Health and Environ., 1985—; mem. consumer adv. pool FDA; adv. bd. Childbirth Edn. Assn., 1980-85. Served with USNR, 1965-70. Decorated Letter of Commendation. Mem. Am. Coll. Nurse-Midwives (chmn. profl. affairs com. 1975-80), Nurses Assn. Am. Coll. Obstetricians and Gynecologists (charter), Aircraft Owners and Pilots Assn., Gt. Plains Perinatal Orgn., Alpha Tau Delta. Author articles in field; patentee teaching model.

STIDGER, RUTH WILLMAN, editorial director, author; b. Rodney, Iowa, Sept. 20, 1939; d. Kenneth Wilbur and Eileen Lucille (Walton) W.; m. Jerry Edgar Saylor; children—Ellen Joyce, Susan Grace; m. 2d. Howe Carson Stidger. Student U. Iowa, 1957-58, Iowa State U., 1964-65, Northwestern U., 1967-68; B.S., Columbia Pacific U., 1983, M.S., 1984. Field mgr. Saul Cohen Realty, Gary, Ind., 1965-67; editor Equitable Ins. Co., Gary, 1967-68; staff editor Cahners Pub., Chgo., 1968-70; features editor McGraw Hill, Chgo., 1970-71; owner Internat. Services, Brighton, U.K., 1971-73, editorial dir Tech. Pub. Co., N.Y.C., 1975-86; owner Ruth W. Stidger & Assocs., Dallas, 1987—. Author: Cost Reduction from A to Z, 1975, Inflation Management, 1976, The Competence Game, 1981, 187 Ways to Amuse a Bored Cat, 1983, Business Basic French, Spanish, and German, 1986; editor-in-chief Better Roads Mag.; editorial dir. Gas Industries Mag. Recipient Jesse H. Neal Editorial award Am. Bus. Press, N.Y.C., 1983, 1969, Jesse H. Neal cert. of merit, 1978, 80. Mem. MENSA, N.Y. Bus. Press Editors (pres. 1980-81), Am. Bus. Press Editorial Com. (chairperson 1980-81). Office: Ruth W Stidger & Assocs 6301 Gaston Ave Suite 400 Dallas TX 75214

STIDNICK, LORI ANN, natural gas company executive; b. Panama City, Fla., May 17, 1959; d. Wesley Charles Jr. and Doris Joan (Fushak) S. BSBA, U. South Ala., 1981. Flight dispatcher Thunderbird Airways, Inc., Houston, 1981-82; producer relations rep. Am. Natural Resources, Houston, 1983-85; trans. and exchange rep. Tenneco Gas Transp., Houston, 1985—. Mem. Natural Gas Men Houston, Natural Gas Men New Orleans, Nat. Assn. Female Execs., Nat. Trans. & Exchange Assn. Republican. Roman Catholic. Club: Houston Cosmopolitan. Home: 9449 Briar Forest Dr #1813 Houston TX 77063 Office: Tenneco Gas Transp 1010 Milam T-1515A Houston TX 77001

STIELOW-LEACH, FAY ANN, interior designer; b. Oostburg, Wis., Apr. 20, 1939; d. Arnold Lloyd and May Annette (Steenweg) Wykhuis; m. Curtis G. Stielow, June 16, 1961 (div. 1978); m. Harrison Langford Leach, July 11, 1987. Student, Carroll Coll., 1957-58; BS, U. Wis., 1961; postgrad., U. Calif., Long Beach, 1962-63. Tchr. Long Beach Jordan High Sch., 1961-64, Shoales Jr. High Sch., Milw., 1964-66, McPherson Jr. High Sch., Orange, Calif., 1966-69; realtor Myers and Hill, Vienna, Va., 1971-74; sales rep. Ryland Homes, Manassas, Va., 1974-76, Fairfield Homes, Woodbridge, Va., 1976-79; v.p. Fairfield Design Studio, Woodbridge, 1980-86, pres., 1986—. Mem. No. Va. Builders Assn., Prince William County C. of C. (com. chairperson 1984-87). Presbyterian. Office: Faifield Design Studio 14824 Build America Dr Woodbridge VA 22191

STILES, LOIS ANN, small business owner; b. Nickelsville, Va., Sept. 12, 1945; d. Lee Edward and Mary Pauline (Compton) White; m. Gilbert J. Stiles Jr., Sept. 12, 1965. BS in Mgmt., Worcester State Coll., 1980. Office mgr. EPA, Washington, 1963-74; sec. U.S. Army Map Service, Office Econ. Opportunity, HEW, EPA, Washington, 1963-74; self employed word processor Westboro, Mass., 1980-81; instr. Grafton (Mass.) Job Corps, 1981-82; owner Better Office Support Services, Inc., Westboro, 1982—. Home: 54 Arch St Westboro MA 01581 Office: Better Office Support Services Inc 19 W Main St Box 656 Westboro MA 01581

STILLINGS, IRENE CORDINER, club woman; b. Boston, Aug. 17, 1918; d. Matthew Wilson and Susan F. (Mason) Cordiner; student Radcliffe Coll., 1936-39; diploma Burdett Coll., 1941; m. Gordon A. Stillings, May 13, 1945; children—David Gordon, Susan Irene. Sec., bookkeeper Boston Refrigerator Co., 1941-42; sec., tchr. Burdett Coll., 1942-44; sec., bookkeeper Gertrude Rittenburg, Boston, 1944-46. Town chmn. Heart Fund, Woodland, Maine, 1953-61; Brownie leader Girl Scouts U.S.A., 1954-58; pres. Woodland Woman's Club 1961-63; sec. PTA, 1961-62; chmn. Baileyville Superintending Sch. Com., 1962-64; chmn. women's activities Nat. Found., East Washington County, 1959-61; pres. Hosp. Aid, 1961-63; chmn. Newcomers Coll. group YWCA, 1965-66, chmn. theatre group, 1968-70, pres. Suburbanites, 1970-71; Stamford chmn. Expt. in Internat. Living, 1965-68; bd. dirs. YWCA of Stamford, chmn. devotion, 1970-88, ann. Antique Show benefit, 1970-77. Mem. Mass. Hort. Soc., St. Luke's Guild (treas. 1954-63), Theta Alpha Chi. Episcopalian. Clubs: Radcliffe; Stamford Woman's (treas. 1975-79, program com., co-chmn. Am. home dept. 1974, 75, pres. 1981-83, dir. 1985-87, 2d v.p. fin. 1987-89, chmn. bldg. investment 1979-81). Home: 277 West Hill Rd Stamford CT 06902

STILLMAN, ANNE WALKER, fashion designer; b. Amsterdam, Apr. 15, 1951; came to U.S., 1953; d. Edmund and Mary (Gwathmey) S. Student Barnard Coll., 1968-72. Pres., designer Sofia & Anne, Ltd., Bethel, Ct. and N.Y.C., 1978—; designer Sofia & Anne Sportknit, 1983—, Sofia & Anne Children's Wear, 1985—, Go Cashmere for L'Zinger by Sofia & Anne, 1986. Office: Sofia & Anne 37 W 39th St New York NY 10018

STILLMAN, ELINOR HADLEY, lawyer; b. Kansas City, Mo., Oct. 12, 1938; d. Hugh Gordon and Freda (Brooks) Hadley; m. Richard C. Stillman, June 25, 1965 (div. Apr. 1975). BA, U. Kans., 1960; MA, Yale U., 1961; JD, George Washington U., 1972. Bar: D.C. Lectr. in English CUNY, N.Y., 1963-65; asst. editor Stanford (Calif.) U. Press., 1967-69; clk. to judge U.S. Dist. Ct. D.C., Washington, 1972-73; appellate atty. Nat. Labor Relations Bd., Washington, 1973-78; asst. to solicitor gen. U.S. Dept. Justice, Washington, 1978-82; supr. appellate atty. NLRB, Washington, 1982-86, chief counsel to mem. bd., 1986-88, chief counsel to chmn. bd., 1988—. Mem. ABA, D.C. Bar Assn. (steering com., adminstrv. law and agy. practice 1984—), Order of the Coif, Phi Beta Kappa. Democrat. Office: Nat Labor Relations Bd 1717 Pennsylvania Ave NW Washington DC 20570

STILLMAN, MARTHA, interior designer; b. Chgo., Nov. 8, 1924; d. Frederick Arthur and Eva Mable (Ihle) Niestadt; m. Charles Harvey Stillman, Sept. 6, 1947; 1 child, Ann Elizabeth. Student, Beloit (Wis.) Coll., 1943-45; BS in Interior Design/Architecture, Northwestern U., 1947. Interior designer Interiors - Martha Stillman, New Canaan, Conn., 1961—; cons. in field. Pres. Wilmette Jrs. Infant Welfare Soc., 1953-60; mem. women's bd. Chgo. Infant Welfare Soc., 1957-60, Women's Rep.; advisor Girl Scouts U.S.A. Mem. Assn. Interior Designers (sec., bd. govs. 1964-75), Am. Soc. Interior Designers, Phi Beta Phi. Republican. Mem. United Ch. of Christ. Clubs: Woodway Country (Darien, Conn.); Skytop (Pa.). Home and Office: 301 W Hills Rd New Canaan CT 06840

STILLMAN, MARY ELIZABETH, librarian, administrator, educator; b. Phila., Oct. 31, 1929; d. Ernest E. and Rosalie (Burhans) Stillman; B.A., Wilson Coll., Chambersburg, Pa., 1950; M.S., Drexel U., Phila., 1952; Ph.D. (fellow), U. Ill., 1966. Librarian, USAF, 1953-63, Export-Import Bank U.S., 1965-68; asst. prof. Drexel U., 1968-72; mem. faculty Albright Coll., Reading, Pa., 1972-87, prof., librarian, 1975-87, spl. asst. to pres., 1987—; editor Drexel Library Quar., 1969-72; cons. research info. system Social and Rehab. Service, 1972-74; del. Pa. Gov.'s Conf. on Libraries, 1977; chmn. Pa. Library Week, 1978, 79; shareholder Reading Library Co., 1980—; mem. long-range planning com. Reading Pub. Library, 1982—, trustee, 1985—; pres. Reading Library, 1985—. Bd. dirs. Reading YWCA, 1981-83. Mem. ALA (reviewer Subscription Books Bull. 1969—), Pa. Library Assn. (dir. pub. relations task force 1974-79, editor bull. 1973-79, treas. colloquium on info. retrieval 1978-79), AAUP. Contbr. articles to profl. jours. Home: 1375 Pershing Blvd Apt 102 Reading PA 19607 Office: Albright Coll Reading PA 19604

STILLMAN, STEPHANIE MATUSZ, computer contract company executive; b. Middlesex County, N.J., July 16, 1946; d. William Stephan Matusz and Mary Jane (Van Horn) Falger; m. Dennis Edison DeMercer, Aug. 22, 1970 (div. 1977); m. Richard Alan Stillman, May 10, 1980; 1 child, Taylor Edison. B.A., Moravian Coll., 1968. Tchr., Hawaii Edn. Dept., Kohala, 1968-71; acct. exec. with various ins. agys., N.J., 1975-79; div. mgr. E.T. Lyons & Assoc., New Brunswick, N.J., 1979-80; sr. personnel adminstr. Systemp, Inc., New Brunswick, 1980-84; br. mgr. Officeforce, Inc., Cedar Knolls, N.J., 1984; pres., chief exec. officer The Resource Group, Inc., Cambridge, Mass., 1985—. Bd. dirs., pres. Rutgers-Livingston Day Care Ctr., Piscataway, N.J., 1978-80. Mem. Cambridge C. of C., Smaller Bus. Assn. New Eng., Data Processing Mgmt. Assn., Assn. Women in Computing. Republican. Avocations: skiing; travel. Office: The Resource Group Inc PO Box 2327 Cambridge MA 02238

STILSON, PHYLLIS VERONICA, nursing administrator; b. Queens, N.Y., Oct. 26, 1947; d. Edward T. and Veronica (Barr) Pisano; m. Gregory Lee S., June 11, 1983; stepchildren: Kenneth Ward, James Erik. Diploma, Cen. Islip Sch. Nursing, 1968; AA, Mt. San Antonio Coll., 1976; BS in Health Scis. Adminstrn., Chapman Coll., 1982; MEd, Nat. U Los Angeles, 1986. Registered nurse. Staff, head nurse Cen. Gen. Hosp., Plainview, N.Y., 1968-71; staff, charge nurse Pomona Valley (Calif.) Hosp., 1971-73; asst.

charge nurse HMO Clinic, Pomona, 1973-75; instr. Valley Coll. Med./Dental Careers, North Hollywood, Calif., 1975-85; asst. dir. nursing edn. Valley Coll. Med./Dental Careers, North Hollywood, 1984-85, dir. nursing edn., 1985-87; health care coordinator/case mgr. U.S. Adminstrs., Calabasas, Calif., 1987-88; supr. utilitzation review CIGNA Health Plan, Glendale, Calif., 1988—. Mem. Calif. Vocat. Nurse Educators.

STIMPSON, CATHARINE ROSLYN, English language educator, writer; b. Bellingham, Wash., June 4, 1936; d. Edward Keown and Catharine (Watts) S. A.B., Bryn Mawr Coll., 1958; B.A., Cambridge U., Eng., 1960, M.A., 1960; Ph.D., Columbia U., 1967. Mem. faculty Barnard Coll., N.Y.C., 1963-80; prof. English, dean of grad. sch., vice provost grad. edn. Rutgers U., New Brunswick, N.J., 1980—; chmn. bd. scholars Ms. Mag., N.Y.C., 1981—. Author: Class Notes, 1979; founding editor: Signs: Jour. Women in Culture and Society, 1974-81; book series Women in Culture and Society, 1981. Chmn. N.Y. Council Humanities, 1984-87, Nat. Council Research on Women, 1984—; bd. dirs. Stephens Coll., Columbia, Mo., 1982-85. Hon. fellow Woodrow Wilson Found., 1958; Fulbright fellow, 1958-60; Nat. Humanities Inst. fellow New Haven, 1975-76; Rockefeller Humanities fellow, 1983-84. Mem. MLA (exec. council, chmn. acad. freedom com., 2d v.p.), P.E.N., AAUP, NOW. Democrat. Home: 62 Westervelt Ave Staten Island NY 10301 Office: Rutgers U Office of Grad Dean New Brunswick NJ 08903

STIMSON, DOROTHY BRICKWEDDE, brokerage executive; b. Cin., Dec. 31, 1917; d. Harry Joseph and Marie (Ihlendorf) Brickwedde; m. Harry Poyner Stimson, Aug. 12, 1943 (dec.); children: Harry Richard, Jane Stimson Schweitzer, Cynthia Stimson Howe, Denise Stimson Andersen, Scott R., Jeffrey D.; m. Robert W. Duffield, Oct. 16, 1970. Ph.B., Marygrove Coll., Detroit, 1940; postgrad. U. Mich., N.Y. Inst. Fin., U. Pa., U. Detroit, Oakland U., Wharton Sch. of U. Pa., Butler U. Cert. tchr., Mich. Mem. engring. aide Signal Corps Ground Signal Service, 1941-44; stockbroker Bache & Co., 1960-65; asst. mgr. Paine Webber Jackson & Curtis, Detroit, 1965-70, v.p., 1970—; lectr. in field internat. Pres. Detroit Osteo. Hosp. Aux.; pres. Detroit Osteopathic Women's Club; trustee, 1st pres.' counsel Marygrove Coll., Providence Hosp. Found. Named Outstanding Vol. Nat. Soc. Fund Raising Execs., 1984. Mem. Mich. Women's Osteo. Assn. (pres.), Women in Fin., Mich. Life Underwriters. Republican. Roman Catholic. Clubs: Zonta, Recess, Detroit Golf. Home: 161 Hendrie Blvd Royal Oak MI 48067

STIMSON, MIRIAM MICHAEL, educational administrator; b. Chgo., Dec. 24, 1913; d. Frank Sharpe and Mary Frances (Holland) S.; B.S., Siena Heights Coll., 1936, M.S., Instn. Divi Thomae, Cin., 1939, Ph.D., 1948. Joined Adrian Dominican Sisters, Roman Catholic Ch., 1935; mem. faculty Siena Heights Coll., Adrian, Mich., 1939-68, chmn. chemistry dept., 1948-68, dir. grad. studies, 1978—; research assoc. Fla. State U., Tallahassee, 1969; prof. Keuka Coll., Keuka Park, N.Y., 1969-78; lectr. Canisius Coll., 1961; mem. screening panel NSF, 1963. Speaker Ch. Women United, Penn Yan, N.Y., v.p., 1973-74, pres., 1974-76; chmn. pub. events com. Keuka Coll. Campaign 1970, Penn Yan, 1970-72; mem. Lenawee County Profl. Devel. Policy Bd., 1976—, chmn., 1979-80, mem. Lenawee County Home Health Care Adv. Bd., 1981—, chmn., 1982-86; exec. com., bd. dirs. Mich. Consortium of Substance Abuse Edn., 1984—, v.p. 1986-87, pres. 1987-88. Mem. Am. Chem. Soc., Nat. Assn. Women Deans, Mich. Assn. Women Deans, Am. Assn. Counseling and Devel., Mich. Assn. Counseling and Devel., Am. Assn. Counseling Edn. and Supervision,. Home: 1126 E Siena Heights Dr Adrian MI 49221 Office: 1247 E Siena Heights Dr Adrian MI 49221

STINE, ANNA MAE, publishing company executive; b. Monongahela, Pa., Sept. 6, 1938; d. Carlton Lee and Martha Regina (Graham) S.; B.S. in Edn., Calif. State Coll. (Pa.), 1959; elem. prin. cert. Duquesne U., 1962, masters in elem. edn., 1962; cert. reading specialist U. Pitts., 1963, postgrad., 1963-65. Tchr., student tchr. supr. Upper St. Clair Sch. Dist., Pitts., 1959-65; nat. lang. arts cons. Macmillan Pub. Co., N.Y.C., 1965-75, regional mgr., Riverside, N.J., 1975-78; v.p., nat. sales mgr.East, Macmillan Pub. Co., 1978—. Recipient Robert Hann award Macmillan Pub. Co., 1965, Donald McGrew award 1967, NJRA award, 1985. Mem. Internat. Reading Assn., NEA, Regional Edn. Service Agy., Keystone Reading Assn., Upper St. Clair Tchrs. Orgn. (pres.). Republican. Roman Catholic. Home: 215 Haddon Commons Haddonfield NJ 08033

STINE, JUDITH ANN, travel agency executive; b. Washington, Oct. 25, 1949; d. Wayne Joseph and Lucelia Ann (Miller) Taylor; m. William George Stine Jr., Sept. 19, 1970; children: Joseph William, Emily Christine. Grad. high sch., Machinato, Japan. Sec. U.S. Army, Machinato, 1968-69; exec. sec. Commanding Officer Atlantic Fleet Hdqrs., Norfolk, Va., 1969-70; nursing aide Hillside Nursing Home, Bryan, Ohio, 1976-79; travel by car counselor Bryan Travel Ctr., Bryan, 1981-82, travel cons., 1982-84, ins. agt., 1984—, mgr., 1984—; coordinator, escort Fayette Sr. Citizen Group, Ohio, 1984—; salesman, product devel. Toledo Automobile Club, 1987. Mem. Bus. Adv. Bd. N.W. Tech. Coll., 1988—, Williams County Safety Council, 1988—. Mem. Bryan C. of C. Republican. Baptist. Club: Omnibus (West Unity, Ohio) (sec. 1974-75). Office: Bryan Travel Ctr 1001 W High St Bryan OH 43506

STINE, KAREN ELIZABETH, toxicologist; b. Kansas City, Kans., Apr. 22, 1956; d. Forrest Dale and Betty Jean (Heston) S.; m. Raymond Andrew Jacobs, Jan 7, 1978; 1 child, Melinda. BS, Coll. William and Mary, 1978; MS, U. Va., 1980; PhD, U. N.C., 1985. Research asst. dept. environ. scis. U. Va., Charlottesville, 1978-80; research asst. curriculum in toxicology U. N.C., Chapel Hill, N.C., 1980-84; asst. prof. Clemson U., S.C., 1984-88, Radford (Va.) U., 1988—. Contbr. articles to profl. jours. Govs. Fellow U. Va., 1978-80. Mem. Am. Phys. Soc., AAAS, Sierra Club (conservation co-chair Foothills Group 1985-87). Democrat. Presbyterian. Office: Radford U Dept Biology Radford VA 24142

STINER, LINDA SAYERS, employee assistance executive; b. Galax, Va., Sept. 4, 1941; d. Maynard Hastin Sayers and Ruth Elizabeth (Cornett) James; m. Robert Gray Bruce, Aug. 3, 1963 (div. Oct. 1984) children: Shannon Elizabeth, Robert Gray, Jr.; m. William Evan Stiner, Dec. 24, 1984. BA in Edn., Radford U., 1963. Cert. employee assistance profl., social worker assoc. Tchr. Bristol (Va.) City Schs., 1963-64, Richmond (Va.) City Schs., 1964-65, Pulaski (Va.) County Schs., 1965-66, Bath County Schs., Hot Springs, Va., 1971-72; substitute tchr. Pickins (S.C.) County Schs., 1977-79; dept. mgr. Hampton's, Pickins, 1979; mgr. Mary Stokes Shop, Clemson, S.C., 1980; social worker Pickins County Dept. Social Services, Pickins, 1980-81; pub. info., tng. coordinator East Tex. Council on Alcoholism, Longview, 1982-86; dir. QUEST Meadow Pines Hosp., Longview, 1986—; seminar and workshop leader, 1982—. Editor: (newsletter) UPDATE, 1983-86. Vol. United Way, Longview, 1982-87; bd. dirs. YMCA, Longview, 1984—, Palmer Drug Abuse Program, Longview, 1984-86. Mem. Assn. Labor Mgmt. Cons. on Alcoholism (founder Ark-La-Tex chpt., pres. 1986-87), Nat. Assn. Alcoholism and Drug Abuse Counselors (cert., pres. E. Tex. chpt. 1985-86). Democrat. Presbyterian. Home: 1826 Shenandoah Ct N Longview TX 75605 Office: QUEST 414 E Loop 281 Suite 5 Longview TX 75601

STINSON, KATHARINE, aeronautical engineer; b. Raleigh, N.C., Sept. 18, 1917; d. William Elmond and Mary Katharine (Byrd) S. BSME, N.C. State U., 1941. Aero. engr. mfg. div. FAA, Washington, 1941-73; pvt. practice aviation cons. Glendale, Calif., 1973—; mem. engrs. council Washington. Conrbr. numerous articles to profl. jours. Recipient Disting. Women in Aerospace award Fedn. orgns. Profl. Women, 1984, Aerospace Pioneer award AIAA, 1987. Fellow Soc. Women Engrs. (pres. 1953-55); mem. Phi Kappa Phi, The Ninety Nines. Presbyterian. Lodge: Soroptimists. Home and Office: 318 Mesa Lila Rd Glendale CA 91208

STINSON, MARY FLORENCE, nursing educator; b. Wheeling, W.Va., Feb. 11, 1931; d. Rolland Francis and Mary Angela (Voellinger) Kellogg; m. Charles Walter Stinson, Feb. 12, 1955; children—Kenneth Charles, Karen Marie, Kathryn Anne. B.S. in Nursing, Coll. Mt. St. Joseph, 1953, postgrad., 1983; M.Ed., Xavier U., Cin., 1967; postgrad. U. Cin., 1981. Staff nurse contagious disease ward Cin. Gen. Hosp., 1953-54, asst. head nurse med. and polio wards, 1955, acting head nurse, clin. instr., 1955-56; instr. St. Francis Hosp. Sch. Practical Nursing, Cin., 1956-57; instr. Good Samaritan Hosp. Sch. Nursing, Cin., 1957-65; instr. refresher courses for nurses Cin. Bd. Edn. and Ohio State Nurses Assn. Dist. 8, 1967-70; coordinator sch. health office Coll. Mt. St. Joseph (Ohio), 1969-72, instr. dept. nursing, 1974-79, asst. prof., 1979—. Charter mem. Adoptive Parents Assn. St. Joseph Infant and Maternity Home; active Women's Com. for Performing Arts Series, Coll. Mt. St. Joseph; mem. St. Antoninus Rosary Altar Rosary and Sch. Soc., St. Antoninus Athletic Club, com. chmn., 1969-70; bd. dirs. Coll. Mt. St. Joseph Alumnae Assn., 1982-84, sec., 1968-69, v.p., 1969-70, pres., 1970-71, chmn. revision of constn., 1976-77; homecoming chmn. Coll. Mt. St. Joseph, 1970, co-chmn., 1977; mem. Gamble Nippert YMCA. Mem. Am. Nurses Assn., Ohio Nurses Assn., Southwestern Ohio Nurses Assn., AAUP. Democrat. Roman Catholic. Club: River Squares (v.p. 1967). Home: 5549 Cleander Dr Cincinnati OH 45238 Office: Coll Mt St Joseph 5701 Delhi Mount Saint Joseph OH 45051

STIP, CATHERINE ANN, contracts administrator, interior designer; b. Canton, Ohio, Mar. 10, 1943; d. Joseph, Jr., and Anna Catherine (Wiley) Sekely; 1 child, Arthur Wayne. Student interior design Parsons Sch. Design, Los Angeles, 1984—; student bus. adminstrn. and interior design Orange Coast Coll., 1983—, Univ. Calif., Irvine. Sec. to various execs. Los Angeles area, 1962-70; contracts coordinator Murdock, Inc., Carson, Calif., 1974-75; contracts adminstr. AHF-Ducommun, Gardena, Calif., 1970-74, 78—; owner Catherine Ann Interiors, Huntington Beach, Calif., 1985—; cons. Artistic Interiors, Fountain Valley, 1984, Trans Designs, Ga., 1984-85, numerous others; sponsor Miss Huntington Beach, 1987—. Mem. Nat. Assn. Female Execs., Huntington Beach C. of C., Nat. Secs. Assn. (sec. 1974-75), Childrens Home Soc. Orange County, Am. Bus. Womens Assn. Avocations: art; cooking; sewing; jogging; sailing.

STITES, M(ARY) ELIZABETH, educator; b. N.Y.C., July 28, 1915; d. Otto and Olivia (Stites) Gaertner; m. Raymond S. Stites, Jul. 29, 1938; 1 child: Mary Elizabeth. BArch, NYU, 1940; postgrad., U. Vienna, 1961. Instr. U. Md. Coll. Arts & Scis., College Park, Md., 1949-67, adminstrv. asst., 1959-76; assoc. prof. U. Md. Coll. Arts & Scis., Silver Spring, 1967-76; cons. Md. Coll. Art and Design, Silver Spring, 1976—; asst. organist St. Luke's Church, Bethesda, Md., 1978—; Lectr. religious architecture, history architecture, archtl. studies of Leonardo da Vinci. Contbr. articles to Book of Knowledge Grolier Soc., 1952, New Cath. Ency., 1965. Past mem. Yellow Springs Town Planning Commn. Mem. Coll. Art Assn., Soc. Archti. Historians, Archaeol. Inst. Am., AIA. Episcopalian. Home: PO Box 98 Garrett Park MD 20896

STIVER, INEZETTA OREL ELIASON, accountant; b. Centerville, Ind., Mar. 26, 1916; d. Wood Esta and Pearl Mae (Davis) Eliason; m. Roy Carl Stiver, Nov. 24, 1940. Diploma, Ind. Bus. Coll., 1948. Pvt. practice acctg. Centerville, 1955-87; instr. acctg. Richmond (Ind.) Bus. Coll., 1945-48. Author: Wilderness Opportunity, 1964; columnist Centerville Crusader Silhouettes. Clk. Centerville Christian Ch., 1955-84; bd. dirs. Hist. Centerville Inc., 1969-84, 86—; mem. Centerville Planning Comn., 1975-77, Wayne County (Ind.) Resource Inventory Commn., 1985—. Recipient civic award Centerville Jaycees, 1971, This Is Your Life award, 1978, Scouters Wife Heart of Gold award, 1979, Outstanding Citizen award Centerville Lions Club, 1986. Mem. Nat. Soc. Pub. Accts., Ind. Soc. Pub. Accts., Soc. Ind. Pioneers, Am. Legion Aux., Centerville Women's Cemetary Assn. (treas. 1980—), Alliance Wayne County Mus. (bd. dirs.), DAR, Colonial Dames 17th Century, Daus. Am. Colonists, Studebaker Family Assn., Ind. Genealogy Soc., Ill. Genealogy Soc., Iowa Genealogy Soc., Ohio Genealogy Soc., Md. Genealogy Soc., Del. Genealogy Soc., Pa. Genealogy Soc., Joshua Eliason Family Descendants (historian). Republican. Address: 116 E Plum St Centerville IN 47330

STOCK, PEGGY L., college administrator; b. Jan. 30, 1936; m. Robert J. Stock. BS in Psychology, St. Lawrence U., Canton, N.Y., 1957; MA, U. Ky., 1963, EdD, 1969. Lic. psychologist, Ohio; cert. tchr. learning disabilities, behavioral problems. Instr. research asst. U. Ky., Lexington, 1958-59, mem. faculty, spl. edn., 1963-67; lectr. psych. dept., speech, theater arts U. Cin., 1970-74; assoc. prof., counseling psychologist Montana State U., Bozeman, 1976-77, asst. dean, office of student affairs and services, 1977-79; exec. assoc. to pres. U. Hartford, West Hartford, Conn., 1980-81, v.p. adminstrn., 1981-86; pres. Colby-Sawyer Coll., New London, N.H., 1986—; pres. Midwest Inst. Tng. and Edn., Cin., 1971-76; vis. prof. sociology and edn. Thomas Moore Coll., Ft. Mitchell, Ky., 1970-71. Contbd. articles to profl. jours. Recipient Mental Health award, Lexington, 1966; U. Ky. fellow, 1966-68, United Jewish Com. fellow, 1981. Mem. Am. Council on Edn. (fellow 1979-80), Am. Assn. Higher Edn., N.H. Coll. and Univ. Council. Office: Colby-Sawyer Coll Pres's House New London NH 03257

STOCKANES, HARRIET PRICE, publishing executive, consultant; b. Crawford, Nebr., Oct. 31, 1923; d. Joseph Hartwell and Lyda Marie (Chadderdon) Price; m. Robert Ward O'Brien, Dec. 28, 1946 (div. Aug. 1964); children—Nan O'Brien Beman, Julia O'Brien Domingue, Lewis W.; m. 2d, Anthony Edward Stockanes, Jan. 7, 1966. Student Carleton Coll., 1941-43; A.B., U. Wis., 1945. Sec., Bitker & Marshall, Milw., 1945-46, Hale & Dorr, Boston, 1946-47; underwriter Standard Annuity & Life Ins. Co., Champaign, Ill., 1964-67; sec. U. Ill., Champaign, 1967-75; rights mgr. U. Ill. Press, Champaign, 1975—. Village clk., Park Forest, Ill., 1950-54. Republican. Home: 2201 E Vermont Ave Urbana IL 61801 Office: U Ill Press 54 E Gregory Dr Champaign IL 61820

STOCKDALE, GAYLE SUE, wholesale florist, ornamental horticulturalist; b. Crawfordsville, Ind., July 3, 1955; d. Robert Lavern and Faye Louise (Ball) S. Student St. Joseph's Coll., 1973-74, Purdue U., 1974; BS in Tech. Horticulture, Eastern Ky. U., 1977. Reclamation foreman South East Coal Co., Irvine, Ky., 1977-79; asst. mgr., landscape designer Evergreen Garden Ctr., Lexington, Ky., 1979-80; asst. mgr., landscape designer, head grower South Trail Garden Ctr., Ft. Myers, Fla., 1980-82; floral designer Flowers by Jean, Cape Coral, Fla., 1982-83; floral designer, landscape designer Bev's Greenhouse, Owenton, Ky., 1983-84; co-owner Royalty Wholesale, Lexington, 1984-87, Imperial Fowers and Gifts, Lexington, 1988—. Contbr. poetry to anthologies. Sponsor, Save the Children, Korea, 1986. Moose lodge scholar, 1973. Mem. Nat. Assn. Female Execs. Democrat. Roman Catholic. Avocations: reading, movies, exercise. Office: Imperial Flowers and Gifts 393 Waller Ave Lexington KY 40504

STOCKHAUSEN, SHARRON RENEE, government official, educator; b. Rochester, Minn., Aug. 19, 1948; d. Henry James and Bernice Gertrude (Foltz) LeCocq; m. Harry Stockhausen, May 4, 1968; children: Stacy Ann, Eric David. Student, U. Minn., 1966, Cameron U., 1979, Anoka-Ramsey Coll., 1980-87; BA in Bus., Metro State U., 1988. Cert. contract mgr. Purchasing agt. U.S. Army, Ft. Sill, Okla., 1976-80; procurement asst. Def. Logistics Agy., Mpls., 1980-84, contract adminstr., mgr. equal employment, 1984—; tchr. Anoka (Minn.)-Hennepin Sch. Dist., 1980—. Editor: Comanche County Cookbook, 1978; newspaper columnist, 1979. Founder, pres. Homemaker's Plus Extension Group, Lawton, Okla., 1978; asst. coach men's softball Champlin/Dayton Athletic Assn., Anoka, 1988. Mem. Nat. Contract Mgmt. Assn. (hospitality chmn. 1986-88), Nat. Assn. for Female Execs. Republican. Presbyterian. Home: 14314 Thrush Dr NW Andover MN 55304 Office: Def Logistics Agy Honeywell Plaza MN12-6254 2701 4th Ave S Minneapolis MN 55408

STOCKS, MARY LEE, social worker; b. Marietta, Ohio, Sept. 3, 1949; d. Graham Lee and Virginia Eleanor (Donaldson) S. BA, Marietta Coll., 1971; MSW, Ohio State U., 1985. Lic. social worker, Ohio. Asst. supr. social worker Franklin County Welfare Dept., Columbus, Ohio, 1972-74; social worker Cen. Ohio Psychiat. Hosp., Columbus, 1974-76; aftercare liaison Columbus Area Community Mental Health Ctr., 1976-77, North Cen. Mental Health Ctr., Columbus, 1977-78; social worker Cen. Ohio Psychiat. Hosp., Columbus, 1981-86; program devel. specialist Office of Consumer Services, Ohio Dept. Mental Health, Columbus, 1986—; dir. Improv(e)-Ohio Mental Health Players, Columbus, 1986—; mem. program com. Ohio Welfare Conf., Columbus, 1986—; cons. We Care Network, Cin., 1986-87. Contbr. articles to profl. jours. Vol. Women's Outreach for Women, Columbus, 1984-86; mem. Ohio Com. on Women and Recovery, Ohio, 1986—; mem. All-Ohio Youth Choir Alumni Assn. Mem. Nat. Assn. Social Workers, Nat. Council on Alcoholism, Nat. Alliance for the Mentally Ill, Ohio State U. Schizophrenia Research, Mental Health Program Franklin County (trustee), Mental Health Assn. Ohio (chmn. stigma and mental illness task force, bd. dirs.), Franklin County Humane Soc., Alpha Delta Mu, Gamma Sigma Sigma. Democrat. Presbyterian. Lodges. Order of Job's Daughters, Order Eastern Star. Office: Ohio Dept Mental Health 30 East Broad St Suite 1115 Columbus OH 43215

STOCKTON, BRENDA EVELYN, data processing executive; b. Houston, Feb. 26, 1949; d. Linzell Wilson and Evelyn Roberta (Barculoo) Creel; m. James Harold Stockton, June 8, 1968; children: Matthew James, Martha Erin, Megan Lyn, Molly Kay. Student, U. Tex., 1967-72. Computer programmer Tex. Hwy. Dept., Austin, 1969-71, programmer, analyst, 1971-72; programmer, analyst State of Wyoming, Cheyenne, 1974-75; systems analyst, dir. fin. systems TRW Controls, Houston, 1975-76; data processing mgr. Marathon Gold Corp., Craig, Colo., 1981-83; systems designer Pegasus Data Systems, Craig, 1982-84, cons., tchr., 1983-84; systems analyst Tex. Dept. Mental Health/Mental Retardation, Austin, 1984-85; dir. data processing Williamson County (All County Agys.), Georgetown, Tex., 1985—; tech. cons. Craig Med. Clinic, 1982-85, Georgetown Weekly, 1985—; tech. advisor Tex. Dept. Pub. Safety, Georgetown, 1986—. Author: (weekly column) Austin American/Statesman Newspaper; contbr. articles to profl. jours. Instr. ARC, Austin, 1984-86; advisor Girl Scouts U.S.A., Georgetown, 1985. Mem. Am. Bus. Women Assn., Data Processing Mgmt. Assn., Nat. Assn. Female Execs., Tex. Assn. Govtl. Data Processing Mgrs. (bd. dirs. 1986—). Republican. Episcopalian. Club: 12 O'Clock (Georgetown) (welfare com). Home: 3202 Sierra Dr Georgetown TX 78628 Office: Williamson County Courthouse 8th & Main St Georgetown TX 78626

STOCKTON, KARLA MARLENE, tax accountant, analyst; b. Houston, Apr. 14, 1951; d. A. Joseph and Marian Louise (Crane) White. BBA, U. Houston, 1979. CPA, Tex. Sr. tax acct. Peat Marwick Mitchell and Co., Houston, 1979-82; tax analyst Mitchell Energy and Devel. Corp., The Woodlands, Tex., 1982—. Mem. Am. Inst. CPA's, Tex. Soc. CPA's, Houston Soc. CPA's, Beta Alpha Psi. Republican. Presbyterian. Office: Mitchell Enery and Devel Corp PO Box 4000 The Woodlands TX 77387-4000

STODDARD, LINDA GANDRUD, veterinarian; b. Owatonna, Minn., Apr. 28, 1944; d. Ebenhard S. and Edith M. (Christensen) G.; m. Hannis L. Stoddard, Jr., July 10, 1973; children—Ebenhard C., Ryan M., Dahlen Ross. B.S. in Edn., U. Minn., 1966, B.S. in Vet. Medicine, 1968, D.V.M., 1970. Veterinarian, Dueland Animal Clinic, S.I., N.Y., 1970-72; dir. advt. Gandy Co., Owatonna, 1972-74, corp. dir., 1962—; owner Branford Vet. Clinic, Inc., Fla., 1974-83, Shamrock Vet. Clinic and Fisheries, fish diseases and aquaculture mgmt., Cross City, Fla., 1984—; guest lectr. U. Fla. Coll. Vet. Medicine, 1978-82; tchr. physics Branford High Sch., 1984; vice chmn. Fla. Dept. Edn. State Instructional Materials Council-Sci Grades K-8, 1987-88; adv. com. Anderson Elem. Sch., 1986-88. Grant writer Branford Sch. Adv. Council, 1982-84. State of Fla. grantee, 1983. 84. Mem. AVMA, Suwannee Valley Vet. Med. Assn. (pres. 1980—), Am. Animal Hosp. Assn., Fla. Vet. Med. Assn. (4-H adv. com.), Am. Heartworm Soc., Alpha Delta Kappa. Avocations: reading; music; architecture.

STOEWE, JUDITH KAY, psychiatrist, health science association; b. Nebreska City, Nebr., July 25, 1940; d. Henry Casper and Fern Pearl (Everett) S. Cert. in Nursing, St. Catherines Coll., Omaha, 1961; BA, Barat Coll., 1970; MD, U. Nebr., 1974. RN; diplomate Am. Bd. Psychiatry and Neurology. Intern, then resident Georgetown U., Washington, 1974-77; fellow in child psychiatry Inst. for Juvenile Research, Chgo., 1978-80; exec. v.p. Assocs. in Adolescent Psychiatry, Skokie, Ill., 1980—; pres. med. staff Charter Barclay Hosp., Chgo., 1985-86. Mem. AAAS, AMA, Am. Psychiatric Assn., Ill. Council Child Psychiatry, Alpha Omega Alpha. Democrat. Roman Catholic. Office: Assocs in Adolescent Psychiatry 5360 W Fargo Skokie IL 60077

STOIA, JOAN MCRAE, academic administrator; b. Boston, Sept. 3, 1949; d. Thomas William and Rosalie (Sullivan) McRae; m. Stephen James Stoia, May 30, 1970; 1 child, Kindreth Joan. BA in English, U. Mass., 1971, MS in Labor Studies, 1981. Asst. dir. bachelor's degree program U. Mass., Amherst, 1974-82, dir. cooperative edn. program, 1982—; workshop leader Northeastern U. Ctr. for Cooperative Edn., Boston, 1986-87; vis. faculty mem. Northeastern U. Ctr. for Labor Mkt. Studies, 1987. Bd. dirs. New England Puppetry Series, Inc., Amherst, 1979—. Grantee U.S. Dept. Edn., 1984, 86. Mem. Am. Soc. Tng. and Devel. (Pioneer Valley chpt.), Western Mass. Econ. Devel. Conf., Univ. Women's Profl. Network, Pioneer Valley PC Users' Group. Democrat. Roman Catholic. Home: 45 Ward St Amherst MA 01002 Office: U Mass Coop Edn Career Ctr Amherst MA 01003

STOICA, SUSANA, computer engineer, consultant; b. Tirgu Muresh, Romania, Apr. 26, 1946; came to U.S., 1985; d. Andrei and Clara (Heisikovitsch) Gerson; m. Vladimir Stoica, Sept. 5, 1970; 1 child, Andrei. MS, Polytech. Inst., Bucharest, Romania, 1969, postgrad., 1972-74. Reg. profl. engr., Ont., Can. Jr. research engr. Inst. Computer Research, Bucharest, 1969-72, sr. research engr., 1972-77; engr. Ramzorei Siemens Industry Ltd., Tel Aviv, 1977-78; elec. engr. Control Data Can. Ltd., Toronto, 1979-85; elec. engr. Control Data Corp., Mpls., 1985-86, cons., 1986-87, mgr. support, 1987—. Contbr. articles to profl. jours.; inventor. Mem. IEEE, Assn. Profl. Engrs. Ont.

STOKELY, EDITH MARGARET DAWLEY, medical technologist; b. Manhattan, Kans., Jan. 23, 1922; d. Earle Reed and Marion Erenay (Price) Dawley; m. Raymond Elmer Stokely, Dec. 6, 1942; children: Janet Mary Stokely Roe, Donna Rae Stokely Steward. BS, Kansas State U., 1943. Research technologist Kansas State U., Manhattan, 1942-44; med. technologist Kecoughton (Va.) Sta. Hosp., 1944-45, Cleve. Clinic Blood Bank, 1945-47, Dr. H.G. Miskjian, Cleve., 1947-49, No. Ill. Blood Bank, Rockford, 1969-72, Dr. H.E. Zenisek, Dr. T.R. Glatter, Rockford, 1972-78, Pierce Chem. Co., Rockford, 1978-79, U. Ill. Coll. Medicine, Rockford, 1979—. Mem. Phi Kappa Phi, Omicron Nu, Dynamis, Alpha Xi Delta Alumnae (pres. 1964-66). Methodist. Club: Rockford Amateur Astronomers (sec. 1974-76, 86-88). Home: 5427 Brookview Rd Rockford IL 61107-1659 Office: U Ill Coll Medicine 1601 Parkview Ave Rockford IL 61107

STOKES, BRENDA LINETTE, computer specialist; b. Bklyn.; d. Stanley and Corinne D. (Skeete) Moore; m. Vincent T. Stokes; 1 child, Nathaniel V. BA in Computer Sci., Hunter Coll., 1984. Coll. aide N.Y.C. Employees' Retirement System, 1981-84, asst. retirement benefits examiner, 1984-86, computer assoc. tech. support, 1986-88, computer assoc.-software, 1988—. Asst. dir. Crusaders Choir, Bklyn., 1983—; musical dir. Miller Meml. Ch. of Nazarene, Bklyn. Hunter Coll. scholar, 1979. Mem. Nat. Assn. Female Execs. Home: 353 Hawthorne St Brooklyn NY 11225

STOKES, EARLINE WILLIS, purchasing manager; b. Fountain Inn, S.C., Aug. 5, 1937; d. James Earle and Mary Lee (Williams) Willis; m. Don O. Stokes, Apr. 20, 1956; children: Greg A., Eric D. AS in Purchasing and Material Mgmt., Greenville Tech. Coll., 1982. Purchasing clk. CRYOVAC div. W. R. Grace, Simpsonville, S.C., 1955-68, buyer, 1968-72, purchasing agt., 1972-76, purchasing mgr., 1976—; mem. Chem. Week Adv. Panel, N.Y.C., 1982-84, 88—. Bd. dirs. Leslie C. Meyer Ctr., Greenville, S.C., 1978-80. Mem. Nat. Assn. Purchasing Mgmt. (cert. purchasing mgr. 1983), Purchasing Mgmt. Assn. Carolinas Va. (bd. dirs. upper S.C. chpt. 1976-82, 85-88). Republican. Baptist. Home: 1226 E Georgia Rd Simpsonville SC 29681 Office: CRYOVAC div WR Grace & Co N Maple St Simpsonville SC 29681

STOKES, SHEILA WOODS, personnel administrator; b. Toledo, Ohio, Aug. 6, 1949; d. Willie and Essie (James) Woods; m. George Farrar Stokes, Nov. 30, 1974; 1 child, Ericka Kaye. BE, U. Toledo, 1971; MA Pub. Adminstrn., Ohio State U., 1979; student, Bryn Mawr Coll., 1986. Tchr. Toledo (Ohio) Pub. Schs., 1971-75; ednl. program coordinator Concern, Inc., Elizabeth, N.J., 1975-76; job placement supr. City of Elizabeth, C.E.T.A., N.J., 1976-78; program assoc. Nat. Ctr. for Research in Vocat. Edn., Columbus, Ohio, 1979-80; tng. 0fficer State of Ariz., Phoenix, 1980-84; tng. 0fficer Ariz. State U., Tempe, 1984—, mgmt. intern, 1986-87; vice chairperson State of Ariz. Mgmt. Devel. Program Bd., 1985—; pres. U. Career Women, Ariz. State U., 1986-87. Bd. dirs. Sexual Assault Recovery Inst., Phoenix, 1987—, Phoenix Black Women's Task Force, 1984-86; civilian mem. Phoenix Police Dept., Use of Force and Police Disciplinary Review Bd., 1985—. Black Board of Dirs. honoree 1985; named Outstanding Young Woman Am. 1983. Mem. Am. Soc. for Tng. and Devel., Tri-Univ. Tng. Consortium, Ariz. Roundtable of Trainers, NAACP, Delta Sigma Theta. Democrat. Baptist. Office: Ariz State U Agrl Bld Personne Tng Office Room 172C Tempe AZ 85287

STOKES, THERESA EMMA (TERI), computer company executive; b. Boston, Apr. 9, 1943; d. Saverio L. and Mary Grace (Van Stratum) Santoro; m. Ivan L. Stokes, June 12, 1965 (div. 1977); children: Theresa-Ann, Eric M.; m. Peter R. Yensen, Apr. 30, 1982. BA in Biology, Boston U., 1965; cert. in chemistry and math, Wellesley (Mass.) Coll., 1970; MS in Applied Mgmt., Lesley Coll., 1987. Lic. med. technologist, (ASCP), Mass. Sales supr. Shaklee Products, Concord, Mass., 1972-76; lab. supr. Somerville Hosp. Bioran Med. Labs, Cambridge, Mass., 1976-77, dir. processing and communications, 1977-79; mgr. mktg. communications Digital Equipment Corp., Marlboro, Mass., 1979-81, specialist indsl. research and devel. bus. ops., 1981-83, mgr. internat. pharm. market, 1983-86, bus. mgr. life sci. and research Kodak corp. account team, 1986—. Contbr. articles to profl. jours.; speaker in field. Advisor Jr. Achievement, Marlboro, 1983-85. Mem. DAR, Drug Info. Assn., Assn. Official Analytical Chemists, N.Y. Acad. Scis., Tridelta. Office: Digital Equipment Corp 1250 Pittsford-Victor Rd PO Box 23227 Rochester NY 14692

STOLLER, ALYCE, training and development specialist; b. Far Rockaway, N.Y., Mar. 31, 1955; d. Sam and Shirley (Sherman) Zimmerman; m. Gerald Stoller, June 14, 1984. BA, Coll. S.I. magna cum laude, N.Y., 1977; MS, Herbert H. Lehman Coll. magna cum laude, Bronx, N.Y., 1982; postgrad., Adelphi U. Mgmt. trainee U.S. Postal Service, Jamaica, N.Y., 1982-84, sr. tng., devel. specialist, 1984—; owner, mgr. Applied Action Career Cons., Long Beach, N.Y., 1985—; mem. exec. bd. Intergovernmental Tng. Council of N.Y.-N.J., 1985—. Vol. cons. Bezalel Health Related Facility, Far Rockaway, 1981-85. Mem. Am. Soc. Tng. and Devel., Nat. Assn. Postal Suprs., Nassau County Police Wives Assn. Office: Applied Action 253 W Hudson St Long Beach NY 11561

STOLLER, IRENE DAVIS, librarian; b. Edinburgh, Scotland; d. Ellis and Alice (Davis) Stoller; m. Irving Gitomer, Dec. 23, 1944 (div. 1975); children—David, Jonathan, Philip, Ellen, Daniel. B.A., Rutgers Univ., 1961; M.S. in L.S., Drexel U., 1962. Adminstrv. asst. to dean Drexel Grad. Sch. Library Sci., Phila., 1960, dir. pub. relations, 1961, instr., 1965; dir. Cherry Hill (N.J.) Free Pub Library, 1962-70; library cons., 1970-71; dir. Old Bridge (N.J.) Free Pub. Library, 1971-75; head Central Library, Contra Costa County Library, 1976-79; head Extension Services, Phoenix Pub. Library, 1980; asst. dir. Madison (Wis.) Pub. Library, 1980-84; dir. Paramus (N.J.) Pub. Library, 1984—; instr. Drexel U., Phila. Community Coll., 1968-69, Glassboro State Coll., 1969. Author: The Trustee and Personnel, 1970, rev., 1983. Mem., Burlington County Human Relations Commn.; bd. dirs. Drexel U. Alumni, 1974-76. Mem. ALA, Am. Trustee Assn., N.J. Trustee Assn., SLA, Library Pub. Relations Council, Catholic Library Assn., Jewish Library Assn., N.J. Library Assn. (mem. at large exec. bd. 1972-75, 2d v.p., sec. 1987-88), Camden County Library Assn. (pres. 1968-69), ACLU (exec. bd. So. Jersey), League Women Voters, Women's Polit. Caucus, Beta Phi Mu, Phi Kappa Phi, Club: Zonta (chmn. service project 1965). Address: 76 Hadley Ave Clifton NJ 07015

STOLTZ, MARY CAROLE, savings and loan executive, accountant; b. Kansas City, Mo., Sept. 16, 1952; d. Charles Gregory and Rosemary Elizabeth (Strauss) S. BS in Home Econs., Kans. State U., 1974; BBA in Acctg., Wichita (Kans.) State U., 1978. CPA, Tex. Acct. Litwin Corp., Wichita, 1977-78; supr. Coopers & Lybrand, Dallas, 1978-82; mgr. Fox & Co., Dallas, 1982-85; dir. acquisitions Ind. Am. Savs., Dallas, 1985, sr. fin. officer, treas., 1986-87; chief fin. officer State Fed. Savs. and Loan, Tulsa, 1987—; speaker seminars Small Bus. Adminstrn. Conf., Dallas, Houston and St. Paul, 1985. Mem. Am. Inst. CPA's, Tex. Soc. CPA's, Real Estate Fin. Execs. Assn., Fin. Mgrs. Soc., Inc., Tulsa C. of C. Roman Catholic. Office: State Fed Savs and Loan 502 S Main Mall Tulsa OK 74103

STOLZ, ANDREA LYNN, health facility administrator; b. Butler, Pa., Mar. 11, 1954; d. Edward C. and Carole A. (Wickenhagen) S. BS in Med. Tech., Edinboro (Pa.) State U., 1976; M in Health Adminstrn., Ga. State U., 1982. Med. technologist Cleve. Found., 1976-79, Grady Meml. Hosp., Atlanta, 1979; supr. lab. Ga. Bapt. Med. Ctr., Atlanta, 1979-81; dir. corp. devel. Cen. Med. Ctr. and Hosp., Pitts., 1982-83, v.p. corp. devel., 1983-85; dir. health facilities devel. Charter Med. Corp., Macon, Ga., 1985—. Mem. adv. bd. Alive mag., 1984-85. Mem. Am. Soc. Clin. Pathologists (cert.). Home: 1620 Rembert Ave Macon GA 31201 Office: Charter Med Corp 577 Mulberry St Macon GA 31298

STOLZENBERG, PEARL, fashion designer; b. N.Y.C., Oct. 9, 1946; d. Irving and Anna (Shenkman) S. Student, Fashion Inst. Tech., 1964-66. Textile stylist, designer Forum Fabrics Ltd., N.Y.C., 1966-68; dir. styling Beauknit Corp., N.Y.C., 1969-74; stylist, designer Mi-Bru-San Co., Inc., N.Y.C., 1983-84; gen. mgr. Laissez-Faire Inc., N.Y.C., 1984-85; merchandiser prodn. The Clothing Acad. Inc., N.Y.C., 1986-87; v.p. String of Pearls Knitwear, Inc., N.Y.C., 1988—; cons. Tam O'Shanter Textile Ltd., Montreal, Quebec, 1974-79, Mitsui, Osaka, Japan, 1976-79, Sergio Valente English Town Sportswear, N.Y.C., 1980-84. Democrat. Jewish. Home: 8340 Austin St Apt. 5Y Kew Gardens NY 11415 Office: String of Pearls Knitwear Inc Jelo Fabrics 1350 Broadway New York NY 10018

STONE, CAROLINE FLEMING, artist; b. N.Y.C., Mar. 26, 1936; d. Ralph Emerson and Elizabeth (Fleming) S.; m. Oakleigh B. Thorne, June 1956 (div. 1969); children: Oakleigh, Henry. Student, Art Students' League, 1954-57, 1973-74, Pratt Graphics, 1973-74. one-woman shows include Saginaw (Mich.) Art Mus., 1978, Jesse Besser Mus., Mich, 1979, Washington Art Assn., Conn., Ella Sharp Mus., Mich., 1980, San Diego Pub. Library, Diablo Valley Coll., Calif., 1981, Trustman Gallery Simmons Coll., Boston, 1985; two-man shows include Miriam Perlman, Chgo., 1980, U. Mich., 1981, Mary Ryan, N.Y.C., 1985, Katonah Gallery, N.Y., 1986; juried shows include Silvermine Nat. Printmaking, Conn., 1978, Print Club, Phila., 1981, Trenton State (nat. print exhibn. purchase award), 1982, Minot State Coll., N.D., 1985, Boston Printmakers (jurors commendation award), 1986; group shows include Mus. N.Mex., 1984, Wilhelm Gallery, Houston, 1985, DeCordova and Dana Mus., Nat. Acad. Art, Boston Pub. Library, Mus. Contemporary Hispanic Art, N.Y.C., 1987; invitational shows include Abington Ctr., Pa., Printmaking Workshop, N.Y., 1982; represented in permanent collections Art Inst. Chgo., Mid-West Mus. Am. Art, Ind., Mus. N.Mex., Nat. Mus. Am. Art, Saginaw Mus., Boston Pub. Library, U. Chgo., U. Mich., Exxon Corp. Chase Manhattan Bank, IBM, Mellon Bank; executed murals Revlon Inc. Mem. N.Y. Arts Group, The Kitchen (bd. dirs.). Episcopalian. Home and Office: C Stone Press 80 Wooster St New York NY 10012

STONE, ELAINE MURRAY, author, television producer; b. N.Y.C., Jan. 22, 1922; d. H. and Catherine (Fairbanks) Murray-Jacoby; m. F. Courtney Stone, May 30, 1944; children: Catherine Margaret, Pamela Elizabeth, Victoria Francis. Student, Juilliard Sch. Music, 1939-41; diploma, N.Y. Coll. Music, 1942; licentiate in organ, Trinity Coll. Music, London, 1947; student, U. Miami, 1952, Fla. Inst. Tech., 1963; PhD (hon.), World U., 1985. Organist, choir dir. St. Ingatius Episc. Ch., 1940-44; accompanist Strawbridge Ballet on Tour, N.Y.C., 1944; organist All Saints Episc. Ch., Ft. Lauderdale, 1951-54, St. John's Episc. Ch., Melbourne, Fla., 1956-59, First Christian Ch., Melbourne, 1962-63, United Ch. Christ, Melbourne, 1963-65, piano studio, Melbourne, 1955-70; editor-in-chief Cass Inc., 1970-71; dir. continuity radio Sta. WTAI, AM-FM, Melbourne, 1971-74; mem. sales staff Engle Realty Inc., Indialantic, Fla., 1975-78; v.p. pub. relations Consol. Cybertronics Inc., Cocoa Beach, Fla., 1969-70; writer, producer Countdown News, Sta. KXTX-TV, Dallas, 1978-80; assoc. producer Focus News, Dallas, 1980; host, producer TV show, Focus on History, 1982—, Episc. Digest, 1984—; judge Writer's Contest sponsored Brevard Community Coll. 1987; chmn. Judge;s Fla. Space Coast Writer's Conf. 1987 (v.p. 1985—). Author: The Taming of the Tongue, 1954, Love One Another, 1957, Menéndez de Avilé s, 1968, Bedtime Bible Stories, Travel Fun, Sleepytime Tales, Improve Your Spelling for Better Grades, Improve Your Business Spelling, Tranquility Tapes, 1970, The Melbourne Bi-Centennial Book, 1976, Uganda: Fire and Blood, 1977, Tekla and the Lion, 1981, Illustrated History of Brevard County, 1988; contbr. articles to nat. mags., newspapers including N.Y. Herald Tribune, Living Church, Christian Life; space corr. Religious News Service, Kennedy Space Ctr., 1962-78. Mem. exec. bd. Women's Assn., Brevard Symphony, 1967—; mem. heritage com. Melbourne Bicentennial Commn.; mem. Evangelism Commn. Episc. Diocese Cen. Fla., 1985-87; v.p. Episcopal Churchwomen Holy Trinity Episcopal Ch., Melbourne, 1988—; bd. dirs. Fla. Space Coast Council Internat. Visitors. Recipient 1st place for piano Ashley Hall, 1935-39, S.C. St. Music Contest, 1939, 1st place for piano composition Colonial Suite, Constitution Hall, Washington 1987; numerous other awards. Mem. Nat. League Am. Penwomen (first place awards Tex. 1979, v.p. Dallas br. 1978-80, pres. Cape Canaveral Br. 1988—, organizing pres. Cape Canaveral Br. 1969, pres. 1988-89), Women Communications, DAR (Fla. St. chmn. music 1962-63), Nat. Soc. DAR (organizing regent Rufus/Fairbanks chpt. 1981-85, vice regent 1987—), Children Am. Revolution (past N.Y. St. chaplain), ACSAP, Am. Guild Organists) organizing warden Ft. Lauderdale), Space Pioneers, Fla. Press Women's Assn. Episc., Melbourne br. Am. Assn. U. Women. Home: 1945 Pineapple Ave Melbourne FL 32935

STONE, ELIZABETH WENGER, emeritus dean; b. Dayton, Ohio, June 21, 1918; d. Ezra and Anna Bess (Markey) Wenger; m. Thomas A. Stone, Sept. 14, 1939 (dec. Feb. 1987); children: John Howard, Anne Elizabeth, James Alexander. A.B., Stanford U., 1937, M.A., 1938; M.L.S., Catholic U. Am., 1961; Ph.D., Am. U., 1968. Tchr. pub. schs. Fontana, Calif., 1938-39; asst. state statistician State of Conn., 1939-40; librarian New Haven Pub. Libraries, 1940-42; dir. pub. relations, asst. to pres. U. Dubuque, Iowa, 1942-46; substitute librarian Pasadena (Calif. Pub. Library System), 1953-60; instr. Cath. U. Am., 1962-63, asst. prof., asst. to chmn. dept. library sci., 1963-67, assoc. prof., asst. to chmn., 1967-71, prof., asst. to chmn., 1971-72, prof., chmn. dept., 1972-80, dean Sch. Library and Info. Scis., 1981-83, prof. and dean emeritus, 1983—; founder, exec. dir. Continuing Library Edn. Network and Exchange, 1975-79; founder Nat. Rehab. Info. Ctr., 1977, project mgr., 1977-83; co-chmn. 1st World Conf. on Continuing Edn. for the Library and Info. Sci. Professions, 1984-85. Author: Factors Related to the Professional Development of Librarians, 1969, (with James J. Kortendick) Job Dimensions and Educational Needs in Librarianship, 1971, (with R. Patrick and B. Conroy) Continuing Library and Information Science Education, 1974, Continuing Library Education as Viewed in Relation to Other Continuing Professional Movements, 1975, (with F. Peterson and M. Chobot) Motivation: A Vital Force in the Organization, 1977, American Library Development 1600-1899, 1977, (with others) Model Continuing Education Recognition System in Library and Information Science, 1979, (with M.J. Young) A Program for Quality in Continuing Education for Information, Library and Media Personnel, 1980, (with others) Continuing Education for the Library Information Professions, 1985; editor: D.C. Libraries, 1964-66; contbr. articles to profl. jours. Program mgr. Nat. Rehab. Info. Center, 1977-83; mem. Pres.'s Com. on Employment of Handicapped, 1972-88; pres. D.C. chpt. Am. Mothers, Inc., 1984-86. Recipient Pres.' medal for disting. service Cath. U. Am., 1982. Mem. ALA (council 1976-83, v.p. 1980-81, pres. 1981-82, chmn. Nat. Library Week 1983-85, Lippincott award 1986, hon. life mem.), D.C. Library Assn. (pres. 1966-67), Spl. Libraries Assn. (pres. D.C. chpt. 1973-74), Assn. Am. Library Schs. (pres. 1974), Am. Soc. Info. Sci., Cath. Library Assn. (hon. life 1986), Am. Soc. Assn. Execs., Am. Assn. Adult and Continuing Edn., Internat. Fedn. Library Assns. and Instns. (chmn. Continuing Profl. Edn. Round Table 1985—), Phi Sigma Alpha, Beta Phi Mu, Phi Lambda Theta. Presbyterian. Club: Washington. Home: 4000 Cathedral Ave NW 15B Washington DC 20016 Office: Catholic U Am Washington DC 20064

STONE, GAIL HETZEL, sales and marketing executive; b. Middletown, Conn., Aug. 28, 1950; d. Raymond Francis and June Lavinia (Carlson) Hetzel; m. Stephen Thomas Nyerick (div. Jan. 1977); m. Christopher Odlin Stone, May 14, 1988. BE, U. Conn., 1972. Advt., sales promotion asst. Ames Dept. Stores, Inc., Hartford, Conn., 1973-74; customer service rep. Eli Lilly & Co. Elizabeth Arden Div., Enfield, Conn., 1974-79; announcer Sta. WMLB-FM, West Hartford, Conn., 1978; coordinating producer PM Mag., Hartford, 1979-80, exec. producer, 1981-83; dir. sales mktg. Monitor Prodns., Inc., N.Y.C., 1984-87; program marketing mgr. Conn. Pub. Broadcasting, Hartford, 1988—; pres. GMH Enterprises, Portland, Conn., 1983-88; Forum guest seminar leader for Werner Erhard & Assocs., New Haven, 1985-86; pub. relations com. The Holiday Project, Hartford, 1982-83; asst. at Youth at Risk/The Breakthrough Found., Bridgeport, Conn., 1986. Friend of Goodspeed Opera House, Hartford Stage Company. Mem. Wadsworth Atheneum. Roman Catholic. Club: Greater Hartford Ad. Office: Conn Pub Broadcasting 240 New Britain Ave Hartford CT 06106

STONE, KATHRYN DOLORES, credit union executive; b. Pontiac, Mich., June 12, 1929; d. Durward South and Betty Marie (LaVelle) Young; student public schs.; m. James Macklin Stone, Oct. 19, 1946; children: James Durward, David Allan. With T&C Fed. Credit Union, Pontiac, 1955—, asst. gen. mgr., teller mgr., acctg. mgr., 1972-77, chief fin. officer, 1977—, treas. bd. dirs., exec. gen. mgr., 1977-83, pres., chief exec. officer, 1977—, exec. com. Credit Union Data Acctg. Council, 1972-74, 77—; mem. exec. com. Oakland County (Mich.), chpt. Credit Unions, 1980—; exec. bd. Credit Union Met. Area Advt. Council, Detroit, chmn., 1983—; v.p. Joint Advt. Bd., Flint, Mich., 1983, dir., 1984-87. Chmn. community div. Pontiac United Way, 1972; fin./treas. 125th anniversary celebration City of Pontiac, also chmn. fundraising and promotion. Recipient various service awards, certs. appreciation. Mem. Credit Union Execs. Soc., Jayno Heights Women's Assn., Epsilon Sigma Alpha (chpt. pres. 1966, 76-77, pres. Mich. council 1968-69). Episcopalian. Author manuals, policy books in field. Office: 2525 N Telegraph Rd Suite 200 Bloomfield Hills MI 48013

STONE, MARGUERITE BEVERLEY, former university dean; b. Norfolk, Va., June 10, 1916; d. James L. and Clara (Thompson) S. B.A. in Chemistry, Randolph-Macon Woman's Coll., 1936; M.A. in Student Personnel Adminstrn, Columbia U., 1940, profl. diploma, 1956; L.H.D. (hon.), Purdue U., 1986. Tchr. Norfolk High Sch., 1936-41; instr. Tusculum Coll., 1941-43; asst. dean women U. Ark., 1946-50, assoc. dean women, 1952-54, dean women, 1954-55; asst. dean women Purdue U., 1956-67, assoc. dean women, 1967-68, dean women, 1968-74, dean students, 1974-80, ret., 1980. Author (with Barbara Cook); monograph Counseling Women, 1973. Trustee Katherine S. Phillips Trust Fund, 1978-83; mem. lay bd. St. Elizabeth's Hosp., 1974-80, Salvation Army, Lafayette Art Mus., 1982-85, Crisis Center.; mem. Tippecanoe County Bd. Zoning Appeals, 1982-83, West Lafayette City Council, 1984-88; mem. adminstrv. bd., found. bd. 1st United Meth. Ch., West Lafayette; mem. community adv. com. Purdue U. Sch. Nursing. Served with USNR, 1943-46, 52-55. Recipient Outstanding Woman in Edn. award Coalition of Women's Orgns. in Greater Lafayette Area, 1978, Disting. Alumni award Purdue U., 1980, Disting. Woman award Purdue U., 1980; named Sagemore of the Wabash Gov. Ind., 1980, 85. Mem. AAUW (past pres. Fayetteville, Ark.), Nat. Assn. Women Deans and Counselors (treas., chmn. hdqrs. adv. com. 1973-75, mem. hdqrs. adv. com. 1975-79), Ind. Assn. Women Deans and Counselors, Purdue Women's Caucus, Mental Health Assn., Phi Beta Kappa, Kappa Delta Pi, Omicron Delta Kappa, Pi Lambda Theta, Zeta Tau Alpha, Mortar Bd., Alpha Lambda Delta (v.p. 1975-79). Clubs: Purdue Women's, Parlor. Home: 1807 Western Dr West Lafayette IN 47906

STONE, MARY ALICE, house products company sales organizer; b. Savannah, Ga., Oct. 27, 1940; d. Melvin Theodore and Alice May (Shaw) Pearson; m. Thomas Lanier Stone, Aug. 14, 1960; children: Mary Elizabeth (dec.), Thomas Lanier, Jr., Michael A., Vicki Lynn. Bookkeeper, Radix Microelectronics, Tustin, Calif., 1967-69; owner Smart Set Bookkeeping-Employment Agy., Santa Ana, Calif., 1969-72; cons. Princess House Products, Havelock, N.C., 1973-74, unit organizer, 1974-77, area organizer, New Bern, N.C. and Ga., 1977-82, sr. area organizer, Marietta, Ga., 1982—. Philanthropic chmn. Cystic Fibrosis Found., Tustin, Calif., 1971-72; vol. Craven Cherry Point Child Devel. Ctr., Havelock, 1972, Spl. Olympics, Marietta, 1983-84; choir dir. Christ Episc. Ch., Havelock, 1973; cookie chmn. Craven Country Council Girl Scouts U.S.; active Mother's March of Dimes. Recipient #1 Area award Princess House Field, 1980, #1 Cen. Unit award, 1985, #1 Sr. Area award, 1987, #1 Sr. Area award, 1988; named to Nat. Area Honor Roll Princess House Inc., 1986, 87, named to President's Honor Roll, 1987. Mem. Nat. Female Execs. Assn., Am. Soc. Profl. Exec. Women, Beta Sigma Phi (Woman of Yr. Havelock chpt. 1973), Beta Sigma Phi Internat. (life, order of Rose Degree 1979). Avocations: Swimming; reading; dancing. Office: Princess House Products PO Box 965065 Marietta GA 30066

STONE, PAULA LENORE, lawyer; b. N.Y.C., Nov. 1, 1942; d. Milton H. and Pauline (Smith) Stone; m. Richard J. Chodoff, July 29, 1969 (dec. 1983). AB in Biology, Muhlenberg Coll., 1961; student Lehigh U., 1960, Jefferson Med. Sch., 1961-63; JD, Temple U., 1981. Bar: Pa. 1982. Med. cons. to trial lawyers, Bala Cynwyd, Pa., 1963-85, N.Y., 1985—; sole practice, Bala Cynwyd, 1982-85, N.Y., 1985—; of counsel firm Turrey Kepler, Norristown, Pa., 1985—. Editor Psychopharmacology Abstracts, Cancer Chemotherapy Abstracts, 1961-64; author: (with R. J. Chodoff) Doctor for the Prosecution, 1983. Mem. Assn. Trial Lawyers Am., Coll. Physicians, Phila., ABA, N.Y. Acad. Scis. (adv. com.), Pa. Bar Assn., ACLU. Democrat. Jewish. Address: Suite 8B 870 United Nations Plaza New York NY 10017

STONE, VIVIAN RENE, staff and facilities manager; b. Indpls., Dec. 21, 1957; d. Rhodell and Helena H. (Steidle) S. GED, George Washington, San Francisco, 1976. Cert. CPR, first aid instr. Asst. mgr. Hilton Hotel, San Francisco, 1978-83; dir. front office Meridien Hotel, San Francisco, 1983-84; ops. mgr. Sterns & Grell, San Francisco, 1985-86; exec. staff, bldg. mgr. State Bar of Calif., San Francisco, 1986—. Mem. Assn. Legal Adminstrs., Assn. Law Office Services, Nat. Assn. Female Execs. Democrat. Roman Catholic. Club: Commonwealth of Calif. (San Francisco). Home: 2638 Clement St #1 San Francisco CA 94121 Office: State Bar Calif 555 Franklin St San Francisco CA 94102

STONEKING, CAROLE LYNNE, association executive; b. Detroit, Mar. 28, 1937; d. Robert Frank and Esther Freda (Meier) S. BS, Wayne State U., 1963, MA, 1972. Program dir. Oakland br. YWCA, Clawson, Mich., 1961-63; program dir. no. br. YWCA, Highland Park, Mich., 1964-67; ctr. dir. Macomb br. YWCA, Warren, Mich., 1968-74; exec. dir. YWCA, East Detroit, 1974-79, Jacksonville, Fla., 1979-85; exec. dir. YWCA of the Midlands, Columbia, S.C., 1985-88; pres. Designs to Accommodate Madame Execs. (DAME), Columbia, S.C., 1988—. Chmn. legis. com., mem. steering com. United Way of Midlands, 1986-87; pres. Coalition to Take Back the Night, Columbia, 1987; adv. com. mem. Respite Care Council on Aging, Columbia, 1987—. Recipient Cert. Appreciation Am. Patriotic Commn., Jacksonville, Fla., 1982. Mem. Nat. Assn. YWCA Execs., Mich. Recreation and Park Assn. (registered profl.), Network of Female Execs., Fla. Council for Profl. Fundraisers (bd. dirs. 1983-85), Greater Columbia C. of C. (bd. dirs. 1987—, chair wellness com. 1987, sec. 1988), Greater Columbia chpt. NOW ((v.p. 1987, pres. 1988), Independent Bus. Women (Columbia chpt. treas. 1988), Columbia Network for Female Execs. (com. mem. 1986-87), Cities in Schs. (Columbia) (bd. trustees, 1988). Office: Designs to Accommodate Madame Execs (DAME) 1005 Jackson Ave Columbia SC 29203

STONER, FRANCES WYNETTE, city official, city secretary; b. Lake City, Fla., Oct. 2, 1943; d. Monroe Mattox Neveils and Freda Bryan (Mobley) Neveils Hollingsworth; m. Jerry Kay Stoner, Dec. 16, 1962; 1 child, Wynette Renae. Diploma Massey Bus. Coll., Jacksonville, Fla., 1962; student Alvin Community Coll., Tex., 1980-81. Legal sec. Crofton Holland & Starling, Titusville, Fla., 1962-63, Davis & Katz, Lebanon, Pa., 1963; dep. city clk. City of Titusville, 1964-68, sec., 1968-72; city clk. City of Alvin, Tex., 1974—. Recipient Cert. of Excellence award U.S. Dept. Labor, Washington, 1980. Mem. Assn. City Clks. and Secs., of Tex. (Salt Grass chpt. sec., treas., 1975, pres. 1978), Internat. Inst. Mcpl. Clks., Nat. Purchasing Inst., Alvin C. of C. Club: Soroptimist Internat. of Alvin (sec. 1984-85, v.p. 1985-86). Home: 113 S Jane St Alvin TX 77511 Office: City of Alvin 216 W Sealy St Alvin TX 77511

STONER, SUE, travel consultant; b. Seminole, Okla., June 8, 1942; d. E.D. and Atha Miriah (Brown) Burkhart; m. George M. Stoner, Jr., Sept. 5, 1964; children—Shelby Lynn, Steven Laird. B.A., Howard Payne Coll., 1964. Pres., Travel World, Inc., Gig Harbor, Wash., 1965—; sec.-treas. Travel Stamps, Inc., Gig Harbor, 1978—; pres. In Shape Inc., Gig Harbor, 1988—. Mem. distributive edn. com. Peninsula Sch. Dist., Gig Harbor. Mem. AAUW, Am. Soc. Travel Agts. (com. chmn.), Inst. Cert. Travel Agts. (cert. travel cons., nat. rep.), Assn. Retail Travel Agts. (com. chmn.), Dist. Assn. Gig Harbor Lady Mchts. (v.p.), Gig Harbor C. of C. (tourism com.). Republican. Baptist. Clubs: Dover AFB Officers' Wives (v.p.) (Gig Harbor), Toastmasters (pres. Gig Harbor chpt. 1987) Altrusa (bd. dirs.). Avocations: reading, travel, painting. Home: 15018 Sherman Dr NW Gig Harbor WA 98335 Office: PO Box 427 3116 Judson St Gig Harbor WA 98335

STOOP, NORMA MCLAIN, editor, author, photographer; b. Panama, C.Z., July 20, 1910; b. Harry Edward and Gladys (Brandon) McLain; student Penn Hall Jr. Coll., Carnegie Inst. Tech., New Sch., N.Y. U.; m. William J. Stoop, Jr., Sept. 20, 1932. Contbg. editor Dance Mag., N.Y.C., 1969-71, assoc. editor, 1971-79, sr. editor, 1979—; sr. editor After Dark, 1978-82, also feature writer; also photographer, theater, ballet and film critic; entertainment editor sr. edit. WNYC-AM, 1980-83; chief film critic Manhattan Arts, 1983—, mem. editors panel Antioch U. summer writers workshop, 1988 ; mem. nat. adv. bd. TV Arts Studio, Inc. Mem. Poetry Soc. Am., Acad. Am. Poets, Dance Masters Am., Dance Critics Assn., TV Acad. Arts and Scis., Sigma Delta Chi. Clubs: Overseas Press, Deadline. Contbr. poems to Tex. Quar., Chgo. Rev., N.Y. Times, Arts in Society, Quest, Atlantic Monthly, Christian Sci. Monitor, others, 1958—, essays to Book Week in N.Y. Herald Tribune; represented in Best Poems of 1973, Exhibit of Dance Photography, Harvard U., Tufts Coll., 1975; MacNeil Lehrer News, 1988. Recipient award Dance Tchrs. Club Boston, 1977. Office: 33 W 60th St New York NY 10023

STOPKEY, LINDA JOHANNA, electronics company official; b. Chgo., Mar. 3, 1960; d. Waldemar Dmitro and Lorraine (Bielenberg) S. B.S. in Mgmt. summa cum laude, Tulane U., 1981; M.B.A., U. Tex., 1984. Cost engr. IBM, Austin, 1981-84, cost engring. mgr., 1984-86, pricer, 1986-87, fin. planner, 1987—. Mem. Am. Soc. Women Accts., Am. Mgmt. Assn., Nat. Assn. Female Execs., Jaycees, Beta Alpha Psi, Phi Chi Theta. Office: IBM Dept 631 14F09 44 S Broadway White Plains NY 10601

STORAASLI, MARIE ELIZABETH, medical technologist, educator; b. Milw., June 26, 1945; d. Tollef Bardolf and Ruth Elizabeth (Storvick) S.; B.S. in Med. Tech., Northwestern U., 1967; M.S. in Clin. Sci., San Francisco State U., 1978; m. Jörn Olaf Thomas von Ramm, July 12, 1981; children—Olaf, Karl. Chemist, Rikshospital Sentrallaboratoriet, Oslo, 1967-68; med. technologist Clinic Internal Medicine, Wauwatosa, Wis., 1968-69; med. technologist U. Minn., Mpls., 1969-71; supervisory med. technologist Hoag Hosp., Newport Beach, Calif., 1971-73; supr. hematology Project HOPE, Maceio, Brazil, 1973; staff research asso. dept. medicine U. Calif., San Diego, 1974-77; instr. hematology San Francisco State U., 1977-78; edn. coordinator Sch. Med. Tech., Scripps Clinic and Research Found., LaJolla, Calif., 1978-80; asst. prof. med. tech. U. N.C., Chapel Hill, 1980—. Mem. Durham (N.C.) Arts Council, Project HOPE Alumni Assn. Mem. AAUP, Am. Soc. Clin. Pathology (asso.), Am. Soc. Med. Tech., N.C. Soc. Med. Tech., Triangle Weavers Guild. Republican. Lutheran. Club: Univ. Women's (U. N.C.), Univ. Women's (Duke U.). Home: 3433 Dover Rd Durham NC 27707 Office: U NC Med Sch Wing B 207-H Chapel Hill NC 27514

STOREY, BELINDA ROLFE, pharmacist; b. Hartselle, Ala., June 1, 1960; d. Perry Ray and Julia Ann (Johnson) Rolfe; m. David A. Storey, Aug. 10, 1985. Student, Auburn U., 1978-79; AA in Edn., Calhoun Coll., 1980; BS in Pharmacy, Samford U., 1984. Registered pharmacist, Ala. Pharmacy extern Reynold's Pharmacy, Birmingham, Ala., 1982-84, Weldon's Pharmacy, Hueytown, Ala., 1984, Princeton Hosp.-Birmingham Med.Ctr., Hueytown, Ala., 1984; pharmacy intern Big B Drugs Inc, Hueytown, 1984-85, pharmacist, 1985—; pharmacy cons. Bradford Group, Birmingham, 1986-88. Mem. Ala. Pharm. Assn., Lambda Kappa Sigma, Alpha Omicron Pi. Methodist. Home: 2095 Montreat Circle Vestavia AL 35216 Office: Big B Drugs No 58 Highway 31 S Pelham Plaza Pelham AL 35124

STORIE-PAHLITZSCH, LORI, writer, editor; b. Tryon, N.C., Nov. 22, 1948; d. Hallard Benjamin and Florence (Gilbert) Storie; m. Robert Pahlitzsch, Dec. 30, 1980. MA in Teaching, English, Converse Coll., 1971. Developer writing program Fine Arts Ctr., Greenville, S.C., 1980-81, writer-in-residence, 1981-84; with writing faculty, communications coordinator S.C. Gov.'s Sch. Arts, Greenville, 1981-83; pub. Writers Unltd., Greenville, 1982-86; adv. editor Cripple Creek Rev., 1981-83, 84; coordinator Roger C. Peace Creative Writing Competition, Greenville, 1986. Author poems, stories; contbr. articles to jours.; mem. editorial bd. Emrys Jour., 1987-88; reader Carolina Connections, 1988. Bd. dirs. Concert Ballet, Greenville, 1980-83, Greenville Sister Cities Internat., 1985-87, River Place Festival, 1986. Home and Office: 26 Partridge Ln Greenville SC 29601

STORM, CINDY JEAN, financial planner; b. Milw., Feb. 23, 1955; d. Elroy H. and Faith E. (Price) S.; m. Dennis E. Fischer, June 3, 1983. BBA in Mktg. and Fin., U. Wis., Milw., 1980. Investment advisor The Liberty Group/Women's Fin. Services, Elm Grove, Wis., 1981—; bd. dirs. Wis. Women Entrepreneurs, Milw. Contbr. more than 20 articles to profl. jours. Bd. dirs. Women's Exchange Milw., 1985-87. Mem. Inst. Cert. Fin. Planners (cert.), Internat. Assn. Fin. Planning, Audobon Soc. Home: 15155 W Lisbon Rd Brookfield WI 53005 Office: Liberty Group 13500 Watertown Plank Rd Elm Grove WI 53122

STORM, JANE ALEXANDRA, restaurateur; b. Los Angeles, May 9, 1951; d. Walter Vickers and Lisa (Fontaine) S. Student, U. Denver, 1969-70. Restaurant supr., bookkeeper, property mgr. Western Brass Industries, Torrance, Calif., 1971—; pres. Storm Enterprises, Ind., Breckenridge, Colo., 1981—; ski instr. Keystone Ski Area, Dillon, Colo., 1970-71. Mem. Nat. Restaurant Assn., Colo. Wyoming Restaurant Assn., Women of the Summit. Republican. Office: Storm Enterprises 1309 W Sepulveda Blvd Torrance CA 90501

STORSETH, JEANNIE PEARCE, insurance administrator; b. Casa Grande, Ariz., Sept. 24, 1948; d. Johnnie E. and Barbara (Dismukes) Pearce; m. Bryce Hallice Storseth, Aug. 15, 1981; 1 child, Michael Scott. B.S., U. Ariz., 1979. Mktg. rep. Group Health Coop., Seattle, 1981-83; dist. mgr. Health Plus/Blue Cross, Seattle, 1983-84; mktg. dir. Personal Health, Seattle, 1984-85; sales dir. Cigna Health Plan, Seattle, 1985—. Mem. Wash. Assn. Health Underwriters (v.p.), Am. Coll. Healthcare Mktg., Nat. Assn. Female Execs. Republican. Mem. Christian Ch. Club: Quota (Tacoma). Avocations: oil painting; writing. Office: Cigna Health Plan 701 5th Ave Seattle WA 98104

STORSTEEN, LINDA LEE, librarian; b. Pasadena, Jan. 26, 1948; d. Oliver Matthew and Susan (Smock) Storsteen. AB cum laude in History, UCLA, 1970, MA in Ancient History, 1972, MLS, 1973. Librarian, Los Angeles Pub. Library, 1974-79; city librarian Palmdale City Library (Calif.), 1979—. Adv. bd. So. Calif. Inter-Library Loan Network, Los Angeles, 1979-80; commr. So. Calif. Film Circuit, Los Angeles, 1980—; council South State Coop. Library System, 1981—, chmn., 1982-83, 85-86, 87-88, chmn., 1987-88; pres. So. Calif. Film Circuit, 1985-86; rec. sec. So. Antelope Valley Coordinating Council, Palmdale, 1983-84. Mem. ALA, Calif. Library Assn., Pub. Libraries Exec. Assn. So. Calif., Am. Saddle Horse Assn., Pacific Saddlebred Assn., So. Calif. Saddle Bred Horse Assn. (bd. dirs.). Home: PO Box 129 Palmdale CA 93550 Office: Palmdale City Library 700 E Palmdale Blvd Palmdale CA 93550

STOTLER, ALICEMARIE H., federal judge; b. Alhambra, Calif., May 29, 1942; d. James R. and Loretta M. Huber; m. James A. Stotler, Sept. 11, 1971. BA, U. So. Calif., 1964, JD, 1967. Bar: Calif. 1967, U.S. Dist. Ct. (no. dist.) Calif. 1967, U.S. Dist. Ct. (cen. dist.) 1973, U.S. Supreme Ct., 1976. Dep. Orange County Dist. Atty.'s Office, 1967-73; mem. Stotler & Stotler, Santa Ana, Calif., 1973-76, 83-84; judge Orange County Mcpl. Ct., 1976-78, Orange County Superior Ct., 1978-83, U.S. Dist. Ct. (cen. dist.) Calif., Los Angeles, 1984—. Active numerous civic orgns. Mem. ABA (jud. adminstrn. div., litigation sect.), Fed. Judges Assn., 9th Cir. Judges Assn., Nat. Assn. Women Judges, Orange County Bar Assn. (mem. numerous coms., Franklin G. West award, 1984, Judge of Yr., 1978), Calif. Judges Assn. (mem. numerous coms.), Orange County Trial Lawyers Assn. (bd. dirs. 1975), Calif. Elected Women's Assn. Edn. Research. Office: US Dist Ct 312 N Spring St Los Angeles CA 90012

STOTT, MARY LOU, real estate broker; b. Washington, Mar. 2, 1933; d. Martin Anthony and Mary Louise (Berberich) Dempf; B.S. in Edn., D.C. Tchrs. Coll., 1955; M.S.W., U. Hawaii, 1972; m. George W. Stott, Jr., Aug. 4, 1956; children—Michael, Helen, Tracey Anne. Tchr. public schs., 1955-69; family therapist Catholic Social Service, Honolulu, 1972-74; public relations dir. Sheraton Hotel Disco, 1975; dir. counseling Chaminade U., 1975-76, dir. women's programs, 1976-77; v.p. Stott Real Estate, Inc., Kailua, Hawaii, 1978—; guidance dir. St. Anthony Sch.; condr. U. Hawaii Career Seminar; mem. Gov.'s Com. on Children and Youth, 1974-75. Recipient Fed. grant for services to women re-entering career world, 1976. Mem. Am. Bus. Women's Assn., Acad. Cert. Social Workers, Nat. Assn. Social Workers, Am. Assn. Sex Educators and Counselors, Nat. Assn. Realtors, Hawaii Assn. Realtors, Honolulu Bd. Realtors. Republican. Roman Catholic. Club: Cath. Daus. Home: 360 Dune Circle Kailua HI 96734

STOTTLEMYRE, DONNA MAE, jewelry store executive; b. Mystic, Iowa, Nov. 11, 1928; d. Clarence William and Nina Alene (Millizer) Clark; m. Robert Arthur Stottlemyre, May 8, 1946; children—Roger Dale, Amber Anita, Tamra Collette. Owner, operator Donna's Dress Shop, Unionville, Mo., 1973-76, Donna's Jewelry Box and Bridal Boutique, Unionville, 1978—. Mem. First Baptist Ch., Sunday Sch. and Bible Sch. tchr. Unionville; 4H Club judge County Fair, Unionville. Mem. C. of C. Avocations: sewing; flower arranging. Home: 217 N 14th Unionville MO 63565 Office: Donna's Jewelry and Bridal 1610 Main Unionville MO 63565

STOTZ, NATALIE HAMER, business official; b. Great Falls, Mont., Oct. 22, 1921; d. Arthur C. Hamer and Gertrude H. (Kaufmann) Wallace; m. Theodore Philip Stotz, June 9, 1956. Student Great Falls Comml. Coll., 1939. C.L.U. Br. office cashier Occidental Life Ins. Co., Great Falls, 1939-44; sec. to underwriter, San Francisco, 1944-47; head claims dept. Friedman & Co., San Francisco, 1947-62; adminstrv. asst. to underwriter, San Jose, Calif., 1962—. Mem. Am. Soc. C.L.U.s. Sec.-treas. West Bay Opera Guild, Palo Alto, Calif., 1965-67. Republican. Christian Scientist. Avocation: ballet. Home: 988 N California Ave Palo Alto CA 94303 Office: 333 W Santa Clara St Suite 712 San Jose CA 95113

STOUFF, FAYE, craft association executive; b. Kirkland, Tex., June 27, 1908; d. George Lee and Eliza Ann (Smith) Rogers; m. Emile Anatol Stouff, Mar. 5, 1925 (dec. 1978); 1 child, Nicholas Leonard. Student pub. schs., Fort Worth. Tchr. cane basketry Chetimacha Indian Reservation, Charenton, La., 1953-84, tchr. beadwork, 1969; mgr. Chetimacha Craft Assn., 1970—. Author: Chetimacha Beliefs, 1970; (booklet) History of Indians, 1975. Baptist. Home: Rural Route 2 Box 224 Jeanerette LA 70544

STOUFFER, NANCY KATHLEEN, publishing company executive; b. Hershey, Pa., Feb. 14, 1951; d. William Lawrence Sweeny O'Brian and Edna (Luttrell); m. David Joel Stouffer, July 19, 1980; children: Jennifer Belle, Vance David. Pres. Ande Pub. Co., Inc., Camp Hill, Pa., 1985—, The Book Cook Inc., Camp Hill, Pa., 1988—; cons. Syn-Comm Group, Inc. div. P.O.P., N.Y.C., 1988—. Contbr. articles on dyslexia to popular mags.; author children's books. Exec. researcher com. on advanced studies in learning disabilities Med. and Ednl. Profl., SPECTRA. Republican. Clubs: Pa. Watercolor Soc.; Nat. Mus. Women in Arts.

STOUT, DONNA KARY, manufacturing company sales executive; b. Balt., Aug. 16, 1954; d. Donald Angelo and Anna May (Vollenweider) Kary; m. David M. Stout, Aug. 13, 1977. B of Biology, Western Md. Coll., 1976; MS, George Washington U., 1980. Microbiologist, McCormick & Co., Balt., 1976-79, specifications coordinator, Hunt Valley, Md., 1979-80, supr. tech. services, indsl. bus., Balt., 1980-83, tech. sales services mgr., Hunt Valley, 1984, sales service mgr., 1984-85, product mgr., 1985, sales and mktg. services mgr., 1985-87, account mgr., 1987—. Mem. Inst. Food Technologists.

STOUT, JUANITA KIDD, judge; b. Wewoka, Okla., Mar. 7, 1919; d. Henry Maynard and Mary Alice (Chandler) Kidd; m. Charles Otis Stout, June 23, 1942. B.A., U. Iowa, 1939; J.D., Ind. U., 1948, LL.M., 1954; LL.D. (hon.) Ursinus Coll., 1965, Ind. U., 1966, Lebanon Valley Coll., 1969, Drexel U., 1972, Rockford Coll. (Ill.), 1974, Roger Williams Coll., 1984, Morgan State U., Balt., 1985; U. Md.-Eastern Shore, 1980; D.H.L., Russell Sage Coll., 1966. Bar: D.C. 1950, Pa. 1954. Tchr. pub. schs., Seminole and Sand Springs, Okla., 1939-42; tchr. Fla. A&M U., Tallahassee, 1949, Tex. So. U., Houston, 1949; adminstrv. asst. to judge U.S. Ct. Appeals (3d circuit), Phila., 1949-55; asst. dist. atty., Phila., 1955-59; judge Ct. of Common Pleas, Phila., 1959—. Recipient Jane Addams medal Rockford Coll., 1966, Disting. Service award U. Iowa, 1974; named to Hall of Fame of Okla., Okla. Heritage Soc., 1981. Mem. ABA, Nat. Assn. Women Judges, Nat. Assn. Women Lawyers, Pa. Bar Assn., Phila. Bar Assn. Democrat. Episcopalian. Home: 1919 Chestnut St Apt 2805 Philadelphia PA 19103 Office: Pa Supreme Ct Room 464 City Hall Philadelphia PA 19107

STOUT, LINDA CLARK, insurance company administrator; b. Richmond, Va., Aug. 25, 1947; d. Joe Phillip and Helen Louise (Burton) Clark. BA, Coll. William & Mary, 1969, MEd, 1976. Tchr. Hampton (Va.) High Sch., 1970-76; adminstrv. asst. Meth. Coll., Fayetteville, N.C., 1976-77; supr. field tng. Ins. Services Office, N.Y.C., 1977-84; mgr. insurer support ISOTEL, Inc., N.Y.C., 1984—. Chmn. Congl. Council Trinity Ch., N.Y.C., 1982-84, mem. council, 1980-82, 86—. Mem. AAUW (pres. Hampton chpt. 1975-76). Episcopalian. Office: Comml Risk Services Inc 1500 Forest Ave Suite 120 Richmond VA 23229

STOUTE, MARGUERITE ALLYN, nurse, educator, consultant; b. Bklyn., Aug. 27, 1949; d. Allan Humphrey and Ina Gertrude (Ricketts) S. B.A., Manhattanville Coll., 1973; B.S. in Nursing Edn., NYU-Washington Square, 1981, M.A. in Nursing Edn., 1983. R.N. Researcher Mt. Sinai Hosp., N.Y.C., 1973, Columbia U., N.Y.U., 1973-74; staff/in-charge nurse Kings County Hosp., Bklyn., 1983—; coordinator nursing edn., inservice-staff devel., diabetes educator Bklyn. Hosp., 1986—; cons. Ina Mag Assn., Bklyn., 1984—; adj. prof. N.Y.C. Tech. Community Coll., 1985—. Pres. Scholarship Fund, Nazarene Ch., Bklyn., 1983—; assoc. mem. Bedford Stuyvesant Alcoholic Treatment Ctr., Bedford, Monroe, Bklyn., 1980—; class agt. class of '73, Manhattanville Coll. Served to lt. Nurse Corps USAR. Mem. Am. Nurses Assn., Assn. Diabetes Educators, Nat. Assn. Female Execs., Nat. Entrepreneur Assn., NYU Alumni Assn. Club: Manhattanville (Purchase, N.Y.). Avocations: writing; singing; speaking; teaching. Home: 1158 Bedford Ave Brooklyn NY 11216

STOVER, KIMBERLY ANN, air traffic controller; b. Paola, Kans., July 30, 1962; d. James Delbert and Carolyn Sue (Bradshaw) Bracken; m. Eric Thomas Stover. BS in Respiratory Therapy, Kans. U., 1984. Cert. respiratory therapist, Kans. Cert. repiratory therapist Kans. U. Med. Ctr., Kansas City, 1983-84; air traffic controller FAA, Olathe, Kans., 1984—; co-owner E.T.'s Best Catering, Overland Park, Kans., 1984—. Mem. Profl. Women Controllers. Methodist. Club: RINC (Overland Park). Home: 9219 Swarner Lenexa KS 66219

STOWE, CANDY RENEE, medical technologist; b. Providence, Jan. 3, 1946; d. Grant Forrest and Florence Juanita (Howe) McNally; m. Wayne Stowe, Oct. 24, 1969 (div. Aug. 1977); children: Annette, Alan and Boyd (twins). BS in Med. Tech., U. Kans., 1969. Med. technologist West Tex. Med. Ctr., Abilene, 1968-69; chief technologist Medilab, Abilene, 1969-70, Westwood Med. Lab., Abilene, 1971, Stonewall Meml. Hosp., Aspermont, Tex., 1977-80, West Loop Med. Lab., Houston, 1980; med. technologist Staff Builders, Houston, 1980-81; chief technologist Fondren Med. Lab., Houston, 1980-81; week end med. technologist Pkwy. Hosp., Houston, 1981-84; med. technologist, evening supr. VA Med. Ctr., Houston, 1984—; cons. Antoine Med. Clinic, Houston, 1981-83, CRS Labs., Houston, 1981—. Mem. Am. Soc. Clin. Pathology, Am. Soc. Med. Tech., Nat. Assn. Female Execs. Home: 107 Kiowa Ct Rosharon TX 77583 Office: VA Med Ctr 2002 Holcombe Houston TX 77022

STRACHAN, GLADYS, executive director; b. N.Y.C., Dec. 10, 1929; d. Jacob Allen and Annie Mae (Alston) McClendon; m. Eugene S. Callender (div. 1963); 1 child, Renee Denise; m. John R. Strachan (dec. 1982). Student, NYU, 1947-49. Dep. asst. Presbyn. Ch. of East Africa, Nairobi, Kenya, 1964-67; assoc. for women's program Presbyn. Ch. of U.S., N.Y.C., 1970-83; exec. United Presbyn. Women, N.Y.C., 1983—; cons. Peace Corps, Nairobi, 1964-67, Operation Crossroads Africa, Nairobi, 1964-67, Afro-Am. Ednl. Inst., Teaneck, N.J., 1977-79, various women's orgns. in Asia and Australia. V.p. Addicts Rehab. Ctr. Bd., N.Y.C., 1957—; mem. N.Y. Coalition of 100 Black Women, N.Y.C., 1972—; sec. Harlem Dowling Children's Service Bd., N.Y.C., 1983—; bd. dirs., treas. Bread for the World, Washington, 1983—. Recipient Cert. of citation borough pres. N.Y.C., 1977, Harlem Peacemaking award Harlem Peacemaking Com., 1983. Office: United Presbyn Women 475 Riverside Dr New York NY 10115

STRACHER, DOROTHY ALTMAN, education educator, consultant; b. N.Y.C., May 11, 1934; d. Joseph and Gussie (Newman) Altman; m. Alfred Stracher, July 4, 1954; children: Cameron Altman, Adam Reed, Erica Terri. BA, Bklyn. Coll., 1955; MA, Columbia U., 1957; postgrad., U. Copenhagen, 1958-59; acad. vis., Oxford (Eng.) U., 1973-74; PhD, Hofstra U., 1979. Cert. English and social sci. tchr., N.Y. Coordinator secondary reading Cen. Moriches (N.Y.) Sch. Dist., 1974-78; coordinator reading Ea. Williston (N.Y.) Sch. Dist., 1978-79; specialist reading and writing SUNY, Old Westbury, 1979-81; adj. prof. dept. reading Hofstra U., Hempstead, N.Y., 1979-82; asst. prof. edn. L.I. U., Bklyn., 1982-83, Coll. New Rochelle, N.Y., 1983-85; sr. learning diagnostic specialist child devel. div. L.I. Jewish Hosp., Bklyn., 1985-86; assoc. prof., dir. program for learning disabled coll. students Dowling Coll., Oakdale, N.Y., 1986—; cons. Johnson & Johnson, Inc., Princeton, N.J., 1982—, Sanford (Fla.) Sch. Dist., 1983, Lawrence (N.Y.) Sch. Dist., 1984, Sch. Dist. 7, N.Y.C., 1984—. Author: (with others) First the Fundamentals, 1980, What Do You Call a Well-Behaved Martian? A Manual For Thinkers' Parents, 1981, Integrating Assessment, 1982; editor: Differentiated Curricula, 1986; contbr. articles to profl. jours. Bd. dirs. Roslyn (N.Y.) Sch. Dist., 1975-84, v.p., 1980-82, pres., 1982-84; mem. adv. bd. Children's Sch. Sci., Woods Hole, Mass., 1976-82. Mem. Reading Forum Found., Orton Soc., Internat. Reading Assn., Nat. Assn. for Gifted Edn., League Women Voters (bd. dirs. 1961-70), NOW, Kappa Delta Pi. Home: 47 The Oaks Roslyn NY 11576

STRADER, JACQUELINE W., small business owner; b. Cin., Mar. 15, 1946; d. John Jacob and Joan (Ganne) S.; m. Don Michael Darragh, Sept. 17, 1965 (div. June 1979); children: Sean Marshall, John Cassilly. Lic. real estate agt. Real estate agt. Ken Realty, La Grange, Ga., 1984—; owner, operator Premier Products, Warm Springs, Ga., 1985—. Mem. Warm Springs Mchts. Assn., La Grange C. of C. Home: 30 Buck Smith Rd Hogansville GA 30230 Office: Premier Products Main St Warm Springs GA 30230

STRADER, MARCIA D., technical writer, trainer; b. Myrtle Point, Oreg., Nov. 12, 1955; d. G. Howard and Durelle (Hill) S.; m. D.S. Crawford, Sept. 10, 1982. Student Skagit Valley Coll., Mount Vernon, Wash., 1972-73; B.S., Oreg. State U., 1978, M.Ed., 1979. Grad. teaching asst. dept. English, Oreg. State U., Corvallis, 1978-79, asst. dir. Oreg. State U. Found., 1979-80; documentation specialist Spartin Systems, Houston, 1980-82; owner, mgr., writer TekniKraft, Houston, 1982-87; tech. writer Internat. Civil Aviation Orgn. (div. of U.N.), Jakarta, 1987—. cons. Rice U., Houston, 1981-82. Author numerous tech. manuals on data processing, 1980—; Editor: Introducing Indonesia, 1986; Editor-In-Chief Indonesian Words and Phrases, 1987. Treas. Jakarta Am. Women's Assn., Indonesia, 1985-87; active Jakarta Internat. Community Activity Ctr., 1985—. Mem. Soc. Tech. Communication, Nat. Assn. Female Execs. Avocation: camping. Office: care Marathon Internat-Jakarta PO Box 1228 Houston TX 77251-1228

STRAHL, MARCIA BRUCE, aeronautical engineer; b. Chgo., June 3, 1944; d. Arthur Leroy and Catherine Evelyn (Daubach) Bruce; m. Wayne Arthur Strahl, Dec. 21, 1963 (div. Jan. 1969). BS in Aeronautical Engring., Aero-Space Inst., Chgo., 1969; MS, Northrop Inst. Tech., Inglewood, Calif., 1979. Engr., scientist McDonnell-Douglas Aircraft, Long Beach, Calif., 1969-75; engr., then sr. engineer Westinghouse Elec. Marine Div., Sunnyvale, Calif., 1975-81, engring. supr., 1981-87; engring. sect. mgr. Westinghouse Elec. Systems Div., Lima, Ohio, 1987—; ground instr. Aviation Tng. Enterprises, Chgo., 1966-69. Mem. tech. adv. com. Math, Engring., Sci. Achievement Industry Tech. for Minority Students; scouting coordinator Boy Scouts Am., Santa Clara, Calif., 1980-86. Recipient Disting. Women Recognition Girls' Club of Mid-Peninsula, San Mateo, Calif., 1976, Twin Women in Industry Recognition Santa Clara YWCA, 1985. Mem. AIAA, Soc. Women Engrs. (sect. pres. 1979-80, sect. rep. 1980-81). Republican. Lutheran. Office: Westinghouse Elec Systems 1501 S Dixie Hwy Lima OH 45802

STRAHLE, JULIA ANN, finance company executive; b. Kansas City, Mo., Nov. 8, 1946; d. Richard Henry and Ellen Catherine (Spinner) S.; m. Anthony R. DeFranco, Mar. 21, 1980 (div. Dec. 1986); m. Glin Tatum, Oct. 2, 1987. Student, Southwest Mo. State U., 1963-66, St. John's U., 1985. Sectionhead Weeden and Co., San Francisco, 1969-74; v.p./registered prin. Equitec Fin. Group, San Francisco, 1974-75; sectionhead Weeden and Co., N.Y.C., 1976-78; pvt. practice cons. N.Y.C., 1978-84; pres. Securities Ops. Specialists, Staten Island, N.Y., 1984—. Southwest Mo. State U. scholar, 1963. Mem. Am. Women Entrepreneurs, Nat. Assn. Female Execs.

STRAIT, BENITA (BONNIE) LESSIN, human services administrator; b. N.Y.C., Sept. 11, 1933; d. Michael and May (Lehman) Lessin; m. Marc A. Nerenstone, Feb. 3, 1952 (div. 1974); children: Marti, Stacy, Peter; m. George A. Strait, May 30, 1976. BA, Queens Coll., 1954; postgrad., U. Pitts., 1954-55. Adminstrv. asst. Met. Ednl. Council for Staff Devel., Washington, 1970; program asst. Vol. Action Ctr. Health and Welfare Council of Nat. Capitol Area, Washington, 1971-73, asst. dir. Vol. Action Ctr., 1973-74, dir. Vol. Action Ctr., asst. dir. community services, 1974; assoc. dir. for program devel. Office Vol. Services Dept. Community Affairs, Boston, 1974-75, assoc. dir., coordinator Commonwealth Service Corps. program, 1975-76, dir. Commonwealth Service Corps., 1976; exec. dir. Epilepsy Found. Am., Westlawn, Iowa, 1976-78; vol. coordinator 6th jud. dist. Dept. of Correctional Services, Cedar Rapids, Iowa, 1978—; field instr. Mt. Mercy Coll., Cedar Rapids, 1979—, chair adv. council 1986—; cons. Conference on Aging Dept. Corrections; leader various workshops. Chair legisl., program coms. Leaders in Volunteerism, 1978—; chair com., bd. dirs. Hancher Guild, Iowa City, 1985—; pres. Pub. Concerns Inst., Cedar Rapids, 1986—; chair adv. council for social work Mt. Mercy Coll.; mem. State Adv. Council for Respiratory Care. Mem. Am. Probation and Parole Assn., Am. Corrections Assn. (chair citizens participation com. 1984-86), Nat. Assn. Vols. in Criminal Justice (State of Iowa rep.), Assn. for Vol. Adminstrn. (chair region VIII, co-chair conference 1976), Iowa Corrections Assn.)treas., exec. bd., chair various coms.), Nat. Assn. for Blacks in Criminal Justice. Home: 10 Ridgewood Lane Iowa City IA 52240 Office: 6th Jud Dist Dept Correctional Services 1035 Third Ave 8E Cedar Rapids IA 52403

STRAKOSCH, KATHERINE WENTON, executive recruiter; b. N.Y.C., Oct. 4, 1933; d. William J. and Elsie G. (Sullivan) Wenton; m. Raymond D. Strakosch, Nov. 10, 1956 (div. May 1977); children—Joanne, Mark, Gregory, Karen. B.A. cum laude, Coll. Mt. St. Vincent, 1955. Cert. personnel cons. Vice pres. Dunhill of Greater Stamford, Inc., Wilton, Conn., 1976-80, pres., 1980—; mem. Town of Wilton Personnel Policies Com., 1983—. Pres. bd. dirs. Wilton Playshop, 1971-73, vice chmn. bd. trustees, 1982-86, chmn. 1986-87; mem. Democratic Town Com., Wilton, 1976-79. Mem. Conn. Assn. Personnel Consultants (sec. 1979, mem. ethics com. 1981—, newsletter editor 1980), Nat. Assn. Personnel Consultants. Roman Catholic. Avocations: tennis; travel; reading. Home: 28 Glen Ridge Wilton CT 06897 Office: Dunhill of Greater Stamford Inc 213 Danbury Rd Wilton CT 06897

STRALEY, TINA H., mathematics educator; b. N.Y.C., Sept. 4, 1943; d. Abraham Sidney and Frances (Yankowitz) Handelman; m. William Forest Straley, June 1, 1967 (div. Oct. 1976); 1 child, Jessica Laura. BA with honors, Ga. State U., 1965, MS, 1966; PhD, Auburn (Ala.) U., 1971. Tchr. math. Miami Beach (Fla.) Sr. High Sch., 1966-67; instr. Spelman Coll., Atlanta, 1967-68, Auburn U., 1971-73; asst. prof. Kennesaw Coll., Marietta, Ga., 1973-78, assoc. prof., 1979-84, prof., 1984—, acting chair dept. math., 1987-88; chmn. dept. math. Kennesaw Coll., Marietta, 1988—; research assoc. Emory U., Atlanta, 1978-79. Contbr. articles to profl. jours. Originator state steering com. Futurescape Programs for High Sch. Girls, U. System and Ga. Dept. Edn., 1983-86. Recipient Salute to Women of Achievement award YWCA, Atlanta, 1985; grantee Kennesaw Coll., 1980, AAUW, 1984-85. Mem. Math. Assn. Am. (instl. 1970-71, editor Southeastern Sect. newsletter 1988—, dept. rep. 1979—), Phi Kappa Phi. Office: Kennesaw Coll Marietta GA 30061

STRALKA, MARY JOSEPHA DALY, nurse; b. Flint, Mich., Mar. 27, 1945; d. Thomas Edward and Dorothy Marie (Hanson) Daly; m. Louis Theodore Stralka, June 30, 1967; children: Matthew Albert, Bethany Margaret. BS in Nursing, St. Louis U., 1970, MSN, 1978. Cert. pediatric nurse practitioner. Staff nurse St. Louis U. Hosps., 1966-69; employee health nurse Cardinal Glennon Hosp., St. Louis, 1971, pediatric nurse practitioner, 1972-73, pediatric nursing practitioner, asst. dir. nursing Emergency Dept., 1973-77; clin. preceptor Washington U. Sch. Medicine, St. Louis, 1980—, assoc. dir. nursing Pediatric Nursing Practitioner program, 1979-81, nurse dir., 1981-86; pediatric nurse practitioner Healthkey/Med. Care Group, St. Louis, 1986-87; clin. nurse specialist Barnes Hosp. Home Health, St. Louis, 1987—; pediatric cons. Community Home Health Agy., St. Louis, 1986—. Author: Pediatric Nurse Practitioner, 1970, Compliance Medicines; mem. article rev. bd. Jour. Pediatric Health Care, 1987. Vol. nurse local chs., Grace Hill Neighborhood Health Ctr., St. Louis, 1983-86; bd. sec. Maternal Child Health Council, St. Louis, 1986-87. Fellow Nat. Assn. Pediatric Nursing Assn. and Practitioners (recert. rev. bd.); mem. St. Louis Pediatric Nursing Practitioners Orgn. (treas. 1984, 85, pres. elect 1987), Assn. Faculties of Pediatric Nursing Adminstrn. and Practitioners Programs, Am. Nurses Assn., Mo. Nurses Assn. (primary care spl. interest group). Office: Nurse Practitioner Cons PO Box 31424 Saint Louis MO 63131

STRAND, KRISTINE ELLEN, speech pathologist; b. Chgo., Sept. 14, 1945; d. Leslie and Eleanor C. (Peterson) S. BS, Northwestern U., 1967, MA, 1968; EdD, Boston U., 1982. Speech-lang. pathologist Chgo. Pub. Schs., 1968-69, Ill. Inst. for Devel. Disabilities, Chgo., 1969-72; asst. prof. Northeastern U., Boston, 1972-80, Boston Coll., Chestnut Hill, Mass., 1982—; dir. speech lang. hearing dept. Kennedy Meml. Hosp. for Children, Boston, 1986—; instr. dept. otolaryngology and communication disorders Harvard Med. Sch., Boston, 1982-86; cons. Attleboro (Mass.) Pub. Schs., 1974-78, Applied Lang. Technologies, Boston, 1980-86. Editorial cons. Language, Speech, & Hearing Services in the Schs.; contbr. articles to profl. jours. Bd. dirs. North Park Coll. and Theol. Seminary, Chgo., 1986—; pres. bd. trustees New Eng. Seaman's Mission, Boston, 1980-83. Mem. Am. Speech Lang. Hearing Assn., Mass. Speech Lang. Hearing Assn. (Disting. Service award 1976, Honors of the Assn. award 1986), Internat. Congress for the Study of Child Lang., New Eng. Child Lang. Assn. Office: Kennedy Meml Hosp for Children 30 Warren St Boston MA 02135

STRAND, NANCY MARIE, nurse; b. Phila., Dec. 27, 1926; d. Edward Joseph and Ella Frances (Waldron) McNelis; student in Nursing, Coll. St. Rose, 1944-47; B.S., N.Y.U., 1951, M.A. in Counseling, 1954; m. Bart Strand, Jan. 15, 1955; children—Deirdre, Maureen, Sheila. Staff nurse, relief supr. VA Hosp., Bronx, N.Y., 1947-59; staff nurse Children's Hosp., Buffalo, 1959-61, VA Hosp., Buffalo, 1961-62; with U. Ark. Hosp., 1962-77, asso. dir. nursing, 1966-73, dir. nursing, 1973-77; clin. coordinator nursing VA Hosp., Little Rock, 1977—; mem. nursing curriculum project So. Regional Edn. Bd.; mem. faculty research workshop U. N.C. R.N. Mem. Am. Nurses Assn. (cert. nursing adminstr.), Ark. State Nurses Assn., Nat. League Nursing, Ark. League Nursing (Ann. award of Merit 1971), AAUW. Roman Catholic. Home: 464 Midland Ave Little Rock AR 72205

STRANGE, DOUGLAS HART MCKOY, civic worker; b. Wilmington, N.C., Mar. 16, 1929; d. Adair Morcy and Katie Reston (Grainger) McKoy; student Hollins Coll., 1946-48; m. Robert Strange, July 16, 1949; children—Robert VI, John Allan, Elizabeth Adair, Katherine Grainger. Fin. chmn. and provisional co-chmn. Knoxville Jr. League; former tchr. Bible class, vestrywoman, pres. ch. women Fox Chapel Episcopal Ch.; former chmn. Fox Chapel House Tour; former chmn. altar guild, mem. worship com. bd. dirs. ch. women, St. John's Episcopal Ch.; altar chmn. Episcopal

Diocese of Tenn.; bd. dirs. Dulin Com., Dulin Gallery Art; invitation coordinator Heart Gala Ball, 1985. Recipient cert. of merit Pitts. Heart Fund, 1975, engraved plate Fox Chapel Episcopal Ch., 1976. Mem. Assn. Jr. Leagues Am., Nat. Soc. Colonial Dames Am. (asst. to editor and bus. mgr. newsletter, 1978-79), Knoxville Civic Opera. Republican. Clubs: Cherokee Garden, Nine-o-clock Cotillion, Cherokee Country. Home: 1126 Bordeaux Circle Knoxville TN 37919

STRANSCAK, SANDRA S., public relations executive; b. Lakewood, Ohio, Apr. 14, 1948; d. Frank Steve and Sue (Titel) S. BA, Cleve. State U., 1971. Nurse recruiter The Cleve. Clin. Found., 1973-84, profl. relations mgr., 1985—; assoc. dir. profl. relations HealthAm., Cleve., 1984-85. Editor, reviewer (book): Nurse Recruitment, 1983. Mem. Greater Cleve. Assn. Nurse Recruiters (pres. 1983-84), Am. Hosp. Assn. Soc. Health Care Planning and Mktg., NOW. Democrat. Lutheran. Club: Toastmasters Internat. (Cleve.) (sgt. at arms 1983-84). Home: 5128 Oakmont Dr Lyndhurst OH 44124 Office: Cleve Clin Found 9500 Euclid Ave Cleveland OH 44106

STRASSER, NANCY SOWERS, insurance agent; b. Englewood, N.J., Nov. 10, 1947; d. Forrest Wayne and Eva Marie (Bosstick) Sowers; m. Dermot Macaraugh Ross-Brown, June 3, 1978 (div. Dec. 1980); David Frederick Strasser, Sept. 17, 1982. Diploma, St. Luke's Hosp. Sch. Nursing, St. Louis, 1969; student, U. Colo., 1970-71. Cert. critical care nurse practitioner. Staff nurse ICU, operating room St. Anthony Hosp. Systems, Denver, 1971-75; critical care crisis nurse Comprehensive Nursing Services, Denver, 1977-79; clin. specialist Pepin Distbg. Inc., Denver, 1979-80; asst. adminstr. NE Meml. Hosp., Houston, 1981; dir. nursing Med. Personnel Pool, Ft. Myers, Fla., 1982; head nursing operating room Lee Meml. Hosp., Ft. Myers, Fla., 1982; team leader S. Fla. Artificial Kidney Ctr., Ft. Myers, Fla., 1983; gen. mgr. Nat. Med. Homecare, Inc., Cape Coral, Fla., 1983-86; sales rep. Met. Life Ins. Co., Ft. Myers, 1987—. Mem. Nat. Assn. Female Execs., DAR, Nat. Assn. Life Underwriters. Home: 517 SE 35th St Cape Coral FL 33904 Office: Met Life Ins Co 8250-101 College Pkwy Fort Myers FL 33919

STRATFORD, CAROL ANN DEERING, occupational therapist; b. Columbus, Ohio, Dec. 17, 1946; d. Earl Brent and Gladys May (Wade) Deering; A.A., Brevard Jr. Coll., 1966; B.S., U. Fla., 1968; m. Francis A. Stratford, Jr., Aug. 4, 1973. Staff occupational therapist Hosp. Albert Einstein Coll. Medicine, Bronx, N.Y., 1968-74; sr. research therapist Inst. Rehab. Medicine N.Y. U. Med. Center, N.Y.C., 1975-81, mem. developmental team voice recognition, wheel chair and environ. control system; supr. dept. occupational therapy Danbury (Conn.) Hosp., 1982-84; tech. aids cons., 1984—. Registered occupational therapist. Mem. Am. Occupational Therapy Assn. (resource person in rehab. engring.), Rehab. Engring. Soc. N. Am. Co-author, editor: (monograph) Environmental Control Systems and Vocational Aids for Persons with High Level Quadriplegia, 1979; contbr. articles to profl. jours. Methodist. Home: 16 N State St Dover DE 19901

STRATMAN, MAXINE THEOBALD, banker; b. Brigham, Wis., May 22, 1938; d. Max L. and Gladys B. (Olson) Theobald; student Barneveld (Wis.) public schs.; children—Julie Lynn, Jodie Lynn. With Barneveld State Bank, Ridgeway, Wis., 1956—, beginning in bookkeeping dept., successively teller, asst. br. mgr., mgr. and asst. cashier 1956-80, asst. v.p., br. office mgr., 1980—. Chair Meml. Hosp. Campaign Fund 1980, Ridgeway Salvation Army, 1981—; treas. Methodist Ch. Mem. Iowa County Bankers Assn. (pres. 1984-86), Nat. Assn. Bank Women. Republican. Home: Rt 1 Box 170 Barneveld WI 53507 Office: Barneveld State Bank Main St Ridgeway WI 53582

STRATTON, EVELYN JOYCE, lawyer; b. Bangkok, Thailand, Feb. 25, 1953; came to U.S., 1971; d. Elmer John and Corrine Sylvia (Henricksen) Sahlberg; m. R. Stephen Stratton, June 16, 1973; children: Luke Andrew, Tyler John. A.A., U. Fla., 1973; B.A., Akron U., 1975; J.D., Ohio State U., 1978. Bar: Ohio 1979, U.S. Dist. Ct. (so. dist.) Ohio 1979, U.S. Ct. Appeals (6th cir.) 1983. Teaching asst. history LeTourneau Coll., Longview, Tex., 1973-74; law clk. Knepper, White, Columbus, 1978-79, Crabbe & Brown, Columbus, 1977-79; assoc. Hamilton, Kramer, Myers & Cheek, Columbus, 1980-85; ptnr. Wesp, Osterkamp & Stratton, 1985—; trustee Linc Resources, Columbus, 1980-86, chmn. bd. dirs., 1984-86 ; speaker legal seminars. Worker Republic Party Campaign, Columbus, 1983—; mem. Women's Rep. Rountable, 1984—; Nat. Soc. to Prevent Blindness (devel. com. Ohio devel. affiliate 1987—); vice chmn. fund drive United Way Columbus, 1984; fundraiser Easter Seal Telethon, 1986, Columbus Mus. Art, 1986; bd. sec. Columbus Countywide Devel. Corp., 1987—; candidate for common pleas judge, 1988. Recipient Gold Key award LeTourneau Coll., Gainesville, Fla., 1974; service commendation Ohio Ho. of Reps., 1984. Mem. Am. Trial Lawyers Assn., Columbus Bar Assn. (com. chmn. 1982-84, bd. govs. 1984-88), Ohio Bar Assn., ABA, Ohio Assn. Civil Trial Attys., Columbus Def. Assn., Columbus Bar Found. (trustee 1985—, officer, sec. 1986-87, v.p. 1987—), Am. Arbitration Assn., Columbus Area Women's Polit. Caucus, Women Lawyers Franklin County, Phi Delta Phi (pres. 1982-83). Clubs: Civitan (trustee 1982-83), Exec. Club of Columbus (bd. dirs. 1986—), Chairman's. Office: Wesp Osterkamp & Stratton 42 E Gay St Suite 812 Columbus OH 43215

STRATTON, LOIS JEAN, state legislator; b. Springdale, Wash., Jan. 5, 1927; d. Charles B. and Ann B. (Hill) Brunton; m. Allen F. Stratton, 1946; children—Alan Edward, Kathleen Prater, Mark Charles, Scott D., Karen Jeanne. Student Kinman Bus. U., 1944-45. Democratic precinct committeewoman, Spokane County, Wash., from 1958; mem. Spokane County Dem. Exec. Bd.; alt. del. Dem. Nat. Conv., 1976; co-chmn. Gov. Dixy Lee Ray Com., 1976; committeewoman Wash. State Dem. Com., from 1977; now mem. Wash. Senate, Dist. 3; exec. sec. pub. affairs Kaiser Aluminum & Chem. Corp., Spokane, from 1963; adminstrv. asst., exec. sec. to pres. Expo 74 World's Fair, Spokane. Recipient World's Fair Expo 74 Vol. Service citations Gov. of Wash. and Wash. State Commn., 1974. Mem. Spokane County Dem. Club (sec.), Jane Jefferson Dem. Club (1st v.p.). Roman Catholic. Office: Office of the State Senate State Capitol Olympia WA 98504 Address: 1724 W Mansfield Spokane WA 99205 *

STRAUB, CINDIE TOUSEY, bridal wear designer, manufacturer, mime; b. Gainesville, Fla., June 6, 1960; d. Charles William and Elizabeth Louise (Shannon) T.; m. Matthew Louis Straub, June 2, 1943; children: Lorelei Elizabeth, Lucie Jean. Grad. high sch., Winter Park, Fla. Mime Sea World of Fla., Orlando, 1978-80; mime, owner Wind Mime, Gettysburg, 1980-87; shop owner A Flower A Day, New Oxford, Pa., 1983-86; owner, designer Elegance, New Oxford, 1986—. Co-author: Mime: Basics for Beginners, 1983; numerous copyrights in pantomimes, bridal veil design. Recipient Pa. State Performance award Pa. Culture Arts Assn., 1986; Pa. Hall of Fame, Outstanding Service award Champions of Older Workers. Mem. Nat. Mime Assn. Democrat. Mem. United Ch. Christ. Office: Elegance 2031 Oxford Rd New Oxford PA 17350

STRAUBER, GRACE FRANCES, hospital administrator; b. N.Y.C., Oct. 24, 1927; d. Jerome James and Grace Frances (Martin) S.; B.B.A., Siena Coll., Loudonville, N.Y., 1963; M.H.A., St. Louis U., 1968. Joined Order Franciscan Sisters of Poor, Roman Catholic Ch., 1947; bus. mgr. St. Francis Hosp., Bronx, N.Y., 1954-56; asst. adminstr. St. Clare Hosp., Schenectady, 1956-59, St. Michael's Med. Center, Newark, 1960-61; asst. adminstr. St. Clare Hosp., Schenectady, 1961-65; provincial treas. Province of St. Anthony, Franciscan Sisters of the Poor, 1966-68; gen. treas. Franciscan Sisters of Poor, 1968-70; exec. dir. St. Mary Hosp., Hoboken, N.J., 1971-80, pres., 1980-85, cons., 1986—, bd. dirs., 1970-85; v.p. Gilbert-Tweed Assocs., Inc. Exec. Search cons., 1987—; bd. dirs. St. Anthony Community Hosp., Warwick, N.Y., 1966—, pres. bd., 1980-83; bd. dirs. St. Francis Community Health Center, 1981-85, Hudson Health Systems Agy., 1976-82, St. Francis Hosp., Greenville, S.C., 1987—; dir. Hudson United Bank, 1979—. Named to Hudson County Health Hall of Fame, 1975; named Hudson County Woman of Achievement, 1976; honored by Exec. Women of N.J., 1988. Mem. N.J. Hosp. Assn. (dir. 1977-79), Am. Coll. Hosp. Adminstrs., Am. Hosp. Assn., Cath. Hosp. Assn., Hosp. Fin. Mgmt. Assn., Hosp. Trustees N.Y. State, Nat. Assn. Female Execs., Hudson Hosp. Council, Met. N.Y. Hosp. Fin. Assn., Acad. for Cath. Health Care Leadership, Internat. Health Econs. and Mgmt. Inst. Office: Gilbert Tweed Assoc 630 3d Ave New York NJ 10017

STRAUGHN, CLAIRE VALENCIA LEE, airline official; b. N.Y.C., June 18, 1953; d. William and Marjorie Media (Hoyt) S. BA in Polit. Sci., Bklyn. Coll., 1976, MA in Sociology, 1982. Asst. dir. Prison Reform in Devel. Edn., N.Y.C., 1973-75; researcher N.Y. Pub. Interest Research Group, N.Y.C., 1976; claims developer Social Security Adminstrn., N.Y.C., 1978-83; sales rep. Delta Airlines, Inc., N.Y.C., 1983—. Mem. Sheepshead Bay Citizen Action Com., Bklyn. Democrat. Baptist. Home: 3573 Nostrand Ave Apt 2-D Brooklyn NY 11229

STRAUS, ELLEN SULZBERGER, broadcast executive; b. N.Y.C., Mar. 11, 1925; d. David Hays and Louise (Blumenthal) S.; m. R. Peter Straus, Feb. 6, 1950; children—Diane Straus Tucker, Katherine Straus Caple, Jeanne Straus Tofel, Eric. B.A., Smith Coll., 1945; D.Comml. Sci. (hon.), St. John's U., 1985; L.H.D. (hon.), Franklin Pierce Coll., 1985. Program sec. N.Y.C. LWV, 1945-48; asst. dir. public info. U.S. AEC, 1948-49; campaign mgr. Herbert Lehman for Senate, 1949; fgn. corr. No. N.Y. newspapers, 1950-55; editor McCall's mag., N.Y.C., 1973-76; v.p. Sta. WMCA, 1976, pres., 1985—; chmn. exec. com. N.Y.C. partnership. Author: A Smith College Mosaic, 1974, A Survival Kit for New Yorkers, 1973, The Volunteer Professional: What You Need to Know, 1972, Women's Almanac, 1976, Women Behind Bars (broadcast series on prison reform 1983-84); monthly column McCall's mag, 1972-74. Pres., chairperson Nat. Call for Action, Inc., 1969-75; founder Vol. Profl., Inc., N.Y.C., 1970; aux. policeperson Mounted, Central Park precinct, 1974-77; chmn. pub. safety com. N.Y.C. Partnership, 1981; chmn. communications com. Pres.' Task Force on Pvt. Sector Initiatives, 1982; mem. adv. panel innovation tech. and regional econ. devel. Office of Tech., U.S. Congress, 1983; moderator Corp. in Contemporary Soc. Aspen Inst., 1983; mem. selection com. Dively Bus. award Harvard U., 1985; mem. The Bishop Desmond Tutu So. Africa Refugee Scholarship Program, 1985; mem. State-City Commn. on Integrity in Govt., 1986; mem. site selection com. Democratic Nat. Com., 1986; auxilary police person, 1986. Recipient Woman of Conscience award, 1970, Hannah G. Solomon award, 1972, Nat. Council Jewish Women; recipient Louise Waterman Wise award Am. Jewish Congress, 1971,Medal of Honor Smith Coll., 1971, Am. Inst. Public Service award, 1974, B'nai B'rith Women Dist. One award, 1976; Consumer Crusader award Caveat Emptor Mag., 1978, Abram L. Sachar award Brandeis U., 1980, Amita Golden Lady achievement award, 1981, award for excellence Soc. for Advancement of Travel for the Handicapped, 1982, Olive award Council of Chs. of City of N.Y., 1983, Radio award Am. Women in Radio and TV, 1984, Caring New Yorker award Community Coucil Greater N.Y., 1986, Buddy award Legal Def. Fund NOW, 1987; named Woman of Yr. Ladies Home Jour., 1973, Woman of Outstanding Achievement Women's Equity Action League, 1984. Democrat. Jewish. Office: 1414 Ave of Americas New York NY 10019

STRAUSS, ANNETTE, mayor, public relations consultant; b. Houston, Jan. 26, 1924; d. Jacob B. and Edith (Weinberger) Greenfield; m. Theodore H. Strauss, Sept. 8, 1946; children: Nancy Strauss Halbreich, Janie Strauss McGarr. Student, Rice U., 1940-41; BA in Sociology, U. Tex., 1944; MA in Sociology and Psychology, Columbia U., 1945. Mayor City of Dallas, 1987—. Trustee John F. Kennedy Ctr. Performing Arts; chmn. nat. council Friends of Kennedy Ctr.; devel. bd. U. Tex, Dallas Inst. Humanities & Culture; chmn. bd. TACA; bd. dirs. nat com. Arts with Handicapped, Dallas Symphony Orch., St. Paul hops. Found., Nat. Jewish Hosp., Children's Med. Ctr., Nat. Council Am. Jewish Com., Dallas Vol. Ctr., Dallas UN Assn., Creative Learning Ctr. Dallas, Jewish Fedn. Dallas, Timberlawn Found., Dallas Black Dance Theater, Community Chest Fund, Operation Lift, Women's Ctr. Dallas County; fundraiser for such programs as Downtown Dallas Family Shelter, U. Tex. Health Sci. Ctr., Dallas Assn. Retarded Citizens, Majestic Theatre, Dallas County Heart Found. Fund; former bd. mem. Dallas com. ARC, Planned Parenthood Dallas, Dallas Theater Ctr., Dallas Mcpl. Library Bd., others. Recipient John F. Kennedy Commitment to Excellence award, Headliner's award Press Club, Pro Bene Meritis award U. Tex., James K. Wilson award Dallas Performing Arts, Humanitarian award Nat. Jewish Hosp., Linz award, Brotherhood award Conf. Christians and Jews, Human Relations awards Am. Jewish Com., Zonta award, Arete award; named Women of Yr., Nat. Jewish Hosp.; named to Honor Roll of Vol. Women, Town and Country mag. Mem. Dallas C. of C. (steering com. Leadership Dallas), Dallas Arboretum Soc., Dallas Hist. Soc. Office: Office of the Mayor 1500 Marilla 5EN Dallas TX 75201

STRAUSS, DIANE C., librarian, educator, writer; b. Milw., Feb. 14, 1943; d. Charles Clifton and Olga (Bondeli) Wheeler; m. Robert P. Strauss, Nov. 26, 1969 (div. 1973). BS, U. Wis., Milw., 1966; MS in Library Sci., U. Wis., 1967. Young adult librarian Enoch Pratt Free Library, Balt., 1967-68; materials analyst U. Wis., Madison, 1968-69; legis. librarian Dept. Labor Library, Washington, 1970-72; social scis. librarian U. N.C., Chapel Hill, 1972-75, head bus. adminstrn./social scis. reference dept., 1975—; adj. instr. U. N.C. Sch. Library Sci., Chapel Hill, 1985—. Author: Handbook of Business Information, 1988; also articles. Mem. ALA, Spl. Libraries Assn. (pres. N.C. chpt. 1980-81), N.C. Online Users Group (pres. 1978). Office: U NC Davis Library CB #3912 Chapel Hill NC 27599

STRAUSS, DOROTHY BRANDFON, marital and family therapist; b. Bklyn.; d. Marcus and Beatrice (Wilson) Brandfon; widowed; 1 child, Josette Strauss Elliott. BA, Bklyn. Coll., 1932; MA, NYU, 1937, PhD, 1963. Cert. clin. supr.; cert. marital, family and sex therapist. Instr. Hunter Coll. CUNY, 1960-63; prof. Kean Coll., Union, N.J., 1963-77; pvt. practice and clin. supervision Bklyn. and, N.J., 1970—; researcher NIMH U. Pa., Phila., 1973-82; clin. assoc. prof. psychiatry, Ctr. for Human Sexuality, Downstate Med. Ctr. SUNY, Bklyn., 1974—, assoc. dir. 1974-82; cons. gerontology, 1977—. Contbr. articles on gerontology to profl. jours. Mem. Am. Assn. for Marital and Family Therapy (clin. mem. 1971—, supr. 1981), Am. Assn. Sex Therapists, Counselors and Educators (chairperson task force on supervision 1984-86, chairperson supr. cert. com. 1986—), Am. Psychol. Assn., Kappa Delta Pi, Lambda Delta Theta, Sigma Phi Omega. Home and Office: 1401 Ocean Ave Brooklyn NY 11230

STRAUSS-SONKIN, ANDREA CORRIN, executive; b. Bklyn., Dec. 29, 1959; d. Harvey and Joan (Wolin) Strauss; m. Mark Alan Sonkin, Mar. 21, 1957. Grad. in travel, tourism, Taylor Bus. Sch., 1978-79. Travel agt. Jericho (N.Y.) Travel, 1978-79; group coordinator Group Cons., Inc., Glen Cove, N.Y., 1979-80; dir. Leslie Travel Co., Closter, N.J., 1980-87; pres., chief operating officer Conf. Creators, Inc., Hackensack, N.J., 1987—; telex/time wire transmission operator Western Union, Hempstead, N.Y., 1979; sabre trained agt. Am. Airlines, Inc., Dallas, 1979. Named Profl. Meeting Planner Pointe of Excellence, 1986, 88, Launch of Coact Johnson & Johnson, 1985, 86. Office: Conf Creators Inc 401 Hackensack Ave Hackensack NJ 07601

STRAW, CLAUDIA AUSTIN, accountant; b. Norfolk, Va., Sept. 15, 1955; d. Erle H. Austin and Flora (Old) Dunham; child by previous marriage, Wesley; m. Michael Allen Straw, Aug. 28, 1981. BS in Bus. Adminstrn., Old Dominion U., 1977. CPA, Fla. Staff acct. McDonald's Corp., St. Petersburg, Fla., 1979-82; supr., staff acct. Gregory, Sharer, Quinn, et al, St. Petersburg, 1982-85; acct. Foelgner and Ronz, P.A., St. Petersburg, 1985-88; ptnr. Foelgner, Ronz, Simone & Straw P.A., St. Petersburg, 1988—. Vol. Ronald McDonald House, St. Petersburg. Mem. Am. Inst. CPA's, Nat. Assn. Accts. (bd. dirs. Suncoast chpt. 1986—, outstanding contbr. 1985-86), Fla. Inst. CPA's, Bus. and Profl. Women Assn., Gulf Coast Exec. Women, Nat. Assn. Exec. Women, Old Dominion U. Alumni. Episcopalian. Club: Bally Health (Clearwater, Fla.). Office: Foelgner Ronz Simone & Straw 1700 66th St N PO 40888 Saint Petersburg FL 33743

STRAWINSKY, ELIZABETH ROWE, psychiatrist; b. Gainesville, Fla., Aug. 31, 1925; d. Albert Reed and Elizabeth Ellen (Rowe) Caro; B.S., Coll. William and Mary, 1948; M.D., Med. Coll. Va., 1948; m. Albert Strawinsky, Dec. 28, 1957. Intern, St. Elizabeths Hosp., Washington, 1948-49, resident in psychiatry, 1949-52, clin. dir., 1962-69, dir. forensic [illegible]ams, 1969-73; psychiatrist No. Va. Mental Health Inst., Falls Church, [illegible]—. Recipient Superior Performance award, HEW, 1962. Diplomate Am. Bd. Psychiatry and Neurology. Fellow Am. Psychiat. Assn.; mem. Med. Soc. Va., Washington Psychiat. Soc., Am. Acad. Psychiatry and Law, Am. Group Psychotherapy Assn., Am. Med. Women's Assn., N.Y. Acad. Scis. Democrat. Home: 16000 Bealle Hill Rd Accokeek MD 20607 Office: 3302 Gallows Rd Falls Church VA 22042

STRAWN, FRANCES FREELAND, real estate executive; b. Waynesville, N.C., Nov. 18, 1946; d. Thomas M. and Jimmie (Smith) Freeland; m. David Updegraff Strawn, Aug. 30, 1974; children: Laurel, Kirk, Trisha. AA, Brevard Community Coll., Cocoa, Fla., 1976; postgrad. U. Cen. Fla., 1976-77. acting sr. buyer Brevard County Purchasing Bd. of County Commns., Titusville, Fla., 1971-75; research analyst Brevard Community Coll., Cocoa, 1977-78; realtor assoc., Orlando, Fla., 1979-82; realtor, broker, pres. Advance Am., Inc., Orlando, 1982—. bd. dirs. Vol. Ctr. of Cen. Fla.; program chmn. Young Rep. Women, Orlando, 1983; coordinator Congressman Bill Nelson's Washington Internship Program; co-ticket chmn. Art and Architecture Orlando Regional Hosp.; mem. steering com. Fla. Heritage Homecoming, Orlando, 1987; sec. Mayor's Wife's Campaign Activities, Orlando, 1986-87; bd. dirs. Vol Ctr. Cen. Fla.; vice chmn. Horizon Exec. Bd.; recording sec. Women's Bus. Edn. Council, 1988, mem. adv. bd. , 1987, bd. dirs. 1988—; active calendar com. Women's Resource Ctr.; lectr. Jr. Achievement Mem. Orange County Bar Auxilliary (bd. dirs. 1986-88, corresponding sec. 1987), Creative Bus. Ownership for Women (adv. bd. 1986—), Nat. Assn. Realtors, Orlando Bd. Realtors (grievance com. 1985—), Fla. Assn. Govt. Purchasing (asst. membership chmn. 1971-75), Orlando Area Bd. Realtors (membership com. 1980-84, profl. standards com. 1983-84, lectr. Success Series), Women's Council of Realtors, Women's Exec. Council. Episcopalian. Club: Citrus (Orlando) (social com. 1987—). Avocations: travel, needlepoint, counted cross stitch, canoe trips, backpacking. Home: 121 N Ivanhoe Blvd Orlando FL 32804 Office: Advance Am Inc 1305 E Robinson St Orlando FL 32801

STREAM, PATRICIA ANN, healthcare care consulting company executive; b. Kansas City, Mo., May 3, 1947; d. Roy L. and Lyna H. Fry; m. John A. Stream, May 29, 1971; children: John Jr., Joshua, Amanda. BS in Nursing, U. Calif., 1969; MSEd, Va. Tech., 1983. Staff nurse Downey (Calif.) Community Hosp., 1969-70; staff nurse Alexandria (Va.) Hosp., 1970-71, head nurse, 1971-72, asst. dir. nursing, 1972-76, dir. edn. and tng., 1976-83; exec. dir. Nursing Mgmt. Systems, Washington, 1983-85; v.p. Health M Connection, Falls Church, Va., 1985-88; pres. Stream & Assocs., Woodbridge, Va., 1988—. Contbr. articles to profl. jours. Mem. Am. Soc. Healthcare Edn. and Tng. of Am. Hosp. Assn. (bd. dirs. Va. chpt. 1979-83, nat. bd. dir. 1985—, Distinguished Achievement award 1979, 84, Outstanding Mem. award 1982, Mentorship 1986). Methodist. Office: Health M Connection 11951 Governors Rd Woodbridge VA 22192

STREBEIGH, BARBARA, organization administrator, editor; b. Rye, N.Y., July 29, 1902; d. Harold Strebeigh and Blanche (Pierce) Bonaparte. Student Sargent Sch. Phys. Edn. (now Boston U.), 1923; sculpture student of Alexander Archipenko, 1940-41; student U. Calif.-San Diego Extension, 1924-25. Mem. phys. therapy staff U.S. Marine Hosp., San Francisco, 1923-24; head dept. field hockey Sargent Coll. Camp, N.H., 20 yrs.; dir. Firefly Diabetic Camp for Children, Pa., 1949; from sec. to v.p. to pres. Airedale Terrier Club Am., 1948-85, hon. pres., dir. 1985—; dog show judge, 1950—; bd. dirs. Animal Rescue League, Phila., 1975—. Author: Pet Airedale Terrier, 1960; Your Airedale. Editor newsletters for Airedale Terrier Club Am., 1948-85; contbr. to field hockey guides; columnist for various dog mags. Exhibitor terracotta sculpture in galleries. Mem. All-Am. Hockey Team, 1928-40. Mem. U.S. Field Hockey Assn. (sec. 1937-40, originator former editor Eagle, named to field hockey Hall of Fame, 1988). Republican. Episcopalian. Home: Beaver Hill Rd Birchrunville PA 19421

STREDDE, SHARON, community foundation executive; b. Aurora, Ill., May 24, 1946; m. Edward H. Stredde, Jan. 24, 1969; 1 child, Robert E. BA, U. Ill., 1968. Asst. to State Rep. Sue Deuchler, Aurora, 1980-82; devel. coordinator YWCA, Aurora, 1982-83; corp. sec. Aurora Found., 1986-87, exec. dir., 1987—. Mem. Coop. Planning and Budgeting, Aurora, Aurora Area Fundraisers; bd. dirs. YWCA, Aurora, 1983-86; mem. bd. edn. West Aurora, Ill., 1985—. Mem. Aurora C. of C. Republican. Congregational. Club: AAUW (Aurora) (asst. treas. 1985-86). Lodge: Rotary. Office: Aurora Found 111 W Downer Pl #312 Aurora IL 60506

STREEP, MERYL (MARY LOUISE STREEP), actress; b. Madison, N.J., June 22, 1949; d. Harry Jr. and Mary W. Streep; m. Donald J. Gummer, 1978; children: Henry, Mary Willa, Grace Jane. BA, Vassar Coll., 1971; MFA, Yale U., 1975, DFA (hon.), 1983; DFA (hon.), Dartmouth Coll., 1981. Ind. actress stage, screen 1975—. Appeared with Green Mountain Guild, Woodstock, Vt.; Broadway debut in Trelawny of the Wells, Lincoln Center Beaumont Theater, 1975; N.Y.C. theatrical appearances include 27 Wagons Full of Cotton (Theatre World award), A Memory of Two Mondays, Henry V, Secret Service, The Taming of the Shrew, Measure for Measure, The Cherry Orchard, Happy End, Wonderland, Taken in Marriage, Alice in Concert (Obie award 1981); movie appearances include Julia, 1977, The Deer Hunter, 1978 (Best Supporting Actress award Nat. Soc. Film Critics), Manhattan, 1979, The Seduction of Joe Tynan, 1979, Kramer vs. Kramer, 1980 (N.Y. Film Critics' award, Los Angeles Film Critics' award, both for best actress, Golden Globe award, Acad. award for best supporting actress), The French Lieutenant's Woman, 1981 (Los Angeles Film Critics award for best actress, Brit. Acad. award, Golden Globe award 1981), Sophie's Choice, 1982 (Acad. award for best actress, Los Angeles Film Critics award for best actress, Golden Globe award 1982), Still of the Night, 1982, Silkwood, 1983, Falling in Love, 1984, Plenty, 1985, Out of Africa, 1985 (Los Angeles Film Critics award for best actress 1985), Heartburn, 1986, Ironweed, 1987; TV film The Deadliest Season, 1977; TV mini-series Holocaust, 1978 (Emmy award); TV dramatic spls. Secret Service, 1977, Uncommon Women and Others, 1978. Recipient Mademoiselle award, 1976, Woman of Yr. award B'nai Brith, 1979, Woman of Yr. award Hasty Pudding Soc., Harvard U., 1980, Best Supporting Actress award Nat. Bd. of Rev., 1979, Best Actress award Nat. Bd. of Rev., 1982, Star of Yr. award Nat. Assn. Theater Owners, 1983, People's Choice award, 1983, 85, 86, 87. Office: care Internat Creative Mgmt 40 W 57th St New York NY 10019

STREET, DEBORAH DAISEY, social worker; b. Lewes, Del., June 8, 1957; d. William Harrison and Shirley Corinne (Street) Daisey; m. Gordon William Street, June 21, 1982; 1 child, Dwayne William. BA in Psychology, U. Del., 1979; MSW, Del. State Coll., 1986. Social worker State of Del., Newark, 1979, Dover, 1979-87; social worker, case mgr. State of Del., Milford, 1987—; houseparent part-time Aid to Dover, 1980-84; parent instr. Child Inc., Wilmington, Del. 1988—; social worker De. Adolescent Program, Inc., Dover, 1984-85. Trainer Girl Scouts Am., Chesapeake Bay council, Dover, 1985—. Democrat. Methodist. Lodge: Lioness (bd. dirs. 1988—). Home: RD 4 Box 111A Dover DE 19901 Office: State of Del 11-13 Church St Milford DE 19963

STREETER, ANNE PAUL, state senator; b. Phila., July 21, 1926; s. Henry Neill and Marianne (Harris) Paul; m. Ronald Mather Streeter; children—Jean, Deborah, Stephen, Richard, Jonathan. B.A., Smith Coll., 1948. Tchr. Springside Sch., Phila., 1948-1949, Oxford Sch., West Hartford, Conn., 1949-1950; mem. Conn. Senate, Hartford, 1982-87, dep. majority leader, 1985-87. Mem. West Hartford Town Council, 1973-81, mayor, 1975-81. Named Woman of Year, Jr. C. of C., West Hartford, 1979, Hartford, 1981. Mem. LWV (pres. 1966-67, 1969-72). Republican. Congregationalist. Home: 31 Brookmoor Rd West Hartford CT 06107 Office: Senate State of Conn State Capitol Room 318 Hartford CT 06106

STREIFF, BARBARA JEAN, small business owner; b. Chgo., Mar. 10, 1941; d. Robert Lee and Irene Rosetta (Scott) M.; children from previous marriage: Angela Denise Hopson, Lori Ann Alexander, Bonnie Jean Pettway, George L. Evans II; m. Michael Lee Streiff, July 2, 1987. AS, Joliet Coll., 1977. Customer service rep. No. Ill. Gas Co., Palos Heights, 1967-71; sales coordinator Maday Wholesale Greenhouse, Calumet City, Ill., 1978-82; asst. mgr. Rainbow Rent-a-Car, Honolulu, 1982-83; reservations mgr. Oceans Travel, Inc., Honolulu, 1983-86; owner The Alternative...In Travel, Honolulu, 1986—; owner The Plant Lady, Park Forest, Ill., 1978-81. Contbr. articles on plant care to profl. jours., 1979-82. Mem. Hawaii Visitor's Bur. Republican. Office: The Alternative...In Travel 2424 Koa Ave Honolulu HI 96815

STREISAND, BARBRA JOAN, singer, actress; b. Bklyn., Apr. 24, 1942; d. Emanuel and Diana (Rosen) S.; m. Elliott Gould, Mar. 1963 (div.); 1 son, Jason Emanuel. Student, Yeshiva of Bklyn. N.Y. theatre debut Another Evening with Harry Stoones, 1961; appeared in Broadway musical I Can Get

It for You Wholesale, 1962, Funny Girl, 1964-65; rec. artist Columbia Records; motion pictures include Funny Girl, 1968, Hello Dolly, 1969, On a Clear Day You Can See Forever, 1970, The Owl and the Pussy Cat, 1970, What's Up Doc?, 1972, Up the Sandbox, 1972, The Way We Were, 1973, For Pete's Sake, 1974, Funny Lady, 1975, The Main Event, 1979, All Night Long, 1981, Nuts, 1987; star, producer film A Star is Born, 1976; producer, dir., star Yentl, 1983; TV spls. include My Name is Barbra, 1965 (5 Emmy awards), Color Me Barbra, 1966; Gold record albums include People, 1965, My Name is Barbra, 1965, Color Me Barbra, 1966, Stoney End, 1971, Barbra Joan Streisand, 1972, The Way We Were, 1974, A Star is Born, 1976, Superman, 1977, The Stars Salute Israel at 30, 1978, Wet, 1979, (with Barry Gibb) Guilty, 1980, Emotion, 1984, The Broadway Album, 1986. Recipient Emmy award, CBS-TV spl. (My Name Is Barbra), 1964, Acad. award as best actress (Funny Girl), 1968, Golden Globe award (Funny Girl), 1969, co-recipient Acad. award for best song (Evergreen), 1976, Georgie award AGVA 1977, Grammy awards for best female pop vocalist, 1963, 64, 65, 77, 86, for best song writer (with Paul Williams),1977, Tony award (spl.award), 1970. •

STRENGTH, JANIS GRACE, educator; b. Ozark, Ala., Jan. 31, 1934; d. James Marion and Mary Belle (Riley) Grace; m. Robert Samuel Strength, Sept. 12, 1954; children: Stewart A., James Houston (dec.), Robert David (dec.), James Steven (dec.). BS in Home Econs. and Edn., Auburn U., 1956; MA in Edn., Washington U., St. Louis, 1978, MA in Adminstrn., 1980. Home economist Gulf Power Co., Pensacola, Fla., 1956-59; tchr. sci. Northside Jr. High Sch., Greenwood, S.C., 1961-68; tchrs. home econs. Greenwood High Sch., 1968-70; chairperson dept. sci. Parkway West Jr. High Sch., Chesterfield, Mo., 1975-82; tchr. sci. Parkway West High Sch., Chesterfield, 1982—; chairperson dist. Phys. Scis. Curriculum Com., 1978-85, Sci. Fair Placement Com., 1978-82, Gifted Edn., 1983-84; leader Phys. Sci. Summer Workshops, Safety Sci. Lab. Workshop; sponsor Nat. Jr. Honor Soc., Parkway West Jr. Class. Supt. youth dept. Sunday sch. Greentrails Meth. Ch., sponsor summer camp; vol. fundraiser March of Dimes, Cerebral Palsy, Multiple Schlorosis, Cancer funds; judge Parkway/Monsanto/St. Louis Post Dispatch Sci. Fairs, 1978—; mem. citizens action com. Parkway Sch. Bd., 1980-84. Mem. NEA, Nat. Sci. Tchrs. Assn. Republican. Methodist. Clubs: Greenwood Country, Cherry Hills Country (Glencoe, Mo.); Raintree Country (Hillsboro, Mo.). Office: Parkway West High Sch Clayton Rd Chesterfield MO 63017

STRETCH, SHIRLEY MARIE, marketing educator; b. Wauneta, Nebr., May 6, 1949; d. Lloyd Ray and Roberta Marie (Schroeder) S.; BS, U. Nebr., 1971; MS, Kans. State U., 1972; MBA, Ohio State U., 1977, PhD, 1982. Instr. clothing and textiles Bowling Green (Ohio) State U., 1972-75; grad. adminstrv. asso. Univ. Coll., Ohio State U., 1976-78, 80; asso. mgr. direct mktg. div. Ashland Petroleum Co. (Ky.), 1979-80; asst. prof. clothing and textiles Tex. Tech U., Lubbock, 1980-85; assoc. prof. mktg. Valdosta State Coll., Ga., 1985-87, Calif. State U., Los Angeles, 1987—. Pres., mem. bd. adminstrn. Sunport Condominium. Ednl. Profl. Devel. fellow, 1971-73. Mem. Am. Mktg. Assn., Lubbock Assn. MBA Execs., Nat. Assn. Female Execs., Am. Home Econs. Assn., So. Mktg. Assn., Southwestern Mktg. Assn., Am. Collegiate Retailing Assn., Omicron Nu, Phi Upsilon Omicron. Republican. Methodist. Club: Toastmasters. Home: 9607 E Longden Ave Temple City CA 91780 Office: Calif State U Dept Mktg Los Angeles CA 90032

STRICKER, RUTH ANN, fitness center owner and director; b. Mitchell, S.D., Mar. 12, 1935; d. Peter August and Eleanor (Ellinger) DeBeer; m. David Dean Stricker, Dec. 26, 1958 (div. 1985); children: Kimberly Ann, Mark David. BS, Macalester Coll., 1957. Studied dance and performed professionally U. Hawaii; camp dir. YWCA, Chgo., pvt. girls' camp, Brainerd, Minn.; owner Ruth Stricker's Fitness Unltd., Minnetonka, Minn., 1970-84; owner, dir. Ruth Stricker's The Marsh, Minnetonka, 1984—; adj. prof. St. Mary's Coll., St. Paul, 1987; facilitator Ann. Itasca Conf., Brainerd, 1984—; advisor nat. fitness program Boy's Clubs of Am.; also lectr. and presenter events nationally. Creator registered exercise method Fitness Unltd., 1975. Trustee, Macalester Coll., St. Paul; past bd. dirs. YWCA of Mpls.; mem. Mpls. Urban League, Jr. League Mpls., Minn. Women's Consortium; elder St. Luke Presbyn. Ch., Wayzata, Minn. Recipient Recognition award Mpls. YWCA, 1985, Woman of Achievement honoree Twin Cities West C. of C., 1979, 81, Disting. Citizen Citation, Macalester Coll., St. Paul, 1987. Mem. Am. Soc. Profl. and Exec. Men, Assn. Female Execs., Am. Coll. Sports Medicine, Internat. Dance Exercise Assn., Internat. Racquet Sports Assn., Women's Sports Found., Twin West C. of C., Better Bus. Bur. Presbyterian. Lodge: P.E.O. (pres. 1968-70). Home: 18125 Shavers Ln Wayzata MN 55391 Office: Ruth Stricker's The Marsh 15000 Minnetonka Blvd Minnetonka MN 55345

STRICKLAND, ANITA MAURINE, retired teacher, librarian; b. Groom, Tex., Sept. 24, 1923; d. Oliver Austin and Thelma May (Slay) Pool; m. LeRoy Graham Mashburn, Aug. 12, 1945 (dec. Mar. 1977); 1 child, Ronald Gene; m. Reid Strickland, May 27, 1978. BBA, West Tex. State U., 1962, MEd, 1965; postgrad. in library sci., Tex. Women's U., 1970. Cert. tchr., Tex.; cert. librarian. Employment inteviewer Douglas Aircraft Co., Oklahoma City, 1942-45; cashier, bookkeeper Southwestern Pub. Services, Groom and Panhandle, Tex., 1950-58; acct. Gen. Motors Outlet, Groom, 1958-62; tchr. bus., lang. arts Groom Pub. Schs., 1962-68; bus. tchr., librarian Amarillo (Tex.) Pub. Schs., 1968-81. Vol. Amarillo Symphony, 1980—, Rep. Party, Amarillo, 1981—, Lone Star Ballet, 1981—; docent Amarillo Art Ctr., 1981—, sec., 1987—. Mem. AAUW (legis. com. 1986—), Amarillo C. of C. (vol. women's div. 1981—). Baptist. Home: 6513 Roxton Amarillo TX 79109

STRICKLAND, BUNNY JUMP, caterer, accountant, bridal consultant; b. Athens, Ga., Apr. 12, 1925; d. Claude Arthur and Myrtle Florence (Barnwell) Jump; m. Warren Davis Strickland, Dec. 22, 1945; children—Warren David, Jacque Bonita Niles. A.A., Mercer U., 1969. Bookkeeper Firestone Tires, Jesup, Ga., 1950-61, Rural Electric Assn., Jesup, 1964-67, Jones Ford, Jesup, 1967-69, Wayne TV, Jesup, 1969-82; cosmetologist Laurie's, Jesup, 1961-64; contract caterer ITT-Rayonier, Jesup, 1980—; caterer, food service cons., Jesup, 1982—; bridal cons., floral designer, cake designer, gown seamstress, Jesup, 1962—. Asst. chmn. Bloodmobile Procurement Team, 1958; chmn. fund raising com. PTA, 1958; campaign aide Jones for Ga. Ho. Reps., 1955; hostess Thomas for U.S. Congress, 1982; pres. Band Boosters, 1961; chmn. benevolent com. 1st Bapt. Ch., 1968-75, dir. Sunday Schs., 1956- 68, tchr., 1978—; active Hosp. Aux., Jesup. Winner 1st place in class, Body Building Competition, Dalton, Ga., 1983, 3rd place overall, 1983; placed 2nd Paper Chase Mile Run, 1983. Mem. AAU. Democrat. Club: Jesup Garden (sec. 1974-78, pres. 1977-81). Lodge: Eastern Star. Avocations: oil painting; cooking; sewing; running; body building.

STRICKLAND, CHARLOTTE ROZIER, mortgage banker; b. West Palm Beach, Fla., Dec. 21, 1953; d. Ralph R. and Rebecca (Tromp) Rozier; m. J. Ray Strickland, May 23, 1986. Grad. high sch. Customer service rep. SCN Bank, Columbia, S.C., 1972-74; loan processor Collateral Investment Co., Columbia, 1974-78; br. mgr. Mortgage Corp. of South, Columbia, 1978-82; asst. v.p. Colonial Mortgage Co., Columbia, 1982-87; sr. loan originator Sun Mortage Corp., Columbia S.C., 1987—; fee examiner HUD, Columbia, 1983—. Named an Outstanding Woman of Yr., Heritage World, Columbia, 1981. Mem. Mortgage Bankers Carolinas, Greater Columbia Mortgage Bankers (pres. 1982). Home: 1200 Princeton St Columbia SC 29205

STRICKLAND, HEIDI J., nurse; b. Jamestown, N.Y., Nov. 2, 1946; d. Cecil Eugene and Lena Betty (Luce) Jarrett; m. Ernest Gary Strickland, June 17, 1967; 1 child, Jaret E. AAS, Jamestown Community Coll., 1966; cert. nurse Practitioner, U. Rochester, 1974. Asst. head nurse Brooks Meml. Hosp., Dunkirk, N.Y., 1967-70; clinic nurse Hans Raag, M.D., Forestville, N.Y., 1970-78; nurse practitioner Sugar Grove (Pa.) Med. Ctr., 1978-84; ptnr. Sugar Grove Pharmacy, 1978-84; ind. med. nurse practitioner Jamestown, N.Y., 1984—; owner, mgr., pres. Cassadaga (N.Y.) Pharmacy, Inc., 1984—. Mem. N.Y. State Coalition of Nurse Practitioners (treas. 1985—), U.S. Power Squadron (sec. 1985—), U.S. Tennis Assn. (1983). Democrat. Office: WCA Hosp 207 Foote Ave Jamestown NY 14701

STRICKLAND, NANCY ARNETTE STANLEY, finance executive; b. Smithfield, N.C., Nov. 18, 1949; d. William Bennette and Lola (Holley) Stanley; m. Matthew Theodore Strickland, Dec. 20, 1975; 1 child, William Scott. BS in Math. Edn., N.C. State U., 1972; MBA, U. N.C., 1975. Tchr math. Johnston County High Sch., Smithfield, N.C., 1972-73; office mgr. J.W. Simons, Raleigh, N.C., 1975-76; tchr. math. Cath. High Sch., Pensacola, Fla., 1976-79; fin. analyst Hardee's Food Systems, Inc., Rocky Mount, N.C., 1980-81, sr. fin. analyst, 1981-82, mgr. corp. analysis, 1982-83, dir. corp. planning, 1983-84, dir. fin. planning and analysis, 1984-86, corp. dir. fin., 1986—; mem. corp. contbns. com. Imasco U.S.A., Inc., Rocky Mount, 1984—, mem. exec. adv. bd., 1985—. Mem. Dental Aux., Rocky Mount, 1979—, Nash County Hist. Soc., 1982—, Friends of the Arts, Rocky Mount, 1983—, N.C. Mus. History Assocs., Raleigh, 1984—, Local Area Women's Network, Rocky Mount, 1984—; mem. budget and allocations com. Rocky Mount United Way, 1984-86; mem. exec. com. N.C. Young Dems., Raleigh, 1972-73; mem. fin. com. Rocky Mount Meth. Ch., 1985—. Mem. Nat. Assn. Female Execs., Pi Mu Epsilon, Phi Kappa Phi. Clubs: YWCA, Pilot (Rocky Mount) (v.p. 1984-85). Office: Hardee's Food Systems Inc 1233 N Church St Rocky Mount NC 27801

STRICKLER, DIANA HOLE, investment banker; b. N.Y.C., July 25, 1951; d. Richard Witherspoon and Tacey (Belden) Hole; m. Richard Stoner Strickler Jr., June 11, 1977; children: Maragret Evans Hennen, William Belden. Student Wellesley Coll., 1969-71; B.A., magna cum laude, Williams Coll., 1973; M.B.A., Columbia U., 1979.Comml. officer First Pa. Bank, Phila., 1974-77; cons. Booz Allen & Hamilton, N.Y.C., 1978; v.p. mortgage fin. dept. First Boston Corp., N.Y.C., 1979—. Trustee Williams Coll., 1977-81; bd. dirs. Columbia Bus. Sch. Alumni Assn. Mem. Phi Beta Kappa, Beta Gamma Sigma. Republican. Mem. Reformed Ch. Clubs: Siwanoy Country (Bronxville, N.Y.), Bronxville Field; Madison Beach. Home: 10 The Byway Bronxville NY 10708

STRIKER, JOY ELLEN, quality assurance executive; b. Bucyrus, Ohio, June 12, 1959; d. Arvin Richard and Carol Jean (Speweike) S. AAS Plastics Tech., Ferris State U., 1979, BS in Plastics Tech. Engr., 1984; MBA, New Hampshire Coll., 1988. Mfg. engr. Gen. Motors Steering Gear, Saginaw, Mich., 1978; reliability engr. Kenner Products, Cin., 1979-82; chem. engr. Diamond Shamrock, Cleve., 1982-83; shift supr. Owens-Ill., Newburyport, Mass., 1984-85, quality assurance supr., 1985-87; supr. quality assurance Owens-Brockway, Vacaville, Calif., 1987—. Mem. Soc. Plastic Engrs., Soc. Mfg. Engrs., Am. Soc. Quality Control. Home: 903 Scottsdale Dr Vacaville CA 95688 Office: Owens Brockway 2500 Huntington Fairfield CA 94533

STRINE, NANCY SHAW, municipal administrator; b. Hagerstown, Md., Dec. 10, 1957; d. James F. and Virginia (Messersmith) S. BA in Polit. Sci. cum laude, U. S.C., 1979, M of Pub. Adminstrn. magna cum laude, 1984. Research asst. S.C. State Legislature, Columbia, 1979-80, senate page, 1980; grad. asst. U. S.C., Columbia, 1981-82; legis. liaison, fiscal analyst Fiscal Planning Services, Inc., Washington, 1982; alumni coordinator, fund raiser Sewickley (Pa.) Acad., 1983; community devel. block grant coordinator City of Hagerstown, 1984-86, mgr. Dept. Community Devel., 1987—. Mem. Washington County Hist. Soc., 1985—, Community Housing Resources Bd., Inc., 1985—; Washington County Homebuilders Assn., 1985—, Hist. Preservation Council, Hagerstown, 1985—, Washington County Commn. Women, 1987—, Washington County Task Force for the Homeless, 1987—, Nat. Trust for Hist. Preservation, 1985—; sponsor Citizens Assisting the Sheltered and Abused, Inc., Hagerstown, 1984—, Community Action Council, Inc., Hagerstown, 1984—. Named one of Outstanding Young Women of Am., 1985. Mem. Am. Soc. Pub. Adminstrs., Md. Assn. Housing and Redevel., Nat. Assn. Housing and Redevel. Ofcls., Nat. Assn. Female Execs., Jaycees, Rho Lambda (founder, 1st pres. U. S.C. chpt. 1978-79), Omicron Delta Kappa, Pi Beta Phi, Mortar Bd. Republican. Methodist. Lodge: Zonta. Office: City of Hagerstown 1 East Franklin St Hagerstown MD 21740

STRIN-GOLD, LAURIE MICHELLE, municipal government professional; b. Los Angeles, May 31, 1961; d. Marvin Arthur and Marilyn Barbara (Cohen) Strin; m. Harold Benjamin Gold, Mar. 20, 1983. BS in Polit. Sci., So. Meth. U., 1982, M of Pub. Adminstrn., 1985. Adminstrv. intern City of University Park, Tex., 1983-84; mgmt. asst. city mgr.'s office City of Dallas, 1985-86, adminstrv. asst. fin. dept., 1986—. Mem. women's com. Dallas Theatre Ctr.; del. Tex. Dem. Conv., 1982. Mem. Internat. City Mgmt. Assn., Am. Soc. Pub. Adminstrn., Urban Mgmt. Assts. North Tex. (program, profl. devel. coms.), ACLU, NOW, Greenpeace. Jewish. Office: City of Dallas Fin Dept 1500 Marilla 2CS Dallas TX 75201

STRO, MARY ANNE, educational administrator; b. Chgo., Jan. 19, 1943; d. James Vicent and Edna Marcia (O'Connell) Routson; m. Jack Hugh Stro, June 21, 1969 (div. 1979). B.A., Northeastern Ill. State U., 1968; postgrad. U. Calif.-San Diego, 1969-74; M.S., San Diego State U., 1976; Ed.D., U.S. Internat., 1982. Counselor, Montgomery Jr. High Sch., San Diego, 1971-75, asst. prin., 1975-77, prin., 1982-84; asst. prin. Southwest High, San Diego, 1977-82; dir. curriculum and instrn. Sweetwater Union High Sch., Chula Vista, Calif., 1985—, dir. pub. info. and govt. relations, 1987—; mem. Western Assn. Schs. and Colls. Accredation Team, San Diego, 1982, 83, 84, 86; assessor, dir., trainer San Diego County Leadership Assessment Ctr., 1984—; mem. San Diego Council Adminstrv. Women Edn., 1984—. Active City Chula Vista Human Relation Commn., 1974; treas. South Bay Community Services, Inc., 1985—, pres. exec. bd., 1987—. Recipient Susan B. Anthony award NOW, 1983; twin honoree YWCA, 1986; named Woman of Achievement, Pres.'s Council 1983-84; Exec. Educator 100, 1985. Mem. Am. Bus. Women's Assn. (exec. bd. 1984—, NOW, Assn. Supervision and Curriculum Devel., Assn. Calif. Sch. Adminstrs., Southwest Adminstrn. Assn. (v.p. 1983-84), Mgmt. Assn. Sweetwater Dist. (pres.-elect 1985), Nat. Council Adminstrv. Women Edn. Office: Sweetwater Union High Sch Dist 1130 5th Ave Chula Vista CA 92011

STROER, ROSEMARY ANN, real estate broker; b. N.Y.C., Oct. 1, 1934; d. Joseph and Rose Ann (Maguire) McBrien; m. Charles Stroer, Dec. 6, 1961 (dec. 1976); m. Alfred Britton III, Dec. 25, 1978. BA in English, CUNY, 1958, MA in English, 1973; MA, NYU, 1976. Dir. pub. relations PepsiCo, Purchase, N.Y., 1960-70; dir. student services and publs. N.Y.C. Bd. Edn., 1970-82; cons. pub. relations numerous orgns. including Ford Found., Architects for Social Responsibility, Cathedral St. John the Divine, Hampton Day Sch., Local TV, Inc., N.Y.C., 1975—; real estate broker, consultant Maruko USA, Inc., N.Y.C., 1986—. Author: Work as You Like It, 1979; editor: Holocaust: A Study in Genocide, 1977, Minimum Teaching Essentials, 1980. Spl. rep. Mayor's Task Force on Immunization, N.Y.C., 1982-83; spl. dem. asst. campaign for Ho. of Reps., N.Y.C., 1972. Recipient Order of the Sun award govt. of Peru, 1964, numerous pub. service awards. Mem. Hunter Coll. Alumni Assn., Mus. Modern Art, UNICEF. Roman Catholic. Home: 315 E 68th St New York NY 10021 Office: 9 E 45th St New York NY 10017

STROH, PATRICIA ANN BARBIER, child care center executive; b. Muncie, Ind., June 30, 1946; d. Carl John Barbier and Syble Leola (Rhodes) Barbier Smith; m. David Leroy Stroh, Aug. 6, 1967; children—Todd, Andrea, Nick. B.S., Ball State U., 1967; M.A., 1969. Tchr., Castleton Pre-Sch., Indpls., 1970-71, Collier County Schs., Naples, Fla., 1973-74; owner Castle Pre-Sch., Naples, 1974-77; owner Trinity Schs., Plano, Tex., 1977—; pres., dir. Trinity Pre-Schs., Inc.; adult educator Collier County Schs., Naples, 1977. Contbr. articles to profl. jours. Chmn. pub. relations Bicentennial Com., Naples, Fla., 1974-76; mem. Collier County Conservancy, Naples, 1976; bd. dirs. Big Cypress Nature Center, Naples, 1974-76; pres. PTO, Plano, 1980-81; leader Boy Scouts Am., Naples, 1974-77; trustee United Meth. Ch., 1984—. Mem. Nat. Assn. for Edn. of Young Children, Tex. Lic. Child Care Assn., Tex. Assn. for Edn. Young Children, Dallas Assn. Edn. Young Children, Assn. for Gifted Students, Home Edons. and Co-op Edn. Assn. (pres. 1983-84), Plano Heritage Assn. Clubs: Jr. Women's of Naples, Naples Players, Tex. A&M (pres.).

STROHM, LILLIAN ANN, home economist; b. South Bend, Ind, Oct. 17, 1914; d. John and Sadie (Kelley) Murphy; B.S., Purdue U., 1938; M.A., George Washington U., 1941; m. John Strohm, Sept. 8, 1941; children—Terry, Karen, Robert, Cheryl, Dave, Colleen. Head home econs. dept. USDA, Bainbridge, Ind., 1938-39, home demonstration agt., Vigo County, Ind., 1938-41; homemaking editor Ford Almanac, Woodstock, Ill., 1954—; cons. Nat. Wildlife Mag., 1984-85. Exec. sec., then pres. Woodstock Opera House Community Center, Inc., 1970-80. Purdue U. scholar, 1928-32; USDA fellow, 1939-40. Mem. AAUW, Omicron Nu, Kappa Delta Pi, Alpha Lambda Delta. Roman Catholic. Clubs: Garden (pres. 1985-86), Book (v.p.), Investment (pres. 1984). Address: 515 W Jackson St Woodstock IL 60098

STROM, JANICE DOLAN, nursing director; b. Milw., May 29, 1938; d. William James and Martha Eleanor (Beyerl) Dolan; m. Bengt Olof Strom, Feb. 27, 1965; children: Sonja Michelle, Bengt Joshua. BS in Nursing, Barry Coll., 1959; cert. registered nurse anesthetist, Johns Hopkins U. Hosp., 1965. Dir. nursing Good Shepherd Home, Littleton, Colo., 1980—. Mem. Colo. Nurses Assn., Non-Practicing and Part-Time Nurses Assn. Democrat. Roman Catholic. Home: 6548 S Clayton St Littleton CO 80121 Office: Good Shepherd Home 445 W Berry Ave Littleton CO 80120

STROM, JULIE KAY, advertising executive; b. Oak Park, Ill., July 1, 1947; d. Harry Frank and Janette Henritte (Nomden) Strom; m. Donald Robert Strandell, May 15, 1982; children: Strom Robert, Soni Karin. B.S. in Radio and TV, U. Ill., 1969. Copywriter, Post Keyes Gardner, Chgo., 1969-70; assoc. creative dir. Needham, Harper, Chgo., 1970-75; sr. v.p., creative dir. Benton & Bowles, Chgo., 1975-85; sr. v.p., exec. creative dir DMB&B, Chgo., 1985—. Office: D'Arcy Masius Benton & Bowles 200 E Randolph Dr Suite 7100 Chicago IL 60601-6833

STROMAN, PATRICIA ANN HARRIS, systems analyst; b. Charleston, W.Va., Dec. 2, 1953; d. Paul Frederick and Faye Virginia (Shafer) Harris; m. Harry Jackson Stroman Oct. 23, 1980; children—James Harris, Virginia Louise. A.S., W.Va. Inst. Tech., 1973. Programmer, Carlton Industries, Richmond, Va., 1974-76; cons. SIS Inc., Richmond, 1976-77; team leader State of Va., Richmond, 1977-80, Airline Tariff Co., Dulles Airport, Washington, 1980-82; WITCO Chem. co., Woodcliffe Lake, N.J., 1982-84; cons. ind field 1986; lead analyst Nat. Liberty Corp., 1987—. Mem. Nat. Assn. Female Execs. Republican. Presbyterian. Home: 1022 Winfield Ct Lansdale PA 19446

STROMAN, PATRICIA ANNE, publishing executive; b. Los Angeles, Oct. 19, 1929; d. Thomas Pendleton and Edythe Camille (Buerkle) S.; m. Seymour William Itzkoff, Sept. 7, 1954; children: Julia Louise, Gerald Hill. BA, UCLA, 1951; MA, Columbia U., 1954. Tchr. Metuchen (N.J.) Schs., 1954-55, North Babylon (N.Y.) Schs., 1955-59; violin restorer Northhampton, Mass., 1974—; violinist Wantastignet Chamber Orch., Brattleboro, Vt., 1980—; pub., editor Paideia Pubs., Ashfield, Mass., 1983—. Office: Paideia Pubs PO Box 343 Ashfield MA 01330

STRONG, ALDA (MRS. LAVERN STRONG), community service volunteer, realtor; b. Menan, Idaho, Sept. 22, 1911; d. William D. and Margaret (Hunting) Watson; grad. high school; nat. grad. Realestate Inst., 1977; m. LaVern Strong, June 14, 1930; children—Nalda (Mrs. Richard C. Powell), Harvey, Deanna (Mrs. Douglas Vollmer). Active Internat. Toastmistress Clubs, 1951—, organizer 4 local clubs, pres. council number 9, No. region, 1959-60, parliamentarian No. region, 1960-61; legislative chmn. Idaho Bus. and Profl. Women's Clubs, 1958-59, chmn. pub. relations, 1959-61, pres.; safety chmn. Idaho Gen. Fedn. Women's Clubs, 1960-61, Idaho chmn., 1964, state safety chmn.; sec. dist. South Central Bus. and Profl. Clubs, 1967; pres. 20th Century, Twin Falls, Idaho, 1962-63; bd. dirs. Twin Falls Salvation Army, chmn., 1975-78, life mem. Salvation Army; state rep. to President's Safety Conf. Mich. State U. Organizer 5 safety clubs Nat. Safety Council; safety chmn. So. Idaho Citizens Safety Council; regional dir. Idaho Women's Hwy. Safety Leaders, 1971-74; bd. dirs. Twin Falls Civic Auditorium, 1959-61; chmn. Twin Falls County chpt. Nat. Found.; sec. Idaho Hosp. Auxiliaries, 1959-60; pres. Twin Falls YWCA; mem. Salvation Army (life); sponsor Sigma chpt. Beta Sigma Phi; sec.-treas. Twin Falls County Civil Def.; past pres. Gem. State Writers Guild, editor Gem State News Letter, 1970-71; mem. Nat. Assn. Parliamentarians (Idaho pres. 1977-80). Democratic candidate Idaho Ho. of Reps., 1960. Recipient Certificate of Merit award Nat. Safety Council, 1959; named Woman of Year, Bus. and Profl. Women's Clubs, 1960, Magic Toastmistress Club, Number 1002, No. region, 1959; Disting. Service award Jr. C. of C., 1960, merit award Idaho Safety Council; registered parliamentarian. Mem. Idaho Bd. Realtors (parliamentarian 1976—). Clubs: Greater Fedn. Women (past local pres.); 20th Century Federated (fine arts chmn. 2d v.p.). Lodges: Altrusa (internat. chmn.), Ladies of Elks (past pres.). Home: 833 Shoshone St N Box 31 Twin Falls ID 83301

STRONG, BETHANY JUNE, novelist, publisher, editor; b. Oklahoma City, June 13, 1906; d. Nicholas Henry and Anna Augusta (Spuhler) McLaughlin; m. John Donovan Strong, Sept. 2, 1928; children: Patricia, Virginia. BS in History of Ideas, Johns Hopkins U., 1966. Novelist, freelance writer, pub., editor Parable Press, Amherst, Mass., 1978—; cons. in field. Author: The King's Generalissima, 1976, First Love, 1978, Murder in the Mirror, 1985; also articles. Mem. Nat. Writers Club, Nat. League Am. Pen Women (pres. Conn. Valley br.). Roman Catholic. Avocation: photography.

STRONG, CAROLYN RAY, electronics company official; b. Pasadena, Calif., Jan. 9, 1951; d. Albert Charles and Juliana (Ray) Strong; B.A. in Math., Whitworth Coll., 1973; postgrad. DeVry Inst. Tech., 1975-77; U. Ore., 1986—. Math. and aerospace demonstrator Pacific Sci. Center, Seattle, 1970, 71; component info. specialist Tektronix, Inc., Beaverton, Oreg., 1973-75, tech. writer, 1975-76, tech. publs. group mgr., 1976-79, tech. communications mgr., 1979-85; tech. publs. and computer tng. mgr., 1985-86, mgr. lab. instruments documentation, 1986—; cons. Portland Community Coll., Chemeketa Community Coll. Bd. dirs. First Tech. Fed. Credit Union, 1984—, sec., 1985-86, vice chmn., 1986-87, chmn. 1987—. Mem. Soc. Tech. Communications (sr. mem., sec. Willamette Valley chpt. 1978, treas. 1979, pres. 1979-80). Home: 1325 NW 92d St Portland OR 97229 Office: PO Box 500 Beaverton OR 97077

STRONG, CATHERINE ELLIS, lawyer; b. Albuquerque, July 12, 1950; d. William Henry and Bernadette (Fitzgerald) Ellis; m. Richard Willis Strong, Aug. 5, 1972; 1 child, Andrew Ellis. B.A., Northwestern U., 1972; J.D., Creighton U., 1976. Bar: Nebr. 1976, Wis. 1977, U.S. Dist. Ct. Wis. 1977. Atty., Strong & Strong, Green Bay, Wis., 1978-82, 83—, Condon, Hanaway, Wickert Fenwick & Strong, Ltd., Green Bay, 1982-83; mem. adv. bd. Juvenile Ct., Green Bay, 1978-80; chmn., organizer Juvenile Restitution Project Fundraising campaign, 1981-82, bd. dirs., 1978-81. Bd. dirs. LacBaie council Girl Scouts U.S., 1978-80; bd. dirs. YWCA, 1980-82, mem. membership/mktg. com., 1985-86, mem. fin. com., 1987—; mem. resource devel. div. United Way, 1981-86; pres., bd. dirs. Family Service Assn., Green Bay, 1982-84, Family Service Properties, 1982-84; mem. accreditation task force Family Service Assn., 1986-87, past pres. bd. dirs., 1984-87; bd. dirs. U. Wis. Green Bay Ecumenical Ctr., 1987—. Recipient Appreciation award Ashwaubenon Assn. Spl. Children's Needs, 1980. Mem. ABA, Nebr. Bar Assn., Wis. Bar Assn., Brown County Bar Assn. (mem. Liberty Bell award selection com. 1983), Alpha Phi. Roman Catholic. Office: Strong and Strong Attys 2301 Riverside Dr Green Bay WI 54301

STRONG, GAY, industrial relations and human resources executive; b. Santa Monica, Calif., Jan. 13, 1930; d. Claude Roderick and Katherine Anna (Brown) Riley; student UCLA, 1947-49; A.A., Pierce Coll., Los Angeles, 1969; B.A. in English, Calif. State U.-Northridge, 1973; m. Duane Gordon Strong, Aug. 20, 1949; children—Philip, Katherine, Patricia, Barbara. With credit office, store ops., then asst. personnel mgr. Builders Emporium, Van Nuys, Calif., 1969-74, personnel mgr., 1974-78; dir. indsl. relations GC Internat., Hawthorne, Calif., 1978-81; personnel mgr. Lok Products Co., Fullerton, Calif., 1981-82; chief exec. officer Asset Recovery, Santa Monica, Calif., 1982-83; dir. Human Resource Targeted Coverage, Inc., Glendora, Calif., 1983—; editor house organ, 1983—. Republican. Editor Builders Emporium house organ, 1972-78. Office: 533 W Foothill Blvd. Glendora CA 91740

STRONG, HELEN FRANCINE, lawyer; b. Detroit, Mar. 22, 1947; d. Lonia and Nancy Lula (Proctor) Lanier; m. Douglas Donald Strong, Oct. 26, 1974; children: Douglas Donald, Jennifer Anne, Stephen Lanier. A.B., U. Detroit, 1969, J.D., 1972. Bar: Mich. 1972. Asst. atty. gen. Office of Atty.

Gen., Lansing, Mich., 1972-73; staff atty. Detroit Edison Co., 1973-80; assoc. William C. Gage, P.C., Detroit, 1980-81; sr. assoc. Lewis, White & Clay, P.C., Detroit, 1981—. Bd. dirs. Detroit Inst. Arts, Founders Jr. Council, 1979-85, Founders Soc., 1977—, mem. adv. com. Centennial Com., 1983-86; mem. adv. com. Your Heritage House, Inc., Detroit, 1983-84, bd. dirs., 1985—; com. mem. exhbns. Detroit Hist. Mus., 1984; mem. bd. advisors Detroit Inst. Arts Founders Jr. Council, 1985—; trustee Eton Acad., 1985—. Recipient Cert. for Outstanding Service to Univ. of Detroit Sch. Law, 1972, Service award Detroit Med. Soc., 1986. Mem. ABA, Fed. Bar Assn., Mich. Bar Assn., Detroit Bar Assn., Wolverine Bar Assn., Nat. Bar Assn., Assn. Trial Lawyers Am., Women Lawyers Assn. Mich., Delta Sigma Theta, NAACP. Roman Catholic. Office: 1300 1st Nat Bldg Detroit MI 48226

STRONG, JUDITH ANN, chemist, educator; b. Van Hornesville, N.Y., June 19, 1941; d. Philip Furnald and Hilda Bernice (Hulbert) S.; B.S. cum laude (N.Y. State regents scholar), SUNY, Albany, 1963; M.A., Brandeis U., 1966, Ph.D., 1970. Asst. prof. chemistry Moorhead State U. (Minn.), 1969-73, acting chmn. chemistry dept., 1976, assoc. prof., 1973-81, prof., 1981—, chmn. dept., 1984-86, dean social and natural scis., 1986—. Recipient Tietzen Meml. award SUNY, Albany, 1963; NSF fellow, 1965-67. Mem. Am. Chem. Soc., Assn. Women in Science, Soroptimist Internat., Minn. Acad. Sci., Sigma Xi. Home: 1209 12th St S Moorhead MN 56560 Office: Moorhead State U Acad Affairs Moorhead MN 56560

STRONG, MAYDA NEL, psychologist, educator; b. Albuquerque, May 6, 1942; d. Floyd Samuel and Wanda Christmas (Martin) Strong; 1 child, Robert Allen Willingham. BA in Speech-Theatre cum laude, Tex. Western Coll., 1963; EdM, U. Tex., Austin, 1972, PhD in Counseling Psychology, 1978; lic. clin. psychologist, Colo., 1984; cert. alcohol counselor III, Colo., 1987. Asst. instr. in ednl. psychology U. Tex., Austin, 1974-78; instr. psychology Austin Community Coll., 1974-78, Otero Jr. Coll., La Junta, Colo., 1979—; dir. outpatient and emergency services S.E. Colo. Family Guidance and Mental Health Ctr., Inc., La Junta, 1978-81; pvt. practice psychol. therapy, La Junta, 1981—; exec. dir. Pathfinders Alcohol Dependency program, 1985—. Del. to County Dem. Conv., 1988. Co-star The Good Doctor, Picketwire Theatre, La Junta, 1980, On Golden Pond, 1981, Plaza Suite, 1987, Otero Jr. Coll. Players, 1987. AAUW fellow, 1974-76. Mem. Bus. and Profl. People (legis. chairperson 1982-83, NES chmn. 1982—), Colo. Psychol. Assn. (legis. chmn. for dist.). Contbr. articles in field to profl. publs. Author poems in Chinook: Paths through the Puzzle, Decisions, Passion. Home: 500 Holly Ave PO Box 177 Swink CO 81077 Office: Otero Jr Coll #21 Town Square Mall La Junta CO 81050

STRONG, TINA ELIZABETH, food products company executive; b. Evanston, Ill., Oct. 23, 1934; d. L. Willis Strong and Elizabeth (Kelsey) Cook; m. Roger C. Persons, Dec. 26, 1956 (div. 1968); children: David, Cynthia. BS, U. Wis., 1956; MBA, Lake Forest Coll., 1985. Tchr. Ill., N.J., N.Y. Tchr. Clifton (N.J.) Pub. Sch., 1957, Rochester (N.Y.) Pub. Sch., 1958; adminstrv. asst. Schaeffer Diversified Co. subs. PFI Industries, Cleve., 1970-73; exec. sec. Kitchens of Sara Lee, Deerfield, Ill., 1973-77, customer order supr., 1977-78, buyer purchasing dept., 1978-82, sr. buyer packaging dept., 1982-84, projects mgr. purchasing dept., 1984-86, purchasing mgr. packaging dept., 1986—. V.p. Spares Sunday Evangel. Singles, Glenview, Ill., 1975-76. Mem. Purchasing Mgmt. Assn., Chgo. Regional Purchasing Council, Council of Women (exec. adv. bd. Purchasing World trade jour. 1986—), Packaging Inst., Sara Lee Corp. Purchasing Council, Internat. Record Collectors Assn., Duke Ellington Soc. (bd. dirs.), LWV (chairperson legis. com. 1965-68), Kappa Alpha Theta. Republican. Office: Kitchens of Sara Lee 500 Waukegan Rd Glenview IL 60015

STRONG-TIDMAN, VIRGINIA ADELE, marketing and advertising executive; b. Englewood, N.J., July 26, 1947; d. Alan Ballentine and Virginia Leona (Harris) Strong; m. John Fletcher Tidman, Sept. 23, 1978. B.S., Albright Coll., Reading, Pa., 1969; postgrad. U. Pitts., 1970-73, U. Louisville, 1975-76. Exec. trainee Pomeroy's div. Allied Stores, Reading, 1969-70; mktg. research analyst Heinz U.S.A., Pitts., 1970-74; new products mktg. mgr. Ky. Fried Chicken, Louisville, 1974-76; dir. Pitts. office M/A/R/C, 1976-79; assoc. research dir. Henderson Advt., Inc., Greenville, S.C., 1979-81; sr. v.p., dir. research Bozell, Jacobs, Kenyon & Eckhardt, Inc., Irving, Tex., 1981-86; sr. v.p., dir. research and strategic planning Bozell, Jacobs, Kenyon & Eckhardt, Inc., Atlanta, 1986—; cons. mktg. research Greenville Zool. Soc., 1981. Mem. Am. Mktg. Assn. Episcopalian. Home: 1835 Johnson Ferry Rd Atlanta GA 30319 Office: Bozell Jacobs Kenyon & Eckhardt One Securities Ctr 3490 Piedmont Rd Suite 1400 Atlanta GA 30305

STRONKS, JULIA KAYE, lawyer; b. Nashville, Oct. 25, 1960. BA, Dordt Coll., 1982; JD, U. Iowa, 1985. Bar: Mich. 1985. Intern Johnson County Attys. Office, Iowa City, 1984-85; assoc. Varnum, Riddering, Schmidt & Howlett, Grand Rapids, Mich., from 1985; now dir. family law project clinic U. Mich., Ann Arbor; cons. atty. Mich. Pro Bono Assn., Grand Rapids, 1985—; interim tchr. Calvin Coll., Grand Rapids, 1987—; bus. law instr. Washtenaw Community Coll., Ann Arbor; lectr. seminars on law and edn., 1987—. Contbr. articles to Pub. Justice Report (corr. Assn. for Pub. Justice, 1985—). Vol. Mich. Coalition Against Domestic Violence, Detroit, 1986—. Mem. ABA, Mich. Trial Lawyers Assn., Mich. Bar Assn., Grand Rapids Bar Assn., Mich. Women's Lawyers Assn.

STROOMER, KATHRYN PAULETTE, management analyst, real estate executive; b. Bridgeport, Conn., Feb. 28, 1949; d. Cornelius Jacob and Kathryn Harriet (Novak) S. BA in English, U. Conn., 1972; MBA, U. New Haven, 1987; postgrad., Yale U., 1987. Editorial asst. Golf Digest/Tennis, Norwalk, Conn., 1974; proposal coordinator Sikorsky Aircraft div. United Techs. Corp., Stratford, Conn., 1974-78, procedures analyst, 1979-82, supr. mfg. engrs., systems and procedures, 1982-87, supplier rating analyst, 1987; pres. Equity Enterprises, Ansonia, Conn., 1986—; specialist policy devel. Textron Lycoming, Stratford, 1988—; pres. The Prose Shop, Ansonia, 1986—; fin. cons. A.L. Williams, Atlanta, 1987. Editor (textbook) Flexible Mfg. Systems, 1985. Contbr. community action com., Seymour, Conn., 1986. Mem. Am. Mgmt. Assn., Soc. Mfg. Engrs. (sec. 1984-87), Am. Congress on Real Estate, Nat. Assn. Female Execs., Sikorsky Suprs. (mem. health/welfare com. 1986). Republican. Clubs: CEO (N.Y.C.); Toastmasters (adminstrv. v.p. 1986-87, pres. 1988). Home: PO Box 222 Ansonia CT 06401 Office: Textron Lycoming 550 Main St Stratford CT 06497 also: Equity Enterprises PO Box 286 Ansonia CT 06401

STROTHER, CANDACE LEE, federal agency administrator; b. Detroit, Dec. 26, 1954; d. Everette Glenn and Yvonne Marie (Gardner) S. Grad. studies, Trinity Coll., Oxford, Eng., 1977; BA in English, Econs., Bus. Adminstrn. cum laude, Hillsdale (Mich.) Coll., 1978; postgrad., Harvard U. Bus. Sch., 1987. Reporter Sta. WMWM, Coldwater, Mich., 1978-79; reporter, anchor, producer Sta. WJIM-TV div. CBS-TV, Lansing, Mich., 1979-80; research asst. syndicated columnists Evans & Novak, Washington, 1981; broadcast liaison The Heritage Found., Washington, 1981-83; staff asst. Office Pub. Liaison White House, Washington, 1983-84; sr. analyst Rep. Nat. Com., Washington, 1984; spl. asst. U.S. Trade Rep. White House, Washington, 1984-85; exec. asst. to undersec. Dept. Labor, Washington, 1985-86; dep. asst. sec. Occupational Safety and Health Adminstrn., Washington, 1985—; pres. The Forum, Washington, 1982-84. Asst. to dir. Reagan-Bush Presdl. Campaign, Detroit, 1980. Named Young Careerist Bus. and Profl. Women, 1979. Mem. Reagan Dep. Asst. Secs. Assn. (bd. dirs. 1986—). Republican. Office: Dept of Labor 200 Constitution Ave Washington DC 20013

STROTHER, PAT WALLACE, author; b. Birmingham, Ala., Mar. 11, 1929; d. Claude Hunter and Gladys Eleanor (English) Wallace; student U. Tenn., Knoxville, 1947-51; m. Lee Levitt, 1951 (div. 1957); m. 2d, David G. Latner, 1958 (div. 1968); m. 3d, Robert A. Strother, 1980. Dir. women's programs WGNS Radio, Murfreesboro, Tenn., 1951-52; continuity dir. WMAK Radio, Nashville, 1952-54; asst. editor Civil Service Leader, N.Y.C., 1955-57; adminstrv. sec. Local 237 Teamsters, N.Y.C., 1957-76; works include: House of Scorpio, 1975, This Willing Passion, 1978, The Wand and the Star, 1978; Traitor in My Arms, 1979; The Voyagers, 1980; Once More the Sun, Silver Fire, 1982; My Loving Enemy, Summer Kingdom, 1983; Sweetheart Contract, Shining Hour, Objections Overruled, 1984; Love Scene, Star Rise, Unyielding Fire, 1985, Under the Sign of Scorpio, The Constant Star, A Wife for Ransom, 1986, Grand Design, 1988. Mem. Authors Guild. Democrat.

STROTHERS, ANN LAVINIA, music company executive; b. Pitts., Aug. 10, 1936; d. Eugene Russell and Irene (Hollinger) Davis; m. Henry T. Crane, Sept. 1961 (div. 1975); m. Gerald O. Strothers Sr., May 15, 1981; 1 child, Donald E. Herd. AS in Bus. Admin., Allegheny Community Coll., Pitts., 1985. Dept. mgr. Beerman Stores, Inc., Dayton, Ohio, 1957-67; with credit dept. Rike Kumler, Dayton, 1968-72; with collection dept. Sears, Roebuck & Co., Pitts., 1973-74; clk., then teller Century Fed. [illegible] Assn., Pitts., 1973-79; adminstrv. banking clk. The Mellon Bank, Pitts., 1979-86; pres. PEK Prodns., Pitts., 1983—; bus. cons. Philip Russell and the Gospel Traditions, Pitts., 1984—. Publisher gospel music including recs. My Life is in God's Hands, 1984, Isn't It Good To Be Here, 1985, Rejoice in Heaven, 1986. Advisor to African Heritage Classroom Com. Univ. Pitts., 1987—. Mem. ASCAP, Nat. Music Publishers Assn. Democrat. Mem. African Meth. Episc. Ch.-Zion. Lodge: Daughters of Isis (Commandress local br. 1980-81). Home and Office: 111 St Croix Dr Pittsburgh PA 15235

STROTHMAN, WENDY J., book publisher; b. Pitts., July 29, 1950; d. Walter Richard and Mary Ann (Hodtum) S.; m. Mark Kavanaugh Metzger, Nov. 25, 1978; children—Andrew Richard, Margaret Ann. Student, U. Chgo. Sch. Bus., 1979-80; A.B., Brown U., 1972. Copywriter, mktg. U. Chgo. Press, 1973-76, editor, 1977-80, gen. editor, 1980-83, asst. dir., 1983; dir. Beacon Press, Boston. Mem. editorial bd. Brown U. Alumni Monthly, Providence, R.I., 1983—. Bd. dirs. Editorial Project for Edn., trustee, 1987—. Mem. Renaissance Soc. (bd. dirs. 1980-83). Club: Pubs. Lunch (N.Y.C.). Office: Beacon Press 25 Beacon St Boston MA 02108

STROUD, MEG DANIELSON, nurse; b. Salt Lake City, June 8, 1955; d. Paul Danielson and Bonnie Sue (Anderson) Paul; m. David Howell Stroud. Assoc. degree, Brigham Young U., 1978. RN; cert. Post Anesthesia Nurse. Staff post-anesthesia recovery nurse St. Mark's Hosp., Salt Lake City, 1978-85, asst. coordinator post-anesthesia recovery and mini-stay, 1985-86, coordinator PAR, 1986—. Contbr. certification review texts, articles to profl. jours. Res. dep. sheriff Salt Lake County Sheriff's office, 1980-82. Mem. Am. Soc. Post Anesthesia Nurses (charter, bd. dirs. 1982-83, treas. 1983-85, v.p. 1985-86, pres. 1986-87), Utah Soc. Post Anesthesia Nurses (founding pres. 1982-83), Nat. Assn. Female Execs., Am. Nurses Assn., Utah Nurses Assn. Home: 5362 Old Trenton Way Murray UT 84123 Office: St Mark's Hosp c/o PAR 1200 E 1300 S Salt Lake City UT 84124

STROUSE, CAROL LOUISE KIRCHMAN, vocational educator; b. Bloomsburg, Pa., Sept. 14, 1947; d. George and Jessie Helen (Kitchen) Kirchman; m. William Earle Strouse, June 21, 1965; 1 child, Matthew Alexander. B.S. in Health and Phys. Edn., Lock Haven U., Pa., 1970; M.S. in Phys. Edn., Ind. State U.-Terre Haute, 1976. Cert. tchr. health, phys. edn. and spl. edn., Md. Tchr. phys. edn., Charles County Bd. Edn., LaPlata, Md., 1970-78, tchr. spl. edn., 1978-85, vocat. tchr., 1978-85, work domain coordinator, 1983—, team leader, 1981-84, cons. elementary career edn., 1986—; spl. edn. reading teacher Milton Somers Middle Sch., 1986—; gymnastics instr., coach Charles County Dept. Parks and Recreation, La Plata, 1973-79. Area coordinator Charles County Spl. Olympics, 1976-78, 82-83; coach soccer St. Mary's County Recreation and Parks, Mechanicsville, Md., 1982-84; mem. Charles County Bd. Elections, 1986; del. MSTA, 1987. Recipient Outstanding Coach award Saint Gymnastics Club, Waldorf, Md., 1982; Recognition for Vocat. Guidance Project, Charles County Bd. Edn., 1982. Mem. United Teaching Assns. (faculty rep. 1983-88), Nat. Assn. Female Execs. Democrat. Methodist. Avocations: reading; swimming; cycling; arts and crafts. Home: Route 2 Box 174 Charlotte Hall MD 20622 Office: Charles County Bd Edn Star Rt 5 Box 536 La Plata MD 20646

STRUCKHOFF, ELIZABETH THERESA, health care administrator; b. Washington, Jan. 24, 1948; d. Victor Fred and Julitta Helen S.; m. James Bradford Harris, May 12, 1982. BA, Benedictine Coll., 1969; MBA, St. Louis U., 1976. Staff mgr. Southwestern Bell, St. Louis, 1969-76; bus. mgr. St. Louis County Orthopedic Group, St. Louis, 1976-80; mgr. St. Louis U. Med. Ctr., 1980—. Contbr. articles to profl. jours. Mem. Am. Coll. Med. Group Adminstrs., Met. St. Louis Clinic Mgrs. Assn. (chair 1981), Med. Group Mgmt. Assn. Roman Catholic. Club: Carlyle Sailing Assn. Office: St Louis U Healthline 3663 Lindell Saint Louis MO 63108

STRUTHERS, DEBORAH MARY, medical corporation executive; b. Sydney, N.S.W., Australia, Feb. 4, 1952; came to U.S., 1973; d. Anthony Eric and Mary Patricia (O'Mullane) Gray; m. Theodore Ralph Culbertson, July 31, 1971 (div. 1979); m. Scott Cameron Struthers, Jan. 31, 1981. Student St. Petersburg Jr. Coll., 1978—. Fin. counselor Wuesthoff Meml. Hosp., Rockledge, Fla., 1973-75; adminstrv. dir. Dresden & Ticktin, M.D.s, P.A., St. Petersburg, Fla., 1976-80; exec. dir., v.p. Am. Med. Mgmt., Inc., Clearwater, Fla., 1980—; pres., dir. All Women's Health Ctr., Inc., St. Petersburg, 1980—, All Women's Health Ctr. North Tampa, Inc., Fla., 1980—, All Women's Health Ctr. Tampa, Inc., 1980—, Women's Ob-Gyn Ctr. Countryside, Inc., 1984—, All Women's Health Ctr. Sarasota, Fla., 1980—, All Women's Health Ctr. Ocala, Fla., 1980—, All Women's Health Ctr. Gainesville, Fla., 1981—, Lakeland Women's Health Ctr., Fla., 1980—, Ft. Myers Womens Health Ctr., Fla., 1980—, All Women's Health Ctr. Jacksonville, Fla., 1980—, Nat. Women's Health Services, Inc., Clearwater, Fla., 1983—, D.M.S. of Ft. Myers, Inc., 1985—, Alternative Human Service, 1979; treas., v.p., dir. Birthing Mgmt. Inc., 1985—.

STRYCZEK, SHAWNEE ANN, corporate executive; b. Connellsville, Pa., Sept. 5, 1955; d. Bernard Thomas and Camile Marie (Manzella) S. Student, Wittenberg U., 1972-73; BBA, U. Akron, 1976; postgrad., St. Francis Coll., 1979-81. Sales rep. Liquid Carbonic Corp., Chgo., 1976-82; pres. SMS Bus. Media, Inc., Cleve., 1982—; v.p. Sleepytime Prodns., North Royalton, Ohio, 1986—. Creator copy toothfairy envelope Sleepytime, 1987. Mem. Bus. Forms Mgmt. Assn., Nat. Bus. Forms Assn., Council Small Enterprises, Women. Bus. Ownwers Assn. Roman Catholic. Office: SMS Bus Media Inc 5415 Schaaf Rd Cleveland OH 44131

STRYKER, LINDA PALMER, electronics company executive; b. Cin., Jan. 20, 1949; d. Roger Cooper and Irene Catherine (Riess) Palmer; m. Gregory Stephan Stryker, Sept. 4, 1982. BA in Anthropology, Ohio State U., 1973. Asst. mgr. Johnny Bench Restaurants, Cin. and Florence, Ky., 1975-77; employment mgr. Hilton-Davis Chem. Co. div. Sterling Drug Co., Cin., 1978-81; personnel supr. Square D Co., Florence, 1981-87; gen. mgr. In-Floor Raceway, Oxford, Ohio, 1988—; mem. Job Service Employers' Com. Northern Ky., 1985—; rep. Bus.-Edn. Success Teams (B.E.S.T.) Northern Ky., 1981—. cons. Project Bus./Jr. Achievement Greater Cin., 1982—. Mem. Nat. Mgmt. Assn. (v.p. Cin. 1983-84, pres. 1984-85), Am. Soc. Personnel Adminstrs., Northern Ky. Personnel Mgmt. Assn. (com. chair 1986-87), Greater Cin. Human Resources Assn. Office: Square D Co 5735 College Corder Rd Oxford OH 45056

STRYKER, WENDY ELLISON, nurse; b. Cedar Rapids, Iowa, Aug. 5, 1951; d. Lloyd William and Mary Jean (Hurd) Ellison; m. David A. Stryker, July 21, 1973 (div. Aug. 1980). BS in Nursing, U. Iowa, 1973. Staff nurse Luth. Med. Ctr., Omaha, 1973-74, charge nurse, 1974; staff nurse U. Iowa Hosps., Iowa City, 1974-75; head nurse Oaknoll Retirement Residence, Iowa City, 1975-76; staff nurse Christian Hosp., St. Louis, 1976, head nurse, 1976; head nurse MBSA, St. Louis, 1976-80; charge nurse No. Va. Dr. Hosp., Arlington, Va., 1980-81, asst. head nurse, 1981—. Mem. Nat. League for Nursing, Nat. Assn. Female Execs., Inc., U. Iowa Coll. Nursing Constituent Soc., Alpha Phi., Am. Nursing Assn. Home: 12268 Aztec Pl Woodbridge VA 22192 Office: No Va Dr Hospital 601 S Carlin Springs Rd Arlington VA 22204

STRYSIK, MARGARET, personnel adminstrator, consultant; b. Chgo.; d. Helen (Furgal) S. AA, Loop Jr. Coll., Chgo., 1968; BSBA with honors, Roosevelt U., 1970; MBA, Loyola U., Chgo., 1976; postgrad. in bus., U. Mich., 1977-79. Asst. personnel dir. Fed. Signal, Chgo., 1970-74; compensation mgr. Chgo. Title & Trust, 1974-80; benefits/compensation mgr. Tenneco Automotive, Deerfield, Ill., 1980-81; benefits mgr., personnel mgr. Williams Cos., Tulsa, 1981-83; dir. compensation and benefits Alexian Health Systems, Elk Grove, Ill., 1983-85; benefits mgr. IC Industries, Chgo., 1985-86, AON Corp., Chgo., 1986—; cons. various cos.; mem. steering com. WEB, Chgo., 1986—. Mem. Cert. Employee Benefits Soc., Am. Compensation Assn. (cert. corp. profl.), Midwest Pension Assn., Am. Soc. Personnel Assocs., Soc. Human Resources Profls., MBA Execs., Phi Theta Kappa. Home: 904 S Canfield Park Ridge IL 60068

STUART, ALICE MELISSA, lawyer; b. N.Y.C., Apr. 7, 1957; d. John Marberger and Marjorie Louise (Browne) S. BA, Ohio State U., 1977; JD, U. Chgo., 1980; LLM, NYU, 1982. Bar: N.Y. 1981, Ohio 1982, N.Y. 1982, U.S. Dist. Ct. (so. dist.) Ohio 1983, U.S. Dist. Ct. (so. and ea. dists.) N.Y. 1983. [illegible] Shapiro, Kelm & Warren, Columbus, Ohio, 1982-84, Paul, Weiss, Rifkind, Wharton & Garrison, N.Y.C., 1984-85, Kassel, Neuwirth & Geiger, N.Y.C., 1985-86, Phillips, Nizer, Benjamin, Krim & Ballon, N.Y.C., 1987—. Surrogate Speakers' Bur. Reagan-Bush Campaign, N.Y.C., 1984. Mem. ABA, N.Y. State Bar Assn., Winston Churchill Meml. Library Soc., Jr. League, Phi Beta Kappa, Phi Kappa Phi, Alpha Lambda Delta. Republican. Presbyterian. Club: Women's Nat. Rep. (N.Y.C.). Office: Philips Nizer Benjamin Krim & Ballon 40 W 57th St New York NY 10019

STUART, CHERYL GENEVA, county administrator; b. Prescott, Ark., Nov. 1, 1948; d. Bruce Edward and Mable Cecelia (Cotton) Buford; children: Arthur LeJohn, Rao Littrelle; m. T.R. Stuart; children: Gwendolyn, Robert. BS, Ark. Bapt. Coll., 1971; MSA, Ouachita U., 1976. Lic. social worker, Ark. Counselor Urban League, Little Rock, 1970-74; exec. officer State of Ark., Little Rock, 1975-77, dir. staff devel., 1977-80; dir. job devel. State of Ark., Ft. Smith, 1980-83; county adminstr. Lewisville, Ark., 1983—; mem. Ark. La. Gas Co. consumer bd., 1988—. Bd. dirs. Urban League, Ark., Soc. Area IV Black Caucus, 1985—; dir. youth dept. Bapt. Congress of Christian Edn. State of Ark.; dir. leadership and tng. women's dept. Ark. State Bapt. Consolidated Conv. Mem. NAACP (sec. 1982-83), Dept. Human Services Employees Assn. (v.p. 1985-87), County Adminstrs. Assn. (sec. 1986—), Ark. State Employees Assn. (v.p. 1987—, bd. dirs. 1984—, Outstanding Employee award 1986, 87), Assn. Exec. Females, Alpha Kappa Mu. Democrat. Club: Sophistics. Lodge: Friendship. Home: PO Box 875 Lewisville AR 71845

STUART, JOAN MARTHA, association administrator; b. Huntington, N.Y., June 2, 1945; d. Ervin Wencil and Flora Janet (Applebaum) Stuart; student Boston U., 1963-67. Prodn. asst. Random House, N.Y.C., 1968-69; book designer Simon & Schuster, N.Y.C., 1969-71; feature writer Palm Beach Post, West Palm Beach, Fla., 1971-72; co-founder, communications dir. Stuart, Gleimer & Assocs., West Palm Beach, 1973-84, pres., 1982—; fin. devel. dir. YWCA Greater Atlanta, 1984-86, Ctr. for the Visually Impaired, Atlanta, 1986—; adj. prof. Kennesaw Coll. Mem. crusade com. Am. Cancer Soc. Bd., 1981—; bd. dirs. Theatre Arts Co., 1980-81; community services chmn., bd. dirs. B'nai B'rith Women, 1980-82; chmn. publicity Leukemia Soc. Atlanta Polo Benefit, 1983; com. chmn. Atlanta Zool. Beastly Feast Benefit, 1984; mem. Atlanta Symphony Assocs.; chmn. Salute to Women of Achievement, 1987, 88. Recipient Nat. award B'nai B'rith Women, 1978, Regional award, 1979; cert. of merit Big Bros./Big Sisters, 1976. Mem. Nat. Soc. Fund Raising Execs., Ga. Exec. Women's Network, B'nai B'rith Women. Republican. Jewish. Contbr. articles to profl. jours. Office: Ctr for the Visually Impaired 763 Peachtree St NW Atlanta GA 30308

STUART, JUDITH CAROL, floral wholesale executive, motel owner; b. Hot Springs, Ark., May 27, 1949; d. Willard Aubrey and Lottie Lorene (Glover) Ducé; m. Colbern Cox Stuart Jr., Mar. 26, 1966 (div. Feb. 1970); 1 child, Colbern Cox III. BS, Ouachita Bapt. U., 1973. Owner, operator Siesta Motor Inn, Arkadelphia, Ark., 1970-75; sales rep. M. Goldberg and Co., Memphis, 1975-76; chief exec. officer Decorators Choice, Memphis, 1976-79; v.p. Coronet Ceramics Inc., Baldwin park, Calif., 1979-84; chief exec. officer Stuart-Anthony Inc., Hot Springs, Ark., 1984-85, D.D.S. Inc., Hot Springs, 1985—. Pres. Clark County Meml. Hosp. Aux., 1972-74; fund raiser Clinton for Gov. campaign, Little Rock, St. Judes Reach Hosp., Memphis, 1975-78; mem. panel Predl. Conf. Women Entrepreneurs, Dallas, 1983; judge Miss AM. Pageant System, 1986-87. Mem. Ark. Ark. Furniture Assn., Women Entrepreneurs Am., Bus. and Profl. Women Assn., Ark. Hospitality Assn., Hot Springs C. of C. (ambassador 1983—), Beta Sigma Phi (state chmn.). Lodge: Order Ea. Star. Office: 1312 Central Ave Hot Springs AR 71901

STUART, KATHERINE J., laboratory administrator; b. Dennis, Ky., June 8, 1929; d. Fred and Ida May (Hutchinson) Stuart; m. App Russell, July 28, 1962 (div. 1974). Cert. in stenography, Ashland Bus. Coll., 1947; cert. cosmetology, Crown Beauty Acad., Ironton, Ohio, 1958; AA in Engring., Chabot Coll., Hayward, Calif., 1969; BSBA, U. San Francisco, 1978. Stenographer Ky. Employment Dept., 1947; sec. Ky. Hwy. Dept., Ashland, 1947-48; head bookkeeper Jack's Appliance, Ashland, 1948-52, credit mgr., 1956-62; head bookkeeper Radio Sta. WCMI, Ashland, 1952-54; office mgr. Radio Sta. WTCR, Ashland, 1954-55; piping buyer United Engrs. & Constrn., Phila., 1955-56; resource mgr. Lawrence Livermore Nat. Lab., U. Calif., Livermore, 1962—. Vol. VA, Livermore, 1985—. Named to Hon. Order Ky. Cols. Mem. Am. Bus. Women's Assn. (v.p. 1983-84, pres. 1984-85, Woman of Yr. 1984), Sci. Investments (pres. 1982—), Lawrence Livermore Lab. Women's Assn. (pres. 1981-83, treas. 1984-85), IBM Personal Computer Valley Blue, U. San Francisco Alumni Assn. Avocations: arts, dancing, gardening, theatre, gourmet cooking. Home: 1849 Elm St Livermore CA 94550 Office: U Calif at Livermore Lawrence Livermore Nat Lab PO Box 808 L-113 Livermore CA 94550

STUART, MARIAN RUTH, medical educator; b. Berlin, May 22, 1930; d. Martin Loewenberg and Margot (Jarislowsky) Alexander; m. August D. Stuart, Sept. 26, 1949 (div. Oct. 1976); children: Peter, Laura, Robert. BA summa cum laude, Kean Coll., Union, N.J., 1971; MS in Psychology, Rutgers U., 1973, PhD in Social and Personality Psychology, 1975. Lic. psychologist, N.J. Mental health clinician Rutgers Mental Health Ctr., Piscataway, N.J., 1972-75; staff psychologist St. Clare's Hosp., Denville, N.J., 1975-77; adj. asst. psychologist, prof. psychiatry Rutgers Med. Sch., Piscataway, 1977—; asst. prof. UMDNJ Rutgers Med. Sch., New Brunswick, N.J., 1978-86; clin. assoc. prof. UMDNJ Robert Wood Johnson Med. Sch., New Brunswick, 1986—; pvt. practice clin. psychology, Morristown, N.J., 1976—. Sr. author: (textbook) The Fifteen Minute Hour, 1986, (chpt.) Family Dynamics, 1981; pub. The River Reporter, 1985—; contbr. articles to profl. jours. Mem. adv. com. Dept. on Aging, County of Morris, 1978-81. Grantee Morris County Dept. on Aging, 1976-77. Mem. Am. Psychol. Assn., N.J. Psychol. Assn., Soc. Tchrs. of Family Medicine. Home: 7 Harwich Rd Morristown NJ 07960 Office: UMDNJ Robert Wood Johnson Med Sch Dept Family Medicine One Robert Wood Johnson Pl New Brunswick NJ 08903-0019

STUART, MARILYN BRANT, urban planner; b. Los Angeles, June 24, 1931; d. Robert Alston Brant and Jane (Mann) Ward; m. Otis Chandler, June 18, 1951 (div. June 1981); children: Norman Brant, Narry Brant, Cathleen, Michael, Carolyn; m. Malcolm Stuart, Sept. 5, 1984; stepchildren: Linda, John, David. Student, Stanford U., 1949-51; MA, UCLA, 1975. Exterior planner Summa Corp., Van Nuys, Calif., 1974-77; pres. Urban Design Disciplines, Pasadena, Calif., 1977-82; ptnr. Thornton, Fagan, Brant, Raucoert, Pasadena, 1981-82; pres. Marilyn Brant and Assoc., Los Angeles, 1982-85; com. chair So. Calif. Assn. of Govt., Los Angeles, 1980-85. Dir. Population Crisis Com., Washington, 1973—; chmn. So. Calif. Population Crisis Com., Los Angeles, 1986—; trustee Loyola Marymount Univ., Los Angeles, 1979—. Mem. Am. Planning Assn., Calif. Planning Assn., Urban Land Inst., World Future Soc. Republican. Episcopalian. Office: M Brant Assocs 11560 Beelagio Rd Los Angeles CA 90049

STUART, MARJORIE LOUISE, designer; b. St. Louis, Jan. 7, 1926; d. Herbert Judson and Vesta Jeannette (Winters) Browne; A.B., Fla. State U., 1947; m. John M. Stuart, Dec. 11, 1954; children—Jane Adkins, Alice Stuart, Richard Stuart. Designer of illusions, off Broadway magic show Make Me Disappear, 1969; designer of space stations, 1977—; lectr. on space architecture, 1977—. Mem. Space Studies Inst., Space Frontier Soc., Internat. Brotherhood Magicians, Soc. Mayflower Descendants. Republican. Methodist. Author: (J. Marberger Stuart) You Don't Have to Slay A Dragon, 1975. Illustrator: Harbin on Magic, 1986. Home: 31 Westgate Blvd Plandome NY 11030

STUART, SISTER MARY A., nutrition researcher and educator, nun; b. Chgo., Nov. 27, 1933; d. Arthur Henry and Cecilia Margaret (Studer) S. BS in Biology, Siena Heights Coll., 1962, MS in Sci., 1969; PhD in Human Nutrition, Purdue U., 1983. Registered dietitian; joined Dominican Sisters, Roman Cath. Ch., 1951. Secondary sci. tchr. Academia Sagrado Corazon, Santurce, P.R., 1965-68, 74-79; instr. chemistry Cath. U. of P.R., Ponce, 1968-69; secondary sci. tchr. Centro Educacional de Bonao, Dominican Republic, 1971-74; research fellow Purdue U., West Lafayette, Ind., 1981-83; post-doctoral fellow USDA Human Nutrition Research Ctr., Grand Forks, N.D., 1983-85; post-doctoral fellow U. Ky. Med. Ctr., Lexington, 1985-86, sr. research assoc., 1986; asst. prof., dir. coordinated dietetics program U. Ky., Lexington, 1987—. Contbr. articles to profl. jours. NSF grantee, 1966, 68, 75. Mem. Am. Inst. Nutrition, Am. Dietetic Assn., Ky. Dietetic Assn., Bluegrass Dietetic Assn., Internat. Soc. for Trace Element Research in Humans, Nat. Assn. Research Nurses and Dietitians, Nutrition Today Soc., Omicron Nu, Sigma Xi. Home: 714 Lynn Dr Lexington KY 40504 Office: Univ Ky 212 Funkhouser Bldg Lexington KY 40506-0054

STUART, PAMELA BRUCE, lawyer; b. N.Y.C., Feb. 13, 1949; d. J. Raymond and Marion Grace (Cotins) S. AB with distinction, Mt. Holyoke Coll., 1970; JD cum laude, U. Mich., 1973. Bar: N.Y. 1974, D.C. 1975, U.S. Dist. Ct. D.C. 1979, U.S. Ct. Appeals (D.C. cir.) 1980, U.S. Supreme Ct. 1980. Trial atty., deputy asst. dir. Bur. of Consumer Protection, FTC, Washington, 1973-79; asst. U.S. atty. U.S. Atty's Office, Washington, 1979-85; sr. trial atty. Office of Internat. Affairs, U.S. Dept. Justice, Washington, 1985-87; atty. Ross, Dixon & Masback, Washington, 1987—. Mem. Jud. Conf. of D.C., 1985-88. Mem. Bar Assn. of D.C., Women's Bar Assn. of D.C., Alumnae Assn. of Mt. Holyoke Coll. (bd. dirs.). Home: 4601 Davenport St NW Washington DC 20016 Office: Ross Dixon & Masback 555 13th St NW Columbia Square Washington DC 20004

STUBAUS, KAREN RUTH, university dean; b. Englewood, N.J., June 12, 1950; d. Kenneth L. and Margaret S. (Dunning) S.; B.A. cum laude, Douglass Coll., 1972; M.A., Rutgers U., 1975, Ph.D., 1984; m. Stephen M. Goldfarb, May 6, 1978. Teaching asst. history dept. Douglass Coll., 1973-76; adminstrv. asst. to v.p. univ. personnel Rutgers U., 1976-77; program devel. specialist Bur. Research, N.J. Div. Youth and Family Services, 1977-78; asst. to dean, dir. continuing edn. Coll. Allied Health Scis., Thomas Jefferson U., Phila., 1978-81; exec. asst. Office Vice Chancellor, N.J. Dept. Higher Edn., 1981-82; acad. planning assoc. Rutgers U., New Brunswick, N.J., 1982-84, asst. dean, 1984—. Mem. Am. Hist. Assn., Orgn. Am. Historians, Nat. Coordinating Com. Promotion History (pres. N.J. chpt. 1982), Phi Beta Kappa. Co-editor: The American Revolution: Whose Revolution?, 1977. Home: 20 Aldrich Ave Metuchen NJ 08840 Office: Rutgers U New Brunswick NJ 08903

STUBBEN, DOLUS JANE (D.J.), advertising executive; b. Clovis, N.Mex., Sept. 12, 1951; d. Joseph P. Harmon and Maurine Yvonne (Simmons) McDonald; m. Ronald Patrick Day, Apr. 11, 1970 (div.); m. John David Stubben, Sept. 23, 1979 (div.); 1 child, Patricia Joan. Student West Tex. State U., 1969-70. Instr. Amarillo (Tex.) Coll., 1971-73; advt. cons., Amarillo, 1976-78; advt. mgr. Montgomery Ward, Amarillo, 1978-80; musician Furr's Cafeteria, Amarillo, 1978-80; piano bar musician, comedienne Quigley's Restaurant, Eugene, Oreg., 1980-81, Jolly's Comedy Club, Amarillo, 1986-88, Sheraton Towers of Amarillo, 1988—; owner, mgr. Welcome Pardner!, Amarillo, 1981—; arbitrator Better Bus. Bur., Amarillo, 1978-79. Author: #555 Death Row, 1981 (Nat. Press Women 2d place award, 1981), Dog Pause ..., 1981 (Nat. Press Women 2d place award 1982, Hon. Mention award 1987); It's a Secret, I Can't Tell You, 1984; songwriter and writer poetry. Media chmn. Am. Cancer Soc., Amarillo, 1978-79; media dir. Braley's 4th of July Picnic, Amarillo, 1977-78; media relations com. St. Jude's Hosp. Tex. Com., Amarillo, 1983; Mem. Tex. Press Women (v.p. 1982, state treas. 1986, membership chmn. 1986, 2 First Pl. awards 1987), Amarillo C. of C. (membership com. 1983). Office: Welcome Pardner PO Box 30926 Amarillo TX 79120

STUBBLEFIELD, JENNYE LEE WASHINGTON, home economist; b. Jacksonville, Fla., Mar. 6, 1925; d. Marion and Ira (McCombs) Washington; B.A. in Instn. Mgmt., Tuskegee (Ala.) Inst., 1946; M.S. in Nutrition, Rutgers U., 1966; m. Charles Stubblefield, June 26, 1954. Dietitian, Lincoln Hosp., Durham, N.J., 1946-48; instr. vets. cooking and baking schs., 1948-50; tchr. vocat. foods, cafeteria mgr. William Jason High Sch., Georgetown, Del., 1950-56; asst. dietitian Mercer Hosp., Trenton, N.J., 1957; instr. nutrition St. Francis Hosp. Sch. Nursing, Trenton, 1957-64, Helene Fulde Hosp. Sch. Nursing, Trenton, part-time 1965-71; dir. food service Middlesex County Head Start, New Brunswick, N.J., 1965-66; tchr. foods and nutrition Nottingham Jr. High Sch., Trenton, 1966-71; dir. dept. health, recreation and welfare City of Trenton, 1971-74; dir. Aid to Low Income Alcoholics Mercer County, Trenton, 1974-76; supr. consumer, homemaking, and family life edn. Trenton Bd. Edn., 1976—; co-adj. instr. Douglass Coll., 1964-65; adv. council Sch. Vocat. Edn., Rutgers U., 1977—. Chmn. bd. dirs. United Progress, Inc., Trenton, 1974-76; mem. Trenton City Council, 1976—, Black Women for Democratic Action, 1978—; vice chmn. Mercer County Dem. Com., 1981-83, chmn., 1983; bd. dirs. Trenton chpt. ARC, 1972-77, chmn., 1976—. Mem. Am. Dietetic Assn., Am. Home Econs. Assn., Home Econs. Edn. Assn., Vocat. Edn. Assn., Am. Vocat. Assn., N.J. Assn. Secondary Sch. Prins. and Suprs., Women's Polit. Caucus, NAACP. Home: 21 Alden Ave Trenton NJ 08618 Office: 108 N Clinton Ave Trenton NJ 08609

STUBBLEFIELD, KATHY JO, educator, dairy farmer; b. Murray, Ky., Sept. 6, 1952; d. Billy Joe and Jimmie Lee (Gingles) S. BS in English, Speech, Murray State U., 1974, MS in Speech, 1975. Tchr. Calloway County High Sch., Murray, 1975—; advisor, sponsor student council, sr. class, cheerleaders Calloway County High Sch., Murray, 1984—; dairy farmer, Murray. Past pres. 4-H Council, Calloway County, Ky.; advisor Ky. Jr. Jersey Cattle Club, 1973-78. Named Duchess of Paducah, Mayor of Paducah, Ky., 1972; named to Hon. Order Ky. col., Gov. of Ky., 1987. Mem. NEA, Ky. Edn. Assn., Calloway County Edn. Assn., 1st Dist. English Tchrs. Assn., Am. Jersey Cattle Club (nat. planning coms. 1977-82, chmn. com. 1979), Ky. Jersey Cattle Club (sec.-treas. 1983—), West Ky. Parish Jersey Club (sec.-treas. 1979—). Democrat. Mem. Ch. of Christ. Home: Rt 5 Box 479 Murray KY 42071 Office: Calloway County High Sch 2108 College Farm Rd Murray KY 42071

STUBBS, FRANCES EVELYN, banker; b. N.Y.C., Dec. 7, 1926; d. Cyrilo Juan and Madeline Orenina (Bowman) Lima; student public schs.; diploma Am. Inst. Banking, 1963; m. Andrew Stubbs, Nov. 25, 1946; children—Steven, Andrea. With Home owners Loan Corp., 1944-47, Kay Jewelers, N.Y.C., 1948-58; with Chase Manhattan Bank, N.A., N.Y.C., 1959—, asst. v.p., mgr. comml. loan ops., 1981-83, asst. v.p., mgr. lockbox, 1983-85, tng. coordinator, 1985—. Vice pres. Family Services Westchester, 1983—. Mem. Nat. Assn. Bank Women (chpt. chmn. 1979-80), Westchester County Bankers Assn. (treas. 1979-85), Bus. and Profl. Women New Rochelle (pres. 1983-85), Negro Bus. and Profl. Women New Rochelle (fin. sec. 1980-85). Presbyterian. Office: 1 New York Plaza New York NY 10081

STUCYNSKI, SUSAN MOEN, information systems designer and implementer; b. Mpls., Sept. 25, 1950; d. Lorna M. (Bisek) Moen; m. Steven Louis Stucynski, June 7, 1974. BA in Liberal Arts with highest distinction, U. Minn., 1974; MBA in Acctg. and Pub. Mgmt., U. Pa., 1979. With accounts payable div. Valspar Corp., Mpls., 1974-75; supr. bus. office neurology dept. U. Pa. Hosp., Phila., 1975-77; sr. mgr. mgmt. info. cons. div. Arthur Andersen & Co., Phila., 1979—. Mem. steering com. Garden Ct. Plaza Tenants Assn., Phila., 1977-80; spl. cons. marathon fundraiser Phila. Orch., 1979-84; bd. dirs. Big Bros./Big Sisters, Montgomery County, Pa., 1986—. Named one of Outstanding Young Women of Am. Phila. YWCA, 1983. Mem. Nat. Assn. Female Execs., Phi Beta Kappa. Home: 515 W King Rd Malvern PA 19355 Office: Arthur Andersen & Co 5 Penn Center Plaza Suite 2600 Philadelphia PA 19103

STUDD, KAREN ANNE, arts and drama educator; b. Scranton, Pa., May 15, 1955; d. Howard R. and Rita (Rooney) S. BS, U. Oreg., 1978, MS, 1983; cert. movement analysis, Laban Inst. Movement Studies, 1987. Tchr., performer, choreographer Community Ctr. Performing Arts, Eugene, Oreg., 1978-81; instr. Lane Community Coll., Eugene, 1982, City of Eugene Parks and Recreation Dept., 1979-83; performer Mary Miller Dance Co., Eugene, 1981-83; asst. prof. U. Wis., Stevens Point, 1983—; grad. teaching fellow U. Oreg. Dance Dept., 1981-83. Choreographer Orchestral Bodies, 1984, Undercurrents, 1985 (Am. Coll. Dance Festival award 1985), Meshing, 1986, Tango Tangent, 1987 (Am. Coll. Dance Festival award 1987). Recipient Chanceors Teaching Excellence award, 1986. Mem. Wis. Dance Assn. (bd. dirs. 1986—), Am. Dance Guild. Democrat.

STUDLEY, HELEN ORMSON, artist, poet, writer, designer; b. Elroy, Wis., Sept. 8, 1937; d. Clarence Ormson and Hilda (Johnson) O.; m. William Frank Studley, Aug. 1965 (div.); 1 son, William Harrison. Owner RJK Original Art, Sherman Oaks, Calif., 1979—; designer Aspen Series custom greeting cards and stationery notes, lithographs Love is All Colors, 1982; represented in numerous pub. and pvt. collections throughout U.S., Can., Norway, Sweden, Austria, Germany, Eng., France; author poetry Love is Care, Changes, 1988. Active Luth. Brotherhood, Emmanuel Luth. Ch. Honors include display of lithograph Snow Dreams, Snow Queens at 1980 Winter Olympics, Lake Placid, N.Y., lithograph Summer Dreams, Summer Queens at 1984 Summer Olympics, Los Angeles; named finalist in competition for John Simon Guggenheim fellowship. Mem. Soc. Illustrators, Am. Watercolor Soc., Internat. Soc. Artists, Internat. Platform Assn., Calif. Woman's Art Guild. Club: Sons of Norway. Office: RJK Original Art 5020 Hazeltine Ave Sherman Oaks CA 91423

STUDY, MARY MARGARET (TELLER), small business owner; b. Oklahoma City, Dec. 3, 1945; d. Ernest Leonard and Mary Ann Teller; B.A., U. No. Colo., 1967; M.A. in Public Relations, M.A. in Journalism, Ball State U., 1970; m. Larry Lee Study, Jan. 3, 1970; 1 son, Darren Boyd. Report specialist, adminstrv. specialist, Avionics Research, Ohio U., Athens, 1971-73, exec. sec. dean Coll. Engring. and Tech., 1973-74; instr.-lectr. public relations Sch. Mass Communications, Mara Inst. Tech., Shah Alam, Malaysia, 1974-76; owner-mgr. Alpha Graphics Ltd., Print Media Service Center, Muncie, 1976—; cons. advt. spltys., 1980—; freelance public relations writer, cons., Athens, 1970-74; free lance writer, pub. periodicals on small bus., graphics, advt. Chmn., Oktoberfest, 1979; Muncie Am's. Hometown Taskforce Licensee, 1987-88; vol. WIPB-TV, 1986—, publicity release writer Mcht's Group, Muncie Mall, 1987; mem. Downtown Bus. Council Retail Promotions and Spl. Events Com., 1978-81, chmn., 1979-81; mem. Try Muncie First Com.; mem. Public Relations Task Force, 1972. Mem. Women in Communications (advisor Ball State U. chpt. 1969), C. of C. Muncie-Delaware County (small bus. council 1979), Alpha Gamma Delta. Editor, pub. Muncie Marketeer, 1978. Office: 111 E Adams Muncie IN 47305

STUECK, LOIS ELAINE, association administrator; b. N.Y.C., Nov. 9, 1936; d. Charles Paul, Sr. and Catherine (Wehner) Hillicke; m. Clifford J. Stueck, July 14, 1956; children: Eileen Leech, Kathleen Kane, John, Paul, Florence. BA in French and Spanish Edn., Queens Coll., 1958; MS in Elem. Edn., U. Bridgeport, 1972. Tchr. Bridgeport (Conn.) Sch. System, 1969-81; first selectman Town of Easton, Conn., 1981-85; exec. v.p. Fairfield (Conn.) C. of C., 1985—; mem. adv. com. Inst. Pub. Service U. Conn., 1984. mem. Greater Bridgeport Met. Planning Orgn., 1982-85, Gov.'s Task Force on Pvt. Sector Initiatives, 1985; dir. Conn. Conf. Municipalities, 1982-85; sec. bd. dirs. Council of Small Towns, 1982-85; hon. bd. dirs. Bridgeport Hosp., 1982-85; vol. Easton Ems, Easton Redding Safe Rides, Meals on Wheels. Mem. Conn. Assn. C. of C. Execs., New Eng. Assn. C. of C., U.S. Assn. C. of C., LWV, Fedn. Dem. Women. Roman Catholic. Home: 18 Shields Ln Ridgefield CT 06877

STUEHR, GAIL ANNE, journalist; b. Cleve.; d. Lee R. and Isabel M. (McCaa) Featheringham; children—Laura Lee, David John, Eric William, Andrea Lynne. Student Muskingum Coll., U. Mich.; B.S. in Edn., Kent State U., 1961; postgrad. Case Western Res. U. Corr., Plain Dealer, Cleve., 1971-81, Sun Newspapers, 1971-76; free-lance writer, pub. relations cons., 1971—; editor, writer Case Western Res. U., Cleve., 1979-80, sr. editor, 1980, dir. media relations, 1980-81, dir. pub. relations Sch. Medicine, 1981—. Contbr. articles to profl. jours. and newspapers. Bd. dirs. Greater Cleve. Counseling Service of Greater Cleve. Interch. Council. Recipient Communicators award Women in Communications, Inc., 1982; Amateur Photography Contest winner Cleve. Press, 1978, 79. Mem. Women in Communications, Inc., Press Club of Cleve. (awards com. 1983-88), Internat. Assn. Bus. Communicators, Am. Assn. Med. Colls., Council for the Advance and Support of Edn. Avocations: swimming; fiction writing; travel; photography. Home: 2183 Demington Dr Cleveland Heights OH 44106 Office: Case Western Res U Sch Medicine Rm W174 Cleveland OH 44106

STULL, FAYE ROSE, banker, counselor; b. Longview, Tex., May 24, 1941; d. Oliver C. and Melissa (Blackman) Hunter; m. Billy C. Stull, Sept. 13, 1962; 1 child, Kathleen. BS in Bus. Adminstrn., U. San Francisco, 1976, MA in Psychology, 1985. Official ops. Wells Fargo Bank, San Jose, Calif., 1972-76, official banking service, 1976-79, asst. mgr., 1979-83, loan officer, 1983—; counselor, therapist Caravan House, Palo Alto, Calif., 1984—; counselor El Camino Hosp., Mountain View, Calif., 1985; clin. dir., counselor Drew Health Found. Advisor Jr. Achievement, San Jose, 1979-82; vol. Strawberry Festival, Los Gatos, Calif., 1981; mem. exec. bd. dirs., officer, treas., program com. Shelter Against Violent Environment, Freemont, Calif. Mem. Soc. Cert. Credit Execs., Santa Clara Valley Urban League. Democrat. Methodist. Home: 2460 W Bayshore Rd #7 Palo Alto CA 94303 Office: Wells Fargo Bank 505 California Ave Palo Alto CA 94306

STUMAN-JONES, DOROTHY LUCILLE, civic leader; b. Marianna, Fla., Mar. 30, 1924; d. Thomas Otto and Shandora (Tharpe) Temples; m. Robert B. Stuman Jr., June 17, 1944 (dec. 1980); children: Barbara Ann, Robert B., Cathy Amanda; m. J. Arthur Jones, Aug. 22, 1987 (dec. May 1988). Student, Massey Bus. Coll., 1945-47, Alverson Bus. Coll., 1947-48, Jefferson State Jr. Coll., 1967-68. Dept. head R.P. McDavid & Co., Birmingham, Ala., 1944-45; sec. to pres. Armour & Co., Birmingham, Ala., 1945-49; free-lance interior decorator Birmingham, 1950—; exec. sec. CLP Corp., doing bus. as McDonald's, Birmingham, 1973—. Contbr. short stories to Nat. Clubwoman, (best in category award for Life of Modern Woman). Active Women's Com. Ala. Symphony Orch.; program chmn. Camelia Scholarship Luncheon; pub. chmn. Birmingham Beautification Bd., 1986-87, plant dig chmn., garden club chmn., litter chmn., 1980-88, chmn., 1988—; vol. East End Hosp.; supt. jr. dept. Sunday sch.; membership chmn. Decorator Showhouse Com.; pres. Women's Missionary Union, 1961-65. Mem. Bus. and Profl. Women's Orgn. (dist. dir. 1985-86, pres. Huffman chpt.,1987—), Women's C. of C. (1st v.p. 1987—, pres. 1988—), VFW, LWV, Iris Soc. Thalian Lit. Club. Republican. Lodges: Shriners, Order of Eastern Star (grand chpt. com. mem., worthy matron two terms).Club: Floradora Garden (pres. 1987—). Home: 245 Roebuck Dr Birmingham AL 35215 Office: CLP Corp 124 Summit Pkwy Birmingham AL 35209

STUMBO, ANITA YVONNE, investment industry publishing executive, stockbroker; b. Dallas, Dec. 9, 1948; d. Earnest Eugene and Edna Maureen (Dill) Randall; m. Allen Stumbo, May 20, 1972; children: John Allen, Kelli Cathleen, James Michael. Student North Tex. State U., 1967-69. Mut. fund clk. Republic Nat. Bank, Dallas, 1969-72; asst. sec.-treas. Fund Mgmt. Co., Dallas, 1972-75; v.p., broker Schneider Bernet & Hickman, Dallas, 1975-83; br. mgr. mcpl. bond dept. Bateman Eichler Hill Richards, Dallas, 1983-84; pres. RR Publ. & Prodn. Co., Inc., Dallas, 1984—; stockbroker W.S. Griffith & Co. Inc., Dallas, 1986—; trustee Walnut Hill UMC Found., Dallas, 1984—; registered rep. N.Y. Stock Exchange, Am. Stock Exchange, Chgo. Bd. Options Exchange; assoc. Commodity Futures Trading Commn. Author, pub. book and study course: Winning Big with UIT Commissions, 1984; author, editor, pub.: The UIT Directory, 1984—; author, pub.: Wall Street Minder, 1985-86, The Wall Street Week with Louis Rukeyser (fin. calendar), 1987; contbr. articles to local newspapers, mags. Creator Parent to Parent, Dallas, 1980-84; active Edna Gladney Aux., Dallas; bd. dirs. Assn. Retarded Citizens Dallas, Walnut Hill UMC Creative Salon, Dallas, 1985—. Named Miss Denton, Denton Jr. C. of C., Tex., 1968. Mem. Nat. Assn. Security Dealers (registered rep. 1972—, registered prin. 1979—), Exec. Women Dallas, Dallas Women's C. of C. (bd. dirs. 1982-83). Methodist. Avocations: organ, piano. Office: RR Publication & Prodn Co Inc PO Box 541073 Dallas TX 75254-1073

STUPEC, GERTRAUD BLEY, food research and development executive; b. Lansing, Mich., June 3, 1937; d. Alfred and Marie Margot (Barkow) Bley. BS in Chemistry, Mich. State U., 1959; MBA in Mktg. Econs., U. Ill., Chgo., 1980. Analytical chemist Corn Products Co., Argo, Ill., 1959-67; research chemist Wilson & Co., Chgo., 1967-69; project leader Beatrice Foods Co., Chgo., 1969-81, mgr. research and devel. U.S. food, 1985-87; mgr. mktg. planning Beatrice Food Ingredients, Beloit, Wis., 1981-85; mgr. flavor applications Food Materials Corp., Chgo., 1987—. Patentee reconstitution of pork rinds by extrusion. Mem. Inst. Food Technologists, Planning Forum, Am. Mktg. Assn., Am. Assn. Investors. Republican. Home: 8212 Cromwell Ave Woodridge IL 60517 Office: Food Materials Corp 2711 W Irving Park Rd Chicago IL 60618

STURGEON, SARA SUE, dentist; b. Indpls., Dec. 31, 1950; d. Melvin I. and Velva Ernestine (Coffin) S. B, Ind. U., 1972, DDS, 1976. Gen. practice dentistry Bloomington, Ind., 1976—; cons. dentistry Hospitality House Nursing Home, Bloomington, 1976—, Bloomington Nursing Home, 1976—; team dist. Ind. U. Women's Athletics, 1976—; mem. Ind. State Controlled Substance Adv. Bd., 1986—. Mem. ADA, Am. Assn. Women Dentists, Acad. Sports Dentistry, Am. Assn. Dental Examiners, Ind. State Bd. Dental Examiners, Acad. Gen. Dentistry, Ind. Dental Assn., Cen. Ind. Tennis Assn. (exec. com., treas. 1982-86, bd. dirs.). Club: Ind. U. Varsity. Office: 320 E 6th St Bloomington IN 47401

STURGES, GLORIA JUNE, learning disabilities educator; b. Ingallas, Kans., Nov. 10, 1937; d. Donald Nathan and Dorothy Ellen (Whaley) Kitch; m. W.G. Bray, Jan. 22, 1960 (div. Apr. 1978); children—Lori Lynn, William Don; m. Sidney James Sturges. B.S. in Edn., Southeastern State U., 1959; M.A. in Edn., Webster U., 1975; postgrad. U. Kans., 1978-84, cert. learning disabilities specialty, 1984. Cert. tchr. elem. edn., Colo., Mo., reading and learning disabilities specialist, Mo. Tchr., Jefferson County Schs., Denver, 1959-60, Briggsdale, Colo., 1960-63, Colo. Sch. for Deaf and Blind, Colorado Springs, 1963-66, Bertha Heid Sch., Thornton, Colo., 1966-70; reading specialist Center Sch. Dist., Kansas City, Mo., 1970-78, learning disabilities specialist, 1985—; bus. exec. Sturges Co., Independence, Mo., 1982—. Active ARC, 1984—, Nat. Polit. Action, Kansas City, Mo., 1970—. conference presenter Emporia State U. Recipient Excellence in Edn. award ARC, 1984-85; Outstanding Achievement award Colo. for Deaf and Blind, 1963. Mem. Nat. Assn. Females Execs., NEA, Kappa Delta Pi. Republican. Baptist. Avocations: gourmet cooking; tennis; swimming; antiques. Home: 16805 Cogan Rd Independence MO 64055 Office: Red Bridge Sch 418 E 106th Terr Kansas City MO 64131

STURGIS, KATHY ANN, lawyer; b. N.Y.C., Aug. 28, 1952; d. Irv DeKoff and Belle (Kerner) DeKoff Shouse; m. Radford Russell Sturgis, May 30, 1976. BA, Mt. Holyoke Coll., 1977; JD cum laude, Stetson U., 1986. Bar: Fla. 1986. Family services aide Dept. Health and Rehab. Services, Ft. Myers, Fla., 1974-77; legis. aide Fla. Ho. of Reps., Ft. Myers and Tallahassee, 1977-79; exec. dir. Voluntary Action Ctr., Lee County, Fla., 1979-80; substitute tchr. Lee County Dist. Sch. Bd., Ft. Myers, 1980-81; owner Dance Fitness Unltd., Cape Coral, Fla., 1980-83; law clk. to circuit judges Fla. 20th Jud. Cir., Ft. Myers, 1985; assoc. Peper, Martin, Jensen, Maichel & Hetlage, Ft. Myers, 1986—. Admissions rep. Mt. Holyoke Coll., SW Fla., 1982—; secretariat mem. Gulf Coast Cursillo, Lee County, 1983; campaign coordinator Com. to Retain Judge Sturgis, Lee County, 1982; bd. dirs. Edison Women's Ctr., Lee County, 1978. Charles A. Dana scholar Stetson U., 1985-86. Mem. ABA, Lee County Bar Assn. (chmn. law related edn. com.), Fla. Bar Assn. (law related edn. com. 1987—). Presbyterian. Clubs: Pilot (Ft. Myers), P.E.O. Office: Peper Martin Jensen et al 2125 1st St Fort Myers FL 33901

STURGULEWSKI, ARLISS, state senator; b. Blaine, Wash., Sept. 27, 1927; B.A., U. Wash. Mem. Assembly Municipality of Anchorage; vice chmn. New Capital Site Planning Commn., mem. Capital Site Selection Com.; chmn. Greater Anchorage Area Planning and Zoning Commn.; mem. Alaska State Senate, 1978—. Rep. nominee Office Gov. Alaska, 1986. Address: Office of the State Senate State Capitol Juneau AK 99811

STURM, RUTH FOSTER, lawyer; b. Bklyn., Jan. 3, 1911; d. Ernest and L. Elsie (Foster) Sturm; B.A., Vassar Coll., 1932; LL.B., Columbia, 1935; summer study U. Lausanne (Switzerland), 1929, U. Berlin, 1931. Admitted to N.Y. bar, 1936, pvt. practice N.Y.C., 1936-42, assoc. with Walter F. O'Malley, Esq.; law asst. Ct. of Appeals State N.Y., 1942-44; U.S. Customs Ct., 1944-76. Mem. Gov.'s Com. Edn. and Employment Women, 1964-65, adv. com. Hudson River Valley Commn., 1965-66. Mem. N.Y. County Lawyer's Assn., Fed. Bar Assn., Bus. and Profl. Women's Club Tarrytowns (pres. 1948-50, N.Y. State safety chmn. 1950-52, by-laws chmn. 1953-58, 2d v.p. 1958-60, 1st v.p. 1960-62, pres. 1962-64, parliamentarian 1972-76), Nat. Council Women, Phi Beta Kappa, Kappa Beta Pi. Republican. Presbyn. Author: A Manual of Customs Law, 1974, supplement, 1976; Customs Law and Administration, 1980, 3d edit. 1982, rev. edits., 1983, 84, 85, 86, 87. Home: Hudson House Ardsley-on-Hudson NY 10503

STURNICK, JUDITH ANN, college president, consultant; b. Mankato, Minn., Apr. 9, 1939. B.A. in English and History, U. N.D., 1961; M.A. in English, Miami U., Oxford, Ohio, 1963; Ph.D. in English, Ohio State U., 1967. Vis. asst. prof. U. S.C., Columbia, 1967-68; asst. prof. Ohio State U.-Newark, 1968-69; chmn. dept. English, dir. honors program Capital U., Columbus, Ohio, 1969-78; v.p. acad. affairs S.W. State U., Marshall, Minn., 1978-83; pres. U. Maine-Farmington, 1983-87, Keene (N.H.) State Coll., 1987—. Co-author: Women's Studies Guide, 1979; contbr. articles to profl. jours. Mem. nat. adv. bd. Rural Am. Women, Washington, 1979-85; bd. dirs. United Way, Farmington, 1983—; chmn. fund raising com. Maine Humanities Council, 1984—; chair Nat. Commn. on Women in Higher Edn., 1986-87. Recipient Praestantia award for Outstanding Teaching, Capital U., 1972; Woodrow Wilson fellow, 1961-62, Nat. Def. fellow, 1961-64. Mem. AAUW, Maine Bus. and Profl. Women, Am. Assn. State Colls. and Univs. (nat. bd. dirs. 1986—), Maine Consortium for Health Professions Edn. (trustee, pres.-elect), Nat. Women's Studies Assn. (co-chmn. nat. coordinating council 1977-79), Nat. Council Edn., New Eng. Assn. Schs. and Colls. (chmn. accrediting teams 1985—), Phi Beta Kappa. Lutheran. Home: 100 Main St Farmington ME 04938 Office: Keene State Coll 229 Main Keene NH 03431-4183

STUTMAN, NANCY, calligrapher, graphic designer, educator; b. Detroit, Feb. 26, 1938; d. Albert E. and Pearl P. (Liebovich) Cook; m. William N. Stutman, Oct. 20, 1963; children—Michael, David. Student U. Ill., 1956-58; cert., grad. with honors Tobe Coburn Sch. for Fashion Careers, N.Y.C., 1959. Asst. buyer millinery R.H. Macy Co. Herald Sq., N.Y.C., 1959-60; exec. asst. Doris Weston, N.Y.C., 1960-64; account exec. Promotion Council Am., N.Y.C., 1965; v.p., co-owner Stutman Assocs., Inc., N.Y.C., 1965-83; prin. Nancy Stutman Calligraphics, Chappaqua, N.Y., 1982-87, Encinitas, Calif., 1987—; workshop instr. for calligraphic socs. The Bus. of Calligraphy, 1984—, Internat. Calligraphy Conf., Portland, Oreg., 1987, Washington, 1988; chairperson promotional gifts/lit N.Y. Soc. Scribes Internat. Calligraphy Conf., 1986. Juried show Master Eagle Gallery, N.Y.C., 1982, 85. Coordinator bus. services-donations for auction to send local baseball team to Cuba, 1982; chairperson fundraising tag sale Blythedale Children's Hosp., Valhalla, N.Y., 1983; vol. Am. Cancer Soc., White Plains, 1985-86, New Westchester Orch., 1985; vol. calligrapher Temple Beth El of No. Westchester, Chappaqua, 1978-88, also active sisterhood and brotherhood. Recipient Service award Temple Beth El of No. Westchester, 1982, 85. Mem. Advt. Club Westchester (hon. mem. 1984, bd. dirs. 1985-87, sec. 1986-87, Gold design award 1984, 85, 86, 87, 2 Bronze awards 1986, Hall of Fame award 1985, Chester award 1987), N.Y. Soc. Scribes, Westchester Assn. Women Bus. Owners (bd. dirs. 1981-87, Pres.'s award 1983), Women in Communications, Westchester County C. of C. (vol. Small Bus. Week, chairperson support network 1985). Democrat. Home and Office: 3008 Rana Ct La Costa CA 92008

STUTTMAN, SUZANNE LEE, art administrator; b. N.Y.C., Mar. 17, 1962; d. Martin L. and Frances (Ruberto) S. BA with honors, Skidmore Coll., 1984; MA, Columbia U., 1985. Copywriter Elsevier Sci. Pub. Co., Inc., N.Y.C., 1985-86; promotions assoc. Raven Press, N.Y.C., 1986-87; freelance copywriter N.Y.C., 1987-88; art adminstr. Sotheby's, N.Y.C., 1988—. Mem. Women's Direct Response Group N.Y., Nat. Assn. Female Execs.

STUTZ, SANDRA LEE, real estate developer; b. Bklyn., Feb. 13, 1948; d. Albert and Miriam Stutz. BA, SUNY, Cortland, 1969. Pres., broker Trio Realty Inc., Bklyn., 1974-76; pres. Prominent Properties Inc., Bklyn., 1984—; sponsor 24 Remsen St. Housing Corp., Bklyn., 1982-88, 421-4th St. Housing Corp., Bklyn., 1984-86. Renovator of Landmark Brownstone Builders, 1982-88. Mem. Cert. Real Estate Appraisers, Bklyn. Bd. Realtors, Bklyn. Heights Assn. Home: 24 Remsen St Brooklyn Heights NY 11201

STYLES, MARGRETTA MADDEN, nursing educator; b. Mount Union, Pa., Mar. 19, 1930; d. Russell B. and Agnes (Wilson) Madden; m. Douglas F. Styles, Sept. 4, 1954; children: Patrick, Michael, Megan. B.S., Juniata Coll., 1950; M. in Nursing, Yale U., 1954; Ed.D., U. Fla., 1968; hon. doctorate, Valparaiso U., 1986. Staff nurse VA Hosp., West Haven, Conn., 1954-55; instr. Bklyn. Hosp. Sch. Nursing, 1955-58; supr. North Dist. Hosp., Pompano Beach, Fla., 1961-63; dir. nursing edn. Broward Community Coll., Ft. Lauderdale, Fla., 1963-67; asso. prof. Sch. Nursing, Duke U., Durham, N.C., 1967-69; dir. undergrad. studies Sch. Nursing, Duke U., 1967-69; prof., dean Sch. Nursing, U. Tex., San Antonio, 1969-73; dean, prof. Coll. Nursing Wayne State U., Detroit; prof. nursing U. Calif., San Francisco, 1977—, dean Sch. Nursing, 1977-87; chairperson Com. for Study of Credentializing in Nursing, 1976-79; mem. adv. group div. nursing HEW, 1977; spl. asst. to pres. for health affairs U. Calif. Systemwide, 1979; dir. nursing services U. Calif. Hosps. and Clinics, 1978-87; mem. Nat. Commn. Nursing, 1980—; mem. Calif. Bd. Registered Nursing, 1985—; mem. Sec.'s Commn. on Nursing HHS, 1988—. Author: On Nursing: Toward a New Endowment (Am. Jour. Nursing Book of Yr. award 1982). Recipient Disting. Alumna award Yale U. Sch. Nursing, 1979; Am. Nurses' Found. 1st disting. scholar, 1983. Fellow Am. Acad. Nursing; mem. Nat. Acad. Scis., Am. Nurses Assn. (pres. 1985-87), Sigma Theta Tau. Office: Univ California School Nursing N531C-D Box 0608 San Francisco CA 94143

SUAREZ, MARY ANN RITA, municipal official; b. Phila., July 20, 1953; d. Alfred Patrick and Rita Kathryn (Scanzaroli) S. AS, Harcum Jr. Coll., 1973; BS, Cabrini Coll., 1975. Cert. elem. tchr., Pa. Sec. Sears Roebuck & Co., St. Davids, PA., 1975-80; tchr. Radnor (Pa.) Schs., 1980-83; adminstrv. asst. Telet Word Processing, King of Prussia, Pa., 1983-86; sec. Thornbury Township, Westtown, Pa., 1986—. Author: American Poetry Anthology, 1982. Mem. Nat. Assn. Female Execs., Pa. Local Govt. Secs. Assn., Alumni Admissions Bd. Cabrini Coll., Bus. and Profl. Women. Home: 223 Matthew Rd Merion Station PA 19066

SUAREZ, SALLY ANN, health care administrator, nurse, consultant; b. Jersey City, Jan. 23, 1944; d. Paul John and Gertrude Marie (Clancey) Tevis; m. Angel A. Suarez (div. June 1977); 1 child, Maria E. Diploma, St. Mary Hosp. Sch. Nursing, 1965; BA in Health Edn. and Nursing, Jersey City State Coll., 1966, MA in Health Sci., 1977. Staff nurse St. Mary Hosp., Hoboken, N.J., 1965, Bayonne (N.J.) Hosp., 1966, Jersey City Med. Ctr., 1965-66; adminstr. Hoboken Med. Arts Family Health Ctr., 1969-75; adj. faculty Jersey City State Coll., 1976-77; adminstrv. supr. St. Mary Hosp., Hoboken, 1977-80; dir. North Hudson Commn. Action Corp. Clinic, West New York, N.J., 1979—; instr. nursing St. Mary Hosp. Sch. Nursing; cons. Creative Concepts in Counseling, Rutherford, N.J., 1979-82, Com. for Cytogenetics, Newark, 1986—. Active March of Dimes, Hudson County, 1982—, ARC, Hudson County, 1984—, United Way, 1984—. Mem. Am. Nurses Assn., N.J. Nurses Assn., N.Y. Acad. Scis., Am. Pub. Health Assn., N.J. Pub. Health Assn., Am. Nursing Found., Nat. League Nursing, N.J. Family Planning Forum (exec. com. 1980-86), Family Planning Assn. N.J. (exec. com. 1986—). Democrat. Roman Catholic. Home: 113 Wilson Ave Rutherford NJ 07070 Office: North Hudson Commn Action Corp 5918 Bergenline Ave West New York NJ 07093

SUAREZ-ROGERS, BARBARA JEANNE, pathology supervisor; b. Detroit, Jan. 3, 1938; d. Henry Walter and Vera Kathleen (Cole) Rogers; m. Ralph John Suarez (dec. 1975); children: William, Charles, Michael, Robert. Student, U. Paris, 1984, Wayne State U., 1984; AA, Harbor Coll., 1985. Supr., instructional coordinator Harbor UCLA Med. Ctr., Torrance, Calif., 1974—; owner Photos by Rogers, 1960-65; photo colorist Van Gogh Studio, Chgo. Office: Harbor UCLA Med Ctr 1000 W Carson Torrance CA 90509

SUBAK-SHARPE, GENELL J., editor, writer; b. Great Falls, Mont.; m. Gerald Subak-Sharpe; children—David, Sarah and Hope (twins). B.A., Butler U., 1959; M.S. in Journalism with honors, Columbia U., 1961. Reporter Indpls. Star, 1958-61; copy editor N.Y. Times, 1962-70; exec. editor Family Health mag. (now Health), 1970-74; editor Med. Opinion mag., 1974-77; v.p., editor Biomed. Info. Corp., 1977-84; pres. G.S. Sharpe Communications Inc., N.Y.C., 1981—. Editor: The Compendium of Drug Therapy, 1979; co-editor: The Physicians' Drug Manual, 1981; editor: The Compendium of Patient Information, 1982; author: (with Kathryn Schrotenboer) Freedom From Menstrual Cramps, 1981; editor: The Physicians' Manual for Patients, 1984; author: Overcomming Breast Cancer, 1987, Breathing Easy, 1988; (with James V. Warren) Frontiers in Medicine series, 1984—, (with Joan Ness) The Calcium-Requirement Cookbook, 1985, (with Lois Jovanovic) Hormones: The Woman's Answerbook, 1987, (with Robert Weiss) Columbia University School of Public Health Complete Guide to Health and Well-Being After 50; editoral dir.: Columbia University College of Physicians and Surgeons Complete Home Medical Guide, 1985; founding editor: The Compendium of Drug Therapy, 1979—; The Compendium of Patient Information, 1983—; Being Well, 1983—; Off Hours, 1983—; Health & Nutrition Newsletter, 1984—. Pulitzer Travel fellow Columbia U., 1961-62; recipient Russell L. Cecil Writing award, Arthritis Found., 1972, Mag. Writing award, Am. Dental Soc., 1977, Blakeslee award Am. Heart Assn., 1985. Mem. Authors Guild, Women's Press Club, Nat. Assn. Sci. Writers, Newswomens Club N.Y. Avocations: restorations historic houses, antique collecting. Home: 606 W 116th St New York NY 10027 Office: G S Sharpe Communications Inc 606 W 116th St New York City NY 10027

SUCHANEK, JEANNE ONTKO, society director, consultant; b. Youngstown, Ohio, Oct. 22, 1955; d. Andrew Anthony and Verne Marie (Dickey) Ontko; m. Jeffrey Scott Suchanek, April, 9, 1983. BA, Youngstown State U., 1979, MA, 1981. Mus. asst. The Mahoning Valley Hist. Soc., Youngstown, Ohio, 1977-81; archivist The Ohio Hist. Soc., Columbus, 1981-84, cons., 1984-85, edn. coordinator, 1985-87; dir. The Ohio Mus. Assn., Columbus, 1987-88; div. dir. Ky. Hist. Soc., Frankfort, 1988—; oral history cons., Columubus, 1987. Editor: Local Government Records Handbook, 1984. The Seminar for Hist. Adminstrn. fellow, 1984. Mem. The Nat. Assn. Female Execs., Ohio Assn. Hist. Socs. and Mus., Ohio Mus. Assn., Midwest Mus. Conf., Am. Assn. for State and Local History, Phi Kappa Phi. Democrat. Roman Catholic. Office: Ky Hist Soc Box H Frankfort KY 40602

SUDAKOFF, MARLENE MITCHELL MOOERS, lawyer; b. Mpls., Feb. 22, 1935; d. Henry Joseph and Frances O'Byrne Mitchell; m. Edwin Stanton Mooers II, July 31, 1965 (dec. 1970); 1 child, Edwin Stanton III; m. 2d, Michael Richard Sudakoff, Jan. 22, 1977. JD, U. Minn., 1958. Bar: Minn. 1959, Fla. 1980. Former ptnr. firm Mitchell & Pierce; ptnr. Goldne Apple Dinner Theatre, Mpls., from 1971; now ptnr. firm Ahlquist & Sudakoff P.A., Sarasota, Fla.; bd. dirs. Three Arts Prodns. Inc., Coastal Prodns. Inc. Asst. treas. Miller for Congress campaign, 1974; active Women Minn. Symphony Orch.; bd. dirs., historian Sarasota Opera Soc.; bd. dirs. Fla. Ballet Inc., Women's Ctr., Family Counseling Ctr.; treas. San Remo (Fla.) Assn., 1980-81; 1st woman chmn. bd. trustees Doctors Hosp., Sarasota, 1987-88, bd. trustees, 1988-89; v.p., dir. Project Rainbow, Inc., 1988—. Mem. ABA, Minn. Bar Assn., Fla. Bar Assn., Sarasota County Bar Assn., Am. Judicature Soc., Assn. Trial Lawyers Am., Criminal Cts. Bar Assn., St. Andrew's Soc., English-Speaking Union, Kappa Beta Pi. Club: Sarasota City. Home: 3647 San Remo Terr Sarasota FL 33579 Office: 2088 Hawthorne St Sarasota FL 34239

SUDBRINK, JANE MARIE, sales and marketing executive; b. Sandusky, Ohio, Jan. 14, 1942; niece of Arthur and Lydia Sudbrink. B.S., Bowling Green State U., 1964; student in cytogenetics Kinderspital-Zurich, Switzerland, 1965. Field rep. Random House and Alfred A. Knopf Inc., Mpls., 1969-72, Ann Arbor, Mich., 1973, regional mgr., Midwest and Can., 1974-79, Canadian rep., mgr., 1980-81; psychology and ednl. psychology adminstrv. editor Charles E. Merrill Pub. Co. div. Bell & Howell Corp., Columbus, Ohio, 1982-84; sales and mktg. mgr. trade products Wilson Learning Corp., Eden Prairie, Minn., 1984-85; fin. cons. Merrill Lynch Pierce Fenner & Smith, Edina, 1986—; sr. editor Gorsuch Scarisbrick Pubs., Scottsdale, Ariz., 1988—. Mem. Am. Ednl. Research Assn., Nat. Assn. Female Execs. Lutheran. Home and Office: 1010 N Plum Grove Rd Schaumburg IL 60173

SUDDUTH, MARY HOSSLEY, operation manager; b. Vicksburg, Miss., Sept. 18, 1947; d. Earl Cecil and Elsie Jane (Tucker) Hossley; m. James A. Sudduth, Mar. 7, 1986; stepchildren—Shawn, Bradley. B.S. in Edn., Miss. State U., 1970. Tchr., Columbus pub. schs., Miss., 1972; sec. to pres. Columbus Marble Works, 1972-76; sec. Miss. State U., Miss., 1976-77; sec. J.L. Teel Co., Columbus, 1977; sec. to v.p. Northrup King Co., Columbus, 1977-82; ops. mgr. Yellow Freight System, Columbus, 1982—. Republican. Roman Catholic. Avocations: needlework; sewing; reading; fishing. Home: PO Box 2643 Columbus MS 39704 Office: Yellow Freight System PO Drawer 2188 Columbus MS 39704

SUDERMAN, INEZ ALDENE, real estate broker; b. Bessie, Okla., July 10, 1938; d. Adolph B. and Lea (Wedel) Javorsky; m. Emery Lowell Suderman, July 29, 1960; children—James, Carol, Timothy. B.S. in Edn., Southwestern U., 1960; B.S., Pan Am. U., 1964. Cert. tchr., Okla., Tex. Tchr. various schs., Kansas City, Kans., 1960-61, Grand Junction, Colo., 1961-62, Pharr, Tex., 1962-64; realtor Century 21 Homefinders, McAllen, Tex., 1978-80, Action Realty, McAllen, 1980—; pres. Women's Council Realtors, McAllen, 1983—; dir. McAllen Bd. Realtors; exec. sec., dir. Lone Star Nat. Bank, Pharr, 1986—; chmn. bd. dirs. Gustov Corp., 1987—; ptnr. Lion-Su and Assocs., 1982—, Crossroads, 1984—, Crosstown Properties, 1985—. Chmn. phone ctr. Clements for Gov. campaign, 1982; active Tex. Arts Alliance, 1986—; mem. Hidalgo County Women's Polit. Caucus; mem. Inner Circle Reps., 1985-86; founding bd. dirs. Samaritan Counseling Ctr., 1984-85; bd. dirs. South Tex. Symphony Assn., 1986. Named Outstanding Woman, McAllen C. of C., 1979. Mem. Tex. Assn. Realtors, McAllen Bd. Realtors (treas. 1985), Internat. Platform Assn., Tex. Agri-Woman (1st v.p.), Tex. State Garden Clubs (life, state trustee 1983-89). Am. Osteo. Assn. Aux. (dir. various coms.), Tex. Osteo. Assn. Aux. (pres. 1980). Mennonite. Clubs: Vesta Study (McAllen) (pres. 1983-84), McAllen Fedn. Women's Clubs (pres. 1978-79). Office: Action Realty 2415 N 10th St McAllen TX 78501

SUDLER, BARBARA WELCH, historical society administrator; b. Honolulu, Apr. 20, 1925; d. Leo F. and Barbara Lloyd (Petrikin) Welch; m. James Stewart Sudler, Dec. 30, 1950 (dec. 1982); children—Eleanor, James S.; m. William H. Hornby, Oct. 22, 1983. B.A., U. Colo., 1944. Exec. adminstr. Historic Denver, 1974-79; exec. dir. Colo. Hist. Soc., Denver, 1979-81, pres., 1981—; historic preservation officer State of Colo., Denver, 1983—; dir. Women's Bank, Denver. Editor: Nothing Is Long Ago, 1975. Bd. dirs. Denver Symphony Assn., 1983—, Met. State Coll. Found. Recipient Soroptomist award, 1980, Contbn. to Arts award Big Sisters, 1981, Contbns. to Community award AIA, 1982, Community Service award U. Colo., 1986. Mem. Am. Antiquarian Soc., Nat. Conf. State Historic Preservation Officers, Colo. Hist. Records Commn., Colo. Commn. on Bicentennial of Constitution, Martin Luther King Jr. Holiday Commn. Republican. Episcopalian. Clubs: Denver Country, University. Lodge: Rotary. Home: 180 High St Denver CO 80218 Office: State Hist Soc of Colo 1300 Broadway St Denver CO 80203

SUDOL, VALERIE JEANNE, dance critic; b. Passaic, N.J., Aug. 28, 1951; d. Theodore Valentine and Jeanne (Bastek) Sudol. A.A. cum laude, Ocean County Coll., 1972. Staff writer Daily Observer, Toms River, N.J., 1970-71; staff writer Asbury Park Press (N.J.), 1971-77; freelance writer, 1972—; adminstrv. asst. Burklyn Ballet Theatre, East Burke, Vt., 1978-79; dance critic Star Ledger, Newark, 1978—. Mem. Dance Critics Assn. (fellow Durham, N.C. 1979). Home: 77 Route 537 Colts Neck NJ 07722 Office: Star-Ledger Ledger Plaza Newark NJ 07101

SUEHR, SUSAN LYNN, chemical engineer; b. Pitts., Feb. 19, 1952; d. Robert L. and Betsy (DeMello) S., m. William L. Smallwood, Jr., Oct. 11, 1980; 1 child, Leigha Christine. B.S. in Chem. Engring., U. Pitts., 1974. Engr., Proctor & Gamble, Cin., 1974-75, Green Bay, Wis., 1975-77, project engr., Cin., 1977-81; sr. engr. Johnson & Johnson, North Brunswick, N.J., 1981-85, project mgr., engr., 1985—. Mem. Republican Nat. Com., 1981—; bd dirs. Huntington Park Homeowners Assn., 1983-86, head budget and fin. com., 1983-86, mem. archtl. com., 1983—. Mem. Soc. Women Engrs. (sr.; chpt. pres. 1979-80), Nat. Assn. Female Execs. Republican. Roman Catholic. Club: Sweet Adelines (chpt. historian 1984-86). Avocations: singing women's barbershop; stained glass design; tennis; swimming; aerobics. Office: Johnson & Johnson E1149 501 George St New Brunswick NJ 08903

SUELTENFUSS, ELIZABETH ANNE, university president; b. San Antonio, Apr. 14, 1921; d. Edward L. and Elizabeth (Amrein) S. B.A. in Botany and Zoology, Our Lady of Lake Coll., San Antonio, 1944; M.S. in Biology, U. Notre Dame, 1961, Ph.D., 1963. Joined Sisters of Divine Providence, Roman Catholic Ch., 1939; tchr. high schs. Okla. and La., 1942-49; mem. summer faculty Our Lady of Lake Coll., 1941-49, mem. full-time faculty, 1949-59, chmn. biology dept., 1963-73, pres., 1978—; mem. adminstrv. staff to superior gen. Congregation Divine Providence, 1973-77. Author articles in field. Bd. dirs. KLRN Public TV; bd. dirs. S.W. Research Found.; chmn. edn. com. Pvt. Sector United San Antonio; bd. dirs. Ind. Colls. and Univs. Tex., Inst. Ednl. Leadership, Trim and Swim. Recipient Achievement and Leadership award U. Notre Dame, 1979, Headliner award Women in Communications, 1980, Good Neighbor award NCCJ, 1982, Today's Woman award San Antonio Light, 1982, Outstanding Woman award San Antonio Express-News, 1983; named to San Antonio Women's Hall of Fame, 1985. Mem. AAAS, Am. Soc. Microbiology, AAUP, AAUW, Nat. Assn. Women Religious, Tex. Acad. Sci., San Antonio 100 and Tex. Women's Forum. Club: Zonta (dir., pres. 1982-84, founders' award 1983-84). Address: Our Lady of the Lake U 411 SW 24th St San Antonio TX 78285

SUESS, PATRICIA ANN, manufacturing systems engineer; b. St. Louis, Feb. 11, 1956; d. John Andrew and Betty Lee (Allen) Leonard; m. Robert Gerard Suess, Nov. 24, 1984; 1 child, Laura Elizabeth. BS in Education and Math, U. Mo., 1976, MS in Nuclear Engring., 1981, MS in Indsl. Engring., 1984. Grad. cert. in Artificial Intelligence, Washington U., 1987. Tchr. Math. St. Thomas Aquinas High Sch., Florissant, Mo., 1976-79; instr. computer programming U. Mo., Columbia, 1979-84; sr. engr. McDonnell Aircraft Co., St. Louis, 1984-86, tech. specialist, 1986—; McDonnell Aircraft Co. rep. McDonnell Douglas Corp. Artificial Intelligence External Relations Com., St. Louis, 1987—. Contbr. articles to profl. jours. Mem. Am. Inst. Indsl. Engrs. (bd. dirs., v.p. chpt. devel. 1986-87, sec. 1987-88, v.p. community affairs 1988—, C.D. award of Excellence 1987), Soc. Mfg. Engrs. (cert. of Appreciation 1986-88), Am. Assn. Artificial Intelligence, Nat. Assn. Female Execs., Mensa. Roman Catholic. Club: McDonnell Douglas Corp. Mgmt. Office: McDonnell Aircraft Co Box 516 Saint Louis MO 63166

SUGAR, SANDRA LEE, career counselor; b. Balt., May 18, 1942; d. Harry S. and Edith Sarah (Levin) Pomerantz; m. Fred N. Sugar, Oct. 11, 1963 (div. 1983); children: Gary Lee, Terry Lynn. BS in Edn. and English, Towson State U., 1965; MS in Edn. and Applied Behavioral Scis., Johns Hopkins U., 1986. Chairperson arts exhibit Balt. Arts Festival, 1979; med. interviewer Johns Hopkins Sch. of Hygiene, Balt., 1980-82; copy writer Concepts & Communications, Balt., 1984; instr. art history and world cultures Catonsville Community Coll., Balt., 1981-85; instr. English Community Coll. of Balt., 1981-85; instr. English and math. Info. Processing Tng. Ctr., Balt., 1985; info. specialist Info. of Md. New Directions for Women, Balt., 1986; trainer, job developer Working Solutions, Balt., 1987—; judge nat. high sch. sci. fiction contests. Author poetry collection, juried exhibition, 1979, 80; editor mus. guides' newsletter Guidelines, 1978; painter juried exhibitions, 1979, 80. Docent Balt. Mus. of Art, 1973-86; festival coordinator Internat. Brass Quintet Festival, Balt., 1986; chairperson spl. events Balt. PTA, 1978-82; bd. dirs. Citizens Planning and Housing Assn., Balt., 1980-82; mem. women's com., ctr. stage hand Balt. Ballet, 1979-84, Balt. Symphony, 1979-80. Recipient F.J. Bamberger scholarship, Johns Hopkins U., 1985, Mayoral Vol. of Yr. award Balt. Mus. Art, 1979. Democrat. Jewish.

SUGGS, MARILYN MARGARET, human services administrator; b. Washington, Dec. 20, 1955; d. Frederick Joseph and Barbara Kathryn (Pope) Adler; BS, Mercy Coll., 1977; MEd, Plymouth State Coll., 1979; EdD, Va. Tech., 1983. Tchr. Hardin No. Elem. Sch., Dola, Ohio, 1977; counselor, vocat. specialist Androscoggin Valley Mental Health Center, Berlin, N.H., 1977-79; primary counselor Fairfax Falls Ch. Community Services, Vienna, Va., 1979-81, asst. dir. Community residences, group homes, 1981-85, behavior analyst service bd., 1987—; dir. rehab. therapy and adolescent program Briarwood Hosp., Alexandria, La., 1985-87; bd. dirs. behavior analyst Fairfax/Falls Ch. Community Services, 1987—. Mem. Council Exceptional Children, Am. Assn. Mental Deficiency, Am. Assn. for Counseling and Devel. Roman Catholic. Home: 9106 Ulysses Ct Burke VA 22015

SUGHRUE, KATHRYN EILEEN, state legislator; b. Oketo, Kans., May 2, 1913; d. John and Charlotte Peterman; B.S. in Home Econs., Kans. State U., 1937; M.S. in Adminstrn., Colo. State U., 1962; m. Herbert Sughrue, May 3, 1941; children—Kathleen, Margaret, Patricia, John, Tim. Extension home economist, Ford County, Kans., 1937-41, Dodge City, Kans., 1949-61; dist. supt., asso. state leader Kans. State U., 1962-69; adv. Home Econs. Coll., Andra Pradesh U., Hyderabad, India, 1969; state leader N.D. State U., Fargo, 1969-73; freelance profl. speaker, 1973-76; mem. Kans. Ho. of Reps., 1976—. Vice pres., sec. Ford County Democratic Party. Recipient Top award Kans. 4-H Club Program, Finney County, 1958; Disting. Service award Kans. State U., 1981. Mem. Home Econs. Extension (pres. state chpt. 1957-58), Nat. Home Econs. Assn. (pres. state chpt. 1956-57), Kans. Home Econs. Assn. (pres. 1976-77), Home Econs. Club, Arts Council Speakers Guild, AAUW, Delta Kappa Gamma, Epsilon Sigma Phi (pres. state chpt. 1959-60). Roman Catholic. Clubs: Bus. and Profl. Women's, Women's Democratic. Philomat, PEO. Contbr. articles to mags.

SUGIYAMA, TOKU MARY, school administrator; b. Sacramento, Sept. 6, 1921; d. Sakae and Kuniko (Kosaka) Koda; m. Yone J. Sugiyama, Apr. 5, 1952; m. George Y. Morishita, Mar. 23, 1942; (dec. Mar. 1949); children—Maeona, Carolyn, George. Jr. cert. U. Calif.-Berkeley, 1941; B.A., Towson State U., 1980, M.A., 1984. Tchr., Poston Relocation Ctr., Ariz., 1941-44; purchasing agt. U.S. Dept. Def., Tokyo Ordnance Depot, 1952-56; instr. Ikebana Sogetsu Sch., Tokyo, 1956-67, exec. dir. Sogetsu USA, sch. Japanese flower arrangement, 1967—. Recipient Mohan Sho, Sogetsu Sch., 1960, Sofu Sho, 1967, Flower Arranger of yr. award Nat. Council State Garden Clubs, 1979. Mem. Md. Fedn. Garden Clubs, Ikebana Internat. (charter), Balt.-Kawasaki Sitster City Cultural Com. Home: 959 Ellendale Dr Towson MD 21204

SUITS, DIANE STEWART, librarian; b. Norwich, N.Y., Dec. 9, 1939; d. Clarence Eugene and Margaret Alice (Carr) Stewart; B.S. in Child Devel. and Family Relationships, Cornell U., 1962; m. Allen P. Suits, Nov. 29, 1968; children—Brian, Andrew; stepchildren—Catherine, Valerie, Stephen, Jeanne. Lic. real estate broker, Mass. Kindergarten and elem. sch. tchr., N.Y. and Mass., 1962-70; asst. librarian Brookline (Mass.) schs., 1970-72; tchr. 2d grade, Salem, N.H., 1972-73; sch. librarian, Windham, N.H., 1973-80; librarian Meml. High Sch., Manchester, N.H., 1980—. Mem. NEA, N.H. Edn. Assn., Manchester Edn. Assn., N.H. Ednl. Media Assn., Cornell U. Alumni Admissions Ambassador Network. Home: 38 Bedard Ave Derry NH 03038 Office: Memorial High Sch S Porter St Manchester NH 03103

SUKET, JUDITH ANN, nurse anesthetist, consultant; b. Milton, Mass., Oct. 28, 1942; d. Ralph Eugene and Mary Jane (Hall) S. B.S., St. Joseph Coll., Standish, Maine, 1975; M.S., Lesley Coll., 1986; R.N., Lynn Hosp. Sch. Nursing, 1964. Cert. nurse anesthetist. Staff anesthetist Quincy City Hosp., Mass., 1967-69, clin. instr. sch. nurse anesthesia, 1969-74, asst. dir., 1975-76; staff anesthetist New Eng. Bapt. Hosp., Boston, 1976-82, Met. Anesthesia Assn., Braintree, Mass., 1982-87, Mass. Eye and Ear Infirmary, 1987—; cons. Cosgrove & Eisenberg, Quincy, 1974—. Mem. Am. Assn. Nurse Anesthetists, Am. Soc. Law and Medicine, New Eng. Assembly Nurse Anesthetists (bd. dirs. 1979-85, chmn. 1985—), Mass. Anesthesia Council Edn. (sec. 1978-80), Mass. Assn. Nurse Anesthetists (bd. dirs. 1984—, continuing edn. coordinator 1984—). Clubs: Altrusa Internat. (treas. 1982-83) (Quincy); Yankee Golden Retriever (sec. 1985—) (Andover, Mass.). Avocations: camping; gardening; cross country skiing; golden retrievers. Home: 76 Bicknell St Quincy MA 02169 Office: Mass Eye and Ear Infirmary 243 Charles St Boston MA 02114

SUKOL, SHERRY MERLE, psychologist; b. Phila., June 29, 1951; d. Austin Lewis and Elvera (Promisloff) S.; B.A., Carnegie-Mellon U., 1973; M.S., Ohio U., 1975, Ph.D. in Clin. Psychology, 1978. Clin. fellow psychology Harvard Med. Sch., 1977-78; clin. intern Children's Hosp. Med. Center, Boston, 1977-78; asst. prof. counseling psychologist West Chester (Pa.) State Coll., 1978-79; fellow Counseling Assos., Paoli, Pa., 1979-81; consulting psychologist Interac Community Mental Health Center, Phila., 1979-81; asst. prof. grad. program counseling and human relations Villanova (Pa.) U., 1980-84; pvt. practice psychology, Wayne, Pa., 1980—. Advisor Women Against Rape, Athens, Ohio, 1977. Lic. psychologist, Pa.; cert. sch. psychologist, Pa. Mem. Am. Psychol. Assn., Phila. Soc. Clin. Psychologist, Phi Kappa Phi. Editor: Consumer's Guide to Psychotherapy, 1980. Office: 400 E Lancaster Ave Ave 8 Wayne PA 19087

SULFARO, JOYCE A., school principal; b. Bklyn., Oct. 23, 1948; d. John Joseph and Mildred Ann (Credidio) Carvelli; m. Guy Sulfaro, Aug. 1, 1971; children—Jacqueline A., Kristin Lynn. BA, Molloy Coll., 1970; postgrad. Fla. Atlantic U., 1979-80; MS in Adminstrn. and Supervision, Nova U., 1982. Tutor reading Our Lady of Loretto, Rockville Centre, N.Y., 1969-70; tchr. lang. arts and math. Resurrection Sch., Bklyn., 1970-73; tchr. Annunciation Sch., Hollywood, Fla., 1976-80, prin., 1980-84; tchr. St. Thomas More Sch., 1984-88; writer English curriculum for Jr. High for Archdiocese of Miami, 1979. Travel coordinator/sec. Rego Park (N.Y.) Met. Youth Orgn., 1969-70. Author: (with M. Sue Timmins) The Basket, 1980. Mem. Nat. Council Tchrs. Math., Fla. League Mid. Schs., Cath. Educators Guild Archdiocese of Miami, Nat. Cath. Ednl. Assn., Am. Mus. Natural History. Office: 1104 Waterloo Ct Rocky Mount NC 27804

SULLINS, JILL PACKALES, entrepreneur; b. N.Y.C., Aug. 16, 1945; d. Sidney A. and Shirley June (Burros) Packales; Benjamin J. Hight, July 24, 1971 (div. Dec. 1981); children: David Matthew, Daniel Jeremy; m. H. Garland Sullins, Feb. 8, 1987. Student, Cornell U.; cert. profl. designation in advt., UCLA. Owner Hillside Graphics, Los Angeles, 1973-78, Dallas, 1978—; founding pres. Assn. Women Entrepreneurs Tex., Assn. Women Entrepreneurs Dallas, Inc.; exec. v.p. Nat. Assn. Women Govt. Contractors, Dallas; bd. dirs. Tech. Enterprises Devel. Ctr. U. Tex. Arlington Sch. Engring. Mem. adv. council U.S. Small Bus. Adminstrn., Dallas; mem. steering com. Pres.'s Nat. Initiative Conf. on Women's Bus. Ownership, 1984, Gov.'s Conf. for Minority and Women Owned Bus. Tex.; League of Women Voters. Named Advocate of Yr. U.S. Small Bus. Adminstrn., 1985. Mem. Women in Communications, Ad League of Dallas, Bus. and Profl. Advt. Assn., Dallas Regional Minority Purchasing Council, Nat. Assn. Women Bus. Owners. Office: Hillside Graphics 6720 Robin Willow Ct Dallas TX 75248

SULLIVAN, A(NNA) MANNEVILLETTE, metallurgist, editor; b. Washington, Aug. 18, 1913; d. Francis Paul and Villette (Anderson) Sullivan; student Wellesley Coll., 1931-33; A.B., George Washington U., 1935; postgrad. Cath. U., 1935-36, M.S., U. Md., 1955. Asst. metallurgist, Geophys. Lab., Carnegie Inst. Washington, 1942-45; metallurgist Nat. Bur. Standards, Washington, 1945-46, U.S. Naval Research Lab., Washington, 1947-78; dep. tech. editor ASME Trans., Jour. Engring. Materials and Tech., 1978-81, cons., 1982—. Mem. Am. Soc. Metals, ASTM, ASME, Mensa, Sigma Xi, Alpha Delta Pi. Iota Sigma Pi. Clubs: Toastmasters, Altrusa Internat. Research in fracture of metals with spl. reference to fracture mechanics. Home: 4000 Massachusetts Ave NW Washington DC 20016

SULLIVAN, CARLEY HAYDEN, political party executive; b. Elko, Nev.; student U. Oreg., 1945-47; m. Will Sullivan; children—Blaine Sullivan Rose, Valerie Sullivan Mitchell, Dan, Peggy Sullivan Hagen. Mgmt. asst. State of Nev., Elko, 1967—; sec. Elko County (Nev.) Democratic Central Com., 1972—; treas. Nev. Dem. Com., 1980-82, co-chmn. state conv., 1980, mem. state cons. planning com., 1982; mem. state hosp. adv. bd., 1964-66, adv. council on children and youth, 1970-80; mem. gov.'s State Sch. Survey Com., 1975-77, Gov.'s Drug Abuse Adv. Bd., 1974-76; gov.'s del. to Nev. Library

Conf., 1981; alt. del. White House Conf. on Libraries, 1982; Nev. del. to Presdl. White House Conf. on Children and Youth, 1970; life mem. Gov.'s Youth Traffic Safety Assn.; exec. sec., interim mgr. Elko C. of C., 1961-68. Pres. Elko Dem. Women, 1970; bd. dirs. Elko Dem. Club, 1970-82; chmn. Rural Nev. Mental Health Adv. Bd., 1973-78; bd. Nev. PTA, 1962-72, pres., 1972-74; v.p. Am. Lung Assn. of Nev., 1972-82, pres.-elect, 1982-84, pres., 1984—; coordinator Youth Traffic Safety Confs., 1968-78; bd. mgrs. Nat. Com. Health and Welfare, PTA, 1972-74; adv. bd. Nat. Council Juvenile Ct. Judges, 1972-74; mem. 8 state project Designing Edn. for the Future, 1965-68; Nev. rep. to nat. ALA conv., 1981; vol. Elko Hosp. Aux.; co-chmn. 1st Rural Nev. Women's Conf., 1980; mem. Nev. Adv. Council for Vocat. Tech. Edn., 1982—; mem., Nev. commr./Nat. Council, Future of Women In The Workplace, 1983-1985; Nev. rep. to Nat. Commn. for Eleanor Roosevelt Centennial, 1984-85; del. to Dem. Nat. Conv., 1984; sec./treas. Elko County Dem. Central Com., 1984-86; mem. Nev. State Bd. Edn., 1984—; apptd. to Nev. U.S. Service Acad. Selection Com., 1987; apptd. by Gov. of Nev. to recommendation com. for Nev. Legislature; mem. Nev. State Dem. Central Com. Recipient honors Am. Lung Assn. Nev., C. of C., Nev. Dept. Edn., Gov.'s Office State of Nev.; Citizen of Year Elko County Mental Health Assn., 1985. Mem. Elko Bus. and Profl. Women (state legis. chmn., scholarship award com., del. to nat. conv.), Sigma Kappa.

SULLIVAN, CLAIRE FERGUSON, marketing educator; b. Pittsburg, Tex., Sept. 28, 1937; d. Almon Lafayette and Mabel Clara (Williams) Potter; m. Richard Wayne Ferguson, Jan. 31, 1959 (div. Jan. 1980); 1 child, Mark Jeffrey Ferguson; m. David Edward Sullivan, Nov. 2, 1984. BBA, U. Tex., 1958, MBA, 1961; PhD, North Tex. State U., 1973. Instr. So. Meth. U., Dallas, 1965-70; asst. prof. U. Utah, Salt Lake City, 1972-74; assoc. prof. U. Ark., Little Rock, 1974-77, U. Tex., Arlington, 1977-80, Ill. State U., Normal, 1980-84; prof., chmn. mktg. Bentley Coll., Waltham, Mass., 1984—; cons. Gen. Telephone Co., Irving, Tex., 1983, McKnight Pub. Co., Bloomington, Ill., 1983, dental practitioner, Bloomington, 1982-83, Olympic Fed., Berwyn, Ill., 1982. Contbr. mktg. articles to profl. jours. Named Outstanding Prof., So. Meth. U., 1969-70; Direct Mktg. Inst. fellow, 1981; Ill. State U. research grantee, 1981-83. Mem. Am. Mktg. Assn. (faculty fellow 1984-85), So. Mktg. Assn., Southwestern Mktg. Assn., Sales and Mktg. Execs. Boston, Beta Gamma Sigma. Republican. Methodist. Home: 9 Potter Pond Lexington MA 02173 Office: Bentley Coll Dept Mktg Waltham MA 02254

SULLIVAN, ELAINE MARTHA, insurance company executive; b. Cambridge, Mass., May 8, 1950; d. Timothy Francis and Eleanor (Heaney) S. BS, Salem State Coll., 1972; MEd, Slippery Rock (Pa.) U., 1974; cert., Katharine Gibbs Sch., 1977, Bentley Coll., MA, Emerson Coll., 1986. Ad minstrv. services exec. John Hancock Mut. Life Ins., Boston. Contbr. articles to profl. jours. mem. Town Meeting Members Assn., Lexington, Mass., Town Report Com., Lexington, 1984-86; class agt. Salem (Mass.) State Coll., 1986-87. Named an Outstanding Young Woman of Am., 1982. Mem. Am. Soc. Tng. and Devel., Conservation Edn. Assn. Home: 31 Chase Ave Lexington MA 02173

SULLIVAN, ELEANOR REGIS, editor; b. Cambridge, Mass., Oct. 19, 1928; d. Timothy Joseph and Katherine Irene (Dowd) S. B.S., Salem State Coll., 1950. Tchr. Clinton Grammar Sch., Conn., 1950-53; tchr. Russell Sch., Cambridge, Mass., 1953-57, George Washington Sch., White Plains, N.Y., 1957-60; editorial asst. Pocket Books, Inc., N.Y.C., 1961-62; editor Charles Scribner's Sons, N.Y.C., 1962-69, Davis Publs., Inc., N.Y.C., 1970—; tchr. writing workshops. Author: Whodunit: A Biblio-Bio-Anecdotal Memoir of Frederic Dannay, 1984; editor 15 Ellery Queen anthologies, 10 Alfred Hitchcock anthologies; contbr. stories and articles to mags., newspapers, book. Vol. ARC, St. Albans Naval Hosp., Queens, N.Y., 1968-73; vol. tutor I Have A Dream Program, N.Y.C., 1986—. Mem. Mystery Writers Am. (bd. dirs. 1974-77, 82-85, Ellery Queen award 1987), Dramatists Guild, Am. Film Inst. Democrat. Roman Catholic. Home: 236 E 49th St New York NY 10017 Office: Ellery Queen's Mystery Mag 380 Lexington Ave New York NY 10017 *

SULLIVAN, FRANCES GERALDINE, data processing executive; b. Trenton, N.J., Aug. 10, 1945; d. Jay Joseph and Edna Lucille (Smith) S.; m. Michael Ray Zona, May 3, 1947. BS in Secondary Edn., Pa. State U., 1967; cert. in acctg., U. Pitts., 1981, MBA Exec. Program, 1985. Programmer, analyst switchgear div. Westinghouse, East Pittsburgh, Pa., 1967-74; mgr. MIS specialty metals div. Blairsville, Pa., 1974-77; mgr. fin. systems water reactor div. Monroeville, Pa., 1977-80, mgr. acctg. nuclear energy systems, 1980-81; mgr. gen. acct. corp. data ctr. Pitts., 1981-82, mgr. project planning corp. data ctr., 1982-84, dir. data adminstrn. corp. data ctr., 1984-85, mgr. corp. payrolls corp. data ctr., 1985-87; mgr. product contincency services Corp. Info. Services, 1987—. Co-founder Meyer Park Neigborhood Assn., McKeesport, Pa., 1986. Methodist. Home: 2133 Duquesne Ave McKeesport PA 15132 Office: Westinghouse Corp Data Ctr 1001 Brinton Rd Pittsburgh PA 15221

SULLIVAN, GWYNETTE, civic leader; b. Campbellsville, Ky., Feb. 19, 1949; d. Leslie McCormick and Della Marie (Rodgers) Turner; m. Ronald Lee Sullivan, June 18, 1967; children: Travis Chad, Farrah Shae. Pres. Taylor County Hist. Soc., Campbellsville, 1984—; chair Willowtown Voting Precinct, Campbellsville, 1985—; sec.-treas. dist. Extention Council, Campbellsville, 1985—; dist. area, 1984-87; mem. 4-H Council Taylor County, Campbellsville, 1984—; leader 4-H Clubs, Taylor County, 1967—; market basket surveyor Farm Bur. fedn., Louisville, 1982—, bd. dirs., 1984—; bd. dirs. adv. bd. Ky. Extention Council, 1986—; bd. dirs. Ky. Hist. Confederation, 1985-87, Taylor County Booth at Ky. State Fair, 1987—. Named Mother of Yr., Mt. Washington Bapt. Ch., Raywick, Ky., 1980. Mem. So. States (chmn. 1984-86). Democrat. Baptist. Home: 7660 Saloma Rd Campbellsville KY 42718

SULLIVAN, KATHRYN ALBERS, academic administrator; b. Grosse Pointe Farms, Mich., Oct. 19, 1948; d. Claude W. and Ann L. (Barasovich) Albers; m. Paul J. Sullivan, Dec. 28, 1974. BA in English, Mich. State U., 1970; MBA, Oakland U., Rochester, Mich., 1987. Adminstrv. asst. Arthur Andersen & Co., Detroit, 1970-74; co-dir. World Plan Exec. Council, San Jacinto, Calif., 1977-78; co-chairperson Sacramento, 1978-79; with various firms, Detroit, 1979-83; adminstrv. asst. to provost Oakland Community Coll., Royal Oak, Mich., 1983-85; dir. adminstrv. services Oakland Community Coll., Royal Oak, 1985—. Mem. Mich. Community Colls. Bus. Officers Assn., Am. Assn. of Women in Community and Jr. Colls., Mich. Assn. for Women Deans, Adminstrs. and Counselors, Nat. Inst. for Leadership Devel. (leader). Office: Oakland Community Coll 739 S Washington Royal Oak MI 48067

SULLIVAN, LAURA A., academic administrator; b. St. Louis, Sept. 30, 1953; d. James Leo and Patrcia Catherine (Gibbons) S.; m. Arthur Leroy Gallegos, Sept. 16, 1986. BA in Elem. and Spl. Edn., Regis Coll., 1976; MA in Ednl. Adminstrn., No. Ariz. U., 1983. Tchr. State Schs. for Severly Handicapped, St. Louis, 1977-79; tchr. jr. high spl. edn. Bloomfield (N.M.) Mcpl. Schs., 1979-80; tchr. high sch. and spl. edn., work study coordinator Bloomfield (N.Mex.) Mcpl. Schs., 1982-83, dir. spl. edn., work study coordinator, 1983-84; exec. dir. Region I Ctr. Coop., Bloomfield, 1984—, cons., 1984, trainer, 1984-87. Sec. bd. dirs. 4 Corners Mental Health, Farmington, N.Mex., 1986-87; sec. San Juan County Dem. Party, Farmington, 1985-87; presenter Parents Reaching OUt, Farmington, 1987. Recipient Cert. Appreciation N.Mex. Sec. State, 1986. Mem. N.Mex. Council of Adminstrs. Spl. Edn. (pres. 1986—), Council for Exceptional Children (pres. N.Mex. 1987—), Nat. Assn. of Female Execs., Phi Delta Kappa.

SULLIVAN, LAURA PATRICIA, insurance company executive, lawyer; b. Des Moines, Oct. 16, 1947; d. William and Patricia (Kautz) S. B.A., Cornell Coll., Iowa, 1971; J.D., Drake U., 1972. Bar: Iowa 1972. Various positions Ins. Dept. Iowa, Des Moines, 1972-75; various legal positions State Farm Mut. Auto Ins. Co., Bloomington, Ill., 1975-81, sec. and counsel, 1981—; v.p., sec., dir. State Farm Cos. Found., 1985—; sec. State Farm & Casualty Co., 1987—, State Farm Gen. Ins. Co., 1987—, State Farm Lloyd's Inc., 1987—. Trustee John M. Scott Indsl. Sch. Trust, Bloomington, 1983-86; bd. dirs. Scott Ctr., 1983-86, Bloomington-Normal Symphony, 1980-85. Mem. ABA, Iowa State Bar Assn., Am. Corp. Counsel Assn. Office: State Farm Mut Automobile Ins Co One State Farm Plaza Bloomington IL 61701

SULLIVAN, SISTER MARIE CELESTE, hospital administrator; b. Boston, Mar. 18, 1929; d. Daniel John and Katherine Agnes (Cunniff) S. BBA, St. Bonaventure U., 1965. Joined Order Franciscan Sisters Roman Cath. Ch., 1952; bus. mgr. St. Joseph's Hosp., Providence, 1954-62; asst. adminstr. St. Joseph's Hosp., Tampa, Fla., 1965-70, adminstr., 1970-83, chief exec. officer, 1983—; mem. Adv. Council Hillsborough County, Emergency Med. Planning Council Hillsborough County; coordinator health affairs Diocese of St. Petersburg, 1980—; mem. Fla. Cancer Control and Research Adv. Bd., 1980—; bd. dirs. 1st Fla. Bank, Westshore Div.; gen. councillor Franciscan Sisters of Allegany, 1984-88. Contbr. articles to profl. jours. Trustee St. Francis Med. & Health Ctr., Miami Beach, Fla., 1986—; bd. dirs. local chpt. Am. Cancer Soc. Recipient Humanitarian award Judeo-Christian Health Clinic, Tampa, 1977, Athena award Fla. West Coast chpt. Women in Communications, 1978, Exec. Woman of Yr. award Tampa Bay chpt. Network Exec. Women, 1987. Fellow Am. Coll. Health Care Execs.; mem. Fla. Hosp. Assn. (trustee 1983-87), Am. Mgmt. Assn., Greater Tampa C. of C. (bd. govs. 1982-87). Democrat. Club: Centre (Tampa) (founding bd. govs.). Home: 3001 W Buffalo Ave Tampa FL 33607 Office: St Joseph's Health Care Ctr PO Box 4227 Tampa FL 33677

SULLIVAN, MARILYN MCWILLIAMS, state justice; b. Portsmouth, N.H., Sept. 19, 1923; d. Joseph and Mary (McWilliams) S. A.B. magna cum laude, Radcliffe Coll., 1945; J.D., Columbia U., 1949. Bar: Mass. 1949. Law clk. Mass. Supreme Ct., 1949-51; assoc. Ropes & Gray, Boston, 1951-73; justice land ct. dept. Mass. Trial Ct., Boston, 1973—, chief justice, 1985—. Served to lt. (j.g.) USNR, 1944-46. Mem. Nat. Assn. Women Judges (dir. dist. 1, 1980-82), Abstract Club, Mass. Conveyancers Assn., Mass. Assn. Women Lawyers, Mass. Bar Assn., Boston Bar Assn., Phi Beta Kappa (past pres.). Roman Catholic. Clubs: Radcliffe, Harvard (gov. 1983—) (Boston); Emma Forbes Cary Guild (Cambridge, Mass.), Guild of Our Lady of Ranson. Office: Land Ct Room 408 Old Courthouse Boston MA 02108

SULLIVAN, MELANIE MANARD, real estate broker, consultant; b. New Orleans, Sept. 21, 1943; d. Robert L. and Marguerite (Castiex) Manard; m. Scott Keith Sullivan, 1963; children: Erin, Scott, Jr., Colleen. Student, La. State U., 1961-63, U. New Orleans, 1969. Lic. real estate broker; grad. Realtors inst. Tchr. Jefferson Parish Sch. Bd., Kenner, La., 1964-65; tchr. Jumairah Am. Sch., Dubai, United Arab Emirates, 1970-77, athletic dir., 1973-78; community activities dir. Dubai, United Arab Emirates, 1975-79; tchr. Our Lady of the Lake Sch., Mandeville, La., 1983; real estate broker, asst. mgr. Merrill Lynch Realty, Mandeville, 1980-87; gen. contractor Sullivan Constrn., Mandeville, 1984—; asst. mgr., tng. dir. Weber Realty Group, Mandeville, La., 1987—; lectr. in field. Co-founder, mem. adv. bd. Our Lady of the Lake Cath. Youth Orgn., 1981-82, Middle East Student Council Assn, Dubai, 1972-79, Middle East Fine Arts Assn., Dubai, 1973-79; founder, commr. Middle East Schs. Sports Assn., Dubai, 1971-79. Honored for Outstanding Civic Service Parents Orgn., Dubai, 1979. Mem. Nat. Assn. Realtors, La. Realtors Assn., St. Tammany Bd. Realtors (million dollar salesperson), Women's Council Realtors, Realtors Land Inst. (cert. comml. investor), New Orleans Real Estate Investors Assn. (cons., sec., v.p., dir., 1981-86), Nat. Leadership Congress (speaker, v.p., 1985—), Shelter Industry Trade Assn. (rep. 1986-87), Delta Gamma. Republican. Roman Catholic. Home: 198 Sandra Lee Dr Mandeville LA 70448 Office: Weber Realty Group 701 Mariners Plaza Mandeville LA 70448

SULLIVAN, NANCY JEAN, dean, educator, nurse; b. Riverside, Calif., July 30, 1949; d. Hugh and Mary Kate Fitzpatrick; m. Thomas J. Sullivan. BA, U. Calif., Santa Barbara, 1971; BS in Nursing, No. Mich. U., 1975; MS in Nursing, U. Wis., Madison, 1983. Registered nurse, Mich.; cert. nursing tchr., Mich. Nurse Marquette (Mich.) Gen. Hosp., 1975-83; instr. nursing Bay de Noc Community Coll., Escanaba, Mich., 1983-86, asst. dean of allied health, 1986—. Active Womens Action for Nuclear Disarmament, Marquette, 1986—. Mem. Mich. Nurses Assn., Mich. Council of ADN Dirs., Am. Pub. Health Assn. Democrat. Office: Bay de Noc Community Coll 2001 N Lincoln Escanaba MI 49855

SULLIVAN, PAMELA GRACE, engineer; b. Rio de Janeiro, Brazil, Apr. 11, 1945 (parents Am. citizens); d. Lloyd Charles and Helen Postill Hawken; AS, Long Beach (Calif.) City Coll., 1968; BSME, Calif. State U., Long Beach, 1971, MSME, 1978; m. Charles J. Sullivan, Feb. 22, 1962 (div.); 1 child, Catherine Anne. Engr., Nevada Engring. & Tech. Corp., Long Beach, 1971-79, also sec.; sr. staff engr. Lockheed Missles & Space Co., Sunnyvale, Calif., 1979—. Mem. Am. Soc. for Metals (Chmn.), Soc. Aerospace Materials and Processes Engrs. (chmn.), ASTM (mem. com. publs. 1981-87), AIME, Am. Ceramic Soc., Soc. Women Engrs. Contbr. articles to profl. publs. Home: 544 W Latimer Campbell CA 95008 Office: Lockheed Missles & Space Co 30-20 B/559 1 PO Box 3504 Sunnyvale CA 94086

SULLIVAN, PATRICIA CLARE, hospital administrator; b. Cortland, Nebr., July 2, 1928. R.N. diploma, Mercy Hosp. Sch. Nursing, Denver, 1954; B.S.N., Coll. St. Mary, Omaha, 1955; M.H.A., St. Louis U., 1971, cert. for internal resources for renewal, 1971; cert. in gerontology, U. Nebr., Omaha, 1976. Instr. Mercy Hosp. Sch. Nursing, Des Moines, 1955-58; dir. Mercy Hosp. Sch. Nursing, 1960-64; nursing supr. pediatrics Mercy Hosp., Des Moines, 1955-58; adminstr. Mercy Hosp., 1977—; pres. Mercy Health Ctr. of Central Iowa, 1982—, Mercy Hosp. Med. Ctr., Mercy Found., Mercy Health & Human Services, Mercy Properties, ShareCare Ltd, Mercy Geriatric Services; coordinator rural hosp. nursing, nursing supr. ob-gyn Mercy Hosp., Durango, Colo., 1958-60, nursing supr., Williston, N.D., 1964-65; adminstr. St. Joseph's Mercy Hosp., Centerville, Iowa, 1965-69; resident Peter Bent Brigham Hosp., Boston, 1970-71; in organizational renewal Province of Omaha, 1971-74; dir. community relations Archbishop Bergan Mercy Hosp., Omaha, 1974-77; mem. Province of Omaha Health Services Council, 1958—; provincial chpt. del. Province Omaha, 1970-74. Dir. film depicting tornado strike to Archbishop Bergan Mercy Hosp., 1975, numerous showings, including at Congl. hearing at Pentagon. Del. Mercy Gen. Chpt., 1981—; bd. dirs. Mercy Hosp., Devils Lake, N.D., 1974-82, Sub-Area IV, Iowa Health Systems Agy., 1977—, NCCJ, 1979-84, Health System of Mercy, 1979, Grand View Coll., Des Moines, 1982-87, Des Moines Better Bus. Bur., 1983-85; regional rep. Diocesan Pastoral Council, 1978-80; mem. Mercy Health Conf., 1979-83, Iowa Network Mercy Hosps. 1979—; dir. Central Nat. Bancshares, First Interstate Bank Corp. (formerly Bancshares) Des Moines.; bd. dirs. Convalescent Home for Children, 1980-84, Health System of Midlands, Omaha, 1985-86. Mem. Nat. League for Nursing, Iowa League for Nursing (pres. 1966-69), Iowa Assn. Bus. Industry, Am. Acad. Med. Adminstrs. (pres. Iowa chpt. 1986-87), Omaha League for Nursing (dir. 1976-77), Am. Hosp. Assn., Soc. Advancement Mgmt., Des Moines C. of C. (bd. dirs.), Cath. Health Assn. (bd. dirs. 1986—). Clubs: Trendleaders of Ryan Advs. for Chief Exec. Officers. Office: Mercy Hosp Med Center 6th and University Ave Des Moines IA 50314

SULLIVAN, PATRICIA LANCE, writer, editor; b. Austin, Tex., Feb. 15, 1950; d. Frederick Lee and Betty Ellen (Leonard) Stead; m. John Edward Sullivan, Jan. 1, 1978. Student U. N.Mex., 1967-70; B.A. in English Lit., Calif. State U.-Northridge, 1978; postgrad. Ga. State U., 1987—. Clk., typist Adamson Co., Santa Monica, Calif., 1970-71; graphic artist Hughes Research Labs., Malibu, Calif., 1971-79; sales rep. In This Issue Mag., Costa Mesa, Calif., 1979-80; pub. relations rep. C.E.C., Newport Beach, Calif., 1980-81; freelance writer, Atlanta, 1981—; writer, editor The Preferred Press, Atlanta, 1984-86; editor The Newsletter, Atlanta Occupational Medicine, 1985-86. Editor: Atlanta Professional Women's Directory, 1982-83; columnist Go mag., 1987—; contbr. articles to profl. jours. Pub. relations staff Nat. MS Soc., Atlanta, 1982. Mem. AAUW, Nat. League Am. Pen Women (chmn. state letters com. Ga. 1986—, editor, pub. Pen-Graphs newsletter Atlanta br., chmn. state conv. 1987, state historian 1988), Women in Communications Inc., Village Writers Group, Kappa Kappa Gamma, Sigma Delta Chi. Republican. Presbyterian. Avocations: reading, computing, travel, writing. Home and Office: 3746 Wieuca Rd NE Atlanta GA 30342

SULLIVAN, PATRICIA MALONE, nurse, health science facility administrator; b. New Haven; d. Thomas Michael and Marie Ellen (Quinn) Malone; 1 child, Tara Marie. Assoc. of Nursing cum laude, U. Bridgeport, 1978, BS magna cum laude, 1980; postgrad., Hartford Grad. Ctr. RN. Nurse Yale New Haven Hosp., 1975-83, nurse, mgmt. info. systems implementor, 1985-86, nurse, coordinator nurse recruitment/human resources, 1986—. Mem. Nat. Assn. Health Care Recruiters, Conn. Assn. Nurse Recruiters (chair), Am. Nurse Assn., Nat. Assn. for Female Execs., Conn. Hosp. Personnel Assn. Office: Yale New Haven Hosp 20 York St New Haven CT 06504

SULLIVAN, RUTH CHRIST, social services administrator; b. Port Arthur, Tex., Apr. 20, 1924; d. Lawrence A. and Ada (Matt) Christ; m. William P. Sullivan; children: Julie, Christopher, Eva, Lawrence, Joseph, Lydia, Richard. RN, Charity Hosp., 1944; BS, Columbia U., 1952, MA, 1953; PhD, Ohio U., 1984. Nurse various orgns. La., 1947-50; first pres. Nat. Soc. Autistic Children, 1968-70; founder, dir. Nat. Soc. Autistic Children's Info. and Referal Service, Huntington, W.Va., 1970-79, Autism Services Ctr., Huntington, 1979—; bd. dirs. Rimland Sch. for Autistic Children, 1974—, Bittersweet Farms, Toledo, Ohio, 1979—, U. W.Va. Affiliated Faculty, Morgantown, 1982—, Community Services for Autistic Adults and Children, Rockville, Md., 1985—; chair adv. bd. Autism Tng. Ctr. Marshall U., Huntington, 1983-85, lectr., cons., adj. prof., Marshall U. Contbr. articles to profl. jours. organizer Guyandotte Assn. Improvement and Preservation, Huntington, 1969-75; pres. Coalition for Responsible Regional Devel., Huntington., 1977-82. Served to 1st lt. Army Nurse Corps., 1944-47. Mem. Council for Exceptional Children, Soc. Neuroscience, Tourette Soc., Alliance for Mentally Retarded. Roman Catholic. Office: Autism Services Ctr Douglas Edn 10th Ave and Bruce St Huntington WV 25701

SULLIVAN, SANDRA JONES, designer, design company executive; b. Fredericksburg, Va., Jan. 26, 1948; d. Carle Hamilton and Lily Mae (Rose) Jones; m. Lehmer Kent Sullivan, July 11, 1970; children—Lehmer Cameron, Catherine Hollis. B.S. in Bus. Edn., Longwood, Coll., 1970. Tchr. James Monroe High Sch., Fredericksburg, 1970, Stafford High Sch., Va., 1971-72, 74-76; pres., designer Homespun Elegance Ltd., Fredericksburg, 1980—. Author, designer numerous needlework leaflets including Elegant Ducks, 1981, A Christmas Sampler, 1981, Wedding Folk Art, 1982, Candlewicking for Christmas, 1982, Tea Dyeing, 1982, Willow Tree Sampler, 1984, Antique Flowers, 1984, Cinnamon Stick Christmas, 1985, The Amish, 1985. Mem. jr. bd. Historic Fredericksburg, 1977—. Mem. Needlework Markets Inc., Nat. Needlework Assn., Am. Ind. Designers Assn., Embroiders Guild, Fredericksburg C. of C. Republican. Methodist. Avocations: antiques; gardening. Home: 915-A Sophia St Fredericksburg VA 22405 Office: Homespun Elegance Ltd 915A Sophia St Fredericksburg VA 22401

SULLIVAN, SHAWN ANNE, marketing professional; b. Kansas City, Mo., June 8, 1955; d. Robert John and Kathleen R. (Dalton) S.; children: William Seward Weeks, Megan Kathleen Weeks. Student, Rockhurst Coll., Kansas City, Mo., 1972-74, Avila Coll., Kansas City, Mo., 1974-75. Buyer, asst. mgr. Lower Level Gifts, Kansas City, 1970-73; retail sales mgr., dir. tourism Bully Hill Vineyards, Hammondsport, N.Y., 1975-79; ops. mgr. DST Systems, Inc., Kansas City, 1983-85, sr. broker dealer services rep., 1985—; cons. wine, Kansas City, 1980-83; designer, saleswoman, buyer Daltons Flowers, Overland Park, Kans., 1967-75, 84—. Editor Jour. Vineyard View mag., 1978-79. Mem. local PTA, Kansas City, 1984-87. Home: 1123 E 116th Terr Apt 2 Kansas City MO 64131 Office: DST Systems Inc 301 W 11th St Kansas City MO 64105

SULLIVAN-REEVIS, MAUREEN PATRICIA, college adminstrator; b. Missoula, Mont., Nov. 13, 1946; d. James Edward Sullivan and Theresa Marie (Martin) Woolery; m. Charles Patrick Reevis, Aug. 25, 1981; children: Cynthia Diane, Brenna Colleen, William Patrick. BA in English, Ea. Wash. U., 1983; postgrad. in edn., Mont. State U., 1985-86. Organizer Welfare Rights Orgn., Spokane, Wash., 1970-75; worker Spokane Falls Community Coll., 1973-75; tutor Ft. Wright Coll. Holy Names, Spokane, 1975-77; Title IV programmer Spokane Sch. Dist., 1979-81; substitute tchr. Loyola-Sacred Heart High Sch., Missoula, 1984-85; instr. reading Blackfeet Community Coll., Browning, Mont., 1985-86, grants writer, 1986, program dir., mem. devel. com., 1986; supervising trainer Laubach Literacy Internat., Browning, 1985—, bd. dirs., 1985-86; tutor Blackfeet Literacy Program, Browning, 1985—, lead trainer, 1986 , pres., 1985-86. Mem. Nat. Assn. Female Execs., Internat. Reading Assn. Democrat. Bahai. Home: 2028 20th St San Pablo CA 94806 Office: Blackfeet Literacy Program Box 819 Browning MT 59417

SULTANA, NAJMA, psychiatrist; b. Nirmal, Andhra, India; July 22, 1948; came to U.S. 1973; d. Khaja Moinuddin and Mujib (Unnisa) Begum; m. Khaja Mohiuddin, July 8, 1971 (div. 1978); m. M. Rashid Chaudhry, Oct. 16, 1981. M.B.B.S. Gandhi Med. Coll., Hyderaba, India, 1973. Resident in psychiatry SUNY/Kings County Hosp. Ctr., Bklyn., 1976-78, fellow child psychiatry, 1978-80; asst. clin. physician S. Beach Psychiat. Ctr., S.I., N.Y., 1980-81; asst. clin. prof. SUNY Downstate Med. Ctr., N.Y.C., 1981—; attending psychiatrist King's County Hosp., Bklyn., 1981—. Mem. Am. Psychiat. Assn. Democrat. Muslim.

SULZBY, ELIZABETH FAY, educator; b. Walker County, Ala., Feb. 25, 1942; d. Phillip Glen and Ophelia Sulzby; BA, Birmingham-So. Coll., 1963; MEd, Coll. William and Mary, 1969; PhD, U. Va., 1977; m. Mitchell Frank Rouzie, July 8, 1980; 1 dau., Kiran Elizabeth. Tchr. public schs., 1966-75; instr. Jacksonville (Fla.) U., 1970-71, R.I. Coll., Providence, 1973-74, U. Va., Charlottesville, 1975-77; asst. prof. edn. Northwestern U., Evanston, Ill., 1977-83, assoc. prof., 1983-86; assoc. prof. edn. U. Mich., Ann Arbor, 1986—, also Ctr. for Learning and Schooling, 1986—, combined program in psychology and edn., 1986—, assoc. in linguists, 1987—; cons. in field. Mem. adv. bd. One-To-One Learning Center, Wilmette, Ill., 1980-82, Solomon Schecter Schs., 1985-86, U. Mich. Children's Ctr., 1986—; child devel. cons. Internat. Games, Inc., 1984—; pres. Literacy Devel. and Young Children Spl. Interest Group, 1988—. Woodrow Wilson fellow, 1963-64; Nat. Council of Tchrs. of English grantee, 1980-81, Nat. Inst. Edn. grantee, 1980-82, Spencer Found. grantee, 1981-82, 84-87, Apple Corp. grantee, 1987-88, North Cen. Regional Ednl. Lab., 1988—; Harvard U. honor scholar, 1963-64; NRC living footnote, 1986. Mem. Am. Ednl. Research Assn., Am. Psychol. Assn., Internat. Reading Assn., Nat. Council of Tchrs. of English, Nat. Reading Conf., Soc. Research in Child Devel. Author: Emergent Writing and Reading in 5-6 Year Olds: A Longitudinal Study, Emergent Literacy: Writing and Reading, 1986, mem. editorial bd. research jours. Reading Research Quarterly, Jour. of Reading Behavior; sr. author McGraw-Hill Reading and McGraw Hill English textbook series; contbr. articles to profl. publs. Home: 1555 Scio Church Rd Ann Arbor MI 48103 Office: U Mich Sch Edn Ann Arbor MI 48109

SUMMER, DONNA (LA DONNA ADRIAN GAINES), singer, actress, songwriter; b. Boston, Dec. 31, 1948; d. Andrew and Mary Gaines; m. Helmut Sommer (div.); 1 child, Mimi; m. Bruce Sudano; children: Brooklyn, Amanda. Singer, 1967—; actress: (German stage prodn.) Hair, 1967-75, (Vienna Folk Opera prodns.) Porgy and Bess, (German prodns.) The Me Nobody Knows, (cable TV spl.) Donna Summer Special, 1980; recorded albums including The Wanderer, Star Collection, Love To Love You Baby, Love Trilogy, Four Seasons of Love, I Remember Yesterday, The Deep, Shut Out, Once Upon A Time, Bad Girls, On The Radio, Walk Away, She Works Hard For The Money, Cats Without Claws, All Systems Go; forerunner of current disco style. Named Best Rhythm and Blues Female Vocalist, Nat. Acad. Rec. Arts and Scis., 1978, Best Female Rock Vocalist, 1979, Favorite Female Pop Vocalist, Am. Music Awards, 1979, Favorite Female Vocalist of Soul Music, 1979, Soul Artist of Yr., Rolling Stone mag., 1979; recipient Best Favorite Pop Single award, 1979, Best-selling Black Music Album for Female Artist award Nat. Assn. Record Merchandizers, 1979, Ampex Golden Reel award for album On the Radio, 1979, Best-selling Album for Female Artist, 1980, Ampex Golden Reel award for single On the Radio, 1980, Ampex Golden Reel award for album Bad Girls, Best of Las Vegas Jimmy award for best rock performance, 1980, Grammy award for best inspirational performance, 1984. Office: care Munao Mgmt 1224 N Vine St Los Angeles CA 90038

SUMMERALL, MARY VIRGINIA, advertising agency executive; b. Brownsville, Tex., Aug. 29, 1956; d. James Leon and Bertha (De La Peña) S. AA, Tex. Southmost Coll., 1975; BA, Pan Am. U., 1977; MA, U. Tex., 1982. Program dir. Media Properties, Inc., Brownsville, 1976-79; asst. v.p. Highland Marketing Group, Austin, Tex., 1980-83; chief copywriter Fellers, Lacy & Gaddis, Austin, 1983-86, creative dir., 1986—. Media dir. Citizens for a United Austin, 1981-82; mem. Austin Women's Polit. Caucus, Austin, 1984—. Recipient Gold award 10th Dist. Advt. Fedn., 1984-86, Gold award Austin Advt. Fedn., 1984-86, Telly award Nat. Telly Awards, 1984-86. Mem. Austin Graphic Arts Soc. Democrat.

SUMMERFORD, SHERRY R., brokerage company executive; b. Hartselle, Ala., Jan. 21, 1948; d. James Benton and Lucy Ruby (Speakman) Roberts; m. Robert Copeland Summerford, Mar. 6, 1965 (dec. 1975); children: Cherie, Gina, Robin. Student, Calhoun Community Coll., Decatur, Ala., 1976-77. Collector Credit Bur. of Decatur (Ala.), 1976-78; collector, bookkeeper Wilson Equipment Co., Decatur, 1978; timekeeper Albert G. Smith Constrn. Co., Athens, Ala., 1978-79; bookkeeper, asst. mgr. Hogan's Ready Mix, Hartselle, Ala., 1979-82; rep. Dewline Trucking, Inc., Federalsburg, Md., 1982—; pres. Summerford & Summerford Enterprises Inc., Mgmt. Agy.-Environ., Decatur, 1987. mgr. Sheriff Buford Burgess polit. campaign, Decatur, 1980. Mem. Credit Women of Ala. (pres. 1977-78), Nat. Assn. Female Execs., Decatur C. of C., Nat. Fedn. Ind. Bus., Am. Legion Ladies Aux., North Ala. Traffic Club (v.p. 1988—), Tenn. Valley Traffic Club. Republican. Methodist. Office: Summerford & Summerford Enterprises Inc 2414 Beltline Hwy Decatur AL 35608

SUMMERS, FRANCES PHAYE, vocational rehabilitation consultant; b. Klamath Falls, Oreg., Apr. 15, 1938; d. Phayo Grindol and Frances Ruth (Henry) Pfefferle; m. C. Oakley Summers Jr., Apr. 25, 1953 (div. Sept. 1969); children—Katherine , Anne, Donald O., Wayne P. Grad. in Social Work, Salvation Army Officers Tng. Coll., 1957; BS, U. Oreg., 1983, MS, 1985. Cert. rehab. counselor, Oreg. Exec. dir. Salvation Army, Oreg., Ariz. and Calif., 1957-69, exec. sec. Employment Div., Flagstaff, Ariz., 1970-75, placement specialist , Medford, Oreg., 1975-78; area supr. Workers Compensation Dept., Oreg., 1978-80; vocat. rehab. cons., Siskiyou, Cascade Rehab., Eugene, Oreg., 1980-85; regional mgr. Cooley/Assocs., Eugene, 1985-86; owner, exec. officer Oreg. Vocat. Solutions, Eugene, 1986—; conf. com. chmn. Oreg. Assn. Rehab. Profls., Eugene, 1982, edn. com. chmn. 1988. Bd. dirs. U. Oreg. Parents Assn., 1981-88, pres., 1986-88. Mem. Eugene C. of C., Nat. Rehab. Assn., Oreg. Assn. Rehab. Profls. in Pvt. Sector, Alpha Lambda Delta, Phi Eta Sigma. Contbr. articles to profl. jours. Avocations: swimming, hiking, antiques, boating, classical music, travel., hiking, boating, classical music.

SUMMERS, LINDA SUZANNE (SMIZINSKI), county government official, realtor; b. Chgo., July 7, 1947; d. Bruno Albert and Wanda Casmira (Tarkowski) Smizinski. BA, Loyola U., 1969, MS in Indsl. Relations, 1976. Index clk. City Chgo., 1969-70; job analyst technician Bureau Adminstrn. Cook County Govt., Chgo., 1970-73, job analyst II, 1973-81, job analyst III supr., 1981-86, labor relations officer, 1986—; job analyst Hay Mgmt. Cons., Chgo., 1978-82. Recipient award Nat. Assn. Counties, Chgo., 1986. Mem. Nat. Assn Female Execs., Chgo. Met. Chpt. Intergovtl. Personnel Mgmt. Assn., Nat. Assn. Realtors, Ill. Assn. Realtors, Chgo. Bd. Realtors, Northwest Real Estate Bd., North Side Real Estate Bd. Democrat. Roman Catholic. Club: Chgo. Health. Office: Cook County Govt County Bldg Room 818 118 N Clark St Chicago IL 60602 also: Am Title Realty Co Inc 6253 N Milwaukee Ave Chicago IL 60646

SUMMERS, LORRAINE DEY SCHAEFFER, librarian, association official; b. Phila., Dec. 14, 1946; d. Joseph William and Hilda Lorraine (Ritchey) Dey; m. F. William Summers, Jan. 28, 1984. B.A., Fla. State U., 1968, M.S., 1969. Extension dir. Santa Fe Regional Library, Gainesville, 1969-71; pub. library cons. State Library of Fla., Tallahassee, 1971-78, asst. state librarian, 1978-84; dir. adminstrv. services Nat. Assn. for Campus Activities, Columbia, S.C., 1984-85; asst. state librarian State Library of Fla., Tallahassee, 1985—; cons. in field. Del. Pres.'s Com. on Mental Retardation Regional Forum, Atlanta. 1975; del. Fla. Gov.'s Conf. on Library and Info. Services, 1978. Mem. ALA (orgn. com. 1979-83, council 1982-84, resolutions com. 1983-85), Assn. Specialized and Coop. Library Agys. (dir. 1976-82, chmn. planning and orgn. com. 1976-80, chmn. nominating com., 1980-81, chmn. by laws com. 1985-86 , exec. bd. state library agy sect. 1983-86, pres. 1987-88), Southeastern Library Assn. (exec. bd. 1976-80), Fla. Library Assn. (sec. 1978-79, dir., 1976-80), Am. Soc. Pub. Adminstrn. Democrat. Methodist. Contbr. articles in field. Office: State Library Fla RA Gray Bldg Tallahassee FL 32399

SUMMERS, RETHA, telecommunications executive, counselor; b. Goldsboro, N.C., May 4, 1953; d. Harvey and Aletha (Graham) S. BS in Bus. Adminstrn., N.C. A&T State U., 1975; postgrad., Campbell U. Employment interviewer Employment Security Commn., Kinston, N.C., 1975-77; service rep. Carolina Telephone, Tarboro, N.C., 1977-86, personnel asst., 1986—. Bd. dirs. Young Future Christian Leaders Assn., 1985—. Mem. Am. Bus. Women's Assn. (pres. 1983-84, Banner award, Woman Yr. 1984), Am. Assn. Counseling and Devel., Dale Carnegie Assn. Home: PO Box 366 La Grange NC 28551

SUMMERS, SUE ELLEN, contract analyst; b. Jasper, Ala., Mar. 27, 1959; d. David Jack and Mary Ellen (Stinson) Rowland; m. Dan L. Summers, Sept. 20, 1986. AS, Walker Coll., 1978; BS in Commerce and Bus. Adminstrn., U. Ala., 1980; MBA, Samford U., 1985; postgrad., Birmingham (Ala.) Sch. Law, 1985—. Auditor TVA, Knoxville, 1980-81; contract analyst So. Co. Services Inc., Birmingham, 1981—. Fin. advisor Jr. Achievement of Jefferson County, Inc., Birmingham, 1983-84, project bus. instr., 1988. Mem. Nat. Mgmt. Assn., Fin. Mgmt. Assn. (charter), U. Ala. Commerce Execs. Soc., U. Ala. Nat. Alumni Assn., Greater Birmingham C. of C. (v.p.'s com. 1985), Am. Legion Aux., Walker Coll. Alumni Assn. (exec. bd.). Republican. Methodist. Club: Met. Dinner Greater Birmingham. Home: 1050 Alford Ave Birmingham AL 35226 Office: So Co Services Inc PO Box 2625 800 Shades Creek Pkwy Birmingham AL 35202

SUMMERSELL, FRANCES SHARPLEY, club woman; b. Birmingham, Ala.; d. Arthur Croft and Thomas O. (Stone) Sharpley; student U. Montevallo, Peabody Coll., Nashville; m. Charles Grayson Summersell, Nov. 10, 1934. Partner, artist, writer Asso. Educators, 1959—. Mem. D.A.R., Magna Charta Dames, U. Women's Club (pres. 1957-58), U.D.C. (state historian 1956-58, pres. Robert Emmet Rodes chpt. Tuscaloosa 1953-55), Daus. Am. Colonists (organizing regent Tuscaloosa 1956-63), English Speaking Union, Marquis Biog. Library Soc. (adv. mem.). Vice-chmn. Ft. Morgan Hist. Commn., 1959-63. Mem. Tuscaloosa County Preservation Soc. (trustee 1965-78, service award 1975), W. Ala. Art Assn., Nat. Trust Historic Preservation, Birmingham-Jefferson Hist. Soc. Clubs: Country, University (Tuscaloosa). Co-author: Alabama History Filmstrips, 1961; Viewing Alabama History Filmstrips, 1961; Florida History Filmstrips, 1963; Texas History Filmstrips, 1965-66; Ohio History Filmstrips, 1967 (Merit award Am. Assn. State and Local History 1968); California History Filmstrips, 1968; Illinois History Filmstrips, 1970. Home: 1411 Caplewood Tuscaloosa AL 35401

SUMRELL, JUNE DALE, systems analyst; b. Rockville Centre, N.Y., May 27, 1957; d. Ferrall Nixon and Ann (Bronsky) S. BS, James Madison U., 1979; MBA, Va. Commonwealth U., 1986. Computer systems analyst Robertshaw Controls Corp., Richmond, Va., 1979-87; lead applications analyst, programmer Blue Cross/Blue Shield of Va., Richmond, 1987—. Active Richmond Jaycees, 1986—. Mem. Data Processing Mgmt. Assn. (profile com., reservations com. Richmond br. 1986—), Roundtable Investors (sec.-treas. 1987—), Alpha Gamma Delta Alumnae. Home: 2027 Airy Circle Richmond VA 23233

SUMTER, ELIZABETH ANN, state government official; b. San Diego, Apr. 10, 1959; d. Frank Anthony and Joan Sylvia (Gajdos) Patlyek; m. Terry Eugene Sumter, July 20, 1983. BA, Ea. Ill. U., 1981, MS in Tech. Edn., 1983, MS in Pub. Adminstrn., 1986. Weather forecaster Channel 10 Cable, Bloomington, Ill., 1977-79; coordinator adminstrv. service Dept. Def., Rantoul, Ill., 1979-81, tech. instr., 1981-83; materiels mgmt. Dept. Def., Austin, Tex., 1983-84; sr. personnel rep. Dept. Human Resources City of Austin, 1984-85, program mgr. Gen. Services, asst. dir. Communications Dept., 1987; dir. programs Tex. Treasury Dept., Austin, 1987—. Editor Safety Quar. mag., 1984. Chairperson United Way, Austin, 1986-87, Tex. Response Austin Aid, 1985-86; sec. Wimberly Hills Home Owners Assn. Named Outstanding Young Career Woman of Yr., Bus. and Profl. Women, 1981, Outstanding Toastmaster Yr., Toastmasters, 1981. Mem. Nat. Assn. Female Execs., Wimberly C. of C., Assn. Pub. Adminstrs. Democrat. Roman Catholic. Home: 65 Hill Country Trail Wimberley TX 78676

SUN, LINDA CHRISTINE, development company executive; b. Shanghai, Peoples Republic of China, Mar. 9, 1943; came to U.S., 1961, naturalized, 1972; d. Richard T.L. and Sophie (Hsu) S.; m. Richard Jack Bishirjian, June 24, 1967 (div. 1984); children: Philip Edmund, Maria Stephanie. BA in Biology, Coll. of St. Teresa, Winona, Minn., 1965; MBA in Mktg. Mgmt., Pace U., 1983. Lic. real estate agent, Va., Md. Technician Microbiol. Assocs., Bethesda, Md., 1966-67; accompanist Westchester Conservatory of Music, White Plains, N.Y., 1974-75; research technician Sloan-Kettering Inst., Rye, N.Y., 1976-79; agt. Prudential Ins. Co., Fairfax, Va., 1984-85, The Equitable, Washington, 1986; mktg. mgr. Gen. Devel. Corp., Falls Church, Va., 1986—; agt. Am. Income Life, Arlington, Va., 1987-88; real estate agt. Shannon and Luchs, Washington, 1987—; panelist First Va. Asian Am. Bus. Conf., 1987; ins. broker Prudential Ins. Co. of Am., Greenbelt, Md., 1986—. Fund-raiser Orgn. of Chinese Americans, Washington, 1983—; First Va. Asian Am. Bus. Conf., 1987; coordinator Pace U. Alumni Reunion, Washington, 1987. Recipient scholarships Viterbo Coll., Coll. of St. Teresa, Rosary Coll.; fellowship George Washington U.; Gold medal Nat. Assn. Piano Tchrs. Mem. Pace U. Alumni Assn. (reunion coordinator Washington chpt., 1987), Coll. St. Teresa Alumnae Assn. Democrat. Roman Catholic. Home: 3800 Powell Ln Falls Church VA 22041 Office: Gen Devel Corp 7115 Leesburg Pike Suite 316 Falls Church VA 22041

SUNDA, SHARON RUTH, retail executive; b. Pasadena, Calif., Aug. 19, 1942; d. Omer and Gladys Aleen (Kemp) Wolfe; m. Gary Lewis Sunda, Jan. 31, 1964; children: Bryan, Eric. BA, U. Calif., Santa Barbara, 1964. Cert. elem. tchr., Calif. Tchr. Garden Grove (Calif.) Unified Sch. Dist., 1964-68; pres. Orange County Speaker Inc., Garden Grove, 1972—. Officer Lamplighter Guild/Children's Hosp., Garden Grove, 1970—; pres. PTA, Garden Grove, 1973-81; mem. parent/adv. com. Bolsa Grande High Sch., Garden Grove, 1987—. Mem. Nat. Assn. Music Merchants, Calif. Assn. Ind. Bus., Garden Grove C. of C. (v.p., bd. dirs., appreciation award 1985), Nat. Assn. Female Execs. Clubs: Pinetree Ladies Golf Assn. (Santa Ana, Calif.) (pres. 1978-80), Jobs Daus. (Altadena, Calif.). Lodges: Soroptimists, Altadena Bethel (honored queen 1960-61). Office: Orange County Speaker Inc 13686 Newhope St Garden Grove CA 92643

SUNDERLAND, BARBARA ANNE, international marketing company executive, fund raising executive; b. Providence, R.I., Mar. 7, 1948; d. Everett Swan and Marica Anne (Galgas) S. BA, Brown U., 1977; MPH, U. Tex., 1988; MPH, U. Tex. Sch. Pub. Health, 1987. Cert. fund raising exec. Owner, Barbara Enterprises, Inc., Providence, 1962-78; exec. dir. Houston Area Parkinsonism Soc., 1979-82; pres. Sunderland Assocs., Internat. Mktg., Houston, 1982—; v.p. Van Dyke Travel Agy., Houston, 1983-85; cons. dept. neurology U. Tex. Med. Sch., 1982. Bd. dirs. R.I. Better Bus. Bur., 1975-78. bd. dirs. Am. Epilepsy Found., Houston chpt., 1983—; mem. edn. com. Houston Area Health Care Coalition, 1983; mem. Patient Edn. and Exchange Group, Health Meeting Planners; coordinator Houston Citywide Ways to Really Stop Smoking sponsored by NBC-TV, 1985-86; mem. mayor's Task Force Against Smoking in Pub. Places, City of Houston, 1985-86; bd. dirs. Parkinsonism Support Groups Am., Washington, 1981—; founder, pres. Stroke Found. of Tex., 1984; coordinator Feminist Majority of Houston, 1987. Recipient Jewish Vets. Brotherhood award, 1965, John Philip Sousa Music award, 1966, award J. Arthur Trudeau Ctr. for Retarded, 1975, Cert. of Appreciation City of Houston, 1985, 86, Cert. Appreciation Mayor of Houston and Dir. Health and Human Resources, 1986; recognized as Outstanding Female Bus. Owner, Dept. Labor, 1976. Mem. Nat. Soc. Fund Raising Execs. (spl. event award Houston chpt. 1982, bd. dirs. S.W. chpt., 1980-83, sec. 1982), Internat. Assn. Bus. Communicators, Nat. Assn. Female Execs., Women's Profl. Assn. (bd. dirs. 1980—) Clubs: Brown U. (pres., newsletter editor) (Houston); Forum; Combined Sch. Alumni (bd. dirs. 1978—). Author: The Stillborn and Neo-Natal Death Handbook for Grieving Parents, Professional Medical Support, Family, and Friends, 1987. Home and Office: PO Box 56754 Houston TX 77256 Office: 4950 Woodway Suite 606 Houston TX 77056

SUNDERLAND, BROOKE WILLIAMS (BROOKE W. SIMON), art gallery owner, sculptor; b. Billings, Mont., Dec. 1, 1940; d. Robert James and Harriette Robiard (Lucas) Williams; m. David Kendell Sunderland, Sept. 13, 1975; 1 child, Matthew Mark. BA, U. Colo., 1969. Self-employed tchr. art Boulder, Colo. Springs, 1971-78; prin. Robiard Art Galleries, Colo. Springs, 1978—; founder Quality West Art Gallery Network, Colorado Springs, 1986; bd. dirs. Gallery Contemporary Art U. Colo., Colorado Springs, 1986—. One-woman shows include Saks Gallery, Denver, U. Colo., Boulder and Colorado Springs, Jewish Community Ctr., Denver, Galerie de Tours, San Francisco; represented in permanent collections Mills Coll., Oakland, Calif., Presdl. Collection Israel, Brigham Young U., Robert Louis Stevenson Sch., Pebble Beach, Calif.; subject of numerous articles. Pres. El Paso County Bd. Health, Colorado Springs, 1984-88; chmn. Mayor's task force on Alcoholism, Colorado Springs, 1986; committeewoman El Paso County Reps., Colorado Springs, 1986—; pres. Colorado Springs Rose Soc., 1986—; mem. adv. bd. Pikes Peak Alliance for Mentally Ill, 1985—; bd. dirs. Performing Arts for Youth, Colorado Springs, 1986—, Facts of Life Hotline, Colorado Springs, 1985 , Minority Council for Arts, Colorado Springs, 1985—; co-chmn. Colo. Fedn. of Republican Women (sec. House Dist. #21). Recipient Alumni and Friends award U. Colo., 1981, Regent citation award U. Colo., 1980, Generators award Electricity mag., 1985; named Outstanding Citizen Colorado Springs, 1980. Mem. Nat. Assn. Antique and Art Appraisers Soc., Small Bus. Council (bd. dirs. 1985—), Colorado Springs C. of C. (past chmn. retail council 1986-87), Phi Alpha Theta. Republican. Episcopalian. Club: Country of Colorado Springs. Home: 3103 Springridge Dr Colorado Springs CO 80906 Office: Robiard Art Galleries 230 E Cheyenne Mountain Blvd Colorado Springs CO 80906

SUNDERMAN, MARTHA-LEE, education administrator, editor; b. Norristown, Pa., July 5, 1934; d. William and Anna B. (Zeyn) Taggart; m. James Biscoe, Mar. 2, 1957 (div. 1971); children: Jennifer Lee Burke, Heather McLean; m. F. William Sunderman, May 3, 1980. AB, Beaver Coll., 1955; postgrad., Villanova U., 1967-71. Jr. engr. Philco Corp., Lansdale, Pa., 1955-57; med. research librarian Merck, Sharp, and Dohme, West Point, Pa., 1957-61; asst. to med. advisor Rohm and Haas Co., Phila., 1963; dir. alumnae affairs Beaver Coll., Glenside, Pa., 1964-67; dir. devel. Friends' Cen. Sch., Phila., 1967-71; asst. to dir. Inst. for Clin. Sci., Hahnemann U. Med. Sch., Phila., 1971-88; asst. to dir. Inst. for Clin. Sci. Pa. Hosp, Phila., 1988—; asst. sec. bd. dirs. Inst. for Clinical Sci. Inc., Phila., 1985—. Editorial assoc. Annals of Clinical and Lab. Sci. jour., 1971—. Mem. Beaver Coll. Alumni Assn. (bd. dirs 1986—). Republican. Lutheran. Home: 1833 Delancey Pl Philadelphia PA 19103 Office: Inst for Clin Sci Pennsylvania Hosp Duncan Bldg 301A Philadelphia PA 19102

SUNDER RAJ, MARY, dentist; b. Bangalore, Karnataka, India, May 15, 1944; came to U.S., 1976; d. Govinda and Maggie (Sweeney) Rao; m. Sunder Raj, May 12, 1975; children: Veena , John Vivek, Christina Vinutha. Grad., Mt. Carmel's Sch., Bangalore, India, 1963; BDS, Bangalore Dental Coll., 1968; postdoctoral, SUNY, Buffalo, 1977-80. Intern Bangalore Dental Coll., 1969-70, lectr., 1970-73; lectr. Belgaum (India) Med. Coll., 1970-73; dental surgeon Govt. Karnataka, India, 1973-76; coordinator oral cancer Sloan Keatering, N.Y.C., 1981-85; faculty NYU Dental Sch., 1980—; pvt. practice dentist 1984—. Contbr. numerous articles to profl. jours. Vol. oral hygiene edn., India, 1969-76. People Fund scholar, Bangalore Dental Coll., 1964-68, NIH grantee, 1977-80. Mem. Am. Oral Pathology, Indian Dental Council. Home: 4317 Marathon Pkwy Little Neck NY 11363

SUNDQUIST, BARBARA LOUISE, personnel executive; b. Grand Forks, N.D., Feb. 10, 1934; d. Elmer Ferdinand and Carolyn Johanna (Schmidt) Anderson; student Northwestern U., 1952-53; B.A. cum laude, U. Minn., 1956; m. John Lewis Sundquist, Oct. 13, 1956. Civil service technician Minn. Civil Service Dept., St. Paul, 1956-58; personnel officer Minn. Dept. Hwys., St. Paul, 1959; personnel dir. Minn. State Prison, Stillwater, 1959-67; suggestion system adminstr. Minn. Dept. Adminstrn., St. Paul, 1970-71; dir. Minn. merit system Minn. Dept. Human Services, St. Paul, 1967-77, personnel dir., 1977-79; commr. Minn. Dept. Employee Relations, St. Paul, 1979-82; personnel dir. Minn. Dept. Human Services, St. Paul, 1983—. Recipient cert. of appreciation Internat. Personnel Mgmt. Assn., citation of honor Office of Gov., State of Minn. Mem. Internat. Personnel Mgmt. Assn., Am. Soc. Personnel Adminstrn., Twin City Personnel Assn., Nat. Pub. Employer Labor Relations Assn., St. Paul Personnel Dirs., Alpha Omicron Pi. Republican. Lutheran. Home: 2750 Dale #50 Roseville MN 55113 Office: 654 Cedar St Saint Paul MN 55155

SUNDVICK, LYNN ELIZABETH, office administrator; b. Oceanside, N.Y., Dec. 25, 1960; d. George Theodore Sundvick and Shirley Ann (Sommer) Sundvick-Lippan. AS in Bus. cum laude, Nassau Community Coll., 1980; BS in Mgmt. magna cum laude, L.I. U., 1982. Office mgr. Petrogulf USA, N.Y.C., 1982-83; adminstrv. asst. Hay Mgmt. Cons., N.Y.C., 1983-85; exec. sec. Lane Assocs., Island Park, N.Y., 1985—; cons. Dave Tam Painting Specialists, Bellmore, N.Y. Mem. Nat. Orgn. Female Execs., Profl. Assn. Diving Instrs. (cert. scuba diver), Delta Mu Delta. Home: 1520 Bellmore Ave Bellmore NY 11710

SUNIER, KATHERINE JOHNSON, nurse; b. Chgo., Mar. 16, 1952; d. Frank Richard and Mary Elizabeth (Pierce) J.; m. Richard Joseph Sunier, Oct. 15, 1983; 1 child, Jessica Michelle. B.S. in Nursing, Iowa Wesleyan Coll., 1975; postgrad. Rush U. Staff nurse Rush-Presbyn.-St. Luke's Hosp., Chgo., 1975-78, head nurse cardiovascular thoracic surgeries, 1979-82; staff nurse operating room Lake Forest Hosp., Ill., 1982—. Mem. Assn. Operating Room Nurses, Am. Endurance Ride Conf., Riding for the Handicapped Orgn., Upper Midwest Endurance and Competitive Riding Assn. Avocations: horseback riding; running, aerobics; handcrafts; computers. Home: 6618 88th Ave Kenosha WI 53140

SUNLIGHT, CAROLE, psychologist; b. DuBois, Pa., Aug, 19; d. Andy and Mary Ann Gaborick; Med. Tech., Carnegie Coll., 1959; BA in Psychology, Cleve. State U., 1971; MA in Psychology (Univ. scholar), Pepperdine U., 1973; PhD in Psychology, U.S. Internat. U., 1980. Med. technologist Doctors Piercy, Fertig, Schneider and Doran, Cleve., 1959-67; chief technologist med. dept. U.S. Steel Corp., Lorain, Ohio, 1967-69; office mgr. dept. philosophy and religious studies Cleve. State U., 1969-70; counselor Gardena Valley Counseling Service, Gardena, Calif., 1971-72; clin. intern Pepperdine U. psychology clinic, 1972-73; testing technician Norco-Corona (Calif.) Sch. Dist., 1973; dir. treatment services Unfinished Symphony Ranch, Inc., Agoura, Calif., 1973-77; pvt. practice, Westlake Village, Calif., 1977-78; staff Kaiser Permanente Mental Health Center, 1977—; pvt. practice, Torrance, Calif., 1980—; speaker in field. Bd. dirs. COMOSI Mental Health, Thousand Oaks, Calif., 1977-78. Registered med. technologist. Mem. Am. (sects on psychology of women, clin. neuropsychology, Calif. Psychol. Assn., Los Angeles County (newsletter editor 1982-84) Psychol. Assn., Am. Med. Technologists (Ohio State Soc. Publ. award 1972), Calif. Neuropsychol. Soc., Psychologists for Social Responsibility, NOW, Psi Chi. Office: 765 W College St Los Angeles CA 90012 Office: 19000 Hawthorne Blvd Suite 300 Torrance CA 90503

SUNSTEIN, CAROLYN RUTH NETTER, antique dealer; b. Phila., Jan. 5, 1922; d. Morton Angelo and Dorothy G. (Goldsmith) Netter; B.S. in Edn., Temple U., Phila., 1942; m. Charles Gerstley Sunstein, Aug. 22, 1941; children—Florence Gertsley Sunstein Begun, Lynn Carol, Charles Gerstley, Jr. Antique miniature collector, 1942—; dealer, show coordinator Phila. Miniature Show, 1972—; lectr., appraiser, 1977—; adv. bd. Warmans Antique Guild, 1981. Sec., Adoption Ctr. Del. Valley, 1982—; bd. dirs. Samuel Paley Day Care Ctr., 1942—, Albert Einstein Med. Ctr., 1975 , Nat. Adoption Ctr., 1980—. Mem. Pa. Antique Assn., Nat. Assn. Miniature Enthusiasts, Internat. Guild Miniature Artisans (pres. 1986-88). Republican. Jewish. Office: PO Box 26734 Elkins Park PA 19117

SUP, BERNICE ANN (SUSIE), retail apparel executive; b. Ft. Lupton, Colo., Nov. 9, 1940; d. Pearl M. Hodge and Lorraine L. (Benedict) Hodge-Wiler; m. Gale Lynn Sup, Nov. 11, 1962; children: Lori, Tate, Layne, Amber. BS in Edn., U. Nebr., 1962, postgrad., 1965. Chemist Dorsey Lab., Lincoln, Nebr., 1962; tchr. sci. and math. Shawnee Mission (Kans.) Sch. Dist., 1963-66; tchr. chemistry and math. Wahoo (Nebr.) Pub. Schs., 1967-68; tchr. math. Lincoln Pub. Schs., 1968; buyer, co-owner, v.p., sec. The Hitchin' Post, Lincoln, 1968—. Pres., v.p., sec. Lincoln Symphony Guild, 1984-87; mem. Mayor's Film Com., Lincoln, 1984-87; leader local council Girl Scouts U.S., Lincoln, 1985-86; bd. dirs. Family Service Assn., 1985-87. Mem. Zeta Tau Alpha, Mu Phi. Presbyterian. Club: Lincoln Women's. Home: 2464 Woodscrest Lincoln NE 68502 Office: The Post and Nickel 144 N 14 St Lincoln NE 68508

SUPINSKI, CATHERINE JOSEPHINE CURRAN (MRS. EDMUND SUPINSKI), librarian; b. N.Y.C., Aug. 27, 1915; d. Francis Joseph and Mary (Jordan) Curran; B.A., Hunter Coll., 1936; M.A., Columbia, 1937, B.S. in Library Sci., 1943; m. Edmund Supinski, June 2, 1951. Asst. librarian Nat. Indsl. Conf. Bd., N.Y.C., 1943-48; librarian N.Y. C. of C., N.Y.C., 1948-64, Dumont (N.J.) High Sch., 1964-80. Mem. Spl. Libraries Assn. (N.Y. pres. 1950-51, internat. 2d v.p. 1953-54), ALA, NEA, N.J., Bergen County, Dumont edn. assns., N.J., Bergen County (rec. sec. 1967-68) sch. librarians assns., N.J. Secondary Tchrs. Assn. Home: 30 Kinderkamack Rd Woodcliff Lake NJ 07675

SURFUS, SANDRA SUE, nurse; b. Knoxville, Tenn., Feb. 2, 1941; d. John Adolph and Ella Jane (McKittrick) Schaller; children: Kim Elizabeth, John Scott, Sara Lynn. BS in Nursing, U. Wis., 1963; MS in Nursing, Calif. State U., Los Angeles, 1980. RN, Calif., Wis. Staff nurse U. Hosps./Madison (Wis.) Gen. Hosp., 1963-74; staff nurse Huntington Meml. Hosp., Pasadena, Calif., 1974-80, cardiac rehab. nurse, 1976-80; mgr. cardiac rehab. and fitness ctr. St. Joseph Med. Ctr., Burbank, Calif., 1980—. Mem. Calif. Soc. Cardiac Rehab. (pres. 1984-86), Am. Assn. Cardiovascular Pulmonary Rehab. (founding fellow 1986). Office: St Joseph Med Ctr Cardiac Rehab Buena Vista and Alameda Sts Burbank CA 91505

SURGALLA, LYNN ANN, electronics executive, research biophysicist; b. Chgo., Dec. 12, 1951; d. Michael Joseph and Mary Theresa (Moran) S.; m. Thomas Francis Valone, Aug. 17, 1986. BA in English, Fla. Atlantic U., 1974, BS in Physics, 1979; BA in Sociology, SUNY, Buffalo, 1982, MS in Natural Scis., 1986, PhD in Biophysics, 1987—; MS in Univ. Adminstrn., SUNY Coll., Buffalo, 1984. Tech. writer Roswell Park Meml. Inst., Buffalo, 1975-76; supr. N.E. YMCA, Snyder, N.Y., 1975-77; lab. asst. dept. physics Fla. Atlantic U., Boca Raton, 1978-79; engr. satellite ops. Lockheed Missiles & Space Co., Sunnyvale, Calif., 1979-81; acad. assessor Allen Youth Services Consortium, Buffalo, 1983-84; v.p. Integrity Electronics & Research, Buffalo, 1982—; research assoc. SUNY, Buffalo, 1986—; coordinator election news coverage Erie County, NBC TV Network, N.Y.C., 1976-77; cons. N.Y. State Edn. Dept., Buffalo, 1982-84; research assoc. Health Instruments and Devices Inst., Buffalo, 1986—. Eastman Kodak research fellow, 1986. Mem. AIAA, U.S. Psychotronics Assn. (v.p. nat. assn. 1987—), Bioelectromagnetics Soc., Biomed. Engring. Soc., Soc. for Biomaterials, N.Y. Acad. Sci., World Future Soc., Planetary Assn. for Clean Energy, People for Ethical Treatment of Animals, SUNY Biophysics Grad. Student Assn. (v.p. 1985-86). Democrat. Office: Integrity Electronics & Research 558 Breckenridge St Buffalo NY 14222

SUSMAN, KAREN LEE, lawyer; b. Austin, Tex., Oct. 26, 1942; d. Paul and Dorothy (Goudchaux) Hyman; m. Stephen D. Susman, Dec. 26, 1965; children: Stacy M., Harry P. BA, U. Tex., 1964; JD, U. Houston, 1981. Bar: Tex. 1981; bd. cert. in family law 1987. Tchr. high schs. Houston and Washington, 1964-68; realty broker Susman Realty, Houston, 1968-78; assoc. Saccomanno, Clegg, Martin & Kipple, Houston, 1981-83, Marian S. Rosen & Assocs., Houston, 1983-86; of counsel Webb & Zimmerman, Houston, 1986—. Editor Internat. Law Jour., 1980-81. Bd. dirs. Downtown YWCA, Houston, 1969-74, pres. 1974; bd dirs. Tex. Arts Alliance, Houston, 1975-78, Antidefamation League B'nai Brith, Houston, 1983-86, Lawyers and Accts. for Arts, Houston, 1985—; chmn. PBS TV Art Auction, Houston, 1975; mem. Tex. State Dem. Fin. Council, 1983—, Harris County Dem. Chmn.'s Council, 1984—, Candidate Selection Com., 1986—; bd. dirs. Houston Symphony, 1985—, Houston Grand Opera, 1988, Womens Advocacy Project, 1987—. Fellow Houston Bar Found.; mem. ABA, Tex. Bar Assn., Houston Bar Assn., Gulf Coast Family Law Specialists, A.A. White Soc., U. Houston Alumni (bd. dirs., v.p., sec. 1983—), Phi Delta Phi. Club: Houston. Home: 10 Shadder Way Houston TX 77019 Office: 1990 S Post Oak Blvd Post Oak Cen 14th Floor Houston TX 77056-3814

SUSMAN, VIRGINIA LEHMANN, psychiatrist, educator; b. Bronxville, N.Y., Nov. 30, 1949; d. Arthur Edwin and Jeanne Anne (Uebelacker) Lehmann; m. William Mark Susman, June 24, 1973; 1 child, Julianne Marie. B.A., Fordham U., 1971; M.D., U. Rochester, 1975. Diplomate Am. Bd. Psychiatry and Neurology. Resident Bronx (N.Y.) Mcpl. Hosp. Ctr., 1975-78, asst. dir. psychiat. outpatient dept., 1978-79, assoc. dir. psychiat. outpatient dept., 1979-80, unit chief inpatient dept., 1980-81; unit chief Westchester div. N.Y. Hosp., White Plains, 1981—, acting. dir. med. student edn., 1984—; asst. prof. psychiatry Albert Einstein Coll. Medicine, Bronx, 1979-81, Cornell U. Med. Coll., White Plains, 1981-87, assoc. prof. 1987—; practice medicine specializing in psychiatry, White Plains, 1978—. Contbr. articles to profl. jours. Research grantee Cornell U. Med. Coll., 1982-85; Picker Found. grantee, 1986—. Mem. Am. Psychiat. Assn., Am. Med. Womens Assn., Physicians for Social Responsibility (acting chmn. Westchester County br. 1982). Office: NY Hosp Westchester Div 21 21 Bloomingdale Rd White Plains NY 10605

SUSSMAN, DEBORAH EVELYN, design company executive; b. N.Y.C., May 26, 1931; d. Irving and Ruth (Golomb) S.; m. Paul Prejza, June 28, 1972. Student Bard Coll., 1948-50, Inst. Design, Chgo., 1950-53, Black Mountain Coll., 1950, Hochschule fur Gestaltung Ulm (Fulbright grantee), W.Ger., 1957-58. Art dir. Office of Charles and Ray Eames, Venice, Calif., 1953-57, 61-67; graphic designer Galeries Lafayette, Paris, 1959-60; prin. Deborah Sussman and Co., Santa Monica, Calif., 1968—; founder, pres. Sussman-Prejza and Co., Inc., Santa Monica, 1980—; speaker, lectr. UCLA Sch. Architecture, Archtl. League N.Y.C., Smithsonian Inst., Stanford Conf. on Design, Am. Inst. Graphic Arts Nat. Conf. at MIT, Design Mgmt. Inst. Conf., Mass.; spl. guest Internat. Design Conf., Aspen, Colo., Fulbright lectr., India, 1976; speaker NEA Adv. Council, 1985, Internat. Council Shopping Ctrs., 1986, USIA Design in America seminar, Budapest, Hungary, 1988. Mem. editorial adv. bd. Arts and Architecture Mag., 1981-85, Calif. Mag., Architecture Calif. Recipient numerous awards AIA Nat. Inst. Honors, 1985, 88, Am. Inst. Graphic Arts, Calif. Council AIA, Communications Arts Soc., Los Angeles County Bd. Suprs, Vesta award Women's Bldg. Los Angeles. Mem. AIA (hon.), Am. Inst. Graphic Arts (bd. dirs. 1982-85, founder Los Angeles chpt., chmn., 1983-84, numerous awards), Los Angeles Art Dirs. Club (bd. dirs., numerous awards), Alliance Graphique Internat., Architects, Designers and Planners Social Responsibility, SEGD. Democrat. Jewish. Avocations: Photography. Office: Sussman-Prejza & Co Inc 1651 18th St Santa Monica CA 90404

SUSSMAN, JUDITH ANNE, interior designer; b. N.Y.C., Jan. 9, 1935; d. Samuel and Paula Gordon (Kroll) G.; m. Donald E. Axinn, Mar. 29, 1953 (div. Apr. 1967); children: Meredith, Allison, Michael, Jennifer; m. Sanford Sussman, Nov. 3, 1967. BA, Columbia U., 1955; cert. design, N.Y. Sch. Interior Design, 1974 Interior designer J.C. Penney, Garden City, N.Y., 1974-76, R.H. Macy, Garden City, 1977; pvt. practice interior design Florence, S.C., 1977-78; prin. Judy Sussman Design Works, Phoenix, 1979—; lectr. Scottsdale (Ariz.) Community Coll., 1988-87. Designs represented in Home mag., 1980, Phoenix mag., 1981-87, Phoenix Home & Garden, 1982, 83, 86, 87, Designer mag., 1982. Chmn. Hist. League, Phoenix, 1981-83; mem. Contemporary Forum Bd. Phoenix Art Mus., 1981-87, Heard Mus., Phoenix, 1981-87. Mem. Am. Soc. Interior Design (chmn. assocs. com., awards com., bd. dirs., head assoc. com. of yr. 1983, 1st pl. Residential Design award 1982, 1st pl. Model Home Designer award 1985, 1st pl Nat. award 1987, merit award 1986, 1st pl. Contract Design award 1987), Nat. Home Fashions League, Jewish Bus. and Profl. Women (bd. dirs.), Phoenix C. of C. Democrat. Jewish. Club: Mill River (Muttontown, N.Y.); Village Tennis (Phoenix). Home: 2039 E Pasadena Phoenix AZ 85016 Office: Judy Sussman's Designworks Ltd 2150 E Highland Suite 205 Phoenix AZ 85016

SUSSMAN, VALERIE JOY, librarian; b. Bklyn., Oct. 4, 1946; d. Morris and Beatrice (Rifkin) S. BA, Queens Coll., 1967, MLS, 1970. Tchr. of library Peter Rouget Intermediate Sch. 88, Bklyn., 1970-82, Bronx High Sch. Sci., N.Y., 1982—; conv. presenter L.I. Library Assn., 1984. Co-author sci. curriculum guide, 1982; author math. and sci. bibliography, 1981; contbr. articles to profl. jours. Bd. dirs. Jeffrey P. Cohen Found., Queens, N.Y. 1973-82; active Adlai E. Stevenson Regular Dem. Club, Queens, 1969-82; mem. adv. com. N.Y. State Senator Gary Ackerman, N.Y. State Assemblyman David Cohen, 1980-82. U.S. Dept. Edn. grantee, 1979. Mem. N.Y.C. Sch. Librarians Assn. (conv. presentor 1982, rec. sec. 1978-80, pres. 1982-84, past pres. 1984-86, book rev. com. 1987—), Pequannock Edn. Fund (bd. dirs. 1984—), ALA, N.Y. Library Assn. (conv. presentor 1982, vitality com. 1984-87), Queens Coll. Library Sci. Alumni Assn. (treas. 1979—), N.Y. Sci. Fiction Soc. (exec. bd. 1984—), Masterwork Chorus, Harmony Singers. Jewish. Home: 39 Madison St Pequannock NJ 07440 Office: Bronx High Sch Sci Library 75 W 205th St Bronx NY 10468

SUSZYCKI, LEE HEDY, social work services coordinator; b. Bklyn., Oct. 19, 1939; d. Peter and Mary S. BS, NYU, 1961, MSW, 1963, postgrad. cert., 1986. Cert. social worker. Social worker Columbia-Presbyn. Med. Ctr., N.Y.C., 1963-70, sr. social worker, 1970-84, coordinator adult cardiac services, 1984—; supr. of MSWs Social Work Services Columiba-Presbyn. Med. Ctr., N.Y.C., 1985—; organizer, pres., cons. Nat. Clin. Network for Social Workers on Heart Transplants, N.Y.C., 1986—, cons. Health Care Financing Adminstrn., N.Y.C., 1987—. Mem. Nat. Assn. Social Workers, Acad. Cert. Social Workers, Internat. Soc. Heart Transplantation, Foundation of Thanatology (liaison adv. com.). Home: 330 E 33d St Apt 6-H New York NY 10016 Office: Columbia-Presbyn Med Ctr Social Work Services 622 W 168 St New York NY 10032

SUTCLIFFE, MARILYN CASE, research technician; b. New Haven, Apr. 20, 1936; d. Warren Evans and Esther Mary (Snow) Case; B.A. summa cum laude, U. Bridgeport, 1957; postgrad. Sorbonne, Paris, 1957-58, Duke U., 1958-59; m. William Manchester Sutcliffe, Dec. 27, 1958; children—Stacy Ellen, James Sheldon. Substitute tchr. Broward County, Fla., 1966-67; tchr. chemistry Nova Sr. High Sch., Ft. Lauderdale, Fla., 1967-68; research technician infectious diseases dept. biochemistry VA Med. Center, Nashville, 1968-86, research technician, 1988—. Fulbright scholar, 1957-58; James B. Duke fellow, 1958. Mem. Am. Soc. Microbiology. Republican. Contbr. articles to profl. jours. Home: 6824 Highland Park Dr Nashville TN 37205 Office: 1310 24th Ave S Nashville TN 37203

SUTHERLAND, KATHLEEN MARIE, marketing professional; b. Quonsett Point, R.I., Dec. 26, 1962; d. Peter Joseph and Patricia Ruth (Kelleher) S. BS, Va. Commonwealth U., 1984. Pub. info. asst. Am. Heart Assn. of Va., Richmond, 1983-84; community relations asst. Housing Opportunities Made Equal, Richmond, 1984; mktg. researcher Swarovski Am. Ltd., Cranston, R.I., 1984-85; sales rep. Swarovski Am. Ltd., Mid Atlantic States, 1985-87, Long Island and Conn., 1987—. Asst. youth group activities Shrine of the Sacred Heart-Cath. Youth Group Assn., Mount Washington, Md., 1986-87. Mem. Am. Assn. of Female Execs., Am. Mktg. Assn. Roman Catholic. Clubs: Fencing Club (Towson, Md. and Stonybrook, N.Y.); N.W. Iceskating (Mount Washington); Entrepreneurial (Stony Brook). Home: 5 Sylvan Ln Miller Place NY 11764

SUTHERLAND, MARY SUE, educator; b. Lansing, Mich., Jan. 21, 1941; d. Peter and Martha (Wender) S. BS, Mich. State U., 1962; MS, U. Tenn., 1963; EdD, U. Ala., 1973; MPH, U. Tenn., 1978. Prof. Young Harris (Ga.) Coll., 1964-66; instr. Middle Ga. Coll., Cochran, 1966-70; asst. prof. SUNY, Brockport, 1974-78; assoc. prof. U. Maine, Farmington, 1978-80, Fla. State U., Tallahassee, 1980—; Bd. dirs. Fla. Panhandle Health Ctr., Panama City, Am. Lung Assn. Fla., Tallahassee. Contbr. articles to profl. jours. Cons. Mental Health, Tallahassee, 1980-82, Health Edn. programs across the U.S., 1974—. Recipient J.T. Pouter award Fla. Pub. Health Assn., 1982. Mem. Am. Pub. Health Assn., Soc. Pub. Health, Am. Alliance Health Phys. Edn. Recreation and Dance (Merit award 1980), Fla. Assn. Profl. Health Edn., Am. Soc. Allied Health Educators. Democrat.

SUTHERLAND, ZENA BAILEY, library school educator, columnist, author; b. Winthrop, Mass., Sept. 17, 1913; d. Jack Karras and Lena (Cohen) Baum; m. Roland Bailey, Dec. 19, 1937 (div. 1962); children—Stephen, Thomas, Katherine Bailey Linehan; m. 2d, Alec Sutherland, July 30, 1964. B.A., U. Chgo., 1937, M.A., 1966. Editor, Rev. Bull., U. Chgo., 1958-86, assoc. editor, 1986—; contbg. editor Saturday Rev., N.Y.C., 1966-72; editor children's books, Chgo. Tribune, 1972-85; prof. emeritus Grad. Library Sch., U. Chgo., 1986—; cons. NBC, Chgo., 1968-71. Coauthor reference book: Children and Books, (Pi Lambda Theta award 1974); editor: Children and Libraries, 1981; author or editor 21 other books, various articles. Active U. Chgo. Service League, Neighborhood Club, Hosp. Vol. group, First Unitarian Ch. Recipient Children's Reading Round Table award, 1978; Sutherland Lectureship established U. Chgo., 1981. Mem. ALA (Grolier award 1983, bd. dirs., jury pres.), Internat. Bd. on Books for Young People, Internat. Reading Assn., Internat. Research Soc., Nat. Council Tchrs. English, Internat. Soc. for Research in Children's Lit., Mensa. Beta Phi Mu. Democrat. Clubs: University Women's (London), Quadrangle (Chgo.), Colony (Chgo.). Home: 1418 E 57th St Chicago IL 60637 Office: Grad Library Sch 1100 E 57th St Chicago IL 60637

SUTPHIN, SUSAN COCKRELL, librarian; b. San Antonio, July 26, 1947; d. Alford R. and Eunice (Thigpen) Cockrell. B.A., Huntingdon Coll., 1968; M.L.S., U. N.C.-Chapel Hill, 1969; A.S., Amarillo Coll., 1983; M.A. in Polit. Sci., W. Tex. State U., 1984. Asst. librarian Davidson County Community Coll., 1969-71; acquisitions librarian Central Piedmont Community Coll., 1971-76; tech. librarian Mason & Hanger-Silas Mason Co., Inc., Amarillo, Tex., 1977-88; with Sci. Library U.S. Patent and Trademark Office, 1988—. Republican. Home: 4612 Raleigh Ave #101 Alexandria VA 22304 Office: US Patent and Trademark Office Scientific Library CP3/4 2021 Jefferson Davis Hwy Arlington VA 22202

SUTTER, AILEEN MARIE, executive recruiting specialist; b. Pitts., Mar. 4, 1959; d. Dennis Lee and Nancy Marie (Smith) McIntyre; m. Mark T. Sutter, Sept. 28, 1985. BA, Pa. State U., 1981. Sales clk. Gimbel's, Bethel Park, Pa., 1981-83; sales asst. Harrington, Righter and Parsons, N.Y.C., 1983; account exec. TempsAm., N.Y.C., 1983-86; exec. recruiter Sales Cons., Inc., Red Bank, N.J., 1986, Mgmt. Recruiters, Inc., San Mateo, Calif., 1986—. Mem. Nat. Assn. Female Execs., Mgmt. Recruiters Assn. (cert.). Home: 390 Pompano Circle Foster City CA 94404 Office: Mgmt Recuiters Inc 1900 S Norfolk St San Mateo CA 94403

SUTTER, ANN BLACK, social worker; b. Tulsa, Feb. 20, 1948; d. Harold James and Jessie (Clarke) Black; m. Patrick T. Sutter, Mar., 1968 (div. July 1970); 1 child, Andrew Travis. BS, U. Tulsa, 1972; MSW, U. Okla., 1977. Mental health technician Tulsa Psychiat. Ctr., 1972-76; planning analyst Tulsa Urban Renewal Authority, 1973-76; instr. U. Fla., Gainesville, 1977-82; supr. med. surg., social work Shands Teaching Hosp., Gainesville, 1982; clin. social worker Charter Peachford Hosp., Atlanta, 1983-84; faculty Mercer U., Atlanta, 1985-87; pres. The Social Services Network, Atlanta, 1984—; instr. Mercer U., Atlanta, 1985-87, cons. Scottish Rite Children's Hosp., Atlanta, 1988. Author newspaper series. Mem. Child Adv. Council, Gainesville, 1978-82; bd. dirs., pres. Big Bros. and Big Sisters, Gainesville, 1977-81; fund-raiser Atlanta Dogwood Festival, Atlanta, 1985-86. Mem. Nat. Assn. Social Workers (cert., chmn. North Ga. unit, 1987—, chair SW region 1987, state bd. dirs. 1987—, state pub. relations coordinator 1987—), Am. Bus. Women's Assn., Atlanta Women's Network, Nat. Assn. Self-Employed, Kappa Alpha Theta. Democrat. Unitarian Universalist.

SUTTER, CAROLYN OPTHOFF, real estate executive; b. Kalamazoo, Oct. 9, 1942; d. John Martin and Lorraine Eleanor (Kloosterman) Opthoff; children: Chandra, Stephan. B.S., Calvin Coll., 1964; M.S., Western Mich. U., 1970; M.P.A., Calif. State U., Long Beach, 1982; postgrad., Harvard U., 1986. Dir. library and mus. services City of Long Beach, 1979-81, dir. telecommunications, 1981, gen. mgr. Tidelands Agy., 1982—. Chairwoman Mich. 4th Dist. Tricounty Women's Polit. Caucus, 1972-76; mem. adv. bd. Sch. Bus. Adminstrn., Calif. State U.-Long Beach; bd. dirs. Family Services Agy. Long Beach; mem. Waterfront Ctr. Named an Outstanding Alumni Calif. State U. Long Beach, 1983, Disting. Alumni Western Mich. U., 1985. Mem. Nat. Council for Urban Econ. Devel., Urban Land Inst., Calif. State U.-Long Beach Alumni Assn. Office: 2601 Main Suite 510 Irvine CA 92714

SUTTER, ELIZABETH HENBY (MRS. RICHARD A. SUTTER), civic leader, management company executive; b. St. Louis, May 15, 1912; d. William Hastings and Alvina (Steinbreder) Henby, A.B., Washington U., St. Louis, 1931; m. Richard A. Sutter, June 15, 1935; children—John Richard, Jane Elizabeth, Judith Ann (Mrs. William Hinrichs). Sec.-treas. Sutter Mgmt. Co., St. Louis, Sutter Clinic, St. Louis; v.p. Downtown Med. Bldg., Inc., St. Louis, until 1985. Chmn. com. on mental health AMA Aux., 1960-62, v.p., 1962-63, 64-64, pres. 1965-66, editor Direct Line newsletter, 1967-74; assoc. editor MD's Wife, 1973-80; mem. adv. bd. Deaconess Hosp. Sch. of Nursing, St. Louis; trustee John Burroughs Sch., 1958-61, v.p. 1959, devel. commn., 1960-61; mem. Historic Bldgs. Commn. St. Louis County, 1957—, chmn., 1973—; chmn. Com. for Preservation Children's Teeth; mem. planning bd. Health, Hosp. Health, Welfare Council Met. St. Louis, 1955-64; pres. Aux. Central States Soc. Indsl. Medicine and Surgery, 1960-61; pres. St. Louis County Med. Soc. Aux., 1948-49, Mo. Med. Soc. Aux., 1952-53; sec. St. Louis County Health and Hosp. Bd., 1956-61, chmn., 1961; bd. dirs. Am. Lung Assn. Eastern Mo., exec. com., 1956-85, v.p., 1960-61; pres. Tb and Health Soc. of St. Louis, 1962-65; adv. council vol. services Nat. Assn. Mental Health, 1962-64; bd. dirs. Am. Cancer Soc., St. Louis, exec. com., 1954-64; bd. dirs. Mental Health Assn. St. Louis, 1960-61; mem. Practical Nursing Edn. Council, chmn. exec. com., 1959-60; mem. AMA Council on Mental Health Planning for Nat. Conf. on Mental Health, 1961; mem. adv. com. on women in services Dept. Def., 1969-72, vice chmn., 1971; participant 24th ann. global strategy discussion U.S. Naval War Coll., 1972; bd. govs. Washington U. Alumni, 1970-71, 75—, vice chmn. 1979-80, chmn., 1980-81; trustee Washington U., 1979-81; pres. Washington U. Arts and Scis. Century Club, 1970-71; bd. dirs. St. Louis Conv. and Tourist Bur., 1975-83, sec., 1980-82; bd. dirs. Health Services Agy., 1975-82; mem. East West Gateway Coordinating Council Task Force on Historic Preservation, 1975-81, University City Historic Preservation Commn., 1977; bd. dirs. Whitney Beach III Assn., Longboat Key, Fla., 1984-87; del. Mo. Republican Conv., 1972, 76, 80, 84, del. Nat. Rep. Conv., 1984. Named 1 of 10 Women of Achievement in good citizen category St. Louis Globe-Democrat, 1961; Alumna of Yr., Gamma Phi Beta, St. Louis, 1966; recipient St. Louis County Med. Soc. award of merit, 1964; Disting. Alumni citation Washington U., 1968, Disting. Alumni Service citation, 1977; Life Style award Eastern Mo. chpt. Am. Lung Assn., 1982; Meritorious Service award Am. Park and Recreation Soc., 1985. Mem. Mo. Hist. Soc., St. Louis Symphony Soc., AMA Aux. (hon. life), Mo. Med. Aux. (hon. life), Met. St. Louis Med. Aux. (hon. life). Presbyterian. Endowed Richard A. and Betty H. Sutter Vis. Professorship in Occ. and Insdl. Medicine Washington U., St. Louis. Home: 7215 Greenway Dr Saint Louis MO 63130

SUTTIN, DORIS BETH, real estate broker and developer, mortgage broker; b. Chgo., July 5, 1940; d. Saul S. and Pearl (Goldberg) Siegal; m. Eugene N. Suttin, Feb. 1, 1961 (div. 1968); m. Myron J. Sponder, July 5, 1976 (div. 1977); 1 son, Adam L. B.S., U. Ill.-Urbana, 1961; Lic. real estate broker, Fla. Advt. mgr. Goldblatt Bros. Inc., Urbana, 1961-62; real estate salesperson Grand Bahama Devel. Co., Freeport, Grand Bahama, 1963-65; asst. sales mgr. Coral Beach Ltd., Freeport, 1968-70; owner-mgr. Saul S. Siegal Co., Miami, Fla., 1970-82; developer DLM Partnership, Miami, 1978—; owner, comml. real estate broker Doris B. Suttin Realty, Inc., Miami, 1981—; Miami Design Dist. Assocs. V.p. membership Lowe Art Mus., Friends of Art, U. Miami. Mem. Women in Communications, South Fla. Poetry Inst., Am. Acad. Poets, Vivian Laramore Rader Poetry Group (2d v.p.), Indsl. Assn. Dade County, Nat. Assn. Women Bus. Owners, Mensa. Home: 1063 NE 204 Terr North Miami Beach FL 33179 Office: Doris B Suttin Realty Inc 2875 NE 191st St Suite 815 North Miami Beach FL 33180

SUTTLES, VIRGINIA GRANT, advertising executive; b. Urbana, Ill., June 13, 1931; d. William Henry and Lenora (Fitzsimmons) Grant; student pub. schs., Mahomet, Ill.; m. John Henry Suttles, Sept. 24, 1977; step-children—Linda Suttles, Peg Suttles La Croix, Pamela Suttles Diaz, Randall. Media estimator and Procter & Gamble budget control Tatham-Laird, Inc., Chgo., 1955-60; media planner, supr. Tracy-Locke Co., Inc., Dallas and Denver, 1961-68; media dir., account exec. Lorie-Lotito, Inc., 1968-72; v.p., media dir. Sam Lusky Assos., Inc., Denver, 1972-86; ind. media buyer, 1984—; mktg. asst. mktg. dept. Del E. Webb Communities, Inc., Sun City West, Ariz., 1985—; lectr. sr. journalism class U. Colo., Boulder, 1975-80; condr. class in media seminars Denver Advt. Fedn., 1974, 77; Colo. State U. panelist Broadcast Day, 1978, High Sch. Inst., 1979, 80, 81, 82, 83. Founder, Del E. Webb Meml. Hosp. Found. Mem. Denver Advt. Fedn. (dir. 1973-75, 80-82, exec. bd., v.p. ops. 1980-81, chmn. Alfie awards com. 1980-81, advt. profl. of yr. 1981-82), Denver Advt. Golf Assn. (v.p. 1976-77, pres. 1977-78), Colo. Broadcasters Assn., Sun City West Bowling Assn. (bd. dirs. 1987—), Sun City West Women's Social Club. Republican. Congregationalist. Club: Denver Broncos Quarterback. Home: 21022 Sunglow Dr Sun City West AZ 85375 Office: First of Denver Plaza Bldg 633 17th St Suite 1616 Denver CO 80202

SUTTON, BARBARA POWDERLY, marketing executive; b. Scranton, Pa., Oct. 29, 1940; d. Eugene Thomas and Kathryn Dorothy (Loftus) Powderly; m. Ronald Lewis Sutton, Jan. 7, 1984 (div. Feb. 1985). Student, Miami (Fla.)-Dade Jr. Coll., 1960. Asst. controller Oak Ridge, Inc., Hialeah, Fla., 1959-63; v.p., media dir. Harold Gardner Assocs., Inc., Miami Beach, Fla., 1963-67; media dir., adminstrv. asst. Stern, Hays & Lang Advt., Inc., Miami, 1967-69; exec. asst. Los Angeles Times, 1969-71; media dir., adminstrv. asst. Greenman Advt., Inc., Hollywood, Fla., 1971-73; asst. to gen. mgr. Sta. WGMA-FM, Hollywood, 1974; with acctg. and settlement dept. Fed. Res. Bank, Miami, 1974-75; bus. mgr. Impart Pub. Corp., Reno, 1975-76; adminstrv. asst., office mgr. Edn. Advancement Inst., Reno, 1976-78; ind. contractor Du-Bar Internat., Reno, 1979-80; pres. Capital Advt., Reno, 1980-81; dir. media Mktg. Systems Internat., Reno, 1981-82; owner Dolphin Secretarial Service, Reno, 1982—, Dolphin Services, Reno, 1982—, Powderly Assocs., Reno, 1982—; pres. Bus.-Promotional Services, Inc., Reno, 1986—; speaker Mktg. Fedn., Inc., N.Y.C., 1986; seminar developer and presenter Advt. and Mktg. for Small Bus., U. Nev. Small Bus. Devel. Ctr., 1987. Bd. dirs. March of Dimes, Reno, 1981-82, Teen View Home, Reno, 1987; mem. Presdl. Task Force, Washington, 1983-85. Named one of 2,000 Women of Achievement, London, 1971. Mem. Nat. Assn. Female Execs., Am. Soc. Profl. and Exec. Women, Nat. Assn. Secretarial Services, Reno Women's Network (appointed to Reno Commn. on Status of Women 1987-89, rec. sec., bd. dirs. Entrepreneurial Women of Reno 1987), Gov. Conf. for Women. Republican. Roman Catholic. Club: Bridge. Office: Bus-Promotional Services Inc 100 W Grove St Suite 360 Reno NV 89509

SUTTON, CATHERINE PORTEOUS, artist; b. Memphis, Dec. 12, 1942; d. Thomas Clark and Anna Elizabeth (Colling) Porteous; m. Bromley Oneal Sutton, Nov. 13, 1970. Student, N.C. State U., 1960-62, 64, Memphis Acad. Arts, 1963. Draftsman A.L. Aydelott, Architects and Engrs., Memphis, 1962; floral designer, interior decorator The Patio Gift Shop, Raleigh, N.C., 1964-65; draftsman, map and model maker James B. Godwin & Assocs., Raleigh, 1965-66; city planning technician Stutsman, Kennelly, Neidigh & Assocs., Miami, Fla., 1966-68; mgr., acct. Suttons Motor Ct., Cary, N.C., 1970-76; owner, artist Sutton Studio, Siler City, N.C., 1980—. Recipient four 1st place awards N.C. Wildlife Art Show, 1982-86, two Purchase prizes City of Raleigh Civic Ctr., 1986, 1st place award N.C. Nature Artists Art Show, 1986. Mem. Soc. Animal Artists, N.C. Nature Artists Assn. (rec. sec., bd. dirs. 1987—, 1st place award 1986), N.C. Wildlife Fedn., Nat. Audobon Soc., Defenders of Wildlife, Nat. Wildlife Fedn., Ducks Unlimited, Am. Mus. Natural History, N.C. Zool. Soc., Carolina Raptor Ctr., Am. Birding Assn., N.Y. Zool. Soc., The Portrait Inst. Democrat. Home and Office: Rt 3 Box 249 SR 1506 Siler City NC 27344

SUTTON, CHRISTINE MAE, insurance company executive; b. Bethany, Mo., Feb. 1, 1952; d. Robert Gordon and Geraldine (Johnson) S. BA, William Jewell Coll., Liberty, Mo., 1974. Rater sales Giles Ins. Agy., Pensacola, Fla., 1974; owner Fading Memories Antiques, Dallas, 1975-76; office mgr., v.p. Mid-Am. Nat. Agy., Mission, Kans., 1976-82; exec. sec., then v.p. H & W Underwriters, Fairway, Kans., 1982-84; dir. adminstrn., asst. sec. Am. Continental Life Ins., Kansas City, 1984-87; chief, staff asst. James E. Brady & Co., Kansas City, 1987; spl. project coordinator Lewer Agy., Kansas City, 1987—. Supporter Mission Internat., Kansas City, 1987—; mem. Mothers Against Drunk Driving, Hurst, Tex., 1987—, Rep. Nat. Com., Washington, 1980—; ambassador People to People program, Washington, Europe, 1970. Mem. Nat. Assn. Female Execs., DAR, Phi Gamma Mu. Home: 8230 N Hickory #2029 Kansas City MO 64118 Office: The Lewer Agy 4534 Wornall Rd Kansas City MO 64111

SUTTON, DIANNE FLOYD, human resource developer, consultant; b. Houston, Dec. 6, 1948; d. Osborne English Floyd and Dorothy (Woods) Floyd Brown; m. Thomas Jones Jr., Jan. 1, 1966 (div. 1970); 1 child, Anthony Spencer; m. Ronald N. Sutton Sept. 15, 1984 (dec. 1985). BA in Edn., Harris-Stowe State Coll., 1970; MA in Edn., Washington U., 1974. Recreation leader City of St. Louis, 1967-70; tchr. St. Louis Pub. Schs., 1970-76; investigator EEOC, St. Louis, 1976-79, trainer, course designer, 1979-82, employee devel. specialist, 1982-85; floral designer D.J. & Assocs., Silver Spring, Md., 1979—; employee devel. specialist USDA, Washington, 1985—; human resource developer Suton Enterprises, Washington, 1986—; sr. v.p. M.E.I. Ltd., Bethesda, Md., 1987—; cons. USDA Grad. Sch., Washington, 1984-85, Creative Communications Assn., 1986—, Becknell & Assocs., Albuquerque, 1985—, Mgmt. Learning Systems, Silver Spring, 1986—. Treas. Nat. Urban Affairs Council, St. Louis, 1979; mem. scholarship com. Nat. Black Rep. Council, Washington, 1986; mem. exec. bd. Tng. Officers Conf., 1980—. Mem. Nat. Assn. Female Execs., World Future Soc., Am. Soc. Tng. and Devel. Baptist. Club: Lettumplay (Washington). Home and Office: 5702 Colorado Ave NW Washington DC 20011

SUTTON, DOROTHY LOUISE, educator; b. Cherry Tree, Pa., Nov. 18, 1929; d. Paul and Viola Trudell (Leamer) S.; B.S. in Bus. Edn., Ind. State Coll., 1952; M.Ed., Pa. State U., 1956; postgrad. U. Colo., 1958, Pa. State U., 1964-65, Temple U., 1968, U. Pitts., 1970-72; m. William R. Ferencz, Dec. 28, 1946; 1 dau., Lucinda Kay Rollin. Tchr., Clarion-Limestone Joint High Sch., Strattonville, Pa., 1952-54; faculty Allegheny Coll., Meadville, Pa., 1954-61, Mohawk Valley Community Coll., Utica, N.Y., 1961-64; prof. secretarial sci. Harrisburg (Pa.) Area Community Coll., 1964-87, pres. faculty orgn., 1985-87, ret., 1987. Sec. bd. dirs. ARC, Meadville, 1956-61; mem. Harrisburg Nursing and Health Services Com., 1977-82. Mem. Exec. Women internat. (v.p. 1979-81, pres. 1981), Assn. Info. Systems Personnel (treas. 1981-82), Delta Pi Epsilon. Republican. Roman Catholic. Club: Soroptimist (pres. 1979-81). Home: 4301 Beaufort Hunt Dr Harrisburg PA 17110 Office: 3300 Cameron St Rd Harrisburg PA 17110

SUTTON, GLORIA JEAN, health sciences counselor; b. Salisbury, Md., Oct. 2, 1948; d. Paul Weldon and Doris Mabel (Tribeck) S.; B.S., Towson State U., 1971; M.Ed., Western Md. Coll., 1977, postgrad. in Parks and Recreation, Tex. A&M U., 1987—. Lic. profl. counselor, Tex.; nat. cert. counselor. Tchr., counselor Carroll County Bd. Edn., Westminster, Md., 1971-77; vocat. evaluator Goodwill Industries, Austin, Tex., 1977-78; vocat. rehab. counselor Tex. Rehab. Commn., Austin, 1978-81; health scis. counselor Austin Community Coll. (Tex.), 1981—, part-time instr. allied health scis., cons. vocat. rehab.; pres. Taysa Video. Mem. Internat. Arabian Horse Assn., Am. Horse Shows Assn., Nat. Show Horse Registry, Cen. Tex. Arabian Horse Club. Home: Rt 1 1301 Cardinal Ln Paige TX 78659 Office: Austin Community Coll Riverside Campus 5712 E Riverside Dr Austin TX 78741

SUTTON, MARILYN ROBERTA, insurance company executive; b. Marion, Ohio, May 20, 1947; d. Ralph Edward and Ida Loree (Walker) Hill; m. Joseph Sutton, May 28, 1982; 1 child, Carmen Michelle Lauderdale. BSBA, Franklin U., Columbus, Ohio, 1981; postgrad. in bus. adminstrn., Baldwin Wallace Coll., 1987—. Successively claims examiner, lead examiner, unit supr. claims and customer service, trainer, div. mgr. Nationwide Ins. Co., Columbus, 1968-84; dir. instl. claims Blue Cross & Blue Shield, Cleve., 1984-85, v.p. claims and customer service, 1985—. Mem. Nat. Assn. Female Execs., Greater Cleve. Growth Assn., Black Profls. Assn. (v.p. leadership identification com.). Democrat. Clubs: Women's City, Playhouse. Avocation: golf. Home: 17060 Saratoga Trail Strongsville OH 44136 Office: Blue Cross & Blue Shield of No Ohio 2060 E 9th St Cleveland OH 44115

SUTTON, NORMA J., lawyer, educator; b. Chgo., June 11, 1952; d. Harry and Beatrice (Ross) Sams; 1 son, Edward Michael. B.A., Loyola U., Chgo., 1974, J.D., 1980; M.A., Gov.'s State U., Park Forest, Ill., 1976. Bar: Ill. 1980, U.S. Dist. Ct. (no. dist.) Ill. 1980, U.S. Ct. Appeals (7th cir.) 1980. Tchr., Tri-County Head-Start, Benton Harbor, Mich., 1974; research assoc. CEMREL, Inc., Chgo., 1975-77; law clk. NACOLAH, Chgo., 1977-80; jud. clk. Ill. Jud. System, Chgo., 1980-82; corp. counsel Soft Sheen Products, Inc.,

Chgo., 1982-85; regional atty. Digital Equipment Corp., 1985; cen. area mng. atty., 1986—. Mem. Tuley Park Players Theater Group, Richard B. Harrison Little Theatre Group. Am. Polit. Sci. Assn. fellow, 1974-75; Fred Hampton Meml. scholar, 1977; Loyola U. Alumni scholar, 1977. Mem. ABA (mem. young lawyers div. computer law com. 1987-88), Ill. Bar Assn. (v.p. young lawyers div., community relations council 1987—), Chgo. Bar Assn., Pi Sigma Alpha. Roman Catholic. Home: 1227 W Lunt Apt 1B Chicago IL 60626 Office: Digital Equipment Corp 1155 W Dundee Arlington Heights IL 60004

SUTTON, TERRI LYNN, software engineer; b. Whittier, Calif., Mar. 17, 1957; d. Johnny Cross Sutton and Norma June (Myers) Hamm. AA in Math., Saddleback Coll., 1985; student, Chabot Coll., 1986—. Jr. programmer A.M. Jacquard Systems, Manhattan Beach, Calif., 1980-81; programmer Calif. Bus Systems, Laguna Hills, Calif., 1981-82, MSI Data Corp., Costa Mesa, Calif., 1982-83; programmer analyst Rising Star Industries, Torrance, Calif., 1983-86; sr. software engr. Dorado Systems, Hayward, Calif., 1986-87, Triad Systems, Livermore, Calif., 1987—. Bd. dirs., v.p. Eucalyptus Park Homeowners Assn., Hayward, 1987—. Mem. Forth Interest Group (treas. Silicon Valley chpt. 1986-87, sec., bd.dirs. 1987—). Republican. Office: Triad Systems 3055 Triad Dr Livermore CA 94550

SUTTON-SALLEY, VIRGINIA B., business executive; b. Miami, Fla.; d. Durward Belmont and Sarabelle (Burns) Sutton; student Sullins Coll., Rollins Coll.; m. George H. Salley, Aug. 28, 1961. Asso., jr. partner D.B. Sutton Jewelry Co., Miami, 1948-50; singer (Gloria Manning, profl. name) with Vincent Lopez Orch., Ben Ribble Orch., 1951-60; owner, operator Wiscasset Antiques, 1960-62; owner, mgr., pres. Sutton Manning Corp., 1962—; guest artist WOR-TV, N.Y.C.; currently appearing on club singing engagements, Miami Beach. Co-author: Royal Bayreuth China; contbr. articles to Miami Beach Post. Mem Met. Dade County Zoning Apls. Bd., 1966-70, vice-chmn. 1970-71; mem. pres.'s adv. council Barry Coll., 1978-79; community advisor Beaux Arts, U. Miami, Lowe Art Mus., 1975-78; bd. dirs. Big Bros., 1971-72, Gilded Lilies Dade County Soc. Crippled Children, 1982-83; founder, pres. Theatre Arts League, 1959, Jr. Theatre Guild of Miami, 1961. Mem. Nat. League Am. Pen Women, Am. Guild Variety Artists, Screen Actors Guild, DAR, Soc. Arts and Letters N.Y.C., Women's Guild of U. Miami. Mem. Christian Ch. Clubs: Miami Yacht, Bath, Surf, Indian Creek, Boothbay Harbour Yacht. Contbr. articles to profl. jours. Office: Sutton Manning Corp 100 N Biscayne Blvd Suite 700 Miami FL 33132

SUTTY, BETTY RAE, association executive; b. Columbus, Ga., May 31, 1948; d. Ralph Lanier and Elizabeth Inez (Simpson) Davis; m. Randall Wayne Young, Apr. 2, 1967 (div.); children: Sean, Alicia, Matthew; m. Arthur P. Sutty, July 7, 1984. Grad., Inst. Orgn. in Mgmt., 1986. Asst. exec. v.p. Greater Lafayette C. of C., Ind., 1979-84; program dir. Aurora (Ill.) C. of C., 1984-85; asst. dir. Naperville (Ill.) C. of C., 1985; exec. dir. N.W. Suburban Assn. Commerce and Industry, Schaumburg, Ill., 1985-87; membership rep. Nat. Assn. for Self Employed, Ft. Worth, 1987—; discussion facilitator Inst. Orgn. Mgmt., 1984-85. Contbr. articles to profl. jours. Bd. advisor Boy Scouts Am., Girl Scouts U.S., White County, Ind., 1970-74; chmn. Young People to Re-elect Nixon, White County, 1972; v.p. Women's Rep. Club, White County, 1972-74; state, local dir. Am. Diabetes Assn., Ind., 1977-80. Recipient Designated Resource Person award Sch. Career Bank, 1983-84. Mem. Am. C. of C. Execs., Ill. Assn. C. of C. Execs. Baptist. Club: Women's Forum (chmn. 1985). Avocations: reading, golf, needlepoint, travel. Home: PO Box 957013 Hoffman Estates IL 60195

SVEC, CYNTHIA LILLIAN, business services administrator, building manager; b. Chgo., Jan. 20, 1941; d. George Mitchell Smith and Lillian (Mottl) Smith Trousil; m. 1964 (div. 1975); children—Victoria Lynn, Jacqueline Paige, Alison E. Student public schs., Cicero, Ill. Office mgr. Belmont Industries, Inc., Cicero, Ill., 1958-67; pres., exec., owner August Bus. Service, Inc., LaGrange, Ill., 1975—; v.p. Stewart's Indsl. Service Inc., LaGrange, 1979-83; owner, mgr. LaGrange Profl. Bldg., LaGrange, 1981—. Recipient Beautification award West Suburban C. of C., LaGrange, 1981. Mem. West Suburban C. of C., Midwest Assn. Commerce and Industry. Republican. Roman Catholic. Avocations: interior decorating and design; international travel; parapsychology, astrology; reading. Office: August Business Service Inc 110 N LaGrange Rd LaGrange IL 60525

SVEC, JANICE LYNN, navy enlistedwoman; b. Santa Anna, Calif., May 14, 1948; d. Leonard August Svec and Wanda Marcelle (Richards) McMillon; m. Lewis Eugene Humphrey, May 24, 1974 (div. 1977); 1 child, Jeromy Starbuck Svec. A.A. in Adminstrn. of Justice, Los Angeles Met. Community Coll., 1982; student criminal justice Thomas Edison State Coll., Trenton, 1985—. Adminstrv. supporter Naval Investigative Service, Subic Bay, Philippines, 1979-81; office supr. Naval Communication Ctr., Yokosuka, Japan, 1981-82; chief master at arms Naval Support Facility Security Dept., Diego Garcia, Brit. Indian Ocean Ter., 1982-83, U.S. Navy Drug Rehab. Ctr., San Diego, 1983-85; instr. U.S. Navy, Lakehurst, N.J., 1985-88, supr. Navy Support Office, 1988—. Roman Catholic. Avocations: body building; horseback riding. Home: 120 Village Way Crockett TX 75835 Office: PO Box 578 Lakehurst NJ 08733

SVEINSSON, LINDA RODGERS, computer scientist; b. Tuscaloosa, Ala., July 1, 1938; d. Eric and Sarah Ella (Haughton) Rodgers; B.A. in Math., Birmingham-So. Coll., 1960; M.S. in Indsl. Engring. (NSF trainee 1970-72), U. Ala., 1972; m. Hjalmar Sveinsson, May 29, 1971; children—Martha M. Reed, Stephen R.M. Moreno, III. Systems analyst U. Ala. Med. Center, Birmingham, 1967-69; systems mgr. Internat. Data Systems, New Orleans, 1969-70; computer scientist Computer Scis. Corp., Silver Spring, Md., 1973-76; computer systems specialist System Devel. Corp., McLean, Va., 1976-78; mem. tech. staff Bell Labs., Columbus, Ohio, 1978-85, tech. supr., 1979-85; mgr. bus. devel. No. Telecom, Inc., Research Triangle Park, N.C., 1985—. Mem. Assn. Computing Machinery, Phi Beta Kappa, Alpha Pi Mu. Republican. Methodist. Home: 10409 Byrum Woods Dr Raleigh NC 27612 Office: PO Box 13010 Research Triangle Park NC 27709

SVENDSEN, JOYCE ROSE, real estate company executive; b. Bayonne, N.J., Nov. 26, 1948; d. Peder and Rita Agnes (Bogert) S.; m. Stephen G. Takach, June 22, 1968; 1 child, Mark Stephen. Regional investigator Channel Co., Whippany, N.J., 1977-79; pres. Svendsen Studio, Clifton, N.J., 1979-82, Treasures, Sugar Loaf, N.Y., 1982-85; sales dir. M.L. Levine Real Estate, Clifton, 1985—. Mem. N.J. Assn. Realtors (million dollar sales club 1986, 87), Passaic Valley Bd. Realtors (assoc.), U.S. Coast Guard Aux. Republican. Unitarian. Office: M L Levine Real Estate 822 Clifton Ave Clifton NJ 07013

SVERDLOVE, ZOLITA, artist, printmaker; b. N.Y.C., Feb. 21, 1936; d. Harry and Leah (Rothman) S.; m. Donald Rapp, May 30, 1956; children: Melissa Rapp, Erica Rapp. Cert., Cooper Union Coll., N.Y.C., 1956, BFA, 1977. Chmn. fine arts com. U. Tex., Dallas, 1972-73, exhibits dir., 1973-74; free-lance artist. Prints reproduced in Mondus Artium, 1976; exhibited in group shows: U. Tex., 1973-74, Dallas Mus. Fine Arts (first prize), 1975, Purdue U. (first prize), 1970, Marymount Coll. (hon. mention), 1969. Nat. Endowment Arts grantee, 1973-74. Mem. Los Angeles Printmaking Soc. (bd. dirs. 1981-83, chmn. new mems. 1983), Graphic Arts Council Los Angeles County Mus., Women's Caucus for Arts, Phila. Print Club. Home and Office: 1445 Indiana Ave South Pasadena CA 91030

SVETLOVA, MARINA, ballerina, choreographer, educator; b. Paris, May 3, 1922; came to U.S. from Australia, 1940; d. Max and Tamara (Andreieff) Hartman. Studies with Vera Trefilova, Paris, 1930-36, studies with L. Egorova and M. Kschessinska, 1936-39; studies with A. Vilzak, N.Y.C., 1940-57. Ballet dir. So. Vt. Art Ctr., 1959-64; dir. Svetlova Dance Ctr., Dorset, Vt., 1965—; prof. ballet dept. Ind. U., Bloomington, 1969—; choreographer Dallas Civic Opera, 1964-67, Ft. Worth Opera, 1967-83, San Antonio Opera, 1983, Seattle Opera, Houston Opera, Kansas City Performing Arts Found. Ballerina original Ballet Russe de Monte Carlo, 1939-41; guest ballerina Ballet Theatre, 1942, London's Festival Ballet, Teatro dell Opera, Rome, Nat. Opera, Stockholm, Sweden, Suomi Opera, Helsinki, Finland, Het Nederland Ballet, Holland, Cork Irish Ballet, Paris Opera Comique, London Palladium, Teatro Colon, Buenos Aires, others; prima ballerina Met. Opera, 1943-50, N.Y.C. Opera, 1950-52; choreographer: (ballet sequences) The Fairy Queen, 1966, L'Histoire du Soldat, 1968; tours in Far East, Middle East, Europe, S.Am., U.S.; performer various classical ballets Graduation Ball; contbr. articles to Debut, Paris Opera. Mem. Am. Guild Mus. Artists (bd. dirs.), Conf. on Ballet in Higher Edn., Nat. Soc. Arts and Letters (nat. dance chmn.). Home: Dorset VT 05251 Office: 2100 Maxwell Ln Bloomington IN 47401 also: 25 W 54th St New York NY 10019

SVILAR, CYNTHIA A. DAVIS, pharmaceutical representative; b. Knoxville, Tenn., Feb. 19, 1953; d. James C. and Margaret L. (Rucker) Davis; m. Dennis Michael Svilar, June 28, 1975; children—Kyle M.D. Svilar, Drew S.D. Svilar, Colin M.D. Svilar. B.A., Ind. U., 1978, Cert. in Computers, 1984. Pharm. rep. Merrell Dow, Cin., 1979-86; cons. Aspen Transp., Hobart, Ind., 1984—; adminstr. driver leasing program Goliath Transp. Inc., Hobart, Ind., mgr., Valparaiso, Ind.; pres. SRB Transp., Hammond, Ind., 1985-87. Recipient Pres.'s Pin, Merrell Dow Pharm., 1980, 81, Century Club, 1985. Mem. Nat. Assn. Female Execs., Bus. and Profl. Women, Beta Sigma Phi. Home and Office: 171 Wexford Rd Valparaiso IN 46383

SVOBODA, ELIZABETH JANE, state legislator, sales professional; b. Toledo, Iowa, Nov. 3, 1944; d. Ambrose and Bernadine D. (Doran) Kearney; m. Stanley J. Svoboda, Mar. 31, 1964; children: Brian, Kelly Marie, Jason, Nicholas. Advanced bus. degree, Bus. Inst. Tech., 1986. Sec. to supt. State Juvenile Home, Toledo, 1963-71; with sales dept. Home Interiors & Gifts, Dallas, 1979—; mem. Iowa Ho. of Reps., Des Moines, 1987—. Vol. lobbyist Iowa Citizens for Community Improvement, 1977-85. Named a Tama County Belle Ringer, 1980; named one of Outstanding Young Women Am., 1982. Democrat. Roman Catholic. Office: Iowa Legislature State Capitol Bldg Des Moines IA 50319

SVOBODA, JOANNE DZITKO, artist, educator; b. Jersey City, Dec. 24, 1948; d. John Richard and Joanna Frances (Rygiel) Dzitko; student Parsons Sch. Design, 1966, Kean Coll., 1970; B.A., Jersey City State Coll., 1970, M.A., 1975; postgrad. Tchrs. Coll., Columbia U., 1972; m. Peter W. Svoboda, Sept. 3, 1972; children—Kimberly Anne, Lauren Anne. Art tchr. YMCA, Jersey City, 1966-70, Henry Snyder High Sch., Jersey City, 1970-80; propr., craftsman, instr. Mountain Designers and Craftsmen, Long Valley, N.J., 1977-80; partner, craftsman, instr. Four Seasons Crafts, Chester and Long Valley, 1978-85; designer, estimator, v.p. Estate Contracting Inc., Long Valley, 1978—; tng. specialist Johnson & Johnson Baby Products, Skillman, N.J., 1984—; instr. interior design Jersey City Bd. Continuing Edn., 1974. Trustee, Jersey City Mus. Assn., 1973-79, chmn. fine arts dept., 1972-79; mem. curriculum revision com. Jersey City Bd. Edn., 1976; judge Distributive Edn. Clubs N.J., 1976, 77, 78; mem. Washington Twp. Shade Tree Commn., 1979-81, chmn., 1981; mem. Washington Twp. Hist. Heritage Commn., 1981-85, Washington Twp. Friends of the Library; publicity chmn. Washington Twp. Hist. Soc., 1980-81; mem. choir Our Lady of the Mountain Cath. Ch. Grantee, N.J. State Dept. Edn., 1973; awards N.J. Fedn. Jr. Woman's Clubs: black and white photography, 1979, crafts, 1979, 1st place color photography, 1980, free form, 1981. Mem. Am. Soc. Interior Designers (affiliate), Federated Art Assn. N.J., Art Educators N.J., N.J. Designer Craftsmen. Democrat. Exhibited Courtney Gallery, Jersey City State Coll., 1970, 74, Long Valley, 1979-80; active encouraging establishment of hist. zone Long Valley, landmarks, Jersey City and Washington Twp.; contbr. articles in field to various publs. Home and Office: 180 A Welsh Rd Lebanon NJ 08833

SWADOS, ELIZABETH A., writer, composer, director; b. Buffalo, Feb. 5, 1951; d. Robert O. and Sylvia (Maisel) S. B.A., Bennington Coll., 1972. Composer, mus. dir. Peter Brook, Paris, Africa, U.S., 1972-73; composer-in-residence La Mama Exptl. Theater Club, N.Y.C., 1977—; mem. faculty Carnegie-Mellon U., 1974, Bard Coll., 1976-77, Sarah Lawrence Coll., 1976-77. Author: The Girl With the Incredible Feeling, 1976 (screenplay adaptation 1977), Runaways, 1979, Lullaby, 1980, Sky Dance, 1980, The Beautiful Lady (musical), 1984; composer theatrical scores: Medea, 1972, Elektra, 1970, Fragments of Trilogy, 1974, Trojan Women, 1974, The Good Women of Setzuan, 1975, The Cherry Orchard, 1977, As You Like It, 1979, Haggadah, 1980, (with Garry Trudeau) Doonesbury, 1983; composer, dir., adapter, mem. cast: Nightclub Cantata, 1977; composer, adapter (with Andrei Serban) Agamemnon (on Broadway), 1977, The Incredible Feeling Show, 1979; composer, dir., adapter: Wonderland in Concert, N.Y. Shakespeare Festival, 1978; adapter, dir.: Dispatches, 1979, Lullaby and Goodnight (opera), 1980; adapter: Works of Yehuda Amichi, Book of Jeremiah; composer music for films: Step by Step, 1978, Sky Dance, 1979; composer music for PBS short stories, 1979, CBS-TV and NBC-TV spls., A Year in the Life (miniseries), 1987; composer: Rap Master Ronnie, 1986; performer: Mark Taper Forum, Los Angeles, 1985, Jerusalem Oratorio, Rome, 1985. Recipient Obie award Village Voice, 1972, 77; Outer Critics Circle award, 1977; nominee for Tony awards, 1978; Creative Artists Service Program grantee, 1976; N.Y. State Arts Council playwriting grantee, 1977—; Guggenheim fellow. Mem. Broadcast Music Inc., Actors Equity. Jewish. Home: 112 Waverly Pl New York NY 10011 Office: care Sam Cohen Internat Creative Mgmt Co 40 W 57th St New York NY 10019 •

SWAIN, ANNA CHAMBLEE, marketing consultant, writer; b. N.Y.C., Mar. 31, 1954; B.B.A. in Internat. Mktg., Bernard Baruch U., 1981. Sec. to pres. Bleuette, Inc., N.Y.C., 1970-73; asst. to dir. classified advt. Fairchild Publs., N.Y.C., 1974-75, asst. mgr. real estate advt., 1976-77; asst. to publs. dir. and nat. sales mgr. Lebhar-Friedman Pub., N.Y.C., 1975; asst. account exec. Gaynor & Lucas Advt., N.Y.C., 1976; research analyst, asso. client service rep. Time, Inc., N.Y.C., 1977-80; mktg. cons., N.Y.C., 1980—. Pub. relations liaison Black Liberation Thru Action, Collectiveness and Knowledge, 1979-80. Mem. Am. Soc. Personnel Adminstrn. (pres. Baruch U. chpt. 1980-81; Harry M. Sherman award 1981), Baruch Arts and Letters Soc. (founder), Women for Racial and Econ. Equality, Nat. Assn. Media Women, Nat. Council Culture and Art, Nat. Bus. League, Internat. Arts Forum (founder), Smithsonian Instn., Mark Twain Assn., N.Y. Poetry Forum, Nat. Assn. Media Women. Club: Beaux Arts (N.Y.C.). Office: PO Box 1142 Ansonia Sta New York NY 10023

SWAIN, CLAUDIA JONES, reading demonstration educator, writer; b. Ft. Worth, Dec. 15, 1937; d. Vidal Leonard and Wynona (Dews) Jones; m. Richard E. Swain, Jr., Apr. 28, 1973. B.S., East Tex. Baptist Coll., 1962; M.Ed., North Tex. State U., 1980, Ph.D., 1985. Classroom tchr. several sch. dists., Northeast Houston, Duncanville, Tex., and Dallas, 1962-69; asst. dean students East Tex. Bapt. Coll., Marshall, 1969-70; presch./children's cons. Bapt. Gen. Conv. Tex.-Womans Missionary Union, Dallas, 1970-77; primary classroom tchr. B.F. Darrell Sch., Dallas, 1977-80, 82-83, title I-primary, 1980-82; reading demonstration tchr. Dallas Ind. Sch. Dist. at B.F. Darrell Sch., Dallas, 1983-85, Charles Rice Sch., Dallas, 1985-86; reading tchr. Health Spl. High Sch., 1986—. Author: God Leads His Children, 1979, Looking at Loss, 1988; author curriculum Woman's Missionary Union, So. Bapt. Conv., Birmingham, 1970-80. Mem. Assn. Supervision and Curriculum Devel., Assn. Childhood Edn. Internat., Assn. Tex. Profl. Educators, Internat. Reading Assn., Delta Kappa Gamma (Alpha state scholar 1982), Phi Delta Kappa. Baptist.

SWAIN, NANCY JANE COX (MRS. JAMES OBED SWAIN), retired educator; b. Elwood, Ind., Dec. 19, 1901; d. Alfred Thomas and Emma (Allen) Cox; A.B. with high distinction, Ind. U., 1923, postgrad., 1928; M.A., U. Tenn., 1951, postgrad., 1953; m. James Obed Swain, June 24, 1923; children—J. Maurice, J. Robert. Teaching missionary M.E. Ch., Costa Rica, 1923-28; instr. U. Tenn., Knoxville, 1943, 45, non-resident instr. corr. Extension Div., 1959-71; tchr. Oak Ridge High Sch., 1943-67, Hollins Coll., 1967. Mem. Am. Assn. Tchrs. Spanish and Portuguese, E. Tenn. Edn. Assn., S. Atlantic Modern Lang. Assn., Phi Beta Kappa, Phi Kappa Phi, Sigma Delta Pi, Pi Delta Phi, Pi Lambda Theta. Republican. Methodist. Mem. P.E.O. Home: 414 Forest Park Blvd Apt 622 Knoxville TN 37919

SWAIN, CAROL ROSE, industrial realations executive; b. La Porte, Ind., June 9, 1934; d. Lorenz J. and Agnes C. (Brady) Thode; divorced; children: Rory, Renee. AA in Gen. Studies, Ind. U., South Bend, 1987. Sec. to pres. Berkel Inc., La Porte, 1967-73, supr. personnel, 1973-76, mgr. indsl. relations, 1976-81, v.p. indsl. relations, 1981—. Mem. Am. Soc. Personnel Adminstrn., Ind. Personnel Assn., La Porte Personnel Assn. (pres. 1978-79), Greater La Porte C. of C. (pres. 1980). Republican. Methodist. Office: Berkel Inc One Berkel Dr La Porte IN 46350

SWAN, JACQUELINE ANN, foundation administrator; b. Binghamton, N.Y., May 11, 1950; d. James Leo and Dorothy (Sevara) D.; m. Robert Timothy Wolcott, June 3, 1972 (div. Aug. 1977); children: Accalia D., Timothy P.; m. Clifton H. Swan, July 10, 1987. BA, SUNY, Binghamton, 1972. Social welfare examiner Broome County Dept. Social Services, Binghamton, 1979-82; employment interviewer N.Y. State Dept. Labor, Wellsville, 1983-84; placement specialist Livingston-Wyoming ARC, Mt. Morris, N.Y., 1984—; personnel technician, trainee City of Binghamton, 1980. Mem. Rochester Area Com. on Handicapped, Bus. Edn. Council Livingston and Wyoming Counties. Democrat. Office: Livingston-Wyoming ARC 18 Main St Mount Morris NY 14510

SWANBERG, CAROL JEAN, system administrator, analyst, programmer; b. N.Y.C., Oct. 28, 1961; d. Raymond J. and Florence J. (Pietrowski) S. BS, U. Pitts., 1983. Adminstrv. specialist office admissions and student aid U. Pitts., 1984-85, system adminstr. Joseph M. Katz grad. sch. of bus., 1985—. Contbr. articles to profl. jours. Mem. Nat. Assn. Female Execs. Roman Catholic. Office: Grad Sch Bus U Pitts 315 Mervis Hall Pittsburgh PA 15260

SWANDER, MARTHA JEANNE, comptroller; b. Tiffin, Ohio, Aug. 23, 1954; d. Irvin Martin and Mary Lorena (Anglemeyer) Rathfelder; m. Tom D. Swander, Aug. 19, 1972; 1 child, Jason David. BBA, Tiffin U., 1986. With constrn. dept., assigner, dispatcher Ohio Bell Telephone Co., Tiffin, 1972-75; bus. mgr. Sandusky Valley Ctr., Inc., Tiffin, 1977-87; comptroller Genoa (Ohio) Savs. and Loan Co., 1987—; cons. Sandusky Valley Ctr., Inc., 1987. Solicitor Arthritis Found., Tiffin, 1984, Am. Cancer Soc., Tiffin, 1985, 87, Easter Seals Soc., 1987. Mem. Bus. Women's Inst. (charter mem.), Nat. Assn. for Female Execs., Am. Legion Aux., D.A.V. Aux. (legis. com. 1986—). Republican. Methodist. Home: 17 Tomb St Tiffin OH 44883

SWANSON, BEVERLY JANE, records and information management executive; b. Willmar, Minn., Jan. 27, 1949; d. Vernon Leroy and Betty Arlene (Schockley) Fullerton; m. Roger William Swanson, Mar. 21, 1970; children: Tammy Marie, Randolph William. BS in Speech, Mankato (Minn.) State U., 1971. Mgmt. analyst, records mgr. Minn. Dept. Hwys., St. Paul, 1974-76; chief records mgr. Minn. Dept. Adminstrn., St. Paul, 1977-79; records mgr. City of Mpls., 1980—. Advisory bd. Minn. Hist. Soc., 1981-83. Named Outstanding Records Mgr. of Yr. IRM mag., 1979. Mem. Assn. Records Mgrs. and Adminstrs. (cert., v.p. region IV 1982-86, membership chmn., sec., v.p., pres. Twin City chpt. 1973-79, mr. mcpl. county govt. industry action com. 1987—, chair long range planning com. 1987—, parliamentarian Twin City chpt. 1987—, Chpt. Mem. of Yr. award 1980), Inst. Cert. Records Mgrs. and Adminstrs. Lutheran. Home: 7003 164th Ave NW Anoka MN 55303 Office: City of Mpls 300 City Hall Minneapolis MN 55415

SWANSON, FERN ROSE, retired educator; b. Kalmar Twp., Minn.; d Henry E. and Susie (Hastings) Rose; student Winona (Minn.) Normal Coll., 1918-20; B.S., St. Cloud (Minn.) State Coll., 1955, M.S., 1958; m. Walter E. Swanson, June 24, 1928. Tchr. high sch. English, Latin, Eyota, Minn., 1920-21; tchr. jr. high sch. English, Appleton, Minn., 1921-22; tchr. elementary schs., Harmony, Minn., 1922-23; tchr. high sch. English, Latin, Augusta, Wis., 1923-24, South Haven, Minn., 1924-26; tchr. elementary and high sch. dramatics, Waterville, 1926-27; tchr. elementary schs., South Haven, 1927-41, 43-51, Silver Creek, Minn., 1941-43; tchr. elementary schs., Annandale, Minn., 1951-53, prin., 1953-67; tchr. elementary reading, Belgrade, Minn., 1967-71. Organizer, South Haven council Girl Scouts U.S.A., 1927, leader, 1927-30. Mem. Minn. Elementary Sch. Prins. Assn. (charter mem. 25 Year Club), NEA, Nat. Assn. Elem. Sch. Prins., Ret. Educators Assn. Minn., Minn. Edn. Assn., Nat. Council Tchrs. English, Central Minn. Reading Council (past dir.), Internat., Minn. reading assns., DAR, Ladies of Grand Army Republic (registrar Lookout Circle, dept. pres. Minn. 1974-77, Betsy Ross Club (nat. pres. 1978, historian 1980—), Pioneer Club (historian 1986—), nat. patriotic instr. 1981-84, nat. jr. v.p. 1984-85, nat. council adminstrn. 1985—), Minn. Hist. Soc., Rebekah, Delta Kappa Gamma (past chpt. pres., Minn. Woman of Achievement award 1982). Episcopalian. Club: Nat. Historian Pioneer. Home: 541 Fairhaven Av South Haven MN 55382 Office: South Haven MN 55382

SWANSON, JUDITH ANNE, paralegal, educator; b. Loma Linda, Calif., June 24, 1941; d. Edward Henry and Gertrude Louella (Ary) Gable; m. Dennis Elroy Swanson, Dec. 30, 1966; children: Shellie Jean, Kimberly Anne, Cynthia Lynn. Cert. paralegal, Calif. State U., 1977. Legal sec. Superior Ct., San Bernardino, Calif., 1958-65; King & Mussell, Attys., San Bernardino, 1965-71, George Starr, Atty., Yucaipa, Calif., 1971-74; probate paralegal William J. Brunick, Atty., Redlands, Calif., 1975—; instr. legal office procedures Crafton Community Coll., Yucaipa, 1977—, San Bernardino (Calif.) Valley Coll. Mem. Yucaipa Little Theater, 1973-80. Mem. Nat. Paralegal Assn. (charter), Calif. Bar Assn. (assoc. mem. Estate Planning, Trust and Probate Law sect.). Republican. Lutheran. Clubs: Yucaipa ArtAssn., Fontana Art Assn., Arlington Art Assn., Desert Art Ctr., Loma Linda Lopers. Avocations: oil painting, hiking, camping. Home: 34033 Nebraska Ln Yucaipa CA 92399

SWANSON, KARIN, hospital administrator; b. New Britain, Conn., Dec. 8, 1942; d. Oake F. and Ingrid Lauren Swanson; m. B. William Dorsey, June 26, 1965 (div. 1974); children: Matthew W., Julie I., Alison K. BA in Biology, Middlebury Coll., 1964; MPH, Yale U., 1981. Biology tchr. Kents Hill (Maine) Sch., 1964-66; laboratory instr. Bates Coll., Lewiston, Maine, 1974-78; asst. to gen. dir. Mass. Eye and Ear Infirmary, Boston, 1979-80; v.p. profl. services Portsmouth (N.H.) Hosp., 1981-83; v.p. Health Strategy Assn. Ltd., Chestnut Hill, Mass., 1983-85; v.p. med. affairs Cen. Maine Med. Ctr., Lewiston, 1986—; corporator Mechanics Savs. Bank, Lewiston, 1988—. Mem. Phi Beta Kappa. Home: 4 Bearce Ave Lewiston ME 04240 Office: Cen Maine Med Ctr 300 Main St Lewiston ME 04240

SWANSON, MARY CAMILLE STEWART, editor, writer; b. Mpls., Apr. 11, 1933; d. James Jewell and Camille Beatrice (Madden) Stewart; m. Roger Whitten Swanson, Sept. 11, 1954 (div. Apr. 1976); children—Paul Stewart, Susan Marie; m. 2d, John Elbert Zelenka, June 30, 1978. B.A., U. Minn.-Mpls., 1954, M.A., 1970, Ph.D. in English, 1977; postgrad. Oxford U. (Eng.), summer 1976. Editor, Sun Newspapers, Mpls., 1976-77; teaching assoc. U. Minn.-Mpls., 1977-79; sr. editor Golle & Holmes Fin. Learning Inc., Minnetonka, Minn., 1979-84; freelance editor, writer, Washington, 1984-85. Author: FLS Financial Writing Guide: A Manual of Style for the Securities Industry, 1982; also articles; editor: Securities Basic Study Course, 30 vols., 1979-83; FLS Blue-Sky Guide, 1979; Securities Selling Skills, 1980; Financial Planning Skills, 1981; Securities Prospecting, 1981; Operations Certification, 1983; Series 6 Plus, 1983, Series 22 Plus, 1983. Home: 1 East Pleasant Lake Rd North Oaks MN 55127

SWANSON, NORMA LEE, quality assurance administrator; b. Kokomo, Ind., May 10, 1934; adopted d. Roy and Lora E. (Ewer) Hupp; m. Ray A. Swanson, Nov. 1, 1952 (div. Nov. 1972); children—Michael, Patrick, Lisa, Kelly. Student, St. Mary-of-the-Woods Coll. Nursing staff hosps. in Ill., 1952, 54, med. records adminstr., Ill., Iowa, 1964-77; med. records adminstr. and instrs. hosps., Khamis Mushayt, Saudi Arabia, 1977-80; quality assurance coordinator VA, Murfreesboro, Tenn., 1980-83, hosps. in Tabuk, Saudi Arabia, 1983-84; health systems specialist VA Med. Ctr., Marion, Ind., 1984-86, quality assurance specialist VA dist. 21, St. Louis, 1986—; cons. in field; Mem. Civic Theater, Murfreesboro, Tenn., 1981-84. Author: Adventures of Lee Kelly, 1976; editor: VA newsletter, 1982-83 Contbr. articles to profl. jours. Mem. Internat. Platform Assn., Speakers Bur.-Quality Assurance Assn., Am. Med. Record Assn., Illowa Med. Record Assn. (pres. 1975-77), Iowa Med. Record Assn. (program chair 1975-76), Nat. Assn. Quality Assurance Profls., Nat. Assn. Female Execs., Internat. Platform Assn. Club: Disabled Am. Vets. Comdrs. Lodges: Altrusa. Office: VA Med Ctr Dist 21 Saint Louis MO 63125

SWANSON, ROCHELLE ANITA, public relations program coordinator, lecturer; b. Kenmare, N.D., Apr. 16, 1949; d. Arthur Reuben and Verna Waneta (Nederbo) S. Student Phoenix Coll., 1968-69, Ariz. State U., 1966; B.S. in Pub. Adminstrn., U. Ariz., 1971; postgrad. U. So. Calif., 1973-75. Cert. recreation therapist. Recreation supr., Cypress, Calif., 1971; recreation specialist aide County of Los Angeles Dept. Parks and Recreation, 1972-74, recreation specialist, 1974-82; program coordinator Jesse Owens Games, Atlantic Richfield Co., Los Angeles, 1982-84; pres. Promotional Cons. Services, 1984—; cons. Fountain Val, 1980-82; lectr. U. Redlands, U. So. Calif., Calif. State U.-Northridge; cons. U. So. Calif., various confs. Calif. Spl. Olympics gymnastics chmn., 1972-83, dir. of competition, 1986—, mem. adv. com. gymnastics rules, 1985; So. region volleyball tournament dir., 1984; dir. Orange County Spl. Olympics Track and Field Meet, 1983; Dist. IX bowling chmn. Mentally Retarded Citizens, 1974-84; chmn. bd. First Lutheran Day Sch., 1983-84; mem. council First Luth. Ch., sec., v.p. ch. council, 1986; state bowling commn. handicapper Assn. Retarded Citizens. Recipient awards Los Angeles Basin Parks and Recreation Commn. and Bd., 1982; spl. award Koroibos Found., 1984; Am. Legion award, 1963. Mem. Calif. Park and Recreation Soc. (sec. dist. XIII, 1981, program awards 1984), Sons of Norway, VASA, Chi Kappa Rho. Republican. Contbr. article to profl. jour. Home: 1756 N Verdugo Rd #22 Glendale CA 91208 Office: 1756 N Verdugo Rd #22 Glendale CA 91208

SWANSON, SHARON LOUISE, school nurse; b. Erie, Kans., Dec. 5, 1942; d. Otis Benton and Ruth Louise (George) Brasier; m. Larry Virgil Swanson, June 6, 1965; children—Larry Albert Benton, Todd Allen, Sharese Louise. Student Chanute Jr. Coll., 1960-61; B.S.N., U. Kans., 1964. Staff nurse Kans. U. Med. Ctr., Kansas City, 1964-65, 75-81, practical nurse instr., 1966-68; coordinator mothers day out Overland Park Christian Ch., Overland Park, Kans., 1973-74; office nurse Benjamin F. Hard, Prairie Village, Kans., 1974-79; sch. nurse Shawnee Mission Public Schs. #512, Kans., 1979—. Pres., PTA West Antioch, Merriam, Kans., 1975-76, 76-77; den mother Cub Scouts, 1976; pres. Antioch Presch. PTA, 1973-74, Milburn Jr. High Sch., 1981-82, Shawnee Mission North Patrons Art Gallery, Mission, Kans., 1985-87; pres. Shawnee Mission North Booster Club, 1986-87. Am. Legion scholar, 1960. Mem. Nat. Assn. Sch. Nurses, Kans. Assn. Sch. Nurses, Kans. Assn. Sch. Health, Am. Sch. Health Assn., U. Kans. Alumni, Kans. U. Nursing Alumni (bd. dirs. 1976-77), Phi Kappa Phi. Democrat. Avocations: Boating; reading; gardening; bridge; travel. Home: 10112 W 70th St Merriam KS 66203 Office: Flint Elemn Sch 5705 Flint St Shawnee KS 66203

SWANSON, VICTORIA CLARE HELDMAN, lawyer; b. Dayton, Ohio, Aug. 28, 1949; d. Paul F. and Anne F. (Thomas) Schmitz; m. Louis M. Heldman, Sept. 21, 1971 (div. 1973); m. John Askins, Feb. 28, 1975 (div. 1977); m. Thomas C. Swanson, Feb. 13, 1988. BA in Journalism with distinction, Ohio State U., 1972; JD, U. Detroit, 1975. Bar: Mich. 1975, U.S. Dist. Ct. (ea. and we. dists.) Mich. 1975, U.S. Ct. Appeals (6th cir.) 1977, U.S. Ct. Appeals (3d cir.) 1980, U.S. Supreme Ct. 1983, Colo. 1984, U.S. Ct. Appeals (10th Cir.) 1984. Assoc. Lopatin, Miller, Bindes & Freedman, Detroit, 1973-76; ptnr. Schaden, Heldman & Lampert, Detroit, 1977—; adj. prof. U. Detroit Sch. Law, 1982. Author: (with Richard F. Schaden) Product Design Liability, 1982; contbg. author: Women Trial Lawyers: How They Succeed in Practice and in the Courtroom, 1986. Mem. Mich. Bar Assn., Colo. Bar Assn., Assn. Trial Lawyers Am., Colo. Trial Lawyers Assn., Mich. Trial Lawyers Assn., Lawyer-Pilots Bar Assn. Office: 1731 Emerson Denver CO 80218

SWANT, JOSANNE GLASS, employee relations manager; b. Bangor, Maine, Feb. 4, 1956; d. William Howard and Beatriz Alicia (Ruiz de Zuniga) Glass; m. Mark Allen Swant, Aug. 25, 1979. A.A., DeAnza Community Coll., 1975; B.A. in Sociology, Calif. State U.-Chico, 1978, B.A. in Psychology, 1978. Benefits coordinator Utah Bancorp., Salt Lake City, 1979-80; employee relations mgr. Nat. Semiconductor Corp., West Jordan, Utah, 1980—; advisor, cons. Sandy City (Utah) Personnel Bd., 1981-83. Mem. Am. Soc. Personnel Adminstrn., Utah Personnel Assn. (legis. liason), Mujeres en Progresso. Office: Nat Semiconductor Corp 3333 W 9000 S West Jordan UT 84084

SWANTKO, ANN REBECCA, county government official; b. Danville, Pa., Dec. 23, 1959; d. Michael and Rebecca Louise (Riple) S. BA, Xavier U., Cin., 1982; MBA, Xavier U., 1988. Dir. religious edn. St. Elizabeth Parish, Cin., 1978-82; asst. ops. officer Provident Bank, Cin., 1982-85; corp. systems analyst Chevy Chase (Md.) Savs. and Loan, 1985-86; dep. recorder Hamilton County, Cin., 1986, chief dep. recorder, 1986—. Coordinator campaign United Appeal, 1986, Fine Arts Fund, Cin., 1987. Mem. Internat. Assn. Clks., Recorders, Election Ofcls., Treas., Nat. Assn. Female Execs., Nat. Assn. Counties, Ohio Recorders Assn., Xavier Alumni Assn. Republican. Roman Catholic. Office: Hamilton County Recorders Office 138 E Court St Cincinnati OH 45202

SWART, DEBORAH GAIL, nurse, consultant; b. Queens, N.Y., Dec. 29, 1954; d. Irving ans Miriam (Bernstein) S. Student, SUNY, Stonybrook, 1972-75; AAS, SUNY, Farmingdale, 1978; BSN, Molloy Coll., 1988. Nurse Jamaica (N.Y.) Hosp., 1978, nurse, cardiology room, 1978-82; nurse, emergency room Queens Hosp. and Ctr., 1982, nurse, pediatrics dept., 1982—; cons. Liace, Suffolk, N.Y., 1987. Conductor Oyster Bay VNs, 1988—. Mem. Emergency Nurses Assn., N.Y. State Nurse Assn. Republican. Jewish. Home: 2562 Bellmore Ave Bellmore NY 11710 Office: Queens Hosp Ctr 82-68 164th St Jamaica NY 11432

SWART, SALLY ANN, insurance company executive; b. Jackson, Mich., July 9, 1947; d. Edwin Jay and Betty Mary (Elmer) Lane; m. Jay P. Lepert, Aug. 16, 1969 (div. Aug. 1970); m. Kenneth D. Swart, Apr. 25, 1981. Cert. gen. ins. Ins. Inst. Am., 1972; BA, Western Mich. U., 1969; postgrad. Aquinas Coll., Grand Rapids, Mich., 1985—. Claims rep. Md. Casualty Co., Bloomfield Hills, Mich., 1970-76; comml. lines rep. Campbell Agy., Grand Rapids, Mich., 1976-80, Poggi Harrison Agy., Grand Rapids, 1980-82; property-casualty underwriting supr. Benson Ins. Co., Naples, Fla., 1981-82; rate, issue supr. Am. Bankers Ins. Co., Miami, Fla., 1982-84; bus. analyst Foremost Inst. Co., Grand Rapids, 1984-86; comml. rating supr. Foremost Ins. Co., 1986-87, comml. automation support analyst, 1987-88; mktg. analyst Crum & Forster Ins. Co., 1988—. Writer newsletters DeKoven Found., 1980. Intake counselor Women's Resource Ctr., Grand Rapids, 1977-80; assoc. mem. Community of St. Mary, Racine, Wis., 1979—. Episcopalian. Avocation: reading. Home: 2620 Ridgecroft SE Grand Rapids MI 49506 Office: Crum & Forster Ins Co 300 Galleria Office Ctr Suite 200 Southfield MI 48034 also: Crum & Forster Ins Co 26375 Halsted Rd #120 Farmington Hills MI 48331

SWARTOUT, JEAN ANN, travel agency executive; b. Catskill, N.Y., Feb. 28, 1945; d. Charles Richard and Vera Mildred (Bower) S. Cert. travel cons. Inst. Cert. Travel Agts. Clk., W.T. Grant Co., Albany, N.Y., 1962-63; mail clk. Mchts. Mut. Ins. Co., Albany, 1963-65; bookkeeper Mountain View Coachline, West Coxsackie, N.Y., 1965-73; mgr. Argus Travel, Inc., West Coxsackie, 1973-84; owner, mgr. Country Side Travel, West Coxsackie, 1984-86, ptnr. West Coxsackie, N.Y., 1986—. Mem. Women In Travel Services, Town and Country Bus. and Profl. Women's Club (2d v.p. Coxsackie 1985-87, 1st v.p. 1987—). Roman Catholic. Avocations: music, reading, theatre, travel. Home: Mansion Sq Apt E-4 Coxsackie NY 12051 Office: Country Side Travel Rt 9-W West Coxsackie NY 12192

SWARTZ, ROSLYN HOLT, real estate investment executive; b. Los Angeles, Dec. 9, 1940; d. Abe Jack and Helen (Canter) Holt; m. Allan Joel Swartz, June 2, 1963. AA, Santa Monica (Calif.) Coll., 1970; BA summa cum laude, UCLA, 1975; MA, Pepperdine U., 1976. Cert. community coll. instr., student-personnel worker, Calif. Mgr. pub. relations Leader Holdings, Inc., Los Angeles, 1968-75; sec., treas. Leader Holdings, Inc., North Hollywood, Calif., 1975-81, pres., 1981—; chief exec. officer Beverly Stanley Investments, Los Angeles, 1979—. Condr. An Oral History of the Elderly Jewish Community of Venice, Calif. at Los Angeles County Planning Dept. Library, 1974. Trainer VITA, Los Angeles, 1975; mem. Friends of the Hollywood Bowl; bd. dirs. Am. Friends of Haifa Med. Ctr. Mem. Am. Pub. Health Assn., Am. Pharm. Assn., UCLA Founders Circle, UCLA Alumni Assn., Phi Alpha Theta, Alpha Gamma Sigma, Alpha Kappa Delta, Phi Delta Kappa, Pi Gamma Mu, Phi Beta Kappa. Lodge: Order of Eastern Star.

SWAZEY, JUDITH POUND, institute president; b. Bronxville, N.Y., Apr. 21, 1939; d. Robert Earl and Louise Titus (Hanson) Pound; m. Peter Woodman Swazey, Nov. 28, 1964; children: Elizabeth, Peter. A.B. (scholar), Wellesley Coll., 1961; Ph.D. (Wellesley Coll. Alumnae fellow, NIH predoctoral fellow, Radcliffe Coll. grad. fellow), Harvard U., 1966. Research assoc. Harvard U., 1966-71, lectr., 1969-71, research fellow, 1971-72; cons. com. brain scis. Nat. Research Council, 1971-73; staff scientist M.I.T. Neuroscis. Research Program, 1973-74; assoc. prof. dept. socio-med. scis. and community medicine Boston U., 1974-77, prof., 1977-80, adj. prof. Schs. Medicine and Pub. Health, 1980—; exec. dir. Medicine in the Public Interest, Inc., Boston and Washington, 1979-82; pres. Coll. of the Atlantic, Bar Harbor, Maine, 1982-84, Acadia Inst., Bar Harbor, 1984—. Author: Reflexes and Motor Integration, the Development of Sherrington's Integrative Action Concept, 1969, (with others) Human Aspects of Biomedical Innovation, 1971, (with R.C. Fox) The Courage to Fail, a Social View of Organ Transplants and Hemodialysis, 1975, rev. edit., 1978 (hon. mention Am. Med. Writers Assn., C. Wright Mills award Am. Sociol. Assn.), Chlorpromazine in Psychiatry, a Study of Therapeutic Innovation, 1974, (with K. Reeds) Today's Medicine, Tomorrow's Science, Essays on Paths of Discovery in the Biomedical Sciences, 1978; editor: (with C. Wong) Dilemmas of Dying, Policies and Procedures for Decisions Not to Treat, 1981, (with F. Worden and G. Adelman) The Neurosciences: Paths of Discovery, 1975; contbr. articles to profl. jours.; assoc. editor IRB: A Jour. of Human Subjects Research, 1979—. Mem. Inst. Medicine (mem. health scis. policy bd.), Nat. Acad. Scis., AAAS (mem. com. on sci. freedom and responsibility), Sherrington Soc., Soc. Health and Human Values, Phi Beta Kappa, Sigma Xi. Office: Acadia Inst Bar Harbor ME 04609

SWEASY, JOYCE ELIZABETH, military officer; b. Key West, Fla., Apr. 25, 1948; d. James Alfred and Josephine Mary (Fassel) Messick. BFA, Phila. Coll. Art, 1971; A in Bus. Adminstrn., Howard County Community Coll., 1985. Commd. 1st lt. U.S. Army, 1978, advanced through grades to capt., 1983; technician ADP Harry Diamond Lab., U.S. Army, Adelphi, Md., 1976-78; contract specialist U.S. Army, Adelphi, 1978-84, analyst procurement Lab. Command,, 1984-85, chief competition mgmt. office, spl. competition advocate, 1985—; owner, operator Hand Made 'N, Ellicott City, Md., 1983—. Contbr. numerous articles to profl. jours. Mem. Font Hill Citizens Orgn., Elicott City, 1987—. Mem. U.S. Army Res. Officers Assn, Nat. Contract Mgrs. Assn., Am. Def. Preparedness Assn. Republican. Roman Catholic. Home: 4008 Arjay Circle Ellicott City MD 21043 Office: US Army Lab Command 2800 Powder Mill Rd Adelphi PA 20783

SWEENEY, DOROTHY LOVE, minister, nurse; b. Worcester, Mass., May 22, 1922; d. Joseph Wilfred and Lillian Mary (Fagga) Fournier; children: Helen F. Hunter, Joseph Wayne Jodrey; m. John L. Sweeney, Mar. 15, 1986; stepchildren: Susan, Florence Moreno, Cathleen Bunn, John L., James, Thomas, Robert. Diploma in nursing, St. Mary's Hosp., 1963; ministerial diploma Religious Sci. Internat., 1973, DD, 1982, DD, United Ch. of Religious Sci., 1988. RN, Ga.; ordained to ministry Ch. of Religious Sci., 1980. Dir., Southeast States region VIII, United Ch. of Religious Sci., Beverly Hills, Calif., 1980 (internat. bd. trustees); staff minister World Ministry of Prayer, United Ch. of Religious Sci., Los Angeles, 1980-81, dir., v.p., Los Angeles, 1983-85 ; minister, dir. Golden Circle Ch. of Religious Sci., Santa Ana, Calif., 1981-83; ministerial staff cons. alcohol recovery services Tustin Community Hosp. (Calif.), Villa Recovery Home for Women, Santa Ana. Author: A Time for Healing, 1975; TV ministry: The Hour of New Thought, 1983. Mem. Southeast Clergy of Religious Sci. (sec., v.p., pres. 1974-77). Club: Toastmaster (treas., sec., v.p., pres. 1971-72). Home: 635 Paseo Dela Playa #303 Redondo Beach CA 90277-6547 Office: Founder's Ch Religious Sci 3281 W 6th St Los Angeles CA 90020

SWEENEY, ELIZABETH ANN, medical center executive; b. Birmingham, Ala., Nov. 9, 1946; d. Huretta and Elizabeth (Whisenant) Chappell; m. LeRoy Sweeney, Jr., Nov. 23, 1985; children: Wesley and Hugh L. Mitchell. BSN, U. Ala., 1973, MSN, 1975. Staff nurse VA Med. Ctr., Birmingham, 1972-74; asst. prof. nursing Sch. Nursing U. Ala., Birmingham, 1975-79; coordinator nursing svcs. Central City Mental Health Ctr., Los Angeles, 1979-80; nurse educator VA Med. Ctr., Los Angeles, 1980—; asst. clin. prof. nursing Sch. Nursing U. Calif., Los Angeles, 1984—; asst. dir. edn. and tng. Kaiser Permanente Med. Ctr., Bellflower, Calif., 1988—; Guest faculty mem. Stanford U., Palo Alto, Calif., 1984; mem. conf. faculty United Nurses Assn. Calif., 1982, 83, 87, Calif. Park and Recreation Soc. Conf., Sacramento, 1985, 86; Equal Employment Opportunity investigator VA, Washington, 1985—. Contbr. articles to profl. jours. Recipient Commendation for Superior Performance Fed. Exec. Bd., Los Angeles, 1984. Mem. Ala. Nurses Assn. (exec. bd. dirs. 1976-79). Office: Kaiser Permanente Med Ctr 9400 E Rosecrans Annex bldg Bellflower CA 90706

SWEENEY, ERNESTINE KAY, nurse; b. Savannah, Ga., Oct. 26, 1959; d. James William and Jane Catherine (Brewer) S.; m. John Earl Foshee, Feb. 12, 1983 (div. 1988). A.D. in Nursing Sci., Northwestern State U., Shreveport, La., 1982. R.N., dental asst. Barksdale AFB, Bossier City, La., 1978-79; nurse orthopedics and neurosurgery Bossier Med. Ctr., 1982-87, nurse cardiac med. unit, 1987—. State officer Internat. Order Rainbow for Girls, 1977-80; vol. La. State Spl. Olympics, Bossier City, 1977-78. Mem. Am. Assn. Critical Care Nurses, NOW. Democrat. Roman Catholic. Lodge: Order Eastern Star. Avocations: writing short stories, collecting records, pen and ink sketching. Home: 3314 Schuler Dr Bossier City LA 71111 Office: Bossier Med Ctr 2105 Airline Dr 100 South Bossier City LA 71111

SWEENEY, JULIA, public relations executive; b. Ladonia, Tex., Feb. 2, 1927; d. Albert Earle and Julia (Nunn) S. Grad. Am. Acad., N.Y.C., 1946; student So. Meth. U., 1958-59. Asst. mgr. Ambrosia House, Milw., 1951-56; sec. Neiman-Marcus, Dallas, 1956-70, publicity dir., 1970-74; columnist, feature writer Dallas Times Herald, 1974-81; pres. Callas, Foster & Sweeney, Dallas, 1982—. Bd. dirs. TACA, Dallas Opera Women's Bd., Susan G. Koman Found. for Cancer Research, Boys' Clubs Dallas, Inc.; bd. dirs., 1st v.p. Friends of Dallas Pub. Library; trustee Protection of Animal World Soc.; mem. March of Dimes Women's Aux., Dallas Theater Ctr. Women's Com.; mem. Southwestern hospitality bd. Met. Opera; mem. Dallas Ballet Women's Com. Mem. Dallas C. of C., Dallas Symphony Orch. League, Dallas Mus. Art League, Dallas County Heritage Soc., Charter 100. Episcopalian. Home: Terrace House 3131 Maple Ave Apt 11B Dallas TX 75201 Office: Callas Foster & Sweeney 2515 McKinney Ave Dallas TX 75201

SWEENEY, KATHY A., mortgage banker; b. Butte, Mont., Sept. 6, 1949; d. Raymond and Gladys (Heino) Miner; m. Michael R. Sweeney, Apr. 28, 1979. Student, Ea. Mont. Coll., 1967-70. Cert. real estate agt., Calif. Servicing officer Met. Service Mortgage, Billings, Mont., 1973-78; br. mgr. Bancshares Mortgage, Billings, 1978-79; asst. personnel dir. Air Base Constructors, Ramon, Israel, 1980-81; visa, real estate mgr. Bechtel Employees Credit Union, San Francisco, 1982-83; br. mgr., asst. v.p. Unified Mortgage, Walnut Creek, Calif., 1983-85; br. mgr., v.p. IMCO Realty Services, Inc., Walnut Creek and San Diego, 1985-87; owner, exec. dir. Kathy Sweeney Promotions, Walnut Creek, 1986—; v.p., retail div. mgr. Monument Mortgage, Inc., Walnut Creek, 1987—. Author poetry, 1986. Mem. Nat. Assn. Female Execs., Assn. Profl. Mortgage Women, Calif. Assn. Real Estate lenders (sec. 1987), Women's Network Contra Costa County. Home: 2863 Via Dominguez Walnut Creek CA 94596 Office: Monument Mortgage 1850 Mt Diablo #650 Walnut Creek CA 94596

SWEENEY, MARGARET MARY, hospital administrator, nun; b. N.Y.C., Oct. 24, 1921; d. Jeremiah and Mary Jane (Dougherty) S. M.B.A., St. John's U., 1966; M.S. in Hosp. Adminstrn., Columbia U., 1970; DSc. (hon.), Iona Coll., 1987. Lic. nursing home adminstr., N.Y. joined Sisters of Charity, Roman Catholic Ch., 1946. Adminstrv. asst. St. Vincent's Hosp., N.Y.C., 1966-68, sr. v.p., 1970-80, pres., 1980—; adminstrv. resident Luth. Med. Ctr., Bklyn., 1969-70; trustee St. Joseph's Hosp., Yonkers, N.Y., 1977—, St. Vincent's Hosp., Harrison, N.Y., 1975—; assoc. prof. N.Y.C. Community Coll., 1973-77; preceptor hosp. adminstrn. Baruch U., George Washington U., N.Y.C., 1974-80; mem. bd. govs., trustee Greater N.Y. Hosp. Assn., 1983—. Contbr. articles to profl. jours.; contbr. lecture series. Chmn, St. Joseph's Ch. Parish Council, Greenwich Village, N.Y., 1973; trustee Medic Alert. Fellow Am. Coll. Hosp. Adminstrs.; mem. Hosp. Fin. Mgmt. Assn., N.Y.C. Pub. Health Assn., N.Y. State Hosp. Assn., Delta Mu Delta. Home: 130 W 12th St New York NY 10011 Office: St Vincent's Hosp 153 W 11th St New York NY 10011

SWEENEY, RHETTA BOYD, advertising executive; b. Chipman, N.B., Can., Oct. 25, 1943; d. Harold John Boyd and Tillie Jane Glenn; m. John Ferran Sweeney, Jr., Mar. 6, 1965; children: Sabrina, Alicia, Faith. Student, Harvard U., 1977-85. Pres. Rhetta Internat., Ltd., Hamilton, Mass., 1985—. Recipient Hatch awards, 1986, 87. Mem. Nat. Council of State Garden Clubs. Clubs: North Shore Garden (Beverly, Mass.) (pres. 1986—); Myopia Hunt (Hamilton); Chilton, Boston Symphony (Boston); Garden Club of Am. Home: 24 Meyer Ln Hamilton MA 01936 Office: Rhetta Internat Ltd 164 Bay Rd Hamilton MA 01936

SWEET, CAROL LYNN, compensation analyst; b. N.Y.C., Dec. 11, 1952; d. William John and Vera Edna (Gretschel) Sloan; m. Stanley Karl Sweet, June 16, 1974; children: Kenneth Justin, Kevin David. A.A., Suffolk County Community Coll., 1973; B.S. in Bus. Adminstrn., SUNY-Buffalo, 1980. Internship affirmative action planning Carborundum Bonded Abrasives Co., Niagara Falls, N.Y., 1980; compensation analyst St. Luke's Med. Ctr., Phoenix, 1981—. Mem. Am. Soc. Personnel Adminstrs., Ariz. Hosp. Personnel Assn., Am. Compensation Assn., Am. Mgmt. Assn. Republican. Jewish. Avocations: music, reading, bicycling, swimming, exploring. Home: 1229 E Claire Dr Phoenix AZ 85022 Office: St Luke's Health System 1800 E Van Buren Phoenix AZ 85006

SWEET, DEE (MRS. HERBERT A. SWEET), business executive; b. Muskogee, Okla., June 3, 1913; d. Walter Oliver and Lola R. (Morris) McDaniel; student Butler U., 1931, 33, summer sch. Oxford U.; m. Herbert A. Sweet, Aug. 28, 1935; children—Judee Lo, Jill B. Sweet Bowles. Asst. to interior decorator L.S. Ayres & Co., Indpls., 1930-33; co-dir. Acorn Farm Camp, Carmel, Ind., 1933-77; owner Acorn Farm Antiques, Carmel, 1960—, Acorn Farm Workshops, 1972—; dir. TV programs WFBM, Indpls., 1949-54, WISH, Indpls., 1955-60; lectr. adult edn. Ind. U., Purdue U., 1959-69. Co-author 2 Try It books for children. Mem. Appraisers Assn. Am. (sr.), Appraisers Soc. Am. (sr.), Associated Antique Dealers Am., Am. Camping Assn., Am. Women in Radio and TV, Ind. Hist. Soc., C. of C., Asso. Antique Dealers Am. Author newspaper column Ind. Soc. Auctioneers. Home: 15466 Oak Rd Carmel IN 46032

SWEET, JOANNE RUTH, sales and marketing executive; b. Hudson, N.Y., Aug. 18, 1961; d. Edward Myron and Joy Marie (Hamm) Althizer; m. Dean Richard Sweet, Aug. 21, 1982. Cert., Columbia Green Community Coll. From receptionist to patient asst. rep. Planned Parenthood, 1981-82; office, mgr. bookkeeper Village Plumbing Co., 1982; inventory clk. Hudson (N.Y.) Audio Video Enterprises, 1983-84, computer operator, 1984-85, sales, mktg. rep., 1985—. Pres. Girls Athletic Assn., Philmont, N.Y., 1979. Fellow Nat. Assn. Female Execs. Home: 68 Harry Howard Ave Hudson NY 12534 Office: Hudson Audio Video Enterprises Inc 309 Power Ave Hudson NY 12534

SWEET, JUDITH ELLEN, banker; b. Rouses Point, N.Y., July 16, 1939; d. Elwin Bernard and Anna Maud (Pratt) Clark; m. James Herbert Sweet, Dec. 28, 1968; children: Kara Lynn, Wendy Ann. BA, U. Ottawa, Ont., Can., 1967; BS in Bus. and Pub. Mgmt., SUNY, Utica, 1984; MS in Guidance, SUNY, Plattsburgh, 1970. Cert. fin. planner. Tchr. Assumption of Mary Sch., Redford, N.Y., 1960-63, St. Joseph's Sch., Brookfield, Conn., 1963-65, St. Mary Magdalene Sch., Oakville, Conn., 1965-66; tchr. French and English, No. Adirondack Cen. Sch., Ellenburg, N.Y., 1966-70; substitute tchr. Chateaugay (N.Y.) Cen. Sch., 1971-74, Oneida (N.Y.) City Sch. Dist., 1979-84; fin. counselor The Savs. Bank of Utica, 1985-86, br. mgr., 1986-87; mgr. fin. services, v.p. SBU Ins. Agy., Utica, N.Y., 1988—; facilitator fin. planning workshops The Savs. Bank of Utica, 1985-87; instr. fin. paraplanner course Am. Inst. Banking, Utica, 1987; speaker SUNY Coll. Tech., utica, 1987; adj. faculty Coll. Fin. Planning. Zone chmn. Am. Heart Assn., Oneida, 1977; pres. Parent Tchrs. Orgn., Oneida, 1978-80; 1st v.p. Oneida City Hosp. Aux., 1980-82. Named Booster of Yr., Seneca St. Sch. Parent Tchrs. Orgn., Oneida, 1985. Mem. Inst. Cert. Fin. Planners, Internat. Assn. Fin. Planners, Bus. & Profl. Women's Orgn. (2d v.p. 1987—). Republican. Presbyterian. Clubs: Progress Literary (Oneida) (recording sec. 1982-84), Friends of the Library.

SWEET, LINDA ANN, financial analyst; b. Berea, Ohio, Oct. 4, 1959; d. Allan Richard McAllister and Rosemary (Kroupa) Szucs; m. Kenneth Charles Sweet, Aug. 8, 1980. BA, Baldwin-Wallace Coll., 1984. Acctg. specialist Ameritrust Corp. N.A., Cleve., 1978-84; cost acctg. supr. Ceilcote Co., Berea, 1984-86; fin. analyst Nat. Semiconductor, South Portland, Maine, 1986-88, Hewlett Packard, Rohnert Park, Calif., 1988—. Mem. Nat. Assn. Female Execs. Republican. Home: 401 Countryside Circle Santa Rosa CA 95401 Office: Hewlett Packard Signal Analysis Div 1212 Valley House Dr Rohnert Park CA 94928

SWEET, MARTHA, human resources professional; b. San Francisco, Oct. 21, 1949; d. Charles Aldrich and Elizabeth (Herbert) S.; m. Sherman Samuel Washburn III; 1 child, Sherman Samuel Washburn IV. Student U. Calif., Davis, 1967-69; BS in Adminstrv. Sci., Pepperdine U., 1979. Personnel supr. Calif. Canners & Growers, San Francisco, 1971-74; employee relations and compensation mgr. Xerox Corp., El Segundo, Calif., 1974-84; human resources mgmt. cons., 1984-86, human resources mgr., Switching Systems Div. NEC Am., Inc., Irvine, Tex., 1986—. Mem. Am. Compensation Assn., Am. Soc. Personnel Adminstrn., Dallas Personnel Assn., Human Resources in High Tech., North Dallas Network Career Women, LWV. Republican. Episcopalian. Home: 518 Hunters Glen Lewisville TX 75067 Office: 1525 Walnut Hill Ln Irving TX 75038

SWEET, NEESA FAE, writer; b. Chgo., July 10, 1948; d. Jason J. and Ione D. Sweet. B.A., U. Ill., 1969. Mem. staff HUD, 1969-71; profl. polit. work, 1971-74; tchr. YMCA, 1974-75; writer, communications work Delta Sky Crains Chgo. Bus., Chgo. Sun Times, Chgo. Tribune, also numerous corps. including U.S. Gypsum, Borg Warner, Allstate, Macarthur Found. Recipient award Internat. Assn. Bus. Communicators. Mem. Am. Soc. Journalists and Authors, Ind. Writers Chgo., Am. Soc. Cybernetics, Assn. for Multi Image (bronze award). Club: Chgo. Press. Office: 1931 N Lincoln Park W Chicago IL 60614

SWEET, PATRICIA MAYER, small business executive, consultant; b. Paris, Tex., Sept. 3, 1944; d. Edward and Claire Dorothy (Gade) Mayer; m. David Charles Sweet, July 3, 1965; children: Britton David, Melissa Mayer, Marc Edward, Kathryn Patricia. BA, U. Okla., 1968. Field coordinator Franklin County Dem. Party, Columbus, Ohio, 1976-77, exec. dir., 1977-78; exec. dir. Ednl. Fund LWV of Cleve., 1980—; pres. SPD, Inc., Cleveland Heights, Ohio, 1983—; caseworker Franklin County Children's Services, 1966-67. Mng. editor: The Youth Vote: The Registration and Voting Patterns of Youth Since the Passage of the 26th Admendment, 1984, New Voters Guide to Practical Politics, 1982; A History of the Black Vote, 1988; project mgr.: A Citizen's Guide to Cleveland, 1984. Mem. WomenSpace, Cleve., 1981-88, Heights Community Congress, 1979-88, Citizens' League, Cleve., 1988; campaign coordinator Metzenbaum for Senate, Columbus, 1976; vol. coordinator Rosemond for Mayor, Columbus, 1974, Ohioans for Gov. Gilligan, Columbus, 1974. Mem. Alpha Gamma Delta (Arc of Epsilon Pi). Lutheran. Clubs: City (Cleve.); Severance Athletic (Cleveland Heights). Home: 1210 Oakridge Dr Cleveland Heights OH 44121

SWEETING, LECIA G., marketing analyst, programmer, speech writer; b. Seattle, Nov. 6, 1953; d. Frank Jr. and Lucille Frances (Smith) Cole; children—Stephen Gregory, Christina Marie. Student U. Mich., 1971-73. Statistician, U. Mich. Basketball, Ann Arbor, 1972-74; dance instr. King High Sch., Detroit, 1972; tech. rep. Xerox, Southfield, Mich., 1974-79; data systems analyst Michigan Bell, Southfield, 1979-85, mktg. analyst, 1985—; news broadcaster sta. WDET-FM, 1979—. Author editor newsletter: News for Liberty, 1983; author ednl. game: Bible Pyramid, 1978. Lectr. Am. Cancer Soc., Southfield, 1980—; sign lang. interpreter Bethlehem Temple Ch., 1982-85; vice chmn. bd. dirs. Nat. Amyotrophic Lateral Sclerosis Assn., Mich., 1985. Recipient Good Citizens award, Mich. Bell Telephone, 1984, Scruggs-Patrick Trailblazer award, 1985. Mem. Engring. Soc. Detroit (sci. fair mgr. West Side Schs., 1980, co-dir. judging sci. fair 1985—, civic affairs com. 1985—). Democrat. Avocation: reading. Office: Michigan Bell Telephone 16025 Northland Dr Room 200 Southfield MI 48075

SWEETING, LINDA MARIE, chemist; b. Toronto, Ont., Can., Dec. 11, 1941; came to U.S., 1965, naturalized, 1979; d. Stanley H. and Mary

(Robertson) S.; BSc, U. Toronto, 1964, MA, 1965; PhD, UCLA, 1969. Asst. prof. chemistry Occidental Coll., Los Angeles, 1969-70; asst. prof. chemistry Towson (Md.) State U., 1970-75, assoc. prof., 1975-85, prof., 1985—; guest worker NIH, 1976-77; program dir. chem. instrumentation NSF, 1981-82; vis. scholar Harvard U., 1984-85. Bd. dirs. Chamber Music Soc. Balt. Mem. Md. Acad. Scis. (mem. sci. council 1975-83), Assn. for Women in Sci. (treas. 1977-78), Am. Chem. Soc. (mem. women chemists Com. 1983—), AAAS, Sierra Club, Wilderness Soc. (exec. com. Exptl. NMR Conf. 1985-87), Nature Conservancy, Aircraft Owners and Pilots Assn., Sigma Xi (sec. TSU Club 1979-81, pres. 1987-88, mid-Atlantic nominating com. 1987—, regional dir. 1988-89). Office: Towson State U Dept Chemistry Baltimore MD 21204

SWEETMAN, LORETTA VINETTE, social worker; b. Niagara Falls, N.Y., Sept. 27, 1941; d. Vincent and Loretta Viola (Williams) Leone; m. George W. Sweetman, Sept. 14, 1967 (div. July 1972); children: Loretta, Mary, GiGi. AS, Claremore Jr. Coll., 1975; BS in Sociology, East Cen. State Coll., 1978; MSW, U. Okla., 1980. With Tulsa Dist. Office Corp Engrs., 1975; with practicum placement dept. VA Hosp., Muskogee, Okla., 1979-80; clin. social worker VA Hosp., Sheridan, Wyo., 1980—, St. Joseph Hosp., Ponca City, Okla., 1980; tchr. Sheridan Community Coll., 1983—. Presenter in field. Bd. dirs. Wyo. Health Care, Sheridan, 1982-85, Sr. Citizens Coordinator Council, Sheridan, 1982-84, exec. bd. pres., 1984-87; rep. Sheridan County Hospice Nat. Hospice Mgrs., 1984-87. Named one of Women of the Yr. Sheridan chpt. Bus. and Profl. Women, 1982, one of Women of the Day Sheridan chpt. Bus. and Profl. Women, 1982. Mem. Nat. Assn. Female Execs., Nat. Assn. Social Workers. Democrat. Roman Catholic. Home: 845 W 13th St Sheridan WY 82801

SWEGEL, DOROTHY, personnel service corp. exec.; b. Forest City, Pa., Dec. 23, 1932; d. John J. and Anna T. (Loush) S.; student Chestnut Hill Coll., Phila., 1950-51. Periodicals librarian Charles M. Schwab Meml. Library, Bethlehem (Pa.) Steel Co., 1952-55; with spl. sales Nat. Airlines, Miami, Fla., 1955-58; sr. supr. TWA Ambassadors Club, Kennedy Airport, Jamaica, N.Y., 1959-66; pres. CoverTemp Inc., Gateway Careers, Inc., PC/ Word Pro Center, White Plains, N.Y., 1969—; dir. Gerber Life Ins. Co. Del. White House Conf. Small Bus. 1986; pres. Westchester Council for Arts 1985-87; group chmn. United Way of Westchester, 1987-88; bd. dirs. Westchester County Assn., Westchester 2000, County C. of C., Manhattanville Coll. Entrepreneurial Ctr., Sales and Mktg. Execs. of Westchester. Mem. Adminstrv. Mgmt. Soc., Westchester Women Bus. Owners Assn., Gannett Bus. Roundtable, Coll. of New Rochelle Pres.'s Adv. Council. Republican. Roman Catholic. Lodge: Soroptimist. Office: 235 Main St White Plains NY 10601

SWEGER, GLENDA LEE, educator; b. Harrisburg, Pa., July 26, 1946; d. George Glenn and Bertha Alverta (Kitner) S. BS, Ind. U. of Pa., Indiana, Pa., 1968; MA, Calif. State U., Fullerton, 1981. Cert. tchr. Calif. Tchr. Greensburg-Salem (Pa.) Unifed Sch. Dist., 1968-69, Covina-Valley (Calif.) Unified Sch. Dist., 1969—; bd. dirs. SCSPA, San Diego, 1972-82; publs. advisor Northview High Sch., Covina, 1970—, accreditation chmn. 1987—; lectr. Great Am. Lecture Series, Covina, 1988—. Author: Male & Female Reporters: Differences in Readers' Perceptions, 1981. Active PTA, Covina, 1969—, SPRING, Seal Beach, Calif., 1987—, Orange County AIDS Found., Calif., 1987—, Ellis Island Found., N.Y.C., 1986—, Statue of Liberty Found., N.Y.C., 1984—. Recipient SCV Educators' grant, Covina-Valley Unifed Sch. Dist., 1986. Mem. Nat. Edn. Assn., Calif. Tchrs. Assn., Covina Unifed Edn. Assn., Nat. Council Tchrs of English, Calif. Assn. for Tchrs of English, Calif. Scholastic Press Assn., Columbia Scholastic Press Advisors Assn., Journalism Edn. Assn., So. Calif. Journalism Edn. Assn., So. Calif. Scholastic Press Assn. (sec. 1976-82, bd. dirs.), So. Calif. Scholastic Publs. Assn., Southland Assn. for Tchrs. of English, IUP Alumni Assn., Fullerton Alumni Assn. Democrat. Evagelical Lutheran. Home: 3372 Rowena Dr Rossmoor CA 90720 Office: Northview High Sch 1016 W Cypress Ave Covina CA 91722

SWENINGSON, NANCY WARISCH, city secretary; b. St. Paul, Nov. 29, 1939; d. John W. and Alma L. (Beck) Warisch; m. Emmett Sweningson, May 2, 1959; children: Sue Sweningson Nalepa, Jon Sweningson, Lee, Jay. Grad. high sch., Mpls. City sec. City of Nassau Bay, Tex., 1971—. Mem. Assn. City Clks. and City Secs. Tex. (pres. Salt Grass chpt. 1985), Internat. Inst. Mcpl. Clks. Home: 18164 Martinique Nassau Bay TX 77058 Office: City of Nassau Bay 1800 Nasa Rd 1 Nassau Bay TX 77058

SWENSEN, WILLODEAN THARPE, banker; b. Dale Country, Ala., Feb. 28, 1933; d. Talmadge Porter and Florence (Evans) Tharpe; m. Edward Gustav Swensen Sr., July 9, 1954; children: Edward Gustav Jr., Patricia Swensen Brown. AS, Columbus (Ga.) Coll., 1985, BBA, 1987. Accredited profl. in human resources. Sec. Muskogee Mfg. Co., Columbus, 1952-55; teller First Nat. Bank, Columbus, 1956-71, purchasing agt., 1971-78, personnel asst., 1978-81; asst. personnel officer First Union Nat. Bank (formerly First Nat. Bank), Columbus, 1981—; chairperson Mktg. Edn. Adv. Com., Columbus, 1987—. Mem. Columbus Area Personnel Assn. (bd. dirs.), Am. Soc. for Personnel Adminstrs., Nat. Assn. of Bank Women. Baptist. Lodge: Soroptimist (sec. Columbus 1986). Home: Quail Rise Rt 6 Box 20-A Phenix City AL 36867 Office: First Union Nat Bank of Columbus 101 13th St Columbus GA 31993

SWENSON, ELIZABETH VON FISCHER, psychologist, educator, lawyer; b. Cleve., Mar. 4, 1941; d. William and Cordelia (Thacker) von Fischer; m. Paul F. Swenson, Aug. 26, 1961; children: Karen, Connie, Kirsten. BS, Tufts U., 1963; MA, Case Western Res. U., 1972, PhD, 1974; JD, Cleve. State U., 1985. Bar: Ohio 1986, U.S. Dist. Ct. (no. dist.) Ohio 1986. Prof., chmn. dept. psychology John Carroll U., Cleve., 1979—; law clk. to justice U.S. Dist. Ct. (no. dist.) Ohio, Cleve., 1987. Contbr. articles to profl. jours. Mem. ABA, Am Psychol. Assn., Phi Beta Kappa. Office: John Carroll U Dept Psychology Cleveland OH 44118

SWENSON, MAY, poet; b. Logan, Utah, May 28, 1919; d. Dan Arthur and Margaret (Hellberg) S. B.S., Utah State U., 1939, LittD (hon.), 1987, PhD (hon.), 1987. Editor New Directions Press, 1959-66; mem. staff Breadloaf Writers Conf., 1976. Poet-in-residence, Purdue U., Lafayette, Ind., 1966-67, U. N.C., Greensboro, 1968-69, 75, Lethbridge U., Alta., Can., 1970, U. Calif., Riverside, 1973; Hurst prof. Washington U., St. Louis, 1982; Author: Another Animal, 1954, A Cage of Spines, 1958, To Mix with Time, 1963, Poems to Solve, 1966, Half Sun Half Sleep, 1967, Iconographs, 1970, More Poems to Solve, 1971, (translated from Swedish) Windows & Stones (Tomas Tranströmer), 1972, The Guess and Spell Coloring Book, 1976, New and Selected Things Taking Place, 1978, In Other Words, 1987. Recipient Nat. Inst. Arts and Letters award, 1960; Brandeis U. award, 1967; Disting. Service Gold medal Utah State U., 1967; Shelley Meml. award Poetry Soc. Am., 1968; transl. medal Internat. Poetry Forum, 1972; Bollingen prize in poetry Yale U., 1981; Guggenheim fellow, 1959; Amy Lowell Travelling scholar, 1960; Ford Found. fellow, 1965; Rockefeller Found. fellow, 1967-68; Lucy Martin Donnally fellow Bryn Mawr Coll., 1968-69, McArthur Found. fellow, 1987; Nat. Endowment for Arts grantee, 1974. Fellow Acad. Am. Poets (chancellor 1980); mem. Am. Acad. and Inst. Arts and Letters, Corp. of Yaddo. Home: 73 Boulevard Sea Cliff NY 11579

SWERGOLD, MARCELLE MIRIAM, sculptor; b. Antwerp, Belgium, Sept. 6, 1927; came to U.S., 1939, naturalized, 1947; d. Gillel and Sarah (Matuzewitz) Elfenbein; student NYU, Art Students League, Sculptors Workshop; m. Maurice Swergold, June 12, 1949; children—Diane Botnick, Henry, Gary Swergold, Paul Kogan, George Kogan. Sculptor, 1965—; one-woman exhbns. include: Studio 12, N.Y.C., 1980, 82, 86, Nat. Fedn. Temple Sisterhoods, 1984; group exhbns. include Farleigh Dickinson U., Teaneck, N.J., 1972, Audubon Artist Ann., N.Y.C., 1978-86, Internat. Treasury Fine Arts, Plainview, N.Y., 1979, New Britain (Conn.) Mus., 1980, also Cork Gallery, Lincoln Center, N.Y.C., Allied Artists Nat. Acad. Galleries, N.Y.C., U.S. Custom House, N.Y.C., others; represented in permanent collection New Britain Mus. Am. Art; represented in pvt. collection of Master Moshe Castel, Israel. Recipient Best in Show award for Tetons, Women's Art Gallery, N.Y.C., 1977, 1st prize for sculpture Stanley Richter Assn. Arts, 1985, Vincent Glinski Meml. award Audubon Artists, 1986. Mem. N.Y. Soc. Women Artists (pres. 1979-81, exec. v.p. 1981—), Artists Equity, Contemporary Artists Guild. Home: 43 Paul St Danbury CT 06810 Studio: 246 W 80th St New York NY 10024

SWIBOLD, GRETCHEN ANN, librarian, author; b. Holland, Mich., May 3, 1933; d. Jan B. and Margaret Ann (Raak) Vanderploeg; m. Richard Edward Swibold, Aug. 15, 1955; children—Katharine Margaret, Edward Jan. A.B., Bryn Mawr Coll., 1955; postgrad. U. Ill.-Urbana, 1958-59; M.S., So. Conn. State Coll., 1970; postgrad. Central Conn. State Coll., 1973-82. Editorial asst. Our Wonderful World, Urbana, Ill., 1955-57; editor Spencer Press, Urbana, 1957-58; research asst. U. Ill.-Urbana, 1958-59; librarian Yale U. Polit. Sci. Research Library, New Haven, 1967-71; librarian Canton Elem. Schs. (Conn.), 1971—. Editor: Animals in Action, 1958; Rolling Wheels, 1959; contbr. articles to newspapers and profl. jours. Bd. dirs. Creative Arts Workshop, New Haven, 1967-71; mem. women's com. Yale U. Art Gallery, New Haven, 1967-71; active Democratic Town Com., Canton, Conn., 1973-86, Charter Commn., Canton, 1983-84, Canton Creative Arts Council, 1980-87 (v.p. 1987—); chmn., sec. Bd. Assessors, Canton, 1975-79. Mem. ALA, U. S. Bd. on Books for Young People, Conn. Ednl. Media Assn., Nat. Council Tchrs. English, Conn. Edn. Assn., Delta Kappa Gamma. Democrat. Home: 731 Cherry Brook Rd North Canton CT 06059 Office: Canton Mid Sch Dyer Ave Collinsville CT 06022

SWICEGOOD, LANA SUSAN HAYDEN, small business executive; b. Mebane, N.C., Apr. 25, 1948; d. Lawrence Andrew and Beulah Ann (Williams) Hayden; m. Clarence Edward Swicegood Jr., Apr. 15, 1967; children: Clarence Reginald, Kimberly Ann. BA, Ashemore Bus. Coll., 1968. Filing clk. McLean Trucking Co., Winston-Salem, N.C., 1967-69; acctg. clk. Nationwide Consumer Service, Raleigh, N.C., 1973-78; sr. acctg. clk. Carolina Power & Light Co., Raleigh, 1978-85; mgr., v.p. Swicegood Appraisers, Raleigh, 1985—. Pres. Exchangettes of Greater Raleigh, 1980, sec., 1981, treas., 1982. Recipient Exchangette of Yr. award Exchange Club of Greater Raleigh, 1982. Republican. Methodist. Home: 1408 October Rd Raleigh NC 27614

SWIERZBIN, KATHLEEN M., marketing professional; b. Worcester, Mass., Mar. 3, 1954; d. Francis Vincent and Helen Theresa (Gosk) S. BS in English, Holy Cross Coll., 1976. Copywriter Filene's, Boston, 1976-77; mgr. direct mail Strawbridge and Clothier, Phila., 1977-80; prodn. mgr. W. Atlee Burpee Co., Phila., 1980-83; v.p. prodn. Spiro & Assocs., Phila., 1983—; guest lectr. Temple U., Phila., 1985—. Mem. Advt. Prodn. Club N.Y.C., SE Regional Postal Customer's Council, Graphic Arts Assn. Del. Valley. Democrat. Roman Catholic. Home: 417 S Perth St Philadelphia PA 19147 Office: Spiro & Assocs 100 S Broad St Philadelphia PA 19110

SWIFT, CAROLYN ANN, life insurance company executive; b. Youngstown, Ohio, Jan. 30, 1946; d. John Joseph and Mary Dominica (Ferraro) DeMarco; m. Richard Joseph Swift, May 7, 1965; children: Richard Joseph, Jeffrey John. Student, Life Office Mgmt., Hartford, Conn., 1976. Sec. N.Y. Life Ins. Co., Youngstown, 1964-65; sec. Western Res. Life, Largo, Fla., 1969-74, supr., 1974-78, dept. mgr., 1978-82, asst. sec., 1982-85, asst. v.p., 1985—. Democrat. Lodge: Ladies of Largo Elks (pres. 1977-78, v.p. 1984-85, 88—). Office: Western Res Life 201 Highland Ave Largo FL 34640

SWIFT, EVANGELINE WILSON, lawyer; b. San Antonio, May 2, 1939; d. Raymond E. and Josephine (Woods) Wilson; 1 child, Justin Lee. Student So. Meth. U., 1956-59; LL.B., St. Mary's U., San Antonio, 1963. Bar: Tex. 1963, U.S. Ct. Appeals (5th cir.) 1972, D.C. 1976, U.S. Dist. Ct. D.C. 1976, U.S. Supreme Ct. 1980, U.S. Ct. Appeals (11th cir.) 1981, U.S. Ct. Appeals (10th cir.) 1982, U.S. Ct. Appeals (D.C. cir.) 1982, U.S. Ct. Appeals (fed. cir.) 1983. Atty.-adv. ICC, Washington, 1964-65; staff atty. Headstart Program, OEO, Washington, 1965; exec. legal asst. to chmn., spl. asst. to vice chmn. EEOC, Washington, 1965-71, chief decisions div., 1971-75, asst. gen. counsel, 1975-76; cons. to sec. Employment Standards Adminstrn., Dept. Labor, Washington, 1977-79; ptnr. Swift & Swift, P.C., Washington, 1977-79; gen. counsel Merit Systems Protection Bd., Washington, 1979-86, mng. dir., 1986-87, dir. policy and evaluation, 1987—; chmn. jud. conf. Merit Systems Protection Bd. U.S. Ct. Appeals (fed. cir.) 1983-86, bd. govs., 1984-86, treas., 1987—; guest lectr. Drake U., U. Pa., MIT; mem. U.S. del. 23d Sessions UNESCO Commn. on Status of Women, Geneva, 1970, U.S. Fed. Circut Bar Assn. (bd. govs. 1985-87, treas. 1987—). Recipient Meritorious Service award Fed. Govt., 1967, Fed. Women's award, 1975; Performance award Merit Systems Protection Bd., 1981-86, Gold award 1986; Presdl. CFC award, 1984, 86, EEO award Merit Systems Protection Bd., 1985. Methodist. Office: Merit System Protection Bd Office of Policy and Evaluation 1120 Vermont Ave NW Washington DC 20419

SWIFT, MARY LOUISE, healthcare professional; b. Potsdam, N.Y., June 15, 1940; d. Theodore Hiram and Virginia Hazel (Beebe) Swift; m. Joseph Anthony D'Errico, Sept. 24, 1961 (div. 1975); children: Dawn, Jon. RN, House of Good Samaritan, Watertown, N.Y., 1961; degree in physician's assistance, Duke U., 1973; BS, St. Joseph's Coll., 1982; postgrad. in surgery, Yale U., 1982-83. Charge nurse House of Good Samaritan, Watertown, 1960-61; operating room nurse Deborah Hosp., Brown's Mills, N.J., 1965, Mount Holly (N.J.) Hosp., 1965-66; vis. nurse Vis. Nurse Assn., Jamestown, N.Y., 1966-69; pediatric nurse Office Dr. Lisciandro, Jamestown, 1969-71; physician's asst. in family practice Chateaugay (N.Y.) Clinic, 1974-82; physician's asst. in emergency dept. Alice Hyde Hosp., Malone, N.Y., 1983—. Fellow Am. Assn. Physician's Assts., N.Y. Soc. Physicians' Assts.; mem. Am. Diabetic Assn. (bd. dirs. 11979-81), Am. Cancer Assn. (bd. dirs. 1976-80). Methodist. Home: 9 Halley Dr Malone NY 12953

SWIG, ROSELYNE C., art advisor; b. Chgo., June 8, 1930; m. Richard Swig, Feb. 5, 1950; children—Richard, Jr., Susan, Marjorie, Carol. Student, U. Calif.-Berkeley, UCLA; M.F.A. (hons.), San Francisco Art Inst. Pres. Roselyne C. Swig Artsource, San Francisco, 1977—. mem. bd. trustees San Francisco Mus. Modern Art, U. Art Mus., Berkeley, Calif., Berkeley Found, Calif. State Summer Sch. of the Arts; bd. dirs. Am. Council for the Arts, N.Y.C., San Francisco Opera, Jewish Community Mus.; past pres. San Francisco Art Inst., Arts Commission, San Francisco, Sta. KQED, Pub. Broadcasting System; trustee Mills Coll., Oakland, Calif., 1987—.

SWINGLE, ARTICE MAY, educational administrator, special education educator; b. Schenectady, Jan. 28, 1939; d. Arto Webster and Ida Elzada (Gosnell) S.; m. Richard Henry Burke, July 29, 1961 (div. 1973); children: Richard Robert, Daniel Douglas; m. John Joseph Wordin, Dec. 31, 1974. BS cum laude, Syracuse U., 1961, MS, 1963; cert. adminstr. spl. edn. Calif. State U., Los Angeles, 1976. Lic. marriage, family and child guidance counselor, Calif.; cert. tchr., adminstr., coll.-level instr., Calif.; cert. elem. tchr., spl. edn. tchr., N.Y. Tchr. educable mentally retarded children, chmn. dept. Tully Central Sch., N.Y., 1961-65; therapist, dir. ednl. services Los Angeles Child Achievement Ctr., 1967-70; diagnostic clinic tchr. Diagnostic Sch. for Neurologically Impaired Children So. Calif., Los Angeles, 1970-78; mem. faculty Calif. State U., Los Angeles, 1974, 77; coordinator spl. services Idaho Falls Sch. Dist. 91, Idaho, 1977—; regional coordinator spl. needs low-incidence programs, Idaho Falls Sch. Dists. 91, 59, 60, 93, 1982-86; lectr. to various profl. and community groups. Co-author: Development of Ordinal Scales of Non-Culturally Biased Development Diagnostic Instrument, 1976. Chmn. bd. trustees 1st Congl. Ch., Idaho Falls, 1983-84, moderator, 1984-85; cons. Human Relations Ctr., Woodland Hills Congl. Ch., also former trustee; den leader Great Western council Boy Scouts Am., 1961. N.Y. Regents scholar, 1957-61; research grantee U.S. Dept. Edn. and ESEA. Mem. Idaho Falls Weavers and Spinners Guild (chmn. spinning study group 1983-87), Pi Lambda Theta. Republican. Avocations: spinning, flying. Home: 735 N 900 E Shelley ID 83274 Office: Idaho Falls Sch Dist 91 690 John Adams Pkwy Idaho Falls ID 83401

SWINTON, LISA GRACE THOMPSON, lawyer; b. Kansas City, Mo., Feb. 15, 1958; d. Lee Vertis and Grace Lucile (Thompson) S. BA, Creighton U., 1979, JD, 1983. Bar: Nebr. 1984. Tchr. Kansas City (Mo.) Pub. Schs., 1980; law clk. Ellick, Spire and Jones Law Firm, Omaha, 1981-83; atty. Nebr. Dept. Social Services, Lincoln, 1983—; Mem. judicial nominating com. dist. ct. of Lancaster County, Lincoln, Nebr., 1987—. Named one of Outstanding Young Women of Am., 1981, 84. Mem. Nebr. State Bar Assn., Nebr. Juvenile Justice Assn., Midlands Bar Assn., Alpha Kappa Alpha, Alpha Sigma Nu, Phi Alpha Theta. Democrat. Office: Nebr Dept Social Services 301 Centennial Mall South Lincoln NE 68509

SWISHER, VERNA LOUISE, nursing educator; b. Ridgeway, Pa., July 14, 1937; d. Clifford and Josephine (Hollabaugh) Beck; m. William E. Swisher, May 18, 1957; children—Sharon Louise Cooney, Traci Lynn. R.N., Clearfield Hosp. Sch. Nursing (Pa.), 1960; B.S.N., Pa. State U., 1967; M.Sc. in Nursing, Indiana U. of Pa., 1986. Nurse, Clearfield Hosp., 1960-63, acting head nurse, 1964, asst. instr., 1964-67, med.-surg. instr., 1967-69; med.-surg. instr. Philipsburg State Gen. Hosp. Sch. Nursing (Pa.), 1969-82; med.-surg. instr. Central Pa. Sch. Nursing, 1982—, mem. admissions com., 1982-83, chmn. inservice com., 1982-83, 85-86, 87-88. Tchr., Sunday Sch., Presbyn. Ch., Clearfield, 1970-73; deacon 1st United Presbyn. Ch., 1970-72. Mem. Am. Nurses Assn., Pa. Nurses Women's Assn. (program chair 1988-89), Dist. 5 Nurses Assn. (nominating com.), Philipsburg Nurses Alumnae Assn., Clearfield Nurses Alumnae Assn. (pres. 1982), Nat. League Nursing, Clearfield Bus. and Profl. Womens Club (v.p., 1987-88, pres. 1971-72, 88-89). Republican. Home: 204 Spruce St Clearfield PA 16800 Office: Cen Pa Sch Nursing 110 Lock Lomond Rd Philipsburg PA 16866

SWIT, LORETTA, actress; b. Passaic, N.J., Nov. 4, 1937. Student, Am. Acad. Dramatic Arts, Gene Frankel Repertoire Theatre, N.Y.C. Stage appearances include Same Time Next Year, Any Wednesday, The Mystery of Edwin Drood, toured in Maine; films include Stand Up and Be Counted, 1972, Freebie and the Bean, 1974, Race with the Devil, 1975, S.O.B, 1980, Beer, 1985; co-star: TV series M*A*S*H, 1972-83 (Emmy awards for Outstanding Supporting Actress in a Comedy series 1979-81); TV movies Mirror, Mirror, Valentine, Friendships, Secrets and Lies, Shirts and Skins, Coffeeville, Cagney and Lacey, Games Mother Never Taught You, First Affair, The Execution; star on: maj. dramatic shows and musical variety shows, including Bob Hope Christmas Special. Mem. AFTRA, Screen Actors Guild, Actors Equity. Office: care William Morris Agy 151 El Camino Dr Beverly Hills CA 90212 *

SWITAK, HEATHER JOAN, nurse; b. Sidney, B.C., Canada, Jan. 2, 1947; d. Ernest Francis and Helen Merrielee (Booth) White; m. Robert Arthur Paul Switak, June 29, 1969; children: Daryl Robert Ryan, Devon Arthur Troy. RN, Branson Hosp. Sch. Nursing, Toronto, 1968; BS, Atlantic Union Coll., South Lancaster, Mass., 1974. Staff nurse New England Meml. Hosp., Stoneham, Mass., 1968-69, charge and medication nurse, 1969-70, orientation nurse, 1970-72, team leader, 1972, in-service edn. instr., 1972-74, dir. staff devel., 1974-79, gen. relief supr., 1980-82, psychiatric and substance abuse unit staff and charge nurse,, 1981-82; dir. resident care Rest Haven Lodge, Sidney, B.C., 1982—; conv. speaker Can. Assn. of S.D.A. Nursing Homes, New Brunswick, 1985, B.C., 1986. Mem. Care Adminstrs. Assn. of B.C. (bd. dirs. 1983-86), Victoria Dirs. of Care. Adventist. Office: Rest Haven Lodge, 2281 Mills Rd, Sidney, BC Canada V8L 2C3

SWITALSKI, CHRISTINE C. A., newspaper manager; b. Hamilton, Ont., Canada, June 26, 1954; d. Ross Joseph and Laura Stephanie Robertson; m. Jan Switalski, Dec. 30, 1983; 1 child: Eric Jan. Grad. high sch., Hamilton, Ont., 1973. Customer service supr. The Spectator, Hamilton, 1983-86, customer service mgr., 1986-87, customer and ednl. services mgr., 1987—. Mem. Ontario NIE Assn. Office: The Spectator, 44 Frid St, Hamilton, ON Canada L8N3G3

SWITTEN, MARGARET LOUISE, French language educator; b. Chgo.; m. Henry N. Switten (dec.). B.Mus., Westminster Choir Coll., 1947; B.A., Barnard Coll., 1948; M.A., Bryn Mawr Coll., 1949, Ph.D., 1952. Asst. prof. music and French, assoc. prof., then prof. French Hampton Inst., Va., 1952-63; mem. faculty Mt. Holyoke Coll., South Hadley, Mass., 1963—, Alumnae Found. prof. French, 1975-83, Lucia, Ruth and Elizabeth MacGregor prof. French, 1983-86, Class of 1926 prof. medieval and 18th Century French lang., lit., 1986—, chmn. dept., 1969-76, 82-83. Contbr. articles to profl. jours. Mary Andersen fellow, 1951-52, Fulbright fellow, 1956-57, Am. Council Learned Socs. fellow, 1969-70. Mem. MLA, Am. Assn. Tchrs. French, Medieval Acad., Modern Humanities Research Assn. Office: Mount Holyoke Coll South Hadley MA 01075 *

SWITZ, MARY ANN, funeral home executive; b. Massillon, Ohio, July 1, 1944; d. Harold Homer and Margaret Ann (Abel) Hartel; m. David Lee Switz, Oct. 13, 1962 (div. 1970); children—Bethany Lynne, Philip David. Student Cleve. Inst. Music, 1974-75, Cuyahoga Community Coll., Cleve., 1976-88, Cleve. State U., 1988—. Sec., Calvin Woodward, Atty., Warren, Ohio, 1969-73, Univ. Circle Research Center, Cleve., 1973-74; program coordinator Univ. Circle Center Community Programs, Cleve., 1974-77; bus. office mgr. Johnson-Romito Funeral Homes, Bedford, Ohio, 1977—; dir. music Luth. Ch. of Covenant, Maple Heights, Ohio, 1982-86. Mem. bd., accompanist, keyboard prin., soloist Chagrin Valley Choral Union, and Orch., Cleve., 1981—; accompanist, concertmistress Solon Players Community Theatre and Orch. (Ohio), 1981-83; organist Forest Hill Presbyn. Ch., Cleveland Heights, Ohio, 1987—. Mem. Nat. Assn. Female Execs., Chagrin Valley Choral Union, Am. Guild Organists. Lutheran. Home: 47 Dewhurst Ave Bedford OH 44146 Office: Johnson-Romito Funeral Homes 521 Broadway Ave Bedford OH 44146

SWITZER, KATHRINE VIRGINIA, TV sports commentator, sports marketing executive; b. Amberg, Ger., Jan. 5, 1947; d. Homer and Virginia Irene (Miller) S. B.A., Syracuse U., 1968, M.A., 1972. Indsl. editor Bristol Myers Corp., Syracuse, N.Y., 1968-72; pub. relations coordinator AMF Inc., White Plains, N.Y., 1973-77; mgr. spl. promotions Avon Products, Inc., N.Y.C., 1977-80, dir. media affairs and sports programs, 1980-85, also dir. sports program pub. relations; lectr. in field. Trustee Women's Sports Found.; spl. advisor Pres.'s Council on Phys. Fitness and Sports. Recipient outstanding individual contbn. award Womens Sports Found., 1982, honor fellow award Nat. Assn. for Girls and Women in Sports, 1983, nat. honor award President's Council on Phys. Fitness and Sports, 1984; named Outstanding Female Runner of 1975 Road Runners Club Am., Runner of Decade Road Runners Club Am., 1976. Club: Road Runners of N.Y. Winner N.Y.C. Marathon, 1974. Office: 211 W 56th St New York NY 10019

SWOGER, MARCIA KAY, manager human resources and development; b. Elkins, W.Va., July 26, 1951; d. James H. and Carrie M. (Arnold) Chandler; m. Timothy Mark Swoger, Nov. 19, 1983; children: Carrie, Joshua. AS in Bus., W.Va. Career Coll., 1972; student, W.Va. U., 1980. Fin. aid officer W.Va. U., Morgantown, 1972-73; adminstrv. asst. W.Va. Mountain Lair, Morgantown, 1973-75, res. mgr., 1977-80, facilities mgr., 1980-82, asst. dir., 1982-85; div. mgr. ETCON, Inc., Gainesville, Ga., 1985-88, mgr. human resources and devel., 1988—. Mem. Am. Bus. Women's Assn., Nat. Assn. Female Execs. (Listed in Who's Who in Profl. and Exec. Women, 1987), Am. Cons. League, Am. Soc. Tng. and Devel. Bus. Council Ga. Democrat. Methodist. Office: ETCON Inc Huntington Place Ctr 1879 Buford Hwy Buford GA 30518

SWOLL, MARUTH JEAN, graphic arts company executive, artist; b. Madison, Tenn., Oct. 22, 1946; d. Roy Kenneth and Wilma Jean (Christian) Pace; m. Ronald Lee Swoll, July 3, 1981. BS, Austin Peay State U., 1970; MBA, U. North Fla., 1982. Kitchen designer Gen. Electric Co., Louisville, 1970-74; tchr. phys. edn. Richmond County Bd. Edn., Augusta, Ga., 1974-75; dir. art A.A. Friedman Co., Inc., Augusta, 1975-77; asst. mgr. project design Seaboard System R.R., Louisville and Jacksonville, Fla., 1978-83, mgr. reprographics, 1983-85; owner Marographics, Jacksonville, 1985—; co-owner (with husband) Trifles Restaurant and Lounge. Recipient Gracey award for jewelry art, 1976. Mem. In-Plant Printing Mgrs. Assn., Nat. Assn. Purchasing Mgrs. Republican. Roman Catholic. Clubs: Civitan Internat. (newsletter pub. 1985—), Internat. Aerobatic (sec. 1986—, newsletter editor 1986—), 99's, Women Pilots Assn. Avocations: flying, scuba diving, painting, golf. Home and Office: 4732 Beauchamp Ct Jacksonville FL 32217

SWORD, SANDRA LEE, health science facility administrator; b. LaSalle, Ill., Nov. 5, 1943; d. Laurence Everrett and Irene Roberta (Dobberstein) Hunter; children: Kimberly, Kristine. BS, Coll. St. Francis, Joliet, Ill., 1983, MS, 1986. RN. Dir. nursing Turtle Creek Skilled Home, LaSalle, 1972-74; nurse utilization rev. Peoples Hosp., Peru, Ill., 1974-75; nurse Franciscan Med. Ctr., Rock Island, Ill., 1975-78; head nurse open heart surgery Meth. Med. Ctr., Peoria, Ill., 1978; dir. surg. services Proctor Community Hosp., Peoria, 1978-86, Broward Gen. Med. Ctr., Ft. Lauderdale, Fla., 1986—. Mem. Am. Coll. Health Care Execs., Assn. Operating Room Nurses, Nat. Assn. Female Execs. Office: Broward Gen Med Ctr 1600 S Andrew Fort Lauderdale FL 33316

SWYDAN, ANNE, marketing professional; b. Worcester, Mass., Aug. 7, 1917; d. Shokri K. and Hafeeza (Koury) S. Student, Clark U., Worcester, 1939. Internat. mktg. communications mgr. Norton Co., Worcester, 1954-84; mgr. Swydan Mktg. Communications Internat. Ltd., Worcester, 1984—. Bd. dirs. Friendly House, Worcester, 1940—, Internat. Ctr. of Worcester, 1979—, R.S.V.P., Worcester, 1986—. Mem. Internat. Advt. Assn. (pres. New England chpt. 1985—). Lodge: Soroptimist Internat. Office: Swydan Mktg Communications Internat 61 Hillcroft Ave Worcester MA 01606

SYCHAK, CYNTHIA KAY, lawyer; b. Butler, Pa., Oct. 24, 1953; d. John James Sr. and Josephine Ann (Zambiski) S.; m. Charles Dufur Berry, July 29, 1978; 1 child, John James. Student, Butler Community Coll., 1971-73; BA cum laude, U. Pitts., 1976; JD, Western New England Coll., 1979. Bar: Pa. 1979. Sole practice Butler, 1979—; instr. Butler County Community Coll., 1987—. Pres., bd. dirs. United Way of Butler County, 1983-89, chair bylaws com., 1985-87; chair Edn. Com. Butler County, 1984-87. Senatorial scholar Senate of Pa., 1974-75. Mem. ABA, Pa. Bar Assn., Butler County Bar Assn. (treas. 1985-86). Republican. Roman Catholic. Home: 1220 LaKevue Dr Butler PA 16001 Office: Morgan Ctr Suite 208 Butler PA 16001

SYKES, GWENDOLYN PHEAGIN, academic administrator; b. Franklin, N.C., July 15, 1945; d. James Thomas and Martha (Elliott) P.; m. Samuel Mason Sykes, June 4, 1966; children: James Mason, Melissa Scott. BA, Meth. Coll., Fayetteville, N.C., 1968. Cert. tchr., N.C. Tchr. journalism Cumberland County Schs., Fayetteville, 1968-77; founder, dir. East Coast Cheerleading Camp, Fayetteville, 1970—; dir. publs. Meth. Coll., 1977-85, dir. spl. projects, 1985—, pres. Gwynco products, 1986—; cheerleading, dance coach Meth. Coll., 1979—; cons. N.C. Dept. Pub. Instrn., Raleigh, 1985—; exec. coordinator Nat. Cheerleading Coaches' Confs., Fayetteville, 1986—. Author: Cheerleading Coaches Manual, 1987; editor: (newsletter) N.C. AE Assn. Educators Polit. Action Com. Edn., 1973-76; contbr. articles to profl. jours. Named Outstanding Young Women of Am., 1975, Tchr. of Yr., Pine Forest High Sch., Fayetteville, 1976. Mem. Nat. Assn. Dance/Exercise Instrs., Nat. Assn. Cheerleading Coaches (mem. planning bd. 1986—), N.C. Cheerleading Coaches Assn. (bd. dirs. 1985—), Meth. Coll. Alumni Assn. (sec. 1970-72, pres. 1973-76, bd. dirs. 1976-80, Alumnus of Yr. 1977), Alpha Xi Delta. Democrat. Episcopalian. Home: 444 Morningside Dr Fayetteville NC 28301 Office: Meth Coll 5400 Ramsey St Fayetteville NC 28301

SYLVAN, RITA, painter, photographer, educator, writer; b. Mpls., 1928; children—Paul, Judy, Carolyn. B.A. in Fine Arts magna cum laude, U. Minn., 1948; postgrad. NYU, 1951, 52-53, Bennington Coll., 1983-84; M.A. in Fine Arts and Fine Arts Edn., Columbia U., 1967. Teaching asst. in art history U. Minn., Mpls., 1948-49, guest lectr. dept. humanities, 1948; asst. to Edward Steichen for exhbns. and book Mus. Modern Art, N.Y.C., 1951-53; asst. curator photography, asst. to John I. H. Baur exhbn. and book Revolution and Tradition in Am. Art Bklyn. Mus., 1951; tchr., art cons. Tenafly Adult Community Edn. (N.J.), 1966-77; tchr. art Tenafly Pub. Schs., 1966-78; a founder, tchr. Art Ctr. No. N.J., Englewood, 1957-62, dir. faculty, 1961, tchr., 1957-62, developer speakers bur., 1957; lectr., discussion leader in field; spl. ednl. projects. One-woman shows include: Columbia U., N.Y.C., 1963 Bergen Mus., Paramus, N.J., 1977, Nat. Endowment for Arts; group shows include: N.J. State Mus., 1970, Newark Mus., 1958, 59, 60, Audubon Artists, N.Y.C., 1962, 67, 84, Broward Art Guild, Ft. Lauderdale, Fla., 1981-86, Boca Raton Mus. Art (Fla.), 1984-88, Norton Gallery Art, Palm Beach, Fla., Hollywood Art and Culture Center, Thomas Ctr. Biennial, Gainesville-Tallahassee, 1986, Boca Raton Mus., Fla. Internat. U., others; represented in permanent collections: Rose Mus., Brandeis U.; work subject of profl. publs. Recipient Purchase award Columbia U., 1962, First award for painting Midwest Regional Exhbn., Mpls. Inst. Art, 1949, Nat. Assn. Women Artists award, 1966, Seasoned Eye, Modern Maturity Mag., 1986, award Boca Raton Profl. Artists, numerous others. Mem. Modern Artists Guild Inc. (a founder, trustee), Phi Beta Kappa, Kappa Delta Pi. Home and Studio: 23385 Barlake Dr Boca Raton FL 33433

SYLVESTER, NINA MARIE, sales executive; b. Detroit, Mar. 9, 1956; d. Joseph and Rosa Maria (Russo) Ratta; m. David William Sylvester, July 20, 1974; 1 child, Lynn Marie. Student, Macomb Community Coll., Warren, Mich., 1977-78; lic., Damark Inst. Real Estate, Fraser, Mich., 1976. Acctg. clk. La Salle Machine Tool Inc., Warren, 1973-75; office mgr. sales dept. United Real Estate, Warren, 1975-76; v.p., sales mgr. Wheatley Die Sets, Inc., Roseville, Mich., 1975-85; pres., owner Quality Die Sets, Inc., Mt. Clemens, Mich., 1985—. Recipient cert. Parker Hannifin Fluid Power Hydraulics Co., 1980. Mem. Nat. Assn. Female Execs., Soc. Mfg. Engrs. (sr.). Office: Quality Die Sets Inc 17097 17 Mile Rd Mount Clemens MI 48044

SYMONDS, ELSA ORNELAS (BONNIE), lawyer; b. Mexico City, Mexico, Dec. 15, 1939; came to U.S., 1946 naturalized, 1970; d. Jaime Josue and Esther Barber Ornelas; m. Michael F. Symonds, Sept. 5, 1964; children—Bonnie Michael, Joshua Michael. A.A. (valedictorian), San Antonio Coll., 1960; B.A. summa cum laude, St. Mary's U., 1967, J.D., 1980. Bar: Tex. 1980. Sec., Mexicana Airlines, San Antonio, 1960-65; translator R. F. Barnes Customhouse Brokers, San Antonio, 1969-72; instr. GT Program, Ft. Sam Houston, San Antonio, 1972-77; instr. San Antonio Coll., 1972—; sole practice law, San Antonio, 1981—. Exhibited one-man show Branch Savs. Assn., San Antonio, 1973. Mem., Hispanic Women's Com. San Antonio, 1983—; mem. Alternatives to Juvenile Delinquency Arrest Program, 1981—; mem. Guardianship Adv. Bd., San Antonio, 1983—; mem. Bexar County Women's Polit. Caucus, 1982—; lector, former mem. parish council Holy Spirit Roman Catholic Ch., San Antonio; bd. dirs. San Antonio YWCA. Named Outstanding Woman of Yr. Express-News, 1986, to San Antonio Women's Hall of Fame; recipient Women in Bus. Advocate award SBA, 1987. Mem. San Antonio Bar Assn., Tex. Trial Lawyers Assn., Assn. Trial Lawyers Am., ABA, Democrat. Office: 809 S St Mary's St San Antonio TX 78205-3408

SYMONDS, GENEVIEVE ELLEN, small business owner; b. Wilson Boro, Pa., Mar. 1, 1931; d. Jacob Rush and Ellen Maria (Brackmann) Twining; student Mercer County Coll., 1974, 76; m. Howard Eugene Symonds, May 21, 1950; children—Jess Howard, Bryce Dale. Acct., Miller's Chrysler Plymouth, Glen Gardner, N.J., 1950-55; officer mgr. Centrum Constrn. Corp., Clinton, N.J., 1969-76; owner, mgr. S & S Bus. Services, Clinton, 1976-81, Gen's Shop for Pappagallo, Clinton, 1982-85; owner, mgr. Gen's/Acctg., from 1982; owner-mgr. Glamour Shop, Clinton, 1986—; corp. sec. Nat. Sporting Frat. Ltd. Pres., Lebanon Twp. (N.J.) Vol. Fire Co. Aux., 1960-64, treas., 1964-68; pres. Lebanon Twp. PTA, 1965-69; committeeperson Hunterdon County Republican Party, 1968—, vice chmn., 1974-77; state committeeperson Rep. Party N.J., 1977-81; mem. com. George Washington council Boy Scouts Am., 1974-78; bd. dirs. Hunterdon County Learning Ctr., Califon, N.J., 1984—. Recipient Service award PTA, 1969, Spl. Service award Boy Scouts Am., 1974. Methodist. Clubs: Hunterdon County Women's Rep. (pres. 1970-74, treas. 1978-82), African Safari of N.Y. Weekly columnist Star newspaper, Washington, N.J., 1964-68; monthly columnist What's In The Pot, Today In Hunterdon Mag., 1977-80. Home: Mountain Top Rd RD #3 Glen Gardner NJ 08826 Office: #1 Main St Clinton NJ 08809

SYMONDS, JANA LERAYNE, military officer; b. Jacksonville, Tex., Dec. 27, 1957; d. Kenneth Vernon and Joy Lea (McCormick) Sheppard; m. Jay Loren Tapping, Dec. 17, 1976 (div. Dec. 1978); m. Daniel Reynolds Symonds, March 30, 1987. BA, Sam Houston State U., 1977. Tchr. Conroe (Tex.) Ind. Sch. Dist., 1978-79; commd. ensign USNR, 1979; advanced through grades to lt. USN, 1979; adminstrv. asst. Naval Air Sta., Agana, Guam, 1980-81; intelligence analyst Cmdr. in Chief Pacific Fleet, Pearl Harbor, HI, 1981-84; barracks officer Transient Personnel Unit, Great Lakes, Ill., 1984-87; officer recruiter Navy Recruiting Dist., Columbus, Ohio, 1987—. Mem. Women Officers Profl. Network (mem. chair 1985-86). Republican. Home: 477 Cherry Ravine Westerville OH 43081 Office: USN Recruiting Dist Fed Bldg 200 N High St Columbus OH 43215

SYMONDS, JOHNNIE PIRKLE, retired pscyhologist; b. Wynnewood, Okla., Apr. 5, 1900; d. John Thomas and Lillie Belle (Driver) Pirkle; m. Percival Mallon Symonds, Dec. 25, 1922. BA, U. Tex., 1920, MA, 1921; postgrad. in teaching, Columbia U., 1921-22, 26-27, 28-29, 30-31, NYU, 1975. Research asst. dept. psychology U. Tex., Austin, 1919-21; research assoc. Inst. Ednl. Research Tchrs. Coll. Columbia U., N.Y.C., 1921-22; psychologist Family Service Soc., Yonkers, N.Y., 1937-46; ret., 1960. Editor: Jour. Cons. Psychology, 1937-46; contbr. articles to profl. jours. Mem. Columbia Com. for Community Service, 1972—; active English in Action Program, English Speaking Union, Riverside Ch., N.Y.C., 1974-75, honored 91st anniversary mem., 1981. Mem. Am. Psychol. Assn., N.Y. State Psychol. Assn., Am. Assn. Applied Psychology, AAAS, Edn. Press Assn., World Fedn. Mental Health, AAUW, Pi Lambda Theta, Kappa Delta Pi. Club: Appalachian Mountain (hon. award 50th anniversary mem. 1980). Home: 106 Morningside Dr Apt 71 New York NY 10027

SYROKOMLA, IRENA EWA, accountant; b. Lodz, Poland, May 17, 1947; d. Arkadiusz and Anna (Fularska) Slusarski; divorced; 1 child: Joanna. Student, U. Warsaw, 1965-70, U. Western Ont., 1971-72; BA with Honors, U. Toronto, 1975. Office mgr., acct. Reinforced Earth Co. Ltd., Toronto, 1983-85, mgr. finance, 1985—. Mem. Cert. Gen. Accts. Assn. Toronto (cert.), Mensa. Office: Reinforced Earth Co Ltd, 190 Attwell Dr, Suite 501, Rexdale Can M9W6H8

SYSNIK, MARY ANN, educator, consultant; b. Newark, Jan. 24, 1931; d. Alfred and Mary Josephine (Galante) Francis; m. Joseph Anthony Sysnik, Apr. 15, 1951; 1 child, Joseph Keith. BA magna cum laude, Kean Coll., 1982, cert. in Family Studies, 1982. Cert. nursery, elem. tchr., N.J. Tchr. Happy Time Nursery Sch., West Caldwell, N.J., 1973-74; pediatric asst. to Dr. Sandra Samuels, West Orange, N.J., 1977-81; supr. Babyland Nursery, Inc., Newark, 1982-83; adminstr. Head Start Program, Elizabeth, N.J., 1983-84; dir. Pre-Care Learning Ctr., Orange, N.J., 1984-86; pres. Child Care Mgmt. Corp., West Orange, 1986—, ITP Learning Ctrs., Inc., West Orange, 1986—; cons. East Orange Vets. Hosp., N.J., 1987. Editor (newsletter) Precare Learning, 1984-86; contbr. to New Community Monthly, 1982-83. Den mother Boy Scouts Am., West Orange, 1970-72; vol. clk. Rutgers U. Health Ctr., Newark, 1980; fundraiser New Community Corp., Newark, 1982-83. Mem. N.J. Task Force on Child Care, Ecumenical Child Care Network, Assn. for Childhood Edn. Internat., Nat. Assn. for the Edn. Young Children, Coalition Infant Toddler Educators, Kean Coll. Alumni Assn., Kappa Delta Pi (named to nat. collegiate honor soc.), Alpha Sigma Lambda (named to nat. collegiate honor soc.). Democrat. Roman Catholic.

SYVERSEN, JUDITH SAWYER, nurse, educator; b. Watertown, N.Y., Sept. 21, 1941; d. Arthur Joseph and Florence Pearl (Hockey) Sawyer; m. David Eugene Alhart, June 10, 1961 (div. 1972); children—Randi Lynne, Scott David, Mark David, Janee J.; m. 2d, Robert Gerald Syversen, July 12, 1975; 1 step-dau., Ellen Lorraine. Lic. Practical Nurse, Rochester Gen. Hosp., 1962; R.N., Monroe Community Coll., 1972; B.S., Alfred U., 1979; M.S., SUNY-Buffalo, 1983. R.N., N.Y. Surg. nurse U. Rochester Med. Ctr. (N.Y.), 1972-73; operating room nurse Genesee Hosp., Rochester, 1973-75, inservice instr. operating room, 1975-79; operating room nurse Rochester Gen. Hosp., 1979-81; asst. prof. nursing Alfred U., Rochester, 1981; asst. prof. nursing Monroe Community Coll., Rochester, 1981-84, sec. faculty governance bd., 1983—, program advisor, 1983, sec. curriculum com. nursing dept., 1982-84, student nurse clin. advisor, 1981—, coordinator course, 1983; assoc. prof. nursing Keuka Coll., Keuka Park, N.Y. 1984-87; dir. Isabella Graham Hart Sch. Practical Nursing, Rochester Gen. Hosp., 1987—. Mem. Genesee Valley Nurses Assn., AAUP, Grad. Student Nurse Assn. (pres. SUNY-Buffalo 1981-82), Council Practical Nurse Programs N.Y. St., N.Y. State Council Practical Nursing Programs (exec. bd.) Sigma Theta Tau. Democrat. Club: Sodus Bay Yacht (trustee 1982-83, 85—). Home: 10 White Briar Pittsford NY 14534 Office: Isabell Graham Hart Sch Practical Nursing Rochester Gen Hosp 1425 Portland AVe Rochester NY 14621

SZABO, DAWN ANITA, systems engineer; b. Saginaw, Mich., Nov. 24, 1957; d. Joseph and Beryl R. Szabo. BS, Mich. State U., 1979, elem. edn. cert., 1982, MA, 1985. Elem. tchr. Alief Sch. Dist., Houston, 1982-84; microcomputer instr. O/E Systems, Troy, Mich., 1985; instl. designer Ednl. Devel. Ctr., Lansing, Mich., 1985; systems engr. Electronic Data Systems, Lansing, 1985—. Mem. Nat. Assn. Female Execs., Am. Soc. Tng. Devel., Mich. State Alumni. Home: 1720 Noble Rd Williamston MI 48895 Office: Electronic Data Systems 905 Southland MS1029 Lansing MI 48910

SZABO, DENISE ZAROTNEY, insurance company executive; b. New Britain, Conn., Aug. 3, 1953; d. Henry and Jacquelyn (Frank) Zarotney; m. John Frederick Szabo, June 6, 1981. Student, Tunxis Community Coll., 1972-73. Office adminstr. Lenko Finishing Inc., Plainville, Conn., 1971-75; customer service rep. Aetna Life and Casualty Co., Hartford, Conn., 1975-76; sr. pension analyst Artna Life and Casualty Co., Hartford, Conn., 1976—. Roman Catholic. Club: Tuesday Bowling (Plainville, Conn.) (v.p. 1985-86). Home: 20 Norton Rd Kensington CT 06037 Office: Aetna Life and Casualty Co 151 Farmington Ave Hartford CT 06156

SZABO, TERRY CARPENTER, architect; b. Bangor, Maine, Feb. 14, 1956; d. Peter Steven and Patricia Ann (Hurley) Carpenter; m. Lajos Laszlo Szabo, Sept. 25, 1982; 1 child, Rachel C. BA, U. Calif., Santa Cruz, 1977; MArch, U. Colo., 1981. Registered architect, Ohio. Designer Maxwell Silver Hammer, Boulder, Colo., 1978-81; draftsperson Syd Harrison, Architect, Denver, 1979, Milburn-Sparn, Boulder, 1979-80; asst. designer Skidmore, Owings & Merrill, Denver, 1980-81; designer Taft Attractions Group, Cin., 1982; pvt. practice architecture Columbus, Ohio, 1982-83; architect, designer Bohm-NBBJ, Columbus, 1983-85, Richardson-Smith-Nexus, Columbus, 1985-87; prin. Szabo & Szabo, Columbus, 1987—. Illustrator (children's Book) St. Lawrence Island, 1969. Grantee NSC., 1976; AIA scholar 1975, 80; recipient 1st, 2d and 3d place trophies Cen. Ohio Car Rally Club, Columbus, 1986-87. Mem. AIA (design award 1981), U.S. Inst. Theater Tech. Home: 201 W 4th Ave Columbus OH 43201 Office: Szabo & Szabo 995 Safin Rd Columbus OH 43204

SZALLAI, JANICE HIGGINS, transportation executive; b. N.J., July 23, 1954; d. Robert William and Rosalind G. (Ziemak) H. BS, U. Conn., 1976; M in Regional Planning, U. N.C., 1982. Tchr. Ho-Ho-Kus (N.J.) Pub. Schs., 1978-79, Haworth (N.J.) Pub. Schs., 1979-80; research assoc. Ctr. Urban and Regional Studies U. N.C., Chapel Hill, 1980-82; regional transp. planner N.J. Transp. Council, Newark, 1982-84; sr. transp. analyst Rail Transp. Dept. Port Authority N.Y. and N.J., N.Y.C., 1984-87, program assoc. mgmt. devel. Dept. Tunnels, Bridges and Terminals, 1987—. Co-author: Energy Conservation Through Land Use, 1982. Mem. Am. Planning Assn., Am. Pub. Transit Assn., Women's Transp. Seminar (treas. 1984-85, bd. dirs. 1985-86). Home: 39 Bayberry Dr Somerset NJ 08873 Office: Port Authority NY and NJ Tunnels Bridges Terminals Dept 1 World Trade Ctr 71 W New York NY 10048

SZARO, JUDITH SALOMEA, advertising executive, artist, political worker; b. Elizabeth, N.J., Aug. 2, 1952; d. Albert Stanley and Mary Stella (Turon) S. BA, Douglass Coll., 1974; postgrad., Rutgers U., 1987—; cert. in art, Albert Pels Sch. Art, 1980. Mktg. researcher Phila. Mftr. Mutual Ins. Co., N.Y.C., 1976-78; advt. bd. artist Spiros Assocs., N.Y.C., 1980-82; freelance comml. artist, polit. fundraiser N.J., 1982-85; advt. exec. Grey Advt., Inc., N.Y.C., 1985—. Corr. sec. Greater Elizabeth Democratic Club, Union County, N.J., 1982-85; local fundraiser, campaign promoter Raymond J. Lesniak for N.J. State Senator, 1982-85, fin. sec., 1982-85. Democrat. Roman Catholic. Office: Grey Advt Inc 777 3d Ave New York NY 10017

SZATALOWICZ, VICTORIA LYNN, physician; b. Manhattan, Kans., June 19, 1948; d. Marion Thomas and Helen Maureen Szatalowicz. B.S., U. Wis., 1970; M.D., U. Okla., 1974. Internal medicine intern Duke U., Durham, N.C., 1974-75, jr. asst. resident, 1975-76, sr. asst. resident, 1976-77, clin. fellow nephrology, U. Colo., Denver, 1977-78, research fellow nephrology, 1978-80; physician emergency dept. Encino Hosp. (Calif.), Beverly Hosp., Montebello, Calif., Washington Hosp., Culver City, Calif., med. dir. La Palma Office Am. Emergicenters, Inc., 1984-86, Centincla Hosp. Airport Med. Clinic, 1986—. Mgr. Pacific region Hunger Project Briefing Leaders, Internat., 1983-84; mem. Wash. Hosp. Infectious Disease Com., Culver City, 1982-84. Recipient Mrs. Fay Lester award U. Okla. Med. Sch., 1974; Anesthesiology Directorship scholar Am. Soc. Anesthesiologists, 1972—.Mem. Am. Med. Women's Assn., ACP, Am. Soc. Internal Medicine, Am. Soc. Emergency Physicians, Student Am. Med. Assn., Delta Zeta (v.p. 1969-70). Office: 9601 S Sepulveda Blvd Los Angeles CA 90045

SZCZESNY, FRANCES EVELYN, human resources executive; b. Bklyn., Aug. 23, 1951; d. Charles and Anne Betty (Lerner) Feurman; m. Thomas A. Szczesny, July 15, 1972; 1 child, Spencer Evan. BA in English, SUNY, Buffalo, 1972; MS in Mgmt., Poly. Inst. N.Y., 1977. Editor John Wiley & Sons, Inc., N.Y.C., 1974-76; asst. dir. personnel Vis. Nurse Service N.Y., N.Y.C., 1977-81, dir. employee relations, 1984-87; pres. HRM Services, Marlboro, N.J., 1987—; human resources cons. Vis. Nurses Assn., S.I., 1981-84, Women Aware, Inc., New Brunswick, N.J., 1986-87, Metaplex Mgmt. Services, Inc., Red Bank, N.J., 1987—, Inst. Bus. Careers, Highland Park, N.J., 1987; adj. lectr. Brookdale Coll., Lincroft, N.J., 1987—; adj. lectr. Ocean County Coll., Toms River, N.J., 1988—. V.p. Whitter Oaks Civic Assn., Morganville, N.J., 1980-81. Mem. AAUW, Am. Soc. for Hosp. Personnel Adminstrn., Am. Soc. Personnel Adminstrn. (speaker), Internat. Assn. Personnel Women (speaker, bd. dirs., program chair 1987—), Nat. Assn. Female Execs., Western Monmouth County C. of C. (speaker). Club: Hadassah (Marlboro, N.J.). Lodge: Soroptimists. Home: 45 Georgian Bay Dr Morganville NJ 07751

SZMYT, DAVENA D., retail executive; b. Brockton, Mass., Nov. 18, 1939; d. David Elroy Dart and Lorena (Young) Love; m. Henry Joseph Szmyt, Aug. 3, 1969; children: Paul Scott, Steven Todd, Christopher Henry. Diploma, Peter Bent Brigham Hosp. Sch. Nursing, 1960. Charge nurse Boston Lying-In Hosp., 1960-62; supr. operating room Beverly Hills (Calif.) Doctors Hosp., 1962-64; nurse Peter Bent Brigham Hosp., Boston, 1964-65; organizer, head nurse Boston City Hosp. and Harvard Surg. ICU, Boston, 1967-68; instr. nursing Lawrence (Mass.) Gen. Hosp. Sch. Nursing, 1968-70; asst. dir. nursing, dir. inservice edn. Hunt Meml. Hosp., Danvers, Mass., 1970-77; organizer 1st regional health ctr. Urgent Care Unit, Wilmington, Mass., 1977-80; co-owner, bus. mgr. Freedman Fur Assocs., Inc., Lawrence, Mass., 1980-84, owner, pres., 1984—; owner, pres. Freedman Furs. of N.H. Inc., Plaistow, N.H., 1984—; mem. adv. com. Bradlees Dept. Store Chain, Plaistow, N.H., 1980; bd. dirs. Rockingham County Trust Bk. Founder Timberlane Civic Assn., Plaistow, 1972; founder, past pres., trustee Plaistow Area Commerce Exchange Inc., 1985-86; sec. Plaistow Safety Complex Com., 1984-86, bldg. com. 1985-87; mem. Plaistow Budget Com., 1985, bd. of selectmen, 1985—; sec. property com. First Bapt. Ch., Plaistow, 1986-88; dir. Plaistow Civil Def., 1980-87. Recipient Outstanding Vol. award Gov. N.H., 1986, named one of Outstanding Women Achievement Manchester Union Leader, 1986. Mem. Plaistow Bus. and Profl. Women Fedn. (pres. 1985-86), Plaistow Area C. of C., Master Furrier Guild. Republican. Home: 22 Forrest St Plaistow NH 03865 Office: Freedman Furs of NH Inc 91 Plaistow Rd #4 Plaistow NH 03865

SZPREJDA, EVELYN A., international marketing executive; b. Green Bay, Wis., Nov. 30, 1944; s. John O. and Pearl (Cwiak) S. Student, U. Wis., 1962-63, 67-68, U. Minn., 1975-77; BA, Coll. St. Thomas, 1980, postgrad., 1987—. Various adminstrv. positions Campbell-Mithun Advt., Mpls., 1968-71; adminstrv. asst. Internat. div. First Nat. Bank Mpls., 1971-73; ops. admintr. Far East ops. Medtronic Inc., Mpls., 1973-76, mktg. coordinator, 1976-78, market adminstrn. specialist Internat. div., 1978-79, mgr. internat. market planning and adminstrv. mgr., 1979-80, mgr. internat. market info. and research, 1980-81; dir. market research and planning Gibsongroup, Inc., Mpls., 1981-82; trade ops. devel. mgr. Control Data Commerce Internat., Mpls., 1982-83; mktg. mgr. healthcare products, 1983-84; dir. planning and new program devel. First Internat. Corp., Mpls., 1984-85; mgr. IXI World Trade Corp., 1985-87; instr. Coll. St. Thomas, 1984-85; export cons., 1981—; ptnr. Intermar Group Ltd., 1985—; gen. mgr. the LISAshop, 1986—. Mem. Minn. Gov.'s Task Force on Internat. Bus. Edn., 1983-84, World Time Capsule Fund, 1987—; precinct chairperson Rep. party. Recipient Bus. Woman Leader award YMCA, 1980. Mem. Am. Mktg. Assn., Internat. Advt. Assn., Japan Am. Soc. Minn. (sec. 1981-82), Mpls. C. of C. (world trade com.), Minn. World Trade Assn. (bd. dirs. 1980, pres. 1983—), World Timecapsule Fund (adv. com. 1987—). Roman Catholic. Club: Greenway Athletic. Home and Office: 2438 13th Avenue S Minneapolis MN 55404

TABACHUK, EMELIA, banker; b. Passaic, N.J., Aug. 3, 1926; d. Michael and Fannie (Stefanyk) T.; student Drake Bus. Coll., 1956, N.Y. Inst. Credit, 1978-80. With Marine Midland Bank, N.Y.C., 1946—, adminstrv. asst., 1975-76, ops. asst., 1976-78, comml. banking officer, 1978—, asst. v.p., 1982-85; retired 1985. Mem. Nat. Assn. Bank Women, Nat. Assn. Female Execs., Am. Soc. Profl. and Exec. Women. Home: 78 Stadtmauer Dr Clifton NJ 07013 Office: 140 Broadway New York City NY 10015

TABAKIN, LORAINE SMITH, lawyer; b. Cambridge, Mass., July 2, 1940; d. Albert Frances Smith and Eileen (Mullett) Boynton; m. Frank Tabakin, Sept. 1, 1963; children: Jennifer, Steven. BS, Simmons Coll., 1962; MSW, Columbia U., 1964; JD, U. Pitts., 1976. Bar: Pa. 1976, U.S. Supreme Ct. 1980, U.S. Ct. Appeals (3d cir.), 1984. Psychiat. social worker Altro Health Rehab. Service, N.Y.C., 1964-65, Pitts. Child Guidance Ctr., 1965-67; asst. county solicitor Allegheny County Law Dept., Pitts., 1976-80; assoc. atty. Strassburger, McKenna, Pitts., 1980-83; ptnr. Tabakin, Carroll & Curtin, Pitts., 1984—. Mem. exec. bd. 14th Ward Dem. Club, Pitts., 1972-73, 80-86; bd. dirs. ACLU, Pitts., 1978-82. Mem. ABA, Pa. Bar Assn., Allegheny County Bar Assn. (council family law sect.), Assn. Trial Lawyers Am. Office: Tabakin Carroll & Curtin 1430 Grant Bldg Pittsburgh PA 15219

TABBERT, RONDI JO, accountant; b. Dallas, Mar. 14, 1953; d. Jack H. and June F. (Williams) Russell; m. William Henry Tabbert, Nov. 16, 1979. A.A., Tarrant County Jr. Coll., 1975; B.S. in Bus., U. Tex.-Dallas, 1980; M.B.A., U. Dallas, 1984. C.P.A., Tex. Bookkeeper, Kelly-Moore Paint, Dallas, 1976-78; corp. acct. Gen. Portland, Dallas, 1978-80; chief acct. W.R. Grace & Co., Dallas, 1980-83; controller Little & Assocs., Dallas, 1983-85; prin. Rondi J. Tabbert, CPA, Desoto, Tex., 1985—; accting. instr., Cedar Valley Community Coll., 1987. Weeky fin. columnist De Soto Tribune, 1986—. Mem. Tex. Soc. CPAs, Am. Inst. CPAs, Nat. Soc. Tax Profls., Nat. Assn. Female Execs., Dallas Soc. CPAs (tax edn. com. 1985-86, vice chmn. 1986-87, chmn. 1987—), Am. Women's Soc. CPAs, Am. Bus. Women's Assn. (program com. 1986-87, program chmn. 1987—), DeSoto C. of C. Mem. Libertarian party. Home: 1055 Turner Ave Dallas TX 75208 Office: 911 N Hampton #104 DeSoto TX 75115

TABEN, EVA MARX, librarian, genetic counselor; b. Munich, Germany, Oct. 1, 1937; came to U.S., 1939; d. Karl Jacob and Ruth (Hirschland) Marx; m. Stanley Taben, Aug. 25, 1957; children—Peter, Charles, Elizabeth. B.A., Sarah Lawrence Coll., 1970, M.S., 1971; M.L.S., Columbia U., 1980. Genetic counselor Albert Einstein Coll. Medicine, Bronx, N.Y., 1971-79; spl. services cons. Westchester Library System, Elmsford, N.Y., 1981—. Chairperson bd. dirs. Westchester Ind. Living Ctr., Inc., White Plains, N.Y., 1983—, adv. council Westchester Community Coll. Retirement Inst. Mem. ALA, N.Y. Library Assn., Westchester Library Assn., Westchester Assn. Continuing Edn. Democrat. Jewish. Home: 36 Paddington Rd Scarsdale NY 10583 Office: Westchester Library System 8 Westchester Plaza Elmsford NY 10523

TABER, CAROL A., magazine publisher. AA, Green Mountain Coll., 1965. Network mgr. Media Networks, Inc., 1970-74; N.Y. advt. mgr. Ladies' Home Jour., 1974-79; assoc. publisher, advt. dir. Working Woman, N.Y.C., 1979-83, publisher, 1984—. Address: Working Woman Mag 342 Madison Ave New York NY 10173 *

TABER, LINDA PERRIN, public relations executive; b. Marshalltown, Iowa, Dec. 30, 1941; d. Burr H. Perrin and Luella (Memler); m. Roy Howard Pollack, Oct. 1, 1983; m. Allan D. Taber, Apr. 26, 1969 (div. 1976). B.A., U. Iowa, 1964; M.A., Syracuse U., 1969. Account supr. Ketchum, Macleod & Grove, N.Y.C., 1969-73; v.p. Carol Moberg, Inc., N.Y.C., 1973-78; dir. Ketchum Pub. Relations, N.Y.C., 1979-83; sr. v.p. Ketchum Pub. Relations, 1983—. Mem. Pub. Relations Soc. Am., The Fashion Group, Women Execs. in Pub. Relations, Women in Communications.

TABLEMAN FARRIS, BETH CASSEL, administrative assistant, business manager; b. Phila., May 10, 1948; d. Edward Clayton and Eleanor Adel

(DeGatis) Cassel; m. G. Kent Tableman, Oct. 17, 1969 (div. Feb. 1983); children: Nathan E., Adam R., Katie M., m. Albert W. Farris Jr., July 25, 1987. BS, Pa. State U., 1969; postgrad. in bus., Temple U., 1969-71; postgrad. in paralegal studies, Beal Coll., Bangor, Maine, 1982-84. Cons. Avco Corp., Phila., 1969-72; with sales and mktg. Milton Bradley Co., Phila., 1972-74; owner Reality Mart, Boston, 1974-76; ptnr., bus. mgr., cons.. G. Kent Tableman, DDS, Bangor, Maine, 1976-82; cons. BCT Cons., Bangor, 1978-85; adminstrv. asst. sales Pejepscot Assocs., Bangor, 1984-85; adminstrv. asst., bus. mgr. Resource Devel., Inc., Brunswick, Maine, 1986— Contbr. articles to dental jours. Chairperson Rep. Women, Phila., 1969-74, Citizens Against Damn, Bangor, 1978. Recipient Outstanding Contbn. of Time award Nat. Hemophiliac Assn., 1968, Outstanding Contbn. award Boston U. Dental Sch., 1976, grantee, 1974. Roman Catholic. Home: 1616 River Rd Brunswick ME 04011 Office: Resource Devel Inc 10 Cushing St Brunswick ME 04011

TABNER, MARY FRANCES, educator; b. Rochester, N.Y., Dec. 11, 1918; d. William Herman and Mary Frances (Willenbacher) Arndt; m. James Gordon Tabner, June 27, 1942; 1 child, Barbara Jean. BA, SUNY, Albany, 1940, MA, 1959; postgrad., U. Rochester, Albany, 1944, 45, Northwestern U. (John Hay fellow), Albany, 1963-64, U. Manchester (Eng.), Albany, 1971-72. Tchr. history pub. schs. Mattituck, N.Y., 1940-43, Gorham, N.Y., 1943-46; tchr. pub. schs. Waterford, N.Y., 1949-55; tchr. social studies Shaker High Sch., Latham, N.Y., 1959-83, now also dir. Russian studies seminar, 1959-83, ret., 1983; tchr. ch. history Our Lady of Assumption Ch., Latham. Author bibliographies on Russian history, Am. studies. N.Y. State Regents independent study grantee, 1966. Mem. Nat. Council Social Studies, N.Y. State United Tchrs., Assn. Advancement Slavic Studies, SUNY, Albany Alumni Assn., History and Art Council Albany, Am., N.Y., Capital Dist. councils for social studies, Shaker Heritage Soc. (trustee, guide, tchr.), English Speaking Union, Am. Assn. Ret. Persons. Republican. Roman Catholic. Home: 557 Columbia St Cohoes NY 12047

TABOR, MILA VILLASOR, systems engineer; b. Bacolod City, Philippines, May 5, 1954; came to U.S., 1975; d. Guillermo Piccio and Milagros (Araneta) Villasor; m. Raymond J. Tabor, Dec. 16, 1982. B. in Bus. and Econs., Lewis U., Lockport, Ill., 1977; postgrad. DePaul U., 1983, Nat. Coll. Edn., Evanston, Ill. Dir. Rural Bank of San Fernando, Inc., Cebu, Philippines, 1974—; asst. to prof. Lewis U., 1975-77; pres. Tabor Industries, Chgo., 1978-84; systems programmer Sears Merchandise Group, Chgo., 1984-87; systems engr. Notis Inc., Evanston, 1987—; project mgr. Primary Cons. Services, N.Y.C., 1980-81; group benefit analyst Bankers Life & Casualty, Chgo., 1981-83. Editor, Systems Project, Users Manual Documentation, 1983. Guide Girl Scouts of Philippines, Manila, 1973. Recipient Nat. Observer award Dow Jones/Lewis U., 1977. Mem. Assn. Info. Mgrs., Nat. Assn. Female Execs., Assn. Women in Computing, Phi Gamma Nu (coeditor newsletter 1975-77). Lodge: Soroptimist of Philippines (organizer, dir. 1973).

TABOR, SANDRA L., diversified energy company executive; b. Devils Lake, N.D., Dec. 19, 1954; d. Allen Thomas and LaVonne (Everson) T. BS in Edn., U. N.D., 1977, JD, 1981. Corp. counsel Knife River Coal Mining Co., Bismarck, N.D., 1981-85, corp. counsel, asst. sec., 1985-87; asst. v.p. corp. communications MDU Resources Group, Inc., Bismarck, 1987-88, v.p., 1988—; def. counsel N.D. Army N.G., Bismarck, 1983-87, environ. legal officer, 1987—; legal advisor N.D. N.G. Assn., Inc., Bismarck, 1983—, Mil. Service Club, Inc., Bismarck, 1983—, N.G. Enlisted Assn., Inc., Bismarck, 1984—; spl. asst. atty. gen. State of N.D., Bismarck, 1984—. Contbr. articles to profl. jours. Vol. March of Dimes, Bismarck, 1984—, United Way, Bismarck, 1985—; legal advisor N.D. Spl. Olympics, Grand Forks, N.D., 1987. Decorated 1st Oak Leaf Cluster, Army Commendation medal, Army Achievement medal. Mem. N.D. State Bar Assn. (legis. com., chairwoman corp. and bus. sect. 1983-86), N.D. Lignite Council (chairwoman fed. leasing policy com. 1986-87, Disting. Service award 1987). Republican. Lutheran. Club: Riverwood Golf Assn. (Bismarck) (pres. 1986-87). Office: MDU Resource Group Inc 400 N 4th St Bismarck ND 58501

TACKOVICH, JO ANN, retired tire company executive, fashion and image consultant; b. Hampton, Tenn., May 4, 1938; d. John Paul and Lena Jane (Cooke) Greer; m. Sidney Clayton Jones, Dec. 22, 1956 (div. Apr. 1959); 1 child, Randall; m. Martin David Tackovich, June 18, 1966. Student U. Arkon, 1974-75. Cert. profl. sec. Tech.-chem. sec. Goodyear Tire & Rubber Co., Akron, 1959-69, corp. law sec., 1969-75, corp. law paralegal, 1975-81, consumer relations profl., 1981-87; owner, pres. Exclusively Jo Ann, fashion image and wardrobing cons., Akron, 1986—. Mem. Akron Women's Network (founder 1978, mem. bd. 1978-81, sec.-treas. 1978-80). Republican. Avocations: fashion, running, aerobics, weight lifting, reading. Home: 1052 N Portage Path Akron OH 44313 Office: Exclusively Jo Ann 1835 W Market St Akron OH 44313

TAFFET, ELIZABETH ROSE, national fund raising consultant; b. Bklyn., July 10, 1934; d. Morris and Sylvia (Samovitz) Gropper; m. Arthur S. Taffet, June 11, 1953 (div. Dec. 1982); children—George, Allen, Mimi. Cert. in Fin. Planning Adelphi U., 1979-84, Clark U., Worcester, Mass., 1952-53, Philanthropy Tax Inst., N.Y.C., 1981, 84. Research dir. Douglas Lawson, Inc., N.Y.C., 1979-80; dir. planned giving Jewish Nat. Fund, N.Y.C., 1980-81, nat. dir. major gifts and bequests, 1981-85, Deferred Planning Concepts, 1985—, Planned Giving Concepts, 1986—; asst. coordinator Found. Caucus White House Conf. Library and Info. Services, 1979; account exec. Juvenile Diabetes Research, Miami, 1979; preparer planned giving instruments Care, Inc., N.Y.C., 1979. Research editor Foundation 500, 1979. Vice pres. Hadassah, Oceanside, N.Y., 1975, also editor newspaper; community rep. Middle States Evaluation Com., Oceanside, 1976; pres. Oceanside council PTA, 1977, also editor newsletter; mem. Adult Edn. Adv. Com., Oceanside, 1978, dir. Women's Orgn. Yeshiva U., 1987—. Mem. Nat. Soc. Fund-Raising Execs., N.Y. League of Bus. and Profl. Women, Nat. Speakers Assn., Internat. Assn. Fin. Planning, Women in Fin. Devel., Am. Women's Econ. Devel. Assn., Women's Econ. Devel. Assn. Corp., N.Y. Planned Giving Assn., Nat. Assn. Female Execs. Democrat. Home: 135 Irma Dr Oceanside NY 11572

TAFT-PRATER, SUSAN MERRITT, insurance company executive; b. Kenosha, Wis., Sept. 11, 1948; d. Thomas Samuel and Alice Marion (Muszynski) Merritt. BA in Polit. Sci., U. Wis.-Parkside, 1970. Adminstrv. asst. Owen Steel Co., Columbia, S.C., 1970-72; asst. So. dist. mgr. Internat. Salt Co., Atlanta, 1972-75; policyholder service mgr., field underwriter mgr. Montgomery Ward Ins. co., Chgo., 1975-78; dist sales mgr. Montgomery Ward Ins. co., Oakland, Calif., 1975-78; exec. mktg. mgr. Unigard Ins. Co., San Jose, Calif., 1978-80; asst. v.p. Fin. Guardian, Inc., Kansas City, Mo., 1980-82; sr. v.p. Allied Assocs., Inc., Santa Clara, Calif., 1982-85; dir. account devel. Woodsmall Pub. Risk Services, Kansas City, Mo., 1985—; exec. dir. Mid Am. Regional Council Ins. Trust, 1987—. Democrat. Roman Catholic. Office: MARCIT 300 Rivergate Ctr 600 Broadway Kansas City MO 64105

TAGGART, VALERIE MANNING, judge; b. Cranbrook, B.C., Can., Aug. 9, 1926; d. Viril Zenis and Jessie Manson (Burgess) Manning; m. Kenneth Elliot Meredith, Sept. 7, 1949 (div. 1976); children—Deborah, Guy, Daphne; m. John David Taggart, June 18, 1981, LL.B., U. B.C. Cert. barrister, solicitor. Assoc. Meredith & Co., Vancouver, 1949-50; research assoc. Fulton Cumming & Co., Vancouver, 1972-74; acting dir. Continuing Legal Edn., Vancouver, 1974-76; exec. dir. Law Found., Vancouver, 1976-80; judge, Vancouver, 1980—; chmn. Family Court Com., Vancouver. Pres. Jr. League, Vancouver; v.p. B.C. Cancer Found., Vancouver; bd. dirs. United Way, Vancouver. Served as wren W.R.C.N.S., 1944-45. Mem. Provincial Judges Assn., Gamma Phi Beta. Avocations: golf; skiing; gardening; fishing. Office: Provincial Ct, 814 Richards, Vancouver, BC Canada V6J 2K3

TAGLIARINO, MARY BETH, entomologist, federal agency administrator; b. Stanford, Tex., June 7, 1955; d. John Joseph and Jayne-a-Beth (Darnabee) T. Bachelor's degree, Tex. A&M, 1978, Master's degree, 1980. Port of entry officer USDA, APHIS, PPQ, Houston, 1981-85; domestic officer 1st class USDA, APHIS, PPQ, Thonotosassa, Fla., 1985—. Home: 6510 Brandon Circle Riverview FL 33569 Office: PO Box 249 Thonotosassa FL 33592

TAGLIO, LESLIE WYNN, cosmetic company executive; b. Inglewood, Calif., Sept. 29, 1954; d. Bud Peter E. and Georgia Mae Taglio. AA, Sierra Coll., 1974; BA, U. Calif., Davis, 1976. Store mgr. Joseph Magnin, San Francisco, 1978-80; spl. events coordinator Macy's of Calif., San Francisco, 1980-81; ptnr. DR Assocs., San Francisco, 1981-88; sales rep. Prestige Fragrances Ltd., San Francisco, 1984—; cons. Closetmaid Inc., Fla., 1984-86, Word Processing Services, San Francisco, 1986-87. Mem. San Francisco Vol. Symphony League, Jr. League of San Francisco, Am. Soviet Youth Orch. com., 1988; chairperson Children's Garden, San Francisco, 1985, Youth Advocates, San Francisco, 1986. Mem. Nat. Assn. Profl. Women, Delta Delta Delta. Club: Spinsters (San Francisco) (pres. 1987-88).

TAGUE, JEAN RUTH, recreational educator; b. Kirkman, Iowa, Dec. 20, 1927; d. Clifford and Ruth (Morgan) T. B.S., Drake U., 1950; M.A., Columbia U., 1955; Ph.D., U. So. Calif., 1968. Cert. therapeutic recreation specialist. Lectr. dept. recreation, UCLA, 1960-64; pres. Creative Leisure Planning, Inc., Los Angeles, 1965-70; prof. Calif. State U., Northridge, 1970-79; prof., chmn. dept. recreation Tex. Woman's U., Denton, 1979—; cons. in field. Editor mag. Programming Trends in Therapeutic Recreation 1980—. Innovative Recreation Programs grantee U.S. Office Edn., Washington, 1983—; Therapeutic Recreation Training grantee U.S. Office Edn., Washington, 1975—. Mem. Nat. Recreation and Park Assn. (bd. dirs. 1977-80), Gerontological Soc., Nat. Council on Aging, Tex. Therapeutic Recreation Section (pres. 1982-83), Calif. Therapeutic Recreation Section (bd. dirs. 1982-83; outstanding recreator, 1978), Nat. Therapeutic Recreation Soc. (pres. 1974-75, Citation for Dedicated Leadership and Service, Disting. Service award). Home: 2225 E McKinney Denton TX 76201 Office: Tex Woman's U Dept Recreation Box 23717 Denton TX 76204

TAINER, EVELINA MARGHERITA, economist; b. Turin, Piedmont, Italy, June 14, 1958; came to U.S., 1962; d. Daniel L. and Onorina M. (Zocovich) T. BA, U. Ill., Chgo., 1979, MA, 1980, PhD, 1985. Economist 1st Nat. Bank Chgo., 1980-85, sr. economist, 1985—; economist Fed. Res. Bank Chgo., 1985; instr. Chgo. State U., 1980, Oakton Community Coll., Des Plaines, Ill., 1981, Chgo. City Coll., 1984; adj. asst. prof. U. Ill.-Chgo., 1987-88; vis. lectr. Ill. Inst. Tech., 1987. Mem. Am. Econ. Assn., Nat. Assn. Bus. Economists (pres. fin. round table 1986—), Com. on Status of Women in Econ. Professions, Chgo. Assn. Bus. Economists, Omicron Delta Epsilon. Roman Catholic. Office: 1st Nat Bank Chgo One 1st Nat Plaza Suite 0476 Chicago IL 60670-0476

TAIRA, FRANCES SNOW, nurse educator; b. Glasgow, Scotland, Feb. 27, 1935; came to U.S., 1959, naturalized, 1964; d. Thomas and Isabel (McDonald) Snow; m. Albert Taira, June 20, 1962; children—Albert, Deborah, Paul. B.S.N., U. Ill., 1974, M.S.N., 1976; Ed.D., No. Ill. U., 1980. Staff nurse various hosps., 1959-73; instr. nursing Triton Coll., 1976-81; asst. prof. nursing Loyola U., Chgo., 1981—. Mem. Am. Nurses Assn., Ill. Nurses Assn., U. Ill. Nursing Alumni Assn., Sigma Theta Tau, Phi Delta Kappa. Roman Catholic. Author: Aging: A Guide for the Family, 1983, Home Nursing: Basic Rehabilitation Care of Adults, 1986; contbr. articles to profl. jours. Home: 404 Atwater Ave Elmhurst IL 60126 Office: Loyola U Lake Shore Campus 6525 N Sheridan Rd Chicago IL 60626

TAJON, ENCARNACION (CONNIE) FONTECHA, retired educator, association executive; b. San Narciso, Zambales, Philippines, Mar. 25, 1920; came to U.S., 1948; d. Espiridion Maggay and Gregoria (Labrador) Fontecha; m. Felix B. Tajon, Nov. 17, 1948; children: Ruth F., Edward F. Teacher's cert., Philippine Normal Coll., 1941; BEd, Far Eastern U., Manila, 1947; MEd, Seattle Pacific U., 1976. Cert. tchr., Philippines. Tchr. pub. schs. San Narciso and Manila, 1941-47; coll. educator Union Coll. Manila, 1947-48; tchr. Auburn (Wash.) Sch. Dist., 1956-58, Renton (Wash.) Sch. Dist., 1958-78; owner, operator Manila-Zambales Internat. Grill, Seattle, 1980-81; Connie's Lumpia House and Ethnic Restaurant, Seattle, 1981-84; founder, pres. Tajon-Fontecha, Inc., Renton, 1980—, United Friends of Filipinos in Am. Found., Renton, 1985—; founder Tajon Fontecha Permanent Scholarship Fund of U. Wash. Filipino Alumni Assn., 1978; U. Wash. Alumni Assn. Endowed Scholarship Fund. Bd. dirs. women's div. Global Ministries United Meth. Ch., 1982-84; bd. dirs. Renton Area Youth Services, 1980-85; mem. Mcpl. Arts Commn. Renton, 1980—; chair fundraising steering com. Washington State Women's Polit. Caucus, 1984—. Recipient spl. cert. of award Project Hope, 1976, U.S. Bicentennial Commn., 1976, UNICEF, 1977; named Parent of Yr. Filipino Community of Seattle, Inc., 1984. Mem. U. Wash. Alumni Assn. (life), U. Wash. Filipino Alumni Assn. (pres. Wash. State chpt. 1985-87), NEA, Renton Retired Tchrs. Assn., Wash. State Edn. Assn., Am. Assn. Retired Persons, Nat. Retired Tchrs. Assn., Renton Hist. Mus., United Meth. Women, Pres.'s Forum, Alpha Sigma, Delta Kappa Gamma. Democrat. Home and Office: 2033 Harrington Pl NE Renton WA 98056

TALAB, ROSEMARY STURDEVANT, library/media, educational technology specialist, educator; b. Rochester, Minn., Oct. 6, 1948; d. Raymond C. and Inga E. (Sattre) Sturdevant; m. Dan H. Talab, July 9, 1980; children: Grant, Pat. B.A., Wichita State U., 1971; M.A. in Library Sci. Edn., M.A. in Audio Visual Edn., Ariz. State U., 1975; Ph.D., U. So. Calif., Los Angeles, 1979. Tchr. Smith Ctr. (Kans.) schs., 1971-73; intern, then asst. Mesa Community Coll., Sacaton, Ariz., 1975-76; sr. researcher, U. So. Calif., 1977-79; asst. prof. Portland (Oreg.) State U., 1980-81, audiovisual coordinator Hollywood Presbyn. Med. Ctr., Los Angeles, 1981-84; asst. prof. Coll. Edn., Kans. State U., 1984—; cons., com. mem. Med. Audiovisual Consortium, Los Angeles, 1982-84. Recipient award U. So. Calif. Alumni Assn., 1977, plaque of appreciation, Faculty Senate Gila River (Ariz.) Career Ctr., 1976; Educare scholar, 1977-79. Mem. Computer Users in Edn., ALA, Mid-Continental Med. Library Assn., Assn. Ednl. Communications and Tech. (chairperson copyright com.), Am. Film Inst., Kans. Assn. for Edn. Com. and Tech. (bd. dirs. 1987—, Cert. Appreciation 1985-87), Kans. Assn. Sch. Librarians, Pi Lambda Theta, Kappa Delta Pi, Alpha Phi. Author: Commonsense Copyright, 1986, Copyright and Educational Media, A Guide to Fair Use and Permissions Procedures, 1988. Contbr. numerous articles to profl. jours., books. Office: Kans State U Dept Curriculum Instrn Manhattan KS 66506

TALBOT, PAMELA, public relations executive; b. Chgo., Aug. 10, 1946. BA in English, Vassar Coll., 1968. Reporter Worcester, Mass. Telegram and Gazette, 1970-72; account exec. Daniel J. Edelman, Inc., Chgo., 1972-74, account supr., 1974-76, v.p., 1976-78, sr. v.p., 1978-83, exec. v.p., 1983—, exec. v.p., gen. mgr., 1984—. Office: Daniel J Edelman Inc 211 E Ontario St Chicago IL 60611 *

TALBOTT, LINDA HOOD, educator, foundation executive, communications executive; b. Kansas City, Mo., Dec. 29, 1941; d. Henry H. and Helen E. (Hamrick) Hood; B.A. with highest distinction, U. Mo., 1962, M.A. (grad. fellow), 1964, Ph.D., 1973; postgrad. (postdoctoral fellow) Harvard U. Inst. Ednl. Mgmt., 1974; m. Thomas H. Talbott, Mar. 5, 1965. Prof. English, Met. Jr. Coll., Kansas City, Mo., 1963-67; prof. English, Queensborough Community Coll., Bayside, N.Y., 1967-68; prof. English, editor Nassau Rev., Nassau Community Coll., Garden City, N.Y., 1968-69; prof. English, adminstr. Lesley Coll., Cambridge, Mass., 1969; founding editor Tempo mag. and devel. officer U. Mo., Kansas City, 1969-76, dir. spl. projects Office of Chancellor, 1976—, adj. prof. edn., 1975—; pres. Talbott & Assocs., Kansas City, 1975—; exec. dir. Clearinghouse for Midcontinent Founds., Kansas City, 1975-85, pres., 1985—; dir. Kansas City Power and Light Co., 1983; lectr., cons. in field; mem. gov's adv. task force on literacy State of Mo., 1987—. Bd. dirs. exec. com. United Community Services/Heart of Am. United Way, 1974-82; mem. exec. com. The Central Exchange, 1978-85; bd. dirs. The Central Exchange Programming Corp., 1984—, Women's Employment Network, Kansas City, 1985—; mem. exec. com. Dimensions Unltd., Kansas City, 1973-77; commr. Kansas City Commn. on Status of Women, 1978-82; adminstrv. dir. Mid-Am. Assembly on Future of Performing Arts, 1979; chmn. Internat. Women's Yr. in Mid-Am. Symposium, 1975; del. Nat. Women's Conf., Houston, 1977; bd. advisors Ctr. for Mgmt. Assistance, Kansas City, 1979—; bd. advs. Kansas City Arts council, 1980-85, Long Term Care Project for Elderly Nat. Demonstration, Mid-Am. Regional Council, 1981-86, Women's Resource Service, U. Mo., Kansas City, 1981-85; hon. dir. Rockhurst Coll., 1977—; hon. trustee Truman Med. Ctr. Found., 1980—; bd. dirs. Greater Kansas City Mental Health Found., 1980-85, Starlight Theatre Assn., 1980—; bd. advisors Greater Kansas City Community Found., 1980-85; cons. R.A. Long Found., 1982—; mem. Community Care Funding Partners Council, 1982—; trustee Bus. and Profl. Women's Found., 1988—; mem. soc. fellows Nelson-Atkins Mus. Art, 1988—. Named Kansas City Tomorrow Leader, 1978; Chi Omega Pub. Service award, 1962; Outstanding Young Woman of Mo., 1967; Woman of the Yr. award, VFW, 1972; Outstanding Achievement award, U. Mo., Kansas City Sch. Edn., 1973; publ. awards, Nat. and Regional Council for Advancement and Support of Edn., 1971, 72, 73; Regional Citizen of Yr. award Mid Am. Regional Council, 1982; Am. Inst. for Public Service award, 1982; Outstanding Career Achiever in Greater Kansas City, Mo. Gen. Assembly citation, 1985; Harvard U. fellow, 1974, others. Mem. Am. Assn. Higher Edn. (coordinator 1973-75), AAUW, Council for Advancement and Support of Edn., Council on Founds., Women and Founds./Corp. Philanthropy, Soroptimist Internat., Mortar Bd., Phi Kappa Phi, Phi Theta Kappa, Phi Delta Kappa, Pi Lambda Theta, Delta Kappa Gamma, Chi Omega. Presbyterian. Clubs: Univ. Women's, Woodside Racquet, Kansas City, Mission Hills Country, Central Exchange. Author: The Community College in Community Service, 1973; Grantmaking in Greater Kansas City: The Philanthropic Impact of Foundations, 1976-80; editor, pub.: The Directory of Greater Kansas City Foundations, 1986, 88; editor: The Foundation Exchange, 1976—; A History of the University of Kansas City: Prologue to a Public University, 1976; A Brief History of Philanthropy in Kansas City, 1980; The Case for the Community Foundation, 1981; Perspectives on Trusteeship for the 80s, 1981; contbr. articles to profl. jours. Office: PO Box 22680 Kansas City MO 64113-0680

TALESE, NAN AHEARN, publishing company executive; b. N.Y.C., Dec. 19, 1933; d. Thomas James and Suzanne Sherman (Russell) Ahearn; m. Gay Talese, June 10, 1959; children: Pamela Frances, Catherine Gay. B.A., Manhattanville Coll. of Sacred Heart, 1955. Fgn. exchange student 1st Nat. City Bank, London and Paris, 1956; editorial asst. Am. Eugenics Soc., N.Y.C., 1957-58, Vogue mag., N.Y.C., 1958-59; copy editor Random House Pub., N.Y.C., 1959-64; assoc. editor Random House Pub., 1964-67, sr. editor, 1967-73; sr. editor Simon & Schuster Pubs., N.Y.C., 1974-81; v.p. Simon & Schuster Pubs., 1979-81; exec. editor, v.p. Houghton Mifflin Co., N.Y.C., 1981-83, v.p., editor-in-chief, 1984-86, v.p., pub., editor-in-chief, 1986-88; sr. v.p. Doubleday & Co., N.Y.C., 1988—. Home: 109 E 61st St New York NY 10021 Office: Doubleday & Co 666 Fifth Ave New York NY 10103

TALL, SUSAN CAROLINE HALL, manufacturing consultant; b. Kingsport, Tenn., Apr. 28, 1959; d. Charles Murrel and Martha Louise (Tuggle) Hall; m. John Higley Tall, Apr. 5, 1959. BS in Civil Engring., Tenn. Technol. U., 1980. Trainee mfg. mgmt. program Gen. Electric Co., De Kalb, Ill. and Malvern, Pa., 1981-83; systems analyst Gen. Electric Co., Malvern, 1983-85, mgr. prodn. planning, 1985-86; supervisory cons. Coopers and Lybrand, Phila., 1986—. Mem. Am. Soc. Quality Control, Am. Prodn. and Inventory Control Soc. Presbyterian. Office: Coopers and Lybrand 2400 Eleven Penn Ctr Philadelphia PA 19103

TALLCHIEF, MARIA, ballerina; b. Fairfax, Okla., Jan. 24, 1925; d. Alexander Joseph and Ruth Mary (Porter) T.; m. Henry Paschen, Jr., June 3, 1957; 1 child, Elise. DFA (hon.), Lake Forest (Ill.) Coll., Colby Coll., Waterville, Maine, 1968, Ripon Coll., 1973, Boston Coll., Smith Coll., 1981, Northwestern U., Evanston, Ill., 1982, Yale U., 1984, St. Mary-of-the-Woods (Ind.) Coll., 1984, Dartmouth Coll., 1985. Ballerina Ballet Russe de Monte Carlo, 1942-47; with N.Y.C. Ballet Co., 1947-65, prima ballerina, 1947-60; former artistic dir. Lyric Opera Ballet Chgo.; founder Chgo. City Ballet, 1979—; prima ballerina Am. Ballet Theatre, 1960. Guest star, Paris Opera, 1947, Royal Danish Ballet, 1961. Named Hon. Princess Osage Indian Tribe, 1953; recipient Disting. Service award U. Okla., 1972, award Dance mag., 1960, Jane Addams Humanitarian award Rockford Coll., 1973, Bravo award Rosary Coll., 1983, award Dance Educators Am., 1956, Achievement award Women's Nat. Press Club, 1953, Capezio award, 1965, Leadership for Freedom award Roosevelt U. Scholarship Assn., 1986. Mem. Nat. Soc. Arts and Letters.

TALLETT, ELIZABETH EDITH, biopharmaceutical company executive; b. London, Apr. 2, 1949; d. Edward and Edith May (Vickers) Symons; m. Martin Richard Tallett, Oct. 30, 1970; children: James Edward, Alexander Martin. BS with honors, U. Nottingham (Eng.), 1973. Mgmt. services mgr. Warner-Lamber (UK), Eastleigh, Eng., 1973-77, strategic planning mgr., 1977-81; internat. dir. strategic planning Warner-Lambert, Morris Plains, N.J., 1981-82, corp. dir. strategic planning, 1982-84; dir. mktg. ops. Parke-Davis, Morris Plains, 1984-87; exec. v.p. therapeutic products Centocor, Malvern, Pa., 1987—. Contbr. articles to profl. jours. Mem. Ch. of Eng.

TALLEY, CAROL LEE, editor; b. Bklyn., Sept. 10, 1937; d. George Joseph and Viola (Kovash) T.; children—Sherry, Jill, Scott. Student, U. Ky., 1955-57, Ohio U., 1957-58. Reporter Easton (Pa.) Daily Express, 1958-60; reporter N.J. Herald, 1962-64, edn. editor, 1964-66; reporter Daily Advance, Dover, N.J., 1966-68; polit. editor, investigative reporter Daily Advance, from 1969, mng. editor, 1974-81; editor Evening Sentinel, Carlisle, Pa., 1982—; Mem. A.P. Task Force N.J., 1970, Pa. Associated Press Mng. Editor's Bd. Dirs. Recipient pub. service awards Nat. Headliners, 1971, Sigma Delta Chi, 1971, George Polk Meml. award for local reporting, 1974, Dew Meml. award Pa. Newspaper Pub.'s Assn., 1985. Mem. Nat. Women's Press Assn., Pa. Newspaper Editors Soc., Sigma Delta Chi. Office: 457 E North St Carlisle PA 17013

TALLEY, RONDA CAROL, educational administrator; b. Glasgow, Ky., Nov. 21, 1951; d. Jack Howard and Ronda Mae (McCoy) T. B.S., Western Ky. U., 1973; M.Ed., U. Louisville, 1974, Ed.S., 1976; Ph.D., Ind. U., 1979. Spl. edn. tchr. Jefferson County Public Schs., Louisville, 1973-76; research assoc. U. Calif., Riverside, 1977, Ind. U., Bloomington, 1977; adminstrv. intern Bur. Edn. Handicapped, HEW, Washington, 1978-81; adj. prof. dept. spl. edn. U. Louisville, 1981-83; adj. prof. Spalding U., 1984-86; coordinator assessment/placement services exceptional child edn. Jefferson County Public Schs., Louisville, 1981-86, coordinator instrnl. support services and placement, 1986—; founder, pres. Tri-T Assocs., 1982—. Sta. WHAS Crusade for Children grantee, 1974-76; Bur. Edn. for Handicapped student research grantee, 1978; cert. sch. psychologist. Mem. Am. Psychol. Assn. (chmn. adminstrs. sch. psychol. services), Am. Ednl. Research Assn., Nat. Assn. Sch. Psychologists, Women in Sch. Adminstrn., Ky. Assn. Sch. Adminstrs., Ky. Assn. Psychology in the Schs. (past pres.), Council Exceptional Children, AAUP, Phi Delta Kappa, Kappa Delta. Republican. Methodist. Editor: Special Education in Transition: Administrator's Handbook on Integrating America's Mildly Handicapped Students, 1982. Home: 9104 Hurstwood Ct Louisville KY 40222 Office: Jefferson County Pub Schs 4409 Preston Hwy Louisville KY 40213

TALLICHET, JAN BOWEN, service executive; b. Dallas, Sept. 7, 1936; d. Gordon Dilworth and Mary Kate (Butcher) Bowen; m. Harry Eugene Evans, Sept. 25, 1954 (div. 1961); m. Julian Camille Tallichet Jr., June 3, 1967; children: Kimberly Elaine, Alan Keith, Mark Ashby, Camille Anne. Student, North Tex. State U., 1964-65. Owner, mgr. Evans Bus. Services, Dallas, 1962-67, Sanborn's Travel Ctr., San Antonio, 1967-84; group br. mgr. Sanborn's Travel, San Antonio, 1984—. Bd. dirs. Salvation Army Aux., San Antonio, 1975. Mem. Inst. Cert. Travel Agts. (cert.), Soc. Incentive Travel Execs., Am. Soc. Assn. Execs. (assoc.), Tex. Soc. Assn. Execs. (assoc.), San Antonio Women in Travel (1st v.p. 1983-84), Freedom's Found. of Valley Forge (life), Altrusa Club. Republican. Mem. Ch. of Christ. Clubs: Woman's of San Antonio (pres. 1974, 76), Opti-Mrs. of San Antonio (pres. 1972-73). Home: Enchanted River Estates Bandera TX 78003 Office: PO Box 2069 Bandera TX 78003

TALLMADGE, KATHLEEN ANN, utility management consultant; b. July 11, 1947; d. John Joseph and Elizabeth (Yesilonis) T. AA, Hudson Valley Community Coll., 1970; BS in Mgmt., Coll. St. Rose, Albany, N.Y., 1979; MBA, Rensselaer Polytech. Inst., 1984. Chief telephone technician N.Y. State Pub. Service, Albany, 1973-79, utility mgmt. analyst, 1979-86; utility mgmt. cons. PMC Mgmt. Cons., Inc., Three Bridges, N.J., 1986-87, Theodore Barry & Assocs., N.Y.C., 1987—. Mem. Bus. and Profl. Women's Orgn., (v.p. 1985-86), Rensselaer Polytech. Inst. MBA Assn. Democrat.

TALLMAN, BONNIE GOLDMAN, lawyer; b. Trenton, N.J., Feb. 11, 1950; d. Norman and Sylvia (Azarchi) Goldman; m. Irving W. Tallman, Jr., Jan. 10, 1982. B.A. magna cum laude, Boston U., 1972; J.D., New Eng. Sch. Law, Boston, 1976. Bar: N.J. 1977, U.S. Dist. Ct. N.J. 1977, U.S. Supreme Ct. Law clk. Superior Ct., Mt. Holly, N.J., 1976-77; asst. county prosecutor Burlington County, Mt. Holly, 1977-82, chief trial atty., 1981-82; ptnr. Goldman and Goldman, Robbinsville, N.J., 1982—; mcpl. ct. judge, N.J., 1986—; police instr. Burlington County Pub. Safety Ctr. (N.J.), 1977-82 lectr. seminars on juvenile and criminal justice, 1978-81. Speaker Community Vols. in Edn., 1979-81; mem. Bordentown 300th Com. Recipient award of appreciation for instrn. Burlington County Fire Acad., 1980; cert of appreciation Legal Secs. Assn., 1980; cert of achievement Pemberton Twp. Police Dept. (N.J.), 1982. Mem. Burlington County Bar Assn. (Robert Criscuolo Lawyer of Yr. award 1982, trustee, 1981, 88), N.J. Bar Assn., Mercer County Bar Assn., ABA, Assn. Trial Lawyers Am., Am. Arbitration Assn. (arbitrator), Bordentown Hist. Soc. (exec. com.) rec. sec. 1981), Sarah Seidel Sisterhood. Jewish. Office: Goldman and Goldman Route 526 PO Box 174 Robbinsville NJ 08691

TALLY, LURA SELF, state legislator; b. Statesville, N.C., Dec. 9, 1921; d. Robert Ottis and Sara (Cowles) Self; A.B., Duke U., 1942; M.A., N.C. State U., Raleigh, 1970; m. J.O. Tally, Jr., Jan. 30, 1943 (div. 1970); children—Robert Taylor, John Cowles. Tchr., former guidance counselor Fayetteville (N.C.) city schs.; mem. N.C. Ho. of Reps. from 20th Dist., 1971-83, chmn. com. higher edn., from 1975, also 1980-83, vice chmn. com. appropriations for edn., 1973-86; state senator from 12th Dist. N.C., 1983-87; chmn. N.C. Senate Com. on Natural Resources, Community Devel. and Wildlife, 1987. Past pres. Cumberland County Mental Health Assn., N.C. Historic Preservation Soc.; trustee Fayetteville Tech. Inst., 1981-86; mem. Legis. Research com. Mem. Am. Personnel and Guidance Assn., Fayetteville Bus. and Profl. Women's Club, Kappa Delta, Delta Kappa Gamma. Methodist. Club: Fayetteville Woman's (past pres.). Office: NC Legis Bldg W Jones St Raleigh NC 27611

TALMA, LOUISE J., composer, educator; b. Arcachon, France, Oct. 31, 1906. Student, Inst. Mus. Art, N.Y.C., 1922-30; pupil, Isidore Philipp and Nadia Boulanger, Fontainebleau Sch. Music, 1926-39; B.Mus., NYU, 1931; M.A. in Music, Columbia U., 1933; L.H.D. (hon.), Hunter Coll, CUNY, 1983; D.Arts (hon.), Bard Coll., 1984. Tchr. Manhattan Sch. Music, 1926-28, Fontainebleau Sch. Music, summers 1936-39, 78, 81-83, 87; mem. faculty Hunter Coll., 1928—, prof. music, 1952-76, prof. emeritus, 1976—; Clark fellow Scripps Coll., 1975; Sanford fellow Yale, 1976; mem. Pres.'s Circle, Hunter Coll., 1977; Bd. dirs. League ISCM. Compositions include: (with Thornton Wilder as librettist) opera The Alcestiad, premiered Frankfurt, West Germany (Marjorie Peabody Waite award Nat. Inst. Arts and Letters 1960); 2 piano sonatas, 6 études for piano, 1 string quartet, 1 sonata for violin and piano, Toccata for orch., Dialogues for piano and orch., Clarinet Quintet; chamber opera Have you heard? Do you know?, Diadem; Flute Quartet; Full Circle for Chamber Orch. Recipient Koussevitzky Music Found. commn., 1959, Nat. Fedn. Music Clubs award, 1963, Nat. Assn. Am. Composers and Condrs. award, 1963, Sibelius medal, 1963, numerous others.; Guggenheim fellow, 1946, 47; sr. Fulbright research grantee, 1955-56; Nat. Endowment of the Arts grantee, 1966, 75. Fellow Am. Guild Organists; mem. League of Composers (dir. 1950—), Fontainebleau Fine Arts and Music Assn. (trustee 1950, v.p. 1982-86), Edward MacDowell Assn. (corporate mem.), A.S.C.A.P., Am. Inst. Arts and Letters, Phi Beta Kappa, Sigma Alpha Iota (hon.). Office: care Am Music Ctr 250 W 54th St New York NY 10019

TALMADGE, SHARON SUE, municipal government official; b. Ft. Belvoir, Va., Jan. 5, 1950; d. Walter Harvey and Genevieve (Harrison) Hall; m. Glen R. Talmadge, April 22, 1972; 1 child, Stacy Lynn. Cert. latent print examiner. Fingerprint tech. FBI, Washington, 1970-71; supr., latent print examiner Balt. Police Dept., 1971—; lectr. in field various orgns. Recipient Law Enforcement medal Md. Soc. SAR, 1981, Bronze Star, Balt. Police Dept., 1981. Mem. Internat. Assn. for Identification (pres. Chesapeake Bay div. 1984-85). Republican. Office: Balt Police Dept 601 E Fayette St Baltimore MD 21202

TALTY, LORRAINE CAGUIOA, accountant; b. Makati, Manila, Philippines, July 3, 1957; came to U.S., 1973, naturalized, 1983; d. Leon Perez and Asuncion (Rodriguez) Caguioa; m. Kevin Michael Talty, Jan. 23, 1982. BBA in Acctg. magna cum laude, Chaminade U., Honolulu, 1979. Office mgr., comptroller Caro of Honolulu, 1976-82; acct. David Schenkein, CPA, Latham, N.Y., 1984-86; sales rep. Caromat Corp., Torrance, Calif., 1985-86; owner Kevlor Internat., mfrs. rep. agy., Fairport, N.Y., 1985—; acct. Cortland L. Brovitz & Co., CPA's, Rochester, N.Y., 1986-87; pvt. practice acctg., Fairport, 1986—. Newsletter editor Country Knolls West Civic Assn., Clifton Park, 1984-85, civic com. rep., 1985-86. Home: 34 Cambridge Ct Fairport NY 14450

TAMBURINE, JEAN HELEN, sculptor, painter, illustrator; b. Meriden, Conn., Feb. 20, 1930; m. Eugene E. Bertolli. Student, Art Students League, N.Y.C., 1948-50; student of Jon Corbino, John Groth, Carlo Ciampaglia, Elisabeth Gordon Chandler. Exhibited group shows Rockport (Mass.) Art Assn., North Shore Arts Assn., Gloucester, Mass., George Walter Vincent Mus., Springfield, Mass., Hudson Valley (N.Y.) Art Assn., Pearl S. Buck Found., Phila., Am. Artists Profl. League, N.Y., Acad. Artists Assn., Springfield, Pen and Brush, N.Y.; heritage bronze commd. by Wallingford (Conn.) Pub. Library, 1986; represented in permanent collections Conn. State Library, Middletown, Nashville Pub. Library, Strong Sch., Hartford, Conn., L'Heure Joyeux, Paris; also pvt. collections; author: Almost Big Enough, 1963, I Think I Will Go to the Hospital, 1965, How Now, Brown Cow, 1967. Recipient Assoc. Members prize Acad. Artists, Founders prize Pen and Brush, 1981, 1st prize for sculpture Arts and Crafts Assn. of Meriden, Conn.; named to Meriden Hall of Fame. Mem. Rockport Art Assn. (Martha Moore Meml. award 1983), North Shore Arts Assn., Acad. Artists Assn., Salmagundi Club, Am. Artists Profl. League, Am. Medallic Sculpture Assn., Internat. Platform Assn., Authors Guild.l, 1965, How Now, Brown Cow, 1967. Home and Office: The Bertolli Studio 73 Reynolds Dr Meriden CT 06450 also: PO Box 740 Rockport MA 01966

TAMBURO, CONSTANCE DOLORES, sales representative; b. Englewood, N.J., Oct. 6, 1940; d. Anthony M. and Carmella (Masci) Merlino; m. Vincent A. Tamburo, Aug. 4, 1962; children—Robert M., Theodore V. A.B., Chatham Coll., 1962. Cert. tchr. Tchr., Fox Chapel and Penn Hills, Pa., 1962-64, 73-76; real estate agt. Koenig & Strey, Lake Forest, Ill., 1977-79; sales rep. Commerce Clearing House, Chgo., 1980—. Docent, Midwest Mus. Am. Art, Elkhart, Ind., 1980-84; pres. Pitts. Opera Guild, 1972-76; mem. Pitts. Opera Aux., 1986—. Andrew Smalley scholar, 1960, 61, 62. Mem. Nat. Orgn. Female Execs., AAUW (v.p. Lake Forest 1976-79), Art Inst. Chgo., Pitts. Peace Inst., Christ Child Soc., Chatham Coll. Alumnae Assn. (exec. bd. 1986-87), Mortar Board. Roman Catholic. Avocation: Tennis. Home: 1124 Aline Ct South Bend IN 46614

TAMEN, HARRIET, lawyer; b. Yonkers, N.Y., May 17, 1947; d. Saul and Lily (Balglau) Tamen. A.B., Bryn Mawr Coll., 1969; J.D., George Washington U., Washington, 1973. Bar: N.Y. 1974, U.S. Dist. Ct. (so. dist.) N.Y. 1975. Atty., W.T. Grant, N.Y.C., 1974-76; atty. City of N.Y. Office Econ. Devel., Div. Real Property, N.Y.C., 1977-81; atty. Credit Lyonnais Bank, N.Y.C., 1981-86, Chase Manhattan Bank, 1986—. Bd. dirs. Dromenon Theatre, N.Y., 1980-86; bd. dirs. Nat. Dance Inst., N.Y., 1982, chmn. bd. dirs., 1984-87; del. exchange program Women in Law, South Am., 1987—; mem. campaign staff Ed Koch for Mayor, N.Y.C., 1977. Mem. ABA, Bar Assn. City of N.Y.

TAMNEY, MARY MARGARET, financial analyst; b. Poughkeepsie, N.Y., May 1, 1951; d. John Francis and Elizabeth B. (Bohlinger) Finn; m. Joseph M. Tamney, July 29, 1972; children: Jason M., Kyleen M. AA, Dutchess Community Coll., Poughkeepsie, 1971; BS, Marist Coll., Poughkeepsie, 1985, MS, 1985—. With Dutchess Bank and Trust Co., Poughkeepsie, 1971—, personnel asst., 1976-82, personnel officer, 1982-84, acctg. supr., 1984-85, asst. controller, 1985—; tchr. Am. Inst. Banking, Poughkeepsie, 1987—. Mem. Spackenkill PTA, Poughkeepsie, Marist Coll. Adv. Bd.; chair employee campaign Poughkeepsie United Way, 1982-85, Hudson Valley Blood Drive, Poughkeepsie, 1982-85; active Dutchess County Youth Hockey. Honoree YMCA Salute to Women in Industry, 1987. Mem. Nat. Assn. Banking Women, Am. Inst. Banking, Alpha Sigma Lambda. Democrat. Roman Catholic. Office: Dutchess Bank and Trust Co 285 Main Mall PO Box 1271 Poughkeepsie NY 12602

TAMULEVICH, JANET ANN, small business owner; b. Chgo., Dec. 17, 1948; d. Edward and Eleanor (Elf) Runis; m. Thomas W. Tamulevich, June 15, 1968; children: Christopher, Andrew. Student, Lowell (Mass.) State Coll., 1966-68; BS summa cum laude, Worcester (Mass.) State Coll., 1980. Pres. Light Control System, Inc., Tyngsboro, Mass., 1980—. Named one of 100 Interesting Women Boston Woman mag., 1988. Office: Light Control Systems Inc 2 Bridgeview Cr Tyngsboro MA 01897

TAN, JULIA, cardiologist, internist; b. Kunming, China, Mar. 1, 1943; came to U.S., 1949, naturalized, 1961; d. Pia Chu and Alice (Wong) Tan; A.B., Wilson Coll., 1965; M.D., Med. Coll. Pa., 1969. Intern, resident Med. Coll. Va., Richmond, 1969-71; resident N.Y. Med. Coll. Hosps., 1971-73; resident in cardiology Case-Western Res.-Cleve. Met. Gen. Hosp., 1973-75; practice medicine specializing in internal medicine and cardiology, Visalia, Calif., 1975—, pres. Julia Tan, M.D., Inc.; dir. CCU Visalia Community Hosp., 1975-85; mem. staffs Kaweah Delta Dist. Hosp., Visalia Community Hosp.; cons. staff Exeter Meml. Hosp., Tulare Dist. Hosp.; mem. Calif. 9th Dist. Med. Quality Rev. Com., 1976-83. Diplomate Am. Bd. Internat. Medicine. Fellow Am. Coll. Cardiology (assoc.); mem. Am. Heart Assn. (dir. Central Valley chpt. 1975-80), Calif. Med. Assn., AMA, Tulare County Med. Soc. Office: 1827 S Court St Suite C Visalia CA 93277

TAN, LILY, textile executive; b. Medan, Sumatra, Indonesia, Aug. 10, 1947; came to U.S., 1968; d. Eng Chuan and Sor Choo (Peh) T. BA, I.K.I.P., Medan, 1967, Gustavus Adolphus Coll., St. Peter, Minn., 1972; MM, U. So. Calif., Los Angeles, 1974. Adminstrn. officer Lloyds Bank, Los Angeles, 1974-80; v.p. Comml. Flooring Assn., Marina Del Rey, Calif., 1981-83; contract mgr. Harbinger Co., Los Angeles, 1983-86; v.p. regional sales Princeton Techs., Ltd., Los Angeles, 1986-87; dir. export services Bentley Mills, Inc., City of Industry, Calif., 1987—. Mem. Network Exec. Women in Hospitality. Office: Bentley Mills Inc 14641 E Don Julian Rd City of Industry CA 91746

TAN, SHIRLEY CHUA, small business owner; b. Manila, Philippines, Dec. 15, 1964; came to U.S., 1985; d. Benito C. and Rosita (Chua) T. Cert. in full charge bookkeeping, Coll. of Guam, Tamuning, 1985; grad., Golden Gate U., 1988. Purchasing mgr. Standard Plytrade Corp., Tamuning, 1981-85; owner Export Mgmt., San Francisco, 1985—, Silk Accents, San Francisco, 1986—. Helper John Riordan Bd. Dirs. City Coll. San Francisco, 1986. Mem. Nat. Assn. of Female Execs., Asian Bus. League of San Francisco, Asian Bus. Assn. Office: 888 Brannan St Suite 275 San Francisco CA 94103

TANAKA, DIANE EMI, marketing professional, consultant; b. Detroit, Feb. 2, 1952; d. Akira and Judith Hisae (Doue) T.; m. Dale William Ma, June 21, 1980. BA, U. Calif., 1974. Graphic artist Scott Printing and Advt., Van Nuys, Calif., 1974-75; media buyer Erwin Wasey, Inc., Los Angeles, 1975-76; account supr. Saatchi and Saatchi DFS, Torrance, Calif., 1976-85; dir. sales, organizational cons. Par Excellence, Inc., Sherman Oaks, Calif., 1982—, mktg. cons., 1985—; dir. AAA Fast Food, Inc., North Hollywood, Calif., 1985—. Advt. mgr. Bob Scott for Assembly, Van Nuys, Calif. 1976. Mem. Women's Referral Service, Inc., Los Angeles County Mus. of Art, Pacific Asian Mus. Art. Republican. Methodist. Club: Calypso Sailing. Home and Office: Par Excellence Inc 13944 Valley Vista Blvd Sherman Oaks CA 91423

TANAKA, LEILA CHIYAKO, lawyer; b. Honolulu, Mar. 11, 1954; d. Masami and Bernice Kiyoko (Nakamura) T. BA in Japanese Lang., Am. Studies with distinction, U. Hawaii, Manoa, 1977; JD, U. Santa Clara, 1980. Bar: Hawaii 1980, U.S. Dist. Ct. Hawaii 1980. Sole practice 1980-81; law clk. to judge State Cir. Ct. judge (2d cir.), Wailuku, Maui, Hawaii, 1981-82; spl. dep. atty. gen. Dept. of Atty. Gen., Hawaii, 1983, dep. atty. gen., 1983—; br. chief Hawaii Housing Authority, 1987—, housing unit supr., eviction hearings trial examiner, Hawaii Housing Authority, 1986—. Mem. ABA, Assn. Trial Lawyers Am., Pacific Rim Found., Orgn. Women Leaders, Phi Kappa Phi. Democrat. Buddhist. Office: State of Hawaii Atty Gen's Office 465 S King St Kekuanao'a Bldg Rm 200 Honolulu HI 96813

TANCS, LINDA ANN, paralegal technician; b. Elizabeth, N.J., Sept. 27, 1963; d. Tibor Louis and Rose (Cecere) T. Student, U. Warwick, Coventry, Eng., 1984; BA, Rutgers Coll., 1985. Sales asst. McCrory Corp., Union, N.J., 1980-83; sales assoc. People Express Airlines, Newark, 1984-85; substitute tchr. Roselle Park (N.J.) Schs., 1984-85; editorial asst. Enslow Pubs., Hillside, N.J., 1985; paralegl technician Fox and Fox, Counsellors at Law, Newark, 1985-88; paralegal technician, asst. legal services coordinator Vol. Lawyers for Arts, N.Y.C., 1988; corp. paralegal Wilentz, Goldman & Spitzer, Woodbridge, N.J., 1988—. Editor German newsletter Der Trichter, 1984-85. Mem. Nat. Assn. Female Execs., Phi Beta Kappa, Phi Sigma Iota, Delta Phi Alpha. Republican. Club: Adventure on a Shoestring (N.J.). Home: 411 Roosevelt St Roselle Park NJ 07204

TANCZAK-DYCIO, MARY, physician; b. Rybnyky, Ukraine, July 10, 1922; came to U.S., 1950, naturalized, 1955; d. Basil and Helen (Cisyk) Tanczak; student U. Lviv, 1940-41, Med. Sch., 1942-44, U. Erlangen (Germany), 1945-49; m. George Dycio, Nov. 11, 1949; children—George Myron, Mark Roman. Resident, Contagious Disease Hosp., Belleville, N.J., 1951-52; intern Mercy Hosp., Canton, Ohio, 1952-53, resident anesthesia, 1952-55; practice medicine specializing in anesthesiology, 1955-58; mem. staff Irvington (N.J.) Gen. Hosp., 1955-58; staff St. Mary's Gen. Hosp., Lewiston, Maine, 1958—, chief anesthesia dept., 1960—, also dir. Sch. Nurse Anesthetists. Fellow Am. Coll. Anesthesiologist; mem. AMA, Am.-Ukrainian, Maine. Androscoggin County med. socs. Office: 300 Pine St Lewiston ME 04240 also: 3 Bayberry Ln Lewiston ME 04240

TANDY, JESSICA, actress; b. London, Eng., June 7, 1909; d. Harry and Jessie Helen (Horspool) T.; m. Jack Hawkins, 1932 (div. 1940); 1 dau., Susan (Mrs. John Tettemer); m. Hume Cronyn, 1942; children: Christopher Hume, Tandy. Student, Dame Alice Owens Girls Sch., Ben Greet Acad. Acting, 1924-27; LL.D., U. Western Ont., 1974; LHD (hon.), Fordham U., 1985. Dramatic adviser Goddard Neighborhood Center, N.Y.C., 1948. First profl. acting role in: Manderson Girls; later appeared in: London debut in The Rumor, 1929; Comedy of Good and Evil, 1929, Alice Sit-By-The-Fire, 1929, Yellow Sands, 1929; other theatre appearances in Twelfth Night, 1930, Man Who Pays the Piper, Autumn Crocus, Port Said, 1931; various engagements, Old Vic, London, including Midsummer Night's Dream, Hamlet, King Lear, 1933-40; first stage appearance U.S., 1930; on Broadway in Time and Conways, 1938, White Steed, 1939, Yesterday's Magic, 1942, Streetcar Named Desire, 1947, Four Poster, 1951-53, Madame Will You Walk, 1953, The Honeys, 1955, A Day by the Sea, 1955, The Man in the Dog Suit, 1958, Five Finger Exercise, 1959, The Physicists, 1964, Noel Coward in Two Keys, 1974; played in Mpls. Hamlet, Three Sisters, Death of a Salesman, 1963, Rose, 1981; Foxfire; in The Glass Menagerie; summer theatre prodns. The Caucasian Chalk Circle, 1950-55; appeared: Triple Play, 1958-59, Big Fish, Little Fish, London, 1962; (with husband) reading tour U.S. Face to Face, 1954; A Delicate Balance, 1966-67, The Miser, 1968, Heartbreak House, Shaw Festival, 1968, Tchin-Tchin, Chgo., 1969, Camino Real, Lincoln Center, N.Y.C., 1970, Home, Morosco, N.Y., 1971, All Over, N.Y.C., 1971; (with husband) in) Samuel Beckett festival, Lincoln Center, N.Y.C., 1972, tour Promenade All, 1972-73, Not I, 1973; limited concert recital tour Many Faces of Love, 1974, 75, 76, also Seattle Repertory theatre; tour (with Husband) Noel Coward in Two Keys, 1975; appeared in Eve, Stratford (Ont.) Festival, 1976; played Mary Tyrone in Long Day's Journey into Night, Theater London, Ont., Can., 1977; star of The Gin Game, at Long Wharf Theatre, New Haven, 1977, Golden Theatre, N.Y.C., 1978; on tour in U.S., Toronto, London, USSR, 1978-79, Rose, Cort Theater, N.Y.C., 1981; appeared (with husband) in Foxfire, Stratford Festival, Ont., 1980, The Guthrie Theatre, Mpls., 1981, Ahmanson Theatre, Los Angeles, 1985-86, Ethel Barrymore Theatre, N.Y.C., 1982-83; in The Glass Menagerie, Eugene O'Neill Theatre, N.Y.C., 1983-84; off-Broadway in Salonika, 1985; (with husband) in The Petition, Golden Theatre, N.Y.C., 1986; motion pictures include A Light in the Forest, 1958, Valley of Decision, Green Years, Desert Fox, The Birds, 1962, Butley, 1973, Honky Tonk Freeway, 1980, Garp, 1981, Still of the Night, 1981, Best Friends, 1982, The Bostonians, 1983, Cocoon, 1984, Sullivan Street, 1986, Batteries Not Included, 1986, The House on Carroll Street, 1988; TV prodns. Portrait of a Madonna, 1948, Christmas 'Till Closing, 1955, Marriage; series, 1954, The Fallen Idol, 1959, The Moon and Sixpence, 1959, Tennessee Williams' Faces of Love, 1977, The Gin Game, 1979, Foxfire, 1987. Recipient Antoinette Perry award for performance in Streetcar Named Desire, 1948; recipient Twelfth Night Club award for Five Finger Exercise, 1960, bronze medallion (with husband) for performance in The Four Poster Comedia Matinee Club, 1952, Obie award for Not I, 1973, Drama Desk award for Happy Days and Not I, Creative Arts award Brandeis U., 1978, Antoinette Perry (Tony) award for The Gin Game, 1978, Drama Desk award, 1978, Los Angeles Critics award, 1979, Sarah Siddons award, 1979; named to Theatre Hall of Fame, 1979; recipient Antoinette Perry award for Foxfire, 1982. Office: 63-23 Carlton St Rego Park NY 11374 *

TANG, VICTORIA, accountant; b. Cambridge, Mass., Oct. 26, 1961; d. Arthur Y.C. and Pauline (Yee) T. BA, Framingham State Coll., 1984. Electronic technician Diode, Inc., 1980-84, tchr., lab. aide, 1984; order entry processor Scandinavian Design Corp., Natick, Mass., 1984-85, order entry supr., 1985-86, acct., 1986-87, fin./payroll asst., 1987—. Active Greenpeace, Mass., 1982-85, Cousteau Soc., Mass., 1982-85, Humane Soc., Framingham, 1982-85. Mem. Nat. Assn. Female Execs. Club: Sierra. Office: Scandinavian Design 603 Worcester Rd Natick MA 01760

TANKOOS, SANDRA MAXINE, court reporting executive; b. Bklyn., Nov. 12, 1936; d. Samuel J. and Ethel (Seltzer) Rich; m. Kenneth Robert Tankoos, Mar. 17, 1957; children: Robert Ian, Gary Russell, Jenine Sheryl. AA, Stenotype Inst., 1957; BA, Queens Coll., 1969; MA, C.W. Post Coll., 1973. Cert. stenotype reporter, 1959. Ct. reporter free lance, N.Y.C., 1957-70; tchr. Spanish, various high schs., L.I., 1970-76; pres. Tankoos Reporting, N.Y.C., 1976—, Ar-Ti Recording, Mineola, N.Y., 1977—. Contbr. articles to profl. jours. V.p., bd. dirs. Temple Sinai, Roslyn Hts., N.Y., 1979—, Liberal Jewish Day Sch., W. Hempstead, 1984—, LWV, Roslyn, 1969-75, NOW, Nassau County, 1975-77. Mem. Nat. Assn. Shorthand Reporters, Principal's Assn. Club: Numismatic (pres. 1973-78). Avocations: writing, piano. Home: 77 Shepherd Ln Roslyn Heights NY 11577 Office: Ar-Ti Recording Inc 223 Jericho Turnpike Mineola NY 11501 also: Tankoos Reporting Co 150 Nassau St New York NY 10038

TANNEN, RICKI LEWIS, lawyer, writer; b. N.Y.C., Apr. 29, 1952; d. Paul and Lillian (Singer) Lewis; m. Marc Jay Tannen, Aug. 25, 1972; children—Laine Amy, Adam Jesse. B.A. in History U. Fla., 1975, M.Ed. in Linguistics, 1981, J.D. with honors, 1981. Bar: Fla. 1982. Tchr. Oak Hall Pvt. Sch., Gainesville, Fla., 1976-79; atty., jud. clk. U.S. Dist. Cts., Miami, Fla., 1981-82; assoc., representing Ft. Lauderdale News and Sun-Sentinel newspaper Ferrero, Middlebrooks, Strickland & Fischer, Ft. Lauderdale, Fla., 1982—; mem. gender bias study commn. Fla. Supreme Ct., 1986, apptd. commr., 1987—; co-chmn. 1986 Fla. Bar Media Law Conf.; research coordinator Ctr. for Govtl. Responsibility, Gainesville, 1979-81. Editor: Elderly Law in Florida, 1982. Contbr. articles to profl. jours. Mem. ABA, Fla. Bar Assn., Am. Fedn. Trial Laws, Fla. Assn. Women Lawyers. Office: Ferrero Middlebrooks Strickland & Fischer 707 SE 3d Ave Fort Lauderdale FL 33316

TANNENBAUM, BERNICE SALPETER, association executive; b. N.Y.C.; d. Isidore and May Franklin; B.A., Bklyn. Coll.; m. Nathan Tannenbaum; 1 son, Richard Salpeter. Mem. exec. bd. Nat. Conf. Soviet Jewry; chmn. Commn. on the Status of Women of the World Jewish Congress; mem. exec. bd. Am. sect. World Jewish Congress, chmn. internat. affairs com.; mem. Zionist Gen. Council; chmn. Am. sect. World Zionist Orgn.; bd. govs., mem. gen. assembly Jewish Agy.; bd. dirs., v.p. United Israel Appeal, Jewish Nat. Fund; mem. exec. com. Am. Zionist Fedn.; mem. Conf. of Pres. of Maj. Jewish Orgns.; nat. pres. Hadassah, N.Y.C., 1976-80, immediate past pres., 1980—; nat. chmn. Hadassah Med. Relief Assn.; mem. Jewish Telegraphic Agy.; bd. govs. Hebrew U. Office: 50 W 58th St New York NY 10019

TANNER, COURTENAY TYLER, real estate executive; b. Ft. Lewis, Wash., Aug. 20, 1948; d. Henry Samuel and Dorothy Elizabeth (Connor) Tyler; m. Richard Brevard Tanner, May 25, 1974; children: Timothy Tyler, Richard Brevard Jr. BA in Teaching, Sam Houston State U., 1970. Tchr. Livingston (Tex.) Ind. Sch. Dist., 1970-71, San Antonio Acad., 1972-74; substitute instr. McKinney (Tex.) Job Corps, 1975-77, 80-82; demonstrator, salesperson Krups-McBride & Allen, Dallas, 1983-85; salesman, agt. Fenwick & Assocs. Realtors, Dallas, 1985-87; coordinator corp. mktg. Remax Preston Rd. North Realtors, 1987—. Touring docent Dallas County Heritage Soc., 1975-83, docent candelight tours Christmas Festival, 1977-87, salesman on-site tickets 1981-83, chmn.-elect, 1984, chmn., 1985, chmn. decorations 1986-87; v.p. 101 Club Dallas County Hist. Soc., 1983-84; chmn. women's com. Wayback House, Inc., Dallas, 1985-86, v.p., 1986-87; sec. Women's Wayback House Bd., Dallas, 1983-84, v.p., 1984-85, pres., 1985-86; artists chmn. Irish Fair com. Women's Com. of Dallas Ballet, 1985-86; mediator Neighborhood Youth Services, Richardson, Tex., 1986-88; vol. Office of Internat. Affairs, Dallas, 1988; active Jr. League of Richardson, 1984-88; leader, pack com. Cub Scouts Boy Scouts Am., 1981-83, 86—. Recipient Gold Pin award Dallas County Heritage Soc., 1986. Mem. Nat. Assn. Realtors, Tex. Assn. Realtors, Greater Dallas Bd. Realtors. Roman Catholic. Clubs: P.E.O. (Dallas) (chaplain 1983-84), Young Lawyer's Wives Inc. (Dallas) (Women's Wayback chmn. 1982-83, luncheon chmn. 1983-84, v.p. ways and means 1984-85).

TANNER, HELEN HORNBECK, historian; b. Northfield, Minn., July 5, 1916; d. John Wesley and Frances Cornelia (Wolfe) Hornbeck; m. Wilson P. Tanner, Jr., Nov. 22, 1940 (dec. 1977); children—Frances, Margaret Tanner Tewson, Wilson P., Robert (dec. 1983). A.B. with honors, Swarthmore Coll., 1937; M.A., U. Fla., 1949; Ph.D., U. Mich., 1961. Asst. to dir. pub. relations Kalamazoo Pub. Schs., 1937-39; with sales dept. Am. Airlines Inc., N.Y.C., 1940-43; teaching fellow, then teaching asst. U. Mich., Ann Arbor, 1949-53, 57-60, lectr. extension service, 1961-72, asst. dir. Ctr. Continuing Edn. for Women, 1964-68; project dir. Newberry Library, Chgo., 1976-81, research assoc., 1981—; dir. D'Arcy McNickle Ctr. for Indian History, 1984-85; cons., expert witness Indian treaties; mem. Mich. Commn. Indian Affairs, 1966-70. Author: Zespedes in East Florida 1784-1790, 1963, General Green Visits St. Augustine, 1964, The Greeneville Treaty, 1974, The Territory of the Caddo Tribe of Oklahoma, 1974; editor: Atlas of Great Lakes Indian History, 1987. NEH grantee, 1976. Mem. Am. Soc. Ethnohistory (pres. 1982-83), Am. Hist. Assn., Conf. Latin Am. History, Soc. History Discoveries, Can. Cartographic Assn., Chgo. Map Soc., Fla. Hist. Soc., Hist. Soc. Mich. Home: 1319 Brooklyn Ave Ann Arbor MI 48104 Office: The Newberry Library 60 W Walton St Chicago IL 60610

TANNER, JANET WITTE, investment company executive; b. Buffalo, Dec. 21, 1944; d. Michael and Louise Witte; B.A. in Econs., Mt. Holyoke Coll., 1966; M.B.A., Columbia U., 1971. Security analyst, acting head research dept. Am. Security and Trust Co., Washington, 1967-69; mgr. commonstock analysis Aetna Life & Casualty, Hartford, Conn., 1971-73, dir. fin. analysis, 1974-76, asst. v.p., 1976-82; pres. Tanner Capital Corp., Boston, 1982—; bd. dirs. U.S. Council for Program for Advancement Comml. Tech. between U.S. and India; guest lectr. Mt. Holyoke Coll., Harvard Bus. Sch.; guest panelist MIT Enterprise Forum. Chmn. YWCA fin. com., 1980-82; bd. dirs. Hartford Ballet, exec. com., 1977-81; corp. adv. bd. Mt. Holyoke Coll., 1982; bd. dirs. Parents and Children's SErvices, Boston. Chartered fin. analyst. Home: 5 Spruce Ct Boston MA 02108 Office: Exchange Place 32nd Floor Boston MA 02109

TANNER, JOAN E., artist; b. Indpls., Nov. 25, 1935. BFA, U. Wis., 1957. Mem. exhbns. and acquisitions com. Santa Barbara (Calif.) Mus. Art, 1969, mem. adv. and selections com. 1120 Artists' space, 1979, mem. jury panel Art Scene, 1986; founder Santa Barbara Contemporary Arts Forum, 1976, bd. dirs., 1976-81, mem. exec. com., 1977-81, pres., 1983; mem. adjudication panel Dance Alliance, Santa Barbara, 1985; lectr. workshop/conf. Los Angeles State Coll., 1986; jury panelist Abrams prize The Womens' Ctr., U. Calif. at Santa Barbara, 1986, with workshop for Abrams prize, 1987, presenter Coll. Creative Studies, 1988, lectr. dept. art, 1988; vis. artist resident Ill. State U., Normal, 1987. One-woman shows include Santa Barbara Mus. Art, 1967, 79, 86, Esther Bear Gallery, Santa Barbara, 1969, 74,

Lafayette (Ind.) Mus. Art, 1973, Ruth Schaffner Gallery, Santa Barbara, 1982, Risser Gallery, Pasadena, Calif., 1983; exhibited in group shows at Lytton Art Ctr., Los Angeles, 1968, Inst. Contemporary Art, Boston, 1968, Santa Barbara Mus. Art, 1969, 76, 80, 83, Fine Arts Gallery San Diego, 1969, Esther Bear Gallery, 1971, 75, Baxter Art Gallery/Calif. Inst. Tech., P)asadena, 1972, Los Angeles Valley Community Coll., Van Nuys, Calif., 1974, Art Gallery/SUNY, Potsdam, 1975, Bob Tomlinson Gallery, Albuquerque, 1976, Indpls. Mus. Art, 1981, San Francisco Mus. Modern Art Rental Gallery, 1982, Las Vegas (Nev.) Mus. Art, Univ. Art Mus., U. Calif.-Santa Barbara, 1983; performed at Santa Barbara Contemporary Arts Forum., 1985, Koslow Rayl Fine Art, Los Angeles, 1988; represented in permanent collections Atlantic Richfield Corp., Denver and Los Angeles, Ivest-Wellington Fund, Boston, The Home Hosp., Lafayette, Santa Barbara Mus. Art, Univ. Art Mus., U. Calif.-Santa Barbara. Bd. dirs. Children's Creative Project, Santa Barbara, 1974, Flintridge Found., South Pasadena, Calif., 1988; mem. community promotions com. City of Santa Barbara, 1982. Home: 624 Olive Rd Santa Barbara CA 93108

TANNERY, JOEL HOWARD, service executive; b. Lawton, Okla., June 12, 1946; d. Otto Porter and Leslie (Reynolds) Howard; m. Dick W. Tannery, Aug. 24, 1967 (div. May 1980); children: Micah B., Richard W. BS in Edn., U. Okla., 1968. Secondary sch. tchr. Oklahoma City Pub. Sch., 1968-71; asst. ticket mgr. athletic dept. U. Okla., Norman, 1971-76; acct. mgr. Metro Advt., Oklahoma City, 1980-81; gen. mgr. Retirement Inns Am., Inc., Oklahoma City, 1981-84; exec. dir. Southmark/Retirement Inn, Ft. Worth, 1984—; cons. Retirement Assocs., Inc., Ft. Worth and Seattle, 1985-86, Southmark/AutumnWest, Ft. Worth and Salt Lake City, 1986—. Columnist weekly newspaper, 1981-84. Mem. pub. relations com. LWV, Lawton, Okla., 1978-79; camapign coordinaotr various candidates, Okla., 1977-80; bd. dirs., fund raiser Vol. Action Ctr., Lawton, 1978-80. Mem. Nat. Assn. Female Execs., Jr. League (pub. relations com.), Ft. Worth C. of C. (action ambassador). Republican. Presbyterian. Club: PEO (Lawton). Office: Retirement Inn at Western Hills 8000 Calmont Ave Fort Worth TX 76116

TANOUS, HELENE MARY, physician; b. Zanesville, Ohio, Oct. 22, 1939; d. Joseph Carrington and Rose Marie (Mokarzel) Tanous; B.A., Marymount Coll., 1961; M.D., U. Tex., 1967. Intern, County Hosp., Los Angeles, 1967-68; resident in radiology U. So. Calif. Hosp., Los Angeles, 1969-71; practice medicine specializing in radiology, Los Angeles, 1972-73; instr. radiology U. So. Calif. Med. Sch., Los Angeles, 1971-72; asst. prof. diagnostic radiology Baylor Med. Sch., Houston, 1973-75; dir. med. student elective in diagnostic radiology Ben Taub Hosp., Houston, 1973-75; pvt. practice diagnostic radiology, Largo, Fla., 1975—; asst. prof. diagnostic radiology U. South Fla. Med. Sch., 1980—; dir. med. student edn. in Diagnostic Radiology. Pres., founder Children's Advocates, Inc.; bd. dirs. Fla. Endowment for Humanities, 1979-83. Diplomate Am. Bd. Radiology. Mem. AMA, So. Med. Assn., Fla. Med. Assn., Internat. Platform Assn., L'Alliance Francaise of Tampa (bd. dirs. 1984—, pres. 1985-87), Fedn. Alliances Francaises U.S.A. (bd. dirs. 1987—). Office: U South Fla Med Sch Dept Radiology 12901 N 30th St Box 17 Tampa FL 33612

TANSEY, IVA LEE MARIE, state legislator; b. Elyria, Ohio, Jan. 6, 1930; d. Edwin Jacob and Fern L. (McKee) Law; student Lorain Bus. Coll., 1965; m. Charles J. Tansey, Sept. 7, 1948; children—Mark, Dennis, Richard. Sec., Vermilion (Ohio) High Sch., 1959-64; exec. sec. Vermilion C. of C., 1964-67; br. sec., asst. mgr. Cardinal Fed. Savs. & Loan Assn., 1967-76; mem. Ohio Ho. of Reps., 1977-88; Republican. Congregationalist. Office: State House Columbus OH 43215

TANZER, DEBRA ANN, personnel director; b. North Riverside, Ill., June 22, 1958; d. Frank John and Sue Ann (Ulchar) Veselsky; m. Raymond Carl Tanzer, Apr. 7, 1984. BS in Bus., Western Ill. U., 1980. Employee relations supr. Mylstar Electronics, Northlake, Ill., 1980-84, MCR Products Inc., Chgo., 1984—. Office: MCR Products Inc 2324 S Kenneth Ave Chicago IL 60623

TAPP, ELISE MARIE, software training company executive; b. Detroit, Feb. 10, 1950; d. George M. and Simonne Marie (Auger) Bergeron; m. Darrell Owen Tapp, Jan. 21, 1983. B.A., U. Mich.; M.A. in Adminstrn., Eastern Mich. U. Cert. tchr., Mich., Tex. With Xerox Corp., Dallas, 1979-81; program instr. Digital Switch Corp., Dallas, 1981-83; software instr. Businessland, Houston, 1983-84;, pres. BusinessWare Learning Ctrs., Inc., Houston, 1985—; with Bus. Software Support, Houston, 1984—; cons. Compaq Computer Co., Houston, 1984—, Tenneco Inc., Houston, 1985—, Exxon, Houston, 1986. Mem. Info. Ctrs. Mgmt. Assn., Ind. Computer Cons., Assn. Profl. Educators. Republican. Roman Catholic. Office: BusinessWare Learning Ctrs Inc 6575 West Loop S Suite 220 Bellaire TX 77401

TARASCON-AURIOL, REGINE GINETTE, research chemist; b. Oran, Algeria, Mar. 6, 1957; came to U.S., 1981; m. Jean-Marie Tarascon, Sept. 5, 1981. BS in Phys. Chemistry, U. Abidjan, Algeria, 1977; MS in ChemE, U. Bordeaux, 1981. Vis. scientist Cornell U., Ithaca, N.Y., 1981; mem. tech. staff AT&T Bell Labs., Murray Hill, N.J., 1982—. Contbr. articles on microlithography to profl. jours. Mem. Am. Chem. Soc., Internat. Soc. for Optical Engring., Materials Research Soc. Home: 149 Clover Hill Rd Millington NJ 07946 Office: AT&T Bell Labs 600 Mountain Ave Murray Hill NJ 07974

TARBOX, KATHARINE RIGGS, investor relations executive; b. N.Y.C., Feb. 8, 1948; d. Henry Fisk and Mary (Powell) T.; m. Jeremy M.F. Warner, Sept. 25, 1975 (div. Nov. 1982); m. Donald O. McLeod, May 25, 1983. BA in Econs., Wellesley Coll., 1970. Cash mgr., specialist Citibank, N.A., N.Y.C., 1970-75, sr. account mgr., 1975-77; cash mgr. Chesebrough Ponds, Inc., Greenwich, Conn., 1977-79, mgr. investor relations, 1979-82; dir. investor relations Chesebrough Ponds, Inc., Westport, Conn., 1982-86; v.p. investor relations Colgate-Palmolive Co., N.Y.C., 1987—. Alumnae gov. Westover Sch., Middlebury, Conn., 1987—. Mem. Nat. Investor Relations Inst. (dir. N.Y.C. chpt. 1981-82). Office: Colgate-Palmolive Co 300 Park AVe New York NY 10022

TARDIF, MONIQUE BERNATCHEZ, Canadian legislator; b. Que., Can., Jan. 8, 1936; d. Henri and Aline (LaRue) B.; m. Louis Tardif (dec.); children: François, Michel, Dominique, Danielle (dec.). Student, Laval U. Dir. for consumer protection Que. Auto Club, 1976-80; mem. Can. Ho. of Commons, 1984—. Mem., bd. dirs. Les Grands Ballets Canadiens, Montreal, 1969-70. Mem. Progressive Conservative Party. Roman Catholic. Office: House of Commons, Room 325 Confederation Bldg, Ottawa, ON Canada K1A 0A6 *

TARLTON, SHIRLEY MARIE, college dean; b. Raleigh, N.C., Aug. 8, 1937; d. Lloyd E. and Mary O. (Suycott) Tarlton; diploma Peace Coll., Raleigh, N.C., 1957; BA in French, Queens Coll., Charlotte, N.C., 1960; MS in Library Sci., U. N.C., Chapel Hill, 1966. Head tech. services div. U. N.C., Charlotte, 1961-68, asst. librarian, 1961-63; asso. dir. tech. services Winthrop Coll. Library, 1968-73, acting dir., 1971, 73-74, dean library services, 1974—; mem. bd. Southeastern Library Network; mem. council Online Computer Library Center. Mem. ALA, Southeastern N.C., S.C., Metrolina Library Assn., Rock Hill C. of C., Sigma Pi Alpha, Phi Theta Kappa, Beta Phi Mu, Phi Kappa Phi. Home: 7406 Windyrush Rd Charlotte NC 28226 Office: Winthrop College Rock Hill SC 29733

TARNOSKI, LORI M., clothing company executive; b. 1940. With V F Corp., Wyomissing, Pa., 1961—, adminstrv. asst. to v.p., 1970-73, asst. sec., 1973-74, sec., 1974—, v.p., 1979—. Address: VF Corporation 1047 N Park Rd Wyomissing PA 19610 *

TARPLEE, SUE CURRIE, health care executive; b. Herkimer, N.Y., Mar. 14, 1954; d. Andrew Grey and Doris Lee (Himelein) Currie; m. Ronald Joe Tarplee, Nov. 9, 1985. BS, U. Pitts., 1976; MHA, Ind. U.-Purdue U., Indpls., 1981. Registered record adminstr. Asst. dir. patient affairs Deaconess Hosp., Evansville, Ind., 1976-77; cons. Blue Cross/Blue Shield, Indpls., 1977-82; with Ernst & Whinney, Indpls., 1983-85, mgr., 1985-87, sr. mgr., 1987—. Contbr. articles to mag. Liaison Pan Am. Games, Indpls., 1986-87. Mem. Network Women in Bus. (com. 1986—), Cen. Ind. Med. Records Assn. (bd. dirs. 1982-86, pres. elect 1988—), Am. Med. Records Assn. Episcopalian. Home: 298 Lake Dr Greenwood IN 46142 Office: Ernst & Whinney 1 Indiana Sq Suite 3400 Indianapolis IN 46204

TARR, MARGO PAQUETTE, marketing and public relations director; b. Hull, Que., Can., Sept. 26, 1934; d. Alfred W. and Germaine (albert) Paquette; divorced; children: Caroline, William L. Jr., Julie. Student, Thomas Coll., 1974, U. Cin., 1981-82. Dir. pub. relations, editor Cin. Bd. Realtors, 1974-82; dir. mktg./pub. relations Chelsea Moore Co., Cin., 1982—. dir. pub. relations Greater Cin.-Japan Sister City Program; bd. govs. Arthritis Found.; mem. Action & Friends of Covington, Riverside Civic Assn., Greater Cin. Apt. Assn.; interpreter World Figure Championships, Cin. Mem. No. Ky. C. of C. (econ. devel. issues com.), Sales and Mktg. Assn./Home Builders, The Heimlich Inst., Cin. Editors Assn. (bd. dirs.). Home: Governor's Point 323 E Second St Covington KY 41011 Office: Chelsea Moore Co 105 W Fourth St Cincinnati OH 45202

TARRANT-FITZGERALD, MAUREEN, hospital marketing director; b. N.Y.C., Mar. 18, 1955; d. Kevin Barry and Alberta Ann (Manitt) Tarrant; m. John Patrick Fitzgerald, June 23, 1979. BA, SUNY, 1977; MBA, Boston U., 1981. Info. asst. Blue Cross-Blue Shield, Washington, 1977-78; service coordinator Kelly Health Care, Boston, 1978-81; dir. Am. Med. Personnel Services, Denver, 1981-82, dir. clinics Rocky Mountain Hosp., Denver, 1982-83, adminstrv. officer Rocky Mountain Hosp., 1983-85; dir. mktg. Porter Meml. Hosp., Denver, 1985-87, v.p. mktg. Rose Med. Ctr., Denver, 1987—; cons. Arapahoe Med. Found., Englewood, Colo., 1983-84; mem. adj. faculty Regis Coll. Denver, 1985—. Site coordinator 9 Health Fair, Denver, 1982-83. Mem. Am. Mktg. Assn., Am. Coll. Health Care Marketers, Am. Hosp. Assn., Soc. for Planning and Mktg., Soc. for Pub. Relations Mktg., Denver C. of C. (ambassador 1982-84), AMA-Acac. Health Services & Mktg. (pres. Colo. chpt.). Democrat. Roman Catholic. Office: Rose Med Ctr 4567 E 9th Ave Denver CO 80220

TARS, SANDRA EMILIE, psychologist; b. Westfield, Mass., June 20, 1944; d. Martin and Emilie Helen (Pietrowski) Eidinger; m. Arvo Tars, June 24, 1967; children: Eric Sven, Karl David. BA magna cum laude, Cornell U., 1966; PhD, U. Mich., 1972. Licensed psychologist, N.Y. Intern Ypsilanti (Mich.) State Hosp., 1967-69; intern counselling div. U. Mich., Ann Arbor, 1969-71, research investigator Inst. Gerontology, 1971-74, lectr. psychology dept., 1972-73; assoc. psychologist Hutchings Psychiat. Ctr., Syracuse, N.Y., 1973-74, mental health team leader, 1974-77, chief psychologist, 1977—; instr., asst. prof. SUNY Health Sci. Ctr., Syracuse, 1973-85, clin. assoc. prof., 1985—; training program dir. Nat. Inst. Mental Health-funded Clin. Geropsychology Internship Program (Hutchings Psychiatric Ctr.). Contbr. articles to profl. jours. Bd. dirs. Alethea, Ctr. for Death and Dying, Syracuse, 1979-82, sec. 1981. Mem. N.Y. Psychol. Assn. (chair legal/legisl. com. 1986—), Cen. N.Y. Psychol. Assn. (pres. 1981-84, Disting. Contbn. award 1988), Am. Psychol. Assn., Assn. Upstate N.Y. Dirs. of Psychology (sec., treas. 1983-85, pres. 1986-87), Gerontol. Soc. of Am. Home: 202 Byron Rd Fayetteville NY 13066 Office: Hutchings Psychiat Ctr 625 Madison St Syracuse NY 13210

TARSELL, THOMASINE MISSOURI, insurance brokerage executive, financial advisor; b. Shamokin, Pa., Sept. 27, 1941; d. Walter Thomas and Missouri Elizabeth (Haas) T.; m. David Charles Cohen, Aug. 13, 1969 (div. Jan. 1982). Grad. Phoenixville Area High Sch., Pa. Cert. ins. counselor. Mfrs. rep. Ardlee Assocs., Phila., 1963-66; v.p. mktg., nat. sales mgr. Marlee Creations, Phila., 1965-66; owner Schneider, Hill & Spangler, 1966-68; account exec., ins. broker Schaprio-Shadline & Balser, Inc., Balt., 1968-71; gen. mgr., ins. broker Bruce Ins. Corp., Balt., 1971-77; founder, chief exec. officer Tomco Ins. Corp. and Tomco Money Mgmt. Corp., Towson, Md., 1977—; exec. v.p. 7 Services Inc., Balt., 1984—; dir. Care First Health Maintenance Orgn., Balt., now advisor; founder, exec. First Comprehensive Directory of Women Owned Businesses in State Md., 1983—, First Women in Exporting Trade Mission, 1985—; chairperson Bus. Ptnrs. Inc., 1987—. Founder, treas. Pooling of Women Entrepreneurial Resources Polit. Action Com., 1984—; mem. Md. Indsl. Devel. Fin. Authority, 1987—, Small Bus. Adv. Council trade policy matters, U.S. Dept. Commerce, 1987—. Named Woman of Yr., Nat. Assn. Women Bus. Owners, 1981, Woman Bus. Advocate of Yr., SBA, 1984. Mem. Ind. Ins. Agts. Assn., Cert. Fin. Planners Assn., Nat. Assn. Women Bus. Owners, Minority Bus. Council Md. (bd. advisors), U.S. Small Bus. Adminstrn. (counselor, lectr.). Republican. Lutheran. Avocations: golf; racquetball; reading; sailing; boating. Office: Tomco Ins Corp 660 Kenilworth Dr Suite 101 Towson MD 21204

TARVER, MAE-GOODWIN, consulting company executive; b. Selma, Ala., Aug. 9, 1916; d. Hartwell Hill and R. Louise (Wilkins) T.; B.S. in Chemistry, U. Ala., 1939, M.S., 1940. Project supr. container shelflife Continental Can Co., Inc., Chgo., 1941-48, project engr. stats., 1948-54, quality control cons., research statistician, 1954-77; pres., prin. cons. Quest Assocs., Park Forest, Ill., 1978—; adj. assoc. prof. biology dept. Ill. Inst. Tech., Chgo., 1957-81. Bd. dirs. Ash Street Coop., Park Forest, Ill., 1976-85. Fellow Am. Soc. Quality Control (Joe Lisy award 1961, Edward J. Oakley award 1975, E.L. Grant award 1983); mem. Inst. Food Technologists, Soc. Women Engrs., Am. Statis. Assn., Park Forest C. of C. (pres. 1986), Sigma Xi. Home: 130 26th St Park Forest IL 60466

TARVER, SHERRY LYNN, chemist; b. Cleve., July 1, 1957; d. John and Lorene (Baugh) Ivy; m. Thomas Wesley Tarver, Jan. 24, 1987. BS, Notre Dame Coll., 1978. Chemist I Union Carbide Corp., Parma, Ohio, 1977-81; chemist II Standard Oil Research and Devel., Warrensville, Ohio, 1981-85, chemist specialist, 1985—, minority recuiter, 1986—; sci. and math. tutor, Shaker Heights, Ohio, 1982. Mem. Am. Chem. Soc., Black Profl. Assn. (sec. 1982), Women in Sci. Engring. Math. Consortium Ohio, Iota Sigma Pi. Democrat. Pentecostal. Lodge: Toastmasters. Home: 747 E 96th St Cleveland OH 44108 Office: Standard Oil Research and Devel 4440 Warrensville Ctr Rd Warrensville OH 44128

TARWATER, LUCY MARGARET SNIDER, electronics company owner; b. Phila., Sept. 15, 1954; d. John Norton and Lucy (Ogle) Snider; m. Keith Allen Tarwater, Feb. 14, 1985 (div. Sept. 1982); 1 child, Michelle Antonia DiAngelo. Student, Pa. State U., 1973-74, Our Lady of Angels, 1974-75, Walters State Community Coll., 1981-83. Account rep. Taylor Hosp., Ridley Park, Pa., 1979-82; bookkeeper Sta. WVTN-FM, Gatlinburg, Tenn., 1982-84; acctg. clk. Dominion Auto, Sevierville, Tenn., 1983-85; owner Valley Distbg. Services, Sevierville, 1985—. Active Amateur Radio Emergency Service. Mem. Nat. Assn. Female Execs. (state rep. 1985), Nat. Wildlife Fedn., Nat. Audubon Soc., Amateur Radio Relay League (lic.). Republican. Methodist. Home and Office: Valley Distbg Services Rt 7 Box 314 Sevierville TN 37862

TASHJEAN, CATHERINE RICHARDSON, librarian; b. St. Paul; d. James A. and Katherine D. (Connolly) Richardson; m. John Tashjean, June 2, 1962. BS in Library Sci., Coll. St. Catherine, St. Paul, 1949. Asst cataloguer Loyola U., Chgo., 1949-50; jr. librarian sch. engring. U. Minn., Mpls., 1950-51, cataloguer law sch., 1951-53, librarian sch. journalism, 1953-62; reference librarian FHA, Washington, 1966; acquisitions librarian Canisius Coll., Buffalo, 1966-71; staff librarian Manhattanville Coll., Purchase, N.Y., 1972-73, acting dir., 1974-75, dir., 1975-78; librarian U.S. Office Personnel Mgmt., Washington, 1978—. Mem. Soc. for History in Fedl. Govt., Delta Phi Lambda. Office: US Office Personnel Mgmt 1900 E St NW Washington DC 20415

TASHJIAN, JULIA ZAKARIAN, state official; b. Providence, June 8, 1938; d. Harry and Eliza (Kaffeian) Zakarian; m. James Samuel Tashjian, Nov. 29, 1959; children: Sherri Lynn, James Edward, Lisa Helene, Charles Harry. Dep. registrar of voters Town of Windsor, Conn., 1968-82; chmn. jury com. Town of Winsdor, Conn., 1969-75; adminstrv. asst. State and Urban Devel. Com., 1965-75, Govt. Adminstrn. and Policy Com., 1975-76, Human Services Com., 1977-78; spl. asst. fin. com. Conn. Legislature, 1979-81, interim intern coordinator, 1979-81; sec. of state State of Conn., Hartford, 1982—; adminstrv. asst. House Asst. Majority Leaders, 1981. Mem. Democratic State Central Com., 1978-82; del. Dem. Nat. Conv., 1980, 84, Dem. Nat. Party Conf., 1981. Mem. Nat. Assn. Secs. of State (exec. com., chmn. by-laws com., sec. 1986, v.p. 1987). Office: Sec of State Office Capitol Ave Hartford CT 06106

TASKA, EILEEN RUTH, therapist, sculptor; b. Bklyn., May 22, 1932; d. Henry Austin and Mildred Elinore (Deisseroth) Johnson; m. Frederick Anton Taska, May 27, 1956 (Jan. 1974); children: Lynn Suzanne, Todd Walker, Heidi Gaye, Gretel Nell. Student, The Cooper Union, N.Y.C., 1954, 55; studies with mem. of Nat. Sculpture Soc., N.Y.C., 1969-72; student, Yale U., 1972-74; BA, Goddard Coll., 1973; MS, Coll. New Rochelle, 1974; PhD, Union Grad. Sch., Cin., 1975. Free-lance graphic artist Greenwich, Conn., 1956-68; pvt. practice psycho-ednl. therapist Greenwich, 1975—; lectr., presenter of workshops and numerous demonstrations in field, Tex., Chgo., N.Y., N.J., Vt., Mass., Wis., 1975—. Exhibited in shows in Vt., Conn., Mass., N.Y., 1971-80; represented in numerous pvt. collections; inventor in field. Club: Midday (Stamford, Conn.). Home and Office: 1035 North St Greenwich CT 06831

TASSONE, GELSOMINA (GESSIE), metal processing executive; b. N.Y.C., July 8, 1944; d. Enrico and A. Cira (Petriccione) Gargiulo; children: Ann Marie, Margaret, Theresa, Christine; m. Armando Tassone, Mar. 20, 1978. Student, Orange County Community Coll., 1975-79, Iona Coll., 1980—. Head bookkeeper Gargiulo Bros. Builders, N.Y.C., 1968-72; pres., owner A&T Iron Works, Inc., New Rochelle, N.Y., 1973—, Gessie Realty, New Rochelle, N.Y., 1980-86, Majestico Iron Works, Inc., N.Y.C., 1980—, A&G Distbg. of West, New Rochelle, 1987—, A&T Contractors Greater N.Y., N.Y.C., 1987—. Recipient Profl. Image award Contractors Council Greater N.Y.C., 1986; Named Businesswoman of Yr., Contractors Council Greater N.Y.C., 1985; company named a Successful Small Bus. Co., Westchester County C. of C./SBA, 1986. Mem. Am. Inst. Steel Constrn. Inc., Am. Welding Soc., Real Estate and Bldg. Servivces, Occupational Safety & Health Adminstrn., Assn. Bus. & Profl. Women in Constrn., Westchester Assn. Women Bus. Owners, The Am. Inst. (N.Y. chpt.). Office: A & T Iron Works Inc 25 Cliff St New Rochelle NY 10801

TASTO, MONICA MAE, auditor; b. Madison, Minn., Jan. 20, 1962; d. Lawrence August and Helen Catherine (Kunz) T. BS in Acctg., Moorhead State U., 1984; postgrad., U. Minn. CPA, Minn. Acct. Gelco Corp., Eden Prairie, Minn., 1984-85; intermediate auditor Minn. Charitable Gambling Bd., St. Paul, 1985-86; jr. auditor Def. Contract Audit Agy., Mpls., 1986—. Mem. Am. Soc. Women CPA's, Am. Inst. CPA's, Minn. Soc. CPA's. Roman Catholic. Home: 11131 Xavier Circle Bloomington MN 55437

TATARA, DEBORAH LYNNE, electronics executive; b. Champaign, Ill., Aug. 15, 1958; d. Ronald Fred and Irene Elsa (Pilz) Spamer; m. Richard Michael Tatara, Oct. 19, 1985. BS in Computer Sci., Ill. Inst. Tech., 1979; M of Mgmt., Northwestern U., 1984. Applications programmer Techs. AT&T, Lisle, Ill., 1980-81, product planner, 1981-82; tech. cons. Techs. AT&T, Chgo.; supr. Data Systems div. AT&T, Lisle, 1984—, dist. mgr. data systems group. Mem. Nat. Assn. Female Execs. Republican. Lutheran. Office: AT&T 4513 Western Ave Lisle IL 60532

TATE, EVELYN RUTH, real estate broker; b. Ottumwa, Iowa, Sept. 21; d. Frank Edward and Ella Belle (Smith) Ross; student public schs., Huntington Park, Calif.; m. William Tate (dec.); 1 son, William. Owner, mgr. Evelyn R. Tate Realty Co., Sherman Oaks, Calif., 1943-53, Beverly Hills, Calif., 1942—; owner, mgr. Evelyn Tate Fine Arts, San Francisco, 1976—; mgr. Beverly Hills Galleries, Hyatt Regency Hotel, San Francisco, 1979—, mgr. art gallery Fairmont Hotel; owner, mgr. Tate Gallery, St. Frances Hotel, San Francisco, Hyatt Regency Hotel San Francisco, Fairmont Hotel, Dallas. Mem. Nat. Assn. Female Execs., The Exec. Female. Home: 999 Green St Apt 1003 San Francisco CA 94133

TATE, MARGARET JANE, dietitian, nutritionist; b. Omaha, Sept. 21, 1950; d. William Brownlee and Louisa Kay (Smith) Hargleroad; m. David Edward Tate, Oct. 21, 1983. BS, U. Nebr., Omaha, 1972; MS, Colo. State U., 1979. Registered dietitian. Dietetic intern Peter Bent Brigham Hosp., Boston, 1972-73, jr. research dietitian, 1973-76; teaching asst. Colo. State U., Ft. Collins, 1976-77, 1977; health program supr. Larimer County Health Dept., Ft. Collins, 1977-83; nutrition cons. Colo. Dept. Health, Denver, 1983—; nutritionist spl. study Harvard Sch. Pub. Health, Boston, 1976, Student Health Program for Migrant Farmworkers and Rural Poor, Denver, 1977; faculty affiliate Colo. State U., 1981-87; cons. Golden West Nursing Home, Ft. Collins, 1982-83. Contbr. articles to profl. jours. Mem. adv. com. USDA Nutrition Edn. and Tng. Program Colo. Pvt. Schs., Denver, 1979-80, residence council Larimer County Dept. Human Devel., Ft. Collins, 1980-82, community action bd., 1982; Denver chpt. Head Start Program health adv. com., 1985—; chmn. Home Econs. Program adv. com. Aurora pub. schs., Aurora, Colo., 1985-86; mem. Healthy Moms/Healthy Babies Coalition, Denver, 1985-86; bd. dirs. Vol. Clearing House, Ft. Collins, 1982-83. March of Dimes fellow in maternal nutrition U. N.C., 1982. Mem. Denver Dietetic Assn. (chmn. allied health and dietetic practice group com. 1985-86, pres.-elect 1986-87, pres. 1987—, dietitian of yr. 1986), Colo. Dietetic Assn. (legis. network coordinator 1982-84, pres.-elect 1983-84, pres. 1984-85, licensure com. chmn. 1984-86, del. ADA house of dels. 1986—, chmn. policies, procedures and bylaws com. 1985-86, chmn. council on dists. 1986—, dietitian of yr. 1987), No. Colo. Dietetic Assn. (pres.-elect 1981-82, pres. 1982-83), Colo. Pub. Health Assn. (sec. 1985-87, dir.-at-large 1987—), Am. Dietetic Assn. (editor Pub. Health Practice Group newsletter editor 1985-86, chmn.-elect 1986-87, chmn. 1987—, Mary C. Zarasky scholar 1982), Am. Pub. Health Assn., Soc. Nutrition Edn. (state legislature com. coordinator 1982-85). Office: Colo Dept Health 4210 E 11th Ave Denver CO 80220

TATE, MERZE, educator; b. Blanchard, Mich., Feb. 6, 1905; d. Charles H. and Myrtle Katora (Lett) T.; B.A. Western Mich. U. 1927; M.A. Columbia U. 1930, B.Litt. Oxford U. 1935, Ph.D. Harvard U. 1941; LL.D. (hon.) Morgan State U., Bowie State Coll. 1977, Lincoln U. 1978; D.H.L., Havard U., 1986. Tchr., Crispus Attucks High Sch., Indpls. 1927-32, Barber Scotia Coll. Concord, N.C. 1935-36, Bennett Coll. 1936-41, Morgan State U. 1941-42; faculty Howard U. 1942-74, now prof. emeritus; Fulbright prof. India 1950-51. Fellow and grantee in field; recipient Nat. Urban League Disting. Achievement award 1948; Western Mich. U. Disting. Alumna award 1970; Mayor of Detroit award 1978; Am. Black Artist's Pioneer award 1978; award The Prometheans, Inc., 1980; Am. Assn. State Colls. and Univs. award, 1982. Mem. Am. Hist. Assn., Assn. Study Afro-Am. History, AAUW (Disting. Mem. award D.C. chpt. 1983), Phi Beta Kappa, Alpha Kappa Alpha (3d fgn. fellow), Pi Gamma Mu. Roman Catholic. Clubs: Radcliffe of Washington, Harvard of Washington, Writers, Howard U. Women's, Howard U. Retirees, Bridge Builders, Bridge Eights. Author: The Disarmament Illusion—The Movement for a Limitation of Armaments to 1907, 1942, The United States and Armaments, 1948, The United State and the Hawaiian Kingdom, 1965, Hawaii: Reciprocity or Annexation 1968, Diplomacy in the Pacific, 1973; contbr. numerous articles to profl. jours.

TATE, SHEILA BURKE, former press secretary to First Lady, public relations executive; b. Washington, Mar. 3, 1942; d. Eugene L. and Mary J. (Doherty) Burke; m. William J. Tate, May 2, 1981; children: Hager Burke Patton, Courtney Paige Patton. BA in Journalism, Duquesne U., 1964; postgrad. in mass communications, U. Denver, 1975-76. Research asst. Westinghouse Air Brake Co.; asst. account exec. Falhgren and Assos.; copywriter Ketchum, MacLeod and Grove, 1964-66; account exec. Burson-Marsteller Assocs., Pitts., 1967; sr. v.p. Burson-Marsteller Assocs., Washington, 1985-87; public relations mgr. Colo. Nat. Bank, Denver, 1967-71; account exec. Hill and Knowlton, Inc., Houston, 1977-78; v.p. Hill and Knowlton, Inc., Washington, 1978-81; dep. to the chmn. Hill and Knowlton Inc., Washington, 1987-88; press sec. to First Lady White House, Washington, 1981-85; press sec. George Bush for Pres. Campaign, 1988; bd. dirs. Corp. for Pub. Broadcasting. Mem. Nat. Press Club, Nat. Press Found. (bd. dirs.). Republican. Clubs: Duquesne U. Century, F Street, Washington Golf and Country. Office: Hill & Knowlton Inc Wash Harbour 901 31st St NW Washington DC 20007

TATE-AUSTIN, PRISCILLA LILLIAN, infosystems specialist, bank officer, magazine editor; b. Dallas, May 4, 1949; d. Raymond Lee and Lillian Margaret (Cullum) Tate; m. Russell Tate-Austin, Apr. 30, 1983. BA in History, Duke U., 1971; postgrad., Freie Universitat, West Berlin, Germany, 1971-73; MA in Art History, Duke U., 1974; postgrad., Columbia U., 1974-77. Music tchr. Paul Lobe Musikschule, West Berlin, Germany, 1972-73; telemarketing Campaign Communications Inst., N.Y.C., 1977-80; exec. interviewer Louis Harris Assocs., N.Y.C., 1980-81; personnel prodn. mgr. Schulman Ronca and Bucavalas, N.Y.C., 1981-82; mktg. support rep. Axxa Corp., N.Y.C., 1982-83; MIS assoc. E.F. Hutton, N.Y.C., 1983-84; asst. v.p. Mfrs. Hanover Trust, N.Y.C., 1984-88; sr. editor PC mag., N.Y.C., 1988—; pres. Power User Group N.Y.P.C., 1983-87. Author: (with others) The Triumph of Patience, 1977; contbg. editor: Computer Equipment Buyer's Guide, 1987-88. Fundraiser John Anderson Unity Campaign, N.Y., 1980; deacon The Riverside Ch., N.Y., 1982-83. Fulbright fellow, 1971, Columbia fellow, 1974. Mem. Micro Mgrs. Assn. (exec. bd. dirs. 1987), Women in Data Processing (network chmn. 1983-84), N.Y. Personal Computer User (SIG Head 1983-87), Info. Ctr. Mgrs. N.Y. Democrat. Home: 160 Riverside Dr New York NY 10024 Office: PC Mag/Ziff Davis Pub Co One Park Ave New York NY 10016

TATELBAUM, BRENDA LOEW, publisher; b. Boston, Apr. 1, 1951; d. Kenneth F. and Florence (Rosoff) Loew; m. Ira R. Tatelbaum, Aug. 1970 (div. May 1983); children: Laura Rani, Max Loew. BA, Boston U., 1971, postgrad., 1980-83; MA, Brown U., 1973. Cert. English, speech tchr., Mass. Library asst. John D. Rockefeller Library, Providence, 1973; speech therapist Dartmouth (Mass.) Pub. Schs., 1974-79; pub., editor Eidos mag., Boston, 1984—; pres., treas., bd. dirs. Brush Hill Press, Inc., Boston, 1984—; founder Tatelbaum Assoc. Pub. Relations & Fund Raising, Boston, 1987—; speaker in field; active fund raising and pub. relations Bill Baird AIDS Awareness Fund, 1987—, Boston U. Ad Hoc Com. for Reproductive Freedom, Boston, 1987—. Author: Eden Poems, 1982, Life Evolves From Living, 1983; short stories; editor: Boston Collection of Women's Poetry, 1983; contbr. articles to profl. jours. Media coordinator Emerson Coll. Polit. Awareness Orgn.-Safer Sex March, Boston, 1987. Fellow World Lit. Acad., Internat. Biog. Assn.; mem. Nat. Assn. for Female Execs., Internat. Women's Writing Guild, Nat. Coalition Against Censorship, ACLU, Civil Liberties Union Mass., Mass. Assn. Older Ams., People for the Am. Way, Hadassah, Nat. Kidney Found., Am. Biog. Inst. Research Assn. (assoc., hon. advisor 1987). Club: Poetry New Eng. (Cambridge, Mass.). Home: 367 Brush Hill Rd Milton MA 02186 Office: Brush Hill Press Inc Box 96 Boston MA 02137-0096

TATEM, NANCY GAUER, nursing services director; b. Newark, N.J., Aug. 16, 1942; d. Harry and Jean (Hill) Gauer; m. H. Randolph Tatem, 3d, Sept. 14, 1963 (div. 1979); children—Jeffrey Randolph, Kyra Elizabeth. RN, Hahnemann U., 1963; BS in Nursing, Gwynedd-Mercy Coll., Gwynedd, Pa., 1984. Cert. gerontol. nurse Am. Nurses Assn., 1985. Med.-surg. nurse Hahnemann U., Phila., 1963-65; health info. coordinator Nat. Found. March of Dimes, Bucks County, Pa., 1977-78; nurse/instr. Upjohn, Doylestown, Pa., 1978-80; head nurse Doylestown Manor (Pa.), 1980-82; surg. asst. AJL Simoes Assocs., Lansdale, Pa., 1982-84; dir. nursing Doylestown Manor, 1984-85; co-founder, dir. nursing services, pres. exec. bd. Services T.H.E. Respite, alternative adult day program, Mechanicsville, Pa., 1986—; vol. nurse ARC, Bucks County, 1977-80. Com. mem. Bucks County Hist. Soc., 1972-78; founding mem. PAK Teen Drug and Alcohol Program, 1976-78; bd. dirs. Bucks County chpt. March of Dimes, 1979-80. Mem. Bucks County RN's Assn. (sec. 1980-84), Pa. Nurses Assn., Forum for Advancement Nursing Excellence, 1984—, Am. Nurses Found, Pa. Adult Day Care Assn., Nat. Gerontol. Nursing Assn., Cen. Bucks C. of C., Sigma Theta Tau (Iota Kappa chpt.). Republican. Presbyterian. Club: PEO. Home: 54 Spring Dr Doylestown PA 18901 Office: T H E Respite Route 413 PO Box 294 Mechanicsville PA 18934

TATSUI-D'ARCY, SUSAN KATHLEEN, entrepreneur; b. Los Angeles, Sept. 25, 1956; d. Paul M. and Sumi Jenny (Kawana) Tatsui; m. Robert Stephen D'Arcy. BA in Psychology, U. Calif., Santa Cruz, 1978. Owner, dir. R.E.C. Day Camp Inc., Santa Cruz, 1979-86; owner, coordinator Profl. Tutoring Program, Santa Cruz, 1980-86, Ski Club for Kids, Santa Cruz, 1981-86; mktg. dir. Just in Case Data Products, Santa Cruz, 1984-86; owner, designer Knock on Wood Designs, Santa Cruz, 1986—; dir., treas. Strata Mktg., Santa Cruz, 1984-86, Custom Computer Mktg., Santa Cruz, 1986—; cons. in field, 1986—. Author: Working Woman's Wedding Planner, 1987, (edni. software) Progressive Preschool, 1988. Mem. C. of C. Republican. Office: Knock on Wood Designs PO Box 2988 Santa Cruz CA 95063

TATUM, ELIZABETH RUTH, insurance company sales manager; b. Pennsauken, N.J., June 29, 1933; d. Edward Rigby and Ruth C. (Schrepple) Fox; m. (dec. 1954); children: Susan Lynn Simpson, Mark Alan, Sharon Elizabeth Portales. RN, U. Pa., 1953; MA in English, Fla. Atlantic U., 1975. CLU. Nursing instr. W. Jersey Hosp., Camden, N.J., 1953-54; staff various USAF hosps., 1954-61; tchr. North Palm Beach (Fla.) Pvt. Sch., 1963-77; field agt. N.Y. Life Ins. Co., West Palm Beach, Fla., 1979-80; bus. agt. Nationwide Ins. Co., North Palm Beach, 1979-80; recruiting mgr. Nationwide Ins. Co., Columbus, Ohio, 1980-82; sales service mgr. Nationwide Ins. Co., Orange, Calif., 1982-87; bus. agt. mgr. Nationwide Ins. Co., Woodland Hills, Calif., 1987—. Bd. dirs. Met. Women's Ctr., Columbus, 1980-82; fund raiser Ohio Dominican Coll., 1981. Mem. CLU Assn., Adminstrv. Mgmt. Soc., Bus and Profl. Womens Assn. (named Woman of Yr. 1981-82), Phi Kappa Phi. Republican. Home: Nationwide Ins Co 21450 Burbank Blvd Woodland Hills CA 91367 Office: Nationwide Ins Co 21031 Warner Ctr Ln Woodland Hills CA 91367

TATUM, GLORIA JEAN, social worker; b. Colbert, Ga., Aug. 20, 1948; d. John Henry and Rosa Lee (Hitchcock) Curry; m. William Robert Tatum, Nov. 21, 1972; children: William Robert III, Alonzo Delarrence. BA, Spelman Coll., 1971; MSSW, U. Louisville, 1979. Accounts receivable clk. Gold Kist, Inc., Athens, Ga., 1971-72; U.S. pub. health rep. Dept. Pub. Health, Chgo., Atlanta, 1972-73; field researcher U.S. Census Bur., Chgo. and So. Ind., 1975-76; social worker Jefferson County Fiscal Ct., Louisville, 1978—; active community outreach services Jefferson County Dept. Human Services, Louisville, 1985—. Group work leader Up Black Emphasis on Adoptions, Inc., Louisville, 1982—; mem. vis. com. U. Louisville Bd. Overseers, 1985—; mem. gov's. A-Plus Program Advocacy Group for Ednl. Excellence in Ind. Mem. Nat. Assn. Social Workers, Nat. Assn. Female Execs., Acad. Cert. Social Workers, Spelman Coll. Alumni Assn., U. Louisville, Alumni Assn. Democrat. Baptist. Avocations: fishing, cycling, reading, especially econ. and med. writings. Home: 21 W Robin Rd New Albany IN 47150

TATUM, JULIA SEARS, real estate professional; b. Parkersburg, W.Va., Nov. 6, 1957; d. Robert and Rebecca (Nuzum) Sears; m. R. James Tatum, June 23, 1984. B in English Lit., Bus., La. State U., 1980. Lic. real estate salesperson, La. Agt. residential sales ERA Realty, Baton Rouge, 1980-83; mgr. sales Fairwood West Residential Devel., Baton Rouge, 1984-85; regional leasing exec. Maurin-Ogden Developers, New Orleans, 1985—. Office: Maurin-Ogden Developers 7924 Wrenwood Blvd Suite C Baton Rouge LA 70809

TAUB, MARCIA JEAN, marketing and display design executive; b. N.Y.C., Oct. 9, 1957; d. Ronald Herbert and Ethel Betty (Flecker) T. Student, Northwestern U., winter 1975, summer 1978; BA, U. Denver, 1979; M of Mgmt. and Human Resource Devel., Nat. Coll. Edn., Evanston, Ill., 1983. Account exec. creative displays div. Saatchi and Saatchi, London, 1980-85; cons. Mktg. Services Group, Chgo., 1987—; display mgr. Max Factor & Co., Stamford, Conn., 1985-87. Vol. Haddasah, N.Y., Jewish United Fund. Mem. Am. Mktg. Assn., Cosmetic Exec. Women, Point-of Purchase Advt. Inst., Chgo. Bus. Women of Pi Beta Phi (pres. Chgo. chpt. 1983-85), Phi Alpha Theta. Clubs: Carlton (Chgo.); Merchandising Exec.

TAUB (BLAKELY), MARILYN LORRAINE, marketing professional; b. N.Y.C., Apr. 11, 1934; d. Arthur Harris and Fannie (Moiseff) Prushan; m. Morton Taub, Oct. 26, 1952 (div. Mar. 1985); children: Steven W., Sheri L.; m. Richard Blakely, June 23, 1985. BS, U. Md., 1974, MS, 1977. Bookkeeper Joseph McGillura Inc., N.Y.C., 1951-52; sec. U.S. Panama Canal Co., Balboa, Republic of Panama, 1953-54; water project asst. Environ. Action Found., Washington, 1978-79; copy editor Assoc. Ofcl. Analytical Chemists, Arlington, Va., 1980-82, mktg. mgr., 1982—. Mem. Council Engring and Sci. Socs., Am. Soc. Assn. Execs. Democrat. Jewish. Office: Assn Analytical Chemists 1111 N 19th St Suite 210 Arlington VA 22209

TAUBER, INGRID DIANE, clinical psychologist; b. Washington, Jan. 30, 1952; d. Laszlo Nandor and Lilly Katherine (Manovill) T.; B.A., Boston U., 1973; M.A., U. Md., 1976; Ph.D., Calif. Sch. Profl. Psychology, 1980. Counselor youth services Area B Community Mental Health Center, Washington, 1974-76; psychology intern Gladman Meml. Hosp., Oakland, Calif., 1976-77, San Francisco Gen. Hosp., 1976-77; pre- and post-doctoral trainee VA Med. Center, San Francisco, 1977-81; pvt. practice clin. psychology, San Francisco, 1977-88; bd. dirs. No. Calif. Holocaust Ctr., tchr. psychol. testing VA Med. Ctr., bd. overseers Tauber Inst. Holocaust Studies, Brandeis U. Lic. psychologist, Calif. Mem. Am. Psychol. Assn., Calif. Psychol. Assn., Am. Orthopsychiat. Assn., Assn. Mental Health Affiliation with Israel. Home: 2090 Green St 26 San Francisco CA 94123 Office: 348 Spruce St San Francisco CA 94118

TAUNTON, KATHRYN JAYNE, accountant; b. Thomaston, Ga., Nov. 3, 1953; d. Mack Doudal and Martha Jayne (Goolsby) T. AA, Cypress Coll., 1973; BA in Accounting, Calif. State U., 1977. Circulation clk. Buena Park Library Dist., Buena Park, Calif., 1973-76; account supr. Orange County State Employees Credit Union, Santa Ana, Calif., 1977-78, Santa Ana City Credit Union, 1978-79; self employed Reliable Credit Union Service, Buena Park, 1979—. Democrat.

TAVARES, MARIANNE CYNTHIA, marketing company executive; b. Cambridge, Mass., Aug. 29, 1956; d. Manuel Simoes and Dorothy Mary (Martin) T. B.S., Framingham State Coll., 1978. Telemarketing rep. Waters Assocs., Milford, Mass., 1977-82, mktg. research analyst, 1982-84; mktg. info. services mgr. Millipore Corp., Bedford, Mass., 1984-85, communications mgr., 1986—. Trustee, Yankee Village Condominiums, Acton, Mass., 1985-86, com. chairperson, 1986-87; vol., group leader CODE Hotline, 1984—, bd. dirs. 1986. Mem. Am. Mktg. Assn., Am. Mgmt. Assn. Republican. Roman Catholic. Avocations: Photography; travel. Home: 1 Townhouse Ln Unit 3 Acton MA 01720 Office: Millipore Corp 80 Ashby Rd Bedford MA 01730

TAYLOR, ADRIENNE ELIZABETH, nurse, administrator; b. Orange, N.J., Nov. 12, 1956; d. William Ernest and Madelyn Louise (Ruso) T. BS in Nursing, Georgetown U., 1978; MPH, Columbia U., 1986. RN, N.Y. Staff nurse Lenox Hill Hosp., N.Y.C., 1978-80, sr. staff nurse, 1980-82, asst. patient care coordinator, 1982-83, quality assurance coordinator, 1983-86, asst. v.p. nursing, 1986—. Mem. AAUW, Am. Hosp. Assn., Am. Mgmt. Assn., Georgetown U. Alumni Assn., Sigma Theta Tau. Democrat. Roman Catholic. Club: N.Y. Road Runners. Home: 460 E 79th St Apt 12F New York NY 10021 Office: Lenox Hill Hosp 100 E 77th St New York NY 10021

TAYLOR, ALISON JEAN, mortgage officer, financial planner; b. Ann Arbor, Mich., Aug. 30, 1952; d. William Ralph and Janice Gwynne (Lowe) T. BS in Human Nutrition, U. Md., 1977. With Nat. Heart Assn., Bethesda Md., 1977-78; food technician Meat Sci. Research Lab. USDA, Beltsville, Md., 1978-79; statis. asst. Food Consumption Research Group USDA, Hyattsville, Md., 1979-80; fin. planner Investors Diversified Services, Bethesda, Md., 1981-82, FSC Securities Corp., Silver Spring, Md., 1982-86, Internat. Money Mgmt. Group, Greenbelt, Md., 1986—; v.p. Wallace Mortgage Co., Inc., Silver Spring, 1983-86; real estate agt. Classic Properties, Inc., Landover, Md., 1983—; mortgage officer United Security Mortgage Corp., Kensington, Md., 1986—. Mem. Internat. Assn. Fin. Planners, Am. Inst. Mortgage Brokers, Nat. Assn Realtors, Am. Dietetic Assn., D.C. Dietetic Assn. Republican. Home: 13101 Dauphine St Silver Spring MD 20906

TAYLOR, ANN LOUISE, marketing executive; b. Fairmont, Minn., Aug. 8, 1937; d. Eugene and Celia Ethel (Fulton) Lundahl; m. James Harold Taylor, May 23, 1959; children: Kimberly Taylor Locey, Jayme K. BA in Edn., U. Minn., 1959; postgrad., Am. Inst. Banking, 1985—. Tchr. Nokomis Jr. High Sch., Mpls., 1959-61, Helen Keller Mid. Sch., Easton, Conn., 1973-75; photojournalist Suburban & Wayne Times, Berwyn, Pa., 1975-80; cons. pub. relations Fla. Internat. Bank, Miami, Fla., 1981-84, dir. mktg. Fla. Internat. Bank, Miami, 1984—. Contbr. articles to profl. jours. Adv. bd., community participation Dade County Pub. Schs., 1987—. Mem. Am. Inst. Banking (v.p. mktg. 1986-87), Am. Soc. Tng. and Devel., Nat. Assn. Bank Women, Am. Pen Women/Miami, Women in Communications (pres. 1987-88), Greater South Dade C. of C. (bd. dirs. 1987—). Republican. Presbyterian. Club: Founders of South Dade (pres. 1987—). Office: Fla Internat Bank 17945 Franjo Rd Miami FL 33157

TAYLOR, ANNA DIGGS, federal judge; b. Washington, Dec. 9, 1932; d. Virginius Douglass and Hazel (Bramlette) Johnston; m. S. Martin Taylor, May 22, 1976; children: Douglass Johnston Diggs, Carla Cecile Diggs. BA, Barnard Coll., 1954; LLB, Yale U., 1957. Bar: D.C. 1957, Mich. 1961. Atty. Office Solicitor, Dept. Labor, W, 1957-60; asst. prosecutor Wayne County, Mich., 1961-62; asst. U.S. atty. Eastern Dist. of Mich., 1966; ptnr. Zwerdling, Maurer, Diggs & Papp, Detroit, 1970-75; asst. corp. counsel City of Detroit, 1975-79; U.S. dist. judge Eastern Dist. Mich. Detroit, 1979—; adj. prof. labor law Wayne State U. Law Sch., Detroit, 1976. Trustee Receiving Hosp. Detroit, Episcopal Diocese Mich., Detroit Symphony, Sinai Hosp., United Found., Community Found. Southeastern Mich., Orch. Hall, Detroit, Greater Detroit Health Council. Mem. Fed. Bar Assn., Nat. Lawyer's Guild, State Bar Mich., Wolverine Bar Assn., Women Lawyers Assn. Mich. Democrat. Episcopalian. Office: US Dist Ct 231 W Lafayette Blvd 740 US Courthouse Detroit MI 48226

TAYLOR, ARLENE ROSE, nursing administrator; b. Calgary, Canada; d. Leslie Warren and Kathleen (Cafferky) T.; m. Jack Fabiani, May 2, 1974 (div. Apr. 1987). BS, Loma Linda U., 1964; MS, Columbia Pacific U., 1983. RN, Calif. Staff RN Meml. Mission Hosp., Ashville, N.C., 1964-65, USPHS Hosp., Shiprock, N. Mex., 1965-67; pub. health nurse Salt Lake City Health Dept., 1967-70; pub. health nurse supr., acting dir. Napa County (Calif.) Health Dept., 1970-74; nursing cons. North Bay Regional Ctr., Napa, Calif., 1976-79; nursing quality assurance coordinator St. Helena Hosp., Deer Park, Calif., 1978—, dir. infection control, 1980—, adminstrv. dir. nursing services, 1985—; pres. Taylor Ednl. Enterprises, 1987—; cons., guest lectr. Pacific Union Coll. , Angwin, Calif., 1978—; preceptor dept. nursing Sonoma State U., 1982—. Vol. Napa County ARC, 1970—; lectr. Napa County Am. Heart Assn., 1970—; bd. dirs. sta. KCDS, Angwin, Calif., 1981—. Mem. Assn. Seventh-day Adventist Nurses (chair continuing edn. 1976—) , Calif. Assn. Quality Assurance Profls., Assn. Practioners of Infection Control, Wine Country Infection Control Practioners Assn., Mensa. Republican. Office: St Helena Hosp and Health Ctr PO Box 99 Deer Park CA 94576

TAYLOR, BARBARA ALDEN, public relations executive; b. Dallas, Aug. 21, 1943; d. Harold Earl and Sally Alden (Howard) T.; BA, Smith Coll., 1965; MA, Antioch Coll., 1971. Vol., Peace Corps, India, 1966-68; tchr. Upper Merion Sch. Dist., King of Prussia, Pa., 1969-70; tchr. Cheltenham Sch. Dist., Elkins Park, Pa., 1970-74; pub. relations dir. Princess Hotels Internat., N.Y.C., 1974-75; chmn. Taylor & Hammond Ltd., N.Y.C., 1975-84; pres. Doremus/Marketshare, 1984-86; sr. v.p. Doremus Porter Novelli, N.Y.C., 1986—. Bd. dirs. Madison Square Boys' and Girls' Club N.Y., 1978—, also mem. women's bd. Boys' Club N.Y. Mem. Women in Communications, Pub. Relations Soc. Am., Soc. Am. Travel Writers, Advt. Women N.Y. Clubs: Doubles Internat., Smith Coll. Club N.Y., Jr. League City N.Y. Avocations: tennis, walking. Office: Porter Novelli 1633 Broadway New York NY 10019 *

TAYLOR, BARBARA JEAN, insurance industry association executive; b. White Plains, N.Y., Feb. 3, 1933; d. Charles George and Gladys Isobel (Winch) Watkins; B.A. in English, SUNY, New Paltz, 1974; m. Richard Taylor, Apr. 10, 1955 (div. 1977); children—Mark Evan, Linda Elizabeth, Janice Barbara, Nancy Jane. Advt. copywriter McCann-Erickson, N.Y.C., 1953-55, newspaper reporter Patent Trader, Mt. Kisco, N.Y., 1962-63, Evening Star, Peekskill, N.Y., 1963-65; founding editor The Yorktowner (N.Y.), 1965-66; gen. news reporter Westchester/Rockland (N.Y.) newspapers, 1966-70, bur. chief, editor No. Westchester Bur., 1970-72; communications specialist fed. Community Devel. Program, Yorktown, 1975-77; asso. dir. N.Y. State Petroleum Council (arm of Am. Petroleum Inst. trade assn.), N.Y.C., 1977-85; v.p. consumer affairs and edn. Ins. Info. Inst., 1985—; founder, mgr. speakers bur. in field; freelance writer for New Dawn, Feminist Bull., The Entertainer; tchr. creative writing adult edn. classes; speaker civic and edn. groups. Bd. dirs. Food for the Hungry; adv. Citizens Commn. on Urban Renewal. Mem. Nat. Assn. Female Execs., NOW, Soc. Consumer Affairs Profls., Home Economists in Bus., Nat. Assn. Ins. Women, Ins. Consumer Affairs Exchange, Nat. Bus. Edn. Assn., Women in Communication, Am. Council on Consumer Interests, Publicity Club of N.Y., Bus. and Profl. Women. Jewish.

TAYLOR, BARBARA JOAN, consulting company executive; b. Dover, Pa., July 23, 1944; m. Daniel F. Taylor (div. 1983); children: Daniel Jr., Russell. Student, U. Md., 1968-81; BA, Columbia Pacific U., 1982, MBA, 1983. Assoc. dir. adminstrv. computer ctr. U. Md., College Park, 1964-81; regional mgr. Systems & Computer Tech. Corp., Malvern, Pa., 1981-85; pres. Lenders Fin. Group, Huntington Beach, Calif., 1985-87, Orange County Bus. Devel. Ctr., Huntington Beach, 1987—. State of Calif. grantee, 1987. Mem. Women in Bus. (dir. 1987—), Ind. Writers of So. Calif. (treas. 1987—), Tex. Instruments Users Group (sec.-treas. so. Calif. region 1986—), Orange County C. of C. (com. chairperson 1986—). Office: Orange County Bus Devel Ctr 523 N Grand Ave 1st Floor Santa Ana CA 92701

TAYLOR, BETTY ANN, American Red Cross administrator; b. Greentown, Ohio, May 26, 1929; d. Ivan Ronald and Ruth Marie (Martin) Daily; 1 child, K. Dean. A.A., Walsh Coll., 1973; student Aultman Hosp., Canton; Ohio, 1949, 50-51; B.A., Malone Coll., 1979; postgrad. other colls., univs. Caseworker ARC, Canton, 1968-73, asst. exec. dir., 1978-80, exec. dir., 1980—, family service officer ARC Nat., Washington, 1979—. Service in numerous disasters in Vietnamese Refugees-Indiantown Gap, Pa., W.Va., Md., Ala., Tex. P.R., N.C., Miss., Ohio; 1st dir. of Canton Red Cross Rape Crisis Ctr., 1975. Recipient award for Community Action, Gov. State of Ohio, 1973; Vice Pres.'s award Nat. ARC, 1985; Vol. Service award Rotary Club of Canton, 1985. Mem. Ohio Citizens Council, Nat. Assn. Social Workers, Nat. Assn. Female Execs. Republican. Office: ARC Canton Chpt 618 Second St NW Canton OH 44703

TAYLOR, BETTY JO, film executive, producer, writer, director; b. Dallas, Feb. 10, 1933; d. William Samuel and Donna Mazie (Lester) Taylor. B.Journalism, U. Tex., 1955. Reporter Dallas Times Herald newspaper, 1955-56; editor Republic Nat. Life, Dallas, 1956-59; dir. media Presbyn. Ch. U.S., Nashville, Atlanta, 1959-70; mgr. communications Coca-Cola USA, Atlanta 1970-81; creative dir. The Bloom Cos., Dallas, 1981-82; pres. The Communications Dept., Inc., Dallas, 1982—; founding bd. dirs. IMAGE Media Ctr., Atlanta, 1978-80; pres., bd. dirs. Women in Film, Atlanta, 1979-81. Author: Where The Clock Walks, 1963; writer, producer, dir. corp. and ednl. films, 1970—; screenings at nat., internat. festivals. Former bd. dirs. Religion in Am. Life, N.Y.C., 1970. Recipient ADDY award for best black-white consumer advt. campaign, Am. Advt. Fedn., 1967; spl. award for film, for Juvenile Diabetes Found, 1980, nat. award for film for United Ways Am, 1980; 4 CINE Golden Eagles for best Am. nontheatrical films; awards from N.Y., Am., Chgo., San Francisco, and other film festivals, 1970—. Mem. Dallas Communications Council, Women in Communications, Pub. Relations Soc. Am. Democrat. Presbyterian. Home: 7603 Bryn Mawr Dallas TX 75225

TAYLOR, CAROLYN ANNE, insurance executive, health promotion administrator; b. Greensboro, N.C., Aug. 11, 1947; d. Charles William and Edna Marie (Zaoralek) Reavis. BS cum laude, U. Minn., 1969, MBA cum laude, 1973. Instr. St. Paul Bus. Coll., 1969-72; mgr. client programs Price-Wilson, Ltd., Toronto, Can., 1972-76; v.p. health cons. programs CDP Assocs., Inc., Atlanta, 1976-86; v.p. ops. Ctr. for Corp. Health Promotion Travelers Ins. Co., Reston, Va., 1987—; cons. Nat. Cancer Inst., 1976-86, Med. Coll. Wis., 1986-87, U. Mass., 1985-87, M.D. Anderson Tumor Inst., Houston, 1986-87; bd. dirs. Campbell Communications Inc., Bethesda, Md. Co-editor: Breast Cancer Digest, 1983; contbr. numerous articles to profl. jours.; researcher for book Business Logistics, 1973. Mem. Assn. Community Cancer Ctrs.; treas. Inverness Homeowners Assn., Potomac, Md., 1982-84. Office: Ctr Corp Health Promotion 1850 Centennial Park Dr #520 Reston VA 22091

TAYLOR, CAROLYN SUE, trade association executive; b. Shattuck, Okla., Jan. 26, 1936; d. Mack Russell Heiserman and Helen Fay (Sills) Landon; m. George Raymond Taylor, Sept. 11, 1955; children: Pamela Sue, Mark Edward (dec.). Student, Okla. State U., Stillwater, 1954-55, So. Meth. U., 1987, 88. Asst. sales mgr. Red Comet, Inc., Littleton, Colo., 1955-57; sec. Continental Oil Co., Ponca City, Okla., 1967-70; exec. sec. Citizens' Utilities Co., Stamford, Conn., 1970-73; corp. sec. Guaranty Trust Co., Ponca City, Okla., 1973-75; co-owner The Place, Columbus, Tex., 1978-81; owner Pat Walker's Figure Salon, Columbus, 1982-83; office mgr. H.F. Halcom, Atty. at Law, Columbus, 1982-86; exec. v.p. Columbus Area C. of C., 1986—. Bd. dirs. Colo. Count Mental Health/Retardation, Columbus, 1981-85; sec. Colo. County Cancer Soc., Columbus, 1983-86; mem. Inst. for Orgn. Mgmt. So. Meth. U. Mem. Am. C. of C. Execs., Tex. C. of C. Execs., Gulf Coast Chamber Execs., Nat. Assn. Female Execs. Republican. Methodist. Club: Pilot of Columbus (pres.-elect 1985-86, pres. 1986-87). Office: Columbus Area C of C 435 Spring St PO Box 343 Columbus TX 78934

TAYLOR, CORA HODGE, social worker; b. Fayetteville, N.C., Nov. 25, 1942; d. John Marlin and Cora Louise (Mitchell) Hodge; B.S., N.C. Coll., Durham, 1963; M.S.W., U. N.C., Chapel Hill, 1965; m. Charles L. Taylor, June 26, 1965; children—Charles L., John M. Clin. social worker VA Hosp., Bedford, Mass., 1965-68, 73-79; chief social worker Regional Health Center, Wilmington, Mass., 1978-79; clin. social worker VA Hosp., Bedford, Mass., 1979—; field instr. Boston U. Sch. Social Work, 1979-87, Smith Coll. Sch. of Social Work, 1986— ; instr., cons. primary care residents Tufts U. Med. Sch., Regional Health Center, Wilmington, Mass., 1978-79. Mem. Town Meeting, Billerica, Mass., 1981—; precinct clk., 1981, 82, precinct chmn., 1984, 85, 86; deacon First Congl. Ch., 1986—. Recipient Superior Performance award VA Hosp., Bedford, 1966, 84, 85, 86. Mem. LWV (dir. 1970-73), Acad. Cert. Social Workers, Nat. Assn. Social Workers. Home: 35 Wildwood Rd Pinehurst MA 01866 Office: 200 Springs Rd Bedford MA 01730

TAYLOR, DELLA MAE, nurse; b. Johnson City, Tenn., Apr. 15, 1932; d. Lee Roy and Honolulu Cornelius (Holly) Brewer; R.N., Meml. Hosp., Johnson City, 1953; student E. Tenn. State U.; diploma newspaper writing Newspaper Inst. Am., 1968; B.S., Steed Coll., 1978; postgrad. Emmanuel Sch. Religion, 1986—; m. John R. Taylor, Jr., Feb. 12, 1955 (dec. Oct., 1986); children: Aliesa Benea, Celeste Taylor. R.N., Tenn. Pediatric polio head nurse Meml. Hosp., Johnson City, 1953-54; staff nurse VA, Mountain Home, Tenn., 1954-55, 1961-64, part-time pvt. duty. 1964-78; staff nurse Meml. Hosp., Clarksville, Tenn., 1955-56; pediatric nurse U.S. Army Hosp., Augsburg, Germany, 1957-61; RN for life ins. exams, Jonesboro, Tenn., 1978—; instr. nursing, 1986—; owner Mama Bear's Fudge. Pres., Pageants III, Jonesboro, 1980-82; coordinator Pageants III Nationwide Youth Scholarship Pageant Corp., 1980-82. Chmn. precinct, 15th Dist. Democratic Com., 1977-78; mothers' chmn. Washington County March of Dimes; youth coordinator Washington County Heart Assn.; chmn. Dr. Charles Underwood Scholarship Fund, 1984. Recipient 2d prize for party time sausage pie Litton. Mem. Nurses Christian Fellowship, E. Tenn. State U Alumni Assn., Steed Coll. Alumni Assn., Nat. Assn. Female Execs., Unicoi C. of C., U.S. Pageants Assns., Bus. and Profl. Women's Club. Washington County Farm Bur. Democrat. Baptist. Home: Rt 8 Box 37 Taylor Dr Jonesboro TN 37659

TAYLOR, DIANA LYNN, sales representative; b. Greensburg, Pa., May 25, 1957; d. Alfred Lawrence Jr. and Garnet Elizabeth (Rahl) T. BSBA, W.Va. Wesleyan Coll., 1979. Sales asst. Liberty Mut. Ins. Co., Dallas, 1979-83, Knoll Internat., Dallas, 1983-84, sales rep. Pentel of Am., San Antonio, 1984-87, Max Factor & Co., Dallas, 1987—. Mem. AAUW, Nat. Assn. Female Execs. Club: Cimarron (Dallas). Home and Office: 2228 Cedarbrush Dr Carrollton TX 75006

TAYLOR, DOROTHY HARRIS, real estate broker; b. Richmond, Va., Nov. 3, 1931; d. Edgar Alan and Sadie (Wheeler) Harris; m. Gethsemane Jess Taylor (dec. Nov. 1964); children: Marlene J., Eric M., Andre E. Student, L.I. U., 1959, John J. Criminal Coll., 1974, Queen's Coll., 1983, 87—, St. John's U., 1984, 86. Lic. real estate broker. Toll collector Port of N.Y. Authority, N.Y.C., 1967-80, tolls dispatcher, 1967; sales exec. Flushing

Tribune, 1979; real estate salesperson Parkfield Realty, Queens Village, N.Y., 1982-83, Arro of Queens, 1983-84; real estate broker Arro of Queens, Queens Village, 1984-85, residential appraiser, N.Y.C., 1986—. Mem. Queens Council on Arts, 1987, Nat. Arbor Day Found., North Shore Animal Shelter League; mem. com. for disabled children Queens Coll.; charter mem. Nat. Mus. Women in Arts. Mem. Nat. Assn. Female Execs. (network dir. 1983-84), Am. Assn. Ret. Persons, Nat. Assn. of Unknown Players for Film, TV, and Print Modeling Arts, Inc. (charter), United Christian Evangelistic Assn. Democrat. Clubs: Dorcas Soc. (Bklyn.) (pres. 1957-58), Queens Coll. Women's. Lodges: Order Eastern Star, Heroines of Jericho, Lady of Knights. Avocations: gardening, crocheting, reading, contesting, interior decorating.

TAYLOR, ELAINE CLAIRE NELSON, experimental psychologist; b. Meadville, Pa., Dec. 2, 1927; d. John David and Martha Margaret (Zurfluh) Nelson; m. John Edward Taylor, Sept. 10, 1949 (div. 1970); children: Jenny L., Jess N. BS, Pa. State U., 1949; MA, Bowling Green State U., 1951; PhD, State U. Iowa, 1954. Sr. scientist Human Resources Research Orgn., Alexandria, Va., 1954-57, cons., 1960-63, sr. staff scientist, 1967-84; independent cons., Carmel Valley, Calif., 1984—; cons. FMC Ordnance Engring., San Jose, Calif., 1977-80, RCA Edn. Programs, Cherry Hill, N.J., 1976; cons. McFann-Gray Assocs., Monterey, Calif., 1984-85, The Woodside Summit Group, Mountain View, Calif., 1984-85, The Nellie Thomas Inst., Monterey, 1984—. U.S. Army Tng. Mgmt. Inst., Fort Eustis, Va., 1975-76, Calif. Dept. Mental Hygiene, Sacramento, 1972. Author tech. papers, book chpts. Sec., Property Owners' Assn., Carmel Valley, 1962-63; mem. adv. com. Monterey Peninsula Water Mgmt. Dist. (Calif.), 1984-87. NIMH grantee, 1972-74. Fellow Am. Psychol. Assn. (pres. div. mil. psychology, 1978-79, sec.-treas. 1975-77, editor newsletter 1973-75); mem AAAS, Human Factors Soc., Sigma Xi. Democrat. Home: 18 Meadow Pl Carmel Valley CA 93924

TAYLOR, ELIZABETH, actress; b. London, Feb. 27, 1932; d. Francis and Sara (Sothern) T. Student, Byron House, Hawthorne Sch., Metro-Goldwyn-Mayer Sch. Motion pictures include Lassie Come Home, 1942, There's One Born Every Minute, 1942, The White Cliffs of Dover, 1943, Jane Eyre, 1943, National Velvet, 1944, Life With Father, 1946, Courage of Lassie, 1946, Cynthia, 1947, A Date With Judy, 1948, Julia Misbehaves, 1948, Little Women, 1948, Conspirator, 1949, The Big Hangover, 1949, Father of the Bride, 1950, Father's Little Dividend, 1950, A Place in the Sun, 1950, Love is Better Than Ever, 1951, Ivanhoe, 1951, Elephant Walk, 1954, Rhapsody, 1954, Beau Brummel, 1954, The Last Time I Saw Paris, 1955, Giant, 1956, Raintree County, 1957, Cat on a Hot Tin Roof, 1958, Suddenly Last Summer, 1959, Holiday in Spain, 1960, Butterfield 8, 1960 (Acad. award best actress), Cleopatra, 1962, The V.I.P.'s, 1963, The Sandpiper, 1965, Who's Afraid of Virginia Woolf (Acad. award 1966), Taming of the Shrew, 1967, The Comedians, 1967, Reflections in a Golden Eye, 1967, Dr. Faustus, 1968, Boom!, 1968, Secret Ceremony, 1968, The Only Game in Town, 1969, X, Y and Zee, 1972, Under Milk Wood, 1971, Hammersmith is Out, 1972, Night Watch, 1973, Ash Wednesday, 1974, The Driver's Seat, 1975, The Blue Bird, 1976, A Little Night Music, 1977, Victory at Entebbe, 1977, The Mirror Crack'd, 1980, Return Engagement (TV), 1979, Between Friends, 1983, Malice in Wonderland (TV film), 1985, North and South (TV miniseries), 1985; Broadway debut in The Little Foxes, 1981; narrator film documentary Genocide, 1981; appeared in play Private Lives, 1983; Hotel (TV series), There Must Be a Pony (TV film), Poker Alice (TV prodn.); author: (with Richard Burton) World Enough and Time; poetry reading, 1964, Elizabeth Taylor, 1965, Elizabeth Taylor Takes Off-On Weight Gain, Weight Loss, Self Esteem and Self Image, 1988. Active philanthropic, relief, charitable causes internationally; initiated Ben Gurion U.-Elizabeth Taylor Fund for Children of the Negev, 1982; nat. chmn. Am. Found. AIDS Research, 1985—. Named Comdr. Arts and Letters (France), 1985; awarded Legion of Honor (France), 1987. Office: Chen Sam & Assocs Inc 315 E 72d St New York NY 10021

TAYLOR, ELIZABETH JANE, investment consultant, real estate company executive; b. Tiffin, Ohio, Oct. 27, 1941; d. Albert Joseph Lucas and Mary Jane Siebenaller-Swander; m. Gaylen Lloyd Taylor, July 11, 1977. Student, Heidelberg Coll., 1961, Austin Community Coll., Tex., 1983-84. Cons., Hypnosis Conn., Ohio and Tex., 1967—; dir. regional mktg. Sibrow, Inc., Ottawa, Can., 1981-83; realtor assoc. Alliance Sales, Austin, 1985—; prin., Taylor & Assocs., Internat. Mktg. & Bus. Devel., Hong Kong, U.S., 1980—; tchr. mktg. and bus. develop., 1980—. Author: profl. column Austin Women Mag., 1984-86; (poetry) Letters from Home, 1986. Vice pres. Am. Congress on Real Estate, 1982-83; arbitrator Better Bus. Bur., 1984—; mem. speakers bur. Austin Woman's Ctr., 1985—; v.p. Austin World Affairs Council, 1984—; mem. adv. panel Austin Woman Mag., 1984-86. Nominated to Tex. Womens Hall of Fame, 1984. Mem. Nat. Assn. Female Execs. (network dir. 1980—). Avocations: writing, behavior research. Home: 3406 Danville Dr Cedar Park TX 78613

TAYLOR, ELLEN BORDEN BROADHURST, civic worker; b. Goldsboro, N.C., Jan. 18, 1913; d. Jack Johnson and Mabel Moran (Borden) Broadhurst; student Converse Coll., 1930-32; m. Marvin Edward Taylor, June 13, 1936; children—Marvin Edward, Jack Borden, William Lambert. Bd. govs. Elizabethan Garden, Manteo, N.C., 1964-74; mem. Gov. Robert Scott's Adv. Com. on Beautification, N.C., 1971-73; mem. ACE nat. action com. for environ. Nat. Council State Garden Clubs, 1973-75; bd. dirs. Keep N.C. Beautiful, 1973-85; mem. steering com., charter mem. bd. dirs. Keep Johnston County (N.C.) Beautiful, 1977-88; life judge roses Am. Rose Soc.; chmn. local com. that published jointly with N.C. Dept. Cultural Resources: An Inventory of Historic Architecture, Smithfield, N.C., 1977; co-chmn. local com. to survey and publish jointly with N.C. Div. Archives and History: Historical Resources of Johnston County, 1980-86. Mem. Nat. Council State Garden Clubs (life; master judge flower shows), Johnston County Hist. Soc. (charter), Johnston County Arts Council (bldg. com. 1960-65, trustee 1960-88, chmn. 1969-70, steering com., Spl. award for projects of Pub. Library Johnston County & Smithfield 1987), N.C. Geneal. Soc. (charter), Johnston County Geneal. Soc. (charter), Hist. Preservation Soc. N.C. (life), N.C. Art Soc. (life). Democrat. Episcopalian. Clubs: Smithfield (N.C.) Garden (charter; pres. 1969-71), Smithfield Woman's (v.p. 1976), DAR (organizing vice-regent chpt. 1976), Gen. Soc. Mayflower Descs. (life), Descs. of Richard Warren, Nat. Soc. New Eng. Women (charter mem. Carolina Capital chpt.), Colonial Dames Am. (life), Magna Charta Dames, Nat. Soc. Daus. of Founders and Patriots Am. Home: 616 Hancock St Smithfield NC 27577

TAYLOR, FAITH JOHNSON, small business owner; b. St. Louis, July 4, 1940; d. James Oliver and Irma (Clay) Johnson; m. Matthew Taylor, Apr. 12, 1961; children: Ronald Matthew, Niché Eugenie, Maret Alise. Cert., Vonderschmit's, St. Louis, 1961; student, Forest Park Community Coll., St. Louis, 1961-62, Florissant (Mo.) Valley Coll., 1986-87. Sec. Jewish Voc. and Employment, St. Louis, 1966-68; instr. No. Systems, Alliance for Community, St. Louis, 1968-69; personnel asst. Cen. States Diversified, St. Louis, 1969-71; indsl. relations asst. Combustion Engring., St. Louis, 1971-73; asst. to gen. mgr. Sta. KEZK Radio, Clayton, Mo., 1973-81; secretarial asst. Universtiy City (Mo.) Sch. Dist., 1980-83; traffic mgr. Sta. KY98 Radio, St. Louis, 1981; sales asst. Sta. KMOV-TV, St. Louis, 1983—; prin., pres. Creative Weddings, St. Louis, 1985—; cons., coordinator Creative Weddings, St. Louis, 1985—. Incorporator Alliance for Community Control, St. Louis, 1968-69, bd. dirs., founder and contributions, 1967; vol. St. Catherine's Ladies Sociality, St. Louis, 1980—, Young Dems. of Mo., St. Louis, 1987; mem. St. Thomas Ladies Guild, Florissant, Mo., 1984—, Our Lady of Providence Club, St. Louis, 1965-66, St. Vincent DePaul Soc., St. Louis, 1983-84. Mem. Nat. Assn. Female Execs., Florissant Valley C. of C. Democrat. Roman Catholic. Clubs: Ladies Sociality (Pagedale, Mo.) (v.p. 1983-84); Just Us (St. Louis) (treas. 1975). Office: Creative Weddings 7584 Olive Rm 206 Saint Louis MO 63130

TAYLOR, FANNIE TURNBULL, educator; b. Kansas City, Mo., Sept. 11, 1913; d. Henry King and Fannie Elizabeth (Sills) Turnbull; m. Robert Taylor, Dec. 2, 1938 (div. 1974); children: Kathleen Muir Taylor Isaacs, Anne Kingston Taylor Wadsack. BA, U. Wis., 1938; LHD (hon.), Buena Vista Coll., Storm Lake, Iowa, 1975. Mem. faculty U. Wis., Madison, 1941—, prof. social edn., 1949—, emeritus, 1979—, dir. Wis. Union Theatre, 1946-66, coordinator univ. systems arts council, 1967-70, assoc. dir. Ctr. Arts Adminstrn., 1970-72, coordinator Consortium Arts Ctr., 1976-84; cons. in field. Author: (handbook) The Arts as a New Frontier, also articles. Program dir. music Nat. Endowment Arts, 1966-67, program info. dir., 1972-76; bd. dirs. Wis. Arts Council, 1964-72, Wis. Found. Arts, 1976—, Madison Civic Music Assn., 1976-84, Madison Children's Mus., 1983-86; council chair Elvehjem Mus. Art, 1976—; mem. grant rev. com. Madison Civic Ctr., 1981-86, Madison Civic Ctr. Found., 1985—; bd. dirs. Wis. chpt. Nature Conservancy, 1963-84, chmn., 1976-77; bd. dirs. Shorewood Hills Found., 1976—, pres., 1976-81. Recipient Oak Leaf award Nature Conservancy, 1981. Fellow Wis. Acad. Scis., Arts and Letters; mem. Assn. Coll., Univ. and Community Arts Adminstrs. (exec. dir. 1970-72, Fannie Taylor award 1972), Am. Assn. Dance Cos. (bd. dirs. 1967-72), Nat. Assn. Regional Ballet (bd. dirs. 1975-77), Nat. Guild Community Schs. Arts (bd. dirs. 1977-80), Women in Communications (Writers' Cup 1980), U. Wis. Alumni Assn. (Disting. Service award 1979). Clubs: Madison Civics (pres. 1969-70), Madison, Univ. (pres. 1982-85), Blackhawk. Home: 1213 Sweet Briar Rd Madison WI 53705 Office: U Wis 5525 Humanities Madison WI 53706

TAYLOR, GRACE ELIZABETH (BETTY) WOODALL, law educator, law library administrator; b. Butler, N.J., June 14, 1926; d. Frank E. and Grace (Carlyon) Woodall; m. Edwin S. Taylor, Feb. 4, 1951 (dec.); children: Carol Lynn Taylor Crespo, Nancy Ann. AB, Fla. State U., 1949, MA, 1950; JD, U. Fla., 1962. Instr. asst. librarian Univ. Libraries, U. Fla., 1950-56, asst. law librarian, 1956-62; dir. Legal Info. Ctr., 1962—, prof. law, 1976—; cons. law libraries; chmn. LAWNET network legal info. Fla. Legislature Lewis scholar, 1946-50. Contbr. numerous articles on automation and law to library publs. Nat. Endowment for Humanities grantee, 1981-82; Council Library Resources grantee 1984-86. Mem. Am. Assn. Law Libraries (exec bd.), Am. Assn. Law Schs., ABA, Am. Soc. Info. Scis., Fla. Library Assn, Online Computer Library Council (past pres. users council), West Law Adv. Bd. Democrat. Methodist. Office: U Fla Legal Info Ctr Gainesville FL 32611

TAYLOR, JANELLE DIANE WILLIAMS, writer; b. Athens, Ga., June 28, 1944; d. Alton L. and Frances (Davis) Williams; m. Michael H. Taylor, Apr. 8, 1965; children: Angela Michelle, Alisha Melanie. Student, Augusta Coll., 1980-81. Orthodontic nurse Athens, 1962-65, Augusta, Ga., 1969-72; med. research technologist Med. Coll. Ga., Augusta, 1977-79; writer Ga., 1978—; bd. dirs. Jo Beth Williams Romance Screenplay Award; lectr. writing Augusta Coll., other schs. and workshops, 1982—. Author: Savage Ecstasy, 1981, Valley of Fire, 1984, First Love, Wild Love, 1984 (Maggie award 1984), Golden Torment, 1984 (Reviewer's Choice award Romantic Times 1984), Savage Conquest, 1985, Stolen Ecstasy, 1985, Moondust and Madness, 1986, Sweet, Savage Heart, 1986 (Golden Pen cert. 1986), Destiny's Temptress, Defiant Ecstasy, 1982, Forbidden Ectasy, 1982, Brazen Ecstasy, 1983, Tender Ecstasy, 1983, Love Me with Fury, 1983, Bittersweet Ectasy, 1987, Wild Is My Love, 1987, Fortune's Flames, 1988, Passions Wild and Free, 1988; contbr. How to Write a Romance and Get It Published, 1983, 2d. edit., 1984, Candlelight, Romance and You, 1983, My First Real Romance, 1985; also articles. Recipient Romantic Times Trophy award for best Indian series, 1985, Sioux Sacred Medicine Wheel and Cheyenne Redtail Hawk feather Coup hon. Gray Eagle Sioux Indian Series, 1983-84; cert. of merit Am. Univ. Women, 1986; named to Romantic Times Writer's Hall of Fame, 1988. Mem. Romance Writers Am., Western Writers Am., Sci. Fiction Writers Am., Ga. Romance Writers Am., Southeastern Writers, Authors League/Authors Guild, Augusta Author's Club. Republican. Baptist. Office: PO Box 11646 Augusta GA 30917-1646

TAYLOR, JANICE QUINTINA, personnel director; b. Vicksburg, Miss., Sept. 14, 1954; d. James Oscar and Annie Pearl (Smith) Taylor. BBA, Tuskegee Inst., 1977. Shift supr. Talon Textron, Morton, Miss., 1977-79; mgr. quality control Talon Textron, Lake City, S.C., 1979-81; dir. human resources, personnel rep. La-Z Boy East, Florence, S.C., 1981-88—; dir. human resources Charleston Marriott, North Charleston, S.C., 1988—. Sec. Florence Vocat. Rehab. Bd., 1984-88; mem. Florence County Bd. Health, 1985-88, eBushua Found, Florence, S.C. Mem. Area VIII Pvt. Industry Council, NAACP (asst. sec. Florence br. 1987—), Nat. Assn. Female Execs., Delta Sigma Theta. Democrat. Baptist. Lodge: Order Eastern Star. Home: 7930 St Ives Rd Apt J-1 North Charleston SC 29418

TAYLOR, JEAN FRANCES, educator; b. Wilmington, N.C., Mar. 20, 1938; d. Lee McKinley and Dorothy (Hankinson) T. AB, Greensboro (N.C.) Coll., 1959; M of Math., U. S.C., 1969. Cert. tchr., N.C. Assoc. caseworker Dept. Pub. Welfare, Laurinburg, N.C., 1959-60; tchr. math. Scotland County Schs., Laurinburg, 1960-61; tchr. math. New Hanover County Schs., Wilmington, 1961-66, 69—, supr. math., 1967-68; asst. planner math. curriculum New Hanover County Schs., 1982-83, calculus curriculm State Dept. Pub. Instrn., Raleigh, N.C., 1984-85; mem. editorial rev. panel Nat. Council Tchrs. Math., Reston, Va., 1982-87. Mem. edn. com. Dept. Human Relations, Wilmington, 1985-86; vol. Friends of Pub. Radio, Wilmington, 1985-87; treas. precinct 17 Wilmington Dems., 1986-87. Recipient Gov.'s award Bus. Com. Math Sci. Edn., Raleigh, 1983, N.C. Presdl. award, 1987. Mem. NEA, N.C. Assn. Educators (bldg. rep., treas. 1970-77), Nat. Assn. Tchrs. Math., N.C. Assn. Tchrs. Math. (ea. pres. 1974-76), Am. Fedn. Tchrs., Delta Kappa Gamma, Phi Delta Kappa. Home: 110 Parkwood Dr Wilmington NC 28403 Office: John T Hoggard High Sch 4305 Shipyard Blvd Wilmington NC 28403

TAYLOR, JERI CECILE, producer, writer; b. Evansville, Ind., June 30, 1938; d. William Edward Taylor and Ruah Loraze (Brackett) Suer; m. Dick Enberg, Sept. 19, 1959 (div. 1977); children: Jennifer, Andrew, Alex; m. David Moessinger, Oc.t 11, 1986. Student, Stevens Coll., 1955-56; AB in English, Ind. U., 1959; MA in English, Calif. State U., Northridge, 1967. Lectr. English Calif. State U., 1967-69; dir. Oxford Theatre, Los Angeles, 1972-78. Producer, writer Quincy series, 1980-83, Blue Thunder series, 1984, movie A Place to Call Home, 1987, Magnum, P.I. series, 1987—; dir. Quincy multiple episodes, 1980-83; producer TV pilots and movies, 1984-87. Mem. Writers' Guild Am. (award 1982), Dir. Guild Am., Am. Fedn. TV & Radio Artists. Office: Universal TV 100 Universal Plaza Universal City CA 91608

TAYLOR, JILL OLSEN, lawyer, artist; b. Logan, Utah, June 1, 1955; d. Keith Conrad and Norma Elveda (Correll) Olsen; m. Bruce T. Taylor, July 3, 1979; children—Jenny, Benjamin, Christina. B.A. summa cum laude, Brigham Young U., 1977; J.D., Brigham Young U., 1980. Bar: Utah, 1980. Dep. county atty., Emery County, Utah, 1980-81; corp. atty. Physicians Emergency Service, Price, Utah, 1981—. Bd. dirs., pres. Covered Bridge Canyon Homeowners Assn., 1983—. Mem. Utah State Bar Assn., ABA, Order of Barristers (mem. nat. bd. govs.), Phi Kappa Phi. Republican. Mormon.

TAYLOR, JOANNA WANDA, philatelist, show promoter; b. Jersey City, May 17, 1942; d. Jan and Victoria Pelagia (Malecki) Sliski; m. Phillip Gray Vincent, Dec. 22, 1961 (div. May 1969), 1 child, Laurie Yvonne; m. Scott Harry Taylor, Jan. 5, 1970, 1 child, Joanna Victoria. BS in Microbiology, U. Md., 1966. Sanitarian Prince Georges County Dept. Health, Cheverly, Md., 1968-72; co-founder Scojo Stamps, Ridgely, Md., 1972—; co-founder, promoter S & S Enterprises, Balt., 1974—; auction agt. Scott H. Taylor, Ridgely, 1979—. Recipient Merchandising Excellence award at Nat., '81 Show, Ameripex '86 (Internat. Stamp Show), Bootholder. Mem. Am. Stamp Dealers Assn. (life), Am. Philatelic Soc. (life, expertizer), Scandinavian Collectors Club, Republican. Club: Tidewater Stamp (sec. 1985) (Easton, Md.). Avocations: gardening; crafts. Office: Scojo Stamps PO Box 423 Ridgely MD 21660

TAYLOR, J(OCELYN) MARY, museum administrator, zoologist, educator; b. Portland, Oreg., May 30, 1931; d. Arnold Llewellyn and Kathleen Mary (Yorke) T.; m. Joseph William Kamp, Mar. 18, 1972. B.A., Smith Coll., 1952; M.A., U. Calif., Berkeley, 1953, Ph.D., 1959. Instr. zoology Wellesley Coll., 1959-61, asst. prof. zoology, 1961-65; assoc. prof. zoology U. B.C., 1965-74; dir. Cowan Vertebrate Mus., 1965-82, prof. dept. zoology, 1974-82; collaborative scientist Oreg. Regional Primate Research Ctr., 1983-87; prof. (courtesy) dept. fisheries and wildlife Oreg. State U., from 1984; dir. Cleve. Mus. Nat. History, 1987—; adj. prof. dept. biology Case Western Res. U., 1987—. Assoc. editor Jour. Mammalogy, 1981-82. Contbr. numerous articles to sci. jours. Fulbright scholar, 1954-55; Lalor Found. grantee, 1962-63; NSF grantee, 1963-71; NRC Can. grantee, 1966-84; Killam Sr. Research fellow, 1978-79. Mem. Soc. Woman Geographers, Am. Soc. Mammalogists (1st v.p. 1978-82, pres. 1982-84), Australian Mammal Soc., Cooper Ornithol. Soc., Soc. Study of Reprodn., Northwest Sci. Assn. (trustee 1980-83), Sigma Xi. Episcopalian. Office: Cleve Mus Natural History Wade Oval University Circle Cleveland OH 44106

TAYLOR, JUNE MARIE, logistics administrator; b. Duluth, Minn., July 11, 1954; d. John Leo and Olive Mae (Howell) Rogalla; m. Bruce Alan Taylor, Feb. 2, 1973 (div. July 1974); m. William Robert Taylor, Jr., June 8, 1978. BS in Bus. Mgr., Wright State U., 1986, postgrad., 1987. Receptionist McLean Constrn. Co., Superior, Wis., 1972; sec. USAF Civil Service, various locations, 1972-79; specialist trainee logistics mgmt. Wright-Patterson AFB, Ohio, 1979-82; installation mobility officer Norton AFB, Calif., 1982-84; mgr. dep. program for logistics Wright-Patterson AFB, 1984—. Key worker Combined Fed. Campaign, Wright-Patterson AFB, 1984. Named one of Outstanding Young Women Am., 1984. Mem. Soc. Logistics Engrs., Nat. Assn. for Female Execs., Am. Legion (sec. Proctor, Minn. chpt. 1970-71), 4-H (v.p. Adolph, Minn. 1971-72). Republican. Methodist.

TAYLOR, KENDALL FRANCES, arts administrator, educator; b. N.Y.C., May 9; d. Alexander and Sophie (Tannenbaum) Finne; m. David R. Garner, Nov. 23, 1979; BA, Fairleigh Dickinson U., Rutherford, N.J., 1962; MA, Vanderbilt U., 1963, MAT, 1964; MA, Syracuse U., 1977, PhD, 1979. Lectr., U. Md., 1964-71; writer, producer Stas. KNBC-TV, KTTV-TV, KPIX-TV, 1971-73; dir. Brainerd Art Gallery SUNY, Potsdam, 1979-80, chmn. Council of SUNY Gallery and Exhibit Dirs., 1979-80; asst. prof. Grad. Sch. George Washington U., 1980—; dir. traveling exhbn. program Library of Congress, 1980-84; dir. Arts Mgmt. Assocs., Washington, 1984—; acad. dir. Washington Seminar Program in Art and Architecture, The Am. U., 1988—; nat. speaker represented by Ross Assocs. Speakers Bur., N.Y.C. Author: (with Lila Weingarten) Arts and Crafts in Los Angeles, 1974, Never Separate from the Heart: The Life and Work of Philip Evergood, 1987; contbr. articles to profl. jours. Field rep. N.Y. State Council on the Arts, N.Y.C., 1980—; mem. steering com. Women Adminstrs. in Higher Edn. Adminstrn., Washington, 1983-84. Ford Found. fellow, 1963-64, Syracuse U. Florence fellow (Italy), 1974-75; Smithsonian fellow, 1977-78. Mem. Am. Assn. Mus. (mem. accreditation com. 1983—, chmn. Women Mus. Dirs. Caucus 1983-84, reviewer Mus. Assessment program 1984), Coll. Art Assn., Nat. Assn. Women Deans & Adminstrs. (presider conf. 1984, 85), Writers Guild Am. Democrat. Jewish. Home: 1841 Columbia Rd NW Washington DC 20009

TAYLOR, LINDA JEAN, small grains and specialty crop analyst; b. Buffalo, May 30, 1959; d. Alfred James and Ileane (Kunold) Taylor. BA, Kalamazoo Coll., 1980; M in Internat. Bus. Studies, U. S.C., 1982. Fin. analyst Gen. Motors Co., Detroit, 1978-79; researcher Traverse Bay Regional Planning Commn., Traverse City, Mich., 1979-80; intern OCFIBRAS subs. Owens Corning Fiberglas, São Paulo, Brazil, 1981-82; internal auditor Monsanto Co., St. Louis, 1982-85, fin. services mgr., 1985-87, internat. fin. analyst, 1987-88, small grains and specialty crop analyst, 1988—; instr. bus. Jr. Achievement, 1987-88. Mem. presdl. adv. com. on coll. investment in South Africa, Kalamazoo Coll., 1980; mem. Council on Internat. Affairs. Mem. Nat. Networking, St. Louis Assn. Credit mgmt. Home: 507 E Sarah Ln Creve Coeur MO 63141 Office: Monsanto Co 800 N Lindbergh Blvd Saint Louis MO 63167

TAYLOR, LINDA KLARE, accountant; b. Schulenburg, Tex., July 19, 1947; d. William Buske and Ottilia Ann (Kleckar) K.; m. Thomas Joe Taylor, Dec. 12, 1975. BS in Math., S.W. Tex. State U., 1969; MS in Accountancy, U. Houston, 1974. Math. tchr. Clear Creek High Sch., League City, Tex., 1969-73; acct. Marathon Oil Co., Houston, 1975-79, acctg. supr., 1979-87; acctg. rep. Marathon Internat. Oil Co., Houston, 1987—. Mem. Petroleum Accts. Soc. Houston (bd. dirs. 1986—, sec. 1987-88). Roman Catholic.

TAYLOR, LISA SUTER, museum director; b. N.Y.C., Jan. 8, 1933; d. Theo and Martina (Weincerl) von Bergen-Maier; m. Bertrand L. Taylor III, Oct. 30, 1968; children: Lauren, Lindsay. Student, Corcoran Sch. Art, 1958-65, Georgetown U., 1958-62, Johns Hopkins U., 1956-58; D.F.A. (hon.), Parsons Sch. Design, 1977, Cooper Union, 1984. Adminstrv. asst. President's Fine Arts Com., 1958-62; membership dir. Corcoran Gallery Art, 1962-66; program dir. Smithsonian Instn., 1966-69; dir. Cooper-Hewitt Mus. Decorative Arts and Design, Smithsonian Instn., 1969-87, dir. emeritus, 1987—; Mem. adv. bd. Art Deco Soc., Fashion Inst. Tech., N.Y., Living Stage, Washington, Moore Coll. Art; mem. vis. com. Bank St. Coll.; cons. U. Cin. Grad. Sch. Art and Architecture; mem. Mayor's Adv. Council on Design. Co-dir. (film) A Living Museum, 1968; editor: Urban Open Spaces, 1979, Cities, 1981; The Phenomenon of Change, 1984, Housing: Symbol, Structure, Site, 1988. Recipient Thomas Jefferson award, 1976; Bronze plaque Johns Hopkins YMCA, 1958; medal of honor Am. Legion, 1951; Bronze Apple award Am. Soc. Indsl. Designers, 1977; named Trailblazer of Yr. Nat. Home Fashion League, 1981, Mcpl. Art Soc. award 1987, Joseph Henry medal, 1987, Dame of Honour Order of St. John of Jerusalem. Mem. Am., N.Y. State, N.Y.C. museum assns., Art Mus. Dirs. Assn., Mcpl. Arts Soc., Central Parks Conservancy, Am. Craftsmans Council, Archtl. League, Ceramics Circle, Needle and Bobbin Club, Smithsonian Instn. (Exceptional Service award 1969, Gold medal 1972, hon., woman's council award 1979), Am. Soc. Interior Designers (hon.), AIA (hon.). Home: Seven Gates Farm Vineyard Haven MA 02568 Office: Cooper-Hewitt Mus 2 E 91st St New York NY 10128-9990

TAYLOR, LUCILLE MARIE, insurance company administrator; b. Youngstown, Ohio, Oct. 16, 1939; d. Victor Emanuel Scarpine and Elizabeth (Louise) Partezana; m. Norman Eugene Taylor, May 15, 1961 (div.); children: Mark Eugene, Stephen Emanuel. RN, St. Elizabeth Med. Ctr., Youngstown, 1960. RN, Ohio. Surg. nurse St. Elizabeth Med. Ctr., Youngstown, 1960-62, Ohio State U. Hosp., Columbus, 1962-65; surg. supr. Salem (Ohio) City Hosp., 1965-66; mgr. divisional claims Equitable Life Assurance, Youngstown, 1967-84; 2d v.p. Dun & Bradstreet Plan Services, Youngstown, 1984-86, regional v.p., 1986—. Democrat. Roman Catholic. Office: Dun & Bradstreet Plan Services 5500 Market St Youngstown OH 44512

TAYLOR, MARGARET TURNER, clothing designer, economist; b. Wilmington, N.C., May 7, 1944. A.B. in Econs., Smith Coll., 1966; M.A. in Econ. History, U. Pa., 1970, now Ph.D. candidate in City and Regionel Planning. Tchr. Jefferson Jr. High Sch., New Orleans, 1966-69; instr. econs. U. Tex.-El Paso, 1974-75; adj. prof. econs., Salisbury State Coll., (Md.), 1976-78; prin. mgr., designer Margaret Norriss, women's clothing, Salisbury, Md., 1980—; planner at Wharton Ctr. Applied Research, Phila., 1985-86; planning cons., freelance writer.

TAYLOR, MARGARET UHRICH, college official, consultant; b. Lebanon, Pa., Nov. 27, 1952; d. William Murray and Anne (Shultz) Uhrich; m. Timothy Norman Taylor, Sept. 29, 1979; 1 child, Walter Marshall. B.A., Shippensburg U., 1974. Adminstrv. asst. Patriot-News Co., Harrisburg, Pa., 1974; reporter Pub. Opinion sect., Chambersburg, Pa., 1975-78; assoc. editor, Miami bur. chief OAG, Inc., N.Y.C., 1978-79; pub. affairs dir. Wilson Coll., Chambersburg, 1980—, co-founder women in transition program, 1985, lectr. in communications, 1986—; adj. faculty Shippensburg U., Pa., 1981—. Founding mem. Commonwealth Assn. Students, 1972; charter mem. Friends of Fulton County Library, McConnellsburg, 1975; founder Unforgettable Charity Ball, Chambersburg, 1983-86 ; active Gotemba Sister-City Com., Borough of Chambersburg, 1981—; cons. dir. Straight Love Franklin County, Chambersburg, 1982-83; founder Women's Network Franklin County, 1982—; bd. dirs. Fulton County Med. Ctr., 1987—. Mem. Soc. Profl. Journalists (treas. Central Pa. chpt. 1981-82, v.p. 1982-83, pres. 1983-84, chmn. freedom of info. com. 1980-81, chpt. del. nat. conv. 1977), Women in Communications, Pa. Pub. Relations Soc., Chambersburg Area C. of C. (active Leadership Com. 1985—). Home: PO Box 552 Hustontown PA 17229 Office: Wilson Coll Pub Affairs Office 1015 Philadelphia Ave Chambersburg PA 17201

TAYLOR, SISTER MARIE DE PORRES, religious organization administrator; b. Los Angeles, May 27, 1947; d. James Sam Taylor and Isabel (McCoy) Clark. BA, Marylhurst (Oreg.) Coll. for Lifelong Learning, 1970; MA, San Francisco State U., 1976; MPA, Hayward (Calif.) State U., 1986.

Cert. secondary tchr., Calif. Tchr., counselor Holy Names High Sch., Oakland, Calif., 1970-79; assoc. pastor St. Benedict Ch., Oakland, 1979-83; dir. Black Caths. Diocese of Oakland, 1982—; exec. dir. Nat. Black Sisters Conf., Oakland, 1982—; coordinator conf. Joint Conf. of Black Priests, Sisters and Bros., Oakland, 1982-87; facilitator Nat. Black Cath. Congress, Balt., 1986-87; conf. designer, cons. Denver Black Caths., 1986; cons. Sacramento Black Caths., 1986; preacher in ch. Author: Lenten Reflections, 1987; editor (book) Tell It Like It Is, 1987. Bd. dirs. Holy Names Coll., Oakland, 1987—; 1st vice chmn. bd. dirs. Police Activities League, Oakland, 1987—; chmn. bd. dirs. Bay Area Black United Fund, Oakland, 1987—; chmn. bd. dirs. com. for urban renewal Oakland Citizens, 1987—. Recipient Rose Casanave award Black Cath. Vicariate, 1982, Outstanding Community Service award, United East Oakland Clergy, 1983, Outstanding Community Leader award Bay Area Links, 1984; named Woman of Yr., YWCA, 1987. Mem. Am. Home Econs. Assn., United East Oakland Clergy (pres. 1980-84), Nat. Assn. of Black Cath. Adminstrs., Nat. Black Sisters Conf., Nat. Assn. of Female Execs. Democrat. Roman Catholic. Club: Ladies of Peter Claver (Oakland) (chaplain 1984-85). Office: Nat Office Nat Black Sisters Conf 3014 Lakeshore Ave Oakland CA 94610

TAYLOR, MARY JAN LIPTHRATT, public relations specialist; b. Brunswick, Ga., Mar. 14, 1955; d. C. Donald and Virginia Dare (Browher) Lipthratt; m. Kevin Patrick Taylor, Oct. 16, 1982. A.B.J. magna cum laude, U. Ga., 1977. Asst. editor Coastal Media, Inc., St. Simons Island, Ga., 1977-81; dir. research Glover Printing Co., Brunswick, Ga., 1982-83; dir. pub. relations Joseph Citron, M.D., P.C., Atlanta, 1984-85; dir. mktg. and pub. relations Cob Gen. Hosp., Austell, Ga., 1985—. Mem. communications com., newsletter editor Brunswick-Glynn County Clean Community Commn., Brunswick, 1983. Club: Toastmasters Internat. Mem. Women in Communications, Am. Soc. Hosp. Mktg. and Pub. Relations, Pub. Relations Soc. Am. Phi Kappa Phi, Kappa Tau Alpha. Home: 887 Regal Path Ln Decatur GA 30030 Office: Cobb Gen Hosp 3950 Austell Rd Austell GA 30001

TAYLOR, MARY JOAN, lawyer; b. Kenton, Ohio, Dec. 24, 1926; d. Maurice A. and Martina (Dolan) McMahon; student St. Mary Springs Coll., 1944-45; Asso. Degree in Bus. Adminstrn. Franklin U., 1946-49; J.D. with high distinction, Ohio No. U., 1951; postgrad., U. Wyo., 1954-56; m. Edward McKinley Taylor, Jr., Apr. 23, 1952; 1 dau., Mary Margaret. Admitted to Ohio bar, 1951; gen. practice law, Kenton, 1951-52, Wichita Falls, Tex., 1953—; ptnr. law firm Taylor and Taylor, Dayton, Ohio, 1957—; law librarian Franklin U., 1948-49. Trustee, Harrison Twp., 1980- . Mem. Ohio Bar Assn., Montgomery County Law Library Assn., Ohio No. U. Alumni Assn. (sec. Miami Valley 1958-60), Iota Tau Lambda, Kappa Beta Pi. Club: Soroptimist. Address: 7417 N Main St Dayton OH 45415

TAYLOR, MARY ROSE, television anchor, journalist; b. Denver, May 26, 1945; d. Walter Gorringe and Marylynn (Eusterman) King; m. Charles Peete Rose, Aug. 10, 1968 (div.); m. 2d, Charles McKenzie Taylor, Feb. 26, 1983; stepchildren—Andrew McKenzie, Camille Taylor McDuffie. BA in Polit. Sci., U. N.C., 1967. Researcher, CBS-TV News, N.Y.C., 1968-71; assoc. producer BBC-TV Documentaries, N.Y.C., London, 1971-73; assigment editor Sta. WNEW-TV Metromedia, N.Y.C., 1973-74; documentary producer PBS, N.Y.C., Washington, 1974-76; producer, assigment editor Sta. WTOP-TV Post-Newsweek, Washington, 1976-77; anchor, reporter KTUL-TV News, Tulsa, 1978-79; anchor, reporter Gannett Broadcasting Sta. WXIA-TV, Atlanta, 1980-84; cons. producer documentary film Pumping Iron, N.Y.C., 1975-76; cons. producer Marshall McLuhan-the Man and his Message, N.Y.C., Toronto, 1982-85. Trustee Met. Atlanta Crime Commn.; mem. com. Gannett Community Service Awards. Recipient 1st place State UPI award, Ga., 1982. Mem. Am. Women in Radio TV, Nat. Acad. TV Arts & Scis., Sigma Delta Chi. Roman Catholic. Researcher: File on the Tsar, 1980-81; researcher on cities European Economic Community, German Marshall Fund, 1976; dir. Oh, Canada, Eh!, 1986, Tom Wolfe's New York-The City of Ambition, 1987. Office: 375 Pharr Rd Suite 217 Atlanta GA 30305

TAYLOR, MAXINE MALOY, comptroller; b. Hartford, Ala., Nov. 10, 1947; d. William Emmet and Maggie (Moody) M.; m. Jerome Taylor, Oct. 11, 1963 (div. Jan. 1983); children: Tanya, Greg. Cert., MacArthur Tech., 1973; A, LBW Jr. Coll., 1981; BS, Troy State U., 1985. Route auditor Nat. Security Ins., Elba, 1973-74; bookkeeper S.D. O'Neal Pub. Acct., Opp, Ala., 1975-77; office mgr., acct. Booth Tractor Co., Opp, 1977-79; acct. TPS Inc., Andalusia, Ala., 1979-86; mgmt. cons., internal auditor Ala. Credit Union League, Birmingham, 1986-88; comptroller, gen. mgr. Montgomery (Ala.) County Employees Credit Union, 1988—. leader, coordinator Girl Scouts, Opp, 1975; active Woodley Baptist Ch., Montgomery, 1987. Mem. Nat. Assn. Accts., Nat. Assn. Female Execs., Phi Theta Kappa. Home: 2188 Mona Lisa Dr Montgomery AL 36111 Office: Montgomery County Employees Credit Union 305 S Lawrence St PO Box 1667 Montgomery AL 36192

TAYLOR, MERRILY ELLEN, university librarian; b. Winchester, Mass., May 24, 1945; d. Philip Forbes and Ruth Ellen (Piper) T. A.A., St. Petersburg Jr. Coll., 1965; B.A., U. South Fla., 1967, M.A., 1973; M.S. in L.S., Fla. State U., 1968. Reference librarian U. South Fla. Library, Tampa, 1968-69, head circulation dept., 1969-74, head collection devel., 1974-77; asst. to univ. librarian Yale U. Library, New Haven, 1977-78; dir. services group Columbia U. Libraries, N.Y.C., 1978-82; univ. librarian Brown U., Providence, 1982—; pres. Consortium R.I. Acad. and Research Libraries, 1985-87. Author: The Yale University Library 1901-1978, 1978; author, editor: Remembering P.D. Ouspensky (exhbn. catalog), 1978. Acad. Library Mgmt. intern Council on Library Resources Washington, 1976. Mem. ALA, R.I. Library Assn. (chmn. pub. relations com. 1985), Research Libraries Group (bd. govs. 1982—, chmn. pub. services com. 1984-86), Assn. Research Libraries (com. on library edn., adv. com. pub. services self study program 1982-84), com. on Gov. policy 1986—, bd. mem. 1986—, Nat. Trust for Historic Preservation, Providence Preservation Soc., Jane Austen Soc. N.Am. Democrat. Methodist. Home: 55 Charlesfield Providence RI 02906 Office: Brown Univ Library Box A Rockefeller Library Providence RI 02912

TAYLOR, NANCY CAROL, printing estimating manager; b. Passaic, N.J., Feb. 8, 1940; d. Harold Clifton Taylor and Carol (Lein) Waring; m. Emil Brian Ludy, June 10, 1960 (div. Aug. 1971); children: Robin Lee, Brian Clifton, Mark Emil. BFA, Ill. Wesleyan U., 1962. Head estimating dept. Logan Printing Co., Peoria, Ill., 1973-81; estimating mgr. Johnson Cover Co., Houston, 1981-82; estimator Hearn Lithography, Houston, 1982-83; sales, estimator, prodn. coordinator Wadell's Lithographing, Houston, 1983; estimator Chas. P. Young, Houston, 1983-85; dir. estimating Reunion Graphic Art Printer, Grand Prairie, Tex., 1985-86; estimating mgr. Performance Printing, Dallas, 1986—. Pres. Universalist Unitarian Ch., Peoria, 1981, v.p., worship trustee, search com. chmn., 1973-81; pres. Cen. Ill. Area Council of Universalist-Unitarian Assn., 1980-81, bd. mem. Cen. Midwest dist.; pres. Unitarian Universalist Womens Fedn., Peoria and Bloomington, Ill., 1970's; v.p., bd. dirs. ACLU, Peoria, 1970's; worship com. chmn. First Unitarian Ch., Houston, 1982-85; bd. dirs. First Jefferson Unitarian Universalist, 1988, also chair sanctuary com. Democrat. Club: Servetus (program pres. 1983-84). Home: 1708 Park Vista Dr #3102 Arlington TX 76012 Office: Performance Printing Co Inc 1306 Motor Circle Dallas TX 75207

TAYLOR, NANCY CLAIRE, insurance executive; b. Orange, Tex., Jan. 12, 1952; d. Larry Lee and Betty Ruth (Estes) Duhon; m. James Tunney Taylor, Jr., Apr. 22, 1972 (div.); children: Avy Heather, Holly-Nan. Program dir. YMCA, Orange, Tex., 1977-79; personnel sec. Bapt. Hosp., Beaumont, Tex., 1979-83, adminstrv. sec. for human resources, 1983-85; exec. sales rep. Colonial Life & Accident Ins. Co., Beaumont, 1985, sales dir., 1985-87, regional sales dir., 1987, mktg. specialist, 1987—. Chmn. Orange County Clean Community; bd. dirs. O.C. Tex. Youth Symphony, 1987-88, v.p. 1988—. Mem. Beaumont C. of C., Orange C. of C., Jaycees (bd. dirs. 1986—), Proudest Crowd. Republican. Mem. Ch. of Christ. Avocations: singing, dancing, exercise, decorating, little theatre. Office: Colonial Life & Accident Ins Co 1495 N 7th St Suite 4 Beaumont TX 77702

TAYLOR, PATRICIA ANN TATE, management consultant; b. Cleve., Jan. 13, 1954; d. John Henry and Catherine Carolyn (Johnson) Tate; m. Terrence Alan Taylor, Aug. 1976 (div. Mar. 1981). BA, Case Western Res. U., 1977; MBA, Harvard U., 1985. Acct. Standard Oil Co., Cleve., 1977-79, budget analyst, 1979-80, adminstr., 1981-83; cons. Deloitte Haskins & Sells, Detroit, 1984, Cresap, McCormick & Paget, Washington, 1985-87, U.S. GAO, Washington, 1987—. Mem. adv. bd. Cornell U., 1981-83, Nat. Assn. Engring. Adminstrs., 1981-83. Nat. Achievement scholar, 1972; fellow Harvard U., 1983. Mem. Black MBA Assn. Baptist. Office: Cresop McCormick & Paget 441 G St NW Washington DC 20537

TAYLOR, RAMONA G., financial services company executive; b. Dallas, 1930. Student So. Meth. U. Sec. Lomas & Nettleton Fin. Corp., Dallas, Lomas & Nettleton Mortgage Investors, Affiliates of Lomas & Nettleton Fin. Corp., L&N Housing Corp. Office: Lomas & Nettleton Fin Corp PO Box 655644 Dallas TX 75265-5644

TAYLOR, ROSANNE CAPPIELLO, training consultants executive; b. Darby, Pa., June 14, 1945; d. Frank S. and Louise Ann (Moreschi) Cappiello; m. A. Jeffrey Taylor, Apr. 27, 1984; stepdau., Jackie. A.B., Immaculate Coll., 1967; Cert. Bus., Villanova U., 1977; postgrad. in Bus. Adminstrn., Wilmington Grad. Sch., 1980-81. Clk. typist AMP Products Corp., Valley Forge, Pa., 1975-76, sales corr., 1976-77, tng. coordinator, 1977-78, supr. and trainer, 1978-80, sales rep., 1980-83, asst. product mgr., 1983-85; dir. mktg. Spitz Space Systems, Chadds Ford, Pa., 1985-86; pres., owner R.C. Taylor & Assocs. Tng. Cons., West Chester, Pa., 1986—. Chmn. Friends for Maggie Found., West Chester, 1984-85; mem. Main Line Women's Network, Women's Referral Network (co-founder), Step-up Support Group for Step-parents, Bus. and Profl. Women, Nat. Assn. Female Execs. (area dir. 1982—), Women in Electronics, Del. C. of C., Delaware County C. of C., Westchester C. of C. Republican. Roman Catholic. Avocations: racquetball; bicycling; reading; cooking. Home: 20 Cannon Hill Rd West Chester PA 19382 Office: R C Taylor & Assocs 20 Cannon Hill Rd West Chester PA 19382

TAYLOR, ROWENA JEANETTE, nurse administrator; b. Sioux City, Iowa, June 18, 1924; d. Antone Raymond and Edith (Pomeroy) Burgess; m. Carl O. Benson, Dec. 18, 1945 (dec. Aug. 1956); children: Jeoffrey, Carla; m. William Rolland Taylor, Aug. 27, 1958; children: Linda, Patricia, Dennis, William. RN, Nebr. Meth. Sch. Nursing, 1945; BS in Nursing, Calif. State U., Fresno, 1972. Head nurse Meth. Hosp., Omaha, 1945-47; sch. nurse Pepperdine Coll., Los Angeles, 1947-50, Needles (Calif.) Sch. Dist., 1950-53, staff nurse dept. devel. services Porterville (Calif.) Devel. Ctr., 1953-56, dir. nursing edn., 1950-61, asst. supr. nursing services, 1961-72, program dir., 1972-77, clin. dir., 1977-84; exec. dir. dept. devel. services Lanterman Devel. Ctr., Pomona, Calif., 1984—. Mem. adv. bd. Career and Continuing Edn., Pomona, 1986—. Mem. Nat. Assn. Supts. of Pub. Resdl. Facilities, Am. Assn. on Mental Deficiency, Am. Legion Aux. Democrat. Methodist. Home and Office: 3530 Pomona Blvd Box 100 Pomona CA 91769

TAYLOR, SANDRA LOUISE, nurse; b. Jacksonville, Fla., Jan. 27, 1960; d. Lonnie James and Inez (Sands) Taylor. A.D.N., Fla. Jr. Coll. Sch. Nursing, 1981. R.N., Fla. Nursing service technician Bapt. Med. Ctr., Jacksonville, 1980-81, staff nurse, 1981—, staff nurse rep. staff nurse com. Democrat. Baptist. Home: Route 2 PO Box 542-A Macclenny FL 32063 Office: Bapt Med Ctr 800 Prudential Dr Jacksonville FL 32207

TAYLOR, STEPHANIE BARNETT, research assistant, consultant; b. Los Angeles; d. Richard Allan and Marian J. (Gray) T. BA, U. So. Calif., 1976, MS, 1986, PhD, 1988. Tchr. Mid City Alternative Sch., Los Angeles, 1977-79; program counselor Student Athletic Academic, Los Angeles, 1979-81; learning specialist Academic Achievement Program, Los Angeles, 1982-83; research asst. U. So. Calif., Los Angeles, 1983-88; cons. Whittaker Health Services, Los Angeles, Traveler's Managed Care, Los Angeles. Pres. Luth. Ch. Women, St. Mark's Ch., Los Angeles, 1982—; chairperson Strike com. SAG, Hollywood, Calif., 1980; founder St. Mark's Dance Acad. Recipient Scholarship State of Calif., 1972, Luth. Ch. Am. Grant, 1977. Mem. NAACP, Internat. Reading Assn., Screen Actors Guild (nat. bd. dirs. 1979-82), Am. Fedn. TV and Radio Artists. Democrat.

TAYLOR, SUSANNE GREGORY, security company executive; b. New Haven, July 19, 1946; d. Frederick Miles and Meriel (Marston) G.; m. Louis Rome, July 21, 1971 (div.); m. Mark Francis Taylor, Sept. 11, 1982. BA, George Washington U., 1969. Licensed pvt. detective, Conn. Personnel dir. NESS Corp., Milford, Conn., 1974-78, v.p., 1978-85, pres., 1985—. Editor NESS newsletter. Mem. Am. Soc. for Indsl. Security, Am. Soc. for Personnel Adminstrn., Am. Mmgt. Assn. (pres. assn.), Conn. Bus. and Industry Assn., Young Pres.'s Orgn. Office: NESS Corp 7 Lafayette St Milford CT 06460

TAYLOR, TINA LAVEL, personnel executive; b. Houston, Aug. 5, 1963; d. Joseph Carroll and Alice Mae (Chavis) T. BBA magna cum laude, Lamar U., 1985. Personnel specialist City of Port Arthur, Tex., 1985-87, asst. dir. personnel, 1987—. Mem. Nat. Assn. Female Execs., Phi Kappa Phi, Beta Gamma Sigma, Alpha Lambda Delta, Alpha Mu Alpha, Delta Sigma Pi. Democrat. Roman Catholic. Home: 3143 E 15th St Port Arthur TX 77640 Office: City of Port Arthur 444 4th St Port Arthur TX 77640

TAYLOR-HEINEBACK, BARBARA, public relations strategist; b. N.Y.C.; d. John H. and Robella (Wilson) Taylor; m. BoAxel Heinebäck (div.); 1 child, J. ERik Axel. Degree in Swedish, U. Stockholm; BA in TV Communications, Howard U. Officer adminstr. Am. Freedom from Hunger Found., Washington, 1969; researcher CBS News, Washington, 1969-72; free-lance writer Sveriges Radio and daily newspaper, Stockholm, 1972-76; press officer to First Lady White House, Washington, 1976-79; cons. pub. affairs, media relations 1979-81; mgr. pub. relations dept. Communications Satellite Corp., Washington, 1981—. Bd. dirs. Washington Urban League. Mem. Am. Women in Radio and TV., Pub. Relations Soc. Am.

TAYLOR-LITTLE, CAROL J(OYCE), state legislator, real estate agent; b. Berkeley, Calif., Aug. 13, 1941; d. Harold Robert and Marjorie Evelyn (Strawn) Hochmuth; m. Nicholas G. Kappas, Aug. 29, 1959 (div. Sept. 1980); children—Anthony N., Katherine M.; m. Donald L. Little, June 19, 1982. Student in real estate Red Rocks Community Coll., 1978; cert. degree adminstrn. non-profit agys. Met. State Coll., Denver, 1981, postgrad. in urban studies and polit. sci., 1981—. Lic. in real estate, Colo. Recreation instr. North Jefferson Recreational Dist. (Colo.), 1970-82; real estate sales agt. Crown Realty/Better Homes & Gardens, Arvada, Colo., 1979—; mem. Colo. Ho. of Reps., Denver, 1982-84, 84-86, 86-88, House majority whip, 1984-86; mem. Colo. Commn. on Women, Denver, 1979-80. Chairperson Med. Malpractice Task Force; vice chmn. Victims' Assistance Adv. Council; mem. Met. Air Quality Council; mem. human services community adv. bd. Met. State Coll. Mem. Merit Appeals Bd., Arvada, 1980-82. Named Woman of Yr., Beta Chi chpt. Beta Sigma Phi, 1968; recipient Outstanding Service award Jefferson County Bd. Realtors, 1978, Outstanding Legislator award Colo. Mental Health Assn., 1985, Legislator of Yr., Colo. Chiropractic Assn., 1986, Legislative award Colo. Nurses Assn., 1987. Mem. Nat. Conf. State Legislators (vice chmn. commerce labor and regulation), Nat. Fedn. Bus. and Profl. Women's Clubs, Inc., Nat. Fedn. Republican Women, Colo. Hist. Soc., Arvada C. of C. (bd. dirs., Image award 1980), Arvada Ctr. for Arts and Humanities. Office: Colo State Ho of Reps State Capitol Denver CO 80203

TAYLOR-NASH, RITA CONSTANCE, equal opportunity manager, proprietor; b. Chgo., Nov. 26, 1949; d. James and Minnie Mary (Lucas) Taylor; m. Anderson Renee Nash, Aug. 26, 1978. B.A. in Sociology, U. Chgo., 1971; M.A. in Sociology, U. Mich., 1972. Claims adjustor Social Security Adminstrn. Chgo., 1973-74; instr. sociology Ill. Central Coll., East Peoria, 1974-75; equal opportunity specialist EEOC, Chgo., 1977-78; EEO adminstr. IIT Research Inst., Chgo., 1978-81; mgr. equal opportunity programs Health Care Service Corp. (Blue Cross/Blue Shield of Ill.), Chgo., 1981—; proprietor Baskin-Robbins 31 Ice Cream Store. Ill. State scholar, 1967-71; Opportunity scholar, U. Chgo., 1967-71; scholar Transitional Yr. Program Yale U., 1966; Rackham fellow, U. Mich., 1971-72. Mem. Affirmative Action Assn. (1st v.p. 1980—, dir. 1980—, pres. 1986—), Chgo. Area Assn. for Affirmative Action and Compliance. Club: Ruth Circle.

TAYLOR-YOUNG, OLIVIA, communications specialist; b. Providence, Nov. 13, 1937; d. Samuel J. Young and Ida (Shapiro) Samuel; m. Kirk H. Taylor, Dec. 15, 1978; children: Robert, Steven, Gary; stepchildren: Julie, Rochelle. Student, U. Conn., 1959, City Coll. San Francisco, 1974-75. Co-founder, dir. pub. edn. Vanished Children's Alliance, San Jose, Calif., 1976-85; with mktg. communications dept. Vitamin Research Products, Mountain View, Calif., 1986-87; specialist market communications Krames Communications, Daly City, Calif., 1987—; cons. in field. Author: The Child Snatchers, 1982.

TCHERKASSKY, MARIANNA ALEXSAVENA, ballerina; b. Glen Cove, N.Y., Oct. 28, 1952; d. Alexis and Lillian (Oka) T.; m. Terrence S. Orr. Student, Washington Sch. Ballet (scholar), 1965-67, Sch. Am. Ballet and Profl. Children's Sch., 1967-70; pupil of, Edward Caton. Appeared with Bolshoi Ballet in Ballet Sch., 1961, 62, N.Y.C. Ballet in A Midsummer Night's Dream, 1963; profl. debut with Andre Eglevsky Ballet Co., 1968; mem., Am. Ballet Theatre, 1970—, soloist, 1972-78, prin. dancer, 1978—, guest appearances throughout U.S. and in Europe, also on TV. Winner Nat. Soc. Arts and Letters competition 1967. Ford Found. scholar, 1967-70. Office: care Am Ballet Theatre 890 Broadway New York NY 10003 *

TEACH, JOAN KRAUSS, school administrator; b. Norristown, Pa., Jan. 19, 1939; d. Alton L. and Eva L. (Fleck) Krauss; m. Richard D. Teach, July 2, 1980; children: Brett David, Danette Suzanne, Alian Diahanne, Kurt Jarred. BS, Wittenberg U., 1960; MS, Purdue U., 1966; PhD, Ga. State U., 1978. Cert. tchr., Ga. Tchr. Columbus (Ohio) Pub. Schs., 1960-61, Romney (Ind.) Pub. Schs., 1961-63; adminstrv. asst. Newell C. Kephart Achievement Ctr. for Children, 1963-66; instr. Practicum in Programming and Educating the Slow Learner, 1964-66; cons. Bd. Cooperative Ednl. Services, N.Y. Spl. Edn. Dept., Buffalo, 1968-70; instr. Ga. State U., Atlanta, 1975-76; diagnostic specialist Howard Sch., Atlanta, 1974-79; dir. Lullwater Sch., Decatur, Ga., 1979—; program coordinator Project ACTION, Atlanta, 1976-79; hearing officer City Schs. Decatur, 1977-79; seminar leader, Decatur, 1986, 87. Contbr. profl. jours., books, 1969—; speaker numerous profl. orgns., 1977—. Developer child service program Christ United Presbyn. Ch., 1978-80, elder, 1978-80; mem. Decatur Devel. Authority, Decatur Area Network. Mem. Inst. Devel. Ednl. Activities, Assn. Individually Guided Edn., Child Advocacy Coalition, Council for Exceptional Children (Ga. rep. 1979-81, pres. Ga. div. for learning disabilities, 1980-82), Nat. Assn. Edn. Young Children, Decatur Bus. Profl. Women, Atlanta Women's C. of C., Bus. and Profl. Women's Club (v.p. 1987-88, pres. 1988—), Atlanta Area Computer Educators, Pi Lambda Theta, Chi Omega. Office: Lullwater Sch 705 S Candler St Decatur GA 30030

TEAFORD, JANE BROWN, state legislator; b. Hunter, Kans., July 1, 1935; d. Fred Welch and Antoinette Prendergast (Lawson) Brown; m. William John Teaford, Feb. 8, 1959; children: Sarah Ellen, Phillip Allen. BS, Kans. State U., 1957. Agt. home econs. Wabaunsee County Extension Council, Alma, Kans., 1957-59; library clk. Downers Grove (Ill.) Pub. Library, 1959-61, U. Ill. Library, Champaign, 1961-62; mem. Iowa Gen. Assembly, Des Moines, 1985—. Bd. dirs., v.p. LWV Iowa, 1973-79, pres., Des Moines, 1979-81, dir. Iowa caucus info. project, 1983-84; mem. Black Hawk County Bd. Social Welfare, Iowa, 1983-84, Profl. and Occupational Regulation Commn., Des Moines, 1983-86. Mem. NAACP (life). Democrat. Methodist. Home: 3913 Carlton Dr Cedar Falls IA 50613 Office: Iowa Ho of Reps State Capitol Des Moines IA 50319

TEAGUE, RICHALYN ELAINE, school system administrator; b. Cleburne, Tex., Nov. 21, 1941; d. Richard F. and Dorothy (Allen) Johnston; m. William E. Houser, May 27, 1962 (dec. Mar. 1982); children: Bryan Allen, Barbara; m. Marvin O. Teague, July 2, 1988. BA in Biology, Edn., Baylor U., 1962; MS in Edn., Adminstn., Tex. So. U., 1977; postgrad., U. Houston, 1981. Tchr. English Manhattan (Kans.) Pub. Schs., 1962-63; tchr. biology Houston Pub. Schs., 1972-75, coordinator instructional sci., 1975-76, tchr. gifted and talented, 1976-79, cons. tchrs., 1979-81, adminstr. program, 1981-82; coordinator instructional dept. Magnet Schs., Houston, 1982-85, asst. prin., 1985-88; dean of instruction, fiscal policy specialist Tex. Edn. Agy., Austin, 1988—; cons. magnet schs. Washington D.C. Pub. Schs., 1984-85; bd. dirs. Local Close=Up Found., Washington 1982-86. Mem. Tex. Assn. Secondary Prins., Houston Assn. Sch. Adminstrs., Tex. Council Women Sch. Exec. Democrat. Home: 1122 Colorado #1409 Austin TX 78701 Office: 1701 N Congress Austin TX 78701

TEASLEY, DEBORAH JOANN, health care administrator; b. Orlando, Fla., May 26, 1951. Diploma, Piedmont Hosp. Sch. Nursing, 1972; BS in Nursing, U. Tex., Galveston, 1978, MS in Nursing, 1980; PhDin Health adminstrn. edn., Tex. A&M U., 1986. Cert. critical care nurse. Staff nurse Barnes Hosp., St. Louis, 1972-74; head nurse Galveston County Meml. Hosp., Texas City, Tex., 1974-79; instr. Alvin (Tex.) Community Coll., 1980-81; instr. U. Tex. Med. Sch., Galveston, 1981-82, asst. prof., 1982-84, asst. dir. nursing, 1984-85; dir. nursing U. Tex. Med. Br., Galveston, 1985-86; assoc. exec. dir. West Jersey Health System, Camden, N.J., 1986-88; exec. dir. West Jersey Hosp., 1988—; tech. advisor videotape on nursing, 1985. Author (book chpt.) Mgmt. Concepts for Nurses, 1987; also articles. Vol. counselor Galveston Rape Crisis Ctr., 1979-80; chairperson task force on abused women NOW, Houston, 1982-83. Recipient Outstanding Faculty award U. Tex., Galveston, 1982; Kempner Found. grantee, 1983. Mem. Nat. Assn. Female Execs., Am. Orgn. Nurse Execs. (legis./regulations com.), Am. Heart Assn. (bd. dirs. Texas City chpt. 1975-77), Sigma Theta Tau, Beta Sigma Phi. Office: West Jersey Health System Mt Ephraim and Atlantic Ave Camden NJ 08104

TEBBETTS, DIANE RUTH, librarian, educator; b. Buffalo, N.Y., May 3, 1943; d. Bernard John and Ruth Amy (Arlin) T.; BA cum laude, U. N.H., 1965; MLS, Simmons Coll., 1972, DA, 1985; MLA, Boston U., 1978. Cataloging library asst. U. N.H., 1965-71, asst. reference librarian, 1971-81, asst. dir., 1981-86; assoc. dir. 1986—, asst. prof., 1971-78, assoc. prof., 1978-87, prof. 1987—; reviewer NEH, 1982—. N.H. Council Humanities grantee, 1979-81. Mem. New Eng. Library Assn. (bd. dirs. 1981-83, v.p. 1985-86, pres. 1986-87), Assn. Coll. and Research Libraries, NEC (pres. 1984-85), N.H. Library Assn. (v.p. 1977-78, pres., 1978-79), ALA, N.H. Conf. on Library and Info. Services, New Eng. Microcomputer Users Group (bd. dirs. 1985-86, v.p. 1986-87, pres. 1987—), New Eng. Library Info. Network (bd. dirs. 1987—). Contbr. in field. Home: 2 Anita St Rochester NH 03867 Office: U NH Library Adminstrn Office Durham NH 03824

TEDDER, JANE ANN, portfolio manager; b. Stillwater, Okla., Oct. 1, 1942; d. Robert M. and Guila M. (Harp) Pyle; children: Troy, Jay, Kira. B in Music Edn., Okla. State U., 1964; diploma in trust banking, Northwestern U., 1979; diploma in sr. mgmt. banking, Rutgers U., 1982. Asst. trust officer Douglas County Bank, Lawrence, Kans., 1975-76, trust officer, 1976-83, v.p., 1978-83; portfolio mgr. Security Mgmt. Co., Topeka, 1983—; vis. lectr. Kans. U., Lawrence, 1986-87. Trustee Plymouth Congl. Ch., Lawrence, 1981-83, moderator, 1984; dir. Ecumenical Christian Ministries Kans. U., Lawrence, 1984-88. Fellow Life Mgmt. Inst. Office: Security Mgmt Co 700 Harrison Topeka KS 66636

TEDESCO, REBECCA SMITH, temporary help service company executive; b. Gulfport, Miss., Jan. 17, 1946; d. Benjamin Edwin and Marguerite (Moore) Smith; divorced; 1 child, Heather Chi. B.A., Maryville Coll., Tenn., 1967; B.Ed., U. Tenn.-Chattanooga, 1968. Sales rep. Xerox Corp., Richmond, Va., 1973-75; stockbroker Moseley, Hallgarten, Washington, 1975-77; DC mgr. Tele Sec. Temporary Personnel, Washington, 1977-79; sales mgr. SelecTemps, Inc., Washington, 1980-81; gen. mgr. MBA Office Temps, Vienna, Va., 1981-82; owner, pres. Ameritemps, Inc., Washington, 1982—; pres., owner AmeriTech Services, Inc., Washington, Ameriperm, Inc., Washington. Mem. Met. Washington Temporary Services Assn. (pres. 1986-88), Nat. Assn. Temporary Service (ethics com.), Greater Washington Bd. Trade, D.C. Conv. Visitors Bur. Democrat. Presbyterian. Avocation: writing. Home: 6315 Chaucer Ln Alexandria VA 22304 Office: Ameritemps Inc 1100 17th St NW #607 Washington DC 22036

TEED, C. CASON, author; b. Dallas, Mar. 9, 1941; d. Jack Charles and Gladys (Swope) Cason; m. William Banta, Feb. 19, 1971 (div. 1977); children: Bayard Swope and Bret Cason (twins); m. John E. Teed, 1978 (dec. 1979). B.A., Newcomb Coll., 1962; M.A., Middlebury Coll., 1963; postgrad.

Sorbonne, Paris, 1964, U. Dijon (France), 1967, So. Meth. U., 1987—. Lectr. in langs. U. Houston, 1965-66, 79-82; tour guide Mus. Fine Arts, Houston, 1975-81; now freelance lang. writer. Author: Guidebook for American Bar Association; Walking Tour of Museum of Fine Arts, Houston, 1981; Conversational Spanish for Medical and Allied Health Personnel, 1983. Vol. translator Ben Taub Hosp., Houston, 1968-70. Govt. of Spain travel stipend, 1962. Mem. AAUP, Soc. Profl. Journalists, Kappa Kappa Gamma. Episcopalian. Home and Office: 6124 Sherry Lane Suite 168 Dallas TX 75225

TEED, PATRICIA JONES, university administrator; b. Pampa, Tex., Nov. 29, 1940; d. Clifford Frank and Mary (Abbott) Jones; m. John Edson Teed, Oct. 8, 1966 (div. 1971); 1 son, Arthur Mayo. B.A. cum laude, Rice U., 1962; Ph.D., 1971; M.A. Emory U., 1963. Asst. to pres. The Crispin Co., Houston, 1970-75; research assoc. Solar Lab., U. Houston, 1975-76, coordinator Half Century Program, 1976-78, dir. camp/community relations, 1978-79, exec., dir., 1979-82, asst. chancellor, 1982-84; v.p. univ. affairs SUNY, Stony Brook, 1984—. Dir., v.p. Alliance Francaise de Houston, Inc., 1973-76; vice chmn. Nice-Houston Sister City Assn., 1975-77; dir. CrimeStoppers, Inc., 1980-82. Fulbright scholar, U.S. Govt., 1963; decorated Palmes Academiques, French Govt., 1979. Mem. Council for Aid and Support Edn., Cultural Arts Council Houston, Fulbright Alumni Assn., Phi Kappa Phi, Pi Delta Phi. Office: SUNY VP Univ Affairs Stony Brook NY 11794

TEETERS, LINDA MARIE, educator; b. Cin., Aug. 22, 1945; d. Irvin Louis and Shirley H. (Huenefeld) T. Cert. dental asst. U. N.C., 1973. Pharmacy intern Edward W. Wolff Pharmacy, 1963-67; dental asst. to various dentists, 1967-73; coordinator dental asst. clinics Hamilton County (Ohio) Bd. Health, 1973-76; dental coordinator Western Hills Vocat. High Sch., Cin., 1976—, chmn. adv. bd. for dental program, 1976—; mem. Ohio Commn. Dental Assisting Certs., 1981—. Mem. Delhi Civic Assn., 1988—. Mem. Am. Dental Assts. Assn. (3d dist. trustee 1984-86), Ohio Dental Assts. Assn. (pres. 1982-83, editor newsletter 1979-84), Cin. Dental Assts. Assn. (pres. 1971-72, 77-78). Democrat. Roman Catholic. Club: Internationally Yours (pres. local chpt. 1985—, historian internat. chpt. 1986—, 1st v.p. internat. bd. 1987—). Home: 5260 Old Oak Trail Apt 66 Cincinnati OH 45238 Office: 2144 Ferguson Rd Cincinnati OH 45238

TEETERS, NANCY HAYS, economist; b. Marion, Ind., July 29, 1930; d. S. Edgar and Mabel (Drake) Hays; m. Robert Duane Teeters, June 7, 1952; children: Ann, James, John. A.B. in Econs., Oberlin Coll., 1952, LL.D. (hon.), 1979; M.A. in Econs., U. Mich., 1954, postgrad., 1956-57, LL.D. (hon.), 1983; LL.D. (hon.), Bates Coll., 1981, Mt. Holyoke Coll., 1983. Teaching fellow U. Mich., 1954-55, instr., 1956-57; instr. U. Md. Overseas, Germany, 1955-56; staff economist govt. fin. sect. Bd. Govs. of FRS, Washington, 1957-66; mem. bd. Bd. Govs. of FRS, 1978-84; economist (on loan) Council Econ. Advs., 1962-63; economist Bur. Budget, 1966-70; sr. fellow Brookings Instn., 1970-73; sr. specialist Congl. Research Service, Library of Congress, Washington, 1973-74; asst. dir., chief economist Ho. of Reps. Com. on the Budget, 1974-78; v.p., chief economist IBM, Armonk, N.Y., 1984—. Author: (with others) Setting National Priorities: The 1972 Budget, 1971, Setting National Priorities: The 1973 Budget, 1972, Setting National Priorities: The 1974 Budget, 1973; contbr. articles to profl. publs. Recipient Comfort Starr award in econs. Oberlin Coll., 1952; Disting. Alumnus award U. Mich., 1980. Mem. Nat. Economists Club (v.p. 1973-74, pres. 1974-75, chmn. bd. 1975-76, gov. 1976-79), Am. Econ. Assn. (com. on status of women 1975-78), Am. Fin. Assn. (dir. 1969-71). Democrat. Home: 243 Willowbrook Ave Stamford CT 06902 Office: IBM Old Orchard Rd Armonk NY 10504

TEFFERTELLER, RUTH SINOVOY (MRS. RALPH B. TEFFERTELLER), social worker; b. Albany, N.Y., Aug. 28, 1917; d. Samuel and Jennie (Katz) Sinovoy; B.A., N.Y. State Coll. for Tchrs., 1939; postgrad. Iowa U., 1939-40; M.S.W., Columbia, 1955; m. Ralph B. Tefferteller, Sept. 5, 1941. Social worker A.R.C., St. Louis, Denver, Roswell, N.Mex., Ft. Bragg, N.C., 1942-46; dir. Children's div., camp dir., program dir., dir. spl. project for delinquency prevention and control Henry Street Settlement, N.Y.C., 1946-68; asst. chief Unitarian-Universalist Service Com. Project in Vietnam, in cooperation with U.S. AID Mission, 1968-71; assoc. area dir. Danvers-Salem area Mass. Dept. Mental Health, 1971-78, area dir., 1978-86, ret.; cons. Astor Project, 1961-62. Recipient Florence Luscomb award for outstanding achievement, 1980; Edward C. O'Keefe award, 1986. Mem. Nat. Assn. Social Workers, Nat. Acad. Social Workers, Nat. Conf. Social Welfare, Internat. Conf. on Social Welfare. Contbr. articles to profl. jours. Address: 127 Front St Marblehead MA 01945

TEICHLER-ZALLEN, DORIS, geneticist; b. Bklyn., Mar. 7, 1941; d. David Moses and Bessie Gertrude (Lesser) Teichler; m. Richard Henry Zallen, Feb. 2, 1964; children: Jennifer Ann, Avram Alexander. BS, Bklyn. Coll., 1961; AM, Harvard U., 1963, PhD, 1966. Postdoctoral fellow U. Rochester, N.Y., 1966-69, asst. prof., 1969-70, fellow pediatrics/genetics, 1977-83; asst. prof. Nazareth Coll. Rochester, N.Y., 1977-83; assoc. prof. Va. Tech. U., Blacksburg, Va., 1983—. Editor: Science and Morality, 1982; contbr. articles to profl. jours. Bd. dirs. YMCA, Squires Ctr., 1986—, Blacksburg Jewish Ctr., 1986—. Mem. AAAS, Am. Soc. of Human Genetics, Hastings Ctr. (assoc.), Phi Beta Kappa, Sigma Xi. Office: Va Tech U 351 Lane Hall Blacksburg VA 24061

TEIG, CAROL DIANE, hospital executive; b. Vallejo, Calif., Aug. 2, 1948; d. Vernon E. and Lillian A. (Johnson) T. BA cum laude, Washington U., St. Louis, 1970, MA, 1971, M in Health Adminstrn., 1983. Editor, writer Envirodyne Engrs., St. Louis, 1972-82; adminstrv. resident Jewish Hosp. St. Louis, 1983-84, dir. planning, 1984-86, v.p. planning/mktg., 1986—. NDEA fellow, 1971. Mem. Am. Mktg. Assn. Office: The Jewish Hosp of St Louis 216 S Kings Hwy Saint Louis MO 63110

TEITZ, BETTY BEATRICE GOLDSTEIN, interior designer; b. Rochester, N.Y., Mar. 10, 1914; d. Albert Stanley and Dora (Finestone) Gould; m. Milton A. Nusbaum, Apr. 10, 1943 (dec. Nov. 1956); 1 dau., Alberta Joyce Nusbaum Duckman; m. Harry Teitz, Dec. 28, 1959. Student Rochester Bus. Inst., 1932-34, Rochester Inst. Tech., 1950-51, Columbia U., 1957-58. Owner design studio, Rochester, 1957; trainee W.J. Sloane, 1958; head design dept. Mason Furniture Co., Fall River, Mass., 1959; pvt. practice interior design, Providence, 1961-65; pres. Indesign Inc., Newport, R.I., 1974—; designer guest house U.S. War Coll., Newport, 1969-70; lectr. Navy Wives U.S.A. Staff asst. Motor Corps Grey Lady Rochester chpt. ARC, 1941-46, active Newport chpt.; Gray Lady vol. Genesee Hosp., Rochester, 1945-55, mem. Rochester Planned Parenthood, 1945-48; active Mental Health Clinic Newport; mem. Citizens Adv. Com., Newport, 1967-78; mem. yachting com. Am.'s Cup Race, summer 1950. Recipient Centennial Pageant Scenic award Rochester, 1948; ARC awards, 1943-53, 10 yr. service pin Genesee Hosp., 1955, Blue Ribbon awards for flower show arrangements, 1950, 52, 55. Mem. Am. Inst. Interior Designers, Constrn. Specifications Inst. R.I. (sec.), Preservation Soc. Newport County, Newport C. of C. (bldg. com.). Club: Flower City Garden (past v.p. Rochester). Home and studio: 29 Rovensky Ave Newport RI 02840 Office: 10 Long Wharf Mall Newport RI 02840

TEIXEIRA, CATHY ANN, corporate executive; b. East Hartford, Conn., Sept. 12, 1956; d. Joseph R. and Shirley (Landry) T. BA in Psychology cum laude, East Conn. State U., 1978; MS in Mgmt. cum laude, Rensselaer Poly. Inst., 1983. Personnel generalist Conn. Transit, Hartford, 1978-82; supr. receiving J.C. Penney Catalog, Manchester, Conn., 1982-83, supr. inventory control, 1983-84; mgr. telephone sales ctr. J.C. Penney Telemktg., Manchester, 1985; mgr. mdse. fulfillment Avon Direct Response, Hampton, Va., 1985-86; mgr. order processing Avon Direct Response div., Hampton, 1986-87, mgr. customer service, telephone sales ctr., 1987-88; mgr. customer relations Chadwick's of Boston, Stoughton, Mass., 1988—. Mem. Nat. Assn. Exec. Women, Data Entry Mgmt. Assn., Am. Mgmt. Assn. Club: Exchange (Hampton). Office: Chadwick's of Boston 179 Campanelli Pkwy Stoughton MA 02072

TEIXEIRA, JACQUELINE LEAH, dietitician; b. San Bernardino, Calif., Aug. 27, 1946; d. William Arthur Hitt and Ruth (Goldie) Williams; m. Manuel Cotta Teixeira, July 20, 1966; children: Manuel Douglas, Johnny Ray, Casey Tyrone, Natalee Kristine. Cert. in Dietetics, U. N.D., 1985. Dietary supr. Palm Haven Convent Hosp., Manteca, Calif., 1984—. Home: 1031 Carmel Manteca CA 95336

TEJEDA, ANNE ELIZABETH DEAN, restaurant and hotel executive; b. Harrisburg, Pa., Mar. 8, 1957; d. Thomas Allen and Elizabeth Walden (Rubey) D. BA with high honors, Ohio State U., 1979. Asst. mgr. Summerhouse Corp., Rehoboth, Del., 1981-82, Strattons Restaurant/Grill, Los Angeles, 1985-86; with service dept. Michael's Restaurant, Santa Monica, Calif., 1985-86; asst. mgr. Hillcrest Country Club/Tennis, Los Angeles, 1986—; dept. supr. L'Ermitage Hotel, Beverly Hills, Calif., 1987—; dest asst. Olympic Games ABC Sports, Los Angeles, 1984. Vol. UCLA Med. Ctr, 1983-84; interviewer Los Angeles Olympic Com., 1984; adminstr., vol. Internat. Med. Corps, Los Angeles, 1984-85. Named Outstanding Vol., UCLA Med. Ctr., 1983. Mem. Nat. Assn. Female Execs. Republican. Methodist.

TELEGA, MILDRED C., sales executive; b. Sewickley, Pa., Sept. 16, 1953; d. Mitchell Richard and Ruth (Decker) Telega. B.S. in Edn., Calif. U., Pa., 1975, M.Ed., 1976. Speech pathologist Community Devel. Ctrs.-Highland Park Ctr., Pitts., 1975-78, supr. program services, 1978-79, program dir., 1979-81, asst. dir. for program services, 1981-83; augmentative communication cons. Adaptive Communication Systems Inc., Clinton, Pa., from 1983; pres. Augmentative Communication Cons. Inc., 1987—. Mem. Am. Speech & Hearing Assn., Assn. for Persons with Severe Handicaps, Allegheny Assn. Retarded Citizens. Avocations: reading; painting. Home: 309 Colony W Dr Caraopolis PA 15108 Office: Augmentative Communication Cons Inc 354 Hookstown Grade Rd Clinton PA 15026

TELEGO, TACY COOK, government public affairs officer; b. Orono, Maine, Nov. 5, 1946; d. Charles T. and Virginia Louise (Totman) Cook; m. Dean Jeffery Telego, May 21, 1983; m. Glenn Allen Yachachak, Sept. 1965 (div. Sept. 1968). B.A., Douglass Coll., Rutgers U., 1968; M.S., Am. U., Washington, 1972. Writer, editor USAF Research and Analysis, Pentagon, Washington, 1968-69; editor Challenge mag. HUD, Washington, 1969-74, pub. info. officer, San Francisco, 1974-75; pub. affairs officer Treasury Bur. Alcohol, Tobacco and Firearms, Chgo., 1975-76, Washington, 1976-78; pub. affairs officer Def. Mapping Agy., Washington, 1978-80; dir. legis. and pub. affairs Mil. Sealift Command, U.S. Navy, Washington, 1980—; owner, mgr. Peacock Internat. Enterprises, Bethesda, Md., 1981—. N.J. Soc. Indsl. Editors scholar, 1968. Mem. Federally Employed Women (editor News & Views, 1977-80; recipient Barbara B. Tennant award 1983), Pub. Relations Soc. Am. (accredited; chpt. v.p. 1981-82; service awards 1978-85), Washington Women in Pub. Relations (founder). Republican. Episcopalian. Clubs: Nat. Press. Home: 4 Sangamore Ct Bethesda MD 20816 Office: US Navy Mil Sealift Command 4228 Wisconsin Ave NW Washington DC 20016

TELESHA, MEREDITH CAROL, employment specialist and training coordinator; b. Hershey, Pa., Oct. 24, 1948; d. Carl Eugene and Ada Kann (Wagner) Cope. Cert., York Thompson Bus. Coll., 1967; student, Pa. State U., 1972, Elizabethtown Coll., 1978. Sec. The Milton S. Mershey Med. Ctr. of Pa. State U., Hershey, 1967-74, personnel asst., 1975-80, employment specialist, 1980-81, employment specialist, training coordinator, 1981-87, employmnet specialist procedures analyst, 1987—; speaker at high schs., bus. schs.; conductor of in-house tng. programs. Mem. Bus. Adv. Com., Hershey, 1978—; sec. Employee Safety Com., Hershey, 1981—; mem. Com. for the Disabled, Hershey, 1986; cons. Right-to-Know Task force, Hershey, 1987—; mem. presdl. task force, 1980-86, Nat. Rep. Com., Pa. Rep. Com. Served with USAR, 1973-76. Recipient Problems of Democracy study award Am. Legion, 1965, Cert. of Merit Gov. of Pa., 1965. Mem. Leadership Found., U.S. Senatorial Club, Am. Bus. Women's Assn. (recording sec. 1979-80, 82-83, v.p. 1980-81, pres. 1981-82, treas. fall frolics 1982), Nat. Secs. Assn., Am. Soc. Personnel Amdminstrn. Lutheran. Lodges: Women's Auxillary to Elks, Order Rainbow. Home: 2267 E Harrisburg Pike Middletown PA 17057 Office: The Milton S Hershey Med Ctr PO Box 850 Hershey PA 17033

TELIS, KAREN ANNE, lawyer; b. Cleve., Mar. 6, 1949; d. Jason Carl and Laura (Katz) Bleiweiss; m. Sherman H. Telis, July 23, 1972; children: Alexander Lee, Michael Charles. BA, Case Western Res. U., 1971; MA, Brown U., 1973; JD, George Washington U., 1979. Bar: D.C. 1979. Tchr. Laurel Sch., Shaker Heights, Ohio, 1973-76; assoc. Fried, Frank, Harris, Shriver & Jacobson, Washington, 1979-83; atty. Genex Corp., Rockville, Md., 1983-84; assoc. Spriggs, Bode & Hollingsworth, Washington, 1984-87, Davis, Graham & Stubbs, Washington, 1987—; guest lectr. George Washington U. Law Sch., Washington, 1983—. Editor George Washington U. Law Rev., 1978. Kenyon Fellow, Brown U., 1972. Mem. D.C. Bar Assn., Womens Bar of D.C., Order of Coif, Phi Beta Kappa. Office: Davis Graham & Stubbs 1200 19th St NW Suite 500 Washington DC 20036-2402

TELLER, DAVIDA YOUNG, psychology, physiology and biophysics educator; b. Yonkers, N.Y., July 25, 1938; d. David Aidan and Jean Marvin (Sturges) Young; m. David Chambers Teller, June 18, 1960 (div. May 1986); children: Stephen, Sara. BA, Swarthmore Coll., 1960; PhD, U. Calif., Berkeley, 1965. Lectr., research prof. U. Wash., Seattle, 1965-69, asst. prof. psychology, physiology and biophysics, 1969-71, assoc. prof., 1971-74, prof., 1973—; research affiliate Regional Primate Research Ctr., Child Devel. and Mental Retardation Ctr.; mem. com. on vision Nat. Acad. Scis.-Nat. Research Council, 1971—, vision research program com. Nat. Eye Inst. and NIH, 1973-76, Assn. Research in Vision and Ophthalmology, program com. Visual Psychophysics and Physiol. Optics, 1973-75, visual scis. B study sect. NIH, 1981-85, chmn. 1983-85; U. Wash. appointments include chmn. Univ. Com. on Vision, 1971; mem. Univ. Council on Women, 1971-76, Faculty Senate Spl. Com. on Faculty Women, 1972-75, ad hoc com. Evaluation of Dir. of Black Studies Program, 1976, faculty adv. bd. Women Studies, 1980-82, ad hoc com. to search for Chmn. Psychology, 1981, standing com. Women Studies, 1982-83, faculty senate council on Grants and Contract Research, 1985—, Univ. Acad. Council, 1986—; dept. psychology appoints include Exec. Com., 1973-75, 77-79; chmn. Budget and Facilities Com., 1979-81; mem. ad hoc com. Staff Employment, 1982-83; honors advisor and dir. Honors Program, 1982—; mem. planning com. 1984-87; reviewer for the following granting agys. NSF, Exptl. Psychology and Visual Sci. B Study Sects. of NIH, Nat Research Council of Can., U.S.-Israel Binational Sci. Found., The Thrasher Research Fund; visited sites for Nat. Inst. Neurol. Diseases and Stroke, Nat. Eye Inst., Vision B. Study Sect. Mem. editorial bd. Infant Behavior and Development, 1981-85, Behavioral Brain Research, 1984-87, Vision Research, 1985—, Clinical Vision Sciences, 1986-87; contbr. numerous articles to profl. jours.; patentee in field. Recipient Sabbatical award James McKeen Cattell Fund, 1981-82. Fellow AAAS, Optical Soc. Am.; mem. Assn. Research in Vision and Ophthalmology, Assn. Women in Sci., Am. Acad. Ophthalmology (Glenn Fry award 1982). Office: U Wash Dept Psychology NI-25 Seattle WA 98195

TELLER, JANE SIMON, sculptor; b. Rochester, N.Y., July 5, 1911; d. Joseph and FLorence (Miller) Simon; m. Walter Magnes Teller; children: Raphael, Joseph, David, Walter. Student, Rochester Inst., Skidmore Coll.; BA, Barnard Coll., 1933. One woman shows include N.J. State Mus., Trenton, 1976 (Purchase Prize 1971, 79), Queens Coll. Gallery, 1981, Mabel Smith Douglass Library Women Artists Series, 1984, Robeson Gallery, Rutgers U., 1986, Skidmore Coll., 1986, The Noyes Mus., 1987, Montclair Mus., 1987; represented in pub. collections Montclair Art Mus., Skidmore Coll., Barnard Coll., Princeton U. Art Mus., Newark Mus., Prudential Life Ins. Co., U.S. Embassy, Japan, Rockefellr U. Fellow N.J. State Council on the Arts, 1985-86; recipient award for Outstanding Achievement in Visual Arts Women's Caucus for Art, Houston, 1988. Mem. Artists Equity, Sculptors Guild, Am. Art Therapy, Princeton Art Assn. Home: 200 Prospect Ave Princeton NJ 08540

TELLO, DONNA, accounting company executive; b. Annapolis, Md., Mar. 23, 1955; m. Gregory Tello, July 5, 1975 (div. 1978); m. Dennis R. Thompson, Apr. 1, 1987; children: Jesse Elliott Timothy Tello, Kimbrelle Shey Thommasson. Owner, tax strategist Tax Savers, San Diego, 1981—; owner, mgr. All Around Bookkeeping, San Diego, 1983—. Libertarian party candidate for state assembly, 1984. Mem. Internat. Platform Soc., Inland Soc. Tax. Cons., Nat. Taxpayers Union, Nat. Assn. Enrolled Agts., Calif. Assn. Enrolled Agts., Mensa (columnist on taxes in monthly newsletter, treas. San Diego chpt. 1985-87). Club: Toastmasters (ednl. v.p. Liberty chpt. 1987). Home and Office: 3835 Merivale Ave San Diego CA 92116

TEMKIN, MAIRLYN LISA, cardiologist, educator; b. Bklyn., June 8, 1954; d. Max Temkin and Sarah (Braun) T. B.A., Johns Hopkins U., 1975; M.D., med. Coll. Pa., 1979. Diplomate Am. Bd. Internal Medicine. Intern internal medicine Nassau County Med. Ctr., East Meadow, N.Y., 1979-80; resident internal medicine, 1980-82, cardiology fellow, 1982-84; research asst. Johns Hopkins U., Balt., 1973-74; clin. supr. SUNY-Stony Brook Med. Sch., 1981-82, asst. clin. instr., 1984—; asst. dir. cardiology Brookhaven Meml. Hosp Med Ctr Patchogue, N.Y., 1984-87; med. dir. cardiac rehab., 1987—. Chmn. physician's edn. com. Suffolk County chpt. Am. Heart Assn., 1984—, bd. dirs., 1985—. Mem. ACP Am. Heart Assn., AMA, Am. Coll. Cardiology. Office: Brookhaven Meml Hosp Med Ctr Dept Cardiology Patchogue NY 11772

TEMPLE, PAULETTE DENISE, housekeeping service administrator; b. Haines City, Fla., Oct. 21, 1958; d. Robert Lee and Annie Lucy (Daniels) Jordan; m. Larry Donell Cooper, July 29, 1979 (div. July 1980); 1 child, Tijuana Patrice; m. Duane Arnold Temple, Aug. 21, 1982; 1 child, Duane Arnold II. Housekeeper Grenelefe (Fla.) Resort, 1976-77, supr., 1977-79, asst. exec. supr., 1979-84, exec. housekeeper, 1984-85; dir. housekeeping Vistana Resort, Lake Buena Vista, Fla., 1985—. Recipient Merit award Nat. Timeshare Council, 1987, 88, Nat. award, 1987. Mem. Nat. Exec. Housekeepers Assn. (rec. sec. 1981-83, 85-87, v.p. 1987-88, pres. 1988), Nat. Assn. Female Execs. Democrat. Baptist. Home: 728 Crescent Valley Ranch Rd Davenport FL 33837 Office: Vistana Resort PO Box 22051 Lake Buena Vista FL 32830-2051

TEMPLEMAN, JANE FRUDDEN, architect; b. Greene, Iowa, June 29, 1931; d. Clyde Marvin and Maude Alice (Perrin) Frudden; m. Clyde Cliffton Templeman, July 24, 1954 (div. 1986); children: David C., Anne, Mark C. BArch, Iowa State U., 1953. Registered architect, Kans. Architect in tng. Howard, Needles, Tammen & Bergendoff, Kansas City, Mo., 1977-83, dir. specifications, 1983-86, architect-project mgr., 1986-88; project mgr. quality assurance Hellmuth, Obata. Kassebaum, Kansas City, Mo. Mem. AIA, Constrn. Specifications Inst. (chmn. nat. spectext com. 1984-87, no. cen. region dir. 1987, recipient Pres.'s Plaque 1986). Republican. Presbyterian. Club: Toastmasters (pres. 1984-85). Office: Hellmuth Obata Kassebaum 323 W 8th St Suite 700 Kansas City MO 64105

TENDLER, MARGE, data processing executive; b. N.Y.C., Apr. 18, 1948; d. James L. and Jeanette T. (Boyd) Pappas; m. Steven H. Tendler, May 7, 1969 (dec. Jan. 1981). BA, NYU, 1971; MBA, U. Rochester, 1981. Cert. in data processing. System analyst Travellers Ins., Hartford, Conn., 1970-73; programmer, analyst Eastman Kodak, Rochester, N.Y., 1973-74; EDP auditor Ernst and Whitney, Los Angeles, 1974-75; system engr. Computer Task Group, various cities, 1976-83, tech. mgr., 1976-83, sales rep., 1976-83, br. mgr., 1976-83; pres. The Software Builders, Inc., Los Angeles, 1984-85; v.p. Data Dimensions, Inc. (acquired The Software Builders, Inc.), Harbor City, Calif., 1985—. Office: Data Dimensions Inc 24404 S Vermont Harbor City CA 90710

TENNANT, MARY JO, educator; b. Tacoma, Jan. 6, 1938; d. Glenn Everett and Adelia Maurine (Converse) Sigler; m. Charles Edward Tennant, June 27, 1959; children: Stephen Victor, Catherine J. Ziarnowski, Susan M., William G. AB, Cornell U., 1959; MT, U. Ariz., 1976. Tchr. Yuma (Ariz.) Dist. 1, 1975-77, Children's Way Sch., Fairfax, Va., 1977-78, St. Michael Sch., Annandale, Va., 1978-84; substitute tchr. Conejo Valley Unified Dist., Thousand Oaks, Calif., 1985; tchr. English Newbury Park High Sch., 1986-87, Redwood Intermediate Sch., Thousand Oaks, 1987—; mem. secondary schs. com. Cornell U., Cornell Club of Washington, 1979-84, Cornell Club So. Calif., 1984—; v.p. sch. bd. Am. Sch. Vientiane, Laos, 1973-74, sec. sch. bd., 1972-73. Neighborhood chmn. Ariz. Cactus-Pine council Girl Scouts U.S., 1974-77, bd. dirs., 1976-77. Recipient Service award Lao Mil. Wives, 1974. Mem. Alpha Phi (dist. alumnae chmn. 1985—). Republican. Roman Catholic. Avocations: reading, sewing, walking. Home: 1317 Breckford Ct Westlake Village CA 91361 Office: Redwood Intermediate Sch 233 W Gainsboro Rd Thousand Oaks CA 91360

TENNEY, DELLA WOOTEN, court reporter, writer; b. Chattanooga, May 5, 1930; d. Charles Madison Wooten and Belle (Davis) Knight; m. Gene William Ailor, Aug. 2, 1948 (div. May 1959); children—Linda Hughie, Sandra Barnwell, Angela Ailor; m. Frank Leonard Stilin, Feb. 21, 1964 (div. Apr. 1971); 1 child, Andrew; m. Edward Jewett Tenney, II, Feb. 17, 1983; stepchildren—Cyndra Fontaine, Edward B. II, Jill. Grad. Gregory Bus. Coll., Knoxville, Tenn., 1950-52; student U. S.C., 1958-59, Stenotype Inst., Jacksonville Beach, Fla., 1972-74, Lippert Sch. Ct. Reporting, Plainview, Tex., 1974. Cert. court reporter, Ga., Fla., Tenn., Guam, N.H. Former personal sec. to lt. gov. of Ga., Atlanta; legal sec. Witt-Gaither-Abernathy, Chattanooga, 1971-72; pres. Accurate Reporting Service, Chattanooga, 1975-78; dean, chief exec. officer The Stenotype Ctr., Chattanooga, 1978-79; ofcl. ct. reporter Guam Superior Ct., 1979-80, N.H. Superior Ct., Concord, 1980—. Author, editor, pub. Basic Stenotype Manual, 1979. Sec., Am. Cancer Soc., Aiken, S.C., 1952-53; campaign mgr. election com. for supt. edn., Aiken, 1954. Mem. N.H. Shorthand Reporters Assn. (sec., v.p.), Nat. Shorthand Reporters Assn., Nat. Assn. Female Execs. Republican. Roman Catholic. Club: Kaypro Users Group. Avocations: traveling; reading; book collecting; motorcycling; photography. Home: PO Box 322 River Rd Claremont NH 03743 Office: NH Superior Ct 163 N Main St Concord NH 03743

TENNY, JOYCE MCCORMICK, professional public relations writer; b. Kenosha, Wis., May 14, 1920; d. William John and Mildred (Johansen) Yanny; m. John McCormick, May 1, 1943 (div. 1952); m. Robert Mack Tenny, Aug. 21, 1954. BS in Journalism, U. Wis., Madison, 1945. Reporter United Press, Madison, 1944-45; picture page editor Louisville Times, 1945-47; pub. relations writer Am. Cancer Soc., N.Y.C., 1947-54, Nat. Multiple Sclerosis Soc., N.Y.C., 1954-60; ptnr. Tenny Lehmann Assoc., Poughkeepsie, N.Y., 1960-66; pub. relations writer Med. Coll. Pa., Phila., 1967-80; profl. pub. relations writer Phila., 1980—. One-woman show includes Pietrantonio Gallery, N.Y.C., 1956; contbr. articles to jours. including N.Y. Times, AMA News, etc. Publicity chmn. N.Y. State Dem. Party, 1958-60, Unitarian Ch., Germantown, Pa., 1965-78. Recipient 1st Prize award IBM Tropy Show, 1958. Mem. AAUW (publicity chmn. Phila. br. 1960—), Med. Coll. Pa. Aux. Democrat. Unitarian.

TENOPYR, MARY LOUISE WELSH (MRS. JOSEPH TENOPYR), psychologist; b. Youngstown, Ohio, Oct. 18, 1929; d. Roy Henry and Olive (Donegan) Welsh; AB, Ohio U., 1951, MA, 1951; PhD, U. So. Calif., 1966; m. Joseph Tenopyr, Oct. 30, 1955. Psychometrist, Ohio U., Athens, 1951-52, also housemother Sigma Kappa; personnel technician to research psychologist USAF, 1953-55, Dayton, Ohio, 1952-53, Hempstead, N.Y.; indsl. research analyst to mgr. employee evaluation N.Am. Rockwell Corp., El Segundo, Calif., 1956-70; asso. prof. Calif. State Coll.-Los Angeles, 1966-70; assoc. research educationist UCLA, 1970-71; program dir. U.S. CSC, 1971-72; dir. selection and testing AT&T, N.Y.C., 1972—; lectr. U. So. Calif., Los Angeles, 1967-70; vice chmn. research com. Tech. Adv. Com. on Testing, Fair Employment Practice Commn. Calif., 1966-70; adviser on testing Office Fed. Contract Compliance, U.S. Dept. Labor, Washington, 1967-73. Pres., ASPA Found.; mem. Army Sci. Bd. Fellow Am. Psychol. Assn. (bd. profl. affairs, edn. and training bd., mem. council reps., pres. div. indsl. organizational psychology); mem. Eastern Psychol. Assn., Am. Soc. Personnel Adminstrn. (bd. dirs. 1984-87), Nat. Acad. Sci. (coms. on ability testing, math. and sci. edn., panel on secondary edn.), Soc. Indsl. and Organizational Psychology (Recipient Profl. Practices award 1984), Nat. Council Measurement in Edn., Psychomatic Soc., Met. N.Y. Assn. Applied Psychology, Am. Ednl. Research Assn., Sigma Xi, Sigma Kappa, Psi Chi, Alpha Lambda Delta, Kappa Phi. Editorial bd. Jour. Applied Psychology, 1972-87; contbr. chpts. to books and articles to profl. jours. Home: 557 Lyme Rock Rd Bridgewater NJ 08807 Office: 1 Speedwell Ave Morristown NJ 07960

TEPP, CYNTHIA KAYE, sportscaster; b. Chgo., Aug. 23, 1957; d. Lawrence Joseph and Daisy Delores (Bruske) T. Student, Ohio State U., 1975-78; BA, Columbia Coll., Chgo., 1979. Desk asst. Sta. WLS-TV, Chgo., 1978-80; co-host Different Drummer program Sta. WBBM-TV, Chgo., 1979; sports reporter Sta. KTVK-TV, Phoenix, 1980-81, Sta. Kool-TV, Phoenix, 1981-83, Sta. WNEV-TV, Boston, 1983-85; sports anchor Sta. KSNW-TV, Wichita, Kans., 1986-88, Sta. KMOV-TV, St. Louis, 1988—. Recipient Hon. Mention award for best sports feature Ariz. AP, Phoenix, 1983; 2d pl. Ariz. Press Club, Phoenix, 1983. Mem. Am. Women in Radio and TV,

Alpha Phi. Roman Catholic. Office: Sta KMOV-TV One Memorial Dr Saint Louis MO 63101

TEPPER, BLOSSOM WEISS, psychologist; b. Bklyn., Oct. 15, 1921; d. Meyer and Anna (Lax) Weiss; m. Louis Tepper, Apr. 17, 1942 (dec. Aug. 1978); children: Irene Tepper Homa, Allan M. BA, Bklyn. Coll., 1942; MEd, Lehigh U., 1962, EdD in Clin. and Counseling Psychology, 1967. Lic. psychologist, Pa.; cert. sch. psychologist, Pa. Tchr. sci., guidance counselor Blue Mountain Sch. Dist., Schuylkill Haven, Pa., 1958-64; successively grad. asst., instr., asst. prof. Lehigh U., Bethlehem, Pa., 1964-71; dir. home and sch. visitor project Luzerne County Schs., Wilkes-Barre, Pa., 1968-71, also adj. prof. Wilkes Coll., Wilkes-Barre, 1969-71; clin. psychologist base service unit, dir. Schuylkill County Mental Health/Mental Retardation, Pottsville, Pa., 1971-72; clin. psychologist Northampton County Mental Health/Mental Retardation, Easton, Pa., 1972-75, clin. psychologist, specialist mental retardation and devel. disabilities, cons. community living program for mental retardation, Bethlehem and Easton, 1975—. Fellow Pa. Psychol. Assn.; mem. Am. Personnel and Guidance Assn., Pa. Personnel and Guidance Assn., Am. Psychol. Assn., Eastern Psychol. Assn., Am. Assn. Mental Deficiency, Am. Assn. Psychiat. Services for Children, Pa. Assn. Sch. Psychologists (charter), Nat. Register Mental Health Providers in Psychology, Am. Assn. Higher Edn. (charter, life), Hadassah (life). Developer exptl. program tng. sch. social workers. Home: Bridle Path Woods Apt C12 Bethlehem PA 18017 Office: Northampton County Dept Human Services Gov Wolf Bldg Mental Health Unit 3d Floor Easton PA 18042

TERBORG-PENN, ROSALYN MARIAN, historian, educator; b. Bklyn., Oct. 22, 1941; d. Jacques Arnold Sr. and Jeanne (Van Horn) Terborg; 1 dau., Jeanna Penn. B.A. in History, Queens Coll., CUNY, 1963; M.A. in History, George Washington U., 1967; Ph.D. in Afro-Am. History, Howard U., 1978. Day care tchr. Friendship House Assn., Washington, 1964-66; program dir. Southwest House Assn., Washington, 1966-69; adj. prof. U. Md.-Balt. County, Catonsville, 1977-78, Howard Community Coll., Columbia, Md., 1970-74; prof. history Morgan State U., Balt., 1969—, project dir. oral history project, 1978-79; project dir. Assn. Black Women Hist. Research Conf., Washington, 1982-83. Author: (with Thomas Holt and Cassandra Smith-Parker) A Special Mission: the Story of Freedmen's Hospital, 1862-1962, 1975. Editor (with Sharon Harley) The Afro-American Woman: Struggles and Images, 1978, 81; (with Sharon Harley and Andrea Benton Rushing) Women in Africa and The African Diaspora, 1987. History editor Feminist Studies, 1984—. Founding mem. Howard County Commn. for Women. Ford Found. fellow, 1980-81, Smithsonian Instn. fellow, 1982, Howard U. grad. fellow in history, 1973-74, recipient Rayford W. Logan Grad. Essay award Howard U., 1973. Mem. Assn. Black Women Historians (co-founder, 1st nat. dir. 1980-82, nat. treas. 1982-84, cert. outstanding achievement 1981), Am. Hist. Assn. (mem. com. on women historians 1978-81), Orgn. Am. Historians (mem. black women's history project adv. com. 1980-81), Alpha Kappa Alpha. Office: Morgan State U Baltimore MD 21239

TERET, TOBY FRIEDMAN, sales representative for graphic arts printer, accountant; b. Bklyn., Apr. 16, 1945; d. Herbert and Judith (Shapiro) Friedman; m. Lester Norris Friedman, Nov. 1, 1962 (div. Nov. 1964); m. Steven Roy Teret, Sept. 15, 1968 (div. May 1974); children: George Friedman, Carrie Teret. BS in Acctg. magna cum laude, Bklyn. Coll., 1984. Adminstrv. supr. VA Hosp., N.Y.C., 1976-79; account exec. Crafton Graphic Co., N.Y.C., 1980-85, account mgr., 1985-86, sales rep., asst. sec., 1988—; sales rep. Penn Colour Graphic, N.Y.C., 1986-88; mem. edn. com. Women In Prodn., 1982—; profl. singer. Mem. Am. Inst. Graphic Arts. Jewish. Home: 3395 Nostrand Ave Brooklyn NY 11229 Office: Crafton Graphic Co Inc 229 W 28th St New York NY 10001

TERKOWITZ, ROBERTA STURGIS, computer systems consultant; b. New London, Conn., Nov. 1, 1951; d. Harlan Mower and Agnes (Mahan) Sturgis; m. Ralph Steven Terkowitz, July 7, 1979; children: Michael Sturgis, Jeffrey Mahan. AB, Middlebury Coll., 1973. Planning analyst Provident Mut. Life Ins. Co., Phila., 1973-75; research room asst. U. Cambridge (Eng.), 1975-76, systems rep. Burroughs Corp., McLean, Va., 1976-78; systems analyst The Washington Post, 1978-80; systems engring. mgr. Memorex Corp., McLean, 1980-87; storage product mgr. Amdahl Corp., Washington, 1987—; speaker govt. Expo '86, Computer Measurement Group Confs., 1981—. Editor: Computer Measurement Group '86 Conference Proceedings, 1986; contbr. articles to profl. jours. Mem. Computer Measurement Group (vendor program chmn. Washington nat. capital area 1985-86, co-program chmn. internat. conf. 1986—). Home: 1324 Ranleigh Rd McLean VA 22101 Office: Amdahl Corp 4801 Massachusetts Ave NW Suite 600 Washington DC 20016

TERPENING, VIRGINIA ANN, artist; b. Lewistown, Mo., July 17, 1917; d. Floyd Raymond and Bertha Edda (Rodifer) Shoup; m. Charles W. Terpening, July 5, 1951; 1 child by previous marriage, V'Ann Baltzelle Diatrick. Studies with Wiliam Woods, Fulton, Mo., 1936-37; student Washington U. Sch. Fine Arts, St. Louis, 1937-40. Exhibited in one-woman shows at Culver-Stockton Coll., Canton, Mo., 1956, Creative Gallery, N.Y.C., 1968, The Breakers, Palm Beach, Fla., 1976; others; exhibited in group shows Mo. Ann., City Art Mus., St. Louis, 1956, 65, Madison Gallery, N.Y.C., 1960; Ligoa Duncan Gallery, N.Y.C., 1964, 78, Two Flags Festival of Art, Douglas, Ariz., 1975, 78-79, Internat. Art Exhibit, El Centro, Calif., 1977, 78, Salon des Nations, Paris, 1985, UN World Conference of Women, Narobi, Kenya, 1985; lectr. on art; jurist for selection of art for exhibits Labelle (Mo.) Centennial, 1972; chmn. Centennial Art Show, Lewiston, 1971, Bicenntenial, 1976; dir. exhibit high sch. students for N.E. Mo. State U., 1974; supt. ann. art show Lewis County (Mo.) Fair; executed Mississippi RiverBoat, oil painting presented to Pres. Carter by Lewis County Dem. Com., Canton, 1979. Mem. Lewistown Bicentennial Hist. Soc. Recipient cert. of merit Latham Found., 1960-63, Mo. Women's Festival Art, 1974, Bertrand Russell Peace Found., 1973, Gold Medallion award Two Flags Festival Art, 1975, Safeco purchase award El Centro (Calif.) Internat. Art exhibit, 1977; 1st pl. award LaJunta (Colo.) Fine Arts League, 1981; diploma Universita Delle Arti, Parma, Italy, 1981; Purchase award Two Flags Art Festival, 1981; award Assn. Conservation and Mo. Dept. Conservation Art Exhbt., 1982; paintings selected for Competition '84 Guide by Nat. Art Appreciation Soc., 1984; 1st pl. award New Orleans Internat. Art Exhibit, 1984, with Am. Women Artists at United Nations Conf. on Women, Nairobi, Kenya, 1985, Two Flags Festival of Art, 1986; named artist laureate, Nepenthe Mondi Soc., 1984, cert. on Arts for the Parks Nat., 1987. Mem. Artist Equity Assn., Inc., Internat. Soc. Artists, Internat. Platform Assn., Nat. Mus. Women in Art (charter), Animal Protection Inst. Mem. Disciples of Christ Ch. Address: Lewistown MO 63452

TERPENNING, MARILOU, oncologist, educator; b. Jersey City, Sept. 20, 1949; d. Clarence DeWitt and Wilma Elizabeth (Coulson) T.; m. Paul Thomas Carter, June 30, 1977 (div. July 1982); 1 child, Paul Thomas Carter Jr. BA with honors, Rutgers U., 1971; MMS, U. Medicine and Dentistry N.J., Piscataway, 1974; MD, Washington U., St. Louis, 1976. Diplomate Am. Bd. Internal Medicine, Am. Bd. Med. Examiners; cert. Med. Oncology. Intern, then resident in internal medicine U. Mich. Med. Ctr., Ann Arbor, 1976-79; fellow in hematology/oncology UCLA, 1979-82; asst. prof. in residence UCLA Sch. Medicine, 1982—; staff physician hematology and med. oncology Sepulveda (Calif.) VA Med. Ctr., 1982—, chief, dir. immunoregulations lab., dir. hematology/oncology ambulatory care, 1982—; cons. UCLA Ctr. for Health Scis., 1986—. Contbr. articles to profl. jours. Grantee Calif. Inst. for Cancer Research, 1982, VA, 1982-86; Damon Runyon-Walter Winchell fellow, 1981-82; recipient Nat. Research Service award NIH, 1979-82. Mem. Am. Coll. Physicians, Am. Soc. Clin. Oncology, Am. Med. Women's Assn., Los Angeles Med. Women's Assn., Phi Beta Kappa. Democrat. Presbyterian. Office: Sepulveda VA Med Ctr 16111 Plummer St Sepulveda CA 91343

TERRAS, AUDREY ANNE, mathematics educator; b. Washington, Sept. 10, 1942; d. Stephen Decatur and Maude Mae (Murphy) Bowdoin. B.S. with high honors in Math., U. Md., 1964; M.A., Yale U. 1966, Ph.D., 1970. Instr. U. Ill., Urbana, 1968-70; asst. prof. U. P.R., Mayaguez, 1970-71; asst. prof. Bklyn. Coll., CUNY, 1971-72; asst. prof. math. U. Calif.-San Diego, La Jolla, 1972-76, assoc. prof., 1976-83, prof., 1983—, vis. positions MIT, fall 1977, 83, U. Bonn (W.Ger.), spring 1977, Inst. Mittag-Leffler, Stockholm, winter, 1978. Inst. for Advanced Study, spring 1984; dir. West Coast Number Theory Conf., U. Calif.-San Diego, 1976, AMS joint summer research conf., 1984; lectr. in field. Author: Harmonic Analysis on Symmetric Spaces and Applications, Vol. I, 1985, Vol. II, 1988; assoc. editor Trans. Am. Math. Soc. Contbr. articles and chpts. to profl. publs. Woodrow Wilson fellow, 1964; NSF fellow, 1964-68; NSF grantee Summer Inst. in Number Theory, Ann Arbor, Mich., 1973; prin. investigator NSF, 1974—. Fellow AAAS; mem. AAAS (nominating com. math. sect.), Am. Math. Soc. (com. employment and ednl. policy com. on coms., council, transactions editor), Math. Assn. Am., Soc. Indsl. and Applied Math., Assn. for Women in Math., Assn. for Women in Sci. Research in harmonic analysis on symmetric spaces and number theory. Office: U Calif San Diego Dept Math C-012 La Jolla CA 92093

TERREBONNE, ANNIE MARIE, medical technologist, educator; b. Isola, Miss., Mar. 17, 1932; d. Tommy Wiley and Alpha Cora (Whitfield) P.; m. Frank Paul Terrebonne, May 7, 1960. A.A., Co-Lin Jr. Coll., 1950; B.S., Miss. State U., 1952; grad. Knoxville Gen. Hosp. Sch. Med. Tech., 1953. Cert. Nat. Cert. Agy. Med. Lab. Personnel. Med., x-ray and EKG technician Layman-Saffold Clinic, Knoxville, Tenn., 1952-55; med. technologist in bacteriology St. Dominic's Hosp., Jackson, Miss., 1956-58; parasitologist Oschner's Clinic and Hosp., New Orleans, 1959-65; sr. med. technician II spl. hematology dept. U. Tex. Med. Br., Galveston, 1969—, mem. research and devel. staff, 1974—, instr. med. tech. students, 1981-86, instr. med. students, residents, and hematology fellows, 1987—. Contbr. articles to profl. jours. Mem. Am. Assn. Med. Technologists, Galveston Dist. Soc. Med. Technologists, Tex. Soc. Med. Technologists, Am. Soc. Clin. Pathologists (cert.), Mental Health Assn. Galveston County, Miss. State U. Alumni. Democrat. Methodist. Clubs: Loyalty, Found. for Christian Living, Positive Thinkers'. Lodge: Order of Eastern Star. Home: 353 Ling Dr Hitchcock TX 77563 Office: U Tex Med Br Spl Hematology Dept 425 Clin Sci Bldg 300 University Blvd Galveston TX 77550

TERRELL, ANNTOINETTE YVONNE, loan executive; b. San Leandro, Calif., Apr. 3, 1963; d. Cleo Visor Dunn; 1 child, Darnell Terrell-Fryer. BS, Calif. State U., 1985, postgrad, 1985—. Cert. loan rep. Teller Wells Fargo Bank N.A., Hayward, Calif., 1980-85; banking svcs. rep. II Union City, Calif., 1985-87; banking svcs. officer San Ramon, Calif., 1987—. Mem. Nat. Assn. Female Execs., San Ramon Mktg. Assn. Home: 3868 Oakes Dr Hayward CA 94542 Office: Wells Fargo Bank NA 3111 Crow Canyon Pl San Ramon CA 94585

TERRELL, ELLEN LARUE, nurse; b. Youngstown, Ohio, Apr. 26, 1953; d. Jesse Jr. and Mattie Mae (Gamble) Thomas; m. Don Mitchell Terrell; children: Dayna, Saunja, Zakkiyyah, Dontaira. Diploma, Sharon (Pa.) Gen. Hosp. Sch. Nursing, 1986; AA, Youngstown (Ohio) State U., 1986. RN, Ohio. Sr. clk. record room St. Elizabeth, Youngstown, 1973-79; sch. nurse Youngstown Bd. Edn., 1982-84; critical care nurse Western Res. Care System, Youngstown, 1986—. Remedial tchr., instr. Youngstown Employment and Tng. Consortium, 1983. Bus. and Profl. Women's Found. scholar, 1985. Mem. Ohio Nurse's Assn., Mahoning-Trumbull Council Black Nurses, NAACP, Youngstown Area Urban League. Baptist. Home: 2291 Volney Rd Youngstown OH 44511

TERRELL, MARGUERITE HARRIS, personnel administrator; b. Athens, Ga., Sept. 11, 1941; d. John Charles and Marguerite Jane (McNair) Harris; m. Ronald A. Terrell, Aug. 27, 1965; children: Holley Jane, Jake. BA, Wesleyan Coll., Macon, Ga., 1963. Caseworker supr. fraud and abuse unit Dougherty County Dept. of Family and Children Services State of Ga., Albany, 1966-81; personnel adminstr. Hill & Foss, Inc., Norcross, Ga., 1982—. Sponsor fund Nat. Rep. Congl. Com., Washington, 1983-87. Mem. Nat. Assn. of Convenience Stores, Ga. Assn. of Convenience Stores, Nat. Assn. for Female Execs., Am. Bus. Women's Assn., Ga. PTA. Republican. Baptist. Club: Norcross Blue Devil (bd. dirs. 1986-87). Lodge: Daughters of the Nile. Home: 2412 Wagon Trace Duluth GA 30136 Office: Hill & Foss Inc 5995 Financial Dr Norcross GA 30071

TERRELL, TRACY ANN, infosystems specialist; b. Washington, July 18, 1963; d. Richard Austin and Jewel Altamai (Caliver) T. BBA cum laude, Howard U., Washington, 1984; postgrad., Johns Hopkins U., 1988. Programmer, analyst C&P Telephone Co., Silver Spring, Md., 1984—. Recipient Avon Products Inc. scholarship, 1982. Mem. Nat. Assn. Female Execs., Assn. Computing Machinery. Democrat.

TERRIS, LILLIAN DICK, psychologist, association executive; b. Bloomfield, N.J., May 5, 1914; d. Alexander Blaikie and Herminia (Doscher) Dick; B.A., Barnard Coll., 1935; Ph.D., Columbia U., 1941; m. Louis Long, Apr. 22, 1935 (dec. Sept. 11, 1968), 1 son, Alexander Blaikie Long; m. Milton Terris, Feb. 6, 1971. Instr. psychology Sara Lawrence Coll., Bronxville, N.Y., 1937-40; jr. personnel tech. SSA, Washington, 1941; sr. personnel clk. OWI, N.Y.C., 1941-43; dir. profl. examination service Am. Public Health Assn., N.Y.C., 1943-70, pres., 1970-79, pres. emeritus, 1979—; assoc. editor Jour. Public Health Policy, 1979—; bd. dirs. Profl. Exam. Service, Vis. Nurse Assn., Chittenden County, Vt. Recipient Nat. Environ. Health Assn. award, 1976; Cert. of Service award Am. Bd. Preventive Medicine, 1979. diplomate Am. Bd. Examiners in Profl. Psychology. Fellow Am. Psychol. Assn.; mem. Am. Public Health Assn., N.Y. State Psychol. Assn., Am. Coll. Hosp. Adminstrs. (hon. fellow), Phi Beta Kappa, Sigma Xi. Contbr. articles in field to profl. jours. Home: 208 Meadowood Dr South Burlington VT 05403 Office: 475 Riverside Dr New York NY 10027

TERRY, ELLEN COLEMAN, real estate executive; b. Paris, Tex., June 11, 1939; d. Rodgers G. and Brown (Dodson) Coleman; children: Todd, Amy. AA, Christian Coll., Columbia, Mo., 1959; BA, So. Meth. U., 1961. Tchr. Cooper High Sch., Abilene, Tex., 1961-63; tchr. Hockaday Sch., Dallas, 1963-66, travel cons., 1975-76; real estate agt. Coldwell-Banker, Dallas, 1976-79; pres., ptnr. Terry, Abio & Adleta, Realtors, Dallas, 1979-81; owner, pres. Ellen Terry, Realtors, Inc., Dallas, 1981—; bd. dirs. Tex. Commerce Bank Dallas. Bd. dirs. Swiss Ave. Counseling Ctr., Dallas Challenge, Susan G. Komen Found., Suicide Crisis Ctr.; mem. adv. com. Crystal Charity Ball. Recipient Disting. Alumni award So. Meth. U., 1985, Disting. Alumnae award Columbia Coll., 1986. Mem. Nat. Assn. Realtors, Tex. Assn. Realtors, Greater Dallas Bd. Realtors (Easterwood cup for Outstanding Realtor 1984), Dallas Women's Council of Realtors, Leadership Tex., Leadership Dallas, Nat. Women's Econ. Alliance (bd. govs.), Pi Beta Phi (Community service award 1985-86, sr. alumnae group). Home: 3510 Turtle Creek Suite 17C Dallas TX 75219 Office: 5401 N Central Suite 225 Dallas TX 75205

TERRY, HILDA, cartoonist, computer animator; b. Newbury Port, Mass., June 25, 1914; d. Charles Zachary Fellman and Annie Tillie Aronson; m. Gregory D'Alessio, June 11, 1938 (div.). dir. Art, Ltd. Desk-Top Pub., 1987—. Creator Teena comic, King Features Syndicate, 1941-64; creator computer animations and graphics for electronic scoreboards for Kansas City (Mo.) Royals, Nassau Coliseum, Long Island, N.Y., Aloha Stadium, Honolulu, Denver Mile High, Meadowland and Giants Stadium, N.J., Arlington Park Race Track, Ill., Hollywood Park Race Track, Calif., AT&T InfoQuests, N.Y.C., others, 1979—; dir. Hilda Terry Gallery, 1960—; author: Baseball Lights Up. Bd. dirs. Prescott Neighborhood House, N.Y.C., 1950—. Recipient Clean Plate Cartoon award N.Y. Times, 1940, Wohelo award Camp Fire Girls, 1950. Mem. Nat. Cartoonists Soc. (Best Animator Cartoonist Rubin award 1980), Internat. Women Writers Guild, Internat. Animated Film Assn., N.Y. MAC Users Group-Writers Spl. Interest Group. Home and Office: 8 Henderson Pl New York NY 10028

TERRY, LEE MARION, employment company executive; b. Tuatapere, N.Z., May 4, 1937; d. Andrew and Edna (Jordan) Mathieson; came to U.S., 1967; m. Richard Lee Terry, Oct. 26, 1967 (div.). A.A., Southland Coll., Invercargill, N.Z., 1953. Owner, pres. Bruce Personnel Service Inc., San Mateo, Calif., 1978—; lectr. Mem. Calif. Assn. Personnel Cons. (past pres.), Nat. Assn. Personnel Cons. (dir. 1981-83), Calif. Employment Assn. (J.R. Pierce award 1976, Jean Widdicombe award 1979, 84), Nat. Assn. Female Execs., Nat. Assn. Personnel Cons. (sec. 1985-86), Am. Soc. Profl. and Exec. Women, Adv. Council Status of Women. Club: Pena Taurina Sol y Sombra (San Francisco). Office: Bruce Personnel Service 493 Seaport Ct Suite 102 Redwood City CA 94063

TERRY, MARY SUE, state official, lawyer; b. Martinsville, Va., Sept. 28, 1947; d. Nathaniel Chatham and Nannie Ruth T. B.A., Westhampton Coll., 1969; M.A., U. Va., Charlottesville, 1970, J.D., 1973. Bar: Va., 1973. Asst. commonwealth's atty. Patrick County, Va., 1973-77, mem. house dels., 1977-85; ptnr. B.H. Cooper Farm, Inc., Stuart, Va., from 1978, Terry & Rogers, Stuart, Va., from 1978; atty. gen. State of Va., Richmond, Va., 1986—; dir. First Nat. Bank of Stuart. Mem. Piedmont Planning Dist. Crime Commn., 1974-77; bd. dirs. West Piedmont Health Planning Council, 1975-77; bd. dirs. Patrick Henry Mental Health Ctr., 1975-77; mem. Pres. Bd. Advisors Ferrun Coll., Va., 1978-83; bd. dirs. Va. YMCA, 1980—; trustee U. Richmond, Va., 1980—; chmn. Gov.'s Task Force to Combat Drunk Driving, 1982. Recipient Service to Youth award Va. YMCA, 1981, Disting. Alumna award U. Richmond, 1984. Mem. Va. Trial Lawyers Assn., ABA, Omicron Delta Kappa. Democrat. Baptist. Office: Atty Gen Va 101 N 8th St Richmond VA 23291 *

TERWILLIGER, NORA BARCLAY, marine biologist; b. Hartford, Conn., Oct. 9, 1941; d. Edward Elwin and Marjorie (Scribner) B.; m. Robert Chapman Terwilliger, May 9, 1967; children: Kelly Jean, Robert Barclay. BS, U. Vt., 1963; MS, U. Wis., 1965; PhD, U. Oreg., 1981. Research asst. Boston U., 1967-69; research asst. U. Oreg., Charleston, 1971-78, research assoc., 1981—; instr. State of Oreg., Coos Bay, 1974-75, S.W. Oreg. Community Coll., Coos Bay, 1980-81; vis. scientist Marine Biol. Assn., Plymouth, Eng., 1983-84; vis. investigator Friday Harbor Labs., 1986, 87; cons. Coos Bay Sch. Dist., 1975-76. Contbr. articles to profl. jours. Mem. AAAS, Am. soc. Zoologists, We. Soc. Naturalists, Phi Beta Kappa. Home and Office: Oreg Inst Marine Biology Charleston OR 97420

TESCHENDORF, BONNIE EVA, physical therapy educator; b. Buffalo, Nov. 3, 1943; d. Clarence and Mary (Dancey) Herbst; m. Melvin C. Teschendorf, Aug. 15, 1970. BS, NYU, 1965; M in Health Adminstrn., New Sch. for Social Research, 1981; cert. gerontology, U. Mich., 1983; postgrad., Columbia U. Cert. phys. therapist, N.Y., N.J., Calif. Staff phys. therapist Inst. Rehab. Medicine, N.Y.C., 1965-68; chief phys. therapist Scripps Clinic and Research Found., La Jolla, Calif., 1968-70; sr. phys. therapist St. Vincent's Med. Ctr., N.Y.C., 1970-73; pvt. practice phys. therapy N.J., 1974-75; dir. phys. therapy asst. program Union Coll., Cranford, N.J., 1979-81; mgr. allied health services Community Health Care, Orange, N.J., 1981-83; asst. prof., assoc. dir. phys. therapy program Columbia U., N.Y.C., 1983—; cons. Van Dyk Manor Nursing Home, Montclair, N.J., 1983—, cons. West Side Fedn. Srs., N.Y.C., 1984-86. Mem. editorial bd. newsletter on aging; contbr. articles to profl. jours. Recipient Brookdale award, 1985. mem. Am. Phys. Therapy Assn. (chmn. edn. specialization com., chmn. task force sect. on geriatrics 1986—, pres. 1988—). Republican. Home: 72 Lakewood Dr Denville NJ 07834 Office: Columbia U 630 W 168th St New York NY 10032

TESELLE, GRACE HILL, writing and design company executive; b. Gibsonia, Pa., Feb. 10, 1928; d. Harold Alton and Hulda Leota (Fisher) H.; m. Virgil Wilbur TeSelle; children: Luanne Elizabeth, Virginia Ellen, Gary John. BS in Commerce, Grove City Coll., 1949; legal asst. cert., George Washington U., 1977. Tchr. bus. dept. Chicora (Pa.) High Sch., 1949-52; sec. Dept. State, Washington, 1952-55; legal adminstr. Petroleum Mktg. Corp., McLean, Va., 1972-77, Rees, Broome and Birken, P.C., McLean, 1977-78; legal asst. Stephens and Krebs Law Firm, McLean, 1978-83; designer, co-owner TeSelles Frame Shop, Falls Church, Va., 1981—; pres., owner Artselle Writing and Design, Falls Church, Va., 1983—; bd. dirs., advisor Mus. One, Inc., Washington, 1984—. Editor/Pub.: Showcase and Art Digest; contbr. articles to profl. jours. Precinct chair election bd., Falls Church, 1968-73; bd. mgrs. Fairfax County Br. YWCA, Donn Loring, Va., 1984— (vol. awards 1985, 86). Mem. Bus. and Profl. Women-McLean Club (newsletter editor 1983-85, pub. relations chair 1985-86, named Va. State Editor of Yr. 1983-84), Internat. Assn. Gerontol. Entrepreneurs (bd. dirs.), Nat. Writers Club, Washington Ind. Writers, Nat. Capitol Area Paralegal Assn. (chair No. Va. chpt. 1979-82), Women's Network-YWCA (editor 1983-87), Assn. Part-Time Profls., Network Entrepreneurial Women, Nat. Alliance Homebased Bus., Va. Assn. Female Execs., Fairfax County C. of C. Republican. Methodist. Home and Studio: 7437 Nigh Rd Falls Church VA 22043

TESSA, MARIAN LORRAINE, talk show host, writer and producer; b. N.Y.C., Sept. 23, 1950; d. Sylvester Joseph and Emma Carol (Chimento) T. BA in English, SUNY, Cortland, 1972; postgrad., N.Y. Sch. Broadcasting, 1972-73. Writer CBS, N.Y.C., 1972-75; show host Manhattan Cable, N.Y.C., 1975—; writer, producer, host Staten Island Cable, 1988. Spokesperson Miss Universe/Miss U.S.A. Beauty Pageants, 1976, promotion benefits; guest appearances include David Susskind Show, 1978, ABC Wide World Spl., 1978, The Joe Franklin Show, 1980, The You Show, 1979, Natural Living Program, 1981; talk show host Kaleidoscope, 1983-85; voice over on cable TV,1975—; performer Broadway in the Streets, 1969; photographic model Penzo Spagnoli Gallery, Florence Italy, 1984; photography shows San Francisco, N.Y.C. and London, 1988. Recipient Forensic award. Mem. TV Acad. Arts and Scis. Home: 302 96th St Suite 3S Brooklyn NY 11209

TESSIER, SUSAN ANNMARIE, accountant; b. Attleboro, Mass., Aug. 24, 1950; d. Albert Louis and Dorothy Florence (Simoneau) T. BBA in Acctg. cum laude, Western Conn. State U., 1983. Clk. typist Hartford (Conn.) Nat. Bank, 1969; delivery logger United Parcel Service, Hartford, 1969-70; bookkeeper, clk. Harris Office Equipment, Hartford, 1970-72; accounts receivable analyst Pratt & Whitney Aircraft, East Hartford, Conn., 1973-74; jr. cost acct. Cushman Chuck Industries, Inc., Hartford, 1976-77; staff acct. Berkshire Transformer Corp., Kent, Conn., 1978-83; materials mgr. Berkshire Transformer Corp., Kent, 1983-84; pvt. practice acct. Lakeville, Conn., 1984—. Artist: (graphic art) Undulation, 1965 (nat. art award 1966). Mem. Nat. Soc. of Tax Profls., Salisbury Conn. C. of C. (sec. 1987-88, treas. 1988—), Delta Mu Delta. Office: Acctg Services Main St Lakeville CT 06039

TESTA, SHARON ANNE, business consultant; b. Lawrence, Mass., Mar. 6, 1948; d. Joseph Robert and Carmela Mary (Palermo) T.; 1 child, Michael Antony. AA, Middlesex Community Coll., 1977; BS in Bus. Edn., Salem State coll., 1981; MBA, N.H. coll., 1985. Sec. Atty. Gen. of Mass., Boston, 1968-69; legal asst. to pvt. atty. Lawrence, 1969-81; owner, bus. cons. M.T. Assocs., Salem, N.H., 1981—; instr. Castle Jr. Coll., Windham, N.H., 1986—, No. Essex Community Coll., Haverhill, Mass., 1987—. Mem. Nat. Assn. Bus. Educators, Nat. Assn. Female Execs., N.H. Coll. Alumni Assn. Democrat. Roman Catholic. Office: MT Assocs PO Box 679 Danville NH 03819

TETA, ROSEMARIE FRANCES STACEY, financial company executive; b. Chester, Pa., July 4, 1955; d. Robert Francis and Sarah A. (Meer) Stacey; m. Nicholas C. Teta, Aug. 5, 1978; children: Monica, Laura. BS in Acctg. and Econs., Widener U., 1976. Staff auditor Touche Ross & Co., Phila., 1976-79; chief acct. Hay Assocs., Phila., 1979-80; tax mgr. Avtex Fibers Inc., Valley Forge, Pa., 1980-82; mgr. treasury ops. Avtex Fibers Inc., Valley Forge, 1982-85, dir. treasury ops., 1985-86; corp. cash mgr. Comcast Corp., Bala Cynwyd, Pa., 1986—. Mem. Nat. Assn. Accts. (bd. dirs. 1976-80), Nat. Corp. Cash Mgrs Assn. Republican. Roman Catholic. Home: 991 Maule Ln West Chester PA 19382 Office: Comcast Corp One Belmont Ave Suite 200 Bala Cynwyd PA 19004

TETERYCZ, BARBARA ANN, entrepreneur, advertising executive; b. Chgo., Jan. 23, 1952; d. Sylvester and Anne (Deutsch) T.; m. Robert Nathan Estes, Oct. 13, 1984. BA, U. Ill., 1974; postgrad. Parkland Coll., 1975-76, U. Ill., 1976-77. Teller, First Fed. of Champaign, Ill., 1974-75; cashier Kroger Co., Champaign, 1975-77; merchandise rep. RustCraft Greeting Cards, Champaign, 1977-78; sales rep. Hockenberg-Rubin, Champaign, 1978, John Morrell & Co., Champaign, 1978-80; account exec. Sta. WICD TV, Champaign, 1981-86; owner Left-Handed Compliments, Champaign; creator 1987, 88 left-handed calendar. Contbg. editor mag. Champaign County Bus. Reports, 1986. Vol. Am. Cancer Soc., 1985, U. Ill. Alumni Assn., 1985-88, Coms. to Elect and Re-elect Beth Beauchamp to City Council, Champaign, 1984, 87. Ill. State scholar, 1970-74. Mem. Ad Club of Champaign (finalist several copywriting contests), Internat. Platform Assn., Entrepreneurs Roundtable (founding), Women's Bus. Council, Urbana C. of C., Champaign C. of C. (pub. relations com., pres.'s club), Nat. Assn. Female Execs., Alpha

Omega. Roman Catholic. Avocations: reading, writing, bicycling, bodybuilding. Home: 1615 Harbor Point Dr PO Box 873 Champaign IL 61820

TEWS, KATHLEEN, youth association executive; b. Martins Mill, Tex., Dec. 23, 1921; d. Caleb and Ethie (Goolsby) Bass; m. Earl William Tews, Oct. 23, 1952 (dec. May 1981). MusB, Baylor U., 1942; postgrad., Harvard U., 1979, 83, 85, Dana U., 1981. Field exec. Girl Scouts U.S., San Antonio, 1949-51; exec. dir. Girl Scouts U.S., Texarkana, Tex., 1951-75, Toledo, 1975-82, San Antonio, 1982—; selections chmn. participants Girl Scouts Am. Internat. events, 1959-75; nat. sec. Assn. Girl Scout profl. workers, 1966-72; monitor, trainer new execs. Girl Scouts U.S., N.Y.C., 1970's. Pres. Music Guild and Community Chorus, Texarkana, 1962-70; mem. Opera Guild, N.Y.C., San Antonio. Mem. Baylor U. Alumni Assn., AAUW, NOW. Democrat. Baptist. Lodges: Altrusa (pres. 1960-62), Zonta (com. chmn. 1976-85). Home: 5909 Luther Ln Dallas TX 75225

TEWS-YOCUM, EVE LYNN, insurance adjuster; b. Berea, Ohio, Aug. 11, 1956; d. Clee Cliffton Leatherman and Marlene J. (Shepard) Findlay; m. James Edward Tews, May 24, 1975 (div.); m. Bryan E. Yocum, Aug. 29, 1987; children—James Wesley Tews, Dianne Marie Yocum. Grad. high sch. Sec., Toensmeier Adjustment, Allentown, Pa., 1974-78, adjuster, 1978-81; resident adjuster Gemmill Adjustment, Reading, Pa., 1981-84; ins. adjuster/owner E.L. Tews Adjustment, Allentown, 1984—. Mem. Lehigh Valley Claims Assn. (pres. 1986—), Nat. Assn. Self-Employed, Nat. Assn. Female Execs., Reading Claims Assn., Lehigh Valley Claims Assn. (sec., 1st. v.p. 1984-85, pres. 1985-86). Democrat. Avocations: aerobics; reading; crocheting.

TEXIDOR, MARGARET STRACHAN, medical educator, researcher; b. Boston, Jan. 14, 1945; d. William Henry and Marjorie Weld Strachan. Diploma in nursing, 1965; AS, Allan Hancock Coll., 1972; BA, LaVerne U., 1974; MA, U. New Orleans, 1975, PhD, 1983. RN, La. Instr. services coordinator Mercy Hosp., New Orleans, 1977-80; assoc. dir. nursing adminstrn. Touro Infirmary, 1980-81; nurse Orleans Parish Schs., 1981; cert. mental health counselor New Orleans, 1980—; research asst. coll. edn. U. New Orleans, 1982-83; from research assoc. to asst. prof. research dept. anesthesiology Tulane Med. Sch., New Orleans, 1984—. Contbr. research articles to profl. jours.; mem. editorial bd. Internat. Jour. Med. Psychotherapy, 1986—. Served to col. USAR, 1964—. Mem. Reserve Officers Assn. (editor newspaper), Am. Bd. Med. Psychotherapists (clin. assoc.), Am. Mental Health Counselors Assn. (com. chair 1985—), La. Mental Health Counselors Assn. (pres. 1987-88), Am. Acad. Pain Mgmt. (mem. profl. adv. bd. 1987—), Am. Soc. Anesthesiologists, Sigma Theta Tau, Kappa Delta Pi, Phi Kappa Phi. Mailing address: PO Box 8063 New Orleans LA 70182-8063 Office: Tulane Med Sch 1430 Tulane Ave New Orleans LA 70112

THAGARD, SHIRLEY STAFFORD, sales and marketing executive; b. Detroit, Nov. 29, 1940; d. Walter Jay Stafford and Marjorie Gertrude (LaRa) Stafford Goode; m. Charles Wendell Thagard, Sept. 21, 1963; children: Grayson Jay, Devon Charles. Assoc. Bus., Webber Coll., 1961; cert. Pierce Coll., 1973. Dir. pub. relations Miami Herald, Fla., 1963-67; pres. Thagard Enterprises, Woodland Hills, Calif., 1980—; v.p. mktg. R.T. Durable Med. Products, Inc., Miami, also Woodland Hills, 1983-85; investment cons., lectr. investments Palisades Fin. Services, Sherman Oaks, Calif., 1985-86; v.p. real estate investments, M.W. Palmer and Assocs., 1986-87, with real estate sales dept. Country Club West Realtors, 1987—; ind. lectr. women's issues and children's health care, 1980—. Editor, pub. Pediatric Network, 1980-85. Contbr. articles to various jours. Creator Med. Moppets healthcare teaching tools, 1983. Chairperson Los Angeles County Mental Health (Expressing Feelings), 1985-87; ind. lobbyist for child abuse legislation Calif. Legislature, 1985—. Recipient commendation Los Angeles City Council, 1983, Calif. Congresswoman Bobbi Fiedler, 1984. Mem. Nat. Assn. Female Execs., San Fernando Valley Bd. Realtors, Assn. Care of Children's Health, Am. Bus. Women's Assn., Pilot Internat. (pub. relations com. 1985-86, San Fernando Valley club commendation 1985), Nat. Assn. Edn. Young Children, Direct Mktg. Council Los Angeles. Avocations: travel, writing. Office: PO Box 8396 Calabasas CA 91302

THAL, ANNE ELISE, hospice director, psychotherapist, consultant; b. Toledo, Aug. 3, 1945; d. William S. and Florence Marian (Salzman) T. AB, U. Chgo., 1966, AM, 1968; postgrad. in bus. adminstrn. U. South Fla., 1982-83. Lic. clin. social worker, Ill., Fla. Research assoc. Hills County Schs., Tampa, Fla., 1972-73; exec. dir. Suicide/and Crisis Ctr., Tampa, 1973-74, bd. dirs., 1972-81, v.p., 1977-79; exec. dir. Tampa Jewish Social Service, 1974-83; pvt. practice psychotherapy, Tampa, 1977—; exec. dir. Hospice of Hillsborough, Inc., 1987—; founder, pres. The Playmakers, Inc., Tampa, 1981-83, dir. mgmt./devel., 1983-85; lectr. Field Inst., U. South Fla., Tampa, 1975-83; cons. in fields; profl. actress, 1962-82. Chmn. Hills County Crisis Council, Tampa, 1975-77; mem. adv. bd. Sr. Resource Ctr., Tampa, 1976-82, Hillsborough Info. Line, Tampa, 1978-82. Named Outstanding Bd. Mem., Suicide and Crisis Ctr., Tampa, 1978; One of 33 Women to Watch, Tampa Tribune, 1982; NIMH fellow, 1967-68. Fellow Acad. Cert. Social Workers (diplomate in clinical social work); mem. Nat. Assn. Social Workers, Network Exec. Women, NOW. Office: 601 S Magnolia Tampa FL 33606

THALER, ELIZABETH BARBARA, industrial relations specialist; b. Freeport, N.Y., Jan. 5, 1959; d. Joseph and Hilda (Engelstein) T. BA in Polit. Sci., SUNY, Binghamton, 1981; MEd in Indsl. Counseling, Northeastern U., Boston, 1986. Dir. spl. events Mass. Cystic Fibrosis Found., Wellesley, 1982-84; human resources adminstr. Gen. Cinema Corp., Chestnut Hill, Mass., 1984-85; career planning coordinator Northeastern U., 1985-86; corp. trainer Sentry Ins. Co., Concord, Mass., 1986-87; sr. tng. specialist Mass. Fin. Services Co., Boston, 1987—; freelance career counselor, Watertown, Mass., 1986-87. Editor: Employee Orientation Handbook, 1986; assoc. editor: (newsletter) Sentry Ctr. East, 1987. Mem. Am. Soc. Tng. and Devel., Kappa Delta Pi. Office: Mass Fin Services 200 Berkeley St Boston MA 02116

THALER, LEDA SUSAN, hospital marketing and public relations executive; b. Mpls., Oct. 24, 1949; d. Jere and Dorothy Beverly (Kaplan) T. BS in Journalism, U. Colo., 1971. Fashion copywriter The Denver Dept. Stores, Denver, 1973-75; promotion coordinator Cinderella City Mall, Denver, 1976-77; dir. mktg. University Hills Mall, Denver, 1977-79; asst. dir. devel. Sewall Rehab. Ctr., Denver, 1980-82; promotions specialist Bonfils Theatre, Denver, 1982-83; writer, editor The Children's Hosp., Denver, 1983-84, mktg. specialist, 1984-86, asst. dir. mktg. and pub. relations, 1987—. Recipient Grand Alfie award Denver Advt. Fedn., 1975, Addy award Am. Advt. Fedn., 1986, Gold Leaf award of merit Colo. Hosp. Assn., 1986. Mem. Am. Mktg. Assn., Pub. Relations Soc. Am.

THALL, LETTY DERMAN, social services administrator; b. New Orleans, Jan. 6, 1947; d. Herbert and Mary Virginia (Coughlin) Derman; m. Bruce Louis Thall, June 23, 1968; children: Gregory Coughlin, Mary Courtney. B.A., Skidmore Coll., 1968; M.S.S., Bryn Mawr Coll., 1974. Trainer, cons. Bell Telephone Co., Phila., 1968-71; policewoman Phila. Police Dept., 1971; planning cons. Health and Welfare Council, Phila., 1974-75; dir. WOAR, Phila., 1975-77; program coordinator Hall-Mercer Ctr., Phila., 1978-80; div. dir. and planner Community Services Planning Council, Phila., 1980-85; exec. dir. Delaware Valley Child Care Council, 1986—; pres. bd. CHOICE, 1977-80; alumni com. mem. Community Leadership Seminars, Phila., 1978-83. Coordinator Shirley Chisholm for Pres., Miami, Fla., 1972; fin. dir. Bill Gray for Congress Com., Phila., 1978; co-chairperson Marion Tasco for City Commr., Phila., 1983; mem. Phila. Mayor's Commn. for Women, 1980-85, vice-chair., 1983-85; bd. dirs. City Parks Assn., 1986—, Ctr. Responsible Philanthropy, 1987—. Mem. Mid Atlantic Assn. for Tng. and Counseling (trainer, group facilitator 1979—), Women's Way (co-founder; bd. dirs. 1975-81), Delaware Valley Assn. for Edn. Young Children, Nat. Assn. Social Workers, Assn. for Creative Change. Democrat. Office: 121 N Broad St 5th Floor Philadelphia PA 19107

THARP, TWYLA, dancer, choreographer; b. Portland, Ind., July 1, 1941; 1 son, Jesse. Student, Pomona Coll.; grad., Barnard Coll.; D of Performing Arts (hon.), Calif. Inst. Arts, 1978, Brown U., 1981, Bard Coll., 1981; LHD, Ind. U., 1987; DFA, Pomona Coll., 1987; studies with, Richard Thomas, Merce Cunningham, Igor Schwezoff, Louis Mattox, Paul Taylor, Margaet Craske, Erick Hawkins. With Paul Taylor Dance Co., 1963-65; freelance choreographer with own modern dance troupe and various other cos. including Joffrey Ballet and Am. Ballet Theatre, 1965—; teaching residencies various colls. and univs. including U. Mass., Oberlin Coll., Walker Art Ctr., Boston U. Choreographer: Tank Dive, 1965, Re-Moves, 1966, Forevermore, 1967, Generation, 1968, Medley, 1969, Fugue, 1970, Eight Jelly Rolls, 1971, The Raggedy Dances, 1972, As Time Goes By, 1974, Sue's Leg, 1975, Push Comes to Shove, 1976, Once More Frank, 1976, Mud, 1977, Baker's Dozen, 1979, When We Were Very Young, 1980, Amadeus, 1984, White Nights, 1985, (film) Hair, 1979, (video spls.) Making Television Dance, 1977, CBS Cable Confessions of a Corner Maker, 1980, (Broadway shows) Sorrow Floats, 1985, Singin' In The Rain, 1985. Recipient Creative Arts award Brandeis U., 1972; Dance mag. award, 1981; Univ. Medal for Excellence, Columbia U., 1987. Office: Twyla Tharp Dance 853 Broadway Suite 1708 New York NY 10003

THATCHER, KRISTINE MARIE, actress, writer; b. Lansing, Mich., June 22, 1950; d. Joseph and Marjory Suzanne (McKeone) Schneider; m. Timothy T. Thatcher, Apr. 24, 1971 (div. Nov. 1977). Grad. high sch., Lansing. Appeared numerous theatre prodns. including Hunting Cockroaches, The Taming of the Shrew, Angel Street, The Real Thing, The Life and Adventures of Nicholas Nickleby, The Browning Version, Twelve Pound Look, You Never Can Tell, A Tinker's Dam, Boy Meets Girl, Custer, A Doll's House, As You Like It, Merton of the Movies, The Nerd, Translations, Arms and the Man, Of Mice and Men, Cat on a Hot Tin Roof, Macbeth, The Threepenny Opera; TV appearances include Trial of the Moke, Hyde and Seeke, Another World, Search for Tomorrow, Modern Parenting; playwright: The Adventures of Captain Karma, 1976, Michigan Bio (The Rustic Village), 1983, Niedecker, 1985, (with Larry Shue) Looking for Tina Meyer, 1985; honorary mem. Milw. Repertory Theater. Mem. Actors' Fund Am., N.Y.C., 1985—, Dem. Nat. Com., Washington, 1988—; vol. Greenpeace, Chgo. and Washington, 1987-88. Nominated for Plays in Process Theatre Communications Group, 1987, Joseph Kesselring award Nat. Arts Club, 1987. Mem. Actors Equity Assn., AFTRA, Dramatists' Guild, Soc. Stage Dirs. and Choreographers, Inc. Roman Catholic. Home and Office: 6722 N Bosworth Ave Chicago IL 60626

THATCHER, MARY JO, television producer; b. Des Moines, Dec. 24, 1951; d. Ben and Barbara Jean (Ward) Thatcher; student Citrus Coll., 1970-72. Actress, various parts, incl. part in Helter Skelter, 1975; exec. producer TV commls., with Denny Harris Inc. of Calif., Los Angeles, 1977-86; packaging, producing TV commls., corp. films & ind. productions, Rider & Thatcher Film.. Mem. Screen Actors Guild, Am. Film Instit., Assn. Ind. Comml. Producers, Women in Film, NOW. Office: 202 Main St Suite 5 Venice CA 90291

THAWLEY, MARY NANCY, sales professional; b. Cambridge, Mass., Oct. 20, 1947; d. George Clifton and Mary Agnes (Glennon) T. BA, U. Mass., Boston, 1969; postgrad., Northeastern U., 1981; studied with Joanne Rathe, Cambridge, 1984, studied with Ulrike Welsch, 1986. Tchr. Boston Sch. Com., 1969; rep. Nynex Info. Resources Co., Lynn, Mass., 1970—; photographer, sports reporter South End News, Boston, 1983-85; photographer sports Lynn Sunday Post, 1986—; photographer Boston Celtics, 1985—. Contbr. articles to profl. jours. Active Johnson-Humphery Dem. campaign for Pres. of U.S., Winchester, Mass, 1964, McGovern Dem. campaign for Pres. of U.S., Boston, 1972; founding mem. Rainbow Coalition, Boston, 1982; mem., photo contbr. New England Sports Mus., 1985—; photographer Joe Kennedy campaign, Cambridge, 1986, 88, Michael Kane campaign, Boston, 1987; spokesperson Berkeley residents Tenants Orgn., Boston, 1987, also chmn. 1988. Hon. fellow John F. Kennedy Library (founding mem.); mem. Associated Photographers Internat., Nat. Press Photographers Assn., Communications Workers Am., Nat. Marfan Found., Greater Lynn Camera Club. Roman Catholic. Home: 40 Berkeley St Apt 207 Boston MA 02116

THAXTON, VERA, home economics educator; b. Wenatchee, Wash., Aug. 15, 1933; d. Charles Clay and Ruth Ellen (Parsons) T. A.A., Mt. San Antonio Coll., 1954; B.A., San Diego State U., 1956; M.S., U. Ill.-Urbana, 1958. Cert. secondary tchr., Calif. Child welfare worker I, Lucas County (Ohio) Child Welfare, Toledo, 1958-60; home econs. instr. Bridgewater (Va.) Coll., 1960-62; licensing caseworker I, Los Angeles County Dept. Charities, Bur. Licensing, 1962-63; home econs. tchr. Pomona (Calif.) Unified Sch. Dist., 1963-69, Sonora (Calif.) High Sch., 1969-71, Banning (Calif.) High Sch., 1971-73, Coachella High Sch., Thermal, Calif., 1974—. Sec., La Quinta Property Owners Assn., 1979-82, 83-84. Mem. AAUW, Am. Home Econs. Assn., Calif. Home Econs. Assn. (dist. past pres., treas.), Nat. Assn. Edn. Young Children, Calif. Assn. Edn. Young Children, Future Homemakers Am. (sponsor), Fgn. Affairs Council. Republican. Presbyterian. Club: U. Ill. Alumni (past treas.). Home: PO Box 85 La Quinta CA 92253 Office: 83-800 Airport Blvd Thermal CA 92274

THAYER, JANE See WOOLLEY, CATHERINE

THAYER, JILL SHELDON, agriculture educator; b. Anchorage, Nov. 13, 1953; d. Averill Sheldon and June (Eliason) T. BS, U. Ala., Fairbanks, 1979, MS, 1982; postgrad., U. Calif., Santa Barbara. Cert. sea and shore survival instr., wildlife rehabilitator. Research assoc., coordinator U. Alaska, Fairbanks, 1979-82; gardening, natural resource agt., asst. prof. extension U. Alaska, Sitka, 1982—; coordinator Student Symposium on Alaska's Aquatic Resources, 1987-88. Contbr. articles to mags. and profl. jours. Mem. downtown revitalization com., Sitka, 1984-85, overall econ. planning com., Sitka, 1984-85; mem. steering com. Symposium on Econ. Future of Southeast Alaska; adv. council mem. Sitka Community Schs., 1983—, Adult Basic Edn. Program, Sitka, Telephone Utilities of Northland, Sitka, 1987—; mem. Sitka Disaster Preparedness Council, Sitka, 1986—; coordinator Sitka Community Fair, 1982-84. Recipient Community Gardeing Assn., 1985. Mem. Nat. Assn. Extension 4H Agts., Nat. Assn. Agrtl. Agts., Nat. Safety Council (Community Safety award Woman's Nat. Div. 1986), NW Assn. Marine Educators, Internat. Assn. Sea Survival Tng., Alaska Natural Resource and Outdoor Edn. Assn., Nature Printing Soc., N.Am. Fruit Explorers, Sikta C. of C., Epsilon Sigma Phi. Lodge: Rotary. Office: Coop Extension Service 4 Lincoln St Room 207 Sitka AK 99835

THAYER, NANCY GAIL, public relations and marketing executive; b. Framingham, Mass., Sept. 10, 1961; d. Robert Howard and Jeanette Nancy (Semonian) Hedges; m. John Louis Thayer, Aug. 24, 1985. AS in Bus., Newbury Coll., 1986. Clk. typist Integral Data Systems, Milford, N.H., 1980; sec. CW Conf. Mgmt. Group, Framingham, 1980-82, adminstrv. asst., 1982-84; mktg. services mgr. IDG Conf. Mgmt. Group, Framingham, 1984—, mgr. pub. relations and non-exhibit sales, 1987—; campus dir. asst. Newbury Coll., Framingham, 1986—. Mem. Am. Soc. Assn. Execs., Nat. Assn. Expo. Mgrs. Roman Catholic. Home: 180 Village St Medway MA 02053

THAYER, WANDA E., business owner; b. Tuscaloosa, Ala., July 27, 1943; d. Herman Springer and Anita (Rogers) Parker; m. Cameron Jones (div. 1976); children—Bryan Keith, Kimberly Ann. Student Foothills Jr. Coll., Palm Beach Jr. Coll. Co-owner Aluma Loc Awning, San Jose, Calif., 1964-67; sec.-treas. A&A Air Conditioning, Boca Raton, Fla., 1968-76; pres. Personalized Air Conditioning, Inc., Boca Raton, 1978—. Chmn. BACPAC, 1979-81; bd. dirs. SAFEPAC, 1983—, Boca Raton United Way, 1984—; mem. bd. of rules and appeals City of Boca Raton, 1986; appointed to Boca Raton Planning and Zoning Bd., 1986—; dep. mayor City of Boca Raton, 1987-88; bd. dirs. Cities in Schs., Inc., 1987—. Mem. Boca Raton C. of C. (dir., treas. 1986-87), Fla. Atlantic Builders Assn. (past 2d v.p., past sec.; Assoc. of Yr. 1983), Nat. Fedn. Ind. Bus., Fla. Air Conditioning Contractors Assn., Better Bus. Bur. Democrat. Lutheran. Avocations: tennis; travel; reading. Home: 149 NW 70th St #205 Boca Raton FL 33432 Office: Personalized Air Conditioning 121 NW 11th St Boca Raton FL 33432

THEBOLT, CATHERINE OLIVIA, health educator; b. Mt. Shasta, Calif., Mar. 23, 1952; d. George Jr. and Olivia Angelina (Marconi) Thebolt; m. Stephen Albert Minall, Jul. 20, 1974 (div. June 1985); m. John David Princell, Sept. 15, 1985; 1 step-daughter, Cori. BA, U. Calif., Berkeley, 1974; postgrad., Dominican Coll., 1974-75. Cert. health/fitness instr., Am. Coll. Sports Medicine. Tchr Marin County Schs., San Rafael, Calif., 1975-77; tchr., counselor McCloud (Calif.) High Sch., 1977-79; cons., owner Corporate Image Inc., San Francisco, 1980-83; owner Sweat Shop, Grand Junction, Colo., 1983-85; cons. Hilltop Rehab. Hosp., Grand Junction, Colo., 1983-86, Attention Youth, Grand Junction, Colo., 1985; supr. Mesa Devel. Services, Grand Junction, Colo., 1985-86; producer talent Sta. KJCT-TV, Grand Junction, Colo., 1984-86; wellness coordinator St. Mary's Hosp., Grand Junction, Colo., 1985—. co-author: Ageless, 1985, It's Up To You, 1986, Heart Smart, 1987. Council mem. Am. Lung Assn, 1986—; bd. dirs. Nat. Council Alcoholism, 1986—; curriculum advisor Mesa County Schs., 1987. Mem. Am. Coll. Sports Medicine, Assn. Fitness Bus., Nat. Wellness Inst. Democrat. Roman Catholic. Home: 2504B Rose Dr Grand Junction CO 81503 Office: St Marys Hosp 7th and Patterson Grand Junction CO 81501

THEESFELD, CAROLE ANN, educator; b. Elmwood Park, Ill., Apr. 29, 1943; d. Howard Maurice and Ann (Romcoe) Kumlin; m. David Alan Theesfeld, Aug. 7, 1965; children: Michael Dean, Michelle Sue. BS in Edn., Ill. State U., 1965; MS in Math. Edn., U. Ill., 1968. Cert. tchr., Ill. Tchr. math. Fremd High Sch., Palatine, Ill., 1965-70, Harper Jr. Coll., Palatine, 1970—; tchrs. aide math. Arlington Heights (Ill.) Grade Schs. Dist. 25, 1976-82; tchr. math. Rolling Meadows (Ill.) High Sch., 1982-83, East Leyden High Sch., Franklin Park, Ill., 1983-84, Addison (Ill.) Trail High Sch., 1984—; dir. plays Addison Trail High Sch., 1984—. Author: Essentials of Algebra (TRB), 1987. Mem. Nat. Council Tchrs. Math., Ill. Council Tchrs. Math, Kappa Mu Epsilon. Lutheran. Club: Addison Trail Fishing (sponsor run 1985—). Home: 712 N Kennicott Arlington Heights IL 60004 Office: Addison Trail High Sch 213 N Lombard Addison IL 60101

THEIM, DONNA JEANNE, financial analyst; b. Troy, N.Y., Dec. 29, 1944; d. Paul F. and Marie H. (Kelly) Coddington; m. Harold D. Theim, Oct. 19, 1968; children: Paul J., Debra A., Cindy J., Christine M. BS in Acctg., Rochester Inst. Tech., 1967; postgrad. in bus., Syracuse U., 1984—. CPA, N.Y. Acct. Cortland L. Brovitz, CPA, Rochester, N.Y., 1967-68, Robfogel Mill Andrews Corp., Rochester, 1968-69; sr. acct. Sidney Z. Galinsky, Rochester, 1969-74; owner True Impressions, Rochester, 1974-79; tax acct. Security Trust Co., Rochester, 1979-81; staff acct. N.Y. State Electric and Gas Corp., Ithaca, 1981-83, sr. acct., 1983-86, sr. tax analyst, 1986-87; sr. tax acct. Goulds Pumps Inc., Seneca Falls, N.Y., 1987—; mem. N.Y. State Electric and Gas Corp. Speakers Club, 1985—. Dir. Nutrition Program for Elderly in Tompkins County Inc., Ithaca, 1986—. Mem. Nat. Assn. Accts. (pres. 1986-87), Am. Inst. CPA's, N.Y. State Soc. CPA's. Home: 396 Applegate Rd Ithaca NY 14850 Office: Goulds Pumps Inc Seneca Falls NY 13148

THEIS, ANNE, communications director; b. Buffalo, Minn., Feb. 27, 1956; d. Alan Anthony and Kathryn Mae (Fiemeyer) T.; m. Stephen John Koller, June 23, 1984. BA in Mass Communications, St. Cloud State U., 1979. Publs. coordinator St. Cloud (Minn.) Hosp., 1979-82; dir. communications Franciscan Sisters Health Care, Little Falls, Minn., 1982—; bd. dirs. St. Cloud Hosp. Employees Credit Union, v.p. 1984-85, pres. 1986-87. Ofcl. Minn. State High Sch. Volleyball League, 1978—; with pub. relations St. Cloud Area United Way, 1980-82, Morrison County United Way, Little Falls, 1986-88. Mem. Minn. Council Hosp. Mktg. and Pub. Relations (treas. 1986, past pres. 1988), Am. Soc. Hosp. Mktg. and Pub. Relations (dir. region 6 1988—, Wis. Hosp. Pub. Relations and Mktg. Soc., Forum Exec. Women, Profl. Women's Orgn., St. Cloud C. of C. (com. mem.). Roman Catholic. Office: Franciscan Sisters Health Care Inc 116 8th Ave SE Little Falls MN 56345

THELIAN, LORRAINE, public relations executive; b. N.Y.C., Jan. 13, 1948; d. Anthony G. and Inez (Gelfo) Bufano; m. Helmuth Thelian, Sept. 11, 1942. BA, Molloy Coll., 1969. Account coordinator Basford Pub. Relations, N.Y.C., 1969-71; from asst. account exec. through v.p. Paluszek & Leslie Assoc., N.Y.C., 1971-74; v.p., assoc. dir. Ketchum Pub. Relations, Washington, 1985—; mem. Washington Bd. Trade, 1987—. Mem. Pub. Relations Soc. Am. (accredited, chmn. accreditation com. Washington chpt. 1987—), Washington Communications Assn. Roman Catholic. Office: Ketchum Public Relations 1625 Eye St Washington DC 20006

THEODORATUS, NOTHING KATHLEEN, communications company credit executive, free-lance writer; b. Sacramento; d. Hilario Ernesto and Otillia (Kraft) Uribe; m. Robert James Theodoratus; children: Sarah Elena, Amelia Elizabeth, Demetri Hilario. BA, Sacramento State Coll., 1962. Bus. mgr. Rev. Pub., Ft. Collins, Colo., 1979-82; collection specialist Everitt Lumber Co., Ft. Collins, 1983-85; credit mgr. Tel-Share US, Inc., Ft. Collins, 1987—; freelance writer Ft. Collins, 1966—; mem. readability editing div. VCH Opportunity Ctr., Ft. Collins, 1970-86. Contbr. articles to profl. jours., mags. and newspapers. V.p. Larimer County Dem. Party, Ft. Collins, 1976-78. Office: Tel-Share US Inc 2601 S Lemay Suite 37 Fort Collins CO 80525

THEODORE, CRYSTAL, artist, retired educator; b. Greenville, S.C., July 27, 1917; d. James Voutsas and Florence Gertrude (Bell) T.; AB magna cum laude, Winthrop Coll., 1938; MA, Columbia U., 1942, EdD, 1953; postgrad. U. Ga., 1947. Instr. art Winthrop Coll., 1938-43; prof. art, head dept. Huntingdon (Ala.) Coll., 1946-52; prof. art, head dept. E. Tenn. State U., 1953-57; prof. art, head dept. Madison Coll., 1957-68; vis. prof. art World Campus Afloat, Chapman Coll., Calif., 1967; prof. art James Madison U., Harrisonburg, Va., 1968-83, ret. Bd. dirs. Rockingham Fine Arts Assn., 1980-85, Women's Coop. Council Harrisonburg and Rockingham County, 1976-79; cons. Valley Program for Aging Services, 1976. Served with USMCR, 1944-46. Gen. Edn. Bd. of Rockefeller Found. fellow, 1952-53; award Carnegie Found. Advancement of Teaching, 1947, 48, 49, 50; Ednl. Found. Program grantee AAUW, 1981-82. Mem. AAUW (cultural interests rep., dir. 1980-82, 1985—), League of Women Voters, Mensa, Kappa Delta Pi, Kappa Pi, Delta Kappa Gamma, Eta Sigma Phi, Pi Lambda Theta. Democrat. Lutheran. Contbr. articles to profl. jours.; paintings in regional and nat. exhbns. Home: Route 5 Box 202 Harrisonburg VA 22801

THEODORE, JASMINA ALEXANDRA, lawyer, economist; b. Kenosha, Wis., June 2, 1955; d. Sima Vladimir and Maria Therese (Churamowicz) Todorovic. B.A. U. Wis.-Parkside, 1973, M.S. in Econs., U. Wis.-Madison, 1975, J.D., 1979. Bar: Calif. 1980, Wis. 1980. Assoc. Latham & Watkins, Los Angeles, 1980-83; asst. counsel Union Oil Co. of Calif., Los Angeles, 1983—; journal referee Jour. Econ. Behavior and Orgn., Los Angeles, 1982—; guest lectr. law, econs. Claremont (Calif.), McKenna Coll. 1982—. Commisioner, Utility Adv. Bd., Pasadena, Calif., 1986—. Mem. State Bar Calif., Wis. Bar Assn., Town Hall of Calif., ABA.

THERRIEN, EILEEN MARIE, youth minister; b. St. Petersburg, Fla., Oct. 5, 1956; d. Joseph Clark and Elsie Faye (Sargent) Cornwell; m. Frederic Howard Therrien, Nov. 27, 1981; children: Rachel Jean, Alexander Joseph. BA, Barry U., 1978. Religion tchr. Madonna Acad. for Girls, Hollywood, Fla., 1978-79; assoc. youth dir. Diocese of St. Petersburg, 1979-82; youth minister St. Paul's Cath. Ch., Tampa, Fla., 1982—; speaker Nat. Cath. Young Adult Ministry S.E. Regional Conf., Norfolk, Va., 1986; cons. Diocese os St. Petersburg Youth Office, 1982-87. Mem. Nat. Assn. Female Execs. Democrat. Roman Catholic.

THEUSCH, COLLEEN JOAN, computer and laser company executive; b. Milw., Dec. 18, 1932; d. Christian Charles and Marie (Fons) T.; m. Edward S. Anderson, Apr. 8, 1978 (dec. Oct. 1984). BEd, Coll. Racine, 1961; MA in Math., U. Detroit, 1966; PhD in Math., Mich. State U., 1971. Instr. Coll. Racine, Wis., 1970-71; sr. research assoc. Richman Co., Cleve., 1971-84, Laser CAM Systems Inc., Cleve., 1984—; part-time faculty Cleve. State U., 1971-72; cons. Custom Cut Technologies, Cleve., 1986-87. Active Beck Ctr. for Cultural Arts, Lakewood, Ohio, 1980—. NSF grantee, 1963-66. Mem. Am. Math. Soc., AAUW, Mensa, Intertel. Roman Catholic. Home: 22962 Maple Ridge Rd #206 North Olmsted OH 44070 Office: Laser CAM Systems Inc 1600 E 55th St Cleveland OH 44103

THEVENET, SUSAN MARIE, lawyer; b. San Antonio, Apr. 6, 1950; d. Stanley Edward and Marie Therese (Hulsebosch) T.; m. Paul Steven Casamassimo, June 28, 1975 (div. 1981). B.A., Pa. State U., 1971; M.A.,

Georgetown U., 1973; J.D., U. Iowa, 1978. Bar: Colo. 1979, U.S. Dist. Ct. Colo. 1979. Legis. asst. Am. Assn. Dental Schs., Washington, 1973-74; civil rights investigator Cedar Rapids Human Rights Commn., 1974-75; assoc. Shoemaker & Wham, Denver, 1979; vis. prof. U. Colo. Coll. Law, Boulder, 1980; assoc. Smart, DeFurio & McClure, Denver, 1979-85, ptnr., 1985-87; bd. dirs. Smart, DeFurio, McClure, Thevenet & Sandler P.C., 1987—. Co-author; Iowa Law Rev., 1977, editor-in-chief, 1977-78. Mem., officer Iowa Women's Polit. Caucus, 1974. Mem. ABA, Colo. Bar Assn. (mem. grievance policy com. 1982-84), Denver Bar Assn. Republican. Roman Catholic. Office: Smart DeFurio McClure Thevenet and Sandler 1120 Lincoln St Suite 1600 Denver CO 80203

THIBEAULT, DALE WILKINS, construction services executive, consultant; b. Manchester, Conn., Sept. 10, 1938; d. Edgar Thomas Richard Wilkins and Jessie Morgan Roberts; widowed; children: Craig, Fleur, Clayton, Danielle. Student, U. Hartford, 1960, Long Beach Community Coll., 1972, Flat River Community Coll., 1974, Santa Rosa Community Coll., 1978. Asst. adminstr. Enfield (Conn.) Extended Care Facility, 1967-68; asst. v.p. Lewten Industries, Inc., Hartford, Conn., 1968; office mgr. Buell-Lungren-Todd, Long Beach, Calif., 1969-73; dir. 8 country region East Mo. Community Action Agy., Flat River, 1974-75; sales mgr. Western region A-L Woodworks, Inc., Lynwood, Calif., 1975-77; corp. sec., controller X-L Homes, Inc., Santa Rosa, Calif., 1978-82, Northridge Corp., Santa Rosa, 1980—; pres. Thibeault & Assocs., Ltd., Santa Rosa, 1984—; v.p. RGS Devel., Inc., Santa Rosa, 1986—. Author or co-author various tng. manuels. Mem. Gov.'s Adv. Bd., Jefferson City, Mo., 1974-75, Southeastern Mo. Regional Rev. Bd., Cape Girardeau, 1973-75; pres., founder Vols. in Action, Cape Girardeau, 1974-75; sec. LWV, Manchester, Conn., 1963, NOW, Cerritos, Calif., 1971-73; den leader, coach Boy Scouts Am., Conn. and Calif., 1965-73. Recipient Achievement awards U. Mo., 1974, Lincoln U., 1974, Regional Area on Aging, Kansas City, Mo., 1974, Inst. Real Estate Mgmt., Sacramento, Calif., 1983. Mem. Rural Builders Council, Sonoma County Apt. Assn., North Coast Builders Exchange, Nat. Assn. Female Execs., Windsor C. of C. Republican. Episcopalian. Lodges: Elks, Peacemakers. Office: Thibeault & Assocs Ltd 3070 Cleveland Ave Santa Rosa CA 95401

THIELE, GLORIA DAY, retired librarian; b. Los Angeles, Sept. 4, 1931; d. Russell Day Plummer and Dorothy Ruby (Day) Th.; m. Donald Edward Cools, June 13, 1953 (div.); children—Michael, Ramona, Naomi, Lawrence, Nancy, Rebecca, Eugene, Maria, Charles. B.Mus., Mt. St. Mary's Coll., Los Angeles, 1953. Library asst. Anaheim (Calif.) Pub. Library, 1970-73, head Biblioteca de la Comunidad, 1973-74, children's library asst., 1974-76, children's br. specialist, 1976-78, children's librarian, 1978-81; head children's services Santa Maria (Calif.) Pub. Library, 1981-85; cons. Literature Continuum, Santa Maria Sch. Dist., 1981-85; cons. Organizational Ch.-Sch. Library, Los Angeles, 1980; guest lectr. children's lit. Allan Hancock Coll., Santa Maria, 1981-85. Library liaison Casa Amistad Community Service Group, Anaheim, 1973-74; mem. outreach com. Santiago Library System, Orange County, 1973-74, mem. children's services com., 1971-81; mem. Community Services Coordinating Council, Santa Maria, 1982-85; chairperson children's services com. Black Gold Library System, 1983-84; cons. children's library programs, 1986—; profl. storyteller, 1987—. Mem. ALA, Calif. Library Assn., So. Calif. Council Lit. for Children and Young People, Women's Network, Delta Epsilon Sigma. Republican. Roman Catholic. Club: Minerva (Santa Maria).

THIELE, IRMA E., educator; b. Buffalo, Sept. 26, 1918; d. Charles Adolph and Elizabeth Gertrude (Rauschnick) Gritzke; m. George Adolph Burgasser, Sept. 8, 1938 (dec. May 1973); children: Joanne Burgasser Gatz, Patricia Burgasser Doebler, Raymond, George Charles; m. Eugene W. C. Thiele, June 29, 1976 (dec. Apr. 1980); stepchildren: Claudia LoJacano, Janet Leslein, Marion Bay. BS in Edn., SUNY, Buffalo, 1964, MA in Supervision, 1968, postgrad., 1977, 82-83, 87. Cert. elem. tchr., supr., sch. prin., in early childhood. Sec. to office mgr. AM&A's Dept. Store, Buffalo, 1935-39; tax preparer IRS, North Tonawanda, N.Y., 1958-59; tchr. Niagara Falls (N.Y.) Bd. Edn., 1964—; head tchr. math. and lang. arts summer sch. Niagara Falls Bd. Edn., 1977, head tchr. sci., 1985; dir. on youth bd., North Tonawanda, 1982-86. Numerous offices PTA, North Tonawanda, 1945-58; leader Girl Scouts U.S., North Tonawanda, 1947-52; chmn. local Eisenhower for U.S. Pres. campaign, North Tonawanda, 1956, March of Dimes, North Tonawanda and Niagara Falls, 1956-57; mem. Luth. Women's Missionary League, Pres. Reagan's Task Force, DeGraff Hosp. Aux.; Sunday sch. tchr. Luth. Ch., supt. Vacation Bible Sch. Mem. Assn. Supervision and Curriculum Devel., Bus. and Profl. Women, Early Childhood Assn., EKNE, SUNY at Buffalo Alumni Assn., Kappa Delta Phi. Republican. Home: 1315 Nash Rd North Tonawanda NY 14120

THIELEN, LOIS ANN, newspaper reporter; b. St. Cloud, Minn., Feb. 1, 1954; d. Joseph and Bernette Mary (Moeller) T. BA in English and History, Coll. St. Benedict, St. Joseph, Minn., 1976; coursework in mass communications, St. Cloud State U., 1977-81. Reporter Sauk Centre (Minn.) Herald, 1977, 1987—; reporter, photographer Stearns-Morrison Enterprise, Albany, Minn., 1977-83, advt. mgr., 1982-83; freelance writer The Land, Mankato, Minn., 1983-85; pub. St. Joseph Jour., 1987. Editor ethnic, heritage cookbook The Melting Pot, 1985; co-founder literary arts mag. Studio One, 1976. Mem. Stearns (Minn.) County Hist. Soc., 1984-87; organizer, worker Albany area combined fund drive, 1981-83. Women of Today scholar St. Cloud State U., 1980. Mem. Nat. Assn. Female Execs., Jaycee Women/Women of Today (local officer Holdingford area 1983-87), Minn. Jaycee Women (editor Newslet, state officer 1984-85). Roman Catholic. Home: Rt 1 Box 44 Grey Eagle MN 56336

THIELEN, MARY JEAN, educational administrator; b. Flint, Mich., Dec. 2, 1942; d. John Sr. and Mary (Henzarek) Hrinevich; m. Harold R. Thielen, April 12, 1969. AA, Flint Community Jr. Coll., 1962; BA cum laude, Mich. State U., 1964, MA, 1967. Tchr. Flint Community Schs., 1964-69; grade head Brookside Sch. Cranbrook, Bloomfield Hills, Mich., 1969-71; sci. tchr. St. Ann Sch., Cleveland Heights, Ohio, 1971-72; grade head Hathaway Brown Sch., Shaker Heights, Ohio, 1972-77; coordinator of admissions Brandon Hall Sch., Atlanta, 1977-80, dir. admissions, 1980—, exec. staff officer, 1984-86, dean of sch., 1987—; supr. student tchrs. U. Mich., Flint, 1964-69; mem. steering com. on Piaget Cleveland (Ohio) Council of Pvt. Schs., 1975; sch. chmn. accreditation com. So. Assn. Colls. and Schs., Atlanta, 1986-88. Fund raiser United Way, Flint, 1963, Am. Cancer Soc., Bloomfield Hills, Mich., 1970; sch. chmn. Scottish Rite Hosp., Atlanta, 1977; sec. Dunwoody Manor Homeowners, Norcross, Ga., 1982-84; mem. Deerfield Homeowners, Dunwoody, Ga., 1984-87. Named scholar Jennings Found., 1976. Mem. Nat. Council Tchrs. Math., Nat. Assn. Ind. Schs., Mich. State U. Alumni, Kappa Delta Pi. Republican. Roman Catholic. Home: 5390 Bannergate Dr Alpharetta GA 30201 Office: Brandon Hall Sch 1701 Brandon Hall Dr Atlanta GA 30350

THIERSTEIN, EMMA JOAN, lawyer, technical information specialist; b. Newton, Kans., Oct. 5, 1937; d. William and Emma Voth; m. Eldred A. Thierstein, Mar. 17, 1959; children—Joel, Gretchen. A.B. in Chemistry, Bethel Coll., North Newton, Kans., 1958; grad. Kans. U., 1958; J.D., U. Ky., 1976. Bar: Ky. 1976, D.C. 1979, Mich. 1979, U.S. Patent Office 1979. Pub. sch. tchr., Woodstock, Nfld., Can., 1960-61; lab. technician Procter & Gamble, Cin., 1966, tech. info. specialist, mgr., Cin. and Brussels, 1967-72, summer 1974; patent examiner U.S. Govt., Washington, 1976-78; asst. patent atty. Upjohn Co., Kalamazoo, 1978-84, asst. patent counsel, Parke Davis div. Warner Lambert, Ann Arbor, Mich., 1984—. Mem. Mich. bd. SSS. Mem. Ky. Bar Assn., D.C. Bar Assn., Mich. Bar Assn., Am. Patent Lawyers Assn., Women Lawyers Assn. S.W. Mich., Phi Alpha Delta Internat. (sec.-treas. 1973-74). Home: 2636 Lakeshore Dr Hillsdale MI 49242 Office: Warner Lambert 2800 Plymouth Rd Ann Arbor MI 48105

THIGPEN, JANET MELVIN, home economics educator; b. Live Oak, Fla., July 17, 1952; d. Herman Dewitt and Mary (McClellan) Melvin; m. Marvin Ray Thigpen, Oct. 24, 1952; children: Jason Ray, Russell Neil. AA, North Fla. Jr. Coll., 1972; BS, Fla. State U., 1980, MS, 1987. Instr. visually handicapped adults North Fla. Jr. Coll., Madison, 1980-81; extension agt. Fla. Cooperative Extension Service, Madison, 1981-87; vocat. tchr. home econs. Volusia County Sch. Bd., Daytona, Fla., 1987—; coordinator Madison County 4-H, Madison, 1981-87. Mem. Nat. Assn. Extension 4-H Agts., Am. Home Econs. Assn. Democrat. Baptist. Office: YWCA 344 S Beach St Daytona Beach FL 32014

THOM, LILIAN ELIZABETH, educator; b. Georgetown, Guyana, July 11, 1937; came to U.S., 1976; d. William Buller and Venus Henrietta (Albert) Thom. M.S., Adelphi U., 1982. Tchr. home econs. St. Philip's Govt. Sch., Georgetown, 1960-62, tchr. elem. edn. St. Philip's Govt. Sch., Georgetown, 1962-75; sr. mistress, tchr., St. Barnabas Govt., Georgetown, 1975-77; day care edn. asst. Community Sponsors, Bklyn., 1978; tchr., supr. edn. St. Mark's Sch., Bklyn., 1978-82; instr. resource room Jr. High Sch. #44, N.Y.C., 1982—; tutor dressmaking Carnegie Sch. Home Econs., Georgetown, 1960, tutor St. Barnabas Govt., Georgetown, 1975-76, evening class Taylor Bus. Sch., Manhattan, N.Y., 1983. Sec., mem. Friends St. George's Cathedral, Georgetown, 1958—. Mem. United Fedn. Tchrs., Nat. Assn. Female Execs., Guyana Tchrs. Assn. Anglican.

THOMA, JANET HOOVER, editor, writer; b. Pitts., Apr. 17, 1937; d. Wayne George and Elizabeth (Coopernail) Hoover; m. John Barry Thoma, Nov. 25, 1961; children—Christine Lynne, Janet Elizabeth, Heidi Ann. B.A. in English, Ohio U., 1959, M.S. in Journalism, 1983. Asst. editor David C. Cook Pub., Elgin, Ill., 1977-78, assoc. editor, 1978-79, editor Chariot Books, 1979-80, mng. editor, 1980-84; sr. acquisitions editor Thomas Nelson Pubs., Nashville, 1984—; cons. children's books, 1983; speaker in field. Author: (with Maggie Mason) Esther, 1978; author series: Buddy Books, 1978; contbr. articles to Christian Herald Mag., Moody Monthly, Bookstore Jour. Bd. dirs. Jr. League Kansas City (Mo.), 1975-76; mem. mayor's com. Alt. Futures for Kansas City, 1976; mem. adv. bd. Elgin Community Coll., 1983. Mem. Mortar Bd. Republican. Episcopalian. Home and Office: 1307 Little John Dr Elgin IL 60120

THOMAS, ANDRA CAROL, scientific studies administrator, registered nurse; b. Decatur, Ill., Dec. 7, 1948; d. Elmer Jr. and Mary Katherine (Patteson) T. Diploma in Nursing, Barnes Hosp. Sch. Nursing, 1969; student, U. Md., 1971-72, Johns Hopkins U., 1976-79, Coll. Notre Dame, Md., 1980-81, SUNY, 1981—. Staff nurse operating rooms Johns Hopkins Hosp., Balt., 1971-72, head nurse operating rooms, 1972-81; clin. rep. Intec Systems, Inc., Pitts., 1981-83, mgr. clin. research, 1983-85; mgr. clin. research implantable defibrillation devices Cardiac Pacemakers, Inc., St. Paul, 1985, mgr. clin. programs, 1985-88, mgr. sci. studies, 1988—. Mem. Pitts. Ballet Theater Guild, 1981-84; aux. vol. St. Margarets Meml. Hosp., Pitts., 1984-85. Mem. Am. Heart Assn. Clin. Councils, Assn. Operating Room Nurses, Am. Mgmt. Assn., Nat. Assn. Female Execs., N.Am. Soc. of Pacing and Electrophysiology. Office: Cardiac Pacemakers Inc 4100 Hamline Ave N Saint Paul MN 55112

THOMAS, ANN LOUISE, personnel services administrator; b. West Green, Ga., Sept. 5, 1930; d. Alpheus Albert and Martha Josephine (Williams) Hazard; div.; children—Rodney, Michael, Karen. Student Wayne State U., 1948-50, Harlem Sch. Nursing, N.Y.C., 1951, Wayne County Community Coll., 1969, Henry Ford Community Coll., 1970. Nat. recruiting dir. Internat. Personnel, Detroit, 1962-69; EEO recruiting specialist Blue Cross/Blue Shield Mich., Detroit, 1969-72; assoc. dir. Detroit Indsl. Mission, 1972-76; personnel adminstr. Parke-Davis div. Warner & Lambert Co., Detroit, 1976-79; adminstr. Comprehensive Health Services Detroit, 1979—. Organizer, planner Focus Hope, Detroit, 1970, bd. dirs., 1970—; advisor-cons. Mich. Inter-Collegiate Black Bus. Students Assn., Detroit, 1970-74; co-founder, mem. Detroit Metro EEO Forum, 1973—; chair bd. dirs. Eastwood Clinics, Detroit, 1986—; active in civil rights movement, 1970's—. Named one of 10 Outstanding Detroit Women, Detroit News, 1972. Democrat. Avocations: travel; gourmet cooking; reading; stamp collecting; classical and jazz music. Home: 17334 Santa Rosa Dr Detroit MI 48221

THOMAS, ANNE CAVANAUGH, lawyer; b. Louisville, July 13, 1950; d. Harry Edward and Martha Mae (Marks) Cavanaugh; m. Andrew Dennis Thomas, Aug. 16, 1975; 1 child by previous marriage, Shelley Anne. BA with honors, Ind. U. S.E., Jeffersonville, 1973; JD, Ind. U., Bloomington, 1976. Bar: Ind. 1976. Staff counsel Teamsters Local 215, Evansville, Ind., 1976-81; sole practice, Evansville, 1981—; instr. U. Evansville, 1976-77; hearing mem. Indsl. Bd. Ind., 1984—. Bd. dirs. Big Bros./Big Sisters of Southwestern Ind., Inc., Evansville, 1977—, v.p., 1982-84; mediator City of Evansville and Fraternal Order Police, 1982; bd. dirs. Evansville EPA, 1988—. Mem. ABA, Ind. State Bar Assn. (mem. council young lawyers sect. 1981-84, author column Res Gestae 1983-84), Evansville Bar Assn. (co-chmn. young lawyers sect. 1983, dir. 1984-85, 86-88, chmn. Lawyers Assistance Program 1985—), Legal Services Organ. Ind. Bd. Dirs. 1987—, dir. Evansville Enviromental Protection Agy. 1988—; Democrat. Office: 405 Court Bldg 123 NW 4th St Evansville IN 47708

THOMAS, BARBARA SINGER, banker, attorney; b. N.Y.C., Dec. 28, 1946; d. Jules H. and Marcia (Bosniak) Singer; m. Allen Lloyd Thomas, Mar. 12, 1978; 1 child, Allen Lloyd Jr. B.A. cum laude, U. Pa., 1966; J.D. cum laude (John Norton Pomeroy scholar 1968-69, editor law rev. 1968-69, Jefferson Davis prize public law 1969), N.Y. U., 1969. Bar: N.Y. 1969. Assoc. Paul, Weiss, Rifkind, Wharton & Garrison, N.Y.C., 1969-78; assoc. Kaye, Scholar, Fierman, Hayes & Handler, N.Y.C., 1973-77, ptnr., 1978-80; commr. SEC, Washington, 1980-83; pres. Samuel Montagu Holdings Inc., N.Y.C., 1984-86; regional dir. Asia Pacific Samuel Montagu Ltd., London, 1984-86; sr. v.p., group head The Internat. Pvt. Bank, Bankers Trust Co., N.Y.C., 1986—; mem. Council on Fgn. Relations; adv. council K.H.D. Deutz Am. Corp., KHD Deutz, N.Y.C.; trustee Inst. East-West Securities Studies, N.Y.C. Mem. adv. council Women's Econ. Roundtable; mem. internat. adv. bd. Am. U.; mem. Women's Forum Women's Trusteeship Los Angeles, N.Y.C.; bd. dirs. N.Y.C. Opera; gov. U. Pa. Joseph H. Lauder Inst. Mgmt. and Internat. Studies; mem. bd. overseers Sch. Arts and Scis.; trustee Pace U., Youth for Understanding, U. Pa. Alumni Assn., Washington Opera, Fin. Women's Assn., N.Y. Law Rev. Alumni Assn.; mem. adv. com. Nat. Mus. of Women's Art; mem. internat. com. N.Y.C. Ballet. Recipient award for outstanding service in govt. Fin. Mktg. Council Greater Washington, 1982, Woman of Achievement award WETA-FM, 1983; named one of Outstanding Young Women in Am., 1981, mem. of Men and Women Under 40 Changing Am., Esquire Mag., 1984, Baylor U. Woman of Yr., 1987. Mem. Young Pres.'s Orgn., ABA, Washington Bar Assn., (sect. on corp., banking and bus. law), N.Y. State Bar Assn., Internat. Bar Assn., Assn. Bar City N.Y. (chmn. corp. law com. 1979-80), Global Econ. Action Inst., Order of Coif, Econ. Club of N.Y., Nat. Assn. Female Execs. (bd. dirs.). Home: 791 Park Ave New York NY 10021 Office: Bankers Trust Co 280 Park Ave New York NY 10017

THOMAS, BETH EILEEN WOOD (MRS. RAYMOND O. THOMAS), editor; b. North Vernon, Ind., May 12, 1916; d. Fayette J. and Emma J. (Ream) Wood; m. Raymond O. Thomas, Feb. 28, 1941; 1 son, Stephen W. Comml. diploma, Bedford High Sch., 1934; student, Lockyear Bus. Coll., 1936. Sec. WPA, Vincennes, Ind., 1935-36, Evansville, Ind., 1937-38, Indpls., 1939-41; sec. to adj. AAF Storage Depot, Indpls., 1941-44; sec. Coll. Life Ins., Indpls., 1957-58, Indpls. Sch. Bd., 1958-59; classified office mgr. North Side Topics Newspaper, Indpls., 1960-67. Editor: Child Life Mag, Indpls., 1967-71, Brownie Reader, 1971-73, Children's Playmate mag, Indpls., 1968—; editorial assoc.: Saturday Evening Post, Indpls., 1971; exec. editorial dir.: Jack and Jill mag, 1971—, Young World mag, 1971-79, Child Life mag, 1971—, Design mag, 1977-80, Turtle Mag. for Presch. Kids, 1979—, Humpty Dumpty's mag, 1980—, Children's Digest, 1980—; exec. editorial dir. juvenile mags., Children's Better Health Inst., Indpls. Mem. Women in Communications, Indpls. Press Club. Club: Thetis. Home: 6172 Compton B Indianapolis IN 46220 Office: Children's Better Health Inst 1100 Waterway Blvd Box 567 Indianapolis IN 46206

THOMAS, BETTY, actress; b. St. Louis. BFA, Ohio U. Former sch. tchr; co-star Hill St. Blues, from 1981; Joined Second City Workshop, Chgo.; appeared on Second City TV, 1984; appeared in after sch. spl. The Gift of Love, 1985, Prison of Children, 1986. Appeared in The Fun Factory game show, 1976; in TV film Outside Chance, 1978, Nashville Grab, 1981, When Your Lover Leaves, 1983; star TV series Hill Street Blues, 1981-87 (Emmy nominations 1981, 82, 83). Emmy Best Supporting Actress, 1985. Office: care Internat Creative Mgmt 8899 Beverly Blvd Los Angeles CA 90048 •

THOMAS, BETTY JANE SUTPHIN, county official; b. Floyd, Va., June 21, 1938; d. Paul Reece and Minnie Hazel (Pugh) Sutphin. Student, U. Va., 1986. Dep. sherrif City of Floyd, 1960-72; adminstrv. asst. Montgomery County, Va., 1972-76, asst. co-adminstr., 1976-81, chief adminstrv. officer, 1981—; guest lectr. Va. Poly. Inst. and State U., Blacksburg, Ferrum (Va.) Coll., Radford U. Contbr. articles to profl. jours.; coordinator/participant film: Montgomery County Economic Development, 1984. Named Montgomery County Woman of Yr., 1982. Mem. Va. Assn. County Adminstrs. (exec. bd. 1988-89), Nat. Assn. County Adminstrs., Am. Soc. Pub. Adminstrn. (bd. dirs., exec. council 1988-89), Va. Criminal Justice Service Commn., SW Va. Econ. Devel. Commn., SE Regional Internat. City Mgrs. Assn. (exec. bd. 1988-89), Va. Local Govt. Mgmt. Assn. (pres. 1989-90), Valley Clk.'s Ann. Baptist. Club: Women's. Lodge: Lady of Moose. Home: 355-A Cherokee Dr Christianburg VA 24073 Office: Montgomery County Courthouse PO Box 806 Christianburg VA 24073

THOMAS, CAROLYN ELISE, educator; b. Mt. Clemens, Mich., Mar. 8, 1943; d. Jack W. and Agnes E. (Anderson) T.; B.A., Western Mich. U.; M.S., U. Wash.; Ph.D., Ohio State U. Instr., U.Idaho, 1966-70; asst. prof. phys. edn. Denison U., Brockport State U., 1972-73; asst. prof. SUNY, Buffalo, 1973-76, asso. prof., 1976—, chmn. dept. phys. edn., 1976-83, chmn. dept. phys. therapy and exercise sci., 1983—. Mem. Philosophic Soc. for Study Sport, Nat. Assn. Sport and Phys. Edn., Soc. Health and Human Values, Nat. Assn. Phys. Edn. in Higher Edn. Author: Sport in a Philosophic Context, 1983; editor: Aesthetics and Dance, 1980. Office: 405 Kimball Tower SUNY Buffalo NY 14214

THOMAS, CATHRYN CAROL, municipal official; b. Rochester, N.Y., June 4, 1958; d. Donald Bartlett and Nancy Jane (Noble) T. BA in Communications, SUNY, 1980. Graphic designer Webster (N.Y.) Pennysaver, 1980, Sykes Datatronics, Rochester, 1980-81, Xerox Corp., Webster, 1981-82, Downtown Publ., Rochester, 1982; mgr. graphic design Type II, Rochester, 1983; town clk., tax receiver Town of Webster, N.Y., 1984—. Mem. Webster Village Band, 1974—, Classical Quintet, Rochester, 1985—, Webster Rep. Com., 1986—; past treas. Webster Vol. Fireman's Band. Mem. State Assn. Women Officeholders, Nat. Assn. Female Execs., Assn. Records Mgrs., N.Y. State Tax Receiver Assn. (treas. 1985-87, sec. 1987—), N.Y. State Town Clk.'s Assn. (dist. dir. 1987—), Monroe County Town Clk.'s Assn. (sec. 1987—). Home: 47 Dunning Ave Webster NY 14580 Office: Town of Webster 1000 Ridge Rd Webster NY 14580

THOMAS, CHARLOTTE W(ILLIAMSON), accounting firm executive, consultant; b. Atlanta, June 15, 1941; d. James Otis and Katie Gold (Hobbs) Williamson; m. Jesse E. Thomas, Feb. 28, 1965; children—Angel Ann Thomas Fannin, Jesse Andre. Student Ga. State U., 1968, Edison Coll., 1983. Cost ascertainment ofcl. Post Office Dept., Atlanta, 1963-67; auditor IRS, Chamblee, Ga., 1968-78; pres. Cons. Acctg. Services, Ltd., Atlanta, 1979—, franchiser, 1983. Editor Acctg. Services, 1983; editor tax preparation tng. program, 1983; creator Five Dollars Research Program, 1983. Bd. dirs. SWAYBO, Atlanta, 1979. Mem. Nat. Assn. Accts., Nat. Assn. Female Execs., Nat. Inst. Accts. Democrat. Baptist. Club: Old Nat. Garden (College Park, Ga.). Home: 5570 Scofield Rd College Park GA 30349 Office: 151 Ellis St NE Suite 514 Atlanta GA 30303

THOMAS, CLARA MCCANDLESS, emeritus English language educator, biographer; b. Strathroy, Ont., Can., May 22, 1919; d. Basil and Mabel (Sullivan) McCandless; m. Morley Keith Thomas, May 23, 1942; children: Stephen, John. B.A., U. Western Ont., London, 1941, M.A., 1944; Ph.D., U. Toronto, 1962; DLitt (hon.), York U., 1986. Instr. English U. Western Ont., London, 1947-61, U. Toronto, 1958-61; asst. prof. English York U., Toronto, 1961-68; prof. York U., 1969-84, prof. emeritus, 1984—; acad. adv. panel Social Scis. and Humanities Research Council, 1981-84; mem. Killam Awards Selection Bd., 1978-81. Author biography of Anna Jameson, 1967, biography of Egerton Ryerson, 1969, biographies of Margaret Laurence, 1969, 75, biography of William Arthur Deacon, 1982; mem.: (editorial bd.) Literary History of Canada, 1980—. Grantee Can. Council, 1967, 73; grantee Social Sci. and Humanities Research Council Can., 1978-80. Fellow Royal Soc. Can.; mem. Assn. Can. Univs., Tchrs. English (pres. 1971-72), Assn. Can. and Que. Lit., Bus. and Profl. Women's Club, Assn. for Can. Studies. New Democratic. Office: York Univ, 305 Scott Library, 4700 Keele St, Downsview, ON Canada M3J 2R2

THOMAS, CLAUDIA LYNN, orthopedic surgeon; b. N.Y.C., Feb. 28, 1950; d. Charles Mitchell and Daisy Mae T; m. Maxwell Delaine Carty, Aug. 24, 1985. BA, Vassar Coll., 1971; MD, Johns Hopkins U., 1975. Diplomate Am. Bd. Orthopedic Surgery. Intern Yale-New Haven Hosp., 1975-76, resident in surgery, 1976-77, resident in orthopaedic surgery, 1977-80; orthopaedic trauma fellow Md. Inst. Emergency Med. Services Systems, Balt., 1980; asst. prof. orthopaedic surgery Johns Hopkins Hosp., 1981-85, Balt. City Hosp., 1981-85; mem. staff Children's Hosp., Provident Hosp. (both Balt.). Mem. AMA, Eastern Orthopaedic Assn., Yale Orthopaedic Assn., Newington Alumni Assn., Nat. Med. Assn., Monumental Med. Assn. (v.p. 1983-85), Johns Hopkins Minority Faculty Assn. (pres. 1983-85). Author: (with A.A. White, M.M. Panjabi) Clinical Biomechanics of the Spine, 1978; (with P. Leppert, E. Siff, C. Thomas) Being a Woman: Your Body and Birth Control, 1979. First black female orthopedic surgeon; contbr. articles to profl. jours. Democrat. Office: St Thomas Hosp 50 Estate Thomas Suite 202 Saint Thomas VI 00801

THOMAS, CLAUDIA WENZEL, foundation administrator; b. Ft. Sill, Okla., Sept. 15, 1947; d. George Herman and Eva Harriet (Feyereisen) Wenzel; m. Charles Ferdinand Glass III, Dec. 13, 1969 (div. 1972); m. Clifton Boyd Thomas Jr., April 7, 1973; children: Jessica Diane, Gavin Boyd. BS, Fla. State U., 1969. Province pres. Alpha Chi Omega Fraternity, Inc., Indpls., 1981-83, asst. collegiate v.p., 1983-85, nat. v.p., sec., bd. dirs., 1985—; chmn. personnel com., adminstrv. com., trustee, dir. of endowment, Alpha Chi Omega Found., Inc., Indpls., 1985—, sec.-treas., 1987. Events chmn. Jr. Women's Club, Glen Ellyn, 1974-77; treas. Glen Ellyn Panhellenic Assn., 1981—; bd. dirs. Westfield Parent Tchrs. Club, Glen Ellyn, 1982—, Glen Crest Student Tchrs. Parents, Glen Ellyn, 1986-87. Republican. Lutheran. Club: Newcomer's Club (Glen Ellyn).

THOMAS, DEBI, ice skater; b. Poughkeepsie, N.Y., Mar. 25, 1967; d. McKinley and Janice Thomas; married. Student, Stanford U. Competitive figure skater 1972—; winner U.S. Figure Skating Championship, 1986, 88, Women's World Figure Skating Championship, 1986; winner bronze medal Olympic Games, 1988. Recipient, Am. Black Achievement Award, Ebony mag. Address: care U S Figure Skating Assn 20 1st St Colorado Springs CO 80906 •

THOMAS, DIANE WELCH, marketing professional; b. Chgo., July 2, 1952; d. William Bernard and Dorothy Jane (McDonough) Welch; m. Kent Livingston Thomas, Oct. 2, 1976; 1 child, Jack. BA in Liberal Studies, U. Del., 1975. Dir. mktg. IGP, Washington, 1977-81; v.p. ACI Mktg. Services, Chgo., 1981—; cons. A.B.E., Chgo., 1986—. Recipient 1st Place award PIMA, 1985, Excellence in Direct Response award APAIGA, 1985, 86. Mem. Chgo. Assn. Direct Mktg. Republican. Office: ACI Mktg Services Inc 600 W Fulton St Chicago IL 60606

THOMAS, DONNA MARIE GOREE, sales executive; b. Albany, N.Y., Dec. 31, 1958; d. William Hampton Goree and Ruby Volina (Gilliam) Berry; m. Jonathan Leonardo Thomas, June 28, 1985. AAS, Corning Community Coll., 1979; BSBA, Elmira Coll., 1982. Adminstrv. asst. IMC Modeling, N.Y.C., 1982, asst. gen. mgr., 1982-83, gen. mgr., 1983-84; adminstrv. asst. Hicks and Greist Advtg., N.Y.C., 1984-85; adminstr. asst. Revlon Inc., N.Y.C., 1984-85, sales rep., 1985-86, dist. mgr., 1986—. Mem. Tenant Assn., Lefrak City, N.Y., 1987. Named one of Outstanding Young Women Am., 1986. Mem. NAACP, Nat. Urban League. Democrat. Member of African Methodist Episcopal. Home: 9602 57th Ave. Rego Park NY 11368

THOMAS, D(ORIS) JULIENNE, pastoral psychotherapist, therapist; b. St. Charles, Mo., June 8, 1936; d. Austin H. and Doris Mary (McQueen) T.; m. J. Myron Auld; children: Gahlen Crawford, Lana Julienne Petersen, Thomas Glenn Crawford. BA, Park Coll., 1979; MDiv., Midwestern Bapt. Theol. Sem., 1979; DMin., San Francisco Theol. Sem., 1982. Ordained to ministry

Bapt. Ch., 1977. Pastoral psychotherapist The Counseling Inst., Kansas City, Mo., 1979-87, dir. resourceing div.; owner, dir. Plaza Marriage and Family Ctr., Kansas city, Mo., 1987—; freelance writer; cons./speaker in field. Editor LifeBldg. Newsletter, 1984-87. Republican. Office: Plaza Marriage and Family Ctr 411 Nichols Rd Suite 235 Kansas City MO 64112

THOMAS, ELIZABETH WADSWORTH, analytical chemist, pharmacologist; b. Washington, May 23, 1944; d. John Golden and Una Francis (Agnew) Wadsworth; m. Alford Mitchell Thomas, June 6, 1970; 1 child, Edward Bryan. BS, East Carolina U., 1966; PhD, U Va., 1970. Postdoctoral fellow Sch. Medicine U. Va., Charlottesville, 1970-72; lectr. chemistry U. Wis., Kenosha, 1972-74; research assoc. Sch. Medicine Northwestern U., Chgo., 1974-75; analytical chemist Abbott Labs., North Chicago, Ill., 1975-80; sr. pharmacologist Abbott Labs., Abbott Park, Ill., 1980-86, group leader, 1987—; chairperson arrangement com. Acad. Pharm. Scis., 1985, midwest regional meeting Am. Pharm. Assn., 1985. Contbr. articles to profl. jours. Mem. Am. Chem. Soc., Internat. Soc. for Study of Xenobiotics, Sigma Xi (pres. Abbott chpt. 1982-83). Home: 38660 Shagbark Ln Wadsworth IL 60083 Office: Abbott Labs Dept 99P AP-4 Abbott Park IL 60064

THOMAS, ELLEN DILLON, marketing executive; b. Nashville, Oct. 29, 1958; d. William Wesley and Ellen Wallace (White) Dillon; m. James Anderson Thomas, June 20, 1981; 1 child, Warner Grant. BS, Vanderbilt U., 1980; MBA, 1981. Mktg. dir. corr. banking div. U.S. Bank, Nashville, 1981-83; advt. dir. Jacques-Miller, Inc., Nashville, 1983-86; sec., treas. Silver Lining, Inc., 1982—, owner, Vol. Ventures Inc., 1987—. Mem. Am. Mktg. Assn. (pres. elect Nashville chpt.), Pi Beta Phi. Mem. Christian Ch. Avocations: gardening, skiing, travel. Home: 716 Cantrell Ave Nashville TN 37215 Office: PO Box 159009 Nashville TN 37215

THOMAS, ELLEN MCVEIGH, human resource executive; b. Manchester, N.H., Aug. 14, 1952; d. John Joseph and Margaret Mary (Devan) McVeigh; m. Stephen David Thomas, Nov. 6, 1983. BS, St. Anselm Coll., 1974; postgrad. in Bus. Adminstrn., Rivier Coll., 1988. Asst. dir. admissions Cath. Med. Ctr., Manchester, 1975-76, dir. admissions, 1976-77, adminstrv. coordinator, 1978-80, asst. dir. personnel, 1981-83, personnel mgr., 1983-85, dir. personnel, 1985-86, v.p. of human resource, 1986—; mgmt. cons. Porter-McGee, Manchester, 1983-85, Creative Entermainment Corp., Manchester, 1981—. Bd. dirs. Anselmian Summer Theatre, Manchester, 1973-76; bd. dirs. Big Bros./Big Sisters of Greater Manchester, 1987—, N.H. Performing Arts Ctr., 1988. Mem. N.H. Soc. for Healthcare Personnel Adminstrn. (treas. 1983-84, v.p., 1984-85, pres. 1985-86), Manchester Soc. Personnel Adminstrs., N.H. Hosp. Assn. (council for mgmt. and recruitment task force 1984—). Office: Cath Med Ctr 100 McGregor St Manchester NH 03102

THOMAS, ESTHER MERLENE, educator; b. San Diego, Oct. 16, 1945; d. Merton Alfred and Nellie Lida (Von Pilz) T. AA, Grossmont Coll., 1966; BA, San Diego State U., 1969; MA, U. Redlands, 1977. Cert. elem. and adult edn. tchr. Tchr. Cajon Valley Union Sch. Dist., El Cajon, 1969—. Contbr. articles to profl. jours. Mem. U.S. Senatorial Club, Washington, 1984—; mem. Lakeside (Calif.) Centennial Com., 1985-86; hon. mem. Rep. Presl. Task Force, Washington, 1986. Mem. Nat. Tchrs. Assn., Calif. Tchrs. Assn., Cajon Valley Educators Assn., Christian Bus. and Profl. Women, Lakeside Hist. Soc. Republican. Home: 13594 Hwy 8 Apt 3 Lakeside CA 92040 Office: Flying Hills Elem Sch 1251 Finch St El Cajon CA 92020

THOMAS, ETHEL COLVIN NICHOLS (MRS. LEWIS VICTOR THOMAS), educator; b. Cranston, R.I., Mar. 31, 1913; d. Charles Russell and Mabel Maria (Colvin) Nichols; Ph.B., Pembroke Coll. in Brown U., 1934; M.A., Brown U., 1938; Ed.D., Rutgers U., 1979; m. Lewis Victor Thomas, July 26, 1945 (dec. Oct. 1965); 1 child, Glenn Nichols. Tchr. English, Cranston High Sch., 1934-39; social dir. and adviser to freshmen, Fox Hall, Boston U., 1939-40; instr. to asst. prof. English Am. Coll. for Girls, Istanbul, Turkey, 1940-44; dean freshman, dir. admission Women's Coll. of Middlebury, Vt., 1944-45; tchr. English, Robert Coll., Istanbul, 1945-46; instr. English, Rider Coll., Trenton, N.J., 1950-51; tchr. English, Princeton (N.J.) High Sch., 1951-61, counselor, 1960-62, 72-83, coll. counselor, 1962-72, sr. peer counselor, 1986—. Mem. NEA, AAUW, Nat. Assn. Women Deans Adminstrs. and Counselors, Am. Assn. Counseling and Devel., Bus. and Profl. Women's Club (named Woman of Yr., Princeton chpt. 1977), Met. Mus. Art, Phi Delta Kappa, Kappa Delta Pi. Presbyn. Clubs: Brown University (N.Y.C.); Nassau.

THOMAS, FLORENCE KATHLEEN, army officer; b. Torrington, Conn., June 20, 1945; d. James Dudley and Nova Lee (Campbell) T. B.A. in Mass Communications, U. Tex.-El Paso, 1970; M.A. in Adminstrn. of Justice, Wichita State U., 1984. Commd. 2d lt. U.S. Army, 1969, advanced through grades to lt. col., 1987; chief ops. tng. devels. U.S. Mil. Police Sch., Ft. McClellan, Ala., 1979-80; exec. officer criminal investigation div. Kaiserslautern, Germany, 1980-82; comdr. criminal investigation div. Nuernberg Field Office, Fed. Republic Germany, 1982-83; corrections officer Forces Command, Provost Marshal, Ft. McPherson, Ga., 1985; chief law enforcement mgmt. div., 1985-87, chief evaluations, exercise div., dir. ops., 1987—; mil. cons. law enforcement activities, 1977—. Mem. Assn. U.S. Army, Nat. Assn. Female Execs., U.S. Golf Assn., Mid-Ga. Women's Golf Assn., Am. Correctional Assn. Avocation: running; golf; fishing. Home: PO Box 45 APO NY 09063 Office: HQ USAREUR DCSOPS APO NY 09043

THOMAS, FRANCES ANN, manufacturing professional; b. Pensacola, Fla., Nov. 24, 1949; d. Elmer Howard and Rozella Ann (Miller) Jenkins; m. Paul Norman Thomas, Nov. 17, 1977 (div. Sept. 1983). BA in Biology, U. Calif., San Diego, 1971; MBA in Fin., Golden Gate U., 1984. Mfg. foreman Aerojet Gen. Corp., Sacto, Calif., 1977—. Served to capt. USAF, 1972-77. Mem. Profl. Women in Nat. Def., Nat. Assn. for Female Execs. Democrat. Lutheran. Home: 9152 Kendrick Way Orangevale CA 95662 Office: ASPC Hazel and Hwy 50 Folsom CA 95630

THOMAS, FRANCES ELIZABETH, telecommunications specialist; b. Phila., Sept. 25, 1953; d. William Samuel and Norma Jean (Harllee) Gist; m. Stanley Edward Thomas, Mar. 18, 1972 (div. July 1980). BA in Mgmt. with honors, Rutgers U., 1982; MBA in Computer & Info. Scis., Temple U., 1984. Word processing supr. Deleuw, Cather/Parsons, Phila., 1978-81; cons. Small Bus. Devel. Ctr., Temple U., Phila., 1983; weekend coordinator Ballard, Spahr, Andrews & Ingersoll, Phila., 1980-85, telecommunications specialist, 1987—; telecommunications specialist Electronic Data Systems, Southfield, Mich., 1985-86. Mem. Nat. Assn. Female Execs., Inc., Assn. MBA Execs., Inc. Democrat. Baptist.

THOMAS, GAYLE ELAINE, trade company executive; b. Independence, Mo., Oct. 17, 1946; d. James Morris and Thelma (Juanita) T.; m. Gerald Ernest Bell (div. 1974); 1 child, Kenneth Bradley; m. Evan Edward Cochrane, Dec. 6, 1980. AA, Spokane (Wash.) Falls Community Coll., 1969; BA, Whitworth Coll., 1972. Agt., mgr. personal lines Nationwide Ins. Co., Columbus, Ohio, 1972-77, Rogers & Rogers, Inc., Spokane, 1977-81; treas. Cochrane & Co., Spokane, 1980—, also bd. dirs.; owner, broker Jones & Mitchell/Thomas Ins. Assn., Spokane, 1981—, also bd. dirs.; mgr. import/export, pres. Gayle's Ltd., Spokane, 1986—, also bd. dirs.; instr. Ind. Agts. Assn. Wash., Spokane, 1978-86. Mem. exec. com. Deaconess Hosp. Found., Spokane, 1981—; tchr. Franklin Dance Sch. for Children, Spokane, 1985—; ednl. reader Planned Parenthood of Spokane, 1983—; bd. dirs. Colonial Clinic Rehab. Ctr., Spokane, 1985—; trustee St. George's Prep. Sch., Spokane, 1985-88, chmn. devel., 1986-87, chmn. mktg., 1987-88. Recipient Leadership award, Spokane YWCA, 1983, 84. Fellow, mem. Bus. Ptnrs., Inc., Inland N.W. World Trade Council, Am. Bus. Women's Assn. (chmn. 1982—, 86, Fund Raising award 1984, 85), Action Women's Exchange (charter 1978, 85), Profl. Resource Options (bd. dirs., founder 1983, Founder award 1986). Republican. Clubs: Spokane Country, Spokane Racquet. Lodge: Order of Eastern Star. Office: Gayle's Ltd PO Box 3321 Spokane WA 99220

THOMAS, GEORGIA MAE, service executive; b. Racine, Wis., Sept. 22, 1939; d. Arthur E. and Alma S. (Baker) Bengtson; m. Monroe Thomas, Aug. 1, 1968. Diploma, Swedish Hosp. Sch. Nursing, Mpls., 1960; BA, U. Wis., Kenosha, 1972. RN. Staff nurse The Swedish Hosp., Mpls., 1960-61; staff nurse, head nurse, supr. St. Luke's Hosp., Racine, Wis., 1961-70; instr. St. Luke's Sch. Nursing, Racine, 1970-74; v.p. Quality Services, Inc., Racine, 1974-80, Cardinal Profl. Bldg. Maintenance and Supplies, Cardinal Express, Racine and Milw., 1980—; del. White House Conf. Small Bus., 1986, exec. bd. Wis. Gov.'s Conf. Small Bus., 1987. Vol. St. Luke's Hosp. Aux., Racine, 1985—; bd. dirs. Rep. Fedn., Racine County, 1986—; mem. Bus. Ptnrs. Inc., Washington, 1987. Mem. Wis. Women Entrepreneurs (legis. chair Milw. 1986-87, pres. 1988-89), Ind. Bus. Assn. Wis. (bd. dirs. 1988-91), Nat. Fedn. Ind. Bus., Nat. Assn. Women Bus. Owners. Lutheran. Home: 1564 Maria St Racine WI 53404 Office: Cardinal Express Inc 1515 16th St PO Box 1885 Racine WI 53401

THOMAS, GEORGIE A., state official. B.A., Cornell U., 1965; M.B.A., Columbia U., 1973. Asst. portfolio mgr. Money Mgmt. dept. R.W. Pressprich & Co., Inc., N.Y.C., 1968-71; portfolio analyst Bache & Co., N.Y.C., 1971-72; with Exxon Corp., N.Y.C., 1973-76, consolidation analyst Treas. dept., 1975-76; treas. Penntech Papers, Inc., N.Y.C., 1976-79; budget dir. Yankee Publishing Inc., Dublin, N.H., 1982-85; treas. State of N.H., Concord, 1985—; mem. econ. growth and productivity and tech. coms. Bus. Research Adv. Council of Bur. Labor Statistics, 1978-79; mem. alumni counseling bd. Columbia U. Bus. Sch., 1973-79. Editor: Jour. World Bus., Columbia Bus. Sch. Mem. Fin. Women's Assn. N.Y. (mem. exec. bd. 1977-78), Womens Econ. Roundtable. Club: Cornell of Fairfield County (Conn.). Home: Ashley Rd Antrim NH 03440 Office: State NH State House Annex Room 121 Concord NH 03301 *

THOMAS, GLADYS ROBERTS, communications executive; b. Washington, Oct. 17, 1934. BA, Bryn Mawr Coll., 1956. Pub. relations mgr. Am. Internat. Group, N.Y., 1978-80, dir. corp. communications, 1980—. Mem. Pub. Relations Soc. Am., Women Execs. in Pub. Relations, Insurers Pub. Relations Council. Republican. Club: India House (N.Y.). Office: Am Internat Group 70 Pine St New York NY 10270

THOMAS, GLORIA JEAN, human resources administrator; b. Moscow, Tenn., June 20, 1954; d. Carrie (Thomas) Jordan. BBA, Memphis State U., 1975. Mgmt. asst. 1st Tenn. Nat. Corp., Memphis, 1976-79, specialist employee benefits, 1979-81; specialist benefits Memphis State U., 1981-83; mgr. benefits Regional Med. Ctr. Memphis, 1983-85, dir. personnel ops., 1985—; Bd. dirs. Mid-South Regional Sickle Cell Council, Memphis, 1984-85, Sr. Citizen Service, Memphis, 1987; com. co-chair Sta. WKNO Action Auction, Memphis, 1987. Mem. Am. Compensation Assn., Tenn. Soc. for Health Care Homan Resources Adminstrn., West Tenn. Seoc. for Health Care Human Resources Adminstrn., Coalition for 100 Black Women (v.p., bd. dirs. 1983-86), Delta Sigma Theta. Office: Regional Med Ctr Memphis 877 Jefferson Memphis TN 38103

THOMAS, HAZEL LOUISE, military officer, chaplain; b. Newark, Feb. 21, 1947; d. George Calvin and Louise Belle (Eaken) T. BA in Music Edn., Glassboro (N.J.) State Coll., 1969; MDiv, Drew Theol. Sch., 1973; ThM, Princeton Sem., 1975. ordained to ministry United Meth. Ch. as deacon, 1971, as elder, 1974. Youth pastor Wesley United Meth. Ch., Phillipsburg, N.J., 1969-71; pastor Sandyston-Walpack United Meth. Chs., Branchville, N.J., 1971-75, Wesley United Meth. Ch., Belleville, N.J., 1975-78, Asbury United Meth. Ch., Paterson, N.J., 1978-79, Cokesbury (N.J.) United Meth. Ch., 1979-82; commd. lt. USN, 1982; chaplain Naval Hosp., Great Lakes, Ill., 1982-84, USS Samuel Gompers, San Francisco, 1984-86, Marine Corps. Air Sta., Beaufort, S.C., 1986-88, Naval Res. Support Hosp. Unit, Kearney, N.J., 1988—; pastor Diamond Hill United Meth. Ch., Berkeley Heights, N.J., 1988—; counselor Clergy Cons., Madison, N.J., 1971-78; chair N.J. Conf. of United Meth. Ch., 1980-82; cons. chaplain Family Service Ctr., Beaufort, 1982-84; mem. adv. com. N.J. Council Chaplains, Trenton, N.J., 1977-82, 86—. Served to lt. USN, 1982—. Mem. Women Officers Network, Bus. and Profl. Women's Assn., Delta Omicron. Democrat. Home: 96 Ferndale Dr Berkeley Heights NJ 07922 Office: 105 Diamond Hill Rd Berkeley Heights NJ 07922

THOMAS, HELEN A. (MRS. DOUGLAS B. CORNELL), journalist; b. Winchester, Ky., Aug. 4, 1920; d. George and Mary (Thomas) T.; m. Douglas B. Cornell. B.A., Wayne U., 1942; LL.D., Eastern Mich. State U., 1972, Ferris State Coll., 1978, Brown U., 1986; L.H.D., Wayne State U., 1974, U. Detroit, 1979. With UPI, 1943—; wire service reporter UPI, Washington, 1943-74; White House bur. chief UPI, 1974—. Author: Dateline White House. Recipient Woman of Year in Communications award Ladies Home Jour., 1975, 4th Estate award Nat. Press Club, 1984; named to Mich. Women's Hall of Fame, 1986. Mem. Women's Nat. Press Club (pres. 1959-60), Am. Newspaper Women's Club (past v.p.), White House Corrs. Assn. (pres. 1976), Sigma Delta Chi (fellow, Hall of Fame), Delta Sigma Phi (hon.). Home: 2501 Calvert St NW Washington DC 20008 Office: 1400 I Street Washington DC 20005

THOMAS, JACQUELYN MAY, librarian; b. Mechanicsburg, Pa., Jan. 26, 1932; d. William John and Gladys Elizabeth (Warren) Harvey; m. David Edward Thomas, Aug. 28, 1954; children—Lesley J., Courtenay J., Hilary A. B.A. summa cum laude, Gettysburg Coll., 1954; student U. N.C., 1969; M.Ed., U. N.H., 1971. Librarian, Phillips Exeter Acad., Exeter, N.H., 1971-77, acad. librarian, 1977—, chair governing bd. child care ctr., 1987—; chair Com. to Enhance Status of Women, Exeter, 1981-84; dir. Loewenstein Com., Exeter, 1982—; pres. Cum Laude Soc., Exeter, 1984-86. Editor: The Design of the Library: A Guide to Sources of Information, 1981, Rarities of Our Time: The Special Collections of the Phillips Exeter Academy Library. Trustee, treas. Exeter Day Sch., 1965-69; mem. bd. Exeter Hosp. Vols., 1954-59; mem. Exeter Hosp. Corp., 1978—; mem. bldg. com. Exeter Pub. Library, 1986—; chair No. New Eng., Council for Women in Ind. Schs., 1985—; Chmn. Lamont Poetry Program, Exeter, 1984-86. N.H. Council for Humanities grantee, 1981-82; Nat. Endowment Humanities grantee, 1982. Mem. ALA, New Eng. Library Assn., N.H. Ednl. Media Assn., New Eng. Assn. Ind. Sch. Librarians, Am. Assn. Sch. Librarians (program com. for non-pub. sch. sect. 1985—), Phi Beta Kappa. Home: 16 Elm St Exeter NH 03833 Office: The Library Phillips Exeter Acad Exeter NH 03833

THOMAS, JANICE LINDA, communication executive; b. Brockton, Mass., Oct. 25, 1949; d. George Sidney Jr. and Jean Louise (Currier) McLean; children: Michell, Kristin. Student, Boston State Coll., 1967-68; BA magna cum laude, Framingham State Coll., 1976. Public info. officer Mass. Dept. Edn., Bur. Fire Tng., Sudbury, Mass., 1976-77, dir. info., 1977-78; public info. officer Internat. Soc. Fire Service Instrs., Hopkinton, Mass., 1976-79; asst. editor Internat. Assn. Fire Chiefs, Washington, 1979-80; mgr. Fire Edn. Resource Network, 1980-82, Fed. Emergency Mgmt. Agy., Office of Planning and Edn., U.S. Fire Adminstrn.; cons. Paradigm, Inc., Potomac, Md., 1981-82; cons. Energy, Mgmt. and Mktg. div. IMR Corp., Falls Church, Va., 1982-84; ind. cons. Thomas Communication Services, 1984—; lectr. in field. Active Youth Adv. Commn. City of Columbia, Mo., 1987—; precinct leader for local, congressional campaigns, 1970-74. Recipient Spl. award, 7th Annual Public Fire Educators Conf., 1981, Ark. Traveler award, 1982, Ill. Spark Plug award, 1982. Mem. NOW, Am. Mgmt. Assn., Internat. Assn. Bus. Communicators, Nat. Assn. Female Execs., Washington Women in Public Relations, Women in Communications. Unitarian Universalist. Contbr. articles to profl. jours. Office: Thomas Communication Services 2004 S Deerborn Circle Columbia MO 65203-1984

THOMAS, JEANNE GEARHART, financial services executive; b. East Orange, N.J., Oct. 16, 1955; d. William Wright and Charlotte (Schamber) Gearhart; m. James William Thomas, Aug. 12, 1978. BSMA, Bucknell U., 1977; MBA, Villanova U., 1985. CLU. Pension actuarial analyst Fidelity Mutual Life Ins. Co., Radnor, Pa., 1977-78; dist. agt. Prudential Ins. Co. Am., Ithaca, N.Y., 1978-80; mgr. continuing edn. programs Am. Soc. CLUs and Chartered Fin. Cons., Bryn Mawr, Pa., 1980-81, asst. dir. continuing edn. programs, 1982-84, dir. continuing edn., 1985—, also bd. dirs. Contbr. articles to profl. jours. Mem. Phila. Assn. Life Underwriters, Am. Soc. CLU's & Chartered Fin. Cons. (bd. dirs. Phila. chpt.). Republican. Presbyterian. Home: 104 Barley Mill Rd Wallingford PA 19086

THOMAS, JOYCE CAROL, author; b. Ponca City, Okla., May 25, 1938; children—Monica, Gregory, Michael, Roy. B.A., San Jose State U., 1966; M.A., Stanford U., 1967. Former asst. prof., later prof. San Jose State U.; vis. prof. English, Purdue U., 1984. Author: (poetry) Bittersweet, 1973, Black Child, 1981, Inside the Rainbow, 1982, (novels) Marked by Fire (Nat Book award), 1982, Bright Shadow, 1983, Water Girl, 1986, The Golden Pasture, 1986. Office: care Internat Creative Mgmt Inc 40 W 57th St New York NY 10019

THOMAS, LEONA MARLENE, medical records educator; b. Rock Springs, Wyo., Jan. 15, 1933; d. Leonard H. and Opal (Wright) Francis; m. Craig L. Thomas, Feb. 22, 1955 (div. Sept. 1978); children—Peter, Paul, Patrick, Alexis. B.A., Govs. State U., 1982, MHS, 1986; cert. med. records adminstrn. U. Colo., 1954. Dir. med. records dept. Meml. Hosp. Sweetwater County, Rock Springs, 1954-57; staff assoc. Am. Med. Records Assn., Chgo., 1972-77, asst. editor, 1979-81; asst. prof. Chgo. State U., 1984—; statistician Westlake Hosp., Melrose Park, Ill., 1982-84. Co. pres. Ill. Dist. 60 PTA, Westmont, Ill., 1972. Mem. Am. Med. Records Assn., Ill. Med. Records Assn., Chgo. and Vicinity Med. Records Assn. Democrat. Methodist. Home: 6340 F Americana Dr Apt 1101 Clarendon Hills IL 60514 Office: Chgo State U Coll Allied Health 95th at King Dr Chicago IL 60608

THOMAS, LUCILLE COLE, librarian; b. Dunn, N.C., Oct. 1, 1921; d. Collie and Minnie (Lee) Cole; m. George Browne Thomas, May 24, 1943; children—Ronald C., Beverly G. Effatt. B.A., Bennett Coll., 1941; M.A., N.Y.U., 1955; M.S., Columbia U., 1957. Tchr., Bibb County Bd. Edn., Macon, Ga., 1947-55; librarian Bklyn. Pub. Library, 1955-56; librarian N.Y.C. Bd. Edn., Bklyn., 1956-68, supr. libraries, 1968-77, dir. elem. sch. libraries, 1977-83; program dir. Weston Woods Inst., Weston, Conn., 1984-85; founder Sch. Library Media Day, N.Y. State, 1973; cons. Putnam Pub. Group, N.Y.C., 1983, bd. examiners N.Y. City Bd. Edn., 1983; dir. Am. Reading Council, N.Y.C., 1976—; mem. adv. bd. Regents' Adv. Council on Learning Tech., Albany, N.Y., 1982—; adj. prof. CUNY, 1987—; coordinator UNESCO/Internat. Assn. Sch. Librarians Book Program for devel. countries, 1980—; trustee N.Y. Met. Reference and Research Library Agy., N.Y.C., 1979-83; liaison Freedom to Read Foundation. Editor: Insight, 1974. Contbr. articles to profl. publs. Treas., Bklyn. Home for Aged Commn., 1967—, vestry mem. St. John's Episcopal Ch., Bklyn., 1988—. Recipient Disting. Alumna award Bennett Coll., 1981; Edn. award Bus. and Profl. Women's Club, Bklyn., 1983; Merit award Bklyn. Council Suprs., 1983, Achievement award Columbia U. Sch. Library Services, 1987, Grolier Found. award, 1988. Mem. ALA (councilor 1980—, exec. bd. 1985—, chair Nominations and Spl. Assignments Com. 1987-88, chair Hqtrs. Library Rev. Accountability Com. 1987-88), Internat. Fedn. Library Assns. (sec. sch. libraries sect. 1985—), Internat. Assn. Sch. Librarianships (coordinator UNESCO gift book program 1980—), N.Y. Library Assn. (pres. 1977-78, Appreciation cert. 1983, pres. sch. library media sect. 1973-74, Outstanding Achievement award 1984, Achievement award 1988), N.Y. Library Club (pres. 1977-78), N.Y.C. Sch. Librarians Assn. (pres. 1970-72), Bklyn. Hist. Soc., Schomburg Soc., Schomburg Commn., N.Y. Coalition of 100 Black Women, Gould Found. Friends. Democrat. Episcopalian. Club: Women's City of N.Y.C. (bd. dirs. 1986—, vice chmn. edn. com. 1987—). Home: 1184 Union St Brooklyn NY 11225

THOMAS, LUCY HARRISON, radio producer; b. Washington, Dec. 19, 1946; d. Thomas Collins and Marylou (Wright) Harrison; m. Robert Lawrence Kurt III, Apr. 12, 1969 (div. 1976); 1 child, Mark Collins. BA, Boston U., 1968, postgrad., 1972-73; student Teaching English as Second Lang. cert. program, U. Calif., Berkeley, 1987—. Research asst. Harvard U., Cambridge, Mass., 1968-69; vol. tchr. U.S. Peace Corps, Liberia, 1969-71; producer Sta. KGO-Radio, San Francisco, 1977-79, freelance producer, 1979-83, exec. producer, 1983—. Mem. Am. Women in Radio and TV. Taoist. Office: Sta KGO-Radio 900 Front St San Francisco CA 94111

THOMAS, MABLE, state legislator; b. Atlanta, Nov. 8, 1957; d. Bernard and Madie Thomas. BS in Pub. Adminstrn., Ga. State U., 1982, postgrad., 1983—. With acctg. dept. Trust Co. Bank, Atlanta, 1977; recreation supr. Sutton Community Sch., Atlanta, 1977-78; data transcriber Ga. Dept. Natural Resources, Atlanta, 1978-79; clk. U.S. Census Bur., Atlanta, 1980; laborer City of Atlanta Parks and Recreation, 1980-81; student asst. Ga. State U., Atlanta, 1981-82; state rep. Ga. House Reps., Atlanta, 1984—; mem. exec. com. Ga. Legis. Black Census, Atlanta, 1985—. Mem. adv. youth council Salvation Army Bellwood Club, 1975; founder Vine City Community Improvement Assn., Atlanta, 1985; mem. Neighborhood Planning Unit, Ga. State U. Adv. Bd. of Comprehensive Youth Services, 1988—, Nat. Black Woman's Health Project, Ga. Housing Coalition; actively involved in Say No to Drugs Program; bd. dirs. Am. Cancer Soc., 1988—. Recipient Bronze Jubilee award City of Atlanta Cultural Affairs, 1984, Disting. Service award Grady Hosp., 1985, Human Service award for community and political leadership for disadvantaged, 1986, Exceptional Service award Young Community Leaders, 1986, Citizenship award Salvation Army Club; named Outstanding Freshman Legislator, 1986, one of Outstanding Young People of Atlanta, 1987. Mem. Ga. Assn. Black Elected Officials (mem. housing and econ. devel. com.), Conf. Minority Pub. Adminstrn. (Outstanding Service award), Nat. Polit. Congress Black Women (bd. dirs.). Democrat. Methodist. Home: PO Box 573 Atlanta GA 30301

THOMAS, MARGARET FLORENCE, stockbroker; b. Laurium, Mich., May 26, 1944; d. Charles and Irma Margaret (Seppala) T. Grad. high sch., Calumet, Mich. Registered rep. Nat. Assn. Security Dealers. Investment exec. Foste Marshall/Shearson Am. Express, Seattle, 1980-86, Oberweis Securities, Oconomowoc, Wis., 1986-87; v.p. investments Internat. Commodities, Seattle, 1987—. Mem. Milw. Bond Club, Nat. Assn. Female Execs. Republican. Presbyterian. Home: PO Box 2133 Redmond WA 98073 Office: Motorola Inc 11911 NE 1st St Suite 304 Bellevue WA 98005

THOMAS, MARGARET JEAN, clergywoman, religious research consultant; b. Detroit, Dec. 24, 1943; d. Robert Elcana and Purcella Margaret (Hartness) T. BS, Mich. State U., 1964; MDiv, Union Theol. Sem., Va., 1971. Ordained to ministry United Presbyn. Ch., 1971. Dir. research bd. Christian edn. Presbyn. Ch. U.S., Richmond, Va., 1965-71; dir. research gen. council Presbyn. Ch. U.S., Atlanta, 1972-73; mng. dir. research div. support agy. United Presbyn. Ch. U.S.A., N.Y.C., 1974-76; dep. exec. dir. gen. assembly mission council United Presbyn. Ch. U.S.A., 1977-83; dir. N.Y. coordination Presbyn. Ch. (U.S.A.), 1983-85; exec. dir. Minn. Council Chs., Mpls., 1985—, 1985—; vice moderator permanent jud. commn. Presbyn. Ch. U.S.A., 1985—; sec. com. on ministry Twin Cities Area Presbytery Ch., Mpls., 1985—; bd. dir. joint religious legis. coalition, 1985—; bd. dirs. Franklin Nat. Bank, Mpls. Contbr. articles to profl. jours. Mem. adv. panel crime/victim services Hennepin County Atty.'s Office, Mpls., 1985-86, Police/Community Relations Task Force, St. Paul, 1986; bd. dirs. Minn. Foodshare, Mpls., 1985—, Minn. Coalition on Health, St. Paul, 1986—, Twin Cities Coalition for Affordable Health Care, 1986-87. Mem. Nat. Assn. Ecumenical Staff, Religious Edn. Assn. (sec. 1974-76), People for the Am. Way, NOW (Outstanding Woman of Minn. 1986), Amnesty Internat. Democratic Farm Laborer. Office: Minn Council of Chs 122 W Franklin Ave #100 Minneapolis MN 55404

THOMAS, MARJORIE BEKAERT, lawyer, television syndicator; b. N.Y.C., Jan. 3, 1947; d. Charles J. and Marjorie (Dew) Bekaert; m. Bryan M. Thomas. BA with honors, Duke U., 1969; JD, U. Fla., 1976. Bar: Fla. 1976. Assoc. van den Berg, Gay & Burke, Orlando, Fla., 1976-79; mng. ptnr. Thomas and Thomas, P.A., Orlando, 1979—; chief exec. officer Ivanhoe Communications Inc., Orlando, 1982—. Fellow NEH, 1979. Mem. Fla. Bar Assn., Orange County Bar Assn. (chmn. estate planning com. 1982), Fla. Assn. for Women Lawyers (pres. 1982), Fla. Exec. Women (pres. 1981), Order of Coif. Democrat. Home: 242 Chase Ave Winter Park FL 32789 Office: Ivanhoe Communications 401 S Rosalind Suite 100 Orlando FL 32801

THOMAS, MARJORIE OLIVIENE, health care administrator; b. Spaldings, Jamaica, Sept. 5; came to U.S., 1971; d. Cedrick Milo and Avis Clair (Morgan) West; m. Carol Oswald Thomas, Sept. 10, 1977; children—Chandra, Brian. A.A., Kendall Coll., 1973; B.S., U. Ill.-Chgo., 1975; M.P.A., Roosevelt U., 1977. Asst. to dir. utilization rev. Bellevue Hosp., N.Y.C., 1977-81, risk mgr., 1981-83, assoc. dir./dir. quality assurance, 1983-85; dir. risk mgmt. Adminstrs. for the Professions, Inc., Manhasset, N.Y., 1985—. Mem. Am. Soc. for Healthcare Risk Mgmt., Assn. Hosp. Risk Mgmt. N.Y. Mem. Christ Temple. Avocations: cooking; reading; writing.

THOMAS, MARLO (MARGARET JULIA), actress; b. Detroit, Nov. 21, 1943; d. Danny and Rose Marie (Cassanti) T.; m. Phil Donahue, May 22, 1980. Ed., U. So. Calif. Theatrical appearances in Broadway prodn. Thieves, 1974, London prodn. Barefoot in the Park, Broadway play Social Security, 1986; star: TV series That Girl, 1966-71; appeared in TV films: The Last Honor of Kathryn Beck, 1984, Consenting Adults, 1985, Nobody's Child, 1986; conceived book and record, starred in TV spl. Free to Be. . . You and Me, 1974 (Emmy for best children's show); films include Thieves, 1977; author: Free to Be...A Family, 1987. Recipient George Foster Peabody award; Tom Paine award Nat. Emergency Civil Liberties Com. Office: care Michael Ovitz Creative Artists Agy Inc 1888 Century Park E Suite 1400 Los Angeles CA 90067 *

THOMAS, MARTHA JANICE, ground transportation company executive; b. Hyden, Ky., Aug. 30, 1949; d. John Maynard and Nell (Hensley) Baker; m. Robert Eugene Ripberger, May 23, 1970 (div. April 1982); children: Amy Elizabeth, Robert Eugene II; m. Jerry Allen Thomas, Jan. 23, 1984. Grad. high sch., Indpls., 1967. Sub-distbr., salesperson Jhirmack, Indpls., 1978-79, real estate salesperson Heritage Estates, Brownsburg, Ind., 1979-81; br. mgr. Home Mark, Inc., Indpls., 1981-82; trade broker The Trade Arranger, Indpls., 1982-84; owner AAA Delivery System, Inc., Indpls., 1984—; participant Women's Initiative Conf., 1985—. Mem. mktg. com. Indpls. Conv. and Visitors Bur., 1984—. Mem. Nat. Assn. Women Bus. Owners, Nat. Passenger Traffic Assn., Nat. Assn. Female Execs., Nat. Def. Transp. Assn., Airport Mgr.'s Club. Office: Indpls Internat Airport Box 51613 Indianapolis IN 46251

THOMAS, MARTHA KATE, financial planner, consultant; b. Phila., May 30, 1942; d. John Doench and Kate Fanning (Walker) McCrumm. Student, Mt. Holyoke Coll., 1960-62; BA, Swarthmore Coll., 1964. Vol. US Peace Corps., Nepal, 1966-68; dir. pub. affairs US Peace Corps., Chgo., 1968-69; dir. western region Am. Freedom Hunger Found., Washington and Chicago, 1969-74; v.p. fin. edn. program devel. Inst. Devel. Econ. Affairs Service Inc., Nederland (Colo.) and Washington, 1974-86; fin. planner Waddell and Reed, Boulder, Colo., 1986—; cons. Family Relations Ctr., Boulder, 1985—; bd. dirs. Tibetan Found., N.Y.C., 1970-85. Dir. Boulder Offender Aid and Restoration Project, 1985-87; active Leadership Boulder, 1988. Mem. Ambassadors Club Boulder C. of C., Boulder Bus. & Profl. Women. Democrat. Mem. Unity Ch. Club: Flatirons Ski (bd. dirs., chmn. membership 1987—). Office: Waddell and Reed 5505 Arapaho Boulder CO 80303

THOMAS, MARTHA WETTERHALL, advertising agency executive; b. Ann Arbor, Mich., Aug. 23, 1949; d. Roy Christner and Doreen (Armstrong) Wetterhall; m. James William Thomas, May 22, 1982. BA cum laude, U. Mich., 1971. Copywriter McCaffrey & McCall, N.Y.C., 1972-76, Cunningham & Walsh, N.Y.C., 1976-78; sr. copywriter Grey/2 Advt., N.Y.C., 1978-79, Symon, Thomas & Hilliard, N.Y.C., 1979-82; exec. v.p., creative dir. Thomas & Thomas Advt., N.Y.C., 1983—. Writer, producer 1st paid TV advt. campaign for art mus., 1985. Recipient Encore award N.Y. Arts and Bus. Council, 1985, Effie award Am. Mktg. Assn., 1987, Telly award for local and regional TV commls., 1988. Mem. Advt. Women of N.Y., Am. Women's Econ. Devel. Corp., Ad Net (2d v.p.). Office: Thomas & Thomas Advt Inc 432 Park Ave S New York NY 10016

THOMAS, MARY ANN MCCRARY, education advisor; b. Washington, Feb. 11, 1935; d. Frank Robert and Mary (Davison) McCrary; m. John Ralph Thomas, Sept. 30, 1961; children: Robert Davison, John Shannon, Kristen Aldridge. BA, U. Calif., Berkley, 1956; MA, UCLA, 1959. Cert. tchr., Calif. Supr. Pacific Bell, San Francisco, 1962-67; advisor gifted, talented San Rafael (Calif.) City Schs., 1973—. Pres. San Rafael PTA Council, 1981-84, outstanding service award, 1983, San Rafael High Sch. Site Council, 1985—; pres. bd. dirs. Marin Wildlife Ctr., 1979-85. Recipient Golden Bell award, Marin Community Found., 1987. Mem. Calif. Assn. Gifted, Calif. Assn. Tchrs. English. Republican. Episcopalian. Home: 70 Windsor Ave San Rafael CA 94901 Office: Davidson Mid Sch 280 Woodland Ave San Rafael CA 94901

THOMAS, MARY BARTON, marriage and family counselor; b. Sherman, Tex., Nov. 4, 1954; m. William M. Thomas, 1978; children: William David, Sarah Elizabeth. BS in Social Sci. and Elem. Edn., Southeastern Okla. State U., 1976; MEd in Ednl. Diagnosis and Psychology, Abilene Christian U., 1979; postgrad. North Tex. State U., 1982—. Lic. profl. counselor, Tex.; basic, intermediate, advance and instrs. certs. Tex. Commn. on Law Enforcement Officer Standards and Edn. With Dallas Police Dept., 1979-86, police officer, 1979-86, staff counselor, investigator, 1981-86; spl. edn. coordinator Savoy (Tex.) I.S.D., 1987—. Recipient Life Saving award Dallas Police Dept., 1983, Safe Driving award, 1985. Delta Kappa Epsilon scholar, 1973, Red River Valley Hist. scholar, 1975-76. Mem. Internat. Law Enforcement Stress Assn., Dallas Psychol. Assn., Am. Assn. Counseling and Devel., Tex. Mcpl. Police Assn., Dallas Police Assn., Nat. Assn. Female Execs., Dallas Mus. Art., Hist. Preservation League of Dallas, Nat. Trust Hist. Preservation, Dallas County Heritage Soc., Tex. Hist. Found., Smithsonian Inst. Nat. Assn., Friends of Kennedy Ctr., Young Rep. Nat. Fedn., Dallas County Rep. Assembly, Nat. Rep. Senatorial Com., Nat. Rep. Congl. Com., Kappa Delta Pi, Phi Alpha Theta. Home: 1800 Crescent Dr Sherman TX 75090 Office: PO Box 446 Savoy TX 75479

THOMAS, NANCY DENECE, manufacturing company executive; b. Long Beach, Calif., Feb. 20, 1959; d. Alan Tuthill and Barbara Jean (Rush) T. V.p. BTE, Inc., Long Beach, 1978-82; v.p., gen. mgr. BTE, Inc., Huntington Beach, Calif., 1982—; pres. Omni Label, Inc., Huntington Beach, 1986—; co-owner LeMac Leasing, 1986—. V.p. Long Beach Spl. Charities, Inc., 1987; pres. Long Beach Spl. Charities, Inc., 1988. Mem. Nat. Assn. Female Execs., Nat. Office Products Assn., Young Execs. Forum, Am. Med. Rec. Assn. Office: BTE Inc 5672 Bolsa Ave Huntington Beach CA 92647

THOMAS, PATRICIA ANNE, law librarian; b. Cleve., Aug. 21, 1927; d. Richard Joseph and Marietta Bernadette (Teevans) T.; B.A., Case Western Res. U., 1949, J.D., 1951. Admitted to Ohio bar, 1951, U.S. Supreme Ct. bar, 1980; librarian Arter & Hadden, Cleve., 1951-62; asst. librarian, then librarian IRS, Washington, 1962-78; library dir. Adminstrv. Office, U.S. Cts., 1978—. Mem. Am. Assn. Law Libraries, Law Librarians Soc. D.C. (pres. 1967-69). Office: US Cts Adminstrv Office Washington DC 20544

THOMAS, PATRICIA GRAFTON, educator; b. Michigan City, Ind., Sept. 30, 1921; d. Robert Wadsworth and Elinda (Oppermann) Grafton; student Stephens Coll., 1936-39, Purdue U., summer 1938; B.Ed. magna cum laude, U. Toledo, 1966; postgrad. (fellow) Bowling Green U., 1968; m. Lewis Edward Thomas, Dec. 21, 1939; children—Linda L. (Mrs. John R. Collins), Stephanie A. (Mrs. Andrew M. Pawuk), I. Kathryn (Mrs. James N. Ramsey), Deborah. Tchr., Toledo Bd. Edn., 1959-81, tchr. lang. arts Byrnedale Sch., 1976-81. Dist. capt. Planned Parenthood, 1952-53, ARC, 1954-55; mem. lang. arts curriculum com. Toledo Bd. Edn., 1969, mem. grammar curriculum com., 1974; bd. dirs. Anthony Wayne Nursery Sch., 1983—; bd. dirs. Toledo Women's Symphony Orch. League, 1983—, sec., 1985—. Mem. Toledo Soc. Profl. Engrs. Aux., Helen Kreps Guild, AAUW, Toledo Artists' Club, Spectrum, Friends of Arts, Phi Kappa Phi, Phi Delta Kappa, Kappa Delta Pi, Pi Lambda Theta (chpt. pres. 1978—), Delta Kappa Gamma (chpt. pres. 1976-78, area membership chmn. 1978-80, 1st place award for exhbn. 1985). Republican. Episcopalian. Home: 4148 Deepwood Lane Toledo OH 43614

THOMAS, SUSANNE TOMLINSON, psychologist; b. Dallas, Dec. 29, 1948; d. Thomas Alfred and Patricia (P.) Tomlinson; divorced; children: John T. Yasinski, Julie A. Yasinski, Stephen E. Yasinski. BA in Bus. Adminstrn., U. Ariz., 1969, MA in Bus. Adminstr., 1970, MA in Psychology, 1971, PhD in Psychology, 1987. Pvt. practice psychology and psychotherapy; counselor to profl., coll. and Olympic athletes, 1972—. Past v.p. Educate People to Protect Innocent Children. Mem. DAR, Delta Gamma. Lodge: Daughters of Nile. Office: 2301 E Sunset Las Vegas NV 89119

THOMAS, TERESA ANN, microbiologist, educator, consultant; b. Wilkes-Barre, Pa., Oct. 17, 1939; d. Sam Charles and Edna Grace Thomas. B.S. cum laude, Coll. Misericordia, 1961; M.S. in Biology, Am. U. Beirut, 1965; M.S. in Microbiology, U. So. Calif., 1973. Tchr., sci. supr., curriculum coordinator Meyers High Sch., Wilkes-Barre, 1962-64, Wilkes-Barre Area Public Schs., 1961-66; research assoc. Proctor Found. for Research in Ophthalmology U. Calif. Med. Center, San Francisco, 1966-68; instr. Robert Coll. of Istanbul (Turkey), 1968-71, Am. Edn. in Luxembourg, 1971-72, Bosco Tech. Inst., Rosemead, Calif., 1973-74, San Diego Community Coll. Dist., 1974-80; prof. math.-sci. div. Southwestern Coll., Chula Vista, Calif., 1980—, pres. acad. senate, 1984-85, del., 1986—; mem. steering com. project CREATE Southwestern Coll.-Shanghai Inst. Fgn. Trade; coordinator Southwestern Coll. Great Teaching Seminar, 1987, 88, coordinator scholars program, 1988—; mem. exec. com. Acad. Senate for Calif. Community Colls., 1985-86, Chancellor of Calif. Community Colls. Adv. and Rev. Council Fund for Instrnl. Improvement, 1984-86; adj. asst. prof. Chapman Coll., San Diego, 1974-83; asst. prof. San Diego State U., 1977-79; chmn. Am. Colls. Istanbul Sci. Week, 1969-71; mem. adv. bd. Chapman Coll. Community Center, 1979-80; cons. sci. curriculum Calif. Dept. Edn., 1986—; mem. Chula Vista Internat. Friendship Commn., 1987-90; pres. Internat. Relations Club 1959-61; mem. San Francisco World Affairs Council, 1966-68; chmn. land use, energy and wildlife com. Congressman Duncan Hunter's Environ. Adv. Council, 1982-84; v.p. Palomar Palace Estates Home Owners Assn., 1983-85, pres. 1987—. NSF fellow, 1965; USPHS fellow, 1972-73; Pa. Heart Assn. research grantee, 1962; named Southwestern Coll. Woman of Distinction, 1987. Mem. Am. Soc. Microbiology (life), Nat. Sci. Tchrs. Assn. (internat. com., coordinator internat. honors exchange lectr. competition sponsored with Assn. Sci Educators Great Britain, 1986), Nat. Assn. Biology Tchrs., Soc. Coll. Sci. Tchrs. (Calif. membership coordinator 1984—), S.D. Zool. Soc., Calif. Tchrs. Assn., NEA, Am. Assn. Community and Jr. Colls., MENSA, Arab Am. Med. Assn., Am.-Lebanese Assn. San Diego (chmn. scholarship com., pres. 1988—), Am. U. of Beirut Alumni and Friends of San Diego (1st v.p. 1984—) Kappa Gamma Pi (pres. Wilkes-Barre chpt. 1963-64, San Francisco chpt. 1967-68), Sigma Phi Sigma. Club: Am. Lebanese Syrian Ladies (pres. 1982-83). Office: Southwestern Coll 900 Otay Lakes Rd Chula Vista CA 92010

THOMAS, VIRGINIA LEE, microscopist; b. Traer, Iowa, Sept. 22, 1916; d. Paul and Zenaide (Kahler) T.; grad. Gates Coll., 1939, U. Mich., 1943. Spectrographer Rock Island (Ill.) Arsenal, 1943-45; electron microscopist U.S. Rubber Research Labs., Passaic, N.J., 1945-54; group leader Interchem. Research Labs., N.Y.C., 1954-62; research scientist Am. Standard Research Lab., Piscataway, N.J., 1962-68; lectr., supr. microscopy U. Medicine and Dentistry, Rutgers U. Med. Sch., Piscataway, 1968-84; cons. on electron and light microscopy. Active Westfield Human Rights, Plainfield Joint Def., Rainbow Food Coop, ACLU. Fellow N.Y. Microscopical Soc. (pres. 1960-61, Ashby award 1962); mem. Electron Microscopical Soc. Am., N.Y. Soc. Electron Microscopists. Clubs: Sierra, Porsche Club Am., Nat. Wildlife Assn., Nature Conservancy. Contbr. chpts. to books in field, articles to profl. jours. Home: 268 Main St Hinton WV 25951

THOMAS-BUCKLE, SUZANN REMINGTON, public policy and planning educator; b. Elizabeth City, N.C., Jan. 22, 1945; d. James Ernest Thomas and Marion (Blackwell) Dodson; m. Leonard Gould Buckle, June 4, 1966. B.A. in English Lit., Wellesley Coll., 1962-66; Ph.D. in Urban Studies and Planning, MIT, 1974. Instr. pub. policy and planning MIT, Cambridge, 1970-74, asst. prof., 1974-78, assoc. prof., 1978-85; community and environ. mediator, 1984—; assoc. prof., dir. law, policy and soc. programs Northeastern U., Boston, 1985—; research assoc. John F. Kennedy Sch. Govt., Harvard U., Cambridge, 1979-81; cons. U.S. Dept. Labor, Nat. League of Cities, 1971-76, Mus. Fine Arts, Boston, 1972-75; reporter ABA, Washington, 1973-77; research cons. U.S. Dept. Justice, Washington, 1975-76; chmn. trustees Am. Legal Studies Assn., 1987—; mem. Forum on Negotiation, Harvard Law Sch., also adv. bd. specialization in negotiation Program on Negotiation. Author: Bargaining for Justice, 1977; Standards Related to Planning for Juvenile Justice, 1980; mem. editorial bd. Law and Society Rev., 1985—; publisher: Legal Studies Forum and Transformations, 1987—; contbr. articles to profl. jours. Trustee Mass. Council for Pub. Justice, Boston, 1982 . Recipient Everett Moore Baker award MIT, 1972; Eli Lilly postdoctoral fellow, 1974; German Marshall fellow, 1979. Mem. Am. Sociol. Assn., Soc. Profls. in Dispute Resolution, Law and Soc. Assn., Soc. for Study of Social Problems. Office: Northeastern U Programs in Law Policy and Soc Boston MA 02115

THOMAS-BUDD, VALERIE LANE, marketing professional; b. Los Angeles, Feb. 5, 1963; d. William J. and Doris P. (Patopoff) T.; m. Robert Paul Budd, July 11, 1987. BA in Mktg., Calif. State U., Fullerton, 1985. Model, sales Nordstrom, Cerritos, Calif., 1983; sec. John R. Hundley, Inc., Downey, Calif., 1981-83; mktg. dir. Office of Extended Edn., Fullerton, 1983-85; sales rep. Harris Lanier, Tustin, Calif., 1985-87; SW mktg. mgr. Polaroid, Santa Ana, Calif., 1987—; com. chair Women in Sales, Orange County, 1985-87; alumni rep. Sales and Mktg. Inc., Orange County, 1984-87. Mem. Orange County Young Reps., 1986-87, Newport Area Preferred Profls., Newport, Calif., 1986-87; provisional mem. Jr. League of Orange County, 1987. Recipient Leadership award Jr. Achievement, 1981, Women in Sales scholarship, 1984; named #1 Salesman in Office, Harris Lanier, 1986. Mem. Sigma Kappa, Pi Sigma Epsilon (pres. 1983-85, Heitz award 1984), Bus. Week (chmn. 1985). Mem. Corona Del Mar Community Ch. Home: 2424 Naples Newport Beach CA 92660 Office: Polaroid 3232 MacArthur Santa Ana CA 92799

THOMAS-LOTHERY, HELEN OLGA, school system administrator, educator; b. Cleve., Feb. 22; d. Joseph Turner Thomas Jr. and Rebecca Alice (Cowan) Thomas-Cotton; m. Lewis Monroe Lothery, Nov. 24, 1951; children: Sharon, Angela. BS, Western Mich. U., 1950; MEd, Wayne State U., 1958, Edn. Specialist, 1982, postgrad., 1987—. Cert. elem.-secondary tchr., Mich. Librarian Detroit Pub. Schs., 1950-53, fine arts specialist, 1954-68, media specialist, 1968-71, media/fine arts specialist, 1971-72, staff devel. adminstrator, 1977-83, administrator, 1983—; adj. prof. Marygrove Coll., Detroit, 1987; mem. task force Crisis Intervention, 1977-83; cons. Nat. Staff Devel. Assn., 1982, Am. Bus. Women's Assn., 1985. Contbr. articles to profl. jours. Nat. pres. Squaws, Inc., Pitts., 1972; chair hostess div. United Negro Coll. Fund, 1984. Mem. Profl. Women's Network, Nat. Assn. Sch. Prins., Am. Bus. Women, The Northeasterners, Phi Delta Kappa (Wayne State U. chapt. Educator of Yr. 1988), Pi Lambda Theta, Beta Pi. Episcopalian. Club: The Detroit Study (pres. 1980-82). Home: 2981 Collingwood Detroit MI 48026 Office: Areac-Detroit Pub Schs 14111 Puritan Detroit MI 48227

THOMASON, ANN WENNINGER, public relations and marketing executive; b. Bucyrus, Ohio, June 22, 1934; d. Clifford Earl and Helene (Hall) Wenninger; m. Lyon Burks Hutcherson Jr., June 9, 1956 (div. Mar. 1976); children: Steven Burks, Leighan Hutcherson Hunt, Michael Hall; m. William Olin Thomason, Nov. 24, 1977. Student, U. Ky., 1952-56; profl. cert., N.Y. Sch. Interior Design, 1963. Prin. Ann Hutcherson Interiors, Glasgow, Ky., 1963-76; part-owner Bucky Farnor & Assocs. (flower, gift and design shop), Nashville, 1977-81; owner, sec., treas. William Thomason & Assocs., Nashville, 1981-85, v.p. pub. relations, 1986-87, exec. v.p., 1988—; presenter in field, 1963—; v.p. Headliner Lectures, Inc. Developer gift line "Annotations". Active Nashville Symphony Guild, pres., 1982-83, mem. exec. com., bd. dirs., 1979-86, chmn. decorations, 1986, chmn. pub. relations com. 1987 Symphony Ball; projects chairperson Tenn. Homecoming '86, Nashville, 1985-86; co-chairperson Heart Gala, Mid. Tenn. Heart Assn., Nashville, 1985; active Nashville Symphony Assn., including bd. dirs., 1982—, spl. events com.; mem. adminstrv. bd. West End United Meth. Ch.; founder, bd. dirs. Tree Found., Inc.; mem. steering com. Cumberland Valley Girl Scout Council, 1987—. Recipient Ky. Col. award Gov. Ky., 1968, Outstanding Vol. award Nashville Symphony Guild, 1979, cert. recognition Nashville Symphony Assn., 1983; named to Outstanding Young Women Am., U.S. Jaycees. Mem. Nashville C. of C., Nat. Assn. for Female Execs., Peak Investment Club. Republican. Methodist. Club: The Cumberland (Nashville). Office: William Thomason & Assocs 2323 Hillsboro Rd Suite 402 Nashville TN 37212

THOMASSON, ELIZABETH STEPHENS, electronics company executive; b. Abbeville, S.C., Sept. 15, 1948; d. Walton Murph and Mary Grace (Porter) Stephens; m. Michael Thomasson (div. Oct. 1982); children: Bryan Rakestraw, Brice Rakestraw, Katie, Sally. Student, Dekalb Community Coll., Decatur, Ga., 1974-76. Sec. Atlanta Water Works, 1968-69; housemother Meth. Children's Home, Decatur, 1970-72; prin. Contract Cleaning Service, Stone Mountain, Ga., 1975-76; seamstress Arrow Co., Buchanan, Ga., 1977-82; prin. Word Perfect Co., Roswell, Ga., 1982-83; sales mgr. So. Exchange, Norcross, Ga., 1983-87; co-mgr. The Network Group, Norcross, 1987; prin. The Electronic Exchange, Norcross, 1988—. Office: The Electronic Exchange 4405 International Blvd Suite B109A Norcross GA 30093

THOMASSON, SYLVIA MCCARDEL, human service administrator, educator; b. Telogia, Fla., July 31, 1938; d. Allison Chesley and C.A. Victoria (Elmore) McCardel; m. Ray Gerald Thomasson, Sept. 20, 1956; children: Victoria Lee, Donna Ray, Cathy Lynn, Charles Jack II. BS in Edn., Fla. So. Coll., 1968; MA in Counseling and Guidance, U. So. Fla., 1972, SEd in Counseling and Guidance, 1974; DEd, Nova U., 1982. Nat. cert. counselor. Counselor Pasco-Hernando Community Coll., Brooksville, Fla., 1974-77, coordinator counseling, 1977-78, dean North Campus, 1978-82, dir. title III dist. office, Dade City, Fla., 1982-84, dir. human services, New Port Richey, Fla., 1984-86, dean student services, 1986—; chmn. staff and program devel. com., 1984-85. Communication chmn. Am. Heart Assn. of Fla., St. Petersburg, 1982—, mem. state and local bd., 1981; sponsor Human Service Club, New Port Richey, 1984-86. Mem. Internat. Soc. for Coll. and Univ. Planning, Nat. Assn. Human Services Educators, So. Assn. Human Services Educators, Fla. Assn. of Community Colls., Am. Assn. Counseling and Devel., Phi Delta Kappa. Democrat. Baptist. Club: Music (Brooksville) (v.p. 1983-84, pres. 1984-85). Avocations: lecturing, writing, collecting art, music. Home: 4320 White Rd Brooksville FL 34602 Office: Pasco-Hernando Community Coll 7025 State Rd #587 New Port Richey FL 33552

THOMPSON, A. LEIGH, tape company executive; b. St. Louis, Nov. 9, 1954; d. Bill Cleveland and Lois Ann (Hough) Thompson; m. Francis Thomas Campos, May 26, 1980 (div. Apr. 1986). A.A. in English, St. Louis Community Coll., 1975; B.S. in Psychology magna cum laude, Lawrence U., 1977. Cert. tchr. spl. edn. Caterer, St. Louis, Appleton, Wis., 1973-77; tchr., therapist The Day Sch., Chgo., 1977-78; mktg. service supv. Market Facts, Inc., Washington, 1978-80; sales promotion mgr. Gentec/Foremost-McKesson, San Francisco, 1981-82; sales trainer, specialist TimeMed (formerly Profl. Tape), Burr Ridge, Ill., 1982—; trainer Dimensions of Profl. Selling, 1984—; speaker in field. Softball coach Police Activities League, San Francisco, 1986. Recipient Take-Me-Along Winner award TimeMed, 1984, Ring Club award, 1984, 87; Lawrence U. grantee, 1976, 77. Mem. Nat. Assn. Profl. Salespersons (pub. relations com. 1985—), Nat. Assn. Female Execs., Lawrence Univ. Alumni (recruiter 1985—), Mortar Bd. Alumni (treas. 1975-77), Phi Theta Kappa. Roman Catholic. Club: Telegraph Hill. Avocations: skiing, modern dance, hiking, racquetball, running, reading, writing. Home: 2601 Chestnut St #1 San Francisco CA 94123 Office: TimeMed 144 Tower Dr Chicago IL 60521

THOMPSON, ANNE ELISE, judge; b. Phila., July 8, 1934; d. Leroy Henry and Mary Elise (Jackson) Jenkins; m. William H. Thompson, June 19, 1965; children: William H., Sharon A. B.A., Howard U., 1955, LL.B., 1964; M.A., Temple U., Phila., 1957. Bar: D.C. bar 1964, N.J. bar 1966. Staff atty. Office of Solicitor, Dept. Labor, Chgo., 1964-65; asst. dep. public defender Trenton, N.J., 1967-70; mcpl. prosecutor Lawrence Twp., Lawrenceville, N.J., 1970-72; mcpl. ct. judge Trenton, 1972-75; prosecutor Mercer County, Trenton, 1975-79; U.S. dist. judge Dist. of N.J., Trenton, 1979—; vice chmn. Mercer County Criminal Justice Planning Com., 1972; mem. com. criminal practice N.J. Supreme Ct., 1975-79, mem. com. mcpl. cts., 1972-75; v.p. N.J. County Prosecutors Assn., 1978-79; chmn. juvenile justice com. Nat. Dist. Attys. Assn., 1978-79. Del. Democratic Nat. Conv., 1972. Recipient Assn. Black Women Lawyers award, 1976, Disting. Service award Nat. Dist. Attys. Assn., 1979, Gene Carte Meml. award Am. Criminal Justice Assn., 1980, Outstanding Leadership award N.J. County Prosecutors Assn., 1980, John Mercer Langston Outstanding Alumnus award Howard U. Law Sch., 1981; also various service awards; certs. of appreciation. Mem. Am. Bar Assn., Fed. Bar Assn., N.J. Bar Assn., Mercer County Bar Assn. Democrat. Office: 343 US Courthouse 402 E State St PO Box 401 Trenton NJ 08608 *

THOMPSON, ANNE MARIE, newspaper publisher; b. Des Moines, Feb. 7, 1920; d. George Horace and Esther Mayer Sheely; m. J. Ross Thompson, July 31, 1949; children—Annette McCracken, James Ross. B.A., U. Iowa, 1940; postgrad. U. Colo., 1971. Co-pub. Baca County Banner, Springfield, Colo., 1951-54; pub. Rocky Ford (Colo.) Daily Gazette, 1954—. Mem. Colo. Ho. of Reps., 1957-61; Colo. presdl. elector, 1972; chmn. Colo. adv. com. SBA, 1979-81. Recipient Community Service award Rocky Ford C. of C., 1975; named Colo. Woman of Achievement in Journalism, 1959; Colo. Bus. Person of Yr., Future Bus. Leaders of Am., 1981; elected to Colo. Community Journalism Hall of Fame, 1981. Mem. Nat. Fedn. Press Women (dir. 1971-81), Nat. Newspaper Assn. (Emma C. McKinney award 1984), Inland Daily award 1984), Inland Daily Press Assn., Colo. Press Assn. (dir. 1981-83), Colo. Press Women, PEO, Bus. and Profl. Women's Club, AAUW. Republican. Methodist.

THOMPSON, ANNIE LAURA, foreign language educator; b. Henderson, Tenn., July 8, 1937; d. Wesley Sylvester and Letha Irene (Jones) T.; m. Edward L. Patterson, June 7, 1980. BA, U. Ala., 1959; MA, Duke U., 1961; PhD, Tulane U., 1973. Instr. Spanish lang. U. Miss., Oxford, 1960-64; instr. Auburn (Ala.) U., 1964-66; teaching asst. Tulane U., New Orleans, 1966-70; assoc. prof. Spanish lang. Delgado Coll., New Orleans, 1970—; instr. Spanish for Physicians and Med. Persons Tulane U., La. State U. Med. Eye Ctr., Ochsner Clinic and Hosp. Author: Religious Elements in the Quijote, 1960, The Attempt of Spanish Intellectuals to Create a New Spain 1930-36, 1973; asst. editor The Crusader, 1961-64. Alt. mem. La. Coastal Commn., 1987—; del. Women's State Rep. Conv., 1987; mem. Women for Better La., Alliance for Good Govt., 1987—, La. Coastal Adv. Council, 1988. Recipient Outstanding Tchr. award Delgado Coll. Student Govt. Assn., 1974; Woodoow Wilson fellow, 1959-60; NDEA fellow, 1968-69. Mem. AAUP, South Cen. MLA, South Atlantic MLA, So. Conf. Lang. Tchrs., Spring Fiesta Assn., Women for A Better La., Alliance for Govt., Phi Beta Kappa, Phi Alpha Theta, Sigma Delta Pi. Mem. Ch. of Christ. also: 7008 Memphis St New Orleans LA 70124 Office: 615 City Park Ave New Orleans LA 70119

THOMPSON, BARBARA JEAN, controller; b. Newport Beach, Calif., Jan. 31, 1964; d. Michael Sullivan Smith and Patricia Anne (Limacher) Wofle; m. Larz "O" Thompson, Sept. 8, 1984. Grad. high sch., Newport Beach, Calif. Sec. Interstate Engring., Anaheim, Calif., 1983, Wolfe Lumber Co., Newport Beach, Calif., 1983-84; acct. Wolfe Lumber Co., Newport Beach, 1984, controller, corp. sec., 1984—; corp. sec./treas. S.W. Jr. Enterprises, Inc., 1986—, also bd. dirs. Advisor Newport Harbor High Sch. Cheerleaders, Newport Beach, 1986—. Mem. Gamma Phi Beta. Republican. Mormon. also: Lake Elsinore CA 92330 Office: Wolfe Lumber Co 901 Dover Suite 200 PO Box 8751 Newport Beach CA 92658-8751

THOMPSON, BARBARA LYNN, account executive; b. Neptune, N.J., Sept. 14, 1963; d. Edmund Leonard III and Betty Ann (Stewart) T. BS in Mktg. and Mgmt., Bloomsburg U., 1985. Lic. realtor, N.J. Resident advisor Bloomsburg (Pa.) U., 1983-85; sales rep. N.J. Natural Gas. Co., Wall, 1985-86; account exec. Shepard's/McGraw-Hill, Colorado Springs, 1987—; cons. resumres Thompson Resumes Unltd., Monmouth Beach, N.J., 1985—. Recipient Lynn Larrison Meml. award Larrison Found., 1981, Keith Alston Meml. award Alston Orgn., 1981. Mem. Nat. Assn. Female Execs., Am. Mktg. Assn., Alpha Sigma Alpha (class pres. 1983). Republican. Methodist. Club: Ocean Grove Women's (award 1981). Home: PO Box 155 Monmouth Beach NJ 07750 0155

THOMPSON, CAROL CROSS, university administrator; b. Washington, Mar. 28, 1941; d. John Walker and Brunhilde (Oakleaf) Cross; m. Kingman B. Brown, Oct. 31, 1959 (div. 1968); children: Karen Bliss, David Michael; m. William Ensign Thompson, Oct. 21, 1979. BS, U. Md., 1971. Mgmt. cons. UNCO, Inc., Systems Interface, Bldg. Maintenance Service Co., Washington, 1972-76; dir. devel. The Nat. Eye Found., Washington, 1976-78; campaign coordinator D.C. chpt. ARC, Washington, 1978-80; founder, exec. dir. Help the Aged U.S., Washington, 1980-82; corp. and found. officer ann. and capital campaign Trinity Coll., Hartford, Conn., 1985-87; dir. corp. and found. relations U. Conn., Storrs, 1988—. Mem. U. Hartford Art Sch. Aux.,

1984—; mem. Leadership Greater Hartford, 1986, mem. task force, 1987; bd. dirs. Parents Anonymous, 1987—. Mem. Nat. Soc. Fundraising Execs. (cert., chair conf. Conn. chpt. 1986, pres. 1987—, nat. bd. dirs. 1987—). Home: 57 Breezy Knoll Avon CT 06001 Office: U Conn Storrs CT 06268

THOMPSON, CARYN ELIZABETH, banker; b. Palo Alto, Calif., Mar. 22, 1954; d. Robert Louis and Harriet Elizabeth (Jeffs) Hildebrand; m. Terence William Thompson, Aug. 30, 1975; children: Cory Elizabeth, Christopher William. Student, U. Ariz., 1972-75; BS, Ariz. State U., 1979, MBA, 1984. Asst. treas. Great Western Bank, Phoenix, 1984-85; asst. v.p. Citibank (Ariz.), Phoenix, 1985-87; v.p. Nat. Processing Co., Phoenix, 1987—. Dem. precinct committee-person, dist. 26, Phoenix, 1983; registrar Ariz. State Govt., 1980. Mem. Nat. Assn. Female Execs., Nat. Assn. Banking Women (bd. dirs. 1985), Ariz. Bank Assn. (bank rep.), Delta Gamma. Democrat. Home: 202 W Lawrence Rd Phoenix AZ 85013 Office: Nat Processing Co 16402 N 28th Ave Phoenix AZ 85023

THOMPSON, CHRISTINE EPPS, librarian; b. Ft. Worth, Nov. 1, 1940; d. John Robert Epps and Eva May (Taylor) Epps McKee; m. Robert Edgar Thompson Jr., Sept. 28, 1957; children: Thomas Len, Robert Keith. BA, North Tex. State U., 1964, MA, 1966, MLS, 1970. Teaching asst. North Tex. State U., Denton, 1964-65, library clk., 1968-70; librarian Tarleton State U., Stephenville, 1970-83; teaching asst. Tex. Woman's U., Denton, 1983-84; head original cataloging dept. Tex. A&M U. Library, College Station, 1984-85, acting head processing div., 1985-86, head original cataloging/copy cataloging dept., 1986-88. Author: The Works of Zbigniew K. Brzezinski; Mgmt. Information Systems Bibliography; Decision Support Systems: A Bibliography, 1980-84; spl. editor Reference Services Rev., 1986; contbr. numerous articles to profl. jours. Mem. ALA, Assn. Coll. Research Libraries, Tex. Library Assn. (chmn. scholarship com. 1980-81, chmn. intellectual freedom com. 1983-84), Tex. Assn. Coll. Tchrs. (exec. bd. 1980-81, 87-88, nomination com. 1983-84), chmn., Com. for Acad. Freedom and Defense, 1987-88, Am. Mgmt. Assn. Democrat. Baptist.

THOMPSON, DIANNE BRITT, health and management consultant; b. Pinehurst, N.C., Aug. 13, 1948; d. Paul Raymond and Sarah (Jackson) Britt; m. Hugh Edward Thompson, May 25, 1969; children: Michelle, Steve, Merideth. Diploma in nursing, Hamlet (N.C.) Sch. Nursing, 1969; diploma in nursing mgmt., Duke U., 1978; BA in Mgmt., St. Joseph Coll., Windam, Maine, 1985. RN, N.C. RN N.C. Bapt. Hosp., Wintston-Salem, 1969-74; dir. nursing Convalescence Nursing Home, Sanford, N.C., 1974-76; dir. med./surg. nursing Wake Med. Ctr., Raleigh, N.C., 1976-85; cons. Va., N.C., 1979—; leader seminars, 1980—; instr. Beauti Control, Dallas, 1983—, nat. exec. dir., 1984—. Choir dir. Grace Bible Ch., Staunton, 1986—. Named Pastor's Wife of Yr. Christian Womanhood mag., 1984. Republican. Baptist. Club: Country (Staunton). Home and Office: Rt 1 Box 157 Mount Sidney VA 24467

THOMPSON, DONNA MARIE, data processing administrator, consultant; b. L.I., N.Y., July 27, 1956; d. Raymond Joseph and Sally Rose (Freda) Pontecorvo; m. Gary Richard Thompson, Mar. 15, 1981; children: Alexander J., Jessica Anne. BA, Drew U., 1978; MBA, Seton Hall U., 1986. Lic. tchr., N.J. Restaurant mgr. Strade, Inc., Elmwood Park, N.J., 1976-78; client field rep. Union Photo Co., Clifton, N.J., 1979-80; client service rep. Automatic Data Processing Corp., Clifton, 1980-82, software support specialist, 1982-84, supr. support, 1984-86, mgr. support, 1986-87, mgr. product, 1987—. Vol. Chitton Meml. Hosp., Pequannock, N.J., 1970-74. Mem. Am. Mgmt. Assn., Nat. Assn. Female Execs., Beta Gamma Sigma. Democrat. Roman Catholic. Office: Automatic Data Processing Corp 1 ADP Blvd Roseland NJ 07068

THOMPSON, DOROTHY BROWN, writer; b. Springfield, Ill., May 14, 1896; d. William Joseph and Harriet (Gardner) Brown; m. Dale Moore Thompson, July 2, 1921; 1 child, William B. (dec.) AB., U. Kans., 1919. Began writing professionally, 1931; contributed verse to nat. mags. and newspapers including Saturday Rev., Saturday Evening Post, Va. Quar. Rev., Poetry, Commonweal, Good Housekeeping and others, author research articles for various hist. jours.; poems pub. in over 200 collections and textbooks; mags. and textbooks pub. in Eng., Australia, N.Z., Can., India, Sweden; 25 in Braille. Author: (poetry) Subject to Change, 1973. Leader poetry sect. Writers' Conf., U. Kans., 1953-55, McKendree Coll., 1961, 63, Creighton U., Omaha, 1966; lectr. writers' conf. U. Kans., 1965, Am. Poets Series, Kansas City, Mo., 1973; mem. staff Poets Workshop, Cen. Mo. State U., 1974; poet-in-schs. residency for Mo. State Council of Arts, 1974. Recipient Mo. Writers' Guild Award, 1941, Poetry Soc. Am., nat. and local awards. Mem. Diversifiers, Poetry Soc. Am., Nat. Soc. Colonial Dames, First Families of Va. (Burgess for Mo.). Mem. Christian Ch. Clubs: Woman's City, Filson (Louisville). Address: 221 W 48th St Apt 1402 Kansas City MO 64112

THOMPSON, FRANCES ANN, ESL educator; b. Havre, Mont., Nov. 2, 1945; d. William Compton and Bess Irene (Harrison) T. B.A. in English, U. Tex.-Arlington, 1967; M.A. in English, East Tex. State U., 1973, Ed.D. in Elem. Edn., 1983. Cert. tchr. all levels and ESL, Tex. Kindergarten tchr. Mrs. Schaeffer's Sch., Arlington, 1967-68; tchr. English, Crystal City Ind. Sch. Dist., Tex., 1969-71; elem. and English tchr. Mirando City Ind. Sch. Dist., Tex., 1974-81; ESL tchr. Como-Pickton Ind. Sch. Dist., Como, Tex., 1981—. Contbr. articles to profl. jours., also poetry to Poor Richard's Poetry, 1968 (1st Pl. award). Mem. Tex. State Tchrs. Assn., Phi Kappa Theta. Republican. Baptist. Avocations: crochet; reading; crafts; needlework. Office: Como-Pickton Ind Sch Dist PO Box 18 Como TX 75431

THOMPSON, GERALDINE JUDITH, educational administrator; b. London, Apr. 27, 1942; d. Thomas John and Edyth Margaret (Walker) Bray; came to U.S., 1960; BA magna cum laude, Smith Coll., 1963; M.A., U. London, 1974; m. Kenneth Stuart Thompson, Mar. 20, 1965; 1 child, Kirsten Deborah. Asst. to pres. Internat. Schs. Services, N.Y., 1963-66; program dir. Noise Abatement Soc., London, 1972-73; asst. dir. African Imprint Library Services, Mt. Kisco, N.Y., 1974-77; sr. v.p., dir. coll. programs Am. Inst. for Fgn. Study, Greenwich, Conn., 1977—; contbr. Coutry Index, Los Angeles, 1982— . Trustee Richmond Coll., 1982—. Mem. Nat. Assn. Fgn. Student Affairs. Club: Smith of Westchester County. Contbr. New Horizons in Education, 1965. Home: Holly Hill Ln Katonah NY 10536 Office: Am Inst Fgn Study 102 Greenwich CT 06830

THOMPSON, HAZEL PAULISON (RUSTY), educational administrator; b. Passaic, N.J., Feb. 4, 1928; B.S. in Edn., Glassboro Coll., 1949; M.A. in Adminstrn. and Supervision, Columbia U., 1960; m. W. Stuart Thompson; 3 children. Tchr., Ridgewood (N.J.) Bd. Edn., 1949-61; tchr. Bloomfield (N.J.) Bd. Edn., 1964-66, reading specialist, 1966-70, adminstrv. asst. in curriculum and instrn., 1970-82, asst. to supt. and dir. personnel, 1982—, also coordinator recruitment, affirmative action officer for hiring policies and procedures; TV coordinator between sch. dist. and N.J. Public TV. Elder, Ref. Ch. in Am. Mem. N.J. Assn. Curriculum Devel., Am. Assn. Curriculum and Supervision, Am. Assn. Sch. Personnel Adminstrs., Mid-Atlantic Assn. Sch. Coll. Univ. Staffing, NEA N.J. Edn. Assn., Internat. Reading Assn., N.J. Reading Tchrs. Assn. Co-author numerous curriculum guides and writings for title funds. Certified as prin., supr., N.J., sch. adminstr., specialist in reading, lang. arts, kindergarten through 12th grades, curriculum devel., kindergarten through 12th grades, adminstrv. supervision for classroom instruction, kindergarten through 12th grades, elem. and secondary libraries coordination. Home: Jacquelin Ave Ho-Ho-Kus NJ 07423 Office: 155 Broad St Bloomfield NJ 07003

THOMPSON, HEIDI COGEAN, manufacturing executive; b. Warwick, R.I., Feb. 16, 1957; d. Wallace William and Ilse Margarete (Götz) Cogean; m. Benton Joseph Thompson Jr., Sept. 13, 1981. AA, Community Coll. of R.I., 1977; BS in Mgmt., R.I. Coll., 1979. Mgr. Fotomat Store, Raynham, Mass., 1979-80, mgr. adminstrn., 1980-82; supr. prodn. Honeywell Info. Systems, Boston, 1982-83, sr. supr. prodn., 1983-84, mgr. quality and tng., 1984-85, adminstr. material control, 1986-87; mgr. planning engring. Sheldahl, Nashua, N.H., 1987—. Tchr. children's Christian doctrine St. Kevin Ch., 1979. Mem. Phi Theta Kappa. Roman Catholic. Club: Bunty Lee Sch. Horsemanship (Derry, N.H.). Office: Skeldahl 100 Northeastern Blvd Nashua NH 03061

THOMPSON, HELEN VIRGINIA, nurse; b. Frederick, Md., May 14, 1941; d. William Linwood and Bertha Mae (Horman) T. BS, Frostburg (Md.) State U., 1963; diploma, Broofs AFB Sch. Aerospace Medicine, 1969, Frederick meml. Hosp. Sch. Nursing, 1968; MA, W.Va. Grad. Studies, 1985. Staff RN, asst. charge nurse Frederick Meml. Hosp., 1968-69; classroom instr. Charleston (W.Va.) Area Med. Ctr. Sch. Anesthesia, 1973-79, asst. dir., 1975-79; staff anesthetist Herbert J. Thomas Meml. Hosp., South Charleston, W.Va., 1979—; counselor Women's Counseling Ctr., Charleston, 1982-85; tchr. Woodburn jr. High Sch., Balt. Chair W.Va. Nurses Polit. Action Com., 1983—. Named Politically Active Nurse of Yr. State of W.Va., 1985. Mem. Assn. Mil. Surgeons U.S., Am. Nurses Assn., Am. Assn. Nurse Anesthetists, NRA, Nat. Guard Assn. Democrat. Mem. Disciples of Christ. Home: Rt 1 Box 166 Walton WV 25286 Office: Herbert J Thomas Meml Hosp MacCorkle Ave SW South Charleston WV 25309

THOMPSON, JACQUELINE DALE, property management business owner; b. Fargo, N.D., Dec. 27, 1950; d. John Seth and Mary Ellen (Pentecost) Thompson; children—Nicholas, Samantha. B.S., N.D. State U., 1973. With music dept. Nels Vogel, Moorhead, Minn., 1973-75; owner Dale Mgmt., Fargo, 1975—. Bd. dirs. Rape and Abuse Crisis Ctr., Fargo, 1984—, Dakota Montessori Sch., 1980-82; mem., past officer Fargo-Moorhead Chamber Chorale, 1980—, Worship Work Area 1st United Meth. Ch., 1988—; mem. Citizens for a Real Choice, Fargo, 1982—; apptd. Rental Housing Bd. of Rev., Moorhead, Minn., 1987—, active Landlord-Tenant Task Force, Fargo, Fargo/Moorhead United Way; vol. Hot Line, 1974-79. Mem. Women's Network Red River Valley, NOW, Nat. Assn. Female Execs., Fargo/Moorhead Apt. Assn. (bd. dirs., pres. 1983-84, sec.-treas. 1982-83, lobbyist 1983, 85, 87), N.D. Apt. Assn. (bd. dirs. 1982—, v.p. 1987—, sec.-treas. 1982-85), AAUW, LWV, PEO, Phi Kappa Phi, Sigma Alpha Iota. Methodist. Avocations: jazzercise, biking, singing, hot air ballooning. Home: 411 Lindenwood Dr Fargo ND 58103 Office: Dale Management PO Box 7303 Fargo ND 58103

THOMPSON, JAYNE AUDREY, lawyer; b. Albert Lea, Minn., Aug. 19, 1939; d. John Blain and Harriet Ordella (Blume) Roberts; m. Paul L. Kuennemeier, Feb. 14, 1987; children—Theresa Brown, Laura Thompson, Jennifer Thompson. B.A., Hamline U., 1961; M.Ed., U. Minn., 1965; J.D., No. Ky. U., 1979. Bar: Ohio 1979. Tchr., U.S. Army Mil. Schs., Wuerzburg, W.Ger., 1962-63, St. Paul Pub. Schs., 1961-62, 63-65, Parkway Sch. Dist., St. Louis, 1965-66; tchr.'s aide U. Cin., Cin. Pub. Schs.; tchr. Wyoming (Ohio) Pub. Schs., 1966-68; substitute tchr. Lockland, Greenhills and Finneytown, Ohio, 1968-70; corp. atty. Eagle Savs. Assn., Cin., 1979; sole practice, Cin., 1980—. Author: Changing Attitudes through Literature, 1965; editor: (TV tape) Around the World with Literature, 1964. Reader, Clovernook Home for Blind; trustee No. Hills Unitarian Ch.; pres. Cin. Unitarian Universalist Council; v.p. UN Info. Com.; mem. Met. Area Religions Coalition Council; co-leader Girl Scouts U.S.A.; mem. Finneytown PTA; mem. Citizens Com. on Justice and Corrections; mem. allocations bd. children's services United Appeal; bd. dirs. Mental Health Services N.W. Mem. ABA, Ohio Bar Assn., Cin. Bar Assn., Assn. Trial Lawyers Am., LWV. Republican. Clubs: Singletons, Cingles (treas.), Zonta. Home: 8393 Sailboat Ln Maineville OH 45039

THOMPSON, JEAN DUNIVANT, medical alumni association director; b. Wright City, Mo., June 21, 1927; d. Claude Lawrence Dunivant and Lela Snow (Niblack) Dunivant-Shears; m. John Goral, Feb. 5, 1946 (div. Nov. 1978); 1 child, Daniel; m. Paul W. Thompson, June 23, 1984. Student, U. Md. Br. mgr., dist. sec. Singer Co., Balt., 1969-71; sec. to exec. v.p. Balt. Fed. Savs., 1971-74; exec. dir. med. alumni assn. U. Md., Inc., Balt., 1974—. Patron Balt. Symphony Orch.; bd. dirs. McHenry Theater Restoration Project; mem. Fed. Hill and Fells Point Preservation Soc., Preservation of Md. Antiquities. Mem. Md. Soc. Assn. Execs., Am. Bus. Women's Assn., Assn. Am. Med. Colls., Nat. Preservation Soc. Republican. Office: U Md Med Alumni Assn 522 W Lombard St Box 2198 Baltimore MD 21230

THOMPSON, JOAN ANDRÉ, charitable organization executive; b. Troy, Ohio, Apr. 4, 1934; d. Ralph Arnold and Helen Glendora (Donavan) Moyer; m. John Allen Thompson, Feb. 24, 1955; children: Katherine, Julie, Scott. A in Bus., Clark Coll., Springfield, Ohio, 1976. Dept. sec. Ohio State U., Columbus, 1956-62; pres. Ohio Assn. for Retarded Citizens, Columbus, 1985—; mem. adv. bd. Dept. Mental Retardation and Devel. Disabilities, State of Ohio, Columbus, 1985-86; mem. nominating com. Assn. Retarded Citizen. Served as cpl. WAC, 1953-55. Named Outstanding Vol., State of Ohio, 1983. Mem. Ohio Devel. Disabilities Planning Council, Ohio Legal Rights Commn., Am. Legion. Republican. Lodge: Lioness. Home: 8090 Ulery Rd New Carlisle OH 45344

THOMPSON, JOAN ANN, educator; b. Jamaica, N.Y., July 29, 1946; d. John Joseph and Elizabeth Ann (Foley) Murphy; divorced; children: Jennifer Christine, Kimberly Alyson. BA, SUNY, 1968; MA, Adelphi U., 1972. Cert. secondary tchr. Math tchr. Cen. High Sch. Dist. #1, Valley Stream, N.Y., 1968-73, Los Angeles City Unified Sch. Dist., 1973-75; math tchr. Campbell Hall, North Hollywood, Calif., 1975-87, chair math. dept., 1979-87. Room mother Sherman Oaks (Calif.) Luth. Childrens Ctr., 1985-86; vol. Girl Scouts U.S.A., North Hollywood, 1985—. NSF grantee, 1971-72, 85. Mem. Nat. Council Tchrs. Math., Calif. Math. Council. Republican. Roman Catholic. Home: 5319 Coldwater Cyn Unit E Van Nuys CA 91401 Office: Campbell Hall 4533 Laurel Canyon Blvd North Hollywood CA 91607

THOMPSON, JOANNE, artist, porcelain manufacturing company executive; b. Chgo., Nov. 2, 1922; d. George A. and Mary Louise Thompson; student U. Colo., Boulder, 1940-42; divorced; children—Barrett, Marc, Stacy. Ind. pub., distbr. limited edition prints. Exhibited group shows Nat. Arts Club Gallery, N.Y.C., 1965-69; Mus. Fine Arts, Springfield, Mass., 1965-70; Am. Artists Profl. League Grand Nat., N.Y.C., 1966-70; Hammond Mus., Westchester, N.Y., 1968; owner, artist, tchr. Joanne Thompson Studio, Scottsdale, Ariz., 1979—. Mem. Am. Artists Profl. League, Artists Guild Chgo., Acad. Artists. Author, illustrator: Fun to Sketch With Pencil and Crayon, 1973; illustrator Love Circles, 1978. Office: PO Box 4042 Scottsdale AZ 85261

THOMPSON, KAY ELLEN, municipal official; b. Berkeley, Calif., Aug. 24, 1942; d. Samuel Clinton and Joyce N. (Slatter) McMullen; children: Christian Leigh, Sean Samuel, Gregg Brady. Student, U. Pacific, 1960-61, Coll. San Mateo, 1961-62, West Valley Coll., San Jose, Calif., 1962-64, No. Nev. Community Coll, 1973. Sales person Lillian's, Elko, Nev., 1957-62; sec. Western Electric, Sunnyvale, Calif., 1963-66; salesperson Avon, San Jose, 1969-72; ceramics designer sold at Lillian's, Elko and San Jose, 1971-72; advisor Summer Playscheme, Edinburgh, Scotland, 1973; gen. supr. Elko County Fair Exhibits, 1977-79; columnist Elko Daily Free Press, 1977-81; tchr. needlework No. Nev. Community Coll., Elko, 1974-84; owner Stockmen's Beauty Salon, Elko, 1981-83; legal sec. Woodbury and Torvinen, Elko, 1982-84; from sec. to exec. sec. Elko Conv. and Visitors Authority, 1984-85, adminstrv. asst., 1985, acting adminstr., 1986, exec. dir., 1986—. Author: (poems) Heartstrings; designer needlework (Silver Thimble award 1980), murals for St. Pauls Episcopal Ch., Elko; editor Rotary newsletter, 1980. Mgr. Nev. Assembly candidate campaign, Elko, 1980; co-chmn. Jr. Golf Program, Elko, 1981-82; trustee Elko County Library, 1983-84; pres. PEO chpt. A, 1979. Mem. Internat. Assn. Auditorium Mgrs., Nat. Assn. Female Execs., Am. Soc. Assn. Execs., Nev. Soc. Assn. Execs. Democrat. Presbyterian. Home: 649 1st St Elko NV 89801 Office: Elko Conv and Vis Authority 700 Moren Way Elko NV 89801

THOMPSON, KRISTEN RUTH, management consultant; b. Greenfield, Mass., Mar. 4, 1952; d. Ernest James and Helena Julia (Prondecki) T. BA, U. Mass., 1974; postgrad., Worcester (Mass.) Polytechnical Inst., 1976; postgrad. study in law, U. Idaho, 1986—. Sales engr. Mobil Oil Corp., Valley Forge, Pa., 1978-80; mgr. engring. Idaho Nat. Engring. Lab., Idaho Falls, Idaho, 1980-86; cons. engring. Idaho Research Found., Moscow, 1986—; cons. Scientech, Inc., Idaho Falls, 1985—; advisor Congressman Richard Stallings, Washington, 1985—; advisor sci. and tech. com. U.S. Ho. of Reps., Washington, 1985—. Chmn. bd. trustees 1st Congl. Ch. of Idaho Falls, 1985. Grantee Steele Reese Found., Salmon, Idaho, 1985. Mem. Am. Nuclear Soc. (assoc.), ABA (student div.), Soc. Women Engrs. (author jour., v.p. Idaho chpt. 1982), Idaho Acad. Sci. Democrat. Lodge: Order Eastern Star. Home: PO Box 3421 Moscow ID 83843

THOMPSON, LAURA ANN, radiologist; b. Ann Arbor, Mich., Aug. 8, 1950; d. John Morgon and Dorothy Georgene (Kinne) T.; m. Ruben Archilla. BS, Fla. Presbyn. Coll., 1972; MD, Tulane Sch. Medicine, 1976. Intern St. Vincent's Hosp. and Med. Ctr., N.Y.C., 1976-77, resident in radiology, 1977-80, resident in nuclear medicine, 1980-81; fellowin nuclear medicine UCLA Sch. Medicine, Los Angeles, 1981-82; assoc. radiologist Western Radiologic Med. Group, Culver City, Calif., 1982-85; radiologist Western Radiologic Med. Group, Culver City, 1985-88; ptnr. Western Radiology Med. Group, Inc., Culver City, 1988—; radiation safety officer Brotman Hosp., Culver City, 1985—, dir. diagnostic radiology, Brotman Hosp., 1986. Mem. Am. Assn. Women Radiologists. Democrat. Office: Western Radiologic Med Group 9801 Washington Blvd #1528 Culver City CA 90230

THOMPSON, LAVERNE ELIZABETH THOMAS, English language educator; b. Bklyn., July 17, 1945; d. Roscoe Lee and Mary Elizabeth (Blackwell) Thomas; m. Robert Louis Thompson, Sept. 28, 1968. BA in English, Speech, Bluffton Coll., 1967; MS in Ednl. Adminstrn./Supervision, U. Dayton, 1977. Cert. sch. prin., Ohio; cert. secondary sch. supr., Ohio; cert. realtor, Ohio. Instr. English, speech Piqua (Ohio) Cen. High Sch., 1967-68; instr. Lima (Ohio) Sr. High Sch., 1968-77, Shawnee High Sch., Lima, 1977-86; grad. asst. U. Toledo, 1986—. Editor Higher Edn. newsletter, 1987. Bd. dirs. Lima YWCA, 1971; co-chair Brotherhood Dinner, Lima, 1976. Mem. Va. Assn. New Homemakers Am. (pres. 1962), New Homemakers Am. (nat pres. 1963); Phi Delta Kappa (charter mem. west cen. Ohio chpt.). Home: 24501 W River Rd Perrysburg OH 43551

THOMPSON, LILLIAN HURLBURT, communications company executive; b. Bennington, Vt., Apr. 27, 1947; d. Paul Rhodes and Evelyn Arlene (Lockhart) Hurlburt; m. Wayne Wray Thompson, June 28, 1969. BS, Skidmore Coll., 1969; MS, U. So. Miss., 1975. Communication cons. Southwestern Bell Telephone, San Antonio, 1978-80; acct. exec. C&P Telephone, Washington, 1980-82, Am. Bell, Washington, 1983; staff mgr. AT&T Info. Systems, Rosslyn, Va., 1984; mgr. sales intermediary mktg. dept. Bell Atlantic Corp., Silver Spring, Md., 1984—. Home: 9203 St Marks Pl Fairfax VA 22031 Office: Bell Atlantic 8630 Fenton St 12th Floor Silver Spring MD 20910

THOMPSON, LINDA LEE, educational consultant; b. Ottumwa, Iowa, Sept. 21, 1940; d. Clarence Adelbert and Ollie Mae (Easley) Andrews; m. Richard Bruce Thompson, Aug. 13, 1961 (div. Nov. 1986); children: Bruce Edward, Curtis Lowell. BA, U. No. Iowa, 1961; postgrad., U. Wis., 1962-66, U. Ariz., 1967-68. Cert. tchr. Math. tchr. Franklin Jr. High Sch., 1961-63; tchr., head math. dept. LaFollette High Sch., Madison, Wis., 1963-67; cons., editor, writer Tucson, 1968—; cons. Ariz. State Dept. Edn., Phoenix, 1981. Author: General Mathematics, 1977; co-author: Consumer Mathematics (2d edition), 1986, McGraw-Hill Mathematics, 1987, You, The Consumer, 1987, Business Mathematics, 1988; contbr. articles to Scholastic Math mag. Chairperson, bd. dirs. Tucson Jr. Strings, 1981-84; com. mem. Rincon/Univ. High Sch. Drug Impact Group, Tucson, 1986—; mem. Univ. High Sch. Parents Bd. Mem. Math. Assn. Am., Nat. Council Tchrs. Math., Nat. Council Suprs. Math., Ariz. Assn. Tchrs. Math. Home and Office: 3340 E 3d St Tucson AZ 85716

THOMPSON, LISA CAROLYN, human realtions professional; b. Long Beach, Calif., Oct. 6, 1952; d. Warren Lester Jones and Virginia Lorraine (Torgeson) Goettleman; m. Robert Clifton Thompson, Mar. 15, 1980 (div. 1987); children: Carolyn Lorraine, Ashley Christina. Grad. high sch., Beaverton, Ore.; student, Portland Community Coll., 1970-72, Foothill Jr. Coll., 1976. Payroll clk. Fireside Thrift Co., Redwood City, Calif., 1976-79, asst. mgr. payroll, 1979-82, mgr. payroll dept., 1982, mgr. personnel/payroll dept., 1982-83, mgr. human resources, 1983-86, asst. v.p. human resources, 1986—. Mem. Am. Mgmt. Assn., Am. Soc. Personnel Adminstrn., Redwood City C. of C. Republican. Episcopalian. Office: Fireside Thrift Co 5600 Mowry School Rd Suite 200 Newark CA 94560

THOMPSON, LYNN ANNE, personnel director; b. Pitts., May 6, 1952; d. Robert Allen and Dolores Ann (D'Ippolito) Bettis; m. Norman Clyde Thompson, Dec. 9, 1944. Student, Slippery Rock State U., 1970-71, U. Calif., Riverside, 1986—. Typist, clk. County of Riverside, Calif., 1976-78; clk. Corban Armco, Inc., Riverside, 1979-80, sr. acctg. clk., 1980-82; bookkeeper, sec. Pacific Clay Products, Inc., Corona, Calif., 1982-85, mgr., personnel support, 1985—. Mem. Nat. Assn. Female Execs., Am. Soc. Personnel Adminstrs., Personnel and Indsl. Relations Assn., Indsl. Relations Research Assn., Calif. Trucking Assn. Avocations: reading, gardening, camping. Office: Pacific Clay Products Inc PO Box 1149 Corona CA 91718

THOMPSON, MARGUERITE MYRTLE GRAMING (MRS. RALPH B. THOMPSON), librarian; b. Orangeburg, S.C., Apr. 23, 1912; d. Thomas Laurie and Rosa Lee (Stroman) Graming; B.A. in English cum laude, U. S.C., 1932, postgrad., 1937; B.L.S., Emory U., 1943; m. Ralph B. Thompson, Sept. 17, 1949 (dec. Oct. 1960). Tchr. English public high schs., S.C., 1932-43; librarian Rockingham (N.C.) High Sch., 1943-45, Randolph County (N.C.) Library, Asheboro, 1945-48, Colleton County (S.C.) Library, Walterboro, 1948-61; dir. Florence (S.C.) County Library, 1961-78. Sec. com. community facilities, services and instns. Florence County Resources Devel. Com., 1964-67; vice chmn. Florence County Council on Aging, 1968-70, exec. bd. 1968-82, bd. treas., 1973-75, bd. sec., 1976-77, bd. v.p., 1979; mem. Florence County Bicentennial Planning Com., 1975-76; mem. relations and allocations com. United Way, 1979-80. Named Boss of Year Nat. Secs. Assn., 1971. Mem. ALA (council 1964-72), Southeastern, S.C. (pres. 1960, chmn. assn. handbook revision com. 1967-69, 80, sect. co-chmn. com. standards for S.C. public libraries 1966-75, fed. relations coordinator 1972-73, planning com. 1976-78) library assns., Greater Florence C. of C. (women's div. chmn. 1969-70, dir. 1975-77), Southeast Regional Conf. Women in Chambers Commerce (dir. 1970-71), Florence, Bus. and Profl. Women's Club (2d v.p. 1975-76, Career Woman of Year 1974, parliamentarian 1980-81, chmn. scholarship com. 1981-82), Delta Kappa Gamma (county chpt. charter pres. 1963-65, treas. 1966-70, chmn. com. on expansion 1977-80, 82-84, state chpt. chmn. state scholarship com. 1967-73, state 2d v.p. 1971-73, state 1st v.p. 1973-75, state pres. 1975-77, chmn. policy manual 1977-81, chmn. adv. council 1978-85, chmn. fin. com. 1981-83, parliamentarian 1987—, dir. SE Region 1978-80, coordinator SE Regional Golden Anniversary Conf. 1979, internat. scholarship com. 1970-74, internat. exec. bd. 1975-77, 78-80, internat. adminstrv. bd. 1978-80, internat. constn. com. 1980-82, internat. achievement award com., 1986-88). Methodist (chmn. ch. library com. 1965-71, chmn. com. ch. history, 1968-69, sec. adminstrv. bd. 1979-82). Club: Florence Literary (sec. 1964-66, 79-82, pres. 1970-72). Home: Route 2 Box 1000 Apt 8B Orangeburg SC 29115

THOMPSON, MARGUERITE THERESA, college administrator; b. N.Y.C., June 21, 1932; d. Emil and Marguerite Theresa (Slevin) Nering; m. Thomas Frederick Thompson, June 22, 1958. Student, Woods Secretarial Sch., 1949-50, Hofstra Coll., 1950-52. Exec. sec. Nat. Can Corp., N.Y.C., 1951-54, Checkmaster, Inc., N.Y.C., 1954-55, John Wiley Publishers, N.Y.C., 1955-58, McGraw Hill Corp., N.Y.C., 1958-62; ex. sec. job corp ctr. Fed. Electric Corp., Edison, N.J., 1962-67; prin. sec. speech and hearing ctr. Rutgers U., New Brunswick, N.J., 1967-80, prin. sec. ctr. computer info. services, 1980-81, tech. adminstr. lab computer sci. research, 1981—; Instr. secretarial procedures Fed. Electric Corp., Edison, 1962-63. Chair Pub. Relations Commn. Piscataway Twp., N.J., 1987—; mem. Presdl. Task Force, Washington, 1980—. Mem. Nat. Assn. Female Execs. Republican. Lutheran. Lodge: Order Eastern Star (Worthy Matron Highland Park chpt. 1976-77, pres. Past Matron and Past Patrons Assn., 1980-81). Office: Rutgers The State U of NJ PO Box 879 Piscataway NJ 08855-0879

THOMPSON, MAVIS SARAH, physician; b. Newark, June 22, 1927; d. Nathaniel Albert and Mavis Carolyn (Smart) T.; B.A., CUNY, 1947; M.D., Howard U., 1953; m. James Blaize, Apr. 17, 1955; children—Clayton, Marcia, Sidney, Ronald, Kevin. Intern, then resident in internal medicine Kings County Hosp., Bklyn., 1953-57; practice medicine specializing in internal medicine, Bklyn., 1957-76; med. dir. Lyndon B. Johnson Health Complex, Inc., Bklyn., 1970-71, 74-76; sch. med. insp. N.Y.C. Bd. Edn., Bklyn., 1962-85; family physician Kingsboro Med. Group, Bklyn., 1976-85;

tchr. dept. nursing Medgar Evers Coll., 1975-76; mem. adv. com. Gerontol. Services Adminstrn. program New Sch. Social Research, N.Y.C.; cons. in field. Bd. dirs. Camp Minisink, 1973—; active local Boy Scouts Am.; lic. lay reader St. George's Epls. Ch., Bklyn., vestry mem., 1985—. Recipient Community Service award St. Mark's Meth. Ch., N.Y.C., 1973; Alberta T. Kline service award Camp Minisink, 1980. Mem. Am. Public Health Assn. (pres. Black caucus health workers 1976-77), Nat. Med. Assn., Am. Mgmt. Assn., Am. Geriatrics Soc., Am. Med. Women's Assn., Kings County Med. Soc., Delta Sigma Theta. Episcopalian. Contbr. articles to med. jours. Office: 1000 Church Ave Brooklyn NY 11218

THOMPSON, MICHELLE, pharmaceutical sales professional; b. Ft. Campbell, Ky., Aug. 19, 1961; d. Kent Christensen and Ida Louise (Mortensen) T. BS in Biology, Utah State U., 1983. Pvt. practice collector delinquent accounts Sandy, Utah, 1979-83; salesperson automobiles Spartan AMC-Jeep-Renault, Murray, Utah, 1983-84; rep. pharmaceutical sales Lederle Labs., Salt Lake City, 1984—. Republican. Mormon. Home: 863 W Clover Meadow Dr Murray UT 84123 Office: Lederle Labs 6312 S Fiddler's Green Circle Suite #430N Englewood CO 80111

THOMPSON, PAMELA KAY, director human resources; b. Wilmington, Ohio, Feb. 18, 1951; d. Robert L. and Ruth Marie (Roberts) T. BS in Bus. Mgmt. cum laude, Webster U., 1984. Personnel asst. Buckeye Molding Co., New Vienna, Ohio, 1978-81; benefit counselor Benefit Communications, Inc., St. Louis, 1982-84; personnel dir. United Mo. Bank of St. Louis, 1984-87; dir. human resoures Becton Dickinson Accu-Glass, St. Louis, 1987—. Named one of Outstanding Young Women of Am., 1986. Mem. St. Louis Women's Commerce Assn., Internat. Assn. of Personnel Women, St. Louis Personnel Assn. (bd. dirs., project chairperson 1987-88), Human Resources Mgmt. Assn. of Greater St. Louis, Am. Inst. of Banking (bd. dirs., chairperson of benefit, compensation and selection coms., 1986-87), Am. Assn. Indsl. Mgmt. (chairperson banking benefit & compensation task force 1985—), Mo. Women's Action Fund. Republican. Home: 745 W Oak Dr Saint Louis MO 63122 Office: 10765 Trenton Ave Saint Louis MO 63132

THOMPSON, PHEBE KIRSTEN, physician; b. Glace Bay, N.S., Can., Sept. 5, 1897; d. Peter and Catherine (McKeigan) Christianson; M.D., C.M. Dalhousie U., Halifax, N.S., 1923; m. Willard Owen Thompson, M.D., June 21, 1923 (dec. Mar. 1954); children—Willard Owen, Frederic, Nancy, Donald. Came to U.S., 1923, naturalized, 1937. Intern Children's Hosp., Halifax, N.S., 1922-23; asst. biochemistry, dept. applied physiology Harvard Sch. Pub. Health, 1924-26; asst. and research fellow in medicine, thyroid clinic, Mass. Gen. Hosp., Boston, 1926-29; asst. in metabolism dept. (endocrinology) Rush Med. Coll. of U. Chgo. and The Central Free Dispensary Chgo., 1930-46; assoc. with husband in practice medicine, Chgo., 1947-54; mng. editor Jour. Clin. Endocrinology and Metabolism, 1954-61, cons. editor, 1961-65; editor Jour. Am. Geriatrics Soc., 1954-82; cons. editor Endocrinology, 1961-65; free-lance editor and writer. Recipient Thewlis award Am. Geriatrics Soc., 1966; cert. of appreciation Am. Thyroid Assn., 1966. Fellow Am. Med. Writers' Assn. (adv. com. 1955-60, v.p. Chgo. 1962), Am. Geriatrics Soc., Gerontological Soc. Am.; mem. Endocrine Soc., AAAS, Am. Genetic Assn., Am. Pub. Health Assn., Ill. Pub. Health Assn., Ill. Acad. Scis., Art Inst. Chgo. (life), Chgo. Hist. Soc. (life). Clubs: Univ.; Harvard; Canadian (corr. sec. 1968-73; mem. bd. 1973-76). Address: 4250 N Marine Dr #613 Chicago IL 60613

THOMPSON, RANDI EILEEN, public relations executive; b. Summit, N.J., June 25, 1952; d. Henry Gilbert and Betty Jane (Fritz) T.; m. Ronald W. Moreland, June 3, 1984; 1 child, LindseyAllison Thompson-Moreland; stepchildren: Michael C. Moreland, Susan J. Moreland. B.A. in Arts and Humanities, U. Md., 1973, M.A. in Communications, 1975. Radio intern Democratic Nat. Com., Washington, 1974; newsletter intern Marriott Corp., Washington, 1974; instr. interpersonal communication U. Md., College Park, 1974-75; assoc. Porter, Novelli & Assocs., Washington, 1975-78, sr. assoc., 1978-80, v.p., research dir., 1980-81, v.p., gen. mgr., Los Angeles, 1981-83, sr v.p., gen. mgr., 1983-86, exec. v.p., Western regional mgr. Doremus Porter Novelli, Los Angeles, 1986—. Mem. Pub. Relations Soc. Am., Am. Assn. Bus. Communicators, Am. Mktg. Assn., Am. Pub. Health Assn., Los Angeles Advt. Women. Democrat. Office: Doremus Porter Novelli 11755 Wilshire Blvd Los Angeles CA 90025

THOMPSON, ROBERTA ANN (BOBBI), small business owner; b. Dayton, Ohio, Oct. 15, 1946; d. Robert Alvin and Lois G. (Hockett) Netzley; m. David Vornholt, Sept. 1966 (div. 1972); 1 child Pamele J.; m. William Lee, Mar. 17, 1972 (div. Jan. 1988). Student, Ohio State U., 1964-66. Pres., owner Aviation Sales, Inc., Vandalia and Miamisburg, Ohio, 1986—; v.p. Argo Comml. Ventures, Inc., Dayton, Ohio, 1988—; chief exec. officer, pres. Condor Aviation Enterprises, Dayton, 1988—. Feature writer Times Publ. mag. Mem. Rep. Nat. Com.; cand. Montgomery County Commr.; trustee, treas. United Cerebral Palsy; bd. dirs. Wright B. Flyer, v.p., hon. aviator, 1985, Women's Air and Space Mus., Nat. Aviation Hall Fame. Mem. Nat. Assn. Female Execs., U.S. C. of C., Ohio C. of C. (task force mem. internat. tort, civil legis., ins. protection, bd. dirs.), Aircraft Owners and Pilots Assn., Dayton Entrepreneurs Bus. Round Table, Nat. Fedn. Ind. Bus. (hon.), Nat. Air Transp. Assn. (trustee, chmn. 1986 awards com.), Dayton Area C. of C. (chmn. transp. com., legis. and govtl. affairs transp. com., program com., bd. dirs.), Ohio Small Bus. Council (bd. dirs., nat. delegate to White House Conf., U.S. chamber dir.), South Metro Dayton Area C. of C. (pres. elect). Republican. Clubs: 500, Aero (Washington); Dayton Airport Mgmt. Office: Argo Comml Ventures Inc 2541 Far Hills Ave Suite 202 Dayton OH 45419

THOMPSON, ROMA JO, social services coordinator; b. Ligonier, Pa., July 15, 1936; d. Joseph Clark and Dorcas Dorothy (Wolford) Mickey; m. R. Jan Thompson, June 9, 1957; children: Randy Jan, Robin Jeffrey, Reis Jay. BS in Elem. Edn., Manchester Coll., 1975; M in Child Care Adminstrn., Nova U., 1987. Nursery sch. dir. Manchester Community Day Care, North Manchester, Ind., 1971-73; tchr. Met. Sch. Dist., Wabash, Ind., 1975-78; adminstr. Ch. World Service/Christian Rural Overseas Program, New Windsor, Md., 1978-81; hostess refugee camp Ch. World Service, Somalia, Africa, 1982; dir. Coop. Disaster Child Care, New Windsor, 1983-87; speaker Internat. Conf., Washington, 1985; cons. Sesame Street TV, N.Y.C., 1984. Columnist weekly article Lead Time mag., 1986. Rep. Ch. Women United, N.Y.C., 1983-87, exec. council, 1988, ecumenical chmn., Md., 1983-87; vol. instr. ARC, 1985-87. Quick Study grantee Disaster Emergency, 1986. Mem. Exec. Women, Nat. Assn. Edn. Young Children (leader workshop 1985), Nat. Vol. Orgns. Active in Disaster (speaker 1984). Democrat. Mem. Ch. of Brethren. Home: 6650 W Butler Dr #8 Glendale AZ 85302

THOMPSON, ROSEMAE M. SCHENCK, hospital executive; b. Hannibal, Mo., Apr. 17, 1923; d. Raina and Mallie Elizabeth (Dickerson) Murphy; m. Albert F. Schenck, July 26, 1942 (dec.); children—Loretta Schenck Grunden, Elizabeth Schenck Barnes; m. Herbert J. Thompson, Dec. 24, 1983. Instr. airplanes Curtiss Wright Aircraft Co., 1942-45; bookkeeper Internat. Shoe Co., Hannibal, Mo., 1951-65; purchasing agt. Levering Hosp., Hannibal, 1967—. Mem. Am. Legion Aux. (past aux. pres.); Assn. Hosp. Purchasing Materials Mgmt. Greater St. Louis, N.E. Mo. Med. and Dental Soc. (past pres.), Bus. and Profl. Women (past pres.), Epsilon Sigma Alpha (past pres. Loveland, Colo.), Bowling Assn. Monday Night Hannibal Ladies League (pres. 1969-81). Home: Ideal Villa Sub Div 158 Janapas Dr Hwy 61 S Hannibal MO 64301-9603 Office: 1 Levering Ln Hannibal MO 63401-9603

THOMPSON, SANDRA ANNEAR, linguistics educator; b. Cleve., July 6, 1941. BA in Linguistics, Ohio State U., 1963, MA, 1965, PhD, 1969. Instr. linguistics Ohio State U., Columbus, 1965-66; instr. English Binat. Lang. Ctr., Taipei, Republic of China, summer 1966; asst. prof. linguistics UCLA, 1968-74, assoc. prof., 1974-78, prof., 1978-86; prof. U. Calif., Santa Barbara, 1986—; vis. asst. prof. linguistics Linguistic Inst., Linguistic Soc. Am., Ohio State U., Columbus, summer 1970, vis. assoc. prof., SUNY, Oswego, summer 1976, prof., UCLA, summer 1983; cons. Info. Scis. Inst., U. So. Calif., Los Angeles, 1982—. Assoc. editor North-Holland Linguistics Series, 1977-80, Studies in Language companion series, 1979—; Lang., 1976-79, Studies in Lang., 1977—, Papers in Linguistics, 1980-84; co-editor: Discourse Perspectives on Grammar series; mem. editorial bd.: Pragmatics and Beyond series, 1988—; U. Calif. Publs. in Lingusitics series, 1983—, Papers in Pragmatics, 1986—; contbr. articles to profl. jours. Recipient Disting. Teaching award UCLA Alumni Assn., 1984; grantee NSF, 1976-80, 80-82, Am. Philos. Soc., 1977-78, U.S. Office Edn., 1977-79, Wenner-Gren Found., 1983—; Netherlands Inst. for Advanced Study fellow, 1984-85, Guggenheim fellow, 1988—. Address: U Calif Santa Barbara Santa Barbara CA 93106

THOMPSON, STACY JO, food brokerage company executive; b. Mpls., Apr. 24, 1958; d. H.A. and Violet (Calhoun) T.; m. Clark David Champeau, Dec. 19, 1987. BA, Gustavus Adolphus Coll., 1980; MA in Psychology, Mankato (Minn.) State U., 1986. Behavioral analyst Christian Concern Inc., Mankato, 1977-79; regional sales mgr. No. Star Co., Mpls., 1979-83; nat. sales mgr. Med-Diet Labs., Mpls., 1982-84; indsl. sales mgr. Lampson and Tew Brokerage Co., Mpls., 1984-87; territorial sales mgr. Nabisco Brands, Mpls., 1987—; ind. contractor, cons. Sol-nuts Inc., St. Joseph, Wis., 1986—; cons. small cos. in food industry, 1986—. Active Aid to Retarded Citizens. Mem. Nat. Assn. Female Execs., Am. Assn. Cereal Chemists, Indsl. Food Technologists, Minn. Indsl. Suppliers Assn. Republican. Lutheran.

THOMPSON, SUSAN LYNNE, cosmetics executive; b. Flint, Mich., Apr. 30, 1950; d. John Seth and Doris Adelia (Almeling) T. BS in Edn., Cen. Mich. U., 1971; MFA, Eastern Mich. U., 1974; diploma in art, Universita Per Straneri, Perugia, Italy, 1972; postgrad., Princeton Theol. Sem., 1987—. Art tchr. Lapeer (Mich.) Pub. Sch. System, 1974-75; beauty advisor Estée Lauder, Inc., Chgo., 1975-77; acct. coordinator Estée Lauder, Inc., Peoria, Ill., 1977-78; acct. exec. Estée Lauder, Inc., St. Louis, 1978-81; regional mktg. mgr. Estée Lauder, Inc., Oklahoma City, 1981-86; regional acct. mgr. Estée Lauder, Inc., St. Louis, 1986—; instr. art therapy Oak Theraputic Sch., Chgo., 1975-76. Recipient 1st Place award Flint Inst. Art, 1972; named one of Outstanding Young Women Am., 1983. Republican. Presbyterian. Home: 306 Emmons Apt 7B Princeton NJ 08540 Office: Estée Lauder Inc 252 A Greenyard Dr Ballwin MO 63011

THOMPSON, TARA DENISE, advertising professional; b. Borger, Tex., June 7, 1962; d. Sammy Jo and Jeannean (Johansen) T. AA, Tex. State Tech. Inst., 1982. Art dir. Dalco Athletic Lettering, Garland, Tex., 1983-85; office mgr. Jean West Enterprises, Dallas, 1985-86; dept. adminstr. Dean Witter Reynolds, Inc., Dallas, 1986-87; info. specialist, pub. relations asst. Anderson Fischel Advt., Dallas, 1986-87, supr. info. ctr., asst. prodn., 1987—. Mem. Nat. Assn. Female Execs. Office: Anderson Fischel 5151 Belt Line Rd #700 Dallas TX 75240

THOMPSON, TINA DIANE, editor; b. Los Angeles, Aug. 20, 1950; d. Gordon W. Thompson and F. Eileen (Knoles) Thompson-Baschky; m. Rainer Freytag, Aug. 17, 1985. BA in Journalism, Calif. State U., Long Beach, 1976. Editorial asst. Systems and Energy and Quest Mags. TRW, Redondo Beach, Calif., 1977-78, assoc. editor Systems and Energy Mag., 1978-81, assoc. editor Quest Mag., 1978-84, editor Editions, Tech. Briefs, 1983-84; promotional writer TRW Mktg. Communications, Redondo Beach, 1984-85; editor TRW Space Log, Redondo Beach, 1985—; v.p. pub. relations Sounds of Space Group, San Bernardino, Calif., 1985—. Author: We've Proven It Can Fly, 1987; author, producer (records) Sounds of Saturn, 1982, Sounds of Space, 1985; contbr. articles to profl. jours. Recipient Pro award Los Angeles Publicity Club, 1981, Maggie award West Coast Mag. Pubs., Manhattan Beach, Calif., 1981. Mem. Internat. Assn. Bus. Communicators (Gold Quill award 1980, Helios award 1984), Aviation Space Writers Assn. (Co. Communications award 1979), Sigma Delta Chi. Office: TRW Space and Tech One Space Park Redondo Beach CA 90278

THOMPSON, VICKIE LEE, construction materials company executive; b. Lincoln, Nebr., Oct. 15, 1950; d. Gilbert Lyle Thompson and Lila Mae (Camp) Fuller; 1 child, Julia Morgan. BA, San Diego State U., 1976. Sales sec. Millard (Nebr.) Lumber Co., 1969-72; sales asst. Am. Forest Products Co., National City, Calif., 1972-74; wood products mgr. Flintkote Supply Co. subs. Genstar, San Diego, 1976-81; coordinator, contractor sales Wickes Lumber Co., Las Vegas, 1982; mgr. Desert Wholesale Co., Las Vegas, Nev., 1982-84; mng. ptnr. Sun Bldg. Materials, Las Vegas, 1984—. Mem. Nat. Assn. Women in Constrn. (treas. 1984-85), Credit Mgrs. Assn., Western States Roofing Contractors Assn. Office: Sun Bldg Materials 4770 W Reno Ave Las Vegas NV 89118

THOMPSON, VIRGINIA ELIZABETH, city official; b. Greensburg, Pa., July 18, 1919; d. Michael Rocco and Louise Margaret (Occhiuzzi) Santoro; m. Murrell Robert Thompson, Apr. 7, 1942 (dec.); children—Sharon Virginia, Murrell Robert Jr. Cert. mcpl. clk. Office mgr. Thomas Drug Store, Greensburg, Pa., 1937-46, O'Malley Builders Hardware, Phoenix, Pa., 1961-68; co-owner The Triangle, Latrobe, Pa., 1946-59; clk. City of Tempe, Ariz., 1968-78, 82—. Author: City of Tempe Records Management Manual, 1984, City of Tempe Legislative History (software), 1986, City of Tempe Election Officers Manual, 1988. Mem. adv. bd. Tempe Salvation Army, 1975-78,d. dirs. ARC, 1982-85; mem. exec. bd. Theodore Roosevelt council Boy Scouts Am., 1975-78; mem. Tempe Hist. Soc., 1975—; charter mem. Fine Arts Ctr. of Tempe, 1982—; sec. Tempe Sister City Corp., 1969-78, historian, 1982—. Bd. dirs. East Valley Cath. Social Services Agy., 1987—. Recipient spl. award Bob Finch Post Am. Legion, Tempe, 1972. Mem. Internat. Inst. Mcpl. Clks. (bd. dirs. 1978), Ariz. Mcpl. Clks. Assn. (pres. 1974-76), Am. Bus. Women's Assn. (sec. 1974-75, v.p. 1976-77; Woman of Yr. 1972). Roman Catholic. Club: Ladies Sodality. Lodges: Zonta (v.p. 1985-86, pres. 1986-87), Ladies Aux. Elks. Avocations: genealogy, reading, music, antiques collecting. Office: City of Tempe 31 E 5th St PO Box 5002 Tempe AZ 85281

THOMPSON, VIVIAN OPAL, nurse; b. Lebanon, Va., Nov. 30, 1925; d. Luther Smith and Cora Belle (Baugh) Thompson; R.N., Knoxville (Tenn.) Gen. Hosp., 1947. Supr. obstetrical dept. Knoxville Gen. Hosp., 1947-48; gen. duty nurse Clinch Valley Clinic Hosp., Richlands, Va., 1948-52, supr., 1957-61, 68-78, 78—; indsl. nurse, Morocco, Africa, 1952-56; charge nurse Bluefield Sanitarium, W.Va., 1961-65, Rochingham Meml. Hosp., Harrisonburg, Va., 1965-68. Democrat. Presbyterian. Home: 205 Pennsylvania Ave Richlands VA 24641

THOMPSON, YVONNE ELIZABETH, business executive; b. Charleston, S.C., Jan. 10, 1948; d. Lurie Darwin and Constance (Morrison) Thompson. B.A. in Polit. Sci., Fisk U., 1969; M.B.A., U. Calif.-Berkeley, 1975. Gen. mgr. Ventures Mgmt. Co., San Francisco, 1974-75; pres. The Venture Group, Inc., San Francisco, 1975-80; pres. Puget Sound Pet Supply Co., Oakland, Calif., 1976-80; v.p. Fulcrum Venture Capital Co., Washington, 1980-81; v.p. mktg. Gen. R.R. Equipment & Services, Inc., East St. Louis, Ill., 1981—; participant Career Pathfinders, St. Louis pub. schs. 1986—. Mem. Gov.'s Club, Springfield, Ill., 1984—; bd. dirs. Arthritis Found., St. Louis, 1985—; mem. adv. council U.S. SBA, 1979-80; vice chmn. Minority and Female Bus. Enterprise Council, Chgo., 1984-86; mem. small bus. com. Minority Bus. Brain Trust, Ho. of Reps., Washington, 1979—. Mem. Nat. Assn. Female Execs., Profl. Women in Constrn., NAACP, Alpha Kappa Alpha. Club: Citizens for Thompson. Avocations: art collecting; travel; skiing; tennis. Home: 4501 Lindell Blvd Saint Louis MO 63108 Office: Gen RR Equipment & Services Inc PO Box 159 East Saint Louis IL 62202

THOMPSON-BOCA, RUTH ANN, mortgage service company executive; b. Long Beach, Calif., Sept. 2, 1955. Student pub. high sch., Anaheim, Calif. Buyer, merchandiser Chic Accessories, Lakewood, Calif., 1974-81; exec. recruiter Appleton & Assocs., Newport Beach, Calif., 1981-82, Exec. Search and Placement, Lakewood, Calif., 1982-83; owner, pres. Desert Document Services, Inc., Tempe, 1983—, The Mortgage Banking Inst., Inc., Tempe, 1984—; also bd. dirs. The Mortgage Banking Inst., Inc.; exec. recruiter Corp. Job Bank, Inc. (subs. Desert Document Services, Inc.), Tempe, Ariz., 1987—. Recipient Cert. of Completion First Interstate Bank, 1983, Keye Prodn. Ctr., 1986. Mem. Nat. Assn. Women Bus Owners, Assn. Profl. Mortgage Women, Young Mortgage Bankers Assn., Ariz. Mortgage Bankers Assn., Mortgage Bankers Assn. of Am. Office: Desert Document Services Inc 455 S 48th St Suite 108 Tempe AZ 85281

THOMSEN, JEAN LOUISE, real estate agent, artist, writer; b. Williamsport, Pa., June 9, 1931; d. Alfred Robert and Ivy Mariam (Middleton) Miller; m. Stephen John Thomsen, Dec. 27, 1970; children—Denise Raymond Barnes, Suzette Nunez; stepchildren—Kari Thomsen, Elizabeth Thomsen. B.A., Vassar Coll., 1976; M.A., State Coll. New Paltz, 1980. Tchr. art City of Poughkeepsie Sch., N.Y., 1977-78; manpower program coordinator Dutchess County Office Human Resources, 1978-83; pub. assistance examiner Dutchess County Dept. Social Services, 1983-84; real estate sales/agt. N.J. Anderson Assocs., Fountain Hills, Ariz., 1985—; tchr. oil painting, 1987—; writer, acquisitions Eleanor Roosevelt's Val Kill, Hyde Park, N.Y., 1981-85. Exhibited Plaza Gallery, Scottsdale, 1988—; exhibited in several juried art shows. Rep. Com. on Handicapping and Affirmative Action, 1978-84; mem. Vassar Coll. Friends of Art Gallery, Poughkeepsie, 1975—; sec. Rural Dutchess Econ. Devel. Corp., Poughkeepsie, 1983—; coordinator Fountain Hills Art League; docent Scottsdale Ctr. for theArts, 1987-88. Mem. N.Y. State Bd. Realtors, Scottsdale Artists League, Dutchess County Art Assn. (past bd. dirs.), Nat. Writers Club. Club: Vassar (Poughkeepsie) (area rep.). Home: 16119 E Cholla Dr Fountain Hills AZ 85268

THOMSEN, PAULA JOAN, account executive; b. Long Beach, Calif., Dec. 1, 1961; d. Peter Steven Polchert and Joan Marilyn (Perrin) Rockwell; m. Mark Thomas Thomsen, Jan. 17, 1981 (div. Jan. 1987), 1 child, Abby Marie. Student, Calif. State U., 1979-80, Inst. Children Lit., Conn., 1987—. Dist. mgr. sales Olan Mills, Inc., Scottsdale, Ariz., 1982-84; mgr. retail merchandising Max Factor and Co., Hollywood, Calif., 1984-87; sr. account exec. Transworld Systems, Inc., Long Beach, Calif., 1987—. Active mem. PTA, Long Beach, 1986—, World Wildlife Fund, Washington, 1986—. Mem. Nat. Assn. Female Execs., Cousteau Soc., Smithsonian Assn, Amnesty Internat., Met. Mus. Art. Republican. Roman Catholic. Home: 822 E Carson St Long Beach CA 90807-2903 Office: Transworld Systems Inc 3605 Long Beach Blvd Suite 332 Long Beach CA 90807

THOMSON, BARBARA PARKER, accountant; b. Bklyn., Dec. 11, 1940; d. Sidney and Eve (Rabinowitz) Schiffman; m. Samuel Robert Parker, Sept. 10, 1960 (div. 1971); children: Jean, Steven, Arthur; m. Malcolm Thomson, June 24, 1979. BA, U. Denver, 1964; MBA, NYU, 1977. CPA, N.Y. Acctg. audit supr. Coopers & Lybrand, N.Y.C., 1977—; treas., bd. dirs. 120 Owners Corp., N.Y.C., 1985-87. Treas. Fund for the Translation of Jewish Lit., N.Y.C., 1986—. Mem. Am. Inst. CPA's, N.Y. State Soc. CPA's. Republican. Jewish. Home: 120 Central Park S New York NY 10019 Office: Coopers & Lybrand 1251 Ave of the Americas New York NY 10020

THOMSON, GRACE MARIE, nurse, minister; b. Pecos, Tex., Mar. 30, 1932; d. William McKinley and Elzora (Wilson) Olliff; m. Radford Chaplin, Nov. 3, 1952; children—Deborah C. Thomson Meshirer, William Earnest. Assoc. Applied Sci., Odessa Coll., 1965; extension student U. Pa. Sch. Nursing, U. Calif.-Irvine, Golden West Coll. RN, Calif., Okla., Ariz., Md., Tex. Dir. nursing Grays Nursing Home, Odessa, Tex., 1965; supr. nursing Med. Hill, Oakland, Calif.; charge nurse pediatrics Med. Ctr., Odessa; dir. nursing Elmwood Extended Care, Berkeley, Calif.; surg. nurse Childrens Hosp., Berkeley; med-surg. charge nurse Merritt Hosp., Oakland, Calif.; adminstr. Grace and Assocs.; active Watchtower and Bible Tract Soc.; evangelist for Jehovah's Witnesses, 1954—.

THOMSON, THYRA GODFREY, former state official; b. Florence, Colo., July 30, 1916; d. John and Rosalie (Altman) Godfrey; m. Keith Thomson, Aug. 6, 1939 (dec. Dec. 1960); children—William John, Bruce Godfrey, Keith Coffey. B.A. cum laude, U. Wyo., 1939. With dept. agronomy and agrl. econs. U. Wyo., 1938-39; writer weekly column Watching Washington pub. in 14 papers, Wyo., 1955-60; planning chmn. Nat. Fedn. Republican Women, Washington, 1961; sec. state Wyo. Cheyenne, 1962-86; mem. Marshall Scholarships Com. for Pacific region, 1964-68; del. 72d Wilton Park Conf., Eng., 1965; mem. youth commn. UNESCO, 1970-71, Allied Health Professions Council HEW, 1971-72; del. U.S.-Republic of China Trade Conf., Taipei, Taiwan, 1983; mem. lt. gov.'s trade and fact-finding mission to Saudi Arabia, Jordan, and Egypt, 1985. Recipient Disting. Alumni award U. Wyo., 1969, Disting. U. Wyo. Arts and Scis. Alumna award, 1987; named Internat. Woman of Distinction, Alpha Delta Kappa; recipient citation Omicron Delta Epsilon, 1965, citation Beta Gamma Sigma, 1968, citation Delta Kappa Gamma, 1973, citation Wyo. Commn. Women, 1986. Mem. N.Am. Securities Adminstrs. (pres. 1973-74), Nat. Assn. Secs. of State, Council State Govts. (chmn. natural resources com. Western states 1966-68), Nat. Conf. Lt. Govs. (exec. com. 1976-79). Home: 3102 Sunrise Rd Cheyenne WY 82001

THOMSON, VIRGINIA WINBOURN, history educator, author; b. Oakland, Calif., Aug. 6, 1930; d. Harry Linn and Jennie Cook (Vineyard) T. A.A., San Mateo Coll., 1948; B.A., San Jose State Coll., 1951; M.A., U. Calif.-Berkeley, 1952. Cert. secondary tchr., Calif. Social sci. tchr. Capuchino High Sch., San Bruno, Calif., 1952-54, Watsonville High Sch., Calif., 1954-87; saleswoman and storyteller Home Interiors, San Mateo, 1963-64. Author: The Lion Desk, 1965; Short Talks Around The Lord's Table, 1985. Recipient Silver Pitcher award Home Interiors, 1964. Mem. Nat. Geog. Soc. (life), AAUW (life), Nat. Writers Club Christian Writers Guild, Calif. Alumni Assn. (life), Phi Alpha Theta. Republican.

THOMSON-KEITH, ELAINE AUDREY, nurse, hospital administrator; b. Portage la Prairie, Man., Can., Oct. 2, 1939; came to U.S., 1961; d. Melvin George and Iverna Mary (Hall) T.; m. Samuel Roddey Keith, July 2, 1983. Diploma in nursing Children's Hosp., Winnipeg, Man.; B.S. in Nursing, Tex. Woman's U.-Houston. R.N., Man., Mo., Mich., Tex. Staff nurse Children's Hosp., Winnipeg, 1960-61; supr. operating room and recovery room Children's Mercy Hosp., Kansas City, Mo., 1961-62, asst. dir. nursing, 1967-72; asst. head nurse Baylor U. Med. Ctr., Dallas, 1962-63; head nurse Univ. Hosp., Ann Arbor, Mich., 1965-67; adminstrv. supr. Methodist Hosp., Houston, 1977—, coordinator and tchr. cert. classes for nurses, 1979; presentations in field. Vol. for blood pressure screening and teaching Greater Houston area Am. Heart Assn., 1976—; CPR instr. and trainer, Houston, 1979—. Named Outstanding Houston Profl. Woman, Fedn. Houston Profl. Women, 1983. Mem. Am. Nurses Assn. (council nursing adminstrn. 1983—), Assn. Operating Room Nurses (cert.; charter mem. and chmn. Southfield chpt. 1965-67, com. chmn. Greater Kansas City chpt. 1963-64, dir. Greater Kansas City chpt. 1967-73, com. chmn. Greater Houston chpt. 1974-76, 77-78, 80-81, 83-84, pres. Greater Houston chpt. 1982-83, chmn. nat. com. on edn. 1981-82, chmn. nat. congress planning com. 1983, nat. dir. 1984-86, nat. nursing practices com. 1987—), Am. Nurses Found. Century Club, Lion's Eye Bank (life). Republican. Presbyterian. Home: 702 Woodhorn Ct Houston TX 77062 Office: Meth Hosp 6565 Fannin Houston TX 77030

THON, MARSHA LORRAINE, protocol specialist; b. Waltham, Mass., July 7, 1941; d. Harold R. and Geraldine Gile; married; 1 child, Ann Thomas. AA, Pierce Bus. Coll., 1961; BA in Bus. and Psychology, Boston U., 1963; postgrad., Calif. State U., UCLA, U. So. Calif. Interpreter internat. div. First Nat. Bank of Boston, 1960-61; salesperson, mktg. div. Litton Industries, Beverly Hills, Calif., 1961-71; counselor, dir. admissions, dir. The Fashion Inst. of Design and Merchandising, Los Angeles, 1972-87; owner, pres. Let's Begin with the Basics, Newhall, Calif., 1987—; cons., speaker, educator Henry Mayo Newhall (Calif.) Meml. Hosp., 1987—; speaker numerous colls., high schs., clubs, orgns. Active Santa Clarita Valley Coll. Of Canyons. Mem. Nat. Assn. Bus. Execs., Nat. Assn. Female Execs., Leads Club, Santa Clarita Valley C. of C., Beta Sigma Phi. Republican. Lodge: Soroptimist.

THOR, LINDA M., college president; b. Los Angeles, Feb. 21, 1950; d. Karl Gustav and Mildred Dorrine (Hofius) T.; m. Robert Paul Huntsinger, Nov. 22, 1974; children: Erik, Marie. BA, Pepperdine U., 1971, EdD, 1986; MPA, Calif. State U., Los Angeles, 1980. Dir. pub. info. Pepperdine U., Los Angeles, 1971-73; pub. info. officer Los Angeles Community Coll. Dist., 1974-75, dir. communications, 1975-81, dir. edn. services, 1981-82, dir. high tech., 1982-83, sr. dir. occupational and tech. edn., 1983-86; pres. West Los Angeles Coll., Culver City, Calif., 1986—; bd. dirs. Calif. Industry Edn. Council, West Los Angeles Coll. Found., Tech. Exchange Ctr. Editor: Curriculum Design and Development for Effective Learning, 1973; author: (with others) Effective Media Relations, 1982. Recipient Delores award for Outstanding Contbn. to Edn. Pepperdine U., 1986, Alumni Medal of Honor, Pepperdine U., 1987. Mem. Calif. Community Colls. Chief Exec. Officers, Calif. Community Colls. Occupational Edn. Coalition, Culver City C. of C. (bd. dirs. 1986—). Lodge: Optimists. Office: West Los Angeles Coll 4800 Freshman Dr Culver City CA 90230

THORBURN, KIM MARIE, internist, educator; b. San Francisco, May 11, 1950; d. Jack Donald and Margaret Marie (Carpenter) T. BA, Stanford U.,

1971; MD, U. Calif., San Francisco, 1976. Diplomate Am. Bd. Internal Medicine. Intern Highland Gen. Hosp., Oakland, Calif., 1976-77, resident in internal medicine, 1977-78; resident in internal medicine U. Calif., San Francisco, 1978-79, asst. clin. prof., 1979-84; asst. clin. prof. medicine U. Calif., Irvine, 1984-87; assoc. prof. U. Hawaii, 1987—; physician Jail Med. Services, San Francisco, 1979-80; staff physician Calif. State Prison, San Quentin, 1980-83, Calif. Instn. for Men, Chino, 1983-84; chief med. officer Calif. Rehab. Ctr., Norco, 1985, Calif. Instn. for Men, Chino, 1986-87; med. dir. Hawaii Dept. of Corrections, 1987—; cons. Task Force Licensure of Correctional Med. Facilities, Calif. Bd. Corrections, 1983, panel on irritant chems. Nat. Acad. Scis., Washington, 1983; chmn. plenary session panel World Congress Prison Health Services, 1983; seminar chmn. Nairobi Forum End of Decade of Women, 1985. Contbr. articles on prison medicine and riot control methods to profl. jours. Advisor Amnesty Internat., 1982—. Recipient cert. of appreciation Men's Adv. Council of San Quentin Prison, 1982; winner awards in surfing; Kellogg Nat. Leadership fellow, 1983-86. Fellow ACP; mem. Hawaii Med. Assn., Calif. Med. Assn. (chmn. task force on health care standards for juvenile detention ctrs. 1983-84, chmn. corrections and detentions health care com. 1986-87), Am. Correctional Health Services Assn. (pres. Calif. chpt. 1984, nat. treas. 1985-89), Internat. Council Prison Med. Services (treas.), San Bernardino County Med. Soc., San Francisco Med. Soc. (del. to Calif. Med. Assn. 1983), Honolulu County Med. Soc., Honolulu Orgn. Women Leaders. Democrat. Office: Oahu Community Correctional Ctr 1922 Kamehameha Hwy Honolulu HI 96819 also: Dept Corrections State Hawaii 677 Ala Moana Blvd Honolulu HI 96813

THORN, SUSAN HOWE, interior designer; b. Washington, Apr. 22, 1941; d. James Bennett Cowdin and Lois (Fiesinger) Howe; A.B. cum laude, Syracuse U., 1962; postgrad. N.Y. Sch. Interior Design, 1965, lighting design Parsons Sch. Design, 1975-77; m. William D. Thorn, June 22, 1963; children—Melissa Ann, William David. Owner, designer Susan Thorn Interiors, Inc., Cross River, N.Y., 1965—; designer total bldg. Cooper Labs, Bedford Hills, N.Y., 1973, total redesign Nycrest Corp., Cold Spring, N.Y., 1973-75, showrooms, model rooms stylist and coordinator France Voiles Co. Inc., N.Y.C., 1976, total design new corp. hdqrs. in Gen. Dynamics Bldg. (with Marjorie Borradaile Helsel), Robert E. Eastman Co., N.Y.C., 1967, Cummin & Friedland Capital Corp., 1982; designer offices, stores, employee areas comml., public, residential clients, including Waccabuc (N.Y.) Country Club, 1969, S. Salem (N.Y.) Library; instr. adult edn. dept. John Jay High Sch., Jr. League No. Westchester, Caramoor Mus.; speaker civic orgns. Mem. Am. Soc. Interior Designers (profl.), Internat. Assn. Lighting Designers (asso.). Episcopalian. Club: Waccabuc Country; Decorators (N.Y.C.). Writer weekly decorating column in The Patent Trader, 1965-66; contbr. articles to newspapers. Home: Route 121 Cross River NY 10518

THORNE, LAURA SYLVIA, chef; b. N.Y.C., Mar. 23, 1956; D. Robert B. and Mignon L. (Fendler) T. Student, SUNY, Binghamton, 1974-76, Calif. Culinary Acad., 1981-82. Chef Royale Fish Restaurant, East Hampton, N.Y., 1979-85, Coast Grill Restaurant, Southampton, N.Y., 1985-88; owner C.J. Thorne Restaurant, Bridgehamtpon, N.Y., 1988—; chef, cons. cookbooks. Named one of 10 Am. Female Chefs, Town and Country mag., 1985; featured in Sunday N.Y. Times mag., 1986. Home: 229 Kings Point Rd East Hampton NY 11937 Office: CJ Thorne Restaurant PO Box 1558 Bridgehampton NY 11932

THORNHILL, LOIS, photographer; b. Boston, Apr. 7, 1945; d. Fred S. and Mary (Evans) T.; B.A., Middlebury Coll., 1966; postgrad. U. St. Thomas, Houston, 1967-69; M.A., N.Y. U., 1971; cert. in graphic design U. Calif.-Santa Cruz, 1983; m. Edward J. McCluskey, Feb. 14, 1981. Research technician dept. virology Baylor Sch. Medicine, Houston, 1966-68; with Kelly Girls, Palo Alto, 1971-72; slide curator dept. art Stanford (Calif.) U., 1972-80; founder, pres. Stanford Design Assocs., Palo Alto, 1981—; cons. copy and museum photography; designer, producer custom lecture slides. Mem. Smithsonian Assos., Coll. Art Assn. Am. Home: 895 Northampton Dr Palo Alto CA 94303 Office: PO Box 60451 Palo Alto CA 94306

THORNLOW, CAROLYN, law firm administrator, consultant; b. Kew Gardens, N.Y., May 25, 1954. B.B.A. magna cum laude, Bernard M. Baruch Coll., 1982. Gen. mgr. Richard A. Ramm Assocs., Levittown, N.Y., 1972-78; adminstr. Tunstead Schechter & Torre, N.Y.C., 1978-82, Cowan Liebowitz & Latman, P.C., N.Y.C., 1982-84, Rosenberg & Estis, P.C., N.Y.C., 1984-85; controller Finkelstein, Borah, Schwartz, Altschuler & Goldstein, P.C., N.Y.C., 1986—; pres. Concinnity Services, Hastings, N.Y., 1984—; instr. introduction to law office mgmt. seminars Assn. Legal Adminstrs., N.Y.C., 1984. Contbr. numerous articles to profl. jours. Mem. N.Y. Assn. Legal Adminstrs. (v.p. 1982-83), Internat. Assn. Legal Adminstrs. (asst. regional v.p. 1983-84, regional v.p. 1984-85), Adminstrv. Mgmt. Soc. (cert.), ABA, Mensa, Beta Gamma Sigma, Sigma Iota Epsilon.

THORNTON, CATHERINE LEE, electrical engineer; b. Baton Rouge, Mar. 19, 1938; d. Jess Brooks and Charlene (Roemer) Thomas; m. Thomas Holman Thornton, Apr. 21, 1963; children: Thomas Holman III, Patricia Ann. BA in Math., Vanderbilt U., 1960; MS in Math., Northwestern U., 1961; PhD in Engring., UCLA, 1976. Research engr. Jet Propulsion Lab., Pasadena, 1961-76, mem. tech. staff, 1977-79, mgr. deep space network advanced systems program, 1980-82, dep. mgr. tracking systems and applications sect., 1982—. Contbr. articles to profl. jours. Bd. trustees Arcadia Presbyn. Ch., 1986-89, elder, lay counselor. Mem. IEEE, AIAA, Am. Geophys. Union, Sigma Xi, Phi Beta Kappa.

THORNTON, LINDA, lawyer; b. Salt Lake City, Sept. 16, 1951; d. Bruce G. and Betty (Junker) Thornton; m. Steven A. Broiles, Aug. 29, 1982; 1 child, David Thornton. BA, U. Calif.-Irvine, 1972; JD, Loyola U., Los Angeles, 1976. Bar: Calif. 1977. Dep. dist. counsel South Coast Air Quality Mgmt. Dist., El Monte, Calif., 1977-79; atty. So. Calif. Edison Co., Rosemead, Calif., 1979-80; assoc. firm Best, Best & Krieger, Los Angeles, 1981-83; ptnr. firm Dunne, Phelps, Mills, Stall & McCord, Los Angeles, 1983; assoc. Law Offices Robert L. Baker, Pasadena, Calif., 1983-86. Mem. ABA, Los Angeles County Bar Assn., Bus. Trial Lawyers Assn. Office: 100 North Hill Ave Suite A Pasadena CA 91106

THORNTON, YVONNE SHIRLEY, physician, musician; b. N.Y.C., Nov. 21, 1947; d. Donald E. and Itasker F. (Edmonds) T.; B.S. in Biology, Monmouth Coll., 1969; M.D., Columbia U., 1973; m. Shearwood McClelland, June 8, 1974; children—Shearwood III, Kimberly Itaska. Resident in ob-gyn Roosevelt Hosp., N.Y.C., 1973-77; fellow maternal-fetal medicine Columbia-Presbyn. Med. Center, N.Y.C., 1977-79; commd. lt. comdr. M.C., USN, 1979; asst. prof. ob-gyn Uniformed Services U. Health Scis., 1979-82, Cornell U. Med. Coll., N.Y.C., 1982—; dir. clin. services dept. ob-gyn N.Y. Hosp.-Cornell Med. Center, 1982—; asst. attending N.Y. Lying-In Hosp., 1982—; staff Nat. Naval Med. Center, Bethesda, Md.; saxophonist Thornton Sisters ensemble, 1955-76.; vis. assoc. physician The Rockefeller U. Hosp., 1986—. Diplomate Am. Bd. Ob-Gyn, Nat. Bd. Med. Examiners. Fellow Am. Coll. Obstetricians and Gynecologists, Am. Coll. Surgeons; mem. AMA, N.Y. Acad. Medicine, Am. Fertility Soc., Soc. Perinatal Obstetricians, Am. Fedn. Musicians. Lambda Sigma Tau. Democrat. Baptist. Office: 525 E 68th St New York NY 10021

THORSEN, NANCY DAIN, real estate broker; b. Edwardsville, Ill., June 23, 1944; d. Clifford Earl and Suzanne Eleanor (Kribs) Dain; m. David Massie, 1968 (div. 1975); i dau., Suzanne Dain Massie; m. James Hugh Thorsen, May 30, 1980. B.Sc. in Mktg., So. Ill. U., 1968, M.Sc. in Bus. Edn., 1975; grad. Realtor Inst., Idaho, 1983. Cert. resdl. and investment specialist. Personnel officer J.H. Little & Co. Ltd., London, 1969-72; instr. in bus. edn. Spl. Sch. Dist. St. Louis, 1974-77; mgr. mktg./ops. Isis Foods, Inc., St. Louis, 1978-80; asst. mgr. store Stix, Baer & Fuller, St. Louis, 1980; assoc. broker Century 21 Sayer Realty, Inc., Idaho Falls, Idaho, 1981—. Bd. dirs. Idaho Vol., Boise, 1981-84, Idaho Falls Symphony, 1982; pres. Friends of Idaho Falls Library, 1981-83; chmn. Idaho Falls Mayor's Com. for Vol. Coordination, 1981-84. Recipient Idaho Gov.'s award, 1982, cert. appreciation City of Idaho Falls/Mayor Campbell, 1982, 87; named to Two Million Dollar Club, Three Million Dollar Club, 1987, Century 21 Internat. Gold Assoc. award, 1987; named Top Investment Sales Person for Eastern Idaho, 1985. Mem. Idaho Falls Bd. Realtors (chmn. orientation 1982-83, chmn. edn. 1983), So. Ill. U. Alumni Assn. Clubs: Newcomers, Civitan (Idaho Falls) (Civitan of Yr. 1986, 87). Office: Century 21 Sayer Realty Inc 403 First St PO Box 1606 Idaho Falls ID 83403

THORSON, MARCELYN MARIE, applied art educator; b. Houston, Dec. 18, 1927; d. Oliver Herbert and Helene Marie (Brown) Fritts; m. Edward L. Thorson, June 16, 1956. BS, Pratt Inst., N.Y.C., 1950. Cert. home economist, tech. tchr. Apparel designer Dallas Sportswear Co., 1954-64, Srader Sportswear Co., Dallas, 1964-65; instr., coordinator apparel design program and pattern design program El Centro Coll., Dallas, 1966-88; cons. computer research Camsco, Inc., Richardson, Tex., summer 1976-77; project devel. coordinator state grant Fashion Design Series, North Tex. State U., summer 1978-79, instr. Indsl. Tng. Lab., summer 1978. Instr. Adult Christian Edn. Found., Bethel Bible Series, Luth. Ch., 1965-80. Mem. Costume Soc. Am., AAUW, Am. Home Econs. Assn., Tex. Jr. Coll. Tchrs. Assn., The Fashion Group (edn. com. 1975—, scholarship chmn. 1975-85, dir. fashion mus. 1963-65, Silver Tray award 1965), Assn. Coll. Profs. Textiles and Clothing. Republican. Home: 11229 Lanewood Circle Dallas TX 75218

THOURP, SHERRY YEAGER, television location manager; b. Port Arthur, Tex., Dec. 2, 1942; d. James Elmer and Rosemary (Kaiser) Yeager; m. William B. Thorup Jr., Jan. 26, 1968 (div. Nov. 1985); children: Tammy Lee, William B. III, John Edward, James Ray, Kai Barrett. Degree, Port Arthur (Tex.) Bus. Coll., 1960-61; student, Broward Community Coll., Davie, Fla., 1980. Location mgr. commercials, features, television episodes various television and film production cos., Fla., Mich., Calif., N.Y., 1983—; prod. asst. (television movie) Where The Boys Are Tri-Star ITC Prodns., Hollywood, Calif., 1983; location mgr. (television show) 22 episodes Miami Vice Universal Studios, Miami Beach, Fla., 1984-85; location mgr. (movie) Revenge of the Nerd II: Nerds in Paradise 20th Cent. Fox, Fort Lauderdale, Fla., 1986; profl. still photographer, 1973—. Contbr. photos to various newspapers, mags., 1980—. Com chmn. Beaux Arts Assn., Fort Lauderdale, 1970-77; chmn. bd. dirs. Festamare Sailing Regatta, Fort Lauderdale, 1981-82. Mem. Teamsters Union. Club: Women's Propeller (Fort Lauderdale) (chmn., pres. 1975-78). Home: 2251 SW 27 Ln Fort Lauderdale FL 33312

THRAILKILL, FRANCIS MARIE, college president; b. San Antonio, Sept. 21, 1937; d. Franklin E. and Myrtle M. (Huggins) T. B.A. cum laude, Coll. New Rochelle, N.Y., 1961; M.A., Marquette U., Milw., 1969; Ed.D., Nova U., Ft. Lauderdale, Fla., 1975. Joined Ursuline Order of Sisters, Roman Catholic Ch., 1955; tchr. Ursuline Acad., Dallas, 1961-64; prin. Ursuline Acad., 1970-77; vice prin. Ursuline Acad., New Orleans, 1965-70; pres. Springfield (Ill.) Coll., 1978-87, Coll. of Mt. St. Joseph, Ohio, 1987—. Trustee Western Hamilton County Econ. Council, Found. Ind. Colls.; mem. Leadership Cin.; bd. dirs. Dan Beard Council, Joy Outdoor Edn. Ctr., Community Mut. Blue Cross/Blue Shield. Mem. Assn. Cath. Colls. and Univs., Assn. Governing Bds. of Colls. and Univs., Assn. Ind. Colls. and Univs., Greater Cin. Corsortium Colls., Nat. Assn. Ind. Colls. and Univs., Ohio Bd. Regents, Council Ind. Colls. Office: Coll of Mt St Joseph Office of Pres Mount Saint Joseph OH 45051

THRALL, MARY ANNA HULL, veterinarian; b. Montreal, Que., Can., July 4, 1944; d. John Floyd and Mariella (Godfrey) Hull; B.A., U. Evansville, 1966; D.V.M., Purdue U., 1970; M.S., Colo. State U., 1977; m. F.G. Freemyer, Mar. 21, 1975; children—Joseph Paul, Anna Marie, Sarah Elizabeth, Clarissa Catherine. Pvt. vet. practitioner Eldred Animal Hosp., Greeley, Colo., 1970-74; resident in clin. pathology Colo. State U., Fort Collins, 1974-77; asst. prof. clin. pathology, 1978-84, assoc. prof., 1984—, dir. lab., 1981-84. Mem. Am. Coll. Vet. Pathologists, AVMA, Colo. Vet. Med. Assn., Am. Animal Hosp. Assn., Colo. Vet. Med. Assn., Am. Animal Hosp. Assn., Am. Soc. Vet. Clin. Pathology, Womens Vet. Med. Assn., Colo. Soc. Cytology, Colo. Assn. Continuing Med. Lab. Edn., Am. Soc. Cytotechnology, Assn. Am. Vet. Med. Colls., Phi Kappa Phi, Phi Zeta. Office: Colo State U Dept Pathology Fort Collins CO 80523

THRASHER, LEE-HOPE, real estate broker, municipal official; b. Norfolk, Va., Apr. 30, 1954; d. Harold Morgan and Emma (Reid) T. BA in Sociology, Old Dominion U., 1977. Lic. real estate broker. Eligibility worker Social Services, Chesapeake, Va., 1977-79; counselor Tidewater Regional Group Home Commn., Chesapeake, 1979-82; agt. real estate sales Greenbrier Realty Co. Inc., Chesapeake, 1982-85, real estate broker, 1985—; cons. Real Estate Cons. Inc., Virginia Beach, Va., 1986—; coordinator victims and witnesses Commonwealth Atty.'s Office City of Virginia Beach. Leader 4-H, Chesapeake, 1973—. Mem. Tidewater Bd. Realtors, Va. Bd. Realtors, Nat. Assn. Realtors, Va. Council Social Welfare. Office: Real Estate Cons Inc 1217 Battlefield Blvd N Chesapeake VA 23320

THRESHMAN-VENEGAS, CLARA INEZ, languages consultant, translator, trainer; b. Bogota, Colombia, Mar. 16, 1959; d. Peter Paul and Pauline Diana (Anchique-Abadia) Threshman-Venegas. Degree in Criminal Justice-Law Enforcement, Norwalk Coll., 1978; Degree in Sociology, Sacred Heart U., 1979; degree in Sociology and Spanish, So. Conn. U., 1980; student, Yale U., 1980-82; postgrad., St. Thomas U. Profl. translator Yale U., Saab Scania of N.Am. and Sowers Lewis & Wood Internat. Mgmt. Cons., Conn., 1979-81; ind. instr. English to Latin Am. physicians Yale U., 1984, dir., instr. Med. Spanish Programs, 1982-85; developer, tchr. emergency med. Spanish programs N.E. region USAF Aux., 1985; founder, developer Med. Communications Learning Ctr.-Sch. Medicine U. Miami, Fla. Author: (books, cassettes and manuals) Emergency Medical Spanish Program Levels I and II, 1985. Mem. The Bach Soc. Miami. Mem. Nat. Assn. Female Execs., Am. Translation Assn., Linguistic Soc. Am., Literary Market Place. Republican. Roman Catholic. Clubs: Alliance Française, German Am. Office: 7925 NW 12th St Suite 111 Miami FL 33126

THROOP, BEATRICE TERRY, educator; b. Raymond, Ill.; d. John Charles and Therese (Mathis) Terry; B.E., Ill. State U., 1930; M.S. (fellow), U. Chgo., 1938; postgrad. U. Oreg., summer 1939, Oreg. State U., summer 1953, Colo. U., summers 1955-56, U. Caen (France), summers 1965-66, U. Md., summer 1963, 65-66; m. Vincent Medville Throop, May 29, 1940 (dec. Oct. 1968); children—Medville Jay, Alice Milberry, David Edmund, Annette Beatrice, Vincent Julian. Tchr., Lima (Peru) High Sch., Women's Fgn. Missionary Soc. of Meth. Ch., 1930-36; instr. Stephens Coll., 1938-40; tchr. public schs., Portland (Oreg.) Air Base, 1941; bibliographer Library of Congress, Washington, 1960-61; tchr. Prince George's County Schs., Brandywine, Md., 1961-77; George Washington U., summers 1967-69, 73-74. Bd. dirs. Suitland Manor Owners Assn., 1981—, sec., 1984—. Mem. AAUW, Assn. Am. Geographers, NEA, Md. Edn. Assn., Prince George's County Tchrs. Assn., Am. Assn. Tchrs. Spanish and Portuguese, Alliance Francaise, Sigma Delta Epsilon. Contbr. articles to local publs. Home: 6100 Westchester Park Dr #1104 College Park MD 20740

THROWER, MELODY MARCUM, manufacturing company executive; b. Norman, Okla., Aug. 23, 1953; d. Leroy Jr. and Laquawana Sherry (McClure) Marcum; m. Alan Linn Thrower, June 16, 1972 (div. Sept. 1984); 1 child, Marca Lee. Student, U. Okla., 1971-73, 76-83. Lic. real estate broker. Ptnr. Alan Thrower Oil and Gas Co., Norman, 1979—; asst. to athletic ticket mgr. U. Okla., Norman, 1979-84; asst. mgr. ops. Smith Barney Harris Upham Co., Oklahoma City, 1984-86; adminstr. Tankless Water Works Inc., Norman, 1986-87, v.p., 1987—. Fund raiser Norman Regional Hosp.; vol., worker Dem. Campaign, Cleveland County, Okla., 1986; spl. project panel Moore-Norman Vocat. Sch., 1986; mem. Assistance League Norman. Mem. Nat. Assn. for Female Execs., Nat. Collegiate Coll. Assn. (Award Merit 1979), Norman C. of C. Club: Varsity "O" (Norman) (sec. 1975-84). Office: PO Box 1713 Norman OK 73070

THRYFT, ANN R., marketing communications manager; b. San Francisco, Dec. 22, 1950; d. William Boyd and Margaret Evelyn (Wilson) T.; m. Alfred Stephens Nelson, May 15, 1971 (div. 1983); m. Mark J. Tussman, Mar. 2, 1985 (div. 1988). BA in Anthropology, Stanford U., 1976. Cert. bus. communicator U.S.A. Mktg. communications specialist Franklin Electric, Sunnyvale, Calif., 1981-82; advt. specialist Lear Siegler Inc., Menlo Park, Calif., 1982-83; mktg. communications mgr. Buscom Systems, Santa Clara, Calif., 1983-84; corp. communications mgr. Nat. Tech. Systems, Calabasas, Calif., 1985-86; mktg. communications mgr. FORTH, Inc., Manhattan Beach, Calif., 1986—; cons. in field. Contbr. article to profl. jour. Mem. Bus.-Profl. Advt. Assn. (bd. dirs. 1987-88), Stanford Alumni Assn., Publicity Club of Los Angeles, Phi Beta Kappa. Avocations: hist. research, researching religious history, poetry, writing fiction. Office: FORTH Inc 111 N Sepulveda Manhattan Beach CA 90266

THUEN, JUDY MORGON, chemist, editor; b. Pasadena, Calif., Nov. 30, 1953; d. Ralph Eugene and Loretta Clementine (Bray) Morgon; m. Eric Thuen, June 19, 1976. AA, Pasadena City Coll., 1974; BS in Biol. Scis., U. Calif., Irvine, 1976, BA in Psychology, 1976. Chemist Diamond Shamrock, Redwood City, Calif., 1976-78; chemist II Narmco Materials/Celanese, Costa Mesa, Calif., 1978-81; chief fin. officer Applied Polymer Tech., Inc., Carlsbad, Calif., 1980-84; database mgr., editor, publisher Internat. Plastics Selector, Inc., San Diego, 1985—; cons. Xscribe Corp., San Diego, 1986. Patentee in field. Mem. Soc. Plastics Industry, Soc. Plastics Engrs., Soc. Advancement Materials and Process Engring., Nat. Assn. Female Execs., Nat. Shorthand Reporters Assn. Republican. Office: IPS 9889 Willow Creek Rd San Diego CA 92126

THUESTAD, LORI LYNN, small business owner; b. Elgin, Ill., June 21, 1957; d. Harry Ashbaugh and Patricia Ann (Porter) Burnidge; m. Ronald Bernard Thuestad, Jan. 26, 1981; children: Rebecca Ann, Patricia Ann. Grad. high sch., Elgin, 1975. lic. real estate, 1987. Pres., owner Ashbaugh Stable, Elgin, 1975—; rep. sales Pace Constrn. Co., Elgin, 1986—; co-mgr. horse shows Impressive Farm, Elgin, 1984—. Republican. Roman Catholic. Home: 1594 Mark Ave Elgin IL 60123 Office: Pace Constrn Co 450 Shepard Dr Elgin IL 60123

THURBER, MARY B. O'DELL, multiple association executive, political consultant, writer; b. Columbus, Nebr., Aug. 28, 1930; d. Harry C. and Helen A. (Cherny) Brown; m. Robert A. O'Dell, July 26, 1953 (div.); children—Christopher, Mark, Paul; m. Marvin D. Thurber, Aug. 30, 1986. B.A. in Elem. Edn., U. Colo., 1952, Tchr. elem. pub. schs., Kirkwood, Mo., 1952-55; news editor Aurora (Colo.) Sun, 1972-76; cons. various Congl. coms., 1976—; exec. dir. Colo. Assn. Tobacco and Candy Distbrs., 1977—, Colo. Assn. Indsl. Bankers, 1982—, Colo. Fin. Services Assn., Denver, 1982—; exec. dir. Okla. Assn. Tobacco and Candy Distbrs., 1985—; cons. pub. relations; dir. Consumer Credit Counseling Service; dir. Sec. State's Bus. Adv. Council. Pres. Aurora JayCee-ettes, 1960; citywide chmn. March of Dimes, 1961; chmn. bd. dirs. Metro Denver Sewage Disposal Dist. No. 1, 1974-76, dir., 1967-86; mem. Colo. Com. on Women, 1974, Aurora Citizens Adv. Budget Com., 1980-81; bd. dirs. Home Neighborly Service; mem. Arapahoe County Republican Exec. Com., 1974-81, 85-86; pres. Aurora Rep. Women's Club, 1974-76; vice chmn. 62d state rep. dist., 1982-83. Named Colo. TAN activist of Yr., Tobacco Inst., 1980, 82; recipient J. Ernest O'Brien Meml. award Nat. Assn. Tobacco Distbrs., 1981; Leo Marks award Colo. Assn. Tobacco and Candy Distbrs., 1986; key to City of Aurora City Council, 1976. Mem. Colo., Soc. Assn. Execs., Am. Soc. Assn. Execs., P.E.O., AAUW, LWV, Pi Lambda Theta, Tau Beta Sigma. Presbyterian. Avocations: music, swimming, reading mysteries. Home: 2848 S Kenton Ct Aurora CO 80014 Office: 1390 Logan St Suite 304 Denver CO 80203

THURMAN, JUDITH, writer; b. N.Y.C., Oct. 28, 1946; d. William A. and Alice (Meisner) T. B.A., Brandeis U., 1967. Adj. lectr. CUNY, Bklyn. Coll., 1973—. Author: (poetry) Putting My Coat On, 1972, Flashlight, 1976, (biography) Isak Dinesen: The Life of a Storyteller, 1982 (Am. Book award 1983), (essays) I Became Alone, 1975, (children's book) Lost and Found, 1978, The Magic Lantern: How Movies Got to Move, 1979; editor: (with Lilian Moore) To See the World Afresh, 1974; contbr. articles to profl. jours. NEH fellow, 1980. *

THURMAN, KAREN, state senator; b. Rapid City, S.D., Jan. 12, 1951; d. Lee Searle and Donna (Altfillisch) Loveland; m. John Patrick Thurman, 1973; children—McLin Searl and Liberty Lee. B.A., U. Fla., 1973. Mem. Dunnellon City Council (Fla.), 1974-82; mayor of Dunnellon, 1979-81; mem. Monroe Regional Med. Ctr. Governancy Com.; mem. Comprehensive Plan Tech. Adv. Com.; del. Fla. Democratic Conv.; Dem. Nat. Conv., 1980; mem. Regional Energy Action com.; mem. Fla. State Senate, 1982—. Recipient Service Above Self award Dunnellon C. of C., 1980; Regional Planning Council Appreciation for Service award. Mem. Dunnellon C. of C. (dir.), Fla. Horseman's Children's Soc. (charter). Episcopalian. Office: Fla Senate State Capitol Tallahassee FL 32301 *

THWEATT, CAROL FRANCES, lawyer; b. Memphis, Sept. 16, 1944; d. Russell E. and Serene (Swords) T.; divorced; children: Rachel, Jeffrey. BA, Memphis State U., 1966; JD, U. Miss., 1981. Bar: Miss. 1981. Bur. chief The Comml. Appeal, Memphis, 1966; editorial asst. Ill. Cen. R.R., Chgo., 1966-68; staff atty. clin. programs Univ. Miss. Law Ctr., University, 1982, coordinator legal info. and referral for elderly, 1982-85; spl. asst. atty. gen. Office of Atty. Gen., Jackson, Miss., 1985-86; sr. atty. State of Miss. Dept. Mental Health, Jackson, 1986—. Mem. Neshoba County Bar Assn. (pres. 1981), So. Inst. Aging (bd. dirs.), So. Gerontol. Soc. (program com.), Phi Alpha Delta. Republican. Presbyterian. Office: Dept Mental Health 1500 Woolfolk Bldg Jackson MS 39201

THWEATT, KATHRYN ANN, public relations executive; b. Little Rock, Oct. 14, 1952; d. George B. and Elizabeth Sue (Walker) T.; children: Steven Dandridge, Laura Angeline. BA in pub. relations and mass communications, William Jewell Coll., 1984. Owner Just Tennis, Lafayette, La., 1973-78; aerobic instr. Rhythmic Aerobics, Little Rock, 1979-82; pub. relations mgr. Kansas City (Mo.) Conv. and Visitors Bur., 1983-87; pub. relations and mktg. mgr. Shreveport (La.)-Bossier Conv. and Tourist Bur., 1985—; publicity dir. Super Derby Festival, Shreveport and Bossier, 1985—; pub. relations chairperson S.E. Tourism Soc., Atlanta, 1986—; 1988 spl. events mgr. Ga's Stone Mountain Park. Writer, cons. Super Derby Festival mag., 1985-87; dir., writer: (audio visual show) Rollin' Out the Red, 1986 (Image award 1986). Mem. publicity com. Sesquicentennial Commn., Shreveport, 1986; publicity com. chairperson Bossier Clean City Commn., 1986—; mem. evangelism com. 1st United Meth. Ch., Shreveport, 1987. Mem. Advt. Fedn. Am. (Image award 1986), Pub. Relations Soc. Am., Travel Industry Am., Am. Bus Assn., Nat. Tour Assn., S.E. Tourism Soc. (pub. relations chairperson 1986—, Best Brochure Series award 1986, Best Promotional Program award 1986), La. Travel Promotion Assn. (coop. mktg. chairperson 1987). Democrat. Home: Stone Mountain Inn Stone Mountain GA 30086 Office: Stone Mountain Park PO Box 778 Stone Mountain GA 30086

THYS, KAREN ANN BAILEY, marketing professional; b. Hobart, Ind.; d. Cecil Alonzo and Florence Elizabeth (Cihonski) Bailey. B.S. in Bus. Adminstrn. and Econs., Regis Coll., 1982. Various acctg. and fin. positions, Chgo. and Denver, 1975-78; fin. analyst II, Adolph Coors Co., Golden, Colo., 1979-82, distbr. econs./expansion analyst, 1982-83, supr. young adult mktg., 1983-84, sr. distbr. econs./expansion analyst, 1984-86, area sales mgr., San Diego, 1986-88, regional mktg. mgr., 1988—.

TIBBETTS, SUSAN MARILYN, forensic scientist; b. Holyoke, Mass., Mar. 6, 1961; d. Robert H. and Marilyn E. (Long) T. BS in Biology, L.I. U., 1983; MS in Forensic Chemistry, Northeastern U., 1985. Intern in forensic sci. Westchester County, Valhalla, N.Y., 1984; forensic chemist K-Chem. Labs., Boston, 1985; asst. forensic scientist Westchester County Dept. Labs. and Research, Valhalla, 1986-88, forensic scientist, 1988—; lectr. Crime Scene Sch. FBI, Valhalla, 1987. Mem. Am. Acad. Forensic Scis., Northeastern Assn. Forensic Scis., Nat. Assn. Female Execs., Northeastern U. Justice Alumni Assn. Office: Westchester County Dept Labs and Research Grasslands Reservation Valhalla NY 10595

TIBERIO, FAITH KUHRT, metal stamping company executive; b. St. Augustine, Fla., Jan. 23, 1926; d. Raymond Theodore and Marguerita (Phillips) Kuhrt; student John B. Stetson U., 1944-45; B.A., Boston U., 1965, M.A., 1967; m. Joseph William Tiberio, May 18, 1945; children—Frederick Morris, Faith Phillips. With Western Union, Phila., 1943-44, So. Bell Telephone Co., St. Augustine, 1944-45; co-founder, mgr. Ty-Car Mfg. Co., Holliston, Mass., 1946-49; partner Century Mfg. Co., Holliston, 1949—, dir., 1970—; v.p. Ty-Wood Corp., Holliston, 1965—. Trustee, Hillside Sch., 1977-80, Mass. 4-H Found.; pres. New Eng. Women, Worcester Colony, 1986-88; vice chmn. pres.'s com. Framingham State Coll. Mem. Bus. and Profl. Women's Club, DAR (state regent 1977-80, nat. curator gen. 1980-83). Club: Framingham Women's Republican (pres. 1983-84). Office: Ty-Wood Corp 383 Fiske St Holliston MA 01746

TIBURZI, ANITA M(ARIE), marketing and public relations firm executive, consultant; b. Englewood, N.J., Aug. 14, 1944; d. August Robert and Gunvor Inga Britt (Dahlberg) T.; m. Stephen F. Johnson, Aug. 3, 1973; 1 child, James Wood. B.A., U. Stockholm, 1966; postgrad. Centre Universitaire Mediterrannee, Nice, France, 1967. Dir. corp. communications Kenton Corp., N.Y.C., 1968-72; dir. bus. devel. L.M. Rosenthal, N.Y.C., 1972-73; cons. Monsanto Corp., Simplicity Corp., Helena Rubenstein, N.Y.C., 1973-78; v.p. Perrier Group, Greenwich, Conn., 1978-83; pres., owner Atwood Internat. Inc., N.Y.C., 1983—; cons. mktg./pub. relations and creative spl. events, etc.; dir. Salt-Free Gourmet Corp., N.Y.C.; trustee Philharmonia Virtuosi, N.Y.C., 1985—. Patentee ednl. toy. Com. mem. Am. Cancer Soc., N.Y.C., 1975—, Millay Colony for Arts, N.Y.C., 1977—, Just One Break, Inc., N.Y.C., 1978—; mem. Inner Circle Republican Com., Washington, 1984—, The Seeing Eye Orgn., N.J., 1986—. Episcopalian. Avocations: art and antique collecting; historical preservation and conservation; riding; tennis. Office: Atwood Internat Inc 22 E 72d St New York NY 10021

TICHMAN, NADYA ERICA, violinist; b. Freeport, N.Y., June 12, 1958; d. Herbert L. and Ruth (Budnevich) T.; B.Mus., Curtis Inst. Music, 1980. Violinist, Aspen Music Festival 1975, 76, Opera Co. Phila. 1978, 79, Concerto Soloists of Phila. 1979-80, Santa Fe Opera Orch. 1979-81, San Francisco Symphony 1980—, Grand Teton Music Festival 1982—, Chamber Music West, 1986; numerous solo and chamber music recitals; co-dir. Chamber Music Sundaes, San Francisco; violinist, Donatello String Quartet.

TICKTIN, STEPHANIE, lawyer; b. Los Angeles, Feb. 20, 1955; d. Theodore J. and Eleanor Carol Ticktin. B.A. cum laude, UCLA, 1979; J.D., Southwestern U. Sch. Law, 1982. Bar: Calif. 1982; lic. FCC gen. radiotelephone with radar endorsement. Assoc. Hillsinger & Costanzo, Los Angeles, 1987—. Editor-at-large The Commentator, 1981-82. Mem. elections com. Southwestern Student Bar Assn., Los Angeles, 1980. Byron Holland hon. scholar, 1977. Office: Hillsinger & Costanzo 3055 Wilshire Blvd Los Angeles CA 90010

TIDBALL, M. ELIZABETH PETERS, physiology educator; b. Anderson, Ind., Oct. 15, 1929; d. John Winton and Beatrice (Ryan) Peters; m. Charles S. Tidball, Oct. 25, 1952. B.A., Mt. Holyoke Coll., 1951, L.H.D., 1976; M.S., U. Wis., 1955, Ph.D., 1959; Sc.D., Wilson Coll., 1973; D.Sc., Trinity Coll., 1974, Cedar Crest Coll., 1977, U. of South, 1978, Goucher Coll., 1979; H.H.D., St. Mary's Coll., 1977; Litt.D., Regis Coll., 1980; D.Litt., Coll. St. Catherine, 1980; H.H.D., Hood Coll., 1982; L.L.D., St. Joseph Coll., 1983; L.H.D., Skidmore Coll., 1984, Marymount Coll., 1985, Converse Coll., 1985; D.Sc., St. Mary-of-The-Woods Coll., 1986; L.H.D., Mt. Vernon Coll., 1986. Teaching asst. physiology dept. U. Wis., 1952-55, 58-59; research asst. anatomy dept. U. Chgo., 1955-56, research asst. physiology dept., 1956-58; USPHS postdoctoral fellow NIH, Bethesda, Md., 1959-61; staff pharmacologist Hazleton Labs., Falls Church, Va., 1961; cons. Hazleton Labs., 1962; asst. research prof. dept. pharmacology George Washington U. Med. Center, 1962-64, assoc. research prof. dept. physiology, 1964-70, research prof., 1970-71, prof., 1971—; Cons. FDA, 1966-67, assoc. sci. coordinator sci. assocs. tng. program, 1966-67; mem. com. on NIH tng. programs and fellowships Nat. Acad. Scis., 1972-75; faculty summer confs. Am. Youth Found., 1967-78; founder, convenor Summer Seminars for Women Am. Youth Found., 1988—; cons. for instl. research Wellesley Coll., 1974-75; exec. sec. com. on edn. and employment women in sci. and engring. Commn. on Human Resources, NRC/Nat. Acad. Scis., 1974-75, vice chmn., 1977-82; cons., staff officer NRC/Nat. Acad. Scis., 1974-75; cons. Woodrow Wilson Nat. Fellowship Found., 1975—, NSF, 1974—, Assn. Am. Colls., 1986—; Lucie Stern Disting. vis. prof. in natural scis. Mills Coll., 1980; scholar in residence Coll. Preachers, 1984, Salem Coll., 1985; disting. scholar in residence So. Meth. U., 1985; cons. Assn. Am. Colls. Project on Status and Edn. of Women, 1986—; rep. to D.C. Commn. on Status of Women, 1972-75, nat. panelist Am. Council on Edn., 1983—; panel mem. Congl. Office of Tech. Assessment, 1986-87. Contbr. sci. articles and research on edn. of women to profl. jours.; mem. editorial bd. Jour. Higher Edn, 1979-83, cons. editor, 1984—; mem. editorial adv. bd. Religion and Intellectual Life, 1983—. Trustee Mt. Holyoke Coll., 1968-73, vice chmn., 1972-73, trustee fellow, 1988—; trustee Hood Coll., 1972-84, 86—, exec. com., 1974-84; overseer Sweet Briar Coll., 1978-85; trustee Cathedral Choral Soc., 1976—, pres. bd. trustees, 1982-84; trustee Skidmore Coll., Saratoga Springs, N.Y., 1988—; councillor Coll. of Preachers, 1979-85, chmn., 1983-85; trustee Washington Cathedral Found., 1983-85, mem. exec. com., 1983-85, bd. vis. Salem Coll., 1986—; ctr. assoc. Nat. Resource Ctr., Girls Clubs Am., 1983—. Shattuck fellow, 1955-56; Mary E. Woolley fellow Mt. Holyoke Coll., 1958-59; USPHS postdoctoral fellow, 1959-61; recipient Alumnae Medal of Honor Mt. Holyoke Coll., 1971, Chestnut Hill Medal for Outstanding Achievement Chestnut Hill Coll., Phila., 1987; named Outstanding Grad. The Penn Hall Sch., 1988. Mem. AAAS, Am. Physiol. Soc. (chmn. task force on women in physiology 1973-80, com. on coms. 1977-80), Am. Assn. Higher Edn., Mt. Holyoke Alumnae Assn. (dir. 1966-70, 76-77), Histamine Club, Sigma Delta Epsilon, Sigma Xi. Episcopalian. Home: 4100 Cathedral Ave NW Washington DC 20016 Office: George Washington U Med Ctr 2300 I St Nw Washington DC 20037

TIEDEMAN, MICHELE LORNA, finance company executive; b. Buffalo, Feb. 11, 1945; d. Woodrow W. and Olive L. (Spinks) T.; m. Daryl Danylak, Mar. 2, 1968 (div. Oct. 1978); children: Mikol Stephon, Gregory David; m. Charles E. Dahlquist, Apr. 6, 1987. Student, U. Buffalo, 1963, Niagara County Community Coll., 1978-82; cert., N.Y. Inst. Fin., 1983. Registered investment advisor; enrolled agt. Adminstrv. asst. Buffalo and Erie County Hist. Soc., 1963-69; adminstrv. asst. Char-Dahl Inc., Lockport, N.Y., 1978—, corp. sec./treas., 1979—; gen. ptnr. M.L. Tiedeman and Co., Lockport, N.Y., 1981—. Vol. ARC, Lockport, 1985—; sec. Niagara County Snowmobile Fedn., Lockport, 1975-76, pres., 1977-78; mem. Canal Spotlight Com. Historic Lockport, Inc. Mem. Nat. Soc. Pub. Accts. (del. at large), Nat. Assn. Enrolled Agts., N.Y. Assn. Enrolled Agts., N.Y. Soc. Ind. Pub. Accts., Nat. Soc. Female Execs. (network chpt. chairperson), Lockport/Ea. Niagara C. of C. (govtl. affairs. com. 1985, bd. dirs. 1987-88, treas. 1988—). Republican. Lutheran. Club: Olcott Snowmobiling (N.Y.) (corr. sec. 1973-76). Office: ML Tiedeman and Co 6850 Akron Rd Lockport NY 14094

TIEGEN, ELAINE MALIN, accounting company executive; b. Elizabeth, N.J., May 22, 1944; d. Bernard Edwin and Estelle (Radin) Malin; m. Robert A. Tiegen, Feb. 2, 1973 (div. Nov. 1975); 1 child, Heike-Ann M. BS in Acctg., Fairleigh Dickinson U., Madison, N.J., 1966. CPA, Fla. Staff auditor Peat, Marwick, Mitchell and Co., Miami, 1968-69; sr. staff auditor J.H. Cohn and Co., CPA's, Newark, N.J., 1969-71; with Clarence Rainess and Co., CPA's, N.Y.C., 1971-73; spl. asst. to sr. ptnr. Wiener, Stern and Hantman, CPA's, Miami, 1973-74; sr. specialist Laventhol & Horwath, Coral Gables, Fla., 1974-78, supr. dept. total acctg. services, 1978-79, mgr., 1979, head dept., 1980-83; prin. Elaine Malin Tiegen CPA, PA, Miami, 1983—; v.p. So. Fla. Interprofl. Council, 1984-85, pres., 1985-86; mem. small bus. rep. of adv. council Fed. Res. Bank of Atlanta, 1986—, chmn. 1988—. Mem. Am. Women's Soc. CPA's, Am. Soc. Women Accts (chpt. pres. 1975-76; Fla. Acct. of Yr. award 1976), Am. Inst. CPA's (small bus. council 1984-87, small bus. taxation com. 1987—), Fla. Inst. CPA's (recipient Disting. Service award Dade County chpt. 1980, 81, 82, gov. 1983-85, pres. chpt. 1984-85), Am. Arbitration Assn., Mensa. Office: 5401 Collins Ave #149 Miami Beach FL 33140

TIEGERMAN, ELLEN MORRIS, speech educator, school system administrator; b. N.Y.C., July 3, 1949; d. Morris and Rita (Levy) Jacobs; divorced; children: Jeremy Shimon, Jonathan David. BA, Bklyn. Coll., 1971, MS, 1974; M of Philosophy, CUNY, N.Y.C., 1978, PhD, 1979. Instr. Queens Coll., Flushing, N.Y., 1974, 77-81; pvt. practice speech pathology 1977—; adj. asst. prof. Marymount Coll., N.Y.C., 1980, C.W. Post Coll., Greenvale, N.Y., 1981; adj. asst. prof. Adelphi U., Garden City, N.Y., 1981, asst. prof., 1981-85, assoc. prof., 1985—, dir. presch. language program, 1983-85, dir. speech and hearing ctr., 1982-85; exec. dir. The Sch. for Lang. and Communication Devel., North Bellmore, N.Y., 1985—; language cons. Iris Hill Nursery Sch., Queens Children Psychiat. Hosp.; language cons., research and clin. coordinator Herbert Birch Sch. for Exceptional Children, 1979-80; language cons., coordinator home tng. program Great Neck Sch. Dist., 1979-80; cons. dir. language and communication services Anderson Sch. for Profoundly Impaired, 1980-81; lectr. in field. Co-author: (with R. Goldfarb) Autism, Encyclopedia on Education 1984, (with D. Bernstein) Language and Communication Disorders in Children, 1985, (with D. Fraser) Babysignals, 1987; contbr. articles to profl. jours. Bd. dirs. Nassau/Suffolk Soc. for Autistic Children, 1982-84. Mem. N.Y. State Speech and Hearing Assn. (registration com. conv. chair 1981-82, conv. chair 1982-83, chair com. on continuing edn. 1982-83, co-chair com. on continuing edn. 1983-84), L.I. Speech and Hearing Assn. (del. for colls. and univs. 1982-83, v.p. 1983-84, conv. chair 1984). Home: 4 Grace Ct N Great Neck NY 11021 Office: Sch for Language and Communication Disorders 10 Campbell St New Hyde Park NY 11040

TIEGS, CHERYL, model, designer. d. Theodore and Phyllis T. Student, Calif. State U., Los Angeles. Profl. model, appearing in nat. mags., including, Time, Life, Bazaar, Sports Illustrated, Glamour; appeared weekly on ABC's Good Morning America; also appearing in TV commls., Cheryl Tiegs line of signature sportswear at Sears, Roebuck & Co., Cheryl Tiegs nationally-distributed line of women's eyeglass frames. Author: The Way to Natural Beauty, 1980. Address: care Eileen Ford 344 E 59th St New York NY 10022

TIEMEYER, HOPE ELIZABETH JOHNSON, retired advertising company executive, club woman; b. Ft. Wayne, Ind., May 20, 1908; d. Edward Tibbens and Burton (Meyers) Johnson; m. Edwin H. Tiemeyer, Oct. 30, 1929 (dec. Apr. 1955); children—Ann Elizabeth (Mrs. G. L. Lewin, Jr.), Edwin Houghton (dec.). BA, U. Cin., 1932. Pres., owner Mail-Way Advt. Co., Cin., pres., 1955-87. Regent, Cin. chpt. D.A.R., 1956-58, chmn. nat. sch. survey com., 1961-62, nat. vice chmn. Americanism Manual for Citizenship, 1962-65, Continental Congress program com., 1962-65, Congress Marshall Com., 1966-68, mem. Congress hostess com., 1969-77; rec. sec. Nat. Chmn.'s Assn., 1969-71, pres. Ohio State Officers Club, 1975-77; sr. nat. membership chmn. Children Am. Revolution, 1958-60, sr. nat. rec. sec., 1960-62, nat. chmn. Mountain Sch., 1962-64, hon. sr. nat. v.p., 1963-64, sr. nat. 1st v.p. 1964-66, sr. nat. pres., 1966-68, hon. nat. life pres., 1970—, 1st v.p. Nat. Officers Club, 1965-69, pres., 1970-73, hon. sr. life pres. Ohio soc.; hon. life mem. Ohio Congress PTA, treas., 1957-62, v.p., dir. dept. health, 1962-63; hon. life mem. Nat. Congress PTA; life mem. Kappa Alpha Theta Mothers Club, pres., 1958-59; v.p. women's com. Cin. Symphony Orch., 1964-65; pres. U. Cin. Parents Club, 1959-61, v.p., 1963-64; area chmn. State House Conf. on Edn., 1953; dir. AAUW, 1963-64; mem. Cin. Social Health Bd., 1950—, exec. com., 1965-70, v.p., 1973-75, treas., 1975-78, life trustee, 1978—; pres. Singleton's of Cin. Club, 1969-71, 73-76, mem. travel bd., 1973—, pres., 1973-74, art com., 1971—, mem. membership com., 1973-78; pres. Newtown Garden Club, 1947-49, City Panhellenic Assn., 1951-52, Ohio Hobby Club, 1958-59, Sigma Nu Mothers Club, 1963-65, pres. Alumnae chpt. Alpha Omicron Pi, 1930-32, nat. admissions com., 1933-35; life mem. Craftshops for Handicapped; chmn. Amelia Earhart Fellowship com. Zonta Club, Cin., 1963-64, program chmn., 1964-65, orientation chmn., 1965-67, internat. relations chmn., 1967-68, dir., 1969-74, mem. exec. com., 1969-74, mem. nat. nominating com., 1970-74, v.p., 1971-73; mem. music com., mem. tea room com. Cin. Woman's Club, 1969—; treas. Queen City chpt. Nat. Assn. Parliamentarians, 1965-69, v.p. Greater Cin. area women's chpt. Freedoms Found. at Valley Forge, 1975-77, sec. 1977-79, pres., 1978-80; mem. Covington-Cin. Suspension Bridge com., 1987—. Mem. Nat. Platform Assn., Nat. Gavel Assn., English Speaking Union. Recipient Jonathon Moore citation and award Ind. Soc. S.A.R., 1967; Good Citizenship medal Nat. Soc., 1967; named Ky. col. Club: Town. Home: 2786 Little Dry Run Rd Cincinnati OH 45244 Office: 229 426-30 Plum St Cincinnati OH 45202

TIENDA, MARTA, demographer, educator; b. Tex. Ph.D. in Sociology, U. Tex., 1976. From asst. prof. to prof. rural sociology U. Wis., Madison, 1976-87; vis. prof. Stanford U., 1987; prof. sociology U. Chgo., 1987—; assoc. dir. Population Research Ctr. Co-author: Hispanics in the U.S. Economy, 1985, Divided Opportunities, 1988; contbr. articles to profl. jours. Mem. Am. Sociol. Assn., Population Assn. Am., Internat. Union for the Sci. Study Population, Nat. Council on Employment Policy, Population Assn. Am. (adv. com.). Office: U Chgo Dept Sociology Chicago IL 60637

TIFFANY, MARY MARGARET, communications company executive; b. Carbondale, Pa., May 19, 1947; d. Curtis Hilton and Margaret Mary (Livsey) Abney; m. Richard Allen Tiffany, Aug. 13, 1976; children: Colleen Denise O'Day, Thomas Edward O'Day. Dir. pub. info. Parkland Healthcare Ctr., Orlando, Fla., 1980-82; mgr. personnel RCS, Inc., Orlando, 1982-84; mgr. adminstrv. services AT&T, Orlando, 1983-84, mgr. tng. programs, 1984-86, mgr. mktg., 1986-88; owner, pres. Tng. Plus, Orlando, 1986—. Mem. Rep. Women Fla., Orlando, 1985-87, Goals 2000 Health and Human Services Task Force; bd. dirs. Am. Diabetes Assn., Orlando, 1987. Recipient Appreciation award Vietnam Vets. Assn., 1983. Mem. Nat. Assn. Female Execs., Adminstrv. Mgmt. Soc., Orlando C. of C. (chairperson bus. after hours com. 1986, orange juice forum com. 1986). Republican. Roman Catholic. Home: 3488 Exeter Ct Orlando FL 32812 Office: Tng Plus Inc 111 N Orange Ave Suite 1325 Orlando FL 32801

TIFT, MARY LOUISE, artist; b. Seattle, Jan. 2, 1913; d. John Howard and Wilhelmina (Pressler) Dreher; m. William Raymond Tift, Dec. 4, 1948. B.F.A. cum laude, U. Wash., 1933; postgrad., Art Center Coll., Los Angeles, 1945-48, U. Calif., San Francisco, 1962-63. Art dir. Vaughn Shedd Advt., Los Angeles, 1948; asst. prof. design Calif. Coll. Arts and Crafts, Oakland, Calif., 1949-59; coordinator design dept. San Francisco Art Inst., 1959-62. Subject of cover story, Am. Artist mag., 1980, studio article, 1987; one woman shows, Gumps Gallery, San Francisco, 1977, 1986, Diane Gilson Gallery, Seattle, 1978, Oreg. State U., 1981, group shows include, Brit. Biennale, Yorkshire, Eng., 1970, Grenchen Triennale, Switzerland, 1970, Polish Biennale, Crakow, 1972, Nat. Gallery, Washington, 1973, U.S.-U.K. Impressions, Eng., 1988; represented in permanent collections, Phila. Mus. Art, Bklyn. Mus., Seattle Art Mus., Library Congress, Achenbach Print Collection, San Francisco Palace Legion of Honor. Served to lt. USNR, 1943-45. Mem. Print Club Phila., World Print Council, Calif. Soc. Printmakers, Phi Beta Kappa, Lambda Rho. Christian Scientist. Home: 150 Seminary Dr #1E Mill Valley CA 94941 Office: 112 Industrial Center Bldg Sausalito CA 94965

TIGHE, MAUREEN ANNE, health care administrator; b. New Haven, July 15, 1952; d. John Joseph and Gertrude Ellen (Vancky) McCarthy. BA in Sociology cum laude, Emmanuel Coll., 1974; MBA, Columbia U., 1979, MPH, 1982. Asst. to dir. community health Somerville (Mass.) Hosp., 1974-75; asst. to exec. dir. Cath. Med. Ctr., Jamaica, N.Y., 1975-77; adminstrv. resident Lenox Hill Hosp., N.Y.C., 1979-80, planner, 1980-82, asst. v.p., 1982-86; dir. planning New Rochelle (N.Y.) Hosp., 1986—. Mem. Am. Hosp. Assn. Soc. Health Planning and Mktg., N.Y. Soc. Health (trustee, chmn. program planning com. 1987). Home: 520 E 84th St 3H New York NY 10028

TIKALSKY, SUSAN M., soil scientist; b. Milw., Apr. 8, 1954; d. Donald Joseph and Betty Lou (Barthels) T.; m. Albert Charles Friedman, Aug. 11, 1984; children: Emma Rose, Joseph. BS in Soil Sci., U. Wis., 1976, MS in Soil Sci., Resource Mgmt., 1981. Soil scientist Soil Conservation Service USDA, Sparta, Wis., 1978; wetlands cartographer Dept. Natural Resources State of Wis., Madison, 1979-80; ind. environ. cons. Madison, 1981-83; research asst. U. Wis., Madison, 1981-83; environ. scientist Wis. Power and Light Co., Madison, 1983-87, dir. environ. affairs, 1987—. Mem. Soil Conservation Soc. Am. (chair legis. com. 1986—), Utility Air Regulatory Group, Land-Water Conservation Coalition, Raptor Edn. Rehab. Assn. (bd. dirs. 1985—). Office: Wis Power and Light Co 222 W Washington Ave Madison WI 53703

TIKELLIS, PAMELA SUZANNE, lawyer; b. Lawrence, Kans., Aug. 9, 1952; d. Ignatius James and Elizabeth (Deery) Tikellis; m. John Heggie Small, Mar. 5, 1982. BA in Psychology, Manhattanville Coll., 1974; MA in Psychology, New Sch. for Social Research, 1976; JD, Del. Law Sch., 1982. Bar: Del. 1982, U.S. Dist. Ct. Del. 1983. Law clk. to presiding justice Ct. of Chancery, Wilmington, 1982-83, assoc. Biggs & Battaglia, Wilmington, 1983-87, assoc. Greenfield and Chimicles, Wilmington, 1987—. Mng. editor Del. Law Sch. Law Rev., Wilmington, 1981-82. Mem. Jr. League of Wilmington, 1982—. Mem. ABA, Del. State Bar Assn. Republican. Roman Catholic. Home: 209 Edgewood Rd Wilmington DE 19803

TILDEN, KAREN ANN, electro-optical engineer; b. Melton, Suffolk, Eng., Aug. 11, 1958; d. Eugene Francis and Janet Caroline (Marsh) T.; m. Steven Lee Allen, Jan. 1, 1983; children: Katherine Mikaela Tilden Allen, Nicholas Lee Tilden Allen. BS, U. Lowell, Mass., 1981; MS, U. Calif., San Diego, 1987. Sr. engr. Convair div. Gen. Dynamics, San Diego, 1981-83, 85—. Mem. Optical Soc. San Diego, Internat. Optical Engring. Soc. Office: Gen Dynamics Convair Div PO Box 85357 MZ42-6210 San Diego CA 92138

TILGER, JUSTINE THARP, research director; b. New Point, Ind., Sept. 11, 1931; d. Joseph Riley and Marcella Lorene (King) Tharp; m. Clarence A. Tilger II, Aug. 22, 1959 (div. Nov. 1972); children: Evelyn Mary, Clarence Arthur III, Joseph Thomas. AB, U. Chgo., 1951; BA, St. Mary's Coll., Notre Dame, Ind., 1954; MA, Ind. U., 1962, PhD, 1971. Mem. Sisters of the Holy Cross, Notre Dame, 1954-58; teaching fellow Ind. U., Bloomington, 1959-61; asst. editor Ind. Mag. History, Bloomington, 1962-64; bookkeeper Touche Ross, Boston, 1974-77; mgr. account services Harvard U., Cambridge, Mass., 1977-81; dir. research and records Bentley Coll., Waltham, Mass., 1982-84; dir. support services Sta. WGBH-TV, Boston, 1985; dir. research Tufts U., Medford, Mass., 1986—; cons. Laduke Assocs., Framingham, Mass., 1972-74, New Eng. Ballet, Sudbury, Mass., 1981-82. v.p. Potter Rd. Sch. Assn., Framingham, 1968-69; chmn. vols. St. Anselm's, Sudbury, 1970-71. Mem. Am. Soc. for Info. Sci, Council for Advancement and Support Edn., New Eng. Online User's Group, Soc. for Competitor Intelligence Profls., Mass. Bus. and Profl. Women (sec. 1981-82), Mensa. Democrat. Roman Catholic. Club: Gem (Framingham) (sec. 1981-83). Home: 15 Auburn St #6 Framingham MA 01701 Office: Tufts U Packard Hall Medford MA 02155

TILIPKO, LAURA, nursing administrator, educator, consultant; b. N.Y.C., Mar. 16, 1953; d. Peter and Alfreda (Jankowski) T. BA in Polit. Sci., Lebanon Valley Coll., 1975; MS, Pace U./N.Y. Med. Coll., 1979, cert. nurse practitioner, 1979; MPA, Baruch Coll., 1986. RN, N.Y. Staff nurse ICU New York Hosp., N.Y.C., 1979-80; family nurse practitioner Roosevelt Hosp., N.Y.C., 1980-81; adult nurse practitioner Bellevue Hosp., N.Y.C., 1981-82; nursing supr. St. Barnabas Hosp., N.Y.C., 1982-84; asst. dir., project dir. Met. Hosp., N.Y.C., 1984-85; asst. adminstr., dir. nurses No. Dutchess Hosp., Rhinebeck, N.Y., 1985—; advisor nursing curriculum Dutchess Community Coll., Poughkeepsie, N.Y., 1985; advisor Ulster Community Coll., Stone Ridge, N.Y., 1985; advisor econs. com. SUNY-New Paltz, 1986. Mem. com., faculty Am. Heart Assn., Poughkeepsie, 1985-86, chmn. nursing edn. com.; bd. dirs. Rhinebeck Day Care Ctr., Hospice of Dutchess Ct. Mem. Am. Nursing Assn. (cert. family nursing practice), Sigma Theta Tau, Pi Gamma Mu. Avocations: scuba diving, skiing, swimming. Home: RD #3 PO Box 149 Rhinebeck NY 12572

TILLEMANS, PATRICIA LOUISE, psychiatric social worker; b. Milbank, S.D., June 12, 1937; d. Patrick Henry and Gwendolyn Faye (Schultz) T. BA, Mt. St. Mary's Coll., Los Angeles, 1966; MSW, U. So. Calif., 1978; postgrad., Cambridge Grad. Sch. Psychology, Los Angeles, 1986—. Cert. teacher, Calif.; lic. clin. social worker, Calif.; diplomate clin. social work. Social worker Good Shepherd Residence, San Francisco, Los Angeles, Chgo., 1967-75; coordinator Status Offender Detention Alternative Program, Los Angeles, 1976; clin. social worker Long Beach (Calif.) Neuropsychiat. Inst., 1978-81; supr. Gateways Conditional Release Program, Los Angeles, 1981-85; dir. Gateways Mentally Disordered Offenders Program, Los Angeles, 1985—; pvt. practice Los Angeles, 1981—; mem. legis. com. Mental Health Council, Los Angeles, 1982-84. Mem. Fellowship of Reconciliation, Los Angeles, 1981—. Mem. Nat. Assn. Social Workers (cert., steering com. 1982-84), Forensic Mental Health Assn. Democrat. Roman Catholic. Office: Gateways Satellite 437 N Hoover Los Angeles CA 90004

TILLERY, LINDA ANN, nurse; b. Wichita, Kans., Dec. 9, 1951; d. J.B. and Letha Ann (Summerhill) Belk; m. Maurice Odell Tillery, May 29, 1969; children: Kevin Bartlett, Angela Wynelle. BS with honors in Nursing, Ark. Tech. U., Russellville, 1981; postgrad. in nursing U. Cen. Ark., Conway, 1988—. RN, Ark. Staff nurse St. Mary's Hosp., Roswell, N.Mex., 1981-82; nursing dir. Lane's Rest Home, Caraway, Ark., 1982-83; charge nurse Hilhaven Nursing Home, Little Rock, 1983; staff devel. instr. Benton Services Ctr. (Ark.), 1983—. Democrat. Baptist. Home: 1122 Sunset Benton AR 72015 Office: Benton Services Ctr Benton AR 72015

TILLINGHAST, META IONE, civic worker; b. Newark, Nov. 14; d. Ralph Vincent and Florence Virginia (MacDonald) Muldoon; student Leland Powers Sch. of Spoken Word, Boston; m. Frederick William Tillinghast; children—Anne (Mrs. Robert Riley), Patricia (Mrs. Charles McLaughlin). Bd. dirs. Balt. chpt. ARC, 1955-58, chmn. Queen Anne's chpt. 1964-66, nat. bd. govs., 1966-69, Md. state fund chmn., 1969-71, Delmarva div. chmn. mems., funds, 1971-73, vols., 1971-74, coordinator community relations Eastern area, 1975-76; chmn. vols. nat. field office (now Eastern field office) ARC, Alexandria, Va., 1976-83, regional chmn. Eastern ops., 1983-86, chmn. vols. Del. chpt., 1986-88, chmn. vols. Nat. Historic Resources, 1986—, mem. nat. hist. resource com.; dir. ch. plays; chmn. United Fund Baltimore County (Md.) Women's div., 1950. Named vol. of year Md., ARC, 1965; recipient award Gen. Fedn. Women's Clubs, 1952. Mem. Md. No. Dist. Fedn. Women's Clubs (pres. 1953-55). Clubs: Women's Glyndon (pres. 1949-51), Talbot County Women's (pres. 1962-64), Women's Ten Hills (pres. 1940-42). Home: Nesbit Rd Rt 3 Box 24 Queenstown MD 21658

TILLMAN, HOPE NELSON, librarian; b. Balt., Sept. 8, 1941; d. Richard Nelson and Hope (Sturtevant) T.; m. Gregory E. Nagy, Dec. 11, 1962 (div.); children—Ilona Kimberly, Paul Gregory; m. 2d, William W. Buckley, Nov. 18, 1977 (div.). Student Goucher Coll., 1959-60, Middlebury Coll., 1960-62; A.B., U. Pa., 1964; M.L.S., Rutgers U., 1966; M.B.A., Rider Coll., 1979. Library trainee Free Library Phila., 1965; jr. librarian Trenton Pub. Library (N.J.), 1968, br. librarian, 1968-69; reference librarian Rider Coll., Lawrenceville, N.J., 1970-82, coordinator info. services, 1982—. Editor: Education Libraries, 1986-88. Mem. Spl. Libraries Assn. (Princeton-Trenton chpt. bus. mgr. 1981-82, pres. 1984-85, chair-elect spl. libraries assn. edn. div., 1987-88, chair, 1988—), AAUP (Rider Coll. chpt. corr. sec. 1974-75, 85-86, treas. 1982-85, fin. sec. 1986-87, v.p. 1987-88, pres. 1988—), N.J. Library Assn., ALA, Govt. Documents Assn. N.J. Unitarian. Home: 16 Alyce Ct Lawrenceville NJ 08648 Office: Rider Coll Library 2083 Lawrenceville Rd Lawrenceville NJ 08648

TILLMAN, MARY ANNE TUGGLE, pediatrician; b. Bristow, Okla., Sept. 4, 1935; d. Thomas Gus and Ruthie (English) Tuggle; B.S., Howard U., 1956, M.D., 1960; postgrad. Harvard Grad. Med. Sch., 1965; m. Daniel Tillman, Apr. 20, 1957; children—Dana, Daniel. Intern, Homer G. Phillips Hosp., St. Louis, 1960-61, resident pediatrics, 1961-63; practice medicine, specializing in pediatrics, St. Louis, 1963—; dir. nurseries Homer G. Phillips Hosp., St. Louis, 1964-79, St. Louis City Hosp., 1979-85; mem. staffs St. Louis Children's, Deaconess, Barnes, Jewish hosps.; asst. prof. Washington U. Sch. Medicine, St. Louis, 1963—, pediatric cons. Project Head Start, 1969—. Recipient Woman of Year award Zeta Phi Beta, 1970; Woman of Achievement, St. Louis Globe Democrat, 1982. Diplomate Am. Bd. Pediatrics. Fellow Am. Acad. Pediatrics (nat. com. adoptions 1969—); mem. Am., Nat. med. assns., Am. Med. Women's Assn. Presbyterian. Contbr. articles to profl. publs. Home: 26 Washington Terr Saint Louis MO 63112 Office: Northland Office Bldg 330 W Florissant at Lucas Hunt Saint Louis MO 63136

TILLMAN, MARY NORMAN, urban affairs consultant; b. Atlanta, Jan. 31, 1926; d. Mary Nellie Shehee; B.A., Morris Brown Coll., 1947; postgrad. U. Minn., 1964, Old Dominion U., 1975; m. James A. Tillman, Jr., Apr. 11, 1952; children—James A., Gina G. Asst. bus. mgr. Morris Brown Coll., Atlanta, 1947-53; race relations and urban affairs cons. Tillman Assos. Cons. Social Engrs., Atlanta and Syracuse, N.Y., 1963—, sr. partner, treas., from 1965, now pres.; clin. prof. United Theol. Sem., New Brighton, Minn.; adj. prof. Gordon-Conwell Theol. Sem., South Hamilton, Mass. Mem. adv. council to urban ministries dept. So. Bapt. Conv.; bd. dirs. Christian Council Met. Atlanta, Tillman Inst. Human Relations. Mem. Tidewater Assn. Public Adminstrs. (dir.), Am. Acad. Consultants, Nat. Black Writers Consortium (v.p.), Joint Ctr. for Polit. Studies. Author: What is Your Racism Quotient?, 1964; (with James A. Tillman, Jr.) Why America Needs Racism and Poverty, 1972; (with J.A. Tillman, Jr.) Black Intellectuals, White Liberals and Race

Relations: An Analytic Overview, 1973;What Is Your Exclusivity Quotient, 1978; also articles. Office: 1765 Glenview Dr SW Atlanta GA 30331

TILLMAN, MAYRE LUTHA, political consultant; b. Dover, Fla., Aug. 24, 1928; d. Luther E. and Marietta T. Wheeler; student Fla. State U., 1945-46, Alladin Bus. Coll., 1963-64; m. Paul D. Tillman, Apr. 7, 1947 (div.); children—Daniel Paul, Shayla Denise Tillman Nail. Credit investigator Maas Bros., Tampa, 1946-47; sec.-bookkeeper Dover Sch., 1950-53; adminstrv. asst. Dave Gordon Enterprises, Tampa, 1965-68; office mgr. Bumby & Stimpson, Inc., Plant City, Fla., 1968-70; tax clk., clk. of circuit ct. Hillsborough County (Fla.) Courthouse, 1970-73; adminstr. property mgmt. Tampa-Hillsborough County Expressway Authority, 1973-74; exec. asst. Fla. Democratic Party, Tallahassee, 1976-78; adminstrv. asst., office mgr. E. F. Hutton & Co., Tampa, 1979-80; cons. politics, meeting planning, Dover, 1980—; consumer advocate Fla. Dept. Ins., Tampa, 1982-84; real estate devel. specialist Dept. Bus. Regulations, Div. Land Sales, Condominiums and Mobile Homes, 1985—. Precinct 721 committeewoman Hillsborough County Dem. Exec. Com., 1964—, sec., 1965-68, state committeewoman, 1974-77, 80-84, state liaison for county conv., 1979; pres. Dem. Women's Clubs Fla., 1979-81, bd. dirs., 1969—, chmn. polit. action com., 1985-87, chmn. campaign com., 1985-87; Fla. coordinator for ERA, Dem. Nat. Com., 1982; active Dem. Exec. Com. Fla., 1974-84, vice chmn. 7th Congl. Dist. on Central Com., 1974-76, 80-84, nat. committeewoman for Fla., 1980-84; chmn. So. region Nat. Fedn. Dem. Women, 1981-82, mem. nat. credential com., 1980; mem. Duke U. Forum on Presdl. Nominations; candidate Fla. Ho. of Reps., 1980; participant Fla. Gov.'s Challenge Conf., Fla. Endowment for Humanities, 1981; mem. hon. bd. Dr. Martin Luther King, Jr. Commemoration and Black History Month Celebration, 1986. Named Hon. Col., State Miss., 1980, State Ky., 1981. Mem. Fla. Fedn. Bus. and Profl. Women's Clubs (pres. Plant City club 1967-69, dist. com. chmn. 1969-71, organizer chmn. talent bank 1970, state chmn. legis. 1970-73, chmn. state conv. 1982), East Hillsborough County Hist. Soc., Plant City Women's Club (parliamentarian 1980-82). Home: PO Box 97 Dover FL 33527

TILSON, KATHERINE ANNE, medical practice manager; b. Cin., Mar. 21, 1951; d. Paul Joseph Walter and Anne Elizabeth (Kleemann) Centner; m. Dennis Bascombe Tilson, II, June 8, 1974. B.S. in Nursing, Med. Ctr. U. Kans.-Kansas City, 1973; M.B.A., Avila Coll., 1983. R.N., Kans., Mo. Staff nurse U. Kans. Med. Ctr., Kansas City, 1973-76, Menorah Med. Ctr., Kansas City, 1976-78; nursing coordinator Kelly Health Care, Inc., Kansas City, 1978, nursing supr., 1978-79, br. mgr., service dir., 1979-83; mgr. ServiceMaster Home Health Care Services, Kansas City, 1983, adminstr., 1983-84; cons. Am. Nursing Resources, Inc., Kansas City, 1984, adminstr. Am. Nursing Resources Home Health Agy., Inc., 1985-88, exec. dir. Am. Nursing Resources, Inc., Kansas City, Mo., 1984-88, exec. dir. 1987—, med. practice mgr. Drs. Brothers and Centner, Kansas City, 1988—; jr. faculty liaison for home health nursing practice residency tng. program S.S.M. Family Practice, Kansas City, 1982-83; mem. in-home services com. Johnson County Area Agy. on Aging, 1982-83. Mem. Challinor Guild, St. Andrew's Episcopal Ch., 1981—, choir, 1980—, Scola Cantorum, 1984-85, Metro Discharge Planners Group, 1985—, Mayor's Corps of Progress for Greater Kansas City, 1980-83. Mem. Broadway Bus. Assn., Mid-Am. Regional Council (in-home services task force 1980—, in-home services com. 1979—), Kansas City Regional Home Health Assn. (bd. dirs. 1979-83, mem., chmn. coms.), Kansas City C. of C. Republican. Avocations: piano; singing; sailing; swimming; sports; sewing; gardening. Home: 4600 W 66th St Prairie Village KS 66208 Office: Drs Brothers and Centner 2727 Main Suite 201 Kansas City MO 64108

TILTON, BERNICE ELIZABETH SHEPPARD (MRS. EARLE BARTON TILTON), civic worker; b. Chgo.; d. Samuel Charles and Elizabeth (Keith) Sheppard; Mus.B., Wis. Coll. Music, 1954; m. Earle Barton Tilton, Mar. 12, 1940. Performed as soloist and two-piano team for orgns., Ill., Wis., Fla., 1947—. Pres., Symphony Club, Clearwater, Fla., 1958-60; founder Mus. Arts Soc., Clearwater, 1960, pres., 1960-62, 81-83; chpt. pres. Delta Omicron, 1964-66, Fla. chmn. alumnae-at-large, 1965-67, internat. v.p. alumnae, internat. bd. dirs., 1967-71; pres. Fla. West Coast Panhellenic Assn., 1967-68, chpt. adv. bd., 1968—. Bd. dirs. Clearwater Community Concert Assn., 1963-74. Recipient Gold Star Delta Omicron, 1967, Recognition award, 1971. Mem. Nat. Soc. Arts and Letters (local sec., v.p. 1972-73), Henry Solomon Lehr Soc. (life), Delta Omicron (alumnae chpt. pres. 1973-74, 81-84, rec. sec. 1985-88). Home: 6 Belleview Blvd Apt 608 Belleair FL 34616

TILTON, ELMIRA FAYE, state legislator; b. Ft. Fairfield, Maine, Nov. 4, 1950; d. Joseph Edward McLaughlin and Thurley Fay (Adams) Allen; m. Edward Brian Smallwood, June 28, 1971 (dec. July 1979); 1 child, William Joseph; m. David Brown Tilton, Sr., Oct. 8, 1982. Elected mem. N.H. State Legislator, Concord, 1986—; mem. N.H. State Legis. coms. Staff Devel. Com., Salem, 1980-87, Conservation Commn., Salem, 1985-87, sec. Salem Boys and Girls Club, 1982—; vice chair Greater Salem Chem. People Task Force, 1983-85. Democrat. Roman Catholic. Club: Garden (Salem). Address: 227 Main St Salem NH 03079

TIMM, JEANNE ANDERSON, musician; b. Sioux City, Iowa, Aug. 15, 1918; d. Milton Earnest and Hazel Fern (Cunningham) Anderson; B.Mus., Morningside Coll., Sioux City, 1940; postgrad. Eastman Sch. Music, La. State U.; m. Everett L. Timm, Aug. 5, 1940; children—Gary Everett, Laurance Milo. Prof. woodwind instruments Morningside Coll., 1943-45, 48—; staff flutist Sta. KSCJ, Sioux City, 1941; prin. flutist Sioux City Symphony, 1943-45; vis. flutist New Orleans Philharm., New Orleans Opera Orch; prof. flute and chamber music La. State U., 1968—; cons., clinician flute cos.; editor Armstrong Edu-tainment Co., 1976—; flutist Baton Rouge Little Theater, summers 1965-81. Mem. Nat. Assn. Wind and Percussion Players, Nat. Flute Assn., Music Educators Nat. Conf., Music Tchrs. Nat. Assn., La. Music Educators Assn., Baton Rouge Music Club, Pi Kappa Lambda, Mu Phi Epsilon. Roman Catholic. Home: 465 Magnolia Woods Baton Rouge LA 70808 Office: La State U 269 Music and Dramatic Arts Bldg Baton Rouge LA 70803

TIMMERMAN, LINDA DAVIS, academic dean; b. Dallas, Dec. 6, 1946; d. James Neal and Judy (Ray) Davis; m. Richard W. Kendall, Sept. 4, 1965 (div. Feb. 1971); m. David William Timmerman, July 31, 1973; 1 child, Bradley William. AA, Navarro Coll., 1980; BS, East Tex. State U., 1981; MA, U. Tex., Tyler, 1985. Asst. sec. of bd. Dallas County Community Coll. Dist., 1975-78; asst. to pres. Navarro Coll., Corsicana, Tex., 1978-81, dir. pub. info., 1981-84, dir. continuing edn., 1984-86, dean of acad. services, 1986—. Chmn. Corsicana Chamber Breakfast Com., 1984-86, Corsicana Ann. Event, 1983, v.p. 1987; cons. Leadership Corsicana Curriculum Com., 1986. Mem. Tex. Jr. Coll. Tchrs. Assn. Democrat. Methodist. Home: Rt 2 Box 5 Corsicana TX 75110 Office: Navarro Coll 3200 W 7th Corsicana TX 75110

TIMMERMANN, SANDRA, educational gerontologist, communications specialist; b. Orange, N.J., Mar. 25, 1941; d. Bernhard and Matilda (Schaaf) T.; m. George W. Bonham. BA with honors, U. Colo., 1963; MA, Columbia U., 1967; EdD, 1979. Account exec. Rowland Co., N.Y.C., 1964-67; dir. pub. info. The N.Y. TV Network. SUNY, N.Y.C., 1967-72; asso. Hoefer/Amidei Pub. Relations/Mktg., 1972-74; asso. dean Inst. Lifetime Learning, Am. Assn. Ret. Persons, Washington, 1974-76, dir. Inst., 1976-84, dir. geriatric edn., 1984-86 ; exec. dir. Peninsula Ctr. for the Blind, Palo Alto, Calif., 1986-88; dir. western states region Am. Found. for the Blind, San Francisco, 1988—; bd. dirs. Calif. Council of Gerontology and Geriatrics, 1988-90; edn. and tng. cons. Am. Soc. on Aging; mem. tng. com. Nat. Ctr. for Black Aged; mgr. older adults sect. HEW Lifelong Learning Project; cons. Brookdale Ctr. on Aging, Hunter Coll.; cons. to bus. and industry; adv. com. nat. project on counseling older people Am. Personnel and Guidance Assn.; nat. adv. com. vocat. edn. and older adults U.S. Dept. Edn. Trustee, chmn. adv. com. on later years Am. Found. for the Blind. Kellogg fellow. Mem. Am. Assn. Adult and Continuing Edn. (editor Edn. and Aging newsletter, chmn. commn. on aging, bd. dirs.), Coalition Adult Edn. Orgns. (dir., pres. 1984-85), Pi Beta Phi, Pi Lambda Theta, Kappa Delta Pi, Phi Delta Kappa. Club: Capital Speakers. Contbr. articles to profl. jours. Home: 371 Cypress Point Rd Half Moon Bay CA 94019

TIMMERMANS, DEANNA D., pharmacist, advertising executive; b. Rapid City, S.D., Feb. 5, 1939; d. Bernard Briggs and Luella (Olson) Dodds; B.S., State U. Iowa, 1961; m. John J. Timmermans, June 24, 1961 (dec. Oct. 1978); 1 son, Jeffrey Jay. Pharmacist, Race Drug, Ketchikan, Alaska, 1961-63, St. Vincent's Hosp., N.Y.C., 1965-66, S.I. Hosp., 1966-71; pharm. market research analyst William Douglas Mc Adams, N.Y.C., 1980-82; account exec. pharm. advt. Dorritie & Lyons, N.Y.C., 1982-84, account supr., 1984-88, v.p./account supr., 1988— . Mem. Jr. Guild S.I., 1970-75 ; treas. Women's Guild S.I. Mental Health Assn., 1970-71; toy chmn. Christ Ch. Day Sch. Fair, N.Y.C., 1971. Mem. Women for Rockefeller, S.I., 1970; mem. com. Republican party, Richmond County, 1970-71; chmn. credentials com. Women's Rep. Conf., Phila., 1972; mem. Met. Rep. Club, 1972—; bd. dirs. Women's Aux. N.Y. U. Coll. Dentistry, sec., 1974, treas., 1974-76, v.p., 1976-78 ; bd. dirs. Yorkville Civic Council, 1977-78, Knickerbocker Greys; bd. dirs., mem. exec. com. Burden Center for Aging, 1977—; coordinator congl. life St. Peter's Luth. Ch., 1976-77, dir. vols., 1977-78, ch. council, 1979-81; active Muscular Dystrophy Assn. Telethon Fund, 1978—. Mem. Pharm. Soc. State N.Y., Assn. Hosp. Pharmacists, Am. Pharm. Assn., Iowa Pharm. Assn., Pharm. Advt. Council, Acad. Pharm. Scis., Fgn. Policy Assn., Parents League N.Y., Aircraft Owners and Pilots Assn., Jr. League City N.Y. (bd. mgrs., exec. com.), Kappa Alpha Theta Alumni Assn., Kappa Alpha Theta (past v.p.), Kappa Epsilon. Lodge: Rotary. Home: 400 E 56th St New York NY 10022 Office: Dorritie & Lyons 655 3rd Ave New York NY 10017

TIMMERMANS-WILLIAMS, GRETCHEN, psychotherapist; b. Portland, Oreg., May 13, 1938; d. Philip Anthes and Ione (Wedemeyer) Briegleb; m. Perry Ralph Timmermans, Apr. 11, 1964 (div. Nov. 1981); 1 child, Alexander Spencer; m. Richard C. Williams, Nov. 26, 1983. BA in Psychology, Whitman Coll., 1960; MS in Psychology, Tulane U., 1962. Cert. jr. coll. tchr. Calif., 1966; cert. marriage, family, child counselor, Calif., 1980. Research asst. Naval Personnel Research Dept., San Diego, 1966-69; systems analyst Logicon, Inc., San Diego, 1969-71; psychol. tech. Pain Unit, VA Med. Ctr., La Jolla, Calif., 1972-76, coordinator, 1976-80; asst. dir. Pain Ctr., Scripps Meml. Hosp., La Jolla, 1980-83; psychotherapist Pain Mgmt. Program Spalding Rehab. Hosp., Denver, 1985; sec., treas. Clin. Data Network, Inc., Broomfield, Colo., 1983—; adminstrv. asst. Pain Rehab. Program Meml. Hosp., Boulder, Colo., 1986—. Research scientist articles for jour., Pain, 1975—. Vol. Health Fair, Broomfield, 1983-87; participant Great Peace March for Global Nuclear Disarmament, 1986. Named one of Outstanding Young Women Am., 1978. Mem. Internat. Assn. for Study of Pain (founding), Am. Pain Soc. (standards com. 1982), Western U.S.A. Pain Soc. (program chair 1981-82, treas. 1982-83). Democrat. Mennonite. Office: Meml Hosp 311 Mapleton Ave Boulder CO 80302

TIMMINS, LOIS FAHS, lecturer, writer, consultant; b. N.Y.C., July 3, 1914; d. Charles Harvey and Sophia (Lyon) Fahs; m. James W. Timmins, Aug. 12, 1942 (div.); children—Nancy Timmins Kirk, Kathy. BS in Edn., Northwestern U., 1935; MA, Columbia U., 1936, EdD, 1941. Instr., Mt. Allison U., Sackville, N.B., Can., 1936-39; asst. prof. Willimantic (Conn.) State Tchrs. Coll., 1941-43 (now named Eastern Conn. State U.); social dir. UNESCO, Mondsee, Austria, summer, 1950; asst. prof. Tex. Woman's U., Denton, 1953-57; profl. staff Timberlawn Psychiat. Hosp., Dallas, 1957-80; dir. Communication Studies, Dallas, 1972—; profl. speaker, Dallas, 1980—. Author: Swing Your Partner, 1939, Understanding Through Communication, 1972, Life Time Chart, 1978, Cassettes: Making Friends with All Your Feelings, 1984, The Mirrors Inside You, 1984, Ambivalance, 1985, (booklet) Finding Words for Your Feelings, 1985, (6 cassette album) Our Secret World of Feelings, 1986; contbr. articles to profl. jours. Recipient citation Nat. Therapeutic Recreation Soc., 1976, Top Rating Profl. Speakers Showcase award Internat. Platform Assn., 1982. Mem. Internat. Assn. Ind. Pubs. Home: 6145 Anita St Dallas TX 75214-2612

TIMMONS, EVELYN DEERING, pharmacist; b. Durango, Colo., Sept. 29, 1926; d. Claude Elliot and Evelyn Allen (Gooch) Deering; m. Richard Palmer Timmons, Oct. 4, 1952 (div. 1968); children: Roderick Deering, Steven Palmer. BS in Chemistry and Pharmacy cum laude, U. Colo., 1948. Chief pharmacist Meml. Hosp., Phoenix, 1950-54; med. lit. research librarian Hoffman-LaRoche, Inc., Nutley, N.J., 1956-57; staff pharmacist St. Joseph's Hosp., Phoenix, 1958-60; relief mgr. various ind. apothecaries, Phoenix, 1960-68; asst. then mgr. Profl. Pharmacist, Inc., Phoenix, 1968-72; mgr. then owner Mt. View Pharmacy, Phoenix and Paradise Valley, Ariz., 1972—; pres. Ariz. Apothecaries, Ltd., Phoenix, 1976—; mem. profl. adv. bd., bereavement counselor Hospice of Valley, 1983—; mem. profl. adv. bd. Upjohn Health Care and Services, Phoenix, 1984-86; bd. dirs. Am. Council on Pharm. Edn., Chgo., 1986—. Author poetry; contbr. articles to profl. jours. Mem. Scottsdale (Ariz.) Fedn. Rep. Women, 1963; various other offices Rep. Fedn.; mem. platform com. State of Ariz., Nat. Rep. Conv., 1964; asst. sec. Young Rep. Nat. Fedn., 1963-65; active county and state Rep. coms. Named Outstanding Young Rep. of Yr., Nat. Fedn. Young Reps., 1965, Preceptor of Yr., U. Ariz./Syntex, 1984; recipient Disting. Public Service award Maricopa County Med. Soc., 1962, Disting. Alumni award Wasatch Acad., 1982, Leadership and Achievement award Upjohn Labs., 1985-86, Outstanding Achievement in Profession award Merck, Sharp & Dohme, 1986. Fellow Am. Coll. of Apothecaries (v.p. 1982-83, pres. 1984-85; chmn. bd. dirs. 1985-86, adv. council 1986—, Chmn. of Yr. 1980-81 Victor H. Morganroth award 1985); mem. Ariz. Soc. of Hosp. Pharmacists, Am. Pharmacy Assn., Ariz. Pharmacy Assn. (Service to Pharmacy award 1976, Pharmacist of Yr. 1981), Maricopa County Pharmacy Assn. (pres. 1977, Service to Pharmacy award 1977), Am. Soc. of Hosp. Pharmacists, Aux. to County Med. Soc. (pres. 1967-68), Am. Aircraft Owners and Pilots Assn., Nat. Assn. of Registered Parliamentarians. Lodge: Civinettes (pres. Scottsdale chpt. 1960-61). Avocations: flying, skiing, swimming, backpacking, hiking. Home: 5302 N 69th Pl Scottsdale AZ 85253 Office: Mt View Pharmacy 10565 N Tatum Blvd Suite B-118 Paradise Valley AZ 85253

TIMMONS, MARY ANN MIKKELSON, marketing executive; b. Sharon, N.D., Oct. 12, 1950; d. Roy Marvin and Alice Harriet (Brun) Mikkelson; m. Larry H. Riehl, June 21, 1970 (div. Jan. 1981); m. David E. Timmons, Jan. 1, 1983. AS, Wahpeton State Sch. Sci., 1970. Cert. Profl. Ins. Woman. Sec. Pioneer Mut. Life Ins., Fargo, N.D., 1970-72, asst. dir. sales promotion and advt., 1972-75, asst. mktg. sec., 1975-77, mktg. sec., 1977-85, coordinator mkgt. adminstrn., 1985—. Bd. dirs. West Fargo Jaycettes, 1972-80. Mem. Sales and Mktg. Execs., Ins. Women Fargo-Moorhead (several offices 1970-86), Fargo C. of C. (chmn. ambassador). Club: Toastmasters. Office: Pioneer Mut Life Ins Co 203 N 10th St Fargo ND 58102

TIMOTHY, MEGAN D'EWES, hotel executive; b. Masvingo, Zimbabwe, June 21, 1943; came to U.S., 1964; d. Noel Esmond and Helen Simpson (Steyn) T. Professiona equestrienne Rhodesian Horse Soc., Zimbabwe, 1956-64; actress, folk singer and stuntwoman Los Angeles, 1965-71, archtl. glassworks designer and restorer, gourmet caterer, 1971-83; owner, operator La Maida House Hotel, North Hollywood, Calif., 1983—.

TINGEY, CAROL, psychologist, educator; b. St. James, Mo., Sept. 24, 1933; d. Willis Alma and Lola (Madsen) Tingey; B.S. magna cum laude, U. Utah, 1970, M.Ed., 1971, Ph.D., 1976; children—Richard, Blaine, James, Neil, Trish. Tchr. public schs., Salt Lake City, 1970, spl. edn. tchr., 1971-72; clin. instr. spl. edn. U. Utah, Salt Lake City, 1972-74; dir. staff devel. Utah State Tng. Sch., American Fork, Utah, 1974-75; asst. prof. spl. edn. U. No. Iowa, Cedar Falls, 1975-77; asst. prof. spl. edn. Trinity Coll., Washington, 1977-78; asst. prof. spl. edn. of severely handicapped George Mason U., Fairfax, Va., 1978-79; assoc. prof. edn. and tng. physically and multi-handicapped Northwestern State U. of La., Natchitoches, 1979-81; assoc. prof. spl. edn. Ill. State U., Normal, also coordinator program for physically handicapped, 1981-83; assoc. prof. psychology Utah State U., Logan, 1983—; bd. dirs. Nat. Down Syndrome Congress; researcher, cons. in field. Fellow Am. Assn. on Mental Deficiency (sec. Utah chpt. 1975, edni. chmn. region VIII 1976-77, treas. edn. div. 1979-80), mem. Assn. for Severely Handicapped, Council for Exceptional Children (pres. Utah chpt. 1974-75), Assn. for Retarded Citizens, Phi Delta Kappa, Phi Kappa Phi. Author: Home and School Partnerships in Exceptional Education; Handicapped Infants and Children: Handbook for Parents and Professionals; New Perspectives on Down Syndrome; Down Syndrome: A Resource Handbook; Early Intervention--Hands on Strategies; contbr. articles to profl. jours.; recorded albums: Self Help Skills, Adaptive Behavior; Socialization Skills; Adaptive Behavior; Daily Living Tasks, Housekeeping Skills, Vocational Awareness, Community Helpers; editorial adv. bd. Exceptional Parent mag. Home: 1565 Rose Orchard Circle Logan UT 84321 Office: Utah State U 174 Devel Ctr/Handicapped Persons Logan UT 84322

TINKER, DEBRA ANN, health facility administrator; b. Cleve., June 27, 1951; d. Keith Donald and Rita Patricia (Rowinski) T.; m. Charles Earl Enos, Aug. 6, 1983; children: Christopher Tinker Enos, Matthew Tinker Enos. BS in Edn. cum laude, Ohio U., 1973; postgrad., Chapman Coll., 1984—. Tchr. English, remedial reading Northmont Jr. High Sch., Clayton, Ohio, 1973-76; dance instr. Schehera's Studio, Dayton, Ohio, 1974-76; substitute tchr. Knox County Schs., Mt. Vernon, Ohio, 1976; tchr. English, remedial reading Ohio Youth Commn., Massillon, Ohio, 1977; coordinator spl. needs program Knox County Joint Vocat. Sch., Mt. Vernon, 1977-82; life ins. sales Belding and Assocs., Mt. Vernon, 1980-82; student control officer Naval Air Tng. Unit, Sacramento, 1982-85; dir. Navy Counseling and Assistance Ctr., Charleston, S.C., 1985—. Leader Girl Scouts Am., Dayton, Ohio counsel, 1975-76, mem., cons. North Charleston, S.C., 1987—; exec. producer Mt. Vernon AWARE, 1977-81; mem. Navy Family Advocacy Support Team, Charleston, 1985—, Navy Alcohol and Drug Adv. Council, Charleston, 1985—; bd. dirs. Exchange Club Ctr. for the Prevention of Child Abuse, Charleston, 1987—. Served to lt. USNR, 1982—. Mem. Charleston Women Officer's Assn., S.C. Mental Health Counselors' Assn., Soc. Mayflower Descendants, Mensa, Kappa Delta Pi. Independent. Lutheran. Home: 202 Brailsford Rd Summerville SC 29483 Office: Counseling & Assistance Ctr Naval Base Code N56 Charleston SC 29408-5100

TINSLEY, RHONDO RAE, labor union administrator; b. Alliance, Neb., May 14, 1946; d. Vincent Leroy and Gloria Irene (Osborn) Rosenberger; m. Dennis Lynn Tinsley, Feb. 14, 1965; children: Erin Tinsley Hessheimer, Blake. BS in Elem. and Spl. Edn., Chadron (Neb.) State Coll., 1973, MS in Sch. Adminstrn., 1975. Sec. Chadron High Sch., 1968-71, Chadron State Coll., 1971-72; dir. Pioneer Sch. for Spl. Children, Chadron, 1972-75; tchr. Lincoln (Neb.) Pub. Schs., 1975-77, counselor, 1977-84; exec. dir. Fremont (Calif.) Unified Dist. Tchrs. Assn., 1984—; cons. in field. Mem. Review Panel Regional Ctr. Office of Mental Retardation, Lincoln, 1982-83; dist. rep. Dem. Cen. Com., 1983-84. Mem. NEA (profl. staff orgn.), Neb. Interchange (pres.1982-84), Lincoln Edn. Assn. (pres. 1983-84). Congregationalist. Home: 37777 Carriage Circle Fremont CA 94536 Office: Fremont Unified Dist Tchrs Assn 4531 Eggers Dr Fremont CA 94536

TINUCCI, GEORGIA MAE, small business owner, designer; b. Chgo., May 12, 1930; d. Philip Arthur and Lillian Georgia (Lish) Sandblom; m. Raymond Peter Tinucci, Aug. 21, 1954. Student, Bradley U., 1948-51. Comml. artist Patton, Haggerty & Sullivan, Chgo., 1951-53; color cons. Crafton & Assocs., Chgo., 1953-55; tchr., mgr. publicity Tinucci Music Ctr., Elmwood Park, Ill., 1966-81; pres. Cove Wax Works, Melrose Park, Ill., 1981—. Republican. Home: 1092 Jamey Ln Addison IL 60101 Office: Cove Wax Works 2311 W Main St Melrose Park IL 60160

TIPTON, JENNIFER, lighting designer; b. Columbus, Ohio, Sept. 11, 1937; d. Samuel Ridley and Isabel (Hanson) T.; m. William F. Beaton., Aug. 29, 1976. B.A., Cornell U., 1958. Lighting designer Paul Taylor Dance Co., Twyla Tharp and Dancers, 1965, Pa. Ballet Co., 1966, Macbeth, Am. Shakespeare Festival, Stratford, Conn., Harkness Ballet Co., 1967, Dan Wagoner Dancers, Richard II, Love's Labour's Lost, Am. Shakespeare Festival, HB Studios N.Y., 1968, Horseman Pass By, Fortune Theatre, Les Grands Ballet Canadiens, Yvonne Rainer Co., City Center Joffrey Ballet, Our Town Anta Theatre, 1969, Anta Theatre Dance Series, 1971, 72, Eliot Feld Ballet Co., Am. Ballet Theatre from 1971; numerous ballets include Airs, Amnon V'Tamar, Bach Partita, The Little Ballet, N.Y. Export: OP Jazz, Triad, Kazuko Hirabayashi Dance Co., A Ballet Behind the Bridge, Negro Ensemble Co., Delacorte Dance Festival, Houston Ballet Co., 1972, Nat. Ballet Co., Hartford Ballet Co., Celebration: The Art of Pas de Deux, Jerome Robbins, Jose Limon Dance Co., 1973, Tempest, Macbeth, Midsummer Night's Dream, N.Y. Shakespeare Festival-Newhouse Theatre, The Killdeer, Newman Theatre, Jerome Robbins' The Dybbuk, N.Y.C. Ballet, Dreyfus in Rehearsal, Barrymore Theatre, 1974, San Francisco Ballet Co., Anthony Tudor's The Leaves Are Fading, Am. Ballet Theatre, Habeas Corpus, Martin Beck Theatre, Murder Among Friends, Biltmore Theatre, 1975, Rex, Lunt-Fontanne Theatre, For Colored Girls Who Consider Suicide When the Rainbow is Enuf (Drama Desk award), Booth Theatre, Cleve. Ballet Co., Mikhail Baryshnikov's The Nutcracker, Am. Ballet Theatre, 1976, The Landscape of the Body, Newman Theatre, The Cherry Orchard (Drama Desk award, Tony award 1977), Agamemnon, Beaumont Theatre, Happy End, Martin Beck Theatre, Agamemnon, Delacorte Theatre, 1977, Museum, Public Theatre, Runaways, Public Theatre and Plymouth Theatre, All's Well That Ends Well, Taming of the Shrew, Delacorte Theatre, After the Season, Academy Festival Theatre, A Month in the Country, Williamstown Theatre Festival, Mikhail Baryshnikov's Don Quixote, Am. Ballet Theatre, The Goodbye People, Westport Playhouse, Funny Face, Buffalo Studio Arena, Drinks Before Dinner, Public Theatre, Alice in Wonderland, The Pirates of Penzance, Public Theatre, 1978, Lunch Hour, 1980, Billy Bishop Goes to War, 1980, The Sea Gull, 1980, Sophisticated Ladies, 1981, The Wake of Jamie Foster, 1982, Uncle Vanya, 1983, Orgasmo Adulto Escapes from the Zoo, 1983, Baby with the Bathwater, 1984, Hurlyburly, 1984, Whoopie Goldberg, 1984, Endgame, 1984, The Ballad of Soapy Smith, 1984; assoc. dir. Goodman Theatre, Chgo.; lighting instr. Yale U. Sch. Drama. Recipient Creative Arts award Brandeis U., 1981. Office: care The Joffrey Ballet 130 W 56 Street New York NY 10019 *

TIPTON, JO ANN, marketing professional; b. New Castle, Ind., July 26, 1950; d. Dan Buford and Doris Kathryn (Pfenninger) T. BBA, Ball State U., 1972; A in Computer Tech., Ind. Vocat. Tech. Coll., 1986. Cash margin bookkeeper Merrill Lynch Pierce Fenner & Smith, Indpls., 1972-73; tax specialist Burger Chef Systems, Inc., Indpls., 1973-74, legal staff acct., 1974-76, paralegal, law librarian, 1977-79, acctg. supr., 1980-82; mktg. coordinator Norris Food Service, Inc., Beech Grove, Ind., 1983-84, mktg. dir., 1985—, also bd. dirs., 1985—. Named one of Outstanding Young Woman in Am., 1975, 76, 85. Mem. Altrusa, Delta Zeta (bd. dirs. Ball State U. 1985—). Republican. Presbyterian. Club: Ind. Flame Fantasy (chmn. 1977, treas. 1978—). Office: Norris Food Service Inc PO Box 500 Beech Grove IN 46107

TIPTON, PEGGY ANN, accountant; b. Sainte Genevieve, Mo., Oct. 5, 1960; d. Louis August and Elizabeth Jane (Klein) Wipfler; m. David Lee Tipton, Mar. 31, 1985; children: Jessica Elizabeth, Amanda Lee. BS in Acctg., S.E. Mo. State U., 1982. Jr. acct. Vernon E. Heck, CPA, St. Louis, 1982-83; acct. Taylor, Morley, Simon, Inc., St. Louis, 1983-84; acctg. mgr. Spielberg Mfg. Co., Antonia, Mo., 1984-85; acct., bus. mgr. Places for People, Inc., St. Louis, 1985-86; mgr. acctg. Christian Bd. Publ., St. Louis, 1986—. Mem. Nat. Assn. Accts., Nat. Assn. Female Execs. Roman Catholic. Home: Rt 3 Box 261C Festus MO 63028 Office: Christian Bd Publ 1316 Convention Plaza Saint Louis MO 63166

TIRAKIS, JUDITH ANGELINA, financial company executive; b. Bristol, Conn., Oct. 11, 1938; d. Dante and Ines (Paravella) Follandri; m. George Tirakis, July 15, 1967. BA, St. Joseph Coll., West Hartford, Conn., 1956-60; postgrad., St. Joseph Coll., 1960-61. With Engelhard Minerals and Chem. Corp., Menlo Park, N.J., 1964-67; supr. Sci. Info. Ctr. Ciba Geigy Pharm. Co., Summit, N.J., 1967-78; records mgr. research info. Ortho Pharm. Corp. div. Johnsn & Johnson, Raritan, N.J., 1978-86; v.p., records mgr. AMBAC Indemnity Corp., N.Y.C., 1986—. Mem. Assn. Records Mgrs. and Adminstrs., Drug Info. Assn., Am. Mgmt. Assn., Nat. Assn. Female Execs., Assn. Image and Info. Mgmt. Office: AMBAC Indemnity Corp 1 State St Plaza New York NY 10004

TIRRELL, JANET ANTHONY, public relations generalist; b. Piedmont, Calif., July 13, 1938. BA in Polit. Sci., U. Calif., Berkeley, 1961, MA in Edn., 1968; postgrad. in bus. adminstrn., Fordham U. Tchr. English Orinda Union Sch. Dist., Calif., 1962-68; coordinator ednl. research, edn. counselor Hill & Knowlton Inc., N.Y.C., 1968-70; cons., writer Ednl. Systems & Designs, Westport, Conn., 1974; writer, producer Producers Row Inc., N.Y.C., 1975. Recipient Helms award, 1963 (All-American 1956-60).

TISCHER, MAE MARION, state legislator, businesswoman; b. Sleepy Eye, Minn., Oct. 16, 1928; d. Paul Fredrick and Frieda (Macho) Lowinske; children—Brad, Becky, Mark, Daniel, Kathleen, Julie. Farmer, Meeker County, Minn., 1949-60; homesteader, Susitna Valley, Alaska, 1961-64; ptnr., owner Mobile Home Movers, Anchorage, 1963-72, Tischer's Burner Service, Anchorage, 1963-72; dist. dir. Muscular Dystrophy Assn. Alaska, 1974-82; mem. Alaska Ho. of Reps., 1982—, chmn. health, edn. and social services com., 1983-84, mem. rules com., 1983-84, fin. subcom. budget oversite and corrections, 1983-84. Organizer Alaska Mobile Home Dealers Assn., Anchorage, 1967; organizer, chmn. Montana Mothers' Club, Montana Creek, Alaska, 1962; organizer, bd. chmn. Barrier-Free Recreation, Inc., Anchorage, 1977; organizer Youth against Dystrophy, Anchorage, 1975. Recipient Regional Spl. Events award Muscular Dystrophy Assn., Anchorage, 1978-79, 80; Humanitarian Recognition award Sta. KIMO-TV, Anchorage, 1982; Humanitarian Dedication award Internat. Firefighters Assn., Anchorage, 1981; citation for Humanitarian Efforts, Alaska State Legislature, 1981. Mem. Commn. Opportunities for Handicapped, Anchorage Republican Women's Club. Lodges: W.O.O.M., Am. Legion Aux. Office: Alaska Ho of Reps Pouch V Juneau AK 99811

TISDALE, LEE W., insurance executive; b. Alexandria, Va., Feb. 18, 1949; d. Eustace Conway Moncure and Adelaide (Hill) Waller; m. G. Randall Tisdale, July 2, 1977; 1 child, R. Brian. BA, Emory & Henry Coll., 1970; postgrad., Coll. Charleston, 1975-76, Mercer U., 1986. Mgr. prodn. Carolina Nat. Mortgage div. C&S Nat. Bank, Charleston, S.C., 1976-79; br. mgr. Mortgage Guarantee Ins. Corp., Tampa, Fla., 1980-83; regional dir. wholesale loans Cen. Fed. Mortgage Co., Tampa, Fla., 1983-84; regional mgr. underwriting Investors Mortgage Ins. Co., Atlanta, 1985; mgr. underwriting Verex Assurance Corp., Atlanta, 1986—; guest speaker various groups, 1977—; instr. S.C. Real Estate Licensing Bd., 1978-79, Horry Georgetown Tech. Edn. Ctr., Myrtle Beach, S.C., 1978-79. Contbr. articles to profl. jours. Mem. Mortgage Bankers Assn. Republican. Episcopalian. Office: Verex Assurance Corp 5775 Peachtree Dunwoody #300C Atlanta GA 30342

TISINGER, CATHERINE ANNE, college president; b. Winchester, Va., Apr. 6, 1936; d. Richard Martin and Irma Regina (Ohl) T. BA, Coll. Wooster, 1958; MA, U. Pa., 1962, PhD, 1970; LLD (hon.), Coll. of Elms, 1985. Provost Callison Coll., U. of Pacific, Stockton, Calif., 1971-72; v.p. Met. State U., St. Paul, 1972-75; v.p. academic affairs S.W. State U., Marshall, Minn., 1975-76, interim pres., 1976-77; dir. Ctr. for Econ. Edn., R.I. Coll., Providence, 1979-80; v.p. acad. affairs Cen. Mo. State U., Warrensburg, Mo., 1980-84; pres. North Adams State Coll., Mass., 1984—; cons. North Cen. Assn. Colls. and Schs., 1980-84, New Eng. Assn. Schs. and Colls., 1978-79, 85—, Minn. Acad. Family Physicians, 1973-77; mem. adv. bd. First Agrl. Bank, North Adams, 1985—; pres. No. Berkshire Cooperating Colls., 1986—. V.p. Med. Simulation Found., 1986—; bd. dirs. Williamstown Concerts, 1988—. Mem. No. Berkshire C. of C. (bd. dirs. 1984—, v.p. 1986—). Avocations: fiber/textile arts, photography, choral and instrumental music. Office: North Adams State Coll Office of Pres North Adams MA 01247

TITCOMB, LEANNE GRAY, educator; b. Lawrence, Kans., Oct. 1, 1949; d. Theodore John and Alice Lorraine (Carlson) G.; m. Leslie Burton Titcomb, Feb. 13, 1988. BS in Edn., U. Kans., 1971; BS in Theology, Way Coll. Bibl. Research, Rome City, Ind., 1979; MEd, E. Carolina U., Greenville, N.C., 1982. Tchr. 6th grade Mendon-Union Schs., Ohio, 1971-72, Wayne Twp. Schs., Dayton, Ohio, 1972-75, Newport News (Va.) Schs., 1975-76; educator presch. and teens Way Coll. Bibl. Research, 1979-81; word processor State Hosp., Denton, Tex., 1981-82; engring. sec. Parsons Brinderhoff/Ranco, Columbus, Ohio, 1983-86; legal sec. Dennis Bezanson, Atty., South Portland, Maine, 1986; tchr., coordinator gifted/talented students Sch. Adminstrv. Dist. 15, Gray, Maine, 1987—. Mem. Maine Tchrs. Assn., Maine Educators Gifted and Talented. Republican. Office: SAD 15 Gray ME 04039

TITTERINGTON, ROBIN JANE, rehabilitation administrator, educator; b. Niskayuna, N.Y., Dec. 31, 1954; d. Walter Jay Sr. and Martha (Whitaker) T. BA in Psychology, St. Andrews Coll., 1977; MA in Deafness Rehabilitation, NYU, 1979. Counselor Floyd Jr. Coll., Rome, Ga., 1979-80; program coordinator Atlanta Ctr. Ind. Living, 1980-87; dir. Ga. Interpreting Services Network, Atlanta, 1987—; adj. instr. DeKalb Coll., Clarkston, Ga., 1984—; v.p. Total Living Community, Atlanta, 1984; bd. dirs. Stagehands, Atlanta, 1986—. Active Atlanta Humane Soc., 1986—; bd. dirs. Stagehands, Inc., 1986—. Recipient Deaf Woman of Yr. award Quota Club, 1980, Handicapped Profl. Woman of Yr. award Pilot Club, 1987. Mem. Ga. Assn. Deaf (exec. sec. 1983-87), Ga. Registry Interpreters for the Deaf. Methodist. Home: 1741 Lee St Decatur GA 30035 Office: Ga Interpreting Services Network 878 Peachtree St #707 Atlanta GA 30309

TITTERTON, ELIZABETH ANN, educator, retired; b. Paterson, N.J., Nov. 26, 1935; d. Robert Bouton and Helen (Fitzpatrick) T. BS, Fla. State U., 1957. Cert. tchr. Tchr. Bennett Elem. Sch., Ft. Lauderdale, Fla., 1957-87, team chair, 1985-87. Mem. Ft. Lauderdale PTA, 1957-87, faculty rep., 1982-87. Named Tchr. of Yr., Bennett Elem. Sch., 1986-87. Mem. Delta Kappa Gamma (v.p. 1972-74, parliamentarian 1978-80, numerous chair positions), Upsilon Sigma Alpha (pres., numerous offices). Republican. Episcopalian. Home: 1613 NE 18th St Fort Lauderdale FL 33305

TITUS, PAMELA LOUISE, real estate broker; b. Ft. Wayne, Ind., Aug. 15, 1953; d. Gene W. Eby and Louise Miller. B.S. in Speech and Hearing, Purdue U., 1975, M.S. in Speech Pathology with highest distinction, 1976. Speech pathologist Speech Pathology Assocs., Houston, 1977-80; profl. recruiter Diversified Human Resources Group, Houston, 1980-81, Key Personnel Pty., Ltd., Sydney, Australia, 1981-82; computer sales rep. ComputerLand, Houston, 1982-84; broker Coldwell Banker Comml. Real Estate Services, 1985—. Mem. Tex. Assn. Realtors, Houston Bd. Realtors, Internat. Coucil Shopping Ctrs.; Club: Houston Realty Breakfast. Presbyterian. Home: 11711 Memorial #112 Houston TX 77024 Office: Coldwell Bankers 2500 West Loop S Houston TX 77027

TOAL, JEAN HOEFER, lawyer, state representative; b. Columbia, S.C., Aug. 11, 1943; d. Herbert W. and Lilla (Farrell) Hoefer; m. William Thomas Toal; children—Jean Hoefer, Lilla Patrick. B.A. in Philosophy, Agnes Scott Coll., 1965; J.D., U. S.C., 1968. Bar: S.C. Ptnr. firm Belser, Baker, Barwick, Ravenel, Toal & Bender, Columbia, 1970-88; assoc. justice, S.C. Supreme Ct., 1988—; mem. S.C. Ho. of Reps., 1975-88, chmn. house rules com., constitutional laws subcom. house judiciary com.; mem. parish council and lector St. Joseph's Cath. Ch. Mng. editor S.C. Law Rev. Bd. visitors Clemson U., 1978; parliamentarian S.C. Democratic Conv.; bd. trustees Columbia Mus. Art. Mem. Columbia Bus. and Profl. Women (named Career Woman of Yr. 1974). Other: SC Supreme Ct PO Box 11330 Columbia SC 29211

TOBE, SUSAN BRING, lawyer; b. N.Y.C., 1949; d. Ira and Sylvia (Stevelman) Bring; m. Richard M. Tobe, 1980. B.A., State U. Coll., Buffalo, 1971; J.D., SUNY-Buffalo, 1974. Bar: N.Y. 1975, U.S. Dist. Ct. (we. dist.) N.Y. 1976. Asst. gen. counsel Carborundum Co., Niagara Falls, N.Y., 1974-75; asst. corp. counsel City of Buffalo, 1975-78; atty.-advisor U.S. Dept. HUD, Buffalo, 1978-81; asst. atty. gen. State of N.Y., Buffalo, 1981—; supervising atty. Pub. Interest Law Clinic, 1982; program lectr. St. Law Inst., N.Y., 1978; guest lectr. various high schs., colls., 1975—; dir. SUNY Sch. Law Alumni Assn., Buffalo, 1979-82. Vol. Leukemia Soc., Buffalo, 1981—, United Way Campaign, Buffalo, 1977, 88, Friends Community Music. Sch., Buffalo, 1984—; com. person Democratic Party, Buffalo, 1976-78; com. mem. Instnl. Advancement State U. Coll. at Buffalo, 1987—. Mem. Erie County Bar Assn., N.Y. Civil Liberties Union, ABA, Women Lawyers of Western N.Y., N.Y. State Bar Assn. (profl. ethics com. 1984-87, profl. discipline com. 1986—), State Univ. Coll. Buffalo Alumni Assn. (bd. dirs. 1984-86, v.p. 1986-88, pres. 1988—). Office: NY State Atty Gen's Office Dept Law 125 Main St Buffalo NY 14203

TOBER, BARBARA D. (MRS. DONALD GIBBS TOBER), editor; b. Summit, N.J., Aug. 19, 1934; d. Rodney Fielding and Maude (Grebbin) Starkey; m. Donald Gibbs Tober, Apr. 5, 1973. Student, Traphagen Sch. Fashion, 1954-56, Fashion Inst. Tech., 1956-58, N.Y. Sch. Interior Design, 1964. Copy editor Vogue Pattern Book, 1958-60; beauty editor Vogue mag., 1961; dir. women's services Bartell Media Corp., 1961-66; editor-in-chief Bride's mag., N.Y.C., 1966—; dir. Gen. Brands Corp., sec.-treas.; adv. bd. Traphagen Sch.; coordinator SBA awards; Am. Craft Council Mus. Assoc., 1983—, benefit food com. chmn., 1984-87. Author: The ABC's of Beauty, 1963, China: A Cognizant Guide, 1980, The Wedding . . . The Marriage . . . And the Role of the Retailer, 1980, The Bride: A Celebration, 1984. Mem. Nat. Council on Family Relations, 1966; nat. council Lincoln Center Performing Arts, Met. Opera Guild; mem. NYU adv. bd. Women in Food Service, 1983; NYU Women's Health Symposium: Steering Com., 1983—. Recipient Alma award, 1968, Penney-Mo. award, 1972, Traphagen Alumni award, 1975, Diamond Jubilee award, 1983. Mem. Fashion Group, Nat. Home Fashions League (v.p., program chmn.), Am. Soc. Mag. Editors, Am. Soc. Interior Designers (press mem.), Intercorporate Group, Women in Communications (60 yrs. of success award N.Y. chpt. 1984), Nat. Assn. Underwater Instrs., Pan Pacific and S.E. Asia Women's Assn., Asia Soc., Japan Soc., China Inst., Internat. Side Saddle Orgn., Millbrook Hounds, Golden's Bridge Hounds, Wine and Food Soc., Chaines des Rotisseurs (chargée de press) (bd. dirs.), Dames d'Escoffier, Culinary Inst. Am. Home: 620 Park Ave New York NY 10021 Office: Bride's Magazine 350 Madison Ave New York NY 10017

TOBEY, JEAN CARLA, clinical pathologist, educator; b. Owosso, Mich., Aug. 18, 1952; d. Floyd Carl and Betty Jean (Crugher) T.; m. Paul D. Brindza, Oct. 6, 1976 (div. June 1982). BS in Vet. Medicine, Mich. State U., East Lansing, 1974, DVM, 1975, PhD, 1986. Gen. practice vet. medicine specializing in small animals Batavia, Ill., 1976-80; research assoc. dept. Micro and Pub. Health Mich. State U., East Lansing, 1980-81, research assoc. dept. Physiology, 1981-82, postdoctoral fellow, 1982-85, instr., resident dept. pathology, 1987—. Contbr. articles to profl. jours. Cardiovascular postdoctoral fellow NIH, 1982-83; recipient Nat. Research Service award NIH, 1984-85, Resident grantee Solvay Vet. Inc., 1986. Mem. AVMA, Chgo. Vet. Med. Assn., Ill. State Vet. Med. Assn., Soc. Neurosci. (Nat. and Mich. chpt.), Am. Soc. Vet. Clin. Pathology, Phi Kappa Phi, Phi Zeta. Home: 2520 Harding Ave Lansing MI 48910 Office: Mich State U Dept Pathology East Lansing MI 48824

TOBIAS, CYNTHIA LEE, computing manager, consultant; b. Dayton, Ohio, July 6, 1945; d. Raymond W. and Dorothy T.; m. Riaz A. Gondal, July 4, 1981. BS in Spanish, Georgetown U., 1967; MA in Sociology, U. Chgo., 1969, PhD in Sociology, 1977; MS in Indsl. Engring., U. Ariz., 1986. Lectr. Bayero U., Nigeria, Africa, 1977-78, cons. socioecons. Chevy Chase, Md., 1979-83; research assoc. U. Ariz., Tucson, 1984-87, dir. med. computing, 1987—; prin. Intertech Assocs., Tucson, 1987—; cons. World Bank, Washington, 1979-83, USDA, Pakistan, 1982, Confacs Group, Tucson, 1987. NIMH grantee, 1969-72; fellow Orgn. of Am. States, 1974-75. Mem. IEEE, Inst. Indsl. Engrs., Human Factors Soc., Ops. Research Soc. of America. Democrat. Office: U Ariz Coll Medicine Office Med Computing Room2104 Tucson AZ 85724

TOBIAS, LESLIE JOY, sales executive; b. Bklyn., Feb. 26, 1961; d. Robert Palmer and Helen Gloria (Rosenberg) T. BSBA, U. Tex., Dallas, 1985; postgrad., E. Tex. State U., 1988—. Dir., owner Leslie Tobias & Assocs., Dallas, 1981-85; account coordinator Kelémata, Dallas and N.Y.C., 1985-86; territory mgr. Kelémata, Dallas, 1987—; speaker in field. Vol. various polit. campaigns, Dallas. Mem. Mktg. Club. Republican. Jewish. Home: 6630 Eastridge #133 Dallas TX 75231

TOBIN, ILONA LINES, psychologist, counselor, educator, consultant; b. Trenton, Mich., Apr. 15, 1943; d. Frank John and Marjorie Cathalean (Lines) Kotyuk; m. Roger Lee Tobin, Aug. 20, 1966. B.A., Eastern Mich. U., 1965; M.A., 1968; M.A., Mich. State U., 1975; Ed.D., Wayne State U., 1978. Tchr., counselor Willow Run Pub. Schs., Ypsilanti, Mich., 1966-72; prof. Macomb County Community Coll., Mt. Clemens, Mich., 1974-79; psychotherapist Identity Center, Inc., Mt. Clemens, 1974-79; dir. treatment Alternative Lifestyles, Inc., Orchard Lake, Mich., 1979-80; psychologist Profl. Psychotherapy and Counseling Ctr., Farmington Hills, Mich., 1980-83; pvt. practice clin. psychology, Birmingham, Mich., 1983—; lectr. Wayne State U., Detroit, 1977—; recruitment dir. Upward Bound Eastern Mich. U., Ypsilanti, 1969-72. Creator Doc's Dolls, 1986. Pres. Hair Prep., 1987; co-chmn. Birmingham Families in Action, 1982-83; bd. dirs. HAVEN-Oakland County's Physical and Sexual Abuse Ctr. and Oakland Area Counselors Assn., 1984-85; mem. exec. bd., v.p. personnel Birmingham Community Women's Ctr., 1984-85, also dir.; mem. adv. bd. Woodside Med. Ctr. for Chemically Dependent Women, 1984-86 . NIMH fellow, 1976-78; Wayne State U. scholar, 1976-78. Mem. Am. Psychol. Assn., Mich. Psychol. Assn., Am. Assn. Sex Educators, Counselors and Therapists, Am. Assn. for Counseling and Devel., Pi Lambda Theta, Phi Delta Kappa. Unitarian. Clubs: Birmingham Bus. Womens.

TOBIN, ROSEMARIE, underwriter; b. Harborne, Birmingham, Eng., Jan. 17, 1960; came to U.S., 1969; d. John Tobin and Rose (Conlon) T. BS in Bus. Adminstrn., Northeastern U., 1984. Telephone specialist John Hancock Mut. Life Ins. Co., Boston, 1984, acctg. technician, 1984-85, asst. underwriter, 1985-87, assoc. underwriter, 1987—. Roman Catholic. Home: 80 Hawthorn Rd Braintree MA 02184 Office: John Hancock Mut Life Ins Co 1 John Hancock Pl Boston MA 02117

TOBOLOWSKY, SARAH, retired librarian; b. Dallas; d. A.B. and Lena (Skibell) T. B.A., So. Meth. U., 1934, M.A., 1938; M.S. in Library Sci., Columbia U., 1952; postgrad. U. So. Calif., Northwestern U., U. Hawaii, Boston U. Sch. tchr. Dallas Ind. Sch. Dist., 1935-80, ret. 1980; sch. librarian Benjamin Franklin Jr. High Sch., Dallas, 1957-80, ret. 1980; instr. North Tex. State U., 1966-70. Honors Day speaker Tex. Woman's U., Denton, 1981. Mem. NEA (life), ALA (joint com. mem. with NEA), Am. Assn. Sch. Librarians (regional bd. dirs.), Dallas Classroom Tchrs. Assn. (pres. 1952-54), Tex. Classroom Tchrs. Assn. (legis. chmn. 1952-53, adv. bd. 1953-55), Tex. State Tchrs. Assn. (life), Tex. Library Assn., Dallas Sch. Librarians (pres. 1947-49), Delta Kappa Gamma (chpt. pres. 1956-58, state pres. 1963-65, State Achievement award 1963, Internat. Achievement award 1984; internat. pres. 1980-82), Kappa Kappa Iota. Home: 6838 Orchid Ln Dallas TX 75230

TOCKLIN, ADRIAN MARTHA, insurance company executive; b. Miami, Fla., Aug. 4, 1951; d. Kelso Hampton and Patricia Jane (Crook) Cook Atkins; m. Gary Michael Tocklin, Nov. 23, 1974. B.A., George Washington U., 1972. Regional claim examiner Interstate Nat. Corp., St. Petersburg, Fla., 1973-74; branch supr. Underwriter's Adjusting Co. subs. Continental Corp., Tampa, Fla., 1974-77, asst. dir. edn. tng. adminstrn., N.Y.C., 1977, asst. regional mgr. adminstrn. ops., Livingston, N.J., 1977-78, br. mgr., Paramus, N.J., 1978-80, sr. v.p. mktg., N.Y.C., Piscataway, N.J., 1980-84, regional v.p., mgr., Livingston, N.J., 1984-86, exec. v.p., 1986—, also dir.; pres. U.S. Protection Indemnity Agy., Inc., N.Y.C., 1983-85, also dir.; bd. dirs. Underwriters Adjusting Co., Arbitration Forums, Inc., Tarrytown, N.Y., 1986—; v.p. Continental Risk Services, Inc., Hamilton, Bermuda, 1983-86; editor-in-chief Profl. Ins. Bulletin Update, N.Y.C., 1977-79. Mem. YWCA Acad. Women Achievers. Mem. Nat. Assn. Ins. Women (Outstanding Ins. Woman in N.Y.C.), NOW. Democrat. Lutheran. Office: Underwriters Adjusting Co One Continental DrS Cranbury NJ 07940

TODA, SALI, financial consultant; b. Jersey City, Feb. 17, 1941; d. Samuel Rubin and Bella (Margulies) Arginteanu; m. Harold K. Toda, Sept. 27, 1968; 1 child from previous marriage, Caia K. Maglinao. BA, U. Hawaii, 1972, MA in Linguistics, MA in Japanese, 1973; PhD in Psycholinguistics, U. East Ga., 1978. CLU; chartered fin. cons. Agt. Aetna Life Ins. Co., Honolulu, 1977-81; ins. specialist Prudential Bache Securities, Honolulu, 1981-83; v.p. TNT Assocs. Inc., Honolulu, 1982—; instr. PSI World, Hawaii State Prison, 1976—, Life Underwriter's Tng. Council, Honolulu, 1981-83, Hawaii Chpt. CLU's, Honolulu, 1983. East West Ctr. grantee, 1972-73. Mem. Am. Soc. CLU's and Chartered Fin. Cons., Million Dollar Round Table, Nat. Assn. Life Underwriters, Assn. Bus. and Profl. Women, Mensa (proctor 1978—, local sec., pres. Hawaii chpt. 1985—), Phi Beta Kappa. Office: TNT Assocs Inc 1040 S King St Suite 101 Honolulu HI 96814

TODD, IMO KELLAM, insurance association executive; b. Mobile, Ala., Dec. 26, 1943; d. Claude Moore and Minnie (Barth) Kellam; m. Jordan A.M. Todd, Sept. 29, 1962 (Div. 1972); 1 child, Shannon Elise. BA, Wesley U., 1963; BS, U. Montevallo, 1966; MBA, U. Ga., 1974. Exec. asst. Baumhauer-Croom Ins., Mobile, Ala., 1963-73; v.p. acct. exec. Haas & Dodd Ins., Atlanta, 1973-78; asst. prof. U. Ga., 1973-79; v.p. acct. exec. Fickling & Walker Ins. Agy., Atlanta, 1978-81; exec. v.p. Profl. Ins. Agts. Ga., Atlanta, 1981—; dir. southeastern ins. conf. U. Greensboro, 1984-87; lectr. in field. Author: How to-of Education, 1984; editor monthly ins. mag.; contbr. articles to profl. mags. Campaign mgr. Cystic Fibrosis, Atlanta, 1975; chmn. annual fund raisers Spl. Olympics, 1983—. Named Speaker of Yr. Speakers Unltd., 1979, Atlanta's 1 in 100 Women, City of Atlanta, 1984. Mem. Am. Soc. Assn. Execs., Nat. Soc. Execs., U.S. Women's C. of C., Nat. Assn. Ins. Women (Ins. Woman of Yr. award 1973-74), Atlanta Assn. Ins. Women. Republican. Office: Profl Ins Agts Ga 1165 Northchase Pkwy Suite 140 Marietta GA 30067

TODD, JOYCE ANDERSON, social service agency director; b. Lumberton, N.C., June 2, 1940; d. Irvin L. and Esther (Huggins) Anderson; m. William H. Strickland, Dec. 9, 1960 (div. Oct. 1976); 1 child, William (dec.); m. John Wendell Todd, July 6, 1979; 1 stepchild, Stephanie Leigh. B.A., Coker Coll., 1960. Social worker Horry County Dept. Social Services, Conway, S.C., 1962-66, casework supr., 1966-73, county dir., 1973—. Mem. S.C. Assn. County Human Service Adminstrs., S.C. County Dirs. and Suprs. Assn., Am. Pub. Welfare Assn., Child Welfare League Am. Democrat. Baptist. Avocations: cooking; snow skiing; golf. Office: Horry County Dept Social Services PO Drawer 1465 Conway SC 29526

TODD, NORMA JEAN ROSS, retired government official; b. Butler, Pa., Oct. 3, 1920; d. William Bryson and Doris Mae (Ferguson) Ross; student spl. courses Pa. State U., 1944-46, Yale U., 1954-57; m. Alden Frank Miller, Jr., Apr. 16, 1940 (dec. Feb. 1975); 1 son, Alden Frank III; m. 2d, Jack R. Todd, Dec. 23, 1977. Exec. mgr. Donora (Pa.) C. of C., 1950-57, Donora Community Chest, 1950-57; office mgr. Donora Golden Jubilee, 1951; staff writer Herald-Am., Donora, 1957, city editor, 1957-70; asso. editor Daily Herald, Donora, 1970-73; service rep. Pitts. Teleservice Center, Social Security Adminstrn., HHS, 1977-83. Mem. Mayor's Adv. Council, Donora, 1965-69, Citizens' Adv. Council, Donora, 1965-69; mem. Donora Bd. Edn., 1954-60, pres., 1960; mem. Donora Borough Council, 1970-72; bd. dirs. Mon Valley chpt. ARC, 1964—, sec. bd., 1966—; bd. dirs. Washington County Tourism Agy., 1970—, sec., 1972—; bd. dirs. Washington County History and Landmarks Found. 1971 80, sec., 1975-80; bd. dirs. Mon Valley council Camp Fire Girls, 1965-79, Mon Valley Drug and Alcoholism Council, 1971-78; bd. dirs. United Way Mon Valley, 1973-82, chmn. pub. relations, 1973-74. Recipient Fine Arts Festival of Pa. Poetry first prize award Fedn. of Women's Clubs, 1987. Mem. Pa. Soc. Newspaper Editors, Pitts. Press Club, Donora C. of C. (pres. 1971-72), DAR (regent Monongahela Valley chpt. 1974-77), Washington County Poetry Soc. (pres. 1967-69), Washington County Fedn. Women's Clubs (rec. sec. 1964-66). Clubs: Order Eastern Star (worthy matron 1966-67), White Shrine of Jerusalem (high priestess 1973-74), Order of Amaranth (royal matron 1966, dist. dep., grand rep. W.Va. 1979-80), Donora Forecast (pres. 1962-63), Donora Unidon (pres. 1965-66, 56-57). Home: Overlook Terr Donora PA 15033 also: 1310 McKean Ave Donora PA 15033

TODD, RENATE KLÖPPINGER, financial executive, consultant; b. Bensheim, Fed. Republic of Germany; came to U.S., 1976; d. Heinrich and Gertrud (Schubert) K.; 1 child, Christopher. BS, Goethe U., Frankfurt, Federal Republic of Germany, 1973, MS in Psychology, 1976; MBA in Finance, UCLA, 1981. Treasury analyst intern Carnation Internat., Los Angeles, 1980-81; corp. fin. assoc. Drexel Burnham Lambert, Inc., N.Y.C., 1981-83; v.p. Fulcrum Venture Capital Corp., Washington, 1983-88, Citibank Leveraged Capital, Frankfurt, Fed. Republic Germany, 1988—; Bd. dirs. Applied Intelligent Systems, Inc., Ann Arbor, Mich., PKS, Inc., Maecomp, Inc. Com. mem. Nat. Assn. of Investment Cos., Washington, 1984—; com. mem. D.C. Com. for Women, Washington, 1986—. Recipient Sister Cities Internat. award, 1981. Mem. OEF Internat. Women in Bus. (cons. 1986, advisor/small bus. San Jose, Costa Rica, 1986), Phi Beta Kappa (named Outstanding Member 1981).

TODD, SANDRA BEAN, communications and public relations executive; b. Brainard, Minn., Jan. 14, 1945; d. Roger Allan and Sara Jeann (Hinde) Bean; 1 son from previous marriage, Richard Jaeger; m. Mark Todd, Dec. 23, 1978; 1 son, Kevin Witt. A.B. in Journalism, U. Ga., 1967. Cert. French tchr., Ga. Editorial asst. Am. Physical Therapy Assn., Washington, 1975-78; pub. relations dir. Chesapeake Bay GSC, Wilmington, Del., 1978-80; editor Am. Life Ins. Co., Wilmington, 1980-82, mgr. publs., 1982-87; info. officer Baha'i World Centre, 1988—; mem. steering com. Internat. Women's Conf., Phila., 1987. Mem. Internat. Assn. Bus. Communicators (accredited), Wilmington Women in Bus. (bd. dirs. 1987—), Phi Kappa Phi.

TODD, SANDRA JO, librarian; b. Cairo, Ill., Aug. 24, 1946; d. Ralph Morrell and Dorothy Alice (Harris) Pattengill; m. William Thomas Smith Todd, Feb. 1, 1969; children: William Michael, Ryan Christopher. BS in Edn., U. Mo., Columbia, 1968; MEd, U. Mo., 1969. Cert. primary, secondary tchr., library media specialist. Substitute tchr. San Diego Unified Sch. Dist., 1969-70; instr. Childbirth Edn. Assn., San Diego, 1971-74; substitute tchr. Leeward Sch. Dist., Waipaihau, HI, 1976-78, Papillion (Nebr.)-La Vista Sch. Dist., 1978-80; campus librarian Met. Tech. Community Coll., Omaha, 1980-84; substitute tchr. Alexander M. Patch High Sch., Vaihingen, Fed. Republic Germany, 1985; librarian, media specialist Alexander M. Patch Elem. Sch., Vaihingen, 1985-86; head librarian Rocky Run Intermediate Sch., Chantilly, Va., 1986—. Co-author manual: Public Relations for Secondary School Media Centers, 1986. Mem. Springfield (Va.) Youth Club, 1986—, W. Springfield High Sch. sports booster club, 1986—, PTA, Springfield, 1986—, Women's Leadership Identification Program, Nebr., 1983-84. Mem. NEA, Va. Edn. Assn., Fairfax County Edn. Assn., Nat. Library Assn., Va. Ednl. Computing Assn. (governing bd. 1987), Library and Info. Tech. Assn., Southeastern Library Assn., Va. Library Assn., Am. Assn. Sch. Librarians, Soc. Sch. Librarians Internat. Democrat. Baptist. Clubs: Pentagon Ski, Navy Officer Wives. Home: 6416 Brentford Dr Springfield VA 22152 Office: Rocky Run Intermediate Sch 4400 Stringfellow Rd Chantilly VA 22021

TODD, SHIRLEY ANN, educational counselor; b. Botetourt County, Va., May 23, 1935; d. William Leonard and Margaret Judy (Simmons) Brown; m. Thomas Byron Todd, July 7, 1962 (dec. July 1977). B.S. in Edn., Madison Coll., 1956; M.Ed., U. Va., 1971. Cert. tchr., Va. Elem. tchr. Fairfax County Sch. Bd., Fairfax, Va., 1956-66, 8th grade history tchr., 1966-71, guidance counselor James F. Cooper Intermediate Sch., McLean, Va., 1971-88, dir. guidance, 1988—; chmn. mktg. Lake Anne Joint Venture, Falls Church, Va., 1979-82, mng. ptnr., 1980-82. Del. Fairfax County Republican Conv., 1985. Fellow Fairfax Edn. Assn. (mem. profl. rights and responsibilities commn. 1970-72, bd. dirs. 1968-70), Va. Edn. Assn. (mem. state com. on local assns. and urban affairs 1969-70), NEA, No. Va. Counselors Assn. (hospitality and social chmn., exec. bd. 1982-83), Va. Counselors Assn. (exec. com. 1987), Va. Sch. Counselors Assn., Am. Assn. for Counseling and Devel. Baptist. Club: Chantilly Nat. Golf and Country (v.p. social 1981-82) (Centreville, Va.). Avocations: golf, tennis. Home: 6543 Bay Tree Ct Falls Church VA 22041 Office: James F Cooper Intermediate Sch 977 Balls Hill Rd McLean VA 22101

TODD COPLEY, JUDITH ANN, materials scientist and mechanical engineering educator; b. Wakefield, West Yorkshire, Eng., Dec. 13, 1950; came to U.S., 1978; d. Marley and Joan Mary (Birkinshaw) Booth; m. David Michael Todd, June 17, 1972 (div. June 1981); m. Stephen Michael Copley, Aug. 3, 1984. BA, Cambridge (Eng.) U., 1972, MA, PhD, 1977. Research asst. Imperial Coll. Sci. and Tech., London, 1976-78; research assoc. SUNY, Stonybrook, 1978; research engr. U. Calif., Berkeley, 1979-82; asst. prof. materials sci. and mech. engring. U. So. Calif., Los Angeles, 1982—; mem. task force Materials Property Council, N.Y.C., 1979—. Contbr. articles to profl. jours. Recipient Faculty Research award Oak Ridge (Tenn.) Nat. Lab., 1986,Brit. Univs. Student Travel award 1972, Brit. Fedn. Univ. Women award 1972; Kathryn Kingswell Meml. scholar 1972. Mem. AIME (research award, 1983), ASTM, Soc. Women Engrs. (sr.), Am. Soc. Metals Internat. (chmn. Los Angeles chpt. 1986—, council mem. materials sci. div. 1984—), Electron Microscopy Soc. Am., Assn. Women in Sci., Hist. Metallurgy Soc., Nat. Soc. Corrosion Engrs. (Seed Grant award 1983), Microbeam Analysis

Soc. Home: 4029 Via Nivel Palos Verdes Estates CA 90274 Office: U So Calif Dept Materials Sci Los Angeles CA 90089-0241

TOENSING, VICTORIA, lawyer; b. Colon, Panama, Oct. 16, 1941; d. Philip William and Victoria (Brady) Long; m. Trent David Toensing, Oct. 29, 1962 (div. 1976); children—Todd Robert, Brady Cronon, Amy Victoriana; m. Joseph E. diGenova, June 27, 1981. B.S. in Edn., Ind. U., 1962; J.D. cum laude, U. Detroit, 1975. Bar: Mich. 1976, D.C. 1978. Tchr. English Milw., 1965-66; law clk. to presiding justice U.S. Ct. Appeals, Detroit, 1975-76; asst. U.S. atty. U.S. Atty.'s Office, Detroit, 1976-81; chief counsel U.S. Senate Intelligence Com., Washington, 1981-84; dep. asst. atty. gen. criminal div. Dept. Justice, Washington, 1984—. Contbg. author: Fighting Back: Winning The War Against Terrorism; contbr. articles to profl. jours. Founder, chmn. Women's Orgn. To Meet Existing Needs, Mich., 1975-79; chmn. Republican Women's Task Force, 1979-81; bd. dirs. Project on Equal Edn. Rights, Mich., 1980-81, Nat. Hist. Intelligence Mus., 1987—. Recipient Spl. Commendation award Office U.S. Atty. Gen., 1980, Agy. Seal medallion CIA, 1986. Mem. ABA (standing com. on law and nat. security, council criminal justice sect., adv. bd. com. complex crimes and litigation, vice chmn. white collar crime com.). Office: Dept Justice Criminal Div 10th & Constitution Ave NW Washington DC 20530

TOEPFER, SUSAN JILL, editor; b. Rochester, Minn., Mar. 9, 1948; d. John Bernard and Helen Esther (Chapple) T.; m. Lorenzo Gabriel Carcaterra, May 16, 1981; children: Katherine Marie, Nicholas Gabriel. B.A., Bennington Coll., 1970. Mng. editor Photoplay Mag., N.Y.C., 1971-72; free-lance writer, N.Y.C., 1972-78; TV week editor N.Y. Daily News, N.Y.C., 1978-79, leisure editor, 1979-82, features editor, 1982-84, arts and entertainment editor, 1984-86, exec. mag. editor, 1986-87; sr. writer People Mag., 1987—. Democrat. Presbyterian. Office: People Mag Time-Life Bldg Rockefeller Ctr New York NY 10020

TOFANI, LORETTA A., journalist; b. N.Y.C., Feb. 5, 1953; d. Lucio M. and Olga R. (Danise) T. B.A., Fordham U., 1975; M.J., U. Calif., 1976. Reporter UPI, Los Angeles, 1977, Washington Post, D.C., 1978-87, Phila. Inquirer, 1987—. Author: newspaper series Rape in the County Jail, 1982 (Pulitzer Prize for local investigative reporting 1983, Soc. Profl. Journalists award for general reporting 1983, Investigative Reporters and Editors Bronze medal 1983, Henry Miller award for enterprise reporting 1983, Robert F. Kennedy citation for reporting on the disadvantaged 1983). Fulbright scholar Japan-U.S. Ednl Commn., Tokyo, 1983; recipient Mark Twain award, 1981, 82, Front Page award Washington-Balt. Newspaper Guild, 1980, 81, 82. Roman Catholic. Home: 2124 O St NW Washington DC 20037 Office: Philadelphia Inquirer 400 N Broad St Philadelphia PA 19101

TOKAR, MAUREEN TANSEY, architect; b. Cin., Mar. 4, 1931; d. Bernard Joseph and Cecile Marie (Sunman) Tansey; B.S. in Architecture, U. Cin., 1955; m. Edward Tokar, June 29, 1974. Job capt. Hixson, Tarter & Merkel, Cin., 1964-68; dir. interior architecture Ferry & Henderson, Springfield, Ill., 1968-72; project coordinator Skidmore, Owings & Merrill, Chgo., 1972-76; rev. architect Ill. Capital Devel. Bd., Chgo., 1977-82; v.p. Planning and Design Cons., 1975—. Active, Art Inst. Chgo. Mem. AIA, Chgo. Women in Architecture, Alpha Omicron Pi. Club: Chgo. Altrusa.

TOLCHIN, SUSAN JANE, public administration educator, writer; b. N.Y.C., Jan. 14, 1941; d. Jacob Nathan and Dorothy Ann (Markowitz) Goldsmith; m. Martin Tolchin, Dec. 23, 1965; children: Charles Peter, Karen Rebecca. B.A., Bryn Mawr Coll., 1961; M.A., U. Chgo., 1962; Ph.D., N.Y.U., 1968. Lectr. in polit. sci. City Coll., N.Y.C., 1963-65, Bklyn. Coll., 1965-71; adj. asst. prof. polit. sci. Seton Hall U., South Orange, N.J., 1971-73; assoc. prof. polit. sci., dir. Inst. for Women and Politics, Mt. Vernon Coll., Washington, 1975-78; prof. pub. adminstrn. George Washington U., Washington, 1978—; editorial bd. mem. Policy Studies Rev., Tempe, Ariz., 1982—. Co-author (with Martin Tolchin): To The Victor: Political Patronage from the Clubhouse to the White House, 1971, Clout-Womanpower and Politics, 1974, Dismantling America-The Rush to Deregulate, 1983, Buying Into America-How Foreign Money Has Changed the Face of Our Nation, 1988. Pres. Wyngate Elem. Sch. PTA, Bethesda, Md., 1981-82; county committeewoman Democratic Party, Montclair, N.J., 1969-73. Dilthey fellow George Washington U., 1983, Aspen Inst. fellow, 1979; named Tchr. of Yr., Mt. Vernon Coll., 1978; recipient Founder's Day award NYU, 1968. Mem. Am. Polit. Sci. Assn. (pres. Women's Caucus for Polit. Sci. 1977-78), Am. Soc. Pub. Adminstrn. (chairperson sect. Natural Resources and Environ. Adminstrn. 1982-83). Democrat. Jewish. Office: George Washington U Dept Pub Adminstrn Washington DC 20052

TOLEGIAN, KATHLEEN WALKER, realtor; b. Providence, June 17, 1944; d. Robert Edward Walker and Mary Antoinette (Brouillard) Holl; m. Eugene Sergei Tolegian, Dec. 3, 1966 (div. 1987); children: Elisabeth Ani, Aram Eugene. Student, East L.A. Coll., 1970-71, Pan American, 1962-63. Sec. 3M Co., Los Angeles, 1963-68; office adminstr. Imperial Clin. Lab., Inc., Lynwood, Calif., 1978-80, v.p., chief fin. officer, 1980-87; realtor Bliss Keeler, Inc., San Marino, Calif., 1986—. Co-chmn. program Los Angeles chpt. Foothill affiliate Am. Diabetes Assn., 1987. Mem. White Ho. Confederacy Mus. (founding), Nat. Assn. Realtors, Calif. Assn. Realtors, Braille Aux. Pasadena (corr. sec, 1984, rec. sec. 1985). Republican. Presbyterian. Office: Bliss Keeler Inc 2486 Huntington Dr San Marino CA 91108

TOLER, MELISSA ANN, health organization executive; b. Carrollton, Mo., Nov. 18, 1953; d. Billy Gene and Sarah Ann (Schnell) T. Diploma, Newman Hosp. Sch. Nursing, 1974; student, Christopher Newport Coll., 1979-80; BA in Bus. Mgmt. with honors, U. South Fla., 1983; MBA in Health Services Mgmt., Fla. Inst. Tech., 1987. With U.S. Navy Nurse Corps, Orlando, Fla., 1974-76, Portsmouth, Va., 1976-78; adminstr. Wooten, Honeywell, Kest & Martinez, Orlando, 1983-84; dir. physician recruitment CIGNA Health Plan of Fla., Inc., Orlando, 1984-86, dir. recruitment and provider relations, 1986-87; program mgr., Diabetes Treatment Ctr. at Orlando Regional Med. Ctr., 1987—. Served to LCDR USNR, 1978—. Mem. Fla. Hosp. Assn., Nat. Assn. Female Execs., Phi Kappa Phi, Beta Gamma Sigma, Sigma Iota Epsilon. Republican. Avocations: swimming, scuba diving. Office: Orlando Regional Med Ctr Diabetes Treatment Ctr 1414 S Kuhl Ave Orlando FL 32806-2093

TOLIVER, C. R., fashion coordinator; b. Chgo., Aug. 4, 1952; d. William Saunders and Amo B. (McWhorter)-Evans; m. Steve N. Toliver, July 2, 1969 (div. July 1980); 1 child, Stephanie Monique. Telephone operator Ill. Bell Telephone Co., Chgo., 1979-82; owner, pres. Ceci, fashion coordinating, Chgo., Lacquered Images, Ltd., 1979—; chmn. Adaptations, entertainment service and cons. firm, not-for-profit, 1984—. Mem. Cosmopolitan C. of C., Notaries Assn. Ill., Am. Mus. Natural History, Am. Film Inst., Nat. Assn. Female Execs. Democrat. Roman Catholic.

TOLL, ROBERTA DARLENE (MRS. SHELDON S. TOLL), social worker; b. Detroit, May 14, 1944; d. David and Blanche (Fischer) Pollack; B.A., U. Mich., 1966; M.S.W., U. Pa., 1971; m. Aug. 11, 1968; children—Candice, John, Kevin. Dir. counselors Phila. Family Planning, Inc., 1971-72; psychologist Lafayette Clinic, Detroit, 1972-73; social worker Project Headline, Detroit, 1973-75; pvt. practice social work, Bloomfield Hills, Mich., 1975—; adj. prof. U. Detroit, Oakland Community Coll. Bd. dirs. Detroit chpt. Nat. Council on Alcoholism. Cert. social worker, Mich. Fellow Masters and Johnson Inst.; mem. Nat. Assn. Social Workers. Democrat. Club: Franklin Hills Country. Home and Office: 640 Lone Pine Hill Rd Bloomfield Hills MI 48013

TOLLETT, EILEEN RICE, business owner, consultant; b. Little Rock, Mar. 28, 1947; d. Charles J. and Mary Lois (Carroll) Rice; m. Billy E. Tollet, Aug. 16, 1969; 1 child, Casey Elaine. BSE, U. Cen. Ark., 1969; MLA, So. Meth. U., 1972; PhD, U. Tex., Dallas, 1981. Pub. relations field cons. Ark. Lung Assn., Little Rock, 1969; instr. McKinney (Tex.) Job Corps Ctr. for Women, 1970-75; staff U. Tex., Dallas, 1976-77, research asst., 1978, 78-79, 79, teaching asst., 1979, research asst., 1980, teaching asst., 1980, 81; owner, operator Tollett Typing & Cons., Allen, Tex., 1977-87; copy editor Developmental Learning Materials, Allen, 1981-84; staff editor Population Inst., So. Meth. U., 1984. V.p. Allen Pub. Library Bd., 1980-87, sec., 1983-86; guest lectr. Heard Mus., 1985; advisor to bd. dirs. Country Day Montessori Sch., Allen, 1980-81, bd dirs., 1979-80; treas. Montessori Parents Assn., Allen, 1979-80; bd. dirs. Inspired Tchrs. Studio, Inc., Dallas, 1979-80; advisor Allen Pub. Library regarding ref. materials collection on Am. Indians, 1979-80, bd. dirs., 1980—; mem. Allen City Council, 1976-78, Collin County Open Space Bd., 1988, bond com., 1987-88; underwriter Heard Natural Sci. Mus. Biology Camp, 1983, 84. UN and Population Inst. scholar, Europe, 1973; bd. dirs., sec. Allen Info. and Referral, 1987. Mem. Am. Bus. Women's Assn. (Woman of Yr. 1987), Alpha Chi. Democrat. Address: PO Box 235 Allen TX 75002

TOLLETT, GLENNA BELLE, accountant, mobile home park operator; b. Graham, Ariz., Dec. 17, 1913; d. Charles Harry and Myrtle (Stapley) Spafford; m. John W. Tollett, Nov. 28, 1928; 1 child, Jackie J., 1 adopted child, Beverly Mae Malgren. Bus. cert., Lamson Coll. Office mgr, Hurley Meat Packing Co., Phoenix, 1938-42; co-owner, sec., treas. A.B.C. Enterprises, Inc., Seattle, 1942—; ptnr. Bella Investment Co., Seattle, 1962—, Four Square Investment Co., Seattle, 1969—, Warehouses Ltd., Seattle, 1970—, Tri State Partnership, Wash., Idaho, Tex., 1972—; pres. Halycon Mobile Home Park, Inc., Seattle, 1979—; co-owner, operator Martha Lake Mobile Home Park, Lynwood, Wash., 1962-73. Mem. com. Wash. Planning and Community Affairs Agy., Olympia, 1981-82, Wash. Mfg. Housing Assn. Relations Com., Olympia, 1980-84; appointed by Gov. Wash. to Mobile Home and RV Adv. Bd., 1973-79. Named to RV/Mobile Home Hall of Fame, 1980. Mem. Wash. Mobile Park Owners Assn. (legisl. chmn., lobbyist 1976-85, cons. 1984, pres. 1978-79, exec. dir. 1976-84, This is Your Life award 1979), Wash. Soc. of Assn. Execs. (Exec. Dir. Service award 1983), Mobile Home Old Timers Assn., Mobile Home Owners of Am. (sec. 1972-76, Appreciation award 1976), Nat Fire Protection Assn. (com. 1979-86), Aurora Pkwy. North C. of C.)sec. 1976-80), Fremont C. of C. Republican. Mormon. Home: 18261 Springdale Ct NW Seattle WA 98177 Office: ABC Enterprises Inc 3524 Stone Way N Seattle WA 98103

TOLLEY, CAROLYN JACKSON, audiologist, audiometric service executive; b. DeQueen, Ark., Aug. 27, 1953; d. Carlton Conway and Charlie Mae (Chaney) Jackson; m. Philip Austin Tolley, June 25, 1977. BSE, U. Ark., 1975; MS (grantee), So. Methodist U., 1979. Tchr. of deaf Mo. State Sch. for the Deaf, Fulton, 1975-76, Tex. Regional Day Sch. for the Deaf, Kenedy, 1976-77; clin. audiologist E.N.T. Surg. Assn., Richardson, Tex., 1979-81; indsl. audiologist, pres. Audiometric Services, Inc., Dallas, 1982—. Mem. Tex. Safety Assn. (dir. 1983—, officer 1988—), Nat. Hearing Conservation Assn. (bd. dirs. 1985—, pres. elect 1988), Am. Speech Lang. Hearing Assn. (cert. clin. competence in audiology), Am. Soc. Safety Engrs., Am. Indsl. Hygiene Assn. Avocations: sailing, travel. Office: Audiometric Services Inc 2718 Hollandale Suite 200 Dallas TX 75234

TOLLEY, EMELIE ALICE, designer, color consultant, writer; b. Bklyn.; d. Albert Edward Tolley and Myra (Polley) Tolley Kilthau. Student, Wellesley Coll., 1946-48, N.Y. Sch. Interior Design, 1948-49. Fabric coordinator Celanese Corp., N.Y.C., 1955-57; fabric editor Seventeen mag., N.Y.C., 1957-62; v.p., accout supr. Benton and Bowles, N.Y.C., 1962-72; corp. fashion dir. Texfi-Industries, N.Y.C., 1972-75; color dir. The Color Box, N.Y.C., 1976—; designer fabric, wallpaper, kitchen accessories. Founder, editor Living with Herbs newsletter, 1980-86; co-author: Kitchen Detail, 1980, Herbs- Gardens, Decorations, Recipes, 1985; contbr. articles to decorating mags. Mem. Herb Soc. Am. Office: Herb Designs Inc PO Box 1332 Southampton NY 11968

TOLLIVER, DEBRA HELENA, real estate executive; b. N.Y.C., Mar. 13, 1960; d. Benjamin Ernest and Albertina (Bermudez) T.; children: Marcos Anthony, Carlos Felipe. Student, SUNY, Albany, 1977-78. Lic. real estate broker. Assoc. E.R.A. Cupo/Tag Realtors, Jersey City, 1985—. Mem. Realtor Polit. Action Com., Hudson County, N.J., 1985-87. Served with USMC, 1978. Mem. Nat. Bd. Realtors, Jersey City Bd. Realtors, Multiple Listing Service. Office: ERA Cupo/Tag Realtors 15 Nardone Pl Jersey City NJ 07306

TOLLIVER, DOROTHY OLIVIA GREENWOOD, social services administrator; b. Cleve.; d. Enoch Greenwood and Olivia Smith; m. Stanley E. Tolliver Sr.; children: Stephanie, Sherrie, Stanley. BS, Kent State U., 1980; MA in Supervision Edn., Baldwin Wallace U., 1980, post masters cert. in Gerontology, 1985; postgrad., U. Akron, 1987. Cert. family life educator. Elem. and music tchr. Cleve. Bd. Edn., 1945-52, music tchr. jr. high, 1964-68, tchr. high sch. social studies and music, 1982-85; dir. Parent Info. Ctr., Cleve., 1962—; tchr., ptnr. Project Bus., Cleve., 1982-84; free-lance cons., lectr., 1962—. Mem. citizen's adv. bd. Juvenile Ct. Cuyahoga City, Cleve., 1973-86; mem. adv. bd. Upward Bound, Cleve., 1982—; mem. county youth service bd. County Commr., Cleve., 1982—. Mem. AAUW, Nat. Council on Family Relations, Nat. Assn. Social Workers, Am. Assn. Counseling and Devel., Gerontol. Soc. Am., Ohio Council for Social Studies, LVW, Cleve. Bar Aux., Ch. Women United. Congregationalist. Office: Parent Info Ctr PO Box 1893 Cleveland OH 44106

TOLLIVER, NILA MOZINGO, pastoral care educator, chaplain; b. Charleston, W. Va., Aug. 7, 1928; d. Samuel Franklin and Lulu Myrtle (Foster) Mozingo; m. Robert Fulton Tolliver, July 29, 1944; children—Trulafaye, Samuel Robert, Dorothy Charlene. Cert. clin. pastoral educator, chaplain; ordained minister Ch. of God, 1972. A.A., Gulf-Coast Bible Coll., Houston, 1969; B.A., Houston Baptist U., 1971; M.A., Anderson (Ind.) Sch. Tehology, 1978, LHD Houston Grad. Sch. Theology. Adminstr. Houston Christian Mission, 1967-70; adminstr. group home Roanoke City Welfare Dept. (Va.), 1971-73; tchr. Nicholas County Schs., Summersville, W.Va., 1973-76; adminstr. Group Home, Hillcrest Girls Home, Anderson, Ind., 1976-78; instr. Gulf-Coast Bible Coll., Houston, 1979-83; prof., Houston Baptist Grad. Sch. Theology, 1983—, cons. chaplaincy Harris County (Tex.) Hosp. Dist., Houston, 1979—; chaplain Tex. Inst. Rehab. Research, 1979—part time, Ben Taub Gen. Hosp., 1978—, San Jacinto Bus. and Profl. Women, 1979-82 (all Houston); chairperson SETEX Bd. Christian Edn., Ch. of God, Seoul, 1987; dir. chaplain interns AMI Park Plaza Hosp., Houston, AMI Heights Hosp. Contbr. articles to religious publs. Mem. state com. Am. Cancer Soc., 1983. Named Tchr. of Yr., Bay Ridge Christian Coll., Kendalton, Tex., 1980. Mem. Assn. Clin. Pastoral Edn., Coll. Chaplains (nominating com. 1983), SE Texa Assn. Chaplains (sec.-treas. 1982, pres. 1984), Christian Assn. Psychol. Studies, Hosp. Christian Fellowship. Clubs: Women of Ch. of God (sec. 1964-66) (Anderson). Home: 1700 W TC Jester #2117 Houston TX 77008-3276 Office: Houston Grad Sch Theology 1129 Wilkins St Suite 200 Houston TX 77030

TOLL-REED, MARTHA PITKIN, banker; b. Danbury, Conn., Aug. 5, 1957; d. O. Wolcott Jr. and Susan (Kelley) Toll; m. William Preston Reed Jr., Jan. 4, 1986. BS in Resource Econs., U. N.H., 1979; MA in Econs., Brown U., 1983. Research assoc. Nat. Econ. Research Assocs., N.Y.C., 1979-81; 2d v.p. The Chase Manhattan Bank, N.Y.C., 1984-87; asst. v.p. Kansallis-Osake-Pankki, N.Y.C., 1987—. Bd. dirs. 541 8th St. Owners Corp., Bklyn., 1986—. Mem. Alpha Zeta. Democrat. Office: Kansallis Osake Pankki 575 Fifth Ave New York City NY 10017

TOM, ELIZA, college administrator, marketing executive; b. N.Y.C., Apr. 9, 1963; d. Henry G.F. and Gloria (Lui) T. BBA, Bernard M. Baruch Coll., 1984. Office asst. Bernard M. Baruch Coll., N.Y.C., 1984-85, asst. registrar, 1985—; v.p. Tridium, Inc., N.Y.C., 1986—. Active Asian Pacesetters, N.Y.C., 1986—. Mem. Nat. Assn. Female Execs., Asian Fin. Soc.

TOMAS, WANDA BRICE, computer executive; b. Nacogdoches, Tex., Mar. 3, 1942; d. James Ernest and Sally Rebekah (Summerville) Brice; m. Paul Elliot Pitt (div. 1964); 1 child, Jon F.; m. Michael S. Thomas, Nov. 2, 1973; children: Michael J., Michele. BA in Polit. Sci., Rutgers U., 1976. Data processing district mgr. Modern Am. Co., Dallas, 1966-73; v.p. Exec. Fringe Benefits, Freehold, N.J., 1973-76; mem. exec. staff mgmt. info. systems adminstrn. Carterfune Communications, Inc., Dallas, 1976-77; mgr. Mobil Oil Corp., Dallas, 1977-78; pres., chief exec. officer Legal Documentation Systems, Inc., Dallas, 1978—; bd. dirs., exec. v.p. Tex.-Sun Realty, Inc., Dallas, 1984-86, Integrated Elec. Supply, Inc., Dallas; co-owner Barnes Maintenance Services Inc., 1987—. Tex. Del. White House Conf. on Small Bus., Washington, 1986, appointed alt. del. by Tex. gov. Mark White; patron com. women's aux. March of Dimes, Dallas, 1984—; mem Mayor's Task Force for City Bond Election, Dallas, 1985, steering com. Tex. Conf. on Small Bus., Austin, 1987. Mem. Nat. Assn. Women Bus. Owners (pres. 1987—, bd. dirs. 1985—), Exec. Women of Dallas (pres. 1987, bd. dirs.), Assn. Women Entrepreneurs of Dallas, Mortgage Bankers Assn.; North Dallas C. of C. (mem. small bus. panel, Small Bus. Woman of Yr. 1987). Democrat. Methodist. Clubs: 2001 Women's (Dallas) (charter steering com. 1984), University (Dallas) (racquetball com. 1985). Office: Legal Documentations Systems Inc 2001 Bryan Tower #3857 Dallas TX 75201

TOMASEVIC, GORDANA, finance company executive; b. Nish, Yugoslavia, Oct. 21, 1943; came to U.S., 1971; d. Branko Stojanovic and Mirijana Zivkovic Sucevic; m. Tomo Tomasevic, Apr. 11, 1978; children: Danijela Djulejic, Nenad Tomasevic. Assocs. in Bus., U. Belgrade, 1963. Controller Govt. Health Inst., Belgrade, Yugoslavia, 1963-71; office clk. Mortgage Guaranty Ins. Corp., Milw., 1973-78, collector, 1978-80, sr. account servicer, 1980-83; collection mgr. Federated Fin. Savs. & Loan, Butler, Wis., 1984-85; collection mgr., asst. v.p. Federated Fin. Savs. & Loan, Elm Grove, Wis., 1985—. Active Ch. Women's Orgn. St. Nickolas Serbian Orthodox Ch., Cudahy, Wis., pres. 1984, 85, camp sec., 1986-87, nat. treas., 1984-87. Republican. Home: 960 Bobolink Dr Brookfield WI 53005 Office: Federated Fin Savs & Loan 945 Elm Grove Rd Elm Grove WI 53122

TOMASULO, VIRGINIA MERRILLS, lawyer; b. Belleville, Ill., Feb. 10, 1919; d. Frederick Emerson and Mary Eckert (Turner) Merrills; m. Nicholas Angelo Tomasulo, Sept. 30, 1952; m. Harrison I. Anthes, March 5, 1988. B.A., Wellesley Coll., 1940; LL.B., Washington U., St. Louis, 1943. Bar: Mo. 1942, U.S. Ct. Appeals (D.C. cir.) 1958, Mich. 1974, U.S. Dist. Ct. (ea. dist.) Mo. 1943, U.S. Supreme Ct. 1954, U.S. Tax Ct. 1974, U.S. Ct. Appeals (6th cir.) 1976. Lawyer, Dept. of Agr., St. Louis and Washington, 1943-48, Office of Solicitor, also lawyer Chief Counsel's Office, IRS, Washington and Detroit, 1949-75; assoc. Baker & Hostetler, Washington, 1977-82, ptnr., 1982—. Sec., S.W. Day Care Assn., Washington, 1971-73. Mem. ABA, Bar Assn. D.C., D.C. Bar Assn., Mo. Bar Assn., Fed. Bar Assn. Episcopalian. Clubs: Nat. Lawyers, Wellesley (Washington). Office: Baker & Hostetler 1050 Connecticut Ave NW Suite 1300 Washington DC 20036

TOMASZ, MARIA, chemist; b. Szeged, Hungary, Oct. 18, 1932; came to U.S., 1956, naturalized, 1963; d. Ivan and Margit Okalyi; diploma chemistry, Eotvos U., Budapest, 1956; Ph.D., Columbia U., 1962; m. Alexander Tomasz, 1956; children—Martin, Julie. Research assoc. Rockefeller U., N.Y.C., 1962, NYU, 1962-66; vis. research assoc. N.Y. Blood Ctr., 1966; asst. prof., then assoc. prof. Hunter Coll., CUNY, N.Y.C., 1966-79, prof., 1979—. Grantee NSF, USPHS. Mem. Am. Chem. Soc., Fedn. Am. Biol. Socs., Biophys. Soc., N.Y. Acad. Scis., Sigma. Author papers in field. Office: Hunter Coll 695 Park Ave New York NY 10021

TOMEI, ANGELA CORINNE, medical technologist; b. Bklyn., June 5, 1957; d. Leo James and Nina Angela T.; m. John C. Robinson, Sept. 27, 1987. BS, St. John's U., 1979, MS, 1985. Exec. sec. Stead-fast Temporaries, Inc., N.Y.C., 1975-79; med. technologist Winthrop-U. Hosp., Mineola, N.Y., 1979—; co-ordinator, founder Nat. Med. Lab. Week Winthrop-U. Hosp., Mineola, 1981—; staff contbr. Winthrop-U. Hosp. Newsletter, Mineola, 1981—; lectr. guest seminar C.W. Post Coll., Westbury, N.Y. 1986—; chmn. com. to petition salary increases, Winthroe-U. Hosp., 1987. Author: (poetry) Our World's Best Loved Poems, 1984 (2d place merit cert. 1983). Contbr. articles to profl. jours. Singer Blessed Sacrament Ch. Choir, Bklyn., 1971-73; mem. Mothers Against Drunk Driving, 1985-87, Nat. Rep. Congl. Com., 1984-86, Am. Health Found., 1986-87, DAV, 1984-87; fundraiser Statue of Liberty/Ellis Island Found., 1985-86, Hands Across Am., 1986. Recipient Cert. of Merit, State Senate-7th Dist., 1985. Mem. Am. Soc. Clin. Pathologists (registered), Empire State Assn. Med. Tech. (chmn. govt. liaison com., Outstanding Med. Tech. Student award 1979, Nassau/Suffolk chpt. founding officer 1985-86, bd. dirs., seminar moderator, 1985-87, pres.-elect 1986-87), Theta Phi Alpha (alumni chmn. 1976-77, marshal/parliamentarian 1977-78, alumni/collegiate rep. 1986-87), Pres. Soc. Alumni Assn..

TOMICH, LILLIAN, lawyer; b. Los Angeles, Mar. 28, 1935; d. Peter S. and Yovanka P. (Ivanovic) T. AA, Pasadena City Coll., 1954; BA in Polit. Sci., UCLA, 1956, cert. secondary teaching, 1957, MA, 1958; JD, U. So. Calif., 1961. Bar: Calif. Sole practice, 1961-66; house counsel Mfrs. Bank, Los Angeles, 1966; ptnr. Hurley, Shaw & Tomich, San Marino, Calif., 1968-76, Driscoll & Tomich, San Marino, 1976—; dir. Continental Culture Specialists Inc., Glendale, Calif. Trustee, St. Sava Serbian Orthodox Ch., San Gabriel, Calif. Charles Fletcher Scott fellow, 1957; U. So. Calif. Law Sch. scholar, 1958. Mem. ABA, Calif. Bar Assn., Los Angeles County Bar Assn., Women Lawyers Assn., UCLA Alumni Assn., Town Hall and World Affairs Council, Order Mast and Dagger, Iota Tau Tau, Alpha Gamma Sigma. Office: 2297 Huntington Dr San Marino CA 91108

TOMISKA, CORA LORENA, civic worker; b. Fontana, Calif., July 30, 1928; d. Riley Royston and Winifred Lillian (Humphry) Green; A.A., Chaffey Jr. Coll., 1948; B.A., Calif. State Coll., San Bernardino, 1976, post-grad., 1976—; m. Joseph Frank Tomiska, June 19, 1950; children—Jo Ann, William Joseph, Robert Royston, Charity Lillianne, Angelina Kathleen. Owner Tomiska Aviaries, Fontana, 1963—. Pres. Redwood PTA, 1976, Sequoia Jr. High PTA, 1969-70, Fontana Council PTA, 1972-74; mem. exec. bd. 5th Dist. PTA, 1972-83, historian, 1976-79, v.p., dir. health, 1979-81, v.p., dir. parent edn., 1981-83; mem. Redwood PTA; sec. consol. projects adv. com. Fontana Unified Sch. Dist., 1972-81, sec. family life edn. project, 1982-86; mem. Mayoral Candidacy Com., 1978: counselor jr. gardening Fontana Redwood Blue Jays, 1964-83; pres. Fontana Garden Club, 1974-77; vol. Fontana Youth Service Center, Am. Heart Fund, Am. Cancer Soc., Christian Youth Edn., Valley Bible Ch., Fontana United Way; scholarship chmn. San Bernardino Valley dist. Calif. Garden Clubs, 1974-83; sec.-treas. Fontana Family Service Agy., 1976-79, pres., 1980-82; mem. Arthritis Found.; mem., personal care provider, estate mgr., Fellowship of the Living Water, 1984—. Recipient 1st place award Calif. Jr. Flower Shows, 1969-73. Mem. ARC, San Bernardino County Mus. Assn., Fontana Hist. Soc., AAUW (edn. chmn. 1981-82), Am. Fedn. Aviculture. Address: 8365 Redwood Ave Fontana CA 92335

TOMLIN, LILY, actress; b. Detroit, 1939. Student, Wayne State U.; studied mime with Paul Curtis, studied acting with Peggy Feury. Appearances in concerts and colls. throughout U.S.; TV appearances include Lily Tomlin, CBS Spls., 1973, 81, 82; 2 ABC Spls., 1975; formerly cast mem. The Music Scene, Laugh In; motion picture debut in Nashville, 1975 (N.Y. Film Critics award); also appeared in The Late Show, 1977, Moment by Moment, 1978, The Incredible Shrinking Woman, 1981, Nine to Five, 1980, All of Me, 1984, Big Business, 1988; one-woman Broadway show Appearing Nitely, 1977 (Spl. Tony award), The Search for Signs of Intelligent Life in the Universe (Drama Desk award, Outer Critics Circle award, Tony award 1986), 1985; recs. include This is a Recording, And That's The Truth, Modern Scream, On Stage. Recipient Grammy award 1971, 5 Emmy awards for CBS Spl. 1973, 81, Emmy award for ABC Spl. 1975. Address: PO Box 27700 Los Angeles CA 90027

TOMLINSON, DONNA LYNN, travel service executive; b. Oklahoma City, Oct. 2, 1951; d. Don Lee Parks and Patsy Ann (Davis) Stanley; m. Thomas Clayton Kemp, Oct. 31, 1971 (div. Aug. 1978); children: Lori, Melanie, Chad. Grad. high sch., Oklahoma City. Dir. sales NW Investors, Hilton Inn, Oklahoma City, 1979-82, Quality Inn Cen., Oklahoma City, 1982-83; ptnr., exec. Hotel Connection, Oklahoma City, 1983—; owner Tomlinson Tour & Travel, Edmond, Okla., 1988—. Mem. Country Music Assn., Nat. Assn. Female Execs., Hotel-Motel Assn. Democrat.

TOMLINSON-KEASEY, CAROL ANN, psychology educator; b. Washington, Oct. 15, 1942; d. Robert Bruce and Geraldine (Howe) Tomlinson; m. Charles Blake Keasey, June 13, 1964; children: Kai Linson, Amber Lynn. BS, Pa. State U., 1964; MS, Iowa State U., 1966; PhD, U. Calif., Berkeley, 1970. Lic. psychologist, Calif. Asst. prof. psychology Trenton (N.J.) State Coll., 1969-70, Rutgers U., New Brunswick, N.J., 1970-72; assoc. prof. U. Nebr., Lincoln, 1972-77; prof. U. Calif., Riverside, 1977—, assoc. dean coll. humanities and social scis., 1986—. Author: Child's Eye View, 1980, Child Development, 1985; also numerous chpts. to books; articles to profl. jours. Recipient Disting. Tchr. award U. Calif., 1986. Mem. Am. Psychol. Assn., Soc. Research in Child Devel., Riverside Aquatics Assn. (pres. 1985). Office: U Calif Dept Psychology Riverside CA 92521

TOMPANE, MARY BETH, management consultant; b. Hollywood, Calif., Sept. 27, 1928; d. Richard Earl and Mary Elizabeth (McGregor) Goss; A.A., Phoenix Coll., 1948; postgrad. No. Ariz. U., Ariz. State U., 1946-55; M.Banking Mgmt., U. Calif., Riverside, 1973; m. Eugene F. Tompane, Nov. 4, 1950; children—Michael, Richard, Donald, John. Mgmt. analyst, 1955-69; dept. head Boswell Hosp., Sun City, Ariz., 1969-72; non profit orgn. cons., Phoenix, 1972—; travel agt., Phoenix and Tempe, Ariz., 1972-81; interim exec. dir. Girl Scouts U.S.A., from 1981; mem. nat. women's bd. Northwood Inst., 1980—. Pres. YWCA of Maricopa County, 1962-65, Phoenix Day Nursery, 1965-67, Anytown USA, 1967-69, Friends of Thunderbird, 1975-77, Family Service Phoenix, 1980; Horizona chmn. Bicentennial City of Phoenix, 1974-76; bd. dirs. Tempe United Way, 1981-86, Tempe Regional Valley of the Sun United Way, 1986—, Tempe Community Council, 1982-85. Named Woman of Year, Phoenix, 1965. Mem. Internat. Assn. Vol. Edn., Dirs. of Vols., Am. Assn. Assn. Execs. Republican. Episcopalian.

TOMPKINS, LESLIE ELIZABETH, advertising executive; b. Evanston, Ill., Mar. 11, 1958; d. Ross Harrison Tompkins Jr. and Celia Jean (Price) Jayson. BA in Communications, Mt. Vernon Coll., 1981. Personnel counselor Logan Tech. and Profl. Services, Arlington, Va., 1981-82; adminstrv. asst. Allied Bendix Aerospace, Arlington, 1982-85; personnel mgr. Advantage, Inc., Washington, 1985-86; account exec. Mgmt. Recruiters Internat., Washington, 1986, Media Sales Group, Washington, 1987; print media coordinator Shannon and Luchs, Bethesda, Md., 1988—. Home: 1400-20th St NW Washinton DC 20036 Office: 6410 Rockledge Dr Suite 300 Bethesda MD 20817

TOMPKINS, LINDA JOY, marketing specialist; b. Des Moines, Oct. 3, 1951; d. Matthew M. and Mary Louise (Foutch) Starkovich; m. James E. Tompkins, July, 1980; children: Edward Matthew, Mary Margaret. Student, Grandview Coll., 1970-74, Drake U., 1975-77. Intermediate trainer Standard Oil/Amco, Chgo. and Des Moines, 1974-75; underwriter, examiner Aetna, Des Moines and Kansas City, Mo., 1975-77; office mgr. Ann Jones Personnel, Kansas City, 1977-78, Randal Kiene, DDS, Kansas City, 1979-82; dir. mktg. Tompkins Assocs., Inc., Lee's Summit, Mo., 1984—. Active Jr. Women's Symphony Alliance, Kansas City, 1986—, Rep. Nat. Com., 1982—. Mem. Am. Philatelic Soc. Roman Catholic. Club: Lakewood Oaks Golf. Home: 151 NE Edgewater Dr Lee's Summit MO 64063 Office: State College PA 16803

TOMPKINS, PAMELA SUE, land manager; b. Duncan, Okla., May 3, 1955; d. Henry Oliver and Patsy Jean (Fulton) T. Student, U. Okla., Norman, 1977-79. Stenographer Gulf Oil Corp., Oklahoma City, 1977-78, accounts payable clk., 1978, sr. clk., 1978-80; in-training landman O-Tex Energy Inc., Oklahoma City, 1980-81; jr. landman, lease records supr HG&G Inc., Oklahoma City, 1981-82; land analyst Wilshire Oil Co. Tex., Oklahoma City, 1982-84; land mgr. Berry Petroleum Corp., Oklahoma City, 1984—. Commr. Oklahoma City Planning Commn., 1987-88; mem. Oklahoma City Plan Update Steering Com.; pres. Gatewood Neighborhood Assn., 1987-88, dist. steering com. Mem. Am. Planning Assn., Oklahoma City Assn. Petroleum Landmen. Republican. Baptist. Home: 1226 NW 22nd St Oklahoma City OK 73106

TOMS, KATHLEEN MOORE, nurse; b. San Francisco, Dec. 31, 1943; d. William Moore and Phyllis Josephine (Barry) Stewart; RN, AA, City Coll. San Francisco, 1963; BPS in Nursing Edn., Elizabethtown (Pa.) Coll., 1973; MS in Edn., Temple U., 1977; MS in Nursing, Gwynedd Mercy Coll. 1988; m. Benjamin Peskoff; children from previous marriage: Kathleen Marie Toms, Kelly Terese Toms. Med.-surg. nurse St. Joseph Hosp., Fairbanks, Alaska, 1963-65; emergency room nurse St. Joseph Hosp., Lancaster, Pa., 1965-69, blood, plasm and components nurse, 1969-71; pres. F.E. Barry Co., Lancaster, 1971—; dir. inservice edn. Lancaster Osteo. Hosp., 1971-75; coordinator practical nursing program Vocat. Tech. Sch., Coatesville, Pa., 1976-77; dir. nursing Pocopson Home, West Chester, Pa., 1978-80, Riverside Hosp., Wilmington, Del., 1980-83; assoc. Coatesville VA Hosp., 1983—; chief Nurse, 1984—; with VA Cen. Office; trainee assoc. chief Nursing Home Care Unit, Washington; mem. Pa. Gov.'s Council on Alcoholism and Drug Abuse, 1974-76; mem. Del. Health Council Med.-Surg. Task Force, 1981—; dir. Lancaster Community Health Center, 1973-76; lectr. in field. Served to maj. Nurse Corps, USAR, 1973—. Decorated Army Commendation medal; recipient Community Service award Citizens United for Better Public Relations, 1974; award Sertoma, Lancaster, 1974; Outstanding Citizen award Sta. WGAL-TV, 1975; U.S. Army Achievement award, 1983. Mem. Elizabethtown, Temple U. Alumni Assns., Pa. Nurses' Assn. (dir.), Sigma Theta Tau, Iota Kappa. Inventor auto-infuser for blood or blood components, 1971. Home: 400 Summit House 1450 West Chester Pike West Chester PA 19380 Office: Coatesville VA Med Ctr Black Horse Pike Coatesville PA 19320

TOMSIC, LINDA JEAN, educator; b. Canonsburg, Pa., Jan. 20, 1952; d. Frank Joseph and Jean Marie (Imperatore) T. BS in Edn., Duquesne U., 1972; MEd, U. Pitts., 1976, postgrad. Tchr. Canon McMillan Sch. Dist., Canonsburg, Pa., 1972-84, 1984—; bd. govs. Duquesne U., 1985—, exec. bd. dirs. 1985-86; basic leader trainer Great Book Found., Canonsburg, 1986—. Mem. Assn. Supervision and Child Devel., Doctoral Assn., Phi Lambda Theta (corr. sec. 1987—), Delta Zeta (pres. 1981-82, 1987—). Home: 158 E College St Canonsburg PA 15317

TONELLI, EDITH ANN, art gallery director, art historian; b. Westfield, Mass., May 20, 1949; d. Albert Robert and Pearl (Grubert) T. B.A., Vassar Coll., 1971; M.A., Hunter Coll., 1974; Ph.D., Boston U., 1981; grad., Mus. Mgmt. Inst. U. Calif.-Berkeley, 1981. Arts curriculum coordinator Project SEARCH, Millbrook, N.Y., 1972-74; curator DeCordova Mus., Lincoln, Mass., 1976-78; dir. art gallery, asst. prof. art U. Md., College Park, 1979-82, dir. mus. studies program, 1979-82; project dir. Summer Inst. Artists U. Md., 1981-82; dir. Frederick S. Wight Art Gallery, 1982—; adj. asst. prof. art UCLA, 1982—; reviewer pub. programs NEH, 1977—. Author exhbn. catalogs. Fellow Nat. Endowment Arts, 1981; predoctoral fellow Smithsonian Instn., 1979; doctoral and teaching fellow Boston U., 1974-76; mem. Helen Squire Townsend fellow Vassar College, 1971-72; recipient dissertation award Boston U. Vis. Com., 1979. Mem. Am. Assn. Museums, Coll. Art Assn., Women's Caucus for Art, Am. Fedn. Arts(advisor profl. tng.), Assn. Art Mus. Dirs. (trustee 1987—), Am. Studies Assn., Art Table Inc. Office: UCLA Wight Art Gallery 1100 Gallery Bldg 405 Hilgard Los Angeles CA 90024

TONER, CAROLYN YAKEL, interior designer, consultant; b. Brawley, Calif., Feb. 13, 1928; d. Henry Roy Yakel and Merry Alyce (Cain) Yakel-Jordan; m. Richard Francis Toner, Oct. 30, 1955 (div. 1968); children: Thomas Kevin, Stephen Gary. AA, Pasadena City Coll., 1948; cert., Rudolph Schaeffer Sch. Design, 1968; cert. Urban Planning, U. Calif., Berkeley, 1980. With personnel Los Angeles Times, 1948-55; pvt. practice designor Corte Madera, Calif., 1968-74, 86—; interior designer Ethan Allen, Mill Valley, Calif., 1974-76; mgr. store planning Gen. Mills Subsidiary, Hayward, Calif., 1977-80; with constrn. bidding, contracting Golden Gate Bridge Dist., San Francisco, 1983-86. Actress TV show Executives Unlimited. Bd. dirs. Christmas Tree Hilldwellers, Corte Madera, 1986-87. Mem. Am. Soc. Interior Designs (assoc., advt. chair 1986, survey team leader 1986), Designers Lighting Forum, Mycol. Soc., Nat. Assn. Female Execs. Home: 14 Summit Dr Corte Madera CA 94925

TONEY, EDNA, playwright, actress; b. N.Y.C., Mar. 22, 1914; d. Henry and Frieda (Berger) Greenfield; m. Anthony Toney, Apr. 8, 1947; children—Anita Karen, Adele Susan. Student New Theatre Sch., 1936; Columbia U., 1953-55, New Sch. Social Research, 1975. Actress WPA Theatre Project, N.Y.C., 1937; writer Kraft Music Hall, N.Y.C., 1946; writer, producer, actress schs., community ctrs., colls., libraries, etc., 1972-82; playwright Meet Miss Lucy Stone (video prons. written, starring Edna Toney 1988), Lincoln Ctr. Library's Museum of the Performing Arts, 1977, Baby Brother Prodn., Mid-Hudson Arts and Sci. Ctr., Poughkeepsie, N.Y., 1980; writer, dir., actress, producer Katonah Community Theatre, N.Y., 1984; columnist Queries and Theories. Author: Once Told Tales, 1967, How to Become a Famous Playwright, 1987; featured in The Rosenbergs: Collected Visions of Artists & Writers by Rob Okun, 1988. Benefit performance Meet Miss Lucy Stone, North Westchester-Putnam County Women's Resource Ctr., Mahopac, N.Y., 1986. Recipient acting awards 10th Annual Arts Festival, 1976. Mem. NOW, Women's Internat. League Peace and Freedom, SANE, Katonah Gallery. Democrat. Avocations: swimming. Home: 16 Hampton Pl Katonah NY 10536

TONG, LORETTA H. F., manufacturing company administrator; b. San Francisco, Sept. 7, 1948; d. Jack and Lucille Fong; m. Benjamin Robert Tong, Feb. 7, 1975. BA, San Francisco State U., 1971, postgrad. Exec. mgr. Calif. Woodworking, Inc., Daly City, Calif., 1981—; cons. nutrition and health Pola Products, San Francisco, 1980—. Adminstrv. coordinator Inst. for Cross-Cultural Research, San Francisco, 1985—; mem. Chinese for Affirmative Action, San Francisco, 1987—, San Francisco Mus. Soc. Mem. Am. Anthrop. Soc., Am. Assn. Home Economists, Consumers Union, Asian Law Caucus. Democrat.

TONJES, MARIAN JEANNETTE BENTON, reading educator; b. Rockville Center, N.Y., Feb. 16, 1929; d. Millard Warren and Felicia E. (Tyler) Benton; m. Charles F. Tonjes (div. 1965); children: Jeffrey Charles, Kenneth Warren. BA, U. N.Mex., 1951, cert., 1966, MA, 1969; EdD, U. Miami, 1975. Dir. recreation Stuyvesant Town Housing Project, N.Y.C., 1951-53; tchr. music., phys. edn. Sunset Mesa Day Sch., Albuquerque, 1953-54; tchr. remedial reading Zia Elem. Sch., Albuquerque, 1965-67; tchr. secondary devel. reading Rio Grande High Sch., Albuquerque, 1967-69; research asst. reading Southwestern Coop. Ednl. Lab., Albuquerque, 1969-71; assoc. dir., vis. instr. Fla. Ctr. Tchr. Tng. Materials U. Miami, 1971-72; asst. prof. U.S. Internat. U., San Diego, 1972-75; prof. edn. Western Wash. U., Bellingham, 1975—; vis. prof. adult edn. Palamar (Calif.) Jr. Coll., 1974; reading supr. Manzanita Ctr. U. N.Mex., Albuquerque, 1968; mem. numerous coms. at Western Wash. U.; dir. summer study in Eng. at Oxford U., 1975—; speaker, cons. in field. Author: (with Miles V. Zintz) Teaching Reading/Thinking Study Skills in Content Classrooms, 2d rev. edit. 1987; contbr. articles to profl. jours. Mem. English Speaking Union/Dartmouth House, London. Recipient Disting. Tchr. award Western Wash. U., 1981; TTT grantee; NDEA fellow Okla. State U. Mem. Am. Reading Forum (chmn. bd. dirs. 1983-85), Internat. Reading Assn. (travel interchange and study tours com. 1984-86, non-print media and reading com. 1980-83, workshop dir. S.W. regional conf. 1982, 85, English Speaking Union tchr. yr. com. 1988-90), Nat. Assn. Primary Edn. (Eng.), Nat. Council Tchrs. English, United Kingdom Reading Assn. (speaker), PEO (past local pres.), English Speaking Union, Phi Delta Kappa (local chpt. nominating com. 1984, alt. del. 1982), Delta Delta Delta. Republican. Office: Western Wash U Dept Edn Bellingham WA 98225

TONUCCI, ELIZABETH FOX, college official; b. Hartford, Conn., Feb. 19, 1944, d. Wesley Vincent and Gertrude Clarissa (Sibley) Birge; m. Armand William Tonucci, July 8, 1967 (div. Jan. 1983); children: Karen, Katherine. BS in Elem. Edn., U. Conn., 1966; cert. profl. in human resources, Personnel Accreditation Inst. Tchr. Salem (Conn.) Elem. Sch., 1966-67, John Fitch Sch., Windsor, Conn., 1967-69; dir. vols. Manchester (Conn.) Meml. Hosp., 1979-86; mgr. personnel Shipman & Goodwin, Hartford, 1986-87; dir. personnel St. Joseph Coll., West Hartford, Conn., 1987—. Mem. Citizens Adv. Com. for Ednl. Goals, Manchester, 1980-81, Manchester Human Relations Commn., 1982-85; co-chmn. Manchester Interracial Council, 1981-84. Mem. Am. Soc. for Personnel Adminstrn., So. New Eng. Coll. and Univ. Personnel Assn., Personnel Mgmt. Assn. Cen. Conn. (chmn. profl. devel./accreditation 1986-87, sec. 1988). Democrat. Congregationalist. Home: 21 Croft Dr Manchester CT 06040 Office: St Joseph Coll 1678 Asylum Ave West Hartford CT 06117

TOOP, GILLIAN V., educator; b. Taunton, Somerset, England, Apr. 15, 1946; came to U.S., 1953, naturalized; d. Gilbert Harry and Vera (Beech) Yard; m. George C. Toop Jr., June 24, 1967; 1 child, Kevin George. Cert. elem. and secondary tchr. N.J., Pa. Tchr. Pa. Pub. Schs., 1967-70, 1971-73; tchr. Big Spring (Tex.) Ind. Schs., 1970-71, Voorhees (N.J.) Twp. Schs., 1974-76; tchr., team leader Fairfax County Pub. Schs., Reston, Va., 1981—; part time cons. tchr. Fairfax County Schs., 198. Contbr. articles to profl. jours. V.p., pub., editor Women of Alluvium, Voorhees, 1976-78; chmn. Lakeside Cluster Assn., Reston, Va.; mem. exec. bd. PTA, Reston, 1985-87, Historic Preservation. Grantee Honeywell Corp., 1987. Mem. NEA, Smithsonian Assocs., Sigma Delta Pi, Sigma Kappa Nat. Sorority (v.p. scholarship 1965-67). Office: Dogwood 12300 Glade Dr Reston VA 22091

TOOTE, GLORIA E. A., lawyer, developer, columnist; b. N.Y.C., Nov. 8, 1931; d. Frederick A. and Lillie M. (Tooks) Toote. Student, Howard U., 1949-51; J.D., NYU, 1954; LL.M., Columbia U., 1956. Bar: N.Y. 1955, U.S. Dist. Ct. (so. and ea. dists.) N.Y. 1956, U.S. Supreme Ct. 1956. With firm Greenbaum, Wolff & Ernst, 1957; mem. editorial staff Time mag., 1957-58; asst. gen. counsel N.Y. State Workmen's Compensation Bd., 1958-64; pres. Toote Town Pub. Co. and Town Sound Studios, Inc., 1966-70; asst. dir. Action Agy., 1971-73; asst. sec. Dept. HUD, 1973-75; vice chmn. Pres.'s Adv. Council on Pvt. Sector Initiatives, 1983-85; housing developer 1976—; pres. Trea Estates and Enterprises, Inc.; newspaper columnist. Former bd. dirs. Citizens for the Republic, Nat. Black United Fund, Exec. Women in Govt., Am. Arbitration Assn., Consumer Alert; bd. overseers Hoover Inst.; vice chair Nat. Polit. Congress of Black Women; former mem. Council Econ. Affairs, Rep. Nat. Com.; pres. N.Y.C. Black Rep. Council; exec. trustee Polit. Action Com. for Equality. Recipient citations Nat. Bus. League, Alpha Kappa Alpha, U.S. C. of C.; YMCA World Service award. Mem. Nat. Assn. Black Women Attys., N.Y. Fedn. Civil Service Orgns., Nat. Assn. Real Estate Brokers, Nat. Citizens Participation Council, Nat. Bar Assn., Delta Sigma Theta, others. Address: 282 W 137th St New York NY 10030

TOPHAM, DIANNE MARIE, university executive; b. Dallas, Apr. 7, 1958; d. Dain S. and Marjorie (Gannon) Hancock. Student, So. Ill. U., 1980. Ops. mgr. Processing Mgmt. Systems, Phoenix, 1981-86; prodn. mgr. Pandick Techs., Los Angeles, 1986-88; univ. adminstr. U. of Phoenix, 1988—. Vol. Make-A-Wish Found., Los Angeles, 1986—. Mem. Nat. Fund Raising Execs., Nat. Assn. Female Execs. Office: U Phoenix 125 Baker St Costa Mesa CA 85040

TOPINKA, JUDY BAAR, state legislator; b. Riverside, Ill., Jan. 16, 1944; d. William Daniel and Lillian Mary (Shuss) Baar; B.S., Northwestern U., 1966; 1 son, Joseph Baar. Features editor, reporter, columnist Life Newspapers, Berwyn and LaGrange, Ill., 1966-77; with Forest Park (Ill.) Review and Westchester News, 1976-77; coordinator spl. events Dept. Fedn. Communications, AMA, 1978-80; research analyst Senator Leonard Becker, 1978-79; mem. Ill. Ho. of Reps., 1981-84; mem. Ill. Senate, 1985—(pub. health com., ins., pensions and licensing com, judiciary I com., senate transp. com., appropriations I com.), mem. Nat. Assn. State Racing Commrs., co-chmn. Citizens Council on Econ. Devel., U.S. Commn. for Preservation of Am.'s Heritage Abroad, serves on legis. ref. bur., senate select. com. on Ill. Pension Funds in No. Ireland, select com. on Kansas City to Chgo. rte. corridor; former mem. minority bus. resource ctr. adv. com. U.S. Dept. Transp.; mem. adv. bd. Nat. Inst. Justice. Founder, pres., bd. dirs. West Suburban Exec. Breakfast Club, from 1976; Republican candidate Ill. Senate, 1984; chmn. Ill. Ethnics for Reagan-Bush, 1984; mem. Ill. Gov.'s Task Force on Horse Racing.

TOPJIAN, MENA ROSE, educator; b. Cambridge, Mass., Sept. 7, 1936; d. Daniel and Siran T. B.S. in Edn., Boston U., 1958, M.Ed. in Sch. Librarianship, 1966. Tchr., Deep River Elem. Sch., Conn., 1958, Prospect Sch., Beverly, Mass., 1959, Oak Grove Sch., North Miami Beach, Fla., 1960, Franklin Sch., Lexington, Mass., 1961-83, Bowman Sch., Lexington, 1983—. Author articles and reports in field of Native Am. studies. Mem. Nat. Council Social Studies Tchrs., Mass. Council Social Studies Tchrs., NEA, Mass. Tchrs. Assn., Lexington Tchrs. Assn., Pan Am. Soc., Cultural Survival Soc. Club: Victorian, World Affairs Council (Boston); Peabody Mus. (Cambridge, Mass.). Home: 36 F Jacqueline Rd Waltham MA 02154 Office: Bowman Sch Lexington MA 02154

TOPPE, MELANIE WILSON, accountant; b. Macon, Ga., Apr. 28, 1949; d. Jesse Franklin and Allene (House) Wilson; m. William Hscass, Aug. 25, 1973 (div. Jan. 1977); m. Jonathan Richard Toppe, Feb. 14, 1981; 1 child, Jessica Leah. BBA, Stetson U., 1971. CPA, Fla. Exec. trainee Maas Bros., Tampa, Fla., 1971-73; asst. buyer Robinsons Dept. Store, St. Petersburg, Fla., 1973-75; buyer Burdine's Dept. Store, Clearwater, Fla., 1975-77; v.p. fin. L.J. Levy, Inc., Largo, Fla., 1977-81; audit sr. Ernst and Whinney, St. Petersburg, Fla., 1981-85; audit supr. Peat Marwick Main, St. Petersburg, 1985-86; dir. fin. adminstrn. St. Petersburg Housing Authority, 1986-88, cons., 1987—; audit, tax mgr. Joslin and Assoc., PA, St. Petersburg, 1988—. Speaker "Planning in the 80's", 1985. Chmn. audit com. United Way, 1986; speaker St. Pete Jr. League, 1985, fin. com., 1985—, treas. thrift shop, 1985, devel. com., 1986—, chmn. comp. com. 1988—. Mem. Fla. Inst. CPA's, Am. Inst. CPA's, Pi Beta Phi (pres. 1984, 86). Clubs: St. Pete Pan Hellenic (pres. 1986, 87), St. Pete Yacht, Presidents. Home: 210 14th Ave N Saint Petersburg FL 33701 Office: Joslin and Assocs PA 1212 66th St N Saint Petersburg FL 33710

TOPPIN, MARTHA DOERR, secondary educator; b. Los Angeles, Aug. 20, 1935; d. Albert Edward and Harriet Doerr. BA, U. Calif., 1957, MA, 1966, cert. tchr., 1968. Program asst. Inst. Internat. Edn., San Francisco, 1961-65; tchr. Vallejo (Calif.) Unified Schs., 1968-69; tchr. Mt. Diablo Unified Sch. Dist., Olympic High Sch., Concord, Calif., 1969-84, Oak Grove Intermediate Sch., Concord, Calif., 1977-84; tchr. Crane Sch., Santa Barbara, Calif., 1984-85, Pine Hollow Intermediate Sch., Concord, 1985—. Contbr. articles to profl. jours. Mem. Calif. Council for Social Studies (no. regional v.p., exec. com. 1976-78, editor newsletter 1975-80), Nat. Council for Social Studies, Phi Delta Kappa, Alpha Delta Kappa. Office: Pine Hollow Intermediate Sch Pine Hollow Rd Concord CA 94521

TORANI, LISA MOORADIAN, public relations/meeting planning consultant; b. St. Louis, Mar. 10, 1953; d. Leonard and Alice (Jamochian) Mooradian; m. Joseph Anthony Torani, July 30, 1983. BA in Communications, St. Louis U., 1975. Med. news writer St. Louis Med. Ctr., 1975-77; pub. info. coordinator St. Louis Assn. for Retarded Citizens and Rainbow Village, 1977-79; dir. pub. relations David Birenbaum & Assocs., St. Louis, 1979-83; dir. meetings and convs. The Bus. Council of N.Y. State, Inc., Albany, 1984—. Mem. Soc. Assn. Execs. of Upstate N.Y. (dir. 1987—), Am. Soc. Assn. Execs., Nat. Assn. Female Execs. Mem. Armenian Ch. Home: 12 Wildwood Ct Clifton Park NY 12065

TORBERG, VIRGINIA HUBBARD, wood carver, soap manufacturer; b. Mpls., May 8, 1922; d. Albert Jerry and Thaaline (Hauge) Hubbard; student pub. schs., Mpls., U. Minn.; m. Bernie R. Torberg, Sept. 18, 1948; children—Steven M., Richard L., Robin S., Peter L., Daniel J. Propr., North Country Soap, Lyndale, Minn., 1973—; partner Country Woodcraft, Lyndale, 1964—; demonstrator soapmaking, wood carving; designer, producer Woodcraft Carving Kit, 1971—; carvings exhibited: Sons of Norway, Mpls., Lutheran Brotherhood Gallery, Mpls., 1975. Pres. local PTA, 1968; mem. Independence (Minn.) Bicentennial Commn. Mem. Minn., Minnetonka (charter) hist. assns., Minn. Valley Restoration Project, Nat., Minn. woodcarvers assns., Nat. Carvers Museum, Smithsonian Assocs., Mus. Store Assn. (assoc.), Am. Heritage Assn., Audubon Soc., Weaver's Guild, Internat. Platform Assn., LWV. Christian Scientist. Clubs: Garden, Lit., Spinner's, Order Eastern Star. Author: Why Carve Just One?, 1970; Country Pattern Book for Woodcarving, 1972; Something About Soap, 1973; also articles. Address: 7888 County Rd 6 Maple Plain MN 55359

TORETTI, CHRISTINE JACK, gas company executive; b. Pitts., Feb. 24, 1957; d. Samuel Williams and Nell Jacqueline (Gibson) Jack; m. Micheal Joseph Toretti, Aug. 15, 1981; children: Joseph Jack, Maxwell Jack. BS in Commerce, U. Va., 1981. Ptnr. C & N Co., Indiana, Pa., 1972—; v.p. S. W. Jack Drilling Co., Indiana, 1984—; owner J&J Enterprises Inc., Indiana, 1987—; bd. dirs. The Savings and Trust Co. of Pa. Bd. mgrs. U. Va., 1984—; trustee Chi Omega Found., Cin., 1984—; pres. Found. Indiana U. of Pa., 1984—, YMCA of Indiana County, 1985—. Republican. Presbyterian. Club: Zonta (treas. 1986—). Home: 57 S Ninth St Indiana PA 15701 Office: S W Jack Drilling Co 43 S Ninth St Indiana PA 15701-0697

TORF, JANE HAMILTON, antique store owner; b. Marshall, Ill., Aug. 29, 1916; d. George and Ethel Rosa (Bennett) Beuhler; m. Allen Britt Hamilton, Feb. 26, 1940 (dec. 1957); children: Judith Carol, Janet Clare; m. Al Torf, Nov. 6, 1965. Student, Art Sch., Chgo., 1935. Sales rep. Marshall Field & Co., Chgo., 1935-40; owner Hamilton House Antique Store, Glendora, Calif., 1951-88; lectr. on antiques, 1958-70. Mem. Internat. Soc. Appraisers (cert.), Am. Soc. Appraisers, Nat. Assn. Dealers, Antique Assn. So. Calif. (v.p. 1965-67). Democrat. Methodist.

TORINESE, MARILYN ROSE, professional association executive; b. N.Y.C., Oct. 11, 1948; d. Anthony Joseph and Anne (Cosenza) Cutrona; m. Constantino L. Torinese, Feb. 28, 1986. Supr. Am. Express Co., N.Y.C., 1967-76; assoc. dir. ASME, N.Y.C., 1978-84, mgr. ops. and support, 1986-87, dir. ops./support/adminstrn., 1987—; mgr. regional office Autex Systems, N.Y.C., 1985-86; cons. Autex Systems, N.Y.C., 1986. Mem. ASME (exec. affiliate), Nat. Assn. for Female Execs. Office: ASME 345 E 47 St New York NY 10017

TORME, MARGARET ANNE, public relations executive, communications consultant; b. Indpls., Apr. 5, 1943; d. Ira G. and Margaret Joy (Wright) Barker; children—Karen Anne, Leah Vanessa. Student Coll. San Mateo, 1961-65. Pub. relations mgr. Hoefer, Dieterich & Brown, San Francisco, 1964-73; v.p., co-founder, creative dir. Lowry & Ptnrs., San Francisco, 1975-83; pres., founder Torme & Co., San Francisco, 1983—; cons. in communications. Mem. Pub. Relations Soc. Am., San Francisco Advt. Club, North Bay Advt. Club (bd. dirs.), San Francisco C. of C.(outstanding achievement award for women entrepreneurs 1987). Office: 414 Jackson St San Francisco CA 94111

TORRE, ELIZABETH LASSITER, social worker, educator; b. Winston-Salem, N.C., June 17, 1931; d. Vernon Clark and Mary (Pfohl) Lassiter; m. Mottram Peter Torre, Apr. 13, 1957 (dec.); m. Andrew Joseph Reck, June 17, 1987. student Wellesley (Mass.) Coll., 1948-49; B.A., Duke U., 1952; M.R.E., Union Theol. Sem., 1957; M.S.W., Tulane U., 1966, Ph.D., 1972; cert. social worker, La. Field dir. undergrad. admissions Duke U., Durham, N.C., 1952-53; head tchr. primary dept. Riverside Ch., N.Y.C., 1957-60; instr. Sch. Social Work, Tulane U., New Orleans, 1966-72, assoc. prof., 1972—, coordinator Indsl. Social Work Program, 1982—; non-govtl. orgn. rep. UNICEF, World Fedn. Mental Health, 1957-61; cons. to v.p. community affairs WETA, Washington, 1979; cons. Office Spl. Symposia and Seminars, Smithsonian Instn., Washington, 1979-86. Treas., N.Y. Jr. League, 1961-62, v.p., 1962-63; bd. dirs. Community Vol. Services, New Orleans, 1965-68; mem. profl. adv. com. Project Pre-Kindergarten, Orleans Parish Sch. Bd., New Orleans, 1967-69; mem. adv. bd. DePaul Community Mental Health Center, New Orleans, 1971-72; mem. citizens adv. com. Orleans Parish Juvenile Ct., New Orleans, 1970-73; mem. Council on Social Work Edn. Task Force on Prevention, 1981—; mem. New Orleans Women's Coalition Task Force on Employers and Working Parents, 1985—. NIMH grantee; Summer Inst. grantee Nat. Endowment Humanities, 1982. Mem. Council Social Work Edn., Nat. Assn. Social Workers (bd. dirs. La. chpt. 1987—), Am. Orthopsychiat. Assn., AAUP, World Future Soc., Phi Beta Kappa. Office: Tulane U Sch Social Work New Orleans LA 70118

TORRES, CYNTHIA ANN, banker; b. Glendale, Calif., Sept. 24, 1958; d. Adolph and Ruth Ann (Smith) T. AB, Harvard U., 1980, MBA, 1984. Research assoc. Bain & Co., Boston, 1980-82; assoc. Goldman, Sachs & Co., N.Y.C., 1984-88, v.p., 1988—. Mem. judiciary rev. bd. Bus. Sch. Harvard U., Boston, 1983-84. Rockefeller Found. scholar, 1976; Harvard U. Ctr. for Internat. Affairs fellow, 1979-80; recipient Leadership award Johnson and Johnson, 1980; by Council for Opportunity in Grad. Mgmt. Edn. fellow, 1982-84. Mem. Acad. Polit. Sci. Club: Harvard of N.Y.C. (mem. schs. com. 1985—). Office: Goldman Sachs & Co 85 Broad St New York City NY 10004

TORRES TUCKER, RITA MARIA, engineer; b. San Antonio, Tex., Oct. 15, 1954; d. Enrique and Lily Erencstina (Ramirez) Torres; m. Howard Wayne Ybarbo, July 8, 1976 (div. Mar. 1978); 1 child, Jennifer Rose; m. Gary Dwayne Tucker, May 26, 1985; 1 stepson, Marshall Austin Tucker. BS in Engring. Sci., Trinity U., 1978; MS in Engring. Adminstrn., St. Mary's U., 1987. Lic. profl. engr., Tex. Engr. Southwestern Bell Telephone Co., San Antonio, 1978—; regional chair Mathcounts of Tex., San Antonio, 1983, state chair, 1987-88; mentor Harlendale Ind. Sch. Dist., San Antonio,

1987—;. Judge Alamo Regional Acad. of Sci. and Engring., San Antonio, 1984-86, Tex. Acad. Decathlon, San Antonio, 1986; sgt. at arms, mentor Baexar chpt. St. Mary's U., San Antonio, 1987—. Mem. Profl. Engrs. in Industry (vice chair region III 1986-87, chmn. 1988), Tex. Soc. Profl. Engrs. (chair edn. 1983-84, Engr. for a Day 1981-86), Tex. Soc. Telephone Engrs. (San Antonio chpt. sgt.-at-arms 1988-89), Nat. Soc. Profl. Engrs. (Young Engr. of Yr. award 1988), Profl. Women S.We. Bell. Home: 5847 Sundance Lane San Antonio TX 78238 Office: Southwestern Bell Telephone Co 10100 Reunion Place Room 435E San Antonio TX 78216

TORRIERO, DOLORES FRANCES, public administrator; b. Bklyn., Mar. 5, 1957; d. Robert Nicholas and Naomi (Abrahms) T. BA, SUNY, Oswego, 1979; MPA, Kent State U., 1982. Research assoc. Clemans, Nelson and Assocs., Columbus, Ohio, 1983; labor relations asst. to mayor's office City of Cleve., 1983-84, labor relations officer utilities dept., 1984—. Pres., charter mem. SouthWest Unitarian Universalist Ch. Mem. Ohio Pub. Employer Labor Relations Assn. (sec.-treas.), Pub. Sector Labor Relations Assn., Internat. Personnel Mgmt. Assn. Home: 931 Tollis Pkwy Broadview Heights OH 44147 Office: Dept Pub Utilities 1201 Lakeside Ave Cleveland OH 44114

TORVIK, PATRICIA ANN, health facility executive; b. Ivanhoe, Minn., Oct. 3, 1938; d. Carl Elmo and Wilma Gertrude (Weigert) Nyhus; m. Peter John Torvik, Sept. 20, 1958; children: Peter John, Jr., Carl Fredric. BS, Wright State U., 1972, MEd, 1977; PhD, Ohio State U., 1983. Tchr. Dayton (Ohio) Pub. Schs., 1972-78; teaching asst. Ohio State U., Columbus, 1978-80; supr. teaching Dayton Mental Health Ctr., 1980-82, program dir., 1982-84, asst. to supt., 1984-86, supt., 1986—; clin. prof. Schs. Medicine and Profl. Psychology, Wright State U., Dayton, 1986—. Bd. dirs. Met. Chs. United, Dayton, 1978-86; mem. Dayton Women's Coalition, 1984—; office chairperson Montgomery County United Way, Dayton, 1986—. Named one of Ten Top Women local newspapers, 1985. Mem. Internat. Assn. Psychosocial Rehab. Services, Assn. Mental Health Adminstrs., Ohio Assn. Mental Health Adminstrs., Ohio Supt.'s Assn. Democrat. Presbyterian. Home: 2000 Harvard Blvd Dayton OH 45406 Office: Dayton Mental Health Ctr 2611 Wayne Ave Dayton OH 45420

TOSH, JUANITA PRILLAMAN, tire company executive; b. Axton, Va., Jan. 13, 1930; d. Stuart Owen and Ann Halvorsen (Jamison) Prillaman; attended public schs., Bassett, Va.; m. James Cleavon Tosh, June 5, 1961; children—Rebecca Ann Craze, Cheryl Sue Layton, Mark Cleavon. Owner, Russ Auto Service Co., Norfolk, Va., 1954-59; v.p. Russ & Prillaman Auto Service Inc., Collinsville, Va., 1959-68; co-owner John Allen Estates, Collinsville, 1975—; v.p. Town Gun Shop, Collinsville, 1983—; owner Tosh Tire Town, Collinsville, 1969—; sec.-treas. Cash Oil Sales Inc., Collinsville, Va., 1982-85. Mem. Retail Mchts. Assn., Va. Tire Dealers and Retreaders Assn., Nat. Tire Dealers and Retreaders Assn., Nat. Alliance Stocking Gun Dealers. Baptist. Home: 208 Ferndale Dr Collinsville VA 24078

TOSH, NANCY PECKHAM, magazine editor; b. Clinton, Iowa, May 5, 1932; d. George Taylor, III and Mildred Amelia (Smallfeldt) Peckham; m. David Warren Tosh, July 5, 1958 (div. Dec. 1978); children—Murray, Warren, Amy. Student, Sullins Coll., Bristol, Va., 1950-52; B.A. in Journalism, State U. Iowa, 1954. Copywriter Sears, Roebuck & Co., Chgo., 1954-58; copywriter, staff writer Clapper Pub. Co., Inc., Park Ridge, Ill., 1973-76, copy editor Crafts 'N Things mag., 1976-77, asst. editor, 1977-79, editor, 1979—. Mem. P.E.O., Gamma Alpha Chi, Phi Theta Kappa. Republican. Home: 1804 S Prospect Park Ridge IL 60068 Office: Crafts 'N Things Mag 14 Main St Park Ridge IL 60068

TOTH, ANNE PATTEN, convalescent center executive; b. Bridgeport, Conn., Dec. 14, 1947; d. Albert Allen and Harriet Ellen (Leib) Garofalo; m. Kevin Randall Meyer, July 29, 1967 (div. June 1972); 1 child, Nicole Marie; m. Michael Edward Toth, Oct. 6, 1978; children: Alexis Patten, Aaron Michael. Student Quinnipiac Coll., Wharton Sch., Harvard Bus. Sch. Programmer, Save the Children, Westport, Conn., 1966-69; systems analyst Burndy Corp., Norwalk, Conn., 1969-70; pvt. practice systems analyst cons., Fairfield, Conn., 1970—; adminstrv. asst. Southport (Conn.) Manor, 1974-75, adminstr., chief exec. officer, 1975—, pres. 1987—. Chpt. pres. Am. Field Service, Greens Farms, Conn., 1984-86; chairwoman Daffodil Festival, Am. Cancer Soc., Fairfield, 1984; chairwoman Gourmet Gala March of Dimes, Stamford, Conn., 1985. Mem. Young Pres. Orgn., Fairfield C. of C. (treas. 1986), Am. Coll. Health Adminstrs. (cert.), Concerned Women's Colleagues, Am. Mgmt. Assn. Democrat. Roman Catholic. Club: YWCA-100 Com. (bd. dirs. 1982—). Avocations: scuba diving, skiing, swimming, horseback riding, travel. Home: 160 Farmstead Hill Rd Fairfield CT 06430 Office: Southport Manor Convalescent Ctr 930 Mill Hill Terr Southport CT 06490

TOTH, JUDITH COGGESHALL, state legislator; b. Rochelle, Ill., Oct. 21, 1937; d. Dr. and Mrs. R.J. Coggeshall; children—Christina, Adriana. Student Mexico City Coll. (U. of Americas), 1956-57; B.A. in Latin Am. Studies, Northwestern U., 1959; postgrad. Georgetown U., 1960-61, U. Andes, Bogota, Colombia, 1965-66, Montgomery Coll., 1980-81, U. Md., 1981-83; M.P.H., Johns Hopkins U., 1984. Bookkeeper, salesperson, professional model, dental asst. and sec., 1955-64; instr. polit. sci. and history U. of the Andes, 1964-66; legis. liaison and office mgr. Emergency Com. for Gun Control, 1968-69; cons. to Internat. Study Ctr., 1968, Pres.'s Commn. on the Causes and Prevention of Violence, 1969; researcher Assoc., Ideas, Inc., 1970-71; v.p. Polit-Econ, Inc., 1971-74; mem. Md. Gen. Assembly, Annapolis, 1975—, mem. various coms., Gov.'s Commn. on Hispanic Affairs, 1979—, chmn. Joint Com. on Medicaid, 1980-82; mem. Task Force to Rev. Hosp. Regulations, 1980-82; cons. in field; mem. adv. com. to NASA, 1976-82; mem. Md. Hist. Trust, 1982—; appointee Washington Met. Council of Govts., 1975—, mem. pub. safety policy com., 1985—. Bd. dirs. Md. Assn. of the Deaf, 1979-82, Citizens Transp. Coalition, 1971-73; pres. Montgomery County Civic Fedn., 1973-74, Washington Met. Congress of Citizens, 1971-73, Cabin John Park Citizens Assn., 1970-72, founding editor Cabin John Village News; founder, co-chmn. Montgomery County Coalition of Pres.'s, 1973-74; mem. adv. com. on the Potomac River, Montgomery County Council, 1970-71; bd. govs. ACLU of Md., 1970-73; mem. environ. groups; bd. dirs. Nat. Consumer Orgn. for Hearing Impaired, 1979-80; active numerous Democratic campaigns in local, state and nat. elections, 1956—; founding mem. Alliance for Dem. Reform, Montgomery County, 1968; Dem. precinct chairperson Cabin John-Bannockburn Estates, 1969-74; mem. Dem. polit. orgns. Recipient numerous award from assns., fedns., socs., Washington Star Cup for Civic Activity, 1974. Mem. Nat. Conf. of State Legislatures (state-fed. assembly, com. on transp. and communication), Nat. Orgn. Women Legislators, Women's Legis. Caucus, Am. Pub. Health Assn., Kappa Kappa Gamma. Office: Lowe House Office Bldg Annapolis MD 21401

TOTTY, SHIRLEY JEAN, social service agency administrator; b. Bentonville, Ark., Oct. 15, 1937; d. Raymond Dock and Mae Belle (Jackson) Edwards; m. Walker Stevenson Totty, Mar. 4, 1961; children: Michael Kevin, Gregory Alan. BA, U. Ark., 1959. Welfare worker Dept. Pub. Welfare State of Tenn., Memphis, 1959-62; social worker Western State Hosp., Bolivar, Tenn., 1962-65, Miss. State Hosp., Whitfield, 1965-68, Dept. Human Resources, Kansas City, Kans., 1968-69; coordinator R.S.V.P. Positive Maturity, Inc., Birmingham, Ala., 1972-73, dir. R.S.V.P., 1973-76, 77-80, dir. nutrition, 1976-77, exec. dir., 1981—. Mem. Mayor's Council for Betterment of Handicapped, Birmingham, 1983-87; chmn. exec. dirs. Birmingham United Way, 1984-85; Gov.'s Task Force Community Partnerships, 1984; chmn. Ala. Office Voluntary Participation, Montgomery, 1983-84; v.p. Access Unltd., Birmingham, 1986-87. Mem. Nat. Council Aging, So. Gerontol. Soc. (bd. dirs. 1985-87), Ala. Gerontol. Soc., Ala. Assn. R.S.V.P. (pres. 1979-80), Vis. Nurses Assn. (bd. dirs. 1985-87), Older Women's League. Baptist. Home: 2105 Vicki Dr Birmingham AL 35235 Office: Positive Maturity Inc 3600 8th Ave S Suite 301 Birmingham AL 35222

TOUCHTON, CYNTHIA VILLARREAL, interior designer; b. Tampa, Fla., Mar. 19, 1949; d. Jose Garza and Maria (Jordon) Villarreal; m. Robert Allen Touchton, Dec. 2, 1972 (div. Dec. 1975). BS, Fla. State U., 1971. Interior designer Ethan Allen Carriage House, Pinellas Park, Fla., 1971-72, Jame Interiors, St. Petersburg, Fla., 1972-75; design dir. Whitehall Interiors, Inc., Largo, Fla., 1975-79; pres. Archtl. Interior Designers, Palm Harbor, Fla., 1979—; adv. bd., instr., prof. St. Petersburg Jr. Coll., Clearwater, Fla., 1973-83. Big sister Big Bros./Big Sisters of Pinellas County, Largo, 1987; mem. St. Petersburg Symphony Guild. Mem. Am. Soc. Interior Designers. Office: Archtl Interior Designers Inc 988 US Hwy 19 S Palm Harbor FL 34684

TOULOUSE-KORNS, JEANNE LORRAINE, electronics manager; b. Inglewood, Calif., Sept. 16, 1958; d. Alfred Robert and Beverly Ann (Moon) Toulouse; m. Peter Holland Haas, Mar. 20, 1981 (div. Oct. 1984); m. Douglas Havens Korns, Nov. 16, 1985. BA with honors, U. Calif., Santa Cruz, 1981. Tech. librarian Amdahl Corp., Sunnyvale, Calif., 1977-80, programmer analyst, 1981-82; systems engr. Santa Clara, Calif., 1982-86; systems programmer UNISYS Corp., Santa Clara, 1986, mgr. tech. support services, 1986-88; planner sales and service Apple Computer, Cupertino, Calif., 1988—. Republican.

TOUPS, LAURA LOUISE, civil engineer; b. Houston, Nov. 24, 1953; d. Delma David and Bernice Luce (Roger) T. BS in Secondary Edn., U. Tex., 1978, BS in Engring. Sci., 1983. Tchr. earth sci. Anderson High Sch., Austin, Tex., 1978-80; staff engr. Urban Engring. Group, Austin, 1983-87; mng. ptnr. Urban Design Group, Austin, 1987—. Treas. Designer's Space Inc., Austin, 1980-86; commr. Water and Wastewater Commn., Austin, 1986—, Downtown Commn., 1986—. Mem. ASCE, Urban Land Inst. Office: Urban Design Group 4412 Spicewood Springs Rd #800 Austin TX 78759

TOURETZ, LILLIAN CAROLE CONRAD, psychotherapist; b. N.Y.C., Oct. 17, 1923; d. Philip and Rose Helen Stetsky; B.A., Hunter Coll., 1944; M.S.W., N.Y.U., 1968; m. Martin Conrad, June 3, 1944; children—David, Donna; m. 2d, Arthur Touretz, May 28, 1977. Asst. mgr. N.Y.C. Housing Authority, 1946-49; pres. Profl. Workers AFL-CIO, 1947-49; lectr., cons. in field, 1952-78; psychotherapist Pelham (N.Y.) Family Service, 1968-77; pvt. practice psychotherapy, Hartsdale, N.Y., 1977—; field instr. Adelphi U., 1972-77. Chmn. United Jewish Appeal; v.p. regional bd. B'nai B'rith, chpt. pres. B'nai B'rith, 1981-84, pres. Council of Pres. Mem. Nat. Assn. Social Workers, Soc. Clin. Social Work Psychotherapists, Hunter Coll., N.Y.U. alumni assns. Democrat. Address: 55 Edgewood RD Hartsdale NY 10530

TOVSEN, JOAN ESTHER, relocation and welcome service executive; b. Chgo., Dec. 3, 1950; d. Oliver Kermit and Josephine Esther (Daleo) T.; m. Ralph Jones, May 1976 (div. 1977). Student, Anchorage Community Coll., U. Alaska, 1969-78. Procurement and legal clk. Bur. Land Mgmt., Anchorage, 1973-78; pres. Anchorage Welcome Service, 1978—, pres., cons. Anchorage Relocation Ctr., 1980—; pres. Alaskan Hospitality and Relocation Services, 1984—; lectr. in field. Editor: Anchorage Blue Book: A Guide to Public Services and Resources, 1980—, The Anchorage Economic Compass: A Socio Economic Profile, 1980—; pub.: Community Blue Book Map and Guide, Anchorage and Eagle River, Alaska, The Anchorage Bowl Wall Map, others. Municipality of Anchorage grantee, 1981-82. Mem. City Hostess Internat. Assn. (pres. 1982-83), Advt. Fedn. Alaska (sec. 1982, bd. dirs.), Anchorage C. of C. (co-chmn. hospitality com.), Anchorage Conv. and Visitors Bur. Mem. Worldwide Ch. of God. Home: PO Box 9-1975 Anchorage AK 99509 Office: Country Village Ctr 3136 Seward Hwy Anchorage AK 99503

TOWER, ELIZABETH ANN, public health physician; b. Cleve., Aug. 1, 1926; d. Robert Fry and Edna (Koppenhafer) Bincham; m. John Cramton Tower, Sept. 2, 1949; children: Christina, Charles, Stephen, Alice. BA, Vassar Coll., 1947; MD, Western Reserve, 1951; MPH, U. of Washington, 1984. Intern and resident in internal medicine New Haven Hosp., 1951-53; gen. practice medicine Anchorage, 1954-64; editor Ala. State Med. Assn., Anchorage, 1959-65; regional health office control program State of Ala. div. Pub. Health, Anchorage, 1964-83, coordinator hepatitis B, 1983-84, med. epidemiologist, 1985-86; vol. communicable disease control Arctic Investigations Lab., Anchorage, 1986-87. Contbr. articles to profl. jours. Club: Nordic Ski (pres. 1970). Home: 6761 Roundtree Anchorage AK 99516

TOWER, JOAN PEABODY, composer, educator; b. New Rochelle, N.Y., Sept. 6, 1938. B.A., Bennington Coll., 1961; M.A., Columbia U., 1964, D.M.A., 1978. Pianist, Da Capo Chamber Players, 1969-84; compositions include: Amazon II (premiered by Hudson Valley Philharmonic), Sequoia (premiered by Am. Composers Orch.); Breakfast Rhythms, Black Topaz, Amazon (original scoring for quintet), Fantasy (cello concerto), Fantasy (clarinet and piano), Cello Concerto, Piano Concerto; works recorded; commns.: Contemporary Music Soc., Jerome Found., Mass. State Arts Council, Schubert Club St. Paul, Richard Stoltzman, St. Louis Symphony, Fromm Found., Nat. Endowment Arts; assoc. prof. Bard Coll., N.Y.C., from 1972; composer-in-residence St. Louis Symphony, 1985-87. Recipient N.Y. State Council for Arts award, 1980; award in music Am. Acad. and Inst. Arts and Letters, 1983; Guggenheim fellow, 1976; Nat. Endowment Arts fellow, 1974, 75, 80, 84, Koussevitzky Found. grantee, 1982. *

TOWEY, MARIE ELIZABETH, nursing administrator, educator; b. Salem, Mass., Jan. 13, 1934; d. Daniel and Mary Catherine (Buckley) Linehan; m. Carroll Francis Towey, Aug. 24, 1957; children—Mary Ellen Towey Roth, Michael Carroll, Kevin James. Diploma Burdett Coll., 1952; R.N., Salem Hosp. Sch. Nursing, 1955; postgrad. Boston Coll. Sch. Nursing, 1956-61; B.S., Salem State Coll., 1975, M.Ed. in Health Counseling and Guidance, 1978. R.N., Mass., Va., D.C, Md. Staff nurse Salem Hosp. and Mass. Gen. Hosp., 1955; nursing instr. Salem Hosp. (Mass.), 1955-59, med. nursing supr., 1960-61; staff nurse Twin Oaks Nursing Home, Danvers, Mass., 1961-71, Mt. Pleasant Hosp., Lynn, Mass., 1971; social worker, nurse NIMH Tng. Grant, Malden Ct. Clinic (Mass.), 1972-73; region IV coordinator North Shore Council on Alcoholism, Danvers, 1973-74; community mental health nurse Danvers-Salem Community Mental Health Resources Unit, Salem, 1974-78; nurse instr. Med. Aid Tng. Sch., Washington, 1978-79, Fairfax County Div. Continuing Edn. med. div., Woodson High Sch. (Va.), 1979-80; dir. nursing and health services ARC, Alexandria, 1980-81; dir. nursing services Med. Personnel Pool, Alexandria, 1981-82, adminstr., 1982-84; adminstr. ambulatory care ctr. Medic 24-Ltd., Baileys Crossroads, Va., 1984—; adminstr. Am. Med. Services, Springfield, Va., 1984-85; dir. nursing service Camelot Hall Nursing Facility, Arlington, Va., 1985-86, Clinton Convalescent Ctr., Md., 1986; sr. med. rev. specialist Intracorp, Falls Church, Va., 1986—; lectr. in field. Co-author planning grant in mental health and mental retardation, 1978. Sec. Mass Soc. of D.C., area chmn. Burke Centre Conservancy (Va.), 1981-88 ; mem. town meeting Danvers Town Govt., 1971-78; pres. Mass. Region IV Mental Health and Mental Retardation Adv. Council, 1977-78; sec., treas. Mass. Area Bd. Coalition, 1977-78; trustee Danvers State Hosp., 1977-82; community mental health resources devel. unit com. chmn. Danvers-Salem Area Mental Health Retardation Bd., 1973-78, pres., 1975-77; chmn. emergency med. services com. North Shore Council on Alcoholism, 1972-76; mem. adv. com. for adult edn. North Shore Region, 1974-75; mem. Danvers Task Force on Deinstitutionalization, 1975-76; bd. dirs. Archdiocesan Council Cath. Nurses, 1969-72. Recipient Merit and Appreciation certs. various agys., socs. and hosps. Mem. Am. Nurses Assn. (membership com. 1983—), Va. Nurses Assn. (hospitality com. 1983), Va. Assn. Home Health Agys. (chmn. region I legis., rep. 1984-86), D.C. Nurses Assn. (conf. com. 1982), Health Adminstrs. Assn. of Nat. Capitol Area, Salem Hosp. Alumnae Assn. (past treas. and chmn. program 1956-58, 60-64), Alexandria C. of C. Republican. Club: Danvers Garden (pres., chmn. civic beautification 1972-77). Home: 10639 Canterberry Rd Fairfax Station VA 22039 Office: Intracorp 5205 Leesburg Pike Falls Church VA 22041

TOWNE, CLAUDIA CIACCO, data processor; b. N.Y.C., Apr. 6, 1945; d. Francesco and Angelina (Gaultieri) Ciacco; B.A., Hunter Coll., N.Y.C., 1966; M.B.A., U. Conn., 1986; m. Gene Leonard Towne, Dec. 23, 1967. Graphics systems analyst Mergenthaler Linotype Co., N.Y.C., 1966-68; systems analyst Service Bur. Corp., Honolulu, 1968-71; systems and programming mgr. Automatic Data Processing, Inc., N.Y.C., 1971-79; info. systems mgr. Berol USA, Danbury, 1979-84; corp. dir. mgmt. info. systems IPCO Corp., White Plains, N.Y., 1985—. Bd. dirs. Greater Danbury Area Jr. Achievement, 1980-83. Mem. Data Processing Mgmt. Assn.

TOWNE, DOROTHEA ALICE, III, chiropractor; b. Easton, Ill., Feb. 1, 1910; d. Elnathan and Fairy Alice (Downey) T. D.C., Cleveland Chiropractic Coll., Los Angeles, 1954, Ph.C., 1955, B.S., 1977; student U. Wash., 1928-30; B.A. magna cum laude, U. So. Calif., 1946. Indsl. relations dir. Standard Paper Box Corp., Los Angeles, 1943-54; asso. dean acad. [illegible] Cleveland Chiropractic Coll., 1956-75, dean, tech., 1976-82, dir. clin. scis., 1972-78, emerita, 1981—; naturopath, 1986—; lectr. in field; numerous radio and TV appearances Composer: (with L. Mayberry) The Presidents Parade. Contbr. to poetry anthologies. Recipient numerous awards including appreciation award San Francisco Bay Research Assn., C.S. Cleveland, Sr., award for outstanding service, 1984. Fellow Internat. Chiropractors Assn., Idaho Assn. Naturopathic Physicians (bd. dirs. 1986, 87-88), Gamma Phi Beta, Psi Chi, Sigma Chi Psi. Address: E 508 Eaton Ave Spokane WA 99218

TOWNER, NAOMI WHITING, fiber artist, educator; b. Providence, May 8, 1940; d. Basil J. and Nellie (Woolhouse) Whiting; B.F.A. in Textile Design, R.I. Sch. Design, 1962; postgrad. (Textron fellow) Foreningen Handarbetets Vanner, Stockholm, 1962-63; M.F.A. in Textile Design, Rochester Inst. Tech., 1965. Internat. studies with faculty Ill. State U., People's Republic of China 1986; Teaching grad. asst. Sch. Am. Craftsmen, Rochester (N.Y.) Inst. Tech., 1963-65, instr. textile design, summer 1964; instr. Ill. State U., Normal, 1965-68, asst. prof., 1968-72, assoc. prof., 1972-76, prof. art, 1976—; lectr. various art guilds and schs., 1967—; dir. workshops on weaving and textile design, 1964—. One person shows art fabrics include: Fox Valley Art League, St. Charles, Ill., 1968, Fine Arts Ctr. Clinton (Ill.), 1971, Old Town Gallery, St. Charles, Mo., 1973, Lincoln Coll., Lincoln, Ill., 1974, Craft Alliance Gallery, St. Louis, 1974, Unitarian Ch., Bloomington, Ill., 1975, The Art-In, Riverton, Wyo., 1975; numerous group shows including: Mus. Contemporary Crafts Fabrics Internat. travelling exhibit, 1961-62, Security Trust Co., Rochester, N.Y., 1965, Ill. State U., Normal, 1965-68, 71, 73-86, Old Town Art Ctr., Chgo., 1967, Brooks Meml. Art Gallery, Memphis, 1967, Lakeview Ctr. for Arts, Peoria, Ill., 1967-68, Ill. State Mus., 1968, Wis. State U., Oshkosh, 1969, Art Inst. Chgo., 1971, No. Ill. U., DeKalb, 1971, U. Mass. Art Gallery, Amherst, 1972, Evansville (Ind.) Mus. Arts and Scis., 1973, 88, Eureka Coll. (Ill.), 1973, Mills Coll., Oakland, Calif., 1974, Columbus (Ga.) Mus. Arts and Crafts, 1974, Wright Art Center, Beloit (Wis.) Coll., 1975, Lowe Art Mus., U. Miami (Fla.) Goldstein Gallery, 1976, U. Minn., St. Paul, 1977, Paul Sargent Gallery, Eastern Ill. U., Charlestown, 1977, Boise (Idaho) State U., 1978, Cin. Art Mus., 1978, Kearney (Nebr.) State Coll. Art Gallery, 1979, Coll. Art Gallery, 1979, Rahr-West Mus., Manitowoc, Wis., 1979, Ill. State Mus., Springfield, 1979, No. Calif. Handweavers, Inc., San Mateo, 1979, Ill. Arts Council Gallery, Chgo., 1979, Tex. Tech U., Lubbock, 1980, Caterpillar Internat., Peoria, Ill., 1980, No. Ill. U., Midwest Constructed Fibers, 1940-80, travelling exhibit, 1980-82, Loveland (Colo.) Mus., 1981, Ft. Collins (Colo.) Mus., 1981, Fiber Art Trends, 1982, Pyramid Arts Ctr., Rochester, 1983, U. Wis.-Green Bay travelling exhibit, 1984-85, Ariel Gallery, Naperville, Ill., 1984, Premonitions, Nashville, 1985, Ill. State Fair Profl. Art Exhbn., Springfield, 1986 (1st place award craft media, merit award 1987), 7th ann. Cen. Ill. Arts Consortium Visual Arts Touring Exhbn., 1984-86 (merit award), Juror's Exhbn.: New Dimensions in Fiber II, Coll. Du Page, Ill.; represented in permanent collections Ill. State Mus., Springfield, Washington U., St. Louis, Eureka (Ill.) Coll., corp. and pvt. collections; juror exhbns. Recipient numerous awards including Silver Shuttle award U. Rochester, 1964, Owens-Corning Fiberglas competition, 1964, award of excellence Ill. Craftsmen's Council Invitational, 1967, Merit award Springfield Art Assn., 1976, Hon. mention Tchr. of Yr. awards, 1986; grantee Handweavers Guild Am. and Ill. Arts Council, 1975-78. Mem. Am. Crafts Council, Midwest Weavers Conf., Am. Fedn. Tchrs., AFL-CIO, Handweavers Guild Am. (rep. 1973-77, bd. dirs. 1978-80), ACLU, Surface Design Assn. Contbr. articles on textile design and weaving to profl. publs.; editor Fiber News, 1975-85; mem. editorial bd. Ars Textrina, 1985—. Home: 610 E Taylor St Bloomington IL 61701 Office: Ill State U Art Dept Normal IL 61761

TOWNS, KATHRYN LOUISE, educational psychology educator; b. Jamestown, N.Y., May 24, 1923; d. Ronald Earl and Ethel Louise (Peterson) T.; divorced; children: Michael, Kristin, Rhonda, Ann. BS in Edn., Miami (Ohio) U., 1944; MEd, Pa. State U., 1965, PhD, 1970. Cert. tchr., Ohio, Pa. Statistician Scripps-Howard, Miami, 1943-44; mathemetician Linde Air Corp., Buffalo, 1944; cost acct. Standard Brands, Terre Haute, Ind., 1945-46; tchr. Ohio and Pa. pub. schs., 1952-64; assoc. prof. ednl. psychology Pa. State U., Harrisburg, 1968—; cons. Pa. sch. dists., 1970—, Danforth Found., Harrisburg, 1985-88; bd. dirs. Potential Reentry Opportunities in Bus. and Edn., Harrisburg. Bd. dirs. Pa. United Way, Harrisburg, 1985—, Tri-County United Way, Harrisburg, 1984-87, Women's Agenda, Phila., 1984—. Served as seaman USN, 1944-45. Recipient 1st Service to Women award Pa. Commn. for Women, 1986. Mem. AAUW, Am. Ednl. Research Assn., Am. Psychol. Assn., EPA, Assn. Woman Psychologists (membership file com. 1981-87), Nat. Women's Studies Assn. (co-convenor 1982-84). Office: Pa State U Capital Coll Middletown PA 17057

TOWNSEND, ALAIR ANE, city official; b. Rochester, N.Y., Feb. 15, 1942; d. Harold Eugene and Dorothy (Sharpe) T.; B.S., Elmira Coll., 1962; M.S., U. Wis., 1964; postgrad. Columbia U., 1970-71; m. Robert Harris, Dec. 31, 1970. Asso. dir. budget priorities Com. on Budget, U.S. Ho. of Reps., Washington, 1975-79; dep. asst. sec. for budget HEW, Washington, 1979-80, asst. sec. for mgmt. and budget, 1980-81; dir. N.Y.C. Office Mgmt. and Budget, 1981-85; dep. mayor for fin. and econ. devel. City of N.Y., 1985—. Mem. Am. Soc. Public Adminstrn., Women's Forum, Nat. Acad. Pub. Adminstrn., Fin. Women's Assn. N.Y.

TOWNSEND, DEANNE MARIE, management consultant; b. Morgantown, W.Va., Oct. 2, 1941; d. Woodrow W. and Theresa M. (Von Bank) Gordon; m. George J. Warren Jr., Aug. 1963 (div. Nov. 1964); m. Harold E. Townsend, Oct. 16, 1965; children: Shannon M. Townsend Kinaman, G. Reneé Townsend Den Uyl. AA in Bus. Sci., Goldenwest Coll., 1978; cert. in personal mgmt. and employee relations, U. Calif., Irvine, 1979; BBA, U. Redlands, Calif., 1980. Asst. to v.p. data processing Kawasaki Motors Corp., U.S.A., Santa Ana, Calif., 1971-77, personnel adminstr., 1977-78; personnel dir. So. Calif. div. Trans Union Credit Info., Fullerton, Calif., 1978-81; owner, operator J&D Assocs., Garden Grove, Calif., 1981—; freelance writer Garden Grove, 1981—; writer and editor data engring. dept. Rockwell Internat., Anaheim, Calif., 1982-83. Author: The Bible Diary, 1983. Mem. Assn. Profl. Cons. (sec. 1985—). Republican. Clubs: Toastmasters Internat. (pres. 1984-85), Paul Revere. Home and Office: J&D Assocs 2166 W Broadway Suite 544 Anaheim CA 92804

TOWNSEND, JANE KALTENBACH, zoologist, educator; b. Chgo., Dec. 21, 1922; B.S., Beloit Coll., 1944; M.A., U. Wis., 1946; Ph.D., U. Iowa, 1950; m. 1966. Asst. in zoology U. Wis., 1944-47; asst., instr. U. Iowa, 1948-50; asst., project assoc. in pathology U. Wis., 1950-53; Am. Cancer Soc. research fellow Wenner-Grens Inst., Stockholm, 1953-56; asst. prof. zoology Northwestern U., 1956-58; asst. prof. to assoc. prof. zoology Mt. Holyoke Coll., South Hadley, Mass., 1958-70, prof., 1970—, chmn. biol. scis., 1980-86. Fellow AAAS (sect. sec. biol. sci. 1974-78); mem. Am. Assn. Anatomists, Am. Inst. Biol. Scis., Am. Soc. Zoologists, Corp. of Marine Biol. Lab., Sigma Xi, Phi Beta Kappa. Office: Mount Holyoke Coll Dept of Biology South Hadley MA 01075

TOWNSEND, JOCELYN F., health facility administrator; b. Union Parish, La., Nov. 7, 1932; d. Allen Walter and Florine (Ross) T.; widowed; children: Delaine, Guy. BSN, Northwestern State U., 1954; MA in Pub. Health, U. Calif., Berkeley, 1965; PhD, Paideia of Calif., 1978; cert. in religious studies, Wolsey Hall, Oxford, Eng., 1987. RN; cert. ins. rehab. specialist. Pub. health nurse Alameda County Heatlh Dept., Oakland, Calif., 1962-64; asst. prof. dept. psychiatry La. State U., New Orleans, 1965-75; project dir. Am. Pub. Health Assn., Washington, 1975-77; exec. v.p. Health U., Washington, 1978-82; dir. rehab. service G. Pierce Wood Meml. Hosp., Arcadia, Fla., 1983-86; coordinator Manatee Glens Corp., Brandenton, Fla., 1986—; cons. Health Positive, Fla., 1985—; chmn. Fla. State Rehab. Dirs. Task Force, 1986. Contbr. articles to profl. jours. Tchr. Trinity United Meth. Sch., Bradenton, 1987. Fellow Royal Soc. Health, Am. Pub. Health Assn.; mem. Nat. Rehab. Assn., Nat. Rehab. Assn. Adminstrs. Home: PO Box 194 Longboat Key FL 33548 Office: Manatee Glens Corp Glen Park Adult Life Skills Ctr PO Box 9478 Bradenton FL 33506

TOWNSEND, MARJORIE RHODES, aerospace engineer, business executive; b. Washington, Mar. 12, 1930; d. Lewis Boling and Marjorie Olive (Trees) Rhodes; m. Charles Eby Townsend, June 7, 1948; children: Charles

Eby Jr., Lewis Rhodes, John Cunningham, Richard Leo. BEE, George Washington U., 1951. Registered profl. engr., D.C. Electronic scientist Naval Research Lab., Washington, 1951-59; research engr. to sect. head Goddard Space Flight Ctr.-NASA, Greenbelt, Md., 1959-65, tech. asst. to chief systems div., 1965-66, project mgr. small astronomy satellites, 1966-75, project mgr. applications exploration missions, 1975-76, mgr. preliminary systems design group, 1976-80; aerospace and electronics cons. Washington, 1980-83; v.p. systems devel. Space Am., 1983-84; aerospace cons. Washington, 1984—. Patentee digital telemetry system. Decorated Knight Order Italian Republic, 1972; recipient Fed. Women's award., 1973, Eur. Culture Assn. award, Rome, 1974, Engr. Alumni Achievement award George Washington U., 1975, Gen. Alumni Achievement award, 1976, Exceptional Service medal NASA, 1971, Outstanding Leadership medal, 1980. Fellow IEEE (chmn. Washington sect. 1974-75), AIAA (chmn. nat. capitol sect. 1985), Washington Acad. Sci. (pres. 1980-81); mem. AAAS (council del. 1985-88), N.Y. Acad. Sci., Am. Geophy. Union, Soc. Women Engrs., Sigma Kappa, DAR, Daus. Colonial Wars, Mensa. Republican. Episcopalian. Home: 3529 Tilden St NW Washington DC 20008

TOWNSEND, PAMELA GWIN, business educator; b. Dallas, Aug. 24, 1945; d. William Thomas and Doris (Gwin) T. B.A. with distinction in Econs. (Univ. scholar), U. Mo., Kansas City, 1977, M.B.A. (Outstanding Acctg. Grad.), 1980. Real estate sales assoc. KEW Realtors, Austin, Tex., 1967-70; staff mktg. asst. Lincoln Property Co., Dallas, 1970-72; dir. mktg. Commonwealth Devel. Co., Dallas, 1972-73; v.p. market analysis Fin. Corp. N.Am., Kansas City, 1973-75; asst. prof., dir. dept. acctg. Park Coll., Parkville, Mo., 1980—, on leave to Kansas U. Ph.D. program. Mem. Friends of Art, Nelson Gallery; mem. Mo. Repertory Theater Guild; underwriter Folly Theater. C.P.A., Kans.; lic. real estate broker, Tex., Mo., Kans. Mem. Am. Inst. C.P.A.s, Kans. Soc. C.P.A.s, Mo. Soc. C.P.A.s, Am. Acctg. Assn., Nat. Assn. Accts., Nat. Tax Assn., Am. Fin. Assn., Beta Alpha Psi Alumnae (pres. 1982), Beta Gamma Sigma, Phi Kappa Phi, Omicron Delta Epsilon, Alpha Chi Omega, Mortar Bd. Episcopalian. Columnist: Tax Tips, Platte County Gazette, 1981. Home: 2604 University St Lawrence KS 66044 Office: U Kans Summerfield Hall Lawrence KS 66044

TOWNSEND, RHONDA JOYCE, small business owner; b. Dayton, Ohio, Aug. 10, 1960; d. Newman Jr. and Bedelia Belle (Hymes) T. AAS, Sinclair Community Coll., 1984; student, Capital U., 1987—. Clk. Bowman Funeral Chapel, Dayton, Ohio, 1979-80, Math Dept. Otterbein Coll., Westerville, Ohio, 1980; asst. sec. Bethel Bapt. Ch., Dayton, 1982-84; apprentice typographer J&L Graphics, Dayton, 1984; typesetter Design Graphics, Dayton, 1984-86; print shop asst. Fletchers' Printing Service, Dayton, 1986; owner Grapes Graphics, Dayton, 1983—; mgr., graphic arts technician Curry Printing, Dayton, 1987—; cons. career day Nettie Lee Roth Intermediate Magnet Sch., 1987; artist, keyline type designer logo 1988 Night Run of Dayton. Editor: 90th Anniversary at Bethel, 1983; editor/pub. (newsletter) Dayton Urban League, 1987. Bd. dirs. Bethel Bapt. Fed. Credit Union (asst. treas. 1987); mem. Bethel Bapt. Gospel Ensemble (treas.). Democrat. Club: Women Inter. Bowling Conf. Home: 4144 Shenandoah Dr Dayton OH 45417

TOWNSEND, SUSAN ELAINE, social service institute administrator, hostage survival consultant; b. Phila., Sept. 5, 1946; d. William Harrison and Eleanor Irene (Fox) Rogers; m. John Holt Townsend, May 1, 1976. BS in Secondary Edn., West Chester State U., 1968; MBA, Nat. U., 1978; PhD in Human Behavior, La Jolla U., 1984. Biology tchr. Methacton Sch. Dist., Fairview Village, Pa., 1968-70; bus. mgr., analyst profl. La Jolla Research Corp., San Diego, 1977-79; pastoral asst. Christ Ctr. Bible Therapy, San Diego, 1980-82, also bd. dirs.; v.p., pub. relations World Outreach Ctr. of Faith, San Diego, 1981-82, also bd. dirs.; owner, pres., cons. Townsend Research Inst., San Diego, 1983—; teaching assoc. La Jolla U. Continuing Edn., 1985—. Author: Hostage Survival-Resisting the Dynamics of Captivity, 1983; contbr. articles to profl. jours. Religious vol. Met. Correctional Ctr., San Diego, 1983—, San Diego County Jail Ministries, 1978—. Served to comdr. USN, 1970-76, USNR, 1976—. Mem. Naval Res. Assn. (life), Res. Officers Assn. (Outstanding Jr. Officer of Yr. 1982), Navy League U.S. (life), West Chester U. Alumni Assn., Nat. U. Alumni Assn. (life), La Jolla U. Alumni Assn., Gen. Fedn. Women's Clubs (pres. Peninsula club 1983-85, pres. Parliamentary law club 1984-86), Calif. Fedn. Women's Clubs (v.p.-at-large San Diego dist. 25 1982-84). Office: 1060 Alexandria Dr San Diego CA 92107

TOWNSEND, TERRY, publisher; b. Camden, N.J., Dec. 14, 1920; d. Anthony and Rose DeMarco; B.A., Duke U., 1942; m. Paul Brorstrom Townsend, Dec. 8, 1961; 1 son, Kim. Public relations dir. North Shore Univ. Hosp., Manhasset, N.Y., 1955-68; pres. Theatre Soc. L.I., 1968-70; pres. Townsend Communications Bur., Ronkonkoma, N.Y., 1970—, L.I. Communicating Service, Ronkonkoma, 1977—; columnist, writer L.I./Bus., Ronkonkoma, 1970-75, pub., 1978—; pub. L.I. Bus. Newsweekly, 1978—; v.p. Parr Meadows Racetrack, Yaphank, N.Y., 1977. Assoc. trustee North Shore U. Hosp., 1968—; bd. govs. Adelphi U. Friends Fin. Edn., 1978-85; chmn. ann. archtl. awards competition N.Y. Inst. Tech., 1970-83; trustee Dowling Coll., 1984—, L.I. Fine Arts Mus., 1984-85; bd. dirs. Family Service Assn. Nassau County, 1982—; dinner chmn. L.I. 400 Ball, 1987. Recipient Media award 110 Center Bus. and Profl. Women, 1977; named First Lady of L.I., L.I. Public Relations Assn., 1973; Enterprise award Friends of Fin. Edn., 1981; L.I. Loves Bus. Showcase Salute, 1982; Community Service award N.Y. Diabetes Assn., 1983; Disting. Long Islander in Communications award L.I. United Epilepsy Assn., 1984. Mem. Public Relations Soc. Am. (pres. L.I. chpt. 1979). Office: L I Bus 2150 Smithtown Ave Ronkonkoma NY 11779

TOWNSEND, TERYL ARCHER, artist, educator; b. Coronado, Calif., May 9, 1938; d. Robert Lee and Elizabeth (Archer) T.; children: Shawn Elizabeth, Don Philip Jr. Studies with Chen Chi, Millard Sheets, Edgar Whitney, Carl Molno, Glen Bradshaw, Maubry Brown, Edward Betts, Robert E. Wood., 1971—. Free-lance tchr. Nantucket, Mass. and Conn., 1974—. Designer book covers. Recipient Merit award Art League Houston, 1975, 77, 82, 3d place award Nat. Small Painting Show, 1976, Merit award So. Watercolor Soc., 1977. Mem. Am. Watercolor Soc., Nat. Watercolor Soc., Rocky Mountain Nat. Watermedia Soc. (Century award 1974, 77), Southwestern Watercolor Soc. (awards 1974-76, 78, 84), Nantucket Artists Assn. (bd. dirs., advisor, exec. com. 1986—, Merit award 1980, 82, 83, 86), Houston Watercolor Soc. (v.p., pres. 1974-75, advisor profl. standards 1976-82, various awards 1975-76, 82-83), Nantucket C. of C., Houston C. of C. (advisor cultural com. 1975-76). Episcopalian. Home: PO Box 2802 Nantucket MA 02584

TOWSON, DOROTHY BUDREAU, corporate training consultant; b. Savannah, Ga., Oct. 13, 1947; d. Remer Lane and Dorothy (Griffin) Budreau; m. Louis Albert Towson, Dec. 21, 1969; children: Wendy Rebecca, Jonathan Louis. BS in Nursing, Fla. State U., 1969; MEd, U. Cen. Fla., 1979. RN, Fla. Dir. nursing Amelia Island Care Ctr., Fernandina Beach, Fla., 1976-77; asst. prof. nursing Brevard Community Coll., Cocoa, Fla., 1977-80, mem. adv. com. Sch. Nursing, 1985-87; acting dir. personnel, recruitment coordinator Holmes Regional Health Care Systems, Melbourne, Fla., 1980-82, assoc. dir. nursing, 1982-83, dir. corp. ednl. services, 1983-86; exec. dir. Ind. Psychiat. and Psychol. Assocs., Inc., Indian Harbour Beach, Fla., 1986—; pres. Devel. Strategies, Inc., Satellite Beach, Fla., 1986—. Contbr. articles to profl. jours. Councilwoman City of Satellite Beach, 1987—; bd. dirs. Brevard County Library, 1988—. Mem. Fla. Soc. Healthcare Edn. and Tng., Cen. Fla. Healthcare Educators (pres. 1985-86), Greater South Brevard C. of C. (chmn. bus. and edn. com. 1986-87, participant Leadership South Brevard 1985-86, Sigma Theta Tau. Republican. Episcopalian. Club: Exchange of South Beaches (Brevard County). Lodge: Soroptomist. Home: 560 Glenwood Ave Satellite Beach FL 32937 Office: Devel Strategies Inc 1275 S Patrick Dr Suite I Satellite Beach FL 32937

TOYSER, FRANCINE, home remodeling equipment company executive; b. Chgo., Feb. 13, 1946; d. Angelo Ralph and Gilda (Stellato) Trozzolo; m. Frank J. Amabile, Apr. 12, 1970 (div. Sept. 1977); 1 child, Laura Rose; m. Richard Walter Toyser, Aug. 26, 1978; step-children—Tammy J., Wendy J. A.A., Coll. of St. Francis, Joliet, Ill., 1967. Tech. writer GTE, Northlake, Ill., 1976-78; dir. services Lion-Hearted Remodeling, Inc., Elmhurst, Ill., 1978-85, corp. sec., 1978—; pres., chief exec. officer Pride Kitchens & Baths, Inc., Villa Park, Ill., 1985—. Mem. Nat. Assn. Remodeling Industry, Nat. Kitchen and Bath Assn., Nat. Assn. Female Execs. Republican. Roman Catholic. Avocation: sailing.

TRACHTENBERG, SELMA HARRIS, educator; b. Troy, N.Y., Nov. 7, 1924; d. Hyman and Rose (Kutler) Harris; m. David Trachtenberg, May 27, 1945; children—Carl Harris, Bruce Sheldon. B.E., State U. Coll., Oneonta, N.Y., 1945, postgrad. State U. Coll., New Paltz, N.Y., 1968-77. Jr. high sch. tchr., Dolgeville, N.Y., 1945-46, Ravena, N.Y., 1946-49; intermediate tchr. Acad. Ave. Sch., Middletown, N.Y., 1963-80. Pres., Sisterhood Temple Sinai, 1956-57; voters service chmn. LWV, 1956-58; sec. Middletown chpt. Hadassah, 1958-61, HMO chmn., Gainesville, Fla. chpt., 1980-83; pres. Sisterhood Temple B'nai Israel, Gainesville, 1982-83; v.p. U. Fla. Law Wives, 1980-81. Mem. Delta Kappa Gamma (membership chmn. Middletown chpt. 1972-78, coordinating com. Gainesville chpt. 1981-83). Club; Women's U. of Middletown (pres. 1967).

TRACY, MARY ELIZABETH, librarian; b. Joliet, Ill., Aug. 18, 1922; d. Charles Joseph and Catherine (Fay) Tracy; B.A. cum laude, Coll. St. Francis, 1944; M.A., Rosary Coll., 1958. Tchr., librarian Joliet pub. schs., 1944-52, 54-61, Am. schs., Bremerhaven and Frankfurt, Germany, 1952-54; librarian Cen. Campus Joliet Twp. High Sch., 1961-86; chmn. Joliet Local Archives Com., 1981-87. Sec., v.p., and mem. adv. bd. Alumnae of the Coll. of St. Francis. Mem. Am., Ill. Library Assns., Ill. Assn. for Media in Edn., Ill. Audio-Visual Assn., Will County Library/Media Assn. (pres. 1976), Joliet Jr. Cath. Woman's League (pres. 1950-51), Joliet Area Hist. Soc. (bd. advisors 1986—). Home: 1010 Glenwood Ave Joliet IL 60435

TRADUP, JANETTA FREEMAN, nursing educator; b. Pawhuska, Okla., Jan. 12, 1951; d. Foy Eugene and Cora Ellen (Anderson) Freeman; m. Steven William Tradup, Aug. 10, 1969 (div. Oct. 1977); 1 child, Gregory Mark. AD in Nursing, U. Albuquerque, 1979; BS in Nursing, West Tex. State U., 1982; MS in Nursing, U. Tex. Health Sci. Ctr., 1984. Staff nurse Lubbock (Tex.) Gen. Hosp., 1979-80, charge nurse, 1980-82; staff nurse Meth. Hosp., Lubbock, 1982; head nurse Tex. Tech. U. Health Sci. Ctr., Lubbock, 1983; instr. Meth. Hosp. Sch. Nursing, Lubbock, 1985—; sec. Meth. Hosp. faculty, Lubbock, 1985-86. Com. mem. Boy Scouts Am., Lubbock, 1982; caseworker Family Outreach, Lubbock, 1986. Mem. Am. Nurses Assn. (cert. high risk perinatal nurse), Tex. Nurses Assn. (faculty cons. student's assn. 1986—), Tex. Perinatal Assn., Council on Maternal Child Nursing, Tex. Nurses Assn. (treas. local dist. 1986), Nat. League Nursing, Tex. League Nursing, Sigma Theta Tau. Home: 4209 40th St Lubbock TX 79413 Office: Meth Hosp Sch Nursing 2002 Miami Lubbock TX 79410

TRAHAN, ELLEN VAUNEIL, non-profit association executive; b. Rosie, Ark., June 30, 1941; d. Jess James Ross and Ellen Alabama (Spears) Massey; m. Terrance Dale Trahan, June 9, 1961; children: Ginny-Marie, Anthony Scott, Julie Jeanette. BA in Home Econs., Magic Valley Christian Coll., Albion, Idaho, 1962; BA in Psychology, Pepperdine U., 1966; postgrad., Willamette U., 1983-84; MBA, Chaminade U., Honolulu, 1985. Social worker Los Angeles Dept. Social Service, 1966-70; adminstr. Socialization Ctr. Marion County Mental Health Clinic, Salem, Oreg., 1973; social service worker Fairview Hosp. and Tng. Ctr., Salem, 1973-85; exec. dir. Autistic Vocat. Edn. Ctr., Honolulu, 1986—. Mem. bus. adv. com. Supported Employment Task Force, Goodwill Corp, 1986-87; orgn. cons. Fairview Parents Club, Salem, 1977-85; advisor Honolulu Dept. Health Community Service to Developmentally Disabled, 1986—. Mem. Nat. Assn. Female Execs., Nat. Soc. Autistic Citizens, Assn. Retarded Citizens. Home: 250 Ohua Ave 3E Honolulu HI 96815 Office: Autistic Vocat Edn Ctr 1903 Palolo Ave Room C-9 Honolulu HI 96816

TRAINOR, AGNES MARIE, aviation economist; b. Washington, Nov. 14, 1951; d. William Ernest and Agnes Rose (Drew) T.; B.A., Trinity Coll., Washington, 1973. With FAA, U.S. Dept. Transp., Washington, 1973-75, CAB, Washington, 1975-82; sr. air transport ofcl. Internat. Civil Aviation Orgn., Montreal, Que., Can., 1982-86, U.S. Dept. Transp., 1986—; multilateral internat. negotiations expert witness on air carrier selection and airline mergers; pvt. pilot. asso. transp. research bd. Nat. Acad. Scis. Mem. Internat. Aviation Club, Aero Club Internat. (pres. 1983-86). Roman Catholic. Home: 4436 Reservoir Rd NW Washington DC 20007 Office: 400 7th St SW Washington DC 20590

TRAINOR, LILLIAN (MIDGE), elections official; b. Norma, N.J., Oct. 30, 1936; d. Loenell Lesley and Lillie Ara (Kenyon) Barber; m. Arthur James Trainor, Mar. 9, 1959; children: Michael, Arthur, Lynn Marie. Student pub. schs., Pleasantville, N.J. Chair Burlington County Bd. Elections, Mount Holly, N.J., 1978-81, commr. of registration, 1981-83, chair, 1983—. Vice chair, mem. exec. bd. Burlington County Dem. Com., 1977—; chair Southampton Twp. Dem. County Com., 1976-79, Bd. County Convassers, Mount Holly, 1978—; v.p. Southeastern Dem. Coalition, 1977—; mgr. Florio for Gov. Campaign, N.J., 1980, Carter for Pres. Campaign, Burlington County area, 1980; del. Dem. Nat. Conv., 1984. Served with WAC, 1955-57. Mem. N.J. State Assn. Election Ofcls., VFW Aux. Club: Big Six (pres. 1973-79). Avocations: accordian, piano, birdwatching, reading. Home: 20 Pleasant St Vincentown NJ 08088 Office: Bd Elections 49 Rancocas Rd Mount Holly NJ 08060

TRANSOU, LYNDA LEW, advertising art administrator; b. Atlanta, Dec. 11, 1949; d. Lewis Cole Transou and Ann Lynette (Taylor) Putnam. B.F.A. cum laude, U. Tex.-Austin, 1971. Art dir., The Pitluk Group, San Antonio, 1971, Campbell, McQuien & Lawson, Dallas, 1973-74, Bozell & Jacobs, Dallas, 1974-75; art dir., ptnr. The Assocs., Dallas, 1975-77; art dir. Belo Broadcasting, Dallas, 1977-80; creative dir., v.p. Allday & Assocs., Dallas, 1980-85; owner Lynda Transou Advt. & Design, 1986—. Recipient Merit award N.Y. Art Dirs. Show, 1980; Gold award Dallas Ad League, 1980, Silver award, 1980, Bronze award, 1981, 82, 2 Merit awards Houston Art Dirs. Club, 1978-86; Merit award Broadcast Designers Assn., 1980, 82; Merit awards Dallas Ad League, 1978, 87; Silver award Houston Art Dirs. Show; Gold award Tex. Pub. Relations Assn., 1982, 85; Gold award N.Y. One Show, 1982, others. Mem. Dallas Soc. Visual Communications (Bronze award 1980, Merit awards, 1978-86), Delta Gamma (historian 1969-70).

TRAPP, MONICE MARIE, small business owner; b. Fargo, N.D., Dec. 13, 1960; d. Robert Riley and Greta Mildred (Lee) Fahey; m. Lawrence William Trapp Jr.; 1 child, Elizabeth Marie. Student, No. Va. Community Coll., Manassas, 1985—. Office mgr. Nat. Lithograph, Inc./Metrotel., Inc., Vienna, Va., 1982-87; proprietor No. Va. Bus. Service, Manassas, 1987—. Republican. Episcopalian. Club: Va. Falconry (sec./treas. 1987—). Home and Office: 9749 Zimbro Ave Manassas VA 22110

TRASK, BETTY M., journalist; b. Laconia, N.H., Jan. 28, 1928; d. James Edwin and Clemency (Anstey) Burbank; m. Allison Keith Trask, June 28, 1947; children: Frank Edwin, Michael Thomas, Rory Scott, Allison Keith, Jr. Women's editor Laconia Evening Citizen, 1966-70, county editor, 1970—; mem. adv. bd. N.H. Vocat.-Tech. Coll., Laconia, 1972-78; treas. N.H. Commn. on Status of Women, Concord, 1974-76; mem. state adv. bd. N.H. Vocat.-Tech. Coll. and Inst., Concord, 1981-84. Bd. dirs. Laconia Salvation Army, 1973—, Belknap Easter Seals, 1980—; trustee Gilford Village Knolls, Inc., N.H., 1985—; mem. task force for alcohol and drug abuse N.H. Gov.'s Commn. on Criminal Adminstrn. and Juvenile Delinquency, 1969-71. Recipient Recognition award Laconia Lions Club, 1977, Lakes Region Citizenship award N.H. Vocat. Tech. Coll., 1978. Mem. Internat. Platform Assn., Sigma Delta Chi. Republican. Avocations: travel, photography. Home: RFD 6 Box 408 Laconia NH 03246 Office: 120 Liberty Hill Rd Gilford NH 03246

TRATTNER, JUANITA TAMMY, advertising executive; b. Balt., Aug. 19, 1960; d. Stephen William and Juanita Frances (Moore) T. Owner Sunshine Prodns., Ocean City, Md., 1980-83; advt. mgr. Oceana mag., Ocean City, 1980-88, gen. mgr., 1988—; promotions coordinator Ocean Plaza Mall, Ocean City, 1984-86, Plata Grande Inc., Ocean City, 1986—; owner Down Under Inc., Ocean City, 1987—; mktg. cons. The Courtesy Shop, Ocean City, 1982—, Embers Restaurant, 1987—, Tiffany's Night Club, 1987—. Mem. Chesapeake Publishing Assn. (mktg. task group), Nat. Assn. Female Execs., U.S. Jaycees. Home: 6509 Ocean Pines Berlin MD 21811 Office: Oceana Mag PO Box 2070 MBS Ocean City MD 21842

TRAURIG, LEONA, researcher, orthomolecular therapist; b. Chgo., Aug. 14, 1934; d. Daniel and Sonia (Lemson) Leviton; m. Walter Bernard Traurig, Nov. 6, 1955; children—Marcia, William, Donald. R.N., Jackson Meml. Hosp., Miami, Fla., 1955. Asst. charge nurse labor and delivery Jackson Meml. Hosp., 1955-56; dir. employee health services Larkin Gen. Hosp., Miami, 1972-73; med. examiner, Miami, 1973-82; pres. Miami Med. Assocs., 1982—; cons. Life Extension Found., Hollywood, Fla., 1982—; organizer-vol. Sch. Systems Clinics, Dade County, Fla., 1970-79; cons. Girl Scouts Am., 1968-74, Home for Aged, 1979—(both Miami). Contbr. articles to profl. jours. Vol. examiner Am. Cancer Soc., Miami, 1982—; vol. counselor health fairs Am. Heart Assn., Miami, 1980-83; vol. coordinator summer camp clinics clinics Girl Scouts U.S.A., Miami, 1971-73. Recipient Best All Round Nurse award Alumnae Assn. Jackson Meml. Hosp., 1955; Appreciation award Dade County (Fla.) Sch. Bd., 1979. Mem. Am. Heart Assn., Am. Nurses Assn., Nat. Bus.-Profl. Assn., Ctr. Chinese Medicine, Life Extension Found. Democrat. Jewish. Address: 13149 SW 91 Ct Miami FL 33176

TRAVERS, JUDITH LYNNETTE, human resource management executive; b. Buffalo, Feb. 25, 1950; d. Harold Elwin and Dorothy (Helsel) Howes; m. David Jon Travers, Oct. 21, 1972; 1 child, Heather Lynne. BA in Psychology, Barrington Coll., 1972; cert. in paralegal course, St. Mary's Coll., Moraga, Calif., 1983; postgrad., Southland U., 1982-84. Exec. sec. Sherman Weeks, P.A., Derry, N.H., 1973-75; corp. asst. sec. Mason-McDuffie Co., Berkeley, Calif., 1975-82; paralegal asst. Blum, Kay, Merkle & Kauftheil, Oakland, Calif., 1982-83; exec. v.p. Western Med. Personnel Inc., Concord, Calif., 1983—; pres. All Ages Sitters Agy., Concord, 1986—. Vocalist record album The Loved Ones, 1978. Vol. local Congl. campaign, 1980, Circle of Friends, Children's Hosp. No. Calif., Oakland, 1987—. Mem. Nat. Assn. Female Execs., Am. Assn. Respiratory Therapy, Calif. Soc. Respiratory Care, Am. Mgmt. Assn., Gospel Music Assn., Palomino Horse Breeders Am., DAR, Barrington Oratorio Soc., Alpha Theta Sigma. Republican. Baptist. Home: 3900 Brown Rd Oakley CA 94561 Office: Western Med Personnel Inc 1820 Galindo St Suite 225 Concord CA 94520

TRAVIS, ARLENE CAREY, home preservationist; b. Malden, Mass., Feb. 25, 1935; d. Mickey H. and Diana (Berns) Carey; ; m. Larry Travis, May 29, 1955; children: Steven, Peter. BS in Edn., Framingham Coll.; postgrad., Tufts U., Mass. Sch. Art. Pres. Mansions & Millionaires, Great Neck, N.Y., 1973—. Author: Mansions and Millionaires. Office: Mansion & Millionares Po Box 252 Greenvale NY 11548

TRAVIS, DAWNA LEE, information systems educator, consultant, author, editor; b. Geneva, N.Y., Feb. 25, 1949; d. Arthur J. and Nancy L. (Trice) T.; m. Andrew Dewire, Aug. 10, 1985; 1 child, Travis. BS, SUNY, Albany, 1970, MS in Computer Sci., 1974; MBA, Northeastern U., 1978. Programmer State Bank, Albany, N.Y., 1970-72, State of N.Y. Dept. Transp., Albany, 1972-73; system analyst State of N.Y. Dept. Tax, Albany, 1973-75; sr. fin. systems analyst TRW-United Carr, Burlington, Mass., 1975-78; sr. cons. Mgmt. Decision Systems, Waltham, Mass., 1978-82; mgr. client services Mgmt. Decision Systems (presently Info. Resources Inc.), Chgo., 1982-84; asst. prof. Bentley Coll., Waltham, 1984—; editor, author The James Martin Productivity Series, Boston, 1987—; systems cons., Boston, 1984—; DSS cons., Sun Refining and Mktg., Phila., 1984—. Office: Decision Tree Assn 26 Crestwood Dr Wellesley MA 02181

TRAVIS, JOAN FAYE SCHILLER, lawyer; b. Chgo., Mar. 15, 1939; d. Jack and Betty (From) Schiller; Ph.B. in Psychology, Northwestern U., 1969; J.D., John Marshall Law Sch., Chgo., 1981; children—Jeffrey Bernard, Leonard Edwin, Elizabeth Sue. Elem. sch. tchr., Chgo., 1970-72; admitted to Ill. bar, 1981, U.S. Ct. Appeals, 1981, U.S. Dist. Ct. bar, 1981, U.S. Ct. Mil. Appeals, 1982, Wis. bar, 1986, U.S. Supreme Ct. 1986; sole gen. practice, Park Ridge, Ill.; asst. corp. counsel Village of Skokie (Ill.); freelance writer, 1971-77; speaker, lectr. in field. Chmn. Consumer Affairs Commn., Skokie; Niles Twp. collector. Mem. ABA, Ill. Bar Assn., Chgo. Bar Assn., Def. of Prisoners Com., N.W. Suburban Bar Assn. (parliamentarian), North Suburban Bar Assn. (pres.), Women's Bar Assn., Assn. Trial Lawyers Am., Ill. Trial Lawyers Assn., Nat. Acad. TV Arts and Scis., Delta Theta Phi. Jewish. Author numerous articles in field. Office: 1550 N Northwest Hwy Park Ridge IL 60068

TRAVIS, NANCY, marketing executive, program administrator; b. Brownwood, Tex., Feb. 29, 1936; d. John Clyde and Annie (Bynum) Goosby; m. Floyd J. Travis (div. 1983); children: J. Barrett, Timothy Allen. BS, U. Tex., 1962; MS, U. So. Calif., 1976. Adminstr. U.S. Army Dept. Continuing Edn., Fed. Republic Germany, 1975-79; dir. Clear Creek County (Colo.) Dept. Community Edn., 1980-83, Dept. Social Services, Central City, Colo., 1980-82; program dir. Am. Ednl. Complex, Killeen, Tex., 1983-85; dir. mktg. Herring Marathon Group, Killeen, 1985-87; program dir. Am. Ednl. Complex Pacific Far East Campus, 1987—; lectr. and cons. in field. Author: English Text, 1985; editor: Training in Communication Skills, 1985. Bd. dirs. Bluebonnet council Girl Scouts Am., Cen. Tex., 1986-87, Am. Heart Assn., 1986-87; mem. Dem. Cen. Com., Colo., 1982-83; advisor Ethiopian Ministry Social Welfare, Addis Ababa, 1971-74. Recipient Comdrs.' award U.S. Army, 1987. Mem. Assn. Am. Bus. Women, Tex. Assn. Single Adults, Internat. Council Shopping Ctrs. (Merit award 1986), Mil. Educators and Counselors Assn., Delta Kappa Gamma.

TRAYLOR, CHERIE LEE, psychiatric social worker; b. Oswego, N.Y., June 20, 1944; d. Donald Elton and Harriette (Lee) Gais; BA, SUNY, Buffalo, 1966, MSW, 1972; m. Jean LaRue Traylor, Jr., Nov. 11, 1965 (div. Dec. 1970). With Psychiat. Clinic, Buffalo, 1967-70; psychiat. social worker Hillcrest Childrens Ctr., Washington, 1972-74; asst. dir. outpatient services Comprehensive Community Mental Health Ctr. #2, Seat Pleasant, Md., 1974-77; psychiat. social worker Arlington (Va.) Mental Health Ctr., 1977-78, So. Calif. Permanente Med. Group, San Diego, 1978—; pvt. practice psychotherapy La Jolla, Calif., 1983—; NIMH fellow, 1970-72. Mem. Nat. Assn. Social Workers (cert.), Nat. Assn. Black Social Workers. Democrat. Club: Foxtrappe (Washington).

TRAYLOR, CLAIRE GUTHRIE, state senator, teacher; b. Kansas City, Mo., Jan. 18, 1931; d. Frank and Janet Guthrie; m. Frank A. Traylor, 1954; children—Nancy, Frank, Susan, David. B.S., Northwestern U., 1952; M.A., Washington U., St. Louis, 1955. Primary sch. tchr., 1955-57; mem. Colo. Ho. of Reps., 1978-82, majority caucus chmn., 1980-82; mem. Colo. State Senate, 1982—, mem. Colo. Commn. on Aging, Colo. Commn. on Children and Families, Colo. Housing Fin. Authority Bd., Colo. Guaranteed Student Loan Bd., Colo. Industrial Commn. Adv. Com., Colo. Internat. Trade Adv. Commn., Colo. Capital Complex Commn., C. of C. (Colo.), Wheat Ridge, Golden, Arvada, Lakewood, Jefferson County, Republican Central Coms., Jr. League, Clear Creek (Colo.) Valley Med. Aux., pres. bd. Highland West-Highland So. (Colo.). Presbyterian. Office: State Capitol Bldg Denver CO 80203 *

TREADWAY, SUSAN MARIE, technical writer; b. West Palm Beach, Fla., June 14, 1951; d. Karl Paul and Margaret Elizabeth (Ross) Casseur; m. Oscar Gaines Owen, June 7, 1969 (div. 1979); 1 child, Angela (dec.); m. Ronald Jay Treadway, Nov. 22, 1980; children: Cassandra Erin, Kimberly Dawn. Student, Craven Community Coll., Havelock, N.C., 1981, Mid. Ga. Tech. Inst., Warner Robins, 1987—. NDI radiographer Space Sci. Services, Inc., Riviera Beach, Fla., 1968-69; with Hayes Internat. Corp., Napier Field, Ala., 1970-71; operating room tech. Flowers Hosp., Dothan, Ala., 1971-73, inventory programmer Bari Co., Niles, Ill., 1985-86; tech. writer Jana, Inc., Warner Robins, Ga., 1987—. Author: Reflections of Feelings, 1980. Family services asst. coordinator USAF, 1987.Served to sgt. USMC,1978-83. Presbyterian. Club: Mensa. Home: 102 Woodfield Dr Warner Robins GA 31088 Office: Jana Inc 151 S Houston Lake Rd Warner Robins GA 31088

TREBILCOT, JOYCE, feminist philosopher, educator; b. San Diego, Feb. 15, 1933; d. Earl and Angela (Dameral) T. B.A. in Philosophy, U. Calif.-Berkeley, 1957; M.A., U. Calif.-Santa Barbara, 1966, Ph.D., 1970. NEH teaching fellow Bryn Mawr Coll., 1967-69; vis. scholar/tchr. women studies U. N.Mex., Albuquerque, 1977-78; assoc. prof. philosophy Washington U.,

St. Louis, 1977—, coordinator women's studies, 1980—; vis. prof. feminist thought Wheaton Coll., Norton, Mass., 1979-80. Author: (pamphlet) Taking Responsibility for Sexuality, 1983, (collection) Radical Lesbian Essays, 1989; editor: Mothering: Essays in Feminist Theory, 1984, spl. issue Jour. Social Philosophy, 1984; mem. editorial bd. Hypatia: Jour. Feminist Philosophy, 1977—, Social Theory and Practice, 1979—, Jour. Social Philosophy, 1981—; contbr. essays to jours. NEH fellow, 1974-75; Washington U. grantee. Mem. Soc. for Women in Philosophy, Nat. Women's Studies Assn., Am. Philos. Assn., Am. Soc. Social Philosophy (dir. 1982). Office: Washington U Campus Box 1073 Saint Louis MO 63130

TREDEAU, DEBRA LOUISE, nurse; b. Milford, Mass., Sept. 28, 1954; d. Peter Albert and Juliette Marie (Duquette) Polostri; m. John Paul Tredeau, Sept. 22, 1979. BS, Boston Coll., 1976. RN Norwood Hosp., Norwood, Mass., 1976-77, Milford-Whitville Regional Hosp., 1977—. Roman Catholic. Home: 137 Freedom St Hopedale MA 01747

TREE, MARIETTA PEABODY, city planner; b. Lawrence, Mass.; d. Malcolm Endicott and Mary Elizabeth (Parkman) Peabody; m. Desmond FitzGerald, Sept. 2, 1939; 1 dau., Frances; m. Ronald Tree, July 28, 1947; 1 dau., Penelope. Student, La Petite Ecole Florentine, Florence, Italy, 1934-35, U. Pa., 1936-39; LL.D., U. Pa., 1964; L.H.D., Russell Sage Coll., 1962, Bard Coll., 1964, Hobart and William Coll., 1967; LL.D., Drexel Inst. Tech., 1965; LL.D. hon. degrees, Franklin Pierce Coll., Coll. New Rochelle, Skidmore Coll. With hospitality div. Office Coordinator Inter-Am. Affairs, 1942-43; researcher Life mag., 1943-45; mem. Fair Housing Practices Panel, N.Y.C., 1958; mem. bd. commrs. N.Y.C. Commn. on Human Rights, 1959-61; U.S. rep. to Human Rights Commn. of UN, 1961-64; mem. U.S. del. UN, 1961; U.S. rep. Trusteeship Council of UN with rank of ambassador, 1964-65; mem. staff U Thant, UN Secretariat, 1966-67; partner Llewelyn-Davies Assocs. (city planners), 1968-80; dir. Llewelyn-Davies, Sahni, Inc., Pan Am. Airways, N.Y.C., CBS; trustee U.S. Trust Co. N.Y.; sr. cons. Hill & Knowlton, Inc.; editor-at-large Archtl. Digest. Del. N.Y. State Constl. Conv., 1967; mem. N.Y. State Democratic Com., 1954-60; mem. civil rights com. Dem. Adv. Council, 1959-60; a founder Sydenham Hosp., interracial hosp., N.Y.C., 1943; past bd. dirs. UN Assn., Citizens Housing and Planning Council, Center Internat. Studies-NYU; bd. dirs. Winston Churchill Found.; mem. Am. council for Ditchley Cooper-Hewitt Mus.; chmn. Citizens Com. for N.Y.C.; chmn. Friends of Arthur Ross Gallery, U. Pa. ; bd. dirs. Franklin D. Roosevelt Four Freedoms Found., Marconi Internat. Found., Council Am. Ambassadors, Fund for Free Expression, Am. Friends of Australia Nat. Gallery. Mem. Pilgrim Soc., Council Fgn. Relations. Episcopalian. Home: One Sutton Pl South New York NY 10022

TREECE, MALRA CLIFFT, educator, author; b. Oxford, Ark., Nov. 19, 1923; d. Joseph A. and Ruth (Thompson) Clifft; B.S., Ark. State U., 1947; M.A., Memphis State U., 1956; Ph.D., U. Miss., 1971; m. Guy Treece, Jan. 18, 1946; children—Diana, Mark David. Prof. bus. communication Memphis State U., 1957—. Recipient Nat., State, Mid-South Poetry awards. Mem. Am. Bus. Communication Assn., Tenn. Poetry Soc., Phi Kappa Phi, Delta Pi Epsilon. Methodist. Author: Communication for Business and the Professions, 1978; 2d edit., 1982, 3d edit., 1986, 4th edit., 1989; Successful Business Communication, 1980, 2d edit., 1984, 3d edit., 1987; Effective Reports, 1982, 2d edit., 1985; contbr. articles to profl. jours. Home: 1064 Estate Memphis TN 38119 Office: Memphis State U 317 Bus Adminstrn Bldg Memphis TN 38152

TREHY, JOAN ELLEN, aerospace company executive; b. N.Y.C., Jan. 28, 1942; d. William Ignatius T. and Winifred Ann (Dodge) Campbell. BS, SUNY, Oneonta, 1963; postgrad., Chapman Coll., Orange, Calif., 1987—. Tchr. third grade Elwood Sch. Dist., Huntington, N.Y., 1963-64; asst. to exec. v.p. Conover-Mast Div., Cahners Publ., N.Y.C., 1964-71; prodn. coordinator The Dreyfus Corp., N.Y.C., 1971-75; sales supr. Gorsuch Ltd., Vail, Colo, 1976-77; asst. sec. Vail Nat. Bank, 1977; subcontract adminstr. Ford Aerospace Corp., Newport Beach, Calif., 1978-83, sr. subcontract adminstr., 1983—. Active Street People In Need Minstry to feed the homeless, Our Lady Queen of Angels Ch., Newport Beach, 1987—. Mem. Purchasing Mgmt. Assn. Orange County, Nat. Assn. Purchasing Mgmt. Republican. Roman Catholic. Toastmasters (Newport Beach) (treas. 1985-86, sec. 86-87). Home: 102 Stanford Irvine CA 92715 Office: Ford Aerospace Corp Ford Rd Newport Beach CA 92658-8900

TREI, ALICE ROSALIE, retired occupational therapist; b. Estonia, Oct. 17, 1909; d. Prüdu and Müna (Kraun) Roost; came to U.S., 1929, naturalized, 1938; certificate occupational therapy, Columbia U., 1948; B.S., N.Y. U., 1954; m. Peter Trei, Sept. 20, 1928 (dec. Jan. 1962); children—Astra (Mrs. Felix Bottenhorn), Alan. Occupational therapist N.Y. State Psychiat. Inst., N.Y.C., 1948-53, head occupational therapist, 1953-79; clin. instr. occupational therapy Columbia U., 1966-79. Recipient Outstanding Employee award N.Y. State Dept. Mental Hygiene, 1975. Mem. Am., N.Y. State (treas. 1959-62, 69-73) occupational therapy assns., Met. N.Y. Dist., World Fedn. Occupational Therapists. Home: 15 Sickles St New York NY 10040

TREIMAN, JOYCE WAHL, artist; b. Evanston, Ill., May 29, 1922; d. Rene and Rose (Doppelt) Wahl; m. Kenneth Treiman, Apr. 25, 1945; 1 child, Donald. A.A., Stephens Coll., 1941; B.F.A. (grad. fellow 1943), State U. Iowa, 1943. Vis. prof. San Fernando Valley State Coll., 1968; lectr. UCLA, 1969-70; vis. prof. State U. Calif., Long Beach, 1977. One man shows include Paul Theobald Gallery, Chgo., 1942, John Snowden Gallery, Chgo., 1945, Art Inst. Chgo., 1947, North Shore Country Day Sch., Winnetka, Ill., 1947, Fairweather-Garnett Gallery, Evanston, 1950, Edwin Hewitt Gallery, N.Y.C., 1950, Palmer House Galleries, Chgo., 1952, Glencoe (Ill.) Library, 1953, Elizabeth Nelson Gallery, Chgo., 1953, Charles Feingarten Gallery, Chgo., 1955, Cliff Dwellers Club, Chgo., 1955, Fairweather-Hardin Gallery, Chgo., 1955, 58, 73, 81, Marian Willard Gallery, N.Y.C., 1960, Felix Landau Gallery, Los Angeles, 1961, 64, Adele Bednarz Gallery, Los Angeles, 1969-71, 74, La Jolla (Calif.) Mus., 1962-72, Palos Verdes (Calif.) Art Mus., 1976, Forum Gallery, N.Y., 1963, 66, 75, 81, Tortue Gallery, Santa Monica, Calif., 1980, 83, 86, Schmidt-Bingham Gallery, N.Y.C., 1986, 88Fairweather-Hardin Gallery, Chgo., 1986; numerous exhbns. including Carnegie Internat., 1955, 57, Met. Mus., 1950, Whitney Mus., 1951, 52, 53, 58, Art Inst. Chgo., 1945-59, John Herron Art Inst., 1953, Library of Congress, 1954, Cocoran Gallery, 1957, Pa. Acad. Fine Arts, 1958, Mus. Modern Art, 1962, Am. Acad. Arts and Letters, N.Y.C., 1974, 75, 76, Retrospective Exhbn., Mcpl. Art Gallery, Los Angeles, 1978; represented in permanent collections Kemper Ins. Co., Chgo., Met Mus. Art, N.Y.C., Denver Mus. Art, State U. Iowa, Ill. State Mus., Long Beach (Calif.) Mus., Whitney Mus. Am. Art, N.Y.C., Tupperware Art Mus., Orlando, Fla., Art Inst. Chgo., Utah State U., Abbott Labs., Oberlin Allen Art Mus., Internat. Mineral Corp., Pasadena Art Mus., U. Calif. at Santa Cruz, Grunwald Found., UCLA, Santa Barbara Mus. Art, Calif., Oakland Mus., Calif., Security Pacific Nat. Bank, Los Angeles, Rochester (N.Y.) Art Mus.; pub. collections include Art Inst. Chgo., Whitney Mus., Met. Mus., Santa Barbara (Calif.) Mus., Portland (Oreg.) Mus. Recipient numerous awards including Logan purchase prize Art Inst. Chgo., 1951, Martin B. Cahn prize, 1959, 60, Pauline Palmer prize, 1953, Saratosa Am. Painting Exhbn. award, 1959, Ford Found. purchase prize, 1960, Purchase prize Ball State Coll., 1961, prize La Jolla Art Mus., 1961, Purchase prize Pasadena Art Mus., 1961; Tiffany fellow, 1947; Tupperware Art Fund fellow, 1955; Tamerind Lithography fellow, 1961. Address: 712 Amalfi Dr Pacific Palisades CA 90272

TREINAVICZ, KATHRYN MARY, programmer analyst, computer consultant; b. Brockton, Mass., Nov. 25, 1957; d. Ralph Clement and Frances Elizabeth (O'Leary) T. BS, Salem State Coll., Mass., 1980. Tchr., Brockton Pub. Schs., 1980-81; instr. Quincy CETA Inc., Mass., 1981-82; programmer systems Architects Inc., Randolph, Mass., 1982, programmer analyst, Dayton, Ohio, 1982-84; sr. programmer analyst System Devel. Corp., Dayton, 1984-86; project mgr. Unysis Inc., Dayton, 1986-87; software engr. Systems and Applied Scis. Corp., 1987—. Mem. Nat. Assn. Female Execs. Democrat. Roman Catholic. Avocations: Steven King novels, needlepoint, knitting, crocheting.

TREISTMAN, JOAN MARION, marketing research company owner; b. N.Y.C., Jan. 4, 1945; d. Ludwig and Helene (Reichenberg) Nussbaum; m. Norman Walter, Jan. 22, 1967; Michelle, Eva. Student, Syracuse U., 1961-63; BA, CCNY, 1965; MBA, U. Chgo., 1969. Field dir. Marketscope, N.Y.C., 1965-67; project dir. Marplan, Chgo., 1967-69; sr. analyst Quaker Oats, Chgo., 1969-70; owner, pres. JMT Assocs., Oakland, N.J., 1970-74; prin., exec. v.p. Perciption Research Services, Inc., Englewood Cliffs, N.J., 1974-87; ptnr., prin. Treistman & Stark Mktg., Inc., Palisades Park, N.J., 1987—; seminar leader Am. Mgmt. Assn., N.Y.C., 1973-75. Mem. Am. Mktg. Assn. (chmn. dir. com. 1981-87, bd. dirs. N.Y. chpt. 1987, Outstanding Service award, 1984, 85, 86, 87), Advt. Research Found. (various coms.), Advt. Women of N.Y.(various coms.), U. Chgo. Women's Bus. Group. Jewish. Home: 109 Thackeray Rd Oakland NJ 07436 Office: Treistman & Stark Mktg Inc 410 Broad Ave Palisades Park NJ 07650

TREJO, ANN HELENE, educational loan program executive; b. Tucson, Sept. 28, 1947; d. John H. and Ann L. (Mulkey) Bright; m. Ray L. Trejo, Oct. 16, 1963; children: Michael, John. BS in Bus. Adminstrn., No. Ariz. U., 1979. Guidance specialist Pima County Career Guidance Project, Tucson, 1973-76; counselor fin. aid No. Ariz. U., Flagstaff, 1976-79; officer fin. aid U. Nev., Reno, 1979-80; adminstr. fin. aid Ariz. State U., Tempe, 1980-81; assoc. exec. dir. Ariz. Loan Mktg. Corp., Phoenix, 1981-85; exec. dir. Ariz. Ednl. Loan Program, Phoenix, 1985-86; dir. fin. services Superior Tng. Service, Phoenix, 1987—; trainer Ariz. Assn. Student Fin. Aid Adminstrn., 1980—; regional rep. Nat. Council Higher Edn. Loan Programs, 1983—; dir. Statewide Career Opportunities Postsecondary Edn., Phoenix, 1983—. Recipient DuBois Found. award, 1976-79, Thompson Meml. Leadership award, 1985-86. Mem. Nat. Assn. Student Fin. Aid Adminstrs., Nat. Assn. Female Execs., Western Assn. Student Fin. Aid Adminstrs. Home: 3625 S Judd St Tempe AZ 85282 Office: Superior Tng Services 1817 N 7th St Suite 150 Phoenix AZ 85006

TRELEASE, JULIA BAINBRIDGE, pharmaceutical company executive; b. N.Y.C., Nov. 23, 1937; d. James Woodrow and E. Blanche (Wagner) Mathews; m. David Justin Trelease, July 19, 1969 (div. June 1982); children: Justin Rogers, Charity Woodrow. Student, Carnegie-Mellon U. (formerly Carnegie Inst. Tech.), 1955-57; cert. in mgmt., Elmhurst (Ill.) Coll., 1986. Asst. editor Playboy Mag., Chgo., 1968-69, assoc. editor, 1969-70; freelance writer, editor Park Ridge, Ill., 1970-80; market researcher Trendex, Inc., Park Ridge, 1980-81; adminstrv. asst. Master Health Services, Inc., Arlington Heights, Ill., 1981-84; v.p. Mediclinic Devel. Corp., Arlington Heights, 1984-87, Gynex, Inc., Des Plaines, Ill., 1983-86; corp. sec. Gynex, Inc., Deerfield, Ill., 1986—; sec.-treas. Inst. Med. Research, Arlington Heights, 1983—. Treas. Troop 76 Boy Scouts Am., Park Ridge, 1983-86. Mem. Mensa. Home: 612 S Cumberland Ave Park Ridge IL 60068 Office: Gynex Inc 570 Lake Cook Rd Deerfield IL 60015

TREMAIN, JULIA F., nurse; b. Chgo., Aug. 9, 1935; d. John Martin and Marcella (Mnikolaicik) Rechul; m. Gerald Tremain, June 7, 1957; children: Robert, Stephen, Catherine, John. Student, DePaul-St. Mary of Nazareth Sch. of Nursing, 1952-55. RN, Ill., Wash. Staff RN St. Mary of Nazareth Hosp., Chgo., 1955-58, Resurrection Hosp., Chgo., 1959-78; staff RN, nurses supr. St. Anne's Hosp., Seattle, 1978—. Mem. Am. Nurses Assn. Roman Catholic. Home: Werik Apt Bldg 7030-15 NW Seattle WA 98117

TREMULIS, ELIZABETH PICKETT, social worker; b. N.Y.C., June 3, 1928; d. Ralph Edgar and Helen Margaret (Richardson) Pickett; B.A., Stanford U., 1950; M.A., U. Chgo., 1951; m. Demosthenes Tremulis, Dec. 22, 1951; children—Michael Sarantos (dec.), Andrea, Peter Alexander, William Stephen. Caseworker, Family Service Bur., United Charities of Chgo., 1951-54; social worker North Suburban Spl. Edn. Dist., Highland Park, Ill., 1970-72, Sch. Dist. 28, Northbrook, Ill., 1969-70, 72—; cons. St. David's Nursery Sch., 1968, Highland Park Community Nursery Sch., 1969-70, Ravinia Nursery Sch., 1970. Mem. Highland Park Caucus Com., 1977-79; mem. Highland Park Landmark Preservation Com., 1979-80; bd. dirs. Highland Park Community Nursery Sch., 1964-65, Northbrook YMCA, 1961-63. Mem. Acad. Cert. Social Workers, Nat. Assn. Social Workers, Nat., Ill. assns. sch. social workers, Ill. Soc. Clin. Social Work, Council for Exceptional Children. Mem. staff Sch. Social Work Jour., 1979-81. Home: 466 Laurel Ave Highland Park IL 60035 Office: 1600 Walters Ave Northbrook IL 60062

TRENGA, MARIA R., financial executive; b. Bklyn., June 11, 1957; d. Gaetano S. and Maria Teresa (Fantasia) T. BS in Acctg., Bentley Coll., 1980; MBA, Babson Coll., 1982. Acct. Boston Gas Co., 1980-82; supr. cost acctg. W.R. Grace and Co., Cambridge, Mass., 1983-85; mgr. fin. ops. Lustre Inc., Boston, 1985—. Roman Catholic. Home: 983 Broadway Somerville MA 02144

TRENT, JOYCE MILLER, librarian; b. Dayton, Ohio, Dec. 7, 1946; d. Fielding Leo and Joyce (Henry) Miller; m. Robert Cody Trent, Mar. 17, 1973; children—Michael Frederick Cody, Paul Templeton, Mark Fielding. B.A., Stephen F. Austin State U., 1969; M.L.S., U. Tex., Austin, 1975. Pub. service librarian Deer Park Pub. Library, Tex., 1969-73; system interlibrary loan librarian San Antonio Pub. Library, 1975-76; dir. system, county librarian Atascosa County Library System, Jourdanton, Tex., 1976-81; library dir. Leon Valley (Tex.) Pub. Library, 1981—. Biweekly columnist N.W. Leader, 1981—. Pres. parish council St. Brigid's Ch., San Antonio, 1980-81; del. Met. Congl. Alliance, San Antonio, 1982—; mem. civic affairs com. Tex. Sesquicentennial Com., Leon Valley, 1984—. Mem. ALA, Tex. Library Assn. (treas. dist. 10, vice chair-elect, then chair), Leon Valley Bus. and Profl. Assn., San Antonio Geneal. Hist. Soc. (sec. 1977-78). Democrat. Roman Catholic. Home: 5903 Forest Rim San Antonio TX 78240 Office: Leon Valley Pub Library 6500 Evers Rd San Antonio TX 78238

TRENT, NELLIE JANE, psychologist; b. St. Louis, July 5, 1921; d. Richard Wesley and Helen Elizabeth (Kuhn) Mellow; A.B., Wellesley Coll., 1943; M.A., Washington U., St. Louis, 1944; m. John Brabson Trent, Apr. 9, 1946; children—Elizabeth Mellow (Mrs. Peter D.W. Heberling), John Brabson. Lic. psychologist, Mo. Tchr., Mary Inst., St. Louis, 1944-46; grad. asst. psychology dept. Washington U., 1963-65; psychologist Kirkwood (Mo.) Sch. Dist., 1965-75; psychologist, chmn. spl. services Ladue Jr. High Sch., St. Louis. 1975-83; pvt. practice psychology specializing in gerontology, counseling elderly and aging, 1983—; instr. psychology Meramec Community Coll., St. Louis, 1969-70; instr. spl. edn. St. Louis U., 1970. Founder, pres. Greater St. Louis Women's Assn. of Freedoms Found. at Valley Forge, 1968; residential chmn. St. Louis and St. Louis County United Fund, 1968; v.p. Wellesley Coll. Class of '43, 1973-78. Founder, pres. bd. Ladue Chapel Nursery Sch., 1957-59, bd. dirs., 1985-87, chmn. pictorial directory of Ladue Chapel, 1984, ordained elder/trustee, chmn. lay visitors com., 1985-87; mem., sec. long-range planning com. Ladue Chapel, 1976-79; mem. St. Louis Presbyn. Council on Aging; bd. dirs. Washington U. Campus, YMCA, YWCA, Campbell House, Girls Home, Multiple Sclerosis Soc. St. Louis, Internat. Inst. Advanced Studies, YMCA/YWCA of Washington U; mem. Council on Aging, Presbytery of Elijah Parish Lovejoy. Recipient Wellesley Coll. award of year, 1968; Liberty Bowl, Freedoms Found., 1968. Lic. psychologist, Mo. Mem. Am. Psychol. Assn., Mo. Psychol. Assn., Nat. Assn. Sch. Psychologists (charter), Mo. Assn. Sch. Psychologists (charter), Soc. St. Louis Psychologists, Assn. Children with Learning Disabilities, Council Exceptional Children, Am. Personnel and Guidance Assn., St. Louis Jr. League (dir. 1950-53), Mo. Hist. Soc. (pres. women's assn. 1964-66, trustee soc. 1968-71), Kirkwood Community Tchrs. Assn. (dir. 1970-75), Mo. State Tchr. Assn., Ladue Community Tchr. Assn.. Home: 70 Fair Oaks Saint Louis MO 63124 Office: Ladue Jr High Sch 9701 Conway Rd Saint Louis MO 63124

TRENT, ROSE MARIE, accounting firm executive; b. Chgo., July 10, 1943; d. William and Katherine (Kristman) Schweitzer; divorced; children: Anna Marie, Tracy Neal, Jeffrey Earl, Stoney Alexander, Sunny Eric. Student, LaSalle Extension U., Chgo., 1966-69; BS, Cen. State U., Edmond. Okla., 1982. Pres. J & R Ranch, Inc., Yukon, Okla., 1972—, My-Co Acctg. Plus, Inc., Yukon, 1982—; v.p. Hillman's Taxidermy Studio, Inc., Yukon, 1976-82, Reliable Lawn Care, Inc., Yukon, 1982—; bd. dirs. South Tex. Electric, Houston, 1977-82, 33 Welding, Inc., Kingfisher, Okla., 1982—, B & B Air Express, Inc., Oklahoma City, 1984—. Mem. Am. Bus. Women's Assn., Nat. Soc. Pub. Accts., Okla. Soc. Pub. Accts., Nat. Taxidermists Assn. Avocations: hunting, fishing, boating. Home: 819 Poplar Yukon OK 73099 Office: J & R Ranch Inc PO Box 850708 Yukon OK 73085

TRENTANOVE, JAYNE MARIE, communications executive; b. Bklyn., Aug. 18, 1957; d. Giulio Cesare and Madeline Marie (Motto) T. BS in Journalism, U. Md., 1978. Promotions asst. Ringling Bros.-Barnum & Bailey, Washington, 1979-80; mktg. coordinator Thomson McKinnon Securities, Inc., N.Y.C., 1980-82; mktg. and communications coordinator Belzona Molecular, Inc., Uniondale, N.Y., 1982-84; dir. communications Sonitrol Corp., Alexandria, Va., 1985—; mktg. and advt. cons. On The Move, Washington, 1985—. Mem. Internat. Assn. Bus. Communicators, Alexandria Profl. Women's Assn. Roman Catholic.

TREPP, PHYLLIS DAKIN, sales executive, b. Newport News, Va., Oct. 6, 1956; d. Wallace Frank and Annette Kirkland (Dakin) T.; m. Brent Alan McIver, May 1, 1982 (div. Jan. 1983). AS in Bus. Adminstrn., Franklin U., 1978; BA in Bus. Adminstrn., Ottawa U., Phoenix, 1985. Cashier Stumps Supermarket, Reynoldsburg, Ohio, 1975; pvt. practice designer, seamstress Whitehall, Ohio, 1975-78; asst. mgr. So-Fro Fabrics, Columbus, Ohio, 1977-79; rental sales agt. Germain Lincoln-Mercury, Columbus, Ohio, 1979-80; supr. First Fed. Savs. & Loan, Bexley, Ohio, 1980-81; asst. to mgr. Hunter Savs. Assn., Gahanna, Ohio, 1981-82; cert. new account rep. CSRIII Home Fed. Savs., Phoenix, 1982-86; account rep. The Fifth Third Bank of Columbus, Gahanna, 1986-87; reporter Inst. Fin. Edn., Phoenix, 1983-86, Home Fed. Savs., Phoenix, 1983-86. Author: Consumer Guide to Savings, 1985; editor yearbook: Trans Am. Club of America Mid-Ohio Chapter, 1979; editor reference manual; The Quick Reference Guide, 1982. Recipient New Idea awards Home Fed. Savs., 1984. Mem. Nat. Assn. Female Execs. Presbyterian. Office: Fifth Third Bank 191 Granville St Gahanna OH 43230

TREPPLER, IRENE ESTHER, state senator; b. St. Louis County, Mo., Oct. 13, 1926; d. Martin H. and Julia C. (Bender) Hagemann; student Meramec Community Coll., 1972; m. Walter J. Treppler, Aug. 18, 1950; children: John M., Steven A., Diane V., Walter W. Payroll chief USAF Aero. Chart Plant, 1943-51; enumerator U.S. Census Bur., St. Louis, 1960, crew leader, 1970; mem. Mo. Ho. of Reps., Jefferson City, 1972-84; mem. Mo. Senate, Jefferson City, 1985—, sec. minority caucus. Mem. Oak-Le-Mehl Republican Club, Concord Twp. Rep. Club; alt. del. Rep. Nat. Conv., 1976, 84; charter mem., bd. dirs. Windsor Community Ctr. Mem. Nat. Order Women Legislators (rec. sec. 1981-82, pres. 1985), Nat. Fedn. Rep. Women. Republican. Mem. Ch. of Christ. Office: Mo State Senate State Capitol Bldg Room 424 Jefferson City MO 65101

TRESMONTAN, OLYMPIA DAVIS, psychotherapist, marriage and family counselor; b. Boston, Nov. 27, 1925; d. Peter Konstantin and Mary (Hazimanolis) Davis; B.S., Simmons Coll., 1946; M.A., Wayne State U., 1960; Ph.D. (Schaefer Found. grantee), U. Calif., Berkeley, 1971; m. Dion Marc Tresmontan, Sept. 15, 1957 (dec. Mar. 1961); m. 2d, Robert Baker Stitt, Mar. 21, 1974. Child welfare worker San Francisco Dept. Social Service, 1964-66; sensitivity tng. NSF Sci. Curriculum Improvement Study, U. Calif., Berkeley, 1967-68; individual practice psychol. counseling, San Francisco, 1970—; dir. Studio Ten Services, San Francisco, Promise for Children, San Francisco, 1981—, tchr. U. Calif. extension at San Francisco, 1971-72, Chapman Coll. Grad. Program in Counseling, Travis AFB, 1971-74; clin. cons. Childworth Learning Ctr., San Francisco, 1976-80; cons. project rape response Queen's Bench Found., San Francisco, 1977. Active Friends San Francisco Pub. Library, Internat. Hospitality Com. Bay Area; bd. dirs. Childworth Learning Center, 1976-80. Mem. Am. Psychol. Assn., Am. Orthopsychiat. Assn., Am. Assn. Marriage Counselors, Calif. Assn. Marriage, Family and Child Therapists. Club: Commonwealth. Author: (with J. Morris) The Evaluation of A Compensatory Education Program, 1967; (Karplus edit.) What is Curriculum Evaluation, Six Answers, 1968. Home: 2611 Lake St San Francisco CA 94121

TREVINO, EVA TERESA PEREZ GARCIA, real estate broker; b. Laredo, Tex., Aug. 5, 1930; d. Luis and Amelia (Ramon) Perez Garcia; m. Oscar T. Treviño, Nov. 12, 1950; children: Armandina, Oscar Jr., Lucia, Ana, Maria, Luis, Jose. Student, Our Lady of Victory, Ft. Worth, Tex., Our Lady of the Lake, San Antonio. Cert. real estate broker. Real estate agt. Deanie Owens Co., San Antonio, 1978-81; real estate broker Hallmark Bradfield, San Antonio, 1981-84; owner, real estate broker Eva. P. Treviño Realtors, San Antonio, 1984—, Distinctive Properties, San Antonio, 1985—, Southpark Realtors, San Antonio, 1987—. Mem. leadership group Mex.-Am. Legal Def. and Ednl. Fund; bd. dirs. Girl Scouts USA San Antonio Council. Mem. Nat. Assn. Real Estate Brokers, Women's Council Realtors, Tex. Real Estate Assn., San Antonio Bd. Realtors. Roman Catholic. Club: Pan Am. League. (San Antonio) (pres. 1984-86). Home and Office: PO Box 28324 San Antonio TX 78228

TRIBBLE, HARRIETT GEE, government official; b. Charleston, S.C., Sept. 19, 1944; d. John Thomas III and Alice G. (Easterling) Forehand; 1 child, Gary Warren Gee Jr. BA, U. Ala., 1977, MBA, 1983. With U.S. Army Materiel Command, Huntsville, Ala., 1967—; dir. Mgmt. Engring. Agy., 1984—. Pres. Huntsville Women's Ctr., 1977; treas., mem. exec. bd. Hope Pl., Huntsville, 1987-88. Mem. Am. Soc. Mil. Comptrollers (1st v.p. 1987, pres. 1988), Assn. U.S. Army, Am. Mgmt. Assn., Huntsville Mus. Art, Huntsville Lit. Assn. Republican. Baptist. Home: 702 Versailles Dr Huntsville AL 35803 Office: US Army Materiel Command Mgmt Engring Agy 4940-B Research Dr Huntsville AL 35805

TRICARICO, LINDA MARIE, fashion designer; b. Bklyn., June 8, 1961; d. John William and Phyllis Jean (D'Addario) T. Student, Bucks County Community Coll., 1978-79, Fashion Inst. Tech., 1979-80. Mgr. retail, 1980-83; coordinator sales and design Sure Snap Corp., N.Y.C., 1983-84; asst. designer E.S. Sutton Inc., N.Y.C., 1984-86; designer Good 'N Plenty Inc., N.Y.C., 1986—; free-lance illustrator, designer. Contbr. fashion trend reports, Milan, Italy, 1984, Rome, 1985, Milan and Florence, Italy, 1986, London and Paris, 1987. Mem. Fashion Soc., Nat. Assn. Female Execs. Democrat. Roman Catholic. Avocations: fashion design, illustration, travel. Home: 322 E 82nd St Apt GC New York NY 10028

TRICKEL, MARY E., academic administrator, controller; b. Elizabeth, N.J., Aug. 4, 1940; d. James Franklin and Helen Mary (McGuire) Marken; m. Francis William Trickel, Aug. 20, 1960; children: Debra, Anne, Mary, Ellen. AAS in Acctg., Middlesex Coll., 1977; BS in Acctg., Rutgers U., 1979; MBA, Fairleigh Dickinson U., 1982. Sec. Cities Service Research and Devel., Cranbury, N.J., 1969-70; with Essex Chem. Corp., Clifton, N.J., 1970-84, controller, until 1984; mgr. acctg. Eco Lab, Inc., Woodbridge, N.J., 1984-87; controller Middlesex Coll., Edison, N.J., 1988—, adj. prof., 1980—; bus. cons. Rutgers U., New Brunswick, N.J., 1979—; career cons. Mem. exec. bd. Middlesex Coll. Found., 1982—; mem. adv. bd. The Berkeley Sch., N.Y.C., 1986—. Recipient Berkeley Schs. Alumni of Yr. award, 1987. Mem. Nat. Assn. Accts. (ednl. dir. 1980-83), Nat. Assn. Female Execs., N.J. Assn. Notary Pubs., Quill & Ink, Middlesex Coll. Alumni Assn. (founding pres.), Delta Mu Delta. Roman Catholic. Avocations: writing, word games. Home: 37 Hillside Ave Sayreville NJ 08872 Office: Middlesex Coll PO Box 3050 Edison NJ 08818

TRIHAS, MARIA, airline executive; b. Athens, Greece, Jan. 10, 1942; came to U.S., 1963; d. Stelios Garyfalidakis and Kaliopi Anagnostaki; m. Lefteris Trihas, Oct. 20, 1963; children: Anastasia, Christina. Student, NYU, 1963-66, cert. in travel, tourism, 1972. Sec. Dorothy Gray, N.Y.C., 1965-66; sec. Olympic Airways, N.Y.C., 1966, supr., 1967-70, supr. purchasing, 1971-77, mgr. purchasing, 1977—; cons. Philoptochos Soc. Archdiocesan Cathedral, N.Y.C., 1987—. Singer radio, Athens, 1962; actress Athens Tragas Theater, 1962; announcer station WEVD Athas Show, 1965.

TRIMBLE, CELIA DENISE, lawyer; b. Clovis, N.Mex., Mar. 3, 1953; d. George Harold and Barbara Ruth (Foster) T.; m. Grady Brian Jolley, Aug. 9, 1980. B.S., Eastern N.Mex. U., 1976, M.A., 1977; J.D., St. Mary's U., San Antonio, 1982. Bar: Tex. 1982, U.S. Dist. Ct. (no. dist.) Tex. 1983, U.S. Ct. Appeals (5th cir.) 1985, U.S. Supreme Ct. 1986. Instr. English, Eastern N.Mex. U., Portales, 1977-78; editor Curry County Times, Clovis, 1978-79; assoc. Schulz & Robertson, Abilene, Tex., 1982-85, Scarborough, Black, Tarpley & Scarborough, 1985-87; ptnr., Scarborough, Black, Tarpley & Trimble, 1988—; instr. legal research and writing St. Mary's Sch. Law, 1981-82. Legal adv. to bd. dirs. Abilene Kennel Club, 1983-85. Recipient Outstanding Lawyerof Abilene, 1988. Mem. ABA, State Bar Tex., Am. Trial Lawyers Assn., Tex. Trial Lawyers Assn., Tex. Criminal Def. Lawyers Assn.,

Abilene Bar Assn. (bd. dirs. 1985-86, 87-88, sec./treas. 1985-86), Abilene Young Lawyers Assn. (bd. dirs. 1985-86, 87—, treas. 1985-86, pres.-elect 1987-88, pres. 1988—), NOW, ACLU, Phi Alpha Delta. Office: Scarborough Black Tarpley & Scarborough 500 Alexander Bldg 104 Pine St Abilene TX 79604

TRIMBLE, JANA DENMAN, training manager; b. Houston, Mar. 9, 1955; d. Peyton Linwood and Paula Gene (Wilroy) Denman; m. Dale L. Trimble, May 25, 1985. B.A., U. Houston, 1981, M.Ed., 1984, postgrad. in instrnl. tech., 1985—. Cert. social sci. tchr., Tex. With Highlands Ins. Co., Houston, 1976-78, Cowen, Rowles, Winston, brokerage firm, Houston, 1978; high sch. tchr. Alief Ind. Sch. Dist., Houston, 1981-83; internal tng. coordinator Community Health Computing, Houston, 1983-85; mgr. product tng. and documentation, 1985—. Republican. Home: 9407 Roos Houston TX 77036 Office: Community Health Computing 5 Greenway Plaza #2000 Houston TX 77046

TRIMBLE, LORA NELLE GARRETSON (MRS. JAMES CURTIS TRIMBLE), writer; b. Wichita Falls, Tex., Aug. 12, 1935; d. Jesse Columbus and Alma Geneva (Higgenbottom) Garretson; m. James Curtis Trimble Sr., Sept. 4, 1954; children: James Curtis Jr., Mary Kristi. Student, Sul Ross State Tchrs. Coll., 1954, Midwestern U., 1956; BA, So. Meth. U., Dallas, 1961. Free-lance writer, 1961-67; dir. Royal Lane Lang. Ctr., Dallas, 1969-77; English lang. tchr. to fgn. adults, 1969-77. Mem. Theta Sigma Phi.

TRIMBLE-SCHAFFHAUSEN, JANE IMBS, apparel manufacturing company executive; b. Paris, France, Sept. 17, 1929; came to U.S., 1939; d. Bravig and Valeska (Balbarishky) Imbs; m. Henry W. Trimble, Oct. 4, 1984; children—Wellington D. Watters, Valeska A. Watters. M.B.A., Vassar Coll., 1951. Pres., Village Store, Birmingham, Mich., 1953-67, N.Y.C., 1961-77; pres. Belle France, Inc., N.Y.C., 1974-82, chmn., 1982—. Recipient Entrepreneur Woman's award Women in Bus., 1981. Mem. Phi Beta Kappa. Office: Belle France Inc 530 7th Ave New York NY 10018

TRIMPER, TERRY, public relations executive; b. North Tonawanda, N.Y., Sept. 25, 1959; d. Frank Andrew and Gloria Ann (Liebig) T. BA in Journalism, Ohio State U., 1982; postgrad. in law and bus. adminstrn., Capital U., Bexley, Ohio, 1984—. With pub. affairs dept. U.S. Army C.E., Cin., 1980-84; sr. staff writer Am. Electric Power, Lancaster, Ohio, 1984-86, programs coordinator, 1986—. Asst. leader Girl Scouts Am., Cin., 1983-84; mem. Cin. Updowntowners, 1983-84; mem. community relations com Fed. Exec. Bd., Cin., 1983-84; active Big Bros./Big Sisters, Cin., 1983-84, Fairfield County United Way, Lancaster, 1985. Recipient Am. Jurisprudence award Lawyers Coop. Pub. Co., Columbus, Ohio, 1985; Ohio State U. R. Piergallini scholar, 1981. Mem. Women in Mining (pres. Ohio chpt. 1988), ABA (student), Nat. Assn. for Female Execs., Ms. Found. for Women, Fairfield County C. of C. (mem. women's div.), Ohio State U. Alumni Assn. Methodist. Home: 1984 Heathcliff Dr Apt 2A Columbus OH 43209 Office: Am Electric Power 161 W Main St Lancaster OH 43130

TRIPLETT, JULIA MARIE HAUTER, school system administrator; b. Washington, Iowa, Oct. 14, 1929; d. Andrew John and Emile Mathilda (Chemlar) Hauter; m. George Howard Triplett, May 28, 1950; children: Pamela Marie, James Edward. BA, U. No. Iowa, 1950; MEd, Ea. Ill. U., 1971, advanced teaching cert., 1974. Tchr. Manning (Iowa) Pub. Schs., 1950-54, Jefferson Sch., Omaha, 1954-56; editor Okla. State U., Stillwater, 1956-57; religious edn. dir. Eliot Unitarian Pre-Sch., Kirkwood, Mo., 1957-63; gifted tchr. Arcola and Charleston (Ill.) Grade Sch., 1967-74; ednl. cons. Ill. State Bd. Edn., Springfield, 1974-85; dir. Ednl. Service Ctr., Rantoul, Ill., 1985—; asst. regional supt. Champaign-Ford Counties, Rantoul, 1987—; workshop presenter Nat. Headstart Assn., Denver, 1978, Internat. Reading Assn., Anaheim, Calif., 1987. Active Mahomet (Ill.) Community Theatre; chair bd. dirs. Urbana (Ill.) Unitarian Ch. Recipient Service award Mahomet Community Theatre, 1982; named Outstanding Educator, Champaign Urbana News Gazette, 1983. Mem. Ill. Reading Council (treas. 1981-83, Service award 1983, 86), Illini Reading Council (pres. 1979-80), Phi Delta Kappa (pres. 1979-81). Democrat. Home: 44 Golf Dr Mahomet IL 61853 Office: Ednl Service Ctr #13 200 S Fredrick Rantoul IL 61866

TRIPP, JEAN WARRICK, nurse, educator; b. Smithfield, N.C., Aug. 12, 1945; d. Almond Rexford and Ann Ruth (Lancaster) Warrick; m. Phillip Melvin Tripp, Nov. 21, 1981; children: Christopher, Jay. Practical nurse lic., Lenoir Community Coll., 1978; A in Nursing, Pitt Community Coll., 1979; BS in Profl. Arts, St. Joseph's Coll., 1985. RN, cert. nurse adminstrn., cert. tchr. Allied health instr. Lenoir Community Coll., Kinston, N.C., 1980-85; nurse educator Guardian Care Nursing Home, Kinston, 1982-84; health occupations tchr. Pitt County Schs., Ayden, N.C., 1985—; advisor state bd. Health Occupations Students Am., Raleigh, 1986—; regional leadership chairperson Health Occupations Educators, Greenville, N.C., 1986—; nat. chairperson health Occupations Profl. Devel., Greenville, 1986—. Mem. N.C. Health Occupation Tchrs. Assn. (chairperson profl. devel. 1986-88), N.C. Vocat. Assn. (regional rep.), Am. Vocat. Assn. (nat. com., chairperson profl. devel.). Democrat. Baptist. Home: Rt 2 Box 305 Grifton NC 28530

TRISTANO, SANDRA, lawyer; b. Chgo., Aug. 30, 1951; d. Elias and Shirley (Wood) Snitzer; m. Michael Eugene Tristano, Sept. 29, 1979. B.A., Cornell U., 1973; J.D., Washington U., St. Louis, 1977. Bar: Ill. 1977, U.S. Dist. Ct. (cen. dist.) Ill. 1977. Staff atty. Ill. Dept. Pub. Aid, Springfield, 1977-80; gen. counsel Ill. Dept. Energy and Natural Resources, 1980—; pro bono vol. Vols. for Justice, Springfield, 1983—. Mem. ABA, Ill. Bar Assn., Sangamon County Bar Assn. Home: 39 Inverness Rd Springfield IL 62704 Office: Ill Dept Energy and Natural Resources 325 W Adams Springfield IL 62706

TRITEL, BONNIE LEE, artists representative; b. Oak Park, Ill., Apr. 22, 1952; d. Clarence Clifford and Kathryn (Grant) Bridwell; m. Jeffrey Robert Tritel, Aug. 17, 1985; 1 child, David. Adminstr. Tritel Studios, Grass Valley, Calif., 1983—. Republican.

TRIVISON, MARGARET ANN, librarian; b. Cleve., Aug. 9, 1942; d. Amilio S. and Louise (Zaccagnini) Trivison. B.A., Notre Dame Coll. (Ohio), 1964; postgrad. Columbia U., 1965; M.S. in Library Sci., Case Western Res. U., 1969. Instr., Cath. Bd. Edn., Cleve., 1964-66; sch. librarian Cleve. Bd. Edn., 1966-69; reference librarian Cuyahoga County Library, Cleve., 1969-71; librarian III, San Diego County Library, San Diego, 1971—; library coordinator, 1971-83, govt. documents librarian, 1982-83, outreach services, 1983-85, dir. adult literacy project, 1985-87, media coordinator, 1987—; dist. humanities adv. bd. San Diego Community Coll. Mem. Calif. Library Services Bd., Sacramento, 1978-82. Mem. Calif. Library Assn., ALA, UN Assn. Democrat. Club: San Diego Mus. Art. Address: 6216 Agee St Apt 115 San Diego CA 92122

TROFINO, JOAN ALHANATI, health care facility administrator; b. N.Y.C.; d. Manoel and Mary (Yurecic) Alhanati; m. Michael Trofino, Sept. 28, 1968. BS in Nursing, Adelphi Coll., 1955-59; MS in Nursing, Adelphi U., 1967; MEd, Columbia U., 1987, EdD, 1988. Supr. obstetrics Wyckoff Hosp., Bklyn., 1960-61; instr. Brookdale Hsop., Bklyn., 1962-64, supr. surgery, 1964-65; dir. nursing emergency room and outpatient dept. Hackensack (N.J.) Hosp., 1969-72; dir. nursing Raritan Valley Hosp., Greenbrook, N.J., 1972-74; v.p. patient care Riverview Med. Ctr., Red Bank, N.J., 1974—. Contbr. articles to profl. jours. Named Nurse Adminstr. of Yr. Mgmt. Forum N.J. State Nurses Assn., Trenton, 1985. Fellow Am. Orgn. Nurse Execs.; mem. Orgn. Nurse Execs. N.J. (legis. chmn. 1981—), Soc. Nursing Service Adminstrs. N.J. (pres. 1980), Nat. Ctr. Nursing Research, NIH, Bethesday, Md. (mem. adv. council), Nat. League for Nursing (bd. dirs.), Sigma Theta Tau. Home: 19 Wildhedge Ln Holmdel NJ 07733 Office: Riverview Med Ctr 35 Union St Red Bank NJ 07701

TROIANO, THERESA MARIE, advertising professional; b. Winthrop, Mass., May 25, 1963; d. Robert Francis and Karen Joan (Andrews) T. BS, Springfield (Mass.) Coll., 1985. Layout prodn. artist Tello's, Cambridge, Mass., 1985-87; asst. to prodn. supr. May Co., Los Angeles, 1987; freelance graphic designer Los Angeles, 1987-88; advt. asst. L.A. Gear, Los Angeles, 1988—; graphic designer, pres. Lá Physique, Los Angeles, 1988—. Mem. Graphic Artist Guild. Home: 512 Ave G Apt #309 Redondo Beach CA 90277 Office: LA Gear 4221 Redwood Ave Los Angeles CA 90066

TROISE, AUDREY HELENA, lumber company executive; b. Schenectady, Sept. 22, 1934; d. George H. and Emma (Relyea) Flavin; student pub. schs., Mechanicsville, N.Y.; m. Frank Troise, Aug. 1, 1964. Steno-sec. Gen. Electric Co., Waterford, N.Y., 1951-52; sec. Taft Hotel and Republic Pictures, N.Y.C., 1952-54; sec. Walter Schneider Assocs., Inc., N.Y.C., 1954-57; sec. William G. Moore & Son Inc. of Del., N.Y.C., 1957-64, corp. sec., dir., 1965-69, v.p., dir., 1969-76, pres., owner, 1976—. Mem. Am. Wood Preservers Assn., Soc. Am. Mil. Engrs., Assn. Bus. and Profl. Women in Constrn., Assn. of Women Bus. Owners.

TROISI, BARBARA DAVIES, reading specialist; b. Rahway, N.J., June 16, 1937; d. Thomas Edward and Ruth Marie (Ohlott) Davies; BS, N.Y.U., 1959, postgrad., 1981—; (dissertation in progress); MA, Fairleigh Dickinson U., 1979; m. Frank X. Troisi, Aug. 22, 1959; children: Pamela Ann, Morgan Andrew. Tchr. English, Cliffside Park (N.J.) Sr. High Sch., 1959-62; reading tchr. Pascack Valley Regional High Sch., Hillsdale, N.J., 1976-78, reading specialist, 1979—; cons. in field. NYU Alumni Scholar, 1955-59; Alcoa scholar, 1955-59; recipient Founders Day award NYU, 1959. Mem. N.J. Assn. Learning Cons., N.J. Reading Assn., Nat. Council Tchrs. English, Internat. Reading Assn., Assn. for Supervision & Curriculum Devel., Kappa Delta Epsilon. Republican. Roman Catholic. Clubs: Jr. Women's of Upper Saddle River, Women's of Upper Saddle River. Contbr. articles to profl. jours. Avocations: writing children's and short stories. Office: Pascack Valley Regional High Sch Piermont Rd Hillsdale NJ 07642

TROLMAN, ARLENE DIANE, psychotherapist, nursing educator, small business owner; b. N.Y.C., June 25, 1937; d. Jerome Richard and Jessie Helen (Levy) Bachner; m. David Steven Trolman, June 9, 1957 (div. 1973); children: Mark, Michael, Debra. BS in Nursing, Adelphi U., 1960, MS, 1964; MEd, Columbia U., 1978, EdD, 1981; cert., Inst. Behavior Therapy, N.Y.C., 1985. Instr. Sch. Nursing Adelphi U., N.Y.C., 1973-75, assoc. prof., 1975—; educator Inservice Sagamore Children's Ctr., Melville, N.Y., 1973-75; pres. Ea. Coastal Cruisers, Inc., Southampton, N.Y., 1985—, Hampton's Bluewater Charters, Inc., Southampton, 1986—. Mem. Am. Nurses' Assn., Nat. League Nursing, Advs. for Child Psychiat./Mental Health Nursing, Sigma Theta Tau.

TROOP, JUDITH ANN, small business owner; b. Weston, W.Va., Sept. 12, 1940; d. James Loyal and Thelma Francis (Skinner) Burkhart; children: John, Francis, Susan, Matthew. Student, S.W. Jr. Coll., Chgo., 1970-72, U. Ill., 1978-79; cert. in paralegal, Roosevelt U., 1982. Sign painter Signs by Judy, Chgo., 1960-80; police officer Dept. Police City of Chgo., 1970—; owner, operator A Profl. Process Service, Chgo., 1982—. Mem. Nat. Tree Farmers Assn., Nat. Assn. Process Servers. Democrat. Office: A Profl Process Service PO Box 8019 Chicago IL 60680-8019

TROSCLAIR, SUSAN JEANNE, musician, educator; b. Kingsport, Tenn., Dec. 8, 1945; d. Lee George and Helen Lucile (Pratt) Davy; m. Richard T. Trosclair, June 28, 1969; 1 child, Kyle Lee. MusB, Oberlin Coll. Conservatory of Music, 1967. Music tchr., piano technician Kingsport, 1967-69, Knoxville, Tenn., 1969-73, Duluth, Ga., 1973-76, Spanish Fort, Ala., 1976—; soloist Kingsport Symphony Orch., 1967, Mobile Piano Ensemble, 1982, duo artist, 1984, 86; adjudicator various musical events in Fla., Ala. La., 1979—. Mem. Music Tchrs. Nat. Assn., 1974—, Ala. Music Tchrs. Assn. (2d v.p. 1984-86, pres. 1986-88, coordinator local affiliates 1982-84), Baldwin County Music Tchrs. Assn. (charter mem., pres. 1978-80, 1983-85, treas. 1982-83), Mobile Music Tchrs. Assn. (parliamentarian, 1979-81, Sonata Com. chmn. 1984-86), Nat. Guild Piano Tchrs. (chmn. Spanish Fort audition ctr. 1980—). Republican. Mem. Assemblies of God Ch. Home: 4 Yankee Trove Spanish Fort AL 36527

TROTTER, DEBRA MILLS, educator; b. Tallahassee, Aug. 16, 1953; d. Hugh Roland and Alfreddia (Gainous) Mills; m. Gary Lionel Trotter, June 20, 1980; 1 child, India Ashlei. BA, Spelman Coll., 1975; MFA, Cranbrook Acad. Art, 1977. Cert. tchr., Fla. Art librarian Spelman Coll., Atlanta, 1973-74; asst. instr. children's art program Cranbrook Acad., Bloomfield Hills, Mich., 1975-76; coordinator ednl. program Loch Haven Art Ctr., Orlando, Fla., 1977-78; tchr. art Orange County Pub. Schs., Orlando, 1978-80; comml. artist Fla. Sun Review News, Orlando, 1978-80; tchr. art Crealde Art Ctr., Orlando, 1979; artist D. Mills-Trotter Inc., Ft. Lauderdale, Fla., 1986—; tchr. Broward County Schs., Ft. Lauderdale, 1980—; vendor D. Mills-Trotter Inc., Ft. Lauderdale, 1988—; instr. supr. Orange County Schs., Orlando, 1978-80. One-woman shows include Broward County Main Library, 1987, Von D. Mizell Ctr., 1982; designer costumes for Kids Stuff (musical), 1986, Costumes kids, 1986; vis. artist Sistrunk Hist. Festival, 1987, also judge, 1985; judge Promenade Arts Festival, 1986. Ann. Sistruck Festival. Mem. evaluating team accrediation high sch., Palm Beach, Fla. 1982; bd. dirs. Lauderhill Arts Council. Mem. Broward Tchrs. Union, Am. Fedn. Tchrs., Nat. Assn. Female Execs., Interested Members Performing Arts Ctr. Team. Democrat. Methodist. Home: 7139 NW 49th St Lauderhill FL 33319

TROTTER, DONNA MARY, commercial artist; b. Burlington, Vt., Aug. 22, 1962; d. Earl D. and Martha L. (Lapointe) T. AS, Champlain Coll., 1987. Customer service rep. McAuliffe, Inc., Burlington, 1981-84; asst. pub. relations dir. Am. Nat. Telcom, Los Angeles, 1985; travel agent Travel with DJ, Montpelier, Vt., 1986; free lance comml. artist Burlington, Vt., 1985—. Vol. Vt. Spl. Olympics, 1985-86, Flynn Theatre for the Performing Arts, Burlington, 1986-87. Merchants Trust Co. grantee, 1986, 87; Father Gerald Dupont Meml. scholar St. Michael's Coll., Winoski, Vt., 1987. Roman Catholic. Home: 40 Staniford Rd Burlington VT 05401

TROUT, MARGIE MARIE MUELLER, civic worker; b. Wellston, Mo., Apr. 27, 1923; d. Albert Sylvester and Pearl Elizabeth (Jose) Mueller; student Webster Coll., 1944-45; cert. genealogist Bd. Cert. Genealogy; m. Maurice Elmore Trout, Aug. 24, 1943; children—Richard Willis, Babette Yvonne. Sec. offices Robertson Aircraft Corp., St. Louis, 1942; speed lathe and drill press operator Busch-Selzer Diesel Engine Co., St. Louis, 1942-43; Cub Scout den mother, Vienna, Austria, 1953-55, Mt. Pleasant, Mich., 1955, London, 1956-57; leader Nat. Capitol council Girl Scouts U.S.A., Bethesda, Md., 1963-65; co-chmn. Am. Booth YWCA and Red Cross Annual Bazaars, Bangkok, Thailand, 1970-72; worker ARC, Vientiane, Laos, 1959-60, Bangkok, 1970-72; activities co-chmn., exec. bd. mem. Women's Club Armed Forces Staff Coll., Norfolk, Va., 1975-77; mem. Am. Women's Clubs, Embassy Clubs, Internat. Women's Clubs Vienna, 1952-55, London, 1956-59, Vientiane, 1959-61, Bangkok, 1969-72, Munich, Germany, 1965-69, Norfolk, 1975-77. Crochet articles exhibited Exhibition of Works of Art by the Corps Diplomatique, London, Eng., 1958. Home: 6203 Hardy Dr McLean VA 22101

TROUT, RUTH BEELER, newspaper editor; b. Kansas City, Mo., July 19, 1922; d. Maxwell Newton and Mary H. (Springer) Beeler; m. Weber F. Trout, Aug. 15, 1942 (div. 1968); 1 child, James J. Student, U. Kans., 1939-42, U. Wis., 1941; BA in Journalism, U. Denver, 1946. Reporter Topeka State Jour., 1942-43; freelance writer Dallas, Houston and Denver, 1945-67; pre-sch. tchr. Mimi's Merri Mornings Nursery Sch., Park Ridge, Ill., 1958-67; reporter, feature writer Park Ridge Advocate, 1967-75, editor, 1975-86; community editor Pioneer Press Cen. Group of Papers, Park Ridge, 1986—. Contbr. articles to med. jours. Founding mem. Park Ridge Hist. Soc.; mem. pub. relations com. Park Ridge YMCA, past dir. Mem. Chgo. Headline Club (ethics com. 1984—), Profl. Journalism Soc. (past bd. dirs., sec.), Park Ridge C. of C. (pub. relations com. 1985—), DAR, Sigma Delta Chi. Republican. Baptist. Office: Pioneer Press 130 S Prospect Ave Park Ridge IL 60068

TROUTMAN, KATHRYN KRAEMER, small business owner; b. Balt., Oct. 5, 1947; d. Edward Fillmore and Bonita (Dick) K.; m. Allen Charles Troutman, May 12, 1974; children: Allen Christopher, Emily Kathryn, Lauren Marie. Student, Columbia Union Coll., Takoma Park, Md., 1966-68, U. Md., 1970-72. V.p. Law Directories, Inc., Washington, 1970-73; real estate developer Balt., 1980—; pub. Workbooks, Inc., Washington, 1979—; founder, pres. The Resume Place, Inc., Washington, Balt., Boston, Va., 1973—; instr. Montgomery Community Coll., Gaithersburg, Md., 1980-81; guest speaker U. Balt. Law Sch., 1979, George Washington U., Washington, D.C., 1985-88; cons., lectr. Psychiat. Inst., Washington, 1982, Hanover Shoes, Pa., 1984, Dept. Energy, Dept. Agriculture, others. Editor, creator: The 171 Reference Book, 1979; editor Nat. Bar Examiner, 1971-73. Mem. Nat. Assn. Women Bus. Owners (sec. 1972-75, founding bd.), Balt. C. of C., Washington D.C. C. of C. Republican. Home: 17 Seminole Ave Baltimore MD 21228 Office: The Resume Pl Inc 1800 I St NW Washington DC 20006

TROUTWINE-BRAUN, CHARLOTTE TEMPERLEY, psychologist, educator, clergywoman; b. Newton, Mass., Nov. 27, 1906; d. Joseph and Libbie (Kempton) Temperley; BS, Simmons Coll., 1927; postgrad. Boston U., 1947-49; MA, Northeastern U., 1966; BES, Internat. Ch. Ageless Wisdom, 1981; m. Arklay S. Richards, Nov. 28, 1928 (div. 1942); children—Whitman Albin, Lincoln Kempton, Sylvia Caroline; m. 2d, Harry Troutwine, May 3, 1945 (div. 1954); m. 3d, Charles E. McCrum, 1961 (div. 1965); m. 4th, Lester Lewis Walsh, Feb. 16, 1968 (div. Feb. 1972); m. 5th, George Braun, Feb. 6, 1975 (dec. Oct. 1975). Pvt. sec. pres. Hygrade Sylvania Electric Corp. Salem, Mass., 1927-28; pvt. and dept. exec. sec. Dr. Stanley Cobb, Bullard prof. neuropathology Harvard U. Med. Sch., 1928-31; part-time work, various positions, 1931-51; exec. dir. Postgrad. Med. Inst., 1951-57; mgr. Postgrad. Information Services, Lederle Labs. div. Am. Cyanamid Co., Pearl River, N.Y., 1957-60; exec. sec. postgrad. med. edn., Hahnemann Med. Coll. and Hosp. also exec. dir. Mary Bailey Inst. Cardiovascular Research, 1961; counselor, tchr. psychology Holliston High Sch., 1965-66. Caseworker Friends of Framingham Reformatory; counselor Falmouth (Mass.) High Sch., 1966-74; psychotherapist Hallgarth Clinic, 1975—. Speaker for Am. Epilepsy League. Mem. Mass. Tchrs. Assn. (life), Spiritual Frontiers Assn. (life), N.E.A. (life), Nat. Ret. Tchrs. Assn. (life), Nat. Assn. Sch. Counselors (charter, life), Assn. Research Enlightenment, Soc. Mayflower Descs. (life), Simmons Coll. Alumnae Assn., AAUW, Med. Soc. Execs. Assn. (emeritus), Am. Soc. Psychical Research, States Med. Postgrad. Assn. (past sec.), Mass. Psychol. Assn., Am. Spiritual Healing Assn. (healing mem., mem. adv. bd.), Spiritual Frontiers Fellowship (life), World Fedn. Healers (healer mem.), Mass. Healers Assn. Author articles in med. and spiritual fields. Mem. Soc. of Friends. Home: 83 Falmouth Ct Bedford MA 01730

TROVER, ELLEN LLOYD, lawyer; b. Richmond, Va., Nov. 23, 1947; d. Robert Van Buren and Hazel (Urban) Lloyd; m. Denis William Trover, June 12, 1971; 1 dau., Florence Emma. A.B., Vassar Coll., 1969; J.D., Coll. William and Mary, 1972. Asst. editor Bancroft-Whitney, San Francisco, 1973-74; owner Ellen Lloyd Trover Atty.-at-Law, Thousand Oaks, Calif., 1974-82; ptnr. Trover & Fisher, Thousand Oaks, 1982—; bd. dirs. Burco Mfg., Los Angeles. Editor: Handbooks of State Chronologies, 1972. Trustee, Conejo Future Found., Thousand Oaks, 1978—, vice chmn., 1982-84, chmn., 1984—; pres. Zonta Club Conejo Valley Area, 1978-79; trustee Hydro Help for the Handicapped, 1980-85. Mem. Conejo Simi Bar Assn. (pres. 1979-80, dir. 1983-85), Ventura County Bar Assn. (state del. 1984), State Bar Calif., Va. State Bar, Phi Alpha Delta. Democrat. Presbyterian. Home: 11355 Presilla Rd Camarillo CA 93010 Office: Trover and Fisher 1107E Thousand Oaks Blvd Thousand Oaks CA 91362

TROWELL-HARRIS, IRENE, nurse; b. Aiken, S.C., Sept. 20, 1939; d. Frank and Irene (Battle) Trowell; m. Benoni Harris, Oct. 2, 1978 (div. May 1983). BA, Jersey City State U., 1971; RN, Columbia Hosp., 1959; MPH, Yale U., 1973; MEd, Columbia U., 1983, EdD, 1983. Staff nurse Talmadge Hosp., Augusta, Ga., 1959-60; head nurse N.Y. Hosp., N.Y.C., 1960-64; pediatric supr. Brookdale Hosp., N.Y.C., 1964-66; adminstr. HHA Maimonides Hosp., Bklyn., 1966-71; adminstr., coordinator Misericordia Hosp., Bklyn., 1974-85; policy devel. Am. Nurses Assn., Kansas City, Mo., 1985—; mem. adj. grad. faculty U. Mo., Kansas City. Contributing editor Jamaica Times Mag., 1978-85; contbr. articles to profl. jours. Mem. leadership com., chief of staff to Gov. N.Y., Latham., 1986—; AIDS advisor ARC, 1987—. Served to lt. col. N.Y. ANG, 1963—. Mem. Am. Nurses Assn. (congl. dist. coordinator 1981-85, task force on AIDS 1986—), N.Y. State Nurses Assn., Am. Pub. Health Assn., Nat. Guard Assn. U.S., Res. Officers Assn. (life), NAACP (life), Kappa Delta Pi. Democrat. Baptist. Club: Yale (N.Y.C.). Home: 7040 N Bales Apt 235 Gladstone MO 64119-1247 Office: Am Nurses Assn 2420 Pershing Rd Kansas City MO 64108

TROXELL, REBECCA LYNNE, information systems professional; b. Winston-Salem, N.C., July 23, 1959; d. John Cline and Elevee Era (Ammons) T. BS, U. N.C., 1983. Instr. Guilford Tech. Community Coll., Jamestown, N.C., 1982; info. system staff AT&T Tech., Greensboro, N.C., 1983—. Mem. Nat. Assn. Female Execs., Quill & Scroll, Am. Clogging Hall fo Fame, Clog Leaders Orgn. Am., N.C. Clogging Council. Republican. Club: Deep River Cloggers (dir. 1987—).

TROY, JANE CAROLYN, government official; b. Washington, Nov. 11, 1935; d. John and Allene (Parry) T.; With Overseas Pvt. Investment Corp., Washington, 1966—, dep. dir., now regional mgr. Africa and Middle East Internat. div. Office: 1615 M St NW Washington DC 20527

TROYER, SUSAN CAROL, health facility executive; b. Peoria, Ill., Mar. 14, 1944; d. Robert Emmanuel and Ethel Mae (Yordy) T. BA, Goshen Coll., 1966; MS, Ill. State U., 1972. Tchr., guidance counselor pub. schs. Ill. and Wiesbaden, Fed. Republic of Germany, 1966-70, 72-73; faculty/residence advisor Mennonite Hosp. Coll. Nursing, Bloomington, Ill., 1970-72; asst. dir. student personnel services Luth. Gen. Hosp., Park Ridge, Ill., 1973-77; adminstrv. asst. nurse recruitment Mt. Sinai Hosp., Chgo., 1977-80; dir. nursing resources St. Margaret Hosp., Hammond, Ind., 1980-85; dir. profl. resources St. Catherine Hosp., East Chicago, Ind., 1985-86; regional dir. profl. resources Lakeshore Health System, N.W. Ind., 1986—; adj. faculty Nat. Coll. Edn., Evanston, Ill., 1985—. Mem. Am. Mktg. Assn., Nat. Assn. for Health Care Recruitment. Mennonite. Clubs: Lake Shore Ski, East Bank (Chgo.). Home: 155 N Harbor Dr Apt 3314 Chicago IL 60601

TRUAX, SUZY, office complex and secretarial service executive; b. Reno, Dec. 10, 1939; d. James A. and J. Sue (Hawkins) Smith; A.A. in Bus., Truckee Meadows Community Coll., 1977; div.; children—Coleen Sue, Kevin Todd. Owner, operator The Exec. Center, Reno, 1980—. Mem. Reno-Sparks C. of C., Am. Bus. Women's Assn. (past pres. Washoe Zephyrs chpt.), Nat. Assn. Secretarial Services, Bricklin Internat. (nat. bd. dirs.), Nor-Cal Bricklin Owners Assn. Democrat. Club: Reno Ad (exec. sec.). Office: 1105 Terminal Way Suite 202 Reno NV 89502

TRUDEL, LYNNE FRANCES, sales manager; b. Boston, Feb. 8, 1953; d. Charles Frances and Nora (Lardner) O'Neill; m. Robert Trudel (div. 1983). Student, Massasoit Community Coll., 1971-72, Newbury Jr. Coll., 1977-78, New Eng. Sch. of Art and Design, 1981. Sales rep. Scandinavian Design, Natick, Mass., 1981-82; asst. mgr. Scandinavian Design, Natick, 1982-83, mgr., 1983-84; office div. mgr. Scandinavian Design Gallery, Washington, 1984-85; regional mgr. desks and furnishings div. Scandinavian Design, Laurel, Md., 1985-86; gen. mgr. Washington, Md. and Va. area Scandinavian Design, Natick, Mass., 1986; sales mgr. Myers Ethan Allen, Hyannis, Mass., 1987—; mgr. retail devel. Roman Research, Norwell, MA, 1988—. Mem. Greater Washington Bd. of Trade, Bus. and Profl. Womans Club of Cape Cod, Cape Cod Womans Orgn. Home: 248 Camp St U-3 West Yarmouth MA 02673 Office: 46 Accord Park Dr Norwell MA 02061

TRUE, CLAUDIA, geologist; b. Kingsville, Tex., Sept. 15, 1948; d. Elmer Conrad and Gift Jeanette (Haralson) T.; m. Michael Frank Driggs, Mar. 31, 1983. B.A. in Geology, Trinity U., 1971; M.S. in Geology, Pa. State U., 1978. Research aide Tex. Bur. Econ. Geology, Austin, 1972-73; coal petrologist coal research sect. Pa. State U., University Park, 1974-77; cons. in coal petrology, University Park, 1975-77; coal geologist U.S. Geol. Survey, Denver, 1977-80; prodn., exploration geologist Mobil Alternative Energy, Inc., Denver, 1980-85; prodn. geologist Mobil Oil Corp., Denver, 1986—; art cons.; speaker in field. Contbr. articles to profl. publs. Mem. Am. Assn. Profl. Geologists, Am. Inst. Profl. Geologists, RMAG, AIME, Denver Coal Club (program chmn. 1984-85, bd. dirs. 1985-87), Soc. Organic Petrolgists, Women in Mining (scholarship awards chmn., tech. adviser 1986-87, sec. 1987-88, v.p. 1988—). Republican. Methodist. Avocations: arts; music; travel; photography. Home: 5210 Tabor St Arcadia CO 80002 Office: Mobil Oil Corp PO Box 5444 Denver CO 80217

TRUE, JEAN DURLAND, entrepreneur, oil company executive; b. Olney, Ill., Nov. 27, 1915; d. Clyde Earl and Harriet Louise (Brayton) Durland; student Mont. State U., 1935-36; m. Henry Alfonso True, Jr., Mar. 20, 1938; children: Tamma Jean (Mrs. Donald G. Hatten), Henry Alfonso III, Diemer Durland, David Lanmon. Ptnr., True Drilling Co., Casper, Wyo., 1951—, True Oil Co., Casper, 1951—, Eighty-Eight Oil Co., 1955—, True Geothermal Energy Co., 1980—, True Ranches, 1981—; officer, dir. Toolpushers Supply Co., Casper, White Stallion Ranch, Inc., Tucson; dir. Belle Fourche Pipeline Co., Casper, Black Hills Trucking, Smokey Oil Co., True Geothermal Drilling Co., True Wyo. Beef; dir. White Stallion Ranch, Tucson. Mem. steering com. YMCA, Casper, 1954-55, bd. dirs., 1956-58; mem. exec. bd. trustees Gottsche Rehab. Ctr., Thermopolis, Wyo., 1966—, v.p., 1973—; mem. adv. bd. for adult edn. U. Wyo., 1966-68; mem. Ft. Casper Commn., Casper, 1973-79; bd. dirs. Mus. of Rockies, Bozeman, Mont., 1983-87. Mem. Nat. Fedn. Rep. Women's Clubs; del. Rep. nat. conv., 1972. Mem. Rocky Mountain Oil and Gas Assn., Casper Area C. of C., Alpha Gamma Delta. Episcopalian. Club: Casper Country, Petroleum Women's (Casper). Home: 6000 S Poplar St Casper WY 82601 Office: Rivercross Rd PO Box 2360 Casper WY 82602

TRUESDELL, CAROLYN GILMOUR, lawyer; b. Oak Park, Ill., July 15, 1939; d. William Bonney and Gladys (Chapman) Gilmour; m. J. Richard Cheney, June 26, 1982; children by previous marriage—Kelly Elizabeth, Robin Suzanne. Student Stanford U., 1957-59; B.A., Case Western Res. U., 1961; J.D., U. Houston, 1975. Bar: Tex. 1975. Law clk. Chief Judge John R. Brown, U.S. Ct. Appeals, 5th Cir., Houston, 1975-76; assoc. Vinson & Elkins, Houston, 1976-83, ptnr., 1983—. Mem. ABA, Nat. Assn. Bond Attys. Office: Vinson & Elkins 3300 First City Tower 1001 Fannin Houston TX 77002

TRUETT, GAYLE CALHOUN, childhood and elementary educator; b. Montgomery, Ala., Oct. 3, 1949; d. Charles Fitzhugh and Alice Brenise (Varnadore) Calhoun; m. Bertram Sharon Truett, May 24, 1969; children: Deborah Lynn, Jonathan Corey. BS with honors, Auburn U., 1984; MEd with honors, Troy State U., 1987. Cert. childhood and elem. tchr., Ala. Tchr. presch. Aldersgate Meth. Ch., Montgomery, 1977-80; tchr. kindergarten Ridgecrest Bapt. Ch., Montgomery, 1980-82; tchr. 1st grade Vaughn Rd. Elem., Montgomery, 1982-83; tchr. kindergarten Fews Elem., Montgomery, 1983-84; tchr. 2d grade St. James Elem., Montgomery, 1984—. Mem. Brighton Estates Assn., Montgomery, 1980—, Bell Rd. YMCA, Montgomery, 1984—; mem., tchr. Ridgecrest Bapt. Ch., Montgomery, 1980—;. Named one of Outstanding Young Women in Am., 1986. Mem. Ala. Assn. for Young Children (Outstanding State Student in Early Childhood 1984), Kappa Delta Pi, Gamma Beta Phi. Democrat. Baptist. Home: 2037 Edinburgh Ct Montgomery AL 36116

TRUFFELMAN, JOANNE, advertising company executive, consultant; b. N.Y.C., Sept. 22, 1943; d. Henry and Selma (Schwartz) T. Student, Queens Coll., 1960-63. Asst. clk. prodn. Maxwell Sarkheim Co., N.Y.C., 1960-63; mgr. prodn. Sherman Sackheim Co., N.Y.C., 1963-67; v.p., mgr. prodn. Wells, Rich, Green Inc., N.Y.C., 1967-77; v.p., dir. creative services McDonald and Little Inc., Atlanta, 1977-82; mgr. graphic and bottler advt. services Coca-Cola USA, Atlanta, 1982-86; owner, pres. T.G. Madison Adv. Services, Atlanta, 1986—, MCTYPE, Atlanta, 1987—. Mem. Humane Soc., Friends Atlanta Zoo, 1987—; vol. United Way. Mem. Gravure Advt. Council, Gravure Tech. Assn., Atlanta Art Dirs. Club, Advt. Club, Print Prodn. Club. Office: TG Madison Inc 3210 Peachtree Rd NE Atlanta GA 30305

TRUITT, PHYLLIS LYNN, financial officer, accountant; b. Evansville, Ill., Aug. 25, 1945; d. Richard Lynn and Mary Louise (Christmas) McNabb; m. Curtis Michael Truitt, July 3, 1964; children: Erick Todd, Michael Sean. Assoc. Bus. Acctg., U. So. Ind., 1983. Bookkeeper Evansville Printing Corp., 1967-69; asst. controller, office mgr. Peerless Pottery, Evansville, 1969-79; credit, office mgr. Shelby Steel, Inc., Evansville, 1979-87; corp. credit, collections mgr. Atlas Van Lines, Inc., Evansville, 1987—. treas. Concordia Lutheran Ch., Evansville, 1984-85; active Ohio Valley Hospice, Evansville, 1985-87. Mem. Nat. Assn. Credit Mgrs. (bd. dirs. 1986—), Women's Credit Group NACM (membership chmn. 1986-87), Aid Assn. Lutherans (treas. 1986-87), Women's Group Nat. Assn. Credit Mgrs., Nat. Orgn. Female Execs. Democrat. Club: Toastmasters. Home: 1819 Sweetser Ave Evansville IN 47715 Office: Atlas Van Lines Inc 1212 Saint George Rd PO Box 509 Evansville IN 47703

TRULLEY, CYNTHIA GENE, photographic company executive; b. Coldwater, Mich., Apr. 24, 1948; d. Richard M. Conrad and Marielle A. (Agnew) Agans; divorced; children: Robert C. Jr., Richard P. Grad. high sch., Crown Point, Ind. Office mgr. McClenthen Motors, Crown Point, 1971-74; payroll clk. Burrell Colour, Inc., Crown Point, 1974-75, bookkeeper, 1975-78, controller, 1978-86, ops. mgr., 1986—. Mem. Assn. Profl. Color Labs. (regional coordinator 1987—), Photo Mktg. Assn. Republican. Roman Catholic. Office: Burrell Colour Inc 1311 Merrillville Rd Crown Point IN 46307

TRUMAN, RUTH, administrator, writer, lecturer, consultant; b. Ashland, Ky., Oct. 5, 1931; d. Rexford Maitland and Allene G. (Barber) Dixon; B.S., Taylor U., 1952; M.S., Calif. State U., 1967; Ph.D. in Higher Edn., UCLA, 1978; m. Wallace Lee Truman, June 5, 1952; children—Mark, Rebecca, Timothy, Nathan. Tchr. Atco (N.J.) Elem. Sch., 1954; tchr. home econs. Chatham (N.J.) High Sch., 1955; counselor, instr. Citrus Coll., Azusa, Calif., 1967-70; dir. counseling Calif. Luth. Coll., Thousand Oaks, Calif., 1971-74; cons. Women's Ednl. Improvement Program, Los Angeles, 1978-80; women's center facilitator Mt. San Antonio Coll., Walnut, Calif., 1981-82; free-lance writer, lectr., cons., 1982-83; coordinator Cancer Mgmt. Network, U. So. Calif., 1983, assoc. dir. office cancer communications Comprehensive Cancer Ctr., 1984—; dir. Cancer Info. Service Calif., U. So. Calif., 1985-86; dir. cert. programs Calif. State U., Fullerton, 1986-88, dir. program services, extended edn., 1988—. Trustee Baker Home for Ret. Ministers, Rowland Heights, Calif., 1982—; chmn. Com. Status and Role of Women, Pacific and Southwest Conf., United Meth. Ch., 1980-82, mem. Bd. Higher Edn., 1983-84; mem. exec. com. Ventura County Council Drug Abuse, 1972-73. Mem. UCLA Doctoral Assn., Phi Delta Kappa. Democrat. Methodist. Author: How To Be A Liberated Christian, 1981; Spaghetti From the Chandelier, 1984; Mission of the Church College, 1978; Underground Manual for Ministers' Wives and Other Bewildered Women, 1974. Home: 2814 E Roberta Dr Orange CA 92669

TRUPIN, ELIZABETH, literary agent; b. Phila., Jan. 23, 1945; d. Charles and Elizabeth (Cleary) Hobbs; m. John F. Wallace, Jan 28, 1967 (div. July 1974); m. James E. Trupin, Nov. 16, 1974; stepchildren: Joshua, Jessica. BA, West Chester State Coll., 1966; MA, U. Del., 1968. Asst. ciculation mgr. The Am. Scholar, Washington, 1968-70; adminstrv. asst., psychology SUNY, Stony Brook, 1970-71; asst. contracts mgr. New Am. Library, N.Y.C., 1971-72; asst. editor Fawcett Pubs., N.Y.C., 1973; lit. agt. Mary Yost Assocs., N.Y.C., 1974-75, JET Lit. Assocs., N.Y.C., 1976—. Home and Office: 124 E 84th St 4A New York NY 10028

TRUSSEL, NANCY LYNNE, small business owner; b. Bklyn., July 10, 1950; d. Howard Franklin and Eleanor (Leister) T.; m. James G. Cullen, Oct. 13, 1985. BA with honors, L. I. U., 1972; BA, SUNY, Fredonia, 1974. Tng. asst. Peat Marwick Mitchell and Co., N.Y.C., 1974-76; dir. human resources Automatic Data Processing, Inc., Clifton, N.J., 1976-83, Litton Computer Services, Fairfield, N.J., 1984-85; mgmt. tng. mgr. Beneficial Corp., Peapack, N.J., 1986; owner Trussel Assocs., Bloomfield, N.J., 1986—; video producer Armstrong Info. Services, N.Y.C., 1985—. Mem. Internat. TV Assn., Am. Soc. Tng. and Devel., N.Y. Orgn. Devel. Network, Nat. Soc. Performance and Instrn. Office: 606 Bloomfield Ave Suite 5 Bloomfield NJ 07003

TRUSZKOWSKI, BERNICE GERTRUDE, equipment lease consultant, broker; b. Balt.; d. Aloysius Walter and Gertrude J. (Brzozowski) T.; m. Philip Donald Wahlmark, Apr. 16, 1977. BS, Towson State U., 1969; MFA, Ariz. State U., 1973, postgrad. sch. bus., 1982. Lic. mortgage broker; cert. lease profl. Gen. mgr. Fed. Lease Sales, Millbrae, Calif., 1973-76; asst. rental mgr. Rossi Ford, Scottsdale, Ariz., 1977-78; gen. lease mgr. Western States Leasing, Scottsdale, 1979; owner Equipment Funding Ltd., Scottsdale, 1979—. Chmn. Cancer Soc. Mem. Nat. Assn. Bus. Women, Phoenix C. of C., Western Assn. Equipment Lessors (regional chair 1983-84, vice chair regulation 1984, vice chair service 1985, bd. dirs. 1986-87, dir. 1986-87). Lodge: Civitan. Office: PO Box 985 Phoenix AZ 85252

TRYON, GEORGIANA SHICK, psychologist; b. Glendale, Calif., Mar. 28, 1945; d. Norman Alton and Nancy Emily (Shaffer) Shick; m. Warren W. Tryon, July 31, 1970; 1 child, Elizabeth. B.A., Pa. State U., 1966; M.A., Kent State U., 1969, Ph.D., 1971. Lic. psychologist, N.Y. Psychologist to outpatients N.Y. Hosp., N.Y.C., 1971-72; dir. Counseling Ctr., Fordham U., N.Y.C., 1972-75, Bronx, N.Y., 1975—; pvt. practice psychology, Briarcliff Manor, N.Y., 1973—. Author, editor: The Professional Practice of Psychology, 1986. Contbr. articles to psychology jours. Mem. Am. Psychol. Assn., Assn. for Advancement Behavior Therapy, Nat. Assn. Women Deans, Counselors and Adminstrs., Eastern Psychol. Assn., N.Y. State Psychol. Assn. Club: Metro Masters Swim (N.Y.C.). Avocation: master swimmer. Office: Fordham U 226 Dealy Hall Bronx NY 10458

TSAI, ELIZABETH TAN, lawyer; b. Roxas City, Philippines, Nov. 6, 1940; naturalized U.S. citizen, 1973; d. Vicente Robles and Rosario (Gonzaga) Tan; A.A. with honors, U. Philippines, Iloilo City, 1958; B.S. in Jurisprudence, LL.B. (Coll. of Law Golden Jubilee scholar), 1962; LL.M. (Univ. fellow), Yale U., 1965; m. Nien-Tszr Tsai, Dec. 2, 1967; children—Pearl Tan, Andrew Tan. Admitted to Philippine bar, 1963, Calif. bar, 1973, D.C. bar, 1974; assoc. firm SyCip, Salazar, Luna & Assocs., Manila, 1963-64; editor Lawyers Coop. Pub. Co., Rochester, N.Y., 1965-71; individual practice law, San Diego, 1973-74; atty.-adv. Div. Investment Mgmt., SEC, Washington, 1977-81, spl. counsel, 1981—. Mem. U. Philippines Alumni Assn. of Met. Washington Area (1st v.p. 1986-87). Democrat. Mem. Chinese Christian Ch. Recent decisions editor Philippine Law Jour., 1961-62; assoc. editor Philippine Internat. Law Jour., 1963-64. Office: 450 5th St Washington DC 20549

TSCHINKEL, SHEILA LERNER, banker, economist; b. N.Y.C., Nov. 21, 1940; d. Abraham and Mira (Nevelova) Lerner; m. Paul Tschinkel, Aug. 11, 1963 (div. 1978). B.A., Hunter Coll., 1961; M.A., Yale U., 1963, postgrad., 1967-68. Asst. prof. U. Alaska, Fairbanks, 1963-65, U. Conn., Storrs, 1967-68; instr. Yale U., New Haven, 1968-69; asst. v.p. Fed. Res. Bank, N.Y.C., 1970-79; v.p., dir. global asset mgmt. Chase Manhattan Bank, N.Y.C., 1979-81; exec. v.p. MPH Commodities Corp., N.Y.C., 1982-83; sr. v.p., dir. research Fed. Res. Bank, Atlanta, 1984—. Mem. Com. on Future of South. Fellow Yale U., 1961-63, Ossabaw Island Project, Ga., 1977. Mem. Am. Econ. Assn., So. Econ. Assn., Money Marketeers N.Y. (bd. govs. 1979-82), Phi Beta Kappa. Office: Fed Reserve Bank 104 Marietta St Atlanta GA 30303

TSCHINKEL, VICTORIA JEAN, environmental and technology consultant, former state official; b. Mt. Vernon, N.Y., Oct. 30, 1947; d. William Aaron and Edith (Meyerson) Nierenberg; m. Walter Rheinhardt Tschinkel, June 15, 1968; 1 child, Erika Lotte Elizabeth. A.B. in Zoology, U. Calif.-Berkeley, 1968. Biologist, librarian Tall Timbers Research Sta., Tallahassee, 1970-74; field insp. Trustees for Internal Improvement Trust Fund, Tallahassee, 1974-76; environ. specialist Dept. Environ. Regulations, Tallahassee, 1976; asst. to sec. Dept. Environ. Regulations, 1976-77, asst. sec., 1977-81, sec., 1981-87; sr. cons. Landers and Parsons, 1987—; mem. energy research adv. bd. Dept. Energy, 1979-86; mem. adminstrv. toxic substances adv. council EPA, 1982-84; dir. Environ. and Energy Inst., Washington, 1984—; mem. Gas Research Adv. Council, Chgo., 1983—, NRC, Washington, 1983—, Space Applications Bd., 1983-85; mem. adv. panel on energy in city bldgs. Office Tech. Assessement, 1980-81; mem. adv. bd. Solar Energy Inst., 1985; mem. Electric Power Research Inst. Adv. Council, NAS site selection com. for superconducting supercollider; mem. adv. council Environ. Protection Research Inst.; mem. adv. com. Nuclear Facility Safety, 1988—; bd. dirs. Fla. Defenders of the Environment, 1987—, 1000 Friends of Fla., 1988—. Mem. Capital Womens Network, Tallahassee, 1983-84, Community Adv. Bd., Ctr. for Profl. Devel., 1983-84. Named North Fla. Pub. Aminstr. of Yr., Am. Soc. Pub. Adminstrs., 1984. Mem. Women Execs. in State Govt., Nat. Acad. Pub. Adminstrn. Office: Landers Parsons & Uhlfelder PO Box 271 Tallahassee FL 32302

TSCHUDIN, GENEVIE NAOMI, former nurse, anesthetist, writer; b. Shelley, Idaho, Feb. 28, 1906; d. Willard Joseph and Naomi Elzada (Lawrence) Goff; m. Paul Tschudin (dec. Nov. 1973). R.N., Latter Day Saints Nurses Tng. Sch., 1923. Sch. nurse, Salt Lake City, 1923-24; nurse for children's orphanage, Salt Lake City, 1924-25; head nurse supt. Hull Hosp., Ypsilanti, Mich., 1930-36; founder unit for contagious diseases Latter Day Saints Hosp., Salt Lake City, 1936-39; chief nurse, anesthetist ob-gyn Jamaica Hosp., N.Y., 1936-39, nurse anesthetist in operating room, 1941; anesthetist ob-gyn Lenox Hill Hosp., N.Y.C., 1939, 41-71; nurse anesthetist operating room Queens Gen. Hosp., Jamaica, 1940. Author (poetry): U.S. Nurses Poetry, 1940 (1st prize). Mem. Fla. State Poets Assn. Republican. Mormon. Club: Poetry Appreciation (Ocala, Fla.). Avocation: writing. Home: 1130 NE 12th Ave Ocala FL 32670

TSE, DAPHNE CHIU-FUN, biochemist; b. Hong Kong, Mar. 11, 1939; came to U.S., 1958, naturalized, 1971; d. Kwong Chiu and Yee Wan (Choy) Hui; B.S., UCLA, 1962; m. Tim Tse, Feb. 1, 1964; children—Anthony, Eric. With Baxter Hyland Div., Inc., Glendale, Calif., 1963—, sr. research scientist, 1979-81, research mgr., 1981—. Recipient Inventor's award Baxter Travenol Co., 1979, 84, 85. Mem. Am. Chem. Soc., Internat. Soc. Thrombosis and Hematology, Am. Heart Assn., AAAS. Methodist. Author articles in field; patentee in field. Office: 1710 Flower Ave Duarte CA 91010

TSE, WINNIE MAN-NAI, technology research and development director; b. Hongkong, Feb. 12, 1953; d. Pui Hong and Yee Mei (Yip) T.; m. Kin Ping Cheung, Aug. 3, 1980. BA in Biology, NYU, 1977, MBA in Info. Systems, 1979. Teller The Hong Kong & Shanghai Banking Corp., Hong Kong, 1973-74; editorial asst. NYU, 1977; bookkeeper Sports Time Industries, Bklyn., 1977-78; programmer, cons. NYU, 1978-79; systems analyst, programmer GMS Systems, Inc., N.Y.C., 1979-80, sr. system cons., 1980-83, project mgr., 1983-84; dir. product devel. Powerbase Systems, Inc., N.Y.C., 1984-86; dir. tech. research and devel. Equitable Fin. Cos., N.Y.C., 1986—; Contbr. articles to profl. jours. Mem. Soc. Info. Mgmt., Assn. Computing Machine, IEEE Computer Soc.

TUBBERT, MARGARET A., biology educator; b. Syracuse, N.Y.; d. Robert Frederick and Jane Agnes (Healy) T. BA in Biology, Syracuse U., 1962; MS in Biology, Northwestern U., 1966; MA in Cell Biology, SUNY, Buffalo, 1972, PhD in Cell Biology, 1973. Lab. asst. biology Utica (N.Y.) Coll. Syracuse U., 1962; instr. Onondaga Community Coll., Syracuse, 1964-66, asst. prof., 1966-68, assoc. prof., 1968-76, prof., 1976—, chmn. biology dept., 1981-84; researcher embryogenesis Utica (N.Y.) Coll. of Syracuse U., 1962; established, coordinator Pre-biotech. Option, Onondaga Community Coll., 1984—; cons. NASA Life Sci. Program in Space, 1975. Molecular Biology Tng. fellow SUNY, Buffalo, 1970-72; scholar Summer Inst. Biotech., U. Rochester, N.Y., 1986; recipient Chancellor's award SUNY, 1980, Onondaga Community Coll. Trustees' Recognition award, Syracuse, 1980. Mem. AAAS, N.Y. Acad. Scis., Beta, Beta, Beta. Republican. Roman Catholic. Home: 4250 Onondaga Blvd Syracuse NY 13219 Office: Onondaga Community Coll Onondaga Hill Campus Syracuse NY 13215

TUCCERI, CLIVE KNOWLES, library administrator, science educator, educational consultant; b. Bryn Mawr, Pa., Apr. 20, 1953; d. William Henry and Clive Ellis (Knowles) Hulick; m. Eugene Angelo Tucceri, Sept. 1, 1984; stepchildren—Heather Deann, Christopher Eugene; 1 child, Clive Edna. BA in Geology, Williams Coll., 1975; MS in Coastal Geology, Boston Coll., 1982. Head sci. dept. Stuart Hall Sch., Staunton, Va., 1975-77; sci. faculty William Penn Charter Sch., Phila., 1977-79; sci. faculty Tower Sch., Marblehead, Mass., 1982-86; sci. faculty Bentley Coll., Waltham, Mass., 1986-88; adminstrv. dir., co-founder Stout Aquatic Library, Nat. Marine and Aquatic Edn. Resource Ctr., Wakefield, R.I., 1982—. Bd. dirs. People against Rape, Staunton, 1976-77. Mem. Nat. Marine Edn. Assn. (sec. 1986-87, chpt. rep. 1987—), Assn. for Supr. and Curriculum Devel., Mass. Marine Educators (pres. 1987—, bd. dirs. 1983—), Cousteau Soc., Oceanic Soc., Woods Hole Oceanographic Inst., Internat. Oceanographic Found., AAUW (bd. dirs., br. pres.-elect 1975-77, v.p. 1985-86, sec. 1986-87), Mass. Environ. Edn. Soc. (bd. dirs. 1985-88), Sigma Xi. Episcopalian. Avocations: renovating old homes; sailing, gardening; reading. Home and Office: 15 Berwick Terr Longmeadow MA 01106

TUCHMAN, BARBARA WERTHEIM, historian, author; b. N.Y.C., Jan. 30, 1912; d. Maurice and Alma (Morgenthau) Wertheim; m. Lester R. Tuchman, 1940; children: Lucy, Jessica, Alma. B.A., Radcliffe Coll., 1933; D.Litt., Yale U., Columbia U., Harvard U. Research asst. Inst. Pacific Relations, N.Y.C., 1934, Tokyo, 1935; editorial asst. The Nation, N.Y.C., 1936, Spain, 1937; staff writer War in Spain, London, 1937-38; Am. corr. New Statesman and Nation, London, 1939; with Far East news desk, OWI, N.Y.C., 1944-45; Jefferson lectr., 1980. Author: The Lost British Policy, 1938, Bible and Sword, 1956, The Zimmerman Telegram, 1958, The Guns of August, 1962 (Pulitzer prize), The Proud Tower, 1966, Stilwell and the American Experience in China, 1971 (Pulitzer prize), Notes from China, 1972, A Distant Mirror, 1978, Practising History, 1981, The March of Folly, 1984, The First Salute, 1988; contbr. to Fgn. Affairs, N.Y. Times, others. Trustee Radcliffe Coll., 1960-72, N.Y. Public Library, 1980—. Decorated Order Leopold 1st class Belgium. Fellow Am. Acad. Arts and Letters (pres. 1978-80), Smithsonian Council, AAAL (Gold medal for history 1978); mem. Authors Guild (treas.), Authors League (council), Soc. Am. Historians (pres. 1971-73). Club: Cosmopolitan. Home: Cos Cob CT 06807 Office: care Russell & Volkening 50 W 29th St New York NY 10001

TUCKER, ANNETTE LA VERNE, nurse, health care administrator; b. N.Y.C.; d. Roy L. and Gwendolyn (Cush) Tucker; 1 child, Aaron Nathaniel. Diploma in Nursing, Misericordia Sch. Nursing, 1976; BS in Health Care Adminstrn. with distinction, Iona Coll., 1984; MSP, New Sch. for Social Research, 1988. Cert. long term care mgmt., 1988. Charge nurse med. Jacobi Hosp., 1976-77; charge nurse pediatrics Bronx (N.Y.) Mcpl. Hosp., 1977-78, asst. head nurse neonatal ICU, 1978-83, coordinator utilization rev., 1983-84; charge nurse hematology Van Etten Hosp., Bronx, 1984-85; asst. dir. Salem Home Care, N.Y.C., 1985-87, dir., 1987—. Mem. Nat. Assn. Female Execs., Harlem Health Forum Council, Home Care Field Practice Com., Home Care Council N.Y.C. Home: 800 Concourse Village West #20A Bronx NY 10451

TUCKER, BEVERLY SOWERS, information specialist; b. Trenton, N.J., Dec. 1, 1936; d. Eldon Jones and Verbeda Eleanor (Roberts) Sowers; m. Harvey Richard Tucker, Dec. 27, 1958 (div. Nov. 1983); children: Randall Richard, Brian Alan. BS in Chemistry with distinction, Purdue U., 1958; MS in Geology, No. Ill. U., 1985; postgrad., Rosary Coll., 1986—. Asst. research librarian CPC Internat., Argo, Ill., 1958-62; chem. patent searcher Chgo., 1962-66; info. specialist C. Berger & Co., Wheaton, Ill., 1986, Amoco Corp., Naperville, Ill., 1987—. Alpha Chi Omega grantee, 1985. Mem. Spl. Libraries Assn., Ill. Fedn. Women's Club (treas. 5th dist. 1979-81, Outstanding Jr. Clubwoman award 1979-80), Garden Club Council Wheaton (pres. 1981-82), Alpha Lambda Delta, Delta Rho Kappa, Theta Sigma Phi, Alpha Chi Omega. Republican. Presbyterian. Clubs: Wheaton Jr. Woman's (pres. 1977-78, Single Parent scholarship 1984), Gardens Etc. (pres. 1978-79). Home: 1507 Paula Wheaton IL 60187 Office: Amoco Corp PO Box 400 Warrenville Rd and Mill St Naperville IL 60566

TUCKER, DEBORAH MERRELL, communications executive; b. Washington, Oct. 27, 1952; d. Howard McKeldin Tucker and Julia (Merrell) Harris. AA in History, Mt. Vernon Coll., 1974; BSBA in Internat. Mgmt., Georgetown U., 1977. Mgr. mktg. com. Fairchild Space & Electronics, Germantown, Md, 1971-81; mgr. fin. com. Fairchild Industries, Germantown, 1981-83, mgr. investor relations, 1983-86; dir. investor relations Fairchild Industries, Chantilly, Va., 1986-87; dir. corp. communications Fairchild Industries, Inc., Chantilly, 1987—. Mem. Nat. Investor Relations Inst., Nat. Investor Relations Inst. (pres. Capitol Area chpt., 1985), Aerospace Council of Aerospace Indsl. Assn. Republican. Episcopalian. Office: Fairchild Industries Inc PO Box 10803 Chantilly VA 22021

TUCKER, FLORENCE DENSLOW, retired government official; b. Greenville, Miss., Nov. 12, 1925; d. Victor Amos and Martha Buchannan (Binkley) Denslow; m. Joseph Nathaniel Tucker Jr., Nov. 9, 1946 (dec.); children: Joseph Nathaniel III, Frederick Steven, James Denslow; m. Noel Francis Parrish, June 25, 1983 (dec. Apr. 1987). Diploma piano, Ward-Belmont Coll., Nashville, 1945; studied piano with Michael Field, N.Y.C., 1945-46; B of Music Edn., Delta State U., Cleveland, Miss., 1960; MS in Counseling, U. So. Miss., 1971; EdD, George Washington U., 1982. Tchr. music Gulfport (Miss.) pub. schs., 1959-63; recreation therapist VA Hosp., Gulfport, 1964-70; edn. counselor USAF, Miss. and Japan, 1971-74, edn. services officer, Republic of Korea, 1974-75, asst. dir. sr. tng. CAP nat. hdqrs., 1975-77; EEO officer D.C. Dept. Labor, 1977-80; bur. chief complaints processing and adjudication Office EEO, U.S. Geol. Survey, Reston, Va., 1980-82, mgr. human resources, Dept. Interior, 1982-84; internat. forum coordinator Pres.'s Com. on Employment of Handicapped, 1985; commr. Alexandria Commn. on Aging, Va., 1985—, chmn. edn. and cultural affairs com., sec., 1987—; vis. prof. Kunsan Tchrs. Coll., Kunsan Jr. Coll., 1974-75; apptd. mem. del. People-to-People Internat. Ambassador Program, Beijing, Peoples Republic China and Hong Kong, 1988; workshop leader, cons. and lectr. in field; bd. dirs. Wake Assocs., Ltd., Washington, 1980-84. Columnist on aging issues, Alexandria (Va.) Gazette-Packet; contbr. articles to profl. jours. Organizer, pres. Gulfport chpt. Parents-Without-Ptnrs., 1962-64; charter mem. Westminster Presbyn. Ch., Gulfport, 1961; mem. Nat. Council on Aging. Recipient Outstanding Vis. Prof. award Kunsan Tchrs. Coll., 1974, Kunsan Jr. Coll. award for promoting tchr. exchange program, also certs. of commendation. Mem. Women in Communication, Nat. Assn. Female Execs., Am. Soc. Profl. and Exec. Women, NATO Def. Coll. Anciens Assn. U.S., Phi Delta Kappa. Club: Aging Issues and The Famous Tuskegee Pilots World War II. Home: Stonehurst 9302 Arlington Blvd Fairfax VA 22031

TUCKER, FRANCES GAITHER, marketing educator, researcher, cons.; b. Pittsfield, Mass., June 7, 1947; d. William Brian and Elizabeth (Walker) Gaither; m. James Burke Tucker, June 14, 1969; children: Lauren Jessica, Lindsey Anne. B.A., Wellesley Coll., 1969; M.B.A. with honors, Boston U., 1974; Ph.D., Ohio State U., 1980. Adminstrv. asst. Bolt Beranek & Newman, Cambridge, Mass., 1969-72; research assoc. Ohio State U., Columbus, 1974-79; asst. prof. Syracuse U. (N.Y.), 1979-86, assoc. prof., 1986—. Janesville-Dewitt Cen. Sch. Dist. Coms. Reviewer, contbr. articles profl. jours. Named Outstanding Young Women in Am., 1983; doctoral fellow Richard D. Irwin Found, 1978. Mem. Am. Mktg. Assn. (local officer 1979-83), Council Logistics Mgmt. (various coms. 1978—, doctoral research fellow 1978), . Club: Syracuse Wellesley. Office: Syracuse U Sch Mgmt Syracuse NY 13244

TUCKER, FRANCES LAUGHRIDGE, civic worker; b. Anderson, S.C., Dec. 4, 1916; d. John Franklin and Sallie V. (Cowart) Laughridge; m. Russell Hatch Tucker, Aug. 30, 1946 (dec. Aug. 1977); children—Russell Hatch, Pamela H. Student U. Conn., 1970, Sacred Heart U., Fairfield, Conn., 1977, 79, Fairfield U., 1978, U. S.C., 1984. Sec. to atty., Asheville, N.C., 1935-37; sec. to gen. mgr. Ga. Talc Mining & Mfg., Asheville, 1937-42; sec. engring. dept. E.I. duPont de Nemours, Wilmington, Del., 1942-46. Chmn. radio com. D.C. chpt. ARC, 1947-48, bd. dirs., Beaufort County chpt., 1982-87, chmn. pub. relations, 1982-87, Hilton Head Island, S.C., 1980-87; mem. pub. relations com. United Fund, Westport-Weston, Conn., 1968-69; bd. dirs. communications media St. Luke's Episcopal Ch., Hilton Head Island, 1980—; media pub. relations Bloodmobile Hilton Head Hosp. Aux., 1984—. Clubs: Sea Pines Golf; Princeton of N.Y.C. Home: 13 Willow Oak Rd Hilton Head Island SC 29928

TUCKER, GEORGINIA MAY PETHERAM (MRS. RALPH J. TUCKER), home economics consultant, author; b. Hanford, Wash., Jan. 14, 1911; d. George Thomas and Emily (Russett) Petheram; B.S., Wash. State U., 1933; m. Ralph J. Tucker, Sept. 22, 1940 (div. Apr. 1954). Trainee, Cascadian Hotel, Wenatchee, Wash., 1933-35; food mgr. Roosevelt Hotel, Seattle, 1936-40, Rhodes Dept. Store Seattle, 1940-43; with U.S. Govt. survey Affect of Food on the Aging, 1951; food mgr. Boise Hotel (Idaho), 1953-57; food research Western Internat. Hotels, Seattle, 1957-59, asst. dir. food and beverage, 1959-66; dir. housekeeping Century Plaza Hotel, Los Angeles, 1966-75, ret., 1975; now cons.; instr. exec. housekeeping Pepperdine U.; instr. Golden Gate U. Hotel and Restaurant Sch., career devel. program Cornell U. Hotel and Restaurant Sch. Bd. mem. Com. of Profl. Women Los Angeles Symphony, 1971-72; docent, mem. bd. Filoli nat. trust. Recipient

Disting. Home Econs. Alumnus award Wash. State U., 1978. Mem. Nat. Exec. Housekeepers Assn. (chpt. bd. mem. 1969-72, sec. 1969-70), Nat. Assistance League (mem. nat. bd. 1963-64), Home Economists in Bus. (nat. directory chmn. 1965), Am. Home Economists Assn., Wash. State Home Economists Assn., Alpha Delta Pi. Episcopalian. Club: Soroptimist (1st v.p. 1967-71, pres. 1971-72) (Beverly Hills, Calif.). Author: The Science of Housekeeping, 1970; The Professional Housekeeper, 1975. Home and Office: 25 Arroyo Ct #3 San Mateo CA 94402

TUCKER, HELEN WELCH, writer; b. Raleigh, N.C., Nov. 1, 1926; d. William Blair and Helen (Welch) T.; B.A., Wake Forest Coll., 1946; postgrad. Columbia U., 1957-58; m. William T. Beckwith, Jan. 9, 1971. Reporter, Burlington (N.C.) Times-News, 1946-47, Twin Falls (Idaho) Times-News, 1948-49, reporter Idaho Statesman, Boise, 1950-51; copy writer Sta. KDYL, Salt Lake City, 1952-53; copy supr. Sta. WPTF, Raleigh, 1953-55; reporter Raleigh Times, 1955-57; editorial asst. Columbia U. Press, 1959-60; dir. publicity and publications N.C. Mus. Art, Raleigh, 1967-70; author books: The Sound of Summer Voices, 1969, The Guilt of August Fielding, 1971, No Need of Glory, 1972, The Virgin of Lontano, 1973, A Strange and Ill-Starred Marriage, 1978, A Reason for Rivalry, 1979, A Mistress to the Regent, 1980, An Infamous Attachment, 1980, The Halverton Scandal, 1980, A Wedding Day Deception, 1981, The Double Dealers, 1982, Season of Dishonor, 1982, Ardent Vows, 1983; Bound by Honor, 1984; contbr. short stories to nat. mags. Recipient Disting. Alumni award in Journalism, Wake Forest U., 1971. Episcopalian. Home: 2930 Hostetler St Raleigh NC 27609

TUCKER, JANEE MICHELLE, technical services consultant; b. New Orleans, Apr. 12, 1946; d. Walbert Francois and Pauline (Mathieu) Mercadel; m. Robert Do Qui, Apr. 25, 1969 (div. June 1978); 1 child, Robert; m. Robert Houston Tucker Jr., June 24, 1979; 1 child, Ian. Student, Los Angeles City Coll., 1965; studied with Lee Strasberg, Actors Studio West, Los Angeles, 1966. Image cons. various polit. candidates New Orleans, 1970-73; staff producer Essence of Life Kwanza Found., New Orleans, 1976, Vanderhorst Tng. Systems, New Orleans, 1983; program coordinator Popeye's Famous Fried Chicken, New Orleans, 1977-85; cons. Tucker & Assocs., New Orleans, 1980-84, pres., chief operating officer, 1985—. Bd. dirs. New Orleans City Ballet, Daishiki Theater of New Orleans; mem. Met. Area Com., Planned Parenthood Advocacy Com. New Orleans. Named Person to Watch New Orleans mag., 1985; recipient Outstanding Women-Owned Bus. Enterprise Award U.S. Dept. Transp., 1986. Mem. Nat. Coalition of 100 Black Women (3d v.p. Greater New Orleans), Women's Am. ORT, Nat. Bus. League, Nat. Assn. Female Execs. Democrat. Home: 3610 Carondelet St New Orleans LA 70115 Office: 210 Baronne St Suite 608 New Orleans LA 70112

TUCKER, JOYCE ELAINE, lawyer, state human rights administrator; b. Chgo., Sept. 21, 1948; d. George M. and Vivian Louise T. B.S., U. Ill., 1970; J.D., John Marshall Law Sch., 1978. Bar: Ill. 1978. Substitute tchr. Chgo. Public Schs., 1970-71; mental health specialist Tinley Park (Ill.) Dept. Mental Health, 1970-74; coordinator Title VII Program, Ill. Dept. Mental Health, Chgo., 1974-76, chief mental health equal employment opportunity officer, 1976-79; acting dir. Ill. Dept. Equal Employment Opportunity, Chgo., 1979-80; dir. Ill. Dept. Human Rights, Chgo., 1980—. Mem. Nat. Bar Assn., Cook County Bar Assn. (Spl. Achievement award 1980), Am. Bar Assn., Chgo. Bar Assn. Mem. African Methodist Episcopal Ch. Other: 619 Stratton Office Bldg Springfield IL

TUCKER, JOYCE KATHRYN CASATO, marketing executive; b. Grantwood, N.J., Mar. 12, 1942; d. Frank Eugene and Eleanor Marion Susan (Kuhn) Casato; children: Brian Straehley, Lynsey Weckman. Student, MacMurray Coll., 1960-62, Chamberlain Sch. Retailing, Boston, 1962; BFA in Visual Communications magna cum laude, Kean Coll., 1984. Asst. buyer Thalhimer Bros., Richmond, Va., 1962-63; ready to wear buyer Hahnes, Newark, 1963-68; RTW buyer Sterns, Paramus, N.J., 1968-69; art dir. Conpac Corp., Warren, N.J., 1984 . Community liaison Jr. League Summit, 1978; area coordinator United Way, Summit, 1975; instr. Downs Syndrome Children, Murray Hill, N.J., 1976; steering com. Nat. Assn. for Prevention Child Abuse, Summit, 1977. Mem. N.J. Art Dirs. Club, Sigma Alpha Lambda, Alpha Lambda Sigma, Phi Kappa Phi. Republican. Presbyterian. Clubs: Woman's (v.p. 1974), Summit Tennis. Home: 26 Sunset Dr Summit NJ 07901 Office: Conpac Corp 50 Mount Bethel Rd Warren NJ 07060

TUCKER, LINDA LEE, association executive; b. Bristol, Conn., Dec. 13, 1944; d. Archibald Hall and Colema Dorothy (Dickey) Souard; m. Robert James Tucker, Nov. 26, 1966; 1 child, Janeea Lynn. Grad. high sch., Bristol. Exec. sec. engring. Gen. Electric Co., Ludlow, Vt., 1962-72, prodn. expediter, 1972-73; free-lance photojournalist Ludlow, 1973-76; editorial asst. Black River Tribune, Ludlow, 1976-82, bus. mgr., 1982-84; advt. dir. The Vt. Standard, Woodstock, Vt., 1984-85; v.p., pub. New Eng. Appraisers Assn., Ludlow, 1985—. contbr. articles to profl. jours. Mem. sch. bd. Ludlow Elem. Sch., 1978-82; treas. Ludlow Bapt. Ch., 1978—, youth leader, 1984—. Mem. Nat. Assn. Female Exec. Republican. Baptist. Office: New Eng Appraisers Assn 5 Gill Terr Ludlow VT 05149

TUCKER, LINDA WISE, real estate operations manager; b. Prospect, Tenn., Oct. 3, 1955; d. Johnnie Ester and Hattie Will (Gatlin) Wise; m. Marc Lory Tucker, June 9, 1979. BS, U. Ala., Florence, 1977. Fin. counselor U. Tenn. Hosp., Memphis, 1978-81; credit mgr. Wilson Electronics, Las Vegas, 1981-82; office mgr. Upjohn Healthcare Services, Abilene, Tex., 1982-83, Computer Optical Products, Chatsworth, Calif., 1983-84; ops. mgr. Merrill Lynch Realty, Woodland Hills, Calif., 1984—; v.p. Marlin Corp., Las Vegas, Nev., 1980—, Futura Services, Woodland Hills, 1988—. Mem. Nat. Assn. Meeting Planners, Nat. Assn. Female Execs., LWV. Jewish. Lodge: Rotary. Home: 22291 Cass Ave Woodland Hills CA 91364-3009 Office: Merrill Lynch Realty 5959 Topanga Canyon Blvd Suite #150 Woodland Hills CA 91367

TUCKER, LYDIA ADKINS, purchasing agent, traffic manager; b. Rocky Mount, N.C., Dec. 5, 1958; d. Henry W. Jr. and Carol Ann (Forbes) Adkins; m. Stephen J. Tucker, June 21, 1980 (div. Sept. 1982). AS in Bus. Adminstrn. with high honors, Vance-Granville Community Coll., Henderson, N.C., 1988. Purchasing agt., traffic mgr. Eastern Block, Inc., Henderson, 1984—. Mem. Vance County Humane Soc., Henderson, 1986, Student Vets. Club, Henderson, 1986, Foster Parents Plan, 1987—. Served to sgt. USAF, 1977-81. Mem. Nat. Assn. Female Execs., Assn. Am. Notaries (notary pub.), Foster Parents Plan. Democrat. Baptist. Home: PO Box 1462 Henderson NC 27536 Office: Eastern Block Inc US 1 Business S Henderson NC 27356

TUCKER, MARCIA, museum director, curator; b. N.Y.C., Apr. 11, 1940; d. Emanuel and Dorothy (Wald) Silverman; student Ecole du Louvre, Paris, 1959-60; B.A., Conn. Coll., New London, 1961; M.A., Inst. Fine Arts, N.Y. U., 1969; hon. doctorate San Francisco Art Inst. Curator, William N. Copley Collection, N.Y.C., 1963-66; editorial asso. Art News mag., N.Y.C., 1965-69; collection cataloger Alfred H. Barr, Jr., N.Y.C., 1966-67, catalog raisonée Howald Collection Am. Art, Ford Found., Columbus (Ohio) Gallery Fine Arts, 1966-69; curator painting and drawing Whitney Mus. Am. Art, N.Y.C., 1969-77; dir./founder The New Museum, N.Y.C., 1977—; faculty U. R.I., Kingston, 1966-68, City U. N.Y., 1967-68, Sch. Visual Arts, 1969-73, Columbia U. Sch. Arts and Scis., N.Y.C., 1977; guest lectr. San Francisco Art Inst., Yale U., Balt. Mus. Art, Art Inst. Chgo., Smithsonian Instn., Princeton U.; U.S. commr. 1984 Venice Biennale Mem. Coll. Art Assn., Am. Assn. Mus. (dir.), Phi Beta Kappa. Author: Anti-Illusion: Procedures/Materials, 1969; Catalogue of Ferdinand Howald Collection, 1969; Robert Morris, 1970; The Structure of Color, 1971; James Rosenquist, 1972; Bruce Nauman, 1973; Al Held, 1974; Richard Tuttle, 1975; Early Work by 5 Contemporary Artists, 1977; Bad Painting, 1978; Barry Le Va, 1979; John Baldessari, 1981; Not Just For Laughs: The Art of Subversion, 1981; Earl Staley. 1973-83, 1984; Paradise Lost/Paradise Regained, 1984; Art After Modernism: Rethinking Representation, 1984; Choices: Making An Art Out of Everyday Life, 1986; Blasted Allegories: An Anthology of Writings by Contemporary Artists, 1987; Markus Raetz: In the Realm of the Possible, 1988; catalog for Am. exhbn. at Venice Biennale; also articles. Office: New Mus of Contemporary Art 583 Broadway New York NY 10012

TUCKER, MELODY SUE, health care administrator; b. Louisville, Nov. 9, 1947; B.S., Ind. U., 1970; M.P.A., Ariz. State U., 1985. Trainer, U.S. Office Edn. Alcohol and Drug Abuse Prevention Program, Chgo., 1974-77; coordinator prevention activities for alcohol, drug abuse, and mental health prevention activities Ariz. Dept. Health Services, Phoenix, 1978-83, contracts coordinator, 1983-84, trainer, 1984-85; planning analyst Community Hosps. of Central Calif., 1985-87; adminstrv. dir. Women's Health Ctr., Tulare (Calif.) Dist. Hosp., 1987—; owner Phoenix Designs, 1988—; cons. various human service orgns., 1976—. Mem. staff Ariz. Gov.'s Task Force on Alcohol and Hwy. Safety, 1982; bd. overseers Calif. Sch. Profl. Psychology. Home: 1729 E Cross Tulare CA 93274 Office: Tulare Dist Hosp 869 Cherry St Tulare CA 93274

TUCKER, MIRIAM HELEN, military supply specialist; b. Toledo, July 4, 1950; d. Ambrose Jacob and Helen Ann (Sturtz) Depinet; m. James Ronald Tucker, July 29, 1978; children: Christopher, Matthew, Richard. BA, Mary Manse Coll., Toledo, 1972. Elem. sch. tchr. St. Rose Sch., Perrysburg, Ohio, 1972-78; agent Prudential Ins. Co., Toledo, 1978-79; sales clk. Foxphoto Co., Toledo, 1978-81; receptionist WGTE-FM, Toledo, 1979-80; store mgr. Stuarts (div. Petries Corp.), Texarkana, Tex., 1984-85; supply mgmt. intern U.S. Army Material Command, Texarkana, 1985-86; gen. supply specialist U.S. Army Tank and Automotive Command, Warren, Mich., 1986—. Mem. Am. Legion. Democrat. Methodist. Lodge: Order Ea. Star. Home: 2484 Coy Ferndale MI 48220

TUCKER, ROSARIO CAPARO, financial planner, consultant; b. Arequipa, Peru, July 5, 1950; came to U.S., 1977; d. Jose David and Maria D. (Rivera) Caparo; m. Pedro O. Bachoir, June 21, 1966 (div. 1972); children: Pedro Oscar, Jose Alejandro. Student, Cath. U., Arequipa, 1969, Harvard U., 1977, Boston U., 1977. Tchr. bus. skills Internat. Library, Arequipa, 1973-74; exec. sec. bilingual Aceros Arequipa, 1974-78; field underwriter N.Y. Life Ins. Co., Los Angeles, 1980—; cons. bilingual program Madison Park High Sch., Boston, 1977, Spl. Services, Paramount, Calif., 1980—; presenter seminars, Paramount, 1985-87. Author poetry; (play) When the Bells Ring Twelve, 1977 (3d Place Nat. award 1977). Mem. Iberoam. Writers U.S. (honor recital poem 1986), Assn. Peruvian Secs., Nat. Assn. Female Execs., Los Angeles Life Underwriters (Nat. quality award 1985), Peruvian C. of C. (v.p. 1984, dir. 1987-88). Republican. Roman Catholic. Club: Interam. (Los Angeles). Office: NY Life Ins Co 5757 Wilshire Blvd Suite 900 Los Angeles CA 90036

TUCKER, SHERRY ELIZABETH, lawyer; b. Guilford County, N.C., July 25, 1947; d. Raymond Jacob and Irma (Davis) T. BA in Sociology, U. N.C., Asheville, 1973; MA in Sociology, Appalachian State U., 1974; JD, N.C. Central U., 1977. Bar N.C., 1978; individual practice law, Chapel Hill, N.C. 1978—; co-owner, founder Elegance Jewelry, Chapel Hill, N.C., Life Systems, Inc., Chapel Hill. Mem. Am. Bar Assn., N.C. State Bar, N.C. Bar Assn. Office: 800-D Franklin Square Chapel Hill NC 27514

TUCKER, SUSAN C., state legislator; b. Winfield, Kans., Nov. 7, 1944; d. Allen and Jeanne (Lawrence) Shaffer; m. Mike A. Tucker, Dec. 2, 1967; children: Mark, David. Student, U. Nigeria, 1965; BA, Mich. State U., 1966. English tchr. Lexington (Mass.) High Sch., 1966-69; legis. aide Mass. Legislature, Boston, 1980-82; mem. Ho. of Reps. Mass. Great and Gen. Ct., Boston, 1983—, vice chair edn. com., chair spl. commn. on child abuse, mem energy com., ethics com.; chair Mass. Caucus Women Legislators. V.p. Mass. LWV, Boston, 1977-80. Recipient Environ. Schievement award Environ. Lobby Mass., 1984. Mem. Nat. Women's Polit. Caucus. Democrat. Office: Mass State House R 473-C Boston MA 02133

TUCKER, TERESA MCLEOD, educator; b. Portsmouth, Va., Nov. 7, 1954; d. Lou Carroll and Frances (Long) McLeod; m. William Jeffrey Tucker, June 16, 1974; children: Amberly Daye, Ashlee Nicole. Grad. high sch. Instr. adult basic edn. Mitchell Coll., Statesville, N.C., 1984-85; instr. compensatory edn. Mitchell Coll., Statesville, 1985—. Vol. Village Place Spl. Olympics, Statesville, 1988; service unit dir. Catawba Valley Area council Girl Scouts Am., 1987-88; leader Brownies Am., 1986-88 (named Leader Yr. 1988). Mem. Iredell County Childrens Mus. Home: Rt 16 Box 303 Statesville NC 28677-9663

TUCKER, WANDA HALL, writer; b. Los Angeles, Feb. 6, 1921; d. Frank Walliston and Hazel Gladys (Smith) Hall; AA, Citrus Coll., 1939; m. Frank R. Tucker, Apr. 16, 1943; children—Frank Robert, Nancy Irene. Society editor Azusa (Calif.) Herald, 1939-42, editor, 1942-43; city editor San Marino (Calif.) Tribune, 1943-45; editor Canyon City (Calif.) News, 1953; reporter Pasadena (Calif.) Star-News, 1953-73, city editor, 1973-75, day mng. editor, 1975, mng. editor, 1975-81, sr. mng. editor, 1981-84, dir. internship program, 1976-79, mem. editorial bd., 1982-84; editor, assoc. pub. Foothill Inter-City Newspapers, 1984-86; communications cons., Palm Desert, Calif., 1986—. Mem. rent rev. commn. City of Palm Desert, Calif.; bd. dirs. Silver Spur Ranch Assn. Recipient writing award Calif. Newspaper Pubs. Assn., 1965; named Woman of Year, Pasadena Women's Civic League, 1974, Pasadena chpt. NAACP, 1977, Emer Bates Meml. award, 1981. Mem. Nat. Soc. Newspaper Columnists, Sigma Delta Chi. Clubs: Desert Press; Greater Los Angeles Press (writing awards 1971-72).

TUFENKJIAN, CAROL LYNN, academic program administrator; b. Syracuse, N.Y., July 6, 1957; d. James Ashod and Laura (Keledjian) T. BS in Health Edn. and Health Scis. summa cum laude, SUNY, Cortland, 1979, MS in Health Edn. summa cum laude, 1983, postgrad. in adminstrn., 1984—. Health educator LaFayette (N.Y.) Sch. Dist., 1979-84; regional field coordinator Med. Coll. Cornell U., N.Y.C., 1984—. Instr. Syracuse ARC. Named one of Outstanding Young Women of Am., Gen. Fedn. Women's Clubs, 1983-84. Mem. N.Y. State Fedn. Profl. Health Educators, Am. Student Assn. (sec. 1983-87). Club: Updowntowners (Syracuse). Home: 104 Aspen St Liverpool NY 13088 Office: Dept Pub Health 411 E 69th St New York NY 10021

TUFT, MARY ANN, association executive; b. Easton, Pa., Oct. 11, 1934; d. Ben and Elizabeth (Reibman) T. B.S., West Chester (Pa.) State Coll., 1956; M.A., Lehigh U., 1960. Cert. assn. exec. Nat. trainer Girl Scouts U.S.A., N.Y.C., 1965-68; cons. Nat. League for Nursing, N.Y.C., 1968-69; exec. dir. Nat. Student Nurses Assn., N.Y.C., 1970-85; mem. Commn. on Dietetic Registration, Am. Dietetic Assn., 1981-85; pres. Specialized Cons. Ltd., 1983-85; exec. dir. Radiol. Soc. N.Am., Oak Brook, Ill., 1985-88; v.p. Chgo. Sinai Cong., 1988—. Bd. dirs. Nurses House, Inc., 1981-85; bd. dirs. Chgo. Sinai Cong., 1987—. Kepner-Tregoe scholar, 1966. Mem. Am. Soc. Assn. Execs. (dir. 1980-83, bd. trustees for cert. 1980-83, vice chmn. 1983-84), N.Y. Soc. Assn. Execs. (pres. 1978-79, dir. 1975-78, First Outstanding Exec. award 1982), Continuing Care Accreditation Assn. (bd. dirs. 1983-85), Specialized Cons. in Nursing (faculty). Office: Radiol Soc N Am 1415 W 22d St Oak Brook IL 60521

TUKE, OTHELIA STANLEY BEATRICE, service executive; b. Prague, Czechoslovakia, Nov. 14, 1923; came to Can., 1952; d. Rudolph and Othelia Frances (Pecha) T.; m. A. Pelican, Feb. 19, 1953 (dec.); 1 child, Othelia Renata Tuke-Pelican. PhD, Charles' U., Prague, 1951. With counter-espionage service U.S. Army, 1951-52; tchr. langs. Can., S.Am. and France, 1956-59; counselor Brampton (Ont.) Family Service, 1959-61; founder, pres. Single Profl. & Bus. People, Toronto, Ont., Can., 1962—; Expert guest on TV and radio talk shows. Author: Methods of Ideological Subversion, 1954; (under pseudonym Dr. Fren): Learned Incompatibilities Between Men and Women, 1964. Mem. Can. Assn. Selective Introduction Services (pres. 1984), Ont. Assn. Selective Introduction Services (pres. 1984). Home: 30 Kew Beach Ave, Toronto, ON Canada M4L 7B7 Office: 2498 Yonge St, Toronto, ON Canada M4P 2H8

TULECKE, ROSE OSBORNE, writer, editor; b. Newton, Kans., Dec. 3, 1942; d. Donald A. and Helen M. (Hartman) Osborne; B.S., U. Kans., 1964; m. Jerome B. Tulecke, June 7, 1965; children—Mark, Linda. Free-lance writer Fort Worth Mag., 1973-77, asso. editor, 1980-81, editor, 1981-84; free-lance writer, 1984—; instr. media communications Tex. Christian U., Ft. Worth, 1984-85; publs. coordinator, editor United Way Met. Tarrant County, 1985—; assoc. editor Tarrant County Med. Soc. Physician, Ft. Worth, 1977-79; editor Focus, Harris Hosp. mag., Ft. Worth, 1979-80. Leader, Girl Scouts U.S.A., 1978-81. Recipient Anson Jones award for excellence in coverage of health industry Tex. Med. Assn., 1984. Mem. Pub. Relations Soc. of Am., Women in Communications, Tarrant County Med. Soc. Aux. Home: 7609 Skylake Dr Fort Worth TX 76179 Office: United Way Met Tarrant County 210 E 9th St Fort Worth TX 76102

TULL, THERESA ANNE, foreign service officer; b. Runnemede, N.J., Oct. 2, 1936; d. John James and Anna Cecelia (Paull) T. B.A., U. Md., 1972; M.A., U. Mich., 1973; postgrad. Nat. War Coll., Washington, 1980. Fgn. service officer Dept. State, Washington, 1963—, dep. prin. officer, Brussels, Saigon, Danang, 1973-75; prin. officer Cebu, Philippines, 1977-79; dir. office human rights, 1980-83; charge d'affaires, Am. Embassy, Vientiane, Laos, from 1983; ambassador to Guyana, 1987—. Recipient Civilian Service award Dept. of State, 1970, Meritorious Honor award, 1977. Mem. Am. Fgn. Service Assn. Club: Cathedral Choral Soc. (Washington). Home: care Waldis 416 N Washington Ave Moorestown NJ 08057 Office: Am Embassy Box V APO San Francisco CA 96346 *

TULLER, WENDY JUDGE, foundation administrator; b. Cranston, R.I., Dec. 17, 1943; d. Alfred Carmen and Anna Louise (Waterman) Judge. A.B., Brown U., 1965; M.L.S., U. R.I., 1969. Librarian, Providence Public Schs., 1965-69; mgr. various locations Xerox Corp., 1969-75; mgr. Carter Hawley Hale Stores, Inc., Los Angeles, 1976; cons. Sibson & Co., Inc., Princeton, N.J., 1976-78; coordinator Atlantic Richfield Co., Los Angeles, 1978-87; pres. Found. for Ednl. Excellence, 1987—. Mem. Am. Soc. Personnel Adminstrn., Am. Soc. Tng. and Devel., Internat. Assn. Personnel Women, AAUW (v.p. local chpt. 1979-80). Club: Los Angeles Athletic. Home: 222 S Figueroa St Los Angeles CA 90012

TUMELSON, BETSY MARTIN, consulting and training company executive; b. Paris, Tenn., July 29, 1943; d. Frank and Bassie Destine (Moore) Martin; m. Ronald Adrian Tumelson, Dec. 14, 1963; children: Arlene Dawn Dettler, Gretchen Loraine, Ronald Adrian, Karen Destine. BS in Human Relations Organ. Behavior, U. San Francisco, 1982; MS in Human Resource Mgmt. Devel., Chapman Coll., 1984. Cert. orgn. cons. Cons. to city mgr. Heidelberg Am. Community, Fed. Republic Germany, 1979-80; cons., trainer U.S. Army Organizational Effectiveness Ctr. and Sch., Ford Ord, Calif., 1980-84; instr. Hartnell Coll., Salinas, Calif., 1985-87; expert community leader Dept of Def., Washington, 1983—, pres. Betsy Tumelson Cons., Monterey, Calif., 1980-84, Systems Excellence, Monterey, 1984—; dir. tng. Mgmt. Inst. Monterey, 1986—, dir. coordinator Salinas C. of C., 1987; bd. dirs. Leaderspirit; prin. cons. Smith/Trahern Mansion, Clarksville, Tenn., 1986—. Author: Moving In and Moving Up, 1982, Managerial Competencies, 1982, Volunteer Motivational Index, 1981. Organizer, facilitator Legis. Forum; Pacific Bell Host, Salinas, 1987, Mayoral Forum: Leadership Salinas, Monterey, 1987; founder chmn. Ad Hoc Group Women's Issues, Heidelberg, Fed. Republic Germany, 1979-80. Named one of Outstanding Young Women of Am., Heidelberg Am. Community, 1976; recipient Outstanding Community Service award Heidelberg Am. Community, 1980, High Achievement recognition Womens' History Week Com., Fort Ord, Calif., 1985, Outstanding achievement award Federal Womens' Program, Fort Ord, 1987. Mem. Nat. Assn. Female Execs., Profl. Women's Network (membership com.). Democrat. Methodist. Club: German/American (chmn. protocol, hospitality) (Heidelberg), American Woman's (Heidelberg). Home: 54 Castro Rd Suite A 3784 Monterey CA 93940 Office: Systems Excellence SYSTEX 177 Webster St Suite 1784 Monterey CA 93940

TUNG, ROSALIE SUET-YING, educator; b. Shanghai, China, Dec. 2, 1948; came to U.S., 1975; d. Andrew Yan-Fu and Pauline Wai-Kam (Cheung) Lam; B.A. (Univ. scholar), York U., 1972; M.B.A., U. B.C., 1974, Ph.D. in Bus. Adminstrn. (Univ. fellow, Seagram Bus. fellow, H.R. MacMillan Family fellow), 1977; m. Byron Poon-Yan Tung, June 17, 1972; 1 dau., Michele Christine. Lectr., diploma div. U. B.C., 1975, lectr. exec. devel. program, 1975; prof. mgmt. Grad. Sch. Mgmt., U. Oreg., Eugene, 1977-80; vis. scholar U. Manchester (Eng.) Inst. Sci. and Tech., fall 1980; vis. prof. UCLA, spring 1981, Harvard U., 1988; prof. mgmt. Wharton Sch. Fin., U. Pa., Phila., 1981-86; disting. prof. bus. adminstrn., dir. internat. bus. ctr. U. Wis., Milw., 1986—. Mem. Acad. Internat. Bus. (treas.), Acad. Mgmt. (bd. govs.),Internat. Assn. Applied Psychology, Am. Arbitration Assn. (comml. panel arbitrators). Roman Catholic. Author 7 books; contbr. articles to profl. jours. Office: U Wis-Milw Sch Business PO Box 742 Milwaukee WI 53201

TUNKIEICZ, MARY URSULA, farm company executive, clown; b. Chgo., Sept. 28, 1937; d. Gunnar and Jennie Adella (Howe) Gram; student public schs., Mich. and Ill.; m. Charles Tunkieicz, Feb. 23, 1957; children—Charlene, John, Jennie, Robert. Vice pres. Charles Tunkieicz Farms, Inc., Kenosha, Wis., 1972—, sec., 1972-80, sec.-treas., 1980—, v.p., sec., 1982-86, chmn. bd., 1985-86; clown Kenosha Unified Sch. Dist., 1979—; dir. I Am Sorry God, Somers Clowns Circus film, Alpha Film Corp.; clown ambassador Cousin Otto's Alley #22, Franzen Bros. Traveling Circus, Delavan, Wis. Leader for cooking Somers 4-H Club, 1974-75, clown project leader, 1976-80; chairperson Kenosha Farm Bur., 1975-78, pres. women's group, 1982-84; pres. Homemakers Club, 1986. Mem. Somers Clowns Clubs (dir.), Soc. Am. Magicians, Wis. Magical Entertainers Club. Democrat. Roman Catholic. Lodges: Moose, Eagles. Contbr. poetry to various pubs. Home: 8410 W 60th St Kenosha WI 53142 Office: 8418 38th St Kenosha WI 53142

TUNNELL, ELIZABETH ANN, government agency administrator; b. Stamford, Tex., Sept. 8, 1937; d. John James and Nona Elizabeth (Jones) Holden; m. Robert Bruce Hays, July 23, 1955 (div. Aug. 1969); children: Susan, Lisa; m. Jim W. Tunnell, May 27, 1972; children: Kathy, Jamie, Larry, Melanie. Cert. in employee relations law. Exec. sec. Brazosport Ind. Sch. Dist., Freeport, Tex., 1958-71; exec. asst. OEO, Dallas, 1971-73; exec. asst. U.S. Dept. Energy, Dallas, 1973-75, program analyst, 1975-79, mgr. state energy conservation programs, 1979-81; mgr. employee relations U.S. Telephone, Inc., Dallas, 1981-85; pres. Employee Relations Cons., Garland, Tex., 1985-87; adminstrv. officer U.S. Immigration and Naturalization Service, Dallas, 1987—. Editor trade mag. TESA Talks, 1971; contbr. articles to profl. mags. Pres., bd. dirs. Homeowners Assn., Garland, 1974, 84-87; tchr. Meth. Ch., Freeport, 1960-71. Mem. Am. Mgmt. Assn., Am. Soc. Tng. and Devel., Fed. Exec. Women (co-organizer local chpt. 1972-73), Am. Soc. Personnel Adminstrn., Council on Union-Free Environment, Tex. Ednl. Secs. Assn. (1st v.p. 1969-71). Office: Immigration/Naturalization Service 1825 Market Ctr Suite 500 Dallas TX 75207

TUNNEY, ARLENE ROCHELLE, architect; b. N.Y.C., Apr. 6, 1946; d. Samuel and Lillian (Koenigsberg) Kohnop; m. Hugh L. Tunney Jr., Mar. 15, 1968 (dec. Mar. 1977). BFA, Pratt Inst., 1966. Registered architect, N.Y., Conn. Prin. Tunney Assocs., Killingworth, Conn., 1973—. Contbr. archtl. plans to mags. Pres. Creative Arts Council, Killingworth, 1984-85, mem. Recipient awards Western Wood Products, 1984; design named Best Radio/Tv Sta. Design Broadcast Engrs., 1976. Mem. AIA, Conn. Soc. Architects (chmn. edn. com. 1984-86), Killingworth C. of C. Club: Duck Island Yacht (Westbrook, Conn.). Office: 306 Pine Orchard Rd Killingworth CT 06417

TUÑON, BETTY JACKSON JONES, nursing administrator; b. Fayetteville, Pa., Feb. 1, 1933; d. Alexander and Lucetta (Fields) Jackson; m. Carlos Tunon. BS, Coppin State Coll., 1970, MEd, 1971; AA, Community Coll. Balt., 1975; BS in Nursing, Coll. Notre Dame, Balt., 1985. Asst. chief nurse Md. Pen. Hosp., Balt., 1981-84; relief sr. nurse Walter P. Carter Ctr., Balt., 1985-87; dir., chief exec. officer E.D.C. Inc., Balt., 1984—; nurse cons. Guardian Health, Balt., 1984—. Mem. Lennard Neighborhood Assn., 1985; block capt. Edgewood Neighborhood Assn., 1985—; organizer Swann Uplands Community Assn., 1986. Mem. Am. Assn. Retired Persons. Home: 601 Lennard St Baltimore MD 21229

TURBEVILLE, DONNIE BAILEY, property developer; b. Gastonia, N.C., June 30, 1947; d. Morrison Landy Bailey and Donie (Shults) Denton; m. Ernest M. Kiser, Dec. 31, 1966 (div. Dec. 1976); children: Kelly Dawn, E. Michael II; m. William S. Turbeville Jr., May 23, 1981. AS in Comml. Edn., U. S.C., 1977, BS in Office Adminstrn., 1985, postgrad., 1987—. Asst. office/warehouse mgr. New Holland div. Sperry Rand, Charlotte, N.C., 1968-72; office mgr. Bruce Flemming & Assocs., Inc., Columbia, S.C., 1972-78; personnel asst. Richtex Corp., Columbia, 1977-79; bookkeeper Ener-Tech, Inc., Columbia, 1979-81; exec. tech. asst. to v.p. Wilbur Smith &

Assocs., Inc., Columbia, 1979-84; mktg. coordinator Stevens & Wilkinson, Inc., Columbia, 1984-85; dir. property devel. Columbia Met. Airport, 1986—; chmn. mktg. com. mem. Nat. Assn. Fgn. Trade Zones, Washington, 1986—, recruitment com. Midlands Internat. Trade Club; mem. Bus. Edn. Adv. Council, Irmo, S.C., 1985—. Author: Mixed Emotions (poetry), 1981, book of cross-stitch graphs, 1982, eight theatrical plays, 1977-86. Active vol. Richland-Lexington Council on Aging, Columbia, 1983—, Citizens Advocating Decency and Revival of Ethics, Columbia, 1987—; adv. council mem. Univ. S.C., 1984—; various duties Dutch Fork Christian Ch., Irmo, 1976—; mem. Irmo High Sch. Athletic Booster Club. Recipient Columbia's Woman of Yr. award Midlands Tech. Coll., 1986. Fellow Cert. Profl. Sec. Acad.; mem. Midlands Internat. Trade Club, Nat. Assn. Women in Constrn. (chmn. edn. com. Columbia chpt.), Lexington Bus. Industry Council (sec.), Cen. Midlands Export Promotion Steering Com., Lexington C. of C., Univ. S.C. Alumni Assn., Golden Key Nat, Honors Soc. Home: 3605 Harrogate Rd Columbia SC 29210-4827 Office: Columbia Met Airport 3000 Aviation Way West Columbia SC 29169-2190

TURCHUK, JULIA GRACE, multi-media director, artist; b. Yonkers, N.Y., Apr. 24, 1945; d. Elsie Riley; 1 dau., Felicia Eve. Student Sch. Visual Arts, 1964, 74, 81, 83, Am. Art Sch.,. 1962. Artist, Burt Wenk Studio, N.Y.C., 1966, Metro Seliger, N.Y.C., 1967; Freelance artist, art dir. 1492 Prodns., N.Y.C., 1967-70; art dir. Laser, Aniforms Prodns., N.Y.C., 1970-71, Aniforms, Melandrea, Prodns., N.Y.C., 1972-73; owner, dir. Coopdesign Studio, N.Y.C., 1974—; dir. co-producer various ednl./sci. confs., internat. showings, 1976—. Group show: Para Art, 1977; contbg. artist to mags.; photographer video works. Recipient Bronze medal Internat. Film and TV Festival, 1978, Info. Film Producers of Am., 1978; Silver medal Info. Film Producers Am., 1980; Presdl. Sports award Roller Skate, 1982. Mem. Nat. Assn. Female Execs. Club: Laces Roller Skate (instr. N.Y.C. 1986—). Home: 313 E 10th St New York NY 10009

TURCK, KATHRYN MARY, casualty insurance specialist; b. N.Y.C., June 28, 1950; d. John James and Gladys Lucy (Campkin) Delaney; m. Thomas Herbert Turck, July 11, 1970 (div. Mar. 1983). BBA, Baruch Coll., 1978; MBA, NYU, 1985. Asst. underwriter INA Ins. Co., N.Y.C., 1970-71; underwriting agt. Huntington T. Block Ins., Washington, 1971-73; account exec. Herbert L. Jamison & Co., N.Y.C., 1973-80; mgr. casualty ins. ITT Corp., N.Y.C., 1980—. Sec. Food and Justice Program-Riverside, N.Y.C., 1987-88. Mem. CPCU Soc. (v.p. N.Y. chpt. 1985-86, pres. 1987-88), Risk and Ins. Mgmt. Soc., Assn. Profl. Ins. Women, Nat. Assn. Female Execs., Beta Gamma Sigma. Home: 345 E 80th St New York NY 10021 Office: ITT Corp 320 Park Ave New York NY 10021

TURCOTTE, MARGARET JANE, nurse; b. Stow, Ohio, May 17, 1927; d. Edward Carlton and Florence Margaret (Hanson) McCauley; R.N., St. Thomas Hosp., Akron, Ohio, 1949; m. Rene George Joseph, Nov. 24, 1961 (div. June 1967); 1 son, Michael Lawrence. Mem. nursing staff St. Thomas Hosp., 1949-50; pvt. duty nurse, 1950-57; polio nurse Akron's Children Hosp., 1953-54; mem. nursing staff Robinson Meml. Hosp., Ravenna, Ohio, 1958-67, head central service, 1963-67; supr. central service Brentwood Hosp., Warrensville Heights, Ohio, 1967, emergency med. technician. Mem. St. Thomas Hosp. Alumni Assn. Democrat. Roman Catholic. Home: 6037 Highview St Lot 14-F Ravenna OH 44266 Office: 4110 Warrensville Center Rd Warrensville Heights OH 44122

TURECK, ROSALYN, concert artist, author, editor, educator; b. Chgo., Dec. 14, 1914; d. Samuel Tureck and Mary (Lipson) Tureck-Wise; (w. 1964). Studies with Sophia Brilliant-Liven, 1925-29, with Jan Chiapusso, 1929-31, with Gavin Williamson, 1931-32; BA cum laude, The Juilliard Sch. Music, 1935; studies with Olga Samaroff; MusD (hon.), Colby Coll., 1964, Roosevelt U., 1968, Wilson Coll., 1968, Oxford U., Eng., 1977, Music and Arts Inst., San Francisco, 1987. Mem. faculty Phila. Conservatory Music, 1935-42, Mannes Sch., N.Y.C., 1940-44, Juilliard Sch. Music, N.Y.C., 1943-55, Columbia U., N.Y.C., 1953-55; prof. music, lectr. U. Calif., San Diego, 1966-72; vis. prof. Washington U., St. Louis, 1963-64, U. Md., 1981-85; vis. fellow St. Hilda's Coll., Oxford (Eng.) U., 1974, hon. life fellow, 1974—; vis. fellow Wolfson Coll., Oxford, 1975—; lectr. numerous ednl. instns., U.S. and Eng., Spain, Denmark, Holland, Can., Israel, Brazil, Argentina; hon. mem. adv. council Ams. for Music Library, Hebrew U., Israel.; bd. dirs., founder Internat. Bach Soc., 1966—, Inst. for Bach Studies, 1968—; founder Tureck Bach Players, 1955, London, 1981, New York, Tureck Bach Inst., Inc., 1981, Symposia 1983, 84, 86—. Debut 2 solo recitals, Chgo., 1924; soloist Chgo. Symphony Orch., 1926, 2 all-Bach recitals, Chgo., 1930; N.Y.C. debut Carnegie Hall with Phila. Orch., 1936; series 6 all-Bach recitals, Town Hall, N.Y.C., 1937, ann. U.S.-Can. tours, 1937—, ann. series 3 all-Bach recitals, N.Y.C., 1944-54, 59—; European debut Copenhagen, 1947; organizer, dir. soc. for performance internat. contemporary music: Composers of Today, Inc, 1951-55; extensive European tours, 1947—; condr., soloist, London Philharmonia, 1958, founder, dir., Tureck Bach Players, London, 1957, N.Y.C., 1981, Bach festivals cities, Eng., Ireland, 1959—; TV series Well-Tempered Clavier, Book I, Granada TV, Eng., 1961; BBC series Well-Tempered Clavier, Books 1 and 2, 1976; numerous TV appearances, U.S., 1961—, including Wm. F. Buckley's Firing Line, 1970, 85, 87, Today Show, Bach recitals on piano, harpsichord, clavichord, antique and electronic instruments, 1963—; world tours in Far East, India, Australia, Europe, 1971, S.Am., Europe, Israel, Turkey, Spain, 1986; N.Y.C. series, Met. Mus. Art and Carnegie Hall, 1969—; appeared with leading orchs. U.S., Can., Europe, South Africa, S.Am., Israel; recs. for HMV, Odeon, Decca, Columbia Masterworks., condr., soloist, Israel Philharmon., Tel Aviv, Haifa and Kol Israel orchs., 1963, Israel Festival, Internat. Bach Soc. Orchs., 1967, 69, 70, Washington Nat. Symphony, 1970, Madrid Chamber Orch., 1970, Tureck Bach Players, London, 1957—, N.Y. 1981, 84, 85; author: An Introduction to the Performance of Bach, 3 vols, 1960; contbr. articles to various mags.; editor: Bach-Sarabande, C minor, 1960, Tureck Bach Urtext Series: Italian Concerto, Schirmer Music, Inc., 1983, Lute Suite, E minor, 1984, C minor, 1985, Paginini-Tureck—Moto Perpetuo, A. Scarlatti—Air and Gavotte; films: Fantasy and Fugue: Rosalyn Tureck Plays Bach, 1972, Rosalyn Tureck plays on Harpsichord and Organ, 1977, Joy of Bach, 1978, Camera 3: Bach on the Frontier of the Future, CBS film, Ephesus, Turkey, 1985; numerous recs. Decorated Officers Cross of the Order of Merit Fed. Republic Germany, 1979; recipient 1st prize Greater Chgo. Piano Playing Tournament, 1928; Winner Schubert Meml. Contest, 1935, Nat. Fedn. Music Clubs Competition, 1935; Phi Beta award , 1946, 1st Town Hall endowment award, 1937; NEH grantee; named Musician of Yr., Music Tchrs. Nat. Assn., 1987. Hon. fellow Guildhall Sch. Music and Drama; mem. Royal Mus. Assn. London, Am. Musicological Soc., Inc. Soc. Musicians (London), Royal Philharmonic Soc. London, Sebastian Bach de Belgique (hon.), New Bach Soc., Oxford Soc. Clubs: Cosmopolitan (N.Y.C.), Bohemians (N.Y.C.) (hon.). Office: c/o Columbia Artists Mgmt 165 W 57th St New York NY 10019

TURK, DONNA CAROL, retail company executive, athletics official; b. Corona, Calif., May 30, 1953; d. Frank Joseph and Patsy Jean (Wood) T. Student in computer programming, Ivy Tech., 1987. Cert. emergency med. technician, Ind. Asst. tng. supr. Hdqrs. Ayr-Way Stores, 1972-74, area mgr. hardlines West region, 1974-75, area mgr. softlines West region, 1975-77, tng. supr. Hdqrs., 1977, exec. devel. program supr. Hdqrs., 1977-78, systems trainer Hdqrs., 1978-80, asst. teleprocessing coordinator Hdqrs., 1980-81, teleprocessing technician Hdqrs., 1981-82; data ctr. supr. Indpls. distbn. ctr. Target Stores, Indpls., 1982—. Silent ptnr., owner Olympic West Judo and Karate Sch.; chairperson Mgrs. Com. for U.S. Judo Inc. 1984-85; mgr. Women's USA Judo team for Can., 1983, Women's USA Dutch Open Team, 1983, Women's USA Can. Cup, 1984, USA Women's team to German Open, 1985, USA Men's and Women's team to Austrian Open, 1986, USA Women's team to Pan Am. Games, 1987; chairperson Pan Am. Games Organizing Com. for Sport Judo, 1987; coach Women's Judo team at Nat. Sports Festival, 1983. Named State judo champion 48 kilos, 1976, 79-83, Sr. Female Competitor Yr. Ind., 1979, 81-82, Nat. Sombo Champion 46 kilos, 1983, Nat. Sombo Champion 46 kilos, AAU, 1984, Nat. Judo champion masters div. 48 kilos, 1984; recipient Bronze medal Sr. Judo Nats., 1981, silver medalist Pan Am. Games, U.S. Open Women's Judo, 1981, Pan Am. judo trials, 1983, Gold medal Pan Am. Sombo trials, 1983; selected for Brit. Open Women's judo team, 1981; named to Nat. Judo team, 1981-83. Mem. Nat. Assn. Female Execs. Office: Target Stores 7551 W Morris St Indianapolis IN 46231

TURK, REGINA LOUISE BRUMFIELD, communications and marketing company consultant; b. New Orleans, July 13, 1955; d. Horace James and Audrey Ernestine (Glass) Brumfield; m. Ralph Norman Menetre III, Aug. 27, 1977 (div. Aug. 1980); m. Jerry Douglas Turk, Apr. 15, 1981.; 1 child, Beau Menetre; stepchildren: Laura Eunice Odom, Jerry Ryan, Kelly Langston. Student, La. State U., 1973-75; cert. Bank Mktg., U. Colo., 1985. Cert. Sr. Trng. Cons. Process Communication Mgmt. Asst. br. mgr. First Bank, Covington, La., 1975-77; bookkeeper St. Tammany Sch. Systems, Covington, La., 1977-79; with Livingston Bank, Denham Springs, La., 1979-80; bus. devel. officer La. Nat. Bank, Baton Rouge, 1980-81; exec. v.p. Jerry Turk & Assocs., Inc., Baton Rouge, 1981-87; pres. Kahler/Turk Communications, Inc., Baton Rouge, 1987—. Coach YMCA Basketball team, 1985-87. Recipient award for Outstanding Achievement Behavioral Cons. Carlson Learning Co., 1986. Mem. Nat. Assn. Women in Radio Broadcasting (hon.), Nat. Assn. Collegiate Secs. Home: 19312 Deer Park Baton Rouge LA 70817 Office: Kahler/Turk Communications Inc 7924 Wrenwood Suite A Baton Rouge LA 70817

TURKEL, ANN RUTH, psychiatrist, psychoanalyst; b. N.Y.C., Nov. 28, 1928; d. Henry Lewis and Betty (Rosensweig) T.; m. Leon Lefer, July 4, 1954; 1 child, Heidi Sara. AB, Barnard Coll., 1947; MD, Albany Med. Coll., 1952; cert. psychoanalyst, William Alanson White Inst. Diplomate Am. Bd. Psychiatry and Neurology, 1958. Attending psychiatrist St. Vincent's Hosp., N.Y.C., 1962—; supervising analyst, supr. psychotherapy William Alanson White Inst. Psychoanalysis, Psychiatry & Psychology, N.Y.C., 1977—; pvt. practice psychiatry N.Y.C., 1957—; asst. clin. prof. psychiatry Coll. Physicians and Surgeons Columbia U., N.Y.C., 1981—; expert on women's issues for media. Asst. editor News for Women in Psychiatry, 1982—; contbr. articles to profl. jours. Fellow Am. Acad. Psychoanalysis (editor Acad. Forum 1976—, trustee 1982-85), Am. Psychiat. Assn. (assoc. editor The Bull. 1964—, chair N.Y. com. on women 1978-85); mem. Internat. Fedn. Psychoanalytic Socs. (sec.-gen. 1983—), World Fedn. for Mental Health, Assn. Women Psychiatrists. Home and Office: 350 Central Park W New York NY 10025

TURLEY-GRINE, ELIZABETH JANE, residential services specialist; b. Beresford, S.D., Apr. 5, 1933; d. Albert and Myrtle (Boster) Nelsen; m. Michael O. Turley, Sept. 20, 1967 (div. 1975); m. Alfonso G. Grine, Mar. 21, 1980; 1 child, Deborah. BA, St. San Antonio, 1965; postgrad., Chaffey Coll., 1965-67. Cert. residential specialist; cert. psychiat. technician. Supr. Pacific State Hosp., Pomona, Calif., 1953-65; owner, operator Turley-Grine, Pomona and La Mirada, Calif., 1965—; adv. cons. Merci, Alhambra, Calif., 1986, Inland Counties, San Bernardino, Calif., 1970-75. Served as pvt. U.S. Army, 1950-52. Named Outstanding Provider, Inland Counties Regional Ctr., San Bernardino, 1974, Outstanding Provider, Eastern Los Angeles Regional Ctr., Alahambra, 1985, State Council Devel. Disabilities, 1986. Republican. Home and Office: 14324 San Ardo Dr La Mirada CA 90638

TURNBULL, DOREEN JOYCE, EDP consultant; b. Evanston, Ill., Jan. 10, 1938; d. Dale M. and Juliet L. (Van Buskirk) T. B.S. in Bus. Mgmt., Calif. State Poly., Pomona, 1969; M.A. in Mgmt., Claremont Grad. Sch., 1984. Sr. systems analyst Sunkist Growers Inc., Sherman Oaks, Calif., 1968-74; EDP systems analyst Ralphs Grocery Co., Compton, Calif., 1974-77; propr. DJT Cons., 1977-80; project mgr., sr. systems analyst, Xerox Corp., Pasadena, Calif., 1980-84; project mgr. DHL Corp., San Bruno, Calif., 1984-86; propr. DJT Cons., 1986; MIS acct. rep., Westinghouse Marine div., Sunnyvale Calif., 1986—. Mem. Data Processing Mgmt. Assn. (chpt. dir., sec.), Am. Mgmt. Assn., Nat. Assn. Female Execs., Women in Mgmt., IS/DP Alumni Assn. (dir.). Club: Altrusa (past treas., past sec.) (Arcadia, Calif.). Home and Office: 760 Edgemar Ave Pacifica CA 94044

TURNER, ANDREA J, corporate services administrator, educator; b. Warren, Ohio, May 24, 1942; d. Nicholas V. and Dulinda L. (Vigorito) Liberator; m. James D. Brown, July 25, 1964 (div. 1981); children: Jamie Lynn Harner, Duane David; m. Mark S. Turner, June 26, 1982; stepchildren: Tammy M., Kathleen J. BS in Edn., Kent State U., 1964, postgrad., 1975-77. Lic. health maintenance orgn. agt. Tchr. math. Bedford (Ohio) Schs., 1964-65; claims examiner John Hancock Ins. Co., Cleve., 1965; asst. to dir. budget Cole Nat. Corp., Cleve., 1965-66; tchr. Streetsboro (Ohio) Schs., 1966-81; claims examiner Adminstrv. Service Cons., Broadview Heights, Ohio, 1981-82; sr. claims approver Enterprise Group Planning, Beachwood, Ohio, 1981-83; mgr. claims Selman and Co., Beachwood, 1983-85, Metlife Healthcare Network, Beachwood, 1985-86; supr. benefits Revco Drug Corp. Office, Twinsburg, Ohio, 1987—. Sec. Community Improvement Corp., 1970s; mem.-at-large Streetsboro Mothers Club, 1970s; sec. Streetsboro Zoning Commn., 1970s; candidate Fin. Dir. Streetsboro, 1970s. Mem. Nat. Assn. Female Execs., Northeastern Ohio Claim Assn. (sec. 1986-87).

TURNER, CAROLINE JACKSON, association executive; b. Rush Springs, Okla., Mar. 19, 1936; d. Johnny and Dorothy Mildred (Morgan) Jackson; m. Robert Elam Turner, May 17, 1957; children: John Robert, Lisa Suzanne Michalak, Mark Andrew. AS, Ventura (Calif.) Coll., 1982. Sec. Mobil Oil Co., Ventura, 1956-60; exec. sec. Loma Linda (Calif.) U., 1968-70, dir. alumni affairs, 1970-72; office mgr. Robert E. Turner DDS, Oxnard, Calif., 1972-82; exec. dir. Santa Barbara-Ventura County Dental Soc., Ventura, 1982—. Mem. allocations com. Santa Barbara United Way, 1986—; bd. dirs. regional occupational program Ventura County Supt. Schs., Oxnard, 1986—. Mem. Compononent Soc. Execs. of the Calif. Dental Assn. (pres. 1986—), Nat. Assn. Female Execs. Republican. Club: Desk and Derrick (Ventura) (pres. 1959-60). Home: 2628 Captains Ave Port Hueneme CA 93041 Office: Santa Barbara-Ventura County Dental Assn 1607 E Thompson Blvd Ventura CA 93001

TURNER, CATHY, retail manager; b. Denison, Iowa, June 1, 1951; d. Teddy Junior and Ruth F. (Paulsen) Cornelius; m. Billy Don Turner, July 3, 1975 (div. Dec. 1979); 1 child, Michelle Suzanne. B.A., U. Iowa, 1973. Asst. store mgr. Casual Corner, Houston, 1975-77, store mgr., 1977-80, dist. mgr., Tampa, Fla., 1980-81, regional mgr., Boca Raton, Fla., 1981—; bd. dirs., sec. Galleria Mall, Houston, 1979-80. Mem. Nat. Assn. Female Execs., Gamma Phi Beta. Lutheran. Avocations: water skiing, skiing, softball. Office: Casual Corner 277 Town Center at Boca Boca Raton FL 33431

TURNER, CHERI ANNE, financial paraplanner, securities agent, real estate agent, musician; b. Spring City, Pa., Apr. 7, 1949; d. Harold William and Evelyn Virginia (Wagner) T. Student Syracuse U., 1967-69; Cert. Fin. Paraplanner, Coll. Fin. Planning, Denver, 1988. Pub. relations mediator Don Poindexter & Assocs., St. Petersburg, Fla., 1969-72; exec. sec. Honeywell Inc., Largo, Fla., 1972-75; sec., design coordinator SCM Design Ctr., Syracuse, N.Y., 1975-76; personnel dir. Jay Galbraith's Penthouse, St. Petersburg, 1977-79; cert. fin. paraplanner R. A. Siebern & Assocs., St. Petersburg, 1982-87, pres. C.A. Turner Services Inc., 1987—, music dir. Capt. Anderson Cruises, Clearwater, Fla., 1982—; real estate sales rep. McCormack/Terwilliger Assocs., St. Petersburg, 1984-87, Hampton Realty, St. Petersburg, 1987—, Corwin Realty Inc., St. Petersburg 1988—; registered rep. gen. securities Mut. Benefit Fin. Service Co. Inc., Tampa, Fla., 1985—; music dir. Capt. Anderson Cruises, Clearwater, Fla., 1982—; pres. CA Turner Services, Inc., Palm Harbor, Fla., 1987—; pvt. practice music tchr., Largo, 1964—. Composer, illustrator children's music book: Ditties for Kiddies, 1980. Mem. Nat. Assn. Female Execs., Inst. Cert. Fin. Planners (counsel adminstr. 1988—), Am. Soc. Notaries, Hospitality Industry Assn. Inc., Nat. Assn. Security Dealers, U.S. Figure Skating Assn. (preliminary test judge 1975—), Sun Coast Figure Skating Club. Avocations: figure skating, music, fishing, gemology, rock hounding. Office: CA Turner Services Inc 4161 103d Ave N Clearwater FL 34622

TURNER, CLAUDIA MARJORIE, corporate education specialist; b. Summit, N.J., Oct. 28, 1939; d. Claude Swanson and Mary Marjorie (Whitfield) Finney; m. Samuel Hamilton Turner, Feb. 10, 1984; children: Gayle Lois Dotson, Gary William Dotson. BS, D.C. Tchrs. Coll., 1974; MEd, U. Md., College Park, 1981. Office mgr. Univ. Legal Services, Washington, 1969-1975; from asst. dir. continuing edn. to assoc. dean Strayer Coll., Washington, 1976-81; div. mgr. edn. Wang Labs., Inc., Bethesda, Md., 1982-86, div. mktg. support dir., 1986—; cons. World Bank, The Office, TRW Washington Group, South Western Pub. Co., Washington, 1978-84. Mem. continuing edn. adv. bd. U. D.C., 1985; advisor Washington area Upward Bound Program; v.p. Plyers Mill Crossing Homeowners Assn., Silver Spring, Md. Democrat. Baptist. Office: Wang Labs Inc 7500 Old Georgetown Rd Bethesda MD 20814

TURNER, DENISE MICHELLE, special education educator; b. Yonkers, N.Y., Nov. 22, 1951; d. George Henry and Lillian Estelle (Crier) T. BA in Psychology, Manhattanville Coll., 1973; MA in Edn., NYU, 1974. Cert. elem. tchr., spl. edn. tchr., learning disabilities, N.Y. Tchr. Adult Edn. Program, Yonkers, 1973-74; tchr., tutor Graham Home for Children, Hastings, N.Y., 1974-77; counselor, tchr. Youth Employment Tng. Program, Yonkers, 1977-79; tchr., tutor Nepperhan Community Ctr., Yonkers, N.Y., 1980-81; tchr. Ednl. Opportunity Ctr., Yonkers, 1979-80; tchr. spl. edn. Yonkers Bd. Edn., 1974—; dir., supr., tchr. Community Meml. Ch. Tutorial Program, 1973-75; cons. Lifestyles Enterprise, Yonkers, 1987—; pres., counselor Deja Ltd. Inc., Yonkers, 1985—. Chairperson, Westchester Womens Polit. Black Caucus, Yonkers, 1979; organizer voter registration drive, Westchester County, 1976-78. NYU fellow, 1974; recipient cert. Achievement City of Norwalk, Conn., 1980, Achievement award Womens Civic Club o Nepperhan Inc., Yonkers, 1981. Mem. NEA, N.Y. State United Tchrs., Yonkers Fedn. Tchrs., Yonkers Assn. Minority Sch. Educators, Black Alumni Assn. Manhattanville Coll., Delta Sigma Theta. Clubs: Westside Polit., Christian Youth Fellowship (Yonkers) (bd. Christian edn. pres. 1973-75). Home: 380 N Broadway C-5 Yonkers NY 10701

TURNER, ELIZABETH ADAMS NOBLE, management conultant; b. Yonkers, N.Y., May 18, 1931; d. James Kendrick and Orrel (Baldwin) Noble; B.A., Vassar Coll., 1953; M.A., Tex. A&I U., 1964; m. Jack Rice Turner, July 11, 1953; children—Jay Kendrick, Randall Ray. Ednl. cons. Noble & Noble Pub. Co., N.Y.C., 1956-67; psychometrist Corpus Christi Guidance Center, 1967-70; psychologist Corpus Christi State Sch., 1970-72, dir. programs, 1972, dir. vol. service, 1972-76, dir. research and tng., 1977-79; program cons. Tex. Dept. Mental Health and Mental Retardation and Corpus Christi State U., 1976-77; coordinator vols. Summer Head Start Program, Corpus Christi, 1967. Chmn. spl. gifts coml United Way, Corpus Christi, 1970; mem. Corpus Christi City Council, 1979-81; mayor pro tem Corpus Christi, 1981-85, mayor, 1987—; co-owner Turner, Whittle & Tate, Inc., Realtors. Leadership Corpus Christi, Com. of 100—Goals for Corpus Christi; mem. adv. bd. U. Tex.; bd. dirs. Coastal Bends Council Govts., Conv. and Tourist Bur., Big Bros., YWCA, Corpus Christi Hearing and Speech, C. of C., Food Bank, Harbor Playhouse, Coastal Bend Mental Health Assn., Suicide Prevention Inc., Tb Assn., Corpus Christi Mus., Leadership Tex. Class 1, Gov.'s Commn. Women, Art Mus. S. Tex., Corpus Christi; bd. govs. Southside Community Hosp., 1st Nat. Gulfway Bank. Admiral Tex. Navy. Recipient Love award YWCA, 1970, Careers award, 1988. Mem. Tex. Psychol. Assn. (pres., mem. exec. bd.), Psychol. Assos. (pres.), Tex. Mcpl. League, Jr. League Corpus Christi, Tex. Bookman's Assn., C. of C. (dir.), Tex. Assn. Realtors, Kappa Kappa Gamma. Clubs: Corpus Christi Country, Corpus Christi Yacht, Junior Cotillion, Corpus Christi Press. Home: 4466 Ocean Dr Corpus Christi TX 78404

TURNER, FRANCES BERNADETLE, clergyman, lecturer, author; b. Superior, Wis., June 28, 1903; d. Fyler Bedell and Eleanor Dolores (Donaly) Rainsford; m. Delos Ashley Turner, Dec. 8, 1936. BS in Edn., U. Minn., 1926; MA in Sociology, Northwestern U., 1938; postgrad. social service adminstrn., U. Chgo., 1941-44; PhD in Sociology and Social Work, Washington U., St. Louis, 1948. Ordained to ministry Episc. Ch., 1986; ordained Episc. deacon Diocese of Chgo., 1988. Tchr. high sch. Bessemer, Mich., 1924-28; field rep. nat. staff ARC, 1929-36, chpt. exec. sec. Kans., Wash., Nev., 1929-36; psychiat. social worker Chgo. State Hosp. and Ill. Inst. Research, 1938-41; chief social service Dixon (Ill.) State Hosp., 1945; assoc. prof. sociology and social work Ariz. State Coll., Tempe, 1946-56; student counselor nursing schs. Good Samaritan Meml. Hosps., Phoenix, 1946-56; ordained minister Divine Sci. Ch., 1965; founder Divine Sci. Ctr., Evanston, Ill., 1965; pastor Divine Sci. Ch., Roanoke and Evanston, Ill., 1971-72; comdr. chapel service Carrillo Hotel, Santa Barbara, Calif., 1979-80; resident counselor Retirement Home, Wichita, Kans., 1974-76; instr. div. continuing edn. Marquette U., 1976, 81-82, Calif. State U., 1976; chaplain Hillcrest Retirement Home, Boise, Idaho, 1986-87, North Shore Retirement Hotal, Evanston, Ill., 1987—; lectr. in field. Author: Happy Is the Man, 1965, God-centered Therapy, 1968, Faith of Little Creatures, 1972, Prosperity and the Healing Power of Prayer, 1984; contbr. articles and poetry to newspapers and mags. Bd. dirs. Maricopa council Campfire Girls, Phoenix, 1955-61. Fellow Am. Sociol. Assn.; mem. Nat. Assn. Social Workers, Assn. Cert. Social Workers, Am. Assn. Marriage Counselors, Internat. Assn. Women Ministers, Am. Assn. Pastoral Counselors, Nat. League Am. Pen Women, Kans. Authors Club, World Poetry Soc., Divine Sci. Internat. Fedn., Internat. New Thought Alliance, Ret. Officers Assn. (aux.), St. Hilda's Guild, Channel City Women's Forum, Santa Barbara, Calif. Club: Daus. of Nile. Home: 1611 Chicago Ave Evanston IL 60602 Office: 5555 N Sheridan Rd Apt 1816 Chicago IL 60640

TURNER, JANICE MARIA, occupational therapist; b. Washington, Oct. 15, 1951; d. Alvin McShayne and Catherleen (Edwards) Harvey; m. Gary Harold Turner, Jan. 28, 1950; children: Gary Harold, Ashely Tiara. BS, U. LaVerne, 1973; MS, Western Mich. U., 1976. Staff therapist D.C. Gen. Hosp., Washington, 1976-78, chief therapist pre-vocat. evaluation, 1978-81; chief occupational therapy VA Med. Ctr., Washington, 1981-86; ind. contract therapist Washington, 1986—; contract therapist Vis. Nurses Assn., Washington, 1983—; cons. SunShine Multi-Service Inc., Washington, 1985-86; mem. admissions bd. occupational therapy Howard U., Washington, 1983-85. Mem. Capital View Bapt. Ch., Washington, 1961, PTA, Washington, 1986. Mem. Am. Occupational Therapy Assn., Arthritis Found. Allied Health (sec. 1977-80), D.C. Occupational Therapy Assn. (co-chairperson continuing edn. com. 1981-82). Democrat. Baptist. Home: 2927 W Street SE Washington DC 20020

TURNER, JOY TILSON, sales executive; b. Greeneville, Tenn., Aug. 13, 1945; d. Raymond Arthur and Dorothy Elizabeth (Inscore) Tilson; m. Steven Kent Turner, June 21, 1969 (div. June 1972); 1 child, Chantelle Leigh. Cert. in secretarial sci., Greeneville Bus. Coll., 1964; student, Ga. State U., 1969-70. Clk. typist to dean of women and sec. to registrar Tusculum Coll., Greeneville, Tenn., 1964-66; clk. typist, stenographer, sec. Huyck Formex, Greeneville, 1966-69; adminstrv. asst. Ga. State U., Atlanta, 1969-70; credit clk. USS Agr. Chems., Atlanta, 1971; from sec. to sales mgr. MECO Corp., Greenville, 1971—. Mem. Nat. Assn. of Female Execs., Nat. Secs. Assn. Internat. (past sec. and pres. Greeneville chpt. 1967-74), Color Marketing Group. Republican. Presbyterian. Home: 101 W Grove St Greeneville TN 37743

TURNER, JULIANA MARGARET, photographer; b. Columbus, Ohio, Nov. 21, 1927; d. William Coulter and Mildred Lavinia (Dickey) Gage; m. Gerry ALan Turner, June 10, 1920 (dec. 1982); children: Steven Lee, Jill Allison, Christopher Alan. Student, Ohio State U., 1945-48. Mgr. circulation Design mag., Columbus, Ohio, 1958-60; creative asst. to editor Design mag., Columbus, 1960-64; asst. to advt. mgr. Ohio Farmer mag., Columbus, 1964-65; ptnr. Creative Assocs., Westport, Conn., 1966-82, pres., 1982—. Photographs in permanent collection at Norwalk Camera Club; photos used in posters, calenders. Mem. Westport Hist. Commn., 1973-78; bd. dirs. Westport-Weston chpt. Am. Cancer Soc., 1970-71; co-chmn. Stop Smoking Clinic, Westport. Recipient numerous awards for photography. Mem. Assoc. Photographers Internat., Older Women's League, Nat. Assn. Female Execs., Fairfield Hort. Soc., Norwalk Camera Club. Republican. Congregationalist. Home and Office: Creative Assocs 12 Edge Hill Ln Westport CT 06880

TURNER, JUNE MCHENRY, small business owner; b. Bridgeton, NJ, June 10, 1934; d. Lester Swain and Margaret Eleanor (Mather) McH.; divorced; 1 child, Mary Ann Turner Lukas. Grad. high sch., Bridgeton. Owner Surfside Marina and Restaurant, Sea Bright, N.J., 1975-78, Snelling Temporaries, Sarasota, Fla., 1986-87, Snelling & Snelling Employment Service, Sarasota, 1984—. Mem. Sarasota C. of C., Nat. Assn. Female Execs., Women's Owners Network. Republican. Presbyterian. Clubs: Alturas of Sarasota, The Meadows; Navesink Country (Middleton, N.J.); Seaview Country (Absecon, N.J.). Lodge: Zonta. Office: Snelling & Snelling Employment Service 4000 S Tamiani Trail Suite 400 Sarasota FL 33581

TURNER, KAREN M., news/public affairs director; b. Trenton, N.J., May 23, 1954; d. Arthur H. and Gloria (Scott) Turner. AB, Dartmouth Coll., 1976; JD, Northwestern U., 1979; MS, Columbia U., 1985. Staff dir. ABA, Chgo., 1980-84; intern Manhattan Community Bd. #7, N.Y.C., 1984-85, Newsweek mag., 1985, Greater Media, Inc., East Brunswick, N.J., 1985-86; news reporter, anchor Sta. WCTC, New Brunswick, N.J., 1986-87; news/pub. affairs dir. Sta. WIZF-FM, Erlanger, Ky., 1987—. Bd. dirs. Hyde Park-Kenwood Community Health Ctr., Chgo., 1983-84, NIA Comprehensive Ctr. for Devel. Disabilities, Chgo., 1982-84. RCA/NBC Broadcast fellow. Mem. Cook County Bar Assn., Dartmouth Alumni Council (exec. commn. Hanover, N.H. 1982-85), Dartmouth Black Alumni Assn. (sec. Hanover 1979-85), Greater Cin. Assn. Black Communicators (exec. com.), Nat. Black Assn. Journalists (founding), Greater Cin. Assn. Radio News Dirs. (founding), Phi Alpha Delta. Author, editor: Model Lawyers Guide to Legal Services, 1983; co-author: The Father of Black Aviation, Legal Self-Help is on the Way; editor: Lawyers See Yourselves as Others See You: Feasibility Study on Institutional Advertising, 1984, Everybody's mag. Office: Sta WIZF-FM 100 Commonwealth Ave Erlanger KY 41018

TURNER, KATHLEEN, actress; b. Springfield, Mo., June 19, 1954; m. Jay Weiss, 1984; 1 child, Rachel Ann. Student, Central Sch. of Speech and Drama, London, Southwest Mo. State U.; M.F.A., U. Md. Various theater roles, Broadway debut: Gemini, 1978; appeared in TV series The Doctors, from 1977; films include Body Heat, 1981, The Man With Two Brains, 1983, Crimes of Passion, 1984, Romancing the Stone, 1984, Prizzi's Honor, 1985, The Jewel of the Nile, 1985, Peggy Sue Got Married, 1986, Julia and Julia, 1988, Switching Channels, 1988. Office: care The Gersh Agy Inc 222 N Canon Dr Beverly Hills CA 90210

TURNER, LOIS LOUISE, college administrator; b. Peoria, Ill., Feb. 24, 1931; d. William Henry and Dorothy Louise (Binns) Suter; m. Harold Eugene Turner, June 24, 1950; children—Linda S. Turner Oliver, Michael E. Student pub. schs., Peoria. Dir. ops. student ctr., Bradley U., Peoria, 1980—, producer dinner theaters, 1981-85; producer Madrigal Dinner, Peoria, 1985-86. Mem. Assn. Coll. Unions Internat., Nat. Assn. Female Execs., Bowling Propr.'s Assn. Am., Peoria Bowling Assn., Republican. Methodist. Club: Quail Meadow Country. Lodge: Moose. Avocations: golf, bowling, camping. Home: 502 W Gift St Peoria IL 61604 Office: Bradley U Student Ctr 915 Elmwood St Peoria IL 61625

TURNER, MARTA DAWN, religious organization administrator; b. Morgantown, W.V., Oct. 7, 1954; d. Trubie Lemard and Dorothy Genevieve (Helmick) T.; m. David Michael Dunning, Mar. 1, 1980. Student, Royal Acad. Dramatic Art, London, 1975; BA with honors, Chatham Coll., 1976; grad. cert. in arts adminstrn., Adelphi U., 1982; MA Devel. Drama, Hunter Coll., 1988. Cert. video prodn. specialist. cons. resource ctr., summer ch. program N.Y.C. Presbytery, 1986—; asst. dir./dir. Riverside Communications, N.Y.C., 1985—. Exec. producer video projects including Hispanic City Sounds, Time for Peace, Silhouette, 1985—; asst. dir./dir. video series Riverside at Worship, 1985—. Mem. Presbyn. Peace Makers, 1985—; bd. dirs. Trinity Presbyn. Ch., N.Y.C, 1980—. Mem. Am. Diabetes Assn., Japan Karate Assn., W.Va. Soc. N.Y.C. (bd. dirs. 1986-87). Home: 540 W 55th St #6V New York NY 10019 Office: NYC Presbytery 7 W 11th St New York NY 10011

TURNER, MARY PAULINE CURTIS (MRS. JAMES CASTLE TURNER), artist; b. Lincoln, Nebr., Feb. 14, 1916; d. William Clapp and Nellie (Lee) Curtis; student Wilson Tchrs. Coll., 1940, Corcoran Sch. Art, 1950-54, Am. U., 1955; m. James Castle Turner, Apr. 14, 1934; children—Vivian Lee Turner Polak, Daniel Castle, Brian, Lisa, Lauran. Exhibited at Corcoran Gallery, 1951, Rockville Art Center, 1968, bronze sculpture of Esther Peterson, asst. sec. labor under Kennedy and Johnson at Rehoboth Beach Art League, 1968; retrospective one-man show Labor Tng. Center, Washington, 1978; art tchr. for ret. persons Sargent House Project, 1965-69. Housing chmn. LWV, 1950; U.S del. Trade Union Conf., Blackpool, Eng., 1977; mem. budget com. D.C. Schs., 1969; mem. D.C. Council Arts and Humanities, 1974; membership chmn. Mus. African Art, 1974—; bd. dirs. Washington Ballet, 1976-82; pres. Whitehall Condominium Assn., Bal Harbour, Fla. Recipient Ronshein award, 1951, prizes Corcoran Sch., 1951, Washington Area award, 1952. Episcopalian (vestry 1969-71, pres. all women's activities 1969, mem. ch. centennial com.). Home: 15101 Interlachen Dr Apt 317 Silver Spring MD 20906

TURNER, MONICA GOIGEL, ecologist; b. N.Y.C., Dec. 9, 1958; d. Peter Joseph and Dorothy Ann (Burger) Goigel; m. Michael G. Turner, Aug. 28, 1982. BS, Fordham U., 1980; PhD, U. Ga., 1985. Environ. specialist U.S. Nat. Park Service, Washington, summer 1981; grad. non-teaching asst. U. Ga., Athens, 1980-83, research asst. Inst. Ecology, 1983-85, postdoctoral research assoc. Inst. Ecology, 1985—. Editor: Landscape Heterogeneity and Disturbance, 1987. Mem. Internat. Assn. Ecology, Internat. Assn. Landscape Ecology (program chair U.S. chpt. 1986—), Internat. Soc. Ecol. Modeling, AAAS, Am. Inst. Biol. Scis., Ecol. Soc. Am., Phi Beta Kappa, Phi Kappa Phi. Roman Catholic. Office: Oak Ridge Nat Lab Environ Scis Div Oak Ridge TN 37831-6038

TURNER, NANCY DEE, marketing professional; b. Poukeepsie, N.Y., Aug. 20, 1946; m. W.W. Turner. RN, U. Ariz., 1964-69; BSBA, U. Phoenix, 1982. Technician Rocky Mountain Geochem., Tucson, 1969-70; technician EFCO Lab., Tucson, 1970-71, asst. mgr., 1971-78; quality control chemist Anamax, Tucson, 1978-79; gen. mgr. EFCO Labs., Tucson, 1979-82, Am. Analytical Labs., Tucson, 1983-84; mktg. mgr. SW region Analytical Techs., Inc., Tucson, 1984—. Vol. ARC, Tucson, 1979-82. Mem. Am. Bus. Women's Ann., Ariz. Assn. Cert. Labs. (pres. 1981-85), Am. Oil Chemists Soc. Republican. Home: PO Box 36385 Tucson AZ 85740 Office: Analytical Techs Inc 21135 48th St Suite 107-110 Tempe AZ 85282

TURNER, PAMELA WALKER, retired educational administrator; b. Montgomery, Ala., July 28, 1943; d. Frederick J. and Yvonne L.B. (Chaplin) Walker; B.A. in Econs., Wellesley Coll., 1965; S.M. in Mgmt., Sloan Sch., MIT, 1971; m. F. Cort Turner, III, Oct. 19, 1968; children—Frederica Chaplin, F. Cort, IV. Cons. energy econs. Arthur D. Little, Inc., Cambridge, 1965-67; mem. corp. orgn.-info. staff, dept. mgr. mktg. div. Soc. Nationale de Siderurgie, Algiers, Algeria, 1970-72; dir. recruitment and placement, Sloan Sch. Mgmt., M.I.T., 1975-79, mgr. accelerated master's program, 1978-79, dir. external relations, 1979-82, lectr. in mgmt., 1978-82; cons. in field. Treas., Buckingham, Browne & Nichols Parents Assn., P.A., 1984-86; treas., bd. dirs. Ten Ten Meml. Dr. Corp., 1984—. Clubs: Wellesley Coll. (Boston); Longwood Cricket, Cambridge Skating (pres. 1983—), Badminton and Tennis. Address: 4 Fayerweather St Cambridge MA 02138

TURNER, SANDRA STEPHENS, publisher, writer; b. Oneida, Tenn., Aug. 21, 1945; d. Ray and Gladys (Tinch) Stephens; m. Kenneth Leon Turner, June 28, 1975; 1 child, Erin Lee. BA in Liberal Arts, U. Tenn., 1965, MS in Communications, 1974. Reporter Herald-Citizen, Cookeville, Tenn., 1966, Tennessean, Nashville, 1966-67; tchr. York Inst., Jamestown, Tenn., 1967-69, Clarkrange (Tenn.) High Sch., 1971, 73; editor Campbell County Times, LaFollette, Tenn., 1972; writer, editor TVA, Chattanooga, 1974-78; publisher, editor Singles Scene, Crossville, Tenn., 1981—. Contbr. articles to various jours. Home: PO Box 454 Crossville TN 38555 Office: Singles Scene PO Box 454 Crossville TN 38555

TURNER, SHIRLEY ANN, small business owner; b. Westfield, N.Y., July 9, 1947; d. Newton Harold and Marian Elizabeth (Adams) Spinks; m. Dale Edward Turner Sr., NOv. 7, 1966; children: Dixie Lynn, Dale Edward II, Ross Andrew. Student, Burton Beauty Acad., 1966, Carroll, 1966. Cosmetologist Jewels Beauty Salon, Wauchula, Fla., 1966-67; owner Shirleys Beauty Salon, Zolfo Springs, Fla., 1967-70, Country Quality Markets Inc., Wauchula, 1979—, Country Kitchen, Wauchula, 1980-82, Homade Sandwiches, Wauchula, 1982—. Sponsor pioneer days Vol. Fire/Sheriff Dept., Wauchula 1986-87, Supt. Schs., Hardee County 1985-87. Mem. Nat. Assn. Female Execs., Nat. Assn. Profl. Cosmetologists. Democrat. Baptist. Office: Country Quality Market Inc PO Box 161 Wauchula FL 33873

TURNER, SHIRLEY SUE, medical technologist, laboratory adminstrator; b. Danbury, Iowa, Nov. 17, 1935; d. Wilmer and Aleva Alice (Diment) Earnest; cert. med. tech. St. Joseph Mercy Hosp. Sch. Med. Tech., 1956; student Nebr. State Tchrs. Coll., 1953-55; m. Edmund Bruce Turner, Sept. 30, 1965; 1 dau., Lisa Kay. Gen. lab. technician Magic Valley Meml. Hosp., Twin Falls, Idaho, 1956-57, Buena Vista County Hosp., Storm Lake, Iowa, 1957-59, Rockwood Clinic, Spokane, Wash., 1969-60; lab., x-ray technician Greene County Hosp., Jefferson, Iowa, 1961-65; chief technologist Gt. S.W. Gen. Hosp., Grand Prairie, Tex., 1965-71; technologist spl. chemistry dept., electrophoresis and autoanalyzers, Internat. Clin. Labs., Fort Worth, 1971-73; supr. chemistry dept. Pathology Assos. of Tex., Fort Worth, 1973-75; chief technologist Dallas-Ft. Worth Med. Center, Grand Prairie, Tex., 1975—; mem. med. lab. technician adv. bd. El Centrol Community Coll., Dallas. Mem. Am. Soc. Clin. Pathologists (affiliate mem., cert. med. technologist), Am. Soc. Med. Technologists. Republican. Methodist. Address: 3544 Granada Fort Worth TX 76118

TURNER, TAMARA ADELE, medical librarian; b. Seattle, Mar. 27, 1940; d. Fredrick Patrick and Florence Elfreda (Puntenney) T. B.A., U. Wash., 1972, M.L.S., 1974. Staff librarian Rainier Sch., Wash. State Library, Buckley, 1974-77; dir. med. library Children's Hosp. and Med. Ctr., Seattle, 1977—. U.S. Dept. Edn. fellow, 1973-74. Mem. Wash. Med. Librarians Assn., Seattle Area Hosp. Library Consortium (pres. 1980), Med. Library Assn., Spl. Libraries Assn., Am. Soc. Info. Sci. (pres. Pacific northwest chpt. 1987-88). Home: 1931 E Calhoun Seattle WA 98112 Office: Childrens Hosp and Med Ctr PO Box 5371 Seattle WA 98105

TURNER, TINA (ANNA MAE BULLOCK), singer; b. Brownsville, Tenn., Nov. 26, 1939; m. Ike Turner, 1956. (div. 1978); children: Craig, Ike Jr., Michael, Ronald. Singer with Ike Turner Kings of Rhythm, and Ike and Tina Turner Revue; appeared in films: Gimme Shelter, 1970, Soul to Soul, 1971, Tommy, 1975, Mad Max Beyond Thunderdome, 1985; concert tours of Europe, 1966, Japan and Africa, 1971; albums with Ike Turner include Hunter, 1970, Ike and Tina Show II, Ike and Tina Show, 1966, Ike and Tina Turner, Bad Dreams, 1973, solo albums include Let Me Touch Your Mind, 1972, Tina Turns the Country On, 1974, Rough, 1978, Airwaves, 1979, Private Dancer, 1984, Break Every Rule, 1986; performed with USA for Africa on song We are The World, 1985. Recipient Grammy award, 1972, 85 (three), 86. Address: care Roger Davies Mgmt 3575 Cahuenga Blvd W Los Angeles CA 90068

TURNER, VALARIE ENGLISH, electronics company administrator; b. Chgo., June 15, 1957; d. Benjamin and LaVelma (Gaddis) English; m. John D. Turner, Aug. 23, 1986. BA, Northwestern U., 1979; MBA, Western Ill. U., 1981. Acct. exec. AT&T, Oakbrook, Ill., 1981-83; buyer Westinghouse Electric Corp., Pitts., 1983-84; sr. buyer Westinghouse Electric Corp., Hunt Valley, Md., 1984—. Mem. Smithsonian Institute, Washington, 1987. Mem. Nat. Assn. Black MBA's, Nat. Urban League. Club: Toastmasters. Home: 127 Ivanhoe St #201 SW Washington DC 20032 Office: Westinghouse Electric Corp 1601 Knecht Ave Baltimore MD 21227

TURNER, VALERIE, vocational counselor; b. Jersey City, Apr. 24, 1957; d. Matthew Carver and Miriam (Phillips) T. BS, Howard U., 1979; MA, NYU, 1981. Cert. vocat. evaluator. Deafness con. N.Y. Soc. for the Deaf, N.Y.C., summer 1981; supr. evaluation services Goodwill Industries of Greater N.Y., Astoria, N.Y., 1981-83; field interviewer Rutgers U., New Brunswick, N.J., 1983; vocat. testing specialist Altro Health and Rehab., Bronx, N.Y., 1983-86; deafness cons. Henry Austin Mental Health Ctr., Trenton, N.J., 1986—; vocat. counselor and coordinator for job placement adv. bd. Kessler Inst. for Rehab., West Orange, N.J., 1987—; ptnr. Finger Singers Mus. Entertainment Service, N.Y.C., 1984-86. Deafness adv. Hudson County Human Services Adv. Council, 1985—. Named Woman of Achievement Hudson County Jersey Jour., 1984; recipient Am. Legion award Jersey City Pub. Sch. System, 1975. Mem. N.Y. City Black Deaf Advs. (office holder), Am. Deafness and Rehab. Assn., Coalition on Sexuality and Disability, Deaf Pride, Inc. Democrat. Home: 132 Armstrong Ave Jersey City NJ 07305 Office: Kessler Inst for Rehab 240 Central Ave East Orange NJ 07018

TURNER-ERFORT, VIRGINIA LORRAINE, zoo official; b. Monticello, Ill., Mar. 29, 1957; d. Richard Glen and Norma Jane (Kimble) Turner; m. Richard Vincent Erfort, Oct. 1, 1983. BS in Animal Sci., U. Ill., 1980; postgrad., Ill. Inst. Tech., 1986—. Sr. lab. technician Continental Grain Co., Libertyville, Ill., 1982-84; sales rep. Burns Vet. Supply Co., Glenview, Ill., 1984-85; coordinator animal adoption Brookfield Zoo Chgo. Zool. Soc., 1985—. Mem. Am. Assn. Zool. Parks and Aquariums, Am. Soc. Animal Sci., Nat. Assn. Female Execs., Kappa Kappa Gamma Alumni Assn. Democrat. Methodist. Office: Chgo Zool Soc Brookfield Zoo Brookfield IL 60005

TURNER-JOHNSTON, RENEE JULIE, graphics company administrator; b. New Orleans, Sept. 7, 1958; d. Howard Jacob Jr. and Joyce Maxine (Davis) Turner; m. Reginald Philip Johnston. Cert., New Orleans Ctr. for Creative Arts, 1976; BFA, Xavier U., New Orleans, 1980; MFA, Pratt Inst., 1982. Office mgr. Teleprompter New Orleans, 1980; mgr. prodn. Gt. Graphics, N.Y.C., 1981—; ptnr. The Graph Co., N.Y.C., 1987—; adminstrv. asst. Morris Jumel Mus., N.Y.C., 1981; adminstr., copywriter Art Fried Graphics, N.Y.C., 1982. Designer (poster) Nat. Handicapped Soc. (1st pl.) 1976; (mag. cover) Audio-Visual Communication, 1985. Vol. 9th Ward Citizen Voters League, New Orleans, 1974-80. Named an All-Am. Media Star Audio-Visual Communication, 1985. Mem. Computer Soc. of IEEE, Mgmt. Graphics Computer Users Group, Multi-Image in N.Y., Nat. Assn. Female Execs. Democrat. Home: 431 Clermont Ave Apt #3 Brooklyn NY 11238 Office: The Graph Co PO Box 723 Bowling Green Sta New York NY 10274

TURNER-PARSONS, BARBARA, social services administrator; b. St. Joseph, Mo., May 31, 1949; d. Dean Deforrest and Wanda Mae (Elder) Turner; children: Charles Aaron Parsons, Brandon Dean Parsons. BS in Secondary Edn., Northwest Mo. State U., 1976, MS in Home Econ. Edn., 1983. Custom decorator J.C. Penney Co., St. Joseph, Mo., 1976-78; instr. vocat. home econs. Craig (Mo.) R-III Sch., 1979-80, Nodaway Holt R-VII Sch., Graham, Mo., 1980-85; regional ctr. dir. Displaced Homemaker Ctr., Maryville, Mo., 1985-88, Rolla, Mo., 1988—; mem. adv. com. Literacy Plus, 1987. Co-sponsor, co-planner Neighbors Helping Neighbors - Farm Crisis Group for Northwest Mo., St. Joseph, 1986—; mem. Project Serve, v.p. 1986-88. Recipient Outstanding Pub. Service award Mo. Home Econs. Tchrs. Assn., AAUW. Mem. Am. Vocat. Assn., Mo. Vocat. Assn., Four State Regional Displaced Homemakers Network (sec./treas. 1987-88), Women's Career Network, YWCA Legislative Network. Home: 1815 Belmont Ct Rolla MO 65401 Office: Rolla Area Vocat Tech Sch 1304 E 10th St Rolla MO 31436-4372

TURNER-WALLS, VALERIE, criminal investigator, urban planner, educator; b. Chgo., June 12, 1957; d. Clifford Turner and Eliza (Kaywood) Turner; m. Lucious Gerald Walls, Jr., Nov. 17, 1984; 1 child, Alexander Gerald Walls. BS, Ill. State U., 1979; MA in Urban Planning and Policy, U. Ill., Chgo., 1983; postgrad. John Marshall Law Sch., Chgo., 1985—. Cert. tchr., Ill. Tchr., Chgo. Bd. Edn., 1979-84; ops. mgr. Allstate Ins. Co., Skokie, Ill., 1980; research asst U. Ill., Chgo., 1981-83; urban planner/cons. Village of Robbins, Ill., 1981-83; auditor Leadership Council, Chgo., 1982-83; criminal investigator Dept. Justice, Chgo., 1984-87, intelligence research specialist, 1987—; tchr., cons. Bryant & Stratton Coll., Chgo., 1983. Mem. legal com. Chgo. Urban League, 1983; chairperson juvenile advocacy unit Robbins Econs. Devel. Corm., 1983; active NAACP. Ill. Govs. summer fellow, 1978. Mem. Fed. Law Enforcement Officers Assn., Nat. Assn. Female Execs., Fed. Criminal Investigators Assn., Chgo. Bar Assn., Federalist Soc., Black Law Students Assn., Am. Planning Assn., Alpha Kappa Alpha, Phi Alpha Delta. Avocations: tennis, reading, traveling.

TURNEY, EMMA LEE PRESLAR, publisher, show producer; b. Van Buren, Ark., Sept. 27, 1928; d. Wray Preslar and Ann Lorraine (Faulkner) Preslar Rutherford. Student Tusla U., 1945. Owner Antiques Prodns., Houston and Round Top, Tex., 1963—, Creative Press, Houston and Round Top, 1978—, S.W. Antiques News/SWAN, Houston and Round Top, 1983—. Author: Antiques Business as a Lifestyle, 1978; contbr. articles to jours. in field. Recipient Round Top-Carmine 4-H award, 1986, Fayette County Friend of 4-H Grand award, 1987. Active Friends of Winedale, Friends of Festival Inst., Round Top. Home: PO Box 66402 Houston TX 77006

TURNIPSEED, PAMELA JEAN, insurance company executive; b. Lake Arrowhead, Calif., Mar. 28, 1947; d. Robert Earl and Dean Ann (Pitcher) T. BA, U. Calif., Santa Barbara, 1970. Claims adjuster Allstate Ins. Co., Los Angeles, 1970-74; claims mgr. Allstate Ins. Co., Honolulu, 1974-78, Tucson, 1978-79, Las Vegas, 1979-81, San Diego, 1981-83, Santa Ana, Calif., 1983-86; owner, pres. Creative Settlements, Honolulu, 1986—; mgmt. cons. Peak Performance Systems, HonoluLu, 1986—. Mem. Nat. Assn. Female Execs., Nat. Assn. Life Underwriters. Office: Creative Settlements 1221 Kapiolani Blvd Suite 815 Honolulu HI 96814

TUROCK, BETTY JANE, information scientist, educator; b. Scranton, Pa., June 12; d. David and Ruth Carolyn (Sweetser) Argust; B.A. magna cum laude (Charles Weston scholar), Syracuse U., 1955; postgrad. (scholar) U. Pa., 1956; M.L.S., Rutgers U., 1970, Ph.D., 1981; m. Frank M. Turock, June 16, 1956; children—David L., B. Drew. Library and materials coordinator Holmdel (N.J.) Public Schs., 1963-65; story-teller Wheaton (Ill.) Public Library, 1965-67; ednl. media specialist Alhambra Public Sch., Phoenix, 1967-70; br. librarian, area librarian, head extension service Forsyth County Public Library System, Winston-Salem, N.C., 1970-73; asst. dir. Montclair (N.J.) Public Library, 1973-75, dir., 1975-77; asst. dir. Monroe County Library System, Rochester, N.Y., 1978-81; asst. prof. Rutgers U. Grad. Sch. Communications, Info. and Library Studies, 1981-87, assoc. prof. 1987—; dir. Grass Roots, Inc., Montclair, 1974—; vis. prof. Rutgers U. Grad. Sch. Library and Info. Studies, 1980-81. Trustee, Raritan Twp. (N.J.) Public Library, 1961-62; mem. Bd. Edn. Raritan Twp., 1962-66; mem. Title VII Adv. Bd., Montclair Public Schs., 1975-77; ALA mem. coordinating council Task Force on Women, 1978-84; treas. Social Responsibilities Round Table, 1978—. Named Woman of Yr., Raritan-Holmdel Woman's Club, 1975. Mem. ALA (councilor 1984—), Public Library Assn., NOW, Rutgers U. Grad. Sch. Library and Info. Studies Alumni Assn. (pres. 1977-78), Phi Theta Kappa, Psi Chi, Beta Phi Mu, Pi Beta Phi. Unitarian. Author: Serving Older Adults, 1983; editor: The Bottom Line, 1984—; contbr. articles to profl. jours. Home: 11 Undercliff Rd Montclair NJ 07042 Office: Rutgers U 4 Huntington St New Brunswick NJ 08903

TURZINSKI-CLASON, PATRICIA ANN, business consultant; b. Milw., Nov. 11, 1950; d. Richard James and Doris Lorene (Smith) Turzinski; student U. Wis., Milw., 1968-69; m. Steven W. Clason, June 1, 1986. Supr. mortgage servicing A.L. Grootemaat & Sons., Milw., 1969-72; legal sec., 1973; exec. sec. Plastronics Inc., Milw., 1974; mgr. mortgage servicing Universal Mortgage Co., Milw., 1975; mgr. Outpost Natural Foods Coop., Milw., 1975-76; owner Genesis, Milw., 1976-79; owner Manifestation Mgmt. Inc., Milw., 1979—, Great Ideas! Speakers Bur. and Meeting Planning Cons., 1983—; owner Ctr. for Creative Learning, Milw., 1983—; founder Women's Resource Network Milw.; pres., bd. dirs. Woman to Woman Inc., 1983—, conf. coordinator, 1984; co-founder Save-A-Farm, Inc.,Tai Chi Chuan Center, Milw.; instr. Cardinal Stritch Coll., Marquette U., Waukesha County Tech. Coll., Mt. Mary Coll. Mem. Wis. Profl. Speakers Assn. (bd. dirs. 1984-87), Nat. Speakers Assn., Meeting Planners Internat., Assn. Advancement Human Animal Bond (pres., bd. dirs.). Author articles, cassette tapes in field. Address: 2437 N Booth St Milwaukee WI 53212

TUTELMAN, JACKI DEENA, textile company executive, consultant; b. Roslyn, N.Y., Nov. 14, 1954; d. Paul and Elaine (Kligman) T. BS in Mass Communications, Emerson Coll., Boston, 1976. Group buyer European and Am. designer collections for women Bloomingdale's, 1976-86; v.p. Jakob Schlaepfer, Inc., St. Gallen, Switzerland, N.Y.C., 1986—. Mem. Fashion Group, Emerson Coll. Alumni Assn. Democrat. Jewish.

TUTHILL, VANIE IRENE, financial administrator; b. Bklyn., Sept. 14, 1950; d. Peter George and Irene E. (Psaki) Peters; m. Kenneth Henry Tuthill, Dec. 4, 1971; children: Bernadette, Alyssa. AA, SUNY, Cobleskill, 1970. Fin. adminstr. Tuthill Petroleum, Inc., Calverton, N.Y., 1980—, Riverhead Oil Products, Inc., Calverton, 1980—, Tuthill Enterprises, Ltd., Calverton, 1979—, Peconic Petroleum, Inc., Calverton, 1985—. Inventor in field. Mem. East End Women's Network, Riverhead C. of C., Oil Heat Inst. L.I., Empire State Petroleum Assn. Greek Orthodox. Club: Riverhead Commodore (pres. 1983-84). Office: Tuthill Petroleum Inc 420 Edwards Ave Calverton NY 11933

TUTTLE, CHRISTINE ANN, communications specialist, entrepreneur; b. Claremont, N.H., Oct. 31, 1954; d. Doris Louise (Lepicier) Tuttle. Cert., Mary Hitchcock Meml. Hosp. Sch. Histol. Technique, Hanover, N.H., 1974; BA, U. R.I., 1978, cert. in counseling alcoholics and other drug users, 1979. Dental sec., receptionist Pasco Dental Ctrs., New Port Richey, Fla., 1983; pharmacy technician Community Hosp., New Port Richey, 1984; med. sec. The Med. Ctr. At Walnut, Garland, Tex., 1984-85; ctr. mgr. Sheppard Dental Ctrs., Garland, 1985-86; bus. mgr. Horizon Dental Ctrs., Mesquite, Tex., 1986-87; communications specialist Garland Police Dept., 1987—. Mem. Am. Bus. Women's Assn. (chairpreson membership com. 1985-87), Alpha Psi Omega. Roman Catholic.

TUTTLE, DONNA FRAME, government official; m. Robert Tuttle. Former tchr. Los Angeles sch. system; undersec. Dept. Commerce, head U.S. Travel and Tourism Adminstrn., Washington, 1984—. Office: Dept Commerce US Travel & Tourism Adminstrn 15th & Constitution Ave NW Washington DC 20230

TUTTLE, DOROTHY EDITH LORNE, writer, communications consultant; b. Seattle, Dec. 7, 1916; d. William Henry and Maude alice (Fuller) T. Student U. Wash., 1936-37, U. Richmond, 1946, Stanford U., 1945-46; Banking/Econs. grad. Am. Inst. Banking, 1941; B.A., Am. U., Washington, 1955; postgrad. Mich. State U., 1960-61; grad. nat. security mgmt. Indls. Coll. Armed Forces, 1969. Pub. relations dir. Mich. Council State Coll. Pres., Lansing, 1961; pub. relations dir. woman's div., dir. weekly press and small dailies Republican Nat. Com., Washington, 1962-64; pub. info. officer, div. dir., br. chief Dept. Navy, Washington, 1965-71; info. and editorial specialist Assn. Am. R.R.s, Washington, 1973-75; writer, communications cons. DELT Communications Serives, Washington, Ithaca, Mich., 1976-84; internat. press corr. and editor USIA, 1948-59; freelance writer and communications cons., Ithaca, 1984—. Editor USA Life, 1950, Navy Mgmt. Rev., 1965-69; contbr. articles to nat. to nat. periodicals and govt. publs. Mem. pres.'s circle Am. U.; mem. Republican Congl. Com. Served with USN-USCG, 1942-46. Am. Inst. Banking fellow, 1936-42; recipient Outstanding Performance award Navy Bur. Supplies and Accounts, 1966; Superior Accomplishment award and Cash award Dept. Navy, Washington, 1967, Fed. Civilian Service award, 1969, Civilian Meritorious Service award, 1971. Mem. Nat. Press Club, Am. Newspaper Women's Club (1st v.p., dir.), AAUW, Am. Legion, Res. Officers Assn., Internat. Fedn. Univ. Women, Washington Press Club (officer, com. mem.), Am. U. Alumni Assn., Stanford U. Alumni Assn., Mich. State U. Alumni Assn., Women in Communications, Inc. Republican. Episcopalian. Home: 636 N Baldwin Rd Ithaca MI 48847

TUTWILER, MARGARET DEBARDELEBEN, treasury official; b. Birmingham, Ala., Dec. 28, 1950; d. Temple Wilson and Margaret (DeBardeleben) Tutwiler, II. Student, Finch Coll., 1969-71; B.A., U. Ala., 1973. Sec. Ala. Republican Party, Birmingham, 1974; scheduler Pres. Ford Com., Birmingham, 1975-78; exec. dir. Pres. Ford Com. Ala., Birmingham, 1976; pub. relations rep. NAM for Ala. and Miss., Birmingham and Washington, 1977-78; dir. scheduling George Bush for Pres. Com., Houston and Washington, 1978-80; spl. asst. to Pres. Reagan and exec. to Chief of Staff The White House, Washington, 1981-85; asst. sec. Dept. Treasury, 1985—. Republican. Episcopalian.

TWA, INEZ LOUISA ARBUTHNOT, writer; b. Boulder County, Colo., Nov. 9, 1905; d. George John and Nancy Louisa (Brammeier) Arbuthnot; student Coll. Commerce, Stockton, Calif., 1929; m. Norman Osbert Twa, Nov. 7, 1929 (dec.); children—Lois, Gordon, Audrey. Office positions, U.S. and Can., 1929-57; with FAA, 1957-75, sec. CAA, Grand Junction, Colo., 1957-63; adminstrv. asst. to dist. chief FAA, Reno, 1963-65, mgmt. tech./specialist area office, Salt Lake City, 1965-68; mgmt. specialist, asst. motor fleet mgr. Dept. Transp., Los Angeles, 1968-72, regional motor fleet mgr. Rocky Mountain Region, Denver, 1972-75, ret., 1975; author short stories pub. 1977—; editor Buckingham Gardens News and Revs. newsletter, 1984-86; contbr. stories to Colo. Old Times Mag., Denver Post newspaper. Active Mental Health Assn., 1958-63, Republican Party. Recipient award C. of C., 1963; service citation CSC, 1975. Mem. Profl. Secs. Internat., Arbuthnot Family International Assn. Aurora Geneal. Soc., Nat. Mus. Women in the Arts (charter). Presbyterian. Home: 800 S Ironton St #95 Aurora CO 80012

TWISS, MAURINE CHRISTMAN, consultant, public relations, author's editor; b. Westervelt, Ill., July 4, 1919; d. Paul and Leota Madge (Jenkins) Christman; student Ill. Wesleyan U., 1937-39; m. Armin Russel Twiss, Oct. 16, 1937; 1 child, Belinda Sue Twiss Allison. Copywriter, Montgomery Ward Corp., Chgo., 1939-41; editorial copy desk Chgo. Tribune, 1948-49; women's editor Jackson (Miss.) Daily News, 1950-54, feature editor, 1954-55; dir. public info. U. Miss. Med. Center, Jackson, 1955-73, dir. spl. services, 1973-78; cons. public relations, author's editor, Jackson, 1978—. Publicist, Miss. Heart Assn., 1953-70, bd. dirs., 1972-78, mem. So. regional evaluation subcom. Am. Heart Assn., 1970-74, chmn., 1973-74; mem. City of Jackson Planning Bd., 1974—; mem. City of Jackson Zoning Bd., 1976-79, 81-86, chmn., 1978-79, 85-86, chmn. comprehensive plan, 1982-88; mem. adv. council Miss. Employment Security Commn., 1978-79, Southeastern Regional Med. Library Program, 1970-72; pres. Miss. Women's Cabinet of Public Affairs, 1963-64; bd. dirs. New Stage, 1965—, pres., 1974-78; bd. dirs. Jackson Arts Alliance, 1979-83, pres., 1981-82. Recipient citation Miss. Assn. Mental Health, 1956, Service to Field award Public Relations Assn. Miss., 1981, numerous state, nat. awards for excellence in writing; named Woman of Achievement, Miss. Press. Women, 1973. Mem. Assn. Am. Med. Colls. Group on Public Relations (chmn. 1967-68, Disting. Service award 1978), Nat. Fedn. Press Women (regional chmn. 1961-65), Miss. Press Women (pres. 1958-60). Democrat. Club: Country of Jackson. Home: 1738 Douglass Dr Jackson MS 39211

TWISS, WANDA MAY, interior designer; b. Marengo, Ind., Oct. 28, 1934; d. Gamford Ingle and Anjie Pearl (Beld) Tate; m. Eugene Clyo Twiss, Nov. 27, 1952; children: Sheryll Lynn, Carol Ann. Student pub. schs., Newcastle, Ind. Decorator Decorating Den, Leesburg, Fla., 1970-85, franchise owner, 1983—, regional coordinator, instr., 1984—, designer, 1985—. Mem. Ch. of Nazarene. Home: Rural Rt 1 Box 1348 Weirsdale FL 32695 Office: Decorating Den 1031 W Main St Leesburg FL 32748

TWOMEY, JANET LOUISE WILKOV, banker; b. Washington, Oct. 17, 1952; d. Harry and Minnie S. Wilkov; m. Thomas N. Twomey, June 6, 1981. Student, Inst. d'Etudes Politiques, Paris, 1972-73; AB, Mt. Holyoke Coll., 1974; MBA, Columbia U., 1980. Corp. lending officer Chem. Bank, N.Y.C., 1980-84; asst. v.p. SE Bank, N.A., Melbourne, Fla., 1984-85, v.p., dept. mgr. corp. bank, 1985-87; sr. v.p. Chem. N.J. Corp., 1987—. Mary Vance Young scholar Mt. Holyoke Coll., 1972, Falk Found scholar Mt. Holyoke Coll., 1974. Mem. Commerce and Industry Assn. N.J. Club: Mt. Holyoke Coll. (South Hadley, Mass.) (class treas. 1984—).

TWYNER, ALEXIS CHERYLE, special education educator; b. Iowa City, Iowa, Sept. 19, 1946; d. Lafayette James and Rosemary Lucille (Roberts) T.; B.A. in Edn. and History, U. Iowa, 1964-68; M.A. in Reading and Learning Disabilities, Marycrest Coll., 1971; Ph.D. in Adminstrn., U. Iowa, 1978. Tchr. Pleasant Valley Community Sch. Dist., LeClaire, Iowa, 1968-73; reading specialist Lincoln Elem. Sch., 1973-75; specific learning disability tchr. North High Sch., Davenport, 1975—; adult edn. instr. Davenport Community Sch. Dist., 1980—. Mem. NEA, Iowa State Edn. Assn., Davenport Edn. Assn., Internat. Reading Assn., Assn. for Children with Learning Disabilities, Pi Lambda Theta. Republican. Office: 626 W 53d St Davenport IA 52804

TYAU, GAYLORE CHOY YEN, business educator, academic administrator; b. Honolulu, May 13, 1934; d. Moses M.F. and Bessie (Amana) T. BS, U. Calif., Berkeley, 1956, MBA, 1959. Cert. bus. tchr., Calif. Tchr. bus. Richmond (Calif.) Union High Sch., 1959-64, Westmoor High Sch., Daly City, Calif., 1964—; instr. City Coll. San Francisco, 1978—; office mgr. P.F. Freytag Assocs., San Francisco, 1978—. Coordinator Pacific Telephone Co.'s Adopt-a-Sch. Program, Colma, Calif, 1987. Mem. Nat. Bus. Edn. Assn., Calif. Bus. Assn. (chairperson program com. 1979, mem. program com. 1981-82, grantee), Am. Vocat. Assn., Assn. for Supervision and Curriculum Devel., Western Bus. Edn. Assn., City Coll. Faculty Assn., Jefferson Union High Sch. Dist. Tchrs. Assn., Beta Phi Gamma. Republican. Episcopalian. Home: 4050 17th St #1 San Francisco CA 94114

TY-CASPER, LINDA, author; b. Manila; came to U.S., 1956; d. Francisco Figueroa and Catalina Viardo (Velasquez) Ty; m. Leonard R. Casper, July 14, 1956; children: Gretchen, Kristina. AA, U. Philippines, 1951, Ll.B., 1955; Ll.M., Harvard U., 1957. Author: The Transparent Sun, 1963, The Peninsulars, 1964, The Secret Runner, 1974, The Three-Cornered Sun, 1979, Dread Empire, 1981, Awaiting Trespass, 1985, Fortress in the Plaza, 1985. Mem. Boston Authors Soc., Filipino Am. Women Network (recipient lit. award 1985), Philippine P.E.N., P.E.N. Women. Roman Catholic. Home: 54 Simpson Dr Saxonville MA 01701

TYLER, ANNE (MRS. TAGHI M. MODARRESSI), author; b. Mpls., Oct. 25, 1941; d. Lloyd Parry and Phyllis (Mahon) T.; m. Taghi M. Modarressi, May 3, 1963; children: Tezh, Mitra. B.A., Duke U., 1961; postgrad., Columbia U., 1962. Author: novels If Morning Ever Comes, 1964, The Tin Can Tree, 1965, A Slipping-Down Life, 1970, The Clock Winder, 1972, Celestial Navigation, 1974, Searching for Caleb, 1976, Earthly Possessions, 1977, Morgan's Passing, 1980, Dinner at the Homesick Restaurant, 1982, The Accidental Tourist, 1985, Breathing Lessons, 1988; contbr. short stories to nat. mags. Home: 222 Tunbridge Rd Baltimore MD 21212

TYLER, CYNTHIA ANN, office administrator; b. Muskegon, Mich., Jan. 7, 1958; d. Donald Joseph and Bonnie Lou (Miller) Kandalec; m. Michael Lee Tyler, Dec. 1, 1979; children: Rebecca Lynn, Diane Elizabeth, Michael David. A in Bus. Adminstn., Muskegon Bus. Coll., 1978. Acct. Landman, Latimer, Clink & Robb, Muskegon, 1978-83; office adminstr. Culver, Lague & McNally, Muskegon, 1983—; mem. secretarial adv. com. Muskegon Bus. Coll., 1987—. Mem. Nat. Assn. Legal Adminstrs. (Western Mich. chpt.). Roman Catholic. Office: Culver Lague & McNally 500 Terr Plaza PO Box 386 Muskegon MI 49443

TYLER, DARLENE JASMER, dietitian; b. Watford City, N.D., Jan. 26, 1939; d. Edwin Arthur and Leola Irene (Walker) Jasmer; B.S., Oreg. State U., 1961; m. Richard G. Tyler, Aug. 26, 1977; children—Ronald, Eric, Scott. Clin. dietitian Salem (Oreg.) Hosp., 1965-73; sales supr. Sysco Northwest, Tigard, Oreg., 1975-77; clin. dietitian Physicians & Surgeons Hosp., Portland, Oreg., 1977-79; food service dir. Meridian Park Hosp., Tualatin, Oreg., 1979—. Registered dietitian. Mem. Am. Dietetic Assn., Oreg. Dietetic Assn., Portland Dietetic Assn., Am. Soc. Hosp. Food Service Adminstrs. Episcopalian. Home: 12800 SE Nixon Ave Milwaukie OR 97222 Office: 19300 SW 65th St Tualatin OR 97062

TYLER, GAIL MADELEINE, nurse; b. Dhahran, Saudi Arabia, Nov. 21, 1953 (parents Am. citizens); d. Louis Rogers and Nona Jean (Henderson) T. AS, Front Range Community Coll., Westminster, Colo., 1979; BS in Nursing, U. Wyo.; R.N., Colo. Ward sec. Valley View Hosp., Thornton, Colo., 1975-79; nurse Scott and White Hosp., Temple, Tex., 1979-83, Meml. Hosp. Laramie County, Cheyenne, Wyo., 1983—. Mem. Critical Care Assn. Avocations: collecting international dolls; sewing; reading; traveling.

TYLER, JANICE ELAINE, elementary educator; b. St. Louis, Jan. 21, 1950; d. Albert Frank DeBrecht and Corinne Loraine (Reaper) Fossell; m. Patrick Dennis Tyler, June 24, 1972; 1 child, Bethany Ann. BE, U. Mo., St. Louis, 1972; postgrad., Tex. Weslyn Coll., 1985, 86. Tchr. Berkeley (Mo.) Sch. Dist., 1972-77, Arlington (Tex.) Ind. Sch. Dist., 1981—. Capt. Crime Watch program, Arlington, 1985—. Mem. Tex. State Tchrs. Assn., Workshop Way Educators, Delta Zeta. Roman Catholic. Home: 3705 Pimlico Dr Arlington TX 76017

TYLER, JOANNA ARMIGER, research and counseling psychologist; b. Balt., Jan. 23, 1943; d. William James Armiger and Marie Eileen (Edmonds) Lowery; A.A., Coll. San Mateo, 1968; B.A. cum laude in Psychology, San Jose State U., 1971, M.A. in Psychology, 1973; Ph.D. in Human Devel. Psychology (grad. fellow), U. Md., 1977; m. Richard Ridley; 1 son, Christopher Blair. Research asst., instr. U. Md., 1973-77; adj. asst. prof. Catonsville (Md.) Community Coll., 1973-78; sr. research analyst Teledyne Brown Engring., Rockville, Md., 1976-78; tech. mgr. Applied Mgmt. Scis., Silver Spring, Md., 1978-82; research project mgr. Arbitron Co., Laurel, Md., 1982-83; pvt. practice psychology, Columbia, Md., 1978—; conf. presenter; coordinator review panel VA grant proposals rev. NIH, 1983—; coordinator/moderator psychology lecture series. Smithsonian Inst.; cons. Mem. Howard County Drug Abuse Adv. Council, 1980-83, Howard County Mental Health Adv. Council, 1983-85. Cert. community coll. tchr. and counselor, Calif.; lic. psychologist, Md. Mem. Md. Psychol. Assn., Am. Psychol. Assn., Phi Kappa Phi. Democrat. Contbg. editor to Md. Psychol. Assn. newsletter, 1980-85; contbr. articles to profl. jours. and newspapers. Office: Columbia Med Ctr 11055 Little Patutent Pkwy Suite 201 Columbia MD 21044

TYLER, PHYLLIS STEPHANIE, monument company executive; b. Johnstown, N.Y., Dec. 16, 1943; d. Emerson Stevens and Doris Christina (Busse) T.; Student SUNY, Cortland, 1962-63, Syracuse U., 1981. Foreperson, Letter Memls., Johnstown, N.Y., 1963-67, mgr. alternate days Cherry Valley Memls., 1965-67; salesperson Castle Monument Co., Waltham, Mass., 1967-69, mgr. retail br., 1968; owner, mgr., carver Kellogg Memls., Mexico, N.Y., 1969—. Mem. Vol. Ambulance Corps; trustee Village of Mexico, 1971-77, dep. mayor, 1976-78; mem. Mexico Acad. and Central Sch. Occupational Adv. Council, 1983—; deacon 1st Presbyterian Ch., 1971-72, trustee, 1973-74, ruling elder, 1975-79, 82—; Republican committeeperson Town of Mexico. Recipient various Skiing medals and trophies; named Unsung Heroine, Central N.Y. chpt. NOW, 1982. Mem. Monument Builders N. Am., N.Y. Monument Builders Assn. (dir. 1984—), Greater Mexico C. of C., Assn. Profl., Managerial and Exec. Women. Club: Order Eastern Star. Designer and creator memls. and cast bronze art pieces. Home and Office: 5358 Academy St Mexico NY 13114

TYLER, THERESA CAMPBELL, hospital program administrator; b. Knoxville, Sept. 22, 1935; d. R. Lynn and Theresa (Hudson) Campbell; m. H. Park Tyler, Oct. 12, 1956; children: Victor Hudson, Lynn Campbell, Amie Holmes. BS in Med. Tech. summa cum laude, U. Tenn., 1956. Med. technologist, instr. Knoxville and Hamilton, Ohio, 1956-61; program coordinator YWCA St. Joseph County, South Bend, Ind., 1971-74, dir. fin. devel., 1979-80, exec. dir., 1980-84, capital campaign exec. dir., 1984-85; addictions planner Ind. Dept. Mental Health, Indpls., 1974-75; coordinator community services No. Ind. Drug Abuse Services, Indpls., 1974-78; pub. relations coordinator, resource devel. specialist Mental Health Ctr. St. Joseph County, South Bend, Ind., 1978-79; exec. dir. Big Bros./Big Sisters Elkhart (Ind.) County, 1985-87; foundation dir. St. Joseph Hosp., Mishawaka, Ind., 1987—. Trustee, South Bend (Ind.) Community Sch. Corp., 1972-76; mem. Human Rights Commn., City of South Bend, 1978-87; bd. dirs. YWCA, 1966-71, The Art Ctr., Inc., 1973-75, Vol. Action Ctr., 1965-80. Office: St Joseph Hosp 215 W 4th St Mishawaka IN 46544

TYNG, ANNE GRISWOLD, architect; b. Kuling, Kiangsi, China, July 14, 1920; d. Walworth and Ethel Atkinson (Arens) T. (parents Am. citizens); 1 child, Alexandra Stevens. A.B., Radcliffe Coll., 1942; M.Arch., Harvard U., 1944; Ph.D., U. Pa., 1975. Assoc. Stonorov & Kahn, Architects, 1945-47; assoc. Louis I. Kahn Architects, 1947-73; pvt. practice architecture Phila., 1973—; adj. assoc. prof. architecture U. Pa. Grad. Sch. Fine Arts, 1968—; assoc. cons. architect Phila. Planning Commn. and Phila. Redevel. Authority, 1952-54, Mill Creek Redevel. Plan, 1954; vis. disting. prof. Pratt Inst., 1979-81, vis. critic architecture, 1969; vis. critic architecture Rensselaer Poly. Inst., 1969, 78, Carnegie Mellon U., 1970, Drexel U., 1972-73, Cooper Union, 1974-75, U. Tex., Austin, 1976; lectr. Archtl. Assn., London, Xian U., China, Bath U., Eng., Mexico City; panel speaker Nat. Conv. Am. Inst. Architects, N.Y.C., 1988, also numerous univs. throughout U.S. and Can.; asst. leader People to People Archtl. del. to China, 1983. Subject of films Anne G. Tyng at Parsons School of Design, 1972, Anne G. Tyng at University of Minnesota, 1974, Connecting, 1976, Forming the Future, 1977; work included in Smithsonian Travelling Exhbn., 1979-81, 82; contbr. articles to profl. publs.; prin. works include: Walworth Tyng Farmhouse (Hon. mention award Phila. chpt. AIA 1953); builder (with G. Yanchenko) Probability Pyramid, Nat. Math. Conf., Smithsonian Mus. Am. History, 1984. Graham Found. for Advanced Study in Fine Arts fellow, 1965, 79-81. Fellow AIA (Brunner grantee N.Y. chpt. 1964, 83, dir., mem. exec. bd. Phila. chpt., 1976-78; mem. NAD (asso.), Nat. Assn. Archtl. Historians, C.G. Jung Center Phila. (planning com. 1979—), Form Forum (co-founder, mem. planning com. 1978—). Democrat. Episcopalian. Home: 2511 Waverly St Philadelphia PA 19146 Office: Univ Pa Dept Architecture Grad Sch Fine Arts Philadelphia PA 19107

TYRRELL, KARINE, documentation analyst; b. Saarbrucken, Germany, Nov. 4, 1940; came to U.S., 1968, naturalized, 1978; d. Eduard and Charlotte (Faber) Ambrosius; B.A., McMaster U., Can., 1964; M.A., So. Ill. U., 1972, Ph.D., 1984; m. James Tyrrell, Aug. 27, 1964 (div. 1979); 1 child, Dalton. Tchr., Hamilton (Ont., Can.) Sch. Bd., 1964-65, Ottawa (Ont., Can.) Sch. Bd., 1966-68; research asst. U.S. Grant Assos., So. Ill. U., Carbondale, 1973-74, teaching asst. 1974-77, dissertation fellow, 1977-78; tech. writer Action Data Services, St. Louis, 1979-80, Boeing Computer Services, Wichita, Kans., 1980 . Home: 9459 E Skinner St Wichita KS 67207 Office: PO Box 7730 M/S K79-51 Wichita KS 67277-7730

TYSINGER, GLENDA ANN, accounting executive, consultant; b. Lexington, N.C., Apr. 3, 1948; d. Travis Elwood and Gladys Marie (Carter) T. AA, Montgomery Coll., Rockville, Md., 1980; BS, U. Md., 1984. Adminstrv. asst., acct. Earth Satellite, Washington, 1980-82; asst. controller Gen. Maintenance Co., Washington, 1982-84, Harvey Constrn. Co., Rockville, 1984-86; acctg. mgr. Christopher Cos., Vienna, Va., 1986—; cons. Lui & Assocs., Washington, 1976—, PG County Task Force, Upper Marlboro, Md., 1979-81, STK, Inc., Washington, 1982-86, Design Ctr., Washington, 1984-86. Active various pol. campaigns, Fairfax county schls.; leader Girl Scouts U.S., Gaithersberg, Md., 1980—. Mem. Nat. Bus. Women's Assn., Am. Soc. Notaries. Republican. Roman Catholic. Office: Christopher Cos 8290 Old Courthouse Rd Vienna VA 22180

TYSON, ANN WILLIAMS, engineer; b. Greensboro, N.C., Oct. 28, 1957; d. Jesse Williams and Donza (Beane) T. BS in Chem. Engring., N.C. State U., 1980. Assoc. engr. radiol. support Carolina Power and Light Co., Raleigh, N.C., 1981-82, engr. engring. quality assurance, 1982-85, sr. engr. nuclear fuels sect., 1985—. Mem. Am. Nuclear Soc., Am. Inst. Chem. Engrs., Energy Info. Forum. Office: Carolina Power and Light Co PO Box 1551 Raleigh NC 27602

TYSON, CHRISTINE BOULOS, travel agency owner; b. N.Y.C., Dec. 16, 1949; d. John and Gloria (Sada) Boulos; m. Joseph E. Tyson, Nov. 28, 1970 (div. May 1983); children: Tracey Cynthia, Alexis Christen. Travel agt., Breech Acad., Overland, Kans., 1981; student, Am. Airlines Sch., Arlington, Tex., 1982. Note loan officer First Nat. City Bank, N.Y.C., 1971-73; advt. exec. T-Views, Inc., Danbury, Conn., 1978-80; real estate assoc. Curtiss & Crandon, New Milford, Conn., 1979-81; travel agt. mgr. Burke's Travel Ctr., New Milford, 1981-82, travel agt. owner, 1982—; lectr. in field. Creator Bus. Network, "The Business Scene", 1987—; author: Travel Minutes, 1984. Mem. New Milford Hosp. Aux., 1985—; bd. dirs. Housatonic Shepaug Valley United Way, 1987—. Recipient Career Appreciation Plaque N.E. Utilities, New Milford, 1985, 86, 87. Mem. Am. Soc. Travel Agts., Space, Greater Danbury Bus. Assn. (v.p. 1988, mem. of the month award 1986), New Milford C. of C. (bd. dirs., membership chmn. 1985—, v.p. 1988—). Home: 299 Aspetuck Rd New Milford CT 06776 Office: Burkes Travel Ctr Inc 516 Danbury Rd New Milford CT 06776

TYSON, CICELY, actress; b. N.Y.C.; d. William and Theodosia Tyson; m. Miles Davis, 1981. Student, N.Y. U., Actors Studio; student hon. doctorates, Atlanta U., Loyola U., Lincoln U. Former sec., model; cofounder Dance Theatre of Harlem; bd. dirs. Urban Gateways. Stage appearances include: The Blacks, 1961-63, off-Broadway, Moon on a Rainbow Shaw, 1962-63, Tiger, Tiger, Burning Bright, Broadway; star: film Sounder, 1972; other film appearances include Twelve Angry Men, 1957, Odds Against Tomorrow, 1959, The Last Angry Man, 1959, A Man Called Adam, 1966, The Comedians, 1967, The Heart is a Lonely Hunter, 1968, The Blue Bird, 1976, The River Niger, 1976, A Hero Ain't Nothin' but a Sandwich, 1978, The Concorde-Airport 79, 1979; TV appearances include: series East Side, West Side, 1963; spl. TV films The Autobiography of Miss Jane Pittman, 1973, 1974, A Woman Called Moses, 1978, The Marva Collins Story, 1981, Benny's Place, 1982; TV series Roots, 1977, King, 1978; TV movie Just An Old Sweet Song, 1976; named best actress for Sounder, Atlanta Film Festival 1972, Nat. Soc. Film Critics 1972, nominee best actress for Sounder, Acad. awards 1972, Emmy award for best actress in a spl. 1973. Trustee Human Family Inst.; trustee Am. Film Inst. Recipient Vernon Price award, 1962; also awards NAACP Nat. Council Negro Women; Capitol Press award. Office: care Triad Artists 10100 Santa Monica Blvd 16th Floor Los Angeles CA 90067

TYSON, CYNTHIA HALDENBY, college adminstrator; b. Scunthorpe, Lincolnshire, Eng., July 2, 1937; came to U.S., 1959; d. Frederick and Florence Edna (Stacey) Haldenby; children: Marcus James, Alexandra Elizabeth. BA, U. Leeds, Eng., 1958, MA, 1959, PhD, 1971. Lectr. Brit. Council, Leeds, 1959; faculty U. Tenn., Knoxville, 1959-60, Seton Hall U., South Orange, N.J., 1963-69; faculty, v.p. Queens Coll., Charlotte, N.C., 1969-85; pres. Mary Baldwin Coll., Staunton, Va., 1985—; bd. dirs. Am. Frontier Culture Edn., Staunton, 1986—; commr. Am. Council on Edn./Commn. on Higher Edn. and Adult Learner, Washington, 1981—. Contbr. articles to profl. jours. Commr. Va. Internat. Trade Commn., Richmond, 1987—; trustee Woodrow Wilson Birthplace Found., Staunton, 1985—; bd. dirs. United Way, Staunton, 1986—. Fulbright scholar, 1959; Ford Found. grantee Harvard U., 1981; Shell Oil scholar Harvard U., 1982. Fellow Soc. for Values in Higher Edn.; mem. Am. Mgmt. Assn. (council ops. enterprise 1985—), So. Assn. Colls. for Women (pres. 1980-81). Republican. Presbyterian. Office: Mary Baldwin Coll Office of the Pres Staunton VA 24401

TYSON, HELEN FLYNN, civic leader; b. Wilmington, N.C.; d. Walter Thomas and Fannie Elizabeth (Smith) Flynn; Student Guilford Coll., Am. U., Washington; m. James Franklin Tyson, Dec. 25, 1940 (dec.). Auditor, Disbursing Office, U.S. Civil Service, AUS, Ft. Bragg, N.C., 1935-46, chief clerical asst. Disbursing Office, Pope AFB, N.C., 1946-49, asst. budget and acctg. officer, 1949-55, supervisory budget officer hdqrs. Mil. Transport Command, USAF, 1955-57, budget analyst Hdqrs. USAF, Washington, 1957-74, ret. Active Arlington Com. 100, Ft. Belvoir, U.S. Army Engr. Center, Civilian-Mil. Adv. Council, Salvation Army Women's Aux., Inter-Service Club Council of Arlington; pres. Operation Check-Mate Council of Arlington, 1981; friend of Arlington County Library. Recipient awards U.S. Treasury, 1945, 46, U.S. State Dept., 1970; Good Neighbor award Ft. Belvoir Civilian-Mil. Adv. Council, 1978; awards U.S. First Army, 1973, ARC, 1977; named Arlington Woman of Yr., 1975; recipient Cert. of Recognition, 1981, Vol. Activists award Greater Washington Met. Area, 1981. Mem. Nat. Fedn. Bus. and Profl. Women's Clubs, Am. Assn. Ret. Fed. Employees, Am. Soc. Mil. Comptrollers (outstanding mem. award Washington chpt. 1988), Nat. Assn. Female Execs., Am. Inst. Parliamentarians, Guilford Coll. Alumni Assn., N.C. Soc. Washington, Altrusa Internat., Alexandria (Va.) City Hosp. Found., Arlington Hosp. Found. Home: 4900 N Old Dominion Dr Arlington VA 22207

TYSON, MARQUETA NEAL, utilities executive; b. Hampton, Va., Sept. 6, 1954; d. Henry McNeal and Mozelle (Moore) T. BA, Hampton U., 1976; MS, Syracuse U., 1977. Media coordinator dept. nursing Hampton (Va.) U., 1973-75, instr., 1977-80; advt. fellow Ogilvy and Mather, N.Y.C., summer 1975; reporter, photographer The New Jour. and Guide, Norfolk, Va., 1976; mktg. and sales promotion rep. Gen. Electric, Cin., 1980-83, operational planning specialist, 1983-86, quality specialist, 1986—; owner BMW Travel, Cin., 1981—, Pulse Communications, Cin., 1983-85. Author: (newsletter) Flightlines, 1985—; producer, host: (TV show) Pulse, 1983-85; host: (TV show) NAACP Show, Cin., 1980; contbr. articles to Applause mag. Pub. relations dir. polit. campaign, Cin., 1987; career mentor Coll. Mt. St. Joseph, Cin., U. Cin.; bd. dirs. Women Helping Women. Recipient Mentor award Coll. Mt. St. Joseph, 1986, Achievement award NAACP, Cin. br., 1987; named one of Outstanding Young Women of Am., Cin., 1983. Mem. Women in Communications, Delta Sigma Theta (sec. Cin. chpt. 1986). Home: 9103 Constitution Dr Cincinnati OH 45215 Office: Gen Electric 111 Merchant St Cincinnati OH 45246

TYSON, MARY (MRS. KENNETH W. THOMPSON), artist; b. Sewanee, Tenn., Nov. 2, 1909; d. Stuart L. and Katherine Tyson; student Grand Central Sch. Art, 1928-30, Eastport Sch. Art, 1928, New Sch. Social Research, 1975-76; m. Kenneth W. Thompson, Oct. 1, 1931; children—Kenneth Stuart, Loran Tyson. Exhibited one-man shows: Montross Gallery, N.Y.C., Bruce Mus., Greenwich, Conn., Present Day Club, Princeton, N.J., Pen and Brush Club, N.Y.C., Bodley Gallery, N.Y.C.; exhibited group shows: Balt. Water Color Club, Phila. Watercolor Club, Addison Gallery, Andover, Mass., Bklyn. Mus., Coll. Arts Assn., Morton Gallery, N.Y.C., St. Louis Mus. Contemporary Art, Government House, Nassau, Pen and Brush Club, N.Y.C. (22 awards), New Rochelle (N.Y.) Art Assn., Allied Artists, Knickerbocker Artists, Katherine Lorillard Wolfe, Nat. Arts Club, Lobster Pot Gallery, Nantucket, Am. Watercolor Soc., Easthampton Guild Hall (award), Nantucket Artists Assn.; represented in permanent collections: Guild Hall Mus., Easthampton, Monterey (Calif.) Peninsula Mus., Nantucket Artists Assn., Harrison Meml. Library, Carmel, Calif. Mem. Am. Watercolor Soc., Pen and Brush Club, Nat. Arts Club. Address: 20 W 11th St New York NY 10011

TYSON, PAMELA ANN, state official; b. Teaneck, N.J., June 17, 1953; d. Theodore Randall and Barbetta (Plescia) T. BA cum laude, SUNY, Stony Brook, 1977; MSW, U. Conn., 1984. Cert. social worker, Mass. Dir. Stony Brook Women's Ctr., N.Y., 1974-75, Lab. Behavior Assessment, Stony Brook, 1975-78; social worker Mass. Soc. Prevention Cruelty Children, Holyoke, Mass., 1979-83; exec. dir. New Eng. Learning Ctr. Women in Transition, Greenfield, Mass., 1983-85; dir. Western Mass. Exec. Office Human Services, Springfield, 1985—, spl. asst. to sec., 1986—; bd. dirs., com. chmn. Hampshire Council Children, Northampton, Mass., 1980-82; founder Ann Western Mass. Confs. on Human Services. Contbr. articles to profl. jours. Founder Franklin County Women's Issues Network; chmn. Springfield Homeless Coalition, Western Mass. Hispanic Adv. Commn.; mem. Mass. Rural Devel. Com., Franklin County Mental Health Task Force, Hampshire/Franklin County Sexual Abuse Task Force, Mass. Human Services Providers, Mayor's Task Force on Deinstitutionalization, Mayor's Task Force on Early Intervention, Springfield Homeless Human Rights Commn., Nat. Com. Prevention Child Abuse, Assn. Advancement Behavior Therapy Social Work Group for Study Behavioral Methods, Franklin County Charter Commn.; bd. dirs. Springfield Infant Mortality and Teenage Pregnancy Coalition. Democrat. Presbyterian. Lodge: Zonta. Avocations: movies, reading. Office: Western Mass Exec Office Human Services 436 Dwight St 3d Floor Springfield MA 01103

TYSON, PHOEBE WHATLEY, painter, artist; b. Wichita Falls, Tex., May 5, 1926; d. Mertic Boyd and Susie Phoebe (Creath) Whatley; student Abilene Christian U., 1943-45; B.A., North Tex. State U., 1946, M.A., 1951; m. Josiah William Tyson, Jr., Dec. 20, 1946; children—Josiah William III, Phoebe Creath Tyson McDavid. Elem. art tchr. Ft. Worth Ind. Sch. Dist., 1946-47; pvt. tchr. art, Haskell, Tex., 1948-50; painter watercolors, acrylics, Seabrook, Tex., 1971-79; exhibitor Biennial Exhbn., Nat. League Am. Pen Women, Kennedy Center, Washington (award of distinction), 1976, Rocky Mountain Nat. Watermedia Exhbn., Golden, Colo., 1977, 82, 85, Univ. Ave Ch. of Christ, Austin, Tex. Water Quality Assn. Recipient purchase prize San Antonio McNay Art Mus., 1985. Mem. McLean (Va.) Art Club (pres. 1970-71), Nat. League Am. Pen Women (nat. art bd. 1972-74, Tex. v.p. 1972-74, Meml. br. pres. 1976-78), Art League Houston, AAUW (v.p. Austin 1955-56), Nat. Watercolor Soc. (assoc.), Watercolor Art Soc. Houston, San Antonio Watercolor Group, Waterloo Watercolor Group, Tex. Watercolor Soc. (Purchase prize). Mem. Church of Christ. Home: 8600 Appalachian Austin TX 78759

TYSON, SHIRLEY ANN, hospital administrator; b. Columbiana, Ohio, Nov. 24, 1934; d. Kenneth Goerge and Sarah Ann (Gray) T. Diploma Nursing, Youngstown Hosp. Assn. Sch. Nursing, 1956; BS in Nursing, Youngstown State U., 1970; MBA, Baldwin-Wallace Coll., 1986. RN, Ohio, Calif. From staff to head nurse Youngstown (Ohio) Hosp. Assn., 1956-61; staff nurse Cedars of Lebanon Hosp., Los Angeles, 1961-63; night supr. Kaiser Found. Hosp., Los Angeles, 1963-66; supr. inservice edn. Salem (Ohio) Community Hosp., 1966-72, dir. personnel, 1972-78, asst. adminstr., 1978—; instr. part time Kent State U., Salem, 1980-84. Mem. adv. bd. Kent State U., Salem, 1987—; adminstrv. advisor Med. Explorers Scout Troupe, Salem. Mem. Am. Orgn. Nursing Execs., Ohio League Nursing (state dir. 1981-82), Northeast Ohio Nursing Service Adminstrs. (sec. 1982-83), Columbiana Bus. and Profl. Women (pres. 1983-85). Lutheran. Office: Salem Community Hosp 1995 E State St Salem OH 44460

TYTLER, LINDA JEAN, marketing executive, state legislator; b. Rochester, N.Y., Aug. 31, 1947; d. Frederick Easton and Marian Elizabeth (Allen) Tytler; m. George Stephen Dragnich, May 2, 1970 (div. July 1976). AS, So. Sem., Buena Vista, Va., 1967; student U. Va., 1973; student in pub. adminstrn. U. N. Mex., 1981-82. Spl. asst. to Congressman John Buchanan, Washington, 1971-75; legis. analyst U.S. Senator Robert Griffin, Washington, 1975-77; ops. supr. Pres. Ford Com., Washington, 1976; office mgr. U.S. Senator Pete Domenici Re-election, Albuquerque, 1977; pub. info. officer S.W. Community Health Service, Albuquerque, 1978-83; cons. pub. relations and mktg., Albuquerque, 1983-84; account exec. Rick Johnson & Co., Inc., Albuquerque, 1983-84; dir. mktg. and communications St. Joseph Healthcare Corp., 1984—; mem. N.Mex. Ho. of Reps., Santa Fe, 1983—, vice chmn. appropriations and fin. com., 1985-86, interim com. on children and youth, 1985-86, mem. edn. com., voters and election com., 1987-88; adv. mem. legis. edn. study com.; chmn. Rep. caucus, 1985—; mem. hosp. cost containment task force Nat. Conf. State Legislatures; del. to Republic of China, Am. Council of Young Polit. Leaders, 1988. Bd. dirs. N. Mex. chpt. ARC, Albuquerque, 1984. Recipient award N.Mex. Advt. Fedn., Albuquerque, 1981, 82, 85, 86, 87. Mem. Am. Soc. Hosp. Pub. Relations (cert.), Nat. Advt. Fedn., Soc. Hosp. Planning and Mktg., Am. Mktg. Assn. Republican. Baptist.

TZENG, MARIAN C., pediatrician; b. Taipei, Taiwan, Aug. 23, 1949; came to U.S., 1974; d. Muran and Onai Chen; m. Stephen S. Tzeng, Aug. 28, 1973; children—Grace Alice, Christine. M.D., Taipei Med. Coll., 1974. Diplomate Am. Bd. Pediatrics. Resident in pediatrics Coll. Medicine and Dentistry of N.J., Newark, 1976-79; fellow in pediatric infections Newark Beth Israel Hosp., 1978-79, mem. staff, 1979-81; Care for Handicapped Children fellow Cleve. Met. Gen. Hosp., 1981-82; clin. instr. St. Luke's Hosp., Cleve., 1982-83, Case Western Res. U. Sch. Medicine, 1982-83; practice medicine specializing in pediatrics, Monterey Park, Calif., 1983—; mem. staffs Garfield Med. Ctr., Beverly Hosp., Valley Vista Hosp. Mem. Am. Acad. Pediatrics. Office: 1900 S Atlantic Blvd #3 Monterey Park CA 91754

UDIN, SUSAN BOYMEL, neurobiology educator; b. Phila., Aug. 11, 1947; d. Jules and Pauline (Friedman) Boymel; m. David Udin, June 3, 1967; children—Rachel, Michael. B.S., MIT, 1969, Ph.D., 1975. Sr. staff scientist Nat. Inst. Med. Research, London, 1978-79; asst. prof. neurobiology SUNY-Buffalo, 1979-85, assoc. prof., 1985—. Contbr. articles to profl. jours. NIH grantee, 1980—; Nat. Acad. Sci. grantee, 1980; March of Dimes grantee, 1983-85; Burroughs Wellcome travel grantee, 1980, 81. Mem. Nat. Eye Inst. Visual Scis. B. Study Sect. 1986—, Women in Neurosci., Soc. for Neurosci., AAAS, Sigma Xi. Avocations: embroidery, gardening. Office: SUNY Dept Physiology Buffalo NY 14214

UDOW, ROSALYN LONG, education and civil liberties specialist, lecturer, lobbyist, local government official; b. Malden, Mass., Jan. 17, 1926; d. Harry A. and Anna Florence (Jacobson) Long; m. Alfred Bernard Udow, Nov. 16, 1951; children—Marianne, Henry Adam. Student Bennington Coll., Vt., 1943-45; A.B., U. Mich, 1947. Exec. dir. N.Y. State Com. for Legal Abortion, 1971, N.Y. State Coalition for Family Planning, N.Y.C., 1971-76; dir. govt. policy affairs Planned Parenthood of N.Y.C., 1976-80; N.Y. regional dir. People for the Am. Way, N.Y.C., 1981-84; dir. edn. and pub. affairs Nat. Coalition Against Censorship, N.Y.C., 1985—; coordinator Hofstra U. Sch. Bd. Forum, Hempstead, N.Y., 1985-87; trustee, bd. vice chair Nassau Community Coll., Garden City, N.Y., 1984—. Editor: Great Neck Regional Plan, 1966; (with others) This is Great Neck, 1956. Contbr. articles to profl. publs. Founder, voters service chair LWV, Great Neck, N.Y., 1954-59; bd. dirs. N.Y. State LWV, 1962; chair Village of Great Neck Planning Bd., 1959-66; sec. Great Neck Regional Planning Bd., 1960-66; trustee, pres. Great Neck Bd. Edn., 1966-70; bd. dirs. Planned Parenthood, Nassau County, N.Y., 1980-83, Family Planning Advocates of N.Y. State, 1980—, Nat. Coalition Against Censorship, N.Y.C., 1983—, Citizens for Family Planning, N.Y. State, 1982—; mem. nat. advance team Ferraro V.P. Campaign, 1984. Recipient Margaret Sanger award Family Planning Advocates of N.Y. State, 1980; Eleanor Roosevelt award Am. Jewish Congress, 1982. Mem. ACLU, Govt. Affairs Profls., Intellectual Freedom Found. Avocations: watercolors, horticulture, monotype. Home: 3 Bly Ct Great Neck NY 11023 Office: Nat Coalition Against Censorship 132 W 43d St New York NY 10036

UEHLING, BARBARA STANER, educational administrator; b. Wichita, Kans., June 12, 1932; d. Roy W. and Mary Elizabeth (Hilt) Staner; m. Stanley Johnson; children: Jeffrey Steven, David Edward. B.A., U. Wichita, 1954; M.A., Northwestern U., 1956, Ph.D., 1958; hon. degree, Drury Coll., 1978; LL.D. (hon.), Ohio State U., 1979. Mem. psychology faculty Oglethorpe U., Atlanta, 1959-64, Emory U., Atlanta, 1966-69; adj. prof. U. R.I., Kingston, 1970-72; dean Roger Williams Coll., Bristol, R.I., 1972-74; dean arts scis. Ill. State U., Normal, 1974-76; provost U. Okla., Norman, 1976-78; chancellor U. Mo.-Columbia, 1978-86, U. Calif., Santa Barbara, 1987—; sr. vis. fellow Am. Council Edn., 1987; cons. higher edn. State of N.Y., 1973-74; cons. North Central Accreditation Assn., 1975-86; mem. nat. educator adv. com. to Comptroller Gen. U.S., 1978; mem. commn. on mil.-higher edn. relations Am. Council on Edn., 1978-86; bd. dirs. Merc Bancorp, Inc., 1979-86, Meredith Corp., 1980—. Author: Women in Academe: Steps to Greater Equality, 1978; contbr. articles to profl. jours. Bd. dirs., chmn. Nat. Ctr. Higher Edn. Mgmt. Systems; bd. dirs. Am. Council on Edn., 1979-83, treas., 1982-83; trustee Carnegie Found. for Advancement of Teaching, 1980-86; mem. adv. com. Nat. Ctr. for Food and Agrl. Policy; bd. dirs. Resources for the Future; mem. NCAA Select Com. on Athletics, 1983-84, NCAA Presdl. Commn.; mem. Nat. Council on Ednl. Research, 1980-82; mem. Bus.-Higher Edn. Forum, Am. Council on Edn. Social Sci. Research Council fellow, 1954-55; NSF fellow, 1956-57; NIMH postdoctoral research fellow, 1964-67; named one of 100 Young Leaders of Acad. Change Mag. and ACE, 1978; recipient Alumni Achievement award Wichita State U., 1978, Alumnae award Northwestern U., 1985. Mem. Am. Assn. Higher Edn. (dir. 1974-77, pres. 1977-78), Western Coll. Assn. (pres.-elect 1988), Sigma Xi. Office: U Calif Santa Barbara Office of Chancellor Cheadle Hall Santa Barbara CA 93106

UFFMAN, DEBRA DAWN, insurance broker; b. Washington, Mo., Nov. 27, 1953; d. Robert Lee and Joyce Dean (Richardson) U. BS in Bus., So. Mo. State U., 1976. Underwriter Crum & Foster Ins. Co., Indpls., 1976-79, Safeco ins. Co., Kansas City, Mo., 1979-80; underwriter, marketing INA Ins. Co., Kansas City, Mo., 1980-81; in marketing Fireman's Fund Ins. Co., Kansas City, 1981-83; nat. sales dir. Fireman's Fund Ins. Co., San Francisco, Calif., 1983-85; asst. marketing v.p. Great Control Ins. Co., Peoria, Ill., 1985-86; asst. v.p., comml. mgr. Gilbert-Magrill Ins. Co., Kansas City, Mo., 1986—; cons. Ins. Agt. Orgn., Lake Ozark, Mo., 1983-84, local bus., Jefferson City, Mo., 1983-84. Author: Top 20 Brokers, 1984, Money/Religion, 1975. Mem. Dancofran Com., Kansas City, 1987—, Comets Blazer Orgn., Kansas City, 1986—, S. Platte County Athletic Group, 1986. Mem. Women's C. of C., Kansas City Ins. Women (regional rep. 1983-84), Indep. Ins. Agts. (recipient mktg. award 1980), Young Agts., Cert. Ins. Counelors Soc. Sigma Kappa. Democrat. Methodist. Home: 4368 NW 82nd Kansas City MO 64151 Office: Gilbert-Magill Ins Co 1220 Washington Kansas City MO 64105

UFFNER, BETH MARILYN, television and film agent; b. N.Y.C., Sept. 30, 1942; d. George and Lillian Elizabeth (Becker) U.; 1 child, Darlene. BA, NYU, 1964. Asst. producer Tony Awards, N.Y.C., 1967-69; assoc. producer Emmy Awards, Los Angeles, 1969-74; casting dir. Barney Miller, Hollywood, Calif., 1974-76; casting exec. NBC-TV, Burbank, Calif., 1977; dir. comedy devel. Warner Bros. TV, Burbank, 1977-79; agt., exec. Internat. Creative Mgmt., Los Angeles, 1979-82; v.p. MTM Enterprises, Studio City, Calif., 1982-85; pres. Beth Uffner & Assocs., Studio City, 1985—. Office: Beth Uffner & Assocs 12725 Ventura Blvd Studio City CA 91604

UGAI, SUSAN MARIE, lawyer; b. North Platte, Nebr., Jan. 4, 1956; d. Norman F. and Alice T. (Nakada) U. BA, U. Nebr., 1978, JD, 1981. Bar: Nebr. 1981, U.S. Dist. Ct. Nebr. 1981, U.S. Ct. Appeals (8th cir.) 1986, U.S. Supreme Ct. Law clk. intern Nebr. Dept. Aging, Lincoln, 1979-81; city atty. City of North Platte, 1981-85; legal services developer Nebr. Dept. Aging, Lincoln, 1985-86; asst. atty. gen. Nebr. Dept. Justice, 1986—. Mem. adv. bd. Salvation Army, North Platte, 1981-85; chmn. edn. and prevention com. Sexual Assault Task Force, 1984-85; mem. North Platte Area Women's Council, 1983-85; mem. Women in Transition/Displaced Homemaker Adv. Bd., 1982-85; bd. dirs. Camp Fire Girls, Inc., 1st v.p. 1986-88; bd. dirs. Job Outfitters, chair, 1986—; mem. planning div. United Way. Mem. ABA (exec. com. young lawyers div. com. on delivery legal services to elderly 1983-87), Nat. Inst. Mcpl. Law Officers (chmn. Nebr. 1983-85), Nebr. State Bar Assn. (co-vice chairperson young lawyers sect. com. on delivery legal services to elderly 1981—), Nat. Fedn. Bus. and Profl. Women (local treas. 1984-85, dist. YCW chmn. 1984-85, State PAC chmn. 1985-86). Democrat. Episcopalian. Office: Nebr Dept Justice 2115 State Capitol Lincoln NE 68509

UGISS-ALTIERI, CAROLYN, real estate consulting and development company executive, broker; b. Scott Field, Ill., Nov. 19, 1947; d. Philip Patrick and Marcia (Truxton) U.; m. Donald R. Altieri, Dec. 12, 1982. B.S., Cornell U., 1969. Lic. real estate broker, N.Y., Colo.; lic. real estate salesperson, Calif. Pub. relations dir. Smoke Watchers Internat., N.Y.C., 1969-73; mktg. dir. Environ. Research & Devel., N.Y.C., 1973-76; exec. v.p. CPC/Corp. Planners and Coordinators, Inc., N.Y.C., 1976—, dir. subs. cos.; dir. Beri, Inc., Salem, Oreg. Mem. Real Estate Bd. N.Y. Club: Cornell of Fairfield County (Conn.). Office: CPC Corp Planners and Coordinators 645 Fifth Ave 21st Floor New York NY 10022

UHLENBECK, KAREN KESKULLA, mathematician, educator; b. Cleve., Aug. 24, 1942; d. Arnold Edward and Carolyn Elizabeth (Windeler) Keskulla; m. Olke Cornelis, June 12, 1965 (div.). B.S. in Math., U. Mich., 1964; Ph.D. in Math., Brandeis U., 1968. Instr. math. MIT, Cambridge, 1968-69; lectr. U. Calif.-Berkeley, 1969-71; asst. prof. U. Ill.-Urbana, 1971-78; assoc. prof., then prof. U. Ill.-Urbana, Chgo., 1977-83; prof. U. Chgo., 1983-88; Sid Richardson Centennial Chair in Math. U. Tex., 1988—. Author: Instantons and Four Manifolds, 1984. Contbr. articles to profl. jours. Fellow Sloan Found., 1974-76, MacArthur Found., 1983; grad. fellow NSF, 1964-68. Mem. Nat. Acad. Scis., Alumni Assn. U. Mich. (Alumnae of Yr. 1984), Am. Math. Soc., Am. Women in Math., Phi Beta Kappa. Office: Math Dept U Tex Austin TX 78712

UHRIG, BARBARA LOUISE, secondary school special education professional; b. Ft. Wayne, Ind., Feb. 20, 1942; d. Joseph and Charlotte (Masursky) Schuster; m. Donald Komito, Aug. 21, 1960 (div. Sept. 1969); m. James Warren Uhrig, June 5, 1970. BS, Miami U., Oxford, Ohio, 1967; MS, Butler U., 1972. Lic. profl. tchr. Tchr. learning disabilities Indpls. Pub. Schs., 1969-79, dept. chairperson, 1979—. Mem. Learning Disabilities Council (pres. 1987—), Ind. Assn. for Children and Adults with Learning Disabilities (v.p. 1984—). Democrat. Jewish. Home: 7367 E 16th Indianapolis IN 46219 Office: NW High Sch 5525 W 34th St Indianapolis IN 46225

UHRMAN, CELIA, artist, poet; b. New London, Conn., May 14, 1927; d. David Aaron and Pauline (Schwartz) U. BA, Bklyn. Coll., 1948, MA, 1953; PhD, U. Danzig, 1977; postgrad. Tchrs. Coll., Columbia U., 1961, CUNY, 1966, Bklyn. Mus. Art Sch., 1956-57, PhD (hon.), LittD, 1973; cert. Koret Living Library U. of San Francisco, 1982. One-woman shows: Leffert Jr. High Sch., Bklyn., 1958, Flatbush C. of C., N.Y.C., 1963, Conn. C. of C., New London, 1962; exhibited in group shows: Smithsonian Instn., Washington, 1958, Springfield (Mass.) Mus. Fine Arts, 1959, Bklyn. Mus., 1959, Old Mystic (Conn.) Art Center, 1959, Carnegie Endowment Internat. Center, N.Y.C., 1959, Lyman Allyn Mus., New London, 1960, Palacio de La Virrelna, Barcelona, Spain, 1961, YMCA, Bklyn., 1962, UFT Art Exhibit, N.Y.C., 1963, Soc. of 4 Arts, Palm Beach, Fla., 1964, Perspective 68, Monte-Carlo, Monaco, 1968, George W. Wingate High sch., Bklyn., 1967, Premier Salon Internat., Charleroi, Belgium, 1968, Palme d'or Beaux Arts, Monte-Carlo, 1970, 72, Dibuix-Joan Miro Premi Internacional, Barcelona, 1970; N.Y. Art Festival, 1970, Internat. Platform Assn. Art Show, Washington, 1971, 73, Ovar Mus., Portugal, 1974, others; represented in permanent collections: Bklyn. Coll., Ch. of Evangel, Bklyn.; tchr. N.Y.C. Sch. System, 1948-82; ptnr. Uhrman Studio, 1973-83). hon. rep. U.S., Centro Studi E Scambi Internazionali, Rome, mem. Internat. Com., 1969. Hon. life mem. World Poetry Day Com., Inc. and Nat. Poetry Day Com., 1977. Recipient award Freedoms Found., George Washington medal of honor, 1964, Diplome d'Honneur Palme d'Or des Beaux Arts Exhbn., Monaco, 1969, 72, Diploma and Gold medal, Centro Studi E Scambi Internazionali, 1972; decorated Order of Gandhi Award of Honour, Knight Grand Cross, 1972; personal poetry certificate WEFG Stereo, 1970; Gold Laurel award Esposizione Internazionale D'Art Contemporain, Paris, 1974; named Poetry Translator Laureate World Acad. Lang. and Lit., 1972, Poet of Mankind Acad. Philosophy, 1972; cert. of appreciation Bd. Edn. of N.Y.C., 1982. Fellow World Lit. Academy Eng.; mem. Internat. Arts Guild (comdr. 1966—), World Poetry Soc. Intercontinental (rep. at large 1969—), Internat. Acad. Poets (founding fellow), N.Y. Artists Equity. Author: Poetic Ponderances, 1969, A Pause for Poetry, 1970, Poetic Love Fancies, 1970, A Pause for Poetry for Children, 1973, The Chimps Are Coming, 1975, Love Fancies, 1987. Home: 1655 Flatbush Ave Apt and Studio C106 Brooklyn NY 11210

UHRMAN, ESTHER, artist, writer, retired social worker; b. New London, Conn., July 7, 1921; d. David Aaron and Pauline (Schwartz) U. Grad. Traphagen Sch. Fashion, 1955; Diploma Di Benemerenza, Centro Studi E Scambi Internat., Rome, 1972, Diploma Academia Leonardo Da Vinci, 1980; A.A., N.Y.C. Community Coll., 1974; cert. in labor relations Cornell U., 1976, cert. unemployment ins. advocate, 1984; Ph.D., Danzig U., Poland, 1977; Ph.D. (hon.) World Acad. Langs. and Lit., 1977. Self-employed writer, artist, Bklyn., 1954—; social worker N.Y. State, Bklyn., N.Y.C., 1959-76; ptnr. Uhrman Studio, Bklyn., 1973-83. Author: Gypsy Logic, 1970, From Canarsie to Masada, 1978, Mitras II, 1988; (radio play) Holland 2067, 1971 (Golden Windmill award 1970); asst. editor: Inside Detective, 1977; contbr. articles to profl. jours.; two-man art shows include Ligoa Duncan Gallery, N.Y.C., 1960, New London C. of C., 1962, Flatbush C. of C., 1963, Uhrman Studio, 1973-83; exhibited in group shows at Traphagen Sch. Fashion, N.Y.C., 1954-55, Carnegie Endowment Internat. Ctr., N.Y.C., 1959, Exposcion De Obras, Palacio De La Virreina, Barcelona, Spain, 1961, Smithsonian Inst., Washington, 1962, Cape May (N.J.) County Lighthouse, 1965, N.Y. Art Festival, 1970, Premier Internacional Dibuix, Barcelona, 1970, Internat. Platform Assn., Washington, 1972-73. Recipient Civilian Service award U.S. Army, 1944, five N.Y. State awards, 1962-65, Silver medal Verso Mexico, 1968, cert. Stamp Designs, 1968, cert. Merit Rassegna Internazionale D'Arte Grafica, Ovar Mus., Portugal, 1974, cert. Merit 26th Exposition D'Arte Contemporain, Luxemborg, 1974. Fellow World Literary Acad., Internat. Acad. Poets (co-founder). Mem. AFL-CIO, Internat. Arts Guild (commandeur, Diplome D'Honneur award 1976), N.Y. Artists Equity Assn., World Poetry Soc. Intercontinental, Dist. Council 37 Retirees. Avocations: walking, theatre, anthropology. Home and Office: 1655 Flatbush Ave Apt C106 Brooklyn NY 11210

UITERMARK, HELEN JOAN, computing services executive; b. Zandvoort, Netherlands, May 4, 1941; came to U.S., 1968, naturalized, 1977; d. Peter Theodore and Maria Francisca (Castien) U.; ed. London, Ont., Can. With Drug Trading Co., London, 1957-59, Richard-Wilcox, London, 1959-62, Friden Bus. Machines, Toronto, Ont., 1962-68, Permatex, West Palm Beach, Fla., 1968-70, Singer Bus. Machines, London, Ont., Can., 1970-72, Los Angeles, 1972-74; with Safariland Leather Co., Monrovia, Calif., 1974-81, v.p. adminstrn., 1975-81; ind. systems analyst, Los Angeles, 1981-83; owner Timor Computing Services, Azusa, Calif., 1983—; exec. dir. Forum Internat., 1983—. Mem. Forum Internat., Aircraft Owners and Pilots Assn.

ULAGARAJ, SANTHI, computer programmer, analyst; b. Kadaiyanodai, Tamil Nadu, India, June 25, 1947; arrivd in Can., 1975; Can. citizen.; d. Velayutham and Shunmuga Sundaram (Pichandy) Kumarandy; m. Muniyandy S. Ulagaraj, Sept. 2, 1970; children: Monika, Vasu. Grad. high school, Tamil Nadu. Key punch clk. Bell Can., Montreal, Que., Can., 1976-81, AGT Province of Alta., Edmonton, 1981-85; computer programmer, analyst Province of Alta., Edmonton, 1985—. York Elem. Sch. PTA, Edmonton, 1986—. Mem. Assn. Computing Machinery. Office: Alta Govt Telephones, 12G ATT 10020 100 St, Edmonton T5J 0N5, Can

ULICHNY, BARBARA L., state legislator; b. Milw., June 10, 1947; d. Clarence and Karmen (Egge) Seybold. BA in Econ., Northwestern U., 1969. Tchr. Nicolet High Sch., Milw., 1969-74; adminstr. bicentennial City of Milw., 1975-76; program staff YWCA, Milw., 1976-78; mem. Wis. Assembly, Madison, 1978-84, Wis. Senate, Madison, 1984—; chmn. senate com. econ. devel., crime victim's council. Mem. Common Cause, Italian Community Ctr., Profl. Dimensions, Wis. Heritages, Watertower Landmark Trust, Milw. Task Force on Rape/Sexual Assault and Domestic Violence, Hist. Lower E. Side Neighborhood Assn.; adv. bd. ctr. study of entrepreneurship Marquette U.; bd. dirs. Milw. Ballet, Visiting Nurses Corp. Recipient Pub. Interest award Ctr. for Pub. Representation, 1977, Wis. Women's Polit. Caucus award, 1979, 81, Woman of Yr. award, NOW, 1980, Nat. Orgn. Victim Assistance award, 1981, Meritorious Service award Phi Kappa Phi, 1984. Mem. Nat. Conf. State Legislature (com. fed. taxation, trade and econ. devel.), Council State Govt. (bus. devel. task force), Wis. Women's Network, LWV. Democrat. Lutheran. Office: Wis State Senate PO Box 7882 Madison WI 53707-7882 also: 3063 N Murray Ave Milwaukee WI 53211

ULLMAN, MARIE, manufacturing company executive; b. Linlithgo, N.Y., Mar. 19, 1914; d. Max and Sarah (Jaffe) Michaelson; R.N., Bklyn. Hosp., 1935; m. Robert Ullman, Aug. 15, 1935. Pres., sec.-treas. Ullman Devices Corp., Ridgefield, Conn., 1938—; dir. State Nat. Bank Conn., Ridgefield. Mem. C. of C. Ridgefield, Bklyn. Hosp. Nurses Alumnae. Home: 43 Chestnut Hill Rd Wilton CT 06897 Office: PO Box 398 Ridgefield CT 06877

ULLO, CATHERINE A., process engineering supervisor; b. Corpus Christi, Tex., Nov. 26, 1950; d. Robert William and Sophia Lee (Rasco) Rasmussen; m. Fred Goodman, Jan. 17, 1970 (div. 1979); children: Christopher, Clinton, Aryn, Jason. BSChemE, U. Wyo., 1981. Process engr. Mostek, Colorado Springs, Colo., 1981-85; supr. process engring. United Technologies Microelectronics Ctr., Colorado Springs, 1985—. Fellow Elecrochem. Soc. Republican.

ULMER, HARRIET GLASS, health services adminstrator; b. St. Louis, June 7, 1940; d. Melvin Gabriel and Deenie Joy (Laskowitz) Shcolnik; m. Allen L. Glass, Sept. 4, 1956 (div.); children—Bonnie Nielson, Bernard J., Laura L.; m. 2d, Raymond A. Ulmer, Feb. 26, 1980 (div.). A.B. in English, UCLA, 1976; M.P.A. in Health Services Adminstrn., U. So. Calif., 1980. Regional project coordinator Kaiser Found. Health Plan, Los Angeles, 1977-80; dir. planning and mktg. Hosp. of Good Samaritan, Los Angeles, 1981, v.p. mktg. and bus. devel., 1981-86; cons. healthcare Laventhol & Horwath, Los Angeles, 1986-87; Western regional dir. provider services Provident Life and Accident Ins. Co., Los Angeles, 1987—; cons. Humana Corp., Los Angeles Health Planning and Devel. Agy. Mem. Coro Assocs.; mem. Los Angeles Area Planning Com. Mem. Am. Hosp. Assn., Am. Coll. Healthcare Execs., Women in Health Adminstrn., Healthcare Execs. of So. Calif., So. Calif. Soc. for Hosp. Planners, Am. Soc. Hosp. Planning, Am. Mktg. Assn. (founder, pres. health care div. So. Calif. chpt. 1984-85), Am. Heart Assn. (chmn. pub. policy edn. com. Greater Los Angeles affiliate 1982-84), Acad. Health Services Mktg. (nominating com. 1985, award coordinator and presentation com. 1987), U. So. Calif. Health Services Adminstrn. Alumni Assn. (treas. 1983-84, v.p. 1984-85). Other: 1914 Corinth #204 Los Angeles CA 90025-5535

ULRICH, GERTRUDE ANNA, retired nurse; b. Steinauer, Nebr., Oct. 19, 1922; d. Fred, Jr. and Matilda (Rinne) U.; R.N., Lincoln (Nebr.) Gen. Hosp., 1960; postgrad. Wesleyan U., Lincoln, 1960-61, B.S. in Natural Scis., 1972; postgrad. U. Nebr., 1967-68, Omaha U., 1966. Instr. Lincoln (Nebr.) Gen. Hosp. Sch. Nursing, 1960-61, 66-67; staff nurse Lincoln Gen. Hosp., 1961-62, 68-71; missionary nurse to Turkey, United Ch. Bd. World Ministries, N.Y.C., 1963-64, camp nurse Girl Scouts U.S.A., Nebraska City, Nebr., summer 1964; staff nurse Homestead Nursing Home, 1964-66; nursing supr. Tabitha Home, Lincoln, 1972-80, med. record supr., 1975-80; evening nursing supr. Homestead Nursing Home, Lincoln, 1980-87. Lincoln Found. ednl. grantee, 1971; named Nurse of Week, Sta. KFOR, 1973, 76. Mem. Am. Nurses Assn. Mem. Reformed Ch. Am. Home: 410 S 41 Lincoln NE 68510

ULWELLING, EILEEN IBANEZ, technologist, analyst; b. San Francisco, May 18, 1957; d. Gary Marzan and Josie (Gomez) Ibanez; m. Brice Bernard Ulwelling, May 9, 1987. BS in Microbiology, UCLA, 1980. Med. technologist Northride (Calif.) Hosp., 1981-84; programmer, analyst Northrop Corp., Hawthorne, Calif., 1984-87, Union Bank, Monterey Park, Calif., 1987-88; applications analyst FHP Inc., Costa Mesa, Calif., 1988—. Mem. Calif. State Med. Technologists, Associated Clin. Pathologists, Women in Mgmt., Associated Med. Technologists. Clin. Chemists. Home: 8204 Flowerwood Avenue Orange CA 92669 Office: FHP Inc 1620 Sunflower Ave Bldg A Costa Mesa CA 92626

UMBDENSTOCK, JUDY JEAN, educator, farmer; b. Aurora, Ill., Feb. 12, 1952; d. Alfred Alloyuisious and Mary Emma (Orha) U. AA, Elgin (Ill.) Community Coll., 1972; AS, 1973; BA, Aurora U., 1977. Cert. secondary tchr., Ill. Phys. edn. tchr., head volleyball and track coach St. Laurence Sch., Elgin, 1970-75; asst. coach varsity basketball East Aurora High Sch., 1976-77; jr. varsity coach softball St. Charles (Ill.) High Sch., 1978-79, phys. edn. tchr., 1978-79; head coach volleyball and basketball, math. tchr. Canton Jr. High Sch., Elgin, Ill., 1979-82; varsity coach volleyball and softball Elgin High Sch., 1982-85, phys. edn. tchr., 1982-86; elem. phys. edn. tchr. Sch. Dist. U-46, Elgin, 1986—; substitute tchr. Elgin, St. Charles and Burlington (Ill.) High Sch., 1977-78; referee sports Elgin and St. Charles Area High Sch., 1970—; cons. Draft and Carriage Horse Assn., Kane and Dupage Counties, 1981—. Leader, youth counselor 4-H (farming and animal husbandry), Northern Ill. area, 1970—; campaign supporter state and local Reps. for re-election, Kane county, 1974-86. Served with U.S. Army, 1976-77, with USNR, 1981-87. Named one of Outstanding Young Women Am., 1983; Elgin Panhellenic Soc.scholar, 1972. Mem. NEA, Nat. Farmers Orgn. (pub. relations 1967-80), Airplane Owners and Pilots Assn., Am. Assn. Health, Phys. Edn. and Recreation, Ill. Edn. Assn., Elgin Tchrs. Assn., Ill. Coaches Orgn., Am. Draft Horse Assn., Kane County Tchrs. Credit Union. Clubs: Barrington (Ill.) Carriage, 99's Women's Pilot Assn. Home: 8N011 Umbdenstock Rd Elgin IL 60123 Office: Sch Dist U-46 E Chicago St Elgin IL 60120

UMPHRESS, AGNES ELLEN, clin. therapist; b. Ashland, Oreg., June 27, 1925; d. Charles Albert and Mabel (Rice) White; B.A., Willamette U., 1947; M.S.W., U. Wash., 1961; m. Rupert Hampton Umphress, Jan. 20, 1962. Supr., Harry & David, Medford, Oreg., 1947-56; med. social worker Oreg. Welfare Commn., 1956-59; clin. therapist U. Wash., 1961-68; chief therapist Children's Home Soc. Wash., Tacoma, 1968-78; co-owner, therapist Counseling Resource Center, Inc., Chehalis, Wash., 1979—; adv. bd. Child Abuse Program, 1974-78, Sexual Assault Program, 1977-78, Family Planning Assn., 1975-80. Cert. Acad. Cert. Social Workers. Mem. Nat. Assn. Social Workers, Nat. Assn. Clin. Social Workers, Am. Assn. Psychiat. Services for Children, Am. Orthopsychiat. Assn. Republican. Club: Sertoma. Contbr. articles to profl. jours. Research on therapeutic programs in technologically advanced and Third World nations. Home: 625 Tauscher Rd Chehalis WA 98532 Office: 118 N Market Blvd Chehalis WA 98532

UNDERHILL, ANNE BARBARA, astrophysicist; b. Vancouver, B.C., Can., June 12, 1920; d. Frederic Clare and Irene Anna (Creery) U. BA, U. B.C., 1942, MA, 1944; PhD, U. Chgo., 1948; DSc (hon.), York U., Toronto, Ont., 1969. Sci. officer Dominion Astrophys. Obs., Victoria, B.C., 1949-62; prof. astrophysics U. Utrecht, The Netherlands, 1962-70; lab chief Goddard Space Flight Ctr./NASA, Greenbelt, Md., 1970-77, sr. scientist, 1978-85; hon. prof. U. B.C., Vancouver, 1985—. Author: The Early-type Stars, 1966; author/editor: B Stars with and without Emission Lines, 1982, O, Of and

Wolf-Rayet Stars, 1988; contbr. articles to profl. jours. Fellow NRC, 1948, Can. Fedn. Univ. Women, 1944, 47. Fellow Royal Soc. Can., Royal Astron. Soc.; mem. Internat. Astron. Union (pres. commn. #36 1963-66), Am. Astron. Soc., Can. Astron. Soc. Anglican. Office: U of Brit Columbia, Dept of Geophysics and Astronomy, Vancouver CANADA V6T 1W5

UNDERKOFLER, JOYCE MARIE, nursing home administrator; b. Buffalo Center, Iowa, Apr. 21, 1933; d. George Stephen and Mary Elizabeth (Leslie) U. RN, Mercy Sch. of Nursing, Cedar Rapids, Iowa, 1953; credential, U. Minn., 1981. Lic. nursing home adminstr., Minn. Nurse Mercy Hosp., Des Moines, 1953-55, St. Francis Hosp., Grinell, Iowa, 1955-57, St. Josephs Hosp., Brainerd, Minn., 1957-67; adminstr. Cedarbrook Manor, Deerwood, Minn., 1967-73; dir. Region V Area Agy. on Aging, Staples, Minn., 1973-75; adminstr. Martin Luther Manor, Bloomington, Minn., 1975-86; exec. v.p. long term care Ebenezer Soc., Mpls., 1986-88; adminstr. Lakeshore Luth. Home, Duluth, Minn., 1988—. Mem. sr. citizens adv. council to Bloomington City Council, 1980-83; treas. Friends of Minn. Valley, Bloomington, 1982—. Mem. Minn. Assn. Homes for Aging (bd. dirs. 1983—, sec., treas. 1985—), Bloomington C. of C. (treas. 1984-86, Leadership Bloomington award 1985). Roman Catholic. Club: Mpls. Torch (sec. 1984-88). Office: Lakeshore Luth Home 4002 London Rd Duluth MN 55804

UNDERLAND-ROSOW, VICKI LOUISE, psychotherapy consultant; b. Moline, Ill., Dec. 4, 1947; d. Arthur Underland and Virginia (Walsh) Severson; m. Richard Francis Rosow, Jan 15, 1972; children: Michael, Katherine. BS, Mankato State U., 1968; MSW, U. Mich., 1977; postgrad., Union for Experimental Colls. and Univs. Social worker Welcome Community Group Homes, Mpls., 1974; instr. U. N.D., Grand Forks, 1975-77; programs specialist U. Mich., Ann Arbor, 1977-79; psychotherapist Park-Nicollet Clinic, St. Louis Park, Minn., 1979-82; asst. prof. Colls. of St. Catherine and St. Thomas, St. Paul, 1982-83; clin. instr. Sch. Social Work U. Minn., Mpls., 1980—; co-dir. Wo/mens Renewal, Mpls., 1983—; pvt. practice psychotherapy Mpls., 1982—; facilatator, cons. Anne Wilson Scheaf Assn., Boulder, Colo., 1982—; cons. Minn. Dept. Edn., St. Paul, 1981-82. Mem. Nat. Assn. Social Workers. Office: 4530 Excelsior Blvd Saint Louis Park MN 55416

UNDERWOOD, PATRICIA RUTH, educator, consultant; b. Lubbock, Tex., Dec. 7, 1939; d. Thomas S. Underwood and Lilian (Baker) Davis. BS in Nursing, U. Colo., 1962; MA, NYU, 1965; D Nursing Sci., U. Calif., San Francisco, 1978. Lectr. U. San Francisco, 1969-73; clin. specialist Langley Porter Inst., San Francisco, 1973-79; clin. prof. U. Calif., San Francisco, 1979—; cons. VA, Western Region, 1975—, Hasegawa Hosp., Japan, 1984—, dept. nursing Tel Aviv U., 1986—. Mem. Am. Nurses Assn., Calif. Nursing Assn. (pres. 1983-85), Sigma Theta Tau. Democrat. Home: 5160 Diamond Heights Blvd #C105 San Francisco CA 94131 Office: U Calif San Francisco Dept Mental Health Community Adminstrv Nursing San Francisco CA 94143

UNDERWOOD, SHIRLEY DIANE, educator; b. Long Beach, Calif., May 3, 1944; d. Elmer Earl and Geneva (Ingram) Boyd; m. Berdett P. Underwood, Mar. 25, 1983. AA, Compton Jr. Coll., 1964; BA, U. Calif., Fullerton, 1983. Cert. tchr. Assn. Christian Schs. Internat. Sec. Orange (Calif.) Christian Sch., 1977-79; tchr. Calvary Christian Sch., Stanton, Calif., 1980-82, Garden Grove (Calif.) Christian Sch., 1983—. Republican. Mem. Assembly God Ch. Home: 2400 E Lincoln #114 Anaheim CA 92806 Office: Garden Grove Christian Sch 13201 Century Blvd Garden Grove CA 92643

UNFRIED, DONA LEE, clergywoman, realtor; b. Los Angeles, Oct. 11, 1928; d. Howard Peter and Helyn Grace (Howson) Wraith; student Santa Monica State Coll., 1948; grad. Unity Sem., 1973, D.D., 1981; diploma in hypnotherapy Ft. Worth Inst., 1970; m. Sept. 1, 1950 (div. 1969); children—Robert F., Teri Lynn. Mgmt. personnel Pacific Telephone, Sacramento, 1947-68; mgr. Match-O-Mates, Ft. Worth, 1968-70; ordained to ministry Unity Ch., 1973; minister Unity Village Chapel, Kansas City, Mo., 1972-75; sr. minister Unity Ch., Overland Park, Kans., 1975-76; sr. minister, chmn. bd. Unity Ch. of Light, Longview, Tex., 1976-83; realty mgr. Realty World, Longview, 1976-83; v.p. Century C-21, 1982; owner employment agy., La Jolla, Calif., 1984-87; interviewer Census Bur., U.S. Gov. Dept Commerce, Los Angeles, 1987—; tchr. in field; condr. workshops; counselor. Mem. Indsl. relations com., public relations com. Longview C. of C., 1981; bd. dirs. Gateway Found., Sacramento. Mem. Internat. New Thought Alliance, Nat. Assn. Realtors, Tex. Assn. Realtors, Million Dollar Club, Nat. Assn. Female Execs., Assn. Unity Chs., Longview Assn. Realtors, Longview Bd. Realtors (chmn. edn. com. 1982). Club: Toasmistresses (pres. Limerick club 1967; numerous speaking awards 1966-72. Home: 500 Hill St Santa Monica CA 90405

UNGARO, JOAN, theater director and writer; b. Bronx, Jan. 8, 1951; d. John Daniel and Alice Cecilia (Murray) U. BA, Thomas More Coll., 1971; postgrad., Hunter Coll., 1972. Asst. lit. editor The Nation, N.Y.C., 1973-74; coordinating editor Psychology Today, N.Y.C., 1977-81; writer Village Voice, N.Y.C., 1982-83, 87—; producer various prodns. N.Y.C., 1983, stage mgr. various theaters, 1981—, dir. various fields, 1986—. Mem. Ensemble Studio Theatre. Roman Catholic. Home and Office: 251 W 89th St Apt 5D New York NY 10024

UNGARSOHN, LORI SUE, small business owner; b. N.Y.C., Jan. 23, 1956; d. Harry and Eva (Beckerman) U. AA, Sullivan County Community Coll., 1976; BA, SUNY, Stony Brook, 1978. Pvt. practice photography South Fallsburg, N.Y., 1974-76; free-lance reporter N.Y.C., 1976-77; pres. Nation-Wide Reporting and Conv. Coverage, Inc. and affiliate, Simultaneous Wireless Interpretations, N.Y.C., 1985—. Contbr. articles to profl. jours., 1983—. Mem. Nat. Assn. for Female Execs., Smithsonian Inst., Phi Beta Kappa. Republican. Jewish. Home: 200 E 94th St Apt 404 New York NY 10028 Office: Simultaneous Wireless Interpretations 350 Broadway Suite 1108 New York NY 10013

UNGER, BARBARA FRANKEL, educator, poet; b. N.Y.C., Oct. 2, 1932; d. David and Florence (Schuchalter) Frankel; B.A., CCNY, 1955, M.A., 1957; advanced cert. NYU, 1970; children—Deborah, Suzanne. Grad. asst. Yeshiva U., 1962-63; edn. editor County Citizen, Rockland County, N.Y., 1960-63; tchr. English, N.Y.C. Pub. Schs., 1955-58, Nyack (N.Y.) High Sch., 1963-67; guidance counselor Ardsley (N.Y.) High Sch., 1967-69; prof. English, Rockland Community Coll., Suffern, N.Y., 1969—; poetry fellow Squaw Valley Community of Writers, 1980; writer-in-residence Rockland Ctr. for Arts, 1986; author: Basement (Poems 1959-65), The Man Who Burned Money, Inside the Wind; contbr. poetry to over 40 lit. mags., including: Kans. Quar., Carolina Quar., Beloit Poetry Jour., Minn. Rev., Poet and Critic, The Nation, Poetry Now, Invisible City, Thirteenth Moon, So. Poetry Rev., Mass. Rev., Nebr. Rev., Wis. Rev.; The Man Who Burned Money, 1981; contbr. to Anthology Mag. Verse, Yearbook Am. Poetry, 1984; Ragdale Found. fellow, 1985. Nat. Endowment for Humanities grantee, 1975; SUNY Creative Writing fellow, 1981-82; Edna St. Vincent Millay Colony fellow, 1984; poetry readings in colls. and libraries throughout N.Y. and elsewhere; critical reviewer Contact II; finalist W.Va. Writing Competition, 1982. Mem. Poets and Writers, Poetry Soc. Am., Writers' Community; honorable mention Chester Jones Nat. Poetry Contest; fiction appeared in True to Life Adventure Stories. Office: Rockland Community Coll 145 College Rd Suffern NY 10901

UNGER, MARIANNE LOUISE, computer graphics artist, consultant; b. Reading, Pa., June 8, 1957; d. Paul Richard and Virginia Ruth (Moyer) U. BS in Art Edn., Kutztown U., 1982. Art tchr. 7 local sch. dists., Reading, 1982-83; sec. Berks Cable, Reading, 1983-84, project asst. new bus. devel., 1984-85; art educator Reading Area Community Coll., Reading, 1983—; pres. Marianne Unger Computer Graphics, Reading, 1985—; cons. in field. Grantee NET Ben Franklin Advanced Tech. Ctr., 1986-87. Mem. Nat. Computer Graphics Assn., Berks Women's Network, Berks County C. of C. Office: 1313 Good St Reading PA 19602

UNGER, MARY ANN, artist, sculptor. B.A. magna cum laude, Mt. Holyoke Coll., 1967; postgrad. U. Calif.-Berkeley, 1968; M.F.A., Columbia U., 1975. Tchr. elem. art Adirondack Central Sch. (N.Y.), 1970-71; tchr. art therapy program, children Columbia Presbyn. Med. Ctr., 1974; instr. intaglio techniques Printmaking Workshop, N.Y.C., 1974-75; instr. ceramics, children Third St. Music Settlement, N.Y.C., 1976-77; instr. ceramic sculpture Coll. Mt. St. Vincent, N.Y.C., 1977; instr. etching, studio founds. Montclair State Coll. (N.J.), 1977-78; instr. sculpture, 3-D design Kutztown State Coll. (Pa.), 1979; mem. faculty, adult degree program Goddard Coll. (Vt.), 1979-80; vis. artist, lectr., various schs., 1979-81. One-woman shows: Mt. Holyoke Coll., South Hadley, Mass., 1967, Columbia U., 1975; 10 Downtown, N.Y.C., 1977, CUNY Grad. Ctr., N.Y.C., 1982, 55 Mercer, N.Y.C., 1983, John Jay Coll., N.Y.C., 1984, Tweed Courthouse, N.Y.C., 1985, Sculpture Ctr., N.Y.C., 1986; group shows include: Aldrich Mus. Contemporary Art, Ridgefield, Conn., 1977, Boulder Arts Center, 1979, Hudson River Mus., Yonkers, N.Y., 1981; Bronx River Restoration Center, N.Y.C., 1983, Sculpture Center, N.Y.C., 1983; represented in permanent collections: E. F. Hutton, Inc., Best & Co., Columbia U., N.Y.C., Mt. Holyoke Coll., Printmaking Workshop; also pvt. collections. Subject of profl. publs.; Recipient numerous awards in field.

UNGER, PAMELA GALE, physical therapist; b. Allentown, Pa., Mar. 7, 1954; d. Franklin Alfred and Doris Ardell (Keim) Fenstermacher; m. Jeffrey Michael Unger, Apr. 23, 1977; children: Stephanie Anne, Jeremy Tod. Student, U. Pitts., 1972-74; BS, U. Pa., 1976. Cert. phys. therapist. Phys. therapist St. Joseph Hosp., Reading, Pa., 1976-78, clin. coordinator phys. therapy, 1977-78; phys. therapist Berks Vis. Nurse, Home Health Agy., Reading, 1978-81; dir. phys. therapy Leader Nursing and Rehab. Ctr., Laureldale, Pa., 1981-84; cons. phys. therapy Profl. Home Health Care Agy., West Reading, Pa., 1982—; dir. phys. therapy Martin, McGough & Eddy Phys. Therapy Services, Somerset, Pa., 1984-85, dir. ea. region, wound care specialist, 1986—; cons. wound care Allegheny and Chesapeake Phys. Therapists, Inc., Johnstown, Pa., 1986—; chief investigator project research Phys. Therapy Found., Alexandria, Va., 1986—, U. Pitts., 1986—. Coach Kutztown (Pa.) Area High Sch., 1985—, chmn. membership com. Kutztown Area Hist. Soc., 1982-84. Grantee Phys. Therapy Found., 1986-88. Mem. Am. Phys. Therapy Assn., Pa. Phys. Therapy Assn. (chmn. continuing edn. com. 1987—). Republican. Mem. United Ch. of Christ. Lodge: Lioness (treas. Bowers, Pa. club 1984—). Home: 443 Wentz St Kutztown PA 19530 Office: Martin McGough and Eddy Office Research and Clin Programs Kutztown PA 19530

UNGER, WENDY SUE, public relations professional; b. N.Y.C., Mar. 28, 1949; d. Harold Milton and Caryl (Rose) Unger. BA, U. Miami, Fla., 1970. Salesperson Jordan Marsh, Miami, Fla., 1970-71, mgmt. trainee, 1971-72, personnel trainer, 1972-74, 74-75; personnel trainer Thalheimers, Richmond, Va., 1974; hotel mgr. Royal Palm Hotel, Miami Beach, Fla., 1975-82, pub. relations cons., 1982—; mgmt. trainee Flagler Fed. Savs. and Loan, Miami, Fla., 1982, community relations officer, 1982—; distbr. Spicers Internat., Oglesby, Ill. Mem. Miami Beach Commn. on Women, 1981-84, Miami's For Me. Mem. Pub. Relation Soc. Am., Bus. and Profl. Women Assn., Miami Beach C. of C., Miami Beach Jaycee Women (charter pres. 1979). Democrat. Jewish. Club: Koach-Hadassah (Miami Beach). Home: 555 NE 15th St #15D Miami FL 33132

UNRUH, LINDA LUELLA, government research consultant, legislative aide; b. Los Angeles, Dec. 4, 1955; d. Jesse Marvin and Virginia June (Lemon) U. BA, U. Calif., Davis, 1976; postgrad., Georg August U., Goettingen, Fed. Republic Germany, 1978. Sr. admissions coordinator Sacramento Med. Ctr., 1976-78; field dir. U.S. Census Bur., Los Angeles, 1979-80; staff asst. The White House, Washington, 1980-81; asst. to speaker Calif. State Assembly, Los Angeles, 1981-86; cons. Calif. Assembly Office of Research, Sacramento, 1987—. Mem. exec. com. Calif. Dems., 1983-87; dir. People in Progress, Inc., Los Angeles, 1986-87. Mem. Coalition of Labor Union Women (exec. bd. dirs. 1982-87), Los Angeles County Fedn. of Labor (del. 1982-87), U.S. Youth Council (del. 1985—). Home: 2100 Blanche Rd Manhattan Beach CA 90266 Office: Assembly Office of Research Sacramento CA 95814

UNSER, BARBARA ANN KREISLE, controller, consultant; b. Hawesville, Ky., Mar. 12, 1936; d. Darwin George and Esther Bell (Mosbey) Kreisle; m. Curtis Franklin Wardrip, Oct. 3, 1953 (div. Apr. 1978); children: Angela Gay Wardrip Cox, Tina Darlene Wardrip Pepito; m. Jan Frederick Unser, June 20, 1987. BA, Bellarmine Coll., 1974. Bookkeeper Custom Photo Art Service, Louisville, 1964-67; dir. pupil personnel Jefferson County Bd. Edn., Louisville, 1967-70; with steel sales Wheeling-Pitts. Steel, Louisville, 1978-81; salesperson Med-Am. Steel Co., St. Louis, 1978-81, Jones and Laughlin Steel, Louisville, 1981-84, Charlestowne Furniture, St. Louis, 1984-87; account exec. Sta. WKCM Radio, Hawesville, 1984-87; controller Joseph H. Vatterott & Bldg. Co., St. Louis, 1987—; photo negative retoucher Custom-Photo Art Service, Louisville, 1965-67; communications counselor Jones & Laughlin Steel, Louisville, Ky., 1978-81; cons., advisor Cox Bros. Door Co., St. Louis, 1986—. Republican. Baptist. Home: 2380 Brook Dr Florissant MO 63033 Office: Mid-America Steel Corp 962 Hays Ave Saint Louis MO 63130

UNTERBERGER, BETTY MILLER, history educator, writer; b. Glasgow, Scotland, Dec. 27, 1923; d. Joseph C. and Leah Miller; m. Robert Ruppe, July 27, 1944; children: Glen, Gail, Gregg. B.A., Syracuse U., N.Y., 1943; M.A., Harvard U., 1946; Ph.D., Duke U., 1950. Asst. prof. E. Carolina U., Greenville, 1948-50; assoc. prof., dir. liberal arts ctr. Whittier Coll., Calif., 1954-61; assoc. prof. Calif. State U.-Fullerton, 1961-65, prof., chmn. grad. studies, 1965-68; prof. Tex. A&M U., College Station, 1968—; vis. prof. U. Hawaii, Honolulu, summer 1967, vis. disting. prof. U. Calif., Irvine, 1987—; mem. adv. com. fgn. relations U.S. Dept. State, 1977-81, chair, 1981; mem. U.S. Dept. Army Hist. Adv. Com., 1980-82; commr. Nat. Hist. Publs. and Records Commn., 1980—. Author: America's Siberian Expedition 1918-1920: A Study of National Policy, 1956, 69 (Pacific Coast award Am. Hist. Assn. 1956); editor: American Intervention in the Russian Civil War, 1969, Intervention Against Communism: Did the U.S. Try to Overthrow the Soviet Government, 1918-20, 1986; contbr.: Woodrow Wilson and Revolutionary World, 1982; editorial adv. bd.: The Papers of Woodrow Wilson, Princeton U., 1982; bd. editors: Diplomatic History, 1981-84, Red River Valley Hist. Rev., 1975-84. Trustee Am. Inst. Pakistan Studies, Villanova U., Pa., 1981—. Fellow Woodrow Wilson Found., 1979; named Disting. Teacher State of Calif. Legislature, 1966; recipient All-Univ. Disting. Teaching award Tex. A&M U., 1975. Mem. Am. Hist. Assn. (chair 1982-83, nominating com. 1980-83), Orgn. Am. Historians (govt. relations com.), Soc. Historians of Am. Fgn. Relations (exec. council 1978-81, 86-89, govt. relations com. 1982-84, v.p. 1985, pres. 1986), Rocky Mountain Assn. Slavic Studies (program chair 1973, v.p. 1973-74), So. Hist. Assn., Asian Studies Assn., NOW, LWV, AAUW, Beyond War, Audubon Soc., Phi Beta Kappa. Office: Tex A&M U College Station TX 77843

UNTERBRINK, NANCI LORINE, banker; b. Longmont, Colo., June 19, 1953; d. James Thomas and Opal Berdena (Abraham) Atkinson; m. Donald Dee Unterbrink, June 21, 1975 (div. Aug. 1982). BA, Ea. Ill. U., 1975. Cert. secondary sch. tchr., Ill. Substitute tchr. Neoga (Ill.) Jr. High Sch., 1975-76; pub. relations Ill. Capital Devel. Bd., Springfield, 1976-79; realtor Century 21 Evans Real Estate, Springfield, 1979-81; deli mgr. Eisner Food Store, Springfield, 1981-83; loan processor Firstbank Mortgage Co., Springfield, 1983-84, closing coordinator, 1984-85, loan originator, 1985—, br. mgr., 1986—; fin. dir. Springfield Realtors Orientation, 1986-87. Dir. bd. dirs. Lincolnfest, chmn. Lincolnfest Roving Entertainers, Springfield, Ill., 1980-84, Lincolnfest Gt. Parade, 1984-86, Lincolnfest Pub. Relations, 1987; chmn. Springfield Realtors United Way, 1987. Recipient Outstanding Achievement award Firstbank Mortgage Co., 1985. Mem. Women in Mgmt., Mortgage Bankers of Am., Nat. Assn. Realtors, Ill. Assn. Realtors, Women Realtors (pres. 1979-81). Democrat. Lutheran. Office: Firstbank Mortgage Co 1625 S 6th St Springfield IL 62703

UNTERMEYER, SALLE PODOS, lawyer; b. Bklyn., Oct. 1, 1938; d. David Meyer and Rose (Ifshin) Garber; m. Steven Maurice Podos, June 20, 1959 (div. Dec. 1978); children—Richard Lance Podos, Lisa Beth Podos; m. Walter Untermeyer, Jr., May 2, 1982. B.A., Vassar Coll., 1959; M.A., Brandeis U., 1960; J.D., Columbia U., 1977. Bar: N.Y. 1978. Assoc., Paul, Weiss, Rifkind, Wharton & Garrison, N.Y.C., 1977-79; gen. counsel v.p., sec. MacAndrews & Forbes Group, Inc., N.Y.C., 1979-81; sr. assoc. Sage Gray Todd & Sims, N.Y.C., 1981-84, Proskauer Rose Goetz & Mendelsohn, N.Y.C., 1984-87; lawyer for the homeless, 1987—. Class fund-raising chmn. Vassar Coll., 1977-80; bd. dirs. Vassar Club N.Y., 1978-80; chmn. women's div. U.S. Senate Campaign, 1970; regional chmn. U.S. Presdl. Campaign, 1972; chmn. State Rep.'s Campaign, 1973; del.-elect Interim Democratic Conv., 1974, Lawyers Com. for Gov. Carey, 1978; chmn. Mo. state legis. Nat. Council Jewish Women, 1969-75, mem. nat. affairs com., 1969-77, chmn. Mo. juvenile justice project, 1970-75, mem. legis. coordinating com. Midwestern region, 1971-75, mem. nat. task force on constl. rights, 1974-77; v.p., bd. dirs. St. Louis Jewish Community Relations Council, 1970-75, chmn. ch.-state and Black Jack Amicus Curiae coms.; v.p., bd. dirs. St. Louis chpt. Am. Jewish Com., 1969-75, chmn. urban affairs and placement for ex-offenders coms., mem. com. on status of women, 1974-77; mem. legis. liaison Coalition for Environment, St. Louis, 1970-74; bd. dirs. St. Louis Jewish Community Ctrs. Assn., 1970-74, chmn. urban affairs and legis. affairs coms.; bd. dirs. St. Louis Jewish Family and Children's Service, 1972-74, chmn. welfare rights and health services coms.; bd. dirs. Glaucoma Found., 1986—; vol. coordinator Poor People's Campaign, 1968; founder, bd. dirs. Consumer's Assn., 1967-69; founder, chmn. Urban Corps program St. Louis Mayor's Com. on Youth, 1969-72; panelist White House Conf. on Children and Youth, 1970, 72, White House Conf. on Aging, 1974, founder, bd. dirs. Mo. chpt. PEARL (Pub. Edn. and Religious Liberty), 1972-75. Woodrow Wilson Found. fellow, 1959; NDEA fellow, 1959. Mem. Assn. Bar City N.Y. (mem. continuing legal edn. com., com. on lecture), ABA, N.Y. State Bar Assn. Home: 950 Park Ave New York NY 10028

UNZ, SUSAN LOUISE M., information specialist; b. Portsmouth, Va., Oct. 15, 1955; d. Anthony Joseph Michnowicz and Barbara Ann (Hurd) Andrianos. BA in History, SUNY, Geneseo, 1977; MS in Edn., SUNY, Oswego, 1983. Cert. tchr., N.Y. Tchr. Solvay (N.Y.) Sch. Dist., 1978-83; data requirements specialist Gen. Electric Co., Syracuse, N.Y., 1984—. Tutor Literacy Vols., Syracuse, 1986—. Mem. Gen. Electric Foreman's Assn. Roman Catholic. Home: 214 Lafayette Rd Syracuse NY 13205 Office: Gen Electric Co Syracuse NY 13221

UPBIN, SHARI DOLORES KIESLER, theatrical producer; b. N.Y.C., June 18, 1941; m. Hal J. Upbin, May 29, 1969; 3 children. Master tap instr. Asst. 1st Black-Hispanic Shakespeare prodn. Julius Caesar, Coriolanus at Pub. Theatre, N.Y., 1979; dir., choreographer Matter of Opinion, Village Gate, N.Y., nat., internat. cos., 1979-82, Side by Side, Sondheim Forum Theatre, N.J., 1981; producer, dir. Vincent, The Passions of Van Gogh, N.Y., 1981; producer Bojangles, The Life of Bill Robinson, Broadway, 1984, Captain America, nat. Am. tour; dir. Fiddler on the Roof, Cabaret, Life with Father, Roar of the Grease Paint, regional theatre. Founded Queens Playhouse, N.Y., Children's Theatre, Flushing, N.Y.; mem. Willy Mays' Found. Drug Abused Children. Recipient Jaycees Service award Jr. Miss Pageants Franklin Twp., N.J., 1976. Mem. Internat. Platform Assn., Soc. Stage Dirs. Choreographers, Actors Equity Assn., Villagers Barn Theatre (1st woman pres.), Drama League N.Y. Home and Office: 45 E 89th St New York NY 10128

UPDEGRAFF, BARBARA GAIL, photographer; b. Utica, N.Y., Mar. 22, 1947; d. Reginald Kenyon Patrick and Emily Marie (Navarro) Lozito; m. Lawrence Distefano (div. Feb. 1977); children: Derrick Distefano, Trevor Distefano; m. Gordon Lee Updegraff, Sept. 10, 1977; 1 child, Brandon Lee. Student, Pace Coll., 1972-74, Mercy Coll., 1983-85. Cert. photographer, N.Y. Sec.-treas. G.L. Updegraff and Co. Inc., Baldwin Place, N.Y., 1978—, Gluco Inc., Baldwin Place, 1986—; freelance photographer Mahopac, N.Y., 1986—; photographer Bixler Real Estate, Carmel, N.Y., 1987. One-woman shows include Catskill Ctr. Photography, Woodstock, N.Y., 1986, Rotating Gallery, West N.Y. State, 1986. Recipient cert. Achievement Putnam Arts Council. Mem. Profl. Photographers Am., Catskill Ctr. Photography, Photog. Eye (v.p. 1986-87), Friends of Photography (family), Putnam Arts Council (family, bd. dirs. 1986—, coordinator gallery 1986-87, cert. Achievement), Mercy Photo Club (pres. 1984-85), New Eng. Camera Club. Home: 28 Tamarack Rd Mahopac NY 10541 Office: GL Updegraff and Co Inc PO Box 160 Baldwin Place NY 10505

UPDIKE, HELEN HILL, economist, consultant, educator; b. N.Y.C., Mar. 27, 1941; d. Benjamin Harvey and Helen (Gray) Hill; m. Charles Bruce Updike, Sept. 7, 1963; children: Edith Hill, Nancy Lamar. B.A., Hood Coll., 1962; Ph.D., SUNY-Stony Brook, 1978. Asst. prof. Suffolk U., Boston, 1965-67; lectr. SUNY-Stony Brook, 1969-75, vis. asst. prof., 1977-78; asst. prof. U. Mass., Boston, 1975-77; asst. prof. Hofstra U., Hempstead, N.Y., 1978-85, assoc. prof., 1985—, chmn. dept. econs. and geography, 1981-84; assoc. dean Hofstra Coll. Hofstra U., 1984-87; pres. Interfid Capital Corp., 1987—; dir. Rapid-Am. Corp., 1979-87; cons. environ. econs., 1973-87., McCrory Corp., 1987—, Fabergé, Inc., 1987—. Author: The National Banks and American Economic Development, 1870-1900, 1985. Trustee, v.p. L.I. Forum for Tech., 1979-85; trustee Madeira Sch., Greenway, Va., N.Y. Outward Bound Ctr., H.B. Earhart; mem. nat. adv. bd. Outward Bound. H.B. Earhart fellow Georgetown U., 1962-63; Georgetown U. fellow, 1963-64. Mem. AAAS, Am. Econ. Assn. Office: Interfid Capital Corp 1 Dag Hammarskjold Plaza 47th Floor New York NY 10017

UPHOLD, RUTH ESTHER, physician, educator; b. Huron, S.D., Sept. 4, 1945; d. William Blaine and Alice Lillian (Butz) U.; divorced. BS, U. Calif., San Francisco, 1967; MD, Tufts U., 1974. Diplomate Am. Bd. Emergency Medicine. Emergency dir. Webber Hosp., Biddeford, Maine, 1975-78; resident in emergeny medicine Valley Med. Ctr., Fresno, Calif., 1978-80; dir. emergency dept. Med. Ctr. Hosp. Vt., Burlington, 1980—; asst. prof. U. Vt. Coll. Medicine, Burlington, 1980—. Contbr. articles to profl. jours. Mem. adv. com. Sexual Assault, Burlington, 1982-84; mem. com. Fatal Accident Rev., Burlington, 1982-87; chair com. Vt. affiliate Am. Heart Assn., Shelburne, Vt., 1983—. Mem. AMA, Emergency Med. Soc. (Vt. chpt. co-chair med. control com. 1982—, adv. council, 1981-83), Am. Coll. Emergency Physicians, Vt. State Med. Soc. Republican. Office: Med Ctr Hosp Vt Dept Emergency Colchester Ave Burlington VT 05401

UPJOHN, MARY KIRBY, educator; b. Kansas City, Mo., Sept. 30, 1948; d. William Bryant and Mary Analaura (Harrington) U.; B.A., Pomona Coll., 1970; M.S., Boston U., 1977. Dir. product devel. and promotion Urban Systems, Inc., Cambridge, Mass., 1970-73; pres., co-founder Funktions, Inc., Watertown, Mass., 1973-75; mng. editor Decade Mag., Boston, 1978-79; assoc. prof. Boston U. Coll. Communication, 1978-87, mem. exec. com., 1986—; sr. analyst Urban Systems Research and Engring., Cambridge, 1988—; cons. Urban Systems Research and Engring., 1975—, bd. dirs., 1982—; cons. Economica, Inc., Goodmeasure, Inc. Recipient Matrix award, 1987, awards of merit New Eng. Newspaper Execs., 1978, 79, 80, 81, 82, 83, 85, Women Grad. award Boston U., 1981. Mem. Women in Communications, Inc. (Nat. Outstanding Adviser award 1980, 81, 83 v.p. Boston chpt. 1981-82, pres. 1983, nat. v.p. 1986-88), Informational Film Producers Assn., Pomona Coll. Alumni Assn. (bd. mem. New Eng. chpt.). Author: Urban Homsteading: A Guide for Local Officials, 1978; (with Kathleen Heintz) Neighborhood Planning Primer, 1979; (with others) Television Literacy, 1981; prin. author Case Study of the Alaska National Communication Program. Home: 39 Marion Rd Watertown MA 02172 Office: Urban Systems Research and Engring 2067 Massachusetts Ave Cambridge MA 02140

UPPLEGER, RUTH SIMPSON, magazine and newspaper controller; b. Grand Ridge, Fla., Dec. 1, 1943; d. Chester Leon and Nellie Ada (Middleton) Jeter; m. James Bernard Simpson, Sept. 14, 1962 (div. 1984); children: Tonya Ruth, Michael James; m. Lawrence Franklin Uppleger, Jan. 25, 1986. Student Chipola Jr. Coll., 1961-62, Canal Zone Coll., 1971-73; BBA, Austin Peay State U., 1985. Bookkeeper, Leaf Chronicle, Clarksville, Tenn., 1976-78, office mgr., 1978-81, asst. controller, 1981-84; controller Music City News, Gallatin News Examiner, Nashville Record, Hendersonville Star News (subs. Multimedia Inc.), Nashville, 1984—. Mem. Nat. Assn. Accts., Nat. Assn. Female Execs. Democrat. Baptist. Club: Civitan (officer, bd. dirs.). Avocations: hiking, dancing, reading, horticulture. Home: 356 Dunbar Cave Rd Clarksville TN 37043

UPRIGHT, DIANE WARNER, art gallery director; b. Cleve., June 9, 1947; d. Rodney Upright and Shirley (Warner) Lavine. Student, Wellesley Coll., 1965-67; BA, U. Pitts., 1969; MA, U. Mich., 1973, PhD, 1976. Asst. prof. U. Va., Charlottesville, 1976-78; assoc. prof. Harvard U., Cambridge, Mass.,

1978-83; sr. curator Ft. Worth Art Mus., 1984-86, dir. Jan Krugier Gallery, N.Y.C., 1986—. Author: Morris Louis: The Complete Paintings, 1979, Ellsworth Kelly: Works on Paper, 1987, various exhbn. catalogues; contbr. articles to art jours. Mem. Coll. Art Assn., Art Table, Inc. Office: Jan Krugier Gallery 41 E 57th St New York NY 10022

UPSHAW-GONZALEZ, LISA GAYE, systems analyst; b. Alamogordo, N.Mex., June 27, 1959; d. James Leroy Upshaw and Margaret (Shackelford) Carrell; m. Michael J. Zamora, Nov. 3, 1976 (div. July 1983); 1 child, Jeremy Brandon; m. Eddie Gonzalez, Mar. 19, 1984. BS in Bus. Computer Systems, U. N.Mex., 1983. Govt. and large account system analyst Office Systems, Alburquerque, 1982-84; sr. system analyst, nat. accounts mgr. Bell Atlantic/CompuShop, Houston, 1984—; cons. Bell Atlantic Pres.' Club, Dallas, 1986-87, 88, Bell Atlantic Leaders Club, 1986, 87. Chmn. publicity Ronald McDonald House, Alburquerque, 1982, chairwoman spl. events, 1983; chairwoman Rep. Vol. Community, Houston, 1986; sponsor Houston Ballet, Theatre of Arts, Fundraising Heart Assn. Mem. Nat. Assn. Female Execs. (network dir. 1987-88), Assn. Info. System Profls., Houston Areal League Personal Computer Specialists, NOW, VFW. Home: 17731 December Pine PO Box 11211 Spring TX 77391-1211 Office: Bell Atlantic/CompuShop 4111 Directors Row Houston TX 77092

UPSHAW-MCCLENNY, LOUISE ADAMS, marketing and sales professional; b. Chgo., Aug. 16, 1953; d. Aubrey Russell Jr. and Evelyn Adams (Torbert) U.; m. Bruce Barron McClenny, Oct. 2, 1976. BA, Auburn U., 1975, M in French Studies, 1976. Fin. asst. Elf Aquitaine Oil & Gas, Houston, 1977-79; sales coordinator Hotel Meridien Houston, 1979-80, sales rep., 1980-81, sales mgr., 1981-82; sales mgr. Four Seasons Hotel, Houston Ctr., Houston, 1982-84, nat. sales mgr., 1984-85, dir. sales, 1985-86, dir. sales, mktg., 1986—. Co-author: Foreign Languages and International Trade: A Global Perspective. Mem. L'Alliance Francaise de Houston, 1977—. Mem. Hotel Sales and Mktg. Assn. (bd. dirs. 1982-83), Meeting Planners Internat. (sec. 1985-86, bd. dirs. 1986—), Downtown Houston Assn., Tex. Exec. Women (v.p. 1985, sec. 1986). Unitarian. Office: Four Seasons Hotel Houston Ctr 1300 Lamar Houston TX 77010

UPSHUR, CAROLE CHRISTOFK, psychologist, educator; b. Des Moines, Oct. 18, 1948; d. Robert Richard and Margaret (Davis) Christofk; A.B., U. So. Calif., 1969; Ed.M., Harvard U., 1970, Ed.D. (NIMH fellow), 1975; 1 dau., Emily. Planner, Mass. Com. on Criminal Justice, Boston, 1970-73; licensing specialist, planner, policy specialist Mass. Office for Children, Boston, 1973-76; asst. prof. Coll. Public and Community Service, U. Mass., Boston, 1976-81, assoc. prof., 1982—, chmn. Center for Community Planning, 1979-81, 84-86; cons. to govt. and community agys. on mental health and social service policy and mgmt., 1970—; cons. Harvard Family Research Project, 1983-86; sr. research assoc. U. Mass. Med. Sch., 1983-86, assoc. in pediatrics, 1986—; adj. prof. Heller Sch. Social Welfare, Brandeis U., 1985—. Lic. psychologist, Mass. Mem. Am. Psychol. Assn., Am. Assn. Mental Deficiency. Cons. editor: Mental Retardation. Office: U Mass Coll Public and Community Service Boston MA 02125

URBACH, PHYLLIS ANN, clothing executive; b. Mpls., June 29, 1936; d. Charles George and Mildred Eileen (Conover) Rose; m. Thomas Arnold Andersen, Sept. 14, 1953 (div. Apr. 1970); children: Debra, Ramona, David, Mark, Brad, Michael; m. Robert Dale Urbach, Feb. 12, 1978 (dec. Feb. 1979). Student, Normandale Coll., 1976-77. Owner, pres., artist Andersen Originals Inc., Burnsville, Minn., 1966-84; activities dir. Lake View Nursing Home, Mpls., 1977-78; owner, pres. designer Lady Huntress Fashions, Edina, Minn., 1983—; substitute tchr. Burnsville Sch. Dist., 1977-79. Editor: Jim Peterson Outdoor News, 1985-86; patentee canvas paint tote, 1985. Leader Cub Scouts Am., Girl Scouts USA, 4-H Club, Burnsville, 1965-68; spiritual instr. Burnsville Jr. High and Newbrighton Sr. High, 1975-81; developer, promoter Mpls. Aquatennial Bicentennial, Mpls., 1975-76; vol. cons. various women's entrepreneurial Orgns., Mpls. Recipient Merit award Mpls. Aquatennial, 1975. Mem. Women's Entrepreneur's Network, Bus. and Profl. Women's Assn., Ducks Unltd. (chmn. Minn. Valley Womnen's chpt.), Internat. Platform Assn., VFW, Nat. Sporting Goods Assn. Home and Office: 4050 Grainwood Trail NE Prior Lake MN 55372

URBAN, JO ANN REBECCA, transportation company executive; b. Allentown, Pa., Aug. 24, 1936; d. Joseph Leo and Anna Roslyn (Loftus) McLaughlin; student Drakes Secretarial Sch., 1952-54; m. Victor John Urban, Oct. 3, 1959; 1 son, Victor John. With Armstrong Trucking, Westinghouse Electric, N.Y.C., 1955-58, various trucking cos. including Long Transp., Jersey Truck Center, South Kearny, N.J., 1958-73; terminal mgr. Midwest Seaboard Transp. div. Midwest Emery, Dana Transport, Perth Amboy, N.J., 1973-76; pres. F.P.R. Express, Inc., South Kearney, 1979—; cons. women in transp. field. Active cub scout com. Hazlet chpt. Boy Scouts Am., 1974-75. Mem. Nat. Assn. Female Execs., N.J. Motor Truck Assn., N.J. Transp. Brokers Assn. (charter mem.). Office: Jersey Truck Ctr Rm 15 South Kearny NJ 07032

URBAN, MARY H(ELEN), educator; b. Newark, June 2, 1942; d. John and Helen (Smrha) U. BS in Edn., SUNY, Geneseo, 1965; MRE, Boston U., 1967, MSW, 1979. Dir. Christian edn. Holy Trinity Luth. Ch., Buffalo, 1970-73; coordinator telephone counseling services Crisis Services, Buffalo, 1973-77; coordinator tng. Sch. Social Work Boston U., 1979-81, asst. prof. and coordinator social work program, 1986—; pvt. practice social work Boston, 1979—; cons. Boys and Girls Clubs, Boston, 1986—. Tchr./trainer staff N.E. region Head Start, 1987—. Mem. Nat. Assn. Social Workers (cert., chair ethics com.). Office: Boston U MET Coll 755 Commonwealth Ave Boston MA 02215

URDA, MARGARET MARY, consumer products company executive; b. Norwalk, Conn., Sept. 29, 1952; d. John and Eileen Marie (Barton) U. BS, Western Conn. State U., 1974; MS, U. Bridgeport, 1976. Tchr. Bethel (Conn.) Middle Sch., 1974-78; tng. cons. Learning Systems div. Xerox Corp., Stamford, Conn., 1978-79; supr. sales tng. Tesa Corp., Denville, N.J., 1979-80; tng. specialist Reader's Digest, Pleasantville, N.Y., 1981-84; sr. tng. specialist SCM Corp., Ossining, N.Y., 1984-86; mgr. tng. and devel. Durkee-French Foods Inc., Paramus, N.J., 1986—; speaker in field. Mem. Am. Soc. Tng. Devel. (v.p. programming com. so. Conn. chpt. 1984, advisor to pres. 1985, 86, 87, asst. regional dir. 1987-88). Roman Catholic. Office: Durkee-French Foods Inc Mack Centre II One Mack Ctr Dr Paramus NJ 07652

URDANG, NICOLE SEVERYNA, psychotherapist; b. N.Y.C., May 16, 1953; d. Laurence and Irena Urdang; B.A. in Psychology, U. Conn., 1974; M.S. in Marriage and Family Counseling, So. Conn. State Coll., 1980; m. Mark Alan Criden, Mar. 1, 1980; children: Madelaine, Maxwell. Co-mng. editor CBS Almanac, Essex, Conn., 1975; psychiat. aide Inst. of Living, Hartford, Conn., 1975-76; supr. Alcohol Aftercare Center, Middletown, Conn., 1977-78; interim dir. Alcoholism Services Orgn., New Haven, 1978; alcoholism program coordinator Yale-New Haven Hosp., 1978-80; pvt. practice psychotherapy, New Haven, 1980-81, Buffalo, 1981—; radio psychotherapist Sta. WKBW, Buffalo, 1982-84; vol. counselor Norwich State Hosp., 1973-74, Planned Parenthood, 1975, Wesleyan U. Women's Ctr., 1977-78, New Haven Women's Ctr., 1979; lectr. in field. Author poems; columnist Met. Community News, 1985. Mem. Am. Assn. Counseling and Devel., Planned Parenthood, Am. Mental Health Counselors Assn., Nat. Assn. Anorexia Nervosa and Associated Disorders, Am. Assn. Sex Educators, Counselors and Therapists, N.Y. Acad. Scis., NOW, Inst. Rational-Emotive Therapy (assoc. fellow, supr.).

UREEL, PATRICIA LOIS, retired manufacturing company executive; b. Detroit, Nov. 29, 1923; d. Peter Walter and Ethel Estelle (Stewart) Murphy; grad. Detroit Bus. Inst., 1941; student Wayne State U., 1942, U. Detroit, 1943, U. Miami, 1945-46; m. Joseph Ralph Ureel, Jan. 4, 1947; children—Mary Patricia, Ronald Joseph. Exec. sec. to chmn. bd. and pres. Detroit Ball Bearing Co. of Mich., 1965-67; exec. sec. to partner charge Mich. dist. Ernst & Ernst, Detroit, 1967-71, Clubs of Inverrary, Lauderhill, Fla., 1971-72, partner charge of group Coopers & Lybrand, Miami, Fla., 1972-74; corp. sec., personnel mgr. Sanford Industries, Inc. and 4 subsidiaries, Pompano Beach, Fla., 1974-81; corp. sec., asso. Asphalt Assos., Ft. Lauderdale, 1982-86. Named Sec. of Yr. for City of Detroit, 1966; cert. profl. sec. Mem. Nat. Secs. Assn., Women's Econ. Club Detroit. Republican. Roman Catholic. Club: Moose. Home: 5375 SW 40th Ave 101 Fort Lauderdale FL 33314

URMER, DIANE HEDDA, management firm executive, financial officer; b. Bklyn., Dec. 15, 1934; d. Leo and Helen Sarah (Perlman) Leverant; m. Albert Heinz Urmer, Sept. 2, 1952; children: Michelle, Cynthia, Carl. Student U. Tex., 1951-52, Washington U., St. Louis, 1962-63; BA in Psychology, Calif. State U.-Northridge, 1969. Asst. auditor Tex. State Bank, Austin, 1952-55; v.p., controller Enki Corp., Sepulveda, Calif., 1966-70, also dir., 1987—; v.p., fin. Cambia Way Hosp., Walnut Creek, Calif., 1973-78; v.p., controller Enki Health & Research Systems, Inc., Reseda, Calif., 1978—, also dir. Contbr. articles to profl. jours. Pres. Northridge PTA, 1971; chmn. Northridge Citizens Adv. Council, 1972-73. Mem. Women in Mgmt. Club: Tex. Execs. Avocations: bowling, sailing, handcrafts, golf. Office: Enki Health and Research Systems Inc 6660 Reseda Blvd #203 Reseda CA 91335

URSINI, JOSEPHINE LUCILLE, lawyer; b. N.Y.C., Sept. 17, 1952; d. Edilio R. and Lucille V. (Ciufo) U.; m. Kenneth A. Krantz. B.S., Boston Coll., 1974; J.D., NYU, 1977. Bar: Md. 1977, D.C. 1978, Va. 1987. Law clk. trial div. U.S. Ct. Claims, Washington, 1977-78; assoc. Fried, Frank, Harris, Shriver, Kampelman, Washington, 1978-83; prin. Dickstein, Shapiro & Morin, Washington, 1983-85; sole practice, 1985-88; dir. of claims Price Waterhouse Govt. Contractor Cons. Service, 1988—. Contbr. articles to profl. jours. Mem. ABA, D.C. Bar Assn., Fed. Bar Assn. Roman Catholic. Georgetown Gilbert and Sullivan Soc. (dir.). Home: 4523 Pickett Rd Fairfax VA 22032 Office: 6500 Rock Spring Dr Bethesda MD 20817

USHER, ELIZABETH HOWARD, educator, writer; b. Lakewood, Ohio; d. George James and Mary Margaret (Strothard) U. AA, Pine Manor Coll., 1968; BA, Western Coll., 1970. Cert. English and Spanish tchr., Ohio. Dir. drama, tchr. English Harding Mid. Sch., 1970-85, Lakewood High Sch., 1985—. Author poems; contbr. articles to profl. jours. Jennings Found. scholar, 1981-82. Mem. Nat. Council English Tchrs., Mensa. Republican. Home: 18101 Clifton Rd Lakewood OH 44107

USHER, PHYLLIS LAND, state official; b. Winona, Miss., Aug. 29, 1944; d. Sandy Kenneth and Ruth (Cottingham) L.; m. William A. Usher. B.S., U. So. Miss., Hattiesburg, 1967; M.S. (Title II-B fellow 1968-69), U. Tenn., Knoxville, 1969; postgrad. Purdue U., Ind. U., Utah State U. Librarian, Natchez (Miss.)-Adams County schs., 1967-68; materials specialist Fulton County Bd. Edn., Atlanta, 1969-71; cons. div. instructional media Ind. Dept. Public Instrn., Indpls., 1971-74, dir. div., 1974-82, dir. fed. resources and sch. improvement, 1982-85; acting assoc. supt. Ind. Dept. Edn., 1985; sr. officer Ctr. for Sch. Improvement, Ind. Dept. Edn., 1985—; pres. bd. dirs. INCOLSA, mcpl. corp., 1980-82; v.p., sec.-treas. Usher Funeral Home, Inc.; mem. task force sch. Libraries Nat. Commn. Libraries and Info. Sci.; dir., v.p. NU Realty Corp.; cons. in field. Mem. Gov. Inst. Conf. Children and Youth Task Force. Recipient citation Internat. Reading Assn., 1975. Mem. ALA, Nat. Assn. State Ednl. Media Profls., West Deanery Bd. Edn., Indpls. Archdioces, Delta Kappa Gamma. Adv. bd. Booklist. Office: Room 229 State House Indianapolis IN 46204

USHIJIMA, CAROL M., utility executive; b. Santa Monica, Calif., Mar. 15, 1958; d. Tadami Ernie and Jean Miyoko (Miwa) U. BA in Econs. and History, UCLA, 1979. Research asst. Nat. Econ. Research Assocs., Los Angeles, 1979-80; jr. adminstrv. asst. Office of City Administrv. Officer City of Los Angeles, 1980-81, jr. adminstrv. asst. Dept. Water and Power, Water Exec. Office, 1981-82, cons. energy utilization Dept. Water and Power, Conservation Div., 1982-87, sr. utility conservation rep., supr. mktg. services, Systems Devel. Div., 1987—. Mem. allocations com. region V United Way, Los Angeles, 1986—; team leader LADWP Asian Community Affiliates, Los Angeles, 1984-85; bd. dirs. West Los Angeles Japanese Am. Citizens League, 1984—. Marina Mercy Hosp. scholar, 1975; recipient Outstanding Community Service award West Los Angeles Japanese Am. Citizens League, 1986. Mem. Asian Pacific Women's Network, Nat. Assn. Female Execs., Leadership Edn. for Asian Pacifics, Assn. Profl. Energy Mgrs., Profl. Women's Network (chairperson LADWP system devel. div. 1986-87), Calif. Scholarship Fedn. (life). Methodist. Office: Los Angeles Dept Water & Power PO Box 111 Room 1169 Los Angeles CA 90051

USHIJIMA, JEAN MIYOKO, city official; b. San Francisco, Feb. 14, 1933; d. Toyoharu George and Frances Fujiko (Misumi) Miwa; m. Tad E. Ushijima; 1 child, Carol M. B.S., U. San Francisco, 1981. City clk. City of Beverly Hills, Calif., 1973—. Bd. dirs. West Los Angels Japanese Am. Citizens League, 1979—, pres., 1988; bd. dirs. Leadership Edn. for Asian Pacifics, 1985—. Mem. Acad. Advanced Edn., City Clks. Assn. Calif. (pres. 1986), Calif. Women in Govt. (program chmn. 1978-79), Leadership Edn. for Asian Pacific (chmn. bd. 1987), League Calif. Cities (admisntrv. services com. 1982-86), Internat. Inst. Mcpl. Clks. (bd dirs. 1988). Avocations: reading, Japanese dancing. Office: City Clerk 450 N Crescent Dr #102 Beverly Hills CA 90210

USHIO, JUDITH SMITH, business executive; b. Los Angeles, Sept. 28, 1949; d. Stanford Groesbeck and MaryEllen Howell (Stoddard) Smith; m. David Evan Ushio, Sept. 19, 1969; Misti, Jocelyn, Cassandra, Nathaniel. Student, Brigham Young, 1967-69. Head teller Am. Savs. and Loan, Provo, Utah, 1969-71; sec. Riggs Bank, Washington, 1971-72; research assoc. Human Resources Corp., San Francisco, 1976-77; exec. v.p. MESA Services Internat., Reston, Va., 1983—; trustee Hosp. Corp Am., Reston, 1986—; bd. dirs. Reston Bd. of Commerce, Reston, 1986—. Bd. dirs. Reston Homeowners Assn., Reston, 1977-83, chmn. 1979-83; pres. Young Womens Youth Orgn., Reston, Herndon, 1986—. Named Citizen of Yr. Reston Times Newspaper, 1981, one of Outstanding Young Women of Yr., 1982; recipient Most Influential Citizen of Reston award Reston Times Newspaper, 1983. Democrat. Mormon. Home: 11100 Wedge Dr Reston VA 22090 Office: MESA Services Internat 11333 Sunset Hills Rd Reston VA 22090

USINGER, JANE ELIZABETH, management consultant, educator; b. E. Chicago, Ind., Sept. 20, 1951; d. Richard Lewis and Vera Wheeler (Nickell) U.; m. Dennis Joseph Goginsky, May 16, 1987. BA in Edn., Purdue U., 1973, MS in Edn. with honors, 1974; MBA, DePaul U., Chgo., 1983. Cert. tchr. Tchr. neurologically impaired Stewart Jr. High Sch., Tacoma, 1974-75; supr., adminstr. Seattle Crisis Clinic, Inc., 1975-78; program coordinator State Dept. Pub. Instrn. ESD 121, Seattle, 1978-80; sales rep. N.W. Airlines, Chgo., 1980-81; tng. coordinator Montgomery Ward, Inc., Chgo., 1981-83; tng. mgr. Calvary Hosp. and Palliative Care Inst., N.Y.C., 1983-85; prin. Omega Assocs., Atlanta, 1985—; mem. continuing edn. faculty Kennesaw (Ga.) Coll., Trident Tech. Coll., Charleston, S.C.; bd. dirs. Ga. Image Cons., Atlanta. Author: One in Fifty, 1978; contbr. articles and poetry to various mags; inventor wheelchair laptray (Purdue Commendation award), 1973. Vol. Rape Relief Ctr., Chgo., 1981-83, AIDS Speakers Bur., 1987—; bd. dirs. Puget Sound chpt. Big Sisters, Seattle, 1975-77. Mortar Bd. fellow, 1973-74. Mem. Am. Soc. Tng. and Devel. (membership com. 1982-83), Fedn. Bus. Profl. Women (chair 1979-80, young career woman program, Young Career Woman award Wash. chpt. 1979), Orgn. Devel. Network, Bus. Network, Atlanta C. of C., Am. Assn. U. Women, Nat. Orgn. Women, Nat. Speakers Assn., Kappa Delta Pi. Roman Catholic. Home: 1194 Moss Bluff Mount Pleasant SC 29464 Office: Omega Assocs Atlanta GA 30301

USSERY, LUANNE, business communicator; b. Kershaw, S.C., Feb. 20, 1938; d. Ralph Thurston and Mary Elizabeth (Haile) U. B.A., Winthrop Coll., 1959. Assoc. editor Kershaw News Era, 1959-61; advt. saleswoman Nonpareil newspaper, Council Bluffs, Iowa, 1961-67; mag. editor Mutual of Omaha-United of Omaha Life Ins. Co., 1968-78, asst. v.p., 1977-82, 2d v.p., 1982-87. Editor: The Presbyterian, Presbytery of Missouri River Valley, Omaha, 1984-88. Elder, clk. of session First Presbyn. Ch. U.S.A., Council Bluffs; chair communications com. Presbytery of Missouri River Valley, 1985-87, moderator, 1988—; trustee Christian Home Assn./Children's Sq. U.S.A., Council Bluffs, 1985-88. Mem. Internat. Assn. Bus. Communicators (sec. chpt. 1971, pres. 1972, Communicator of Yr. 1973), Ins. Consumer Affairs Exchange.

UTHGENANNT, LISA JUDITH CROWE, manufacturing company human resource executive; b. Concord, Mass., Sept. 26, 1960; d. Arthur Samuel and Mary French (Clayton) Crowe; m. James Arthur Uthgenannt, May 24, 1987. BA in Psychology, Muhlenberg Coll., 1983; postgrad., Rensselaer Poly. Inst., 1983—. Employee relations intern Gen. Electric Plastics, Pittsfield, Mass., 1985; human resources mgr. Ceramaseal, Inc., New Lebanon, N.Y., 1985—. Democrat. Episcopalian. Office: Ceramaseal Inc PO Box 260 New Lebanon NY 12125

UTLEY, DONNA LAVELLE, hospital administrator; b. Tulare, Calif., June 30, 1948; d. Donald Raymond and Vivian Lee (Baber) Rogers; B.S., Calif. State U., Fresno, 1970; M.P.A., U. So. Calif., 1985; m. July 23, 1970. Resources and devel. asst. Concentrated Employment Program, Fresno, Calif., 1970-72; personnel analyst Fresno County Personnel Dept., 1972-74; personnel mgr. Fresno County Health Dept., 1974-79; personnel dir. Merced (Calif.) Community Med. Ctr., 1979-81; dir. human resources Bay Area Hosp., Coos Bay, Oreg., 1981-85; asst. adminstr. human resources, St. Elizabeth Med. Ctr., Yakima, Wash., 1985—; Bd. dirs., chmn. Personnel com. Enterprise for Progress in the Community, 1987-88. Mem. Wash. Soc. Hosp. Personnel Adminstrn., Am. Soc. Healthcare Human Resources Adminstrn., Cen./S.E. Wash. Healthcare Personnel Dirs. Assn. (pres. 1987-88), Pacific N.W. Personnel Mgmt. Assn.. Republican. Methodist. Office: 110 S 9th Ave Yakima WA 98902

UTSLER, DONNA LYNN, electronics buyer, design consultant; b. Dallas, June 11, 1944; d. John Andrew and Winona (Stewart) Vitkovits; m. William N. Utsler, 1964 (div. Dec. 1975); children: Darrell Wayne, Shannon Elizabeth. B in Arts and Scis., SW Tex. State U., 1980. Data transcriber IRS, Austin, Tex., 1972-75; bookkeeper, sales rep. The Toggery, Austin, 1975-76; design cons. Donna Utsler Decorating Den, Austin, 1985—; commodity mgr. Tex. Instruments, Austin, 1976—. Stage mgr. Zachary Scott Community Theater, Austin, 1976-77; co-chamn. decorating com. Women's Art Guild, Austin, 1987—. Mem. Nat. Assn. Female Execs., Austin Purchasing Mgmt. Assn. (chmn. electronic buyers com. 1984), Alpha Chi. Office: Decorating Den 2014 Crystal Shore Austin TX 78728

UTZ, DOROTHY DUNBAR, school counselor; b. Marietta, Ohio, Aug. 13, 1927; d. John Williams Ellis and Esther (Fry) D.; m. John Paul Utz; children: Richard Allen, David John, Jon Christian, Nancy Anne. BS cum laude, Ohio State U., 1948; MEd, Bowling Green U., 1967, postgrad.; postgrad., Miami U. Ohio. Cert. tchr. home econs., ednl. counselor, Sch. Supr., Ohio. Home econs. tchr. Hamilton Twp. Schs., Franklin County, Ohio, 1948-51, Bloom Twp. Schs., Seneca County, Ohio, 1951-52; home econs. tchr. Bucyrus City (Ohio) Schs., 1968-72, sch. counselor, 1972—; kindergarten initiator Parents, Attica, Ohio, 1957. Chief Ohio Clan, Dunbar, 1983—; active Chem. Dependency Network, Bucyrus. Ohio State U. scholar, Columbus, 1944. Mem. Nat. Assn. Female Execs., Ohio Sch. Counselors, Delta Kappa Gamma, Phi Delta Kappa, Alpha Lamda Delta, Phi Upsilon Omicron, Omicron Nu. Republican. Club: Lutheran Daughters (New Washington Ohio) (treas. Ohio 1954). Home: 15449 E County Rd 58 New Washington OH 44854 Office: Bucyrus City Schs 245 Woodlawn Ave Bucyrus OH 44820

UTZ, SARAH WINIFRED, nursing educator; b. San Diego, Nov. 2, 1921; d. Frederick R. and Margaret M. (Gibbons) U.; B.S., U. Portland, 1943, Ed.M., 1958; M.S., UCLA, 1970; Ph.D., U. So. Calif., 1979. Clin. instr. Providence Sch. Nursing, Portland, Oreg., 1946-50, edn. dir., 1950-62; edn. dir. Sacred Heart Sch. Nursing, Eugene, Oreg., 1963-67; asst. prof. nursing Calif. State U., Los Angeles, 1969-74, assoc. prof., 1974-81, prof., 1981—, assoc. chmn. dept. nursing, 1982—; cons. in nursing curriculum, 1978—; past chmn. ednl. adminstrs., cons., tchrs. sect. Oreg. Nurses Assn., past pres. Oreg. State Bd. Nursing; mem. research program Western Interstate Commn. on Higher Edn. in Nursing; chmn. liaison com. nursing edn. Articulation Council Calif. Served with Nurse Corps, USN, 1944-46. HEW grantee, 1970-74, Kellogg Found. grantee, 1974-76, USDHHS grantee, 1987—; R.N., Calif., Oreg. Mem. Am. Nurses Assn., Calif. Nurses Assn. (edn. commr. region 6 1987—, co-chair edn. interest group region 6 , 1987—), Am. Ednl. Research Assn., AAUP, Town Hall Calif., Phi Delta Kappa, Sigma Theta Tau. Formerly editor Oreg. Nurse; reviewer Western Jour. Nursing Research. Home: 1409 Midvale Ave Los Angeles CA 90024 Office: 5151 State University Dr Los Angeles CA 90032

UZENDA, JARA CARLOW, technical writer; b. Brookline, Mass., May 24, 1946; d. Roscoe William and Gloria Pauline (St. Jacques) Carlow; m. William ANthony Perry, June 1, 1963 (dec. Dec. 1971); children: Troy Anthony, William Lance; m. Richard Paul Matsumoto Sr., May 24, 1981; 1 child, Richard Paul Jr. Student, R.I. Jr. Coll., 1965-67, U. R.I., 1967-68; BS in Journalism, U. Colo., 1975, MS in Telecommunications, 1978. Mktg. mgr. Humidor Smoke Shoppes, Warwick, R.I., 1965-69; telecommunication cons. Arthur D. Little, Inc., Boston, 1976-78; dir. research Horizon House Internat., Boston, 1978-80; market analyst Internat. Telecommunications, Boulder, Colo., 1980-81; field service engr. Allied Info. Systems, Boulder, 1981-83; gen. ptnr. Kentucky Gold Ltd., San Jose, Calif., 1984; sr. tech. writer Paradyne Corp., Largo, Fla., 1984-86; sales and mktg. Piedmont Airlines Golf Resort Directory, Myrtle Beach, S.C., 1986-87; cons. Data Security, Little River, S.C., 1987—; vis. prof. Prescott Coll., Flagstaff, Ariz., 1972; film dir. Niel Minority News, Estes Park, Colo., 1973-74; featured artist Denver Post, 1973; spl. expert Latin Am. Telecommunications, Washington, 1980. Author: Electronic Fund Transfer, 1978; contbr. articles to Flatiron Mag., Telecommunications Mag., Security Management Mag. Grantee Nat. Endowment Arts, 1973. Mem. Council Internat. Relations & UN Affairs, Internat. Relations Club, Soc. Women Engrs., U. Colo. Alumni Assn., Mortar Bd. Lodge: Optimists. Home: PO Box 603 Little River SC 29566

VAASSEN, ROSETTI GAYL, product manager; b. Leon, Iowa, May 4, 1956; d. Gaylord S. Hart and Wilmetta LouAnn (Watkins) Waddell; m. Robert Gilbert Vaassen; 1 child, David Michael. BA in Math., Graceland Coll., 1977; MBA, Coll. St. Thomas, 1987. Engr. Northwestern Bell, Des Moines, 1977-79; mgr. distbn. engring. Northwestern Bell, Dubuque, Iowa, 1979-81; mgr. constrn. Northwestern Bell, Waterloo, Iowa, 1981-84; mgr. bus. devel. Northwestern Bell, Mpls., 1984-85; product mgr. U.S. West, Mpls., 1985—; instr. Project Bus. Dubuque, 1980-81. Advisor Jr. Achievement, Des Moines, 1978-79. Mem. Soc. Women Engrs., U.S. West Women. Home: 17123 Round Lake Rd Eden Prairie MN 55346 Office: Northwestern Bell 100 S 5th St Room 770 Minneapolis MN 55402

VAGNEUR, KATHRYN OTTO, accountant, rancher, author; b. Aurora, Ill., Feb. 23, 1946; d. Harold William and Afton (Bryner) Otto; m. Gerald Ronald Terwilliger, Oct. 19, 1968 (div. 1974); 1 dau., Jocelyn Marie; m. Clyde O. Vagneur, Aug. 24, 1979. BS in Math., U. Utah, 1968; MS in Agribus. Mgmt., Ariz. State U., 1979. CPA, Colo. Computer systems designer U. Utah Libraries, Salt Lake City, 1966-68; research asst. in computer systems Carnegie-Mellon U., 1968-70; owner, mgr. Evening at Arthurs Restaurant, Aspen, Colo., 1973-76; self-employed tax cons. Phoenix, 1977-78; with Touche Ross & Co., Colorado Springs, Colo., 1978-82; ptnr., fin. mgr. V Bar Lazy V Ranch, Peyton, Colo., 1978—; ptnr. Vagneur & Firth, Colorado Springs, 1982—; pres. The Marlwood Corp., Colorado Springs; chmn. Excellence in Bus. Seminar Series, 1987-88. Chmn. bd. dirs. Pikes Peak Ctr.; del. Rep. State Conv., 1982, White House Small Bus. Conf., 1986; bd. dirs. Springs Into Action Econ. Devel. Strategy, 1987-88; mem. Gov.'s Econ. Devel. Action Council, 1987; 4-H leader. Mem. Am. Inst. CPAs, Nat. Soc. Accts. for Coops., Colo. Soc. CPAs, Nat. Assn. Accts., Jr. League, Am. Salers Assn., Nat. Cattlemen's Assn. (featured speaker 1986 Beef Profit Conf.), Nat. Fedn. Ind. Bus., Colorado Springs C. of C. (com. chmn.), Am. Quarter Horse Assn., Beta Alpha Psi, Alpha Zeta. Author: A Financial Analysis of Cooperative Livestock Marketing, 1978; contbr. articles to mags. Home: 14725 Jones Rd Peyton CO 80831 Office: Vagneur & Firth 830 N Tejon Suite 303 Colorado Springs CO 80903

VAI, MARJORIE THERESA, language educator, administrator, author; b. Jersey City, Feb. 24, 1947; d. Mario and Grace (Nolan) V.; m. Sener R. Erturkmen, Mar. 11, 1978; 1 child, Daniel V. AB, Rutgers U., 1968; MA, NYU. Instr. Am. Coll. Greece, Athens, 1974-76, N.Y. Inst. Tech., N.Y.C., 1977-79; product mgr. Litton Ednl. Pubs. Internat., N.Y.C., 1979-81; dir. product devel. Atlantis Publishers, N.Y.C., 1981-82; instructional design cons., N.Y.C., 1982-87; instructional designer/author courseware English on Call!, McGraw-Hill Pubs., N.Y.C., 1988; dir. English Lang. Inst., acting chair lang. dept. The New Sch., N.Y.C., 1988—; freelance writer Dow Jones Inc., South Brunswick, N.J., 1983, 84. Author: (with L. Ferreira) Read On! Speak Out!, 1979; contbg. editor Dowline Mag. Mem. TESOL. Home: 491 12th St Brooklyn NY 11215

VAIL, BEVERLY MAY, industrial, statistical engineer; b. Arlington, Va., June 4, 1962; d. Thomas Lennington Curtis and Nancy Elizabeth (Overton) V. BS in Indsl. Engring., Ops. Research, Va. Poly. Inst., 1984; postgrad., Drexel U., 1987—. Quality engr. Burroughs Corp. (name now UNISYS), Paoli, Pa., 1984-87, statis. process control engr., 1987—. Mem. NSPE, Inst. Indsl. Engrs. Office: UNISYS 2476 Swedesford Rd Paoli PA 19301

VAIL, IRIS JENNINGS, civic worker; b. N.Y.C., July 2, 1928; d. Lawrence K. and Beatrice (Black) Jennings; grad. Miss Porters Sch., Farmington, Conn.; m. Thomas V.H. Vail, Sept. 15, 1951; children—Siri J., Thomas V.H. Jr., Lawrence J.W. Exec. com. Garden Club Cleve., 1962—; mem. women's council Western Res. Hist. Soc., 1960—; mem. jr. council Cleve. Mus. Art, 1953—; chmn. Childrens Garden Fair, 1966-75, Public Square Dinner, 1975; bd. dirs. Garden Center Greater Cleve., 1963-77; trustee Cleve. Zool. Soc., 1971—; mem. Ohio Arts Council, 1974-76, pub. sq. com. Greater Cleve. Growth Assn.; mem. endangered species com. Cleve. 200 Soc. Recipient Amy Angell Collier Montague medal Garden Club Am., 1976, Ohio Gov.'s award, 1977. Episcopalian. Clubs: Chagrin Valley Hunt, Cypress Point, Kirtland Country, Union, Colony, Women's City of Cleve. (Margaret A. Ireland award). Home: Hunting Valley Chagrin Falls OH 44022

VAIL, LINDA DIANNE, interior designer; b. Wellsville, N.Y., Aug. 13, 1947; d. Wirt Edward and Doris Marie (Eldridge) Washburn; m. Burr DeForest Vail III, Nov. 21, 1966; 1 child, Adrienne Elizabeth. BS, U. Vt., 1974. Cert. interior designer. Interior designer Freeman French Freeman, Architects, Burlington, Vt., 1978-80; pres. The Lone Arranger Inc., Burlington, 1980-81; interior designer Alexander Truex DeGroot, Burlington, 1981-85; v.p. Architecture/Interior Design Assocs. Inc., Burlington, 1985—. Author: Dining on Deck, 1986. Chmn. interiors com. Flynn Theatre for Performing Arts, Burlington, 1984-86, mem. bldg. com., 1982-86. Mem. AIA (affiliate Vt. chpt., corr. mem. interiors com.), Am. Soc. Interior Designers, Inst. Bus. Designers, Nat. Trust Historic Preservation. Home: RD Box 2598 Charlotte VT 05445 Office: AIDA Inc 212 Battery St Burlington VT 05401

VAIL, PHYLLIS, library director; b. Warwick, N.Y., Nov. 12, 1926; d. Harry Wisner and Gladys (Van Arsdale) V. AB, U. Mich., 1948; MLS, Pratt Inst., 1977. Dir. library U.S. Trust Co., N.Y., 1969-74; bus. and legal librarian Fla. Atlantic U., Boca Raton, Fla., 1975-77; dir. Okeechobee County (Fla.) Pub. Library, 1977-80, Jefferson Twp. Pub. Library, Oak Ridge, N.J., 1981—. Contbr. articles to profl. jours. Mem. ALA, N.J. Library Assn., Delta Zeta. Democrat. Home: 54 Southern Ln Warwick NY 10990 Office: Jefferson Twp Pub Library Weldon Rd Oak Ridge NJ 07438

VAILE, JEAN ELIZABETH, association executive; b. Cut Bank, Mont., July 18, 1938; d. Leo M. and Evelyn A. (Hensrude) Baker; m. Alvin L. Vaile (div.); children—Arthur Henry, Sheila Jean, Leo Michael. Student Kinman Bus. Sch., 1956-57, Fresno City Coll., 1975-76, U. San Francisco, 1980, State Center Community Coll., Fresno, Calif., 1981-82. Lic. life disability ins. agt., real estate agt., Calif.; notary pub., Calif. Mgr., Glacier Drug, Browning, Mont., 1958-60, Club Cafe, Browning, 1960-67; office mgr. J.C. Penny Co., Mont., 1967-69, Bob Ward & Sons, Inc., Missoula, Mont., 1970-73; acct. Sun Fruit, Ltd., Fresno, 1973-76; bus. adminstr. Assn. for Retarded Citizens, 1976-82; adminstrv. asst. to sr. v.p. Guarantee Savs., Fresno, 1985—; Amway distbr., 1975—; owner part-time income diversification and 2d income devel. bus. Chmn. supervisory com. Fresno Consumers Credit Union, 1979; voting mem. two social service health orgns., 1979—. Mem. Republican Presdl. Task Force. Lutheran. Club: Toastmasters. Home: 2007 E Austin Fresno CA 93726

VAINIO, MARIE OPYRCHAL, communications company executive; b. Detroit, May 27, 1951; d. Anthony and Virginia Elizabeth (Kendorski) Opyrchal; m. David Gerard Vainio, Dec. 29, 1979; children: Lauren Marie, David Anthony. Student, Wayne State U., 1969-71; BBA, Western Mich. U., 1973. Corp. auditor Dept. Revenue State Ill., Chgo., 1974-75; research analyst NPD Research, Schaumburg, Ill., 1975-77; state mktg. dir. Tele-Communicators, Inc., Butte, Mont., 1977-87; advt. mgr. Am. Eyecure, Butte, Mont., 1987—. Mem. Mont. Cable TV Assn. (bd. dirs. 1980-82, pres. 1982-83), Jr. League Butte. Roman Catholic.

VAKIL, VIRGIE MAY, lawyer; b. Hershey, Pa., Oct. 4, 1943; d. John Henry and Mary Dorothy (Phillips) Tshudy; m. Hassan C. Vakil, Mar. 9, 1967; children—Jeffrey Jahan, Mark Mehdi. Diploma in nursing Harrisburg Hosp. (Pa.), 1964, Ga. State U., Atlanta, 1970; B.A. summa cum laude, West Chester State U., 1976; J.D., Temple U., 1981. R.N., Pa., Ga. Nurse, Allegheny Gen. Hosp., Pitts., 1964-66; nurse Piedmont Hosp., Atlanta, 1966-67, instr. nursing, 1968; utilization rev. analyst Blue Cross/Blue Shield Del., Wilmington, 1971; sole practice, Media, Pa., 1982-87; assoc. Gibbons, Buckley, Smith, Palmer & Proud, P.C., Media, 1987—. Contbg. author: Practices, 1983, Nurses Legal Handbook, 1985. Bd. dirs. women in bus. com. Delaware County C. of C., 1981-85; Republican committeewoman Upper Providence Twp. (Pa.), 1982-86 ; bd. dirs. Community Care Programs, 1986—, Upper Providence Citizens Assn., 1987—. Mem. ABA, Pa. Bar Assn., Assn. Trial Lawyers Am., Delaware County Bar Assn. (chmn. med./dental law com. 1985—), LWV, Psi Chi, Pi Gamma Mu, Phi Alpha Delta. Republican. Home: 690 Meadowbrook Ln Moylan PA 19065 Office: 113 N Olive St Media PA 19063

VALAD, PAULA TOLTESY, international organization executive; b. Bklyn., Sept. 17, 1938; d. Paul Joseph and Hattie Wood Toltesy; B.A., Goucher Coll., 1960; cert. of accomplishment in editorial practices U.S. Dept. Agr. Grad. Sch., 1972; postgrad. George Washington U., Am. U., 1960—; 1 son, Hossain M. Sec., IBRD, Washington, 1960-70, tech. editor, 1970-74, evaluation officer, 1975-83, loan officer Eastern Africa Country Programs Dept., 1983-87; ops. officer, East Asia and Pacific Projects Dept., 1987, projects officer, Asia Country Dept., 1987—; vice-chmn., coordinator career devel. and day care coms., consultation com. Staff Assn., 1973-74. Chmn. subcom. on mobility of status of women working group Personnel Classification Rev. Panel, vice chmn. task force on legal aspects of taxation and pensions, 1981-82, alt. chmn. job grading rev. panel, 1986-88. Mem. Soc. Internat. Devel., Assn. Women in Devel. Clubs: Toastmasters. Home: 5221 Marlyn Dr Bethesda MD 20816 Office: 1818 H St NW Washington DC 20433

VALANCE, MARSHA JEANNE, library director, story teller; b. Evanston, Ill., Aug. 2, 1946; d. Edward James, Jr. and Jeanne Lois (Skinner) Leonard; m. William George Valance, Dec. 27, 1966 (div. 1976); 1 dau., Marguerite Jeanne. Student Northwestern U., 1964-66; AB, UCLA, 1968; MLS, U. R.I., 1973. Children's librarian trainee N.Y. Pub. Library, N.Y.C., 1968-69; reference librarian Action Meml. Pub. Library (Mass.), 1969-70; mgr. The Footnote, Cedar Rapids, Iowa, 1976-78; assoc. editor William C. Brown, Dubuque, Iowa, 1978-79; library dir. Dubuque County Library, Dubuque, 1979-81; library dir. G.B. Dedrick Pub. Library, Geneseo, Ill., 1981-84; library dir. Grand Rapids Pub. Library, Minn., 1984—; workshop coordinator, participant, sect. chmn. profl. confs. Co-author: Mystery, Value and Awareness, 1979; Pluralism, Similarities and Contrast, 1979; contbr. articles to publs. Troop leader Mississippi Valley Council Girl Scouts U.S.A., Cedar Rapids, 1976-78; mem. liturgy com. St. Malachy's Roman Catholic Ch., Geneseo, 1983; com. judging clinic 4-H, Moline, Ill., 1984; trustee KAXE No. Community Radio, 1986—, ICTV, 1988-90; sec. Grand Rapids Community Services Council, 1986; coach Itasca County 4-H Horse Bowl Team, 1987; organizer Grand Rapids Storyfest, 1987; program chmn. Spotlight on Books Conf., 1989—. Iowa Humanities Bd. grantee, 1981, Minn. Library Found. grantee, 1985, 86, 87, Blandin Found. grantee, 1986, Arrowhead Regional Arts Council grantee, 1987. Mem. ALA, Minn. Library Assn., Iowa Libraries of Medium Size (sec. 1981), Northlands Storytelling Network (bd. dirs. 1988-90), Nat. Assn. Preservation and Perpetuation Storytelling, NCIC, Alliance Info. and Referral Services, DAR (constn. chmn. 1983-84), Am. Morgan Horse Assn., Mississippi Valley Morgan Horse Club, North Cen. Morgan Assn., Alpha Gamma Delta. Club: Geneseo Jr. Women's (internat. chmn. 1983-84). Home: 1405 7th Ave SE Grand Rapids MN 55744-4083 Office: 21 NE 5th St Grand Rapids MN 55744

VALDES, BEATRIZ, social services administrator; b. Havana, Cuba, July 30, 1952; d. Camilo Antonio and Josefa (Saud) V. BS, Fla. Internat. U., 1978. Tchr. Sts. Peter and Paul Sch., Miami, Fla., 1974-76; med. social worker Mercy Hosp., Miami, Fla., 1978-79, oncology social worker, 1979-84, dir. social services, 1984—; owner, ptnr. Social Work Registry and Cons., Inc. Vol. numerous coms. Am. Cancer Soc., Miami, 1982—. Am. Cancer Soc. fellow, 1983. Mem. South Fla. Soc. Oncology Social Workers, Fla. Soc. Dirs. Hosp. Social Work, Nat. Soc. Hosp. Social Work Dirs. Home: 741 SW 27th Rd Miami FL 33129 Office: Mercy Hosp 3663 S Miami Ave Miami FL 33133

VALDES, DIANE GRACE, marketing and sales executive; b. Maspeth, N.Y., Apr. 20, 1948; d. Alfred Otto and Charlotte Florence (Bronnenkant) Bruggeman; m. Julius Valdes, Apr. 4, 1971. A.A.S., Queensborough Community Coll., 1967; B.S., Nova U., 1979. Jr. acct. Exxon, N.Y.C., 1967-69; acct. BRM Assos., N.Y.C., 1969, Texaco, N.Y.C., 1969-74; supr. Eutectic, Flushing, N.Y., 1974-76; regional industry dir. Am. Express, N.Y.C., 1976-83; v.p. Eastern Exclusives, Boston, 1983—; pres. The Mktg. Dept., 1985-86, sr. v.p., gen. mgr. Rogers Merchandising Inc., 1986—. Author tng. manual, Travel newsletter, 1982. Active Murray Hill Community, 1982, 7 E. 35th Coop, 1983. Recipient VISTA award Am. Express, 1983. Mem. Am. Soc. Travel Agts (tour relations com. 1983), Am. Hotel and Motel Assn., Am. Film Assn., Am. Mgmt. Assn., Sigma Mu Omega (pres. Bayside, N.Y. 1966-67). Home: 7 E 35th St New York NY 10016

VALDES-DAPENA, MARIE AGNES, pediatric pathologist, educator; b. Pottsville, Pa., July 14, 1921; d. Edgar Daniel and Marie Agnes (Rettig) Brown; m. Antonio M. Valdes-Dapena, Apr. 6, 1945 (div. Oct. 1980); children: Victoria Maria Valdes-Dapena Hiltebeitel, Deborah Anne Valdes-Dapena Malle, Maria Cristina Valdes-Dapena, Andres Antonio, Antonio Edgardo, Carlos Roberto, Marcos Antonio, Ricardo Daniel, Carmen Patricia Valdés-Dapena Fater, Catalina Inez, Pedro Pablo. BS, Immaculata Coll., 1941; MD, Temple U., 1944. Diplomate: Am. Bd. Pathology. Intern Phila. Gen. Hosp., 1944-45, resident in pathology, 1945-49; asst. pathologist Fitzgerald Mercy Hosp., Darby, Pa., 1949-51; dir. labs. Woman's Med. Coll. Pa., Phila., 1951-55; instr. pathology Woman's Med. Coll. Pa., 1947-51, asst. prof., 1951-55, assoc. prof., 1955-59; assoc. pathologist St. Christopher's Hosp. for Children, Phila., 1959-76; dir. sect. pediatric pathology U. Miami-Jackson Meml. Hosp., Miami, 1976-81, pediatric pathologist, dir. div. edn. in pathology, 1981—; cons., lectr. U.S. Naval Hosp., Phila., 1972-76; instr. pathology Sch. Medicine U. Pa., 1945-49; instr. Sch. Medicine U. Pa. (Sch. Dentistry), 1947, Sch. Medicine U. Pa. (Grad. Sch. Medicine), 1948-55, vis. lectr., 1960-62; asst. prof. Temple U. Med. Sch., 1959-63, assoc. prof., 1963-67, prof. pediatrics, 1967-76, prof. pathology and pediatrics, 1981—; prof. pathology and pediatrics U., Miami, 1976—; cons. pediatric pathology div. med. examiner Dept. Pub. Health Phila., 1967-70; mem. perinatal biology and infant mortality research and tng. com. Nat. Inst. Child Health and Human Devel., NIH, 1971-73; mem. sci. adv. bd. Armed Forces Inst. Pathology, 1976-82; assoc. med. examiner, Dade County, Fla., 1976—; chmn. med. bd. Nat. Sudden Infant Death Syndrome Found., 1961-81, 87, pres., 1984-87, chmn. bd., 1985-88. Contbr. articles to profl. jours. NIH grantee. Mem. U.S. and Can. Acad. Pathology (pres. 1980-81), Coll. Physicians Phila., Internat. Assn. Pediatric Pathology, Dade County Med. Soc., Alpha Omega Alpha. Roman Catholic. Home: 1245 Thrush Ave Miami Springs FL 33166 Office: U Miami Sch of Med Dept Pathology PO Box 016960 Miami FL 33101

VALENCIA, SANDRA LEE, public relations executive; b. Pittston, Pa., May 1, 1960; d. John Anthony and Angeline (Maira) Sellani; m. Ruben Ruiz Valencia, Aug. 10, 1985. Bs in Music Therapy, Coll. Misericordia, Dallas, Pa., 1982; cert. profl. designation in pub. relations, UCLA, 1987. Cert. adult edn. instr., Calif. Music/recreation therapist Children's Services, Wilkes-Barre, Pa., 1983; music/recreation therapost Wyoming Valley Clinic, Wilkes-Barre, 1983-84; dir. activities Oakview Convalescent Hosp., Glendora, Calif., 1984-85; dir. community relations Oakview Convalescent Hosp., Glendora, 1985-86; dir. pub. relations Oakview Health Care, Inc., Covina, Calif., 1986—; tchr. adult edn. Citrus Community Coll., Azusa, Calif.; freelance writer; patient activities cons., Oakview Health Care, Inc. Author: (ednl. game series) Play on Words, 1985. Mem. Health Care Pub. Relations & Mktg. Assn., Sigma Phi Sigma. Republican. Home: 14515-2 Woodland Dr Fontana CA 92335 Office: Oakview Health Care Inc 706-A E Arrow Hwy Covina CA 91722

VALENSTEIN, KAREN, investment company executive; Ed. Conn. Coll., Hawthorne Coll., postgrad. NYU; div.; 2 children. Former mcpl. analyst Bank of N.Y., Citibank; with Lehman Bros. Kuhn Loeb Inc., v.p., to 1983; 1st v.p. E.F. Hutton Group, Inc., N.Y.C., 1983—. Office: E F Hutton Group Inc 31 W 52nd St New York NY 10019

VALENTE, BENITA, lyric soprano; b. Delano, Calif.; d. Lawrence Guiseppe and Severina Antonia (Masdonati) V.; m. Anthony Phillip Checchia, Nov. 21, 1959; 1 son, Peter. Grad., Curtis Inst. Music, 1960; studied with, Chester Hayden, Martial Singher, Lotte Lehmann, Margaret Harshaw. Met. Opera debut, 1973; leading roles in: Orfeo, Rigoletto, Traviata, Idomeneo, Marriage of Figaro, Faust, La Boheme, Falstaff, Turandot, Magic Flute, Rinaldo, Pelléas et Mélissande, Deidamia; appeared throughout U.S. and Europe, in operas and symphonies. Winner Met. Opera Council Audition 1960. Recs. for Columbia Records, Desmar Records, RCA, Pantheon. Mem. Phila. Cosmopolitan Club, Phila. Chamber Music Soc. (music adv.com.).

VALENTE, PATRICIA LUCILLE, academic counselor; b. Chgo., June 30, 1940; d. Joseph James and Mae L. (Durand) V.; m. Robert J. Maxwell, Jan. 19, 1963 (div. Feb. 1974); children: Kim Maxwell, Robert Maxwell; m. Robert W. Witzke, Aug. 4, 1977. BA, No. Ill. U., 1962, MS, 1967; MS, George Williams Coll., 1976. Cert. sex educator, sex therapist. Tchr. English Hinsdale (Ill.) High Sch., 1963-69; tchr. English Morton Coll., Cicero, Ill., 1969-71, counselor, sex therapist, 1971—; cons. West Chgo. (Ill.) Community High Sch., 1965-66; mem. north cen. visitation team Ill. State Dept. Edn., Springfield, 1968; presenter in field. Author: (with others) Community College Career Alternatives, 1981, The WOW Group: The New Frontier, 1984. Named Educator of Yr., Morton Coll., 1979. Mem. CWP (exec. bd. dirs. 1983—), ASSECT, IGPA, AGPA. Roman Catholic. Home: 17 W 507 Portsmouth Dr Westmont IL 60559 Office: Morton Coll 3801 S Central Ave Cicero IL 60650

VALENTINE, LINDA JEANNE KROES, apparel manufacturing company executive; b. Kalamazoo, Mar. 9, 1950; d. Keith Edward and Delores June (Burpee) Kroes; student Mich. State U., 1969-70; B.B.A., Western Mich U., 1974; M.B.A., Loyola U. Chgo., 1980; m. Clark McCray Valentine, Jr., Apr. 17, 1971. Sr. tng. specialist Montgomery Ward & Co., Chgo., 1976-79, salary adminstrn. specialist, 1979-80; compensation analyst Hart Schaffner & Marx, Chgo., 1980-81, corp. compensation mgr., 1981-83, corp. compensation and human resource systems mgr., 1983—. Mem. Am. Compensation Assn., Chgo. Compensation Assn., Human Resource Systems Profls., Internat. Assn. Personnel Women, Human Resource Planning Soc., Nat. Assn. Female Execs., M.B.A. Network, Loyola Grad Sch. Bus. Alumni Assn., NOW.

VALENTINE, LINDA WEAVER, lawyer; b. Indpls., Sept. 15, 1956; d. Charles Allen and Lenora Weaver. A.B. in Journalism magna cum laude, Ind. U., 1980, J.D. magna cum laude, 1982. Bar: Ind. 1983, U.S. Dist. Ct. (so. dist.) Ind. 1983, U.S. Ct. Claims 1983, U.S. Tax Ct. 1983, U.S. Ct. Mil. Appeals 1983, U.S. Ct. Appeals (7th cir.) 1983. Assoc. Bose McKinney & Evans, Indpls., 1983—; instr. Am. Inst. for Paralegal Studies, 1988—; lectr. Ind. Continuing Edn. Forum, 1988; judge Ind. U. Sch. Law Moot Ct. Competitions, 1986-88. Mem. Soc. Profl. Journalists, ABA, Ind. Bar Assn., Indpls. Bar Assn. Pi Beta Phi. Republican. Baptist. Office: Bose McKinney & Evans 11 N Pennsylvania St Indianapolis IN 46204

VALENTINE, MARJORIE PARKS, psychologist, consultant; b. Chattanooga, Apr. 20, 1928; d. Leon C. and Marjorie (Atlee) Parks; m. Andrew Jackson Valentine, July 20, 1949; children—Rawson J., Atlee Ann, Sarah. B.A., U. Tenn., 1949; M.A., George Washington U., 1954; Ph.D., Am. U., 1977. Lic. psychologist, D.C., 1981, Ill., 1987. Sch. psychologist Escambia County Schs., Pensacola, Fla., 1962-65, dir. Headstart Program, 1965; sch. psychologist Arlington (Va.) Pub. Schs., 1966-79; instr. U. Va. Regional Ctr., 1975-76; research affiliate Program on Women, Northwestern U., 1979-82; assoc. Cassell, Rath and Stoyanoff, Ltd., Evanston, Ill., 1981-85 ; pvt. practice psychologist, 1987—; adj. faculty Seabury-Western Seminary, 1984—. Pres. bd. dirs., exec. com. Chicago Commons Assn., 1980—. Mem. Am. Psychol. Assn., Ill. Psychol. Assn. Republican. Episcopalian. Club: Junior League of Evanston. Address: 1091 Sheridan Rd Winnetka IL 60093

VALENTINO, VIVIAN, advertising executive; b. Camaguey, Cuba, Mar. 1, 1952; came to U.S., 1966; d. Federico and Delia Margarita (Gutierrez) Diaz; divorced; 1 child, Yamberli Nichole; m. Walter Valentino, Aug. 2, 1978. BA, Montclair (N.J.) State U., 1978. Mgr., pub. relations asst. Intar Theatre, N.Y.C., 1976-84; advt. agy. mgr. Valentino Media Buying Service, Miami, Fla., 1986—. Fundraiser Nat. Puerto Rican Forum, N.Y.C., 1982-85. Mem. Camara de Comercio Latina. Home: 9960 SW 102 Ave Rd Miami FL 33176

VALENZUELA, DEBRA GUADALUPE, utility company executive; b. San Antonio, Mar. 7, 1957; d. Isaac Rosales and Jesusa (Escobar) V. BBA, St. Mary's U., San Antonio, 1979. Personnel asst. Union Camp Corp., San Antonio, 1979-82; benefits adminstr. City Water Bd., San Antonio, 1982-85, personnel and safety specialist, 1985—; bd. dirs. San Antonio Water Bd. Fed. Credit Union. Mem. Am. Water Works Assn., Nat. Assn. Female Execs., Nat. Notary Assn. Democrat. Roman Catholic. Office: City Water Bd PO Box 2449 1001 E Market San Antonio TX 78298

VALERIO, HELEN JOSEPHINE, restaurant company executive; b. Chelsea, Mass., Nov. 23, 1938; d. William P. and Helen (Hoffman) Kazukonis; m. Michael A. Valerio, Oct. 6, 1957; children—Michael A., Laura L., Linda M. Acct., Piece O Pizza, of Am. Inc., Arlington, Mass., 1958-63; treas. Papa Gino's of Am., Inc., Needham Heights, Mass., 1963—, sr. v.p., 1980-81, exec. v.p., 1981—; chmn. bd. Helen Broadcasting. Bd. dirs. Cath. Charitable Bur. Boston, Family Counseling Service Boston; chmn. Nat. Adv. Council Women's Ednl. Programs; trustee Nichols Coll., Dudley, Mass. Mem. Nat., Mass. restaurant assns., Fin. Execs. Inst., Small Bus. Adminstrn. (nat. adv. council). Roman Catholic. Clubs: Weston Community League, St. Julia's Women's (pres. 1977-78). Lodge: Dames of Malta. Home: 1064 Grove St Framingham MA 01701 Office: 600 Providence Hwy Dedham MA 02026

VALERIO, KAREN THERESA, telecommunications manager; b. Calgary, Alta., Can., Oct. 24, 1955; came to U.S., 1958; d. Eugene Frank and Anne (Kuri) V. Student U. Minn., Mpls., 1974-77, Loyola U., Chgo., 1981-82. Word processor IDS, Mpls., 1973-76; sec. MCI Telecommunications, Mpls., 1977-79, coordinator, Chgo., 1979-81, supr., 1981-83, ops. mgr., Los Angeles, 1983-85, customer service mgr., 1985-88; regional support mgr., 1988—. Mem. Nat. Assn. Female Execs., Humane Soc. U.S. Roman Catholic. Avocations: bicycling, reading, cooking. Home: 3539 Sawtelle Los Angeles CA 90066 Office: MCI Telecommunications 6101 W Centinela Culver City CA 90230

VALERY, LENORE DOROTHY, health services executive; b. Liberty, N.Y., June 20, 1947; d. Isaac and Eva (Kanter) V. Diploma, Kree Electrolysis, N.Y.C., 1967, Traphagen Fashion Design Sch., N.Y.C., 1969, Hoffman Electrolysis, N.Y.C., 1970, Internat. Sch. Esthetics, N.Y.C., 1971. Pres. Lenore D. Valery, Ltd., N.Y.C., 1973—. Fellow Soc. for Clin. and Med. Electrologists (cert.); mem. Internat. Guild Profl. Electrologists, Skin Care Assn. Am. Home and Office: 119 W 57 St New York NY 10019

VALETTE, REBECCA MARIANNE, educator; b. N.Y.C., Dec. 21, 1938; d. Gerhard and Ruth Adelgunde (Bischoff) Loose; m. Jean-Paul Valette, Aug. 6, 1959; children: Jean-Michel, Nathalie, Pierre. B.A., Mt. Holyoke Coll., 1959, L.H.D. (hon.), 1974; Ph.D., U. Colo., 1963. Instr., examiner in French and German U. So. Fla., 1961-63; instr. NATO Def. Coll., Paris, 1963-64, Wellesley Coll., 1964-65; asst. prof. Romance Langs. Boston Coll., 1965-68, assoc., 1968-73, prof., 1973—; lectr., cons. fgn. lang. pedagogy; Fulbright sr. lectr., Germany, 1974; Am. Council on Edn. fellow in acad. adminstrn., 1976-77. Author: books including Modern Language Testing, 1967, 77, French for Mastery, 1975, 81, 88, Contacts, 1976, 81, 85, C'est comme ça, 1978, 86, Spanish for Mastery, 1980, 84, Album: Cuentos del mundo hispánico, 1984, French for Fluency, 1985, Situaciones, 1988; contbr. numerous articles to fgn. lang. pedagogy and lit. publs. Mem. MLA (chmn. div. on teaching of lang. 1980-81), Am. Council on Teaching Fgn. Langs., Am. Assn. Tchrs. French (v.p. 1980-86), Am. Assn. Tchrs. German, Phi Beta Kappa, Alpha Sigma Nu. Home: 16 Mount Alvernia Rd Chestnut Hill MA 02167 Office: Boston Coll Lyons 311 Chestnut Hill MA 02167

VALIANT, EVA MARIE, account executive; b. Rahway, N.J., Dec. 6, 1958; d. Genare and Catherine (Speeshock) V. BA in Psychology, Rider Coll., 1980. Supr. service Altair Airlines, Tampa, Fla., 1981-83; mgr. sales Arrow Air, Tampa, Fla., 1983-85; account exec. Purolator Courier Corp., Tampa, Fla., 1985-87, Edison, N.J., 1987-88; profit freight systems Purolator Courier Corp., Newark, 1988—. Home: 1 John St PO Box 694 Carteret NJ 07008

VALIMONT, CONSTANCE MARIE, marketing research company executive; b. Philipsburg, Pa., Dec. 10, 1948; d. Levaud C. and Helen Ann (Lucas) V.; m. Stephen D. Pedersen, Dec. 30, 1967 (div. Dec. 1982). Student, Fla. State U., 1966-67; AA in Bus. Adminstrn., St. Petersburg Jr. Coll., 1973; BBA in Mktg. and Mgmt., U. So. Fla., 1976. Sec. service club U.S. Army Spl. Services, Fed. Republic Germany, 1970-71; jr. adminstr. E-Systems Inc., St. Petersburg, Fla., 1968-76; adminstrv. sec. Abcor Inc., Wilmington, Mass., 1977-78; asst. to controller Kneissl of Am., Merrimack, N.H., 1978-79; sales coordinator Skandinavia Inc., Londonderry, N.H., 1979-80; cons. Norfell Inc., Chelmsford, Mass., 1980-81; mgr. mktg. services Swix Sport U.S.A., Chelmsford, 1981-85; mgr. adminstrv. services Davidson-Peterson Assocs. Inc., York, Maine, 1985-87, project mgr., 1987—. Active Biden for Pres. campaign, Manchester, N.H., 1987. Mem. Seacoast Communications Network (treas.), N.H. Seacoast Tourism Council, Seacoast Postal Cusomer Council (sec.), Seacoast Bus. and Profl. Womens Club, Phi Kappa Phi, Beta Gamma Sigma. Democrat. Roman Catholic. Home: 17 Cushing Rd Newmarket NH 03857 Office: Davidson-Peterson Assocs Inc PO Box 350 Bragdon Commons York ME 03909

VALK, ELIZABETH, magazine publisher; b. Winston-Salem, N.C., Apr. 29, 1950; d. Henry Lewis and Elizabeth (Fuller) V. BA, Hollins Coll., 1972; MBA, Harvard Bus. Sch., 1979. Clin. adminstr. Mass. Gen. Hosp., Boston, 1973-77; asst. to circulation dir. Time Mag.-Time Inc., N.Y.C., 1979-80, 81-82; circulation dir. Fortune Mag.-Time Inc., N.Y.C., 1982-84, Sports Illustrated-Time Inc., N.Y.C., 1984-85, Time Mag.-Time Inc., N.Y.C., 1985-86; publisher Life Mag.-Time Inc., N.Y.C., 1987—. Bd. trustees Hollins Coll., 1987—. Office: Life Mag Time & Life Bldg 1271 Ave of the Americas New York NY 10020

VALK, SHIRLEY ROUNELLE, construction company executive; b. Trenton, Mich., Feb. 18, 1948; d. Granvel William and Blance Lophia (Pratt) Curtis; m. Billy Lee Baker, July 23, 1983; children: Jennifer Dawn Beedy, Joshua Mark. Grad. high sch., Whittier, Calif. Telephone operator Gen. Telephone Co., Whittier, 1967-68; bookkeeper Major Motor Supply Co., Downey, Calif., 1971-73; owner, mgr. Shirley's Daycare, Riverside, Calif., 1971-80; office mgr. Dr. Mastakas, Kingman, Ariz., 1981-84; fin. officer, co-owner Affordable Constrn. Co., Kingman, 1988—; with Steel Roof Systems, Riverside, cons. Mary Kay Cosmetics, Riverside. Mem. Nat. Assn. Female Execs., MADD. Democrat. Lutheran. Home: 13543 Avenal Hesperia CA 92345 Office: Steel Roof Systems 10447 Arlington Ave Riverside CA 92505

VALLARTA-SHORTER, KATHLEEN MAE, physical therapist; b. Freeport, Ill., Nov. 7, 1950; d. Roy Rudolph and Lois Marie (Pfile) Vallarta; m. Douglas Roy Stone, June 3, 1972 (div. July 1980); 1 child, Ryan Douglas; m. John William Shorter, Oct. 19, 1986. BS in Physical Medicine, U. Wis., 1973, postgrad. cert. in phys. therapy. Phys. therapist City View Nursing Home, Madison, Wis., 1973-75; staff phys. therapist Muhlenberg Med. Ctr.,

Bethlehem, Pa., 1975-77; phys. therapist Valley Group Physical Therapy Assocs., Bethlehem, 1978-80, Bethlehem Area Sch. Dist., 1980, Vis. Nurse Assn. of Bethlehem, 1980; staff phys. therapist Easton (Pa.) Hosp., 1980-85, coordinator of clin. edn., sr. staff phys. therapist, 1985-87, acting chief phys. therapist, 1987, chief phys. therapist, 1987—; clin. faculty supr. Temple U., Phila., 1985—; clin. field instr. U. Pitts., 1986—, various other colls. Mem. Am. Phys. Therapy Assn. (orthopedic, neurology and geriatric sects.), Pa. Phys. Therapy Assn. Republican.

VALLBONA, RIMA-GRETEL ROTHE, Spanish educator, writer; b. San José, Costa Rica, Mar. 15, 1931; d. Ferdinand Hermann and Emilia (Strassburger) Rothe; BA/BS, Colegio Superior de Señoritas, San José, 1948; diploma U. Paris, 1953; diploma in Spanish Philology, U. Salamanca, Spain, 1954; MA, U. Costa Rica, 1962; D in Modern Langs., Middlebury Coll., 1981; m. Carlos Vallbona, Dec. 26, 1956; children: Rima-Nuri, Carlos-Fernando, María-Teresa, María-Luisa. Tchr., Liceo J.J. Vargas Calvo, Costa Rica, 1955-56; faculty U. St. Thomas, Houston, 1964—, prof. Spanish, 1978—, head dept. Spanish, 1966-71, chmn. dept. modern fgn. lang., 1978-80; vis. prof. U. Houston, 1975-76, Rice U., 1980-81, U. St. Thomas, Argentina, summer 1972, Rice U. program in Spain, summer 1974. Mem. scholarship com. Inst. Hispanic Culture, 1978-79, 88, chmn., 1979, bd. dirs., 1974-76, chmn. cultural activities, 1979, 80, 85; bd. dirs. Houston Pub. Library, 1984—. Recipient Aquileo J. Echeverria Novel prize, 1968; Agripina Montes del Valle Novel prize, 1978; Jorge Luis Borges Short Story prize, Argentina, 1977; lit. award SW Conf. Latin Am. Studies, 1982; Constantin Found. grantee for research U. St. Thomas, 1981; Ancora lit. award, Costa Rica, 1984. Mem. MLA, Am. Assn. Tchrs. Spanish and Portuguese, Houston Area Tchrs. of Fgn. Langs., S. Cen. MLA, SW conf. Orgn. Latin Am. Studies, Latin Am. Studies Assn., Inst. Internat. de Lit. Iberoam., Latin Am. Writers Assn. of Costa Rica, Inst. Hispanic Culture of Houston, Casa Argentina de Houston, Inst. Lit. y Cultural Hispanico, Phi Sigma Iota, Sigma Delta Pi (hon.). Roman Catholic. Club: Nat. Writers. Author: Noche en vela, 1968, Yoland Oreamuno, 1972, La obra en prosa de Eunice Odio, 1981, Baraja de Soledades, Las Sombras que perseguimos, 1983; (short stories) Polvo de camino, 1971, La Salamandra rosada, 1979, Mujeres y agonias, 1982, Cosecha de pecadores, 1988; mem. editorial bd. Letras Femeninas, U.S.; co-dir. Foro Literario, Uruguay, Alba de América; contbr. numerous articles and short stories to lit. mags. Home: 3002 Ann Arbor St Houston TX 77063 Office: 3812 Montrose Blvd Houston TX 77006

VALLEAU, NORMA KATHRYN SASS, lawyer; b. Dearborn, Mich., Mar. 9, 1933; d. Norman Ralph and Dorothy Lorraine (Mullreed) Sass; m. Kenneth William Valleau, Sept. 2, 1953 (div. 1956); children—Bobbee Leota Kovar, Carla Renee Margolis; m. 2d John Henry Metz, July 15, 1983. A.S., Henry Ford Coll., 1974; B.S., Western State Coll., Fullerton, Calif. 1980, J.D., 1980. Bar: Ind. 1981. Actress, singer, dancer Kennedy Artists, N.Y.C., 1960-78; actress Eastside/Westside Repertory, N.Y.C., 1960-63, Herbert Berghof Studios, N.Y.C., 1963-64; legal intern Screen Actors Guild, Hollywood, Calif., 1978-80; ptnr. Metz & Valleau, Indpls., 1981-82; law clk. U.S. Bankruptcy Ct., Indpls., 1982-85; atty. legal div., bankruptcy specialist FDIC, 1985-87, sr. ptnr. Valleau, Coney & Metz, Indpls., 1987—; program dir. Lawyers in the Classroom project, N.Y. State Bar Assn., 1977; outstanding dir. Fullerton Children's Theatre, 1979. Mem. Friends of Benjamin Harrison House, Indpls., 1983—, Indpls. Hist. Soc., 1983—; instr. Free U., Indpls., 1983; v.p. Women's Caucus, Fullerton, Calif., 1978-81. Women's Caucus Book scholar, 1978-80. Mem. ABA, Ind. Bar Assn., Indpls. Bar Assn., Screen Actors Guild, Actors Equity Assn., Am. Guild Variety Artists, AFTRA, DAR (Caroline Scott Harrison chpt.). Lutheran. Home: 3663 N Pennsylvania Indianapolis IN 46205 Office: Valleau Coney & Metz 3663 N Pennsylvania -B Indianapolis IN 46205

VALLERY, JANET ALANE, industrial hygienist; b. Lincoln, Nebr., Apr. 4, 1948; d. Gerald William and Lois Florence (Robertson) V.; B.S., U. Nebr., Lincoln, 1970; diploma Bryan Meml. Sch. Med. Tech., Lincoln, 1971. Med. technologist Lincoln Gen. Hosp., 1971-72; congressional sec., 1973; lab. scientist Nebr. Dept. Health, 1973-79; sr. safety indsl. hygienist Nebr. Dept. Labor, 1979-85; indsl. hygienist U.S. Dept. Labor OSHA, 1985—; cons. in field. Mem. Am. Conf. Govt. Indsl. Hygienists, Am. Soc. Clin. Pathologists (assoc.), Arabian Horse Assn. Nebr., Nebr. Dressage Assn., Am. Indsl. Hygiene Assn., Am. Legion Aux. Republican. Methodist. Home: 4900 S 30th St Lincoln NE 68516 Office: 6910 Pacific St Rm 100 Omaha NE 68106

VALO, CAROLYN ROSE, hospital medical records director; b. Mpls., Dec. 29, 1952; d. Pierson John and Dancia (Bubalo) Kirk; m. David Allen Valo, Oct. 12, 1985. A.A.S., St. Mary's Jr. Coll., 1977; B.A., Metro State U., 1982. Cert. Am. Med. Record Assn. Sec. Nat. Assn. Ind. Businessmen, Mpls., 1969-70; clk., typist, data clk. Mpls. Health Dept., 1970-75, health info. mgr., 1977-84; faculty asst. St. Mary's Jr. Coll., Mpls., 1976-77, adj. faculty, 1978—; client service rep. Code 3 Health Info. Systems 3M, Mpls., 1984-85; asst. dir. med. records Fairview-Southdale Hosp., Mpls., 1985, dir. med. records, 1985—, mem. Patient Care Task Force; adj. faculty Moorhead Area Vocat. Tech. Inst., 1986—; mem. faculty St. Catherine's Coll., St. Mary's Campus, 1987; pvt. practice cons. Ambulatory Care, Mpls., 1983; cons. severity systems, quality assurance Mediqual Systems Inc., 1988, speaker profl. groups in field. Contbr. articles to profl. jours. Mem. Am. Med. Record Assn. (appeals panel), Minn. Med. Record Assn. (pres. 1984-85, award, dir.), Twin Cities Women in Computing, Assn. Record Mgrs. and Adminstrs., Nat. Assn. Female Execs. Home: 1897 Carroll Ave Saint Paul MN 55104 Office: Fairview-Southdale & Ridges 6401 France Ave S Minneapolis MN 55435

VALO, MARTHA ANN, hospital dietary official; consultant; b. West Aliquippa, Pa., Apr. 6, 1938; d. George and Susan Helen (Pollak) V.; m. John Daniel Dempsey, Dec. 17, 1974. B.S., Carlow Coll., 1960; postgrad. U. Pa. Registered dietitian. Food service mgr. Stouffer's Mgmt. Co., Phila., 1960-76; restaurant mgr. Strawbridge & Clothier, Phila., 1976-78; food service dir. Saunders House, Phila., 1978-80; dir. dietary services Kennedy Meml. Hosp., U. Med. Ctr., Stratford, N.J., 1980—; cons. dietitian Pinecrest Nursing Home, Sewell, N.J., 1980—; chmn. N.J. Hosp. Assn. Dietary Group Purchasing, Princeton, 1980—; adj. faculty Camden County Coll., Blackwood, N.J., 1985—. Mem. Am. Dietetic Assn., N.J. Dietetic Assn., Phila. Dietetic Assn., So. N.J. Nutritional Council, Am. Soc. for Hosp. Food Service Adminstrs. Home: 43 Harwood Ln Clementon NJ 08021 Office: Kennedy Meml Hosps Univ Med Ctr 18 E Laurel Rd Stratford NJ 08084

VALONE, MELISSA BRIANA, audio-visual company executive; b. Austin, Tex., Dec. 10, 1950; d. James Floyd and Elizabeth (Emerson) V. m. Don Shuwarger, Oct. 31, 1981. B.A., U. Colo., 1974. Studio mgr. United Audio Rec., San Antonio, 1974-76; co-owner Cat Tracks, San Antonio, 1976-78, Houston, 1978-82, v.p. Cat Tracks, Inc., Houston, 1982—, pres., 1983—. Recipient 1st, 2d and 3d place awards for audio-visual prodn., 5W's award 1984, 85, 86, 87 Internat. Assn. Bus. Communicators, Houston, 1983, merit award, 1984; 1st place Addy award San Antonio Advt. Fedn., 1978, 79, 2 awards of excellence, 1977, Best of Tex. award Tex. Pub. Relations Assn., others. Mem. Audio Engrng. Soc., Houston Advt. Fedn., Assn. for Multi-Image, Women in Communications (bd. dirs., 1st place Matrix award Houston chpt. 1984, 85, 86, 87). Home: 16325 Brook Forest Dr Houston TX 77059 Office: Cat Tracks Inc 11328 S Post Oak Rd Suite 104 Houston TX 77035

VAMBERY, MARIE JOSEPHE, drug company executive, consultant; b. Oran, Algeria, Aug. 3, 1950; d. Jean and Santina (Linteris) Radenac; m. Robert George Vambery, Mar. 5, 1976. Lic. in English, U. Paris, 1969; M.B.A., Ecole de Haut Enseignement Commercial, Paris, 1971, Columbia U., 1973. Brand supr. Procter & Gamble Co., Paris, 1973-76; product mgr. L'Oreal Co., N.Y.C., 1976-77; sr. product mgr. Block Drug Co., Inc., Jersey City, 1979-81, dir. new products, 1981-87, product group mgr., 1987—; sr. product mgr. CPC Internat. Best Foods, Englewood Cliffs, N.J., 1979-81. Author: Marketing in the French Tire Industry, 1971. Fulbright Found. scholar, 1971; Johnson Wax Found. fellow, 1971, French Govt. Fgn. Office fellow, 1972. Mem. Am. Mgmt. Assn., Am. Mktg. Assn. Club: Essex County Country (West Orange, N.J.). Home: Wildwood Ave Llewelyn Park West Orange NJ 07052 Office: Block Drug Co Inc 257 Cornelison Ave Jersey City NJ 07302

VAN AMAN, CONSTANCE SUE, data processing manager; b. South Bend, Ind., Oct. 5, 1953; d. Jack Vernon and Phyllis Henrietta (Smith) Hess; m. Dale Patrick Vanaman, Oct. 15, 1976; (div. 1985); children: Troy Alan, Chad James. ADP, Ind. Vocat. Tech. Coll., 1981. Programmer Triad-Utrad, Huntington, Ind., 1980-81; project mgr. K-Mart Corp., Fort Wayne, 1981—; prof. Ind. Vocat. Tech. Coll., Fort Wayne, 1981—. Bd. dirs. Stop Child Abuse and Neglect Orgn., Fort Wayne, 1985-87. Fellow Nat. Assn. Female Execs.; mem. Soc. to Advance Total User Systems (bd. dirs. 1985—). Democrat. Methodist. Avocations: piano, music, interior decorating, tennis. Home: 123 N Indiana Ave Auburn IN 46706 Office: K-Mart Corp Ferguson Rd Box 359 Fort Wayne IN 46801

VANAMAN, LINDA BELL, telecommunications company executive; b. Lexington, Ky., Aug. 13, 1941; d. William Herald and Velma (Hill) Bell; m. Thomas Clark Vanaman, Mar. 1962 (div. Dec. 1983); children: Thomas Randolph, John Tyler. BA magna cum laude, Duke U., 1982. Office mgr., then personnel asst. Foam Design, Inc., Research Triangle Park, N.C., 1982-84; staffing-recruiting specialist Sumitomo Electric RT, Inc., Research Triangle Park, 1985-87; coordinator relocation and immigration No. Telecom Inc., Research Triangle Park, 1987-88, mgr. staffing services, 1988—. Mem. exec. bd. Spouse Employment Assistance Program, Research Triangle Park, 1987—; bd. dirs. Durham Chamber Pvt. Industry Council, 1985-87, Triangle Area Bus. Advisory Council, 1986-87; v.p. adv. bd. Duke U. Art Mus., 1986-87. Mem. Am. Soc. Personnel Adminstrs., Durham Triangle Personnel Assn. (v.p. 1987-88, pres.-elect 1988—). Home: 3102 Eubanks Rd Durham NC 27707 Office: No Telecom Inc 4001 E Chapel Hill-Nelson Hwy PO Box 13010 Research Triangle Park NC 27709

VAN ANDEL, BETTY JEAN, household products company executive; b. Mich., Dec. 14, 1921; d. Anthony and Daisy (Van Dyk) Hoekstra; A.B., Calvin Coll., 1943; m. Jay Van Andel, Aug. 16, 1952; children—Nan Elizabeth, Stephen Alan, David Lee, Barbara Ann. Elementary sch. tchr., Grand Rapids, Mich., 1943-45; service rep. and supr. Mich. Bell Telephone Co., Grand Rapids, 1945-52; bd. dirs. Amway Corp., Grand Rapids, 1972—. Treas., LWV, 1957-60; chmn. Eagle Forum, Mich., 1975—; bd. dirs. Christian Sch. Ednl. Found., Pine Rest Christian Hosp., Grand Rapids Opera, 1982, exec. com. Mem. Nat. Trust Hist. Preservation, St. Cecelia Music Soc., Smithsonian Assos. Republican. Club. Women's City of Grand Rapids Home: 7186 Windy Hill Rd SE Grand Rapids MI 49506 Office: PO Box 172 Ada MI 49301

VAN ANDEL-GABY, BARBARA A., marketing professional; b. Grand Rapids, Mich., May 9, 1962; d. Jay and Betty Jean (Hoekstra) Van Andel; m. Richard Douglas Gaby, June 29, 1985. BA, Hope Coll., 1983; MBA, Ind. U., 1985. Mktg. intern Marriott Corp., Bethesda, Md., 1984; mgmt. specialist Amway Corp., Grand Rapids, Mich., 1985-87; sales mgr. Amway Grand Plaza Hotel, Grand Rapids, 1987—. Bd. dirs. Better Bus. Bur. of Western Mich. Mem. Nat. Assn. Female Execs., Assn. MBA Execs., Am. Mktg. Assn. Republican. Home: 6749 Ada Dr Grand Rapids MI 49506 Office: Amway Corp 7575 E Fulton Ada MI 49355

VAN ANTWERPEN, REGINA LANE, underwriter, insurance company executive; b. Milw., Aug. 16, 1939; d. Joseph F. Gagliano and Sophia B. (Johannik) Wolfe; widowed; children: Thomas II, Victoria. Student, U. Wis., Milw., 1954-57. Vol. tchr. St. Eugene Sch., Milw., 1968-72; office mgr. Gardner Beuder Inc., Milw., 1972-80; mfg. rep. Rosenbloom & Co., Chgo., 1980-81; spl. agt. Northwestern Mut. Life, Milw., 1981—; registered rep. Northwestern Mut. Life Equities Inc., Milw., 1985—. Author (poetry) One More Time Its Christmas, 1978, True Friendship, 1979. Mgr. Sch. Bd. Elections, Fox Point, 1969; v.p. Suburban Rep. Women's CLub, Milw., 1968-72. Mem. Milw. Life Underwriters, Women's Life Underwriters (v.p. 1982-83), Legis. Orgn. Life Underwriters, Nat. Assn. Securities Dealers (lic.). Republican. Roman Catholic. Office: Northwestern Mut Life 7545 North Point Washington Rd Milwaukee WI 53217

VAN ARK, JOAN, actress. d. Carroll and Dorothy Jean (Hemenway) Van A.; m. John Marshall, Feb. 1, 1966; 1 child, Vanessa Jeanne. Student, Yale Sch. Drama. Appeared at Tyrone Guthrie Theatre, Washington Arena Stage, in London, on Broadway; appeared in plays: Barefoot in the Park; School for Wives; Rules of the Game; Cyrano de Bergerac; Ring Round the Moon; appeared on TV series: Temperatures Rising; We've Got Each Other; Dallas; Knots Landing, 1979—; motion pictures for TV: The Judge and Jake Wyler, 1972; Big Rose, 1974; Shell Game, 1975; The Last Dinosaur, 1977; Red Flag, 1981; TV miniseries: Testimony of Two Men, 1978. Recipient Theatre World award, 1970-71, Los Angeles Drama Critics Circle award, 1973. Mem. Actors Equity Assn., SAG, AFTRA. Club: San Fernando Valley Track. Office: care William Morris Agy Inc 151 El Camino Beverly Hills CA 90212 *

VANBARRIGER, CAROL LYNNE, healthcare consultant; b. Connellsville, Pa., Apr. 26, 1941; d. Charles Lynn and Iola Grace (Sembower) Sliger.; m. George Van Barriger, May 27, 1966 (div. Feb. 1972). RN, Montefiore Hosp., 1962; BS, Coll. St. Francis, 1985; postgrad, Nat. Coll. Edn., 1987—. Pub. health nurse Kendall County Health Dept., Yorkville, Ill., 1970-72; team leader Edward Hosp., Naperville, Ill., 1972-73; emergency nurse Cen. Dupage Hosp., Winfield, Ill., 1973-74; staff nurse and head nurse Palos Community Hosp., Palos Heights, Ill., 1974-77, surg. nurse, 1977-82; auditor Med-Charge Analysis, Chgo., 1982-83; mgr. Intracorp CIGNA, Glen Ellyn, Ill., 1983-86, Metlife Healthcare Network, Schaumburg, Ill., 1986; project mgr. Healthcare Intermediaries, Lombard, Ill., 1986-88; dir., provider services Multicare HMO, Chicago, IL, 1988—; Mem. group comparison studies healthcare delivery/costs USSR, 1981, China, 1982, England, 1985. V.p. Indian Oak Condominium Assn., Bolingbrook, Ill., 1972-76; treas. Hickory Heights Condominium Assn., Hickory Hills, Ill., 1978-83, bd. dirs. 1983-87. Mem. Nat. Assn. Quality Assurance Profls., Ill. Assn. Quality Assurance Profls., Midwest Assn. Billing Auditors (treas. 1986-87), Nat. Assn Female Execs., Ill. Nurses Assn., Women's Health Exec. Network. Home: 9450 Greenbriar Dr Hickory Hills IL 60457

VAN BRONKHORST, ERIN MARIE, journalist, educator; b. Seattle, June 24, 1949; d. John and Edna Marie (de la Torre) Van B.; m. Steven G. Buty, Apr. 25, 1987. B.A. in History, U. Wash., 1971, M.Bus. and Econs. Journalism (Bus. and Econs. Reporting fellow), 1982. News writer Sta. KIRO-TV, Seattle, 1970-71; newswoman AP, Seattle and Olympia, Wash., 1971-73; editor, co-pub. Pandora Women's News Jour., Seattle, 1973-76; polit. writer Fairbanks (Alaska) Daily News-Miner, 1976-77; reporter Seattle Post-Intelligencer, 1977-79, copy editor, 1979-83; vis. asst. prof. communication arts Gonzaga U., Spokane, Wash., 1983-84; copy editor Tacoma News Tribune, 1984-88; writer Seattle Bus. Jour.; tchr. news writing YWCA, 1974. Recipient Hearst monthly award for spot news, 1977; 1st place for page layout Nat. Fedn. Press Women, 1984. Mem. Wash. Press Assn., Phi Beta Kappa. Author: (with Cara Peters) How to Stop Sexual Harassment: Strategies for Women on the Job, 1980. Home: 620 W Mercer Pl #1A Seattle WA 98119

VAN BRUNT, MARCIA ADELE, social worker; b. Chgo., Oct. 21, 1937; d. Dean Frederick and Faye Lila (Greim) Slauson; student Moline (Ill.) Pub. Hosp. Sch. Nursing, 1955-57; B.A. with distinguished scholastic record, U. Wis., Madison, 1972, M.S.W. (Fed. tng. grantee), 1973; M.O.E. Bartholomew; children—Suzanne, Christine, David. Social worker div. community services Wis. Dept. Health Social Services, Rhinelander, 1973, regional adoption coordinator, 1973-79, chief adoption and permanent planning no. region, 1979-82, asst. chief direct services and regulation no. region, 1983-84, adminstr., clin. social worker No. Family Services, Inc.; counselor, public speaker, cons. in field of clin. social work. Home: 5264 Forest Ln Rt 1 Rhinelander WI 54501 Office: Box 237 Rhinelander WI 54501

VAN CASPEL, VENITA WALKER, financial planner; b. Sweetwater, Okla.; d. Leonard Rankin and Ella Belle (Jarnagin) Walker. Student, Duke, 1944-46; B.A., U. Colo., 1948, postgrad., 1949-51; postgrad., N.Y. Inst. Fin., 1962. Cert. fin. planner. Stockbroker Rauscher Pierce & Co., Houston, 1962-65, A.G. Edwards & Sons, Houston, 1965-68; founder, pres., owner Van Caspel & Co., Inc., Houston, 1968—, Van Caspel Wealth Mgmt.; owner, mgr. Van Caspel Planning Service, Van Caspel Advt. Agy.; owner Diamond V Ranch; dir. MBank; Moderator PBS TV show The Money Makers and Profiles of Success, 1980; 1st women mem. Pacific Stock Exchange. Author: Money Dynamics, 1975, Dear Investor; The New Money Dynamics, 1978, Money Dynamics for the 1980's, 1980, The Power of Money Dynamics, Money Dynamics for the New Economy, Money Dynamics for the 1990's; editor: Money Dynamics Letter; columnist The Sat. Evening Post. Bd. dirs. Boy Scouts Am., Horatio Alger Assn., Robert Schuller Ministries. Recipient Matrix award Theta Sigma Phi, 1969, Horatio Alger award for Disting. Americans, 1982, Disting. Woman's medal Northwood Inst., 1986, George Norlin award U. Colo. Alumni Assn., 1987. Mem. Internat. Assn. Fin. Planners, Inst. Cert. Fin. Planners, Phi Gamma Mu, Phi Beta Kappa. Methodist. Office: Van Caspel & Co Inc 1300 Post Oak Blvd 22nd Floor Houston TX 77056

VANCE, CARRIE TEMPLE, nurse; b. Jackson, Miss., Nov. 20, 1944. A.A. in Nursing, San Joaquin Delta Coll., Stockton, Calif., 1974; BA in Health Service Adminstrn., St. Mary's Coll., Moraga, Calif., 1978; MS in Nursing Adminstrn. and Music, PhD in Music Performance, Columbia Pacific U., 1985. Lic. nurse, Calif. Staff nurse Dameron Hosp., Stockton, Calif., 1976-77, charge nurse, 1977-80, supr. nursery, 1980—. Mem. San Joaquin Gen. Hosp. Delta Coll. Nurse Alumni Assn., Soc. Nursing Service Adminstrs., Nat. Assn. Female Execs., Columbia Pacific U. Alumni Assn., Nat. Assn. Neonatal Nurses, St. Mary's Coll. Alumni Assn. Seventh-day Adventist. Office: Dameron Hosp Assn 525 W Acacia St Stockton CA 95203

VANCE, KATHERINE MCCORMICK, lawyer; b. Missoula, Mont., Nov. 30, 1953; d. John Thomas and Camilla (McCormick) V.; m. G. Bruce Sewell, May 1, 1982. B.A., St. Lawrence U., 1976; J.D., Tulsa U., 1979. Bar: Okla. 1979. Pvt. practice, Tulsa, 1979-84; estate adminstr. U.S. Bankruptcy Ct. Eastern Dist. Okla., 1984-87; asst. U.S. trustee region 20 Exec. Office for U.S. Trustees, Dept. Justice, Tulsa, 1987—. Mem. Women's Concerns Forum, Tulsa, 1981-84; mem. Task Force on Domestic Violence, Tulsa, 1981-84; pres. Democratic Women's Action Group, Tulsa, 1983-84; mem. Okla. Dem. Task Force on Women, 1984. Mem. ABA, Okla. Bar Assn. (dir. young lawyers div. 1983-88), Okla. Trial Lawyers Assn. (membership com. 1984), Tulsa County Bar Assn., Tulsa Women Lawyers Assn. (exec. com. 1984). Democrat. Episcopalian. Office: US Trustee Office 3130 US Courthouse Tulsa OK 74103

VANCE, ZINNA BARTH, artist, writer; b. Phila., Sept. 28, 1917; d. Carl Paul Rudolph Barth and Dorothy Ellice (Wilson) Hart; m. Nathan E. Curry (div. 1959); m. Samuel Therrel Vance, Dec. 2, 1960; children: Barry, Scott Hart. BS in Edn. summa cum laude, Southwestern U., Georgetown, Tex., 1965; MA in Communications, U. Tex., 1969. Cert. in teaching langs., Tex. Freelance writer various publs., 1946-56; assoc. editor, newspaper Canacao Clipper, Philippines, 1956-58; dir. Region One Tex. Fine Arts Assn., Austin, 1962-63; sec. Tex. Fgn. Langs. Assn., 1967; publicity dir. Burnet (Tex.) Creative Arts, 1983—; freelance portrait artist, Liberty Hill, Tex.; owner Gallery Zinna Portrait Studio, Liberty Hill, Tex., 1978—; artist registry Hill Country Arts Found., Ingram, Tex., 1984—; art columnist two newspapers Burnet, 1983—. Contbr. numerous articles to profl. jours.; exhibited in pvt. and corp. collections; illustrator children's books; numerous one-woman shows. Active Hill Country Arts Found., 1978—, Burnet Creative Arts, 1980—, Hill Country Council of Arts, 1986—. Named one of Tex. Emerging Artists Hill Country Arts Found., 1985; Featured as Cover story Philippines Internat. mag., 1957. Mem. Nat. Mus. Women in Arts (charter mem.), Nat. Portrait Inst., Alpha Chi, Phi Kappa Phi. Republican. Episcopalian. Home: Rt 2 Box 135 Liberty Hill TX 78642

VANCINA, EDLYN JEAN, skin care consultant, problem solver; b. Joliet, Ill., Jan. 3, 1954; d. Edward Joseph and Marilyn Sophia (Fleischauer) V.; m. Joseph Lawrence Scott, May 12, 1986. BS in Edn., No. Ariz. U., 1976. Cons. skin care Mary Kay Cosmetics, Dallas, 1980-85; make-up artist Christian Dior, El Segundo, Calif., 1985—; make-up cons. Biotherm Cosmetics, 1986—; make-up artist Janet Sartin Inc., N.Y.C., 1988; promotional rep. Clientele, Inc., Miami, Fla., 1988—; asst. mktg. Halston Fragrance, 1987, Deneuve Fragrance, 1987, Ralph Lauren Fragrance, 1987, Fendi Fragrance, 1987; mem. career mktg. bd. Mademoiselle mag., N.Y.C., 1987—. Mem. Am. Bus. Women's Assn., Flagstaff, Ariz. C. of C. (hon. Sawdust Art Festival Queen). Episcopalian. Home and Office: 22024 Antigua Mission Viejo CA 92692

VAN CLEAVE, KIRSTIN DEAN (KIT), writer, educator, publishing executive; b. Ft. Worth, Jan. 9, 1940; d. Henry Shibley and Lola Kathryn (Wimberly) van C. BA in Journalism, North Tex. State U., 1961; MA in English, U. Houston, 1972; DL in English, London Inst., 1973. Reporter Associated Gen. Contractors News Service, Houston, 1961-62; dir. pub. relations Diboll Advt. Agy., Tex., 1963-64; writer Goodwin, Dannenbaum, Littman and Wingfield Advt. Agy., Houston, 1964-65; reporter Houston Tribune, 1965-68; copywriter sales promotion dept. Gulf Pub. Co., 1968-70; Houston editor, then mng. editor Metrobeat, Dallas, 1970; editor publs., dir. pub. relations, press rep. Baroid div. NL Industries, Inc., Houston, 1973-74; presdl. speechwriter Gulf Oil Co., 1974-76; chief exec. officer Inner-View Pub. Co., Houston, 1980—; mem. faculty U. Houston; past mem. faculty Coll. of Mainland, Texas City, Tex., St. Agnes Acad., Houston. Author: They Still Do, 1973, Folklore of Texas Cultures, 1975, (poetry) Day of Love (set into a song cycle which was nominated for Pulitzer prize in Mus. Composition), 1978, Amourette, 1979, Laurels, 1980; librettist: Four Songs (composer Thomas Pasatieri), 1980; editor Inner-View mag., Houston; columnist: Houston Home & Garden, Houston Guide, Scene mag., In Houston, Billboard; contbr. articles to mags. Regional coordinator South and S.W. region, leader Houston chpt. Guardian Angels. Recipient Mayor's Vol. award City of Houston, 1988, Excellence in Journalism award Houston Exec. Adv. Council, 1986, 1st Place award Harris County Med. Soc., 1986, Clean Houston Pub. Service award, 1986-87; named one of fifty Most Interesting Houstonians, City Mag., 1985. Mem. S.W. C. of C., Houston C. of C., AAUP, Music Critics Assn., Internat. Assn. Bus. Communicators, Am. Soc. Authors and Journalists, World Tae Kwon Do Fedn., Cha Yon Ryu Black Belt Assn., Nat. Women's Martial Arts Fedn., Tex. Press Assn., Houston Press Club. Home: PO Box 66156 Houston TX 77266

VAN CURA, JOYCE BENNETT, librarian, educator; b. Madison, Wis., Mar. 25, 1944; d. Ralph Eugene and Florence Marie (Cramer) Bennett; m. E. Jay Van Cura, July 5, 1986. B.A. in Liberal Arts (scholar), Bradley U., 1966; M.S. in L.S., U. Ill., 1971. Library asst. research library Caterpillar Tractor Co., Peoria, Ill., 1966-67; reference librarian, instr. library tech. Ill. Central Coll., East Peoria, 1967-73; asst. prof. Sangamon State U., Springfield, Ill., 1973-80, assoc. prof., 1980-86; head library ref. dept. Ill. Inst. Tech., 1987—; convenor Council II, Ill. Clearinghouse for Acad. Library Instrn., 1978; presentor 7th Ann. Conf. Acad. Library Instrn., 1977, Nat. Women's Studies Assn., 1983, others; participant Gt. Lakes Women's Studies Summer Inst., 1981. Democratic precinct Committeewoman, 1982—. Pres., Springfield chpt. NOW, 1978-79. Ill. state scholar, 1962-66; recipient Am. Legion citizenship award, 1962; cert. of recognition Ill. Bicentennial Commn., 1974; invited Susan B. Anthony luncheon, 1978, 79. Mem. ALA, Ill. Library Assn. (presentor 1984) Ill. Assn. Coll. and Research Libraries (bibliog. instrn. com.), Am. Fedn. Tchrs., AAUW (chmn. standing com. on women Springfield br., mem. com. on women Ill. state div.), Nat. Women's Studies Assn. (presentor 1983, 84, 85) Springfield Art Assn., Nat. Trust Historic Preservation, Women in Mgmt., Beta Phi Mu. Reviewer Library Jour., Am. Reference Books Ann. Contbr. article in field to publ. Home: 535 N Michigan #1614 Chicago IL 60611-3810 Office: Ill Inst Tech Paul Galvin Library Chicago IL 60616

VAN DAM, DARLENE LAURA, computer executive; b. San Francisco, Feb. 10, 1948; d. Clyde LeRoy and Edna Lee (Alderman) Whitfield; m. Donald R. Van Dam, Oct. 14, 1974; children: Jeffrey Thomas, Laura Anne. BA in Psychology cum laude, Calif. State U., Northridge, 1974. Cert. elem. tchr., Calif. Tchr. Los Angeles Unified Sch. Dist., 1977-80; systems programmer Gen. Electric Info. Services, Rockville, Md., 1980-83, mgr. tng. MCI, Arlington, Va., 1983-84; task mgr. Network Solutions, Inc., Vienna, Va., 1984, div. dir., 1984-87, v.p., 1987—; instr. data processing Litton Data Command, Agoura, Calif., 1980; cons. Deltak, Atlanta, 1984—, MCI, Arlington, 1985-86, Riggs Bank, Washington, 1986—; bd. dirs. Computer & Office Project Enterprise, Gaithersburg, Md. Mem. Ariz. Council Child Care, Phoenix, 1975-77; fund-raiser Juvenile Diabetes Assn., Washington; com. mem. PTA, Gaithersburg. Mem. Balt.-Washington Instrs. Soc., Washington Info. Ctr. User Group, SAS User Group, Bus. and Profl. Women's

Orgn. Republican. Jewish. Home: PO Box 159 Gaithersburg MD 20877 Office: Network Solutions Inc 8229 Boone Blvd 7th Floor Vienna VA 22180

VANDAME, LYNN MICINSKI, manufacturing company executive; b. South Bend, Ind., May 23, 1954; d. Harry Patrick and Shirley Ann (Kaysen) Micinski; m. Danny Lee VanDame, Nov. 27, 1982; children—Helen Michele, Katrina Ann. A.Applied Sci., Tex. State Tech. Inst., 1974; completion cert. McLennan Community Coll., 1978; B.S., Purdue U., 1982. Lic. practical nurse; registered animal technician. Personnel mgr. Mott's, Inc., Waco, Tex., 1974-76; sr. quality assurance operator M & M Mars Candy, Waco, 1976-77; research asst. Purdue U., West Lafayette, Inc., 1980, 82-84; quality assurance supr. Gen. Foods Mfg. Corp., Lafayette, Ind., 1985-88; quality assurance mgr. Fasson- Roll div., Ft. Wayne, Ind., 1988—. Contbr. articles to various publs. Mem. Inst. Food Technologists, Leather Artisans Internat., Lafayette Kennel Club, Am. Soc. for Quality Control. Alpha Zeta. Democrat. Roman Catholic. Avocations: leathercraft; raising, training, and breeding Appaloosa horses and Siberian Huskies. Home: Box 5215 Lafayette IN 47903 Office: Fasson Roll Div 3011 Independence Dr Fort Wayne IN 46808

VAN DE BOVENKAMP, SUE ERPF, charitable organization executive; b. N.Y.C.; d. George Norton and Bettina Lions (Hearst) Mortimore; student Gardner Sch., Art Students League, Cooper Union; m. Armand Grover Erpf, 1965; children: Cornelia Aurelia, Armand Bartholomew; m. Gerrit Pieter Van de Bovenkamp, Aug. 11, 1973. Pres. Armand G. Erpf Fund, N.Y.C., 1971—; founder, hon. chmn. Erpf Catskill Cultural Ctr., 1972—. Bd. advisors, founder N.Y. Zool. Soc., 1971—, William Beebe fellow, 1983—; fellow in perpetuity Met. Mus. Art, 1977; life fellow Pierpont Morgan Library, 1974—; mem. council of friends Whitney Mus. Am. Art, 1971-77; mem. Whitney Circle, 1978—; bd. dirs. Catskill Ctr. for Conservation and Devel., 1983-86; mem. adv. council, dept. art history and archaeology Columbia U., 1972—, established univ. seminar on uses of oceans, 1977, mem. adv. council Translation Ctr., 1986; life conservator N.Y. Pub. Library, 1980; fellow Frick Collection; 1971—; mem. council Agribus. Council, Inc., 1979-87; founder, life mem. World Wildlife Fund, 1973—, bd. dirs., 1984—; mem. pres.'s council Columbia U., 1973-78. Life mem. Mus. City N.Y., 1972—, mem. pres.'s council, 1971—. Mem. N.Y. Acad. Scis., The Planetary Soc. Office: The Armand G Erpf Fund 640 Park Ave New York NY 10021

VAN DEMARK, RUTH ELAINE, lawyer; b. Santa Fe, N. Mex., May 16, 1944; d. Robert Eugene and Bertha Marie (Thompson) Van D.; m. Leland Wilkinson, June 23, 1967; children—Anne Marie, Caroline Cook. A.B., Vassar Coll., 1966; M.T.S., Harvard U., 1969; J.D. with honors, U. Conn., 1976. Bar: Conn. 1976, U.S. Dist. Ct. Conn. 1976, Ill. 1977, U.S. Dist. Ct. (no. dist.) Ill. 1977, U.S. Supreme Ct. 1983, U.S. Ct. Appeals (7th cir.) 1984. Instr. legal research and writing Loyola U. Sch. Law, Chgo., 1976-79; assoc. Wildman, Harrold, Allen & Dixon, Chgo., 1977-84, ptnr., 1984—. bd. dirs., sec. Systat, Inc., Evanston, Ill. Assoc. editor Conn. Law Rev., 1975-76. Mem. adv. bd. Horizon Hospice, Chgo., 1978—; del.-at-large White House Conf. on Families, Los Angeles, 1980; mem. adv. bd. YWCA Battered Women's Shelter, Evanston, Ill., 1982-86; vol. atty. Pro Bono Advocates, Chgo., 1982—, bd. dirs. Friends of Pro Bono Advocates Orgn.; bd. dirs. New Voice Prodns., 1984-86, Byrne Piven Theater Workshop, 1987—; founder, bd. dirs. Friends of Battered Women and their Children, 1986-87. Mem. ABA, Ill. Bar Assn., Conn. Bar Assn., Chgo. Bar Assn., Appellate Lawyers Assn. Ill. (bd. dirs. 1985-87), Women's Bar Assn. Ill., AAUW, Jr. League Evanston (chair State Pub. Affairs Com. 1987-88, Vol. of Yr. 1983-84). Clubs: Chgo. Vassar (pres. 1979-81), Cosmopolitan (N.Y.C.). Home: 1127 Asbury Ave Evanston IL 60202 Office: Wildman Harrold Allen & Dixon 1 IBM Plaza Chicago IL 60611

VANDENBERG, SISTER PATRICIA CLASINA, hospital administrator; b. N.Y.C., Mar. 15, 1948; d. Paul John and Alice Margaret (Walters) V. BS in Nursing cum laude, Hunter Coll., 1970; MHA, Duke U., 1979. Nurse critical care staff Roosevelt Hosp., N.Y.C., 1967-69, St. Vincent's Hosp., N.Y.C., 1970; nurse specialist, instr. Meth. Hosp. Bklyn., 1970-71; cons., instr. St. John's Hosp., Anderson, Ind., 1972; nurse critical care, ambulatory services Mt. Carmel Med. Ctr., Columbus, Ohio, 1974-77; v.p. clin. services, apostolic devel. Holy Cross Hosp., Silver Springs, Md., 1979-83; pres., chief exec. officer St. Alphonsus Regional Med. Ctr., Boise, Idaho, 1983—, trustee, 1983—; trustee Holy Cross Hosp., Blue Cross Idaho, Boise, 1986—. Mem. task force United Way, Boise, 1985; bd. dirs. ARC, Boise, 1984-85. Mem. Idaho Hosp. Assn. (trustee), Greater Boise C. of C. (bd. dirs. 1987), Sigma Theta Tau. Roman Catholic. Office: St Alphonsus Regional Med Ctr 1055 N Curtis Rd Boise ID 83706

VANDER, BARBARA J., controller; b. Junction City, Kans., Mar. 7, 1955; d. Atlas Vander and Jacklon C. (Midkiff) Clement; m. Ronald Albert Nipper, Nov. 13, 1982. BS in Bus. Adminstrn. in Acctg., La. State U., 1977, MBA, 1980, MS in Acctg., 1981. CPA, La., Tex. Performance auditor, budget officer City of Shreveport, La., 1978-79; staff acct. Memaca Petrolium Co., Baton Rouge, 1979-81; auditor Ernst & Whinney, CPA, New Orleans, 1981-82, Arthur Young, CPA, San Antonio, 1982-83; controller APS Systems and Data Terminal Corp., San Antonio, 1983—. Mem. Stewardship com. Grace Luth. Ch., San Antonio, 1986—; adv. CPA Santonio Clean & Beautiful Program, 1985. Mem. Nat. Assn. of Accts, (social dir. 1986—), Am. Assn. of Women Accts. (corr. sec. 1986—, treas. 1986—), Am. Inst. CPA's (San Antonio chpt. chair young CPA Invol.), Tex. Soc. CPA's, Beta Gamma Sigma, Pi Tau Pi. Democrat. Baptist. Home: 13702 Bellcrest San Antonio TX 78217 Office: APS Systems 4242 Piedras Dr E Suite 200 San Antonio TX 78228

VANDERBILT, GLORIA MORGAN, artist, actress, fashion designer; b. N.Y.C., Feb. 20, 1924; d. Reginald Claypoole and Gloria (Morgan) V.; m. Pasquale di Cicco (div.); m. Leopold Stokowski, 1945 (div. 1955); children—Stanislaus, Christopher; m. Sidney Lumet, 1956 (div.); m. Wyatt Emory Cooper, 1963; children—Carter V. (dec.), Anderson H. Attended, Mary C. Wheeler, Miss Porter's schs.; studied acting with, dir. Sanford Meisner, beginning 1955. Exhibited in one-man shows at Rabun Studio, N.Y.C., 1948, Bertha Shaeffer Gallery, N.Y.C., 1954, Juster Gallery, N.Y.C., 1956, Hammer Gallery, N.Y.C., 1966, 68, Cord Gallery, N.Y.C., 1966, Washington Gallery Art, 1968, Neiman-Marcus, Dallas, 1968, Vestart Gallery, N.Y.C., 1969, Parish Museum, Southampton, N.Y., also in Nantucket, Mass., Houston, Reading, Pa., Monterey, Calif., Nashville; exhibited in group shows, Washington Gallery Art, 1967, Hoover Gallery, San Francisco, 1971, stage career; acted in summer stock prodn. The Swan; made Broadway debut in The Time of Your Life, 1955; other stage appearances include Picnic, 1955, The Spa, 1956, Peter Pan, 1958, The Green Hat; made TV debut in Tonight At 8:30; other TV appearances include Colgate Comedy Hour, 1955, Flint and Fire on U.S. Steel Hour, 1958, Family Happiness on U.S. Steel Hour, 1959, Very Important People; appeared in film Johnny Concho, 1955; dir. design film, Riegel Textile Corp., N.Y.C., from 1970; designer stationary and greeting cards, Hallmark Co., fabrics, Bloomcraft Co., bed linens, Martex Co., table linens, Peacock Co., Gloria Vanderbilt jeans; also china, glassware, scarves. Recipient Sylvania award 1959, Fashion award Neiman-Marcus 1969. Author: Love Poems, 1955, (with Alfred Allen Lewis) Gloria Vanderbilt Book of Collage, 1970, Woman to Woman, 1979, Once Upon a Time: A True Story, 1985; author: (with Alfred Allen Lewis) play Three by Two, early 1960's, Black White, White Knight, 1987; poems and short stories. Mem. Actors Equity, Screen Actors Guild, AFTRA, Authors League Am., Am. Fedn. Arts. *

VANDER GOOT, MARY E., psychologist, educator; b. Orange City, Iowa, Feb. 5, 1947. AB, Calvin Coll., 1968; MA, PhD, Princeton U., 1971. Lic. psychologist, Mich. Psychologist Bd. Edn. for the Borough of North York, Toronto, Ont., Can., 1971-76; prof. psychology Calvin Coll., Grand Rapids, Mich., 1976—; pvt. practice psychology Psychology Assocs., P.C., Grand Rapids, 1978—. Author: A Life Planning Guide for Women, 1982, Piaget as a Visionary Thinker, 1985, Narrating Psychology, 1987, Healthy Emotions, 1987. Mem. Nat. Assn. Female Execs., Am. Psychol. Assn. Club: Older Women's League. Home and Office: 1000 Parchment Dr SE Grand Rapids MI 49506 Office: Calvin Coll Dept Psychology Grand Rapids MI 49506

VANDERHOST, LEONETTE LOUISE, psychologist; b. Phila., June 11, 1924; d. Charles and Pauline (McGhaney) V. BA, Hunter Coll., 1945; MA, NYU, 1979, PhD, 1986. Lic. psychologist, N.Y. Intern staff Lincoln (Ill.) State Sch., 1951-52; staff Evansville (Ind.) State Hosp., 1953-54, Children's Guidance Ctr., Dayton, Ohio, 1954-56; psychotherapist Hempstead (N.Y.) Consultation Services, 1963-66; staff, sr. psychologist Hillside Hosp., Glen Oaks, N.Y., 1957-69; sr. psychologist, chief West Nassau Mental Health Ctr., Franklin Sq., N.Y., 1959-63; pvt. practice psychologist N.Y.C., 1959—; cons. Big Sisters, N.Y., 1960-62, Health Ins. Planning, N.Y., 1962-64, Head Start, N.Y., 1967-73. Mem. Am. Psychol. Assn., Am. Orthopsychiatric Assn.

VANDERLINDEN, CAMILLA DENICE DUNN, human resource executive, educator; b. Dayton, July 21, 1950; d. Joseph Stanley and Virginia Danley (Martin) Dunn; m. David Henry VanderLinden; Oct. 10, 1980; 1 child, Michael Christopher. Student, U. de Valencia, Spain, 1969; BA, U. Utah, 1972, MS, 1985. Asst. dir. Davis County COmmunity Action Program, Farmington, Utah, 1973-76; dir. South County Community Action, Midvale, Utah, 1976-79; supr. customer service Ideal Nat. Life Ins. Co., Salt Lake City, 1979-80; mgr. customer service Utah Farm Bur. Mutual Ins., Salt Lake City, 1980-82; quality assurance analyst Am. Express Co., Salt Lake City, 1983-86, quality assurance and human resource specialist, 1986-88; mgr. quality assurance & engrng. Am. Express Co., Denver, 1988—. Republican. Home: PO Box 246 Farmington UT 84025 Office: Am Express Travel Related Services Co Inc 181 Iverness Dr W Englewood CO 80112-3100

VAN DER POL, DENISE MARIE, rehabilitation center executive; b. Santa Ana, Calif., Nov. 25, 1955; d. A.C. Murhyle and Mary Carolyn (Steiner) Sales. Student, Fullerton (Calif.) Community Coll., 1975-76, Saddleback Coll., Mission Viejo, Calif., 1979-81, U. Alaska S.E., 1988. Grant evaluator Calif. Dept. Edn., Sacramento, 1981; credential specialist Calif. Assn. Alcohol and Drug Counselors, Newport Beach, 1981-83; rehab. counselor Orange County Halfway House, Anaheim, Calif., 1981-83; alcohol edn. instr., group facilitator Safety Cons. Services, Westminster, Calif., 1981-83; dir. counseling Cascade Rehab. Ctr., Anchorage and Juneau, Alaska, 1984-86; owner, dir. counseling S.E. Rehab. Services, Juneau, 1986—; program coordinator Statewide Conf. Foster Parent Devel., Orange County, 1981. Commr. Capistrano Unified Sch. Dist. Rev. Bd., 1980; bd. dirs. Gastineau Human Services, Juneau, 1988. Mem. Nat. Rehab. Assn., Nat. Assn. Rehab. Profls. in the Pvt. Sector, Calif. Assn. Alcohol and Drug Educators, Saddleback Coll. Alumni Assn., Ducks Unltd., Nat. Fedn. of Independent Bus. Club: Rotary. Office: Southeast Rehab Services 130 Seward St Suite 212 Juneau AK 99801

VANDERPOOL, NANCY LEE, insurance broker; b. Lynwood, Calif., Aug. 19, 1948; d. Marty A. and Marie T. (Cody) Cubellis; m. Hoyt K. Vanderpool, Feb. 15, 1969; children: Hoyt K. III, Brandan S. BSBA, Woodbury Coll., 1969. Asst. office mgr. So. Calif. Cooks Assn., Los Angeles, 1968-74; ptnr. Vanderpool & Assocs., Santa Anna, Calif., 1974-78; v.p. Vanderpool & Vanderpool Ins. Services Inc., Tustin, Calif., 1983—. Precinct capt. Huntington Park (Calif.) Reps.; active youth soccer, Anaheim, Calif., 1979—. Mem. Nat. Assn. Female Execs., Nat. Fedn. Ind. Businesswomen, Nat. Assn. Life Underwriters, Orange County Assn. Health Underwriters (speaker 1986—), Orange County Employee Benefit Council. Roman Catholic. Office: Vanderpool & Vanderpool 14751 Plaza Dr Suite D Tustin CA 92680

VAN DER WOUDE, MARY ELIZABETH, French hornist, writer, educator; b. Grand Rapids, Mich., Dec. 1, 1939; d. John William and Elizabeth (ten Hoor) Monsma. French horn studies with Philip Farkas, Chgo., 1957-64; French horn studies with Lorenzo Sansone, N.Y.C., 1964-67; BS, Chgo. City Coll., 1965; BA, St. Xavier Coll., Chgo., 1968; postgrad. in piano, Am. Conservatory of Music, Chgo., 1974-76, postgrad. in French horn, 1983-84. French hornist Grand Rapids Symphony Orch., 1955-57, Grand Rapids Chamber Orch., 1955-57, Chgo. Civic Orch., 1958-60, Chgo. Chamber Orch., 1959-64; composer French horn texts Summy-Birchard Co., Evanston, Ill., 1960-62; composer, writer Charles Colin, Inc., N.Y.C., 1961-65; free-lance musician St. Louis, 1970-71; composer French horn Fema Publs. div. Interlochen Press, Naperville, Ill., 1974-75; French hornist Bach & Madrigal Soc., Phoenix, 1977-80, Ariz. Ballet, Phoenix, 1977-80, Phoenix Chamber Orch., 1977-80; freelance French hornist, writer Phoenix, 1987—. Contbr. articles to profl. jours. Mem. Am. Fedn. Musicians, Chgo. Fedn. Musicians, Phoenix Fedn. Musicians. Home and Office: PO Box 37562 Phoenix AZ 85069-7562

VAN DEVANTER, SUSAN EARLING, health care marketing executive; b. Washington, Dec. 12, 1960; d. Willis and Ann Pemberton (Cutler) Van D. BA, Skidmore Coll., 1983. Customer service rep. GTE-Sprint, Arlington, Va., 1984; mktg. rep. TDX Systems, Inc., Vienna, Va., 1984-85, sr. sales rep., 1985; account exec. TDX Systems, Inc., Norfolk, Va., 1986; mktg. cons. Mktg. Inst. Internat. Corp., Herndon, Va., 1986-88; mktg. coordinator Nat. Rehab. Hosp., Washington, 1988—. Editor bus. and econs. newspaper, 1983. Vol. Rep. Nat. Com., Washington, 1981; mem. Friends of the Kennedy Ctr., Washington, 1987—. Nat. Assn. Female Execs., Am. Soc. Assn. Execs., Am. Mktg. Assn. (Washington chpt.), Acad. Health Services Mktg. Episcopalian. Office: Nat Rehab Hosp 102 Irving St NW Washington DC 20010

VANDEVER, LOIS ARLENE LAYCOCK, nurse; b. Milw., Apr. 17, 1931; d. Russell Dana and Thelma Elizabeth (Strodthoff) Laycock; B.S.N., U. Denver, 1959; pediatric nurse practitioner U. Colo., 1970; m. Mar. 1957 (div. 1981); 1 son, Vincent James. Staff nurse Denver Public Schs., 1959-64; coordinator health services Cherry Creek Schs., Englewood, Colo., 1970-73; cons. U. Colo. Sch. Nursing, Colo. Bd. Nursing, Denver, 1975-79; wellness seminar developer, speaker, freelance writer, columnist, cons. various bus.'s, industries, colls., 1980—; pres. Invest in Yourself,1980; instr. various colls.; cons. in field; monitor, mem. rewrite com. nurse practice act com. Colo. Bd. Nursing; chmn. fund raiser event Colo. Woman's Coll.; lay minister Stephen Series. Mem. Nat. Assn. Female Execs., U. Denver Alumni Club, Mile High Alumni, Non-Practicing and Part-Time Nurses Assn. (lobbyist), Nat. Assn. Pediatric Nurse Practitioners and Assocs., Am. Nurses Assn., Colo. Nurses Assn., Friends U. Denver Sch. Nursing (dir.), Centennial C. of C. (numerous com. appointments), Instr. Noetic Scis. Republican. Episcopalian. Clubs: Colo. Columbine Dollogy (officer), Rocky Mountain Standard Schnauzer, Zonta (officer and dir.) (Englewood-Littleon), Denver Minikins, Zonta (dir. Englewood-Littleton). Editorial bd. Nursing, 1970-75; pioneer nurse practitioner program in public schs.; co-author: Invest in Yourself, 1982. Home: 7900 W Layton Ave #836 Littleton CO 80123 Office: PO Box 3493 Littleton CO 80161

VAN DOREN, META WESTFALL, music educator; b. Atkinson, Nebr., Sept. 26, 1902; d. George Elbert and Myrtle AnnaLee (Mackrill) Westfall; m. Paul VanDoren, June 24, 1926; 1 child, Meta Joan Gay. Teaching and music credential San Diego State Coll.; student piano and organ U. Hawaii; organ student U. Calif.-San Diego. Tchr. music pub. schs. Los Angeles, Pasadena, Chula Vista, Oceanside, Calif.; tchr. piano, organ, Calif.; chmn. auditions Nat. Piano Tchrs.; organist, choir dir. various chs. Co-author: Folk Songs of the United States, Calif. State Series. Music scholar Inst. Nat. Bellas Artes, Mexico City, 1956, Royal Acad. Music, London, 1960, Vienna Music Acad., 1962, Nazionale di Cecilia, Rome, 1966, Konserratorium, Lucerne, Switzerland, 1970, Royal Music Conservatory, Brussels, 1971. Mem. Am. Coll. Musicians (cert.), Nat. Guild Mus Tchrs. (Hall of Fame). Lodge: Daus. of Nile. Home: 602 S Nevada St Oceanside CA 92054

VAN DUYN, MONA JANE, poet; b. Waterloo, Iowa, May 9, 1921; d. Earl George and Lora G. (Kramer) Van D.; m. Jarvis A. Thurston, Aug. 31, 1943. B.A., U. No. Iowa, 1942; M.A., U. Iowa, 1943; D.Litt. (hon.), Washington U., St. Louis, 1971, Cornell Coll., Iowa, 1972. Instr. English U. Iowa, 1943-46, U. Louisville, 1946-50; lectr. English Univ. Coll., Washington U., 1950-67; poetry readings 1970—; poetry editor, co-pub. Perspective, A Quar. of Lit., 1947-67; lectr. Salzburg (Austria) Seminar Am. Studies, 1973; adj. prof. poetry workshop Washington U., Spring 1983; vis. Hurst prof. Washington U., 1987. Poet-in-residence, Breadloaf Writing Conf., Mass., 1974, 76; author: Valentines to the Wide World, 1959, A Time of Bees, 1964, To See, To Take, 1970, Bedtime Stories, 1972, Merciful Disguises, 1973, Letters from a Father and Other Poems, 1983. Recipient Eunice Tietjens award, 1956, Helen Bullis prize, 1964, 76, Harriet Monroe award, 1968, Hart Grane Meml. award, 1968, Borestone Mountains 1st prize, 1968, Bollingen prize, 1970, Nat. Book award, 1971, Loines prize Nat. Inst. Arts and Letters, 1976, Sandburg prize Cornell Coll., 1982, Shelley Meml. prize Poetry Soc. Am., 1987; grantee Nat. Council Arts, 1967; grantee in poetry NEA, 1985; Guggenheim fellow, 1972; fellow Acad. Am. Poets, 1980. Mem. Nat. Inst. Arts and Letters, Acad. Am. Poets (chancellor 1985).

VAN DYKE, EVELYN JEAN, aircraft company executive; b. Chgo., Jan. 30, 1938; d. Ralph Siegers and Clara Sylvia (Wesselius) Simpson; m. Arthur Stenberg, Dec. 15, 1956 (div. Nov. 1962); children: Arthur Ralph Stenberg, Scott Marshall Stenberg. From clk. to supr. Hughes Aircraft Co., El Segundo, Calif., 1962-73, head govt. property adminstrn., 1973-78, mgr. transp. and warehousing, 1978-81; mgr. materials mgmt. ops. Hughes Aircraft Co., Canoga Park, Calif., 1981—. Summer missionary European Bible Missions, Czechoslovakia, 1985. Republican. Home: 2619 Deerwood Simi Valley CA 93065

VAN DYKE-COOPER, ANNY MARION, financial company executive; b. Howard, Ont., Can., Sept. 30, 1928; d. Anthony and Anna (Koolen) Van D.; m. John Arnold Cooper, Apr. 9, 1983. C.F.A., U. Va., 1969; B.A., Sir George Williams U., 1959. Tchr., Lanoraie Sch. Bd., 1946-47; sec. Can. Nat. Rys., Montreal, Que., Can., 1947-51; sec. Sorel Industries Ltd., Sorel, Que., Can., 1952-53; with Bell Investment Mgmt. Corp. and BIMCOR, Inc. subs. Bell Canada, Montreal, 1953-83; portfolio mgr. U.S. Equities, 1971-83; v.p. investments, dir. Cooper, Van Dyke Assocs. Inc., Birmingham, Mich., 1983—. Mem. Inst. Chartered Fin. Analysts (trustee 1979-80), Fin. Analysts Soc. Detroit, Montreal Soc. Fin. Analysts (program chmn., pres. 1974-75), Can. Council Fin. Analysts (vice-chmn. 1976-77), Fin. Analysts Fedn. (treas. 1977-78, vice chmn. 1978-79, chmn. 1979-80). Home: 1660 Apple Ln Bloomfield Hills MI 48013 Office: 1100 N Woodward Ave Birmingham MI 48011

VANE, MARY KATHLEEN, chemist, chemical company executive; b. Washington, Apr. 27, 1951; d. Calvin Chaplin and Grace Rachel (Van Zant) V. BS with honors, Cornell U., 1973. Research chemist DuPont Co., Wilmington, Del., 1973-75, tech. service rep., 1976-77; mktg. rep. DuPont Co., N.Y.C., 1978-79, sales rep., 1979-80, mktg. supr., 1980-81; strategic planner DuPont Co., Wilmington, 1981-83; mktg. mgr. DuPont Co., N.Y.C., 1983-86; bus. mgr. DuPont Co., Wilmington, 1986—; lectr. Cornell U., Ithaca, N.Y., 1974—, mem. adv. council, 1986—. Vol. Congressman Bill Green's campaign, N.Y.C., 1984, 86; sponsor Christian Children's Fund, Richmond, Va., 1986—. Mem. Nat. Assn. Female Execs., Underfashion Club. Republican. Methodist. Office: DuPont de Nemours Textile Fibers Dept Chestnut Run Plaza Laurel Run Bldg Po Box 80 705 Wilmington DE 19898

VANE, SYLVIA BRAKKE, anthropologist, cultural resource management company executive; b. Fillmore County, Minn., Feb. 28, 1918; d. John T. and Hulda Christina (Marburger) Brakke; m. Arthur Bayard Vane, May 17, 1942; children—Ronald Arthur, Linda, Laura Vane Ames. A.A., Rochester Jr. Coll., 1937; B.S. with distinction, U. Minn., 1939; student Radcliffe Coll., 1944; M.A., Calif. State U.-Hayward, 1975. Med. technologist Dr. Frost and Hodapp, Willmar, Minn., 1939-41; head labs. Corvallis Gen. Hosp., Oreg., 1941-42; dir. lab. Cambridge Gen. Hosp., Mass., 1942-43, Peninsula Clinic, Redwood City, Calif., 1947-49; v.p. Cultural Systems Research, Inc., Menlo Park, Calif., 1978—; pres. Ballena Press, Menlo Park, 1981—; cons. cultural resource mgmt. So. Calif. Edison Co., Rosemead, 1978-81, San Diego Gas and Elec. Co., 1980-83, Pacific Gas and Elec. Co., San Francisco, 1982-83, Wender, Murase & White, Washington, 1983—, Yosemite Indians, Mariposa, Calif., 1982-84, San Luis Rey Band of Mission Indians, Escondido, Calif., 1986—, U.S. Ecology, Newport Beach, Calif., 1986—, Riverside County Flood Control and Water Conservation Dist., 1985—. Author: (with L.J. Bean), California Indians, Primary Resources, 1977, The Cahuilla and the Santa Rosa Mountains, 1981. Contbr. chpts. to several books. Bd. dirs. Sequoia Area council Girl Scouts U.S., 1954-61; bd. dirs., v.p., pres. LWV, S. San Mateo County, Calif., 1960-65, cons. San Francisco council Girl Scouts U.S., 1962-69. Fellow Soc. Applied Anthropology; mem. Southwestern Anthrop. Assn. (program chmn. 1976-78, newsletter editor 1976-79), Am. Anthropology Assn., Soc. for Am. Archaeology. Mem. United Ch. of Christ. Office: Ballena Press 823 Valparaiso Ave Menlo Park CA 94025

VANEK, EUGENIA POPORAD, medical educator, consultant; b. Cleve., June 23, 1949; d. George and Anna P. (Dumitru) Poporad; B.S., Case-Western Res. U., 1970; M.A. (fellow), Boston U., 1972; Ed.D., U. Rochester, 1974; m. John Albert Vanek, Aug. 28, 1971; children—Matthew Dumitru, Jessica Petera. Tchr. Cleveland Heights (Ohio) High Sch., 1970; instr. Monroe Community Coll., Rochester (N.Y.) Inst. Tech., 1972-74; asst. prof. med. edn. research Case-Western Res. U., Cleve., 1974-80, asst. prof. family medicine, 1979-80, asst. clin. prof. community dentistry, 1978-87; adj. prof. Goddard Coll., Plainfield, Vt., 1980-81; ednl. cons. 1980—; with Cleve. Clinic Ednl. Found., Case Western Res. U. Med. Sch. Chmn. Northeastern Ohio alumni scholarship admissions com. U. Rochester, 1974-76, 1979-80; active N.E. Ohio affiliate Am. Heart Assn., 1977; mem. Task Force on Heart Disease in Young; trustee Oberlin (Ohio) Early Childhood Center, 1980-83, Oberlin Friends of Pub. Library, 1982-84. Ednl. cons. study fellow, 1977; active Lorain County Bd. of Health, 1986—. Mem. Health Scis. Communication Assn. Author: In Piagetian Research: Compilation and Commentary, Vol. 4, 1976; contbr. numerous articles to various publs. Home and Office: 46 Stewart Ct Oberlin OH 44074

VANESS, MARGARET HELEN, artist, consultant; b. Seattle; d. Paul Edward and Alma Magdalena Lauch; B.F.A., U. Wash., Seattle, 1970, 71, M.F.A., 1973; cert. bus. Drexel U., Phila., 1975; m. Gerard Vaness; children—Bette, Bruce, Barbara, Helen-Cathleen. Teaching asst. Sch. Art, U. Wash., 1971-73; illustrator DuPont Co., Wilmington, Del., 1973-74, Boeing Vertol Co., Phila., 1974-75; illustrator, program mgr. Boeing Co., Seattle, 1978-84; judge art shows, 1969—; executed mural for Dr. L. Mellon-Boeing Vertol Med. Center, 1974; commd. by USIA, 1973. Mem. Coll. Art Assn., Soc. for Tech. Communication, Photog. Soc. Am. (area rep. 1985—), U. Wash. Alumni Assn. (life), U. Wash. Arboretum Found. (unit pres. 1981-83), Nat. Mus. of Women in the Arts (charter mem.), Lambda Rho (past pres.). Address: 17128 2d Ave SW Seattle WA 98166

VAN GEMERT, MARIE ESTHER, health foundation executive; b. Momence, Ill., Feb. 10, 1938; d. Earl Ester and Anna Marie (France) Bartholomew; m. Charles E. Van Gemert, July 23, 1960 (dec. Sept. 1986); children: Judith Ann, Charles Earl. Student, Roosevelt U., 1957-58, No. Ill. U., 1957-59; BA in Social Sci., Gov.'s State U., 1981, MA in Sociology, 1982. Tchr. elem. schs.; social worker State Fla. Dept. Rehab., Jacksonville, 1960-64; exec. dir. Am. Lung Assn. of NW Ind., Merrillville, 1983-85, Hemophilia Found. of Ill., Chgo., 1985—. Mem. AAUW, Chgo. Soc. Assn. Execs., Nat. Soc. Fund Raising Execs., Nat. Hemophilia Found., Profl. Staff Orgn. (sec. 1986-87), Nat. Acad. TV Arts and Scis. Roman Catholic. Lodge: Zonta. Home: 314 Osage Park Forest IL 60466 Office: Hemophilia Found of Ill 332 S Michigan Ave Suite 812 Chicago IL 60604

VANGER, RACHEL JUSTINE, restaurant owner; b. Sacramento, Calif., Oct. 2, 1961; d. Milton Isadore and Elsa (Oribe) V.; m. David Keith McHaffey. BA, Wellesley (Mass.) Coll., 1983; MPS, Cornell U., 1986. Hostess, cashier Hotel Northampton, Mass., 1983-84; grad. teaching asst. Hotel Sch. Cornell U., Ithaca, 1985-86; co-owner, operator ARAD Ventures Inc. doing bus. as Arigato Japanese Steak House, Rochester, N.Y., 1986—. Office: ARAD Ventures Inc Arigato Japanese Steak House 2720 W Henrietta Rd Rochester NY 14623

VANGHEL, RUTH MARGARET, advertising agency administrator; b. Buffalo, Apr. 12, 1950; d. Russell Short and Emma Pleasant (Wear) Garrick; m. Jeffrey George Vanghel. Grad. high sch., Williamsville, N.Y. Sec. McKesson and Robbins Drug Co., Cheektowaga, N.Y., 1972-78; sales rep. Nasco Inc., Springfield, Tenn., 1978-80; telemktg. sales rep. L.M. Berry and Co., Williamsville, 1980-81, mgr. telemktg. sales unit, 1981-83, mgr. sales div., 1984—; grad. asst. Dale Carnegie Inst., Buffalo, 1985. Mem. Nat. Assn. Female Execs. Home: 129 Beale Ave Cheektowaga NY 14225 Office: LM Berry Co 1219 N Forest Rd Williamsville NY 14221

VAN GILDER, BARBARA JANE DIXON, interior designer, consultant; b. South Bend, Ind., Dec. 6, 1933; d. Vincent Alan and Wanda Anita (Rapell) Dixon Van Gilder; student Mich. State U., 1951-55; postgrad. St. Mary's Coll., 1956-57, N.Y. Sch. Design, 1956-58; m. Erwin Dalton VanGilder, May 25, 1959; children: Eric Dalton, Marc David. Factory color cons. Smith-Alsop Paint Co., Terre Haute, Ind., 1955-56; archtl. design cons., Mishawaka, Ind., 1956-58; residential-comml. designer, South Bend, Chgo., 1958-63; designer industrialized housing industry, Ga., Fla., Ind., Mich., 1962—; design cons. Skyline Corp., Ind., Calif., Pa., 1962-66; v.p. design Treasure Chest Corp., Sturgis, Mich., 1969, also dir.; pres., dir. Sandpiper Art, Inc.; v.p. T.C.I. Ltd.; design cons. C.O. Smith Ind. Peachtree Housing, Moultrie, Ga., Nobility Homes, Ocala, Fla.; head merchandising and design Sandpiper Originals, clothing boutique, 1978-87; pres., owner mktg. design firm, 1987—; currently pub. relations ofcl. Am. Mktg. Assn., adj. tchr. Lakeshore Sch. System. also coordinator trade show displays; nat. advt. rep. Studebaker-Packard Corp., Mercedes Benz, Clark Equipment, 1959-63; writer series on decorating for 2 Mich. newspapers, 1961-63; participant TV show Know Your Decorator, Calif. and Maine, 1962, 77. Officer, Shoreham Village (Mich.) Bd. Zoning, 1960-63. Named Woman of Year, Profl. Model's Club, 1952; recipient 1st pl. furniture design hardwoods Nat. Hardwoods Assn., 1956; 1st pl. Best in Show award, Louisville, Atlanta, 1964-65, 66, 69, 70-74, 76; others. Mem. Design Council Industrialized Housing (award 1974), Nat. Soc. Interior Designers, Mich. State U. Alumni Assn., Internat. Platform Assn., Internat. Biog. Assn. Contbg. editor Skyliner mag., 1962-66; permanent guest editor, contbr. Today's Home mag., 1974—. Home: 3630 S Lakeshore Dr St Joseph MI 49085 Office: PO Box 244 Stevensville MI 49127 also: PO Box 1100 Dunedin FL 33528

VAN HAMEL, MARTINE, dancer; b. Brussels, Nov. 16, 1945. Student, Nat. Ballet Sch. Can. Debut with Nat. Ballet Can., 1963; guest dancer Royal Swedish Ballet, Royal Winnipeg Ballet, Joffrey Ballet; with Am. Ballet Theatre, 1970—, soloist, 1971-73, prin. dancer, 1973—; created leading female roles in Estuary (Lynn Taylor-Corbett), Bach Partita (Twyla Tharp), Field, Chair, and Mountain (David Gordon), Push Comes to Shove (Twyla Tharp), Sphinx (Glen Tetley); choreographer Amnon V'Tamar, many others; founder New Amsterdam Ballet, N.Y.C. Winner Gold medal internat. competition, Varna, Bulgaria, 1966, Prix de Varna for best artistry all categories, 1966; recipient Cue mag. award, 1976, Dance mag. award, 1983. Office: care Am Ballet Theatre 890 Broadway New York NY 10003 *

VAN HEMERT, JUDY, electronic manufacturing company executive, educator, sheet metal fabrication company executive; b. Dallas, Feb. 8, 1947; d. Marion Everett and Thelma Rhea (Robinson) Van H.; children—Christopher Martin, Matthew Everett. B.A., Vanderbilt U., Nashville, 1969; cert. lang. therapist Scottish Rite Hosp., Dallas, 1971. Cert. secondary tchr., Tex., cert. Lang. therapist. Lang. therapist Scottish Rite Hosp., Dallas, 1970-72, The Winston Sch., Dallas, 1975-82; mktg., purchasing S.V. Mfg., Richardson, Tex., 1982-84; pres. Bullet Electronics, Rockwall, Tex., 1984—; owner C-Power, Inc. Elder Presbyn. Ch. Named Miss Park Cities. Mem. Assn. Women Entrepreneurs of Dallas, Nat. Assn. Women Bus. Owners, Small Bus. Owners, Tex. Bus. Council, Rockwall C. of C. (exec. bd. dirs.). Republican. Avocations: golf; tennis. Office: C-Power Products Inc 2007 Industrial Ln Rockwall TX 75087

VAN HÖECKE, PATRICIA MCREYNOLDS, marketing executive, consultant; b. Wichita, Kans., Feb. 17, 1947; d. Emery LeRoy and Margaret Glyn (Wiman) McReynolds; m. Larry D. Sprowls, May 25, 1968 (div. 1979); 1 child, Scott Wiman; m. John W. Van Höecke, Nov. 30, 1985. BA, So. Nazarene U., 1968; postgrad., Trinity U., 1974; MBA, Tex. Christian U., 1980. Mktg. cons. Images, Ft. Worth, 1978-81; group v.p. mktg. USAA Group, San Antonio, 1981-83; pres. Images II, Inc., San Antonio, 1984—, Marshall, Van Höecke, et. al., San Antonio, 1986—; cons. Water Parks, Inc., Venture Group, Inc., 1987, Kathmar Luggage. Bd. dirs. Multiple Sclerosis Soc., Tarrant County, Tex., 1980-82, Community Guidance Ctr., Bexar County, Tex., 1982-85, Women's Ctr., San Antonio, 1984-85. Named Editor of Yr. Internat. Assn. of Bus. Communicators, 1974; recipient Golden Quill award Internat. Assn. of Bus. Communicators, 1983.

VAN HOOK, CAROLE MARIE, social worker, educator; b. Colfax, Wash., June 3, 1948; d. Kenneth Richard and Ruth Helen (Cawley) Morris; m. Peter James Van Hook, Mar. 8, 1969; children: Michael, Lisa, Emily. BS, Lewis and Clark Coll., 1969, MAT, 1969; MSW, U. Utah, 1988. Cert. elem., secondary tchr. Calif., Utah. Multimedia specialist Pacific Telephone, San Francisco, 1969; tchr. elem. St. Patrick's Sch., Rodeo, Calif., 1969-70; tchr. English John Muir High Sch., Martinez, Calif., 1970-71; tchr. remedial reading Emmett (Idaho) Sch. Dist., 1976-80; tchr. English Granite Sch. Dist., Salt Lake City, 1980-81; tchr. Rowland Hall St. Marls Sch., Salt Lake City, 1981-86; social worker Family Support Cen., Salt Lake City, 1986, Salt Lake City Alcohol and Drug Treatment Cen., 1987—; tchr., counselor Rivendell Child and Adolescent Psychiat. Ctr., West Jordan, Utah, 1986—; bd. dirs. edn. com. Planned Parenthhood, Salt Lake City, 1986—. Mem. Child Abuse Prevention Task Force, Salt Lake City 1986-87. Mem. Nat. Assn. Social Workers. Episcopalian. Home: 3101 S 3340E Salt Lake City UT 84109

VAN HOOZER, JEAN ELIZABETH, auditor, credit union executive; b. Marlow, Okla., May 4, 1932; d. Thomas Osa and Gladys Mamie (Sample) McCarley; student Okla. Baptist U., Shawanee, 1951-52; B.S. in Bus Adminstrn., Cameron U., Lawton, Okla., 1978; m. Teddy Gene VanHoozer, Sept 2, 1952; children—Dewayne, David, Nancy. With Lawton (Okla.) Public Schs., 1952-68, bus. office mgr., 1960—, auditor, 1968—; mgr. Lawton Tchrs. Fed. Credit Union, Lawton, 1968—. Mem. Nat. Edn. Credit Union Council, Data Processing Mgmt. Assn., Okla. Public Acct. Democrat. Baptist. Club: Altrusa. Office: 1806 Liberty St Lawton OK 73501

VAN HORN, ANDREA LEE, retail executive; b. Bethlehem, Pa., June 5, 1952; d. William Peter and Mildred (Moyer) Van H. BA in Psychology, Bucknell U., 1974. From asst. buyer to div. mgr. Kaufmann's Inc., Pitts., 1974-81; buyer Winkelman's Stores, Inc., Detroit, 1981-84, Hit or Miss Inc., Stoughton, Mass., 1984-87, Womens Splty. Retailing, Enfield, Conn., 1987—. Republican. Presbyterian. Home: 471 Nassau Dr Springfield MA 01129 Office: Womens Splty Retailing 107 Phoenix Ave Enfield MA 06082

VAN HORN, SUSAN, commercial photographer; b. Montevideo, Uruguay, Oct. 11, 1953; d. Robert Earl and Maryjane Bodell (Kozen) Van H. Student, Calif. State U., Hayward, 1971-73, Otis Parsons Sch. Design, 1984-85, Barnsdall Arts Ctr., 1985—. Acct. exec. Kessler & Eisele, Los Angeles, 1977-80; v.p., photographer Hershey Assocs., Los Angeles, 1980-83; pres. Van Horn Photography, Los Angeles, 1983—. Artist, pub. Fine Arts Prints, 1987—. Mem. Ctr. for Environ. Edn.. Mem. NOW, Women Photographers in Am., Am. Soc. Mag. Photographers, Friends of Photography, Internat. Sculpture Inst., Blvd. Bus. Assn. (bd. dirs.), Animal Protection Inst., Assn. Research and Enlightenment, Am. Crafts Council, Mus. Women in Arts (charter mem.), Edgar Cayce Found., Internat. Assn. Bus. Communicators (Bronze Quill award 1986). Democrat. Office: Van Horn Photography 3427 Glendale Blvd Los Angeles CA 90039

VANHOVE, LORRI KAY, lawyer, financial services executive; b. Madison, S.D., Dec. 10, 1956; d. Robert Harold Vanhove and Doris Darlene (Beck) Vanhove Strub. BS, S.D. State U., 1979; JD, U. Neb., 1982. Bar: S.D. 1982, U.S. Dist. Ct. S.D. 1982, Minn. 1985. Cons. fin. planning Fed. Land Bank of Omaha, 1982-85; mgr. advanced fin. planning IDS Fin. Services Inc., Mpls., 1985—. Speaker various civ. groups. William Holt scholar U. Neb., 1980, Yale C. Holland scholar U. Neb., 1981. Mem. ABA, S.D. Bar Assn. (contr. articles to jour.), Minn. Bar Assn., Hennipen County Bar Assn., Phi Delta Phi. Home: 7360 Gallager Dr #323A Edina MN 55435 Office: IDS Fin Services Inc IDS Tower Minneapolis MN 55474

VAN HOWE, ANNETTE EVELYN, real estate agent; b. Chgo., Feb. 16, 1921; d. Frank and Susan (Linstra) Van Howe; B.A. in History magna cum laude, Hofstra U., 1952; M.A. in Am. History, SUNY-Binghamton, 1966; m. Edward L. Nezelek, Apr. 3, 1961. Editorial asst. Salute Mag., N.Y.C., 1946-48; asso. editor Med. Econs., Oradell, N.J., 1952-56; nat. mag. publicist Nat. Mental Health Assn., N.Y.C., 1956-60; exec. dir. Diabetes Assn. So. Calif., Los Angeles, 1960-61; corporate sec., v.p., editor, public relations dir. Edward L. Nezelek, Inc., Johnson City, N.Y., 1961-82; mgr. condominium, Fort Lauderdale, Fla., 1982-83; dir. Sky Harbour East Condo, 1983-88; substitute tchr. high schs., Binghamton, N.Y., 1961-63. Bd. dirs. Broome County Mental Health Assn., 1961-65, Fine Arts Soc., Roberson Center for Arts and Scis., 1968-70, Found. Wilson Meml. Hosp., Johnson City, 1972-81, Found. SUNY, Binghamton; trustee Broome Community Coll., 1973-78; v.p. Broward County Commn. on Status of Women, 1982—; bd. dirs. Ft. Lauderdale Women's Council of Realtors, 1986—, Broward Arts Guild, 1986; grad. Leadership Broward Class III, 1985, Leadership Am., 1988; trustee Unitarian-Universalist Ch. of Ft. Lauderdale, 1982—. Mem. AAUW (legis. chair Fla. div. 1986-87), Am. Med. Writers Assn., LWV (dir. Broome County 1969-70), Alumni Assn. SUNY Binghamton (dir. 1970-73), Am. Acad. Polit. and Social Sci., Nat. Assn. Female Execs., Am. Heritage Soc., Nature Conservancy, Nat. Hist. Soc., Ft. Lauderdale Women's Council Realtors (corr. sec.), Alpha Theta Beta, Phi Alpha Theta, Phi Gamma Mu. Clubs: Binghamton Garden, Binghamton Monday Afternoon, Acacia Garden (pres.); 110 Tower; Tower Forum; Downtown Council. Editor newsletter Mental Health Assn., 1965-68, newsletter Unitarian-Universalist Ch., weekly 1967-71, History of Broome County Meml. Arena, 1972. Home: 2100 S Ocean Dr Fort Lauderdale FL 33316 Office: 2230 SE 17th St Fort Lauderdale FL 33316

VANKIRK, MARSHA LAUTERBACH, legal professional; b. Worchester, Mass., Nov. 23, 1949; d. Robert Emil and Jane (Stonerod) Lauterbach; m. Thomas Lee Vankirk, Jan. 5, 1980 (div. 1983). BS in Sociology, U. Pitts., 1975. Stock trader Pitts. Nat. Bank, 1970-73; research assoc. U. Pitts., 1974; sr. legal asst. Buchanan Ingersoll, P.C., Pitts., 1975—. Contbr. to profl. jour. Mem. citizens review com. United Way Allegheny County, 1987—; adv. bd. Renaissance Too, 1986—; bd. dirs. United Mental Health, Inc., 1986—. Mem. Pitts. Paralegal Assn. (v.p. 1977-80). Democrat. Presbyterian. Office: Buchanan Ingersoll PC 600 Grant St 57th floor Pittsburgh PA 15219

VAN LAMMEREN, PATRICIA C., insurance company underwriting manager; b. Kansas City, Kans., Aug. 13, 1959; d. Jerry L. and Ella L. (Kelly) Watson; m. William A. Van Lammeren, July 19, 1981 (div. Aug. 1984); 1 child, Andrea Renee Van Lammeren. B in Bus. Studies, U. Mo., Kans. City, 1982. Sec. Allstate Ins. Co., Overland Park, Kans., 1978-81; rotation mgr. Allstate Ins. Co., Overland Park, 1981-82, underwriter, 1982-85, market underwriter, analyst, 1985-86, territorial underwriting mgr., 1986-88, accelerated mgmt. claim tng., 1988—. Mem. Nat. Assn. Female Execs. Democrat. Methodist.

VANLEEUWEN, LIZ SUSAN (ELIZABETH), farmer, state legislator; b. Lakeview, Oreg., Nov. 5, 1925; d. Charles Arthur and Mary Delphia (Hartzog) Nelson; B.S., Oreg. State U., 1947; m. George VanLeeuwen, June 15, 1947; children—Charles, Mary, James, Timothy. Secondary sch. and adult tchr., 1947-70; news reporter, feature writer The Times, Brownsville, Oreg., 1949—; co-mgr. VanLeeuwen Farm, Halsey, Oreg.; mem. Oreg. Ho. of Reps., 1981—; weekly radio commentator, 1973-81. Mem. E.R. Jackman Found., PTA, sch. adv. com.; precinct committeewoman; founder Linn County Ct.-Apptd. Spl. Advs. Recipient Outstanding service award Oreg. Farm Bur., 1975, Oreg. Farm Family of Yr. award, 1983; Chevron Agri. Spokesman of Yr. award, 1975. Mem. Oreg. Women for Agr. (pres.), Oreg. Women for Timber, Linn-Benton Women for Agr. (pres.), Linn County Farm Bur., Linn County Econ. Devel. Com., Grange, Am. Agri-Women, Nat. Conf. State Legislature's Agr. and Food Policy Com. Republican. Office: Capitol Bldg H382 Salem OR 97310

VAN LEEUWEN, PATRICIA ANN SZCZEPANIK, research specialist; b. Chgo., May 27, 1939; d. Marion Edward and Ruth Hazel (Brophy) Szczepanik; m. G. Dale Van Leeuwen, May 27, 1978. BS in Chemistry, U. Ill., Urbana, 1961; MPH, U. Ill., Chgo., 1987. Research asst., research assoc. BIM div. Argonne (Ill.) Nat. Lab., 1961-76, biochemist, 1976-82; biochemist RER div. Argonne Nat. Lab., 1980-82; research assoc. U. Ill. Coll. Pharmacy, Chgo., 1982-87; research specialist U. Ill. Sch. Pub. Health, Chgo., 1987—; research assoc., asst. prof. Dept. Medicine U. Chgo., 1976-80. Contbr. 48 articles to sci. jours. Mem. Am. Assn. Study Liver Disease, Am. Soc. Mass Spectometry, Nat. Environ. Health Assn., Air Pollution Control Assn., Am. Chem. Soc. Episcopalian. Office: U Ill Sch Pub Health Environ and Occupational Health Scis Dept PO Box 6998 Chicago IL 60680

VAN LEUVEN, HOLLY GOODHUE, social scientist, consultant, researcher; b. Salem, Mass., Dec. 2, 1935; d. Nathaniel William and Elizabeth VanClowes (Crowley) Goodhue; m. John Jamison Porter, II, Oct. 16, 1954 (div. 1974); children: Donald J. II, Nathaniel G., Alison A. Dionne, Erin E.; m. Robert Joseph VanLeuven, Dec. 31, 1976. BA with honors, Western Mich. U., 1971, MA with honors, 1975. Exec. dir. Community Confrontation and Communication Assocs., Grand Rapids, Mich., 1969-73; coordinator tng., research Nat. Ctr. for Dispute Settlement, Washington, 1973; tng. dir. Forest View Psychiat. Hosp., Grand Rapids, 1974; case coordinator Libner, Van Leuven, & Kortering, P.C., Muskegon, Mich., 1982-87; pres. Genesis Cons. Group, Muskegon, Mich., Phoenix, 1987—; talk show host Sta. WTRU-TV, Muskegon, 1985; cons. U.S. Dept. Justice, Washington, 1969-73, No. Ireland Dept. Community Relations, Belfast, 1971; jury selection cons. various law firms in Midwest, 1975—. Contbr. articles to profl. jours. Bd. dirs. Planned Parenthood Western Mich., Grand Rapids, 1964-72, Jr. League Grand Rapids, 1955—, YFCA, Muskegon, 1981-83, Girl Scouts U.S., 1988—; chmn. Student Showcase, Inc., Muskegon, 1983—; candidate for Mich. State Rep. 97th Dist., Muskegon, 1978; pres. Planned Parenthood Assn., Muskegon, 1980. Mem. Am. Sociol. Assn., Am. Soc. Trial Cons. Clubs: Muskegon Country, Century; Women's City (Grand Rapids). Lodges: Zonta, Compass. Home: 966 Mona Brook Rd Muskegon MI 49441

VAN LOAN, MARY KIRKWOOD (MARY K. TWIDDY), personal financial counseling officer, educator, author; b. Mitchell, S.D., Dec. 18, 1934; d. Robert Campbell and Virginia Viola (Bates) Kirkwood; m. Richard Rodman Van Loan, July 11, 1959 (div. 1977); children—Richard Rodman, Lynn Virginia, Robert Edward; m. John William Twiddy, Aug. 23, 1980; stepchildren—John Peter, Susan Twiddy Slink. B.A. in English, Mt. Holyoke Coll., 1956; postgrad. in Secondary Edn., Boston U., 1957-58. Cert. fin. planner, tax preparer. English tchr. Castilleja Sch. for Girls, Palo Alto, Calif., 1956-57, Andrew Warde High Sch., Fairfield, Conn., 1958-60; substitute tchr. Town of Greenwich, Conn., 1974-79; co-owner, developer Assoc. Budget Cons., Greenwich, 1979-80; personal fin. counseling officer Union Trust Co., Greenwich, 1980—; instr. fin. planning adult edn., Greenwich, 1983—. Author various articles. Officer, Young Republicans, Greenwich, 1961-62; mem. Greenwich council Boy Scouts Am., 1968—, exec. bd., 1985—, asst. treas. 1986—, Explorer post advisor banking and fin., 1986-87. Recipient awards Boy Scouts Am., 1974. Mem. Internat. Assn. Fin. Planning (chmn. So. Conn. Chpt. 1986-87, pres. 1985-86, sr. adv. bd. 1987—), Inst. Cert. Fin. Planners (bd. dirs. Westchester, Rockland, Fairfield socs. 1985—, sec. 1987-88), Nat. Assn. Bank Women, Lower Fairfield County Estate Planning Council, AAUW, Mt. Holyoke Fairfield Villages Alumnae Assn., Nat. Assn. Female Execs. Mormon. Avocations: handcrafts; sports; travel. Home: Old Forge Rd Greenwich CT 06830 Office: Union Trust Co 1 Lafayette Pl Greenwich CT 06830

VANMEER, MARY ANN, publisher, writer, researcher; b. Mt. Clemens, Mich., Nov. 22; d. Leo Harold and Rose Emma (Gulden) VanM.; stepmother Ruth (Meek) VanM. Student Mich. State U., 1965-66, 67-68, Sorbonne U., Paris, 1968; B.A. in Edn., U. Fla., 1970. Pres. VanMeer Tutoring and Translating, N.Y.C., 1970-72; freelance writer, 1973-79; pres. VanMeer Publs., Inc., Clearwater, Fla., 1980—, VanMeer Media Advt., Inc., Clearwater, 1980—; exec. dir., founder Nat. Ctrs. for Health and Med. Info., Inc., Clearwater, 1982-87; pres. Health and Med. Trends, Inc. 1987—. Author: Traveling with Your Dog, U.S.A., 1976; How to Set Up A Home Typing Business, 1978; Freelance Photographer's Handbook, 1979; See America Free, 1981; Free Campgrounds, U.S.A., 1982; Free Attractions, U.S.A., 1982; VanMeer's Guide to Free Attractions, U.S.A., 1984; VanMeer's Guide to Free Campgrounds, 1984; DUI Survival Manual, 1987; The 'How to Get Publicity for Your Business' Handbook, 1987; pub. Nat. Health and Med. Trends Mag., 1986—. Pub. info. chairperson, bd. dirs. Pinellas County chpt. Am. Cancer Soc., Clearwater, 1983-84, 86-88. Mem. Am. Booksellers Assn., (PACT) Performing Arts, Concert, and Theatre, Author's Guild. Republican. Office: VanMeer Publs Inc PO Box 2138 Clearwater FL 34617 also: Nat Ctrs for Health and Med Info Inc PO Box 389 Clearwater FL 34617

VAN METER, CHRISTINE MARY, nurse, educator; b. Paterson, N.J., Dec. 29, 1951; d. Joseph Charles and Marion Elizabeth (Tacq) Babcock; m. Robert Allen Van Meter, Mar 16, 1974 (div. 1985); 1 son, Daniel Joseph. B.S. in Phys. Edn., U. Oreg., 1973; B.S. in Nursing, Russell Sage Coll., Troy, N.Y., 1980; MS in nursing U. Portland, 1986. R.N., N.Y., Wash., Oreg. Nurse, Albany (N.Y.) Med. Ctr. Hosp., 1979-80, Kadlec Med. Ctr., Richland, Wash., 1980—; instr. nursing Columbia Basin Coll., Pasco, Wash., 1982—, coordinator paramedic program, 1983—, instr. advanced cardiac life support, 1982, 83—; trustee mid-Columbia Emergency Med. Services Council . Kellas scholar, 1980; W.K. Kellogg fellow, 1985-86. Mem. Am. Nurses Assn., Wash. Edn. Assn., Sigma Theta Tau. Home and Office: 1845 D Peachtree Ln Richland WA 99352

VAN METER, LINDA LIESELOTTE, psychologist, consultant; b. N.Y.C., Feb. 27, 1950; d. William Dirk and Gretel Lieselotte (Dietrich) Groon; m. William Isaac Van Meter, May 22, 1976; children: Matthew William, Alisa Lieselotte. BA in Psychology, East Stroudsburg State Cll., 1972; MA in Psychology, Marywood Coll., 1985. Intern Pocono Hosp., East Stroudsburg, Pa., 1971-72; caseworker, therapist Mental Health/Mental Retardation of Carbon, Monroe and Pike Counties, Stroudsburg, Pa., 1972-76; psychologist Pocono Neuropsychiat. Ctr., East Stroudsburg, Pa., 1976-87; psychologist, clin. suprs. Pocono Neuropsychiat. Ctr., East Stroudsburg, 1987-88; psychologist, cons. Coll. Hill Med. Ctr., East Stroudsburg, 1986—; cons. Winco Health Care and Cons., Inc., East Stroudsburg, 1986—. Mem. Biofeedback Soc. Am., Pa. Psychol. Assn., Pa. Soc. Behavioral Medicine and Biofeedback, Psi Chi. Lutheran. Club: Pocono Environ. (East Stroudsburg). Home: 80 Clermont Ave Stroudsburg PA 18360 Office: College Hill Med Ctr 329 E Brown St East Stroudsburg PA 18301

VAN NAME, JUDITH ANN, economist, educator; b. Cin., July 14, 1945; d. Glen Albert and Lena Anna (Woerner) Beyring; B.S., Miami U., Oxford, Ohio, 1967; M.S., Ohio State U., 1968. Instr. home econs. U. Del., Newark, 1968-71, asst. prof., 1971-77, assoc. prof. Coll. Human Resources, 1977—, chmn. textiles, design and consumer econs., 1978-83; dir. Computer Input Services, Inc. Pres., White Haven Poconos Homeowners Assn., 1975-76, dir., 1976-79. HEW grantee, 1974-76, Dept. Health, Human Services grantee, 86-88. Mem. Am. Home Econs. Assn., Am. Assn. Univ. Profs., Am. Council Consumer Interests, Assn. for Fin. Counseling and Planning Edn., Phi Upsilon Omicron. Author: (with James D. Culley and Barbara H. Settles) Understanding and Measuring the Cost of Foster Family Care, 1975; contbr. articles and revs. to profl. jours. Home: 125 Dallam Rd Newark DE 19711 Office: Textiles Design and Consumer Econs U Del Newark DE 19716

VANN-CHENAULT, SUSAN KAY, comptroller; b. Portsmouth, Va., Mar. 21, 1954; d. William Harry and Eleanor Josephine (Bond) Vann; m. Timothy Alan Chenault, Feb. 28, 1981. BA, Coll. William & Mary, 1976; postgrad., Coll. Notre Dame of Md., Balt., 1985—. Mgmt. analyst Hdqrs. Communication Electronics Command, Ft. Monmouth, N.J., 1978-81, Defense Depot, Tracy, Calif., 1981-83, Hdqrs. First U.S. Army, Ft. Meade, Md., 1983-87. Dir. youth program Pinecrest Bapt. Ch., Portsmouth, 1976-78, Harmony Bapt. Ch., Stockton, Calif., 1982-83; mem. Big Bros.-Big Sisters Am., Monmouth, N.J., 1979-81; foster parent Social Services, Anne Arundel County, Md., 1986-87. Recipient Spl. Act award Hdqrs. First U.S. Army, 1985, 86, Exceptional Performance Hdqrs. First U.S. Army, 1985, 86; named one of Outstanding Young Women Hdqrs. First U.S. Army, 1985, one of Outstanding Young Suprs. Mem. Soc. Mil. Comptrollers. Southern Baptist. Home: 1522 Wampanoag Dr Severn MD 21144 Office: Hdqrs First US Army AFKA RM M Fort Meade MD 20755-7000

VAN NESS, STELLA ANN, nurse, medical care consultant; b. Glens Falls, N.Y., May 9, 1955; d. Willie Leroy and Lillian Frances (Baker) Cleveland; m. Edward Leo Van Ness, July 21, 1973; children: Kristi Marie, Edward Leo Jr. AS, Adirondack Community Coll., 1982. Unit clk. Glens Falls Hosp., 1975-82, RN, 1982; RN cardiac care unit Phoenix Gen. Hosp., 1982-83; RN Scottsdale (Ariz.) Meml. Hosp., 1983; med. review coordinator Ariz. Physician IPA, Phoenix, 1983-84; adminstr. Am. Health Group Inc., Phoenix, 1984-87; pres., chief exec. officer of ops. Action Health Care Inc., Phoenix, 1987—. Home: 119 W Villa Theresa Dr Phoenix AZ 85023 Office: Action Health Care Inc 301 E Bethany Home Rd Suite C-278 Phoenix AZ 85012

VAN NORMAN, PEGGY SHINN, social worker; b. Seattle, Dec. 31, 1951; d. Albert William and Betty Jane (Richardson) Shinn; m. Timothy S. Van Norman, Aug. 2, 1980; children: Megan Ann, Michael Frederick. BS in Social Work, Calif State U., Sacramento, 1974. Crisis interventionist Suicide Prevention Service, Sacramento, Calif., 1971-74; pre-parole counselor Calif. State Med. Facility, Vacaville, Calif., 1973-74; mental health specialist Warm Hands Co., Sacramento, 1974; site mgr. Sr. Now Generation, Tucson, 1974-78; personnel cons. Republic Personnel, Tucson, 1978-79; habilitation specialist Rehab. & Work Adjustment Ctr., Tucson, 1979-82; social worker Flower Square Healthcare, Tucson, 1984—. Recipient Job Tng. Partnership Act grant Pima County, Tucson, 1984. Mem. Nat. Assn. of Social Workers, Am. Soc. on Aging. Democrat. Office: Flower Square Healthcare 2502 N Dodge Blvd Tucson AZ 85716

VAN NOY, CHRISTINE ANN, executive assistant; b. Oakland, CA, Mar. 25, 1948; d. Julio Ceaser and Bernice Thelma (Rose) Lucchesi; m. David Craik Van Noy, July 10, 1971; children: James Allan, Joseph Julio. Student, U. Calif., Berkeley, 1971-73. Exec. sec. Kaiser Permanente Med. Care Program, Oakland, 1966-76; owner Secret Closet Boutique, Moraga, Calif., 1972-82; owner, operator The Wordshop, Moraga, 1976-86; owner, cons. Van Noy & Assocs., Moraga, 1979—; exec. sec. to sr. v.p., regulation mgr. Kaiser Permanente Med. Care Program, 1986—; instr. U. Calif., Santa Cruz, 1983-84, Diablo Valley Coll., Concord, Calif., 1984; cons. Nat. Alliance Homebased Businesswomen, San Francisco, 1981-84. Author: Homebased Business Guide, 1982, (with others) Women Working Home, 1982. Mem. bd. Moraga Sch. Dist., 1985, Calif. Federated Jr. Women's Clubs, 1972-77; bd. dirs. Orinda/Moraga Recreational Swimming Assn., 1984-85, St. Mark's United Methodist Ch., Moraga, 1983-84; mem. bd. Protect Our Nation's Youth Baseball Assn., 1987-88. Democrat. Roman Catholic. Home: 181 Paseo Del Rio Moraga CA 94556 Office: Kaiser Permanente Med Program 1924 Broadway Oakland CA 94556

VAN NOY, LINDA INEZ, position classification specialist; b. Neptune, N.J., Oct. 25, 1949; d. Roy and Isabelle Maime (Lawrence) Williams; m. George Ingram, Oct. 11, 1969 (div. 1973); m. Irving Van Noy, Dec. 10, 1982. A.A., Brookdale Coll., N.J., 1978; B.S., U. Md., 1985. Sec., Dept. of Army, Ft. Monmouth, N.J., 1967-78, exec. sec., 1978-79, intern, 1979-81, equal opportunity mgr., Adelphi, Md., 1981-85, personnel mgmt. specialist, from 1985, now position classification specialist; founder Profl. Outlook, 1987—. Named Outstanding Young Woman of Am., 1984. Mem. Federally Employed Women Inc. (pres. Adelphi chpt. 1987-88), Nat. Assn. Female Execs., Occupational Services Inc. (bd. dirs. 1980-81). Democrat. Am. Baptist. Avocation: bowling. Home: 3927 Blackburn Ln Apt 43 Burtonsville MD 20866 Office: Lab Command 2800 Powder Mill Rd Adelphi MD 20783

VAN ORDEN, PHYLLIS JEANNE, librarian, educator; b. Adrian, Mich., July 7, 1932; d. Warren Philip and Mabel A. Nancy (Russell) Van O. BS Ea. Mich. U., 1954; AMLS, U. Mich., 1958; EdD, Wayne State U., 1970. Sch. librarian East Detroit (Mich.) Pub. Schs., 1954-57; librarian San Diego Pub. Library, 1958-60; media specialist Royal Oak (Mich.) Pub. Schs., 1960-64; librarian Oakland U., Rochester, Mich., 1964-66; instr. Wayne State U., Detroit, 1966-70; asst. prof. Rutgers U., New Brunswick, N.J., 1970-76; prof. library science Fla. State U., Tallahassee, 1977—, assoc. dean for instrn., 1988—. Editor: Elementary School Library Collection, 1974-77; author: Collection Program in Schools, 1988. Recipient Fla. State Library grant, 1984, 88, Fla. Dept. Edn., 1986. Mem. Assn. Library Service to Children (past pres.), Library Resources and Technical Services Div. Am. Library Assn. (Blackwell/North Am. Scholarship award 1983), Pi Lambda Theta. Office: Fla State U Sch Library and Info Studies Tallahassee FL 32306

VANOVER-BREWER, THELDA OLLIE, computer hardware and software sales executive; b. Miami, Fla., Apr. 13, 1951; d. Lee Alan and Thelda Frances (Stone) Vanover; m. Steven D. Rasbach, Jan. 15, 1977 (div. Sept. 1979); m. Darrell Steven Brewer, Apr. 13, 1985; 1 child, Travis Cristian. Student bus. Miami-Dade Community Coll., 1969-71; Notary public, lic. real estate broker, mortgage broker, Fla. Sales mgr. All-Am. Properties, North Miami, Fla., 1978-80; ptnr. H.V.L.L., Inc., Miami, Fla., 1980-82; v.p. Action Title Co., Miami, 1982-85; owner Unltd. Connections, Miami, 1984—; systems cons., computer sales and services Login Systems, Ft. Lauderdale, Fla., 1985—; cons. to new small businesses, Miami, 1984-87. Writer Unltd. Connections News, 1985. Democrat. Avocations: painting, sewing, tennis, country cooking. Office: Login Systems 5440 NW 33d Ave Suite 112 Fort Lauderdale FL 33309

VAN PATTEN, ELIZABETH, communications and marketing consultant; b. Schenectady, N.Y., Aug. 25, 1945; d. Eben Ellsworth and Agnes Frances (O'Connell) Van Patten. BFA, Ithaca Coll., 1967; postgrad., Baruch Coll., 1967, New Sch. Social Research, 1967, NYU, 1967, NYU, 1978-80. V.p. Child Research Service, N.Y.C., 1972-81; pres. Van Patten Research, N.Y.C., 1981—; v.p. Nova Research Inc., N.Y.C., 1986-88; producer, dir. film and video prodns. Producer films on women's rights and achievements. Mem. Am. Mktg. Assn., Qualitative Research Cons. Assn.

VAN PELT, VALERIE RUTH, contracts administrator; b. Knoxville, Tenn., May 30, 1960; d. John Bishop and Annie Marie (Tucker) Van P. AS in Liberal Sci., St. Mary's Coll., Raleigh, N.C., 1980; BS in Pol. Sci. and Criminal Justice, U. N.C., 1982; cert., Nat. Ctr. Paralegal Tng., Atlanta, 1982. Asst. bookkeeper Chapel Hill (N.C.) Country Club, 1983-84; contracts adminstr., paralegal Carolina Power and Light Co., Raleigh, 1984; paralegal SAS Inst., Inc., Cary, N.C., 1984-86, fed. govt. contract negotiator, 1986—. Author: fed. gov. contracts manual. Mem. Cary Jaycee Women. Democrat. Presbyterian. Office: SAS Inst Inc One SAS Circle Box 8000 Cary NC 27512-8000

VAN RAALTE, POLLY ANN, educator; b. N.Y.C., Sept. 22, 1951; d. Byron Emmanuel and Enid (Godnick) Van R.; student U. London, 1972; BA, Beaver Coll., 1973; MS in Edn., U. Pa., 1974, postgrad. in edn., 1975—; postgrad. in spl. edn. West Chester State Coll., 1975-77. Title I reading tchr. Oakview Sch., West Deptford Twp. Sch. Dist., Woodbury, N.J., 1974-75, Title I reading supr., summer 1975; lang. arts coordinator Main Line Day Sch., Mitchell Sch., Haverford, Pa., 1975-76; reading supr. Salvation Army, Phila., summer 1976; reading Huntingdon Jr. High Sch., Abington (Pa.) Sch. Dist., 1976-78; reading specialist No. 2 Sch., Lawrence Pub. Sch., Inwood, N.Y., 1978-87; reading specialist Hewlett Elem. Sch., Hewlett-Woodmere Pub. Sch., Hewlett, N.Y., 1987—; instr. reading and spl. edn. dept. Adelphi U., 1979—; cons. to sch. dists.; advisor Am. Biog. Inst., Inc.; speaker at reading convs. Coordinator, Five Towns Young Voter Registration, Hewlett, N.Y., summer, 1971; chmn. class fund Beaver Coll., also mem. internat. relations com. U. Pa. scholar, 1977-78. Mem. Internat. Reading Assn., Wis. Reading Assn., Nat. Council Tchrs. English, Nassau Reading Council, N.Y. Reading Assn., Council Exceptional Children, Nat. Assn. Gifted Children, Am. Assn. of the Gifted, Nat./State Leadership Tng. Inst. on the Gifted and Talented, Children's Lit. Assembly, N.Y. State English Council, Assn. Curriculum Devel., Am. Israel Pub. Affairs Com., New Leadership com. of Jewish Nat. Fund, Nat. Polit. Action Com, Am. Friends of Hebrew U. (torch com.), Technion Soc., Am. Friends David Yellin Tchr's. Coll., Am. Friends Ben Gurion U., Am. Friends Israel Philharmonic, Cooper-Hewitt Mus., Mus. Modern Art, Met. Mus. Art, Whitney Mus., Phila. Mus. Art, Smithsonian Inst., Friends of Carnegie Hall, Friends of Am. Ballet Theatre, U. Pa. Alumni Assn. N.Y.C., Pi Lambda Theta, Kappa Delta Pi (sec.). Club: Human Relations (sec.). Home: 26 Meadow Ln Lawrence NY 11559 Office: Hewlett Elem Sch Broadway and Herkimer St Hewlett NY 11557

VANREKEN, MARY K., clinical psychologist; b. East Grand Rapids, Mich., Dec. 13, 1947; d. Donald L. and Elsa M. (DeWind) vanR. Cert. Trinity Christian Coll., 1967; B.A. magna cum laude, Hope Coll., 1969; M.A., Appalachian State U., 1970; Ph.D., Purdue U., 1977. Lic. psychologist, Tenn., Ga. Vis. asst. prof. psychology Ind. U., Bloomington, 1977-78; asst. prof. Ind. State U.-Terre Haute, 1978-80; psychologist Valley Psychiat. Hosp., Chattanooga, 1980-82, adolescent program dir., 1983, chief psychologist, 1982-84; pvt. practice, Chattanooga, 1982—; adv. council Family and Children's Services, Chattanooga, 1981-85. Named Outstanding Young Woman, Ind. State U., 1979. Mem. Am. Psychology Assn., Assn. for Women in Psychology, Southeastern Psychol. Assn., Tenn. Psychol. Assn. (chmn. continuing edn. ctr. 1988—, Ga. Psychol. Assn., Chattanooga Area Psychol. Assn. (treas. 1983, ethics com. 1984-86), NOW (treas. Tenn., 1983-85, sec. Tenn. 1985-86), Women's Network of Chattanooga, Chattanooga Bus. and Profl. Women, LWV, Psi Chi. Democrat. Methodist. Avocation: photography, bicycling. Office: Northgate Psychology Group Suite 301 1 Northgate Park Chattanooga TN 37415

VAN RUYVEN, BEVERLY RAE, postal service administrator; b. Red Deer, Alta., Can., Oct. 7, 1956; d. Robert F. and Betty J. (Wolcott) George; m. Andreas M. Van Ruyven; children: Nicholas, Jessica. BA, U. Victoria, B.C., 1979. Flight attendant Can. Pacific Airlines, Vancouver, 1979-80; sales rep. Xerox Can., Vancouver, 1980-82; sales rep. Canada Post Corp., Vancouver, 1982-83, maj. account exec., 1983-85, sales mgr., 1985—. Mem. Sales and Mktg. Execs. Mem. Social Credit Party. Roman Catholic. Office: Can Post Corp, PO Box 2110, Vancouver, BC Canada V6B 4Z3

VAN SCHAICK, JENNIE R., marketing professional; b. Sidney, N.Y., Sept. 2, 1945; d. Karl L. and Anna M. (Bennet) Van S. BS, Hartwick Coll., 1967; MA, Webster U., 1985. Med. technologist Ellis Hosp., Schenectady, N.Y., 1968; research technician Gen. Electric R&D Ctr., Schenectady, 1968-71; tech. rep. Gen. Sci. Corp., Bridgeport, Conn., 1971-72; mktg. asst. The London Co., Cleve., 1972-75; project mgr. Radiometer A/S, Copenhagen, 1976-80; mgr. European mktg. Radiometer A/S, London, 1980-82; gen. mgr. Instrumentation Lab., Inc., The Netherlands and Fed. Republic Germany, 1983-86; internat. mktg. mgr. Ciba Corning Diagnostics Inc., Oberlin, Ohio, 1986—; lectr. European Mgmt. Assn., Brussels, Belgium, 1985; mem. trade com. The Hague, Netherlands, 1985-86. Mem. Soc. Clin. Pathologists (cert.), Am. C. of C., The Am. Women's Club.

VAN SETERS, VIRGINIA ANN, writer; b. Columbia, S.C., Apr. 11, 1947; d. Garret and Virginia Carolina (Motley) Van S. BA in Journalism, U. S.C., 1968. Research div. publs. editor Coll Bus. Adminstrn. U. S.C., Columbia, 1969—; editorial adv. bd. Studies in Econ. Analysis jour. U. S.C., Columbia, 1979—. Author: 22 Object Talks for Children's Worship, 1986, 2d edit. 1987, 26 Object Talks for Children's Worship, 1988; contbr. articles to profl. jours. and consumer mags. Singer Beulah Bapt. Ch., 1959—, tchr. 1973—, pianist 1975—, substitute children's minister, 1980—; supr. children's counselors Billy Graham Evangelistic Assn., Columbia, 1987. Home: 245 Chateau de Ville Columbia SC 29204 Office: Univ SC Coll Bus Adminstrn Columbia SC 29208

VANSICKLE, BARBARA JEAN, computer programmer; b. Parkersburg, W.Va., Oct. 18, 1948; d. Robert Syrl and Evelyn June (Anderson) McGraw; m. John Vernon Morrison Jr., Oct. 7, 1968 (dec. June 1981); children: John Vernon III, Deborah Margarette; m. Danny Ray Vansickle, Oct. 1, 1983. AS, Shawnee State Community Coll., 1984; student, Ohio U., 1985. Keypunch operator Columbus (Ohio) Mut. Life Ins. Co., 1966-67, Steele Data Processing, Washington Court House, Ohio, 1971-74; data entry operator F&R Lazarus, Columbus, 1978-79; clk. III Parker Hannifin Corp., Waverly, Ohio, 1979-80; computer programmer Shawnee State U., Portsmouth, Ohio, 1981—; instr. part-time Southeastern Bus. Coll., Portsmouth, 1982-83. Mem. Valley High Sch. PTA, Lucasville, Ohio, 1982-85; pres. Valley High Sch. Band Boosters, 1986-87, v.p., 1985-86. Mem. Data Processing Mgmt. Spl. Interest Group for Edn., Data Processing Mgmt. Assn., Digital Equip. Corp. Users Soc. (assoc.). Republican. Home: Rt 4 Box 540-C Lucasville OH 45648 Office: Shawnee State U 940 Second St Portsmouth OH 45662

VAN SICKLE, BETSY DOLORES, university sports information official; b. Pitts., Nov. 26, 1952; d. Francis Anthony and Betty Dolores (Varhol) Bjalobok; m. Gary Alyn Van Sickle, Sept. 1, 1984; 1 child, Michael Andrew. B.S., Edinboro U., 1973. Tchr. English and journalism Canon McMillan Schs., Canonsburg, Pa., 1974-75, Sto-Rox High Sch., McKees Rocks, Pa., 1975-76; asst. sports info. dir. Duquesne U., Pitts., 1976-78; acting sports info. dir. Old Dominion U., Norfolk, Va., 1978-79; sports info. dir. Marquette U., Milw., 1979—; press officer U.S. Olympic Com. for Pan Am. Games, Caracas, Venezuela, 1983, for Nat. Sports Festival, Indpls., 1982. Editor: Basketball Media Guide (Best in Nation award Coll. Sports Info. Dirs. Am.), 1981, also other press guides on athletics. Mem. pub. relations com. Wis. Spl. Olympics, Madison, 1983—. Named one of Outstanding Young Women Am., 1981; recipient Cert. Leadership award YWCA, 1986. Mem. Coll. Sports Info. Dirs. Am. (numerous publ. awards 1980—), Women in Communications (co-editor newsletter 1982-84), U.S. Basketball Writers Assn., Women's Sports Found., Milw. Pen and Mike Club, Milw. Advt. Club.

VAN SLETT, KAREN ANN, researcher, nurse; b. Milw., Sept. 13, 1950; d. Theodore Ernst and Regina Viola (Orlikowski) Voss; m. Gene Francis Van Slett, Nov. 6, 1971. BS, U. Wis., Milw., 1972. RN, Wis., Calif. Nursing instr. County Hosp. Sch. Nursing, Milw., 1973-75; nursing supr. Project Involve, Milw., 1976-77; pub. health nurse Home Kare, Inc., San Jose, Calif., 1977-78; br. mgr. Quality Care, Inc., San Jose, 1978-79; ops. mgr. Cardiodyne Gen., Los Gatos, Calif., 1979-83; clin. research assoc. Barnes-Hind, Inc., Sunnyvale, Calif., 1983-86, Genentech, Inc., 1986—. Mem. Assocs. Clin. Pharmacology, Nat. Assn. Female Execs. Democrat. Mem. Friends of Berkeley Shakespeare Festival. Home: 44467 Arapaho Ave Fremont CA 94539

VAN TIEM, DARLENE MIRIAM, corporate executive, educator; b. Detroit, Jan. 18, 1942; d. Norman O. and Miriam (Scoots) Roff; m. Phillip Michael Van Tiem, Apr. 4, 1964; children: Bradford Michael, Adrienne Miriam. BA, Albion Coll., 1963; MA, Mich. State U., 1965; MEd, Marygrove Coll., Detroit, 1974; PhD, Wayne State U., 1986. Instr. pub. schs. Lansing, St. Clair Shores, and Grosse Pointe, Mich., 1963-75; instr. Wayne County Community Coll., Detroit, 1975-80; asst. prof., dir learning skills ctr. Marygrove Coll., Detroit, 1978-86; sr. analyst tech. and tng. group Gen. Physics Corp., Warren, Mich., 1986-87; mgr. curriculum adminstrn. and tech. tng. Troy, Mich., 1987—; cons. MCI Telecommunications, Southfield, Mich., 1983-85. Lector, Eucharistic Minister St. Clare of Montefalco Ch., Grosse Pointe Park, 1980—, sec. five year planning commn. Mem. Am. Soc. Tng. and Devel. (treas. 1985-86, 1st v.p. 1987, pres. 1988, book reviewer newsletter 1983-84), Nat. Assn. Devel. Edn. (mem. adv. bd. 1984-86, research com. 1981-86, new directions task force, 1985-86), Mich. Devel. Edn. Consortium (founder, 1st pres. 1984-86), Soc. Mnfg. Engrs. (sr. mem. 1986), Soc. Automotive Engrs., Pi Lambda Theta, Alpha Lambda Delta, Pi Beta Phi.

VANTOAI, TARA TRAN, agronomist; b. Longxuyen, Vietnam, July 14, 1947; m. Norman N. Vantoai, July 17, 1975; children: Anna Kimberly, Alan Vicent. BS in Agronomy, Nat. Inst. Agrl., Saigon, 1972; MS in Agronomy, Cornell U., 1978; PhD in Agronomy, Ohio State U., 1982. Instr. Nat. Inst. Agrl., Saigon, 1972-75; grad. research asst. Cornell U., Ithaca, N.Y., 1976-80; grad. research asst. Ohio State U., Columbus, 1980-82, research assoc., 1982-84; plant physiologist Soil Drainage unit USDA Agrl. Research Service, Columbus, 1984—; adj. asst. prof. Ohio State U., 1984—. Contbr. articles to profl. jours. Mem. Am. Soc. Agronomy, Am. Soc. Plant Physiologist, Internat. Soc. Plant Molecular Biology, Crop Sci. Soc. Am., Midwestern EEO Adv. Com., Sigma Xi. Mem. United Ch. Christ. Office: USDA/ARS Soil Dranage Unit 590 Woody Hayes Dr Columbus OH 43210

VANTREASE, ALICE TWIGGS, marketing executive; b. Augusta, Ga., Mar. 29, 1943; d. Samuel Warren and Harriett Alice (Wright) Twiggs; m. John Mulford Marks, July 8, 1964 (div. Oct. 1972); children—John Mulford, Sarah Elizabeth; m. James David Vantrease, May 9, 1980 (div. Mar. 1988). Student Winthrop Coll., 1961-62, Augusta Coll., 1962-64. Sales staff Chalker Publ. Co., Waynesboro, Ga., 1972-74; with Creative Displays, Inc., Tuscaloosa, Ala., 1974-78; sales mgr. GMC Bdcasting, Chattanooga, 1978-80; corporate sales, mktg. dir. Creative Displays Inc., Augusta, 1980-83; pres. Creative Mktg. Services, Augusta, 1983—. Bd. dirs. Better Bus. Bur., 1987-88. Mem. Outdoor Advt. Suppliers Assn. (pres.), Nat. Speakers Assn., Am. Mgmt. Assn., Am. Assn. Coop Advt. Profls., Outdoor Advt. Assn. Am., Outdoor Advt. Suppliers Assn. (v.p. 1984-87, pres. 1987—, editor newspaper 1985—). Instr., Small Bus. Devel. Council, Augusta, 1985-86. Episcopalian. Club: Jr. League. Avocations: Painting; writing. Home: 2927 Lake Forest Dr Augusta GA 30909 Office: Creative Mktg 825 Russell St Augusta GA 30914-2247

VAN UMMERSEN, CLAIRE A(NN), university official, biologist; b. Chelsea, Mass., July 28, 1935; d. George and Catherine (Courtovich); m. Frank Van Ummersen, June 7, 1958; children: Lynn, Scott. BS, Tufts U., 1957, MS (Am. Cancer Soc. grantee), 1960, Ph.D., 1963; SD (hon.), U. Mass., 1988. Research asst. Tufts U., 1957-60, research assoc., 1960-67, grad. asst. in embryology, 1962, postdoctoral teaching asst., 1963-66, lectr. in biology, 1967-68; asst. prof. biology U. Mass., Boston, 1968-74; asso. prof. U. Mass., 1974-86, asso. dean acad. affairs, 1975-76, assoc. vice chancellor acad. affairs, 1976-78, chancellor, 1978-79; dir. U. Mass. Environ. Sci. Ctr., 1980-82; cons. Mass. Bd. Regents, 1981-82; asst. Lancaster Course in Ophthalmology, Mass. Eye and Ear Infirmary, 1962-69, lectr., 1970—; reviewer HEW. Assoc. vice chancellor acad. affairs Mass. Bd. Regents for Higher Edn., 1982-85, vice chancellor for mgmt. systems and tele-communications, 1985-86; chancellor U. System of N.H., 1986—. Recipient Disting. Service medal U. Mass., 1979. Mem. AAAS, Am. Soc. Zoologists, Soc. Devel. Biology, Phi Beta Kappa, Sigma Xi. Office: Dunlap Ctr Durham NH 03824

VAN VLACK, MELVA BULLINGTON (MRS. WILLIAM CLARK VAN VLACK), retired home economist; b. Vesta Community, Charleston, Ark., Apr. 3, 1909; d. Baxter Lee and Ella Emma (McConnell) Bullington; B.S., U. Ark., 1932, M.S., 1965; postgrad. U. Calif. at Berkeley, 1939, U. Ala., 1948, Jacksonville State U., 1949; m. William Clark Van Vlack, Aug. 9, 1946. Home econs. instr., Prairie Grove, Ark., 1932-33; elementary tchr., Liberty-Tulsa County, Okla., 1933-34; home demonstration agt., Magnolia, Ark., 1934-36, Hope, Ark., 1936-39, Pine Bluff, Ark., 1939-47; jr. high sch. home econs. instr., Atalla, Ala., 1949-57; extension home economist, Ft. Smith, Ark., 1957-75. Ofcl. home econs. div. Ark.-Okla. Livestock Show and Fair, Ft. Smith U., 1958-72. Recipient Distinguished Service award Nat. Assn. Extension Home Economists, 1970. Mem. Am. Home Econs. Assn., Ark. Assn. Extension Home Economists (dist. counselor), Bus. and Profl. Women Pine Bluff and Ft. Smith, Sebastian County 4-H Club Found. (life), Epsilon Sigma Phi, Delta Gamma Sigma, Delta Sigma Delta. Methodist. Clubs: Sorosis (Magnolia); Soroptimist, Altrusa. Home: PO Box 245 Charleston AR 72933

VAN VRANKEN, LEAH, graphic designer; b. Stockton, Calif., Sept. 20, 1953; d. Edward and Ethelyn Helen (Epperson) V. BA in Art, English, San Diego State U., 1976, postgrad., 1987; postgrad., Boston Archtl. Ctr., 1981, UCLA, 1986. Layout designer Harvard U. News Office, Cambridge, Mass., 1981-82; graphic designer Harvard U. Office of U. Publs., Cambridge, 1982-84; creative dir. Pepperdine U. Publs. Office, Malibu, Calif., 1984-88; prin. Leah Van Vranken Design, Carmel, Calif., 1988—; instr. Harvard U. Extension, 1983; cons. designer Martin & Soares, Inc., Monterey, Calif., 1979-88. Mem. Univ. Coll. Designers Assn. (Award of Excellence 1985), Council for Advancement Support Edn. (Silver Medal 1986, Bronze Medal 1988), People in Communication Arts, Alpha Phi (v.p. 1973-74). Roman Catholic. Office: PO Box 2842 Carmel CA 93921

VAN WAGNER, NANCY LEE, educator; b. Bklyn., Aug. 8, 1938; d. Antonio and Julia Kathryn (Frieri) Mercaldo; m. Anthony Burton Van Wagner (div. May 1979). Student, Pine Crest Bible Inst., 1959-62; BA, Roberts Wesleyan Coll., 1964; MEd, Mich. State U., 1970; diploma in legal assistance, Oakland U., 1984. Elem. tchr. Clark Lake (Mich.) Sch. Dist., 1965-66, Holly (Mich.) Sch. Dist., 1966-69, Clarkston (Mich.) Sch. Dist., 1969—; legal asst. intern George Dovas, Southfield Mich., summer 1984. Precinct del., mem. exec. com. Oakland County Democratic Com., 1986—; Sunday sch. leader Brightmoor Tabernacle. Mem. NEA, Mich. Edn. Assn., Clarkston Edn. Assn. (region 7 del. to Mich. Edn. Assn. 1981—). Home: 8564 Elizabeth Lake Rd PO Box 402 Union Lake MI 48085 Office: Pine Knob Elem Sch 6020 Sashabaw Rd Clarkston MI 48085

VAN WART, GAY ANN, hospital contract administrator; b. Detroit, Jan. 19, 1937; d. Edwin Pelham and Gay Martin (Teasdale) Baugher; m. Calvin Thomas Van Wart, June 3, 1956 (div. Apr. 1971); children: Brenda Kay, Pamela Gay, Charles Wayne (dec.). Student, Draughon's Bus. Coll., 1955-56, Richland Coll., 1977-78. Adminstr. asst. L-M Div. Ford Motor Co., Dallas, 1967-73; asst. sec. TCC, Inc., Dallas, 1973-74; asst. gov., affairs dir. Flower Mound New Town, Lewisville, Tex., 1974-75; asst. dir. of fund raising Yale U., New Haven, Conn., 1976-78; mgr. customer service Blue Cross Blue Shield of Tex., Dallas, 1978-81; sr. assoc. Abrams, Warrick & Winstead, Dallas, 1981-82; account exec. CIGNA Health Plan, Dallas, 1982-84; sales mgr. Whittaker Health Services, Los Angeles, 1984-87; dir. contracting City of Hope Nat. Med. Ctr., Duarte, Calif., 1987—; sec. Forward Looking Strategies Coalition, Los Angeles, 1987-88. Bd. dirs., chmn., Mothers Against Drunk Drivers, Dallas, 1981-84; pres. Remove Intoxicated Drivers, Dallas, 1981-84; founder Dallas County Driving While Intoxicated Task Force, Dallas, 1983; fundraiser Dallas Met. Opera, 1982. Mem. Bus. and Profl. Women (sec. v.p. Los Angeles chpt. 1985-88, Dallas chpt. 1983-84), High Quality Child Care Coalition, Am. Mktg. Assn., Soc. for Health-care Planning & Mktg. Republican. Episcopalian. Home: 3450 Fairpoint St Pasadena CA 91107

VAN ZANDT, ELAINE MARIAN, computer programmer; b. Albany, N.Y., Jan. 21, 1945; d. Joseph John and Katherine Mary (Fisher) DeRusso; m. Walter F. Mucha, 1966 (div. 1978); 1 child, Walter David; m. Lloyd Van Zandt, Mar. 23, 1979; 1 stepson, Mark. Student, Albany Med. Ctr. Sch. Nursing, 1962-63, Hudson Valley Community Coll., 1965, Albany Bus. Coll., 1974-76. Licensed practical nurse. Various positions Sterling Drug, Inc., Rensselaer, N.Y., 1964-78; data entry operator N.Y. State Higher Edn. Services Corp., Albany, 1979; computer operator N.Y. State Dept. Mental Hygiene, Albany, 1979-81, computer program trainee, 1981-82; computer programmer N.Y. State Office of Mental Health, Albany, 1982-85, sr. computer programmer, analyst, 1985—. dir. nursery, deaconess New Life Assembly of God, East Greenbush, N.Y., 1987. Office: NY State Office of Mental Retardation and Devel Disablities 800 N Pearl St Albany NY 12204

VAN ZANDT MORRIS, LINDA, public information official; b. Somerville, N.J., Dec. 9, 1956; d. John B. and Mabel Irene (Wilson) Van Zandt; m. Stephen E. Morris, Oct. 2, 1982. BA in English, Rutgers U., 1979. Journalist Somerset Messenger-Gazette, Somerville, 1979-84; pub. info dir., editor newsletter Somerset County Bd. Chosen Freeholders, Somerville, 1984—. Mem. publicity com. Am. Heart Assn., Somerville, 1985—. Mem. Pub. Relations Soc. Am., Nat. Assn. County Info. Officers, N.J. Assn. Pub. Info. Officials, Phi Beta Kappa. Home: 723 Drake Ave Middlesex NJ 08846 Office: Somerset County Pub Info PO Box 3000 Somerville NJ 08876

VARALLO, DEBORAH GARR, construction executive; b. Nashville, Feb. 14, 1952; d. August Anthony and Kathleen Marie (Baltz) Garr; m. James Edward Varallo, May 6, 1978. BS in Secondary Edn., Baylor U., 1976. With pub. relations dept. Hermitage (Tenn.) Landing, 1976-77; salesperson Elm Hill Meats, Nashville, 1977-78; asst. dir. ARC, Nashville, 1978-81; sales mgr. Varallo Foods, Inc., Nashville, 1981-85; salesperson Mid. Tenn. Equipment, Nashville, 1985-86, Garr Equipment Co., Mt. Juliet, Tenn., 1986—. Mem. adv. com. Hemophilia Adv. Bd. Tenn. Health and Environment, 1986—; chmn. Mid-Cumberland chpt. Hemophilia Found., 1986—. Recipient Outstanding Vol. award Mid-Cumberland Chpt. Hemophilia Found., 1985, Metro Council Dirs. Vols. Nashville, 1987. Mem. Nat. Assn. Profl. Saleswomen (v.p. Nashville chpt. 1986-87, pres. 1987—, chair nat. com. for membership retention 1987—, chair nat. task com. 1988), Nat. Assn. Female Execs., Nashville Assn. Mfrs. Reps. (pres. 1979-81), Assn. Builders and Contractors (program dir. Tenn. chpt. 1986-87, membership com.), Am. Rental Assn., Wilson County Home Builders Assn. (membership com. 1988). Club: Toastmasters (Nashville) (charter, pres. 1986-87). Home: 425 Beacon Hill Dr Nashville TN 37122

VARELLAS, SANDRA MOTTE, lawyer, judge; b. Anderson, S.C., Oct. 17, 1946; d. James E. and Helen Lucille (Gilliam) Motte; m. James John Varellas, July 3, 1971; children: James John III, David Todd. BA, Winthrop Coll., 1968; MA, U. Ky., 1970, JD, 1975. Bar: Ky. 1975, Fla. 1976, U.S. Dist. Ct. (ea. dist.) Ky. 1975, U.S. Ct. Appeals (6th cir.) 1976, U.S. Supreme Ct. 1978. Tchr. Midway Coll., Ky., 1970-72; adj. prof. U. Ky. Coll. Law, Lexington, 1976-78; instr. dept. bus. adminstrn. U. Ky., Lexington, 1976-78; atty. Varellas, Pratt & Cooley, Lexington, 1975—; Fayette County judge exec., Ky., 1980—; hearing officer Ky. Natural Resources and Environ. Protection Cabinet, Frankfort, 1984-88. Committeewoman Ky. Young Dems., Frankfort, 1977-80; pres. Fayette County Young Dems., Lexington, 1977; bd. dirs. Ky. Dem. Women's Club, Frankfort, 1980-84; grad. Leadership Lexington, 1981; chairwoman Profl. Women's Forum, Lexington, Ky., 1985-86. Named Outstanding Young Dem. Woman, Ky. Young Dems., Frankfort, 1977, Outstanding Former Young Dem., Ky. Young Dems., 1983. Mem. ABA, Ky. Bar Assn. (treas. young lawyers div. 1978-79, long range planning com., 1988-89), Fla. Bar, Fayette County Bar Assn. (treas. 1977-78, bd. govs. 1978-80), LWV (nominating com 1984-85). Club: Philharm. Women's Guild (Lexington, Ky.) (bd. dirs. 1979-81, 86-89). Office: Varellas Pratt & Cooley 167 W Main St Lexington KY 40507

VARGA, ROBERTA ODELL, management consultant; b. Oklahoma City, Oct. 26, 1925; d. Ira Ellsworth and Elizabeth (Brandon) Odell; m. Stephen Ivan Varga, Oct. 20, 1956; children: Patricia Ann Butowick, Diane Lyn Sancer. PhB, Northwestern U., 1980. Mgr. Velsicol Chem. Corp., Chgo., 1959-69; mgr. Borg-Warner Corp., Chgo., 1969-84, cons., 1985—; com. mem. Borg-Warner Found., Chgo., 1970—. Contbr. articles to profl. jours. Mem. contbns. com. Borg-Warner Found., Chgo., 1970—. Mem. ABA, Assn. Records Mgrs. and Adminstrs., Chgo. Office Automotive Roundtable (chmn. 1986). Unitarian. Office: Borg-Warner Corp 200 S Michigan Ave Chicago IL 60604

VARGAS, LENA BESSETTE, nursing administrator; b. Hardwick, Vt., Dec. 26, 1922; d. Leon Alphonse and Dorilla Leah (Boudreau) Bessette; m. Jose Emilio Vargas, Sept. 3, 1949; children—Jose Emilio, Maria del Carmen, J. Ramon, Vicente Andres, Yolanda Teresa. B.S. in Nursing Edn., U. Vt., 1949. Instr. basic nursing Mary Fletcher Hosp., Burlington, Vt., 1947-49; clin. instr. St. Francis Hosp., Evanston, Ill., 1949-50; nurse participant streptomycin therapy research H.M. Biggs Meml. Hosp., Ithaca, N.Y., 1950-51; supr. ancillary personnel Providence Hosp., Washington, 1953-55, asst. dir. nursing, 1965—. Mem. council, del. cooperative congress Greenbelt Coop., Savage, Md., 1983—; bd. dirs. Providence Hosp. Fed. Credit Union, Washington, 1977-80, v.p. bd. dirs., 1983-85. Mem. AAUW (chmn. various coms.), Nat. League for Nursing, Christ Child Soc. Roman Catholic. Avocations: bridge, travel, real estate, horseback riding. Home: 10706 Keswick St Garrett Park MD 20896 Office: Providence Hosp 1150 Varnum St Washington DC 20017

VARMECKY, BETTY JO, electronic instrumentation executive; b. Tulsa, Jan. 22, 1927; d. Walter Jonathon and LaVinia (Clear) Eyestone; m. Joseph Dean Varmecky, Jan. 11, 1947; children—Joseph Dean Jr., Diane Louise, David Charles. Student U. Tulsa, 1945, Okla. State U., 1946. Sec. Tri-State Instrument Lab. Inc., Tulsa, 1959-75, pres., 1975—. Mem. Instrument Soc. Am. Democrat. Christian Scientist. Avocations: travel; exercise; reading. Office: Tri-State Instrument Lab Inc 6801 E 15th St Tulsa OK 74112

VARNER, CHARLEEN LAVERNE MCCLANAHAN (MRS. ROBERT B. VARNER), educator, administrator, nutritionist; b. Alba, Mo., Aug. 28, 1931; d. Roy Calvin and Lela Ruhama (Smith) McClanahan; student Joplin (Mo.) Jr. Coll., 1949-51; B.S. in Edn., Kans. State Coll. Pittsburg, 1953; M.S., U. Ark., 1958; Ph.D., Tex. Woman's U. 1966; postgrad. Mich. State U., summer, 1955, U. Mo., summer 1962; m. Robert Bernard Varner, July 4, 1953. Apprentice county home agt. U. Mo., summer 1952; tchr. Ferry Pass Sch., Escambia County, Fla., 1953-54; tchr. biology, home econs. Joplin Sr. High Sch., 1954-59; instr. home econs. Kans. State Coll., Pittsburg, 1959-63; lectr. foods, nutrition Coll. Household Arts and Scis., Tex. Woman's U., 1963-64, research asst. NASA grant, 1964-66; asso. prof. home econs. Central Mo. State U., Warrensburg, 1966-70, adviser to Colhecon, 1966-70, adviser to Alpha Sigma Alpha, 1967-70, 72, mem. bd. advisers Honors Group, 1967-70; prof., head dept. home econs. Kans. State Tchrs. Coll., Emporia, 1970-73; prof., chmn. dept. home econs. Benedictine Coll., Atchison, Kans., 1973-74; prof., chmn. dept. home econs. Baker U., Baldwin City,

Kans., 1974-75; owner, operator Diet-Con Dietary Cons. Enterprises, cons. dietitian, 1973—. Mem. Joplin Little Theater, 1956-60. Mem. NEA, Mo., Kans. state tchrs. assns., AAUW, Am., Mo., Kans. dietetics assns., Am., Mo., Kans. home econs. assns., Mo. Acad. Scis., AAUP, U. Ark. Alumni Assn., Alumni Assn. Kans. State Coll. of Pittsburg, Am. Vocat. Assn., Assn. Edn. Young Children, Sigma Xi, Beta Sigma Phi, Beta Beta Beta, Alpha Sigma Alpha, Delta Kappa Gamma, Kappa Kappa Iota, Phi Upsilon Omicron. Methodist (organist). Home: Main PO Box 1009 Topeka KS 66601

VARNER, NELLIE MAE, real estate investment broker; b. Lake Cormorant, Miss., 1935; d. Tommie and Essie (Davis) V.; m. Louis S. Williams (div. Feb. 1964). AA, Highland Park Community Coll., 1956; BS, Wayne State U., 1958, MA, 1959; PhD, U. Mich., 1968. Tchr. pub. schs. Detroit Bd. Edn., 1959-64; spl. asst. to dean Coll. Lit., Sci. and Arts U. Mich., Ann Arbor, 1968-70, faculty assoc. Ctr. Russian and Ea. European Studies, asst. prof. polit. sci., 1968-79, dir. affirmative action programs, 1972-75, assoc. dean Grad. Sch., 1976-79; research assoc. Russian Research Ctr., research fellow Ctr. Internat. Affairs Harvard U., Cambridge, Mass., 1970-71; assoc. sales Real Estate One, Farmington, Mich., 1971-75; v.p. Strather & Varner, Inc., Southfield, Mich., 1978—; chmn. Mich. Real Estate Adv. Bd., Lansing, 1979-80; bd. dirs. Community Investment Adv., Washington, Am. Inst. for Bus., Detroit, New Detroit, Inc.; del. White House Conf. on Small Bus., 1980. Bd. regents U. Mich., Ann Arbor, 1980—; bd. dirs. Highland Park YMCA, 1980-82, Hartford Credit Union; chmn. bd. dirs. Hartford Head Start Agy. Wilton Park fellow, 1969, Social Sci. Research Council tng. fellow, 1970-71; U. Mich. grantee, 1970-71. Mem. Nat. Assn. Realtors, Mich. Assn. Realtors, NAACP, S. Oakland County Bd. Realtors, Nat. Assn. Women Bus. Owners, Phi Kappa Phi, Pi Sigma Alpha, Delta Sigma Theta (bd. dirs. Detroitchpt.). Democratic. Baptist. Office: Strather & Varner Inc 3000 Town Ctr #2460 Southfield MI 48075

VARSA, MARILYN D., educational and career consultant; b. N.Y.C., May 22, 1938; d. Irving and Hannah (Grand) Edelman; m. George G. Varsa, Feb. 3, 1968; 1 child, Craig Steven. BS, Columbia U., 1956; MA, Hunter Coll., 1985. Pres. GMC Universal Ltd., N.Y.C., 1972—, Derek Street, Inc., N.Y.C., 1974—; ednl. and career cons. Goddard-Riverside Community Ctr., N.Y.C., 1986—. Home: 525 E 86th St New York NY 10028 Office: GMC Universal Ltd 310 Madison Ave New York NY 10017

VASARKOVY, DIANE ROSE, computer systems administrator; b. Newark, June 5, 1943; d. William Louis and Laura Veronica (Fischer) V.; children: Robert Frank Montoya, Richard Michael Montoya. Student, San Antonio Coll., 1970-73; BBA, U. Tex., San Antonio, 1981. Cert. in gen. ins. Ins. Inst. Am.; cert. in data processing Inst. for Cert. Computer Profls. Data control clk. AEC, Albuquerque, 1966-67, programmer, analyst Hillcrest State Bank, Dallas, 1967-69, Alamo Nat. Bank, San Antonio, 1969-71; sr. programmer, analyst S.W. Info. Mgmt. Systems, San Antonio, 1971-74; systems analyst United Services Automobile Assn., San Antonio, 1974-81, project mgr., 1981-86, dir. mktg. systems, 1986—; v.p., bd. dirs. United Services Automobile Assn. Fed. Credit Union, 1979-84; bd. advisors Computer Bus. Mgmt. Ctr. San Antonio, 1986—, St. Phillips Coll., San Antonio, 1987. Mem. San Antonio Computer Profls., Data Processing Mgmt. Assn. (dir. San Antonio chpt. 1975-77, 82, sec. 1982-83, pres. 1986), Women in Info. Processing. Home: Rt 5 Box 5352 Boerne TX 78006 Office: USAA USAA Bldg D-3-W San Antonio TX 78288

VASHRO, MAXEEN LAVERE, small business owner; b. Mpls., Mar. 13, 1951; d. Max Lee and Helen LaVere (Knudtson) Murray; divorced, Apr. 1985; children: Courtney, Genell. Student, U. Minn., 1970-73, Mankato State U., 1973-74; BA in Theater Arts, U. Calif., Long Beach, 1975. Fitness cons. Fitness Plus, Mpls., 1981-83; dance, fitness instr. Sivanich Sch. Music and Dance, Mpls., 1983; founder, owner Body To The Max, Mpls., 1983—; fitness cons. Twin Town Treatment Ctr., St. Paul, 1986—, 3R's Treatment Ctr., Mpls., 1985—. Author, cheorographer Health and Recovery Program, 1983; choreographer, tchr. ednl. program on tape for aerobic instrs., 1981—. Chmn. Dance for Heart, Am. Heart Assn., 1984, 86. Mem. Internat. Dance Exercise Assn., Profl. Dance Tchrs. Assn., Phi Beta (sec. 1980-82), Kappa Delta (nat. v.p. 1980-82). Home: 315 Cottage Downs Hopkins MN 55343 Office: Body To The Max 1304 University Ave NE Minneapolis MN 55413

VASQUEZ, JUNE FILIPKOWSKI, psychologist; b. Willimantic, Conn., May 29, 1943; d. John T. and Sabina (Yaskinowsky) Filipkowski; m. Alphonse T. Vasquez, Apr. 19, 1938; 1 child, Cathleen. BA, Boston U., 1965, MA, 1967; PhD, Rutgers U., 1975. Adj. asst. prof. psychology Lehman Coll., Bronx, N.Y., 1981-82, Iona Coll., New Rochelle, N.Y., 1981-82; adj. lectr. Manhattan Coll., N.Y.C., 1980-81; asst. psychologist Great Neck, N.Y.; lectr. in psychology Manhatten Coll., Riverdale, N.Y., 1980-81. Mem. legisl. com. PTA, Larchmont, 1980—. Mem. Am. Psychol. Assn., N.Y. State Psychol. Assn., LWV (bd. dirs. 1979). Home: 7 Nassau Rd Larchmont NY 10538 Office: 935 No Blvd Great Neck NY 11021

VASS, JOAN, fashion designer; b. N.Y.C., May 19, 1925; d. Max S. and Rose K.; children by previous marriage—Richard, Sara, Jason. Student Vassar Coll., 1941; B.A., U. Wis., 1946. Pres., Joan Vass Inc., N.Y.C., 1977—. Recipient Prix de Cachet, Prince Machiabelli, 1980; Coty award, 1979; Disting. Woman in Fashion award Smithsonian Instn., 1980. Office: Joan Vass Inc 117 E 29th St New York NY 10016

VASS, LISA TAYLOR, software executive; b. Balt., Dec. 17, 1953; d. George Henry and Cannie Marion (Chandler) Mueller; m. Garry James Vass, June 28, 1981; 1 child, Carmen Abigail. BFA, Towson State Coll., Balt., 1975; student, Columbia U., 1986. Pres. Emmet/Taylor Assocs., Balt., 1976-78; mgr. Mothercare, Gaithersburg, Md., 1979-80; asst. mgr. Stein's, Arlington, Va., 1980-81; pres. Telemachus Software Assocs., West New York, N.J., 1982—. Author play, Money, 1977; composer of songs. Bd. dirs. Columbia Community Theatre, Md., 1972-76; v.p. PTA, West New York, 1987, treas., 1988. Mem. Am. Women Entrepreneurs Assn., Am. Entrepreneurs Assn., Metro Opera Guild, Assn. Research and Enlightenment. Democrat. Club: Wagner Soc.

VASSAR, TINA MARRIE, nurse; b. Portsmouth, Va., Oct. 29, 1956; d. John Dixie and Hazell (Barr) V. BS in Nursing, Radford U., 1979; MS in Nursing, U. Va., 1983. Staff nurse U. Va. Hosp., Charlottesville, 1979-80, head nurse, 1980-83; cardiothoracic surgery clin. nurse specialist N.C. Meml. Hosp., Chapel Hill., 1983—; adj. instr. U. N.C. Sch. Nursing, Chapel Hill, 1986—. Bd. dirs. ARC, Chapel Hill. Mem. Am. Nurses Assn. (bd. dirs., research chmn. Dist. II 1984—), Am. Assn. Critical Care Nurses (bd. dirs., workshop chmn. Triangle chpt. 1984-85, chpt. treas. 1986-87), Alpha Delta Pi. Republican. Baptist. Avocations: swimming, music. Office: NC Meml Hosp Manning Dr Chapel Hill NC 27514

VAUGHAN, MARILOU TAYLOR, magazine editor; b. Detroit; d. Robert Adams and Dorothea (Trauffer) Taylor; B.A., Eastern Mich. U., 1958; postgrad. Stanford U., 1959; m. David Rodman Vaughan, Jan. 2, 1960. Asst. editor Smithsonian mag., Washington, 1974-76; assoc. editor New West mag., Beverly Hills, Calif., 1976-77, Archtl. Digest, Los Angeles, 1977-79; editor Bon Appetit mag., Los Angeles, 1979-85; sr. editor Los Angeles Times Mag., 1985-86; editor West coast Family Circle mag., 1986—. Mem. Am. Assn. Mag. Editors. Office: Family Circle Mag 6100 Wilshire Blvd Suite 720 Los Angeles CA 90048

VAUGHAN, MARTHA, biochemist; b. Dodgeville, Wis., Aug. 4, 1926; d. John Anthony and Luciel (Ellingen) V.; m. Jack Orloff, Aug. 4, 1951; children—Jonathan Michael, David Geoffrey, Gregory Joshua. Ph.B., U. Chgo., 1944; M.D., Yale U., 1949. Intern New Haven Hosp., Conn., 1950-51; research fellow U. Pa., Phila., 1951-52; research fellow Nat. Heart Inst., Bethesda, Md., 1952-54, mem. research staff, 1954-68; head metabolism sect. Nat. Heart and Lung Inst., Bethesda, 1968-74; acting chief molecular disease br. Nat. Heart, Lung and Blood Inst., Bethesda, 1974-76, chief cell metabolism lab., 1974—; mem. Metabolism Study Sect. NIH, 1965-68. Mem. editorial bd. Jour. Biol. Chemistry, 1971-76, 80-83, 88—; mem. editorial adv. bd. Molecular Pharmacology, 1972-80; contbr. articles to profl. jours., chpts. to books. Bd. dirs. Found. Advanced Edn. in Scis. Inc., Bethesda, 1979—, exec. com., 1980—, treas., 1984-86, v.p. 1986-88, pres. 1988—; mem. Yale U. Council com. med. affairs, New Haven, 1974-80. Recipient Meritorious Service medal HEW, 1974, Disting. Service medal HEW, 1979, Commd. Officer award USPHS, 1982. Mem. Nat. Acad. Scis., Am. Soc. Biol. Chemists (chmn. pub. com. 1984-86), Assn. Am. Physicians, Am. Soc. Clin. Investigation. Home: 11608 W Hill Dr Rockville MD 20852 Office: Nat Heart Lung and Blood Inst Bldg 10 Room 5N-307 NIH Bethesda MD 20892

VAUGHAN, PEGGY THORPE, personnel interviewer, home economist; b. Emporia, Va., May 12, 1942; d. Neuit Henry Thorpe Sr. and Ruth Ethel (Harris) Thorpe Harrell; m. Joseph Kelley Vaughan, Dec. 21, 1962; children: Jody, Thorpe, Andy. BS in Home Econs. Edn., Longwood Coll., 1964. Lic. tchr. Tchr. spl. edn. Emporia Elem. Sch., 1964-65; tchr. home econs. Southampton High Sch., Courtland, Va., 1965-66, Greensville High Sch., Emporia, 1968-69; elem. grade tchr. Roanoke Christian Sch., Roanoke Rapids, N.C., 1979-80; part-time instr. Halifax Community Coll., Weldon, N.C., 1969-80, Southside Va. Community Coll., Alberta, Va., 1984-85; interviewer U.S. Dept. Commerce, Charlotte, N.C., 1984—; consumer council rep. Farm Fresh Supermarkets, 1986-88, regional rep., 1988—; judge Future Homemakers Am./Home Econs. Related Occupations contest Deep Creek High Sch., Norfolk, Va., 1988. Vol. Am. Cancer Soc. Bazaar, 1987—; mem. Va. Bluegrass and Country Music Found., Richmond, 1988—; v.p. Emporia Jr. Women's Club, 1965-69, Greenville County Hist. Soc., 1988; com. chmn. Emporia Federated Garden Club, 1967-69; co-chmn. campaign Henry Howell for Gov., 1969-78. Named one of Outstanding Young Women of Am., 1978. Mem. Am. Home Econs. Assn., Va. Home Econs. Assn. (spl. edn. sect. 1964-65, Tidewater Home Economists (pres. 1986-88), Home Economists in Homemaking (yr. book chmn. 1979), United Daus. Confederacy (com. chmn. 1986—, recording sec. 1987—), Emporia Hist. Soc. (com. chmn. 1985—), Archeol. Soc., Early Am. Soc., Am. Rose Soc. Baptist. Lodges: Rotary (surrogate mother for Mexican Rotary exchange student 1987—), Order o Ea. Star (officer 1988). Home: 204 Battery Ave Emporia VA 23847

VAUGHN, ELEANOR, state legislator; b. Troy, Idaho, Nov. 12, 1922; m. Benjamin Vaughn Sr.; 3 children. Grad., Kinman Bus. U. Mem. Mont. State Senate. Democrat. Home: 251 Mahoney Rd PO Box 45 Libby MT 59923 *

VAUGHN, ELLEN LORA, utility company executive; b. Xenia, Ohio, Mar. 24, 1950; d. Bruce Howard and Jessie (Whitehair) McPhaden; m. James David Vaughn, July 12, 1969 (div. Mar. 1977). BA, Whitman Coll., 1972; MBA, City Univ., Bellevue, Wash., 1987. Adminstrv. asst. protocol dept. Expo '74, Spokane, Wash.; orner PR Plus, Bellingham, Wash., 1977-81; coordinator corp. relations Puget Power Co., Bellingham, 1981—. Mem. Whatcom Mus. Commn., Bellingham, 1985—, pres., 1985-87; mem. Wash. State Ins. Commrs. Tort Study Group, Olympia, 1987—; mem. exec. bd. dirs. United Way of Whatcom County, 1984-87. Mem. N.W. Electric Light and Power Assn., Whatcom C. of C., Whatcom Women in Bus. (pres. 1980-82). Office: Puget Power Co PO Box 1078 Bellingham WA 98227

VAUGHN, GAIL MORRIS, psychologist; b. Pomona, Calif., Dec. 15, 1946; d. Donald Duvall and Margaret Pearl (Shelton) Nance; m. Donald Gene Proffitt, June 3, 1967 (dec. Nov. 1973); 1 child, David Wayne; m. James Lewis Vaughn III, Sept. 21, 1985. BS in Nursing, William Jewell Coll., 1977; MA in Human Relations, Webster U., 1983; PhD, Golden State U., 1986; cert., Neuro-Linguistics Inst., 1984. RN. Mo. Nurse Kansas City hosps., 1977-81; counselor Yokefellows Mid-Am., Kansas City, 1981-83; psychotherapist, owner Christian Crisis Counseling, Liberty, Mo., 1983—; seminar speaker, Mo. Co-chmn. treatment com., media com. U.S. Attorney's Task Force Drug Abuse, Kansas City. Named a Woman of Achievement Mid-Continent Council Girl Scouts USA, 1987. Mem. Adolescent Resource Network, Nat. Assn. Female Exec., Nat. Assn. Women Bus. Owners, Nat. Council Alcoholism (Kansas City bd. dirs.), Network Profl. Children Of Alcoholics Kansas City (pres. 1986-87), Mo. Assn. Alcoholism Counselors, Met. Child Abuse Network. Office: Christian Crisis Counseling 1201 W College Liberty MO 64068

VAUGHN, LESLEY MILLER MEHRAN, lawyer; b. Eng., Aug. 24, 1944; came to U.S., 1952; d. Victor Raymond and Daphne (Trecker) Miller; m. G.R.C. Mehran, June 29, 1966 (div. Jan. 1978); children: Diana, Mark, Rawley, Peter; m. John Spencer Vaughn, Aug. 6, 1983. Cert., U. Geneva, 1965, U. Paris, 1966; BS, U. Calif., Berkeley, 1967; JD, Loyola U., Los Angeles, 1982. Bar: Calif. 1982, U.S. Ct. Appeals (9th cir.) 1984. Assoc. Finley, Kumble, Wagner, Heine, Underberg, Manley & Casey, Los Angeles, 1982-83, Smith & Holland, Los Angeles, 1983-86, Lawler, Felix & Hall, Los Angeles, 1986—. Contbr. articles to profl. jours. Mem. ABA, Calif. Bar Assn., Phi Alpha Delta. Republican. Presbyterian. Home: 930 Afton Rd San Marino CA 91108 Office: Lawler Felix & Hall 700 S Flower St Los Angeles CA 90017

VAUGHN, MARY, health care facilities exec.; b. Trafford, Ala., Apr. 20, 1930; d. Grover Webster and Vivian Lenora (Dorman) V.; student Birmingham Bus. Coll., 1952, Howard Coll., 1959, U. Ala., 1960, 62, Balboa Intermediate Care Facility, San Diego, 1969-76; certificate in therapeutic activities tng. Grossmont Adult Sch., 1975; m. James T. Lovvorn, Mar. 1952 (div. 1959). Owner, pres., treas. Balboa Manor Inc. and Balboa Manor Health Facility, San Diego, 1969-79. Charter pres. Quota Club of Birmingham (Ala.), 1967-68; lt. gov. 8th dist. Quota Internat., 1968-69; supr. adv. com. to Jim Bates, 4th Dist. Supr. San Diego County, 1973—; mem. San Diego County Com. on the Handicapped, 1979—; mem. support com. Community Video Center, pub. access TV, 1979—. Pres., bd. dirs. Girls Club San Diego, 1987-88. Recipient Safety award Indsl. Indemnity, 1973, 75, cert. of appreciation Jim Bates, 1975, 11th Woman award Women's Internat. Ctr., 1988; named Citizen of Month Congl. Service award, 1987; notary pub., cert. nursing home adminstr., Calif. Mem. Am. Health Care Assn., Am. Coll. Nursing Home Adminstrs., Am., Calif. nursing home assns., Com. of 100 of San Diego Klee Wyk Soc., San Diego Opera, Bus. and Profl. Women's Club (pres. Birmingham chpt. 1967-69), San Diego Mus. Natural History, San Diego Mus. of Man, Nat. Notary Assn. Republican. Methodist. Author: Exploring Mental Therapy. Home: 2804 C St San Diego CA 92102

VAUGHN, MARY KELLEY, savings and loan executive, consultant; b. N.Y.C., Mar. 25, 1959; d. Clarence Breck and Jean Ann (Jacobs) Kelley; m. Michael Wayne Vaughn, May 28, 1957. BS, U. Ala., Birmingham, 1982; MBA, Sanford U., 1986. Mgr. Collateral Investment Co., Birmingham, Ala., 1982-84, L.M. Berry Yellow Pages, Birmingham, 1984-86; legal asst. Sirote-Permutt, et al., Birmingham, 1986-87; mgr. Ala. Fed. Savs. and Loan, Birmingham, 1987—. Home: 1709 Brookview Trail Birmingham AL 35216

VAUGHN, NOEL WYANDT, lawyer; b. Chgo., Dec. 15, 1937; d. Owen Heaton and Harriet Christy (Smith) Wyandt; m. David Victor Koch, July 18, 1959 (div.); 1 child, John David; m. Charles George Vaughn, July 9, 1971. BA, DePauw U., 1959; MA, So. Ill. U., 1963; JD, U. Dayton, 1979. Bar: Ohio 1979, U.S. Dist. Ct. (so. dist.) Ohio 1979, U.S. Cir. Ct. (6th cir.) 1987. Communications specialist Charles F. Kettering Found., Dayton, 1968-71; tchr. English Miami Valley Sch., Dayton, 1971-76; law clk. to judge Dayton Mcpl. Ct., 1978-79; coordinator Montgomery County Fair Housing Ctr., Dayton, 1979-81, 85—; atty. Henley Vaughn Becker & Wald, Dayton, 1981—; lectr. Wright State U., Dayton, 1965-67. Chmn. Dayton Playhouse, Inc., 1981—; pres. Freedom of Choice Miami Valley, Dayton, 1980-83, 86-87; bd. dirs. ACLU, Dayton, 1982-86; com. mem. Battered Woman Project-YWCA, Dayton, 1983-84; pres. Legal Aid Soc. Dayton, 1983-84; chmn. Artemis House, Inc., 1985—; bd. dirs. Miami Valley Arts Council, 1985-86. Recipient Order of Barristers award U. Dayton, 1979. Mem. ABA, Dayton Bar Assn. (chmn. delivery legal services com. 1983-84), Ohio FAIR Plan Underwriting Assn. (bd. govs. 1986—). Home: 3700 Wales Dr Dayton OH 45405

VAUGHN, REBECCA ELIZABETH, banker; b. Pascagoula, Miss., June 13, 1944; d. Walter Edward and Elizabeth (Norwood) Nettles; m. Gerald Glen Vaughn June 2, 1963 (dec. Nov. 1981); children: Angie, Chad, Bethany. Student, Sch. Bank Mktg., U. Colo., 1974-75, Mktg. Mgrs. Sch., U. Wis., 1978; grad., La. State U., 1987. Bookkeeper Trustmark Nat. Bank, Brookhaven, Miss., 1963-64, with ops., 1964-65, teller, note teller, 1966-68, asst. cashier, 1969-73, asst. v.p., 1974-78, v.p. mktg., 1978-88, sr. v.p., 1988—; bus. cons. Project Bus. div. Jr. Achievement, Brookhaven, 1984-86. Editor: (newsletter) Vault Talk, 1971—; contbr. articles to jours. Bd. dirs. Miss. Econ. Council, Brookhaven, 1976-77. Named one of Outstanding Young Women Am., 1968, 69, 70, 71, Young Career Woman, 1971. Mem. Brookhaven/Lincoln County C. of C., Bank Mktg. Assn. (bd. dirs. 1981-83, 85-87, named to exec. com. Pres. Club 1983), Nat. Assn. Bank Women, So. Fin. Exchange (mktg. com. 1985-88), Beta Sigma Phi. Baptist. Home: Rt 8 Box 408 Brookhaven MS 39601 Office: Trustmark Nat Bank PO Box 539 148 S Whitworth Ave Brookhaven MS 39601

VAUGHT, BETTE JENNE, medical association executive; b. Farmington, Mo., Dec. 19, 1924; d. Walter and Emma (Coleman) Aubuchon; m. Charles Vaught, 1948 (div.); 1 child, Charles R. Sec. Internat. Brotherhood Elec. Workers, Milw., 1952-54, Milw. Braves, 1956-57; sec. Am. Osteopath Assn., Chgo., 1958-68, coordinator conv., 1968-78; exec. dir. Am. Coll. Gen. Practitioners, Osteopathic Medicine and Surgery, Arlington Heights, Ill., 1978—; cons. Am. Acad. Disability Physicians, Chgo., 1988—. Mem. Nat. Assn. Female Execs., Am. Soc. Assn. Execs., Chgo. Soc. Assn. Execs., Profl. Conv. Med. Assn. Democrat. Roman Catholic. Home: 491 Le Parc Buffalo Grove IL 60089 Office: Am Coll Gen Practitioners 2045 S Arlington Heights Rd Arlington Heights IL 60005

VAUGHT, JANET MAUREEN BURGER, city official; b. Indpls., Jan. 23, 1952; d. Clifford Robert and Opal June (McKinnon) Burger; m. Charles H. Vaught, Jr., Sept. 15, 1977; children: Patricia Lynn, Jennifer Leigh. BS in Edn., So. Ill. U., 1974, MS in Edn., 1984. Registered mcpl. clk.; cert. mcpl. clk. Research asst. So. Ill. U., Carbondale, 1974, sec., 1974-75, researcher, 1976; sec. City of Carbondale, 1976-77, dep. city clk., 1977-79, city clk., 1979—. Vol. Girl Scouts Am.; bd. dirs. LWV, 1988). Ill. tchr. edn. scholar State of Ill., 1970. Mem. Internat. Inst. Mcpl. Clks. (bd. dirs. 1988), Nat. Bus. Edn. Assn. (award of merit 1974), Ill. Bus. Edn. Assn. (scholar 1973), So. Ill. Bus. Edn. Assn., Mcpl. Clks. Ill. (pres. 1987), Carbondale Bus. Profl. Women (2d v.p. 1987), Delta Pi Epsilon, Pi Omega Pi, Pi Lambda Theta, Kappa Delta Pi. Methodist. Avocations: travel, reading, being with children. Home: 620 Glenview Dr Carbondale IL 62901 Office: City of Carbondale PO Box 2047 Carbondale IL 62902

VAUX, DIANE RITCHEY, clinical psychologist; b. Cambridge, Mass., Nov. 2, 1942; d. John Arthur and Frances (Curtis) Ritchey; m. Walter Gregson Vaux, Jan. 15, 1983. BA, Ind. U., 1964, MA, 1965; MS, Drexel U., 1968, U. Pitts., 1975; PhD, U. Pitts., 1979. Lic. psychologist, Pa. Tchr. secondary Pitman (N.J.) High Sch., 1965-66; jr. cataloguer Drexel Library, Phila., 1966-67; reference librarian Free Library of Phila., 1968-69, coordinator young adult services, 1969-72; mental health therapist S.W. Communities Mental Health/Mental Retardation Ctr., Pitts., 1977-82; coordinator stepfamily services Families in Transition, Pitts., 1982-85; pvt. practice specializing in psychology Murrysville, Pa., 1985—. Charter mem. West Pa. Task Force on Women and Addictions, Pitts., 1981-86. Fellow Am. Psychol. Assn., Pa. Psychol. Assn.; mem. Acad. of Family Psychology, Am. Assn. of Marital and Family Therapists (clin.). Home: 3491 Ivy Ln Murrysville PA 15668 Office: 3205 Sardis Rd Murrysville PA 15668

VAVRICK, ELLAN FINMAN, insurance company executive; b. Pensacola, Fla., Aug. 28, 1943; d. Maurice Max Finman and Rosalie (Buchman) Rotwein; m. Samuel Dunham Harris Jr., Dec. 30, 1971 (div. Feb. 1982); children Marcia Harris Francis, Julie Harris Prommasit; m. Richard Anthony Vavrick, Mar. 12, 1987. AA, Pensacola (Fla.) Jr. Coll., 1967; BA, U. W. Fla., 1970. Registered health underwriter; cert. fin. planner Nat. Assn. Securities Dealers. Exec. asst. Amy's Shop's, Inc., Pensacola, Fla., 1961-68; exec. asst. to pres. Pensacola Rug & Shade, Co., Pensacola, 1968-69; account exec. WBOP radio, Pensacola, 1971; owner, artist Grand Lagoon Gallery, Pensacola, 1971-77; sales rep. in tng. Travelers Ins. Co., Pensacola, 1977-78, agy supr., 1978-80, prodn. mgr., 1980-85; dir. disability income sales Pan-Am. Lif Ins. Co., New Orleans, 1985—; instr. mktg. Life Office Mgmt Assn., Pan Am., New Orleans, 1986-87; mem. Ins. Commrs. Cost Containment com., Baton Rouge, 1986-87; speaker Internat. Assn. Fin. Planners workshop, New Orleans, 1986, La. State Health Underwriters conv., Baton Rouge, 1986. Contbr. articles to profl. jours.; author: (monthly column) Panorama, 1985-87. bd. dirs. La. Multiple Sclerosis Soc., New Orleans, 1985-87, U.S. Councils of Navy League, Pensacola, 1980-84, v.p. 1985; mem. museum expansion com., U.S. Naval Aviation Museum Found., Pensacola, 1984; ops. officer Assn. Naval Aviation, New Orleans, 1987; bd. dirs. mentor program Covenant House New Orleans, 1987—. Mem. U.S. Marine Corps Assn. (life), Inst. Cert. Fin. Planners, Nat. Assn. Health Underwriters, Beta Sigma Phi. Republican. Roman Catholic. Clubs: Ikebana Internat. (Pensacola) (exhibition chair 1974-77, treas. 1975, sec. 1976); Krewe of Shangri-La (New Orleans). Home: 3025 Esplanade Ave New Orleans LA 70119 Office: Pan Am Life Ins Co 601 Poydras St 12 Floor New Orleans LA 70130

VAZQUEZ, BARBARA LINDER, home economist; b. Hartwell, Ga., June 8, 1944; d. Ezra and Claurdie Mae (Linder) Rucker; m. Raul Enrique Vazquez, Aug. 8, 1970 (div. July 1982). BS, Morris Brown Coll., Atlanta, 1966; MS, Hunter Coll., 1974. Dietitian N.Y.C. Hosps., Bronx, 1966-68; home economist N.Y.C. Dept. Social Services, 1968-74, supervising home economist, 1974—; home nursing instr. ARC, N.Y.C., 1968—. Named one of Outstanding Young Women of Am., 1970. Mem. Am. Home Econs. Assn., Nat. Assn. Female Execs., Morris Brown Coll. Alumni Assn. N.Y. (corr. sec. 1984—, Profl. Citation 1983, Outstanding Service award 1985, Outstanding Alumna and Spl. Recognition award 1988), Alpha Kappa Alpha. Democrat. Baptist. Home: 121 Mount Hope Pl Bronx NY 10453 Office: NYC Dept Social Services Div Home Economics 109 E 16th St New York NY 10003

VEGA, KAY MAYFIELD, shopping mall manager, real estate entrepreneur; b. Madison, Ind., Jan. 26, 1947; d. George A. and Charlotte M. (Pickett) Mayfield; m. D. Edwin Vega, Aug. 6, 1966 (dec. Aug. 1979); children: Eric, Martina. Grad. high sch., Madison, 1965. Cert. shopping ctr. mgr.; lic. real estate broker. Advt. salesperson Madison Courier & Weekly Harold, 1966-68; salesperson Combined Ins., Madison, 1968-71, Sun Country Builders, Clermont, Fla., 1973-76; mall mgr. Clearwater (Fla.) Assocs., 1981—; owner, pres. Payment Ctrs., Inc., Clearwater, 1983-85; pres. Pinellas Electronics Assocs., Inc., Clearwater, 1985—. Correspondent, co-host TV program, Clearwater, 1984-85. Pres. Parent Tchrs. Fellowship, Largo Christian Sch., Clearwater, 1986-87; mem. sponsorship com. Celebrity Golf Tournament-Alcohol Community Treatment Services, Tampa, Fla., 1986; mem. Clearwater Community Relations Bd., 1985—. Mem. Internat. Council Shopping Ctrs., Fla. Council Shopping Ctrs., Nat. Assn. Female Execs., Contractors and Builders Assn., Clearwater C. of C. (chmn. sponsorship Aquafest 1986, mem. cen. area council 1987-88, govt. affairs council 1987-88). Republican. Lodge: Independent Order of Foresters. Office: Clearwater Assocs Mgmt Office #9 Sunshine Mall Clearwater FL 34616

VEGTER, AMY HOFMAN, data processing manager; b. N.Y.C., July 12, 1956; m. Roy J. Vegter, Dec. 25, 1977. BA, SUNY, Binghamton, 1976; MS, Columbia U., 1978; MBA, SUNY, Albany, 1984. Asst. librarian Paine Webber Inc., N.Y.C., 1978-80; asst. librarian cataloging dept. SUNY, Albany, 1980-82; customer service rep. BRS, Latham, N.Y., 1982-84, coordinator med. products devel., 1984, mgr. med. product devel., 1984-86, mgr. database design and devel., dir. database prodn. and on-line quality control, 1987—. Mem. Am. Mgmt. Assn., Spl. Libraries Assn., Nat. Assn. Female Execs. Home: 11 Ashford Ln Niskayuna NY 12309 Office: BRS 1200 Rt 7 Latham NY 12110

VEIR, MAGGIE, fashion designer; b. Pasadena, Calif., Feb. 11, 1956; d. Robert Edwin and Barbara Ann (Hunt) V. Student, Mission Design Sch., South Pasadena, Calif., 1972-74, San Diego State U., 1975-76, Phila. Coll. Textiles, 1977; BFA, Parsons Sch. Design, N.Y.C., 1979. Designer Charlotte Ford, N.Y.C., 1979-80, Adolfo Sport, N.Y.C., 1980-81; pvt. practice designer N.Y.C., 1981-83; v.p. design, merchandising G.V. Sport, N.Y.C., 1983-84; dir. design R.R.J. Industries, N.Y.C., 1985-87, Herman Geist, N.Y.C., 1987—; cons. New Mints, N.Y.C., 1980-84, Dolphin, N.Y.C., 1980-81, Regardé, N.Y.C., 1982-84. Designer quilts Family History, Basketweave, 1976, weaving mobile Suspention, 1974, raku pottery Tea Set, 1976, clothing Silk Cocoon and Suede, 1978-79. Pres. Christopher St. Central Block and Merchants Assn., N.Y.C., 1984-85, founding mem. Fedn. to Preserve Greenwich Village Waterfront and Great Port, N.Y.C., 1986-87; dir. Hist. Plaque

Designation Project, N.Y.C., 1984-87; chairperson Christopher St. Fair, N.Y.C., 1987. Mem. Nat. Assn. Female Execs. Democrat. Presbyterian. Home: 110 Christopher St #40 New York NY 10014

VELA, CELIA TOMACITA, federal agent; b. Bremerton, Wash., Mar. 29, 1953; d. Jesse and Maria Juana (Lujan) Ramirez; m. Pedro Vela, Jr., Oct. 6, 1979 (dec. 1983). BS in Criminal Justice, San Diego, 1975, postgrad., 1976-78. Cert. explosive instr. Fed. agt. Alcohol, Tobacco & Firearms, Treasury Dept., Phoenix, 1978-82, San Diego, 1982-87, vault custodian, 1982-87, destruction officer, 1982-87, recruiter, 1984-87, explosive instr., 1986—, arson investigator, 1985—, naval intelligence agt. Naval Intelligence Service, 1987—, recruiter, 1987—. Author recruitment manual: How to Fill Out 171, 1985. Local Bd. Selective Service System, Chula Vista, Calif., 1985—. Served with USAR, 1976-78. Recipient Outstanding Performance award Treasury Dept., 1981, Spl. Achievement award, 1986. Mem. Nat. Assn. Arson Investigators, Nat. Assn. Treasury Agts., Internat. Assn. Bomb Technicians and Investigators, Nat. Assn. Female Execs. Roman Catholic. Club: St. Mary's Women Choir (National City). Avocations: violin, running, swimming, bicycling. Office: Alcohol Tobacco and Firearms 880 Front St Room 6N16 San Diego CA 92188

VELARDI, JOAN LOUISE, corporate marketing executive; b. Ridgewood, N.J., June 12, 1959; d. Ignatius E. and Mary Elizabeth (Porto) V. BA in Chemistry, Coll. Holy Cross, 1981. Sales rep. Stauffer Chem., Westport, Conn., 1981-86; mktg. asst. to v.p. comml. devel. Internat. Flavors and Fragrances, N.Y.C., 1986-87; mktg. mgr. DeZaan Inc. (div. W.R. Grace), Fort Lee, N.J., 1987—. Mem. Ingredient Food Technologists, Am. Assn. Cereal Chemists, Nat. Assn. Female Execs. Roman Catholic. Home: 164 Diamond Bridge Ave Apt 18 Hawthorne NJ 07506 Office: DeZaan Inc 1 Bridge Plaza N Fort Lee NJ 07024

VELASCO, VIVIAN ROSE LACONICO, controller; b. Manila, Philippines, Nov. 22, 1965; came to U.S., 1983; d. Napoleon Buenaventura and Pacita (Laconico) V. BS in Bus. Econs., U. Philippines, 1983. Receptionist Halston Enterprises, N.Y.C., 1984; fin. officer Lady Godiva Ltd./Veena for Diva, Inc, N.Y.C., 1984-87; asst. comptroller, office mgr. Veena For Diva, Inc., N.Y.C., 1987—. Dancer Folk Lorico Filipino Dance Co. of N.Y.C, 1984—, asst. treas., 1986, bd. dirs., treas., bus. mgr., 1988—. Home: 58-14 43rd Ave #3B Woodside NY 11377

VELASQUEZ, PATTI A., lawyer; b. Reno, Aug. 18, 1955; d. Nat Edward Velasquez and Shirley June Tombs. BA magna cum laude, Duke U., 1977; JD, Yale U., 1980. Bar: Ill. 1980, U.S. Dist. Ct. (no. dist.) Ill. 1980, U.S. Tax Ct. 1981, U.S. Ct. Appeals (7th cir.) 1981, Fla. 1984, U.S. Dist. Ct. (so. dist.) Fla. 1985, U.S. Ct. Appeals (11th cir.) 1985. Assoc. Sonnenschein, Carlin, Nath & Rosenthal, Chgo., 1980-83; sole practice Palm Beach, Fla., 1984-85; assoc. Honigman Miller Schwartz and Cohn, West Palm Beach, Fla., 1985-86; mem. Honigman Miller Schwartz and Cohn, West Palm Beach, 1987—; bd. dirs. Gulfstream Goodwill Industries. Bd. dirs. Jr. League of te Palm Beaches; v.p. Choral Soc. Palm Beaches; vice-chmn. Palm Beach Gardens Code Enforcement Bd. Mem. ABA, Palm Beach County Bar Assn., Phi Beta Kappa. Democrat. Home: 3896 Begonia St Palm Beach Gardens FL 33410-5608 Office: Honigman Miller Schwartz & Cohn 1655 Palm Beach Lakes Blvd Suite 600 West Palm Beach FL 33401

VELLER, MARGARET PAXTON, physician; b. Beaver Dam, Ky., Dec. 14, 1925; d. Darrell K. and Gladys (Myers) V.; B.A., Vanderbilt U., 1947, M.D., 1950. Intern, resident Vanderbilt U. Hosp., Nashville, 1950-54; practice medicine, 1954—. Mem. Am., Miss. (com. maternal and child care 1956-72), Homochitto Valley med. assns., Miss. Obstet. and Gynecol. Soc., Phi Beta Kappa, Alpha Omega Alpha. Baptist. Club: Pilgrimage Garden. Home: 28 S Circle Dr Natchez MS 39120 Office: Natchez Med Clinic 49 Sgt S Prentiss Dr Natchez MS 39120

VELTMAN, HENRIETTA, social worker; b. Muskegon, Mich., May 17, 1928; d. Douglas and Minnie (Achterhof) V. Student Chgo. Sch. Nursing, Hope Coll., Holland, Mich.; DD (hon.) Milw. Bible Inst. (now Grace Bible Coll.). Ordained to ministry. Social worker Salvation Army, Holland, Mich., 1961—. Mem. Nat. Assn. Female Execs. Republican. Avocations: photography; reading. Home: 148 W 16th St Holland MI 49423 Office: The Salvation Army 4 E 9th St Holland MI 49423

VELTMAN, JAMIE DAWN, pilot; b. Clarksburg, W.Va., Nov. 20, 1958; d. Charles Leslie Akers and Mary Kelly (Gerrard) Williamson; m. Gregory David Veltman, June 9, 1979 (div. May 1987); 1 child, Christina Dawn. Cert., West. Fla. Helicopters, 1986; cert. flight tng., Bell Helicopter Textron, 1986. Cert. rotocraft-helicopter flight instr. Pvt. practice helicopter comml. pilot services, flight instr. Largo, Fla., 1986—. Mem. Concerned Women for Am. Mem. The Whirly-Girls, Inc., Internat. Women Helicopter Pilots, Am. Helicopter Soc., Inc., Aircraft Owners and Pilots Assn. Republican. Home and Office: 821 Jacaranda Dr Largo FL 34640

VELUSWAMY, ANGAMMAL NANJAPPASARI, psychiatrist; b. Coimbatore, India, Feb. 22, 1940; came to U.S., 1964, naturalized, 1976; d. P. and Parvathi (Krishnaswamy) Nanjappasari; m. V.P. Veluswamy, Apr. 23, 1965; children: Murali, Asha. MD, U. Madras, India, 1963. Intern, Troy, N.Y., 1964-65; resident in psychiatry Clinton Valley Ctr., Pontiac, Mich., 1966-69, staff psychiatrist, 1969-76; chief substance abuse program VA Hosp., Allen Park, Mich., 1976-78; pvt. practice psychiatry, Southfield and Mt. Clemens, Mich., 1978—; mem. staff Kingswood Hosp., Ferndale, Mich., St. Joseph Hosp., Mount Clemens. Mem. Am. Psychiat. Assn., Mich. Psychiat. Assn., Mich. Neuropsychiat. Hosp. and Clin. Physicians (pres. 1978-79). Home: 2150 Shore Hill West Bloomfield MI 48033 Office: 30161 Southfield Rd Southfield MI 48076

VENDLER, HELEN HENNESSY, literature educator, poetry critic; b. Boston, Apr. 30, 1933; d. George and Helen (Conway) Hennessy; 1 son, David. A.B., Emmanuel Coll., 1954; Ph.D., Harvard U., 1960; Ph.D. (hon.), U. Oslo; D.Litt. (hon.), Smith Coll., Kenyon Coll., U. Hartford, Union Coll., Columbia U. Instr. Cornell U., Ithaca, N.Y., 1960-63; lectr. Swarthmore (Pa.) Coll. and Haverford (Pa.) Coll., 1963-64; asst. prof. Smith Coll., Northampton, Mass., 1964-66; asso. prof. Boston U., 1966-68, prof., 1968-85; Fulbright lectr. U. Bordeaux, France, 1968-69; vis. prof. Harvard U., 1981-85, Kenan prof., 1985—, assoc. acad. dean, 1987—, sr. fellow Harvard Soc. Fellows, 1981—; poetry critic New Yorker, 1978—. Author: Yeats's Vision and the Later Plays, 1963, On Extended Wings: Wallace Stevens' Longer Poems, 1969, The Poetry of George Herbert, 1975, Part of Nature, Part of Us, 1980, The Odes of John Keats, 1983, Wallace Stevens: Words Chosen Out of Desire, 1985, Harvard Book of Contemporary Am. Poetry, 1985; editor: Voices and Visions: The Poet in America, 1987, The Music of What Happens, 1988. Fulbright fellow, 1954; AAUW fellow, 1959; Guggenheim fellow, 1971-72; Am. Council Learned Socs. fellow, 1971-72; NEH fellow, 1980, 85; Overseas fellow Churchill Coll., Cambridge, 1980; recipient Lowell prize, 1969, Explicator prize, 1969, award Nat. Inst. Arts and Letters, 1975; Nat. Book Critics Circle award, 1980. Mem. MLA (exec. council 1972-75, pres. 1980), English Inst. (trustee 1977-85), Am. Acad. Arts and Scis., Norwegian Acad. letters and Sci., Phi Beta Kappa. Home: 16 A Still St Brookline MA 02146 also: Warren House Harvard U Cambridge MA 02138

VENINGA, KAREN ANN, human service facility administrator; b. Marshalltown, Iowa, Sept. 19, 1944; d. Pieter and Katherine (Borchardt) Smit; m. Robert Louis Veninga, Dec. 29, 1967; 1 child, Brent Karl. BS in Biology, Sioux Falls Coll., 1967; MPH in Pub. Health Nutrition, U. Minn., 1976. RN, Minn. Staff nurse intensive coronary care Midway Hosp., St. Paul, 1967-68; occupational health nurse, curriculum coordinator, instr. Mounds-Midway Sch. Nursing, St. Paul, 1968-74; lectr. Dept. Nursing Coll. St. Catherine, St. Paul, 1976-77; instr. Dept. Nursing St. Olaf Nursing, Northfield, Minn., 1978-86; dir. human resources Bapt. Hosp. Fund, Inc., St. Paul, 1986-88; coordinator recruitment and retention HealthEast, Midway Hosp., St. Paul, 1988—; cons. N.D. Health Care Assn., Bismarck, 1980. Author: article book Readings in Community Health Nursing, 1986; also contbr. nutritional health care articles to profl. jours. Pres. Brimhall Elem Sch. PTA, St. Paul, 1977-78; cons. Soc. for Nutrition Edn. to March of Dimes, Mpls., 1978; chairperson worship com. Centennial United Meth. Ch., St. Paul, 1985-87. Mem. Am. Nurses Assn., Minn. Nutrition Council (chairperson edn. com. 1979-80), Twin City Health Care Personnel Assn., Sigma Theta Tau. Methodist. Office: Midway Hosp HealthEast 1700 University Ave Saint Paul MN 55104

VENINGA, LOUISE ANN, trade association executive; b. Dallas, Aug. 3, 1948; d. Frederick William and Dolores M. (Meehan) V.; m. Benjamin R. Zaricor, Dec. 23, 1971; children: Tanya, Carl. BA, Webster Coll., 1970; MA, Washington U., St. Louis, 1972. Bd. dirs., v.p., founder Fmali Corp., Santa Cruz, Calif., 1973—. Author: The Ginseng Book, 1973, The Golden Seal Book, 1975. Mem. Monterey Bay Internat. Trade Assn., Herbal Trade Assn. (sec., treas. 1979). Office: Fmali Corp 831 Almar Ave Santa Cruz CA 95060

VENNARD, LAURA JEANNE, investment company executive; b. N.Y.C., July 30, 1950; d. James Francis and Jeanne (Brown) V. BA, SUNY, Albany, 1972; M in Mgmt., Simmons Coll., 1978. CPA, Mass. Acct. Moseley, Hallgarten & Estabrook, Boston, 1973-78, Coopers & Lybrand, Boston, 1978-81; treas. Tucker Anthony Realty Corp., Boston, 1981—; v.p. Tucker Anthony & R.L. Day, Inc., Boston, 1981—. Treas. Indsl. Coop. Assn., Somerville, Mass., 1982-86; mem. loan fund bd. Revolving Loan Fund, Somerville, 1982-86. Mem. Am. Soc. CPA's, Mass. Soc. CPA's. Office: Tucker Anthony & RL Day Inc One Beacon St Boston MA 02108

VENNÉ, PAMELA EILEEN, personnel manager; b. Alton, Ill., Dec. 25, 1948; d. Everett C. and Flossie E. (Maynard) Auer; m. Jim Venne, May 1, 1971 (div. 1975); m. W. David Snyder, Feb. 13, 1982 (div. July 1986); 1 child, Amissa Lynn. BS, North Cen. Coll., 1971; postgrad. U. Wis., 1974, St. Louis U., 1975, U. Utah, 1978. Credit and collection mgr. Ziegler Candy Co., Milw., 1972-73; personnel asst. Erie Mfg. Co., Milw., 1973-75; personnel mgr. Foods Service Mgmt., St. Louis, 1975-77; personnel dir. Ireco Chems., Salt Lake City, 1978-79; supr. Kelly Services, Salt Lake City, 1979; div. personnel mgr. Southland Corp., Dallas, 1979—. Chmn. Polit. Action Com., Dallas, 1982—. Mem. Dallas Personnel Assn. (exhibits dir. 1982-83, v.p. 1984-85, treas. 1985-86), Am. Soc. Personnel Adminstrs., Nat. Assn. Female Execs. Office: The Southland Corp 3636 Mckinney Dallas TX 75221

VENNING, ELEANOR HILL, ret. biochemist; b. Montreal, Que., Can., Mar. 16, 1900; d. George William and Elsie Annette (Kent) Hill; B.A., McGill U., Montreal, 1920, M.S.C., 1921, Ph.D. in Exptl. Medicine, 1933; m. E. A. Venning, June 29, 1929. Assoc. prof. exptl. medicine McGill U., 1950-60, prof., 1960-65; dir. endocrine labs. Royal Victoria Hosp., Montreal, 1950-65. Fellow Royal Soc. Can.; emeritus mem. Can. Soc. Biochemistry, Can. Soc. Physiology, Endocrine Soc. U.S. (Fred Comad Koch award 1962), N.Y. Acad. Scis., Can. Soc. Endocrinology and Metabolism. Contbr. chpts., numerous articles to profl. publs.

VENNOCHI, JOAN LOBIONDO, journalist; b. N.Y.C., Jan. 27, 1953; d. John Joseph and Martha Diane (Homick) LoBiondo; m. Thomas Michael Vennochi, Feb. 19, 1977. B.S., Boston U., 1975; J.D., Suffolk U., 1984. Editor Thomaston (Conn.) Express, 1975; staff reporter Danbury (Conn.) News-Times, 1975-77; mem. Spotlight Team Boston Globe, 1977—, staff reporter, gen. assignment Spotlight Team, 1981-83, polit. reporter City Hall bur., 1983-84, bur. chief, 1984, State House bur. chief, 1985—. Recipient Pulitzer prize for local investigative reporting, 1980. Office: 135 Morrissey Blvd Boston MA 02107

VENTOSA, CARMEN, computer programmer; b. Havana, Cuba, Apr. 10, 1960; d. Armando Ventosa and Irene Ortega. BS in Computer Scis., CUNY, 1985. Computer sci. programmer Fed. Reserve Bank, N.Y.C., 1985—. Recipient Achievement award AT&T Info. Systems Labs., N.Y.C., 1985. Mem. Nat. Assn. Female Execs., Inc., Fed. Reserve Club N.Y. Home: 119 Ellwood St Apt 2C New York NY 10040

VENTRESCA, DEBORAH ANNE, nurse; b. Boston, Oct. 12, 1948; d. H. Vincent and M. Helen (Butler) Strout; m. Anthony L. Ventresca Jr.; 1 child, Amy L. AS in Nursing, North Shore Community Coll., 1980; BS in Nursing summa cum laude, U. Mass, 1986, postgrad., 1988—. Staff nurse J.B. Thomas Hosp., Peabody, Mass., 1980-87; staff nurse home health J.B. Thomas Home Care/Vis. Nurses, Peabody, 1987; staff devel coorinator Lenox Hill Nursing and Rehabilitative Care Facility, Lynn, Mass., 1987-88; community health nurse J.B. Thomas Health Care, Peabody, 1988—. Vol. nurse Make Today Count, Beverly, Mass., 1982-84; nurse admission assessment Hospice North Shore, 1983, vol. coordinator, 1983-84, bd. dirs., 1984-86; bd. dirs. Am. Cancer Soc., Lynn, 1987—. Mem. Sigma Theta Tau. Republican. Club: Lothrop (Beverly). Home: 30 Boyles St Beverly MA 01915 Office: JB Thomas Home Health Care 100 Lowell St Peabody MA 01960

VENTRY, CATHERINE VALERIE, lawyer; b. Bronxville, N.Y., Feb. 19, 1949; d. Victor and Catherine Regina (Dillon) V. AB in Logic and Philosophy, Vassar Coll., 1971; postgrad., Boston U., 1972; JD, N.Y. Law Sch., 1978. Bar: N.Y. 1979, U.S. Dist. Ct. (so. and ea. dists.) N.Y. 1979. Adj. asst. prof. John Jay Coll. of Criminal Justice, N.Y.C., 1978-80; adj. asst. prof. bus. law Coll. Mount St. Vincent Lehman Coll., N.Y.C., 1978-82; staff atty. City of N.Y. Dept. Housing Preservation and Devel. Litigation Bureau, N.Y.C., 1981-84; sole practice Congers, N.Y., 1984—; Tax editor Prentice-Hall Pub. Co., Englewood Cliffs, N.J., 1980-81. Mem. N.Y. State Bar, Rockland County Women's Bar, Rockland County Bar Assn., MENSA. Office: 2 Congers Rd New York NY 10956

VENTULETH, CINDY LEE, operations analyst, editor; b. Santa Monica, Calif., Apr. 6, 1951; d. Wendell E. and Constance E. (Talbert) V. BA in History, Calif. State U., Northridge, 1974, MA in History, 1982, BA in English, 1986. Adminstrv. ops. analyst, mng. editor Santa Susana Press Calif. State U., 1984—, teaching asst., 1987—. Santa Monica Tchrs. Assn. scholar, 1971. Mem. Calif. Women Higher Edn., Bibiographic Soc. Calif. State U., Nat. Wildlife Assn., Save the Children. Republican. Office: Calif State U Library 18111 Nordhoff St Northridge CA 91330

VERANO, BEVERLY JO, lawyer, accountant; b. Lafayette, Ind., Nov. 7, 1950; d. John Peter and Josephine Annetta (Horney) Speicher; m. Roger Wayne Huffer, June 28, 1969 (div. 1977); m. Hugh Tabor Verano, Jr., Dec. 20, 1981. BS magna cum laude, San Diego State U., 1974; JD, U. San Diego, 1980; LLM in Taxation, Boston U., 1981. Bar: Calif. 1981, Mass. 1982; CPA, Calif. Hon. acctg. intern Price Waterhouse & Co., San Diego, 1973, tax acct., 1974-77; law clk. Ball, Hunt, Hart Brown & Baerwitz, Beverly Hills, Calif., 1979; tax research asst. to Boris I. Bittker, Yale U. Law Sch., New Haven, 1979-80; assoc. Holzwarth & Schoellerman, Newport Beach, Calif., 1981-83; tax planning cons. CIGNA Corp., Newport Beach, 1983-84; acting tax mgr. Arthur Anderson & Co., Costa Mesa, Calif., 1984; pres. CFG Planning Group, Irvine, Calif., 1985-87; assoc. Fiore & Nordberg, Newport Beach, 1987—; instr. cert. program in fin. planning U. Calif., Irvine, 1987—. Mng. research editor U. San Diego Law Rev., 1979-80; author audio recs., mag. article. Mem. ABA (tax sect., subcom. estate planning for the executive and prof.), Calif. Bar Assn. (com. on taxation, estate planning, probate com.), Orange County Bar Assn. (estate planning and probate com., taxation com.), Orange County Women Lawyers, Calif. Soc. CPA's, Women in Bus. (fin. com.), Beta Alpha Psi, Phi Kappa Psi. Republican. Baptist. Home: 24 Springwood Irvine CA 92714 Office: Fiore & Nordburg 4631 Teller Ave Suite 120 Newport Beach CA 92660

VERBOFSKY, MARNIE ROSALYN, clinical laboratory executive, industrial film producer; b. Pitts., Aug. 14, 1946; D. Isadore and Ethelee (Rosenberg) Verbofsky; Student, U. Ill., 1964-65, Roosevelt U., 1965-66. Payroll adminstr. Cushman Belmont, Chgo., 1966-68; asst. credit mgr. Bailey Beauty Supply, Chgo., 1968-73; corp. asst. sec. Med. Analytics, Inc., Chgo., 1973-74; nat. satellite field coordinator Metpath, Inc., Hackensack, N.J., 1974-77; area dir., regional sales mgr. Nat. Health Labs. div. Revlon, Inc., San Mateo, Calif., 1977-78; v.p., ptnr. COMUTEC, Agoura, Calif., 1978—; pres. Abused Drugs Lab., Inc., Chatsworth, Calif., 1983—; trainer Small Bus. Adminstrn. Legis. appointee to Calif. State Conf. on Small Bus., 1980, 81, bd. govs. Roar Found. Shambala Preserve, 1986, 87. . Recipient Award of Merit, SBA, 1982; Cert. of Appreciation, Pierce Coll., 1982, Western Regional Los Angeles C. of C., 1983, others. Mem. Clin. Lab. Mgmt. Assn., Nat. Speakers Assn. Republican. Home: 22330 Victory #806 Woodland Hills CA 91367 Office: 9176 Independence Ave Chatsworth CA 91311

VERDI, CHARLOTTE THERESA, nurse, health educator, counselor; b. N.Y.C., Mar. 2, 1948; d. Joseph Charles and Vincenza (Taormina) V. BA in Psychology, Marymount Manhattan Coll., 1976; MA in Health Edn., NYU, 1977. Registeres nurse, Bellevue Sch. Nursing, 1969. Head nurse chest div. Bellevue Hosp., N.Y.C., 1969-72; team leader, sr. nurse NYU Hosp., 1972-78; supr. intensive care N.Y. Infirmary, N.Y.C., 1978; pvt. duty case cons. N.Y. State Registry, N.Y.C., 1978—; nursing edn. supr. instr., substance abuse cons. Met. Hosp. Ctr., N.Y.C., 1979—; pvt. practice alcoholism and substance abuse cons. N.Y.C., 1986—; counselor Verdi Inst. Health, Edn., Counseling and Theraputics, N.Y.C., 1988—; substance abuse cons. Americans for Substance Abuse Prevention, N.Y.C., 1985—. Contbr. articles to profl. jours. Mem.N.Y. State Nurses Assn. (task force cons. 1983—), N.Y. Fedn. Alcoholism Counselors (edn. cons. N.Y.C. chpt. 1975—), N.Y. Heart and Lung Assn. (nurse cons. 1983—), N.Y. Fedn. Profl. Health Educators (health edn. cons. 1978—), Am. Nurses Assn., Nat. Assn. Female Execs., Nat. Orgn. Italian Am. Women. Home: 331 E 29th St Apt 4P New York NY 10016

VERDUIN, BERT M., real estate executive; b. Benton, Ark., Feb. 9, 1947; d. Elvis Lee and Helen Lee (McBride) Moses; m. Michael Hankins, May 23, 1970; children—Valerie Ann, Clinton Logan. A.A.S., Brookhaven Coll., 1982. Acct., Realty Devel. Corp., Dallas, 1970-77; owner, mgr. Tax Service, Dallas, 1977-83; sr. v.p., controller Realty Devel. Corp., Dallas, 1983-87; pres. Strobe Mgmt. Services, Inc., Dallas, 1987—. Republican. Mem. Ch. of Christ. Avocations: reading; crafts. Office: Strobe Mgmt Services Inc 8131 LBJ Freeway Suite 200 Dallas TX 75251

VERDUIN, BETTY RUTH, nurse, karate school administrator; b. Muskegon, Mich., Feb. 6, 1938; d. Frances (Walter) Burwell Anderson; adopted d. Clarence Earl and Melba Lanea (Hallman) Monticue; m. Robert Visscher Verduin, July 28, 1962; children—Mark, Scott, Kurt. Diploma Augustana Hosp. Sch. Nursing, Chgo., 1958; student U. Mich., 1977-81. Registered profl. sch. nurse, 1976. Nurse, Meml./Mercy Hosp., St. Joseph, Mich., 1958-73; dir. health services Lakeshore Schs., Stevensville, Mich., 1974-81; dir. nurses Shoreham Terr. Nursing Home, St. Joseph, 1981-82; dir. Beverly Home Health of St. Joseph, 1982-85; clinic dir. MARCHA (Migrant & Rural Community Health Assn.), Benton Harbor, Mich., 1986-88, dep. dir., 1988—; owner, chief black belt instr. The Unicorn Acad. of Traditional Tae Kwondo Karate, St. Joseph, 1984—. Sec. Berrien County Heart Unit, 1978-80. Named Foster Parent of the Yr. Dept. Social Services, Benton Harbor, 1975; recipient cert. of Appreciation Mich. Heart Assn., 1979. Mem. Nat. Assn. Female Execs., Universal Tae kwondo Assn. Republican. Avocations: oil painting, horse back riding. Home: 1574 Oak Terr Saint Joseph MI 49085 Office: Unicorn Acad Traditional Taekwondo Karate 2640 W John Beers Rd Stevensville MI 49127

VERDUIN, CLAIRE LEONE, publishing company executive; b. Chgo., Mar. 23, 1932; d. David R. and Helen (Vande Velde) Ellman; m. J. Richard Verduin, Aug. 25, 1956 (Mar. 1979); children: Pamela A., Paul D., Beth L. Verduin Cain. BBA, U. Wis., 1954. Editorial asst. Brooks/Cole Pub. Co., Pacific Grove and Monterey, Calif., 1973-74, project devel. editor, 1974-85, editor, 1978-85, mng. editor, 1985—. Treas. Am. Field Service, Pacific Grove, 1978; mem. Pacific Grove Sch. Bd., 1983. Mem. Am. Assn. for Counseling and Devel., Nat. Assn. Human Service Educators, Acad. Criminal Justice Scis., Am. Soc. Criminology. Office: Brooks/Cole Pub Co 511 Forest Grove Pacific Grove CA 93950

VERGARI, JANE D'APICE, retail executive; b. Yonkers, N.Y., June 29, 1950; d. John Dominic and Jeanne (Romano) D'Apice; m. Bohn Carl Vergari, Aug. 20, 1972; children: Bohn, Jr., Carl Andrew. BA in Psychology, Coll. of New Rochelle, 1971. Asst. buyer Bloomingdale's, N.Y.C., 1971-72; exec. recruiter Bus. Careers, Inc., N.Y.C., 1972-81; ptnr., v.p Herbert Mines Assoc., N.Y.C., 1981—. Mem. Nat. Retail Merchants, Fashion Group. Republican. Roman Catholic. Office: Herbert Mines Assoc 780 Third Ave New York NY 10017

VERGERONT, SUSAN BOWERS, state legislator, public relations consultant; b. Milw., Nov. 30, 1945; d. Arthur William and Mary (Oberly) Bowers; m. David J. Vergeront, May 2, 1945; children: Margaret, John W., David E. BS, U. Wis., 1967. Research assoc. Wis. Legis. Council, Madison, 1967-70; exec. dir. Grafton (Wis.) C. of C., 1978-80; account exec. Vollrath & Assocs., Sheboygan, Wis., 1981-84, now of counsel; mem. Wis. Assembly 1984—; dir. Rep. Assembly Campaign Com.; mem. Wis. State Bd. Am. Legis. Exchange Council, Madison, 1985-87. Bd. dirs. Women's Bus. Initiatives Corp., Milw., 1987—,Manitou Council Girl Scouts U.S.A., Manitowic, Wis., 1984-87, Ozaukee Council on Alcohol and Drug Abuse. Named One of Outstanding Young Women Am. Grafton Jaycettes, 1980, Outstanding Young Wisconsinite, Wis. Jaycees, 1981. Mem. Nat. Conf. State Legislators (nat. com.), U.S. Jaycees (life), Grafton C. of C. (v.p. 1980-81). Presbyterian. Office: Wis State Legislature PO Box 8953 Madison WI 53708

VERGO, JANET, personnel consulting executive; b. Huntington, N.Y., May 14, 1961; d. John and Nina (Firenze) V. BS, Boston U., 1985. Cert. trainer Marriott, Inc., Arlington, Va., 1985-87; pres. Vergo Enterprise, Herndon, Va., 1985—; personnel cons. Albers Corp., Washington, 1987—; cons. City Sch. Dist., Rochester, N.Y., 1985—, The McCandless Co., Herndon, 1986, assoc. Fin. Placement Network, Washington, 1988—. Producer video: Grimefighters, 1984. Mem. Health Plus (bd. dirs.), Nat. Assn. Female Execs. Home: 3312 Stone Heather Ct Herndon VA 22071 Office: Albers Corp 1700 k St NW Washington DC 20006

VERLINDE, BEVERLY JANE, university administrator; b. Visalia, Calif., Feb. 9, 1952; d. Clayton Howard and Beverly Jane (Spomer) Ford; m. Larry Wayne Verlinde, June 19, 1971 (div. May 1980); children: Krista Elizabeth, Julie Marie (dec.). BS in Human Relations and Organizational Behavior, U. San Francisco, 1984; postgrad., Calif State U., Chico. Asst. to dir. Sacramento Savs. and Loan, 1976-79; dir. human resources Goodwill Industries, Tucson, 1979-81; dir. employee assistance program Calif. State U., Chico, 1983—, mem. child day care provisions com., child abuse/neglect com.; spl. asst. to dir. personnel Tucson Electric Power Co., Tucson, 1978-79, v.p., dir. human relations. Co-chair heart at work program Am. Heart Assn., co-chair conf. com. Butte County Child Abuse Council; vice chair City of Chico Affirmative Action Com.; mem. task force Butte County Alcohol and Drug Adv. Bd., Chico; chair edn. com., speakers bur. Alt. Choice Team. Calif. State U. grantee, 1985; Lt. Merton Rawlins scholar, 1987. Mem. Employee Assistance Soc. of N.Am. (chmn. credential com.), ALMACA, Calif. State Univ. Women's Council. Home: 678 Eastwood Ave Chico CA 95928 Office: Calif State U 101 Salem St Suite 3 Chico CA 95929-0111

VERMEULE, EMILY TOWNSEND (MRS. CORNELIUS C. VERMEULE III), classicist, educator; b. N.Y.C., Aug. 11, 1928; d. Clinton Blake and Eleanor (Meneely) Townsend; m. Cornelius C. Vermeule III, Feb. 2, 1957; children: Emily Dickinson Blake, Cornelius Adrian Comstock. A.B., Bryn Mawr Coll., 1950; student, Am. Sch. Classical Studies, Athens, 1950-51, St. Anne's Coll., Oxford U., 1953; M.A., Harvard, 1954; Ph.D., Bryn Mawr Coll., 1956; D. Litt., Douglass Coll., Rutgers U., 1968, Tufts U., 1980, U. Pitts., 1983, Bates Coll., 1983, U. Miami, Oxford, Ohio, 1986; LL.D., Regis Coll., 1971; D. Fine Arts, U. Mass, Amherst, 1971; D.Litt., Smith Coll., 1972, Wheaton Coll., 1973, Trinity Coll., 1974; L.H.D., Emmanuel Coll., 1980. Instr. in Greek. Bryn Mawr Coll., 1956-57; instr. Wellesley (Mass.) Coll., 1957-58, prof. art and Greek, 1965-70, chmn. dept. art, 1966-67; asst. prof. classics Boston U., 1958-61, asso. prof. classics, 1961-65; fellow for research Boston Mus. Fine Arts, 1965—; James C. Loeb vis. prof. classical philology Harvard, 1969, dir. univ. Cyprus expdn., 1971—, Samuel and Doris Zemurray Stone-Radcliffe prof., 1970—; Sather prof. U. Calif. at Berkeley, 1975; Geddes-Harrower prof. Greek art and archaeology U. Aberdeen, 1980-81; Bernhard vis. prof. Williams Coll., 1986. Author: Euripides V. Electra, 1959, Greece in the Bronze Age, 1964, The Trojan War in Greek Art, 1964, Götterkult, 1974, Toumba tou Skourou, The Mound of Darkness, 1975, Death in Early Greek Art and Poetry, 1978, (with V. Karageorghis) Mycenaean Pictorial Vase-Painting, 1982; Contbr. articles to profl. jours. judge Nat. Book Award, 1977. Recipient Gold medal for distinguished achievement Radcliffe Coll. Grad. Soc., 1968; Guggenheim fellow, 1964-65. Fellow Soc. Antiquaries, Brit. Acad. (corr.), German Archaeol. Inst. (corr.); mem. Am. Inst. Archaeology, Am. Acad. Arts and Scis., Am. Philos. Soc. (v.p. 1978-81), Am. Philol. Assn. (Charles J. Goodwin award of merit 1980), Classical Assn. New Eng., Smithsonian Council (bd. scholars 1983—), Hellenic Soc., Classical Assn., Library of Congress. Office: Harvard U Dept Classics 319 Boylston Hall Cambridge MA 02138

VERMILYEA, GAIL DIANNA, computer software company executive, information systems consultant; b. Poughkeepsie, N.Y., Mar. 13, 1942; d. George Smith and Sarah Eustice (Dugan) V. B.A., Seton Hill Coll., 1964; postgrad. Am. U., Washington, 1966-71. Programmer/analyst Dept. Defense, Washington, 1964-67; cons., mgr. Control Data Corp., Rockville, Md., 1967-71, 72-82, The Netherlands, 1971-72, Mpls., 1982-84; cons., officer Vertek Assocs., Washington, 1984-86, 87—; v.p. QINT Database System Corp., Washington, 1986-87; com. mem. Initial Graphics Exchange Specification Standards Com., Nat. Bur. Standards, Gaithersburg, Md., 1986— vice-chmn. Common Data System Lang./End User Facility Com., Washington, 1978-82; research assoc. Nat. Bur. Standards, Gaithersburg, 1986—. Bd. dirs. Bethesda Overlook Condo Bd., Bethesda, Md., 1985-87, Seton Hill Coll. Alumnae, Greensburg, Pa., 1978-84; trustee Seton Hill Coll., 1986—. Recipient Profl. Services Outstanding Achievement award Control Data Corp., Mpls., 1976, 78. Mem. Assn. Computing Machinery, IEEE., Nat. Assn. Female Execs. Roman Catholic. Avocations: tennis; skiing; travel. Home: 5300 Pooks Hill Rd Bethesda MD 20814 Office: Vertak Assocs 5300 Pooks Hill Rd Bethesda MD 20814

VERNA, MARILYN ANN, educator; b. Bklyn., July 15, 1944; d. Angelo and Mary Setaro V. BS, St. John's U., 1966; MS, Bklyn. Coll., 1970; diploma, Coll. of Staten Island, 1978. Tchr. Bd. Edn., N.Y.C., 1966—; acting asst. prin. Bd. Edn., Bklyn., 1973-74, P.S. 176 K, Bklyn., 1979-81; travel cons. Deville Travel, Bklyn., 1984—; tchr. linker United Fedn. Tchrs., Bklyn., 1985—; mem. Dist. 20 Curriculum Com., Bklyn., 1980—. Contbr. articles to profl. jours. Election inspector United Dem. Orgn., Bklyn., 1968-83. Impact II Bd. Edn. grantee, 1987, N.Y. State Edn. Dept. grantee, 1987. Mem. Assn. Tchrs. N.Y. (Educator of Yr. award 1985), N.Y. City Math Tchrs., Cath. Tchrs. Assn., Nat. Council Math. Tchrs., Internat. Assn. Travel Agents. Home: 1821 W 9th St Brooklyn NY 11223

VERNICK, ANDREA MERRILL, cosmetic company advertising executive; b. Newark, Nov. 18, 1949; d. Harold David and Ada Beatrice (Lipnik) V.; B.A., Sch. Communications, Am. U., 1971. Clerical Asst. promotion dept. Estee Lauder, Inc., N.Y.C., 1971-72, dir. promotions, 1975-82, dir. promotions and coop. print advt., 1982-83, exec. dir. promotions and coop. print advertising, 1983-88, v.p. promotions and co-op advt., 1988—. Mem. Nat. Assn. Female Execs., Am. U. Alumni Assn. Home: 311 E 71st St New York NY 10021

VERPLANKE, ANNA LOUISE, nutritionist; b. Camden, Tenn., Mar. 22, 1935; d. Wiley Leonard and Rosa Belle (Clark) Noles; m. Edward Ely Verplanke, Jul. 19, 1953; children: Rose Anne & Mary Anne (twins), Julia Edwina. Student, U. Fla., 1976-77; B of Restaurant and Hotel Mgmt., Purdue U., 1983. Cert. Dietetic Food Service Mgmt. Chef., asst. mgr. Paducah (Ky.) Country Club, 1955-65, Drew (Miss.) Country Club, 1965-71; dir. food service Lexington House Inc., Crestwood, Ill., 1971-73; chef, asst. mgr. Burlington (Iowa) Country Club, 1973-76; dir. dietetics Rosewood Convalscent Ctr., Memphis, 1976-80; dir. food service Carolina Village Inc., Hendersonville, N.C., 1980—; cons. Dearfield Episcopal Home, Asheville, N.C., 1981; mem. organizing com. Satellite Food Program Elderly, Memphis, 1978. Vol. NRC, Paducah, 1961-65; troop leader Girl Scouts Am., Drew, 1968-71. Mem. Nat. Dietary Mgrs. Assn. (pres. 1984-86), Nat. Assn. Female Execs., bus. and Profl. Women's Club (Woman Day 1985). Democrat. Baptist. Home: 23 Appleblossom Ln Hendersonville NC 28739 Office: Carolina Village Inc 600 Carolina Village Rd Hendersonville NC 28739

VER STEEG, DONNA LORRAINE FRANK, nurse, sociologist, educator; b. Minot, N.D., Sept. 23, 1929; d. John Jonas and Pearl H. (Denlinger) Frank; B.S. in Nursing, Stanford, 1951; M.S. in Nursing, U. Calif. at San Francisco, 1967; M.A. in Sociology, UCLA, 1969, Ph.D. in Sociology, 1973; m. Richard W. Ver Steeg, Nov. 22, 1950; children—Juliana, Anne, Richard B. Clin. instr. U. N.D. Sch. Nursing, 1962-63; USPHS nurse research fellow U. Cal. Los Angeles, 1969-72; spl. cons., adv. com. on physicians' assts. and nurse practitioner programs Calif. State Bd. Med. Examiners, 1972-73; asst. prof. UCLA Sch. Nursing, 1973-79, assoc. prof., 1979—, asst. dean, 1981-83, chmn. primary ambulatory care, 1976-87, assoc. dean, 1983-86; co-prin. investigator PRIMEX Project, Family Nurse Practitioners, UCLA Extension, 1974-76; assoc. cons. Calif. Postsecondary Edn. Commn., 1975-76; spl. cons. Calif. Dept. Consumer Affairs, 1978; accredited visitor Western Assn. Schs. and Colls., 1985—; mem. Calif. State Legis. Health Policy Forum, 1980-81. Named Outstanding Faculty Mem., UCLA Sch. Nursing, 1982. Fellow Am. Acad. Nursing; mem. AAAS, Am. Pub. Health Assn., Am. Soc. Law and Medicine, Nat League Nursing, Calif. League Nursing, Soc. Study Social Problems, Assn. Health Services Research, Am., Calif. (pres. 1979-81) nurses assns., Am. Sociol. Assn., Stanford Nurses Club, Sigma Theta Tau. Contbr. articles to Gerentol. Soc. Am. jour., N.Am. Nursing Diagnosis Assn. jour., chpts. to books. Home: 708 Swarthmore Ave Pacific Palisades CA 90272 Office: UCLA Sch Nursing 10833 LeConte Ave Los Angeles CA 90024-1702

VESPERI, MARIA DAVOREN, anthropologist, educator, journalist, gerontology specialist; b. Worcester, Mass., June 24, 1951; d. Arthur Ernest and Mary Elizabeth (Davoren) V.; 1 chile, Corinna Aline Calagione. BA, U. Mass., 1973; MA, Princeton U., 1975, PhD, 1978. Vis. asst. prof. anthropology, U. South Fla. Grad. Coll., Tampa, 1978-81, adj. asst. prof. anthropology, 1981—; vis. asst. prof. anthropology New Coll., Sarasota, 1985-86; cons., writer St. Petersburg Times (Fla.), 1980, staff writer, 1981-87, editorial dept. 1986—, editorial bd., 1988—; project dir. folk arts documentary supported by Nat. Endowment for Arts; cons. hist. photo exhibit Mus. Fla. History. Active Gray Panthers. Commonwealth scholar, U. Mass., 1969-73; Princeton U. fellow, 1973-75, NIH Pub. Health Service research fellow, 1976-78; doctoral dissertation grantee NSF, 1975-76, grantee Adminstrn. on Aging, 1975-76, Nat. Endowment for Arts, 1983. Mem. Am. Anthropol. Assn., Gerontol. Soc. Am., N.Y. Acad. Scis., Soc. Humanistic Anthropology (program chairperson 1987), Assn. for Anthropology and Gerontology (newsletter editor 1982-87, pres.-elect 1987), Nat. Council on Aging, Fla. Press Club, Phi Beta Kappa, Alpha Lambda Delta. Author: City of Green Benches: Growing Old in a New Downtown, 1985. Contbr. articles to publs. in field. Home: 1209 Alcazar Way S Saint Petersburg FL 33705 Office: PO Box 1121 Saint Petersburg FL 33731

VEST, MARLYN MARIE, marketing professional, consultant; b. Pensacola, Fla., July 29, 1947; d. Arthur Frederick and Marlyn (Shaw) Farwell; m. Bill Robert Vest, Oct. 25, 1969; 1 child, Scott Brian. BS in Recreation Adminstrn., U. Fla., 1969; MS in Continuing and Vocat. Edn., U. Wis., 1976. Recreation supr. Beloit Recreation Dept., Wis., 1969-70; recreation therapist Mendota Mental Health Inst., Madison, Wis., 1970-75; acting unit chief Mendota Deaf Treatment Ctr., Madison, 1976; instr. U. Wis., Madison, 1977; dir. activity and rehab. therapy Mendota Mental Health Inst., Madison, 1976-87; cons. therapies Dept. Health and Social Services, Madison, 1976-87; mgr. mktg. Badger State Industries, Madison, 1987—; preceptor U. Wis., Madison, 1984-87; clin. asst. prof. U. Wis., Milw., 1983-87; dir. tourism and recreation adv. com. Madison Area Tech. Coll., 1987—; lectr. in field. Contbr. articles to profl. jours. Instr., advocate Tourette Syndrome Assn., Wis. chpt., 1981—. Recipient Gov.'s Merit award State Wis. Dept. Health and Social Service, Madison, 1982, Exceptional Performance award, 1981, 83, 86. Mem. Wis. Parks and Recreation Assn. Therapeutic Soc. (chmn. 1970, Outstanding Contbns. to Field award 1979), Wis. Parks and Recreation Assn. (service recognition award 1985), Dane County Recreation Coordinating Council (chmn. 1974), P. Lambda Theta Nat. Honor Assn. Methodist. Avocations: travel, cross-country skiing, wind surfing, gardening, canning. Home: 21 Aarback Rd Cambridge WI 53523 Office: Badger State Industries 2565 E Johnson St Madison WI 53704

VEST, MARY ELIZABETH, transportation company official; b. Roanoke, Va., Nov. 19, 1954; d. Robert Ellsworth and Margaret (Taylor) V. Student, St. Andrew's Coll., Laurinburg, N.C., 1972-74, U. S.C., 1976. Mng. editor Richlands (Va.) News-Press, 1976-78, Delmarva News, Millsboro, Del., 1979-83; ops. mgr. Mer-Lou Transp. Inc., 1983—; part-time journalism tchr. Del. Tech. and Community Coll., 1981-83; profl. cons. sch. publs.; dir. Millsboro Hut, Inc. Recipient awards for spot news, series, and photo story, Va. Press Assn., 1977; award for layout, design, photo series, feature series, and editorials Md.-Del.-D.C. Press Assn., 1980, 81, 82. Mem. Sigma Delta Chi. Roman Catholic. Home: 41 C Blue Teal Rd Selbyville DE 19975 Office: Box 247 Millsboro DE 19966

VETRANO, J. BEA, marketing professional; b. Bronx, N.Y., May 17, 1956; d. Joseph J. and Rose Faith (Ventigli) V.; m. Raymond Tiberge, Feb. 14, 1988. BA in Mktg. and Mmgmt., Rider Coll., 1980. Sales rep. Office Products div. IBM Corp., Lawrenceville, N.J., 1980-81; asst. product mgr. Hunt Mfg. Co., Phila., 1981-84; acct. exec. Mktg. Group, Ft. Washington, Pa., 1984-87; coordinator mktg. and pub. relations Matrix Devel. Group, Cranbury, N.J., 1987—. Active Bus. Vols. for the Arts. Mem. Nat. Assn. Female Execs. Episcopalian. Home: 25B Darien New Hope PA 18938 Office: Matrix Devel Group Forsgate Dr CN 4000 Cranbury NJ 08512

VETTER, BETTY MCGEE, nonprofit corporation executive; b. Center, Colo., Oct. 25, 1924; d. William Allen and Bonnie Hunsaker McGee; m. Richard C. Vetter, Sept. 4, 1951; children: David Bruce, Richard Dean, Robert Alan. B.A., U. Colo., 1944; M.A., Stanford U., 1948. Chemist Shell Devel. Co., Emeryville, Calif., 1944-45; instr. Fresno State Coll., 1948-50, Far Eastern div. U. Calif., 1950-51; adj. prof. Am. U., Washington, 1952-64; part-time U. Va., Arlington, 1952-64, U. Md. Ext. div., College Park, 1960-61; exec. dir. Commn on Profls. in Sci. and Tech. (formerly Sci. Manpower Commn.), Washington, 1964—. Editor: Sci., Engring., Tech. Manpower Comments, 1965—. Served with U.S. Naval Women's Res., 1944-45. Mem. Manpower Analysis and Planning Soc., AAAS. Home: 4779 N 33d St Arlington VA 22207 Office: 1500 Massachusetts Ave NW Suite 831 Washington DC 20005

VETTER, LOUISE BERTHA CAROLINE, psychologist, researcher, consultant; b. Davenport, Iowa, Nov. 26, 1937; d. Louis Anderson and Alice Charlotte (Vick) V. BS in Home Econs. Edn., Iowa State U., 1959, MS in Psychology, 1962; PhD in Counseling, Psychology, Ohio State U., 1968. Lic. psychologist, Ohio. Research assoc. U. Mo. Family Study Ctr., Kansas City, 1965-66; grad. research assoc. Nat. Ctr. for Research in Vocat. Edn., Ohio State U., Columbus, 1966-68, research specialist, 1968-77, sr. research specialist, 1977-88, sr. researcher emeritus, 1988—; prin. LCBVentures, Columbus, 1988—; cons. editor Career Devel. Quar., 1987—. Contbr. articles to profl. jours. Pres. Ohio Women, Inc., Columbus, 1983-85. Fellow Am. Psychol. Assn.; mem. Vocat. Edn. Equity Council, Am. Assn. for Counseling and Devel., Am. Vocat. Assn., Phi Kappa Phi (pres. Ohio State U. chpt. 1986-87).

VETTER, MARY MARGARET (PEGGY), investment manager financial consultant; b. Richmond, Va., June 7, 1945; d. Robert Joseph and Miriam Thomas V.; B.A., Cath. U. Am., 1967; M.B.A. with distinction, N.Y.U., 1978; m. Dimitri Yannacopoulos, May 24, 1980. Asst. to controller N.C. Trading Co., N.Y.C., 1972-74; asst. controller Shaheen Natural Resources Inc., N.Y.C., 1974-76; fin. coordinator mining div. Nat. Bulk Carriers, Inc., N.Y.C., 1976-77; corp. cons. mktg. and strategic planning Gen. Electric Co., Bridgeport, Conn., 1978-80; v.p., internat. mktg. strategy Bankers Trust Co., N.Y.C., 1980-83; fin. cons. Shearson Lehman/Am. Express, Stamford, Conn., 1984—. Bd. dirs. South Central Conn. Emergency Med. Services Council. Named Woman of Yr., N.Y.U. Alumnae Assn., 1978. Mem. Fin. Women's Assn. N.Y., Women in Mgmt., Beta Gamma Sigma. Republican. Roman Catholic. Home: 11 Don Bob Rd Stamford CT 06903 Office: 5 High Ridge Park Stamford CT 06905

VEZEAU, SISTER JEANNETTE EVA, college president; b. Rochester, N.H., May 11, 1913; d. Edward U. and Laura Ann (Richey) V. B.S., Boston U., 1948, M.Ed., 1955, Ed.D., 1960; D.H.L. (hon.), Notre Dame Coll., 1985. Joined Sisters of Holy Cross, 1933; tchr. high sch. Manchester, N.H., 1937-45, North Grosvenordale, Conn., 1945-49, New Bedford, Mass., 1949-57; prin. St. George High Sch., Manchester, 1960-64; supr. schs. Sisters of Holy Cross in New Eng., Pittsfield, N.H., 1964-67; pres. Notre Dame Coll., Manchester, 1967-85; mem. Christian Unity Commn., 1965-71, Diocesan Sch. Bd. Manchester, 1965-71; adv. bd. Elliott Sch. Nursing, Manchester, 1966-76; mem. exec. bd. N.H. Coll. and Univ. Council, 1967-85 treas., 1978-85; mem. exec. bd. Council for Better Schs. in N.H., 1975-78; bd. incorporators Cath. Med. Center, 1978; mem. Gov.'s Commn. on Post Secondary Edn., 1973-84, vice chmn., 1977-79; incorporator Amoskeag Savs. Bank. Author: (with others) 10,000 Legal Words, 1971. Recipient Woman of Achievement award N.H. Fedn. Bus. and Profl. Women's Clubs, Inc., 1974. Mem. Am. Council Edn. Address: 181 Hall St Manchester NH 03104

VEZINA, MONIQUE, Canadian government official; b. Rimouski, Que., Canada, July 13, 1935; m. Jean-Yves Parent; 4 children. Mem. cabinet, minister external relations, mem. Parliament, Govt. of Canada, Ottawa, Ont., 1984-86, minister supply and services and receiver gen., 1986-87; minister of state for transport Govt. of Canada, 1987-88, minister of state for employment and immigration, 1988—. Chmn. parents com. Lower St. Lawrence Sch. Bd., 1964-67; bd. dirs., pres. Assoc. Family Orgns., Que., Can., 1974-81; nat. pres. Dames Helene de Champlain, 1976-79; pres. Fedn. des Caisses populaires Desjardins du Bas St-Laurent, 1976-84, Girardin-Vaillancourt Found., 1981-84; bd. dirs. Confedn. des Caisses populaires et d'economies Desjardins, 1977-84, Societe immobiliere du Que., 1984; mem. Conseil a superieur de l'education du Que., 1978-82, chmn. secondary sch. bd., 1978-82; dep. bd. chmn. Regie de l'assurance automobile du Que., 1978-81; chmn. bd. dirs. Institut cooperatif Desjardins, 1978-81. Office: Parliament Bldgs, Ottawa, ON Canada K1A 0A6 *

VIACAVA, LILLIAN D., librarian; b. Bklyn.; d. Frank and Camille (Raffetto) V. B.A., Coll. New Rochelle, 1951; M.S. in Library Service, Columbia U., 1954. Reference librarian Iona Coll., New Rochelle, 1954-59, asst. librarian, 1960-75, assoc. librarian, 1976—. Mem. ALA, AAUP, Cath. Library Assn. Westchester Library Assn. (chair coll. sect. 1978-79), Am. Soc. Info. Sci, Spl. Libraries Assn. Office: Iona Coll Ryan Library New Rochelle NY 10801

VICKERS, MONTEZ MOSER, public relations executive; b. North Miami, Fla., Oct. 12, 1953; d. William Thomas and Merrill Catherine (Small) Moser; m. Lewie Marks Vickers, Jan. 17, 1987; 1 stepson, Christopher. BA in Communications magna cum laude, U. Ala., 1981. Admissions clk. Bapt. Med. Ctr.-Montclair, Birmingham, Ala., 1971-72; bus. mgmt. technician U.S. Small Bus. Adminstrn., Birmingham, 1972-79; intern Totalcom, Inc., Tuscaloosa, Ala., 1980-81; writer Birmingham (Ala.) Mag., 1981-82; dir. pub. relations, copywriter Gillis, Townsend and Riley Adv., Birmingham, 1982-83; free-lance copywriter Birmingham, 1983-85; adminstrv. sec. U. Ala., Birmingham, 1983-85; dir. pub. relations Enterprise (Ala.) State Jr. Coll., 1985—. Contbr. numerous articles to various mags., 1981-85. Mem. Coffee County Humane Soc., 1985-86, Nat. Council for Community Relations, bd. dirs. Nat. Spring Chicken Festival, Enterprise, 1986. Mem. Dothan Advt. Fedn., Nat. Assn. Female Execs., Hunter-Jumper Assn. Ala. (3 state championships 1983), Am. Bus. Womens Assn. (sec. enterprise chpt.). Baptist. Club: Coffee County Arts Alliance. Office: Enterprise State Jr Coll Hwy 84 S Enterprise AL 36331

VICKERS, NAOMI R., real estate executive; b. Anderson, Ind., Mar. 13, 1917; d. Floyd Leroy and Gertrude Marie (Richards) Stamm; m. Robert Ross Vickers (dec.); children—Robert V. Vickers, Richard R. Vickers, Philip L. Vickers, Denise (Mrs. Jack L. Healey). Sec., treas. Vickers Fine Homes, Anderson, 1951—, Vickers Apts., 1956—; sec., treas. Comml. Bldgs., 1958—. Mem. Toy Collectors Am. (antique toy train collector). Mem. Order Eastern Star, White Shrine, Madison County Shrine. Home: 2003 E 7th St Anderson IN 46012 Office: 724 Alhambra Dr Anderson IN 46012

VICKERS, PATSY, correctional services chaplain; b. Douglas, Ga., Dec. 29, 1949; d. Guy and Thelma (Wilcox) V. BS, SUNY, Brockport, 1976; MS, Atlanta U., 1980. Supr. vol. services N.Y. State Dept. of Corrections, Sonyia, 1983-86; chaplain Wallkill (N.Y.) Correctional Facility, 1986—. Office: Wallkill Correctional Facility PO Box 86B Wallkill NY 12589

VICKERY, BYRDEAN EYVONNE HUGHES (MRS. CHARLES EVERETT VICKERY, JR.), library services administrator; b. Belleview, Mo., Apr. 18, 1928; d. Roy Franklin and Margaret Cordelia (Wood) Hughes; m. Charles Everett Vickery, Jr., Nov. 5, 1948; 1 dau., Camille. Student Flat River (Mo.) Jr. Coll., 1946-48; B.S. in Edn., S.E. Mo. State Coll., 1954; M.L.S., U. Wash., 1964; postgrad. Wash. State U., 1969-70. Tchr., Ironton (Mo.) Pub. Schs., 1948-56; elem. tchr. Pasco (Wash.) Sch. Dist. 1, 1956-61, jr. high sch. librarian, 1961-68, coordinator libraries, 1968-69; asst. librarian Columbia Basin Community Coll., Pasco, 1969-70, head librarian, dir. Instructional Resources Center, 1970-78, dir. library services, 1979-87, assoc. dean library services, 1987—; chmn. S.E. Wash. Library Service Area, 1977-78, 88—. Bd. dirs. Pasco-Kennewick Community Concerts, 1977—, pres., 1980-81, 87-88; bd. dirs. Mid-Columbia Symphony Orch., 1983—; trustee Wash. Commn. Humanities, 1982-85. Author, editor: Library and Research Skills Curriculum Guides for the Pasco School District, 1967; author (with Jean Thompson), also editor Learning Resources Handbook for Teachers, 1969. Recipient Woman of Achievement award Pasco Bus. and Profl. Women's Club, 1976. Mem. AAUW (2d v.p. 1966-68, corr. sec. 1969), Wash. Dept. Audio-Visual Instrn., ALA, Wash. Library Assn., Am., Wash. assns. higher edn., Wash. State Assn. Sch. Librarians (state conf. chmn. 1971-72), Tri-Cities Librarians Assn., Wash. Library Media Assn. (community coll. levels chmn. 1986-87), Am. Assn. Research Libraries, Soroptimist Internat. Assn. (rec. sec. Pasco-Kennewick chpt. 1971-72, treas. 1973-74, pres. 1978-80), Columbia Basin Coll. Adminstrs. Assn. (sec.-treas. 1973-74), Pacific N.W. Assn. Ch. Libraries, Women in Communications, Pasco Bus. and Profl. Women's Club, P.E.O. Beta Sigma Phi, Delta Kappa Gamma, Phi Delta Kappa (sec. 1981-82, Outstanding Educator award 1983). Home: 4016 W Park St Pasco WA 99301 Office: Columbia Basin Community Coll 2600 N 20th Ave Pasco WA 99301

VIDAVER, VIRGINIA SEWELL, nurse, educator; b. Jackson, Tenn., Feb. 11, 1934; d. Clyde Stetzel and Martha Virginia (Moore) S.; m. Robert M. Vidaver, May 27, 1960; children: Mary Martha, Robert Clyde, Patrick Sewell, John Bathory. BS, Union U., 1955; M in Nursing, Yale U., 1958; MEd, Columbia U., 1982; postgrad., Va. Commonwealth U., 1986—. Mem. edn. com. Norfolk Com. for Prevention of Child Abuse, 1982—; organizer, mem. Healthy Mothers Healthy Babies Coalition, Norfolk, 1983—; chair mgmt. adv. com., bd. dirs. Pride in Parenting, 1984-86 (mem. 1986—). Mem. Am. Nurses' Assn. (state fin. com. 1983, state del. 1986, local bd. mem. 1987—), Nat. Assn. Childbearing Ctrs., Nat. League for Nursing, Nat. Assn. for Home Care, Nurses Assn. of Am. Coll. of Obstetricians and Gynecologists, Va. Perinatal Assn., Va. League for Nursing Legis. Com., Va. Nurses Assn. (bd. dirs. Tidewater chpt. 1987—), Sigma Theta Tau (pres. local chpt. 1985—, state co-chair 1986—), Kappa Delta Pi. Democrat. Office: Old Dominion Univ Dept Nursing Norfolk VA 23508

VIDOVIC, AGNES ANN, physical education educator; b. Chgo., Jan. 28, 1929; d. Joseph and Mary (Kirincic) Radich; m. Martin P. Vidovic, Sept. 14, 1957; children—Janice Geralyn, Christopher Martin. A.A., Wilson Jr. Coll., 1949; B.S., U. Ill.-Urbana, 1951; M.S., W.Va. U., 1952; postgrad. numerous univs. Instr., ARC, 1947-49, YMCA, Chgo., 1953-55, YWCA, Chgo., 1956-57, Chgo. Park Dist., 1951; waterfront dir. Clearwater Camp for Girls, Minocqua, Wis., 1955; instr. U. Chgo. Lab. Sch., 1952-54, Lindblom High Sch., Chgo., 1954-62; chair girls' dept. phys. edn. Hubbard High Sch., Chgo., 1962-63, Morgan Park Acad., Chgo., 1965-67; prof. phys. edn. Truman Coll., Chgo., 1967—; judge/referee Ill. High Sch. Assn., 1969-74; ednl. film distbr. U.S. Gymnastics Fedn. Women's Com., 1969-72; timer/scorer Midwest Open Gymnastics Championship for Women, 1969-70; vol. lectr. Mayfair Coll. Adult Edn., 1968-74, cons. 1968-73; voting rep. Chgo. City Colls. Faculty Council, 1983-85; mem. Nat. Bd. Women Athletics, 1974-80. Bd. dirs. Mothers Assn. U. Ill., 1977—, chair fall conf., 1983, 2d v.p., 1984-85; mem. choir Assumption Cath. Ch., Chgo., 1953-59, St. Monica Cath. Ch., Chgo., 1968-71; mem. 41st Ward Women's Democratic Orgn.; faculty rep. Truman Coll. Community Council, 1981-83. State of Ill. scholar, 1949-51; Oscar Mayer scholar, 1962; recipient 25-Yr. Service award ARC, 1984. Mem. AAHPER and Dance (life; charter 500, Nat Intramural Sports Council 1967-71), Nat. Dance Assn. (higher edn. div.), Ill. Assn. Health, Phys. Edn., Recreation and Dance. Democrat. Club: St. Monica Women's (Chgo.). Office: Truman Coll 1145 W Wilson Ave Chicago IL 60656

VIEHMYER, LAURA LACY, human resources executive; b. Balt., Oct. 3, 1955; d. Edward Earl Viehmyer and Barbara Anne (Lacy) Hough; m. James E. Vaughn, July 3, 1982; 1 child, Edward Andrew Vaughn. BA in Psychology and Edn. summa cum laude, U. Md., Balt., 1976. Personnel analyst, then sr. personnel analyst Seminole County Bd. County Commrs., Sanford, Fla., 1978-81; dir. personnel Piezo Tech., Inc., Orlando, Fla., 1981-84; mgr. human resources adminstrn. Travelers/EBS, Inc., Maitland, Fla., 1984—; cons. Orlando C. of C., 1984, Orlando Sci. Ctr., 1987. U. Md. scholar, 1974, Univ. Student scholar, 1974. Mem. Am. Soc. Personnel Adminstrn. (dist. dir. 1987, conf. com. mem. Fla. State Conf. 1985, 86, 88, conf. chairperson, 1987), Fla. Pub. Personnel Assn., Cen. Fla. Personnel Assn. (chpt. pres. 1985-86, bd. dirs. 1983-87, Personnel Exec. of Yr. 1985), Psi Chi, Phi Kappa Phi. Baptist. Office: Travelers/EBS Inc 2701 Maitland Ctr Pkwy Maitland FL 32751

VIENNE, DOROTHY TITUS, school principal; b. Buffalo, May 8, 1939; d. Robert Paul and Bertha (Wissman) Titus; m. Richard Paul Vienne, Aug. 27, 1960; children: Richard Paul Jr., Kerstina Elaine. BS in Elem. Edn., SUNY, Brockport, 1960; MS in Elem. Edn., SUNY, Buffalo, 1964; postgrad., U. Buffalo, 1968-76, Canisius Coll., 1978. Cert. elem. tchr., N.Y. Elem. tchr. Lancaster (N.Y.) Cen. Schs., 1960-62, reading tchr., 1962-68, reading specialist, 1968-76; program supr. Kenmore-Town of Tonawanda, Kenmore, N.Y., 1976-79, 81-86; coordinator pupil personnel services Assn. for Retarded Children, Buffalo, 1980-81; prin. Kenmore-Town of Tonawanda Union Free Sch. Dist., Kenmore, 1986—; speaker Summer Inst. for Prins., 1987. Mem. steering com. Western N.Y. Prins. Ctr., Buffalo, 1986-87; bd. dirs. Lift Counseling Service, Elma, N.Y., 1980-87. Mem. Assn. for Supervision and Curriculum Devel., Sch. Adminstrs. N.Y. State, Phi Delta Kappa. Republican. Methodist. Home: 50 Gaylord Ct Elma NY 14059 Office: Kenmore Town Tonawanda Schs 250 Athens Blvd Buffalo NY 14223

VIGIL, CAROL JEAN, lawyer; b. Santa Fe, Oct. 24, 1947; d. Martin Jr. and Evelyn (Abeita) V.; m. Philip D. Palmer, Dec. 16, 1977; 1 child, Erika L. BS, U. N.M., 1974, JD, 1978. Bar: N.M. 1979. Fellow in Indian law Indian Pueblo Legal Services, Santa Ana Pueblo, N.M., 1978-80; appellate div. clk. to atty. gen. State of N.Mex., Santa Fe, 1980-84; sole practice Santa Fe, 1984-87; tribal atty. Tesuque Pueblo, N.M., 1985—; tribal prosecutor Eight No. Indian Pueblo Council Child Abuse Prosecution Project, San Juan Pueblo, N.M. 1986—. Sec. No. N.M. Legal Services, Santa Fe, 1981-82, chmn., 1982-83, vice chmn. 1984-85; bd. dirs. Santa Fe Mountain Ctr., 1985-86; bd. dirs., sec., treas., Pueblo Ins. Agy., 1985-86. Mem. ABA, N.M. Bar Assn. (pro bono com. 1987-88, chair elect independent law sect. 1987-88), Indian Bar Assn., Delta Theta Phi. Democrat. Roman Catholic. Home and Office: 214 McKenzie Santa Fe NM 87501

VIGIL, TERRY ANNE, college official; b. Detroit, July 25, 1946; d. Charles Howard and Margo (Carroll) Peake; A.B., Brown U., 1968; M.R.P., Syracuse U., 1970; m. Roy Max Vigil, June 27, 1970; children—Kiara Maria, Ryan Howard. Planner, Mass. Dept. Community Affairs, Boston, 1970-72; regional planner Bur. Transp. Planning and Devel., Mass. Dept. Public Works, Boston, 1972-79; supr. State Transp. Plan Staff for Bur. Transp. Planning and Devel. in cooperation with Exec. Office Transp. and Constrn., Boston, 1979-81; pres., chmn. bd. Kidpool, Inc., 1982-83; planning cons., freelance writer, 1982; grants dir. Bridgewater (Mass.) State Coll., 1982—. Sec.-treas. Brookline Council for Planning and Renewal, 1980-82, vice chmn., 1979-80; founder, treas. Friends of Lost Pond, Chestnut Hill, Mass., 1981—; pres. Chestnut Hill Village Assos., 1974-76. Mem. AAUW, Assn. Women Deans, Adminstrs. and Counselors, Women's Transp. Seminar Greater Boston. Christian Scientist. Author: Citizen's Transportation Handbook, 1975; Regional Transportation Plan Guidelines, 1978; I-93 Joint Transportation Study, 1980. Home: 10 Craftsland Rd Chestnut Hill MA 02167

VIGIL-GIRON, REBECCA D., secretary of state; b. Taos, N. Mex., Sept. 4, 1954. Grad., N. Mex. Highlands Univ. Sec. of state of New Mex., Santa Fe. Democrat. Office: Office of the Sec of State 400 State Capitol Santa Fe NM 87503 *

VIGNOCCHI, MADALENA JOAN, accountant; b. Lake Forest, Ill., July 2, 1952; d. Anthony and Juanita Dolly (Thompson) V.; m. Thomas Stanley Lawrence, Nov. 21, 1981; children: David, Michael. BS in Fin., U. Ill., 1973. CPA, Ill. Staff acct. Ernst & Whinney, Chgo., 1974-75, in-charge acct., 1975-76; semi-sr. internal auditor McGraw-Edison Co., Elgin, Ill., 1976-77, tax acct., 1977-79; sr. tax analyst Safety Kleen Corp., Elgin, 1980-84, acctg. supr., 1984-85, mgr. capital budget, property acct., 1985—. Mem. Am. Inst. CPA's, Women in Mgmt. (pres. No. Fox Valley chpt. 1984-86), Ill. CPA's. Roman Catholic. Office: Safety Kleen Corp 777 Big Timber Rd Elgin IL 60123

VIGNOS, SUSAN LOUISE, municipal government official; b. Canton, Ohio, June 9, 1958; d. Edward Henry and Helen (Paulus) Hawkins; m. Richard Charles Vignos, Sept. 9, 1978 (div. Oct. 1987); children: Andrea Lynn, Jacquelyn Marie. Student, Bowling Green (Ohio) State U., 1976-78, Kent (Ohio) State U., 1978-81, Walsh Coll., 1982—. Coordinator admissions Valley View Nursing Home, Akron, Ohio, 1978-79; adminstrv. asst. Manor Care Nursing Home, Akron, 1979-81; corp. auditor city income tax dept. City of Canton, 1982, clk., investor treasurer's dept., 1982-83, chief dep. treas., 1983-85, city treas., 1985—. With USNR, 1988—. Mem. Ohio Mcpl. Treas. Assn., Nat. Mcpl. Treas. Assn. U.S. and Can. (legis. com.), Mcpl. Fin. Officers Assn., NE Ohio Tax Adminstrs., Ohio Mcpl. League, Canton Jaycees, City Club Canton. Episcopalian. Club: Canton Exchange (sec.). Home: 1714 Harvard Ave NW Canton OH 44703 Office: City of Canton 218 Cleveland Ave Canton OH 44702

VIKING, NANCY LEE, festival management consultant; b. St. Paul, Nov. 2, 1943; d. Clarence Lee and Helen Voila (Olson) Law; m. Don Stuart Johnson, Aug. 1, 1963 (div. 1967); 1 child, Eric Don; m. Robert Edward Viking, Dec. 31, 1985. Student, U. Minn., 1961-62. cert. Festival Exec. degree, Purdue, 1986. Adminstrv. asst. St. Paul Winter Carnival Assn., 1966-67, First Bank St. Paul, 1967-69; festival mgr. Mpls. Aquatennial Assn., 1969-86; adminstrv. coordinator Internat. Festivals Assn., Mpls., 1970-83; parade coordinator City of Santa Ana (Calif.) Community Events Ctr., 1986—. Pub. relations dir. Minn. Little Gophers Baseball Team, Mpls., 1983-86. Mem. Internat. Festivals Assn. (bd. dirs. 1986-87), Minn. Press Club, Pub. Relations Soc. Am., Mpls. Chinese Am. Assn. of Minn., Exec. Women in Tourism, Mpls./Iberaki (Japan) Sister City Assn. Republican. Lutheran. Lodge: Zonta.

VILLA, JOAN, management consultant, writer, poet, educator; b. San Mateo, Calif., June 14, 1949; d. Leonard Charles and Angeline Josephine (Arena) Calabrese; m. Anthony Q. Villa, Jan. 20, 1973. B.S. in Exceptional Child Edn., State U. Coll. at Buffalo, 1973; M.S. in Edn., Nova U., 1978. Cert. tchr. pre-sch., elem., N.Y., emotionally handicapped, jr. coll. adminstrn., supr., Fla. Tchr. emotionally disturbed Sch. Bd. Broward County, Ft. Lauderdale, Fla., 1974-79; adj. prof. U. La Verne, Calif., 1979, 80; sr. coordinator Personal Dynamics Inst. Minn., 1978-85; adj. prof. Nova U., Davie, Fla., 1981—; resident mgr. Personal Dynamics Inst., 1985; pres., owner Personal & Profl. Devel. Ctr., Coral Springs, Fla., 1979—; sponsor continuing profl. edn. program Fla. State Bd. Accountancy, Gainesville, 1982—; apptd. Fla. teaching profl.-NEA Women's Leadership Tng. Cadre, 1980. Contbr. articles to profl. jours. Mem. edn. task force Ft. Lauderdale/Broward County C. of C., 1985, mem. small bus. coalition, 1984; recipient Outstanding Young Woman of Am. award, 1984; coordinator Exceptional Child week Council for Exceptional Children, 1979, communications chmn., 1977-78, sec., 1976-77. Recipient Appreciation award Am. Soc. Tng. and Devel., Broward-Palm Beach chpt., 1983, Dedicated Service award, 1983, regional chpt. excellence award, 1983, chpt. of the yr. award, 1983, Nat. Profl. Contbn. award, 1983, Outstanding Leadership award, 1982, Outstanding Service award, 1981, others. Mem. Am. Soc. Tng. and Devel. (region IX conf. strategic planning chmn., 1984, strategic planning chmn., nat. issues chmn. 1985), (Broward-Palm Beach chpt. exec. bd., 1984, pres. 1983, mem.ship chmn., 1981) Classroom Tchrs. Assn. (bldg. chmn., 1976-79), Fla. Freelance Writers Assn., Pompano Beach C. of C., Ft. Lauderdale C. of C., Assn. Profl. Saleswomen, Network Connection, Women in Sales Assoc., NEA. Clubs: Coral Springs Exec., Women's Exec. Avocations: bicycling; reading; rug hooking; leather craft; dancing. Home: 8811 NW 21st St Coral Springs FL 33065 Office: Personal and Profl Devel Ctr 1439 S Pompano Pkwy Suite 301 Pompano Beach FL 33069

VILLALÓN, SILVIA DURÁN, real estate executive; b. La Havana, Cuba, Apr. 7, 1941; d. Mario Andrés and Ondina (Paredes) Durán; m. Jose R. Garrigó, Apr. 5, 1959 (div. Oct. 1983); children: Jose R., Silvia M., Jorge I.; m. Andrés Villalón, Aug. 17, 1984. BS, Instituto Del Vedado, La Havana, 1958; AA, Miami Dade Community Coll., 1984. Pres. Silvia Garrigo Interiors, Key Biscayne, Fla., 1974-87, Garrigo, Duran & Assocs., Realtors, Key Biscayne, 1976-87; v.p. The Royal Poinciana Group, Inc., Cape Coral, Fla., 1984-87; pres. Sailfish Co., Realtors, Cape Coral, 1986-87, Poinciana Realty of Cape Coral, Inc., Cape Coral, 1987—, The Tile Wholesaler, Inc., Cape Coral, 1987—. Home: 600 Grapetree Dr 3C-S Key Biscayne FL 33149 Office: 1110 Pine Island Rd #9 Cape Coral FL 33909 also: 1321 Hancock Bridge Pkwy Cape Coral FL 33904

VILLANI, SUSAN, school administrator; b. Bklyn., July 4, 1950; d. Jerry C. and Helen (Hartzman) V.; BA, Harpur Coll., SUNY, Binghamton, 1970; MEd, Tufts U., 1971; C.A.G.S., Northeastern U., 1979, EdD, 1983; children: Evan, Adria. With Havils Jewelers, Riverhead, N.Y., 1958-71, Meenan Oil Co., Hicksville, N.Y., 1967; substitute tchr. Somerville (Mass.) Public Schs., 1971; tchr. Batchelder Sch., North Reading, Mass., 1971-78; prin. Hazard Elem. Sch., Wakefield, R.I., 1978-85, Lincoln Sch., Winchester, Mass., 1985-88, Thoreau Sch., Concord, Mass., 1988—; cert. instr. Parent Effectiveness Tng., 1977; program adv. bd. Prin.'s Ctr. Harvard U., 1987—; con., workshop presenter on monitoring and career devel. Mem. Bus. and Profl. Women (Young Career Woman of R.I. 1979), Young Career Women of R.I., North East Coalition of Edn'l. Leaders (pres. 1981-83), Mass. Assn. Elem. Sch. Prins., Nat. Assn. Elem. Sch. Prins., Nat. Assn. Secondary Sch. Prins. (assessor for adminstr. assessments, Assn. Supervision and Curriculum Devel., Am. Assn. Sch. Adminstrs., Am. Ednl. Research Assn., Kappa Delta Pi, Phi Delta Kappa. Home: 16 Dee Rd Lexington MA 02173 Office: 161 Mystic Valley Pkwy Winchester MA 01890

VILLARREAL, MARY KATHERINE, corporate risk manager; b. Port Arthur, Tex., Aug. 6, 1957; d. Elias and Thelma C. (Palmer) V. BBA, Secondary Edn. Cert., Lamar U., 1979. Asst. adminstr., legal sec. Ross, Griggs & Harrison Law Firm, Houston, 1980-83; risk mgr. Mariner Corp., Houston, 1983-88, v.p. human resources, 1988—; grad. asst. Dale Carnegie Inst., Houston, 1984-86. Campaign coordinator United Way. Houston, 1984-87. Mem. Nat. Safety Council, Tex. Hotel/Motel Assn., Tex. Safety Council, Nat. Assn. Female Execs. Roman Catholic. Office: Mariner Corp 1700 W Loop South #900 Houston TX 77027

VILLAVECCHIA, ROBERTA LEE GRIFFIN, systems engineering executive; b. Los Angeles, Oct. 25, 1938; d. John Martin and Eleanor (Long) Griffin; divorced; children: Candace, Robert, Kathy, Joan, Lisa, Barbara; married. Student, Trinity U., San Antonio, 1970; BA, Brooks Inst. at Santa Barbara, Calif., 1976. Systems engr. Bendix Corp., Cape Kennedy, Fla., 1964-71; asst. dir. Confederate Air Force Mus., Harlingen, Tex., 1976-84; systems engr. Calcutron Corp., Houston, 1984-86; gen. mgr. Jiffco Systems, Inc., Houston, 1986-87; major account rep. Western Union Corp., Houston, 1987—; cons. Confederate Air Force Mus., Rio Computers, San Antonio, 1984—. Author: History of the Ghost Squadron, 1977; asst. editor CAF Dispatch, 1978-83; contbr. articles to Flypast Mag., Time-Life Series on WWII War in the Air, 1978; patentee lab. glassware for Project Apollo, 1966. Bd. dirs. CAF Flying Mus., 1970. Recipient Merit awards Profl. Photographers Am., 1977, Gold Medal photography award Los Angeles County Fair, 1976. Mem. Houston Air Cargo Assn., Houston World Trade Assn. Republican. Roman Catholic. Home: 8517 Hearth Dr #21 Houston TX 77060 Office: Western Union Corp 1415 N Loop West Suite 300 Houston TX 77008

VILLENEUVE, EVA ZOPHIA, nutritionist, hospital administrator; b. St. Neotts, Eng., Sept. 5, 1947; came to Can., 1952; m. John William Villeneuve; children: Tyson, Sarah. BA, U. Toronto, 1969; BEd, Ont. Coll. Edn., 1970; B of Home Econs., U. B.C., 1977. Cert. dietitian, tchr. Tchr. Lincoln County Sch. Bd., St. Catharines, Ont., 1970-72, Ottawa (Ont.) Sch. Bd., 1973; dietetic intern Vancouver (B.C.) Gen. Hosp., fall 1977-78, clin. dietitian renal and cardiac wards, 1979-81; out-patient dietitian St. Paul's Hosp., Vancouver, fall 1978-79; dir. dietary services Versa Services at Mt. St. Joseph Hosp., Vancouver, 1981—; speaker in field. Rep. Lincoln County Sch. Bd., st. Catharines, 1972, 78-79. Mem. B.C. Dietitians and and Nutritionists Assn. Roman Catholic. Office: Mt St Joseph Hosp, 3080 Prince Edward St, Vancouver, BC Canada V5T 3N4

VILLINES, DEBIANNE, health care coordinator; b. Buffalo, Apr. 2, 1955; d. Louis David Lo Vallo and Virginia Iona (Tagg) Du Bois, m. John Clay Villines, Jan. 17, 1973 (div. Oct. 1984); 1 child, Coop Joshua. AS in Nursing, Ga. State U., 1976, BSN, 1981; MN, Emory U., 1984. Cert. in neonatal intensive care. Charge nurse Crawford Long Hosp., Atlanta, 1976-78; staff nurse specializing in Ob-Gyn Atlanta, 1978-79; staff nurse specializing in neonatal care Northside Hosp., Atlanta, 1979-80, asst. unit mgr. specializing in neonatal care, 1980-86; coordinator intensive care units Scottish Rite Children's Hosp., Atlanta, 1986—; chmn. ethics com. Northside Hosp., 1983-86; profl. relations com. Scottish Rite Children's Hosp.; Ga. Nurses' Polit. Action Com.; Ga. rep. Mead Johnson Symposium Perinatal Med., 1982; lectr. in field, 1985-88. Named to Dean's List, Mortar Bd. Ga. State U. Mem. Ga. Nurses' Assn., Ga. Nurses for Life, Ga. Perinatal Assn., Ga. Women's Health Adminstrn. Network, Nat. Assn. Neonatal Nurses, Nurses' Assn. Am. Coll. Obstetrics and Gynecologists. Republican. Club: Masterpeace (Atlanta). Home: 4501 Dobbs Crossing Marietta GA 30068 Office: Scottish Rite Children's Hosp 1001 Johnson Ferry Rd Atlanta GA 30063

VILLONE, MARYANN, hospital admininstrator; b. Clifton, N.J., Jan. 11, 1951; d. Edward J. and Joan C. (Strominski) Kraiger: m. Dennis Alan Villone, May 3, 1975; children: Dennis Edward, Richard Alan. AAS, County Coll. Morris, N.J., 1971. RN. ICU charge nurse Morristown (N.J.) Meml. Hosp., 1972-74, supr. hemodialysis units, 1974-77, 79-87, cardiac nurse, 1978-79, night supr. nursing div., 1987—. Active Chester PTA, N.J., 1985—. Mem. N.J. Renal Network (med. rev. bd. 1985-87, council on quality assurance 1985-87), Am. Nephrology Nurses Assn., Nat. Assn. Female Execs., Orgn. Nurse Execs. N.J., Council Mid. Nurse Mgrs., Am. Nephrology Nurses Assn. Home: Rural Rt 2 PO Box 621C Chester NJ 07930 Office: Morristown Mem Hosp 100 Madison Ave Morristown NJ 07960

VILSECK, KATHLEEN ORA, small business owner; b. Harlingen, Tex., Aug. 25, 1951; d. Clarence Wayne and Gloria Antoinette (Wallace) Haley; m. Francis Joseph Moltz, Sept. 15, 1973 (June 1980); m. Jan Thomas Vilseck, April 24, 1986; 1 child, Robert. BBA in Mgmt., Tex. A&I U., 1975. Purchasing clk. Tex. A&I U., Kingsville, 1977-80, adminstrv. clk., 1980-83, dir. of purchasing and supplies, 1983-87; owner Unique Interiors, Kingsville, 1987; with order entry dept. Consol. Systems Inc., Memphis, Tenn, 1987—.

VINCENT, CLARE, museum curator; b. Jersey City, Aug. 30, 1935; d. Harold and Lorena (Cole) V. AB, Coll. William and Mary, 1958; MA, NYU, 1963; cert. mus. tng., Met. Mus. Art and Inst. Fine Arts, 1963. Cataloguer slides Cooper Union Sch. Architecture, 1959-60; asst. to curator decorative arts Cooper Union Mus. Arts of Decoration, 1960-61; curatorial asst. western European arts Met. Mus. Art, N.Y.C., 1962-67, asst. curator, 1967-72, assoc. curator European sculpture and decorative arts, 1972—; cons. to catalogue of antique sci. instruments Adler Planetarium, Chgo., 1984—. Author: European Clocks in New York Collections, 1972, Rodin at the Metropolitan Museum art, 1981; contbr. in field. Mem. Antiquarian Horological Soc. (v.p. Am. sect. 1977—), N.Y. Acad. Sci. (vice chmn. history of sci. and tech. sect. 1988—), Furniture History Soc., Société Internationale de l'Astrolabe, Internat. Union History and Philosophy of Sci. (sci. instrument commn.), History Sci. Soc., Renaissance Soc. Am., Coll. Art Assn. Home: 326 E 85th St New York NY 10028 Office: Met Mus Art 5th Ave and 82d St New York NY 10028

VINCENT, DONNA MARIE, marketing professional, educator; b. Lake Charles, La., July 26, 1958; d. Ronald Gene and Margie (Broussard) V. BS in Gen. Studies, La. State U.; PhD in Communications, U. So. Miss. Dir. pub. service Sta. KLCL, Westlake, La., 1978-79; producer, account exec. Cablevision, Baton Rouge, 1979-81; co-editor, co-pub. Conoco, Lake Charles, 1982-85; dir. mktg. Shaw Assocs., Hattiesburg, Miss., 1986—; intern BBC, Birmingham, Eng., 1985, Yorkshire TV, Leeds, Eng., 1985; adj. faculty William Carey Coll., Hattiesburg, 1986. Media coordinator Artists Civic Theater and Studio, Lake Charles, 1983-84. Recipient Ted Turner Excellence award, 1981, 7 other awards for producing TV sports programs; scholar Rotary Internat., 1984-85. Mem. Speech Communication Assn., La. Press Women. Republican. Roman Catholic. Home: 4711 W Braddock Rd #10 Alexandria VA 22311

VINCENT, JULIE LEE, industrial engineer; b. Medford, Oreg., Dec. 22, 1944; d. Gerald Talifero and Lois (Lindsey) Latham; m. Dennis Robert Vincent, Sept. 10, 1966; children: Carrie Liane, Sarah Jean. BS in Gen. Engring., Oreg. State U., 1966, MS in Indsl. Engring., 1968. Corp. indsl. engr. project leader Tektronix, Portland, Oreg., 1978-81; mgr. mfg. resource planning tng. Tektronix, Beaverton, Oreg., 1981-83; materials mgr., engr. computer systems Tektronix, Wilsonville, Oreg., 1983-86, mgr. procurement div. graphics worksta., 1986-88; mgr. reconditioned products Tektronix, Wilsonville, 1988—; tech. rev. Brigham Young U. Mfg. Consortium, Provo, Utah, 1981-83. Mem. Soc. Mfg. Engrs. (treas. 1982-83), Inst. Indsl. Engrs. Office: Tektronix Wilsonville Park PO Box 1000 Wilsonville OR 97070

VINCENT, M. DIANE, mental health administrator; b. Sandusky, Mich., Jan. 20, 1943; d. Frank Sherman and Ethyl Marie (Paige) Reiner; Ph.B., Wayne State U., 1965; M.A., Oakland U., 1978; m. Gerald Vincent, 1963 (div. 1978); children—Melissa, Michael, Geoffrey; m. Ronald W. Marr, 1985. Caseworker, State of Mich., 1965-66; therapist Project Fresh Start, Dept. Labor Spl. Project, Detroit, 1966-68; probation officer Recorders Ct., Detroit, 1968; dir. Hotline, Birmingham, Mich., 1971-75; exec. dir., v.p., bd. dirs. Square Lake Counseling Ctr., Ltd., Bloomfield Hills, from 1975, now chief exec. officer; dir. Common Ground, Inc., 1975-80; pres. Whethersfield Assocs., consultants, 1980-84; mem. coordinators council Oakland County Office of Substance Abuse Services, 1972-80; mem. adv. bd. Health Mgmt. Services, 1986—; sec.-treas. EAP, Inc., 1985-87; cons. employability programming for women, 1979—, Booth Communications, 1982-84; mem. Oakland County Prosecutor's Task Force on Child Molesters, 1978; bd. dirs. Community Action Council. Trainer, empathy trainers; mem. Gov.'s Task Force Substance Abuse Prevention, 1972; sec. bd. dirs. Mich. Assn. Crisis Centers, 1972-75; mem. Substance Abuse Adv. Council, 1980-85; bd. dirs. Madrigal Chorale of Southfield, 1984—; mem. adv. bd. Woodside Hosp., 1984 , Common Ground, 1980—; sec. bd. dirs. Madrigal Chorale. Cert. social worker, Mich. Mem. Mich. Assn. Substance Abuse Program Dirs., Am. Assn., Counseling and Devel. Mich. Assn. Program Dirs. Mich. Alcohol and Addiction Assn., Assn. Labor Mgmt. Adminstrs. and Cons. on Alcoholism. Co-author: Prosecuters Handbook To Prevent Child Molesting; A Guide to Public Access in Cable Television. Home: 1727 Washington St Birmingham MI 48009 Office: 2550 S Telegraph St Bloomfield Hills MI 48013

VINE, JANET DIANA, educator, author; b. Albany, N.Y., Apr. 6, 1937; d. Harold Arthur and Dora Mary (Meyer) Vine; B.A., Syracuse U., 1959; M.A., SUNY, 1964. Tchr. English, Herbert Hoover Jr. High Sch., Kenmore, N.Y., 1959-66; tchr. Kenmore East Sr. High Sch., 1966—, chmn. dept. English, 1970-83; cheerleading coach, 1959-77; sr. asso. Write Assos., 1982—. Mem. Am. Fedn. Tchrs., N.Y. State United Tchrs., Kenmore Tchrs. Assn., NEA, Authors Guild, Nat. League of Am. Pen Women (pres. Western N.Y. br. 1984-86), Assn. Profl. Women Writers, The Write People, Nat. Council Tchrs. English, AAUW, Pi Lambda Theta, Eta Pi Upsilon, Sigma Kappa. Methodist. Club: Kenmore Women Tchrs. Bowling Assn. (pres. 1983-84). Author: English: A Comprehensive Review, 1982; Discovering Literature, Reading Guide and Review Tests, 1968; Exploring Literature, Reading Guide and Review Tests, 1968; contbr. articles to newspapers and mags. Office: 350 Fries Rd Tonawanda NY 14150

VINES, DIANE WELCH, psychotherapist, educator; b. Rochester, Minn., Apr. 3, 1945; d. Howard Henshel and Edna (Steck) Welch; m. Ted Kerzie. B.A., St. Petersburg Jr. Coll., 1964; B.S. magna cum laude, Vanderbilt U., 1967; M.A. with honors, N.Y.U., 1973; postgrad. Boston U.; 1 son, Juan Antonio. Coordinator emotionally disturbed children unit state hosp., Phila., 1967-68; instr. nursing Mt. Sinai Hosp. Sch. Nursing, N.Y.C., 1968-69; asst. dir. nursing Vista Hill Psychiat. Hosp., Chula Vista, Calif., 1969-70; chmn. dept. New Rochelle (N.Y.) Hosp. Sch. Nursing, 1970-71; part-time staff nurse Manhattan Bowery Project, N.Y.C., 1971-72; evening supr. state hosp. for emotionally disturbed children and adolescents, 1972-73; psychotherapist Albert Einstein Med. Center, Bronx, 1973-74; instr. Faulkner Hosp. Sch. Nursing, Boston, 1974-75; instr. students preparing for licensure exam. Mass., Boston, 1974-75; pvt. practice psychotherapy, co-founder Beacon Assos., Brookline, Mass., 1976—; dir. ambulatory nursing Boston Children's Hosp. Med. Center, 1975-78; asst. prof. grad. program psychiat. community mental health nursing, Boston, 1978—; White House fellow, spl. asst. to sec. edn., Washington, 1982-83; dir. Nat. Adult Literacy Initiative, U.S. Dept. Edn., 1983-85; dir. spl. programs Calif. State U., 1985—; pvt. practice psychotherapy, WLA, 1986—; adv. com. Mass. Bd. Registration in Nursing; co-founder sexual abuse program Children's Hosp. Med. Center, Boston, 1977, cons., 1978; psychiat. nurse cons. Criminal Victimology Cons., Inc., Boston, 1978. Active, YMCA, Germantown, Pa.; vol. activities dir. Boys' Club, National City, Calif. Recipient Nat. Research Service award, 1981; cert. psychiat. nurse, psychotherapist, Mass.; cert. secondary sch. tchr., Pa. Mem. Am. Nurses Assn., Am. Orthopsychiat. Assn., Nurses United for Reimbursement of Services, Advanced Council on Psychiat. Mental Health Nursing (Am. Nurses Assn.), AAUW, Advocates for Child Psychiat. Nursing, Am. Sociol. Assn., Sigma Theta Tau (treas. 1966-67), Contbr. articles to profl. jours. Home: 2606 Purdue Ave Los Angeles CA 90064 Office: Calif State U 400 Golden Shore Long Beach CA 90802

VINESETT, ELIDA SANTO, infosystems specialist; b. Coco Solo, Republic of Panama; m. James C. Vinesett; children: Karen D., Richard J. BS, San Diego State U., 1979; MBA, Old Dominion U., 1986. Data processing computer op. County of San Diego, 1976-78; programmer I City of Chesapeake, Va., 1979-81; programmer analyst CDI Computer Dynamics, Virginia Beach, Va., 1981-82; sr. systems analyst CBN Christian Broadcasting, Virginia Beach, 1983—. Recording sec. Women's Aglow Fellowship, Chesapeake, 1986—, v.p., 1987-88, Concerned Women for Am., 1987; pres. PTA, San Diego, 1975; co-founder Women's Support Group, Chesapeake, 1988—. Mem. Nat. Assn. Female Execs., AAUW (chmn. exec. bd.), Women's Network of Hampton Rds. Lodge: Toastmasters (treas. speech club Norfolk chpt. 1988—). Home: 520 Peren Ave Chesapeake VA 23330 Office: CBN Christian Broadcasting Virginia Beach VA 23465

VINEYARD, GERRY LYNN LESTER, educator; b. Monroe, La., Aug. 28, 1938; d. A.J. and Mattie Lou (Oliver) Lester; B.A., NE La. U., 1959, M.A., 1963; student Saltillo Tchrs. Coll., Mex., Southwestern Theol. Sem., Ft. Worth; m. Percy Ray Vineyard, July 7, 1962; children—William Webster, Margaret Loraine, Elizabeth. Tchr. West Monroe (La.) Jr. High Sch., 1959-61, Crosley Elementary Sch., West Monroe, 1961-62, Ouachita (La.) Parish Jr. High Sch., 1963-65, Ponchatoula (La.) High Sch., 1968-69, Natalbany (La.) Bapt. Sch., 1970-74, Madisonville (La.) Jr. High Sch., 1975-80, Covington (La.) High Sch., 1980—. Nat. Def. Act grantee, 1960. Mem. Council Exceptional Children, Assn. Children with Learning Disabilities, La. Edn. Assn., NEA, DAR (state chmn. 1972-75, librarian 1976-78). Democrat. Baptist. Clubs: Les Mesdames, Womans Missionary Union. Office: PO Box 838 Covington LA 70440

VINSON, MARGARET CAROLYN, petroleum properties broker; b. Waco, Tex., May 29, 1942; d. Presley Ewing and Margaret Helen (Pond) V.; m. Robert C. L. Robertson II, Aug. 27, 1960 (div. July 1964); children—Lisa Lee Robertson Meador, Laura Ellen. Student U. Tex., 1960-61, Art Ctr. Sch., Los Angeles, 1962-63, Massey Bus. Coll., 1964, Inst. Energy Devel., Houston, 1980. Sec., chmn. bd. Continental Oil Co., Houston, 1964-68; exec. asst. Reading & Bates, Houston, 1969-71; prodn. coordinator King Resources Co., Denver, 1974-75; adminstrv. asst. Astrodamain Corp., Houston, 1976-78; exec. asst. Lucey Products Co., Houston, 1978-80; self-employed as petroleum properties broker, Houston, 1980—. Instr., Jefferson and Weld County 4-H, Colo., Denver, 1972-74; precinct chmn. Macey for Mayor Campaign, Houston, 1981; mem. steering com. Tim Hearns Benefit, Houston, 1982; vol. Am. Heart Assn., Houston, 1983. Mem. Am. Assn. Petroleum Landmen, Houston Assn. Petroleum Landmen, Corpus Christi Petroleum Assn. Presbyterian.

VINSON, SANDRA TIPTON, sales executive; b. San Pedro, Calif., July 30, 1951; d. Densial Owen and Bonnie Rhea (Lloyd) Tipton; m. Gary Wayne Wood, June 26, 1970 (div. 1981); 1 child, Rebekah Dawn; m. George William Vinson, Apr. 10, 1982. Student, State Coll. Ark., 1969-70, U. Ark., Little Rock, 1970, 79-81. Co-owner, mgr. Wood Pharmacy, Cabot, Ark., 1976-81; asst. mgr. BP's, Little Rock, 1981-83; sales mgr. The Creative Circle, Little Rock, 1983-84, Littleton, Colo., 1984-85; sales mgr. The Creative Circle, Marietta, Ga., 1985-86, regional sales dir., 1986—. Troop leader Girl Scouts U.S., Calico Rock, Ark., 1972-75; judge Cobb County Jr. Miss Pageant, Marietta, 1988; vol. Am. Cancer Soc., Marietta, 1988. Mem. C. of C., Bus. and Profl. Women. Democrat. Baptist. Home: 2238 Oakrill Ct Marietta GA 30062 Office: Creative Circle 15777 S Broadway Gardena CA 90248

VINTON, DOLORES (DEE) ANNE, corporation executive, consultant; b. Chgo., Oct. 8, 1930; d. Roy A. and Hattie Anne (Younger) Berg; m. Charles J. Vinton, Sept. 29, 1951 (div. 1968); children—Sharon Anne, Charles Daniel. Student Ariz. State U., 1967, Ednl. Inst. Am. Motel and Hotel Assn., 1977; diploma Wine Inst., San Francisco, 1974. Cert. in food service sanitation. Actress, Bobbie Ball Agy., Scottsdale, Ariz., 1966-77; recreation supr. pub. relations dept. City of Tempe (Ariz.), 1966-68; mgr. pub. facilities Sky Chefs, Tulsa and Phoenix, 1970-78; sr. food service dir. Saga Corp., San Francisco, 1978—, also job bank dir. for hiring handicapped, 1982—. Bd. dirs. Ariz. Cactus Pine council Girl Scouts U.S.A., 1961-64, dist. chmn., 1964; mem. com. Scottsdale Town Enrichment Program, 1965; mem. Mayor's Com. Hiring of Handicapped, San Francisco, 1983. Recipient Disting. Pub. Service award City of Scottsdale, 1965; Life Saving award City of Phoenix, 1970; cert. of merit Gov.'s Com. Hiring of Handicapped, 1979, 81; cert. of appreciation Careers Abound, 1982, award for support employment of disabled youth, 1983; named Calif. Small Employer of Yr., Calif. Gov.'s Com., 1982; named Employer of Yr., Goodwill Industries, 1982. Mem. AFTRA, Nat. Assn. Female Execs., Nat. Assn. Bus. and Profl. Women. Clubs: Commonwealth, Golden Gate Tennis (San Francisco). Home: 550 Battery Apt 2003 San Francisco CA 94111

VIOLETTE, DIANE MARIE, government agency administrator; b. Pontiac, Mich., Apr. 19, 1958; d. Bernard Desmond and Mary Virginia (Bartosh) V.; m. Glenn Martin Payette, Apr. 18, 1987. BA in Journalism, Mich. State U., 1980; postgrad., Air Force Inst. Tech., 1981-86; cert. in govt. contracts and mgmt., UCLA, 1987; postgrad., Calif. State U., Northridge, 1987—. Contract adminstr. Def. Contract Adminstrn. Services Mgmt. Area, Van Nuys, Calif., 1980-84, adminstrv. contract officer, 1984-88; pres. def. contracting Diane Violette & Assocs., Van Nuys, 1987—. Contbr. articles to profl. jours. Mem. Am. Businesswomen's Assn., Nat. Contract Mgmt. Assn., Kappa Tau Alpha.

VIPPERMAN, CAROL FAYE, consultant; b. Renton, Wash., Feb. 24, 1948; d. James Riley and Lydia Bobbyette (Caldwell) V.; divorced. BA, U. Wash., 1970. Service rep. Liberty Mut. Ins. Co., Seattle, 1970-72; group sales mgr. John A. Tetley Co., Seattle, 1972-76; regional sales mgr. Harrison Hotel, Seattle, 1976-78; pres. Carol Vipperman Inc., Seattle, 1978—; bd. advisers No. Sun, Inc., Lynnwood, Wash., 1983-84, W.I.S.E., Bellevue, Wash., 1984-85; mem. mktg. adv. bd. Seattle office Deloitte Haskins & Sells. Author: Solution to Sales Problems, 1983, Marketing You Services, 1987; contbr. articles to profl. jours. Bd. dirs. Alki Found., Seattle, 1984, Seattle Enterprise Ctr.; advocate Seattle Children's Home, 1984; chmn. Wash. State Small Bus. Improvement Council, 1986—; participant White House Conf. on Small Bus., 1986; mem. adv. bd. Sound Savs. & Loan, Washington State Commn. on Efficiency and Accountablity in Govt. Mem. Travellarians (pres. 1974-75), Sales and Mktg. Execs. (pres. 1980-81), Internat. Transactional Analysis Assn. (cert. 1982—), Women Bus. Owners (co-founder 1979-80), Greater Seattle C. of C. (vice chmn. 1984-86 bd. trustees). Democrat. Clubs: Seattle; Rainier. Office: 1932 1st Ave Suite 609 Seattle WA 98101

VIRGA, KAREN FAYE, physical therapist; b. San Jose, Calif., Apr. 14, 1951; d. Nicholas and Edna Faye (Bishop) Chimento; m. Richard Virga, June 22, 1975; children: Jason, Justin. BS, NYU, 1975; MA, Columbia U. Lic. phys. therapist, N.Y., Conn. Phys. therapist Burke Rehab. Ctr., White Plains, N.Y., 1975-79, Danbury (Conn.) Ortho. Assocs., 1980—; lab instr. neurobiology NYU, 1978-79; lectr. Danbury Orthopedic Assocs., 1983—; pvt. practice phys. therapy, N.Y. and Conn., 1975—; ptnr., officer Concepts in Total Health, Avon, Conn., 1986—; evaluation specialist Worklab, Inc., Danbury, 1988—; bd. dirs. Back Sch., Danbury Orthopedic Assocs., 1985—. Contbr. articles to profl. jours. Mem. Am. Phys. Therapy Assn., Arthritis Found., Paraplegic Found. Democrat. Home: 12 Kilian Dr Danbury CT 06811 Office: Danbury Orthopedic Assocs 73 Sandpit Rd Danbury CT 06811

VIRTUE, JOYCE SWAIN, nutritionist, educator, program director; b. San Antonio, Apr. 13, 1936; d. Gladstone Benjamin and Delphine (Tafolla) Penaloza; m. Nick Virtue, Sept. 16, 1963; children: Eugene Michael, David Alexis, Paul Nicholas. Student, San Antonio Coll., 1952; BA, PhD, Internat. U. Nutrition Edn., Huntington Beach, Calif.; postgrad., Internat. Coll. Applied Nutrition, 1981, Johns Hopkins U., 1984—. Clin. nutritionist, staff educator Optimum Health Labs., Encino, Calif., 1980; dir. nutrition and food sci. Ford-Kennedy Labs., Reseda, Calif., 1980-82; dir. nutritional therapeutics Nutritional Sci. Testing Labs., Sherman Oaks, Calif., 1982-85; intern Parkwood Community Hosp., Canoga Park, Calif., 1983-84; fellow Bryn Mawr (Pa.) Community Hosp., 1983-84; health educator Calif. State U., Northridge, 1981, various gynecologists, obstetricians; dir. nutritional therapeutics Silver Virtue Med. and Nutrition Group, Los Angeles; cons. Physicians Labs., Santa Monica, Calif. and N.Y.C., 1980-82, Lopapa Inst. of Allergy and Immunology, Los Angeles; past nutritionist, make-up person Mary Tyler Moore; appeared numerous radio and TV talk shows. Author (with Sally Struthers): The Natural Beauty Book, 1979; contbr. articles to profl. jours. Mem. Nat. Adv. Council Met. U. of Southwest, Phoenix. Recipient Golden Eagle award NOSOTROS, 1980. Mem. Am. Coll. Nutrition, Internat. Coll. Applied Nutrition, Internat. Acad. Med. Preventics, Am. Soc. Parenteral and Enteral Nutrition. Office: 11611 San Vicente Blvd Los Angeles CA 90049

VISCONTI, JANNA PEARL, lawyer, artist; b. N.Y.C., Dec. 17, 1952; d. Stanley Schwartz and Marion Sue (Wasserman) Goldstein; m. Richard D. Visconti, Dec. 31, 1985. B.F.A., Pratt Inst., 1975; J.D., St. John's U., 1979. Bar: N.Y. 1979, Ariz. 1982, Conn. 1987. Assoc. firm Rogers & Wells, N.Y.C., 1979-82, Snell & Wilmer, Phoenix, 1982-85, Cummings & Lockwood, Stamford, Conn., 1985—. Mem. Friends of Vol. Bur., Phoenix, 1983-84. Mem. ABA (real property section), N.Y. State Bar Assn., Nat. Assn. Bond Lawyers, State Bar Ariz., Episcopalian. Office: Cummings & Lockwood 10 Stamford Forum Stamford CT 06904

VITA, DIANA, aerobics instructor; b. N.Y.C., Aug. 22, 1955; d. Michael Joseph and Lillian Diana (Mandracchia) V. B.A., CUNY, 1978. Cert. aerobic instr. Instr. aerobics and slimnastics YMCA, Bklyn., 1981-83; owner, mgr. Diana Vita's Aerobic Dance Studio, Bklyn., 1983—. Instr., Sch. Settlement, Bklyn., 1982-83, 85, Mut. of N.Y. (MONY), N.Y.C., 1983, ITT, N.Y.C., 1983-86, Pratt Inst., Bklyn., 1985—. Mem. Aerobics and Fitness Assn. Am. Office: Diana Vita's Aerobic Dance Studio 776A Manhattan Ave Brooklyn NY 11222

VITA, JACQUELINE DUNN, legislative aide; b. Bklyn., Feb. 5, 1958; d. Richard William and Gertrude Ann (Zmudnovich) Martin; m. Thomas William Vita, Oct. 12, 1985. BA in Art Edn., Molloy Coll., 1980; postgrad., L.I. U., 1982-86. Credit interviewer Bloomingdale's, Garden City, N.Y., 1977-82; substitute tchr. Diocese of Rockville Ctr., N.Y., 1980; counselor fin. aid Molloy Coll., Rockville Ctr., 1980-81, counselor fin. aid and admissions, 1981-84, exec. dir. alumni affairs, 1984-88; legis. aide Sen. John R. Dunne, Garden City, N.Y., 1988—; L.I. rep. Area Ind. Colls., N.Y.C., 1982-84, N.Y. State Fin. Aid Adminstrn., N.Y.C., 1980-81; vice-chairperson N.Y.S. Bd. Higher Edn. Services Corp., Albany, 1979-81. Active Nassau County Rep. Coms., 1982—. Mem. Council for Advancement Higher Edn., Middle States Assn. (steering com. commn. on higher edn. 1984-86). Roman Catholic. Home: 166 Spencer Ave Lynbrook NY 11563

VITAL, TINA JEAN, chemical engineer; b. Atlantic City, Dec. 22, 1953; d. Andrew and Dorothy (Clark) Vital; B.S., U. Pitts., 1976; M.S. in Chem. Engring., Lehigh U., 1979; postgrad. U. Md., 1985—. Engring. intern Hoffman LaRoche, Inc., Nutley, N.J., summer, 1980; control engr. Exxon Chem. Ams., Baytown, Tex., 1980-83; applications engr. combustion engring. Simcon, Bloomfield, N.J., 1983-85. Mem. Soc. Women Engrs., Am. Inst. Chem. Engrs., Am. Chem. Soc., Nat. Soc. Profl. Engrs. Contbr. articles to profl. jours.

VITALE, ANNA M., construction company executive, real estate management executive; b. Newark, July 17, 1942; d. Andrew and Pearl (Chelak) Franchak; m. Frederick R. Vitale, May 7, 1961; children—F. Richard, J. Steven, J. Christipher. Student Trenton State Coll., 1967-68. Vice pres. Vitran, Inc., Allentown, N.J., 1972-80, pres., 1980—, also dir.; ptnr. Hampton Manor Ltd., Mt. Holly, N.J., 1983—, also dir.; mgr., owner LaChez Salon, Allentown, 1966-76, Colonial Manor Salon, Jacobstown, N.J., 1977-88. Mem. U.S. Trotting Assn., N.J. and Pa. Racing Commn., Am. Soc. Noteries, Internat. Platform Assn. Home: RD 1 Box 111-5 Wrightstown NJ 08562

VITALE, CONCETTA, college administrator, nurse; b. New Kensington, Pa., May 21; d. Theodore R. and Anna Marie (Pecoraro) V.; m. Joseph Lewis Hlafcsak, Mar. 19, 1983; children—Susan, Judith. Diploma in Nursing, Mercy Hosp. Sch. Nursing, 1960; B.S., U. Pitts., 1973, M.S. in Nursing, 1975, postgrad., 1985. Staff nurse Mercy Hosp., Pitts., 1960-61, 67-68, VA Hosp., Butler, Pa., 1961-62, VA Hosp., Pitts., 1962-67; faculty Catherine McAuley Sch. Practical Nursing, Pitts., 1968-73; pvt. duty nurse Mercy Hosp., Pitts., 1973-75; faculty U. Pitts., 1975-77; clin. specialist John J. Kane, Hosp., 1977-78; nurse clinician Western Psychiat. Inst. and Clinic, U. Pitts., 1978-81; dir. nursing Community Coll. Allegheny County-Boyce Campus, Monroeville, Pa., 1981-88; asst. dean instrn. Community Coll. Allegheny County, Center North, Pitts., 1988— ; mem. adv. com. Butler County Community Coll.; mem. craft adv. com. Forbes Rd. E. Area Vocat. Tech. Sch., Monroeville, 1981. Vol. Pitts. Action Against Rape, 1977, 78. Mem. Am. Nurses Assn., Pa. Assn. Assoc. Degree Nurse Educators (sec. 1983-87), Sigma Theta Tau (sec. Eta chpt. 1984-86). Roman Catholic. Avocations: skiing; hiking; biking. Home: 926 S Aiken Ave Pittsburgh PA 15232-2212 Office: Community Coll Boyce Campus Allegheny County 595 Beatty Rd Monroeville PA 15146

VITALE, LINDA BEIER, advertising agency executive; b. Dover, N.J., Oct. 27, 1944; d. Helmuth and Frieda (Griesbach) Beier; m. Lawrence C. Vitale, Aug. 27, 1972; 1 child, Leslie Catherine. BA, Roanoke Coll., 1966. Jr. copywriter Leber, Katz, Paccione, N.Y.C., 1967-69; promotional writer Doyle Dane Bernbach, N.Y.C., 1969-73, 75-76; copywriter DKG Advt., N.Y.C., 1973-75; promotional writer Wells, Rich, Greene Advt., N.Y.C., 1976-78, v.p., 1979-87; copy chief The Widmann Co., N.Y.C., 1987—; sr. copywriter Batton, Barton, Durstein & Osborne, N.Y.C., 1978-79. Recipient several awards N.Y. Art Dirs. Club. Republican. Lutheran. Home: 1 Kitchell Rd Convent Station NJ 07961 Office: The Widmann Co 12 E 41st St New York NY 10017

VITENAS, BIRUTE KAZLAUSKAS, systems engineer; b. Los Angeles, Feb. 12, 1949; d. Vincent and Valeria (Dambrauskaite) Kazlauskas; B.S. in Stats., Stanford U., 1970; M.S. in Ops. Research, Columbia U., 1972; postgrad. Rutgers U., 1976; m. Almis T. Vitenas, July 4, 1970; 1 son, Aleksas Joseph. Mem. of tech. staff-switching maintenance Bell Labs., Holmdel, N.J., 1970-71, mem. tech. staff PAR Radar Evaluation, Whippany, N.J., 1971-74, mem. tech. staff, operator services planning, Holmdel, 1974-77, supr. operator services planning, 1977-81, dept. head network project planning, 1981-83; asst. to v.p. customer systems AT&T Info. Systems, Lincroft, N.J., 1983-85; dir. tech. program analysis AT&T Bell Labs, 1985-86, exec. dir. resource planning, 1986—. Mem. Ops. Research Soc. Am., Am. Statis. Assn. Republican. Roman Catholic. Office: AT&T Bell Labs Holmdel NJ 07733

VITTADINI, ADRIENNE, fashion designer; b. Gyor, Hungary; came to U.S., 1957; d. Alexander and Aranka (Langhiel) Toth; m. Gian Luigi Maria Vittadini, 1972; 1 stepchild, Emanuele. Ed., Moore Coll. Art, Phila. Designer Rosanna-Warneco, N.Y.C., 1970-76; v.p. for design Kimberly Knitwear-Gen. Mills, N.Y.C., 1976-78; chmn. bd. Adrienne Vittadini Inc., N.Y.C., 1979—. Recipient Design award Retail Fashion Authorities Am., 1979, Outstanding Phila. Fashion Designer award Council for Labor and Industry, Phila., 1984, Coty Am. Fashion Critics award, 1984. Office: Adrienne Vittadini Inc 575 7th Ave New York NY 10018

VITTER, PATRICIA BUTLER, lawyer; b. Gainesville, Fla., Dec. 31, 1951; d. Robert Hardy and Charleton (Galloway) Butler; m. William R. Vitter, Dec. 2, 1978; 1 son, Robert S. B.S.Ed., Fla. State U., 1973, J.D., 1975. Bar: Fla. 1976. Jud. asst. 2d Dist. Ct. Apls., Lakeland, Fla., 1976-77; atty. Charles Mixon, Tampa, 1977-79; sole practice, Inverness, Fla., 1979-86; ptnr. Bradshaw, Mountjoy & Vitter, Inverness, 1986—. Bd. dirs. Withlacochee Area Legal Services, Ocala, Fla., 1980-82; trustee Central Fla. Community Coll., Ocala, 1984, vice chmn. bd. trustees, 1985-87, chmn. bd. trustees, 1987—; mem. regional citizens adv. council Withlacochee Regional Planning Council, 1982-84. Mem. Fla. Bar Assn., ABA, Citrus County Bar Assn., Tri County Bar Assn., Citrus County C. of C., Beta Sigma Phi. Democrat. Methodist. Club: Altrusa. Home: Henderson Trail Inverness Fl 32650 Office: 209 Courthouse Square PO Box 881 Inverness FL 32651

VITTI, MADELYN MARIE, accounting service company executive; b. Stamford, Conn., Jan. 17, 1960; d. Nazzareno James and Anna Marie (Forlenzo) V. B.B.A. in Acctg., U. No. Fla., 1982. Acctg. mgr. Shawnee Airlines, Miami, Fla., 1978-80; night auditor Inn at Baymeadows, Jacksonville, Fla., 1981-83; asst. cashier Capital Bank, Miami, 1983-85; founding pres. Acctg. for Small Bus., Inc., Jacksonville, 1985-87, chmn. bd., 1985, treas., 1985-86; v.p., acct. Acctg. for You, Inc., 1987— (purchaser Acctg. for Small Bus. Inc.). Mem. Nat. Soc. Pub. Accts., Fla. Assn. Indep. Accts. Republican. Lutheran. Avocations: swimming, tennis. Office: Accounting for You Inc 9140 Golfside Dr 4-S Jacksonville FL 32216

VIXIE, ANNE CHRISTINE, infosystems specialist; b. Whittier, Calif., Jan. 3, 1943; d. Orvin Leroy Vixie and Viola Jean (Sharp) Langowski; m. Gordon Allred Isbell, Apr. 13, 1960; children: Shannon, Gordon Jr., Allison. AA, Fullerton Coll., 1970; BA, Calif. State U., Fullerton, 1972, MLS, 1975. Acquisitions librarian Longview (Wash.) Pub. Library, 1974-76; communications specialist NW Pub. Power Assn., Vancouver, Wash., 1976-78; bus. resources supr. Lamb-Weston, Inc., Tigard, Oreg., 1978-84; owner Anne Vixie Bus. Research, Beaverton, Oreg., 1984-85; mgr. info. services AT&E Labs., Inc., Beaverton, 1985—. Mem. Spl. Libraries Assn., Wash. County Coop. Library, Oreg. Online Users Group. Republican. Unitarian. Office: AT&E Labs Inc 1400 NW Compton Dr#300 Beaverton OR 97006

VLAHAC, MARY ANN RITA, market research consultant, small business owner; b. Bridgeport, Conn., June 11, 1954; d. John S. and Catherine R. (Landor) V.; m. James Thomas Westerman, May 13, 1978; 1 child, Christopher James. A.S., Housatonic Community Coll., 1974; B.S., U. Conn., 1976; M.B.A., U. Bridgeport, 1980. Market research Remington Arms/du-Pont, Bridgeport, 1976-79; sr. market research staff Pitney Bowes, Stamford, Conn., 1979-86; mktg. research mgr. People's Bank, Bridgeport, 1986—; v.p. mktg. Mar-Kris Trading Co., Stratford, Conn., 1985—; owner Gewgaw, Stratford, 1980—; ptnr. Glass & Crafts, Bridgeport, 1980—. Stained glass artist. Adv., Housatonic Community Coll., 1985-86. Mem. U. Conn. Alumni Assn., U. Bridgeport Alumni Assn., Housatonic Community Coll. Alumni Assn., Conn. Crafts Guild, Stratford Hist. Soc. Avocations: art, music, classic film, acting, writing. Home: 545 Windsor Ave Stratford CT 06497

VLASSARA, HELEN, physician, educator, researcher; b. Athens, Greece, July 3, 1947; came to U.S., 1974; d. Vassilios and Asteria (Petropoulou) V.; m. Anthony Cerami, May 1, 1981. M.D., Med. Sch. Athens, 1973. Postdoctoral fellow Rockefeller U., N.Y.C., 1974-76, research assoc., 1980-82, asst. prof., 1983—; intern, resident in internal medicine Columbia U. Coll. Physicians and Surgeons, N.Y.C., 1976-79; endocrinology fellow N.Y. Med. Ctr., N.Y.C., 1980-82; physician assoc. Rockefeller U. Hosp., N.Y.C., 1981—; attending physician Cornell U. Med. Sch., N.Y.C., 1984—. Author research papers. Mem. Am. Coll. Physicians and Surgeons, Am. Diabetes Assn., N.Y. Clin. Diabetes Assn., European Assn. for Study of Diabetes. Office: Rockefeller U 1230 York Ave New York NY 10021

VOCHT, MICHELLE ELISE, lawyer; b. Detroit, Sept. 27, 1956. BA with honors, U. Mich., 1978; JD, Wayne State U., 1981. Bar: Mich., U.S. Dist. Ct. (ea. and we. dist.) Mich., U.S. Ct. Appeals (6th cir.), 1981. V.p., sec. Roy, Shecter & Vocht PC, Birmingham, Mich., 1981—. Mem. com. for re-election of current Mich. Supreme Ct. Justice, 1986, exec. bd. Birmingham Women's Community Ctr., 1987-88. Mem. ABA, Assn. Trial Lawyers Am., Mich. Trial Lawyers Assn., Women Lawyers Assn. Mich., Oakland County Trial Lawyers Assn (exec. bd. dirs. 1982-84, 88—), State Bar Assn. Mich. (chmn. gen. practice section 1984-86, sec. 1982-83, vice-chmn. 1983-84, mem. civil procedure com. 1982-84, assoc. mem. lawyers and judges assistance com., 1988—, hearing panelist atty. discipline bd., 1982—), Am. Inn of Ct. (barrister 1984-87). Roman Catholic. Home: 901 N Adams Birmingham MI 48008 Office: Roy Shecter & Vocht PC 877 S Adams Suite 302 Birmingham MI 48011

VOEKS, VIRGINIA WILNA, educator; b. Champaign, Ill., May 9, 1921; d. B. Forrest and Dorothy (Wade) V.; B.S. summa cum laude, U. Wash., 1943, M.S., 1944; Ph.D., Yale U., 1947; m. William McBlair IV. Research asso. Yale U., New Haven, 1944-45; asst. prof. U. Wash., 1947-49; asst. prof. San Diego State U., 1949-55, asso. prof., 1955-58, prof., 1958-71, prof. emeritus, 1971—. Recipient Pres. medal U. Wash., 1943; Sterling award Yale, 1945. Fellow N.Y. Acad. Scis., Am. Psychol. Assn. (sec.-treas. div. I 1965-77, editor Newsletter); mem. Western Psychol. Assn., AAUP, AAAS, Nat. Geog. Soc., Psychonomic Soc. (charter), UN Assn. San Diego, U.S. Olympic Soc., San Diego Ballet Assn. (charter), Jacques Cousteau Soc. (charter), Am. Bible Soc., Union of Concerned Scientists, Com. for Nuclear Responsibility, Save the Redwoods League (life), Nat. Wildlife Fedn., Assoc. Council Arts, Phi Beta Kappa, Sigma Xi, Psi Chi (pres. U. Wash. chpt. 1942-44), Phi Kappa Phi, Sigma Epsilon Sigma, Alpha Lambda Delta. Episcopalian. Club: Heritage. Author: On Becoming an Educated Person, 1957, 64, 70, 79; contbr. article to Internat. Ency. Social Scis., 1971; contbr. articles to profl. jours. Editorial bd. Teaching Psychology. Home: PO Box 877 4319 Explorer Rd La Mesa CA 92044 Office: San Diego State U Dept Psychology San Diego CA 92182

VOELCKERS, GWENN, health care facility executive; b. Mineola, N.Y., Sept. 20, 1954; d. William Warner and Barbara Anne (Walters) V. BS in Mgmt., Nazareth Coll., Rochester, N.Y., 1976. Pub. relations asst. Arts Council, Rochester, 1976-77; dir. gallery Genesee Country Mus., Mumford, N.Y., 1977-79; dir. pub. relations Planned Parenthood, Rochester, 1979-83; dir. community relations Rochester United Meth. Home (RUMH), 1983-85; v.p. mktg., devel. Wesley-on-East (formerly RUMH), 1985—; mem. Pub. Relations Soc. of Am., Rochester; mem. pub. relations com. United Meth. Assn. Health Welfare Ministries, Dayton, Ohio, 1987—. Contbr. articles The Gleaner mag., 1975-76. Chmn. dist. United Way, Rochester, 1985-87; vol. companion Compeer, 1982; bd. dirs., polit. action com. Family Planning Advocates, 1981-82. Mem. Nat. Soc. Fundraising Execs. (officer Rochester chpt. 1985), Pub. Relations Soc. Am. (program com. 1987—), Upstate N.Y. Hosp. Pub. Relations Council, Mktg. Communicators Rochester, Grantmakers Forum Rochester, C. of C. Women's Council, Rochester Area Assn. Homes Services for Aging (mktg. com. 1987—), Nazareth Coll. Alumni Assn. (bd. dirs. 1981). Office: Wesley-on-East 630 East Ave Rochester NY 14607-2194

VOELKER-CORBY, CATHERINE ANGELA, banker; b. St. Cloud, Minn., May 30, 1957; d. Francis Hilmer and Ludmila Angela (Padrnos) Voelker; m. Michael Edward Corby, Sept. 30, 1953; 1 child, Bennett Francis Corby. BA in Econs. and Bus., Macalester Coll., 1979; MBA in Mktg., Columbia U., 1983. Asst. to dir. Bus. Econs. Edn. Found., St. Paul, 1978-80; asst. pub. relations I. C. System, Inc., St. Paul, 1980-81; info. cons. Booz, Allen & Hamilton Inc., N.Y.C., 1983-85; v.p. Chem. Bank, N.Y.C., 1985-88, First Fidelity Bancorporation, Phila., 1988—; bd. dirs. Non-Traditional Employment for Women, N.Y.C. dir. pub. relations Berg for Congress campaign, St. Paul, 1979-80. George F. Baker scholar, 1978. Mem. Phi Beta Kappa, Beta Gamma Sigma. Club: MONI Ptnrship (presiding officer 1986—). Home: Sutton Towers #211-B Collingswood NJ 08107 Office: First Fidelity Bancorp Planning 10th Floor Fidelcor Broad and Walnut Sts Philadelphia PA 19109

VOGEL, MALVINA GRAFF, video and infosystems specialist; b. N.Y.C., May 5, 1932; d. Daniel Louis and Rose Miriam (Kanarick) Graff; m. Seymour Vogel, Jan. 27, 1952 (div.); children: Howard Ferris, Hal Steven, Scott Leslie, David Michael, Lisa Gayle. AB, Hunter Coll., 1952, postgrad., 1953. Cert. tchr., N.Y., N.J. Tchr. Norwood (N.J.) Pub. Schs., 1952-53, Farmingdale (N.Y.) Pub. Schs., 1953-55; researcher, writer Sy Vogel Realty, Commack, N.Y., 1965-67; writer-editor E.D.L.-McGraw Hill, N.Y.C., 1967-73; writer ednl. programs Ednl. Concepts, Inc., Babylon, N.Y., 1973-75, Instructional Concepts, Inc., New Hyde Park, N.Y., 1973-75; editor-in-chief Waldman-Playmore Pub. Co., N.Y.C., 1976-83; v.p. creative services Kid Stuff/GameTek, Inc., Plantation, Fla., 1983—. Author short stories, reading and social studies programs; adaptor lit. classics for children; editor over 200 books for children and adults, 20 quiz game shows for computer disks. Pres. Old Bethpage Elem. Sch. PTA, 1967-71; founder, pres. women's aux. Plainview, N.Y. Little League, 1968; scholarship chair Plainview-Old Bethpage Scholarship Fund, 1972-73. Scholarship for children's writing, Hofstra U., 1975. Mem. Nat. Assn. Female Execs., Soc. Children's Book Writers, Women in Communications, Soc. Preservation of English Lang. and Lit. Home: 9225 NW 45th St Sunrise FL 33351 Office: GameTek Inc 150 S Pine Island Rd Plantation FL 33324

VOGEL, MARY STALGAITIS, dentist, dental educator; b. Hazleton, Pa., Aug. 2, 1949; d. Joseph George and Sylvia (Nicholas) Stalgaitis. B.S., Pa. State. U., 1974; D.M.D., U. Pitts., 1974. Dental extern Home for Crippled Children, Pitts., 1973-75; pres. Mary Vogel, D.M.D., P.C., Pitts., 1976—; asst. clin. prof. Sch. Dental Medicine U. Pitts., 1974—; panel discussant on Women's Careers, Pa. Sect. Edn., Indiana U. Pa. Demonstrator dental procedures TV, 1981. Troop leader Girls Scouts U.S.A., Forrest Hills, P.A., 1983; active health fair booth Women's Task Force on Alcoholism, Pitts., 1982; keynote speaker Marian High., Tamaqua, Pa., 1981. Mem. Am. Assn. Women Dentists (v.p. Pitts. br. 1982-83), ADA, Pa. Dental Assn. (del. 1980), East End Pitts. Odontol. Soc. (pres. 1978-79), Acad. Oral Medicine, (Sr. Dental Student award 1974), U. Pitts. Dental Alumni (exec. com. 1977—), Nat. Assn. Women's Bus. Owners. Roman Catholic. Club: Equicess. Home and Office: Suite 340 Gateway Towers Pittsburgh PA 15222

VOGEL, WILLA HOPE, restaurateur; b. Valley Falls, Kans., Jan. 14, 1929; d. Henry Ray Tosh and Freda Alice (Brunton) Jackson; m. David L. Vogel, Dec. 25, 1943 (dec. 1987); children: Randall Daniel, Diana. Grad. high sch., Topeka, Kans. Owner, mgr. Drapery Shop, Topeka, 1956-68, Plantation Steak House, Topeka, 1962—, North Star Supper Club, Topeka, 1972—. Mem. Kans. Restaurant Assn., Topeka Restaurant Assn. Office: Plantation Steak House 6646 N Topeka Blvd Topeka KS 66617

VOGELGESANG, SANDRA LOUISE, federal government official; b. Canton, Ohio, July 27, 1942; d. Glenn Wesley and Louise (Forry) Vogelgesang; m. Geoffrey Ernest Wolfe, July 4, 1982. BA, Cornell U., 1964; MA, Tufts U., 1965, MA in Law and Diplomacy, 1966, PhD, 1971. With Dept. State, Washington, 1975—, policy planner for sec. state and European Bur., 1975-80, dir. Econ Analysis Office, Orgn. Econ. Coop. and Devel., 1981-82, econ. minister U.S. Embassy, Ottawa, Can., 1982-86, dep. asst. sec. Internat. Orgn. Affairs Bur., 1986—; bd. dirs. Edward R. Murrow Ctr. for Pub. Diplomacy, Fletcher Sch., Medford, Mass., 1978—; bd. advisors Am.'s Soc., N.Y.C., 1986—. Author: Long Dark Night of the Soul, The American Intellectual Left and the Vietnam War, 1974, American Dream-Global Nightmare: The Dilemma of U.S. Human Rights Policy, 1980. Recipient Meritorious Service awards, 1973, 74, 82, 83, 86, Disting. Honor award, 1976 Dept. State, Pres.' Disting. Service award, 1985. Mem. Council on Fgn. Relations. Home: 5330 Wapakoneta Rd Bethesda MD 20816 Office: Internat Orgn Affairs Bur 2201 C St NW Washington DC 20520

VOIGHT, ELIZABETH ANNE, lawyer; b. Sapulpa, Okla., Aug. 6, 1944; d. Robert Guy and Garnetta Ruth (Bell) Voight; m. Bodo Barske, Feb. 22, 1985; 1 child, Anne Katharine. B.A., U. Ark.-Fayetteville, 1967, M.A., 1969; postgrad. U. Hamburg (W.Ger.), 1966-67; J.D., Georgetown U., 1978. Bar: N.Y. 1979. Lectr. German, Oral Roberts U., Tulsa, 1968-69; tchr. German, D.C. pub. schs., 1971-73; instr. German, Georgetown U., Washington, 1973-74, adminstrv. asst. to dean Sch. Fgn. Service, 1974-77; law clk. Cole & Corette, Washington, 1977-78; atty. Walter, Conston, Alexander & Green, P.C., N.Y.C., 1978-88; sole practice, Munich, Fed. Republic Germany, 1988—. Translator articles for profl. jours. Chmn. regional screening Am. Field Service, N.Y.C., 1981-86. German Acad. Exchange Program fellow, 1966-67. Mem. Assn. Bar City N.Y., ABA, Internat. Fiscal Assn., Phi Beta Kappa, Kappa Kappa Gamma. Office: c/o Barske, Rottenbuchstrasse 529, 8032 Munich, Graefelfing Fed Republic Germany

VOIGHT, NANCY LEE (MRS. JAY VAN HOVEN), counseling psychologist; b. Kansas City, Mo., Nov. 24, 1945; d. Paul and Leona Alvina (Schultz) V.; B.A., Wittenberg U., 1967; M.A., Ball State U., 1971; Ph.D., Mich. State U., 1975; m. Jay Van Hoven, June 27, 1975; children—Joshua, Janna, Lydia. Tchr. lang. arts Ashland (Ohio) City Schs., 1967-68; tchr. English, Speedway (Ind.) City Schs., 1969; basic literacy instr. Army Edn. Center, Gelnhausen, W. Ger., 1969-70; individual assistance Bethel Home for Boys, Gaston, Ind., 1970-71; counselor Wittenberg U. Ohio, 1971-72; staff psychologist Ingham County Probate Ct., Lansing, Mich., 1972-74; asst. prof. U. N.C., Chapel Hill, 1975-79, counseling psychologist, 1976-79; psychologist for employee devel. Gen. Telephone Electronics, No. Region Hdqrs., Indpls., 1979-80; behavioral sci. coordinator Family Practice Center, Community Hosp., Indpls., 1980-82; media psychologist Sta. WIFE, Indpls., 1981-82; asst. dir. Chapel Hill Counseling Center, 1980-86; dir. Behavior Therapy Ctr., Indpls., 1982-86; treas. Med. Specialty Disability Ins. Corp., Indpls., 1982-86; psychologist Alternatives to Boys Sch., 1983-85; staff psychologist Meth. Hosp. Ind., 1985-86; psychologist Dept. Corrections State of Mich., Kincheloe, 1986—; advisor Sex Info. and Counseling Center, Chapel Hill, 1977-79. Chmn. housing bd. U. N.C., 1976-79. Office Edn. grantee, 1977-78, 78-80; Spencer Found. young scholars grantee. Mem. Am. Psychol. Assn., Ind. Psychol. Assn., Mich. Psychol. Assn., Assn. Advancement Behavior Therapy, Inst. Rational Living, Soc. Behavioral Medicine, Am. Assn. Marriage and Family Therapists. Lutheran. Author: Becoming, 1978; Becoming: Leader's Guide, 1978; Becoming Aware, 1979; Becoming Informed, 1979; Becoming Strong, 1979; also articles. Home: Box 326 DeTour Village MI 49725 Office: Kinross Corrections Facility Health Services Kincheloe AFB MI 49788

VOIGT, CYNTHIA, author; b. Boston, Feb. 25, 1942; d. Frederick C. and Elise (Keeney) Irving; married, 1964 (div. 1972); m. 2d Walter Voigt, Aug. 30, 1974; children: Jessica, Peter. B.A., Smith Coll., 1963. High sch. tchr. English Glen Burnie, Md., 1965-67; tchr. English Key Sch., Annapolis, Md., 1968-69, 71-79, tchr., chmn., from 1981. Author: (children's books) Homecoming, 1981, Tell Me If Lovers Are Losers, 1982, Dicey's Song, 1982 (Newbery medal 1983), The Callendar Papers, 1983, A Solitary Blue, 1983, Building Blocks, 1984, Jackaroo, 1985, The Runner, 1985, Come a Stranger, 1986, Izzy, Willy Nilly, 1986, Stories About Rosie, 1986, Sons From Afar, 1987, Tree By Leaf, 1988. Office: care Atheneum Pubs Juvenile Publicity Dept 866 3d Ave New York NY 10022 *

VOIVODAS, GITA KEDAR, market research professional; b. Baroda, Gujarat, India, May 2, 1942; came to U.S., 1962; d. Kedarnath and Emily Nirmala (Lederer) Kulshreshtha; m. Constantin Voivodas, May 12, 1972 (dec. 1973). BS, Maharaja Sayajirao U., 1960; postgrad., Cornell U., 1962; MA, Stanford U., 1963; PhD, Columbia U., 1977. Teaching fellow Child Devel. Ctr., N.Y.C., 1964-67; research asst. Tchrs. Coll. Columbia U., N.Y.C., 1972-76; asst. prof. Fordham U., N.Y.C., 1977-84; cons. Liebling Assocs., N.Y.C., 1985—; dir. research Louis Harris and Assocs., N.Y.C., 1986-87; pres. Profl. Papers Assocs., N.Y.C., 1983—; cons. Child Trends Inc., Washington 1979, dir. numerous profl. confs., N.Y.C. 1977-83. Guest editor: Jour. Edn. Psychol., 1976-84; contbr. articles to profl. jours. Cons. Sex Discrimination Assistance Ctr., Columbia U. 1979, Women's Action Alliance, 1979, Project Right-to-Read, Fordham U. 1979-80, N.Y. State Nat. Abortion Action League, 1986—, mem. exec. bd. Early Childhood Edn.

Council, 1977-84. Fellow U.S. Office Edn. 1972-76; grantee Fordham U. 1981. Mem. Am. Ednl. Research Assn., Soc. Research Child Devel., Nat. Soc. Study Edn., Am. Mktg. Assn., Nat. Assn. Female Execs. Office: Profl Papers Assocs 390 Riverside Dr #14B New York NY 10025

VOLK, HELEN D(OHRAU), lawyer; b. Cornwall, N.Y., Sept. 18, 1947; d. Francis Robert, Sr., and Marion (Mitchell) Dohrau. B.S. cum laude, SUNY-Potsdam, 1969; J.D., Albany Law Sch., 1973. Bar: N.Y. U.S. Dist. Ct. (no. dist.) N.Y., U.S. Supreme Ct. Tchr., Greece Central Sch. Dist., N.Y., 1969-70; atty. mcpl. affairs N.Y. State Dept. Audit and Control, Albany, 1973-75, sr. atty., 1979-81, legis. liaison, 1981; counsel N.Y. State Emergency Control Bd. for City of Yonkers, Albany, 1975-79; asst. counsel N.Y. State Edn. Dept., Albany, 1981—; mem. com. on character and fitness, 3d Jud. Dept., Albany, 1980—; adj. prof. Russell Sage Coll., Troy, N.Y., 1978-80. Contbr. article to legal publ. Vol. March of Dimes, Latham, N.Y., 1980-84, pub. TV Sta. WMHT-TV, Schenectady, 1979—; soloist Hamilton Presbyn. Ch., Calvary Meth. Ch.; community vol. coordinator Singles Outreach Support; bd. dirs. Point of Woods Condominiums, 1984—, chmn. litigation com., 1986—, pres., 1987—. Featured alumna SUNY-Potsdam Alumni Assn., 1983. Mem. N.Y. State Bar Assn. (mcpl. law sect. chmn. 1983-85, ho. of dels. 1985-87, 1st vice chair and fiscal officer 1981-83, 2d vice chair 1979-81, sec. 1978-79, exec. com. 1976-87, membership com. 1987—, media awards com. 1987—), Women's Bar Assn. State of N.Y. (chpt. organizer 1977, v.p. 1983-84, legis. chair 1982-83, dir. 1977-82), Am. Soc. Pub. Adminstrn., Exec. Women in Govt. Democrat. Mem. Reformed Ch. Am. Clubs: Zonta (bd. dirs. Albany 1980-82, 83-85), Bus. and Profl. Women, Kripalu Yoga Fellowship. Office: NY State Education Dept 138 EB Albany NY 12234

VOLK, PATRICIA GAY, advertising company executive, writer; b. N.Y.C., July 16, 1943; d. Cecil Sussman and Audrey Elaine (Morgen) Volk; m. Andrew Blitzer, Dec. 21, 1969 (div.); children—Peter Morgen, Polly Volk. B.F.A. cum laude, Syracuse U., 1964; student, Sch. Visual Arts, N.Y.C., 1968, New Sch., N.Y.C., 1975, Columbia U., 1977—. Art dir. Appelbaum & Curtis, N.Y.C., 1964-65, Seventeen Mag., Triangle Publs., N.Y.C., 1966-68; copywriter Doyle, Dane, Bernbach, Inc., N.Y.C., 1969—, also sr. v.p., creative mgr., 1969-87, sr. v.p.- assoc. creative dir., 1987—. Author: The Yellow Banana (Word Beat Press Fiction Book award 1984), 1985, White Light, 1987; contbr. articles and short stories to profl. and popular publs. Recipient Stephen E. Kelly award, 1983, various Andy, Clio, Effie and One Show awards, 1970—. Mem. Author's Guild.

VOLKERT, DORIS CAMPBELL, microbiologist; b. Youngstown, Ohio, Apr. 1, 1923; d. Frank Dickson and Frances Fitzgerald (Baker) Campbell; B.S., Pa. State U., 1944; M.S. in Bacteriology, U. Pitts., 1950; m. Charles Fredric Volkert, Oct. 11, 1947; children—Fredric Campbell, Christy Campbell. Research asst. N.Y. State Dept. Health, Albany, 1944-48; research fellow West Penn Hosp., Pitts., 1948-50; office mgr. West Penn Dailies, Gibsonia, 1960-64; assoc. prof. biology Monmouth Coll., West Long Branch, N.J., 1965—; microbiologist Paul Kimball Hosp., Lakewood, N.J., 1970—. Pres., North Suburban Fine Arts League, Richland, Pa., 1958-59. NASA grantee, 1960-61. Mem. Am. Soc. Med. Tech., AAUP, N.Y. Acad. Sci., Am. Soc. Microbiology, Am. Women in Sci., Theobald Smith Soc., Phi Sigma, Beta Beta Beta. Clubs: Monmouth College Faculty, Zonta. Home: 2031 New Bedford Rd Spring Lake Heights NJ 07762 Office: Monmouth Coll Biology Dept Cedar Ave West Long Branch NJ 07764

VOLKIN, HILDA APPEL, artist, sculptor. BS, Mass. Coll. Art; MAT, Radcliffe Coll.; postgrad., UCLA, Tamarind Inst., Albuquerque. Dir. Fuller Lodge Art Ctr., Los Alamos, N.Mex. One- and two-person shows include Mass. Coll. Art, Boston, Gov.'s Gallery, Santa Fe, Mayville (N.D.) State Coll., U. Portland, Oreg.; group shows include Cleve. Mus. Art, Santa Fe Festival of the Arts, Bergen Community Mus., Paramus, N.J., Mus. Albuquerque, Gov.'s Gallery, State Capitol, N.Mex., Mus. Fine Arts, Santa Fe, Printmakers, SPAR Nat., Shreveport, La.; prin. works include Regal Plastics Co., Albuquerque, N.Mex. State U., Las Cruces, Congregation Albert, Albuquerque; represented in permanent collections Cleve. Mus. Art (awards), Mus. Albuquerque, U. N.Mex. Art Mus., Massillon (Ohio) Mus. (awards), Beth Israel-West Temple, Cleve., Los Alamos High Sch., Los Alamos Nat. Lab., Pub. Service Co. N.Mex., Sunwest Bank, Albuquerque, Moncor Bank, Albuquerque, Albuquerque Bank, also pvt. collections. Recipient awards Nat. Assn. Women Artists, Canton (Ohio) Art Inst., Purchase award. Mem. Albuquerque Mus. Soc. Layerists-Multi Media.

VOLKMANN, FRANCES COOPER, psychologist, educator; b. Harlingen, Tex., May 4, 1935; d. Edward O. and Elizabeth (Bass) C.; m. John Volkmann, Nov. 1, 1958; children—Stephen Edward, Thomas Frederick. A.B. magna cum laude, Mt. Holyoke Coll., 1957; M.A., Brown U., 1959, Ph.D., 1961; DSci., Mt. Holyoke Coll., 1987. Research assoc. Mt. Holyoke Coll., South Hadley, Mass., 1964-65; lectr. U. Mass., Amherst, 1964-65, Smith Coll., Northampton, Mass., 1966-67; asst. prof. Smith Coll., 1967-72, assoc. prof., 1972-78, prof. psychology, 1978—, dean faculty, 1983—; vis. assoc. prof. Brown U., Providence, 1974, vis. prof., 1978-82; vis. scholar U. Wash., Seattle, summer 1977. Contbr. articles to profl. jours. Trustee Chatham Coll., 1987—. USPHS fellow, 1961-62; NSF grantee, 1974-78; Nat. Eye Inst. grantee, 1978-82. Fellow Am. Psychol. Assn., AAAS, Optical Soc. Am.; mem. Eastern Psychol. Assn., Soc. Neurosci., Psychonomic Soc., Assn. Research in Vision and Ophthalmology. Home: 40 Arlington St Northampton MA 01060 Office: Smith Coll Northampton MA 01063

VOLLAND, CAROL TASCHER, financial services executive; b. Morris, Ill., Mar. 23, 1935; d. Murl Elvyn and Helen Marie (Lindquist) Tascher; m. George William Volland, Aug. 12, 1978. Student Monmouth Coll., 1953-55; B.S. in Interior Design, U. Ill., 1957; postgrad. Art Inst. Chgo. Evening Sch., 1959-62. Lic. real estate broker, ins. and securities broker, Colo., Ill. Archtl. and interior designer Peoples Gas Light & Coke Co., Chgo., 1957-65, consumer lectr., corp. architect and interior designer, 1965-70, dir. home planning bur., 1970-74; corp. fashion coordinator Ozite Corp. div. Brunswick Corp., Libertyville, Ill., 1974-75, dir. pub. relations, 1975-77, contract sales mgr., 1977-78; pres. Volland & Assocs., Lakewood, Colo., 1982—; mem. corp. responsibilities bd. Brunswick Corp. Internat., 1976-77. Author: Creative Moneystretchers for the Home, 1973. Mem. Nat. Home Fashions League (exec. v.p. 1977-78), Am. Soc. Interior Designers, Women in Communications, LWV, Nat. Trust Hist. Preservation, Genesee Found. Republican. Methodist. Club: Altrusa of Jefferson County. Home: 1962 Montane Dr E Golden CO 80401 Office: Volland and Assocs 143 Union Blvd Suite 900 Lakewood CO 80228

VOLPE, LORETTA ANN, advertising agency executive, lecturer; b. N.Y.C., Feb. 27, 1954; d. Eugene Francis and Marie Antoinette (Pati) Volpe. A.S., S.I. Coll., 1974; B.B.A., Bernard Baruch Coll., 1976, M.B.A., 1982. Media planner Ted Bates, N.Y.C., 1975-77; media supr. Foote, Cone & Belding Advt. Agy., N.Y.C., 1977-81; dir. planning and media ops. SSC&B Advt. Agy., N.Y.C., 1981-88; sr. v.p., dir. media Lintas, N.Y.C., 1988—; adj. lectr. Bernard Baruch Coll., N.Y.C., 1978-83. Mem. Bernard Baruch Coll. Alumni Assn. of N.Y.C. (bd. dirs. 1979—). Democrat. Roman Catholic. Office: Lintas New York 1 Dag Hammerskjold Plaza New York NY 10017

VOLTZ, JEANNE APPLETON, magazine editor, writer, food consultant; b. Collinsville, Ala., Nov. 12, 1920; d. James Lamar and Marie (Sewell) Appleton; m. Luther Manship Voltz, July 31, 1943 (dec. Aug. 1977); children—Luther Manship, Jeanne Marie. A.B., U. Montevallo, Ala., 1942. Corr., The Birmingham (Ala.) News, 1939-42; reporter The Press-Register, Mobile, Ala., 1942-45; reporter, feature writer The Miami Herald, 1947-53, food editor, 1953-60; food editor Los Angeles Times, 1960-73, Woman's Day, N.Y.C., 1973-84; free-lance writer, food cons., N.Y.C., 1984—; instr. wine and food in civilization UCLA, 1972-73; expert witness Senate Com. on Nutrition and Health, Ft. Lauderdale, Fla., 1980; adj. prof. Home Econs. Hotel Mgmt. NYU, 1987-88. Author: The California Cookbook, 1970 (Tastemaker award 1970); The Los Angeles Times Natural Foods Cookbook, 1974; The Flavor of the South, 1976 (Tastemaker award 1976), An Apple A Day, 1983; Barbecued Ribs and Other Great Feeds, 1985. Mem. Met. Mus. Art, N.Y.C., 1975. Recipient Vesta award Am. Meat Inst., 1962-72; Alumni of Yr. award U. Montevallo, 1981. Mem. Les Dames d'Escoffier (dir. 1976, pres. 1985-86), Inst. Food Technologists, Soc. Nutrition Edn., Women in Communication, Soc. Women Geographers, Internat. Assn. Cooking Profls., N.Y. Acad. Scis., Phi Tau Sigma. Democrat. Methodist.

VON BUDDE, BRIGITTE ROSEMARIE, translator, librarian; b. Frankfurt, Fed. Republic Germany, Sept. 13, 1952; came to U.S., 1973.; BA, Norwich U., 1977; MLS, SUNY, Albany, 1978. Librarian Murray (Ky.) State U., 1981-82, Memphis State U., 1983-84, N.D. State U., Fargo, 1984-86; translator Fargo, 1982—; cons. U. Fla. Astronomy Lab., Gainesville, 1980. Mem. Am. Translators Assn. Home and Office: 812 7th St N Fargo ND 58102

VON DER HEYDE, JANE COWAN, lawyer; b. N.Y.C., Apr. 3, 1949; d. Matthew Jennings and Camilla (Cowan) von der H.; m. David Morrison Lindley, June 12, 1971; children—Camilla, Carolyn. B.A., Barnard Coll., 1971; J.D., Boston U., 1974. Bar: N.Y., 1975. Assoc., Skadden Arps Slate Meagher & Flom, N.Y.C., 1974-80; v.p. and gen. counsel Gen. Occidental Inc. and related cos., N.Y.C., 1980-84; sr. v.p., gen. counsel G.O. Holdings, Mgmt. Inc. and related cos., N.Y.C., 1984—; dir. Grand Union Co., Elmwood Park, N.J., 1982—. Editor Boston U. Law Rev., 1973-74. Mem. ABA, Assn. Bar City N.Y. Office: GO Holdings Mgmt Inc 650 Fifth Ave New York NY 10019

VON DOHRMANN, JEAN ANN, finance company executive; b. Aitkin, Minn., Jan. 3, 1933; d. Gordon Richard and Almira Esther (Youngberg) Tully; m. Harry Robert Ellis, Aug. 11, 1951 (div. Nov. 1967); children: Bradley Dale Ellis, Jeffrey Duane Ellis, Susan Leslie Ellis; m. Kurt Karl von Dohrmann, Dec. 22, 1967 (dec.). Student, San Antonio Coll., 1964-66; BA, U. Alaska, 1975. With admissions and med. records dept. USPHS Hosp., Barrow, Alaska, 1965-66; sec., bookkeeper Fuller O'Brien Corp., Anchorage, 1966-68; office mgr. Comml. Contractors Inc., Anchorage, 1968-74; staff acct. Mukluk Frieght Lines, Anchorage, 1975; property mgr. Hayes Alm Investments, Anchorage, 1975-81; bus. mgr. Joe L. Hayes Investments, Anchorage, 1981—; legis. aide Speaker of House Joe Hayes, Juneau, Alaska, 1983; bd. dirs. Alaska Continental Bank, Anchorage; treas., bd. dirs. Holden, Hackney & Breeze Inc., Anchorage, 1987—. Commr. Alaska Commn. Status Women, Anchorage, 1978-81; mem. Mayor's Budget Adv. Commn., Anchorage, 1980-82; chmn. dist. 12 Anchorage Reps., 1982-85. Mem. Am. Soc. Women Accts. (pres. 1983-84), Rep. Assn. Bus. and Profl. Women, Horizons Unltd. (Anchorage pres. 1979-80). Home: 1405 W 16th Ave Anchorage AK 99501 Office: Joe L Hayes Investments 307 E Northern Lights #201 Anchorage AK 99503

VON FURSTENBERG, DIANE SIMONE MICHELLE, fashion designer; b. Brussels, Belgium, Dec. 31, 1946; came to U.S., 1969; d. Leon L. and Liliane L. (Nahmias) Halfin; m. Eduard Egon von Furstenberg, July 16, 1969 (div.); children—Alexandre, Tatiana. Student, U. Madrid, 1965-66, U. Geneva, 1966-68. Founder, pres. Diane von Furstenberg Studio, N.Y.C., 1970—; pres. Diane Von Furstenberg Ltd., N.Y.C. Office: Diane Von Furstenberg Studio 745 Fifth Ave 24th Floor New York NY 10151 *

VON GENCSY, EVA, dancer, choreographer, educator; b. Csongrad, Hungary, Mar. 11, 1924; came to Can., 1948; d. Joseph and Valery Von G.; m. John S. Murray, May 13, 1957 (div. 1967). Student V.G. Troyanoff, Russian Ballet Acad., Budapest, Hungary, 1934-41, Szineszegyesuleti Iskola (Theater Sch.), 1941-44; diploma Royal Acad. Dance, London, 1953. Solo debut Salzburg Landes Theater, Austria, 1945-47; soloist Royal Winnipeg Ballet, Can., 1948-53; with Ballets Chiriaeff TV Co. (name changed to Les Grands Ballets Canadiens), 1953-57; TV performer, 1957-70; jazz instr. Banff Sch. Fine Arts, summers 1962-75; founder, dir. jazz workshop Saidye Bronfman Ctr., Montreal, Que., Can., 1965-72; with Les Grands Ballets Canadiens, 1962-72; co-founder, artistic dir., resident choreographer Les Ballets Jazz de Montreal Sch. and Co., 1972-79; choreographer; adjudicator dance festivals. Past bd. dirs. Dance in Can. Recipient Best Dancer award French TV, 1967, Queen's medal, 1977. Mem. L'Union des Artistes, ACTRA and Equity (hon.). Home: 3650 Mountain St Apt 508, Montreal, PQ Canada H3G 2A8

VON HOLT, LAEL POWERS, psychotherapist, psychiatric social worker; b. Boston, Apr. 9, 1927; d. Merritt Adams and Rea Francisca (Hunt) Powers; BA, U. Mass., 1950; MSW, U. Mo., 1972, postgrad., 1978; postgrad. Menninger Found., Topeka, 1977-85; m. Henry William Von Holt, Jr., Sept. 18, 1954; children—Gardner, Dudley, Edward. Psychiat. social worker N.Y. Dept. Mental Hygiene, Wingdale, 1950-51, Mass. Dept. Mental Health, Worcester, 1951-54; instr., social worker U. Oreg., Eugene, 1954-59; psychiat. social worker Mo. Dept. Mental Health, Fulton State Hosp., 1973-81, Columbia (Mo.) Regional Hosp. Psychiat. Services, Inc., 1977-82, Family Mental Health Ctr., Jefferson City, Mo., 1982—; field instr. U. Mo., Columbia, 1988. Bd. dirs. PTA, 1970-74, 77-78; mem. health com. Boone County Community Services Council, 1975-76; vol. Meals on Wheels, 1972-73, 76-79; den mother Boy Scouts Am., 1968-69, 71-72; mem. by-laws com. Springdale Neighborhood Assn., 1977. Diplomate Internat. Acad. of Behavioral Medicine Counseling and Psychotherapy; named Social Worker of Yr. Cen. Mo., 1986. Mem. Nat. Assn. Social Workers, Acad. Cert. Social Workers, Registry Clin. Social Workers, LWV (city council observor 1976-82, chmn. local action com. 1979-80, sec. 1974-77, chmn. Observer Corps 1981-83, chmn. com. mental health 1988—), Kappa Kappa Gamma. Republican. Methodist. Club: Stephens Coll. Faculty Wives (pres. 1979-80). Home: 378 Crown Point Columbia MO 65203 Office: Family Mental Health Ctr 1905 Stadium Jefferson City MO 65101

VON RAFFLER-ENGEL, WALBURGA, linguist, kinesicist, educator; b. Munich, Germany, Sept. 25, 1920; came to U.S., 1949, naturalized, 1955; d. Friedrich J. and Gertrud E. (Kiefer) von R.; m. A. Ferdinand Engel, June 2, 1957; children: Lea Maxine, Eric Robert von Raffler. D.Litt., U. Turin, Italy, 1947; M.S., Columbia U., 1951; Ph.D., Ind. U., 1953. Freelance journalist 1949-58; mem. faculty Bennett Coll., Greensboro, N.C., 1953-55, Morris Harvey Coll., Charleston, W.Va., 1955-57, Adelphi U., CUNY, 1957-58, NYU, 1958-59, U. Florence, Italy, 1959-60, Istituto Post Universitario Organizzazione Aziendale, Turin, 1960-61, Bologna Center of Johns Hopkins U., 1964, Vanderbilt U., Nashville, 1965—; prof. linguistics Vanderbilt U., 1977-85, prof. emerita, sr. research assoc. Inst. Pub. Policy Studies, 1985—, dir. linguistics program, 1978-86; chmn. com. on linguistics Nashville U. Ctr., 1974-79; Italian NSF prof. Psychol. Inst. U. Florence, Italy, 1986-87; prof. NATO Advanced Study Inst., Cortona, Italy, 1988; prof. linguistics Shanxi U., Peoples Republic China, 1985; vis. prof. U. Ottawa, Ont., Can., 1971-72, Inst. for Lang. Scis., Tokyo, 1976; grant evaluator NEH, NSF, Can. Council; manuscript reader Ind. U. Press, U. Ill. Press, Prentice-Hall; cons. Trinity U., Simon Frazer U. Author: Il prelinguaggio infantile, 1964, The Perception of Nonverbal Behavior in the Career Interview, 1983, 2d edit., 1985; co-author: Language Intervention Programs 1960-74, 1975; editor, co-editor 12 books; author film and videotape; contbr. over 300 articles to profl. and popular publs. Recipient grants from Am. Council Learned Socs., grants from NSF, grants from Can. Council, grants from Ford Found., grants from Kenan Venture Fund, grants from Japanese Ministry Edn., grants from NATO, grants from Finnish Acad., grants from Meharry Med. Coll., grants from Internat. Sociol Assn., grants from Internat. Council Linguists, grants from Tex. A&M U., grants from Vanderbilt U., grants from others. Mem. AAUP, Internat. Linguistics Assn., Linguistic Soc. Am. (chmn. Golden Anniversary film com. 1974) Internat. Sociol. Assn. (session chmn. profl. conf. 1983), Internat. Assn. for Applied Linguistics (com. on discourse analyses, sessions chmn. 1978), Lang. Origins Soc. (exec. com. 1982—, chmn. internat. congress, 1987), Internat. Sociol. Assn. (research com. for sociolinguistics, session co-chmn. internat. conf. 1983), Internat. Assn. for Study of Child Lang. (v.p. 1975-78, chmn. internat. conf. 1972), Inst. for Nonverbal Communication Research (workshop leader 1980-81), Tenn. Conf. on Linguistics (pres. 1976), Southeastern Conf. on Linguistics (hon. mem. 1985), Semiotic Soc. Am. (organizing com. Internat. Semiotics Inst. 1981), Kinesics Internat. (pres. 1988). Office: Vanderbilt Univ Box 26B Nashville TN 37235

VON STADE, FREDERICA, mezzo soprano; b. Somerville, N.J., June 1, 1945; m. Peter Elkus, 1973; children: Jennie, Lisa. Student, Mannes Coll. Music, N.Y.C., Ecole Mozart, Paris. Former nanny, salesgirl; sec. Am. Shakespeare Festival. Debut in Die Zauberfloete with Met. Opera, 1970, later resident mem.; appeared with opera cos. including Paris Opera, San Francisco Opera, Salzburg Festival, London Royal Opera, Spoleto Festival, Boston Opera Co., Santa Fe Opera, Houston Grand Opera, La Scala; recital artist, soloist with symphony orchs.; appeared in operas The Marriage of Figaro, Faust, The Magic Flute, Don Giovanni, Tales of Hoffman, Rigoletto, Der Rosenkavalier, The Seagull, Werther, The Barber of Seville; albums Frederica Von Stade Sings Mozart-Rossini Opera Arias, French Opera Arias, Pelleas and Melisande, Idomeneo, La Sonnambula. Mem. Am. Guild Mus. Artists. Roman Catholic. Office: care Columbia Artists Mgmt 165 W 57 St New York NY 10019

VON ZWEHL, JOANNE, real estate executive; b. Flushing, N.Y., Sept. 27, 1959; d. Joseph and Noreen (O'Gorman) Von Z. BBA, Ft. Lewis Coll., 1981. Lic. realtor, real estate broker. Loan cons. Verex Assurance, Inc., Jericho, N.Y., 1981-83; prin. various real estate corps., N.Y.C., 1982-84; pres. All Island Appraisal Firm, Melville, N.Y., 1984—, All Island Building Corp., Melville, N.Y., 1984—; pres., broker Cayman Realty, Melville, 1984—; pres., constrn. supr. CMS Quality Devel. Corp., Melville, 1986—; pres. R.D.A. Enter of N.Y., Farmingdale, N.Y., 1987—; owner Varn Products Co. Ltd, Manchester, Eng., 1982—, Varn Products Co., GMBH, Dusseldorf Fed. Republic. Germany, 1982—; broker State of N.Y. Dept. Real Estate, 1983—. Fellow Nat. Assn. Female Execs.; mem. Animal Protection Inst. of Am., N.Y. State Assoc. Realtors, Inc., Multiple Listing Service of L.I., Inc., Am. Power Boat Assn. Republican. Roman Catholic. Home: 12 Cross St Port Washington NY 11050 Office: RDA Enter of NY 431 Conklin St Farmingdale NY 11735

VOORHIES, BARBARA, anthropology educator. BS in Geology magna cum laude, Tufts U., 1961; PhD in Anthropology, Yale U., 1969. Lectr. So. Conn. State Coll., New Haven, 1969; asst. prof. San Diego State Coll., 1969-70; vis. prof. U. Calif., Santa Barbara, 1970-71, asst. prof., 1971-77, assoc. prof., 1977-82, prof., 1982—, chair dept. anthropology, 1985-87; field asst. U.S. Geol. Survey, 1961; research asst. Peabody Mus. Natural History, Yale U., 1963-65; with archeol. survey Caribbean Research Ctr., Guatemala; with excavations dept. anthropology Yale U., San Felipe, Guatemala, 1966-68; archeol. researcher NSF, Chiapas, Mex., 1973, 78-79, New World Archeol. Found., 1977, Nat. Geog. Soc., Chiapas, 1981, 83, 88. Author (with M. Kay Martin): La Mujer: Un Enfoque Antropológico, 1978; editor spl. issue Am. Antiquity, 1977. Fellow Am. Anthrop. Assn.; mem. Soc. for Am. Archaeology, Sociedad Mexicana Antropología, Sigma Xi (pres. local chpt. 1981-82). Office: U Calif Santa Barbara Dept Anthropology Santa Barbara CA 93106

VOORLAS, LANAY LUSSIER, systems control specialist; b. Racine, Wis., Aug. 17, 1952; d. Lawrence Joseph and Evelyn Marie (Howe) Lussier; m. Peter Gust Voorlas, Sept. 7, 1975. Student pub. schs., Racine. Records clk. Wis. Natural Gas Co., Racine, 1972-74, systems control specialist, 1974—. Home: 3171 Lathrop Ave Racine WI 53405 Office: Wis Natural Gas Co 233 Lake Ave Racine WI 53401

VORBEAU, BARBARA ELAINE, corporate librarian; b. Laconia, N.H., Mar. 19, 1943; d. Raymond Sheldon and Grace Josephine (Moses) Kimball; m. David Vorbeau, Nov. 1, 1964 (div. 1983); children: Joyce Elaine, Judy Elizabeth. BEd, Plymouth (N.H.) State Coll., 1965; AA in Library Sci., U. N.H., 1979; MLS, U. R.I., 1983. Library vol. Goffstown (N.H.) Sch. Dist., 1973-76; library tech. asst. Merrimack Valley Coll., U. N.H., Manchester, 1976-78; library asst. N.H. State Library, Concord, 1978-82, Wang Inst. Library, Tyngsboro, Mass., 1982-83; library tech. asst. Wang Labs., Lowell, Mass., 1983; serials/document delivery librarian Digital Equipment Corp., Merrimack, N.H., 1984—; cons. Goffstown Congl. Ch. Library, 1980-82. mem., chmn. Goffstown Mothers Club, 1974-80; mem. Goffstown Congl. Ch. Choir, 1977-88, ch. sch. tchr., mem. Mission Com., 1986-88. Mem. N.H. Library Assn. (spl. libraries group 1986—), Spl. Libraries Assn., Beta Phi Mu. Lodge: Order Eastern Star. Office: Digital Equipment Corp MK01-1/K11 Continental Blvd Merrimack NH 03054

VOSNIADOU-PAPANICOLAS, STELLA, psychologist; b. Athens, Greece, Nov. 26, 1946; came to U.S. in 1967.; d. Socrates and Alice Vosniadou; m. Costas N. Papanicolas; children: Lito, Irene. BA, Brandeis U., 1971; MA, Columbia U., N.Y.C., 1973; PhD, Clark U., 1979. Asst. prof. Ctr. Study Reading U. Ill., Champaign, 1979—. Editor: Similarity and Analogical Reasoning, 1987. Contbr. articles to profl. jours. Mem. Am. Edn. Research Assn., Soc. Research Child Devel., Am. Psychol. Assn. Office: U Ill 51 Gerty Dr Champaign IL 61820

VOSS, CAROLYN JEAN, nursing educator; b. Battle Creek, Mich., Dec. 28, 1937; d. Melvin O. and Ruth A. (Armantrout) Buck; m. Calvin W. Voss, Sept. 17, 1978. B.S. in Nursing, Walla Walla Coll., 1973; M.A. in Nursing, Ball State U., 1975, Ph.D. in Nursing Adminstrn. and Health Edn., Columbia Pacific U., 1983. ICU staff relief charge nurse Portland Adventist Hosp., 1971-72; ICU charge nurse, staff nurse Kettering Med. Ctr., 1973-74; instr. Andrews U., Berrien Springs, Mich., 1975-77; asst. dir. nursing Hinsdale Hosp. (Ill.), 1977-78; instr. nursing St. Luke's Sch. Nursing, Racine, Wis., 1978-86; cons. VNA, Racine, 1986—; instr. Mifton Coll., 1979-82, Mt. Sinai Coll., Ladysmith, Wis., 1983. Author: Poetry for High School Studies, 1955. Bd. dirs. Racine chpt. Am. Cancer Soc., 1980; instr. CPR ARC, Racine, 1980—. Mem. Nat. League Nursing, Assn. Seventh-Day Adventist Nurses.

VOSS, KATHLEEN MARIE, human resources executive; b. Chgo., Jan. 31, 1947; d. Walter Arthur Voss and Kathryn Lorriane (Dempsey) Egerer; m. Peter Alan Grossman, Sept. 9, 1984. Diploma, Michael Reese Sch. Nursing, 1968; BA, DePaul U., 1978; MBA, U. Chgo., 1980. Staff nurse Michael Reese Hosp., Chgo., 1968-69, Mercy Hosp., Chgo., 1969-71; charge nurse Ravenswood Hosp., Chgo., 1971-74; head nurse Northwestern Meml. Hosp., Chgo., 1974-77; corp. personnel specialist Jewel Cos., Inc., Chgo., 1980-82; mgr. employment and benefits services Jewel Food Stores, Melrose Park, Ill., 1982-83, dist. personnel mgr., 1983-85; mng. assoc. Exec. Assets Corp., Chgo., 1985-87, v.p., 1987-88; founder, prin. The Voss Group (human resource cons.), Evanston, Ill., 1988—; speaker in field. Bd. dirs. Youth Job Ctr. of Evanston, Ill., 1984—. Mem. Am. Coll. Healthcare Execs., Women Health Exec. Network, Am. Coll. Healthcare Execs., Women Health Execs. Network, Carer Mgmt. Univ. Chgo. Women's Bus. Group. Avocation: dog training. Home and Office: The Voss Group 801 Hinman Evanston IL 60202

VOSS, ROSEMARY JEAN, real estate executive; b. Milw., Feb. 10, 1946; d. William Bernard and Priscilla Eugenie (Pendleton) V. BS, U. Wis., Oshkosh, 1969; M, Calif. State U., Long Beach, 1975. Cert. real estate broker, Calif. Tchr. Long Beach Unified Sch. Dist., 1969-71, 72-76, U.S. Dept. Def., San Vito, Italy, 1971-72; salesperson Century 21 Sparrow, Long Beach, 1976-78; broker, owner Century 21 A Marketpl., Long Beach, 1978—; tchr. Long Beach City Coll., 1984—. Fund raiser Easter Seals, Long Beach, 1978—; dir. fund raising Sarah Ctr., Long Beach, 1984—. Mem. Nat. Assn. Realtors, Nat. Million Dollar Round Table, Fedn. Internationale des Administrateurs de Biens Conseils Immobiliers, Sales and Mktg. Execs. Long Beach, Long Beach Bd. Realtors (1st v.p., 2d v.p.), Long Beach C. of C. (women's council), Nat. Assn. for Female Execs. Office: Century 21 A Marketplace 4600 E Pacific Coast Hwy Suite 8 Long Beach CA 90804

VOSSELER, HARRIET ELAINE, federal program recruiter; b. Columbus, Nebr., Aug. 19, 1928; d. Franz Wilhelm and Ruby Mabel (Koch) Luchsinger; m. Erwin Gene Vosseler, Oct. 10, 1948 (div. 1965); children: Linda Kay, David Gene, Cheryl Lynn, Judith Ann, Martin Paul. Student, Midland Luth. Coll., Fremont, Nebr., 1946-47, Fresno (Calif.) City Coll., 1972-73, Calif. State U., Fresno, 1973-78, UCLA, 1983. Missionary Luth. Ch. Am., Guyana, 1951-54; salesperson Liberty House div. AMFAC, Inc., Honolulu, 1962-63; clk. Fresno City Unified Sch. Dist., 1965-67; clerical asst. Calif. State U., 1967-78; mgr. Shortstop, Fresno, 1978-79; vol. Peace Corps, Jamaica, 1979-82; recruiter Peace Corps, Los Angeles, 1982-87, Ednl. Resource Devel. Trust, Los Angeles, 1988—; mem. So. Calif. Peace Corps Service Council, 1983—. Contbr. numerous articles to profl. jours. Mem. com. on missions 1st. United Meth. Ch., Santa Monica, Calif., 1984-85; active Nat. Alliance for Mentally Ill, Calif. Alliance for Mentally Ill, Nat. Com. Preserve Social Security and Medicare, Smithsonian Instn. Mem. NOW, Am. Assn. Retired Persons, Nat. Assn. Female Execs. Democrat. Home: 1074 Elkgrove Ave #1 Venice CA 90291

VOTTERO, DIANE MARIE, sales executive; b. Danville, Pa., Aug. 10, 1950; d. Stephen Dominic and Josephine Delores (LaCross) V. BS in Edn. summa cum laude, East Stroudsburg (Pa.) U., 1972; MS in Edn., Temple U., Phila., 1979; postgrad. in bus. adminstrn., St. Joseph's U., Phila., 1982—. Cert. tchr. Tchr. Allentown (Pa.) Sch. Dist., 1972-79; sales mgr. Olan Mills Portrait Studio, Whitehall, Pa., 1979-80; sales rep. Challenge Industries, Reading, Pa., 1980-82; telephone account rep. Donnelley Directory, Reading, 1982-84, telephone account exec., 1984-85, account rep., 1985-87, account exec., 1987—. Tchr. adult edn. St. Paul's Cath. Ch., Allentown, 1975-78, vocalist, guitarist, 1978—. Mem. Nat. Assn. Female Execs., Kappa Delta Pi. Club: Emmaus (Pa.) Road Runners. Office: Donnelley Dir Allentown PA 18103

VOURNAS, ANASTASIA PETROW, marketing executive; b. Washington, Aug. 28, 1946; d. George Christian and Helen Jean (Petrow) V.; B.A., U. Denver, 1969, M.B.A., 1970. From account coordinator to account exec. Young & Rubicam, Inc., N.Y.C., 1971-77; account mgr. Compton Advt., Inc., N.Y.C., 1977-78; account supr. SSC&B, Inc., N.Y.C., 1978-80; v.p., account supr. Benton & Bowles, Inc., N.Y.C., 1980-82; mktg. cons. Phoenix House Found., Inc., Warner Communications Inc., N.Y.C., 1982-84; v.p. Am. Express Travel Related Services Co., Inc., N.Y.C., 1984—. Democrat. Home: 230 E 50th St New York NY 10022 Office: 200 Vesey St New York NY 10285

VOUTYRAS, JEANETTE, hospital administrator; b. Leerdam, The Netherlands, July 30, 1952; came to U.S., 1965; d. Gysbert and Johanna (Bolle) Vandenoever; m. Gregory Scott Voutyras, Aug. 31, 1974; children: Johanna Nora, Gina Nicole. BS, Ohio U., 1974; MS, Cleve. State U., 1977. Cert. bioanalyst lab. dir. Med. technologist VA Med. Ctr., Cleve., 1976-79; chief technologist Southgate Med. Lab., Cleve., 1979-80; dir. lab. services Northeastern Ohio Gen. Hosp., Madison, 1980-85, dir. ancillary services, 1985—. Vol. Am. Cancer Soc., Cleve., 1984, ARC, Cleve., 1985—; active March of Dimes, Cleve., 1987—; bd. dirs. Lake County Council on Aging, Painesville, Ohio, 1987—. Mem. Am. Soc. Clin. Pathologists (cert.), Am. Soc. Med. Technologists. Republican. Office: Northeastern Ohio Gen Hosp 2041 Hubbard Rd Madison OH 44057

VOWELL, EVELENE C., real estate broker; b. Hickman, Ky., May 11, 1940; d. Haughty Chester and Lottie Bell (Williams) Craddock; m. Darrell Odine, Dec. 27, 1959; children—Amy Darlene, Kerry Don, Dai Keith. Student Memphis State U., 1976-85; cert. Grad. Realtors Inst., 1987. Lic. real estate affiliate broker. County agrl. sec. Extension Service, Hickman, Ky., 1957-59; payroll sec. Roper Pecan Co., Hickman, 1961-63; PR3 inspector Gen. Electric Co., Memphis, 1969-71; sec. Swift and Co., Memphis, 1971-73; affiliate broker John R. Thompson Realtors, Memphis, 1976-83, Crye Leike Realtors, Memphis, 1983—. Named Million Dollar Seller, Crye Leike Realtors, Memphis, 1984, 85. Mem. Memphis Bd. Realtors. Club: Ind. Order Foresters (Memphis). Home: 2808 Charles Bryan Rd Memphis TN 38134

VOWELS, ELEANOR ELAINE, speech pathologist; b. Pitts., Mar. 10, 1937; d. Arnett Lloyd and Amanda (Anthony) Wooding; B.S. in Psychology, Howard U., 1962, PhD, 1988; M.A. in Speech Pathology and Audiology (Vocat. Rehab. fellow 1965-67), Catholic U. Am., 1967; postgrad. U. Md.; m. Aug. 27, 1960; 1 son, David Scott. Speech pathologist Prince George County (Md.) Diagnostic Teaching Center, 1967-70; speech pathologist Dept. Human Resources D.C., 1970-72, dir. speech pathology and audiology, 1972—; dir. speech pathology and audiology children and youth project D.C. Gen. Hosp., 1972—, dir. handicapped infant intervention project, 1977—, dir. tng. grant, 1980—; v.p. D.C. Consortium Handicapped Children's Programs, 1979, pres., 1980. Pres., D.C. Area chpt. Children Internat. Summer Villages, Inc., 1981, 82-83, mem. expansion com., trustee-at-large Nat. Children's Internat. Summer Villages, Inc. 1982—, also mem. long range planning com.; chmn. com. on handicapped Commn. Pub. Health, 1982, advisor to commr., 1986—; mem. Mayor's Com. on the Handicapped, 1986—, Devel. Disabilities Council, 1986—. HEW Bur. Edn. grantee, 1977—. Mem. Am. Speech and Hearing Assn. (cert. clin. competence), D.C. Assn. Retarded Citizens (dir. 1972—), D.C. Speech and Hearing Assn., Md. Speech and Hearing Assn., Nat. Assn. Retarded Citizens, Zeta Phi Beta. Democrat. Baptist. Producer audio visual slide presentations on handicapped children, 1962, 70. Home: 7718 Jaffrey Rd Fort Washington MD 20744 Office: Commn of Pub Health 1875 Conneticut Ave NW Washington DC 20009

VRANA, MAULFREY STEWART, public relations and advertising agency executive; b. Omaha, Mar. 11, 1933; d. Roland Augustus and Marian Youel (Thompson) Stewart; B.Sc. in Edn., U. Nebr., Omaha, 1953; m. Laird B. Fisher, Aug. 7, 1958; children—Stephen Laird, Andrew Scott, Pamela Jane; m. 2nd Theodore W. Vrana, Nov. 27, 1982. Editor Exec. mag., Omaha, 1978-81; communications dir. Century 21, 1976-78; public relations exec. Easter Seal Soc., 1981-82; owner Muffy Fisher Assos., 1976—; editor, pub. Time Manager, 1982-87; feature editor Lincoln Mag., 1988—. Author: Cash in Your Closet, 1984; co-author: Alive and Writing in Nebraska, 1986. Recipient merit mother award Nebr. Mothers Assn., 1985. Bd. dirs. United Way, Lincoln Found., Lincoln Symphony Guild; active ARC pub. relation commn. Lincoln/Lancaster; mem. fin. com. 1st Plymouth Ch., Fellowship Chs., Asst. League. Mem. Nat. League Am. Pen Women (Nebr. state pres.), Pub. Relations Soc. Am., Am. Soc. Tng. and Devel., Lincoln C. of C., Nebr. Travel Industry Council, TWIG Daniel Network, Wooden Spoon, Nebr. Writers Guild., Nat. Speakers Assn., Gen. Fedn. Women's Clubs. Lodge: PEO. Republican. Address: 3260 Van Dorn Lincoln NE 68502

VREELAND, DIANA DALZIEL, magazine editor; b. Paris, France; d. Frederick Y. and Emily Key (Hoffman) Dalziel; m. Thomas Reed Vreeland, Mar. 1, 1924 (dec. 1966); children: Thomas Reed, Frederick D. Fashion editor Harper's Bazaar, 1939-62, columnist, 1936-38; with Vogue mag., 1962—, editor-in-chief, 1962-71, cons. editor, 1971—; Cons. Costume Inst., Met. Mus. Art, 1972. Author: (with Hemphill) Allure, 1980; D.V. (Plimpton and Hemphill), 1984. Decorated Legion of Honor France; recipient award N.Y. Fashion Designers, 1963, Chevalier de L'Ordre National de la Merite, 1970, Woman of Yr. award Westchester County Fedn. Women's Clubs, 1979, Pres.' Fellow's award R.I. Sch. Design, 1979, Rodeo Dr. award, 1983, Am. Ann. award Council of Fashion Designers, 1984, Chevalier des Arts et Lettres Ministry of Culture, France, 1984, Fellow for Life award Met. Mus, N.Y.C., 1986. Office: Met Mus Art Costume Inst 1000 Fifth Ave New York NY 10028

VREELAND, ELEANOR P., publishing company executive. BS, Queens Coll., 1952; MBA, NYU, 1958. With Peck & Peck, 1947-58; pub. relations dir. Bklyn. Pub. Library, 1960-65; v.p., treas., cons. St. John's Library Cons., Inc., 1965-67; advt. and publicity dir. Frances Denny, 1967-68; product mgr. Macmillan Library Services, 1960-69; dir. mktg. Strechert-Hayner, 1971-79; pres. Katharine Gibbs Schs., 1981—; with Macmillan, Inc., N.Y.C., 1971—, v.p., 1981—. Office: Macmillan Inc 866 Third Ave New York NY 10022 *

VROOMAN, JOAN JEFFERSON, editor, free-lance writer; b. Toronto, Ont., Can., Oct. 6, 1929; came to U.S., 1951, naturalized, 1962; d. Arthur Richard and Ivy Lillian (Umpleby) Jefferson; m. Gerald Willard Ames, Aug. 11, 1952 (div. 1962); children: Susan D., Michael G., Dianne E., Kathleen E.; m. William Chester Vrooman, Aug. 24, 1963; 4 stepchildren. ARCT, Royal Conservatory Music, Toronto, 1946; student Victoria Coll. of Toronto U., 1947-51. Community living editor Cortland Standard Printing Co., (N.Y.), 1962—; bd. dirs., pres. County Communications Council, Cortland, 1970-80; lectr. in field. Named Woman of Achievement Cortland County Women, 1985. Bd. dirs. Cortland County C. of C., 1976-8; adv. bd. Aid to Women Victims of Violence, Cortland, 1978; counselor Finger Lakes Assn., Penn Yan, N.Y., 1980—; bd. dirs. 1890 House Mus., Cortland, 1984—; sec., 1988—. Club: Zonta (bd. dirs. 1978—. Republican. Episcopalian. Home: 721 Lime Hollow Rd Cortland NY 13045 Office: Cortland Standard Printing Co 110 Main St Cortland NY 13045

VUCANOVICH, BARBARA FARRELL, congresswoman; b. Camp Dix, N.J., June 22, 1921; d. Thomas F. and Ynez (White) Farrell; m. Ken Dillon, Mar. 8, 1950 (div. 1964); children: Patty Dillon Cafferata, Mike, Ken, Tom, Susan Dillon Stoddard; m. George Vucanovich, June19, 1965. Student, Manhattanville Coll. of Sacred Heart, 1938-39. Owner, operator Welcome Aboard Travel, Reno, 1968-74; Nev. rep. for Senator Paul Laxalt 1974-82; mem. 98th-100th Congresses from 2d Nev. dist., 1983—; mem. coms. interior and insular affairs, house adminstrn. Pres. Nev. Fedn. Republican Women, Reno, 1955-56; former pres. St. Mary's Hosp. Guild, Lawyer's Wives. Roman Catholic. Club: Hidden Valley Country (Reno). Office: US Ho of Reps 312 Cannon House Office Bldg Washington DC 20515 *

VUCKOVICH, CAROL YETSO (MRS. MICHAEL VUCKOVICH), librarian; b. East Liverpool, Ohio, Sept. 23, 1940; d. Stephen A. and Louise (Sever) Yetso; B.S., Geneva Coll., 1966; M.L.S., U. Pitts., 1968; m. Michael Vuckovich, Sept. 24, 1970. Computation analyst Crucible Steel div. Colt Industries, Midland, Pa., 1958-62; library dir. Community Coll. Beaver County, Monaca, Pa., 1968—, instr. human anatomy and physiology, 1970—. Mem. Am. Library Assn., Pa. Library Assn., Spl. Libraries Assn., Am. Inst. Biol. Scis., Am. Anti-Vivisection Soc., Nat. Wildlife Fedn., Coll. and Research Libraries. Home: 21 Elm St Midland PA 15059

VUICH, ROSE ANN, state legislator; b. Cutler, Calif.; d. Obren and Stana V. Ed. Cen. Calif. Community Coll. Mem. Calif. Senate from 15th dist., 1976—. Mem. Nat. Soc. Pub. Accts., Beta Sigma Phi. Democrat. Office: Office of the State Senate State Capitol Sacramento CA 95814 *

WACHBRIT, JILL BARRETT, accountant, leasing company executive; b. Ventura, Calif., May 27, 1955; d. Preston Everett Barrett and Lois JoAnne (Fondersmith) Batchelder; m. Michael Ian Wachbrit, June 21, 1981; 1 child, Michelle. AA, Santa Monica City Coll., 1975; BS, Calif. State U., Northridge, 1979; M in Bus. Taxation, U. So. Calif., 1985. CPA. Supervising sr. tax acct. Peat, Marwick, Mitchell & Co., Century City, Calif., 1979-82; sr. tax analyst Avery Internat., Pasadena, Calif., 1982-83; tax mgr., asst. v.p. First Interstate Leasing, Pasedena, 1983—. Republican. Jewish.

WACHNER, LINDA JOY, apparel marketing and manufacturing executive; b. N.Y.C., Feb. 3, 1946; d. Herman and Shirley W.; m. Seymour Applebaum, Dec. 21, 1973 (dec. 1983). BS in Econs. and Bus., U. Buffalo, 1966. Buyer Foley's Federated Dept. Store, Houston, 1968-69; sr. buyer R.H. Macy's, N.Y.C., 1969-74; v.p. Warner div. Warnaco, Bridgeport, Conn., 1974-77; v.p. corp. mktg. Caron Internat., N.Y.C., 1977-79; pres. U.S. div. Max Factor & Co., Hollywood, Calif., 1979-82, pres., chief ops. officer, 1982-83; pres., chief exec. officer Max Factor & Co. Worldwide, 1983-84; mng. dir. Adler & Shaykin, N.Y.C., 1984-86; owner, pres., chief exec. officer Warnaco Inc., N.Y.C., 1986—; bd. dirs. Standard Brands Paints, Reebok Shoes Internat.; mem. bus. adv. council City of Los Angeles, U. So. Calif. Sch. Bus. Adminstrn.; mem., chmn. trade promotion U.S.-Philippines Bus. Com. Presdl. appointee Adv. Com. for Trade Negotiations; trustee Martha Graham Ctr. Contemporary Dance, Inc.; mem. U.S.-Philippines Bus. Com.; mem. bd. trustees U. Buffalo Found. Recipient Silver Achievement award Los Angeles YWCA; named Outstanding Woman in Bus., Women's Equity Action League, 1980, Woman of Yr., MS. Mag., 1986; honoree Nat. Women's Forum, 1986. Mem. Young Pres.'s Orgn., Com. of 200, Am. Mgmt. Assn., Am. Apparel Mktg. Assn. (bd. dirs.), Los Angeles C. of C. (bd. dirs.). Republican. Jewish. Office: Warnaco Inc 90 Park Ave New York NY 10016 also: Warnaco Inc 11111 Santa Monica Blvd Los Angeles CA 90025

WACHS, KATE MARY, psychologist; b. Chgo., Aug. 27, 1951; d. Charles Herbert and Rose Ann W. BA magna cum laude, Rosary Coll., 1974; MA, U. S.D., 1976, PhD, 1980. Licensed psychologist, Ill., Mich. Asst. clin. psychologist Lewis & Clark Mental Health Ctr., Yankton, S.D., 1977-78; intern clin. psychology Rush Presbyn. St. Luke's Med. Ctr., Chgo., 1978-79, house staff in psychology, 1979-80; psychologist Bay Med. Ctr., Bay City, Mich., 1980-83; pvt. practice psychology Mich., 1983-86, Chgo., 1984—; pres. IntiMate Introduction Service, Inc., Advanced Degrees Introductions, Inc.; columnist Chgo. Life Mag., 1984—, Women In Mgmt. Newsletter, 1984-86, Amplifier, 1986—; editor articles for local and nat. pubs.; guest on local and nat. radio and TV programs, 1982—. Mem. Assn. for Media Psychology (bd. dirs. 1985—), Am. Psychol. Assn. (bd. dirs. Div. 46 1986—, chmn. ethics/guidelines com. 1986-87, chmn. membership com. 1987—, liaison to Pub. Info. Com. 1987—), Am. Pain Soc., Women in Mgmt. (Women Achievement award entrepreneurial contbns. 1987). Office: 1030 N State Suite 7C Chicago IL 60610

WACHSMAN, KATHRYN MARY, lawyer; b. Providence, Oct. 27, 1949; d. Anthony and Mayme D'Agostino; m. Harvey F. Wachsman, Jan. 31, 1976; children: Dara Nicole, David Winston, Jacqueline Victoria, Lauren Elizabeth, Derek Charles. BA in Math., Avila Coll., 1971; JD, Washburn U., 1974. Bar: Conn., N.Y., Fla., D.C., Kans. Assoc. firm Pegalis & Wachsman, Great Neck, N.Y., 1978—. Mem. ABA, N.Y. State Bar Assn., Conn. Bar Assn., Fla. Bar Assn., D.C. Bar Assn., N.Y. State Trial Lawyers Assn., Nassau County Bar Assn., Kans. Bar Assn., Am. Coll. Legal Medicine (assoc. in law), Assn. Trial Lawyers Am. Office: Pegalis & Wachsman PC 175 East Shore Rd Great Neck NY 11023

WACHTEL, WENDIE LYNN, investment banker; b. Washington, July 5, 1953; d. Sidney B. and Irma (Schocken) W. Mgr. trading dept. Wachtel and Co., Inc., Washington, 1967-74, v.p., 1974—; dir. Fla. Glass Industries, Inc., Miami, Valkyrie Fin. Group, Washington, Applidata Inc., Alexandria; workshop leader The Entrepreneurship Inst., Washington, 1982. Mem. Nat. Assn. Securities Dealers (vice chmn. bus. conduct com. 1984, Security Traders Assn. of Washington (pres. 1980-82), Nat. Security Traders Assn., Bond Club of Washington. Office: Wachtel and Co Inc 1101 14th St NW Washington DC 20005-5680

WACHTELL, ESTHER, music center executive; b. N.Y.C., June 30, 1935; d. Victor and Rnoda (Wolin) Pickard; m. Thomas Wachtell, Jan. 27, 1957; children—Roger Bruce, Wendy Anne, Peter James. B.A., Conn. Coll., 1956; M.A., Cornell U., 1957. Exec. dir. Performing Tree, Los Angeles, 1978-79; dir. tech. assistance Calif. Arts Council, Los Angeles and Orange Counties, 1979-81; coordinator vol. activities Music Ctr. Los Angeles, 1974-83, coordinator spl. projects, 1980-84; dir. devel. Music Ctr. Unified Fund, Los Angeles, 1984—; arts mgmt. cons., lectr. So. Calif., 1975-82. Bd. dirs. Los Angeles, Philharmonic, 1973-75; bd. govs. Performing Arts Council, Los Angeles, 1975—; vice. chmn. Am. Council for Arts, 1979—; mem. fin. com. Com. to Reelect Tom Bradley, Los Angeles, 1978; trustee Coro Found., 1979-85, Orthopaedic Hosp., Los Angeles, 1980—, Claremont McKenna Coll., 1983—; commr. Calif. Council for Humanities, 1984—; mem. adv. bd. May Co., 1985. Recipient Eve award Assistance League Los Angeles, 1978, Activist award Broadway Dept. Stores, 1980, Recognition award Big Sisters Los Angeles, 1982, Presdl. citation Music Ctr., 1982, 84, Portfolio award Exec. Women, 1985. Mem. Phi Beta Kappa. Republican. Club: Regency (Los Angeles). Home: 35 Crest Rd E Rolling Hills CA 90274 Office: Music Ctr fLos Angeles 135 N Grand Ave Los Angeles CA 90012

WACHTER, MICHELLE RENEA, state government agriculture administrator; b. Madison, Wis., Nov. 3, 1959; d. Thomas John Triggs and Patricia Yvonne (Elder) Severson; m. Daniel James Wachter, Sept. 25, 1982; children: Nicole, Brody. Grad. high sch., Oregon, Wis. Crime info. technician Wis. Dept. Justice, Madison, 1978-79; pension technician CUNA Mut. Ins. Soc., Madison, 1979-80; adminstrv. asst. Wis. Dept. Agriculture, Madison, 1980—. Contbg. author: Am. Anthology of Poems, 1987. Mem. Nat. Assn. Female Execs. Home: PO Box 222 193 N Kerch St Brooklyn WI 53521 Office: Wis Dept Agr 801 W Badger Rd Madison WI 53713

WACHTER, WANDA VALERIE, accountant; b. Enda, Okla., Dec. 5, 1952; d. Robert J. and Jean M. (Debold) W.; B.B.A. with honors, George Washington U., 1978. With Telesec Temporaries, Falls Church, Va., 1972; mgmt. accountant Am. Assn. Coll. Registrars and Adminstrs., Washington, 1973; accountant technician Am. Council on Edn., Washington, 1973-74, Naval Regional Med. Center, Washington, 1974-77, Immigration and Naturalization Service, Washington, 1978; staff accountant Assn. Advancement of Med. Instrumentation, Roslyn, Va., 1978-79, Honeywell Info. Systems, Inc., McLean, Va., 1979-80; asst. controller Fairmac Realty Corp., Arlington, Va., 1980-82; prin. D.J. Wachter, Inc., Arlington, 1983—.

WACKER, MARGARET MORRISSEY, communications executive; b. Washington, Dec. 12, 1951; d. Warren Ernest Clyde and Ann Romeyn (MacMillan) Wacker. B.A., Carnegie Mellon U., 1974. Promotion specialist Millipore Corp., Bedford, Mass., 1974-77, corp. communications mgr., 1982—, dir. communications Lab. Products div., 1981-82; dir. advt. IVAC div. Eli Lilly Co., San Diego, 1977-79, dist. sales mgr., Los Angeles, 1979-80; bus. unit mgr. Sage div. Orion Research, Cambridge, Mass., 1980-81; counselor to handicapped individuals in bus. Mem. Internat. Assn. Bus. Communicators. Democrat. Episcopalian. Avocations: painting; sewing. Home: 99 Pond Ave Unit 322D Brookline MA 02146 Office: Millipore Corp 80 Ashby Rd Bedford MA 01730

WADDEY, SHERYL DIANE, operations administrator; b. Houston, Oct. 31, 1955; d. Melvin Otto and Merle Darlene (Dussetschleger) Krezer; m. Byron Thomas Waddey, Apr. 12, 1986. BS, Tex. A&M U., 1978. Cert. secondary tchr. math. and psychology, Tex. Instr. math. LaPorte (Tex.) Ind. Sch. Dist., 1978-84; acct., adminstrv. asst. HDR Techserv, Inc., Dallas, 1984-86, mgr. ops., 1986-87; office mgr. HDR Engring. Inc., Dallas, 1987—. Advisor edni. tour., 1981-83, mem. textbook com. State of Tex., 1983-84; coach Dallas Softball Assn., 1985-86. Lutheran.

WADDINGTON, BETTE HOPE (ELIZABETH CROWDER), violinist; b. San Francisco, July 27, 1921; d. John and Marguerite (Crowder) Waddington; BA in Music, U. Calif. at Berkeley, 1945, postgrad.; postgrad. (scholarship) Juilliard Sch. Music, 1950, San Jose State Coll., 1955; MA in Music, San Francisco State U., 1953; violin student of Joseph Fuchs, Melvin Ritter, Frank Gittelson, Felix Khuner, Daniel Bonsack, D.C. Dounis, Naoum Blinder, Eddy Brown; life cert. music and art Calif. Jr. Coll. Violinist Erie (Pa.) Symphony, 1950, Dallas Symphony, 1957, St. Louis Symphony, 1958—. Cert. gen. elem. and secondary tchr., Calif.; cert. jr. coll. librarian. Toured alone and with St. Louis Symphony U.S., Can., Middle East, Japan, China. Mem. Am. Musicians Union (St. Louis and San Francisco chpts.), U. Calif., San Francisco State Univ. Alumni Assn., San Jose State Univ. Alumni Assn., Sierra Club (life), Alpha Beta Alpha. Avocations: travel, art and archeology history, drawing, painting. Office: St Louis Symphony Orch Powell Hall Grand Ave and Delmar Blvd Saint Louis MO 63103

WADDLE, AUDREY STERLING, rehabilitative nurse; b. Gloucester County, Va., June 20, 1932; d. James Edward and Ethel Hayden (Williams) Sterling; RN, Riverside Sch. Profl. Nursing, 1952; student Hampton Inst., 1971-72, Thomas Nelson Community Coll., 1973; BS in Health Adminstrn., St. Joseph's Coll., 1980; m. Travis Gene Waddle, May 4, 1952; children: Pamela Gayle Waddle Furr, Anita Darlene Smith. Cert. trainer, course developer, supr. trainer, Va. Head nurse Riverside Hosp., Newport News, 1953, Onslow County Hosp., Jacksonville, N.C., 1954; pvt. duty, relief dir. Gray's Clinic & Hosp., Springhill, La., 1955-57; gen. duty nurse Eastern State Hosp., Williamsburg, Va., 1957-58, head nurse, 1958-59, nurse supr., 1959-65, mental health nurse instr. and tng. coordinator, 1982-88, chmn. ward manual com., 1967-81, RN coordinator, 1988—. Adv. bd. and selection com. Lafayette Practical Nurse Program, Williamsburg, 1972-82; mem. State of Va. Dept. Mental Health/Mental Retardation Individualized Treatment Planning Com., 1979-80; chmn. Eastern State Hosp. United Fund drive, 1978-79; mem. G.S.H. Tardive Dyskinesia Tng. Com., 1988—. Registered profl. nurse, Va.; U. Md. grantee, 1964. Mem. Am. Nurses Assn. (cert.), Va. Govt. Employees Assn., Nat. Soc. Registered Nurses. Presbyterian. Developer psychiat. practical nurse program Eastern State Hosp., 1967; co-author manuals. Home: 108 Underwood Rd Williamsburg VA 23185 Office: Drawer A Williamsburg VA 23187

WADE, BETH GROBE, social agency adminstrator; b. Victoria, Tex., Sept. 8, 1942; d. Chester Allen and Evelyn Ann (Paul) Grobe; m. Harold Dean Wade, June 24, 1961; children: Len, Lorie, Jonathan, Jennifer, Julie. BA, Lubbock Christian Coll., 1977, MA, Tex. Woman's U., 1985, postgrad., 1987—. Tchr. Lubbock (Tex.) Christian Sch., 1975-77; biofeedback therapist Christian Care Ctr., Mesquite, Tex., 1978-79; counselor, tchr. Ft. Worth Christian Sch., 1980-84, dir., counselor Richland Hills Ch. of Christ Community Care Ctr., Ft. Worth, 1985—; part-time tchr. Dallas Christian Sch., 1977-79; seminar speaker Richland Hills Counseling Ctr., Ft. Worth, 1985—; counselor, cons. Christs' Haven for Children, Keller, Tex., 1984-87; condr. parenting seminars Richland Hills Ch. of Christ, Ft. Worth, 1980-87, marriage enrichment seminars, 1985-87. Den mother Boy Scouts Am., Iuka, Miss., 1968-69; leader Brownie Scouts, Dallas, 1977-79; bd. dirs. Christmas Providers, N.E. Tarrant County, Tex., 1986-87; mem. Cancer Crusade, Mother's March of Dimes, 1980-87; treas. PTA, Burnsville, Miss., 1979, v.p. PTO, Fort Worth Christian, 1981-82. Mem. Internat. Assn. Marriage and Family Counselors, Am. Assn. Christian Counselors, Alpha Chi, Associated Women for Christian Edn. Republican. Mem. Ch. of Christ. Clubs: Creative Arts Guild, PTO (v.p. 1980-82) (Ft. Worth). Office: Richland Hills Community Care Ctr 6250 NE Loop 820 Fort Worth TX 76118

WADE, BETTY ANN, educational administrator; b. Wheatland, Wyo., June 13, 1951; d. Marvin William and Margaret Edith (Fullmer) Arland; m. George Franklin Wade, June 10, 1977; 1 child, Leigh Ruth. BA, Hamline U., 1976, postgrad., 1988. Program and community devel. Washington County Hist. Soc., Stillwater, Minn., 1976-77; coordinator communication ctr. William Mitchell Coll. Law, St. Paul, 1979-83, dir. personnel and adminstrv. services, 1983—; piano tchr. Barta Sch. Music, Scottsbluff, Nebr., 1970-74; tchr. Platte Valley Arts Orgn., Scottsbluff, 1974; cons. Nat. Inst. for Trial Advocacy, St. Paul, 1985, bd. dirs., nominating com. V. Group Health, Inc. Active Mounds Park Acad. Parents Assn., Maplewood, Minn., 1984—; pub. relations coordinator Shakespeare & Co. Theatre, White Bear Lake, Minn., 1975-78; Diocesan regional del. St. John's Episc. Ch., White Bear Lake, 1986—, choir mem., 1984-86. Mem. Coll. and Univ. Personnel Assn., Internat. Assn. Personnel Women. Office: William Mitchell Coll Law 875 Summit Ave Saint Paul MN 55105

WADE, CHRISTINE BLAIR, food company executive, writer; b. Palmetto, Ga., Sept. 20, 1943; d. Harvey Leonard and Winnie Mae (Turpen) Blair; m. Howard Alexander Wade, July 27, 1961 (div. Aug. 1979); children: Sharon Lynne, Donnie Brian. Student, Clayton State Coll., 1984; exec. devel. cert., Dale Carnegie, Smyrna, Ga., 1986. Sec. to gen. mgr. Dixie Frozen Foods, Inc., Peachtree City, Ga., 1961-64, office supr., 1964-67, corp. officer, asst. sec., 1967-69; dir. gen. acctg. Hi-Brand Foods, Peachtree City, 1967-78, dir. adminstrn., 1978-83, v.p. adminstrn., 1983-87, div. v.p. info. systems, 1987—; speaker Peachtree City Elem. Sch., 1980, West Ga. Coll., 1987. Author numerous poems. Mem. com. Adopt-A-Sch. Fed. Program, Fayette County, Ga., 1986-87; pres. McIntosh Pilot Club, 1989, mem. media com. McIntosh High Sch. PTC, 1988; vice chmn. adv. com. Fayette County United Way, mem. dist. admissions com. Mem. Dale Carnegie Inst. (participant, exec. image, Best Presentation award 1986), Common (IBM User's Group), Fayette County C. of C. (pub. relations rep. 1987, chmn. pub. relations 1988, econ. devel. com., nominating com. for new dirs., bd. dirs. 1988-90). Democrat. Baptist. Clubs: Pilot Internat., McIntosh Pilot (Peachtree City) (charter, officer). Home: PO Box 2167 Peachtree City GA 30269 Office: Hi-Brand Foods PO Box 2048 Peachtree City GA 30269

WADE, GAIL LORETTA, corporate exercise company executive, computer consultant; b. Richmond, Va., Apr. 3, 1954; d. Joseph Louis Thompson and Mae Frances (Fries) McCoy; m. Leon Wade, Dec. 27, 1975; children: Chrystyna, Charyssa. Student Fayetteville State U., 1976-80; BS in Natural Sci., Edison State Coll., 1985. Lab. technician Am. Hoescht Corp., Branchburg, N.J., 1980-83; asst. mgr. Atlas Door Corp., Edisn, N.J., 1984-86; chief of staff Winebow, Inc., Hohokus, N.J., 1986-87; pres. GDN Data Systems, New Brunswick, 1985—; regional mgr. Personalized Aerobics, East Brunswick, N.J.., 1987—. Contbr. poetry to mags. Mem. Nat. Assn. Female Execs., Black Women's Network Assn. (exec. bd. dirs.), N.J. Bus. Women's Assn. Democrat. Roman Catholic. Home: 260 Delavan St New Brunswick NJ 08901

WADE, JANICE ELIZABETH, musician, educator, conductor; b. Decorah, Iowa, May 20, 1937; d. Lloyd Edward and Viviah Lois (Caskey)Richards; children: Kendall Anne, Craig Patrick. B in Music Edn., Drake U., 1959, M in Music Edn., 1960. Pvt. tchr. music Des Moines, 1960-87; asst. prof. music Wartburg Coll., Waverly, Iowa, 1987—; prin. 2d violin Des Moines Symphony, 1965-87, negotiating team, 1983-87, chmn. players' com., 1978-85; tchr. instrumental music Des Moines Pub. Schs., 1966-76; music dir. conductor Des Moines Community Orch., 1976-87; concertmaster Bijou Players, Des Moines, 1980—; dir., conductor Wartburg Community Symphony, 1987—. Contbr. articles to profl. jours. Active Planned

Parenthood. Office: Wartburg Coll Dept Music 222 9th St NW PO Box 1003 Waverly IA 50677

WADE, JULIA HOWARD, interior designer; b. Alexandria, La., Dec. 2, 1928; d. Samuel Eugene and Louis D'Or (Moore) Howard; B.A., Baylor U., 1948; student La. Coll., 1946; m. Nelsyn Ernest Brooks Wade, June 29, 1948; children—Sylvia Laureen, Lisa Frances, William Alan, David Eugene. Organizer, dir. Children's Theatre, San Augustine, Tex., 1948-52; tchr. English San Augustine High Sch., 1948; partner, decorator, advt. mgr., buyer Nelsyns Furniture Store, San Augustine, 1958—; lectr. in field. Hist. chmn. 8-County Deep East Tex. Devel. Assn., 1975; bd. dirs. San Augustine Public Library, 1980-82, pres., 1984-85; bd. devel. E. Tex. Bapt. Coll., 1978-82. Named Outstanding Small Retailer, S.W. Home Furnishings Assn., 1979; Pres.'s award, C. of C., 1973; Rotary award, 1980, Outstanding Dealer, Kirsch, 1985. Mem. C. of C. (v.p. 1972-77, co-recipient Outstanding Citizens award 1987), S.W. Home Furnishings Assn. (cert.), Nat. Assn. Retail Dealers of Am., Nat. Assn. Female Execs., Tex. Old Missions and Forts Restoration Assn., Nat. Trust Hist. Preservation, Baylor U. Alumni Assn., Tex. Forestry Assn., DAR (chmn. Constn. com. 1980—, writer, dir. U.S. Constn. 200th Anniversary drama 1987), San Augustine County Hist. Soc., Internat. Platform Assn. Republican. Baptist. Clubs: Heritage (pres. 1963), Bible (pres. 1953, 57). Lodge: Gideons (v.p. and program chmn. aux. 1986—). Home: 412 Baxter Ln San Augustine TX 75972 Office: 128 E Columbia St San Augustine TX 75972

WADE, KIMM HECHLER, finance company executive; b. Phila., June 1, 1961; d. Edwin Charles and Janice Louise (Lurcott) Hechler; m. Robert Erwin Wade, May 2, 1986; 1 child, Jessica Nichole. Student, Ohio U., 1979-82; BBA, Nat. U., 1985—. Loan closer Nat. City Fin., San Diego, 1983; loan counselor Merrill Lynch Mortgage, San Diego, 1983-84, new loan set up, 1984-85, data base control specialist, 1985-86, project analyst, 1986, research analyst, 1986-87; impound adminstr. Wells Fargo Mortgage, San Diego, 1987, systems liaison, 1987—. Chaplain Job's Daughters, Columbus, 1973-74; exchange student Am. Field Service, Holland, 1978. Mem. Nat. Assn. Female Execs., Summit Orgn. Republican. Methodist. Home: 3033 Forrester Ct San Diego CA 92123 Office: Wells Fargo Mortgage 404 Camino Del Rio S San Diego CA 92108

WADE, MARY CARROLL, pyschologist, educator, government official; b. Rome, Ga., Sept. 1, 1909; d. Seaborn Rosa and Dollie Savannah (Hill) Carroll; student Maryville Coll., 1926-28, B.A., 1931; postgrad. U. of the South, summer, 1938; M.A., George Washington U., 1948; Ed.D., Am. U., 1970; lic. psychologist, Washington; m. Richard Rudolph Wade, Apr. 1, 1967 (dec.). Tchr., Hawkins County, Tenn., 1934-36, Pittman Center, Tenn., 1937-38, Chattanooga, 1938-42, Meigs County, Tenn., 1936-37; with War Dept., Washington, 1942-43; library asst. Library of Congress, Washington, 1943-44; planner, U.S. Govt. Printing Office, Washington, 1944-67, planner-in-charge, 1967-72, chief marginally forms continuous forms sect., Specifications Div., 1972-80, chmn. Fed. Women's Program, 1972-73; cons. psychologist Va. Vocational Rehab. Dept., 1954-57; lectr. Montgomery Coll., Rockville, Md., 1981-82; freelance writer and lectr., 1982—; lectr. Fed. Office Systems Expo, 1982, No. Va. Community Coll., 1984. Bd. dirs. United Cerebral Palsy, D.C., 1970-82; active ARC; hon. staff mem. Tenn. State Senator Annabelle Clement O'Brien, 1982. Recipient United Service Orgn. award, 1946; Superior Service award, U.S. Govt. Printing Office, 1963, 66, 67, 68, Spl. Achievement award, 1971-72, named Woman of the Yr. Fairfax County Bus. and Profl. Womens' Club, 1986, others. Mem. Am. Psychol. Assn., Va. Psychol. Assn., D.C. Psychol. Assn., Soc. for Personnel Adminstrn., Nat. Vocat. Guidance Assn., Am. Personnel and Guidance Assn., Pub. Personnel Assn., Franklin Tech. Soc., Bus. Forms Mgmt. Assn. (rec. sec. 1980-81), Am. U. Alumni Assn., George Washington U. Alumni Assn., Maryville Coll. Alumni Assn., Nat. Trust Historic Preservation, Poetry Soc. Va., Va., Nat. Assn. Ret. Fed. Employees (rec. sec. 1984-86), Am. Assn. Ret. Persons, Smithsonian Assocs., Kappa Delta Epsilon, Psi Chi, Phi Delta Gamma (pres. Beta chpt., nat. council rep.). Presbyterian. Clubs: Toastmasters (v.p. No. Va. chpt., pres. 1985-86), Wash. of Printing House Craftsmen, Wash. Litho, George Washington Univ., Americana (pres., v.p., sec., treas., council 1986-87), Altrusa, (corr. sec. 1982-84, rec. sce. 1984-85), Columbian Women, (corr. sec. 1984-85, pres. 1987—), Club Council of Alexandria (rec. 1983), Fairfax County Bus. and profl. Women's (recording sec. 1973-74, v.p. 1974-75, pres. 1975-76). Contbr. articles to profl. jours.

WADE, MARY LOUISE POWELL, minister; b. Springfield, Ohio, Sept. 25, 1932; d. Gamaliel Wyatte Holmes and Lucy Maxwell (Sloan) Powell; m. Walter B. Wade, Aug. 25, 1956 (div. July 1980); children: Susan Sloan Wade Massey, Holly Bibb Wade Crane, Walter Wyatte. AA Meridian Jr. Coll., 1951; B.A., U. So. Miss., 1953, M.A., 1954; counselor cert. U. So. Ala., 1979; student Columbia Theol. Sem., Decatur, Ga., 1984-85; grad. St. Paul Theol. Sem., Kansas City, Mo., 1987. Ordained minister Presbyn. Ch., 1987. Speech therapist Moultrie Ga. Speech Clinic, 1954-55, U. Tenn. Speech and Hearing Center, 1955-56, Jackson County Exceptional Sch., 1957-58; vending machine sales Morrisons Co., Pascagoula, 1974; newspaper dealer, Clarion Ledger, Jackson, Miss., 1974-75; audiologist, hearing aid salesman Beltone Co., Hattiesburg, Miss., 1975-77; receptionist Singing River Mental Health Services, Pascagoula, 1977; youth services counselor Jackson County Youth Ct., Miss. Dept. Youth Services, Pascagoula, 1977-84, also chief counselor, probation officer; night mgr. N.E.W.S. Shelter for Battered Women, 1985-87; youth minister Grace Presbyn. Ch., Kansas City, 1985-86; stated supply pastor Argentine Presbyn. and John Calvin Presbyn. chs., Kansas City, Kans., 1987-88. Neighborhood chmn. Girl Scouts, 1958-68; trombonist Gulf Coast Symphony, 1981-84; asst. coach Aquatic Club swim team, 1960-70; dir. youth choir 1st Presbyn. Ch., Pascagoula; instr. water safety ARC; rape crisis counselor Gulfcoast Women's Center, Biloxi, Miss.; mem. Pas-Point Singers. Mem. Miss. Assn. Clin. Counselors, State Employees Assn. Miss. Democrat. Home: 909 Bales Kansas City MO 64127

WADE, MERRY GAYLE, educational administrator; b. Salem, Ill., Nov. 30, 1937; d. Clinton Lee Annis and Marcella Claris (Clemins) Allen; children: Marvin, Angel Wade Loucks, Mark, Matt. BA, U. Colo., 1970, MA, 1973, EdS, 1976. Adminstrv. asst. U. Iowa, Iowa City, 1960-62; substitute tchr. Lebanon (Ind.) Sch., 1962-64; tchr. Foothills Elem. Sch., Lakewood, Colo., 1971-76; prin. Copeland (Kans.) Elem. Sch., 1976-83, Washington Elem. Sch., McPherson, Kans., 1983-87, McPherson Mid. Sch., 1987—; presenter in field. Leader 4-H Club, Copeland, 1976-83; mem. Copeland Recreation Commn., 1976-80; choir dir. Christian Ch., Copeland, 1976-78; dir. Copeland Community Theatre, 1980-83. Named Kans Outstanding Rural Sch. Adminstr. Kans. State U., 1981; recipient Exec. Educator 100 award, 1987. Mem. Kans. Assn. Elem. Sch. Prins. (dist. IV Outstanding Adminstr. award 1981, pres. 1986-87), Kans. Internat. Reading Assn. (sec.1979-81), Western Kans. Reading Council (pres. 1978-79), United Sch. Adminstrs. (exec. bd. 1987-88), Phi Delta Kappa (v.p. Western Trails chpt. 1980-81, Reed internat. seminar scholar 1987, appreciation of service award 1987). Home: 201 Center St McPherson KS 67460 Office: McPherson Mid Sch 700 E Elizabeth St McPherson KS 67460

WADE, SALLY KOETTING, infosystems executive; b. Phila., Aug. 17, 1953; d. John Lawrence and Mildred Leone (Wahlert) Koetting; m. Richard C. Corson, Feb. 5, 1977 (div. Feb. 1981); m. David R. Wade, Oct. 2, 1987. BA, Grove City Coll., 1975; postgrad., Carnegie-Mellon U., 1987—. Supr. office services Dravo Corp., Pitts., 1975-77, compensation analyst, 1977-79, supr. employee info. ctr., 1979-82, project mgr., 1982-84, mgr. employee relations, infosystems, 1984—. Vol. ticket sales Allegheny Brass Band, Pitts., 1985—. Mem. Assn. Human Resource Systems Profls. (bd. dirs. Pitts. chpt. 1985-86, pres. 1986-87, Mem. of Yr., 1986), Pitts. Personnel Assn. Republican. Methodist. Home: 45 Tommy Dr Pittsburgh PA 15236 Office: Dravo Corp One Oliver Plaza Pittsburgh PA 15222

WADE, SARA THOMASON, health care executive, real estate broker; b. New Albany, Miss., Jan. 30, 1936; d. James Henderson and Rosabel (Purvis) Thomason; m. John Smith Wade, Sr., Dec. 23, 1956 (div. Oct. 1968); children—John Smith, Kimberly Rose. B.S., Blue Mountain Coll., Miss., 1957; M.Ed., U. Miss., 1973; M.A., Central Mich. U., 1976, PhD Calif. Coast U., 1986. Cert. med. technologist, cytotechnologist. Cytotechnologist, Huntsville (Ala.) Hosp., 1958; bench technologist North Miss. Med Ctr, Tupelo, 1960-61, ednl. coordinator Sch. Med. Technology, 1961-70, adminstrv. dir., 1970—; med. technologist S.J. McDuffie, M.D., Nettleton, Miss., 1970—; cons. med. tech. Miss. State U., Starkville, 1973—, Clay County Hosp., West Point, Miss., 1983; lectr. workshops. Author: Management, 1983; Quality Circles Training Manual, 1983. Mem. Miss. Soc. Med. Tech. (state pres. 1979-80, dist. pres. 1977, dir. 1970-72, 76-78), Am. Soc. Med. Tech. (del. 1976-80), Am. Soc. Cytotechnologists (state rep.). Republican. Methodist. Clubs: Tupelo Running (dir. 1982-83), Miss. Magnolia Quality Circles (dir. 1983-84, pre. elect 1984-85, pres. 1985-86), Tupelo Soroptimist (sec. 1982-84, dir. 1981-82, pres. elect 1984-86, prs. 1986-88), Alpha Mu Tau. Home: 3 Songbird Ln Tupelo MS 38801 Office: North Miss Med Ctr 830 S Gloster St Tupelo MS 38801

WADE, SUZANNE, systems analyst; b. Chgo., Dec. 29, 1938; d. Edward Peter and Dorothy Rose (Hamerly) Traxel; m. Robert Gerald Wade (div. Feb. 1980); children: Peter John, Robert Gerald Jr., Suzette Marie, Francesca Louise, Elizabeth Rose. AA, Orange Coast Coll., 1980; BA, Calif. State U., Fullerton, 1985. Analyst data info. Motorola, Mesa, Ariz., 1972-75; planner prodn. Ford Aerospace, Newprt Beach, Calif., 1975-79; supr. prodn. control Shiley, Inc., Irvine, Calif., 1979-81; mgr. bus. systems Hughes Aircraft Co., Fullerton, 1981-85; systems specialist Long Beach, Calif., 1985—; lectr. to clubs, classes Calif. State U., Fullerton, 1984-85. Author: (manual) Data Services, 1985; columnist, 1984-85. Mem. Am. Prodn. and Inventory Control Soc., Nat. Assn. Female Execs., Los Angeles Aerospace and Def. Spl. Interests Group (steering com., publicity chmn. 1987—). Methodist. Club: Toastmasters (Long Beach) (treas. 1986—). Home: 2299 Legion Dr Apt #402 Signal Hill CA 90806

WADEKAMPER, BARBARA JEAN, small business owner; b. Joplin, Mo., Sept. 2, 1940; d. Lloyd Harry and Olga Julianda (Pomerenke) Cline; m. Lon Gene Wadekamper, Oct. 10, 1958 (div. 1982); children: Scott Dean, Lonette Lea Wadekamper Wright. Grad. high sch., Yakima, Wash.; student, Blue Mountain Community Coll., Pendleton, Oreg., 1975-85. Bookkeeper Betz-Wadekamper Farms, Hermiston, Oreg., 1970-71; office mgr. Louthan's IGA, Hermiston, 1974-76; rancher, farmer The Ranch, Hermiston, 1970-81; co-owner Western Alfalfa, Inc., Irrigon, Oreg., 1973-81; co-owner, operator Brown's Auto & Truck Stop, Irrigon, 1981-88. Chmn. Irrigon Watermelon Festival, 1984—; bd. dirs. Morrow County (Oreg.) Med. Bd., 1987—; active Yakima (Wash.) Cancer Soc., 1954-70. Mem. Irrigon C. of C. (organizer, 1987—), Theta Rho. Republican. Lutheran. Club: Jr. Women's (Union Gap, Wash.). Lodges: Rebekah (Decoration of Chivalry), Lioness. Home: PO Box 648 Rt 2 Box 323 Irrigon OR 97844 Office: Brown's Auto & Truck Stop PO Box N (Hwy 730) Irrigon OR 97844

WADESON, HARRIET, psychotherapy educator; b. Washington; children: Lisa Sinrod, Eric Sinrod, Keith Sinrod. BA, Cornell U., 1952; MA, Goddard Coll., 1975; MSW, Catholic U., 1976; PhD, Union Grad. Sch., 1978. Research psychologist NIMH, Bethesda, Md., 1962-75; pvt. practice psychotherapy 1965—; assoc. prof. U. Houston/Clear Lake, 1978-80, U. Ill. at Chgo., 1980—; cons., lectr. in field. Author: Art Psychotherapy, 1980, The Dynamics of Art Psychotherapy, 1987; contbr. articles to profl. jours. Mem. Am. Art Therapy Assn. (exec. bd., chair pubs. 1983-87, chair research 1987—, Research award 1978), Nat. Assn. Social Workers, Am. Psychol. Assn., Nat. Women's Studies Assn., Am. Acad. of Psychotherapists, Am. Orthopsychiat. Assn., Finish Art Therapy Assn. (hon.). Office: U Ill at Chgo Box 4348 MC 036 Chicago IL 60680

WAELSCH, SALOME GLUECKSOHN, genetics educator; b. Danzig, Germany, Oct. 6, 1907; came to U.S., 1933, naturalized, 1938; d. Ilyia and Nadia Gluecksohn; m. Heinrich B. Waelsch, Jan. 8, 1943; children—Naomi Barbara, Peter Benedict. Student, U. Konigsberg, Ger., U. Berlin; Ph.D., U. Freiburg, Ger., 1932. Research assoc. in genetics Columbia U., 1936-55; assoc. prof. anatomy Albert Einstein Coll. Medicine, 1955-58, prof., 1958-63, prof. genetics, 1963—, chmn. dept. genetics, 1963-76; mem. study sects. NIH. Research, numerous publs. on devel. genetics. Fellow Am. Acad. Arts and Scis.; mem. Nat. Acad. Scis., N.Y. Acad. Scis. (hon. life), Am. Soc. Zoologists, Am. Assn. Anatomists, Genetics Soc., Soc. Devel. Biology, Am. Soc. Naturalists, Am. Soc. Human Genetics, Sigma Xi. Office: Albert Einstein Coll Medicine Dept Genetics 1300 Morris Park Ave Bronx NY 10461

WAELTY, BEATRYCE ANN, rubber and tire company executive; b. Mpls., Aug. 25, 1938; d. Paul Peter and Marion Ann (Hopkins) Heltemes Jerome; m. Thomas K. Hallcock, June 21, 1963 (div. 1977); m. Waldo G. Waelty, Apr. 7, 1979; children—Thomas J.P., Shawn M. (dec.), Kimberley A., Scott E. A.A., Stephens Coll., 1958; B.S., U. San Francisco, 1986. Mgr., Shasta Valley Realty, Weed, Calif., 1978-79; sec., account clk. Area Agy. on Aging, Weed, Calif., 1980-81; data reductionist Aerojet Tactical Co./Aerojet Strategic Propulsion Co., Sacramento, 1982-84; documentation coordinator, 1984, documentation supr., 1984—. Lodge: Order Eastern Star (worthy matron). Avocations: Gardening; needlepoint; carpentry. Home: 1806 Sheffield Way Roseville CA 95678 Office: Aerojet Strategic Propulsion Co Hwy 50 and Hazel Ave Sacramento CA 95813

WAGENBERG, CHARLOTTE B., human resources executive. BA, U. Conn., 1968; MS, Yeshiva U., 1972; MEd, Columbia U., 1976, EdD, 1984. Tchr. N.Y.C. Bd. Edn., 1970-75; edn. cons. 1976-77; program cons. Chase Manhattan Bank, N.Y.C., 1977-78; asst. tng. mgr. St. Luke's Hosp. Ctr., N.Y.C., 1978-81; corp. dir. tng. and devel. St. Luke's-Roosevelt Hosp. Ctr., N.Y.C., 1981-85, assoc. v.p., human resources devel., 1985—; asst. prof. sch. pub. adminstrn. NYU, 1985—. Recipient Disting. Adj. Faculty award NYU Grad. Sch. Pub. Adminstrn., 1987. Mem. Am. Soc. for Tng. and Devel., Tng. Dirs. Forum. Office: St Luke's Roosevelt Hosp Ctr Amsterdam Ave at 114th St New York NY 10025

WAGNER, ALLISON JEAN, vocational nurse; b. Los Angeles, Calif., Dec. 14, 1960; d. Kurt Joseph and Barbara Jean (Wallace) Wagner. A.A./B.A., U. of the Pacific, 1979-83; L.V.N., Maric Coll., 1984-85. Lic. vocat. nurse. Editor/distbr. Winning Images, Beverly Hills, Calif., 1985-86; med. cons. Ctr. for Spl. Surgery, Los Angeles, 1985—; publicist You're Becoming, Los Angeles, 1986. Mem. Calif. Theatre Council, Los Angeles, 1986; Phoenix Art Mus., 1987-88. Recipient Multiple Athletic awards, scholastic awards, The Buckley Sch. Mem. Nat. Assn. Female Execs., Alpha Chi Omega. Methodist. Club: Mary Duque Guild. Avocations: tennis; weight training; scuba diving; racquetball; golf. Office: Ctr for Spl Surgery 1125 S Beverly Dr Suite 505 Los Angeles CA 90035-1148

WAGNER, DOROTHY MARIE, court reporting service executive; b. Milw., June 8, 1924; d. Theodore Anthony and Leona Helen (Ullrich) Wagner; grad. Milw. Bus. U., 1944; student Marquette U., U. Wis., Milw. Stenographer, legal sec., Milw., 1942-44; hearing reporter Wis. Workmen's Compensation Dept., 1944-48; ofcl. reporter to judge Circuit Ct., Milw., 1952-53; owner, operator ct. reporting service Dorothy M. Wagner & Assocs., Milw., 1948—; guest lectr. ct. reporting Madison Area Tech. Coll., 1981—. Recipient Gregg Diamond medal Gregg Pub. Co., 1950. Mem. Nat. (registered profl. reporter, certificate of proficiency), Wis. shorthand reporters assns., Am. Legion Aux., Met. Milw. Assn. Commerce. Roman Catholic. Home: 214 Williamsburg Dr Thiensville WI 53092 Office: 135 Wells St Suite 400 Milwaukee WI 53203

WAGNER, ELIZABETH ANN, manufacturing and financial consultant; b. Crowder, Okla., Nov. 21, 1934; d. William Robert and Lillian Edna (Scott) Bristow; m. Richard Arthur Wagner, June 25, 1955 (div. Sept. 1961); children: Kathleen Elizabeth, Richard Arthur Jr. Student, UCLA, 1961, Compton City Coll., 1963, 65. Controller Artistic Brass div. Norris Industries, Los Angeles, 1967-72; controller Classic Brass div. FamilianCorp., Carson, Calif., 1973; internal auditor Van Nuys, Calif., 1974; controller Dyna div. Compton, Calif., 1975; v.p. fin. Electronic Applications Co., El Monte, Calif., 1977-84; fin. cons. El Monte, Calif., 1984—, also bd. dirs.; owner Western Gen. Services, Diamond Bar, Calif., 1980—; pres. Calif. Transformers, El Monte, 1982-84, U.S. Relays, El Monte, 1982-84, fin. cons. 1984—; pres. Pacific Wing and Rotor, Long Beach, Calif., 1982-83. Active Downey (Calif.) Community Theater, 1961-65. Mem. Nat. Assn. Relay Mfrs., People for the Am. Way, Greenpeace. Republican. Club: Quota (treas. 1967) (Downey). Home: 259 N Rock River Dr Diamond Bar CA 91765

WAGNER, FLORENCE, telecommunications executive; b. McKeesport, Pa., Sept. 23, 1926; d. George and Sophia (Petros) Zeleznik; B.A. magna cum laude, U. Pitts., 1977, M.P.A., 1981; m. Francis Xavier Wagner, June 18, 1946; children—Deborah Elaine Wagner Franke, Rebecca Susan Wagner Schroettinger, Melissa Catherine Wagner Good, Francis Xavier, Robert Francis. Sec. to pres. Tube City Iron & Metal Co., Glassport, Pa., 1944-50; cons. Raw Materials, Inc., Pitts., 1955; gen. mgr. Carson Compressed Steel Products, Pitts., 1967-69; partner Universal Steel Products, Pitts., 1970-71; gen. mgr. Josh Steel Co., Braddock, Pa., 1971-78; owner Wagner's Candy Box, Mt. Lebanon, Pa., 1979-80; borough sec./treas. Borough of Pennsbury Village, Allegheny County, Pa., 1980—; ptnr. Tele-Communications of Am., Burgettstown, Pa., 1984-86; trustee Profit-Sharing trust, Pension trust; mem. Foster Parents, Jefferson Twp. Planning Commn., Washington County, Pa. Mem. Pitts. Symphony Soc., Pitts. Ballet Theater Guild. Mem. Soc. Pub. Adminstrn. (founder U. Pitts. br.), Acad. Polit. Sci., U.S. Strategic Inst., Southwestern Pa. Sec. Assn., AAUW, Alpha Sigma Lambda (past treas., sec., pres.) Republican. Roman Catholic. Home: RD 2 Box 105 Lee Rd Burgettstown PA 15021 Office: 6 Pennsberry Blvd Pittsburgh PA 15205

WAGNER, IRENE MARY, accountant; b. Syracuse, N.Y., Feb. 3, 1958; d. Harold J. and Dorothy T. (Richmond) W. BS, Elmira Coll., 1980. CPA, N.Y. Staff acct. Randolph & Carpenter CPA's, Ithaca, N.Y., 1980-86, Sciarabba, Walker & Co. CPA's, Ithaca, 1986—. Bd. dirs., sec. Salvation Army Women's Aux., Ithaca, 1986-88; bd. dirs., treas. Hospicare of Tompkins County, Ithaca, 1988-89; deaconess Bethel Grove Bible Ch., 1988. Mem. N.Y. State Soc. CPA's, Am. Inst. CPA's, Nat. Assn. Accts. (Ithaca chpt., v.p. communications 1986-88, treas. 1986-88, bd. dirs. attendance 1988—).

WAGNER, JACQUELINE ANN, city planner; b. N.Y.C., B.S. magna cum laude in Bus. Adminstrn., N.Y. Inst. Tech., 1974; M.B.A., Nova U., 1976, D.B.A., 1981. Asst. to v.p. sales Gianinni Sci. Corp., N.Y.C., 1964-67; planning analyst City of Hollywood (Fla.), 1968-72, zoning adminstr., 1973-77, city planner, 1977-80, prin. planner, 1980—; staff adv. Planning and Zoning Bd., City Commn. adj. prof. mgmt. Boward County (Fla.) Community Coll., 1981—; adj. prof. bus. policy M.B.A. program Nova U., Ft. Lauderdale, Fla., 1982. Youth adv., counselor St. John's Episcopal Ch., Hollywood, 1973-75. Mem. Acad. Mgmt., Am. Inst. Planners, Fla. Planning and Zoning Assn., Am. Soc. Public Adminstrs., Internat. Platform Assn. Club: Zonta. Home: PO Box 292637 Davie FL 33329 Office: 2600 Hollywood Blvd Hollywood FL 33020

WAGNER, JANET BEVERLY, teacher; b. Newark, Jan. 24, 1945; d. Albert Marcus and Helen Ilona (Straka) W.; m. Joseph Richard Federico, Apr. 22, 1967 (div. May 1977). BA in Elem. Edn., Coll. William Paterson, 1967, postgrad. Bookkeeper 1st Nat. State Bank N.J., Newark, 1962-63; tchr. elem. Stockton Sch. East Orange (N.J.) Bd. Edn., 1967-68, Gillette (N.J.) Sch., 1968-69, Irvington (N.J.) Bd. Edn., 1969—; adminstr. Panacea Studio Dance Arts and Fitness, Westfield, N.J., 1983—. Vol. Irvington Gen. Hsop., 1968, Elizabeth (N.J.) Gen. Hsop., 1988. Coll. William Paterson scholar, 1989. Mem. NEA, N.J. Edn. Assn., Irvington Edn. Assn. (rep. 1985-86), Irvington Bus. and Profl. Women's Club, N.J. Opera Soc., Silva Mind Control Internat. (life), Theta Delta Rho. Republican. Home: 1380 North Ave Apt 616 Elizabeth NJ 07208 Office: Irvington Bd Edn 1150 Springfield Ave Irvington NJ 07111

WAGNER, JUDITH BUCK, investment advisory firm executive, banker; b. Altoona, Pa. Sept. 25, 1943; d. Harry Bud and Mary Elizabeth (Rhodes) B.; m. Mark S. Foster, June 17, 1967 (div. 1977); m. Joseph E. Wagner, Mar. 15, 1980; 1 child, Elizabeth. BA in History, U. Wash., 1965; grad. N.Y. Inst. Fin., 1968. Chartered fin. analyst; registered Am. Stock Exchange; registered N.Y. Stock Exchange; registered investment advisor. Security analyst Morgan, Olmstead, Kennedy & Gardner, Los Angeles, 1968-71; research cons., St. Louis, 1971-72; security analyst Boettcher & Co., Denver, 1972-75; pres. Wagner Investment Counsel, 1975-84; chmn. Wagner & Hamil, Inc., Denver, 1983—; chmn., bd. dirs. The Women's Bank, N.A., Denver, 1977—, organizational group pres., 1975-77; chmn. Equitable Bankshares Colo., Inc., Denver, 1980—; bd. dirs. Equitable Bank of Littleton, 1983—, pres., 1985; bd. dirs. Colo. Growth Capital, 1979-82; lectr. Denver U., Metro State, 1975-80. Author: Woman and Money series Colo. Woman Mag., 1976; moderator 'Catch 2' Sta. KWGN-TV, 1978-79. Pres. Big Sisters Colo., Denver, 1977-82, bd. dirs., 1973—; bd. fellows U. Denver, 1985—; bd. dirs. Red Cross, 1980, Assn. Children's Hosp., 1985, Colo. Health Facilities Authority, 1978-84, Jr. League Community Adv. Com., 1979—, Brother's Redevel., Inc., 1979-80; mem. Hist. Paramount Found., 1984, Denver Pub. Sch. Career Edn. Project, 1972; mem. investment com. YWCA, 1976—; mem. adv. com. Girl Scouts U.s.; mem. agy. relations com. Mile High United Way, 1978-81, chmn. United Way Venture Grant com., 1980-81; fin. chmn. Schoettler for State Treas., 1986; bd. dirs. Downtown Denver Inc., 1988—. Recipient Making It award Cosmopolitan Mag., 1977, Women on the Go award, Savvy mag., 1983, Minouri Yasoni award, 1986, Salute Spl. Honoree award, Big Sisters, 1987; named one of the Outstanding Young Women in Am., 1979; recipient Woman Who Makes A Difference award Internat. Women's Forum, 1987. Fellow Fin. Analysts Fedn.; mem. Women's Forum of Colo. (pres. 1979), Women's Found. Colo., Inc. (bd. dirs. 1986—), Denver Soc. Security Analysts (bd. dirs. 1976—, v.p. 1980-81, pres. 1981-82), Leadership Denver (Outstanding Alumna award 1987), Pi Beta Phi (pres. U. Wash. chpt. 1964-65). Office: Wagner & Hamil Inc 410 17th St #840 Denver CO 80202

WAGNER, JUDITH L., government official; b. Washington, Feb. 26, 1947; d. Henry C. and Pauline O. (Woodruff) W.; B.S., Madison Coll., 1968; M.S.A., George Washington U., 1970. Mgmt. analyst Office Sec. Army, Washington, 1968-73, U.S. Secret Service, Washington, 1973-74, chief mgmt. programs and studies br., mgmt. and orgn. div., 1974-77, chief paperwork mgmt. br., 1977-78; chief mgmt. and orgn. div. U.S. Mint, Washington, 1978-79, asst. dir. mgmt. services, 1979—. Collegiate profl. teaching cert., Va. Mem. Am. Soc. Public Adminstrn., Am. Mgmt. Assn., Am. Assn. Budget and Program Analysis, Fed. Exec. Inst. Alumni Assn. Office: 633 3d St NW Washington DC 20220

WAGNER, JULIA A(NNE), retired editor; b. Alexandria, Va., Feb. 15, 1924; d. Luigi and Domenica (Di Giammarino) Coppa; Widowed. B.A., George Washington U., 1948, M.A., 1950. With U.S. Govt., Washington, 1941-55, publs. editor, 1951-55; editorial asst. Dell Pub. Co., N.Y.C., 1956-59, mng. editor, 1959-72, editor-in-chief, 1973-87. Mem. Am. Fedn. Astrologers. Democrat. Roman Catholic.

WAGNER, LOUISE HEMINGWAY BENTON, educational company executive; b. Chgo., July 29, 1937; d. William and Helen (Hemingway) Benton; student Skidmore Coll., 1955-57; B.A. in English, Finch Coll., 1960; m. Ralph C. Wagner, May 23, 1979. Pub. relations asst. Look mag., N.Y.C., 1960-62, Compton Ency., Chgo., 1962-63; mktg. services Ency. Brit. Press, Chgo., 1963-66; dir. exhibits Ency. Brit. Ednl. Corp., Chgo., 1966-70, v.p. mktg. services, 1970-83, chmn. bd. dirs., 1983-87, vice chmn. 1988—. Bd. dirs. Chgo. Lying-In Hosp., Cradle Soc., Evanston, Ill., Reading is Fundamental, Chgo.; mem. women's bd. U. Chgo.; governing mem. Orchestral Assn. Chgo., Art Inst. Chgo. Mem. ALA, Assn. for Edn. Communication Tech. Episcopalian. Clubs: Racquet, Mid-Am., Arts (Chgo.); Country of Fairfield (Conn.); Thorngate Country (Deerfield, Ill.). Office: Ency Brit Edn Corp 310 S Michigan Ave Chicago IL 60604

WAGNER, MARCIA ELLEN, probation officer; b. Van Wert, Ohio, July 18, 1938; d. Gaylord Dwight and Marcella Ferne (Febes) Lee; m. Timon Wagner, Jan. 5, 1959(dec. Feb. 1977); children: Ray, Becky (dec.), Elaine, Andrew. Student, Ind. U. Telecommunication sec. Walston and Co., Ft. Wayne, Ind., 1961-67; mgr. Western Union, Ft. Wayne, 1968-69; sec. Allen Circuit Ct., Ft. Wayne, 1970-71, probation officer, 1971-79, chief probation officer, 1979—; program dir. Allen County Community Corp., Ft. Wayne, 1985—. Commr. Met. Human Relation Commn., Ft. Wayne, 1984—. Mem. Ind. Corrections Assn. (pres. 1979), Am. Probation and Parole, Nat. Assn. Female Execs., Am. Corrections Assn. Republican. Lutheran. Office: Allen County Adult Probation 602 1/2 S Calhoun St Fort Wayne IN 46802

WAGNER, MARJORIE COOGAN DOWNING, retired educational association administrator; b. N.Y.C., Mar. 16, 1917; d. Charles A. and

Marguerite C. (Ohl) Coogan; m. John Wagner, June 6, 1974; children—Francis, Margaret, Nicholas. B.A., Coll. Mt. St. Vincent, 1938; M.A., Cath. U. Am., 1939; Ph.D., Yale, 1942; LL.D., Chapman Coll., 1975. Dean Sarah Lawrence Coll., Bronxville, N.Y., 1961-65; dean of faculty Scripps Coll., Claremont, Calif., 1965-71, Frederick Hard prof. English Lit., 1971-74; pres. Calif. State Coll. Sonoma, Rohnert Park, 1974-76; vice chancellor faculty-staff affairs Calif. State U., Long Beach, 1976-80; dir. Insts. for Chief Acad. Officers, Am. Council Edn., 1980-84; cons. Ednl. Inst.; sr. adv. com. Nat. Commn. on State Colls. and Univs., 1985-86. Bd. dirs. United Way, 1975; trustee Mt. St. Mary's Coll., Los Angeles, 1979—, Council on Adult and Experimental Learning, 1986—. Mem. Western Coll. Assn. (dir. 1969-71), Western Assn. Schs. and Colls. (sr. commn. 1968-71, 76-83), Am. Council Edn. (dir. 1977-79, commn. on leadership). Home: 2326 Mark West Springs Rd Santa Rosa CA 95404

WAGNER, MICHELLE ANN, public relations executive, sales representative; b. Athens, Ohio, Mar. 16, 1963; d. David Bowman and Ann (Snee) W. BS, Fla. State U., 1985; postgrad., Ga. State U. Admissions recruiter Kennesaw Coll., Marietta, Ga., 1985-87, Am. Coll. Applied Arts, Atlanta, 1987—; sales cons. Darby Printing Co., Atlanta, 1987. Artist exhibit Calligraphy: The Artwork, 1986. Vol. Atlanta Human Soc., 1986—; fundraising chmn. Atlanta Seminole Booster Assn., 1987; exhibit coordinator Friends of Alphabet, Atlanta, 1986-87. Mem. Nat. Assn. Female Execs., So. Assn. Collegiate Registrars and Admissions Counselors (cover artist Ga. chpt. 1985-87, Cert. Appreciation for Outstanding Contbns. 1987), Ga. Assn. Collegiate Registrars and Admissions Counselors (resolutions com. 1986-87), Cobb County Counselors Assn. (del. Marietta chpt. 1985-87), Kappa Alpha Theta (officer promotions and spl. events). Republican. Baptist. Home: 2214 Peachtree Rd #A6 Atlanta GA 30309 Office: Am Coll Applied Arts 3330 Peachtree Rd Atlanta GA 30328

WAGNER, SUE ELLEN, state legislator; b. Portland, Maine, Jan. 6, 1940; d. Raymond A. and Kathryn (Hooper) Pooler; m. Peter B. Wagner, 1964: children—Kirk, Kristina. B.A. in Polit. Sci., U. Ariz., 1962; M.A. in History, Northwestern U., 1964. Asst. dean women Ohio State U., 1963-64; tchr. history and Am. govt. Catalina High Sch., Tucson, 1964-65; reporter Tucson Daily Citizen, 1965-68; mem. Nev. Assembly, 1975 83; now mem. Nev. Senate from 3d dist. Author: Diary of a Candidate, On People and Things, 1974. Mem. Reno Mayor's Adv. Com., 1973-84; chmn. Blue Ribbon Task Force on Housing, 1974-75; mem. Washoe County Republican Central Com., 1974-84, Nev. State Rep. Central Com., 1975-84; mem. Nev. Legis. Commn., 1976-77; del. social service com. Council State Govts.; v.p. Am. Field Service, 1973, family liaison, 1974, mem.-at-large, 1975. Kappa Alpha Theta Nat. Grad. scholar, also Phelps-Dodge postgrad. fellow, 1962; named Outstanding Legislator, Nev. Young Republicans, 1976. One of 10 Outstanding Young Women in Am. Mem. AAUW (legis. chmn. 1974), Bus. and Profl. Women, Kappa Alpha Theta. Episcopalian. Office: Office of the State Senate State Capitol Carson City NV 89710 Other Address: 845 Tamarack Dr Reno NV 89509 *

WAGNER, SYLVIA RAE, human resource executive; b. Mitchell, S.D., Feb. 14, 1949; d. Robert Henry and Rose Ann (Heiter) W. BA, U. S.D., 1971; MA, Okla. State U., 1974. Tchr., Ft. Riley Jr. High Sch., Junction City, Kans., 1971-72; instr. Okla. State U., Stillwater, 1972-74; communications specialist St. Paul Cos., 1974-76, mgmt. tng. supr., 1976-80, asst. to v.p. human relations, 1981-82; personnel officer Western Life Ins. Co., 1982-85, sr. personnel officer, 1985-86, v.p. human resources, 1987-88, v.p. corp. services, 1988—; cons. Mgmt. Assistance Project, Mpls., 1980-86; instr. Nat. Coll. Bus., St. Paul, 1974-75; mem. Minn. Coalition on Health Employer Corp. Council, 1986—, vocat. adv. com., 1986—. Bd. dirs. KOPE, St. Paul, 1980-87, sec.-treas., 1985-87; mem. Nat. Women's Polit. Caucus, Mpls., 1982—, Minn. Women's Consortium; bd. dirs. Women's Theatre Project, 1986—, Minn. Ins. Info. Ctr., 1986—, Met. East Devel. Ptnrship, 1987—. U. S.D. scholar, 1967-71. Mem. Am. Soc. Personnel Adminstrn., Am. Soc. Tng. and Devel., Woodbury C. of C. (bd. dirs.), Mortar Bd., Phi Beta Kappa, Alpha Lambda Delta. Home: 76 Carla Ln Little Canada MN 55109 Office: Western Life Ins Co PO Box 64271 Saint Paul MN 55164

WAGNER PERKINS, JANE TIFFANY, home economist; b. Kalamazoo, Nov. 5, 1904; m. Willard B. Dean; children: Sally, Diana; m. Albert R. Perkins; stepchildren: John, Nancy. Student, Iowa State U., Ames; BS, Columbia U.; postgrad., Art Inst. Chgo., 1924-26, Simmons Coll., Boston, 1926. Instr. home econs. Audubon, Iowa, 1928-29; field supr. Certo Corp., Rochester, N.Y., 1929; home services dir. Consol. Gas Co., 1929-32, Servel Corp., Inc., 1935-41; dir. Women's Service Ctr. Chgo. Daily News, 1942; dir. Home Econs. Standard Brands of N.Y.C., 1942-50; dir. Women's War Activities NBC-TV, 1950; food editor Am. Home Mag., 1950, 1950-57; home services dir. Gas Appliance Mfrs., N.Y.C., 1950-57. Author: Cookbook for Consolidated Gas. Radio chmn. United Council of Churchwomen, 1943-50. Recipient Centennial award City of Iowa City, 1957. Mem. Am. Home Econs. Assn., Home Economists in Bus. (chmn. 1937), Advt. Women's Club (bd. dirs.), Press Club. Episcopalian. Clubs: Orienta Beach Tennis; La Jolla Beach Tennis, Pi Beta Phi.

WAGNON, JOAN, state legislator; b. Texarkana, Ark., Oct. 17, 1940; d. Jack and Louise (Lucas) D.; m. William O. Wagnon Jr., June 4, 1964; children: Jack, William O. III. BA in Biology, Hendrix Coll., Conway, Ark., 1962; MEd in Guidance and Counseling, U. Mo., 1968. Sr. research technician U. Ark. Med. Sch., Little Rock, 1962-64; sr. research asst. U. Ark. Med. Sch., Columbia, Mo., 1964-68; tchr. No. Hills Jr. High Sch., Topeka, 1968-69, J.S. Kendall Sch., Boston, 1970-71; counselor Neighborhood Youth Corps, Topeka, 1973-74; exec. dir. Topeka YWCA, 1977—; mem. Kans. Legislature, 1983—. Mem. Health Planning Rev. Commn., Topeka, 1984-85. Recipient Service to Edn. award, Topeka NEA, 1979, Outstanding Achievement award, Kans. Home Econs. Assn., 1985; named Woman of Yr. Mayors Council Status of Women, 1983; named one of Top Ten Legislators Kans. Mag., Wichita, 1986. Mem. Topeka Assn. Human Service Execs. (pres. 1981-83), Topekans for Ednl. Involvement (pres. 1979-82), Golden City Women's Forum. Democrat. Methodist. Lodge: Rotary. Home: 1606 Boswell Topeka KS 66604 Office: Topeka YWCA 225 W 12th St Topeka KS 66612

WAGO, MILDRED HOGAN, publican; b. N.Y.C., Aug. 16, 1918; d. Andrew James and Gunhild (Olsen) Hogan; m. Charles Leonard Wago, Nov. 24, 1949; children: Linda G., Charlene C. Grad. high sch., White Plains, N.Y. Clk. Met. Life Ins. Co., N.Y.C., 1938-50; publican Town of North Castle, Armonk, N.Y., 1961—. Mem. N.Y. State Assn. Receivers and Collectors (v.p. 1983—), Westchester County Assn. Receivers and Collectors (pres. 1987—), Nat. Assn. Exec. Females. Republican. Home: 3 Wago Ave Armonk NY 10504

WAHL, JOAN CONSTANCE, tech. writer, editor; b. Phila., Dec. 23, 1921; d. Frank L. and Sara E. (Timoney) O'Brien; B.A., Rosemont Coll., 1943; postgrad. U. Calif., Los Angeles, 1960-61; m. John Carl Wahl, Jr., Dec. 31, 1943 (div. 1959); children—John, Mark, David, Lawrence, Thomas, Jeanne, Madeleine Sophie, Eugene. Substitute tchr. Los Angeles City Bd. Edn., 1961; editor, proofreader Renner/Cal-Data Corp., Los Angeles, 1962-63; editor, tech. writer Volt Tech. Corp., 1964-66; sr. tech. editor, writer, project editor Aerospace Corp., El Segundo, Calif., 1966—. Sect. chmn. United Way, Los Angeles, 1963-64; mem. communications com. St. Paul the Apostle Roman Cath. Ch., Westwood, Calif., 1976-78. Recipient Outstanding Service award United Way, 1964. Mem. Soc. Tech. Communications (sr.), Aerospace Women's Com., Mental Health Assn. Los Angeles County, Kistler Honor Soc. Contbr. articles to profl. jours. Office: Aerospace Corp M3/377 2350 El Segundo Blvd El Segundo CA 90245

WAHL, ROSALIE E., judge; b. Gordon, Kans., Aug. 27, 1924; children: Christopher Roswell, Sara Emilie, Timothy Eldon, Mark Patterson, Jenny Caroline. B.A., U. Kans., 1946; J.D., William Mitchell Coll. Law, 1967. Bar: Minn. 1967. Asst. state pub. defender Mpls., 1967-73; clin. prof. law William Mitchell Coll. Law, 1973-77; assoc. justice Minn. Supreme Ct., St. Paul, 1977—. Fellow Am. Bar Found; mem. ABA (chmn. sect. legal edn. and bar admissions, accreditation com., criminal justice sect., individual rights and responsibility sect.), Minn. State Bar Assn. (com. legal assistance to disadvantaged), Am. Judicature Soc., Nat. Assn. Women Judges, Nat. Assn. Woman Lawyers, Minn. Women Lawyers Assn., Am. Law Inst. Office: Minn Supreme Ct 230 State Capitol Saint Paul MN 55155

WAHL, SUZANNE MARIE, flight attendant; b. Flint, Mich., Jan. 16, 1952; d. Robert Leslie and Patricia Ann (McGriff) Blanckaert; m. David Lee Zeigler, Sept. 4, 1977 (div. Nov. 1983); m. Thomas Lee Wahl, Mar. 18, 1984. BS in Criminal Justice, Mich. State U., 1973; cert. in mgmt., Bradley U., 1976. Dir. pub. safety Ill. Cen. Coll., East Peoria, 1975-78; reservations agt. Ozark Airlines, Peoria, Ill., 1978-84; supr. reservations Ozark Airlines, St. Louis, 1984-86; flight attendant TransWorld Airlines, St. Louis, 1986—; v.p. Forcom, St. Louis, 1984-86, Video Alternatives, 1986—. Home: 1692 Kircher Saint Charles MO 63303

WAHONICK, NANCY ANNE, communications consultant and educator; b. Baldwin, Fla., Aug. 20, 1935; d. Herbert A. and Jeannette (Rainer) Pope; m. Donald R. Wahonick July 3, 1955 (div. 1975); children—Donald R., Bobbie Ruth. B.A., Cleve. State U., 1976; M.A., St. Louis U., 1980. Vice pres. communications Nat. Benevolent Assn., St. Louis, 1976-85; prof., dir. communications dept. Maryville Coll., St. Louis, 1984—. Editor mag. Family Talk, 1976-84; contbg. author: Religious Public Relations Handbook, 1983; contbr. articles to profl. jours.; contbg. author: All God's Children, 1979. Media liaison Reagon/Bush Innagural Com., Washington, 1981; religious press rep. Carter/Ford Debates, 1976; trustee W. Shore Chorale, Lakewood, Ohio, 1972-76; mem. Lakewood Ohio Civil Service Commn., 1973-74, Arts and Edn. Com. and Mo. Arts Council, 1979-81; pub. relations dir. Crestwood Children's Theatre, 1980-83; mem. long range planning com. Webster Groves Christian Ch., St. Louis; bd. dirs., ch. sch. dir. Lakewood Christian Ch., Cleve., 1959-76. Recipient Hinkhouse-DeRose award for exhibits and displays, 1982, for Film Caring Changes, 1984; award Women in Communication, 1984; Outstanding Alumnae award, Cleve. State U., 1976; Bus. and Profl. Women scholarship award, 1975; Lakewood Coll. Club Career Advancement scholar, 1975; State of Ohio Career Advancement grantee, 1975; Cleve. State U. Literary award, 1974. Mem. Religious Pub. Relations Council (treas. 1980-82), Assoc. Ch. Press (dir. 1980-82), Pub. Relations Soc. Am., Women in Communications. Mem. Christian Ch. Club: St. Louis Press. Office: Maryville Coll 13550 Conway Rd Saint Louis MO 63141

WAHRMUND, ALICE MAE, tax specialist, consultant; b. Kerrville, Tex., June 28, 1960; d. Russell A. and Ada Mae (Montel) Dickey; m. Charles Dennis Wahrmund, Aug. 14, 1978; 1 child, Richard James. Student, Barbizon Sch., San Antonio, 1977, Durham Bus. Coll., 1979, Nat. Tax Tng. Sch., Monsey, N.Y., 1981. Clk. Anthony's, Kerrville, Tex., 1977-78; mgr. Irongate Apts., Austin, Tex., 1979-80; sec. bd. dirs. Art World Security, Inc., Kerrville, 1983—; pres. Four Seasons Bus. Services, Inc., Kerrville, 1983—; owner A&R Bus. Service, Kerrville, 1985—, Howdy Greeters, Kerrville, 1988—. Mem. TAPA, Nat. Soc. Pub. Accts. Office: Four Seasons Bus Service Inc 516 Sidney Baker Kerrville TX 78028

WAINESS, MARCIA WATSON, legal administrator; b. Bklyn., Dec. 17, 1949; d. Stanley and Seena (Klein) Watson; m. Steven Richard Wainess, Aug. 7, 1975. Student, UCLA, 1967-71, 80-81, Grad. Sch. Mgmt. Exec. Program, 1988, grad. Grad. Sch. Mgmt. Exec. Program, 1988. Office mgr., paralegal Lewis, Marenstein & Kadar, Los Angeles, 1977-81; office mgr. Rosenfeld, Meyer & Susman, Beverly Hills, Calif., 1981-83; adminstr. Rudin, Richman & Appel, Beverly Hills, 1983; dir. adminstrn. Kadison, Pfaelzer, Los Angeles, 1983-87; exec. dir. Richards, Watson and Gershon, Los Angeles, 1987—; faculty mem. UCLA Legal Mgmt. & Adminstrn. Program, 1983, U. So. Calif. Paralegal Program, Los Angeles, 1985; mem. adv. bd. atty. asst. tng. program, UCLA, 1984—. Mem. adv. bd. UCLA Atty. Asst. Tng. Program., 1984—. Mem. ABA (chmn. Displaywrite Users Group 1986, legal tech. adv. council litigation support working group 1986-87), State Bar Calif., Los Angeles County Bar Assn. (exec. com. law office mgmt. sect.), Assn. Profl. Law Firm Mgrs., Assn. Legal Adminstrs. (asst. regional v.p. Calif. 1987-88, regional v.p. 1988-89, pres. Beverly Hills chpt. 1985-86, membership chmn. 1984-85, chmn. new adminstrn. sect. 1982-84). Office: Richards Watson and Gershon 333 S Hope St 38th Floor Los Angeles CA 90071

WAINWRIGHT, HILDA ALEXANDER, service executive, small business owner; b. Teheran, Iran, June 18; came to U.S., 1945, naturalized 1947; d. Mamikon and Balasan (Carapetyan) Ohanian; m. Boris Alexander, May 27, 1945 (dec. Aug. 1961); children: Ronald Boris, Douglas Haig; m. Richard A. Wainwright, Feb. 18, 1977. Student, Ecole Jean D'Arc, Teheran, 1945, Brown Bus. Sch., 1947, Gemological Inst. Am., 1963, Banford Acad. Styling, 1950. Design stylist Elizabeth Arden, N.Y.C., 1949-52; owner, mgr. Randough, N.Y.C., 1960; sales rep. Roux Labs., Jacksonville, Fla., also N.Y.C., 1968-71, Mackey Internat. Airline, Ft. Lauderdale, Fla., 1971-73; owner, mgr. CIR-Q-TEL Inc., Kensington, Md., 1980—, exec. v.p., pres., 1982-84, treas., 1984—; owner franchises Hairperformers Hair Salons; pres. H.A.W. Enterprises. Pres. Armenian Gen. Benevolent Union, N.Y.C. and Fla., 1945—. Clubs: Washington Speakers, Black Tie, Chevy Chase Women's, Columbia Country. Lodge: Old Crows. Avocations: tennis, gardening, painting in oil and acrylic, bridge, languages. Home: 3333 University Blvd W #212 Kensington MD 20895 Office: CQT Electronics Inc 6600 Virginia Manor Rd Beltsville MD 20705

WAIT, NANCY LOUISE, artist; b. Chgo., Dec. 1, 1949; d. Franklin Wait and Frances McCarthy; m. Jerry Brody, Sept. 10, 1978 (div. 1982). Student, Carnegie-Mellon U., 1967-69, Royal Acad. Dramatic Art, London, 1970-72. Actress Eng., 1972-77; free-lance artist, illustrator N.Y.C., 1980—; instr. N.Y. Sch. Interior Design, 1985. Exhibited in group shows at Keane Mason Gallery, N.Y.C., 1983 (1st prize); commd. to paint Mohammed Ali, 1980, 2 kings of Afghanistan and Alan Greenspan. Pres. local Block Assn., Manhattan, N.Y.; vol. Beth Israel Hosp., N.Y.C., 1986; mem. Ctr. for Peace through Culture, N.Y.C.

WAITE, ELLEN JANE, library director; b. Oshkosh, Wis., Feb. 17, 1951; d. Earl Vincent and Margaret (Luft) W.; m. Thomas H. Dollar, Aug. 19, 1977 (div. July 1984). BA, U. Wis., Oshkosh, 1973; MLS, U. Wis., Milw., 1977. Head of cataloging Marquette U., Milw., 1977-82; head catalog librarian U. Ariz., Tucson, 1983-85; assoc. dir. libraries Loyola U., Chgo., 1985-86, acting dir. libraries, 1986-87, dir. libraries, 1987—; cons. Loyola U., Chgo., 1984, Boston Coll., 1986. Contbg. author: Research Libraries and Their Implementation of AACR2, 1985; author: (with others) Women in LC's Terms: A Thesaurus of Subject Headings Related to Women, 1988. Mem. ALA. Office: Loyola U Cudahy Library 6525 N Sheridan Rd Chicago IL 60626-5385

WAITE, GLORIA E., optometrist; b. Rochester, N.Y., May 12, 1943; d. Warren Henry and Frieda (Plapp) Horn; B.S., U. Calif., Berkeley, 1965, O.D., 1966; m. Ray L. Waite, Aug. 20, 1966. Pvt. practice optometry, Pinole, Calif., 1977—; asst. clin. prof. Sch. Optometry, U. Calif.-Berkeley, 1983—. Recipient Cert. of Appreciation Richmond Unified Sch. Dist., 1978-81. Mem. Alameda-Contra Costa Counties Optometric Soc. (dir. 1975-83, pres. 1981-82), Calif. Optometric Assn. membership div. exec. com. 1978-83, Speaker award 1979-82), Pinole-Hercules C. of C. (dir. 1977-83), AAUW (mem. Richmond-El Cerrito chpt. hosting com. 1978, treas. 1979), Am. Optometric Assn., Calif. Optometric Assn. (membership div. 1978-87, chmn. membership div. 1978-88, trustee). Republican. Lutheran. Clubs: Soroptomists (chmn. El Pinablo nominating com. 1980, Woman of Achievement award 1977), Rotary (Pinole). Contbr. articles in field to profl. publs. Office: 635 Tennent Ave Pinole CA 94564

WAITE, SALLY GRIFFITH, lawyer; b. Newark, Ohio, July 20, 1946; d. John Gerald and Mildred Marie (Shorts) Griffith; m. David R. Middleton, June 4, 1967 (div. Jan. 4, 1977; 1 son, Brock David. BA, Berea Coll., 1968; JD, Stetson U., 1978. Bar: Ind. 1979. Tchr., Troy Public Schs. (Ohio), 1968-70; labor relations atty. Bethlehem Steel Co., Chesterton, Ind., 1978-79; union relations atty. Gen. Electric Co., Cin., 1979-81, mgr. employee relations, 1981-83, mgr. employee relations, community relations, Tiffin, Ohio, 1983-85, mgr. profl. relations Aerospace Electronics Systems dept., 1985-86, mgr. employee relations electronics lab., 1986-88, mgr. union relations lighting div., Cleve., 1988—. Mem. ABA, Ind. Bar Assn., Seneca County Personnel Assn., Indsl. Mgmt. Council Tiffin, Phi Delta Phi. Republican. Methodist. Home: 2833 Courtland Blvd Shaker Heights OH 44122 Office: Gen Electric Lighting div Nela Park Cleveland OH 44122

WAITE, SCOTIA BALLARD KNOUFF, criminal justice specialist; b. Willis Wharf, Va., Apr. 8, 1909; d. Warren Alan and Lotta Mondora (Chard) Ballard; B.L.I., Emerson Coll., 1931; M.Ed., Boston U., 1933; diploma Sch. Social Work, Columbia U., 1939; m. William Francis Knouff, Oct. 9, 1943 (dec. Jan. 1968); children—Mary Francis Knouff Linn, Warren Irving Knouff; m. 2d Frederick Waite, Jan. 3, 1976. Dir., Mathews County (Va.) Relief Office, 1932-35, Rappahanock County Relief Office, 1935-36, dir. relief offices Norfolk County and City of S. Norfolk (Va.), 1936-37, case worker Henry Watson Children's Aid Soc., Balt., 1937, with New Orleans Council Social Agys., 1938-40, dir. Council Social Agenices, Syracuse, NY, 1940-44, asst. dir. Detroit Council Social Agys., 1944-45, tech. cons. juvenile delinquency Dept. Justice, Washington, 1948-50, instr., dir. Sociology Research Lab. CCNY, 1950-55, faculty dept. Sociology Adelphi U., 1955-63; dir. research and staff devel. Nassau County (N.Y.) Probation Dept., 1963-78; co-dir. Improving Victim Services Through Probation project Am. Probation and Parole Assn. of Aberdeen (N.C.) and Blackstone Inst. of Washington, 1978-80; cons. criminal justice, Pinehurst, N.C., 1980—; examiner Nat. Commn. on Accreditation for Corrections, 1979—; adj. asso. prof. Sch. Criminal Justice, C.W. Post Coll., L.I.U., 1967—; tech. cons. Nat. Inst. Corrections, 1983; mem. Child Placement Rev. Com. Moore County, N.C.; chmn. Youth Services Commn. Moore County. Mem. Nat. Republican Com. Recipient Outstanding Achievement award C.W. Post Coll. Sch. Criminal Justice, 1977, Spl. award Nassau County Probation Dept., 1978. Mem. Am. Probation and Parole Assn. (Walter Dunbar award 1977), Am. Correctional Assn., Northeastern Assn. Correctional Educators, Tex. Correctional Assn., AAUW. Episcopalian. Clubs: Pinehurst Country. Author numerous reports in corrections, victim services. Home: PO Box 456 McDonald Rd Pinehurst NC 28374

WAITE, SHIRLEY ELEANOR, retired nurse and administrator; b. Gloucester, Mass., Jan. 4, 1925; d. Walter Dunlap and Ida Estelle (Robinson) Collins; R.N., Truesdale Hosp. Sch. Nursing, Fall River, Mass., 1946; student Miami Dade Community Coll., 1963-68, Fla. Internat. U., Miami, 1974-77; cert. in nursing adminstr., 1980; m. Horatio Simmons Waite, Feb. 15, 1946; children—Bruce F., Cheryl J. Waite Kapit, Charles W., David W., Gayle I. Staff nurse, St. Luke's Hosp., New Bedford, Mass., 1946; nurse premature and new born nursery Union Hosp., Fall River, Mass., 1947-48; supr. Newport (R.I.) Hosp., 1951-52; staff nurse, supr. Jackson Meml. Hosp., 1953-63; supr. Meml. Hosp., Hollywood, Fla., 1964-65; supr., asst. dir. nursing, dir. nurse recruitment Cedars of Lebanon Health Care Center, Miami, Fla., 1966-77; head nurse North Miami Gen. Hosp., 1978; v.p. nursing service DeSoto Meml. Hosp., Arcadia, Fla., 1978-87; mem. adv. com. South Fla. Community Coll.; Charlotte Vo-Tech. Sch., DeSoto LPN Sch.; 2d v.p. Cedars of Lebanon Credit Union. Notary pub., Fla., geog. rep. Desoto County commn. Future of Nursing in Fla. Mem. Nat. League Nursing, Fla. League Nursing, Fla. Orgn. Nursing Execs., Charsoto Council Continuing Edn. for Nurses (pres. 1981-82), Dade County Practitioners in Infection Control (past v.p.). Home: Route 1 Box 411 Herbert Rd Arcadia FL 33821 Office: PO Box 2180 Arcadia FL 33821

WAITERS, GAIL ELENORIA, public administrator; b. Kansas City, May 15, 1954; d. Lloyd Winfred and Lenora (Sampson) W. BA in Mass Communication, Calif. State U., Hayward, 1981; MPA, Calif. State U., 1988. Undergrad. admissions specialist Calif. State U., Hayward, 1972-74, registration coordinator, 1974-82; adminstrv. analyst U. Calif., Berkeley, 1982-85; program mgr. City of Sunnyvale (Calif.), 1985—. Bd. dirs. YWCA, Berkeley, 1983-85, treas., 1985. Mem. Internat. Assn. Bus. Communicators, Nat. Forum for Black Pub. Adminstrs., Orgnl. Devel. Network, Internat. City Mgmt. Assn. Democrat. Baptist. Office: City of Sunnyvale PO Box 3707 Sunnyvale CA 94086-3707

WAITS, DOROTHY THERESA, accountant; b. N.Y.C., May 24, 1940; d. Michael Joseph and Elizabeth Mary (Urban) Hronec; m. John Patrick Waits, Oct. 29, 1960. BA in Econs., Hunter Coll., 1969. Controller Ambassador Emil Mosbacher Jr., N.Y.C., 1968-81; tax accountant Richard Leibner, CPA, N.Y.C., 1981-87; tax mgr. Investors Records Corp., N.Y.C., 1987—. Mem. Nat. Assn. Female Execs., N.Y. Soc. Ind. Accts. Democrat. Roman Catholic. Home: 150 Myers Ave Hicksville NY 11801 Office: Investors Records Corp 250 W 34th St Suite 3331 One Penn Plaza New York NY 10119

WAITZ-HALPERIN, ESTHER, sportswear manufacturing company executive; b. Allentown, Pa., Aug. 17, 1925; d. Abraham and Sadie (Ostrow) Waitz; m. Marvin Goldberg, 1947 (div. 1957); m. Bernard Halperin, June 15, 1963 (dec. 1964); children—Richard Goldberg, Jonathan Halperin; m. Abe Krantz, June 19, 1974 (div. dec. 1985). B.A., Moravian coll., 1948; M.S., Temple U., 1962. Pre-sch. tchr. Jewish Community Ctr., Allentown, 1955-63, summer camp tchr. 1955-63; kindergarten tchr. Jewish Day Sch., Allentown, 1962; pres. Halsen Products, Inc., Slatington, Pa., 1964—. Chmn. Allentown United Way, 1966-81; subscriber Met. Opera, N.Y.C., 1974—. Mem. Atlantic Apparel Assn., Lehigh Valley Needle Trades (bd. dirs. 1964-80, chmn. Pa. apparel week 1969), Pi Delta Epsilon. Republican. Clubs: Hadassah, ORT (Allentown). Lodge: Shriners. Avocations: opera; ballet; dancing; travel. Home: 3717 Congress St Allentown PA 18104 Office: Halsen Products Inc 216 Cherry St Slatington PA 18080

WAJDA, GERALYN, salesperson; b. Chgo., Sept. 17, 1954; d. Robert Joseph Sr. and Shirley Ann (Super) Zeinz; m. Paul B. Wajda, Feb. 21, 1981. AAS in Interior Design, Harper Jr. Coll., 1973, AA, 1975; BFA in Interior Design, No. Ill. U., 1976. Salesperson Homemakers, Inc., Schaumburg, Ill., 1972-73; interior designer John M. Smyth Co., Chgo., 1973-75; clk. Mdse. Mart, Chgo., 1977; space planner Richmond Manhoff & Marsh, Chgo., 1977; paste-up artist Paddock Pubs., Arlington Heights, Ill., 1977; interior designer Boise Cascade, Itasca, Ill., 1977-85, salesperson, 1985—. Mem. Profl. Inst. Bus. Designers, IFMA (No. Ill. Chpt.). Home: 1340 Rosita Dr Palatine IL 60067 Office: Boise Cascade 800 W Bryn Mawr Itasca IL 60143

WAKE, MARVALEE HENDRICKS, zoology educator; b. Orange, Calif., July 31, 1939; d. Marvin Carlton and Velvalee (Borter) H.; m. David B. Wake, June 23, 1962; 1 child, Thomas A. BA, U. So. Calif., 1961, MS, 1964, PhD, 1968. Teaching asst./instr. U. Ill., Chgo., 1964-68, asst. prof., 1968-69; lectr. U. Calif., Berkeley, 1969-73, asst. prof., 1973-76, assoc. prof., 1976-80, prof. zoology, 1980—, chmn. dept. zoology, 1985—, assoc. dean Coll. Letters and Sci., 1975-78. Editor, co-author: Hyman's Comparative Vertical Anatomy, 1979; co-author: Biology, 1978; contbr. articles to profl. jours. NSF grantee, 1978—; Guggenheim fellow, 1988-89. Fellow AAAS, Calif. Acad. Scis.; mem. Am. Soc. Ichthyology and Herpetology (pres. 1984, bd. govs. 1978—), Internat. Union Biol. Scis. (U.S. Nat. Com. 1986-92). Home: 999 Middlefield Rd Berkeley CA 94708 Office: Univ Calif Dept Zoology Berkeley CA 94720

WAKELEE, ADAH MAE, microbiologist; b. Conneaut, Ohio, Apr. 6, 1935; d. Walter Ivan and Arleen Louise (Beach) Terrill; B.S. in Med. Tech., Wittenberg U., 1960; m. Robert L. Wakelee, Jr., May 23, 1963; children—Kieth Robert, Kent Walter. Staff technologist, Mercy Hosp. Lab., Springfield, Ohio, 1959-63, Grant Hosp. Lab., Columbus, Ohio, 1963-64, J. Mark Handley, M.D., Santa Maria, Calif., 1965-69; microbiologist Rome (N.Y.) City Hosp. Lab., 1972-79; chief technologist MDS Health Systems Inc. (formerly Lorkim Labs.), Rome, 1980-85; asst. lab. supr. Slocum Dickson Med. Group, 1985—; cons. in microbiology Rose Hosp., Rome, Slocum-Dickson Med. Group, Utica, N.Y. Mem. Oneida County Profl. Adv. Council, 1977, 78; trustee Rome Acad. Scis., 1978—, pres., 1979-81; mem. Rome Mayor's Water Com., 1983-85; Cert., registered Am. Soc. Clin. Pathologists; lic. clin. med. technologist, Calif. Mem. Am. Soc. Clin. Pathology, Am. Soc. Microbiology, N.Y. State Assn. Public Health Labs., Mohawk Valley Engrs. Exec. Council (chmn. 1981-82, sec. 1983-84), AAUW (pres. Rome br. 1980-82). Republican. Congregationalist. Clubs: Order Eastern Star, Daus. of the Nile. Determined causes of illnesses, Rome, 1975, Holland Patent (N.Y.) area, 1976; co-author article in field for profl. jour. Home: 123 Glen Road S Rome NY 13440

WALBRAN, BONNIE (JANE) BREAUX, psychologist; b. Little Rock, Feb. 23, 1938; d. Bertin Joseph and Jeanne Rita (LaNasa) Breaux; A.B. cum laude, Vassar Coll., 1960; Ph.D., Washington U., 1975; postgrad. St. Louis U.; m. Jon A. Newell, July 21, 1984; children by previous marriage—Stephanie Jane, Alexa Suzanne. Research asst. Milbank Meml. Fund, Hudson River St. Hosp., Poughkeepsie, N.Y., 1960-61, Tufts U. Med. Sch., Boston, 1961-62, Harvard U. Sch. Public Health dept. epidemiology, Boston, 1962-64; research asst. Washington U. Sch. Medicine dept. psychiatry, St. Louis, 1965-69, 75-77, research asso., 1978-79; dir. New Hope Learning Center, St. Louis U., 1979-81; unit psychologist, coordinator psychol. services St. Louis Developmental Disabilities Treatment Ctr., 1981-88; psychologist, habilitation mgr. Alton (Ill.) Mental Health and Devel. Ctr., 1988—; instr. Webster Coll. Mem. Am. Psychol. Assn., Am. Assn. Mental Deficiency, Valley Sailing Assn., Sigma Xi. Democrat. Contbr. articles in field to profl. jours. Home: 215 Jefferson Rd Webster Groves MO 63119 Office: Alton Mental Health Ctr 4500 College Ave Alton IL 62002

WALCOTT, ARDELL WILLIAMS, bank executive; b. Savannah, Ga., June 3, 1945; d. Willie Mae (Smalls) Smith; m. Randall Walcott, Sept. 16, 1963; children: Darrell, Kevin. AA, Clayton State Coll., 1980; student, Ga. State U., 1980-82. Telephone operator N.Y. Telephone, N.Y.C., 1966-68; bank teller Chem. Bank, Bklyn., 1969-73; asst. v.p. Citizens & So. Nat. Bank, Atlanta, 1973—. Bd. dirs. West End Merchants Assn., Atlanta, 1985—; bd. mgrs. of Butler St. YMCA, Atlanta, 1985—; treas. com. to elect Michael Hightower, College Park, Ga., 1986—, College Park NAACP, 1987. Mem. Am. Bus. Women's Assn. (treas. 1985-86, del. 1986, pres. 1986-87, Women of Yr. 1988—, Bus. Assoc. of Yr. 1988—), Atlanta Urban Bankers Assn. Democrat. Baptist. Home: 2766 Dodson Lee Dr East Point GA 30344 Office: Citizens & So Nat Bank 2523 Bolton Rd NW Atlanta GA 30318

WALD, FRANCINE JOY WEINTRAUB (MRS. BERNARD J. WALD), physicist; b. Bklyn., Jan. 13, 1938; d. Irving and Minnie (Reisig) Weintraub; student Bklyn. Coll., 1955-57; B.E.E., CCNY, 1960; M.S., Poly. Inst. Bklyn., 1962, Ph.D., 1969; m. Bernard J. Wald, Feb. 2, 1964; children—David Evan, Kevin Mitchell. Engr., Remington Rand Univac div. Sperry Rand Corp., Phila., 1960; instr. Poly. Inst. Bklyn., 1962-64, adj. research asso., 1969-70; lectr. N.Y. Community Coll., Bklyn., 1969, 70; instr. sci. Friends Sem., N.Y.C., 1975-76, chmn. dept. sci., 1976—. NDEA fellow, 1962-64. Mem. Am. Phys. Soc., Am. Assn. Physics Tchrs., Assn. Tchrs. in Ind. Schs., N.Y. Acad. Scis., Nat. Sci. Tchrs. Assn., AAAS, Sigma Xi, Tau Beta Pi, Eta Kappa Nu. Home: 520 LaGuardia Pl New York NY 10012

WALD, PATRICIA MCGOWAN, federal judge; b. Torrington, Conn., Sept. 16, 1928; d. Joseph F. and Margaret (O'Keefe) McGowan; m. Robert L. Wald, June 22, 1952; children—Sarah, Douglas, Johanna, Frederica, Thomas. B.A., Conn. Coll., 1948; LL.B., Yale U., 1951; H.H.D., Mt. Vernon Jr. Coll., 1980; LLD, George Washington Law Sch., 1983, CUNY, 1984, Notre Dame U., 1985, Georgetown U., 1987. Bar: D.C. 1952. Clk. U.S. Ct. of Appeals Judge Jerome Frank, 1951-52; asso. firm Arnold, Fortas & Porter, Washington, 1952-53; mem. D.C. Crime Commn., 1964-65; atty. Office of Criminal Justice, 1967-68, Neighborhood Legal Service, D.C., 1968-70; co-dir. Ford Found. Project on Drug Abuse, 1970, Center for Law and Social Policy, 1971-72, Mental Health Law Project, 1972-77; asst. atty. gen. for legis. affairs U.S. Dept. Justice, Washington, 1977-79; judge U.S. Ct. of Appeals, D.C. circuit, 1979-86, chief judge, 1986—. Author: Law and Poverty, 1965; co-author: Bail in the United States, 1964, Dealing with Drug Abuse, 1973; contbr. articles on legal topics. Trustee Ford Found., 1972-77, Phillips Exeter Acad., 1975-77, Agnes Meyer Found., 1976-77, Conn. Coll., 1976-77; mem. Carnegie Council on Children, 1972-77. Mem. ABA (bd. editors ABA Jour. 1978-84), Am. Law Inst. (council 1979—, exec. com. 1985—), Inst. Medicine, Phi Beta Kappa. Office: 3832 US Courthouse John Marshall Pl Washington DC 20001 also: US Ct of Appeals US Courthouse 3rd & Constitution Ave NW Washington DC 20001

WALD, SYLVIA, artist; b. Phila., Oct. 30, 1915. Ed., Moore Inst. Art, Sci. and Industry. Exhibited one-woman shows, U. Louisville, 1945, 49, Kent State Coll., 1945, Nat. Serigraph Soc., 1946, Grand Central Moderns, N.Y.C., 1957, Devorah Sherman Gallery, Chgo., 1960, New Sch., 1967, Book Gallery, White Plains, N.Y., 1968, Benson Gallery, Bridgehampton, L.I., 1977, Knoll Internat., Munich, Germany, 1979, Amerika Havs, Munich, 1979, Aaron Berman Gallery, N.Y.C., 1981, group shows, Nat. Sculpture Soc., 1940, Sculpture Internat., Phila., 1940, Chgo. Art Inst., 1941, Bklyn. Mus., 1975, Library of Congress, 1943, 52, 58, Smithsonian Instn., 1954, Internat. Print Exhbn., Salzburg and Vienna, 1952, 2d Sao Paulo Biennial, 1953, N.Y. Cultural Center, 1973, Mus. Modern Art, N.Y.C., 1975, Benson Gallery, Bridgehampton, L.I., 1982, Dumon-Landis Gallery, New Brunswick, N.J., 1982-83, Suzuki Gallery, N.Y.C., 1982, Sid Deutch Gallery, N.Y.C., 1983, Aaron Berman Gallery, N.Y.C., 1983, Full House Gallery, Kingston, N.J., 1984, others; represented in permanent collections, Aetna Oil Co., Am. Assn. U. Women, Ball State Tchrs. Coll., Bibliotheque Nationale, Paris, Bklyn. Mus., Howard U., State U. Iowa, Library of Congress, U. Louisville, Nat. Gallery, Mus. Modern Art, Phila. Mus., N.C. Mus., Rose Mus. Art at Brandeis U., Whitney Mus., N.Y.C., Finch Coll. Mus., N.Y.C., U. Nebr., Ohio U., U. Okla., Princeton, Victoria and Albert Mus., Walker Gallery, Worcester (Mass.) Art Mus., Guggenheim Mus., N.Y.C., Grunewald Mus., U.Calif. Los Angeles, Rutgers Mus., N.J., Aschenbach Collection Mus., San Francisco, Grunewald Coll. Mus. UCLA; Contbr. to profl. publs. Address: 417 Lafayette St New York NY 10003

WALDAU, HELEN FRANCES, educator; b. Torrington, Conn., Mar. 21, 1925; d. Teofil and Michaelena (Plaga) Budney; B.A., U. Conn., 1953, 6th yr. certificate, 1968; M.A., U. Hartford; divorced; children—Geoffrey, Christopher, Peter, Sandra. Mem. faculty Hopewell Sch., Glastonbury, Conn., 1966—; tchr. academically talented, Glastonbury, 1982-85; dir. Apple Computer Project, 1984; supr. U. Conn. open edn. interns, 1971-75. Fellow U. Conn., 1967-68. Mem. NEA, Conn., Glastonbury edn. assns., Greater Conn. Council for Open Edn. (charter), Glastonbury Task Force for Gifted Edn., Conn. Tchrs. Center for Humanistic Edn., Psi Upsilon Omicron. Home: 1808 Main St Glastonbury CT 06033

WALDAUER, KAREN, publisher; b. N.Y.C., Jan. 13, 1938; d. Max and Sylvia Gordon; student CCNY, 1955-58; m. Charles Waldauer, May 8, 1958; children—Jan, Kim. Head art dept. Bohanon Printing, Syracuse, N.Y., 1960-64, A.S. Barnes Co., 1964-65; prodn. dir., regional editor, mng. editor Rutgers U. Press, 1965-68; pres. Middle Atlantic Press, Wallingford, Pa., 1968-84; pres. Valley Del Publs., 1984—; pub. cons. Wilmington (Del.) News Jour., Corp. Service Co. Bd. dirs. Sch. in Rose Valley. Mem. Pubs. Alliance, Phila. Pubs. Group, Small Mag. Pubs. Group, Brandywine Valley Press Assn. Clubs: Phila. Skating, Skating of Radnor (past pres.). Office: 840 E St Rd PO Box 31 Westtown PA 19395

WALDECK, JACQUELINE ASHTON, author; b. Chgo.; d. John and Maria Teresa (Arneri) Ashton; m. William George Waldeck, Sept. 20, 1947 (div. June 1964). BA, U. Colo., 1948; postgrad. Tex. Agrl. & Mech. U., 1970. Staff and vol. writer Montrose Daily Press, Colo., 1949-66; feature editor Fiesta Mag., Boca Raton, Fla., 1971-76; free-lance writer, historian, pub., lectr., Boca Raton, 1971—. Author: Boca Raton from Pioneer Days, 1980, Boca Raton: A Romance, 1981, Boca Raton Pioneers and Addison Mizner, 1984; also numerous mag. articles. Sec. Tri-County Mental Health Assn., Montrose, 1964-65; pub. relations chmn. Montrose County chpt. ARC, 1950-63; bd. dirs. Friends Boca Raton Mus. Art, 1983-84; mem. Friends Boca Raton Library, Friends Caldwell Play House, Boca Raton, 1983—. Mem. Nat. League Am. Pen Women (br. v.p. 1984-88, Nat. Biennial award for non-fiction article 1984), Nat. Soc. Arts and Letters (chpt. bd. dirs. 1983-88, pub. relations chmn. drama, music, dance, arts and letters contests 1984-88), Fla. Hist. Soc., Boca Raton Hist. Soc., Greater Boca Raton C. of C. Avocations: dancing, psychology, anthropology, international relations, history. Home: 398 W Camino Real Apt 1 Boca Raton FL 33432

WALDEN, AMELIA ELIZABETH (MRS. JOHN WILLIAM HARMON), author; b. N.Y.C.; d. William A. and Elizabeth (Wanner) W.; m. John William Harmon, Feb. 9, 1946 (dec. 1950). B.S., Columbia U., 1934; cert., Am. Acad. Dramatic Arts. Author: Gateway, 1946, Waverly, 1947, Sunnycove, 1948, Skymountain, 1950, A Girl Called Hank, 1951, Marsha, On-Stage, 1952, Victory for Jill, 1953, All My Love, 1954, Daystar, 1955, Three Loves Has Sandy, 1955, The Bradford Story, 1956, I Found My Love, 1956, My Sister Mike, 1956, Palomino Girl, 1957, Flight Into Morning, 1957, Today is Mine, 1958, Queen of the Courts, 1959; duo of novels An American Teacher: Where Is My Heart?, 1960; How Bright the Dawn, 1962, A Boy to Remember, 1960, Shadow on Devils Peak, 1961; trilogy The American Shakespeare Festival: When Love Speaks, 1961; So Near the Heart, 1962, My World's the Stage, 1964, My Dreams Ride High, 1963, To Catch A Spy, 1964, The Spy on Danger Island, 1965, Race the Wild Wind, 1965, The Spy with Five Faces, 1966, In Search of Ophelia, 1966, A Spy Called Michel-E, 1967, A Name for Himself, 1967, The Spy Who Talked Too Much, 1968, Walk In A Tall Shadow, 1968, A Spycase Built For Two, 1969, Same Scene, Different Place, 1969, The Case of the Diamond Eye, 1969, Basketball Girl of the Year, 1970, What Happened to Candy Carmichael?, 1970, Valerie Valentine is Missing, 1971, Stay to Win, 1971, Play Ball, McGill, 1972, Where was Everyone when Sabrina Screamed?, 1973, Go, Phillips, Go, 1974, Escape on Skis, 1975, Heartbreak Tennis, 1977; Amelia Walden collection personal, profl. papers, original manuscripts, research data established at, U. Oreg., Eugene, 1982, pioneer young adult novel. Home: 89 N Compo Rd Westport CT 06880

WALDER, DEBBY JEAN, nursing service administrator, nurse, educator; b. Watertown, S.D., Nov. 25, 1947; d. James Russell and Gladys Elizabeth (Owen) W. B.S. in Nursing with honors, S.D. State U., 1970; M.S. in Nursing, U. Minn., 1977. Staff nurse VA Med. Ctr., Mpls., 1970-71, instr., 1971-75, coordinator, 1976-77, trainee-assoc. chief nursing service for edn., 1977; assoc. chief nursing service for edn. VA Med. Ctr., Wilmington, Del., 1977-80; assoc. Chief nursing service for edn. VA Med. Ctr., Richmond, Va., 1980-83; chief nursing service VA Med. Ctr., Huntington, W.Va., 1983-85, VA Med. Ctr., Cin., 1985-87; quality mgmt. analyst VA Hosp., Madison, Wis., 1987—; adj. faculty Med. Coll. Va., Richmond, 1980-82; basic cardiac life support instr.-trainer Am. Heart Assn., Richmond, 1980-83; clin. prof. Marshall U. Sch. Nursing, Huntington, 1983—. Mem. task force Richmond Area chpt. Am. Heart Assn. Recipient Outstanding Cardio-pulmonary Resuscitation Instr. award Richmond Area chpt. Am. Heart Assn., 1982, Achievement award VA Med. Ctr., Richmond, 1983, recognition award for excellence in mgmt. VA Med. Ctr., Huntington, 1983; Bush Found. fellow, 1975-76. Mem. Nat. League for Nursing, Am. Hosp. Assn., Am. Soc. Nursing Service Adminstrs., Phi Kappa Phi, Sigma Theta Tau (Phi chpt. scholar 1969-70), Pi Lambda Theta. Roman Catholic. Office: VAH 2500 Overlook Terr Madison WI 53704

WALDMAN, DIANE, museum deputy director; b. N.Y.C., Feb. 24, 1936; m. Paul Waldman, 1957. B.F.A., Hunter Coll., 1956; M.A., Inst. Fine Arts, NYU, 1965, postgrad. With Solomon R. Guggenheim Mus., N.Y.C., 1965—, asst. curator, 1967-69, assoc. curator, 1969-71, curator exhbns., 1971-81, dir. exhbns., 1981-82, dep. dir., 1982—; Mem. adv. bd. Skowhegan Sch. Painting and Sculpture. Author: monographs Roy Lichtenstein. 1971, Ellsworth Kelly: Drawings, Collages and Prints, 1971, Joseph Cornell, 1977, Anthony Caro, 1982, Willem de Koonig, 1988; contr. articles to profl. jours. Am. commr. to Biennale Sydney, 1988; mem. adv. bd. Ctr. Internat. Am. Relations, Am. Soc.; mem. com. internat. Musee d'Art Moderne; mem. N.Y. State Gov.'s Task Force on Asbestos, 1987—. Mem. Am. Assn. Mus. (mus. accreditation com.), Internat. Council Mus., Internat. Com. for Mus. and Collections Modern Art, Internat. Adv. Bd. ROSC, Ireland, Louis Comfort Tiffany Found. (trustee), Am. Soc. Safety Engrs. Office: Solomon R Guggenheim Mus 1071 Fifth Ave New York NY 10128

WALDMAN, JUDITH L., clinical psychologist; b. N.Y.C., Aug. 28, 1942; d. Abraham and Adele Pauline (Wolitzer) W. B.S., SUNY-New Paltz, 1964; M.A., Hofstra U., 1975, M.A., 1980, Ph.D., 1983. Cert. tchr., psychologist. Tchr. North Babylon, N.Y., 1964-79; psychologist, Schwartz & Assocs., Brightwaters, N.Y., 1982—, N.Y. Mental Health Services, Bay Shore and Bethpage, N.Y., 1985—. Mem. Am. Acad. Psychotherapists, Am. Psychol. Assn., N.Y. State Psychol. Assn., Suffolk County Psychol. Assn. Home: 9 Hiawatha Rd Babylon NY 11702 Office: NY Mental Health Services 140 S Windsor Ave Brightwaters NY 11718

WALDMAN, REBECCA, art dealer; b. Phila., July 11, 1947; d. Frank Cooper and Bernice Silverstein Lewis; m. Michael J. Waldman, June 27, 1982. B.A., NYU 1969, M.A., 1971, now doctoral candidate; Owner, operator Gallery Rebecca Cooper, Washington and N.Y.C., 1974-80; pres. Rebecca Cooper, Inc., N.Y.C., 1980—; N.Y. Mayor's Adv. Com. on Interior Furnishings and Design Industry, 1981-82; hon. program chair N.Y. Assn. Woman Bus. Owners-Artsroundtable, 1980; mem. exec. bd., sec. assocs. Am. Craft. Mus.; lectr. Collectors Circle. Mem. Princess Grace Found., Whitney Mus. Circle of Friends, Guggenheim Mus. Assocs. Com., N.Y.C. Ballet Guild, Am. Fedn. Art (nat. patron), Mus. Mod. Art, Met. Mus. Art. Home: 27 E 65th St New York NY 10021

WALDOCH, LAUCHLIN TENCH, lawyer; b. Gainesville, Fla., Nov. 7, 1951; d. Benjamin M. and Mary Catherine (McInnis) Tench; m. Stehpan Lawrence Waldoch, June 28, 1980; children: Catherine Ashley, Alexander Dawkins Pickney. BA cum laude, Tulane U., 1973; JD with honors, U. Fla., 1978. Bar: Fla., 1978, U.S. Dist. Ct. (no. and mid. dists.) Fla. 1978 , U.S. Ct. Appeals (5th and 11th cirs.) 1978. Aide Fla. Supremem Ct. Justice James C. Adkins, Tallahassee, 1970-80; ptnr. Dell, Graham, Willcox, Barber and Henderson, Gainesville, 1981-87, Messer, Vickers, Capparelo, Freach and Madsen, Tallahassee, 1987—. Mem. Vol. Bar Assn. Youth Judicial Cir. (cert. appreciation). Mem. ABA (litigation sect. Fla. bar appellate rules com. 1984—), Fla. Bar Assn., Fla. Defense Lawyers Assn., 8th Jud. Cir. Bar Assn (bd. dirs. 1986-87). Democrat. Presbyterian. Office: Messer Vickers Caparello French and Madsen PO Box 1876 Suite 701 First Fla Bank Bldg Tallahassee FL 32302-1876

WALDORF, JEAN MOSELEY, publishing executive; b. Montgomery, Ala., Mar. 15, 1942; d. Max H. and Lillian (Campbell) Moseley; m. Ronald C. Waldorf, May 1983; children—Kathleen, Michael and Patrick Kotecki. Student U. Ala., 1959, U. Ill., 1960-63, Troy State U., 1972-74. Supr. dept. advt./layout Champaign-Urbana (Ill.) Courier, 1959-63; freelance advt. promotional work, 1963-68; freelance advt., Memphis, 1968-70; owner, operator Books-N-Things, Montgomery, 1970-73; advt. mgr. Daily Sentinel Star, Grenada, Miss., 1974-76; advt sales mgr. Sta. WRIL-FM, Grenada, 1977; owner, publisher, editor The Copper Era, Greenlee County, Ariz., 1977—; pres. New Horizons Pub. Co., Inc., Ariz. Corp., 1983—. County chmn. March of Dimes, Grenada; bd. dirs. Downtown Prescott Bus. Assn., Prescott, Ariz., 1982, Graham/Greenlee Counseling Ctr., 1987-88; job tng. partnership act Greenlee County Bd. Dirs., 1984. Recipient Jaycee's Disting. Young Woman award, Montgomery, 1972, State of Ala., 1972, Nat. Found. March of Dimes Vol. Appreciation award, 1973, Community Involvement award Ariz. Newspaper Assn., 1986, Blue Ribbon award Nat. Newspaper Assn., 1988. Mem. Miss. Presswomens Assn., Nat. Press Women's Assn., Miss. Advt. Execs., Nat. Advt. Execs. Assn., Ariz. Newspapers Assn., Nat. Press Assn. Republican. Roman Catholic. Clubs: Ala. Fedn. Women's, Soroptimist Internat. Home: PO Box 1357 Clifton AZ 85533 Office: 55 N Coronado Blvd Clifton AZ 85533

WALDRON, GAILYN LEE, architect; b. Bradford, Pa., Oct. 10, 1951; d. Jerome and Joan (Isroff) Weinberg. B.A., Stephens Coll., Columbia, Mo., 1972; M.A. in Architecture, U. Colo., 1973, in Solar Architecture, Ariz. State U., 1976. Jr. planner Beardsley David Assocs., Inc., Denver, 1972; land planner, landscape architect David Clinger Assocs., Lakewood, Colo., 1973; land planner Benedict Assocs., Inc., Aspen, Colo., 1973-75; co-founder, ednl. dir. Roaring Fork Resource Ctr., Aspen, 1973-79; design guidelines coordinator Green Valley Rancy, Denver, 1981; with Skidmore, Owings & Merrill, 1981-83; prin. archtl. planner, designer GW Designs, GW Equity, Aspen and Denver, 1981—; cons. to gov.'s office State of Calif., 1979; energy cons. Pitkin County, 1973. Author: Solar Architecture, 1975. Editor Sun Jour., 1973-78. Mem. Downtown Denver, Ind. Mem. AIA, Am. Planning Ctr., Internat. Solar Soc., Colo. Solar Energy Soc. Avocations: triathletics.

WALDRON, MARGARET ANN, food consultation director; b. Ft. Collins, Colo., July 14, 1927; d. Charles Gehlert and Katharine (Graham) Humphrey; m. David Waldron (div.); 1 child, Sara Waldron Stotts; m. Gene Tepper. BS, Cornell U., 1950; diploma, La Jarenne, Paris, 1978. Assoc. food editor McCall's mag., N.Y.C., 1951-54; food cons. Paris, 1954-56; TV producer Gen. Foods, N.Y.C., 1956-58; with Calif. Foods Research Inst., San Francisco, 1960, Cunningham & Walsh Advt., San Francisco, 1960-63, J. Walter Thompson, San Francisco, 1964; prin. Maggie Waldron Assocs., San Francisco, 1965-73; with Ketchum Communications, San Francisco, 1973—; dir., sr. v.p. Ketchum Food Ctr., San Francisco. Author: Fire and Smoke, 1980. Mem. Am. Inst. Wine and Food (patron, bd. dirs. nat. chpt. 1984-86), San Francisco Profl. Food Soc. (founding mem.), Women's Forum. Democrat. Presbyterian. Home: Kappas Marina Gate 6 E Pier 29 Sausalito CA 94965 Office: Ketchum Communications 55 Union St San Francisco CA 94111

WALDSMITH, MARY LOUISE, lawyer; b. Chgo., Feb. 22, 1956; d. Herman William Waldsmith. BS in Journalism, Ariz. State U., 1977, JD, 1980. Bar: Ariz. 1980, U.S. Dist. Ct. (so. dist.) Ariz. 1980. Asst. counsel USN Office of Gen. Counsel, San Diego, 1983-85, Long Beach, Calif., 1985; counsel USN Office of Gen. Counsel, China Lake, Calif., 1985-87; sr. atty., advisor U.S. Army Health Command, San Antonio, 1987—. Editor Teen Gazette, 1976-77, (law sch. newspaper) The Devil's Advocate, 1978-80. Served to capt. JAGC, U.S. Army, 1980-83. Named one of Outstanding Young Women of Am., 1983. Office: Office Staff Judge Advocate Health Services Command Fort Sam Houston TX 78234

WALENTIK, CORINNE ANNE, pediatrician; b. Rockville Centre, N.Y., Nov. 24, 1949; d. Edward Robert and Evelyn Mary (Brinskele) Finno; m. David Stephen Walentik, June 24, 1972; children: Anne, Stephen, Kristine. AB with honors, St. Louis U., 1970, MD, 1974. Diplomate Am. Bd. Pediatrics, Am. Bd. Neonatal and Perinatal Medicine. Resident in pediatrics St. Louis U. Group Hosps., 1974-76, fellow in neonatology, 1976-78; neonatologist St. Mary's Health Ctr., St. Louis, 1978-79; co-dir. neonatal unit St. Louis City Hosps., 1979-84, dir. neonatal unit, 1983-85; dir. neonatalogy St. Louis Regional Med. Ctr., 1985—; asst. prof. pediatrics St. Louis U., 1980—; supr. nursery follow up program Cardinal Glennon Children's Hosp., 1979—. Contbr. articles to profl. jours. Mem. adv. com. Mo. Perinatal Program., 1983-86. Fellow Am. Acad. Pediatrics; mem. Mo. Perinatal Assn. (pres. 1983), Nat. Perinatal Assn. (council 1984-87), Mo. State Med. Assn., St. Louis Met. Med. Soc. Roman Catholic. Home: 7234 Princeton Ave University City MO 63130 Office: St Louis Regional Med Ctr 5535 Delmar Blvd Saint Louis MO 63112

WALKE, JEAN HOLLAND, software systems engineer, computer systems consultant; b. Detroit, May 16, 1950; d. Harold Ferguson and Anne (Kostrick) Holland; m. Le Verne Douglas Rizor, June 19, 1971 (div. Aug. 1977); 1 child, James Delbert; m. Sanford E. Walke, III, Aug. 23, 1980. Student U. Mich., 1968-71; B.B.A., Eastern Mich. U., 1980. Office mgr. Mich. Testing Engrs., Inc., Ann Arbor, 1972-75, Constrn., Testing & Inspection, Inc., Ann Arbor, 1977-78; pvt. practice word processor, Ann Arbor, 1978-81; systems analyst ADP Network Services, Dearborn and Ann Arbor, 1981-84; tech. mgr. ADP Dealer Services, Southfield, Mich., 1984-85; engring. supr. Applicon-Schlumberger, Ann Arbor, 1985-86; pvt. practice computer systems cons., 1986—; v.p., dir. Bay & Tool Rental, Inc., Ann Arbor, 1977-83; v.p., dir., cons. Am. Lender Services, Inc., Ann Arbor, 1984—. Named Steward of the Meet, Criterium du Quebec, 1977; recipient award of appreciation City of Grayling, Mich., 1978; 6th Overall Nat. Championship for Co-Drivers, Sports Car Club Am., 1979; named tech. cons. ofyr. Mich. region ADP Network Services, Ann Arbor, 1982. Mem. Nat. Assn. Female Execs., Sports Car Club Ann Arbor (pres. 1973-74). Republican. Presbyterian. Club: Ralligators (treas. 1973-74) (Dearborn, Mich.). Avocations: contract bridge; sports car rallying. Home: 3509 Hillside Dr Ypsilanti MI 48197 Office: Am Lender Services Inc 2010 Hogback Rd Suite 6 Ann Arbor MI 48105

WALKER, ALICE MALSENIOR, author; b. Eatonton, Ga., Feb. 9, 1944; d. Willie Lee and Minnie (Grant) W.; m. Melvyn R. Leventhal, Mar. 17, 1967 (div. 1977); 1 dau., Rebecca Walker Leventhal. B.A., Sarah Lawrence Coll., 1966; Ph.D. (hon.), Russell Sage U., 1972; D.H.L. (hon.), U. Mass., 1983. Author: Once, 1968, The Third Life of Grange Copeland, 1970, In Love and Trouble, 1973, Langston Hughes, American Poet, 1973, Meridian, 1976, I Love Myself When I Am Laughing, 1979, You Can't Keep a Good Woman Down, 1981, The Color Purple, 1982, In Search of Our Mothers' Gardens, 1983, Good Night, Willie Lee, I'll See You in the Morning, 1979, Revolutionary Petunias, 1974, The Life of Thomas Lodge, 1974, Horses Make a Landscape Look More Beautiful, 1984, Living By the Word: Selected Writings, 1988. Recipient Lillian Smith award, 1979; recipient Rosenthal award Nat. Inst. Arts and Letters, 1973, Guggenheim Found. award, 1979, Am. Book award, 1983, Pulitzer prize, 1983. Address: care Washington Square Press 1230 6th Ave New York NY 10020 also: care G K Hall 70 Lincoln St Boston MA 02111 *

WALKER, ALMA JANE, communications executive; b. Buffalo, June 17, 1925; d. Louis S. and Mary Ann (Scherrer) Eichinger; m. Henry G. Walker, Oct. 1, 1951; children: Cynthia, Henry G. III, Catherine. Student, George Washington U., 1947-50. Adminstrv. asst. to sec. to Pres. The White House, Washington, 1945-51; TV producer CBS News and Pub. Affairs, N.Y. and Washington, 1951-53; producer NBC-TV, Washington, 1953-56; pvt. practice cons. media prodn. and pub. relations Washington, Paris and London, 1959-63; co-owner Walker Broadcasting Corp., Ft. Pierce, Fla., 1965-69; mgr. pub. affairs Sta. WPLG-TV, Miami, Fla., 1971-80; v.p. W&W Properties (formerly I&W Properties, Ltd.), Miami and Hollywood, Fla., 1975—; pres. AVC Prodns., Miami, 1980—, W. & W. Communications, 1986—. Recipient Ohio State award Ohio State U., Columbus, 1976, Iris award Nat. Assn. TV Program Execs., Miami, 1976, Edward R. Murrow award Radio/TV News Dirs. Syracuse (N.Y.) U., 1977. Mem. Nat. Acad. TV Arts and Scis. (bd. govs. 1975—, Emmy award 1975-76, 79). Home: 1424 W 28th St Sunset #1 Miami Beach FL 33140 Office: W&W Properties 5920 Rodman St Hollywood FL 33023

WALKER, ANNIE PING, retail administrator; b. Nanking, Peoples Republic of China, Jan. 9, 1949; came to U.S., 1969; d. Ho-Hsi and Wen-Fong (Hu) Chi; m. Charles A. Walker, Sept. 23, 1967; children: Dennis Allen, Doris Ann. Student, Fgn. Coll., Taipei, Republic of China, 1968. Clk. sales Navy Exchange, Kenitra, Morocco, 1972-75; clk. customer service Yokosuka, Japan, 1975-78; dept. supr. Pearl Harbor, Hawaii, 1978-79, mgr. location sales, 1980-81, mgr. sales, 1981-83, mgr. retail ops., 1983-85; mgr. retail ops. San Diego, 1985-86; mgr. regional sales Brigade Brands Ltd., Dallas, 1987—. Lodge: Soroptimists. Home: 2106 Greenstone Tr Carrollton TX 75010 Office: Brigade Brands Ltd PO Box 117863 Carrollton TX 75011

WALKER, BERNADETTE MARIE, municipal agency professional; b. Detroit, Apr. 2, 1960; d. Charles Legreair and Dorris Willedith Walker. BA, U. Detroit, 1982. Asst. pub. service attendant Detroit Zool. Park, 1979-85; clk. Dept. Pub. Works, City of Detroit, 1985-86, sr. clk., adminstrv. liaison complaint service reps., 1986—. Mem. women's and young adult coms. NAACP, Detroit, 1986—, co-advisor youth council, 1987; mem.-at-large Mus. African-Am. History, adminstrv. sec. Christian Ed. Ministry-New Prospect, 1986; contbg. supporter Detroit Assn. Black Orgns. Mem. Assn. Mcpl. Profl. Women (assoc.), SCLC, NAACP (life). Democrat. Baptist. Home: 20040 Snowden Detroit MI 48235 Office: City of Detroit Dept Pub Works Two Woodward Ave Detroit MI 48226

WALKER, BETSY ELLEN, computer products and services company executive; b. Atlanta, Sept. 14, 1953; d. John Franklin and Betty Louise (Brown) Walker. B.A. summa cum laude, Duke U., 1974; M.B.A., Harvard U., 1978. Mgmt. trainee, First Atlanta, 1974, officer, 1975-76; analyst Coca Cola, Atlanta, 1977; bus. ansyst Am. Mgmt. Systems Inc., N.Y.C., 1978-80, prin., 1981, v.p., dir. fin. services group, 1982—. J. Spenser Love fellow Harvard U., 1976. Mem. Phi Beta Kappa, Pi Mu Epsilon. Clubs: Harvard Bus. Sch., Downtown Athletic (N.Y.C.). Office: Am Mgmt Systems Inc 2 Rector St New York NY 10006 also: Am Mgmt Systems Inc 1777 N Kent St Arlington VA 22209

WALKER, CAROL ANN, real estate broker, consultant; b. Zurich, Mont., July 25, 1937; d. Thomas Hugh and Iona (Williams) Murphy; m. Fred A. Shelton, Jan. 18, 1970 (div. May 1974); children: F. Kevin, Kelly Andrew; m. Gene Glen Walker, Feb. 17, 1977; children: Jesse Clayton, Dylan Buck, Kimberly Brooke. AA, Ricks Coll., 1958. Mgr. div. Am. Western Life Ins. Co., Salt Lake City, 1966-70; real estate broker Profl. Investment Cons., Salt Lake City, 1974-78; investment counselor Profl. Investment Cons., Idaho Falls, 1978—; owner Fin. Freedom Enterprises, Idaho Falls, 1987—; bd.

dirs. Gen. Agts. and Mgrs. Assn., 1968-70. Author: How To Succeed In Business Without Being a Man, 1979; contbr. articles to various jours. Pres. Ensign Jr. High Sch. PTA, Salt Lake City 1977; chmn. Making Am. Confs., Idaho Falls 1986; mem. Bi-Centennial Constitution Commn., Idaho Falls, 1987; pres. Jr. Achievement, Idaho Falls 1980-81; bd. dirs. Utah Tech. Coll., 1972-77. Mem. Sales and Mktg. Exec. (Salesman Yr. 1978), Salt Lake City, Devel. Workshop Inc., Idaho Falls, Salt Lake Bd. Realtors, Nat. Assn. Securities Dealers. Republican. Mormons. Home: 7050 Val Verde Idaho Falls ID 83401 Office: Walker Investments 7050 Val Verde Idaho Falls ID 83401 also: Fin Freedom Enterprises 132 N Woodruff Idaho Falls ID 83401

WALKER, CAROLINE ANN, auditor; b. Seattle, Nov. 16, 1944; d. Charles Leonard and Ann Phyllis (Dziedzic) W.; B.A. in Econs., U. Wash., 1966; M.A. in Econs., UCLA, 1968; grad. Dale Carnegie Course in Effective Speaking and Human Relations, 1986.; m. James C. Sudduth, Mar., 1971 (div. Mar. 1978). Regional economist U.S. Army C.E., Los Angeles, 1969-70, Seattle, 1971-73, 78-79; econ. analyst Library of Congress, Congl. Research Service, Washington, 1970-71; project coordinator Pierce County (Wash.) Wash., Alaska Regional Med. Program, 1974-75; market adminstr. Pacific N.W. Bell Telephone Co., Seattle, 1979, staff specialist, 1979-83, project mgr., 1983, mgr. internal auditor, 1983-87; auditor City of Seattle, 1987—; staff specialist AT&T, 1983; lectr. 13th Ann. Pacific N.W. Regional Econ. Conf., 1979. Campaigner mem. Republican Nat. Com. Cert. info. systems auditor. Mem. Inst. Internal Auditors Alumni Assn. U. Wash., EDP Auditors Assn. Clubs: Wash. Athletic, Women's University. Won appeal against Sec. of Wash. State on anti-fluoridation measure, 1976. Home: 1700 Taylor Ave N #403 Seattle WA 98109 Office: City of Seattle 107 Municipal Bldg Seattle WA 98104

WALKER, CAROLYN, state legislator; b. Yuma, Ariz.. State rep. Ariz., 1983-86, state senator. Democrat. Address: PO Box 4382 Phoenix AZ 85030 *

WALKER, CAROLYN ANN, telephone company official; b. Lynchburg, Va., July 24, 1945; d. Charlie Stencil and Virginia May (Scruggs) W.; student No. Va. Community Coll., 1972—. Long distance operator C & P Telephone, Arlington, Va., 1966-69, employment interviewer, 1969-75, supr. service order typists, 1975-76, govt. liaison, Washington, 1976-78, staff supr., Silver Spring, Md., 1978-82, Washington, 1982-83; staff supr. Bell Atlantic Network Services, Inc., Silver Spring, 1984—. Adv., exec. adv. Jr. Achievement. Mem. Nat. Assn. Female Execs. Office: 13100 Columbia PIke Chesapeake Complex Silver Spring MD 20904

WALKER, CAROLYN PEYTON, English educator; b. Charlottesville, Va., Sept. 15, 1942; d. Clay M. and Ruth (Newman) Peyton; BA in Am. History and Lit., Sweet Briar Coll., 1965; cert. in French, Alliance Francaise, Paris, 1966; EdM, Tufts U., 1970; MA in English and Am. Lit., Stanford U., 1974, PhD in English Edn., Stanford U., 1977. Tchr. Elem. and jr. high schs. in Switzerland, 1967-69; tchr. elem. grades Boston Sch. System, 1966-67,69-70; Newark (Calif.) Unified Sch. System, 1970-72; instr. div. humanities Canada Coll., Redwood City, Calif., 1973, 76-78; instr. Sch. Bus., U. San Francisco, 1973-74; evaluation cons. Inst. Profl. Devel., San Jose, Calif., 1975-76; asst. dir. Learning Assistance Ctr., Stanford U., Calif., 1972-77, dir., 1977-84, lectr. Sch. Edn., 1975-84, dept. English, 1977-84, supr. counselors, tutors and tchrs., 1972-84; assoc. prof. dept. English, San Jose State U., Calif., 1984—; dir. English dept. Writing Ctr., 1986—, dir. Steinbeck Research Ctr., 1986-87; head cons. to pres. to evaluate coll.'s writing program, San Jose City Coll., 1985-87; cons. U. Tex., Dallas, 1984, Stanford U., 1984, 1977-78, CCNY, 1979, U. Wis., 1980—, and numerous testing programs; pres. San Diego State U., 1982, Ednl. Testing Service, 1985—, also to numerous universities and colls.; pres. Waverley Assocs., ednl. cons., 1980—; condr. reading and writing workshops, 1972—; reviewer Random House Books, 1978—, Research in the Teaching of English, 1983—; cons. Basic Skills Task Force, U.S. Office Edn., 1977-79, Right to Read, Calif. State Dept. Edn., 1977-82 , Program for Gifted and Talented, Fremont (Calif.) Unified Sch. Dist., 1981-82; bd. dirs. high tech. sci. ctr., San Jose, 1983-84. Recipient award ASPIRE (federally funded program), 1985, two awards Student Affirmative Action, 1986, award Western Coll. Reading & Learning Assn., 1984. and numerous other awards and grants; Mem. MLA, Calif. Profs. of Reading, Western Coll. Reading Assn. (treas. 1982-84, bd. dirs. 1982-84), Nat. Council Tchrs. English, No. Calif. Coll. Reading Assn. (sec.-treas. 1976-78), Am. Assn. U. Profs., Jr. League Palo Alto (bd. dirs. 1977-78, 83-84), ; vol. fund-raiser, Peninsula Ctr. for the Blind, Palo Alto, Calif., 1982—, The Resource Ctr. for Women, Palo Alto, 1975-76.. Author: (with Patricia Killen) Handbook for Teaching Assistants at Stanford University, 1977; How to Succeed As a New Teacher: A Handbook for Teaching Assistants, 1978; (with others) Academic Tutoring at the Learning Assistance Center, 1980, Writing Conference Talk: Factors Associated with High and Low Rated Writing Conferences, 1987; contbr. articles to profl. jours. Home: 2350 Waverley St Palo Alto CA 94301 Office: San Jose State U English Dept San Jose CA 95192

WALKER, CEIL THOMAS, advertising executive; b. Charleston, W.Va., Dec. 28, 1952; d. Paul Stephen Thomas and Lois Ann Sowers Kraemer; m. V. Deloss Walker, Dec. 30, 1979; children: Deloss Thomas, Cecilia Lona. Student, Stephens Coll., Columbia, Mo., 1970-71, Bradley U., 1971-72; BA, U. South Fla., 1974. Dir. NFL properties & Pro Mag. Tampa Bay (Fla.) Buccaneers, Tampa, Fla., 1975-77; dir. mktg. Memphis Rogues, 1977-78; dir. pub. relations Racquet Club of Memphis, 1978-81; sr. v.p. ops., treas. Walker & Assocs., Memphis, 1985—, also bd. dirs. Chmn. Memphis Symphony Ball, 1984; Epicurean chmn. Memphis Symphony, 1985; bd. dirs. Memphis Devel. Found., 1987-89, Memphis Symphony League, 1983, 85, pres. elect 1987, pres. 1988; mem. inaugural com. Gov. Ned McWherter, 1987; active LeBonheur Children's Hosp. Club. Mem. Pub. Relations Soc. Am., Memphis Advt. Fedn.. Presbyterian. Clubs: Chicakasaw Country, Racquet of Memphis, Summit, Petroleum (Memphis). Home: 485 Ripplebrook Rd Memphis TN 38119 Office: Walker & Assocs 50 N Front St Memphis TN 38103

WALKER, CONSTANCE MAXFIELD, management consultant; b. Washington, Mar. 16, 1949; d. Orville Eldred and Rose Mary (Stiarwalt) Maxfield; m. Robert Charles Kneip, III, Aug. 21, 1971 (div. Apr. 1981); 1 dau., Stephanie Alexandra; m. Richard Howard Cowles, May 16, 1981 (dec.); m. Phillip Walker, July 25, 1985. Clk.-typist HEW, Social Security Adminstrn., New Orleans, 1971-72, service rep., 1972-73; mgmt. analyst Office Comptroller of Currency, Treasury Dept., Washington, 1974-77; dir. mgmt. analysis div. U.S. Customs, New Orleans, 1978-80, mgmt. analyst, Houston, 1980-81, program analyst, 1981-82, chief data processing br., 1982-83, chief mgmt. analysis br., 1983-85; pres. Constance Walker Assocs., Inc., 1985—. Author: MBO Handbook, 1979, Professional Problem Solving, 1985, The Productivity Ascent, 1987, Participative Problem Solving: A Guide for Work Teams, 1988; (with others) Program Management Handbook, 1983, Introduction to Employee Involvement, 1985; contbr. numerous articles to profl. jours. Mem. Friends of Stehlin Found., 1982—, Friends of the Cabildo, 1978-80. Named Customs Woman of Yr., U.S. Customs, 1979, recipient Outstanding Performance award, 1979, 80, 81, 82, 83, 84, 85; named Fed. Exec. Bd. Woman of Yr., 1979; recipient Outstanding Service award Office of Sec. of Treasury, 1976; Cora Bell Wesley scholar, UDC, 1969. Mem. Assn. for Quality and Participation, Treasury Hist. Assn., DAR, Daus. Rep. of Tex., Daus. 1812. UDC, Va. Tech. Alumni Assn., Delta Zeta. Episcopalian. Home: 1711 Mission Springs Dr Katy TX 77450 Office: Constance Walker Assocs Inc 1500 S Dairy Ashford Suite 102 Houston TX 77077

WALKER, DARCY LYNN, banker; b. Chgo., June 29, 1949; d. Blake Mitchell and Dorothy Virginia (Schlickan) Walker. BA, Yale U., 1971; MBA, Wharton Sch., 1971, U. Pa., 1973. Lending officer Citibank N.Y., N.Y.C., 1973-75; lending officer Citibank Houston, N.Y.C., 1975-79; v.p., dir. corp. tng. Citibank N.Y., N.Y.C., 1979-82; v.p., dir. Bankcard credit policy Citicorp Credit Services Inc., N.Y.C., 1982-84, v.p., dir. nat. collections, 1984-87; bus. mgr. Liquid Markets Citibank Investment Bank, N.Y.C., 1987—. Bd. advisor Girl Scout Council Greater N.Y., 1982-84. Mem. Fin. Women's Assn. Republican. Methodist. Clubs: Tuxedo (N.Y.); Jr. League, Yale (N.Y.C.). Office: Citibank 399 Park Ave New York NY 10042

WALKER, DELORES ANNE, bank executive, foundation administrator; b. Teaneck, N.J., Aug. 31, 1935; d. Stanley and Helen (Fischer) Lewandowski; (div. 1972); children: Debra Walker Fredericks, Scott Donald. AA, Pasadena (Calif.) City Coll., 1972; BSA with honors, UCLA, 1976. Cert. tchr., Calif. Regional controller Hyatt Med. Mgmt., Encino, Calif., 1970-78; asst. adminstr., controller Med. Ctr. Encino, Encino, 1978-80; dir. fin., Planned Parenthood Fedn., N.Y.C., 1981-86, chief fin. officer, 1986—; vols. Am. Greater N.Y., 1986-87; v.p. corp. fin. Covenant House, 1987—. Mem. Nat. Bus. Educators Assn., NOW, Hosp. Fin. Mgmt. Assn. Home: 456 Grand Ave 7A Leonia NJ 07605 Office: Covenant House 440 Ninth Ave New ork NY 10001

WALKER, ELAINE NOGAY, media executive; b. Ogden, Utah, Aug. 6, 1951; d. William Anthony and Mary Agnes (Sagan) Nogay; m. Charles Dorian Walker; children: Erin Michelle, Evan Todd. Student, U. Md., 1969-72. Legis. aid and press aid U.S. Congressman Bud Shuster, Washington, 1974-75; adminstrv. aide to pres. A.S. Nemir Assn., Washington, 1975-76; congl. liaison Can Mfrs. Inst., Washington, 1976-80; housing program mgr. Calif. Assn. Realtors, Los Angeles, 1980-82; press sec. Los Angeles Council Pres., 1982-85; dir. communications Pvt. Sector Systems, Los Angeles, 1985-86, Los Angeles West C. of C., 1986; pub. affairs and editorial mgr. Sta. KHJ-TV, Los Angeles, 1986—; producer Pub. Affairs Talk Show Sta. KHJ-TV, 1986-87, Group W Cable TV Talk Show, Santa Monica, Calif, 1986; creator, producer, host Family Talk Show, Sta. KHJ-TV, 1987—; instr. Atwater Elem. TV Class, Los Angeles, 1986-87. Author: Directions For Solving The Housing Crunch, 1981. Mem. adv. council Retired Sr. Vol. Program, 1987; sec. Hollywood Little Red Schoolhouse PTA, 1987-88. Mem. Radio and TV News Assn., Women in Pub. Affairs, Nat. Assn. Female Execs. Club: Greater Los Angeles Press. Office: Sta KHJ-TV 5515 Melrose Ave Los Angeles CA 90038

WALKER, ELJANA M. DU VALL, civic worker; b. France, Jan. 18, 1924; came to U.S., 1948; naturalized, 1954; student Med. Inst., U. Paris, 1942-47; m. John S. Walker, Jr., Dec. 31, 1947; children—John, Peter, Barbara. Pres., Loyola Sch. PTA, 1958-59; bd. dirs. Santa Calus shop, 1959-73; treas. Archdiocese Denver Catholic Women, 1962-64; rep. Cath. Parent-Tchr League, 1962-65; pres. Aux. Denver Gen. Hosp., 1966-69; precinct committeewoman Arapahoe County Republican Women's Com., 1973 74; mem. re-election com. Arapahoe County Rep. Party, 1973-78, Reagan election com., 1980; block worker Arapahoe County March of Dimes, Heart Assn., Hemophilia Drive, Muscular Dystrophy and Multiple Sclerosis Drive, 1978-81; cen. city asst. Guild Debutante Charities, Inc. Recipient Distinguished Service award Am.-by-choice, 1966; named to Honor Roll, ARC, 1971. Mem. Cherry Hills Symphony, Lyric Opera Guild, Alliance Franciase (life mem.), ARC, Civic Ballet Guild (life mem.), Needlework Guild Am. (v.p. 1980-82), Kidney Found. (life), Denver Art Mus., U. Denver Art and Conservation Assns. (chmn. 1980-82), U. Denver Women's Library Assn., Chancellors Soc, Passage Inc. Roman Catholic. Clubs: Union (Chgo.); Denver Athletic, 26 (Denver); Welcome to Colo. Internat. Address: 6185 S Columbine Way Littleton CO 80121

WALKER, ETHEL GORDON, medical technologist; b. Chgo., Apr. 25, 1939; d. Edward and Sophia Mildred (Siegel) Gordon; m. Howard Walker, Jan. 28, 1962; children—Dina, Gordon. B.S., U. Ill., 1960; postgrad. in med. tech. Northwestern U., 1961. Registered med. technologist. Standards technologist Coll. Am. Pathologists, Chgo., 1964-65; med. technologist Western Electric Co., Chgo., 1965-66; mgr. North Shore Travel Shop, Winnetka, Ill., 1978-81; with sales and mktg. dept. Xonics Med. Systems, Des Plaines, Ill., 1981-82, v.p. Ctr. for Mammography, Inc., Northfield, Ill., 1983-85; ptnr. SK Cons., Cary, Ill., 1985-88; program adminstr. MacNeal Hosp. Comprehensive Cancer Ctr., 1988—. Active Nat. Abortion Rights Action League, 1974—; bd. dirs. LWV, 1975; mem. nat. women's com. Brandeis U., 1980—. Mem. Am. Hosp. Assn., Soc. Study Breast Disease, Nat. Alliance of Breast Cancer Orgns., Nat. Assn. Female Execs. Democrat. Jewish. Office: MacNeal Hosp 3249 S Oak Park Ave Berwyn IL 60402

WALKER, EVELYN, retired educational television executive; b. Birmingham, Ala.; d. Preston Lucas and Mattie (Williams) W.; AB, Huntingdon Coll., 1927, postgrad. Cornell U., 1927-29, spl. courses U. Ill., 1955, MA, U. Ala., 1963; LHD, 1974. Speech instr. Phillips High Sch., Birmingham, 1930-34; head speech dept. Ramsay High Sch., Birmingham, 1934-52; chmn. radio and TV, Birmingham Pub. Schs., 1944-75, head instructional TV programming services, 1969-75; Miss Ann, broadcaster children's daily radio program, Birmingham, 1946-57; producer Our Am. Heritage radio series, 1944-54; TV staff producer programs shown daily Ala. Pub. TV Network, 1954-75; past cons. Gov.'s Ednl. TV Legislative Study Com., 1953; nat. del. Asian-Am. Women Broadcasters Conf., 1966; past chmn. Creative TV-Radio Writing Competition. Mem. Emerita Nat. Def. Adv. Com. on Women in Services; past TV-radio co-chmn. Gov.'s Adv. Bd. Safety Com.; past TV chmn. Festival of Arts; past audio-visual chmn. Ala. Congress, also past mem. Birmingham council P.T.A.; media chmn. Gov.'s Commn. on Yr. of the Child; bd. dirs. Women's Army Corps Found. Recipient Alumnae Achievement award Huntingdon Coll., 1958; Tops in Our Town award Birmingham News, 1957; Air Force Recruiting plaque, 1961; Spl. Bowl award for promoting arts through Ednl. TV., 1962; citation 4th Army Corps., 1962; cert. of appreciation Ala. Multiple Sclerosis Soc., 1962; Freedoms Found. at Valley Forge Educator's medal award, 1963; Top TV award A.R.C., 1964; Ala. Woman of Achievement award, 1964; Bronze plaque Ala. Dist. Exchange Clubs, 1969; cert. of appreciation Birmingham Bd. Edn., 1975; Obelisk award Children's Theatre, 1976; 20-Yr. Service award Ala. Ednl. TV Commn.; key to city of Birmingham, 1966; named Woman of Yr., Birmingham, 1965; named Ala. Woman of Yr., Progressive Farmer mag., 1966; hon. col. Ala. Mem. Am. Assn. Ret. Persons, Ala. Assn. Ret. Tchrs., Huntingdon Coll. Alumnae Assn. (former internat. pres.), Former Am. Women in Radio and TV, Ala. Hist. Assn., Arlington Hist. Assn. (dir., pres. 1981-83, bd., dirs. Arlington Antebellum Home and Gardens), Magna Charta Dames (past state sec.-treas.), DAR (former pub. relations com. Ala., TV chmn., state program chmn. 1979-85, state chmn. Seimes Microfilm com. 1985-88, state chmn. Motion Picture, Radio TV com. 1988—), Colonial Dames 17th Century, U.S. Daus. 1812 (past state TV chmn.), Daus. Am. Colonists (past 2d v.p. local chpt., state chmn. TV and radio), Ams. Royal Descent, Royal Order Garter, Plantagenets Soc. Am., Salvation Army Women's Aux., Symphony Aux., Humane Soc. Aux., Eagle Forum, Nat. League Am. Pen Women, Com. of 100 Women (bd. dirs.), Royal Order Crown, Women in Communications (past local pres., nat. headliner 1965), English Speaking Union, Birmingham-Jefferson Hist. Soc., Delta Delta Delta (mem. Golden Circle). Methodist. Clubs: Downtown, Birmingham Country, The Club. Home: 744 Euclid Ave Mountain Brook Birmingham AL 35213

WALKER, GAIL JUANICE, electrologist; b. Bosque County, Tex., Sept. 3, 1937; d. Hiram Otis and Hazel Ruth (Carmichael) Gunter; cert. Shults Inst. Electrolysis, 1971; children—Lillian Ruth, Deborah Lynn. In quality control Johnson & Johnson, San Angelo, Tex., 1962-70; owner, pres., electrologist Ariz. Inst. Electrolysis, Scottsdale, 1979—; ednl. cons. Gail Walker's Internat. Sch. Electrolysis, Tokyo, 1980; area corr. Hair Route mag., 1981; participant continuing edn. program in electrology Shelby State Coll., 1981. Editor Electrolysis World. Cert., Pvt. Bus. and Tech. Schs., State of Ariz. Mem. Ariz. Assn. Electrologists (pres. 1980—), Am. Electrolysis Assn., Internat. Guild Profl. Electrologists, Nat. Fedn. Ind. Businessmen, Ariz. Assn. Electrologists (organizer 1980). Republican. Baptist. Club: Order of Eastern Star.

WALKER, GAIL ROBERTSON, educational services executive; b. Rutherfordton, N.C., Feb. 25, 1941; d. George Edward Sr. and Lillian Juanita (Phillips) Robertson; m. Jerry Richard Walker Sr., Nov. 9, 1940; children: Jerry Richard Jr., Jon Robertson, Derek Grant. BEd, Western Carolina U., 1963, MEd, 1978. Tchr. Martinsville (Va.) City Schs., 1963-64, Cleveland County Schs., Shelby, N.C., 1970-80, Wake County Schs., Raleigh, N.C., 1980-84; pres., owner Triangle Edn. Services Inc., Raleigh, 1984—; mem. N.C. Quality Assurance Commn., Raleigh, 1978-81; speaker in field. Producer, dir. radio program, 1974. Mem. N.C. Friendship Force to Republic of China, 1986; bd. dirs. Inner Wheel, Raleigh, 1985, Info. Network, Raleigh, 1987. Mem. Nat. Edn. Assn. (Hilda Maehling fellow), N.C. Assn. Classroom Tchrs. (human relations award 1980), Cleveland County Assn. Educators (pres. 1978-79), Internat. Reading Assn. (state young authors com. 1987—, state legis. chairperson), Assn. Supervision/Curriculum Devel., Raleigh/Wake Internat. Reading Assn. (v.p. elect 1988-89), Nat. Assn. Female Execs., Phi Delta Kappa. Democrat. Presbyterian. Lodge: Soroptimist (bd. dirs. 1988). Home: 8817 Trailing Cedar Dr Raleigh NC 27612

WALKER, GERRI HENDRICKS, education association administrator; b. Phila., July 14, 1944; d. Charles George and Ethel Viola (Lee) Hendricks; m. Reginald Edmond Walker, June 1, 1964; children: Rana, Tschaka. BA, U. Pitts., 1966; MEd, Temple U., 1975. Pre-sch. tchr. Sch. Dist. Phila., 1966-68, personnel trainee, 1969—, personnel examiner, 1971, ednl. adminstr., 1971-76; employment supr. Camden (N.J.) County Coll., 1978-79; personnel adminstr. Sch. Dist. Phila., 1980-82; asst. dir. personnel U. Pa., Phila., 1982-83, mgr. employment, 1983-85; dir. innovation and staff devel. Community Coll. Phila., 1985-88; with cabinet Mayor's Office Phila., 1988—; adj. faculty U. Pa., Antioch U., Phila. Ctr., 1982—; pres. The Walker Group Mgmt. Cons., Phila., 1986—; bd. mem. Citizens Com. on Pub. Edn. in Phila., 1985-88. Bd. dirs. Stage East Repertory Theater, Phila., 1974-77, Women's Campaign Fund, Harrisburg, Pa., 1986—, CHOICE; treas. Communicomp Communications Sch., Phila., 1978-80; v.p. Met. YWCA, Phila., 1981-85; bd. dirs. Pa. Women's Campaign Fund, Harrisburg, Pa., 1986—; chair Phila. CARE's for Africa, 1987—; mem. Educators to Africa, 1970-72; council pres. Internat. Trng. in Communications, Inc. Mem. Am. Soc. Tng. and Devel., Assn. Black Women in Higher Edn., Phila. Human Resources Planning Group, Internat. Platform Assn., Nat. Polit. Caucus Black Women, Delta Sigma Theta. Democrat. Club: Rainbow (Phila.). Office: 1660 Mcpl Services Bldg Philadelphia PA 19102-1684

WALKER, GRACE MARIA, printing broker, consultant; b. Smithfield, N.C., Feb. 12, 1940; d. William Nathanial and Martha (Barnes) W.; 1 child Marc Sandridge. Student, CUNY, 1956-60. Cert. journeyman printer, N.Y. Prodn. mgr. VA Graphics, N.Y.C., 1964-68; ind. contractor N.Y.C., 1968-70; pres. GS Graphics, N.Y.C., 1970-78; ind. contractor Los Angeles, 1978-83; account exec. Stationers Corp., Commerce, Calif., 1983-85; chief exec. officer Grace Walker & Assocs., Los Angeles, 1985—. Mem. Printing Industries Am., Printing Industries So. Calif., Rep. Inner Circle. Democrat. Home: 1236 S Bedford St Los Angeles CA 90035 Office: Grace Walker & Assocs 1236 S Bedford St Los Angeles CA 90035

WALKER, JO ANN HOOVER, nurse anesthetist; b. St. George, Kans., Dec. 20, 1931; d. Joel Louis and Juanita Fern (Shelton) Hoover; R.N., Stormont-Vail Sch. Nursing, 1952; cert. registered nurse anesthetist Charity Hosp. Sch. Anesthesia for Nurses, 1969; m. Rankin T. Walker, Jr., Nov. 27, 1955; 1 dau., Victoria Ann. Office nurse, med. sec., asst. office mgr. Manuel De J. Castillo, M.D., Los Angeles, 1952-60; office nurse, med. sec., David Brobeck, M.D., Inglewood, Calif., 1959-60; emergency rm. nurse Centinela Hosp., Los Angeles, 1963-64; staff nurse Bd. Nat. Missions, United Presbyn. Ch., Ganado Mission, Ganado, Ariz., 1964-67; surg. intensive care nurse VA Hosp., Albuquerque, 1969; staff cert. registered nurse anesthetist U., N.Mex. Hosp., Albuquerque, 1969—. Mem. N.Mex. Assn. Nurse Anesthetists (pres.), Am. Assn. Nurse Anesthetists, Am. Bus. Women's Assn. (treas. 1983-84). Republican. Presbyterian. Home: 225 Sycamore St NE Albuquerque NM 87106 Office: 2211 Lomas Blvd NE Albuquerque NM 87106

WALKER, JOSEPHINE GREGORY, postal service administrator; b. Staten Island, N.Y., Nov. 13, 1936; d. Joseph and Tommie (Gregory) Snoddy; m. Theodore Walker, July 4, 1954 (div. 1962); children—Ted Vance, Tony Vincent. Student Kent State, Cuyahoga Community Coll. Supr. East Cleve. br. U.S. Postal Service, 1980-82, supt. Beachwood (Ohio) br., 1982-84, acting mgr. Garfield Heights (Ohio) br., 1984-85, mgr. Bay Village (Ohio) br., 1985—. Assoc. editor Women's Newsletter U.S. Postal Service, 1978-79. Panelist Affirmative Action com., 1988—. Recipient Spl. Achievement award U.S. Postal Service, 1982, Women's Program award, 1979. Mem. Internat. Platform Assn. Democrat. Roman Catholic. Lodge: Zonta (bd. dirs. local club). Avocations: bowling, reading. Home: 19955 Rockside Rd Bedford OH 44146-2074 Office: US Postal Service Bay Village Br 27106 E Oviatt Bay Village OH 44140

WALKER, KATHELEEN MARIE, home economics educator; b. New Iberia, La., Oct. 23, 1942; d. Dennis Faulk and Della Marie (Romero) Bourque; children: Wesley Graham, Cinnamon Jill. BS, La. State U., 1964, MS, 1970, EdD, 1977. Asst. home economist La. State U. Extension Service, Opelousas, 1964-70, assoc. home economist, 1970-75, home economist, parish chmn., 1975—. Named an Outstanding Young Woman of La. Jaycee-Jaynes, 1975; recipient Opelousas Citizen of Yr. award, 1981. Mem. Nat. Assn. Extension Home Economists, La. Assn. Extension Home Economists (pres. elect 1988), La. Home Econs. Assn. (disting. service recipient, 1985), Am. Home Econs. Assn., Gen. Fedn. Womens' Clubs (jr. dir. 1974-76, chairperson visual arts com. 1976-78, chairperson home life com. 1972-74), La. Fedn. Womens' Clubs (pres. 1970-72), Epsilon Sigma Phi (state pres. 1985-86, so. regional dir. 1986-88). Roman Catholic. Home and Office: 2070 Hwy 749 Suite A Opelousas LA 70570

WALKER, LINDA LOU, business owner; b. Billings, Mont., June 6, 1950; d. John Harvey and Virginia Arleen (Gilbert) Schafer; m. John Harry Walker Jr., Aug. 2, 1971; children: Gregory Allen, Christina Wendy, John Harry III. Student, Mendocino Jr. Coll., U. Md. Paymaster Chevy Chase (Md.) Country Club, 1970-71; mgr. tax dept. Beneficial Fin., Inc., Ukiah, Calif., 1982-84; with payroll dept. Lopez Farm Labor Contractor, Hopland, Calif., 1982-85; owner Walker Bookkeeping and Tax Service, Ukiah, 1984—. Chmn. Sch. Site Council, Hopland, 1982-84, Dist. Adv. Council, Ukiah, 1984-88. Fellow Calig. Tax Preparers Program; mem. Calif. Assn. Compensatory Edn., Calif. State Bd. Edn. (reviewer 1986). Home and Office: 160 Jefferson Ukiah CA 95482

WALKER, LYNDA KAY, lawyer; b. Orlando, Fla., Aug. 2, 1956; d. Leon David and Margaret Alice (McKay) W. BS in Indsl. Mgmt., Auburn U., 1978; JD cum laude, Samford U., 1981. Bar: Ala. 1981. Asst. counsel AmSouth Bank N.A., Birmingham, Ala., 1981-84; counsel Nat. Realty Com., Washington, 1985—. Assoc. editor Cumberland U. Law Rev., 1980-81; editor, writer Nat. Realty Com. newsletter,1985—. Mem. The Tax Coalition, Washington, 1986—, Women in Govt. Relations, Washington, 1986—, Joint Real Estate Tax Commn., Washington, 1985—, Urban Land Inst., Washington, 1985—, Potomac Group, Washington, 1986—, New Dem. Forum, Washington, 1985—. Named one of Outstanding Young Women in Am., 1980, 85. Mem. ABA (taxation law sect., real estate tax problems com., real property, probate and trust law sect., corp., banking and bus. law sect.), Ala. Bar Assn., Young Men's Bus. Club (sec. 1983-84), League of Women Voters (vice chmn. 1984), Ala. State Soc., Phi Delta Phi. Democrat. Methodist. Home: 2032 Belmont Rd NW 412 Valley Vista Washington DC 20009 Office: Nat Realty Com 1250 Connecticut Ave NW Suite 630 Washington DC 20036

WALKER, LYNN LOUISE, lawyer, women's health activist; b. Orange, Calif., July 20, 1951; d. James Ross and Velma Louise (Koontz) W.; B.A., Calif. State U., Fullerton, 1973; secondary edn. cert. Chapman Coll., 1975; J.D., Western State U., 1984; 1 son, Tru. Health staff Feminist Women's Health Center of Orange County (Calif.), 1974-76, dir., 1976-82. Community organizer Women Against Violence Against Women, Orange County, 1975-76; bd. dirs. Nat. Abortion Fedn., 1978-79, Anaheim Free Clinic, 1984, Feminist Women's Health Center of Orange County. Recipient Margret Sanger award Fedn. of Feminist Women's Health Centers, 1976. Mem. Internat. Law Soc., NOW, Internat. Childbirth Edn. Assn., Am. Public Health Assn., Nat. Assn. Parents and Profls. for Safe Alternatives in Childbirth, Assn. for Childbirth at Home Internat., Abortion Rights Movement. Home: 601 N Clementine Anaheim CA 92805

WALKER, MARILYN KAY, government research analyst; b. Greeley, Colo., July 21, 1950; d. George R. and Elise M. (Jones) W. BS, Ohio State U., 1972. Research analyst U.S. Dept. Justice, Washington, 1972—.

WALKER, MARY ALICE, educator; b. Warrenton, Ga., Feb. 5, 1941; d. Pierce and Bessie (Pitts) Hill; B.S., Brockport State U., 1963; M.Ed., Nazareth Coll., Rochester, N.Y., 1975; cert. sch. adminstrn. Brockport State U., 1984; m. James Walker, June 29, 1963. Tchr., Jonathan Child Sch.,

Rochester, N.Y., 1963-66; dir. Work Edn. Teaching Center, Rochester, 1966-68; tchr. Project Follow Through, John Williams Sch., Rochester, 1968-77, tchr. reading, 1977-86; adminstrv. specialist Rochester City Sch. Dist., 1986—. Treas., United Ch. Ministry, Rochester; chmn. bd. Rochester Opportunities Industrialization Center; active N.Y.-Wash. Missionary Soc.; sec., bd. dirs. Martin Luther King Ctr. Mem. Reading Tchrs. Assn., Sch. Administrs. Assn. N.Y. State, Assn. Sch. adminstrs Rochester, assn. Supervision and Curriculum Devel. Methodist-Episcopal. Address: 797 Arnett Blvd Rochester NY 14619

WALKER, MARY ELLA, nurse; b. St. Louis, Aug. 23, 1945; d. Earl Earnest and Myrtle Emma (Agnew) W.; B.S. in Nursing, Tex. Christian U., 1967; M.S. in Nursing, U. Tex., 1972, Ph.D., 1976. Staff nurse, asst. head nurse, head nurse Barnes Hosp., St. Louis, 1967-71; staff nurse Brackenridge Hosp., Austin, Tex., 1972; research asso. U. Tex. System, 1973-74; research asso. Center Study of Human Resources, Austin, 1975-76, So. Regional Council, Inc., Atlanta, 1975-76; nurse cons. Tex. Med. Found., Austin, 1976-77; vis. lectr. U. Wis., Oshkosh, 1977-78; program dir. S.W. Rural Health Field Services Program Nat. Rural Center, Austin, 1977-78; program dir. Tex. Rural Health Field Services Program, 1979-85; program devel. officer Tex. Office of Rural Health, 1987; health care cons., 1986—; lectr. U. Tex., 1979-85, 87-88. Mary Gibbs Jones scholar, 1976; Meadows fellow, 1983-85. Fellow Am. Acad. Nursing; mem. Am. Nurses Assn., Nat. Rural Health Assn., Sigma Theta Tau, Phi Kappa Phi. Contbr. articles in field to profl. jours.

WALKER, MARY L., lawyer; b. Dayton, Ohio, Dec. 1, 1948; d. William Willard and Lady D. Walker. Student, U. Calif., Irvine, 1968; BA in Biology/Ecology, U. Calif., Berkeley, 1970; postgrad., UCLA, 1972-73; JD, Boston U., 1973. Bar: Calif. 1973, U.S. Supreme Ct. 1979. Atty. Southern Pacific Co., San Francisco, 1973-76; from assoc. to ptnr. Richards, Watson, & Gershon, Los Angeles, 1976-82; dep. asst. atty. gen. lands div. U.S. Dept. Justice, Washington, 1982-84; dep. solicitor U.S. Dept. Interior, Washington, 1984-85; asst. sec. of energy, environment, safety and health U.S. Dept. Energy, Washington, 1985-87; spl. cons. to chmn. Law Engring., Atlanta, 1988—. Mem. Calif. Bar Assn., Nat. Fedn. Rep. Women, World Affairs Council, Renaissance Women. Office: Law Engring 1000 Abernathy Rd NE Atlanta GA 30328

WALKER, MOIRA KAYE, sales executive; b. Riverside, Calif., Aug. 2, 1940; d. Frank Leroy and Arline Rufina (Roach) Porter; m. Timothy P. Walker, Aug. 30, 1958 (div. 1964); children: Brian A., Benjamin D., Blair K., Beth E. Student, Riverside City Coll., 1973. With Bank of Am., Riverside, 1965-68, Abitibi Corp., Cucamonga, Calif., 1968-70, Lily div. Owens-Illinois, Riverside, 1970-73; salesperson Lily div. Owens-Illinois, Houston, 1973-77; salesperson Kent H. Landsberg div. Sunclipse, Montebello, Calif., 1977-83, sales mgr., 1983-85; v.p., sales mgr. Kent H. Landsberg div. Sunclipse, Riverside, 1985—. Mem. Nat. Assn. Female Execs., Women in Paper (treas. 1978-84). Democrat. Lutheran. Office: Kent H Landsberg div Sunclipse 1180 Spring St Riverside CA 92507

WALKER, NANCY EILEEN, public relations executive, marketing consultant; b. Gary, Ind., Oct. 6, 1947; d. Thomas Jackson and Marjorie Catherine (Mann) W. BA in Speech, U. Wis., 1969. Copywriter Sears, Roebuck & Co., Chgo., 1969-70; v.p. Brave New Workshop, Inc., Mpls., 1971-81; mktg. communicatins dir. NOVUS Inc., Mpls., 1981—; pvt. practice New'sprint, Mpls., 1984—; bd. dirs. Brave New Workshop, Inc.; advt. cons. Tuthill's Gen. Store, Mpls., 1984—. Mem. Pub. Relations Soc. Am.

WALKER, NAOMI WARREN, electronics analyst, consultant; b. Chgo., Dec. 23, 1932; d. Chester Nelson and Eula Elizabeth (Ellenberger) Warren; m. Dale Eugene Walker, June 28, 1953 (dec. Aug. 1968); 1 child, Diana Lynn. BS, Ariz. State U., 1972; postgrad., UCLA, 1976, Calif. State Poly U., Pomona, 1978, Pepperdine U., 1987—. Contract specialist Gen. Electric Co., Ontario, Calif., 1966-69; exec. asst. Data Design Labs, Cucamonga, Calif., 1969-70; office mgr. Ralph M. Parsons Co., Pasadena, Calif., 1974-76; pvt. practice cons. Claremont, Calif., 1976-79; sr. analyst Xerox Corp., El Monte, Calif., 1979—; instr., mem. bus. adv. council, Mt. San Antonio Coll., Walnut, Calif., 1975—; v.p. Warren Automotive, Pomona, 1972-84; cons. in field. Docent Ariz. State U. Art Gallery, 1971-74. Mem. Am. Soc. of Profl. and Exec. Women, Nat. Assn. of Female Execs., Women in Mgmt. (assoc.), Phi Chi Theta, Sigma Iota Epsilon. Republican. Presbyterian. Home: 1014 West Arrow Hwy #C Upland CA 91786

WALKER, NORMA ELIZABETH PEDEN, educator; b. Grove City, Pa., Sept. 26, 1921; d. David Stanton and Mary Louella (Giebner) Peden; B.S., Indiana U. of Pa., 1958; M.S., Pa. State U., 1961, Ph.D., 1968; m. Charles Linn Walker, May 14, 1940 (dec.); children—Edward Erdman, Charles Linn, Rebecca Walker Mihelcic, Ellen Walker Torrey (dec.), Esther Walker Habla, Charlotte Walker Whatley; m. Russell Gras, Sept. 17, 1983. Homemaking tchr. Marion Center (Pa.) Area High Sch., 1958-60, tchr., head homemaking dept., 1961-63; grad. research asst. Pa. State U., 1960-61, instr., 1963-68; assoc. prof. clothing and textiles Tex. Tech. U., 1968-69, asso. prof., chmn. clothing and textiles, 1969-70, prof., chmn., 1970-75, Margaret W. Weeks prof., 1975-77; prof. consumer services Indiana U. of Pa., 1977-83. Vol. Oakwood Family Hosp., 1977-78, v.p. vol. orgn., 1977-78, pres., 1978. Mem. AAUW, Am. Cancer Soc., Am. Assn. Textile Chemists and Colorists (council for profl. devel. 1973-75), Am. Home Econs. Assn. (ofcl. bd. 1973-75, state adv. student membership sect. 1979-83), ASTM, Assn. Coll. Profs. Textiles and Clothing (sec. 1977, rep. central region 1976-78), Indiana County Hist. Soc. (curator of costume), Pierian Sorosis Study Club (pres. 1986-87), Kappa Delta Pi, Kappa Omicron Phi, Delta Kappa Gamma, Phi Delta Kappa. Republican. Methodist (bd. edn. Western Pa, lay del. ann. conf. Western Pa., mem. Council of Ministries, various bds. and coms., commn. missions and benevolence, chmn. Martus Circle, 1986—). Club: Current Events (pres.). Home: 3007 55th St Lubbock TX 79413

WALKER, PAMELA DREXEL, arts executive; b. Providence, Jan. 14, 1943; d. John Rozet and Noreen (Stonor) Drexel; children—Andrew B.H., James Drexel. B.A., Sarah Lawrence Coll., 1964; M.A., New Sch. Social Research, 1967. Psychotherapist, Pacific Psychotherapy, San Francisco, 1970-77; pres. Western Opera Theater, San Francisco, 1975-77; sr. adviser Trans Century Found., Washington, 1977-79; dir. cultural programs Ptnrs. of the Americas, Washington, 1979-80; pres. PDW Assocs., Washington, 1980—; cons. mgmt. Ministry Culture People's Republic of China, 1988; exec. dir. Arts Internat., Washington, 1983-86, N.Y. Internat. Festival of Arts, Inc., N.Y.C., 1986-87, pres. PDW Assocs, Washington; evaluator Nat. Endowment Arts, 1978—. Assoc. producer Women Behind Bars NBC-News documentary, 1987-88. Bd. dirs. The House Found., N.Y.C., Acad. London, Crossways Prodns. Office: PDW Assocs Nat Inst for Music Theater J F Kennedy Ctr Performing Arts Washington DC 20566

WALKER, PATRICIA LILLIAN, editor; b. Chgo., Jan. 2, 1943; d. Robert Warren and Virginia Margaret Walker; B.A., U. Ill., 1965; M.S. in Communications, Mich. State U., 1967; m. Peter Klaus Jeziorski, Aug. 28, 1971; 1 son, Peter. Reporter, Chgo. Tribune, 1967-69, Metalworking News, Chgo., 1969-71; mng. editor Am. Metal Market and Metalworking News, N.Y.C., 1971-74, editor-in-chief, 1974-87; pres. Exec. Press Inc., 1981-84; trustee Inst. Archeo-Metall. Studies; bd. dirs. Copper Club. Office: 7 E 12th St New York NY 10003

WALKER, PEGGY JEAN, social work agency administrator; b. Carbondale, Ill., Aug. 9, 1940; d. George William and Lola Almeda (Black) Robinson; children—Edith Nell and Keith Alan. B.A., So. Ill. U., 1962, Ph.D., 1986; M.S.W., Washington U., St. Louis, 1967. Caseworker, casework supr. Ill. Dept. Public Aid, 1964-71; child welfare adminstr. Ill. Dept. Children and Family Service, 1971-75; mem. faculty social work program So. Ill. U., 1975-79; exec. dir. Western div. Children's Home Soc. of Fla., Pensacola, 1979—; appointed to Ill. Juvenile Justice and Delinquency Prevention Adv. Council, 1978-79; adj. adv. bd. dept. social work U. West Fla., 1982—. Bd. dirs. Hoyleton (Ill.) Children's Home, 1975-79; mem. Leadership Fla., 1988—. Mem. Nat. Assn. Social Workers, Acad. Cert. Social Workers, Council Social Work Edn., Fla. Assn. Health and Social Services. Presbyterian. Club: Pensacola Yacht. Home: 107 Florida Ave Gulf Breeze FL 32561 Office: 5375 N 9th Ave Pensacola FL 32504

WALKER, RENEE KELLEY, educational administrator; b. Macon, Ga., June 26, 1961; d. Joseph A. and Grace (Fountain) Kelley; m. Anthony Scott Walker, June 22, 1986; children: Brian David, Brendan Scott. A.S., Macon Jr. Coll., 1980; B.S., Ga. Coll., 1982, M.S., 1985. Dir., prin., Briarwood Acad., Macon, 1982—, tchr. annex program, 1985—; tchr. sci. Macon Youth Devel. Ctr., 1983—. Recipient Excellence award Bd. Dirs. Briarwood Acad., 1983. Mem. NEA, Correctional Edn. Assn., Nat. Council Social Studies, Ga. Correctional Assn. Office: Briarwood Acad 800 Lackey Dr Macon GA 31206

WALKER, RUTH ANN, journalist; b. Elmhurst, Ill., June 22, 1954; d. Robert F. and Jeanne (Carsman) W. AB, Oberlin (Ohio) Coll., 1976. Staff reporter Aiken (S.C.) Standard, 1977-78; various editing and writing positions Christian Sci. Monitor, Boston, 1978-83, bus. corr., 1983-85, editorial writer, 1985-88, asst. editor, 1988—. Recipient Exceptional Merit Media award Nat. Women's Polit. Caucus, 1987. Christian Scientist. Home: 26 Waverly St #402 Brighton MA 02135

WALKER, RUTH FERGUSON, banker; b. Richmond, Ohio, Oct. 10, 1922; d. Edgar Lemoin and Gertrude Elizabeth (Harbourt) Wilson; m. Howard W. Ferguson, June 4, 1946 (dec. Oct. 1967); 1 child, Charlotte Ruth Ferguson Saunders; m. Maynard W. Walker, Mar. 17, 1969. Student, Asbury Coll. Teller Miners Mechs. Bank, Steubenville, Ohio, 1941-46; clk., mgr. data processing Jefferson County Treas., Steubenville, 1946-51; asst. bookkeeper Asbury Coll., Wilmore, Ky., 1952-59; office mgr. Arthur O. Hall, P.A., Columbus, Ohio, 1959-64; v.p. Diamond Savs. and Loan Co., 1964—, Findlay, Ohio, 1984—. Mem. Columbus Symphony League, 1987—. Republican. Methodist. Lodge: Zonta (internat. pres. 1988—).

WALKER, SALLY BARBARA, glass company executive; b. Bellerose, N.Y., Nov. 21, 1921; d. Lambert Roger and Edith Demerest (Parkhouse) W.; diploma Cathedral Sch. St. Mary, 1939; A.A., Finch Jr. Coll., 1941. Tchr. interior design Finch Coll., 1941-42; draftsman AT&T, 1942-43; with Steuben Glass Co., N.Y.C., 1943—, exec. v.p., 1959-62, exec. v.p. ops., 1962-78, exec. v.p. ops. and sales, 1978-83, exec. v.p., 1983—. Mem. Fifth Ave. Assn. Republican. Episcopalian. Clubs: Rockaway Hunting, Lawrence Beach, U.S. Lawn Tennis, Colony, English-Speaking Union. Home: 116 E 66th St New York NY 10021 Office: 715 Fifth Ave New York NY 10022

WALKER, SALLY WARDEN, state legislator; b. Wilmette, Ill., Feb. 5, 1929; d. Sydney C. and Florence (Collins) Warden; m. O.B. Walker, Dec. 28, 1948; children: Richard, Christine, Nancy, Catherine, Sara. Student, William Jewell Coll., 1947-48. Commr., chmn. Univ. Pl. Parks and Recreation Bd., Tacoma, 1979-85; mem. Wash. Ho. of Reps., 1985—, environ. affairs, edn., and commerce and labor coms. Formerly vol. dir. Pierce County Rep. Party, del. Pierce County Conv., precint committeewoman 28th dist., 1978—; past bd. dirs. Town Hall Lecture Series; former dir. Christian Edn., mem. vestry St. Mary's Episc. Ch. Recipient Woman of Community award Inter-Chpt. Council Am. Bus. Women's Assn., 1986, Achievement award Puget Sound Inter-Chpt., Golden Acorn award PTA. Mem. Tacoma/Pierce County C. of C., Lakewood C. of C., LWV. Clubs: 28th Dist. Rep., Lakewood Rep. Women's. Home: 4617 Bellview St W Tacoma WA 98466 Office: House Office Bldg Olympia WA 98504

WALKER, TEMMY NATALIE, real estate company executive; b. Chgo., Mar. 18, 1935; d. George and Arlene (Cook) Rubenstein; m. Robert Harold Walker, June 2, 1957; children—Scott Graham, April Michele, Jillian Barri. B.A., U. Ill., 1957. Lic. real estate broker, Calif. Pres., Temma Creative Art, Chgo., 1957-72; real estate salesperson Harleigh Sandler, Los Angeles, 1973-74, real estate mgr. Fred Sands Realtors, Los Angeles, 1974-76, v.p., 1976-80, sr. v.p., 1980-86; co-owner James R. Gary & Co., Ltd. Est. 1986—; guest writer Los Angeles Times, 1979—, San Fernando Valley Daily News, 1979—. Mem. Nat. Assn. Realtors (fed. dist. coordinator 1983—), Calif. Assn. Realtors (dir. 1980—, regional v.p. 1987), San Fernando Valley Bd. Realtors (dir. 1980—, exec. com. 1982—, v.p. 1985, pres. 1986). Home: 5026 Veloz Ave Tarzana CA 91356 Office: James R Gary & Co Ltd East 4400 Coldwater Cyn Suite 100-155 Studio City CA 91604

WALKER, WENDY DIANA KNIGHT, insurance company specialist; b. Elizabeth, N.J., Nov. 11, 1961; d. William Henry Jr. and Catherine Lillian (Fulton) Knight; m. George Russell Walker, Jr., Oct. 25, 1986. Student, U. Warwick, Eng., 1981-82; BA, Duke U., 1983. Lic. real estate agent. Underwriter Chubb & Son, Inc., N.Y.C., 1983-86; sr. underwriter Atlantic Mut. Ins. Cos., N.Y.C., 1986-87, producer specialist, 1987-88, underwriting supr., 1988—. Tchr. internship program Howard U., N.Y.C., 1986. Mem. Nat. Assn. Realtors, Assn. Profl. Ins. Women, Nat. Assn. Female Execs., Oranges/Maplewood Bd. Realtors, St. John's Choir. Democrat. Episcopalian. Home: 486 Valley Rd West Orange NJ 07052 Office: Atlantic Mut Cos 195 Broadway New York NY 10007

WALKER, YVONNE MARGARET, comedy show producer, director, talent manager; b. Herrin, Ill., June 14, 1950; d. Dale Eugene Walker and Bette Ruth (Leavelle) Lerma. Cert. in writing, Palmers Writer Sch., 1971. Store mgr. Volume I Books, Chgo., 1969-71; sec. Emporium Dept. Store, San Francisco, 1972-74; store mgr. Little Prof. Books, Daly City, Calif., 1974-75; talent agt. Walker Talent Mgmt., San Francisco, 1973-79; copywriter ETC Advt., San Francisco, 1974-79; events coordinator Legendary Events, San Francisco, 1979-83; freelance copywriter San Francisco, 1983-84; exec. producer Starburst Comedy, San Francisco, 1984—; artist mgmt., pres. Laughing Stock Ltd., San Francisco, 1987—; producer Santa Cruz (Calif.) Comedy Competition, 1987—. Columninst comedy mag., 1987—. Democrat. Office: Laughing Stock PO Box 31248 San Francisco CA 94131

WALKER-ANDERSON, GAY ELLEN, travel consultant; b. Columbus, Ga., Nov. 28, 1957; d. Dale Ray and Barbara Joyce (Rothaermel) W.; m. Donald A. Anderson, April 25, 1987. BA in Zoology, Ohio Wesleyan U., 1980; diploma, Balboa Inst. of Travel, 1987. Research asst. Cleve. Clinic Found., 1980-81; repair mgr. Hood Sailmakers, Annapolis, Md., 1981-82; floor mgr. Shore Sails, Annapolis, 1982-85; service mgr. North Sails San Diego, 1985-87; travel cons. Balboa Travel, San Diego, 1987—; sail repairer for Stars and Stripes America's Cup races, 1986-87. Mem. Am. Soc. Travel Agts. Unitarian. Club: San Diego Yacht, Calif. Dressage Soc. Home: 4745 Del Monte Ave San Diego CA 92107 Office: Balboa Travel 3211 Holiday Ct La Jolla CA 92037

WALKER BROTMAN, LAUREN RAE, construction executive; b. Warren, Ohio, Jan. 18, 1949; d. Cecil Clair Schrecengost and Lottie Beatrice (Prichard) Wolfcale; m. Chester W. Walker (div. 1977); children: Shaunna Lea, Paul Wood; m. Carl S. Brotman, Apr. 19, 1984. Grad., Sch. Cosmetology, 1970. Cosmetologist various places, Rutherfordton, N.C., 1971-77; office mgr. Consolidated Freight, Charlotte, N.C., 1978-79; cosmetologist, mgr. Command Performance, Gastonia and Charlotte, N.C., 1979-81; cosmetologist various places, Charlotte, 1981-82; sales rep. Statewide Inc., Charlotte, 1982—, v.p. new constrn., 1985—. Mem. Charlotte Apartment Assn., Charlotte Home Builders Assn. Jewish. Club: Chelsea. Office: L S Walker Assocs 6101 Idlewild Rd Suite 204 Charlotte NC 28212

WALKER-COOKE, CATHY LOU, free-lance designer, calligrapher, small business owner; b. Sacramento, Aug. 4, 1955; d. John Louis and Mary Lou (Sherrod) W.; m. Amos Everett Cooke, Apr. 5, 1986. Student, San Jose State U., 1973-76, Consumnes River Coll., 1985-86. Adminstrv. sec. Boise Cascade, Portland, Oreg., 1977-78, Transam. Corp., San Francisco, 1979-81; documents examiner SBA, Sacramento, 1983-86; conf. registrar Calif. Assn. Hosps., Sacramento, 1986-87; prin. Cathy's Calligraphy, Sacramento, 1987—; loan cons. SBA, Pa., Mich., Ga., 1985-86. Co-author, proofer handbook Foreclosure Handbook, 1981; contbr. articles to profl. jours. V.p. Black Student Union, Hiram Johnson, Sacramento, 1972-73; vol., mem. Sacramento Black Women's Network, 1987—; mem. Young Adult Ushers, Shiloh Bapt. Ch., Sacramento, 1985—, Sacramento Component Choir, 1986. Democrat. Office: Cathy's Calligraphy 8163 Pixley Way Sacramento CA 95828

WALKER-LEWIS, ROSALIND GISELE, advanced quality engineer; b. Memphis, July 1, 1960; d. Joseph Louis and Georgia (Whitaker) Walker; m. Rudolph Clifton Lewis; 1 child, Damon Walker. BS in Indsl. Engring., U. Louisville, 1982. Engring. asst. Naval Ordnance Sta., Louisville, 1981-82; grad. research asst. U. Louisville, 1982-83; quality control engr. Gen. Electric, Utica, N.Y., 1984-86; advanced quality engr. Gen. Electric Co., Utica, N.Y., 1986—. Mem. Am. Soc. Quality Control (programs chair 1986-87, sec. 87-88), Gen. Electric Profl. Women's Assn. (social chair 1986-87, assoc. chair 1987-88). Baptist. Club: Charms. Home: 4 Butternut Rd New Hartford NY 13413

WALKER-SMITH, ANGELIQUE KETURAH, minister, religious organization administrator; b. Cleve., Aug. 18, 1958; d. Roosevelt Victoreold and Geneva (Willis) Walker; m. R. Drew Smith. BA, Kent State U., 1980; M in Div., Yale U., 1983. Prodn. asst. Sta. WFSB-TV, Hartford, Conn., 1980-81; assoc. min. Convent Ave. Bapt. Ch., N.Y.C., 1981-82, Horace Bushnell United Ch. Christ, Hartford, 1981, 83; overseas leader Operation Crossroads Africa, N.Y.C., 1983-86; assoc. pastor Cen. Bapt. Ch., Hartford, 1983-86; exec. dir. Trenton (N.J) Ecumenical Area Ministry, 1986—; co-mem. team seminars Princeton Sem. Continuing Edn., 1987—. Contbr. articles to profl. jours. Pub. relations coordinator Urban League, Cleve., 1979-80, staff mem., 1979, 81-83; subcom. chmn. Mayor's Task Force on Hunger/Homelessness, Trenton, 1986—; mem., minister Hartford Action Plan on Infant Health, 1984-86; mem. NAACP, Hartford, 1981-85. Recipient Mercer County Recognition award Mercer County Exec., 1987. Mem. Ptnrs. in Ecumenism (officer for internat. affairs 1986—), Nat. Assn. Ecumenical Staff (sec. 1987—), Women in Communications, Minister Council-Am. Bapt. Chs. (v.p. Hartford 1984-86), Commn. on Local and Regional Ecumenism, Black Women in Ministry (founder, coordinator Hartford chpt. 1984-86), Nat. Bapt. Conv. U.S.A. Inc., Am. Bapt. Chs., Blue Key. Office: Trenton Ecumenical Area Ministry 2 Prospect St Trenton NJ 08618

WALKER-TAYLOR, YVONNE, academic official; b. New Bedford, Mass., Apr. 17; d. Dougal Ormonde and Eva Emma (Revallion) Walker; m. Robert Harvey Taylor (dec.). B.S., Wilberforce U., 1936; M.A., Boston U., 1938; Edn. Specialist, U. Kans., 1964; L.H.D. (hon.), Morris Brown Coll., 1985; Dr. Pedagogy (hon.), Medaille Coll., 1985, Northeastern Coll., 1985. Asst. acad. dean Wilberforce U., Ohio, 1967-68, v.p., acad. dean, 1973-83, provost, 1983-84, pres., 1984-87. Bd. dirs. Nat. Commn. on Coop. Edn., 1977-82, 83—, United Way, Xenia, Ohio, 1985—; chmn. culture planning council Nat. Mus. Afro-Am. History; sec. Greene Oaks Health Ctr., 1983-87; bd. trustees, Dayton Art Inst. Named Woman of Yr., Met. Civic Women's Assn., Dayton, 1984, one of Top Ten Women, Dayton Newspapers-Women's Coalition, Dayton, 1984, Outstanding Woman of Yr., Iota Phi Lambda, Dayton, 1985; recipient Drum Major for Justice award So. Christian Leadership Conf., 1986. Mem. Com. on Ednl. Credit and Credentials of the Am. Council on Edn., Alpha Kappa Alpha. African Methodist Episcopalian. Club: Links (past pres.). Home: 1279 Wilberforce-Clifton Rd Wilberforce OH 45384 Office: Wilberforce Univ Brush Row Rd Wilberforce OH 45384

WALL, ANN MANN, publisher, consultant; b. Richmond, Va., Apr. 27, 1944; d. William Hodges Jr. and Ann Scott (Vaughan) Mann; m. Byron Emerson Wall (div.). BA, Tulane U., 1966; MA, St. John's Coll., Santa Fe, 1972. Mem. editorial staff House of Anansi Press Ltd., Toronto, Ont., Can., 1968—, bd. dirs., 1971—, pres., publ., 1974—; mem. adv. panel The Can. Council, Ottawa, 1985-86; bd. dirs. Books Can. Inc., Toronto, 1975-76, Assn. for Export of Can. Books, Ottawa, 1981-85. Editor: Mindscapes: Poems by Zieroth, Jiles, Musgrave, Wayman, 1971; speaker in field. Mem. Assn. Can. Pubs. (v.p. 1977-78, 86-87, chmn. literary press group 1978-79, chmn. coll., scholarly sect. 1980-82), Assn. Can. Studies, Assn. Can. Studies in the U.S. Home: 14 Summerhill GDNS Apt 1, Toronto, ON Canada M4T 1B4 Office: House of Anansi Press Ltd, 35 Britain St, Toronto, ON Canada M5A 1R7

WALL, CAROLYN R., communications executive; b. Springfield, Mass., July 2, 1942; d. Amedio G. and Celestina F. (Penna) Raimondi; m. Peter M. Wall, Oct. 24, 1964 (div. 1972); children—Christina, Suzanne; m. Warren J. Keegan, June 17, 1984. A.B., Trinity Coll., Washington. Advt dir. Beldoch Industries, N.Y.C., 1972-74; promotion dir. "W" Fairchild Pubs., N.Y.C., 1974-76; v.p., pub. Adweek, N.Y.C., 1976-83; assoc. pub. N.Y. Mag., N.Y.C., 1983-84, pub., 1984-85; exec. v.p. consumer div. Murdoch Mags., 1985-87; v.p., gen. mgr. Sta. WNYW, N.Y.C., 1987—. Mem. bus. adv. bd. Lubin Schs. of Bus., Pace U., 1982-88. Mem. Advt. Women of N.Y. (bd. dirs., pres. 1981-83). Democrat. Roman Catholic. Office: Sta WNYW 205 E 67th St New York NY 10021

WALL, CHARLEEN TYSON, infosystems specialist; b. Sellersville, Pa., Nov. 15, 1955; d. Willard Kulp and Ruth Ann (Moyer) Tyson; m. Daniel Edward Wall, June 4, 1983. BS in Computer Sci., Bridgewater (Mass.) State Coll., 1982-86; postgrad., Simmons Coll., 1986—. Word processing sec. Mass. Tchrs. Assn., Boston, 1975-79, asst. supr. word processing, 1979-83, supr. word processing, 1983-84, word processing systems analyst, 1984—. Active Soc. for the Preservation of New England Antiquities. Mem. Internat. Soc. Wang Users, Nat. Assn. Female Execs., Assn. MBA Execs., Inc., Bus. Sci. Internat. (office of future panel), Pilgrim Soc. Democrat. Home: 338 Thomas Clapp Rd Scituate MA 02066 Office: Mass Tchrs Assn 20 Ashburton Pl Boston MA 02108

WALL, ELEANOR ANN, construction company executive; b. Birmingham, Ala., Nov. 28, 1932; d. F.J. and Flossie Eleanor (Thompson) Shelton; m. Frank Gillis Wall, Jr., Aug. 23, 1953; children: Patti Ann, Frank Gillis III, Eleanor Lee. Grad. pub. high sch., Birmingham. Asst. mgr. Telco Credit Union, Birmingham, 1951-59; jobsite officer mgr. Marbury-Pattillo Constrn. Co., Birmingham, 1961-70; sec.-treas. W & P Constrn. Co., Leeds, Ala., 1971-74, Springhill Constrn. Co., Leeds, Ala. and McIntyre, Ga., 1974—; Attendant Computers in Constrn. Seminar, Atlanta, 1982, Ga. Unemployment Compensation Seminar, Savannah, 1986, Ga. Sales and Use Tax Seminar, Atlanta, 1986, Kirby Bldg. Seminars. Sponsor Little League Girls and Boys Softball, Wilkinson County, Ga.; sponsor, donor McIntyre May Day, McIntyre Library, Wilkinson County 4H Clubs; mem. Friends of the Library, Irwinton, Ga.; bd. dirs. Oceans of Amelia Assn., 1987—, sec., 1988—. Mem. Nat. Assn. Exec. Secs., Nat. Assn. Female Execs., Am. Inst. Profl. Bookkeepers, Am. Soc. Concrete Constrn., Ga. Mining Assn. Republican. Baptist. Club: Ga. Bulldog (Athens, Ga.). Lodge: Elks. Home: Springhill Farm Rt 1 Box 273 Irwinton GA 31042 Office: Springhill Constrn Co Hwy #57 McIntyre GA 31054

WALL, MARY ANN, infosystems specialist; b. Somerville, Mass., Oct. 15, 1940; d. Joseph James and Rita Coleman (Hayes) Moran; m. Peter F. Wall, Oct. 20, 1962. BA in Math., Emmanuel Coll., Boston, 1962; MS in Computer Sci., Worcester Poly. Inst., 1984. Statistician U.S. Dept. Health, Edn. and Welfare, Winchester, Mass., 1962-68; math programmer U.S. Army, Natick, Mass., 1968-75, chief systems and programs, 1975-86, dir. info. mgmt., 1986—. Contbr. articles to profl. jours. Vol. Danforth Mus. Art, Framingham, Mass., 1985—. Mem. Assn. for Computing Machinery, Fed. Info. Processing Council of N.Eng. (pres., program chmn., exec. bd. 1976—). Office: US Army RD&E Ctr Kansas St Natick MA 01760

WALL, MURIEL FRANCES, intercultural researcher; b. N.Y.C., Apr. 24, 1929; d. Charles and Fae (Zelesnick) Goldberg; m. George Jack Wall, Aug. 27, 1950; children—Barron Steven, Yvette Love, Suzanne Blondie. B.A., Hunter Coll., 1951; M.L.S., Rutgers U., 1969; Ed.D., NYU, 1979. Tchr. pub. schs., N.Y.C., 1951-60, multimedia tchr., 1960-65, media specialist, 1965-69; media cons. Hunter Coll. Tchrs. Library, N.Y.C., 1969-71; intercultural media dir. Rutgers U., New Brunswick, N.J., 1971-75; intercultural cons., dir. Info. Cons. Assocs. ICA Pub., Hackensack, N.J., 1975—; media cons. Union City Bd. Edn. (N.J.), 1969-70; media cons. Project Best, N.Y.C., 1969-71; media researcher, cons. Dissemination Ctr., Bronx, N.Y., 1972-73. Editor newsletters; author monographs. Pres. Parent-Tchr. Orgn., Teaneck, N.J., 1965. Mem. ALA, Tchrs. of English to Speakers of Other Langs., Latin Americanist Ctr. for Latin Am. Studies, Global Perspectives Info. Exchange. Democrat. Jewish. Club: Singles Travel (pres. Hackensack 1983-84). Office: ICA Pubs Info Cons Assocs 232 Boulevard Hasbrouk NJ 09999

WALL, PHYLLIS ANNE, marketing professional; b. Boston, Sept. 29, 1957; d. Frederick Leonard and Alice (Keedy) W.; children: Brendan

Nathaniel, Michael John. Student, U. Mass., 1978-80. Rep. customer service GTE Sprint (formerly So. Pacific Communications Corp.), Washington, 1982-83, sr. customer service rep., 1983-84; from specialist customer care to sr. sales rep. GTE Sprint, Boston, 1984, account rep., 1984-85, select account mgr., 1985; nat. account exec. Nynex Corp., Boston, 1985-86; dir. mktg. and corp. sales Stonington Inst., North Stonington, Conn., 1986-88, dir. sales adminstrn., 1988—. Complaint mediator Mass. Atty. Gen.'s Office, Boston, 1979-80; citizen rep. State Adv. Com. on Substance Abuse, Boston, 1979-81; mem. Concerned Citizens for Drug Abuse Prevention, Hanover, Mass., 1978-79; supporter Columbia (Conn.) Youth Recreation Council, 1986—, Slater Meml. Mus., Norwich, Conn., 1986—. Mem. Conn. Assn. Labor/Mgmt. Alcohol Counselors. Office: Stonington Inst Swantown Hill Rd North Stonington CT 06359-0216

WALLACE, BARBARA FAITH, linguistics educator; b. N.Y.C., Dec. 15, 1952; d. Robert Earl and Faith Willi (Jones) Wallace Riggold; m. Glenn Ronald Gadsden, Feb. 14, 1980 (div. 1982); children: Faith Willi; m. Melvin Wilson Orr, June 8, 1984 (div. 1986); children: Theodora-Michele Alexandria. Diploma, U. London, 1977; MA, CUNY, 1981, M Philosophy, 1981. Tchr. linguistics Queens Coll., N.Y.C., 1979-80, John Jay Coll., N.Y.C., 1981-82, CCNY, 1981-84, N.Y.C. Bd. Edn., 1986—; language arts dir. Coll. New Rochelle/Harlem, N.Y.C., 1982-84; prison instr. LaGuardia Community Coll., 1984-85, Higher Edn. Devel. Fund, Bronx, N.Y., 1984-85. Contbr. articles to profl. jours. Council Internat. Edn. Exchange grantee, 1974; Brit. Fedn. U. Women scholar, 1976; faculty fellow CUNY, 1977-81. Mem. Linguistic Soc. Am. (travel grant 1978), Modern Lang. Assn., Am. Dialect Soc., Nat. Council Tchrs. Eng., Internat. Apple Core Assn. Jehovah's Witness. Home: 10 W 135 St New York NY 10037-2625 Office: Henry Highland Garnet Sch Success 175 W 134 St New York NY 10030

WALLACE, BARBARA LIVINGSTONE, business executive; b. Edmore, Mich., Apr. 7, 1941; d. Nuel Nichols and Ruth Lucille (Purdon) Donley; m. James Louis Wallace; 1 child, Wendy Ruth Borden. B.A., Mich. State U., 1964; postgrad. Central Mich. U., 1975-76. Social worker, asst. to bd. Oesterlin Home for Children, Springfield, Ohio, 1967-70; office mgr. Farmers Ins. Group, Boulder, Colo., 1971-74; adminstrv. asst. to dean Ferris State Coll., Big Rapids, Mich., 1974-77; exec. dir. crime prevention grant 720 Lilac, Big Rapids, 1980; exec. dir. Mich. Coalition to Prevent Shoplifting, 1981; exec. dir. Mecosta County Area C. of C., Big Rapids, Mich., 1982—; sec. West Mich. Crime Prevention Assn., Grand Rapids, Mich., 1980-85; state adv. bd. Distributive Edn. Clubs of Am., 1980-86; tech. asst. Nat. Coalition to Prevent Shoplifting, 1981; lectr. crime prevention, 1980—; awards chmn. Internat. Soc. Crime Prevention Practitioners, Louisville, 1984; nominations chmn. Internat. Soc. Crime Prevention Practitioners, Louisville, 1984., various chairmanships, 1982—. Author, editor newsletter: Ferris State Pharmacy Alumni, 1974-77, Mich. Coalition to Prevent Shoplifting, 1980, Mecosta County Area C. of C., 1982—. Author mag.: Michigan Backroads, 1979. Mem., co-chmn. fundraising Mecosta County Gen. Hosp. Aux., Big Rapids, 1978; crime prevention com. Mich. Commn. on Criminal Justice, Lansing, 1979-83; trustee cemetary bd. City of Big Rapids, 1979-84; sec. Big Rapids Ind. Devel. Corp., 1982—; mem. Republican Women's Task Force, Lansing, 1982—, Mecosta County Council for the Arts, Big Rapids, 1982—; bd. dirs. Mecosta County Council for the Humanities, Big Rapids, 1983-84; West Central Mich. Community Growth Alliance Task Force, 1984—, Mich. Leadership Found. of Hugh O'Brien Youth Found., 1986—, Town Council, Big Rapids, 1985—; v.p. GFWC-MI Edn. Found., 1985—. Recipient Vol. of Yr. award Internat. Soc. of Crime Prevention Practitioners, 1982; Outstanding Leadership award, Nat. Crime Prevention Coalition, 1980; Outstanding Service award Distributive Edn. Clubs Am., Mich. chpt., 1983. Mem. Gen. Fedn. Women's Clubs (pres. Mich. chpt. 1984-86, bd. dirs. 1984—, nat. pub. affairs dept. chmn. 1986—), Mich. State C. of C., Mich. State C. of C. Execs. (bd. dirs. 1984—, scholar 1984, sec. 1986, treas. 1987), U.S. C. of C., Big Rapids Women's Club (pres. 1978-80), W.Mich. Tourist Assn. (bd. dirs., 1985—), Mich. Sesquicentennial Commn., Omicron Delta Kappa.

WALLACE, BONNIE ANN, biophysics educator, researcher; b. Greenwich, Conn., Aug. 10, 1951; d. Arthur Victor and Maryjane Ann W. B.S. in Chemistry, Rensselaer Poly. Inst., 1973; M.Philosophy, Yale U., 1975, Ph.D. in Molecular Biophysics and Biochemistry, 1977. Postdoctoral research fellow Harvard Med. Sch., Boston, 1977-78; asst. prof. dept. biochemistry and molecular biophysics Columbia U., N.Y.C., 1979-86, assoc. prof. 1986 ; prof. dept. chemistry, dir. Ctr. for Biophysics Rensselaer Poly. Inst., 1987—; vis. scientist MRC Lab. Molecular Biology, Cambridge, Eng., 1978. Contbr. numerous articles to profl. jours. Jane Coffin Childs fellow, 1977-79; recipient Irma T. Hirschl award, 1980-84; Camille and Henry Dreyfus Tchr.-Scholar award, 1986. Mem. N.Y. Acad. Scis. (chmn. biophysics sect. 1983-85, adv. bd. 1986), Aspen Ctr. for Physics Fellowship, 1986, Biophys. Soc. (nat. council, Dayhoff award 1985), Am. Chem. Soc., Am. Crystallographic Assn., Sigma Xi, Phi Lamda Upsilon. Office: Rensselaer Poly Inst Dept Chemistry Troy NY 12180-3590

WALLACE, DEBORAH ARLENE, nurse; b. Atlanta, May 28, 1952; d. Russell George and Ruth Evelyn (Inzen) W.; 1 child, Matthew Paul. RN, Ga. Bapt. Sch. Nursing, Atlanta, 1973, Cert. RN Anesthesia, 1985; BS in Nursing, SUNY, Albany, 1984. Registered Nurse Anesthetist. Charge nurse ob-gyn Ga. Bapt. Hosp., Atlanta, 1973-74; charge nurse plastics, orthopedics, radical cancer postop patients Drs. Meml. Hosp., 1974-75, mem. IV unit, 1981-84; charge nurse Henrietta Egleston Hosp., 1975-81; cert. registered nurse anesthesia VA Hosp., Decatur, Ga., 1985-86; nurse anesthesia Snellville (Ga.) Anesthesia Services, 1986—. Sponsor Friends of Atlanta Zoo, 1988—. Mem Ga. Assn. Nurse Anesthetists, Ga. Assn. Nurses, Phi Theta Kappa. Republican. Baptist. Club: FOZA (Atlanta). Home: 863 Brandy Oaks Ln Stone Mountain GA 30088 Office: Snellville Anesthesia Services 2161 Scenic Hwy Snellville GA 30278

WALLACE, DOROTHY MAE ADKINS, educator; b. Danville, Va., Nov. 14, 1941; d. George Burton and Ruby Mae (Law) A. BS, Radford Coll., 1964; MS in Bus. Edn., Va. Poly. Inst., 1966. Grad. teaching asst. Va. Poly. Inst., Blacksburg, 1964-65; prof. bus. Chowan Coll., Murfreesboro, N.C., 1965—; chairperson dept. bus. Chowan Coll., Murfreesboro, 1985—. Contbr. articles to profl. jours. Mem. Northampton County Hist. Soc., Jackson, N.C., 1979—; treas., sec. Woodland (N.C.) Community Club, 1979—, Woodland Civic Club, 1979—. Mem. Am. Acctg. Assn. Democrat. Baptist. Office: Chowan Coll Jones Dr Murfreesboro NC 27855

WALLACE, ELAINE MARIA, osteopathic physician and surgeon; b. Newark, May 15, 1954; d. Clarence Rufus and Camille (Mobilia) W. BS, U. Miss., 1976; DO, U. Health Scis., 1980. Intern Lakeside Hosp., Kansas City, Mo., 1980-81; research asst. sch. pharmacology U. Miss., Oxford, 1979-80; practice medicine specializing in osteopathic medicine Kansas City, Mo., 1980—; physician well baby clinics Kansas City Pub. Health Dept., 1980-83, emergency room Lakeside Hosp., Kansas City, 1980-82; physician, dir. Rape Crisis Ctr. Lakeside Hosp., 1980—; lectr. U. Health Scis., Kansas City, 1982—; chmn. osteopathic medicine dept. U. Health Sci. Med. Sch., 1987—. Exec. producer Bast records Anne Steward Sweet Inspirations, 1987. Recipient DAR Good Citizen award, 1972, Golden Poet award World Poetry Assn., 1987; named Prof. of Yr., U. Health Scis., 1988. Mem. AMA, Am. Osteo. Acad., Am. Osteo. Assn., Mo. Osteo. Assn., Am. Med. Women's Assn., Nat. Bd. Osteo. Med. Examiners, Sigma Sigma Phi, Delta Omega. Office: U of Health Scis 2105 Independance Ave Kansas City MO 64124

WALLACE, JANE HOUSE, geologist; b. Ft. Worth, Aug. 12, 1926; d. Fred Leroy and Helen Gould (Kixmiller) Wallace; A.B., Smith Coll., 1947, M.A., 1949; postgrad. Bryn Mawr Coll., 1949-52. Geologist, U.S. Geol. Survey, 1952—, chief Pub. Inquiries Offices, Washington, 1964-72, spl. asst. to dir., 1974—, Washington liaison Office of Dir., 1978—. Recipient Meritorious Service award Dept. Interior, 1971, Distinguished Service award, 1976. Mem. geol. socs. Am., Washington (treas. 1963-67), Sigma Xi (asso.). Home: 3003 Van Ness St NW Washington DC 20008 Office: Interior Bldg 19th and C Sts NW Washington DC Mail Address: US Geol Survey 103 Nat Center Reston VA 22092

WALLACE, JANE YOUNG (MRS. DONALD H. WALLACE), editor; b. Geneseo, Ill., Feb. 17, 1933; d. Worling R. and Margaret C. (McBroom) Young; m. Donald H. Wallace, Aug. 24, 1959; children: Robert, Julia. B.S. in Journalism, Northwestern U., 1955, M.S. in Journalism, 1956. Editor house organ Libby McNeill & Libby, Chgo., 1956-58; prodn. editor Instns. Mag., Chgo., 1958-61; food editor Instns. Mag., 1961-65, mng. editor, 1965-68, editor-in-chief, 1968-85; editor Restaurants and Instns., 1970-85, editorial dir., 1985—, assoc. pub., 1985—; editorial dir. Hotels and Restaurants Internat. Mag., 1971—, Foodservice Equipment Specialist Mag., 1975—; v.p. Cahners Pub. Co., 1982; cons. Nat. Restaurant Assn., dir., 1977-82; cons. Nat. Inst. for Foodservice Industry.; vis. lectr. Fla. Internat. U., 1980. Editor: The Professional Chef, 1962, The Professional Chef's Book of Buffets, 1965, Culinary Olympics Cookbook, 1985, Academy of American Culinary Foundation Cookbook, 1985, American Dietetic Association Foundation Cookbook, 1986. Contbr.: restaurant chpt. World Book Ency, 1975, Food Service Trends, American Quantity Cooking, 1976. Mem. com. investigation vocat. needs for food service tng. U.S. Dept. Edn., 1969; mem. Instnl. Food Editors' Conf., 1959—, pres., 1967; mem. hospitality industry edn. adv. bd. Ill. Dept. Edn., 1976, mem. adv. bd. Ill. sch. foodservice, 1978; mem. corp. adv. bd. Am. Dietetic Assn. Nutrition Found., 1981; trustee Presbyn. Ch., Barrington, Ill., 1983-85; trustee Culinary Inst. Am., 1987. Recipient Jesse H. Neal award for best bus. press editorial, 1969, 70, 73, 76, 77, 79, 82; named Outstanding Woman Northwood Inst., 1983. Fellow Soc. for Advancement Foodservice Research (dir. 1975—, sec. 1980); mem. Internat. Foodservice Mfrs. Assn. (Spark Plug award 1979), Nat. Assn. Foodservice Equipment Mfrs., Am. Bus. Press Assn. (chmn. editorial com. 1978), Am. Inst. Interior Designers (asso.), Women in Communications (v.p. Chgo. 1957-58), Ivy Soc. Restauranteurs of Distinction (co-founder 1970—), Am. Dietetic Assn. (hon.), Roundtable for Women in Food Service (bd. dirs. 1980-84), Les Dames d'Escoffier (charter mem.), Culinary Inst. of Am. (ambassador, trustee 1987), Brotherhood of Knights of Vine (Gentlelady award 1980, 81), Gamma Phi Beta, Kappa Tau Alpha. Home: 186 Signal Hill Rd Barrington IL 60010 Office: Restaurants & Instns 1350 E Touhy Ave Box 5080 Des Plaines IL 60018

WALLACE, JOAN S., government administrator, social scientist; b. Chgo., Nov. 8, 1930; d. William Edouard and Esther (Fulks) Scott; m. John Wallace, June 12, 1954 (div. Mar. 1976); children—Mark, Eric, Victor; m. Maurice A. Dawkins, Oct. 14, 1979. A.B., Bradley U., 1952; M.S.W., Columbia U., 1954; postgrad., U. Chgo., 1965; Ph.D., Northwestern U., 1973; H.H.D. (hon.), U. Md., 1979, L.H.D. (hon.), Bowie State Coll., 1981. Lic. psychologist, social worker. From asst. prof. to assoc. prof. U. Ill.-Chgo. 1967-73; assoc. dean, prof. Howard U., Washington, 1973-76; v.p.-programs Nat. Urban League, N.Y.C., 1975-76; v.p. adminstrn. Morgan State U., Balt., 1976-77; asst. sec. adminstrn. USDA, Washington, 1977-81; adminstr. Office Internat. Cooperation and Devel., USDA, Washington, 1981—; speaker in field. Contbr. articles, chpts. to profl. publs. Chair Binat. Agrl. Research and Devel. Found. Recipient Disting. Alumni award Bradley U., 1978, Meritorious award Delta Sigma Theta, 1978, award for leadership Lambda Kappa Mu, 1978, award for outstanding achievement and service to nation Capital Hill Kiwanis Club, 1978, Links Achievement award, 1979, Presdl. Rank for Meritorious Exec., 1980, Cert. of Honor Delta Sigma Theta, 1982, Community Service award Alpha Phi Alpha, 1987. Mem. Am. Psychol. Assn., Am. Consortium for Internat. Pub. Adminstrn. (exec. com., governing bd.), Soc. Internat. Devel. (Washington chpt.), Sr. Exec. Assn., Nat. Assn. Social Workers, Soc. for Internat. Devel., AAAS, Soc. Internat. Devel., White House Com. on Internat. Sci., Engring. and Tech., Nat. Assn. of Social Workers, Am. Evaluation Assn., Consortium Internat. Higher Edn. (adv. com.), Pi Gamma Mu. Episcopalian. Lodge: Toastmasters (hon. mem.). Home: 4141 N Henderson Arlington VA 22203 Office: USDA Internat Cooperation & Devel 14th and Independence Ave SW Washington DC 20250

WALLACE, MARTHA REDFIELD, management consultant; b. Omaha, Dec. 27, 1927; d. Ralph J. and Lois (Thompson) Redfield. BA, Wellesley Coll., 1949; MA in Internat. Fin., Tufts U., 1950; LittD (hon.), Converse Coll., 1975; LLD (hon.), Occidental Coll., 1975, Pace U., 1975, Manhattan Coll., 1977. Instr. in econs., asst. to dean Fletcher Sch. Econs., Tufts U., 1950-51; economist Dept. State, Washington, 1951-53; with RCA Internat., 1954-55; mem. editorial staff Fortune mag., 1955-57; with IBM, 1960-61; asst. dir. corp. devel. Time, Inc., 1963-67; dir., bd. dirs. Henry Luce Found., Inc., N.Y.C., 1967-83; pres. Redfield Assocs., N.Y.C., 1983—; bd. dirs. Am. Express Co., Bristol-Myers Co., Chem. N.Y. Corp.; bd. dirs. N.Y. Stock Exchange, 1977-83, mem. surveillance com., 1985—; mem. Conf. Bd., 1974—, Nat. Com. on U.S.-China Relations, 1975—, Temporary Commn. on City Fins., 1975-77, Brit.-N.Am. Com., 1976—, Trilateral Commn., 1978-84; chmn., trustee Trust for Cultural Resources of City N.Y., 1977-81; mem. Adv. Com. on Adminstrn. of Justice, 1981-82; mem. social services vis. com. dept. polit. sci. MIT; mem. vis. com. dept. social scis. U. Chgo., 1980-84; treas. Nat. Com. for United States-China Relations, 1987—; mem. adv. com. Fletcher Sch. Law and Diplomacy, Tufts U.; mem. Sr. Bus. Adv. Council, Pres.'s Council and Adv. Group. Trustee Williams Coll., 1974-86, trustee emeritus, 1986—, citizens budget commn., 1976—, Internat. House, Greater N.Y. Councils, Boy Scouts Am.; bd. dirs. Am. Council on Germany, Greater N.Y. Fund/United Way, 1974-86, Legal Aid Soc., Regional Plan Assn., 1985-88, Citizens Crime Commn. N.Y.C., Inc., 1983—, N.Y.C. Partnership, 1980-85, Council Fgn. Relations, Inc., 1972-82; chmn. N.Y. Rhodes Scholars Selection Com., 1983-86, membership council Whitney Mus.; mem. Bretton Woods Com., 1987. Wellesley Coll. Durant scholar, 1949. Mem. Am. Judicature Soc. (bd. dirs. 1978—, v.p., exec. com. 1978-81, chmn. 1981-83), Council on Founds. (bd. dirs. 1971-77), Found. Ctr. (bd. dirs. 1971-77), Japan Soc. (bd. dirs. 1975—, chmn. 75th Anniversary Fund 1982-83), Am. Council on Germany (bd. dirs. 1980—), World Resources Inst., Asia Soc. (mem. pres.'s council, mem. Asian agenda adv. group), N.Y. Racing Assn. (bd. dirs. 1976—), Acad. Polit. Scis., Saratoga Reading Rooms, Inc., Fairbank Ctr. for East Asian Studies, Phi Beta Kappa Assocs., Phi Beta Kappa. Clubs: River, Bd. Room, Economic, Wellesley. Home and Office: 435 E 52d St New York NY 10022

WALLACE, MARY ELISABETH, political science educator; b. Oak Park, Ill., July 27, 1910; d. Malcolm William and Lillie May (Pitkin) W. B.A., U. Toronto, Ont., Can., 1931, Diploma in Social Sci., 1935; B.A., Oxford U., 1934; Ph.D., Columbia U., 1949. Social worker, 1935-45; mem. staff Sch. Social Work, U. Toronto, 1945-46; from lectr. to prof. polit. sci. U. Toronto, 1946-76, prof. emeritus polit. sci., 1976—. Editor: Readings in British Government, 1948; author: Goldwin Smith: Victorian Liberal, 1957; The British Caribbean: From the Decline of Colonialism to the End of Federation, 1977. Contbr. articles to learned jours. Fellow Royal Soc. Can.; mem. Toronto Symphony Orch. Assn., Can. Nature Fedn., Can. Assn. Internat. Affairs, Can. Wildlife Fedn. Mem. Liberal Party. Mem. United Ch. Can. Avocations: ornithology, music. Home: 421 Heath St E, Toronto, ON Canada M4G 1B4

WALLACE, PAULA KATHLEEN, computer consultant; b. San Diego, June 3, 1951; d. Paul W. and Betty J. (Moore) W. Auditor Stinson Beach (Calif.) Water Dist., 1978-83; mgr. support and tng. McClure Mgmt. Systems, Larkspur, Calif., 1984-86; owner Wallace & Assocs., Novato, Calif., 1986—; instr. Calif. CPA Soc., Palo Alto, 1985—. Mem. Nat. Assn. Female Execs. Office: Wallace & Assocs 8 Los Cedros Dr Novato CA 94947

WALLACE, PHYLLIS ANN, educator; b. Balt.; d. John L. and Stevella (Parker) W. B.A., NYU, 1943; M.A., Yale, 1944, Ph.D., 1948. Economist, statistician Nat. Bur. Econ. Research, 1948-52; lectr. Coll. City N.Y., 1948-51; asso. prof. econs. Atlanta U., 1953-57; econ. analyst U.S. Govt., 1957-65; chief tech. studies U.S. Equal Employment Opportunity Commn., Washington, 1966-69; v.p. research Met. Applied Research Center, N.Y.C., 1969-72; now prof. Sloan Sch. Mgmt. Mass. Inst. Tech., Cambridge; dir. State St. Bank and Trust Co., Stop and Shop. Cos., Boston, Tchrs. Ins. and Annuity Assn. Am., N.Y. Trustee Brookings Instn., Washington; mem. Minimum Wage Study Commn., Pres.'s Pay Adv. Com. Mem. Indsl. Relations Research Assn. (pres. 1988). Home: 780 Boylston St Apt 15-H Boston MA 02199 Office: Mass Inst Tech Sloan Sch Mgmt Cambridge MA 02139

WALLACE, WANDA A., accounting educator, consultant, researcher; b. Kindley AFB, Bermuda, Aug. 19, 1953; d. Wayne R. and Alice L. (Anderson) Wilson; m. James J. Wallace, Nov. 3, 1972. B.B.A. magna cum laude, Tex. Christian U., Ft. Worth, 1972; M. Profl. Accountancy, 1974; Ph.D., U. Fla., 1978. Audit staff mem. Arthur Andersen & Co., Ft. Worth and Hartford, Conn., 1972, Ernst & Ernst Co. (now Ernst & Whinney), Jackson, Miss., 1973; research asst. U. Fla., Gainesville, 1976-77; instr. U. Ariz., Tucson, 1978; prof. U. Rochester (N.Y.), 1978-82; Corrigan prof. So. Meth. U., Dallas, 1982-85; Deborah D. Shelton systems prof. accounting Tex. A & M U., 1985—; cons. regression Price Waterhouse, N.Y.C., 1979—; cons. continuing edn. Peat, Marwick, Mitchell & Co., N.Y.C., 1980-81; cons. statis. techniques in litigation support Peterson & Co. Cons., Chgo., 1983—; cons. Arthur Andersen & Co., 1983—. Contbr. monographs, articles to profl. publs.; mem. editorial bd. Auditing: A Jour. of Practice and Theory, 1982—, others; author: Handbook of Internal Accounting Controls, 1984, Auditing, 1986. Mem. Fulbright scholars screening com., 1985-87, chmn., 1987—. Recipient First Lit. award Am. Woman's Soc. C.P.A.s, 1981, 84, Wildman Gold medal, 1981, Cert. Disting. Performance, Inst. Mgmt. Acctg., 1980; grantee Peat, Marwick, Mitchell & Co., 1979-80, 82. Mem. Am. Acctg. Assn. (nat. council 1982-84, 87-88, auditing sect. sec.-treas. 1983-84, chair govt. and non-profit sect. 1987-88), Inst. Internal Auditors (bd. regents 1982-84, Gold Medal 1981). Lutheran. Office: Tex A&M U Coll Bus Adminstrn Dept Acctg College Station TX 77843

WALLACH, ROCHELLE LAMM, financial services executive, publisher, author; b. Fargo, N.D., Apr. 16, 1948; d. Barney Eyles and Marion LaVerne (Peterson) Lamm; m. Alan Victor Wallach, Apr. 26, 1978; 1 child, David-Andrew. B.A., Loretto Heights Coll., 1970; M.B.A., U. Denver, 1980. Cert. fin. planner. Inst. salesman Kraft Foods, Inc., Ft. Worth, 1973-75; dir. adminstrn. Coll. Fin. Planning, Denver, 1975-77; regional v.p. Oppenheimer Mgmt., N.Y.C., 1977-80; exec. v.p., nat. sales mgr. Integrated Resources, Inc., N.Y.C., 1980-86; pres. Lamm Wallach Communications Group, Inc., Denver, 1985-87, AAL Advisors, Inc./AAL Distributors, Inc., Appleton, Wis., 1987—. Author, pub.: On the Road Again, How to Succeed in the Competitive World of Wholesaling, 1985; author: On the Road Again, A Success Guide for Business Women Who Travel, 1985; author, producer video: Nanny Comes to Your House, How to Take Care of Your Newborn, 1986. Named Disting. Alumna, U. Denver, 1985. Mem. Inst. Cert. Fin. Planners, Internat. Assn. Fin. Planning (speakers bur.). Avocations: travel; writing; fishing; private pilot. Office: AAL Distbrs Inc 222 W College Ave Appleton WI 54914

WALLACH, SUSAN SILVERMAN, advertising executive, entrepreneur; b. N.Y.C., June 25, 1956; d. Marvin Edward and Sondra (Sherr) Silverman; m. Jordan L. Wallach, Jan. 7, 1978; 1 son, Michael Phillip. B.S. in Advt., U. Fla., 1976. Copywriter, Fla. Sun Mktg., Sarasota, 1976-77; editor Sarasota Mag., 1977; sr. account exec. Sawyer & Assocs. Advt., Sarasota, 1977-80; mktg. dir. Investment Seminars, Inc., Bradenton, Fla., 1981; pres., account exec. Ward & Wallach Advt., Sarasota, 1981-85; v.p., account exec. Collateral Inc., Sarasota, 1985-86, dir. v.p. SBV Advt. Fedn., Sarasota, 1979-86; chief exec. officer Wallach Advt., Sarasota, 1986—. Copywriter advertisement Civilized Carpet Sale, 1983 (first pl. Addy award 1984). Precinct rep. Sarasota County Republican Exec. Com., 1980-83; mem. Sarasota County Civic League, 1984—. Jewish. Avocations: music, film.

WALLACK, RINA EVELYN, lawyer; b. Pitts.; d. Erwin Norman and Gloria A. (Schacher). AD in Nursing, Delta Coll., 1973; BS cum laude in Psychology, Eastern Mich. U., 1980; JD cum laude, Wayne State U., 1983. Registered nurse Mich.; bar: Calif. 1983. Psychiat. head nurse Ypsilanti State Hosp., Mich., 1973-77, instr., nursing educator, 1977-80; teaching asst. contracts Wayne State U., Detroit, 1981-83; legal asst. Wayne County Prosecutor's Office, 1982-83; atty. NLRB, Los Angeles, 1983-86, Paramount Pictures Corp., Los Angeles, 1986—. Contbr. articles to profl. jours. Instr., ARC, Mich., 1978-80. Recipient Am. Jurisprudence Book award, 1983; Order of Coif, 1983. Mem. ABA, Am. Trial Lawyers Assn., Mich., Calif. bar assns. Avocations: shooting, movies, dancing, reading, photography. Office: Paramount Pictures Corp 5555 Melrose Ave Los Angeles CA 90038

WALLAR, VIVIAN FAY, educator; b. Orlando, Fla., Apr. 26, 1945; d. Len Joel and Vera (Cox) Lester; m. Donald Elbert Wallar, Nov. 21, 1973; children: Don II, Jason Kyle. BS, Southern Coll., Collegedale, Tenn., 1968; MA, Loma Linda (Calif.) U., 1972. Tchr. So. Calif. Conf. Seventh Day Adventists, Lynwood, 1968-71, Long Beach, 1980-83, West Coving, 1983—; prin. So. Calif. Conf. Seventh Day Adventists, Lynwood, 1972-73; assoc. supt. edn. So. Calif. Conf. Seventh Day Adventists, Glendale, 1973-74; tchr. Southeastern Calif. Conf. Seventh Day Adventists, Riverside, 1971-72, Garden Grove, 1974-77; tchr. Wash. Conf. Seventh Day Adventists, Shelton, 1977-80. Republican. Home: 4363 Fruit St LaVerne CA 91750

WALLEN, PAULA GAIL, mortgage company executive, real estate developer; b. Dayton, Ohio, Sept. 23, 1953; d. Clarence W. Kirkpatrick and Alpha Nadine (Wilson) Louthan; m. William H. Wallen, Aug. 2, 1969; children: William James, William H. II, Christopher Aaron. Cert. in real estate law, Sinclair U., 1977; cert. in residential specialists, Dayton Real Estate Tng., 1981, cert. in real estate appraisal, 1982. Real estate assoc. Kimberlin & Assocs., Middletown, Ohio, 1977-78, Oyer, Inc., Middletown, 1978-79; br. mgr. Courtney Duff & Assocs., Inc., Middletown, 1979-81; real estate assoc. Ungar Realty, Franklin, Ohio, 1981-82; pres. Federated Mktg. Inc., Franklin, 1982—; pres., chief exec. officer Federated Mortgage Corp., Centerville, Ohio, 1984—, Ameri-Cor Land Title Agy., Centerville, 1983-87; chmn., chief exec. officer Federated Mortgage Corp. Devel., Centerville, 1986—, Federated Mortgage Corp. Leasing, Centerville, 1986—; cons. mortgage banking Cin. Post, 1985—. Contbr. articles to profl. jours. Active For Love of Children, 1986—; founder benefit underprivileged children Christmas celebration, 1986. Recipient Profl. of Yr. Commendation, Mayor of Dayton, Ohio, 1986. Mem. Nat. Assn. Realtors, Ohio Realtors Assn., Middletown Bd. Realtors (assoc.), Inst. Real Estate Appraisers, Dayton C. of C. Republican. Club: Million Dollar (Columbus, Ohio). Office: Federated Mortgage Corp 2440 Brittany Ct Centerville OH 45459

WALLER, CLAUDIA CRONIN, association director; b. Detroit, Nov. 10, 1939; d. Arthur Dennis and Elizabeth Claudia (McDermid) Cronin; m. John Delano Waller, Aug. 11, 1962; children: Mark Christopher, John Joseph, Michael Dennis, Brian Francis. BS in Nursing, St. Mary's Coll., Notre Dame, Ind., 1962; postgrad., U. Va., 1981-83. Nurse, supr., instr. St. Joseph Hosp., South Bend, Ind., 1962-65; researcher Arlington (Va.) Cablevision, 1973-75; cons. Luzier Personalized Cosmetics, Kansas City, Mo., 1975-83; specialist govt. relations Nat. Sch. Bds. Assn., Alexandria, Va., 1983-85; asst. dir. Ctr. for Law and Edn., Washington, 1985; exec. dir. Am. Assn. Children's Residential Ctrs., Washington, 1985—; Lobbyist Va. Sch. Bds. Assn., 1979-83, Nat. Sch. Bds. Assn., Washington, 1981-83. Author (newsletter) Residential Treatment News, 1985—. Vice chmn. Alexandria City Sch. Bd., 1973-82; mem. Va. Spl. Edn. Adv. Com., Richmond, Va., 1980-84; trustee No. Va. Community Coll., Annandale, Va., 1982—, Alexandria Police Youth Camp, 1987—. Named Woman of Month, Alexandria Woman's Commn., 1979. Mem. Meeting Planners Internat., Greater Washington Soc. Assn. Execs., Nat. Assn. Female Execs., AAUW (lobbyist 1982-84), LWV (chair com. 1974-76). Democrat. Roman Catholic. Home: 5943 Kelley Ct Alexandria VA 22312 Office: Am Assn Children's Residential Ctrs 440 First St NW Suite 310 Washington DC 20001

WALLER, JOYCE ELAINE, financial planner; b. Joliet, Ill., May 6, 1944; d. George Robert and Lorene (Jennings) Cotter; m. Robert L. Waller, Oct. 21, 1967; children: Debra Ann, John Robert Hardin. BA, No. Ill. U., DeKalb, 1966; postgrad., No. Ill. U., 1970-72; Cert. in Fin. Planning, Coll. for Fin. Planning, Denver, 1987. Cert. fin. planner. Psychologist trainee Dwight (Ill.) Reformatory for Women, 1966; psychologist, diagnostic team supr. Ill. Dept. Corrections, Joliet, 1967-72; tax preparer H & R Block, Aurora, Ill., 1981-83; fin. planner Waller Fin. Services, Plainfield, Ill., 1977-86; adminstrv. asst. Joan Baurer & Co., Inc., Crystal Lake, Ill., 1981-83; fin. plan writer Tax & Investment Strategies, Naperville, Ill., 1983-85; tax preparer Talman Home Savs. & Loan, Chgo., 1986; fin. planner IDS Fin. Svcs., Inc., Joliet, Ill., 1986—. Mem. Plainfield band Boosters, Ill., Plainfield PTO, 1987. Mem. Internat. Assn. Fin. Planners, Inst. of Cert. Fin. Planners. Methodist. Club: Jesse Walker UMC (treas. 1984-87). Home: 613 Park Ln Plainfield IL 60544 Office: IDS Fin Services Inc 611 W Jefferson St Shorewood IL 60436

WALLER, JULIA REVA, college work study program professional, financial aid counselor; b. Chgo., Aug. 24, 1950; d. Katie Lee (Waller) Richmond; 1 child, Kevin. B.A. in Psychology, Calif. State U.-Sacramento, 1982; M.A. in Edn., Calif. Poly State U.-San Luis Obispo, 1987. Youth supr.

State of Ill., Chgo., 1972-74, caseworker, 1974-79; re-entry counselor Calif. State U., Sacramento, 1980-82, fin. aid advisor, 1981-83; fin. aid counselor Calif. Poly. State U., San Luis Obispo, 1983-87; mgr. coll. work study program, 1987. Treas, Detroit Area Neighborhood Council, Sacramento, 1981-82; mem. Operation PUSH, Chgo., 1971-76, Calif. Homemakers Assn., Sacramento, 1980-82, NAACP, San Luis Obispo. Marrion Muddox scholar, 1983-84; Herbert E. Collins scholar, 1984-85; Programs for Adult Students Admission and Re-entry scholar, 1981-82. Mem. Nat. Assn. Female Execs., Calif. Assn. Counseling and Devel., Western Assn. Student Fin. Aid Adminstrs., Calif. Assn. Student Fin. Aid Adminstrs., Calif. Black Faculty and Staff Assn. Pentecostal. Avocations: Directing plays; drama; book collecting. Office: Calif Poly State University San Luis Obispo CA 93407

WALLER, LAURA RHODES, financial planner; b. Bklyn, July 17, 1945; d. Seymour J. and Florence (Kaufman) Rhodes; m. Edward M. Waller, Jr., June 18, 1982; children: Melissa Leigh Wax, Jonathan David Wax, Lauren Elizabeth. BA, Tulane U., 1966, MSW, 1968; cert. fin. planning, Coll. Fin. Planning, Denver, 1982. Therapist Adult Mental Health Ctr., St. Petersburg, Fla., 1971-77; fin. planner Raymond, James & Assocs., Tampa, 1978-84; pres. Laura Waller Advisors, Inc., Tampa, 1984—. Contbr. to Handbook of Financial Planning, 1987. Mem. Inst. Cert. Fin. Planners (nat. bd. dirs., so. regional dir. 1982-87), Internat. Assn. Fin. Planning (pres. Tampa Bay chpt. 1986), Network of Exec. Women (recipient Recognition award 1986), Tampa C. of C. (com. for Homeless of Tampa 1986-87), Athena Soc., Phi Beta Kappa. Democrat. Jewish. Home: 3609 Watrous Tampa FL 33629 Office: Laura Waller Advisors Inc 201 E Kennedy Suite 1109 Tampa FL 33602

WALLER, LOU A., advertising executive, creative director; b. Oklahoma City, Nov. 21, 1938; d. Paul Travis and Deborah Frances (Heep) Lower; m. John H. Waller, Mar. 1, 1961; children: Jennifer L., David A. BS, U. Okla., 1960; Assoc. Applied Arts, Ind. Tech. Coll., 1980. Cert. practitioner neurolinguistic programming; registered nurse. Operating room nurse various hosps., Ind., Ohio, Okla., 1961-78; acct. exec. Ash Advt., Elkhart, Ind., 1980; v.p., creative mgr. NPC Printing Co., Niles, Mich., 1981-84; owner, pres., creative dir. NPC Communications of Ind., Inc., South Bend, 1984—; adj. assoc. prof. advt. art design U. Notre Dame, Ind., 1985-86. Featured in Success Story ann. report, Ind. Tech. Coll., South Bend, 1986. Mem. Am. Mktg. Assn. (dir. Michiana chpt. 1982-86), Nat. Assn. Neuro-Linguistic Programming, Women Bus. Owners Michiana (steering com. 1986, logo design 1987). Republican. Clubs: Knollwood Country (Granger, Ind.); The Pickwick (Niles, Mich.). Office: NPC Communications of Ind Inc 300 N Michigan South Bend IN 46601

WALLER, WILHELMINE KIRBY (MRS. THOMAS MERCER WALLER), civic worker, organization official; b. N.Y.C., Jan. 19, 1914; d. Gustavus Town and Wilhelmine (Claflin) Kirby; m. Thomas Mercer Waller, Apr. 7, 1942. Ed., Chapin Sch., N.Y.C. Conservation chmn. Garden Club Am., 1959-61, pres., 1965-68, chmn. nat. affairs, 1968-74, dir., 1969-71; mem. adv. com. N.Y. State Conservation Commn., 1959-70; mem. Nat. Adv. Com. Hwy. Beautification, 1965-68; trustee Mianus River Gorge Conservation Com. of Nature Conservancy, 1955—, Arthur W. Butler Meml. Sanctuary, 1955-79; mem. Rachel Carson council Nat. Audubon Soc., 1964—; v.p. Bedford (N.Y.) Farmers Club, 1954-74; dir. Westchester County Soil and Water Conservation Dist., 1967-74; adviser N.Y. Gov.'s Study Commn. Future of Adirondacks, 1968-70; adv. com. N.Y. State Parks and Recreation Commn., 1971-72; adv. com. to sec. state UN Conf. Human Environment, 1971-72; mem. Pres.'s Citizens Adv. Com. on Environ. Quality, 1974-78. Mem. planning bd., Bedford, 1953-57; mem. Conservation adv. council, Bedford, N.Y., 1968-70, Westchester County Planning Bd., 1970-88; bd. govs. Nature Conservancy, 1970-78; Mem. Lyndhurst council Nat. Trust for Historic Preservation, 1965-74; bd. dirs. Scenic Hudson, Inc., 1985—. Recipient Frances K. Hutchinson medal Garden Club Am., 1971, Holiday mag. award for beautiful Am., 1971, Conservation award Am. Motors Corp., 1975. Mem. Nat. Soc. Colonial Dames, Huguenot Soc. Am., Daus. of Cincinnati. Address: Tanrackin Farm Bedford Hills NY 10507

WALLERSTEDT-WEHRLE, JOANNA KATHERINE, poet, writer, lyricist; b. Columbus, Ind., Sept. 14, 1944; m. Jason W. Wehrle, June 24, 1979; children: Christian J., Michelle L., Gina R. Student, Ind. U., Indpls., 1967-69. Former model, bookkeeper, employment counselor, exec. sec. Contbr. poems to various publications; composer (with others) popular songs. Address: 4141 N Elmhurst Dr Indianapolis IN 46226

WALLIN, JUDITH KERSTIN, pediatrician, educator; b. Paris, Apr. 23, 1938; came to U.S., 1938; d. Theodore Bror and Ella Charlotte (Butler) Wallin. BS in Chemistry, Elizabethtown (Pa.) Coll., 1960; MD, Temple U., 1964. Diplomate Am. Bd. Pediatrics. Diplomate Am. Bd. Pediatrics. Intern Bellevue Hosp., N.Y.C., 1964-65, resident specializing in pediatrics, 1965-67, attending pediatrician, 1967—; instr. pediatrics, NYU, 1967-71, asst. prof. clin. pediatrics, 1971-74, assoc. prof., 1974—. Trustee Elizabethtown Coll., 1988—. Recipient Educate for Service through Profl. Achievement award, O.F. Stambaugh Alumni award Elizabethtown Coll., 1978. Home: 300 E 33d St New York NY 10016 Office: Bellevue Hosp Dept Pediatrics 27th St and 1st Ave New York NY 10016

WALLING, GEORGIA, psychotherapist b. Cedarhurst, N.Y.; d. William English and Anna (Strunsky) W.; student U. Paris, 1931-32, Vassar Coll., 1932-34; BA, Rollins Coll., 1935; MA, Columbia U., 1937, MS in Social Work, 1947. Caseworker, Family Service Soc., Atlanta, 1948-49, Bklyn. Bur. Social Service, 1951-53, Inwood House, N.Y.C., 1954-58; sr. psychiat. casework therapist Childrens Village, Dobb's Ferry, N.Y., 1959-60; asso. staff mem. Postgrad Center for Mental Health, N.Y.C., 1960-65; pvt. practice psychotherapy and psychoanalysis, N.Y.C. Mem. Nat. Assn. Social Workers, N.Y. State Soc. Clin. Social Work Psychotherapists, Postgrad. Psychoanalytic Soc., Acad. Cert. Clin. Social Workers, Nat. Accreditation Assn. for Psychoanalysis.

WALLING, SUSAN EILEEN FEMRITE, interior designer; b. Glenwood, Minn., Oct. 4, 1944; d. Sigvold Elmer and Sally Evangeline (Amundson) Femrite; B.S., U. Minn., 1966, cert. interior design, 1980; m. Greg Thomas Walling, Aug. 13, 1966; children—Christopher, Kari. Tchr., Roseville (Minn.) Public Schs., 1966-68, St. Louis Park (Minn.) Public Schs., 1968-73; interior designer Sue Walling Interiors, Edina, Minn., 1978-81; pres., interior designer SW Design, Inc., Mpls., 1981—. Pub. in Designer Mag., 1983, 84, 85. Active, Children's Health Center Aux., Friends of Mpls. Art Inst.; bd. life and growth Mt. Olivet Lutheran. Ch. Mem. Am. Soc. Interior Designers (assoc.). Club: Edina Country (swim club bd.). Office: 925 Southgate Office Plaza 5001 W 80th St Minneapolis MN 55437

WALLIS, ELIZABETH SUSAN, air traffic control specialist; b. Tulsa, Dec. 20, 1953; d. Ralph David and Margaret Ella (Nolen) W. Student, Drury Coll., 1972-73; BS, U. Ark., 1976. Resident asst. U. Ark., Fayetteville, 1974-76; placement interviewer Okla. Employment Service, Tulsa, 1977-78; air traffic control specialist FAA Houston, 1978-84, regional staff specialist, Los Angeles, 1984-85, plans and programs specialist, Olathe, Kans., 1985, supervisory air traffic control specialist, 1985-87; FAA quality assurance specialist FAA Cen. Region, 1987—. Bd. dirs. Westmont Homes Assn., 1987—. Mem. Profl. Women Controllers (charter, cen. regional area dir. 1985-86, nat. sec. 1987—), Air Traffic Control Assn. Avocation: travel. Office: FAA Cen Region Hdqrs Air Traffic Div 601 W 12th Kansas City MO 64106

WALLIS, JOANNA, data processing executive; b. Washington, Nov. 10, 1944; d. John Howard and Suzanne (Waters) Phinney; m. Mark Harvey Wallis, Sept. 3, 1967 (div. June 1978); 1 child, Shane Michael. BA, Russell Sage, 1966. Research chemist Lockheed Calif. Co., Burbank, 1966-67; scientific programmer Lockheed Missiles & Space, Sunny Valley, Calif., 1967; mem. tech. staff Analysts Internat. Corp., Los Angeles, 1967-69; mem. staff Computer Scis. Corp., El Segundo, Calif., 1969-73, customer systems rep., 1975-78, br. support mgr., 1978-80, dist. systems mgr., 1980-82, dist. prof. service mgr., 1982-83, mgr. infonet support ctr., 1983-84, S.W. div. mgr. application micro computers, 1984-87, mem. adv. staff, 1987—. Republican. Home: 3209 S Walker San Pedro CA 90731 Office: Computer Scis Corp 2100 E Grand Ave El Segundo CA 90245

WALLISON, FRIEDA K., lawyer; b. N.Y.C., Jan. 15, 1943; d. Ruvin H. and Edith (Landes) Koslow; m. Peter J. Wallison, Nov. 24, 1966; children—Ethan S., Jeremy L., Rebecca K. A.B., Smith Coll., 1963; LL.B., Harvard U., 1966. Bar: N.Y. 1967, DC 1982. Assoc. Carter, Ledyard & Milburn, N.Y.C., 1966-75; spl. counsel, div. market regulation Securities & Exchange Commn., Washington, 1975; exec. dir., gen. counsel Mcpl. Securities Rulemaking Bd., Washington, 1975-78; ptnr. Rogers & Wells, N.Y.C. and Washington, 1978-83, Jones, Day, Reavis & Pogue, Washington, 1983—; mem. Govtl. Acctg. Standards Adv. Council, Washington, Nat. Council on Pub. Works Improvement, Washington. Mem. Nat. Council Govtl. Acctg., Nat. Assn. Bond Lawyers, Fed. Bar Assn., ABA, N.Y.C. Bar Assn. Office: Jones Day Reavis & Pogue Metropolitan Sq 1450 G St NW Suite 600 Washington DC 20005

WALLSKOG, JOYCE MARIE, nursing educator, psychotherapist; b. Melrose Park, Ill., Apr. 20, 1942. BSN, Alverno Coll., 1977; MSN, U. Wis., Milw., 1982. RN, Wis.; cert. psychotherapist, Wis. Staff nurse St. Mary's Hill Hosp., Milw., 1977-78; Staff nurse Waukesha (Wis.) Meml. Hosp., 1978-80, clin. nurse specialist, 1980-87; asst. prof. nursing Marquette U., Milw., 1986—; psychotherapist Psychiat. Assocs. Comprehensive Services, Ltd., Milw., 1982-85; nurse psychotherapist Counseling and Wellness Ctr., Waukesha, 1982—; cons. Alverno Coll., Milw., 1983-84, Health Care Cons., Sussex, Wis., 1985—; coordinator Waukesha Premenstral Syndrome Program, 1980—. Contbr. articles to profl. jours. Bd. dirs. Waukesha County Mental Health Assn., 1982; mem. Waukesha County Unified Services, 1984; advisor Resolve Through Sharing, 1986—, Women's Health Services, 1987—. Mem. Am. Nurses Assn. (council psychiat and mental health nursing), Wis. Nurses Assn. (rep. Wis. Coalition on Sexual Misconduct by Psychotherapists and Counselors 1988—), Forum for Death Edn. and Counseling, Sigma Theta Tau, Delta Upsilon Sigma. Office: Marquette Coll Nursing Milwaukee WI 53233

WALSCH, NELLIE LEE, steel warehousing executive; b. Garrison, Ky., Mar. 18, 1920; d. Thomas Edgar and Essie Beatrice (Akers) Martin; student public and pvt. schs., also various coll. courses; m. Herman W. Walsch, Nov. 19, 1949; 1 son, Daniel Lee. With United Iron & Metal Co., Inc., Balt., from 1946, office mgr., bookkeeper div. Curtis Steel products Co.; corp. sec., bookkeeper Marlen Trading Co., Inc., Balt., Chesapeake Internat. Corp., Balt.; bookkeeper Curtis Export Corp., Balt., LSL Assos., Balt. Democrat. Methodist. Office: 4101 Curtis Ave Baltimore MD 21226

WALSCHLEGER, DONNA LORETTA, insurance professional; b. Springfield, Ill., Oct. 4, 1948; d. Donovan Edgar and Mary Ellen (Howell) Davis; m. Ted B. Walschleger, Oct. 19, 1968; children: Elizabeth Anne, Rachel Susan, Julie Marie. Postgrad., Sangamon State U., 1982—. Clk. Village of Sherman, Ill., 1973-77; from sec. to asst. dir. casualty claims Horace Mann Ins. Co., Springfield, 1982-86; agt. State Farm Ins. Co., Sherman, 1986—; broker Raynolds Realty, Springfield, 1975-85. Mem. Nat. Assn. Realtors, Springfield Assn. Ins. Women (Exec. of Yr. 1986). Home: 22 Somerset Sherman IL 62684 Office: State Farm Ins 134 N First St Sherman IL 62684

WALSH, ALISON CLARA, manufacturing company executive; b. Lewiston, Maine, Dec. 1, 1961; d. Dwight Rolfe and Jane Rae (McKee) W.; m. Mark E. McCarty, July 16, 1988. Student, Amherst Coll., 1979-81; BS, MIT, 1988. Mgr. ops. Charleswater Products, Inc., West Newton, Mass., 1981-86; comptroller Charleswater Products, Inc., West Newton, 1986—. Mem. steering com. Jobs for New Ams., Brookline, Mass., 1984-85; organizer, editor newsletter Newton Open Channels, 1981-82; adv. bd. Barry L. Price Rehab. Ctr., West Newton, 1983—. Mem. Nat. Assn. Female Execs. Mem. United Ch. of Christ. Office: Charleswater Products Inc 93 Border St West Newton MA 02165

WALSH, ANNMARIE HAUCK, research firm executive; b. N.Y.C., May 5, 1938; d. James Smith and Ann-Marie (Kennedy) Hauck; m. John F. Walsh, Jr., June 20, 1960; children: Peter Hauck, John David. B.A., Barnard Coll., 1961; M.A., Columbia U., 1969, Ph.D., 1971. Sr. staff mem. Inst. Pub. Adminstrn., N.Y.C., 1961-72, pres., 1982—; dir., assoc. prof. Ctr. for Urban and Policy Studies, CUNY Grad. Ctr., N.Y.C., 1972-79; dir. Gov.'s Task Force on Regional Planning, N.Y., Conn., N.J., 1979-81; cons. urban and regional mgmt. UN, 1966-70, cons. pub. enterprise and bond fin., 1978—. Author: Urban Government for Zagreb, Yugoslavia, 1968, Urban Government for Lagos, Nigeria, 1968, Urban Government for the Paris Region, 1968, The Urban Challenge to Government: An International Comparison of Thirteen Cities, 1969, The Public's Business: Politics and Practices of Government Corporations, 1978, 2d edit, 1980; editor: Agenda for a City, 1970. Bd. dirs. Pub. Enterprise Project, Twentieth Century Fund, 1972-76; bd. dirs. Ralph Bunche Inst., UN, 1978-82. Herbert Lehmann fellow, 1966-69. Mem. Regional Plan Assn. (bd. dirs. 1987), Nat. Acad. Pub. Adminstrn. (panel mem. on govt. corps., ADP mgmt. deregulation in govt., civil service reform, NASA reorgn.), Phi Beta Kappa. Office: Inst Pub Adminstrn 55 W 44th St New York NY 10036

WALSH, BEATRICE METCALFE PASSAGE, civic worker; b. Schenectady, N.Y., Mar. 6, 1917; d. William Riley and Jessamine (Littlefield) Passage; student Western Res. U., 1941-42, Cleve. Community Coll., 1980—; m. Thomas Joseph Walsh, July 12, 1941; 1 dau., Joan Beatrice (Mrs. Peter Michael Waltz). Vol. worker ARC, 1941-46, 47-53; leader council Cleve. Beachwood (Ohio) Girl Scouts, 1952-57; vol. worker Community Chest, 1947-50; mem. women's com. Cleve. Orch., 1962—; Am. Red Cross, 1963—; ladies program chmn. Am. Chem. Soc., 1960, Am. Inst. Chem. Engrs., 1961, ladies program conv. com., 1969; mem. Orange Community Arts Council, 1969—, Pepper Pike Civic League, 1966—; ladies program co-chmn. Nat. Heat Transfer Conf., 1964; mem. women's com. Chagrin Valley Little Theater; mem., corr. sec. exec. bd. Case Western Res. U. Mem. Nat. Huguenot Soc., Nat. Soc. Founders and Patriots, Nat. Soc. New Eng. Women (sec. Cleve. Colony 1980—), Shaker Heights LWV, Case Faculty Wives (pres. 1958-59), Western Res. Rep. Women's Club, DAR, (Shaker chpt., corr. sec. 1962-64, registrar 1964-69, publicity chmn. 1968-70, chaplain 1969-71, librarian 1972-73, vice regent 1973-74, regent 1974-76, dir. 1985—, del. state conv. 1963, 64, 66, 69, 73, 74, 75, chmn. reception, del. nat. conv. 1964, 73, 74, 75), Friends of Orange Community Library, Daus. Am. Colonists (regent Charter Oak chpt. 1977-79, parliamentarian 1981-86), Nat. Soc. Daus. of Founders and Patriots Am., Order Crown of Charlemagne, Soc. Magna Charta Dames, Nat. Soc. New Eng. Women, Colonial Dames 17th Century, (corr. sec. 1985—), Nat. Soc. Women Descs. of Ancient and Honorable Arty. Co., Nat. Soc. Daus. 1812, Early Settlers of the Western Res., Western Res. Hist. Soc., Garden Center Greater Cleve. Presbyterian. Clubs: Blackbrook Country, Landerhaven Golf, Moreland Hills Golf, Landerwood Swim, Suburban Garden, Green Valley Garden (club rep. 1972-73, corr. sec. 1976-77, pres.); Case-Western Res. U. (exec. bd. 1981—); Univ. Women's. Home: 32555 Creekside Dr Pepper Pike Cleveland OH 44124

WALSH, CHERYL LEE, marketing communications manager; b. Lawrence, Mass., Mar. 11, 1954; d. Leo Emmanuel and Doris Marion Walsh. Cert. English, Wroxton Coll., Oxford, Eng., 1974; B.A. in Journalism/English, U. Mass., 1975; M.B.A., Suffolk U., 1982. Public relations staff Eastern States Expn., Springfield, 1976; dir. pub. relations Newbury Jr. Coll., Boston, 1976-79; assoc. dir. univ. relations, coordinator spl. events U. Mass., Amherst, 1979-84; dir. communications Wang Inst. Grad. Studies, Tyngsboro, Mass., 1984-85; mktg. communications mgr. IHRDC, 1985-86, Lisp Machine, Inc., Andover, Mass., 1986-87; mktg. communications BBN Labs, Inc., 1987—. Contbg. editor: Your Career in Public Relations, 1983. Mem. Western Mass. Commn. on Tourism, Boston, 1983-84; bd. dirs. Amherst C. of C., 1979-81. Mem. Publicity Club Boston, Inc. (v.p. membership 1983-84, co-chmn. bell ringer judging event 1986). Roman Catholic. Office: BBN Labs Inc 33 Moulton St Cambridge MA 02238

WALSH, DIANE, pianist; b. Washington, Aug. 16, 1950; d. William Donald and Estelle Louise (Stokes) W.; m. Henry Forbes, 1969 (div. 1979); m. Richard Pollak, 1982. MusB, Juilliard Sch. Music, 1971, MusM, Mannes Coll., 1982. N.Y.C. debut Young Concert Artists Series, 1974; founder Mannes Trio, 1982; appearances include: Kennedy Ctr. for Performing Arts, Washington, 1976, Met. Mus., N.Y.C., 1976, Wigmore Hall, London, 1980 (with Mannes Trio) Lincoln Ctr.'s Alice Tully Hall, Library of Congress, 1987; appeared with maj. orchs. worldwide, including St. Louis Symphony, Indpls. Symphony, San Francisco Symphony, Buffalo Philharm., Bavarian Radio Symphony of Munich, Berlin Radio Symphony, Radio Symphony Frankfurt, Radio Symphony Stuttgart; has toured Europe, N.Am., S.Am., Cen. Am.; recs. for Nonesuch Records, 1980, 82, Book-of-Month Records, 1985; mem. piano and chamber music faculty Mannes Coll. Music. Recipient 3d prize Busoni Internat. Piano Competition, Italy, 1974, 2d prize Mozart Internat. Piano Competition, Salzburg, Austria, 1975, 1st prize Munich Internat. Piano Competition, 1975, Naumburg Chamber Music award, 1986; Nat. Endowment Arts. grantee, 1981.

WALSH, GERRY O'MALLEY, lawyer; b. Houston, Dec. 22, 1936; d. Frederick Harold and Blanche (O'Malley) W. B.S., U. Houston, 1959; J.D., S. Tex. Coll. Law, 1966. Bar: Tex. 1966, U.S. Dist. Ct. (so. dist.) Tex. 1967, (we. dist.) Tex. 1976; cert. elem. tchr. Tex. Elem. tchr. Houston, 1959-65; instr. bus. law U. Houston, 1966-67; sole practice, Houston, 1966—; lectr. legal, jud. and civic orgns. Adviser, den mother Sam Houston council Boy Scouts Am.; mem. Mus. Fine Arts. Recipient den mother award Sam Houston council Boy Scouts Am. Mem. Houston Zool. Assn., Houston Archeol. Soc., Bus. and Profl. Women's Assn. (Woman of Yr. 1973), ABA, Am. Judicature Soc., Tex. Criminal Lawyers Assn., Harris County Criminal Lawyers Assn., Tex. Trial. Lawyers Assn., State Bar Tex., Houston Bar Assn., U. Houston Alumni Assn., So. Tex. Coll. Law Alumni Assn., Nat. Criminal Def. Lawyers Assn., Zeta Tau Alpha (best mem. and rec. sec. 1958), Sigma Chi (award 1958). Office: 505 Westcott Suite 307 Houston TX 77007

WALSH, JANET LAURENTIA, human resources manager, educator; b. Lowell, Mass., June 22, 1954; d. William P. and Ruth (Laird) W. BA in Econs., Bucknell U., 1976; MBA in Mgmt., Loyola Coll., Balt., 1982. Mgr. human resources P.H.H. Group Inc., Balt., 1982-84; mgr. employee relations The Am. Sterilizer Co., Erie, Pa., 1984-86; mgr. U.S. personnel Soc. for Worldwide Interbank Fin. Telecommunications, Culpeper, Va., 1987—; instr. Gannon U., Erie, 1985-86, Howard Community Coll., Columbia, Md., 1979-84. Pres. adv. com. on Bus. and Econ. Affairs U. Md., 1978-79. Mem. Am. Soc. Personnel Adminstrs., Employment Mgmt. Assn., Alpha Lambda Delta, Alpha Sigma Nu. Club: Bucknell Alumni (pres. 1977-80). Office: Soc Worldwide Interbank Fin Telecommunications 2005 McDevitt Dr Culpeper VA 22701

WALSH, JULIA MONTGOMERY, investment banking executive; b. Akron, Ohio, Mar. 29, 1923; d. Edward A. and Catherine Skurkay Curry; m. John G. Montgomery, Apr. 7, 1948 (dec. 1957); children: John, Stephen, Michael, Mark; m. Thomas M. Walsh, May 18, 1963; 1 child, Margaret; stepchildren: Mary F., Patrick J., Kathleen Carr, Thomas D., Joan Cassedy, Daniel, Ann Walton; BBA magna cum laude, Kent State U., 1945, LLD, 1967; postgrad. Harvard U., 1962; LLD Smith Coll., 1983. Dir. Fulbright Program, Ankara, Turkey; personnel officer Am. Consulate Gen., Munich, Fed. Republic of Germany; sr. v.p., registered rep. Ferris & Co., 1955-74; vice chmn. Ferris & Co., Inc., 1974-77; chmn. Julia M. Walsh & Sons, Inc., Washington, 1977-83; mng. dir. Julia M. Walsh & Sons (div. Tucker Anthony & R.L. Day, Inc.), Washington, 1984—; bd. dirs. Pitney Bowes, Stamford, Conn.; mem. Services Policy Adv. Com. to U.S. Trade Rep., Small Bus. Com. Fed. Res. Bank Richmond, Investment Banking Adv. Com. Am. Stock Exchange, former gov. and exchange ofcl.; trustee Dole Commn.; mem., dir. exec. com. Greater Washington Bd. of Trade; panelist TV program Wall Street Week. Bd. dirs. Nat. Bd. of Shrine of Immaculate Conception, Neighborhood Econ. Devel. Corp. D.C.; trustee Kent State U. Found., Nat. Assn. Bank Women, Mount St. Mary's Coll., Emmitsburg, Md., S.I.A. Inst., Wharton Bus. Sch. U. Pa.; past trustee Georgetown U.; mem. adv. bd. First Am. Bank; former trustee Simmons Coll., Boston. Roman Catholic. Office: Tucker Anthony & RL Day Inc 1050 Connecticut Ave #490 Washington DC 20036

WALSH, LAUREL KIMBROUGH, real estate executive, accountant; b. Detroit, Nov. 10, 1941; d. Edwin Price and Margaret Edna (Roberts) Kimbrough; m. Thomas Edward Walsh Jr., June 13, 1964; children: Heather Ann, Jennifer. BA, Duke U., 1963; postgrad., Ariz. State U., 1979-82. Mgmt. trainee Citicorp N.Am., N.Y.C., 1964-65; asst. head dept. bus. devel. United Jersey Banks, Hackensack, 1965-66; sr. tax acct. Henry & Horn, CPA's, Scottsdale, Ariz., 1980-84; v.p., controller Nat. Portfolio, Inc., Scottsdale, 1984—. Mem. Scottsdale Leadership Program, 1988. Mem. Am. Inst. CPA's, Ariz. Soc. CPA's, Ariz. Duke Alumni (local exec. com.), Scottsdale C. of C. (govt. affairs com. 1988—), Beta Gamma Sigma. Office: Nat Portfolio Inc 8300 N Hayden Rd #100 Scottsdale AZ 85258

WALSH, LYNN DREWE, business and management educator; b. N.Y.C., May 8, 1946; s. John Martin and Adele Bertha (Hofmann) W.; 1 child, Matthew Adam. AB in English, North Cen. Coll., Naperville, Ill., 1968; MS in Counselor Edn., L.I. U., 1972; PhD in Organizational and Adminstrv. Studies in Higher Edn., NYU, 1984. Cert. tchr. secondary English, N.Y. Research asst. in chemistry North Cen. Coll., 1965-66; tchr. English, math. and sci. Marshall Jr. High Sch., Columbus, Ga., 1968-69; asst. to dir. continuing edn., adult studies evening div. and summer sch., C.W. Post Ctr., L.I. U., Greenvale, N.Y., 1969-71, asst. to v.p. for adminstrn., 1971-72; asst. to dean instrn., counselor Student Problem Solving Ctr., Nassau Community Coll., Garden City, N.Y., 1972-73; acad. adminstrv. assoc. SUNY, Old Westbury Coll., 1973-77, dir. instrnl. support, 1977-78, asst. v.p. for acad. affairs, 1978-81, acting v.p. for student devel., 1981-82, exec. asst. to pres. for instl. planning and devel., exec. dir. Old Westbury Found., 1982-84, assoc. v.p. for acad. affairs, and spl. asst. to pres. for planning, 1984-87, prof. bus. mgmt., 1987—; adj. assoc. prof. higher edn. NYU, 1985—; mem. L.I. Regional Adv. Council on Higher Edn. Task Force on Acad. Affairs, 1973-87. Contbr. articles to profl. publs. Recipient Outstanding Contbn. to Student Govt. award Student Govt. Assn., SUNY, Old Westbury Coll., 1981, citation for excellence in performance Dept. Counseling and Guidance, Grad. Sch. Edn., C.W. Post Ctr. L.I. U., 1972, Chancellor's award for excellence in profl. service SUNY, 1980, cert. of appreciation Grad. Student Orgn., NYU, 1987. Mem. Am. Assn. Higher Edn., Am. Assn. Univ. Adminstrs., Am. Ednl. Research Assn. (first chairperson grad. student div. J 1982-84, co-chairperson grad. student program com. for 1983 ann. meeting 1982—), Phi Delta Kappa, Phi Lambda Theta. Office: SUNY-Old Westbury Old Westbury NY 11568

WALSH, MARGARET M., answering service executive; b. Appleton, Wis., Nov. 26, 1920; d. Eugene J. and Anna M. (Finnegan) W.; student U. Wis. Extension, 1939, Spencerian Coll., 1940-41. Pres., owner Tel/Sec Inc., Appleton, 1949—; dir. Assoc. Appleton Bank. Founder, chmn. C.L.A.S.P., Inc. Mem. ATAE Inc. (pres. 1972-73), Sales and Mktg. Assn. NE Wis. (pres. 1979-80). Republican. Roman Catholic. Club: Riverview Country (pres. 1982-83). Home: 465 Meadows Dr Appleton WI 54915 Office: Tel/Sec Inc 516 W 6th St Appleton WI 54911

WALSH, MARILYN, lawyer, broadcasting company executive; B.A., Grinnell Coll., 1950; J.D., N.Y. U., 1957, LL.M., 1958, M.B.A., 1963. With U.S. Trust Co., 1951-53, Irving Trust Co., 1953-57; tax atty. Davies, Hardy, Ives and Lawther, 1958-64; with CBS, Inc., N.Y.C., 1964—, sr. tax atty., 1965-66, tax counsel, 1966-67, asst. treas., dir. tax sect., 1967-72, corporate v.p., dir. taxes, 1972—. Office: CBS Inc 51 W 52nd St New York NY 10019 *

WALSH, MARY D. FLEMING, civic worker; b. Whitewright, Tex., Oct. 29, 1913; d. William Fleming and Anna Maud (Lewis) Fleming; B.A., So. Meth. U., 1934; LL.D. (hon.), Tex. Christian U., 1979; m. F. Howard Walsh, Mar. 13, 1937; children—Richard, Howard, D'Ann Walsh Bonnell, Maudi Walsh Roe, William Lloyd. Pres. Fleming Found.; v.p. Walsh Found.; partner Walsh Co.; mem. Lloyd Shaw Found., Colorado Springs, Big Bros. Tarrant County; guarantor Fort Worth Arts Council, Schola Cantorum, Fort Worth Opera, Fort Worth Ballet, Fort Worth Theatre, Tex. Boys Choir; hon. mem. bd. dirs. Van Cliburn Internat. Piano Competition; co-founder Am. Field Service in Ft. Worth; mem. Tex. Commn. for Arts and Humanities, 1968-72, mem. adv. council, 1972-84; bd. dirs. Wm. Edrington Scott Theatre, 1977-83, Colorado Springs Day Nursery, Colorado Springs Symphony, Ft. Worth Symphony, 1974-81; hon. chmn. Opera Ball, 1975, Opera Guild Internat. Conf., 1976; co-presenter (with husband) through Walsh Found., Tex. Boy's Choir and Dorothy Shaw Bell Choir ann. presentation of The Littlest

Wiseman to City of Ft. Worth; granter with husband land and bldgs. to Tex. Boy's Choir for permanent home, 1971, Walsh-Wurlitzer organ to Casa Manana, 1972. Sem. Recipient numerous awards, including Altrusa Civic award as 1st Lady of Ft. Worth, 1968; (with husband) Disting. Service award So. Bapt. Radio and Television Commn., 1972; Opera award Girl Scouts, 1977-79; award Streams and Valleys, 1976-80; named (with husband) Patron of Arts in Ft. Worth, 1970, Edna Gladney Internat. Grandparents of 1972, (with husband) Sr. Citizens of Yr, 1985; Mary D. and Howard Walsh Meml. Organ dedicated by Bapt. Radio and TV Commn., 1967, tng. ctr. named for the Walshes, 1976; Mary D. and Howard Walsh Med. Bldg., Southwestern Bapt. Theol. Sem.; library at Tarrant County Jr. Coll. N.W. Campus dedicated to her and husband, 1978; Brotherhood citation Tarrant County chpt. NCCJ, 1978; Spl. Recognition award Ft. Worth Ballet Assn.; Royal Purple award Tex. Christian U., 1979; Friends of Tex. Boys Choir award, 1981; appreciation award Southwestern Bapt. Theol. Sem., 1981, B. H. Carroll Founders award, 1982; numerous other award for civic activities. Mem. Ft. Worth Boys Club, Ft. Worth Children's Hosp., Jewel Charity Ball, Ft. Worth Pan Hellenic (pres. 1940), Opera Guild, Fine Arts Found. Guild of Tex. Christian U., Girl's Service League (hon. life, hon. chmn. Fine Arts Guild Spring Ballet, 1985), AAUW, Goodwill Industries Aux., Child Study Center, Tarrant County Aux. of Edna Gladney Home, YWCA (life), Ft. Worth Art Assn., Ft. Worth Ballet Assn., Tex. Boys Choir Aux., Friends of Tex. Boys Choir, Round Table, Colorado Springs Fine Art Center, Am. Automobile Assn., Nat. Assn. Cowbelles, Ft. Worth Arts Council (hon. bd. mem.), Am. Guild Organists (hon., Ft. Worth chpt.), Rae Reimers Bible Study Class (pres. 1968), Tex. League Composers (hon. life), Chi Omega (pres. 1935-36, hon. chmn. 1986), others. Baptist. Clubs: The Woman's (Club Fidelite), Colorado Springs Country, Garden of Gods, Colonial Country, Ridglea Country, Shady Oaks Country, Chi Omega Mothers, Chi Omega Carousel, TCU Woman's. Home: 2425 Stadium Dr Fort Worth TX 76109 Home: 1801 Culebra Ave Colorado Springs CO 80907

WALSH, MAUREEN MARIE, marketing and management consultant; b. Dubuque, Iowa, Apr. 16, 1949; d. Michael Eugene and Rosemary Veronica (Anthony) W. BA, U. Wis., 1972, MBA in Mktg., 1976. Gen. mgr. Phila. Theatre Co., 1976-78; dir. mktg. Children's Theatre Co., Mpls., 1978-80, Bkly. Acad. Music, 1980-81, Joffrey Ballet, N.Y.C., 1981-82; account exec. Ogilvy & Mather Dir., N.Y.C., 1982-83; pres. Walsh Ptnrs., N.Y.C. and Phila., 1983—; Mem. faculty Temple U., Phila., 1976-78; asst. prof. Bklyn. Coll., 1982-84, Adelphi U., N.Y.C., 1980-84; cons. Minn. Arts Bd., 1978-80, Yellow Springs Inst., Phila., 1981—, Genesis New Age Ctr., Phila., 1988—, New Frontier mag., Phila., 1988—. Campaign mgr. for county freeholder, N.J., 1977; bd. dirs. 6 arts orgns., N.Y.C., 1983—. Home: 277 W 10th St Apt 7E New York NY 10014

WALSH, MONICA MARY, public relations executive; b. Neptune, N.J., Feb. 19, 1952; d. Edward Leo and Ruth Claire (Sandford) W.; m. Stanley Julius, June 8, 1974 (div. June 1976). BA in English, Chestnut Hill Coll., 1974. Reporter, feature writer Daily Observer, Toms River, N.J., 1974-76; dir. pub. info. N.J. Dept. Edn., Trenton, 1976-78; press sec. N.J. Gen. Assembly Majority, Trenton, 1978-83; sr. v.p. The Marcus Group, Inc., Trenton and Secaucus, N.J., 1983—; cons. various campaigns, 1983—. Recipient Iris award Internat. Assn. Bus. Communications, 1987. Mem. Internat. Assn. Bus. Communicators (trustee Women's Polit. Action com. N.J. chpt. 1986—, Iris award 1987). Democrat. Roman Catholic. Home: 104A Library Pl Princeton NJ 08540 Office: The Marcus Group Inc 226 W State St Trenton NJ 08608

WALSH, PEARL JERI LANE, editor, writer; b. Los Angeles, Nov. 9, 1914; d. John H. and Bertha (Frisch) Lane, cert. in pub. relations U. Calif. at Los Angeles, 1973; student Stanford U., 1964, U. So. Calif., 1939, Calif. State U.-Northridge, 1973; m. John Edward Walsh, Sept. 1951; 1 son, John Edward; 1 son by previous marriage, David Lane Nittinger. Tech. editor The Rand Corp., Santa Monica, Calif., 1947-50, Naval Weapons Center, China Lake, Calif., 1950-54; cons. editor Hawaiian Sugar Planters Exptl. Sta., Honolulu, 1964-65; tech. editor Mobil Research Corp., Dallas, 1967-68; tech. writer RCA Electromagnetic and Aviation Systems Corp., Van Nuys, Calif., 1968-71; free-lance editor McGraw-Hill Pub. Co., N.Y.C., 1950—; tech. writer C.E., U.S. Army, Los Angeles, 1974—; sr. writer U. Calif. Neuropsychiat. Inst. Program, Los Angeles, 1972-74; freelance supervisory editor Goodyear Pub. Co. subs. Prentice Hall Co., Palisades, Calif., 1971-80; pres. OR-Stat, Inc., Tarzana, Calif., 1960-67. Cert. travel cons.; recipient Outstanding award Naval Ordnance Test Sta., 1952; Spl. Act award Army Corps. Engrs., 1975. Mem. Soc. for Tech. Communication (sr.; publicity chmn. 26th internat. conf., mgr. nat. publicity com. 1984-85, pub. relations Los Angeles chpt. 1969—), So. Calif. Bookbuilders Assn. Publicity Club Los Angeles, Women in Communications, Am. Med. Writers Assn., Med. Mktg. Assn., Metric Assn. Author: Composition Standards, 1951; On Preparing Technical Papers, 1971. Inventor ratchet for Coxhead Varitype machine. Home: 8633 Balboa Blvd Unit 5 Northridge CA 91325 Office: 300 N Los Angeles St Los Angeles CA 90012

WALSH, SUSAN FRANCES, psychiatric social worker; b. Fostoria, Ohio, Apr. 5, 1943; d. Edward Doty and Frances Elizabeth (Storey) W.; B.S., Ind. U., 1965; A.M., U. Chgo., 1968, Ph.D., 1984. Instr. social work Northwestern U. Med. Sch., also staff social worker Northwestern Meml. Hosp., Chgo., 1968-75; pvt. practice psychotherapy, Chgo., 1974—; asso. dept. psychiatry Northwestern U., also coordinator outpatient services Inst. Psychiatry, Northwestern Meml. Hosp., 1975-84, asst. to dir. Inst. Psychiatry, 1984-85; lectr. U. Chgo., 1984-86 ; field instr. U. Chgo., U. Ill., Chgo. Circle; pres. Susan F. Walsh, Ph.D. Ltd. Mem. Nat. Assn. Social Workers. Research on alternative to psychiat. hospitalization. Home: 3150 N Lake Shore Dr Chicago IL 60657 Office: 333 E Ontario St Chicago IL 60611

WALSH-JONES, PAMELA LEIGH, geologist; b. Frankfurt, W.Ger., July 1, 1957; d. William Walker and Gertraude Liebhilde (Hille) Walsh. B.S., Va. Poly. Inst., 1979; m. Malcolm Stuart Jones, June 2, 1984. With Esso Exploration, Houston, 1979-80; well logging engr. Core Labs., Houston, 1980-81, instr., Dallas, 1981-82, geologist, geochemist, Dallas, 1982—. Lutheran.

WALSTON, LYNN MAURYNE, banker; b. Indpls., Mar. 20, 1956; d. Frank, Jr. and Lula Lenora (Adams) Jameson; m. Gregory D. Walston, July 2, 1977 (div. Mar. 1985); children—Tamara J., Stacey V. Assoc. degree Ind. U., 1978; bus. mgmt. degree Ind. U./Purdue U.-Indpls., 1987. With Mchts. Nat. Bank, Indpls., since 1976—, bus. devel. officer, since 1982—, br. mgr., since 1982—, asst. v.p., since 1985—. Troop leader local Girl Scouts U.S., 1983—; vol. Planned Parenthood, Indpls., 1985—; treas. Riverside Park United Methodist Ch., 1984—. Recipient Vol. Service award Indpls. Humane Soc., 1983, Girl Scouts Just Friends Program, Indpls., 1985. Mem. Nat. Assn. Bank Women (scholar 1983, 85), Indpls. Urban Bankers (assoc. v.p. 1986, v.p. 1987), Nat. Assn. Female Execs. Democrat. Avocations: aerobics; bowling; reading. Home: 3211 N Sharon Ave Indianapolis IN 46222 Office: Merchants Nat Bank 950 N Shadeland Ave Indianapolis IN 46219

WALTER, BEVERLY TONEY, cosmetic company executive; b. Comfort, W.Va., Mar. 27, 1946; d. Charles Leftridge Toney and Ruth Areta (Leadingham) Dail; divorced; children: Beth Yvonne Walter, Nathan Andrew Walter. Hon. Degree, Westmoreland Community Coll. Mgr. dist. Nutri-Metrics, 1974-76; regional mgr. Nutri-Metrics, Inc., 1976-78; sr. regional mgr. Nutri-Metrics, Inc., City of Industry, Calif., 1978-82, mgr. corp. sales, 1982-84, v.p. sales and mktg., 1985-87, exec. v.p., chief operating officer, 1987—; owner, mgr. Here's To Your Health Store, Latrobe, Pa., 1977-82; pres. Beverly T. Walter Seminars Internat., Latrobe, 1970—; prodn. owner Aries & Co., speaking orgn., Pomona, Calif., 1987—. Speaker Sen. Campbell Conv. on Women, Los Angeles, 1987-88. Spiritualist. Club: Los Angeles Bus. and Profl. Women's. Home: 23 Los Coyotes Dr Pomona CA 91766 Office: Nutri-Metics Internat 19501 E Walnut Dr City of Industry CA 91749

WALTER, CHRYSANDRA LOU, national park superintendent; b. Toledo, Nov. 29, 1947; d. Richard Lambert Walter and Winifred May (Buckley) Moore. BA, San Jose State U., 1969. Park ranger Point Reyes (Calif.) Nat. Seashore, 1969-70; education specialist Pacific Northwest Region, Nat. Parks Service, Seattle, 1970-73; interpretive specialist Manhattan Sites unit N.Y.C. Nat. Parks), N.Y.C., 1973-76; chief of interpretation George Washington Meml. Pkwy., Washington, 1976-78; mgr. San Francisco Area Golden Gate Nat. Recreation area, 1978-82; park supt. Lyndon B. Johnson Nat. Hist. Park, Johnson City, Tex., 1982-84; dep. supt. Gateway Nat. Recreation Area, N.Y.C., 1984-85; park supt. Lowell (Mass.) Nat. Hist. Park, 1985—. Bd. dirs. Merrimack Reperetory Theatre, Lowell, 1985—, Lowell Girls' Club, 1984—, Tully/Tsongas Found., Lowell, 1985—; chmn. bd. dirs. Women in the Wilderness, San Francisco, 1981-82. Mem. Lowell C. of C. (bd. dirs., sub-chairwoman Women's com., 1985—). Republican. Methodist. Club: Johnson City Women's (pres. 1984). Lodge: Rotary (Lowell). Office: Lowell Nat Park 171 Merrimack Lowell MA 01852

WALTER, CLAIRE MARGARET, free-lance writer; b. Bridgeport, Conn., Sept. 9, 1943; d. Oscar and Louise (Laden) W.; m. Burns E. Cameron, Apr. 20, 1973 (div. 1985); 1 child, Andrew Cameron-Walter. BA, Boston U., 1965. Asst. editor U.S. Camera & Travel, N.Y.C., 1964-67; mng. editor Ski, Ski Bus. jours., N.Y.C., 1967-71; dir. ski mktg. services Davis Pub. Relations, N.Y.C., 1971-73; sales promotion specialist Swissair, N.Y.C., 1973-75; free-lance writer N.Y.C., 1975—. Author: The Young People's Illustrated Dictionary of Skiing, 1978, Winners: The Blue Ribbon Encyclopedia of Awards, 1981, Pennsylvia's Historic Restaurants and their Recipes, 1986. Commr. Hoboken (N.J.) Hist. Dist. Commn., 1978—; dir. com. Brownstone Revival, N.Y.C., 1985—. Mem. U.S. Ski Writers Assn., Soc. Am. Travel Writers, Aviation/ Space Writers Assn., Soc. Am. Travel Writers, Ea. Ski Writers Assn. Home and Office: 939 Bloomfield St Hoboken NJ 07030

WALTER, MADALINE REEDER, management consultant; b. Kansas City, Mo., Nov. 20, 1944; d. Douglas Lee and Madaline (Brown) Reeder; m. Steven L. Walter, Feb. 12, 1966 (div. July 1978); children: Lee, Sean, Seth, Muffy. AA, Bradford Coll., 1964; BS in Edn., Kansas U., 1966. Youth coordinator Adventure Unlimited, Kansas City, 1972-74; exec. dir. Council on Edn., Kansas City, 1976-82; mgmt. specialist MBS Inc., Leawood, Kans., 1982-83; pres., prin. founder Strength Inc., Shawnee Mission, Kans., 1983—. Local chmn. Gov.'s Conf. on Edn., Kansas City, 1976; mem. Gov.'s Commn. on Children and Youth, Jefferson City, Mo., 1979-82. Mem. Nat. Assn. Female Execs., Multi-Level Mgmt. Inventory Network of Cons., Operational Politics/Women on the Way Up, Kappa Kappa Gamma, Friends of Art. Lodge: Rotary. Office: Strength Inc 4210 Shawnee Mission Pkwy Shawnee Mission KS 66205

WALTER, MARY ELLEN, hardware supply executive; b. New Brighton, Pa., May 6, 1942; d. Robert C. and Louise S. (Matterness) Snyder; grad. Butler Community Coll.; married; 1 child. Cert. customer service exec. Sec., Fretz-Moon Tube Co., East Butler, Pa., 1960-63; sec. in advt. and fin. Am. Hardware Supply Co., Butler, Pa., 1963-75, customer service mgr., 1976—. Mem. Am. Soc. Profl. and Exec. Women, Nat. Assn. for Female Execs., Nat. Wildlife Fedn., Nat. Audubon Soc., YMCA, YWCA, Telecommunications Mgmt. Assn., Butler County Humane Soc., Western Pa. Conservancy, Internat. Customer Service Assn. Democrat. Roman Catholic. Home: 356G Whitestown Rd Butler PA 16001

WALTER, MAY ELIZABETH, retail company executive; b. N.Y.C.; d. Peter J. and Elizabeth (Shaub) W.Co-founder, treas., exec. v.p., vice chmn. Mut. Buying Syndicate, Inc., 1931-65; pres. Retail Marketers Advt., Inc., N.Y.C., 1966-67, cons., adviser, 1968-71. Sec., trustee, mem. exec. com. Am. Crafts Council, N.Y.C., 1962-77, hon. trustee, 1977—; adv. council Snite Mus. Art, U. Notre Dame. Recipient Salute to Women award Republican Women in Bus. and Professions, 1962. Home: 923 Fifth Ave New York NY 10021

WALTER, NANCY ANN, personnel administrator, state agency administrator; b. Indpls., Nov. 7, 1945; d. Kenneth Seerley and Genevieve Altha (Stout) Foltz; m. Donald Joseph Walter, June 14, 1974. BS with honors, Mich. State U., 1974. Personnel sec. Eli Lilly & Co., Indpls., 1964-72; personnel officer Mich. Dept. Commerce, Lansing, 1974-76, personnel dir., 1982-84; personnel officer, mgr. Mich. Dept. Civil Service, Lansing, 1976-81; personnel dir. Mich. Bur. of State Lottery, Lansing, 1981-82; personnel dir. Mich. Dept. Agr., Lansing, 1984-86, asst. to dir., 1986-87. Tchr., vol. ARC, 1972-76; vol. Radio Talking Book WKAR, East Lansing, 1984—. Mem. Internat. Personnel Mgmt. Assn. (cen., internat. regions), Am. Soc. Personnel Adminstrn., Am. Soc. Tng. and Devel., Produce Mktg. Assn. Democrat. Office: Mich Dept Agr PO Box 30017 Lansing MI 48909

WALTER, NOLA JANICE, rental company administrator, artist; b. Eau Claire, Wis., Mar. 29, 1934; d. Robert Emmet and Adeline Victoria (Johnson) Rossman; student Dist. 1 Tech. Inst., Eau Claire, 1977-78; 1 dau., Rhea Carol. Exec. sec. W.H. Hobbs Supply Co., Eau Claire, 1952-54; jr. accountant C.A. Irwin Co., Eau Claire, 1954-61; legal sec. various attys. in Eau Claire, Mpls., 1963-73; office mgr. Bearson-Steinmetz Rentals, Eau Claire, 1974-85; freelance artist, 1980—. Recipient Gregg Shorthand certificate of merit, 1952, certs. of award in oil painting, 1977, 78; Gold, Silver and Bronze awards in competitive dancing, 1979, 80, 81, 82, 83, 84. Mem. Nat. Wildlife Fedn., Am. Antiques and Crafts Soc., Smithsonian Assos., Am. Film Inst. Democrat. Congregationalist. Home: 825 Barland St Eau Claire WI 54701 Office: 315 E Madison St Eau Claire WI 54701

WALTERS, ANNA LEE, writer, educational administrator; b. Pawnee, Okla., Sept. 9, 1946; d. Luther and Juanita Mae (Taylor) McGlaslin; student U. N.Mex., 1977—; m. Harry Walters, June 1965; children—Anthony, Daniel. Dir. Navajo Community Coll. Press, Tsaile (Navajo Nation), Ariz., 1982—; contbg. author: The Man to Send Rainclouds, 1974, Warriors of the Rainbow, 1975, Shantih, 1976, The Third Woman, 1979, The Remembered Earth, 1979, American Indians Today, Thought, Literature, Art, 1981; co-author textbook: The Sacred Ways of Knowledge, Sources of Life, 1977; author: The Otoe-Missiouria Tribe, Centennial Memoirs, 1881-1981, 1981; Earth Power Coming, 1983; The Sun is Not Merciful, 1985, Ghost Singer, 1988; contbr. articles to jours.; guest editor Frauen Offensive, 1978; also poet, feature writer. Recipient Am. Book award The Before Columbus Found., 1986, Virginia Scully McCormick Lit. award, 1986. Office: Navajo Community Coll Press Tsaile AZ 86556

WALTERS, BARBARA, television journalist; b. Sept. 25, 1931; d. Lou and Dena (Selett) W.; m. Lee Guber, Dec. 8, 1963 (div. 1976); 1 dau., Jacqueline Dena; m. Merv Adelson, May 10, 1986. Grad., Sarah Lawrence Coll., 1953; LHD (hon.), Ohio State U., Marymount Coll., Tarrytown, N.Y., 1975, Wheaton Coll., 1983. Former writer-producer WNBC-TV; then with sta. WPIX and CBS-TV; joined Today Show, 1961, regular panel mem., 1963-74, co-host, 1974-76; newscaster ABC Evening News (now ABC World News Tonight), 1976. Contbr. to ABC programs Issues and Answers; appears on prime-time ABC entertainment spls.; co-host ABC TV news show 20/20; moderator syndicated TV program Not For Women Only. Author: How To Talk With Practically Anybody About Practically Anything, 1970. Contbr. to Reader's Digest. Hon. chmn. Nat. Assn. Help for Retarded Children, 1970. Recipient award of yr. Nat. Assn. TV Program Execs., 1975, Emmy award Nat. Acad. TV Arts and Scis., 1975; Mass Media award Am. Jewish Com. Inst. Human Relations, 1975; Hubert H. Humphrey Freedom prize Anti-Defamation League-B'nai B'rith, 1978; Matrix award N.Y. Women in Communications, 1977; Barbara Walters' Coll. Scholarship in Broadcast Journalism established in her honor Ill. Broadcasters Assn., 1975; named to 100 Women Accomplishment Harper's Bazaar, 1967, 71, One of Am.'s 75 Most Important Women Ladies' Home Jour., 1970, One of 10 Women of Decade Ladies' Home Jour., 1979, One of Am.'s 100 Most Important Women Ladies' Home Jour., 1983, Woman of Year in Communications, 1974; Woman of Year Theta Sigma Phi; Broadcaster of Yr. Internat. Radio and TV Soc., 1975; named one of 200 Leaders of Future Time Mag., 1974, One of Most Important Women of 1979 Roper Report, One of Women Most Admired by Am. People Gallup Poll, 1982, 84. Office: ABC News 1330 Ave of Americas New York NY 10019 *

WALTERS, DONNA CHERYL, deaf services director; b. Los Angeles, Mar. 1, 1946; d. Sheila Doreen Carroll; m. Roland Walters Jr., May 17, 1986; children: Randall, Reginald, Natalie, Christina. BS in Nursing, Boston U., 1967. Pub. health nurse D.C. Health Dept., Washington, 1970; staff nurse Psychiat. Inst. Washington, 1971, head nurse, 1972, group leader, patient adv., 1973; campus minister Tom Skinner Assocs., Washington, 1975-80; adminstr. deaf services Mcpl. Health Services, Inc., Balt., 1980-85; dir. deaf services Balt. Med. System, Inc., 1985—; mem. adv. bd. Cen. Interpreter Referral Service, 1986—; mem. adv. bd. for health studies AA degree program, Gallaudet U., Washington, 1986—. Author (songbook) Lift Up Your Hands Vol. I, 1976, Lift Up Your Hands Vol. II, 1978, You've Got a Song, 1979. Served to lt., USN, 1967-69. Grantee Chesapeake Edn. & Research Trust, 1983, Robert Wood Johnson Found., 1985—. Democrat. Presbyterian. Home: 9515 Mellenbrook Rd Columbia MD 21045 Office: Balt Med System Inc 3411 Bank St Baltimore MD 21224

WALTERS, GWEN ANN, small business owner, operator; b. Denver, Dec. 24, 1938; d. Jack and Mae (Braddy) Carson.; m. Dan Walters, Mar. 13, 1960 (div. Apr. 1975); children: Daniel Scott, David Allen. Diploma Secretarial Adminstrn., Colo. State U., 1959. Mgr. sales Tessier & Assocs., Phoenix, 1974-75; adminstrv. asst. John Senseney, Phoenix, 1975-77; acct. Greyhound Corp., Phoenix, 1977-79; pres. A GOS Co., Mesa, Ariz., 1979—; v.p., sec. Intercontinental Telecommunications, Mesa, 1983—, Steel Cool Bldgs.; cons. Ariz. Inst. Electrolysis, Scottsdale, 1979-87, Esthetics Mktg., Scottsdale, 1986—; bd. dirs. Nat. Food Service, Scottsdale. Mem. Nat. Assn. Sec. Services, Met. Ariz. Sec. Services, Assn. Info. Systems Profls., Ariz. Practicing Accts., Mesa C. of C., Chandler C. of C. Republican. Lodge: Zonta. Office: A GOS Co 1660 S Alma School Rd #205 Mesa AZ 85202

WALTERS, JUDY HARUE, lawyer; b. Columbus, Ohio, Mar. 1, 1953; d. Leon Kurtz and Sadae (Yamamoto) W. Student, Princeton U., 1971-73, 74-75; AB, U. Calif., Berkeley, 1977; JD, Harvard U., 1981. Bar: Calif. 1981, U.S. Dist. Ct. (cen. dist.) Calif. 1981. Assoc. Sheppard, Mullin, Richter & Hampton, Los Angeles, 1981-87, Paul, Hastings, Janofsky & Walker, Santa Monica, Calif., 1987—. Mem. ABA, Los Angeles County Bar Assn., Women Lawyers Assn. of Los Angeles, Princeton Profl. Women, Phi Beta Kappa. Democrat. Office: Paul Hastings Janofsky & Walker 1299 Ocean Ave 5th Floor Santa Monica CA 90401

WALTERS, KAY LYNN, software development company executive; b. Big Spring, Tex., Nov. 27, 1942; d. Lesley Albert and La Verne (Holden) Clawson; BA in English, U. Tex., Arlington, 1974; MBA, So. Meth. U., 1978; children: David Ryan, Stephen Paul. Programmer, Bank of A. Levy, Oxnard, Calif., 1966-68; project leader 1st Data Processing, Big Spring, 1968-70, Results, Inc., Dallas, 1970-72; dir. application systems ENSERCH Corp., Dallas, 1973-80; mgr. devel. Performance Assos., Inc., Plano, Tex., 1980-81; sr. v.p. Directions, Inc., Dallas, 1981—. Mem. So. Meth. U. MBA Assn. Baptist. Office: 15301 Dallas Pkwy Suite 400 LB 23 Dallas TX 75248

WALTERS, LINDA ANN, nursing educator; b. Los Angeles, Sept. 3, 1940; d. Thomas and Lolita (Llora) Walters. B.S., Adelphi Coll., 1963; M.A., Columbia U., 1969; Ph.D. candidate NYU. R.N., N.Y. Pediatric sr. nurse NYU Med. Ctr., 1963-65; pediatric nurse clinician, clin. researcher Sloan-Kettering Inst., N.Y.C., 1965-67; pediatric instr. Montefiore Hosp. Affiliation, Bronx, N.Y., 1967-69; clin. nurse specialist in maternal and child health North Shore Hosp., Manhasset, N.Y., 1969-71; asst. prof. maternal and child health Bronx Community Coll., 1971-77; asst. prof. maternal and child health Pace U., Pleasantville, N.Y., 1977—; cons. research found. CUNY, 1978-79; writer Profl. Examination Service, N.Y.C., 1983—. Contbr. articles to profl. jours. Dist. bd. Health Systems Agy., N.Y.C., 1976-82; steering com. dist. bd. Comprehensive Health Planning, N.Y.C., 1973-76. Mem. AAUP, Nurses Assn. of Am. Coll. Obstetricians and Gynecologists, Nat. League Nursing, Am. Nurses Assn. (cert. in maternal and child health), Sigma Theta Tau, Delta Delta Delta. Democrat. Roman Catholic. Lodge: K.C. Office: Pace U Grad Div Nursing Bedford Rd Pleasantville NY 10570

WALTERS, MARY COON, justice state supreme court; b. Baraga, Mich., Jan. 29, 1922; d. Marvin Leonard and Nancy C. (Conway) Coon; m. Asa Lane Walters, July 9, 1952 (dec. June 1974); 1 child, Mark Richard. J.D., U. N.Mex., 1962. Bar: N.Mex. 1962, U.S. Supreme Ct. Pvt. practice Albuquerque, 1962-71, 73-78; judge 2d Jud. Dist. N.Mex., Albuquerque, 1971-72; judge N.Mex. Ct. Appeals, Santa Fe, 1979-81, chief judge, 1981-83; justice N.Mex. Supreme Ct., Santa Fe, 1984—. Served with Women's Airforce Service Pilots, 1943-44, USAF, 1951-55. Mem. ABA, N.Mex. Bar Assn., Albuquerque Bar Assn., Santa Fe Bar Assn. Democrat. Roman Catholic. Office: N Mex Supreme Ct PO Box 848 Santa Fe NM 87504 also: New Mexico Supreme Ct Santa Fe NM 87503

WALTERS, MARY KATHERINE, small business owner; b. Lima, Ohio, July 13, 1951; d. Robert Arthur and Lyla Faye (Steinwinder) Horstman; m. Dennis R. Siebeneck, Aug. 16, 1969 (div. 1975); children: Jaimine Lee, Jason Robert; m. Wayne Lee Walters, Aug. 3, 1978. Grad. high sch., Ottawa, Ohio. With sales Pixler Men's Wear, Defiance, Ohio, 1975-76; mgr. Lauber's, Archbold, Ohio, 1976-78; adminstrv. asst. Western Union, Indpls., 1980-82, rep. service, 1981-83, rep. sales, 1983-84; owner TeleComp Systems Inc., Carmel, Ind., 1984—. Den mother Boy Scouts Am., Carmel, 1979-82, leader, 1981-82. Mem. Retail Mchts Assn. (pres. 1986), C. of C. Home: 11289 Wood Creek Dr Carmel IN 46032 Office: TeleComp Systems Inc 101 E Carmel Dr Suite 103 Carmel IN 46032

WALTERS, SUZANNE WEINMAN, purchasing agent; b. Cleve., Oct. 9, 1941; d. Earl Edward and Marie (Hirt) Weinman; m. Jerry B. Walters, May 13, 1961; children: Michael Alan, Michele Ann. Grad. high sch., Cleve. Various clerical positions Greensboro, N.C., 1965-70; acctg. sec. Coop. Savs. and Loan, Wilmington, N.C., 1970-74; acctg. clk. Diamond Shamrock Chem. Corp., Castle Hayne, N.C., 1975-78, purchasing sec., 1978-83, buyer, 1983—. Home: 26 Magnolia Dr Rocky Point NC 28457 Office: Occidental Chem Co PO Box 368 Castle Hayne NC 28429

WALTHER, ZERITA, paralegal; b. N.Y.C., Nov. 22, 1927; d. James Alexander and Sarah Rebecca (Esperance) Potter; m. George P. Walther II, Dec. 30, 1946; children: Joseph, Leona. BS in Edn., Met. Inst., London, 1973; cert. in labor studies, Cornell U., 1979; paralegal cert., Manhattanville Coll., 1984. Tchr. OEO, L.I. City, N.Y., 1966-69, Washington Bus. Inst., N.Y.C., 1969-70; editorial asst., feature writer N.Y. Times, N.Y.C., 1973-85; legal asst., supr. Marcus, Rippa & Gould, White Plains, N.Y., 1985—; casting cons. Am. Model Agy., N.Y.C., 1961-62, casting cons., 1962-63; bd. dirs., cons. Rockingchair Press News Service, Elmsford, N.Y., 1978—. Sec. Women of Westchester, 1978-80; coordinator Elmsford chpt. Women in Self Help, 1982—; mediator, vol. Better Bus. Bur., White Plains, 1983-85, Westchester Mediation Ctr., Yonkers, N.Y., 1988—; legis. asst. to 12th dist. Westchester County legislator, White Plains, 1984—. Lily Endowment Found. and Smithsonian Inst. scholar Sarah Lawrence Coll., summer 1979. Mem. Nat. Paralegal Assn. Democrat. Roman Catholic. Office: Marcus Rippa & Gould 4 Cromwell Pl White Plains NY 10601

WALTON, AMANDA LORETTA, educator; b. Millen, Ga., Sept. 16, 1941; d. Willie and Gussia (Wilson) Jones; m. Van L. Walton, July 3, 1966; children: Myshiel Alston, Van Lawrence Walton Jr. AA in Liberal Arts, Manhatten Community Coll., 1975; BA in Polit. Sci., York Coll., 1980; M, City Coll. of N.Y., 1983, postgrad., 1985. Teacher asst. Pub. Sch. 200, Manhatten, 1970-73; aux. trainer Pub. Sch. 132, N.Y.C., 1974-81; tchr. Pub. Sch. 274, Bkyln., 1981—; ednl. cons., Queens, N.Y., 1981—. Mem. legisl. adv. com., Albany, N.Y., 1981, Queens Village Bellrose Dems., Queens Village, 1983. Mem. Internat. Reading Assn., Manhattan Reading Council, Nat. Assn. for Female Execs., Inc. Democrat. Roman Catholic. Home: 221-39 112 Ave Queens NY 11429

WALTON, BARBARA GAYLE, nurse, consultant; b. Detroit, Jan. 6, 1955; d. Calvin Arthur and Harriet Jane (Best) Lepien; m. Larry Austin Walton, Oct. 11, 1980. Student, Mich. State U., 1973-76; diploma, Henry Ford Hosp. Sch. Nursing, 1978, BS, Columbia Pacific U., 1987, MS, 1987. Staff nurse Univ. Hosp., Ann Arbor, Mich., 1978-79, nurse clinician, 1979-81; charge nurse Vet.'s Adminstrn. Med. Ctr., Ann Arbor, 1981-82; instr. edn. Saline (Mich.) Community Hosp., 1982-84, asst. dir. edn., 1984-87; client, devel. specialist Commn. on Profl. and Hosp. Activities, Ann Arbor, 1987—; Co-founder NurseWise Inc., Ann Arbor, 1986—. Mem. Kidney Disease Adv. Com., Mich. Dept. Pub. Health. Mem. Am. Assn. Critical Care Nurses (cert., bd. dirs. and Washtenaw County chpt. 1986-88), Mich. Soc. Health Edn. and Tng., Soc. Pub. Health Educators, Mich. Nurses Assn., Am. Assn. Neurosurgical Nurses, Nat. Assn. Female Execs., Am. Bus. Women's Assn. (Maia chpt.). Home: 860 E Forest Ypsilanti MI 48198 Office: Nurse Wise Inc 1495 Cobblestone Ann Arbor MI 48108

WALTON, BEVERLY RAY, association administrator; b. Milw., Feb. 2, 1960; d. George Britain Jr. and Marie Elena (Ward) W. BBA, East Carolina U., 1982; MBA, Meredith Coll., 1985. Sales cons. Paul B. Williams, Inc., Raleigh, N.C., 1985-87; personnel cons. Quality Personnel, Inc., Raleigh, 1987; acct. exec. Greater Raleigh C. of C., Raleigh, 1987—; mentor Wake County Career Beginnings Program. Mem. Nat. Assn. Profl. Saleswomen (v.p. 1987—), Greater Raleigh C. of C. (Ambassador 1986—). Republican. Baptist. Home: 6205 H North Hills Dr Raleigh NC 27609 Office: 800 Salisbury St Raleigh NC 27602

WALTON, CARMELITA NOREEN, nurse; b. Chgo., Nov. 15, 1926; d. Elmo Augusta and Evelyn Mae (Terry) Desobrey; student St. Marys Coll., U. Notre Dame, 1943-45; grad. Cook County Sch. Nursing, 1949; student DePaul U., 1978-79; children from previous marriage—Michael Jerome. Head nurse, supr., nurse clinician Cook County Hosp., Chgo., 1951-71; supr. U. Chgo. Hosps./Clinics, 1963-68; dir. nursing Woodlawn Child Health Center, Chgo., 1968-69; dir. nursing prison health care Cermak Health Services, Cook County Jail, Chgo., 1973—; con. surveyor Nat. Commn. on Correctional Health Care. Recipient Superior Pub. Service award City of Chgo., 1984. Mem. Am. Nurses Assn. (cert. in nursing adminstrn., mem. Council Nursing Adminstrn.), Ill. Nurses Assn., Nat. League Nursing, Am. Pub. Health Assn., Am. Correctional Health Services Assn. Democrat. Roman Catholic. Home: 5050 LakeShore Dr S Apt 1608 Chicago IL 60615 Office: 2800 California Ave S Chicago IL 60608

WALTON, DANNA MOORE, lawyer; b. Texas City, Tex., Mar. 27, 1950; d. Dan Milton and Bennie Jo (Ellis) Moore; m. George Alan Walton, June 6, 1981; children—Jonathan Alan, Marleta Jo. B.A., Baylor U., 1971, J.D., 1974. Bar: Tex. 1974. Tchr., Alvin Ind. Sch. Dist. (Tex.), 1972; atty. Shell Oil Co., Houston, 1975-77, asst. cop. sec., 1977-81, atty., 1981-86, legal mgr., 1986—. Tchr., dir. So. Main Bapt. Ch., Houston, 1975—; pres. bd. dirs. Beckford Homeowners Assn., Houston, 1977-79. Mem. ABA, State Bar Tex., Houston Bar Assn., Houston Young Lawyers Assn., Phi Delta Phi (pres. 1977-78; Outstanding Mem. 1975). Home: 13003 Birch Grove Houston TX 77099 Office: Shell Oil Co 800 Louisiana St Houston TX 77002

WALTON, KAREN KAY, managing director; b. Brownwood, Tex., Sept. 24, 1944; d. Samuel Emmett and Crystal (Fine) W. BA, U. Tex., 1966; MBA, San Jose State U., 1978. Unit dir. ARC, Korea, 1966-67; program supr. Seoul, Korea, 1968-69, asst. dir., 1969-70; div. rep. Hartford, Conn., 1970-71, asst. div. mgr., 1971-72, asst. to mgr., 1972-73; asst. nat. dir. Blood Services Donor Resources Devel., Washington, 1973-76, tng. cons. Washington, 1976; dir. personnel tng. and devel. Burlingame, Calif., 1978-79, asst. mgr. service to divs. and chpts., 1979-83, mng. dir., 1983—; personnel asst. Nauta-Line Houseboat Co., Nashville, 1967-68; tng. cons. Am. Red Cross, Washington, 1976; research project dir. Calif. High Sch. Bus. Edn. Depts. Evaluation, 1977; long range planning cons. Calif. Nurses Assn., San Francisco, 1980. Mem. Rep. presdl. task force, Washington, 1980-82; mem. LWV, San Jose, Calif., 1980-83; exec. com. Am. Cancer Soc., San Jose, 1980-83. Mem. Beta Gama Sigma, Phi Mu. Club: Commonwealth of Calif. Office: ARC 1870 Ogden Dr Burlingame CA 94010

WALTON, PEGGY ANN, communications consultant, radio show host and producer, realtor; b. Raymore, Mo., Dec. 8, 1932; d. Harry Francis and Esther (Wolf) Moneymaker. B.S. in Home Econs. cum laude, U. Nebr.-Omaha, 1954. Lic. salesman real estate, Va. Asst. dir. Dairy Council, Omaha, 1954-57; home economist Nebr. Wheat Commn., Lincoln, 1957-64; mgr. consumer info. Chem. Mfrs. Assn., Washington, 1964-81; Realtor, Town and Country Properties, Falls Church, 1981—; exhibits coordinator-cons. Nestle Coordinating Ctr. for Nutrition, Washington, 1981-86; host-producer Consumer Aware show Sta. WGTS-FM, Takoma Park, Md., 1983—; retailer and marketer Bloomingdales and Nordstrom, Tyson Ctr., Va., 1986—; participant Internat. Trade Fair, Lausanne, Switzerland, 1959, South Am. nutritionists, 1960, Internat. Trade Fair, Cairo, 1961; product-acceptance explorer Nebr. Dept. Agr., Central and S.Am., 1962. Recipient First Place award in audio-video Am. Soc. Assn. Execs., 1979; named Friend of Extension, Dept. Agr., 1980. Mem. Am. Women in Radio and TV (nat. membership chmn. 1964-65), Am. Women in Radio and TV (Nebr. chpt. pres. 1962-64), Home Economists in Bus. (nat. sec. 1965-67, chmn. conv. program 1970), Nat. Home Fashions League (nat. sec. 1971-72, exec. v.p. 1972-73, local dir. 1967-69, Outstanding Mem. 1972), Nat. Fedn. Press Women (charter; Newsletter award 1976), Nat. Fedn. Press Women, Capital Press Women (bd. rep. 1973-74, radio award 1984), Soc. Consumer Affairs Profls.

WALTON, SANDRA STEVENSON, personnel manager; b. Richmond, Va., May 14, 1949; d. William Blake Jr. and Frances (Brock) Stevenson; divorced; 1 child, Evan. BSBA, Va. Commonwealth U., 1981. Office personnel employment mgr. Reynolds Metals Co., Richmond, 1977-78, mgmt. info. sci. personnel mgr., 1978-79, hdqrs. personnel mgr., 1981—. Mem. career devel. council J. Sargeant Reynolds Community Coll., 1980-81; mem. task force CETA Consortium, 1980-82; mem. bus. adv. council Va. Dept. Rehab. Services, 1982-85; arbitrator Better Bus. Bur., 1985—. Recipient Cert. Appreciation and Recognition, Va. Dept. Rehab. Services, 1982, 83, Gov.'s Adv. Council, 1983. Baptist. Clubs: Westwood Racquet, Forest Heights Garden (pres. 1977-79). Office: Reynolds Metals Co 6601 W Broad St Richmond VA 23230

WALZ, BETTY MARION, personnel service executive, dental management consultant; b. Big Timber, Mont., July 23, 1934; d. Milton Sureno and Donna Marion (Chapel) Willard; m. John William Walz, Aug. 30, 1963 (div. 1977); children—Mrs. Jemell Guiles, Mrs. Shawn Hooks. Registered dental asst., Calif. Dental asst. various offices, Seattle and San Diego, 1953-75; dental office mgr. various offices, San Diego, 1975-80; dental mgmt. cons., San Diego, 1980-81; founder, pres. Profl. Fill-Ins/PFI Personnel Services, San Diego, 1980—. Mem. adv. bd. San Diego Community Coll. Dist., 1982—; leader San Diego-Imperial council Girl Scouts U.S., 1959-69; youth chmn. Jr. Women's Club, Chula Vista, Calif., 1968; vol. Flying Samaritans, 1975, 76, 82, 83. Recipient State Service award Jr. Women's Club, 1968, Girl Scouts Service award Jr. Women's Club, 1968. Mem. San Diego County Dental Assts. Soc., So. Calif. Dental Assts. Assn. (del. 1985), Am. Dental Assts. Assn., Nat. Assn. Women Bus. Owners (2nd v.p. San Diego chpt. 1986-87), Beta Sigma Phi. Republican. Mem. Religious Sci. Ch. Avocations: oil paintng; fishing; walking; travel. Home: 4201 Bonita Rd #238 Bonita CA 92002 Office: PFI Personnel Services 1081 Camino del Rio S #221 San Diego CA 92108

WALZER, LISA ROBIN, architect; b. N.Y.C., Dec. 30, 1955; d. Morris and Rita Nirenberg; m. Andrew Walzer, May 17, 1986. BArch, Syracuse U., 1978. Registered architect, N.Y. Jr. designer RBS&D, N.Y.C., 1979-81; intermediate designer The Eggers Group, N.Y.C., 1981-82; sr. designer Ferrenz, Taylor & Clark, N.Y.C., 1983-85; project designer Perkins & Will, N.Y.C., 1985; project mgr. Soo Kim Assn., N.Y.C., 1985-87; ptnr. Walzer Davids Assocs., N.Y.C., 1987—. Mem. AIA. Home: 239 E 79th St New York NY 10021

WAMBACH, CATHERINE LOUISE, advertising agency executive; b. Aberdeen, Md., Jan. 28, 1956; d. Richard W. and Ann (Stutts) W. BA, Cornell U., 1978. Reporter San Diego Daily Transcript, 1978-80; reporter, editor The Beacon, San Diego, 1980-82; dir. corp. communications M.D.I., Inc., National City, Calif., 1982-84; prin. CW Communications, San Diego, 1984; account exec. Sippel and Assocs., Del Mar, Calif., 1984-86; pres. Wambach, Leap, Dunning and Stopper, San Diego, 1986—; cons. dir. San Diego Archtl. Club, 1985-87. Mem. Ocean Beach Planning Bd., San Diego, 1980. Mem. Computer and Electronics Mktg. Assn. (treas., v.p. 1984-86, pres. 1986-87). Club: San Diego Press. Office: Wambach Leap Dunning Stopper 9601 Aero Dr Suite 200 San Diego CA 92123

WAMBLES, LYNDA ENGLAND, academic administrator, consultant; b. Nashville, Dec. 30, 1937; d. Henry Russell and Doris Olivia (Stuart) England; m. Byron Adolph Wambles, Sept. 3, 1965; 1 child, Teri Leigh Moore Wambles Taylor. Student, U. Tenn., 1964-65, 73-74, Washington U., St. Louis, 1984-86. Cert. profl. sec. Exec. sec. Gen. Truck Sales, Knoxville, Tenn., 1972-74; asst. to dean Coll. Law U. Tenn., Knoxville, 1974-76; office mgr. Washington U. Sch. Bus., St. Louis, 1977-78, registrar, dir. info. systems, 1978-83, asst. dean for faculty and adminstrn. services, 1983-86; cons. in field St. Louis, 1978-86, Overland Park, Kans., 1986—; cons. in field, St. Louis, 1978—; lectr. div. continuing edn. Washington U., St. Louis, 1978-80. Author: (with others) Procedures Manual and Information for State Guaranty Associations, 1987. Active United Way of Greater Knoxville, 1973-74; leader lunch participant YWCA, St. Louis, 1981-83. Fellow Acad. Cert. Profl. Secs.; mem. Profl. Secs. Internat., Nat. Secs. Assn. (Tenn. div. Sec. of Yr. 1975), Assn. Info. Systems Profls. Republican. Presbyterian. Home and Office: 8425 W 113th St Overland Park KS 66210

WAMMACK, KARIN ELISABETH, public health physician; b. Spokane, Wash., Nov. 29, 1952; d. Lewis Oren and Ruth Louise (Weber) W. BS, Ea. Wash. U., 1977; MD, Loma Linda U., 1981. Diplomate Nat. Bd. Pub. Health. Intern Riverside Gen. Hosp., Calif., 1981-82; resident Kaiser Found. Hosp., Fontana, Calif., 1982-84; perdiem So. Calif. Permanente Med. Group, Fontana, 1982-84; pub. health physician Firebaugh (Calif.) Health Ctr. Fresno County Dept. Health, 1984—; governing bd. dirs. Dos Palos Meml. Hosp., 1986—; peer review team Fresno County Dept. Health, 1986. Preceptor nurse practitioner program Calif. State U., Fresno, 1984—, UCLA Family Medicine, 1986. Mem. AMA, Am. Acad. Family Practice, Am. Med. Women's Assn. (br. treas 1986-87), Nat. Rural Health Assn., N.Y. Acad. Sci., Fresno Madera Women Physicians Assn. (treas. 1986-87), AAUW, DAR. Democrat. Roman Catholic. Lodge: Rotary. Home: 125 S Granada #42 Madera CA 93637 Office: Firebaugh Health Ctr 1133 P St Firebaugh CA 93622

WAMPLER, BARBARA BEDFORD, entrepreneur; b. New Bedford, Mass., July 23, 1932; d. William and Mary (Fitzpatrick) Bedford; m. John H. Wampler, Oct. 21, 1950; children: John H. Jr., William C., James B., Robert T. AS, Tunxis Community Coll., 1975. Lic. real estate agt., Mass. Counselor Wampler Counseling Rehab. Services, Farmington, Conn., 1975-85; owner, mgr. Wampler Mktg., Farmington, 1980-84, Earth Campgrounds I and II, Otis, Mass., 1984—; pres., mgr. Earth Works, Otis, Mass., 1984—. Contbr. articles to profl. jours. Faculty scholar U. Hartford, 1976. Mem. Bus. Mgrs. Assn., Nat. Campground Owners Assn., Mass. Assn. of Campground Owners. Home: POBox 690 Rt 8 Otis MA 01253 Office: Earth Works PO Box 690 Rt 8 Otis MA 01253

WANG, GALINDA YU, small business owner; b. Taipei, Republic of China, Nov. 4, 1949; d. Chen and Malinda Wang; m. Paul Tchao, Sept. 14, 1986. Student, Fashion Inst. Tech., 1974. Designer textiles Veldor, N.Y.C., 1974-78; fashion designer Galinda, N.Y.C., 1978-79; owner, designer La Chine Classic Inc., N.Y.C., 1979—. Mem. Orgn. Chinese-Am. Women (founder). Home: 340 E 64th St #11S New York NY 10021 Office: La Chine Classic Inc 1411 Broadway New York NY 10018

WANG, JOSEPHINE L. FEN, physician; b. Taipei, Peoples Republic of China, Jan 2, 1948; came to U.S., 1974; d. Pao-San and Ann-Nam (Chen) Chao; m. Chang-Yang Wang, Dec. 20, 1973; children: Edward, Eileen. MD, Nat. Taiwan U., Taipei, 1974. Diplomate Am. Bd. Pediatrics, Am. Bd. Allergy and Immunology. Intern Nat. Taiwan U. Hosp., 1973-74; resident U. Ill. Hosp., Chgo., 1974-76; fellow Northwestern U. Med. Ctr., Chgo., 1976-78, instr. pediatrics, 1978—; cons. Holy Cross Hosp., Chgo., 1978—, Meth. Hosp. Ind., 1979—, St. Anthony Hosp., 1985—. Mem. Am. Acad. Allergy. Office: 9012 Connecticut Dr Merrillville IN 46410 also: 4901 W 79th St Burbank IL 60459

WANGER, SHELLEY ANTONIA, magazine editor; b. Los Angeles, July 4, 1948; d. Walter and Joan (Bennett) W. Student, Vassar Coll., 1966-68; BA, Sarah Lawrence Coll., 1970. Asst. to editor N.Y. Rev. of Books, N.Y.C., 1975-82; articles editor House & Garden mag., N.Y.C., 1982—; cons. editor Conde Nast's Traveler, 1987—. Office: House & Garden 350 Madison Ave New York NY 10017

WANGSGARD, LYNNDA M., librarian, dairy farmer; b. Ogden, Utah, Mar. 17, 1948; d. Samuel Lynnwood and Mildred (Masters) W. B.S., Weber State Coll., 1970; M.Library and Info. sci., Brigham Young U., 1976, M.P.A., 1983. Cert. secondary tchr., Utah. Intermural mgr. Weber State Coll., Ogden, 1969-70; fine arts librarian Weber County Library, Ogden, 1970-79, asst. library dir., 1979-85, dir., 1985—; mng. ptnr. Wangsgard Dairies, Huntsville, Utah, 1979—; del. Utah Gov.'s Conf. on Libraries, Salt Lake City, 1979; project dir. Utah Endowment for Humanities, Salt Lake City, 1979-80; mem. Utah Adv. Com. on Libraries and Info. Sci., Salt Lake City, 1980—; cons. Weber State Coll., 1983. Joint author Utah Plan for Library and Information Services, 1982. Chmn. Weber County Affirmative Action Com., 1972-76; mem. Utah Farm Bur., Salt Lake City, 1979—; bd. dirs. Weber LWV Ogden, 1983—. Recipient Beginning Profl. award Mountain Plains Library Assn., 1979; named Woman of Yr. YWCA No. Utah, 1988; Utah Endowment for Humanities project grantee, 1978-80. Mem. ALA (council 1984-88), Mountain Plains Library Assn., Utah Library Assn. (dir. 1982-83, research award for jour. article 1983), Freedom to Read Found., Ogden C. of C. (women's council 1983—), AAUW, Phi Kappa Phi, Phi Beta Mu. Lodge: Rotary. Home: 2737 Harrison Blvd Ogden UT 84403 Office: Weber County Library 2464 Jefferson Ave Ogden UT 84401-2488

WANLAND, RUBY EVELYN, educator; b. Orlando, Fla., July 30, 1937; d. Algot Waldemar and Lydia Albertina (Mattson) W. AA, Cottey Coll., 1957; BA, So. Ill. U., 1959; MA, Nova U., 1983. Cert. tchr. social studies secondary edn., Fla. Tchr. Howey-in-the-Hills (Fla.) Acad., 1959-63, North Miami (Fla.) Sr. High Sch., 1963-70, Northwestern Sr. High Sch., Miami, Fla., 1970—; tchr. rep. north Dade Area PTA bd., chairperson human relations council North Miami Sr. High Sch., 1968-70; sponsor Close-Up Northwestern Sr. High Sch., Washington, 1970-73, county Silver Knights, Miami, 1970—, chmn. 5-yr. evaluation So. Assn. Schs. and Colls., 1975, chmn. social studies dept., mem. curriculum council, mem. faculty council, 1975—, peer tchr., 1981-83, 85; adj. tchr. Dade Acad. Teaching Arts Miami (Fla.) Beach Sr. High, 1987. Author ednl. packages for schs. Active Dem. campaigns, North Miami, 1975-76, 80-81; vol. voter registration Northwestern Sr. High Sch., Miami, 1975—. Recipient recognition award Dade County Sch. Bd., 1971-72, award Northwestern Sr. High Sch. PTO, 1973-77, 86; named Tchr. of Yr., Northwestern Sr. High Sch., 1986; Dade Bar Assn. scholar, 1965. Mem. Nat. Social Studies Council, Fla. Social Studies Council, Dade County Social Studies Council, United Tchrs. Dade (rep. 1968, 74-79, human relations council 1968-70, del. Fla. Edn. Assn. 1980, 83-84, tchr. rep., sabbatical leave com., professionalization of edn. task force 1986-87, award 1968, 73), AFL, Fla. Trails Assn., Appalachian Trail Conf. Presbyterian. Home: 911 N E 141st St North Miami FL 33161

WANNEMACHER, PATRICIA COLLEEN, electrical contractor; b. Bloomington, Ill., Mar. 17, 1931; d. William and Louise (Ehrmantraut) O'Neil; m. Louis J. Wannemacher, Feb. 5, 1951; children—Steven, John, Jo Ann Reidy, Karen Arseneault. Grad. high sch., Bloomington. Ptnr., Wannemacher Electric, Bloomington, 1961-67, v.p. Wannemacher Electric, Inc., Bloomington, 1967-82, pres., 1982—. Mem. McLean County Bd., Ill., 1972-80, chmn. fin. com., 1978-80; mem. assoc. bd. Ill. Wesleyan U., Bloomington, 1984—; co-chmn. Children's Christmas Party for Unemployed, Bloomington, 1982—; mem. United Pvt. Industry Council, Pekin, Ill., Econ. Devel. Council Bloomington-Normal; mem. community bd. St. Joseph's Med. Ctr., Bloomington. Mem. McLean County C. of C. (pres. 1982-83), McLean County Elec. Contractors Assn., Ill. Assn. Women Contractors (1st v.p.). Republican. Roman Catholic. Avocations: reading, cooking, travel. Office: Wannemacher Electric Inc 210 Stillwell St PO Box 3726 Bloomington IL 61702

WANTMAN, LINDA KAISER, family therapist; b. Long Island City, N.Y., Aug. 15, 1944; d. Fred and Catherine (Helmken) Kaiser; m. Stuart Charles Wantman; children: Julie, Daniel. BA, Colby Coll., 1966; MLS, Long Island U., 1977; MEd, Temple U., 1982, PhD, 1986. Tchr. Levittown (N.Y.) Pub. Schs., 1966-67, Ellenville (N.Y.) Cen. Schs., 1967-68, Northport (N.Y.) Pub. Schs., 1968-73; librarian Delaware Valley Coll., Doylestown, Pa., 1977-79; family therapist Inst. for Comprehensive Family Therapy, Spring House, Pa., 1983—, assoc. faculty mem., 1986—; pvt. practice family therapy Spring House, 1986—; mem. adv. bd. Parents Network, Ambler, Pa., 1987—. Mem. Am. Assn. Marriage and Family Therapists, Phi Beta Kappa, Phi Delta Gamma. Home: 8 Farber Dr PO Box 340 Chalfont PA 18914

WARBRITTON, PATRICIA ANN, travel agency administrator; b. Glendale, W.Va., Jan. 27, 1949; d. Wilbert and Arlene Margaret (Nagel) Miner; m. David Scott Warbritton, July 6, 1974; children: Jeffrey Scott, Jason Patrick. BA, U. Fla., 1971. Exec. dir. Brandon (Fla.) Cultural Ctr., 1981-84; account mgr. Tampa (Fla.) Travel Service, Inc., 1986—. Mem. exec. com. Hillsboro County Reps., 1986-87; bd. dirs. Hillsboro County Bd. Children's Services, Tampa, 1986—, Bloomingdale Little League, Brandon, 1987—. Mem. Greater Brandon C. of C., Jr. Service League, Fla. Fedn. Women's Clubs (Judy M. Martin award 1985, vice dir. Jr. clubs 1986-88, dir. 1988—). Republican. Methodist. Home: 2821 Fairway View Dr Valrico FL 33594

WARD, BARBARA CONNER, risk management professional, consultant; b. Plainview, Tex., Apr. 13, 1940; d. William Elbert and Sarah Pauline (Lovell) Conner; m. Dalton L. Ward, Sept. 13, 1958 (div. 1987); children: Dana Renyce, Lisa Suzaune. Student, Wharton (Tex.) Jr. Coll., 1978-82; BS, U. Houston, 1982. Office adminstr., cashier Interstate Securities, Odessa, Tex., 1964-65; dept. asst. supr. Ft. Bend Ind. Sch. Dist., Sugar Land, Tex., 1974-78; organ. cons. B.C. Ward Enterprises, Inc., Sugar Land, 1982-86; ins. sales, cons. Multi-Ins. Service Co., Houston, 1986-87; coordinator flexible benefits Tex. Sch. Services Found., 1987—; risk mgmt. cons. 1988—. Host parent Am. Field Service, Houston, 1980; elder First Presbyn. Ch., Sugar Land, 1982-85; community liaison Ft. Bend Assn. Retarded Citizens, 1984—, fundraiser, 1985-87, Vol. of Yr., 1985; bd. dirs. Youth Opportunities Unltd., Richmond, Tex., 1985. Recipient Service award Richmond State Sch., 1985-87. Mem. Tex. Investors Tng. Enterprises (sec. 1986-87), Houston Assn. Life Underwriters. Republican.

WARD, BETHEA, artist, small business owner; b. Montgomery, Ala., July 6, 1924; d. Charles E. and Lucy (Walter) W. BFA, Syracuse U., 1946; postgrad., Trinity U., San Antonio, 1965, 66, 68, San Antonio Art Inst., 1967, Houston Mus. Fine Arts Sch., 1973-75. Interior designer Davison-Paxon, Atlanta, 1946-47; assoc. prof. interior design U. Tex., Austin, 1947-51; interior designer Heminways-Bundrick, Shreveport, La., 1951-55; draftsman, supr. Ark. Fuel subs. Cities Service Co., Shreveport, 1955-82; visual artist, owner Tex. Notables Studio-Gallerie, Houston, 1983—. Juried shows include (watercolor paintings) Midland (Tex.) Art Fest. (2d place award, 1962), 35th Ann. Local Artist Exhbn., San Antonio (Wofford award 1965), Wichita, Kas. Centennial Nat. Exhbn. (inclusion award 1970), Cen. Tex. Hist. on Canvas Exhbn. (1st place award TFAA 1972), Star of Republic Mus., Washington, Tex., San Antonio Pub. Library, Houston Pub. Library, Harris Co. Heritage Soc.; group exhibits include U. Houston, 1986; contbr. ink drawing to Southwestern Hist. Quarterly, 1977; commns. include drawing for Moody Found. of Galveston; one person shows include Star of the Republic Mus., Houston Pub. Library, Harris County Heritage Soc. Recipient Award of Distinction Juried Art Fair, Houston Internat. Festival, 1987, numerous awards for watercolor paintings. Mem. Hoover Watercolor Soc. (founding mem. 1952), Watercolor Art Soc. Houston (chmn bd. social chmn., sec., co-founder), Art League Houston, Columbus (Tex.) C. of C., Cultural Arts Council Houston, Coppini Acad. Fine Arts (life), Tex. Arts Alliance, Tex. Commn. on the Arts, Southwestern Watercolor Soc. (founding mem., pub. chmn.), Tex. State Hist. Assn., Tex. Hist. Found., Nat. Mus. of Women in the Arts, Cultural Arts Council of Houston. Republican. Presbyterian. Home and Studio: Tex Notables Studio-Gallerie 9614 Valverde St Houston TX 77063

WARD, CYNTHIA VAUNE, editor; b. Boston, May 9, 1958; d. John Peter and Joyce (Maunder) W. BA in Polit. Sci., Chinese, Wellesley Coll., 1981. V.p. publs. Western Monetary Cons., Ft. Collins (Colo.) and Washington, 1984—; sr. editor, columnist Conservative Digest, Washington, 1985—; mng. editor Am. Press Internat., Washington, 1987—. Office: Conservative Digest/ Am Press Internat 1210 National Press Bldg Washington DC 20045

WARD, DIANE KOROSY, lawyer; b. Cleve., Oct. 17, 1939; d. Theodore Louis and Edith (Bogar) Korosy; m. S. Mortimer Ward IV, July 2, 1960 (div. 1978); children: Christopher LaBruce, Samantha Martha; m. R. Michael Walters, June 30, 1979. AB, Heidelberg Coll., 1961; JD, U. San Diego, 1975. Bar: Calif. 1977, U.S. Dist. Ct. (so. dist.) Calif. 1977. Ptnr. Ward & Howell, San Diego, 1978-79, Walters, Howell & Ward, A.P.C., San Diego, 1979-81; mng. ptnr. Walters & Ward, A.P.C., San Diego, 1981— ; dir., v.p. Oak Broadcasting Systems, Inc., 1982-83; dir. Elisabeth Kubler-Ross Ctr., Inc., 1983-85; sheriff Ranchos del Norte Corral of Westerners, 1985-87; trustee San Diego Community Defenders, Inc., 1986-88. Pres. bd. dirs. Green Valley Civic Assn., 1979-80; trustee Palomar-Pomerado Hosp. Found., chmn. deferred giving, 1985—; trustee Episcopal Diocese of San Diego. Mem. ABA, Rancho Bernardo Bar Assn. (chmn. 1982-83), Lawyers Club San Diego, Profl. and Exec. Women of the Ranch (founder, pres. 1982—), San Diego Golden Eagle Club, Phi Delta Phi. Republican. Episcopalian. Club: Soroptimist Internat. (pres. chpt. 1979-80). Home: 16503 Avenida Florencia Poway CA 92064 Office: Walters & Ward 11665 Avena Pl Suite 203 San Diego CA 92128

WARD, DORIS ELIZABETH, biologist, educator, counselor; b. Charlotte N.C., Jan. 11, 1935; d. James Hopkins and Florie Kathryn Cofield; B.S., Howard U., 1966, postgrad. 1967-70; M.Ed. in Guidance and Counseling, Bowie State U., 1985; postgrad. U. Md., Summer 1985, George Washington U., 1985, 87; EdS, George Washington U., 1987; m. Eddie Eugene Ward, Sept. 18, 1954; children—Eddie Eugene, Tanya Devonne, Tracia Lynnore, Tamara Elizabeth. Cert. sci. tchr. and guidance counselor, Md. Med. technician U.S. Dept. Agr., Washington, 1958-64, biol. lab. technician, Bethesda, Md., 1964-65; histologic tech. lab. instr. Howard U., Washington, 1966-67; biologist (histopathology technician) NIH, Bethesda, 1969-71; tchr. Our Lady Queen of Peace Sch., Washington, 1972-74; program analyst/mgmt. analysis HHS, Washington, 1974-82; career planning counselor Prince Georges Community Coll., Largo, Md., 1985—. Hospice vol.; mem. United Communities Against Poverty, Inc., 1982; developer, facilitator bereavement support ministry St. Joseph's Ch., Landover, Md., 1984; cons./vol., career counselor for transition and spl. needs populations Cerebral Palsy Assn. Prince Georges County, 1986. Recipient Tchr. Appreciation award Our Lady Queen of Peace Sch., 1974. Mem. Am. Vocat. Assn., Am. Soc. Clin. Pathologists, Am. Assn. for Counseling and Devel., Nat. Career Devel. Assn., Chi Sigma Iota. Democrat. Roman Catholic. Home: 13003 Keverton Dr Upper Marlboro MD 20772

WARD, EDITH, information resources specialist; b. N.Y.C., July 17, 1928; d. Max and Rose (Loth) Halpern; m. Benjamin Ward, Oct. 23, 1949. MA, CUNY, 1948; MLS, Columbia U., 1967. Indexer Project Urbandoc, N.Y.C., 1967-69; cataloger McKinsey and Co., N.Y.C., 1969-70, mgr. tech. services, 1970-71, mgr. library, 1971-72; info. resource cons. various orgns., 1972-77; transnat. corps. affairs officer UN Ctr. Transnat. Corps., N.Y.C., 1977-88, sr. officer, 1988—. Mem. ALA, Am. Soc. Indexers, Am. Soc. Info. Sci., Assn. Info. Mgrs., Spl. Libraries Assn. Office: UN Ctr Transnat Corp Affairs DC2-1312 New York NY 10017

WARD, ETTIE, legal educator, lawyer, consultant; b. N.Y.C., Oct. 10, 1951; d. Jacob Benjamin and Hilda (Meltzer) W.; m. Alexander Rosenzweig, Nov. 13, 1977; 1 child, Robert Harry. AB, Barnard Coll., 1971; JD, Columbia U., 1974. Bar: N.Y. 1975, U.S. Dist. Ct. (so. and ea. dists.) N.Y. 1975, U.S. Ct. Appeals (2d cir.) 1975, U.S. Supreme Ct. 1979. Assoc. Kaye, Scholer, Fierman, Hays & Handler, N.Y.C., 1974-82; asst. prof. law St. John's U., Jamaica, N.Y., 1983—; reporter U.S. Ct. Appeals (2d cir.) Com. Pretrial Phase of Civil Litigation, 1984-86, 2d cir. Standing Com. on Improvement of Civil Litigation, 1986—. Mem. Selective Service Bd., 1985—. Mem. ABA, Assn. Bar of City of N.Y., Fed. Bar Council. Democrat. Jewish. Office: St John's U Law Sch Grand Central and Utopia Pkwys Jamaica NY 11439

WARD, JANE PAMELA, psychiatric social worker; b. Sioux City, Iowa, Feb. 10, 1948; d. Robert James and Alice Noreen (Gullickson) Ward. BA, Wartburg Coll., 1970; MSW, U. Iowa, 1975. Psychiat. therapist Community Mental Health Center of Scott County, Davenport, Iowa, 1975-76, coordinator of consultation and edn., 1976-77; dir. social work program Viterbo Coll., LaCrosse, Wis., 1977-79; asst. exec. dir., dir. social services Bremwood Luth. Children's Home, Waverly, Iowa, 1979-82; exec. dir. Three Crosses Ranch, Strawberry Point, Iowa, 1982-83; psychiat. pvt. practice and cons., 1983—; adj. prof. U. No. Iowa, Cedar Falls, 1983; asst. prof. U. Wis.-Oshkosh, 1984—; mem. Gov.'s Commn. Planning Com. for Conf. on Children, Iowa, 1976; cons. South Cen. Community Justice Planning Commn., La Crosse, 1977, Viterbo Coll., 1979. Mem. Nat. Assn. Social Workers (dir. 1978-79), Bi-County Mental Health Assn. (dir. 1976), Acad. Cert. Social Workers (diplomate), Nat. Registry Clin. Social Workers (diplomate). Lutheran. Office: 324 Clow Faculty Dept Social Work U Wisconsin Oshkosh WI 54901

WARD, JEANNE PATRICIA, family counselor, consultant; b. Bklyn., Mar. 23, 1945; d. James Joseph and Grace Frances (Brennan) Lawton; m. Robert L. Bucher, June 11, 1966 (div. Aug. 1977); children—Barbara Anne, Laura Jeanne; m. Charles F. Ward Jr., Aug. 19, 1983. B.A. in Edn., St. Catherine's Coll., St. Paul, 1966; M.A. in Counseling and Psychology, Coll. St. Thomas, St. Paul, 1972. Tchr., Mpls. Pub. Schs., 1966-70; tchr. spl. edn. Duval County Schs, Jacksonville, Fla., 1977-79; instr. Fla. Jr. Coll., Jacksonville, 1977—; sch. counselor Duval County Schs., Jacksonville, 1979-83; pvt. practice family counseling, Jacksonville, 1983—; cons. direct mktg. tng. design and devel. Am. Transtech, Jacksonville, 1985-87; founder, dir. Divorce Ministry Diocese of St. Augustine, Jacksonville, 1979-83; Fla. del. White House Conf. on Families, 1980; regular panelist WJXT, Channel 4, Jacksonville, 1982—. Author curriculum. Bd. dirs., chmn. personnel com. Child Guidance Clinic, Jacksonville, 1977—; bd. dirs. Girls Club of Jacksonville, 1981-83; chairperson Mayors Commn. on Status of Women, Jacksonville, 1985-87; dir. tng. and staff devel. City of Jacksonville, 1986-87; chmn. task force Corp. Child Care, 1985—; cons. Fla. Community Coll., 1988—. Bd. dirs. YWCA. Mem. AAUW, Nat. Assn. Female Execs., ASTD, Nat. Council of Family Relations, Phi Delta Kappa. Democrat. Roman Catholic. Club: N.E. Fla. Soc. Parents of Visually Impaired Children (program chmn. 1985—). Home: 1651 Flager Ave Jacksonville FL 32207 Office: Fla Community Coll Jacksonville 101 W State St Jacksonville FL 32202

WARD, JUDITH LINDA BURTON, clinical psychologist; b. Des Moines, Apr. 20, 1953; d. Jack Duane and Carolyn Strimple Gillespie Burton; adopted dau. David Marvin Ward. B.A. in Psychology, Alma Coll., 1975; M.A. in Clin. Psychology, Marshall U., 1978; doctoral studies, U. Denver, 1988—. Psychology intern children's unit Community Mental Health Ctr., Huntington, W.Va., 1977; sr. therapist, adult out-patient unit Jefferson County Comprehensive Mental Health Ctr., Steubenville, Ohio, 1978-81, acting unit chief, 1981-82; prin. psychologist Martha's Vineyard Mental Health Ctr., Edgartown, Mass., 1982-87; cons., condr. workshops in field. Mem. Am. Psychol. Assn. (assoc.). Democrat.

WARD, KAREN GRAFF, public relations executive; b. Phoenix, Nov. 14, 1948; d. Charles Wesley and Doris Mae (Walker) Graff; m. Raymond Edward List, Sept. 2, 1972; m. Forrest Herndon Ward, Aug. 8, 1982 (div. July 1986). B.S., Ohio U., 1970; cert. in French, Italian, Internat. House, Rome, 1972; postgrad. U. Calif.-Berkeley, 1974, 78. Lic. ins. agent, Pa., 1975. Bilingual personnel agt. Kaiser Engrs. of Italy, Sardinia and Rome, 1970-74; agt. Lincoln Nat. Life Ins., Harrisburg, Pa., 1975-76; adminstrv. mgr. Peabody Office Furniture, Boston, 1976-78; mktg. dir., commd. sales Western Contract Furnishers, San Francisco, 1978-81; free lance cons. interior design and comml. Furnishings, San Francisco, 1981-82; dir. sales, mktg. Romex Sentinel Systems, Stockton, Calif., 1982-83; pres. owner Madison Ave. West, Stockton, 1983—; gen. mgr. Stockton Auto Ctr., Stockton, 1987-88; dir. pub. relations Stockton Women's Network, 1986—, Jr. Achievement San Joaquin, Stockton, 1986—, YMCA San Joaquin, 1984-88; bd. dirs. Women's Ctr. San Joaquin, 1984—; cons., lectr. in field. Planning Commr. City Stockton, 1985—. Re cipient Disting. Leadership award Nat. Assn. Community Leadership Orgn., 1986, Disting. Grad. Achiever Jr. Achievement 1985; Woman of Achievement Bus. & Profl. Women, 1984, 85; named one of Outstanding Young Women in Am., 1981. Mem. Nat. Fedn. Bus. and Profl. Women, Am. Mktg. Assn., Stockton C. of C., Nat. Assn. Exec. Females, Am. Assn. Univ. Women, Am. Bus. Women Assn., Leadership Stockton Alumni Assn. (bd. dirs. 1986-87), Chi Omega Alumnae. Republican. Presbyterian. Avocations: traveling, reading, cooking, boating. Office: Madison Ave West 242 N Sutter Suite 501 Stockton CA 95202

WARD, KARYN ANDRO, accountant; b. Dallas, Oct. 22, 1959; d. Paul John Andro; m. William Warren Ward, Aug. 2, 1986. BS, N. Tex. State U., 1982, MS, 1985. CPA, Tex. Staff acct. Baird, Kurtz & Dobson CPAs, Dallas, 1983-86; sr. tax acct. Electronic Data Systems, Dallas, 1986-87, Arthur Andersen & Co., Washington, 1987—. Vol. Dallas Suicide and Crisis Ctr., 1985-87; Sunday sch. tchr. Holy Trinity Cath. Ch., Dallas, 1986. Mem. Tex. Soc. CPAs, Dallas Soc. CPAs, Delta Zeta Alumnae Assn. (v.p. programs). Republican.

WARD, MARGARET MOTTER, violist, violinist; b. Grand Rapids, Mich., Sept. 21, 1928; d. Gerrit and Dorris Alberta (Gilbert) VanRingelesteyn; student Mich. State U., 1946-49; Mus.B., Eastman Sch. Music, U. Rochester, 1952; m. Robert Paul Ward, June 17, 1978; children—Eva Lynne Motter, Phoebe Motter Baldini, Antonia Motter Gorman, Charles Frederick Motter. Violinist, violist Grand Rapids (Mich.) Symphony, 1942-51; violist faculty quartet Mich. State U., 1947-49, Rochester (N.Y.) Philharm., 1951-53; instr. violin and viola U. N.C., Chapel Hill, 1953-56; violist Miami (Fla.) Symphony, 1962-64, LaQuartette, Miami, 1963-64; prof. violin and viola Conservatoire Nationale du Liban, Beirut and violist chamber orch. and quartet of Lebanese Conservatory, Beirut, 1964-66; pvt. tchr. violin and viola, Washington, 1967-78, 85—; instr. viola Montgomery Coll., 1970-74; violist Kennedy Center Opera House Orch., Washington, 1971-85 , Wolf Trap Filene Center Orch., Vienna, Va., 1971-83, Balt. Symphony, 1973-74, Am. Camerata for New Music, Wheaton, Md., 1974-85; founder, violist New Stringart Quartet, 1982-84; faculty D.C. Youth Orch. Program, 1985—; mem. Amateur Chamber Music Players, Inc. Mem. Suzuki Assn. of the Ams., Am. String Tchrs. Assn. (pres. Md./D.C. chpt.). Home: 1101 Playford Ln Silver Spring MD 20901

WARD, MILLICENT DENISE, communications executive; b. San Antonio, May 25, 1955; d. Oscar Melvin and Zelma Darling (White) W.; m. Robert Lloyd Johns, Feb. 14, 1984. Student, East Carolina U., 1973-75, Allen Hancock Coll., 1975-76, San Francisco City Coll., 1980-81. Video coordinator Dean Witter, San Francisco, 1977-78; with sales, tng. dept. Gen. Electrnoics Systems, Berkeley, Calif., 1978-82; mktg. rep., salea person Pacific Video Resources, San Francisco, 1982-83; client services rep. Realtime Video, San Francisco, 1983, San Francisco Prodn. Group, San Francisco, 1983—; Videographer OCCUR Oakland City Council Redevel., Berkeley, 1981; video editor Gen. Electronics Systems-N.Y. Hosp. Project, 1982. Mem. Internat. TV Assn., Minorities and Women in TV Networks (bd. dirs. 1983-85), Women in Telecommunications (bd. dirs. 1983-85). Democrat. Club: San Francisco Croquet (bd. dirs. 1983-85). Office: San Francisco Prodn Group 550 Bryant St San Francisco CA 94107

WARD, NANCY ELIZABETH, production executive, print consultant; b. Lima, Ohio, July 28, 1942; d. Marion Delbert Staup and Virginia Louise (Conner) Staup Meyers; m. Terry David Crider, Sept. 20, 1960 (div. 1972); children—Cristina, Heather, Jay; m. Kenneth Earl Ward, Dec. 20, 1980. Student in mktg., Edison State U., 1974-78; student in print mgmt., Cin. Tech. Coll., 1980-81. Prodn. dir. Lark Communications, Asheville, N.C., 1981-84, TMI Pub., Charlotte, N.C., 1984-85; prodn. mgr. print and advt. Uptons, Atlanta, 1985-86; sales mgr. Comdata Corp., 1987—; advisor graphics Western Carolina U., Culowhee, N.C., 1983. Prodn. dir. book: Fiberarts Design Book 2, 1982, Quiltmakers Art, 1983. Republican. Methodist. Avocations: antique collector; furniture refinishing; piano; ballet. Home: 1018 Autumn Crest Ct Stone Mountain GA 30083

WARD, NANCY P., answering service executive; b. Orange, N.J., June 14, 1938; d. Robert and Adele (Byrne) Prescott; m. Robert A. Ward, Jr., Oct. 3, 1964; children—Victoria, Jennifer, Robert, B.A., Wellesley Coll., 1960. Editorial asst. McGraw Hill Pub. Co., N.Y.C., 1960-61, Harper & Row Pub., N.Y.C., 1961-63; asst. office mgr. Hornblower Weeks/Hemphill-Noyes, N.Y.C., 1963-65; asst. sales mgr. Chemway Corp., Wayne, N.J., 1965-68; owner All Hours Answering Service (N.J.), 1968—; sec., v.p., dir. CGW Enterprises Advt. Agy., Butler, N.J., 1970—; v.p., dir. Litho Four Printing, Butler, 1970-87, B.E.K., Inc., Butler and Wayne, N.J., 1970—; v.p., dir. N.J. Exchanges, Inc., Ridgewood, 1983—. Co-pres. Kinnelon Elem. Home and Sch. Assn. (N.J.), 1977-78, v.p., 1976-77; mem. Kinnelon Drug Adv. Council, 1979-82; troop leader Girl Scouts U.S.A., Kinnelon, 1982-84. Mem. Pompton Lakes C. of C., Oakland C. of C., West Milford C. of C., N.J. Mfrs. Assn. Republican. Episcopalian. Clubs: Wellesley of N.J.; Women of Smoke Rise (Kinnelon). Home: 393 Ski Trail Kinnelon NJ 07405 Office: All Hours Answering Service 817 Ringwood Ave Pompton Lakes NJ 07442

WARD, RACHEL, actress; b. Eng., 1957; m. Bryan Brown; 1 dau. Former model; movie debut in Three Blind Mice; other movies include: Night School, 1981, Sharky's Machine, 1981, Dead Men Don't Wear Plaid, 1982, The Final Terror, 1984, Against All Odds, 1984, Fortress, 1985; TV miniseries: The Thorn Birds, 1983. Office: care Triad Artists Inc 16th Floor 10100 Santa Monica Blvd Los Angeles CA 90067 *

WARD, VERNETTA LAVERN, foundation adminstrator, lay organization official; b. Detroit, Sept. 29, 1948; d. Henry Hilery and Arnetta Melvyn (Williams) Brown; m. Santonius R.L. Ward; children: Lawrence, Terrence, Kimberley, Shinese, Racquel, Tiffany. BA, U. Detroit, 1980; postgrad., Wayne State U., 1981. LPN, Mich. LPN various hosps., Detroit, 1971-77; sch. health worker Detroit Bd. Edn., 1977-80; med. tech. instr. Detroit Inst. Commerce, 1980-82; tchr., adminstrv. asst. Greater Grace Acad., Detroit, 1982-84; instr. med. sci. Cambridge Bus. Sch., Detroit, 1984-86; prog. dir. YWCA of Greater Milw., 1986—; pastoral minister St. Elizabeth/St. Gall Ch., Milw., 1987—. Author: (plays) Family Affair, 1987, Working at the Y, 1988. Pres. Parents Against Violence Emerge, Milw., 1987—; coordinator Students Against Violence Emerge; presenter Women to Women, Inc., Milw., 1987; sponsor St. Elizabeth/St. Gall Youth Club, 1987—, Little Sis. Club, 1987—; producer, dir. Vel-Phillips Talent Ensemble, 1987—; sponsor, group ldr. Explorers Boy Scouts Am.; coach girls basketball YWCA, 1987; co-dir. God Is For Teens; facilitator local Christian leadership inst., 1988. Recipient Appreciation awards St. Gall Youth Group, 1988, Shade Tree Women's Ctr., 1987. Mem. Nat. Assn. Female Execs., Nat. Black Ministers. Democrat. Roman Catholic. Clubs: Photo, Ebony, Women. Home: 1411 W Atkinson Milwaukee WI 53206 Office: St Elizabeth/St Gall YWCA 128 W Burleigh 3940 N 21st St Milwaukee WI 53212

WARD, VIRGINIA ANN, advertising and sales executive; b. East Orange, N.J., Nov. 27, 1946; d. Bernard A. and Doris R. (Keegan) W.; m. J. Clarke Baker, Mar. 9, 1968 (div. Apr. 1980); children: J. Richard Baker, M. Theresa Baker, J. Gordon Baker, Lesley S.K. Baker. BA, St. Mary's Coll., Notre Dame, Ind., 1968; postgrad., U. Chgo., 1968-69; MBA, U. Rochester, 1980. Spl. programs coordinator Am. Library Assn., Chgo., 1969-70; documentation specialist Xerox Corp., Rochester, N.Y., 1980-82; advt. and sales promotions mgr. Hewlett-Packard, Ft. Collins, Colo., 1982—; cons. Ft. Collins Light and Power, 1986. Bd. dirs. Centennial Blend Chorus, Sweet Adelines, Ft. Collins, 1986; v.p. Council of Adoptive Parents, Rochester, 1975; active Leadership of Ft. Collins, 1986-87; mem. Ft. Collins Library Bd., 1987—. Roman Catholic. Club: Writers of the Round (Ft. Collins.). Office: Hewlett-Packard 3404 E Harmony Rd Fort Collins CO 80525

WARD, VIRGINIA LEE, consumer foods company executive; b. Grand Forks, N.D., Aug. 16, 1944; d. Vernol Lee Smith and Betty Louise (Scott) Perrin; m. William Edward Ward, Jr., July 23, 1977; children—Brian Scott Green, William E. Ward III, Andrew T. Ward, Wendy Helen Ward. B.S., U. N.D., 1966. Cert. tchr. Tchr. Ind. Sch. Dist. 279, Osseo, Minn., 1966-68; various mktg. mgmt. and human resource positions, IBM, 1973-81; dir. human resource planning The Pillsbury Co., Mpls., 1981-82, v.p. human resources, 1982—; trustee Voyageur Outward Bound, Mpls., 1981—; mem. human resource com. Nat. Food Processors, Washington, 1984—; bd. dirs. Secural Cos. Mem. benefit com. Children's Cancer Research, Mpls., 1985; fund raiser United Arts Council, St. Paul, 1985; mem. exec. com. Pillsbury PAC, 1984—; mem. Minn. Women's Polit. Campaign Fund, 1983—, bd. dirs., 1985—; mem. Women's Econ. Roundtable, 1986—. Recipient Leadership award Pillsbury Exec. Office, 1985, IBM Achievement award, 1981, Sioux Alumni award U. N.D., 1986. Mem. Am. Soc. for Personnel Adminstrn., Am. Mgmt. Assn., Human Resource Planning Soc. (pres. 1987—, bd. dirs. 1982—, mem. exec. com., 1982—). Republican. Episcopalian. Clubs: Somerset (St. Paul); Mpls. Athletic. Avocations: backpacking, running, golfing, flyfishing, wildlife conservation. Home: 8580 Alverno Ave West Inver Grove Heights MN 55075 Office: The Pillsbury Co 200 S 6th St Minneapolis MN 55402

WARDELL, PAULA LOUISE, business consultant; b. Upland, Calif., June 19, 1952; d. Ted Abrose and Arla Dean (Hickman) W. Degree in fin., Ottawa U., Kansas City, Mo., 1984. Sportswear buyer Kline-Kinsler, Los Angeles, 1975-77; merchandiser Remar's Women's Apparel, Los Angeles, 1977-80, Judy Ann of Calif., Los Angeles, 1980; with cosmetics sales dept. Jones Stores, Kansas City, 1982-84; mgr. cosmetics dept. Woolf Bros., Kansas City, 1984-85; dir. ops. Panache Chocolatier, Kansas City, 1985-86; prin. cons., owner Wardell and Assocs., Kansas City, 1986—. Asst. co-chairperson Folly Theatre, Kansas City, 1981; mem. budget com. United Community Services, Kansas City, 1982. Mem. Nat. Assn. Female Execs., Nat. Assn. Women Bus. Owners. Club: The Establishment (Kansas City) (chairperson 1987). Office: Wardell and Assocs 218 Delaware Suite 206 Kansas City MO 64105

WARDEN, CAROLYN MARIE, financial institution executive; b. Detroit, Oct. 29, 1956; s. William Haxton and Shirley Marie (Pressel) Warden. Student U. Heidelberg (W.Ger.), 1976; B.A., Albion Coll., 1978; postgrad. Xavier U., 1979, 83. Acct. Profl. Mgmt. Cons., Cin., 1978-79; examiner Nat. Credit Union Adminstrn., Grand Rapids, Mich., 1979-80, consumer examiner, Cin., 1980-82, fin. examiner, 1982; chief operating officer Emery Employees Fed. Credit Union, Cin., 1982-84; treas. Jefferson Bldg. and Savs. Bank, 1984-85, cons. and regional dir. Midwest Fed Comp, Inc., Cin., 1985-87, v.p. sales and mktg., Arlington, Va., 1987—. Contbr. articles to newspapers and mags. Chmn., Kappa Alpha Theta Alumnae Philanthropies, Cin., 1980-82, editor, 1982-84, chmn. ways and means com. 1984-85. Receipient Ann McFarland Timmerman Service award, 1987; Webster scholar, 1977; Albion Coll. honor grantee, 1974-77. Mem. Cin. Profl. Mgrs. Assn. (chmn. 1982-86). Club: Bankers of Cin. Home: 6075 Joust Ln Alexandria VA 22310 Office: 2700 S Quincy St #440 Arlington VA 22206

WARDLAW, BARBARA ANNE, service executive; b. Reno, Dec. 12, 1958; d. Donald Bee Ricketts and Mary Ellen (Nance) Braley; m. Jon Keith Wardlaw, June 5, 1982; 1 child, Jennifer Marie. BA, U. Nev., 1982. Teller First Nat. Bank San Jose, Calif., 1977-80; customer service rep. Group W. Cable TV, Reno, 1982-83; v.p. ops. Phone-A-Gram System, Reno, 1983—. Active Muscular Dystrophy telethons San Jose, Reno, 1972—. Mem. Nat. Assn. Female Execs. Republican. Home: 330 Sells St Sparks NV 89431 Office: Phone-A-Gram System Inc 1201 Corporate Blvd Reno NV 89502

WARDLE, RHEA ROSE, educator, counselor; b. Springfield, Mass., Aug. 10, 1951; d. Morris Harry and Josephine Naomi (Kazeroid) Kalman; m. Steven Robert Wardle, Apr. 29, 1983. BS in Secondary Edn., U. Conn., 1973; MEd in Counseling, Springfield (Mo.) Coll., 1978. Tchr. Kiley Jr. High Sch., Springfield, 1973-77, Hazelwood High Schs., St. Louis, 1977—; counselor Hazelwood High Sch. Tchr. Never Too Old To Read, Springfield, 1974-77; organizer Adopt-A-Grandparent, St. Louis, 1979-81, Scholarship Run-Walk, St. Louis, 1988; counselor Drug Addiction Clinic, St. Louis, 1978-80. Fellow NEA, Nat. Council Tchrs. English, Greater St. Louis Tchrs. English, Assn. for Curriculum and Supervision. Home: 1535 Surfside Dr Saint Louis MO 63138 Office: Hazelwood East High Sch 11300 Dunn Rd Saint Louis MO 63138

WARD-MCDUFFIE, KAY FRANCES, educator; b. Chgo., Aug. 10, 1947; d. Thomas David and James Ola (Suddoth) W. BS in Edn., Chgo. State U., 1971, MEd, 1977; cert. paralegal, Roosevelt U., 1987. Cert. tchr., paralegal. Operator Ill. Bell Telephone Co., Chgo., 1966-67; data entry operator Credit Bur. Cook County, Chgo., 1968-71; tchr. Chgo. Bd. Edn., 1971—; tutor coordinator Scanlan Elem. Sch., Queen of Peace High Sch., Chgo., 1973-75. Hostess Beth Eden Bapt. Ch. (pres. 1978-86, industrious aid 1987); Ch. rep. NAACP, Chgo., 1980-84; fin. sec. Morgan Park Civic League, Chgo. Recipient Disting. Service Scroll Scanlan Sch. PTA, 1972. Mem. Chgo. State U. Alumni Assn. (v.p., dir. 1980-84), Chgo. Area Reading Assn., Phi Delta Kappa. Democrat. Home: 12854 S Throop St Calumet Park IL 60643

WARD-MCLEMORE, ETHEL, research geophysicist, mathematician; b. Sylvarena, Miss., Jan. 22, 1908; d. William Robert and Frances Virginia (Douglas) Ward; B.A., Miss. Woman's Coll., 1928; M.A., U. N.C., 1929; postgrad. U. Chgo., 1931, Colo. Sch. Mines, 1941-42, So. Meth. U., 1962-64; m. Robert Henry McLemore, June 30, 1935; 1 dau., Mary Frances. Head math. dept. Miss. Jr. Coll., 1929-30; instr. chemistry, math. Miss. State Coll. for Women, 1930-32; research mathematician Humble Oil & Refining Co., Houston, 1933-36; ind. geophys. research, Tex. and Colo., 1936-42, Ft. Worth, 1946—; geophysicist United Geophys. Co., Pasadena, Cal., 1942-46; tchr. chemistry, physics, Hockaday Sch., Dallas, 1958-59, tchr. math., 1959-60; tchr. chemistry Ursuline Acad., Dallas, 1964-67, Hockaday Sch., 1968-69; geophys. cons., Dallas, 1957-77; bd. dirs. Geol. Info. Library of Dallas. Mem. Am. Math. Soc., Math. Assn. Am., Am. Geophys. Union, Seismol. Soc. Am., Soc. Exploration Geophysicists, AAAS, Soc. Indsl. and Applied Math., Am. Chem. Soc., Inst. Math. Statistics, Tex Acad. Sci., Sigma Xi. Contbr. various articles to profl. jours.; author: China, 1983; also annotated bibliographies of sedimentary basins, 1981, 83. Home: 11625 Wander Ln Dallas TX 75230

WARDRIP, CAROL ANN, university secretary; b. Reno, Nov. 23, 1938; d. Thomas Henry and Alice Viola (Brooks) Dwyer; m. William G. Davis (dec.); 1 son, William; m. 2d, Robert Wardrip (div.); children—Jacqulyn Lee, Robert Lewis Jr. Cert. Reno Bus. Coll., 1956, UCLA Law Library Cataloging, 1966. Supervising sec. Farmers Ins. Group Br. Claims Office, Eureka, Calif., 1957-60; legal sec. various firms, Eureka, 1960-64; jury commr., law librarian, Humboldt County, Calif., 1964-66; sec., adminstrv. aide Humboldt State U. Marine Lab., Trinidad, Calif., 1966—. Recipient commendation Humboldt County Commn. on Status of Women, 1983; citation Internat. Women's Ctr., Santa Cruz, Calif., 1984. Mem. Calif. State Employees Assn. (chpt. sec. 1977-78, chpt. treas. 1983-85, newsletter editor 1978-82), Calif. Jury Commr.'s Assn. (bd. dirs. 1966), Am. Assn. Law Libraries. Democrat. Participated in legal action to ensure privacy rights for jurors, State of Calif., 1965-66. Home: PO Box 402 Trinidad CA 95570 Office: Humboldt State U Marine Lab PO Box 690 Trinidad CA 95570

WARE, BARBARA ANN SCOTT, construction executive; b. Bklyn., Feb. 17, 1955; d. Dudley and Marian (James) Scott; m. Morris Ware Sr.; children: Michele, Morris, Jr. Grad. high sch., Roosevelt, N.Y. cert. energy auditor, N.Y. Community aide Roosevelt (N.Y.) Schs., 1974-76; tchrs. aid Salvation Army, Hempstead, N.Y., 1976-78; asst. dir. NOW, Mineola, N.Y., 1978-80; co-owner JOW, Hempstead, N.Y., 1980—. Bd. dirs. Long Island Women's Equal Opportunity Council, 1981—; mem. adv. bd. N.Y. State Dept. of Social Services, 1986; chair Long Island Affirmative Action Program, Inc., 1986. Mem. Assn. Minority Entrepreneurs.

WARE, CONSTANCE EVERETT, college administrator; b. Mineola, N.Y., Mar. 8, 1931; d. Charles Knox and Adele Constance (Shields) Everett; m. Richard Henry Ware, Sept. 26, 1953; children—Stephen Everett, Robert Francis, II, Philip Charles. B.A., Manhattanville Coll., 1952. Assoc. dir. devel. Trinity Coll., Hartford, Conn., 1974-77, dir. devel., 1977-83, v.p. devel., 1983—; lectr. Hartford Grad. Ctr., 1980—, Council Advancement and Support Edn., Washington, 1984; cons. Manhattanville Coll., Purchase, N.Y., 1985; cons. in field. Corporator Inst. of Living, Hartford, 1979—; bd. dirs. Greater Hartford ARC, 1980-84; trustee Convent Sch. of Sacred Heart, N.Y.C., 1978-82; v.p. Hartford Architecture Conservancy, 1975-83. Recipient Women in Leadership award YMCA, 1978, Vol. Recognition award United Way, 1980, Fellowship Leadership Conf. award Carnegie Found., 1978. Mem. Assn. Am. Colls. (nat. devel. com. 1978), Council Advancement and Support Edn. (participant conf. sr. devel. officers 1981), Nat. Soc. for Fund Raising Execs (v.p. Hartford chpt. 1979-80). Republican. Roman Catholic. Clubs: University (Hartford); Princeton (N.Y.C.); Algonquin (Boston); Metropolitan (San Francisco). Avocations: travel; tennis; gardening. Office: Trinity Coll 300 Summit St Hartford CT 06106

WARE, MICHELLE, information systems programmer, analyst; b. Boston, Oct. 15, 1960; d. Alan Mills Ware and Ruthann (Yackley) Ware Barker. BS in Mgmt. Info. Systems, U. Nev., Las Vegas, 1982, MBA, 1988. Programmer Systems Integration Mgmt. Co., Las Vegas, 1983—, project leader, 1986—. Troop leader Girl Scouts U.S., Las Vegas, 1984-85. Mem. Nat. Assn. Female Execs., DEC User Soc. Republican.

WARES, LYDIA JEAN, marketing professional, fashion designer; b. Dawajaic, Mich., Mar. 26, 1947; d. Milton Arnold and Maxine (Claughton) W.; 1 child, Kaliq Rahshan. B, Purdue U., 1973, M, 1974, PhD, 1981. Mgr. mktg. Ind. Gas Co., Indpls., 1983—; fashion designer Lydia Jean Inc., Indpls., 1985—; commentator numerous fashion shows. Hostess Paul Robeson Conf., 1976; storyteller Black Culture Ctr., 1976; mem. Mayor's Black History Com., Indpls., 1979; hostess Children's Mus. Named Miss Black Greater Lafayette, 1972; fellow Tobe-Coburn Fashion Inst., 1973, Purdue U., 1977. Mem. Ind. Home Economist in Bus. (chmn. local arrangements com. exec. bd. 1983—), Ind. Home Econs. Assn., Am. Home Econs. Assn., Indpls. Profl. Assn. (bd. dirs. 1986—), Nat. Assn. Female Execs., Delta Sigma Theta. Office: Ind Gas Co 1630 N Meridian St Indianapolis IN 46202

WARFEL, (MARTHA) KAY, speech pathologist, educational evaluator; b. Lancaster, Pa., Mar. 2, 1955; d. Orlene Dickenhart and Martha (Herr) W.; m. C. Robert Paul III, Aug. 15, 1987. BS, Pa. State U., 1976; MEd, U. Oreg., 1979; MBA, Iona Coll., 1986. Cert. clinician. Speech pathologist Lancaster-Lebanon Intermediate Unit #3, East Petersburg, Pa., 1976-78, Mapleton (Oreg.) Sch. Dist., 1978-79, Douglas Edn. Service Dist., Sutherlin, Oreg., 1979-80, Bethel Sch. Dist., Eugene, Oreg., 1980-81, N.Y.C. Bd. Edn., Bronx, 1981-85; speech, lang. evaluator Com. On Spl. Edn., Bronx, 1985—; speech pathologist Eugene Speech and Hearing Ctr., 1980; instr. sensory impairments Manhattan Coll., Riverdale, N.Y., 1987—; press officer 1988 USA Olympic Track and Field Trials. Vol. Rep. Nat. Com., Lancaster, 1972, Spl. Olympics, 1976—, Lane County Prisons, Eugene, 1979. Mem. Am. Speech-Lan.-Hearing Assn., Am. Mktg. Assn. Methodist. Home: 209 Garth Rd 6H Scarsdale NY 10583 Office: Com on Spl Edn 750 Baychester Ave New York NY 10475

WARFIELD, JANET SMITH, lawyer; b. Phila., Sept. 6, 1936; d. Norman Perry and Dorothy Imogene (Warfield) Smith; m. Alexander Stilwell Traub, III, Mar. 22, 1958 (div. May 1979); children—William Fairley, Stephen Alexander, Russell Perry. BA, Swarthmore Coll., 1958; JD with honors, Rutgers U.-Camden, 1980. Bar: N.J. 1980. Research asst. Towers Perrin Forster & Crosby, Phila., 1959-61; research asst. Cumberland Advisors, Vineland, N.J., 1973-78; law clk., assoc. Cooper Perskie, April Niedleman Wagenheim & Weiss, Atlantic City, 1979-83; title examiner N.J. Realty Title Ins. Co., Toms River, 1984-86; v.p., in-house counsel, Chelsea Title and Guaranty Co., Northfield, 1986—. Am. Field Service exchange student, 1953; mediator Community Justice Ctr. Mem. ABA, N.J. Bar Assn., Atlantic County Bar Assn., Community Justice Inst., Pi Sigma Alpha. Office: Chelsea Title & Guaranty 1418 New Rd Northfield NJ 08225

WARING, VIRGINIA, publisher, musician; b. Dinuba, Calif., Oct. 18, 1915; d. M. Rene and Elma (Merritt) Clotfelter; m. Livingston Hawley Gearhart, Feb. 28, 1940 (div. 1953); 1 child, Paul Alexander; m. Frederic Malcolm Waring, Dec. 2, 1954; 1 child, Malcolm Merritt. BA and MusB, Mills Coll., 1937; piano student of Robert Casadesus, Paris, 1937-39. Mem. 2-piano team Morley & Gearhart, 1940-53; owner Interior Design Assocs., East Stroudsburg, Pa., 1962-68; creative costume designer Fred Waring's Pennsylvanians, 1969-83, asst. condr. and mistress of ceremonies, 1980-83; chmn. bd. Fred Waring Enterprises, Delaware Water Gap; pres., owner Shawnee Press, Inc., Delaware Water Gap, Pa., 1983—; artistic dir. Fred Waring Summer Workshop, Pa. State U., 1985. Rec. artist (Morley and Gearhart) 4 Two-Piano Record Albums (Columbia Records and Omni Sound). Founding bd. dirs. Child Help U.S.A., 1965—; pres. bd. trustees Joanna Hodges Piano Competition, Palm Desert, Calif., 1983, 84, 85; bd. dirs. Palm Valley Sch., Palm Springs, Calif., 1967, 68, 69; founding bd. dirs. Pocono Arts Ctr., Stroudsburg, Pa., 1965-75. Mills Coll. scholar, 1934, 35, 36, 37; Fleischman Trustee Fund scholar, 1937-39. Mem. Am. Soc. Interior Designers, Music Pubs., Ch. Music Pubs. Assn., ASCAP. Republican. Avocations: needlework, reading, tennis, golf. Home: The Gatehouse Shawnee-on-Delaware PA 18356 Office: Shawnee Press 1 Waring Dr Delaware Water Gap PA 18327

WARNATH, MAXINE AMMER, organizational psychologist, educator; b. N.Y.C., Dec. 3, 1928; d. Philip and Jeanette Ammer; m. Charles Frederick Warnath, Aug. 20, 1952; children—Stephen Charles, Cindy Ruth. B.A., Bklyn. Coll., 1949; M.A., Columbia U., 1951, Ed.D., 1982. Lic. psychologist, Oreg. Various profl. positions Hunter Coll., U. Minn., U. Nebr., U. Oreg., 1951-62; asst. prof. psychology Oreg. Coll. Edn., Monmouth, 1962-77; assoc. prof. psychology, chmn. dept. psychology and spl. edn. Western Oreg. St. Coll., Monmouth, 1978-83, prof. 1986—, dir. organizational psychology program 1983—; pres. Profl. Perspectives, Salem, Oreg., 1987—; cons., dir. Orgn. Research and Devel., Salem, Oreg., 1982—, seminar leader Endeavors for Excellence program. Author: Power Dynamism, 1987. Mem. Oreg. Psychol. Assn. (pres. 1980-81, pres.-elect 1979-80, legis. liaison 1977-78), Am. Psychol. Assn. (com. pre-coll. psychology 1970-74), Western Psychol. Assn. Office: Orgn Research and Devel 708 Rural Ave S Salem OR 97302

WARNER, BETTY ANN, medical education consultant; b. Pocatello, Idaho, Oct. 19, 1945; d. Donald L. and Virginia (Hale) Jones; m. Robert B. Warner, June 11, 1966; children: Alison Diane, Megan Beth. BS in Edn., Butler U., 1968; MS, U. Ill., 1976. Tchr. biology Indpls. Pub. Schs., 1968-72; instr. biology Coll. Lake County, Grayslake, Ill., 1973-80, dir. Learning Ctr., 1980-83; dir. edn. Am. Coll. Chest Physicians, Park Ridge, Ill., 1983-86; dir. owner Continuing Med. Edn. Assocs., Libertyville, Ill., 1986—; dir. continuing edn. Acad. Gen. Dentistry, 1987—; founder Chgo. Area Devel. Educators, Grayslake, 1982. Editor newletter, 1987. Mem. Am. Soc. Assn. Execs., Alliance Continuing Med. Edn., Women in Mgmt., Greater Chgo. Med. Soc. Execs., Chgo. Soc. Assn. Execs.

WARNER, CAROLYN, business and marketing consultant; b. Ardmore, Okla., Aug. 2, 1930; d. Senator Uriah Thomas and Mary Wilma (Tullis) Rexroat; m. Ronald H. Warner, Dec. 28, 1950; children: Cathy Ann, Caron Suzanne, Steve Van, Constance Kay, Christopher John, Christi Mary. Student, U. Okla., 1948-50; BA, Stephens Coll. Radio work 1946; children's dramatic program WKY, Oklahoma City, 1947; producer and host Coffee with Carolyn; producer and host Guest Room, The Best Years, Thru the Looking Glass Sta. WKY-TV, Oklahoma City, 1948; polit. speaker for Gov. Roy Tunrer, U.S. Senator Robert Kerr, U.S. Senator Elmer Thomas Okla., 1943-50; v.p., treas. Warners Furniture & Interiors, Phoenix, 1953—; supt. of Pub. Instrn. Ariz., 1974-86. Kappan editorial cons. Phi Delta Kappa edn. mag. Mem. Nat. Commn. Pub. Service; dem. candidate U.S. Senate, Ariz., 1976; gov. of Ariz., 1986; Phoenix Union Dist. Bd. of Trustees, 1968-73, pres. com. Paperwork Reduction, bd. trustees; Gov.'s commn. on Ariz. Environ.; Ariz.-Mexico Commn.; Ariz. Bd. Regents, 1974-86; Ariz. Community Coll. Bd.; cons. Nat. Sch. Bds. Assn.; v.p. Ariz. Sch. Bds. Assn.; bd. dirs. Jobs for Am.;s Grads., Pres.'s commn. on Fin. Elementary and Secondary Edn., Council of CHief State Sch. Officers; founder, charter mem. Ariz. Ednl. Found.; chairperson Presdl. Classroom for Young Ams. bd. of advisors; mem. nat. commn. on Higher Edn., United Meth. Ch. Mem. Council of Chief State Sch. Officers, Western Correctional Assn. Clubs: Phoenix Execs. (pres.), Dem. Women's, LWV, Nat. Conf. of Christians and Jews, Nucleus, Phoenix Met. C. of C. Office: Carolyn Warner & Assocs 5245 N 21st St Phoenix AZ 85016

WARNER, JANET CHARMAINE, administrative analyst; b. Atlanta, Nov. 25, 1949; d. Roderick Mark Warner and Janet Lillian (Crawl) Shortt. BA, Clark Coll., 1971; MA, Atlanta U., 1974. Lead tchr. Model Cities Program, Atlanta, 1971-72; research asst. So. Regional Council, Atlanta, 1973-74; statis. analyst Dept. Pub. Safety, Atlanta, 1974-85; adminstrv. analyst Bur. Water, Atlanta, 1985—; cons. Atlanta U., 1975, Youth Motivation Task Force, Ft. Valley, Ga., 1987-88. Vol. Andrew Young Campaign for Congress, Atlanta, 1978. Mem. So. Sociol. Soc. (pres. 1974), Urban and Regional Info. Assn., Nat. Assn. Female Execs. (pres. 1984), Assn. Systems Mgmt., Alpha Kappa Alpha (grad. advisor 1980-85). Democrat. Roman Catholic. Office: Bur Water 236 Forsyth St Suite 320 Atlanta GA 30303

WARNER, KATHLEEN MARIE, marketing professional; b. Jeanette, Pa., Sept. 13, 1947; d. Henry and Mabel (Boston) Faletto. Prin. Kathleen Warner, Inc., Los Angeles, 1976-83, 85—; pres. Kathleen Warner Prodns., Durango, Calif., 1981-85; sales mgr. Pacific Data Services, Inc., Dallas, 1986-88; dir. corp. div. Louis Newman Galleries, Beverly Hills, Calif., 1988—; teaching cons. Jr. Achievement, Los Angeles, 1986-88. Chmn. Durango City Arts Commn., 1985-86. Mem. Los Angeles World Affairs Council, Nat. Assn. Female Execs., Nat. Assn. Women Bus. Owners. Office: PO Box 1090 Culver City CA 90232

WARNER, KATHLYN MARY, government personnel management supervisor; b. Pueblo, Colo., Mar. 11, 1952; d. Russell Schirmer Noll Sr. and Ruth Oleta (Nelson) Noll Crump; m. Patrick Vincent Warner, July 30, 1982; stepchildren: David John, Erik Patrick. Student, U. So. Colo., 1970-72. Personnel asst. U.S. Postal Service, Colorado Springs, Colo., 1978-81, supr. employment and services, 1981-87; mgr. personnel services U.S. Postal Service, Van Nuys, Calif., 1987—; personnel action instr. U.S. Postal Service, San Bruno, Calif., 1979-80, mem. Western region hiring practices audit team, 1980-84, EEO affirmative action coordinator, Colorado Springs, 1981-86, human resources info. systems coordinator, 1986—; mem. negotiating team for labor/mgmt. contract with U.S. Postal Service, 1987. Guest speaker pres.'s com. Employment of the Handicapped, Nat. Conv., Denver, 1987.; developer, speaker various tng. sessions, 1987—. Named Fed. Employee of Yr. Govt. Employees Ins. Co., 1986. Mem. Nat. Assn. Female Execs., Nat. Assn. Postal Suprs. Home: PO Box 7372 Van Nuys CA 91409 Office: US Postal Service 15701 Sherman Way Van Nuys CA 91409-9461

WARNER, LAVERNE, educator; b. Huntsville, Tex., Aug. 14, 1941; d. Clifton Partney and Velma Oneta (Steely) W. BS, Sam Houston State U., 1962, EdM, 1969; PhD, East Tex. State U., 1977. Cert. elem. sch. tchr., Tex. First grade tchr. Port Arthur (Tex.) Ind. Sch. Dist., 1962-64; kindergarten tchr. Burlington (Vt.) Community Schs., 1964-66; first grade tchr. Aldine Sch. Dist., Houston, 1967-68; music tchr. Crawfordsville (Ind.) Community Schs., 1968-71; prof. Elem. Edn. Sam Houston State U., Huntsville, 1975—; chair Faculty Senate Sam Houston State U., 1986-88. Author: (with P. Berry) Tunes for Tots, 1982, (with K. Craycraft) Fun with Familiar Tunes, 1987; contbg. editor for Good Apple, Inc., Carthage, Ill., 1986—; contbr. over 40 articles to profl. jours. Mem. Huntsville City Parks Bd., 1986—; bd. dirs. Huntsville Leadership Inst., 1986-88, chmn. adv. bd. 1987-88, chmn. 1987-88; Community Child Care Assn. Huntsville, 1988—. Mem. Tex. Assn. Coll. Tchrs. (life, past pres.), Nat. Assn. for the Edn. of Young Children (life), Tex. Elementary-Kindergarten-Nursery Educators (state pres. 1982-84), Phi Delta Kappa (area 3H coordinator 1986—), Sam Houston Assn. for Edn. Young Children (charter). Democrat. Mem. Ch. of Christ. Club: Sam Houston Univ. Women (pres. 1985-86). Office: Sam Houston State U Coll Edn and Applied Sci Huntsville TX 77341

WARNER, MARGO C., physical therapist, small business owner; b. Benton Harber, Mich., Mar. 3, 1946; d. Donald C. and Nancy (Filstrup) Clark; m. H. William DeVitt, Aug. 26, 1967 (div. Aug. 1980); children: Nancy, Barbara; m. Jerry L. Warner, Nov. 28, 1986. Student, U. Wis., 1968. Staff therapist Madison (Wis.) Gen. Hosp., 1968-70, Sage Massage Home, Milw., 1971-74; staff therapist Glenfield Health Care, Milw., 1974-82, rehab. dir., 1982; co-owner Wis. Therapy Services, Milw., 1982-84; owner Milw. Therapy Services, 1984—; cons. family health plan HMO, Milw., 1985—; mem. SE Wis. Health System Plan Home Health, Milw., 1985-86. Advisor Kind Care-Day Care Adult, Milw., 1985-86. Mem. TEMPO, Wis. Phys. Therapy Assn. (com. chmn. Madison chpt. 1978, Disting. Service award 1981). Republican. Home: 4811 N Cumberland Blvd Whitefish Bay WI 53217 Office: Milw Therapy Services 5464 N Port Washington Rd Glendale WI 53217

WARNER, MARY GWEN, accountant; b. Richton, Miss., Dec. 7, 1938; d. Hughie G. and Ora Lee (Kittrell) Edwards; m. Thomas E. Warner, Dec. 10, 1960; children: Anthony, David, Sean. Student, U. Ala., Mobile, 1956-59. Controller Giddens & Rester Theatres, Mobile, 1960-84; acct. Gulf Lumber Co., Mobile, 1984—; corp. sec. Edwards Drugs, Lucedale, Miss., 1978—, Air-Sho, Inc., Mobile, 1980-87. Mem. Am. Soc. Women Accts. (pres. 1988), Exec. Women Internat. (treas. 1988), Mobile Mardi Gras Soc. Democrat.

WARNICK, PATRICIA ANN, health care executive; b. Shenandoah, Pa., Sept. 30, 1948; d. Alfred Samuel and Anna Patricia (Knapp) Warnick. RN, Coatesville (Pa.) Hosp., 1972; BS in Sociology, St. Joseph's U., 1980, MS in Health Adminstrn., 1982. Staff nurse Presbyn. Hosp.-U. Pa. Med. Ctr., Phila., 1972-75, 87—, asst. nurse mgr. ICU, 1975-76, staff nurse emergency room, 1976-78, 80-81, hospice nurse, 1978-80, asst. nurse mgr. emergency room, 1981-82, clin. specialist emergency dept. and ambulatory care, 1982-83, dir. hospice services and asst. dir. Presbyn. Home Health, 1983-87, nurse emergency dept., 1987—; clin. preceptor Villanova U., Pa., 1985-86; mem. ethics com. Presbyn. Hosp., U. Pa. Med. Ctr., 1986—, mem. nursing practice com., 1986-88, asst. dir. Presbyn. Home Health, 1983-87. Vol. nurse ARC; chmn. service and rehab. com. Am. Cancer Soc., Phila., 1987—. Mem. Oncology Nurses Soc., Nat. Nursing Assn., Nat. Assn. Female Execs., Nat. Hospice Orgn., Pa. Hospice Orgn. (mem. ethics com.), Emergency Nurses Assn., Alpha Sigma Lambda. Democrat. Roman Catholic. Home: 7400 Haverford Ave E-206 Philadelphia PA 19151 Office: Presbyn U Pa Med Ctr 51 N 39th St Philadelphia PA 19104

WARNKEN, VIRGINIA MURIEL THOMPSON, social worker; b. Anadarko, Okla., Aug. 13, 1927; d. Sam Monroe and Ruth L. (McAllister) Thompson; A.B., Okla. U., 1946; M.S.W., Washington U., 1949; m. Douglas Richard Warnken, Sept. 16, 1957; 1 son, William Monroe. Med. social cons. Crippled Children's Services, Little Rock, 1950-54; supr. VA Hosp., Little Rock, 1954-55; asst. prof. U. Tenn. Sch. Social Work, Nashville, 1955-57; dir. social services N.Y. State Rehab. Hosp., Rockland County, 1957-58; asst. prof. U. Chgo. Sch. Social Service Adminstrn., 1958-59; free lance editor, 1960—; instr. evening div. Coll. of Notre Dame, Belmont, Calif., 1967-68; asso. Mills Hosp., San Mateo, Calif., 1978—; med. aux. Community Hosp., Pacific Grove, Calif., 1980—. Com. mem. C. of C. Miss Belmont Pageant, 1971-84, co-chmn., 1975-78. U.S. Children's Bur. scholar, 1947-49. Mem. Assn. Crippled Children and Adults (dir. 1952-55), Assn. Mentally Retarded (dir. 1953-55), Am. Assn. Med. Social Workers (practice chmn. 1954-55), Nat. Assn. Social Workers (dir. 1962-66), Acad. Cert. Social Workers, Am. Assn. Med. Social Workers, Nat. Rehab. Assn., Am. Psychol. Assn., Am. Orthopsychiat. Assn., Council Social Work Edn. Democrat. Presbyterian. Clubs: Carmel Valley Golf and Country, Peninsula Golf and Country, Monterey Golf and Country (Palm Desert, Calif.). Author: Annotated Bibliography of Medical Information and Terminology, 1956. Address: 1399 Bel Aire Rd San Mateo CA 94402

WARNS, MARIAN KINCAID, labor relations arbitrator, psychology educator; b. Louisville, Oct. 3, 1923; d. Horace L. and Laura (Law) Kincaid; BA, U. Louisville, 1944, MEd, 1972, PhD, 1976; m. Carl Arthur Warns, Jr., Sept. 14, 1946. Asst. tng. dir. Richard Store Co., Miami, Fla., 1947-48; personnel and tng. dir. Kaufman Straus Co., Louisville, 1948-52; tchr., asst. coordinator Ahrens Trade High Sch., 1952-56; personnel, tng. dir. H.P. Selman Co., 1956-57; research asso. in arbitration Carl A. Warns Jr., 1957-64; indsl. psychology cons. Raymond Kemper & Assos., 1970-72; instr. psychology U. Louisville, 1972-76, adj. prof. indsl. psychology, 1983—; pvt. practice labor relations arbitrator, 1971—. Mem. Nat. Acad. Arbitrators (gov.), Am. Psychol. Assn., N.Y. Acad. Scis., Mortar Bd., Indsl. Relations Research Assn., Phi Kappa Phi, Psi Chi. Episcopalian. Contbr. articles in field to profl. jours. Home and Office: 312 Brunswick Rd Louisville KY 40207

WARREN, ANTOINETTE DEBORAH, investigation services executive; b. St. Louis, Apr. 12, 1949; d. Atkins Wilbert and Olivette Lorraine (Jones) W. BA in Sociology, Fontbonne Coll., 1973; postgrad., Martin Luther King, Jr. Ctr. for Non-Violent Social Change, Atlanta, 1982. Lic. pvt. investigator, Calif., sch. adminstr., Calif. Dep. juvenile officer St. Louis Juvenile Ct., 1973-75; ct. investigator, dep. sheriff Mobile (Ala.) County Mcpl. Ct., 1975; adminstrv. asst. Oakland (Calif.) Community Alternative Program, 1976-77; coordinator ct. liaison and intake Project EDEN Inc., Hayward, Calif., 1977-78; probation officer fed. cts. U.S. Dept. Justice, St. Louis, 1978-83; pres. Warren & Assocs., Emeryville, Calif., 1983—; adminstr. The Warren Inst., Emeryville, 1986—; founder Black Bus. Exchange, Oakland, 1984—; pvt. investigator Fund for Profl. Pvt. Investigators, Oakland, 1985; panelist Black Advs. in State Service, Oakland, 1986; advisor career Alumnae Resources, Oakland, 1986-87. Recipient award Human Devel. Corp., 1972, award Nat. Assn. Negro Bus. and Profl. Women, 1987. Mem. Am. Soc. for Indsl. Security, Assn. for Non-Violent Social Change, Am. Youth Found., Continental Socs., Assn. Lic. Investigators. Baptist. Office: Warren & Assocs 5901 Christie Ave Suite 403 Emeryville CA 94608

WARREN, DEBRA LYNN, social worker; b. Great Lakes, Ill., Sept. 22, 1960; d. Robert Ellis and Julia Marie (Brugioni) Warren; m. James Edward Schelinski, July 30, 1983. B.A. in Psychology, Lake Forest Coll., 1981, B.A. in Sociology and Anthropology, 1981; M.A., U. Chgo., 1983, postgrad. 1983—. Cert. social workers, Ill. Therapist/intake coordinator Bradley Counseling Ctr., Lake Villa, Ill., 1983-85; dir. North Suburban Counseling & Therapeutic Services, Lake Bluff, Ill., 1985—; cons. mem. Cons. Resource Assn., Lake Forest, 1985—; cons., pub. speaker various orgns. Author: The Highwood Centennial History Book, 1987; co-author: (with Virginia Smiley) screenplay, Robots, 1986. Sec. Regione Emilia Romagna del Nord Am. in the Chgo. Italian Consular Dist.; vol. coordinator Dem. Com. to Re-elect the Pres., Highland Park, 1980; religious edn. instr. St. James Ch., Highwood, Ill., 1979-86; vice chmn. Youth Service Network, Gurnee, Ill., 1985-86, chmn., 1986-87; bd. dirs. Lake County Domestic Violence Task Force, Waukegan, 1984—; chmn. centennial com. City of Highwood; mem. joint civic com. Italian Americans. Mem. Acad. Cert. Social Workers, Nat. Assn. Social Workers, Ill. Soc. Clin. Social Work, Nat. Assn. Female Execs., Nat. Registry of Health Care Providers in Clin. Social Work. Democrat. Roman Catholic. Office: North Suburban Counseling & Therapeutic Services 11 N Skokie Hwy Lake Bluff IL 60044

WARREN, JEAN ELISE, sales executive; b. Atlanta, Apr. 27, 1953; d. Harry Davenport and Jean Elise (Sackett) W. BA, Converse Coll., 1975. Sales rep. Parke-Davis & Co., Greenwood, S.C., 1975-77, profl. sales rep., 1977-80, sr. profl. sales rep., trainer, 1980-87; sales rep. Durr-Fillauer Med., Inc., Birmingham, Ala., 1987—. Class agt. Converse Coll., 1975-81; mem. Spinster's Cotillion, Birmingham, Ala., 1976-84; vol. Birmingham Children's Hosp., 1976-86. Mem. Jr. League Birmingham. Republican. Presbyterian. Club: Millionaire's, Parke-Davis Gainer's. Home: 2505 Montevallo Rd #9 Birmingham AL 35223 Office: Durr-Fillauer Med Inc 107 Walter Davis Dr Birmingham AL 35209

WARREN, JEAN ELIZABETH, hospital executive; b. Phila., May 17, 1930; d. William Lawrence and Julia Evelyn (Bell) Hall; m. George Howard Warren, Mar. 4, 1949 (div. Apr. 1962); children—Bruce Eric, Adrienne Lynn. Student York Coll., 1977; Managerial Studies cert., Hofstra-Cornell Univs., 1979. Telephone operator N.Y. Telephone Co., Bklyn., 1952-61; telephone operator N.Y.C. Health and Hosp. Corp., Jamaica, N.Y., 1961-67, clinic supr., 1967-69, adminstrv. asst., 1969-74, acting asst. dir. grants, N.Y.C., 1974-76, Women, Infants and Children's program dir., Jamaica, 1976—; mem. health adv. bd. South Jamaica Ctr. for Children and Parents, 1978—. Recipient Significant Service award South Jamaica Ctr. for Children, 1978, 80, 84, 87, 88, Merit cert. N.Y. State Assembly, 1982; mem. Internat. Platform Assn., nutrition com. Queens Interfaith Network, Cen. Queens Task Force for the Homeless; Recognition award Queens Hosp. Ctr., 1982, 86, 87. Mem. Nat. Assn. Female Execs., N.Y. State Women Infant Children's Assn., Queens Zeta Amicae of Zeta Phi Beta (Amica of Yr. 1988). Democrat. Lutheran. Avocations: travel; cooking; sewing; swimming. Office: Queens Hosp Ctr WIC Program 114-02 Guy R Brewer Blvd Jamaica NY 11434

WARREN, JUNE ROCHELLE, state official; b. Detroit, Mar. 23, 1935; d. Frank J. and Lula B. Warren; B.S. in Occupational Therapy, Wayne State U., Detroit, 1959. Rehab. counselor, So. Calif., 1966-71; rehab. supr. Calif. Dept. Rehab., 1971-75, asst. dist. adminstr., 1975-76, dist. adminstr., Riverside, 1976-79, Los Angeles, 1979-81, asst. to dep. dir. adminstrv. services, Sacramento, 1981-82, chief rehab. engring. sect., 1983-85; chief of centralized services, field operation div., 1985—; mem. Los Angeles County Commn. Disabilities, 1979-81. Mem. Nat. Rehab. Assn., Nat. Rehab. Counselor Assn., Alpha Kappa Alpha. Methodist. Home: 8963 Amoruso Ave Fair Oaks CA 95628 Office: 830 K St Mall Sacramento CA 95814

WARREN, LORETTA AILEEN, nursing consultant; b. Greeley, Colo., Dec. 6, 1942; d. John E. and F. Aileen (Pearson) Carlson; m. Fred J. Warren, Dec. 29, 1965 (div. Apr. 1979); children: Heather A., Holly A. Diploma, Swedish Hosp., Mpls., 1965; BS in Nursing summa cum laude, Met. State Coll., 1976. RN. Staff nurse Weld County Gen. Hosp., Greeley, 1965-66; staff and charge nurse Bethesda Hosp., Denver, 1966-74; staff nurse Porter Hosp., Denver, 1974-76; mental health nurse II Arapahoe Mental Health, Littleton, Colo., 1976-78; co-founder Rocky Mountain Women's Ctr., Denver, 1978-80; mental health nurse III Park East Mental Health, Denver, 1980-82; owner Cons. in Health and Healing, Denver, 1980—; clin./staff supr. Safe House for Battered Women, Denver, 1982-83, Gateway Battered Women's Shelter, Aurora, Colo., 1982-83; seminar coordinator and workshop presentor, 1978—. Mem. Colo. Coalition for Domestic Violence Legislation, Denver, 1978-83, Coalition against Violence against Women, Denver, 1980-82, various orgns. against wife and child abuse, 1980—. Mem. Colo. Nurses Assn. Democrat. Office: Consultants in Health and Healing 1818 Vine Denver CO 80206

WARREN, MARY FRANCES, computer information analyst; b. Stockton, Calif., July 19, 1951; d. Rupert Burke Andrews and Sally Lee (Crowl) Barrell; m. Jerry Delwin Warren, Mar. 11, 1977 (div. Sept. 1986). Student, U. Calif., 1970-72; AA, Calif. State Coll., 1985. Supr. line ops. Bay Area Rapid Transit Dist., Oakland, Calif., 1972-76; travel agt. Greyhound Lines Inc., San Francisco, 1977-78; residence service advisor mktg. PT&T, Oakland, 1979-82; IBM mainframe cons. Info. Systems Orgn. div. Pacific Bell, Concord, Calif., 1982-85; analyst data network Info. Systems Orgn. div. Pacific Bell, San Ramon, Calif., 1985—. Mem. Big Bro./Big Sisters Am., Oakland, 1977—; mem. Pacheco (Calif.) Town Council, 1986—. Mem. Women in Telecommunications (lectr. 1986—). Democrat. Episcopalian. Office: Pacific Bell 2600 Camino Ramon Room BWC25 San Ramon CA 94583

WARREN, PEGGY MILLS, university administrator; b. Greenville, N.C., Oct. 24, 1939; d. Zeno and Lizzie (Mayo) Mills; m. Don R. Warren Sr.; children: Don R. Jr., Donna W. Student, East Carolina U., 1977, Pitt Community Coll., 1977-80. Various clerical positions Va., 1958-66; with quality control dept. Nat. Spinning, Washington, N.C., 1967; sec. Albemarle Paper Co., Pactolus, N.C., 1967-68; adminstrv. asst. trust dept. N.C. Nat. Bank, Greenville, 1968-72, loan processor, 1972-76; benefits adminstr. East Carolina U. Sch. Medicine, Greenville, 1976—; prin. Peggy's Antiques and Collectibles, Greenville, 1986—. Mem. State Employees Assn. N.C. (sec., treas. 1985-86, del. 1986), Clin. Adminstrv. Mgrs. (chair 1984-85), Women's Network, Women Bus. Owners (sec. 1987—). Republican. Home: Route 5 Box 465 Greenville NC 27834 Office: East Carolina U Sch Medicine Moye Blvd Brody Bldg Greenville NC 27858-4354

WARREN, RITA SIMPSON, manufacturing company executive; b. Borger, Tex., Jan. 17, 1949; d. William D. and Bobbie J. (Hindman) S.; m. Harry E. Warren, Jr., June 10, 1978. BA in Sociology, U. Tex., 1977; MBA, North Tex. State U., 1982. V.p. communications Tetra Pak Inc., Dallas, 1977-85; v.p. mktg. Devex Inc., Dallas, 1986-87; v.p. designs and markets pressure measurement devices Neotech Industries, Inc., Irving, Tex., 1987—. Recipient various awards Dairy and Food Industries Supply Assn., 1979, 84, Soc. Visual Communication, 1979, Dallas Ad League TOPS, 1984. Mem. Pub. Relations Soc. Am., Internat. Assn. Bus. Communicators, Jaguar Owners Assn. S.W. (co-pres. 1979-83), Tex. chpt. Mktg. Communications Execs. Internat. Republican. Club: Tex. T Register (MG). Avocations: classic European automobiles, vintage car racing, gardening. Office: Neotech Industries Inc 8150 Springwood Dr Suite 150 Irving TX 75063

WARREN, SALLY ANN, management consultant; b. Detroit, Nov. 22, 1943; d. Kenneth Wayne and Ann (Trimble) W. BA, Swarthmore (Pa.) Coll., 1965; MA, Stanford (Calif.) U., 1968. Analyst Aerospace Tech. Div. Library of Congress, Washington, 1965-67; mgmt. trainee Bank of Boston, 1969-72; internat. officer Bank of Boston, London, 1972-74; asst. v.p. Bank of Boston, Hong Kong, 1974-76; dep. mgr. 1st Nat. Bank Boston (Hong Kong) Ltd., Hong Kong, 1974-76; v.p. Salomon Bros., N.Y.C., 1977-81; pvt. practice mgmt. cons. N.Y.C., 1981—; exec. sec. Conf. Bd. Chmn., N.Y.C., 1985—; acting dir. career planning and placement office Swarthmore Coll., 1984-85. Chmn. beautification com. East 63d St Block Assn., N.Y.C., 1981—; elected mem. N.Y.C. Dem. County Com., 1983; career counselor, bd. dirs. N.Y. State Council Econ. Edn., N.Y.C., 1983—, exec. com., chmn. nominating com.; bd. mgrs. Swarthmore Coll., 1988—. Mem. Swarthmore Coll. Alumni Council (pres. 1985-87, mgrs. council 1988), Swarthmore Coll. Class 1965 (pres. 1980—), The Asia Soc. (vol. 1981—).

WARREN, TERESA YOUNG, marketing professional; b. San Diego, Jan. 9, 1958; d. Dwight Arthur and Harriett Elida (Porter) Young; m. E. Thomas Warren Jr., Dec. 26, 1981; 1 child, Andrew Thomas. BA in Liberal Studies, San Diego State U., 1981. Account exec., prodn. mgr. Berkman and Daniels, San Diego, 1981-83; account exec. Bill Bailey Communications, La Jolla, Calif., 1983-84; dir. mktg. Jennings, Engstrand and Henrikson, San Diego, 1984—. Mem. telethon com. March of Dimes, San Diego, 1984-86; bd. dirs. exec. com. San Diego Council of Camp Fire, 1988—. Mem. Nat. Assn. Law Firm Mktg. Adminstrs., Advt. Club San Diego. Home: 7020 Gardenia Ct Carlsbad CA 92009 Office: Jennings Engstrand and Henrikson 2255 Camino del Rio South San Diego CA 92108

WARREN, VIRGINIA GOOLEY, audiologist, educator; b. Lynn, Mass.; d. Charles A. and Gertrude Jane (Lundrigan) Gooley; m. Geoffrey Michael Warren, Oct. 14, 1945; children: Patricia Ann, Barbara Jean. BA, Marymount Coll., 1960; MA, U. So. Calif., Los Angeles, 1965, PhD, 1972. Lic. audiologist, Calif. Instr. Marymount Coll., Palos Verdes, Calif., 1960-65; chair speech dept. Marymount Coll., Palos Verdes, 1965-68; clin. audiologist Los Angeles Otosurgical Group, 1968-70; staff audiologist Childrens Hosp., Los Angeles, 1970-73; asst. prof. Calif. State U., Long Beach, 1973-75, dir. speech and hearing clinics, 1975-78, 79-82, chair dept. communicative disorders, 1980-82, assoc. dean humanities dept., 1982—, prof. communicative disorders, 1984—; bd. dirs. Rainbow Services, San Pedro, Calif., 1985—. Author: Fundamentals of Speech, 1964; contbr. articles to prolf. jours. Mem. Los Angeles County Com. on Aging, 1982—; bd. dirs., pres. Harbor View House, San Pedro, Calif., 1984—. Fellow Soc. for Ear, Nose, and Throat Advances in Children; Mem. AAUW (Status of Women award 1985), Am. Speech and Hearing Assn., Calif. Speech and Hearing Assn., Calif. Women in Higher Edn. (chpt. pres. 1982-84, state pres. 1987—). Office: Calif State Univ Sch Humanities Long Beach CA 90840

WARWICK, DIONNE, singer; b. East Orange, N.J., Dec. 12, 1941; m. Bill Elliott (div. 1975); 2 sons. Ed., Hartt Coll. Music, Hartford, Conn. As teen-ager formed Gospelaires, then sang background for rec. studio, 1966; debut, Philharmonic Hall, N.Y. Lincoln Center, 1966; appearances include London Palladium, Olympia, Paris, Lincoln Ctr. Performing Arts, N.Y.C.; records include I'll Never Love This Way Again, That's What Friends are For; albums include Valley of the Dolls and Others, 1968, Promises, Promises, 1975, Dionne, 1979, Then Came You, Friends, 1986, Reservations for Two, 1987; TV appearances Sisters in the Name of Love, 1986; screen debut The Slaves, 1969, No Night, So Long, also, Hot! Live and Otherwise; co-host: TV show Solid Gold; host: TV show A Gift of Music, 1981; star: TV show Dionne Warwick Spl. Recipient Grammy awards, 1969, 70, 80. Address: care Arista Records Inc 6 W 57th St New York NY 10019 *

WASHINGTON, BARBARA JEAN WRIGHT, personnel administrator; b. Chgo., July 31, 1946; d. Jacob Henry and Barbara Mae (Pearson) Wright; m. Paul Joseph Washington Jr., Sept. 6, 1969; children: Paul Joseph, Barbara Jeanine, Nyree Jeanine. Student, Bethel Coll., 1964-66; Grad., Bus. Methods Inst., Chgo., 1967; cert. in real estate, Prince George Coll., 1976; student, U. Md., 1978-79, Germanna Community Coll., Orange, Va., 1985-86. Payroll clk. Carson Pirie Scott & Co., Chgo., 1965-67; underwriter Zurich Ins. Co., Chgo., 1967-68; receptionist, sec. Roosevelt U., Chgo., 1968-69; sales rep. Avon Co., Crofton, Md., 1973-75; dist. mgr. Avon Co., Washington, 1975-77; office mgr. Bailey, Banks & Biddle, Landover, Md., 1974-76; teller Md. Nat. Bank, Riverdale, 1977; subs. tchr. Prince Georges Sch. System, New Carrollton, Md., 1977-80; from dept. mgr. to mgr. personnel Montgomery Ward, Inc., Fredericksburg, Va., 1980-87; employee personnel specialist Dept. of Navy, Crystal City, Va., 1987—; diamond counselor Montgomery Ward, Inc., Fredericksburg, 1981-83; employer adv. mem. Va. Employment

Commn., Fredericksburg, 1983-87; advisor bus. edn. Fredericksburg and Germanna Colls., 1983-87. Adv. counsel Germanna Community Coll., Orange, Va., 1986; chairperson Spotsylvania County Vocat. and High Sch., Fredericksburg, 1985; bd. dirs. Fredericksburg Area Food Clearing House; mem. Spotsylvania County Vocat. Adv. Council. Named Retail Pace Setter Rappahannock area United Way, 1986; recipient Meritorious Service in Bus. award AME Meth. Ch., 1985. Mem. Am. Soc. Personnel Adminstrs., Nat. Assn. Female Execs., Beta Kappa. Democrat. Home: 6036 Battlefield Green Dr Fredericksburg VA 22401

WASHINGTON, DEBRA M., news editor, free-lance writer; b. Chgo., Jan. 27, 1954; d. Henry Eugene McGrew and Martha Elizabeth (Craig) Jackson. BA, Pepperdine U., 1975; cert. mgmt. effectiveness, U. So. Calif., 1986. Editor Sears, Roebuck & Co., Los Angeles, 1976-77; asst. editor Union Bank, Los Angeles, 1978-80; asst. editor employee newsletter Lockheed Calif. Co., Burbank, 1980; asst. editor, prromotion copywriter Los Angeles Times, 1980-84; news editor employee publ. GasNews, periodically writer and editor weekly newsletter, editor FYI daily news bulletin So. Calif. Gas Co., Los Angeles, 1984—; freelance writer Jenesis, Altadena, Calif., 1986—; columnist Star-News, Pasadena, Calif., 1987—. Recipient 1st place PRISM award, 1983, PRISM Merit award, 1986 Pub. Relations Soc. Am., Award of Excellence, 1983, Award of Merit, 1984 Greater Los Angeles Press Club. Mem. Internat. Assn. Bus. Communicators (pres. 1982, 4 Merit awards, 2 Gold Quill awards of merit, 6 Silver awards of excellence, 5 Bronze Quill awards, others). Home: 49 W Terrace St Altadena CA 91101 Office: Socal Gas Co 720 W 8th St Los Angeles CA 91001

WASHINGTON, EMELDA OLEVIA, service executive; b. New Orleans, July 18, 1927; d. Lawrence Coleman and Irma (Lewis) Flores; m. Abraham Washington, June 14, 1948; children: Venessa, Killian. Student, So. U., Baton Rouge, 1944-46, Xavier U., New Orleans, 1953-54, Dominican Coll., 1971-72; BS, Wayne State, 1973. Home counselor Housing Authority of New Orleans, 1949-50; with tenant relations Housing Authority, New Orleans, 1958-69; assoc. dir. Catholic Charities, New Orleans, 1969-77; dir. Carrollton Hollygrove Sr. Ctr., New Orleans, 1977—; del. Nat. Inst. Sr. Ctr., 1986—. Corr. sec. La. League Good Govt., 1970-73; organizer, advisor Treme Sr. Citizens, 1970-74; chmn. Helping Hands Com. Little Flower of Jesus Ch., 1971-77; v.p. Girl Friends Inc., 1972-76; bd. dirs. Vol. and Info. Agy., 1973-75; bd. dirs., treas. Community Access Corp.; bd. dirs., sec. Friends of Zoo; bd. dirs., v.p. Human Service on Cable; bd. dirs., pres. Girl Friends Inc.; bd. dirs., pres. Gold of Carrollton; past pres. Palm Air Civic Assn. Recipient Cert. Merit, 1973, Cert. Appreciation Boy Scouts Am., 1975, Archdiocese award. Mem. Adult Day Care Assn., Mental Health Assn. La., Mental Health Assn. New Orleans, Nat. Postal Alliance. Democrat. Roman Catholic. Home: 9514 Palmetto St New Orleans LA 70118 Office: Carrollton-Hollygrove Sr Ctr 3300 Hamilton St New Orleans LA 70118

WASHINGTON, PATRICIA LEATREAL, educator, consultant; b. Md., Apr. 30, 1947; d. William Howard and Dorothy Lee Long; m. Robert Levi Reed, July 4, 1967 (dec. 1969); m. Lindsay Washington, Oct. 2, 1976; 1 child, Ryan Lewis. M.A. in Adminstrn. and Supervision, Morgan State U., 1977. Tchr. Balt. City Pub. Schs., 1967-69, 72-81, tchr. gifted children, 1981—; tchr. pvt. sch., Balt., 1969-72, cons. gifted and talented, 1982-85, instructional specialist, Balt. City Pub. Schs., 1985—. Md. Writing Project, Balt. Acad. Scis; dir. Sch. for Gifted and Talented Students. Author curriculum unit: William Shakespeare, 1984, Drug Abuse Education, 1985, Computer Programming for Gifted Students, 1987. Dir-at-large Provinces Civic Assn., 1978-80. Recipient Tchr. of Yr. award NEA, 1971; Funds for Ednl. Excellence grantee, 1986. Mem. NEA, State Md. Internat. Reading Assn., Olympics of the Mind Assn., Nat. Assn. Gifted Children, Phi Delta Kappa. Democrat. Baptist. Club: Bridge (v.p. 1980-84). Lodge: Eastern Star. Avocations: tennis; swimming; chess; ice skating; coin collecting.

WASHINGTON, VIVIAN EDWARDS, social worker, former govt. ofcl.; b. Claremont, N.H., Oct. 26, 1914; d. Valdemar and Irene (Quashie) Edwards; A.B., Howard U., 1938, M.A., 1946, M.S.W., 1956; m. George Luther Washington, Dec. 22, 1950; 1 son, Valdemar Luther. Tchr., guidance counselor, sch. social worker, asst. prin., prin. Edgar Allan Poe Sch. Program for Pregnant Girls, Balt., 1939-73; cons. Office Adolescent Pregnancy Programs, HEW, Washington, 1978-80, program devel. specialist, 1980-81; exec. dir. Balt. Council on Adolescent Pregnancy, Parenting and Pregnancy Prevention Inc., 1982-86, cons., 1986—; cons. to adolescent parents. Bd. dirs. Nat. Alliance Concerned with Sch.-Age Parents, 1970-76, pres., 1970-72; Author: I Am Somebody, I Am Me, 1986; bd. dirs. YWCA, Balt., 1966-69, United Way Central Md., 1971-80; bd. visitors U. Balt., 1978-80; adv. commn. on social services City of Balt., 1978-85, Govs. Council on Adolescent Pregnancy, 1986; chmn. Md. Gov.'s Commn. on Children and Youth, 1972-77, active 1987. Recipient Alumni award Howard U. Sch. Social Work, 1966; Clementine Peters award United Way, 1980; Sojourner Truth award Nat. Bus. and Profl. Women, 1979; Vashti Turley Murphy award Balt. chpt. Delta Sigma Theta, 1981; Balt.'s Best Blue and Silver award, 1983, Pvt. Sector Vol. Service award Pres. Reagan, 1984; Paul Harris fellow Balt. Rotary, 1985; United Way Community Service award, 1985; Equal Opportunity award Balt. Urban League, 1987. Mem. Nat. Assn. Social Work, LWV, Nat. Council Negro Women (life), Balt. Urban League, Balt. Mus. Art, Delta Sigma Theta (nat. treas. 1958-63, Las Amigas service award Balt. chpt. 1973). Democrat. Episcopalian. Club: Pierians. Contbr. articles to profl. jours. Home: 3507 Ellamont Rd Baltimore MD 21215

WASINGER, VIRGINIA LEE, quality engineer; b. Paris, Tex., Sept. 21, 1932; d. Theo Lee and Elizabeth Virginia (Cartter) White; B.B.A., Tarleton State U., 1978; children—Janet Wasinger Dickson, James, Richard, Lee Anne, Cynthia. Counselor, Nat. Bus. Con., Dallas, 1969; indsl. relations mgr. Voltaic Internat. Corp., 1969-71; property mgr. Sky-Harbour Lake Property, Granbury, Tex., 1974-75; owner Granbury Picture Framing, 1973-76; quality engr., documentation specialist Brown & Root Constrn., Glen Rose, Tex., 1979-83; quality assurance engr. UE&C, N.H., 1983—. Mem. Am. Assn. for Quality Control. Home: PO Box 129 Church and Warnock Bluffdale TX 76433

WASKO, CASSIE HORTON, newspaper editor; b. Raleigh, NC, Feb. 26, 1949; d. Harry Perryman and Doris (Goerch) Horton; m. Peter Jerry Wasko, June 21, 1967; children: Peter Jerry Jr., Carl Goerch. Student, Campbell Coll., 1967-68, Wilson Tech. Inst., 1968-69. Reporter The News-Jour., Raeford, N.C., 1977-79, The Sandhill Citizen, Southern Pines, N.C., 1979, The Chatham Record, Pittsboro, N.C., 1980-86; news editor The Chatham Record/ The Chatham News, Pittsboro, N.C., 1986—. Vice chmn. Pittsboro (N.C.) Bicentennial Com., 1986—; bd. dirs., sec. East Chatham Med. Ctr., Pittsboro; bd. dirs., com. chmn. Hospice Chatham County, Pittsboro, 1984—; bd. dirs. Chatham County Home Health, Pittsboro, 1987—. Mem. N.C. Press Assn. (News Writing award 1982, 83, Editorial Writing award, 1987). Democrat. Methodist. Club: Pittsboro Bridge. Home: 400 Credle St Pittsboro NC 27312 Office: The Chatham Record Courthouse Sq Pittsboro NC 27312

WASS, HANNELORE LINA, educator; b. Heidelberg, Germany, Sept. 12, 1926; came to U.S., 1957, naturalized, 1963; d. Hermann and Mina (Lasch) Kraft; m. Irvin R. Wass, Nov. 24, 1959 (dec.); 1 child, Brian C.; m. Harry H. Hisler, Apr. 13, 1978. B.A., Tchrs. Coll., Heidelberg, 1951; M.A., U. Mich., 1960, Ph.D., 1968. Tchr. W. Ger. Univ. Lab. Schs., 1958-60; mem. faculty U. Mich., Ann Arbor, 1958-60, U. Chgo. Lab. Sch., 1960-61, U. Mich., 1963-64, Eastern Mich. U., 1965-69, prof. ednl. psychology U. Fla., Gainesville, 1969—; cons., lectr. in thanatology. Author: The Professional Education of Teachers, 1974; Dying-Facing the Facts, 2d edition, 1987; Death Education: An Annotated Resource Guide, 1980; Death Education: An Annotated Resource Guide, vol. 2, 1984; Helping Children Cope With Death, 2d edit., 1984; Childhood and Death, 1984. Founder, editor Death Studies, 1977—; cons. editor Ednl. Gerontology, 1977—, cons. editor Death, Aging, and Health Care, Hemisphere Pub. Corp. and Harper and Row; contbr. articles to profl. jours. Mem. Am. Psychol. Assn., Gerontol. Soc., Internat. Work Group Dying, Death and Bereavement (bd. dirs.), Assn. Death Edn. and Counseling (bd. dirs.). Methodist. Home: 6014 NW 54 Way Gainesville FL 32606 Office: U Fla 1418 Norman Hall Gainesville FL 32611

WASSERMAN, ELVIRA, psychiatrist, psychotherapist; b. N.Y.C.; d. Charles W. and Zena (Berlin) W.; A.B., Hunter Coll., 1933; M.D., Women's Med. Coll. Pa., 1938; cert. N.Y. Sch. Psychiatry, 1962, Postgrad. Center for Mental Health, 1965; children—James G. Wallach, Lewis R. Wallach. Intern, Wilkes Barre (Pa.) Gen. Hosp., 1938-39; resident Creedmoor State Hosp., N.Y.C., 1959-62, supervising psychiatrist, 1962-65; practice medicine specializing in psychiatry, psychoanalysis and hypnoanalysis, N.Y.C., 1959-76, specializing in family, marital, and child therapy, and metaphysical psychotherapy, West Palm Beach, Fla., 1976—; asst. prof. guidance and counseling L.I.U., 1972-76; med. dir. Long Beach Mental Health Clinic, 1965-70, West Nassau Mental Health Clinic, 1970-76. Mem. Am. Psychiat. Assn., Internat. Soc. Clin. and Exptl. Hyponosis, Soc. Med. Analysts, N.Y. Council Child Psychiatry, Nat. League Am. Pen Women.

WASSERMAN, MARLIE P(ARKER), publisher; b. Chgo., Feb. 14, 1947; d. Theodore E. and Faye (Beller) Parker; m. Mark Wasserman, Nov. 24, 1968; children—Aaron David, Danielle Elizabeth. B.A., Duke U., 1969; M.A., Old Dominion U., 1970. Editor, U. Chgo. Press, 1970-78; sr. editor Rutgers U. Press, New Brunswick, N.J., 1978-83, asst. dir. and editor-in-chief, 1983-87, assoc. dir., editor-in-chief, 1987—. Office: Rutgers U Press 109 Church St New Brunswick NJ 08901

WASSON, BELINDA MARIE, travel agency executive; b. Winchester, Ky., July 16, 1959; d. Woodie Keith and Vivian Frances (Estes) W. Student, Midway Coll., 1977-79; cert. in travel, Pacific Travel Sch., Santa Ana, Calif., 1980. Travel agt. Trips and Tours Internat., Lexington, Ky., 1980-81; group travel sales Bluegrass Auto Club Travel Agy., Lexington, 1982-84; conv. and group sales Commonwealth Travel Agy., Lexington, 1984—. Contbg. writer, editor Traveling Times Inc.; editor-in-chief (newsletter) Bus. Travel Update. Vol. March Dimes, Lexington, 1986-87, Cen. Ky. Reps., 1980, 84; daily worker Wooford Sr. Citizens Ctr., Versailles, Ky., 1978. Mem. Nat. Tour Assn. Republican. Mormon. Club: Woodford Dance (Versailles). Home: 1189 Millcreek Dr Lexington KY 40502 Office: Commonwealth Travel 160 Moore Dr Lexington KY 40503

WASSON, HELEN SHIELDS, city clerk; b. Kosciusko, Miss., July 30, 1928; d. Richard L. and Estelle (Ryle) Shields; m. Timothy C. Wasson, Oct. 5, 1946; 1 child, Deborah Kaye Wasson Dean. Acct. Attala Butane Co., Kosciusko, 1946-55; stenographer U.S. Govt., Tachikawa, Japan, 1955-56; with acctg. dept. First Fed. Savs., Wichita Falls, Tex., 1960-63; note teller Fed. Credit Union, Vandenburg, Calif., 1963-64; bookkeeper Alaska Nat. Bank, Eielson AFB, 1970-73; acct. Peoples Bank of Miss., Kosciusko, 1974-76; acct. City of kosciusko, 1976-82, city clk., tax collector, 1982—. Mem. Internat. Clks. Assn., Miss. Mcpl. Assn., Miss. Mcpl. Clks. Assn., Attala C. of C. United Methodist. Club: New Book LOvers. Home: Rt 2 PO Box 16G Kosciusko MS 39090 Office: 220 W Washington Ave Kosciusko MS 39090

WATANABE, RUTH TAIKO, music historian, library science educator; b. Los Angeles, May 12, 1916; d. Kohei and Iwa (Watanabe) W. B.Mus., U. So. Calif., 1937, A.B., 1939, A.M., 1941, M.Mus., 1942; postgrad., Eastman Sch. Music, Rochester, N.Y., 1942-46, Columbia U., 1947; Ph.D., U. Rochester, 1952. Dir. Sibley Music Library Eastman Sch. of Music, Rochester, N.Y., 1947-84; prof. music bibliography Eastman Sch. of Music, 1978—, historian, archivist, 1984—; adj. prof. Sch. Library Sci. State U. Coll. at Geneseo, 1975-83; coordinator adult edn. program Rochester Civic Music Assn., 1963-75; lectr. on music, book reviewer, 1966—; program annotater Rochester Philharmonic Orch., 1959—. Author: Introduction to Music Research, 1967, Madrigali—II Verso, 1978; editor: Scribners New Music Library, vols. 2, 5, 8, 1973, Treasury of Four Hand Piano Music, 1979; contbr. articles to profl. jours., contbr. symphony orchs. of U.S., 1986, internat. music jours. Mem. overseers vis. com. Baxter Sch. Library Sci., Case Western Res. U., 1979-85. Mem. AAUW (Pa. Del. fellowship. 1949-50, 1st v.p. Rochester 1964-65, mem. N.Y. state bd. 1965-66, mem. nat. com. on soc.'s reflection on arts 1967-69, nat. com. Am. fellowships awards 1969-74, br. pres. 1969-71, hon. co-chair Capitol Fund Drive, 1986—), Internat. Assn. Music Libraries (2d v.p. commn. on conservatory libraries, commn. research libraries), Am. Musicol. Soc., Music Library Assn. (v.p. 1968-70, citation 1986), Music library Assn. (mem. editorial bd. 1967—), Music Library Assn. (pres. 1979-81), ALA, Music Librarian Assn./Internat. Assn. Music Libraries (joint com., 1986-87), Civic Music Assn. Rochester, Phi Beta Kappa, Phi Kappa Phi, Mu Phi Epsilon (gen. chmn. nat. conv. 1956, nat. librarian 1958-60, recipient citation 1977), Pi Kappa Lambda (sec. 1978—), Delta Phi Alpha, Epsilon Phi, Delta Kappa Gamma (parliamentarian 1986—). Club: Soroptimist (chmn. North Atlantic Conf. 1961, pres. 1964-66), Univ. (Rochester). Home: 111 East Ave Apt 610 Rochester NY 14604 Office: Eastman Sch Music Rochester NY 14604

WATERMAN, DEBORAH ANN, lawyer; b. Columbus, Ohio, Dec. 4, 1956; d. William Vance and Frances Aileen (Raines) Waterman. BA, Coll. William and Mary, 1978, JD with honors, Ohio State U., 1981. Bar: Ohio 1981, W.Va. 1982. Researcher econ. issues Ohio Ednl. Broadcasting Network Columbus, 1980; assoc. Goodwin & Goodwin, Charleston, W.Va., 1981-83, Jenkins, Fenstermaker, Krieger, Kayes & Farrell, Huntington, W.Va., 1983-85; ptnr. Rhoads & Waterman, 1985—. Scholar Marshall-Wythe Sch. Law, Williamsburg, Va., 1979. Mem. ABA, W.Va. Bar Assn. (domestic law com. of legis. adv. group 1982), Pike County Bar Assn. (pres. 1986, 87), Ohio State Bar Assn., Environ. Law Assn. (treas. Ohio State U. 1978-80), Internat. Law Soc. Pi Delta Phi (pres. coll. chpt. 1977-78), Kappa Delta (chmn. 1977-78). Office: 118 E 2d St Waverly OH 45690

WATERS, ELLEN MAUREEN, publishing executive, writer; b. Liberty, Ill., Aug. 19, 1938; d. Charles Francis and Virginia Elizabeth (Robinson) Linker; m. Gerald Louis Waters, Jan. 18, 1957; children: Tamara, Gerri-Layne, Christina, Andrea. Student, Baker U., 1977-82, 88—. Typesetter, reporter Baldwin (Kans.) Ledger, 1967-73; editor Wellsville (Kans.) Globe, 1973-74; asst. registrar Baker U., Baldwin City, 1975-77, registrar, 1977-82; editorial asst. Intertec Pub., Overland Park, Kans., 1984-85; mng. editor Southwind Pub. Co., Overland Park, 1985—; freelance writer, Baldwin City, 1974-75, Carrollton, Ky., 1983; owner, operator Watermarks Editorial Service, Overland Park. Contbr. articles to tech. publs. Mem. Nat. Writers Club (manuscript critic ghostwriter 1987—), Pi Gamma Mu. Office: 9021 Wedd Overland Park KS 66212 Office: Southwind Pub Co 4551 W 107th Suite 343 Overland Park KS 66207

WATERS, GAIL PATRICIA, military officer; b. Antigo, Wis., Nov. 27, 1957; d. Joe Edward and Joan Eva (Carpenter) W. BBA, U. Montevallo, 1980; postgrad., U. Okla., 1986—. Commd. 2d lt. USAF, 1980, advanced through grades to capt., 1984; chief mgmt. engring. br. RAF Upper Heyford, Eng., 1980-81, comdr., 1981-82; organl. action officer Hdqtrs. Strategic Air Commd., Offult AFB, Nebr., 1982-83, chief manpower programmer, 1984-86; edn. industry student Honeywell Inc., USAF Inst. Tech., Clearwater, Fla., 1986-87; comdr. Mgmt. Engring. Squadron, Goodfellow AFB, Tex., 1987—. Vol. Spl. Olympics, Omaha, 1984-86, Pinellas County Vol. Assn., Clearwater, 1987, Pub. Schs. San Angelo, Tex., 1988. Mem. Inst. Indsl. Engrs., Nat. Assn. Female Execs., Air Force Assn., Co. Grade Officer's Assn. (rep. 1982—), Am. Soc. Mil. Comptrollers. Republican. Baptist. Office: Det 12 3314 MES/CC Goodfellow AFB TX 76908-5000

WATERS, MAXINE, state legislator; b. St. Louis, Aug. 15, 1938; d. Remus and Velma (Moore) Carr; m. Sidney Williams, July 23, 1977; children by previous marriage—Edward, Karen. Grad. in sociology Calif. State U., Los Angeles. Former tchr. Head Start; mem. Calif. Assembly from dist. 48, 1976—, Democratic caucus chair, 1984. Mem. Dem. Nat. Com.; del. Dem. Nat. Conv., 1980; mem. Nat. Adv. Com. for Women, 1978— . Office: Calif State Assembly State Capitol Sacramento CA 95814

WATKINS, CYNTHIA ANN, controller; b. San Bernardino, Calif., May 15, 1951; d. Donald Eugene and Bobbie Ann (Hamilton) Carlson; m. Ed Dean Watkins, Aug. 23, 1986; children by previous marriage: Matthew Lynn Burmaster, Gary Scot Burmaster. Student, Calif. State U., Sacramento, 1969-72. Asst. supr. Crocker Nat. Bank, Carmichael, Calif., 1972-79; sales asst. Merrill Lynch, Sacramento, 1979-82; owner Offices Works Ltd., Fair Oaks, Calif., 1982-84; v.p. ops. Balanced Energy Systems Tech., Sacramento, 1983-85; acctg. cons. Sacramento, 1985—; controller Ergos Corp., Sacramento, 1986—; cons. in field. Founding mem. Christ Community Ch. Singles Ministry, Carmichael, 1978-80; paraprofl. counselor Christ Community Ch., Carmichael, 1979-83; treas. Camps Farthest Out Inc., No. Calif., 1984-86, chmn., 1986—, voting del., 1987. Democrat. Mem. Christian Ch. Club: Exec. of Sacramento (founding mem., bd. dirs.). Office: Ergos Corp 1830 15th St Suite 150 Sacramento CA 95814

WATKINS, GAYLE LYNN, military officer; b. San Francisco, Aug. 20, 1956; d. Charles Edward and Constance (Campbell) W.; m. Andrew Thomas Chmar, Feb. 22, 1980. BA in Biology, Gettysburg Coll., 1978; MBA, Harvard U., 1985. Comd. 2nd lt. U.S. Army, 1978, advanced through grades to capt., 1981; with 7th Inf. Div., Ft. Ord, Calif., 1978-82; asst. prof. leadership and mgmt. U.S. Mil. Acad., West Point, N.Y., 1985—. Office: US Mil Acad Behavioral Scis and Leadership Dept West Point NY 10996

WATKINS, PIA MARIE, mechanical engineer; b. Kingston, Jamaica, July 24, 1964; came to U.S., 1978; d. Edwin Horatio and Kathleen (Martin) W. BSME with honors, U. Miami, Coral Gables, Fla., 1985. Analytical engr. Pratt and Whitney Corp., West Palm Beach, Fla., 1985—. Bd. dirs. Jupiter (Fla.) Homeowners Orgn. Mem. ASME (assoc., sec. 1984-85), Soc. Women Engrs. (Service Award Fla. chpt. 1986). Home: 193 Maplecrest Circle Jupiter FL 33458 Office: Pratt and Whitney PO Box 2691 West Palm Beach FL 33402

WATKINS, SABRINA SUE, drilling engineer; b. Stillwater, Okla., Nov. 13, 1958; d. Herbert Edmond and Sue Elizabeth (Cleveland) W. BSCE, Lehigh U., 1981. Registered engr.-in-tng., La. Assoc. engr. Conoco, Inc., New Orleans, 1981-82, prodn. engr., 1982-84, drilling engr., 1984-88; sr. drilling engr. Conoco, Inc., Houston, 1988—. Leader Girl Scouts U.S., New Orleans, 1982-87. Mem. Soc. Petroleum Engrs. Office: Conoco Inc PO Box 2197 600 N Dairy Ashford Offshore Bldg Suite 1058 Houston TX 77252

WATKINS, SALLY MARIE, nursing administrator; b. Roswell, N.Mex., Aug. 17, 1954; d. William Chester and Pauline Ruth (Cumpsten) Allbright; divorced; 1 child, Avery Marie. BS in Nursing, U. Tex., Houston, 1976; MS, U. Utah, 1986. Staff nurse Univ. Hosp., Salt Lake City, 1976-77, 78-79, head nurse, 1980-84, dir. nursing, 1984—; asst. head nurse St. Lukes Hosp., Boise, Idaho, 1977-78; adj. asst. dir. parent-child div. coll. nursing U. Utah; lectr. in field. Mem. Healthy Mothers/Healthy Babies Coalition Utah, Salt Lake City, 1986—; troop leader Girl Scouts USA, Salt Lake City, 1987—. Mem. Am. Nursing Assn., Am. Orgn. Nursing Execs., Nurses Assn. of Am. Coll. Ob-Gyn, Utah. Perinatal Assn. (sec. 1988—), Utah Nurses Assn. (pres. dist. 1 1988—), Sigma Theta Tau. Office: Univ Hosp 50 N Medical Dr Salt Lake City UT 84132

WATKINS, SARA VAN HORN, oboist, conductor; b. Chgo., Oct. 12, 1945, d. John Edward and Virginia Pentland (Marthens) W.; B.Mus., Oberlin Conservatory Music, 1967; m. John Shirley-Quirk, Dec. 29, 1981; children: Benjamin Watkins Shirley-Quirk, Emily Sara Watkins Shirley-Quirk. Prin. oboist Honolulu Symphony Orch., 1969-73, Nat. Symphony Orch., Washington, 1973-81; solo oboist, condr., Europe, U.S., 1981—; featured on album Tit-for-Tat (A Celebration) Music by Benjamin Britten. Mem. Chgo. Fedn. Musicians, London Musicians Union.

WATKINS, SUE IRENE, hospital official; b. Canton, Ga., July 31, 1963; d. Lloyd Eldrin and Era (McWhorter) W. AA, Reinhart Coll., Waleska, Ga., 1982; AB, U. Ga., 1984, postgrad. in edn., 1988—; MS, Valdosta State Coll., 1985. Sec. various orgns., 1980-84; grad. asst., then instr. Valdosta (Ga.) State Coll., 1984-85; intern orgn. devel. Owens-Ill, Valdosta, 1985; intern personnel South Ga. Med. Ctr., Valdosta, 1985; staff devel. mgr. St. Mary's Hosp., Athens, Ga., 1985—. Instr.-trainer CPR Ga. affiliate Am. Heart Assn., Athens, 1985—; first aid instr. Ga. affiliate ARC, Athens, 1986—. Mem. Ga. Adult Edn. Assn., Am. Psychol. Assn., Nat. Exec. Female, Phi Beta Kappa, Phi Kappa Phi, Golden Key. Baptist. Home: 1569 Cleveland Rd Bogart GA 30622

WATKINSON, AMY JOELA, marketing professional, consultnat; b. Balt., Oct. 14, 1952; d. Seymore and Marion Estelle (Weismann) Josephson; m. Wayne B. Watkinson, Sept. 8, 1973. BA magna cum laude, U. Calif., San Diego, 1983; MPH, Yale U., 1985. Exec. asst. Morristown (N.J.) Meml. Hosp., 1975-78; v.p. Mountain Cons., N.Y.C., 1982-83; staff asst. Yale U. Sch. Medicine, New Haven, 1984-85; cons. health sysems Travelers Ins., Hartford, Conn., 1985-87; sr. devel. cons. Aetna Life & Casualty, Hartford, 1987-88; dir. mktg. and community outreach APT Found., New Haven, Conn., 1988—; cons. Cigna, Bloomfield, Conn., 1985. Vol. Mercy Hosp., San Diego, 1981-82. Named Mental Health Vol. of Yr. Mercy Hosp., 1982. Mem. Nat. Assn. for Female Execs., ALMACA. Office: Apt Found 904 Howard Ave New Haven CT 06105

WATKINSON, PATRICIA GRIEVE, museum director; b. Merton, Surrey, Eng., Mar. 28, 1946; came to U.S., 1972; d. Thomas Wardle and Kathleen (Bredl) Grieve. BA in Art History and Langs. with honors, Bristol U., Eng., 1968. Sec. Mayfair Fine Arts and The Mayfair Gallery, London, 1969-71; adminstr. Bernard Jacobson, Print Pub., London, 1971-73; freelance exhbn. work, writer Kilkenny Design Ctr., Davis Gallery, Irish Arts Council in Dublin, Ireland, 1975-76; curator of art Mus. Art, Wash. State U., Pullman, 1978-83, dir., 1984—; asst. prof. art history Wash. State U., Pullman, 1978. Co-author, co-editor: Gaylen Hansen: The Paintings of a Decade, 1985. Mem. Assn. Coll. & Univ. Museums and Galleries (western regional rep. 1986-88), Art. Mus. Assn. Am. (Wash. state rep. 1986—), Internat. Council Museums (modern art com. 1986—), Wash. Mus. Assn. (bd. dirs. 1984-87), Am. Fedn. Arts (western freg. rep. 1987—). Office: Mus of Art Wash State U Pullman WA 99164-7460

WATROUS, JOAN CHEEVERS, state government legislative administrator; b. Binghamton, N.Y.; d. Thomas Joseph and Antoinette Marie (Casella) Cheevers; divorced; children: Susan Marie, Stephen Richard. BA, SUNY, Binghamton, 1963; MS, Syracuse U., 1974. With guest relations dept. NBC Studios, N.Y.C.; host/producer talk show Stas. WCNY-TV and WNYS-TV, Syracuse, N.Y., 1971-73; dir. pub. relations N.Y. Urban Devel. Corp., Radisson, N.Y., 1973-75; mgr. mktg. Sta. WUNC, Chapel Hill, N.C., 1975-77; account exec. Sta. WPTF-TV, Raleigh, N.C., 1977-79; v.p. Broome County C. of C., Binghamton, 1980-84; dir. mktg. Pub. Broadcasting Co., Binghamton, 1984-86; dep. dir. N.Y. Senate Commerce Com., Albany, 1986—; community ambassador to West Pakistan; mem. regional adv. bd. SBA, 1988—. Bd. dirs. Tri-Cities Opera Co., Binghamton, 1980—; mem. Vestal (N.Y.) Jr. League. Mem. SUNY-Binghamton Alumni Assn. (bd. dirs., past pres.), SUNY-Binghamton Found. Roman Catholic. Home: 2417 High Ave Vestal NY 13850 Office: NY Senate Commerce Com 905 LOB Albany NY 12247

WATSKY, DONNA LOUISE, microbiologist; b. Lackawanna, N.Y., Aug. 4, 1944; d. Fred and Ida Caroline (Columbus) Kubiak; B.S., SUNY, Buffalo, 1966; M.S., Med. Coll. Va., Va. Commonwealth U., 1971; m. Michael Jay Watsky, Nov. 29, 1972; children—Joel Frederick, Tema Marie. Blood bank technician St. Joseph Mercy Hosp., Ann Arbor, Mich., 1966-67, asst. supr. chemistry, 1967-69; nightshift technologist St. Marys Hosp., Richmond, Va., 1969-71; supr. microbiology Anne Arundel Gen. Hosp., Annapolis, Md., 1971—, tchr. microbiology to nursing students, 1971-72; clin. instr. med. lab. tech. Prince Georges Community Coll., 1975-79; clin. rotation instr. med. tech. program U. Md., 1982—. Mem. Am. Soc. for Med. Tech., Md. Soc. Med. for Tech. (dir. 1981-82, pres. elect 1988), Am. Soc. Microbiology, Omicron Sigma. Home: 290 G Hilltop Ln Annapolis MD 21403 Office: Anne Arundel Gen Hosp Franklin and Cathedral Sts Annapolis MD 21401

WATSON, BARBARA CHRISTIE, furniture manufacturing executive; b. Seattle, Nov. 24, 1939; d. Lynn Gilbert and Maxine Bessie (Slaight) Murray; m. Grahame Edward Watson, Sept. 9, 1960; children—Sherian, Ruth, Heidi, Keith. Student pub. schs., Seattle. Draftsman, Boeing Co., Seattle, 1958-60; sec., treas. Watson & Assocs. Inc., Bainbridge Island, Wash., 1960—. Sec. Bainbridge Island Planning Adv. Council, 1972-74; mem. Econ. Devel. Council of Kitsap County, 1983. Mem. Bainbridge Island C. of C. (v.p. 1973, pres. 1974). Republican. Office: 12715 Miller Rd NE Bainbridge Island WA 98110

WATSON, BARBARA K., publishing executive; b. Iowa Falls, May 2, 1943; d. Kenneth Scott and Ruth Frances (Beed) Titus; m. Eddie L. Watson, Dec. 27, 1962 (div. Mar. 1984); children: John Lee, Donna rae. Student, Amarillo Coll., 1960-62, Tex. Women's U., 1962-63. Sec. Phillips Petroleum Co., Amarillo, Tex., 1960-62; exec. sec. Am. Airmotive, Miami, Fla., 1963-64; sec. U.S. Army, Ft. Bragg, N.C., 1965-66, Ft. Sill, Okla., 1967; office mgr. Travel & Meeting Planners, Daytona Beach, Fla., 1971-72; owner, mgr. Creative Crafts, Enterprise, Ala., 1974-79; artist, pubs. The Brushworks, Ontario, Calif., 1980—; judge Orange County (Calif.) Fair, 1985, 86, 87, 88; nationwide art seminar instr., 1979—; product cons. Binney and Smith, Easton, Pa., 1985-87, Blair Art Products, Twinsburg, Ohio, 1986-87. Artist, publ. (instrn. book) A Bit of Barb, Vol. I, 1980, Vol. II, 1982, The Color Book, 1986, Our World of Angels, Vol. I, 1986, Vol. II, 1987, (book) Its Really Acrylic, 1988; pub. Birds and Beasts Vol. I, 1983, Vol. II, 1984; contbr. articles to profl. jours. Leader Girl Scouts Am., Enterprise, Ala., 1973-74. Served with USNR, 1960-64. Recipient 2d Place award Coffee County Art Show, Elba, Ala., 1980, 1st Place award Piney Woods Art Festival, Enterprise, 1981. Mem. Nat. Soc. of Tole and Decorative Painters (judge cert. program, 1983, 84, 86, 88, edn. com. 1982-83, founder Barefoot Tolers chpt., 1978, recipient Master Decorative Artist award 1982). Republican. Club: Luncheon Pilot (pres. 1977-78) (Enterprise). Home: 5610 Howard Ave Ontario CA 91761 Office: The Brushworks PO Box 9311 Ontario CA 91762

WATSON, CAROL, accountant; b. Nagoya, Japan, Apr. 10, 1957; came to U.S., 1957; d. Crestle and Annie Lee (Brown) W. Student, U. Md., 1975-77, Prince Georges Community Coll., 1979; BS, Bowie (Md.) State Coll., 1981. Operating acct. Maritime Adminstrn., Washington, 1981-85; supervisory cost acct. Dept. Transp., Office of Sec. of Transp., Washington, 1985-87; operating acct. spl. programs and analysis sect. U.S. Dept. Treasury, Washington, 1987, operating acct. U.S. Mint, 1987—; tax cons. H&R Block, Washington, 1982-84. tutor Hine Jr. High Sch., Washington, 1985-86; citizen ambassador All China Women's Fedn., Boise, 1987. Served with USAFR, 1985—. Mem. Nat. Assn. Female Execs., Assn. for Profl. And Exec. Women. Democrat. Home: 117 Panorama Dr Oxon Hill MD 20745 Office: US Mint 633 3d St NW Washington DC 20220

WATSON, CAROL DIANE, educator; b. Akron, Ohio, Oct. 30, 1946; d. Donald Devere and Edwina Marie Watson; B.A., U. Akron, 1968; M.A., Stanford U., 1975; Ph.D., Columbia U., 1980; 1 son, Thomas Tarikh Korula. Staff psychologist NYU Dental Sch., 1979-80; asst. prof. Grad. Sch. Mgmt., Rutgers U., Newark, 1980-88 ; assoc. prof. Sch. Bus., Rider Coll., Lawrenceville, N.J., 1988—; vis. asst. prof. Amos Tuck Sch. Bus. Adminstrn., Dartmouth Coll., Hanover, N.H., 1981-82. Mem. Am. Psychol. Assn., Acad. of Mgmt. Contbr. articles to profl. jours. Office: Rider Coll Sch Bus Lawrenceville NJ 08648

WATSON, CATHERINE SUSAN, savings and loan executive; b. East St. Louis, Ill., Jan. 22, 1953; d. James Francis and Helen Lorraine (Cease) Galvin; m. Thomas Alan Watson, Sept. 8, 1978 (dec. Apr. 1986). BSBA, So. Ill. U., 1976. FSLIC clk. Illini Fed. Savs. and Loan Assn., Fairview Heights, Ill., 1973-76, loan officer, 1976-78; br. mgr., asst. v.p., asst. sec. Roosevelt Fed. Savs. and Loan Assn., Chesterfield, Mo., 1978-85, br. support and tng. adminstr., asst. v.p., 1985—. Lodge: Elks (ladies com. chair 1987—). Office: Roosevelt Fed Savs and Loan 900 Roosevelt Pkwy Chesterfield MO 63017

WATSON, CHARLOTTE ALLENE, social service administrator; b. Hobbs, N.Mex., Sept. 7, 1953; d. Charles Ernest Watson and Bennie Allene (Johnson) Huddleston. Student, Austin Coll., 1981. Csrt. peace officer, Tex., cert. indsl. firefighter. Technician quality control Tex. Instruments, Inc., Sherman, 1972-77, specialist tng. and devel., 1977-84, indsl. hygiene technician, 1984-86; exec. dir. My Sisters' Place-Yonkers (N.Y.) Women's Task Force, 1986—; co-founder Grayson County Women's Crisis Line, Inc., Sherman, also bd. dirs. Res. officer Sherman Police Dept., 1985-86; vol. Bella Abzug for Congress, 1986; mem. legis. com. Westchester Coaltion Family Violence Agys., 1986; founding mem. Coalition for Responsible Govt. Funding N.Y., 1987—; mem. adv. bd. Women's Info. Network, 1988—; bd. dirs. Greater Westchester Human Rights Fund, 1987, Lebian/Gay Democrats Tex., 1980-86, Tex. Lesbian/Gay Rights Advs., 1980-86, N.Y. State Coalition Against Domestic Violence, chmn. membership com., 1988—. Mem. NOW (chpt. pres. 1978-81), Nat. Coalition Against Domestic Violence. Home: 247 E 235th St New York NY 10470 Office: Yonkers Women Task Force Inc PO Box 1245 Yonkers NY 10702

WATSON, CHRISTINE DONNA, accounting manager, consultant; b. Carmel, Calif., Dec. 20, 1958; d. Thomas Harold and Barbara Glee (Leedom) W. BA in Bus. Adminstrn., Suffolk U., 1980, MBA, 1981. CPA. Office acct. Deloitte Haskins and Sells, Boston, 1979-81; staff auditor Wolf and Co. Mass., Boston, 1981-82; controller Capron Lighting and Sound Co., Needham, Mass., 1982-83, BFC Enterprises, Inc., Boston, 1983-84; mgr. acctg. Hersey Products Inc., Dedham, Mass., 1984-87; cons. Grinnell Fire Protection System, Cleveland, N.C., 1987—; sr. acct. The Pathfinder Fund, Watertown, Mass., 1988—; cons. Boston Waterfront Realty, 1979-80, Ctr. Design Industry Schedule, 1981-82, Harvard U., 1981-83, Brigham and Women's Hosp., 1983-84. Served with Mass. N.G., 1977—. Recipient Mass. Medal Merit, 1987; fellow Suffolk U. 1980. Mem. Nat. Assn. Accts., Nat. Assn. Women Accts., Mass. Soc. CPA's., Nat. Speleological Soc. Clubs: Tech Squares, Boston Grotto.

WATSON, CLAIRE, sales professional; b. Selma, Ala., Aug. 21, 1936; d. Leslie Warren and Norma (Green) W.; children: Susan, Steven. BS, U. Ala., 1958; postgrad., Volusia Coll., 1970, Seminole Coll., 1978. Sec., treas. Watson Sales Co., Maitland, Fla., 1963-80; pres. Watson Sales Co., Altamonte Spring, Fla., 1980—; v.p., owner S&C Assocs., Altamonte Spring, 1984—; sec., bd. dirs. Fla. Bus. and Industry Recycling Program, 1987—. Pres. English Estates Civic Assn., Maitland, 1961; bd. dirs. Fla. Symphony, Orlando, 1960-70, PESO, Orlando, 1969-70. Named one of Outstanding Young Women Yr., Jr. League, 1968, Outstanding Young Women Am., 1970. Mem. Fla. Soft Drink Suppliers (pres. 1983-84), Ala. Soft Drink Suppliers (pres. 1984-85), Chi Omega Alumnae Assn. Presbyterian. Club: Citrus. Home: 108 Camphor Tree Ln Altamonte Springs FL 32714 Office: 224 W Center St Suite 1016 Altamonte Springs FL 32714

WATSON, DIANE EDITH, state legislator; b. Los Angeles, Nov. 12, 1933; d. William Allen Louis and Dorothy Elizabeth (O'Neal) Watson. B.A., UCLA, 1956; M.S., Calif. State U., Los Angeles. Tchr., sch. psychologist Los Angeles Unified Sch. Dist., 1960-69, 73-74; assoc. prof. dept. guidance Calif. State U., Los Angeles, 1969-71; health occupations specialist Bur. Indsl. Edn., Calif. Dept. Edn., 1971-73; mem. Los Angeles City Bd. Edn., 1975-78; mem. Calif. Senate from dist. 28, 1978—, chairperson health and welfare com., Legis. Black Caucus, joint commn. pub. rights and commn. on tchr. equality. Author: Health Occupations Instructional Units-Secondary Schools, 1975; Planning Guide for Health Occupations, 1975; co-author; Introduction to Health Care, 1976. Del. Democratic Nat. Conv., 1980. Recipient Mary Church Terrell award, 1976, Brotherhood Crusade award, 1981; named Alumnus of Yr., UCLA, 1980, 82, Senator of Yr., Calif. Trial Lawyers, 1982. Mem. Calif. Assn. Sch. Psychologists, Los Angeles Urban League, Calif. Tchrs. Assn., Calif. Commn. on Status Women. Roman Catholic. Office: Office of the State Senate State Capitol Sacramento CA 95814 •

WATSON, DIANE RITTENHOUSE, sales executive; b. Englewood, N.J., Mar. 2, 1949; d. George Virgil Rittenhouse and Lois Carol (McHale) Wagner; m. David Stewart Watson; children—David Stewart III, Michael Rittenhouse. Student La. State U., 1967-68, 68-74. With sales and mgmt. depts. Motorola C & E Inc., El Segundo, Calif., 1976-79; sales engr. CSC Inc., Anaheim, Calif., 1979-81; br. mgr. Executone, Anaheim, 1982-83; cons. Bryson-Watson Cons. Co., Anaheim, 1983-84; dist. mgr. GTE Sprint Communications, Gardena, Calif., 1984-86; v.p., regional sales mgr. Home Savs. of Am., Savs. of Am. and Ahmanson Mortgage Co., Irwindale, Calif., 1986—. Sponsor, Sta. KCET-TV, Los Angeles, 1985-86, M.A.D.D., 1985-86; membership dir. Los Angeles Racquet Club, 1974-76. Mem. Internat. Orgn. Women in Telecommunications (1st v.p. 1984, founder Alpha chpt., pres. 1982, 83, nat. dir. fin. 1984-85), Women in Sales, Women in Mgmt. Republican. Mem. Ch. of Religious Sci. Club: Toastmasters (sec. 1980-81). Avocation: tennis, bridge, bicycling, jogging. Home: 2261 Ardemore Dr Fullerton CA 92633 Office: Home Savs of Am 1001 Commerce Dr Irwindale CA 91706

WATSON, EUGENIA GLADYS, retired education educator; b. Bridgeport, Conn., Oct. 1, 1919; d. Samuel and Lucy Ellen (Allen) Baskerville; m. James Mervyn Watson, Apr. 28, 1943; children: James M., Donald E., Charles A. BS, N.C. A&T State U., 1941; MEd, Bridgewater (Mass.) State Coll., 1964, postgrad., 1968-70; postgrad., Boston U., 1968, Howard U., 1970, U. Conn., 1971. Cert. bus. adminstrn., English, elem. edn. educator. Tchr. San Mateo (Calif.) County Sch. System, 1959-61, Brockton (Mass.) Sch. System, 1963-68; night instr. Brockton Bus. Coll., 1964-68; asst. prof. edn. Bridgewater State Coll., 1968-85, lectr., 1972-85, student-tchr. supr., 1985-86; lectr. on African history and culture to women's ch. orgns., Brockton, 1972-85, Brockton High Sch., 1984, on African art Bridgewater Library, 1980, Brockton Art Mus., 1983. Trustee Brockton Library System, 1977—; mem. adv. com. Brockton Art Mus., 1979—, clk., dir. Brockton Continental Cable TV Pub. Access, 1979—; trustee, pulpit asst. Lincoln Congl. Ch., Brockton, 1980—. Recipient citation of honor Am. Mothers Assn., 1976, 79, Brockton NAACP, 1986. Mem. NEA (Mass. minority rep. 1980), Mass. Tchrs. Assn. (bldg. rep. 1976-79, Disting. Service award 1976-79), Bridgewater State Coll. Alumni Assn. (Outstanding Service award), Delta Kappa Gamma (chmn. world fellowship 1983-85, edn. com. Alpha Kappa chpt. 1986—). Democrat. Clubs: Links (Middlesex City, Mass.) (pres. 1969-71, historian); Jack and Jill Am. (Newton, Mass.) (pres. 1967-69, assoc.). Home: 474 Pearl St Brockton MA 02401

WATSON, GEORGIA BROWN, author; b. Atlanta; d. George C. and Willie (Willingham) Watson; B.S., Ga. So. Coll., 1946; M.A., George Peabody Coll., Vanderbilt U., 1947, Ph.D., 1949. Tchr., Ga. pub. schs., 1931-42; prof. psychology Ga. So. Coll., Statesboro, from, 1949, now emeritus prof., emeritus chmn. psychology dept.; postdoctoral research fellow Yale U., 1961-62. Served to maj. WAC, 1942-46. Mem. Internat. Platform Assn. Methodist. Author: How to Enjoy Retirement: Climb a Tree and Holler, 1979, Life in the Retirement Bed of Roses, 1982, Retirement Tracks: After Showing the Wisdom of Age, Leave in a Hurry, 1984, World War II in a Khaki Skirt, 1985, Doses of Humor to be Taken by Citizens of Mature Age, 1988; also articles. Home: 4 Preston Dr Statesboro GA 30458

WATSON, GEORGIANNA, librarian; b. Lock Haven, Pa., Feb. 18, 1949; d. George and Anna (Eisenhower) Rhine; children: Sharga Nicolle, George Winfield-Martin. BA in Edn., Lock Haven State U., 1971; MLS, Brigham Young U., 1978; M in Pub. Adminstrn., John Jay Coll. Criminal Justice, N.Y.C., 1986. Tchr. Mifflin County Sch. Dist., Lewistown, Pa., 1971-72; librarian Shiprock Boarding Sch. Bur. Indian Affairs, Shiprock, N.Mex., 1972-79, Ft. Sill Indian Sch. Bur. Indian Affairs, Lawton, Okla., 1979-80; librarian U.S. Mil. Acad., West Point, N.Y., 1980-83, head pub. services, library, 1983—; mem. N.Y. State adv. council for use of govt. documents. Mem. Southeastern N.Y. Library Resource Council (mem. continuing edn. com., chairperson govt. documents interest group), Southeastern N.Y. Reference Library Interest Group, Am. Soc. Equine Appraisers (cert.), Am. Quarter Horse Assn., Internat. Arabian Horse Assn., Pi Alpha Alpha. Republican. Home: 237 Plains Rd Walden NY 12586 Office: US Mil Acad Dept Army West Point NY 10996-1799

WATSON, HELEN RICHTER, educator, ceramic artist; b. Laredo, Tex., May 10, 1926; d. Horace Edward and Helen Mary (Richter) Watson. B.A., Scripps Coll., 1947; M.F.A., Claremont Grad. Sch. and U. Ctr., 1949; postgrad. Alfred U., 1966; Swedish Govt. fellow Konstfackskolan, Stockholm, 1952-53. Mem. faculty Chaffey Coll., Ontario, Calif., 1950-52; chmn. ceramics Mt. San Antonio Coll., Walnut, Calif., 1955-57; prof., chmn. ceramics dept. Otis Art Inst., Los Angeles, 1958-81; mem. faculty Otis-Parsons Sch. Design, 1983-88, ret. 1988 ; studio ceramic artist, Claremont, Calif. and Laredo, Tex., 1949—; design cons. Interpace, Glendale, Calif., 1963-64; artist-in-residence Claremont Men's Coll., 1977. Claremont Grad. Sch. fellow, 1948-49; Swedish Govt. grantee, 1952-53; recipient First Ann. Scripps Coll. Disting. Alumna award, Claremont, 1978. Mem. Artists Equity, Nat. Ceramic Soc., Am. Craftsmen's Council, Los Angeles County Mus. Art, Mus. Contemporary Art Los Angeles. Republican. Episcopalian. Address: 220 Brooks Ave Claremont CA 91711 Address: 1906 Houston St Laredo TX 78040

WATSON, JACKIE RIEVES, human relations and business educator; b. Gainsville, Tex., July 25, 1945; d. Jack Henry and Wilma May (Griffin) R.; m. Hal Watson Jr.; children, Hal, Amy, Anne. BS, U. Tex., 1979; MEd, North Tex. State U., 1980, PhD, 1985. Instr. Tarrant County Jr. Coll., Hurst, Tex., 1978-80; research assoc. health sci. ctr. U. Tex., Dallas, 1979-80; mgmt. devel. intern Zale Corp., Dallas, 1980-81; cons. Assocs. in Communications and Tng., Dallas, 1982—; prof. human relations and bus. Amber U., Garland, Tex., 1983—; pvt. practice career counselor, Dallas, 1986—; mgmt. cons. Xerox Corp., Bell Hellicopter, Sun Oil, Halliburton, Trammel Crow, Motorola Corp., 1983—. Mem. Dallas Mus. Fine Arts; vol. RISD Child Safe Program, Dallas, 1985-87, Am. Heart Assn., Dallas, 1986, Dallas Leukemia Soc., Dallas, 1982-87. Recipient Pres.' Research award Tex. Assn. Community Service and Continuing Edn., 1986; HEW grantee, 1979-80. Mem. Am. Mgmt. Assn., Am. Soc. Tng. and Devel., Analytical Psychology Assn. Democrat. Methodist. Home: 9629 Spring Branch Dallas TX 75238 Office: Amber U 1700 Eastgate Garland TX 75041

WATSON, JUANITA, nursing educator; b. Ephrata, Pa., July 5, 1946; d. Harry Augustus and Dorothy Mae (Leisey) Watson. Diploma in Nursing, Reading Hosp., 1967; B.S. in Nursing, U. Pa., 1970, M.S. in Nursing, 1973; postgrad. NYU, 1980—. Staff nurse Hosp. U. Pa., Phila., 1967-72; clin. nurse Student Health Hosp., U. Pa., Phila., 1972-73; instr. nursing Thomas Jefferson U., Phila., 1973-76, asst. prof. nursing, 1976-82; dir. continuing edn. St. Agnes Med. Ctr., Phila., 1982-87, dir. edn., 1987—. Nurses Ednl. Funds scholar, N.Y.C., 1968, Alumni Assn. scholar Reading Hosp. Sch. Nursing, 1968. Mem. Pa. Nurses Assn. (treas. Phila. dist. 1974-78), Nat. League Nursing, Sigma Theta Tau (chpt. treas. 1972-74), Pi Lambda Theta. Democrat. Lutheran. Home: G107 Country Sq Apts Stratford NJ 08084 Office: St Agnes Med Ctr 1900 S Broad St Philadelphia PA 19145

WATSON, KATHARINE JOHNSON, art museum director, art historian; b. Providence, Nov. 11, 1942; d. William Randolph and Katharine Johnson (Badger) W.; m. Paul Luther Nyhus, Dec. 17, 1983. B.A., Duke U., 1964; M.A., U. Pa., 1967, Ph.D. (Kress Found. fellow, Chester Dale fellow), 1973. Teaching asst. U. Pa., 1966-67; instr., curator exhbns. U. Pitts., 1969-70; curator of art before 1800 Allen Meml. Art Mus., Oberlin, Ohio, 1973-77; lectr. Oberlin Coll., 1973-77; dir. Bowdoin Coll. Mus. Art, Brunswick, Maine, 1977—; trustee Mus. Art of Ogunquit, Regional Art Conservation Lab., Williamstown. Author: Pietro Tacca, 1983; author text for exhbn. catalogues; co-editor: Allen Meml. Art Mus. Bull, 1974-77; contbr. articles to profl. jours. Am. Council Learned Socs. fellow, 1977-78; Villa I Tatti fellow, 1977-78. Mem. Assn. Art Mus. Dirs., Am. Assn. Museums, Maine Art Commn., Coll. Art Assn. Office: Bowdoin College Museum of Art Walker Art Bldg Brunswick ME 04011

WATSON, KITTIE WELLS, speech communication educator; b. Newburgh, N.Y., July 31, 1953; d. Cody Usry and Bettie Richards (Todd) Watson. AA, Gainesville Jr. Coll., 1973; BS, U. Ga., 1975; MA, Auburn U., 1977; PhD, La. State U., 1981. Cert. tchr., Ga. Grad. teaching asst. Auburn U. (Ala.), 1975-77, instr., 1977-79; instr. Tulane U., New Orleans, 1979-81, asst. prof. speech communication, 1981-85, assoc. prof., 1985—, also acting head dept. speech communication, 1981-83, chmn. dept., 1982-84, assoc. dir. Inst. for Study Intrapersonal Processes; staff writer and reviewer Prentice-Hall, Wm. C. Brown, Addison Wesley pub. cos.; exec. v.p. SPECTRA Communication Assocs., pres. SPECTRA Creations; co-owner operator Rainbow River Studios. Mem. editorial bd. several jours. Author: Instructional Objectives and Evaluation, 1980, Effective Listening, 1983, Groups in Process, 3d edit., 1987; contbr. numerous articles to scholarly jours.; creator audio and video tapes: Watson-Barker Listening Test; Willing Yourself to Listen. Mem. Am. Council for Career Women, task force nat. tchr. cert. examination Ednl. Testing Service, recipient Mortar Bd. Teaching Excellence award Tulane U., 1982; Achiever award Am. Council for Career Women, 1987; Ralph Nichols Research award, 1988; inducted Listening Hall Fame 1988. Mem. Inst. Study of Intrapersonal Processes (assoc. dir.), Speech Communication Assn., Internat. Communication Assn., Am. Soc. Tng. and Devel. (v.p. profl. devel.), So. Speech Communication Assn., Eastern Speech Assn., Am. Soc. Tng. and Devel., Internat. Listening Assn. (1st. v.p., mem.-at-large, chmn. research com., Research award 1985), Delta Delta Delta. Home: 701 Jefferson Ave Metairie LA 70001 Office: Tulane U Dept Communications Newcomb Hall New Orleans LA 70118

WATSON, LORI ANNE, business owner; b. Washington, Mar. 31, 1962; d. Katie Lucille Nance Jones. Student, Coll. Boca Raton, Fla., Broward Community Coll., Fla. Internat. U. Sales asst. Fla. Export, 1984-85; sales asst., bartender Norwegian Cruise Lines, 1984-85; asst. mgr., cruise hostess Admiral Cruise Lines, 1985-86; sales asst. Fla. Export, Miami, Fla., 1986—; pres., owner Global Ship Services, Inc., Miami, 1986—; crew welfare sec. Norwegian Caribbean Cruise Lines, Miami, 1984-85, crew welfare rep., 1984-85. Active Big Bros./Big Sisters Miami. Mem. Nat. Assn. Female Execs. Clubs: Miami Propeller, Bon vi'bons. Home: 150 SE 25th Rd 6J Miami FL 33129 Office: Global Ship Services Inc 530 Biscayne Blvd #206 Miami FL 33132

WATSON, MARSHA JEAN, writer; b. Kansas City, Kans., July 18, 1957; d. John Stanley and Doris Jean (Elliott) W. Student, U. Mo., Kansas City and Columbia, 1977-85. Pres. Watson Writing Services, Boston, 1983—. Contbr. articles, fiction and poetry to mags. and jours. Vol. Human Rescue Inc., Kansas City, 1979-81. Mem. Nat. Writers Club, Nat. Assn. Female Execs. Republican. Home: 47 Rockaway St Apt 3 Lynn MA 01902

WATSON, MARY STONE, speech and drama educator; b. Marcellus, N.Y., May 24, 1909; d. James Horace and Ethel (Cowles) Stone; B in Oral English, Syracuse U., 1931; MA, U. Md., 1965; m. Harry P. Watson, June 27, 1936; children—Ruth Watson Lancaster, Robert S., Rollin J., Harry P., Douglas J., Donald M., Sara L. High sch. tchr. English, speech, drama, N.Y., Pa., Md., 1931-37, 62-64; prof. speech Essex Community Coll., Baltimore County, Md., 1965-79, part-time instr., former head speech and drama dept.; lectr., condr. workshops in communications and therapeutic communication, 1965—; producer, anchor person Cable TV show The Best Is Yet To Be, 1981-82. Vol. day care and summer camp YMCA; active 2d Presbyn. Ch., Balt. Home: 108 W 39th St Apt 8 Baltimore MD 21210

WATSON, MURIEL ANITA ELLIS, budget analyst, consultant; b. Oklahoma City, Dec. 24, 1951; d. Hughes Van Sr. and Mable Vivian (Withers) Ellis; 1 child from previous marriage, Meyanna Kamilah. BS in Bus. Adminstrn., U. No. Colo., 1973; M of Urban Adminstrn. and Urban Affairs, U. Colo., Denver, 1978, postgrad., 1987. Extension agt. Colo. State U., Denver, 1974-75; grad. asst. U. of Colo., Denver, 1975-76, legis. intern, 1976; sec. Regional Transportation Dist., Denver, 1976-78; bus. planning specialist Colo. Econ. Devel. Assn., Denver, 1978; presdl. mgmt. intern Bur. of Reclamation, Dept. of Interior, Denver, 1978-80; chief program and budget staff Bureau of Land Mgmt., Dept. of Interior, Denver, 1980-83; cost analyst, comptroller US Air Force Acctg. and Fin. Ctr., Denver, 1983-84, budget analyst, comptroller, 1984—; bd. dirs. Colo. State Bd. of Social Work Examiners, Denver, 1986—, Am. Found. for Research in Consumer Protection; cons., co-founder Women's Network and Resource Consortium of Colo., Denver, 1987—. Parish council com. mem., lector, eucharistic minister Cure d' Ars Catholic Ch., Denver, 1981—; sec., chmn. nominating com., bd. dirs. Urban League of Met. Denver, 1983—; adv. bd. Montbello Rainbow Assn., Denver, 1983—; vol. Girl Scouts of Am., Denver, 1983—; sec., bd. dirs. Blessed Sacrament Sch. PTA, Denver, 1986—; vol. Western States Black Women in Bus., Denver, 1986; vol. United Negro Coll. Fund, Denver, 1986—. Named Colorado fellow U. of Colo., 1976, Outstanding Contbn. to the Minority Bus. Community Colo. Econ. Devel. Assn., 1978; recipient Kenneth J. Hansen Scholarship award, 1972, Presdl. Mgmt. Intern award, 1978, Alpha Kappa Alpha Book award, 1970. Mem. Nat. Assn. for Female Execs., Am. Soc. Mil. Comptrollers, Presdl. Mgmt. Intern Alumni Group, Fed. Women's Program (subcom. mem. 1980-83), Black United Dedicated Govt. Employees, Am. Assn. State Social Work Bds. (bd. dirs.). Democrat. Roman Catholic. Clubs: Sippers N'Sliders; Nat. Brotherhood of Skiers. Office: USAF Acctg and Fin Ctr Bldg 444 CWBP Lowry AFB CO 80279

WATSON, NANCY LOUISE, editor; b. Mpls., Apr. 25, 1948; d. Roland S. and Kathleen M. (DeSpain) Roemer; m. Richard C. Watson, Sept. 2, 1981. PhB in Communications, Northwestern U., 1980; postgrad., Roosevelt U., 1987—. Exec. editor AMA, Chgo., 1970—. Freelance writer Pioneer Press, Evanston, Ill., 1978-80. Active Humane Soc. Am., Smithsonian Inst. Roman Catholic. Office: AMA 535 N Dearborn St Chicago IL 60610

WATSON, OLIVIA JEANETTE WARREN, statistician; b. Memphis, Sept. 11, 1942; d. Robert Lee and Ethel Mae (Pugh) Warren; m. Matthew Emrey Watson II, July 12, 1966 (div. 1975); children: Matthew, Angela. BBA, Memphis State U., 1985. Adminstrv. officer CNS Assocs., Memphis, 1963-65; asst. station coordinator Urban League, St. Louis, 1965-67; asst. leasing specialist Ford Motor Credit Co., L.I., N.Y, 1968-78; mem. constrn. acctg. staff TVA, Knoxville, 1978-80; energy cons., computer operator Memphis, 1980-86; statistician Chattanooga, 1986—. Mem. NAACP, Memphis, 1966—. Mem. Nat. Assn. Female Execs., Soc. Minority Employees. Republican. Baptist. Home: 409 Cameron Circle Apt 1403 Chattanooga TN 37403

WATSON, PATRICIA DILLON, state education administrator, educator; b. Rochester, N.Y., July 11, 1936; d. Joseph Bernard and Ruth Magdalena (Panzlau) Dillon; m. Robert Alexander Watson III; children: Robert Alexander IV, Michael Patrick. AB, Cath. U. of Am., Washington, 1958; MA, Cath. U. of Am., 1970; MS, Johns Hopkins U., Balt., 1984. Cert. advanced profl. teacher, supr., Md. Tchr. Regina High Sch., Hyattsville, Md., 1958-59; exec. asst. alumni assoc. Cath. U. of Am., Washington, 1959-61; tchr. Blessed Sacrament Sch., Washington, 1973-78, Prince George's County, Upper Marlboro, Md., 1961-67; instrl. supr. Prince George's County, Upper Marlboro, 1967-73, tchr. talented, gifted, 1978-85; curriculum specialist Md. State Dept. of Edn., Balt., 1985—; instr. Johns Hopkins U., Balt., 1984—; presenter Econ. Edn. Leadership Program, Annapolis, Md., 1986; cons. PBS Video, Alexandria, Va.; mem. elem. edn. adv. com. Loyola Coll., Balt. Sec. Sch. Bd. Blessed Sacrament Sch., Washington; Merit Badge counselor, Boy Scouts Am., Washington, 1983-86. Mem. Assoc. for Curriculum Devel., Nat. Council for Social Studies, Md. Council for Social Studies, Md. Council of English Tchrs. (pres. 1968-69). Republican. Roman Catholic. Home: 6676 32 Place NW Washington DC 20015 Office: Md State Dept of Edn 200 W Baltimore St Baltimore MD 21201

WATSON, ROBERTA CASPER, lawyer; b. Boise, Idaho, July 11, 1949; d. John Blaine and Joyce Lucile (Mercer) C.; m. Robert George Watson, July 22, 1972; 1 child, Rebecca Joyce. BA cum laude, U. Idaho, 1971; JD, Harvard U., 1974. Bar: Mass. 1974, U.S. Dist. Ct. Mass. 1975, U.S. Supreme Ct. 1979, U.S. Ct. Appeals (1st cir.) 1979, U.S. Tax Ct. 1979, Fla. 1985, U.S. Dist. Ct. (mid. dist.) Fla. 1985, U.S. Dist. Ct. (so. dist.) Fla. 1987. Assoc. Peabody & Brown, Boston, 1974-78, Mintz, Levin, Cohn, Ferris, Glovsky & Popeo, Boston, 1978-84; sr. dir. Wolper Ross & Co., Miami, 1983-85; assoc. Trenam, Simmons, Kemker, Scharf, Barkin, Frye & O'Neill P.A., Tampa, Fla., 1985-87, ptnr., 1988—. Author articles in profl. jours. Pres. Performing Arts Ctr. of Greater Framingham, Mass., 1983; bd. dirs. Northside Community Mental Health Ctr., Tampa chpt. Am. Heart Assn., Tampa chpt. Lupus Found. Am.; mem. South Fla. Employee Benefits Council; trustee Unitarian Universalist Found., Clearwater, Fla. Mem. ABA (tax sect.), Hillsborough County Bar Assn., Fla. West Coast Employee Benefits Council. Republican. Unitarian Universalist. Club: Tampa. Lodge: Order Eastern Star. Home: 124 Adalia Ave Tampa FL 33606 Office: Trenam Simmons Kemker et al 2700 Barnett Plaza Tampa FL 33601

WATSON, SHARON GITIN, psychologist, administrator; b. N.Y.C., Oct. 21, 1943; d. Louis Leonard and Miriam (Myers) Gitin; m. Eric Watson, Oct. 31, 1969; 1 child, Carrie Dunbar. B.A. cum laude, Cornell U., 1965; M.A., U. Ill., 1968, Ph.D., 1971. Psychologist City N.Y. Prison Mental Health, Riker's Island, 1973-74; psychologist Youth Services Ctr., Los Angeles County Dept. Pub. Social Services, Los Angeles, 1975-77, dir. clin. services, 1978, dir. Youth Services Ctr., 1978-80; exec. dir. Crittenton Ctr. for Young Women and Infants, Los Angeles, 1980—. Contbr. articles to profl. jours. Pres. Calif. Assn. Services for Children, 1986-87, chmn. program com. 1985-

86, chmn. mgmt. info. services com., 1984-85, sec., treas., chmn. budget and fin. com., chmn. membership com., 1983-84; mem. community adv. com. Div. of Adolescent Medicine, Children's Hosp. of Los Angeles; mem. bd. dirs. Los Angeles Children's Roundtable; co-chair Los Angeles Children's Services Planning Council; pres. Assn. Children's Services Agys. So. Calif., 1984-85, sec., 1981-83; mem. Parents Council, Westridge Sch. for Girls; bd. dirs. Adolescent Pregnancy Child Watch. Mem. Am. Psychol. Assn., Am. Mgmt. Assn., Cornell Alumni Assn. of So. Calif., Nat. Conf. Social Welfare. Club: Pasadena (Calif.) Figure Skating (pres. 1985-87). Home: 4056 Camino Real Los Angeles CA 90065 Office: Crittenton Ctr for Young Women and Infants 234 E Avenue 33 Los Angeles CA 90031

WATSON, SUZANNE MARIE-CLAIRE, marketing executive; b. Toronto, Ont., Can., Jan. 16, 1946; d. William Gordon and Jeanne Marie (Roy) W.; m. George Michael Laszloffy, Sept. 15, 1983; 1 child, Michael Leonard. Student, Ryerson Poly. Inst., Toronto, 1966. Catalogue copywriter Sears Ltd., Toronto, 1966-69, buyers asst., 1969-70, sales promotion coordinator, 1970-73; tech. writer Xerox Can., Inc., Toronto, 1973-75, adminstrv. asst., 1975-76, data systems support specialist, 1976-82, tng. support analyst, 1982-85, product specialist, 1985-87, mgr. sales promotion, 1987—. Liberal. Roman Catholic. Clubs: Toastmasters, Leaside badminton (sec. 1974-76) (Toronto). Home: 835A Millwood Rd, Toronto, ON Canada M4G 1W5 Office: Xerox Canada Inc, 5650 Yonge St, North York, ON Canada M2M 4G7

WATT, MOLLY LYNN, educational consultant; b. Danbury, Conn., Jan. 9, 1938; d. Paul Ross and Denise (Dryden) Lynn; m. Daniel Watt, Apr. 26, 1970; children: Robin Flanagan, Kristin Lynn Gustafson. MA, Antioch Coll., 1963; BS cum laude, Lesley Coll., 1970, cert. advanced study, 1979. Tchr. Brookline (Mass.) Pub. Schs., 1970-80; co-founder Tchr. Ctr., Brookline, 1971; adminstr. Amherst (Mass.) Pub. Schs., 1980-81; dir. Ednl. Alternatives, Antrim, N.H., 1980—; sr. assoc. Edn. Devel. Ctr., 1986—; mem. adj. faculty Lesley Coll., Keene State Coll., Union Coll., Antioch Coll.; cons. to Computer Camps Internat., Bolt Beranek & Newman, Tech. Edn. Research Ctrs. Nat. Hands-on Workshops; mem. edn. adv. com. Apple Co.; co-leader The Logo and Computers in Edn. workshop, Beijing, Peoples Republic of China, 1986. Co-author: Teaching with Logo, 1986, Welcome to Logo, 1984; columnist Teaching and Computers mag.; contbr. chpts. to books, articles to profl. publs. Bd. mem. N.H. Assn. for Computers in Edn., chmn. publs. com. Danforth grantee. Mem. Nat. Assn. Elem. Sch. Prins., N.H. Assn. Elem. Sch. Prins., Assn. for Supervision and Curriculum Devel., Am. Assn. Tng. and Devel., New Eng. Coalition Ednl. Leaders. Democrat. Mem. Soc. of Friends. Address: Gregg Lake Rd Antrim NH 03440

WATTERS, MARIANNE GIBSON, bank administrator; b. Gastonia, N.C., Dec. 29, 1954; d. Marion Eugene and Mary Louise (McSwain) Gibson; m. Clyde Stewart Fentress, Dec. 15, 1979 (div. 1981); m. James Patrick Watters, Aug. 30, 1986. BA, Gardner Webb Coll., 1978; postgrad., Cape Fear Tech. Cert. respiratory therapist. Pvt. practice piano tchr. Wilmington, N.C., 1979-86; respiratory therapist New Hanover Meml. Hosp., Wilmington, 1980-85; paralegal Michael R. Mitwol Offices, Wilmington, 1985-87; adminstrv. asst. Community Bank of Forest, Va., 1987—. Mem. Am. Inst. Banking, Nat. Orgn. Exec. Women, Nat. Guild Piano Tchrs., Alpha Psi Omega, Lynchburg Advt. Club. Democrat. Home: Rt 2 Box 346 Evington VA 24551 Office: The Community Bank of Forest Route 221 Forest VA 24551

WATTERSON, BETSY SUSANNE, corporate executive, cosmotologist; b. LaGrange, Ga., Jan. 23, 1964; d. Henry Max and Hilda Voncile (Patridge) Shelnutt; m. David Lee Watterson, July 18, 1956. Cert. cosmetology, Troup Tech. Hair designer Vaden Horne Hair Design, LaGrange, 1983; cons. Bee Discount, Morton Grove, Ill., 1983-84; make-up artist Carson Pirie Scott, Chgo., 1984-85, Ill. mktg. dir. Pivot Point Internat., Inc., Chgo., 1985-86, nat. mktg. mgr., 1986-87; sales, service rep. Newell Corp., Freeport, Ill., 1987—. Contbr. articles to newspapers. Recipient Citizenship award. Fellow Young Exec. Club of Beauty and Barber Supply Inst. Home: 9451 W Maple Rosemont IL 60018 Office: Newell Corp Freeport IL 61032

WATTS, DORIS EARLENE, retired librarian; b. Palatka, Fla., Jan. 7, 1923; d. Charles Franklin and Elouise A.C. (Hagler) Foster; m. Fernand Cortez Watts, Aug. 30, 1950 (dec. 1955); children: Varick Steven, Franklin Cortez. A.B., Howard U., 1950; postgrad., Cath. U. Am., 1960-61, Cath. U. Am., 1965. Clk. War Dept., Washington, 1942-46, VA, Washington, 1949; editorial clk. Dept. Army, Washington, 1950-52; clk. Dept. Army, 1953-59, Dept. Commerce, Washington, 1959; with ICC, Washington, 1959—, librarian, to 1983. Recipient Spl. Achievement award ICC, 1983; recipient Spl. Achievement award, 1984. Mem. ALA, Delta Sigma Theta. Democrat. Methodist. Home: 2502 Perry St NE Washington DC 20018

WATTS, EMILY STIPES, educator; b. Urbana, Ill., Mar. 16, 1936; d. Royal Arthur and Virginia Louise (Schenck) Stipes; m. Robert Allan Watts, Aug. 30, 1958; children: Benjamin, Edward, Thomas. Student, Smith Coll., 1954-56; A.B., U. Ill., 1958, M.A. (Woodrow Wilson Nat. fellow), 1959, Ph.D., 1963. Instr. in English U. Ill.-Urbana, 1963-67, asst. prof. English, 1967-73, assoc. prof., 1973-77, prof., dir. grad. studies dept. English, 1977-79; bd. dirs. U. Ill. Athletic Assn., chmn., 1981-83; mem. faculty adv. com. Ill. Bd. Higher Edn., 1984—, vice chmn., 1986-87, chmn., 1987-88. Author: Ernest Hemingway and The Arts, 1971, The Poetry of American Women from 1632 to 1945, 1977, The Businessman in American Literature, 1982; contbr. articles on Jonathan Edwards, Anne Bradstreet to lit. jours. John Simon Guggenheim Meml. Found. fellow, 1973-74. Mem. Authors Guild, Ill. Writers Assn., Phi Beta Kappa, Phi Kappa Phi. Republican. Presbyterian. Home: 1009 W University Ave Champaign IL 61821 Office: U Ill 208 English Bldg Urbana IL 61801

WATTS, HEATHER, ballerina; b. Long Beach, Calif., Sept. 27, 1953; d. Keith Nevin and Sheelagh Maud (Woodhead) W. Student, Sch. Am. Ballet, N.Y.C. mem. corps de ballet N.Y.C. Ballet Co., 1970-78, soloist, 1978-79, prin., 1979—; dir. N.Y. State Summer Sch. of Arts Sch. of Dance, Saratoga Springs, from 1982. Created roles in George Balanchine's Robert Schumann's Davidsbündlertänze, Peter Martin's Rossini Pas de Deux, Lille Suite, Suite from Histoire du Soldat, Calcium Light Night, Sonate di Scarlatti, Concerto for Two Solo Pianos, Tango, A Schubertiad, Song of the Auvergne, Ecstatic Orange, Jerome Robbins' Piano Pieces, Chamber Works, I'm Old Fashioned, & The Four Seasons; PBS-TV appearances include Bournonville Dances, The Magic Flute, A Choreographer's Notebook (all Dance in America series), and Lincoln Center Special: Balanchine Celebrates Stravinsky. Recipient Dance Mag. award, 1985; L'Oreal Shining Star award, 1985, Lions of the Performing Arts award N.Y. Pub. Library, 1986. Address: care NYC Ballet NY State Theater Lincoln Ctr New York NY 10023 also: care Sharon Wagner Artists Service 150 West End Ave New York NY 10023

WATTS, HELENA ROSELLE, military analyst; b. East Lynne, Mo., May 29, 1921; d. Elmer Wayne and Nellie Irene (Barrington) Long; m. Henry Millard Watts, June 14, 1940; children—Helena Roselle Watts Scott, Patricia Marie Watts Foble. B.A., Johns Hopkins U., 1952, postgrad., 1952-53. Assoc. engr., Westinghouse Corp., Balt., 1965-67; sr. analyst Merck, Sharp & Dohme, Westpoint, Pa., 1967-69; sr. engr. Bendix Radio div. Bendix Corp., Balt., 1970-72; sr. scientist Sci. Applications Internat. Corp., McLean, Va., 1975-84; mem. tech. staff The Mitre Corp., McLean, 1985—; adj. prof. Def. Intelligence Coll., Washington, 1984-85. Contbr. articles to tech. jours. Mem. IEEE, AAAS, Nat. Mil. Intelligence Assn., U.S. Naval Inst., Assn. Old Crows, Mensa, N.Y. Acad. Sci. Republican. Roman Catholic. Avocations: photography, gardening, reading. Home: 4302 Roberts Ave Annandale VA 22003 Office: The Mitre Corp W442 7525 Colshire Dr McLean VA 22102

WATTS, JOYCE LANNOM, university administrator; b. Los Angeles, June 1, 1942; d. Kenneth Loren and Elsie (Weston) Lannom; m. John Ransford Watts, Dec. 20, 1975. B.A. cum laude, Calif. State U.-Long Beach, 1976; MBA, Northwestern U., 1987. Exec. asst. to pres. Calif. State U.-Long Beach, 1964-75, exec. dir. alumni affairs, 1976-79; mem. staff vice chmn. U.S. Commn. Civil Rights, 1975-76; regional adminstr. Career Research, Chgo., 1979-81; 2d v.p. No. Trust Co., Chgo., 1981-84; asst. dean, dir. career devel. and placement Kellogg Grad. Sch. Mgmt., Northwestern U., Evanston, Ill., 1984—. Mem. internat. bd. Chgo. Met. YMCAs; mem. bd. Community Adv. Council for Programs on Women, Northwestern U. Mem. Employment Mgmt. Assn., Coll. Placement Council, Midwest Coll. Placement Assn., Women in Mgmt. (pres.-elect 1988, Woman of Achievement award 1987), Dorothy L. Sayers Soc. Home: 614 Forest Ave Evanston IL 60202

WATTS, KAREN, nurse; b. Savannah, Ga., Dec. 2, 1956; d. Spencer Ashton and Helen May (Conners) Smith; m. Thurman Richard Watts, Feb. 6, 1955. AS, Armstrong State Coll., 1977, BS in Nursing, 1980. Cert. critical care nurse. Staff nurse Mem. Med. Ctr., Savannah, 1978-81, head nurse, med. floor, 1981, clinician, critical care, 1981-82, head nurse, critical care, 1982-83, clinician, critical care, 1985—; patient-clinical educator Candler Gen. Hosp., Savannah, 1983-85; instr. Am. Heart Assn., 1985—, affiliate faculty, 1986—. Contbr. critical care program to Orientation Manual, 1985. Mem. Am. Assn. Critical Care Nurses, Sigma Theta Tau. Republican. Roman Catholic. Home: One Fox Squirrel Dr Savannah GA 31406 Office: Mem Med Ctr Inc 4700 Waters Ave Savannah GA 31404

WATTS, LOU ELLEN, educator; b. Conway, S.C., Sept. 23, 1940; d. Bernie Louis and Dallie Ellen (Lemons) Overhultz; m. Ervin William Watts, Feb. 3, 1963; children: William Ashley. B in Music Edn., La. State U., 1962; postgrad. U. Ga., 1965; MEd, U. Ariz., 1987. Cert. elem. tchr., music tchr., Ind., Ga., La., Ariz. Music tchr. Westchester Twp. Sch., Chesterton, Ind., 1963-64; music cons. Clayton County Sch., Jonesboro, Ga., 1964-66; elem. and chorus tchr. Tucson Unified Sch. Dist., 1979—, intermediate head div. tchr., music cons., 1983-84, chorus dir., 1979-84, music tchr. mid. sch., 1987—; teacher, cons. archaeology, 1983—. Author (tchr./student manuals): Archaeology is More Than a Dig; contbr. articles to profl. jours. Pres., fine arts chmn., cons. Sahuaro Jr. Women's Club, Tucson, 1970-74; state consumer chmn., music award chmn. Ariz. Fedn. of Women's Club, 1970-72; mem. Tucson Panhellenic Council, 1971-72; project chmn. Southwest Children's Exploratory Ctr., Tucson. Tucson Enrichment Fund grantee, 1983—. Recipient Clubwoman of the Year Ariz. Fedn. Jr. Women's Club, 1972. Mem. NEA, Nat. Audubon Soc., Nat. Sci. Tchr. Assn., Music Educators Nat. Conf., Ariz. Edn. Assn., Ariz. Sci. Tchr.'s Assn. (Search for Excellence in Sci. award 1985), Tucson Edn. Assn., DAR, So. Ariz. Arabian Horse Assn., Delta Kappa Gamma, Sigma Alpha Iota. Home and Office: 8740 E Summer Terr Tucson AZ 85749

WATTS, MARY ANN, educator; b. Harrisburg, Pa., Sept. 13, 1927; d. Major Allan and Ellana Susan (Robinson) Brown; m. Spencer R. Watts, June 23, 1951; children: Shelley Lynn, Allison Dee, Howard Allan. BS, Cheyney U., 1949; student, Temple U., 1965-67, Pa. State U., 1969-72. Tchr. Harrisburg Sch. Dist., 1949-51, 59-69, Balt. Sch. Dist., 1951-57, tchr. Reading (Pa.) Sch. Dist., 1969—, mem. sch. dist. dress and discipline code com., 1977-79; corr. Hamburg Item. Mem. Bernville Borough Council, 1976—, v.p., 1988—; treas. Berks County Boroughs Assn., 1977—. Mem. NEA, Pa. Edn. Assn., Reading Edn. Assn., Berks County Boroughs Edn. Assn., Pa. Elected Women's Assn., NAACP, LWV, Delta Sigma Theta. Democrat. Mem. United Ch. Christ. Clubs: Bernville Woman's (pres. 1978-80, 86-88, Woman of Yr. 1985), GNO of Harrisburg. Office: Reading Sch Dist 8th and Washington Sts Reading PA 19602

WATTS, MICHELLE MARIE, chemist; b. Cleve., Oct. 31, 1951; d. Samuel Purcell and Winifred Marie (Dominick) W. BS in Chemistry, Bowling Green (Ohio) State U., 1974; MBA in Mktg., Xavier U., 1980. Chemist Ashland Chem. Co., Dublin, Ohio, 1974-80, Sherex Chem. Co., Dublin, 1980—. Inventor amine oxides, 1981. Tutor Upward Bound, Ohio Wesleyan Coll., 1982—. Named one of Outstanding Young Women Am., 1986; recipient Service award Upward Bound, 1985, 86. Mem. Am. Chem. Soc., Am. Mgmt. Assn., Nat. Assn. Female Execs., Alpha Kappa Alpha. Office: Sherex Chem Co 5777 Frantz Rd Dublin OH 43017

WATTS, VIVIAN EDNA, state legislator; b. Detroit, June 7, 1940; d. Edward William and Dorothy Beatrice (Price) Walker; m. David Allan Watts, Jan. 30, 1960; children—Cynthia, Jeffery. B.A., U. Mich., 1962. Pres., Fairfax Area LWV, 1975-77; dir. research Fairfax C. of C., 1977-79; legis. aide U.S. Congress, 1980, Va. Gen. Assembly, 1980-81; legislator Va. Ho. of Dels., 1982-86; sec. Transp. and Pub. Safety, State of Va., 1986—; chmn. joint com. on in-state tuition, 1983. Editor, chmn. report Sch. Closing Task Force, 1978. Bd. dirs. Pre-Paid Legal Services, 1983—. Gov.'s Regulatory Reform Adv. Bd., 1982—. No. Va. Community Coll. Child Care Bd., 1980—; exec. bd. Nat. Capital United Way, 1976—; chmn. Tax and Revenue of Fairfax Fiscal Commn., 1978; founding mem. Fairfax Com. 100, 1975; chmn. 1978 Sch. Bond Referendum, 1978; mem. Gov.'s Cabinet; cons. Arthur Young & Co., 1985-86; child care bd. No. Va. Community Coll., 1980-85. Named Fairfax County Citizen of Year, Washington Star, 1978, Citizen of Yr. Annandale (Va.) C. of C., 1986. Mem. No. Va. Consortium for Continuing Higher Edn. (dir.), Friends of Victim Assistance Network (dir.), No. Va. Coalition for Children (dir.), Bus. and Profl. Women (Woman of Yr. 1983), Woman Execs. in State Govt. Democrat. Unitarian.

WATZ, DEBORAH KAREN, food products executive; b. N.Y.C., Jan. 22, 1950; d. Stephen Peter Perkowski and Lillian Natalie Jurgan; m. Martin Charles Watz, Feb. 4, 1984. BS in Nutrition, Rutgers U., 1972, postgrad. in fragrance and odor chemistry, 1974; postgrad., Arthur D. Little Mgmt. Edn. Inst., Cambridge, Mass., 1980. Lic. nutritionist. Flavor chemist Meer Corp., North Bergen, N.J., 1972-76, Haarman & Reimer Corp., Springfield, N.J., 1976-77; dir. flavor and fragance div. S.B. Penick div. CPC Internat., Orange, N.J., 1977-78; flavor chemist Anheuser Busch Inc., St. Louis, 1978-82; instr. food service mgmt. Onondaga Community Coll., Syracuse, N.Y., 1983-84; food prodn. mgr. A.R.A. Health Care Nutrition Services, Newport News, Va., 1984-88; pres., owner My Maid Profl. House Cleaners Inc., St. Louis, 1988—. Vol. Meals on Wheels, Syracuse, 1982-84. Republican. Roman Catholic. Home: 1528 Indian Hill Ln Manchester MO 63021

WAUGH, CAROL-LYNN RÖSSEL, writer, artist; b. Staten Island, N.Y., Jan. 5, 1947; d. Carl Frederick Leopold and Muriel Alice (Kiefer) Rössel; m. Charles Gordon Waugh, Nov. 11, 1967; children—Jenny-Lynn, Eric-Jon Rössel. B.A. in Humanities, SUNY-Binghamton, 1968; M.A. in Art History, Kent State U., 1979. Sewing instr. Singer Co., Augusta, Maine, 1971-72; instr. art history U. Maine, Augusta, 1977; art instr. Adult Edn., Winthrop, Maine, 1978; pvt. practice writer, artist, Winthrop, 1973—. Author: Petite Portraits, 1982; My Friend Bear, 1982; Octagon Houses of Maine, 1982; Teddy Bear Artists, 1984; (with Susanna Oroyan) Contemporary Artist Dolls, 1986; editor (with Isaac Asimov and Martin H. Greenberg) anthologies: The Twelve Crimes of Christmas, 1981, 2d edit. 1982, Japanese, Italian, Swedish edits.; Big Apple Mysteries, 1982, Japanese edit.; Show Business Is Murder, 1983, German edit.; Thirteen Horrors of Hallowe'en, 1983; Murder on the Menu, 1984; (with B. Pronzini and M.H. Greenberg) Manhattan Mysteries, 1987; (with M.H. Greenberg and Frank D. McSherry, Jr.) Murder and Mystery in Boston, 1987; (with H.H. Greenberg and Isaac Asimov) Hound Dunnit, 1987; (with M.H. Greenberg) The New Adventures of Sherlock Holmes, 1987; Murder and Mystery in Chgo., 1988, The Sport of Crime, Purr-fect Crime; co-author short story (in anthology); contbr. chpts. to books on dolls; reviewer children's books, art books, books about bears for various mags. and Sunday Sun-Jour., Lewiston-Auburn, Maine; authority on teddy bears; contbr. articles on dolls, teddy bears, antiques to mags.; lectr. in fields; sculptor original artist dolls, 1973—; designer original teddy bears produced by House of Nisbet, Avon, Eng., 1987, collector's plates for Brimark, Ltd., 1986; exhibited watercolor paintings and photography. Justice of Peace, Kennebec County, Maine, 1972-78; mem. Kennebec County Democratic Com., Augusta, 1972-80, 88. Buttonwood scholar, N.Y. Stock Exchange, 1964-68, 70-71; recipient awards for original artist dolls, awards for color photography Nat. Fedn. Press Women, 1987. Mem. Soc. Children's Book Writers, Original Doll Artist Council Am., Mystery Writers Am. Home: 5 Morrill St Winthrop ME 04364

WAUGH, SHEILA LOUISE, academic department director; b. Toronto, Ont., Can., June 21, 1938; d. George Lyman and Isobel Farrell (Griffiths) Duff; m. Douglas Oliver William Waugh, Jan. 16, 1971. BS, McGill U., 1960; MS, Dalhousie U., 1962. Lectr. U. Victoria, B.C., Can., 1963-64; sec. Parliament of Can., Ottawa, Ont., Can., 1964-66, Assn. Canadian Med. Colls., Ottawa, 1966-70; asst. mgr. Campus Bookstore, Kingston, Ont., 1973-75; head credentials sec. Royal Coll. Physicians and Surgeons Can., Ottawa, 1975—. Founding editor Assn. Can. Med. Colls. Newsletter, 1967-70; contbr. articles to profl. jours., 1965-85. Sec. Nat. Capital Arts Alliance, 1964-65; local, regional exec. New Dem. Party, 1962-70; v.p. Women's Aid, 1971-73; bd. dirs. John Howard Soc., 1971-74. Home: 183 Marlborough Ave, Ottawa Can K1N 8G3

WAX, ROSALIE HANKEY, anthropologist, educator; b. Des Plaines, Ill., Nov. 4, 1911; d. Richard B. and Anna (Orb) Hankey; m. Murray L. Wax, Mar. 5, 1949. B.A. in Anthropology, U. Calif.-Berkeley, 1942; Ph.D., U. Chgo., 1950. Acad. teaching asst. anthropology U. Chgo., 1946-47, instr. social scis., 1947-49, asst. prof., 1950-57, examiner Coll. Social Scis., 1947-55, chmn. Coll. Social Scis., 1956; dir. Workshop on Am. Indian Affairs U. Colo., 1959-69; research assoc. Ogala Sioux Ednl. Research Project Emory U., 1962-64; assoc. prof. U. Kans., 1964-69, prof., 1970-73, assoc. dir. Indian Edn. Research Project, 1966-69; prof. dept. anthropology and sociology Washington U., St. Louis, 1973-77; vis. lectr. U. Miami, 1959-62. Author: Magic, Fate and History: The Changing Ethos of the Vikings, 1969; Doing Fieldwork, Warnings and Advice, 1971. Rockefeller Found. Humanities fellow, 1981-82; grantee in field. Fellow Am. Anthrop. Assn., AAAS (councilor 1973-74), Soc. Study Social Problems; mem. Am. Ethnol. Soc., Central States Anthrop. Soc., Soc. Applied Anthropology. Office: Washington U Dept Anthropology Saint Louis MO 63130

WAY, CAROL JANE, nonprofit administrator; b. Providence, Jan. 24, 1940; d. Wilfred Bartholomew and Lillian Elizabeth (Tainsh) Martineau; m. Paul Howard Way, June 28, 1958 (div. 1986); children: Laura L. Way Jordahl, P. Craig, Victoria L. Way Hermansen, J. Brent. EdB, R.I. Coll., 1960; postgrad., U. R.I., 1960; MPA, Mankato (Minn.) State U., 1978; postgrad., Universidad Internacional, Mexico City, 1985. Cert. in secondary edn.; lic. in real estate. Tchr. pub. secondary schs. Scotia, N.Y., 1962-64, 67-68, Schenectady, N.Y., 1968-69; reporter, freelance writer The Long Islander newspaper, Huntington, N.Y., 1969-71; tchr. pub. secondary schs. Avon, Conn., 1971-72; asst. to dir. Ret. Sr. Vol. program, Hartford, Conn., 1972-73; dir. pub. info. Mankato Schs., 1974-78; tchr. pub. secondary schs. Fairfield, Conn., 1979-80; assoc. dir. YWCA of Greater Bridgeport, Conn., 1980-81; dir. alumni relations Sacred Heart U., Fairfield, 1982-84; exec. dir. Westport (Conn.) C. of C., 1986-88, West Hartford (Conn.) C. of C., 1988—; bd. dirs. Child Guidance Ctr. of Greater Bridgeport, 1986—; mem. corp. support com. Voluntary Action Ctr. of Mid-Fairfield and Norwalk, Conn., 1986—; participant English Inst. SUNY chpt. N.Y. State Tchrs. Assn., 1964. Contbr. articles to mags. and newspapers. Lt. gov. R.I. Girls' State, Providence, 1955, mem. Housewives for Rockefeller and Schenectady Reps., 1964; registered lobbyist various non-partisan groups, Minn. and Washington, 1975-78; chairwoman Blue Earth County (Minn.) Reps., 1975-78; town com. Fairfield Reps., 1980-83. Mem. Nat. Assn. Bus. Economists, Nat. Assn. Female Execs., AAUW (life, bd. dirs. 1963-81, nat. legis. com. 1976-78, 80-83), Women in the Arts (charter), Fairfield Network Exec. Women, Women in Mgmt. Episcopalian. Lodge: Rotary. Home: 48 Gate Ridge Rd Fairfield CT 06432 Office: West Hartford C of C 948 Farmington Ave West Hartford CT 06107

WAY, MATLYNN BRYANT, school counselor; b. New Bern, N.C., Dec. 30, 1957; d. Harold and Arabelle (Bulluck) Bryant; m. Leroy Way Jr., April 6, 1985. BS in Spl. Edn., East Carolina U., 1980, MEd, 1983. Cert. curriculum specialist, N.C. Tchr. of handicapped Bertle County Schs., Windsor, N.C., 1980-82; counselor New Bern-Craven Co. Schs., 1982-85, guidance supr., with dropout prevention, 1987—; job placement specialist Coastal Carolina Community Col., Jacksonville, N.C., 1985-86; chmn. Bertle County Spl. Olympics, Windsor, 1981-82. Chmn. Student Union Minority Arts Com. East Carolina, Greenville, 1979-80; big sister, Big Bros., Big Sisters of the Lower Neuse, New Bern, 1984-85, bd. dirs., 1988; mem. Onslow County Council on Women, Jacksonville, 1985-86; v.p. Craven County Com. for Children; elder, deacon Presbyn. Ch. Mem. N.C. Sch. Counselor Assn., N.C. Assn. for Counseling and Devel., N.C. Ednl. Office Personnel, N.C. Dropout Prevention Assn., Assn. for Supervision and Curriculum Devel., N.C. Assn. Educators, Tri-County Counselors Assn. (sec. treas. 1984-85), Nat. Assn. Female Execs., Gamma Beta Phi, Kappa Delta Pi, Alpha Kappa Alpha (membership chmn. 1979-80, corr. sec., 1986—). Democrat. Home: PO Box 2241 New Bern NC 28560 Office: New Bern-Craven Co Schs 3600 Trent Rd New Bern NC 28560

WAYLOR, CHERYL WATSON, insurance services company owner, consultant; b. Montreal, Que., Can., Sept. 8, 1943; came to U.S., 1954; d. Alan Douglas and Jean Mary (Hughes) Watson; m. Joseph Robert Earl Waylor, Apr. 5, 1969 (div. Feb. 1979). B.B.A., Ga. State U., 1980, postgrad. Supr. div. Liberty Mut., Atlanta, 1969-76; instr. ins. DeKalb Community Coll., Clarkston, Ga., 1978-79; mgr. div. Kemper Group, 1979-85; cons. Waylor & Assocs., Overland Park, 1986—; owner, pres. h.m.s. Co., Ins. Services, Overland Park, 1986—; lectr. in field; ins. cons. Fortune and Co. Risk Mgrs. Inc. Contbr. articles to profl. jours. Vol. Boy Scouts Am., Girl Scouts U.S., Leukemia Soc. Am., 1987. Polit. speaker coordinator Kemper Group, Overland Park, 1982, 85, Ins. Women Greater Kansas City, 1986; vol. explorer Boy Scouts Am., 1987; vol. Girl Scouts U.S.A. Leadership Devel., 1987—. Mem. Ins. Women of Greater Kansas City-Nat. Assn. Ins. Women (bd. dirs. 1985-86, v.p. 1987-88, pres.-elect 1988—, Rookie of Yr. 1985, Best Speaker in Communicate with Confidence Speakoff, Kansas City, State Mo. 1987), Nat. Assn. Women Bus. Owners. Republican. Club: Toastmasters Internat. (area 7 gov. 1986-87, adminstrv. v.p. 1986, v.p. edn. 1987, pres. 1988, div. O., best evaluator 1985). Avocations: sky diving, fencing, running, reading, travel. Office: 6901 W 63d St Suite 121 Shawnee Mission KS 66202

WAYMIRE, ROBERTA ARLENE, construction company executive; b. Wimbledon, N.D., June 20, 1936; d. Gaylord and Huldah Evelyn (Ekstrand) Thorne; student Brigham Young U., 1953-54; m. Kenneth L. Waymire, Feb. 26, 1955; children—Thorne L., Kent L. Reporter, Democrat Herald, Albany, Oreg., 1955-56; with Waverly Constrn. Co., Inc., Tigard, Oreg., 1964—, v.p., 1982—. Mem. Portland Metro Homebuilders Assn. Republican. Home and Office: 8735 SW Curry Dr #B Wilsonville OR 97070

WAYNE, KYRA PETROVSKAYA, author; b. Crimea, USSR, Dec. 31, 1918; came to U.S., 1948, naturalized, 1951; d. Prince Vasily Sergeyevich and Baroness Zinaida Fedorovna (Fon-Haffenberg) Obolensky; m. George J. Wayne, Apr. 21, 1961; 1 child, Ronald George. B.A., Leningrad Inst. Theatre Arts, 1939, M.A., 1940. Actress, concert singer, USSR, 1939-46; actress, U.S., 1948-51; enrichment lectr. Royal Viking Line cruises, Alaska-Can., Greek Islands-Black Sea, Russia/Europe, 1978-79, 81-82, 83-84, 86-87. Author: Kyra, 1959; Kyra's Secrets of Russian Cooking, 1960; The Quest for the Golden Fleece, 1962; Shurik, 1971; The Awakening, 1972; The Witches of Barguzin, 1975; Max, The Dog That Refused to Die, 1979 (Best Fiction award Dog Writers Assn. Am. 1980); Rekindle the Dreams, 1979, Quest for Empire, 1986. Founder, pres. Clean Air Program, Los Angeles County, 1971-72; mem. women's council KCET-Ednl. TV. Served to lt. Russian Army, 1941-43. Decorated Red Star, numerous other decorations USSR; recipient award Crusade for Freedom, 1955-56; award Los Angeles County, 1972. Mem. Soc. Children's Book Writers, Authors Guild, P.E.N., UCLA Med. Faculty Wives (pres. 1970-71, dir. 1971-75) UCLA Affiliates (life), Los Angeles Lung Assn. (life), Friends of the Lung Assn. (pres. 1988), Idyllwild Sch. Music, Art and Theatre Assn. (trustee 1987). Home: 234 S Rimpau Blvd Los Angeles CA 90004

WAYNE, LARISA ALEXANDER, civil engineer; b. Moscow, May 30, 1955; came to U.S., 1979; d. Alexander Haim and Rachel (Rizhik) Vainshtub. ŽCE, Moscow Civil Engring. Sch., 1977; postgrad., Parsons Sch. Interior Design, 1982-83. Civil engr. N.Y.C. Dept. Environ. Protection, 1980-84; civil engr., insp. constrn. N.Y.C. Dept. Parks, 1984—. Vol. Jewish Nat. Fund, 1985, Jewish Mus., 1986. Home: 141 E 89th St Apt 4C New York NY 10128

WAYNER, DONNA SHPIKULA, audiologist, educator, consultant; b. Chgo., Mar. 22, 1940; d. Taras and Mary (Bass) Shpikula; m. Peter C. Wayner Jr., Jan. 26, 1963; children: Peter Charles III, Taras Jon, Elizabeth Michele. BA, Clarke Coll., 1961; MA, Northwestern U., 1962; PhD, Rensselaer Poly. Inst., 1979. Audiology intern VA Hosp., Chgo., 1962-63; rehab. audiologist Hartford (Conn.) Hearing League, 1963-64; clin. audiologist Albany (N.Y.) Med. Ctr. Hosp., 1972-76; asst. prof. surgery Albany Med. Coll., 1981-88; coordinator, audiologist Hearing Rehab. Ctr. at Albany Med. Ctr., 1981-87, dir., 1987—; assoc. prof. surgery Albany Med. Coll., 1988—; adj. prof. Coll. of St. Rose, Albany, 1979—; founder, profl. advisor

Hearing Endeavor for Albany Region, 1983—. Author: Journey Through Our Town, 1984. Leader Latham (N.Y.) troop Girl Scouts of U.S., 1977-86. Mem. Am. Speech, Lang. and Hearing Assn. (cert.), Am. Acad. Otolaryngology, Acad. Rehabilitative Audiology, N.Y. State Speech and Hearing Assn. Roman Catholic. Office: Albany Med Ctr Hearing Rehab Ctr New Scotland Ave Albany NY 12208

WEARING, MARY ANN SHIRLEY, banker; b. Hartford, Conn., Dec. 8, 1949; d. Philippe Eugene and Irene Yolande (Beaulieu) Boutin; m. John P. Quinn, Sept. 28, 1968 (div. Oct. 1978); children: Shaun Philippe Quinn, Amanda Irene Quinn, Sara Helen Quinn; m. Michael D. Wearing, Dec. 22, 1979. Student in bus., N.H. Tech. Inst., 1981—; cert. in mgmt., Ctr. Fin. Studies, Fairfield, Conn., 1986; cert. in banking, N.H. Sch. Savs. Banks, 1987. Office mgr. Montgomery Ward, Portsmouth, N.H., 1977-79; paralegal Rinden Profl. Assn., Concord, N.H., 1979-81; with Concord Savs. Bank, 1981—, with loan originations dept., 1982-84, mgr. mortgage servicing, 1984-85, officer loan servicing, 1985—; voice trainer, Lyndonville, Vt., 1974-77; cons., Concord, 1987—. Dir. music Burke Mountain Theater, 1976; v.p. St. Johnsbury Players, 1977. Mem. Nat. Assn. Banking Women, Am. Inst. Banking (mem. edn. com. 1985—), Am. Mortage Assn. (mem. servicing com. 1988—), Nat. Assn. Female Execs. Roman Catholic. Club: Pittsfield (N.H.) Players. Home: Parade Rd Barnstead NH 03218 Office: Concord Savs Bank 45 N Main St Concord NH 03301

WEATHERBEE, LINDA, insurance executive; b. Decatur, Ill., July 20, 1956; d. Carl and V. Lucile (Westwood) W. BA, James Millikin U., 1977; postgrad., Ill. State U., 1981-82. CLU; chartered fin. cons.; FLMI. Fin. analyst State Farm Life Ins., Bloomington, Ill., 1979-82; supr. State Farm Life Ins., Austin, Tex., 1982-86; asst. supt. State Farm Life Ins., Salem, Oreg., 1986—. Rep. vol., Bloomington, 1982; tutor adult edn. program Chemeketa Community Coll., Salem, 1986, 87; tchr. high sch. religion course, Salem, 1987—. Mem. Adminstrv. Mgmt. Soc., Life Office mgmt. Assn., Williamette Soc. CLU and ChFC (bd. dirs. 1987—), Am. Horse Show Assn. Mormon. Club: N.W. Horse Council (Oreg.). Office: State Farm Ins 4600 25th Ave NE Salem OR 97313

WEATHERFORD, DORIS LINDA, political consultant, author; b. Jasper, Minn., Sept. 20, 1943; d. Harry D. and Leona M. (Schultz) Barge; m. Roy Carter Weatherford, Feb. 8, 1966; 1 child, Margaret Marie. BA, Arkansas Tech. Coll., 1965; postgrad., Brandeis U., 1965-66, Harvard U., 1969. Researcher U.S. News and World Report mag., Washington, 1966-68; tchr. Bridgewater (Mass.)-Raynham Regional High Sch., 1968-72; free-lance polit. cons. Tampa, Fla., 1976—; state campaign mgr. Clean-Up '84 Petition Drive, Tampa, Castor for Commr. of Ed., Tampa, 1986; field mgr. Kennedy for Pres., Tampa, 1980, Sheldon for Cong., 1982. Author: Foreign and Female, 1986. Active Dem. Com., Tampa, 1974—, local PTA; sec. Hillsborough County Commn. on Status of Women, Tampa, 1977-79; treas. Fla. Consumer Action Network, Orlando, 1983-85; pres. Women's Polit. Caucus, Tampa, 1980-82. Recipient Outstanding Personal Contribution award Hillsborough County Commrs., 1983; named Poet Laureate of Ybor City Ybor City C. of C., 1987. Mem. Authors Guild/Authors League. Democrat. Club: Women's of Tampa. Home and Office: 5425 County Rd 579 Seffner FL 33584

WEATHERSPOON, J. VANESSA, real estate investor; b. Prairie View, Tex., Dec. 15, 1957; d. Lindsey and Josie (Barnes) W. BA in Math., Spelman Coll., 1980; BS in Indsl. Engring. Tech., Marietta, Ga., 1982. Asst. prodn. supr. Kraft Foods, Decatur, Ga., 1982-84; quality control mgr. Advo Systems, Inc., Atlanta, 1984-85; agy. ops. mgr. Equitable Fin. Services Co., Omaha, 1985-88; pres., owner VaNes Enterprises Inc., College Park, Ga., 1988—; administr. agy. ops. Equitable Fin. Cos. Mem. Nat. Council Negro Women, Bus. and Profl. Women, Inst. Indsl. Engrs., Alpha Kappa Alpha. Office: VaNes Enterprises Inc 1745 Phoenix Blvd Suite 160 College Park GA 30349

WEATHERUP, WENDY GAINES, insurance agent, writer; b. Glendale, Calif., Oct. 20, 1952; d. William Hughes and Janet Ruth (Neptune) Gaines; m. Roy Garfield Weatherup, Sept. 10, 1977; children—Jennifer, Christine. B.A., U. So. Calif., 1974; Lic. ins. agt. Ins. agt. Gaines Agy., Northridge, Calif., 1974—. Mem. Nat. Assn. Female Execs., U. So. Calif. Alumni Assn., Alpha Gamma Delta. Republican. Methodist. Avocations: photography; travel; writing novels; computers. Home: 17260 Rayen St Northridge CA 91325 Office: Gaines Agy 8448 Reseda Blvd Northridge CA 91324

WEAVER, BARBARA FRANCES, librarian; b. Boston, Aug. 29, 1927; d. Leo Francis and Nina Margaret (Durham) Weisse; m. George B. Weaver, June 6, 1951; 1 dau., Valerie S. Clark. B.A., Radcliffe Coll., 1949; M.L.S., U. R.I., 1968; Ed.M., Boston U., 1978. Head librarian Thompson (Conn.) Public Library, 1961-69; dir. Conn. State Library Service Center, Willimantic, 1969-72; regional adminstr. Central Mass. Regional Library System, Worcester, 1972-78; asst. commr. of edn., state librarian N.J., Trenton, 1978—; pres. Val-A, Inc., Thompson, Conn., from 1980; lectr. Simmons Coll., Boston, 1976-78. Mem. ALA, N.J. Library Assn., Chief Officers State Library Agys. Office: NJ State Library Dept of Edn 185 W State St Trenton NJ 08625-0520

WEAVER, CYNTHIA GAIL, lawyer; b. Radford, Va., Apr. 10, 1958; d. Walter Scott and Ruth E. (Conner) W. A.B. with honors, Coll. William and Mary, 1980; J.D., Mercer U., 1983. Bar: Ga. 1983, Va. 83, U.S. Tax Ct. 1983, U.S. Supreme Ct. 1987. Assoc., Heard Leverett & Phelps, P.C., Elberton, Ga., 1983—. Named one of Outstanding Young Women of Am., 1987. Mem. Ga. Women's Lawyers Assn., Nat. Assn. Female Execs., Va. Bar Assn., Ga. Bar Assn., Ga. Trial Lawyers Assn., Elberton Bar Assn. (sect. treas. 1986-87, v.p. 1987-88), Assn. Trial Lawyers Am., ABA, Phi Delta Phi. Democrat. Methodist. Club: Elberton Country. Avocations: numismatics; tennis; golf; skiing; softball. Home: 750 Fleming Rd C-1 Elberton GA 30635 Office: Heard Leverett & Phelps 25 Thomas St Elberton GA 30635-0399

WEAVER, DAWN LERENE, printing company executive; b. Lancaster, Pa., May 22, 1948; d. James Fisher and Sarah Helen (Hanna) W.; m. June 28, 1970 (div. 1980); children: James Russell, Jennifer Adele. Student, St. Petersburg Jr. Coll., 1966-67, Millersville (Pa.) U., 1967-68. Prin. Dawn's House of Ceramics, Bird-in-Hand, Pa., 1969-79; paste-up artist Lancaster Newspapers, 1970-73; art dir. Wickersham Printing, Lancaster, 1974-75; customer service account mgr. Intelligencer Printing Co., Lancaster, 1975-81; salesperson Veitch Printing Corp., Lancaster, 1981-84, dist. mgr., 1984—. Mem. Nat. Assn. Female Execs. Republican. Lutheran. Home: 4 N School Ln Lancaster PA 17603 Office: Veitch Printing Corp 1740 Hempstead Rd Lancaster PA 17601

WEAVER, DONNA RAE, college administrator; b. Chgo., Oct. 15, 1945; d. Albert Louis and Gloria Elaine (Graffis) Florence; m. Clifford L. Weaver, Aug. 20, 1966; 1 child, Megan Rae. BS in Edn., No. Ill. U., 1966, EdD, 1977; MEd, De Paul U., 1974. Tchr. Richards High Sch., Oak Lawn, Ill., 1966-71, Sawyer Coll. Bus., Evanston, Ill., 1971-72; asst.prof. Oakton Community Coll., Morton Grove, Ill., 1972-75; vis. prof. U. Ill. at Chgo., 1977-78; dean Mallinckrodt Coll., Wilmette, Ill., 1978-83; assoc. v.p. campus dir. Nat. Coll. Edn., Chgo., 1983—; cons. Nancy Lovely and Assocs., Wilmette, 1981-84, N. Cen. Assn., Chgo., 1982—;bd. dirs. El Valor Corp., 1985-87. Contbr. articles to Am. Vocat. Jour., Ill. Bus. Edn. Assn. Monograph, Nat. Coll. Edn.'s ABS Rev. Mem. New Trier Twp. Health and Human Services Adv. Bd., Ill., 1985—; bd. dirs. Open Lands Project, 1985-87, Kenilworth Village House, 1986-87. Recipient Achievement award for Outstanding Performance in Edn., Women in Mgmt., 1981; Am. Bd. Master Educators charter disting. fellow. Office: Nat Coll Edn 18 S Michigan Ave Chicago IL 60603

WEAVER, ELIZABETH, financial service marketing executive; b. N.Y.C., Apr. 29, 1958; d. Leonard Joseph and Marie (Kelly) W.; m. Charles Theodore Sporing, Nov. 14, 1982. BA, Marist Coll., 1980; MBA, Adelphi U., 1986. Asst. mktg. Shearson Loeb Rhoades, N.Y.C., 1980-81; asst. v.p. mktg. E. F. Hutton, Garden City, N.Y., 1981—. Mem. Newcomer's Assn., Rockville Ctr., N.Y., 1982. Mem. Nat. Assn. Female Execs. Republican. Roman Catholic. Avocations: cross-country skiing, all-terrain vehicle riding. Office: E F Hutton 1225 Franklin Ave Garden City NY 11530

WEAVER, GLENDA ROSE, nurse; b. Liberty, Tex., Jan. 2, 1944; d. Glenn Wood and Esther Augusta (Becker) W.; student Lamar U., 1961-62; diploma Hotel Dieu Sch. Nursing, 1963; B.S., St. Joseph's Coll., North Windham, Maine, 1986. Cert. nurse adminstr. Supr. Kersting Meml. Hosp., Liberty, Tex., 1963-65; sch. nurse Liberty Ind. Sch. Dist., 1965-71; dir. nursing service Chambers Meml. Hosp., Anahuac, Tex., 1971-76; asst. dir. nursing service North Shore Med. Plaza, Houston, 1976-78; dir. nursing service Kelsey-Seybold Clinic, Houston, 1978-82; nurse specialist-adminstrn. Baylor U. Coll. Medicine, Houston, 1982—. Mem. Tex. Hosp. Assn.-Nursing Service Adminstrs., ARC (past county first aid chmn. and disaster nurse chmn.). Methodist. Home: 2501 Westridge #49 Houston TX 77054 Office: 1200 Moursund Suite 191A Houston TX 77030

WEAVER, KAREN, educator; b. Chestnut Hill, Pa., May 25, 1958; d. Robert Everett and Joanne (Mateer) W. BS, Lock Haven U., 1980; MS, Purdue U., 1983. Instr. phys. edn., head coach field hockey and Lacrosse Salisbury (Md.) State Coll., 1982-87; head field hockey coach Ohio State U., 1987—; dir. Karen Weaver's Field Hockey Camp, Salisbury 1987—; cons. goalkeeping various high schs. and colls. 1978—. Contbr. articles to profl. jours. Named Coach Yr., USA Today Newspapers, 1986. Mem. Coll. Field Hockey Coaches Assn. (pres. 1986—, chmn. ethics com. 1985-87), U.S. Field Hockey Assn. (chmn. indoor hockey com. 1984—), Nat. Collegiate Athletic Assn. (selection com. 1984—). Democrat. Presbyterian. Home: 710 Ferndale Rd Salisbury MD 21801 Office: Salisbury State Coll Athletic Dept Salisbury MD 21801

WEAVER, MARGUERITE (PEGGY) MCKINNIE, plantation owner; b. Jackson, Tenn., June 7, 1925; d. Franklin Allen and Mary Alice (Caradine) McKinnie; children: Lynn Weaver Hermann, Thomas Jackson Weaver III, Franklin A. McKinnie Weaver. Student, U. Colo., 1943-45, Am. Acad. Dramatic Arts, 1945-46, S. Meisner's Profl. Classes, 1949. Actress theatrical cos., Can., New Eng., N.Y.C., 1946-52; mem. staff Mus. Modern Art, N.Y.C., 1949-50; editor radio/TV Sta. WTJS-AM-FM, Jackson Sun Newspaper, 1952-55; columnist Bolivar (Tenn.) Bulletin-Times; owner Heritage Hall Plantation, Hickory Valley, Tenn. Chmn. Ho. of Reps. of Old Line Dist. Hardeman Countyy, Tenn., 1985—; founder, hon. bd. dirs. Paris-Henry County (Tenn.) Arts Council, 1965—; charter mem. adv. bd. Tenn. Arts Commn., Nashville, 1967-74, Tenn. Performing Arts Ctr., Nashville, 1972—; chmn. Tenn. Library Assn., Nashville, 1973-74; regional chmn. Opera Memphis, 1979—; patron Met. Opera Nat. Council, N.Y.C., 1980—. Mem. Am. Women in Radio and TV, Internat. Platform Assn., DAR. Methodist. Clubs: Jackson Golf and Country, English Speaking Union, Summit (Memphis). Avocations: horseback riding, travel, theatre, visiting art museums, golf. Home: Heritage Hall Heritage Farms Hickory Valley TN 38042

WEAVER, MARILYN ROSADO, financial executive; b. Camden, N.J., Sept. 30, 1944; d. Joaquin Victor Rosado and Isabel (E'del) Kelley; m. John L. Weaver, June 20, 1964; children: John, Cindy, Sherry. AS in Acctg., St. Joseph's U., 1985. Staff acct. Campbell Chevrolet, Runnemede, N.J., 1961-62; supr. banking dept. RCA Service Co., Cherry Hill, N.J., 1963-65; pres., cons. J&L Acctg. Services, Cherry Hill, 1966-77; from staff acct. to v.p. fin. Learn Inc., Mt. Laurel, N.J., 1978-86; pres., cons. J&L Computer Services, Cherry Hill, 1986—; cons. J&L Computer Services, Cherry Hill, 1983-87. Mem. Nat. Assn. Accts. (v.p. edn., devel. dir.), Nat. Assn. Female Execs., Controllers Council.

WEAVER, MOLLIE LITTLE, lawyer; b. Alma, Ga., Mar. 11; d. Alfred Ross and Annis Mae (Bowles) Little; m. Jack Delano Nelson, Sept. 12, 1953 (div. May 1970); 1 dau., Cynthia Ann; m. 2d, Hobart Ayres Weaver, June 10, 1970. B.A. in History, U. Richmond, 1978; J.D., Wake Forest U., 1981. Bar; N.C. 1982, Fla. 1983; Cert. profl. sec.; cert. adminstrv. mgr. Supr., Western Electric Co., Richmond, Va., 1952-75; cons., owner Cert. Mgmt. Assocs., Richmond, 1975-76; sole practice, Ft. Lauderdale, Fla., 1982-86, Emerald Isle, N.C., 1986—. Author: Secretary's Reference Manual, 1973. Mem. adv. council to Bus. and Office Edn., Greensboro, N.C., 1970-73, adv. com. to bus. edn. Va. Commonwealth U., Richmond, 1977. Recipient Key to City of Winston-Salem, N.C., 1963; Epps award for scholarship, 1978. Mem. ABA, N.C. Bar Assn., Fla. Bar Assn., Carteret County Bar Assn., Word Processing Assn. (v.p., founder Richmond 1973-75), Adminstrv. Mgmt. Soc. (com. chmn. Richmond, 1973-75), Phi Beta Kappa, Eta Sigma Phi, Phi Alpha Theta. Republican. Home: 807 Ocean Dr Emerald Isle NC 28557

WEAVER, PAMELA SUE, insurance company supervisor; b. Sylvania, Ohio, June 9, 1962; d. Frank D. and L. Kay (Truesdell) W.; m. Edward L. Groskopf, Dec. 19, 1981 (div. 1984). Student pub. schs., Phoenix. Lic. property and casualty ins. agt., Ariz. Sr. rater, coder St. Paul Ins., Phoenix, 1980-83; asst. underwriter CIGNA Ins. Co., Phoenix, 1983; supr. comml. lines Eagle Star Ins. Co., Scottsdale, Ariz., 1984-86; asst. underwriter comml. lines dept. Nautilus Ins. Co., Scottsdale, 1986-87; underwriter comml. lines dept. Nautilus Ins. Co., 1987—. Home: PO Box 31307 Phoenix AZ 85046

WEAVER, PATTI ANN, bank examiner; b. Port Hueneme, Calif., Sept. 3, 1956; d. Henry Elbert and Ruth Elizabeth (Davidson) W.: m. Terry Lee Quanstrom, Feb. 22, 1988. BBA in Mktg., Cen. State U., 1978. Clk., typist govt. grade-2 FAA, Oklahoma City, 1978-79; bank examiner trainee govt. grade-5 FDIC, Austin, Tex., 1979-84; bank examiner govt. grade-12 FDIC, Tulsa, 1984-87; bank examiner govt. grade-14 FDIC, Dallas, 1987—; instr. div. bank supervision FDIC, Washington, 1985-87, coordinator personal computers, Dallas, 1986-87. Mem. Nat. Assn. Female Execs. Democrat. Baptist. Lodge: Order Eastern Star (assoc. matron 1979).

WEAVER, SIGOURNEY (SUSAN WEAVER), actress; b. N.Y.C., 1949; d. Sylvester (Pat) Weaver and Elizabeth Inglish; m. James Simpson, 1984. B.A., Stanford U.; M. in Drama, Yale U. First profl. theater appearance in The Constant Wife, 1974; other roles in Beyond Therapy, Hurlyburly, 1984, The Merchant of Venice, 1987; films include: Alien, 1979, Eyewitness, 1981, Deal of the Century, 1983, The Year of Living Dangerously, 1983, Ghostbusters, 1984, Aliens, 1986, Half Moon Street, 1986, One Woman or Two, 1987. Office: Internat Creative Mgmt care Sam Cohn 40 W 57th St New York NY 10012 *

WEAVER, STACEY ELIZABETH, airline executive; b. Pitts., Mar. 30, 1947; d. Charles W. and Charlotte E. (Williams) Vollmer; m. John W. Beck, Jan. 1, 1981. BA, Mt. Holyoke Coll., 1969; MS, U. Pa., 1970; MBA, So. Meth. U., 1982. Engr. Westinghouse Elec. Corp., Pitts., 1971-73, Combustion Engring, Inc., Windsor, Conn., 1973-75; energy cons. Reddy Communications, Inc., Greenwich, Conn., 1975-77; dir. communications Vermont Nuclear Power Corp., Rutland, Vt., 1977-80; mgr. pub. info. Tex. Mcpl. Power Agy., Arlington, 1980-82; sr. fin. analyst AMR Corp./ Am. Airlines, Ft. Worth, 1982-84, mgr. AAdvantage program, 1984-85, dir. investor relations, 1985—. Author: Nuclear Energy Debate Book, 1977. Campaign worker Hutchison for Congress, Dallas, 1982; pres. Nuclear Energy Women, Washington, 1975-77. Fellow Nat. Sci. Found. U. Pa., 1969, Dresser Found. So. Meth. U., 1982; named Top Investor Relation Professional, 1987. Mem. Am. Inst. Wine and Food (treas. 1985—), Sigma Xi. Office: AMR Corp MD 2D58 Dallas-Fort Worth Airport PO Box 619616 Dallas TX 75261-9616

WEAVER, VIRGINIA DOVE, museum executive; b. Westerly, R.I.; d. Ronald Cross and Elva Gertrude (Burdick) Dove; m. Water Albert Weaver, Jr. (div. Apr. 1982); children—Marshall Gueringer, Claudia Cross, Leila Jane. B.A., Tulane U., 1973; M.A., 1977. Dir. volunteers Hermann Grima Historic House, New Orleans, 1976-77; adminstrv. analyst City Chief Adminstrv. Office, New Orleans, 1977-83; dir. public relations New Orleans Mus. Art, 1983—. Coeditor: Letters From Young Audiences, 1971; contbr. articles to profl. jours. Bd. dirs. New Orleans chpt. Young Audiences, Inc., 1968-77; co-chmn. New Orleans Symphony Book Fair, 1973-74; mem. city council investigative panel SPCA, New Orleans, 1981-82; nat. public relations chmn. Nat. Soc. Daughters of Founders and Patriots Am., 1985—. Nat. Council Jewish Women grantee, 1977. Mem. Pub. Relations Soc. Am. (So. Classics anvil award 1985, 87, So. Classics award Excellence 1986), La. Press Assn. (assoc.), La. Travel and Promotion Assn., Deep South Hotel/Motel Assn., La. Restaurant Assn. Episcopalian. Bd. dirs. Symphony Womens Com., 1982-86; mem. steering com. Mayors Arts Task Force, New Orleans, 1978-79. Clubs: Orleans (fine arts com., spring lecture series 1988—); Le Petit Salon (chmn. publicity for 150th anniversary 1988). Avocation: Piano. Home: 7478 Hurst St New Orleans LA 70118 Office: New Orleans Mus Art PO Box 19123 New Orleans LA 70179

WEBB, ALANA DAVIS, dietitian, consultant; b. Rosenberg, Tex., Nov. 25, 1956; d. Andrew J. and Jorene (Tarver) Davis; m. Michael A. Webb, Apr. 11, 1982. BS, Tex. Women's U., 1978. Lic. dietitian, Tex. Clin. dietitian Seton Med. Ctr., Austin, Tex., 1979-84; pres., chairperson bd. dirs. Austin Nutrition Cons., Inc., 1984—; chief of nutrition Tex. Youth Commn., Austin, 1985—; staff dietitian Austin Eating Disorders Clinic, 1984—; cons. Tex. Sch. for Deaf, Austin, 1985—, Tex. Instruments, Austin, 1985—, W/C Health Maintenance Program, Austin, 1984—. Mem. com. to combat nutrition misinfo., 1985-86, Dial a Dietitian com., 1985—, chairperson bylaws com., 1980-82, 1986—, pub. affairs com., 1980-81; mem. Austin Area Cystic Fibrosis Found., 1980—, parent edn. taskforce Am. Heart Assn., 1981-83; mem. Tex. State Bd. Examiners of Dietitians, 1988. Jewel Taylor Family Trustfund scholar, Tex. Women's U., 1978. Mem. Am. Dietetic Assn. (Young Dietitian of Yr. 1986), Tex. Dietetic Assn. (bd. dirs. 1985-86, chairperson div. nutrition consultation and pvt. practice), Austin Dietetic Assn. (pres. 1985-86), Gov.'s Interagy. Council Nutrition and Fitness, Alpha Chi, Phi Upsilon Omicron. Home: 414 Yucca Round Rock TX 78681 Office: Cent Tex Nutrition Cons 4107 Medical Pkwy Suite 214 Austin TX 78756

WEBB, ALICE ELIZABETH SAVAY, therapist; b. Laredo, Tex.; d. Albert Charles and Elizabeth Mary (Barnett) Savay; m. Edwin O. Webb (div. 1974); children: Kelly O., Alysha. BA, Tex. Tech. U., 1970; MSW, Our Lady of the Lake U. of San Antonio, 1975; postgrad., The Inst. for Advanced Study of Human Sexuality, 1980-83. Med. social worker med. br. U. Tex., Galveston, 1976-78, coordinator, psychotherapist The Gender Clinic, 1978-80, renal social worker, 1981-83; pvt. practice sex therapy San Francisco, 1980-81; psychotherapist Family Service Ctr. of Galveston County, 1983-86; pvt. practice sex therapy, psychotherapy Galveston, 1986—; cons. sex therapy The Women's Internat. Treatment Ctr., Deer Park (Tex.) Hosp., 1986—. Contbr. articles to Archives of Sexual Behavior. Campaign office coordinator Ben Barnes for Gov., Brownwood, Tex., 1972; campaign organizer Barefood Sanders for U.S. Senate, Cen. Tex., 1972; chair fund drive Am. Heart Assn., Brown County, Tex., 1973. Mem. Am. Assn. Sex Educators, Counselors and Therapists (life), Nat. Assn. Social Workers, Assn. of Sexologists, Harry Benjamin Internat. Gender Dysphoria Assn., Inc.(charter). Democrat. Office: 1917 Broadway Suite 2 Galveston TX 77550

WEBB, BETTY JO, school administrator; b. Plain Dealing, La., Apr. 6, 1945; d. Joe and Georgia V. (Little) W; 1 child, Arthur Ray. B.A. in Sociology, U. Minn., 1967, M.A. in Edn. Adminstrn., 1973, postgrad. 1979—. Social worker Pillsbury Services, Mpls., 1967-68, Hennepin County, Minn., 1968-69; social worker Mpls. Pub. Schs., 1969-72, asst. prin., 1972-81, prin., 1981—; compliance specialist Mpls. Schs., 1976-78. Bd. dirs. Domestic Abuse Project, Mpls., 1985, St. Mary's Grad. Ctr., Katahdin Youth Ctr.; active Bus. Econ. Edn. Found., St. Paul; choir dir. Wayman Ch., Mpls. Mem. Nat. Assn. Secondary Sch. Prins., Minn. Assn. Secondary Sch. Prins., Nat. Alliance Black Sch. Educators, Mpls. Prins. Forum, Internat. Platform Assn., Phi Delta Kappa. Baptist. Avocations: golf; fishing; tennis; piano; singing. Home: 3668 Brookdale Dr Minneapolis MN 55443 Office: Mpls Pub Schs Franklin Jr High 1501 Aldrich Ave Minneapolis MN 55411

WEBB, KATHARINE, counselor; b. Bklyn., Sept. 13, 1931; d. Joseph Norris and Thelma (Black) Norris Sharpton; m. John James Webb, May 25, 1956 (div. Aug. 1971); children—John, Tyra, Lori. B.S. in Home Econs., Hunter Coll., 1954, M.S. in Home Econs., 1957; M.S. in Guidance and Counseling, Western Mich. U., 1969; Ph.D. in Guidance and Psychol. Services, Ind. State U., 1972. Tchr. home econs. N.Y.C. Bd. Edn., Bklyn., 1954-65, counselor, 1965-68; counselor Ind. State U., Terre Haute, 1970-72; assoc. prof. counselor edn. SUNY-Brockport, 1972-79; mem. N.Y. State Commn. of Correction, Albany, 1979-85; dir. guidance and counseling N.Y. State Dept. Correctional Services, 1985—; mediator, arbitrator Community Dispute Ctr., Rochester, N.Y., 1973-79; mediator, fact-finder N.Y. State Pub. Employees Relations Bd., Albany, 1975-79. Pres. bd. dirs. Brockport Childcare Ctr. (N.Y.), 1973-74, Nat. Migrant Found., Inc., Albany, 1983-84; bd. dirs. YWCA of Rochester (N.Y.), 1975-77. Recipient cert. recognition YWCA of Rochester, 1975, cert. disting. service Urban League Rochester, 1976, award for disting. spl. programs SUNY Office Spl. Programs, Albany, 1978, award for support and contbns. Rochester Ednl. Opportunity Ctr., 1978, award for service Mental Health Assn. Rochester, 1979, Disting. Alumni award Ind. State U., 1986. Mem. Am. Correctional Assn., N.Y. State Personnel and Guidance Assn. (v.p. for profl. services 1979-80), Am. Assn. Counseling and Devel., Pub. Offender Counselor Assn., Assn. for Non-White Concerns, 100 Black Women, Delta Kappa Gamma Soc., Delta Sigma Theta. Democrat. Roman Catholic.

WEBB, LAURA LEE, design and development company executive; b. Columbus, Ohio, Feb. 23, 1953; d. Richard L. and Ferrel L. (McCray) Zeimer; divorced; children: Edward M., Daniel L. Grad. high sch. Sr. v.p., gen. mgr. Indsl. Computer Designs, Inc., Westlake Villa, Calif., 1979—. Office: Indsl Computer Designs Inc 31264 Labaya Dr Westlake Villa CA 91362

WEBB, MARY LOUISE, dollhouse and miniatures shop owner; b. Richmond, Va., June 8, 1947; d. Arthur and Joyce Ray (Allard) Mandella; m. Richard F. Lobasso, Dec. 31, 1974 (div. 1981); m. Keith William Webb, Jan. 3, 1985, 1 child, Darryll. Grad. high sch., Richmond. Model tchr. House of Albert, West Palm Beach, Fla., 1972-74; owner AAA Employment, Melbourne, Titus, Fla., 1974-85, AAA Temp, Melbourne, Merritt Island, Titusville, Fla., 1974-85; owner, pres. All Through the House, Melbourne, Fla., 1986—; pres. AAA Temp Inc., St. Petersburg, Fla., 1980-83. Office: All Through the House 720 E New Haven Ave Suite 11 Melbourne FL 32901

WEBB, SHARON LYNN, writer; b. Tampa, Fla., Feb. 29, 1936; d. William Wesley Talbott and Eunice Geraldine Tillman; m. W. Bryan Webb, Feb. 6, 1956; children—Wendy, Jerri, Tracey. Student Fla. So. Coll., 1953-56, U. Miami, 1962; ADN, Miami-Dade Sch. Nursing, 1972. Freelance writer, 1960-66; registered nurse South Miami Hosp., 1972-73, Union Gen. Hosp., Towns County Hosp., Blairsville, Ga., 1973-81. Author: RN, 1981, Earthchild, 1982, Earth Song, 1983, Ram Song, 1984, Adventures of Terra Tarkington, 1985, Pestis 18, 1987; over 40 short stories. Mem. Author's Guild/League, Sci. Fiction Writers Am. (south/central dir., bd. dirs.).

WEBBER, MARGARET BROWN, civic worker; b. McIntosh, Fla., Dec. 24, 1913; d. William Randolph and Roberta (Farra) Brown; m. William Beverly Webber, Oct. 24, 1938; children—William Beverly, Robert Franklin, Betsey Farra, Bruce Randolph. Student Converse Coll., 1930-32; B.A., Coll. William and Mary, 1934. Co-founder Multnomah Play Sch., Portland, Oreg., 1948; mem. Washington County Juvenile Adv. Com., Tri-County Community Council, Portland; bd. dirs. YWCA, Portland, 1964-79, mem. world service council, 1977—; bd. dirs. Tigard Community Youth Services, Codero House; mem. long-range planning com. Tigard Sch. Dist.; mem. budget and eval. coms. United Way, Columbia-Willamette, Portland, 1971-83; mem. Jud. Fitness Commn.; bd. dirs. Portland Youth Philharmonic; bd. assocs. Linfield Coll., McKinnville, Oreg. Recipient Lay Educator of Yr. award Tigard (Oreg.) Sch. Dist., 1969; Excellence in Action award Delta Kappa Gamma, Beaverton, Oreg., 1980. Democrat. Methodist.

WEBBER, MARGARET ELISABETH ROSE, health care facility administrator; b. Tokyo, Nov. 17, 1935; came to U.S., 1940; d. Lawrence and Caroline Brownell (Averill) Rose; m. Christopher Lawrence Webber, Apr. 7, 1958; children: Michael James, Elisabeth Rose, Lawrence Andrew, Caroline Margaret. Sec. credit dept. Scribner Bookstore, N.Y.C., 1956; sec. imports Oxford U. Press, N.Y.C., 1956-58; dir. patient services and profl. programs Am. Cancer Soc. Westchester County, N.Y., 1976-78; coordinator hospice vols. St. Luke's Hosp., N.Y.C., 1979-82; dir. vol. services St. Barnabas

Hosp., Bronx, 1982-84, Montefiore Med. Ctr., Bronx, 1984—. Mem. Greater N.Y. Assn. Dirs. Vol. Services in Health Care Facilities (sec. 1986-87, pres.-elect 1988), N.Y. State Assn. Dirs. Vol. Services, Am. Soc. Dirs. Vol. Services of Am. Hosp. Assn., Assn. Vol. Adminstrs. Democrat. Episcopalian. Office: Montefiore Med Ctr 111 E 210th St Bronx NY 10467

WEBER, BARBARA, financial executive; b. Bryn Mawr, Pa., Feb. 12, 1939; d. John Patrick and Margaret Veronica (Clune) Burke; m. Francis Owen Weber, Oct. 28, 1978; children—Richard, Jennifer, Charles, John, Deborah. B.A., Rosemont Coll., 1960. Broker, Jefferson Standard, Bethesda, Md., 1975-77; sr. v.p. Wallace Fin. Group, Bethesda, 1977-83; dir. agencies Home Life Ins. Co., Bethesda, 1983-84; pres. Md. Fin. Group, Balt., 1984—. Mem. Nat. Republican Congl. Com., 1986. Mem. Gen. Agts. and Mgrs. Assn. (treas.), Nat. Assn. Life Underwriters, Nat. Assn. Securities Dealers, Balt. Estate Planning Council, Balt. Assn. Fin. Planners, Internat. Assn. Fin. Planners. Roman Catholic. Club: Hunt Valley Country. Avocations: swimming; horseback riding. Home: 15 Glen Lyon Ct Phoenix MD 21131 Office: Md Fin Group 9515 Deereco Rd SUite 601 Timonium MD 21093

WEBER, BARBARA M., sales executive; b. Oneonta, N.Y., Apr. 27, 1945; d. Peter J. and Helen (Bettiol) Macaluso; m. Peter Biddle Weber, July 29, 1972. Student, SUNY, Cortland, 1963-67; AAS in Merchandising and Retail Mgmt., SUNY, Mohawk Valley. Service cons. N.Y. Telephone, Albany, N.Y., 1966-68; sr. service advisor N.Y. Telephone, Albany, 1970-73; data communications instr. AT & T, nationwide, 1968-70; equipment mgr. Rushmore & Weber, Albany, 1978-82; v.p. ops. Rushmore & Weber, 1983—, gen. mgr., v.p., 1987—, also bd. dirs. Republican. Roman Catholic. Club: Schuyler Meadows Country. Home: PO Box 236 Newtonville NY 12128 Office: Rushmore & Weber Inc 272 Wolf Rd PO Box 757 Latham NY 12110

WEBER, BEVERLY JO, secondary educator; b. Cin., Nov. 16, 1933; d. Lawrence John and Laura Lucille (Collins) Nieman; m. Vernon Emil Weber, June 12, 1954; children: Lawrence, Terrence, Teresann, Anthony, Heidi. BA, Ursuline Coll., 1976. Cert. tchr., Ohio. Tchr. 5th grade St. Ladislaus, Columbus, Ohio, 1954-55; tchr. Immaculate Conception, Highland Park, Ill., 1956-57; substitute tchr. St. Francis Assisi, Gates Mills, Ohio, 1966-76; substitute tchr., counselor, social studies chair St. Paschal Baylon Sch., Highland Heights, Ohio, 1977-87; supr. student tchrs. Notre Dame Coll. for Women, South Euclid, Ohio, 1987—; bd. dirs. Glen Oak Schs., Gates Mills, Ohio, 1976-78, History Day, Cleve., 1978; mem. Cleve. Diocesan Social Studies Text Evaluation Team. Mem. Nat. Council Social Studies, Nat. Cath. Edn. Assn., Ohio Council for Social Studies, Diocesan Social Studies Tchrs. Assn., Gt. Cleve. Council Social Studies, Cleve. Mus. Art. Roman Catholic. Clubs: Mother's, Gilmour. Home: 5363 W Mill Dr Highland Heights OH 44143 Office: Notre Dame Coll Dept of Edn 4545 College Rd South Euclid OH 44121

WEBER, CAROL A., associate publisher; b. Washington, May 3, 1940; d. Harry Lee and Rosa Lee (McCannon) Almond; m. Romann H. (John) Weber, Aug. 6, 1966; 1 son, Romann Matthew. B.A. in English, Madison Coll. (now James Madison U.), 1962. Gen. assigment reporter Roanoke Times (Va.), 1962-64; gen. assignment reporter Miami Herald (Fla.), from 1964, successively edn. writer, investigative reporter, asst. city editor, Broward editor, to 1982, asst. mng. editor features, 1982-84, assoc. pub., 1985—. Mem. Com. of 100, bd. advisors com. 100; bd. dirs. Mus. Art, Broward Performing Arts Found., Inc.; bd. govs. Ft. Lauderdale C. of C., Philharmonic Orch. of Fla.; trustee Vinnette Carroll Repertory Co., Salvation Army Bd. Recipient various state, nat. awards for writing; named Woman of Yr., Women in Communication, Broward County, Fla., 1981. Office: The Miami Herald 1520 E Sunrise Blvd Fort Lauderdale FL 33304

WEBER, CHARLENE LYDIA, social worker; b. Phila., Mar. 2, 1943; d. Walter Gotlieb and Dorothy (Peart) W.; m. Billy Mack Carroll, Oct. 3, 1959 (div. Sept. 1974); children: Dorothy Patricia, Robert Walter, Lydia Baker, Billy Bob, Elizabeth Louise; m. John Edward Thomaston, Sept. 26, 1974 (div. July 1986). BSW with honors, Coll. Santa Fe, 1983; MSW, N.Mex. Highlands U., 1988. Client service agt. I Social Services div. Dept. Human Services, Albuquerque, 1975-78, client service agt. IV, 1978-83; social worker II Social Services div. Dept. Human Services, Bernalillo, N.Mex., 1983, social worker III, 1983—. Mem. Nat. Assn. Social Workers, N.Mex. Council on Crime and Deliquency, Albuquerque Retarded Assn., Child Welfare League. Democrat. Home: 72 Umber Ct Rio Rancho NM 87124 Office: Dept Human Services div Social Services PO Box 820 Bernalillo NM 87004

WEBER, DOROTHY MARGARET, savings and loan association executive; b. Wagoner, Okla.; children: R. Alan, Robert L. Student, Okla. State U., 1966-67, U. No. Iowa, 1968; M with hons. in mktg., Am. Inst. Banking, 1980. Dir. pub. relations and promotions Arts Council, Oklahoma City, 1972-78; dir. advt. pub. relations Fidelity Bank, N.A., Oklahoma City, 1978-80; acct. supr. Rozier, Sumner & Berry, Inc., Oklahoma City, 1980-82; account exec. Strong/Hill Advt. Agy., Inc., Oklahoma City, 1982-84; v.p., dir. mktg., advt and sales Continentinal Fed. Savs. and Loan Assn., Oklahoma City, 1984—. Bd. dirs. Okla. Alliance for Arts Edn., A Project of John F. Kennedy for Performing Arts, 1986-88, Cen. Okla. Multi-Media Assn., 1977-78, Art Inst. Okla., 1976-80; mem. adv., planning coms. Expectations '77; mem. mktg. com. Okla. Theater Ctr., 1987; mem. Arts Communications Team; mem. pub. relations steering com. Okla. State High Sch. Theater Festival; co-chmn. Nat. Conf. Arts and the Bicentenncial Graphics Design com., Arts '76; ch-chmn. pub. relations steering com. Allied Arts Found. Ann. Fund Drive, 1978, mem. 1973; moderator Am. Inst. Discussion, 1981—; mem. planning com. First Ann. Tri-City Ballet Festival; mktg. cons. Ballet Okla., 1974-79. Recipient ADDY awards, 1980-88, Silver medal Graphex, 1983, Outstanding Creative Design award Warred Paper Co., 1986. Mem. Am. Inst. Banking, Fin. Instns. Mktg. Assn., Bank Mktg. Assn., Bus. and Profl. Advt. Assn. (regional conf. com. 1982), Pub. Relations Soc. Am. (assoc.), Bus. and Profl. Women (adv. bd., chmn. legis. com., co-chmn. pub. relations com.), Oklahoma City Advtg. Club. Home: 3808 NW 6th St Oklahoma City OK 73116

WEBER, JANET M., nursing school administrator; b. Lansdale, Pa., Mar. 12, 1936; d. Russell H. and Naomi (Moyer) W. Diploma in nursing, Washington County Hosp. Sch. Nursing, 1959; B.S. in Nursing, Grace Coll., 1960; M.Ed., Duquesne U., 1969. Staff nurse, supr. Murphy Med. Ctr., Warsaw, Ind., 1959-60; coll. nurse Grace Coll., Winona Lake, Ind., 1959-60; med. surg. nursing instr. Washington County Hosp. Sch. Nursing, Hagerstown, Md., 1961-64; pvt. duty nurse Washington County Hosp., Hagerstown, 1964; chmn. found. of nursing Presbyn. Univ. Hosp. Sch. Nursing, Pitts., 1964-72; curriculum coordinator Albert Einstein Med. Ctr. Sch. Nursing, Phila., 1972-73; assoc. dir. Albert Einstein Med. Ctr. Sch. Nursing, 1973-74, acting dir., 1974, dir., 1974-87; cons. Md. Bd. Higher Edn., 1981-82. Author: The Faculty's Role in Policy Development, 1981, Assisting Students with Educational Deficiencies, 1975. Mem. Pa. League Nursing (pres. 1982-86, bd. dirs. Area I 1974-76), Washington County Hosp. Nurses Alumni Assn. (pres. 1962-64), Nat. League Nursing (bd. rev. 1980-84, chmn.-elect Council Diploma Programs 1985-87), Am. Hosp. Assn. Assembly Hosp. Schs., Hosp. Assn. Pa. (sec. council hosps. with schs. nursing 1979), Grace Coll. Alumni Assn., Duquesne U. Alumni Assn. Republican. Home: 5640 Arbor St Philadelphia PA 19120

WEBER, JANET MARIE, utilities company administrator; b. Rodney, Can., Apr. 2, 1938; d. Gordon Albert and Magdelene Cecil (Coleman) Bondy; m. Leonard Henry Weber, Apr. 16, 1955; children: Leonard G., Terrance H., Douglas T., Michael J. Comml. III, Bulmer Bus. Coll., Windsor, Ont., 1955. Clk. Oakville (Ont.) Hydro-Elec. Commn., 1962, collection clk., collection supr., accounts receivable supr., customer accounts supr., 1987—. Office: Oakville Hydro-Elec Commn, 2350 Trafalgar Rd, PO Box 1900, Oakville CAN L6J 5E3

WEBER, JOAN JULIA, management consultant; b. St. Louis, Mar. 13, 1941; d. Orville Otto and Doris Ethel (Wehmeier) W. Student, Sorbonne U., Paris, 1962; BA, Wellesley Coll., 1963; MBA, St. Louis U., 1984. Asst. buyer Filene's, Boston, 1963-65; asst. dir. spl. events Famous Barr Co., St. Louis, 1965-72; exec. dir. Mo. Am. Revolution Bicentennial Commn., Jefferson City, 1973; pub. relations counselor Coca-Cola Account of Infoplan Internat., Inc., St. Louis, 1975-76; pub. relations account supr. The Pub. Relations Ctr., Chgo., 1978; bus. programs dir. Continuing Edn. Dept. Washington U., St. Louis, 1980-81; mgmt. cons. St. Louis Small Bus. Devel. Ctr. of St. Louis U., 1983-84, dir. cons. services, 1984-85, dist. dir., 1985—; selection com. Women Bus. Owners Conf., St. Louis, 1984—; adv. com. Minority Bus. Devel. U.S. Dept. Commerce, St. Louis, 1985, Human Resources Systems, St. Louis U., 1985; selection com. Midwest Venture Capital Conf., St. Louis, 1987. Founder, chair St. Louis Women's Polit. Caucus, 1971-72; pres. Planning and Environ. Research Inst., Mo. and Ill., 1972-74; bd. dirs. Met. Zool. Park and Mus. Dist., St. Louis, (treas. 1976-79, 1981-82, sec. 1980-81, v. chmn. 1982-83, chmn. 1983-84). Recipient Bus. in the Arts awards Esquire Mag. Bus. Com. for the Arts, 1974, Golden Quill award St. Louis Women Bus. Owners, 1985, St. Louis Paving Block award Nat. Assn. Women Bus. Owners, 1986. Mem. Mo. Venture Capital Forum, St. Louis-Lyon (France) Sister Cities Inc. (chmn. commerce com. 1984—). Home: 4501 Lindell Blvd Saint Louis MO 63108 Office: St Louis Small Bus Devel Ctr 3642 Lindell Blvd Saint Louis MO 63108

WEBER, LINDA FICKLIN, therapist; b. Columbia, Mo., Mar. 11, 1926; d. Nathan Clyde and Helen Othelia (Erickson) Ficklin; m. Joseph Ralph Weber, Sept. 29, 1946; children: Barry, Cynthia, Amy, Gwen. BA cum laude, Elmhurst Coll., 1968; MS, No. Ill. U., 1975. Tchr. Dist. #45 Schs., Villa Park, Ill., 1968-74, counselor, 1974-84; counselor, therapist Linda Weber & Assocs., Villa Park, 1982-85; adminstrv. sec. D.C. chpt. Ch. of the Brethren, Washington, 1985-88, nat. bd., exec. bd., del.; pastoral counselor Washington Pastoral Service, 1988—. Mem. Women for a Meaningful Summit, Washington, 1985, core group Nat. Bd. YWCA, Washington, 1985—. Mem. Am. Assn. Pastoral Counselors, Am. Assn. Counseling and Devel., NOW, Womaen's Caucus, Alpha Xi Delta. Home: 2130 P St NW #524 Washington DC 20037 Office: Washington Pastoral Counseling Service Washington DC 20002

WEBER, LINDA RAE, insurance company executive; b. Montclair, N.J., May 2, 1943; d. Alfred H. and Marguerite (Campbell) Mildon; 1 child, Matthew. Project mgr. Colonial Life Ins. Co., Parsippany, N.J., 1968-79, Newsweek, Livingston, N.J., 1979-80; mgr. data processing Scholastic Co., Englewood Cliffs, N.J., 1980-81, Royal Life Ins. Co., N.Y.C., 1981-83; v.p. Charter Security Life Ins. Co., Chatham, N.J., 1983-84, Met. Security Life Ins. Co., Chatham, N.J., 1984-85, Western Nat. Life Ins. Co., Pine Brook, N.J., 1985-87; sr. v.p. adminstrn. and info. services Am. Centennial Ins. Co., Wilmington, Del., 1987—. Mem. Data Processing Mgmt. Assn. Home: 16 Gregory Terr Bloomfield NJ 07003 Office: 1st Del Fin Group 1100 Carr Rd Wilmington DE 19809

WEBER, LISA ANN, nurse supervisor; b. Wellington, Kans., Jan. 7, 1964; d. Paul Raymond and Neila Janell (Scott) W. Lic. Practical Nurse, Barton County Community Coll., 1983, A in Nursing, 1984; BS in Nursing, Wichita State U., 1986. RN, Kans. Lic. practical nurse Cen. Kans. Med. Ctr., Great Bend, 1983-84, RN, 1984; nurse, patient care supr. St. Francis Regional Med. Ctr., Wichita, Kans., 1984-87. Big Sister Big Bros./Big Sisters of Am., Wichita, 1987. Mem. Sigma Theta Tau. Democrat. Roman Catholic. Home: 7007 Briarwood Wichita KS 67212

WEBER, MARGARET LAURA JANE, accountant; b. Fairview, Mo., Jan. 4, 1933; d. Mert James and Margaret Orr (Mortensen) Joel; m. James E. Jennings, Mar. 1953 (div.); children: James Edward Jennings, Janie Lea Franks, David Alan Jennings; m. Albert H. Weber, June 1956; children: Luhwanna Stonecipher, Margaret Anne Shadwick. AA, Crowder Coll., Mo., 1972; postgrad. Mo. So. Coll., 1985. Teller, First State Bank, Joplin, Mo., 1951-53; clk. Mo. Lic. Dept., Joplin, 1954-57, U. Mo. Ext. Dept., Neosho, 1967-68; cashier Crowder Coll., Neosho, Mo., 1968-83, acct., 1983—. Mem., Newton County Welfare Com., 1984—. Mem. Am. Bus. Women's Assn. (Woman of Yr. 1982, Bus. Assoc. of Yr. 1987), Nat. Assn. Female Execs., Mo. Assn. Community Jr. Colls. (bd. dirs. 1978-82). Republican. Baptist. Home: Rt 6 Box 197 Neosho MO 64850 Office: Crowder Coll 601 Laclede Ave Neosho MO 64850

WEBER, MARY ELLEN HEALY, economist; b. San Francisco, May 28, 1943; d. Ignatius Bernard and Grace Marie (Hogan) Healy; B.A., Dominican Coll., 1965; postgrad. U. Mex., 1967, (vis. scholar) Stanford U., 1969-70, Cath. U. Chile, 1970-71, U. Chile, 1971-72; Ph.D., U. Utah, 1974; m. Stephen Francis Weber, Dec. 21, 1971. U. Utah teaching fellow, 1965-68; asst. prof. Smith Coll., 1972-75; country economist World Bank, IBRD, 1975-76; sr. economist Internat. Research & Tech. Corp., McLean, Va., 1976-78; dir. regulatory analysis, chief economist OSHA, U.S. Dept. Labor, Washington, 1979-84; pres. Weber Software Enterprises, 1984—, Web-Wolf Data Systems, Inc., 1986—. Social Sci. Research Council fgn. area fellow 1969-71. Mem. Am. Econ. Assn., Nat. Economists Club, Soc. Govt. Economists, Washington Women's Network. Roman Catholic.

WEBER, MARY HELEN, lawyer; b. Chgo., Sept. 24, 1950; d. Frank Joseph and Mary Helen (Suchy) Kryda; m. Roger Alan Weber, Aug. 11, 1973. B.A., Wellesley Coll., 1972; M.A., Harvard U., 1973; J.D., U. Cin., 1976. Bar: Ohio 1976, U.S. Dist. Ct. (so. dist.) Ohio 1976, U.S. Ct. Appeals (6th cir.) 1976, U.S. Tax Ct. 1977. Law clk. to judge U.S. Dist. Ct. (so. dist.) Ohio, Cin., 1976-77; atty. Cin. Dist. Counsel's Office, IRS, Cin., 1977-82, sr. atty., 1982-85, dep. regional counsel for tax litigation Central Region, 1985—. Contbr. articles to legal jours. Recipient Spl. Achievement Performance Bonus award Chief Counsel's Office, IRS, Washington, 1983, 86, 87, High Quality Increase award, 1982; Atty. of Quarter award Central Region Chief Counsel's Office, IRS, 1981; nominee Younger Fed. Lawyer award Fed. Bar Assn., 1983, 84; nominee James E. Markham Jr. award IRS, 1982. Mem. Order of Coif, ABA, U. Cin. Law Alumni Assn. (v.p., trustee 1983-85), Phi Beta Kappa. Clubs: Wellesley Coll. (pres. 1982-83), Radcliffe Coll. (treas. 1979-84), Harvard (bd. dirs. 1986—). Office: IRS Regional Counsel's Office 550 Main St Room 7510 Cincinnati OH 45202

WEBER, MOLLY SMITH, editor; b. Durham, N.C., Sept. 4, 1957; d. H. Ralph and Sally Ann (Simmons) Smith; m. Walter Charles Weber, July 13, 1985. BA in Psychology, Yale U., 1979; MA in Edn., Stanford U., 1980. Dir. aquatics SUNY, Purchase, 1980-81; sales rep. Prentice-Hall, Inc., Englewood Cliffs, N.J., 1981-83; sales rep. West Edn1. Pub., St. Paul, 1983-85, acquisitions editor, 1985—. Active Dem. Polit. Campaigns, 1987—; mem. Nat. Dem. Com. Mem. Am. Mgmt. Assn., NOW. Avocations: swimming, snow and water skiing, running, photography. Home: 309 E 70th Terr Kansas City MO 64113 Office: West Pub Co PO Box 411628 Kansas City MO 64141

WEBER, PATRICIA LOUISE BRADEN, marketing educator; b. Ft. Wayne, Ind., Oct. 31, 1945; d. Walter Frederick and Margaret June (Houk) Nagel, Jr.; m. Joseph Lou Braden, Aug. 23, 1969 (div. Feb. 1975); m. 2d, Walter Jacob Weber, Jr., July 20, 1981. B.S. in Bus. Adminstrn. with distinction, Ind. U., 1967, M.B.A., 1969, D.Bus.Adminstrn., 1973. Staff research assoc. div. research Sch. Bus. Adminstrn., Ind. U., Bloomington, 1967-70; adj. asst. prof. mktg. Coll. Bus., Eastern Mich. U., Ypsilanti, 1970, assoc. dean Coll. Bus., 1981-87; dir. Ctr. for Entrepreneurship, 1987—; mem. research faculty Grad. Sch. Bus. Adminstrn., U. Mich., Ann Arbor, 1970-81, asst. dir. div. research, 1980-81, adj. assoc. prof. mktg., 1974-81; subprogram coordinator Coastal Zone research Mich. Sea Grant Program, Ann Arbor, 1977—; mem. steering com. Minority Tech. Council Mich., Ann Arbor, 1982-83; mem. resource adv. com. Mich. changing economy program Mich. Dept. Commerce, Lansing, 1975-76; mem. subcoms. on competitive position, econ. growth and diversification, and statis. data Mich. Econ. Action Council, Lansing, 1975-76; dir. many sponsored research projects, cons. to govt., industry, bus. firms and profl. groups, 1970—. Author: Technological Entrepreneurship, 1977; (with Ramesh Gurnani) Data Processing in the Tax Function, 1980, also numerous tech. reports and articles in profl. jours. Program advisor Mich. Council for Arts, Detroit, 1978; bd. dirs. Child and Family Services of Washtenaw, Ann Arbor, 1983—, chmn. devel. com., 1984—. Mem. AAAS, Am. Inst. for Decision Scis. (chmn. Mktg. Track, Midwest AIDS), Am. Mktg. Assn. (chpt. v.p., dir. 1976-80, chmn. program com. 1977-78, editor chpt. membership directory 1977, Marketeer 1975-77; chpt. cert. of recognition 1976-79), Am. Statis. Assn., Internat. Council for Small Bus. (exec. adv. com. 1974-75), Mich. Tech. Council (mem. state bd. dirs, chmn. bd. dirs. so. cen. 1986—, research adv. bd. 1982-84), Soc. Automotive Engrs. (assoc. mem.; co-chmn. socio-tech. com. 1982—, sessions chmn. internat. congress 1982), Greater Detroit C. of C. (econ. devel. strategic planning com. 1982—), Eastern Mich. U. Women's Assn. (pres.-elect 1983—), Mich. Hist. Soc., Ann Arbor Art Assn. (dir., treas. 1980—), DAR, Alpha Gamma Delta, Beta Gamma Sigma, Omicron Delta, Alpha Lambda Delta. Home: 550 Cliffs Dr N 202C Ypsilanti MI 48198 Office: Ea Mich U Ctr for Entrepreneurship 121 Pearl St Ypsilanti MI 48197

WEBER, SUSAN LEE, marketing consultant; b. Honolulu, Nov. 30, 1948; d. Kenneth Charles and Valerie (June) W. BBA, San Jose (Calif.) State U., 1970; postgrad., U. Calif., Berkeley, 1972-73, Pepperdine U., 1977-78; Cert. in Mktg., Harvard U. Small bys. organizer VISTA, Roseville, N.C., 1970-72; cosmetics buyer USN Commissary Supply, Oakland, Calif., 1972-74; cosmetics product mgr. Shaklee Corp., San Francisco, 1974-76; mktg. mgr. Max Factor, Inc., Hollywood, Calif., 1976-81; v.p. electronic mktg. Bank of Am., San Francisco, 1981-83, v.p. bank card merchandising, 1983-85, v.p., upscale mktg., sales, 1985-88; mng. prin. Mktg. Fundamentals, San Francisco, 1988—. Mem. Am. Mktg. Assn., Bay Area Women's Network, Nat. Assn. Female Execs. Republican. Presbyterian. Office: Mktg Fundamentals 1 Hallidie Plaza Suite 701 San Francisco CA 94102

WEBSTER, BEVERLEY CARLOTTA, dietitian, food service director; b. Georgetown, Guyana, Mar. 2, 1957; d. Percival Augustus and Urmia Angela (Van Leesten Fox) Cummings; m. Curtis Charles Webster, Nov. 20, 1982. BS in Dietetics, Coll. Misericordia, 1979; MS in Dietetics, Marywood Coll., Scranton, 1982. Dietetic intern Scranton State Gen. Hosp., 1979-80; community service dietitian Maternal Health Services, Hazleton, Pa., 1980; dir. food service Leader Nursing Home, Bethlehem, Pa., 1980-81; clin. dietitian Grandview Hosp., Sellersville, Pa., 1981-83; chief clin. dietitian Pottsville (Pa.) Hosp. and Warne Clinic, 1983-84; dir. food service HCA Raulerson Hosp., Okeechobee, Fla., 1985-87; dir. food and nutritional services AMI Meml. Hosp. of Tampa, 1987—; cons. Greenview Nursing Home, Orwicksburg, Pa., 1983-84. Mem. Am. Dietetic Assn., Fla. Dietetic Assn. Roman Catholic. Club: Home Econs. (Dallas, Pa.). Home: 12130 74th St N Pinebrook Estates Largo FL 34649

WEBSTER, LINDA KRISTOF, lawyer, army officer; b. Corpus Christi, Tex., Aug. 29, 1956; d. Paul Judson and Shirley Helen (Fitzgerald) Adams; m. Noel Ray Webster, Nov. 19, 1977; children: David Ray, Ryan Douglas. B.A. in History and Geography with highest honors, cert. secondary social studies, U. Okla., 1978; J.D., U. Tex., 1981; postgrad. U.S. Army Judge Adv Gen's Sch., 1988. Bar: Tex. 1981. Entered as capt. U.S. Army, 1982; asst. Staff Judge Adv., Ft. Hood, Tex., 1982-85, prosecutor, 1982-83, legal asst., 1983-84, claims officer, 1985; asst. staff judge advocate, Ft. McClellan, Ala., 1985-88, claims cfficer 1985, adminstrv. law officer, 1986, prosecutor, 1987-88. Contbr. articles to legal jours. Mem. ABA, Tex. Bar Assn., Assn. Am. Trial Lawyers, Am. Bus. Women's Assn. Democrat. Office: Judge Adv Gen's Sch Charlottesville VA 22903

WEBSTER, NANCY JOAN, employee relations administrator; b. Geneva, Ohio, Jan. 21, 1949; d. Arthur Clair and Alice Mary (Falk) Eisbrenner; m. Bruce Alan Webster, June 15, 1968; children—Teresa Lynn, Melanie Marie. B.A. in Bus. Mgmt., Hiram Coll., 1985. Placement specialist Goodwill Industries, Ashtabula, Ohio, 1973-77, Ohio Job Service, Ashtabula, 1977-80; employee relations adminstr. RMI Co., Ashtabula, 1980—; EEO affirmative action, 1984—. Pub. relations chmn. Saybrook Elem. Sch. PTO, Ashtabula, 1976-78, carnival chmn., 1975-78, pres. 1976-78; sec. Mallory Sharon Metals Recreational Assn., Ashtabula, 1982-84; mem. job service employer com. Ashtabula County, 1986—, chairperson nominating com., 1988; mem. Youth Citizens Council Planning Com., 1987—; bd. dirs. United Way, Ashtabula County, 1976-79; vice chmn. allocations com., 1978-79, com. mem. priorities, nomination, Ohio Citizens Council, services innovations, 1977-80. Recipient Cert. of Appreciation, Goodwill Industries, 1975, Ashtabula County Vocat. Edn. Sch., 1985. Mem. Ashtabula County Personnel Assn. (v.p. 1987-88, pres. 1988-89), Am. Soc. Personnel Adminstrs. Catholic. Avocations: consumer advocacy, volunteer work, home remodeling and repair. Home: 2105 Anthony Ave Ashtabula OH 44004 Office: RMI Co Metals Reduction Plant E 21 and State Rd PO Box 490 Ashtabula OH 44004

WECK, KRISTIN WILLA, savings and loan association executive; b. Elgin, Ill., Nov. 5, 1959; d. John Francis and Florence Elaine (Ebel) W. BBA, Augustana Coll., Rock Island, Ill., 1981. Lic. real estate salesman, Ill. Intern with investment banking group First Chgo. Bank, London, 1980; intern Prudential-Bache Co., Ft. Lauderdale, Fla., 1981; residential appraiser Fox Valley Appraisal Counselors, Ltd., West Dundee, Ill., 1982-84; asst. real estate loan officer First Nat. Bank, Barrington, Ill., 1982-84; savs. and loan field examiner III Fed. Home Loan Bank, Chgo., 1984—. V.p. Brandywine Condo Assn., Crystal Lake, Ill., 1983. Recipient Outstanding Achievement award Fed. Home Loan Bank Bd., 1985. Mem. Soc. Real Estate Appraisers (candidate). Republican. Lutheran. Home: 435A Brandy Dr Crystal Lake IL 60014 Office: Fed Home Loan Bank 111 E Wacker Dr Suite 800 Chicago IL 60601-4360

WECK, MADONNA MAUREEN, educator; b. Chgo., Dec. 17, 1944; d. John Francis and Gertrude Bernice (Fitzgerald) Casey; m. Larry D. Weck, July 29, 1970; children: Maureen, John, Casey, Kevin, Madonna N., James, Meghan. BA in Elem. Edn., St. Mary's Coll., South Bend, Ind., 1967, MA in Spl. Edn., 1969. Cert. spl. edn., elem. edn., adminstrn., Ill. Elem. tchr. Sch. Dist. 25, Arlington Heights, Ill., 1967-69, 77—, tchr. learning disabilities, 1969-70, reading specialist, 1974-76, intermediate, 1976-77; Active PTA, Arlington Heights, 1979—. Roman Catholic. Club: Our Lady of the Wayside Women's (Arlington Heights). Home: 334 S Belmont Arlington Heights IL 60005

WEDEL, DANA LYN, psychiatric nurse; b. Chgo., Nov. 21, 1952; d. Paul George and Jean Marie (Martin) W.; m. Charles J. Uhlman, Oct. 30, 1987. BA, Temple U., 1977; AS, Community Coll. Phila., 1982; BSN, SUNY, Albany, 1988. Cert. psychiat. mental health nurse. Staff psychiat. nurse Thomas Jefferson Univ. Hosp., Phila., 1982-85, charge nurse, 1985-86, emergency psychiat. nurse, 1986—; presentor at confs., 1983—. Mem. Am. Nurses Assn., Pa. Nurses Assn., Psychiat. Mental Health Nurses Assn. Democrat. Episcopalian. Office: Thomas Jefferson Univ Hosp 111 S 11th St Philadelphia PA 19102

WEDEL, JEANNETTE KATHRYN, association executive; b. Columbus, Wis., Oct. 12, 1937; d. Joseph A. and Margaret Elizabeth (O'Connor) W.; m. Dennis Arnold Olson, April 30, 1983. Student, Prospect Hall, Milw., Wis., 1955-56. Exec. sec. Oscar Mayer & Co., Madison, Wis., 1956-58; adminstrv. asst. Credit Union Nat. Assn., Madison, 1958-69; assoc. Gale Assocs., Washington, 1969-71; asst. dir. Coalition for Rural Am., Washington, 1972-73; devel. officer AAAS, Washington, 1974—; participant Internat. Seminar on Women in Devel., Mexico City, 1975. Editor proceedings and report Role of Sci. and Engring. Socs. in Devel., 1979. Treas. Human Rights Internet, Cambridge, Mass., 1983—, v.p. Woman's Nat. Dem. Club, Washington, 1985—. Mem. Fedn. of Orgns. for Profl. Women (pres. 1981-83), AAAS, Nat. Soc. Fund Raising Execs., Council of Engring. and Sci. Soc. Execs., Am. Mgmt. Assn. Roman Catholic. Office: AAAS 1333 H St NW Washington DC 20005

WEDGWORTH, RUTH SPRINGER, fertilizer company executive; b. Eaton Rapids, Mich., May 10, 1903; d. Clarence P. and Minnie L. (Washburn) Springer; student Mich. State U., 1921-23; LL.D. (hon.), U. Fla., 1965; H.H.D. (hon.), Fla. So. Coll., 1976; m. Herman H. Wedgworth, June 23, 1923; children—Helen Jean, George H., Barbara Ann. Pres., Wedgworth Farms, Inc., Belle Glade, Fla., 1938-80, Wedgworth's Inc., Belle Glade, 1954—, pres. Wedgworth Produce, Inc., Belle Glade, 1955-65; sec. Seminole Life Ins. Co., West Palm Beach, Fla., 1955-65; dir. Fla. Nat. Bank, Belle Glade, 1979—. Mem. Palm Beach County (Fla.) Bd. Edn., 1947-53; bd. dirs. Western Palm Beach County Hosp. Dist., 1940-47; chmn. Highlands Glades Drainage Dist., 1942-68; mem. Gov.'s Com. on Migrant Work, 1942-46; trustee Fla. So. Coll., 1970—; mem. migrant work com. Nat. Council Chs., 1948-56; leadership mem. Boy Scouts Am., 1979. Recipient Award of Merit, Gamma Sigma Delta, 1978; Council of Farmers Cooperatives award, 1979; named Woman of Yr. (Progressive Farmer, 1947), Belle Glade, Fla., 1975, Fla. Agr., 1986, Fla. Woman of Yr. in Agr., 1987; award for excellence in industry and bus. Palm Beach County Com. on Status of Women, 1978; Disting. Service award, Fla. Farm Bur., 1979, Fla. Fruit and Vegetable Assn., 1958; Outstanding Service award for employment and community leadership Everglades Progressive Citizens, 1970; Achievement award, Lions, 1961; inducted to Fla. Agrl. Hall of Fame, 1988. Mem. Fla. Hort. Soc., Fla. Soils Sci. Soc., Beta Sigma Phi. Methodist. Clubs: Belle Glade Women's, PEO, Lions (internat. hon.). Office: 651 NW 9th St Belle Glade FL 33430

WEEDEN, MARCIA MARION, quality assurance director; b. Weymouth, Mass., Oct. 20, 1952; d. Vernon Alden and Marion Charlotte (Norling) W.; m. Frank Robert Hansen, Feb. 19, 1977 (div. 1980). BA in History, U. R.I., 1974, BS in Textiles and Clothing, 1974, postgrad. Cert. quality engr., quality technician. Quality control technician Cranston (R.I.) Print Works-Corp., 1975-77, Murdock Webbing Co., Central Falls, R.I., 1981-82; quality assurance engr. Victor Corp., Westerly, R.I., 1982; quality assurance specialist DCASMA Boston, Providence, 1983—; quality assurance rep. DCASMA Boston, Fall River, Mass., 1986; dir. quality assurance Duro Industries, Inc., Fall River, 1986—. Mem. Cranston chpt. Big Brothers/Big Sisters Am., 1987. Mem. Am. Soc. Quality Control, Am. Assn. Textile Chemists and Colorists. Unitarian Universalist. Office: Duro Industries Inc 110 Chace St Fall River MA 02724

WEEKES, SHIRLEY M., artist; b. Buffalo, May 9, 1917; d. Ray Roscoe and Loretta Marie (Ent) Thompson; grad. Detroit Art Acad., 1939; m. Thomas Weekes, Mar. 27, 1942; children: Judith, Thomas. One woman shows: Frye Mus., Seattle, 1967, 72, Haines Gallery, Seattle, 1973, 75, Challis Gallery, Laguna Beach, Calif., 1970, 72, 74; group shows include: Frye Mus., 1965-69, 71-75, Seattle Art Mus., 1972; represented in permanent collections Frye Mus., Laguna Beach Mus. Art. Mem. San Diego Watercolor Soc. Home: 5093 Aegina Way Oceanside CA 92054

WEEKS, BRIGITTE, book editor; b. Whitchurch, Hants, Eng., Aug. 28, 1943; came to U.S., 1965; d. Jack and Margery May (Millett) W.; m. Edward A. Herscher, Sept. 6, 1969; children—Hilary, Charlotte, Daniel. Student, Univ. Coll. of North Wales, Bangor, 1962-65. Asst. editor Boston Mag., 1966-70; editor Kodansha Internat., Tokyo, 1969-72, Resources for the Future, 1973-74; asst. editor The Washington Post Book World, 1974-78, editor, 1978-88; editor-in-chief Book-of-the-Month Club, N.Y.C., 1988—; pres. Nat. Book Critics Circle, 1984-86. Office: Book-of-the-Month Club 485 Lexington Ave New York NY 10017

WEEKS, JANET HEALY, judge; b. Quincy, Mass., Oct. 19, 1932; d. John Francis and Sheila Josephine (Jackson) Healy; m. George Weeks, Aug. 29, 1959; children: Susan, George. AB in Chemistry, Emmanuel Coll., Boston, 1954; JD, Boston Coll., 1958; LLD (hon.), U. Guam, 1984. Bar: Mass. 1958, Guam 1972. Trial atty. Dept. Justice, Washington, 1958-60, Trapp & Gayle, Agana, Guam, 1971-73; ptnr. Trapp, Gayle, Teker, Weeks & Freidman, Agana, 1973-75; judge Superior Ct. Guam, Agana, 1975—; chmn. task force cts., prosecution and def. Terr. Crime Commn., 1973-76; mem. Terr. Crime Commn. Bd., 1975-76, Guam Law Revision Commn., 1981—; rep. Nat. Conf. State Trial Judges, 1982. Mem. Cath. Sch. Bd. Guam, 1973. Mem. Nat. Assn. Women Judges (charter), Am. Judges Assn., ABA, Fed. Bar Assn. (chpt. sec. 1974), Guam Bar Assn. Club: Internat. (Guam). Office: Superior Ct Guam Judiciary Bldg Agana GU 96910

WEEKS, JULIE RAE, marketing executive; b. Lansing, Mich., Nov. 2, 1957; d. George Compton and Mollie Ray (McKinley) W. BA, U. Mich., 1979, MA, 1981. Field rep. Baker for Pres., Lansing, 1979-80; research asst. Market Opinion Research, Detroit, 1980, research analyst, 1982-84, sr. research asst., 1984-87, dir. of research, 1988—. Republican. Episcopalian. Office: Market Opinion Research 243 W Congress Detroit MI 48226

WEEKS, MARGARET SUZETTE, special education educator; b. Jonesboro, Ark., Mar. 4, 1950; d. Billy Ray Alsup and Marilyn Lee (Finley) Ballinger; m. Larry Charles Land Weeks, July 17, 1971; 1 child, Joshua Land. Student, So. Baptist Coll., 1968-69; B Spl. Edn., Ark. State U., 1972. Cert. tchr., Ark. Elem. sch. tchr. Tuckerman, Ark., 1972-73, Batesville, Ark., 1973-74; high sch. tchr. Walnut Ridge, Ark., 1980-82, 84-86; tchr. Lawrence County Exceptional Sch., Portia, Ark., 1982-84; tchr., bldg. coordinator elem. sch., St. Peters, Mo., 1986—; guest speaker, vol. various orgns., 1976-85. Bd. dirs. Am. Cancer Soc., Walnut Ridge, 1980-86. Mem. NEA, Mo. Ednl. Assn., Ark. Ednl. Assn., Ark. Assn. For Children with Learning Disabilities. Democrat. Presbyterian. Home: 44 Jamaica Saint Peters MO 63376

WEEKS, PATSY ANN LANDRY, librarian, teacher; b. Luling, Tex., Mar. 3, 1930; d. Lee and Mattie Wood (Callihan) Landry; m. Arnett S. Weeks, Dec. 2, 1950; children—Patsy Kate, Nancy Ann, Janie Marie. B.S., Southwest Tex. State U., San Marcos, 1951; M.L.S., Tex. Woman's U., Denton, 1979. Tchr. art, reading, math. Grandview Ind. Sch. Dist., Tex., 1950-52; tchr. phys. edn. Beaumont Ind. Sch. Dist., Tex., 1953; tchr. art, coll. algebra Cisco Jr. Coll., Tex., 1957-58; tchr. remedial reading Taylor County Schs., Tuscola, Tex., 1965-66; tchr. remedial reading Anson Ind. Sch. Dist. Tex., 1971-73; librarian Bangs Ind. Sch. Dist., Tex., 1973-79, learning resources coordinator, 1979—; adv. com. Edn. Service Ctr., 1978-83; coordinator Reading is Fundmental Program, 1978-83. Bd. dirs. Anson Pub. Library, Tex., 1971-72. Exhibitor oil paintings, pastels at Tex. fairs (1st prize 1952, 60). Mem. ALA, Assn. Library Service to children (Caldecott award com. 1986), Am. Assn. Sch. Librarians, Intellectual Freedom Round Table, Tex. Library Assn. (mem. intellectual freedom and profl. responsibility com. 1979-81, mem. Tex. Bluebonnet award com. 1982-85, chair adv. com. 1987, chair children's round table 1987), Tex. Assn. Sch. Librarians (media prodns. award com. 1985-86), Tex. Assn. Improvement Reading, Teenage Library Assn. Tex. (chmn. audio-visual award com. 1984), Tex. Assn. Sch. Library Adminstrs., Tex. State Tchr. Assn. (life), Phi Delta Kappa, Kappa Pi, Alpha Chi, Beta Phi Mu, Delta Kappa Gamma. Baptist. Clubs: Bangs Progressive Women's (treas. 1974-76). Home: 110 Poco St Bangs TX 76823 Office: Bangs Ind Sch Dist PO Box 969 Bangs TX 76823

WEEKS, VIRGINIA LYNN, research and development executive; b. March AFB, Calif., Feb. 6, 1952; d. John Edward and Azella Virginia (Morrill) Anderson; m. Calvin George Weeks, Feb. 14, 1980; children by previous marriage: Raymond Edward, Jerry Glenn Jr. Student, Sinclair Community Coll., 1981-83, U. Tex., San Antonio, 1980. Procur asst. specialized contracting USAF, Wright-Patterson AFB, Ohio, 1973-77; buyer logistics contracting USAF, Kelly AFB, Tex., 1977-81; contract specialist USAF, Wright-Patterson AFB, Ohio, 1981-84; spl. asst. Peace Log, Tehran, Iran, 1977; acting chief of contracts cruise missile program Gen. Dynamics/Convair, San Diego, 1984-86; contracts mgr. VERAC, Inc., San Diego, 1986—; cons. Gen. Dynamics, San Diego, 1985, Efratrom, 1986. Mem. Nat. Assn. Female Execs., Nat. Mgmt. Assn., Nat. Contract Mgmt. Assn. Republican. Office: VERAC Inc 9605 Scranton Rd Suite 500 San Diego CA 92121

WEEMS, CATHLEEN, city official; b. Jasper, Ala., May 28, 1920; d. Rufus Hillard and Mary Elizabeth (Handley) Cornelius; m. Jesse James Weems, Feb. 7, 1942 (dec. 1978); children—Coletta Renea Weems Vest. Student Walker Coll., 1960-61. Teller, Bank Cordova Citizens, Ala., 1938-42; with Indian Head Mills, Cordova, 1943-56, sec. to pres., 1957-59, sec. to So. Dist. pres. Natco Corp., Cordova, 1960-70; asst. to mgr. Health Care Center, HEW, Cordova, 1971-77; exec. dir., mgr. Cordova Housing and Cordova Manor, 1977—; exec. dir. Cordova Housing Authority, 1977—; sec., mgr. Cordova Manor Apts., 1977—; mgr. Cordova Park, 1977-82, Cordova Warrior River Apts., 1977-82. Sec., Citizens Group, Cordova, 1983—; active ARC; mem. Ala. Dept. Econ. and Community Affairs, Montgomery, Vol. & Info. Center of Community Resources, Birmingham; sec. Long Meml. Meth. Ch. Fellow Nat. Assn. Housing Redevel. Officials, Nat. Assn. Female Execs.; mem. Ala. Housing & Urban Devel. Registration, Nat. Assn. Housing & Redevel. Democrat. Clubs: Ladies Aux VFW, Order Eastern Star, Lioness. Avocations: music; travel; aerobics; ceramics. Home: 101 Stewart St Cordova AL 35550 Office: Cordova Housing Authority Rt 2 Cook Blvd Cordova AL 35550

WEESE, CYNTHIA ROGERS, architect, educator; b. Des Moines, June 23, 1940; d. Gilbert Taylor and Catharine (Wingard) Rogers; m. Benjamin H. Weese, July 5, 1963; children: Daniel Peter, Catharine Mohr. B.S.A.S., Washington U., St. Louis, 1962; B.Arch., Washington U., 1965. Registered architect, Ill. Pvt. practice architecture Chgo., 1965-72, 1974-77; draftsperson, designer Harry Weese & Assocs., Chgo., 1972-74; prin. Weese Hickey Weese Ltd., Chgo., 1977—; design critic Ball State U., Muncie, Ind., Miami U., Oxford, Ohio, 1979, U. Wis.-Milw., 1980, U. Ill.-Chgo., 1981, 85, Iowa State U., Ames, 1982, Washington U., St. Louis, 1985. Mem. AIA (dir. Chgo. chpt. 1980-83, v.p. 1983-85, 1st v.p. 1986-87, pres. 1987-88, disting. building awards 1977, 81, 82, 83, 86, interior architecture award 1981, disting. service award 1978), Chgo. Women in Architecture, Chgo. Network, Chgo. Archtl. Assistance Ctr. (bd. dirs.), Nat. Inst. Archtl. Edn. (bd. dirs. 1988—), Alpha Rho Chi. Democrat. Clubs: Arts, Chgo. Archtl. Office: Weese Hickey Weese 9 W Hubbard St Chicago IL 60610

WEGHORST, MARGARET LYNN, telephone company official, educator; b. Pasadena, Calif., Jan. 3, 1948; d. Gerald Robert and Genevieve Marilyn (Scheffler) Eilers: m. Dwight Edward Weghorst, Aug. 20, 1978 (div. Dec. 1982). BS in Mgmt., No. Ill. U., 1970; MBA in Systems, De Paul U., 1984. Lic. real estate broker, Ill. Various managerial positions Ill. Bell Telephone, Chgo., 1970-87, mgr. computer ops., 1987—. Recipient Leadership in Bus. award YWCA, Chgo., 1984. Mem. Computer Ops. Mgmt. Assn. (v.p. 1987-88), Bell Mgmt. Women (pres. Chgo. 1984-85). Roman Catholic. Home: 1105 W Hillgrove Ave La Grange IL 60525 Office: Ill Bell Telephone 3206 W 61st St Chicago IL 60629

WEGLARZ, CINDY SUE, chemical engineer; b. Oak Park, Ill., July 13, 1960; d. Stanley and Anne J. (Koster) W. AS, Triton Coll., 1980; BCE, U. Ill., 1982. Lab. technician Diamond Shamrock, Franklin Park, Ill., 1981, Mazer Chem., Gurnee, Ill., 1983; devel. engr. II Morton Chem., Ringwood, Ill., 1983—. office: Morton Chem 5005 Barnard Mill Rd Ringwood IL 60072

WEGMANN, PAMELA ANN, infosystems executive; b. New Orleans, Oct. 24, 1951; d. Peter Paul and Margaret Rose (Helmke) W. BA, La. State U., 1973. lic. tchr., La. Tchr. Jefferson Parish Sch. System, Gretna, La., 1973-79; field rep. La. Fedn. of Tchrs., Metairie, La., 1979-82; Lexis account rep. Mead Data Cen., New Orleans, 1982-84, sr. account rep., 1984-85; br. mgr. Mead Data Cen., Houston, 1985—. campaign worker Dist. E. Jefferson Parish Sch. Bd. Race, Metairie, 1977, Louis Lambert Campaign for Gov., New Orleans, 1979, Carter for Pres., New Orleans, 1980. Fellow Loyola Inst. of Politics; mem. Info. Industry Assn., Am. Mgmt. Assn. Democrat. Presbyterian.

WEGNER, MARY SUE, nuclear engineer; b. Centralia, Ill., Feb. 27, 1941; d. Clarence Frank and Mabel Arwood (Collie) Wehlage; A.A. in Physics, McLennan Community Coll., 1972; B.S. in Nuclear Engring., Tex A&M U., 1974; postgrad. Ga. Inst. Tech., 1980-81; m. Lloyd Arthur Wegner, May 7, 1961 (div.); children—Diana Teresa, Kathleen Marie, Karl David. Draftsman USAF, Keesler AFB, Miss., 1959-60; clk. Mid-State Electric Co., Alexandria, La., 1963-66; draftsman Dresser Indsl. Valve and Instrument div., Alexandria, 1966-67; aircraft insp. Gen. Dynamics, Waco, Tex., 1968-70; draftsman Lone Star Gas, Waco, 1971-72; nuclear field engr. Gen. Electric Co., Atlanta, 1974-81; reactor systems engr. Nuclear Regulatory Commn., Bethesda, Md., 1981—. Served with USAF, 1959-60. Cert. governance Am. Nuclear Soc. Mem. Am. Nuclear Soc. (N. Ala. chpt. chmn. 1977). Home: 12205 Bond St Wheaton MD 20902 Office: Nuclear Regulatory Commn Office Analysis and Evaluation of Oper ational Data Washington DC 20555

WEH, REBECCA ROBERTON, charter services administrator, computer consultant; b. Colorado Springs, Colo., Sept. 23, 1946; d. Eddie Joseph, Jr. and Roberta Louise (Aucoin) Roberton; m. Allen Edward Weh, July 5, 1968; children—Deborah, Ashley, Brian. B.S., U. N.M., 1969, postgrad. spl. edn., 1970-72, acctg., 1980-82. Tchr., Calvert Acad., Albuquerque, 1971-72, Albuquerque Pub. Sch., 1972-73; staff acct. McCarthy, Weems, C.P.A.s, Albuquerque, 1979-83; v.p., adminstrn. Charter Services, Albuquerque, 1983—; computer programmer various small bus., N.M., 1982—; instr. Computer Software Seminars, 1983—. Designer, developer Computer Programs for Bus., 1984—. Vol., N.M. Kidney Found., Albuquerque, 1972; bd. dir. St. Pius X High Sch. 1981-89, also fin. chmn. 1986-87; mem. City of Albuquerque Beautification Com., 1982-84; vol. U.S. Senator P.V. Domenici Republican campaign, Albuquerque, 1983-84. Mem. Jr. League of Albuquerque (fin. v.p. 1987-88,treas. 1984-85, nominating com. 1985-86, Service award), Kappa Alpha Theta (fin. adv. 1977-78, treas. 1977-82, Outstanding Alumni of Yr. 1980). Roman Catholic. Office: Charter Services Inc PO Box 25604 Albuquerque NM 87125

WEHL, GABRIELLE, lawyer; b. Syracuse, N.Y., July 18, 1952; d. Stanley Alfred and Adeline (Letkiewicz) Urbanowicz; m. Marvin Joseph Wehl Jr., May 27, 1978; 1 child, Marvin Joseph Wehl III. BA in Govt. magna cum laude with highest honors, Sweet Briar Coll., 1974; JD, U. Ala., 1977. Bar: Ala. 1977, U.S. Ct. Appeals (5th cir.) 1978, U.S. Dist. Ct. (so. dist.) Ala. 1979, U.S. Ct. Appeals (11th cir.) 1981, U.S. Dist. Ct. (no. dist.) Ala. 1985. Law clk. to presiding justice 23d Jud. Cir. Ct., Huntsville, Ala., 1977-78; staff atty. Legal Aid Soc. of Mobile County, Ala., 1978-80, Legal Services Corp. of Ala., Mobile, 1980-85; assoc. atty. Bell, Richardson & Sparkman PA, Huntsville, 1985—; speaker Social Security Law Ala. Consortium of Legal Services Programs, Mobile, 1984, sex discrimination law NOW, Huntsville, 1986. Mem. Ala. State Bar Assn., Huntsville-Madison County Bar Assn., Phi Beta Kappa. Democrat. Roman Catholic. Home: 213 Winthrop Dr SW Huntsville AL 35801 Office: Bell Richardson Sparkman 116 S Jefferson St Huntsville AL 35801

WEHRLE, MARTHA GAINES, former state legislator; b. Charleston, W.Va., Nov. 30, 1925; d. Ludwell Ebersole and Betty (Chilton) Gaines; A.B., Vassar Coll., 1948; M.A., Harvard U., 1954; m. Russell Schilling Wehrle, Oct. 16, 1954; children—Michael H., Ebersole Gaines, Katherine S., Philip N., Martha Chilton. Tchr., W.Va. schs., 1949-50, Belmont (Mass.) Day Sch., 1951-53; mem. W.Va. Ho. of Dels., 1974-84, vice chmn. edn. com., 1976, chmn. constl. revision com., 1977-84, mem. fin. com.; dir. Kanawha Bank & Trust Co., 1984—; bd. dirs. McJunkin Corp. Bd. dirs. Kanawha Valley Found., 1987—, Arthur B. Hodges Ctr., Inc.; mem. adv. council W.Va. Woman's Commn. Mem. LWV, Garden Club Am. (chmn. nat. affairs and legis. 1987—). Democrat. Episcopalian. Clubs: Kanawha Garden, Charleston Jr. League.

WEHRMAN, ROSANNA XIMENES, medical social worker; b. San Antonio, June 4, 1949; d. Edward Trevino and Lucrecia (Cano) Ximenes; m. Douglas Eugene Wehrman, Mar. 29, 1972; children: Anastacia Nicole, Russel Eugene. B of Sociology, Southwest Tex. State U., 1970; M of Social Work, Our Lady of Lake Worden Sch. Social Work, San Antonio, 1972. Cert. clin. social worker, advanced clin. practitioner, social worker. Med. social worker U. Tex., Galveston, 1974-76; dir. social services St. Joseph Hosp., Paris, Tex., 1976-77; social worker Denton State Sch., Paris, 1977-78; dir. social services med. plaza Home Health Services, Paris, 1982-83; med. social worker Tex. Dept. Health, Paris, 1983—. Mem. adv. bd. Health Profl. Adv. Com., Paris, 1986—, New Beginnings, Paris, 1985—; bd. dirs. Chance, Inc., Paris, 1986—, chairperson, 1985-86; bd. dirs. Family Haven Family Violence Shelter, Paris, 1985-86. Office: Tex Dept Health 740 SW 6th Paris TX 75460

WEI, KATHERINE, business executive; b. Peking, China, Oct. 4, 1930; came to U.S., 1949, naturalized, 1969; d. Kato and Alice (Chao) Yang Young; m. C.J. Shen (div.); children—Ada, Lawrence, Ava; m. Chung C Wei; children—Larry, Audrea. Diploma in Nursing, Shanghai Nursing Sch., 1949. Adminstr., Med. Office, J.F. Kennedy Airport, 1952-71; dir. pub. relations Falcon Shipping Group, Houston, 1971-80, sr. v.p., 1980-87, chmn. bd., 1987—; lectr. in field. Author: (autobiography) Second Daughter, 1984. Pres., Am. Contract League Charity Found., Memphis, 1984—. Mem. Am. Contract Bridge League. Avocation: bridge. Address: 14 Greenway Plaza Houston TX 77046

WEICK, MARY DENISE, nurse; b. Lake City, Minn., Feb. 12, 1959; d. Harold E. and Dorothy E. Weick. BS in Nursing, Augustana Coll., 1981; postgrad., George Mason U., 1986—. RN, registered emergency med. technician, Minn., D.C. Staff nurse Mayo Clinic Meth. Hosp., Rochester, Minn., 1981-82; pub. health nurse Peace Corps, Bolivar Province, Ecuador, 1982-84; clin. supr. nursing The Washington Home & Hospice, 1985-86; community health nurse D.C. Govt. Dept. Human Services, Washington, 1986—; speaker on nursing Peace Corps, Washington, 1987; speaker City-Wide AIDS Educators, Washington, 1987; translator Spanish Internat. Council Nurse Researchers, Washington, 1987. Asst. coordinator Returned Peace Corps Vols., Washington, 1986—, mem. nat. council, 1986—. Grantee WHO, Quito, Ecuador, 1984. Mem. Am. Nurses Assn., D.C. Nurses Assn., Am. Pub. Health Assn., Kennedy Ctr. Inst., Smithsonian Inst. Republican. Lutheran.

WEIDEL, LYNNE CATHERINE, consulting firm executive; b. Ridley Park, Pa., Sept. 13, 1946; d. Daniel Gossard and Antoinette Marie (Maccinile) W. BA, U. Del., 1968; MHA, U. Minn., 1976. Dir. instl. planning Met. Hosps., Inc., Portland, Oreg., 1979-81, v.p., 1982-83; chief exec. officer Clackamas Health Care Consortium, Portland, 1982-83; prin. Weidel & Assocs., Portland, 1983-88; v.p. Dearing and Assocs., Spokane, Wash., 1988—; sports network coordinator Inst. for Managerial and Profl. Women, Portland, 1980-81; mem. Multnomah sub-area council N.W. Oreg. Health Systems Agy., Portland, 1982-83; preceptor U. Minn., Mpls., 1982—. Coauthor: Marketing Women's Health Care, 1987. Bd. dirs. Portland YWCA, 1983-84, Lake Grove Neighborhood Assn.; vol. Big Sister/Big Brother program. Mem. Am. Coll. Hosp. Execs., Am. Soc. Hosp. Care Planning and Mktg., Oreg. Health Care Planning and Mktg. Assn. (steering com. 1984—). Club: Bergfunde Ski (Portland). Avocations: white water rafting, hiking. Office: Dearing and Assocs S 1414 Bernard Spokane WA 99203

WEIDEMANN, CELIA JEAN, social scientist, international development consultant; b. Denver, Dec. 6, 1942; d. John Clement and Hazel (Van Tuyl) Kirlin; m. Wesley Clark Weidemann, July 1, 1972; 1 child, Stephanie Jean. BS, Iowa State U., 1964; MS, U. Wis.-Madison, 1970, PhD, 1973; postgrad. U. So. Calif., Washington, 1983. Advisor, UN Food & Agr. Orgn., Ibadan, Nigeria, 1973-77; ind. researcher, Asia and Near East, 1977-78; program coordinator, asst. prof., research assoc. U. Wis., Madison, 1979-81; chief institutional and human resources U.S. Agy. for Internat. Devel., Washington, 1982-85, team leader, cons., Sumatra, Indonesia, 1984; dir. fed. econs. program Midwest Research Inst., Washington, 1985-86; pres. Weidemann Assocs., Arlington, Va., 1986—; cons. Internat. Ctr. for Research on Women, Kinshasa Zaire, 1986, U.S. Congress, Aspen Inst., Ford Found., World Bank, Nigeria, Gambia, Indonesia; cons. U.S. Agy. for Internat. Devel., Kenya, Jordan, Global Exchange, 1986-87. Author: Planning Home Economics Curriculum for Social and Economic Development; contbr. chpts. to books and articles to profl. jours. Am. Home Econs. Assn. fellow, 1969-73 (recipient research grant Ford Found. 1987—). Mem. Soc. Internat. Devel., Am. Sociol. Assn., U.S. Dirs. of Internat. Agrl. Programs, Assn. for Women in Devel. (pres.-elect 1988—, founder, bd. dirs.), Internat. Devel. Conf. (bd. dirs., exec. com.), Am. Home Econs. Assn. (Wis. internat. chmn. 1980-81), Internat. Fedn. Home Econs., Pi Lambda Theta, Omicron Nu. Roman Catholic. Avocations: mountain trekking, piano/pipe organ, canoeing, photography, poetry. Home: 2607 N 24th St Arlington VA 22207

WEIDENBRUCH, ANNA MAE, nurse; b. Owosso, Mich., July 26, 1926; d. Robert Harry and Della Jane (Gander) Thompson; m. Manley Lavern Nixon, Aug. 3, 1946 (div. 1961); children: Terry Lee, Douglas Kent, LaVerna Ann, Norma Jean; m. Donald F. Clewley, Aug. 27, 1961 (dec. 1973); m. Heinz Weidenbruch, 1984. Assocs. of Nursing, Lansing (Mich.) Community Coll., 1983. RN, Mich. Staff nurse Sparrow Hosp., Lansing, 1958-62, Ingham Med. Hosp., Lansing, 1962-64, Lansing Gen. Hosp., 1964-66, 1977-88; staff nurse Hazel I. Findlay Country Manor, St. Johns, Mich., 1987—. Democrat. Home: 2123 Northwest Ave Lansing MI 48906 Office: Hazel I Findlay Country Manor 1101 S Scott Rd Saint Johns MI 48879

WEIDENFELD, SHEILA RABB, television producer, author; b. Cambridge, Mass., Sept. 7, 1943; d. Maxwell M. and Ruth (Cryden) Rabb; B.A., Brandeis U., 1965; m. Edward L. Weidenfeld, Aug. 11, 1968; children—Nicholas Rabb, Daniel Rabb. Assoc. producer Metromedia, Inc., WNEW-TV, N.Y.C., 1965-68; talent coordinator That Show with Joan Rivers, NBC, N.Y.C., 1968-71; coordinator NBC network game programs, N.Y.C., 1968-71; producer Metromedia, Inc., WTTG-TV, Washington, 1971-73; creator/producer Take It From Here, NBC (WRC-TV), Washington, 1973-74; press sec. to first lady Betty Ford and spl. asst. to Pres. Gerald R. Ford 1974-77; mem. Pres.'s Adv. Commn. on Historic Preservation, 1977-81; TV producer, moderator On the Record, NBC-TV, WRC-TV, Washington, 1978-79; pres. D.C. Prodns., Ltd., 1978; mem. Sec. State's Adv. Commn. on Fgn. Service Inst., 1972-74. Author: First Lady's Lady, 1979. Mem. U.S. Holocaust Meml. Council, 1987—; corporator, Dana Hall Sch., Wellesley, Mass; bd. dirs. Wolf Trap Found., Women's Campaign Fund, 1978-79; bd. dirs. D.C. Contemporary Dance Theatre, 1986—, D.C. Republican Central Com., 1984—; mem. D.C. Preservation League, 1987—; chmn. C&O Canal Nat. Hist. Park Commn, 1988—. Recipient awards for outstanding achievement in the media AAUW, 1973, 74; named hon. consul of Republic of San Marino to Washington; knighted by Order of St. Agatha, Republic of San Marino, 1986. Mem. Washington Press Club, Am. Newspaper Women's Club, Am. Women in Radio and TV, Nat. Acad. TV Arts and Scis. (Emmy award 1972), Sigma Delta Chi. Home and Office: 3059 Q St NW Washington DC 20007

WEIDENFELLER, GERALDINE CARNEY, speech and language pathologist; b. Kearny, N.J., Oct. 12, 1933; d. Joseph Gerald and Catherine Grace (Doyle) Carney; B.S., Newark State U., 1954; postgrad. Northwestern U., summer 1956, U. Wis., summer 1960; M.A., N.Y. U., 1962; m. James Weidenfeller, Apr. 4, 1964; children—Anne, David. Lic speech/language pathologist, N.J. Speech pathologist Kearny (N.J.) Public Schs., 1954-61, North Brunswick (N.J.) Public Schs., 1961-65, Bridgewater (N.J.) Public Schs., 1969-72; speech therapist Somerset County Ednl. Commn., 1983—; real estate agt., N.J., 1982—; pvt. practice speech therapy, Somerville, N.J., 1980—. Vice pres. Rosary Soc., Hillsborough, N.J., 1986—. Mem. Am. Speech and Hearing Assn., N.J. Speech and Hearing Assn. Roman Catholic. Club: Toastmasters (winner dist. humorous speech contest 1984, sec. 1985, advanced Toastmaster 1986). Home: 3 Banor Dr Somerville NJ 08876

WEIDERSPON, RHONDA KAY, sales professional; b. Loveland, Colo., Jan. 31, 1958; d. Richard Eugene and Gloria Mae (Ackerson) W. BS, Colo. State U., 1982. Sales rep. Parker Livestock Supply, Billings, Mont., 1982-84; dist. sales mgr. Loomix Inc., Arroyo Grande, Calif., 1984—. Democrat. Lutheran. Home: 3860 Kiki Dr Helena MT 59601 Office: Loomix Inc PO Box 490 Arroyo Grande CA 93420

WEIDMAN, TERESA JOSEPHINE, marketing executive; b. Buffalo, Sept. 19, 1960; d. Joseph and Vincenza (Fasone) Pitrola; m. Michael John Weidman, Aug. 20, 1982. BA in Environ. Design and Planning, SUNY, Buffalo, 1983, BSBA, 1985. Systems engr. Electronic Data Systems, Troy, Mich., 1985-86; mktg. coordinator Detroit Tool Industries, Warren, Mich., 1986-87; product adminstr. Automated Mktg. Systems, Southfield, Mich., 1987—. Mem. Nat. Assn. Female Execs., Am. Mktg. Assn., Bus. and Profl. Women U.S.A. Roman Catholic. Home: 3623 Hunter Ave Royal Oak MI 48073 Office: Automated Mktg Systems 26533 Evergreen Rd Suite 400 Southfield MI 48076

WEIGEL, ELSIE DIVEN, publishing executive, writer, editor; b. Phila., May 31, 1948; d. William Bleakley Diven and Elsie May (Betts) Darling; m. John C. Weigel, Dec. 19, 1970 (div. 1979); 1 Child, Kimberly Joy. BA, Am. U., 1970. Editorial asst. Water Pollution Control Fedn., Alexandria, Va., 1970-72; Asst dir. publs. Am. Speech, Hearing, and Lang. Assn., Rockville, Md., 1972-78; editor-in-chief Potato Chip/Snack Food Assn., Alexandria, 1978-79; dir. publs. Nat. Soc. Pub. Accts., Alexandria, 1979-80; editorial project dir. Energy Info. Adminstrn. U.S. Dept Energy, Washington, 1980—. Editor newsletter Rittenhouse Family Assn.; contbr. articles to profl. jours. Mem. Life Skills Ctr. (bd. dirs. 1987—) Washington. Mem. Nat. Assn. Govt. Communicators (Blue Pencil award), Nat. Assn Female Execs., Sigma Detla Chi. Home: 8303 Pondside Terr Alexandria VA 22309 Office: US Dept Energy 1000 Independence Ave Washington DC 20003

WEIGHTMAN, JUDY MAE, lawyer; b. New Eagle, Pa., May 22, 1941; d. Morris and Ruth (Gutstadt) Epstein; children: Wayne, Randall, Darrell. BS in English, California U. of Pa., 1970; MA in Am. Studies, U. Hawaii, 1975; grantee in internat. relations Chaminade U., 1976; JD, Richardson Sch. Law, 1981. Bar: Hawaii 1981. Tchr. Fairfax County Sch. (Va.), 1968-72, Hawaii Pub. Schs., Honolulu, 1973-75; lectr. Kapiolani Community Coll., Honolulu,

1975-76; instr. Olympic Community Coll., Pearl Harbor, Hawaii, 1975-77; lectr. Hawaii Pacific Coll., Honolulu, 1977-78; law clerk to atty. gen. Hawaii and Case, Kay and Lynch and Davis & Levin, 1979-81, to chief judge Intermediate Ct. Appeals, Honolulu, 1981-82; dep. pub. defender Office of Pub. Defender, Honolulu, 1982-84; staff atty. Dept. Commerce & Consumer Affairs, State of Hawaii 1984-86; pres., dir. Am. Beltwrap Corp., 1986—; dir. pre-admission program, asst. prof. William S. Richardson Sch. Law, 1987—. Mem. neighborhood bd. No. 25 City and County Honolulu, 1976-77; vol. Legal Aid Soc., Honolulu, 1977-78; bd. dirs. women's div. Jewish Fedn., Protection and Advocacy Agy.; parent rep. Wheeler Intermediate Adv. Council, Honolulu, 1975-77; Hawaii rep. Metropolis Studios; trustee Carl K. Mirikitani Meml. Scholarship Fund, Arts Council Hawaii, membership dir. ACLU, 1977-78, bd. dirs., Hawaii, 1988—; founder Hawaii Holocaust Project. Community scholar, Honolulu, 1980. Mem. ABA, Hawaii Women Lawyers, Assn. Trial Lawyers Am., Hawaii Bar Assn., Am. Judicature Soc., Richardson Sch. Law Alumni Assn. (alumni rep. 1981-82), Phi Delta Phi (v.p. 1980-81). Democrat. Jewish. Clubs: Hadassah, Women's Guild.

WEIGLE, MARTA, folklorist, educator; b. Janesville, Wis.; d. Richard D. Weigle. Student, St. John's Coll., Annapolis, Md., 1961-62; AB cum laude in Social Relations, Harvard U., 1965; MA, U. Pa., 1968, PhD, 1971. Asst. prof. anthropology and English U. N.Mex., Albuquerque, 1972-77, assoc. prof., 1977-83, prof. anthropology, English and Am. studies, 1983-87, prof. Am. studies and anthropology, 1987—, chmn. dept. Am. studies, 1984—; mgr., co-owner Abacus Books, Inc., 1973-74; rev. panelist NEH; cons. Hispanic heritage wing Mus. Internat. Folk Art, Sante Fe, 1986—; lectr. in field. Author: Follow My Fancy: The Book of Jacks and Jack Games, 1970, The Penitentes of the Southwest, 1970, Spiders and Spinsters: Women and Mythology, 1982, (with David Johnson) Lightning and Labyrinth: An Introduction to Mythology, 1979, At the Beginning: American Creation Myths, 1980, (with Kyle Fiore) Santa Fe and Taos: The Writer's Era, 1982, Hispanic Arts and Ethnohistory in the Southwest, 1983, Two Guadalupes, 1987, (with Peter White) The Lore of New Mexico, 1988; editor: Echoes of the Flute, 1972, The Lightning Tree Southwestern Calendar for 1974, 1973, Hispanic Villages of Northern New Mexico, 1975, The Lightning Tree Bicentennial Southwestern Reader for 1976: An Anthology of Folklore with Weekly Calendar, (with Charles L. Briggs) Hispano Folklife of New Mexico: The Lorin W. Brown Fed. Writers' Project Manuscripts, 1978, New Mexicans in Cameo and Camera, 1985; cons. editor: Chamisal and Penasco: The Farm Security Administration Photography of Russell Lee, 1985, Colonial Frontiers: Art and Life in Spanish New Mexico, 1982-83; assoc. editor Ancient City Press, 1972-74, ptnr., editor, 1981—; assoc. editor: The Lightning Tree, Inc., 1974-76; contbr. numerous articles to revs. and papers to profl. jours. Recipient award of honor Cultural Properties Rev. Com., State of N.Mex., 1976, Zia award N.Mex. Press Women, 1977; grantee Nat. Endowment for Humanities, 1979-81, Exxon Edn. Found., 1979. Bd. dirs. Santa Fe Hist. Soc., 1977-81, Spanish Colonial Arts Soc., 1979—; trustee Am. Folklife Ctr., 1987—. Mem. N.Mex. Folklore Soc. (2d v.p. 1977-78, 1st v.p. 1978-79, pres. 1979-80, Roll of Honor 1978), Am. Folklore Soc. (editor Folklore Women's Communication 1977-79, editor publs., series, vols. 1-8, exec. bd. 1983-86, fellow), Office: U N Mex Dept Am Studies Albuquerque NM 87131

WEIHRER, ANNA LEA, government data processing executive; b. Clarksburg, W.Va., Feb. 28, 1927; d. Roscoe and Catherine Ruth (Waters) Allman; m. Calvin Lawrence Bucklew, Aug. 21, 1947 (dec. 1948); m. Arthur H. Weihrer, Dec. 25, 1950; 1 child, Carol Jo. BA, W.Va. U., 1948, MS, 1949. Instr. W.Va. U., Morgantown, 1948-77; mathematician U.S. Naval Propellant Plant, Indian Head, Md., 1955-62; data processing staff U.S. Pub. Health Service, Washington, 1962-69; asst. prof. George Washington Sch. Medicine, Washington, 1969-71; staff Office Surgeon Gen. Data Systems Agy., Washington, 1971-74; dep. project mgr. Triservice Med. Info. Systems Army, Washington, 1974-87; with Gen. Bus. Services, Inc., Damascus, Md., 1988—. Contbr. numerous articles to profl. jours. Recipient Performance awards U.S. Govt., 1955—. Mem. Assn. Computer Machines, Data Processing Mgmt. Assn., Phi Beta Kappa. Methodist. Office: Gen Bus Services Inc 20271 Goldenrod Ln Germantown MD 20874

WEIL, MILDRED WISHNATT, college dean; b. Newark; d. Benjamin Wishnatt and Esther (Manks) Wilson; m. Philip E. Weil, Dec. 21, 1947 (dec. 1978); children: Ann Dédre, Barbara Jane; m. Herbert Zients, Sept. 8, 1984; children: Michael, Steven. BA, Rutgers U.; MA, NYU, PhD. Prof., assoc. dean to dean William Paterson Coll., Wayne, N.J., 1960-85; dean grad. studies Kutztown (Pa.) U., 1985—; counselor Straight and Narrow, Paterson, N.J., 1980-85. Editor-author: The Sociology of the Arts, 1975, Sociological Perspectives in Marriage and the Family, 1972; author: Marriage, the Family, and Sociology, 1971. Recipient Founders Day award NYU. Mem. Eastern Sociol. Soc., Phi Delta Kappa. Home: 375 Spring Valley Rd Easton PA 18042 Office: Kutztown Univ Grad Ctr Rm 100 Kutztown PA 19530

WEIL, SUZANNE S. FERN, broadcasting executive; b. Mpls., June 22, 1933; d. Maurice and Esther (Sperling) Swiller; m. Fred Weil, Jr., Sept. 14, 1952 (dec. Apr. 1983); 1 dau., Peggy. Student, U. Minn.-Mpls. Coordinator performing arts Walker Art Center, Mpls., 1969-76; dir. dance program Nat. Endowment for Arts, Washington, 1968-78; sr. v.p., mng. dir. Pub. Broadcasting Service, Washington, 1980-81; sr. v.p. programming Pub. Broadcasting Service, 1981—; mem. media adv. com. Am. Inst. Architects, Washington, 1983—; dir. Nat. Arts Adv. Bd., Action for Children's TV, Boston, 1978—; cons. editor Jour. Arts ad Mgmt. and Law, Washington, 1982—. Bd. dirs. Cunningham Dance Found., N.Y.C., 1982—; bd. dirs. Film in the Cities, St. Paul, 1976—, Guthrie Theater, Mpls., 1982—, Twyla Tharp Dance Found., N.Y.C., 1978—; trustee Dance USA, Washington, 1982-83. Bush fellow Harvard U. Inst. for Arts Adminstrn., 1973. Mem. Nat. Acad. TV Arts and Scis. Club: Mpls. Home: 2101 Connecticut Ave NW Washington DC 20008 Office: 1320 Braddock Pl Alexandria VA 22314

WEIL-GARRIS BRANDT, KATHLEEN, art historian; b. Surrey, Eng., Apr. 7, 1934; d. Kurt Hermann and Charlotte (Garris) Weil; m. Werner Brandt, 1982 (dec. 1983). BA with honors, Vassar Coll., 1956; postgrad., U. Bonn, 1956-57; MA, Radcliffe U., 1958; PhD, Harvard, 1966. Asst. prof. NYU, N.Y.C., 1963-67, assoc. prof., 1967-72, prof., 1973—; assoc. prof. NYU Inst. Fine Arts, N.Y.C., 1967-72, prof., 1973—; vis. prof. Harvard U., Cambridge, Mass., 1980; editor in chief The Art Bulletin, N.Y.C., 1977-81. Author: Leonardo and Central Italian Art, 1974, Problems In Cinquecento Sculpture, 1977; author: (with J. d'Amico) The Renaissance Cardinal's Ideal Palace, 1981; contbr. numerous articles to profl. jours. Guggenheim fellow, 1976; grantee Henkel Found., 1987; research award Humboldt Found. 1985; Dist. Teaching award Lindback Found, 1967. Mem. Coll. Art Assn. (bd. dirs. 1973-74, 77-81), Renaissance Soc. Am. (area rep.), Soc. Architl. Historians, Phi Beta Kappa (v.p. 1979-81). Office: NYU Inst Fine Arts 1 E 78th St New York NY 10021

WEIMER, LUCINDA MAY, educator; b. Huntington, Pa., Sept. 20, 1949; d. Arthur Snyder and Elsie Pauline (Treece) Wagner; m. Richard Vincent Weimer Jr., June 4, 1972; 1 child, Chad Andrew. BE, Shippensburg State Coll., 1972; postgrad., Western Md. U. Cert. tchr., Md. Educator phys. edn. Cynthia Warner Sch., Ltd., Takoma Park, Md., 1972-74; educator English Gov. Thomas Jr. High Sch., Frederick, Md., 1974-81; media specialist St. Martins Sch., Gaithersburg, Md., 1981-82; educator English Linganore High Sch., Frederick, Md., 1982-85, Middletown (Md.) Jr. High Sch., 1985-87; work-study coordinator and counselor Frederick County Vocat. Tech. Ctr., Md., 1987—; chair English dept. Middletown Middle Sch., 1986-87—; cons. corp. fitness program Gillette Corp., Rockville, Md., 1981-82, curriculum cons. Lang. Arts Task Force, Frederick, Md., 1985—. Co-author: career curriculum Career Skills Through English, 1983. Coordinator March of Dimes Reading Olympics, Gaithersburg, Md., 1981; rep. Equity comm. Frederick county, 1985-87. Mem. NEA, Supervision and Curriculum Devel, Nat. Council Tchrs. of English, Md. State Tchrs. Assn., Nat. Bd. Cert. Counselors, Alpha Sigma Tau.

WEIN, CYNTHIA ELLEN, marketing executive; b. Takoma Park, Md., Dec. 24, 1957; d. Arthur Benjamin and Mary Louise (Barker) W. BS, Purdue U., 1979; M, Antioch Sch. Law, 1982-83. Mktg. researcher Sheraton, Washington, 1979-80; sales mgr. Sea Pines Plantation Co., Hilton Head Island, S.C., 1980-81; dir. sales Sheraton Potomac Hotel, Rockville, Md., 1981-82, Ritz Carlton Hotel, Washington, 1982-83; pres. Creative Planning Internat., Washington, 1983—; dir. membership Great Inns of America, Annapolis, 1987—. Mem. Meeting Planners Internat., Washington Conv. and Visitors Assn., Greater Washington Soc. of Assn. Execs., Found. for Internat. Meetings (bd. govs. 1985-86). Clubs: Conservative, Purdue (pres. 1982—)(Washington). Office: Creative Planning Internat 1825 Eye St NW #400 Washington DC 20006

WEIN, LIBBY (LILLIAN) RAPHAEL, social worker; b. Phila., Feb. 23, 1934; d. Samuel and Esther (Terry) Raphael; m. Joseph Alexander Wein, June 23, 1957; children: Michele Georgeanne, Paul Frederick. Cert., Franklin Sch. Sci. and Arts, 1955; AA, Santa Monica Coll., 1969; BA cum laude, UCLA, 1976; MSW, U. So. Calif., 1981. Lic. social work, Calif. Med. social worker Midway Hosp., Los Angeles, 1981-82; psychotherapist Airport Marina Counseling Service, Los Angeles, 1981-83; geriatric, psychiat. social worker Sr. Health and Peer Counseling Ctr., Santa Monica, Calif., 1983—; cons. Cedars-Sinai, Los Angeles, 1978, case mgr., 1979; ctr. fellow UCLA, U. So. Calif. Long Term Care Gerontology Ctr., 1985. Mem. Nat. Assn. Social Workers, Soc. Clin. Social Work. Home: 324 S Clark Dr Beverly Hills CA 90211 Office: Sr Health & Peer Counseling Ctr 2125 Arizona Santa Monica CA 90404

WEINBERG, LILA SHAFFER, author, editor. d. Sam and Blanche (Hyman) Shaffer; m. Arthur Weinberg, Jan. 25, 1953; children: Hedy Merrill and Anita Michelle (twins), Wendy Clare. Editor Ziff-Davis Pub. Co., 1944-53; assoc. chief manuscript editor jours. U. Chgo. Press, 1966-80, sr. manuscript editor books, 1980—; mem. faculty Sch. for New Learning DePaul U., Chgo., 1976—; vis. faculty continuing edn. programs U. Chgo., 1984—. Author: (with husband) The Muckrakers, 1961 (selected for White House Library 1963), Verdicts Out of Court, 1963, Instead of Violence, 1963, Passport to Utopia, 1968, Some Dissenting Voices, 1970, Clarence Darrow: A Sentimental Rebel, 1980; contbr. articles and revs. to various publs. Recipient Friends of Lit. award Chgo. Found. Lit., 1980, Social Justice award Darrow Community Ctr., 1980, Disting. Body of Work award Friends of Midwest Authors, 1987. Mem. Soc. Midland Authors (dir. 1977-83, pres. 1983-85, Best Biography award 1980), ACLU, Pioneer Women, Clarence Darrow Commemorative Com., YIVO, Authors' League. Home: 5421 S Cornell Ave Chicago IL 60615

WEINBERG, SYDNEY STAHL, historian; b. N.Y.C., Oct. 2, 1938; d. David Leslie and Berenice (Jarvis) Stahl; B.A., Barnard Coll., 1960; M.A., Columbia U., 1964; Ph.D., 1969; m. Michael Weinberg, Sept. 1, 1957; children—Deborah Sara, Elisa Rachel. Instr. history N.J. Inst. Tech., 1967-69, asst. prof., 1969-72; asso. prof. history Ramapo Coll. N.J., Mahwah, 1972-74, prof., 1974—. Nat. Endowment for Humanities fellow, 1977-78. Mem. Inst. for Research in History, Middle Atlantic Radical Historians Orgn., Am. Hist. Assn., Orgn. Am. Historians, Am. Studies Assn. Author: The World of Our Mothers: The Lives of Jewish Immigrant Women, 1988; contbr. articles to profl. jours. Home: 80 LaSalle St New York NY 10027 Office: Ramapo Coll NJ Mahwah NJ 07430

WEINER, ANNETTE B., anthropology educator; b. Phila., Feb. 14, 1933; d. Archibald W. and Phyllis M. (Stein-Goldman) Cohen; m. Martin Weiner, 1953 (div. 1973); children: Linda Matisse, Jonathan Weiner; m. Robert Palter, 1979 (div. 1982); m. William E. Mitchell, 1987. B.A., U. Pa., 1968; Ph.D., Bryn Mawr Coll., 1974. Vis. asst. prof. Franklin and Marshall Coll., Lancaster, Pa., 1973-74; asst. prof. anthropology U. Tex., Austin, 1974-80, assoc. prof., 1980-81; prof., chmn. dept. anthropology NYU, N.Y.C., 1981—; David B. Kriser prof. NYU, 1985—. Author: Women of Value: Men of Renown: New Perspectives in Trobriand Exchange, 1976, The Trobrianders of Papua New Guinea, 1987; contbr. articles to profl. jours. Guggenheim fellow, 1980; fellow Inst. Advanced Study, Princeton, N.J., 1980-81; grantee Wenner-Gren Found. Anthrop. Research, 1982, 85, 85, NEH, 1976, 85, Am. Council Learned Socs., 1976, NIMH, 1972-73. Fellow Am. Anthrop. Assn., Royal Anthrop. Inst. Gt. Britain and Ireland, Assn. Social Anthropology in Oceania; mem. Soc. Cultural Anthropology (bd. dirs. 1985—), Cibola Anthrop. Assn. (pres. 1977-79), Commn. Visual Anthropology. Home: Pleasant Valley Farm Wolcott VT 05680 Office: NYU Dept of Anthropology 25 Waverly Pl New York NY 10003

WEINER, ELIZABETH MARGARET, writer; b. White Plains, N.Y., July 26, 1948; d. Lawrence Arthur Weiner and Barbara Jane (Dorf) Miltenburger. BA cum laude, Barnard Coll., 1971; MS in Journalism, Columbia U., 1975. Reporter Roll Call Newspaper, Washington, 1973; publicity dir. Nat. Consumer's League, Washington, 1974; reporter Montgomery County Sentinel, Washington, 1975-78, States News Service, Washington, 1978-81, 83; asst. dir. communications Nat. Com. for Responsive Philanthropy, Washington, 1986-87; freelance writer Washington, 1988—. Contbr. articles to profl. jours. Vol. VISTA, Washington, 1967-68; mem. Potomac River Albacore Fleet, Washington, 1987-88. Recipient 1st prize in News Story Weeklies Md.-Del.-D.C. Press Assn., 1975. Democrat. Jewish. Home and Office: 3509 Rodman St NW Washington DC 20008

WEINER, ILENE BERSON, magazine publishing executive; b. Newark, Apr. 29, 1942; d. Irving and Alice Florence (Goodman) Berson; m. Ira Jason Weiner, Feb. 8, 1986. BA, Barnard Coll., 1964; MA, CUNY, 1969. Mgr. advt. prodn. Modern Photography Mag., N.Y.C., 1971-74, mng. editor, 1974-77, dir. prodn., 1977-87; dir. prodn. ABC Consumer Mags., N.Y.C., 1985-87, v.p. prodn., 1987—; musical dir. off-Broadway prodns. Guest columnist Folio mag., Mag. for Design and Prodn., 1987. Mem. Assn. Publ. Prodn. Mgrs., Women in Prodn. (exec. bd. 1983-86).

WEINER-ALEXANDER, SANDRA SAMUEL, critical care nurse, consultant; b. N.Y.C., Jan. 12, 1947; d. Herbert A. and Ruth (Wallerstein) Samuel; m. Neil D. Weiner, June 15, 1969 (div. June 1980); 1 child, Jaime Michelle; m. Robert J. Alexander, Sept. 30, 1984; 1 stepchild, Rob Alexander. BS in Nursing, SUNY, Buffalo, 1968; Cert. in Critical Care, Golden West Coll., 1982; postgrad. UCLA. RN, Pa., Calif. Staff nurse N.Y. Hosp.-Cornell Med. Ctr., 1968-69; head nurse med.-surg. nursing Abington (Pa.) Hosp., 1969; assoc. prof. Sch. Nursing, U. Pa., Phila., 1970; instr. nursing Coll. of Med. Assts., Long Beach, Calif., 1971-72; surg. staff nurse Med. Ctr. of Tarzana, Calif., Cedar-Sinai Med. Ctr., Los Angeles, 1976-80; supr. recovery room Beverly Hills Med. Ctr., Los Angeles, 1981—; med. cons. RJA & Assocs., Beverly Hills, 1984—; instr. CPR, Los Angeles, 1986—. Mem. women's aux. Ctr. Theater Group Vols., Los Angeles, 1986-88. Mem. Am. Nursing Assn., Am. Assn. Critical Care Nurses, Heart and Lung Assn., Post Anesthesia Nurses Assn., U.S. Ski Assn., AAU. Democrat. Jewish. Avocations: skiing, running, traveling, theater, ballet. Home: 529 N Rodeo Dr Beverly Hills CA 90210-3206 Office: Beverly Hills Med Ctr 1177 S Beverly Dr Los Angeles CA 90035

WEINGROFF, DEBORAH MARY, state official; b. Hackensack, N.J., Dec. 23, 1952; d. Michael and Mary (Pokusa) Cajohn; m. Stephen Roy Weingroff, June 5, 1977. B.A., Stockton State Coll., 1976; A.S. Ocean County Coll., 1973. Mem. com. Twp. of Dover Mcpl. Ct., Toms River, N.J., 1973-78; asst. welfare dir. Twp. of Dover, Toms River, 1978—; field rep., state ofl. rental assistance program Dept. Community Affairs, 1988; field rep. State N.J., 1988—. Bd. dirs. Family Planning Ocean County, Toms River, 1977; chmn. Salvation Army, Toms River, 1983-84, sec. adv. bd.; sec. Cen. Ocean City unit Am. Heart Assn. Mem. Ocean Welfare League, Alumni Assn. Ocean County Coll. Mcpl. Welfare Assn. N.J. Jewish. Lodge: Sisterhood. Home: 81 Shady Nook Dr Toms River NJ 08753 Office: Twp of Dover Office Pub Assistance 33 Washington St Toms River NJ 08753

WEINHEIM, DONNA L., advertising executive; b. N.Y.C., Mar. 4, 1951; d. Walter and Eva (Domingo) W. BFA, Rochester Inst. Tech., 1972. Asst. art dir. Ogilvy and Mather, N.Y.C., 1972-76; art dir. Rosser Reeves Inc., N.Y.C., 1976-80; creative dir. Dancer Fitzgerald Sample, N.Y.C., 1980—. Designer (book jacket) Math Anxiety, 1978. Recipient awards including Art Dirs., Andy, Clio, Cannes Film Festival. Home: 345 E 80th St New York NY 12022 Office: DFS Dorland Worldwide Inc 405 Lexington Ave New York NY 10174

WEINHOUSE, IRIS, health science facility director, speech therapist; b. N.Y.C., Dec. 8, 1936; m. David Weinhouse; children Erica, Laura, Amy. BA, Bklyn. Coll., 1957, MA, 1962; PhD, CUNY, 1973. Lic. speech pathologist, N.Y., N.J. Speech pathologist Hosp. for Spl. Surgery, N.Y.C., 1957-58; supr. speech pathology Kings County Hosp., Bklyn., 1958-62; asst. prof. William Patterson Coll., Wayne, N.J., 1972-74; pvt. practice speech therapy Hillsdale, N.J., 1974—; dir. speech clinic Rockland Community Coll., Suffern, N.Y., 1985—; cons. speech pathologist Ramapo Manor Nursing Home, Suffern, N.Y., 1974-79; adj. instr. Montclair State Coll., Upper Montclair, N.J., 1979-84, Bergen Community Coll., Paramus, N.J., 1978—. Author, producer: (audio tapes on accent remediation) Sounds of American English, 1983, Pronunciation of American English, 1986; lectr. (seminars, workshops) Businesses and Corporations-Effective Communication, 1981. Mem. Am. Speech-Lang. Assn. Office: Rockland Community Coll 145 College Rd Suffern NY 10901

WEINKAUF, MARY LOUISE STANLEY, educator; b. Eau Claire, Wis., Sept. 22, 1938; d. Joseph Michael and Marie Barbara (Holzinger) Stanley; B.A., Wis. State U., 1961; M.A., U. Tenn., 1962, Ph.D., 1966; m. Alan D. Weinkauf, Oct. 12, 1962; children—Stephen, Xanti. Grad. asst., instr. U. Tenn., 1961-66; asst. prof. English, Adrian Coll., 1966-69; prof., head dept. English, Dakota Wesleyan U., Mitchell, S.D., 1969—. Mem. Mitchell Arts Council; bd. trustees, The Ednl. Found., 1986—. Mem. Nat. Council Tchrs. English, S.D. Council Tchrs. English, Sci. Fiction Research Assn., Popular Culture Assn., Milton Soc., AAUW (div. pres. 1978-80), S.D. State Poetry Soc. (pres. 1982-83), Delta Kappa Gamma (pres. local chpt., mem. state bd. 1972—, state v.p. 1979-83, state pres. 1983-85), Sigma Tau Delta, Pi Kappa Delta, Phi Kappa Phi. Republican. Lutheran. Office: Dakota Wesleyan U 507 Smith Hall Mitchell SD 57301

WEINS, MARY JUNE, small business owner, accountant; b. Long Beach, Calif., Oct. 1, 1942; d. Roy Chester and Mary Jane (Van Petten) Haslam; m. Charlie Jerome Hutto, Aug. 4, 1961 (div. Jan. 1970); 1 child, William Jerome; m. Robert Spencer, July 26, 1980; children: James Jacob, Joseph John. Student, Compton Jr. Coll., 1962-64, Long Beach City Coll., 1972-77, Napa Coll., 1978-87; cert. in massage therapy, Calistoga Sch. of Massage, 1987. Bookkeeper Muller & King, CPA's, South Gate, Calif., 1961-70; office mgr. A-1 Thread Rolling Co., Inc., South Gate, 1970-78; acctg. supr. Internat. Air Service Co., Inc., Napa, Calif., 1978-80; bus. mgr. Wilson-Cornelius Ford, Vallejo, Calif., 1980-82; controller Campbell's Carpets, Inc., Concord, Ca., 1982-84; owner Herco Bus. Services, Napa, 1984—; employment referral service and mgmt. cons. various automotive dealerships, no. Calif., 1984—. Prayer pal coordinator Pioneer Girls Club, Grace Baptist Ch., Napa, 1982-84. Mem. No. Calif. Motor Car Dealers Assn., Solano Automotive Bus. Women (pres.), Nat. Assn. of Female Execs. Democrat. Baptist. Office: Herco Bus Services 1325 Imola Ave W #618 Napa CA 94559

WEINSHIENK, ZITA LEESON, federal judge; b. St. Paul, Apr. 3, 1933; d. Louis and Ada (Dubov) Leeson; m. Hubert Troy Weinshienk, July 8, 1956 (dec. 1983); children: Edith Blair, Kay Anne, Darcy Jill; m. James N. Schaffner, Nov. 15, 1986. Student, U. Colo., 1952-53; BA magna cum laude, U. Ariz., 1955; JD cum laude, Harvard U., 1958; Fulbright grantee, U. Copenhagen, Denmark, 1959. Bar: Colo. 1959. Probation counselor, legal adviser, referee Denver Juvenile Ct., 1959-64; judge Denver County Ct., 1964-71; Denver dist. judge 1972-79, U.S. dist. judge for dist. Colo., 1979—. Precinct committeewoman Denver Democratic Com., 1963-64; bd. dirs. Crime Stoppers. Named One of 100 Women in Touch with Our Time Harper's Bazaar Mag., 1971. Mem. ABA, Colo. Bar Assn., Denver Bar Assn., Nat. Conf. Fed. Trial Judges, Colo. Women's Bar Assn., Women's Forum of Colo., Harvard Law Sch. Assn., Denver League Women Voters, Order of Coif (hon. Colo. chpt.). Office: US Dist Ct 1929 Stout St Room C-246 Denver CO 80294

WEINSTEIN, CAROLE, training and educational specialist, communications consultant, educator; b. N.Y.C., Dec. 9, 1940; d. Arthur S. and Frances E. (Schwartz) W.; 1 son, Daniel Jason Baldwin. BS Bklyn. Coll., 1965; MS CCNY, 1976; student Columbia U., 1978-79. Cert. tchr. N.Y., 1965, N.J., 1976, Calif., 1977. Tchr. N.Y.C. pub. schs., 1965-69; specialist Human Resources Agy., N.Y.C., 1969-70; adult edn. trainer, cons. Higher Edn. Devel. Fund, N.Y.C., 1970-76, 78-80, CUNY Research Found., N.Y.C., 1980-82; tng. specialist Blue Cross & Blue Shield Co. of Greater N.Y., N.Y.C., 1982-85; ednl. and communications cons. Deloitte Haskins & Sells, Exec. Office, N.Y.C., 1985—; cons., adj. prof. Hunter Coll., N.Y.C., 1975-76, U. San Francisco, 1978, LaGuardia Community Coll., N.Y.C., 1980-81, N.Y.C. Tech. Coll., 1980-82, Pace U., N.Y.C., 1983-84, Baruch Coll., 1984, Grad. Sch. Mgmt. and Urban Professions and Adult div. New Sch. for Social Research, 1984, 85, 86. NYU Grad. Sch. Pub. Adminstrn., 1984, 85, 86, NYU Am. Language Inst., 1979-82. Author: Applied Writing, 1982; contbr. articles to profl. jours.; designer and facilitator profl. tng. programs, speaker at nat. confs. Mem. Nat. Assn. Female Execs., Am. Soc. Tng. and Devel., Am. Assn. Adult and Continuing Edn., Am. Assn. Bus. Communications, Women in Communications, Inc. Democrat. Jewish. Club: Toastmasters. Office: Deloitte Haskins & Sells 1114 6th Ave New York NY 10036

WEINSTEIN, JOYCE, artist; b. N.Y.C., June 7, 1931; d. Sidney and Rose (Bier) W.; student CCNY, 1948-50, Art Students League, 1948-52; m. Stanley Boxer, Nov. 28, 1952. Exhibited in one-women shows: Perdalma Gallery, N.Y.C., 1953-56, L.I. U., Bklyn., 1969, U. Calif.-Santa Cruz, 1969, T. Bortolazzo Gallery, Santa Barbara, Calif., 1972, Dorsky Gallery, N.Y.C., 1972, 74, Galerie Ariadne, N.Y.C., 1975, Gloria Cortella Gallery, N.Y.C., 1976, Meredith Long Contemporary Gallery, N.Y.C. 1978, 79, Martin Gerard Gallery, Edmonton, Alta., Can., 1981, 82, 84, Galerie Wentzel, Cologne, W.Ger., 1982, Haber Theodore Gallery, N.Y.C., 1983, 85, Cologne, W.Ger., 1987, Gallery One, Toronto, Ont., Can., 1983, Paul Kuhn Gallery, Calgery, 1985, Eva Cohn Gallery, Highland Park, Chgo, Ill., 1985, Galerie Wentzell, Cologne, 1987, Meredith Long & Co., Houston, 1988, Hokin Gallery, Miami, 1988; group shows: Marlborough Gallery, N.Y.C., 1968, Bula Mus. Art, Calcutta, India, 1970, Rose Fried Gallery, N.Y.C., 1970, Hudson River Mus., 1971, Dorsky Gallery, 1972, Suffolk Mus., Stony Brook, N.Y., 1972, New York Cultural Center, 1973, Stamford (Conn.) Mus., 1973, Landmark Gallery, N.Y.C., 1974, Women's Interart Center, N.Y.C., 1974, 75, 78, New Sch. Social Research, N.Y.C., 1975, Bklyn. Mus., 1975, Galerie Areadne, N.Y.C., 1975, Fairleigh Dickinson U., Hackensack, N.J., 1976, Gloria Cortella, Inc., 1976, Edmonton Art Gallery Mus., 1977, 77, 83, Northeastern U., Boston, 1977, Lehigh (Pa.) U., 1977, Long Contemporary Gallery, 1977, 78, 79, 80, Mus. Modern Art, N.Y.C., 1981, Galerie Wentzel, Cologne, W.Ger., 1981-85, Martin Gerard Gallery, Edmonton, 1981, Gallery One, Toronto, 1983, 84, Martin Girard Gallery, 1981-84, Haber Theodore Gallery, 1982-85, Queens Mus., N.Y.C., 1984, Jerald Melberg Gallery, Charlotte, N.C., 1984, Edmonton Art Gallery Mus., 1985, Richard Green Gallery, N.Y.C., Centre de Creacio, Barcelona, Spain, 1987, also numerous univs. and colls.; represented in permanent collections: Pa. Acad. Fine Arts, N.J. State Mus., Ciba-Geigy Corp., New Sch. Social Research, Bula Mus. Art, U. Calif., Mus. Modern Art, N.Y.C., McMullen Gallery, Edmonton, Ga., Phoenix Gallery, N.Y.C., 1988, Pumpkin Galler, Ancrom, N.Y., 1988, Provident Nat. Bank, Phila., 1988 others; represented by Paul Kuhn Gallery, Calgary, Alta., Eva Cohon Gallery, Chgo. and Highland Park, Ill., Hokin Gallery, Palm Beach and Miami, Fla., Galerie Ninety-Nine, Miami, Gallery One, Toronto, and Galerie Wentzel, Cologne, W. Ger., Wade Gallery, Los Angeles, Frances Aronson Gallery, Atlanta, Meredith Long and Co., Houston; exec. coordinator Women in Arts Found., Inc., 1975-79, 81-82, coordinating bd., 1983-87. Recipient Lambert Fund award Pa. Acad. Fine Arts, 1955; Susan B. Anthony award NOW, 1983. Home and Studio: 37 E 18th St New York NY 10003

WEINSTEIN, MARCIA LOIS, psychology educator; b. N.Y.C., May 16, 1954; d. Herman Harry and Yetta (Linder) W.; m. Richard Alan Steinbrook, July 21, 1978; 1 child, Hillary Weinstein. BA, Princeton U., 1974; MA, U. Pa., 1975, PhD, 1978. Lic. psychologist, Mass. Asst. prof. psychology Salem (Mass.) State Coll., 1978-84, assoc. prof., 1984—; cons. child care ctr. Salem State Coll., 1978—; staff Malden (Mass.) Hosp., 1982—. Mem. Am. Psychol. Assn., Mass. Psychol. Assn. Jewish. Office: Salem State Coll 252 Lafayette St Salem MA 01970

WEINSTEIN, NANCY ANNE, box mfg. co. exec.; b. Richmond, Va., Oct. 21, 1925; d. Morris Hyman and Bertha (Batkins) W.; cert. commerce, U. Richmond, 1971. With C&O Ry., 1942-57; with Va. folding box div.

WESTVACO, Richmond, 1957-86, supr. acctg. dept., 1971-86. Pres. Highland Springs Civic Assn., 1953-55, Highland Springs Jr. Women's Club, 1951-53; treas. Belmont Meth. Ch., Richmond, 1965-79; mem. budget and allocations com. United Way Greater Richmond, 1981—; trustee Ednl. Found. of Am. Women's Soc. C.P.A.s-Am. Soc. Women Accts., 1982-84. Mem. Am. Soc. Women Accts. (pres. Richmond chpt. 1978-80, chmn. nat. subcom. 1981). Republican. Club: Richmond Coin (past treas.). Home: 3556 Marquette Rd Richmond VA 23234

WEINSTEIN, NANCY LOU, interior designer; b. Covington, Ky., Apr. 8, 1946; m. Mel Weinstein, Sept. 19, 1964; 1 child, Jennifer Nicole. Pvt. practice interior design Long Beach, Calif., 1966; dir. Easter Seals Internat. Design House, 1985. Contbr. articles to mags., newspapers. Named Hon. Order of Ky. Cols., 1959. Mem. Interior Design Soc., Design Internat., Orange County (Calif.) Charter 100, Women in Business, Nat. Assn. of Women Bus. Owners, Long Beach C. of C.

WEINSTEIN, SHARI ALEXANDRA, advertising sales representative; b. Teaneck, N.J., Apr. 10, 1962; d. Jerry Marvin and Rosalyn (Cobb) W. BS in Bus. Adminstrn., Boston U., 1984. Acctg. clk. Flackman, Goodman & Potter, Ridgewood, N.J., 1978-80; human resources asst. Witco Chem. Corp., Paramus, N.J., 1980, 81; fixed assests asst. Flexi-Van Leasing Corp., Hackensack, N.J., 1983, 84; sales asst. Macy's, Paramus, 1984; mktg. rep. Beeper Co., Florham Park, N.J., 1984-85; advt. devel. coordinator Murdoch mags., N.Y.C., 1985-86, mgr. classified advt. sales, 1987—. Mem. Am. Mktg. Assn., Nat. Assn. Female Execs. Home: 185 Prospect Ave Apt 9B Hackensack NJ 07601

WEINSTOCK, ELEANOR, state legislator; b. N.Y.C., Jan. 25, 1929; m. Sander Weinstock; children: Jane, Charles, Ann. BS, Skidmore Coll., 1950. State rep. Fla., 1978-56, state senator, 1986—. Mem. LWV (pres. Fla. 1973-75). Democrat. Jewish. Address: 319 Clematis St Suite 617 West Palm Beach FL 33401 *

WEINTRAUB, AMY, nursing home executive; b. N.Y.C., June 3, 1951; d. Milton and Rosemary (Goodman) W. m. Daniel Droz, Apr. 28, 1974 (div. Feb. 1978); 1 child, Marlana Ruth. BA summa cum laude, Boston U., 1973. Assoc. producer Sta. WNVT-TV, Annandale, Va., 1973-74; assoc. dir. Sta. WTAE-TV, Pitts., 1974-76; producer, dir. Sta. KDKA-TV, Pitts., 1976-78; producer, dir. Sta. WPXI-TV, Pitts., 1978-79, exec. producer, pub. affairs dir., 1979-81; free-lance writer Pitts., 1974-80; v.p. Catherine Manor, Inc., Newport, R.I., 1981-86, pres., 1987—. Writer, producer (film documentary) Walking the Tightrope, 1975 (Golden Quill award 1976); producer, dir. (film documentary) Eyewitness Mag. (Matrix award 1979); author, photographer: Childcare--Where Are You?, 1974. Recipient Nat. Broadcast award Women at Work, 1979, Broadcast Media award U. San Francisco, 1979, Headliner award Pa. AP, 1980. Mem. Guest House Assn. (sec. 1983-85, v.p. 1986), Dramatists Guild, Internat. Women's Writing Guild, Newport Hospitality Assn. (bd. dirs.).

WEINTRAUB, SUSAN GAIL, marketing professional, consultant; b. N.Y.C., Nov. 6, 1959; d. Emanuel Harry and Mabel Alice (Bill) W. BS, Syracuse U., 1981. Sales rep. Sharp Electronics Corp., N.Y.C., 1981-83; communications cons. Coradian Corp., N.Y.C., 1983-84; mktg. cons. Emanuel Weintraub Assoc., Inc., Port Lee, N.J., 1983-87; acct. exec. A.C. Nielsen Corp., N.Y.C., 1987—. Contbr. articles to profl. jours. Mem. Nat. Assn. Female Execs. Jewish. Office: A C Nielsen 1345 Ave of the Americas New York NY 10021

WEINTZ, CAROLINE GILES, advertising consultant, travel writer; b. Columbia, Tenn., Dec. 8, 1952; d. Raymond Clark Jr. and Caroline Higdon (Wagstaff) Giles; m. Walter Louis Weintz; 1 child, Alexander Harwood. AB, Princeton U., 1974; MA, U. London, 1976. Dir. advt. and promotion E.P. Dutton Pubs., N.Y.C., 1977-86; advt. cons. Assn. Jr. Leagues, N.Y.C., 1986—. Author: The Discount Guide for Travelers over 55, 4th edit., 1988. Researcher St. Paul's Nat. Hist. Site and Bill of Rights Mus., Westchester, N.Y., 1986—; mem. Jr. League, Pelham, N.Y. Mem. Authors Guild, Huguenot Soc. Am., Daughters of Cin. Episcopalian. Club: Princeton (N.Y.C.). Home: 444 Wolf's Ln Pelham Manor NY 10803

WEIR, GLORIA JANE (MRS. N. LYLE EVANS), physician; b. Baton Rouge, Jan. 18, 1921; d. Claude Arnold and Peggy (Downing) W.; student Sullins Coll., 1936-37; B.S., La. State U., 1940, M.D., 1943; m. N. Lyle Evans, July 26, 1952; children—Peggy Jane, David Lyle. Intern, Charity Hosp. La., New Orleans, 1944, resident in pediatrics, 1949-50, chief resident, 1950-51; pvt. practice medicine specializing in pediatrics, Baton Rouge, 1952-80; staff mem. Baton Rouge Gen. Med. Ctr., vice chief staff, 1965, vice chief pediatrics, 1969, chief pediatrics, 1970-71, now pediatric cons. Child Day Care Ctr.; mem. staff Our Lady of Lake Regional Med. Ctr., Baton Rouge, chief pediatrics, 1959-60, mem. instl. rev. bd.; mem. staff Women's Hosp., chief pediatrics, 1969-70; vis. staff Earl K. Long Meml. Hosp.; clin. asst. prof. pediatrics La. State U. Med. Sch.; chief med. cons. Disability Determination Services, Baton Rouge Area, State of La. Diplomate Am. Bd. Pediatrics. Fellow Am. Acad. Pediatrics (alt. state chmn. La. chpt. 1975-78); mem. AMA, La. State Med. Soc., East Baton Rouge Parish med. socs., Am. Med. Women's Assn., Baton Rouge Women in Medicine, Baton Rouge Assn. for Retarded Citizens (bd. dirs. 1978-79), La. Heart Assn., Baton Rouge Pediatric Socs., Cancer Soc. Baton Rouge (dir. 1963-67, 76-79), Sullins Alumnae Assn., La. State U. Med. Sch. Alumni Assns., Baton Rouge Symphony Aux. (benefactor), Delta Zeta (mem. house corp.), La. State U. Alumni Fedn. Episcopalian. Club: Harlequins. Home: 5885 Eastwood Dr Baton Rouge LA 70806 Office: 2730 Wooddale Blvd PO Box 66498 Baton Rouge LA 70896

WEIR, VENTANA JILL, management consultant; b. Flint, Mich., June 27, 1946; d. Dale Frederick and Mary-Jo (Gundry) Stanquits. Dir. tng. Bullock's Store, Los Angeles, 1969-70; mgr. tng. and devel. P&O/Princess Cruises, San Francisco, 1970-72; mgr. employee relations Bancroft-Whitney Co., San Francisco, 1972-79; cons., trainer orgn. devel. Levi Strauss & Co., San Francisco, 1979-82; sr. cons. Block-Petrella-Weisbord, San Francisco and N.J., 1982-85; owner, cons. WorkLife, San Francisco, 1985—; conf. speaker with various orgns., 1985-87. Contbr. articles to profl. jours. Mem. Am. Soc. Tng. and Devel., Orgn. Devel. Network, Am. Soc. Personnel Adminstn. Democrat. Office: WorkLife 89 Woodside Dr San Anselmo CA 94960

WEISBERG, RUTH, artist. Laurea in Painting and Printmaking, Acad. di Belle Arti, Perugia, Italy, 1962; BA, U. Mich., 1963, MA, 1965. lectr., demonstrator, juror, curator U. Mich., 1987, 88, U. Hawaii, Honolulu, 1988, Pa. Acad., Phila., 1987, Queens Coll., N.Y.C., 1987, CCNY, 1987, U. Iowa, 1978, 87, U. N.D., Grand Forks, 1987, Fresno (Calif.) Arts Ctr. and Mus., Carnegie Mellon U., Pitts., 1986, 87, U. Tenn., Knoxville, 1986, U. Calif., Santa Cruz, 1985, U. Washington, Seattle, U. Kans., Lawrence, Skirball Mus. Hebrew Union Coll., Los Angeles, Calif. Inst. Arts, Valencia, Otis Art Inst., Los Angeles, Mass. Coll. Art, Boston, Norwegian Graphic Artists' Assn., Oslo, Coll. Art Assn. Conf., Detroit, many others. Solo and two-person exhibitions include: Pollack Gallery, Toronto, 1969, 71, Richard Nash Gallery, Seattle, 1971, 72, 74, Seaberg-Isthmus Gallery, Chgo., 1972, Mcpl. Art Gallery, Oslo, 1972, Triad Gallery, Los Angeles, 1974, Norwegian Graphic Arts Assn., Oslo, 1976, Palos Verdes (Calif.) Art Gallery, 1976, El Camino Coll., Los Angeles, 1977, Oglethorpe U., Atlanta, 1978, Peppers Art Gallery, U. Redlands (Calif.), 1980, Kellas Gallery, Lawrence, Kans., 1979-81, M. Shore and Sons, Santa Barbara, Calif., 1981, U. Richmond, Va., 1985, U. Tenn., Knoxville, 1986, Sierra Nev. Mus. Arts Reno, 1987, The Alice Simsar Gallery, Ann Arbor, Mich., 1968, 69, 72, 74, 77, 88, Associated Am. Artists, N.Y.C., 1987, Jack Rutberg Fine Arts, Los Angeles, 1983, 85, 88; group exhibitions include: Chgo. Art Inst., 1978, E.B. Crocker Art Mus., 1978-80, Contemporary Arts Ctr., New Orleans, 1980, Pratt Graphic Ctr., N.Y.C., 1978-80, U. Art Mus., U. N.M., 1981, Loyola Marymount U., Los Angeles, 1982, Kenkeleba House, N.Y.C, 1984, The Design Ctr., Los Angeles, 1984, Palos Verdes Art Ctr., 1984, Gallery in the Plaza, Security Pacific Bank, Las Angeles, 1985, Thomas Ctr. Gallery, Gainesville, Fla., Associated Am. Artists, N.Y.C, 1987, many others; works published in The Survey Exhibition Catalogues, 1968-88; permanent collections include: The Achenback Found. for Graphic Arts, Fine Arts Mus., San Francisco, Ariz. State U. Mus., Tempe, The Art Inst. Chgo., The Dance Collection, Lincoln Ctr., N.Y.C., Detroit Inst. Arts, Grunwald Found. for Graphic Arts, U. Calif., Los Angeles, The Bibliotheque Nat. France, Paris, Los Angeles County Mus. Art, The Jewish Mus. N.Y.C, The Nat. Gallery, Washington, The Nat. Musl Women in the Arts, many others; contbr. articles to profl. jours. Mem. Coll. Art Assn. (co-chair studion sessions), Tamarind Inst. (mem. nat. adv. bd.), Los Angeles Artists Equity (mem. adv. bd.), Los Angeles Printmaking Soc. Home: 2421 Third St Santa Monica CA 90405 Office: U So Calif Sch Fine Arts Los Angeles CA 90089-0292

WEISBERG, RUTH MAXINE, radio reporter; b. Phila., Pa., May 31, 1956; d. William and Libby (Magness) W.; m. Peter Paul Kerch. BS with honors in Spl. Edn., Pa. State U., 1977. Traffic reporter Shadow Traffic Network, Phila., 1978-82; news anchor Sta. WIFI-FM, Phila., 1982-83; features editor Sta. WPEN, Phila., 1983-85; arts and entertainment editor Sta. WSNI-FM, Phila., 1985-88; Contbg. editor Internat. TV Assn., Phila., 1982—. Contbg. editor monthly ITVA Newsletter. Recipient Miss Am. Pageant scholarship, 1980, Radio Features awards Phila. Press Assn., 1983, AP, 1983, Women in Communications, 1984. Mem. Internat. TV Assn, Narberth Community Theater. Home and Office: 37 Sabine Ave Narberth PA 19072 Office: Sta WSIN-FM Arts and Entertainment Editor 1 Bala Plaza Bala Cynwyd PA 19004

WEISBERGER, BARBARA, choreographer, artistic director, educator; b. Bklyn., Feb. 28, 1926; d. Herman and Sally (Goldstein) Linshes; m. Sol Spiller, Sept. 3, 1945 (div. 1948); m. Ernest Weisberger, Nov. 15, 1949; children: Wendy, Steven. B.S. in Edn., Psychology, Pa. State U., 1945; L.H.D. (hon.), Swarthmore Coll., 1970; D.F.A. (hon.), Temple U., 1973, Kings Coll., 1978, Villanova U., 1978. Founder, dir., tchr. Wilkes-Barre (Pa.) Ballet Theater, 1953-63; founder, dir. Pa. Ballet, Phila., 1962-82, Carlisle (Pa.) Project, 1984—; vice chmn. dance panel Nat. Endowment for the Arts, Washington, 1975-79. Performed with Met. Opera Ballet, N.Y.C., 1937, 38, Mary Binney Montgomery Co., Phila., 1940-42, ballet mistress, choreographer, Ballet Co. of Phila. Lyric Opera, 1961-62, ; choreographic works include Italian Concerto, Bach, Symphonic Variations, Franck; also operas for, Phila. Lyric Opera Co. Ford Found. grantee, 1963, 65, 68, 71, 84; Named Disting. Dau. of Pa., 1974, Disting. Alumna, Pa. State U., 1972; recipient 46th ann. Gimbel Phila. award, 1978. Mem. Psi Chi. Home: 571 Charles Ave Kingston PA 18704 Office: Carlisle Project 9 S Pitt St Carlisle PA 17013

WEISBERGER, TERI MICHAUD, nurse practitioner; b. Waterville, Maine, Dec. 30, 1954; d. Marc Emille and Muriel Phyllis (Grenier) Michaud; m. Steven Ira Weisberger; children: Ryan Robert Freeman, Travis Steven. RN, Ea. Maine Med. Ctr., 1976; cert. family nurse practitioner, U. So. Maine, 1982. RN, Maine, Mo. ICU, emergency room nurse Osteopathic Hosp., Waterville, 1976-77; recovery room nurse Kirksville (Mo.) Osteopathic Hosp., 1977-79; ob-gyn nurse practitioneer Dr. Rudolf Winkelbauer, Brunswick, Maine, 1982-85; family nurse practitioner Dr. Steven Weisberger, Jonesport, Maine, 1985—; med. cons. Jonesport Head Start Program, 1985—. Office: Arnold Meml Med Ctr Main St Jonesport ME 04649

WEISBURGER, ELIZABETH KREISER, chemist, editor; b. Greelane, Pa., Apr. 9, 1924; d. Raymond Samuel and Amy Elizabeth (Snavely) Kreiser; m. John H. Weisburger, Apr. 7, 1947 (div. May 1974); children—William Raymond, Diane Susan, Andrew John. BS, Lebanon Valley Coll., Annville, Pa., 1944; PhD, U. Cin., 1947, DSc (hon.), 1981. Research assoc. U. Cin., 1947-49; col. USPHS, 1951—; postdoctoral fellow Nat. Cancer Inst., Bethesda, Md., 1949-51, chemist, 1941-73, chief Carcinogen metabolism and toxicology br., 1972-75, chief Lab. Carcinogen Metabolism, 1975-81, asst. dir. chem. carcinogenesis, 1981—; lectr. Found. for Advanced Edn. in Scis., Bethesda, 1980—; adj. prof. Am. U., Washington, 1982—. Asst. editor-in-chief Jour. Nat. Cancer Inst., 1971-87; contbr. articles to profl. jours. Trustee Lebanon Valley Coll., 1970—, pres. bd. trustees, 1985—. Recipient Meritorious Service medal USPHS, 1973, Disting. Service medal, 1985; Hillebrand prize Chem. Soc. Washington, 1981. Fellow AAAS (nominating com. 1978-81); mem. Am. Chem. Soc. (Garvan medal 1981), Am. Assn. Cancer Research, Soc. Toxicology, Am. Soc. Biol. Chemists, Royal Soc. Chemistry, Grad. Women in Sci. (hon.), Iota Sigma Pi (hon.). Lutheran. Office: Nat Cancer Inst 9000 Rockville Pike Bethesda MD 20892

WEISE, CELESTA KATHLEEN, information systems specialist; b. Lincoln, Nebr., Apr. 16, 1942; d. Edwin and Alma (Freese) W. BS, U. Nebr., 1962. Systems engr. trainee IBM Corp., Lincoln, 1962-64; assoc. systems engr. IBM Corp., St. Paul, 1964-65; staff instr. IBM Corp., Mpls., 1965-72; sr. mktg. support rep. IBM Corp., Palo Alto, Calif., 1972-74; sr. product adminstr. IBM Corp., White Plains, N.Y., 1974-76; mgr. IMS edn. IBM Corp., San Jose, Calif., 1976-77; mgr. large systems support IBM Corp., Chgo., 1977-79; mgr. advanced edn. ctr. IBM Corp., Dallas, 1979-83; mgr. office systems tech. support IBM Corp., Irving, Tex., 1983-84, mgr. customer support programs, 1984-85, mgr. quality programs, 1985-86, mgr. establishment communications, tech. support, 1986-87, cons. instr. expert system edn., 1987—. Mem. St. Paul's Luth. Ch., Plymouth, Nebr., 1942-85, Preston Hollow Presbyn. Ch., Dallas, 1985-87. Mem. Am. Assn. Artificial Intelligence, Las Colinas Bus. and Profl. Women's Assn., Airline Owners and Pilots Assn., Ninety-Nines, Phi Beta Kappa, Chi Omega. Clubs: Brookhaven Country (Dallas), John Newcombe Tennis (Puerta Vallarta, Mex.); Las Colinas Sports, Am. Airlines Admirals (Irving). Republican. Presbyterian. Office: IBM Corp 1212 Corporate Dr Irving TX 75038

WEISE, JOAN CAROLYN, electronics company administrator; b. Libertyville, Ill., Feb. 3, 1939; d. James Gardner McDearmid and Anne Louise (Quist) Nehls; m. James Edward Weise, Aug. 15, 1959; children: Renee, James, Laura. Student, U. Ill., 1956-58; BA in Edn., Carthage Coll., 1973. Cert. tchr., Ill. Dir. nursery sch. Rosa Kahn Sch., Mundelein, Ill., 1971-73; tchr. Avon Sch., Round Lake, Ill., 1973-77; with customer service, contracts depts. AM Document, Santa Ana, Calif., 1978-81; mgr. customer service Plessey Semicondr., Irvine, Calif., 1981-84, mgr. ops. support, 1984-87; profl. beauty cons. Mary Kay Cosmetics, Irvine, 1987—. chmn. Library Friends, Millburn, Ill., 1969-73, Citizen Sch. Adv., Millburn, 1974-75; leader 4-H, Millburn, 1972-77. Mem. Am. Prodn./Inventory Control, Nat. Assn. for Female Execs.

WEISER, BARBARA S., consulting actuary; b. N.Y.C., Oct. 31, 1944; d. Jack and Lee (Baron) W. B.A., Queen's Coll., 1965. Tchr. math. N.Y.C. High Schs., 1965-67; asst. actuary Buck Cons., N.Y.C., 1968-79; actuarial mgr. A.S. Hansen, Dallas, 1980-82; assoc. cons. actuary, Dallas, 1982-86; cons. actuary, N.Y.C., 1987—. Mem. Am. Acad. Actuaries. Home: 333 E 30th St Apt 18-B New York NY 10016

WEISMAN, BARBARA, lawyer; b. Jersey City, N.J., Jan. 19, 1954; d. Albert and Estelle (Platt) W. B.A. magna cum laude, Douglass Coll., New Brunswick, N.J., 1975; J.D., Seton Hall Law Ctr., Newark, 1979. Bar: N.J. 1979, U.S. Dist. Ct. N.J. 1979, U.S. Supreme Ct. 1986. Law clk. Lamb Hartung Gallipoli & Coughlin, Jersey City, 1977-79; asst. prosecutor Hudson County Prosecutor's Office, Jersey City, 1980-82; atty. N.J. Solicitor's Office Port Authority of N.Y. & N.J., N.Y.C., 1982—. Mem. ABA, N.J. State Bar Assn., Hudson County Bar Assn. Home: 4 Bergen Ct Bayonne NJ 07002 Office: Port Authority of NY and NJ 1 World Trade Ctr New York NY 10048

WEISMAN, DIAN LAUREL, resort management administrator; b. Portsmouth, N.H., Apr. 29, 1956; d. H. Robert and Beatrice Patricia (Pombrio) W.; m. David C. Briskey, Apr. 19, 1980 (div. May 1983); m. Mark E. Miller, Mar. 18, 1988. BA in English, French, Colby Coll., 1978; cert. in real estate, U. Maine, Augusta, 1979. Lic. real estate salesman, Maine. Retail mgr. Consumer Value Stores, Nashua and Hudson, N.H., 1972-74; with real estate sales/mgmt. Carroll Perkins Assocs., Waterville, Maine, 1978-80; real estate salesman Hamel Realtors, Fryeburg, Maine, 1980-83; with bus. mgmt. Forest Glen Inn, North Conway, N.H., 1984; with mgmt. and budget dept. Ea. Slope Inn Assocs., North Conway, N.H., 1984—, Attitash Mt. Village, Bartlett, N.H., 1984—; cons. Cathedral Ledge Resort, Bartlett, 1987—. Contbr.: Infoshare, 1986. Counselor, adv. Carroll County Against Domestic Violence, Conway, 1984-86; mem. career counseling com. Kennett High Sch., Conway, 1987—. Recipient N.E. region Excellence award Am. Land Devel., 1985, nat. award excellence Am. Land Devel., 1985. Mem. Resort Condominiums Internat., Nat. Vacation Ownership Council (N.H. chpt.), Am. Resort & Residential Devel., Nat. Assn. for Female Execs. Republican. Roman Catholic. Club: White Mt. Lioness (North Conway) (pres. 1986—). Home: 4902 Park St Panama City FL 32404 Office: Ea Slope Inn Assocs Main St PO Box 359 North Conway NH 03860

WEISS, BONNIE LYN, sales executive; b. Chgo., Apr. 5, 1950; d. Douglas and Gussie (Shulman) Goldner; m. Jerry K. Weiss, Feb. 17, 1980. BS in Communications, So. Ill. U., 1972. Contract coordinator Travel Enterprises, Chgo., 1974-76; dir. ops. Hawaiian Holidays, N.Y.C., 1976-80; sales mgr. Hyatt Hotels Worldwide Sales, N.Y.C., 1980-83, assoc. dir. of sales, 1983-85; dir. of sales Hyatt Hotels Worldwide Sales Office, N.Y.C., 1985—. Mem. Soc. if Incentive Travel Execs. (membership chmn. 1984-85, member services chmn. 1985, Cert. of Appreciation 1985, 86), N.Y. Soc. of Assn. Execs. (chmn. assoc. mems. adv. com. 1987-88), Sales Exec. Club of N.Y. (Outstanding Achievement award 1986), Meeting Planners Internat., Hotel Sales Mgmt. Assn. Office: Hyatt Hotels Worldwide Sales 675 Third Ave 23d Floor New York NY 10017

WEISS, DEBRA S., construction company executive; b. Three Rivers, Mich., Dec. 4, 1953; d. Harold E. and Winifred (Dunn) W. Student Albion Coll., 1972-73, Lake Superior State Coll., 1974-76; cert. Industrialized Housing Inst., Wausau, Wis., 1975. Lic. builder and mech. contractor, Mich. Sales mgr. Weiss Constrn., Inc., Alanson, Mich., 1976-80; owner, chmn. bd. dirs. Weiss Constrn., St. Ignace, Mich., 1980—; corp. sec., supr. spl. projects Weiss Corp., St. Ignace, 1984—. Bd. dirs. Eastern Upper Peninsula Pvt. Industry Council, Sault Ste. Marie, Mich., 1985-87, pres. 1987—, Downtown Devel. Authority, Mackinaw City, Mich., 1985-87; mem. St. Ignace Zoning Bd., 1984-89, St. Ignace City Council, 1985—; bd. dirs., pres. Eastern Upper Peninsula Pvt. Industry Council. Recipient Ruth Huston Whipple award, 1986, Garden City award, 1986. Mem. NOW, St. Ignace Bus. and Profl. Women (pres. 1980-81; Woman of Yr. 1980, Anna Howard Shaw award 1981, 82), Mich. Fedn. Bus. and Profl. Women. (mem. strategic long range planning com. 1985-87, BPW/USA Strategic Planning com. 1987-89, chmn. issues mgmt. com.; Outstanding Young Career Woman 1982, chmn. 1987-88), Nat. Fedn. Bus. and Profl. Women (long range strategic planning comm., 1987—),Silver Mountain Ski Assn. (bd. dirs. 1982-85), St. Ignace C. of C., St. Ignace Tourist Assn., Upper Peninsula Tourist and Recreation Assn., Silver Mountain Cross Country Club, Nat. Assn. Female Execs. Avocations: skiing, reading, rock repelling. Office: Weiss Constrn 99 Bertrand St Saint Ignace MI 49781

WEISS, DIANE, gift and wardrobe selection service executive; b. Middletown, N.Y., Aug. 12; d. Henry Wolfe and Shirley Angel (Angelowitz) Weiss. B.S., U. Fla., 1975. Assoc. buyer Burdine's Miami, Fla., 1977-78, buyer, mgr., 1978-81; with retail ops. Monet Jewelers, Southeast/Southwest, N.Y.C., 1981-83; pres., owner Present Co., Dallas, 1983—, and Los Angeles, 1986—; designer copyright The Big D.G.O.P.ers, 1984. Fund raiser, 500 Inc, Dallas, 1983—; vote recruiter Concert Hall, Dallas, summer, 1982; active Betty Svboda Council Election, Dallas, winter, 1983; fund raiser Jewish Fedn., Dallas, 1982—. Mem. Los Angeles County Mus. Office: Present Co 1441 Midvale Ave Suite 401 Los Angeles CA 90024 also: PO Box 7488 Beverly Hills CA 90212

WEISS, ELAINE LANDSBERG, community development official; b. N.Y.C.; d. Louis and Sadie Blossum (Schoenfeld); divorced. BA in Philosophy and Polit. Sci., Bklyn. Coll., 1960; postgrad., NYU Law Sch., 1960-62; MA in Sociology, Hunter Coll., N.Y.C., 1969. Social investigator N.Y.C. Dept. Social Services, 1963-64; intern, fellow Eleanor Roosevelt Meml. Found., Nat. Assn. Intergroup Relations Ofcls., 1964-65; asst. dir. housing and asst. project dir. Operation Equality, Nat. Urban League, 1965-67; program assoc. housing div. ch. missions Am. Bapt. Home Mission Socs., 1967-70; pres. E.L. Weiss Assocs., 1970-76; exec. dir. Suffolk Community Devel. Corp., Coram, N.Y., 1976—; mem. citizens adv. com. N.Y.C. Dept. Housing Preservation and Devel.; exec. com. L.I. Community Devel. Orgn.; past 2d v.p. Suffolk Housing Task Force; chmn. Suffolk County Citizens Adv. Com., 1981-82. Recipient cert. of commendation L.I. Council Chs., 1981. Mem. Nat. Assn. Housing Ofcls., N.Y. State Assn. Housing and Redevel. Ofcls., Am. Contract Bridge League (life master). Home: 211 E 18th St New York NY 10003 Office: 625 Middle Country Rd Coram NY 11727

WEISS, KATHLEEN MCKITTRICK, physician; b. Palo Alto, Calif., Oct. 13, 1952; d. Jack Wilson and Amy (Morrison) McKittrick; m. Frederick George Weiss. BS, U. Washington, 1974; MD, U. So. Calif., 1978. Diplomate Am. Bd. Internal Medicine. Intern, then resident Kaiser Found. Hosp., Los Angeles, 1978-81; staff physician North West Permanente, Portland, Oreg., 1981-87; gen. practice internal medicine Newberg, Oreg., 1987—. Mem. ACP, Oreg. Med. Soc., Christian Med. Soc. Office: Newberg Internal Medicine 500 Villa Rd Newberg OR 97312

WEISS, MARILYN MAGALIFF, artist; b. Bklyn., Sept. 4, 1932; d. Max and Anna (Haber) Ackerman; B.S. magna cum laude, N.Y. U., 1953, m. Howard Jerry Weiss, Nov. 24, 1972; children—Jodi Kim Magaliff Gittelman and Barry Todd Magaliff (twins). Exhibited one-woman shows: Alper-Goldberg Gallery, Cedarhurst, N.Y., 1977, Fred Leighton Madison Ltd., 1975, Port Washington (N.Y.) Library, 1974, Adelphi U., 1974, Hewlett Woodmere Library, 1972, Bodley Gallery, N.Y.C., 1983; exhibited in group shows Firehouse Gallery Nassau Community Coll., Garden City, 1971, Palazzio Vechio, Florence, Italy, 1972, Palazzio Nat., Naples, Italy, 1972, Brockton (Mass.) Library, 1972, Roanoke (Va.) Fine Arts Center, 1972, Milliken U., 1972, U. Okla., 1973, Southeastern Ark. Art. and Sci. Center, 1973, Tuskegee Inst., 1974, Albrecht Gallery, 1974, Bergen Community Mus., 1974, 84, 85, Jesse Besser Mus., 1976, Central Wyo. Mus. Art, 1977, U. Wis., 1978, City Gallery, N.Y.C., 1981, Community Mus., 1974, Equitable Gallery, N.Y.C., 1979, Fed. Bldg., N.Y.C., 1979, 81-87, U.S. Painting Exhbn., 83-85, 85-88, Traveling Painting Exhbn. U.S.A., 1972-74, 88—, Traveling Watermedia Exhbn. U.S.A., 1976-78, Oil and Watermedia Exhbn., 1978-80, Cayuga Mus. History and Art, Auburn, N.D., 1983, Stephanie Roper Gallery, 1985, Pace Un. Art Gallery, N.Y., 1988, Maier Mus. Art, Va., 1988, Lever House, N.Y.C., 1988, Sarah Lawrence Coll., 1985, Lighthouse Gallery, Fla., 1986, McPherson Coll., 1986, Schenectady Mus., N.Y., 1987, Alelphi U., N.Y., 1987, Nabisco Art Gallery, N.J., 1987, numerous others. Recipient maj. prize Suburban Art League Ann. Show, 1968, 71; Elizabeth Morse Genius Found. prize for water media, 1983, Cecil Shapiro Meml. award, 1988. Mem. Hempstead Harbor Art Assn., Contemporary Artists Guild, Nat. Assn. Women Artists, Beta Gamma Sigma. Address: 1100 Park Ave New York NY 10128

WEISS, MARTHA MORALES, finance company executive; b. Honduras, May 10, 1943; came to U.S., 1962; d. Camilo and Maria (Morales) Gutierrez; m. Gerald H. Weiss, July 31, 1971; children: Paul J., David F. MS in Math., U. Notre Dame, South Bend, Ind., 1971; MBA, Fairleigh Dickinson U., 1980; PhD, U. Iowa, 1974. Dir. research Wycoff (N.J.) Pub. Schs., 1977-81; mgr. accounts control Deak Perera Wall St., N.Y.C., 1981-82; dir. fin. Concorde/Nopal, N.Y.C., 1982-84; v.p., treas. Gestra, Inc., Hackensack, N.J., 1984—. Democrat. Roman Catholic. Office: Gestra Inc 385 Prospect Ave Hackensack NJ 07601

WEISS, MYRNA GRACE, investment banker; b. N.Y.C., June 22, 1939; d. Herman and Blanche (Stiftel) Ziegler; m. Arthur H. Weiss; children: Debra Anne, Louise Esther. BA, Barnard Coll., 1958; MA, Hunter Coll., 1968; MPA, NYU, 1978. Dir. admissions Columbia Prep. Sch., N.Y.C., 1969-72; dir. PREP counselling NYU, N.Y.C., 1973-74; dept. head Hewitt Sch., N.Y.C., 1974-79; mgr. Met. Ins. Co., N.Y.C., 1979-84; mktg. exec. Rothschild, Inc., N.Y.C., 1984-85; pres. First Mktg. Capital Group Ltd., N.Y.C., 1985-87; ptnr. Lared Group, N.Y.C., 1987—; bd. dirs. First Woman's Bank, Mastermedia, Inc.; advisor Gov.'s Hwy. Safety Com., N.Y.C., 1985—. Bd. dirs. 92d St. YMCA, N.Y.C., 1972—. Mem. Fin. Women's Assn. N.Y. (pres. 1984-85), Women's Forum. Club: Economic of N.Y. (N.Y.C.) (bd. dirs. women's econ. roundtable 1988). Office: 1st Mktg Capital Group Ltd 1056 Fifth Ave New York NY 10128

WEISS, PAULINE EDITH, psychiatrist; b. N.Y.C., Nov. 23, 1931; d. Ellis H. and Freda (Teitlebaum) Liberman; B.A., Bklyn. Coll., 1952, M.S., 1958; M.D., Autonomous U., Guadalajara, Mex., 1973; m. Aaron Weiss, Nov. 26, 1964. Tchr. spl. edn. N.Y.C. Pub. Schs.; attending in psychiatry Roosevelt

Hosp.; practice medicine specializing in psychiatry, N.Y.C.; psychoanalyst Karen Horney Inst.; staff psychiatrist St. Luke's-Roosevelt Hosp. Ctr.; asst. clin. psychiatrist Columbia U. Coll. Phys. and Surg. Recipient cert. of excellence N.Y.C. Bd. Edn. Mem. Am. Psychiat. Assn., Am. Med. Women's Assn., Am. Acad. Psychoanalysis, Assn. Women Psychiatrists. Democrat. Jewish. Office: 240 Central Park S New York NY 10019

WEISS, RHODA ELAINE, hospital administrator, marketing consultant; b. Detroit, Oct. 8, 1949; d. Harold Martin and Mildred (Million) W. BA in Communications, Mich. State U., 1971; MA in Psychology, Antioch U., 1980; postgrad., U. Calif., Berkeley, 1981. Reporter Gannett Newspapers, N.Y.C., 1971-72; editor Luth. Hosp. Soc., Los Angeles, 1973; pub. relations dir. St. John's Hosp., Santa Monica, Calif., 1974-75; pub. relations agt. The Rand Corp., Santa Monica, 1975-76; community relations dir. Torrance (Calif.) Meml. Hosp., 1976-78; asst. adminstr. Sisters of Providence, St. Joseph Med. Ctr., Burbank, Calif., 1978—; cons. Hosp. Home Health Care Agy., Torrance, 1977-87, Beverly Enterprises, Pasadena, Calif., 1985-87, Interactive Health Systems, Santa Monica, 1986, Am. Assn. Homes for Aged, Washington, 1986—, Univ. Hosps. Cleve., 1986—, Kennedy Meml. Hosps., N.J., 1987, Catherine McAuley Health Ctr., Ann Arbor, Mich., 1988—; adj. prof. Pepperdine U., Malibu, Calif., 1984—. Contbr. articles to profl. jours. Bd. dirs. Juvenile Justice Connection Project, Los Angeles, Watts-Willowbrook Boys and Girls Clubs, Watts, Calif.; mem. Hospice Adv. Bd., Torrance; bd. dirs. Holocaust Sites Presentation com., Los Angeles. Recipient 16 Lulu Awards Los Angeles Advt. Women, 1981-86, 4 Maggie Awards Western Pub. Assn., Los Angeles, 1983-84. Mem. Healthcare Pub. Relations and Mktg. Assn. (pres., 25 Golden Adv. awards 1982-88), Women in Communications (pres., Clarion award 1982, 83, 84, 85), Pub. Relations Soc. Am. (bd. dirs., 25 Prisms awards 1981-87), Calif. Hosp. Assn. (bd. dirs.), Hosp. Council of So. Calif. (bd. dirs.), Assn. of Western Hosps. (bd. dirs., 11 Best of West awards 1980-84), Nat. Hospice Orgns. (bd. dirs.), Cath. Health Assn. (recipient Excellence award, 1986, 1988), Internat. Assn. Bus. Communicators (4 Gold Quills, 27 Silver Quills, 56 Bronze Quills 1978-88), Am. Soc. Hosp. Mktg. (15 Touchstone awards 1983-87), Publicity Club (16 PRO awards 1981-88), Women in Health Adminstrn. (mem. chart bd. 1981—, pres. 1985), Am. Mktg. Assn., Am. Soc. for Hospital Planning and Mktg., Am. Soc. for Healthcare, Planning and Mktg., Alpha Delta Pi (alumna pres. 1978-80, local chpt. adv. 1977-81, Outstanding Alumni 1980). Jewish. Club: Health Care Execs. (Los Angeles). Home: 307 Montana #203 Santa Monica CA 90403 Office: St Joseph Med Ctr Buena Vista and Alameda Burbank CA 91505

WEISS, SUZANNE BETH, travel industry executive; b. N.Y.C., Mar. 23, 1954; d. Bert and Estelle (Jaslow) W.; m. Kenneth M. Novak, Dec. 28, 1975 (div. Sept. 1981); m. Kenneth M. Novak, Dec. 28, 1982. BA, U. Rochester, 1976; MBA, U. Chgo., 1980. Mktg. mgr. SPSS, Inc., Chgo., 1979; sr. assoc. John Morton Co., Chgo., 1979-83; product mgr. mileage plus United Airlines, Chgo., 1983-87; dir. mktg., sales Sawtooth Software, Chgo., 1987—. Treas. Rape Victim Advocates, Chgo., 1980-84.

WEISS, THERESA DOMINGUEZ, nurse practitioner; b. Los Angeles, Aug. 16, 1950; d. Richard Joseph and Norma (Romero) Dominguez; m. Fred Toby Weiss, Dec. 5, 1982; 1 stepchild, Rebecca. Grad. in Nursing, Rio Hondo Coll., Whittier, Calif., 1975. RN. Rehab. nurse pediatric and spinal cord Rancho Los Amigos Hosp., Downey, Calif., 1969-75; critical care nurse Beverly Hosp., Montebello, Calif., 1975-78; co-dir. Cardiac Rehab. Ctr., Whittier, 1978-79; jr. faculty medicine U. Calif., Irvine, 1982-84; med. cons., adminstr. Health Mgmt. Ctr., Orange, Calif., 1984-87, Meml. Headache Clinic, Newport Beach, Calif., 1987—; researcher in field; instr. pre-natal care Chope Community Hosp., San Mateo, Calif., 1982, Coastline Coll., Costa Mesa, Calif., 1985—. Mem. Am. Nurses Assn., Calif. Nurses Assn., Calif. Coalition of Nurse Practitioners, Nat. Assn. Female Execs. Office: Meml Headache Clinic 360 San Miguel Ave Suite #603 Newport Beach CA 92660

WEISSMAN, RONEE FREEMAN, tour agency owner, speech pathologist; b. N.Y.C., Apr. 16, 1951; d. Jonas Herbert and Marion (Rosen) Freeman; B.A. magna cum laude, Queens Coll., 1973, M.A. in Speech Pathology, 1978; m. Eugene Weissman, Jan. 28, 1973; children—Ilana Nicole, Adam Scott. Tchr. high sch. speech, theatre and English, N.Y.C., 1973-75; speech pathologist Byram Hills (N.Y.) Sch. Dist., part-time, 1979-80, E. Ramapo Sch. Dist., Rockland, N.Y., 1981-82; speech pathologist Vis. Therapy Assocs., 1983-84; owner, v.p., dir. Weissman Teen Tours, Inc., Ardsley, N.Y., 1974—. Youth dir., Sunday sch. tchr. Temple Israel, New Rochelle. Speech and hearing handicapped cert., speech arts cert., N.Y.; lic. speech pathologist, N.Y. Mem. Am. Speech, Lang. and Hearing Assn. (cert. clin. competency), N.Y. State Speech, Lang. and Hearing Assn., Am. Camping Assn. (cert.), Westchester Assn. Women Bus. Owners, Sales and Mktg. Execs. of Westchester, Phi Beta Kappa, Kappa Delta Pi. Home and Office: 517 Almena Ave Ardsley NY 10502

WEISSMAN, ROZANNE, communications company executive, writer; b. Cleve., Sept. 14, 1942; d. Jack and Gertrude (Hibshman) W. B.S. in Journalism, Ohio U., 1964. Reporter, Fairchild Publs. Inc., Cleve., 1964-66; pub. relations/promotion specialist, feature writer Cleve. Plain Dealer, 1966-67; reporter Drug Research Reports, Washington, 1967, Consumer News Inc., Washington, 1968; dep. press sec. Utah Rep. Wayne Owens, Washington, 1974; investigative reporter Jack Anderson, Washington, 1974-75; lectr. Open U., Washington, 1978-80; spokesperson, media relations/community relations coordinator, head nat. communications network NEA, Washington, 1968-80; dir. pub. affairs Communications Workers Am., Washington, 1981-86; v.p. corp. communications Corp. for Pub. Broadcasting, Washington, 1986. Contbr. writings to coll. textbooks, edn. jours., publs., mags.; co-producer radio/TV series: Rewiring Your World, 1981-84; co-producer play: Lineman and Sweet Lightnin', 1983. Cons. on AIDS and drug abuse Nat. Inst. Drug Abuse. Recipient Feature Writing awards Ednl. Press Assn., awards for articles, pub. relations, advt.; prize for environ./urban renewal proposal Cleve., Cleve. Press, 15 awards for advt., mktg., public relations and public service in 1985. Mem. Nat. Press Club, Am. Mgmt. Assn., Pub. Relations Soc. Am., AFTRA, Nat. Women's Econ. Alliance, Am. Soc. Assn. Execs., Washington Ind. Writers, Internat. Platform Assn. Internat. Policy Inst., Am. Women in Radio-TV, Advt. Club Met. Washington. Democrat. Office: Corp for Pub Broadcasting 1111 16th St Washington DC 20036

WEISSMANN, CAROL S., programmer; b. Anmoore, W.Va., Jan. 20, 1938; d. Russell G. and Agnes (Newlon) Simons; m. Henry David Weissmann; children: Dori, Mark, Denton, Scott. BS, W.Va. Wesleyan Coll., 1960; MBA, SUNY, Binghamton, 1978. Cert. home economist, N.Y. Home economist Oneida County Coop. Extension, New Hartford, N.Y., 1959-60, Steuben County Coop. Extension, Bath, N.Y., 1960-61; tchr. Harpursville (N.Y.) Cen. Sch., 1963-65; v.p., treas. Glen Mar Farms, Inc., Harpursville, 1965-78; systems programmer SUNY, Binghamton, 1978-81; data base technician, systems analyst Norwich (N.Y.) Eaton Pharms., Inc., 1981-83; sr. systems programmer Link Flight Simulation div. Singer Co., Binghamton, 1983—, also link trainer, mem. EEO com., 1985—, also trustee, v.p. community benefit trust fund, 1987—; tchr. substitute Harpursville Cen. Sch., 1965-75; pres., bd. dirs. Broome County Coop. Extension, Binghamton, 1980. Life mem. Harpursville PTA, 1976—; chairperson, sec. Home Econs. Div. Commn., Cornell Coop. Extension, Binghamton, 1978. Mem. AAUW, Assn. of Computing Machinery, Assn. for System Design, Profl. Womens Network, 4th Ann. Conf. for Women (com. rep. 1985-86), Am. Home Econs. Assn., Am. Beef Cattlewomen's Assn. Republican. Methodist. Home: Welton St Harpursville NY 13787 Office: Singer Co Link Flight Kirkwood Industrial Park Binghamton NY 13902

WEISSMANN, HEIDI SEITELBLUM, radiologist, educator; b. N.Y.C., Feb. 4, 1951; d. Louis and June (Joseph) Seitel Bloom; m. Murray H. Weissmann, June 16, 1973; 1 dau., Lauren Erica. B.S. in Chemistry magna cum laude, Bklyn. Coll., CUNY, 1970; M.D., Mt. Sinai Sch. Medicine, N.Y.C., 1974. Diplomate Nat. Bd. Med. Examiners. Intern Montefiore Med. Ctr., Bronx, N.Y., 1974-75, resident in diagnostic radiology, 1975-78 ; fellow in computerized transaxial tomography and ultrasonography N.Y. Hosp.-Cornell U. Med. Ctr., N.Y.C., 1978-79; instr. in radiology and nuclear medicine Albert Einstein Coll. Medicine and Montefiore Med. Ctr., Bronx, 1979-80, asst. prof. radiology and nuclear medicine, 1980-84, assoc. prof. nuclear medicine, 1984—, assoc. prof. radiology, 1986—; adj. attending physician Montefiore Med. Ctr., 1979-87; chmn. Nuclear Medicine Grand Rounds: Greater N.Y., 1980—; physician coordinator Nuclear Medicine Technologist In-Service Tng. Program, 1982-86; cons. NIH, 1984-86, NIH Diagnostic Radiology, 1985-86. Assoc. editor Nuclear Medicine Ann., 5 vols., 1979-84, editor, 3 vols., 1985—; contbr. chpts. to books, articles to jours.; reviewer Jour. of Radiology, 1981—, mem. editorial adv. bd., 1985-86, assoc. editor, 1986—; reviewer. Jour. of Nuclear Medicine, 1981—, Am. Jour. of Roentgenology, 1986—, Gastroenterology, 1986—, Western Jour. of Medicine, 1985—; contbr. audiovisual programs and films. Recipient Saul Horowitz, Jr., Meml. award (Disting. Alumnus award), Mt. Sinai Sch. Medicine, 1980, Pres.' award, Am. Roentgen Ray Soc., 1979, Berta Rubinstein, M.D., Resident award, 1978, others. Mem. Radiol. Soc. N.Am. (mem. subcom. for nuclear medicine of program com., 1981, 82, 83, chmn. 1984, 85, 86), Soc. Nuclear Medicine (trustee 1983-87, 88—, sec.-treas. Correlative Imaging Council 1979-82, exec. bd. 1982-84, pres. 1984-86, mem. acad. council 1980—, task force on interrelationship between nuclear medicine and nuclear magnetic resonance 1983—, gov. Greater N.Y. chpt. 1983-85, treas., 1985-86, 86-87, 2d ann. Tetalman award of Edn. and Research Found. 1982, mem., vice chmn. coms. and subcoms.), Soc. Gastrointestinal Radiologists, Am. Inst. Ultrasound in Medicine, N.Y. Acad. Scis., Assoc. Alumni Mt. Sinai Med. Ctr., Nuclear Radiology Club (chmn. 1983—). Phi Beta Kappa.

WEIZER, JOYCE, lawyer, insurance company executive; b. Phila., Dec. 4, 1954; d. Samuel and Esther (Segal) W. BBA, Temple U., 1976; JD, Villanova U., 1979. Bar: Pa. 1979. Gen. counsel, sec. Zinman Group subs. and affiliates, Jenkintown, Pa., 1979-82; gen. counsel, asst. sec. MFMI subs. and affiliates, Phila., 1982-87, Underwriters Mgmt. Ins. Co., Phila., 1987—; arbitrator Phila. Ct. Common Pleas, 1985—. Mem. ABA, Pa. Bar Assn., Phila. Bar Assn., Mensa, B'nai B'rith Women. Club: Peale (Phila.). Office: Underwriters Mgmt Ins Co 1760 Market St Philadelphia PA 19103

WELBORN, SARAH, real estate broker, marketing and public relations executive, consultant; b. Greenville, S.C., Aug. 19, 1943; d. William Ernest Welborn and Elsie Jocelyn (Bowen) Hemphill; m. Nabil M. Sbitani, June 18, 1958 (dec.); children: Omar N., Ameen N.; m. Christian Heurich, Jr., Apr. 28, 1970 (div. May 1971); m. James Edwin Carroll, Dec. 19, 1974 (div. Jan. 1986); children: Salina J.A. Longo-Carroll. Student, Am. U., 1969-71; cert. in Real Estate, Prince Frederick Community Coll., 1974; cert., Merrill Lynch Relocation Mgmt., 1977, Real Estate Tng. Ctr., 1979, Real Estate Prep., 1981, Moore Sch. of Real Estate, 1982, Nat. Real Estate Sch., 1986. From ad copy writer to head of pub. and govt. relations dept. Lewis, Dobrow and Lamb Advt. and Pub. Relations Co., Washington, 1961-68; broker, sales assoc. Various Real Estate Firms, Reston, Va. and Denver, 1974-84; owner, broker Welborn Properties Realtors and Mktg. Cons., Denver, 1984-86; mktg. mgr., trainer Realty World Western, Berwyn, Ill., 1987—; Chmn. pub. relations com. various realty bds., Reston, Lakewood, Colo., 1975-86; investment cons. J-B Assocs., Inc., Denver, 1984; pub. relations cons. Red River Inns, Rifle, Colo., 1985; telemktg. cons. Assocs. Nat. Mortgage Co., Dallas, 1986; pres. Women's Council Realtors, Jefferson County, Colo., 1985-86. Contbr. articles to profl. jours. Commr. Health and Welfare commn., Alexandria, 1966-68; vol. coordinator Presdl. campaign of George McGovern, 1971-73. Mem. Am. Mensa Soc., West Town Bd. Realtors (chmn. RPAC com. 1987—), Ill. Assn. Realtors, Nat. Assn. Realtors. Democrat. Home: 5333 W 23d Pl Cicero IL 60650

WELCH, ANN-MARIE STEPHENSON, internist; b. Knoxville, Tenn., Aug. 20, 1937; d. Charles Millard and Laura Norwood (Roberson) Stephenson; m. Bruce L. Welch, Aug. 23, 1959. B.S., Duke U., 1959, M.A., 1960; M.D., Johns Hopkins U., 1974. Diplomate Am. Bd. Internal Medicine, 1978. Research asst. in pharmacology Duke U., Durham, N.C., 1960-62, Med. Coll. Va., 1962-64; research assoc. dept. biology Coll. William and Mary, Williamsburg, Va., 1964-66, U. Tenn. Meml. Research Ctr. and Hosp., Knoxville, 1966-69, Md. Psychiat. Research Center, Balt., 1969-70; intern, Yale-New Haven Hosp., 1974-75, resident, 1975-76; resident U. Conn. Health Center, Farmington, 1977-78; practice medicine specializing in internal medicine, New Britain, Conn., 1980—; mem. staff New Britain Gen. Hosp.; 1979—sr. ptnr. Welch Assocs., Kensington, Conn. Co-editor: Physiological Effects of Noise, 1970; co-author research reports in biochem. and pharmacol. fields. Gen. Foods fellow; Fulbright scholar; Internat. Inst. Edn. research scholar; NIH fellow. Mem. Am. Soc. Pharmacology and Exptl. Therapeutics, AAAS, AMA (CSMS alt. del.), Am. Soc. Internal Medicine, N.Y. Acad. Scis., Conn. State Med. Soc. (mem. ho. of dels. 1984-85, council 1985—, sec. 1986—), Hartford County Med. Soc. (mem.-at-large bd. dirs. 1984-85, assoc. councilor to Conn. State Med. Soc. 1985-86, bd. dirs. 1986—, chmn. legis. com. 1987—), Phi Beta Kappa, Sigma Xi. Office: 40 Hart St New Britain CT 06052

WELCH, BETTY LEONORA, accountant; b. Missoula, Mont., July 18, 1961; d. George Oliver and Betty June (Dolton) W. BBA, U. Mont., 1983. CPA, Mont. Staff acct. Ellis & Assocs., Boise, Idaho, 1984; acct. Glacier Electric Coop., Cut Bank, Mont., 1984-86, office mgr., 1986—; income tax cons. Mem. Nat. Assn. Female Execs., Am. Inst. CPA's, Beta Gamma Sigma. Democrat. Roman Catholic. Avocations: skiing, sewing, reading, hunting. Office: Glacier Electric Coop Inc 410 E Main St Cut Bank MT 59427

WELCH, CAROL MAE, lawyer; b. Rockford, Ill., Oct. 23, 1947; d. Leonard John and LaVerna Helen (Ang) Nyberg; m. Donald Peter Welch, Nov. 23, 1968 (dec. Sept. 1976). B.A. in Spanish, Wheaton Coll., 1968; J.D., U. Denver, 1976. Bar: Colo. 1977, U.S. Dist. Ct. Colo. 1977, U.S. Ct. Appeals (10th cir.) 1977, U.S. Supreme Ct. 1981. Tchr., State Hosp., Dixon, Ill., 1969, Polo Community Schs., Ill., 1969-70; registrar Sch. Nursing Hosp. of U. Pa., Phila., 1970; assoc. Hall & Evans, Denver, 1977-81, ptnr., 1981—; mem. Colo. Supreme Ct. Jury Inst., Denver, 1982—; vice chmn. com. on conduct U.S. Dist. Ct., Denver, 1982-83, chmn., 1983-84; lectr. in field; speaker Women and Bus. Conf., Denver, 1982. Pres. elect Family Tree, Inc. Named to Order St. Ives, U. Denver Coll. Law, 1977. Mem. Colo. Def. Lawyers Assn. (treas. 1982-83, v.p. 1983-84, pres. 1984-85), Denver Bar Assn., Colo. Bar Assn. (mem. litigation sect. council 1987—), ABA. Republican. Office: Hall & Evans 1200 17th St Suite 1700 Denver CO 80202

WELCH, JEANNE MARIE, archeologist; b. Ramsey, N.J., Sept. 11, 1923; d. Lynus Randolph and Dorothy Delight (Leighton) Spadon; m. Francis Martin Welch, Dec. 1, 1942; children—James Francis, Michael Leighton. B.A. in English Lit., U. Wash., 1966, M.A. in Anthropology, 1968. Archeol. cons., Curtis, Wash., 1973-75; state archeologist State of Wash., Olympia, 1975-76, state conservator, 1977, dir. Office of Archeology/Hist. Preservation, 1977-81; pres. Western Heritage, Inc., Olympia, 1981—; sec.-treas. N.W. Heritage Found., Olympia, 1981—; lectr. in field; mem. project adv. com. Pacific Sci. Ctr. Trustee Makah Mus. Mem. Soc. Am. Archeology, Am. Soc. Conservation Archeology, Soc. Profl. Archeologists (qualifications rev. bd. 1982-83), Wash. Archeol. Research Ctr. (exec. com. 1985), Assn. Wash. Archeology, Nat. Conf. State Hist. Preservation Officers (past mem. rev. and compliance com.). Democrat. Roman Catholic. Avocations: physical fitness; flying; languages. Office: PO Box 6266 Olympia WA 98502

WELCH, J(OAN) KATHLEEN, dance studio executive; b. Pensacola, Fla., Jan. 28, 1950; d. Leslie Peter and Frances Louise (Hughes) Morales. Salesperson with Arthur Murray Dance Studio, Colo., Fla., Pa. and N.J., 1970-81; sales rep. Warner-Lambert Co., Morris Plains, N.J., 1981-83; supr., mgr. Dance Club Internat., Chatham, N.J., 1983—; judge Nat. Dance Council Am., 1977—; dance coach, 1975—; choreographer, 1971—; competitor, 1972-81. Recipient awards Arthur Murray Studio, 1971-81, 1st place counselor award Arthur Murray All Star Tournament, 1977, various awards Dance Club Internat., 1st place supr., registrar in Tournament Champions, 1984—. Mem. Imperial Soc. Tchrs. of Dancine (assoc. ballroom br., Latin-Am. br), Am. Dance Tchrs. Assn. Inc. Mem. Unity Ch. Home: 117 E Westfield Ave Roselle Park NJ 07204 Office: Dance Club Internat 6 S Passaic Ave Chatham NJ 07928

WELCH, KATHY JANE, oil company official; b. San Antonio, Aug. 5, 1952; d. John Dee and Pauline Ann (Overstreet) W.; m. John Thomas Unger, Jan. 8, 1977. B.A.S. in Computer Sci., So. Meth. U., 1974; M.B.A. in Fin., U. Houston, 1978. Programmer, analyst Tex. Instruments, Houston, 1974-76, project leader, 1976-78, br. mgr., 1978-81; mgr. systems and programming Global Marine, Houston, 1981-84, mgr. office automation, 1984-85, mgr. user systems, 1985-88, dir. MIS, Advanced Tech. div. Browning-Ferris Industries, Houston, 1988 . Mem. Am. Mgmt. Assn., Fedn. Houton Profl. Women, Assn. MBA Execs., Am. Mgmt. Assn., Ops. Research Soc. Am., Assn. Women in Computing (pres. Houston chpt. 1986-87), Mensa, Beta Gamma Sigma. Office: Browning-Ferris Industries PO Box 3151 Houston TX 77253

WELCH, MARY EDDISON, town official; b. N.Y.C., Nov. 17, 1917; d. William Barton and Mary Corbin Eddison; m. E. Sohier Welch, Dec. 27, 1940; children—Edward S., William B., Mary C., Anne E. BA, Bennington Coll., 1940. Adminstr., Mystic Valley Mental Health Ctr., Lexington, Mass., 1970-77; mem. Bd. Selectmen Town of Harvard, Mass., 1980-86. pres. Harvard LWV, 1986-88; bd. dirs. Girl Scouts U.S.A., N.Y.C., 1955-66; trustee Bennington Coll., Vt., 1964-71; bd. dirs. Minute Man Home Care Corp., Lexington, 1977-80, Dana McLean Greeley Found for Peace and Justice, Inc., 1988—; pres. Harvard League of Women Voters, 1986-88. Democrat. Unitarian. Club: Chilton (Boston). Avocation: sailing.

WELCH, MARY-SCOTT, writer; b. Chgo.; d. William Scott and Myrtle (Ferrin) Stewart; A.B. in English, U. Ill.; m. Barrett F. Welch (dec.); children: Farley, Laura Stewart, Margaret, Mary Barrett. Books include: Your First Hundred Meals, What Every Young Man Should Know, The Family Wilderness Handbook, Networking: The Great New Way for Women to Get Ahead; former mem. staff Esquire-Coronet mag., Pageant mag., Look mag.; contbg. editor Glamour mag.; columnist Seventeen mag., McCall's mag., Vogue mag.; contbr. to mags. including Ladies Home Jour., Redbook, Ms., Modern Maturity, Working Woman, Woman's Day. Bd. advisors Inst. Women and Work, Cornell U. Served with USNR. Mem. Authors Guild, Authors League, Women in Communications, Women's Inst. Freedom of Press, NOW (adv. bd.; past coordinator rape prevention com. N.Y.C.), Phi Beta Kappa, Kappa Kappa Gamma, environ. and civil liberties orgns. Home and Office: 30 Waterside Plaza New York NY 10010

WELD, TUESDAY KER (SUSAN KER WELD), actress; b. N.Y.C., Aug. 27, 1943; d. Lathrop Motley and Aileen (Ker) W.; m. Claude Harz, Oct., 1965 (div. 1971); 1 dau., Natasha; m. Dudley Moore, Sept. 20, 1975 (div.); 1 son, Patrick; m. Pinchas Zukerman, Oct. 18, 1985. Attended, Hollywood (Calif.) Profl. Sch. Actress: (TV programs) including Cimarron Strip, Playhouse 90, Kraft Theatre, Alcoa Theatre, Climax, Ozzie and Harriet, The Many Loves of Dobie Gillis, 77 Sunset Strip, The Millionaire, Tab Hunter Show, Zane Grey Theatre, Follow the Sun, Bus Stop, Dick Powell Theatre, Adventures in Paradise, Naked City, Eleventh Hour, DuPont Show of the Month, The Greatest Show on Earth, Mr. Broadway, Fugitive, The Crucible, (films) including debut in Rock, Rock, Rock, 1956, Serial, Rally Round the Flag Boys, The Five Pennies, The Private Lives of Adam and Eve, Return to Peyton Place, Wild in the Country, Bachelor Flat, Lord Love A Duck, Pretty Poison, I Walk the Line, A Safe Place, Play It As It Lays, Because They're Young, High Time, Sex Kittens Go to College, The Cincinnati Kid, Soldier in the Rain, I'll Take Sweden, Who'll Stop the Rain, Looking for Mr. Goodbar, Thief, Author! Author!, Once Upon a Time in America, (TV movies) including Reflections of Murder, 1974, F. Scott Fitzgerald in Hollywood, 1976, A Question of Guilt, 1978, Mother and Daughter: The Loving War, 1980, Madame X, 1981, The Rainmaker, 1982, The Winter of Discontent, 1983, Scorned and Swindled, 1984, Circle of Violence, 1986. •

WELDON, EUNICE BERTHA, government official; b. Westmoreland, Va., July 29, 1941; d. Jesse Arthur and Mary Nannie (Jones) W. Grad., Cortez Peters Bus. Coll.; student, George Washington U. With D.C. Govt., Washington, 1962—, audit verification specialist Dept. Human Services, 1979-80, acting acctg. tech. supr., 1980, acting staff asst., 1980-81, acting program analyst, 1981, audit verification payment specialist, 1981-83, program analyst, 1983—. Mem. Nat. Assn. Female Execs. Baptist. Office: DC Dept Human Services 801 N Capitol NE Washington DC 20001

WELDON, VALERIE SHARLENE, owner needlework mail order business; b. Kansas City, Mo., Oct. 4, 1930; d. James Woodward and Valerie Dorothy (Shannon) W.; m. Donald Charles Krenkel, June 1, 1952 (div. Oct. 1981); children: Sharol Lyn Krenkel, Shannon Leslie Krenkel, Liza Beth Krenkel. BA, U. Kansas City, 1951. Advt. asst. James W. Weldon Metallurgy Lab., Kansas City, 1951-66, researcher, mgr. fgn. purchasing, 1966-75, v.p., 1975-81; pres. Needlepoint, Inc., Jupiter, Fla., 1974—. Editor Needlepoint Bull., 1974—; contbr. articles to profl. jours. Mem. ACLU; county com. mem. Rep. Com. Kansas City, 1966-74. Mem. Am. Assn. Retired Persons. Office: Needlepoint Inc PO Box 1585 Jupiter FL 33468-1585

WELDON, VIRGINIA V., medical school administrator, pediatric endocrinologist; b. Toronto, Sept. 8, 1935; came to U.S., 1937; d. John Edward and Carolyn Edith (Swift) Verral; children: Ann Stuart, Susan Shaefer. A.B. cum laude, Smith Coll., 1957; M.D., SUNY-Buffalo, 1962; L.H.D. (hon.), Rush U., 1985. Diplomate Am. Bd. Pediatrics in pediatric endocrinology and metabolism. Intern Johns Hopkins Hosp., Balt., 1962-63, resident in pediatrics, 1963-64; fellow pediatric endocrinology Johns Hopkins U., Balt., 1964-67, instr. pediatrics, 1967-68; asst. prof. Washington U., St. Louis, 1968-73, assoc. prof. pediatrics, 1973-79, prof. pediatrics, 1979—; v.p. Med. Ctr. Washington U., 1980—, dep. vice chancellor med. affairs, 1983—; gen. clin. research ctrs. adv. com. NIH, Bethesda, Md., 1976-80, research resources adv. council, 1980-84; dir. Centerre Trust Co., St. Louis, Southwestern Bell Corp., Gen. Am. Life Ins. Co. Contbr. articles to sci. jours. Commr. St. Louis Zool. Park, 1983—; bd. dirs. United Way Greater St. Louis, 1978—, St. Louis Regional Health Care Corp. Fellow Am. Acad. Pediatrics, AAAS; mem. Inst. Medicine, Assn. Am. Med. Colls. (del., chmn. council acad. socs. 1984-85, chmn. assembly 1985-86), Am. Pediatric Soc., Nat. Bd. Med. Examiners (bd. dirs. 1987—), Endocrine Soc., Soc. Pediatric Research, AAU (joint com. health policy), Nat. Assn. Biomed. Research (bd. dirs.), St. Louis Med. Soc., Sigma Xi, Alpha Omega Alpha. Roman Catholic. Home: 4444 Lindell Blvd Suite 8 Saint Louis MO 63108 Office: Washington U Sch Medicine Box 8106 660 S Euclid Ave Saint Louis MO 63110

WELHAN, BEVERLY JEAN LUTZ, nursing educator, adminstrator; b. Phila., Dec. 7, 1950; d. Winfield E. and Mary Helen (James) Lutz; m. Joseph Welhan, Jan. 7, 1984; m. Robert John LeBar, Aug. 28, 1971 (div. July 1978); children, James Benjamin, Jillian Grace. Diploma, Montgomery Hosp. Sch. Nursing, 1971; B.S.N., Gwynedd Mercy Coll., 1974; M.Ed., Lehigh U., 1977; M.S.N., Villanova U., 1983. Staff nurse recovery room Montgomery Hosp., Norristown, Pa., 1971-72; charge nurse North Penn Convalescent Residence, Lansdale, Pa., 1972-74; instr. med.-surg. nursing Episcopal Hosp., Phila., 1974-78; staff nurse Montgomery Hosp., Norristown, Pa., 1978-79; asst. dir. nursing edn. Episcopal Hosp., Phila., 1979-85, assoc. dir. nursing edn., 1985—; part-time instr. Pa State U., 1983-84; cons. Leonard M. Amodei, Esquire, Phila., 1980-83, James Ciamaichelo, Esquire, Phila., 1983—. Author: Testing Program for Scherer's Introductory Medical-Surgical Nursing, 1986. Mem. Nat. League Nursing, Am. Nurses Assn., Pa. Nurses Assn. Southeastern Pa. League for Nursing (mem. nominating com. 1982-83, bd. dirs. 1983-85), Montgomery Hosp. Alumni Assn., Sigma Theta Tau, Phi Kappa Phi. Republican. Home: 506 E Godfrey Ave Philadelphia PA 19120 Office: Episcopal Hosp Sch Nursing Front St and Lehigh Ave Philadelphia PA 19125

WELKER, CONNI, ergonomic engineer, consultant; b. Honolulu, Apr. 4, 1945; d. John Connely and Gwendolyn Shirley (Lannom) W.; children: Sean, Christopher, Andrea, Joshua. BS in Psychology, Bloomsburg U., 1976; MS in Ergonomic Engring., Tex. Tech U., 1980. Research assoc. Dept. Indsl. Engring. Tex. Tech U., Lubbock, 1980-82; ergonomic engr. Ethicon, Inc. div. Johnson & Johnson, Somerville, N.J., 1982-86, Bell Labs. div. AT&T, Whippany, N.J., 1986—; pvt. practice cons., Raritan, N.J., 1980—. Author: Industrial Ergonomics, 1985, govt. publ. Male/Female Differences in Performance, 1975. Mem. Human Factor Soc. (vice chmn. indsl. ergonomics tech. adv. group, 1987), Sigma Xi. Home: 30 Doughty St Raritan NJ 08869 Office: AT&T Room 14D-373 Whippany Rd Whippany NJ 07981

WELLER, JANE KATHLEEN, nurse; b. Balt., May 26, 1948; d. Donald Boyd and Jane Lee (Collins) Sealing; m. Richard Earl Weller, Oct. 20, 1973 (div. Dec. 1978); 1 child, Jennifer Lee. AA in Nursing, Essex Community Coll., Balt., 1971; BS in Health, U. Md., 1983. RN, Md. Nurse, adminstr.

supr. Liberty Med. Ctr., Balt., 1971—. Mem. Nat. League for Nursing, Md. League for Nursing, Nat. Emergency Nurses Assn., Md. Emergency Nurses Assn., Nat. Assn. Bus. Women. Lutheran. Home: 6062 Cedarwood Drive Columbia MD 21044 Office: Liberty Med Ctr 2600 Liberty Heights Baltimore MD 21215

WELLER, KIMBERLY ANN, architect; b. Portland, Oreg., May 24, 1954; d. John Howard and Julanne (Chevrier) W.; m. Douglas Hartley Gordon, Aug. 27, 1983. AB in Urban Studies and Italian, Stanford U., 1976; MArch, MIT, 1980. Registered architect, N.Y. Designer, housing analyst The Ehrenkrantz Group, P.C., N.Y.C., 1977-79; assoc. Perkins and Will, N.Y.C., 1980-84; v.p. Architecture for Health, Sci. and Commerce, White Plains, N.Y., 1984—. Co-author: The Grunsfeld Variations, 1981. Mem. MIT Architecture and Planning Alumni Assn. N.Y. (co-founder, steering com. 1982-86), Young Architects Com., Archtl. League N.Y. (co-founder), Phi Beta Kappa. Democrat. Office: Architecture Health Sci Commerce 7-11 S Broadway White Plains NY 10601

WELLES, MELINDA FASSETT, psychologist, educator, consultant, artist; b. Palo Alto, Calif., Jan. 4, 1943; d. George Edward and Barbara Helena (Todd) W.; m. Robert Joseph Sbordone, June 30, 1972 (div. Aug. 1977). Student fine arts San Francisco Inst. Art, 1959-60, U. Oreg., 1960-62; BA in Fine Arts, UCLA, 1964, MA in Spl. Edn., 1971, PhD in Ednl. Psychology, 1976; student fine arts and illustration Art Ctr. Coll. Design, 1977-80. Cert. ednl. psychologist, Calif. Asst. prof. Calif. State U., Northridge, 1979-82, Pepperdine U., Los Angeles, 1979-82; assoc. prof. counseling and spl. edn. U. So. Calif., Los Angeles, 1980—; mem. acad. faculty Pasadena City Coll., 1973-79, Art Ctr. Coll. Design, 1978—, Otis Art Inst. of Parsons Sch. Design, Los Angeles, 1986—, UCLA Extension, 1980-84, Coll. Devel. Studies, Los Angeles, 1980—, El Camino Community Coll., Redondo Beach, Calif., 1982-86; cons. spl. edn.; pub. adminstrn. analyst UCLA Spl. Edn. Research Program, 1973-76; exec. dir. Atwater Park Ctr. Disabled Children, Los Angeles, 1976-78; coordinator Pacific Oaks Coll. in service programs for Los Angeles Unified Schs., Pasadena, 1978-81. Author, Calif. Dept. Edn. tech. reports, 1972-76; editor: Teaching Special Students in the Mainstream, 1981; group shows include: San Francisco Inst. Art, 1960, U. Hawaii, 1978, Barnsdall Gallery, Los Angeles, 1979, 80; represented in various pvt. collections. HEW fellow, 1971-72; grantee Calif. Dept. Edn., 1975-76, Calif. Dept. Health, 1978. Mem. Calif. Assn. Neurologically Handicapped Children, Am. Council Learning Disabilities, Clearing House for Info. on Learning Disabilitics, Calif. Scholarship Fedn. (life), Alpha Chi Omega. Democrat. Office: U So Calif WPH 1101 Univ Park Los Angeles CA 90089

WELLES, NYDIA LELIA CÁNOVAS, psychologist; b. Buenos Aires, Argentina, Mar. 30, 1935; came to U.S., 1967, naturalized, 1977; d. Artemio Tomás and Pura (Martínez) Cánovas; B.A. in Elem. Edn., Nat. Coll. Edn., Evanston, Ill., 1976; M.A. in Counseling Psychology, Northwestern U., 1977, PhD in Counseling Psychology, 1986; m. Lorant Welles, Oct. 21, 1967; 1 son, Lorant Esteban. Tchr. in Argentina, 1954-64; pvt. practice psychology, Argentina, 1964-67; social worker Cath. Charities, Chgo., 1971-75; translator SRA, Chgo., 1975; test adminstr. Ednl. Testing Service, 1975-76; Latin Am. Services supr. Edgewater Uptown Community Mental Health Council, Chgo., 1978-80 ; research asst. Center Family Studies, 1978-79; mem. allocation com. campaign for human devel. Archdiocesis of Chgo., 1985—. Mem. Ill. Assn. for Hispanic Mental Health (co-founder), Phi Delta Kappa. Roman Catholic. Author papers in field. Home: 3110 Hill Ln Wilmette IL 60091

WELLING, JUNE STRATE, business college executive; b. Cardston, Alta., Can., Mar. 13, 1927; d. Clarence H. and Esther (Pack) Strate; m. Woodrow J. Welling, Apr. 13, 1944; children: Terrance, Kent, Annette. BS, Cen. State U., Edmonds, Okla., 1967; M of Bus. Edn., U. Okla., 1970; EdD, Utah State U., 1976. Tchr. bus. edn. U.S. Grant High Sch., Oklahoma City, Okla., 1967-74; lectr. Utah State U., Logan, 1974-76; cons. Cen. Mindanao U., Bukidncn, The Philippines, 1976-78; pres., founder Logan Bus. Coll., 1980—; cons. Small Bus. Mgmt., Logan, 1976, Woman's Ctr. of Utah State U., 1976; instr. flying Utah State Extension, Moab and Vernal, 1980-81. Mem. AAUW (pres. 1984-86, v.p. program com. 1986-87), Nat. Bus. Edn. Assn., Utah Bus. Edn. Assn., Western Bus. Edn. Assn., Utah Proprietary Sch. Assn., Delta Pi Epsilon (recording sec.). Democrat. Mormon. Home: 411 W 100 S PO Box 745 Logan UT 84321 Office: Logan Bus Coll 75 S 400 W Logan UT 84321

WELLINGTON, PATRICIA PADGITT, computer company administrator; b. New Orleans, July 4, 1940; d. Newton and Louise (Nesbitt) Padgitt; m. Duke Wellington, Apr. 9, 1960; children: Kenneth, Scott, Brian. Student, Cornell U., 1958-60, Drake Bus. Sch., N.Y.C., 1960; BA, Ramapo Coll. of N.J., 1979. Cert. housing counselor HUD. Asst. supr. HUD project Fair Housing Council of No. N.J., Hackensack, 1977, project dir., housing counselor, 1979-84; sec. specialist IBM Corp., Franklin Lakes, N.J., 1984—. Active Bergen County council Girl Scouts U.S., Paramus, N.J., 1976-80; vol. Martin Luther King Jr. Meml. Day Care Ctr., Paterson, N.J., 1970-77; trustee No. N.J. Fair Housing Council, 1965-77; bd. dirs. Wyckoff (N.J.) Family YMCA, 1987—. Presbyterian. Office: IBM Corp 400 Parsons Pond Dr Franklin Lakes NJ 07417

WELLMAN, ELIZABETH ANN, travel educator; b. Ft. Campbell, Ky., June 4, 1955; d. Andrew Olan and Betty Jo (Tinsman) Drenkhahn; m. Reynard J. Wellman, Aug. 17, 1982; 1 stepchild, Jennifer. BA in Polit. Sci., Purdue U., 1977. With ops. Bennett Tours, San Francisco, 1977-78; travel agt. Ask Mr. Foster, Chgo., 1978, Bd. of Trade Travel, Chgo., 1978, Longhorn Travel, Austin, Tex., 1979-80; interviewer Tex. Employment Commn., Austin, 1980-81; travel agt. Sanborn's Travel, Austin, 1981; instr. travel Capitol City Trade and Tech. Sch., Austin, 1981—, head travel dept., 1984—. Del. Travis County Dem. Conv., Austin, 1984. Home: 8400 Washita Dr Austin TX 78749

WELLMAN, MARY MARGARET, psychology educator; b. Bklyn., May 20, 1946; d. John F. and Anna H. Haunss; m. Robert J. Wellman. BS, SUNY, Geneseo, 1967; MA, SUNY, Stony Brook, 1970; PhD, U. Conn., 1980. Lic. psychologist, Mass., R.I. Tchr. elem. sch. Kings Park (N.Y.) Schs., 1967-74; reading cons. Thompson (Conn.) Pub. Schs., 1974-81; asst. prof. R.I. Coll., Providence, 1981-87, dir. Sch. Psychology, 1984—, assoc. prof., 1987—; adj. instr. psychology Anna Maria Coll., Paxton, Mass., 1980-82, Worcester (Mass.) State Coll., 1982-84; pvt. practice psychologist, Charlton, Mass., 1982—; cons. psychologist Comprehensive Mental Health Service, Waban, Mass., 1983-85; asst. attending child psychologist McLean Hosp., Belmont, Mass., 1986—. Contbr. articles to profl. jours. Pres. Charlton Hist. Soc., 1977-79. Recipient Disting. Service award Southbridge (Mass.) C. of C., 1980. Mem. Am. Psychol. Assn., R.I. Psychol. Assn., Nat. Assn. Sch. Psychologists, R.I. Sch. Psychologists Assn. (bd. dirs. 1985—), R.I. Assn. Women in Psychology. Office: RI Coll Adams Library 115 Providence RI 02908

WELLS, DONNA FRANCES, distribution company executive; b. Lima, Ohio, Dec. 19, 1948; d. Arthur Robert and Frances Lucille (Knudtson) W.; m. Darrell Donald Erickson, Nov. 26, 1980. Cert., Parks Bus. Sch., 1972; student, Sheridan Coll., 1984—. Dir. purchasing Wolff Distbg., Gillette, Wyo., 1973—. Mem. Nat. Assn. Purchasing Mgmt., Nat. Assn. of Female Execs., Gillette Racing Assn. (aux. v.p. 1986—), VFW Aux., Am. Legion Aux. Home: 105 Sequoia Gillette WY 82716

WELLS, ELAINE LOUISE, state legislator, health care administrator; b. Emporia, Kans., May 26, 1951; d. Walter Lawrence and Ruth Maxine (Mangold) Laue; m. Richard Dean Wells, Sept. 24, 1967; children: Dane Eric, Daric Ean. Student, Washburn U., 1978-85. Asst. activities dir. Brookside Manor, Overbrook, Kans., 1975-76, adminstr., 1976-86; adminstr. Fairlawn Heights, Topeka, 1987—; mem. Ho. of Reps., Topeka, 1987—. Vice chair Osage County (Kans.) Dem. Com., 1982-86; bd. dirs. Osage County Farm Bur., 1986. Mem. Kans. Health Care Assn. (bd. dirs. 1985-87). Home: Rt 1 Box 166 Carbondale KS 66414 Office: Kans State Capitol Room 272 W Topeka KS 66612

WELLS, FAY GILLIS, writer, lecturer, broadcaster; b. Mpls., Oct. 15, 1908; d. Julius Howells and Minnie Irene (Shafer) Gillis; student Mich. State Coll., 1925-28; m. Linton Wells, Apr. 1, 1935 (dec. 1976); 1 son, Linton Wells, II. Free-lance corr. in USSR for N.Y. Herald Tribune and AP, 1930-34, aviation mags., 1930-36; fgn. corr. N.Y. Herald Tribune, 1935-36, spl. Hollywood corr., 1937-38, syndicated boating columnist, 1960-62; contbr. book revs. Saturday Review, 1939-42; dep. chief of mission for U.S. Comml. Co., Portuguese W. Africa, 1942-46; White House corr. Storer Broadcasting Co., 1964-77; aircraft pilot, 1929; designer yacht interiors Alta Grant Samuels, 1958-62; now co-chmn. Internat. Forest of Friendship; hon. co-chmn. Nat. Air Heritage Council; mem. com. to select 1st journalist in space, 1985—. Recipient Sherman Fairchild Internat. Air Safety Writing award, 1965, Amelia Earhart medal, 1967, Golden Age of Flight award Nat. Air and Space Mus.-Dept. Transp., 1984, award Internat. Conf. Women Engrs. and Scientists, 1984. Mem. 1967. Mem. Aviation/Space Writers Assn., Am. Women in Radio and TV (pres. Washington chpt. 1968-69, CBS Charlotte Friel award 1972), Radio-TV Corrs. Assn., White House Corrs. Assn., Aircraft Owners and Pilots Assn., The Ninety-Nines (charter mem.; Most Valuable Pilot, Washington chpt. 1975), OX5 Aviation Pioneers (Outstanding Woman of Year award 1972), Internat. Soc. Woman Geographers, Broadcast Pioneers, Zonta Internat., Nat. Bus. and Profl. Womens Clubs, Nat. League Am. Pen Women, Nat. Aero. Assn. (named elder statesman 1984). Clubs: Georgetown, Overseas Press (founding mem. 1939), Am. Newspaper Women's, Nat. Press, Internat. Forest Friendship (co-gen. chmn. 1976—). Home: 4211 Duvawn St Alexandria VA 22310

WELLS, GERTRUDE BEVERLY, communications consultant; b. Harerhill, Mass., July 14, 1940; d. True Franklyn Wells and Priscilla Eleanor (Browne) Duerstling. BS, SUNY, Fredonia, 1962; MA, Coll. St. Rose, 1969; PhD, U. Mo., 1976. Tchr. speech pathology N.Y. Pub. Schs., Albany and Clifton Park, 1962-70; lectr. SUNY, Albany, 1970-73; asst. prof. Coll. St. Rose, Albany, 1975-77; assoc. prof. U. No. Iowa, Cedar Falls, 1977-78; prof. U. Southwestern La., Lafayette, 1978-85; prof., program dir. Calif. State U. Stanislaus, Turlock, 1985-87; ind. communications cons. Dallas, 1987—. Author: Stuttering Treatment, 1987; contbr. articles to profl. jours. Mem. United Way of Stanislaus County, Modesto, Calif., 1985-87, Stroke Services, Inc., Modesto, 1985-87, Services to Older Adults Advisory Council, Modesto, 1985-87. Mem. Am. Speech Lang. Hearing Assn., Calif. Speech Lang. Hearing Assn., AAUP, Nat. Assn. Women Deans Adminstrs. and Counselors, Kappa Delta Pi. Democrat. Mem. Unitarian Ch. Home and Office: 17725 Windflower #112 Dallas TX 75252

WELLS, KATHY LYNN, educator; b. Charleston, W.Va., June 9, 1958; d. Clarence Eric and Ereinstine Ruth (Adams) W. BS in Secondary Edn., W.Va. U., 1979; MA in Specific Learning Disabilities, W.Va. Coll. Grad. Studies, 1985. Cert. tchr., W.Va.; cert. Educable Mentally Impaired, W.Va.; cert. in behaviorally disorders; cert. in specific learning disabilities. Spl. educator Belle (W.Va.) Elem. Sch., 1979-80, Roosevelt Jr. High Sch., Charleston, 1980-81, George Washington High Sch., Charleston, 1981—; tchr. adolescence care unit Charleston Area Med. Ctr., 1985-86; bd. dirs. Wells and Assocs. Named to Hon. Order Ky. Cols.; named Commodore of the Ship, W.Va. Mem. Charleston Jaycettes. Democrat. Presbyterian. Lodge: Masons (v.p. local chpt. 1984, pres. localchpt. 1986-87). Home: 2999 Pennsylvania Ave Charleston WV 25302

WELLS, KATHY T., nurse; b. Rock Rapids, Iowa, June 26, 1947; d. Gerald Richard and Eva (Day) Travers; divorced; children: Joy Lavone Huggins Parker, Chris William Huggins, Lexa Lyn Huggins. BS in Nursing, Augustana U., 1965; MBA, North Ga. U., 1977. RN Ware Meml. Hosp., Waycross, Ga., 1969-72, Glynn Brunswick Hosp., Brunswick, Ga., 1972-78, Tonner Meml. Hosp., Carrollton, Ga., 1975-78; adminstr., nurse Long County Med. Ctr., Ludowici, Ga., 1978-83; RN, office mgr. Dr. Glenn Carter Office, Hinesville, Ga., 1983—. Mem. research bd. Ga. Cancer Soc., 1978—; mem. Liberty County Red Cross, Hinesville, Ga., 1978—; mem. Child Abuse Council, Ga., 1978—. Served to capt. USN, 1965-69, Vietnam. Mem. Nursing Life Assn., Ga. Nursing Assn., SE Emergency Medicine Assn., Am. Med. Assn. RN's. Methodist. Home: PO Box 904 Hinesville GA 31313 Office: Dr Glenn Carter 303 Fraser Dr Hinesville GA 31313

WELLS, MARILYNN VELMA, service executive; b. Beaumont, Tex., June 28, 1944; d. Freddie Louis and Mercile Velma (Adams) W.; m. Johnny Mitchell (div.); children: Anthony Louis Mitchell, Reginald Allan Mitchell. BS, Calif. State U., Northridge, 1970; MA, Calif. State U., Los Angeles, 1988. Registered dietitian, Calif. Dietitian Martin Luther King Jr. Gen. Hosp., Los Angeles, 1972-76; nutrition specialist Riverside (Calif.) Unified Sch. Dist., 1976-79, Los Angeles Unified Sch. Dist., 1980-81; dir. food service, maintenance and ops. Inglewood (Calif.) Unified Sch. Dist., 1981-84; dir. food services Alhambra (Calif.) Sch. Dist., 1984—. Contbr. articles to profl. jours.; co-director, script writer (motion picture) For Our Customers Sake, 1981. Mem. Calif. Sch. Food Service Assn. (chmn. pub. info. 1986-87), So. Calif. Sch. Food Service Assn. (chmn. pub. info. 1987-88, pres. elect 1988), Calif. Assn. Sch. Bus. Officials, Am. Dietetic Assn., Alhambra Mgmt. Assn. Democrat. Baptist. Home: 5614 Valley Glen Way Los Angeles CA 90043 Office: Alhambra Sch Dist 15 W Alhambra Rd Alhambra CA 91801

WELLS, MARSHA VANSANT, computer specialist, educator; b. Spartanbug, S.C., Feb. 19, 1954; d. Carl Johnson and Martha Elizabeth (Steadman) Vansant; m. Randy Walker Wells, Dec. 6, 1974 (div.); children: Philip Walker, Amanda Leigh. BBA, U. S.C., 1979. Sec. S.C. Dept. Youth Services, Spartanburg, 1975-79; owner, mgr. The Tredmill, Inc., Spartanburg, 1978-80; acct. Reeves Bros., Inc., Spartanburg, 1980-82, sr. acct., 1982-84, programmer, 1984-85; system support rep. Entré Computer Ctr., Spartanburg, 1985-88; systems specialist Dept. Med. Edn., Spartanburg Regional Med. Ctr., 1988—. Adult leader trainer Boy Scouts Am., Spartanburg, 1982. Methodist. Home: 501 Camelot Dr #88 Spartanburg SC 29301 Office: Spartanburg Regional Med Ctr Dept Med Edn 101 E Wood St Spartanburg SC 29303

WELLS, MARY ELIZABETH THOMPSON, psychotherapist; b. Dallas, Oct. 9, 1936; d. Owen Perry and Ruth Marie (Baker) Thompson; children: Tadd Whitney, Britony Ruth. BA in Sociology, Syracuse (N.Y.) U., 1958; MA in Child Devel., Tufts U., 1964, MEd in Counseling Psychology, 1974. Asst. dir. pub. relations Inst. for Crippled and Disabled, N.Y.C., 1958-59; head tchr. Eliot-Pearson Children's Sch., Tufts U., Medford, Mass., 1964-66; psychotherapist Mental Health Ctr. of Greater Cape Ann, Gloucester, Mass., 1974—. Mem. Am. Psychol. Assn., Am. Orthopsychiat. Assn. Clubs: Essex County (Manchester, Mass.); Manchester Yacht. Home: 52 Central St Manchester MA 01944 Office: Mental Health Ctr of Greater Cape Ann Addison-Gilbert Hosp 298 Washington St Gloucester MA 01930

WELLS, MELISSA FOELSCH, foreign service officer; b. Tallinn, Estonia, Nov. 18, 1932; emigrated to U.S., 1936, naturalized, 1941; d. Kuno Georg and Miliza (Korjus) Foelsch; m. Alfred Washburn Wells, 1960; children: Christopher, Gregory. BS in Fgn. Service, Georgetown U., 1956. Consular officer Trinidad, 1961-64; econ. officer mission OECD, Paris, 1964-66; econ. officer London, 1966-71; internat. economist Dept. State, Washington, 1971-73; dep. dir. maj. export projects Dept. Commerce, 1973-75; comml. counselor Brazil, 1975-76; ambassador to Guinea, Bissau and Cape Verde, 1976-77; U.S. rep. to ECOSOC, UN, N.Y.C., 1977-79; resident rep. UNDP, Kampala, Uganda, 1979-81; dir. IMPACT program UNDP, Geneva, Switzerland, 1982-86; ambassador to Mozambique, 1987—. Mem. Am. Fgn. Service Assn. Office: US Ambassador to Mozambique care Dept State Washington DC 20520

WELLS, PATRICIA BENNETT, business administration educator; b. Park River, N.D., Mar. 25, 1935; d. Benjamin Beekman Bennett and Alice Catherine (Peerboom) Bennett Breckinridge; A.A., Allan Hancok Coll., Santa Maria, Calif., 1964; B.S. magna cum laude, Coll. Great Falls, 1966; M.S., U. N.D., 1967, Ph.D., 1971; children—Bruce Bennett, Barbara Lea. Fiscal acct. USIA, Washington, 1954-56; public acct., Bremerton, Wash., 1956; statistician U.S. Navy, Bremerton, 1957-59; med. services accounts officer U.S. Air Force, Vandenberg AFB, Calif., 1962-64; instr. bus. adminstrn. Western New Eng. Coll., 1967-69; vis. prof. econs. Chapman Coll., 1970; vis. prof. U. So. Calif. systems Griffith AFB, N.Y., 1971-72; assoc. prof., dir. adminstrn. mgmt. program Va. State U., 1974-81; assoc. prof. bus. adminstrn. Oreg. State U., Corvallis, 1974-81, prof. mgmt., 1982—, univ. curriculum coordinator, 1984-86, dir. adminstrv. mgmt. program, 1974-81, pres. Faculty Senate, 1981; cons. process tech. devel. Digital Equipment Corp., 1982. Pres., chmn. bd. dirs. Adminstrv. Orgnl. Services, Inc., Corvallis, 1976-83, Dynamic Achievement, Inc., 1983—. Cert. adminstrv. mgr. Pres. TYEE mobile home park. Fellow Assn. Bus. Communication (mem. internat. bd. 1980-83, v.p. Northwest 1981, 2d v.p. 1982-83, 1st v.p. 1983-84, pres. 1984-85); mem. Am. Bus. Women's Assn. (named Top Businesswoman in Nation 1980, Bus. Assoc. Yr. 1986), Assn. Info. Systems Profls., Adminstrv. Mgmt. Soc., AAUP (chpt. sec. 1973, chpt. bd. dirs. 1982, 84-87, pres. Oreg. conf. 1983-85), Am. Vocat. Assn. (nominating com. 1976), Associated Oreg. Faculties, Nat. Bus. Edn. Assn., Nat. Assn. Tchr. Edn. for Bus. Office Edn. (pres. 1976-77, chmn. public relations com. 1978-81), Corvallis Area C. of C. (v.p. chamber devel. 1985-86, pres. 1988—, Pres.' award 1986), Sigma Kappa. Roman Catholic. Lodge: Rotary. Contbr. numerous articles to profl. jours. Office: Oreg State U Coll Bus 418C Bexell Corvallis OR 97331

WELLS, RONA LEE, consumer products company executive; b. Beaumont, Tex., Aug. 23, 1950; d. Ray Peveto and Frances (Manning) Reed; m. Harry Hankins Wells, Mar. 22, 1975. BS in Systems Engring, So. Meth. U., 1972. Registered profl. engr., Tex. With initial mgmt. devel. program Southwestern Bell Corp., Houston, 1972-73, engr. and inventory coordinator, 1973-74, sr. engr. supr., 1974-75, engring. project supr., 1975-77, dist. supr. maj. project, 1977-79, dist. supr. materials, 1979; mgr. field services CNA Fin. Corp., Chgo., 1979-80, mgr., asst. to v.p., 1980, area mgr. support services, 1980-82, area mgr. acctg. services, 1982; dir. bldg. and office mgmt. Kimberly-Clark, Neenah, Wis., 1982-85; ops. specialist Kimberly-Clark, New Milford, Conn., 1985-86, acting supt., 1985, project leader, 1985-88, ops. mgr., 1988—. Mem. Nat. Def. Exec. Res., Washington, 1979—. Named one of Outstanding Young Women of Am., 1978. Mem. Inst. Indsl. Engrs. (sr.), Soc. Women Engrs. (sr.), NSPE, Nat. Assn. Female Execs., Sigma Tau. Home: Rt 2 #7 Hilton Estates Conway AR 72032 Office: Kimberly-Clark Corp 480 Commerce Conway AR 72032

WELLS, VALDA EVELYN, management consultant; b. N.Y.C., June 23, 1935; d. William Frederick and Valda Elva (Baldwin) W.; B.A. in Econs., N.Y. Sch. Social Research, N.Y.C., 1967. With Gen. Electric Co., N.Y.C., 1964-80, cons. internat. trade policy devel., 1973-75, mgr. internat. research programs, 1975-80; pres. Wellspring, N.Y.C., 1980—; co-dir. CW Assocs., 1983—; tchr. profl. communication. Mem. Women Bus. Owners N.Y., Ind. Citizens Research Found, Nat. Assn. Female Execs., Am. Soc. Profl. and Exec. Women, Internat. Platform Assn. Democrat. Presbyterian. Home: 36-19 Bowne St Flushing NY 11354 Office: PO Box 310 Flushing NY 11352

WELLS-LIVERMORE, CRYSTAL JEAN, transportation executive; b. Fresno, Calif., Feb. 14, 1959; d. Goffrie Cylester and Frances Ruth (Metz) Wells; m. Galen Ray Livermore, Jan. 30, 1988. BS in Bus. and Adminstrv. Scis., Calif. State U., Fresno, 1983. Asst. to mgr. Visalia (Calif.) Mcpl. Airport, 1979-80; service rep. Emery Worldwide, Fresno, 1980-85, service supr., 1985—. Mem. Nat. Assn. Female Execs. Home: 4910 N Ninth St Apt 106 Fresno CA 93726 Office: Emery Worldwide 4941 E Anderson Suite 101 Fresno CA 93726

WELNA, SHARON KAY, data processing executive; b. Omaha, Nebr., July 28, 1951; d. Raymond Arthur and Blanche June (Stahlecker) Wahlstrom; m. Gary Hunter Welna, Mar. 23, 1974; children: Matthew Aaron, Michael Arthur. BA, U. Nebr., 1973. Govt. intern State of Nebr., Lincoln, 1972-73; programmer Con Agra, Omaha, 1973-77; systems analyst Cen. Telephone, Lincoln, 1977-79; mgr. data processing St. Joseph Hosp., Omaha, 1979-88, dir. data processing and fin., 1988—. Editor: (book) County Boards Handbook, 1974. Mem. Assn. Systems Mgmt., Data Processing Mgmt. Assn. (exec. forum), Nat. Assn. Exec. Females, Delta Zeta. Republican. Lutheran. Office: St Joseph Hosp 601 N 30th St Omaha NE 68131

WELS, MARGUERITE SAMET (MRS. RICHARD H. WELS), interior decorator; b. N.Y.C.; d. Max and Bertha (Levine) Samet; student N.Y. U., 1937, N.Y. Sch. Interior Design, 1938-41; m. Richard H. Wels, Dec. 12, 1954; children—Susan Rebecca, Amy Elizabeth. Interior decorator—Marguerite Samet, N.Y.C., 1946-60; interior decorator, head Marguerite Samet Assos., 1960—; co-ordinator U.S. Army Spl. Services, 1942-46; cons. United Bowling Centers, Inc., Interboro Gen. Hosp. Active in William Alanson White Inst. Psychiatry, Psychoanalysis and Psychology, Am. Jewish Com., Islands Research Found. Mem. Am. Inst. Interior Designers (exec. bd., v.p. N.Y. Met. chpt.), Democratic Women's Workshop. Jewish. Clubs: Women's City, Woman Pays. Home: 480 Park Ave New York NY 10021

WELSH, CAROL NEISSER, business educator, financial consultant; b. Vineland, N.J., Dec. 16, 1950; d. Wolfgang P. and Eva (Berwin) Neisser; m. Richard H. Welsh, May 30, 1976; children: Richard M., Stephen W. BS, Drexel U., 1972, MBA, 1982. CPA; cert. internal auditor. Staff acct. Laventhal and Horwath, CPAs, Phila., 1972-75; internal auditor Sun Ship Bldg. and Dry Dock, Chester, Pa., 1975-77; cost acct. AHSC div. Harleco, Gibbstown, N.J., 1977-79; cost acctg. supr. E. Merck div. Harleco, Gibbstown, 1979-80; cost acctg. mgr. E.M. Sci. affiliate E. Merck Darmstadt, Gibbstown, 1980-83; lectr. sch. bus. Glassboro (N.J.) State Coll., 1983—; fin. cons. Stageworks Theatre Touring Co., Glassboro, 1986—. Mem. allocations com. United Way, Gloucester County, N.J., 1986; trustee Richwood Presch., N.J., 1985—. Mem. An. Inst. CPA's, N.J. Soc. CPA's, Inst. Internal Auditors, Inst. Mgmt. Accts. Office: Glassboro State Coll Bunce Hall Rt 322 Glassboro NJ 08028

WELSH, DIANE KRESCENT, small business owner; b. N.Y.C., Oct. 4, 1951; d. Francesco and Alvine (Wendell) Biondi; m. Richard Robert Welsh, June 3, 1973. BA, Mercy Coll., 1973; MS, Western Conn. State U., 1975. Adminstr. Medallic Art Co., Danbury, Conn., 1975-76; consumer affairs Ethan Allen, Danbury, 1976-78; adminstr. Gen. Data Communications, Middlebury, Conn., 1978-80; pres. Lady Di, Inc., New Fairfield, Conn., 1985—. Coach Pee Wee Soccer League, New Fairfield, 1985; pres. New Fairfield PTO, 1985-86, 1986-87; vol. Spl. Olympics, New Fairfield. Mem. Nat. Assn. Female Execs. Republican.

WELSH, DONNA BARHAM, financial company executive; b. Aberdeen, Md., Aug. 16, 1956; d. John Ernest and Carol Marie (Preston) Barham; m. James Howard Welsh, Oct. 18, 1980; 1 child, Megan McKenzie. BS, U. Md., 1978. Actuarial analyst S.M. Hyman Co., Balt., 1978-79; plan adminstr. The Stuart Hack Co., Balt., 1979-80, account mgr., 1980-81, account exec., 1981-83, mgr. plan adminstrn., 1983-84, dept. head plan design, 1984-85, owner, v.p., 1985—. Mem. Am. Soc. Pension Actuaries, Alpha Xi Delta (Mason-Dixon alumnae chpt.). Democrat. Roman Catholic. Home: 4238 Darleigh Rd Baltimore MD 21236 Office: The Stuart Hack Co 4623 Falls Rd Baltimore MD 21209

WELSH, JUDITH SCHENCK, educator; b. Patchogue, L.I., N.Y., Feb. 5, 1939; d. Frank W. and Muriel (Whitman) Schenck; B.Ed., U. Miami (Fla.), 1961, M.A. in English, 1968; m. Robert C. Welsh, Sept. 16, 1961; children—Derek Francis, Christopher Lord. Co-organizer Cataract Surg. Congress med. meetings, 1963-76; grad. asst. instr. Dale Carnegie Courses Internat., 1967; adminstr. Office Admissions, Bauder Fashion Coll., Miami, 1976-77, instr. communications, 1977—, also pub. coll. monthly paper; free-lance writer regional and nat. publs.; guest speaker Optifair Internat., N.Y.C., 1980; guest speaker, mem. seminar faculty Optifair West, Anaheim, Calif., 1980, Optifair Midwest, St. Louis, 1980, Face to Face, Kansas City, Mo., 1981. Mem. Nat. Assn. Female Execs., Fla. Freelance Writers Assn., Nat. Writers Club (award), Delta Gamma. Congregationalist. Clubs: Coral Reef Yacht, Riviera Country, Royal Palm Tennis. Co-editor: The New Report on Cataract Surgery, 1969, Second Report on Cataract Surgery, 1974; editor: Surgidev's Cataract Surgery N.O.W., 1982—; contbr. Miami Today, 1985—, Ft. Lauderdale Sun/Sentinel, 1986—, Prime Times, Club Life, Gainesville Sun, The Oklahoman. Home: 1600 Onaway Dr Miami FL 33133 Office: 1600 Onaway Dr Miami FL 33133

WELSH, MARY MCANAW, educator, family mediator; b. Cameron, Mo., Dec. 7, 1920; d. Francis Louis and Mary Matilda (Moore) McA.; m. Alvin F. Welsh, Feb. 10, 1944; children: Mary Celia, Clinton F., M. Ann. AB, U.

Kans., 1942; MA, Seton Hall U., 1960; EdD, Columbia U., 1971. Reporter, Hutchinson (Kans.) News Herald, 1942-43; house editor Worthington Pump & Machine Corp., Harrison, N.J., 1943-44; tchr., housemaster, coordinator Summit (N.J.) Pub. Schs., 1960-68; prof. family studies N.Mex. State U., Las Cruces, 1972-85; adj. faculty dept. family practice Tex. Tech. Regional Acad. Health Ctr., El Paso, 1978-82, Family Mediation Practice, Las Cruces, 1986—. Mem. AAUW (pres. N.Mex. 1981-83), AAUP, N.Mex. Council Women's Orgn. (founder, chmn. 1982-83), LWV, Nat. Council Family Relationships, Am. Home Econs. Assn., Western Gerontol. Soc., Theta Sigma Phi, Delta Kappa Gamma, Kappa Alpha Theta. Democrat. Roman Catholic. Author: A Good Family is Hard to Found, 1972; Parent, Child and Sex, 1970; contbr. articles to profl. jours.; writer, presenter home econs. and family study series KRWG-TV, 1974; moderator TV series The Changing Family in N.Mex./LWV, 1976. Home and Office: PO Box 3483 University Park Las Cruces NM 88003

WELSH, SUE ANGELA, development and fund-raising specialist; b. N.Y.C., Nov. 10, 1938; d. Edward Thomas and Susan Bridget (Swanton) W.; B.A., Immaculate Heart Coll., 1960, Calif. secondary teaching credential, 1961; children—John Francis, Kieron Michael. Secondary sch. tchr. Los Angeles City Schs., 1960-77; field rep. Inter-Study, Los Angeles, 1977-78; dir. devel. pub. relations Immaculate Heart Coll. Ctr. Peace Justice and Global Cooperation, 1988—; dir. devel./community relations Poseidon Center for Troubled Adolescents with Learning Disabilities, Los Angeles, 1979—; dir. devel. Bilingual Found. Arts, 1983—, exec. dir., 1985-88; adminstrv. coordinator Danzantes Unidos, 1978-82. Recipient Pub. Service to Youth in Watts award, 1964, Los Angeles County Human Relations award, 1965, Mexican Folklorico Arts Adv. award, 1979, Vol. Action Center award, 1982. Home: 354 S Harvard Blvd Los Angeles CA 90020

WELTY, EUDORA, author; b. Jackson, Miss.; d. Christian Webb and Chestina (Andrews) W. Student, Miss. State Coll. for Women; B.A., U. Wis., 1929; postgrad., Columbia Sch. Advt., 1930-31. Author: A Curtain of Green, 1941, The Robber Bridegroom, 1942, The Wide Net, 1943, Delta Wedding, 1946, The Golden Apples, 1949, The Ponder Heart, 1954, The Bride of the Innisfallen, 1955, The Shoe Bird, 1964, Losing Battles, 1970, One Time, One Place, 1971, The Optimist's Daughter, 1972 (Pulitzer prize 1973), The Eye of the Story, 1978, The Collected Stories of Eudora Welty, 1980, One Writer's Beginnings, 1985; contbr.: New Yorker. Recipient creative arts medal for fiction Brandeis U., 1966, Nat. Inst. Arts and Letters Gold Medal, 1972, Nat. Medal for Lit., 1980, Presdl. Medal of Freedom, 1980, Commonwealth medal, 1984, Nat. Medal of Arts, 1987. Mem. Am. Acad. Arts and Letters. Home: 1119 Pinehurst St Jackson MS 39202

WENC, KAREN MARIE, cell biologist, researcher; b. Springfield, Mass., May 2, 1954; d. Joseph John and Mildred Mary (Orzech) W. Student, Boston U., 1972-73; AB, Smith Coll., 1976. Research asst. Yale U. Sch. Medicine, New Haven, Conn., 1976-78, Mass. Gen. Hosp., Boston, 1978-80, Beth Israel Hosp., Boston, 1980-85; research assoc. St. Elizabeth's Hosp., Boston, 1985—. Mem. Brookline Town Meeting, Mass., 1985—; bd. dirs. treas. Mass. Jobs With Peace, Boston, 1986—; mem. Adv. Council Pub. Health, Brookline, 1986—. Democrat. Home: 439 Washington St Apt #1 Brookline MA 02146 Office: St Elizabeth's Hosp Biomed Research 736 Cambridge St Boston MA 02135

WEND, JOANNE LENORE, accountant; b. Detroit, Nov. 26, 1960; d. Joseph H. and Eleanor Marie (Hadock) Denys; m. Dennis James Wend, Oct. 8, 1982. BBA in Acctg., Detroit Inst. Tech., 1981. Bookkeeper Swick Bus. Assocs., St. Clair Shores, Mich., 1978-80; cashier St. Joseph Hosp., Mt. Clemens, Mich., 1981-82, jr. acct., 1983-84; acct. Detroit Macomb Hosp. Corp., 1984-85; sr. budget analyst Pontiac (Mich.) Osteo. Hosp., 1986-88; owner Automated Fin. Services, East Detroit, Mich., 1983—. Vol. PIME Missionaires, Fraser, Mich., 1985—. Mem. Nat. Assn. Female Execs., Healthcare Fin. Mgmt. Assn. Roman Catholic. Home and Office: 24613 Brittany St East Detroit MI 48021

WEND, KAREN DEIRDRE, engineer; b. New Hyde Park, NY, Aug. 23, 1962; d. Eric William and Evelyn Dorothy (Caserta) Gormley; m. Eric Richard Wend, Nov. 2, 1985. B, Rochester (N.Y.) Inst. Tech., 1980-85. Cert. mfg. technologist. Mfg. engr. ITT Avionics, Nutley, N.J., 1988—. Mem. Soc. Mfg. Engrs. Office: 14 Oakley Dr Huntington Station NY 11746

WENDEL, FAYE F., coin equipment manufacturing executive; b. Newark, Sept. 16, 1928; d. John Thomas and Sara Rose (Agliozzo) Fiorenza; m. Daniel C. Wendel, Nov. 26, 1949; children—Catherine C., Daniel C. III, Wayne J. Sec., P. Ballantine & Sons, Newark, 1946-49; head hostess, asst. to mgr. Bambergers-Carriage House Restaurant, 1971-74; sec. Peter Wendel & Sons, Inc., Irvington, N.J., 1961-78; sec. Wendel Industries, Inc., Union, N.J., 1978-80, pres., 1980—; pres. D.C. Wendel Corp., 1982—. Tchrs. aide St. Ann Sch.; asst. treas. Ladies Aux. St. Rose of Lima Ch., 1963. Mem. Short Hills Assn., Twig Group of Overlook Hosp., Rotary Assn., Am. Soc. Profl. and Exec. Women. Clubs: Republican, Short Hills Racquet. Home: 33 Quaker Rd Short Hills NJ 07078 Office: 1012 Greeley Ave N Union NJ 07083

WENDER, PHYLLIS BELLOWS, literary agent; b. N.Y.C., Jan. 6, 1934; d. Lee and Lillian (Frank) Bellows; m. Ira Tensard Wender, June 24, 1966; children: Justin Bellows, Sarah Tensard. B.A., Wells Coll., 1956. Asst. advt dir. Book Find Club, N.Y.C., 1957-58; publicity dir. Grove Press, N.Y.C., 1958-61, Dell Pub. Co., N.Y.C., 1961-63; theatrical agt. Artists Agy. Inc., N.Y.C., 1963-68; agt. Wender & Assocs., N.Y.C., 1968-81; writers' agt. Rosenstone/Wender, N.Y.C., 1981—. Bd. dirs. Just Women Inc., Bklyn., 1982, mem. adv. com., 1983-87; bd. dirs. Fortune Soc., N.Y.C., 1977-80; trustee Wells Coll., Aurora, N.Y., 1981—. Mem. Women's Media Group (dir. 1988—). Club: Cosmopolitan (N.Y.C.). Office: Rosenstone/Wender 3 E 48th St New York NY 10017

WENGER, DOROTHY MAE, dietitian; b. Rozel, Kans., Jan. 20, 1917; d. John Edward and Irene Margaret (McElroy) Franz; m. Edward Lawrence Wenger (dec.); 1 child, Edward Lawrence III. Student, Iowa State Tchrs. Coll., Cedar Falls, 1937-39; BS, Lindenwood Coll. for Women, St. Charles, Mo., 1940; postgrad., U. W.Va., 1941, Columbia U., 1945, 47. Registered dietitian. Dietetic intern Mayo Clinic, Rochester, Minn., 1941, Western Pa. Hosp., Pitts., 1941-42; head dietitian, dir. dept. St. Luke's Hosp., Bluefield, W.Va., 1942-44, Monongalia Gen. Hosp., Morgantown, W.Va., 1944-49, Elyria (Ohio) Meml. Hosp., 1949-57; chief dietitian Lakewood Hosp., Cleve., 1957-58; dir. dietary dept. Beach Hosp., Ft. Lauderdale, Fla., 1959-61, North Broward Med. Ctr., Pompano Beach, Fla., 1961-75; chief dietitian North Broward Med. Ctr., Pompano Beach, 1975—; supr. clin. practicum program for student from various schs., including Atlantic Vocat. Sch., Broward Community Coll., Fla. Internat. Coll.; community nutrition lectr. North Broward County Hosp. Dist., 1985—. Developer dietetic course programs for various levels. Guidance vol. children and adults with Dyslexia, 1965—; lector Episcopal Ch., 1986—. Mem. Am. Dietetic Assn., Tri-county Clin. Mgrs., W.Va. Dietetic Assn. (state pres. 1942-44), Greater Miami Dietetic Assn. (adv. com. for dietetic tech. 1974-80), Cons. Dietitians for Long Term Facilities (Fla. state dietetic rep. 1978-79), Fla. Dietetic Assn. (chmn. dist. edn. com. 1975-77). Republican. Clubs: Quota (Morgantown), Triangle (St. Charles).

WENGER, MICHELE JAY, educational administrator; b. Cin., Mar. 29, 1947; d. John Paul and Mildred Elizabeth (Zaus) W.; B.S., U. Cin., 1969, M.Ed., 1970; postgrad Xavier U., 1972-82, Coll. Mt. St. Joseph, 1980-81. With Cin. Public Schs., 1970—, dir. Right to Read, 1972—, project dir. minimum competencies in writing, 1978-81, sex desegregation, 1981-82, assoc. 1984-87. U. Cin. scholar, 1969-70; Betty Jane Hull scholar, 1968. Mem. Internat. Reading Assn., Nat. Coalition Sex Equity for Edn., Assn. Supervision and Carriculum Devel., Phi Delta Kappa (pres. U. Cin. chpt. 1982-84), Kappa Delta Pi (chpt. historian 1983-85). Home: 6308 Eagles Lake Dr Cincinnati OH 45248 Office: 2488 Madison Rd Cincinnati OH 45208

WENGER, NIKI M., educator; b. Cin., June 9, 1940; d. Virgil Linza and Lillian Fern (Marshall) Mason; m. Philip Morgan Wenger, Sept. 1, 1962; children: Mason, Mitchell, Damon. BA in Psychology, U. Miami, 1962; MA in Gifted Edn., W.Va. Coll. Grad. Studies Inst., 1982; PhD in Humanities, W.Va. Tech. U., 1987. Lic. pvt. pilot, 1987. Statistician PIE Freight Co., Akron, Ohio, 1962-63; social worker Akron Welfare Dept., Akron, 1963-64; tchr. gifted children Calhoun County Schs., Grantsville, W.Va., 1978-82, Wood County Schs., Parkersburg, W.Va., 1982-85; computer instr. Parkersburg Community Coll., 1983-85; tchr. basic adult edn. Wood County Schs., Parkersburg, 1984-85; faculty W.Va. Gov.'s Honors Acad., 1985; tchr.-in-space finalist NASA Langley Research Ctr., Hampton, Va., 1985-87; computer cons., Parkersburg, 1982-85; software evaluator Scholastic, Inc., 1984-85; coordinator W.Va. Gifted Child program Mensa, 1982-87. Contbr. articles to profl. jours. Co-founder Northwest Youth Sports Assn., Canal Fulton, Ohio, 1976-77; mem. career adv. network YWCA, Parkersburg, 1983-85; co-host Easter Seals Telethon, 1988; mem. exec. bd., treas. W.Va. Gifted Edn. Assn. Jimmy Dolittle fellow Air Force Assn., 1986; named Woman of Achievement Girl Scouts of Am., 1987; recipient Disting. Service award Muskingum Coll., 1988. Mem. Mensa (proctor 1982-87), Tchr.-in-Space Edn. Found. (treas. 1985—), Intertel, Council for Exceptional Children, Civil Air Patrol (hon. chmn. 1986), Aircraft Owners and Pilots Assn., Ninty Nine's, Phi Delta Kappa (Kermit Cook Address award 1987). Republican.

WENGER, VICKI, interior designer; b. Indpls., Aug. 30, 1928. Ed. U. Nebr., Internat. Inst. Interior Design, Parsons in Paris. Pres., Vicki Wenger Interiors, Bethesda, Md., 1963-71, Washington, 1982—, pres. Beautiful Spaces Inc., Washington, 1982—; chief designer Creative Design, Capitol Heights, Md., 1969-84; lectr. Nat. Assn. Home Builders, 1983—; mem. programs com. D.C. Assn. Home Builders, 1983—. Author-host: (patented TV interior design show) Beautiful Spaces 1984. Designer Gourmet Gala, March of Dimes, Washington, 1986-88; designer decorator showcase Nat. Symphony Orch., Washington, 1983-87, Am. Cancer Soc., Washington, 1983. Mem. Am. Soc. Interior Designers (profl. mem. 1973—; mem. nat. bd. 1973-75, nat. examining com. 1977-78, pres. Md. chpt. 1976, mem. president's barrier free com. 1980), Nat. Trust Hist. Preservation, Smithsonian Instn. (sponsor), Friends of Corcoran Mus. (sponsor), Friends of Kennedy Ctr., Friends of Vieilles Maisons Françaises. Democrat. Presbyterian. Club: Pisces (Washington). Office: Beautiful Spaces Inc 3227 N St NW Washington DC 20007

WENNING, KATHERINE, film editor. d. Henry William and Claire (Schwartz) W.; m. Michael Edward Smith; divorced. AB, Bryn Mawr Coll., 1965; postgrad., Columbia U., N.Y.C., 1966 67. Film editor N.Y.C., 1973—. Author: (ghostwriter) Innovations in the Non-Custodial Treatment of Offenders, 1976; film editor: Hester Street, 1973-74, Girlfriends, 1978, The Bostonians, 1983-84, My Little Girl, 1985-86, Maurice, 1986-87, Slaves of New York, 1988; spl. sequence editor: Reds, 1981; editor TV: King Crab, 1980, Stoned, 1980, Svengali, 1982, Amy and the Angel, 1982, A Very Delicate Matter, 1982, Frank and Fearless, 1982, Revenge of the Nerd, 1983, Cougar, 1983, Pudd'nhead Wilson, 1983, I Want to go Home, 1984, Mom's on Strike, 1984, The Adventures of Con Sawyer and Hucklemary Finn, 1985, Don't Touch, 1985, Welcome Home, Bobby, 1985, The Belarus File, 1985, The Gift of Amazing Grace, 1986, Supermom's Daughter, 1986. Nominated 4 Emmy awards, 1983—. Mem. N.Y. Women in Film (bd. dirs. 1988—), Motion Picture Film and Video Tape Editors Assn., Am. TV Arts Scis. Democrat. Home: 133 W 17th St New York NY 10011

WENSEL, MICHELE ALETA, sales executive; b. Los Angeles, Mar. 28, 1947; d. Marion Thomas and Lillian Abigale (Michel) Burson; m. James Ryan, Nov. 11, 1962 (div. 1964); children: James, Michael, Michelle Elizabeth; m. Charles Alan Wensel, July 8, 1982. AA, Delta Coll., 1979. Process server U.S. Judicial System, Stockton, Calif., 1979-85; sales rep. Hansel & Ortman Cadillac, Stockton, 1985-86; sales exec. Modesto (Calif.) BMW, 1986-87; asst. fin. mgr. Jeff Read Dodge, 1988—. Contbr. photographs to profl. jours. Mem. Nat. Assn. Female Execs., Nat. Assn. Profl. Saleswomen, Network Nat. Geographic, Archeology Inst. Am., Greenpeace, Soc. Prevention Cruelty to Animals. Republican. Moslem. Home: 2121 B St San Diego CA 92102 Office: 2829 National City Blvd National City CA 92050

WENTE, VERGIE DEE, court official; b. Allison, Kans., Apr. 24, 1936; d. Virgil D. and Hazel (Storer) Wennihan; student Colby Community Coll., 1969-70; m. Lloyd Wente, July 23, 1953 (div. May 1966); children—Allen Charles, Rhonda Marie, Daniel Lloyd, Lynne LaRea. Bookmobile librarian N.W. Kans. Library System, Hoxie, 1968-70; clk. Dist. Ct. of Sheridan County, Hoxie, 1970-76; chief clk. 15th Jud. Dist. Kans., Hoxie, 1976—; mem. clks. adv. council Kans. Supreme Ct., 1979—. Honored by chief justice Supreme ct. for outstanding contbns. to Kans. Dist. Ct. Clks. and Adminstrs. Assn., 1981. Mem. Kans. Assn. Dist. Ct. Clks. and Adminstrs. (sec.-treas. 1978, v.p. 1979, pres. 1980, legis. chmn. 1981, chmn. 1982—, Mem. public edn. and info. 1981—, exec. com. 1982-84, President's award 1983), Nat. Assn. Ct. Adminstrs. (dir. 1982-84). Mem. Ch. of Christ. Home: 1417 Sheridan Ave Hoxie KS 67740 Office: Box 753 Hoxie KS 67740

WEPPLER, DEBORAH, nurse; b. Middle Village, N.Y., Jan. 22, 1957; d. John Thomas and Florence Thersea (Gerrain) W. Diploma in nursing with honors, Jackson Meml. Sch. Nursing, Miami, Fla., 1979; BS in Nursing, U. Miami, 1984. Cert. critical care RN. Staff nurse Hollywood (Fla.) Med. Ctr., 1979-80, charge nurse, 1980-82; staff nurse Jackson Meml. Hosp., Miami, 1982-84, assoc. head nurse, 1984—. Mem. Am. Assn. Critical Care Nurses, Soc. Critical Care Medicine. Republican. Roman Catholic. Home: 1161 SW 118th Terr Davie FL 33325 Office: Jackson Meml Hosp 1611 NW 12th Ave Miami FL 33136

WERBLIN, JOAN BRANCH, advertising executive; b. Norwalk, Conn., July 10, 1950; d. Lee Milton and Rita Mary (Mathews) W. BA, Dickinson Coll., 1973. Copywriter Travel Tours, Norwalk, 1977-78; account exec. Am. Media Assocs., Westport, 1979-80; assoc. editor Fairfield County Mag., Westport, 1980-83; editor Italia Mag., Boston, 1983; editorial dir. Whittle Communications, Knoxville, Tenn., 1984-87; creative dir. Gallagher Knetzger, Conshohoeken, Ps., 1987—. Editor: (mag.) Southern Style, 1987; contbr. articles to mags. Mem. Am. Soc. Mag. Editors, Soc. Profl. Journalists, Sigma Delta Chi. Democrat.

WERDEN, SUZANNE E., accountant; b. Detroit, Sept. 24, 1950; d. Edward and Edith (Wagner) Giza; m. Feb. 17, 1983; children: Daniel, Patrick. BS in Economics, Oakland U., Rochester, Mich., 1977. Mgr. St. Joseph Mercy Hosp., Pontiac, Mich., 1977-79; mgr. fin. dept. Hevblein, Inc., Allen Park, Mich., 1979-83; owner Fin. Acctg. Services, Inc., W. Bloomfield, Mich., 1979-87; owner secretarial service Exec. Sec. Plus, Mich., 1988—; cons. J.D. Caton Assocs., W. Bloomfield, 1981-83. vol. probation officer City of Detroit, 1972. Nat. Assn. Female Execs. Republican. Roman Catholic. Office: Fin Acctg Services Inc 6022 W Maple Suite 407 West Bloomfield MI 48033

WERLING, ANITA LAURA, publishing company executive; b. Evansville, Ind., Nov. 26, 1946; d. Kenneth Edward and Carolyn May (Pascoe) W. BA, Ind. U., 1968, MLS, 1971. Asst. reference librarian Fairleigh Dickinson U., Teaneck, N.J., 1971-72; supr. books and series U. Microfilms Internat., Ann Arbor, Mich., 1972-74, mgr. vault investment books and collections, 1975-77, gen. mgr. collections and curriculum products, 1982-83, v.p. collections and curriculum products, 1984-85, v.p. dissertation info. service, 1986-87; pres. CineBooks, Evanston, Ill., 1987—. Pub. (12 vol. book) The Motion Picture Guide, 1985; contbr. articles to profl. jours. HEA fellow Ind. U., 1970-71. Mem. ALA, Direct Mktg. Assn., Info. Industry Assn. Office: Cine Books 990 Grove St Evanston IL 60201

WERNER, DORIS THERESA, electrical engineer; b. St. Johnsburg, Vt., Oct. 24, 1948; d. Gaston Simon and Diana (Rapoza) Couture; m. Gerald Andrew Werner, Mar. 4, 1981; 1 child, Kimberly Anne. AS in Bus., Champlain Coll., 1970; BS in Elec. Engring. Tech., Milw. Sch. Engring., 1983. Lab technician State of Vt., Roxbury, 1969-71; with product control dept. Alloy Products, Waukesha, Wis., 1972-73; with internal sales dept. Husco, Waukesha, 1973-77; office mgr. Hartmann Controls, Hartland, Wis., 1977-78; insp. Donohue & Assocs., Waukesha, 1979-81, team leader, 1983-84; jr. engr. Gen. Electric Corp., Milw., 1984; elec. engr. Empire Generator, Germanton, Wis., 1984-85, Harley Davidson Inc, Milw., 1985—. Active Zool. Soc., Milw. County, 1985—. Mem. Harley Employee Recreation Orgn. Roman Catholic. Home: 15755 Heather Hill Dr Brookfield WI 53005 Office: Harley Davidson 3700 W Juneau Ave Milwaukee WI 53208

WERNER, GLORIA S., librarian; b. Seattle, Dec. 12, 1940; d. Irving L. and Eva H. Stolzoff; B.A., Oberlin Coll., 1961; M.L., U. Wash., 1962; postgrad. UCLA, 1962-63; m. Newton Davis Werner, June 30, 1963; 1 son, Adam Davis. Reference librarian UCLA Biomed Library, 1963-64, asst. head pub. services dept., 1964-66, head pub. services dept., head reference div., 1966 72, asst. biomed. librarian public services, 1972-77, asso. biomed. librarian, 1977-78, biomed. librarian, assoc. univ. librarian, dir. Pacific S.W. regional Med. Library Service, 1979-83; asst. dean library services UCLA Sch. Medicine, 1980-83; assoc. univ. librarian for tech. services, 1983—; adj. lectr. UCLA Grad. Sch. Library and Info. Sci., 1977-83. Mem. ALA, Med. Library Assn., Assn. Acad. Health Sci. Library Dirs. (dir. 1981-83). Editor, Bull. Med. Library Assn., 1979-82, asso. editor, 1974-79; mem. editorial bd. Ann. Stats. Med. Sch. Libraries U.S. and Can., 1980-83; mem. accrediting commn. Western Assn. Schs. and Colls. Office: UCLA Research Library Library Adminstrv Office Los Angeles CA 90024

WERNER, KERRI LYNN, banker; b. Ephrata, Pa., Sept. 10, 1962; d. John Charles Werner and Leilani (Leisey) Eberhart. BA, Franklin and Marshall Coll., Lancaster, Pa., 1984; postgrad. in bus. adminstrn., St. Joseph's U., Phila., 1985—. Cash mgr. Meridian Bank, Reading, Pa., 1984-86, product mgr., 1986-87, credit analyst, 1987—. Mem. Nat. Assn. Female Execs., Phi Beta Kappa. Office: Meridian Bank PO Box 1102 Reading PA 19603

WERNER, PHYLLIS TENGDIN, editor, writer; b. Chgo., Dec. 20, 1923; d. Elmer Theodore and Agnes Minne Tengdin; m. Dean Franklin Werner, Oct. 14, 1945; children—Nancy Werner Bybel, Sallie Werner Wilson, Lynn Werner Driggers, Barbara Werner Douglas. A.A., Kansas City Jr. Coll., 1943; B.A., U. Okla., 1945; postgrad. U. Mo. Asst. prodn. dir. Carter Advt., Kansas City, Mo., 1945; reporter Daily Oklahoman, Oklahoma City, 1946-48; librarian Denver Post, 1948-49; reporter Dispatch Newspapers, North Kansas City, Mo., 1968-69; editor Central States Lutheran, Kansas City, Mo., 1979—, Mo.-Kans. synod supplement Lutheran mag., 1988— ; freelance writer, 1948—; del. to Luth. Ch. in Am. Biennial Convs., 1976, 78, 84. Vice pres. bd. govs. Kansas City Philharm., social chmn., 1980-82; past vice chmn Cockefair Chair (humanities) U. Mo., Kansas City; past pres. Philharm. Guild N.; past mem. Kansas City Mayor's Commn. for Human Relations, mem. commn. Sister Cities; mem. Lyric Opera Guild, Friends of Art, North Kansas City Hosp. Aux., Clay-Platte County (Mo.) Med. Aux. (past v.p.); bd. dirs. Mo. Citizens for Arts; legis. liaison Kansas City Symphony Guild, Kansas Inter-faith Peace Alliance, Luths. for Justice and Peace. Mem. World Assn. for Christian Communicators, Women in Communications, Inc., AAUW (v.p.), Hist. Kansas City Found., NCCJ (dir.), Ecumedia (vice chmn.), Gamma Phi Beta. Club: Central Exchange. Home and Office: 4609 N Main St Kansas City MO 64116

WERNER, SANDRA LOUISE, engineering company executive; b. St. Petersburg, Fla., Mar. 20, 1942; d. Omar Earl and Louvinia Gertrude (Lynn) Powers; m. Richard Joseph Werner, June 10, 1961 (dec. 1983). AA, St. Petersburg (Fla.) Jr. Coll., 1965; BA, U. So. Fla., 1975. Cert. elect., mech. insp. Clk. City of St. Petersburg Police Dept., 1961-63; exec. sec. J.H. Harland Co., St. Petersburg, 1965-70; pres. HWC Engring., Clearwater, Fla., 1984—; bd. dirs. HWC Engring., Clearwater. Youth leader Girl Scouts Am., Pinellas County, Fla., 1972-82, 4-H, 1972-82; mem. Marley Group, St. Petersburg Fine Arts Mus. Mem. IBM Users Group, Clearwater C. of C. Democrat. Clubs: Suncoast Jaguar (St. Petersburg), Fla. Trail Assn. Home: 1694 El Tair Trail Clearwater FL 34625

WERNIKOFF, NANCY KASDON, speech and language pathologist; b. Cleve., Apr. 6, 1938; d. Eli David and Doree (Sands) Kasdon; B.A., N.Y. U., 1962; M.S. in Edn., Queens Coll., 1969; m. Sergio Wernikoff, Oct. 26, 1958; children: Laura Sue, Daniel Mark. Speech pathologist Speech Rehab. Inst., N.Y.C., 1962-63, acting speech supr. speech therapy dept., 1963-65; speech-lang. cons. pre-sch. program Pascack Valley (N.J.) Council Spl. Edn., 1976-77; cons. speech-lang. pathologist Ramsey (N.J.) Public Schs., 1978—; pvt. practice, 1967—; cons. in field. Mem. exec. bd. Archer Nursery Sch., Allendale, N.J., 1973-74; active local Boy Scouts Am., Girl Scouts U.S.A., 1972-78; mem. exec. bd. sisterhood Temple Beth Or, Washington Twp., N.J., 1976-81, mem. exec. bd. Temple Beth Or, 1981—. Recipient Griffith Hughes Meml. prize Washington Sq. Coll. of Arts and Scis., N.Y. U., 1962. Mem. Am. Speech, Lang. and Hearing Assn. (cert.), N.J. Speech Language and Hearing Assn. (chair judiciary com.), Bergen County Speech and Hearing Assn. (co-founder), Speech and Hearing Study Group (co-founder). Home: 42 Somerset Dr Woodcliff Lake NJ 07675

WERNIMONT, CHERYL ANN, postal service administrator; b. Ottumwa, Iowa, May 24, 1944; d. Raymond Peter and Dorothy Grace (Grimes) Greiner; m. Raymond Thomas Wernimont (dec. Nov. 1974); children: Brian Thomas, Cindy Ann. Student, U. Iowa, 1963-65, 87—. Owner, operator Talleyrand Tavern/Cafe, Keota, Iowa, 1970-71; clk. U.S. Postal Service, North Liberty, Iowa, 1971-72; clk., operator letter sorting machine Cedar Rapids, Iowa, 1972-78, supr. mail processing, 1978-79; mgr. customer service Iowa City, Iowa, 1980-86; postmaster Marion, Iowa, 1986—; bd. dirs. U.S. Postal Service Women Program, Cedar Rapids, 1976-78, east Cen. Iowa Postal Customer Council, Cedar Rapids, 1980-87; mem. promotion bd. U.S. Postal Service Upward Mobility, Cedar Rapids. Mem. Am. Bus. Women's Assn. (pres. local chpt. 1981-82, 86-87, v.p. 1982-83, chmn. ways and means com. 1984-85, 87-88, Achievement award 1982, Boss of Yr. award 1983, Woman of Yr. award 1983), Marion C. of C. (ambassador 1986—, exec. dir. 1987—). Democrat. Roman Catholic. Club: Coralville Water Ski (sec. 1984-85). Lodge: Rotary. Office: US Postal Service 1101 6th Ave Marion IA 52302-9998

WERTHEIM, MARY CAROLE, advertising agency executive; b. Albuquerque, Dec. 25, 1939; d. Joseph and Stella (Mensio) May; m. Jerry Wertheim, Aug. 20, 1960; children—Jerry Todd, John Vincent. Student U. N.Mex., 1958-60, George Washington U., 1960-61. Treas. Werthco Ranch, N.Mex., 1972—; billing systems coordinator JGS&W, P.A., Santa Fe, 1973-74; founder, pres. Creative Images, LTD., Santa Fe, 1978—. Past mem. N.Mex. Com. Children and Youth, N.Mex. State Library Com. Recipient numerous awards for advt. prodn., 1978—. Mem. Santa Fe C. of C. (bd. dirs. 1983-88, treas. 1984-86), No. N.Mex. Advt. Fedn. (bd. dirs. 1981-82), Gen. Fedn. Women's Clubs (nat. bd. dirs. 1970-80), N.Mex. Fedn. Women's Clubs (state pres. 1976-78). Avocations: skiing; swimming; reading. Office: Creative Images Ltd 355 E Palace Ave Santa Fe NM 87501

WERTS, EIRENE ELIZABETH, human resources specialist; b. Alton, Ill., Oct. 10, 1954; d. Harry W. and Elizabeth (Englezou) Tsimpris; m. Dwight A. Werts, May 31, 1975 (div. June 1979). Grad. high sch., East Alton-Wood River, Ill. Sec. fin. aids Lewis & Clark Community Coll., Godfrey, Ill., 1972-76; sec. Brass Group Olin Corp., East Alton, Ill., 1976-79; adminstrv. asst. Jonathan's Landing, Jupiter, Fla., 1979-80, personnel adminstr., 1980-81, mgr. personnel, 1981-87, mgr. human resources, 1987—; bd. dirs. Pvt. Industry Cuncil, Palm Beach, Fla., 1983—, vice-chairperson, 1986-87, chairperson, 1987—; mem. Town of Jupiter Merit Adv. Bd., 1984-87. Mem. Am. Soc. Personnel Adminstrs., South Fla. Developers Personnel Assn., Personnel Assn. of Palm Beach County (sec. 1984-86). Democrat. Greek Orthodox. Office: Jonathan's Landing 17290 Jonathan Dr Jupiter FL 33477

WERTZ, ALTA HAPP, artist, educator; b. Kennewick, Wash., Feb. 19, 1921; d. Henry Lewis and Annie Elizabeth (Yates) Leckliter; student Bakersfield Jr. Coll., 1939-40; m. Richard Clarence Smith (div. 1961); children—Robin (Mrs. Bernard Charles Danylchuk), Alan Montgomery, Shelley (Mrs. Thomas William Stoye); m. 2d. William Morris Happ, Jan. 19, 1967 (dec. 1980); m. 3d Harvey William Wertz, Feb. 26, 1984. Instr. oil painting, adult edn. Palomar Coll., San Marcos, Calif., 1958-62; pvt. tchr., lectr. in field, 1962—; one-woman shows The Atheneaum, La Jolla, Calif., 1959, Jeane's Gallery, La Jolla, 1961, Palomar Coll., 1959-61, The Little Galleries, Escondido, Calif., 1964, La Pina Ltd., La Jolla, 1965, 66, 67, Gray's Gallery, Escondido, 1973, Carlsbad Oceanside Art League Gallery, 1973; exhibited in group shows San Diego Mus. Art, San Diego Art Inst., Riverside Mus. Art, San Bernardino Mus. Art, So. Calif. Expn., Del Mar, also various galleries represented in permanent collections; lectr. on psychology and symbology of color in music and art. Active Palomar Hosp. aux., 1957-59; pres. Showcase of Arts, Escondido, 1961-62; rep. to San Diego Council of Visual Arts, 1966-67; mem. Escondido Cultural Arts Com., 1972-73; chmn. Mission Valley (Calif.) Expn. Art, 1967; bd. dirs. Philos. Religious Free Library, 1970-74, Pala Mission Indian Sch., 1965-72. Huntington Hartford Found. fellow, Pacific Palisades, Calif., 1964. Recipient numerous other awards. Mem. San Diego Art Inst., San Diego Art Guild of Fine Arts Soc., San Diego Watercolor Soc., Nat. League of Am. Pen Women (pres. 1974-76), Watercolor West. Home: 11302 Moorpark St North Hollywood CA 91602

WERTZ, JANE KARR, broadcaster; b. Chgo., Aug. 16, 1934; d. Kenneth L. and Catharine C. (Carpenter) Karr; m. Edwin P. Neubauer, Aug. 10, 1956 (div. 1979); children—Kenneth Paul, Kathryn J., Keith E. (dec.); m. Charles W. Wertz, June 21, 1980. B.A., Beloit Coll., 1956. Tchr., Winnebago County Schs., Rockford, Ill., 1956-57; broadcaster Sta. WREX-TV, Rockford, 1964-80; pub. relations dir. Swedish Am. Hosp., Rockford, 1976-80; on-air talent Beloit Cable TV, Wis., 1970-80; broadcaster, program dir. Sta. KSTS-TV, San Jose, Calif., 1981-86; instr. advt. San Jose State U., 1984—. Bd. dirs. Peninsula Ctr. for Blind, Palo Alto, Calif., 1981—. Mem. AFTRA, P.E.O. Sisterhood, Delta Gamma. Republican. Methodist. Home: 1010 Robin Way Sunnyvale CA 94087 Office: Sta KSTS-TV 2349 Bering Dr San Jose CA 95131

WESCHLER, ANITA, sculptor, painter; b. N.Y.C.; d. J. Charles and Hulda Eva (Mayer) W.; married. Exhibited Met. Mus., Mus. Modern Art, Art Inst. Chgo., Pa. Mus. Internat., Am. Acad., Inst. Arts and Letters, Bklyn. Mus., Newark Mus., Carnegie Inst., Whitney Mus. Annuals, museums and galleries, throughout U.S.; represented in permanent collections U. Pa., Met. Mus. Art, Syracuse U., Butler Art Inst., Whitney Mus., Norfolk Mus., Brandeis U., Amherst Coll., Yale U., Wichita State Mus., SUNY Binghamton, U. Iowa, U. Nebr.; 13 one-man shows in N.Y.C., 12 group traveling shows, 30 one-man shows nationwide, 1964—; one-man shows include Birmingham (Ala.) Mus. Art, Main Library, Winston-Salem, N.C., U. Wis., Milw., del., U.S. Com. of Internat. Assn. Art, Fine Arts Fedn. N.Y., creator, plastic resins and synthetic glazes as painting media; author: poetry book Nightshade, A Sculptors Summary. Recipient prizes Corcoran Gallery, San Francisco Mus., Am. Fedn. Arts Traveling Show, Montclair Art Mus.; fellow MacDowell Colony, Yaddo. Mem. Archtl. League, Sculptors Guild (past bd. dirs., treas.), Nat. Assn. Women Artists, Internat. Inst. Arts and Letters, Artist Craftsmen N.Y., Fedn. Modern Painters and Sculptors. Address: 136 Waverly Pl New York NY 10014

WESLEY, MARGARET ANN, aircraft company executive; b. Durant, Okla., Oct. 18, 1943; d. William Earnest and Floye Alyene (McKee) Hudson; m. Freddie Leon Wesley, June 1, 1963; 1 child, Donna Darise. Student, West Tex. State U., 1964, SUNY, Albany, 1987—. Instructional aide West Tex. State U., Canyon, 1961-64; legal asst. John Corlett, Atty., Monte Vista, Colo., 1965; legal sec. Phillips Petroleum Col., Amarillo, Tex., 1966-68; asst. dir. of corp. relations Tandy Corp., Ft. Worth, 1975-76; stenographer Gen. Dynamics, Ft. Worth, 1979, support supply analyst, 1980-81, procurement analyst, 1982, sr. logistics supply analyst, 1983-87, logistics supply rep., 1988—; instr. adult edn. mgmt. Gen. Dynamics, 1985—; tng., devel. seminare Paragon Assoc.; lectr. in field; conductor workshops in field. Designer jewelry. Mem. Nat. Mgmt. Assn. (v.p. mgmt. devel. 1985-88, exec. v.p. 1988—), Nat. Assn. Female Execs., Inst. Cert. Profl. Mgrs., Mensa. Republican. Nazerene. Club: Toastmasters (v.p. 1986—). Home: 3300 Westfield St Fort Worth TX 76133

WESLEY-HOSFORD, ZIA, cosmetics company executive, author, consultant; b. N.Y.C., Mar. 3, 1945; divorced; 1 child, Ariane Lee Heller. Student, Endicott Jr. Coll., 1964, Vidal Sassoon Acad., San Francisco, 1978. Lic. cosmetologist, Calif. Singer, dancer Broadway musicals, San Francisco and Los Angeles, 1969-77; owner, operator Zia Full Service Salon, Sausalito, Calif., 1979-83; pres. Zia Cosmetics, San Francisco, 1983—; instr. skincare Elite Tng. Ctr., San Francisco, 1983-86; cons. Zia Image Consulting, San Francisco, 1980—. Author: Being Beautiful, 1983, Putting on Your Face, 1985 (Bestseller 1986), Face Value, 1986, Skincare for Men Only, 1987, Head to Toe: The Beautiful Body Book, 1988, (video) Great Face, 1987. Co-chmn. Mill Valley (Calif.) Film Festival Guild, 1983-86.

WESLEY-KRUEGER, JONNIE LYNN, crisis center director; b. Bklyn., Mar. 26, 1961; d. Richard David and Ruth Elizabeth (Crist) W.; m. James Wesley Krueger, Sept. 14, 1985. BA, U. Calif., Irvine, 1984. Co-dir. Women's Resource Ctr. U. Calif., Irvine, 1982-83, asst. coordinator Rape Prevention Edn. Program, 1983-84; vol. services coordinator Orange County Sexual Assault Network, Orange, Calif., 1984-86; dir. programs Orange County Sexual Assault Network, Orange, 1986—; Orange county rep. So. Calif. Rape Hotline Alliance, 1985—; cons. Human Services Adv. Bd. Calif. State U. Fullerton, 1986; so. regional rep. Calif. State Coalition of Rape/Crisis Ctrs., 1986-87; advisor Calif. State Assembly Select Com. on Sexual Assault, Sacramento, 1987-88. Mem. Orange County Feminist Network, AAUW (Orange chpt.). Democrat. Presbyterian. Office: OCSAN 172 N Tustin Suite 205 Orange CA 92667

WESMAN, ELIZABETH CLAIRE, personnel/labor relations educator; b. N.Y.C., Aug. 13, 1944; d. Alexander Gregory and Elizabeth Mary (Collins) W.; m. Dana Edward Eischen, June 27, 1976; 1 child, Tamara Elizabeth. A.B., Smith Coll., 1966; M.A., Northwestern U., 1969; Ph.D., Cornell U., 1982. Instr. LeMoyne Coll., Syracuse, N.Y., 1970-75; lectr. Cornell U., Ithaca, N.Y., 1980-81; prof. Syracuse U., 1981—; referee Nat. Mediation Bd., 1981—; mem. labor panel Am. Arbitration Assn. Contbr. articles to profl. publs. Area dir. capital fund drive Smith Coll., 1980. U.S. Dept. Labor fellow, 1979-81; Assn. for Canadian Studies in the U.S. grantee, 1986. Mem. Am. Soc. Personnel Adminstrn. (student advisor 1982—), Indsl. Relations Research Assn., Acad. Mgmt. (state membership com. 1983—, chair com.), Soc. Profls. in Dispute Resolution, Human Resource Mgmt. and Orgn. Behavior Assn., AAUP. Avocations: distance walking, reading, piano. Office: Syracuse U Sch Mgmt 606 Crouse-Hinds Bldg Syracuse NY 13244

WESSEL, GENIE LIPA, nurse, state agency consultant; b. Balt., Mar. 19, 1942. RN, The Johns Hopkins Hosp., Balt., 1963; BS in Nursing, Am. U., 1980; MS, U. Md., 1984. Head nurse The Johns Hopkins Hosp., 1963-66, instr. Sch. of Nursing, 1966-67, instr., 1971-73; staff devel. coordinator Howard County Gen. Hosp., Columbia, Md., 1973-76; supr. sch. health Howard County Health Dept., Ellicott City, Md., 1976-81, coordinator sch. health, 1981-82, asst. to healt officer, 1982-85; nurse cons. Md. State Dept. Health/Mental Hygiene, Balt., 1985—; assoc. U. Md. Sch. Nursing, 1987—; lectr. Howard Community Coll., Columbia, 1984—. Mem. adminstrv. com. Md. Fitness Commn., 1982—, grants com. March of Dimes, 1986—; commr. Howard County Commn. for Women, 1983—; bd. dirs. Md. State Games Commn., 1985—. Recipient vol. award Am. Heart Assn., Balt., 1986. Mem. Am. Sch. Health Assn. (bd. dirs. 1987—, co-chair nurse study com. 1986, budget com. 1986-87), Md. State Sch. Health Council, Md. Pub. Health Assn. (pres. 1986-87), Sigma Theta Tau, Phi Kappa Phi. Home: 10323 Kettledrum Ct Ellicott City MD 21043

WEST, ALEXANDRIA PRIFTIS, insurance company manager; b. Bristol, Pa., Feb. 6, 1957; d. George and Hilde (Heumann) Priftis; m. Stephen Ruppert W.; 1 child, Jonathan. BA in Psychology, Douglass Coll., 1978. Ins. agent Prudential Ins. Co., Bethesda, Md., 1978-81; asst. gen. agent Mass. Mut. Ins. Co., Vienna, Va., 1981—. Mem. Nat. Assn. Female Execs., Nat. Assn. Life Underwriters. Office: Mass Mut Ins Co 8614 Westwood Ctr Dr #700 Vienna VA 22180

WEST, ANITA S., research director, researcher; b. N.Y.C., Oct. 21, 1930; d. Bert S. and Dorothy (Sandler) Wolfe; m. David Lee West, Feb. 18, 1955; children: David R., Laurie D. Student, Columbia U., 1952-55; BA, U. Denver, 1960, MS, 1962, PhD, 1969. Research systems analyst IBM, N.Y.C., 1962-63; research scientist Martin-Marietta, Denver, 1960-62; sr. research scientist Denver Research Inst., U. Denver, 1975-78, head research div., 1978—, dir., chief operating officer, 1986-88; prin. scientist Applied Research Assocs., Denver, 1988—; cons. U.S. Dept. Justice, 1978-87, USAF, Washington, 1972-86, Dept. Army, Washington, 1980, Nat. Inst. Edn., Washington, 1975-85, Nat. Inst. Corrections, Boulder, Colo., 1983-85, NSF, Washington, 1980—. Contbr. numerous articles and tech. papers to profl. jours. Mem. Gov.'s Adv. Commn. Sci. and Tech., Colo., 1978-85, Commn. on Conversion to Metric, Colo., 1981-83; chmn. Rocky Flats Monitoring Com. Evaluation, Colo., 1981-83, chmn. Mayor's Conf. on Women, Denver, 1974. Mem. AAAS, N.Y. Acad. Scis., Sigma Xi (former chpt. pres.). Jewish. Home: 3235 S St Paul Denver CO 80210 Office: Applied Research Assocs 3235 S Saint Paul Denver CO 80210

WEST, ANN EASTERLING, aerospace engineer; b. Cin., Oct. 20, 1951; d. William Dudley and Carol Louise (Chamberlain) Easterling; m. Jeffrey Allan West, Jan. 31, 1976 (div. July 1986); 1 child, Jeremy Allan. BS in Areospace Engring., Auburn U., 1974; postgrad., U. Tenn. Space Inst., Tullahoma, 1974-76; MS in Aviation Sci., MBA, Emory-Riddle Aero. U., 1984. Research engr. Arnold Research Orgn., Tullahoma, 1974-76; structural engr. Aerojet Nuclear Corp., Idaho Fall, Idaho, 1976; flight test engr. Sikorsky Aircraft, West Palm Beach, 1977-87, H-60 project engr., 1987—. Mem. Am. Helicopter Soc. (v.p. Fla. chpt. 1984-85, pres. 1985-88), Soc. Women Engrs., Soc. Flight Test Engrs., Sigma Gamma Tau. Repulican. Home: 2094 Pitts Terrace Stuart FL 34997 Office: Sikorsky Aircraft PO Box 109610 West Palm Beach FL 33410

WEST, ANNA LOUCHHEIM, public relations consultant; b. Phila., Dec. 5, 1953; d. Frank Pfeiffer and Betty (Meinel) Louchheim; BA, Mt. Holyoke Coll., 1975; MS, Boston U., 1980; m. Edward Foulke West, July 6, 1974; children: David Louchheim, Jonathan William. Pub. participation coordinator Delaware Valley Regional Planning Commn., 1975-77; pub. info. rep. New Eng. Power Co., 1977-79; sr. communications cons. Energy Research Group, Inc., 1979-83, v.p., 1983-84; prin. Kearns & West, Inc., 1984—. Mem. Pub. Relations Soc. Am. (former pres. Boston chpt.). Home: 22 Venado Dr Tiburon CA 94920 Office: Kearns & West Inc 50 Osgood Pl Suite 230 San Francisco CA 94133

WEST, BARBARA JO, marketing professional; b. Bishop, Calif., Apr. 10, 1945; d. James Joseph and Inez E. (Fackrell) Carberry; m. Robert M. West, Oct. 1, 1972 (div. 1982); children: N. Dion, W. Todd. BBA, Boise State U. Mktg. asst. H.J. Heinz Co., Boise, Idaho, 1973-74, asst. product mgr., 1975-78, product mgr., 1978-80, sr. product mgr. new products Ore-Ida Brand div., 1980-81, sr. product mgr. product devel. dept. Weight Watchers div., 1981-83; sr. product mgr. Am. Home Products, 1983-84; pres. Barbstac Corp., 1984-86; mgr. mktg./promotions Commtek Publ., 1986-87; dir. mktg. and promotions Commtek Pub., 1987-88; dir. sales promotion McCalls Mag., 19886. Advisor Jr. Achievement, Boise, 1976-77; pub. relations dir. Idaho chpt. Cystic Fibrosis, 1979-80. Recipient Mktg. Achievement award Sales and Mktg. Execs., 1979; Jr. Achievement scholar, 1964. Mem. Am. Mktg. Assn., Idaho Advt. Fedn., Assn. Nat. Advertisers. Democrat. Roman Catholic.

WEST, BARBARA LYNN (BOBBI), management consultant; b. Rockingham, N.C., July 10, 1947; d. Thomas Walter West and Dorothy Mae (Hewitte) Waites; m. Dennis Duane Thomas Dec. 28, 1943 (div.); 1 child, Denise DeAun. Student, U. Mo., 1974. Counselor Snelling and Snelling Co., Bellevile, Ill. and St. Louis, 1969-70; fashion coordinator Country Set Sportswear, St. Louis, 1970-73; asst. buyer, mgr. Famous Barr Dept. Stores, St. Louis, 1974-77; account exec., mgr. Sales Cons., Inc., St. Louis, 1979-86; pres., ptnr. Comprehensive Search, St. Louis, 1987—; Cons., search specialist healthcare mfg. and human resource industries, 1987. Contbr. articles to profl. jours. Mem. Squires and Ladies Charitable Found., St. Louis, 1986—. Mem. Profl. Saleswomen of St. Louis (dir. networking, 1983—), Nat. Assn. Women Bus. Owners, Nat. Assn. Female Execs., St. Louis Ambassador's Orgn. Democrat. Office: Comprehensive Search Specialists Inc 1900 Station Plaza Suite 100 1910 Pine St Saint Louis MO 63103

WEST, BENITA LOUISE, educator; b. Cleve., Mar. 27, 1956; d. Harold Frank and Louise (Kendall) W. BS, Defiance Coll., 1978; MEd, Cleve. State U., 1986. Cert. elem. edn., devel. handicapped educator, learning disabilities educator, Ohio. Clk., typist Cuyahoga Welfare Dept., Cleve., 1973-74; tchr. edn. V.I. Dept. Edn., St. Thomas, Ohio, 1979-85; tchr. Mental Devel. Ctr., Cleve., 1985-87; learning disabilities tchr. Cleve. Pub. Schs., 1987—. tchr., asst. supt. East View United Ch. Christ, Cleve., 1985—. Mem. Am. Fedn. Tchrs. Lodge: Order of Eastern Star. Home: 3455 Milverton Rd Shaker Heights OH 44120 Office: Artemus Ward Elem Sch 4315 W 140th St Cleveland OH 44135

WEST, CAROLYN JO, land development company executive, financial consultant; b. Paducah, Ky., July 4, 1935; d. Joe Ed and Leona (Burks) Holly; m. William B. West, Sept. 28, 1957 (dec.); 1 dau., Holly Lynn Pierce. B.S., Pepperdine U., 1957; postgrad., Calif. State U.-Fullerton, 1965-67. Bookkeeper Quality Produce Co., Santa Ana, Calif., 1957-69; asst. mgr., controller Savi Devel. Corp., Orange, Calif., 1969-75; treas., controller So. Pacific Constrn. Co., Garden Grove, Calif., 1975-77; asst. controller, chief acct. Dunn Properties Corp., Santa Ana, 1977-79; v.p., treas., controller, chief fin. officer Saddleback Assocs. Inc., Santa Ana, 1979 ; cons. Nantell Investments, Fountain Valley, Calif., 1977—; cons., chief fin. officer Gilmer Properties, Orange, 1980—, Churchill Comml. Brokerage Inc., 1987—; cons. investors, land developers., 1977—. Founder Helping Hands, Hillview Acres Children's Home, pres. 1963-67; leader trainer Girl Scouts U.S.A., Orange County, Calif., 1967-70; fund raiser, Orange County Democratic Com., 1968; speaker So. Calif. Women's Ch. Confs.; tchr. Bible classes, Ch. of Christ, Santa Ana and Garden Grove. Recipient outstanding service awards Girl Scouts U.S.A., 1969, Hillview Acres Children's Home, 1971. Mem. Delta Chi Omega (pres. 1954-55). Home: 8763 Rogue River Fountain Valley CA 92708 Office: Saddleback Assocs Inc PO Box 17899 Irvine CA 92713

WEST, CYNTHYA THOMAS, municipal agency administrator; b. Massillon, Ohio, Sept. 12, 1947; d. Anthony Frank and Beverly Elaine Thomas; m. William Alan West, Oct. 13 1985. BS, Kent (Ohio) State U., 1969. Purchasing agt. Masoneilan/Dresser, Houston, 1981-85; buyer pub. works contracts County of Orange, Gen. Services Agy., Purchasing and Material Mgmt., Santa Ana, Calif., 1985—. Assisted in restoration of the Hist. Orange County Courthouse, Santa Ana, 1985-87. Mem. Nat. Assn. Purchasing Mgmt., Purchasing Mgmt. Assn. of Houston (co-chmn. Houston pub. relations com. 1984-85), Purchasing Mgmt. Assn. Orange County (chmn. planning com. 1988—), Nat. Assn. for Female Execs., Calif. Assn. Pub. Purchasing Officers (chairperson conf. registration com. 1986), Friends of San Juan Capistrano Library, Friends of South Coast Repertory and Orange County Performing Arts Ctr. Office: County of Orange General Services Agy Purchasing and Materials Mgmt 1300 S Grand Bldg A Santa Ana CA 92705

WEST, DOTTIE (DOROTHY MARIE MARSH), singer; b. McMinnville, Tenn.; d. William and Pelina (Jones) Marsh; m. William West, 1952 (div. 1972); children: Morris, Kerry, Shelly, Dale; m. Byron A. Metcalf, Aug. 27, 1973 (div. 1981). B.A. in Music, Tenn. Tech. Coll., 1956. Singing debut, WEWS-TV, Cleve., 1956-60; singer 5-piece band, Cross-Country, 1966—; performances include: Grand Ole Opry, 1962—, Memphis Symphony Orch., 1973, Kansas City Symphony, 1961-74; TV appearances include: Good Ole Nashville, Eddy Arnold Spl., Country Hit Parade, Music Country U.S.A., Glen Campbell Show, Mike Douglas Show; rec. artist Staeday Records, 1959-61, Atlantic Records, 1962, RCA, 1962—; albums include: Country Singing Sensation, Greatest Hits, Sound of Country Music, Here Comes My Baby, 1964, Would You Hold it Against Me?, 1966, Forever Young, 1970, Last Time I Saw Him, 1974, All I Ever Need Is You, 1979, What Are We Doin' In Love, 1981. Recipient Grammy award female artist for Here Comes My Baby 1965; named Number One Female Writer in U.S., Billboard mag. 1974; Number One Female Performer in Eng. 1973, 74; Country Music Artist of Yr., British Country Music Assn.; Coca Cola Country Girl 1972. Address: care Agy for Performing Arts 9000 Sunset Blvd Los Angeles CA 90069 *

WEST, JULIA STICKNEY, medical psychotherapist; b. Cambridge, Mass., Oct. 8, 1928; d. Charles Alpheus Jr. and Emily (Preston) Stickney; m. Royal Fontaine West, May 3, 1957; children: Jane Catherine, Philip, Elizabeth, John, Charles Douglas, Thomas. AA, Orange Coast Coll., 1970; BA in Psychology, Calif. State U., Northridge, 1976; MA in Psychology with honors, U.S. Internat. U., 1978; PhD in Psychology, Brunel U., West London, Eng., 1984. Cert. Am. Bd. Med. Psychotherapists. Telephone counselor Am. Cancer Soc., Reseda, Calif., 1974; student trainee, therapist in community psychiatry VA Hosp., Sepulvede, Calif., 1975-76; psychotherapist Family Counselling Ctr., El Cajon, Calif., 1978-79; counselor crisis night-line Brunel U., Uxbridge, Eng., 1981-83; pvt. practice psyhchotherapy Weybridge, 1978-83; clin. psychologist Aromco: Dharan (Saudi Arabi) Med. Ctr., 1984-87; clin. psychologist, cons. Comprehensive Psychol. Services, Mesa, Ariz., 1987-88; pvt. practice med. psychology Mesa, 1988—. Contbr. articles to profl. jours. Cons., Teen Leadership Inst. No. Ariz. U., Flagstaff, 1987; canvassar Ariz. Advs. for Children, Tucson, 1987—; bd. dirs. Tempe (Ariz.) Chem. People, 1988—. Mem. AAUW, Am. Psychol. Assn., Brit. Psychol. Assn. (chartered), Internat. Assn. Applied Psychology, Internat. Assn. Cross-Cultural Psychologists, Ariz. Psychol. Assn., Am. Bus. Women's Assn. (head edn. seminar Tempe 1987). Republican. Lutheran. Home: 12419 Shasta Ct Phoenix AZ 85044 Office: Desert Vista Hosp 570 W Brown Rd Suite 108 Mesa AZ 85201

WEST, KATHRYN MARIE, pianist; b. Lansing, Mich., Apr. 15, 1935; d. Harry Allen and Mabel Agnes (Dyer) Strait; student Central Mich. U., 1952-55, Eastern Mich. U., 1979-81; m. David Roche West, June 11, 1955; children—Julie, Martha, Nancy, Jean, Mark. Profl. accompanist Ann Arbor Civic Theatre, U. Mich. Gilbert and Sullivan Soc., U. Mich. Summer Theater, 1965-72, Comic Opera Guild, 1983, 86-87; duo pianist with Naomi Donaldson, 1970-76, with Margaret Bond, 1972-85; sec. Office of Pres. U. Mich., Ann Arbor, 1976-77, exec. sec., 1978-83; sec. U. Mich. Law Sch., Ann Arbor, 1984—; concerts in Kansas City, Mo., Ohio, Mich. Organist, choir dir. 1st Congl. Ch., Chelsea, Mich., 1987—. Mem. Friends of Four Hand Music, Amateur Chamber Music Players, Sigma Alpha Iota. Home: 1105 Granger Ann Arbor MI 48104

WEST, LOLA C., health care administrator, consultant; b. Bklyn., Aug. 5, 1947; d. George William and Adele (Vaughn) W. BA, CUNY, Bklyn., 1970; M in Urban Planning, CUNY, N.Y.C., 1972. Field analyst Greenleigh Assocs., Inc., N.Y.C., 1971-73; counselor, instr. John Jay Coll. of Criminal Justice, N.Y.C., 1973-74; adminstrv. dir. Langston Hughes Headstart Program of N.Y., N.Y.C., 1975; bldg. adminstr. United Cerebral Palsy Assns. of N.Y. State, Inc., N.Y.C., 1977-79, unit-wide adminstr., 1979-80, dir. Warner community project, 1980-82, asst. regional dir., 1982-85, dir. community residences, 1986—; cons. N.Y.C. Bd. of Edn., Bronx, 1974, The Hawver Group, N.Y.C., 1984, 86, 87, assessor. Bd. dirs. N.Y. Women Against Rape, N.Y.C., 1985-86. Proclamation Lola C. West Day, N.Y.C., 1987. Democrat. Home: 125 Willoughby Ave Brooklyn NY 11205-3726 Office: 330 W 34th St New York NY 10001

WEST, LORETTA MARIE, underwriter; b. N.Y.C., Feb. 2, 1950; d. James L. and Alice (Richardson) West. A.B., Washington Coll., Chestertown, Md., 1972. Cert. profl. ins. woman. Disbursements cashier Middlesex Ins. Co., Concord, Mass., 1972-76, tech. asst., 1976-78, comml. lines underwriter, 1978-83; sr. comml. lines underwriter Sentry Ins. Co., Concord, 1983-86, large acct. underwriter, 1986—. Mem. Framingham Republican Town Com., Greater 12th Precinct Neighborhood Assn.; trustee Prescott Gardens Condos, 1984—. Mem. Nat. Assn. Ins. Women, Mass. Assn. Ins. Women (various coms. Middlesex and South Middlesex chpts., co-dir. South Middlesex chpt. 1986-88, Wonan of Yr. award 1980). Roman Catholic. Home: 6 Prescott St Framingham MA 01701 Office: Sentry Ins Rt 2 Concord MA 01742

WEST, MARCIA ANN, broadcasting executive; b. Seattle, Nov. 27, 1944; d. Byron Hale and Norma Ruth Harvey; B.A., W. Tex. State U., 1966, M.A., 1969; postgrad. U. Colo., 1971-76. Instr. Spanish, W. Tex. State U., 1966-68, U. Evansville (Ind.), 1969-71, U. Colo., Denver, 1971-76; host, co-producer Esta Semana, Sta. KRMA-TV, Denver, 1971-75; asso. editor La Luz mag., 1972-79; producer, broadcaster KOA News, Denver, 1972-76; mgr. public affairs KOA Stas., Denver, 1976-78, program and public affairs dir., 1978-80; dir. pub. affairs Sta. KCNC-TV, 1980—; publicity dir. Barney Ford Meml. Assn., 1976—; cons. in field. Bd. dirs. Cystic Fibrosis Found., Denver Opportunities Industrialization Center; mem. selection com. Minoru Yasui Vol. Awards for Denver; bd. dirs. Denver Better Bus. Bur., 1986—; mem. State Influenza Com. Am. Lung Assn.; adv. to Jr. League; adv. bd. Denver International. Film Festival; mem. selection com. 10th Nat. Abe Lincoln awards; cons. Gov.'s Conf. Library Services. Recipient Abe Lincoln Merit award, 1977; Tummy award Denver Area Journalists Assn., 1972; Silver Bell award Nat. Advt. Council, 1981; Broadcast Preceptor's award San Francisco State U., 1983; named Outstanding Educator U. Colo., Denver, 1976; Outstanding Tchr. Fgn. Lang., W.Tex. State U., 1966; Best Public Affairs Producer, Denver Catholic Register, 1977; chosen media contributions winner Colo. Salute to Women, 1981. Mem. Am. Women in Radio and TV, Nat. Assn. Broadcasters, Colo. Broadcasters Assn., Nat. Alliance Businessmen, Nat. Assn. Program Execs. (selection com. awards 1978), Nat. Broadcasters Assn. for Community Affairs (regional v.p., nat. conf. chairperson 1980-81, pres. 1981-82, exec. com. 1983—; awards for best pub. affairs program, 1984, 85, 86), Nat. Assn. Social Workers (award for improving quality of life through media 1983), Leadership Denver, Denver C. of C. Author articles. Home: 61256 Cherry Creek Denver CO 80206 Office: 1044 Lincoln St Denver CO 80203

WEST, SHARON MARIE, electrical engineer; b. Racine, Wis., May 5, 1959; d. Richard Irving and Virginia Margaret (Hansen) W. BS in Engring., U. Ill., 1981, MS in Engring., 1983. Registered profl. engr., Ill. Teaching asst. U. Ill., Champaign, 1981-83; engring. technician C.E., U.S. Army, Champaign, 1980-83; engr. Ill. Bell Telephone, Chgo., 1983-85, mgr., 1986—. Adminstrv. adviser Jr. Achievement, Downers Grove, Ill., 1985—; sci. fair judge Mus. Sci. and Industry, Chgo., 1985. Mem. Nat. Soc. Profl. Engrs., Western Soc. Engrs., Ill. Soc. Gen. Engrs., Ill. Soc. Profl. Engrs., Soc. Women Engrs., Gamma Epsilon. Republican. Lutheran. Avocations: tennis, golf, jogging, composing music, playing piano. Office: Ill Bell Telephone Co 225 W Randolph St HQ26B Chicago IL 60606

WEST, SHIRLEY JEAN, real estate broker; b. Olney, Tex., July 10, 1937; d. Richard Hiram and Lois Lorene (Collins) Porter; m. George Edgar West, Mar. 22, 1956; children—Richie Lynn, Lori Leanne, Ami Sabrina. Student Odessa Coll., 1955, 56, 78. With Prudential Ins. Co., Odessa, 1955, Amoco Prodn. Co., Odessa, 1955-57, Abilene, Tex., 1957-61; dir. child devel. Crescent Park Bapt. Ch., Odessa, 1973-78; broker Goodwin Real Estate, Odessa, 1978-83, Eidson Wasson Lish Realtors, Odessa, 1983—(sales person yr. 1985-86) . Mem. Odessa Bd. Realtors, Tex. Assn. Realtors, Nat. Assn. Realtors, Women's Council Realtors. Republican. Baptist. Club: Odessa Racquetball and Health. Home: 2408 Quail Park Pl Odessa TX 79761 Office: Eidson Wasson Lish 4200 Maple Odessa TX 79762

WEST, THERESA CATHERINE, financial company executive; b. Vancouver, B.C., Can., Jan. 3, 1957; d. Robert Johnson and Myrna Barbara (McEachern) Thomas; m. Robin Rae West, Apr. 14, 1975 (div. Feb. 1982); children: Nicholas, Tiffaney, Christopher. Student in Mktg. and Mgmt., B.C. Inst. Tech., 1977; student in Pre-Commerce, Douglas Coll., Richmond, B.C., 1979; student in Realty Appraisal and Pre-Commerce, Langara Coll., Vancouver, B.C., 1980-82. Various clerical positions Vancouver, Ont., 1975-80; jr. mortgage underwriter Montreal Trust Co., Ltd., Vancouver, 1980-81; broker Westward Mortgage Realty, Burnaby, B.C., 1982-84; mgr. mortgage dept. Newport Realty Ltd., Vancouver, 1984-85; sr. account rep. Pitney Bowes of Can., Vancouver, 1985-88, sales mgr., 1988—; mortgage cons. William McGregor & Assocs., New Westminster, B.C., 1984; mktg. cons. Can. Fitness, Richmond, 1985. Vol. campaign for premier, Richmond, 1986, campaign for Children's Wish Found. Social Credit. Mem. Sci. of Mind Found. Ch. Club: Toastmasters. Office: Pitney Bowes Can, 3157 Grandview Hwy, Vancouver, BC Canada V3E 1G8

WEST, VALERIE JEANNE, advertising executive; b. Los Angeles, Dec. 14, 1956; d. Charles Harold and Ruth Ann (Pergl) W. BBA, San Diego State U., 1979, MBA in Mktg., 1981. Internal project dir. Decision/Making/Information, Santa Ana, Calif., 1982; project dir. L&J Research, Los Angeles, 1982-84; account exec. Abert, Newhoff & Burr, Los Angeles, 1985—. Pub. relations asst. Philibosian Campaign, Los Angeles, 1984. Republican. Clubs: Toastmasters, Westwood Ski. Office: Abert Newhoff & Burr 2121 Ave of the Stars #1600 Los Angeles CA 90067

WEST, VIRGINIA, artist, educator; b. Boston, May 24, 1924; d. Alexander and Beatrice (Lowe) McWilliam; m. John Barth West, Sept. 4, 1941 (div. 1973); children: John Thomas, Lynnea Christine, Elise Anne, David Lowe,

Michael; m. Frank Martin, Oct. 11, 1974. MFA, Coll. Art Md. Inst., 1974. Instr. Coll. Art Md. Inst., Balt., 1969-82. Author: Finishing Touches for the Handweaver, 1968, Weavers Wearables, 1976, The Virginia West Swatch Book, (ltd. edit.), 1986, Designer Diagonals: A Portfolio of Bias-Designed Clothing, 1988; contbr. numerous articles on weaving. Recipient purchase award Balt. Mus. Art, 1970. Mem. Am. Craft Council (sec. 1968-70, pres. Md. chpt.), Balt. Weavers Guild (hon.), Weavers Guild Pitts. (hon.), Mo. Fiber Artists (life). Episcopalian. Home and Office: 2809 Grasty Rd RFD #8 Baltimore MD 21208

WESTALL, MARTA SUSAN WOLF, librarian; b. Newark, Mar. 25, 1946; d. John Andrew and Gertrude Agnes (Kane) Turk; B.S., Bowling Green U., 1968; M.L.S., U. Tex., 1977; Library asst. serials dept. Bowling Green (Ohio) U. Library, 1968; sch. librarian Brooks Jr. Secondary Sch., Powell River, B.C., Can., 1968-69; asst. librarian U. Mich. Libraries, Ann Arbor, 1970-72; br. librarian Social Work Library, Gen. Libraries, U. Tex., Austin, 1972-75, cons. Center Social Work Research, Sch. Social Work, 1974-75, dir. info. services, 1975-79; asst. dir. Collection devel. Tex. State Library, Austin, 1980—; mem. Nat. Accreditation Com. for Info. and Referral Agys., 1977—; mem. Statewide Devel. Bd. for Establishment Tex. Info. and Referal Orgn., 1976. Bd. dirs. Cystic Fibrosis Found., 1987—, Tex. Embassy Mus., 1986—; v.p., bd. dirs. Austin Rape Crisis Ctr., 1987—. Mem. Spl. Libraries Assn., Am. Soc. Info. Sci., Alliance Info. and Referral Systems (mem. exec. com. Tex., mem. nat. standards com.), ALA, Tex. Library Assn., Austin On-Line Users Group, State Agy. Libraries of Tex. (pres. 1981-83), Assn. Specialized and Coop. Library Agys. (chmn. publs. com. 1982-84), Women's Art Guild, Austin Jr. Forum, Toastmasters Internat. (pres. W. Austin chpt. 1987-88). Mem. editorial bd. Info. and Referral, Jour. Alliance Info. and Referral Systems, 1978—; editor Library Devels., jour. Tex. State Library, 1980—. Home: 8507 Adirondack Cove Austin TX 78759 Office: Tex State Library PO Box 12927 Austin TX 78711

WEST-ALLEN, M. D., communications specialist; b. Riverside, Calif., Aug. 7, 1957; d. Harvey Dennis and Ruth Minnie (Turner) West; m. DeWayne David Allen, Nov. 24, 1979; children: Neel Omar, Vennie Oni, Kimani DeWayne. BS in Journalism, Northwestern U., 1979. Reporter/editor Macon News (Ga.), 1978; bur. reporter Newsweek, Atlanta, 1978; life/style editor LaPorte Herald Argus (Ind.), 1979-80; asst. editor Fairchild Publs., Chgo., 1980-81; editor Kemper Group, Long Grove, Ill., 1981-83; staff specialist corp. relations Allstate Ins. Co., Northbrook, Ill., 1983—; editor/cons. Pres.'s Pvt. Sector Survey on Cost Control, Washington, 1982-83. Mem. Internat. Assn. Bus. Communicators (dir. Chgo. 1983-84, com. chairperson 1982-83, newsletter editor 1984-85), Am. Mgmt. Assn., Delta Sigma Theta (rec. sec. Evanston-North Shore Alumnae chpt. 1983-85, regional rep. 1977-79). Democrat. Roman Catholic. Office: Allstate Ins Co Allstate Plaza N F3 Northbrook IL 60062

WESTBROOK, ANDREA, educational administrator; b. Gainesville, Ga., Mar. 27, 1949; d. Arthur Guy and Hazel Dean (Bradley) Parks; children: Reece, Mary Margaret. AS, Gainesville Jr. Coll., 1969; M in Mktg. Distbn., U. Ga., 1974. Owner, pres. Fashion Consultants, Gainesville, 1975-781; mem. faculty Brenau Coll., Gainesville, 1981-82; coordinator career and profl. devel. and small bus. del. Gainesville Jr. Coll., 1982-85; dir. placement Lanier Area Tech. Sch., Gainesville, 1985—; research coordinator Elrod Mktg., Atlanta, 1976—; cons. Lanier Tech. Found., Gainesville, 1985—. Chmn. Council on Aging, Gainesville, 1985-86, Vol. Gainesville Recognition Celebration, 1985-86. Named Young Career Woman of Ga., Ga. Bus. Profl., 1974; elected to Distributive Edn. Hall of Fame, State Distributive Edn. dept., 1974; recipient cert. of appreciation Vietnam Vets. Leadership, Atlanta, 1984; Kellogg grantee Va. Poly. Inst. and State U., 1985. Mem. Nat. Assn. Female Execs., Ga. Coll. Placement Assn., Nat. Speakers Assn., Gainesville-Hall County C. of C., Am. Assn. Women in Community, LWV. Democrat. Baptist. Avocations: aerobics; dancing; story collecting. Home: 2805 Willow Ridge Dr Gainesville GA 30501 Office: Lanier Area Tech Sch Mundy Mill Rd Oakwood GA 30566

WESTBURY, JUNE ALWYN, Canadian government official; b. Hamilton, N.Z.; came to Can., 1948, naturalized, 1971; d. Philip William and Doris Myrtle (Halcrow) Cantwell; student Brain's Coll., Auckland; voice student of Mina Caldow; m. Peter W.A. Westbury, Oct. 22, 1949; children—Sheila Westbury Raffey, Pamela June, Jennifer Doris. Elected alderman, Ward I, Winnipeg (Man., Can.) City Council, 1969, vice chmn. Centennial Celebrations Com., 1970, mem. various Council coms., including Parks and Recreation, Health and Welfare, Housing and Urban Renewal, Utilities and Personnel, chmn. Health and Welfare Com., 1971, councillor, Roslyn Ward, City of Winnipeg, 1971-77, mem. various times Environ. and Works and Ops. Coms., Winnipeg Police Commn., Winnipeg Heritage Corp., chmn. subcom. on Group Homes, elected Corydon Ward, 1977, chmn. Adv. Com. on Hist. Bldgs., 1979; elected Liberal mem. Legis. Assembly, Man., Ft. Rouge Constituency, 1979-81. Founder, chmn. Laurier Club of Man., 1982—; bd. dirs. Winnipeg Mcpl. Hosps., 1970-79, 85—, chmn., 1971-75, vice chmn., 1977-78. Elected sec. (first woman) Liberal Party of Man., 1968-69, v.p. Liberal Party of Can., 1970-73; Liberal candidate Osborne Constituency, 1973; bd. dirs. Man. Health Orgns., Inc., 1970-76; bd. dirs. Can. Council Christians and Jews, co-chair Central Region, 1986-88, chmn. program com., 1979-85, mem. Central Exec. Com., 1976-85, Nat. Exec., 1979-85; bd. dirs. Age and Opportunity Centres, 1972-76; adv. bd. YWCA, 1972-82; exec. Riverview Community Centre, 1973-74; commr. Nat. Capital Commn., Ottawa, 1976-82, mem. adv. com. on design, 1976-83; ofcl. Man. Track and Field Assn., 1978; mem. Task Force on Maternal and Child Health, 1979-82; dir. Big Sister's Assn., chair publicity com, 1987-88, Epiphany pageant St. Alban's Anglican Ch., 1954-72; pres. Riverview-Ashland Home and Sch. Assn., 1967-69; edn. chmn. Royal Winnipeg Ballet Women's Com., 1967-69. Named Woman of Yr. in Politics and Govtl. Affairs, YWCA, 1979; recipient Melitta achievement award, 1982. Mem. Man. Hist. Soc., Heritage Can. Found. (bd. govs. 1982-86), Rainbow Soc. (v.p.).

WESTENHOFER, FAY LORRAINE, insurance company executive; b. Marshfield, Oreg., Jan. 25, 1942; d. Orville F. and Louisa E. (Becker) Merritt; m. Charles E. Westenhofer, Apr. 20, 1968. A of Risk Mgmt., Ins. Inst., Malvern, Pa., 1984; student, Linfield Coll., McMinnville, Oreg., 1988—. Chartered property casualty underwriter. Sr. claims adjuster Nationwide Ins., Portland, Oreg., 1966-85; liability and employee benefits supr. Convoy Co., Portland, 1985—. Mem. Nat. Assn. Ins. Women (Claims Woman of Yr. 1983), Soc. Chartered Property Casualty Underwriters, Oreg. Casualty Adjuster Assn., Risk and Ins. Mgrs. Soc. Republican. Methodist.

WESTERFIELD DORRELL, GLADYS LUCILE, nurse; b. Danville, Ind., Aug. 13, 1925; d. Hubert Harold and Leona Elizabeth (Schenck) Westerfield; m. Homer Ralph Dorrell, July 20, 1947; children: Harold L., Dale E., Dean A. Diploma in Nursing, Meth. Hosp. Sch. Nursing, 1946; student, U. Indpls., 1978-79. RN, Ind. Staff nurse Meth. Hosp., Indpls., 1946-48; pvt. duty nurse Bloomington (Ind.) Hosp., 1948-49; staff nurse, tchr. Friends United Meeting subs. Mission Hosp., Kaimosi, Kenya, 1956-60; dir. nursing Friends Hosp., Kaimosi, 1962-66; staff nurse Home Care Agy Greater Indpls., 1970-72, hosp. liasion, 1972-79; staff nurse Vis. Nurse Service, Inc., Indpls., 1979-83, coordinator home health aide, 1983—; item reviewer test service Nat. League for Nursing, N.Y.C., 1986. Contbr. articles to profl. jours. Mem. Decatur Twp. Community Choir, Indpls., 1970—; bd. dirs., sec. Friends Apt. Homes, Inc., Plainfield, Ind., 1977-84, pres., 1986-87. United Soc. Friends Women fellow, Plainfield, 1986. Mem. Am. Nurses Assn., Ind. State Nurses Assn. Mem. Soc. of Friends. Club: Gideon's Aux. (Indpls.). Home: 4848 Bellingham E Dr Indianapolis IN 46241 Office: Vis Nurse Service Inc 930 N Illinois Indianapolis IN 46204

WESTERHOLD, RUTH ELIZABETH, psychologist, educator; b. Youngstown, Ohio, Aug. 4, 1926; d. Samuel Gordon and Grace Elizabeth (Green) Meadows; BS, Youngstown U., 1946; postgrad. Ohio U., 1947, U. Ill., 1947-49; PhD, So. Ill. U., 1978; m. Walter Charles Westerhold, June 1, 1949; children: Marsha L., Carl E. Chief clin. psychologist Alton (Ill.) State Hosp., 1952-55; psychologist St. Louis (Mo.) County Spl. Sch. Dist., 1963-68; chief psychologist Kaskaskia Spl. Edn. Dist., Centralia, Ill., 1968-78; dir. learning communications E. Miss. Jr. Coll., Scooba, 1978-83, coordinator instnl. techniques, 1987—, coordinator devel. edn., 1987-88; consulting psychologist div. vocat. rehab. State of Ill., Alton, 1954-55. USPHS fellow, U. Ill., 1947-49. Cert. school psychologist, Mo., Ill. Mem. Am. Psychol. Assn., AAAS, Psi Chi Counselor, lectr., writer child-rearing, family, learning. Home: PO Box 135 Artesia MS 39736

WESTERMANN, MARY LOUISE, medical librarian, educator; b. N.Y.C., Mar. 11, 1953; d. A. Louis and Anne U. (Skelly) Morse; m. Karl S. Westermann, Jan. 18, 1975 (div.). B.S. in Biology, L.I.U., 1975, M.S. in L.S., 1976, M.P.A. in Health Care Adminstrn., 1986. Con. med. librarian Nassau-Suffolk Health Systems Agy., Melville, N.Y., 1976-77; dir. John N. Shell Library Nassau Acad. Medicine, Garden City, N.Y., 1977—; adj. prof. L.I.U., Greenvale, N.Y., 1983—, instr., 1976-83. Editor, Perspectives Health Sci. Libraries, Cath. Library World. Trustee L.I. Library Resources Council, 1986—; bd. dirs. Sr. Connections Program, Adelphi U., 1987—. Recipient E. Hugh Behymer award L.I.U., 1976. Mem. Med. Library Assn. (sec. med. socs. sect. 1981-82, instr. continuing edn. 1982, chmn. med. soc. sect. 1986-87; cert. health scis. librarianship), Spl. Libraries Assn. (sec. L.I. chpt. 1978-80, bd. dirs. 1982-84, pres. elect 1988—), ALA, Cath. Library Assn. (instr. workshop), Suffolk-Nassau on-Line Retrievers (chmn. 1981), Med. and Sci. Libraries of L.I. (pres. 1980-81), Nassau County Library Assn. (chmn. health services com. 1978-81, 83—), L.I. Library Resources Council (bd. trustees 1987—, Adelphi U. Sr. Connections Program (adv. bd. 1987—), Beta Beta Beta, Beta Phi Mu (bd. dirs. Beta Mu chpt. 1987—), Pi Alpha Alpha. Office: Nassau Acad Medicine 1200 Stewart Ave Garden City NY 11530

WESTFALL, CAROL ANN, artist, educator; b. Everett, Pa., Sept. 7, 1938; d. Carroll Francis and Doris Lucille (Hawkins) Dooley; m. Jon David Westfall, Jan. 27, 1962 (div. Aug. 1976); children: Camille, Maigann. BFA, Rhode Island Sch. Design, 1960; MFA, Md. Inst., 1972. Instr. Md. Inst., Balt., 1968-72; prof. fine arts Montclair State Coll., Upper Montclair, N.J.; adj. assoc. prof. Columbia U. Tchrs.' Coll., N.Y.C., 1976-86; artist-in-residence Memphis Coll. Art, 1985, Am. Craft Mus., N.Y.C., 1987; mem. artists in schs. panel N.J. State Council on Arts, Trenton, 1978—; mem. disting. faculty selection com. Montclair State Coll., 1987, v.p. sch. fine and performing arts senate, 1987—; study leader India Tour Textile Mus., Washington, 1987. Co-author: Plaiting: Step by Step, 1976; artistic works exhibited at Lausanne Biennale, 1975, Am. Craft Mus. 1987. Recipient Gov. N.J. Purchase award N.J. State Mus., 1975; Indo-Am. fellow, 1980-81, N.J. State Council on the Arts fellow, 1987; Montclair State Coll. Arts Research grantee, 1987. Mem. N.Y. Rug Soc. Office: Montclair State Coll Dept Fine Arts Upper Montclair NJ 07043

WESTHEIMER, PARTICIA HELEN, business communications consultant; b. Colorado Springs, Colo., Feb. 20, 1943; d. Julius Milton and Ernestine (Hartheimer) W.; m. David M. Shanes, June 27, 1967 (div. 1974). BA magna cum laude, Goucher Coll., 1965; MEd, U.S. Internat. U., 1979. Cert. instr. bus. indsl. mgmt., Calif. Tchr. Park Sch. Balt., 1966-71, Hotton Arms Sch. Girls, Bethesda, Md., 1973-75, Marin County Day Sch., Corte Madera, Calif., 1975-79, La Jolla (Calif.) County Day Sch., 1980-83, pres. Westroots Bus. Writing Systems Inc., La Jolla, 1983—; cons. Southland Corp., Dallas, San Diego, Los Angeles; speaker Strategies for Success, Mpls., 1985-86. Mem. bus. profl. div. United Jewish Fedn., San Diego, 1987. Mem. Am. Soc. Tng. Devel., Nat. Speakers Assn., Nat. Assn. Female Execs., San Diego C. of C. Club: La Jolla Athletic. Home and Office: Westroots Bus Writing Systems 3131A Via Alicante La Jolla CA 92037

WESTHEIMER, (KAROLA) RUTH SIEGEL, psychologist, television personality; b. Frankfurt, Fed. Republic Germany; came to U.S., 1956; m. Manfred Westheimer; children: Miriam, Joel. Grad. psychology, U. Paris Sorbonne; Master's degree, New Sch. for Social Research, N.Y.C., 1959; EdD, Columbia U., 1970. Research asst. Columbia U. Sch. Pub. Health, N.Y.C., 1967-70; assoc. prof. Lehman Coll., Bronx, N.Y., 1970-77; with Bklyn. Coll.; counsellor, radio talk show hostess Sexually Speaking Sta. WYNY-FM, N.Y.C., 1980—; hostess TV series Good Sex, Dr. Ruth Show, Ask Dr. Ruth 1987 . Author: Dr. Ruth's Guide to Good Sex, 1983, First Love: A Young People's Guide to Sexual Information, 1985, Dr. Ruth's Guide for Married Lovers, 1986, autobiography All In a Lifetime, 1987; contbr. articles to mags.; appeared in film A Woman or Two, 1986. Office: King Features Syndicate Inc 235 E 45th St New York NY 10017 *

WESTINGHOUSE, ANNA MARIE, nursing service administrator; b. Cin., Mar. 21, 1931; d. Aaron Fleming Johnson and Violet Naomi (Lee) Venator; m. Edwin Arnold Westinghouse, Sept. 3, 1976 (div. 1982); 1 child, Lynn Ellen. Grad. high sch., Hammond, Ind. Radio interviewer Sta. WYCA-FM, Hammond, 1970-77, Sta. WLNR-FM, Lansing, Ill., 1977-85; dir. Meals-on-Wheels, Home Nursing Service, Hammond, 1983-84, dir. mktg. and pub. relations, 1983-85, asst. exec. dir., 1985-87; adminstr. Dorchester Sr. Retirement Home, Harper Dolton, Ill., 1987—. Contbr. articles on aging, women's rights and minority rights to local newspapers; producer radio programs on women's rights and minority rights, 1983. Mem. Lake County Womens Council, exec. bd., 1976-85. Mem. N.W. Ind. Womens Bur. (exec. bd. 1976-78). Democrat. Club: Toastmasters. Home: 511 Conkey St Hammond IN 46324 Office: Home Nursing Service 111 Sibley St Hammond IN 46320

WESTKELLOGG, CLAUDIA CURRY, lawyer; b. Houston, Feb. 26, 1945; d. Jessie and Dorothy (Brown) Curry; m. George Joseph Westkellogg; 1 child, Danielle Juili. BS in Urban Studies magna cum laude, Pepperdine U., 1974, MPA, 1976; JD, UCLA, 1980. Contact compliance officer Watts Health Found., Los Angeles, 1977-81; dir. World Won for Christ Legal Services, Inglewood, Calif., 1981-83; ptnr. Curry & Johnson-Parker, Inglewood, 1983—; legal counsel World Won for Christ Ministry, Inglewood, 1981—, Paradise Mortuary, Los Angeles, 1987—, Tyscott Records, Indpls., 1986; cons. Kellogg, Lumpkins & Keys, Inglewood, 1985—; vol. probate panel Los Angeles Superior Ct. Law sch. scholar UCLA, 1978. Mem. Calif. Bar Assn., Los Angeles County Bar Assn., Inglewood Bar Assn., Black Women Lawyers, Young Womens Christian Council (pres. Los Angeles chpt. 1974-76), Inglewood C. of C., NAACP. Democrat. Office: Curry & Johnson-Parker 101 N LaBrea Ave #508 Inglewood CA 90301

WESTON, DAWN THOMPSON, artist, researcher; b. Joliet, Ill., Apr. 15, 1919; d. Cyril C. and Vivian Grace Thompson; student (scholar) Penn Hall Jr. Coll., Chambersburg, Pa., 1937-38; B.S., Northwestern U., 1942, postgrad. in reading and speech pathology, 1960-61, M.A. in Edn. Adminstrn., 1970; postgrad. U. Ill., 1964; student Art Inst. Chgo., 1954, Pestalozzi-Froebel, Chgo., 1955, Phila. Inst. for Achievement Human Potential, 1963; m. Arthur Walter Weston, Sept. 10, 1940; children—Roger Lance, Randall Kent, Cynthia Brooke. Therapist, USN Hosp., Gt. Lakes, Ill., 1940-45; tchr. Holy Child and Waukegan (Ill.) High Schs., 1946-54; elem. and jr. high art dir. Lake Bluff (Ill.) Schs., 1954-58; pioneer ednl. dir. Grove Sch. for Brain-Injured, Lake Forest, Ill., 1958-66, now life mem. corp., chmn. bd., 1984-87; one-woman shows: Evanston Woman's Club, Northwestern U., Deerpath Gallery, Lake Forest; The Hein Co., Waukegan; numerous group shows, 1939-76. Represented in permanent collections: ARC, Victory Meml. Hosp., Waukegan, Sierra Assos., Chgo., numerous pvt. collections U.S., Can., Japan, Africa; works include: Poisonous Plants of Midwest set of etchings for Country Gentleman mag., 1956, Clouds mural, 1981; ind. researcher on shifting visual imagery due to trauma, 1982—. Mem. Presdl. Gold Chain, Trinity Coll., 1979. Named Citizen of Yr., Grove Sch., 1978, room at sch. named in her honor, 1982; cert. tchr./adminstr., Ill. Mem. Art Inst. Chgo., Deerpath Art League, Pi Lambda Theta. Methodist (del. Ann. Conf. 1982-88). Research on uneven growth, 1969—. Home and Office: 349 E Hilldale Pl Lake Forest IL 60045

WESTON, JUDITH HELEN, fine arts firm executive; b. Phila., May 18, 1945; d. Kurt Louis and Hilldegard (Salomon) Karo; m. Jeffrey Martyn Weston, May 19, 1968; 1 child, Shaun Alexander. Student Boston U., 1967-70; B.A. magna cum laude, U. Mass.-Boston, 1975. Lab. technician Herbert V. Shuster, Inc., North Quincy, Mass., 1975-77, sr. lab. technician, 1977-78; dir. ocular allergy lab. Eye Research Inst., Boston, 1979-85; cons., 1985; pres. Weston Fine Arts, Braintree, Mass., 1985—. Contbr. chpts. to books, monographs and jour. articles to profl. lit. Democrat. Jewish. Avocation: photography. Office: Weston Fine Arts 244 Middle St Braintree MA 02184

WESTON, PHYLLIS, art gallery director; b. Cleve., Mar. 17, 1921; d. Armin and Wilma H. (Wasserman) Hornstein; m. Leo F. Weston, Oct. 18, 1953; children—H. Todd Cobey, John Cobey. Ed., Simmons Coll., Yale U. Director, AB Closson Jr. Co. Art Gallery, Cin., 1964—; art cons. Proctor & Gamble Co., Cin., 1983—; cons. and lectr. in art. Named Woman of the Yr., 1987. Chmn., founder Enjoy the Arts; founder Cin. Commn. on the arts, the Post Corbett awards; bd. dirs., mem. numerous arts and civic orgns. including Cin. Bicentennial Com., Friends of Cin. Parks, med. arts com. U. Cin. Sch. Medicine. Home: 4 Taft Rd Ln Cincinnati OH 45206 Office: 401 Race St Cincinnati OH 45202

WESTPHAL, RUTH LILLY, educational audiovisual company executive, author, publisher; b. Glendale, Calif., July 27, 1931; d. Glen R. and Margaret E. (John) Lilly; m. H. Frederick Westphal, June 25, 1953. B.A. in Edn., UCLA, 1953; M.A. in Instructional System Tech., Chapman Coll., 1966. Cert. tchr. Calif. Tchr. pub. schs., Los Angeles, Glendale, Whittier, Calif., 1953-65; instuctional systems analyst Litton Industries, Anaheim, Calif., 1965-67; dir. devel. Trainex Corp., Garden Grove, Calif., 1967-69; owner, pres. Concept Media, Inc., Irvine, Calif., 1969—, Westphal Pub., Irvine, 1980—. Co-founder Friends of City Library, LaHabra, Calif., 1960-65; mem. Los Angeles County Mus. Art, 1975—, Laguna Beach Mus. Art, 1979—, Nautical Heritage Soc. Dana Point, Calif. 1982—. Author, editor numerous ednl. filmstrip programs. Author: Plein Air Painters of California: The Southland, 1982 (Western Books award 1982), Plein Air Painters of California: The North, 1986 (Western Books award 1986). Recipient numerous awards Info. Film Producers Am., Internat. Film and TV Festival N.Y., Chgo. Film Festival, Am. Jour. Nursing Media Festival, Author Recognition award U. Calif., 1983. Mem. Nat. Audiovisual Assn., Assn. Media Producers. Avocations: Art history. Office: Concept Media Inc 2493 DuBridge Ave Irvine CA 92714

WESTPHAL-DAVIS, ROXY ANNATTA, consulting company executive; b. Plentywood, Mont., Oct. 2, 1955; d. Jack A. and Betty Lou (Keogh) Westphal; m. Lee C. Gaston, Aug. 22, 1981 (div. 1983); m. Robert J. Davis, Mar. 22, 1985. BS in Bus. Adminstrn., Calif. State U., Sacramento, 1980. Supr. Cal-Farm Ins., Sacramento, 1978-81; with product devel. div. Deltak, Inc., Naperville, Ill., 1981-82, product mgr., 1982-83, mgr. product devel., 1983-84; edn. cons. Interactive Tng. Systems, Cambridge, Mass., 1984; ptnr. Corp. Resource Assocs., Belmont, Calif., 1984-85; pres. Corp. Resource Assocs., Inc., Redwood City, Calif., 1985—; cons. Bank Am., San Francisco, 1984—, First Interstate Services Co., Torrance, Calif., 1985—; bd. dirs. Corp. Resource Assocs., Inc., Redwood City. Mem. AAUW, Am. Electronics Assn., Nat. Assn. Female Execs. Republican. Episcopalian. Office: Corporate Resource Assocs Inc 333 Twin Dolphin Dr #225 Redwood City CA 94065

WETCHER, GOLDIE RAPPAPORT, psychotherapist, clinic administrator; b. Camden, N.J., July 12, 1939; d. Morris G. and Jean (Gordon) Cohen; m. Martin Paul Rappaport, June 7, 1959 (div. 1975); children—Karen Leah, Steven Aaron; m. Kenneth Wetcher, Apr. 11, 1976. B.A., Newcomb Coll., Tulane U., 1961, postgrad. Sch. Social Work, 1963; M.S.W., U. Houston, 1969-70. Psychotherapist Mental Health Mental Retardation, La Marque, Tex., 1970-72; psychotherapist Family Counseling Assoc. and Wetcher Clinic, Houston, 1972—. Organizer Crisis Mgmt. Service, Houston, 1984; active Bay Area Med., Houston, Orgn. Rehab. Tng., Houston; trustee Congregation Shaar Hashalom, Houston, 1984-85. Fellow Nat. Assn. Social Workers, Acad. Cert. Social Workers; mem. Houston Group Psychotherapy Assn. (tng. faculty), Am. Assn. Marriage and Family Therapists, Am. Group Psychotherapy Assn., Phi Beta Kappa, Phi Kappa Phi. Republican. Avocations: water sports; nutrition. Home: 2010 Port Royal Houston TX 77058 Office: Wetcher Clinic 16902 El Camino Real Suite 2C Houston TX 77058

WETHERBY, IVOR LOIS, librarian; b. Louisville, May 22, 1924; d. Luther Silas and Clara Marders (Hite) W.; m. Herbert Charles Howard, July 4, 1947; children: Ivor Jane, Elizabeth Wetherby, John Allen, Luther Hite, Ann Dell. AB, Ky. Wesleyan Coll., 1944; MS in Library Sci., Fla. State U. 1965; SEd, Fla. Atlantic U., 1984. Various clerical and secretarial positions, 1944-50; tchr. Our Lady of Mercy Acad., Louisville, 1963-64; librarian Palm Beach Jr. Coll., Lake Worth, Fla., 1966-78; head librarian Sebring (Fla.) Pub. Library, 1978; health scis. reference librarian Miami (Fla.)-Dade Community Coll., Med. Ctr. Campus, 1978-87; librarian med. library Moncrief Army Community Hosp., Ft. Jackson, S.C., 1987—. Mem. Spl. Libraries Assn., Columbia Area Med. Librarians' Assn., DAR. Episcopalian. Home: 1227 Quail Run Percival Rd at Lake Ave Columbia SC 29206 Office: Moncrief Army Community Hosp PO Box 499 Fort Jackson SC 29207-5720

WETHERELL, CLAIRE, state legislator; b. Flandreau, S.D., Feb. 18, 1919; d. Thomas James and Margaret (Hefron) H.; m. Robert Miles Wotherell (dec. 1943); children: Michael Edward, Dennis Hart, Ellen Ann Hermann, Robert Thomas. Student, U. Calif., Berkeley, 1937-39; RN, Mercy Hosp. Sch. Nursing, 1942. City councilwoman Mountain Home, Idaho, 1971-78; mem. Idaho State Senate. Dem. committeewoman Elmore County, 1955—; vice chmn. Idaho State Dem. Party, 1962-72. Named Disting. Citizen Idaho Daily Statesman, Boise, 1978. Mem. Mountain Home Com. of Fifty, Bus. and Profl. Women (named Woman of Progress, Idaho, 1976), C. of C., Idaho Land Title Assn. (pres. 1971-72). Roman Catholic. Home: 360 E 15th N Mountain Home ID 83647 *

WETHERELL, VIRGINIA BACON, state legislator, engineering company executive; b. Anniston, Ala., May 15, 1947; d. William Dennis and Mary (Perkins) Bacon; children: Virginia Blakely, Page Perkins. BA, Auburn U., 1968; MS, Jacksonville State U., 1971. Tchr. Biology and Physiology Anniston High Sch., 1968-72; planner East Ala. Regional Planning & Devel. Com., Anniston, 1974-82; exec. dir. City-County Drug Abuse Commn., Pensacola, Fla., 1976-82; dir., officer Coastal Transp., Pensacola, 1980-86; elected mem. Fla. Ho. of Reps., 1982—; dir., officer Ammons, Bass, Bass & Boys, Pensacola, 1985-86, Gulf Coast Mortgage & Investments, Pensacola, 1985-86; mktg. adminstr. Baskerville-Donovan Engrs., Pensacola, 1986—; mem. exec. com. Gulf Coast Econs. Club, Pensacola, 1985—, Homeporting Commn., Pensacola, 1985—; chmn. internat. trade and econ. devel. Fla. Ho. of Reps., 1986-88; bd. dirs. Bapt. Health Care Found., Pensacola, 1987—. Bd. dirs. Fla. Council on Asian Affairs, 1985—, Fla. Com. on Future, 1987-88; mem. exec. com. Fla. Dem. Party, 1985—. Named Profl. Leader of Yr. Pensacola C. of C. and Pensacola News Jour., 1981, Fla.'s Outstanding Young Woman Fla. Jaycees, 1982, Woman of Yr. Pensacola Breakfast of Champions, 1983. Mem. Nat. Conf. State Legislatures, Council of State Govt., Fla. Chpt. of Dem. Leadership. Episcopalian. Clubs: Leadership Pensacola (founding mem., pres. 1981), Pensacola Heritage Found. (pres. 1980-82). Home: 1325 North A St Pensacola FL 32501

WETLI, PEGGY MARIE, theater company executive; b. Green Bay, Wis., Oct. 10, 1949; d. Alois Bernard and Viola Marie (Frye) W. Founder, exec. and artistic dir. CLIMB Theatre, St. Paul, 1974—; cons., lectr. U. Minn., St. Paul. Author 14 plays for children and adults. Bd. dirs. Minn. Alliance for Art in Edn., 1978-81. Roman Catholic. Office: CLIMB Theatre 529 Jackson St Suite 227 Saint Paul MN 55101

WETSTONE, JANET MEYERSON, designer, journalist; b. Spartanburg, S.C.; d. Louis Alexander and Ella (Levinson) Meyerson; m. Richard J. Wetstone, Sept. 21, 1947 (div. Dec. 1973); children—John B., Gregory S., Linda Wetstone Sherman. Student U. Mo., 1945-47, Ga. State U., 1970, 80. Interior designer Jan's Interiors, Atlanta, 1965-68; pres. Wetstone Crafts Co., Atlanta, 1968—; instr. women in bus. Emory U., 1972; cons. Plaid Enterprises Inc. Author: Rags to Riches with Mod-Podge, 1969; Specially Yours Decorating With Sheets, 1977; Needle-Podge Book, 1976; Creative Frame Maker, 1972; patentee craft paint, frame maker. Pres. edn. guild Ringling Mus., Sarasota, Fla., 1963-64, chairperson 1st creative art carnival, 1963-64; decorating chairperson Jimmy Carter Election Night, Atlanta, 1976; dir. communications Carter Mondale 1980 Campaign, Atlanta, 1980; chmn. visual arts Sarasota Centennial, 1985-86. Mem. United Inventors and Scientists Am., Women in Film (v.p. 1982-83), Fla. Assn. Realtors, Million Dollar Club, Phi Sigma Sigma. Club: 1980 (Atlanta). Avocations: riding; painting; golf. Home: 3969 Glen Oaks Manor Dr Sarasota FL 33582

WETTERHAHN, KAREN ELIZABETH, chemistry educator; b. Plattsburgh, N.Y., Oct. 16, 1948; d. Gustave George and Mary Elizabeth (Thibault) W.; m. Leon H. Webb, June 19, 1982; children—Leon Ashley, Charlotte Elizabeth. B.S., St. Lawrence U., 1970; Ph.D., Columbia U., 1975. Chemist, Mearl Corp., Ossining, N.Y., 1970-71; research fellow Columbia

U., N.Y.C., 1971-75, postdoctoral fellow, 1975-76; asst. prof. chemistry Dartmouth Coll., Hanover, N.H., 1976-82, assoc. prof., 1982-86, prof., 1986—. Contbr. articles to profl. jours., 1974—. A.P. Sloan fellow, 1981. Mem. Am. Chem. Soc., Am. Assn. Cancer Research, AAAS, N.Y. Acad. Scis. Office: Dartmouth Coll Dept Chemistry Hanover NH 03755

WETZEL, BARBARA JO, nurse; b. Hagerstown, Md., July 12, 1950; d. Vivian (Cunningham) W.; m. Wayne Homens (div. July 1983). Diploma in nursing, Md. Gen. Hosp. Sch. Nursing, 1971. RN Kapiolani Med. Ctr. for Women and Children, Honolulu, 1985—. Home: 1717 Mott Smith Dr #2408 Honolulu HI 96822

WETZEL, DOROTHY LEE, marketing professional, consultant; b. N.Y.C., May 5, 1959; d. Charles Arthur and Marion Daisy (Crooke) W; m. Daniel Sugarman. BA, Tufts U., 1981; MBA, Columbia U., 1983. Assoc. product mgr. Shulton USA, Wayne, N.J., 1983-86; sr. product mgr. Advil Whitehead Labs., N.Y.C., 1986—; cons. Arts and Bus. Council, N.Y.C., 1986—. Mem. Toastmasters Club. Democrat. Unitarian. Office: Whitehall Labs 685 3rd Ave New York NY 10019

WEVER, KAREN LYNN, accountant; b. Indlps., Jan. 3, 1960; d. Duard Eugene and Marcia Kathleen (Brown) W. BS in Acctg., Ball State U., 1982. Claims taker Ind. Employment Security Div., Indlps., 1982-83; acctg. officer Huntington Bank, Noblesville, Ind., 1983—, Hamilton County. Mem. Nat. Wildlife Fedn., Sierra Club. Republican. Methodist. Home: 6806 Reunion Ln Indianapolis IN 46250 Office: Huntington Bank One Wainwright Plaza Noblesville IN 46060

WEXLER, ANNE, government relations and public affairs consultant; b. N.Y.C., Feb. 10, 1930; d. Leon R. and Edith R. (Rau) Levy; m. Joseph Duffey, Sept. 17, 1974; children by previous marriage: David Wexler, Daniel Wexler. B.A., Skidmore Coll., 1951, LL.D. (hon.), 1978; D.Sc. in Bus. (hon.), Bryant Coll., 1978. Assoc. pub. Rolling Stone mag., 1974-76; personnel adviser Carter-Mondale transition planning group, 1976-77; dep. undersec. regional affairs Dept. Commerce, 1977-79; asst. to Pres. of U.S., Washington, 1979-81; pres. Wexler and Assocs., Washington, 1981; now govt. relations and pub. affairs cons., chmn. Wexler, Reynolds, Harrison & Schule, Inc., Washington; bd. dirs. Am. Cyanamid Co., New Eng. Electric System, Monarch Capital Corp., Cambridge Mcht. Bank; mem. vis. com. J.F. Kennedy Sch. Govt., Harvard U. chmn. Dem. Congl. Dinner Com., 1983; bd. dirs. Ctr. for Nat. Policy; bd. advisors Carter Ctr., Emory U.; bd. visitors U. Md. Sch. Pub. Affairs. Named Outstanding Alumna Skidmore Coll., 1972, recipient most disting. alumni award, 1984. Mem. Council on Fgn. Relations., Com. of 200, Nat. Womens Forum. Jewish. Office: 1317 F St NW Suite 600 Washington DC 20004

WEXLER, JACQUELINE GRENNAN (MRS. PAUL J. WEXLER), association executive, former college president; b. Sterling, Ill., Aug. 2, 1926; d. Edward W. and Florence (Dawson) Grennan; m. Paul J. Wexler, June 12, 1969; stepchildren: Wendy, Wayne. A.B., Webster Coll., 1948; M.A., U. Notre Dame, 1957; LL.D., Franklin and Marshall Coll., 1968, Phila. Coll. Textiles and Sci., 1987; D.H.L., Brandeis U., 1968; LL.D., Skidmore Coll., 1967, Smith Coll., 1975; HHD, U. Mich., 1967, U. Ohio, 1976, D.H.L., Carnegie Inst., 1966, Colo. Coll., 1967, U. Pa., 1979; HHD (hon.), U. Hartford, 1987. Tchr. English and math. Loretto Acad., El Paso, Tex., 1951-54; tchr. English and math. Nerinx Hall, St. Louis, 1954-59; tchr. English Webster Coll., 1959-60, asst. to pres., 1959, v.p. devel., 1960, exec. v.p., 1962-65, pres., 1965-69; v.p., dir. internat. univ. studies Acad. for Ednl. Devel., N.Y.C., 1969; pres. Hunter Coll., City U. N.Y., 1969-79, Acad. Cons. Assoc., N.Y.C., 1980-82; pres. NCCJ, 1982—; writer, commentator, cons.; mem. Am. Council on Edn., Commn. on Internat. Edn., 1967; mem. adv. com. to dir. NIH, 1978-80; mem. exec. panel chief naval ops. U.S. Navy, 1978-81; bd. examiners Fgn. Service, Dept. State, 1981-83; dir. Interpublic Group of Cos., Inc., United Techs. Corp.; mem. Pres.'s Adv. Panel on Research and Devel. in Edn., 1961-65; mem. Pres.'s Task Force on Urban Ednl. Opportunities, 1967. Author: Where I Am Going, 1968; contbr. articles to profl. jours. Chmn. bd. dirs. Central Midwestern Regional Ednl. Lab.; bd. dirs. Arts and Edn. Council Greater St. Louis; trustee U. Pa. Recipient NYU Sch. Edn. Ann. award for creative leadership in edn., 1968; Elizabeth Cutter Morrow award YWCA, 1978; named One of Six Outstanding Women of St. Louis Area St. Louis chpt. Theta Sigma Phi, 1963, Woman of Achievement in Edn. St. Louis Globe-Democrat, 1964, Woman of Accomplishment Harpers Bazaar, 1967; Kenyon lectr. Vassar Coll., 1967. Mem. Mo. Acad. Squires, NCCJ (pres. 1982—), Kappa Gamma Pi. Office: Nat Conf Christians and Jews 71 Fifth Ave New York NY 10003

WEXLER, JO SHEILA, advertising and marketing executive; b. Jan. 4, 1946; d. Isadore and Rella (Blaustein) W.; m. John Willis Fuller, Sept. 11, 1965; 1 son, Blair. B.A., Fla. State U., 1965; M.A. (grad. asst.), U. Fla., 1972; postgrad. U. Ga., 1972-73. Fashion artist Furchgott's, Jacksonville, Fla., 1967; advt. and pub. relations mgr. Jacksonville Area C. of C., 1972-74; mktg. dir. Jax Navy Fed. Credit Union, 1974-76; account supr. Abramson/Himelfarb Inc., Washington, 1976-81; v.p. mktg. Morgan Burchette Assocs., Inc., Alexandria, Va., 1981-85; pres. Wexler Mktg. Group, Alexandria, 1985—. Cellist, Jacksonville Symphony, 1967-76; cellist Alexandria (Va.) Symphony, 1987—; Arlington (Va.) Symphony, 1977—, chmn. corp. devel. com., 1983—, bd. dirs., 1984—. Recipient Pres.'s medal Fla. Pub. Relations Assn., 1975. Mem. Am. Mktg. Assn., Women in Advt. and Mktg. (bd. dirs. 1982-85, 86—, secy. 1983-85, pres. 1987—), Phi Kappa Phi. Democrat. Jewish. Office: Wexler Mktg Group Inc 1021 Prince St Alexandria VA 22314

WEY, LIH-ER LIAO, computer analyst; b. Kaohsiung, Republic of China, Dec. 10, 1952; d. Suei-Yung and Luang (Fung) Liao; m. Chin-Long Wey, Mar. 16, 1977; children: Jessica K., Tiffany K. BA, Nat. Cen. U., 1975; MA, Chinese Culture U., 1977; MS, Tex. Tech. U., 1982. Software design engr. Tex. Instrument Inc., Lubbock, 1982-83; system analyst computer lab. Mich. State U., East Lansing, 1983—. Mem. Digital Users Group, Sun Users Group. Office: Mich State U 400 H Computer Ctr East Lansing MI 48824

WEYEN, WENDY LEE, newspaper reporter, writer; b. Indpls., July 29, 1963; d. Harvey Lee and Louise Marie (Eberhart) W. BA in Journalism, BS in Bus., Ind. U., 1985, MBA, 1986; cert., Tilburg (The Netherlands) U., 1985. Cert. internat. bus., Tilburg. Assoc. instr. Ind. U., Bloomington, 1985-86; reporter, staff writer St. Petersburg (Fla.) Times, 1986—; systems cons. Arbutus Yearbook, Bloomington, 1985-86. Poynter scholar St. Petersburg Times, Ind. U., 1984, 85. Mem. Ind. U. Alumni Assn., Beta Gamma Sigma, Phi Beta Kappa. Republican. Lutheran.

WEYGMAN, LORRAINE IRENE, management consultant; b. Toronto, Ont., Can., June 6, 1938; d. Isaac and Thelma (Rosner) W.; 1 child: Joel Mandelbaum. BA in Psychology, York U., Toronto, Can., 1971; MFA, York U., 1979; MEd in Adult Edn., U. Toronto, 1985. Tchr. North York Bd. Edn., Ont., 1957-64; art supr. Vaughn Twp. Sch. Area, Maple, Ont., 1964-69; cons. York Region Bd. Edn., Aurora, Ont., 1969-85; owner, pres. Leah-Lorraine Assocs., Toronto, 1981-87; bd. dirs., trustee Coll. Naturopathic Medicine, Toronto, Condominium Corp., North York; bd. dirs. Can. & Internat. Assn. Women Bus. Owners, North York, North York Bus. Council. Contbr. numerous articles to newspapers, mags., other periodicals. Mem. Ont. Soc. Tng. Devel., Can. Assn. Women Bus. Owners (v.p. 1985—), Fedn. Women Tchrs. Assn., Ont., Personnel Assn. Ont., North York Bus. Assn. Clubs: McGibbon Investment, Univ. Women's (Toronto). Home: 27 Wild Gingerway, Downsview, ON Canada M3H 5W9 Office: Leah-Lorraine Assocs, 27 Wild Ginger Way, Downsview, ON Canada M3H 5W9

WEYMANN, BARBARA LEE, software engineer; b. Santa Monica, Calif., Oct. 18, 1933; d. James Francis and Mary Jane (Martin) McDermott; m. Ray J. Weymann, June 16, 1956; children: Lynn Weymann Walker, Catherine, Steven. BA in Math., Pomona Coll., 1955. Mgmt. trainee Naval Ordnance Test Sta., Inyokern, Calif., 1955-56; programmer Ednl. Testing Service, Princeton, N.J., 1956-58; research analyst Kitt Peak Nat. Obs., Tucson, 1965-75; exec. dir. YWCA, Tucson, 1977-80; systems analyst Bell Tech. Ops. div. Textron, Tucson, 1980-85; software engr. Systems and Software Engring. div. Singer, Tucson, 1985-86, Jet Propulsion Lab., Pasadena, Calif., 1986—. Vice mayor City of Tucson, 1975-77, mem. city council, 1973-77; mem. Ariz. Women's Commn., 1975-76, Commn. to Appoint Appellate Ct. Justices, Ariz., 1980-84, Tucson Water Commn., 1982-86. Mem. Women in Mgmt., Exec. Womens Council (charter). Democrat. Home: 3565 Greenhill Rd Pasadena CA 91107 Office: Jet Propulsion Lab 4800 Oak Grove Pasadena CA 91109

WHALEN, BARBARA LOUISE, health science facility administrator; b. Lynn, Mass., Aug. 30, 1956; d. Henry Francis and Barbara Ann (Driscoll) W. BA, Stonehill Coll., North Easton, Mass., 1978; M of Pub. Adminstrn., U. Mass., 1980. Asst. dir. Div. of Registration, Boston, 1981-83; adminstr. Middlesex Fells Nursing Home, Melrose, Mass., 1983-85, Hunt Nursing and Retirement Home, Danvers, Mass., 1985—. Bd. dirs. Greater Lynn chpt. Am. Cancer Soc., 1984—, Cath. Fmily Services, Lynn, 1984—. U. Mass. fellow, 1979-80. Mem. Am. Coll. Health Care Adminstrs., Mass. Coll. Health Care Adminstrs. (bd. dirs. 1986).

WHALEN, LUCILLE, academic administrator; b. Los Angeles, July 26, 1925; d. Edward Cleveland and Mary Lucille (Perrault) W. B.A. in English, Immaculate Heart Coll., Los Angeles, 1949; M.S.L.S., Catholic U. Am., 1955; D.L.S., Columbia U., 1965. Tchr. elem. and secondary parochial schs. Los Angeles, Long Beach, Calif., 1945-52; high sch. librarian Conaty Meml. High Sch., Los Angeles, 1950-52; reference/serials librarian, instr. in library sci. Immaculate Heart Coll., 1955-58; dean Immaculate Heart Coll. (Sch. Library Sch.), 1958-60, 65-70; assoc. dean, prof. SUNY, Albany, 1971-78, 84-87; prof. Sch. Info. and Library Sci., SUNY, 1984-87; dean grad. programs Immaculate Heart Coll. Ctr., Los Angeles, 1987—; dir. U.S. Office Edn. Instn. Mem. Spl. Libraries Assn. (chmn. com. research 1974-80, chmn. social and human services sect. 1983-84), ACLU, Common Cause, Amnesty Internat. Democrat. Roman Catholic. Home: 320 S Gramercy Pl Apt #101 Los Angeles CA 90020 Office: Immaculate Heart Coll Ctr 10951 Pico Blvd Los Angeles CA 90064

WHALEN, NANA LEE, diet counselor, writer; b. Mullens, W.Va., Nov. 12, 1937; d. Gerald Eugene and Hilda Belle (Fowls) Richards; m. John M. Whalen, Dec. 15, 1959; children: Timothy John, Maria Marye, Angela Sue. BS in Edn., Ohio State U., 1959. Free-lance columnist The Village Voice, Severna Park, Md., 1975-76, The Annapolis (Md.) Evening Capitol, 1977, The Baltimore Sun, 1978-82; counselor, owner Diet Ctr. of Severna Park, 1983—, Worthington (Ohio) Dietcenter, 1985—; mem. Diet Ctr. Nat. Profl. Adv. Bd., 1988—. Author: Whale of a Cookbook, 1978, Whale of a Cookbook II, 1979, Hooked on Seafood, 1982, Strawberries, 1983. Mem. Assn. of Met. Washington Diet Ctr. Owners, Am. Bus. Women's Assn., Kappa Alpha Theta. Methodist. Home: 504 Denington Ln Severna Park MD 21146 Office: Diet Ctr of Severna Park 692 B Ritchie Hwy Severna Park MD 21146

WHALEN-CRUZ, WANDA JO, management analyst; b. Balt., June 16, 1958; d. Ervin David and Joyce Eileen (Hahn) Whalen; m. David Cruz, Apr. 4, 1987. Student, Catonsville Community Coll., 1976-79. Clk. typist Md. State Police, Pikesville, 1975-76; sec. State Hwy. Adminstrn., Balt., 1976-78; sec. U.S. Army C.E., Columbia, Md., 1978-80, Al Batin, Saudi Arabia, 1980-85, Balt., 1985; mgmt. asst. U.S. Army, Ft. Irwin, Calif., 1985, mgmt. analyst, 1985—; equal opportunity counselor U.S. Army, Ft. Irwin, 1986—. Mem. Nat. Assn. for Female Execs., Am. Soc. of Mil. Comptrollers, Federally Employed Women, Federal Women's Program (pres. 1985—, mgr. 1988—). Home: 550 W Fredricks Barstow CA 92311

WHALEY, CHARLOTTE TOTEBUSCH, publisher, editor, writer; b. Pitts., June 21, 1925; d. Charles R. and Elizabeth G. (Dunn) Totebusch; m. Gould Whaley, Jr., Aug. 24, 1951; children—John Gould, Robert Dunn. B.A., So. Meth. U., 1970, M.A., 1976. Editorial asst. Southwest Rev., So. Meth. U., Dallas, 1971-72, asst. editor, 1972-74, assoc. editor, 1974-75, asst. to dir. So. Meth. U. Press, mng. editor Southwest Rev., 1975-81, editor Southwest Rev., 1981-83, asst. dir., editor So. Meth. U. Press, 1981-82, editor, 1982-83; editor/pub. Still Point Press, 1984—. Mem. Book Pubs. Tex. (treas. 1987—), Am. Booksellers Assn., Southwestern Booksellers Assn. (chmn. lit. awards com. 1987-88), Phi Beta Kappa (asst. sec. So. Meth. U. chpt. 1979-82, pres. North Tex. chpt. 1982-84). Home and Office: 4222 Willow Grove Rd Dallas TX 75220

WHALEY, PEGGY ELAINE, editor, publisher; b. Cleveland, Tenn., Nov. 30, 1939; d. Edward Darrell and Pauline (Earley) Ellis; m. Leo Jackson Whaley, Mar. 29, 1957; children—Sherri, Angela, Traci. Student Cleveland Community Coll., 1963-65, Dalton Jr. Coll., 1970-72, also spl. classes. Office mgr. So. Gen. Products, Ringgold, Ga., 1967-73, also corp. officer; office mgr. Joe Goodson, C.P.A., Dalton, Ga., 1974-78; comptroller Profl. C & C., Dalton, 1980-83; owner, operator Whaley & Assocs., Dalton, 1983—; editor, assoc. pub. S.E. Floor Covering, Dalton, 1985-86; carpet market editor Ams. Textiles Internat. Editor, pub. Peggy Whaley News Report, 1982-85; contbg. editor Carpet and Rug Industry, 1974-85, America's Textiles, 1984-85. Publicity dir. LWV, Dalton, 1978-80; mem. bd. Dalton Regional Library, 1981-86, chmn. bd., 1985-86; Republican sec. and v.p., Dalton, 1970-80. Mem. N.Y. Bus. Press Editors, Inc., Nat. Assn. Accts. (v.p. communications 1984-85), Nat. Assn. Floor Covering Women (nat. bd. dirs.), Nat. Assn. Female Execs., Am. Soc. Profl. and Exec. Women, Dalton C. of C. (mem. coms.), World Trade Council (local bd. dirs. 1984—). Club: Pilot. Lodges: Order Eastern Star (past matron), Toastmasters (local v.p. 1984—). Avocations: writing, swimming, tennis. Home: PO Box 191 Cohutta GA 30710 Office: PO Box 205 Dalton GA 30722 also: 300 Emory Sq Suite 106 Dalton GA 30720

WHALEY, SARA STAUFFER, publishing executive; b. Chgo., Apr. 11, 1932; d. Jacob Reiff and Sara Elizabeth (Seal) Stauffer; m. Charles H. Whaley Jr., Feb. 18, 1961 (dec. 1985). BA, U. R.I., 1954, MA, 1962; MA, Middlebury Coll., 1955; MLS, SUNY, Geneseo, 1971; postgrad., Syracuse U., 1963-64. Tchr. French Friends Sch., Wilmington, Del., 1955-57; fgn. service officer U.S. Dept. State, Washington, 1958-60; substitute tchr. Rochester (N.Y.) Pub. Schs., 1961-70; pres., editor, pub. Rush (N.Y.) Pub. Co., Inc., 1975—. Fulbright fellow, 1954-55. Mem. Nat. Women's Studies Assn., Nat. Urban League, Nat. Women's Polit. Caucus, Nat. Orgn. Women, Nat. Assn. Women Bus. Owners, NAACP, Rochester Women's Network. Democrat. Mem. United Ch. Christ. Home: 142 Farmcrest Dr Rush NY 14543 Office: Rush Pub Co Inc PO Box 1 Rush NY 14543

WHAM, DOROTHY STONECIPHER, state legislator; b. Centralia, Ill., Jan. 5, 1925; d. ERnest Jospeh and Vera Thelma (Shafer) Stonecipher; m. Robert S. Wham, Jan. 26, 1947; children: Nancy S. Wham Mitchell, Jeanne Wham Ryan, Robert S. II. BA, MacMurray Coll., 1946; MA, U. Ill., 1949. Counsellor Student Counselling Bur. U. Ill., Urbana, 1946-49; state dir. ACTION program, Colo./Wyo. U.S. Govt., Denver, 1972-82; mem. Colo. Ho. of Reps., 1986-87; mem. Colo. Senate, 1987—, vice chair jud. com., 1987—, mem. capital devel. com., health, environ., welfare and instns. Mem. Civil Rights Commn. Denver, 1972-80; bd. dirs. Denver Com. on Mental Health, 1985—, Denver Symphony, 1985—. Mem. Am. Psychol. Assn., Colo. Mental Health Assn. (bd. dirs. 1986—), LWV. Republican. Methodist. Lodge: Civitan. Home: 2790 S High St Denver CO 80210 Office: State Capitol Room 333 Denver CO 80203

WHARTON, LISA ANN, advertising executive; b. Washington, Pa., Dec. 1, 1958; d. Robert Lucien and Ruth Irene (Beardmore) W. BA in Mass Communications, U. South Fla., 1981. Mgr. mktg. Better Bus. Forms, Pinellas Park, Fla., 1982-85; mgr. corp. advt. Pro Ad Group, St. Petersburg, Fla., 1986; dir. advt. Pursley Advt., St. Petersburg, 1987—; dir. slide presentation Morton Plant Hosp., Clearwater, Fla., 1981; dir. advt. Visual Concepts, St. Petersburg, Fla., 1985-86; dir. mktg. Statue of Liberty com. St. Christopher, Tierra Verde, Fla., 1986. Recipient 1st place for black-and-white photo Scarborough Faire Gallery, 1983. Mem. Internat. Assn. Bus. Communicators, Direct Mktg. Assn., Pinellas Advt. Fedn., NOW, Nat. Assn. for Female Execs. Office: Pursley Advt 5017 Haines Rd Saint Petersburg FL 33714

WHARTON, MARY MERCHANT, educator; b. Martinsburg, W.Va., Nov. 13, 1942; d. Oliver Phillipps and Mary Belle (Maddox) Merchant; m. Stewart Boyd Wharton Jr., Sept. 28, 1963; children: Stewart B. III, Mary Ella Wharton Hoskins. BA in Secondary Edn., Shepherd Coll., 1965, BA in Elem. Edn., 1975. Cert. tchr., W.Va. Tchr. 1st and 2d grade Middleway (W.Va.) Elem. Sch., 1967-72; tchr. 1st grade South Jefferson Elem. Sch., Charlestown, W.Va., 1972-77, tchr. 2d grade, 1977-85, tchr. 3d grade, 1985—. Den mother troop #42 Cub Scouts of Am., Charlestown, 1973-75; leader troop #595 Girl Scouts U.S., Charlestown, 1974-79; leader 4-H Club, Charlestown, 1985-87; active PTA; spl. edn. Sunday Sch. tchr., 1985—; Asbury Children's Council Leader, 1983-85. Mem. NEA, United Daus. of the Confederacy (pres. 1983-87, W.Va. page 1987—), Jefferson County Edn. Assn., W.Va. Edn. Assn., Jaycee-ettes (pres. Charlestown chpt. 1968-70, Jaycee-ette of Yr. 1969), Sigma Sigma Sigma. Democrat. Methodist. Club: Tops (Shenandoah Junction, W.Va.) (correspondence 1987). Home: PO Box 338 Ranson WV 25438

WHATLEY, DEBORAH HINTON, industrial engineer; b. Del Rio, Tex., Apr. 14, 1959; d. Carl Raymond and Elizabeth Ruth (Walters) Hinton; m. Charles Edwin Whatley, Sept. 1, 1979; 1 child: Matthew Charles. AA, Okaloosa Walton Jr. Coll., 1978; BS in Textile Engring., Auburn U., 1982; postgrad., Furman U., 1987—. Maintenance supr. J.P. Stevens, Greenville, S.C., 1982-83, quality control mgr., 1983-88; indsl. engr. Michelin Tire Corp., Greenville, 1988—. Mem. Tau Beta Pi, Phi Psi. Republican. Presbyterian. Home: 107 Brockman Dr Mauldin SC 29662 Office: JP Stevens White Horse Rd PO Box 1026 Greenville SC 29601

WHATLEY, JACQUELINE BELTRAM, lawyer; b. West Orange, N.J., Sept. 26, 1944; d. Quirino and Eliane (Gruet) Beltram; m. John W. Whatley, June 25, 1966. BA, U. Tampa, 1966; JD, Stetson U., 1969. Bar: Fla. 1969, Alaska 1971. Assoc. Gibbons, Tucker, McEwen Smith & Cofer, Tampa, Fla., 1969-71; sole practice, Anchorage, 1971-73; ptnr. Gibbons, Tucker, Miller, Whatley & Stein, P.A., Tampa, 1973-81, pres., 1981—. Bd. dirs. Travelers Aid Soc.; trustee Humana Women's Hosp., Tampa, Keystone United Meth. Ch., 1986—. Mem. ABA, Fla. Bar Assn., Alaska Bar Assn., Tenn. Walking Horse Breeders and Exhibitors Assn. (v.p. 1984-87, dir. for Fla. 1981-87), Fla. Walking and Racking Horse Assn. (bd. dirs. 1988—, pres. 1980-82). Republican. Methodist. Club: Athena (Tampa). Home: PO Box 17595 Tampa FL 33682 Office: 101 E Kennedy Blvd Tampa FL 33602

WHEATLEY, BRIANA MARIE, labor relations professional; b. North Tonawanda, N.Y., Jan. 4, 1942; d. Raymond George and Helen Dorothy (Arnts) Tessmer; m. Donald Paul Wheatley (div. Aug. 1978); children: Deborah, David. AAS in Retail and Promotion, Tobe Coburn Sch., 1963; BS in Personnel Mgmt. with honors, Purdue U., 1973; postgrad., Ind. U., Ft. Wayne, 1983-86. Asst. dir. personnel Ind.-Purdue U., Ft. Wayne, 1973-76; adminstrv. asst. dir. community devel. and planning City of Ft. Wayne, 1976-77; personnel coordinator govt. compliance GTE Ind., Ft. Wayne, 1977, personnel coordinator labor relations, 1977-79, div. mgr. personnel, 1979-82, mgr. compensation and staffing, 1982-83, mgr. labor relations, 1983-84; mgr. employee relations GTE North, Irving, Tex., 1984-87, GTE Supply, Irving, Tex., 1987—; instr. Purdue U., Ft. Wayne, 1978-80. Mem. Pvt. Industry Council, Ft. Wayne, 1982-84, Hanicap Adv. Council, Ft. Wayne, 1977-84. Gov.'s Council on Mgmt. and Labor, Indpls., 1987. Mem. Am. Soc. for Personnel Adminstrs. (trea. 1980-82, bd. dirs. 1982-83), Nat. Assn. for Female Execs., Indsl. Relations Research Assn., Alpha Xi Delta. Republican. Presbyterian. Home: 2831 Timber Hill Dr Grapevine TX 76051 Office: GTE 4500 Fuller Dr Irving TX 75038

WHEATLEY, KATHLEEN NIEHOFF, infosytems specialist, microbiologist; b. Louisville, June 30, 1949; d. Robert Bernard and Carolyn Lee (Lynch) Niehoff; m. Charles Morris Wheatley, Nov. 20, 1970; children: Christopher Scott, Micah Kelty, John Patrick. BS in Med. Tech., Spalding U., Louisville, 1971; MA in Health Services Mgmt. and Human Resources Devel., Webster U., Jeffersonville, Ind., 1987. cert. med. technologist, Calif. Supr. microbiology dept. St. Anthony Hosp., Louisville, 1972-78; microbiologist Bapt. Hosp. East, Louisville, 1981-82; microbiologist, med. technician, student trainer Humana Hosp. Audubon div. Humana, Inc., Louisville, 1982-86; installer software for hosp. systems Humana, Inc., Louisville, 1986—; project dir. lab. installation Medcom (Ulticare) hosp. systems software. Chairperson cultural arts com. Fern Creek Elem. Sch. PTA, Louisville, Ky., 1981-83. Mem. Am. Soc. Med. Technologists, Ky. Soc. Med. Technologists, Am. Soc. Clin. Pathologists (cert. 1971). Roman Catholic. Home: 8000 Perchwood Ct Louisville KY 40291 Office: Humana Inc 500 W Main St PO Box 1438 Louisville KY 40201-1438

WHEATLEY, MARGARET BISSON (PEGI WHITE), small business owner, personnel consultant; b. Washington, Dec. 27, 1941; d. Robert Omer Bisson and Margaret (Dysart) Redfield; m. Richard Withington Wheatley, Jr., June 5, 1971. B.S. in Psychology, Philosophy, Ripon Coll., 1963. Dep. probation officer Orange County, Calif., 1964-71; personnel cons., office mgr. James Holder Placement, San Francisco, 1972-77; owner Margaret Bisson Wheatley Designs, Mill Valley, Calif., 1976—; pres., co-owner, personnel cons. McCall Personnel Services, Inc., San Francisco, 1978—; dir., co-owner MTS/McCall Temporary Service, Inc., San Francisco, 1982—; owner P&L Resources, San Francisco, 1983—; curriculum advisor City Coll. San Francisco, 1987—. Mem. Calif. Assn. Personnel Cons. Republican. Club: Commercial (San Francisco) (bd. dirs. 1986-88). Avocations: tennis; international travel. Office: McCall Personnel Services Inc 369 Pine St Suite 700 San Francisco CA 94104

WHEATLEY, MARY JANE, data processing executive; b. Bedford, Ind., Aug. 10, 1949; d. Robert Marshall and Iona Ruth (Jones) Toliver; m. James Edward Wheatley; children: Stephen Jay, Hannah Lee, Joanna Gayle. BS, Ball State U., 1971; MS in Bus. Edn., Ind. U., 1977. Tchr. 1972-74; exec. sec. Robertson Corp., 1974-80; data processing exec. 1981-87; sec./treas. Robertson Industries, Dallesport, Wash., 1987—. Mem. Brownstown (Ind.) Library Bd.; bd. dirs. Jackson County Girl's Club Am., Jackson County Substance Abuse Task Force. Mem. Forest Products Research Soc. (chair Ohio Valley sect., co-chair nat. meeting 1987), Delta Gamma (treas. 1968-70), Pi Omega Pi, Phi Beta Lambda. Mem. Christian Ch. Club: Hickory Hills Country (Brownstown). Home: 316 Jodi Dr Brownstown IN 47220 Office: PO Box 787 Bedford IN 47421

WHEEL, LESLEY, design firm executive; b. N.Y.C.; d. Lester and Helénè (Nelson) W. BA, Brwyn Mawr Coll. Free-lance theater design N.Y.C., 1957-61; prin. Wheel Gersztoff Friedman Assocs. Inc. (formerly Wheel-Garon Inc.), N.Y.C., 1961-72, pres., 1972—. Mem. Internat. Assn. Lighting Designers (founding, past pres.), Lighting Research Inst. (past bd. dirs.). Office: Wheel Gersztoff Friedman Assocs 12100 Wilshire Blvd Suite 480 Los Angeles CA 90025

WHEELER, BETTY ELLER, foundation administrator; b. Elkin, N.C., Feb. 21, 1938; d. Wade Edward and Dempsie (Smith) Eller; m. Stanley B. Wheeler, May 29, 1959 (div. June 1981); children: Mark Edward, Jonathan Burke. BA in Sociology, Tex. Tech U., 1958, postgrad., 1958-59. Elem. sch. tchr. 1959-60; dist. dir. Camp Fire Girls, 1960-63; child welfare worker Lubbock (Tex.) County Child Welfare, 1964-67; officer Lubbock County (Tex.) Juvenile Probation, 1967-68; vol. staff Nat. Camp Fire Girls, Tex. and N.Mex., 1975-76; cons. social services Milam's Children's Tng. Cen., Lubbock, 1975-76; asst. exec. dir. Lubbock Day Care Assn., 1972-77; cons. fund raising Easter Seal Soc., Lubbock, 1978; dir. Christian Edn. St. Paul's Epis. Ch., Lubbock, 1971-83; interim dir. All Saints Epis. Sch., Lubbock, 1980-81; exec. dir. YWCA Lubbock, 1981—; bd. dirs. Tex. Coalition Juvenile Justice 1986—; adv. council Cultural Affairs Council 1985—, Teen Connection 1987—. Bd. dirs. Lubbock Heritage Soc. 1985—; delegate St. Dem. Conv., Austin 1986; chmn. Elec. Utility Bd. 1982, City-county Health Bd., Citizens Com. for Lubbock County Juvenile Detention Ctr., South Plains Youth Council, Dupre and Parsons Elem. Schs. PTA, Tex. Tech Arts and Scis. Adv. Council, United Way, Lubbock Symphony Guild; del. 1970 Gov.'s Conference on Children and Youth; vol. Salvation Army Soup Kitchen; polit. campaign worker Dem. Party; participant in numerous other civic activities. Named one of Outstanding Young Women Am., Lubbock Bus. and Profl. Women's Club, 1968, Lubbock's Woman of the Yr., Altrusa Club, 1968. Mem. Nat. Assn. YWCA Execs., United Way Exec. Dirs. Assn. (past chmn.), S. Plains Chpt. Nat. Soc. Prevention Child Abuse (bd. dirs.), Interagency Action Council, Exec. Forum., Jr. League (community v.p. 1978-79, exec. com. 2 yrs., bd. dirs. 4 yrs., sustaining advisor 2 yrs.), Delta

Delta Delta (Tex. adv. council). Home: 3310 55th St Lubbock TX 79413 Office: YWCA 3101 35th St Lubbock TX 79413

WHEELER, BONNIE, therapist; b. Hamilton, Ohio, Mar. 25, 1953; d. Philip Thomas and Ruth Charlotte (Weber) W. BA, Kalamazoo Coll., 1975; MA, Western Mich. U., 1978; postgrad., Mich. State U., 1982—. Cert. social worker, Mich. Child care counselor Lakeside Boys and Girls Residence, Kalamazoo, 1975-78; dir. residence hall, counselor Nat. Coll. Edn., Evanston, Ill., 1978-79, dir. housing, counselor, 1979-80, dir. counseling and housing services, 1980-81; masters counselor Family Planning and Prenatal Clinic, Waukegan, Ill., 1981-82; intern crisis counselor ELDIR House Crisis Ctr. and Outpatient Clinic, Saginaw, Mich., 1982-83; mental health therapist Emergency Services, Lansing, Mich., 1984—; counselor Concern, Lansing, Mich., 1986-88, Psychol. and Behavioral Cons., East Lansing, 1987—; adv. programming bd. Mich. State U., East Lansing, 1983-84; vol. counselor Early Intervention Program, Richland, Mich., 1978; leader workshop Mich. State U., East Lansing, 1983, 84, 85; faculty adv. student orgn. Nat. Coll. Edn., Evanston, 1978-81. Presentor, leader Group Mgmt.: A Dynamic Approach, 1984, Team Bldg. and Leadership, 1984, Sex Roles and Lifestyles, 1981, 82, Counseling the Pregnant Teen, 1981. Mem. Am. Assn. Counseling and Devel., Assn. for Humanistic Psychology, Assn. for Humanistic Edn. and Devel., Assn. for Specialists in Group Work, Am. Mental Health Counselors Assn., Assn. for Humanistic Psychology, Looking Glass Music and Arts Assn. (pres. bd. dirs., Best Cookie award 1987), Lansing Folk Song Soc. Home: PO Box 6486 East Lansing MI 48826-6486

WHEELER, CAROL ESTELLE, educational administrator; b. Mobile, Ala., Sept. 9, 1936; d. Frederick G. and A. Estelle (Ryan) W. AB, Maryville Coll., St. Louis, 1958; MA in Philosophy, Georgetown U., 1971; MA in Edn., U. Chgo., 1976. Joined Sisters of Mercy, Roman Cath. Ch., 1959. Tchr. Mercy High Sch., Balt., 1961-68, asst. prin., 1971-72, advisor to beginning tchrs., 1976-77, pres., prin., 1977—; tchr. Bishop Toolen High Sch., Mobile, 1968-69; supr. student tchrs. U. Chgo., 1974-75, adminstrv. asst. MST program, 1975-76; mem. profl. standards and tchr. edn. adv. bd. Md. Dept. Edn., 1984-86. Trustee Loyola Coll., Balt., 1982-88, Mercy Hosp., Balt., 1985—, Cathedral Found. Bd., Archdiocese Balt., 1983—; del. provincial chpt. Sisters of Mercy, Balt., gen. chpt. Sisters of Mercy of the Union. Mem. Mercy Secondary Edn. Assn. (pres. 1983-87), Assocs. Research in Pvt. Edn., Assn. Supervision and Curriculum Devel., Nat. Assn. Secondary Sch. Prins., Nat. Cath. Edn. Assn.

WHEELER, LAURIE JILL, free-lance fashion stylist; b. Evansville, Ind., Feb. 15, 1959; d. Allan Gordon and Emily Ann (Iwen) W. Student, Bennington (Vt.) Coll., 1977-79; BFA, U. Miami, Coral Gables, Fla., 1982; student, Sch. of the Art Inst. of Chgo., 1988—. Prodn. artist Associated Graphic Prodns., Miami, Fla., 1980-82, Soileau Studio, Houston, 1982-83; free-lance designer Wilmington, Del., 1983-85; account coordinator/traffic mgr. Lyons Inc., Wilmington, 1985-87; sales assoc. and asst. visual presentation Talbots, Wilmington and Chgo., 1986—; freelance fashion stylist, 1988—; cons. mktg., fashion designer, Wilmington, 1987—. Mem. Golden Key, Phi Kappa Phi. Republican. Lutheran. Home and Office: 350 W Oakdale #806 Chicago IL 60657

WHEELER, LOTTIE MARIE, insurance specialist; b. Marshall, Tex., June 8, 1933; d. Johnnie and Azell Lois (Stanmore) Wright; m. Ira Brooks, Feb. 17, 1955 (div. 1957); m. Calvin Wheeler, Oct 7, 1957; Carlos Ray, Shannon Rozell. Student, Prairie View (Tex.) Coll., 1951-54, Wiley Coll., 1954-56, Ark. Bapt. Coll., 1961-62. Clk. admissions dept. McRae Sanitorium, Alexander, Ark., 1959-66; med. asst. Dr. Worthie R. Springer, Little Rock, 1966-72; specialist hearings and appeals Blue Cross and Blue Shield, Little Rock, 1972—. Recipient Key to City, Little Rock, 1971, Key to City, Kansas City, 1985, Key to City, Ft. Worth, Tex., 1987. Mem. Gamma Phi Delta (basileus 1971—, regional dir. 1985—, numerous awards). Democrat. Baptist. Lodge: Order Eastern Star (trustee Alexander chpt. 1960—). Home: 4102 Cobb St Little Rock AR 72204

WHEELER, PATTY NASH, newspaper publisher; b. Charlotte, N.C., Jan. 25, 1944; d. Benjamin Marion Nash and Ceil (Sypher) Murphy; m. Rowland McLamb Shelley, Aug. 17, 1968 (div. Feb. 1979); 1 son, Stephen Benjamin; m. 2d Thaddeus Alvin Wheeler, Jr., May 23, 1981. B.A. in Journalism, U. N.C., 1965. Lic. real estate broker, N.C. Reporter, News and Observer, Raleigh, N.C., 1965-67; writer, editor N.C. State U., Raleigh, 1968-70, 72-77; writer, alumni office Northwestern U., Evanston, Ill., 1970-71; dir. info. service N.C. Symphony, Raleigh, 1977-79; writer Carolina Country Mag., Raleigh, 1979-82; pub. Skyland Post, West Jefferson, N.C., 1982—; pres. Blue Ridge Communications, Inc., West Jefferson, 1982—. Bd. dirs. Northwest N.C. Devel. Assn., Winston-Salem, 1983-86, Ashe County Council on Aging, West Jefferson, 1983—; pres. Ashe County chpt. N.C. Symphony, West Jefferson, Raleigh, 1983, Nat. Com. for New River, 1985-87; sec. Ashe County Performing Arts Bldg. Com., 1983—; panelist N.C. This Week Sta. WUNC-TV, 1986—. Mem. N.C. Press Assn., Ashe County C. of C. (bd. dirs. 1983—). Democrat. Episcopalian. Home: PO Box 67 West Jefferson NC 28694 Office: Skyland Post PO Box 67 West Jefferson NC 28694

WHEELER, WENDY ROBIN, computer company executive; b. Washington, Aug. 25, 1953; d. Malcolm Frederick and Aurora Dorothy (Anas) W.; m. Ian Stanley Reid, Aug. 16, 1986; 1 child, Emily Claire. B.A. in Modern Lang. and Lit., Trinity Coll., 1975. Mktg. rep. IBM, Waltham, Mass., 1975-80; product mgr. Prime Computer, Natick, Mass., 1980-82, asst. to pres., 1982-83, dir. product mktg., 1983-86, v.p. systems mktg., 1986, v.p. sales support, 1986—; bd. dirs. Mass. Product Devel. Corp. Named 1984 Woman of Achievement in Bus. and Industry, Boston, YWCA, 1984. Mem. Profl. Council Boston (bd. dirs.), Women in Info. Processing. Office: Prime Computer Inc Prime Park Natick MA 01760

WHEELWRIGHT, ANN COULAM, publishing executive; b. Salt Lake City, Oct. 21, 1920; d. Charles Henry and Georgia (Billings) Coulam; m. Max Wheelwright, May 29, 1939; children: Margaret Ann Wheelwright Parry, Steven C., James C., Catherine Wheelwright Ockey, Scott, Thomas. Student, San Francisco Jr. Coll., 1936-37, Brigham Young U., 1937-39; BA, U. Utah, 1983. Sec.-treas., acct. Wheelwright Lithographing Co., Salt Lake City, 1947-76, Wheelwright Press Ltd., Salt Lake City, 1965—, Wheelwright Pioneer Publications, Salt Lake City, 1972—. Chmn. Salt Lake City PTA, 1954-68, pres. 1968-72; rep. Women's Legis. Council, Salt Lake City, 1968-72; dist. sec. Salt Lake City Reps., 1972-78; missionary, acct. Latter Day Sts. Ch., Toulouse, France, 1978-81, Island of Reunion, France, 1984-86. Home and Office: 1836 Sunnyside Ave Salt Lake City UT 84108

WHELAN, ELAINE GILLIGAN, nurse, educator; b. Waltham, Mass., July 14, 1945; d. Thomas Joseph and Rose C. (Walker) Gilligan; m. James Michael Whelan, May 15, 1971; 1 son, Brian James. BA, Jersey City State U., 1973, MA, 1974; BS in Nursing Pace U., 1977; MS in Nursing, Seton Hall U., 1980. Cert. gerontol. nurse practitioner. Staff nurse Holy Name Hosp., Teaneck, N.J., 1966, instr. nursing, 1967-74; staff nurse St. Elizabeth's Hosp., Brighton, Mass., 1967; assoc. prof. nursing Bergen Community Coll., Paramus, N.J., 1974—; clin. cons. Nurses Reference Library, 1981-83. Contbr. articles to profl. jours. Mem. Am. Nurses Assn. (mem. com. 1975-77), Holy Name Hosp. Alumni Assn., Jersey City State Alumni Assn., Pace U. Alumni Assn., Kappa Delta Pi, Sigma Theta Tau. Roman Catholic. Office: Bergen Community Coll 400 Paramus Rd Paramus NJ 07652

WHELAN, MARIE ELAINE, writer researcher; b. Everett, Mass., Apr. 22, 1952; d. William Francis and Edna Claire (Gardner) Whelan; m. Joseph Ambrose Cota, Sept. 8, 1979; children: G. William Cota, Christopher J. Cota, Katherine C. Cota. With Millipore Corp., Bedford, Mass., 1975-81; freelance writer, researcher Tewksbury, 1981—; corr. The Lowell (Mass.) Sun, 1984-85; writer Merrimack Valley Advertiser, Tewksbury, Mass., 1985-87. Supporter various child abuse prevention programs and youth athletic programs. Mem. Teh Nat. Writer's Club, Soc. for Tech. Communication, Am. Med. Writers' Assn., Soc. of Children's Book Writers, Nat. Assn. for Female Execs. Republican. Roman Catholic. Home: PO Box 534 Tewksbury MA 01876 Office: PO Box 648 Tewksbury MA 01876

WHELAN, SHARON ANN, nurse, educator; b. Owatonna, Minn., Dec. 6, 1944; d. Zenon and Mathilda (Dushek) Hincheski; m. William Earl Jester, Apr. 8, 1938 (dec. Apr. 1977); children: Scott Alan, Michelle Renee. RN diploma, St. Mary's Sch. Nursing, Rochester, Minn., 1965; BS in Nursing, Coll. St. Thomas, 1980; postgrad., U. Minn., 1984; MS in Health Adminstrn., Mankato State U., 1986. Charge nurse, in-service dir. Owatonna Health Care, 1972-74; sch. nurse Medford (Minn.) Pub. Schs., 1974-77; with mgmt. staff Owatonna City Hosp., 1965-77, head nurse intensive care, 1977-80; assoc., dir. patient care services Naeve Health Care Assn., Albert Lea, Minn., 1980-84; nursing instr. Austin (Minn.) Community Coll., 1984-85; sr. mgmt., dir. patient care services Health Cen. Owatonna, 1984—; cons. Ind. Nursing, Owatonna, 1984—, Ambulance Personnel, Owatonna, Albert Lea, 1977-84. Contbr. articles to profl. jours. Brd. dirs. Am. Heart Assn., Southeastern Minn., 1987, People to People, Owatonna, 1986. Recipient Citizen award Medford Pub. Sch., 1962, Women Leader award Health Cen. Corp./YMCA, 1986; grantee Grahm Chalmers Found., 1986. Mem. Nursing Adminstrv. Council of Health Cen. (bd. dirs. 1985—), Am. Orgn. Nurse Execs. (staff dist. 1985-87), Minn. Nurse Execs., Am. Hosp. Assn., The Exec. Female (nat.), Toastmasters Internat., Alumni Assn. St. Mary. Club: Exchange (Owatonna) (fundraiser). Home: 149 River View Dr Monticello MN 55362 Office: Health Cen Owatonna 903 S Oak Owatonna MN 55060

WHELCHEL, SANDRA JANE, writer; b. Denver, May 31, 1944; d. Ralph Earl and Janette Isabelle (March) Everitt; m. Andrew Jackson Whelchel, June 27, 1965; children: Andrew Jackson, Anita Earlyn. BA in Elem. Edn., U. No. Colo., 1966; postgrad. Pepperdine Coll., 1971, UCLA, 1971. Elem. tchr. Douglas County Schs., Castle Rock, Colo., 1966-68, El Monte (Calif.) schs., 1968-72; br. librarian Douglas County Libraries, Parker, Colo., 1973-78; zone writer Denver Post, 1979-81; reporter The Express newspapers, Castle Rock, 1979-81; history columnist Parker Trail newspapers, 1985—; columnist Authorship mag.; contbr. short stories and articles to various publs. including: Empire mag., Calif. Horse Rev., Host mag., Jack and Jill, Child Life, Children's Digest; author (non-fiction books): Your Air Force Academy, 1982; (coloring books): A Day at the Cave, 1985, A Day in Blue, 1984, Pro Rodeo Hall of Champions and Museum of the American Cowboy, 1985, Pikes Peak Country, 1986, Mile High Denver, 1987; lectr. on writing. Mem. Internat. Order of Foresters, Nat. Writers Club (treas. Denver Metro chpt. 1985-86, v.p. membership 1987), Parker Area Hist. Soc. (pres. 1987, 88).

WHERRY, RUTH MARIE, nurse, educator; b. Boone County, Iowa, Aug. 22, 1926; d. Eland Bates and Myrtle (Belle) Gardner; m. John D. Wherry (dec. Nov. 1958); children: Margaret, Martha, John, Marcy; m. Paul Ogilvie, June 1960 (div. July 1966); 1 child, Susan; m. Guy Dickerson, May 23, 1969 (div. Aug. 1974); 1 child, Ronald. RN diploma, Iowa Meth. Hosp., Des Moines, 1947. Pub. health nurse Iowa State Dept. Health Cass County, Atlantic, 1948-49, Iowa State Dept. Health Polk County, Des Moines, 1949-50; office mgr. Dr. Joe Standefer, Des Moines, 1950-52; asst. house supr., coordinator heart sta. Iowa Meth. Hosp., Des Moines, 1952-54; office mgr. Dr. Lyons, Uchiyama & Stewart Olson, Des Moines, 1954-60; instr. lic. practical nurse program Des Moines Adult Edn. Indianola Dist., 1966-67; dir. nursing Hutchison's Nursing Home, Des Moines, 1967-68, Jefferson Homes, Indianola, Iowa, 1969-71; staff nurse, intensive care Des Moines Gen. Hosp., 1975—; instr. critical care nursing Des Moines Gen. Hosp, 1985—. Pres. PTA, Carlisle, Iowa, 1964-65; bd. dirs. Bidwell-Riverside Community Ctr., Des Moines, pres. 1982-84; mem. steering com. Nurses for Harkin 1985, 86, 87, adv. com. Senator Harkin, 1986—. Recipient Citizen award Am. Legion Madrid Post, Napier, Iowa, 1943. Mem. Iowa Nruse's Assn. (various coms. 1984—), Am. Assn. Critical Care Nurses, Am. Nursing Assn., 7th Dist. Iowa Nurses Assn. (chmn. legis. com. 1981-82, pres. 1983—, Nurse of Yr. award 1986), Warren County TB & Health Assn. (pres. 1963-64). Democrat. Home: 2300 Glenwood Dr Des Moines IA 50321 Office: Des Moines Gen Hosp East 12th & Des Moines St Des Moines IA 50309

WHIGHAM, TERRI LEE, marketing executive; b. Riverside, Calif., May 8, 1953; d. Gordon Terrance and Virginia Lee (Warren) W. Student Merced Jr. Coll., 1979. Asst. to pres. BAC-Pritchard, Inc., Merced, Calif.; asst. to pres. Valley Sheet Metal, South San Francisco, Calif.; asst. to supt. Herman Christensen & Sons, San Carlos, Calif.; corp. treas. TransGlobal Mktg. Corp., San Francisco; v.p., sec./treas. D&B Buying Group; pres. Internat. Trading Resources, Internat. Almond Brokerage; exec. dir. Am. Sports Merchandising. Mem. Nat. Assn. Female Execs., Nat. Sporting Goods Assn., Far West Ski Assn. Democrat. Methodist.

WHILEY, JOAN MARGARET, public relations writer, journalist; b. Vancouver, B.C., Can. Jan. 4, 1930; d. Alfred Ernest and Mary Margaret Mathews Scoby; B.A., U. B.C., 1951; m. John D. Whiley, Dec. 21, 1955 (div. Jan. 1965); children—Philip Vincent, Louise Margaret, Anthony John. Writer, Chiswell & Assos. Public Relations, London, 1954-57; freelance writer, 1958-65; writer Nordstrom's, Inc., Seattle, 1965-68; creative supr. Cole & Weber, Inc., Seattle, 1968-71; dir. public affairs Seattle City Light, 1973-78; mgr. mem. relations Wash. Public Power Supply System, Seattle, 1978-82; freelance writer, journalist, contbr. editor Pacific Shipper, 1982—. Mem. bd. Univ. Dist. Community Council, 1979—. Mem. Pub. Relations Soc. Am. (accredited), Seattle Economists Club, Friends of the Earth, Mountaineers. Club: Wash. Athletic. Home: 5823 17th St NE Seattle WA 98105 Office: 1931 Second Ave Seattle WA 98101

WHINERY, DOROTHY COOKE (MRS. JAMES C. WHINERY), association executive; b. Louisville; d. Thomas and Abigail (Latimer) Cooke; B.S. in Music, Drake U., 1935; m. James Curtis Whinery, Oct. 9, 1938 (dec. Oct. 1955); 1 dau., Janet (Mrs. Jock Evan Thompson). Tchr. music pub. schs. Somers, Iowa, 1935-38; asst. buyer Younkers, Inc., Des Moines, 1941-45; nat. exec. sec. Sigma Alpha Iota, Des Moines, 1957—, nat. exec. bd., 1957—, mem. fin. planning group, 1981—. Bd. dirs. Des Moines Civic Music Assn., 1950-53, exec. sec., 1953-65. Recipient Sword Honor, 1950, Rose Honor, 1962, Ring Excellence, 1968, all Sigma Alpha Iota. Mem. Nat. Trust Hist. Preservation, Smithsonian Assos., Met. Mus. Art, Am. Bus. Women's Assn. Included in book Iowa Women at Work, 1979. Home: 1447 57th St Des Moines IA 50311 Office: 4119 Rollins Ave Des Moines IA 50312

WHIPPLE, BARBARA, graphic artist, writer; b. San Francisco, June 16, 1921; d. George Hoyt and Katharine Ball (Waring) W.; B.A., Swarthmore Coll., 1943; B.S., Rochester Inst. Tech., 1956; M.F.A., Temple U., 1961; children by previous marriage: Christine, Katharine; m. Grant Heilman, Aug. 14, 1961; 1 son, Hans. Tchr., Elizabethtown Coll., 1973-76, Franklin and Marshall Coll., 1974-76; grad. asst. Tyler Sch. Art, 1961; graphic artist; condr. workshops Adams State Coll., 1982, Colo. Graphic Arts Center, 1980, 82, Sangre de Cristo Art Ctr., Pueblo, Colo., 1985. One person shows include: Lebanon Valley Coll., 1973, Colo. Mountain Coll., 1979, Foothills Art Center, 1980, 84, Adams State Coll., 1982, 88, North Mus., Lancaster, Pa., 1988, West Nebr. Art Ctr., 1984; numerous invitational and group shows; co-author: Water Media Techniques, 1984; Water Media: Processes and Possibilities, 1986; bibliography: La Revue Moderne, 1969, Am. Artist, 1980, Colorado Outdoors, 1980; contbr. Am. Artist, 1971-80, contbg. editor, 1979-85. Bd. dirs. Swarthmore Coll., 1970-76; pres. Chaffee County LWV, 1980-81. Recipient 1st prize for prints Lancaster Open Juried Show, 1964, Best of Show award Liberal Religious Art, Denver, 1967, 1st prize for drawing Phila. Watercolor Club, 1979, others. Mem.Nat. Assn. Women Artists, Women Artists So. Colo., Associated Artists of San Luis Valley, Foothills Art Center, Colo. Artists Assn., Nat. Mus. of Women in Arts (founding), Chaffee County Council on Arts (pres. 1988). Home: PO Box 609 Buena Vista CO 81211 Office: 429 E Main St Buena Vista CO 81211

WHIPPLE, BEVERLY JEAN, medical clinic administrator; b. Portland, Oreg., Dec. 15, 1952; d. Kenneth C. and Myrtle Irene (Wales) W. Student Yakima Valley Coll., 1970-72; BA in Music with distinction, Cen. Wash. State Coll., 1975. Music tchr. West Valley Sch. Dist., Yakima, Wash., 1976-78; ind. truck driver, 1978-79; disc jockey Towne Plaza Disco, Yakima, 1979-80; co-founder, dir. Feminist Women's Health Ctr., Yakima, 1980-83, Everett, Wash., 1983-84, mem. quality assurance com., 1980—, exec. dir., pres., bd. dirs., 1984-85, v.p. 1985—. Conf. speaker Nat. Abortion Fedn., Atlanta, 1984, mem. conf. faculty; conf. speaker, Nat. Lawyers Guild, Seattle, 1985, Nat. Women's Studies Assn., Seattle, 1985, San Francisco, 1986; inservice speaker Planned Parenthood Affiliates Wash., Olympia, 1985; witness sub-com. on civil and constl. rights U.S. Ho. of Reps., 1985; speaker numerous other civic orgns.; creator video On the Barricades For Abortion Rights: What We've Learned and How We've Won Against the God Squads. Mem. Wash. State Assn. Abortion Providers (organizer, speaker 1987-88). Avocation: keyboard instruments, flute. Office: Feminist Women's Health Ctr 2002 Englewood St Yakima WA 98902

WHIPPLE, CAROL OWEN, rancher, business cons.; b. Amarillo, Tex., Apr. 11, 1940; d. Wiley Ducoe and Marian (Hall) Owen; student U. Ariz., 1957-59, Utah State U., 1960; m. Gordon S. Whipple, Mar. 26, 1980; children—Laura, Katherine, Randall. Owner, operator Creekwood Ranch, farming, horse and cattle breeders, Amarillo, 1960—; dir. Okla. Stud, Inc., Purcell, 1976-78, sec., 1978-80; sec. Rowel, Inc., comml. bldg. and property mgmt., Amarillo, 1975-79, pres., 1979—; owner, operator A New Idea, furniture leasing, 1979-80; pres. Sun Tans Unlimited, Inc., 1979-80; partner Whipple Assos., mgmt. cons., direct sales distbrs., 1981—; tng. cons. Neo-Life Tng. Center, Amarillo. Pres. Amarillo Girl Scout Council, 1974-78. Mem. Am. Soc. Profl. and Exec. Women, Nat. Assn. Female Execs., Am. Quarter Horse Assn., Appaloosa Horse Club, Internat. Entrepreneurs Assn., Nat. Fedn. Ind. Bus., Kappa Alpha Theta. Presbyterian. Home: Route 2 Box 370 Canyon TX 79015 Office: 4551 S Western St Suite 1 Amarillo TX 79109

WHIPPLE, ELEANOR BLANCHE, educational administrator, social worker; b. Bellingham, Wash., June 7, 1916; d. Charles William and Susan Blanche (Campbell) W.; B.A. in Sociology, U. Wash., 1938, M.S.W., 1949; Ph.D., U. Santa Barbara, 1982; m. Robert Auld Fowler, Oct. 1, 1938 (div. 1947); children—Lawrence William, Jeanice Marie Fowler Roosevelt. Lic. clin. social worker. Founder, dir. Camp Cloud's End, Deception Pass, Wash., 1939-42; therapist Family Counseling Service, Seattle, 1949-58; pvt. practice counselling, Burbank, Calif., 1958-60; social service dir. Hollygrove Children's Residential Treatment Center, Hollywood, Calif., 1960-66, exec. dir., 1966-81; adj. faculty Biola U., La Mirada, Calif., 1972-80; dean Grad. Sch. Calif. Christian Inst., Orange, 1981-85, pres., 1985—. V.p., bd. dirs. Christian Fellowship for the Blind, Inc. Mem. Nat. Assn. Social Workers (chartered), Assn. Christian Therapists, Acad. Cert. Social Workers, N.Am. Assn. Christians in Social Work (bd. dirs., disting. service award). Contbr. articles in field to profl. publs. Home: 1105 Mound Ave Apt 9 South Pasadena CA 91030 Office: Calif Christian Inst 1744 W Katella Ave Orange CA 92667

WHIPPLE, JACQUELINE CONANT, writer, media specialist; b. Columbus, Ohio, Mar. 31, 1921; d. William Horace and Gertrude Virginia (Bryant) Conant; A.B. magna cum laude, Mt. Holyoke Coll., 1943; postgrad. Art. Inst. Boston, 1974-79; m. David Collins Whipple, Sept. 6, 1944; children—Nancy, Roger, Leah, Benjamin. Reporter, Scarsdale (N.Y.) Inquirer, summers, 1939-43; scriptwriter radio dept. J. Walter Thompson Co., N.Y., 1943-45; reporter Washington Daily News, 1945-47; broadcast journalist, chief editorial writer Sta. WCRB-AM-FM, Waltham, Mass. and Boston, 1960-67; with Sch. div. Houghton Mifflin Co., Boston, 1967-88; freelance all media; jury chmn. excellence in pub. writing/support of edn. Council for Advancement and Support of Edn., Washington, 1981. Chmn. "Know Your Town"-Waltham LWV, 1951, v.p., 1953; pres. Cohasset (Mass.) PTA, 1963. Recipient Tom Phillips award, UPI Broadcasters of Mass., 1963; cert. of merit Art Inst. Boston, 1976.ons. Democrat. Unitarian. Clubs: Boston Women's City; Cohasset Yacht. Contbr. articles to popular mags. Home: 119 N Main St Cohasset MA 02025

WHISLER, JULIE DAWSON, communications executive; b. Columbia, Tenn., Aug. 28, 1958; d. James Edward and Beverly Ann (Roach) Dawson; m. Eric Wayne Whisler, Nov. 8, 1986. BS, David Lipscomb Coll., 1980. Sales sec. Southwestern Co., Nashville, Tenn., 1980; sec. Muscular Dystrophy Assn., Brentwood, Tenn., 1980-82; sec. No. Telecom, Inc., Nashville, 1982-83, licensing coordinator, 1983-85, specialist internat. mktg., 1985-86, supr. customer relations, 1986—. Vol. Muscular Dystrophy Assn., Nashville, 1982—, camp counselor, 1984-85, 86; pres. Marching Against Dystrophy, Nashville, 1983-85. Named one of Outstanding Young Women of Am., 1985. Office: No Telecom Inc 200 Athens Way Nashville TN 37228

WHITACRE, KAREN LYNN, financial executive; b. Stuttgart, Fed. Republic of Germany, Dec. 25, 1951; d. Eugene Maxwell and Marion Eileen (Jones) W. BS in Acctg. cum laude, Pa. State U., 1973. Auditor Peat, Marwick, Mitchell & Co., Trenton, N.J., 1973-75; chief mgmt. analyst N.J. Housing FIn. Agy., Mercerville, N.J., 1975-81; sales mgr., field underwriter Mut. of N.Y., North Brunswick, N.J., 1981-87; pres. P&R Fin. Services and Tax Planning, East Windsor, N.J., 1984-87; sr. sales trainer Merrill Lynch Pierce, Fenner and Smith, Princeton, N.J., 1987—; instr. Middlesex County Coll., Edison, N.J., 1983. Mem. Am. Inst. CPA's, N.J. Soc. CPA's, Nat. Assn. Female Execs., Am. Women's Soc. of CPA's. Home: 1 Witherspoon Court East Windsor NJ 08520 Office: PO Box 9032 Princeton NJ 08543-9032

WHITAKER, DIANE DANIEL, corporate planner; b. Lacrosse, Wis., Sept. 14, 1956; d. Lewis Edgar and Mary Ann (Wilson) Daniel; m. Ross Ward Whitaker, Feb. 15, 1987. AB, Mt. Holyoke Coll., 1978; MBA, U. Chgo., 1980. Comml. banking officer Marine Bank, N.A., Milw., 1980-84; asst. staff mgr. Wis. Bell, Milw., 1984-87, mgr., 1987—. Mem. fin. com. Great Blue Heron Council, Girl Scouts U.S., Waukesha, Wis, 1983-85, Friends of Ballet, Milw., 1987; sec. Metro. Milw. Civic Alliance, 1983-85. Lodge: Milw. Civitan (pres. 1984-85, sec. 1987). Office: Wis Bell 740 N Broadway Milwaukee WI 53202

WHITAKER, EILEEN MONAGHAN, artist; b. Holyoke, Mass., Nov. 22, 1911; d. Thomas F. and Mary (Doona) Monaghan; m. Frederic Whitaker. Ed., Mass. Coll. Art, Boston. Annual exhibits in nat. and regional watercolor shows; represented in permanent collections, Charles and Emma Frye Mus., Seattle, NAD, U.S. Internat. U., San Diego. Hispanic Soc., N.Y.C., High Mus. Art, Atlanta, U. Mass., Norfolk (Va.) Mus., Springfield (Mass.) Mus. Art, Reading (Pa.) Art Mus., Okla. Mus. Art, St. Lawrence U., Wichita State U., Retrospective show, Founders Gallery U. San Diego, 1988, pvt. collections; author: Eileen Monaghan Whitaker Paints San Diego, 1986. Recipient numerous major awards, including; several awards Allied Artists Am.; Fist Prize Providence Water Color Club; several awards Am. Watercolor Soc.; Wong award Calif. Watercolor Soc.; De Young award Soc. Western Artists; Springville (Utah) Mus. First award; Ranger Fund purchase prize; Orbrig prize NAD; silver medal Am. Watercolor Soc.; Watercolor West. Fellow Huntington Hartford Found., 1964; Walter Biggs Meml. award Nat. Acad. Design, 1987. Academician NAD; mem. Am. Watercolor Soc., Watercolor West (hon.), San Diego Watercolor Soc. (hon.). Home: 1579 Alta La Jolla Dr La Jolla CA 92037

WHITAKER, HELENA MARIE, computer programmer; b. Chgo., Oct. 19, 1953; d. Zdzislaw Teodor and Helena Louise (Jasiorkowska) Korbut; m. Jerry Whitaker, May 23, 1981; 1 child, Sarah Lynn. BS in Math., U. Ill., Chgo., 1977; postgrad., St. Louis U., 1977-78. Commd.2d lt. USAF, 1977, advanced through grades to 1st lt., 1979; systems analyst Air Force Global Weather Cen., Offutt AFB, Nebr., 1978-81; resigned USAF, 1981; sr. sci. programmer, analyst Computer Scis. Corp., NSTL Sta., Miss., 1981-83; supr. data processing Metro Area Transit, Omaha, Nebr., 1983-86; programmer, analyst Creighton U., Omaha, 1987—. Mem. Data Processing Mgmt. Assn. (chmn. calling com., co-chmn. computer graphics contest com.), Omaha Festival Folk Dancers (asst. to dir. 1979-80), Mid-Am. Woodcarvers Assn. Republican. Roman Catholic. Office: Creighton U Computing Adminstv 24th and California Sts Omaha NE 68178-0046

WHITAKER, MARY MANNING, journalist, photographer; b. Marlboro, Mass., Apr. 2, 1947; d. John Francis and Mary Virginia (Bordeleau) Manning; m. Frank D. Whitaker, July 15, 1975 (div. May 1980); 1 child, Michelle. BA in English, U. Nev., 1970. Copy girl Las Vegas Sun, Nev., 1965, reporter, 1966-71, Sunday editor, 1976-78, journalist, 1978—; info. officer Clark County Health Dist., Las Vegas, 1971-73; reporter AP Stanford, San Francisco, 1973-76. Mem. Pen Women of Am., Sigma Delta Chi (bd. dirs. 1986). Democrat. Unitarian. Office: Las Vegas Sun 121 S Highland Dr Las Vegas NV 89127

WHITAKER, REBECCA JANE, information retrieval specialist; b. Terre Haute, Ind., July 31, 1946; d. Prevo Loren and Mary Gorden (Boling) W. BS, Ind. U., 1968, MLS, 1972. Reference librarian Downers Grove (Ill.) High Sch., 1968-70, tchr., resource librarian, 1970-71; librarian, asst. prof. Western Mich. U., Kalamazoo, 1972-80; info. retrieval specialist Ind. Coop. Library Services Authority, Indpls., 1980—; adj. faculty Sch. Library Sci. Western Mich. U., Kalamazoo, 1977-79. Contbr. articles to profl. jours. Mem. ALA (sect. chair 1983-84, div. bd. 198—), Mich. Database Users Group (founder), Ind. Online Users Group (co-founder, bd. ex-officio), Ind. Library Assn., Beta Phi Mu, Pi Lambda Theta. Home: 3470 Sherburne Ln #C Indianapolis IN 46222 Office: Ind Coop Library Services 5929 Lakeside Blvd Indianapolis IN 46278

WHITAKER, SUSANNE KANIS, veterinary medical librarian; b. Clinton, Mass., Sept. 10, 1947; d. Harry and Elizabeth P. (Cantwell) Kanis; m. Daniel Brown Whitaker, Jan. 1, 1977. A.B. in Biology, Clark U., 1969; M.S. in Library Sci., Case Western Res. U., 1970. Regional reference librarian Yale Med. Library, New Haven, 1970-72; med. librarian Hartford Hosp., Conn., 1972-77; asst. librarian Cornell U., Ithaca, N.Y., 1977-78; vet. med. librarian Coll. Vet. Medicine, Cornell U., 1978—; sec. SUNY Council Head Librarians, 1981-83. Mem. Med. Library Assn. (cert., sec.-treas. vet. med. libraries sect. 1983-84, chmn. 1984-85, directory editor 1984—), Med. Library Assn. (upstate N.Y. and Ont. chpt.). Home: 502 The Parkway Ithaca NY 14850 Office: Cornell U NY State Coll Vet Medicine Flower Vet Library Ithaca NY 14853

WHITCOMB, CAROLE JANE BOUGHTON, education association executive; b. Omaha, Dec. 21, 1938; d. Harris Allen and Geraldine Lorraine (Webb) Boughton; (div.); children: Jeffrey Logan, Jennifer Rae. BA, Iowa State U., 1960. Assoc dir. devel. Northwestern U./Northwestern Meml. Hosp., Chgo., 1973-78; assoc. dir. Yale U. "Campaign Yale", New Haven, Conn., 1978-79; dir. major and corp. giving ABA, Chgo., 1979-84; exec. dir. Associated Coll. Ill., Chgo., 1984—; bd. trustee Goodwill Industries, Chgo. 1987—; sec., bd. trustees Found. for Ind. Higher Edn., 1988. Mem. Council Advancement and Support Edn., Nat. Soc. Fund Raising Exec., Exec. Club Chgo. (bd. dirs. 1987—), Econ. Club Chgo. (mem. com. 1984—), University Club Chgo. Club: U. Home: 1120 N Lake Shore Dr Chicago IL 60611 Office: Assoc Coll Ill 150 N Wacker Dr Chicago IL 60606

WHITCOMB, RAE JEAN, medical supplies company executive; b. Sturgis, Mich., Mar. 21, 1940; d. Ralph Wilford and Velma Jeanette (Guernsey) Whitcomb; student Purdue U., 1958-60; M.T., Pontiac Gen. Hosp., 1961; student Robert Morris Coll., 1974-78, Marywood Coll., 1978. Teaching supr. Parkview Meml. Hosp., Ft. Wayne, Ind., 1961-68; sales rep. Gen. Diagnostics, Morris Plains, N.J., 1968-70; chief med. technologist Citizens Gen. Hosp., New Kensington, Pa., 1970-74, Sewickley (Pa.) Valley Hosp., 1974-79; sales rep. Fisher Sci. Co., Pitts., 1979-81, eastern regional sales mgr., 1981-83, biomed. mktg. mgr., 1983-86, mktg. mgr., 1986—. Mem. Am. Soc. Clin. Pathologists, Am. Soc. Med. Tech., Pa. Soc. Med. Tech. Office: 711 Forbes Ave Pittsburgh PA 15219

WHITE, ANNE UNDERWOOD, geographer, consultant, researcher; b. Washington, Sept. 22, 1919; d. Norman and Anne Francis (Bayard) Underwood; m. Gilbert Fowler White, Apr. 28, 1944; children—William D., Mary B., Frances A. B.A., Vassar Coll., 1941. Jr. sociology sci. analyst U.S. Dept. Agr., Washington, 1942; econ. analyst, field examiner Nat. Labor Relations Bd., Washington, 1943-44; research asst. Gilbert F. White, Chgo., East Africa, 1966-72; editor Natural Hazards Research and Info. Ctr., Boulder, Colo., 1976-78; mem. profl. staff Inst. Behavioral Sci. U. Colo., Boulder, 1979—; cons. World Bank, Washington, 1980, U.S. AID, Nairobi, Kenya, 1982. Author: (with Gilbert F. White and David J. Bradley) Drawers of Water: Domestic Water Use in East Africa, 1972. Contbr. chpts. to books, articles to profl. jours. Mem., Boulder County Parks and Open Space Adv. Com., 1976-82, chmn., 1977; mem. Sunshine Fire Protection Dist. Bd., Boulder County, 1981-85, chmn., 1984; chairperson Boulder County Task Force on Services for Elderly, 1984; mem. Plan Boulder County Bd., 1985-88; active mem. Women's Forum of Colo., Denver, 1976—, Women's Democratic Club, Boulder, Plan Boulder County. Mem. Assn. Am. Geographers, Soc. Women Geographers, Colo. Water Congress, Acad. Ind. Scholars. Home: 624 Pearl St Boulder CO 80302 Office: U Colo Inst Behavioral Sci Box 482 Boulder CO 80309

WHITE, BARBARA GRUBB, nurse, educator; b. Churchland, N.C., Feb. 20, 1941; d. Howard Cowan and Beatrice Lowe (Curlee) Grubb; m. Ben Knox White, Apr. 6, 1963. Diploma in nursing, Rowan Meml. Hosp. Sch. Nursing, Salisbury, N.C., 1962; BA, Pfeiffer Coll., 1967; MEd, U. N.C., Charlotte, 1974; EdD, N.C. State U., 1982. Cert. counselor, N.C. Pediatric staff nurse Rowan Meml. Hosp., 1962-63, instr. nursing, 1963-70, assoc. dir. nursing services, 1970-71; sr. instr. Rowan Tech. Coll., Salisbury, 1971-80; clin. nurse specialist VA Med. Ctr., Salisbury, 1980-84, nurse, pub. health coordinator, 1984—; speaker, cons. various orgns. Walter Lowe Tatum scholar, 1959. Mem. Am. Nurses Assn. (cert. community health nurse), Nat. League for Nursing, Rehab. Nurses Assn. (reviewer edn. modules)., Rehab. Nursing Inst. (research task force). Methodist. Office: VA Med Ctr 1601 Brenner Ave Salisbury NC 28144

WHITE, BETTY, actress, comedienne; b. Oak Park, Ill., Jan. 17, 1922; m. Allen Ludden, 1963 (dec.). Student pub. schs., Beverly Hills, Calif. Appearances on radio shows This Is Your FBI, Blondie, The Great Gildersleeve; actress: (TV series) including Hollywood on Television, The Betty White Show, 1954-58, Life With Elizabeth, 1953-55, A Date With The Angels, 1957-58, The Pet Set, 1971, Mary Tyler Moore Show, 1974-77, The Betty White Show, 1977, (TV miniseries) The Best Place to be, 1979, The Gossip Columnist, 1980, (film) Advise and Consent, 1962; guest appearances on other programs; summer stock appearances Guys and Dolls, Take Me Along, The King and I, Who Was That Lady?, Critic's Choice, Bells are Ringing; star: (TV series) The Golden Girls, 1985— (Emmy award for best actress 1986). Recipient Emmy award Nat. Acad. TV Arts Scis., 1975, 76; Los Angeles Area Emmy award, 1952. Mem. Am. Humane Assn., Greater Los Angeles Zoo Assn. (dir.), AFTRA. Office: care William Morris Agy 151 El Camino Beverly Hills CA 90212 *

WHITE, BEVERLY JEAN, state legislator, corrections technician; b. Salt Lake City, Sept. 28, 1928; d. Gustave R. and Helene (Sterzer) Larson; m. M. Floyd White, Apr. 8, 1947; children—Susan White Morris, Douglas Floyd, Robyn White Bauder, David Scott (dec.), Wendy Jo White McCleery. Mem. Utah Ho. of Reps., 1971—; mem. Gov.'s Commn. on Status of Women, 1986—. Bd. dirs. Tooele Valley Regional Hosp., 1987—; Sunday Sch. tchr. Ch. of Jesus Christ of Latter Day Saints. Recipient Legislator of Year award Utah Social Workers, 1982, Woman of Year award Beta Sigma Phi, 1982; named Dem. Legislator of 1987, Utah State Dem. Com. Mem. Nat. Order Women Legislators (past treas.), Utah Orgn. Women Legislators (treas.), Tooele Dem. Women's Orgn., Bus. and Profl. Women's Club. Club: Tooele Womans (past pres.).

WHITE, CATHERINE JANE, nurse; b. Vandling, Pa., Feb. 14, 1937; d. William and Mildred (Wilson) Burt; m. Matteo A. Surico, Nov. 12, 1955 (dec. May 1972); children: Rocco, Matteo, William, Wayne, Mark, Sally, Allen; m. William J. White, July 24,1977; stepchildren: William, Melody, Stephen, Cheryl, Roxanne, Scott, Mark. AAS, Dutchess Community Coll., 1977; BS, SUNY, New Paltz, 1983, MPS, 1985. RN. Nurse Eden Park Nursing Home, Poughkeepsie, 1977-78; nurse Hudson River Psychiat. Ctr., Poughkeepsie, 1978-84, adminstr. nurse, 1984—. Pres. ladies aux. Fairview Fire Co., Poughkeepsie, 1957-58; insp. Bd. of Elections, Town of Poughkeepsie. Republican. Methodist. Lodge: Order Ea. Star (conductress 1983-84). Home: 51 Wilmar Terr Poughkeepsie NY 12601

WHITE, CLARA JO, graphoanalyst; b. County Cherokee, Tex., June 26, 1927; d. William and Elmira (Johnson) Walker; m. Jeff Davis White, May 5, 1950; children: Anita, Jackie, Mona Lisa, Jeris, Gina. Cert., Ft. Worth Bus. Coll., 1947; AA, Riverside City Coll., 1986; cert. mgmt. and supervisory devel., U. Calif., Riverside, 1986. Cert. Graphoanalyst 1977; cert. master graphoanalyst 1979; cert. mus. docent tng., 1977. Owner, pres. White Handwriting Analysis Service, Riverside, Calif., 1982—; lectr., cons. Graphoanalysis, Riverside, 1977—. Asst. editor (commemorative book) Reflections, 1986. Mem. YWCA, Riverside, com. Riverside Mental Health Assn., 1981—; v.p. Heritage House Mus., Riverside, 1981—, co-pres., 1985-86, pres. 1986-87; historian Riverside Juvenile Hall Aux., 1984—, pres., 1987—; vol. teacher's aide County of Riverside Juvenile Ct. Schs., 1979—; mem. Riverside Mus. Assocs., bd. dirs., 1985-87, vol. 1985-88, aux. historian 1984—, pres., 1987-88; mem. Met. Mus. Assocs., 1960—. Recipient Cert. of Merit Riverside County Probation Dept., F.H. Butterfield Sch., 1980; named Vol. of Yr. Riverside City Coll., 1982; named to Hall of Fame Riverside Juvenile Hall Aux., 1984; Golden Poet award, 1987. Mem. Internat. Graphoanalysis Soc. (life, cert. master graphoanalyst; 2d and 1st v.p., pres. So. Calif. chpt., pres. excellence award 1982, 83, 84), Internat. Graphoanalysis Chgo. Soc. (cert. of merit 1981), U.S. Olympic Soc., Nat. Assn. Female Execs., Smithsonian Inst. (assoc.), Riverside C. of C., The Research Council of Scripps Clinic and Research Found. Club: Women's Networking (Riverside). Home and Office: 7965 Helena Ave Riverside CA 92504

WHITE, CYNTHIA ADAMO, psychologist; b. Boston, Jan. 17, 1944; d. Sebastian Anthony and Olga Celia (Rizzo) Adamo; m. Michael Dale White, Aug. 26, 1972. BA, Fla. Atlantic U., 1968; MS, U. Miami, 1970, PhD, 1973. Diplomate Am. Bd. Medicine and Psychotherapists. Dir. program Dade County Youth Services, Miami, Fla., 1973-74; psychologist West Union (Ohio) Community Mental Health Ctr., 1974-75, Longview State Hosp., Cin., 1975-76; health psychologist VA Med. Ctr., Cin., 1976—; psychologist Eating Disorders Clinic U. Cin. Med. Ctr., 1978-83. Mem. Am. Psychol. Assn., Cin. Psychol. Assn. (sec. 1985-86, bd. dirs., 1986—), Sigma Psi. Club: Clifton Track (Cin.); Dayton Bicycle. Office: VA Med Ctr 3200 Vine St Cincinnati OH 45220

WHITE, CYNTHIA CAROL, sales executive; b. Ft. Worth, Oct. 16, 1943; d. Charlie Bounds and Bernice Vera (Nunley) Rhoads; m. Franklin Earl Owen, Oct. 20, 1961 (div. Jan. 1987); children: Jeffrey, Wayne, Valeria Ann, Carol Darlena, Pamela Kay; m. John Edward White, Jan. 1, 1988. Cert. Keypuncher, Comml. Coll., 1963; student, Tarrant County Jr. Coll., 1974-77; BBA in Mgmt., U. Tex., Arlington, 1981. Keypunch operator Can-Tex. Industries, Mineral-Wells, 1966-67; sec. Electro-Midland Corp., Mineral-Wells, 1967-68; exec. sec. to v.p. sales Pangburn Co., Inc., Ft. Worth, 1972-78; bookkeeper, sec. CB Service, Ft. Worth, 1978-82; sales coordinator Square D Co., Ft. Worth, 1982—. Mem. Nat. Assn. Female Execs. Baptist. Home: 916 Bering Hurst TX 76053 Office: Square D Co 5208 Airport Freeway Suite 110 Fort Worth TX 76117

WHITE, DORA ELIZABETH, realtor, broker; b. Chgo., Sept. 6, 1942; d. Wiley Henry and Lillie (Hatcher) Samuels; m. Norman White, Aug. 20, 1960 (div. 1981); children—Pamela Y., Brian L. Cert. in real esate Central YMCA Coll., 1964; Assoc. degree in Real Estate, Triton Coll., 1977; Course I Cert., Realtors Inst. Ill., 1981. Clk. typist Harris Trust & Savs. Bank, Chgo., 1960-67; broker, salesman Penny's Real Estate, Maywood, Ill., 1967-71; closing loan officer Kaufman & Broad Homes, Hinsdale, Ill., 1972-73; ind. real estate broker Chgo. and suburban Ill., 1973-78; owner, broker All Am. Realty, Oak Park, Ill., 1979—. Bd. dirs. Am. Tennis Found. Mem. Nat. Assn. Market Developers (chpt. pres. 1983—), Nat. Assn. Realtors, Ill. Assn. Realtors, Oak Park Bd. Realtors. Office: All Am Realty 56 Chicago Ave Oak Park IL 60302

WHITE, DORIS ANNE, artist; b. Eau Claire, Wis., July 27, 1924; d. William I. and Mary (Dietz) W. Grad., Art Inst. Chgo., 1950. One woman shows, IFA Galleries, Washington, Berestrum Art Center and Museum, Neenah, Wis., Bradley Gallery, Milw.; exhibited in group shows, Ill. Mus., Springfield, 1963, Art Alliance, Phila., 1963, Museum Modern Art, N.Y.C., 1967, Pa. Acad. Fine Arts, Phila., 1963, 64, 66, Art Inst. Chgo., 1963, Met. Museum, 1966, N.A.D., N.Y.C., 1962, 63, 64, 65, 67, Butler Inst. Am. Art, Youngstown, Ohio, 1960, 61, 63, 64, 65, Smithsonian Instn., Washington, 1960, Walker Art Center, Mpls., 1963, 64, Madison (Wis.) Salon Art, 1958-63, 64, Spanish Internat. Pavilion, St. Louis, 1969, Utah State U., Logan, 1969, 70, Cleve. Inst. Art, Miami (Fla.) U., Chautauqua (N.Y.) Art Assn., Soc. Four Arts, Palm Beach, Fla., Instituto de arte de Mexico, others; represented in permanent collection, Butler Inst. Am. Art, Walker Art Center, Milw. Art Center. Recipient Grand award, 1963, Grumbacker award, 1965, Paul Remmy award, 1964; all Am. Watercolor Soc.; Ranger Fund Purchase award; Obrig award both NAD; medal of honor Knickerbocker Artists, 1963; Four Arts award Soc. Four Arts, Palm Beach, 1963. Mem. NAD. Home: 2750 Church Rd Jackson WI 53037

WHITE, DOROTHY JEAN, insurance claims administrator; b. Salinas, Calif., Apr. 15, 1935; d. Emery Ward and Clarine Elaine (Wallace) Bell; m. James Paul White, Dec. 30, 1962. Student, Walla Walla Coll., 1957-58. Office mgr. H. Emmerson and Assoc., Portland, Oreg., 1959-64; mgr. claims prodcedures, documentation, tng. and internal quality control Blue Cross Blue Shield, Portland, Oreg., 1964—. Dir., promotor, fund raiser Statue of Liberty, Portland, 1985, 86. Named Woman of the Yr., Blue Cross of Oreg., 1977. Mem. Oreg. Accident and Health Claims Assn. Home: 895 NW Riverview Ave Gresham OR 97030 Office: Blue Cross and Blue Shield of Oreg 100 SW Market St Portland OR 97207

WHITE, DOROTHY T., nursing educator; b. N.Y.C., Dec. 11, 1923; d. Joseph V. and Pearle E. (Salter) Raymond; diploma in nursing L.I. Coll. Hosp. Sch. Nursing, Bklyn.; B.S., M.A., Ed.D., Columbia U.; diploma, Inst. Ednl. Mgmt., Harvard U., 1982; m. G.M. White, Jan. 5, 1952. Prof. nursing Med. Coll. Ga., Augusta, 1971-77, dean Sch. Nursing, 1971-76; prof. Nova U., Ft. Lauderdale, Fla., 1977-78, dir. The Louise Mellen Inst. Nursing, 1977-78; prof. Calif. State U., Sacramento, 1978-79, chmn. div. nursing, 1978-79; prof. Hunter Coll.-City U. N.Y., Hunter-Bellevue Sch. Nursing, N.Y.C., 1979—, dean, 1979-82; cons. Office of Chancellor, City U. N.Y.; dir. Augusta Radiation Center, 1973-76; govtl. appointee Master Planning Com. for Nursing in Ga., 1971-75. Bd. dirs. Nurses House, Nurse Ednl. Fund (pres. 1986-88); trustee Mt. St. Mary Coll., 1960-61, assoc. trustee, 1961-65. Recipient citation Office of Sec. State of Ga., 1977; Cert. of Appreciation, U.S. Army Health Services Command, 1977. Mem. Group for Advancement in Nursing (founder), Am. Acad. Polit. and Social Scis., AAUW, Am. Assn. Women in Higher Edn., Am. Assn. Female Execs., Am. Assn. Higher Edn., AAUP, Am. Assn. Univ. Adminstrs., Nat. Assn. Women Deans, Adminstrs. and Counselors, N.Y. Acad. Scis. Author papers in field. Office: 440 E 26th St New York NY 10010

WHITE, ELEANOR GREENBERG, state agency administrator; b. Memphis, Sept. 1, 1946; d. Herbert James and Edith (Becker) Greenberg; m. Barry B. White, June 4, 1967; children: Joshua Samuel, Adam Jacob, Benjamin Daniel. AB cum laude, Radcliffe Coll., 1967; M of Pub. Adminstrn., Northeastern U., 1975. Program analyst HUD, Washington, 1967-69; rep. multifamily housing HUD, Boston, 1970-74, sr. rep. multifamily housing, govt. tech. rep., 1974-76, chief multifamily housing programs br., 1976-83, acting dep. dir. housing devel., 1976-83; asst. coordinator housing studies Mass. Dept. Community Affairs, Boston, 1969-70; chief ops. Mass. Housing Fin. Agy., Boston, 1983-86, dep. dir., chief ops., chair inner city taskforce, 1986—; mem. career adv. bd. Radcliffe Coll., Cambridge, Mass., 1980—; mem. tech. adv. com. Mass. Rate Setting Commn., Boston, 1986—; lectr. in field. Bd. dirs. Govt. Ctr. Child Care Corp., Boston, 1977-79. Recipient Services to Humanity award B'nai B'rith New Eng. Realty Lodge, Boston, 1987; Loeb fellow Harvard U., Cambridge, 1978-79. Mem. Nat. Assn. Housing and Renewal Officials, New Eng. Women in Real Estate, Am. Mgmt. Assn., Mass. Assn. Mental Health (tech. adv. com. 1986—, bd. dirs. 1987), Citizens' Housing and Planning Assn. (bd. dirs.). Club: Radcliffe of Boston. Office: Mass Housing Fin Agy 50 Milk St Boston MA 02109

WHITE, ELYSE KAPLAN, consulting executive; b. Washington, Nov. 18, 1949; d. Ira H. Kaplan and Bernice (Klavan) Ousley; m. Lawrence Bernard Werner, July 12, 1970 (div. Sept. 1978); m. William Eugene White, Jan. 4, 1982; 1 child, Ilana Michele. BS, U. Md., 1971, MA, 1975; postgrad., Mich. State U., 1976-79. Tchr. Montgomery County Pub. Schs., Bethesda, Md., 1971-74; grad. asst. U. Md., College Park, 1974-76; instr. Prince Georges Community Coll., Lanham, Md., 1975-76; grad. asst. Mich. State U., East Lansing, 1976-79; organizational devel. specialist Marriott Corp., Washington, 1979-80, dir. corp. orgn., 1980-83; dir. tng. and devel. Goldome, Buffalo, 1984-85; sr. cons. COMSAT, Washington, 1985-86; pres. Competitive Dynamics, Washington, 1986—; fellow Congl. Mgmt. Found., Washington, 1982-83. Bd. dirs. Am. Lung Assn., Buffalo, 1984; cons. ARC D.C. chpt., Washington, 1987. Mem. AAUW (Outstanding Grad. Woman award 1975), Am. Mktg. Assn., Am. Soc. Personnel Adminstrn., Am. Soc. Tng., Nat. Council Career Women, Phi Kappa Phi. Office: Competitive Dynamics 1000 Connecticut Ave NW Washington DC 20036

WHITE, ETHYLE HERMAN (MRS. S. ROY WHITE), artist; b. San Antonio, Apr. 10, 1904; d. Ferdinand and Minnie (Simmang) Herman; ed. pvt. schs., instrs.; m. S. Roy White, Mar. 3, 1924 (dec.); children: Mrs. William Marion Mohrle, Patsyruth Wheeler. Exhibited numerous one-man, group shows, Tex.; represented pub. collections in U.S., pvt. collections in Switzerland, Germany, Sweden. Del. Internat. Com. Centro Studi E. Scambi Internationali. Mem. Anahuac Fine Arts Group, San Antonio, Beaumont, Galveston, Houston art leagues, Daus. Republic Tex., UDC, Pastel Soc. Tex., Watercolor Soc., Nat. League Am. Pen Women, Dallas Tex. Sumie Soc. of Am., Baytown (Tex.) Porcelain Guild. Episcopalian. Mem. Order Eastern Star. Clubs: Fine Arts (Anahuac); Artist and Craftsmen (Dallas). Author, illustrator: Arabella. Author: Poet's Hour. Home: PO Box 176 Anahuac TX 77514

WHITE, FLORENCE HELEN, library director; b. Chgo., Oct. 7, 1932; m. Clyde O. White; children: John, James. Library dir. Carter Lake (Iowa) Pub. Library, 1975—. Pres. Sr. Citizen Meal Site, Carter Lake, 1986-87. Mem. Iowa Library Assn., Iowa Small Library Assn. Home: 3113 Surfwood Dr Carter Lake IA 51510 Office: Carter Lake Pub Library 1120 Willow Dr Carter Lake IA 51510

WHITE, FRANCINE BUSCEMI, lawyer; b. Chgo., Feb. 27, 1956; d. Salvatore and Johanna (Lietzow) Buscemi; m. William White. B.A. in Polit. Sci., Loyola U., Chgo., 1978; J.D., John Marshall Law Sch., 1982. Bar: Ill. 82, U.S. Dist. Ct. (no. dist.), U.S. Ct. Appeals (7th cir.). Law clk. to fed. magistrate U.S. Dist. Ct. (we. dist.) Ill., Rockford, 1982-83; sole practice, gen., Rockford, 1982-84; asst. juvenile pub. defender Winnebago County, Rockford, 1983-84; assoc. trial atty. Lawrence J. Ferolie & Assocs. Ltd., 1984—. Mem. Ill. Indsl. Rules Adv. Com., 1988. Mem. allocations com. United Way, 1986-88. Mem. Winnebago County Bar Assn. (sec. young lawyers div. 1984-85), Ill. Bar Assn. (worker compensation law sect.), Ill. Trial Lawyers Assn., Am. Trial Lawyers Assn., Women Trial Lawyers, Caucus of Am. Trial Lawyers Assn.

WHITE, GERMAINE, account executive; b. Dallas, Jan. 8, 1959; d. Julius Cornelius and Gloria (Smith) White. B.F.A., So. Meth. U., 1980. Cert. tchr., Tex. Resident advisor So. Meth. U., Dallas, 1979-80; student tchr. Dallas Ind. Sch. Dist., Dallas, 1980; sub. tchr. Richardson Ind. Sch. Dist., (Tex.), 1981; contract adminstrs. AFTRA/Screen Actors Guild, Dallas, 1981-84; account exec. WBAP Radio, Dallas, 1984-86; account exec. Western Union Priority Mail, Inc., 1986—; mem. adv. bd. Two Byrds Pub. Co. Vice pres. edn. task force Dallas Urban League, 1983-84; vol. Richardson Symphony Orch. Named one of Outstanding Young Women of Am., 1985, 86. Mem. Assn. Black Communicators (sec. 1983-84, exec. bd.), Music Ednl. Nat. Conf., Assn. Broadcast Execs. Tex., Sociology Club So. Meth. U., Mu Phi Epsilon, Delta Sigma Theta. Office: Western Union Priority Mail Inc 12200 Park Central #120 Dallas TX 75251

WHITE, GINGER GALE, savings and loan association executive; b. Sulphur Springs, Tex.; d. James Maurice and Zettie Faye (Turner) Sheffield; 1 child by previous marriage, Cary Michael; m. Timothy Charles Dyring, June 26, 1987. Student, E. Tex. State U., Commerce, Tex. Mktg. specialist Schlegel Lining Tech., The Woodlands, Tex., 1981-84; account exec. Citicorp Homeowners, Houston, 1984-86; v.p. Houston Savings Assn., 1986—. Mem. Assn. Profl. Mortgage Women, Nat. Assn. Female Execs. Home: 4 North Brook Pebble Ct The Woodlands TX 77380 Office: Houston Savings Assn 1919 Allen Parkway Suite 100 Houston TX 77019

WHITE, GLENDA GALE, corporate executive; b. Newport News, Va., Sept. 24, 1949; d. Paul Oliver and Katherine (Owen) Warden; m. Alan G. White (div. Feb. 1986); children: Kimberly, Paul. AS in Mgmt. magna cum laude, Asnuntuck Community Coll., Enfield, Conn., 1983. Adminstrv. asst. Positions, Inc., Hartford, Conn., 1976-78; office mgr. Mark V Lab., Inc., East Granby, Conn., 1978-83; v.p. fin. and adminstrn., corp. sec./treas. Zwick Am., Inc., East Windsor, Conn., 1984—. Asst. to selectman Town of Suffield, 1983. Republican. Congregationalist. Club: Am. Soc. (Metals Park, Ohio). Home: 31 Bent Rd Windsor CT 06095

WHITE, GLORIA WATERS, university administrator; b. St. Louis County, Mo., May 16, 1934; d. James Thomas and Thelma Celestine (Brown) W.; B.A., Harris-Stowe Tchrs. Coll., 1956; M.A., Washington U., St. Louis, 1963, M. Juridical Studies, 1980; m. W. Glenn White, Jan. 1, 1955; 1 child, Terry Anita White-Finster. Tchr., St. Louis Bd. Edn., 1956-63, psychol. counselor, 1963-67; dir. office spl. projects Washington U., 1967-76, asst. to asso. vice chancellor personnel and affirmative action, 1975-88, vice chancellor for personnel, affirmative action officer, 1988—. Bd. dirs. Am. Assn. Affirmative Action, 1974-77; instl. chair Arts and Edn. Fund, 1975-88; mem. Eastern Dist. Mo. Desegregation and Adv. Com., 1981-82; bd. trustees, Blue Cross/Blue Shield of Mo., 1984—; adv. bd., Tchrs. Ins. Annuity Assn., 1988—. Accredited exec. in personnel; cert. life counselor, life tchr. Recipient citations Urban League, Pres.'s Council Youth Opportunities, Distinguished Alumni award Harris State Coll., 1987. Mem. Coll. and Univ. Personnel Assn. (bd. dirs. 1981-88, pres. 1986-87, 87-88, v.p. research and publs. 1981-85, pres.-elect 1985-86, immediate past pres. 198-88, v.p., Creativity award 1981, Disting. Service award 1983), Am. Soc. Personnel Adminstrn., St. Louis Symphony Soc., Delta Sigma Theta. Roman Catholic. Home: 545 Del Price Ct Saint Louis MO 63124 Office: Box 1184 Saint Louis MO 63130

WHITE, HARRIETTE GEHRINGER, manufacturing company executive; b. Clarksburg, W.Va., Dec. 18, 1925; d. Heister Guie and Mary Cordelia (Franklin) Rhawn; m. James W. Behringer, Nov. 7, 1947 (dec.); children: Cole Franklin, Rocklin Tufts, Marcy Rhawn, Liese Ann; m. Beanman TwittyWhite, Nov. 11, 1977. BS, Northwestern U., 1947; MA, U. Ill., Urbana, 1968. Editor My Weelky Reader Xerox Edn. Publs., Middletown, Conn., 1969-74; with pub. and guest relations dept. Internat. Ctr. Tng. and Mgmt. Devel., Leesburg, Va., 1975—. Author: Hidden Pictures, Animals Say Funny Things, Happy Holidays. Rutherford fellow, 1968. Mem. NOW, Women in Communications (pres. 1970), Pub. Relations Soc. Am. Democrat. Unitarian. Home: PO Box 1010 Leesburg VA 22075 Office: PO Box 2000 Leesburg VA 22075

WHITE, HELEN MURRAY, insurance agency owner, speech consultant; b. Springfield, Mo., June 8, 1933; d. Dorsey L. and Ama M. (Giboney) Murray; m. William C. White Jr., Aug. 8, 1954; children: William C. III, Julie Anne. BS in Edn., S.W. Mo. State U., 1954; postgrad., St. Louis U., 1962; MEd, Drury Coll., 1968. Cert. in speech pathology; chartered property and casualty underwriter; cert. ins. counselor. Tchr. various pub. schs., Mo., Ill., N.J., 1954-60; speech pathologist Spl. Sch. Dist., St. Louis County,, Mo., 1960-62; dir. Springfield (Mo.) Speech and Hearing Ctr., 1963-68; instr. Drury Coll., Springfield, 1968-80; v.p. Bill White Ins. Agy., Springfield, 1970—; ptnr. LearnFest Creative Seminars, Springfield, 1986—; cons. U.S. Med. Ctr. Fed. Prisoners, Springfield, 1970—. Chairperson Greene County Planning and Zoning Commn., Springfield, 1978-82; pres. Greene County Hist. Preservation, 1983-84; bd. dirs. Springfield Community Hosp., 1983—. Mem. Chartered Property Casualty Underwriters (chpt. pres. 1984-85), Cert. Ins. Counselors (bd. dirs., nat. faculty 1986—,), Am. Speech and Hearing Assn., Nat. Colloquium on Underserved Populations, Nat. Assn. Female Execs., Cert. Ins. Service Reps. (bd. dirs. 1988—). Democrat. Unitarian. Club: Network. Office: Bill White Ins Agy 1736 E Sunshine Springfield MO 65804

WHITE, INGRID DIANE, electric utility official; b. Worcester, Mass., Dec. 9, 1950; d. James Richard and Doris Elsie (Sieghardt) W. BA in Afro-Am. Studies, Polit. Sci., U. Mass., 1973; postgrad., U. Mich., 1987—. Adminstrv. asst. W.E.B. DuBois, U. Mass., Amherst, 1970-73; social worker Neighborhood Service Orgn., Detroit, 1974; probation officer City of Detroit, 1974-78; adminstrv. asst. to councilman Detroit City Council, 1978-82; power plant operator Detroit Edison Co., 1982-84, safety analyst, 1984-85, personnel specialist, 1985-87, program coordinator community and govt.

affairs, 1987—. Adminstr. Detroit Edison Polit. Action com., 1987—; active Ga. Prison Observers com., Atlanta, 1971; community organizer Miss. Action for Community Edn., Greenville, 1971-74, Inst. for Black World, Atlanta, 1971-74, Labor Def. Coalition, Detroit, 1971-74; office mgr. Cockrel for Council Campaign, 1977; mem. exec. bd., fundraiser Alliance for a Rational Economy, Detroit, 1978-82; trustee Detroit Inst. for Urban Policy Research, 1980-82; mem. steering com. Detroit Coalition for Nat. Health Service, 1981-82; chmn. planning com. Southeastern Mich. Food Coalition, 1987—; coordinator United Found., Detroit, 1985-86, 88; mem. adv. bd. Motlzn. Disabled Youth Leadership, Detroit, 1986-87; coordinator Cass High Sch. Adopt-A-Sch., Detroit, 1986-87; mem. Allocations panel Detroit Pub. Edn. Fund, 1987-88. mem. Utility Workers Union Am. (sec. local 223, 1983-84), Minority Resource Devel. Orgn. (bd. dirs. 1986-87), Women's Forum. Office: Detroit Edison Co 2000 2d Ave Detroit MI 48226

WHITE, JEAN TILLINGHAST, state senator; b. Cambridge, Mass., Dec. 24, 1934; d. James Churchill Houlton and Clara Jean (Carter) Tillinghast; m. Robert D. Price, May 18, 1957 (div.); m. Peregrine White, June 6, 1970. B.A., Wellesley Coll., 1956. Supr., programmer Lumber Mut. Ins. Co., Cambridge, 1964-70; selectman, chmn. Town of Rindge (N.H.), 1975-80; clk. regulated revenues N.H. Ho. of Reps., Concord, 1978-80, vice chmn. regulated revenues, 1980-82; mem. N.H. Senate, 1982—, chmn. fin. com., v.p., treas. Perry White, Inc., Rindge, N.H., 1970—; dir. Peterborough Savings Bank (N.H.). Chmn., Rindge Friends of Library, 1972. Republican. Unitarian. Office: NH Senate Room 120 Concord NH 03301 Other Address: Hampshire Rd Rindge NH 03461 *

WHITE, JERUSHA LYNN, lawyer; b. Kansas City, Mo., Nov. 30, 1950; d. Riley Vaughn and Edith Blynn (Ringen) W.; m. Larry D. Hancock, Jan. 5, 1969 (div. 1973); m. Stephen Perry Wasson, Nov. 30, 1978 (div. 1985). AS, Mo. State Fair Community Coll., 1974; BS, Cen. Mo. State U., 1978; JD, U. Mo., Kansas City, 1981. Bar: Mo. 1981. With Montgomery Ward & Co., Sedalia, Mo., 1968-69, Parkhurst Mfg. Co., Sedalia, 1969-71, United Farm Agy., Sedalia, 1972-73, Montgomery Ward & Co., 1973-74, Howard Truck & Equipment Co., Sedalia, 1974-75, McGraw-Edison Co., Sedalia, 1975-76, Rival Mfg. Co., Sedalia, 1977-78; buyer Hotel Equipment Co., Century City, Calif., 1978; law clk. Legal Aid of Western Mo., Kansas City, 1979-80, Horowitz & Shurin, P.C., Kansas City, 1980-81; assoc. Steve Borel/Steve Streen, Kansas City, 1982-83; sole practice, Sedalia, 1983-85; ptnr. Cope, Schuber & White, 1985-86; staff atty. Hyatt Legal Services, 1986—. Mem. ABA, Mo. Bar Assn. Democrat. Presbyterian. Home: 5500 NE Scandia Ln, Kansas City 65301 Office: Hyatt Legal Services 5522 NE Antioch Rd Kansas City MO 64119

WHITE, JOY MIEKO, communications executive; b. Yokohama, Japan, May 1, 1951; d. Frank Deforest and Wanda Mieko (Ishiwata) Mellen; m. George William, June 5, 1948. BA in Communications, Calif. State U., Fullerton, 1974, teach. cert., 1977; cert. bus. mgmt., Orange Coast Coll., 1981. Secondary tchr. Anaheim (Calif.) Union High Sch. Dist., 1977-80; tech. writer Pertec Computer Corp., Irvine, Calif., 1980-81; supr. large systems div. Burroughs, Mission Viejo, Calif., 1981-83; mgr. Lockheed div. CalComp, Anaheim, 1983-86; owner, pres. Communicator's Connection, El Toro, Calif., 1986—; lectr. UCLA, 1983—; adj. faculty, coordinator tech. communication program Golden West Coll., Westminster, Calif., 1987—; instr. U. Calif., Irvine, 1987—; condr. numerous workshops, profl. presentations, 1982—. Editor Modeska Wildlife Tucker, 1974. Active Performing Arts, Costa Mesa, 1986—. Mem. Soc. for Tech. Communication (sr., Mem. of Yr. Orange County chpt. 1987), Soc. Profl. Journalists, Nat. Assn. Female Execs. Democrat. Club: 7th Floor Wine (El Toro). Home: 21651 Vintage Way El Toro CA 92630

WHITE, JUANITA GREER, university regent, legislator, educator; b. Atlanta, Nov. 19, 1905; d. Harry Goldsmith and Cleio E. (Greer) Greer; A.B., Agnes Scott Coll., 1926; Ph.D., Johns Hopkins U., 1929; m. Thomas Sherman White, June 6, 1935; 1 dau., Sally M. Prof. biology and chemistry, chmn. dept. sci. Mary Baldwin Coll., 1930-35; instr. anatomy and physiology Bennett Jr. Coll., 1935-38; research chemist Bell Labs., Murray Hill, N.J., 1943, De Luxe Labs., 20th Century-Fox Film Corp., N.Y.C., 43-46; instr. chemistry Hunter Coll. Sch. Gen. Studies, N.Y.C., 1943-44, 49-51; asso. prof. sci. Willimantic (Conn.) State Tchrs. Coll., 1951-52. Mem. Nev. Assembly, 1970-72; mem. exec. bd. ARC, Dutchess County, N.Y., 1940-44, Millbrook (N.Y.) Vis. Nurse Com., 1938-44, 46-50; mem. Nev. Gov.'s Com. on Aging, 1959-66; del. White House Conf. on Aging, 1961; mem. Nev. Gov.'s Com. on Med. Edn., 1963-64; edn. chmn. Nev. Gov.'s Commn. on Status of Women, 1963-66; dir. Nev. Tb and Respiratory Health Assn., 1963-73, pres., 1972-73; Nev. commr. Western Interstate Commn. Higher Edn., 1965-74, mem. exec. com., 1965-74; adv. com. Nat. Def. for Lang. Centers U.S. Office Edn., 1966-67; adv. com. S.W. Regional Lab. Edn. Research, 1967-74, Nev. Higher Edn. Commn., 1963-69, Nev. Edn. Commn., 1965, Clark County Health Planning Council, 1972-76; mem. governing body Clark County Health Services Agy., 1976-79, chmn. plan devel. com., 1977-79; mem. Nev. adv. com. Rural Devel. Program, 1973-74; regent U. Nev., 1963-71, adv. com. Coll. Med. Scis., 1975-83, hon. mem., 1983—; trustee Nevada So. Univ. Land Found., 1966-79. Recipient Disting. Nevadan award U. Nev., 1972; Outstanding Alumna award Agnes Scott Coll., 1980; Juanita White Hall U. Nev. at Las Vegas named in her honor, 1976; Nev. State Med. Coll. Citation, 1988. Mem. AAUW (dir. Nev. state div. 1957-67, state pres. 1963-65, nat. com. on social and econ. issues 1961-63, mem. internat. fellowships award com. 1964-73, chmn. internat. awards com. 1967-73, mem. edn. found. 1967-71), Phi Beta Kappa, Sigma Xi, Beta Sigma Phi (hon.). Republican. Episcopalian. Home: 639 Ave I Boulder City NV 89005

WHITE, JUDITH LOUISE, child services administrator, consultant; b. Lodi, Ohio, Feb. 27, 1939; d. Henry and Charlotte Virginia (Spahr) Schmelzer; m. Downer Dale White, Sept. 4, 1959; children: Mark, Kelly, Kristy, David. AA, Northland Pioneer Coll., Holbrook, Ariz., 1980; postgrad., No. Ariz. U., 1984—, Ariz. State U., 1985—. Tchr. White Mountain Apache Head Start Program, Whiteriver, Ariz., 1976-80, child services coordinator, 1980-87; cons. Nat. Indian Head Starts, 1980—; trainer Indian Child & Family Conf., Phoenix and Albuquerque, 1982-86, Fetal Alcohol Syndrome-Indian Health Services, Whiteriver, 1984—; cons. White Mountain Apache Head Start Resource Access Project, 1984—; assoc. tchr. Northland Pioneer Jr. Coll., Holbrook, Ariz., 1985—; trainer pilot parent program; coordinator Whiteriver Pilot Parents. Mem. Coalition for Chronically Ill Children, Phoenix, 1985—. Mem. Council Exceptional Children, Nat. Assn. for Edn. Young Children, White Mt. Assn. for Edn. Young Children. Avocations: music, reading, spending time with grandchildren. Home: Box 707 Whiteriver AZ 85941 Office: Whiteriver Elem Sch PO Box 190 Whiteriver AZ 85941

WHITE, KATHERINE PATRICIA, lawyer; b. N.Y.C., Feb. 1, 1948; d. Edward Christopher and Catherine Elizabeth (Walsh) W. BA in English, Molloy Coll., 1969; JD, St. John's U., 1971. Bar: N.Y. 1972, U.S. Dist. Ct. (ea. and so. dists.) N.Y., 1973, U.S. Supreme Ct. 1976. Atty. Western Electric Co., Inc., N.Y.C., 1971-79, AT&T Co., Inc., N.Y.C., 1979-83, AT&T Communications, Inc., N.Y.C., 1984—; adj. prof. law N.Y. Law Sch., N.Y.C., 1987-88, Fordham U. Sch. of Law, 1988—. Vol. Sloan Kettering Inst., 1973, North Shore U. Hosp., 1975, various fed., state and local polit. campaigns; judge N.Y. State Bicentennial Writing Competition, N.Y.C., 1977-78; chmn. Com. to Elect Supreme Ct. Judge, N.Y.C., 1982. Mem. Am. Corp. Counsel Assn., N.Y. State Bar Assn. (young lawyers com., bus. and banking law com. real estate law sect., corp. counsel sect.), Nassau County Bar Assn. (membership com., environ. law com., real estate sect., young lawyers sect.), Assn. of Bar of City of N.Y. (adminstrv. law com. 1982-85, young lawyers com. 1976-79, judge nat. moot ct. competition 1979—), Cath. Lawyers Guild for Diocese of Rockville Ctr. (pres. 1980-81), St. John's U. Sch. Law Alumni Assn. (pres. L.I. chpt. 1986-88). Clubs: Metropolitan, Wharton Bus. Sch. N.Y. (N.Y.C.). Home: 5 Starlight Ct Babylon NY 11704 Office: AT&T Communications Inc 32 Ave of the Americas New York NY 10013

WHITE, KATHLEEN MAE, social worker; b. Lamar, Colo., Feb. 12, 1941; d. Cornelius William and Lillian Mae (Oswald) Hogan; A.A., U. Md., 1969; M.S.W., Our Lady of Lake U., 1976; B.S. cum laude, Tex. A. and I. U., 1972; m. Larry F. White, Mar. 30, 1959; children—Thomas William, Richard Edward, Judy Lynn, Ramona Marie. With Vol. Services, ARC, Wright Patterson AFB, Ohio, 1964-65, Randolph AFB, Tex., 1965-66, Sembach AFB, Ger., 1966-69; tchr. St. Augustines Cath. Sch., Laredo, Tex., 1970-71; social worker Tex. Dept. Public Welfare, San Antonio, 1972-74; tchr. Edgewood Ind. Sch. Dist., San Antonio, 1976-78; coordinator teenage mother's sch. Harlandale Ind. Sch. Dist., San Antonio, 1978-83; pvt. practice mental health social work, 1976—. VA stipend, 1975-76. Mem. Acad. Cert. Social Workers, Am. Assn. Social Workers, Am. Bus. Women's Assn., Our Lady of Lake U. Alumni Assn. Republican. Roman Catholic. Home: Rt 3 Box 180 B Cibolo TX 78108 Office: 214 Rosewood Universal City TX 78148

WHITE, KATHY ANN HURST, personnel executive; b. Spur, Tex., Sept. 20, 1944; d. Marion Clinton and Bernice Marie (Justice) Hurst; m. Danney Ray White, Feb. 18, 1968; (div. 1978); children—Andrea Dawn, Amy Michelle. B.A., U. Tex.-Austin, 1967. Civilian personnel, U.S. Army, 1967—, chief classification task force Army Communications Command, Sierra Vista, Ariz., 1978-81, chief position mgmt. and classification Army Health Services Command, San Antonio, 1981-83, chief Balt. field office Civilian Personnel Service, 1983—, U.S. Total Army Personnel Agy., 1987—; speaker at symposia and confs. on women's career devel., equal employment programs; mem. blue-ribbon com. Fed. Women's Program, Ft. Meade, Md., 1984. Active Girl Scouts U.S.A., Ariz. and Tex., 1964-67, 79-81; performer ch. choirs, vocal ensembles, 1976—; asst. dir. youth choir Ch. of Castle Hills, San Antonio, 1981-83; vol. Rock Ch. Ministries, Balt., 1983—; mem. Action Singles, Balt., Va. Internat. exchange fellow Girl Scouts U.S.A., Greece, 1965; recipient awards Dept. of Army. Mem. Nat. Assn. Female Execs., Classification and Compensation Soc., Internat. Personnel Mgmt. Assn., Womens Clubs Am. (bd. adv. editors, named Outstanding Young Woman of Am. 1967). Avocation: doll collecting. Home: 2842 Aspen Hill Rd Baltimore MD 21234 Office: US Total Army Personnel Agy Balt Field Office Ste 1114 31 Hopkins Plaza Baltimore MD 21201-2814

WHITE, LAURA KATHERINE, entrepreneur, color and image consultant; b. Glendale, Calif., Sept. 12, 1959; d. Lawrence Russell Moss and Jane (Olsen) Edwards; m. Nicolas Vincent White, July 21, 1984; 1 child, Nicole Evelyn. AA, Glendale Community Coll., 1979; BAE, Ariz. State U., 1982. Sales rep. Revlon, Inc., N.Y.C., 1983-87; tchr. Glendale Community Coll., 1985; cons. color and image Sunland, Calif., 1986—; model Louise Wells Ltd., Inc., Fullerton, Calif., 1986—; make-up artist, model Loreal, faze 2 and Let's Face It, Encino and Santa Ana, Calif., 1988—; tchr. Burbank and Glendale Parks & Recreation. Mem. Nat. Assn. Female Execs., Kappa Delta. Democrat. Mem. Ch. Religious Scientist.

WHITE, LELA MAE CAWTHRON, construction company consultant; b. Chgo., Feb. 23, 1920; d. Welburn McCoy and Janie Melon (Dunlap) Cawthron; m. James White, Apr. 6, 1962 (div. 1963). AA, Wilson Jr. Coll., 1940; BA, Roosevelt U., 1958. Exec. sec. HEW, Chgo., 1966-70, adminstrv. asst., 1970-72, equal opportunity specialist, 1972-81; cons. Samuels Constrn. Mgmt. & Engrs., Inc., Chgo., 1985—; exec. sec. to bd. dirs. Morgan Park Coop., Chgo., 1949-88. Mem. AAUW, Nat. Assn. Female Execs. Democrat. Club: Les Amies Social (Chgo.) (sec.). Home: 10817 S Bishop St Chicago IL 60643

WHITE, LOIS M., editor; b. Detroit, Aug. 4, 1931; d. Arnold George and Cecyl Abbie (Pond) Barker; m. George White, Sept. 25, 1954; children: Susan, Karen, Michael. Grad. high sch., Detroit. Claim adjuster Detroit Ins. Agy., 1951-54; sec. U.S. Govt. Office, Newport News, Va., 1954-55, Ford Motor Co., Novi, Mich., 1956-58; spl. writer Detroit News, 1977-80; mng. editor Audecibel Mag. div. Nat. Hearing Aid Society, Livonia, Mich., 1980—. Contbr. articles to profl. jours. Office: Nat Hearing Aid Society 20361 Middle Belt Livonia MI 48152

WHITE, LYNNE HANAVAN, television executive; b. Williamsport, Pa., Apr. 14, 1950; d. J. Hanavan and Charlotte (Bagot) White; m. John Croxton Nigg, July 5, 1986; stepchildren: Dorie, Marc, Stacy. BS, U. Kans., Lawrence, 1972. Cons. City div. Pfizer Inc., N.Y.C., 1973-76; account exec. ABC-Radio, Houston, 1976-77; dir. Western region Tex. Pharm. div. Warner Lambert Co., Morris Plains, N.J., 1977-80; assoc. Henri Bollinger Pub. Relations, Hollywood, Calif., 1980-82; sr. publicist Columbia Pictures TV, Burbank, Calif., 1982-84; mgr. media services NBC-TV, Burbank, 1984-88, Lynne White Promotions, Manhattan Beach, 1988—. Writer for mag. The Movie Guide, 1980-82. V.p., bd. dirs. Santa Monica (Calif.) Rep. Club, 1982-85. Mem. Publicists Guild of Am., Acad. TV Arts and Scis. Republican. Presbyterian. Club: Hollywood Womens Press (newsletter award 1985). Office: Lynne White Promotions Manhattan Beach CA 90266

WHITE, MARGITA EKLUND, television association executive; b. Linköping, Sweden, June 27, 1937; came to U.S., 1948; d. Eyvind O. and Ella Maria (Eriksson) Eklund; m. Stuart Crawford White, June 24, 1961 (div. 1987); children—Suzanne Margareta, Stuart Crawford. B.A. magna cum laude in Govt, U. Redlands, 1959, LL.D. (hon.), 1977; M.A. in Polit. Sci. (Woodrow Wilson fellow), Rutgers U., 1960. Asst. to press sec. Richard M. Nixon Presdl. Campaign, Washington, 1960; adminstrv. asst. Whitaker & Baxter Advt. Agy., Honolulu, 1961-62; minority news sec. Hawaii Ho. of Reps., 1963; research asst. to Senator Barry Goldwater and Republican Nat. Com., 1963-64; research asst., writer Free Society Assn., 1965-66; research asst. to syndicated columnist Raymond Moley, 1967; asst. to Herbert G. Klein, White House dir. communications, 1969-73; asst. dir. USIA, 1973-75; asst. press sec. to Pres. Gerald R. Ford, 1975; asst. press sec. to Pres., dir. White House Office of Communications, Washington, 1975-76; commr. FCC, 1976-79; dir. Radio Free Europe-Radio Liberty Inc., 1979-82, vice chmn., 1982; pres. Assn. Maximum Service Telecasters; bd. dirs., ITT, Rayonier Forest Resources Co., Armtek Corp., Washington Mut. Investors Fund; U.S. del. Internat. Telecommunications Union Plenipotentiary Conf., Nairobi, 1982; coordinator TV Operators Caucus, Inc., 1985-88. Mem. George Foster Peabody Adv. Bd., 1979-86. Recipient Disting. Service award U. Redlands Alumni Assn., 1974; Superior Honor award USIA, 1975. Mem. Exec. Women in Govt. (founding mem., sec. 1975), Women's Forum of Washington. Home: 7238 Evans Mill Rd McLean VA 22101 Office: 1730 M St NW Washington DC 20036

WHITE, NANCY, fashion consultant; b. Bklyn., July 25, 1916; d. Thomas J. and Virginia (Gillette) W.; student pvt. schs.; m. Ralph Delahaye Paine, Jr., July 25, 1947 (div. Dec. 1977); m. Clarence J. Dauphinot; children—Gillette Dauphinot Piper, Katharine Delahaye Paine; m. George Key Thompson, Nov. 1978. Fashion editor Pictorial Rev. mag., 1936-40; asst. fashion editor Good Housekeeping mag., 1940-47, fashion editor, 1947-57; asst. editor Harper's Bazaar, N.Y.C., 1957-58, editor-in-chief, 1958-71; fashion dir. Bergdorf Goodman, N.Y.C., 1972-74; dir. Gen. Mills; fashion cons., N.Y.C., 1974—; cons. fashion design Channel 13 Public TV; cons. spl. events Nat. Found. March of Dimes. Former mem. Nat. Council of Arts; mem. women's bd. Lighthouse for the Blind. Decorated knight Order Merit (Italy), Silver medal Merit (Spain); recipient N.Y. Designers award. Mem. Fashion Group (past pres.). Address: 3 E 77 St Apt 5C New York NY 10021

WHITE, NANCY ANN, cultural organization administrator; b. Rochester, N.H., Feb. 19, 1958; d. David Keith and Elizabeth (Gray) W. AS in Human Services, Mass. State Coll., Brockton, 1978; BS in Recreation, Lyndon State Coll., Lyndonville, Vt., 1980. Supr. recreation Newtown (Conn.) Park and Recreation Commn., 1980-81; dir. parks and recreation New Fairfield (Conn.) Park and Recreation Commn., 1981-83, Needham (Mass.) Park and Recreation Commn., 1983—; speaker Gov.'s Alliance Against Drugs, Mass., 1987—. Mem. Nat. Assn. Female Execs., Nat. Park and Recreation Assn. (cert. master profl.), Mass. Park and Recreation Assn. (v.p. 1986-88, pres. 1988-90). Office: Needham Park and Recreation Commn 1471 Highland Ave Needham MA 02192

WHITE, NANCY ELIZABETH, psychotherapist, artist; b. San Angelo, Tex., Feb. 8, 1935; d. John William and Vivian Olive (Harrison) Whitten; m. Kirkwood Coulter Myers, Nov. 25, 1954 (dec.); children—Kirkwood Coulter, Nancy Elizabeth; m. 2d, Robert Arthur White, Apr. 25, 1959 (dec. Oct. 1977); children—Mark Hadley, John Bradford. B.F.A., U. Houston, 1976, M.A., 1978; Ph.D. in Clin. Psychology, Union Experimenting Colls. and Univs., Cin., 1985. Profl. artist, Houston, 1970-77; art therapist Galveston County Hosp., Texas City, Tex., 1976-77; psychotherapist, Houston, 1978—; nat. seminar leader, Houston, 1983—; one-woman shows: Erdon Gallery, Houston, 1971, 72, Houston Bar Ctr., 1971; group shows include: Alfred Lee Gallery, Houston, 1975, Sol Del Rio Gallery, San Antonio, 1976. Recipient Merit award S.W. Watercolor Soc., 1976; 1st prize Jewish Community Ctr., 1976; citation Tex. Fine Arts, 1977; Merit award Watercolor Art Soc. Houston, 1977. Mem. Am. Assn. Marriage and Family Therapy, (clin.), Am. Assn. Sex Educators, Counselors and Therapists (cert.), Internat. Acad. Profl. Counseling and Psychotherapy, Am. Psychol. Assn. (clinical), Am. Art Therapy Assn. (registered art therapist), Watercolor Art Soc. Houston. Republican. Mem. Unity Ch. Clubs: Profit Seekers Investment (treas. 1965-70), Memorial Forest Garden (pres. 1960) (Houston). Home: 9023 Briar Forest Dr Houston TX 77024 Office: 4600 Post Oak Pl Suite 157 Houston TX 77027

WHITE, PAMELA JANICE, lawyer; b. Elizabeth, N.J., July 13, 1952; d. Emmet Talmadge and June (Howlett) W. BA with honors, Mary Washington Coll., 1974; JD, Washington and Lee U., 1977. Bar: Md. 1977, U.S. Dist. Ct. Md. 1978, D.C. 1979, U.S. Dist. Ct. D.C. 1979, U.S. Ct. Appeals (4th cir.) 1979, U.S. Ct. Appeals (D.C. cir.) 1981, U.S. Ct. Claims 1981, U.S. Ct. Appeals (2d cir.) 1983, N.Y. 1983, U.S. Dist. Ct. (so. dist.) N.Y. 1983, U.S. Ct. Appeals (9th cir.), U.S. Supreme Ct. 1981. Assoc. Ober, Kaler, Grimes & Shriver, Balt., 1977-84, ptnr., 1985—; mem. Md. Bd. Bar Examiners, 1986—. Note and comment editor Washington and Lee Law Rev. 1976-77, Washington and Lee Law Council 1983-87, emeritus mem., 1988—. Mem. ABA, N.Y. State Bar Assn., Md. State Bar Assn. (legal edn. sect. council 1987—), D.C. Bar Assn., Balt. City Bar Assn., Fed. Bar Assn., Women's Bar Assn. Md. (treas. 1986-87, v.p. 1987-88, pres.-elect 1988-89, bd. dirs. 1984-86), Md. Assn. Def. Counsel. Presbyterian. Office: Ober Kaler Grimes & Shriver 10 Light St Baltimore MD 21202

WHITE, PATRICIA ANN, management consultant; b. Newark, Oct. 23, 1942; d. Edgar Dennis and Anna Patricia (Simile) Savacool; m. Ronald Lee White, June 16, 1962; children: Lisa Anne, Christopher Lee. BS in Social Sci magna cum laude, Montclair State Coll., 1979; postgrad., Columbia U., 1979-80, New Sch. of Social Research, N.Y.C., 1984, Vt. Coll., Norwich U. Tchr. elem. sch. Absecon (N.J.) Bd. of Edn., 1968-70; sales rep, trainer Savacool Real Estate, Bloomfield, N.J., 1971-73; utilization coordinator Mountainside Hosp., Montclair, N.J., 1973-76; med. asst. Gastroent. Assocs., Montclair, 1976-77; exec. dir. Women Helping Women, Montclair, 1977-80; sr. mgmt. trainer Automatic Data Processing, Inc., Clifton, N.J., 1980-84; sr. mgmt. cons. The Equitable, N.Y.C., 1984-86; dir. mgmt. and orgn. devel. and planning Equicor, Nashville, 1986—; ptnr. The Spectrum Group, Brentwood, Tenn., 1988—; chairperson Women's Bus. Resource Group, N.Y.C., 1986-87; prin. cons. D.R. & W. West Caldwell, N.J., 1985-87. Co-founder Career Women's Network, No. N.J., 1982; bd. dirs., YWCA, Montclair, 1979-81. Mem. Human Resource Planning Soc., Organizational Devel. Network, Am. Soc. of Training & Devel. Democrat. Home: 1323 Robert E Lee Ln Brentwood TN 37027 Office: Equicor 1801 West End Ave Nashville TN 37027

WHITE, PATRICIA SMITH, home economist; b. Greenville, R.I., Dec. 13, 1928; d. Ernest Leslie and Ruth Althea (Leathers) Smith; m. Winfield Horace White III, June 21, 1949 (dec. July 1969); children: Cynthia Ellen, Deborah Lynn (dec.), Brian Winfield. BS in Textiles, Clothing and Related Arts, U. R.I., 1950; MS in Family and Community Devel., U. Md., 1972, PhD in Human Devel. Edn., 1981. Statis. quality control technician Oscar Mayer Meat Packing Co., Chgo., 1954; textile research technician Gillette Research Inst., Rockville, Md., 1965-67; extension agt. home econs. U. Md. Coop. Extension Service, College Park, 1967-77, area extension agt. community resource devel., 1978—; supervising agt. expanded food and nutrition edn. program USDA, Prince George's County, Md., 1969-77, Balt., 1971-72; community nutritionist St. Mary's Assn. Retarded Citizens, Leonardtown, Md., 1983—; agt. trainer U. Md. Coop. Extension Service, 1985. Author: (video) Parliamentary Procedure Instruction, 1987. Initiator, bd. dirs. Friends of Margaret Brent Garden, St. Mary's City, Md., 1983—; bd. dirs. Resource Conservation and Devel. Bd., La Plata, Md., 1986—. Fellow U. Md. Coop. Extension Service, 1971-72; U. Md. grantee, 1977. Mem. LWV (pres. St. Mary's County br. 1987—, Woman of Yr. 1981), AAUW (pay equity com., rep. Md. women com., chair choices St. Mary's County chpt. 1986—, Woman of Yr. 1986, 87, 88), NOW (St. Mary's chpt.), Common Cause, Orgn. to Save Social Security, Md. Community Resource Devel. (charter, chmn. membership, past pres. 1978—), Community Devel. Soc. (publs. com., past chair low income com. 1978—), Am. Home Econs. Assn. (cert., grantee 1982), Am. Inst. Parliamentarians. Democrat. Mem. Unitarian Ch. Club: Toastmasters (Leonardtown) (initiator, ednl. v.p. 1983—). Home: Rt 2 Box 82-1 Leonardtown MD 20650 Office: U Md Coop Extension Service Box 663 State Rt 245 Govtl Ctr Leonardtown MD 20650

WHITE, REGINA JACKSON, social services administrator; b. Lufkin, Tex., Dec. 7, 1957; d. Ewell Arthur and Doris (Harrison) Jackson; m. Kendall R. White, Mar. 17, 1984; 1 child, Rachell Channing. BS in Psychology, Sam Houston State U., 1980; MS in Human Relations and Bus., Abilene Christian U., Garland, Tex., 1982. Cert. social worker, Tex. Mgmt. intern City of Garland, Tex., 1980-84; support services coordinator City of Garland, 1984—. Mem. Community Involvement Coalition of Garland, 1986—. Mem. Nat. Assn. Social Workers, North Tex. Conf. of Minority Pub. Adminstrs. Baptist. Office: City of Garland 701 Clark St Garland TX 75040

WHITE, RUTH MIRIAM WEIHS, trade and fin. co. exec.; b. Vienna, Austria; came to U.S., 1947, naturalized, 1952; d. Hugo and Ilka (Herzog) Weihs; B.A. in Bus. Adminstrn., St. John's U., Shanghai, China, 1947; postgrad. N.Y.U., CCNY; m. Paul White, Sept. 18, 1949. Exec. sec. to chmn. bd. Pan Am. Trade Devel. Corp., N.Y.C., 1947-49, mgr., 1949-53, asst. v.p., 1953-58, v.p., 1958-74, sr. v.p., 1974—; pres. Indsl. Crystal Corp. Office: 2 Park Ave New York NY 10016

WHITE, SANDRA JEANNE, elementary educator; b. Peoria, Ill., May 23; d. Allen Noel Pate and Margaret Lucy (Stout) P.; m. Dale Eugene White Aug. 31, 1957; children—Cynthia Jeanne, Julie Ann Nelson. B.S. in Edn., Western Ill. U., 1967; M.S. in Edn., Ill. State U., 1974. Elem. tchr. Peoria Pub. Schs., 1967—; adj. instr. Ill. Central Coll. Bd. dirs., v.p., chmn. promotions Corn Stock Theatre; chmn. play selection com. Community Children's Theatre; active 1st United Meth. Ch., adminstrv. bd., council ministries, edn. chmn., mem. choir, tchr. Selected for 1981 Social Studies Colloquium Northwestern (Ill.) U., Follett Pub. Co.; Gov.'s Master Tchr. program nominee, 1984. Mem. AAUW, Peoria Edn. Assn., Ill. Edn. Assn., NEA (life), Assn. Supervision, Curriculum Devel., Ill. Assn. Supervision and Curriculum Devel. (editorial bd.), Ill. Assn. Tchr. Educators, Ill. Guidance and Personnel Assn., Delta Kappa Gamma, Phi Delta Kappa (newsletter editor Beta Psi chpt.). Office: 1704 W Aiken Peoria IL 61605

WHITE, SANDRA R., account representative, chemist; b. Houston, Oct. 18, 1948; d. Earl Douglas and Joleta (Phillips) Lively; m. Gerald Robert White, Sept. 30, 1983; children by previous marriage—Laurie Joanna, Jamie Racquel. Student San Jacinto Coll., 1966-68; B.S. in Chemistry, Sam Houston State U., 1970; MBA Houston Bapt. U. Grad. Sch. Bus., 1987. Chemist, Sorbotec, Inc., Houston, 1971-72, Champion Papers, Inc., Pasadena, Tex., 1974-75, Core Labs, Inc., Houston, 1981-82; account rep. Foxboro Co., Houston, 1982-88, mgr. instrumentation and controls product CSI/Instrumatics, Houston, 1988— ; moon rock chemist at Lunar Receiving Lab., Johnson Space Ctr., Brown & Root-Northrup, Houston, 1970-71; salesman Tex. Real Estate Commn., 1972—; mem. Act for Eight Community TV, Cousteau Soc. Charter mem. Nat./State Leadership Tng. Inst. on Gifted and Talented, Ventura, Calif. 1979—; mem. Houston Mus. Natural Sci., Houston Contemporary Arts Mus. Sam Houston State U. undergrad. research fellow in organic chemistry, 1969-70. Mem. Soc. Women Engrs., Nat. Assn. Female Execs., Am. Chem. Soc. (sr. mem.), Instrument Soc. Am., Nat. Mus. for Women in the Arts (charter), Nat. Assn. Corrosion Engrs., Instrument Soc. Am. (sr., bd. dirs. standards practices com. 1987, Standards and Practices com. liason). Republican. Methodist. Club: Christian Women's. Home: 5155 Cripple Creek Houston TX 77017 Office: CSI/Instrumatics PO Box 266724 Houston TX 77207

WHITE, STEPHANIE ALICE, lobbyist, lawyer; b. Schenectady, N.Y., Feb. 22, 1949; d. John Joseph and Elvira Louise (Geelan) Srodoski; m. Earl Timothy White (dec. Dec. 1983); 1 child, Katharine L. B.S., Empire State Coll., SUNY, 1977; J.D. magna cum laude, U. Bridgeport, 1981. Bar: Conn.

1982. Mem. Riccio & White, Bridgeport, Conn., 1982-84; atty. advisor to asst. sec., Office of Civil Rights, Dept. Edn., Washington, 1984-86; minority counsel Com. on D.C., U.S. Ho. of Reps., Washington, 1986-87; mgr. pub. affairs, Pitney Bowes, Inc., Stamford, Conn., 1987—. Named Grad. of Yr. Phi Delta Phi award, 1981. Mem. ABA, D.C. Bar Assn. Republican. Roman Catholic. Home: 109 Ledgebrook Dr Norwalk CT 06854 Office: Pitney Bowes Inc World Headquarters Stamford CT 06926-0700

WHITE, SUSIE ARVILLA, special education teacher; b. Hot Springs, Ark., June 22, 1951; d. Frank Joseph and Helen Arvilla (Small) Sluppick; m. Martin Miller White Jr., June 28, 1980; 1 child, Taylor Eric. MS in Spl. Edn., Henderson State U., 1979. Cert. vocat. evaluator, Ark. Tchr. Magnet Cove (Ark.) High Sch., 1974-76, Cutter Morning Star Sch., Hot Springs, 1976-77; vocat. evaluator Ctr. for Adult Handicapped, Benton, Ark., 1977-79, Hot Springs Rehab. Ctr., 1979-85; tchr. Lake Hamilton Jr. High Sch., Pearcy, Ark., 1985—. Mem. Ark. Children with Learning Disabilities. Democrat. Roman Catholic. Office: Lake Hamilton Sch Dist 105 N Wolf Dr Pearcy AR 71964

WHITE, VICKI G., rehabilitation counselor; b. Austin, Tex., Oct. 12, 1953; d. Ralph and Frances (May) White. BS in Edn. of Deaf, U. Tex., 1974, MEd in Vocat. Rehab. Counseling, 1974. Cert. tchr. of the deaf. Tchr. Tex. Sch. for the Deaf, Austin, 1974-78; vocat. rehab. counselor Tex. Rehab. Commn., Austin and Ft. Worth, 1979-85, 87—; rehab. specialist Regional Rehab. Exchange of S.W. Ednl. Devel. Lab., Austin, 1985-86; cons. 1986—; project coordinator supported employment Vaughn House, Inc., Austin, 1987; vocat. rehab. counselor Tex. Rehab. Commn., Austin, 1987—; vocat. communication specialist, TRC. Contbr. articles to profl. jours. Council mem. Travis County Council for Deaf, Austin, 1980-85; mem. Pub. Responsibility Com. Travis State Sch., Austin, 1985; alt. Pvt. Industry Council, Austin, 1988. Fellow U. Tex. 1978-79; recipient Spl. Merit award Tex. Rehab. Commn., 1984. Mem. Nat. Assn. for Deaf, Nat. Rehab. Assn., Nat. Assn. Female Execs., Am. Deafness and Rehab. Assn., Registry Interpreters for the Deaf. Office: Tex Rehab Comm 2412-A S Lamar Blvd Austin TX 78704

WHITE, VIRGINIA LOU, township official; b. Barberton, Ohio, Oct. 23, 1932; d. Lucius F. and Edith M. (Carlton) Converse; m. Neil Mason White, Sept. 8, 1956; children:William Neil, David Converse, Holly Susanne. BA, Baldwin-Wallace Coll., 1954. Sec. to exec. sec. Adult Edn. Found. (now Inst. for Civic Edn.) U. Akron, 1954-55, office mgr., 1955-57; tchr. bus. edn. Kenmore High Sch., Akron, 1957-59, Elyria (Ohio) Pub. high Sch., 1959-60; charter twp. clk Meridian Twp., Okemos, Mich., 1972—; del., alt. Mich. Rep. Conv., 1972—; pres. Converse Press. Mem. Mid-Mich. chpt. Mother's Against Drunk Driving; sec. Mich. Rep. Issues Com., 1979-80, vice chmn., 1981-87, corr. sec., 1987—; mem. Ingham County Rep. Exec. Com., 1972—; mem. exec. com. Rep. 6th Congl. Dist., 1980—; co-chmn. Ingham County Reagan/Bush Com., 1980-84; active com. Ruppe for Senate, 1982; chmn. Com to Support Police and Fire Mileage, Meridian Twp., 1982; co-chmn. Friends of Capital Area Transp. Authority, 1983; chaplain Mid.-Mich. Rep. Women's Club, 1988—. Mem. Internat. Inst. Mcpl. Clks., Mich. Mcpl. Clks., Mich. Assn. Clks. Mem. Christian Ch. Club: Mich. State U. Women's Sports Booster, Okemos Book. Lodge: Zonta (local pres. 1981-83). Home: 1641 Birchwood Dr Okemos MI 48864 Office: 5151 Marsh Rd Okemos MI 48864

WHITE, WINIFRED DEMAREST (MRS. HERBERT A. WHITE), editor; b. N.Y.C.; d. Peter Edward and Margaret (McLaughlin) Demarest; A.B., Coll. New Rochelle, 1914; postgrad. in journalism Columbia U. Extension, 1916-18; m. Joseph S. Gifford, Aug. 29, 1925 (dec. Feb. 1948); m. 2d, Herbert A. White, Nov. 14, 1964 (dec. Oct. 1972). Tchr. English, speech Bryant High Sch., N.Y.C., 1914-17; asst. to bursar Rockefeller Inst. Med. Research, 1917-26; asst. editor, asst. to exec. sec. AIME, N.Y.C., 1947-59, editor, 1960—; exec. sec. Soc. Women Engrs., N.Y.C., 1961-73, assoc. life mem., 1973—; cons. copy editor IEEE, 1981—; freelance editor miscellaneous papers, 1959—; editorial proofreader, 1978—. Recipient Ursula Laurus citation Coll. New Rochelle, 1977, Angela Merici gold medal, 1984; cert. of recognition and White Glove award Soc. Women Engrs. Editor: Ironmaking Proc., Open Hearth Proc., Honors Book, 1950-63, Proc. Conf. on Women, 1971; copy editor Trans. of ASHRAE, 1976-81. Home: 12 E 97th St New York NY 10029

WHITEBOOK, DENA KOENIGSBERG, psychotherapist; b. N.Y.C.; d. Louis and Yetta (Shapiro) Koenigsberg; B.A., Hunter Coll., N.Y.C., 1940; M.A., Pepperdine U., Los Angeles, 1976; m. Harold Plant, Oct. 30, 1943; children—Janet G., Richard P.; m. 2d, Edward F. Whitebook, Dec. 14, 1963. Sch. tchr., N.Y.C., 1945-47; crisis therapist Los Angeles Suicide Prevention Center, 1964-76; instr. UCLA Extension, 1975-77; pvt. practice psychotherapy, Beverly Hills, Calif., 1977—; dir. counseling Am. Inst. Family Relations, Los Angeles, 1978-82; tchr. human sexuality, clin. supr. LaVerne (Calif.) U. Extension, 1980-82; radio and TV panelist, 1967—; cons. in field. Mem. Am. Assn. Marriage and Family Therapists, Am. Assn. Sex Therapists, Educators and Counselors, Assn. Humanistic Psychology, Am. Assn. Suicidology, Internat. Assn. Suicide Prevention, Calif. Assn. Marriage and Family Therapists. Home: 320 N Maple Dr #405 Beverly Hills CA 90210 Office: 9300 Wilshire Blvd Beverly Hills CA 90212

WHITEHEAD, ARDELLE COLEMAN, advertising and public relations executive; b. Carrollton, Ohio, May 13, 1917; d. James David and Gilsie Dale (Hendricks) Coleman; m. W. Wilson Whitehead, Mar. 9, 1974. B.S., Wittenberg U., 1938. Various advt. agy. and corp. exec. positions, N.Y.C., Los Angeles, until 1966; consumer affairs specialist Jennings/Thompson, Phoenix, 1966-73; pub. communications mgr. Valley Nat. Bank, Phoenix, 1974-76; pres. Whiteheads Inc., Phoenix, 1976—. Author, pub. various advt. booklets. Named Adperson of Yr., Phoenix, 1978. Mem. Women in Communications (chpt. dir. 1977-83, named Woman of Achievement Phoenix chpt. and Far West region 1981), Pub. Relations Soc. Am. (chpt. dir. 1980-84, Percy award for excellence 1985). Clubs: Phoenix Advt. (dir. 1966-76, pres. 1974-75). Home: 337 E Pierson St Phoenix AZ 85012

WHITEHEAD, GERALDINE BOYD, school social worker; b. Syracuse, N.Y., Feb. 28, 1953; d. William Harlis and Mary Lou (Johnson) Boyd; m. William Marcel Whitehead II, Sept. 29, 1979; children: Geri Tahira, William Marcel III. B in Edn., Hamilton Coll., 1975; MSW, Syracuse U., 1979; postgrad., U. Bridgeport, Conn., 1979. Cert. tchr., nursery sch. to 6th grade, N.Y., social worker, Conn. Tchr. City of Utica (N.Y.) Bd. Edn., 1975-76; counselor Hillbrook Detention Home, Syracuse, 1976-79; family counselor II Family Services Woodfield, Bridgeport, 1979-84; sr. probation officer jud. dept. Office of Adult Probation, Bridgeport, 1984-86; sch. social worker, liaison psychiat. day treatment City of Bridgeport Bd. of Edn., 1986—; field instr. Sacred Heart U., Fairfield, Conn., 1980-84. Adv. Hutchings Psychiat. Ctr., Syracuse, 1978; drug core team coordinator United Way of Fairfield County, Bridgeport, 1986—; active Housatonic Girl Scouts Am. Whitney Young fellow, 1977-79; recipient Community Service award Sta. WIXT-TV, 1979; named Outstanding Young Women Am., 1988, Conn. Outstanding Young Citizens award, Conn. Jaycees and Sta. WVIT-TV, 1988. Mem. NEA, Negro Bus. and Profl. Women's Club (Profl. Accomplishment award 1988), Nat. Assn. Black Social Workers, Conn. Assn. Sch. Social Workers, Conn. Probation and Parole Assn., Nat. Black Child Devel. Inst., Nat. Assn. Female Execs. Home: 106B Smoke Valley Rd Stratford CT 06497 Mailing: PO Box 812 Bridgeport CT 06601

WHITEHEAD, HELEN MAY, small business owner, marketing consultant; b. Harrisburg, Pa., Sept. 1, 1951; d. Warren Benjamin Engle and Priscilla Jean (Zinkan) Kohlhaas; m. Darell Roger Whitehead, Jan. 27, 1973; 1 child, Gregory James. AA in Liberal Arts, U. Md.-European div. Germany, 1978; certificado de Suficiencia, U. Zaragoza, Spain, 1978; BS in Mktg., Northeastern U., 1982; BS in Bus. Adminstrn. with high honors, Auburn U., 1983; MBA, Simmons Coll., 1987. Mgr., sales rep. M&S Indian Jewelry, Griesheim, Fed. Republic Germany, 1978-79; message distbn. shift supr. U.S. Air Force, Scott AFB, Belleville, Ill., 1971-75, communications detachment controller U.S. Air Force Europe, Ramstein, Fed. Republic Germany, 1975-78; tng. dept. coordinator Aviation Simulation Tech., Inc., Bedford, Mass., 1982-84; regional sales mgr. Huang's Trading Co., Skokie, Ill, 1984-87; substitute tchr. Hanscom Primary Sch., Bedford, 1986-87, Quincy High Sch., 1987-88; pres., small bus. entrepreneur Uniques, Bedford, 1983-87; speaker in field. Scholarship chairperson Hanscom Officers' Wives Club, Bedford, 1982-84. Served with U.S. Air Force, 1971-78, ETO. Mem. Nat. Assn. Female Execs., Alpha Sigma Lambda. Home: 107 Dundee Rd North Quincy MA 02171-1305

WHITEHEAD, JANICE, real estate consultant; b. Reynolds, Mo., Aug. 7, 1924; d. Horace and Nellie (Ford) W.; m. Frank Bain, Mar. 23, 1960 (div. Sept. 1969); 1 child, Jessica Violet. Cert. in mortgage and fin., Horizon Fin. Inst., Miami, Fla., 1980; cert., Okla. Sch. Real Estate, 1981; cert. in ins., Chase Nat., Springfield, Mo., 1982. Pres. Native Am. Pub., Coalgate, Okla. and Berryville, Ark., 1970—; owner, pres. Land Dealers, Coalgate, 1980-86; pub., editor Distant Drums, Berryville, 1986—; owner, pres. Mortgage Foreclosers, Berryville, 1985—. Editor, pub. Choctaw Jour., 1984, newsletter editor, pub. Distant Drums, 1985—. Project dir. Only Way Indian Bapt. Ch., Keota, Okla., 1985-86. Mem. Nat. Assn. Female Execs., VFW (pres. ladies aux. 1985), DAV, Native Am. Cultural Soc. (nat. dir. 1984—), Chatha Soc. (project dirs. 1984-84), United Rabbit Growers Entity (advisor 1987—). Republican. Office: Mortgage Foreclosers Rural Rt 4 Box 994 Berryville AR 72616

WHITEHEAD, PATRICIA ANN, nurse; b. San Diego, Jan. 31, 1946; d. Normon Clyde and Mary Asunda (Fantoni) Collins; m. George M. Whitehead, June 12, 1966 (div. Mar. 1975); children: Garrett Grafton Rayne, Sharna Raynel. BS in Nursing, Loma Linda (Calif.) U., 1967, MPH, 1971; cert. Pediatric Nurse Practitioner, U. Calif, San Diego, 1979. RN, Calif. Pub. health nurse San Bernadino County, Calif., 1967-72, San Diego County, 1974; sch. nurse, pediatric nurse Vista (Calif.) Unified Sch. Dist., 1974-85; pediatric nurse practitioner Sharp Rees-Stealy Med. Group, San Diego, 1985—. Mem. Pres.'s Council, San Diego, 1984-85. Recipient USPHS scholarship, 1971. Fellow Nat. Assn. Pediatric Nurse Practitioners (cert. chmn. 1987—); mem. San Diego Assn. Pediatric Nurse Practitioners, Mothers Against Drunk Driving. Republican. Office: Sharp Reese Stealey Med Group 8901 Activity Rd San Diego CA 92126

WHITEHURST, SUSAN ALLEN, magazine editor; b. Newport, R.I., Aug. 18, 1954; d. Donald Lewis and Joan (Wardner) Allen; m. John Sanford Whitehurst, Oct. 12, 1974; children: Lindsay Kamer Whitehurst, Elizabeth Chapman Whitehurst. BA in English magna cum laude, So. Methodist. U., 1974; MS in Journalism, Northwestern U., 1975. Mng. editor Microelectronic Mfg. and Testing Lake Pub. Co., Libertyville, Ill., 1978-79; assoc. editor Bldg. Supply News Mag. Cahners Pub. Co., Chgo., 1975-78; sr. editor Security Distbg. and Mktg. mag. Cahners Pub. Co., Des Plaines, Ill., 1979-81, editor, 1981-86, editorial dir. Security Distbg. and Mktg., Security mags., 1986—; co-chair editorial adv. bd. Cahners Pub. Co., Newton, Mass., 1987-88, assoc. pub., 1988—. Recipient Jesse H. Neal award Am. Bus. Press, 1977, 81, 82-84, 86, Editorial Excellence award Am. Soc. Bus. Press Editors, 1982, 83, 85, Peter Lisagor award Soc. Profl. Journalists, 1982. Mem. Nat. Burglar and Fire Alarm Assn. (chair pub. relations com. 1986, Woman of the Yr. 1986), Nat. Fire Protection Assn., Phi Beta Kappa. Office: Cahners Pub Co 1350 E Touhy Ave Des Plaines IL 60018

WHITENIGHT, KATHY ANN, health care administrator; b. Bainbridge, Md., May 21, 1953; d. Herman David and Margie Ann (Dunn) W. AS in Psychology, Ricks Coll., 1973; BS in Psychology, Brigham Young U., 1976, gerontology specialist, 1985, MPA, 1986. Adminstr. Canyon Care Ctr., Idaho Falls, 1976-77; counselor, owner Diet Ctr., Kansas City, 1977-78; exec. asst. sec. Brigham Young U., Provo, Utah, 1978-79; assoc. dir. Multiple Sclerosis Soc., San Francisco, 1979-80; asst. to dean/adminstn. Brigham Young U., 1980—; coll. rep. Brigham Young Spl. Projects, 1985—. Contbr. articles to profl. jours. Social worker Mayor's Com. Hire Handicapped, Idaho Falls 1974. Mem. Adminstv. Mgmt. Soc. Republican. Mormon. Club: Great Salt Lake Dog Tng. Office: Brigham Young U 591 SWKT Provo UT 84602

WHITESIDE, ELIZABETH AYRES, lawyer; b. Columbus, Ohio, Feb. 24, 1960; d. Alba Lea and Virginia (Ayres) W. Student, Ind. U., 1978-80; BFA, U. Wis., Milw., 1982; JD, Ohio State U., 1985. Bar: Ohio, 1985, D.C., 1986, N.Y., 1988, U.S. Dist. Ct. (no. and so. dists.) Ohio, 1986, U.S. Ct. Appeals (6th and D.C. cirs.), 1986, U.S. Tax Ct., 1986. Dep. clk. Franklin County Mcpl. Ct, Columbus, 1981; law clk. Chester, Hoffman & Willcox, Columbus, 1983-84, Porter, Wright, Morris & Arthur, Columbus, 1984; assoc. Squire, Sanders & Dempsey, Columbus, 1985-87, Shearman & Sterling, N.Y.C., 1987—. Mng. editor Ohio State U. Law Jour., 1984-85. Mem. ABA, D.C. Bar Assn., Ohio Bar Assn., Columbus Bar Assn., Am. Judicature Soc., Phi Delta Phi. Republican. Methodist. Home: 260 W 52d St #5-K New York NY 10019 Office: Shearman & Sterling 599 Lexington Ave New York NY 10022

WHITESIDE, PEGGY SUE, civil engineer; b. Madison, Wis., Oct. 29, 1946; d. Clyde Clarence and Naomi Irene (Watt) W. BS in Agr., Civil Engring., U. Wis., 1970. Civil engr. Soil Conservation Service, Madison, Wis., 1970-79; project engr. Ayres Assocs., Eau Claire, Wis., 1979-86; pres. SOCON Engring., Inc., Waunakee, Wis., 1986—. Mem. Am. Soc. Civil Engrs. (pres. 1985-86 NW Wis. branch).

WHITESIDES, ELIZABETH IGLER (MRS. LAWSON EWING WHITESIDES), lawyer, club woman; b. Glendale, Ohio, Oct. 12, 1910; d. Herman Einhaus and Matilda (Voegtle) Igler; LL.B., U. Cin., 1932, J.D., 1967; m. Lawson Ewing Whitesides, June 29, 1935; children—Elizabeth Lawson (Mrs. David Garth Holdsworth), Lawson Ewing. Admitted to Ohio bar, 1932, U.S. Supreme Ct., 1968; pvt. practice law, Cincinnati, 1932—. Mem. Cin. Woman's Club; Town Club, Cin., mem. Glendale Lyceum; pres. Monday Class, Glendale, 1948-49, Glendale Village Gardeners, 1966-67. Mem. Cin. Council on World Affairs. Mem. Cin., Ky. hist. socs., Cin. Bar Assn., Order of Coif, Phi Delta Delta, Kappa Alpha Theta (pres. Cin. alumnae 1954-55). Episcopalian. Address: 840 Woodbine Ave Glendale Cincinnati OH 45246

WHITFIELD, GRACE GARREN, educator, media specialist; b. Morganton, Ga., Feb. 5, 1930; d. Frederick Jay and Bonnie (McDaris) Garren; m. Samuel Roy Whitfield, June 7, 1952; children: Bryan Jay, Sally R. Whitfield Creswell. BS, North Ga. Coll., 1952; MLS, West Ga. Coll., 1978. County clk. Fannin County Govt., Blue Ridge, Ga., 1949-50; tchr., asst. prin. Fannin County Sch. System, Blue Ridge, 1950-52; tchr. Atlanta City Schs., 1953-54, Cobb County Schs., Marietta, Ga., 1955-87; supervising tchr., media specialist Brown Elem. Sch., Smyrna, Ga., 1987—. Sch. rep. Smyrna Clean City, 1984—. Named Tchr. of Yr. Ga., Brown Elem. Sch., 1985. Mem. Ga. Assn. Educators (local pres. 1952-53), Ga. Library Media Dept, So. Assn. Schs. and Colls., Cobb County Assn. Media Specialists, Alpha Delta Kappa (various coms. 1983-85, state pres. 1986-88, advisor internat. conv. 1987). Baptist. Lodge: Order Ea. Star. Home: 2195 Trailwood Dr Smyrna GA 30080 Office: Brown Elem Sch 3265 Brown Rd Smyrna GA 30080

WHITFIELD, LEIGH COSBY, commercial property manager; b. Dallas, Aug. 19, 1952; d. Fred H. and Oneita F. (Needham) C. BA, So. Meth. U., 1974. Lic. real estate broker, Tex.; cert. property mgr. Office mgr. Exec. Enterprises, Inc., Dallas, 1974-78; office mgr. Joe V. Hawn, Jr., Developer, Dallas, 1978-79; assoc. buyer Zale Corp., Dallas, 1979-81; property mgr., supr. Fults Mgmt. Co., Dallas, 1981-84; mgr. Plaza of the Americas, Wynne/Jackson Mgmt. Co., Dallas, 1984-86; v.p. mgmt. Folsom Investments, Inc., Dallas, 1986—. Mem., vol. Dallas Mus. League, 1981-85; mem. Children's Arts & Ideas Found., Dallas, 1985; mem. Dallas Ballet Women's Com. Mem. Inst. Real Estate Mgmt., Bldg. Owners & Mgrs. Assn., Comml. Real Estate Women, Greater Dallas Bd. Realtors. Republican. Mem. Unity Ch. Avocations: floral arranging; antique collections; music performances.

WHITFIELD, SUSAN GANTT, dietary specialist; b. Albemarle, N.C., July 8, 1954; d. William Miles and Mavelene Lee (Scarboro) Gantt; m. Thomas Patrick Whitfield, Mar. 24, 1974; children: Shelly Nicole, Tiffany Lee. Grad. high sch., So. Pines, N.C. Various positions 1972-83; data processing coordinator Charter By-the-Sea Hosp., St. Simons Island, Ga., 1983-85, food service and purchasing specialist, 1985—, dietary specialist, 1985-88. Mem. Dietary Mgrs. Assn. (cert.). Democrat. Methodist. Lodge: Woodman of World. Home: 303 Atlantic Dr Saint Simons Island GA 31522

WHITING, OLLIE BETH, manufacturing executive; b. Oakland, Miss., June 18, 1953; d. Stephen and Lillie (Holman) Brown; m. John H. Whiting, Dec. 23, 1978; children: Dedrick Shaunn, Lakeisha Elizabeth. B in Acctg., U. Miss., 1974; M in Mgmt., U. Ark., 1986. Sr. acctg. clk. Dobbs-Life Savers, Inc., Memphis, Tenn., 1975-78, invoice acct., 1978-79; inventory control leader kimberly Clark Corp., Memphis, 1979-82, cost specialist, 1982-86; cost analyst Litton Microwave Cooking Products, Memphis, 1986-87, fin. analyst, 1987-88; cost, fin. analyst Ga. Pacific Corp., Atlanta, Ga., 1988—. tchr. Middle Baptist Ch., Memphis, 1979—; troop leader Girl Scouts Am., Memphis, 1986—; tutor Memphis City Sch. System, 1985-86; active Gardenview Elem. Sch., Memphis, 1986-87; rep. LeMoyne Owen Coll., Memphis, 1986. Mem. Nat. Assn. Female Execs., Am. Mgmt. Assn., Phi Gamma Nu. Baptist. Club: Toastmasters. Home: 2591 Charlestown Dr #3A College Park GA 30337 Office: Ga Pacific Corp 133 Peachtree NE Atlanta GA 30303

WHITING, SUSAN FRANCES HIGGINS, hosp. public relations adminstr.; b. St. Cloud, Minn., July 6, 1945; d. Daniel Malachy and Mary Frances (Helget) Higgins; B.A. in Speech and Theatre Arts/Journalism, Manakato (Minn.) State U., 1967; m. Ward Harrison Whiting, May 25, 1968; children—Edward James, Ian Daniel. Copywriter, Better Homes and Gardens, Des Moines, 1967-68; asst. editor IBM, Rochester, Minn., 1968-70; publs. editor, dir. pubic relations Hubbard Milling Co., Mankato, 1970-73; instr. speech, dir. pubic relations Ohio No. U., Ada, 1973-79; dir. public relations and devel. St. Luke's Hosp., Maumee, Ohio, 1979—. Mem. Women in Communications, Public Relations Soc. Am., Am. Soc. Hosp. Public Relations, Ohio Soc. Hosp. Public Relations, Am. Mktg. Assn. Roman Catholic. Office: 5901 Monclova Rd Maumee OH 43537

WHITLEY, ELIZABETH DURRELL, association executive; b. Comanche County, Okla., May 2, 1953; d. Jesse W. and Ann (Marshall) W.; B.A. in Polit. Sci. and Am. History, Sweet Briar (Va.) Coll., 1975. Staff asst. scheduling office Office of the Vice Pres., Washington, 1973-74; legis. liaison Cook Industries, 1975-77; dir. scheduling John Warner for Senate campaign, Va., 1978; asst. dir., congressional liaison AIA, 1979; legis. dir. Office of U.S. Congressman Barry M. Goldwater, Jr., Washington, 1980-82; staff asst. to Senator Paul S. Trible, Jr., Washington, 1983-85; exec. v.p. Nat. Council Agrl. Employers, Washington, 1985—; researcher polit. campaigns; fund raiser. Bd. dirs. Am. Council Young Polit. Leaders, 1981-82; chmn. Sweet Briar Washington Job Resources Council, 1975-77. Mem. Women in Govt. Relations, Sweet Briar Alumnae Assn., Washington Jr. League. Republican. Presbyterian. Club: Capitol Hill. Office: 499 S Capitol St Washington DC 20003

WHITLOCK, ELLEN DEAL, non-profit association administrator; b. High Point, N.C., May 8, 1955; d. Raymond Lester Jr. and Dorsey (Crumpler) Deal; m. David Evan Whitlock Sr.; children: David Evan, Jr., Dorsey Virginia, Leslie Ann, John Wilson. Student, Guilford Community Coll., High Point Coll. Small bus. owner High Point, 1974-79; exec. dir. Mental Health Assn., High Point, 1982—. Mem. program com. Guilford County Conf. on Youth, Greensboro, N.C., 1983—; mem. Guilford County Juvenile Delinquency Prevention Com., Greensboro, 1984—; v.p. Jr. League of High Point, 1984-85, chairperson adv. planning com., 1987-88; rep. Inner Agy. Council, High Point, 1985—; chairperson sr. ctr. task force United Services for Older Adults, Greensboro, 1985—; chmn. Guilford County Involvement Council, Greensboro, 1986—; co-chmn. Guilford County Commn. on Needs of Children, Greensboro, 1987—. Mem. Assn. Mental Health Profls., Mental Health Assn. N.C. (exec. dir. rep. 1985—, Spillman award 1986). Republican. Methodist. Office: Mental Health Assn in High Point 305 N Main St High Point NC 27262

WHITLOCK, MARY ELLEN JENKINS (MRS. DOUGLAS WHITLOCK), social worker, travel consultant; b. Brownville, Nebr., Sept. 3, 1906; d. John Crisler and Mabel (Sapp) Jenkins; student Sullins Coll., 1923-24, Ferris Inst., 1924; A.B., Ind. U., 1927; m. Douglas Whitlock, June 18, 1929; children—Douglas Whitlock II, Marilyn Whitlock Long, Sandra (Mrs. Theodore G. Driscoll, Jr.). Case worker Children's Aid Soc., Detroit, 1927-28, head adoption dept., 1928-29; case supr. Asso. Charities Washington, 1929-32; co-owner, sec.-treas. Global Travel, Inc.; travel cons., 1973—. Mem. Women's Inaugural Com., Washington, 1953, 57. Chmn. women's com. Devereux Found., Devon, Pa., 1959-61. Mem. League Rep. Women, Nat. Fedn. Rep. Women, Family Service Assn. of Am., Goodwill Industries Assn., Mental Health Assn., Vis. Nurse Assn.; trustee Family and Child Services, Washington, 1951-65, 1st v.p., 1962-65; v.p. Episcopal Ch. Women of Washington, 1963-69, pres., 1969-72. Recipient award Alpha Omicron Pi, 1963; award Episcopal Diocese Washington, 1972. Mem. Ind. Soc. of Washington (mem. exec. bd. 1932—, award 1962), Ind. U. Alumni Assn., Alpha Omicron Pi. Republican. Episcopalian (vestrywoman 1968-71, 74-79). Clubs: Little Garden (pres. 1938-40), Wednesday (pres. 1940-42) (Sandy Spring, Md.); Internat. Neighbors (1st pres. 1956-58)) (Washington); Women of St. Thomas (pres. 1960-62). Home: The Westchester Apt 504-B 4000 Cathedral Ave NW Washington DC 20016

WHITLOCK, RUTH HENDRICKS SUMMERS, music educator; b. McAllen, Tex., May 10, 1934; d. Harold Glen and Lucile (McKee) Hendricks; B.A. (Theodore Presser scholar), Newcomb Coll., New Orleans, 1955; M.A., Occidental Coll., Los Angeles, 1970; Ph.D. (Mu Phi Epsilon grantee), N. Tex. State U., 1981; m. Robert Edward Whitlock, Jr., June 2, 1972; 1 son, Hal; stepchildren—Karen, Robert Edward, III. Music tchr., choral dir., supr. Tex. public schs., 1955-73; teaching fellow music edn. and choral music. N. Tex. State U., 1973-75; assoc. prof. music edn. Tex. Christian U., Ft. Worth, 1975—, dir. music edn. studies, 1985—; tchr. clinics and workshops; founder, steering com. Tex. Music Edn. Symposia, 1977, 85. Mem. Music Educators Nat. Conf., Am. Choral Dirs. Assn., Tex. Music Educators Conf., Tex. Music Educators Assn., Tex. Choral Dirs. Assn., Pi Kappa Lambda, Mu Phi Epsilon (Outstanding Faculty award 1979). Republican. Episcopalian. Author: Choral Insights-General Edition, 1982; Choral Insights-Renaissance Edition, 1982; Choral Insights-Baroque Edition, 1985; co-author: Guide to Writing Curriculum and Planning Instruction, 1985; Sing, 1988; originator, co-editor: Conscience of a Profession, 1987. Home: 2712 6th Ave Fort Worth TX 76110 Office: Tex Christian U Dept Music Fort Worth TX 76129

WHITLOW, SHARON HOBART, municipal government official; b. Concord, N.H., Dec. 21, 1946; d. Robert Edward and Frances Eleanor (Horne) Hobart; m. David Andrew Whitlow, Dec. 1, 1973 (div. 1988); children: Lindsay Anne, Caitlin Frances. BA, Cen. Mich. U., 1969; M in Pub. Adminstrn., U. Conn., 1971. Research dir. Colo. Mcpl. League, Wheat Ridge, 1971; asst. to town mgr. Town of Vail, Colo., 1971-72; asst. personnel dir. City of Boulder, Colo., 1972-74; acting town mgr. Town of Windham, Maine, 1975; asst. to dir. Greater Portland (Maine) Council of Govts., 1975-79; project coordinator NW Mcpl. Conf., Mt. Prospect, Ill., 1979-80; asst. dir. Birth to Three, Eugene, Oreg., 1981-82; econ. devel. coordinator Lane Council of Govts., Eugene, 1984-88; asst. state dir. Oreg. Small Bus. Devel. Ctr. Network, Eugene, 1988—. Contbr. articles to mags. Bd. dirs. YWCA, Eugene, 1977-78; com. mem. United Way, Portland, 1975, bus. rep., 1986. Mem. Internat. City Mgmt. Assn. (bd. dirs. 1986—, horizons com. 1978-79, chair conf. planning com. 1988), Metro Area Bus. Assistance Group, Oreg. Market Place (bd. dirs., vice chairperson 1987), Council for Econ. Devel. in Oreg. (bd. dirs. 1985—, sec.-treas. 1987-88, v.p. 1988—). Home: 4441 Fox Hollow Rd Eugene OR 97405 Office: Oreg Small Bus Devel Ctr Network 1069 Willamette St Eugene OR 97401

WHITMAN, BETSEY SELLNER, math educator; b. Wilmington, Ohio, Apr. 21, 1938; d. William and Beatrice Elizabeth (Harger) Sellner; m. Harrison Carlton Whitman, Aug. 27, 1960; children: William George, Eliza Jane, Harrison Carlton II, Rebecca Suzanne. BA, Shimer Coll., 1958; MAT, Harvard U., 1959; MA, U. Fla., 1964; PhD, Fla. State U., 1975. Tchr. Conard High Sch., West Hartford, Conn., 1959-62; jr. coll. tchr. Gibbs Jr. Coll., St. Petersburg, Fla., 1964-65; tchr. Notre Dame Acad., St. Petersburg, 1966-67; from instr. to assoc. prof. Fla. A&M U., Tallahassee, 1967-83, prof., chair dept. math., 1983—; Owner, dir. The Math Place, Tallahassee, 1980—. Bd. stewards United Ch. in Tallahassee, 1978—; vol. Big Bend Hospice, Tallahassee, 1982—;. Mem. Nat. Council Tchrs. of Math, Fla. Council of Tchrs. of Math. (editor jours. 1979-85), Math. Assn. Am., Nat. Assn. Mathematicians, Assn. for Women in Mathematics, Women and Math Edn.,

Alpha Kappa. Democrat. Congregationalist. Home: 2228 Shirley Ann Ct Tallahassee FL 32308

WHITMAN, CLEMENTINE MCGOWIN, university administrator, oil company executive; b. Jackson, Ala., Apr. 15, 1943; d. Douglas DeVaughn and Juanita (Spann) McGowin; m. R. Wayne Whitman, Apr. 12, 1968 (div. July 1978). B.S., U. Ala., 1965. Teaching fellow U. Ala.-Tuscaloosa, 1965-68, fiscal asst., 1968-70; adminstrv. asst. U. Ala. Sch. Medicine, Birmingham, 1970-79; exec. asst. to internal medicine chmn. U. Tex. Med. Sch. Houston, 1979-88, mem. employee relations com., 1979-88, sec. com., 1979-82, chmn. com., 1983-84, 85-86; mem. pres.'s employee relations adv. council, 1983— (chmn. 1987-88); exec. asst. to internal medicine chmn. U. Ark. Coll. Medicine, Little Rock, 1988—. Mem. U. Ala. Alumni Assn., U.S. Figure Skating Assn., Boat Owner's Assn. of U.S. Presbyterian. Club: Birmingham Figure Skating. Home: 2200 Andover Sq #1002 Little Rock AR 72207 Office: U Arkansas Coll of Medicine Dept of Internal Medicine 4301 W Markham Slot 640 Little Rock AR 72205

WHITMAN, MARINA VON NEUMANN, economist; b. N.Y.C., Mar. 6, 1935; d. John and Mariette (Kovesi) von Neumann; B.A. summa cum laude, Radcliffe Coll., 1956; M.A., Columbia U., 1959, Ph.D., 1962; L.H.D., Russell Sage Coll., 1972, U. Mass., 1975, N.Y. Poly Inst., 1975, Baruch Coll., 1980; LL.D., Cedar Crest Coll., 1973, Hobart and William Smith Coll., 1973, Coe Coll., 1975, Marietta Coll., 1976, Rollins Coll., 1976, Wilson Coll., 1977, Allegheny Coll., 1977, Amherst Coll., 1978, Ripon Coll., 1980, Mt. Holyoke Coll., 1980; Litt.D., WilliamsColl., 1980; m. Robert Freeman Whitman, June 23, 1956; children—Malcolm Russell, Laura Mariette. Mem. faculty U. Pitts., 1962-79, prof. econs., 1971-73, distinguished pub. service prof. econs., 1973-79; v.p., chief economist Gen. Motors Corp., N.Y.C., from 1979, now group v.p. pub. affairs; sr. staff economist Council Econ. Advisers, 1970-71; mem. U.S. Price Commn., 1971-72; mem. Council Econ. Advisers, Exec. Office of Pres., 1972-73; dir. Mfrs. Hanover Trust Co., Procter & Gamble Co.; mem. President's Commn. for Nat. Agenda for Eighties; mem. Trilateral Commn.; mem. adv. com. on reform internat. monetary system Dept. Treasury, from 1977; mem. Consultative Group on Internat. Econs. and Monetary Affairs (Group of 30), from 1979; econ. adv. com. U.S. Dept. Commerce, from 1979. Bd. overseers Harvard Coll., 1972-78; trustee Princeton U., from 1979. Recipient Columbia medal for excellence, 1973; George Washington award Am. Hungarian Found., 1975; fellow Earhart Found., 1959-60, AAUW, 1960-61, NSF, 1968-70, also Social Sci. Research Council. Mem. Am. Econ. Assn. (exec. com. 1977-80), Commn. on Critical Choices for Ams., Atlantic Council (dir.), Council Fgn. Relations (dir. 1977—), Am. Fin. Assn. (dir. from 1979), Phi Beta Kappa. Author: Government Risk-Sharing in Foreign Investment, 1965; International and Interregional Payments Adjustment, 1967; Economic Goals and Policy Instruments, 1970; Reflections of Interdependence: Issues for Economic Theory and U.S. Policy; also articles; bd. editors Am. Econ. Rev., 1974-77; mem. editorial bd. Fgn. Policy. Office: Gen Motors Corp 3044 W Grand Blvd Detroit MI 48202 *

WHITMER, BARBARA BICAN, foundation director; b. Chardon, Ohio, May 27, 1936; d. Burdell Alvie Bican and Thora Maxine (Garber) Bican, Alvord, Lattimore; m. Tyler Whitmer; children: Paul Sherman, Lisa Michelle. BS in Edn., Miami U., 1958. Tchr. bus. West Geauga High Sch., Chesterland, Ohio, 1958-59, Dixon (Mo.) High Sch., 1959-60; adminstrv. sec. Ill. State U., Normal, 1960-63; pvt. practice realty Bloomington, Ill., 1974-81; dir. Brokaw Found., Bloomington, 1985—; asst. dir. devel. BroMenn Healthcare, Bloomington, 1985—. Mem. Nat. Assn. Hosp. Devel., McLean County Mental Health Assn. (treas. 1969), Bi-Nor Jr. Women's Club (pres. 1971-72, jr. dir. 1972-74), C. of C. (women's div. 1985—, mem. chair), Woman's Club of Bloomington (treas.). Republican. Mem. First Christian Ch. Home: 319 Garfield Dr Bloomington IL 61701 Office: BroMenn Healthcare 807 N Main St Bloomington IL 61701

WHITMIRE, KATHRYN JEAN, mayor of Houston; b. Houston, Aug. 15, 1946; m. James Whitmire (dec.). B.B.A. with honors, U. Houston, 1968, M.S. in Acctg., 1970. C.P.A., Tex. Audit mgr. Coopers & Lybrand, Houston, 1971-76; controller City of Houston, 1977-81, mayor, 1982—; mem. faculty bus. mgmt. U. Houston, 1976-77, mem. adv. com. Coll. Bus. Adminstrn., 1978-80; chmn. standing com. on arts U.S. Conf. Mayors, 1984—. Mem. adminstrv. bd. St. Paul's United Meth. Ch., Houston, 1972-75; bd. dirs., treas. Juvenile Diabetes Found., Houston, 1977; adv. bd. Houston YWCA, 1979-81, Houston Area Women's Ctr., 1978-79. Recipient Disting. Alumna award U. Houston, 1982. Mem. Am. Soc. Women Accts. (bd. dirs. 1972-73), Tex. Soc. C.P.A.s (chpt. bd. dirs. 1973-75). Office: Mayors Office PO Box 1562 Houston TX 77251 *

WHITMORE, BEATRICE EILEEN, labor association administrator; b. Harrisonburg, Va., Mar. 15, 1935; d. Everett Dulaney and Beatrice M. (Shorts) Ott; m. William Eugene Taylor, Sept. 30, 1955 (div. Mar. 1965); children: John David, Mark Wayne; m. Dale Wilford Whitmore, May 3, 1967; 1 child, Theresa Ann. High sch. grad., Harrisonburg. Clk. typist USAF Civil Service, Eglin AFB, Fla., 1956-58, Clark AFB, Phillipines, 1958-60; sec. USAF Civil Service, Wright-Patterson AFB, Ohio, 1960-75, fire insp., 1975-85, sec.-treas. local F-88, 1977-83, pres. local F-88, 1983-85, pres. emeritus, 1985—; fed. staff rep. Internat. Assn. Fire Fighters, Washington, 1985—. Leader, organizer Little Sparkies, Wright-Patterson AFB, 1976-79; den mother Boy Scouts Am., New Carlisle, Ohio, 1963-65. Served with USAF, 1953-55. Mem. Nat. Assn. Female Execs., Inc., Staff Reps. Union. Lodge: Job's Daughters. Home: 2311 Glade Bank Way Reston VA 22091

WHITNEY, CONSTANCE CLEIN, psychologist, consultant; b. Seattle, Nov. 12, 1931; BA, Stanford U., 1952; MA, Washington U., St. Louis, 1977, PhD, 1984; children: Mark R. Wittcoff, Caroline C. Wittcoff. Instr., U. Mo., St. Louis, 1976-78; clin. research asst. med. sch., Washington U., 1977-80; motivation research dir. 1980-84, fellow in bus. mgmt. 1983-86. Bd. dirs., Am. Heart Assn., UN commn. to Eliminate Discrimination; leadership cons., Loyola-Marymount U., Girl Scouts Am. Mem. Bus. and Profl. Women, Am. Psychol. Assn., Calif. Psychol. Assn., Assn. for Advancement Behavioral Therapy, AAUP, Am. Ednl. Research Assn., Internat. Soc. for Polit. Psychology, Am. Soc. Tng. and Devel., Acad. Mgmt., Mt. St. Mary's Coll. Alumni Assn., Stanford Univ. Alumni. Author: Effective Learning Skills, 1977, What is Treatment?, 1977, Social Network Characteristics of Hospitalized Depressed Patients, 1982; writer, dir. film Women and Money: Myths and Realities, 1976. Home: 10601 Wilshire Blvd Los Angeles CA 90024

WHITNEY, JANE, foreign service officer; b. Champaign, Ill., July 15, 1941; d. Robert F. and Mussette (Cary) W. BA, Beloit Coll., 1963; CD, U. Aix, Marseille, France, 1962. Joined Fgn. Service, U.S. Dept. State, 1965, vice consul, Saigon, Vietnam, 1966-68, career counselor, 1968-70, spl. asst. Office of Dir. Gen.,, 1970-72, consul, Stuttgart, Fed. Republic Germany, 1972-74, Ankara, Turkey, 1974-76, spl. asst. Office of Asst. Sec. for Consular Affairs, 1976-77, mem. Bd. Examiners Fgn. Service, 1977-78, 79-81, consul, Munich, Fed. Republic Germany, 1978-79, Buenos Aires, Argentina, 1981-82, ethics officer Office of Legal Adviser, 1982-85, advisor Office of Asst. Sec. for Diplomatic Security, 1985-86, dep. prin. officer, consul, Stuttgart, 1986—. Recipient awards U.S. Dept. State, 1968, 70, 81, 85, 87. Democrat. Roman Catholic.

WHITNEY, MELANIE, postal inspector; b. Beaumont, Tex., Nov. 2, 1954; d. Fred Emory and Betty June (West) W. BA in English, Lamar U., 1977. Social worker Tex. Dept. Human Resources, Beaumont, 1978-82; postal carrier U.S. Postal Service, Nederland, Tex., 1982-84; postal clk. U.S. Postal Service, Beaumont, 1984-85; postal insp. U.S. Postal Inspection Service, New Orleans, 1985—; social work assoc. Tex. Dept. Human Services, Austin, 1982—. Mem. Internat. Assn. Credit Card Investigators. Democrat. Home: 4151 Division St #116 Metairie LA 70002-3247 Office: US Postal Insp Service PO Box 51690 701 Loyola New Orleans LA 70151-1690

WHITNEY, MYRNA-LYNNE, logistics engineer; b. Montreal, Que., Can., May 27, 1942; came to U.S., 1949, naturalized, 1962; d. Edmund W. and Florence S. (Richardson) Prasloski; B.A. magna cum laude, Calif. State U.-Northridge, 1971; M.S., Central Mo. State U., 1975; m. Richard A. Whitney, Jan. 2, 1977. Sec., Rockwell Internat., Canoga Park, Calif., 1962-69, methods and procedures analyst, 1976-77, environ. health and safety engr., 1977-79, system safety engr., 1979-81, developer missile support plan, 1981-84, tech. asst. space shuttle program, 1984; logistics specialist Dept. Air Force, 1984—. Served with USAF, 1971-74; maj. Res., 1975—. Decorated USAF Meritorious Service medal, Air Force Commendation medal. Mem. Am. Soc. Safety Engrs., Soc. of Logistics Engrs., System Safety Soc., Phi Kappa Phi. Office: Air Force Plant Rep Rocketdyne 6633 Canoga Ave Canoga Park CA 91303-2790

WHITNEY, PHYLLIS AYAME, author; b. Yokohama, Japan, Sept. 9, 1903; d. Charles J. and Lillian (Mandeville) W.; m. George A. Garner, July 2, 1925; m. Lovell F. Jahnke, 1950 (dec. 1973). Grad., McKinley High Sch., Chgo., 1924. Instr. dancing San Antonio, 1 yr; tchr. juvenile fiction writing Northwestern U., 1945; children's book editor Chgo. Sun, 1942-46, Phila. Inquirer, 1947, 48; instr. juvenile fiction writing N.Y.U., 1947-58; leader juvenile fiction workshop Writers Conf., U. Colo., 1952, 54, 56. Author: A Place for Ann, 1941, A Star for Ginny, 1942; (vocat. fiction for teenage girls) A Window for Julie, 1943; Red Is for Murder (mystery novel for adults), 1943, The Silver Inkwell, 1945, Willow Hill, 1947, Writing Juvenile Fiction, 1947, Ever After, 1948, Mystery of the Gulls, 1949, Linda's Homecoming, 1950, The Island of Dark Woods, 1951, Love Me, Love Me Not, 1952, Step to the Music, 1953, A Long Time Coming, 1954, Mystery of the Black Diamonds, 1954, The Quicksilver Pool, 1955, Mystery on the Isle of Skye, 1955, The Fire and The Gold (Jr. Lit. Guild), 1956, The Highest Dream (Jr. Lit. Guild), The Trembling Hills (Peoples Book Club), 1956, Skye Cameron, 1957, Mystery of the Green Cat, (Jr. Lit. Guild), 1957, Secret of the Samurai Sword (Jr. Lit. Guild), 1958, The Moonflower, 1958, Creole Holiday, 1959, Thunder Heights, 1960, Blue Fire, 1961, Mystery of the Haunted Pool, 1961 (Edgar award Mystery Writers Am.), Secret of the Tiger's Eye, 1961, Window on the Square, 1962, Mystery of the Golden Horn, 1962, Seven Tears for Apollo, 1963, Mystery of the Hidden Hand, 1963 (Edgar award Mystery Writers Am. 1964), Black Amber, 1964, Secret of the Emerald Star, 1964, Sea Jade, 1965, Mystery of the Angry Idol, 1965, Columbella, 1966, Secret of the Spotted Shell, 1967, Mystery of the Strange Traveler, 1967, Silverhill, 1967, Hunter's Green, 1968, Secret of Goblin Glen, 1968, Mystery of the Crimson Ghost, 1969, Winter People, 1969, Secret of the Missing Footprint, 1970, Lost Island, 1970, The Vanishing Scarecrow, 1971, Listen for the Whisperer, 1971, Nobody Likes Trina, 1972, Snowfire, 1973, Mystery of the Scowling Boy, 1973, The Turquoise Mask, 1974, Spindrift, 1975, Secret of Haunted Mesa, 1975, The Golden Unicorn, 1976, Secret of the Stone Face, 1977, The Stone Bull, 1977, The Glass Flame, 1978, Domino, 1979, Poinciana, 1980, Vermilion, 1981, Guide to Fiction Writing, 1982,, Emerald, 1983,, Rainsong, 1984, Dream of Orchids, 1985, Flaming Tree, 1986, Silversword, 1987, Feather on the Moon, 1988; sold first story to Chgo. Daily News; later wrote for pulp mags., became specialist in juvenile writing, now writing entirely in adult field. Pres. Authors Round Table, 1943, 44; pres. exec. bd. Fifth Annual Writers Conf., Northwestern U., 1944. Recipient Friends of Lit. award contbrs. children's lit., 1943; Reynal and Hitchcock prize ($3000) in Youth Today contest for book Willow Hill; Recipient Today's Woman award Council Cerebral Palsy Auxs., 1983. Mem. Mystery Writers Am. (pres. 1975, Grandmaster award for lifetime achievement 1988). Office: care McIntosh & Otis 310 Madison Ave New York NY 10017

WHITNEY, RUTH ANN ROTUNDO, court social worker, researcher; b. Schenectady, N.Y., July 3, 1945; d. Joseph and Barbara Ruth (Bristol) Rotundo; m. V. Kevin Whitney, Mar. 20, 1976 (dec. Apr. 1981). BA, Mt. Holyoke Coll., 1966; MSW, Simmons Sch. Social Work, 1969. Lic. clin. social worker. Caseworker, supr. Dept. Social Service, Mass. Gen. Hosp., Boston, 1969-75; supr. social work Cambridge (Mass.) Vis. Nurse Assn., 1975-79; sr. social worker, dir. tng. Family Service Clinic, Middlesex Probate and Family Court, Cambridge, 1979—; mem. Middlesex Divorce Research Group, Cambridge, 1980—; cons. The Mediation Group, Brookline, Mass., 1985—; clin. assoc. Simmons Sch. Social Work, Boston, 1971—. Contbr. chpts. to books, articles to profl. jours. Pres. bd. Dept. Social Services, Cambridge-Somerville, 1984—, Mt. Holyoke Coll. Class of '66, 1986—; mem. Instl. Review Bd. Mt. Auburn Hosp., 1980—, Gov's. Commn. on The Unmet Legal Needs of Children, 1987—. Mem. Nat. Social Work Assembly (del. 1987). Democrat. Mem. Soc. of Friends. Office: Ct Clinic Middlesex Probate Ct House East Cambridge MA 02141

WHITNEY, RUTH REINKE, magazine editor; b. Oshkosh, Wis., July 23, 1928; d. Leonard G. and Helen (Diestler) Reinke; BA, Northwestern U., 1949; m. Daniel A. Whitney, Nov. 19, 1949; 1 son, Philip. Copywriter edn. dept. circulation div. Time, Inc., 1949-53; editor-in-chief Better Living mag., 1953-56; assoc. editor Seventeen magazine, 1956-62, exec. editor, 1962-67; editor-in-chief Glamour mag., N.Y.C., 1967—. Mem. Fashion Group, Am. Soc. Mag. Editors (pres. 1975-77), Women in Communication, Matrix award 1980), Alpha Chi Omega. Home: Riverview Rd Irvington-on-Hudson NY 10533 Office: Glamour Condé Nast Bldg 350 Madison Ave New York NY 10017

WHITNEY-TEEPLE, ELIZABETH PERRY, medical information systems director; b. Atlanta, Jan. 9, 1950; d. Robert Perry and Elizabeth Ann (Vanstory) T.; m. Robert A. Whitney, 1986. BS, U. State N.Y., Albany, 1980; M in Health Service Adminstrn., George Washington U., 1983. Enlisted USAF, 1978, advanced through grades to capt.; research asst. NIH, Bethesda, Md., 1980-81; dep. comdr., ops. officer 60th Air Evac Flight, Andrews AFB, Washington, 1981-82; resident med. adminstr. Malcolm Grow Med. Ctr., Andrews AFB, 1982-83; dir. patient affairs USAF Regional Hosp., March AFB, Calif., 1984-85; dir. med. systems USAFR Hosp., March AFB, 1983-87; med. policy liaison officer Office Asst. Sec. of Def., Med. Systems Support Ctr., Falls Church, Va., 1987—; project mgr. VA/Def. Dept. Software Test, March AFB, 1984-86; regional cons. med. systems SAC, March AFB, 1985—. Pub. speaker March AFB, Los Angeles, Riverside, Calif., 1986; leader death & dying seminars, March AFB Community, 1984-85. Mem. Am. Soc. Mil. Surgeons, Am. Coll. Healthcare Execs. Democrat. Office: OASD HA DMSSC/OPAR 5201 Leesburg Pike Suite 500 Falls Church VA 22041

WHITSON, BETTY ANN, educational administrator; b. Canadian, Tex., May 15, 1937; d. Jack H. and Ruth Mary (King) W.; m. Paul R. Caillet, Sept. 18, 1960 (div. 1969). B.A., West Tex. U., 1958; B.S., U. Houston, 1963, M.Ed., 1977, Ed.D., 1979. Cert. tchr., Tex., Md. Tchr., Dalhart High Sch., Tex., 1958-59, Poolesville Jr. High Sch., Md., 1959-60, Southland Elem. Sch., Houston, 1963-76; teaching fellow U. Houston, 1976-79; asst. prin., tchr. Wainwright Elem. Sch., Houston, 1979—; vis. instr. U. St. Thomas, Houston, 1981. Contbr. research articles to profl. publs. Recipient Tchr. of Yr. award Wainwright Elem. Sch. 1982, Best Tchr. Made Mgmt. Program, Dept. Technology, Technology Fair, 1983, Excellence in Teaching award Tex. A&M U., 1985. Mem. Nat. Sci. Tchr. Assn., Computer Educator Assn., NEA, Tex. Edn. Assn., Tex. Classroom Tchrs. Democrat. Presbyterian. Avocations: birding; hiking; reading. Home: 3818 Glen Arbor #6 Houston TX 77025 also: 1 E Wavy Oak Circle The Woodlands TX 77381 Office: Wainwright Elem Sch 5330 Milwee Houston TX 77092

WHITT, MARGARET AGNES TOKARSKI, personnel coordinator; b. Wyandotte, Mich., Sept. 30, 1950; d. Leo Edward and Sophi (Uszynski) Tokarski; m. David L. Whitt, May 22, 1977. AA in Commerce, Henry Ford Community Coll., Dearborn, Mich., 1971; student, Albright Coll., 1979-81; BA, Alvernia Coll., 1988. Sec. the J.L. Hudson Co., Detroit, 1971-72, exec. sec., 1972-74; exec. sec. the J.L. Hudson Co., Ann Arbor, Mich., 1974-77; legal sec. Beaumont, Smith & Harris, Detroit, 1972; sec. Owens-Corning Fiberglass, Toledo, 1977-78; exec. sec. Owens-Corning Fiberglass, Wayne, Pa., 1978-81; adminstrv. asst. GAI-Tronics Corp., Reading, Pa., 1981-84, personnel coordinator, 1984—. Mem. Am. Soc.Personnel Adminstrs., Jr. League of Berks County, Berks Women Network. Republican. Roman Catholic. Home: 205 Cathy Ann Dr Reading PA 19606 Office: Gai-Tronics Corp PO Box 31 Reading PA 19603

WHITTAKER, HELEN DEWITT, library director, educator; b. Darlington, S.C., Apr. 26, 1954; d. Marion Rollins and Margaret (Coleman) DeWitt; m. Gary Scott Whittaker. BA in English, Agnes Scott Coll., 1975; MLS, U. N.C., 1976; MA in Journalism, U. S.C., 1985. Cert. librarian, S.C., N.C., Va. Dir. region Allendale (S.C.)-Hampton-Jasper Regional Library, 1976-77; supr. ops. Pub. Library Charlotte, N.C., 1977-83; dir. Marion (S.C.) County Library, 1983-84; stringer Columbia (S.C.) Newspapers, 1985; dir. Bristol (Va.) Pub. Library, 1986-87; asst. prof. E. Tenn. State U., Kingsport, 1988—. Contbr. articles to profl. jours. Chmn. publicity Bristol Visitors and Conventions Com., 1986, Bristol Leadership Tomorrow, 1987; treas. Charlotte Women's Polit. Caucus, 1982; bd. dirs. Hawkins County chpt. ARC. Mem. ALA, Tenn. Library Assn., Nat. Assn. Female Execs., Marion C. of C., Kappa Tau Alpha. Presbyterian. Home: 116 Willowbrook Dr Kingsport TN 37660 Office: Kingsport U Ctr University Blvd Kingsport TN 37660

WHITTAKER, SHEELAGH DILLON, broadcast executive; b. Ottawa, Ont., Can., Apr. 9, 1947; d. John Dean and E.M. Theresa (Tessie) (Sadlier-Brown) W.; m. Michael James Van Dusen; children: Meghan, Matthew, Daniel John. BSc, U. Alta., Can., 1967; BA, U. Toronto, 1970; MBA, York U., 1975. Sessional lectr. U. Alta., Edmonton, Can., 1967-68; asst. to the provost U. Guelph, Can., 1971-73; economist Ministryof Natural Resources Govt. of Quebec, Can., 1974-75; commerce officer dept. consumer and corporate affairs Govt. of Quebec, Ottawa, 1975-79; dir., mgmt. cons. The Can. Cons. Group, Inc., Toronto, 1979-85; v.p. planning and corp. affairs Can. Broadcasting Corp., Ottawa, Ont., Can., 1985—; dir. The Can. Cons. Group, Inc., Toronto, 1983, Sterling Trust, Toronto, 1987, Can. Advt. Found., Toronto, 1987. Gulf Oil scholar, 1967, Nat. Research Council scholar, 1968; Govt. of Ontario Exchange fellow, 1974. Office: Canadian Broadcasting Corp, 1500 Bronson Ave, Ottawa, ON Canada K1G 3J5

WHITTEMORE, DOROTHY JANE, librarian; b. San Jose, Calif., Nov. 9, 1920; d. Glen James and Jane Dorothy (Katz) Gordon; A.B., San Jose State Coll., 1941, cert. of librarianship, 1942, postgrad., 1952-53; m. Robert Clifton Whittemore, June 15, 1959; children by previous marriage—Stanley Allen Lawton, Shirley Anne (Mrs. Anthony Kopcych). Sch. library supr. Piedmont (Calif.) Sch. Dist., 1942-43; asst. post librarian Presidio of San Francisco, 1943-49; jr. librarian San Jose (Calif.) State Coll., 1951-53; reference librarian Tulane U. Library, New Orleans, 1953-76, acting dir., 1976-78, asst. dir. public service, 1978-80, dir. Norman Mayer Bus. Library, 1980-86, dir. Turchin Library, A.B. Freeman Sch. of Bus., 1986—. New Orleans chpt. LWV, 1964-66, dir. La. chpt., 1967-69, 73—; mem. citizens adv. com. City Planning Commn. of New Orleans, 1965-67; sec. New Orleans chpt. La. Consumers League, 1972-74; active Public Affairs Research Council; mem. adv. council La. State Bd. Nursing, 1977—. Council on Library Resources research grantee, 1972. Mem. Spl. Libraries Assn. (pres. La. chpt. 1975-77, sec.-treas. social welfare sect. 1977-79), La. Library Assn. (chmn. coll. and reference sect. 1968-69, exec. bd. 1973-74), New Orleans Library Club (past pres.), Am. Soc. Info. Sci., Nat. Microfilm Assn. Author: (with others) Citizen's Guide to Louisiana Government, 1969. Home: 7521 Dominican St New Orleans LA 70118 Office: Tulane U AB Freeman Sch Bus Turchin Library New Orleans LA 70118

WHITTEN, CAROL PENDÁS, government official; b. N.Y.C., Dec. 4, 1945; d. Juan Manuel and Loida (Calejo) Pendás; m. Jamie Lloyd Whitten Jr.; 1 child, Joseph Anthony. BS in Home Econs., Barry Coll., 1967, MS in Edn., 1970. Tchr., adminstr. various acads. and schs., Miami, Fla., 1967-78; edn. program specialist women's ednl. equity act program U.S. Dept. Edn., Washington, 1980-81, exec. asst. to dir., Nat. Inst. Edn., 1982-83, spl. asst. to dep. undersec. for mgmt., 1983-84, dir. Office Bilingual Edn., 1985—; congl. liaison officer legis. affairs office U.S. Dept. Labor, Washington, 1984-85. Mem. Rep. Hispanic Assembly, Washington, Rep. Women's Fed. Forum, Washington, Eagle Forum, Renaissance Women. Office: US Dept of Edn Office Bilingual Edn and Minority Langs 300 7th St NW Room 421 Washington DC 20202

WHITTEN, PATRICIA LEE, biologist; b. Melrose Park, Ill., Mar. 15, 1951; d. Donald R. and Frances Elizabeth (Martin) W. BA with high honors, U. Ill., 1973; PhD, Harvard U., 1982. NIMH postdoctoral fellow Yerkes Regional Pvt. Research Ctr., Atlanta, 1982-83; research assoc. Yerkes Regional Primate Research Ctr., Atlanta, 1985-87; vis. asst. prof. dept. anthropology U. Mich., Ann Arbor, 1983-84; assoc. research scientist, Mellon Found. fellow Sch. Medicine Yale U., New Haven, 1984—; lectr. dept. anthropology Yale U., 1987. Contbr. articles to profl. jours. U. Ill. James scholar, 1969-73; Wenner Gren Found. research grantee, 1974. Mem. Am. Assn. Phys. Anthropologists, Internat. Primatological Soc., Am. Soc. Primatologists, Animal Behavior Soc., AAAS, N.Y. Acad. Scis., Phi Beta Kappa. Office: Yale U Sch Medicine Dept Obstetrics and Gynecology 333 Cedar St New Haven CT 06510

WHITTENBORN, BYNAH MAY, international trade specialist; b. Abilene, Tex., Sept. 26, 1948. BA, East Tex. State U., 1973. Mem. inside sales staff Daniel Industries, Houston, 1978-80, asst. mgr. export, 1980-83, export control officer, 1983-85; export cons. Houston, 1985—. Republican.

WHITTIER, SARAJANE, social studies educator; b. North Manchester, Ind., Dec. 17, 1912; d. Charles and Ethel Clo (Free) Leckrone; m. C. Taylor Whittier, June 18, 1934; children—Chip, Tim, Cece, Penny. B.A., U. Chgo., 1934, M.A., 1946. Research sec. Oriental Inst., Chgo., 1935-39; tchr. pub. schs., Flossmoor, Ill., 1939-41, Sta. WSUN-TV, St. Petersburg, Fla., 1955-56, Sta. GWETA-TV, Washington, 1961-62; substitute tchr. pub. schs., Fla. and Md., 1962—. Co-author: Pasture Trails, 1941. Asst. monthly newsletter Supt.'s Digest, 1983-85. Pres., PTA, St. Petersburg, 1960's; Kans. chmn. Friends of J.F.K. Ctr., Topeka, 1969-75, Tex. chmn., San Antonio, 1975-82; guardian Camp Fire Girls, Chgo., 1936-41, bd. dirs. Camp Fire Kans., Tex., La. Gaithersburg, Md., 1958-64; Sunday sch. tchr. Christian Ch., Chgo., 1926-34, chmn. Westbank Forum Ch. Women United. St. Petersburg, 1950-57, pianist, San Antonio, 1975-82. U. Chgo. scholar, 1933-34. Mem. AAUW (past pres., life mem.). Republican. Avocations: acting; music; directing little theatres; photography; world traveling. Home: 756 Fairlawn Dr Gretna LA 70056

WHITTINGTON, MARY JAYNE GARRARD, journalist; b. Monteagle, Tenn., Aug. 13, 1915; d. William Mountjoy and Mabelle Moseley (Smith) Garrard; grad. Nat. Cathedral Sch., 1934; student King-Smith Studio Sch., 1934-35; m. William Madison Whittington, Jr., Dec. 27, 1945; children—Jamie Garrard Whittington Gasner, William Madison, Anna Aven. Contbg. editor Delta Rev., Memphis, 1964-69, Mississippi mag., 1977-82; freelance writer, columnist, Greenwood, Miss., 1956—. Mem. exec. bd. Greenwood Found. Arts, 1962-83; mem. Ctr. Study So. Culture, Oxford, Miss.; bd. govs. Greenwood Little Theatre, 1956-66, 75-82; trustee Ballet Miss.; bd. dirs. Mimi Garrard Dance Co., N.Y.C., Ctr. Study So. Culture, Internat. Ballet Competition IV, Jackson, Miss., Mississippians for Ednl. TV, Friends of Art in Miss., Friends of Art Mus., Naples, Fla. Served to capt. WAC, 1942-45. Mem. Nat. League Am. Pen Women, So. Debutante Assembly, DAR, First Families Va., Delta Cotton Wives, Nat. Soc. Colonial Dames, Order Crown Am. Jr. Aux. (life), Kappa Pi (hon.). Clubs: Arts, Naples, Fla., Greenwood Garden, Greenwood Country. Address: 1000 Grand Blvd Greenwood MS 38930

WHITTLESEY, FAITH RYAN, diplomat; b. Jersey City, Feb. 21, 1939; widow; children: Henry, Amy, William. B.A. cum laude, Wells Coll., 1960; J.D., U. Pa., 1963; postgrad., Acad. Internat. Law, The Hague, Netherlands. Spl. asst. atty. gen. Pa. Dept. Justice, Phila., 1964-65; law clk. to judge U.S. Dist. Ct. (ea. dist.) Pa., 1965-66; spl. asst. atty. gen. Pa. Dept. Public Welfare, 1967-70; asst. U.S. atty. Ea. Dist. Pa., 1970-72; mem. Pa. Ho. of Reps., 1972-76; chmn., vice chmn. Delaware County Council, Media, Pa., 1976-81; mem. firm Wolf, Block, Schorr and Solis-Cohen, Phila., 1980-81; ambassador to Switzerland, Bern 1981-83; asst. to pres. for pub. liaison, mem. sr. staff The White House, Washington, 1983-85; ambassador to Switzerland 1985-88; ptnr. Myerson & Kuhn, N.Y.C., 1988—. Mem. Phi Beta Kappa. Office: Myerson & Kuhn 237 Park Ave New York NY 10017

WHITTLESEY, SUSAN PRIMUS, accountant, rancher; b. Chgo., July 15, 1957; d. Harold Charles and Marilyn Ann (Bernstein) Primus; m. David Clinton Whittlesey, June 1, 1986; 1 child, Seth Mikel. BS in Acctng., Ohio State U., 1978. CPA, Colo. Sr. cost analyst Huntington Nat. Bank, Columbus, Ohio, 1979-81; adminstr. trust tax Huntington Nat. Bank, Columbus, 1981-82; tax specialist Scullion Beekmann and Co., Denver, 1983-85; prin. Susan Primus Whittlesey CPA, Steamboat Springs, Colo., 1985—. Sec./treas. Cow Creek Community Assn., Steamboat Springs, Colo. 1986—. Mem. Am. Inst. CPA'S, Colo. Soc. CPA's, Am. Bison Assn. (bd. dirs. 1987—). Home and Office: 28800 Routt County Rd 43 Steamboat Springs CO 80487

WHITTON, MARY CLARK, marketing professional; b. Charlotte, N.C., Mar. 5, 1948; d. Beaumert Harrison and Daphne Amelia (Clark) W.; m. James Nicholas England, Dec. 28, 1974. BA, Duke U., 1970; MS in Guidance, N.C. State U., 1974, MSEE, 1984. Founder, v.p. Ikonas Graphics Systems, Raleigh, N.C., 1978-82; product mgr. Adage Inc., Boston, 1982-83; cons. Whitland Assocs., Raleigh, 1983-84, 1985; founder, v.p. mktg. Trancept Systems Inc., Raleigh, 1986-87; dir. mktg. Sun Microsystems, Inc., Research Triangle Park, 1987—. Treas. br. com. orgn. YMCA, 1984—. Mem. Assn. Computing Machinery-Siggraph (local chair 1984-86), IEEE, IEEE Computer Soc. of IEEE, Soc. Women Engrs. (pres. ea. N.C. sect. 1985-86, v.p. 1984-85). Club: Tarheel Sports Car (bd. dirs. 1983-85). Office: Trancept Systems Inc 500C Uwharrie Ct Raleigh NC 27606

WHITWORTH, KATHRYNNE ANN, professional golfer; b. Monahans, Tex., Sept. 27, 1939; d. Morris Clark and Dama Ann (Robinson) W. Student, Odessa (Tex.) Jr. Coll., 1958. Joined tour 1959 and; Ladies Profl. Golf Assn.; mem. adv. staff Walter Hagen Golf Co., Wilson Sporting Goods Co. Named to Hall of Fame Ladies Profl. Golf Assn., Tex. Sports Hall of Fame, Tex. Golf Hall of Fame, World Golf Hall of Fame. Mem. Ladies Profl. Golf Assn. (sec. 1962-63, v.p. 1965, 73, pres. 1967, 68, 71, 1st mem. to win over $61,000,000.00). Office: care Ladies Profl Golf Assn 4675 Sweetwater Blvd Sugar Land TX 77478

WIAR, KIMBERLY VARTHIA, executive recruiter; b. Lincoln, Nebr., Mar. 2, 1937; d. Arthur W. and Fern Mary (Bohlman) Voss; m. Harold B. Wiar, m Oct. 12, 1954 (div. 1963); 1 child, Robert H. BA, U. Calif., 1967. Mem. editorial staff U. Chgo. Press, 1969-78, editor, 1975-78; research assoc. Heidrick & Struggles, Inc., San Francisco, 1980-81, research mgr., 1981-83; assoc. Zivic Group, Inc., San Francisco, 1983-85, v.p., 1985-87; prin. Kimberly Wiar & Co., San Francisco, 1987—. Bd. dirs. Oakland (Calif.) Soc. Prevention Cruelty to Animals, 1986—. Mem. Women Health Care Execs., Calif. Exec. Recruiters Assn., Nat. Assn. Female Execs., San Francisco C. of C. (mem. arts and culture council, govt. affairs council). Club: Commonwealth (San Francisco). Home: 10 Milland Dr B-13 Mill Valley CA 94941

WICHERSKI, JANE LENDER, rehabilitation counselor; b. Mpls., Aug. 24, 1939; d. Harold Leroy and Felicitas Jane (Gassere) La Fayette; m. William George Lender, Sept. 25, 1961 (div. Jan. 1981); 1 child, Guy J. Lender; m. Andrew Joseph Wicherski, Feb. 9, 1986. BS in Med. Tech., U. Minn., 1961; MA in Human Devel., St. Mary's Coll., Winona, Minn., 1980. Cert. rehab. cons., Minn. Research scientist exptl. surgery VA Hosp., Mpls., 1965-70, psychiat. technologist counseling, 1979-81, asst. dir. chronic pain program, 1980-81; research scientist U. Minn. Dept. Physiology, Mpls., 1970-79; cons. Vocat. Rehab. Cons., St. Paul, 1981-85, prin., cons., 1985—; cons. Rate Cons., Mpls., 1987. Mem. Assn. Rehab. Counselors Am., Minn. Assn. Rehab. Providers. Lutheran. Office: Vocat Rehab Cons 176 N Snelling Suite 330 Saint Paul MN 55104

WICHMAN FULLER, SARA ELIZABETH, writer; b. Charlevoix, Mich., Sept. 2, 1941; d. Earl Franklin and Naomi Ruth (White) Bacon; m. Rod Roy Wichman, Sept. 2, 1962 (div. 1978); m. Duane Leroy Fuller, Aug. 22, 1986; children: Kimberly Anne, Todd Anthony. BA, Mich. State U., 1963. Freelance writer Portland, 1978—; reporter New Rev., Milw., 1978-79; relocation coordinator Georgia-Pacific Corp., Portland, 1979-82; instr. journalism Clackamas Community Coll., Oregon City, 1983-84, Mt. Hood Community Coll., Gresham, Oreg., 1985; owner Info. Please, Gresham, 1984—; co-owner The Healing Touch, Portland, 1987—. Author: Portland Thrift Store Guide, 1985; editor Movin' On, 1982; contbr. articles to profl. Mem. Willamette Writers, Internat. Assn. Bus. Communicators (Oreg. chpt.). Democrat. Episcopal. Office: The Healing Touch 521 NE Davis Portland OR 97232

WICK, ERIKA ELISABETH, psychologist; b. Basel, Switzerland, July 31, 1937; d. Josef and Martha (Gabriel) W.; came to U.S., 1964, naturalized, 1970; Ph.D., U. Basel, 1964. Prof. psychology St. John's U., Jamaica, N.Y., 1976—. Fellow Acad. Psychosomatic Medicine, Soc. Clin. Exptl. Hypnosis; mem. Am. Psychol. Assn., N.Y. Acad. Sci.; fellow Acad. Psychosomatic Medicine. Office: St John's U Jamaica NY 11439

WICK, SISTER MARGARET, college administrator; b. Sibley, Iowa, June 30, 1942. BA in Sociology, Briar Cliff Coll., 1965; MA in Sociology, Loyola U., Chgo., 1971; PhD in Higher Edn., U. Denver, 1976. Instr. sociology Briar Cliff Coll., Sioux City, Iowa, 1966-71, dir. academic advising, 1971-72; v.p., acad. dean Briar Cliff Coll., Sioux City, 1972-74, 76-84; pres. Colls. of Mid-Am., 1985-87, Briar Cliff Coll., 1987—; bd. dirs. 1st Interstate Bank Sioux City. Active Mission Task Force of the Sisters of St. Francis; mem. Iowa planning com. Nat. Identification Program for Women, 1980-84; bd. dirs. Mary J. Treglia Community House, 1976-84, Marian Health Ctr., 1987—, Iowa Pub. TV, 1987—. Mem. AAUW, Am. Council on Edn., North Cen. Edn. Assn. (cons.-evaluator for accrediting teams 1980-84), Quota Internat. Lodge: Rotary. Home: 4646 Talbot Rd Sioux City IA 51104 Office: Briar Cliff College Office of President 3303 Rebecca Sioux City IA 51104

WICKENHEISER, ELIZABETH RUSSACK, artist, poet, cartographer; b. N.Y.C., Sept. 21, 1914; d. Martin and Nettie (Shako) Russack; m. Herbert Emil Wickenheiser, Oct. 14, 1933 (dec. 1982); children: Georgine Elizabeth Altomare, Alice Emma Martinelli, Herbert Matthias, Phyllis Hope Graudszus, Walter Russack. Student, Sch. Fine and Applied Art Pratt Inst., 1931-33, NYU, 1934. Cartographer U.S. Army Map Service, Washington, 1951-67; asst. curator art exhibits Alexander Gallery, Washington, 1953-54, curator, 1955-60; adv. com. decorations Alexander Gallery, 1960-67, map service exhibits com., 1963-67, sponsor arts club, 1959. One woman shows include 5 at Alexander Gallery, 1954-58, U. Md., 1961, Gurmukh Arts Gallery, 1983; exhibited Met. State annuals, 1952-55, Nat. Collection Fine Arts Smithsonian Inst., 1954, Corcoran Gallery Art, Washington, 1951-55, 58, Washington Water Color Club annual, 1955, 58, Md. Artists annual Balt. Mus. Art, 1956, Psychiat. Inst. Art Assn. Montgomery County, Md., 1981; contbr. Federal Poet (editor 1984-85), Cicada, Haiku Zasshi Zo, Waterways, Green County Council Arts Literary Supplement, Modern Haiku, 1983-87. Supr., sponsor, instr. arts crafts activities Montgomery County, Md.; set up, contbd. numerous local exhibits including AAUW Fellowship Fund, 1947, PTA Kensington (Md.) Schs., Noyes Library, Chevy Chase Library, 1960, 65, 77, 80. Recipient 1st prize pastels, 2d prize drawings AM VETS Army Map Service artists, 1956. Mem. Nat. Fedn. State Poetry Socs., Fed. Poets Washington, Nat. Mus. Women in Arts. Democrat. Home: 10302 Fawcett St Kensington MD 20895

WICKER, KRISTIN LEE, educator, musician; b. Ft. Dodge, Iowa, Nov. 7, 1953; d. Winford Lee and Helen Caroline (Brown) Egli; m. Kirk Michael Wicker, Jan. 1, 1982 (dec. June 1982). AA, Iowa Cen. Coll., 1974; B in Music Edn., Morningside Coll., 1976; M in Mus., U. S.D., 1983. Cert. tchr., Iowa. Tchr. instrumental music Garrigan Affiliated Schs., Algona, Iowa, 1976-77, Sioux City (Iowa) Community Schs., 1977—. asst. prin. bassist Sioux City Symphony, 1974—; freelance bassist, Sioux City, 1976—. Named Tchr. of Yr. Sioux City Community Schs., 1988-89. Mem. NEA, Iowa Edn. Assn., Sioux city Edn. Assn., Iowa Bandmasters Assn., Sioux City Musicians Assn., Zeta Sigma, Mu Phi Epsilon. Republican. Lutheran. Office: Woodrow Wilson Mid Sch 1010 Iowa St Sioux City IA 51105

WICKER, VERONICA DICARLO, judge; b. Monessen, Pa., Nov. 26, 1930; d. Vincent James and Rose Margaret DiCarlo; m. Thomas Carey Wicker Jr.; children: Thomas Carey III, Catherine Wicker Stentiford. B.F.A., Syracuse U., 1952; J.D., Loyola U. of the South, 1966. Bar: La. 1966. U.S. magistrate New Orleans, 1977-79; judge U.S. Dist. Ct. (ea. dist.) La., New Orleans, 1979—. Mem. vis. com. Loyola U. Law Sch. Mem. ABA, Fed. Bar. Assn., La. Bar Assn., New Orleans Bar Assn., Jefferson Parish Bar Aux., Fed. Dist. Judges Assn., Assn. Women Judges, Maritime Law Assn., Assn. Women Attys., Justinian Soc. Jurists, Phi Alpha Delta, Alpha Xi Alpha, Phi Mu. Lodge: Rotary. Office: US Dist Ct C-508 US Courthouse 500 Camp St New Orleans LA 70130

WICKERT, CYNTHIA LEE, non-profit corporation comptroller; b. Fort Sill, Okla., July 20, 1956; d. James Edwin and Ruth Arlene May (Wantz) Haley; m. Steven William Wickert; children: Michael David, Angela Renae. Student, Ill. Cen. Coll., 1973-76. Head bookkeeper The Batchelder Co., Peoria, Ill., 1973-76; acct. Peoria Sch. Med., 1976-78; pub. acct. Al Morganthal, P.A., Phoenix, 1978-80; asst. controller Indsl. Uniform Services, Inc., Phoenix, 1980-81; adminstrv. acct. Maxway, Inc., Ankeny, Iowa, 1981-82; chief acct. Cen. Iowa Employment and Tng. Co., Des Moines, 1982-85; comptroller Proteus Employment Opportunities, Des Moines, 1985—. Treas. Peoria Welcome Wagon, 1975-76. Mem. Accts. Assn. Iowa, Des Moines C. of C. Democrat. Office: Proteus Employment Opportunities Inc 175 NW 57th Pl Box 10385 Des Moines IA 50306

WICKHAM, PATRICIA MARIA-CLAIRE, automotive executive; b. Battle Creek, Mich., May 29, 1951; d. James and Maria (Meertens) Powell; 1 child, Richard James Wickham. BS in Fin., LaSalle U., 1979. Supr. Retail Grocers Inventory Specialists, El Paso, Tex., 1977-79; with GTE Communications, El Paso, 1979-83; master scheduler GTE Network, El Paso, 1983-84; customer svc. mgr. Consolidated Diesel Co., Rocky Mount, N.C., 1984-86, new products mgr., 1986-87; materials mgr. Europe Johnson Controls, Ann Arbor, Mich., 1988—. Fund raiser sickle cell anemia, El Paso, 1978-82, multiple sclerosis, El Paso, 1980-83; advisor Jr. Achievement, El Paso, 1982-84, Rocky Mount, 1984-87. Mem. Am. Prodn. and Inv. Control Soc. (pres. 1984-86), Atlantic Coast Symposium, Nat. Assn. Female Execs. (dir. 1981-82). Democrat. Roman Catholic. Home: 2720 Buff Rd Rocky Mount NC 27803 Office: Johnson Controls, Automotive N.V., Bell Telephonelaan 2, 2440 Geel Belgium

WICKSTROM, CHARLOTTE AMY, federal agency director; b. Sidney, N.Y., Apr. 9, 1944; d. Burt H. and Isabel M. (Plossl) McIntosh; children: Karin E., Erica L. BS, Stanford U., 1965; MS, U. Alaska, 1980. Ops. research analyst Gen. Dynamics Corp., Ft. Worth, 1966-67; chief work authorization USAF, Laughlin AFB, Tex., 1968-69; analyst indsl. engring. USAF, Ft. Richardson, Alaska, 1969-73; chief force devel. U.S. Army Communication Command, Ft. Richardson and Camp Darby (Italy), 1973-79; indsl. engr. U.S. Army Communication Command, Ft. Richardson, 1979-80, chief mgmt. engring., 1980-82, chief engr. design, 1982-83; dir. engr. programs Alaskan Air Command, Elmendorf AFB, 1983—. Judge Alaska Sci. Fair, Anchorage, 1986, 87; rep. Fed. Womens Program, Elmendorf AFB, 1987—. Mem. Am. Inst. Indsl. Engring. (sr.), Nat. Assn. for Female Execs., Aircraft Owners and Pilots Assn., Alaska MacIntosh Users Group, Mensa. Club: 99's.

WICKWIRE, CAROLYN JANE, medical administrator; b. Paris, Tex., Dec. 28, 1936; d. James Ward and Marian (Alexander) Garvin; m. Hubert Martin Wickwire, Aug. 1, 1969. BA with high honors, So. Meth. U., 1958; postgrad., Dallas Theater Center, 1964-68. Sec. to infectious diseases sec. Southwestern Med. Ctr. U. Tex., Dallas, 1958-73, adminstrv. asst. sect. infectious diseases Health Sci. Ctr. U. Tex., Dallas, 1974-75, adminstrv. services officer, 1976-82, exec. asst. to chmn. internal medicine, 1982—, mem. info. systems planning, 1982, mem. telecommunications task force, 1985-87. House mgr. Dallas Theatre Ctr., 1967-68. Mem. Adminstrs. Internal Medicine (bd. dirs. 1982-84), Assn. Am. Med. Colls., Am. Mgmt. Assn., Soc. Theatrical Artists Guidance and Enhancement, Phi Beta Kappa. Office: U Tex Southwestern Med Ctr 5323 Harry Hines Blvd Dallas TX 75235-9030

WICKWIRE, PATRICIA JOANNE NELLOR, psychologist, educator; b. Sioux City, Iowa; d. William McKinley and Clara Rose (Pautsch) Nellor; B.A. cum laude, U. No. Iowa, 1951; M.A., U. Iowa, 1959; Ph.D., U. Tex., Austin, 1971; postgrad. U. So. Calif., UCLA, Calif. State U., Long Beach, 1951-66; m. Robert James Wickwire, Sept. 7, 1957; 1 son, William James. Tchr., Ricketts Ind. Schs., Iowa, 1946-48; tchr., counselor Waverly-Shell Rock Ind. Schs., Iowa, 1951-55; reading cons., head dormitory counselor U. Iowa, Iowa City, 1955-57; tchr., sch. psychologist, adminstr. S. Bay Union High Sch. Dist., Redondo Beach, Calif., 1962—, dir. student services and spl. edn.; cons. mgmt. and edn.; mem. Calif. Interagency Mental Health Council, exec. bd., 1968-72; chmn. Friends of Dominguez Hills (Calif.), 1981—; mem. exec. bd. Beach Cities Symphony Assn., 1970-82. Lic. ednl. psychologist, marriage, family and child counselor, Calif. Mem. AAUW (exec. bd., chpt. pres. 1962-72), Los Angeles County Dirs. Pupil Services (chmn. 1974-79), Los Angeles County Personnel and Guidance Assn. (pres. 1977-78), Calif. Personnel and Guidance Assn. (exec. bd. 1984—, pres. 1988—), Assn. Calif. Sch. Adminstrs. (dir. 1977-81), Los Angeles County SW Bd. Dist. Adminstrs. for Spl. Edn. (chmn. 1976-81), Calif. Assn. Sch. Psychologist (dir. 1981—), Am. Psychol. Assn., Am. Assn. Sch. Adminstrs., Calif. Assn. for Measurement and Evaluation in Guidance (dir. 1981, pres. 1984-85), Am. Assn. Counseling and Devel., Assn. Measurement and Eval. in Guidance (Western regional editor 1987—, conv. chair 1986), Calif. Assn. Counseling and Devel. (exec. bd. 1984—, pres. 1988—), Internat. Career Assn. Network (chair 1985—), Pi Lambda Theta, Alpha Phi Gamma, Psi Chi, Kappa Delta Pi, Sigma Alpha Iota. Contbr. articles in field to profl. jours. Home and Office: 2900 Amby Pl Hermosa Beach CA 90254

WIDDER, BETTE WIENBERG, nursing adminstrator; b. Lafayette County, Mo., June 20, 1929; d. Elmer Arthur and Lorene Mathilda (Bodenstab) Wienberg; m. John Arthur Widder, July 7, 1953; children—John A., Anne Whiteley, Susan Jane, Scott Kevin. R.N. Luth. Hosp. Sch. Nursing, 1950, U. Mo., 1950-53; BA cum laude, Linfield Coll., 1976. R.N., Oreg., N.Y. Acting supr. U. Mo. Hosps., 1951-52; mem. staff Arlington (Va.) Community Hosp., 1960-61, W. Jefferson Gen. Hosp., Marrero, La., 1965, dispensary 8th Naval Dist., 1965; mem. rehab. staff A. Holly Patterson Home, Uniondale, N.Y., 1969-70; mem. staff St. Vincent Hosp. and Med. Ctr., Portland, Oreg., 1972-78, asst. dir. nursing services, 1978—. Founder, editor St. Vincent Nursing Newsletter. Contbr. articles to profl. jours. Leader Girl Scouts U.S.A., Virginia Beach, Va., 1963-64. Mem. AAUW, SEE Internat., Am. Nurses' Assn., Oreg. Nurses' Assn., Oreg. Orgn. for Nurse Execs., Washington County Pub. Affairs Forum. Home: 15095 NW Oakmont Loop Beaverton OR 97006 Office: St Vincent Hosp & Med Ctr 9205 SW Barnes Rd Portland OR 97225

WIDENER, PERI ANN, public relations manager; b. Wichita, Kans., May 1, 1956; d. Wayne Robert and LuAnne (Harris) W. B.S., Wichita State U., 1978; postgrad. Ala. A&M U., 1981. Advt. intern Associated Advt., Wichita, 1978; pub. relations asst. Fourth Nat. Bank, Wichita, 1978-79; mktg. support rep. Boeing Co., Wichita, 1979-83, pub. relations rep., Huntsville, Ala., 1983-85, pub. relations mgr., 1985—. Participant United Way. Preston Huston scholar, Wichita State U., 1978; recipient Best Electronic Ad award Def. Electronics mag., 1982, Best Total Pub. Relations Program award Huntsville Press Club, 1985, Huntsville Media awards, 1986, 87, Huntsville Advt. Fedn. Addys, 1988; named one of Outstanding Young Women of Am., 1986. Mem. Women in Communications, Pub. Relations Council Ala. (bd. dirs. 1985—, State bd. 1988, officer Huntsville chpt. 1984—, Excellence award 1986, Achievement award 1986, Pres.'s award Huntsville chpt. 1985), Internat. Assn. Bus. Communicators (D2 Silver Quills award 1985). Mem. Pub. Relations Soc. Am., Huntsville-Madison County C. of C., Sigma Delta Chi. Club: Hunstville Press. Methodist. Office: The Boeing Co PO Box 1470 Huntsville AL 35807

WIDGER, BEVERLY ANN, retail executive; b. Hanover, N.H., Aug. 6, 1951; d. Norman E. Wilder and Kate (Read) Gauthier; m. Robert L. Widger, Jan. 6, 1976; 1 child, Ann. BS, Plymouth (N.H.) State Coll., 1973, N.Y. Inst. Tech., 1984; postgrad., SUNY, Stonybrook, 1984-85. Cert. tchr., N.H. Tchr. Cornish (N.H.) Elem. Sch., 1973-78; mgr. Children's Place, Lake Grove, N.Y., 1978-81, Yield House, Lake Grove, 1981-85; dist. mgr. Yield House, Merrimack, N.H., 1985-86, dir. store ops., 1986-87; ops. mgr. library services Yankee Book Peddler, Contoocook, N.H., 1987—; career network mem. Plymouth (N.H.) State Coll., 1986—. Named one of Outstanding Young Women Am., 1978. Mem. Nat. Retail Mchts. Assn., Nat. Assn. Female Execs., PTA, Working Parents for Action. Republican. Home: 37 Tanglewood Dr Henniker NH 03242 Office: Yankee Book Peddler Maple St Contoocook NH 13229

WIDGOFF, MILDRED, physicist, educator; b. Buffalo, Aug. 24, 1924; d. Leo and Rebecca (Shulimson) W.; children—Eve Widgoff Shapiro, Jonathan Bernard Widgoff Shapiro. B.A., U. Buffalo, 1944; Ph.D., Cornell U., 1952. Research assoc. Brookhaven Nat. Lab., Upton, N.Y., 1952-54; research fellow Harvard U., 1954-59; asst. prof. research Brown U., Providence, 1959-68; assoc. prof. research Brown U., 1968-74, prof. physics, 1974—. Fellow Am. Phys. Soc.; mem. Sigma Xi, Phi Beta Kappa, Phi Kappa Phi. Office: Brown U Dept Physics Box 1843 Providence RI 02912

WIDING, CAROL SCHARFE, lawyer; b. South Orange, N.J., Dec. 18, 1941; d. Howard Carman and Marjorie (McConaghy) Scharfe; m. C. Jon Widing, July 2, 1966; 1 child, Daniel McClure. BA, Wellesley Coll., 1964; MEd, Harvard U., 1965; JD, Widener U., 1980. Bar: Del. 1981, Pa. 1981, U.S. Dist. Ct. Del. 1981, U.S. Ct. Appeals (3d. cir.) 1983, Conn. 1984. Tchr. elem. schs. Lexington, Mass. and Bryn Mawr, Pa., 1964-68; pvt. tutor Ibadan, Nigeria, 1965; tchr. Phila. Adult Basic Edn. Acad., 1970-72; dep. atty. gen. child protection services Del. Dept. Justice, Wilmington, 1981-83; staff atty. UAW Legal Services, Newark, Del., 1983; assoc. Hebb & Gitlin, P.C., Hartford, Conn., 1985-86, Steinberg & Louden, Hartford, 1987—. V.p. program AAUW, Middletown, Del. 1974; chmn. pub. relations and fundraising Lower New Castle County Med. Ctr., Middletown, 1980. Mem. ABA, Pa. Bar Assn., Del. Bar Assn., Conn. Bar Assn., Hartford County Bar Assn., Hartford Assn. Women Attys. Home: 14 Briar Hill Avon CT 06001 Office: Law Offices of Bruce Louden 99 Pratt St Hartford CT 06103

WIDMAYER, PATRICIA, management consultant; b. Buffalo, Jan. 21, 1943; d. C. Lane and Elizabeth M. (Gillgus) Ramsdell; m. Lawrence C. Widmayer, June 15, 1963; children: Carole Lane, Christopher Almon. BA, Mich. State U., 1966, MA, 1969, PhD, 1971. Instr. Oakland U., Rochester, Mich., 1971-72; research assoc. Office of the Speaker, Lansing, Mich., 1973-75; dist. staff dir. Congressman Bob Carr, Washington, 1975-77; dir. legis. Mich. Dept. Edn., Lansing, 1977-82; dir. policy Office of Gov., Lansing, 1982-83; exec. dir. Gov.'s Commn. on Higher Edn., Lansing, 1983-85; pres. Widmayer and Assocs., Chgo., 1985—; trainer Nat. Women's Edn. Fund, Washington, 1982—; spl. project dir. colo. Commn. on Higher Edn., Denver, 1985-86; cons. Borg-Warner Found., Chgo., 1985-87, MacAuthur Found. 1987, Sears Found. 1987, Donors Forum Chgo., 1986, Associated Colls. Ill., 1986—, Colo. Dept. Edn., 1986—, Nat. Assn. Bank Women, 1987—, DePaul U., 1986—, Dept. of Agri., 1986—, Mich. Community Coll. Assn., 1987—. Author numerous govt. papers, reports, 1977-85; editor report: Putting our minds together, 1984. Vol. cons. to local, state and nat. campaigns and issue coalitions; coordinator Nat. Women's Polit. Caucus of Mich., 1975-80, Mich. Women's Assembly, 1976-84; bd. dirs. Econ. Devel. Corp., East Lansing, Mich., 1979-85. Inst. for Ednl. Leadership fellow George Washington U., Washington, 1978-79. Mem. Am. Assn. Higher Edn., Execs.' Club of Chgo., Delta Delta Delta (officer 1968-85) Lodge: Zonta (officer 1978-81). Home: 420 Church St Evanston IL 60201 Office: Widmayer and Assocs 500 N Michigan #1400 Chicago IL 60611

WIDNALL, SHEILA EVANS, aeronautics educator; b. Tacoma, Wash., July 13, 1938; d. Rolland John and Genievieve Alice (Krause) Evans; m. William Soule Widnall, June 11, 1960; children—William, Ann. BS, MIT, 1960, MS, 1961, PhD, 1964; PhD (hon.), New Eng. Coll., 1975, Lawrence U., 1987. Asst. prof. MIT, Cambridge, 1964-70, asst. prof., 1970-74, prof. aeronautics, 1974—; dir. univ. research U.S. D.O.T., Washington, 1974-75; dir. Chemfab Inc., Bennington, Vt., Aerospace Corp., Los Angeles, Draper Labs., Cambridge, Mass.; bd. trustees Carnegie Corp., 1984—. Contbr. articles to profl. jours.; patentee in field; assoc. editor AIAA Jour. Aircraft, 1972-75, Physics of Fluids, 1981—, Jour. Applied Mechanics, 1983-87; mem. editorial bd. Sci. '85, 1984-86. Chmn. faculty MIT, Cambridge, 1970-81, com. on undergrad. admission and fin. aid, 1982-84; bd. visitors U.S. Air Force Acad., Colorado Springs, Colo., 1978-83. Fellow AAAS (bd. dirs. 1982—, pres. elect 1986-87, pres. 1987-88, chmn. 1988—), Am. Phys. Soc. (exec. com. 1979-82), AIAA (bd. dirs. 1975-77, Lawrence Spery award 1972), Am. Acad. Arts and Scis.; mem. Soc. Women Engrs. (Outstanding Achievement award 1975), ASME, Nat. Acad. Engring. Club: Seattle Mountaineers. Office: MIT 77 Massachusetts Ave Cambridge MA 02139

WIDNER, DEBBIE FROST, foundation executive; b. Silver City, N.Mex., Apr. 20, 1959; d. Joseph Boyd and Edith Irene (Dannelley) Frost; m. Larry Glen Widner, Nov. 26, 1982; children: Amber D'Lynn, Trey Allen. BS in Agr., N.Mex. State U., 1981. Agt. Roosevelt County 4-H N.Mex. State U. Extension Service, Portales, 1982—. producer 4-H videos. Recipient Deans Excellence award N.Mex. State U., 1981. Mem. Nat. Assn. Agrl. Agts., Nat. Assn. Extension 4-H Agts., N.Mex. Assn. Extension 4-H Agts. (sec. 1985-86), N.Mex. Assn. Agrl. Agts. Democrat. Lodge: Order Eastern Star. Office: Roosevelt County Coop Extension Rt 1 Box 78A-1 Portales NM 88130

WIDULSKI, LAURA JEAN, accountant; b. New Rochelle, N.Y., Sept. 5, 1961; d. William Paul and Rosemarie Claire (Biscoglio) W. AS in Acctg., Westchester Community Coll., 1980; BBA in Acctg., Iona Coll., 1982; postgrad. bus. adminstrn. Pace U., 1985—. CPA, N.Y., realtor, 1987. CPA, N.Y.; lic. real estate salesperson. Staff acct. Litton Fin. Services, Stamford, Conn., 1982-83; asst. to controller, acct. Simon & Schuster Pub. Co., N.Y.C., 1983-85; auditor, staff acct. Lombardi & Palazzolo, CPA's, Yonkers, N.Y., 1985-86; owner, pres. Sun N Ski Tours, Inc., Scarsdale, N.Y., 1986—; realtor N. Am. Group, 1987—. Mem. Nat. Assn. Female Execs., Fin. Club Pace U. Republican. Roman Catholic. Avocations: skiing, tennis, running, dancing, singing. Home: Sentry Pl Scarsdale NY 10583 Office: Sun N Ski Tours Inc PO Box 592 Scarsdale NY 10583

WIDUTIS, FLORENCE, educator, author; b. Phila., May 29, 1912; d. Elmer Russell Alburger and Josephine (Reid) Weber; m. Albert Brownell, June 1931 (div. 1934); 1 child, Barbara Dell; m. George W. Widutis, Apr., 1940 (dec. 1959); 1 child, Josephine Puckett. BS magna cum laude, NYU, 1956; MEd, U. Md., 1961; postgrad., St. Louis U., U. Ghana, U. Mexico, %. Opinion analyst UN Info. Office, N.Y.C., 1943; editor, exec. dir. Program Info. Exchange, N.Y.C., 1944-47; faculty Arcane Sch. Meditation, N.Y.C., 1950-53; tchr. secondary schs. N.J. and D.C., 1957-76; editor, pub. Pilgrims, Somerville, NJ, 1956-60, Beautiful Day Books, College Park, Md., 1976—; freelance writer, workshop facilitator, symposium coordinator, lecturer various orgns., various states, 1976—; Editor Internat. Inst. Transpersonal Diplomacy Bd., Hamilton, Va., 1985-87; bd. dirs. Planetary Citizens, NYC, 1978-81, William Penn House, Washington, 1983-84. Author: Here's How It's Done, 1945, Yours Is the Power, 1977, The True Path, 1979; (with Catherine H. Clark) Books for New Age, Children and Youth, 1976, (curriculum) The Person and the Planet, 1980; contbr. various poems, articles on hunger, population, peace, education, smoking and health to profl. jours. Vol. Society Friends Com. on Nat. Legis., 1978, World Hunger Edn. Service, Washington, 1979. Democrat. Mem. Society of Friends. Clubs: Wayfarers, B and B Square Dance (Washington). Home and Office: 3318 Gumwood Dr Hyattsville MD 20783

WIEDEMANN, ANITA MELISSA, computer engineer; b. Knoxville, Tenn., Dec. 21, 1960; d. Tom Stanberry and Patricia Ann (Cox) Collier; adopted d. Samuel A. Collier; m. Jack Hunt Wiedemann, June 11, 1983. BA in Computer Sci., U. Tenn., 1984; MS, U. Cen. Fla., 1988. Computer engineer Martin Marietta Aerospace, Orlando, Fla., 1984—. Mem. Internat. Soc. Optical Engring., Am. Assn. Artificial Intelligence. Home: 6400 Lakeville Rd Orlando FL 32818

WIEDEN, MARION ANNA, microbiologist; b. Cleve., Oct. 16, 1937; d. Joseph Frank and Anna Barbara (Bohac) Rusnak; B.S., U. Ariz., 1959; m. Walter Carl Wieden, Aug. 8, 1959; children—Mark David, Jill Ann, Matthew Joe. MS, PhD Columbia Pacific U., 1987. Microbiologist, St. Mary's Hosp., Tucson, 1961-63, chief microbiologist, 1963-68; chief microbiology sect. VA Hosp., Tucson, 1968—; adj. faculty health related professions U. Ariz., 1986—; chmn. Tucson Inter-hosp. Infections Control Com., 1974-77; mem. clin. lab. adv. bd. Ariz. State Dept. Health Services, 1983—. Registered microbiologist and clin. lab. specialist Nat. Registry, Am. Acad. Microbiology. Mem. Am. Soc. Med. Tech. (liaison officer for VA in Ariz.), Ariz. State Soc. Med. Tech. (Cert. of Merit 1975, 78, 79, 80, 83, 85, Cert. of Achievement 1980; Outstanding Contbns. to Microbiology award 1981, 85, 87, Mem. of Yr. award 1981, state dir. 1976-79, 80-81, program chmn. 1981 conv., gen. chmn. 1983, 85, pres. Tucson chpt. 1980-81), Am. Soc. Microbiology (cert. specialist, chair microbiology sci. assembly 1986-87), Ariz. Soc. Microbiology (program chmn. Tucson br. 1979-81), Am. Pub. Health Assn., Assn. Practitioners in Infection Control, Internat. Soc. for Human and Animal Mycology, Am. Soc. Clin. Pathologists (various coms.), Smithsonian Instn., U. Ariz. Alumni Assn., Coccidioidomycosis Study Group, Med. Mycol. Soc. of Ams., Beta Beta Beta, Alpha Delta Pi. Roman

Catholic. Contbr. articles to profl. jours. Address: 7180 N Cathedral Rock Pl Tucson AZ 85718

WIEDL, SHEILA COLLEEN, biologist; b. Buffalo, Feb. 19, 1950; d. Frank George and Corinne Ruth (Nuskay) W.; B.S., Daemen Coll., 1972; M.S., U. Notre Dame, 1974; Ph.D., SUNY-Buffalo, 1986. Instr., Holy Cross Jr. Coll., South Bend, Ind., 1973-74; research technician SUNY, Buffalo, 1975-78; entomol. asst. N.Y. State Health Dept., 1979-80; entomol. intern Ohio Dept. Health, 1981; prof. natural scis. Trocaire Coll., Buffalo, 1974-85; postdoctoral scientist Am. Cyanamid, Lederle Labs., Pearl River, N.Y., 1985-86, clin. research assoc., 1986—. Mem. N.Y. State Assn. Two-Year Colls., Assn. Gnotobiotics, N.Y. State Archeol. Assn. Roman Catholic. Club: Notre Dame Alumni. Contbr. articles to profl. jours. Home: 298 Country Club Ln Pomona NY 10970-2501 Office: Lederle Labs Middletown Rd Pearl River NY 10965

WIEDLEA, JANE LEACH SMITH, civic worker; b. Battle Creek, Mich., Oct. 14, 1910; d. William Reynolds and Edith Pearl (Leach) Smith; A.B., Battle Creek Coll., 1933; postgrad. U. Mich., 1933; m. Clare Edgar Wiedlea, June 30, 1934; children—William Clare, Jane Reynolds, John Towle. Sch. librarian Willard Library, Battle Creek, 1927-29; desk librarian Battle Creek Coll., 1931-33, instr. history, 1933-35. Mem. Sturgis (Mich.) Public Library Bd., 1950-86, pres., 1955-60, 75-86; mem. Sturgis Hosp. Bd., 1969—, v.p., 1974-85, 87—, pres., 1985-87; pres. Sturgis Hosp. Aux., 1969-70, life mem., 1970—; sec. S.W. Dist. Hosp. Aux. Bd., 1970-74; active St. John's Guild, St. John's Altar Guild; chmn. planning com. centennial yr. Episcopal Diocese of Western Mich., 1874-1974; bd. dirs. James Monroe Meml. Found., 1956-59. Named Citizen of Yr., 1970. Mem. DAR (Amos-Sturgis chpt. regent 1953-55, 73-75, nat. vice chmn. Am. History month 1955-58, citizens steering com. 1959-60, state regent Mich. 1961-64, hon. state regent for life), U.S. Daus. of 1812, Daus. Colonial Wars, Daus. Am. Colonists. Republican. Episcopalian. Club: Polit. Study. Home: 400 Cottage Ave Sturgis MI 49091

WIEDRICH, JOYCE LORRAINE, nurse; b. Rochester, N.Y., June 21, 1952; d. Ernest Lee Wiedrich and Lorraine Maxine (Barth) Mason. Diploma, Highland Sch. of Nursing, 1973; AAS, Monroe Community Coll., 1973; BS in Nursing, U. Rochester, 1978; MS in Nursing, Family Health, U. Rochester, 1981. Cert. nurse practitioner. Staff nurse U. Rochester (N.Y.), 1973-80; nurse practitioner Highland Hosp., Rochester, 1980-85; asst. prof. nursing Monroe Community Coll., Rochester, 1985-86, nurse practitioner Rochester Cardiothoracic Assocs., 1986-87, Dr. Richard H. Feins, Rochester, 1987—; clin. assoc. U. Rochester, 1983—; cons. in nursing Monroe Community Coll., Rochester, 1987. Served with capt. USAR, 1983—. Mem. N.Y. State Nurse Practitioner Coalition (local rep. 1987—), Reserve Officers' Assn., Sigma Theta Tau. Republican. Methodist. Lodge: Eastern Star. Home: 63 Lochnavar Pkwy Pittsford NY 14534 Office: Dr Richard Feins 601 Elmwood Ave Box Surgery Rochester NY 14642

WIEGNER, ELIZABETH ANN, chemist, computer educator; b. Montville, N.J., Mar. 13, 1949; d. Clifford Raymond and Delta Eva (Balliet) W.; m. Fred Kitterle, Mar. 18, 1967 (div. 1973). BA in Chemistry and Psychology, Fla. Atlantic U., 1980; postgrad., Oral Roberts U., 1980-81, Calif. State U., Bakersfield, 1988—. Freelance tech. writer, translator, San Francisco, 1981-82; scientist Bechtel Labs., San Francisco, 1983-86; tech. writer Wilson-Zublin, Inc., Bakersfield, Calif., 1986-87; instr. computer studies Bakersfield Coll., 1987—; air quality technician Arco Oil & Gas Co., Bakersfield, 1987-88; chemist BC Labs. Inc., Bakersfield, 1987—. Mem. Am. Chem. Soc., Am. Running and Fitness Assn. Democrat. Episcopalian. Mailing Address: PO Box 10375 Bakersfield CA 93389-0375

WIEGNER, KATHLEEN KNAPP, magazine writer; b. Milw., Apr. 12, 1938; d. Russell Darwin and C. AngeLyn (Spicuzza) Knapp; m. Edward A. Wiegner, Dec. 16, 1960 (div. 1970); 1 child, Christine Elizabeth. BS, U. Wis., 1960, MA, 1962, PhD, 1967. Instr. U. Wis., Milw., 1964-66, asst. prof., 1967-73; writer, editor Forbes Mag., Los Angeles, 1974-85, bur. mgr., 1985-87, nat. tech. corr., 1987—. Author: (poetry) Encounters, 1972, Country Western Breakdown, 1974, Freeway Driving, 1981. Home: 2444 Cloverfield Santa Monica CA 90405 Office: Forbes Mag 11835 W Olympic #1135 E Los Angeles CA 90064

WIEL, CAROL LEE, sales and marketing executive; b. Washington, Mar. 11, 1943; d. John Myron and Alice Shelton (Trollinger) Ehrmantraut; m. Thomas Theodore, Sept. 5, 1964; children: Jeffrey Scott, Gregory Todd. BA, U. Md., 1964; student Nashville Sch. Art. Tchr. St. Mary's County, Lexington Park, Md., 1965-72; owner, gen. mgr. Standard Sales Co., Nashville, 1977-82; mgr. Aladdin Industries, Nashville, 1982—. Bd. dirs. Nat. Assn. for Sight Conservation and Aid to Blind, Nashville, 1982; paraprofl. counselor Crisis Intervention Ctr.; mem Franklin Rd. Acad. Athletic Boosters, Nashville Sch. Art; dept. chmn. United Way; mem. outreach com. Woodmont Christian Ch. Mem. Am. Telemktg. Assn., Nat. Assn. Female Execs., Nat. Housewares Mfrs. Assn., Nashville Warehouse Investors, Incentive Mfrs. Reps. Assn., Nat. Wildlife Fedn. (assoc.), Delta Gamma Alumnae Assn. Republican. Club: Md. Farms Racquet. Avocations: art and design, poetry, tennis. Home: 6043 Wellesley Way Brentwood TN 37027 Office: Ingram Video Inc 347 Reedwood Dr Nashville TN 37217

WIEMER-SUMNER, ANNE-MARIE, psychotherapist, educational administrator; b. Ger., Mar. 3, 1938; came to U.S., 1949, naturalized, 1956; d. Franz and Margaret (Neubacher) Wiemer; BA, Hunter Coll., 1963; MA, N.Y. U., 1965; cert. Psychoanalytic Individual and Group Therapy, Washington Square Inst. Psychotherapy, 1975, 76; m. Eric Eden Sumner, May 24, 1974; children: Erika, Trevor. Adminstrv. asst., counselor, asst. chmn. admissions N.Y. U., N.Y.C., 1956-69; asst. dean student Hunter Coll., N.Y.C., 1969-71; asso. dean students Cooper Union Advancement Art and Sci., N.Y.C., 1971—; supr. Washington Sq. Inst. for Psychotherapy, N.Y.C., 1977-81; pvt. practice psychotherapy, N.Y.C. Trustee Grace Ch. Sch., 1985—; pres. Washington Sq. Assn., 1987. Mem. Council Psychoanalytic Psychotherapists, Am. Psychol. Assn., Am. Group Psychotherapy Assn., Am. Orthopsychiat. Assn., Internat. Assn. Group Psychotherapy, Nat. Accreditation Assn. and Am. Exam. Bd. Psychoanalysis, N.Y. State Assn. Practicing Psychotherapists, Coll. Placement Council, Eastern Coll. Personnel Officers. Club: City. Home: 7-13 Washington Sq N New York NY 10003 Office: Cooper Union Cooper Sq New York NY 10003

WIENER, ANNABELLE, UN ofcl.; b. N.Y.C., Aug. 2, 1922; d. Philip and Bertha (Wrubel) Kalbfeld; ed. Hunter Coll.; married, Jan. 1, 1941; children—Marilyn Grunewald, Marjorie Petit, Mark. Chmn. UN Dept. Pub. Info., Nongovtl. Orgns. Exec. Com., spl. adviser to sec. gen. Internat. Women's Year Conf.; mem. exec. bd. Nongovtl. Orgns. Com. on Disarmament UN; bd. dirs. World Fedn. UN Assns., also founder, dir. art and philatelic program. Mem. Am. Fedn. Arts, Mus. Modern Art, Musee Nat. Message Biblique Marc Chagall, Am. Philatelic Soc., UN Philatelic Soc., UN Assn. U.S. Address: UN Hdqrs New York NY 10017

WIENER, VALERIE, public relations professional; b. Las Vegas, Oct. 30, 1948; d. Louis Isaac and Tui Ava (Knight) W. BJ, U. Mo., 1971, MA, 1972; MA, Sangamon State U., 1974; postgrad., McGeorge Sch. Law, 1976-79. Producer TV show "Checkpoint" Sta. KOMU-TV, Columbia, Mo., 1972-73; v.p., owner Broadcast Assocs., Inc., Las Vegas, 1972-86; pub. affairs dir. First Ill. Cable TV, Springfield, 1973-74; editor Ill. State Register, Springfield, 1973-74; producer and talent Nev. Realities Sta. KLVX-TV, Las Vegas, 1974-75; account exec. Sta. KBMI (now KFMS), Las Vegas, 1975-79; nat. traffic dir. six radio stas., Las Vegas, Albuquerque and El Paso, Tex., 1979-80; exec. v.p., gen. mgr. Stas. KXKO and KKJY, Albuquerque, 1980-81; exec. adminstr. Stas. KSET AM/FM, KVEG, KFMS and KKJY, 1981-83; press sec. U.S. Congressman Harry Reid, Washington, 1983-86; adminstrv. asst Friends for Harry Reid, Nev., 1986; press sec. U.S. Senator Harry Reid, Washington, 1987-88. Sponsor Futures for Children, Las Vegas, Albuquerque and El Paso, 1979-83; mem. Exec. Women's Council, El Paso, 1981-83, VIP bd. Easter Seals, El Paso, 1982. Named one of Outstanding Young Women of Am., 1982, Outstanding Vol. United Way, El Paso, 1983. Mem. Nat. Mgmt. Assn., Dem. Press Secs. Assn., El Paso Assn. Radio Stas., Nat. Assn. Female Execs., U.S. Senate Staff Club, Sigma Delta Chi. Democrat. Christian Scientist.

WIER, PATRICIA ANN, publishing executive; b. Coal Hill, Ark., Nov. 10, 1937; d. Horace L. and Bridget B. (McMahon) Norton; m. Richard A. Wier, Feb. 24, 1962, 1 dau., Rebecca Ann. B.A., U. Mo., Kansas City, 1964; M.B.A., U. Chgo., 1978. Computer programmer AT&T, 1960-62; lead programmer City of Kansas City, Mo., 1963-65; with Playboy Enterprises, Chgo., 1965-71; mgr. systems and programming Playboy Enterprises, 1971; with Ency. Brit., Inc., Chgo., 1971—; v.p. mgmt. services Ency. Brit. USA, 1975-83, exec. v.p. adminstrn., 1983-84; v.p. planning and devel. Ency. Brit., Inc., 1985, pres. Compton's Learning Co. div., 1985; pres. Ency. Brit. (USA), 1986—; exec. v.p. Ency. Brit., Inc., 1986—; mem. council Grad. Sch. Bus., U. Chgo., Northwestern U. Assocs.; chmn. Compton's Learning Co., 1987—. Bd. dirs. Body Politic Theatre. Mem. Direct Selling Assn. (bd. dirs. 1984—, chmn. 1987—), Women's Council U. Mo. Kansas City (hon. life), Com. 200, The Chgo. Network. Roman Catholic. Office: Ency Brittanica Inc 310 S Michigan Ave Chicago IL 60604

WIER, SANDRA THOMAS, infosytems specialist; b. Richmond, Va., Feb. 23, 1959; d. Clarence Overton and Gale (Anderson) Thomas; m. Frank Roland Wier, June 30, 1984. BS in Bus., Longwood Coll., 1981. With Va. Power (formerly Va. Elec. & Power Co.), Bremo Bluff, 1981—, assoc. budget analyst, 1983-86, planning and tracking bugdet analyst, 1986-87, assoc. project systems analyst, 1987—. Coach Dixie Youth Softball Assn., Dillwyn, Va., 1982-83; team cpt. local chpt. March of Dimes, 1985, 86, 87. Mem. Internat. Facilities Mgmt. Assn., Bldg. Ownwers and Mgrs. Assn., Am. Soc. Profl. and Exec. Women. Methodist. Home: Rte 1 Box 181A Dillwyn VA 23936 Office: Va Power Real Estate Facilities Innsbrook Technical Service Ctr 5000 Dominion Blvd Glen Allen VA 23060

WIERSEMA, CATHERINE B., financial consultant; b. Clermont, Puy De Dome, France, Sept. 28, 1953; came to U.S., 1972; d. Andre Boussard and Luce Auzies; m. Frederik D. Wiersema, June 13, 1987. B, Toulouse U., France, 1972; MBA, Simmons Coll., 1986. Trust asst. Sovran Bank, Richmond, Va., 1974-75, budget analyst, 1975-76, investment officer, 1976-80; asst. v.p. mktg. mgr. Bank of Boston, 1980-81; mgr. sales support Fidelity Investments, Boston, 1981-84, mgr. sales div., 1984-85, asst. v.p. group product mgr., 1985-86, asst. v.p. market mgr., 1986-87; pres. Fin. Sales Cons., Inc., Boston, 1987—; instr. mktg., sales Radcliffe Coll., Cambridge, Mass., 1987—. Counselor Planned Parenthood, Richmond, Va., 1979-80; bd. dirs. Project RAP, Beverly, Mass., 1984-86; mem. com. Boston Children's Mus., 1986—. Club: Boston.

WIESAND, CHRISTINE GLORIA, management consultant, information resource specialist; b. Balt., Oct. 10, 1955; d. Rowland Kenneth and Juliana (Trasarti) Hill; m. William J. Wiesand III, Mar. 26, 1977 (div. 1987). BA in Fgn. Langs., Coll. of Notre Dame, 1977; MBA in Acctg., Loyola Coll., Balt., 1982. Sect. chief internal audit AT&T Tech. Inc., Balt., 1977-83; sr. mgr. electronic data processing auditing Black & Decker Corp., Balt., 1983-87; mgr. mgmt. cons. services, info. resource Price Waterhouse, Balt., 1987—; speaker conf. Computer Audit, Control and Security, Chgo., 1985, North Jersey Inst. Internal Auditors, Newark, 1986. Mem. Electronic Data Processing Auditors Assn., Inst. Internal Auditors, Mid-Atlantic Top Secret User Group, Info. Systems Security Assn., Profl. Certs. Cert. Info. Systems Auditor, Cert. Systems Profl. Democrat. Roman Catholic. Office: Price Waterhouse 7 St Paul St Suite 1700 Baltimore MD 21202

WIESE, KATHLEEN FAYE, nursing administrator; b. Hazen, N.D., Mar. 19, 1957; d. Ben F. and Wilma E. (Buchmann) Thomas; m. Gene P. Wiese, Sept. 1, 1978; 1 child, Adam J. Diploma, Bismarck Hosp. Sch. Nursing, 1977. Cert. critical care nurse; RN. Nurse Hazen Hosp., 1977-78; intensive care nurse Mandan (N.D.) Hosp., 1978-81, intensive care, supr. emergency room, 1981-85, asst. dir. nursing, 1985, dir. patient care services, 1985—, acting adminstr., 1987—; sec. SW Area Health Edn. Ctr. for Advanced Life Support, N.D., 1984-86; mem. Gov.'s Task Force on Advanced Life Support, N.D., 1984-86. Mem. Safety Belt Coalition, N.D., 1987—; mem. ambulance adv. com. Burleigh-Morton County, 1988; hosp. rep. Blue Cross & Blue Shield of N.D.; bd. dirs. Burleigh-Morton div. Am. Heart Assn., 1987—, program chairperson, 1987—, Central N.D. Tumor Registry, 1985—. Mem. Am. Orgn. Nurse Execs., Am. Assn. Critical Care Nurses, Missouri Valley Critical Care Nurses (sec. 1979-80, v.p. 1980-81, pres. 1981-83), N.D. Nurse Adminstrs., N.D. Hosp. Assn. (constitution & bylaws com.), Am. Heart Assn. Democrat. Lutheran. Home: Rt 5 Box 329 Bismarck ND 58501 Office: Mandan Hosp 1000 18th St NW Mandan ND 58554

WIESENBERG, JACQUELINE LEONARDI, lecturer; b. West Haven, Conn., May 4, 1928; d. Curzio and Filmenia Olga (Turriziana) Leonardi; m. Russel John Wiesenberg, Nov. 23; children—James Wynne, Deborann Donna. B.A., State U. N.Y. at Buffalo, 1970, postgrad., 1970-73, 80—. Interviewer, examiner Dept. Labor, New Haven, 1948-52; sec. W.I. Clark Co., Hamden, Conn., 1952-55; acct. VA Hosp., West Haven, 1956-60; acct.-commissary U.S. Air Force Missle Site, Niagara Falls, N.Y., 1961-62; tchr. Buffalo City Schs., 1970-73, 79; acct. Erie County Social Services, Buffalo, 1971-73; lectr., 1973—. Contbr. articles to CAP, U.S. Air Force mag., 1954—. Capt., Nat. Found. March of Dimes, 1969—, com. mem. telethon, 1983-86; den mother Boy Scouts Am., 1961-68; chmn. Meals on Wheels, Town of Amherst, 1975-76; leader, travel chmn. Girl Scouts Am., 1968-77. Mem. Internat. Platform Assn., Am. Astrol. Assn., Western N.Y. Conf. Aging, Epsilon Delta Chi, Alpha Iota. Home: 14 Norman Pl Amherst NY 14226

WIESENFELD, BESS GAZEVITZ, business executive, real estate developer; b. Elizabeth, N.J., May 6, 1915; d. Morris and Rebecca (Sokolov) Gazevitz; m. Benjamin Wiesenfeld, Oct. 23, 1938 (dec.); children: Myra Judith Wiesenfeld Lewis, Elaine Phyllis Wiesenfeld Livingston, Ira Bertram, Sarah Ann Wiesenfeld Wasserman. BFA, N.Y. Sch. Design, N.Y.C., 1982. Real estate devel. Colonia, N.J., 1961—; interior designer 1961—; chair Bess & Co., Phila., 1982—. Mem. Nat. Trust for Hist. Preservation, (assoc.) Am. Soc. Interior Designers, Met. Mus. Art., Mus. Modern Art, Smithsonian Inst., Victorian Soc. of Met. Opera Guild. Republican. Jewish. Home: 374 New Dover Rd Colonia NJ 07067 also: 2320 Old South Ocean Blvd Palm Beach FL 33480

WIESLER, EVELYN LYDIA, stock enforcement investigator; b. Queens, N.Y., Sept. 21, 1959; d. Otto Franz and Lieselotte Elfriede (Prepens) W. BBA, Pace U., 1983, postgrad. Legal sec. Morton A. Luchs Esq., N.Y.C., 1977-78, Mendes and Mount, N.Y.C., 1978; sr. communications analyst N.Y. Stock Exchange, 1978-88, enforcement investigator, 1988—. Mem. Empire Wit, Phi Chi Theta. Lutheran. Home: 61-14 69th Ln Middle Village NY 11379 Office: NY Stock Exchange 11 Wall St New York NY 10005

WIESNER, JOAN RUTH, state senator; b. Passaic, N.J., Feb. 25, 1950; d. Harry James and Ruth Dorothy (Elander) Winslow; m. Albert Frederick Wiesner, III, June 12, 1971; 1 child, Albert Frederick, IV. B.A. in English, U. R.I., 1972. Research asst. Eastern Color and Chem. Co., Providence, R.I., 1972-73; personnel supr. Wiesner Mfg. Co., Providence, 1972-77; mem. R.I. Senate, 1983—; mem. exec. council USDA Research and Conservation and Devel. Council, 1978—. Chmn., Burrillville Republican Town Com., R.I., 1980-83; bd. dirs. Northwest Health and Community Nursing Com., 1984—, No. R.I. Mental Health Assn., Woonsocket, 1984—; mem. exec. com. R.I. Rep. State Central Com., Providence, 1984—. Mem. N. Providence Bus. and Profl. Women's Club. Baptist. Avocations: tennis; skiing; singing. Home: 60 Sherman Farm Rd Harrisville RI 02830 Office: RI State House Smith St Room 21 Providence RI 02864 *

WIESNER, SHARON MARIE, investment banker, oil production executive; b. Omaha, July 16, 1938; d. Ralph Remmington and Evelyn Adeline (Morris) Von Bremer; m. Virgil James Wiesner, Apr. 4, 1959 (div. 1982); children—Scott James, Lydia Marie, Michelle Elizabeth. B.A., Creighton U., 1959; M.A., U. Nebr.-Omaha, 1964, postgrad., 1979-82. Owner, v.p. Wiesner Distbg. Co. Inc., Lincoln, Nebr., 1966-72, Wiesner Tire Co. Inc., Omaha, 1972-75; v.p. Fin. Inc., Omaha, 1975-82; with fin., sales oil Am. Internat. Sales Corp., Dallas, 1982-83; pres. Joint Capital Resources, Dallas, 1983—; Richland Petroleum seminar, 1987; Dresser Atlas Oil, Logging and Geol. Inst., 1987. Editor: Born Rich: A Historical Book of Omaha, 1978. Author: Slanting News, 1959; Critical Study of Iago's Motivation, 1964. Vice pres. Assistance League Omaha, 1973-78; fund raiser Opera Omaha; v.p. women's bd. Omaha Community Playhouse; v.p. Lincoln Symphony Guild, 1966-71; bd. dirs. Omaha Jr. Theatre, 1975-79. Named Outstanding Young Woman Jr. C. of C., Norfolk, Nebr., 1964; recipient Valuable Service awards Lincoln Gen. Hosp., Omaha Community Playhouse. Mem. Omaha Writers Group, The Quill, Landmarks Inc., Nat. Beer Wholesalers, AAUW, Omaha Symphony Guild (v.p. 1973-78), Omaha C. of C., Lincoln C. of C., Brownville Hist. Soc., Brownville Fine Arts Assn., Nebr. Kennel Club, Dalmatian Club Am., Minn.-St. Paul Dalmatian Club, Blue Ribbon Dog Breeders, Beta Sigma Phi, Omicron Delta Kappa, Phi Delta Gamma, Theta Phi Alpha (pres. 1958-59). Club: Womens (v.p. 1966-70). Avocations: painting; music; art; writing. Home and Office: Joint Capital Resources PO Box 12518 Dallas TX 75225

WIEST, ELIZABETH HERMAN, nursing educator; b. Lancaster, Pa., July 3, 1936; d. Paul Lester and Elizabeth MacDonald (Woodburn) Herman; diploma Lancaster Gen. Hosp. Sch. Nursing, 1957; B.S.N., U. Md., 1966, M.S., 1968; Ed.D., U. Wyo., 1980; m. Donald K. Wiest, Mar. 8, 1980. Staff nurse Lancaster Gen. Hosp., 1957-63, Univ. Hosp., Balt., 1965-66; asst. prof. U. Md., Balt., 1967-74; asst. prof. U. Wyo., Laramie, 1974-80, assoc. prof., 1980-83, dir. off-campus nursing programs, 1983—. Bd. dirs., past chmn. bd. Wyo. affiliate Am. Heart Assn., rep. N.W. Regional Heart Com., 1981-85, mem. edn. and community program com., mem. cardiovascular nursing council of Am. Heart Assn.; exec. bd. Western Council Higher Edn. in Nursing, 1982-85; apptd. to Bd. Health City of Laramie. USPHS trainee, 1966-67; Kemper scholar, summer 1969. Mem. LWV, Am. Nurses Assn. (council on continuing edn.), Western Inst. Nursing, Wyo. Nurses Assn. (pres. Dist. 12, bd. dirs.), Nat. League Nursing, Wyo. Commn. Nursing and Nursing Edn. (vice-chmn.), Lancaster Gen. Hosp. Nurses Alumni Assn., Summer Sch. Alumni Assn. Rutgers Summer Sch. Alcohol Studies, U. Wyo. Alumni Assn., Sigma Theta Tau. Republican. Lutheran. Home: 1930 Sheridan Laramie WY 82070 Office: U Wyo Sch Nursing Box 3065 University Station Laramie WY 82071

WIETHOP, ROSE MARIE, financial analyst; b. St. Louis, Aug. 21, 1960; d. Joseph Louis Sr. and Marie Annastasia (Skurat) Difani; m. Brian Vernon Wiethop, June 11, 1983; 1 child, Brian Vernon Jr. BA in Math., Computer Sci. magna cum laude, St. Louis U., 1982, MBA in Fin., 1986. Programmer analyst Anheuser Busch Cos., Inc., St. Louis, 1982-84, systems analyst, 1984-85; fin. analyst Anheuser Busch Inc., St. Louis, 1985-87; treasury analyst Anheuser Busch Cos., Inc., St. Louis, 1987-88; pres. R. Wiethop Cons. Inc., St. Louis, 1988—; lectr. on computer sci. Mem. Women in Bus. Network (research and edn. coordinator 1985, edn. planner 1986). Home and Office: 11114 Wedgestone Ct Saint Louis MO 63126

WIGGENHORN, SUSAN MARIE, telecommunications executive; b. Dayton, Ohio, June 16, 1951; d. Roman Hubert and Ruth Ellen (Bramlage) W. BS in Indsl. Mgmt., Purdue U., 1973; MBA, Ind. U., 1987. Sr. cons. Arthur Andersen & Co., Chgo., 1973-76; mgr. The Ind. Nat. Bank, Indpls., 1976-81; data processing officer Ind. Nat. Bank, Indpls., 1981-84, asst. v.p., 1984—; adjunct prof. telecommunications Ind. U., 1987. Contbr. articles to mags. Mem. fin. com. and council Immaculate Heart of Mary Ch., Indpls., 1985-87. Recipient Meritorious award Ind. Sec. of State, 1986. Mem. Ind. Telecommunications User Assn. (founder, Telecommunications Profl. of Yr. 1986), Network Women in Bus., Ind. U. Alumni Assn. (bd. dirs.), Zeta Tau Alpha.

WIGGERS, CHARLOTTE SUZANNE WARD, magazine editor; b. Cleve., Dec. 14, 1943; d. Raymond Paul and Irene Mary (Knapp) W.; m. John Houston Black, Feb. 1975 (div. 1980). AB, Smith Coll., 1966. Asst. editor The Hudson Rev., N.Y.C., 1966-76; assoc. editor The Print Collector's Newsletter, N.Y.C., 1977-79; copy editor Electronics mag., McGraw-Hill, N.Y.C., 1979-81; sr. copy editor Spectrum mag., N.Y.C., 1981-85; mng. editor Essence mag., N.Y.C., 1985—. Home: 50 W 85th St Apt 5 New York NY 10024 Office: Essence Magazine 1500 Broadway New York NY 10036

WIGGINS, CAROLYN LEE, educator; b. N.Y.C., Dec. 8, 1947; d. Roedolphus and Hattie (Simmons) W. BA, Antioch Coll., 1974, MEd, 1976; LHD (hon.), Ea. Am. U., 1980; postgrad., Fordham U., 1982, U. Santa Barbara, 1986. Cert. tchr., N.Y., Calif. Tchr., Morning Side Day Care Ctr., Inc., N.Y.C., 1969-76; early childhood specialist Laguardia Community Coll., Long Island City, N.Y., 1976-80; dir. Cathedral Pkwy. Pre-Sch., N.Y.C., 1980-82; ednl. cons. Concerned Parents Family Day Care, Bronx, N.Y., 1982-83; asst. exec. dir. Morning Side Head Start, N.Y.C., 1983-86; dir. edn. Concerned Parents Family Day Care, Inc., 1986—; cons. Harlem Interfaith Counseling Service, 1986—; adj. prof. Coll. of New Rochelle Sch. New Resources, 1983—; asst. chancellor Ednl. Theol. Consortium, N.Y.C., 1983—; pres. Ednl. Assocs., N.Y.C., 1985-86. Author workbooks. Mem. Melrose Housing Devel. Block Assn., Bronx, N.Y., 1979—; mem. adv. com. Early Childhood Resource Info. Ctr., N.Y.C., 1984—; chmn. edn. com. Morisanic Urban Renewal Community Orgn., Bronx, 1980—; vice chmn. Concerned Parents Family Day Care, Inc., Bronx, 1984-86; pres. North Atlantic Research Inst., 1986—. Mem. Nat. Assn. Edn. Young Children, Early Childhood Edn. Council N.Y., Assn. Black Women in Higher Edn., Assn. Black Educators of N.Y., United Negro Coll. Fund, Horace Mann Soc. Democrat. Methodist. Avocations: reading, traveling. Office: Concerned Parents Family Day Care Inc 1180 Rev James Polite Ave Bronx NY 10459

WIGGINS, MARIE ELIZABETH, accountant; b. Ft. Thomas, Ky., Feb. 16, 1949; d. Joseph Herbert and Alma Elizabeth (Wolking) Hesselbrock; m. G. Donald Wiggins, May 14, 1977; children: Timothy Donald, Carrie Marie. BBA, U. Cin., 1972, MBA, 1975. CPA. File clk. Cin. Tax Bur., 1967-69; jr. acct. Main Hurdman, Cin., 1969-72; supr. Haines Landen CPA, Cin., 1972-76; mgr. William I. Schoenfeld Co., Dayton, Ohio, 1976—. Contbr. articles to periodicals. Mem. Am. Inst. CPAs, Ohio Soc. CPAs. Mem. Ch. of God. Home: 810 Gondert Ave Dayton OH 45403 Office: William I Schoenfeld & Co 120 W 2d St Suite 1300 Dayton OH 45402

WIGGINS-WALCOTT, GWENDOLYN ANN, financial systems executive, consultant; b. Bklyn., May 25; d. Francis and Ann Lee (Jackson) Wiggins; 1 child, Gabrielle Ann. BA, CUNY; MBA, L.I. U., 1976. Staff acct. Mitchell and Tiros, CPAs, N.Y.C., 1976-77; chief acct. Nat. Commn. on Observance of Internat. Women's Yr., N.Y.C., 1977-78; controller Port Royal Communications, 1978-79; internal auditor Port Authority of N.Y. and N.J., 1979-81, mgr.-in-tng., 1981-83, mgr. fin. systems, 1983—; prin. G.A. Wiggins and Assocs., Bklyn., 1977—. Co-chmn. bd. dirs. Ch. Ushers Assn. of Bklyn. and L.I., 1979-81; mem. Community Planning Bd., Bklyn., 1982-84. Thomas A. Ellis Oratorical scholar, 1968. Mem. Nat. Assn. Black Accts. (regional v.p. 1982-84), Nat. Assn. Accts. (assoc. dir. 1982-84), Fin. Women's Assn., Council Concerned Black Execs. (bd. dirs. 1981-88). Democrat. Baptist. Club: Toastmasters (N.Y.C.). Home: 325 Clinton Ave Suite 8B Brooklyn NY 11205

WIIG, ELISABETH HEMMERSAM, educator; b. Esbjert, Denmark, May 22, 1935; came to U.S., 1957, naturalized, 1967; d. Svend Frederick and Ingeborg (Hemmersam) Nielsen; m. Karl Martin Wiig, June 10, 1958; children—Charlotte E., Erik D. B.A., Statsseminariet Emdrupborg, 1956; M.A., Western Res. U., 1960; Ph.D., Case Western Res. U., 1967; postgrad., U. Mich., 1967-68. Clin. audiologist Cleve. Hearing and Speech Center, 1959-60; instr. dept. phonetics Bergen (Norway) U., 1960-64; asst. prof., dir. aphasia rehab. program U. Mich., 1968-70; asst. prof. Boston U., 1970-73, asso. prof., chmn. dept., 1973-77, prof. dept. communication disorders, 1977-87. Author: Language Disabilities in Children and Adolescents, 1976, Language Assessment and Intervention for the Learning Disabled, 1980, 84, CELF Screening Tests: Elementary and Secondary Levels, 1980, Clinical Evaluation of Language Functions, 1980, 87; Test of Language Competence, 1985; editor: Human Communication Disorders: An Introduction, 1981, 85; contbr. articles to profl. jours. Recipient Metcalf Cup and Prize for excellence in teaching Boston U., 1967. Fellow Am. Speech and Hearing Assn. (cert. clin. competence in speech pathology and audiology); mem. Council Exceptional Children, Internat. Neuropsychology Soc. Address: 7101 Lake Powell Dr Arlington TX 76016

WIK, JEAN MARIE (BECK), library media specialist; b. Aitkin, Minn., Feb. 10, 1938; d. Herman Otto Beck and Ferdina Mathilda (Petersen) Kalt; m. Richard Lyle Wik, Aug. 17, 1958; children: Steven L., Lori Jo. BS, No. State Coll., Aberdeen S.D., 1963; MA, U. Minn., 1972; cert. in media arts,

Mankato State U., 1974. Elem. tchr. Howard Hedger Sch., Aberdeen, S.D., 1958-62; tchr. spl. edn. Westwood Sch., Bloomington, Minn., 1963-64; elem. tchr. Washburn Sch., 1964-71; media generalist elem. and secondary schs., 1972-86, Kennedy High Sch., Bloomington, 1986—; dir. Annehurst Curriculum Classifications System project Bloomington Schs., 1976-85. Mem. Minn. Edn. Assn., NEA, Minn. Ednl. Media Orgn. Club: Christian Women's (Bloomington) (pres. 1972-74, area rep. 1981-85). Office: Kennedy High Sch 9801 Nicollet Ave S Bloomington MN 55420

WIKE, D. ELAINE, business executive; b. Ridgecrest, Calif., Sept. 26, 1954; d. Robert G. and Jimmie Mae (Sallee) Field; student U. Houston, 1975-77; m. Mike Wike, Oct. 14, 1978; children—Mike II, Angelina Elaine, William V., Danielle Elizabeth. Legal sec. Morgan, Lewis & Bockius, Washington, 1977-78; legal asst. Alfred C. Schlosser & Co., Houston, 1972-77, 78-81, Jerry Sadler, atty., Houston, 1982-83; founder, owner DEW Profl. & Bus. Services, Houston, 1979—; office mgr. Law Offices Mike Wike, Houston, 1983—. Treas., Wilhelm Schole Parents Orgn., 1981-82; vol. campaign worker, (Ron Paul for Congress and Reagan for Pres.), 1975, 76; mem. Republican Presdl. Task Force. Mem. Young Ams. for Freedom, Nat. Notary Assn., Nat. Assn. Female Execs., Am. Soc., Notaries. Republican. Mem. Christian Ch. Office: 2421 S Wayside Dr Houston TX 77023

WIKSTROM, LORETTA WERMERSKIRCHEN, artist; b. Willow River, Minn., Mar. 2, 1938; d. Jacob Joseph and Anna Bertha (Doege) Wermerskirchen; m. Donovan Carl Wikstrom, Aug. 16, 1958; children: Bradley Donovan, Kendra Kay, Brock Karl. Student, St. Paul Sch. of Art, 1956-57, U. Minn., 1957-58, Honolulu Acad. of Art, 1963-66, Dayton Art Inst., 1985-87. Exhibited in group shows Sinclair Coll., 1985, Arts Venture, 1985; one woman shows Beavercreek Library, 1986, City of Englewood, 1986. Vol. artist Boy Scouts Am., Charleston, S.C. and Minn., 1967-74; vol. artist, tchr. Girl Scouts Am., O'Fallon, Ill., 1975-76; vol. art judge Pub. elem., Jr. and Sr. High Sch., Charleston and Mascoutah, Ill., 1969-78, Ill. State Hist. Library, Belleville, Ill., 1979, Belbrook (Ohio) High Sch., 1988. Recipient 2d place and hon. mention Nat. Nature and Wildfowl Show, 1987, hon. mention Wyoming (Ohio) Pub. Arts Commn. show, 1987. Mem. Guild S.C. Artists, Charleston Artists Guild, Minn. Artists Assn., Gateway East Artists Guild, St. Louis Artists Guild, Beavercreek Creative Artists Assn. (sec. 1987—, v.p. 1988—), Dayton Soc. Painters and Sculptors. Home: 45 Hawthorne Glen Trail Beavercreek OH 45440

WILBORN, AURELIA, insurance agent, accountant, registered investment adviser; b. Mobile, Ala., Oct. 18, 1948; d. Joseph and Cecilia (Matthews) Dabney; m. Anthony Outten, June 25, 1965; 1 son, Alexander; m. 2d, Donald Wilborn, Sept. 27, 1981. Grad. LaSalle Extension U., Chgo., 1982. Lic. ins. agt. Accounts receivable clk. CNA, Chgo., 1966-68, Maremont, Chgo., 1968-70, Interstate United, Chgo., 1970-75; investment processor Seaway Nat. Bank, Chgo., 1976-86; propr. Wilborn's Bookkeeping & Acctg. Services, Libra Mailing Co. Pollwatcher mayoral election, Chgo., 1983. Mem. Nat. Assn. Female Execs. Baptist, U.S. C. of C.

WILBUR, SANDRA BETH, music company executive; b. Little Rock, May 24, 1946; d. Jerome Seymour and Ruth (Hirsch) Beloff; m. James H. Wilbur, Mar. 23, 1974; children: Jason, Kristina. BA, Sarah Lawrence Coll., 1968; postgrad., U. Calif., Berkeley, 1969; MA, UCLA, 1972. Pres. Gold Std. Music & Prodn., Plainfield, N.J., 1972-82; instr. Am. Guild Authors & Composers, N.Y.C., 1977-81; assoc. music dir. Benton & Bowles Ad Agy., N.Y.C., 1980-82; pres. Sandy Wilbur Music, Inc., N.Y.C., 1982—. Composer, lyricist (songs) Hit'n Run Lover, The Woman In Me. V.p. Plainfield symphony Orch., 1979-81. Recipient Clio award, 1982. Mem. AFTRA, Am. Soc. Authors, Composers and Pubs., Screen Actors Guild, Am. Fedn. Musicians, Songwriters Guild. Office: 48 E 43d St 7th floor New York NY 10017

WILBURN, MARY NELSON, lawyer, writer; b. Balt., Feb. 18, 1932; d. David Alfred and Phoebe Blanche (Novotny) Nelson; A.B. cum laude, Howard U., 1952; M.A., U. Wis., 1955, J.D., 1975; m. Adolph Yarbrough Wilburn, Mar. 5, 1957; children—Adolph II, Jason David. Bar: Wis. 1975, U.S. Supreme Ct 1981. Lectr. U. Wis. Law Sch., 1975-77, 83, 84, 85; atty. adv. Bur. Prisons, Dept. Justice, 1977-82; chmn. Wis. State Parole Bd., Madison, 1986-87; gen. counsel D.C. Bd. Parole, 1987—; commr. The Commn. to Restructure the Interstate Compact, 1988—; mem. Women's Bur., Dept. Labor, 1981-82; mem. Wis. Sentencing Commn., 1986-87. Mem. Madison Met. Sch. Dist. Bd. Edn., 1975-77; assoc. mem. Schutz Am. Sch. Bd., Alexandria, Egypt, 1983-85. Mem. Internat. Assn. Paroling Authorities (exec. v.p. 1987—), Women's Bar Assn., Nat. Bar Assn., ABA, The Links, Inc., Am. Correctional Assn., Nat. Assn. Black Women Attys., Federacion International de Abogadas, Nat. Council Negro Women (commn. on edn.), Howard U. Alumni Assn., Alpha Kappa Alpha. Club: Nat. Lawyers (Washington). Contbr. to Cairo Today, 1983-84. Office: DC Bd Parole 1111 E St NW Suite 600 Washington DC 20004

WILCHER, SHIRLEY J., lawyer; b. Erie, Pa., July 28, 1951; d. James S. Wilcher and Jeanne (Evans) Cheatham. AB cum laude, Mt. Holyoke Coll., 1973; MA, New Sch. Social Research, 1976; JD, Harvard U., 1979. Bar: N.Y. 1980. Assoc. Proskauer Rose Goetz and Mendelsohn, N.Y.C., 1979-80; staff atty. Nat. Women's Law Ctr., Washington, 1980-85; assoc. counsel Com. on Edn. and Labor U.S. Ho. Reps., Washington, 1985—. Editor Harvard U. Civil Rights/Civil Liberties Law Rev., 1978-79; contbr. articles to profl. jours. Nat. bd. dirs. Nat. Polit. Congress of Black Women, Washington, 1985-87; convenor Black Women's Roundtable on Voter Participation, Washington, 1984-85. Mem. ABA, Nat. Bar Assn., Nat. Conf. Black Lawyers (local bd. dirs. 1980-87, nat. bd. dirs. 1986-87). Democrat. Buddhist. Office: Com on Edn and Labor 2181 Rayburn HOB Washington DC 20515

WILCHER, SUSAN BURNS, trade association executive; b. Phila., Oct. 27, 1952; d. Henry E. and Selma R. (Windermann) Burns; m. Thomas E. Wilcher, Oct. 12, 1983. B.A., Lafayette Coll., 1974; J.D., NYU, 1977. Bar: N.Y. 1978. Counsel Ind. Ins. Agts. Am., Inc., N.Y.C., 1977-79, asst. gen. counsel, 1979-83, v.p., corp. sec., 1983—; counsel Ind. Ins. Agts. Am. Ednl. Found., N.Y.C., 1983—; chmn. Legal Com. Future One, N.Y.C., 1982—. Founder Nat. Agents Polit. Action Commn., Washington, 1983. Mem. ABA, N.Y. County Lawyers Assn., Phi Beta Kappa. Contbr. articles to profl. jours.

WILCOX, CATHERINE CECILE SLATTERY, education consultant; b. Norwalk, Conn., Mar. 19, 1942; d. Martin John and Catherine Mary (Creagh) Slattery; m. William Bryan Wilcox, Feb. 18, 1964; children: Catherine Anne, William, Amy, Heather, Alexis. BS in Edn., Western Conn. State U., 1969; MA in Edn., U. Bridgeport, 1976; Cert. in Profl. Edn., So. Conn. State U., 1983. Cert. in Adminstrn. and Supervision. Tchr. West Sch., New Canaan, 1969-83; lectr., cons. IBM, Atlanta, 1984-86, cons., 1986—; writing coordinator South Sch., New Canaan, 1986—; pvt. practice edn. cons. U.S., Mex., Can., 1985—; pres. Coast-to-Coast Consultants, 1986—. Editor: The Other Side of the Coin, 1987. Vol. Stamford Festival of Arts, 1976-86; guide Stamford Nature Ctr., 1982-84. Mem. Assn. for Supervision and Curriculum Devel., Nat. Edn. Assn., Phi Delta Kappa. Roman Catholic. Club: Shippan Racquet (Stamford). Home: 29 Mohegan Ave Stamford CT 06902

WILCOX, COLLEEN BRIDGET, special education administrator; b. Rock Island, Ill., July 24, 1949; d. Wayne Eugene and Virginia Mae (Dewrose) W. B.S., U. Iowa, 1971; M.S., U. Ariz., 1974; PhD U. So. Calif., 1986; ednl. adminstrn. credential U. So. Calif. Asst. dir. parks and recreation City of Moline (Ill.), 1969-74; dir. speech pathology Instituto Guatemalteca Sequiridad, Peace Corps., Guatemala City, 1971-72; speech and lang. specialist Tucson Sch. Dist., 1974-75; aphasia tchr. specialist, itinerant specialist Los Angeles County Schs., 1975-77; program specialist in severe lang. disorder/aphasia Los Angeles County Supt. Schs., 1977-79, program adminstr./communication disorders, 1979-83, mem. budget standards com. 1979-82; mem. credential adv. bd., communications dept. Calif. State U., Los Angeles, 1978, asst. prof., 1977-83, chmn. sabbatical rev. com.; dir. spl. edn. Tucson Unified Sch. Dist., 1983-88; supt. No. Suburban Spl. Edn. Dirs., Highland Park, Ill., 1988—; art dir. the Great Stampede, 1981-83; Bd. dirs. dept. developmental disabilities Assn. Retarded Citizens; bd. dirs. Tuscon Chpt. Diabetes Assn., 1988—, Pima Council on Developmental Disabilities; chmn. spl. edn. adv. council Pima Coll. Spl. Edn.; co-chair Mayor's Com. Constitution Celebration, 1986. Recipient Harriett Rutherford Johnstown award Pi Beta Phi, 1971; Barnes Drill award U. Iowa, 1971; lic. speech pathologist, cert. tchr. speech and hearing therapy, severely handicapped credential, learning handicapped credential, Calif.; cert. speech and lang. therapist, Ariz. Mem. Calif. Speech and Hearing Assn. (exec. council 1986—), Am. Speech and Hearing Assn. (cert. clin. competence in speech pathology, conv. com. 1979, com. on manpower 1982-83, Ariz. legis. councilor 1986—), Jr. League of Tucson (state polit. action delegate 1986), Council Exceptional Children (legis. com.), Pi Beta Phi Alumnae, Phi Delta Kappa. Co-author, illustrator: Let's Share, 1983, Super Soup, 1986, Understanding and Preventing AIDS, 1987. Office: NSSED 760 Red Oak Ln Highland Park IL 60035

WILCOX, EVLYN, city mayor. children: Wayne, Moire, Marlene. Owner, pres. Manpower, Inc., San Bernardino, Riverside, Upland, San Gabriel Valley and Corona, Calif.; mayor City of San Bernardino. Pres. Arrowhead United Way, 1983, campaign chmn., 1981; pres. Community Arts Prodns.; treas., bd. dirs. Nat. Orange Show; bd. dirs. YMCA; bd. councillors Calif. State U., San Bernardino. Named Citizen of Yr. Inland Empire mag., 1979. Mem. Exec. Women Internat. (pres Inland Empire chpt. 1975), Uptown Bus. and Profl. Women. Bus. and Profl. Women USA (pres. San Orco dist.), San Bernardino Area C. of C. (pres. Athena award 1986). Lodge: Zonta Internat. Office: Office of the Mayor 300 North D St San Bernardino CA 92418 *

WILCOX, JOANN ROSE COURT, hospital administrator; b. Detroit, Apr. 6, 1940; d. Harry Clement and Rose Martha (Seide) Court; children from previous marriage: Andrea, Julie, Grant IV. BS in Nursing, U. Mich., 1963; MS in Nursing, Wayne State U., Detroit, 1979. Cert. advanced nurse adminstr. Nurse U. Mich. Hosp., Ann Arbor, 1963, Borgess Hosp., Wayne, Mich., 1964, Annapolis Hosp., Wayne, Mich., 1964-66, Mt. Carmel Mercy Hosp., Detroit, 1966-71; nurse Pontiac (Mich.) Gen. Hosp., 1971-78, dir. nursing, 1978-81, v.p. nursing, 1981-86, v.p. adminstrn., 1986—. Mem. Am. Orgn. Nurse Execs., Mich. Nurses Assn. (pres. 1985—), U. Mich. Alumni Orgn., Wayne State Alumni Orgn., Sigma Theta Tau. Episcopalian. Home: 824 First Milford MI 48042 Office: Pontiac Gen Hosp Seminole at W Huron Pontiac MI 48053

WILCOX, JULIA M., program systems analyst; b. Detroit, Oct. 31, 1958; d. Kenneth Robert and MaryLee (Highsmith) Hartley; m. Jon Gregory Wilcox, Mar. 20, 1982. AS, Oakland Community Coll., Union Lake, Mich., 1982, AA, 1982; BBA, Ea. Mich. U., 1985. Program systems analyst Gen. Dynamics Services Co., Sterling Heights, Mich., 1985-87, Gen. Dynamics Health Network, Inglewood, Calif., 1987—. Mem. Mgmt. Club. Club: Toastmasters (adminstrv. v.p. Mich. chpt. 1987).

WILCZEK, ANNA MARIE, aerospace company executive; b. Tacoma, Aug. 30, 1941; d. George Vincent and Mary Veronica (Linik) Ezell; m. Martin Stephen Wilczek, Oct. 29, 1939 (div. 1973); children: Stephen Joseph, Joanne Helene. Cert., Golden West Coll., 1970; BA in Mgmt., Redlands U., 1987. Supr. dept. Cascade Ins. Co., Tacoma, 1959-64; property mgr. Omnia Properties, N.Y.C., 1964-67; asst. mgr. Mesa Microwave, Santa Ana, Calif., 1966-67; supr. stats. dept. Orange County Sheriff's Dept., Santa Ana, 1967-70; coordinator IMC, Santa Monica (Calif.) Coll., 1970-80; program analyst TRW, Inc., Redondo Beach, Calif., 1980-82, word processing specialist, 1982-83, data mgmt. systems specialist, 1983-85, mgmt. systems adv., 1985—. Mem. Assn. Info. Systems Profls., Nat. Assn. Female Execs. Democrat. Club: Toastmasters. Home: 1238 17th St #6 Santa Monica CA 90404

WILD, HEIDI KARIN, oil company executive; b. Detroit, July 28, 1948; d. Lauren Daggett and Eleanor Stephanie (Churchman) Wild; m. Francis Michael Robinson, Oct. 2, 1982. BS, Western Mich. U., 1971; MBA, U. Hawaii, 1985. Tchr. secondary edn. St. Clair Sch. System, St. Clair Shores, Mich., 1971-74; personnel asst. Union Camp Corp., Kalamazoo, 1974-76; receptionist, typist Pacific Resources Inc., Honolulu, 1976-77, sec., 1977-78, adminstrv. asst., 1978, mktg. and supply analyst, 1978-80, coordinator light product supply and exchange, 1980-81, mgr. product supply, 1981-83, dir. product supply, 1983-85, gen. mgr. light products, 1985, gen. mgr. supply and distbn. 1985-86, mgr. petroleum coordination, 1986-87, acting v.p. supply and distbn., 1987-88, gen. mgr. Hawaii supply, 1988—; bd. dirs. PRI Fed. Credit Union. Mem. U. Hawaii MBA Alumni Group (pres. bd. dirs. 1988—), Hawaii Soc. Corp. Planners, Navy League, Western Mich. U. Alumni Assn., Nat. Assn. Female Execs., Sierra Club, Beta Gamma Sigma. Democrat. Clubs: Petroleum (Los Angeles); Honolulu, PRI Golf. Avocations: golf, travel. Office: Pacific Resources Inc 733 Bishop St Honolulu HI 96813

WILDE, CATHERINE MEDLIN, banker; b. Gastonia, N.C., Feb. 16, 1952; d. Alton Edward and Donnie Ruth (Liles) Medlin; m. Steven C. Wilde. Student, Asheville Buncombe Tech. Coll. Cert. real estate broker. Dealer credit sec. Wachovia Bank and Trust, Asheville, N.C., 1978-82; customer service rep. 1st Comml. Bank, Asheville, 1982-83, asst. br. mgr., 1983-86; asst. v.p. Old Stone Bank, Asheville, 1986—; bd. dirs. instr. Inst. Fin. Edn., Asheville, Am. Inst. Banking, Asheville, 1984-86, pres., 1983-86. Editor Wachovia Western Region newsletter, 1980 (Outstanding Editor award). Mem. Am. Bus. Women's Assn. Club: Altrusa. Office: Old Stone Bank 962 Merrimon Ave PO Box 8472 Asheville NC 28814

WILDE, LAURA FRANCES, industrial engineer; b. Aberdeen, Md., Dec. 2, 1959; d. Lowell Francis and Linda Maria (Wright) Miller; m. Dale Edwin Wilde, Aug. 6, 1983. BS in Indsl. Engring., U. Mo., Columbia, 1981, MS in Indsl. Engring., 1982; postgrad. in acctg., Angelo State U., 1985—. Licensed registered profl. engr., Tex. Engr. assoc. Gen. Telephone of the SW, San Angelo, Tex., 1983-85, sr. planner, 1985, adminstr., 1985-87, project coordinator, 1987—. Editor Mo. Shamrock Student Mag., 1981-82. Parlamentarian Young Homemakers, Wall, Tex., 1985-86; sec. Catholic Daughters of Am., Wall, 1986-87; vice chair FHA adv. council Wall High Sch., Wall, 1986-87. Mem. Tex. Soc. Profl. Engrs. (sec. 1984-85, 87—), Inst. Indsl. Engrs. (sr.), Nat. Assn. Female Execs., Bus. and Profl. Women. Roman Catholic. Office: Gen Telephone of the SW 2701 S Johnson St San Angelo TX 76904

WILDER, ELEANOR MARIE (NORA ROBERTS), writer; b. Washington, Oct. 10, 1950; d. Bernard Edward Robertson and Eleanor Margaret Harris; m. Ronald Eugene Aufdem-Brinke, Aug. 17, 1968 (div. 1985); children: Daniel, Jason; m. Bruce Allen Wilder, July 6, 1985. Grad. high sch., Silver Spring, Md. Legal sec. Wheeler & Korpec, Silver Spring, 1966-68; sec. R&R Lighting, Silver Spring, 1972-75; writer, 1979—. Author: The Heart's Victory, 1982, Golden Medallion, 1982-87, This Magic Moment, 1983, Untamed, 1983, A Matter of Choice, 1984, MacGregor Clan Series, 1985, Hot Ice, 1987, Brazen Virtue, 1988, O'Hurley Series, 1988. First inductee Romance Writers of Am. Hall of Fame, 1986; recipient Waldenbooks award, 1985, 86. Mem. Washington Romance Writers, Romance Writers Am. (charter mem., Golden Medallion 1982-87), Writers' Guild. Democrat. Roman Catholic. Avocations: dancing, reading, films, sailing.

WILDER, JOYCE ANN, lawyer; b. Keene, N.H., Mar. 10, 1950; d. Russell Roland and Theresa Marie (Beauregard) W. Student Bryn Mawr Coll., 1967-69; m. Joseph M. Anderson, May 5, 1984. B.A. magna cum laude, Yale U., 1971; J.D., Cornell U., 1974; LL.M. in Taxation, Boston U., 1977. Bar: N.H. 1974, U.S. Dist. Ct. N.H. 1974, U.S. Tax Ct. 1975, U.S. Ct. Appeals (1st cir.) 1979. Assoc. Bell & Kennedy, Keene, 1974-76; ptnr. Smith, Connor & Wilder, P.C. and predecessor firm Smith, Connor & Wilder, P.C., Nashua, N.H., 1976—, also dir.; dir. Clement Indsl. Park of Hudson, Inc. (N.H.). Bd. dirs. Big Bros./Big Sisters of Nashua, 1982-84. Mem. ABA, N.H. Bar Assn., Assn. Trial Lawyers Am., N.H. Trial Lawyers Assn. Episcopalian. Office: 47 Factory St Nashua NH 03061

WILDER, MARGUERITE ELIZABETH GOLDSWORTHY, musician, educator; b. Marietta, Ga., Aug. 25, 1947; d. Harold Millington and Regina (Benson) Goldsworthy; m. William Ray Wilder Sr., Apr. 11, 1967 (div. Aug 1977); children: Terri Lynn, William Ray Jr. B Music Edn., U. Ga., 1975. Cert. tchr. Band dir. Dekalb (Ga.) County Pub. Schs., 1975-77, Tapp Middle Sch., Cobb County, Ga., 1977-88, Woodward Acad., College Park, Ga., 1988—; Clinician U.S. and Can. Nat. and State Conventions; condr. State-Regional Honor Bands (South-East); judge Concert and marching festivals (southeast). Mem. Music Educators Nat. Conv., Ga. Music Educators Assn. (regional chairperson, Jr. All-state chmn., treas., chmn. music selection com.), Nat. Band Assn., Women Band Dir. Nat. Assn. Office: Woodward Acad 1662 Rugby Ave College Park GA 30337

WILDER, SONIA MARLENA, urban planning specialist; b. Munich; d. Joseph and Rose (Leimseider) W. BS, Towson State U., 1969; MSW, U. Md., 1976; MBA, Loyola Coll., 1980. Licensed clin. social worker, Md. Clin. social worker John Hopkins Hosp., Balt., 1969-79; asst. to dir. human devel. Office of Mayor, Balt., 1980-81; analyst mgmt. Blue Cross/Blue Shield, Balt., 1981-83; dir. planning Wilder Bldg. Co., Balt., 1983-84; officer field ops. adminstrv. Neighborhood Reinvestment Corp., Washington, 1984—; cons. mgmt. Wilder Bldg. Corp. 1984—. Mem. Young Leadership Council Jewish Charities, 1982-84, Chizuk Amuno Cong. 1969—. Mem. Psi Chi, Alpha Sigma Nu. Home: 4900 Cloister Dr Rockville MD 20852

WILDERMUTH, JO VOISARD, publishing company executive; b. Eng., Oct. 17, 1951; came to U.S., 1953; d. James Laverne and Thelma Isobel Joyce (Bradfield) Voisard; m. Rickey Lynn Wildermuth, Aug. 16, 1975; children: Stephanie, Alicia, Richard. AS, Edison State Coll., 1982. Machinist Copeland Corp., Sidney, Ohio, 1974-78; timekeeper Baumfolder Corp., Sidney, 1978-80; engring. clk. Hartzell Fan Co., Piqua, Ohio, 1980-84; cost acct. Broadway Cos., Inc., Dayton, Ohio, 1984-86; dir. projects Antioch Pub. Co., Yellow Springs, Ohio, 1986—; instr. Edison State Coll., Piqua, 1987—; cons. Galsco Inc., Springfield, Ohio, 1987—. Active Ohio United Way. Mem. Am. Bus. Women's Assn. (pres. Sidney chpt. 1987-88, Woman of Yr. 1988), Am. Prodn. and Inventory Control Soc. (adminstrv. asst. 1987-88), Nat. Assn. Female Execs. Republican. Home: PO Box 661 Sidney OH 45365 Office: Antioch Pub Co 888 Dayton St Yellow Springs OH 45387

WILDERMUTH, NANCY JANET, advertising executive; b. Bklyn., Aug. 2, 1956; d. George Frederick and Janet Neumann Wildermuth; student Centenary Coll., 1974-75; B.B.A. cum laude, Adelphi U., 1980. Mktg. adminstr., permissions editor Holt, Rinehart and Winston, CBS, Inc., N.Y.C., 1976-78, 78-79; account exec. N.Y. Yellow Pages, Inc., N.Y.C., 1980-81; account exec. Ad Forum, Inc., N.Y.C., 1981; advt. mgr. P.T.N. Pub. Corp., Woodbury, N.Y., 1982-84; advt. rep. Petersen Pub. Corp., 1984—. Mem. Am. Mktg. Assn., Mktg. and Advt. Club (pres.), Advt. Club N.Y., L.I. Advt. Club, Adelphi U. Alumni (dir.), Sandbar Beach Club (bd. dirs., commodore). Home: 30 Waterside Plaza Apt 37C New York NY 10010

WILDERMUTH, SUSAN DENISE, academic administrator; b. Hudson, N.Y., Oct. 3, 1950; d. Frank Edward Wildermuth and Ruth Erhlen (Corson) Demler. BS, SUNY, New Paltz, 1973; MBA cum laude, Bernard Baruch Coll., 1987. Tchr. Brevard County Sch. Dist., Cocoa Beach, Fla., 1974-76, N.Y. State Dept. Juvenile Correction, Ithaca, 1977; asst. adminstr. St. Luke's/Roosevelt Hosp., New York, 1978-82; asst. to v.p. Ptnrs. in Care, Inc., N.Y.C., 1983-85; mgr. acctg. The Computer Factory, Elmsford, N.Y., 1985-86; asst. budget dir. Polytechnic U., Bklyn., 1986-87, assoc. budget dir., 1987-88, dep. dir. budget and planning, 1988—; cons. mktg. and bus. mgmt. Health Services, Ltd., N.Y.C., 1983-84. judge Cocoa Beach (Fla.) Ann. Art Show, 1975-76, Brevard County Annual Crafts Festival, Merritt Island, Fla., 1976; chair Cocoa Beach Bicentennial Art Show, 1976; mem. N.Y. Pub. Library, 1984—, Mus. Nat. History, 1979—; sec., treas. Tenants Assn., N.Y.C., 1979—. Mem. Nat. Assn. Coll. and Univ. Bus. Officers, Nat. Assn. Female Execs., Greene County Art Guild (lectr. 1977). Democrat. Presbyterian. Home: 448 W 57th St New York NY 10019 Office: Polytechnic U 333 Jay St Brooklyn NY 11201

WILDEY, SHARON ANN, lawyer; b. North Vernon, Ind., June 21, 1943; d. Murrell Edward and Virginia Lorane (Beach) W.; m. Edward Victer Mikesell, Feb. 23, 1975 (div. Apr. 1980); children—Tim, Heather, Brooke, Meredith. B.S., Ind. U., 1972, J.D., 1975. Bar: Ind. Assoc., Luber, Sakaguchi & Wildey, South Bend, 1976-78, Wildey & Forsman, South Bend, 1978-81, now with Adler, Kaplan & Begy ; founder, pres. Women's Legal Clinic, Inc., South Bend, 1980—. Editor Justicia, 1976. Recipient Roses award Ind. U. Women's Studies, 1979. Mem. Ind. Bar Assn., ABA, Assn. Trial Lawyers Am., Ind. Bar Found., Ind. Women's Polit. Caucus. Democrat. Mem. Soc. Friends.

WILDING, DIANE, infosystems specialist, marketing executive, consultant; b. Chicago Heights, Ill., Nov. 7, 1942; d. Michael Edward and Katherine Surian; m. Mafro Georg Wilding, May 7, 1975 (div. 1980). BBA magna cum laude, No. Ill. U., 1963; postgrad., U. Chgo., 1972-74; Cert.German Lang., Goethe Inst., Rothenberg, Fed. Republic Germany, 1984. Lic. cosmetologist; CPA, Ga.; wine connoisseuse. Systems engr. IBm Corp., Chgo., 1963-68; data processing mgr. Am. Res. Corp., Chgo., 1969-72; system research and devel. project mgr. Continental Bank, Chgo., 1972-75; fin. industry mktg. rep. IBM Can., Ltd., Toronto, Ont., 1976-79; cons. regional telecommunications mktg. Control Data Corp., Atlanta, 1980-84; gen. mgr. The Plant Plant, Atlanta, 1985—. Author: The Canadian Payment System: An International Perspective, 1977. Bd. dirs. Easter House Adoption Agy., chgo., 1974-76. Mem. Internat. Brass Soc., Chgo. Council on Fgn. Relations, Goethe Inst., Mensa. Clubs: Ponte Verde (Fla.); Royal Ont. Yacht. Home: PO Box 95189 Atlanta GA 30347 Office: The Plant Plant 500 Lindbergh Dr Atlanta GA 30324

WILES, HILDA LONG, retired educator; b. Bethany, Ohio, Aug. 29, 1915; d. Elmer B. and Elsie (Stabler) Long; m. Kimball Wiles, June 6, 1936 (dec. Feb. 1968); children: David, Jon, Wendy, Ann Kimball. Student, U. Ala., Tuscaloosa, 1939-42; BA, U. Fla., 1960, MA, 1975, EdS, 1977. Cert. tchr., Fla. Classroom tchr. Alachua County Sch. Bd., Gainesville, Fla., 1960-68, curriculum research specialist, 1978-85, tchr. cons., 1985—; tchr., researcher P.K. Yonge Lab. Sch. U. Fla., Gainesville, 1968-74; asst. prin. Westwood Mid. Sch., Gainesville, 1976-77; cons. Am. Sch., Asuncion, Paraguay, 1974, Richland County, Columbia, S.C., 1977-78, Martha Manson Acad., Gainesville, 1978-79. Bd. dirs. Hippodrom State Theatre, Gainesville, 1980-84; mem. child advocacy women council Alachua County, 1978-80. Mem. AAUW, LWV (bd. dirs. Gainesville/Alachua chpt. 1984-86), Assn. Supervision and Curriculum Devel. (bd. dirs. 1981-85), Fla. Assn. Supervision and Curriculum Devel. (state planning 1983), Phi Delta Kappa (pres. 1983-84), Pi Lambda Theta (pres. 1980-81). Democrat. Methodist. Club: Univ. Women.

WILEY, ALICE HAYES, interior designer; b. Evergreen Park, Ill., Nov. 18, 1934; d. Elwin Felton and Ruth (Robertson) W.; m. Jim Lee Potts, June 25, 1960 (div. Oct. 1974); children: Kendall, Stephanie. BA, U. Kans., 1956. Interior designer Alice Wiley Interiors, Mill Valley, Calif., 1964—. Active Jr. League, Children's Theater. Republican. Episcopalian. Home and Office: 196 W Blithedale Ave Mill Valley CA 94941

WILEY, CAROL RICHARDSON, former library administrator; b. Flushing, L.I., N.Y., Jan. 5, 1946; d. Harry Alvin and Claire Amelia (Sepe) Richardson; A.A., Thomas A. Edison State Coll., 1979, B.S.B.A., 1982; m. Bennett John Wiley, Nov. 28, 1965; children—Jennifer, Julianne, Megan Jean. Sec. to dir. clin. investigation CIBA Pharm. Co., Summit, N.J., 1965-67; sec.-treas. Tuxford Corp., Westfield, N.J., 1971-79; dir. Watchung (N.J.) Public Library, 1980-82. Chmn. adult edn. program Wilson Meml. Ch., Watchung, N.J., 1977-81; sec. Watchung Borough Community Chest, 1977-82; mem. Christian Edn. com. Wilson Meml. Ch., 1977-81, mem. exec. bd., 1979, 80; adminstr. Otterbein United Meth. Ch., Lancaster, Pa., 1985—. Mem. ALA, Nat. Assn. Female Execs., N.J. Library Assn., Mensa. Republican. Home: 313A Pierson Rd Lititz PA 17543

WILEY, HANNAH CHRISTINE, dance educator, choreographer; b. Spokane, Wash., Aug. 21, 1950; d. Owen and Martha M. (Spille) W.; m. Robert A. Lyons, 1986. B.A., U. Wash., 1973; M.A., NYU, 1981. Instr. in dance Cornish Inst. Allied Arts, Seattle, 1973-75; dancer, tchr. Ballet Folk Co., Moscow, Idaho, 1975-76; choreographer Empty Space Theatre, Seattle, 1975-77; asst. prof. dance Mt. Holyoke Coll., South Hadley, Mass., 1977-82, assoc. prof., 1982—; vis. prof. dance U. Wash., Seattle, summers 1980-86, assoc. prof., 1982-87, prof., chair of dance, 1987—; artist in resident U. Idaho, Moscow, 1975-76; chairperson Five Coll. Dance Dept., Western

Mass., 1982-87; coordinator New Eng. Coll. dance Festival, Amherst, Mass., 1983-84. Choreographer numerous original ballets, 1977—; manuscript reviewer Schirmer Books, N.Y.C., 1983. Mem. Council on Arts and Humanities, South Hadley, 1981-83. Recipient Research Materials award Capezio Ballet Markers and Ballet Internat., 1982; faculty grantee Mt. Holyoke Coll., 1978, 82, 85, faculty fellow, 1980. Mem. Am. Coll. Dance Festival Assn. (dir. 1983-84), Congress on Research in Dance. Democrat. Unitarian. Office: U Wash Meany Hall AB-10 Seattle WA 98195

WILEY, RITA SCHMITT, social services professional; b. Chgo., Aug. 30, 1941; d. Albert Matthew and Mary Evelyn (Griffin) Schmitt; widowed; children: Brian, Lisa, Matthew, Gregory. BS in Psychology, Marquette U., 1962; MA, Loyola U., Chgo., 1976. Cert. tchr., Ill. Regional cons. Parish Social Ministry Consultation Services Cath. Charities Archdiocese of Chgo., 1986—; mem. service commn. bd. Deanery 1, Lake County, Ill.; mem. bd. PADS Shelter, Lake County; instr. Office for Ministry Formation, Chgo. Editor (brochure/monograph) Modeling Parish Sharing, 1987. Sec. Friends of the Future Scholarship Fund, Palatine, Ill., 1980-86; mem. Art Inst. Chgo., 1984—, Chgo. Council of Fgn. Relations, 1984—, Chgo. Archdiocesan Parish Sharing Commn., 1985—, Cath. Charities USA, Washington, 1986—; cons. St. Thomas Ministry of Care, 1981—, Hispano Community Council, Waukegan, Ill., 1987—; fellow Cath. Charities Legalization Program, 1987. Recipient Cert. Appreciation, Archdiocese Chgo., 1984. Office: Cath Charities 1114 W Grace Chicago IL 60013

WILGENBUSCH, NANCY, college administrator. B magna cum laude, Cath. U.; M, Tex. Women's U.; PhD in Edn., U. Nebr. Dean adult and continuing education then v.p. mktg. and pub. relations Coll. of St. Mary, Omaha, 1975-84; pres. Marylhurst (Oreg.) Coll., 1984—; bd. dirs. PacifiCorp, Portland, Oreg., Mutual of Omaha Fund Mgmt. Co. Commr. Port of Portland; gov's adv. com. on info. systems; bd. dirs. Portland Jr. Achievement. Fellow Am. Leadership forum (founder Oreg. chpt., exec. bd.); mem. Oreg. Ind. Colls. Assn. (pres.), Portland C. of C. (bd. dirs.). Office: Marylhurst Coll Lifelong Learn Office of the Pres Marylhurst OR 97036

WILGOCKI, MARILYN ELKINS, educator; b. Phila., Jan. 6, 1936; d. Samuel Edward and Magdalene Gene (Brennecke) Elkins; m. Edward Frank Wilgocki Jr., June 13, 1959 (dec. July 1986); children: Jennifer Lynne, Victoria Leigh. B of Music Edn., Westminster Coll., 1957; MEd, Pa. State U., 1959. Music tchr. Abington (Pa.) Sch. Dist., 1959-63, Hatboro (Pa.) Horsham High Sch., 1963-65, Sch. Dist. #69, Downers Grove, Ill., 1976-79; dir. ch. music First Congl. Ch., Downers Grove, 1976—; fine arts tchr. Sch. Dist. 41, Glen Ellyn, Ill., 1979—; dir. Quarter Notes, Downers Grove, 1969-82. Composer: (one act musicals) Magic Kazoo, Mother Goose Goes Berserk, Subject to Change, 1970-73; arranger choral music. Mem. NEA, Am. Choral Dirs. Assn., Music Educators Nat. Conf., Am. Guild English Handbell Ringers, Choristers Guild. Republican. Club: Music (Downers Grove) (com. chairperson 1969—). Home: 62 Tower Rd Downers Grove IL 60515 Office: Hadley Jr High Sch 240 Hawthorne Ave Glen Ellyn IL 60137

WILHELM, MARY LOU, librarian; b. Custer, S.D., Sept. 27, 1937; d. John Albert and Mary (Koch) W. BS in Elem. Edn., Concordia Tchrs. Coll., River Forest, Ill., 1960; MS in Library Sci., U. So. Calif., 1966; postgrad., U. Calif., Irvine, 1968-74. Librarian San Marino (Calif.) Pub. Libary, 1964-66; head librarian Orange Coast Coll., Costa Mesa, Calif., 1967-74, assoc. librarian, 1966-67, 74-76; dir. library services Cuesta Coll., San Luis Obispo, Calif., 1976—. Contbr. articles to profl. jours. Mem. AAUW, Calif. Library Assn., Community Coll. Assn. Instrn. and Tech., Faculty Assn. Calif. Community Colls., Sierra Club. Office: Cuesta Coll Library PO Box 8106 San Luis Obispo CA 93403-8106

WILHELM, PAMELA COULTER, nurse; b. Meadville, Pa., Nov. 16, 1954; d. Paul William and Reeda Rowene (Kline) C.; m. Paul Geoffrey Wilhelm, Jan. 20, 1973 (div. 1980); 1 child, Jennifer Leigh; m. John Edward Fargo, June 12, 1981. AN, Greenville (S.C.) Tech. Coll., 1981; BA in Liberal Studies, Limestone Coll., Gaffney, S.C., 1988. RN, S.C. Nurse Meadville (Pa.) City Hosp., 1978-79; staff nurse Spartanburg (S.C.) Regional Med. Ctr., 1979—, Family Med. Ctr., Spartanburg, 1985—; campus nurse U. S.C., Spartanburg, 1986—. Democrat. Methodist. Home: 3981 Cannons Campground Rd Spartanburg SC 29302-9664 Office: Spartanburg Regional Med Ctr 101 E Wood St 3d Ctr Spartanburg SC 29304

WILHELM, STEPHANIE ANNE, optometry technician; b. Inglewood, Calif., Sept. 6, 1950; d. Robert Franklin and Eva Earl (Alexander) Wilhelm. AA in Phys. Therapy, Fullerton Coll., 1978; student, San Antonio Coll., 1973, 80-84, U. Md., 1974-75, City Coll. Chgo., 1974, U. Tex., 1982-84, 87—. Enlisted USAF, 1968, advanced through ranks to staff sgt., 1975, document control clk., Offult AFB, Nebr., 1969-70, personnel adminstr., Japan, 1970-72, mgr. telecommunications, Kelly AFB, Tex., 1972-74; adminstr. acctg. and fin., Crete, 1974-75; instr. arts and crafts Anaheim (Calif.) Parks, Recreation and Arts Dept., 1976, instr. sports, spl. olympics coach 1976; exec. sec. Holovision Internat. Corp., Anaheim, 1976; exec. sec. Link Realtors, Fullerton, Calif., 1976; admissions clk. Fullerton Coll., 1976-77; dir. membership San Antonio Bd. Realtors, 1979-80; mfg. dir. Comp-Data Service, Inc., San Antonio, 1980-84; owner Charter Point Enterprises, San Antonio, 1983; mobile catering co. exec., 1984-86; mgr. food service, 1986-87; optometry specialist Sheppard AFB (Tex.) Tech. Sch., 1986-87; optometry technician, Lackland AFB, Tex. Decorated Air Force Commendation medal. Mem. North San Antonio C. of C., Nat. Assn. Female Execs., Am. Entrepreneurs Assn. Democrat. Roman Catholic. Office: PO Box 380555 San Antonio TX 78280

WILKENING, LAUREL LYNN, university official, planetary scientist; b. Richland, Wash., Nov. 23, 1944; d. Marvin Hubert and Ruby Alma (Barks) W.; m. Godfrey Theodore Sill, May 18, 1974. B.A., Reed Coll., 1966; Ph.D., U. Calif.-San Diego, 1970. Asst. prof., assoc. prof. U. Ariz., Tucson, 1973-80, dir. Lunar and Planetary Lab., head planetary scis., 1981-83, vice provost, prof. planetary scis., 1983-85, v.p. research, dean Grad. Coll., 1985-88; div. scientist NASA Hdqrs., Washington, 1980; provost U. Washington, Seattle, 1988—; vice chmn. Nat. Commn. on Space, Washington, 1984-86; co-chmn. primitive bodies mission study team NASA/European Space Agy., 1984-85; chmn. com. rendezvous sci. working group NASA, 1983-85; mem. panel on internat. cooperation and competition in space Congl. Office Tech. Assessment, 1982-83. Author: (monograph) Particle Track Studies and the Origin of Gas-Rich Meteorites, 1971; editor: Comets, 1982. Mem. Ariz. Gov.'s Adv. Com., 1984-86. U. Calif. Regents fellow, 1966-67; NASA trainee, 1967-70. Fellow Meteoritical Soc. (councilor 1976-80), AAUW; mem. Am. Astron. Soc. (chmn. div. planetary scis. 1984-85), Am. Geophys. Union, AAAS, Internat. Astron. Union (orgn. com. 1979-82), Phi Beta Kappa. Democrat. Office: U Wash Office of Provost Seattle WA 98195

WILKERSON, CAROL LEE, lawyer; b. Atlanta, Feb. 19, 1956; d. Raymond William Jr. and Marianne (Hollingsworth) L.; m. James Michael Wilkerson, May 7, 1988. AB, Duke U., 1978; JD, U. Ga., 1981. Bar: Ga. 1981, U.S. Dist. Ct. (no. dist.) Ga. 1981, U.S. Ct. Appeals (11th cir.) 1981. Staff atty. Kerman & Assocs., Atlanta, 1982; staff atty. Hyatt Legal Services, Atlanta, 1982-84, mng. atty., 1984-86, regional ptnr., 1986-87; mng. atty. Hyatt Legal Services, Smyrna, Ga., 1987—. Named one of Outstanding Young Women of Am., 1983. Mem. ABA, Ga. Bar Assn., Atlanta Bar Assn., Cobb County Bar Assn. Republican. Episcopalian. Home: 175 Westover Ln Marietta GA 30064 Office: Hyatt Legal Services 3236A South Cobb Dr Smyrna GA 30080

WILKERSON, MARJORIE JOANN MADAR, insurance company executive, author, teacher, consultant; b. Spokane, Wash., Dec. 2, 1930; d. Joseph Robert and Margaret Muriel (McKay) Madar; m. Billy E. Wilkerson, Jan. 9, 1953; 1 child, Wesley James McEarl. Student U. Puget Sound, 1948; B.A., UCLA, 1949; postgrad. So. Meth. U., 1958. Mgmt. to agt. Travelers Ins. Cos., Houston and Dallas, 1952-63; sr. account agt. Allstate Ins. Cos., Tacoma, 1966—; cons in field; lectr. various colls. and univs. Author: Sex and Society, 1976. Editor publ. Chiropractic Edn., also newsletter. Pres., co-founder Pierce County Women's Polit. Caucus, Tacoma; newsletter editor bd. Caucus State of Wash., Seattle; lobbiest Caucus and prior for ERA, Olympia, Wash.; citizen lobbiest Worker Right to Know, Olympia, 1984-85; spokesperson Community effort to protect zoning, Gig Harbor, Wash., 1980-84; bd. dirs., sec. Beaumont Art Mus., Tex., 1954-57; pres. Walnut Hill League, N. Dallas, 1957-65; established first Girl Scout Program in Beaumont Girl Scouts U.S., 1955; mem. citizen lobby for higher standards of air quality. Grantee activist to study Washington Commn. for Humanities, 1974-75. Recipient numerous sales awards Allstate Ins. Co.; named Divisional Agt. of Yr., 1984. Mem. Parent's Assn. Wash. State U., Alumni Assn. U. Puget Sound. Home: 5418 Wollochet Dr NW Gig Harbor WA 98335 Office: 15 Oregon Suite 304 Tacoma WA 98409

WILKES, DONNA NATALIE, historian; b. Washington, Feb. 8, 1954; d. Roland A. and Grace D. (Vaughn) W. BS cum laude, Georgetown U., 1977; MA, Harvard U., 1982. Research fellow Sch. Medicine Georgetown U., Washington, 1974, counselor, tutor Office for Minority Students, 1976-77; editor, researcher Ctr. for Applied Psych., Washington, 1978-79; historian U.S. Naval Research Lab., Washington, 1979; freelance editor Washington, 1980-85; cons. historian History Assoc., Inc., Rockville, Md., 1985—, U.S. Dept. Energy, Washington, 1987—, Smithsonian Instn., Washington, 1988—; mem. Nat. Council on Pub. History, Washington, 1985—. Vol., Media Community Relations Com., 1986—, Providence Hosp., 1985; bd. dirs. D.C. Ind. Living Service, Inc., 1982; mem. Mayor's Com. on Handicapped, Washington, 1982, Archdiocesan Com. on Handicapped, Washington, 1981, Planning Com. for UN Day Celebration, Washington, 1981. Grantee NSF, 1980-82, 86; recipient Cert. of Appreciation Fed. Emergency Mgmt. Agy., Washington, 1986, Outstanding Alumni award Georgetown U., 1986, Cert. of Merit Washington Acad. Sci., 1971, Nat. Contbn. award Internat. Yr. of the Disabled Person, 1981; named Washington Woman of Yr., 1987. Mem. History of Sci. Soc., Soc. for History in Fed. Govt., Mensa. Democrat. Roman Catholic. Home: 6236 Eastern Ave NE Washington DC 20011

WILKES, HELEN TOWNSEND, artist; b. El Paso, Tex., 1904; d. Wilber and La Belle Frances (Read) Townsend; B.A., U. Calif., Berkeley, 1926; pupil of Sam. H. Harris, Katherine Shackelford, Robert Frame, Gay Maccoy, Lenard Kester; m. Peter F. Wilkes, 1927 (dec. 1969); children—Peter T. (dec.), Patricia Wilkes Wright; m. 2d, Kenneth Thomas Norwood, Aug. 14, 1978. One-woman shows: St. Mark's Gallery, Altadena, Calif., 1960, 62, 64, Main YWCA Gallery, Glendale, Calif., 1963, Tuesday Afternoon Club Gallery, Glendale, 1964, Glendale Fine Arts Gallery, 1968, Glendale Main Library Gallery, 1966; group exhbns. include: Greek Theatre, Los Angeles, 1961, Santa Paula (Calif.) C. of C., 1961, 63, Gallery Cezanne, Laguna Beach, Calif., 1972-74, Glendale Fine Arts Gallery, 1967-71, Descanco Gardens Guild shows, 1983—, Gallery Highway One, Cayucus, Calif., 1987—; chmn., exhibit dir. Glendale All-City Art Show, 1960; gallery dir. St. Mark's Episcopal Ch., Altadena, 1957-63; coordinator Vincent Price shows, Glendale and Los Angeles, 1964; co-founder, v.p. Glendale Fine Arts Gallery, 1967; bd. dirs. Glendale Art Assn., 1955-56; mem. Gallery Cezanne, 1972-76; art juror, speaker, tchr. in field. Bd. govs. Glendale Symphony Orch. Assn., women's com. Glendale Symphony Orch., Glendale Philharm. Affiliates. Mem. PEO, Group Four Painters (co-founder 1976), Los Angeles Art Assn., Nat. Mus. Women in Arts (charter), Descanso Garden Guild, Contempos, Zeta Tau Alpha. Episcopalian. Address: 1831 Crestmont Ct Glendale CA 91208

WILKEY, YVONNE WILLIAMS, travel agency owner, consultant; b. Waynesville, N.C., Aug. 26, 1950; d. Ebb Columbus and Ruby Lee (Cooper) Williams; m. Rick Conway, July 20, 1968; children: Richard Everette, Kimberly Caroline, Sarah Angela. Student, Tenn. Tech. U., 1973; grad., Inst. Cert. Travel Agts., Wellesly, Mass., 1987. Travel cons. Vacation Travel, Easley, S.C., 1980-82, Exec. Travel, Greenville, S.C., 1982-83; mgr. Daniel Travel, Anderson, S.C., 1983-84; v.p. Greer (S.C.) World Travel, 1984-85; pres. New Horizons Travel, Clemson, S.C., 1985—; cons. and lectr. in field. Mem. Profl. Women in Travel (pres. 1985-88), Am. Soc. Travel Agts., Assn. Retail Travel Agts., Cruise Lines Internat. Assn., Travel Agts. of the Carolinas, Clemson C. of C. (welcome back com. 1987), Assn. of Women Profls. (Clemson). Home: 302 Rock Creek Dr Clemson SC 29631 Office: New Horizons Travel 1103 Tiger Blvd Clemson SC 29631

WILKIE, SALLY JO, health services executive; b. Washington, Pa., Sept. 22, 1939; d. Donald Crawford and Bernice Meryl (Dowler) Ewing; student U. Pitts., Community Coll. of Allegheny County, LaSalle Extension U.; children—Bonnie Vey, L. Craig; m. Robert Wilkie, Aug. 9, 1986. Various secretarial positions U. Pitts. Grad. Sch. Public Health, 1957-65; fellowship sec. Indsl. Health Found., Pitts., 1965-67, asst. office mgr., 1967-71, office mgr., 1971-73, dir. office services, 1973-79, v.p. adminstrn., 1979—, also sec., trustee. Active Exec. Women's Council Greater Pitts. Mem. Nat. Assn. Female Execs., Am. Mgmt. Assn., Pitts. Bus. and Profl. Women's Club. Club: Order Eastern Star. Office: 34 Penn Circle W Pittsburgh PA 15206

WILKINS, ARLENE, social worker; b. Balt., Oct. 20, 1936; d. Joseph Martin and Alice Gertrude (Mickey) Martin Patterson; m. E.J. Wilkins, Jan. 15, 1963; children—Del, Deirdre, Justin, Patrick. B.A., Wilkes Coll., 1959; M.A., U. Pa., 1962. Social worker Children's Service Inc., Phila., 1960-62, Western Psychiat. Inst. and Clinic, Pitts., 1966-67, Bethesda United Presbyterian Ch., Pitts., 1967-70; clin. social worker Allegheny Gen. Hosp., Northview Heights Health Ctr., Pitts., 1967-86. Program chmn. St. Andrew United Presbyn. Ch., Sewickley, Pa., 1981-83. Mem. Nat. Assn. Social Workers, Clin. Social Workers. Republican. Home: 416 College Park Dr Corapolis PA 15108 Office: Allegheny Gen Hosp Social Service Dept 320 E North Ave Pittsburgh PA 15212

WILKINS, CAROLINE HANKE, consumer agency administrator, political worker; b. Corpus Christi, Tex., May 12, 1937; d. Louis Allen and Jean Guckian Hanke; m. B. Hughel Wilkins, 1957; 1 child, Brian Hughel. Student, Tex. Coll. Arts and Industries, 1956-57, Tex. Tech. U., 1957-58; BA, U. Tex., 1961; MA magna cum laude, U. Ams., 1964. Instr. history Oreg. State U., 1967-68; adminstr. Consumer Services Div., State of Oreg., 1977-80, Wilkins Assoc., 1980—; mem. PFMC Salmon Adv. subpanel, 1982-86. Author: (with B. H. Wilkins) Implications of the U.S.-Mexican Water Treaty for Interregional Water Transfer, 1968. Dem. precinct committeewoman, Benton County, Oreg., 1964—; publicity chmn. Benton County Gen. Election, 1964; chmn. Get-Out-the-Vote Com., Benton County, 1966; vice chmn. Benton County Dem. Cen. Com., 1966-70; vice chmn. 1st Congl. Dist., Oreg., 1966-68, chmn. 1968; vice chmn. Dem. Party Oreg., 1968-69, chmn. 1969-74; mem. exec. com. Western States Dem. Conf., 1970-72; vice chmn. Dem. Nat. Com., 1972-77, mem. arrangements com., 1972, 76, mem. Dem. charter commn., 1973-74; mem. Dem. Nat. Com., 1972-77, 85—, mem. size and composition com., 1987—, rules com. 1988; mem. Oreg. Govt. Ethics Commn., 1974-76; del., mem. rules com. Dem. Nat. Conv., 1988. Mem. AAUW, Nat. Assn. Consumer Agy. Adminstrs., Soc. Consumer Affairs Profs., Nat. Fedn. Dem. Women (1st v.p. 1983-85, pres. 1985-87). Lodge: Zonta Internat. Office: 3311 NW Roosevelt Corvallis OR 97330

WILKINSON, DORIS YVONNE, medical sociology educator; b. Lexington, Ky., June 13, 1936; d. Howard Thomas and Regina (Cowherd) W. BA, U. Ky., 1958; MA, Case Western Res. U., 1960, PhD, 1968; MPH, Johns Hopkins U., 1985. Asst. prof. U. Ky., Lexington, 1968-70; assoc. prof., then prof. Macalester Coll., St. Paul, 1970-77; exec. assoc. Am. Sociol. Assn., Washington, 1977-80; prof. med. sociology Howard U., Washington, 1980-84; vis. prof. U. Va., 1984-85; prof. sociology U. Ky., Lexington, 1985—; chmn. panel women in sci. program NSF, Washington, 1976; panelist pub. program div. NEH, Washington, 1976; rev. panelist Nat. Inst. Drug Abuse, Washington, 1978-79; mem. bd. sci. counselors Nat. Cancer Inst., Bethesda, Md., 1980-84. Author: Workbook for Introductory Sociology, 1968; co-editor: The Black Male in America, 1977, Alternative Health Maintenance and Healing Systems, 1987; contbr. articles to profl. jours. Bd. overseers Case Western Res. U., Cleve., 1982-87. Woodrow Wilson fellow, 1959-61; grantee Social Sci. Research Council, 1975, Nat. Inst. Edn., 1978-80, Nat. Cancer Inst., 1986-88, Ky. Humanities Commn., 1988. Fellow Am. Orthopsychiatric Assn.; mem. D.C. Sociol. Soc. (pres. 1982-83), Soc. for Study of Social Problems (v.p. 1984-85, pres. 1987-88), Eastern Sociol. Soc. (v.p. 1983-84, I. Peter Gellman award 1987), Am. Sociol. Assn. (exec. office and budget com., 1985-88, Dubois-Johnson-Frazier award, 1988), N.Y. Acad. Scis., Alpha Kappa Delta (outstanding grad. student 1964). Unitarian. Office: U Ky Dept Sociology Lexington KY 40506

WILKINSON, JESSIE LENORE, data processing executive; b. Balt., Mar. 12, 1957; d. Robert Warren Wilkinson and Eleanor Lambeth (Rankin) Brewster. Programmer, project leader Satbel, Ltd., Johannesburg, Republic of South Africa, 1976-77; sr. programmer Ned Equity, Ltd., Johannesburg, 1977-78; systems analyst, project leader Barlow Rand Computer Services, Johannesburg, 1978-82; sr. systems cons. Viable Info. Processing Systems, Hunt Valley, Md., 1983—. Newsletter editor Md. Assn. Anorexia Nervosa and Bulimia, Balt., 1986, bd. dirs., 1987; mem. Black Sash, Johannesburg, 1980—. Mem. Data Processing Mgmt. Assn. Republican. Methodist.

WILKINSON, MARILYN JO, public relations executive; b. Springfield, Ill., Aug. 19, 1943; d. Milo Benjamin and Alice Virginia (Hott) Watson; m. David Lowell Wilkinson, Mar. 14, 1970; children: Scott; stepchildren: Sarah, Claire. BS in Communications, U. Ill., 1965. Exec. editor, assoc. pub. Hollister Newspapers, Wilmette, Ill., 1966-70; freelance writer, cons. Chgo., 1970-79; mgr. mktg. communications Telecommunications div. Rockwell Internat. Corp., Downers Grove, Ill., 1979-83; editor Telefood Mag., Harcourt, Brace, Jovanovich, Chgo., 1983-84; account exec., supr. Hill & Knowlton, Chgo., 1985-86; sr. v.p. United Dairy Ind. Assn., Rosemont, Ill., 1986. Cons. editor: The Taste of Mexico, 1986. Bd. dirs. Community Family Service and Mental Health Assn., LaGrange, Ill., 1978-83. Mem. Internat. Assn. Cooking Profls., Pub. Relations Soc. Am., Am. Soc. Assn. Execs., Kappa Tau Alpha, Sigma Delta Chi. Office: United Dairy Ind Assn 6300 N River Rd Rosemont IL 60018

WILKINSON, ROSALYN SARAH, university director; b. Sturgis, Mich., Dec. 19, 1936; d. Gordon B. and Marie (Jensen) Schilz; m. Thomas Allan Wilkinson; Dec. 21, 1959; children: Chris, Tedric, Nachelle. Student, Albion Coll., 1955-57; BA, U. Okla., 1959; MA, U. Mo., Kansas City, 1964. Head counselor U. Okla., Norman, 1958-59; pub. relations asst. Coll. Medicine U. Nebr., Omaha, 1959; consumer research analyst Hallmark Cards, Kansas City, Mo., 1960-62; office mgr., counselor Glynn-Mullen Placement Services, Kansas City, 1962-64; dir. vols. Erie County Home and Infirmary, Buffalo, 1973-74; outreach coordinator, pub. info. cons. Erie County Office for Aging, Buffalo, 1975-76; pre-retirement planning coordinator Ctr. for Study of Aging SUNY, Buffalo, 1977-78, mgr. human resources devel. and benifits adminstrn., 1978—; dir. The Leading Edge Tng. Cons., Amherst, N.Y., 1976—; mem. statewide tng. and devel. com. Cen. Adminstrn. SUNY, Albany, 1982-83, statewide benefits com. Cen. Adminstrn. SUNY, Albany, 1983-85, statewide Human Resource and Devel. Transition Team Gov's. Office Employment Relations, Albany, 1984-85, statewide adminstrn. resource system Cen. Adminstrn. SUNY, Albany, N.Y., 1987-88. Editor (tabloid column) To Your Benefit, 1984-87; (booklet) A Guide To Services For Older People In Erie County, 1975, 76, Everything You Wanted To Know About Handicapped Students, 1975, 76; (newspaper) Viewpoint on Aging, 1975-76, also author; author series of brochures, 1975-76; presenter in field. Mem. project grants com., community problem solving com. United Way Buffalo and Erie Counties, 1987-88, communications com. Sweethome Cen. Schs., Amherst, 1979-80, co-pres. PTA Willow Ridge Elem., Amherst, 1972-73, program planning com. Nat. Conf. for Assn. Vol. Adminstrs., 1987. Mem. Am. Soc. Tng and Devel. (pres. Niagra Frontier chpt. 1985-86, chair publicity com. region II conf. Western N.Y., 1987, chmn. chpt. film festival. 1983, various coms., Nat. Acheivement award 1986), Buffalo Area Speakers Assn., U. Buffalo Speakers Bur. Republican. Unitarian. Club: Toastmasters (pres. U. Buffalo club 1987—). Home: 41 Willow Ln Amherst NY 14150 Office: SUNY at Buffalo Personnel Bldg 104 Crofts Hall Buffalo NY 14260

WILKINS-WILDE, MARY JEANNE, small business owner; b. Hayden, Colo., June 20, 1931; d. Charles Manley and Mary M. (Biner) Wilkins; m. Donald Earl Wilde; children: Brian Charles, Andrea Leigh (dec.). BA, U. Colo., 1953, MA, 1956. Cert. elem. tchr., Colo. Elem. tchr. Denver Pub. Schs., 1953-60, tchr. Sta. KRMA-TV, 1959-60, reader asst., 1986—; bd. dirs., corp. sec. and treas. Wilde Inc., Denver, 1963—; corp. sec., asst. Treas. Wilexco, Inc., Denver, 1981—, also bd. dirs.; corp. sec. Indsl. Mech. Devices Corp., Denver, 1986—, also bd. dirs. Editor (newsletter) Arapahoe Assn. for Retarded Children, 1969-71. Chmn. membership com., bd. dirs. U. Denver Women's Library Assn., 1971-73. Mem. Jr. League Denver, Inc. (bd. dirs.), P.E.O. Sisterhood (pres. 1977-79), DAR (registrar Colo. chpt. 1979-83), Kappa Kappa Gamma (sec. and v.p. local chpt. 1976-80). Republican. Club: Ladies of the Petroleum (spl. events 1987-88, pres. 1988—). Home: 5607 Southmoor Circle Englewood CO 80111 Office: Wilde Inc 1660 S Albion St Suite 414 Denver CO 80222

WILKOCZ, JODI BETH, hotel controller; b. Phila., June 22, 1958; d. Fredrick and Rebecca (Shapiro) W. BS in Acctg., U. Del., 1980. CPA, Va. Acct. USDA, Washington, 1980-81; tax acct. Marriott Corp., Washington, 1981-83; asst. hotel controller Marriott Corp., Tampa, Fla., 1983-85, Marco Island, Fla., 1985-86; lead asst. hotel controller Marriott Corp., Orlando, Fla., 1986-87; hotel controller Marriott Corp., Dayton, Ohio, 1987—. Mem. Nat. Assn. Female Execs.

WILKOF, MARCIA VALERIE, educator, consultant; b. Canton, Ohio, Oct. 2, 1950; d. Raymond G. and Rossetta G. (Alpiner) W. AB cum laude, U. Cin., 1972; MS, U. Pa., 1977, PhD, 1982. Instr. bus. Temple U., Phila., 1978-80; vis. lectr. Rutgers U., New Brunswick and Newark, N.J., 1981-82, asst. prof. bus. mgmt., 1982—; vis. asst. prof. U. Pa. 1984-85. Mem. Acad. Mgmt., Am. Soc. for Tng. and Devel., Nat. Head Injury Found. Office: Rutgers U Management Dept New Brunswick NJ

WILKS, JACQUELIN HOLSOMBACK, educator; b. Oakdale, La., Jan. 18, 1950; d. Jack and Ida Mae (Bass) Holsomback; B.S., La. Coll., 1972; M.A.T., Okla. City U., 1982; postgrad. So. Bapt. Theol. Sem., Louisville, 1974, S.E. Mo. State U., 1977; counseling cert. Central State U., Edmond, Okla., 1983; m. Thomas M. Wilks, Jan. 28, 1972; children—Thomas David, Bryan Emerson. Sec. to adminstr. Allen Parish Hosp., Kinder, La., 1968-69; tchr. horseback riding, swimming Triple D Guest Ranche, Warren, Tex., 1969; singer, speaker Found. Singers, including TV and radio appearances, record albums, 1970-71; tchr. English, reading Pine Bluff (Ark.) High Sch., 1972-74; tchr. kindergarten Doyle Elem. Sch., East Prairie (Mo.) R-2 Sch. Dist., 1974-75; tchr. 1st grad Bertrand (Mo.) Elem. Sch., 1975-76; tchr. 6th grade sci. A.D. Simpson Sch., Charleston, Mo., 1976-78; dir. admissions and fin. aid Mo. Bapt. Coll., St. Louis, 1978-80; fin. adminstr. Control Data Inst., Control Data Corp., St. Louis, 1980-81; dir. tutorial services, instr. tutorial methods Okla. Bapt. U., 1981-83 instr. horsemanship St. Gregory's Jr. Coll., 1981; counselor Gordon Cooper Area Vocat. Tech. Sch., 1982-83, Shawnee Jr. High Sch. (Okla.), 1983-85; dir. Resource Ctr., instr. English, St. Gregory's Coll., Shawnee, Okla., 1985—; bd. dirs. Computer Commn. Services Inc., Tulsa; tutor for children under jurisdiction Juvenile Ct., Jefferson County, Ark., 1972-73, leader group counseling/therapy sessions, 1972. Choreographer, First Bapt. Ch. Youth Choir, Pine Bluff; v.p. St. Gregory's Coll. Therapeutic Horsemanship Program, 1981-82; Republican election judge. Recipient Kathryn Carpenter award La. Bapt. Conv., 1971; Real Scope award Realty World, St. Louis, 1980; lic. Realtor, Mo. Mem. Nat. Hist. Soc., Univ. Alliance Okla. Bapt. U., Nat. Assn. Fin. Aid Adminstrs., Nat. Assn. Admissions Counselors, Athenian Lit. Soc., Nat. Geog. Soc., Gamma Beta Phi, Kappa Delta, Phi Kappa Phi. Republican. Baptist. Clubs: Kathryn Boone Music, Civinette Booster. Home: Route 3 Box 143 Shawnee OK 74801 Office: St Gregory's Coll 1900 W MacArthur Shawnee OK 74801

WILL, JESSIE GERMAN, handwriting expert, document examiner; b. Muskogee, Okla., Oct. 8, 1912; d. William Paxton Zacheus and Mabel Gussie (Ward) German; student Ward Belmont Coll., 1929-30, Drake U., 1930-32; B.S., Okla. U., 1933; cert. Internat. Graphoanalysis Soc., 1968, master cert., 1973; m. Edward Ray Will, Sept. 29, 1934; children—Henry German, Margaret Ann Will Cornell. Handwriting expert, document examiner, Tulsa, 1970—; lectr. Oklahoma City U., 1972-78, Tri-County Tech. Sch., Bartlesville, Okla., 1977-81. Pres. local PTA, 1948-49, 55-58; bd. dirs. Tulsa WYWCA, 1963, Tulsa Philharmonic, 1964; mem. nat. panel advisers Nat. Forensic Center. Mem. PEO, (chpt. pres. 1962-63), Internat. Graphoanalysis Soc., Ind. Assn. Questioned Document Examiners (corr. sec. 1976-77), Tulsa Boys Home Women's Assn. (v.p. 1978-79), Internat. Assn. Forensic Scis., Kappa Alpha Theta (pres. alumni assn. 1961, coll. dist. pres. 1961-63), Mu Phi Epsilon. Republican. Mem. Disciples of Christ Ch. Expert witness in fed. cts., Okla., dist. cts. Okla., Kans., Mo., and Ark. Home and Office: 1727 E 31st St Tulsa OK 74105

WILL, MADELEINE C., government official; b. Hartford, Conn., Aug. 9, 1945; married; 3 children. AA, Hartford Coll. for Women, 1965; BA, Smith Coll., 1967; MA, U. Toronto, Can., 1969. Asst. sec. for spl. edn. and rehab. services Dept. Edn., Washington, 1983—; panelist White House Conf. on Aging, 1977; chmn. govt. affairs com. Montgomery County Assn. for Retarded Citizens, 1979; mem. govt. affairs com. Nat. Assn. Retarded Citizens; mem. Pres.'s Task Force on Legal Equity for Women; cons. Rock Creek Found. Office: Dept Edn Spec Edn & Rehab Services 330 C St SW Washington DC 20202

WILL, SUSAN JEAN, nursing educator; b. Toledo, Feb. 26, 1949; d. Edward E. and Vivien R. (Long) Ziemke. BS in Nursing summa cum laude, Capital U., 1971; MS summa cum laude, Ohio State U., 1972; postgrad., Portland State U. Nurse public health Columbus (Ohio) Pub. Health Nursing, 1971-72; clinical specialist Mushingum County Mental Health, Zanesville, Ohio, 1972; cons., evaluator Ohio Dept. Mental Health, Columbus, 1972-73; cons. staff devel. Bethesda Hosp., Zanesville, Ohio, 1972-73; cons. AK. Psychiatric Inst., Anchorage, 1973-77; instr. Anchorage (AK) Community Coll., 1974-77; assoc. prof. Oreg. Health Scis. U., Portland, 1977-81, 1984—; administr. Community Mental Health Services AK Dept. Mental Health, Juneau, 1981-84; cons. Province Ala., Edmonton, Can. 1985-87, Dept Family Nursing 1984-85, Dept Mental Health Nursing 1986—, Oreg. Health Scis. Commr. Planning Commn. Lake Oswego, Oreg. 1982-83. Mem. Am. Nurses Assn., Council Psychiat. Mental Health Nursing, Oreg. Nurses Assn., Sigma Theta Tau. Democrat. Home: 791 4th St Lake Oswego OR 97034 Office: Oreg Health Scis U 3181 SW Sam Jackson Park Rd Portland OR 97201

WILLACY, HAZEL MARTIN, lawyer; b. Utica, Miss., Apr. 20, 1946; d. Julious and Willie Thelma (Barnes) Martin; m. Aubrey Barrington Willacy, Mar. 18, 1967; children: Austin Keith, Louis Samuel. Student Tougaloo Coll., 1963-64; BA in Econs., Smith Coll., 1967; JD, Case Western Res. U., 1976. Bar: Ohio 1976. Labor economist Bur. Labor Stats., U.S. Dept. Labor, 1967-70; assoc. Baker, Hostetler, Cleve., 1976-80; labor relations atty. Sherwin Williams Co., Cleve., 1980-82, asst. dir. labor relations, 1983-87, dir. labor relations, 1987—. Contbr. articles to profl. jours. Trustee, Fedn. Community Planning, vis. com. bd. overseers student affairs Case Western Res. U.; bd. dirs. Cleve. Music Sch. Settlement. Mem. ABA (labor law com.), Ohio Bar Assn. (labor law com.), Cleve. Bar Assn., Order of Coif. Club: Law Wives. Office: 101 Prospect Ave Cleveland OH 44115

WILLADSEN, KAY A., marketing representative; b. Saginaw, Mich., May 11, 1947; d. W. Franklin and Elaine (Simkins) Brooks; m. Michael C. Willadsen, Dec. 5, 1964; children: Michael C., Erik J. AA, McComb Coll., 1973; student Eastern Mich. U., 1977-78, U. Ill., 1979; BBA, Bowling Green State U., 1982; postgrad. Ind. U., 1983-85. Mktg. rep. Credit Bur. of Hancock County, Inc., Findlay, Ohio, 1983-87; account exec. TRW Info. Services, 1987—; treas. Northwest Ohio Consumer Credit Assn., 1988-89. Choreographer dance Flowers and Confusion, 1974. Precinct del. Livingston County Republicans, Hamburg, Mich., 1976, state conv. del., 1976; treas. Hillcrest Gasline Project, Findlay, Ohio, 1984; membership chmn. Am. Bus. Women's Assn. Mem. Nat. Assn. Female Execs., Am. Business Women's Assn. (recording sec. 1986—), Ohio Mortgage Bankers Assn., Findlay Downtown Area Assn. (bd. dirs.), Bowling Green Alumni Assn., Credit Grantors Assn. (dir. 1983-86). Methodist. Club: Women's Lions (dir. 1974-75). Avocations: dance, reading, investments. Home: 3210 Byrnwyck Dr Findlay OH 45840 Office: TRW Information Services 5577 Airport Hwy Suite 205 Toledo OH 43615

WILLARD, NANCY MARGARET, writer, educator; b. Ann Arbor, Mich., June 26, 1936; d. Hobart Hurd and Margaret (Sheppard) W.; m. Eric Lindbloom, Aug. 15, 1964; 1 child, James Anatole. B.A., U. Mich., 1958, Ph.D., 1963; M.A., Stanford U., 1960. Lectr. English Vassar Coll., Poughkeepsie, N.Y., 1965—. Author: poems In His Country: Poems, 1966; Skin of Grace, 1967; A New Herball: Poems, 1968, Testimony of the Invisible Man: William Carlos Williams, Francis Ponge, Rainer Maria Rilke, Pablo Neruda, 1970, Nineteen Masks for the Naked Poet: Poems, 1971, Childhood for the Magician, 1973, The Carpenter of the Sun: Poems, 1974, A Visit to William Blake's Inn: Poems for Innocent and Experienced Travelers, 1981 (Newberry Medal 1982), Household Tales of Moon and Water, 1983; (short stories) The Lively Anatomy of God, 1968; (juveniles) Sailing to Cythera and Other Anatole Stories, 1974, All on a May Morning, 1975, The Snow Rabbit, 1975, Shoes Without Leather, 1976, The Well-Mannered Balloon, 1976, Night Story, 1986, Simple Pictures are Best, 1977, Stranger's Bread, 1977, The Highest Hit, 1978, Papa's Panda, 1979, The Island of the Grass King, 1979, The Marzipan Moon 1981, Uncle Terrible, 1982, Angel in the Parlor: Five Stories and Eight Essays, 1983, The Nightgown of the Sullen Moon, 1983, Night Story, 1986, The Voyage of Ludgate Hill, 1987, The Mountains of Quilt, 1987, Firebrat, 1988; (novel) Things Invisible To See, 1984; illustrator: The Letter of John to James and Another Letter of John to James, 1982. Recipient Hopwood award, 1958, Devins Meml. award, 1967; Woodrow Wilson fellow, 1960; NEA grantee, 1987. Mem. Children's Literature Assn., The Lewis Carroll Soc., The George MacDonald Soc. Office: Vassar Coll Dept English Raymond Ave Poughkeepsie NY 12601

WILLARD, PAMELA LOUISE, resort executive; b. Suffern, N.Y., Nov. 2, 1950; d. Creston Leroy and Claire Dorothy (Earl) Johnston: m. Campbell Dale Willard, Sept. 9, 1979. Student, Daytona Beach Jr. Coll., 1968, Ga. State U., 1969. Supr. research devel. Aetna Life and Casualty Ins. Co., Hartford, Conn., 1974-76, coordinator tng., 1976-77, tng. cons., 1977-79; co-owner Sandy's Housekeeping, Sunriver, Oreg., 1980-82; supr. group billing, coordinator spl. events Amelia Island Plantation, Fernandina Beach, Fla., 1982, conf. coordinator, 1982-83, mgr. catering, 1983-84, dir. conf. services, 1984—. Office: Amelia Island Plantation Amelia Island Pkwy Fernandina Beach FL 32034

WILLARD-GALLO, KAREN ELIZABETH, molecular biologist; b. Oak Ridge, July 8, 1953; d. Harvey Bradford and Isabella Victoria (Rallis) Willard; student in microbiology U. Reading, Eng., 1973-74; A.B. in Biology, Randolph-Macon Woman's Coll., 1975; M.S. in Immunology, Va. Poly. Inst., 1978, Ph.D. in Molecular Biology, 1981; m. James Paul Gallo, July 31, 1982. Grad. teaching asst. Va. Poly. Inst., 1976-78; fellow Research Inst. in Cell Biology, Argonne Nat. Lab., Ill., 1977, lab. resident student assoc., 1978-81, postdoctoral fellow, 1981-82; research assoc. Ludwig Inst. for Cancer Research, Brussels, 1982-85; research scientist Internat. Inst. Cellular and Molecular Pathology, Brussels, Belgium, 1986—; advisor on Immunology WHO, 1987—; cons. in field. Recipient award for teaching excellence Va. Poly. Inst., 1977, 78. Mem. Am. Soc. Cell Biology, Electrophoresis Soc., Internat. Coordinating Com. Human Lymphocyte Protein Database, 1987—. Contbr. chpts., articles to profl. publs.; patentee method for early detection infectious mononucleosis. Home: Ave Chevalier Jehan 117, 1300 Wavre Belgium Office: Internat Inst Cellular and Molecular Pathology Dept Biochem, UCL 7539 Ave Hippocrate, 75 1200 Brussels Belgium

WILLBANKS, JILL ANN, home economics educator; b. Big Spring, Tex., Jan. 22, 1956; d. C.W. and Sue (Sutton) W. BS in Home Econs., Tex. Tech U., 1977. Cert. elem. and secondary tchr., Tex. Home econs. tchr. Spur (Tex.) High Sch., 1978-82, Big Spring (Tex.) High Sch., 1982—; counselor Camp Boothe Oaks Girl Scouts USA, Sweetwater, Tex., 1976-80. Bd. dirs. Big Spring March of Dimes, 1983-86. Mem. Assn. Tex. Profl. Educators, Nat. Wildlife Fedn., Phi Upsilon, Delta Kappa Gamma. Roman Catholic. Home: 2609 Wasson Rd Big Spring TX 79720 Office: Big Spring High Sch 708 11th Pl Big Spring TX 79720

WILLBANKS, SUE SUTTON, investor, writer, artist; b. Luling, Tex., Sept. 24, 1935; d. William Herbert and Melba Ophelia (Ward) Sutton; m. Charles Walter Willbanks, Nov. 21, 1953 (dec. Feb. 1979); children—Jill Ann, Brenda Kay. B.S., Tex. Tech. U., 1955; M.A., U. Tex. Permian Basin, 1980. Cert. secondary, vocat. and elem. tchr., Tex. Tchr., Big Spring Ind. Sch. Dist., Tex., 1964-68, 1972-79, dept. chmn., 1980-82; owner, pres. Sutwill Co., Tucson, Ariz., 1981—; pvt. practice psychotherapy, Tex., Hawaii, 1979—. Author short stories and poems. Contbr. articles to profl. jours. Organizer Silver Heels Vol. Fire Dept., Howard County, Tex., 1970-71; bd. dirs. Permian Basin Planned Parenthood Assn., Odessa, Tex., 1980-82; organist Immaculate Heart of Mary Ch., Big Spring, Tex., 1975-78; Mem. Nat. Assn. Female Execs., Psi Inst. Hawaii, Inst. Noetic Scis., Common Boundary. Methodist. Avocations: interior decorating, acting. Home: 6644 N Amahl Pl Tucson AZ 85704

WILLDEN, DEBORAH HOFFMAN, laboratory executive; b. Norfolk, Eng., July 12, 1956; d. Jay Milton and Gertrude (Lewis) H.; m. Joseph Francis Dau, Jan 27, 1980 (div. Dec. 1982); m. Mark Allen Willden, Dec. 17, 1983. Student, Palomar Coll., 1976, Loma LInda U., 1972; BS, Donsbach U., 1982, MS, 1984, PhD, 1985. Office staff counselor, ednl. opportunites, program and services Palomar Coll., San Marcos, Calif., 1976-78; tech. sec. San Diego, 1978-80; asst. lectr. J.M. Hoffman Nutrition Seminars, Valley Center, Calif., 1980-85; pres. Royal Labs., Inc., San Marcos, Calif., 1985—; ptnr. Profl. Press Pub., Valley Ctr., 1982—. Author: The Raw Food Program, 1984. Republican. Office: Royal Labs Inc 465 Production St San Marcos CA 92025

WILLEN, JILL INEZ, health science association administrator; b. Canton, Ohio, Aug. 17, 1961; d. Milton Leonard and Emily Claire (Steiner) W. BA, Vanderbilt U., 1982; M of Health Adminstrn., Ohio State U., 1984. Adminstrv. resident Aultman Hosp., Canton, Ohio, 1983, adminstrv. asst., 1984-86, asst. v.p., alternative delivery systems, 1986-87; asst. to pres. Mercy Health Care System, Cin., 1987—. Vice chmn. Impact Symposium, 1980-82; asst. advisor Temple Israel Youth Group, 1984; mem. Big Bros./Big Sisters Greater Cin. Mem. Forum Health Care Service Adminstrn., Med. Group Mgmt. Assn., Am. Med. Care and Rev. Assn., Acad. Health Services Mktg., Am. Coll. Health Care Mktg., Jr. League Cin. Home: 425 Missouri Ave #3 Cincinnati OH 45226 Office: Mercy Health Care System 2335 Grandview Ave Cincinnati OH 45206-2280

WILLENZ, NICOLE VALLI, management consultant; b. Washington, May 21, 1958; d. Eric and June Adele (Friedenberg) W. BA in Econs., Boston U., 1980. Legis. aide U.S. Ho. of Reps., Washington, 1980-81; asst. to dir. of communications World Council of Credit Unions, Washington, 1981-82; dir. program services, dir. computer and systems devel. Nat. Industrial Transp. League, Washington, 1982-86; dir. electronic data info. products and services Comtrac/First Nat. Bank Chgo., Chgo., 1987; mgr. Price Waterhouse, Chgo., 1988—. Coordinator seminar series on electronic data info.; contbr. articles to mags. Chair spl. events Folger Shakespeare Theater, Washington, 1980-82; vol. Dollars for Dems., Bethesda, Md., 1980, Holloway for Ho. of Reps. Campaign, Bethesda, 1986, Young Leadership Jewish United Fund, Chgo., 1988. Mem. Am. Nat. Standards Inst. (UN del. 1986—, vice chair ASCX12 internat. project team, 1986— chair transp. project team 1986), Nat. Indsl. Transp. League, Data Interchange Standards Assn., Lincoln Pk. West Civic Assn. Democrat. Jewish. Club: Traffic of Chgo. Office: Price Waterhouse 200 E Randolph Dr Chicago IL 60601

WILLETT, ROSLYN, public relations executive, consultant; b. N.Y.C., Oct. 18, 1924; d. Edward and Celia (Stickler) S.; 1 child, Jonathan Stanley. BA, Hunter Coll., N.Y.C., 1944; postgrad., Columbia U., 1944, CUNY, 1946-47, NYU, 1947-48. Dietitian YWCA, N.Y.C., 1944; tech. and patents librarian Stein Hall & Co., N.Y.C., 1944-46, food technologist tech. services and devel. dept., 1946-48; editor McGraw-Hill, Inc., N.Y.C., 1949-50, Harcourt Brace Jovanovich, Inc., N.Y.C., 1950-54; pub. relations writer Farley Manning Assocs., N.Y.C., 1954-58; cons. pub. relations and food service Roslyn Willett Assocs., Inc., N.Y.C., 1959—; adj. prof. Hunter Coll., 1955-56, Polytech. Univ. N.Y., 1981-82; lectr. in field. chmn. Woman's Polit. Caucus, Inc., N.Y., N.J., Conn., 1971-73; v.p. Mid Hudson Arts and Sci. Ctr., Poughkeepsie, N.Y.; bd. dirs. small bus. task force Assn. for Small Bus. and Professions, 1981-85, Regional Adv. Council Fed. Small Bus. Adminstrn., 1976-78, Rhinebeck Chamber Music Society, 1985-86. Mem. Pub. Relations Soc. Am. (accredited), Food Service Cons. Soc. Internat., N.Y. Acad. Scis., Inst. Food Technologists. Clubs: Paris (N.Y.C.), Publicity (N.Y.C.). Home: Hunn's Lake Rd Stanfordville NY 12581 Office: 441 W End Ave New York NY 10024

WILLETT, WILLIE MAE, educator; b. Brownsville, Tenn., July 21, 1941; d. Joe Louis Hafford and Idella (Reid) Hafford-Keller; m. Lee L. Willett, Sept. 25, 1965; 1 child, Rhonda Lee. BA, Lane Coll., 1964; MS, Eastern Ill. U., 1975; postgrad., Memphis State U., 1982—. Social worker Dept. Children and Family Service, Decatur, Ill., 1964-66; tchr. Decatur Pub. Schs., 1966-75, Memphis City Schs., 1975—; staff devel. coordinator, chmn. dept. Orleans Elem. Sch., Memphis, 1984—; level III career ladder Tenn. State Dept., 1984—; affiliate broker B/W Properties, Memphis, 1979—; cons. Christian Bros. Coll., Memphis, 1986. Bd. dirs. Memphis Urban League, Inc., 1979—; grad. Leadership Memphis, 1980; dir. pub. relations Abe Scharff YMCA, Memphis 1985—; v.p. Local Commn. Excellence in Edu., Memphis, 1985—. Recipient Outstanding Tchr. award Christian Bros. Coll., 1986. Mem. Internat. Reading Assn., United Teaching Profession (faculty rep. 1984), West Tenn. Ednl. Assn., Rotary Assn. for Teacher Excellence (award 1984), Lane Coll. Alumni Assn. (nat. v.p. 1986-89), Alpha Kappa Alpha. Democrat. Methodist. Home: 1923 Tacoma Ave Memphis TN 38116 Office: Memphis City Schs 1400 McMillan St Memphis TN 38116

WILLEY, RUTH, educator; b. North Kingstown, R.I., May 11, 1928; d. Gorton Thayer and Katharine (Lindsay) Lippitt; m. Robert B. Willey, Jan. 14, 1956. BA, Wellesley Coll., 1950; PhD, Radcliffe Coll., 1956. Instr. Wellesley (Mass.) Coll., 1956-57; commercial histologist Triarch Products, Ripon, Wis., 1959-61; asst. prof. Ripon (Wis.) Coll., 1961-63; asst. prof. U. Ill., Chgo., 1965-71, assoc. prof., 1971—; environ. affairs officer 1979-86, Rocky Mt. Biol. Lab., bd. trustees 1975-78, asst. dir. 1962. Author: Microtechniques, 1971; contbr. articles to profl. jours. Advisor Save Dunes Council, Beverly Shores, Ind. 1975—; mem. Nature Conservancy, Washington 1967—. Office: U Ill Dept Biol Sci Box 4348 Chicago IL 60680

WILLIAMS, ANN C., federal judge; b. 1949; m. David J. Stewart. BS, Wayne State U., 1970; MA, U. Mich., 1972; JD, U. Notre Dame, 1975. Asst. U.S. atty. U.S. Dist. Ct. (no. dist.) Ill., Chgo., 1976-85, judge, 1985—; adj. prof., lectr. Northwestern U. Law Sch., Chgo., 1979—. Mem. Fed. Bar Assn., Fed. Judges Assn., League of Black Women, Women's Bar Assn. of Ill. Office: US Dist Ct 219 S Dearborn St Chicago IL 60604 *

WILLIAMS, ANNA FAY, economist, writer; b. Newark, July 23, 1935; d. Haney Fay and Mary Lillian Rodgers; B.S. in Journalism cum laude, U. Minn., 1957; M.A. in Broadcast Film Arts, So. Meth. U., 1968, M.A. econs., 1975; children—Paul C. Friedlander, Mark T. Friedlander. Editor, Richardson (Tex.) News, 1960; asst. editor Sun News, Sun Oil, Dallas, 1960-69; field research dir. Corp. for Public Broadcasting, Dallas-Ft. Worth, 1972-75; pres. Multi-Media, Inc., Dallas, 1968-70; instr. econs. So. Meth. U., Dallas, 1973-74, Richland Coll., Dallas, 1975-78, Northlake Coll., Irving, Tex., 1978-80; exec. and founding editor Solar Engrng. Mag., Dallas, 1975-81; staff economist Keplinger Cos., energy cons., Houston, 1982-85; v.p. Tex. Commerce Bancshares, 1985—; presenter profl. paper 18th Intersoc. Energy Conversion Engrng. Conf., 1983, 19th, 1984. Mem. Internat. Solar Energy Soc. (gen. chmn. ann. meeting Am. sect.), ASHRAE, Assn. Energy Engrs. (hon., chmn. regional tech. programs 1981—), Tex. Solar Energy Soc. (founder, dir. 1978-80), Center for Renewable Resources (officer, dir. 1978-80). Author: The Shared Time Strategy, 1966, Dallas Food Finds, 1974, Handbook of Photovoltaic Applications, 1985; also papers in field. Office: 3621 Wake Forest Houston TX 77098-5500

WILLIAMS, ANNE M., lawyer, librarian; b. Mpls., Dec. 20, 1940; d. Kenneth Paul and Bette Jane (Linne) Martin; div.; children—Kathryn Malaika, Tara Lynn. B.A. cum laude, Mt. Holyoke Coll., 1962; diploma edn. Makerere U. Coll., Kampala, Uganda, 1963; M.L.S., SUNY-Buffalo, 1972, J.D. magna cum laude, 1975. Bar: N.Y. 1976. Tchr., Tchrs. for East Africa Program, Columbia U. and Kenya Govt., Wusi, 1963-65; library asst. N Kumbi Internat. Coll., Kabwe, Zambia, 1965-70; teaching asst. SUNY-Buffalo, 1973-75; law assoc. Phillips, Lytle et al, Buffalo, 1975-79; regional legal advisor U.S. AID, Swaziland, 1979-82, Morocco, 1983-86, Abidjan, Ivory Coast, 1986-88; AID rep., Guinea-Bissau, 1988—. Pres., Parent/Tchr./Student Assn., Buffalo, 1977-78. Recipient Meritorious Honor award U.S. AID, 1981. Mem. ABA, Am. Soc. Internat. Law, Phi Beta Kappa. Episcopalian. Home and Office: Bissau ID Department State Washington DC 20520

WILLIAMS, ANNIE JOHN, educator; b. Reidsville, N.C., Aug. 26, 1913; d. John Wesley and Martha Anne (Walker) W. AB, Greensboro Coll., 1933; MA, U. N.C., Chapel Hill, 1939; postgrad., Appalachian State U., summer 1944, Duke U., summer 1936, Cornell U., summer 1961. Tchr. math. Blackstone (Va.) Coll., 1934-35; tchr. Hoke High Sch., Raeford, N.C., 1935-37, Massey Hill High Sch., Fayetteville, N.C., 1937-42, Alexander Graham Jr. High Sch., Fayetteville, 1942-43, Carr Jr. High Sch., Durham, N.C., 1943-53; supr. math. N.C. Dept. Pub. Instrn., Raleigh, 1959-62; tchr. math. Durham High Sch., 1953-59, 62-78, ret., 1978; vol. in math. N.C. Sch. Sci. and Math., Durham, 1980—; adj. asst. prof. dept. math. and sci. edn. N.C. State U., Raleigh, 1966-73. Author: (with Brown and Montgomery) Algebra, First Course, 1963, Algebra, Second Course, 1963. Recipient cert. of recognition Dept. Math. and Sci. Edn. N.C. State U., 1979, Gov.'s award for outstanding vol. service, 1986; named Vol. of Yr., Key Vol. Program co-sponsored by Vol. Services Bur. and Durham Morning Herald, 1986. Mem. Nat. Council Tchrs. Math. (life, bd. dirs. 1957-60), Math. Assn. Am. (life), N.C. Council Tchrs. Math. (hon. life, W.W. Rankin Meml. award 1975), Internat. Platform Assn., DAR (N.C. chpt. chair Am. History Month 1980-82, corr. sec. 1982-84, chaplain 1984-86, Gen. Davie chpt.), Delta Kappa Gamma, Mu Alpha Theta (hon.). Methodist. Clubs: Pierian Lit. (sec. 1979-80, pres. 1980-81), Durham Woman's (co-chmn. internat. affairs dept. 1985-87). Home and Office: 2021 Sprunt Ave Durham NC 27705

WILLIAMS, ARDELIA RUTH, psychologist; b. Melrose Park, Ill., May 31, 1936; d. Alfred Otto and Pearl Marietta (Coleman) Max; children: Sean, Stewart, Anne Williams. BA in Psychology, St. Mary's Coll., 1975, MA in Psychology, 1979. Psychol. asst. Noel A. Williams, MD, Walnut Creek, Calif., 1977—. Mem. Am. Psychol. Assn., Calif. Psychol. Assn., Marriage Family Child Assn. Republican. Office: 130 La Casa Via Bldg 3 Suite 212 Walnut Creek CA 94598-3056

WILLIAMS, BARBARA A., executive dietitian; b. Fountain Inn, S.C., June 23, 1938; d. John D. Williams and Josephine (Griffin) Bates. BS in Home Econs., W.Va. U., 1963; postgrad., U. Bridgeport, 1988—. Registered dietitian., N.Y. Food service supr. Providence Hosp., Detroit, 1963-64, Met. Hosp., Detroit, 1964-68; exec. dietitian ARA Healthcare Dietitian Services, Armonk, N.Y., 1968—. Mem. Am. Dietitic Assn., Conn. Dietetic Assn., Phila. Dietetic Assn., Nat. Assn. Univ. Women, Zeta Phi Beta. Democrat. Home: 97 Grassy Plain St Apt 18 Bethel CT 06801 Office: ARA Healthcare Nutrition Services 1 Byram Brook Pl Armonk NY 10504

WILLIAMS, BARBARA ANNE, college president; b. Camden, N.J., Oct. 14, 1938; d. Frank and Laura Dorothy (Szweda) Williams. BA cum laude, Georgian Court Coll., 1963; MLS, Rutgers, The State U., 1965; MA, Manhattan Coll., 1973; postgrad., NYU, 1976—. Cert. English tchr., N.J. Joined Sisters of Mercy, 1957. Sec., Camden Cath. High Sch., N.J., 1956-57; registrar Georgian Court Coll., Lakewood, N.J., 1960-66, dir. library services, 1966-74, dean acad. affairs, 1974-80, pres., 1980—; dir. Assn. Ind. Colls. and Univs. in N.J., Ind. Coll. Fund of N.J., N.J. Natural Gas Co., ednl. adv. council N.J. Woman mag., Diocese of Trenton, N.J. Mem. adv. bd. Ocean County Ctr. for Arts, Lakewood, N.J., 1983—; mem. Ocean County Pvt. Industry Council, 1983—. Named Outstanding Woman N.J. Assn. Women Bus. Owners, 1983; recipient Salute to the Policymakers award Exec. Women N.J., 1986, Woman in Leadership award Monmouth Council of Girl Scouts, 1987. Mem. Assn. of Mercy Colls. (pres. 1981-83), Mercy Higher Edn. Colloquium (mem. exec. com. 1980-87), Monmouth/Ocean Devel. Council (bd. dirs. 1981-84, humanitarian 1985), Ocean County Bus. Assn. (trustee 1982-84), Nat. Assn. Ind. Colls. and Univs. (secretariat 1981-83). Home and Office: Georgian Court Coll Lakewood NJ 08701

WILLIAMS, BARBARA ELAINE, publishing company official; b. Bartlesville, Okla., Aug. 12, 1952; d. B. Joe and Roy Marie (Smith) W.; m. Charles M. Ellertson, Apr. 20, 1985. B.A. cum laude, Duke U., 1974. Asst. to bus. mgr. Duke U. Press, Durham, N.C., 1974-75, prodn. asst., 1975-78, assoc. prodn. mgr., 1979-82, jours. mgr., 1982-85; prodn., design mgr. Menasha Ridge Press, 1985—; freelance designer, 1987—; panelist Career Counseling Conf., Durham, 1983, 84, Conf. Editors Learned Jours., 1985, Modern Lang. Assn., 1985. Photographer Latent Image 3, 1976, Latent Image 4, 1978, Latent Image 5, 1980, N.C. Mus. Art Ann. Show, 1978, 79. Mem. Arts Ctr. Gallery Bd.(chmn. selection com. 1985—), Assn. Am. Univ. Presses (jours. com. 1983-85). Democrat. Office: Menasha Ridge Press 109 Britania Ave Durham NC 27704

WILLIAMS, BARBARA IVORY, educational consultant; b. Detroit, Apr. 28, 1936; d. Henry Oliver and Willa Mae (Frazier) I.; m. Alney Elliott Whitener, Jan. 1, 1987. BS, Wayne State U., 1957, MEd, 1960; PhD, U. Washington, 1973. Tchr. Detroit Pub. Schs., 1957-68; program assoc. Mich.-Ohio Regional Lab., Detroit, 1968-70; lectr. predoctoral U. Wash., Seattle, 1970-73; sr. program assoc. Far West Lab. for Ednl. Research and Devel., San Francisco, 1973-76; sr. cons. E.H. White & Co., San Francisco, 1976-77; sr. program assoc. Northwest Regional Lab., Portland, Oreg., 1977-84; arca coordinator Ednl. Testing Service, Washington, 1984-85; edn. group dir. Research and Evaluation Assocs., Washington, 1985-87; ind. cons. Washington, 1987—. Mem. Am. Ednl. Research Assn., Am. Psychol. Assn., Nat. Assn. Black Sch. Educators, Phi Delta Kappa, Alpha Kappa Alpha (pres. Portland chpt. 1980-84). Democrat. Baptist. Home: 408 Critenden St NW Washington DC 20011

WILLIAMS, BARBARA JEAN, typographer, graphic designer; b. Omaha, Nebr., Nov. 25, 1948; d. Arthur M. and Mary E. (Jensen) Pedersen; m. Loren Marion Williams, Dec. 29, 1968; children—Loren Benjamin, Jeffrey Clarke. B.S. in Botany, Iowa State U., 1969; postgrad. U. Nebr., 1969. Substitute tchr. Council Bluffs (Iowa) Pub. Schs., 1969-70; chief telex operator Singerwerke, Blankenloch, W.Ger., 1971-72; sec. Iowa State U., Ames, 1972; tchr. Gaffney (S.C.) Day Sch., 1972-74; composition dir. Kidd's Printing Co., Gaffney, 1979; owner, mgr. Typographics, Gaffney, 1979—; cons., type supplier several cos., 1979—; corr. Cycle News, 1987—. Choir dir. Saint Paul's Lutheran Ch., Gaffney, 1981; choir mem. Liedolsheim (W.Ger.) Gesangverein, 1971-72, Erlenbrunn (W.Ger.) Gesangverein, 1977-78, Limestone Community Chorus, Gaffney, 1987—. Recipient numerous Addy awards for typography and graphic arts, 1981-87. Mem. (charter) Advt. Fed. of Spartanburg, Spartanburg Area C. of C., Nat. Assn. Self-Employed, Jaycees (Gaffney chpt.), Midget-Mini Sprint Connection. Republican. Lutheran. Club: Spartanburg (S.C.) Kennel (sec. 1973-74). Home and Office: Route 2 Box 323 Robbs Sch Rd Gaffney SC 29340

WILLIAMS, BARBARA JEAN, insurance company executive; b. Binghamton, N.Y., Oct. 4, 1948; d. Walter William and Georgia E. (Bentley) Williams; m. Matthew J. Williams. Grad. high sch., Clyde, N.Y. Sec. Allstate Ins. Co., Rochester, N.Y., 1966-69, telephone adjuster, 1969-73, field auto and home adjuster, 1973-75, initial unit mgr., 1975-78; home office trainer Tech-Cor, Wheeling, Ill., 1978-79; security analyst Rochester, 1979-80; unit claim mgr. 1980, dist. claim mgr., 1980-86, property claim mgr., 1987—. Mem. Nat. Assn. Female Execs. Republican. Methodist.

WILLIAMS, BETTY, corporate professional; b. Los Angeles, Nov. 27, 1920; d. John D. Rasmussen and Muriel Grace (Kay) Winters; children—Derek Allen, Diane Lee Gilmore. Student Los Angeles City Coll., 1938-40, Occidental Coll., 1940, Los Angeles Jr. Coll. Bus., 1954-55, Loretta Young Way Sch. Modeling, 1959-61; Fellow of Religious Sci., Ernest Holmes Coll. Sch. Ministry, 1985. Lic. practitioner of religious sci. Exec. sec., asst. mgr. research dept. Los Angeles C. of C., 1957-63; exec. sec. McCann Erickson-Advt., Los Angeles, 1963-66, U. So. Calif., 1966-71, League of Calif. Cities, Los Angeles, 1972-77, Getty Oil Co. Texaco Inc., Los Angeles, 1980-86; exec. sec., writer Soc. West Mag./Patte Barham Edn., Los Angeles, 1977-79, 86-87; owner Faith Enterprises, 1986—; recording sec. So. Calif. Assn. C. of C. Mgrs., 1957-63, San Gabriel Valley Assn. C. of C., 1957-63; asst. mgr. Los Angeles C. of C. Alaska Good Will Tour, 1960. Author poetry, letters to high officials. Charter mem. Republican Presdl. Task Force, Washington, 1982; worker Rep. party, Los Angeles, 1978; mem. church choir Founder's Religious Sci. Ch., 1972-84, sec., practitioner, 1974-84. Mem. Am. Stats. Assn., Am. Mktg. Assn., Internat. Soc. Gen. Semantics, Classroom Tchrs. Gen. Semantics, League of Religious Sci. Practitioners. Avocations: singing; piano; dancing; swimming. Home: 4067 Beltway Dr #138 Addison TX 75244 Office: 2101 Midway Rd #310 Carrollton TX 75006

WILLIAMS, BRENDA PAULETTE, financial consultant, entrepreneur; b. St. Louis, July 7, 1946; d. Herman and Hattie Williams; B.J., Ohio U., Athens, 1969; postgrad. U. Mo., Columbia. Newscaster, Sta. KATZ, St. Louis, 1969-70; reporter, talk show producer/host Sta. KPLR-TV, St. Louis, 1973-74, Stas. KSD-TV and Radio, St. Louis, 1974-77; weekend anchor-reporter Sta. KMBC-TV, Kansas City, Mo., 1977-81, weekday anchor-reporter, 1981-85; pres. H. Pearl Investments, Inc., 1986—, Kansas City Skywave, Inc., 1986—; fin. cons. Merrill Lynch, 1987—. Recipient Cert. of Appreciation St. Louis Urban League-St. Louis Sentinel, 1975, Human Relations award Nat. Assn. Colored Women's Clubs, 1975, Documentary Reporting award Mo. Radio and TV Assn., 1979, Consumer Reporting award Mo. Dept. Consumer Affairs, 1979, Outstanding Achievement in Journalism award Mo. Black Leadership Assn., 1981, Headliner award, 1982; selected for Am. journalists tour of Israel, Israeli Journalist Assn., 1980; Black Achiever award SCLC, 1981. Mem. Alpha Kappa Alpha (Women of Involvement award 1974), Sigma Delta Chi.

WILLIAMS, CAROL J., social work educator; b. New Brunswick, N.J., Aug. 12, 1944; d. Einar Arthur and Mildred Estelle (Clayton) Jorgensen; m. Oneal Alexander Williams, July 4, 1980. BA, Douglass Coll., 1966; MS in Computer Sci., Stevens Inst. Tech., 1986; MSW, Rutgers U., 1971, PhD in Social Policy, 1981. Child welfare worker Bur. Children's Services, Jersey City, 1966-67, Outagamie County Dept. Social Services, Appleston, Wis., 1967-69; supr. WIN N.J. Div. Youth and Family Services, New Brunswick, 1969-70; coordinator Outreach Plainfield (N.J.) Pub. Library, 1972-76; research project dir. County and Mcpl. Govt. Study Commn., N.J. State Legislature, 1976-79; assoc. prof. social work Kean Coll., Union, N.J., 1979—; cons., evaluator Thomas A. Edison Coll., 1977—, mem. acad. council; others; cons. Assn. for Children N.J., 1985-88. Mem. NOW, Council on Social Work Edn., Nat. Assn. Social Workers, Nat. Consumers Union, Kean Coll. Fedn. Tchrs. Democrat. Clubs: Good Sam (Agoura, Calif.); Outdoor World (Bushkill, Pa.). Home: 32 Halstead Rd New Brunswick NJ 08901 Office: Social Work Program Kean Coll Morris Ave Union NJ 07083

WILLIAMS, CHARLOTTE EVELYN FORRESTER, civic worker; b. Kansas City, Mo., Aug. 7, 1905; d. John Dougal and Georgia (Lowerre) Forrester; student Kans. U., 1924-25; m. Walker Alonzo Williams, Sept. 25, 1926; children—Walker Forrester, John Haviland. Trustee, Detroit Grand Opera Assn., 1960-87 , dir., 1955-60; chmn. Grinnell Opera Scholarship, 1958-66; founder, dir., chmn. adv. bd. Cranbrook Music Guild, Inc., 1952-59, life mem., 1952—; bd. dirs. St. Peter's Home for Boys, Detroit, 1951-53, Detroit Opera Theater, 1959-61, Severo Ballet, 1959-61; Detroit dist. chmn. Met. Opera Regional Auditions, 1958-66; patron-mem. Met. Opera Nat. Council; mem. Central Opera Service, Met. Opera Guild; mem. Opera Guild Ft. Lauderdale (Fla.); mem. Friends of Children's Mus. at Singing Pines, Boca Raton Hist. Soc., Greater Miami Opera Guild, Fla. Atlantic U. Found.; past pres. Friends of Caldwell Playhouse, Boca Raton. Mem. Debble-Rand Meml. Service League (life), DAR, English-Speaking Union, Vol. League Fla. Atlantic U., PEO, Order Eastern Star. Home: 1355 Fan Palm Rd Boca Raton FL 33432

WILLIAMS, CHARLOTTE L., secondary educator; b. Greenwood, Miss., July 28, 1951; d. Rex and Nell Marie (Tate) Livingston; m. Jerry L. Williams, Aug. 4, 1973; chilren: Kathryn, Tate. BA, Miss. State U., Starkville, 1973, MEd, 1977; postgrad., Delta State U., Cleveland, Miss., 1980-82. Cert. secondary tchr., Ga. French/Spanish tchr. Indianola (Miss.) Acad., 1973-75; reserve librarian Mitchell Meml. Library Miss. State U., 1977-79; Spanish/Eng. tchr. Armuchee (Ga.) High Sch., 1980-82; Spanish tchr., chmn. fgn. language dept. Midland Valley High Sch., Langley, S.C., 1982-86; Spanish tchr. Westside High Sch., Augusta, Ga., 1986-87, Cass High Sch., Cartersville, Ga., 1987—; vice-chmn. Aiken County Bd. of Edn. Foreign Language in Service, 1982-83, chmn. 1983; pub. chmn. Richmond County Bd. of Edn. Foreign Language Festival, Augusta. Co-leader Martinez chpt. Girl Scouts Am., 1986-87, leader Cartersville, 1987—; area chmn. Augusta Am. Cancer Soc., 1984-87; acolyte mother Aldersgate United Meth., active Augusta Easter Seal Soc., 1982-86. Mem. DAR, Nat. Council of Tchrs. of English, Am. Assn. Tchrs. of Spanish and Portuguese, Am. Council Tchrs. Fgn. Langs., Fgn. Lang. Assn. Ga., Profl. Assn. Ga. Educators, Cartersville-Bartow C. of C. Methodist. Club: Dames Married to Dental Students. Office: Jerry L Williams DMD 310 N Tennessee St Cartersville GA 30120

WILLIAMS, CINDY J., actress; b. Van Nuys, Calif., Aug. 22, 1947; d. Bechard J. and Frances (Bellini) W.; m. William Louis Hudson, May 1, 1982; children: Emily, Zachary. Grad. high sch., Van Nuys. Film appearances include Travels With My Aunt, American Graffiti, The Conversation, More American Graffiti; regular in TV series Laverne and Shirley. Active Actors and Others for Animals, Los Angeles, Greenpeace, Nature Conservancy. Nominated Best Supporting Actress Brit. Acad. Awards, London, 1974; named Honorary Citizen Office of Mayor, New Orleans, 1977, Honorary Mem. Teamsters Union, Milw., 1979, Hon. Texan Office of Gov., Austin, 1987, Disting. Alumni Calif. Jr. Colls., 1987; recipient Hon. Commendation medal U.S. Marine Corps, 1977, Award of Appreciation Blinded Vets Adminstrn., 1979. Democrat. Roman Catholic. Office: care Walt Disney Co 500 S Buena Vista St Burbank CA 91521

WILLIAMS, CYNTHIA DILLON, recreational facility administrator; b. Toccoa, Ga., Apr. 10, 1950; d. John Francis and Mildred Frances (Carroll) D.; m. Dale Edward Williams, Mar. 20, 1970; 1 child, Mary Elizabeth. BS, Brenau Coll., 1983. Program coordinator Rabun County Parks and Recreation Dept., Clayton, Ga., 1977-79, dir., 1979-81; program dir. Toccoa-Stephens County Parks and Recreation Dept., 1973-77, dir., 1981—. Active Leadership Ga., 1986, All Ga. Communities Com., Toccoa, 1987, Toccoa-Stephens County 2000 Com., 1987; coordinator Toccoa Internat. Festival, 1986—, Community Health Awarenes Day, 1987; bd. dirs. Stephens County High Sch. Band Boosters, 1985-87; chmn. Leadership Toccoa-Stephens County, 1987. Mem. Ga. Recreation and Parks Soc. (pres. 1987), Nat. Recreation and Park Assn. (south regional council 1987), Ga. Mcpl. Assn. Democrat. Episcopal. Home: 504 E Tugalo St Toccoa GA 30577 Office: Toccoa-Stephens County Recreation Parks Dept PO Box 159 Toccoa GA 30577

WILLIAMS, DAWN ELLEN, nurse; b. Youngstown, Ohio, Sept. 13, 1955; d. John Ronald and Carol Ann (Fanson) Smith. Student Barry U., 1973-75; BSN, Vanderbilt U., 1978; postgrad. Emory U., 1983-84. Staff nurse Ga. Bapt. Hosp., Atlanta, 1978; staff nurse Protem, Atlanta, 1978-79, dir. nursing, 1979-80; staff nurse telemetry Crawford W. Long Hosp., Atlanta, 1980-81; cardiovascular staff nurse Emory U. Hosp., Atlanta, 1981-83, cardiology staff nurse, 1983-84; ICU-CCU nurse Humana Gwinnett Community Hosp., Snellville, Ga., 1984-85; customer service rep. Adler Instrument Co., Norcross, Ga., 1985-86, purchasing agt., 1986-87. Mem. adminstrv. bd., Meth. youth fellowship, N. Springs Meth. Ch. Mem. Am. Assn. Critical Care Nurses, Gamma Phi Beta, Panhellenic Soc. (sec. Nashville 1976-77). Office: Adler Instrument Co 2745 Wendy West Norcross GA 30071

WILLIAMS, DEBORAH SHANNON, loan officer, consultant; b. St. Louis, Dec. 28, 1951; d. Paul and Milderine (Edwards) Shannon; m. Joseph Monroe Williams, Oct. 29, 1983. BS in Spl. Edn., U. Mo., 1980. Cert. tchr.; lic. real estate broker. Employment specialist Jobs for Mo. Grads., St. Louis, 1980-83; sales cons. City Equity Corp., St. Louis, 1983-85; broker, salesperson Coldwell Banker Real Estate, St. Louis, 1985-86; loan officer Fleet Mortgage Corp., St. Louis, 1986—; author courses on career devel., 1980. Vol. Jr. Olympics Washington U., 1986. Mem. Internat. Assn. Bus. and Fin. Cons., Nat. Assn. Realtors, Nat. Assn. Female Execs., U. Mo. Alumni Assn. Home: 3134 Shenandoah Saint Louis MO 63104

WILLIAMS, DIANE ELIZABETH, data processing professional, state agency executive; b. Bertram, Tex., Sept. 10, 1959; d. Chester Doyle and Hazel Elizabeth (Simpkins) W. Assoc. of Applied Sci. magna cum laude, Temple Jr. Coll., 1980; BS magna cum laude, U. Mary Hardin-Baylor, 1981; MBA, S.W. Tex. State U., 1987. Asst. to bus. mgr. U. Mary Hardin-Baylor, Belton, Tex., 1980-81; adminstrv. data processing programmer Dept. Hwys. and Pub. Transp., Austin, Tex., 1982-83, systems analyst, 1983-84, project mgr., 1984-85, large project devel. mgr., 1985-86, fin. system unit mgr., 1986-88, automation planning and procurement mgr., 1982—; speaker in field, colls. and univs., 1985—. Mem. Nat. Assn. Female Execs., Exec. Women Tex. Govt., MBA Assn., Women in Pub. Sector. Democrat. Mem. Ch. of Christ. Home: 2611 Bee Caves #149 Austin TX 78746 Office: State Tex Dept Hwys Pub Transp 38th and Jackson Austin TX 78701

WILLIAMS, DIANE LYNN, food products executive; b. Burgaw, N.C., Aug. 28, 1951; d. James Clayton and Mary Urilla (Ruddell) W. Student, U. N.C., Charlotte, 1969-72, U. Cin., 1980-81. From salesperson to office mgr. Christian Foods Inc., Wilmington, N.C., 1972-75; sec. Swift Agrl. Chems. Co., Wilmington, 1975-76, Biggers Bros. Inc., Charlotte, N.C., 1976-78; sec. Internat. Salt Co., Charlotte, 1978-79, salesperson sodium sulfate, 1979, ter. mgr., 1979-81; mgr. nat. accounts Internat. Salt Co., Clarks Summit, Pa., 1981—. Chair campaign Internat. Salt Co., United Way, 1984, loaned exec., Lackawanna chpt., Scranton, Pa., 1985; bd. dirs., chair personnel com. United Cerebral Palsy N.E. Pa., Scranton, 1985—; class participant Leadership Lackawanna, 1986-87; mem. long range planning com. Jr. League Scranton, 1986-87, treas., 1987—; advisor youth Calrks Green United Meth. Ch., 1984-85. Recipient Tiger Stock Cash award Akzo Zout Chemi/ISCO, 1985. Mem. Alpha Delta Pi. Republican. Presbyterian. Home: 225 Woodlawn Ave NW Clarks Summit PA 18411

WILLIAMS, DIANNE ELIZABETH, academic program director; b. Cleve., May 5, 1945; d. David Henry and Norma Ida (Hackstedde) Senger; m. Charles R. Williams, Sept. 6, 1969; children: Christopher Sean, Emily Dawn. BS, DePauw U., 1967; MS, U. R.I., 1979; postgrad., Hartford Grad. Ctr., Groton, Conn., 1986. Head nurse, instr. Condell Hosp., Chgo., 1969-72; sch. nurse U.S. Dept. of Defense schs., Yokohama, Japan, 1974-75; assoc. prof. Mohegan Community Coll., Norwich, Conn., 1980-84, dir. nursing, 1984-87, dir. instructional services, 1986—. Mem. Montville (Conn.) Health Care Task Force, 1984-86, LWV, Montville, 1984-86; bd. dirs. Planned Parenthood, New London, Conn., 1984-86, Women's Ctr. S.E. Conn., New London, 1986—, S.E. Conn. Aids Project, 1987—. Served as nurse USN, 1968-69. Mem. Am. Nurses Assn. (del. 1985), Conn. Women Higher Edn., Norwich C. of C. (active leadership program 1987-88), Phi Kappa Phi, Sigma Theta Tau. Republican. Home: 20 Caribou Way Oakdale CT 06370 Office: Mohegan Community Coll Mahan Dr Norwich CT 06360

WILLIAMS, DOLORES LOUISE, telecommunications executive; b. Rockford, Ill., Apr. 20, 1937; d. Arthur F. and Erma Lee (Johnson) Warner; divorced; 1 child, Leona Marie Williams Pierce. BE, Ottawa (Kans.) U., 1959. Cert. tchr., Kans., Tenn. Tchr., acting principal Navajo Indian Reservation, N.Mex. and Ariz., 1959-62; service rep. Ill. Bell., Rockford, 1972-74; sr. service rep. Michigan Bell, Jackson, 1964-67; sr. service rep. South Central Bell, Memphis, 1967-70, unit supr. bus. office, 1974-81; asst. sales mgr. AT&T and South Central Bell, Nashville and Memphis, 1981—; asst. dir. HWPC Child Care Tng. Program, Memphis, 1970-71; dir. Shelby County Headstart, Memphis, 1971-73. Recipient Outstanding Service award Warren Headstart Ctr., Memphis, 1973. Mem. Am. Mgmt. Assn. Jehovah's Witness. Home: 500 Michele Dr Antioch TN 37013

WILLIAMS, DONNA LEE, educator, consultant; b. Pitts., Sept. 16, 1946; d. Arthur Danks and Josephine (Crowe) W.; m. Leo John Sahene, Oct. 23, 1965 (div. 1969). AAS, Community Coll. Allegheny County, 1979. Instr. Community Coll. Allegheny County, Pitts., 1981—, U. Pitts., 1983-86; singles cons./advisor 1983—. Author: Positively Singular: Before We Can Be Happily Married, We Must First Learn How To Be Happily Single, 1981; producer (cable program) Positively Singular, 1981; also designer mdse. Adv. Assn. for Children and Adults with Learning Disabilities, Pitts., 1980-82. Mem. Profl. Singles Assn. (founder, pres. 1985—), Nat. Assn. Female Execs., Nat. Assn. Single Persons (charter), NOW, Phi Theta Kappa. Democrat. Home: 6636 Northumberland St Pittsburgh PA 15217-1313

WILLIAMS, DOROTHY, correctional administrator; b. Dothan, Ala., Jan. 31, 1943; d. Cliff Bostick; m. James A. Williams; children: Angela, Melody, James A. II. BS, Allen U., 1961; MA, U. Ala., 1981; postgrad., Wayne State U., Merrill-Palmer Inst. Cert. tchr., Ala. Tchr. reading, supr. Tuscaloosa (Ala.) City Schs., 1970—. Historian Ala. Assn. Women's and Youth Clubs; mem. Bailey Christian Meth. Episcopal Ch., Tuscaloosa Arts Council. Southeastern Leadership fellow; Ford Found. grantee, 1968. Mem. NEA (state del.), Nat. Assn. Colored Women's Clubs, Las Amigas Federated Club (past pres.), Nat. Council Negro Women, Ala. Edn. Assn., AAUW (bd. dirs.), Profl. Educators Tuscaloosa (bd. dirs.), Zeta Phi Beta. Home: 1 Geneva Dr Tuscaloosa AL 35403

WILLIAMS, DOROTHY ELLEN, educator; b. San Benito, Tex., July 27, 1940; d. Harry James, Jr. and Josephine Louise (Witherwax) W.; B.S., Tex. Woman's U., 1962; M.Ed., Our Lady of Lake Coll., San Antonio; 1968; midmgmt. cert. U. Tex., San Antonio, 1982; Ed.D., Tex. A&M U., 1985. Tchr., coach Harlandale Sch. Dist., San Antonio, 1962-68; instr. Sam Houston State U., Huntsville, Tex., 1968-69; tchr. Harlandale Sch. Dist., 1969-75; asst. athletic dir. San Antonio Sch. Dist., 1975-82; vice prin. M.L. King Middle Sch., San Antonio, 1982-85; prin. Harry Rogers Middle Sch., San Antonio, 1985—. Phi Delta Kappa. Mem. Nat. Assn. Secondary Sch. Prins., Tex. Assn. Secondary Sch. Prins., Nat. Fedn. Bus. and Profl. Women, Phi Kappa Phi, Methodist. Author articles in field. Home: PO Box 21292 San Antonio TX 78221 Office: 314 Galway San Antonio TX 78223

WILLIAMS, EDNA ALETA THEADORA JOHNSTON, journalist; b. Halifax, N.S., Can., Sept. 19, 1923; d. Clarence Harvey and Edna May (Lewis) Johnston; student Maritime Bus. Coll., 1943; m. Albert Murray Williams, Apr. 16, 1949 (dec.); children—Murleta, Norma, Martin, Charla, Kerrick, Renwick, Julia. Typist, Dept. Treasury (Navy), Halifax, 1944-49; with Bedford (N.S.) Mag., Halifax br., 1954-55, Presbyn. Office, New Glasgow, N.S., part-time, 1965-67, Thompson and Sutherland, New Glasgow, part-time, 1967-69; family editor, columnist and reporter New Glasgow Evening News, 1969—. Baptist rep. Pictou County Council of Churches, 1978-82, sec., 1980-82; pres. ch. aux. 2d United Bapt. Ch., 1979-83, organist, 1970—, chorus dir. Men's Choir, 1980—; organist St. James Anglican Ch., 1983-85; provincial pres. Women's Inst. of African United Bapt. Assn., 1983-86; mem. council Halifax YWCA; founding mem. Pictou County YM-YWCA, 1966—, bd. dirs., 1967-77, corr. sec., v.p., 1975-77, 1974-75; past pres., past provincial dir. Home and Sch.; past officer local interracial com.; bd. dirs. Big Bros./ Big Sisters, 1984-86, Pictou County United Way, 1983—, Pallative Care Aberdeen Hosp., 1987—, Black United Front. Mem. Can. Press Assn. Home: 230 Reservoir St, New Glasgow, NS Canada B2H 4K4 Office: Evening News, 352 East River Rd, Glasgow, NS Canada B2H 5E2

WILLIAMS, ELEANOR JOYCE, government air traffic control specialist; b. College Station, Tex., Dec. 21, 1936; d. Robert Ira and Viola (Ford) Toliver; m. Tollie Williams, Dec. 30, 1955 (div. July 1978); children—Rodrick, Viola Williams Smith, Darryl, Eric, Dana Williams Jones, Sheila Williams Watkins, Kenneth. Student Prairie View A&M Coll., 1955-56, Anchorage Community Coll., 1964-65, U. Alaska-Anchorage, 1976. Clk./stenographer FAA, Anchorage, 1964-66, adminstrv. clk., 1966-67, personnel staffing asst., 1967-68, air traffic control specialist, 1968-79, air traffic controller supr., San Juan, P.R., 1979-80, Anchorage, 1983-85, airspace specialist, Atlanta, 1980-83, Washington, 1985—; with FAA, Washington, 1985-87; area mgr. Kansas City Air Rt. Traffic Control Ctr., Olathe, Kans., 1987—. Sec. Fairview Neighborhood Council, Anchorage, 1967-69; mem. Anchorage Bicentennial Commn., 1975-76; bd. dirs. Mt. Patmos Youth Dept., Decatur, Ga., 1981-82. Recipient Mary K. Goddard award Anchorage Fed. Exec. Assn. and Fed. Women's Program, 1985, Sec.'s award Dept. transp., 1985. Mem. Bus. and Profl. Women U.S.A., Inc., Bus. and Profl. Women U.S.A., Inc. (North to the Future club) (charter pres. 1975-76), Blacks In Govt., Nat. Black Coalition of Fed. Aviation Employees (pres. cen. region chpt. 1987—, recipient Over Achievers Award, 1987), Profl. Women Controllers Orgn., Nat. Assn. Female Execs., NAACP. Democrat. Baptist. Avocations: singing; sewing. Home: 10904 Bradshaw St Overland Park KS 66210 Office: FAA 1810 E Loula Olathe KS 66061

WILLIAMS, ELIZABETH GUNDLACH, controller; b. Richmond, Va., Feb. 15, 1944; d. Herman Charles and Dorothy Mary (Hardy) Gundlach; m. Matthew Thomas Williams, July 2, 1966; 1 child, Anne Cary. BA in Psychology, Boston Coll., 1966; MS in Fin., Va. Commonwealth U., 1987. Cert. tchr., Va. Elem. tchr. Charlottesville (Va.) Schs., 1966-67; elem. tchr., coordinator St. Mary's Sch., Richmond, 1968-71; English tchr., coordinator Chesterfield (Va.) County Schs., 1971-79; acct. H.C. Gundlach Co., Richmond, 1979-80, office mgr., 1980-81, treas., mgr., 1981-85; controller Sands Anderson Marks Miller, Richmond, 1985-86; cons. fin. and strategic planning services Richmond, 1986-88; controller Automated Bus. and Computer Solutions and Systems, Alexandria, Va., 1988—; chmn. Textbook Adoption Com., Chesterfield, Va., 1974-75. Sponsor Ameurop Cultural Exchange, Richmond, 1983-84, Fulbright Found., 1985; rep. Richmond Cath. Diocese on Exec. Com. for Ednl. TV, Channel 23, 1968-70. Mem. Nat. Assn. Accts. (pub. relations dir. 1986—), Nat. Assn. Female Execs., Am. Bus. Women's Assn. (v.p. 1983-84, rec. sec. 1983). Home: 2519 Cherrytree Ln Richmond VA 23235

WILLIAMS, ELIZABETH RHONDA, educator, researcher; b. Boston, May 2, 1951; d. Edith Loretta (Burke) Williams; 1 child, Lisa Marie Wheeler. BFA, Tufts U., 1972; MA, Goddard Coll., 1974; EdD, Boston U., 1986; postdoctoral, Harvard U., 1987—. Researcher Harvard U., Cambridge, Mass., 1974-75; educator Boston Pub. Schs., 1975—; educator Roxbury Community Coll., Boston, 1985-86; cons. soc. for intellectual edn., tng. and research Georgetown U., Washington, 1986; cons. Nat. Coalition Bldg. Inst. Inc., Boston U., 1986. Mem. Women and Internat. Devel., Boston U. Women Grads. Club, Soc. for Intercultural Edn., Tng. and Research, Mass. Tchrs. Assn., NOW, New Eng. Womens Studies Assn., Nat. Womens Studies Assn., Cultural Survival, Inc., Tufts Univ. Club, Nat. Assn. of Fgn. Students Affairs, Pi Lambda Theta. Home: 237 Garden St Cambridge MA 02138

WILLIAMS, ERIS ALAIDA ANDERSON, nursing educator; b. Union, N.D., Dec. 8, 1924; d. Andrew O. and Esther Sophia (Johnson) Anderson; m. Ralph Oscar Williams; children—Kandela Groves, Kristie Lampton, Jack Fader. A.D.N. with honors, Everett Community Coll., 1970; B.S.N., U. Wash., 1973, M.S.N. in Adminstrn. and Edn., 1974. R.N., Wash. Nurse obgyn, nursery Island Hosp., Anacortes, Wash., 1966-68; head nurse medications Skagit Valley Hosp., Mt. Vernon, Wash., 1970-71; spl. duty nursing U. Wash. Hosp., 1972-74; asst. dir., dir. edn. Standring Hosp., Seattle, 1974-76; instr. nursing Highline Community Coll., Seattle, 1976-77; dir., coordinator nursing program Grays Harbor Coll., Aberdeen, Wash., 1977—, wrote new ADN program, 1986; apptd. to State Bd. Practical Nurse Examiners, Dept. Licensing, Olympia, Wash., 1978-82; mem. transferability com. Wash. State Community Coll. Nursing Dirs., 1980-85, Wash. State Council on Nursing Edn., 1985—, S.W. Wash. Task Force on Nursing Shortage, 1987—. Mem. Nat. League Nursing, Wash. State Nurses Assn., Am. Nurses Assn., Wash. Edn. Assn., NEA, Wash. State Vocat. Edn. Assn., Wash. State Health Occupations Assn. Lutheran. Home: 234 HoHum Ln Aberdeen WA 98520 Office: Grays Harbor Coll Aberdeen WA 98520

WILLIAMS, ERNESTINE, marketing administrator; b. Cleveland, Miss., Jan. 21, 1950; d. Mason and Jo-ella (Hobbs) W.; m. Eddie Jordan Jr., Mar. 15, 1975 (div. Aug. 1981); 1 child, Sheryce Danita. Student, Bradley U., 1968-70. Utility teller Upper Ave. Nat., Chgo., 1973-74; supr. accounts receivable Claims Processing Corp., Chgo., 1974-76; sr. gen. ledger clk. Yr. Book Med. Pubs., Chgo., 1976-83, coordinator promotions, 1983-86, mgr. mktg. adminstrn., 1986—. Mem. Am. Mgmt. Assn., Chgo. Assn. Direct Mktg., Nat. Assn. for Female Execs., Chgo. Book Clinic. Democrat. Baptist. Home: 3827 W Flournoy Chicago IL 60624

WILLIAMS, EUPHEMIA GOODLOW, nursing educator, consultant; b. Bagwell, Tex., Oct. 17, 1938; d. Otis John and Blanche M. (Pouge) Goodlow; m. James Altrice Williams, July 23, 1960 (div. July 1987); children—Caren, Christopher, Curt, Catherine. B.S., U. Okla., 1961; M.S., U. Colo., 1973, Ph.D., 1981. Staff nurse, head nurse VA Hosp., Oklahoma City, 1961-66; pub. health nurse Oklahoma City-County Health Dept., 1966-70; instr. U. Colo. Sch. Nursing, Denver, 1974-77, asst. prof., 1977-81; assoc. prof., chmn. dept. nursing Cameron U., Lawton, Okla., 1981-82; assoc. prof. nursing Met. State Coll., Denver, 1982-84, chmn. dept. nursing and health care mgmt., 1984-88; prof., head dept. nursing SW Mo. State U., Springfield, 1988—; workshop cons. S.D. State Health Dept., Pierre, 1975-76. Mem. profl. adv. com. Vis. Nurses' Assn., Boulder, 1978-81; mem. citizens adv. com. Boulder High Sch. (Colo.), 1978-79. Predoctoral nurse fellow HEW, 1978. Mem. Am. Nurses Assn., Am. Pub. Health Assn., Nat. League Nursing, Sigma Theta Tau. Democrat. Lutheran. Home: 961 15th St Boulder CO 80302 Office: Met State Coll Box 33 1006 11th St Denver CO 80204

WILLIAMS, FLORA LEONA, economics educator; b. Talahassee, Jan. 21, 1937; d. Noble J. and Dorothy (Rohrer) Rouch; m. Leiw K. Williams, June 26, 1960; children: Chadwick, Lora Lu, Matthew. BS, Manchester Coll., 1959; MS, Purdue U., 1964, PhD, 1969. Tchr., Mishawaka, Ind., 1959-64, West Lafayette, Ind., 1964-68; research asst. Purdue U., West Lafayette, 1968-69, asst. prof., 1969-75, assoc. prof. home econs., 1975—; vis. prof. U. Calif., Davis, 1976; cons. in field. Author: The Family Economy, 1973, Guidelines to Financial Counseling, 1980; contbr. articles to profl. jours. HEW grantee. Mem. Assn. Consumer Research, Am. Econs. Assn., Am. Home Econs. Assn., Am. Council on Consumer Interest, Family and Consumer Research. Home: 3815 Gate Rd Lafayette IN 47905 Office: Purdue U MTHW Hall CSR Dept West Lafayette IN 47907

WILLIAMS, GENA KAY, automotive dealership executive; b. Fairfax, Va., Apr. 12, 1963; d. Leon Ellis and Vena Pearl (Hicks) W. B.S., U. Ariz., 1981; postgrad. Hofstra U., 1983; student in Archtl. Drafting, ITT Tech. Inst., Sacramento, 1988—. Controller TGI Friday's, Tuscon, Ariz., Westbury, N.Y., 1980-83; auto dealer, bus. mgr. Williams, Inc., Hampton, Va., 1983—. ROTC scholar U. Ariz., Tucson, 1979. Mem. Peninsula Assn. Credit Execs., Nat. Assn. Female Execs., Am. Mgmt. Assn., Peninsula Women's Network, Intertel, Triple Nine Soc., Mensa. Republican. Presbyterian. Lodge: Rosicrucians, Martinist. Avocations: photography, skiing. Office: Williams Inc PO Box 9568 Hampton VA 23670-0568

WILLIAMS, GERTIE BOOTHE, retired home school administrator; b. Smithfield, Va., Feb. 6, 1928; d. Claiborne Benton and Elnora Mae (Brown) Boothe; m. Jesse Cary Williams Sr., June 14, 1949; children: Linda, Jesse Cary Jr., Sharon. BS, Va. State Coll., 1945; postgrad., U. Va., 1971; MS, Va. State Coll., 1980. Technician Norfolk (Va.) Naval Base, 1942-43; filing clk. IRS, Bronx, N.Y., 1945-46; tchr. Sussex County, Waverly, Va., 1946-57; supervising tchr. Va. State U., Petersburg, 1957-59; tchr. Petersburg Pub. Schs., 1957-75, coordinator home sch., 1976-86. Mem. Women Robb for Gov. Va., Petersburg, 1979. Recipient vol. service award Cystic fibrosis Found., 1979, cert. appreciation Mental Health Project Cen. State Hosp., 1980. Mem. Va. Edn. Assn., Va. State U. Nat. Assn. (v.p. 1984), NEA, Wives Beaux-Twenty (reporter 1985-87), Jack and Jill Am. Ptnrs. (journalist 1957), Nat. Council Negro Women (local chmn. 1975), Phi Delta Kappa (treas./historian 1978), Kappa Delta Pi (v.p./historian 1981-84), Delta Sigma Theta (pres. 1968-70, initiated "self help teen program, 1970-75). Democrat. Baptist. Clubs: Order Ea. Star (worth matron 1949-50), Links (pres. 1977-79, coordinator "Just Say No", 1986-87). Home: 920 Shields St Petersburg VA 23803

WILLIAMS, GWENDOLYN STEWART, nurse; b. Montgomery, Ala., May 31, 1960; d. Horace Jr. and Janie (Hall) Stewart; m. Ralph Williams Sr., Dec. 22, 1983; 1 child, India Danielle. BS in Nursing, U. Ala., 1982, MS, 1987. RN, Ala. Staff, charge nurse DCH Regional Med. Ctr., Tuscaloosa, Ala., 1982-84; dir. nursing Nursing Home, Northport, Ala., 1984-85; dir. nursing services Greene City Hosp., Eutaw, Ala., 1985-86; staff edn. specialist II Dept. Mental Health and Mental Retardation, Tuscaloosa, 1986—. Named one of Outstanding Young Women of Am., 1985. Mem. Ala. State Nursing Assn. (adminstrv. mem.-at-large 1985-86), Nat. Assn. Female Execs., Jaycettes, Tuscaloosa C. of C. Home: 56 E Lake Tuscaloosa AL 35405

WILLIAMS, HARRIET CLARKE, retired college administrator, artist; b. Bklyn., Sept. 5, 1922; d. Herbert Edward and Emma (Gibbs) W. AA, Bklyn. Coll., 1958; student, Art Career Sch., N.Y.C., 1960; cert., Hunter Coll., 1965, CPU Inst. Data Processing, 1967; student, Chineses Cultural Ctr., N.Y.C., 1973. Adminstr. Baruch Coll., N.Y.C., 1959-85; mktg. researcher 1st Presbyn. Arts and Crafts Shop, Jamaica, N.Y., 1986—; tutor in art St. John's U., Jamaica, 1986—. Exhibited in group shows at Union Carbide Art Exhibit, N.Y.C., 1975, Queens Day Exhibition, N.Y.C., 1980,

1st Presbyn. Arts and Crafts Shop, N.Y.C., 1986, others. Vol. reading tchr. Mabel Dean Vocat. High Sch., N.Y.C., 1965-67; mem. polit. action com. dist. council 37, N.Y.C., 1973-77; mem. negotiating team adminstrv. contracts, N.Y.C., 1975-78; mem. Com. To Save CCNY, 1976-77. Appreciation award Dist. Council 37, 1979. Mem. Artist Equity Assn. N.Y., Nat. Assn. Female Execs., Lakota Devel. Council, Am. Film Inst., Bklyn. Coll. Alumni. Roman Catholic. Office: Baruch Coll 17 Lexington Ave New York NY 10010

WILLIAMS, HAZEL MAY, real estate executive; b. San Diego, Oct. 21, 1926; d. William and Alice May (Yarno) Roth; B.A., San Diego State U., 1946; student West Valley Jr. Coll., 1970-73; grad. Realtors Inst.; m. Shelley S. Williams, Jr., Aug. 24, 1947; 1 dau., Christabel May. V.p. Shelley Williams Assos., Inc., Saratoga, Calif., 1968—. Active Los Gatos chpt. ARC, Community Hosp. Aux., West Valley Republican Women. Named Woman of Yr., Santa Clara chpt. Women's Council Realtors; cert. residential specialist, Realtor and broker; cert. real estate brokerage mgr. Mem. Nat. Assn. Realtors (dir. 1986—), Calif. Assn. Realtors (dir. 1974-79, 84, regional v.p. 1981, dir.-at-large 1983, chmn. policy com. 1985—), Los Gatos-Saratoga Bd. Realtors (ombudsman, pres. 1978, certs. of merit, Realtor of Yr. 1980), San Jose Real Estate Bd., Women's Council Realtors, Calif. Assn. Real Estate Tchrs., DAR (Los Gatos chpt.). Clubs: Saratoga Foothill, San Jose Women's. Office: 12960 Saratoga Sunnyvale Rd Saratoga CA 95070

WILLIAMS, HENRIETTA VER MEER, clinical psychologist; b. Pella, Iowa, Apr. 2, 1924; d. Otto Henry and Dena Catherine (Stadt) Ver Meer; B.A. in Philosophy, U. Iowa, 1944; M.A. in Psychology, U. Ill., 1946, Ph.D. in Exptl. Psychology, 1949; postgrad. in clin. psychology U. Md., 1966-67; m. Richard Hays Williams, Feb. 19, 1971; children—Marylie Catherine Williams Karlovac, Robert Harold, Frank Rendler. Counselor, U. Wis., Madison, 1945-51, lectr. dept. psychology, 1951-52; research psychologist NIMH, Bethesda, Md., 1965-67, postdoctoral intern in clin. psychology, 1967-68; staff psychologist, psychologist-in-charge of div. St. Elizabeth's Hosp., Washington, 1969-72, clin. adminstr., 1972-74; dir. psychol. services Pitt County Mental Health Center, Greenville, N.C., 1974-78; pvt. practice clin. psychology, asso. Nelson Clinic, Greenville, 1978-88, Family Med. Care, 1988—; cons. Alcoholic Rehab. Center, 1977-79, Regional Rehab. Center, Pitt Meml. Hosp., 1977-81, Devel. Evaluation Clinic, Med. Sch., 1980-84; clin. asst. prof. psychology Eastern Carolina U. Sch. Medicine, 1977—. Mem. vestry St. Luke's Episcopal Ch., Rockville, Md., 1968-71; mem. incorporating body, chmn. personnel com. St. Luke's Half-Way Houses, Rockville. Mem. Am. Psychol. Assn., Nat. Register Health Service Providers in Psychology, Phi Beta Kappa, Univ. Condominium Assn. (pres. 1980-82). Democrat. Clubs: PEO. Contbr. articles in field to profl. jours. Home: 111 Cardinal Dr Greenville NC 27858 Office: Nelson Clinic Medical Pavilion Suite 9 Greenville NC 27834

WILLIAMS, IMA JO, home economist, civic worker; b. Bowie, Tex., Feb. 23, 1942; d. Herman Wayne and Clarice (Bilbrey) Tompkins; m. Robert Melvin Williams, Jan. 27, 1963; children—Stacy, Angie, Mark. BS in Home Econs., North Tex. State U., 1963. Home economist Lone Star Gas Co., Dallas, 1963-64, Mich. Consol. Gas Co., Ann Arbor, 1964-65; home econs. tchr. Milan High Sch., Mich., 1965-69; nutrition coordinator Shay Elem. Sch., Harbor Springs, Mich., 1979—; pres. Crooked Tree Arts Council, Petoskey, Mich., 1982-83, v.p. vols., 1983-84, fin. v.p., 1984-85; bd. dirs. Concerned Citizens for Arts, Detroit, 1983-87, regional v.p., 1987—. Author (fairy tale): Petal, 1978. Performer local theatrical prodns., 1982—. Mem. AAUW (chmn. Mich. Ednl. Found. Program com. 1981-83, mem. nat. devel. com. 1983-85, Mich. cultural com. chmn. 1985-87, nat. sub-com. chmn. immigration reform). Republican. Methodist. Clubs: Garden (pres. 1979-81) (Harbor Springs); Antiques (program v.p. 1987—) (Petoskey). Home: 6546 Lower Shore Dr Harbor Springs MI 49740

WILLIAMS, J. LINDA, librarian; b. Bethesda, Md., June 30, 1945; d. Joseph Gordon and Annie Louise (Whitfield) DiMisa; m. Charles Edward Williams, Nov. 2, 1968. BS in Secondary Edn./English and History, Radford U., 1966; MLS, U. Md., 1977; postgrad., Bowie (Md.) State Coll., 1987. Cert. tchr., librarian. Tchr. English, history Prince William County Pub. Schs., Woodbridge, Va., 1967-73; tchr. English Charles County Pub. Schs., Laplata, Md., 1973-76; library media specialist St. Mary County Pub. Schs., Leonardtown, Md., 1977-84; staff specialist Md. State Dept. Edn., Balt., 1985—. Profl. devel. grantee 3M, 1981. Mem. ALA (various divs.), Acacia, Md. Library Assn., Md. Edn. Media Assn. Home: Rt 4 Box 4146 Laplata MD 20646 Office: Md State Dept Edn 200 W Baltimore St Baltimore MD 21201

WILLIAMS, JACQUELINE, university administrator; b. Mobile, Ala., Sept. 19, 1938; d. Zack and Ethel (Powe) W. BS, Ala. State U., 1960, MEd, 1974, EdS, 1981; postgrad., U. Ala. Tchr. pub. schs. City of Mobile, 1960-64; various positions Ala. State U., Montgomery, 1983-84, dir. grants and projects, 1984-88, asst. v.p. for student affairs, 1988—; cons. Bishop State Jr. Coll., Mobile, 1979, Stillman Coll., Tuscaloosa, Ala., 1983. Recipient cert. U.S. Dist. Ct. (mid. dist.) Ala., 1974. Mem. Coalition of 100 Black Women, Phi Delta Kappa, Alpha Kappa Mu, Delta Sigma Theta. Democrat. Methodist. Club: Century. Home: 107 Stuart St Montgomery AL 36105 Office: Ala State U 915 S Jackson St Montgomery AL 36195

WILLIAMS, JERRY RUTH, telephone company manager; b. Bogalusa, La., Sept. 5, 1936; d. Charlie and Procula Marian (Norris) W.; Hutcherson; B.A. magna cum laude, So. U., 1957; M.Ed., U. Mo., St. Louis, 1969; m. Robert P. Williams, Jan. 25, 1959; 1 dau., Michelle Yvette. Tchr. English, New Orleans pub. schs., 1957-59; case worker Mo. Dept. Welfare, St. Louis, 1960-61; tchr. St. Louis pub. schs., 1961-66; counselor Normandy Sch. Dist., St. Louis, 1969-78, dir. alt. learning program, 1975-76; staff trainer Title IX Workshop, 1977; staff supr. service costs Southwestern Bell Telephone Co., St. Louis, 1978-80, customer service supr. bus. installation control, 1980-82; asst. staff mgr. materials mgmt.-methods, 1982-84, customer services staff supr.-tng., 1984-86, mgr.-measurements, 1986—; mem. Southwestern Bell Profl. Women, Southwestern Bell Speakers Bur. Mem. Dist. Council on Ministries; bd. dirs. Wesley Found., Epworth Children's Home. Mem. United Meth. Women (E. Mo. conf. v.p., chair reception com., unit pres. mem. exec. bd.), United Meth. Ch. gen. conf., 1988, Phi Delta Kappa, Alpha Kappa Alpha, Kappa Delta Pi, Alpha Kappa Mu. Methodist. Club: Toastmasters (adminstrv. v.p. 1983-84). Home: 1967 Willow Lake Dr Chesterfield MO 63017 Office: 915 Olive 5th Floor Saint Louis MO 63101

WILLIAMS, JOAN ALICE, federal agency administrator; b. Norfolk, Va., May 15, 1931; d. Bernard Leigh and Alice Eugenia (Ramsey) Scott, Sr.; m. Edward Samuel Brisbane, Sept. 22, 1951 (div. Oct. 1962); children: Darryl Edward Brisbane, Pierre S.Brisbane; m. Luther Williams Sr., Oct. 12, 1963 (div. Sept. 1970); m. Shirley Stanford Moss, Nov. 24, 1979 (div. Feb. 20, 1981). AB in Social Sci., Norfolk State Coll., 1975, MA in Communication, 1978. Cert. in infant nursing. Sch. clk. Norfolk City Schs., 1963-64; clk. U.S. Postal Office, Norfolk, 1964-73, supr., 1973—. Br. sec. (bi-monthly newsletter) Nat. Assn. Postal Suprs., 1983-85. Dir. I. Sherman Greene Chorale, Norfolk, 1972—; vol. Am. Heart Assn., Norfolk, 1983; vol. worker soup kitchen St. Mary's Cath. Ch., Norfolk, 1986, money counter, 1986—; mem. La Gemmes Civic and Social Club, Virginia Beach, Va. Recipient Service award I. Sherman Greene Chorale, 1986. Mem. Nat. Assn. Female Execs., Delta Sigma Theta (treas. 1985-87), Alpha Kappa Delta. Clubs: Toastmistress (council del. regional newspaper 1985), Women's. Lodges: Ladies of Peter Claver, Cath. Daus. of Am. Home: 525 Garren Ave Norfolk VA 23509-1632 Office: Customhouse Post Office 124 Atlantic St Norfolk VA 23514-9998

WILLIAMS, JOY RHONDA, publishing company executive; b. Ipswich, Australia, May 30, 1945; came to U.S., 1954; d. Francis Leon and Ailsa Mary (Bailey) W.; m. Raymond Joel Bennett, Feb. 12, 1962 (div. 1974); 1 child, Melissa Anne Howell. AA in Psychology, DeAnza Coll., Cupertino, Calif., 1974. Exec. sec. Cobilt div. Computervision, Sunnyvale, Calif., 1972-74; tracking system analyst Memorex, Inc., Santa Clara, Calif., 1974-77; computer operator LCS Inc., Sunnyvale, 1977-78; project librarian Logisticon Inc., Sunnyvale, 1978-79, programmer-analyst, 1979-82; sr. programmer-analyst Microvertics, Inc., Mountain View, Calif., 1982-83; sr. systems analyst Data Architects, Inc., San Francisco, 1983-84; tech. editor Sci. Applications Internat. Inc., Los Altos, Calif., 1985-86; owner, pres. Artist Publs. Inc., Cupertino, 1984—. Office: Artist Publs Inc PO Box 466 Cupertino CA 95015-0466

WILLIAMS, JOYCE LORRAINE, small business owner; b. Balt., July 7, 1943; d. George and Priscilla Cecilia (Powell) W.; 1 child, Eric T. Cert. in radiology, Johns Hopkins U., 1971; cert in counseling, Coppin State Coll., 1974; cert. in therapy, Balt. Community Coll., 1975; BS, Antioch U., 1978. Tchr. Batl. City Pub. Schs., 1971; adminstr. Project ADAPT, Balt., 1972-78, CETA Adminstrn., Balt., 1979-81; salesperson Equitable Life Assurance Co., Balt., 1981-82; adminstrv. staff asst. R.J. Washington & Assocs., 1982-83; pres. Best Temporary Services, Inc., Balt., 1983—; Mem. Greater Balt. Com., 1985—, MD/MC Minority Supplier Devel., Balt., 1985—. Sec., treas. Balt County Dems. Inc., 1979. Recipient Presedential Citation Assn. for Equal Opportunity in Higher Edn., 1988. Mem. Minority Bus. Directory (Leadership award 1984), Antioch U. Alumnae Assn. (Extra Mile award 1985). Democrat. Home: 7505 Fairbrook Rd Apt 2D Baltimore MD 21207

WILLIAMS, JUANITA HINGST, clinical psychologist, educator; b. Jackson, Miss., Dec. 17, 1922; d. Henry Christian and Anna (Bryant) Hingst; m. James Brooks Williams, Aug. 29, 1942; children: Karen, Anita, Gretchen, Laura. BA, Rutgers U., 1957; MA, Temple U., 1959, PhD, 1963. Lic. psychologist, Fla. Psychologist VA, Bay Pines, Fla., 1963-64; asst. prof. U. South Fla., Tampa, 1966-70, assoc. prof., 1970-77, prof., 1977-85, emeritus prof., 1985—. Author: (book) Psychology of Women, 1977, 3d edit., 1987; contbr. articles to profl. jours. Mem. NOW, 1987—. Recipient Award of Distinction Athena, 1982, Woman of Distinction Soroptimist, 1987. Fellow Am. Psychol. Assn. Democrat. Office: U South Fla Womens Studies Tampa FL 33620

WILLIAMS, JUDITH L., library administrator; b. Jacksonville, Fla., Sept. 3, 1948; d. Herman D. and Lucille T. (Jaskowiak) W. BA, Fla. State U., 1970, MLS, 1971. From librarian to sr. librarian to asst. dir. to dir. Jacksonville Pub. Libraries, 1971—. Active Jacksonville Community Council. Mem. ALA, Fla. Library Assn., Southeastern Library Assn., League of Women Voters, Jacksonville C. of C. Office: Jacksonville Pub Libraries 122 N Ocean St Jacksonville FL 32202-3374

WILLIAMS, JULIE BELLE, psychiatric social worker; b. Algona, Iowa, July 29, 1950; d. George Howard and Leta Maribelle (Durschmidt) W.; BA, U. Iowa, 1972, MSW, 1973. Lic. psychologist,Minn.; lic. social worker, Iowa. Social worker Psychopathic Hosp., Iowa City, 1971-72, Child Devel. Clinic, Iowa City, 1973; OEO counselor YOUR, Webster City, Iowa, 1972; group therapist Cedar Manor Nursing Home, Tipton, Iowa, 1973; therapist Mid-Eastern Iowa Community Mental Health Ctr., Iowa City, 1973; psychiat. social worker Mental Health Ctr. N. Iowa, Mason City, 1974-79, chief psychiat. social worker, 1979-80; asst. dir. Community Counseling Ctr., White Bear Lake, Minn., 1980-85, dir., 1985—; lectr., cons. in field. NIMH grantee, 1972-73. Mem. Nat. Assn. Social Workers (cert., pres. local chpt.), NOW, Am. Orthopsychiat. Assn., Am. Assn. Sex Educators, Counselors and Therapists, Minn. Women Psychologists, Minn. Lic. Psychologists, Phi Beta Kappa. Democrat. Office: 4739 Division Ave White Bear Lake MN 55110

WILLIAMS, KAREN HASTIE, lawyer; b. Washington, Sept. 30, 1944; d. William Henry and Beryl (Lockhart) Hastie; m. Wesley S. Williams, Jr.; children: Amanda Pedersen, Wesley Hastie, Bailey Lockhart. Cert., U. Neuchatel, Switzerland, 1965; BA, Bates Coll., 1966; MA, Tufts U., 1967; JD, Cath. U. Am., 1973. Bar: D.C. 1973. Staff asst. internat. gov. relations dept. Mobil Oil Corp., N.Y.C., 1967-69; staff asst. com. Dist. Columbia U.S. Senate, 1970, chief counsel com. on the budget, 1977-80; law clk. to judge Spottswood Robinson III U.S. Ct. Appeals (D.C. Cir.), Washington, 1973-74; law clk. to assoc. justice Thurgood Marshall U.S. Supreme Ct., Washington, 1974-75; assoc. Fried, Frank, Harris, Shriver & Kampelman, Washington, 1975-77, 1975-77; adminstr. Office Mgmt. and Budget, Washington, 1980-81; of counsel Crowell & Moring, Washington, 1982, ptnr., 1982—; Bd. dirs. Crestar Fin. Services Corp.; mem. bd. professional responsibility D.C. Ct. Appeals. Assoc. editor Cath. U. Law Review. Bd. dirs. D.C. chpt. ARC, also exec. com.; bd. trustees Nat. Cathedral Sch., Washington; v.p. Greater Washington Research Ctr., also bd. trustees; mem. N.Am. delagation Trilateral Commn. Mem. ABA (pub. contract law sect., vice chmn. legis liaison com.) standing com. membership), Nat. Bar Assn., Washington Bar Assn., Nat. Contract Mgmt. Assn., NAACP (bd. dirs. legal defense fund). Office: Crowell & Moring 1001 Pennsylvania Ave NW Washington DC 20004-2505

WILLIAMS, KATHLEEN ELIZABETH, nurse, health care administrator; b. Darby, Pa., Jan. 29, 1954; d. James Patrick and Kathleen Elizabeth (O'Doherty) Tuppeny; m. Richard Alvin Williams, Dec. 24, 1980; 1 child, Caroline Michelle. BS in Nursing, U. Pa., 1976, MS in Nursing, 1984. RN, Pa., N.J., Va. Staff nurse ICU, Mercy Cath. Med. Ctr., Darby, 1976-77; pub. health nurse Va. Dept. Health, New Castle, 1978-80; pub. health nurse supr. Va. Dept. Health, Covington, Va., 1980-82; clin. intern Gloucester County Health Dept., Woodbury, N.J., 1983-84; discharge planning coordinator St. Agnes Med. Ctr., Phila., 1984-85, dir. home health care, 1985-87; southeastern sales rep. Home Care Info. Systems, Bloomfield, N.J., 1987—; agy. preceptor U. Pa., Phila., 1986-87, Villanova (Pa.) U., 1986. Contbr. chpt. to Home Health Adminstrn., 1987. Leadership scholoar U. Pa., 1983-84. Mem. Am. Nurses Assn., Am. Pub. Health Assn., Nat. Assn. Female Execs., Sigma Theta Tau. Home: 7950 Crossroads Dr #601 North Charleston SC 29418

WILLIAMS, LEONETTE MARY, law librarian; b. Ft. Lauderdale, Fla., Sept. 18, 1952; d. Ralph Edgar and Helen (Pleska) Dorval; m. Boyce Carl Williams, June 7, 1975. BA in English Lit., Upsala Coll., 1974; MLS, U. So. Calif., 1978. Acquisitions librarian U. So. Calif. Law Library, Los Angeles, 1978-85, Head of Tech. Services, 1985—. Mem. Am. Assn. Law Libraries, So. Calif. Assn. Law Libraries (bd. dirs. 1984-88), Am. Soc. Info. Science (pres. Los Angeles chpt. 1982, Mem. of Yr. 1981). Office: U So Calif Law Library University Park MC-0072 Los Angeles CA 90089-0072

WILLIAMS, LORELLE, automobile sales administrator; b. Seattle, June 24, 1945; d. Maximillian Herzig Best and May Best Tompkins; m. Don Armstrong Williams, Apr. 20, 1974. Student, Pasadena City Coll., 1962-64, North Bay Coll., 1963-68, No. Va. Community Coll., 1969-70. Lic. real estate agt., Va. Mgr. personnel City of Los Angeles, 1963-69; sales rep. Bellaire, Inc., Washington, 1969-72; sales mgr., rep. Brown's Volvo and Subaru, Alexandria, Va., 1972—; cons. Herzig and Assocs., Alexandria, 1985—. Mem. Assn. for Research and Enlightenment.

WILLIAMS, LOUISE ANITIA, visual communications consultant; b. Portland, Oreg., Mar. 31, 1942; d. Homer Bruce and Ora Ellen (Diehl) W.; student public schs., Beaverton, Oreg.; 1 dau., Tiffany Joy Wlecial. Med. asst., physicians' practice, 1963-64; adminstrv. asst. St. Vincent's Hosp., 1964-70; salesman, sales mgr., nat. sales mgr. Indsl. Systems, 1970; regional sales mgr. Peel O'Matique, 1971; bus. devel. rep. Imperial Bank, 1971-72; pvt. practice fin. cons., Los Angeles, 1972-73; sales rep. Printing Services, Granada Hills, Calif., 1976; partner Art, Love, Time & Money, Marina City, Calif., 1978-79; pres., sole stock holder Corporate Creative Services, Sherman Oaks, Calif., 1979-85; advt. cons., Orange, Calif., 1985—. Commr. Status of Women, Orange County, 1986-89; mem. Rep. Presdl. Task Force. Served with Hosp. Corps, USN, 1960-63. Named Angel Yr. Childhelp USA, Los Angeles, 1984. Mem. Nat. Assn. Female Execs., Los Angeles Ad Club, Women in Bus., Nat. Assn. Women Bus. Owners, Western Los Angeles C. of C., Sales and Mktg. Execs., Med. Mktg. Assn., Sherman Oaks C. of C. Republican. Mem. Metro Church. Clubs: Buckley Parents Assn., Mid Town Exec. (Los Angeles). Home and Office: 177 S Waterwheel Way Orange CA 92669

WILLIAMS, LULA MAE, nurse; b. Columbus, Ga., Aug. 12, 1947; d. Roosevelt and Lula Belle (Bridges) W. BS in Nursing, Tuskegee Inst., 1970; M of Nursing, Emory U., 1973. Staff nurse VA Med. Ctr., Tuskegee, Ala., 1971-72, clin. specialist, 1974-77; head nurse VA Med. Ctr., Nashville, 1977-81; asst. chief nurse VA Med. Ctr., Poplar Bluff, Mo., 1981-84; assoc. chief nurse VA Med. Ctr., Perry Point, Md., 1984-85, quality assurance coordinator, 1985—. Served to 2d lt. U.S. Army, 1967-70, maj. Res. Mem. Am. Nurses Assn., Nat. Assn. Quality Assurance Profls., Md. Assn. Quality Assurance Profls., Res. Officers Assn., Delta Sigma Theta (Harford County v.p. 1987, treas. 1988). Democrat. Mem. Church of Christ. Office: VA Med Ctr Bldg 5H Perry Point MD 21902

WILLIAMS, LYDIA F., telecommunications company official; b. New Orleans, Aug. 28, 1949; d. Edgar Joseph and Muriel (Bartholomew) W. BS in Math., Xavier U., New Orleans, 1971. Cert. info. systems auditor. Programmer Mountain Bell Telephone Co., Denver, 1973-74, sr. programmer, 1974-77, staff mgr., 1977-81, audit mgr., 1981-87; acctg. mgr. US West Communications, Denver, 1987—; cons. Bartholomew Enterprises, Denver, 1986—. Mem. EDP Auditors Assn. (CISA coordinator), Inst. Internal Auditors, Project Mgmt. Inst., Soc. Info. Mgmt., Data Processing Mgmt. Assn., Nat. Brotherhood Skiers (Nordic dir. 1986—, Pioneer award 1988, Pres.'s award 1987), Black Employees Assn. (editor newsletter 1979-84), Zeta Phi Beta (editor newsletter 1982-84). Democrat. Roman Catholic. Club: Martin Luther King (Denver), Flyers Running (historian 1985-87). Office: US West Communications 930 15th St Room 750 Denver CO 80202

WILLIAMS, LYNDA ELAINE, small business owner; b. Topeka, Aug. 30, 1951; d. James David and Doris Darleen (Davis) Leek; m. Ronald O. Williams, July 10, 1977 (div. Jan. 1987); children: Rebecca Laura, Ryan Christopher. Student, Foothill Jr. Coll., 1969-70, Deanza Jr. Coll., 1971. Designer trainee Douglas Haylock Total Graphics, San Jose, Calif., 1971-78; architect, engr. ARAMCO, Dhahran, Saudi Arabia, 1978-79, creative dir. Material Supply, 1979-83, graphic designer, 1980-84, lectr., 1981-83; owner, designer Creative Designs, Napa, Calif., 1984—; cons. U. Petroleum and Minerals, Dhahran 1982-84, Nat. Paper Products Co., Dammam, Saudi Arabia 1981-84. Artist, designer Saudi Arabian Met/Ocean, 1979. Mem. Nat. Assn. Female Exec., Napa C. of C. Baptist. Club: Toastmaster Internat., (pres. 1982-83, treas. 1981-82). Office: Creative Designs 1524 Jefferson Napa CA 94559

WILLIAMS, M. JANE, marketing and sales manager; b. Salem, Ohio, Aug. 17, 1955; d. Robert Angus and Mary Elizabeth (Riddle) W.; 1 child, Landon Matthew Betsworth. BSBA, Youngstown State U., 1964. Cert. real estate agt. N.C. Corp. acct. Westminster Co., Greensboro, N.C., 1984-86; market analyst Zaremba Coms. N.C., Inc., 1986; sales mgr. Stonehaven Zaremba, Winston-Salem, N.C., 1987; sales and mktg. mgr. Laurel Brook at Adams Farm and Winsor Park R&D Homes, Inc., Greensboro, 1987-88, Westminster County, Greensboro, 1988—. Mem. Profl. Women's Consortium (bd. dirs., pres. elect 1987, pres. 1988—), Nat. Assn. Homebuilders (nat. sales and mktg.), Ambassadors Club-Greensboro C. of C. Unitarian Universalist. Home: PO Box 10224 Greensboro NC 27404

WILLIAMS, MARCIA NADINE, corporate professional; b. Welch, Okla., June 19, 1939; d. Oren Earnest Moore and Bernadine W. (Highsmith) Lawson; m. Morgan T. Williams, Jan. 22, 1957 (div. Feb. 1983); children: Tom, LeAnn, John; m. Darrell D. Moore, Sept. 1, 1985. BS, Fresno State Coll., 1969. Bus. mgr. Pathol. & Clin. Services, Fresno, Calif., 1967—; corp. sec. Golden Valley Transport Inc., Fresno, 1987. Mem. Clin. Lab. Mgmt. Assn., Nat. Assn. Female Execs., Calif. Med. Assts. Assn. (dir.-at-large 1984, chmn. membership com. 1987, Med. Asst. of Yr. 1985), Fresno Women's Network. Democrat. Baptist. Home: 1383 E Ticonderoga Dr Fresno CA 93710 Office: Pathol & Clin Services 2111 E Dakota Fresno CA 93726

WILLIAMS, MARGARET LU WERTHA, nurse; b. Midland, Tex., Aug. 30, 1938; d. Cotter Craven and Mollie Jo (Tarter) Hiett; m. James Troy Lary, Nov. 16, 1960 (div. Jan. 1963); 1 child, James Cotter; m. Terrell C. Williams, Aug. 11, 1985. BS, Tex. Woman's U., 1960; MA, Tchrs. Coll., N.Y.C., 1964, EdM, 1974, doctoral studies, 1981. Nurse Midland Meml. Hosp., 1960-63; instr. Odessa (Tex.) Coll., 1963-67; dir. ADNP Laredo (Tex.) Jr. Coll., 1967-70; asst. prof. Pan Am. U., Edinburgh, Tex., 1970-72; nursing practitioner St. Luke's Hosp., N.Y.C., 1972-79; sgt. Burns Security, Midland, 1979-81; safety compliance officer Area Builders, Odessa, 1981-83; field supr. We Care Home Health Agy., Midland, 1983-87; pres. Nursing Research and Consultation, Stanton, Tex., 1982—; charge nurse Glenwood, A Psychiat. Hosp., Midland, 1987—. Vol. Battered Women's Ctr., Midland, 1987—, IMAGE, Midland, 1970-72; troop leader Girl Scouts U.S., Midland, 1962-72. Recipient Isabelle Hampton-Robb award Nat. League for Nursing, 1976; named one of Outstanding Young Women of Am., 1965. Mem. Tex. Nurses Assn. (pres. dist. 21 1962-65, dist. 32 1970-72), Am. Nurses Assn. (del. 1966-72), Tex. Nurses Assn. (vol. T-Pappin 1987—). Office: Nursing Research and Consultation PO Box 1218 Stanton TX 79782

WILLIAMS, MARILYN, corporate planner, health manager; b. Ashland, Ky., July 28, 1950; d. Charley Thurman and Wilma Margaret (Burke) W. BS, Queens Coll., 1971; MS, U. Ala., Birmingham, 1977. Asst. biochemist So. Research Inst., Birmingham, 1972-75; asst. exec. dir. Jefferson County Med. Soc., Birmingham, 1977-78; dir. project rev. Birmingham Regional Health Systems Agy., 1978-80; v.p. planning and regulation Miss. Hosp. Assn., Jackson, 1980-82; v.p. planning, regulation and data Miss. Hosp. Assn., 1982-85; corp. planning coordinator, acting dir. Inst. for Profl. Devel. Commn. on Profl. and Hosp. Activities, Ann Arbor, Mich., 1986—. Contbr. articles to profl. jours. Mem. allocations com. United Way, Jackson, 1985; bd. dirs. Modern Dance Collective, Jackson, 1985. Richards Co. scholar, 1970; named an Outstanding Young Women of Am., 1974, Woman of Yr. Jackson Bus. and Profl. Women's Club, 1984; recipient Commendation award VA, 1977. Mem. Am. Coll. Healthcare Execs., Am. Hosp. Assn. Soc. Hosp. Planning and Mktg., U. Ala. Alumni Assn. Grad. Program in Hosp. and Health Adminstrn. Democrat. Home: 1116 W Washington Ann Arbor MI 48103 Office: Commn Profl and Hosp Activities 1968 Green Rd PO Box 1809 Ann Arbor MI 48106

WILLIAMS, MARILYN MARIE, radio consulting firm executive; b. Atlanta, Feb. 6, 1954; d. Benjamin Snow and Marjorie Alice (Murphy) Hand; m. Owen Rhys Williams, Aug. 29, 1987. Student W.Va. State Coll., 1971-72, Valley Coll., North Hollywood, Calif., 1973-75, Santa Monica Community Coll., 1983-84. With McKee Baking Co., Collegedale, Tenn., 1971-72; product devel. coordinator Superscope/Marantz, Northridge, Calif., 1972-74; office mgr. Drake-Chenault, Inc., Canoga Park, Calif., 1974-79; music dir. Sta. KIQQ Radio, Los Angeles, 1979-80; traffic dir. Watermark, Inc., North Hollywood, Calif., 1980-81; v.p. ops. Pollack Media Group, Inc., Pacific Palisades, Calif., 1981—, conf. coordinator, 1982—. Vol. big sister Big Sisters Am., 1977—. Recipient Proficiency and Leadership award, 1978, Outstanding Support award Dept. Children's Services. Mem. Meeting Planners Internat. Republican. Episcopalian. Office: Pollack Media Group 984 Monument St Suite 105 Pacific Palisades CA 90272

WILLIAMS, MARTHA LYNN, controller, numismatic executive; b. Dallas, Jan. 21, 1952; d. Joseph Raymond and Lola Betty (Jones) Burress; m. W. Crutchfield Williams II, Aug. 7, 1976. Student Houston Community Coll., 1984. Acctg. staff Met. Rare Coin Galleries, N.Y., 1973-74, Robert L. Hughes, Inc., Atlanta, 1974-75; daconis operator NASA, Houston, 1978-79; controller, fgn. exchange trader Tex. Fgn. Exchange, Houston, 1979-81; bullion trader, acct. Colonial Coins, Houston, 1982-84; controller Houston Numismatic Exchange, 1985-87; sec. City of Clear Lake Shores, Tex., 1987—. Organizer Teen Club, Clear Lake Shores, Tex., 1984; pres. Clear Lake Shores Civic Club, 1984-86; charter sec. Seaside Lioness Club, 1978. Mem. Nat. Assn. Female Execs., Am. Numismatic Assn., Tex. Numismatic Assn. Republican. Methodist. Club: Kemah Bay Garden (treas. 1980). Lodge: Eastern Star (worthy matron 1982-83, sec. 1985-87). Home: 915 Ivy Clear Lake Shores TX 77565 Office: Houston Numismatic Exchange 2486 Times Blvd Houston TX 77005

WILLIAMS, MARY CAROL, minister; b. Greensboro, N.C., Dec. 24, 1953; d. Kenneth and Marth (Harwell) W.; m. Thomas J. Kowalski, May 19, 1979 (div. Apr. 1984); m. George N. Gilbert, Oct. 17, 1987. BA in Religion, Catawba Coll., 1976; MA, Duke U., 1979. Ordained to ministry Meth. Ch., 1977. Assoc. minister Cen. United Meth. Ch., Asheboro, N.C., 1979-81, Trinity United Meth. Ch., Tallahassee, 1981-82; minister Calvary United Meth. Ch., Tallahassee, 1982-86, Hickory Grove/Sedgefield Lakes United Meth. Chs., Greensboro, 1986—; chaplain Jr. Women's Club, Tallahassee, 1982-85; chaplain Moses Cane Hosp., Greensboro, 1986—. Mem. Am. Assn. Pastoral Counselors (student), Bd. Ordained Ministry, Greensboro Meth. Ministers (pres.). Democrat. Home: 1228 Guilford Coll Rd Jamestown NC 27282 Office: Hickory Grove United Meth Ch 5959 Hickory Grove Rd Greensboro NC 27410

WILLIAMS, MARY ELMORE, English and history educator; b. San Angelo, Tex., Sept. 19, 1931; d. Mortimer Taylor and Florrine (Gee) Elmore; m. Mark B. Williams, Sept. 6, 1951; children—John Mark, Mary Jean. A.A., San Angelo Coll., 1950; B.S., Tex. Christian U., 1951; M.S., Corpus Christi State U., 1983; postgrad. U. Chgo., 1954, Princeton U., 1961, Mansfield Coll., Oxford U., 1966. Tchr. 1st grade First Methodist Ch., Dallas, 1951-52; tchr. 8th grade Pleasant Grove Jr. High, Dallas, 1952-54; tchr. history Hamlin Jr. High Sch., Corpus Christi, 1958; tchr. 6th grade St. Christopher's Episcopal Sch., Lubbock, Tex., 1968; tchr. English and history Hamlin Jr. High, Corpus Christi, 1974—, coordinator Adopt-a-School Program, 1983—; cons. KEDT-TV Tex. History series The Lone Star, Corpus Christi, 1984-85; cons. textbook com. Corpus Christi Ind. Sch. Dist., 1983, 86; mem. curriculum writing team Corpus Christi Ind. Sch. Dist., 1985-86. Campaign coordinator Ruth Gill for Mayor, Corpus Christi, 1979; del. Gov.'s Commn. for Women, Corpus Christi Council for Women, San Antonio, 1985; task force rep., Ted Roberts Better Sch. Program, chmn. tchr. com., 1987. Named Outstanding Tchr. Am. History-Tex., DAR, Corpus Christi, 1986; recipient Robert A. Taft accolade for Excellence in Tchng. Govt. and Politics, 1986. Mem. Assn. Curriculum and Devel., Corpus Christi Council Social Studies (v.p. 1981-83), Tex. Council Social Studies (conv. chmn. 1988), Corpus Christi C. of C. (events chmn. 1983), YWCA (v.p., chmn. bldg. com. 1983—), AAUW (v.p. 1983-85, pres. 1986-88), Phi Delta Kappa. Avocations: tennis; reading. Home: 601 Barracuda Pl Corpus Christi TX 78411 Office: Hamlin Jr High Sch 3900 Hamlin Dr Corpus Christi TX 78411

WILLIAMS, MARY IRENE, college administrator; b. Hugo, Okla., June 30, 1944; d. Primer and Hyler B. (Tarkington) Jackson; m. Lee A. Williams (div. June 1981); 1 child, Monica Ariane. BS in Bus. Edn., Langston U., 1967; MS in Bus., Emporia (Kans.) State U., 1973; EdS, U. Nev., Las Vegas, 1977; postgrad., U.S. Internat. U., 1987—. Instr. Spokane (Wash.) Community Coll., 1967-70; tchr. bus. Topeka Pub. Schs., 1970-73; instr. Clark County Community Coll., Las Vegas, 1973—, adminstr., 1978—. Named Educator of Yr. Nucleus Plaza Assn., 1985, New Visions, Inc., 1986. Mem. Internat. Assn. Bus. Communicators, Nat. Bus. Edn. Assn., Internat. Assn. Female Execs. Office: 3200 E Cheyenne Ave North Las Vegas NV 89030

WILLIAMS, MARY JANE, controller; b. Des Moines, Iowa, July 10, 1951, d. Raymond Marvin and Ruth Nann (Flowers) Pallesen; m. Gardner L. Williams II, Aug. 27, 1985. BA in Art History, U. Oreg., 1979, MBA in Fin., 1981. Controller Spectra Physics, Eugene, Oreg., 1979-83; mgr. Price Waterhouse, Portland, Oreg., 1983-85; cons. Williams and Assocs., Portland, 1986; controller High Point Communications, Inc., Portland, 1986—; Adv. bd. Natural Tech., Inc., Beaverton, Oreg. 1986—. Mem. art activities council, Portland Art Mus., 1986-89. Mem. U. Oreg. Alumni Assn. (bd. dirs. 1985—), Phi Beta Kappa, Beta Gamma Sigma. Democrat. Methodist. Club: Portland Golf.

WILLIAMS, MELVA JEAN, oil and gas co. exec.; b. Burke, S.D., June 11, 1935; d. Wayne and Mildred Eva (Graham) Mulholland; grad. Roberta's Finishing Sch., Miami, Fla., 1950, Charron-Williams Comml. Coll., 1954; m. J.B. Williams, Apr. 29, 1977; children—Mark, Doris, Robin, Jeannie. With Southeastern Resources Corp., Ft. Worth and Rising Star, Tex., 1968—, pres., 1979-83, vice chmn. bd., 1983—, also dir.; with Delta Gas Co., Inc., Tchula, Miss., 1973-81, sec., treas., 1974-81, also dir.; with SERPCO, Inc., Fort Worth, 1977—, v.p., 1980-84, pres., 1984—, also dir.; sec., treas. J J & L Drilling Co., Inc., Ft. Worth and Cisco, Tex., 1979-82, also dir.; with Rising Star Processing Corporation, Fort Worth, sec. treas. 1981—, also dir.; with Brownwood Pipeline Corporation, Fort Worth, sec. treas. 1981—, also dir.; gen. partner B & W Real Estate Investments, Nashville, 1980—, F & W Real Estate Investments, Fort Worth, 1981—, Westward Properties, Ft. Worth; bd. dirs. Aero Modifications Internat., Inc., Ft. Worth and Waco, Tex., GeoDyne Inc., Ft. Worth. Republican. Home: 6150 Indigo Ct Fort Worth TX 76112 Office: 2201 Scott Ave Fort Worth TX 76103

WILLIAMS, MELVA L., actress, educator; b. Chgo., June 1, 1925; d. Oscar and Louvonia (Witcher) W. B.Ed., Chgo. State U., 1960, M.S. in Edn., 1967; Ed.D., Nova U., 1979. Musician with instrumental and vocal groups, 1945-60; actress radio, TV, stage and films, 1945—; tchr. Chgo. Pub. Schs., 1960-69, asst. prin., 1969—; mem. Goodman Theatre Repertory Co., Chgo., 1971-72, Milw. Repertory Co., 1974—; choral dir., various locations, 1960—; speech specialist; TV appearances include: The Great Pretender, Under the Biltmore Clock, Jack and Mike series (ABC), Sable series (CBS), Bird of the Iron Feather, Mike Royko at Best, A Matter of Principle; stage appearances include: The Little Foxes, Under Papa's Pictures, The Mouthtrap, The Sunshine Boys, God's Favorite, Raisin in the Sun, Native Son, Royal Family, Assassination (all Chgo.). Author: Soul Talk, 1970; (play) Play Doubletime for Me, 1974. Recipient nomination for Chgo. Emmy award, 1969, Chgo. Jeff award, 1987; named Woman of Distinction in Edn. and Drama, Chgo. Citizens Scholarship Com., 1970; Service awards Model Cities Program, West Side Cluster High Schs., chs. and community orgns., Chgo. Mem. Chgo. State U. Alumni Assn., Nova U. Alumni Assn., Actors Equity, Screen Actors Guild, Am. Fedn. Musicians, AFTRA, Explorers Investment Group (bd. dirs.). Phi Delta Kappa.

WILLIAMS, MELVA MAUREEN, medical technologist; b. New Orleans, Sept. 8, 1958; d. Everett Joseph and Melva Dier (Borris) W. BS, Loyola U., New Orleans, 1982; MT, Touro Infirmary Hosp., 1983. Non-registered lab. technician Alton Ochsner Med. Found., New Orleans, 1981-82, registered med. technologist, 1983-86, med. tech. supr., 1986—. Mem. Am. Soc. Clin. Pathologists (registered med. technologist), Nat. Assn. Female Execs., La. Soc. Prevention of Cruelty to Animals, Humane Soc. of the U.S., Alton Ochsner Med. Found. Soc. Avocations: cooking, reading, stitching, writing, swimming, animals. Home: 1730 Constantinople St New Orleans LA 70115 Office: Alton Ochsner Med Found 1516 Jefferson Hwy New Orleans LA 70121

WILLIAMS, MELVENIA COREAN, college administrator; b. Norway, S.C., Nov. 11, 1945; d. Abe and Rosa Lee (Tyler) W. BS, S.C. State Coll., 1987. With Bright Hope Bapt. Ch., Phila., 1965-66; exec. sec. to pres. Voorhees Coll., Denmark, S.C., 1971-77; sec. to pres. Claflin Coll., Orangeburg, S.C., 1977-84; adminstrv. asst. to pres. Claflin Coll., Orangeburg, 1984—. Recipient cert. of honor for Outstanding Service, Claflin Coll., 1983. Mem. Nat. Assn. Female Execs. AAUW, Zeta Phi Beta, Alpha Kappa Mu. Democrat. Baptist. Lodge: Order of Eastern Star. Home: 897 Magnolia St Orangeburg SC 29115

WILLIAMS, MIKKI D., dance and fitness professional; b. Bronx, N.Y., July 4, 1943; d. Louis Schwartzbaum and Bette (Rubinstein) Rawson; m. Gabriel Michael Durishin, June 25, 1966 (dec. Feb. 1973); 1 child, Jason; m. Anthony John Williams, June 4, 1977. BS, Ithaca Coll., 1965; postgrad., U. New Haven, 1986—. Profl. dancer nightclubs, toured U.S., 1964-72; tchr. high sch. Rye-Neck, Levittown, Milford, N.Y. and Conn., 1965-70; caterer, owner Happy Cooker, Westport, Conn., 1973-79; dance instr., owner A Dance Class, Inc., Westport, 1976—; dance tchr., dir. A Dance Class, Inc., Westport, Conn., 1976-87; choreographer The Mikki Williams Dancers, toured U.S., 1978-87; fitness adminstr. The Body Firm, Inc., Fairfield, Conn., 1980-87; owner Kisses, Inc., Westport, 1982-84; trainer, seminars Mikki Williams Unltd., Westport, Conn., 1987—; mem. adv. bd. Reebok New England, Mass., 1986—; choreographer Mikki Williams Dancers, 1978—; fitness adminstr., cons., speaker, seminar leader, meeting planner Mikki Williams Unltd., Westport, 1980—; dir. dance U. Bridgeport, Conn., 1979; entertainment chmn. Town of Westport, 1985. Choreographer DanceAm. (1st place 1985, 2d place 1986, 3d place 1987), Young Am.'s Nat. Invitational Dance Festival, 1987 (1st place), off-Broadway show; contbr. articles to promotional mags. Mem. gov. bd. Levitt Pavilion Performing Arts, Westport, 1980—, White HouseConf. Small Bus., Boston, 1984-87, chef March of Dimes Gourmet Gala, 1985-87, celebrity waiter Leukemia Soc., 1984-87, Westport-Weston Arts Council, 1976; Levitt Pavilion for Performing Arts (governing bd.), Westport, 1979—, Theatre Artists Workshop, 1985, Entrepreneural Womens Network (pres.) Fairfield Cty, 1985-87. Recipient Brandeis U. local chpt. award, 1980; First Place Honors award Tremaine Nat. Dance Competition, 1984-87, Am. Regional Cuisine award Culinary Inst. Am., N.Y., 1986, 1st pl. award Dance Am., Las Vegas, 1984, New Orleans, 1985, 1st pl. award and gold medal Young Ams. Dance Festival, Calif., Las Vegas, 1986. Mem. Internat. Dance Exercise Assn. (state rep. 1985—), Aerobics and Fitness Assn. Am., Dance Masters Am., Nat. Assn. Female Execs., Am. Coll. Sports Medicine, Southwestern Area Commerce and Industry Assn., Westport Young Women's League, Entreprenurial Womens Network (pres. 1985-87), Dance Educators Am. (seminar leader Tchr. Tng. Sch. Western Ky U. 1981-83) , Profl. Dance Tchrs. Assn., Nat. Assn. of Dance and Affiliated Artists, Profl. Dance Tchrs. Assn. Democrat. Jewish.

WILLIAMS, MILDRED JANE, librarian; b. Charlotte, N.C. Nov. 9, 1944; d. Leonard Augustus and Frances Edith (Long) W. B.A., Pfeiffer Coll., Misenheimer, N.C., 1966; M.S.L.S., U. N.C., 1968. Reference librarian Pub. Library Charlotte and Mecklenburg County (N.C.), 1967-70, assoc. dir., 1974-77; head dept. documents and serials Library of Davidson Coll. (N.C.), 1970-73; acting asst. dir. U. N.C.-Charlotte Library, 1977-78; pub. library cons. N.C. State Library, Raleigh, 1979-80, asst. state librarian, 1980-85, state librarian, 1986—. Mem. N.C. Library Assn. (2d v.p. 1983-85), Southeastern Library Assn., ALA. Democrat. Baptist. Office: State Library 109 E Jones St Raleigh NC 27611

WILLIAMS, MINNIE CALDWELL, retired educator; b. Chapel Hill, N.C., Feb. 25, 1917; d. Bruce and Minnie (Stroud) Caldwell; m. Peter Currington Williams Sr., Aug. 21, 1938; children—Peter Jr., Bruce, James, Jacqueline, Charles. B.S. in English, N.C. Central U., 1938, M.A. in Elem. Edn., 1942; postgrad. U. Ill., 1962, U. South Fla., 1965, Fla. State U., 1967. Cert. elem. tchr., N.C.; cert. spl. edn., Fla. Tchr. Weldon pub. schs., N.C., 1940-60, Pinellas County Sch., St. Petersburg, Fla., 1961-80, reading specialist, 1961-80, spl. edn. tchr., 1961-80. Exec. Democratic committeeman, Pinellas County, Fla., 1983-85, local campaign and poll worker; co-chairperson United Way Com. Recipient Ret. Tchrs. award Dixie Hollins High Sch., 1984; Ret. Tchrs. award NAACP, 1980; Panhellenic Service award Greek Orgn., 1980. Mem. Nat. Assn. Ret. Tchrs., Am. Bus. Women Assn., Profl. Bus. Women, Garden Club of St. Petersburg, Delta Sigma Theta (NAACP rep.), Kappa Delta Pi. Baptist. Avocations: Travel; reading; gardening; arts; bowling. Home: 1726 28th Ave S Saint Petersburg FL 33712

WILLIAMS, NANCY ELIZABETH, nurse, educator; b. Monticello, N.Y., Jan. 29, 1934; d. Irene Louise (Nolan) McCollom; divorced; children: Aaron, Brenda, David, Fred, Raphael, Jeffrey, Laural. BS in Nursing, Ariz. State U., 1970. RN. Nurse St. Lukes Hosp., Phoenix, 1970-71; nurse, midwife Indian Health Service, Hopi Reservation, Ariz., 1971; nurse Scottsdale (Ariz.) Community Hosp., 1972-73, Women's Hosp. at Las Vegas, Nev., 1973-74; charge nurse Tempe (Ariz.) Community Hosp., 1974-75; staff nurse Brotman Meml. Hosp., Culver City, Calif., 1976; supr. dept. obstetrics Stormont-Vail Hosp., Topeka, 1976; dir. nursing Woodland Health Ctr., Topeka, 1976-77; nurse supr. Medicenter of Topeka, 1977; dir. nursing Am. Health Enterprises, Waverly, Kans., 1977; mgr. quality assurance, workshop design, risk mgmt. Kans. Neurol. Inst. of Topeka, 1978—; adj. faculty, chmn. mortality/morbidity dept. Washburn U. Mem. Kans. Assn. of Hosp. Edn. Coordinators, Kans. Orgn. for Nurse Execs., Nurse Educators Today in Topeka. Democrat. Roman Catholic. Home: 2028 Lincoln Topeka KS 66604 Office: Kans Neurol Inst 3107 W 21st St Topeka KS 66614

WILLIAMS, NANCY ELLEN-WEBB, social services administrator; b. Quincy, Ill., Aug. 1; d. Charles and Garnet Naomi (Davis) Webb; m. Jesse B. Williams, Apr. 11, 1959; children: Cynthia L. Williams Clay, Troy Andrea Williams Redic, Bernard Peter. BA, Quincy Coll., 1957; postgrad., Tenn. A&I U., 1961; M Pub. Adminstrn., U. Nev., Las Vegas, 1977; LHD (hon.), U. Humanistic Studies, 1986. Cert. peace officer, Nev. (chmn. Standards and Tng. Com., 1978-81). Tchr. Shelby County Tng. Sch., Memphis, 1957-61; dep. probation officer Clark County Juvenile Ct., Las Vegas, 1961-66, supervising probation officer, 1966-74, dir. probation services, 1974-80, dir. intake admissions, 1980-81, dir. Child Haven, 1981—; mem. Nev. Crime Commn., 1970-81. Author: When We Were Colored, 1986, Dinah's Pain and Other Poems of the Black Life Experience, 1988; contbr. poetry to various mags. Mem. exec. com. Clark County Econ. Opportunity Bd., Las Vegas, 1963-71; chmn. So. Nev. Task Force on Corrections, 1974-81; mem. Gov.'s Com. on Justice Standards and Goals, 1979-81; bd. dirs. U. Humanistic Studies, Las Vegas, 1984—. Recipient Friend of the Golden Gloves award Golden Gloves Regional Bd., 1981, Tribute to Black Women award U. Nev., Las Vegas, 1984. Fellow Am. Acad. Neurol. and Orthopedic Surgeons (assoc.); mem. AAUW, Nat. Council Juvenile Ct. Judges, Nat. Writers Assn. Democrat. Office: Child Haven 3401 E Bonanza Rd Las Vegas NV 89101

WILLIAMS, PATRICIA ANN, insurance company manager; b. Dalton, Ga., July 17, 1950; d. John E. and Cecile (Caylor) W.; m. Perry L. Kiker, May 30, 1970 (div. June 1975). Grad. Dalton High Sch., 1968. Exec. sec. DOM, Inc., Dalton, 1969-77, Dorsett Carpet, Dalton, 1977-79; sales agt. Allstate Ins. Co., Chattanooga, 1979-83, asst. market sales mgr., Jackson, Miss., 1983-84, market sales mgr., Memphis, 1984—. Mem. Life Underwriters Tng. Council, Gen. Agts. and Mgrs. Assn. Republican. Baptist. Club: Memphis Exchange. Avocations: travel; reading; crafts. Home: 2992 New London Dr Memphis TN 38115 Office: Allstate Ins Co Inc 5240 Poplar Ave Memphis TN 38119

WILLIAMS, PATRICIA G., academic administrator; b. Rutherfordton, N.C., May 8, 1951; d. John Otis Hines and Mary Edith (Williams) Smith. BA in Sociology, Bennett Coll., 1972; MS in Counselor Edn., Ill. State U., 1986. Share owner correspondent AT&T, Piscataway, N.J., 1972-75; investigator N.J. Bell Telephone, Newark, 1975-78, asst. staff mgr., 1978-81; hall dir. Bennett Coll. Residential Life, Greensboro, N.C., 1981-83; grad. asst. Ill. State U. Residential Life, Normal, 1983-84, residence hall coordinator, 1984-87, conf. coordinator, summer 1986, facilities coordinator, summer 1987, area coordinator, 1987—; cons. North Cen. Coll. Activities, Naperville, Ill., 1986-87, Westside Unity Ministerial Sch., Detroit, 1987. Sec. to bd. dirs. Neighborhood House, New Brunswick, N.J., 1973; coordinator Ill. State U. Hands Across Am., 1986. Mem. Nat. Assn. Student Personnel Adminstrs., Nat. Assn. Personnel Workers, Ill. Com. on Black Concern in Higher Edn., Nat. Assn. Female Execs., Assn. Psychol. Type, Kappa Delta Mu, Delta Sigma Theta (fin. sec. 1984-85, chairperson fin. com. 1987—). Office: Ill State Univ Residential Life Office Fell Hall Annex Normal IL 61761

WILLIAMS, PATRICIA JEAN, financial planner; b. St. Louis, Sept. 29, 1942; d. A. P. and Mary M. (Teak) Anderson. BA, Fresno (Calif.) State U., 1964; MA, San Jose (Calif.) State U., 1968; EdD, U. No. Colo., 1977. Cert. fin. planner, Calif. From tchr. to asst. prin., supr. East Side Union High Sch. Dist., San Jose, 1964-77; pres. Leadership Devel. Inst., Colorado Springs, Colo., 1977-79; owner The Fern Factory, Santa Ana, Calif., 1979-80; mgr. Intel Corp., Santa Clara, Calif., 1980-81; ptnr. Dahl & Williams, San Jose, 1981-83; pres., ptnr. The Delta Group/Delta Advisors Inc., Los Altos, Calif., 1983—; planning commr. City of Los Altos, 1988—; instr. bus. dept. Foothill Community Coll., Los Altos, 1984—. Chair econ. com. Los Altos City Gen. Plan Rev. Com./2005 Com., 1986-87. Recipient Woman of Achievement award Soroptimists, 1987. Mem. Internat. Assn. Fin. Planners, Los Altos C. of C. Club: Quota (Los Altos) (pres. 1986-87). Office: The Delta Group 167 S San Antonio Suite 7 Los Altos CA 94022

WILLIAMS, PEGGY LENORE, circus executive; b. Madison, Wis., Nov. 5, 1948; d. Richard Eli and Harriet Jane (Edwards) W. Student in speech pathology, U. Wis., 1970; grad., Ringling Bros. Barnum and Bailey Circus Clown Coll., Venice, Fla., 1970. Profl. circus clown Ringling Bros. Barnum and Bailey Circus, Venice, Fla., and throughout U.S., 1970-79, cons. ednl. services dept., 1977—; costume designer clown dept. Ringling Bros. Barnum and Bailey Circus, Venice, Fla., 1979-81; asst. performance dir., publicity cons. Ringling Bros. Barnum and Bailey Circus, Washington, 1981-87; instr., gag writer Ringling Bros. Barnum and Bailey Clown Coll., 1973-85; supr. circus performers, circus cons. Disneyland, Anaheim, Calif., 1987—; circus cons. Sci. Devel. Program, N.Y.C., 1978—; cons., mgr. Disneyland Circus Fantasy, Anaheim, Calif., 1987—; developer spl. circus tours for blind, 1972; tchr. course on circus Fordham U. Grad. Sch. Edn., summer 1985, 86, 87; dir. circus workshop Children's Mus. Manhattan, spring 1987. Author Circus Teaching Unit, 1975—; author, editor braille circus program, 1977—; designer Circus Sch., Library Kit, 1981; performance dir. RBBB Circus Asian tour, 1988. Tchr. swimming to retarded children YMCA, Bethesda, Md., 1980. Richard Lounsbery Found. grantee, N.Y.C., 1987-88. Mem. Nat. Assn. Female Execs., Circus Fans Am. (assoc.). Republican. Mormon. Home: 1909 Jefferson St Madison WI 53711 Office: Ringling Bros Barnum & Bailey 3201 New Mexico Ave NW Washington DC 20016

WILLIAMS, PETRA SCHATZ, antiquarian; b. Poughkeepsie, N.Y., Sept. 2, 1913; d. Grover Henry and Mayme Nickerson (Bullock) Schatz; m. J. Calvert Williams, Nov. 26, 1946; children: Miranda, Frederica, Valerie. AB, Skidmore Coll., 1936; JD, Fordham U., 1940. Founder Fountain House, Phoenix, 1953, Fountain House East, Jeffersontown, Ky., 1966. Author: Flow Blue China, An Aid to Identification, 1971, Flow Blue China II, 1973, Flow Blue China and Mulberry Ware, 1975, Staffordshire Romantic Transfer Patterns, 1979, Staffordshire II Romantic Transfer Patterns, 1986. Past pres. Meml. Hosp. Aux., Phoenix, Heard Mus. Guild, Phoenix; bd. dirs. Ky. Humane Soc. Mem. Nat. Soc. Interior Designers (nat. dir. for Ariz. 1957-58, Ky. 1968, pres. Ky. 1967-68), DAR, Ky. Hist. Soc., Flow Blue Internat. Collectors Club (hon.). Mem. Soc. of Friends. Club: Filson.

WILLIAMS, REGINA MARIA, public relations specialist; b. Queens, N.Y., Sept. 2, 1959; d. Horace Calvin and Shirley Yvonne (Forbes) W. BA in Radio-TV Broadcasting, San Jose State U., 1983. Account exec., sales rep., plant service clk. AT&T, San Jose, 1978-86; coordinator, producer, anchor, writer Sta. KSJS, San Jose, 1981-83; dir. prodn. TV staff, spl. projects, assoc. producer Sta. KNTV, San Jose, 1982-87; asst. coordinator pub. relations San Jose Hosp. Found., 1987—. Mem. Am. Women in Radio and TV, Nat. Assn. Female Execs., NAACP. Democrat. Roman Catholic. Office: San Jose Hosp Found 25 N 14th St Suite 610 San Jose CA 95112

WILLIAMS, RHONA LORAINE, public relations executive; b. Salina, Kans., Dec. 2, 1953; d. Joseph Henry and Constance Loraine (Hill) W. BA, U. Minn., 1975. News reporter, pub. affairs show host Sta. WEYI-TV, Saginaw, Mich., 1975; news anchor, reporter Sta. WOTV-TV, Grand Rapids, Mich., 1975-79; news anchor, reporter, pub. affairs show host Sta. WHAS-TV, Louisville, 1979-81; news anchor, reporter Sta. KCNC-TV, Denver, 1981-84; pub. relations mgr., mktg. asst. Adolph Coors Co., Golden, Colo., 1984-87; dir. pub. affairs Blue Cross/Blue Shield of Colo., Denver, 1987—. Bd. dirs. Urban League of Denver, 1988—, Minority Enterprises Inc., 1988—; mem. com. Denver Dist. Attys. Com. on Crime, 1982—, Denver Victim's Service Ctr., 1988—; co-chmn. Dem. Precinct Caucus, Denver, 1988, alt. del., 1988; mem. Colo. Black Women for Polit. Action, Denver, 1981—. Recipient Kizzy award Black Women's Hall of Fame, Chgo., 1985; CBS News fellow, 1979-81. Mem. Nat. Assn. Female Execs., Minn. Alumni Assn. Office: Blue Cross/Blue Shield of Colorado 700 Broadway Denver CO 80273

WILLIAMS, ROSANA FRISCHE, manufacturing executive; b. Waxahachie, Tex., Feb. 2, 1937; d. John Louis and Ruth (Liggette) Frische; children: Bradley J., John Keith. AA, El Centro Coll., Dallas, 1975; student, U. Tex., Arlington, 1976-78. Inventory control supr. Larkin Co., Waxahachie, 1961-81; sr. software implementation coordinator, cons. FMC Corp., Chgo., 1981-86; project mgr. Nelmor div. AEC Corp., North Uxbridge, Mass., 1986-88; prodn. and inventory control mgr. Larkin Products div. Cooper Industries Inc., Waxahachie, 1988—. Mem. Am. Prodn. and Inventory Control Soc. (cert.). Office: Larkin Products Waxahachie TX 75165

WILLIAMS, ROSE, public relations consultant; b. Chgo., Sept. 24, 1949; d. Bealie and Louise (Billingslea) W.; B.S. in Edn., U. Ill., 1971. Coordinator, mgr. mdsg. Playboy Enterprises, 1970-74; exec. asst. Bank Mktg. Assn., Chgo., 1974-79; dir. mktg. Chgo. Daily Defender, 1979-80; pres. RAW Enterprises, public relations, Chgo., 1980—; mem. speakers bur. Chgo. Bd. Edn., 1981-83; mem. host com., public relations co-chmn., Women's Bur., Dept. Labor, 1979-83; exec. council, chmn. publicity Provident Hosp. Aux., Chgo., 1981—; exec. council, co-chmn, public relations Chgo. PBS Sta. WTTW, 1981-84; mem. faculty Columbia Coll., Chgo., 1987—. Recipient Public Service award Nat. Council Negro Women, 1978, Dept. Labor, 1981, Govs. award PBS Sta. WTTW, 1982. Mem. Nat. Assn. Female Execs. (network dir.), Nat. Assn. Media Women (past 1st v.p. Chgo. chpt.), Chgo. Assn. Commerce and Industry, Cosmopolitan C. of C. (v.p. pub. relations 1984-86, bd. dirs. 1983—, corp. sec. 1986-88, v.p. mktg. 1988, Mem. of Yr. award 1987), Publicity Club Chgo., Chgo. Fashion Exchange, Black Pub. Relations Soc. (treas. 1984-86), Pub. Relations Soc. Am. (co-chmn. minorities com. Chgo. chpt. 1987—, chmn. profl. devel. com. 1988), Chgo. Assn. Black Journalists (asst. editor newsletter), Delta Sigma Theta. Address: 505 N Lake Shore Dr Chicago IL 60611

WILLIAMS, RUTH H., management consultant; b. Bklyn., Mar. 15, 1938; d. Oscar and Lillian (Steinberg) Forster; student schs., Los Angeles; children—Steven, Richard, Michael. Asst. studio mgr. Columbia Records, Los Angeles, 1966-71; West Coast adminstr. Custom div. RCA Records, Los Angeles, 1972-75; studio mgr. Motown Records, Los Angeles, 1975-80; central scheduling supr. Golden West TV/KTLA, 1980-85; ops. mgr. West Hollywood Paper, 1985-86.; ind. cons. mgmt., Los Angeles, 1987—. Mem. Nat. Womens Political Caucus, Mcpl. Elections Com. Los Angeles, Polit. Advocacy com., West Hollywood Neighborhood Council, NOW; del. County Cen. Dem. Com.; alt. 45th Assembly Dist. Los Angeles Dem. Party; past commr. Rent Stabilization Bd. City of West Hollywood; founder, chair Citizens for Srs. Mem. Nat. Acad. Rec. Arts and Scis. Home and Office: 7548 Lexington Ave West Hollywood CA 90046

WILLIAMS, SANDRA WHEELER, commercial artist; b. Glenns Falls, N.Y., Apr. 2, 1957; d. John Wheeler and Phyllis Yoder (Reihl) W.; m. Allen James Gencarelle, Sept. 18, 1980. BA, U. So. Fla., 1981. Mgr. prodn. Skydiving mag., DeLand, Fla., 1982-86; pres. AVOT Industries Inc., Orange City, Fla., 1987—; judge U.S. Parachute Assn., Alexandria, Va., 1982—; pres. Misty Blues All-Woman Skydiving Team Inc., Orange City, 1987—. Home and Office: 549 Daley St Orange City FL 32763

WILLIAMS, SHARON TAYLOR, interior designer; b. Waukegan, Ill., Aug. 23, 1948; d. John Issac and Ruth (Robertson) Williams; B.S. in Bus. Edn. and Interior Design, Western Ill. U., 1970; postgrad. U. Minn., 1975, 79; postgrad. U. Calif., Berkeley. Interior designer masterplan sales and interior design studio Dayton's Dept. Store, St. Paul, 1973-77; owner, pres., dir. interior design The S. Williams Design Group, Mpls., 1977—; mem. faculty dept. applied arts U. Wis.-Stout; mem. faculty U. Calif. pre-college acad. program, 1988—; mfrs. rep. contract and furnishings for instns. Recipient design and sales achievement award Dayton's Dept. Store, 1974. Fellow Internat. Biog. Assn.; mem. Am. Soc. Interior Designers, Mpls. Soc. Fine Arts, Mpls. Inst. Arts, Nat. Assn. Women Bus. Owners, Nat. Assn. Female Execs., Minn. Soc. AIA (interiors com.), Greater Mpls. C. of C., North Suburban C. of C., Alpha Omicron Phi. Methodist.

WILLIAMS, SHIRLEY MAE, non-profit organization administrator, clergywoman; b. Portsmouth, Va., May 17, 1939; d. Sherman James Sheard and Helen Estelle (Weal) Sheard Davidson; m. Boris Eugene Williams, Nov. 2, 1968; children: Raymond, Diana, Paula. AS, Camden County Coll., 1973; BA, Rutgers U., 1976; MA, Antioch U., Phila., 1987; postgrad., Union for Experimenting Colls. and Univs., 1988—. Ordained to ministry Holy Spirit Ch., 1980. Social work technician, nurse's aide Our Lady of Lourdes, Camden, N.J., 1962-71, community relations coordinator, social work asst., 1971-75; dir. Vols. of Am., Camden, 1975-78; tchr. N.J. Dept. Correction, Trenton, 1978-79; asst. exec. dir. Group Homes, Inc., Camden, 1979-81, exec. dir., 1981—; founder, pastor Holy Spirit Cathedral, Mt. Laurel, 1980—; lectr. Camden County Coll., 1977, Rutgers U., 1977; panelist TV programs, 1985. Recipient Solidarity Day award N.J. State Senate, 1985. Mem. Camden County Commn. on Women, LWV. Lodge: Queen Esther (assoc. matron 1983-85). Home: 20 Hunters Dr Mount Laurel NJ 08054 Office: Group Homes Camden County Inc 35 S 29th St Camden NJ 08105

WILLIAMS, SUSAN EILEEN, urban planner; b. Chgo., Dec. 13, 1952; d. Joseph Andrew and Alice (Regnier) W.; 1 child, Ryan Joseph. AA in Polit. Sci., Coll. of Desert, Palm Desert, Calif., 1971; BA in Polit. Sci., U. Calif., Riverside, 1973; M of Pub. Adminstrn., Consortium Calif. State Colls. and Univs., 1982. Planning trainee City of Indio, Calif., 1975-79, assoc. planner,

1979-80, prin. planner, 1980—, prin. planner redevel. agy., 1983—. Mem. Am. Planning Assn., Assn. Environ Profls., Ill. Geneal. Soc., Geneal. Club Am. Roman Catholic. Office: City of Indio 100 Civic Center Mall PO Drawer 1788 Indio CA 92202

WILLIAMS, SYLVIA HILL, museum director; b. Lincoln University, Pa., Feb. 10, 1936; m. Charlton E. Williams. A.B., Oberlin Coll., 1957; Cert. de Francais Parle, Ecole Pract. de l'Alliance Francaise, Paris, 1963; M.A. in Primitive Art, NYU Inst. of Fine Arts, 1975. Program cons. Nat. Assembly for Social Policy and Devel., N.Y.C., 1963-68; account exec. Harry L. Oram, Inc., N.Y.C., 1968-71; Mellon research fellow The Bklyn. Mus., 1971-73, asst. curator, 1973-76, assoc. curator, 1976-78, curator, 1978-83; dir. Nat. Museum of African Art, Smithsonian Inst., Washington, 1983—; lectr. African art New Sch. for Social Research, N.Y.C., 1979-80; adj. asst. prof. NYU, 1980. Author: Black South Africa, Contemporary Graphics, 1976; contbg. author: African Art as Philosophy, 1974. Contbr. articles to Apollo Mag., African Arts, others. Curator, organizer major exbhns. Bklyn. Mus., Nat. Mus. African Art. Nat. Mus. Act grantee (Paris, Tervuren, London), 1974. Mem. African Am. Museums Assn., Assn. Art Mus. Dirs., Assn. Primitive and Pre-Columbian Art (dept. Art History and Archeology, Columbia U.), Am. Assn. of Mus. (exec. council). Office: Nat Mus of African Art Smithsonian Inst Washington DC 20560

WILLIAMS, VERONICA MYRES, psychiatric social worker; b. Shreveport, La., May 11, 1947; d. McEura and Margie Virginia (Reagan) Myres; B.A., La. Tech. U., Ruston, 1969; M.S.W., U. Mich., Ann Arbor, 1977; m. John L. Williams, Jr., Nov. 30, 1969; children—Nicole Leann, Jennifer Lyn, Erica Maria. Probation counselor Citizens Probation Authority, Flint, Mich., 1970-72; unit dir., therapist Services to Overcome Drug Abuse Among Teenagers, Flint, 1972-74; psychiat. therapist Psycho-Therapeutic Treatment Clin., P.C., Flint, 1974-77; psychiat. social worker Hurley Med. Center, Flint, 1977-79; field instr. Sch. Soc. Work, U. Mich., Ann Arbor, 1978-79, 86—; psychiat. social worker Inst. Mental Health, Flint, 1979-81, Psychotherapeutic Treatment Clinic, 1981-83; clin. social worker Flint Bd. Edn., 1979-83; pupil apprasial spl. edn. Caddo Parish Sch. Bd., Shreveport, La., 1983-85; developer dropout prevention program Flint Bd. Edn., 1986—; psychiat. therapist Mott Children's Health Ctr., 1986—. Cert. social worker, Mich. Mem. Nat. Assn. Social Workers, Acad. Cert. Social Workers, Mich. Edn. Assn., NEA. Democrat. Office: Pierson Sch 300 E Mott Flint MI 48505

WILLIAMS, VICKI (JEAN), professional counselor; b. Mt. Vernon, Ohio, June 8, 1958; d. Gerald Eugene and Irene Jeanette (Mickley) W. BA in Psychology, BA in Sociology, Otterbein Coll., 1980; postgrad., Ohio State U., 1984—. Lic. profl. counselor, Ohio. Advocate for mentally retarded NW Ohio Devel. Ctr., Toledo, 1977; live-in counselor with status offeners Mahoning County Residential Youth Ctr., Youngstown, Ohio, 1979; counselor battered women Turning Point, Inc., Marion, Ohio, 1980; residential counselor for juveniles Syntaxis, Ins., Gahanna, Ohio; emergency services social worker/counselor SW Community Health Ctr., Inc., Columbus, 1983-84; child welfare caseworker Franklin County Children's Services, Columbus, 1984-85; group home supr. unruly youth Sunrise House, Inc., Sedalia, Ohio, 1985-86; social worker, staff trainer, coordinator Scioto Village-Riverview Complex Ohio Dept. Youth Services, Delaware, 1986-87; coordinator community services Ohio Dept. Health Employee Assistance Program, Columbus, 1987—; bd. dirs. Ohio Mental Health Assn. Mem. Nat. Assn. Female Execs., Ohio Assn. Counseling and Devel., Nat. Assn. Social Workers. Roman Catholic. Office: Ohio Dept Health Employee Assistance Program 22 E Gay St 7th Floor Columbus OH 43266-0555

WILLIAMS, VIRGINIA WALKER, journalist; b. Walker County, Ala., June 5, 1915; married; 1 child. BA in Elem. Edn., Ala. State U., 1945; MA in Journalism, Marquette U., 1979; postgrad., U. Wis., Milw. Cert. remedial reading specialist, Wis. Tchr. various elem. schs., Ala., 1933-56; reading specialist Milw. Pub. Schs., 1956-69, journalist, editor, 1969-79; journalist Milw. Fire and Police Commn., 1980-85; founder, dir. Echo Writer's Workshop, Milw.; pub. Echo mag.; freelance writer. Contbr. articles to Milw. Jour., Milw. Sentinel, Milw. Community Jour., Wis. Rep. Newspaper, Westside News, An Anthology of Black Writing, New Voices in Am. Poetry, 1985, Quill Book Anthology, 1987. Mem. Conservation Work Project Bd., Milw. Recipient Headliner award, Jack and Jill award, NAACP award, Service Club award, Advt. Club Milw. award. Mem. Nat. Press Women, Wis. Council Writers, Women in Communications, Soc. Profl. Journalists, Adminstrs. Suprs. Council, Phi Delta Kappa, Lambda Kappa Mu, Pi Lamba Theta. Methodist. Club: Milw. Press. Lodges: Zonta. Home: PO Box 2107 Milwaukee WI 53201

WILLIAMS, WENDY LOUISE, engineer; b. Chgo., Aug. 13, 1958; d. Clovis Lee and Shirley (Caffey) W. AA in Merchandising, Fashion Inst. Los Angeles, 1979; BS in Mktg., U. Ill., Chgo., 1984, postgrad., 1984—. Mgmt. trainee ABN-Lasalle, Chgo., 1984-85; systems engr. IBM Corp., Oak Brook, Ill., 1985—. Mem. Nat. Assn. Female Execs. Democrat. Presbyterian.

WILLIAMS, WENDY SUSAN, marketing professional; b. Seattle, Nov. 28, 1954; d. Walter Baker and Marie (Wilson) W. Student, Evergreen State Coll., 1972-74; BA in Japan Area Studies, U. Wash., Seattle, 1976; MBA in Mktg., U. Chgo., 1983. Author: Homestay English, 1979, Zyindex Users Guide, 1984. Walter E. Heller scholar, U. Chgo., 1981, Japan Found. scholar, 1981; grantee U.S. Dept. Edn. Mem. DEC User Soc. Office: Walker Richer & Quinn 2825 Eastlake Ave E Seattle WA 98102

WILLIAMS, YVONNE LAVERNE, education executive, lawyer; b. Washington, Jan. 7, 1938; d. Smallwood Edmund and Verna Lucille (Rapley) W. B.A., Barnard Coll., 1959; M.A., Boston U., 1961; J.D., Georgetown U., 1977. Bar: D.C. 1980. Fgn. service officer USIA, Washington and abroad, 1961-65; dir. women's Africa commn. African-Am. Inst., N.Y.C., 1966-68; assoc. prof. African studies Benedict Coll., Columbia, S.C., 1968-70; press sec. Hon. Walter Fauntroy, U.S. Congress, Washington, 1970-72; dir. African-Am. Scholars Council, Washington, 1972-73; assoc. Leva, Hawes, Symington, Martin, Washington, 1977-79; asst. v.p. Brimmer & Co., Washington, 1980-82; assoc. dir. fed. relations, legal counsel Tuskegee U., Washington, 1982-83, v.p. fed. and internat. relations, legal counsel, 1983—. Vol., mem. Operation Crossroads Africa, N.Y.C. and Washington, 1960—; mem. Mayor's Internat. Task Force, Washington, 1982-83; participant Leadership Am., 1988; alumnae trustee Barnard Coll., 1988—. African Research and Studies Program fellow, Boston U., 1960; Barnard Coll. scholar, 1955-57. Mem. ABA, Nat. Bar Assn., Nat. Assn. Coll. and Univ. Attys., Nat. Assn. State Univ. and Land Grant Colls. Democrat. Club: Barnard (Washington)(bd. dirs. 1986—). Office: Tuskegee U Washington Office Suite 490 11 DuPont Circle NW Washington DC 20036

WILLIAMS-BREESE, MARILYN OLIVE, financial consultant; b. Panama City, Panama, May 5, 1942; d. William Josiah and Millicent Margaret (Vierela) Whinnen; m. William Donald Breese, Dec. 28, 1985; children by previous marriage: Thomas Michael, Timothy Scott, Stacey Suellen. BS in Edn., Ball State U., 1965; MS in Gifted Edn., U. Bridgeport, 1975; postgrad., U. Buffalo, 1975-76. Tchr. elem. Pub. Schs., Ft. Rucher, Ala., 1967, Enterprise, Ala., 1968; tchr. elem. Project Explore, Stamford, Conn., 1974-75; coordinator gifted and talented programs Pub. Schs., Irvington, N.Y., 1976-82; bd. dirs. Programs for Gifted Bd. Cooperative Edml. Services, South Westchester, N.Y., 1977-80; adj. prof. gifted program Manhattanville Coll., Harrison, N.Y., 1978-80; sales assoc. Nat. Pension Services Inc., White Plains, N.Y., 1981-85; pension planner Wimbry Fin. Services, North Salem, N.Y., 1985-88; owner, pres. The Heritage Group Inc., New Milford, Conn., 1988—; cons. Dept. Edn. Gifted & Talented Devel. Ctr., 1980—. Mem. Am. Soc. Pension Actuaries, Nat. Assn. Life Underwriters, Inst. Cert. Fin. Planners (chpt. chmn. program and continuing edn.), Phi Delta Kappa. Home: 19 Maple Dr Vail's Gove Peach Lake NY 10509 Office: Heritage Group 221 Danbury Rd New Milford CT 06776

WILLIAMSON, CONNIE MCDANIEL, home economist; b. Kent, Iowa, Dec. 15, 1943; d. John Nelson and Marjorie Gwendolen (Chandler) Davenport; B.S., Iowa State U., 1965, M.S., 1970; postgrad. U. Tenn., Knoxville, Colo. State U.; m. Gary L. McDaniel, July 31, 1966; 1 dau., Kerstin Ann; m. B.D. Butler, Sept. 15, 1985. Cert. home economist. Tchr. home econs., Iowa, Kans. and Tenn., 1965-78; extension agt. Colo. State U., Ft. Collins, 1978—; tchr. Colo. State U., 1986-87. Mem. NEA, Nat. Assn. Extension Home Economists, Nat. Home Econs. Assn., Nat. Assn. Female Execs., Bus. and Profl. Women. Republican. Methodist. Clubs: Atlantic Golf and Country, Ft. Morgan Country, Order Eastern Star. Author curriculum guides, textbook and instrn. manuals, articles. Home: 194 27th Rd Grand Junction CO 81503

WILLIAMSON, DONNA CONSTANCE, health care products company executive; b. Schenectady, June 6, 1952; d. Albert Carl and Aurelia Alexandra Erickson; m. Scott Howard Williamson, July 24, 1976; 1 child, Erik. B.S., Brown U., 1974; M.S., MIT, 1976. Dir. domestic planning Travenol Labs., Deerfield, Ill., 1980-82, dir. strategic planning, 1982-83; v.p. Baxter Travenol Labs., Inc., Deerfield, 1983-85, v.p. corp. planning and bus. devel., 1983-84, 85-86; pres., chief exec. officer Omnis Surg., Northbrook, Ill., 1985; corp. v.p. Health Cost Mgmt. Group, 1986—. Editorial bd. Strategic Planning Mgmt., 1982—. Chief crusader Crusade of Mercy, Chgo., 1983; regional gov. MIT Sloan Club, Chgo., 1983-85; trustee Brown U., 1987—; bd. dirs. ARC, Chgo., 1984—. Recipient Leadership award YWCA, Chgo., 1980. Mem. The Planning Forum (bd. dirs. 1988—). Club: Econ. (Chgo.). Avocations: cross-country skiing; sailing; bicycling; tennis. Office: Baxter Travenol Labs 1 Baxter Pkwy Deerfield IL 60015

WILLIAMSON, EVANGELINE FLOANN, vocational rehabilitation corporate executive; b. Ft. Wayne, Ind., Nov. 29, 1934; d. David Samuel and Anna Florence (Baker) McNelly; m. Clark Murray Williamson, Dec. 20, 1957 (div. 1964); 1 child, Dawn Valerie (dec.). BA with distinction Transylvania U., 1956. Asst. dir. publs. ABA, Chgo., 1958-66; pres., owner Herringshaw-Smith, Inc., Chgo., 1966-77; internal cons. Monarch Printing Corp., Chgo., 1978-80, Callaghan & Co., Wilmette, Ill., 1980-82; v.p., co-owner Career Evaluation Systems, Inc., Niles, Ill., 1983—; bd. dirs. MarTech Enterprises, Chgo. Author: From Typist to Typesetter, 1978; editor: Transylvania: Tutor to the West (John Wright), 1975; editor, designer: Silvermiths, Jewelers, Clock and Watchmakers of Kentucky, 1785-1900 (Marquis Boultinghouse), 1980; speaker in field; contbr. articles to profl. jours. Bd. dirs., treas. West Central Assn., Chgo., 1976-77; bd. dirs. Martha Washington Hosp., Chgo., 1975-76, Mary Thompson Hosp., Chgo., 1977. Named to Nat. Disting. Registry in Med. and Vocat. Rehab., 1987. Mem. Am. Voc. Assn., Nat. Rehab. Assn., Am. Assn. for Counseling and Devel., World Future Soc., Niles C. of C. Republican. Mem. Christian Ch. Avocations: antique clock and furniture collecting, writing. Office: Career Evaluation Systems Inc 6050 W Touhy Ave Chicago IL 60648

WILLIAMSON, JUANITA V., English educator; b. Shelby, Miss.; d. John M. and Alice E. (McAllister) W. BA, LeMoyne-Owen Coll., 1938; MA, Atlanta U., 1940; PhD, U. Mich., 1961. Asst. prof. English LeMoyne-Owen Coll., Memphis, 1947-56, prof., 1956—, Disting. Service prof., 1980; adj. prof. Memphis State U., 1975—, linguist, summer 1969, 73, 75; vis. prof. Ball State U., Muncie, Ind., 1963-64, U. Tenn., Knoxville, summer 1975; vis. prof. U. Wis., Milw., summer 73, linguist, summer 1966-67; linguist French Inst. Atlanta U., summer 1963, Hampton (Va.) Inst., summer 1964, U. Ark., Pine Bluff, summer 1981. Editor: A Various Language, 1971; contbr. articles to profl. jours. Mem. exec. com. United Way, Memphis, 1953-56; cons. Girl Scouts U.S., Memphis, 1956; bd. dirs. Integration Service, Memphis, 1952-58; mem. exec. com. hist. council United Ch. Christ, 1976. Recipient citation for excellence in edn. Memphis City Council, 1973; fellow Rockefeller Found., 1949-51, Ford Found., 1954; HEW grantee, 1964-68. Mem. MLA (program com., minority affairs com.), Nat. Council Tchrs. English (coll. sect. exec. com. 1976-79), Am. Dialect Soc. (exec. com. 1979-82), Conf. on Coll. Composition and Communication (exec. com. 1969-71), Delta Sigma Theta. Home: 1217 Cannon St Memphis TN 38106 Office: LeMoyne-Owen Coll 807 Walker Ave Memphis TN 38126

WILLIAMSON, JUDY DARLENE GRAHAM, secondary educator; b. Gallipolis, Ohio, Nov. 10, 1948; d. Byron Jr. and Margaret Mae (Bush) Greenlee; m. Lannes Clay Williamson, Aug. 29, 1984. AB, Glenville State Coll., 1970; MA, Marshall U., 1973, postgrad., 1986. Librarian, tchr. Mason County Bd. Edn., Point Pleasant, W.Va., 1970—; acting dir. Mason County Pub. Library, Point Pleasant, 1986-87; cons. Found. for Library Research, Point Pleasant, 1983—. Created the Automated Library System computer software; contbr. articles to profl. jours. Treas. Point Pleasant Emergency Med. Services, Point Pleasant, 1976-82; mem. chpt. 2 com. Mason County Bd. Edn., 1983—, computer com., 1984—; mem. bicentennial steering com. City of Point Pleasant, 1987. Grantee W.Va. Dept. Edn., 1981, 82. Mem. W.Va. Library Assn., W.Va. Edn. Assn., Mason County Reading Council, W.Va. Ednl. Media Assn., Alpha Delta Kappa. Republican. Methodist. Home: 2764 US 35 S Southside WV 25550 Office: Point Pleasant High Sch 2312 Jackson Ave Point Pleasant WV 25550

WILLIAMSON, KATHY ANN, radio station executive, disc jockey; b. Lewiston, Maine, May 7, 1959; d. Cecil Thayne and Patricia Ann (Yokell) Hodgdon; m. John Kevin Williamson, Oct. 9, 1982 (div. Oct. 1986); 1 child, John Marshall. Student, U. Maine, 1977-80. News dir. Sta. WDEA AM & FM (Dudman Corp.), Ellsworth, Maine; prodn. mgr. Stas. WCOU and WAYU (Lowe Group)), Lewiston, Maine, June to Jan. 1986, Sta. WBLM-FM (Fuller Jeffrey Group), 1986-87, Sta. WIGY and WJTO, 1987—; stock voice Sun Video, Portland, 1986—, Kern Media, Sebago Lake, Maine, 1986—, Channel 6 TV, Portland, 1986—; co-owner Travelling Tunes Rd. Show. Vol. literacy programs, Seattle, 1984; participant child devel. program Bur. Mental Retardation, Lewiston, 1987. Office: Sta WBLM Radio 80 Exchange St Portland ME 04101

WILLIAMSON, MIRIAM BEDINGER, medical librarian; b. Asheville, N.C., Nov. 18, 1919; d. Robert Dabney and Mary Julia (Smith) Bedinger; m. Robert Lewis Williamson Sr., June 9, 1944 (div. June 1969); children: Robert Lewis Jr., John Bedinger, Ellen Richmond, Thomas Reid. BA, Agnes Scott Coll., 1941; MS, Presbyn. Sch. Christian Edn., 1943; postgrad., U. Tenn., 1969. Ch. social worker, kindergarten tchr. N.E. Community Ctr., Italian Presbyn. Mission, Kansas City, Mo., 1943-44; med. librarian Blount Meml. Hosp., Maryville, Tenn., 1972—; tchr. vocat. edn. programs, adult reading program Alcoa, Blount County, Maryville sch. systems. Mem. Blount County unit Bread for the World. Grantee Library Medicine, HEW, 1973, HHS, 1981, Blount County unit Am. Cancer Soc., 1982, Blount Meml. Hosp. Aux., 1986-87; recipient Outstanding Service award Vocat. Edn. Dept., 1983, 85. Mem. Med. Library Assn., Tenn. Hosp. Assn., Tenn. Health Sci. Library Assn., Knoxville Area Health Sci. Library Consortium. Democrat. Home: 103 Hopi Dr Maryville TN 37801 Office: 907 E Lamar Alexander Pkwy Maryville TN 37801

WILLIAMSON, MYRNA HENNRICH, army officer; b. Gregory, S.D., Jan. 27, 1937; d. Walter Ferdinand and Alma Lillian (Rajewich) H. B.S. with honors, S.D. State U., 1960; M.A., U. Okla., 1973; grad., U.S. Army Command and Gen. Staff Coll., 1977, Nat. War Coll., 1980. Commd. 2d lt. U.S. Army, 1960, advanced through grades to brig. gen., 1985; bn. comdr. Mil. Police Sch. U.S. Army, Fort McClellan, Ala., 1977-79; chief plans policy and service div. Jl 8th Army U.S. Army, Korea, 1980-81; chief mgmt. support Office Dep. Chief Staff for Research, Devel. and Acquisition U.S. Army, Washington, 1981-82; brigade comdr. U.S. Army, Fort Benjamin Harrison, Ind., 1983-84; comdg. gen. 3d ROTC Region U.S. Army, Fort Riley, Kans., 1984-87; dep. dir. mil. personnel mgmt. U.S. Army, Washington, 1987—; U.S. del. com. on women in NATO Forces, 1986—. Recicpient Disting. Alumnus award S.D. State U., 1984. Mem. Nat. Speakers Assn., Internat. Platform Assn., Assn. U.S. Army, Nat. Assn. Uniformed Services, Phi Kappa Phi. Office: US Army Hdqrs DAPE-MP Washington DC 20310-0300

WILLIAMSON, SHERRI REDIES, county official; b. Charlotte, N.C., Oct. 3, 1953; d. Robert F. and Sara F. (Riley) R.; m. Joe Linwood Williamson, Aug. 21, 1976. B.S. in Geography, East Carolina U., 1976. Trainee, Mecklenburg County, Charlotte, 1978-80; zoning insp. Charlotte-Mecklenburg County, Charlotte, 1980—. Vice-pres. local Homeowners Assn., 1981-84. Mem. N.C. Assn. Zoning Ofcls. (charter). Democrat. Roman Catholic. Club: Women's. Avocations: gourmet cooking; aerobics; gardening; camping; crafts. Office: PO Box 31097 Charlotte NC 28231

WILLIAMSON, VIKKI LYN, finance executive; b. Huntington, W.Va., June 30, 1956; d. Ernest E. and Wanda C. (Cole) W. BA in Secondary Edn., English, Temple U., 1978; postgrad. in Acctg. and Fin., U. Cin., 1984—. CPA, Ohio; cert. tchr., Tenn., Ohio. Tchr. Springfield Christian Acad., Tenn., 1978-79; acctg. asst. Children's Hosp. Med. Ctr., Cin., 1979-84; asst. dir. fin. services U. Cin. Med. Ctr., 1984-85, dir. fin. services, 1985-88, dir. fin. and adminstrn., 1988—; instr. Miami U., Oxford, Ohio, 1984—; bd. dirs. Contemporary Dance Theatre, 1987—. Mem. Healthcare Fin. Mgmt. Assn., Am. Assn. Blood Banks, Ohio Assn. Blood Banks (fin. com. mem. 1986—), Assn. Women Adminstrs. (fin. com. mem. 1987—), U. Cin. Assn. Mid-Level Adminstrs. (bd. dirs. 1987—), Am. Inst. CPA's, Alpha Epsilon Theta, Beta Gamma Sigma, Delta Mu Delta. Office: U Cin Med Ctr Hoxworth Blood Ctr 3231 Burnet Ave ML #55 Cincinnati OH 45267

WILLIAN, CAROL LEE, travel company executive; b. San Mateo, Calif., Mar. 19, 1944; d. Carl and Mildred Lee (Denham) Bergfeld; m. Bryan Gale Willian; 1 child, Craig Philip. BS, Fontbonne Coll., 1966. Tchr. St. Casimir Grade Sch., St. Louis, 1967-73; exec. dir. Indpls. Clean City Com., 1982-85; mktg. dir. D.E. Murphy, Inc., Indpls., 1985-86; corp. sales rep. Ross & Babcock Travel Bur., Inc., Indpls., 1986-88, dir. group incentives, 1988—. Active Jr. League Indpls., 1977—; exec. mem. Nat. Assn. Counties Conf., Indpls., 1987; pres. St. Lukes Home Sch. Assn., 1988-89. Mem. Network Bus. Work. Republican. Roman Catholic. Office: Ross & Babcock Travel Bur Inc 9102 N Meridian Indianapolis IN 46260

WILLINGHAM, JEANNE MAGGART, dance educator, ballet company executive; b. Fresno, Calif., May 8, 1923; d. Harold F. and Gladys (Ellis) Maggart. student Tex. Woman's U., 1942; student profl. dancing schs., worldwide. dance tchr. Beaux Arts Dance Studio, Pampa, Tex., 1948—; artistic dir. Pampa Civic Ballet, 1972—. Mem. Tex. Arts and Humanities, Tex. Arts Alliance, Pampa C. of C. (fine arts com.), Pampa Fine Arts Assn. Office: Pampa Civic Ballet 315 N Nelson Pampa TX 79065

WILLINGHAM, MARY MAXINE, fashion retailer; b. Childress, Tex., Sept. 12, 1928; d. Charles Bryan and Mary (Bohannon) McCollum; m. Welborn Kiefer Willingham, Aug. 14, 1950; children—Sharon, Douglas, Sheila. B.A., Tex. Tech U., 1949. Interviewer Univ. Placement Service, Tex. Tech U., Lubbock, 1964-69; owner, mgr., buyer Maxine's Accent, Lubbock, 1969—; speaker in field. Leader Campfire Girls, Lubbock, 1964-65; sec. Community Theatre, Lubbock, 1962-64. Named Outstanding Mcht., Fashion Retailor mag., 1971, Outstanding Retailer; recipient Golden Sun award Dallas Market, May 1985. Mem. Lubbock Symphony Guild, Ranch and Heritage Ctr. Club: Faculty Women's. Office: 10 Briercroft Ctr Lubbock TX 79412

WILLIS, BETSY BEST, accountant, educator; b. Waco, Tex., Oct. 15, 1948; d. Alfred Clinton and Almarie (Jenson) Best; m. Stephen Vondyl Willis, Aug. 19, 1972; children: Bryan Stephen, Blake Robert, Wendy. BBA, Baylor U., 1971, M of Taxation, 1987. CPA, Tex. Acct. Peat, Marwick, Mitchell, CPA's, Houston, 1971-73, Greenstein, Dulocck & Logan, Waco, Tex., 1973-75, Thomas E. Riggs CPA, Waco, 1976-78, Harris Computer Services, Waco, 1980-82; lectr. Baylor U., Waco, 1975—; pvt. practice acct. Waco, 1982—. Dir. presch. div. 1st Bapt. Ch., Waco, 1979—; cons. Sr. Texan's Employment Program, Waco, 1981—; leader Jr. Great Books Reading Program, Waco, 1981—; mem. Waco Ind. Sch. Dist., 1982—; mem. adv. bd. Baylor U. Grad. Women's Orgn., 1988—. Mem. Am. Inst. CPA's, Tex. Soc. CPA's, Cen. Tex. CPA's, Beta Alpha Psi, Beta GAmma Sigma. Baptist. Club: P.E.O. Sisterhood (Waco). Home: 5305 Lake Highlands Waco TX 76710

WILLIS, CAROL FEALY, interior designer; b. Ft. Lauderdale, Fla., Aug. 5, 1954; d. Jack and Gertrude (Frank) Fealy; m. David Charles Willis. BFA in Indsl. Design, R.I. Sch. Design, 1976. Project designer The Dolan Partnership, Ft. Lauderdale, 1976-81; sr. project designer Lauderdale Design Group, Ft. Lauderdale, 1981-83; pres., owner Carol Fealy, Inc., Ft. Lauderdale, 1983—. Office: 608 E Olas Blvd Fort Lauderdale FL 33301

WILLIS, JANE MARLOW, journalist; b. Brandenburg, Ky., Mar. 8, 1942; d. James Mercer and Thelma (Marlow) W.; B.A., So. Meth. U., 1964; postgrad. (Mark Ethridge fellow), U. N.C., 1966, MS Eastern Ky. U., 1985; mem. staff Meade County Messenger, Brandenburg, 1964—, editor, 1966—, pub., 1978-83; with Peace Corps, Solomon Islands, 1987-88. Former den mother local Cub Scouts; mem. drive com. Patton Museum Fund, 1965; mem. local com. Ky. Bicentennial, 1973; patron Pioneer Playhouse, Danville, Ky., 1972; mem. Brandenburg Vol. Fire Dept., 1975—, chmn. firemen's ball, 1977, chmn. Brandenburg Fire Sch., 1977, cert. fire fighter; group coordinator Brandenburg Unity Festival, 1975-76; participant 1977 inaugural parade, 1977 part-time instr. fire sci. Ky. Dept. Vocat. Edn. Mem. Ky., Western Ky. (pres. 1971) press assns., Nat. Newspaper Assn., Internat. oc. Fire Service Instrs. (charter mem. Ky. chpt., Dixie Firemen's Assn. (sch. com.), DAR, Women of Moose, Mensa, Sigma Delta Chi. Democrat. Methodist. Clubs: Falls City Corvette, Hillcrest Country. Editor: Since April Third, 1975; Meade County Messenger Happy Holidays Cookbook, 1975; Summertime and The Cookin' Is Easy, 1977. Co-author slide presentation, Does A Water Curtain Really Work?. Home and Office: 321 Main St Brandenburg KY 40108

WILLIS, LOUISE MCKINNEY, retired petroleum company executive; b. Cooper, Tex., Nov. 12, 1924; d. Charles Martin and Birdie Floy (Griffin) McKinney; m. Glenn Harry Willis, May 7, 1948; children: Stephen Eric, Susan Renee, Mary Lynn, Glenda Ann. Student U. Okla., 1946-47. Instrument repair technician Tinker Field AFB, Okla., 1943-46; transit check clk. Fed. Res. Bank, Oklahoma City, 1948-50; sec. Southwestern Power Co., Tulsa, 1950-51, U.S. Govt. Agy., New Orleans, 1951-53; dist. mgr. World Book Encyclopedia, Dallas, 1972-78; v.p. Dor-Texan Petroleum, Inc., Dallas, 1980-87, ret., 1987. Mem. Dallas Opera Guild, 1984-85; pres. Dallas PTA, 1965-66, hon. life mem., 1975—; pres. St. Andrews Study Club, Dallas, 1968-69, 87-88; chmn. Cotillion Park Bd., Dallas, 1964-66. Mem. Dallas C. of C. Baptist. Clubs: Petroleum, Dallas Athletic. Lodge: Order of Rainbow Girls (chmn. bd. dirs. 1973-76).

WILLIS, MAXINE FRASURE, paralegal; b. Norman, Okla., Aug. 15, 1953; d. Claude Caswell and Edna Lee (Thomason) Gower; m. Eugene Frasue, Mar. 6, 1954 (div. 1980); children: Steven, James, Cheryl; m. James Emerson Willis, Sept. 7, 1985. Student, U. Okla., 1951-52. Lic. real estate agt., Calif. Legal sec. Peter F. Matranga Esq., El Monte, Calif., 1957-71; supr., bank officer Security Pacific Nat. Bank, Los Angeles, 1971-74; probate paralegal J. Robert Kotchick Inc., El Monte, 1974-76; paralegal, trust adminstr. Security Pacific Nat. Bank, Los Angeles, 1976—, Hawkings Realtors, Temple City, 1979-80; paralegal, office mgr. Anderson, McPharlin & Conners, Los Angeles, 1980—. Mem. Assn. Legal Adminstrs., Los Angeles County Bar Assn. (probate and trust sect.). Republican. Baptist. Home: 1552 Belmont Park Rd Oceanside CA 92056 Office: Anderson McPharlin & Conners 624 S Grand St 19th Floor Los Angeles CA 90017

WILLIS, SUSAN EADIE, nurse, educator; b. Balt., Nov. 17, 1949; d. Donald and Ruth Jacqueline (Hill) Eadie; m. David Larry Willis, July 25, 1970; children—Christopher Michael, Diana Lynn, Patrick Ryan, Cara Michele. A.A., St. Petersburg Jr. Coll., 1969, A.S. in Nursing, 1972; B.A. in Psychology, St. Leo Coll., Fla., 1979; B.S. in Nursing, U. South Fla., Tampa, 1981, now postgrad. in oncology nursing. R.N., cert. vocat. tchr., Fla. Staff nurse Morton Plant Hosp., Clearwater, Fla., 1972-73, 80-82, intravenous therapist, 1973-76; office nurse Dr. William Davis, Clearwater, 1976-80; instr. Pinellas Vocat. Tech. Inst., Clearwater, 1982—; also ARC nurse. Asst. author nursing modules for practical nurse program. Mem. Pinellas County PTA. Mem. Pinellas County Tchrs. Assn., Pinellas Assn. Vocat. Educators, Am. Nurses Assn., Fla. Nurses Assn., Phi Kappa Phi. Republican. Home: 9 Ibis Circle Safety Harbor FL 34695

WILLISCROFT, BEVERLY RUTH, lawyer; b. Conrad, Mont., Feb. 24, 1945; d. Paul A. and Gladys L. (Buck) Williscroft; m. Kent J. Barcus, Oct. 1984. BA in Music, So. Calif. Coll., 1967; JD, John F. Kennedy U., 1977. Elem. tchr., Sunnyvale, Calif., 1968-72; legal sec., legal asst. various law firms, Bay Area, 1972-77; admitted to Calif. bar, 1977; asso. firm Neil D. Reid, Inc., San Francisco, 1977-79; sole practice, Concord, Calif., 1979—; exam. grader Calif. Bar, 1979—; real estate broker, 1980-88; tchr. real estate King Coll., Concord, 1979-80; lectr. in field; judge pro-tem Mcpl. Ct.,

1981—. Bd dirs. Contra Costa Musical Theatre, Inc., 1978-82, v.p. adminstrn., 1980-81, v.p. prodn., 1981-82; mem. community devel. adv. com. City of Concord, 1981-83, vice chmn., 1982-83, mem. status of women com., 1980-81, mem. redevel. adv. com., 1984-86, planning commnr. 1986—; co-chmn. Longshore Morning Forum, Concord, 1980-84; mem. exec. bd. Mt. Diablo council Boy Scouts Am., 1981-85. Named Woman of Achievement, Todos Santos Bus. and Profl. Women, Clayton, Calif., 1980, 81; recipient award of merit, Bus. and Profl. Women, Bay Valley Dist., 1981. Mem. Concord C. of C. (dir., chmn. govt. affairs com. 1981-83, v.p. 1985-87, pres. 1988—, Bus. Person of Yr. 1986), Calif. Women Lawyers, Calif. State Bar, Contra Costa County Bar Assn., Contra Costa Barristers. Clubs: Todos Santos Bus. and Profl. Women (co-founder, pres. 1983-84, pub. relations chmn. 1982-83), Soroptimists (fin. sec. 1980-81). Office: 2151 Salvio St Suite 310 Concord CA 94520

WILLMAN, VICTORIA LYNN (VICKI), business executive, tympanist; b. Helena, Mont., Apr. 21, 1959; d. Glenn Robert and Pearl Elaine (Martin) W. B.S. in Music, Mary Coll., Bismarck, N.D., 1981. Tchr. music Hatton Pub. Schs., N.D., 1981-82; pres., mgr. Bus. Services, Inc., Bismarck, 1982—; prin. tympanist Bismarck-Mandan Symphony Orch., Bismarck, 1982—; free-lance percussionist. Announcer and producer Saturday Classics program and Morning Classics, Prairie Pub. Radio, Bismarck, 1985—. Trustee Bismarck-Mandan Symphony Orch., 1986—. Recipient Miss Congeniality award Bismarck C. of C., 1987; selected Princess of Summer, 1987 Folkfest Pageant. Mem. Nat. Assn. Bus. Commn. Agts. (regional rep. 1984-85), Percussive Arts Soc. Inc., Am. Fedn. Musicians (Local 229). Lutheran. Avocations: travel, jogging, jazz and classical music. Office: Bus Services Inc PO Box 638 1237 W Divide Ave Bismarck ND 58502

WILLS, AUDREY E, bank executive; b. Phila., Mar. 28, 1930; d. Theodore A. and Mary C. (Dixon) W. AA, Villanova, 1966. Operations officer First Pa. Bank, Phila., 1961-66, asst. v.p., div. head, 1966-74, v.p., 1974-85, divisional v.p., 1985—; bd. dirs. Del. Valley Bank Methods Assn., Phila.; cons. Fraud Control Bureau, PHila., 1970—, Hurst Assocs., Springfield, Pa., 1986—, L & L Custom Catering Inc., Frederick, Pa., 1980—. Author: Loss Prevention Awareness, 1979; author and exec. producer of film: Tell it to the Judge, 1986; contbr. articles to various publications; editor: Prevention Awareness newsletter. Mem. Phila. Art Mus. Assn., 1975—; mem. New Hanover Civic Assn., (township, Pa.), 1975 81; mem. Greater Phila. Cultural Alliance, 1976—; mem. Smithsonian Assocs., Washington, 1980—; mem. Paradise (environmental) Watchdogs, Frederick, Pa., 1987; mem. Phila. Clearing House Fraud Commn. (past chmn.). Recipient Cert. of Appreciation Dept. Defense USAF Guard and Reserve, 1985, Cert. achievement Women's Forum YWCA of Phila., 1987. Mem. Pa. Bankers Assn., Am. Mgt. Assn., Am. Inst. of Banking, Bank Adminstrn. Inst., Del. Valley Fin. and Security Officer's Assn. Club: Cen. Perklomen Bus. and Profl. Women. Home: Renninger Rd Frederick PA 19435 Office: First Pa Bank 3020 Market Philadelphia PA 19101

WILLS, JANET RAE, personnel director; b. Webster City, Iowa, Feb. 16, 1947; d. Arthur Rex and Mildred Gladys (Stafford) L; m. Fred A. Wills, Aug. 12, 1967; children: Kent Bradley, Tiffany Jeanne. BA, Upper Iowa U., 1979. Asst. v.p., persnnel officer Security Bank, Marshalltown, Iowa, 1980—. Mem. Am. Inst. Banking (state chair 1986—), Am. Soc. for Personnel Adminstrn. Democrat. Methodist. Home: 201 Santa Barbara Marshalltown IA 50158 Office: Security Bank 11 N 1st Ave Marshalltown IA 50158

WILLS, JULIE ELIZABETH, marketing professional; b. Harrisburg, Pa., July 17, 1959; d. Arthur Belair Jr. and Amy (Chivis) Williams. BS, Pa. State U., Middletown, 1980. Unit supr. CNA Ins., Reading, Pa., 1980-81; comml. casualty analyst Aetna Casualty & Surety and Co., Reading, 1981-83, sr. comml. account rep., 1983-84; comml. account exec. Aetna Casualty & Surety and Co., McLean, Va., 1985-87; ter. mktg. supr. Crum & Forster Comml. Ins., Towson, Md., 1987—. Chairperson United Way of Berks County (Pa.), 1984-85. Mem. Ins. Women of Washington, Am. Soc. Profl. and Exec. Women, Delta Tau Kappa. Presbyterian. Office: Crum & Forster Comml Ins 901 Dulaney Valley Rd Towson MD 21204

WILLS, NASREEN SANAULLA, design company executive, special events planner; b. Bhopal, India, Feb. 23, 1963; came to U.S., 1983; d. Mohamad and Helen (Abraham) Sanaulla; m. Douglass McCall Wills, Feb. 4, 1984. BS, U. Bhopal, 1981; postgrad., George Washington U., 1983-84. Adminstrv. asst. The Georgetown Design Group, Inc., Washington, 1984-85, exec. producer, coordinator spl. events, 1985—. Mem. Friends of Capital Children's Mus., Friends of Kennedy Ctr., Washington Charitable Fund. Mem. Washington Fashion Group, Washington Performing Arts Soc., Internat. Students House Alumni Assn. (fund raiser 1983—). Moslem. Office: The Georgetown Design Group 1301 20th St NW Washington DC 20011

WILLSEY, JOAN CLEE, data processsing executive; b. Cleve., Oct. 5, 1946; d. William and Clarice (Kunkleman) Clee; m. David Brant Hatch, June 17, 1967 (div.); 1 child, Teressa Jean; m. Jere Lee Willsey, Jan. 14, 1984. AA, Monroe Community Coll., 1968; BA, U. Rochester, 1986, MBA, 1987. Office mgr. Borrows Mech., Rochester, 1970-74; computer programmer Xerox Corp., Rochester, 1974-80, fin. analyst, 1980-86, fin. cons., 1986-87, mgr. staff services, 1987—. Mem. Beta Gamma Sigma. Democrat. Club: Toastmasters (v.p. ednl. com.). Office: Xerox Corp Bldg 214-07S 800 Phillips Rd Webster NY 14580

WILLSIE, BERTHA SPOONER, educator; b. Ashville, N.Y., May 15, 1921; d. Frank W. and Jeannette C. (Bergstresser) Spooner; B.A., Coll. Wooster, 1942; A.M., Cornell U., 1947; postgrad. Western Res. U., 1943, U. Buffalo, 1944-45, U. Havana, 1948, St. Bonaventure U., 1964-67; m. Robert L. Willsie, June 30, 1951; 1 dau., Anita Ruth. High sch. English and lang. tchr. Bemus Point High Sch., 1942-47; instr. French and Spanish, Alfred U. Extension, 1948-52; tchr. French, Spanish, Latin Falconer High Sch., 1952-56; tchr. Panama Central Sch., 1958-64; head fgn. lang. dept. Jamestown (N.Y.) Public Schs., 1964-76; instr. Spanish Chautauqua (N.Y.) Instn., 1976—. Mem. Bd. Edn., Chautauqua Central Sch., 1970-77; mem. Marvin Community House. Recipient Scholarships, Coll. Wooster, 1938-42, Cornell U., 1946-47. Mem. N.Y. State Fgn. Lang. Educators Council, Internat. Order King's Daus. and Sons, Chautauqua County Hist. Soc., Fenton Hist. Soc., DAR (chmn. com. on schs.), Phi Beta Kappa, Phi Sigma Iota, Delta Kappa Gamma (chair scholarship com.). Methodist. Club: Eastern Star (dist. dep. grand matron, Chautauqua dist.). Home: Box 155 Stow NY 14785

WILLSON, ALICE FAYE, construction company executive, interior designer; b. Watson, Mo., June 14, 1931; d. Raymond LeRoy and Elsie Christina (Herrmann) Oslin; m. Robert Mitchell Willson, June 8, 1947; children: Pamela Jeanne, Patricia Joanne. Student, Kansas City U., 1957, Miami-Dade Community Coll., 1977. Clk. Interstate Nurseries, Hamburg, Iowa, 1948-51; clk., asst. dept. head Dun & Bradstreet, Denver, 1952; corr. Dun & Bradstreet, Kansas City, 1952-55; from ins. clk. to asst. cashier to mgr. bus. office Kans. U. Med. Ctr., Kansas City, 1956-59; exec. sec. Security Mut. Ins., Miami, Fla., 1960-62; exec. officer, ptnr. Standard Improvement Co., Miami, 1962—; owner A.F.W. Decorators, Miami, 1986—. Asst. troop leader Girl Scouts Am., Kansas City, 1956, troop leader, Miami, 1970; camp worker Miami Dems., 1963-68. Office: Standard Improvement and AFW 7165 SW 47th St Unit 317 Miami FL 33155

WILLSON, JULIE, financial planner, securities broker; b. Stockton, Calif., Jan. 30, 1958. BA, U. Calif., Irvine, 1979. Supr. tng. dept., br. investment officer Am. Savs. and Loan Assn., Whittier, Calif., 1979-83; fin. cons. Shearson Am. Express, Orange, Calif., 1983-84; investment services officer Discount Investments Am. (now Griffin Fin. Services), Long Beach, Calif., 1984-86; account exec. Morgan, Olmstead, Kennedy and Gardner, Newport Beach, Calif., 1986; fin. planner Christopher Weil and Co., Inc., Newport Beach, 1986—; presenter seminars, Long Beach, Newport Beach, 1984—. Contbr. articles on personal fin. to local newspapers. Mem. Inst. Cert. Fin. Planners (cert.), Internat. Assn. Fin. Planners, Bus. and Profl. Women (Young Careerist award 1988), Nat. Assn. Female Execs. Office: Christopher Weil & Co Inc 4400 Macarthur Blvd #150 Newport Beach CA 92660

WILMER, MARY CHARLES, artist; b. Atlanta, Aug. 25, 1930; d. William Knox and Harriott Creighton (Thomas) Fitzpatrick; student Wellesley Coll., 1948-50; A.B., Agnes-Scott Coll., 1970; B.F.A., Coll. of Art, 1974; m. John Grant Wilmer, Dec. 28, 1950; children—John Grant, Knox Randolph, Charles Inman, Mary Catherine; m. 2d, Olin Grigsby Shivers, May 18, 1982. One-woman shows: Image South Gallery, 1974, Aronson Gallery, 1977, 79, Heath Gallery, 1982, Coach House Gallery, 1983; exhibited in group show: Colony Sq., 1975; portrait painter, 1974—. Bd. dirs. Hillside Cottages, 1963-65, Atlanta Child Services, 1965-68, Atlanta Coll. Art, 1965—, Atlanta Puppetry Arts, 1982—; co-chmn. Ga. Commn. Nat. Mus. of Women in the Arts, 1985—. Episcopalian. Club: Piedmont Driving. Address: 1 Vernon Rd Atlanta GA 30305

WILMORE, MARIE MCCLURG, government official; b. Tremont, Ohio, Jan. 27, 1940; d. Charles McClurg and Elsie Louisa (Ridder) McClurg Pearis; m. Jon Frederick Mattfeld, Nov. 30, 1957 (div. 1965); 1 child, Frederick; m. Dhalmas Otto Wilmore, May 29, 1969 (dec. 1982); 1 child, Laura Kathleen. Student No. Va. Community Coll., 1971-75. Clk. stenographer USAF, Wright Patterson AFB, Ohio, 1957-62, sec.-stenographer, 1967-69, sec.-stenographer, Washington, configuration mgmt. specialist, 1970-72; with Dept. Navy, Washington, mgmt. analyst, 1974-82, dep. OEO officer, 1976-77, reports control analyst Naval Air Systems Command, 1977-82, staff asst. to dep. asst. Sec. Navy for res. affairs, 1981-82, petty officer USNR, 1979—; pres. Dhalmar Arabian Farm, Spotsylvania, Va., 1976—. Recipient Zero Defects awards, 1960, 63, 67, Sustained Superior Performance award Dept. Air Force, 1966, Dept. Navy, 1985, Air Force Unit Excellence award, 1969. Mem. Federally Employed Women, Navy Speech Club (v.p. membership com.), Naval Sea Systems Command Computer Club (treas. 1986-88), Va. Arabian Horse Assn., Eastern Amateur Arabian Horse Assn. Baptist. Office: Dept Navy Sea System Command (SEA62Y11L) Washington DC 20362-5101

WILMOTH, DONNA RENÉ, real estate executive; b. Birmingham, Ala., Oct. 7, 1951; d. Preston Cleve and Melba Lorene (Wood) W. BFA, Auburn U., 1974; student in real estate, Richland Coll., 1986-87. Lic. real estate agt., Tex. Adminstrv. asst. Fulton Co., Boston, 1974-75; graphic communicator U. Va. Law Sch., Charlottesville, 1975-76; orientator, cons. Fuji Gakuin and Nisseit Kanagawa Co., Tokyo, 1976-81; comml. real estate agt. Louis G. Reese, Inc., Dallas, 1982-83; investor real estate Donna Wilmoth Investments, Dallas, 1983—; pres. Waterhouse and Assocs., Inc., Dallas, 1984—; comml. and retail leasing agt. Southmark Corp., Dallas, 1986—. Mem. Dallas Mus. Art, Dallas Young Reps., DMA. Republican. Presbyterian. Club: Les Amis Du Vins (Boston).

WILMS, NANCY ANDERSON, dermatologist; b. Battle Creek, Mich., July 19, 1950; d. Harold E. and Mary V. Anderson; m. Dale John Wilms, Sept. 5, 1976. B.A. cum laude, Andrews U., 1972; M.D., Loma Linda U., 1976. Diplomate: Am. Bd. Dermatology, 1982. Intern, Loma Linda U. (Calif.), 1976-77, resident in internal medicine, 1977-78; family practice staff Kaiser Permanente, San Bernardino, Calif., 1978; resident in dermatology Henry Ford Hosp., Detroit, 1978-81, staff, 1981-82; asst. prof. dermatology, pediatrics, pathology Loma Linda U., 1982—; cons. Jerry L. Pettis VA Hosp., Loma Linda, San Bernardino County Hosp., 1982—. Mem. AMA, Calif., Med. Assn., San Bernardino Med. Soc. Republican. Contbr. articles to profl. jours. Office: Faculty Med Offices 11370 Anderson St Suite 2600 Loma Linda CA 92354

WILROY, HIABURNIA GAINES, title insurance company executive; b. DeSoto County, Miss., Apr. 22, 1929; d. Hubert Cornelius Gaines and Mattie Mae (Chamberlin) Gaines Troy; m. Leslie Lee Crawford, June 1, 1947 (div. June 1969); children—Leslie Lee, Jr., Richard Marvin; m. William Edwards Wilroy, Oct. 15, 1970 (div. Dec. 1985). B.B.A., U. Miss., 1979. Cert. profl. sec. Exec. sec. to county agt., Hernando, Miss., 1948-49; legal sec. W.E. Wilroy, Hernando, 1950-51, 53-57; chief clk. DeSoto County Agrl. Stblzn. and Conservation Service, Hernando, 1957-58; legal sec. Wilroy, Wilroy & Hagan, Hernando, 1958-69; corp. officer, asst. v.p. Mid-South Title Ins. Corp., Memphis, 1969—. Docent Ramesses The Great Exhibition. Mem. Profl. Secs. Internat. (treas. Memphis chpt. 1981-82, bd. dirs. 1984-85), Women's Soc. Christian Service (circle chmn. Hernando). Methodist. Club: Garden Study (sec.) (Hernando). Avocations: bridge, reading, needlepoint, knitting. Home: 96 Robinson St E PO Box 63 Hernando MS 38632 Office: Mid-South Title Ins Corp 1200 One Commerce Sq Memphis TN 38103

WILSON, ALICE BLAND, real estate consultant; b. Rainelle, W.Va., Apr. 1, 1938; d. Brady Floyd and Mildred Martha (George) Bland; m. Louis William Groves, Jr., Apr. 20, 1957 (div. 1981); children: Martha Rachel, Leonora Jayne; m. Glen Parten Wilson, Dec. 11, 1982. AB, W.Va. U., 1959, postgrad. in microbiology, 1975-78. Contract adminstr. Washington Plate Glass Co., Washington, 1979-80; mem. acctg. staff Forbes Co., Washington, 1981; customer relations rep. Stern's Co., Washington, 1982; real estate assoc. Merrill Lynch Realty Co., Washington, 1985—. Contbr. articles to Jour. Parasitology, Vol. coordinator John Glenn for Pres. campaign, Washington, 1983-84; co-chmn. hospitality com. Women's Nat. Democratic Club, Washington, 1985—; mem. internat. adv. council ARC, Washington, 1985—. Mem. Washington Assn. Realtors (mem. residential sales com. 1985—). Avocations: flying, aerobics, nature study. Clubs: Million Dollar, Pres.' Home: 433 New Jersey Ave SE Washington DC 20003 Office: Merrill Lynch Realty Co 2305 Calvert St NW Washington DC 20008

WILSON, ALMA D., state supreme court justice; b. Pauls Valley, Okla., May 25, 1917; d. William R. and Anna L. (Schuppert) Bell; m. William A. Wilson, May 30, 1948; 1 child, Lee Anne. AB, U. Okla., 1939, LLB, 1941, JD, 1970. Bar: Okla. 1941. Sole practice Muskegee, Okla., 1941-43; sole practice Oklahoma City, 1943-47, Pauls Valley, 1948-69; judge Pauls Valley Mcpl. Ct., 1967-68; apptd. spl. judge Dist. Ct. 21, Norman, Okla., 1969-75, dist. judge, 1975-79; assoc. justice Okla. Supreme Ct., Oklahoma City, 1983—. Mem. bd. visitors U. Okla., mem. alumni bd. dirs.; mem. Assistance League; trustee Okla. Meml. Union. Recipient Guy Brown award, 1974, Woman of Yr. award Norman Bus. and Profl. Women, 1975; elected to U. Okla. Hall of Fame, 1975. Mem. Garvin County Bar Assn. (past pres.), Okla. Bar Assn. (co-chmn. law and citizenship edn. com.), AAUW, Altrusa, Am. Legion Aux. Office: Okla Supreme Ct State Capitol Room 1 Oklahoma City OK 73105 *

WILSON, ANGELA BARNES, educator; b. Franklin, Va., Dec. 18, 1957; d. Richard Roudolph and Marion Eugenia (Cain) Barnes; m. Steve Edward Wilson, Sept. 25, 1982. Student, E. Carolina U., 1976-79; BS in Biology Edn., Va. Commonwealth U., 1981, postgrad., 1987—; MEd, Va. State U., 1986. Cert. tchr., prin., Va. Tchr. E.W. Wyatt Jr. High Sch., Emporia, Va., 1981-82, King William (Va.) High Sch., 1982-83, Greensville County High Sch., Emporia, 1983—; cons. Writing Across the Curriculum program, Va. State U., Richmond, 1984—; mem. Va. Edn. Assn. Council on Instrn. and Profl. Devel., 1987—. Leader Emporia council Girl Scouts U.S., 1985-86. Mem. NEA, Va. Edn. Assn. (task force on quality edn. 1985-86, sex equality council 1986-87), Greensville Edn. Assn. (dir. pub. relations 1986-87Outsanding Service award 1985), Va. Sci. Tchrs. Assn., Am. Bus. Women's Assn. (program dir. 1984-85, Stephen Bufton Meml. scholar 1986), Nat. Assn. for Curriculum and Supervision, Nat. Assn. Female Execs., Delta Sigma Theta, Phi Delta Kappa. Democrat. Baptist. Home: Rte 3 Box 334 A Emporia VA 23847

WILSON, ANN, singer, recording artist; b. 1950; d. John and Lou Wilson. Ed., Cornish Allied Inst. Fine Arts, Seattle. Lead singer rock group Heart, 1975—. Albums include: Dreamboat Annie, 1975, Magazine, 1975, Little Queen, 1977, Dog and Butterfly, 1978, Bebe le Strange, 1980, Heart Live-Gr, Private Audition, 1982, Passionworks, 1983, Heart, 1985, Bad Animals, 1987; single recs. include: Magic Man, 1976, Barracuda, 1977, Crazy on You, 1976, Straight On, 1978, Even It Up, 1980, Sweet Darlin', 1980, Tell It Like It Is, 1981, Unchained Melody, 1981, This Man is Mine, 1982, City's Burning, 1982, Bright Light Girl, 1982, How Can I Refuse, 1983, Sleep Alone, 1983, Almost Paradise, 1984, The Heat, 1984, What About Love, 1985, Never, 1985, These Dreams, 1986, Nothin' at All, 1986, Alone, 1987, Who Will Run to You, 1987, There's The Girl, 1987, I Want You So Bad, 1988. Office: Suite 333 219 1st Ave N Seattle WA 98109

WILSON, ANN, corrections supervisor; b. Yokohama, Japan, July 29, 1947; d. Woodrow Wilson and Catherine Remson (Lawson) W. BA, William and Penn Coll., 1970. Cert. physical edn., elem. and secondary tchr., Mass. Coach Beaverdale and West Des Moines Girls Softball League, 1987—; correctional supervisor Iowa Correctional Assn. for Women, Mitchellville. Named one of Outstanding Young Women in Am., 1972. Mem. Iowa Correctional Assn., Am. Correctional Assn., Nat. Youth Sports Coaches Assn., Nat. Assn. for Female Execs. Democrat. Episcopalian. Home: 3007 57th St Des Moines IA 50310 Office: Iowa Correctional Assn for Women PO Box 700 Mitchellville IA 50169

WILSON, ANN BOUIE, educational program administrator; b. Birmingham, Ala., Dec. 25, 1948; d. Charles and Annie Laurie (Gainer) Bouie; m. Frederick Myles Wilson Jr., Jan. 11, 1951. BA in Sociology, U. Calif., 1971; MA in Edn., Stanford U., 1972, MA in History, 1977, PhD in Adminstrns. Policy Analysis, 1977. Cert. tchr., Calif. Asst. prof. Calif. State U., San Luis Obispo, 1972-73; social sci. instr. Nairobi Coll., East Palo Alto, Calif., 1973-74; program assoc. Far West Lab., San Francisco, 1977-80; with Nat. Sch. Resource Network, San Rafael, Calif., 1980-81; project dir. Project Interface, Oakland, Calif., 1982—; cons. Del Paso Heights Elem. Sch. Dist., Sacramento, 1983—. Mem. assoc. staff Allen Temple Bapt. Ch., Oakland, 1982—, tchr. noon bible class; mem. Bay Area Black United Fund, Oakland, 1980-81, Oakland East Bay jr. league; mem. edn. com. Bay Area Urban League, Oakland; mem. adv. bd. STEMS Project U. Calif., Berkeley; co-chair Oakland Pub. Schs. Task Force on Racism and Discrimination, Human Relations subcom.; facilitator single subject credential adv. com. Calif. State U., Hayward; bd. dirs. East Oakland Youth Devel. Ctr., East Bay Jr. League; mem.-at-large Am. Baptist Chs. Named one of Outstanding Young Women Am., 1982, 85. Democrat. Baptist. Home: 5514 Picardy Dr Oakland CA 94605 Office: Project Interface 8500 A St Oakland CA 94621

WILSON, BARBARA B., English educator; b. Atlanta, Nov. 20, 1939; d. Henry Lamar and Mary Leila (Westbrooks) Brower; m. Hansel Marvin Wilson, Aug. 31, 1957; children: Thomas Westbrook, Marvin Jeffrey, Susanna Lyne, Mary Jennifer. BA in French, Sorbonne, 1981; BA in English, Ga. Southwestern Coll., 1982, MEd in English, 1983; cert. English, Emory U., 1984; postgrad. in English Edn., Columbus (Ga.) Coll., 1987—. Acctg. educator United Meth. Ch., Monrovia, Liberia, 1975-80; owner, operator The Wordshop Bookstore, Americus, Ga., 1972-75; English educator Riverview Acad., Albany, Ga., 1982; English educator Americus City Sch. System, 1982—, literary coordinator, coach, 1986—. Vol. Am. Cancer Soc., Americus, 1985—, tchr. Americus lst United Meth. Ch., 1981—. Mem. French Hon. Soc., English Hon. Soc., NEA, Ga. Assn. Educators, Americus Hist. Soc., Sigma Chi. Republican. Methodist. Office: Americus High Sch 805 Harrold Dr Americus GA 31709

WILSON, BERTHA, Canadian justice; b. Kirkcaldy, Scotland, Sept. 18, 1923; d. Archibald Wernham and Christina Noble; m. John. Wilson, 1945. MA, Aberdeen (Scotland) U., 1944; parchment, Tng. Coll. Tchrs., Aberdeen, 1945; LLB, Dalhousie U., Halifax, N.S., 1957, LLD (hon.), 1980; LLD (hon.), Queen's U., Kingston, 1983, U. Calgary, 1983, U. Toronto, 1984, U. Alta., 1985, York U., 1986; LHD (hon.), Mt. St. Vincent U., Halifax, 1984; DCL (hon.), U. Western Ont., 1984, U. Windsor, 1985. Bar: N.S. 1957, Ont. 1959. Assoc. Osler, Hoskin & Harcourt, Toronto, 1958-68, ptnr., 1968-75; created Queen's Council Can., 1973; judge Can. Ct. Appeals, Ont., 1975-82, Supreme Ct. Can., Ottawa, Ont., 1982—, Can. Permanent Ct. Arbitration, 1984—. Trustee Clarke Inst. of Psychiatry, 1972-75; trustee Toronto Sch. Theol., 1975-81, mem. exec. com., 1977-81; chmn. Rhodes Scholarship Selection Com., Ont., 1980-84; bd. govs. Carleton U., 1983-85; bd. dirs. Can. Ctr. for Philnthropy, 1981—; mem. jud. com. United Ch. Can., 1985—. Mem. Can. Bar Assn. (mem. nat. council, mem. Ont. council 1970-73). Mem. United Ch. Can. Office: Supreme Ct Can, Wellington St, Ottawa, ON Canada K1A 0J1 *

WILSON, BETTY MAY, finance company executive; b. Moberly, Mo., Mar. 13, 1947; d. Arthur Bunyon and Martha Elizabeth (Denham) Stephens; m. Ralph Felix Martin, Aug. 22, 1970 (div. May 1982); m. Gerald Robert Wilson Sr., Mar. 3, 1984; stepchildren: Gerald Robert Jr., Heather Lynn, Jeffrey Michael. BS in Acctg. and Bus. Adminstrn., Colo. State U., 1969. CPA, Mo. Tax mgr. Arthur Andersen & Co., St. Louis, 1969-75; v.p., asst. sec., dir. taxes ITT Fin. Corp., St. Louis, 1975—; sr. v.p., bd. dirs. Lyndon Ins. Co., St. Louis, 1977—, ITT Lyndon Life Ins. Co., ITT Lyndon Property Ins. Co., St. Louis, 1977—. Mem. Am. Inst. CPA's, Mo. Soc. CPA's, Am. Fin. Services Assn. (chmn. tax com. 1987-88), Tax Execs. Inst. Inc. (bd. dirs. St. Louis chpt., past sec., past. pres.), Mo. Girls Racing Assn. (pres. 1977-82). Baptist. Office: ITT Fin Corp 12555 Manchester Rd Saint Louis MO 63131

WILSON, CAROL, corporate lawyer; b. Rushville, Ill., Feb. 25, 1935; d. William C. and Anna Gertrude (Dace) W.; div.; 1 child, Mark Anthony Wilson Smith. BA, Stanford U., 1955; JD cum laude, U. Ariz., 1971. Bar: Ariz., 1971, U.S. Ct. Appeals (9th cir.), 1971. Ptnr. Browning, Wilson & Hawkins, Tucson, 1972-78, Wilson & Thompson, Tucson, 1978-80, Wilson & Price, Tucson, 1980-83; instr. U. N.C., Charlotte, 1983-86; gen. counsel AlphaGraphics, Tucson, 1986—; judge pro tem Pima County Superior Ct., Tucson, 1982-83. Mem. State Bar Ariz. (civil practice and procedure com.), Pima County Bar Assn. (pres. 1982-83), Order of the Coif. Office: AlphaGraphics Inc 3760 N Commerce Dr Tucson AZ 85705

WILSON, CHARLOTTE JOYCE, financial services executive, marketing and communications consultant; b. Phila., Aug. 4, 1946; d. William and Charlotte Louise (Gettier) Todd; m. Richard Reynolds Wilson, July 12, 1969. BA, Conn. Coll., New London, 1968; MEd, Lehigh U., Bethlehem, Pa., 1973; postgrad. U. Pa., Phila., 1977-79. Cert. tchr., Pa. Coordinator gifted curriculum Lower Moreland Sch. Dist., Huntingdon Valley, Pa., 1972-78; gifted resource dir. North Pa. Sch. Dist., Lansdale, 1978-81; dir. tng. and devel. Federated Investors Inc., Pitts., 1981-82, dir. product info. and market devel., 1982, asst. v.p. product devel., 1983—; mktg. cons. Kans. City Bank & Trust Co., Kansas City, Mo., 1983-84; author and producer film, 1986; communications cons. Republic Nat. Bank, N.Y.C., 1983-84, Union Nat. Bank, Albany, N.Y., 1983-84. Author: A Guide to Marketing Bank Services, 1983; contbr. in field. Bd. dirs. Abraxas Found., Pitts., 1983-87. Recipient Quality Circle Facilitator award Quality Circle Inst., 1982. Mem. Am. Mktg. Assn. (pres. 1986-87, nat. chpt. excellence award 1986-87), Bus. Profl. Advt. Assn. (bd. dirs.), AAUW. Republican. Episcopalian. Clubs: Econs., Advt. (Pitts.). Home: Upper Saint Clair PA 15241

WILSON, DARLENE ANNE, stockbroker; b. Erie, Pa., Nov. 10, 1945; d. Russell Benjamin Ford and Yvonne Norma (Gross) Hall; m. Peter Craig Wilson, Nov. 6, 1965; children: Craig Allen, Dain Walter. Student, Gannon U., Erie, 1963-65; BS in Econs., Christopher Newport Coll., Newport News, Va., 1978; MBA, George Washington U., 1980. Sec. Union Iron Works, Erie, 1963-66; instr. USAF, Columbus, Miss., 1966-68, Selma, Ala., 1969-73; prin. Bus. Sch., Randolph AFB, TX, 1973-76; stockbroker Shearson, Lehman, Hutton Inc. (formerly E.F. Hutton & Co.), Norfolk, Va., 1978—; small bus. cons. San Antonio, 1973-76, Newport News, 1977, Tulsa, 1981—. Mem. Women in Bus. Republican. Lutheran. Club: Quota Internat. (Norfolk) (treas., sec., v.p. 1983—). Home: 125 Wilderness Rd Hampton VA 23669 Office: Shearson Lehman Hutton Inc 101 St Paul's Blvd Norfolk VA 23510

WILSON, DONNA MICHELE, fraternal organization administrator; b. Atlanta, May 5, 1963; d. Terance Lee Wilson and Frances Janette (Hill) Abbuel. Student, West Ga. Coll., 1982. Balance clk. Fin. Data Services, Carrollton, Ga., 1981-83; income auditor Ramada Renaissance Hotel, Atlanta, 1983-87; fin. coordinator Phi Mu Fraternaties, Atlanta, 1987, staff inventory control Consol. Mktg. Inc., Atlanta, 1987—. Fellow Exec. Women. Office: Consol Mktg Inc 1820 Water Pl Suite 250 Atlanta GA 30339

WILSON, DORIS FANUZZI, state agency administrator; b. N.Y.C., Oct. 17, 1935; d. Vitoantonio and Rose (Colavito) Panzarino; children: James Douglas Fanuzzi, Robert Alan Fanuzzi; m. Richard Gerard Wilson, Aug. 21, 1977 (div. 1987). BA cum laude, Hunter Coll., 1956; MA, Montclair State Coll., 1978. Tchr. learning disabilities, cons. Tri-County Ednl. Vocat. High Sch., Totowa, N.J., 1979-80, Fairlawn (N.J.) Bd. Edn., 1982-83, Regional

Child Study Team, Franklin, N.J., 1983-84, curriculum and instrn. div. devel. disabilities N.J. Dpt. Human Servcies, Trenton, 1984—. Mem. Nat. Assn. Female Execs., AAUW, N.J. Assn. Learning Cons., N.J. Assn. Children with Learning Disabilities, N.J. Women's Polit. Caucus. Republican. Home: 333 W State St Apt 6P Trenton NJ 08618 Office: Dept Human Services Div Devel Disabilities 222 S Warren St Trenton NJ 08625

WILSON, ELAINE KAY, marketing executive, health consultant, metaphysician; b. Long Beach, Calif., Nov. 2, 1940; d. Leonard Iven and Mildred Elizabeth (McKay) W. BA, San Jose State U., 1963. Med. technologist Santa Clara County Hosp., San Jose, Calif., 1964-67, Root Scott Lab., San Bernardino, Calif., 1967-70, BioSci. Lab., Van Nuys, Calif., 1970-72, Facey Med. Group, Van Nuys, 1975-86; mktg. exec. Kayson Enterprises, Mt. Aukum, Calif., 1986—; wholistic health practioner Therapy Dynamics Ctr., Diamond Springs, Calif., 1988—. Editor The Gathering Place, 1988—. Republican. Home: PO Box 498 Mount Aukum CA 95656-0498 Office: Kayson Enterprises PO Box 499 8080 Mt Aukum Rd Mount Aukum CA 95656-0499

WILSON, ELIZABETH DOLAN NOLAN, investment company executive; b. Joplin, Mo., Mar. 9, 1909; d. John Lewis and Elizabeth (Hale) Dolan; m. Ralph Lauder Nolan, Oct. 17, 1929 (dec. Aug. 1971); children—Thomas Connor, John Keith; m. Alan Shepherd Wilson, Jr., Jan. 18, 1978 (dec. Oct. 12, 1987). Student Drury Coll., 1927, 28, Kans. State Tchrs. Coll., 1927, 28. Famouse Artists Sch. Illustration and Design, 1960-63, Famous Artists Writers Sch., 1968, Inst. Children's Lit., 1975. Pres. Connor Investment Co., Joplin, 1971-79, also dir. Illustrator: Tales About Joplin, Short and Tall, 1962, 2d edit., 1968, 3d edit., 1988; contbr. poetry, hist. articles and sports columns to profl. jours. Emeritus mem. women's aux. to bd. dirs. Drury Coll. Women's Aux., Springfield, Mo., 1961—, Joplin Hist. Soc. Dorothea B. Hoover Mus., Joplin; committeewoman Republican party, Joplin, 1964; bd. dirs. Spiva Art Ctr., 1956-60, 70-73. Mem. Pi Beta Phi. Republican. Presbyterian. Clubs: Century (Joplin), Twin Hills Golf and Country (Joplin). Avocations: golf; bridge. Home: 1240 Crest Dr Joplin MO 64801 Office: Connor Investment Co Joplin MO 64801

WILSON, EVALYN LEONARD, nurse, consultant; b. Fontana, Calif., June 30, 1951; d. William Robert and Wilda M. (Pirl) L.; m. Steven L. Wilson, Nov. 7, 1987. Diploma, St. Francis Sch. Nursing, 1975; BS in Interior Design, Kans. State U., 1984. Staff nurse St. Francis Regional Med. Ctr., Wichita, Kans., 1973-81; research nurse U. Kans. Sch. Medicine, 1981-82, staff nurse Sierra Vista Hosp., San Luis Obispo, Calif., 1981, Meml. Hosp., Manhattan, Kans., 1981-84, The St. Mary Hosp., Manhattan, 1982-84; med. planner Widom, Wein, Cohen, Los Angeles, 1984-85; facility programmer Am. Med. Internat., Inc., Beverly Hills, Calif., 1985-86; pres. Lyn Leonard & Assoc., Fairway, Kans., 1986—. Mem. Am. Soc. Interior Design (assoc.), Inst. Bus. Designers (affiliate). Avocations: skiing, photgraphy, needlework, sewing.

WILSON, EVELYN GAIL, retail chain official; b. Anniston, Ala., Aug. 9, 1945; d. John Haywood and Letty Bell (Johnson) Wildman; m. Jimmy Ray Rust, June 28, 1960 (dec. Mar. 1970); 1 son, Jimmy Ray (dec.); m. William O. Wilson, Jr., June 26, 1971; stepchildren—Andrew, Angela. Student Gadsden (Ala.) Bus. Coll., 1965, U. Ala.-Birmingham, 1975-76. Cert. profl. sec. Billing clk. Central Photocolor, Anniston, 1963; sec. Ch. of St. Michael and All Angels, Anniston, 1963-66; dist. sec. Ala. Vocat. Rehab. Service, Anniston, 1966-76; personnel adminstr. Super Valu Stores, Inc., Anniston, 1976—; instr. secretarial procedures Anniston Jr. Achievement, 1975; instr. written communication Am. Inst. Banking, 1981-82. Officer, mem. Wellborn Band Boosters, 1978-83, Wellborn Athletic Assn., 1970-88; dir. Boys Club Anniston, Inc., 1972, Anniston Football for Youth, 1975; bd. dirs. United Way of Calhoun County, mem. allocations com., 1985-86, mem. govt. relations com. Ala. Nat. Secs. Assn. scholar, 1963. Mem. Am. Soc. Personnel Adminstrs. (v.p. 1981-82), Internat. Mgmt. Assn. (sec. 1982-83, 1st v.p. 1985-86, sr. v.p. 1986-87, pres. 1987-88), Nat. Secs. Assn. (pres. 1975-76, Sec. of Yr. 1976, 68), Anniston Area C. of C. Episcopalian. Home: 4212 Brian Dr Anniston AL 36201 Office: Super Valu Stores Inc Roberts Dr Industrial Park Anniston AL 36202

WILSON, FRANCES HELEN, occupational therapist; b. Pitts., Oct. 17, 1929; d. J. Vernon and Margaret Hassler (Prugh) Wilson; B.A., Conn. Coll., 1951; advanced standing certificate Columbia Sch. Occupational Therapy, 1953. Therapist, Washington County Soc. Crippled Children and Adults, Washington, Pa., 1953-54; staff therapist Oakland VA Hosp., U. Pitts., 1955-66; supr. Occupational Therapy Clinic, Aspinwall VA Hosp., Pitts., 1966-74, 81-85; supr. Occupational Therapy Clinic, Oakland VA Hosp., Pitts., 1974-80. Active Jr. League Pitts., Inc. Mem. Western Pa. (treas. 1967-69), Am. occupational therapy assns., Presbyterian Univ. Hosp. Pitts. Vol. Assn., 1986—. Republican. Presbyterian. Clubs: Conn. Coll. (treas. 1971—), Twentieth Century (Pitts.). Home: 14 Devon Ln Ben Avon Heights Pittsburgh PA 15202

WILSON, JACKIE LYNN, educator; b. Houston, Sept. 22, 1933; d. John and Elton Jean (Spivey) Harris; B.A., Adelphi U., 1971; M.S., L.I. U., 1974; D.P.A., U. Colo., 1984; children—Robert, Patrick, Gregory. Detective, policewoman Nassau County (N.Y.) Police Dept., 1968-76; asst. prof. criminal justice L.I. U., 1973-76; asso. prof., chmn. dept. criminal justice Met. State Coll., Denver, 1976-85, prof. criminal justice and criminology, 1985—. Served with USAF, 1952-57. Mem. Internat. Assn. Black Women for Criminal Justice (pres.), Am. Criminal Justice Assn., Am. Assn. Criminology, Colo. Prison Assn. (exec. bd.), Colo. Assn. Probation Ofcls. (exec. bd.), Colo. Law Enforcement Officers Assn. (exec. bd.), Delta Sigma Theta, Delta Theta Kappa. Home: 255 Holly St Denver CO 80220 Office: 1000 11th St Denver CO 80204

WILSON, JACQUELINE ETHERIDGE, religious organization executive; b. Washington, Dec. 16, 1937; d. Robert B. and Bessie Lee (Dixon) Etheridge; m. John H. Wilson, Jr., Mar. 2, 1957; children—Margaret Cecelia, John H., Susan Elizabeth, Jacqueline Marie. A.B. in Elem. Edn., Cath. U. Am., 1966; M.Ed. in Adminstrn. and Supervision, Howard U., 1980. Typist law office, 1954-56; clk.-typist U.S. Army Corr. Unit, Pentagon, Washington, 1955; elem. sch. tchr. D.C. Pub. Schs., 1966-79; exec. dir. Office of Black Catholics, Archdiocese of Washington, 1979—; math. resource tchr. Benning Sch., 1966-69; mem. textbook evaluation com. D.C. Pub. Schs., 1971-73, cons. career devel. ctr., 1977-78; lectr. Washington Theol. Union, 1983, Office of Social Devel., 1982, Trinity Coll., 1983-84, Josephite Sem., Washington, 1981; cons. Black Cath. History Research Project, 1983—. Catechist, St. Gabriel Ch., 1963-81, charter mem., pres. parish council, 1971-77; master catechist, cons. Office of Religious Edn., 1981—; charter mem., pres., bd. dirs. Secretariat for Black Catholics, 1974-78; team mem. IMPAC Teen Retreats, 1976-79; mem. com. Africa and diaspora St. Augustine Ch., Washington, 1981—; mem. planning com. March on Washington, 1983; supporter Mt. Carmel Shelter for Homeless Women, 1982—; mem. children's programming adv. com. Sta. WDCA, 1984—; mem. Ctr. for Life Bd. Trustees, Providence Hosp. Editor Black Cath. News, 1979—. Recipient grants and awards D.C. Community Humanities Council, Archdiocese of Washington, Am. Bd. Cath. Missions. Mem. Assn. Supervision and Curriculum Devel., Nat. Black Child Devel. Inst., Nat. Urban League, NAACP, Nat. Assn. Black Cath. Adminstrs. (area coordinator 1977-79, 83—). Democrat. Home: 4342 G St SE Washington DC 20019 *

WILSON, JANE FARISS, girls organization executive; b. Adamsville, Tenn., Mar. 6, 1928; d. Hugh David and Myrtle (Griffin) Fariss; A.A., Sullins Coll., 1947; B.A., U. Tenn., Chattanooga, 1949; postgrad. Scarrit Coll., 1973, Vanderbilt U. Grad. Sch. Mgmt., 1975, U. Chgo, 1977, N.Y.U., 1978, Harvard U. Bus. Sch., 1980, IBM Community Exec. Program; div.; children—David Lamar, Deborah Jane. Field dir., supr. Moccasin Bend council Girl Scouts U.S.A., Chattanooga, 1965-72, field exec. Cumberland Valley council, Nashville, 1972-76, exec. dir. Dogwood Trails council, Springfield, Mo., 1976-80, counselor Project Overview, Chattanooga, 1981, interim exec. dir. Flint River council, Albany, Ga., Pioneer Valley council, Springfield, Mass., Green Hills council, Freeport, Ill., Maumee Valley council, Toledo, Indiana Lakes council, Elkhart, Ind., 1982-85; cons. in field; ch. sch. and religious edn. trainer. Mem. Springfield Community Planning Council, 1977-80. Mem. Adminstrv. Mgmt. Soc., Assn. Girl Scout Exec. Staff, Am. Guild Organists, Fellowship United Meths. in Music Worship and Other Arts, Bus.and Profl. Women, C. of C., AAUW, Sigma Alpha Iota. Clubs: Zonta, Quota. Home and Office: PO Box 94 Osage Beach MO 65065

WILSON, JANET SUE, travel company executive; b. Clarksburg, W.Va., Oct. 28, 1934; d. Glenn Everett and Edna Marie Shaver; m. Alwin D. Wilson, Sept. 21, 1957 (div. Aug. 1959); 1 child, Virginia Marie. Student Davis & Elkins Coll., 1952-54, U. S. Fla., 1981. Travel mgr. Central W.Va. Auto Club, Clarksburg, 1954-57, Peninsula Motor Club, Sarasota, Fla., 1958-63; travel dir. Boyce Travel Agy., Sarasota, 1963-72; pres. Janet Wilson Travel Inc., Sarasota, 1972—; sec. First Step of Sarasota, 1978-79, pres., 1981-85; mem. nominating com. Southeast Fla. Am. Soc. Travel Agts., 1988—. Chmn. Com. for an Elected Sheriff, Sarasota, 1985; bd. dirs. Crimewatch, Sarasota, 1985—; instr. Sarasota Voct. Sch. for Literacy Vols. of Am.; bd. dirs. Floyd Manor Retirement Ctr., Sarasota, Suncoast Travel Assn.; mem. Dem. exec. com. Recipient various awards from airlines and transp. cos. Mem. Internat. Platform Assn., Am. Soc. Travel Agts. (mem. nominating com. North Cen. Fla. chpt, Crest award 1983), Phi Mu. Democrat. Presbyterian. Club: Altrusa (Sarasota) (treas. 1980-81). Avocations: needlepoint, professional sports, books. Home: 6449 Kahana Way Sarasota FL 34231 Office: 2136 Gulf Gate Dr Sarasota FL 33581

WILSON, JANICE DARLENE, computer programmer analyst; b. Audubon, N.J., May 18, 1955; d. Ernest George and Dorothy Antoinette (Miller) Wilson Farrow. BA, Am. U., 1977; MPA, Temple U., 1985. Personnel support specialist Fidelity Bank, Phila., 1981-83, programmer, 1983-86, programmer analyst, 1986-87, sr. programmer analyst, 1987—. Vol. advisor, tutor Library Vols. Am., Camden, N.J., 1985—; supporter Amnesty Internat., Washington, 1987—. Recipient Service award Camden County 4-H, 1986. Mem. Black Data Processing Profls. Phila., Phila. Writers. Democrat. Episcopalian.

WILSON, JANIS KAY, promotion director; b. Anamosa, Iowa, Dec. 28, 1939; d. Clyde S. and Irma L. Wilson. B.F.A., Drake U., 1962. Copywriter, Chase Manhattan Bank, N.Y.C., 1962-66; presentation mgr. Newspaper Advt. Bur., N.Y.C., 1966-71; mktg./promotion mgr. Metromedia, N.Y.C., 1971-74; sr. promotion writer N.Y. Times, 1974-78; dir. mktg. services Crain Communications, N.Y.C., 1978-83; promotion dir., Standard Rate & Data Service div. MacMillan, Wilmette, Ill., 1984-88, circulation dir., 1988—. Mem. Women's Design Group, Mag. Pubs. Assn., Internat. Newspaper Advt. and Mktg. Execs., Internat. Newspaper Pubs. Assn., Assn. Bus. Publs. Republican. Roman Catholic. Home: 927 Suffolk Ct Libertyville IL 60048 Office: Standard Rate & Data Service 3002 Glenview Rd Wilmette IL 60091

WILSON, JEAN MARIE HALEY, civic worker; b. Dallas, Oct. 16, 1921; d. William Eldred and Helen Marie (Littlepage) Haley; B.A., So. Meth. U., 1943; m. Edward Lewis Wilson, Jr., Mar. 19, 1943; children—Edward Lewis III, William Haley, Sarah. Bd. dirs. Dallas Symphony Orch. League, 1963—, sec., 1964-68, 1st v.p., 1968-72, vice-chmn. spl. projects, 1977—, rec. sec., 1984-85, 7th v.p., 1985-86, trustee, 1976—, showhouse chmn., 1987, corresponding sec., 1987-88; v.p. activities Dallas Civic Music Assn., 1986—; precinct chmn. Democratic Party, 1952-62; mem. Dallas County Dem. Exec. Com., 1952-62; bd. dirs. TACA (Com. for Fund Raising of the Arts), 1975—; mem. Southwestern hospitality bd. Met. Opera; charter mem., bd. dirs., North Tex. Herb Club, 1974-78. Mem. Women in Communications, Am. Symphony Orch. Leagues, Herb Soc. Am. (life), Am. Hort. Soc., Pewter Collectors Club Am., Internat. Platform Assn., Le Cercle Francaise of Dallas (hon. chmn. 1985—), Kappa Alpha Theta. Methodist. Home: 3501 Lexington Ave Dallas TX 75205 Office: 2909 Maple Ave Dallas TX 75201

WILSON, JEAN SPANN, real estate executive; b. Murray, Ky., Dec. 29, 1929; s. Cross and Gladys (Miller) Spann; m. Beck B. Wilson, May 26, 1969; m. James F. Williams Jr., Feb. 12, 1949 (dec. 1968); children: James F. III, Johnny W. Student, Murray (Ky.) State Coll. Pvt. practice land developer 1969-79; broker Lake Barkley Realty, Cadiz, Ky., 1979—; bd. dirs. Anderson Shores Corp., Murray, Spann Enterprises, Murray, Pennyrile Bd. Realtors, Princeton, Ky. Exec. com. Ky. Dem., 1987, 1988. Mem. Trigg County C. of C., Am. Assn. Ret. Persons (legis. com. Ky. chpt.). Democrat. Baptist. Home: 104 Canton Blue Springs Rd Cadiz KY 42211 Office: Lake Barkley Realty Main St Cadiz KY 42211

WILSON, JENNIFER LEE, computer programmer; b. Madison, Wis., Apr. 29, 1963; d. John Randall and Susannah Brent (Trimble) W. BS in Math, BS in Computer Sci., Pa. State U., 1985. Computer programmer Pa. Transp. Inst., University Park, 1983-84; computer programmer IBM Corp., Raleigh, N.C., 1983; computer programmer IBM Corp., Boca Raton, Fla., 1984-85, sr. assoc. programer, 1985—. Mem. Assn. Computing Machinery, Nat. Assn. Female Execs., Mortar Bd., Delta Upsilon Soc.

WILSON, JILL BERMAN, management consultant; b. Washington, Nov. 11, 1952; d. William Howard Berman and Jean Burton (Hirsh) Weinberg; m. William D. Wilson, Sept. 18, 1974 (div. Nov. 1978); m. Richard L. Levy, May 25, 1986; children: Scott H., Brenda A. BA in Polit. Sci., George Washington U., 1974; MPA, Am. U., 1978. Adminstrv. officer Inst. for Advanced Studies in Justice, Washington, 1976-78; programs and planning adminstr. Nat. Ctr. for State Courts, Williamsburg, Va., 1978-80; dir. research Nat. Shorthand Reporters Assn., Vienna, Va., 1980-85; pres. Wilson, Levy & Assocs., Plainview, N.Y., 1985—; cons. U.S. Agy. for Internat. Devel., Kingston, Jamaica, 1986—, Nat. Jud. Coll., Reno, Nev., 1981-85. Editor: (book) Introduction to Computer Transcription, 1983; contbr. over 30 articles to profl. jours. Mem. Md. Com. for Children, Balt., 1983-86, L.I. Blood Donor Program, Mineola, N.Y., 1987; bd. dirs. Plainview Library Assn., 1987. Mem. ABA, Nat. Shorthand Reporters Assn., Nat. Assn. Female Execs., Pi Alpha Alpha. Democrat. Jewish.

WILSON, JOAN EMILY, nursing education administrator; b. Plainfield, N.J., May 15, 1937; d. Walter William and Julia (Leahy) W.; m. Charles Morris, Apr. 26, 1968 (dec. Apr. 1977); m. James Wright, Feb. 14, 1981 (dec. Aug. 1981). Diploma, Jersey City Med. Ctr., 1958; BS in Nursing, Ohio Sate U., 1965, M in Nursing, 1966. Staff nurse Overlook Hosp., Summit, N.Y., 1958-63, Dr.'s Hosp., Columbus, Ohio, 1963-64; instr. U. Wash., Seattle, 1966-68, Everett (Wash.) Community Coll., 1968-72; dir. nursing program Tacoma Community Coll., 1972—; mem. Wash. State Bd. Nursing, 1982-87. Trustee Lakewood Hosp., Tacoma, 1986—. Mem. Am. Nurses Assn., Nat. League for Nursing, Am. Fedn. Tchrs., Sigma Theta Tau. Home: 6018 Hillcrest Dr SW Tacoma WA 98499

WILSON, JUDY KATRINA, mental health facility administrator, psychotherapist, researcher; b. Peru, Ind., Feb. 16, 1944; d. Wayne Leroy and Eleanor (McLaughlin) W.; m. James M. Shook, Dec. 30, 1972. BS, Fla. Atlantic U., 1967; MS, Fla. State U., 1975; degree in Edn. Specialist, U. Fla., 1975, PhD, 1985. Mental health counselor Vocat. Rehab., Panama City, Fla., 1968-70; supr., psychotherapist Sabal Palm Treatment Facility, West Palm Beach, Fla., 1970-72; supr., team leader Project CREST, Gainesville, Fla., 1973-76; exec. dir. Mental Health Assn., Ocala, Fla., 1976-78, Rape Crisis/Spouse Abuse Ctr., Ocala, 1978—; pvt. practice in field. Campaign mgr. several polit. candidates, Fla. Named Humanitarian of Yr., Ocala Jaycees, 1981. Mem. Am. Assn. for Counseling and Devel., Am. Mental Health Counselors Assn., Fla. Victim Witness Network, Ocala Bus. Women's Network. Democrat. Methodist. Lodges: Soroptimist (Woman Helping Women award 1983, 84, Sertoma (Service to Mankind award 1983). Home: 721 NE Third St Ocala FL 32670 Office: Creative Services Inc PO Box 2193 Ocala FL 32678

WILSON, KAREN ELAINE, trader; b. Charleston, S.C., June 24, 1964; d. Richard James and Marcia (Burton) W. BS in Applied Math., Indsl. Mgmt. with honors, Carnegie-Mellon U., 1986. Sales asst. IBM Mktg. div., Pitts., 1985; sales, trading Shearson Lehman Bros. Capital Markets, N.Y.C., 1986—. Mem. Young Reps., Vienna, Va. Mem. Delta Delta Delta (pres. 1985-86). Episcopal. Home: 205 E 95th St #15H New York NY 10128 Office: Shearson Lehman Bros World Fin Ctr 200 Vessey St New York NY 10007

WILSON, KAREN MIRTH MCKEE, naval officer; b. Hamdem, Conn., Apr. 13, 1945; d. Benjamin Franklin Moore and Dorothy Martha (Schumacher) Moore Mach-Brandt; AS in Acctg. and Bus. Mgmt., Southwestern Coll., Chula Vista, Calif., 1973; div.; 1 dau., Billie Jo. Enlisted in U.S. Navy, 1963, commd. chief warrant officer, 1979; personnel officer personnel support activity Naval Submarine Base, Groton, Conn., 1979-82; personnel officer USS Fulton, 1982-84; asst. dept. dir. MCA liaison/system mgmt. Enlisted Personnel Mgmt. Center, New Orleans, 1984-86, dir. Pacific fleet surface readiness, 1986-88, personnel officer Naval Oceanographic Office, Bay St. Louis, 1988—. Zone adminstr. Parents Without Ptnrs. Mem. Nat. Assn. Female Execs., Fleet Res. Assn. Republican. Presbyterian. Home: 208 Berry Wood Ct Slidell LA 70461 Office: Naval Oceanographic Office NSTL Bay Saint Louis MS 39522-5001

WILSON, KATHERINE SCHMITKONS, biologist; b. Lorain, Ohio, Jan. 22, 1913; d. H. William and Katherine (Bauman) Schmitkons; AB, Oberlin Coll., 1933; MS, Northwestern U., 1935; PhD, Yale U., 1944; m. George E. Woodin, Nov. 23, 1961. Instr. biology Muskingum Coll., New Concord, Ohio, 1935-40; bot. researcher Yale U., 1941-44, Sessel fellow in biology, 1948-49, instr. biology, 1953-56; biologist div. research grants NIH, Bethesda, Md., 1956-58, scientist adminstr. genetics, 1958-77; ret., 1977; cons., lectr. genetics, 1978—. Recipient High Quality Service award HEW, NIH, 1966. Fellow AAAS, N.Y. Acad. Sci.; mem. Am. Soc. Human Genetics (spl. citation 1973), Genetics Soc. Am. (Service citation 1979), Environ. Mutagen Soc., Am. Inst. Biol. Scis., Am. Genetic Assn., Sigma Xi. Congregationalist. Club: PEO. Author: Botany—Principles and Problems, 6th ed., 1963; contbr. articles to profl. jours. Home: 77 235 Indiana Ave Palm Desert CA 92260

WILSON, KATHRYN ELIZABETH, ticket office manager, consultant; b. Charleston, W.Va., Jan. 23, 1956; d. James Hugh and E. Jeanelle (Hobby) McKinnon; m. Jerry L. Wilson Jr., Nov. 5, 1983. BBA, Memphis State U., 1978. Adminstrv. asst. Memphis State U. Religious Affairs, 1977-78; operator Memphis State U. Word Processing, 1978-79; asst. mgr. Zondervan Family Bookstore, Memphis, 1980; booking agt. Andrus, Blackwood & Co., Memphis, 1980-82; ops. mgr. Victory Communications Sta. WMSO-Radio, Collierville, Tenn., 1982-83; mktg. v.p., mktg. support Encore Prodns., Inc., Oklahoma City, 1983-86; ticket office mgr. Mabee Ctr., Tulsa, 1986-88; box office mgr. Pub. Events Box Office, Okla. City, 1988—; cons. KEM Prodns., Oklahoma City, 1978—, Spring House Assn., Alexandria, Ind., 1980—, Encore Prodns., Inc., Oklahoma City, 1983—, Encore Homes, 1986—. Mem. Box Office Mgrs. Internat. Republican. Baptist. Lodge: Woodmen of World (watchman 1982-83). Home: 6608 Saddleback Dr Oklahoma City OK 73150 Office: Pub Events Box Office One Myriad Gardens Oklahoma City OK 73102

WILSON, LESLIE ANN, labor union executive; b. Malvern, Ark., June 28, 1941; d. Lester Earl and Dovie Inez (Rood) W.; m. Kenneth Ray Mullins, May 31, 1968 (div. May 1972). BBA, Eastern Mich. State U., 1968; student, Washtenaw Community Coll., 1986. Ticket agt. North Cen. Airlines, Ypsilanti, Mich., 1961-67; automobile inspector Ford Motor Co., Ypsilanti, 1967—; pres. Huron Valley Promotions, Canton, Mich., 1981—. Named Best Actress Dale Carnegie Inst., 1982. Mem. UAW (trustee local #898 1978-81, v.p. 1981—), Nat. Assn. Female Execs., Nat. Assn. Talent Dirs., Country Music Assn., Internat. Country Music Buyers Assn., Aircraft Owners and Pilots Assn. Democrat. Seventh Day Adventist. Club: Ann Arbor (Mich.) Flyers. Lodges: Order of Eastern Star, Shriners. Office: Huron Valley Promotions Inc PO Box 87007 Canton MI 48187

WILSON, LINDA JOAN, beverage company executive; b. Morristown, N.J., May 8, 1958; d. Walter Richard and Elvira (Schroeder) Schleicher; m. David Paul Wilson, July 18, 1981; 1 child, Jeffrey Paul. BS in Chem. Engring., U. Ill., 1979; MBA, Lehigh U., 1984. Engr. Air Products & Chems., Inc., Allentown, Pa., 1979-81; project engr. Air Products & Chems., Inc., Allentown, 1981-83, sr. project engr., 1983-84, account mgr., 1984-86; material planner Pepsico-Pepsi Bottling Group, Purchase, N.Y., 1986-87; material planning mgr. Pepsico-Pepsi Bottling Group, Somers, N.Y., 1987-88; bus. mgr. devel. and procurement Pepsi Cola Co., Somers, 1988—; cons. Lotepro Corp., Valhalla, N.Y., 1986. Active St. James Episcopal Ch., Danbury, Conn., 1986—. Recipient Edison Jr. High PTA Scholarship, Wheaton, Ill., 1975. Mem. Nat. Assn. Female Execs., Alpha Xi Delta (pres. 1978). Republican. Episcopal. Club: Jubilation Ski (Allentown) (bd. dirs. 1983-86). Home: 8 Ralto Ct Danbury CT 06811

WILSON, MARGARET JEAN, psychologist; b. Williamston, S.C., May 25, 1929; d. John Wesley and Clara Louise (Knight) W. BA in Psychology, Furman U., 1950; MS in Sch. Psychology, Winthrop Coll., 1974. cert. tchr. psychology, typing, shorthand, elem. edn., elem. guidance counselor. Legal sec. Williams & Henry, Attys., Greenville, S.C., 1950-52; sec. Atlantic Coast Line R.R., Greenville, S.C., 1952-60; exec. sec. to Woodside Mills, v.p., Greenville, S.C., 1960-61; sec., adminstrv. asst. Illinois Cen. R.R., Greenville, S.C., 1961-68; tchr. elem. schs. Greenville, S.C., 1968-73; sch. psychologist Greenville County Schs., 1974—. Mem. Nat. Assn. Female Execs., Nat. Assn. Sch. Psychologists, S.C. Assn. Sch. Psychologists (sec., bd. dirs. 1981-83, cert. for outstanding work 1983), Piedmont Assn. School Psychologists (treas. 1979-81). Southern Baptist. Clubs: Christian Bus., Profl. Women's. Home: 16 S Florida Ave Greenville SC 29611 Office: Greenville County Schs 301 Camperdown Way PO Box 2848 Greenville SC 29602

WILSON, MARGARET SULLIVAN, college dean; b. Norwich, Conn., Mar. 21, 1924; d. John Joseph and Margaret Ellen (Connelly) Sullivan; B.S., Eastern Conn. State U., 1944; M.A., U. Conn., 1949; m. William Robert Wilson, July 20, 1950 (dec.); children—Margaret Ellen, William Robert. Reading cons. Greenwich (Conn.) Pub. Schs., 1948-50; asst. prof. early childhood, chmn. dept. early childhood Eastern Conn. State U., Willimantic, 1967-77, exec. asst. to pres., 1977-78, v.p. adminstrv. affairs, 1978-80, exec. dean, 1980—; commr. Nat. Connm. Prevention Infant Mortality; mem. Norwich Ecox. Devel. Commn.; coordinator Ecumenical Action; dir. Rose City Community Lad Trust Housing; del. White House Conf. on Children, 1970, 80; cons. Windham-Willimantic Child Care, 1971—; corporator Chelsea Groton Savs. Bank, Norwich, Conn. Mem. Conn. Mental Health Bd., 1979-83; mem. adv. bd. Norwich Hosp.; chmn. rev. com. Conn. Health Coordinating Council; mem. Eastern Regional Mental Health Bd., 1976-83, chmn., 1979-81; mem. Norwich Bd. Edn., 1954-69, 80-83, Conn. Democratic Cental Com., 1966-82, Dem. Town Com., 1964-82; chmn. Blue Ribbon Commn. To Establish Goals for U. Conn. Health Ctr., 1975-76. mem. vestry Ch. of Resurrection, Episcopal ch., Norwich; mem. policy adv. com. Conn. Dept. Human Services. Named Citizen of Yr., C. of C., 1970; recipient Disting. Service award Eastern Conn. State U., 1972, Mental Health Bell award Conn. Mental Health Assn., 1972, Valient Women award Council Ch. Women, 1976, Woman of Yr. award Bus. and Profl. Women, 1978, Jefferson award Inst. Pub. Service, 1982. Mem. Norwich Area C. of C. (dir. 1979-81), Greater Willimantic C. of C. (edn. com.), United Ch. Women Conn. (bd. dirs.) AAUW (chair legis. com.). Democrat. Home: 27 Canterbury Turnpike Norwich CT 06360 Office: 83 Windham St Willimantic CT 06226

WILSON, MARGERY LAUREN, editor, writer; b. Oxnard, Calif., Jan. 12, 1951; d. Loren George and Mary Brosius (Samuelson) Wilson; m. David Robert Gommel, Oct. 25, 1970 (div. 1979); 1 dau., Johanna Christina; m. Edward Joseph Kochanowski, Feb. 14, 1988. Student Santa Barbara City Coll., 1968-70, U. Mass., 1983-87. Columnist, Santa Barbara News-Press (Calif.), 1964-65; writer, abstractor Leisure Abstracts and Horseman's Abstracts, Goleta, Calif., 1970-72; editor Winthrop Pubs., Cambridge, Mass., 1979-81; freelance writer, 1964—; with pub. relations dept. MIT, 1987; co-founder, mng. editor Orthodox People Mag., Boston, 1980-84; exec. v.p. Internat. Orthodox Christian Writer's Guild, Cumberland, R.I., 1980-84; lit. cons. Inkfellows, Providence, Cumberland, 1981—. Author: Burgesses of Bucks County, 1983, others; editor Sex Roles and Human Behavior (K.F. Schaffer), 1981. Bd. dirs. youth com. Cambridge YWCA, 1983-84, mem. adv. council afterschool activities, 1983-84. Mem. New Eng. Historic Genealogy Soc., Bucks County Hist. Soc., Internat. Platform Assn., Nat. Assn. to Aid Fat Ams., Girl Scouts U.S.A. Democrat. Eastern Orthodox. Home: 71 Fifth St #1 Cambridge MA 02141 Office: Mass Inst Tech 77 Massachusetts Ave Room 4-237 Cambridge MA 02139

WILSON, MARILY SHARRONN, accountant; b. Seattle, May 27, 1942; d. Jack Edward Murphy and Cora Phyllis Toby; m. Ronald Duncan Nelson, May 5, 1961 (dec. 1966); children: Sharon Louise, Zeatra Corinne, Ronald Stanley; m. Lawrence William Wilson, Feb. 14, 1981. BA, Griffin Murphy

Bus. Sch., 1968. Audit clk. Pay'n' Save Corp., Seattle, 1967; bookkeeper Chromium Co. Inc., Seattle, 1967-70, Sunderland's Wholesale Jewelry, Seattle, 1970-73; staff acct. Helwig, Bulter and Assocs., CPAs, Seattle, 1973-78, Otto R. Enger, Seattle, 1978-85; acct., adminstrv. asst. Majiq, Inc., Redmond, Wash., 1985—; acct., owner Paradise Book-keeping and Tax Service, Mt. Vernon, Wash., 1985—. Home: 1869 Peter Burns Rd Mount Vernon WA 98273 Office: Majiq Inc 8707 148th Ave NE Redmond WA 98052

WILSON, MARJORIE PRICE, physician, university dean; b. Pitts., Sept. 25, 1924; m. Lynn Minford Wilson, Sept. 15, 1951; children: Lynn Deyo, Liza Price. Student, Bryn Mawr Coll., 1942-45; M.D., U. Pitts., 1949. Intern U. Pitts. Med. Center Hosps., 1949-50; resident Children's Hosp. U. Pitts., 1950-51, Jackson Meml. Hosp., U. Miami Sch. Medicine, 1954-56; chief residency and internship div. edn. service Office of Research and Edn., VA, Washington, 1956; chief profl. tng. div. Office of Research and Edn., VA, 1956-60, asst. dir. edn. service, 1960; chief tng. br. Nat. Inst. Arthritis and Metabolic Disease, NIH, 1960-63; asst. to assoc. dir. for tng. Office of Dir. NIH, 1963-64; asso. dir. extramural programs Nat. Library Medicine, 1964-67; asso. dir. program devel. OPPD NIH, Bethesda, Md., 1967-69; asst. dir. program planning and evaluation NIH, 1969-70; dir. dept. instl. devel. Assn. Am. Med. Colls., Washington, 1970-81; sr. assoc. dean U. Md. Sch. Medicine, Balt., 1981-86; vice dean U. Md. Sch. Medicine, 1986-88; pres. Edl. Commn. Fgn. Med. Grads., Phila., 1988—; mem. Inst. Medicine, Nat. Acad. Scis., 1974—; bd. visitors U. Pitts. Sch. Medicine, 1974—; mem.-at-large Nat. Bd. Med. Examiners; mem. adv. com. Md. Cancer Registry; mem. Gov.'s Commn. on Toxic Substances; mem. council of sect. on med. schs. AMA, 1987-88. Contbr. articles to profl. jours. Mem. adv. bd. Robert Wood Johnson Health Policy Fellowships, 1975-87; trustee Analytic Services, Inc., Falls Church, Va., 1976—. Fellow Am. Coll. Physician Execs., AAAS; mem. Assn. Am. Med. Colls., Am. Fedn. Clin. Research, IEEE. Office: Edl Commn Fgn Med Grads 3624 Market St Philadelphia PA 19104-2685

WILSON, MARY EVE, youth librarian, storyteller; b. Nashville, May 23, 1943; d. Alwin Curtis and Mary Usula (Glover) Hutcherson; B.S., Miss. State Coll. for Women, 1965; M.L.S., Vanderbilt U., 1968. Librarian, George Washington Carver High Sch., Newport News, Va., 1968-69; children's, young adult librarian Finkelstein Meml. Library, Spring Valley, N.Y., 1970-77; young adult services specialist Tampa-Hills County Pub. Library System, Tampa, Fla., 1977-82; asst. children's coordinator Sno-Isle Regional Library System, Marysville, Wash., 1985—; adj. prof. Grad. Sch. Library Sci., Fla. State U., 1981. Contbr. articles to profl. jours. Aide to Fla. state senator Betty Castor, 1982-84; vis. prof. Peabody Coll., Vanderbilt U. Mem. Hills County Women's Polit. Caucus, 1980; del. Fla. Conf. on Children and Youth, 1981; bd. dirs. Northside Community Mental Health Complex, Tampa, 1981-84; mem. Fla. Alliance for Responsible Adolescent Parenting, 1978-82. Recipient vol. service award Hills County Children's Services, 1981. Mem. ALA (pres. young adult services div. 1981-82). Democrat. Episcopalian. Office: Sno-Isle Regional Library System PO Box 148 Marysville WA 98270

WILSON, MARY MADGELINE, fashion designer; b. Jamaica, N.Y., Jan. 28, 1956; d. Elbert and Mary Madgeline (Williams) W. Student, CUNY, 1974-75; BFA, Parsons Sch. of Design, N.Y.C., 1978. Asst. designer Girl-Town div. of Genesco, N.Y.C., 1978; men's designer, stylist Coronet Casuals Corp., N.Y.C., 1978-81; designer boyswear Garan, Inc., N.Y.C., 1981-82; head designer youthwear Am. Argo Corp., N.Y.C., 1982—. Mem. The Fashion Soc. (newsletter editor 1986—). Home: 107-03 157th St Jamaica NY 11433 Office: Am Argo Corp 350 Fifth Ave Rm 1400 New York NY 10118

WILSON, MARY RUTH, sales and retail executive, fashion buyer, counselor; b. Washington, May 25, 1935; d. Eugene Marshall and Mary Virginia (Morris) Grinder; m. Willis C. Briggs, June 25, 1955 (div. 1962); 1 child, Scott Dwight; m. Theodore R. Wilson, May 26, 1966 (div. 1980). Student, Principia Coll., 1954-55. Supr. sales Hoover Co., North Canton, Ohio, 1970-72; sales mgr. Gen. Binding Corp., Northbrook, Ill., 1972-77; pres. Custom Products, Inc., Oxon Hill, Md., 1977-83; v.p. Tetra Designs, Inc., Washington, 1983—; sales and pub. relations rep. Banner Glass Inc., Silver Spring, Md., 1984-86; cons., Washington, 1985—. Fin. negotiator: (film) Jules Verne, 1985—. Membership chmn. Coalition New Americans, Washington, 1984, 85; pub. relations rep., liaison Arlington County Condo Assn., The Prospect House, Arlington, Va., 1985, communications and pub. relations rep. Prospect House, 1985; active Beethoven Soc., Washington, Nat. Lyric Opera Soc., Washington. Recipient Golden Triangle sales award Hoover Co., 1971, 72 (1st woman supr.), Donahue award (sales supr. of yr.), Gen. Binding Corp., 1974. Mem. Ins. Women of Montgomery and Prince George's County, Md. (bd. 1984-85, sec. 1986-87), Nat. Assn. Ins. Women, Nat. Press Club, Arlington C. of C., Ind. Ins. Agts. No. Va., Washington and No. Va. Claims Assns., Internat. Platform Assn., Md. Glass Assn. Avocations: writing; theater; importing; artistic endeavors; travel. Home: 808 1200 N Nash St Arlington VA 22209 Office: Tetra Designs Inc The Pavilion at Old Post Office 1100 Pennsylvania Ave NW Washington DC 20004

WILSON, MAUREEN COLETTE, human resources executive; b. Grosse Pointe, Mich., Sept. 16, 1959; d. John Richard and Gertrude (Martz) W. BA in Communications and Psychology, U. Mich., 1981; M in Mgmt., Northwestern U., 1987. Personnel rep. John Nuveen and Co., Inc., Chgo., 1982-85; mgr. human resources Nat. Assn. Realtors, Chgo., 1985—. James B. Angell scholar U. Mich., 1979-80. Mem. Am. Soc. Personnel Adminstrs., Human Resources Mgmt. Assn. Chgo., Internat. Assn. Personnel Women, Phi Beta Kappa, Kappa Tau Alpha. Roman Catholic. Club: U. Mich. Alumni. Home: 21 W Goethe Apt 16 B Chicago IL 60610 Office: Nat Assn Realtors 430 N Michigan Ave Chicago IL 60611

WILSON, MELANIE ANN, clinical psychologist; b. Greenville, Miss., July 13, 1952; d. Charles Marshall and Beverly Ann (Plunkett) W. BA, Lebanon Valley Coll., 1974; MS, Millersville U., 1975; D of Clin. Psychology, Hahnemann U., 1987. Lic. psychologist; cert. sch. psychologist. Sch. psychologist Berks County Intermediate Unit, Reading, Pa., 1976-82; cons. psychologist Family Service of Phila., 1984—; pvt. practice clin. psychology Phila., 1984—; mem. clin. psychology staff Bryn Mawr (Pa.) Hosp. Youth and Family Ctr., 1987—; cons. psychologist Bryn Mawr Hosp. Inpatient Psychiat. Unit, 1987—; cons. psychologist Grad. Hosp. Health and Fitness Ctr., Phila., 1988—. John Frederick Steinman fellow, Lancaster, Pa., 1983-84. Mem. Am. Psychol. Assn. (assoc.), Pa. Psychol. Assn., Phila. Soc. Psychoanalytic Psychology. Democrat. Presbyterian. Home: 1334 Montgomery Ave H-4 Narberth PA 19072 Office: Bryn Mawr Hosp Youth Family Ctr Bryn Mawr PA 19010

WILSON, MOLLIE CROSS HALEY, investment counselor; b. Charlotte, N.C., May 5, 1942; d. Shaffer and Mollie Flournoy (Cross) Haley; B.S. with honors in Bus. Adminstrn., U. Ark., Fayetteville, 1963, M.B.A., 1972, Ph.D. in Fin., 1979; m. Jack E. Grober. Grad. asst. U. Ark., Fayetteville, 1971-73, instr., 1974-79; assoc. Robert E. Kennedy, Inc., Fayetteville, 1971-85; v.p. investment div. Mchts. Nat. Bank, Ft. Smith, Ark., 1979-83; pres. October Money Mgmt., 1983—; fin. cons. for public cos., Ark. Bd. dirs. Ark. Community Found., 1979-83, Ft. Smith Heritage Found., 1979-83. Chartered fin. planner, 1982. Bd. dirs. Ft. Smith Salvation Army, 1982—, vice chmn., 1986-87, chmn. 1987-88; bd. dirs. Comprehensive Juvenile Services, 1984—. Mem. Inst. Chartered Fin. Planners, Internat. Assn. Registered Fin. Planners, Ark. Soc. Fin. Mgrs. (bd. dirs., 1972—), Dallas Soc. Investment Analysts, Fin. Analysts Fedn., Western Ark. Estate Planning Council, Beta Gamma Sigma. Contbr. articles to publs. Home: PO Box 5096 Fort Smith AR 72903 Office: 2220 S Waldron Rd Fort Smith AR 72903

WILSON, MONICA ANN, infosystems specialist; b. Oakland, Calif., Jan. 23, 1958; d. John D. Howell and Eddie Jo (Johnson) Mack; m. Glen Wilson, Mar. 6, 1982; children: Maurice Dujon, Marvin Glen. Student, Laney Coll., Diablo Valley Coll., Chabot Coll. With EG&G, Inc., San Ramon, Calif., 1980-83, programmer/analyst, 1983-84; lead programmer/analyst Computer Synergy, Oakland, 1984-85, project leader, 1985—. Mem. Digital Equipment Users Group, Am. Mgmt. Assn., Nat. Assn. Female Execs., NAACP, Decus Black Users Group (pres., founder Oakland chpt.). Democrat. Pentecostal. Home: 1131 Santa Lucia Dr Pleasant Hill CA 94523

WILSON, ORINE ARAVE, elementary educator; b. Los Angeles, June 17, 1926; d. Nelson Harris and Elizabeth (Daniels) Arave; m. Robert Davis Wilson, Dec. 25, 1948; children: Richard, Adrian, Blake, Penny, Timothy, Lawrence. BBA magna cum laude, Woodbury Coll., Los Angeles, 1946; BS in Elem. Edn., Lewis-Clark State Coll., 1973; MEd, U. Idaho, 1979. Exec. sec. Northwestern Mut. Life Ins., Seattle, 1950-57; sec. Humanities dept. Lewis-Clark State Coll., 1971-73; tchr. Lewiston (Idaho) Sch. Dist., 1973—. Dist. chmn., leader Camp Fire Girls, Lewiston, 1967-68; hon. life mem., pres. local council, sec. state PTA, 1957-68. Gertrude Mellon Dick scholar, Lewiston-Clark State Coll., 1973; named Distinguished Citizen of Yr., VFW, 1964, Young Woman of Yr., Jay-c-ettes, 1966. Mem. NEA, Idaho Edn. Assn., Lewiston Edn. Assn., Idaho Council Tchrs. English Idaho Council Internat. Reading Assn., Hetama Reading Council, Beta Sigma Phi. Mem. Reorganized Ch. of Jesus Christ of Latter-day Saints. Home: 1007 Burrell Lewiston ID 83501 Office: Centennial Sch 815 Burrell Lewiston ID 83501

WILSON, PATRICIA JANE, educator, librarian, educational and library consultant; b. Jennings, La., May 3, 1946; d. Ralph Harold and Wilda Ruth (Smith) Potter; m. Wendell Merlin Wilson, Aug. 24, 1968. B.S., La. State U., 1967; M.S. U. Houston-Clear Lake, 1979; Ed.D., U. Houston, 1985. Cert. tchr., learning resources specialist (librarian), Tex. Tchr., England AFB (La.) Elem. Sch., 1967-68, Edward White Elem. Sch., Clear Creek Ind. Schs., Seabrook, Tex., 1972-77; librarian C.D. Landolt Elem. Sch., Friendswood, Tex., 1979-81; instr./lectr. children's lit. U. Houston 1983-86; with U. Houston/Clear Lake, 1984-87; cons. Hermann Hosp., Baywood Hosp., 1986-87. Trustee, Freeman Meml. Library, Houston, 1982-87, v.p., 1985-86, pres., 1986-87; mem. Armand Bayou Nature Ctr., Houston, 1980—; bd. dirs. Sta. KUHT-TV, 1984-87. Editor A Rev. Sampler, 1985-86; Author: HAPPENINGS: Developing Successful Programs for School Libraries, 1987; contbg. editor Tex. Library Jour., 1988—; contbr. articles to profl. jours. Mem. ALA, Am. Assn. Sch. Librarians, Internat. Reading Assn., Nat. Council Tchrs. English, (Books for You com. 1985—), Tex. Joint Council Tchrs. English, Antarctican Soc., Kappa Delta Pi, Alpha Delta Kappa, Phi Delta Kappa. Methodist. Club: Lakewood Yacht (Seabrook). Home and Office: 1118 Appleford Dr Seabrook TX 77586

WILSON, PATRICIA POPLAR, electrical manufacturing company executive; b. Chgo., Sept. 20, 1931; d. George and Leona (O'Brien) Poplar; BS U. Wash., 1966, MA 1967, PhD 1980; m. Chester Goodwin Wilson, Jan. 30, 1960; children: Susan Spadafora, Chester Wilson. Instr., U. Wash., Seattle, 1967-74; women's editor Nor'westing Mag., Seattle, 1969—; pres. Wilson & Assos. N.W. Inc., Seattle, 1974—; v.p. N.W. Mfg. & Supply, Inc., 1977-87, pres., 1987—; pres. Trydor Sales Alberta Ltd., Can. Mem. Electric League, N.W. Mfg. & Supply. Episcopalian. Club: Seattle Yacht. Author: Household Equipment, Guide to Surplus Equipment. Contbr. articles to profl. jours. Office: 4045 7th Ave S Seattle WA 98108

WILSON, RAMONA GRAHAM, travel agency executive; b. Rochester, N.Y., Nov. 25, 1952; d. Thomas J. and Marie Patricia (Golisano) Graham; m. David M. Wilson, Aug. 18, 1976 (div.). AAS, Monroe Community Coll., Rochester, N.Y., 1983. Nursing mgr. Genesee Health Services, Rochester, N.Y., 1982-84, Methodist Med. Ctr., Dallas, 1984-86; pres. Travel Cons. Am., Inc., Addison, Tex., 1986—.

WILSON, SANDRA FAY, military officer; b. Durham, N.C., Oct. 27, 1957; d. Frederick Edward and Margaret Louise (Benneham) W. BA, U. N.C., 1980; grad. with distinction, Def. Intelligence Coll., Washington, 1988. Commd. 2d lt. USAF, 1980, advanced through grades to capt., 1984; flight comdr. West Berlin, Fed. Republic Germany, 1981-83; officer instr. San Angelo, Tex., 1983-85; chief of ops. prodn. Osan AFB, Republic of Korea, 1985-86, Alexandria, Va., 1986-87; chief of ops. prodn. Hdqrs. USAF Pentagon, Washington, 1987—. Tutor Higher Achievement Program, Washington, 1987; Big Bros./Big Sisters Am., San Angelo, 1984-85, Washington, 1987-88. Mem. Alpha Kappa Alpha. Home: 2801 Park Ctr Dr #A1005 Alexandria VA 22302

WILSON, SANDRA JEAN, psychological examiner, mental health center administrator; b. Kansas City, Kans., Aug. 31, 1946; d. George W. and Jean Lucy (Danforth) Hurst; m. Jimmy Charles Jones, June 11, 1970 (div. Feb. 1980); 1 child, Jason Clifton; m. Virgil Ray Wilson, June 4, 1982; 1 child, Leah Michell. BS, U. Central Ark., 1968; MA, U. Ark., 1973. Psychologist asst. Ark. Children's Colony, Conway, 1968-72, dir. evaluation, 1972-74; coordinator cons. and edn. Human Services Ctr. West Central Ark., Conway, 1974-76; ctr. coordinator Delta Counseling and Guidance Ctr., Dermott, Ark., 1976-79; dir. Southwestern Ark. Counseling and Mental Health Ctr., De Queen, 1979—; treas. Ark. Bd. Examiners in Psychology, 1976-80. Fellow Ark. Psychol. Assn.; mem. Ark. Sch. Psychology Assn., Ark. Behavior Therapy Assn., Am. Psychol. Assn., Spasmodic Dysphonia Assn. Ark., Am. Assn. Children with Learning Disabilities (pres. chpt.). Democrat. Baptist. Avocations: sewing, gardening, crafts. Home: Rt 1 Box 332-OA De Queen AR 71832 Office: SW Ark Counseling Ctr PO Box 459 De Queen AR 71832

WILSON, SANDRA LANDRY, marketing professional; b. East St. Louis, Ill., Apr. 3, 1947; d. Abbie Anthony and Marie Rita (Alcott) Landry; m. Peter Brian Wilson, June 12, 1971; children: Brian Scott Landry-Wilson, Erin Marie Landry-Wilson. BS, Southern Ill. U., 1969; M in Communication, U. Wis., 1970; M of Mgmt., Northwestern U., 1975. Tchr. Madison (Wis.) Pub. Sch. System, 1970-73; mkt. mgr. Santa Fe Industries, Chgo., 1975-80; cons. Frank Lynn and Assocs./Applied Strategies, Chgo., 1980-85; mkt. planner Chgo. Bd. Options Exchange, Chgo., 1985-86; dir. mktg. Arthur Young Internat., Chgo., 1986—. Contbr. articles to profl. jours. Mem. Am. Mktg. Assn., Am. Mgmt. Assn., Pub. Relations Soc. Am., Northwestern Mgmt. Club. Home: 247 E Chestnut #2401 Chicago IL 60611 Office: Arthur Young Internat 1 IBM Plaza Chicago IL 60611

WILSON, SHARONN, automobile rental service executive; b. Bristol, Conn., Oct. 9, 1951; d. Blakeley and Betty-Claire (Botting) W. BA in Fine Arts, Dickinson Coll., 1973; MLS, SUNY, Albany, 1977. Mgmt. trainee Enterprise Rent-A-Car/Leasing, San Bruno, Calif., 1981; asst. mgr. Enterprise Rent-A-Car/Leasing, Berkeley, Calif., 1982; mgr. Enterprise Rent-A-Car/Leasing, San Leandro, Calif., 1982; mgr. Enterprise Rent-A-Car/Leasing, San Francisco, 1983, asst. area mgr., 1984-85, area mgr., 1985—. Mem. council Silver Bay (N.Y.) Assn., 1978—. Home: 835 Vista Montara Circle Pacifica CA 94044 Office: Enterprise Rent-A-Car/Leasing 1133 Van Ness Ave San Francisco CA 94109

WILSON, SHERRIE DARLENE, mortgage banker; b. Jacksonville, Fla., Dec. 17, 1950; d. Joseph Frank and Marguerite Faye (Ponce) Dietz. Student, Fla. Jr. Coll., U. North Fla. Lic. mortgage banker, Fla. Credit investigator Credit Bur. Jacksonville (Fla.), 1968-70; loan processor Tucker Bros., Inc., Jacksonville, 1970-72, Collateral Investment, Jacksonville, 1972-73; personnel officer Barnett Mortgage Co., Jacksonville, 1973-82, v.p., mgr. loan inventory, 1982—. Bd. dirs. Mental Health Assn. Jacksonville, 1982—; vol. counselor Drug Abuse Program, Jacksonville, 1978-80; cons., women's com. rep. Am. Inst. Banking, 1974-81; adv. Community Bd. Bank, 1978; vol. Spl. Olympics, 1979-82. Mem. Young Mortgage Bankers Assn. (pres. 1978-79), Mortgage Bankers Assn. Fla. (bd. govs. 1985-87), Mortgage Bankers Assn. Jacksonville (pres. 1983-84, regional gov. of state assn. 1983-84), Am. Soc. Personnel Adminstrs. (dir. 1979-81). Democrat. Roman Catholic. Office: Barnett Mortgage Co 17 W Adams St Jacksonville FL 32202

WILSON, SUSAN ELLEN, elementary educator; b. Hartford, Conn., Jan. 30, 1948; d. Henry Tracy and Mary Ellen (Kelsey) Bartlett; m. Dennis Lawrence Wilson, Feb. 18, 1979. BA, St. Joseph Coll., 1970; MS, Cen. Conn. State Coll., 1974. Elem. tchr. East Hartford (Conn.) Bd. Edn., 1970—; ptnr. Rainbow Photo, East Hartford, 1982—, Rainbow Farms, East Hartford, 1986—; ptnr. The Country Rainbow, 1987. Democrat. Roman Catholic. Home: 284 Hills St East Hartford CT 06118

WILSON, SYBIL JOSEPHINE (JODY), real estate appraiser, consultant; b. Washington, Apr. 11, 1959; d. Robert Murray and Sybil Josephine (Hetherington) W. Student, Va. Poly. Inst. & State U., 1977-79; BS in Bus. Mgmt., Mary Baldwin Coll., 1987—. Sec., appraiser Milton, Case & Assocs., Lynchburg, Va., 1979-84; appraiser real estate Joseph S. Durrer & Assocs., Roanoke, Va., 1984-86; sr. cons. Laventhol & Horwath, Atlanta, 1986—. Mem. Mortgage Banker Assn. Ga. (affiliate), Am. Inst. Real Estate Appraisers, Soc. Real Estate Appraisers. Office: Laventhol & Horwath 225 Peachtree St NE Suite 2100 Atlanta GA 30303

WILSON, TEDDY, finance and tax consultant; b. Kansas City, Mo., Oct. 20, 1938; d. Lonnie R. and Eva M. (Rice) W.; m. Michael D. Matsik, Dec. 28, 1969 (div. 1981); children: Cynthia, Mary. Student, UCLA, 1956-60, Calif. State U., Los Angeles, 1961-65. V.p., gen. mgr. Stanley S. Adler, Inc., Tarzana, Calif., 1967-83; pvt. practice in fin. and tax cons. Encino, Calif., 1983—; cons. Automac Parking, Inc., Long Beach, 1983—, Protocall, Inc., Signal Hill, Calif., 1982-88. Mem. Beta Alpha Psi. Republican. Presbyterian. Office: 16161 Ventura Blvd 216 Encino CA 91436

WILSON, WILMA RUTH, utility company executive; b. East Chicago, Ind., June 20, 1950; d. William Vernon and Barbara Ann (Carson) Coward; m. Clyde Matthew Wilson, July 30, 1966; children: Dawn, Tracy. BS in Bus. Adminstr., Ind. U., 1980; postgrad. Purdue U., 1984-84. Engring. record clk. No. Ind. Pub. Service Co., Hammond, 1970-72, application credit clk., Gary, 1972-76, asst. to chief clk., 1976-78, personnel rep., 1978-84, system cons., Hammond, 1984—; loaned exec. United Way, 1988; mem. speakers bur., 1983-84; dir. No. Ind. Fed. Credit Union, Merrillville; edn. cons. Gary Vocat. Office Edn. Program, 1985—. Multimedia instr. ARC, Hammond, 1982—; loaned exec. Lake Area United Way, 1984-88. Mem. Ind. U. Alumni Assn. Democrat. Baptist. Clubs: Xinos Beams, La Belle Femmes (Gary)(sec. 1983-84). Avocations: traveling, reading. Home: 3828 W 15th Ave Gary IN 46404 Office: No Ind Pub Service Co 5265 Hohman Ave Hammond IN 46320

WILSON, YOLANDA GAIL, banking specialist; b. Galveston, Tex., Sept. 4, 1961; d. George Wilson and Betty Jean (Crawford) Britton. BS, U. Houston, 1983. Mgmt. trainee Guaranty Fed., Galveston, 1983-84; group supr. Guaranty Fed., Texas City, Tex., 1984-85, dept. supr., 1985—; instr. Inst. Fin. Edn., Galveston County, 1983—. Vol. Harris County Juvenile Ct., Seabrook, 1986—. Mem. Am. Bus. Women's Assn. (v.p., chmn. programming and membership 1986-87, pres. 1987—), Nat. Assn. Bank Women, U. Houston Alumni Orgn. (bd. dirs. Galveston chpt.), Alpha Kappa Alpha. Baptist. Home: 2919 Plymouth Colony Dr Webster TX 77598

WILSON, YVONNE CHANTILOUPE, family counselor; b. Mandeville, Jamaica, Mar. 26, 1944; d. Raphael Wilburn and Leila May (Mahoney) Chantiloupe; m. Robert Lee Wilson, Jr., Dec. 23, 1967 (div. 1978); children: Robert Lee III, Kurt Olaf; m. Godfrey Alexander Phillip, Aug. 29, 1985. AA, Laguardia Community Coll., 1977; BA, Calif. State U., San Bernardino, 1981; MA, Azusa Pacific U., 1983. Lic. marriage, family and child counselor. Social service counselor Casa De San Bernardino, 1978-80; mental health asst. County Mental Health, San Bernardino, 1980-84; instr. Adelphi Bus. Coll., San Bernardino, 1984-85; adminstrv. dir., owner Home Tutoring Service, Rialto, 1984-86; marriage, family counselor Psychology Ctr., San Bernardino, 1983—; pvt. practice marriage, family counseling San Bernardino, 1983—; social service practitioner Dept. Psych. Social. Services, Riverside, Calif., 1985-87; dir. clin. services Inland Empire Residential Ctrs., Mentone, Calif., 1987—; bd. dirs. Sch.. Attendance Rev. Bd., Rialto Sch. Dist., 1978-85, Casa de Ayuda, San Bernardino, 1984-85; mem. adv. bd. Chaffey Coll., Alta Loma, Calif, 1983-84; cons. Daughters United Dept. Pub. Soc. Service, Riverside, 1986—. Mem. Calif. Assn. Marriage and Family Therapists, Calif. State U. Alumni Assn. (sec., treas. 1984-86). Home: 150 E Morgan St Rialto CA 92376

WILSON-REED, JUANITA KAY (NITA), auditor; b. Charleston, Ill., July 27, 1944; d. Charles Edward Gregory and Lois Juanita (Taylor) Gregory-McInturff-Wood; m. Clyde Wilson, Feb. 14, 1976 (div. 1978); 1 child, April Lyn. Student, Eastern Ill. U., Cen. Fla. Community Coll., Lincoln Land Community Coll.; degree in mgmt., Sangamon State U. Supr. fiscal mgmt. Ill. Dept. Cen. Mgmt. Services, Springfield, 1976-79; supr. gen. acctg. systems Ill. Dept. Commerce and Community Affairs, Springfield, 1979-80; supr. support services Ill. Dept. Pub. Health, Springfield, 1980-84; EDP auditor Ill. Dept. Corrections, Springfield, 1984-85; mgr. external auditing Ill. Dept. Pub. Aid, Springfield, 1985—; cons. real estate, Crystal River, Fla., 1969-75. Mem. Data Processing Mgmt. Assn. (regional bd. dirs. 1979—, pres. local chpt. 1985—), Inst. Internal Auditors (bd. dirs. 1984-87, v.p. 1988—), Nat. Assn. Female Execs., Ill. Pub. Health Assn. (chmn. 1986). Baptist. Lodge: Order of Eastern Star. Home: 2800 E Lake Shore Dr Springfield IL 62707-8912 Office: State of Ill Dept Pub Aid 100 S Grand East Springfield IL 62704

WILZACK, ADELE, state health official; Student Loyola Coll., R.N. diploma Mercy Hosp. Sch. Nursing, Balt., 1957; B.S. in Nursing, Mt. St. Agnes coll., 1959; M.S. in Nursing, U. Md., 1960; postgrad. in pub. adminstrn. U. So. Calif., 1976. Staff nurse Mercy Hosp., Balt., 1957-60, supr. non-profl. personnel, 1961-63, asst. dir. nursing services, 1963-65; project nurse operation REASON, Community Action Agy., Health and Welfare Council, Balt., 1965-67; asst. dir. bur. spl. home services Balt. City Health Dept., 1967-72, dir. bur. spl. home services, 1972-74, dir. health services for aging, 1974-76, asst. commr. health services for aging and med. care, 1976-79; asst. sec. for med. care programs Md. Dept. Health and Mental Hygiene, Balt., 1979-83, sec. dept., 1983—; assoc. faculty mem. U. Md. Sch. Nursing; vis. faculty mem. U. Mich. Inst. Gerontology, Ann Arbor; past mem. Md. Gov.'s Task Force on Med. Malprctice Ins., Md. Gov.'s Task Force on Health Care Cost Containment; mem. Gov.'s Commn. on Black and Minority Health, Gov.'s Council on Adolescent Pregnancy, Gov.'s Adv. Bd. for Justice Assistance; past com. mem. and chmn. Central Md. Health Systems Agy.; past com. mem., past subcom. chmn. Md. Med. Assistance Adv. Com.; past chmn. Balt. City Sub-Area Adv. Council; past mem. regional adv. task force Johns Hopkins Hosp., task force on aging U. Md. Recipient award for outstanding contbns. to intergroup relations and dedicated humanitarian service to citizens of Balt. City, Balt. Community Relations Commn., 1978, Alumna of Yr. award Loyola Coll., 1978, Woman Mgr. of Yr., Conf. for Women in State Service, 1981; Merit scholar U. Md. Sch. Nursing. Mem. Md. Pub. Health Assn. (past mem. exec. com.), Am. Pub. Health Assn. (past mem. governing council state affiliate), Balt. City Med. Soc. (past mem. long-term care com.), Sigma Phi Sigma, Sigma Theta Tau. Office: Md Dept Health and Mental Hygiene 201 W Preston St Baltimore MD 21201

WIMBERLY, BEADIE RENEAU (LEIGH), financial services executive; b. Fouke, Ark., Apr. 18, 1937; d. Woodrow Wilson and Grace B. (Winkley) Reneau; m. Benjamin Leon Price, 1954 (div. 1955); m. Elbert William Wimberly, Dec. 16, 1956; children—Stephanie Elaine Wimberly Davis, Jeffrey Scott, Lael Wimberly Carter Alston. Student William & Mary Coll., 1964-65, U. Md.-Ludwigsburg/Stuttgart, 1966-68, Northwestern State U. La., 1973-75, Cornell U., 1979, Leonard Sch., 1983. Cert. ins. agt.; registered gen. securities rep. SEC, registered investment adviser SEC. Internat. trainer of trainers North Atlantic council Girl Scouts, Fed. Republic Germany, 1965-69, 76-78; inventory master The Myers Co., Inc., El Paso, Tex., 1970; abstract asst. Vernon Abstract Co., Inc., Leesville, La., 1970-71; sec. to chief utilities and pollution control Dept. Army, U.S. Civil Service, Ft. Polk, La., 1971-72, asst. to post safety officer, 1972-73, adminstr. tech. Adj. Gen.'s Office, 1973-75, sr. library technician post libraries, 1975, personnel staffing specialist, Stuttgart, Fed. Republic Germany, 1976-79, voucher examiner Fin. and Acctg. Office, Ft. Polk, 1980-81; chief exec. officer Fin. Strategies, Inc., Leesville, La., 1981—, stockbroker, corp. exec., 1983—, mktg. exec., 1983—; labor cons. AFL/CIO, Ft. Polk, 1981—; sr. resident mgr. Anchor Nat. Fin. Services Inc., dir., treas. Wimberly Enterprises, Inc. Bd. dirs. Calcasieu Parish council Boy Scouts Am., 1982-83, active, 1988—; treas. Vernon Parish Hist./Geneal. Soc., 1986-87; pres. Vernon Parish Helpline/Lifeline, 1985; charter mem. Nat. Mus. of Women in the Arts; mem. Vernon Parish Arts Council. Mem. Pilot Internat., Internat. Assn. Fin. Planners, Nat. Assn. Govt. Employees (v.p. Ft. Polk chpt. 1980-81), Internat. Platform Assn., C. of C., Assn. U.S. Army, Am. Assn. Fin. Profls., Nat. Women's Polit. Caucus, Am. Soc. Mil. Comptrollers, LWV-La. (state bd. dirs. 1986-87, treas. Leesville chpt. 1982-87), NOW (Ruston-Grambling chpt.). Republican. Baptist. Club: Toastmasters (named Competent Toastmaster, 1979). Lodge: Rotary (bd. mem.-at-large Leesville club 1988—). Office: Fin Strategies Inc 302 N 5th St Leesville LA 71446

WIMER, CYNTHIA CROSBY, research scientist; b. Boston, Oct. 23, 1933; d. Robert Addison and Hazel Gertrude (Ruggles) Crosby; m. Richard Earl Wimer, Dec. 21, 1957; children: John S., James L., Mark C. BA in Music, Wellesley Coll., 1955; MA in Psychology, McGill U., 1958; PhD in Psychology, Rutgers U., 1961. Research assoc. The Jackson Lab., Bar Harbor, Maine, 1962-69; assoc. research scientist specializing in neurogenetics Beckman Research Inst. of City of Hope, Duarte, Calif., 1969—. Contbr. numerous articles to profl. jours. Home: 386 North Lima Sierra Madre CA 91024 Office: Beckman Research Inst of City of Hope 1450 E Duarte Rd Duarte CA 91010

WIMMER, LAURA LYNNE, public relations specialist; b. Portland, Oreg., Mar. 29, 1958; d. Joseph Ball and Sieglinde Luise (Murschall) W.; m. James Thomas Keppinger, July 4, 1986. BA in Polit. Sci., Vassar Coll., 1980. Publs. specialist Kerr Pubs., Portland, 1981-84; writer, mgr. Profl. Writing Service, Portland, 1984—; pub. relations specialist, counselor Downtown Women's Ctr., Portland, 1987—; freelance The Alliance Newspaper, Portland, 1981-84, Met. Women's Yellow Pages, 1987. Editor Miscellany News, 1979-80, Oreg. Rainbow News, 1984. Polit. cons. Com. to Elect Stan Kahn, Portland, 1984; editor Cawthorne for Commr. Campaign, Portland, 1984; forest service vol. Friends of Bagby Hot Springs, Portland, 1983-87. Mem. Nat. Assn. Female Execs., Women in Communications, Portland C. of C. Democrat. Club: Portland City.

WIMS, LOIS ANN, criminal justice educator; b. Pawtucket, R.I., Oct. 27, 1956; d. Louis Vincent and Ella Noella (Lacroix) W.; m. Normand Edmond Gamache Jr., May 26, 1983; children: Kyle Normand, Ellary Wims. BS summa cum laude, Bryant Coll., 1977; diploma, R.I. Mcpl. Police Acad., Kingston, 1977; MA in Criminal Justice, Salve Regina Coll., 1981; ABD in Psychol., U. R.I., 1988, postgrad. Police officer Cen. Falls (R.I.) Police Dept., 1977-85; part-time instr. sociology and adminstrn. justice Salve Regina Coll., Newport, R.I., 1979-83, instr. criminal justice, 1983—; cons. R.I. Dept. Vocat. Edn., Providence, 1982; lectr. in field. Spokesman R.I. Cesarean Prevention Movement, Providence, 1986-87; actress Pawtucket (R.I.) Community Players, 1983-87 (recipient Gregson award, 1986); treas. Police Relief Assn., Central Falls, 1978-83; vol. R.I. Rape Crisis Ctr., Providence, 1976-77. Named Woman of Yr., Cranston Bus. and Profl. Women, 1987; recipient Young Career Woman award R.I. Bus. and Profl. Women, 1984, commendations for outstanding police work. Mem. Am. Criminal Justice Soc., Frat. Order Police (sec. 1978-83). Roman Catholic. Home: 234 Benedict St Pawtucket RI 02861 Office: Salve Regina Coll Ochre Point Ave Newport RI 02840

WINANDY, CAROL MARIE, designer; b. Chgo., Sept. 8, 1938; d. Thomas Pierre and Marie Ann (Diedling) W. B.A. in Fine Arts, Art Inst. Chgo., 1961; postgrad. U. Chgo., 1961. Dress designer Adrian Tabin, Chgo., 1961-62; lingerie designer Kellwood Co., Chgo., 1962-63, Phill-Maid Co., Chgo., 1963-65, Vassarette div. of Munsingwear, Mpls., 1965-67, O'Bryan Bros., Inc., Chgo., 1967-76; founder, pres. Tatsy Co., Chgo., 1976—; founder Love Pet Co., 1986. Patentee in field. Mem. Fashion Group, Internat. Old Lacers, Thimble Collectors Internat. Office: Tatsy Co PO Box 1401 Des Plaines IL 60017

WINANT, ANAIS, arts administrator; b. Newport, R.I., Feb. 17, 1950; d. Barent Parlee and Laurencia (Brown) W.; m. Edward Scott Williams, Feb. 15, 1985 (div. 1987). BA in Creative Writing, San Francisco State U., 1980. With public relations dept. Magic Theatre, San Francisco, 1980-82; dir. pub. relations, devel. Julian Theatre, San Francisco, 1982-83; mng. dir. Friends of the Phila. String Quartet, Seattle, 1983-85; dir. planning, devel. Seattle Repertory Theatre, 1985—. Active Leadership Tomorrow, Seattle, 1987—, various arts advocacy orgns. Mem. Northwest Devel. Officers, Wash. Touring Artists Coalition. Home: 2908 E Columbia Seattle WA 98122 Office: Seattle Repertory Theatre 155 Mercer St Seattle WA 98109

WINANT, ETHEL WALD, broadcasting executive; b. Worcester, Mass., Aug. 5; d. William and Janice (Woolson) Wald; children: William, Scott, Bruce. BA, U. Calif., Berkeley; MTA, Whittier Coll. Dir. casting Talen Assocs., N.Y.C., 1953-56; assoc. producer Playhouse '90, CBS, Hollywood, Calif., 1956-60; assoc. producer All Fall Down, MGM, Calif., 1960-61; producer Gt. Adventure, CBS, Hollywood, 1961-62; v.p. talent, dir. program devel. CBS, Hollywood, 1962-75; exec. producer Best of Families, PBS, N.Y.C., 1975-77; v.p. talent NBC, Burbank, Calif., 1978—, v.p. mini-series and novels for TV, 1979; sr. v.p. Metromedia Producers Co., 1981—; mem. adv. bd. Ctr. for Advanced Film Studies, Am. Film Inst., 1981—, Procter & Gamble Gt. Am. Women; cons. in field. Exec. producer: (TV movie) A Time to Triumph, 1985. Mem. Pres.'s Commn. for Women; mem. Calif. Arts Council; mem. speakers bur. Braille Inst.; bd. dirs. Circle Reperatory Theatre. Recipient Disting. Alumni award Calif. Community Colls., 1981, Life Achievement award Casting Soc. Am., 1987; named TV Woman of Yr., Conf. Personal Mgrs., 1974. Mem. Nat. Acad. TV Arts and Scis. (exec com. 1981—, bd. govs., Emmy award 1960), John Tracy Clinic, Women in Film (Crystal award 1979), Hollywood Radio and TV Soc. (bd. dirs. 1981—, sec. 1981—). Office: 5746 Sunset Blvd Los Angeles CA 90028

WINCHELL, MARGARET WEBSTER ST. CLAIR, realtor; b. Clinton, Tenn., Jan. 26, 1923; d. Robert Love and Mayme Jane (Warwick) Webster; student Denison U., 1940, Miami U., Oxford (Ohio), 1947, 48; m. Charles M. Winchell, June 7, 1941; children—David Alan (dec.), Margaret Winchell Boyle; m. 2d, Robert George Sterrett, July 15, 1977 (dec. 1985). Saleswoman Fred K.A. Schmidt & Shirmer real estate, Cin., 1960-66, Cline Realtors, Cin., 1966-70; owner, broker Winchell's Showplace Realtors, Cin., 1972—; ins. agt. United Liberty Life Ins. Co., 1966—, dist. mgr., 1967-70, 77-82, regional mgr., 1982—; stockbroker Waddell & Reed, Columbus, Ohio, 1972—, Security Counselors; ins. broker, 1984, gen. agent; dir. Fin. Cons., 1984, 85, 86, 87. Treas., v.p. Parents without Partners, 1969, sec., 1968; pres. PTA; dir. Children's Bible Fellowship Ohio, 1953-76; dir. Child Evangelism Cin.; nat. speaker Child Evangelism Fellowship and Nat. Sunday Sch. Convs., 1955-57; pres. Christian Solos, 1974; chaplain Bethesda N. Hosp. Mem. Nat. Assn. Real Estate Bds. West Shell Realtors (v.p.), Womens Council Real Estate Bd. (treas.). Clubs: Alfonta, Travel go go, Guys and Gals Singles (founder, 1st pres.), Hamilton Singles (pres.). Home and Office: 8221 Margaret Ln Cincinnati OH 45242

WINDER, MARGARET ANNE FORT, educator; b. Charlotte, N.C., Aug. 26, 1933; d. Risden Sherrill and Margaret Elizabeth (Hodges) F.; m. Ralph Eugene Moore, June 19,1954 (div. 1973); m. William Ray Winder Jr., July 24, 1982; children: Ralph Eugene Moore Jr., Melanie Margaret McNutt. BA, Erskine Coll., Due West, S.C., 1955; student, U. South Fla., 1965, 70-71, 74, 86, Furman U., 1975, Fla. So. Coll., 1976, Manatee Community Coll., Bradenton, Fla., 1987. Social worker Dept. Pub. Welfare, Abberville, S.C., 1955-56; teacher Pub. Schs. Polk, Osceola, Hall counties, Fla. Ga., 1957-74; sales rep. Ency. Britannica Ednl. Corp., Chgo., 1974-76; teacher Sarasota County Pub. Schs., Sarasota, Fla., 1976-82; office mgr. Atlantic So. Prodns. Inc., Sarasota, Fla., 1982-84; teacher Sarasota County Pub. Schs., Sarasota, Fla., 1984-85; v.p. Atlantic So. Prodns. Inc., Sarasota, Fla., 1985-87; mgr. rental property self employed, Sarasota, Fla., 1979—; bd. dirs. Village Brooke Condominium Assoc., Sarasota, 1980-82; county del. Fla. Ed. Assoc. Conf., Tampa, 1980; dir student intern teachers, Fla. Pub. Schs., 1971,74,76. Mem. Sarasota Classified Teacher Assoc. (sch. rep. 1980-82). Republican. Home and Office: 4574 W Robin Hood Trail Sarasota FL 34232

WINDSOR, MAURA KATHLEEN, religious organization administrator; b. Youngstown, Ohio, Feb. 8, 1937; d. Harold Cecil and Isabel Dorothy (Donahue) Cowher; m. Charles Robert Windsor, Jan. 23, 1960; children: Terri, Charles Jr., Donald C., David S. BS in nursing, Youngstown State U., 1960; M in Religious Studies, Ursuline Coll., 1982; RN, Youngstown Hosp., 1958; student, Youngstown State U., 1983. RN, Ohio. RN Western Reserve Care System, Youngstown, Ohio, 1958-70, Assumption Nursing Home, Youngstown, Ohio, 1976-82; spl. programs coordinator Mahoning County Alcoholism Services, Youngstown, Ohio, 1987—. Dir. Respect Life Cath. Charities Diocese of Youngstown, 1982—; prin. C.C.D. Holy Family Parish, Poland, Ohio, 1982-83; catechist Holy Family Parish, Poland, 1967—; chmn. bd. dirs. state diocesan Pro-life Convocation Ohio Cath. Conf., Columbus, Ohio, 1985—, asst. dir. exec. com., 1988—; mem. adv. com. to Pro Life com. Nat. Conf. Cath. Bishops, Washington, 1986; co-chmn. Mahoning County Alcohol Services, Youngstown, 1986, Teen Action Day, Youngstown, Just Say No Week, Youngstown; chmn. Mahoning County Crop Walk, Youngstown, 1985; mem. Task Force on Capital Punishment, Columbus, 1986, 87; pres. Poland Baseball Mom's Club, 1976, 77, Poland Football Mom's Club, 1977, 79; mem. Mahoning County Task Force on Drinking/Driving, Ohio Coalition Against Death Penalty, Columbus. Recipient Distinguished Service award Boy Scouts of Am., 1985. Mem. Ohio Nurses Assn., Nat. Assn. Cath. Charities. Home: 7435 Forest Hill Poland OH 44514 Office: Diocese Youngstown Cath Charities 225 Elm St Youngstown OH 44503

WINDSOR, NATALIE PRECKER, broadcast journalist; b. N.Y.C.; d. Bernard and Ruth (Pastor) Precker. BFA, Kent State U., 1974. Radio news anchor various stas., Cleve., Rochester, N.Y., Chgo. and Phoenix, 1974-87; news anchor Sta. KPWR-FM, Los Angeles, 1987—. Para-counselor Los Angeles Free Clinic Helpline, 1984—; para-chaplain Los Angeles Bd. Rabbis, 1986—. Mem. Nat. Assn. Female Execs., Delta Chi. Home: 1800 N Winona Blvd Los Angeles CA 90027

WINE, SHERRY LYNNE, insurance professional, small business owner; b. Roanoke, Va., July 19, 1949; d. Irvin Jr. and Mary Dorothy (Hill) Pearcey; m. John David Wine, Dec. 6, 1969 (div. 1980); 1 child, Bradley Scott. Student, Va. Western Community Coll., 1967-69, New River Community Coll., 1971-72. Lic. ins. broker. Owner Calico Cactus, Radford, Va., 1973-80; mgr. Greenleaf Plant Farms, Stuart, Fla., 1980-81; ins. rep. Gary H. Reaves and Assocs., Roanoke, 1983-85, Prudential Ins. Co., Roanoke, 1985-87, Jefferson Pilot, Roanoke, 1987; owner Avant Gardens, Roanoke, 1987—; ins. broker Roanoke, 1987—. Vol. ARC, Roanoke, 1981. Mem. Nat. Assn. Life Underwriters. Baptist. Office: Avant Gardens 3959 Electric Rd Roanoke VA 24018

WINE-BANKS, JILL SUSAN, lawyer; b. Chgo., May 5, 1943; d. Bert S. and Sylvia Dawn (Simon) Wine; m. Ian David Volner, Aug. 21, 1965; m. Michael A. Banks, Jan. 12, 1980. BS, U. Ill.-Champaign-Urbana, 1964; JD, Columbia U., 1968. Bar: N.Y. 1969, U.S. Ct. Appeals (4th cir.) 1969, U.S. Ct. Appeals (6th and 9th cirs.) 1973, U.S. Supreme Ct. 1974, D.C. 1976, Ill. 1980. Asst. press. and pub. relations dir. Assembly of Captive European Nations, N.Y.C., 1965-66; trial atty. criminal div. organized crime and racketeering sect. and labor racketeering sect. U.S. Dept. Justice, 1969-73; asst. spl. prosecutor Watergate Spl. Prosecutor's Office, 1973-75; lectr. law seminar on trial practice Columbia U. Sch. Law, N.Y.C., 1975-77; assoc. Fried, Frank, Harris, Shriver & Kampelman, Washington, 1975-77; gen. counsel Dept. Army, Pentagon, Washington, 1977-79; ptnr. Jenner & Block, Chgo., 1980-84; solicitor gen. State of Ill. Office of Atty. Gen., 1984-86, dep. atty. gen., 1986-87; exec. v.p., chief operating officer, Am. Bar Assn., Chgo., 1987—. Bd. dirs. Northwestern U. Ctr. Urban Affairs, Internat. Women's Forum, The Chgo. Network; chmn. fund raising com. U. Ill. Coll. Communications. Recipient Spl. Achievement award U.S. Dept. Justice, 1972, Meritorious award, 1973, Cert. Outstanding Service, 1975; decoration for Disting. Civilian Service, Dept. Army, 1979. Fellow Am. Bar Found.; mem. ABA (council sect. litigation 1979-80, chmn. ann. meeting 1982, Pres.'s club Fund for justice and edn.), Ill. Bar Assn., Womens Bar Assn. Ill., Chgo. Bar Assn., Chgo. Council Lawyers. Clubs: Economic, Legal. Office: Am Bar Assn 750 N Lake Shore Dr Chicago IL 60611

WINEKOFF, CONNIE J., accountant; b. Garden City, Mich., Oct. 26, 1962; d. CHarles Richard and Charlotte Ruth (Schroeder) W. A in Commerce, Henry Ford Community Coll., 1986. Office asst. Meyers Jewelers, Westland, Mich., 1979-80; bookkeeper Bank of the Common Wealth, Detroit, 1980-81, Mich. Nat. Bank, Livonia, 1981-82; mgr. acctg. div. Alexsis Risk Mgmt., Livonia, 1982—. Office: 19790 Haggerty Rd Livonia MI 48152

WINER, KAREN MARCIA, theater finance administrator; b. Newark, Oct. 7, 1950; d. Irvin and Nettie Renée (Riesenberg) W. BA, SUNY, Brockport, 1972. Prodn. coordinator Theater dept. SUNY, Brockport, 1970-72; arts cons. Monroe County Pub. Library, Rochester, N.Y., 1972-73; resident stage mgr. Coconut Grove Playhouse, Miami, 1973-76; asst. box office treas. Circle in the Sq., N.Y.C., 1976-80; assoc. producer New Cafe A Go Go, N.Y.C., 1985-86; asst. box office treas. Shubert Orgn., N.Y.C., 1980-87; bookkeeper Jameson Advtg. Inc., N.Y.C., 1988—; assoc. producer New Cafe A Go Go, Vintage, N.Y.C., 1985-86. Mem. Internat. Alliance Stage and Theatrical Employees, Actors' Equity Assn.

WINES, DOROTHY HELEN JONES, attendance agent; b. Detroit, Apr. 18, 1940; d. George W. and Johnnie Beatrice (DeMeyers) Jones; divorced; 1 child, Janeen Michelle Coleman. B, Wayne State U., 1968, M in Guidance and Counseling, 1981. Social worker Wayne County Dept. Social Services, Detroit, 1963-66; attendance agt. Detroit Bd. Edn., 1966—; chair ways and means Tri-State Conf. on Pupil Personnel, Detroit, 1986-87. Pres. Met. Youth Council, 1984—. Mem. NAACP, Am. Bus. Women's Assn., Am. Bridge Assn., Nat. Assn. Female Execs., Phi Delta Kappa. Democrat. Clubs: V.I.P. Bridge, Friday Niter Bridge. Office: Cen High Sch 2425 Tuxedo Detroit MI 48206

WINES, MARCIA CHARLENE, controller; b. Westchester, Pa., May 10, 1950; d. John J. Levchuk and Virginia B. (Klotz) Martin; m. Robert C. Wines, June 17, 1972; children: Kristina R. and Kelly L. BA, Muhlenberg Coll., 1972; MBA, Monmouth Coll., West Long Branch, N.J., 1987. CPA, N.J., Fla. Acct. U.S. Govt., Babenhausen, Germany, 1973-76; tax acct. Nearman & Lents, PA, Miami, Fla., 1977-80; sr. acct., supr. Mishkan, Horowitz & Boaz, PA, Miami, 1980-82; sr. acct. Reydel, Perier & Neral, PA, Belmar, N.J., 1982-84; controller C.J. Hesse, Inc., etal, Belford, N.J., 1984—. Coach Neptune (N.J.) Recreation League, 1986—; trustee United Meth. Homes of N.J., Neptune, 1986—. Mem. Am. Inst. Cert. Pub. Accts., Fla. Inst. Cert. Pub. Accts., N.J. Inst. Cert. Pub. Accts. Methodist. Middletown United (treas.). Home: 507 Glenmere Ave Shark River Hills NJ 07753 Office: CJ Hesse Inc et al PO Box 207 Belford NJ 07718

WINFIELD, BARBARA LABARGE, plastics consultant; b. Potsdam, N.Y., June 27, 1935; d. Clarence Lewis and Barbara (Pelsue) LaB.; m. Armand G. Winfield, July 23, 1966. B.S. in Art Edn., SUNY-Buffalo, 1958, postgrad., summer, 1959; postgrad. Columbia U., summer, 1960. Tchr. art Susquehanna Central Sch. Dist., Binghamton, N.Y., 1958-61, Conard High Sch., West Hartford, Conn., 1961-62, South Congl. Ch., Hartford, Conn., 1962-66; art dir. Fine Art Found. of Conn., Hartford, 1962-66; owner LaBarge Studios, Rocky Hill, Conn. and N.Y.C., 1962-68; pres. LaBarge Industries Ltd., West Babylon, N.Y., 1968-70, Finders Delightful Ltd., West Babylon, 1975-77; sec.-treas. Armand G. Winfield Inc., West Babylon and Santa Fe, N.Mex., 1966—; maker mus. replications for various Am. museums; designer, mfr. fashion jewelry, sculpture, housewares, indsl. products, toys, games, stage sets and costumes; plastics cons. Author, patentee in field. Mem. exec. com. to elect Dora Battle as Mayor of Santa Fe, 1981-82; aux. bd. Santa Fe Crime Stoppers Carnivals, 1983, 84. Recipient cert. of excellence in graphic design, Mead Library of Ideas, 1968. Mem. Soc. Plastics Engrs., (affiliate), Soc. Advancement Material and Process Engring. (dir., co-chmn. membership Rio Grande chpt. 1985-86, sec. 1987), Santa Fe C. of C. Club: Santa Fe Press (bd. dirs. 1983). Home: PO Box 1296 Santa Fe NM 87504 Office: 3 Siler Ln Santa Fe NM 87501

WINFREY, OPRAH, television talk-show hostess; b. Kosciusko, Miss., Jan. 29, 1954; d. Vernon and Vernita (Lee) W. BA in Speech and Drama, Tenn. State U. Reporter, news anchorperson Sta. WTVF-TV, Nashville; news anchorperson Sta. WJZ-TV, Balt., 1976-77, hostess morning talk show People Are Talking, 1977-83; hostess talk show A.M. Chgo. Sta. WLS-TV, from 1984; hostess The Oprah Winfrey Show ABC-TV, Chgo., 1984—. Appeared in films The Color Purple, 1985 (nominated Acad. award), Native Son, 1986; producer, actress: ABC TV movie, The Women of Brewster Place, 1988. Recipient Woman of Achievement award NOW, 1986. Address: care WLS-TV Channel 7 190 N State St Chicago IL 60611 *

WING, JANET ELEANOR SWECDYK BENDT, nuclear scientist; b. Detroit, Oct. 12, 1925; d. Jack and Florence C. (Springman) Sweedyk; m. Philip J. Bendt, Sept. 4, 1948 (div. Jan. 1972); children: Karen Ann Bendt Sox, Paul Philip, Barbara Jean Bendt Medlin, Linda Sue; m. G. Milton Wing, Aug. 26, 1972 (div. Jan. 1987). BSEE with distinction, Wayne State U., 1947; MA in Physics, Columbia U., 1950; postgrad., U. Oreg., 1966-67, U. N.Mex., 1968-71. Research engr. Gen. Motors Corp., Detroit, 1944-48; physicist, mathematician Manhattan Project Columbia U., N.Y.C., 1950-51; mem. research staff Los Alamos (N.Mex.) Nat. Lab, 1951-57, 68—, project leader, 1976-81, asst. group leader, 1980-84, assoc. group leader, 1985—. Bd, dirs., treas. Esperanza Shelter, Santa Fe, N. Mex., 1984—. Mem. Am. Nuclear Soc., AAAS, Women in Sci. and Engring., Los Alamos Women in Sci., Sigma Xi, Tau Beta Pi. Office: Los Alamos Nat Lab Los Alamos NM 87545

WING, KYLENE SCARBOROUGH (MRS. ROBERT L. WING), columnist; b. Charlotte, N.C.; d. Kyle and Tomi (Riggs) Scarborough; grad. Stevens Schs. for Models, 1946-47, Ben Bard Acad. Theatre, Hollywood, Calif., 1952, Nat. Acad. Broadcasting Washington, 1957, UCLA Extension, 1965, Free U. Berlin Otto-Suhrz Inst. Extension, 1966. m. Robert L. Wing, Jan. 16, 1943; children—Susan, Jayme. Columnist, Kylene's Kalifornia Kapers, Inverness, Fla., 1965-66, Kylene's Kontinental Kapers, Berlin, Germany, 1966-68; publicity chmn. Am. Women's Club Founder patron Huntington Hartford Theatre; mem. Concerned Friend Nat. League Families POW-MIA, U.S. Congl. Adv. Bd. Recipient letter of Appreciation USAF, 1973. Mem. Planetary Soc., Hollywood C. of C., Freedom Found. at Valley Forge, Los Angeles World Affairs Council. Presbyn. Clubs: German American Women's, American Women's, American Yacht (all Berlin); Los Angeles Riding and Polo; Air Force Officers Wives; Bel-Air Republican Women's. Address: 3405 Blair Dr Hollywood CA 90068

WING, SARAH WILLIAMSON, psychologist; b. Buffalo, Feb. 11, 1932; d. Charles Hequembourg and Constance (Cook) W. BA in Psychology, Conn. Coll., New London, 1953; MA in Human Relations, Ohio U., 1956; M in Pub. Adminstrn., Pacific Luth. U., Tacoma, 1979; PhD in Psychology, U. Oregon, 1966. Lic. psychologist, Wash. Sch. psychologist Fairborn City Schs., Ohio, 1959-62; grad. asst. U. Oreg., Eugene, 1963-64; sch. psychologist Eugene Pub. Schs., Oreg., 1964-67, Bellevue Pub. Schs., Wash., 1967-70; psychologist Wash. Corrections Ctr., Shelton, 1970-72, Wash. State Reformatory, Monroe, 1972-77, Western State Hosp., Ft. Steilacoom, Wash., 1977-85; pvt. practice psychology Bellevue, 1985—; counselor Project Head Start, Eugene, 1966, 67. Sec. bd. Pacific Luth. Theol. Sem., 1981—; ct. adjucation mem. Luth. Ch. Am., 1980-87; bd. dirs. Ch. Council of Greater Seattle, 1987—; vol. Eastside Domestic Violence Program, Bellevue, 1985—; pres. Puget Sound chpt. Luth. Women's Caucus., Seattle, 1986-88. Recipient Community Service award Internat. Toastmistress Club., 1980. Fellow Am. Orthopsychiat. Assn.; mem. Am. Psychol. Assn., Am. Assn. Correctional Psychology (pres. 1979-81), Am. Assn. of Counseling & Devel., Am. Assn., Pastoral Counselors (mem. task force), Wash. Psychol. Assn. (sec. coping with stress com.). Lutheran. Office: PO Box 5556 Bellevue WA 98006

WINGATE, ELIZA CUNNINGHAM WEEKS, librarian, consultant; b. Washington, Sept. 25, 1943; d. Donald Weeks and Eliza Cunningham (Goddard) Weeks Bacas; m. Paul Shawn Wingate, Sept. 23, 1966; children—Rose Alice, Sierra Laurel. B.A. in Art, U. Calif.-Berkeley, 1965; M.L.S., Drexel U., 1983. Librarian circulation dept. film and resource library Ludington Pub. Library, Bryn Mawr, Pa., 1976-83; head librarian Belmont Hills Pub. Library (Pa.), 1983-86; library dir. San Anselmo (Calif.) Pub. Library, 1986—.; Producer slide/tape: Penguins Don't Have Libraries, 1982. Active Lower Merion Resource Ctr., Bala-Cynwyd, Pa., 1974-76; v.p. Zero Population Growth, Phila., 1977-78; bd. dirs. New Gulph Children's Ctr., 1980-85. Mem. ALA, Calif. Library Assn., Marin Interlibrary Network of Dirs., North Bay Coop. Library System, Beta Phi Mu. Democrat. Office: San Anselmo Pub Library 110 Tunstead Ave San Anselmo CA 94960

WINGATE, VICKI MAREE, accounting administrator; b. Long Beach, Calif., Apr. 3, 1957; d. Jack O. and Peggy M. (Seastrunk) W. BS in Commerce, U. Va., 1979. CPA. Internal auditor S.C. Nat. Bank, Columbia, 1979-80; staff accountant Price Waterhouse & Co., Columbia, 1980-82; auditor S.C. Legis. Audit Council, Columbia, 1982-84; asst. dep. commr. fiscal affairs S.C. Dept. Mental Retardation, Columbia, 1984—. Mem. Am. Inst. CPA's, S.C. Assn. CPA's, S.C. Assn. Govt. Fin. Officers, U. Va. Alumni Assn., Chi Omega. Republican. Presbyterian.

WINGER, DEBRA, actress; b. Cleve., 1955; d. Robert and Ruth W.; m. Timothy Hutton, March 16, 1986; 1 child, Emmanuel Noah. Student Calif. State U.-Northridge. Made 1st profl. appearance in Wonder Woman TV series, 1976-77; appeared TV film Spl. Olympics, 1977; appeared in films Thank God It's Friday, 1978, French Postcards, 1979, Urban Cowboy, 1980, Cannery Row, 1982, An Officer and a Gentleman, 1982, Terms of Endearment, 1983, Mike's Murder, 1984, Legal Eagles, 1986, Black Widow, 1987, Made in Heaven, 1987, Betrayed, 1988. Served with Israeli Army, 1972. Office: care John West PMK Pub Relations Inc 8436 W Third St Suite 650 Los Angeles CA 90048 *

WINGO-DAVIS, MARIAN LEE, feminist therapist; b. Asheville, N.C., Sept. 16, 1944; d. Hugh Albert and Lee Ardis (English) Wingo; B.S. in Edn., Fla. State U., Tallahassee, 1966; M.S. in Human Devel. Counseling with honors George Peabody Coll., 1978; m. H.C. Davis, Aug. 28, 1966; children—Remi, Wade. Feminist therapist, human devel. counselor, San Antonio, 1980-82; dir. women's tng. programs Internat. Trainers, Educators and Cons., Inc., San Antonio, 1980-82, now cons; staff counselor Gulf Coast Family Counseling Agy., Pascagoula, Miss., 1983—; exec. bd. San Antonio Women's Credit Union, 1981—, San Antonio Women's Law Center, 1981—, Battered Women's Shelter of Bexar County, 1981—; co-dir., owner Family Counselors Affiliated, Ocean Springs, Miss.; bd. dirs., owner Marian Wingo-Davis & Assocs., Ocean Springs. Program chmn. Bexar County Women's Polit. Caucus, 1980-81; exec. bd. Gulf Coast Women's Center; bd. dirs. Pascagoula Women's Restitution Center. Recipient Today's Woman award San Antonio Light, Women's Network Profl. Devel. Leadership award, Lic. counselor. Mem. Nat. Feminist Therapist Assn., Assn. Women in Psychology, Town and Country Bus. and Profl. Women (Outstanding Citizen award), Women in Bus., NOW, Tex. Women's Polit. Caucus, Am. Assn. Counseling and Devel., Older Women's League, Am. Soc. Tng. and Devel. (asst. chairperson nat. women's network 1983-85, dir. women's network 1986—, council of networks 1988—, regional coordinator 1981-83), Nat. Assn. Profl. Cons. Methodist. Home: 111 Mark Daniel Circle Ocean Springs MS 39564 Office: 649 Jackson Ave Ocean Springs MS 39567

WINICK, PAULINE, sports, communications executive; b. N.Y.C., Sept. 19, 1946; d. Morris and Frances (Fox) Leiderman; m. Bruce Jeffrey Winick, June 19, 1966 (div. 1977); children—Margot Scott, Graham Douglas. B.A., Bklyn. Coll., 1966; M.A., NYU, 1971; A.S., Miami-Dade Community Coll., 1977. Tchr. N.Y.C. Pub. Schs., 1966-66, 69-74, Bloomington (Ind.) Pub. Schs., 1968-69; producer Sta. WPLG-TV, Miami, Fla., 1975-79; dir. Office of Communications, Metro-Dade County, Miami, Fla., 1979-86; exec. asst. city mgr. City of Miami, 1986; proprietor Pauline Winick and Assocs., 1986—; v.p. for adminstrn. Miami Heat Basketball Team, 1988—. Bd. dirs. Fla. Close-Up, Miami, 1979—, Miami City Ballet, Anti-Defamation League, 1983, LWV, Miami, 1980, Dade Pub. Edn. Fund, 1987—; counselor Dade County Cultural Affairs Council; mem. exec. com. Leadership Miami Conf., 1980-82; bd. dirs. Found. for Excellence in Pub. Edn., 1987—, Miami Arts Exchange, 1987—, Jewish Fedn. TV, 1987—. Mem. Nat. Acad. TV Arts and Scis. (bd. govs. Miami chpt. 1986-88), Fla. Bar Assn. (mem. grievence com.). Home: 11420 SW 72d Ave Miami FL 33156 Office: 330 Greco Ave Coral Gables FL 33146 Office: The Miami Heat The Miami Arena Miami FL 33136-4102

WINJE, BARBARA GAYL, financial executive; b. Elko, Nev., Oct. 5, 1952; d. David Bert and Ardith Eileen (Abbott) Fretwell; m. Lewis Charles Winje, July 13, 1985 (div.); children: Michael Todd, Jeffrey Martin. BA, Cen. Wash. U., 1982; MFin, Seattle U., 1984. Clk. State Wash. Highways, Everett, 1972-73; mgr. Arctic Circle Drive Inn, Everett, 1973-74; operator Gen. Telephone Co., Everett, 1973-74; office mgr. Southland Corp., Bothel, Wash., 1974-76; acctg. mgr. Reinell Boats, Marysville, Wash., 1976-78; v.p. fin. Bayliner Marine Corp., Arlington, Wash., 1978-86; v.p. Pacific Marine Mgmt., Inc., Arlington, 1987—. Mem. Marysville (Wash.) Sch. Dist. Adv. Bd., 1982, Everett (Wash.) Community Coll. Adv. Bd., 1983. Mem. Assn. for Individual Investors, Nat. Assn. Accts., Am. Soc. Profl. Exec. Women. Republican. Mormon. Office: Pacific Marine Mgmt 3210 Smokey Point Dr Suite 200 Arlington WA 98223

WINKEL, NINA, sculptor; b. Germany, May 21, 1905; d. Ernst and Augustine (Bauer) Koch; came to U.S., 1942, naturalized, 1945; student Staedel Mus. Art Sch., 1929-31; D.F.A. (hon.), SUNY, 1985; m. George J. Winkel, Dec. 15, 1934. Trustee, Sculpture Ctr., Inc., N.Y.C., 1946-69, pres., 1970-73, pres. emeritus, trustee, 1974—; one-man shows: Notre Dame U., 1954, Sculpture Ctr., N.Y.C., 1944, 47, 58, 72, Adirondack Mus., Elizabethtown, N.Y., 1976, Ctr. Music Drama Art, Lake Placid, N.Y., 1977, Nat. Savs. Bank, Plattsburgh, N.Y., 1979, Carpenter and Painter Gallery, Elizabethtown, 1982, Allentown (Pa.) Art Mus., 1982, SUNY-Plattsburgh, 1983, 84, SUNY-Albany, 1984, Sculpture Ctr. Inc., N.Y.C., 1984, Winkel Sculpture Ct., 1987; group shows: Met. Mus., Whitney Mus., Pa. Acad., San Francisco Mus., Va. Mus.; hon. adj. prof. SUNY-Plattsburgh, 1983. Juror for sculpture competition Winter Olympics 1980 in Lake Placid, 1978—; trustee Keene Valley Library Assn., 1967—, chmn. bi-centennial com., 1973-77; trustee Adirondack Mus., Elizabethtown, N.Y., 1978—. Recipient Samuel F.B. Morse Gold medal NAD, 1964, Artists Fund prize, 1979, Gold medal, 1982; Founders prize, Mrs. Louis Bennett prize Nat. Sculpture Soc.; Pen's Brush award Pen's Brush club, 1982, Disting. Service award SUNY-Plattsburgh, 1987, Disting. Service award SUNY, 1987. Fellow Nat. Sculpture Soc. (sec. 1965-68, Bronze medal 1967, 71, Purchase prize 1981, Medal of Honor 1988); mem. Nat. Acad. Design (E. Watrous Gold medal 1945, 78, 83), Sculptors Guild, Ctr. Music, Drama and Arts-Lake Placid, Omicron Delta Kappa (hon.). Winkel Sculpture Court, SUNY-Plattsburgh, opened Oct. 1987, contains over 40 pieces of her sculpture. Home: Dunham Rd Keene Valley NY 12943

WINKLER, JUDY KOITER, medical computer specialist; b. Glens Falls, N.Y., Oct. 1, 1953; d. John and Mary Louise (Baker) Koiter; m. Gerhard Winkler, Apr. 10, 1981. BA, U. Colo., 1976; MA, So. Ill. U., 1979. Cert. tchr., Colo. Asst. tchr. Ctr. ESL, Carbondale, Ill., 1978-79; tchr. Austrian Ministry Edn., Vienna, 1979-82; instr. Jefferson County Adult Edn., Wheatridge, Colo., 1983-85; tchr. Spring Inst. Internat. Studies, Denver, 1982-84; tng. specialist Internat. Med. Corp., Denver, 1984-85; rep. applications support Datatron Inc., Tustin, Calif., 1985-86; dir. tng. Computers for Medicine Inc., Riverside, Calif., 1986—; cons. in field. Mem. Am. Soc. Tng. Devel., Nat. Assn. Female Execs. Office: Computer for Medicine Inc 10022 Dufferin Ave Riverside CA 92503

WINKLER, NANCY ANN, bank executive; b. N.Y.C., Feb. 11, 1952; d. Andrew Melvin and Madeline Virginia (Mellon) Nordback; m. Herman Michael Winkler, Oct. 15, 1972; 1 child, Herman Andrew. B.B.A. in Acctg. and EDP, Pace Coll., 1972, M.B.A. in Acctg., 1976. With auditing dept. Bankers Trust Co., N.Y.C., 1972-82, v.p., 1979-82; v.p., unit head First Nat. Bank Chgo., 1982—, unit head ALCO audit 1982-83, sect. head ALCO and service products audit, 1983-84, ALCO and staff depts. audit, 1984-86, mgr. fin. acctg. systems and ops., control dept., 1987—; C.P.A., Ill.; adj. instr. acctg. Pace U., 1977-82; instr. various audit rev. courses, 1980-81; speaker industry confs. Chartered bank auditor. Vestry mem. St. John's Episcopal Ch. Mem. Nat. Assn. Female Execs., Mem. Bank Adminstrn. Inst. (chartered bank auditor study group task force 1978-81, exam. com. 1982-87), Inst. Internal. Auditors (N.Y.C. chpt.), Bus. and Profl. Womens Assn. of NW Suburbs, Nat. Assn. Female Execs. Office: First Nat Bank of Chgo One First Nat Plaza Suite 0319 Chicago IL 60670

WINN, JILL KANAGA KLINE, management executive; b. Oakland, Calif., Jan. 20, 1944; d. Lawrence Wesley and Virginia Louise (Honold) Kanaga; m. Donald Gene Kline, May 30, 1964 (div. 1979); children: Christian Lawrence, Kirsten Michael. Student, Northwestern U., 1961-63, Stella Adler Theater Studio, N.Y.C., 1963-64, Columbia Coll., Chgo., 1970-71. Comml. actress N.Y.C., 1964-77; supr. hostesses Jolly Roger Restaurants, Irvine, Calif., 1978-79; v.p. Mid-Continent Agys., Inc., Glenview, Ill., 1980—, mgr. accounts receivable portfolio program, 1983—, cons., 1985—. Author: Wet Her Down, Charlie, 1970. Recipient Cleo award Am. TV Comml. Festival, 1966. Mem. Nat. Assn. Female Execs., Nat. Assn. Women in Careers, Kappa Kappa Gamma (v.p. Westport, Conn. chpt. 1966). Democrat. Home: 2050 Valencia Northbrook IL 60062

WINN, LANELLE MILDRED, school counselor; b. Amarillo, Tex., Aug. 13, 1929; d. Henry Alton Bassett and Mildred Phyllis Schoening; m. Cecil M. Winn, Mar. 13, 1953; children: Gregory Wayne, Cecelia Jean, Sharon Gail. BA, West Tex. State U., 1951, MEd, 1968. Licensed tchr., Tex.; Licensed counselor, Tex. Tchr. Lazbuddy (Tex.) Ind. Sch. Dist., 1949-50, Carlsbad (N.Mex.) Ind. Sch. Dist., 1951-52, Amarillo (Tex.) Ind. Sch. Dist., 1952-53; research asst. W. Tex. State U., Canyon, 1965-67, field rep., 1968-69; instr. Amarillo Community Coll., 1969-70; vocat. counselor Bay City (Tex.) Ind. Sch. Dist., 1970-73; home sch. coordinator, vis. tchr. Harlandale Ind. Sch. Dist., San Antonio, Tex., 1973-85, counselor, 1985-87. Mem. Am. Assn. Counseling and Devel., Tex. Assn. of Counseling and Devel., Assn. Tex. Profl. Educators, Christian Counselors of Tex., Women In Bus. Baptist. Home: 208 Vivian Lane San Antonio TX 78201

WINN, SHARON KESSLER, consultant, educator; b. Denver, Sept. 29, 1943; d. Chester Milton and Elouise Martha (Rodgers) K.; m. Robert Kirk Winn, June 14, 1969. BA, U. Wis., 1965; MPA, U. Wash., 1972. Research scientist Bettelle, Seattle, Wash., 1973-77; asst. to chief exec. dir. Group Health, Seattle, 1977-79; prin. Winn, Elder & Assocs., Bellevue, Wash., 1979-82; pres. Winn & Assocs., Inc., Seattle, 1982—; clin. assoc. prof. u. Wash., 1975—; cons. Profl. Examination Service, N.Y.C., 1973-79. Contbr. numerous, monographs articles to profl. jours. Mem. bd. tng. commn. United Way, Seattle, 1983-84, fundraiser, 1986. Mem. Greater Seattle C. of C., U. Wash. Alumni Assn. (pres. dept. Health Services 1973), Inst. Mgmt. Cons. (pres., cert.; bd. dirs. NW chpt.). Democrat. Episcopalian. Office: Winn & Assocs Inc 1904 3rd Ave Seattle WA 98101

WINOGRAD, AUDREY LESSER, advertising executive; b. N.Y.C., Oct. 6, 1933; d. Jack J. and Theresa Lorraine (Elkind) Lesser; m. Melvin H. Winograd, Apr. 29, 1956; 1 child, Hope Elise. Student, U. Conn., 1950-53. Asst. advt. mgr. T. Baumritter Co., Inc., N.Y.C., 1953-54; asst. dir. pub. relations and creative merchandising Kirby, Block & Co., Inc., N.Y.C., 1954-56; div. mdse. mgr., dir. advt. and sales promotion Winograd's Dept. Store, Inc., Point Pleasant, N.J., 1956-73, v.p., 1960-73, exec. v.p., 1973-86; pres. AMW Assocs., Ocean Twp., N.J., 1976—. Editor bus. newsletters. Bd. dirs. Temple Beth Am, Lakewood, N.J., 1970-72. Mem. Jersey Pub. Relations & Advt. Assn. (pres. 1982-83), Monmouth Ocean Devel. Council, Monmouth County Bus. Assn. (pres. 1988—, bd. dirs. 1985—), Retail Advt. Conf., N.J. Assn. Women Bus. Owners, Soc. Prevention Cruelty to Animals, Am. Soc. Prevention Cruelty to Animals, Humane Soc., Friends of Animals, Animal Protection Inst. Office: AMW Assocs 10 Pine Ln Ocean NJ 07712

WINSBERG, GWYNNE ROESELER, health care executive; b. Chgo., Nov. 28, 1930; d. Berthold Ernst and Ruth Pearl (Wondrack) Roeseler; m. David Melvin Winsberg, Dec. 1, 1950 (div. Apr. 1984); children: Jeri Lynne, William Franklin. MS, U. Chgo., 1962, PhD, 1967. Asst. prof. Northwestern U., Chgo., 1967-75; assoc. dean Stritch Sch. Medicine, Loyola U., Maywood, Ill., 1975-81; sr. analyst U.S. DHHS, Washington, 1979-81; pres. GRW Assocs., Chgo., 1981—; v.p. Efficient Health Systems, Inc., Skokie, Ill., 1987; sec., trustee NorthCare, Evanston, Ill., 1975-81. Contbr. articles to profl. jours. Adv. Suburban Health Systems Agy., Oak Park, Ill., 1977-81; cons. Met. Chgo. Labor Council, 1983; v.p. New Music Chgo., 1983—; trustee Organic Theater, 1986—. Recipient NEH award, U. Pa., 1974; research fellow USPHS, U. Chgo., 1962-65. Mem. Am. Pub. Health Assn., Ill. Pub. Health Assn., Nat. Acad. Arts and Scis. Democrat. Methodist. Office: GRW Assocs Inc 5533 N Glenwood Chicago IL 60640

WINSETT-YOUNG, VICTORIA LOUISE, advertising company public relations executive; b. Dallas, Feb. 6, 1950; d. Milo Asa and Louise Love (Metcalfe) Winsett; m. Robert Miles Young, May 27, 1983; 1 son, Christopher John Asa. A.A. in Merchandising, Wade's Coll., Dallas, 1970; student So. Methodist U., 1974-78. Copywriter Sugarman Internat., Dallas, 1969-71; promotion dir. Quandrangle, Dallas, 1971-74; account exec. Tracy-Locke, Dallas, 1974-78, account supr., 1978-80, mgr. pub. relations Tracy-Locke/BBDO, 1980-82; dir. pub. relations Cunningham & Walsh, Dallas, 1982-86; owner The Young Co., Dallas, 1986—; cons. pub. relations Krause & Assocs., Dallas, 1982—. Editor, Shop Talk, 1983; author ann. report Nat. Assn. Retarded Citizens, Dallas, 1981; vol. in pub. relations Consumer's Day Fair, Dallas C. of C., 1982; chmn. pub. relations Boys Club Am., Dallas, 1983; assoc. chmn. pub. relations Terrace Homeowners, Dallas, 1983. Mem. Pub. Relations Soc. Am. (assoc.), Tex. Pub. Relations Assn., Women in Communications, Inc. (profl.), Nat. Assn. Female Execs. Episcopalian. Address: 10806 Colbert Way Dallas TX 75218

WINSLOW, HELEN CAUDLE, artist; b. New Salem, N.C., Mar. 24, 1916; d. Rufus Spurgeon and Nellie Sophia (Richardson) Caudle; B.A., Fla. So. Coll., 1936; student Art Students League, 1936-41, Otis Art Inst., Los Angeles, 1954-57; m. Randolph Winslow, Nov. 30, 1940; 1 dau., Joyce. Artist; juried exhbns. include; Frye Art Mus., Seattle, 1960, 62, 65, De Young Mus., San Francisco, 1968, 69, San Bernardino Mus., 1978; one woman shows include: Roberts Gallery, Los Angeles, 1966, Brentwood Gallery, Los Angeles, 1967-68, Vallis & Jensen, San Francisco, 1967, Gallery Fair, Mendocino, Calif., 1968-80, Austin Gallery, Scottsdale, Ariz., 1974-77; pvt. art tchr., 1956—; tchr. summer painting workshop, Rye, Colo., 1972-80. Recipient purchase award Los Angeles Ann. Art Festival, 1956, 2d prize Calif. State Fair, 1965, Wells Fargo award De Young Mus., 1969, 1st prize Beverly Hills Art League, 1974, spl. award San Bernardino Mus., 1978. Fellow Royal Soc. Arts; mem. Art Students League (life), Soc. Western Artists, Los Angeles Art Assn. Featured in article in S.W. Art Mag., 1977. Home: 9934 Westwanda Dr Beverly Hills CA 90210

WINSLOW, MARGARET RUTH, interior designer; b. Waco, Tex., Dec. 3, 1926; d. Ernest Fred and Hattie Henreyetta (Fisches) Stieg; m. Joseph Stanley Winslow, Feb. 11, 1944; children: Iris Lynette, Clinton Alan, Kenneth Lee, Marti Sue. Diploma, LaSalle Extension U., Chgo., 1970. Bookkeeper, acct. Winslow Engring. Co., Oklahoma City, 1965-75; pvt. practice interior designer Oklahoma City, 1984—. Editor, pub.: (calender) Notes & Narrations, 1980-87. Librarian St. Luke's U. Meth. Ch., Oklahoma City. Republican. Club: Les Bon Livres Book (sec. yearbook 1987—). Home and Office: 5817 N Ross Ave Oklahoma City OK 73112

WINSTON, JUDITH ANN, lawyer; b. Atlantic City, Nov. 23, 1943; d. Edward Carlton and Margaret Ann (Goodman) Marianno; B.A. magna cum laude, Howard U., Washington, 1966; J.D., Georgetown U., 1977; m. Michael Russell Winston, Aug. 10, 1963; children—Lisa Marie, Cynthia Eileen. Dir. EEO Project, Council Great City Schs., Washington, 1971-74; legal asst. Lawyers Com. for Civil Rights Under Law, Washington, 1975-77; admitted to D.C. bar, 1977, U.S. Supreme Ct. bar; spl. asst. to dir. Office for Civil Rights, HEW, Washington, 1977-79; exec. asst., legal counsel to chair U.S. EEO Commn., Washington, 1979-80; asst. gen. counsel U.S. Dept. Edn., 1980-86; dep. dir. Lawyers Com. for Civil Rights Under Law, 1986—; edn1. cons., 1974-77; guest lectr. Washington Coll. Law of Am. U. Active NAACP Legal Def. and Ednl. Fund, 1968-79; chair employment discrimination com. Women's Legal Def. Fund, 1979.; Mem. ACLU, (bd. dirs., higher achievement program, trustee Nat. Capital Area), D.C. Bar Assn., Washington Council Lawyers, Washington Bar Assn., Nat. Bar Assn., Fed. Bar Assn., Links Inc., Alpha Kappa Alpha, Phi Beta Kappa, Delta Theta Phi. Democrat. Episcopalian. Author: Desegregating Schools in the Great Cities: Philadelphia, 1970; Chronicle of a Decade 1961-1970, 1970; Desegregating Urban Schools: Educational Equality/Quality, 1970. Home: 1371 Kalmia Rd NW Washington DC 20012 Office: Lawyer's Com for Civil Rights Under Law 1400 Eye St NW Washington DC 20005

WINTER, JOAN ELIZABETH, psychotherapist; b. Aiken, S.C., Feb. 24, 1947; d. John S. and Mary Elizabeth (Caldwell) Winter. BS, Ariz. State U., 1970; MSW, Va. Commonwealth U., 1977. Lic. clin. social worker, Va. Counselor Child Psychiatry Hosp., Phoenix, 1969-70, Ariz. Job Coll., Casa Grande, 1970-71; dir. Halfway House, Richmond, Va., 1971-73; state supr. resdl. treatment, Richmond, 1973-75; psycotherapist Med. Coll. Va., Richmond, 1975-76, Va. Commonwealth U., 1976-77; exec. dir. Family Research Project, Richmond, Va., 1979-81; dir. Family Inst. Va., Richmond, 1980—; examiner, approved supr. Bd. Behavioral Scis., Commonwealth of Va., 1982-86; mem. Avanta Network, Exec. Council and Faculty, Nat. Inst. of Drug Abuse, Research Adv. Com. Author: The Phenomenon of Incest, 1977, The Use of Self in Therapy: The Person and Practice of the Therapist, 1987, Family Life of Psychotherapists, 1987; contbr. articles to profl. jours. Diplomate Nat. Assn. Social Workers; mem. Am. Soc. Cert. Social Workers, Am. Family Therapy Assn., Am. Assn. Marriage and Family Therapy (approved supr.), Avanta Network Faculty. Address: 2910 Monument Ave Richmond VA 23221

WINTERLING, MARY ANN, educational adminstrator; b. Balt., Mar. 15, 1943; d. Leo George and Loretta Catherine (Novak) Winterling; B.A., Coll. Notre Dame, 1965; M.Ed., Johns Hopkins U., 1971, cert. advanced study in edn., 1980. Tchr., Balt. City Pub. Sch. No. 47, Hampstead Hill, 1965-74; asst. prin. Balt. City Pub. Sch. No. 150, Bentalou Elem. Sch., 1974-80, prin., 1980—; asst. prin. sr. tchrs., 1978-79. Sec. S.E. Civic Orgn., 1972-73; mem. Adminstrs. Adv. Council, 1976-79. Mem. Assn. for Supervision and Curriculum Devel., Nat. Assn. Elem. Sch. Tchrs., Nat. Assn. Elem. Sch. Prins., Md. Assn. Elem. Sch. Prins., Assn. Tchr. Educators, Johns Hopkins U. Alumni Assn., Pub. Sch. Adminstrs. and Suprs. Assn., Pi Lambda Theta, Phi Delta Kappa. Democrat. Roman Catholic. Club: Johns Hopkins. Office: 220 N Bentalou St Baltimore MD 21223

WINTERS, ALICE GRAHAM BUTLER (MRS. CARL S. WINTERS), civic worker; b. Linton, Ind., July 5, 1907; d. William Austin and Mary (Inman) Butler; A.B., Franklin Coll., 1932; spl. student U. Rochester, 1929-30, Colgate-Rochester Div. Sch., 1929-30; m. Carl S. Winters, May 23, 1925; children—Barbara (Mrs. Robert Kane), Janet (Mrs. Ralph Kuzmic), Linda (Mrs. Allen F. Jones). Minister junior ch., Jackson, Mich., 1931-39, 1st Bapt. Ch. Oak Park, Ill., 1939-59; lectr. Adult Edn. Council Chgo.; also freelance writer. Organizer, pres. Jackson (Mich.) Peace Council, 1933-35; pres. Jackson County LWV, 1935, Chgo. Drama League, 1948-50, Chgo. Mission Union, 1956-60; treas. Art Assocs. Oak Park, 1961-64; pres. Infant Welfare Soc., 1960-62; mem. Com. of 100, Nat. Council of Chs., 1963—; bd. dirs. Woman's Bd. Salvation Army, Chgo., 1960—, pres. bd., 1969—; bd. dirs. Women's Bd. Mental Health Assn., Chgo.; bd. dirs. Maywood (Ill.) Home and Hosp., 1940-62, v.p. bd., 1958-62; mem. woman's bd. Christian U. of Tokyo, 1963—. Recipient Outstanding Woman award Chgo. Assn. Commerce and Industry, 1976; citation for outstanding contbns. to humanity Franklin Coll., 1978; Disting. Service award Salvation Army Internat., 1980; Cert. of Recognition for outstanding service Comprehensive Community Services of Chgo., 1980; citation for achievement and influence Chautauqua Instn., 1982, Alice and Carl Winters Park named in their honor, 1985. Mem. Delta Zeta, Beta Sigma Phi, Kappa Delta. Clubs: Conference Club Presidents (bd. dirs. 1962—, chmn. pub. relations, sec.); 19th Century Woman's; Garden; Chautauqua (N.Y.) Women's; Oak Park Country; Zonta. Home: 404 N East Ave Oak Park IL 60602 Other: Packard Manor Chautauqua NY 14722

WINTERS, BARBARA JO, musician; b. Salt Lake City; d. Louis McClain and Gwendolyn (Bradley) W. AB cum laude, UCLA, 1960, postgrad., 1961; postgrad., Yale, 1960. Mem. oboe sect. Pasadena (Calif.) Symphony, 1958-60; mem. oboe sect. Los Angeles Philharmonic, 1961—, now prin. oboist., clinician oboe, English horn, Oboe d'amore. Recs. movie, TV sound tracks. Home: 3529 Coldwater Canyon Studio City CA 91604 Office: 135 N Grand Ave Los Angeles CA 90012

WINTERS, BETH ANN, retired association executive; b. Monroe, Mich., June 12, 1918; d. John Joseph and Edith (Golden) Harrington; m. Edward R. Winters, 1979; children James W. Payne III, Michael H., Penelope Ann, Terrence J. Various clerical, bookkeeping and secretarial positions, 1934-58; clk. Monroe County, 1959-63; owner Winters Office Aids, Monroe, 1963-65; acting exec. dir. Monroe County chpt. ARC, 1964, exec. dir., 1964-85, chmn. 1959-62; co-organizer Coordinating Council Agencies, Monroe, 1964. Bd. dirs. Friends Monroe County Zoo Assn., 1958-60, Monroe County Big Bros., 1968, Monroe County OEO, 1969, Mich. Welfare League, 1968, S.E. Mich. Tourist Assn., 1961; chmn. Monroe County Traffic and Safety Com., 1979; mem. Greater Monroe Council Alcoholism; treas. Alcohol and Substance Abuse Ctr., 1979-80. Recipient award ARC, 1960, 62, Camp Fire Girls, 1960; chpt. house named in her honor. Mem. Monroe County His. Soc. (sec. 1964-66), ARC Retirees, Art and Crafts League Monroe (vice chmn. 1958), Monroe County Bus. and Profl. Women, St. Patrick's Soc. Am. Irish (founder 1958, 1st pres. 1958-59), VFW Aux. Democrat. Roman Catholic. Club: Navy Mother's (charter, past dir.). Home: 443 N Macomb St Monroe MI 48161 Office: 421 S Monroe St Monroe MI 48161

WINTERS, DEBORAH ANN, radiologist; b. Garden City, Kans., Aug. 23, 1951; d. Wesley Chester and Ruby Irene (Vaughn) W.; m. Clyde Elam Marlin, Dec. 21, 1975; children: Angela Michelle, Rachel Leanne. B.A. cum laude, So. Missionary Coll., 1973; postgrad. Vol. State Community Coll., 1973-74, Middle Tenn. State U., 1974; M.D., Loma Linda U., 1978. Diplomate Am. Bd. Radiology, Nat. Bd. Med. Examiners. Records librarian Sta. WSMC, Collegedale, Tenn., 1969-71, 1972-73; computer operator Eaton, Yale & Towne, Gallatin, Tenn., 1973-74; resident in radiology Loma Linda U. (Calif.) Med. Center, 1979-82; practice medicine specializing in radiology Middle Tenn. Radiology Assocs., McMinnville.sec. med. staff River Park Hosp., 1988. Active in local Adventist Ch. Mem. Am. Coll. Radiology, Radiol. Soc. N.Am., Warren County Med. Soc. (v.p. 1986, pres. 1987), Tenn. Radiology Soc., Middle Tenn. Radiology Soc., Tenn. Med. Soc., So. Valley Radiol. Soc., Am. Assn. Women Radiologists, Loma Linda U. Women's Med. Aux. Alumni Assn., Nat. Soc. of Tole and Decorative Painters, San Diego Zool. Soc. Office: River Park Hosp Sparta Hwy McMinnville TN 37110

WINTERS, JEANNE HASKELL, home economist; b. Amsterdam, N.Y., Apr. 27, 1944; d. George E. and Helen M. (Stewart) H.; m. William U. Winters, Oct. 18, 1969; 1 child, Daniel W. BS, SUNY, Plattsburgh, 1966, MS, 1971. Cert. home economist. Extension home economist Albany (N.Y.) County Cooperative Extension, 1968-70, Saratoga County Cooperative Extension, Ballston Spa, N.Y., 1970—. Mem. Am. Home Econs. Assn., Nat. Assn. Extension Home Economists (Disting. Service award 1979, Continued Excellence award 1987), N.Y. State Assn. Extension Home Economists (treas. 1974, pres. 1976, Continued Excellence award 1986), Saratoga C. of C. (class II leader 1986-87), Epsilon Sigma Phi (Superior Excellence award 1979). Lodge: Soroptimists. Office: Cornell Coop Extension 50 W High St Ballston Spa NY 12020

WINTERS, JOANNE MARIE, elementary school principal; b. Pitts., June 3, 1947; d. Alexander Xavior and Josephine Ann (Rusciolelli) Wisniewski; m. Patrick John Winters, May 17, 1975; children: Timothy Charles, Julia Gayle, Martin Alexander. BS, Clarion State Coll., 1969; MS, U. Md., 1971, PhD, 1981. Cert. reading specialist, K-12 tchr., 1-8 adminstn./supervision elem. and middle sch., Md. Reading specialist middle and elem. grades Howard County Bd. Edn., Ellicott City, Md., 1971-87, asst. prin. Running Brook Elem. Sch., 1987—; instr. Choppin State Coll., Balt., spring, 1983; speaker Md. State Reading Conv., Timonium, 1987, 88. Sec. Bryant Woods PTA, Columbia, 1985, Running Brook PTA, Columbia, 1987, also 2nd v.p., 1987-88. Mem. Internat. Reading Assn. (mem. Md. State chpt., pres. Howard County chpt. 1976-77, v.p. 1986-87), NEA, Md. Edn. Assn., Howard County Edn. Assn., Assn. for Supervision and Curriculum Devel., Howard County Assn. Elem. Sch. Adminstrs. Democrat. Roman Catholic. Home: 6246 Cricket Pass Columbia MD 21044 Office: Running Brook Elem Sch 5215 W Running Brook Rd Columbia MD 21044

WINTERS, MARY ANN, educational administrator; b. Ancon, Panama, Apr. 28, 1948; came to U.S., 1951; d. Leonard McCrea and Selyn (Martin) W. BA, Mt. St. Vincent, 1971; M of Pub. Sci. in Non-Profit Mgmt., New Sch. Social Research, 1988. Tchr. Incarnation Sch., N.Y.C., 1970-74; co-dir. Washington Heights Ctr. for Action, N.Y.C., 1974-79; dir. Kingsbridge Heights Community Ctr., Bronx, 1975-79; devel. dir. Elizabeth Seton Coll., Yonkers, N.Y., 1982-85, Sch. of Holy Child, Rye, N.Y., 1985—. Mem. Council for Advancement and Support of Edn., Westchester Assn. Devel. Officers (v.p. 1985-87, pres. 1987—), Westchester County Assn. Avocations: sailing, music. Office: Sch of Holy Child Westchester Ave Rye NY 10580

WINTERS, MARY-FRANCES, small business owner; b. Buffalo, Mar. 13, 1951; d. Lawrence A. and Gladys M. (Molock) S.; m. Joseph R. Winters, June 2, 1973; children: Joseph, Mareisha. BA, U. Rochester, 1973, MBA, 1982. Personnel specialist Eastman Kodak Corp., Rochester, N.Y., 1973-79, mgr., 1979-81, sr. market analyst, 1981-84; pres. Winters Group, Rochester, 1984—; Bd. dirs. Eltrex Industries, Rochester. Trustee U. Rochester, 1986—; bd. dirs. Black Bus. Assn., Rochester, 1986—, United Way Greater Rochester, 1984—, Girl Scouts U.S., N.Y.C., 1987—; pres. bd. dirs. Genesee Valley Girl Scouts U.S., 1984-87. Named Bus. Women of Yr. Negro Bus. and Profl. Women's Orgn., Rochester, 1987; recipient Athena award Rochester Area C. of C. Mem. Am. Mktg. Assn., Alpha Kappa Alpha. Methodist. Home: 12 Port Meadow Trail Fairport NY 14450 Office: The Winters Group Inc 14 Franklin St Rochester NY 14604

WINTER-SWITZ, CHERYL DONNA, travel company executive; b. Jacksonville, Fla., Dec. 6, 1947; d. Jacqueline Marie (Carroll) Winter; m. Frank C. Snedaker, June 24, 1974 (div. May 1976); m. Robert William Switz, July 1, 1981. AA, City Coll. of San Francisco, 1986; student, Golden Gate U., 1986—. Bookkeeper, agt. McQuade Tours, Ft. Lauderdale, Fla., 1967-69; mgr. Boca Raton (Fla.) Travel, 1969-76; owner, mgr. Ocean Travel, Boca Raton, Fla., 1976-79; ind. contractor Far Horizons Travel, Boca Raton, Fla., 1979-80; mgr. Tara/BPF Travel, San Francisco, 1981-84; mgr. travel. dept. Ernst & Whinney/Lifeco Travel, San Francisco, 1984-86; ptnr., mgr. Travelmain Ltd., Walnut Creek, Calif., 1986—; instr. Golden Gate U., 1986—. Mem. Amateur Trapshooting Assn., Hotel and Restaurant Mgmt. Club. Republican. Episcopalian. Home: 642 Brussels San Francisco CA 94134 Office: Travelmain Ltd 2121 N California Blvd Suite 280 Walnut Creek CA 94596

WINTHER, VIRGINIA E., clothing executive; b. Cin., Dec. 20, 1959; d. Frederick Bernard and Natalie Jean (Norton) W. A in Mktg., U. Cin., 1979, BA in Communications, 1981. Mgr. mdse. Gold Circle, Cin., 1982-85; account mgr. Calvin Klein Menswear, N.Y.C., 1985—. Mem. Nat. Assn. Female Execs., Summerfair, Inc., Alpha Chi Omega (sect. chmn. 1985—, v.p. 1986-87, pres. 1988). Republican. Presbyterian. Club: Cin. Ski. Home: 3936 Delmar Ave Suite 2000 Cincinnati OH 45211

WINTHROP, BARBARA SEVERY, chef, food consultant; b. Oceanside, Calif., Oct. 30, 1945; d. George Fairburn and Dorothy Mary (Severy) Winthrop. BA, Hunter Coll., 1969. Chair dept. phys. edn. Packer Collegiate Inst., Bklyn., 1969-75; coach, tchr. Chapin Sch., N.Y.C., 1975-81; mgr. Servomation Corp., Stamford, Conn., 1981-82; chef Alpen Pantry, N.Y.C., 1982-83; head chef Bagels & Caviar, Bklyn., 1983-85, Heights Casino, Bklyn., 1985-87, Christopher's Restaurant, N.Y.C., 1987-88, Portland Yacht Club, Falmouth, Maine, 1988—; mem. Mid. States Evaluation, N.Y.C., 1974. Vol. Dem. Party, 1985. Mem. NOW, Audubon Soc., Ms. Found. for Women, Wilderness Soc., Athletic Assn. Ind. Schs. Home: 50 Remsen St Brooklyn NY 11201 Office: Christopher's Restaurant 115 Christopher St New York NY 10014

WINTOUR, ANNA, editor-in-chief; b. Eng., Nov. 3, 1949; came to U.S., 1976; d. Charles and Elinor W.; m. David Shaffer, Sept. 1984; children: Charles, Kate. Student, Queens Coll., 1963-67. Deputy fashion editor Harper's and Queen Mag., London, 1970-76; fashion editor Harper's Bazaar, New York, 1976-77; fashion and beauty editor Viva Mag., New York, 1977-78; contbg. editor fashion and style Savvy Mag., New York, 1980-81; sr. editor N.Y. Mag., 1981-83; creative dir. U.S. Vogue, N.Y., 1983-86; editor in chief British Vogue, London, 1986, House and Garden, N.Y., 1987-88, Vogue, N.Y., 1988—. Office: Vogue Magazine Conde Nast Bldg 350 Madison Ave New York NY 10017

WINTZ, MILDRED MARY, environmental educator; b. Upper Darby, Pa., Feb. 25, 1932; d. George Lee and Mildred Ellen (Deering) Jenkins; B in Applied Arts, U. Pa., 1955; MA in Environ. Edn., Beaver Coll., 1979; EdD Temple U., 1987; m. Donald Wintz, July 31, 1954; children—Lisa Marie, Donald Lee, Donna Lee. Designer, John Reid Interiors, 1955-58; prin. Wintz Assos., Huntingdon Valley, Pa., 1959—; dir. edn. Pennypack Watershed Assn., Huntingdon Valley, 1978—. Instr., CPR and first aid, ARC; trainer Girl Scouts U.S.A., Phila.; mem. environ. adv. commn. Upper Moreland Twp.; mem. Union League Phila. Recipient environ. award Pennypack Watershed Assn.; William Penn award Trefoil Soc., ARC. Cert. in elem. and secondary environ. edn., Pa. Mem. Am. Soc. Interior Designers, Assn. Interpretive Naturalists, Pa. Assn. Environ. Educators, Phila. Art Alliance,

Land Mgmt. Task Force. Republican. Lutheran. Club: Huntingdon Valley Country. Author: Gray Fox Environmental Field Education Programs, 1976; Discovery Trek Environmental Field Education Programs, 1978—. Office: 2955 Edge Hill Rd Huntingdon Valley PA 19006

WINZELBERG, ELISSA F., architect; b. Bklyn., July 14, 1953; d. Emil and Bernice (Kotofsky) W.; m. Howard Jeffrey Cohen, July 9, 1978. BArch, Pratt Inst., Bklyn., 1976; MS in Hist. Preservation, Columbia U., 1978. Licensed architect, N.Y., N.J. Assoc. Beyer, Blinder, Belle, N.Y.C., 1978-86; pvt. practice architecture Kew Gardens, N.Y., 1986—; cons. in field. Mem. AIA, Am. Soc. Interior Designers (interior design project award 1984), N.Y. Soc. Architects.

WIRSIG, JANE DEALY, writer, editor; b. Boston, Aug. 22, 1919; d. James Bond and Anna B. (McQuillen) Dealy; B.A., Vassar Coll., 1941; M.S. (Vassar Coll. fellow 1941-42), Columbia U., 1942; m. Woodrow Wirsig, Dec. 11, 1942; children—Alan Robert, Guy Rodney, Paul Harold. Network radio newswriter CBS, 1942-43; free lance writer articles, short stories various mags., 1942—; editor Vassar Alumnae mag., 1952-53; editor, rewriter Companion in Paris, Woman's Home Companion, 1953-56; editor Wirsig, Gordon & O'Connor, Inc., Princeton, N.J., 1956-58; editorial cons. Ednl. Testing Service, Princeton, 1957-60, dir. publs., 1960-70, exec. dir. info. services and publs., 1971-74, sec. corp., 1974-80. Mem. exec. bd. George Washington council Boy Scouts Am., 1976-80. Mem. Am. Assn. Higher Edn., Greater Princeton C. of C. (dir. 1974-81, v.p. 1976-80, pres. 1980), Phi Beta Kappa. Club: Vassar (Central N.J. v.p. 1955-57). Home: 25 Gordon Way Princeton NJ 08540

WIRT, JEANNETTE MAE, hospital executive; b. Pottstown, Pa., Mar. 9, 1947; d. Harold William and Kathryn (Kleman) Williams; m. Lowell Richard Wirt, July 29, 1967; children: Andrew Lowell, Amy Ruth, Kathryn Elizabeth. Cert. radiographer, Coatesville (Pa.) Hosp., 1967; cert. radiation therapy technologist, Penrose Cancer Hosp., 1970. Staff technologist, instr. Coatesville Hosp., 1967-69, Meml. Hosp., Colorado Springs, Colo., 1969; staff technologist M.S. Hershey Med. Ctr., Pa., 1973; sr. technologist York (Pa.) Hosp., 1973-74, supr., 1974-77, supr. dosimetrist, 1977-83, tech. dir., 1983-87, adminstr. mgr., 1987—; clin. supr. Gwynedd Mercy Coll., Gwynedd Valley, Pa., 1978—; site visitor Joint Rev. Com. in Edn. in Radiologic Tech., Chgo., 1980—; instr. in field., 1984, 86. Bd. dirs., chair nurse's edn. com. Am. Cancer Soc., York, Pa., 1984—, mem. exec. com. 1985—; tchr. Grace Brethren Ch., Dillsburg, Pa., 1974—. Mem. Am. Soc. of Radiologic Technologists (chair task force on radiation therapy), Pa. Soc. Radiologic Technologists (chair legis. com. 1985), Am. Healthcare Radiology Adminstrs., Soc. Radiation Oncology Adminstrs. Republican. Home: 3004 Bedford Pl Rd #6 York PA 17404 Office: York Hosp 1001 S George St York PA 17405

WIRTENBERG, THELMA JEAN (JEANA), marketing executive, research psychologist; b. N.Y.C., Jan. 28, 1950; d. Harold and Pearl Cecile (Hershberg) W. BS in Math. magna cum laude, CUNY, 1971; MA in Psychology, UCLA, 1972, PhD in Psychology, 1979. Social sci. analyst U.S. Commn. on Civil Rights, Washington, 1975-79; research mgr. Nat. Inst. Edn., Washington, 1979-83; market research mgr. AT&T Techs., Parsippany, N.J., 1983-85; market mgr. AT&T Info. Systems, Parsippany, 1985—; cons. Orbit Prodns., Inc., Washington, 1986—; cons. psychology of women div. Am. Psycol. Assn., Washington, 1976-83; Washington area mgr. Inst. Pub. Service, 1982-83. Co-editor: Sex-Role Research: Measuring Social Change, 1983; co-editor Psychology of Women Quar. spl. issue, 1981. Chancellors intern fellow UCLA, 1972-75. Mem. Soc. for Psychol. Study Social Issues (spl. issues dissertation award 1979), Phi Beta Kappa. Democrat. Jewish. Office: AT&T One Speedwell Ave 403C Morristown NJ 07960

WIRTHS, CLAUDINE GIBSON, psychologist, author; b. Covington, Ga., May 9, 1926; d. Count Dillon and Julia (Thompson) Gibson; m. Theodore William Wirths, Dec. 28, 1945; children: William M., David G. AB, U. Ky. 1946, MA, 1948; MEd, Am. U., 1979. Program dir. N.C. League for Crippled Children, Chapel Hill, 1948-49; research psychologist Savannah River Urbanization Studies, Aiken, S.C., 1950-52; research psychologist, cons. various pub. and pvt. agys., S.C., D.C., Md., Bermuda, 1953-79; spl. edn. tchr. Montgomery Pub. Schs., Gaithersburg, Md., 1979-80, coordinator learning ctr., 1980-84; adj. faculty Frederick (Md.) Community Coll., 1985—. Co-author: (with Williams) Lives Through The Years, 1968; author: I Hate School, 1986 (Best Book award ALA 1987), I Need A Job, 1988; contbr. articles to profl. jours. and popular press. Vice chair Def. Adv. Com. Women in Service, Washington, 1960-63, adv. com. Seneca Pk., Montgomery County, 1970-79; adv. bd. Sec. Nat. Resources, Md., 1976-79. Named Outstanding Citizen of County, Aiken, 1954; recipient award Montgomery County Environ. Trust, 1973, 1st pl. award for feature story, Md., D.C., Del. Press Assn., 1980. Mem. Assn. Children with Learning Disabilities, Washington Ind. Writers, Phi Beta Kappa. Episcopalian. Home and Office: PO Box 335 Braddock Heights MD 21714

WISCH, MARILYN JOAN, pension design firm executive; b. Bklyn., Oct. 13, 1942; d. Irving Elmer and Sylvia (Manzar) Chezar; m. Steven Charles Wisch, Sept. 19, 1965 (div. Nov. 1981); 1 child, Beth Allyson. BS, NYU, 1964; MEd, Adelphi U., 1976, paralegal employee benefits program, 1982. Art dir. Doyle Dane & Bernbach, N.Y.C., 1964-69; tchr. Baldwin Sch. Dist., N.Y., 1977; real estate saleswoman Village Homes, Rockville Centre, N.Y., 1978-82; cons., v.p., ptnr., owner Accu-Plan Adminstrs., Inc., Rockville Centre, 1983-87; pres./owner Accrued Benefits Planning Ltd., Rockville Centre, 1987—; paralegal instr. Adelphi U., Garden City, N.Y., 1983—. Poll insp., Baldwin, 1977-78; v.p. Plaza PTA, Baldwin, 1978-79; v.p. Sisterhood, pres. Couples Club, Central Synagogue, Rockville Centre, 1978-81; vol. South Nassau Communities Hosp., Oceanside, N.Y., 1979-81. Mem. Nat. Assn. Female Execs. (network dir. 1985), Am. Soc. Pension Actuaries (coordinator for testing Rockville Centre 1986), Nat. Inst. Pension Adminstrs., Rockville Centre C. of C. (bd. trustees). Democrat. Jewish. Avocations: gardening, reading, seminars, public speaking. Home: 1276 Surrey Ln Rockville Centre NY 11570 Office: Accrued Benefits Planning Ltd 1276 Surrey Ln Rockville Centre NY 11570

WISDOM, GUYRENA KNIGHT, psychologist, educator; b. St. Louis, July 27, 1923; d. Gladys Margaret (Hankins) McCullin; AB, Stowe Tchrs. Coll., 1945; AM, U. Ill., 1951; postgrad. St. Louis U., 1952-53, 58, 62; Washington U., St. Louis, 1959-61; U. Chgo., 1966-67; Drury Coll., 1968; U. Mo., 1971-72; Fontbonne Coll., 1973; Harris-Stowe StateColl., 1974, 81-82. Tchr. elementary sch. St. Louis Pub. Sch. System, 1945-63, psychol. examiner, 1963-68, sch. psychologist, 1968-74, cons. spl. edn., 1974-77, supr. spl. edn. dept., 1977-79, coordinator staff devel. div., 1979-81; pvt. tutor, 1971-72; sch. psychologist, 1984-85; pvt. practice psychologist, St. Louis, 1985-88; assessment specialist St. Louis Regional Ctr. for the Developmentally Disabled, 1988—; instr. Harris Tchrs. Coll., St. Louis, 1973-74, Harris-Stowe Coll., 1979. Contbr. articles to profl. jours. Mem. Nat. Assn. Sch. Psychologists, Mo. Assn. Children With Learning Disabilities, Council for Exceptional Children, Mo. Tchrs. Assn., Assn. Supervision and Curriculum Devel., Pi Lambda Theta, Kappa Delta Pi. Roman Catholic. Home: 5046 Wabada St Saint Louis MO 63113

WISE, EARNESTINE SPRINGER, traffic manager; b. Denton, Tex., Jan. 10, 1941; d. Earnest and Sarah Katherine (O'Neil) Springer; m. Carl L. Carpenter, Dec. 23, 1960 (div. 1971); children—Carl L., Shannon René; m. James Marrion Wise, June 15, 1973. Student So. Meth. U., 1972-74, Brookhaven Jr. Coll., 1980-82, U. Tex.-Dallas, 1982-86. Traffic mgr. Zoecon Corp., Dallas, 1971—. Mem. Am. Soc. Traffic and Logistics (cert. mem.; chpt. bd. dirs. 1982-84), Cert. Claims Profl. Accreditation Council (hon.), Delta Nu Alpha Transp. Club. Democrat. Baptist. Home: 13677 Rawhide Pkwy Dallas TX 75234 Office: Zoecon Corp 12200 Denton Dr Dallas TX 75234

WISE, GINGER WARD, bank executive; b. Edenton, N.C., Jan. 5, 1954; d. Jesse Herman and Mary (Mitchell) Ward; m. Paul F. Wise, June 4, 1977; children: Lindsey Nichole, Paul Matthew. BA, U. S.C., 1976. Mgr. comml. loans First Nat. Bank S.C., Columbia, 1978-81; corp. services sales rep. First Nat. Bank S.C., 1978-80, commercial loans system project mgr., 1980-81; adminstr. asst. C&S Nat. Bank S.C., Columbia, 1981-83, asst. electronic banking officer, 1983-85, electronic banking officer, 1975-76; electronic banking officer C&S Nat. Bank S.C., 1985-86; electronic banking officer, dept. head C&S Nat. Bank S.C., Columbia, 1986—; chair Columbia Postal Customer Council, 1983-85. ch. Contbr. articles to profl. jours. Chair Sch. Improvement Council, West Columbia, 1986—; pres. Wood Elem. Sch. PTA, West Columbia, 1987—. Mem. Luth. Women. Republican. Office: C&S Nat Bank SC 295 Greystone Blvd Columbia SC 29222

WISE, MAUREEN KAMEN, public relations executive, editor; b. Los Angeles, Mar. 26, 1946; d. Murray Morton and Rosalyn Estelle (Horowitz) Kamen; m. Murray Jay Wise, Aug. 7, 1966; children: Stephanie Lauren, Tracey Meredith. BS, Elmira (N.Y.) Coll., 1966. Cert. elem. tchr., N.Y. Tchr. elem Horseheads (N.Y.) Cen. Sch. Dist., 1966-67, East Ramapo Sch. Dist., Spring Valley, N.Y., 1967-69; pub. relations dir. United Jewish Appeal of Rockland, Spring Valley, N.Y., 1971-86; publicity coordinator recreation dept. Town of Ramapo, Suffern, N.Y., 1973; dir., tchr. Pomona (N.Y.) Jewish Cen. Nursery Sch., 1975-78; community resources dir. Planned Parenthood of Rockland, West Nyack, N.Y., 1979-82; owner, pres. Wise Promotions, Spring Valley, 1981—; pub. relations dir. Women's League for Conservative Judaism, N.Y.C., 1985—; bd. dirs. United Jewish Community of Rockland, Rockland City, N.Y., 1976—; mem. chancellor's com. Jewish Theol. Sem., N..Y.C., 1987; founding mem., v.p. Rockland County Tourism Bd., Suffern, 1983-85. Mng. editor Women's League Outlook mag., 1985—; prodn. supr. (baby record book) Welcome to the World, 1985-86; producer, dir. multimedia presentations, theatrical prodns. Mem. citizens adv. com. Rockland County, 1984; mem. United Jewish Appeal. Recipient Woman of Achievement award, J.T. Sem. Torah Fund Campaign, 1986, Disting. Service award Rockland County. Mem. Bus. and Profl. Women (bd. dirs., pub. relations chmn. 1979, 83-86), Pomona Jewish Ctr. (exec. bd.), Rockland Women's Network (In Celebration of Women award for Achievement in Bus., 1984), Westchester-Rockland Women's League (past pub. relations chmn.). Democrat. Club: Elmwood Playhouse (Nyack). Lodge: Hadassah (Rockland). Home: 24 Fairway Oval Spring Valley NY 10977 Office: Women's League for Conservative Judaism 48 E 74th St New York NY 10021

WISHARD, DELLA M., state legislator; b. Bison, S.D., Oct. 21, 1934; d. Ervin E. and Alma J. (Albertson) Preszler; m. Glenn L. Wishard, Oct. 18, 1953; children: Glenda Lee, Pamela A., Glen Ervin. Grad. high sch., Bison. Mem. S.D. Ho. of Reps., Pierre, 1984—. Columnist County Farm Bur., 1970—. Committeewoman state Rep. Cen. Com., Perkins County, S.D., 1980-84. Mem. Am. Legis. Exchange Council (state coordinator 1985—), Fed. Rep. Women (chmn. Perkins County chpt. 1978-84), S.D. Farm Bur. (state officer 1982). Lutheran. Home and Office: PO Box 139 Prairie City SD 57649

WISHNER, KATHLEEN LAMBERT, physician; b. Modesto, Calif., June 11, 1943; d. Henry Oscar Lambert and Alyce (Littlefield) Lambert Daniells; m. Phillip Andrew Harris, Aug. 4, 1961 (div. 1973); children—Jeffrey John, Michael Lambert; m. William Jay Wishner, May 20, 1973. B.A., Calif. State U.-San Francisco, 1963; Ph.D., U. Calif.-San Francisco, 1968; M.D., U. So. Calif., 1976. Diplomate Nat. Bd. Med. Examiners, Am. Bd. Pediatrics, Am. Bd. Pediatric Endocrinology. Intern Children's Hosp. Los Angeles, 1976-77; resident Los Angeles County/U. So. Calif. Med. Ctr., 1977-78; fellow pediatric endocrinology City of Hope/Harbor-UCLA, 1978-79; asst. prof. U. Minn.-St. Paul, 1968-70, U. So. Calif., Los Angeles, 1970-73; teaching assoc. Georgetown U., Washington, 1973-74; staff physician City of Hope Med Ctr., Duarte, Calif., 1979-81; assoc. clin. prof. U. So. Calif., Los Angeles, 1984—; practice medicine specializing in pediatric endocrinology and clin. nutrition, Pasadena, Calif., 1981—cons. Panel on space sta. ops. medicine NASA, Am. Inst. Biol. Scis., 1983-85; sci. adv. bd. NutraSweet Co., 1987—. Contbr. articles to profl. jours. NIH grantee, 1969-73, 69-72, 79-81. Mem. Am. Diabetes Assn. (dir. So. Calif. affiliate 1982-87, pres.-elect 1986-87, dir. Calif. affiliate 1987—, pres.-elect 1987—, nat. bd. dirs. 1988—, publs. com. 1987—, Nat. award 1985), Am. Dietetic Assn. (registered dietitian), Am. Inst. Nutrition, Calif. Med. Assn. (com. on accreditation and certification of continuing med. edn. 1985-87), Los Angeles County Med. Assn. Democrat. Office: Pasadena Diabetes and Endocrinology Med Group 10 Congress St Suite 320 Pasadena CA 91105

WISKERCHEN, KAREN ANN, marketing executive; b. Milw., Apr. 3, 1959; d. Lloyd Henry and Patricia Barbara (Kempski) W. BBA in Mktg., U. Wis., Milw., 1982, MS in Mgmt., 1985. Research supr. Pert Survey Research, Milw., 1981-84; exec. asst. Gen. Split Corp., Milw., 1984-85; research supr. Cramer-Krasselt Advt. Agy., Milw., 1981-85; research mgr. J.J. Keller & Assocs., Neenah, Wis., 1985—. Bd. dirs., mem. activity com., Big Bros. and Sisters, Inc., Appleton, Wis., 1986—. Mem. Nat. Assn. Female Execs., Am. Mktg. Assn., Direct Mktg. Assn. Roman Catholic. Home: 192 Denhardt Ave Neenah WI 54956

WISNER, CYNTHIA ANN, geologist; b. Carthage, Mo., July 7, 1957; d. James William and Billie Ann (Glaze) Schooler; m. David Lee Wisner, Feb. 12, 1983. BS in Geology, Baylor U., 1980; postgrad., Houston Bapt. U., 1986—. Geologist McClelland Engrs., Houston, 1980, Getty Oil subs. Texaco, Houston, 1981-85, Minatome Corp., Houston, 1985-86. Mem. Houston Geol. Soc., Am. Assn. Petroleum Geologists, Delta Gamma. Home: 9507 Wellsworth Houston TX 77083

WISNER, LINDA ANN, advertising agency executive, publishing company executive, interior designer; b. Sidney, N.Y., Apr. 28, 1951; d. Herbert and Ruth (Usher) W. B.A. in Theatre and Art, Macalester Coll., 1973, postgrad. in journalism, 1974; postgrad. in graphic design Mpls. Coll. Art and Design, 1973-74; postgrad. in advtg. and mktg. U. Minn., 1974. Designer, publs. asst. Macalester Coll., St. Paul, 1973-76; designer Stretch & Sew Inc., Eugene, Oreg., 1976-78; free-lance designer, Eugene, 1978-79; owner, creative dir. Wisner Assocs., Eugene, 1979-87, Portland, 1987—, Interludes, Eugene, 1981—; ptnr. Instant Interiors, Eugene, 1979—; mktg. dir. Palmer/Pletsch Assocs., 1988; chmn. Bus. Images Exhibit, Eugene, 1983. Designer, editor booklet series: Instant Interiors, 1979-83 (Woodie award 1980-83); designer, illustrator: Palmer/Pletsch Sewing Books, 1981—. Ambassador, City of Eugene, 1985-87 ; bd. dirs. Maude Kerns Art Ctr., Eugene, 1984-85, Oreg. Repertory Theatre, 1986-87, Oreg. Sales and Mktg. Exec., 1986. Nat. Merit scholar Macalester Coll., 1969. Mem. Designers' Forum (pres. 1983-84, Designer of Yr. 1983), Sales and Mktg. Execs., Graphic Artists Guild, Exec. Bus. Women (pres. 1983-84), Mid Oreg. Ad Club (numerous certs. and trophy 1980-85), Portland Culinary Alliance, Eugene C. of C. (M.V.P. Leadership Program award 1986). Avocations: design; illustration; soft sculpture; event planning; catering.

WISNIEWSKI, DAWN MARIE, engineering firm accounting executive, marketing coordinator; b. Milw., Aug. 16, 1962; d. Richard and Barbara Joan (Hasselmaier) W. Student Sierra Coll, Rocklin, Calif., 1984—. Asst. bookkeeper G & G Enterprises, Ltd., Milw., 1979-80; acctg. asst. Kestly & Co., West Allis, Wis., 1980-81; asst. bookkeeper Republic-Dau, Milw., 1981-82; acctg. supr., data processing coordinator, mktg. coordinator CWC-HDR, Inc. subs. HDR Engring., Inc., Irvine, Calif., 1982—. Mem. Nat. Assn. Female Execs., Data Processing Mgmt. Assn. Avocations: reading, crocheting, sewing, theatre. Office: 2415 Campus Dr Suite 201 Irvine CA 92715

WITCHEL, BARBARA MURIEL, college administrator, gerontology and psychology educator; d. Herman and Ann (Lotto) Goldfein; m. Sam Witchel; children—Alexandra, Gregory, Phoebe, Emmett. B.A., NYU, 1953, M.A., 1955; Ed.D., Rutgers U., 1965. Cert. tchr. kindergarten-8th grade, N.Y. Tchr. pub. schs., Fairlawn and Caldwell, N.J., 1955-62; instr. Rutgers U., New Brunswick, N.J., 1962-64; assoc. prof. Kean Coll., Union, N.J., 1965-67; assoc. prof. gerontology Iona Coll., New Rochelle, N.Y., 1970—; dir. Iona Coll., Rockland Campus, Orangeburg, N.Y., 1983—; reviewer Adminstrn. Aging, Washington, 1979-85, N.Y. State Dept. Edn., Albany, 1983; mem. spl. adv. com. White House Conf. on Aging, 1980-81. Producer, host TV series The New Age: A Focus on the Older American, 1980; dir. spl. edn. program The University of the New Age, 1981-82. Mem. Passaic Bd. Edn., 1966-68, pres., 1967-69. Recipient Service award Passaic Bd. Edn., 1969; fellow Rutgers U., 1962-84; Iona Coll. fellow, Bryn Mawr, Pa., 1985. Mem. Am. Assn. Higher Edn., Gerontol. Soc., AAUP, Phi Delta Kappa, Kappa Delta Pi. Avocations: sculpting; reading science fiction; gardening. Home: 27 Myrtledale Rd Scarsdale NY 10583 Office: Iona Coll-Rockland Campus One Dutch Hill Rd Orangeburg NY 10962

WITH, DAPHNE MARINA, management information analyst; b. St. John's, Can., Dec. 4, 1939; d. Arthur and Evelyn Mary (Kearley) Tuck; m. K. Ritchie D. With, Oct. 26, 1969; 1 child, K.A. Gregory. RN, Toronto (Ont.) East Gen. Hosp., Can., 1960. Various nursing positions Midland, Ont., Toronto, 1960-70; temp. staff Polysar Ltd., Sarnia, Ont., 1977-84, risk mgmt. info. analyst, 1984—. Mem. Progressive Party. Anglican. Office: Polysar Ltd, Vidal St S, Sarnia CAN N7T 7M2

WITHERSPOON, JUANITA MAE NEW, county agency administrator; b. Sylacauga, Ala., July 18, 1944; d. James Wesley and Mabel Saline (Wynn) New; m. Robert James Witherspoon; children: Michael Ranier, Rolan Dion. BA, Talladega Coll., 1967; postgrad., U. Mich., 1968-70, Mich. State U., 1972, 77. Case worker Luth. Children's Friend Soc., Bay City, Mich., 1967-68; sch. social worker Saginaw (Mich.) Pub. Schs., 1968-70, substitute tchr., 1970-71, 79-80; caseworker Youth Protective Services of Saginaw County, 1971-72; coordinator family living resource ctr. Univ. Ctr. Delta Coll., 1973-77; dir. office of pub. guardian, conservator Saginaw County, 1980—. Adv. mem. Temporary Health Care Services, Saginaw, 1985—. Mem. Nat. Assn. Female Execs. (Regional Interagency Com.), Social Service Club Saginaw, Saginaw County Assn. for Retarded Citizens (bd. dirs. 1984—), Zeta Phi Beta (named Zeta of Yr. 1983, treas. 1984-86). Baptist. Lodge: Zonta. Office: Saginaw County Govt 1600 N Michigan Ave Suite 503 Saginaw MI 48602

WITHERSPOON, MARIA BERNARDA PENA, bilingual educator; b. San Cristobal, Dominican Republic, Dec. 20, 1955; came to U.S., 1969; d. Benjamin de Jesus and Belen Pena; m. James Howard Witherspoon, Aug. 6, 1977. AA, Pima (Ariz.) Community Coll., 1980; BS, U. Ariz., 1981, MEd, 1986. Cert. tchr., Ariz. Family counselor El Rio Neighborhood Ctr., Tucson, 1979; pre-sch. tchr. Project Head Start, Tucson, 1980; data collector U. Ariz., Tucson, 1982; bilingual educator Tucson Unified Sch. Dist., 1984—; mem. Spanish Lang. Arts Adoption com. Tucson Unified Sch. Dist. Mem. Task Force on Native Am. Studies, Tucson, 1986. Mem. NEA, Tucson Edn. Assn. (alt. state del., assembly rep.), Nat. Assn. Bilingual Edn., Ariz. Assn. Bilingual Edn., Am. Home Econs. Assn., Nat. Assn. Female Execs. Democrat. Roman Catholic. Home: 516 E Lester St Tucson AZ 85705 Office: Holladay Intermediate Sch 1110 E 33d St Tucson AZ 85713

WITHERSPOON, RUTH CAROLYN SMITH, professional organization administrator; b. Detroit; d. Walker Elliot and Bettie (Cannady) Smith; m. William C. Witherspoon, June 1, 1944; children: William Roger, Linda Carole, David Jerome. BS cum laude, CCNY, 1951, MS, 1956. Office adminstr. Council Fgn. Relations Inc., N.Y.C., 1952-58, asst. treas., 1958-87, comptroller, treas., 1964-68; treas. Fgn. Relations Library, 1966—. Mem. Teaneck (N.J.) Bd. Adjustment, 1977-88. Mem. Nat. Assn. Negro Bus. Profl. Women's Club (nat. fin. sec. 1971—, N.E. dist. fin. sec. 1967-71), Kappa Delta Pi, Beta Alpha Psi. Democrat. Home: 137 Voorhees St Teaneck NJ 07666 Office: Council Fgn Relations Inc 58 E 68th St New York NY 10021

WITHROW, MARY ELLEN, state treasurer; b. Marion, Ohio, Oct. 2, 1930; d. Clyde Welsh and Mildred (Stump) Hinamon; m. Norman David Withrow, Sept. 4, 1948; children: Linda Rizzo, Leslie Legge, Norma, Rebecca. Student, pub. schs., Marion, Ohio. Mem. Elgin Local Bd. Edn., Marion, Ohio, 1969-72, pres., 1972; safety programs dir. ARC, Marion, 1968-72; dep. registrar State of Ohio, Marion, 1972-75; dep. county auditor Marion County (Ohio), 1975-77, county treas., 1977-83; treas. State of Ohio, Columbus, 1983—; chmn. Ohio State Bd. Deposits, from 1983. Mem. Democratic Nat. Com., co-chair farm crisis task force; mem. Met. Women's Ctr.; pres. Marion County Dem. Club, 1976. Inducted Ohio Women's Hall of Fame, 1986; named Outstanding Elected Dem. Woman Holding Pub. Office, Nat. Fedn. Dem. Women, 1987; fellow Women Execs. in State Govt., Harvard U., 1987. Mem. State Assn. County Treas. (legis. chmn. 1979-83, treas. 1982), Nat. Assn. State Treas. (v.p. M.W. region 1983), Nat. Assn. State Auditors Comptrollers and Treas. (2d v.p.), Council of State Govts. (state and fed. affairs com.), Delta Kappa Gamma Internat. (hon. Ohio mem.). Club: Bus. and Profl. Women's. Office: State of Ohio Treasury Dept 30 E Broad St 9th Floor Columbus OH 43215

WITKIN, EVELYN MAISEL, geneticist; b. N.Y.C., Mar. 9, 1921; d. Joseph and Mary (Levin) Maisel; m. Herman A. Witkin, July 9, 1943 (dec. July 1979); children—Joseph, Andrew. A.B., N.Y. U., 1941; M.A., Columbia U., 1943, Ph.D., 1947; D.Sc. honoris causa, N.Y. Med. Coll., 1978. Mem. staff genetics dept. Carnegie Inst., Washington, 1950-55; mem. faculty State U. N.Y. Downstate Med. Center, Bklyn., 1955-71; prof. medicine State U. N.Y. Downstate Med. Center, 1968-71; prof. biol. scis. Douglass Coll., Rutgers U., 1971-79, Barbara McClintock prof. genetics, 1979—. Author articles; mem. editorial bds. profl. jours. Postdoctoral fellow Am. Cancer Soc., 1947-49; fellow Carnegie Instn., 1957; Selman A. Waksman lectr., 1960; Phi Beta Kappa vis. scholar, 1980-81; grantee NIH, 1956—; recipient Prix Charles Leopold Mayer French Acad. Scis., 1977, Lindback award, 1979. Fellow AAAS; mem. Nat. Acad. Scis., Am. Acad. Arts and Scis., Environ. Mutagen Soc., Am. Genetics Soc., Am. Soc. Microbiology, Radiation Research Soc. Home: 88 Balcort Dr Princeton NJ 08540 Office: Rutgers U Waksman Inst Microbiology Piscataway NJ 08854

WITKIN, MILDRED HOPE FISHER, psychotherapist, educator; b. N.Y.C.; d. Samuel and Sadie (Goldschmidt) Fisher; AB, Hunter Coll., MA, Columbia U., 1968; PhD, NYU, 1973; children: Georgia Hope, Roy Thomas, Laurie Phillips; m. Jorge Radovich, Aug. 26, 1983. Head counselor Camp White Lake, Camp Emanuel, Long Beach, N.J.; tchr. econs., polit. sci. Hunter Coll. High Sch.; dir., group leader follow-up program Jewish Vacation Assn., N.Y.C.; investigator N.Y.C. Housing Authority; psychol. counselor Montclair State Coll., Upper Montclair, N.J., 1967-68; mem., lectr. Creative Problem-Solving Inst., U. Buffalo, 1968; psychol. counselor Fairleigh Dickinson U., Teaneck, N.J., 1968, dir. Counseling Center, 1969-74; pvt. practice psychotherapy, N.Y.C., also Westport, Conn.; sr. faculty supr., family therapist and psychotherapist Payne Whitney Psychiat. Clinic, N.Y. Hosp., 1973—; clin. asst. prof. dept. psychiatry Cornell U. Med. Coll., 1974—; asso. dir. sex therapy and edn. program Cornell-N.Y. Hosp. Med. Center, 1974—; sr. cons. Kaplan Inst. for Evaluation and Treatment of Sexual Disorders, 1981—; supr. master's and doctoral candidates, N.Y. U., 1975—; pvt. practice psychotherapy and sex therapy, N.Y.C., also Westport, Conn.; cons. counselor edn. tng. programs N.Y.C. Bd. Edn., 1971-75; cons. Health Info. Systems, 1972-79; vis. prof. numerous colls. and univs.; chmn. sci. com. 1st Internat. Symposium on Female Sexuality, Buenos Aires, 1984; exhibited in group shows at Scarsdale (N.Y.) Art Show, 1959, Red Shutter Art Studio, Long Beach, 1968. Edn. legislation chmn. PTA, Yonkers, 1955; publicity chmn. United Jewish Appeal, Scarsdale, 1959-65; Scarsdale chmn. mothers com. Boy Scouts Am., 1961-64; mem. Morrow Assn. on Correction N.J., 1969—. Recipient Bronze medal for services Hunter Coll.; United Jewish Appeal plaque, 1962; Founders Day award N.Y. U., 1973; diplomate Am. Coll. sexologists. Fellow Internat. Council Sex Edn. and Parenthood of Am. U.; mem. Am. Psychol. Assn., AAUW, Women's Med. Assn. N.Y.C., Am. Coll. Personnel Assn. (nat. mem. commn. II 1973-76), Nat. Assn. Women Deans and Counselors, Am. Assn. Sex Educators, Counselors and Therapists (regional bd., nat. accreditation bd., cert. internat. supr.), Soc. for Sci. Study Sex, Eastern Assn. Sex Therapists, Am. Assn. Marriage and Family Counselors, N.J. Assn. Marriage and Family Counselors, Ackerman Family Inst., Am. Personnel and Guidance Assn., Am., N.Y., N.J. psychol. assns., Creative Edn. Found., Am. Assn. Higher Edn., Assn. Counselor Supervision and Edn., Profl. Women's Caucus, LWV, Am. Women's Med. Assn., Nat. Council on Women in Medicine, Argentine Soc. Human Sexuality (hon.), Pi Lambda Theta, Kappa Delta Pi, Alpha Chi Alpha. Author: 45-And Single Again, 1985. Contbr. articles to profl. jours. and textbooks; lectr. internat. workshops, radio and TV. Office: 35 Park Ave New York NY 10016 Home: 9 Sturges Commons Westport CT 06880

WITKIN-LANOIL, GEORGIA HOPE, psychologist, lecturer, author. Student Wellesley Coll., 1961-63; B.A. in Sociology, Barnard Coll., 1965; postgrad. in elem. edn. Hunter Coll., 1967-69; M.A. in Psychology, New Sch. for Social Research, 1970, Ph.D. in Psychology, 1977. Lic. clin. psychologist, N.Y. State. Asst. producer Grey Advt., N.Y.C., 1966-68; teaching asst. New Sch. for Social Research, 1968-69; adj. lectr. Lehman Coll., CUNY, 1971-72; assoc. prof. dept. social and behavioral sci. SUNY-Valhalla, 1972—, mem. vis. faculty criminal justice dept., 1972—; supr.

residency program human sexuality program Mt. Sinai Sch. Medicine, N.Y.C., 1982—; former mem. vis. faculty U. Conn., NYU Coll. Dentistry, also others; assoc. prof. psychology Westchester Community Coll., Valhalla; presenter at profl. confs., also papers; pvt. practice clin. psychology, Scarsdale, N.Y. and N.Y.C.; appeared on various TV shows including Donahue, Today Show, Hour Mag. Author: The Female Stress Syndrome, 1984 (also Dutch, Japan, German, English, Spanish and Australian edits.); Coping with Stress; Human Sexuality; The Male Stress Syndrome, 1986. columnist Your Emotional Best, Health Mag., also mem. editorial adv. bd.; mem. editorial adv. bd. Jour. Preventive Psychiatry. Contbr. articles to profl. publs., mags. and newspapers. Mem. steering com. Westchester Community Coll. Found., 1973-75. Mem. AAAS, Soc. for Sex Therapy and Research, Westchester County Psychol. Assn., N.Y. Acad. Scis., Am. Assn. Sex Educators, Counselors and Therapists (cert. sex educator; mem. regional bd., exec. com.), Am. Assn. for Profl. Law Enforcement, Mensa, Criminal Justice Educators Assn. N.Y. State, Am. Soc. Criminology, World Future Soc., N.Y. State United Tchrs., Eastern Psychol. Assn., Am. Med. Writers Assn. Home: 8 East 83rd St Apt 3A New York NY 10028-0418 Office: Mt Sinai Med Coll Dept Psychiat New York NY 10053

WITKOWSKI, KATHLEEN CHRISTINE, travel company executive; b. Flushing, N.Y., Jan. 14, 1959; d. Thomas Joseph and Eileen Helen (Regan) W. BBA, Bucknell U., 1981. Sales rep. Graybar Elec. Co., L.I. City, N.Y., 1981-85; sr. systems cons. United Tech. Communications, N.Y.C., 1985-86; nat. accts. mgr. Access Am., N.Y.C., 1986—. Mem. Nat. Assn. Female Execs., Wall Street Network Group. Roman Catholic. Home: 45-32 196th St Flushing NY 11358

WITMER, ROCHELLE CAMPBELL, claims examining supervisor; b. Asheville, N.C., July 23, 1945; d. Gary and Jewell (Hill) C.; m. Kirk Harold Witmer; children: Matthew Colin, Eric Scott. Dégre deuxieme, Université de Strasbourg, Strasbourg, France, 1966; BA, Stetson U., 1967; MA, U. Wis., 1968. Instr. Simpson Coll., Indianola, Iowa, 1968-71; employment interviewer Fla. Employment Service, Ft. Lauderdale, 1972-76; unemployment claims adjudicator Fla. State Bur. of Unemployment Compensation, Ft. Lauderdale, 1976-79; unemployment claims interviewer Bur. of Unemployment Compensation Commonwealth of Pa., Coatesville, 1982-84; office mgr. Campbell and Kim, N.Y.C., 1982; claims examiner Nat. Liberty Corp., Frazer, Pa., 1984-86; claims examining supr. Nat. Liberty Corp., Frazer, 1986—. Designer software: Pre-Sch. Math, 1982. Choir mother Olivet Meth. Ch., Coatesville, 1982—; mem., actress West Chester and Barley Sheaf Players, Lionville, Pa., 1985. Mem. National Orgn. Female Execs. Office: Nat Liberty Corp 20 Moores Rd Frazer PA 19355

WITORT, JANET LEE, lawyer; b. Cedar Rapids, Iowa, Mar. 10, 1950; d. Charles Francis and Phyllis Harriet (Wilber) Svoboda; m. Stephen Francis Witort, Oct. 27, 1979. Student U. Colo., 1968-69, U. Iowa, 1971; B.A., U. No. Colo., 1972; J.D., Loyola U., 1979. Bar: Ill. 1979; U.S. Dist. Ct., 1979; U.S. Supreme Ct., 1987. Paralegal, Fed. Nat. Mortgage Assn., Chgo., 1973-75, Sidley & Austin, Chgo., 1975-76; assoc. Frankel, McKay & Orlikoff, Chgo., 1979-81; atty. Mut. Trust Life Ins. Co., Oak Brook, Ill., 1981-86 ; sr. atty., asst. sec. North Am. Co. for Life and Health Ins., Chgo., 1986— ; bd. dirs. Chgo. Library System, 1988—; Midwest regional dir. Nat. Fedn. Paralegal Assns., Chgo., 1975-76 . Author: (with others) The Legal Assistant-a Self Statement, 1974. Vol., Republican campaign, Chgo., 1974-76; trustee Hinsdale Ill. Pub. Library, 1987—. Mem. ABA, Ill. Bar Assn., Women's Bar Assn., Chgo. Bar Assn., Chgo. Paralegal Assn. (sec. 1973-74), Ill. Paralegal Assn. (v.p. 1975-76), Phi Alpha Delta, Student Bar Assn. (class rep. 1976-77). Republican. Methodist. Office: NAm Co Life & Health Ins 222 S Riverside Plaza Chicago IL 60606

WITSIL, ELIZABETH SMITH ALISON (MRS. WALTER EARLE WITSIL), former social worker; b. Wilmington, Del., Sept. 13, 1909; d. Alexander and Katharine Anna (Smith) Alison; A.B., Wilson Coll., 1931; postgrad. Columbia U., 1934-36; m. Walter Earle Witsil, Aug. 27, 1938 (dec. Feb. 1964); 1 child, Adah Elizabeth Witsil Unger; step-children—Walter Earle, Sarah Virginia Witsil Lloyd. Accounting clk. Remington Rand, Inc., Bridgeport, Conn., 1932-33; social case-worker Bridgeport Br.-New Eng. Home for Little Wanderers, 1933-36; social case worker Conn. Children's Aid Soc., Danbury, 1936-38; dir. membership, pub. relations and publicity YWCA, Bridgeport, 1964-75; dir. cultural tours and vols. Bridgeport Mus. Arts, Sci. and Industry, 1975-83. Mem. Bd. Fin. Fairfield (Conn.), 1955-79; mem. Fairfield Rep. Town Meeting, 1947-55; pres. bd. mgrs. Woodfield Maternity Home and Adoption Service, Bridgeport, 1954-57, mem. corp.; bd. dirs. Vis. Nurse Assn. Bridgeport, United Fund Council Eastern Fairfield County, Bridgeport Council Ch. Women, Child Guidance Center of Bridgeport, Conn. Conf. Social Work, Mountain Grove Cemetery Assn., Bridgeport; v.p. Fairfield Community Services; trustee Greater Bridgeport Symphony Soc., 1978—; mem. Sr. Citizens Tax Relief Com., Fairfield, 1980-85, Sr. Citizens Life Center Study and Bldg. Com., 1981-84; bd. assos. U. Bridgeport; mem. Republican Women's Assn. Fairfield. Mem. AAUW, LWV, DAR, Bridgeport Hosp. Aux. (pres. 1961-63), Delta Kappa Gamma (hon.). Presbyterian (trustee, elder). Clubs: Contemporary (sec. 1957-64, pres. 1976), Wilson Coll. Home: 235 Millard St Apt C3 Fairfield CT 06430

WITT, HELEN MERCER, government official, lawyer; b. Atlantic City, July 13, 1933; m. Edward A. Witt; 5 children. B.A., Dickinson Coll., 1955; J.D., U. Pitts., 1969. Mem. law firms Cleland, Hurtt & Witt, and Witt & Witt, 1970-74; asst. to chmn. U.S. Steel Corp./United Steelworkers Am. bd. arbitration, 1975-82; mem. Nat. Mediation Bd., 1983-88, chmn., 1987—. Office: Nat Mediation Bd 1425 K St NW Washington DC 20572

WITT, SANDRA SMITH, federal agency official; b. Rockwood, Tenn., Aug. 27, 1944; d. William Perry and Imogene (Collins) Smith; children: Whitney, Christian. Student, U. Chattanooga, 1966-67; AS in Nuclear Technology, Chattanooga State Tech. Coll., 1976; BS in Physics, U. Tenn., 1978, MS in Engring. Sci., 1982. Cert. nuclear equipment qualification engr., Ala. Tech. writer, editor Tenn. Blue Cross-Blue Shield, Chattanooga, 1966-68; supr. editing dept. Copr. Law Firm, Chattanooga; asst. physics lab. U. Tenn., Chattanooga, 1977-78; oil field engr. Schlumberger Co., Houston, 1978; research assoc. U. Tenn. Space Inst., Tullahoma, Tenn., 1979-81; sr. project engr. Wyle Labs., Huntsville, Ala., 1981-82; engr. U.S. Dept. Energy, Aiken, S.C., 1983—. Recipient Spl. Service award Dept. Energy, 1986, 87, Career award Nat. Bus. and Profl. Women, 1987; Diuguid fellow, 1976. Mem. Am. Nuclear Soc., Nat. Assn. Female Execs., Phi Theta Kappa (past v.p.), Sigma Pi Sigma.

WITTE, JEANNE M., nurse, health science facility executive; b. Elgin, Ill., June 5, 1938; d. George Frederick and Josephine Agnes (McCarthy) Rumple; children: Cindy, Randy, Terry, Marisue, Corey. Diploma in nursing, St. Francis Coll., 1959. RN; cert. ins. rehab. specialist. Staff nurse St. Charles Hosp., Aurora, Ill., 1960-65; staff nurse OB Copley Hosp., Aurora, 1970-75; dir. nursing North Aurora Ctr., 1975-76; asst. dir. nursing St. Charles Nursing Ctr., Aurora, 1976-77; dir. edn. and rehab. Fox Valley Nursing Ctr., 1976-77; rehab. nurse Chubb Ins., Chgo., 1977-80; regional rehab. supr. CNA, Chgo., 1980-81; catastrophic specialist Crawford & Co., Schaumburg, Ill., 1981-85; regional mgr. AIHRS, Lisle, Ill., 1985—; guest faculty Rehab. Inst. of Chgo., 1981, 85-86; speaker ins. seminars, Chgo. , 1980, 84-85. Bd. dirs. Playmakers, Inc., St. Charles, Ill., 1976-85. Mem. NARPPS, Assn. Rehab. Nurses, Rehab. Ins. Nurses Group, Nat. Assn. Female Execs., Women in Mgmt. Office: AIHRS 901 Warrenville Rd Suite 300 Lisle IL 60532

WITTELES, ELEONORA MEIRA, physicist; b. Jerusalem, July 14, 1938, d. Salomon and Rivka (Komornik) Witteles. B.S., Fordham U., 1962, M.S., 1963; M.S., N.Y.U., 1965; Ph.D. (research fellow), Yeshiva U., 1969. Postdoctoral fellow Bar-Ilan U., Israel, 1969-70, asst. prof., 1970-72; ind. cons., 1972-80; sr. research scientist Atlantic Richfield Co., Los Angeles, 1980-84; sr. scientist Hughes Aircraft Co., El Segundo, Calif., 1984-86; exec. dir. WIT, Palos Verdes, Calif., 1986—. Mem. Am. Phys. Soc., N.Y. Acad. Scis., IEEE, IEEE Engring. in Medicine and Biology Soc., IEEE Magnetics Soc., Com. on Status of Women in Physics. Research on solid state physics, superconductivity, applied material scis., inventor med. instrumentation and cryogenic instrumentation. Home: 4714 Browndeer Ln Palos Verdes CA 90274 Office: WIT 904 Silver Spur Rd Suite #637 Palos Verdes CA 90274

WITTENMYER, JAYN JEFFERS, health science executive; b. Bloomingdale, Ind., Aug. 28, 1937; d. William Hazelton and Pauline (Brading) Jeffers; m. William Ray Wittenmyer, Oct. 18, 1958; children: Andrea, Amera, Adriene. BS in Edn., Ind. State U., 1965; cert. spl. edn., Ball State U., 1966. Exec. dir. Parke County Assn. for Retarded Citizens, Rockville, Ind., 1964-66; field cons. Ind. Assn. Retarded Citizens, Indpls., 1966-68; asst. exec. dir. Wis. Assn. for Retarded Citizens, Madison, 1968-75; exec. dir. Wis. Council on Devel. Disabilities, Madison, 1976—; cons. in field; guest lectr. U. Wis., 1969—. Recipient Pub. Interes award Ctr. Pub. Rep., 1983, Family Support award State of Wis., 1985, day named in her honor Gov. Anthony Earl, 1986. Mem. Nat. Assn. Female Execs., Am. Assn. for Mental Retardation, Assn. for Severe Handicaps. Mem. Soc. of Friends. Lodge: Order Ea. Star. Home: 2614 Lunde Ln Mount Horeb WI 53575

WITTER, DIANA GONSER, public relations professional; b. Omaha, June 5, 1930; d. Bruce Winfred and Helen Marie (Vincent) Gonser; m. Richard P. DeVere, Aug. 30, 1952 (div. 1975); children: Scott Page DeVere, Denise DeVere Bauer, Don William DeVere II; m. Richard S. Witter, June 14, 1986. BS, Ohio State U., 1952. Housing asst. Ohio State U., Columbus, 1952-53; personnel asst. First Community Village, Columbus, 1970-72, adminstrv. asst. to adminstr., 1972-78, pub. relations dir., 1978—. Pres. Jazz Arts Group of Columbus, 1981-83, mem. exec. com. N.W. Kiwanis scholar, 1948. Mem. Mirrors, Chimes and Mortar Bd., Childhood League, Pi Beta Phi. Home: 1235 Lake Shore Dr Columbus OH 43204 Office: First Community Village 1800 Riverside Dr Columbus OH 43212

WITTLER, SHIRLEY JOYCE, former state official, state commissioner; b. Ravenna, Nebr., Oct. 10, 1927; d. Earl William and Minnie Ethel (Frink) Wade; m. LeRoy F. Wittler, Dec. 31, 1946; children: Julie Diane, Barbara Liane. Student, U. Nebr., 1944-47. Real estate saleswoman Harrington Assocs., Lincoln, Nebr., 1965-69; real estate broker Tom Searl Realty, Inc., Cheyenne, Wyo., 1970-76; dep. state treas. Wyo., 1976-78; state treas. 1979-83; now chmn. state tax commn. and bd. equalization State of Wyo. Pres. LWV, Lincoln, 1965-69; bd. dirs. LWV Wyo., 1970-72; fin. chmn. Republican Central Com. Laramie County, Wyo., 1974-76; chmn. Laramie County Pres. Ford Com., 1976; Rep. precinct committeewoman, 1972-77; mem. Laramie County Library Bd., 1976, Community Devel. Adv. Bd., 1974-77. Mem. Cheyenne Bd. Realtors (pres. 1976, Cheyenne Realtor of Yr. 1974), Women's Civic League (treas. 1974, legis. chmn. 1975-76). Lutheran. Home: 204 Park Lane Tower 1717 Alexander St Cheyenne WY 82001 Office: Dept Revenue and Taxation Herschler Bldg Cheyenne WY 82002

WITZ, GISELA, chemist, educator; b. Breslau, Federal Republic of Germany, Mar. 16, 1939; came to U.S., 1955.; d. Gerhardt Witz and Hildegard (Sufeida) Minzak. BA, NYU, 1962, MS, 1965, PhD, 1969. Assoc. research scientist NYU Med. Ctr., N.Y.C., 1970-73, research scientist, 1973-77, asst. prof., 1977-80; asst. prof. Univ. of Medicine and Dentistry of N.J.-Rutgers Med. Sch., Piscataway, N.J., 1980-86, assoc. prof. UMDNJ- Robert Wood Med. Sch., Piscataway, 1986—; cons. Nat. Research Council, Washington, 1982-83, 85-86. Contbr. articles to profl. jours. Recipient Dupont Teaching award, NYU, 1966; Univ. Scholar, Founders Day award, N.Y. U., 1969. Mem. Am. Assn. Cancer Research, Am. Chem. Soc., Soc. Toxicology, N.Y. Acad. Sci., Sigma Xi. Office: U Medicine and Dentistry NJ Robert Wood Johnson Med Sch Piscataway NJ 08854

WITZMAN, AUDREY LORAINE, educator; b. Galva, Ill., July 22, 1937; d. Clarence Gilbert and Gladys Bernice (Westlin) Peterson; m. Thomas A. Witzman, Aug. 10, 1958; children: Johanna Marie, Jocelyn Anne. BA, Eureka Coll., 1958; MEd, Nat. Coll. Edn., 1962; PhD, Northwestern U., 1976. Pub. sch. tchr., Ill., 1958-67; asst. prof. early childhood edn. Northeastern Ill. U., Chgo., 1968-71; developer, owner/dir. Country Woods Nursery Sch. and Day Camp, Valparaiso, Ind., 1971—; prof. early childhood edn. Governors State U., University Park, Ill., 1979-87; edn. cons. Ill. State Bd. Edn., 1987—. Chmn., Porter County (Ind.) Child Protection Team, 1980, 86; bd. dirs. Family House, Valparaiso, 1981-87. Mem. Nat. Assn. for Edn. Young Children, Midwest Assn. Edn. Young Children (co-coordinator conf. Indpls. 1982, Ind. rep. to bd. 1981-83), Ind. Assn. for Edn. Young Children. Republican. Methodist. Home: 450 East 725 North Valparaiso IN 46383 Office: Ill State Bd Edn 100 N First St Springfield IL 62777

WNUKOWSKI, DARLENE ESTHER, systems programmer; b. Stanley, Wis., Apr. 23, 1952; d. George William and Esther (Nisula) W. BS in Math., U. Wis., Eau Claire, 1974. Application programmer U. Wis., Oshkosh, 1974-78, programmer, analyst, 1978, systems programmer, 1978-83; sr. systems programmer Schreiber Foods, Inc., Green Bay, Wis., 1983-86, systems programmer, tech. specialist, 1986—. Mem. Nat. Systems Programmers Assn., The Computer Measurement Group. Lutheran. Office: Schreiber Food Inc PO Box 19010 Green Bay WI 54307-9010

WOEHL, RUTH BARNETT, postal service manager; b. Austin, Tex., Mar. 13, 1931; d. Robert Carroll and Ella Louise (Woelke) Barnett; m. Ernest Edward Woehl, Nov. 24, 1951; children: Kathryn Lavonne, Sandra Gayle, Randall Clay. Sec. Fehr/Granger, Architects, Austin, 1948-51; sr. file control clk. Tex. Edn. Agy., Austin, 1951-59; clk. typist USDA, Austin, 1962-68, Office of Econ. Opportunity, Austin, 1968-69; clk. stenographer Postal Service, Austin, 1969-74; personnel asst. U.S. Postal Service, Austin, 1974-82, tng. and devel. specialist, 1982-87, mgr. Postal Employee Devel. Ctr., 1987—. Leader Girl Scouts U.S.A., Austin, 1959-66. Mem. Nat. Assn. for Female Execs., Am. Bus. Womens Assn. (v.p. 1981-82, chpt. Woman of Yr., 1986), Nat. Assn. of Postal Suprs. Lutheran. Club: Toastmasters (pres. 1977-78).

WOELFLING, MAXINE MARIE, state agency administrator; b. Sharon, Pa., Oct. 26, 1949; d. Max Frank and Mary Theresa (Koch) Tomczak; m. Frank Adam Woelfling, Aug. 17, 1974; children: Andrew, Peter. BS, U. Pitts., 1971; JD, U. Notre Dame, 1974. Bar: Pa. 1974, U.S. Dist. Ct. (mid. dist.) Pa. 1976, U.S. Ct. Appeals (3d cir.) 1976. Asst. atty. gen. Dept. Environ. Resources, Commonwealth Pa., Harrisburg, 1974-81, dir. Bur. Regulatory Counsel, 1981-85; chmn. Environ. Hearing Bd., Commonwealth Pa., Harrisburg, 1985—. Named one of Outstanding Young Women of Am., 1980. Mem. Pa. Bar Assn. (treas. 1986-87, vice-chmn. 1987-88, chmn. 1988, environ. mineral and natural resources law sect.). Democrat. Roman Catholic. Home: 117 Maple Ave Hershey PA 17033 Office: Environ Hearing Bd 101 S 2d St Suites 3-5 Harrisburg PA 17101

WOFFORD, JEAN J., electronics company executive; b. Jewel County, Kans., May 7, 1934; d. Charles Milton and Opal Orpha (Dunn) Anderson; m. Courtney M. Jones, June 10, 1950 (div. 1958); 1 child, Debra Jean Jones; m. W.B. Wofford III, Oct. 26, 1965 (div. 1980); 1 child, Cynthia Treece Wofford. BA in Arts, U. Ill., Chgo., 1977; postgrad., Roosevelt U., 1979. Sales agt. Frontier Airlines, Denver, 1962-65; area sales mgr. Weaver Airline Sch., Chgo., 1965-68; dir. of sales women Culligan Internat. Corp., Northbrook, Ill., 1968-71; owner Beltone Hearing Ctr., Chgo., 1971-78; electronics sales rep. Newark Electronics Co., Chgo., 1980—. Author: Women in Sales, 1970. Republican. Episcopalian. Home: 505 N Lake Shore Dr Chicago IL 60611

WOHLFAHRT, BARBARA ROBBINS, manufacturing company executive; b. Chgo., Oct. 30, 1947; d. Frederick Arthur and Dorothy (Roper) Robbins; m. Timothy Harry Wohlfahrt, Aug. 23, 1969; children: Patricia, Rick, Melinda, Matthew. BSME, U. Wis., 1969. Tech. writer Gilman Engring., Janesville, Wis., 1969-70; sales person Wausau (Wis.) Metals Corp., 1970-71; exec. v.p. Modu-Line Windows, Wausau, 1972-85, Major Industries, Wausau, 1983-88, Republic Industries, Wausau, 1988—; exec. v.p. Prime Cons., Wausau, 1983—. Author: (with E. Jablonski) The Art of Tipping: Customs & Controversies, 1984. Bd. dirs. Luth. Social Services, Wausau, 1975-78, Tippers Internat., Wausau, 1983—. Republican. Lutheran. Home: 3012 Hubbill Ave Wausau WI 54401 Office: Major Industries Inc 7120 Stewart Ave Wausau WI 54401

WOIT, BONNIE FORD, artist; b. N.Y.C., Jan. 19, 1931; d. Gaylon Tracy and Geraldine Ida (Gillespie) Ford; m. Erik Peter Woit; children: Peter, Steven. BA, Allegheny Coll., 1953; postgrad., Harvard U. Extension Courses, 1954-55; student advanced seminars, Silvermine Sch. Art, 1970-72. One-woman shows include U.S. Embassy, Paris, 1969, Galerie La Palette Bleu, Paris, 1970, Silvermine Guild Gallery, New Canaan, Conn., 1974, New Canaan Soc. for Arts, 1978, Olympic Towers, N.Y.C., 1980, Ingber Gallery, N.Y.C., 1981, 84, New Canaan Nature Mus., 1987; group shows include Green Farms Invitational, Conn. (award), 1977, New Eng. Exhbn. at Silvermine (William Lowman award, New. Eng. award 1979), 1978, , Conn. Painters and Sculptors Annual Stamford (Conn.) Mus., 1980, Arteder Exhbn. Bilbao, Spain, 1982, Artists invite Artists, Art Pl., Southport, Conn., 1988; large scale acrylics on canvas in pvt. and pub. collections U.S., France, Denmark, Fed. Republic Germany, Spain. V.p. Silvermine Guild Arts Ctr., 1976-78; pres. Resources Ultd., Darien, Conn., 1970-76, later advisor painting class for handicapped adults. Mem. Inst. for Visual Artists (founder, chmn. 1984—). Democrat. Studio: 559 West Rd New Canaan CT 06840

WOJAHN, R. LORRAINE, state legislator; b. Wash. Mem. Wash. State Ho. of Reps., 1969-76; mem. Wash. State Senate from dist. 27, 1977—, mem. commerce and labor, rules, fin. instrns., ways and means coms. Democrat. Office: Office of the State Senate State Capitol Olympia WA 98504 Other Address: 3592 E K St Tacoma WA 98404 *

WOJCIECHOWSKI, MARGOT JEAN, mineral policy researcher; b. Toronto, Ont., Can., May 4, 1936; d. George Edward and Jessie Julia (McKinnon) Hill; m. Bohdan Wieslaw Wojciechowski, Jan. 29, 1935; children: Peter Witold, Krystyna Teresa. BA with honors, U. Toronto, 1958; MA, Queen's U., 1970. Assessor Treasury Dept. Govt. Ont., Can., 1958-59; economist Dominion Bur. Stats., Ottawa, Can., 1959-62; research asst. Queen's U., Kingston, Ont., 1968-74, Centre Resource Studies Queen's U., Kingston, Ont., 1977-78; asst. dir. Centre Resource Studies Queen's U., Kingston, 1979-86, assoc. dir., 1987—. Author books; contbr. articles to profl. jours. Sec. Kingston Polish Refugee Fund, 1981-87. Mem. Can. Inst. Mining and Metallurgy, councillor 1986-88, (econ. com., publs., chmn. 1987), Prospectors and Developers Assn. Can. Home: RR 6, Kingston Can K7L 4V3 Office: Centre Resource Studies, Queen's U, Kingston Can K7L 3N6

WOJTACH, MARY ANN, telecommunications executive; b. Passaic, N.J., Jan. 13, 1954. EdB, Felician Coll., 1979, postgrad. Tchr. Most Sacred Heart Sch., Wallington, N.J., 1979-80; customer service rep. D. Klein & Sons, Lodi, N.J., 1980-82; supr. telecommunications PVM Oil Assocs., Inc., Ft. Lee, N.J., 1982—. Democrat. Roman Catholic. Home: 35 Dick St Clifton NJ 07013

WOJTAK, RUTH MARIE, retail company executive; b. Kenosha, Wis., Sept. 25, 1956; d. Richard Stanley and Anne Theresa (Steplyk) W. Assoc. Applied Sci., Gateway Tech. Inst., 1976; B.A., U. Wis.-Parkside, 1980. Transp. aide Kenosha Achievement Ctr. (Wis.), 1977; lifeguard U. Wis.-Parkside, Kenosha, 1980, library clk., 1978-80; asst. mgr. K Mart Corp., Troy, Mich., 1980—. Mem. Am. Mgmt. Assn., Distributive Edn. Clubs Am. (parliamentarian 1976), Nat. Assn. Female Execs., U. Wis.-Parkside Alumni Assn., Career Guild. Roman Catholic. Office: K Mart #3441 2300B West Higgins Hoffman Estates IL 60559

WOLANIN, BARBARA ANN BOESE, art curator, art historian; b. Dayton, Ohio, Dec. 12, 1943; d. William Carl and Elisabeth Cassell (Barnard) Boese; m. Thomas R. Wolanin, June 11, 1966 (div. 1980); children: Peter Michael, Andrew Thomas. AB, Oberlin Coll., 1966, AM, 1969; MAT, Harvard U., 1967; PhD, U. Wis., 1981. Dir. children's art classes Allen Art Mus., Oberlin, Ohio, 1967-68; art tchr. Lorain (Ohio) Pub. Schs., 1968-69, Newton (Mass.) Pub. Schs., 1969-71; teaching asst. U. Wis., Madison, 1972-74; asst. prof. art Trinity Coll., Washington, 1978-83; asst. prof. art James Madison U., Harrisonburg, Va., 1983-85; curator Architect of the Capitol, Washington, 1985—; guest curator Pa. Acad. of Fine Arts, Phila, 1980-83. Contbr. articles to profl. jours. Bd. dirs. Janney Extended Day, Washington, 1979-83; hon. bd. mem. Ft. Harrison, Dayton, Va., 1986. Woodrow Wilson fellow, 1967, Kress fellow U. Wis., 1974, Smithsonian fellow, 1976; recipient Faculty Devel. award James Madison U., 1985. Mem. S.E. Coll. Art Assn., Women's Caucus for Art., Am. Assn. Mus., Coll. Art Assn., Phi Beta Kappa (pres. Trinity Coll. 1982-83). Democrat. Episcopalian. Home: 4347 Brandywine St NW Washington DC 20016 Office: U S Capitol Office Architect of the Capitol Washington DC 20515

WOLANSKY, BONNIE KAY, electrical engineer; b. Syracuse, N.Y.; d. Abraham Ghemey and Roslyn (Olum) Greenhouse; m. Bennett Lloyd Wolansky, June 23, 1985. Student, LeMoyne Coll., Syracuse, 1975-76, Upstate Med. Ctr., Syracuse, 1981-82; BS, Ohio State U., 1980; MSEE, Syracuse U., 1983. Project engr. Dynamics Research Corp., Wilmington, Mass., 1983-84; systems engr. AT&T Info. SYstems Labs., Holmdel, N.J., 1984-85; design engr. Goodyear Aerospace Corp., Akron, Ohio, 1985-86; sr. design engr. Ocean Systems div. Gould, Cleve., 1986—. Fellow Masonic Med. Research Lab., Utica, N.Y., 1981. Mem. IEEE, Soc. Women Engrs., Nat. Assn. Female Execs., Mentor User's Group. Office: Gould Ocean Systems div 18901 Euclid Ave Cleveland OH 44117

WOLD, NANA BEHA, social services administrator; b. N.Y.C., Nov. 4, 1943; d. William John and Margaret (Robinson) Beha. BA, Tex. Women's U., 1965; M in Social Welfare, U. Calif., Berkeley, 1967. Psychiat. social worker Mendocino State Hosp., Talmage, Calif., 1967-70, Calif. State Dept. Mental Health, San Diego, 1972-74; supervising psychiat. social worker Calif. State Dept. Health, San Diego, 1974-81; assoc. chief, case mgmt. services San Diego Regional Ctr. Devel. Disabled, 1981—; instr. social work Chapman Coll., San Diego, 1972; mem. adv. com. Community Living Project, San Diego, 1973-76, Sr. Citizens Day Care Ctr., San Diego, 1976-77; mem. Sen. Ellis' Task Force for Devel. Disabled, San Diego, 1984—; co-chair Com. Community Care for Devel. Disabled, San Diego, 1978—. Co-author: Sex Education for the Mentally Retarded, 1975, (pamphlet) Happiness is a Good Home, 1977. Vol. Army Community Services, Ft. Wolters, Tex., 1968-69. Mem. Nat. Assn. Social Workers, Am. Assn. Mental Deficiency. Republican. Roman Catholic. Office: San Diego Regional Ctr Devel Disabled 4355 Ruffin Rd #306 San Diego CA 92123

WOLF, BARBARA ANNE, research administrator, biologist; b. N.Y.C., July 24, 1947; d. Boris and Molly (Gruberg) W.; B.A. magna cum laude (N.Y. State Regents scholar, Stanley Koncal award 1968), Queens Coll., City U. N.Y., 1968; Ph.D. in Biology, M.I.T., 1973; m. Robert Stanley Spiel, Aug. 25, 1973; children—Melissa Heather, Seth Brandon. Research asst. chem. synthesis Sloan-Kettering Inst. for Cancer Research, Rye, N.Y., 1967; teaching asst. cell biology M.I.T., Cambridge, 1969-70, supr. grad seminars, 1972-73; research asst. virology Rockefeller U., N.Y.C., 1973-75, fellow Nat. Cancer Inst., 1975-77, research assoc., oncological studies, summer, 1977; mgr. biol. services Revlon Research Center, Bronx, N.Y., 1977-80, dir. biol. services, 1981—; asso. prof. Coll. Pharmacy St. John's U., Queens, N.Y., 1981—. Mem. Am. Soc. Microbiologists, Soc. Toxicology, Am. Coll. Toxicology, N.Y. Soc. Electron Microscopists, Soc. of Cosmetic Chemists, Genetic Toxicology Assn., Environ. Mutagen Soc., AAAS, N.Y. Acad. Scis., Sigma Xi, Phi Beta Kappa, Beta Delta Chi. Contbr. articles on cell biology and oncology to sci. jours. Office: 2121 Route 27 Edison NJ 08818

WOLF, CAROLE BRUCE, educator; b. Houston, Mar. 20, 1944; d. Victor Van Buren and Susie Ellen (Fuller) Bruce; B.A., Stephen F. Austin State U., 1965, M.A. in English, 1968; Ph.D. in English (Truman Camp fellow), Tex. Tech U., 1982; m. John Charles Wolf, Oct. 21, 1967; children—Allan Bruce, Anne Elizabeth. Tchr. English, Marshall (Tex.) High Sch., 1965-66; teaching asst. in English, Stephen F. Austin State U., 1966-68; tchr. English, Castleberry Ind. Sch. Dist., Ft. Worth, 1968-72; instr. English, South Plains Coll., 1974, 79, 86; instr. English, Tex. Tech U., Lubbock, 1973-79, lectr., 1980—; asst. archivist Southwest collection Tex. Tech. U., 1983-84; archivist Episcopal Diocese of Northwest Tex., 1984—; instr. Tarrant County Jr. Coll., 1969. Vol., Am. Cancer Soc.; leader South Plains council Cub Scouts Am.; pres. S.C. Episcopal Churchwomen, Lubbock, 1982-83, vestryman, 1986—. Mem. South Central Modern Lang. Assn. Episcopalian. Contbr. articles to profl. publs. Home: 3312 40th St Lubbock TX 79413

WOLF, ELIZABETH ANN, project analyst; b. Berkeley, Calif., Oct. 3, 1950; d. Andrew Ross Ferguson and Bertha Margaret (Vuolle) Ross. P-roject analyst Blue Cross/Blue Shield United, Milw., 1976—. driver Meals on Wheels, West Bend, Wis., 1987; tutor Laubach Literacy, Milw. 1982. Mem. Nat. Assn. Female Execs. Home: 7198 N River Dr West Bend WI 53095

WOLF, GERTRUDE OLSHAKER, journalist, poet; b. Bklyn., Sept. 27, 1923; d. Morris and Sarah Olshaker; B.A., Bklyn. Coll., 1944; m. Milton Wolf (div. 1969); children: Carol Jane, Laura Wolf Shur, Nancy Wolf Baumann, David Charles. Dir. prodn. Intersci. Pubs., N.Y.C., 1944; reporter, asst. to editor Somerset Messenger-Gazette, Somerville, N.J., 1944-46; assoc. editor Cosmetic & Drug Preview, 1946; editor-in-chief Citations, Comml. Investment Trust, N.Y.C., 1946-47; reporter, feature writer, asst. theater editor, drama critic Columbus (Ohio) Citizen, 1947-51; advt. copywriter Eaton Paper Corp., Pittsfield, Mass., 1951-52; suburban newspaper corr. Evening and Sunday Bull., Phila., 1966-69; reporter West Chester Daily Local News, 1966-67, Ardmore Main Line Times, 1968; reception desk clk. LaGuardia Med. Group, Jamaica, N.Y., 1971-80; clk. Queensborough Public Library, 1981-87; free-lance journalist, 1987—. Recipient writing awards. Mem. Phila. Press Assn. Author poetry: Golden Tinsel and the Stars, 1980; Seashells at Mantoloking, 1981; The First Snow of Winter, 1983; Lonely Landscape, 1984; Castle of Dreams, 1984; Movie Street Scene, 1985, Surrealistic, 1986. Home: 65-10 Parsons Blvd Apt 1D Fresh Meadows NY 11365-4575

WOLF, ISABEL DRANE, food scientist, government official, consultant; b. Boston, Nov. 21, 1933; d. Louis Andrew and Anna (Whalen) Drane; B.S., Simmons Coll., 1955; M.S., U. Minn., 1971; m. Richard V. Lechowich, Jan. 21, 1983; children—Isabel, August L., Erika M. Wolf. Instr. dept. food sci. and nutrition U. Minn. 1972-79, asst. prof., 1979-81, assoc. prof., 1981—, extension food and nutrition specialist, 1972—; dir. Office of Consumer Advisor U.S. Dept. Agr., 1982-83, adminstr. Human Nutrition Info. Service, 1983-85, pvt. cons., 1985—; dir. mktg., ABC Research Corp., Gainesville, Fla., 1987—. Mem. Inst. Food Technologists, Soc. Nutrition Edn., Nat. Nutrition Consortium, Minn. State Nutrition Council, Am. Home Econs. Assn. Author: (with N.W. Jerome, J.G. McCleery) Help Yourself - Choices in Food and Nutrition, 1981; contbr. articles to profl. jours. Office: ABC Research Corp 3437 SW 24th Ave Gainesville FL 32607

WOLF, JO ANN, educator, writer; b. Peoria, Ill., Oct. 9, 1940; d. Joseph W. and Helen M. (Riedelbauch) W.; divorced, 1978. BS, Bradley U., 1962; MA, Claremont Grad. Sch., 1965. Tchr. Alta Vista (Kans.) High Sch., 1962-64, Davenport (Iowa) Cen. High Sch., 1965-67; prof. Coll. of DuPage, Glen Ellyn, Ill., 1969-88; sec., co-founder Phoenix Rising, Wheaton, Ill., 1984—. Author: Approaches To Individual Writing, 1971, Using Standard Punctuation, 1973, Promises To Keep, 1977; (with others) Living On Purpose, 1987.

WOLF, JOAN LEVIN, ballet educator; b. Richmond, Va., July 28, 1933; d. Simon Jacob and Jean (Sturman) Levin; m. Harold Lawrence Wolf, May 6, 1956; children—Eric Andrew, Elizabeth Ann. Student Coll. William and Mary, 1951-54. Soloist, Richmond Civic Ballet Co., Va., 1949-57, pres., 1955-56; comml. artist Cargill & Wilson Advt. Agy., Richmond, 1954-56; owner Joan Wolf Sch. Ballet, River Edge, N.J., 1957-79, Hillsdale, N.J., 1963—; owner, dir. Joan Wolf Ballet Ensemble, 1964-82; artistic dir., choreographer Joan Wolf Ballet Co., Hillsdale and River Edge, 1972—. Trustee, Hackensack YMHA, 1969-70; bd. dirs. Pascack Valley Mental Health Ctr., 1975-77; chmn. Bikeway Commn. Woodcliff Lake, 1975—; mem. Bergen County Cultural Arts Commn., 1977-80. Recipient cert. of merit as profl. tchr. Nat. Acad. of Ballet, 1960; citation for outstanding cultural contbn. State of N.J., 1981; commendation Bergen County Freeholders, 1981. Mem. Hillsdale C. of C. (pres. 1968-71), Greater Pascack Valley C. of C. (trustee, chmn. Bikeway Commn. 1974—). Subject of book There's Always a Right Job for Every Woman (Roberta Roesch). Home: 12 Anderson Ct PO Box 8588 Woodcliff Lake NJ 07675 Office: 455 Hillsdale Ave Hillsdale NJ 07642

WOLF, KATHLEEN, educational facility owner; b. Port Jefferson, N.Y., Dec. 30, 1942; d. Patrick and Patricia (Neger) Raimond; m. David Wolf, July 5, 1964; children: Ross, Gaelynn, Amanda. BS in Edn., SUNY, New Paltz, 1964. Cert. elem. educator, Fla., N.Y.; cert. early childhood tchr., Fla. Tchr. Mid. Country Sch. Dist., Centereach, N.Y., 1964-66, Mid. Island Sch. Dist., Coram, N.Y., 1970-71, Pasco County Schs., Fla., 1971-79; owner, dir. The Little Learning Pl., Port Richey, Fla., 1979—; tchr. Pasco County Adult Edn., Fla., 1982-86. Mem. Pasco County Bd. Edn., Fla., 1986—. Mem. Nat. Assn. for Edn. Young Children, Fla. Sch. Bd. Assn., Fla. Assn. for Children Under Six, West Pasco Presch. Assn. (treas., pres. 1980—), Delta Kappa Gamma. Republican. Office: The Little Learning Pl 11004 Martha Ave Port Richey FL 34668

WOLF, MARY, training specialist; b. Camden, N.J., July 7, 1938; d. Harry S. and Reba (Braun) Elkins; B.S. in Edn., Temple U., 1960; M.A. in Human Devel., Fairleigh Dickinson U., 1979; children—Alan Eric, Lisa Caryl, Marla Beth. Tchr., Camden High Sch., 1960-61, W. Phila. High Sch., 1961-64; instr. World-Wide Ednl. Services, Newark, 1979; pres. Dynamic Lifestyles, Inc., Belmar, N.J., 1979—; tng. specialist Ocean County Coll., Toms River, N.J., 1979-81; tng. specialist Ocean County Employment and Tng. Adminstrn., Toms River, N.J., 1981-82; mgr. RCA, Eatontown, N.J., 1982-85; adminstr. tng. amd organization devel. GE Astro Space Div., Princeton, N.J., 1985—; cons. in field. Mem. Am. Personnel and Guidance Assn., Am. Soc. Tng. and Devel., Nat. Soc. Performance and Instrn., Nat. Assn. Female Execs., Assn. Humanistic Psychology. Office: GE Astro Space Div PO Box 800 Princeton NJ 08540

WOLF, MARY ZIETLOW, manufacturing company executive; b. New London, Wis., Feb. 26, 1950; d. Gordon Leo and Melane Mary (Simonis) Z.; student U. Wis., Stevens Point, 1968-70, part time, 1977-80; m. Rodney A. Wolf, 1980; children—Dirk, Wayne. Adminstrv. asst. K.F. Kellogg, Northfield, Ill., 1970-74; prodn. mgr. M.R. Ceramics, Inc., Iola, Wis., 1974-77; plant mgr. Weber Tackle Co., Stevens Point, Wis., 1977-81; v.p. Rodmar Co., Amherst Junction, Wis., 1981-85, Rodmar Mfg. Inc., Nelsonville, Wis., 1985—; mgr. Rodmar Acctg. and Tax Services, 1984—; Mem. Tomorrow River Fine Arts Council, sec., 1985—; mem. Tomorrow River PTO, 1987—, v.p. 1987, pres. 1988. Mem. Nat. Assn. Female Execs., Nat. Assn. Tax Practitioners. Roman Catholic. Home: 8946 Loberg Rd Amherst Junction WI 54407 Office: PO Box 68 3000 Hwy 161 Nelsonville WI 54458

WOLF, MONICA THERESIA, procedures analyst; b. Germany, Apr. 26, 1943; came to U.S., 1953, naturalized, 1959; d. Otto and Hildegard Maria (Heim) Bellemann; children: Clinton, Danielle. BBA, U. Albuquerque, 1986. Developer Word Processing Ctr., Pub. Service of N.Mex., Albuquerque, 1971-74, word processing supr., 1974-78, budget coordinator, 1978-80, lead procedures analyst, 1980—; mem. adv. bd., student trainer APS Career Enrichment Ctr. Instr. firearm safety and pistol marksmanship. Mem. Internat. Word Processing Assn. (founder N.Mex. chpt.), Nat. Assn. Female Execs., Nat. Rifle Assn., N.Mex. Shooting Sports Assn. Democrat. Club: Sandia Gun (adv. bd., coach). Home: 305 Alamosa Rd NW Albuquerque NM 87107 Office: 414 Silver Ave SW Albuquerque NM 87103

WOLF, NANCY PATRICIA, clothing buyer; b. Jersey City, Mar. 15, 1953; d. Edwin and Margaret (Boymann) S.; m. Karl Alvin Wolf, May 29, 1976. Student, U. Md., 1973-74. Asst. buyer Sterns, Paramus, N.J., 1983-85; buyer Robinson's of Fla., St. Pete, 1984-87, G. Fox, Hartford, Conn., 1987—. Home: 7 Lang Rd Windsor CT 06095

WOLF, RAMONA MARLIS, assistant human resources officer; b. Reading, Pa., Mar. 22, 1961; d. Charles F. Ginder and Marlis Ursula (Hertrampf) Dietrich; m. Robert Karl Wolf, Apr. 4, 1987. Student, Pa. State U., 1984—. Clerical supr. Security of Am. Life Ins. Co., Reading, Pa., 1980-85; tng. facilitator Meridian Bancorp, Inc., Reading, 1985—. Teen club advisor Boscov's Dept. Store, Reading, 1983-84. Mem. Am. Bus. Women's Assn. (chairperson bull., pres. 1988—), Am. Inst. Banking (bd. govs, chpt. rep., 1985—, v.p. mktg. Berks County chpt. 1988—, AIB'r of Yr. 1986-87). Office: Meridian Bancorp 35 N 6th St Reading PA 19601

WOLF, SHARON VERNA, psychologist; b. Flushing, N.Y., Mar. 11, 1950. Research assoc. Ohio State U., Columbus, 1979-80; asst. prof. Morehead (Ky.) State U., 1980-81; vis. asst. prof. Purdue U., West Lafayette, Ind., 1981-83, N.Mex. State U., Las Cruces, 1983-84; vis. assoc. prof. Calif. State U., Long Beach, 1984—. Contbr. chpts. to books and articles to profl. jours. Recipient NSF fellow, 1977-79. Mem. Am. Psychol. Assn., Soc. for Personality and Social Psychology (cons. editor bull. 1985—), Soc. for Experimental Social Psychology, Midwestern Psychol. Assn., Western Psychol. Assn. Democrat. Office: Calif State Univ 1250 Bellflower Long Beach CA 90840

WOLFE, ANN, sculptor, educator, lecturer; b. Mlawa, Poland, Nov. 14, 1905, came to U.S., 1911, naturalized, 1927; d. Jacob and Sarah Wolfe; m. Mark A. Graubard, Mar. 5, 1927; children—Jane Strovas, Maya Jones. B.A., Hunter Coll., 1926; pvt. study, Manchester, Eng., Paris, 1931-33. Tchr. sculpture Minnetonka Art Center, Minn., 1971-73, pvt classes, Mpls, 1965-70. One man shows include Worcester Art Mus, Mass, 1939, Grace Horne Gallery, Boston, 1941, Whyte Gallery, Washington, 1946, Hamline U., St. Paul, 1951, Walker Art Center, Mpls., 1955, Mpls. Inst. Arts, 1964, Adele Bednarz Galleries, Los Angeles, 1966, Stewardt-Verde Galleries, San Francisco, 1966, Westlake Gallery, Mpls. 1970; represented in numberous group, national and regional exhibitions in N.Y.C., Chgo., Penn. Acad. Fine Arts, Third Sculpture Internat., 1949. Recipient sculpture awards Allied Artists of Am., N.Y.C., 1936, Soc. Wash. Artists, 1944, 45, Mpls. Inst. Arts, 1951, Soc. Minn. Sculptors, 1955. Mem. Soc. Minn. Sculptors. Home: 2928 Dean Pkwy Minneapolis MN 55416

WOLFE, ANTOINETTE, sales executive; b. San Bernadino, Calif., Feb. 7, 1954; d. Dennis and Smila Rose (Janich) Prokopis; m. John Edward Wolfe, Sept. 16, 1972 (div. 1983); children—Jason, Dennis. Student pub. schs., Gary, Ind. With classified advt. sales staff Mpls. Star & Tribune, 1972—, classified field sales rep., 1981—. Recipient Pub.'s award trophy, Mpls Star & Tribune, 1983, Pub.'s Club and award, 1984-85. Mem. Nat. Assn. Female Execs. Democrat. Greek Orthodox. Avocations: horseback riding; writing poetry. Home: 11626 University Ave N 10 Coon Rapids MN 55433 Office: Mpls Star & Tribune 425 Portland Ave S Minneapolis MN 55488

WOLFE, CAROLINE MARGARET, nurse; b. Toledo, Dec. 9, 1943; d. Russet John and Angela Frances (Kelly) DuMont; m. Warren Dwight Wolfe, Dec. 29, 1973; children—Mark Russet, Jeremy Dean, Jason Kelly. Diploma in nursing St. Vincent Hosp., Toledo, 1964; B.S. in Nursing, Mary Manse Coll., Toledo, 1966. Registered nurse, Ohio. Staff nurse, asst. head nurse ICU, Maumee Valley Hosp., Toledo, 1964-69; asst. head nurse hemodialysis Med. Coll. of Ohio, Toledo, 1969-71, head nurse hemodialysis, 1971-73, head nurse renal unit, 1973-75, staff nurse renal unit, 1978-81, transplant nurse coordinator, 1981—. Mem. Am. Nephrology Nurses Assn., N.Am. Transplant Coordinators Orgn., Kidney Found. Northwestern Ohio (pres. 1970-72, sec. 1973-74). Democrat. Avocations: skiing, reading, bowling. Home: 5617 Dianne Ct Toledo OH 43623 Office: Med Coll of Ohio CS 10008 Toledo OH 43699

WOLFE, CONNIE MARIE, accountant; b. Grosse Pointe Woods, Mich., Oct. 3, 1961; d. Charles Edward and Geraldine Charlotte (Wisniewki) W. BBA in Acctg., Adrian Coll., 1983. Staff acct. Forrest J. Williams, CPA, Colorado Springs, Colo., 1984-87; CPA Forrest J. Williams, CPA, 1987—. Gillian scholar. Mem. Nat. Assn. Female Execs., Alpha Kappa Psi (master ceremonies 1982). Democrat. Roman Catholic. Home: 4745 Garden Ranch Dr K-204 Colorado Springs CO 80907 Office: Forrest J Williams CPA 5125 N Union Blvd Suite 7 Colorado Springs CO 80918

WOLFE, CORINNE HOWELL, retired social worker; b. El Paso, Tex., Dec. 15, 1912; d. David Emerson and Clara (Schultz) Howell; B.A., U. Tex., El Paso, 1933; M.S.W., Tulane U., 1944; LL.D. (hon.), N.Mex. State U., 1983; m. Howard Clark Wolfe, Jr., Feb. 29, 1936. Social worker Tex. Dept. Public Welfare, 1933-45, Family Service Assn., Ft. Worth, 1945-46, VA, Dallas, 1946-48; dir. staff devel. and tng. Social and Rehab. Service, HEW, Washington, 1948-72; prof. social work N.Mex. Highlands U., Las Vegas, 1972-82, ret., 1982; cons. social services, social work edn. Mem. adv. panel N.Mex. Community Corrections. Recipient Disting. Service award HEW, 1973; Outstanding Alumni award Tulane U., 1975, Father Reynolds Rivera Humanitarian award Bar Assn., 1987; named N.Mex. Vol. of Yr., 1983. Mem. Nat. Assn. Social Workers (Nat. Social Worker Yr. 1986), Council Social Work Edn. (Disting. Service award 1972), N.Mex. Alliance Mentally Ill, Northern N.Mex. Civil Liberties Union (chair), N.Mex. Human Services Coalition (co-chair), Council Social Work Edn., Am. Public Welfare Assn., Nat. and Internat. Conf. on Social Welfare, Santa Fe Living Treasure. Democrat. Methodist. Contbr. articles to profl. jours. Home: 2509 Avenida de Isidro Santa Fe NM 87505

WOLFE, DEBORAH ANN, lawyer; b. Detroit, May 4, 1955; d. Adam and Mary A. (Smyth) Wolfe; m. Lester D. McDonald, May 23, 1987. Student Ariz. State U.-Tempe, 1973-76; B.A. in Polit. Sci., Bus. Tex. Christian U., Ft. Worth, 1977; postgrad. So. Meth. U., 1977-78; J.D., U. San Diego, 1980. Bar: Calif. 1981, Ariz. 1982. Sole practice, San Diego, 1981-83; ptnr. Kremer & Wolfe, San Diego, 1983-86; assoc. D.Dwight Worden, Solana Beach, Calif., 1986—; judge F. Lee Bailey Moot Ct. Competition, San Diego, 1984. Floutist, San Diego City Guard Band, 1981—, Grossmont Sinfonia, La Mesa, 1982-83; Classical/Chamber Music Quartet, San Diego, 1983. Author: (with Kremer and Craig) Handling Your Own Divorce, 1984. Mem. Assn. Trial Lawyers Am., Calif. Trial Lawyers Assn., San Diego Trial Lawyers Assn. (Outstanding Trial Lawyers award 1987). Republican. Clubs: Lawyers, Dimensions (San Diego). Office: 740 Lomas Santa Fe Dr Suite 102 Solana Beach CA 92705

WOLFE, DEBORAH CANNON PARTRIDGE, government education consultant; b. Cranford, N.J.; d. David Wadsworth and Gertrude (Moody) Cannon; 1 son, Roy. B.S., N.J. State Coll.; M.A., Ed.D., Tchrs. Coll., Columbia U.; postgrad., Vassar Coll., U. Pa., Union Theol. Sem., Jewish Sem. Am.; hon. doctorates, Seton Hall U., Coll. New Rochelle, Morris Brown U.; LL.D., Kean Coll., 1981; L.H.D., Stockton State Coll.; L.L.D., Centenary Coll. Former prin., tchr. pub. schs. Cranford, also Tuskegee, Ala.; faculty Tuskegee Inst., Grambling Coll., NYU, Fordham U., U. Mich., Tex. Coll., Columbia U.; supervision and adminstrn. curriculum devel., social studies U. Ill., summers; prof. edn., affirmative action officer Queens Coll.; prof. edn. and children's lit. Wayne State U., summer; now edn. chief U.S. Ho. of Reps. Com. on Edn. and Labor, 1962—; Fulbright prof. Am. lit. NYU; U.S. rep. 1st World Conf. on Women in Politics; chair non-govtl. reps. to UN (NGO/DPI exec. com.), 1983—; editorial cons. Macmillan Pub. Co.; cons. Ency. Brit.; adv. bd. Ednl. Testing Service; asso. minister First Bapt. Ch., Cranford, N.J.; mem. State Bd. Edn., 1964—; chairperson N.J. Bd. Higher Edn., 1967—; mem. nat. adv. panel on vocat. edn. HEW; mem. citizen's adv. com. to bd. Edn., Cranford; mem. Citizen's Adv. Com. on Youth Fitness, Pres.'s Adv. Com. on Youth Fitness, White House Conf. Children and Youth, 1950, 60, White House Conf. Edn., 1955, White House Conf. Aging, 1960, White House Conf. Civil Rights, 1966, White House Conf. on Children, 1970, Adv. Council for Innovations in Edn.; v.p. Nat. Alliance for Safer Cities; cons. Vista Corps, OEO. Contbr. articles to ednl. publs. Bd. dirs. Cranford Welfare Assn., Community Center, 1st Bapt. Ch., Cranford, Community Center Migratory Laborers, Hurlock, Md.; trustee Sci. Service, Seton Hall U.; mem. Public Broadcasting Authority.; bd. regents Seton Hall U.; sec. Kappa Delta Pi Ednl. Found.; mem. adv. com. Elizabeth and Arthur Schlesinger Library, Radcliffe Coll.; trustee Edn. Devel. Center. Recipient Nat. Achievement award Nat. Assn. Negro Bus. and Profl. Women's Clubs, 1958; Woman of Year award Delta Beta Zeta; Woman of Year award Morgan State Coll.; Achievement award Atlantic region Zeta Phi Beta. Mem. Council Nat. Orgns. Children and Youth, Am. Council Human Rights (v.p.), NCCJ, Nat. Panhellenic Council (dir.), Nat. Assn. Negro Bus. and Profl. Women (chmn. speakers bur.), Nat. Assn. Black Educators (pres.), NEA (life), LWV, N.Y. Tchrs. Assn., Am. Tchrs. Assn., Fellowship So. Churchmen, AAUW (nat. edn. chmn.), AAUP, Internat. Reading Assn., Comparative Edn. Soc., Am. Acad. Polit. and Social Sci., Internat. Assn. Childhood Edn., Nat. Soc. Study Edn., Am. Council Edn. (commn. fed. relations), Assn. Supervision and Curriculum Devel. (rev. council), AAAS (chmn. tchr. edn. com.), Nat. Alliance Black Educators (pres.), NAACP, Internat. Platform Assn., Ch. Women United (UN rep., mem. exec. com.), UN Assn.-U.S.A. (exec. com.), Delta Kappa Gamma Edn. Soc. (chmn. world fellowship com.), Kappa Delta Pi (chmn. ritual com.), Pi Lambda Theta, Zeta Phi Beta (internat. pres. 1954, chmn. edn. found. 1974—). Home: 62 S Union Ave Cranford NJ 07016 Office: CUNY Queens Coll New York NY

WOLFE, HARRIET MUNRETT, lawyer; b. Mt. Vernon, N.Y., Aug. 18, 1953; d. Lester John Francis Jr. and Olga Harriet (Miller) Munrett; m. Charles Briant Wolfe, Sept. 10, 1983. B.A., U. Conn., 1975; postgrad., Oxford U. (Eng.), 1976; J.D., Pepperdine U., 1978. Bar: Conn. 1979. Assoc. legal counsel, asst. sec. Citytrust, Bridgeport, Conn., 1979—; mem. govt. relations com. Electronic Funds Transfer Assn., Washington, 1983—. Mem. Conn. Bar Assn. (mem. legis. com. banking law sect.), ABA, Conn. Bankers Assn. (trust legis. com.), Guilford Flotilla Coast Guard Aux., U.S. Yacht Racing Union, Phi Alpha Delta Internat. (Frank E. Gray award 1978, Shepherd chpt. Outstanding Student award 1977-78). Home: 26 FarmView Dr Madison CT 06443 Office: Legal Dept Citytrust 961 Main St Bridgeport CT 06601

WOLFE, JANICE E., government executive; b. Racine, Ohio, Aug. 25, 1939; d. Donald Clark and Erline (Sargent) W. A.B. in Govt., Ohio U., 1961; J.D., Ohio State U., 1964. Bar: Ohio 1964. Atty. examiner Ohio Dept. Liquor Control, Columbus, 1964; asst. atty. gen., Columbus, Ohio, 1965-72; dist. counsel SBA, 1972-80, dep. dist. dir., Chgo., 1980-83, dist. dir., Washington, 1983-87, dep. assoc. adminstr. bus. devel., 1987—. Recipient SBA awards. Office: SBA 1441 L St NW Washington DC 02416

WOLFE, JEAN ELIZABETH, medical illustrator; b. Newark, Oct. 3, 1925; d. Arthur Howard and Ethel (Harper) Wolfe; B.S., Russell Sage Coll., 1947; student Pratt Inst., 1949-50; diploma U. Rochester Sch. Medicine and Dentistry, 1955; postgrad. (W.B. Saunders fellow), U. Pa., 1955-56, U. Pa., 1980; M.F.A., U. Pa., 1973, M.A. (hon.), 1973. Exhibitor, Pratt Inst. Galleries, Bklyn., 1958, N.Y. Med. Coll., 1958, Assn. Med. Illustrators, 1961-86, AMA, N.Y.C., 1965, Phila., 1965, A.C.S., Atlantic City, 1965, Research Study Club Los Angeles, 1966, Phila. Art Alliance, 1967, 73, U. Pa. Ophthal. Soc., 1967-68, N.J. Med. Soc., 1968, Cayuga Mus. History and Art, 1968, Pensacola Art Center, 1969, FAA Aero. Center, Oklahoma City, 1970, Scheie Eye Inst., 1972-75, Assn. Med. Illustrators Traveling Salon, 1978, Moore Coll. Art, 1985, Mus. of Am. Illustration Soc. of Illustrators, 1986; represented in permanent collections Archives of Med. Visual Resources, Francis A. Countway-Harvard Med. Library, Boston, Mutter Mus., Phila. Coll. Physicians, comprehensive collection of major work donated by Scheie Eye Inst.; contbg. illustrator Adler's Textbook Ophthalmology, 8th edit., 1969. Illustrations in med. books, jours., pharm. house pubs.; instr. Pembroke Coll. Brown U., 1947-49; mem. faculty Kimberley Sch., Upper Montclair, N.J., 1950-52; free lance med. illustration Studio N.Y. Med. Coll., 1956-60; instr. Pratt Inst., 1958-59; asso. in med. illustration U. Pa. Sch. Medicine, 1960-72, research asst. prof. med. art in ophthalmology, 1972-85; free lance med. and sci. illustration, 1985—; guest lectr. Johns Hopkins Med. Sch., 1973, NIH; guest artist USAF, Air Force Acad. and NORAD, 1971. Recipient Merit certificate AMA; Appreciation certificate ACS; 1st prize Pensacola Art Center, Am. Heart Assn., 1969, Gold medal Graphic Arts Soc. of Del. Valley, 1973. Mem. Phila. Art Alliance, Assn. Med. Illustrators (Ralph Sweet, Tom Jones awards, gov. 1970—, chmn. nominating com. 1972-73, vice chmn. bd. govs. 1973-74, chmn. bd. 1974-75), Soc. Illustrators (cert. merit 1986), Graphic Artists Guild, AAUP, Women's Caucus for Art.

WOLFE, JOAN LUEDDERS, non-profit organizations consultant, writer; b. Detroit, May 2, 1929; d. William R. and Mary Lucinda (Deane) Luedders; B.A., in Econs., U. Mich., 1951; D.Public Service (hon.), Western Mich. U., 1973; m. Willard Wolfe, June 26, 1953; children—John Roberts, Peter Harper (dec.). Founder, chmn. West Mich. Environ. Action Council, exec. dir., 1971-73, 1st woman chair, 1977; mem. Mich. Natural Resources Commn., 1973-82; bd. dirs. Dyer Ives Found., 1984—, Mich. Wetlands Found., 1984-88. Author: Making Things Happen: The Guide for Members of Volunteer Organizations, 1981. Pres., Belmont Sch.-Community Club, Newcomers Club Grand Rapids, Grand Rapids Audubon Club, Mich. Pesticide Council. Recipient Environ. Quality award Mich. Soc. Internal Medicine, 1970; Conservation award Am. Motors Corp., 1973; others. Mem. AAAS, Mich. Assn. Vol. Adminstrs., Nat. Audubon Soc. (nat. bd. dirs. 1982-87).

WOLFE, JUDITH ANN, constuction supply company executive; b. Austin, Minn., Mar. 11, 1946; d. Harold Lloyd and Lola Jean Lysne; m. Michael Dennis Wolfe; children: Anthony, Troy, Kimberly, Kelly. Cert. in credit adminstrn., Inst. Credit, Phoenix, 1986, cert. in advanced credit adminstrn., 1987. Credit mgr. Turf Irrigation, Phoenix, 1978—; corp. officer Turf Irrigation, 1978—. Author various wage and edn. surveys, 1987; reporter legis. updates newsletter, 1987. Mem. Nat. Assn. Credit Mgrs. (bd. dirs. 1987—, mem. ednl. group), Nat. Assn. Female Execs., Nat. Assn. Women in Constrn. Republican. Office: Turf Irrigation & Waterworks 3622 S 30th St Phoenix AZ 85040

WOLFE, LAURA CARNES, builder specialist broker; b. Jefferson, S.C., Aug 13, 1936; d. John Howard and Lottie Lula (Killough) Carnes; m. John Beasley Benton (dec. 1970); m. Elton Edwin Wolfe Jr., Apr. 2, 1972 (div. 1976); children: Deborah Elizabeth, Benton Parker. Student, U. S.C., 1955-56. Clk., Sears Roebuck, Florence, S.C., 1954-55; receptionist Am. Textile Mfrs. Inst., Charlotte, N.C., 1961-67, Pilot Life, Charlotte, 1958-60; sec. Chas. T. Main Inc, Charlotte, 1961-67; treas., mgr. Chipper Service, Lancaster, S.C., 1967-68; credit mgr. Buensod Div. Aeronca Inc., Pineville, N.C., 1968-72; export internat. credit analyst Scovill Inc., Monroe, N.C., 1972-87; bus. specialist broker, CPI Assocs., Lancaster, 1987—. Pres. Lancaster County Heart Assn., 1981. Mem. Internat. Assn. Execs. in Fin., Credit and Internat. Bus., Nat. Assn. Credit Mgmt., Am. Legion Aux. Democrat. Baptist. Club: Evening Garden (pres. 1981-83) (Lancaster). Avocations: reading, gardening, travel, swimming. Home: 419 Churchill Dr Lancaster SC 29720

WOLFE, LYNNELLE YVONNE, fast food chain executive; b. Bemidji, Minn., Feb. 23, 1961; d. Max Merideth and Yvonne Carol (Benson) W. Student, Oxford U., 1982; BS, Bemidji State U., 1983. Opening team mem. Internat. Dairy Queen, Inc., Mpls., 1983-84; ops. specialist Am. Dairy Queen Corp. subs. Internat. Dairy Queen, Inc., 1984-87, franchise devel. specialist on franchise sales, 1987—. Recipient Top of Field award, 1984-86. Lutheran. Avocations: softball, travel, reading, dance, spectator sports. Office: Am Dairy Queen Corp 5701 Green Valley Dr Bloomington MN 55437

WOLFE, MARGARET RIPLEY, historian, educator, consultant; b. Kingsport, Tenn., Feb. 3, 1947; d. Clarence Estill and Gertrude Blessing Ripley; B.S. magna cum laude, East Tenn. State U., 1967, M.A., 1969; Ph.D. (Haggin fellow), U. Ky., 1974; m. David Early Wolfe, Dec. 17, 1966; 1 dau., Stephanie Ripley. Instr. history East Tenn. State U., 1969-73, asst. prof., 1973-77, assoc. prof., 1977-80, prof., 1980—. Mem. Tenn. Com. for the Humanities, 1983-85 (exec. council 1984-85). Author: Lucius Polk Brown and Progressive Food and Drug Control, Tennessee and New York City, 1908-1920, 1978, An Industrial History of Hawkins County, Tennessee, 1983, Kingsport, Tennessee: A Planned American City, 1987; contbr. articles to profl. jours. Recipient Disting. Faculty award East Tenn. State U., 1977; East Tenn. State U. Found. research award, 1979, Alumni cert. merit, 1984. Mem. Am. Hist. Assn., Orgn. Am. Historians, So. Assn. Women Historians (pres. 1983-84, exec. com. 1984-86), So. Hist. Assn. (com. on the status of women 1987, program com. 1988), Smithsonian Assocs., ACLU, NOW, Tenn. Hist. Soc., Women in Hist. Profession (coordinating com.). Office: E Tenn State U Kingsport Ctr Kingsport TN 37660

WOLFE, NORMA LEE, construction company executive; b. Seneca, Mo., Mar. 12, 1932; d. Lawrence L. and Stella Mae Arehart; m. R. E. Wolfe, Mar. 7, 1957; children: Alan E., Deborah L. Student pub. schs., Seneca. Corp. sec. Ming of Am., Inc., Prairie Village, Kans., 1969-79, gen. mgr., 1969-75, dir., 1969—; sec.-treas. Alan E. wolfe Equipment & Constrn. Co., Kansas City, Mo., 1973—; commn. officer Joplin (Mo.) Police Dept., supr., 1953-57. Mem. ch. council, treas. Prince of Peace Luth. Ch., Grandview, Mo., 1970-75; mem. Luth. Ch. Women. Democrat. Office: 3001 E 83d St Kansas City MO 64132

WOLFE, RINNA EVELYN, educator; b. Bklyn., May 2, 1925. B.B.A., CCNY, 1957; M.A. in Creative Arts, San Francisco State U., 1966. With Charles Stores, N.Y.C., 1944-54, Raylass Dept. Stores, N.Y.C., 1955-59; classroom and resource tchr. Mt. Diablo Schs. (Calif.), 1960-65, Danville Schs. (Calif.), 1965-67, Berkeley Schs. (Calif.), 1967-80; extension tchr. U. Calif., 1968-78. Author: From Children With Love, 1970; The Singing Pope,

1980 (presented to Pope John Paul, Apr. 1982), Women Taket Care, 1987. Point Found. fellow, 1976. Mem. Am. PEN Women, Nat. Book Assn.

WOLFE, SHANA KAY, accountant; b. Hagerstown, Md., Mar. 3, 1958; d. Frederick John and Beulah Virginia (Keadle) Siponen; m. Robert Anthony Smith, Oct. 2, 1976 (div. 1980); Daryl Lynn Wolfe, Apr. 16, 1983; children: Erin Christine. AA in Acctg., Hagerstown (Md.) Jr. Coll., 1979; BSBA in Acctg., Shippensburg (Pa.) U., 1982. Cert. Mgmt. Accountant, Md., 1982. Acctg. clk. Tristate Elec. Supply Co., Inc., Hagerstown, 1976-82, acctg. supr., 1982-83, acctg. mgr., 1983-87, controller, 1987—. Recipient Student Performance award Inst. Cert. Mgmt. Accts., 1982. Mem. Nat. Assn. Accts. (pres. 1984-85). Democrat. United Methodist. Home: 56 Emerald Dr Hagerstown MD 21740 Office: Tristate Elec Supply Co Inc 1741 Dual Hwy PO Box 469 Hagerstown MD 21741-0469

WOLFE, TRACEY DIANNE, distributing company executive; b. Dallas, June 13, 1951; d. George F. Wolfe and Helen Ruth Cline Lemons; B.S. in Edn. and Social Sci., East Tex. State U., Commerce, 1973, M.S. in Elem. Edn., 1976; 1 son, Bronson Alan. Asst. to dir. student devel. East Tex. State U., 1973-74; corp. sec., v.p. Wolfe Distbg. Co., beer distbrs., Terrell, Tex., 1974—. Mem. Pilot Club Internat., Kappa Delta (alumnae v.p. 1978-79, alumnae treas. 1979-81, province pres. 1980-82). Republican. Methodist. C-lub: Pilot (Terrell). Home: 3316 Lakeside Dr Rockwall TX 75087 Office: 100 Metro Dr Terrell TX 75160

WOLFE-MORGAN, LOIS LOUISE, seminar leader; b. Flint, Mich., Feb. 6, 1948; d. Lawrence Dennis and Muriel Esther (Bill) Lyden; m. Cyril George Wolfe, Sept. 23, 1939 (div. June 1984); m. Michael Henry Morgan III, Jan. 2, 1946; stepchildren: Scott, Erin. A in Bus. Adminstrn., Oakland Community Coll., 1980; student, U. Ala., 1984-85, Cen. Mich. U., 1985-86; BA, Calif. Pacific U., 1988. Various clerical positions U.S. Army Tank-Automotive Command, Warren, Mich., 1966-74, various adminstrv. positions, 1974-75, supr. concepts lab., adminstrv. officer, 1975-79, supr. readiness engring., adminstrv. officer, 1979-80, program dir. exec. devel., employee devel., 1980-85; dir., owner Wolfe Assocs., Plymouth, Mich., 1985—; regional dir. The Effectiveness Inst., Plymouth, 1985—; dir. owner Acad. Funding Inst., Plymouth, 1987—; sr. assoc. Reid & Assoc., Pendleton, S.C., 1985—; trainer, speaker Office of Personnel Mgmt., Chgo., 1985—. Mem. Am. Soc. for Tng. and Devel., Women in Def., Nat. Speakers Assn. (cert. profl.), Profl. Speakers Assn. Mich. Office: Wolfe Assocs PO Box 404 Plymouth MI 48170

WOLFERT, RUTH, therapist; b. N.Y.C., Nov. 10, 1933; d. Ira and Helen (Herschdorfer) W. BS summa cum laude, Columbia U., 1967, postgrad., 1966-68. Pvt. practice therapist N.Y.C., 1972—; dir. Action Groups, N.Y.C., 1974-76, Gestalt Groups, N.Y.C., 1976—; faculty, coordinating bd. Women's Interart Ctr., N.Y.C., 1971-75, bd. dirs.; presenter Stockton (N.J.) State Coll., 1974-75; presenter in field. Contbr. booklet A Consumer's Guide to Non-Sexist Therapy, 1978. Mem. Assn. Humanistic Psychology (bd. dirs. ea. regional network 1981-87, pres. 1985-87), N.Y. Inst. Gestalt Therapy (trainer 1979—, chair workshops program 1979-83, co-chair conf. 1983-85), Assn. Transpersonal Psychology (co-chair N.Y. discussion group 1983-85), N.Y. Acad. Scis. Office: Gestalt Groups 161 E 91st St New York NY 10128

WOLFF, LEA, nuclear industry manager; b. Bklyn., June 16, 1944; d. Murray and Mollie (Braelow) Glassman; m. Jesse S. Wolff, July 2, 1966; children: Marci A., Laura S., Denise C. BA in Econs., Bklyn. Coll., 1974; MBA in Fin., Fairleigh Dickinson U., 1980, MBA in Indsl. Mgmt., 1985. Asst. to exec. v.p. fin. ERS div. Equitable Life Assurance Soc. U.S., N.Y.C., 1977-81; mgr. strategic planning GPU Nuclear Corp., Parsippany, N.J., 1981—. Pres. West Caldwell (N.J.) Residents Assn., AWARE, Newark, 1987—; bd. dirs. West Essex Community Health Services, Inc., Fairfield, N.J., 1987—, Bd. Mem. Inst., Orange, N.J., 1988—; facilitator Bd. Mem. Inst., Project Gro. Mem. Edison Electric Inst. (strategic planning and issues identification coms.). Home: 69 Brian Rd West Caldwell NJ 07006 Office: Gen Pub Utilities GPU Nuclear Corp 1 Upper Pond Rd Parsippany NJ 07054

WOLFF, MARY HELEN, service executive; b. Dayton, Ohio, Jan. 10, 1946; d. Richard Louis and Vera Ann (Nece) W. Student, Cornell U., 1969, U. Dayton, 1966-67. Adminstrv. asst. Sheraton-Dayton Hotel, 1964-69; personnel dir. Park Sheraton Hotel, N.Y.C., 1969-70; asst. catering dir. Marriott's Essex House Hotel, N.Y.C., 1970-71; mgr. program devel. Top Value Incentive Travel, Dayton, 1973-79; mgr. incentive sales Trusthouse Forte Hotels, Chgo., 1979-85; dir. incentive sales Marriott Hotel Corp., Chgo., 1985; dir. internat. incentive sales and mktg. Grand Champions Resorts, Chgo., 1985-88; pvt. practice service executive 1988—; speaker Meeting Planners Internat. Annual Conv., 1985. Sec. Lexington Lane Homeowners Assn., Schaumburg, Ill., 1986; mem. John Lindsey Reelection Campaign, N.Y.C., 1969. Mem. Soc. Incentive Travel Execs., Nat. Assn. Female Execs., Am. Bus. Women's Assn. (sec. 1983-84). Democrat. Roman Catholic. Home and Office: 22 Superior Ct Schaumburg IL 60193

WOLFF, REBECCA ANN, sales professional; b. Dayton, Ohio, Aug. 3, 1957. BS in Chemistry, U. Dayton, 1979; MBA in Mktg., Xavier U., 1986—. Engr. quality control carbon products div. Union Carbide Corp., Clarksburg, W.Va., 1979-81; application rep. carbon and graphite electrodes and specialties ctr. Union Carbide Corp., Parma, Ohio, 1981-83; sales rep. carbon and graphite specialty products Union Carbide Corp., Chgo., 1983; sr. sales rep. chem div. Unocal Corp., Houston, 1984-86; sr. sales rep. indsl. chems. Albright & Wilson Ams., Richmond, Va., 1987—. Mem. Cin. Drug and Chem. Assn.

WOLFF, SIDNEY CARNE, astronomer, observatory administrator; b. Sioux City, Iowa, June 6, 1941; d. George Albert and Ethel (Smith) Carne; m. Richard J. Wolff, Aug. 29, 1962. BA, Carleton Coll., 1962, DSc (hon.), 1985; PhD, U. Calif., Berkeley, 1966. Postgrad. research fellow Lick Obs, Santa Cruz, Calif., 1969; asst. astronomer U. Hawaii, Honolulu, 1967-71, assoc. astronomer, 1971-76; astronomer, assoc. dir. Inst. Astronomy, Honolulu, 1976-83, acting dir., 1983-84; dir. Kitt Peak Nat. Obs., Tucson, 1984-87, Nat. Optical Atronomy Observatories, 1987—. Author: The A-Type Stars—Problems and Perspectives, 1983; (with others) Exploration of the Universe, 1987, Realm of the Universe, 1988; contbr. articles to profl. jours. Research fellow Lick Obs. Santa Cruz, Calif., 1967. Mem. Astron. Soc. Pacific (pres. 1984-86, bd. dirs. 1979-85), Am. Astron. Soc. (council 1983-86), Internat. Astron. Union. Office: Nat Optical Astronomy Obs PO Box 26732 Tucson AZ 85726

WOLFF, SUSAN (JOEY), new products marketing executive; b. N.Y.C., Apr. 11, 1944; d. Seymour Barnett and Julia (Weiner) Joseph; m. Ivan Lawrence Wolff, June 18, 1967; 1 child, Adam Gregory. BS with honors, Cornell U., 1966; MS with honors, NYU, 1968. Mgr. mktg. research Mattel, Inc., Hawthorne, Calif., 1968-74; mgr. new product research Gillette Co., Boston, 1975-76; mktg. mgr. new products AT&T Consumer Products, Basking Ridge, N.J., 1977-81, dir. mktg. Advanced Mobile Phone Service, Inc. subs., Basking Ridge, 1981-83; pres. Wolff Assocs. Inc., Mountain Lakes, N.J., 1983—; mng. dir. Solomon-Wolff Assocs. Inc., Mountain Lakes, N.J., 1984-86, pres., 1981-86. NDEA fellow NYU, 1966-68. Mem. Cornell U. Alumni Assn. (pres. 1981-86), Am. Mktg. Assn. Office: Wolff Assocs Inc 165 Laurel Hill Rd Mountain Lakes NJ 07046

WOLFGRAM, DEBORAH DIANE, date processing executive; b. Iowa City, June 9, 1959; d. William Curtis and Janet (Johnson) McLeod; m. Douglas Edward Wolfgram, Dec. 29, 1987. BS, Calif. State U., Long Beach, 1981; MBA, U. Calif., Irvine, 1986. Sr. v.p. ops., systems and telecommunications Analytic Investment Mgmt., Irvine, 1981—; bd. dirs. Microtex Industries, San Juan Capistrano, Calif. Author: Expert Systems for the Technical Professional, 1987. Mem. Computer Soc. of IEEE, Am. Mgmt. Assn., Phi Eta Sigma, Alpha Lambda Delta. Republican. Presbyterian. Home: 29842 Highview Circle San Juan Capistrano CA 92675 Office: Analytic Investment Mgmt 2222 Martin St Suite 230 Irvine CA 92715

WOLFMAN, BRUNETTA REID, community college president; b. Clarksdale, Miss., Sept. 4, 1931; d. Willie Orlando and Belle Victoria (Allen) Griffin Reid; m. Burton Wolfman, Oct. 4, 1952; children—Andrea, Jefferey. B.A., U. Calif.-Berkeley, 1957, M.A., 1968, Ph.D., 1971; D.H.L. (hon.), Boston, U., 1983; D.P. (hon.), Northeastern U., 1983; D.L. (hon.), Regis Coll., 1984, Stonehill Coll., 1985; D.H.L., Suffolk U., 1985; D.E.T. (hon.), Wentworth Inst., 1987. Asst. dean faculty Dartmouth Coll., Hanover, N.H., 1972-74; asst. v.p. acad. affairs U. Mass., Boston, 1974-76; acad. dean Wheelock Coll., Boston, 1976-78; cons. Arthur D. Little, Cambridge, Mass., 1978; dir. policy planning Dept. Edn., Boston, 1978-82; pres. Roxbury Community Coll., Boston, 1983—; dir. U.S. Trust Bank, Boston, 1982, Am. Council Edn., Harvard Community Health Plan. Author: Roles, 1983. Bd. overseers Wellesley (Mass.) Coll., 1981; bd. dirs. Boston-Fenway Program, 1977, Freedom House, Boston, 1983. Boston Pvt. Industry Council, 1983; bd. dirs. NCCJ, Boston, 1983, co-chair; bd. overseers Boston Symphony Orch., Mus. Fine Arts, Boston; councilor Council on Edn. for Pub. Health. Recipient Freedom award NAACP No. Calif., 1971; Amelia Earhart award Women's Edn. and Indsl. Union, Boston, 1983. Mem. Adult Edn. Assn. U.S.A., Am. Sociol. Assn., Am. Ednl. Research Assn., AAUW, Black Women for Policy Action, 1976, Greater Boston, C. of C. (edn. com. 1982), Pi Lambda Theta, Alpha Kappa Alpha (Humanitarian award 1984). Democrat. Home: 180 Beacon St Boston MA 02116 Office: Roxbury Community Coll 1234 Columbus Ave Boston MA 02119

WOLFORD, ELIZABETH JULE JOHNSON, cardiovascular specialist, ultrasound technologist; b. Breckenridge, Minn., Mar. 3, 1960; d. Clifford Eugene and Diana Mae (Strubel) Johnson; m. Scott Clinton Wolford, Aug. 6, 1983; 1 child, Stephanie Elizabeth. Student, U. N.D., 1978-81; BS in Radiol. Tech., U. Okla., 1983. Registered vascular technologist. Sr. sonographer Oklahoma City Clinic, 1983-85; chief cardiovascular technologist Advanced Cardiovascular Tech., Albuquerque, 1985-87; sr. sonographer Diagnostic Mobile Ultrasound, Inc., 1987—. Mem. Okla. Sonographers Soc., Soc. Non-Invasive Vascular Tech., Soc. Diagnostic Med. Sonographers, Am. Registry Diagnostic Med. Sonographers (cert.), Am. Inst. Ultrasound Medicine, Registry Vascular Technologist. Republican. Methodist. Home: 717 Westview Dr Yukon OK 73099 Office: Diagnostic Mobile Ultrasound Inc 902 S Bryant Edmond OK 73034

WOLICKI, NANCY FRIEDA, lawyer; b. Chgo., Sept. 8, 1953; d. Samuel and Ingrid (Rappel) W.; B.A. in Journalism and Sociology, U. Ariz., 1974, J.D., 1977. Admitted to Ariz. bar, 1977; law clk. firm Verity, Smith & Kearns, Tucson, 1976-77, Ariz. Ct. Appeals, 1977-78; legis. asst. fgn. policy and armed services health, staff atty. Billy Carter investigation to U.S. Sen. Dennis DeConcini, 1979-81; staff dir. Senate Subcom. on Alcoholism and Drug Abuse, Washington, 1981-84; mem. staff Senator Gordon J. Humphrey, Washington, 1984-87; coordinator adv. com. Voluntary Fgn. U.S. Aid, 1987; sr. analyst legal and congressional affairs President's Commn. on the HIV Epidemic, 1987—. Recipient William Spaid Meml. award U. Ariz. Coll. Law, 1977, Senate commendation for Billy Carter investigation, 1980. Mem. Am. Bar Assn., Ariz. Bar Assn., Phi Kappa Phi. Jewish. Office: 531 Hart Senate Office Bldg Washington DC 20510

WOLK, JOAN MARCIA, technical writer, consultant; b. Pitts., Dec. 2, 1947; d. Samuel David and Rhoda (Levy) Kopelman; m. Stephen Selis Wolk, Oct. 25, 1970 (div. Sept. 1977); 1 child, Jason. BA in English, Ohio U., 1969; postgrad. in linguistics, Ohio State U., 1970; MA in Linguistics, U. Mass., 1970. Tchr. English, chmn. dept. English Prince George County Bd. Edn., Upper Marlboro, Md., 1970-73; editor, 1977-81; sr. tech. writer Boeing Computer Services, Vienna, Va., 1981-85, systems analyst electronic pub., 1985-87; mgr. tech. writing VM Software, Inc., Reston, Va., 1987—; cons. tech. writing, Gaithersburg, Md., 1988—. Democrat. Jewish. Avocations: parapsychology/metaphysics, concerts, theater, opera, walking. Home and Office: 13 Story Dr Gaithersburg MD 20878

WOLLITZ-DOOLEY, MARY, psychologist; b. Glendale, Calif., June 30, 1943; d. Paul Edward and Helen Virginia (Jones) Wollitz; m. Paul Anthony Dooley, June 15, 1974. BA, Mundelein Coll., 1966; MA, Butler U., 1971; PhD, Indiana U., 1983. Lic. psychologist, Ind. Tchr. Iowa Catholic Schs., Cedar Rapids and Iowa City, Iowa, 1966-69; dir. adult edn. North Riverside (Ill.), Tecumseh (Mich.) Bds. Edn., 1969-72; cons., tchr. adult edn. div. Archdiocese of Balt., 1972-74; pvt. practice cons., educator Indpls., 1974-76; behavioral clinician Ind. Dept. Corrections, Plainfield, 1976, psychologist, 1984—; research assoc. Ind. U., Bloomington, 1979-80; assoc. instr. Ind. U., Bloomington and Indpls., 1980, 82; editor newsletter Share, 1972-74. Author: Options: A Program Planning Guide, 1973. Mem. Common Cause (Ind. governing bd. 1976, 83), Network, Washington, 1983, Guilford Twp., Plainfield, 1987. Mem. Am. Psychol. Assn. (assoc. 1978-84), Ind. Psychol. Assn., Soc. Psychol. Study Social Issues, Am. Assn. Correctional Psychologists, Audubon Soc., Nat. Wildlife Fedn., Pi Lambda Theta. Democrat. Roman Catholic. Office: Ind Youth Ctr 727 Moon Rd Plainfield IN 46168

WOLNOWITZ-KOMENSKY, CARYN L., marketing professional; b. Bklyn., May 23, 1957; d. Felix and Shirley (Ruback) W.; m. Alan Michael Komensky. BA, N.Y. Inst. Tech., 1981. Div. mktg. mgr. Encyclopaedia Britannica, Floral Park, N.Y., 1983-85; regional mktg. mgr. Encyclopaedia Britannica, Northbrook, Ill., 1985-86; nat. mktg. mgr. Encyclopaedia Britannica, Chgo., 1986—. Internat. Council Shopping Ctrs. Office: Encyclopaedia Britannica USA 310 S Michigan Ave Chicago IL 60604

WOLOSZYNSKI, THERESA E., underwriter; b. Suffern, N.Y., Sept. 9, 1963; d. Edward Victor Woloszynski and Filomena Teresa (Ferreira) Campbell. BS in Bus. Adminstrn., Bryant Coll. of Bus. Adminstrn., 1985. Underwriter Liberty Mut. Ins. Co., Portsmouth, N.H., 1985-86; policies and procedures analyst Liberty Mut. Ins. Co., Boston, 1986-88, industry and regulatory relations analyst, 1988—. Roman Catholic. Office: Liberty Mut Ins Co 175 Berkeley St Boston MA 02117

WOLOTKIEWICZ, MARIAN MARGARET, writer, college administrator; b. Camden, N.J., Apr. 22, 1954; d. Edward J. and Rita J. Wolotkiewicz; m. Paul J. Sagan, Mar. 31, 1984. BA, Mt. Holyoke Coll., 1976; cert. legal asst. tng. program U. Mass., 1975; JD, Suffolk U., 1979. Manuscript editor law div. Little, Brown & Co., Boston, 1979-84; freelance writer/editor, 1985-88; dir. pub. info. Regis Coll., Weston, Mass., 1988—; founder, pres. Barrister Pub. Inc., 1981-88. Chmn. Stow Cable TV Adv. Com., 1983—. Mem. Mass. Bar Assn. (mng. editor tax sect. newsletter 1978-83), Mass. Women's Bar Assn (editor newsletter 1979-83). Office: Regis Coll 235 Wellesley St Weston MA 02193

WOLPE, CLAIRE FOX, civic worker, psychotherapist; b. N.Y.C., June 24, 1909; d. David and Pauline (Hirsch) Fox; A.B., Mills Coll., 1930; M.A., U. So. Calif., 1936, M.S.W., 1965; Ph.D., Marquette U., 1970; postgrad. Smith Coll., summer 1931, Columbia U., summer 1963, U. Mexico City, summer 1964; m. Arthur S. Wolpe, Dec. 25, 1932 (dec. Mar. 1962); children—Ruth (Mrs. Roy Rose), Sheri (Mrs. Jerome Langer). Student advisor Jewish student orgn. UCLA, 1931-33; with Travelers Aid, Los Angeles, 1934; med. social work Los Angeles County Gen. Hosp., 1934-38; with USPHS, 1938; social worker Los Angeles County Health Dept., 1938-39; psychiat. social worker Gateways Psychiat. Hosp. and Mental Health Center, Los Angeles, 1962-63, 65-66; exec. dir. Bay Cities Mental Health Center, Los Angeles, 1966-68; supr. Airport Marina Counseling Service; pvt. practice. Mem. Mayors Com. on Civil Def. 1950-52, Wilshire Coordinating Council, 1954-58; leader Girl Scouts U.S.A., 1954-58; mem. regional bd. NCCJ, 1951-55. Bd. dirs. So. Calif. Mental Health Assn., 1955-58, Los Angeles chpt. A.R.C., 1951-53, Community Relations Conf. So. Calif., 1950-60, Los Angeles Jewish Fedn. Council, 1952-58, B'nai B'rith Anti-Defamation League, 1973—, Hillel Assn., 1973—. Fellow Soc. Clin. Social Workers, Am. Assn. Orthopsychiatry; mem. Nat. Assn. Social Workers, Psychotherapy Assn. So. Calif. (dir. 1967—, pres.-elect 1984), Calif. Marriage, Family and Child Counseling Assn., Am. Group Psychotherapy Assn., Los Angeles Transactional Analysis Soc. (sec.-treas. 1966-68), Psi Chi. Jewish religion. Mem. B'nai B'rith Women. Home and Office: 234 Orange Dr Los Angeles CA 90036

WOLQUITT, ELEANOR ANNA, writer; b. Montreal, Que., Can., Dec. 14, 1922; came to U.S., 1923; d. Herman and Esther (Rothenberg) W. BA, Hunter Coll., 1942. Editor Jean Renoir, Beverly Hills, Calif., 1949-51; story analyst 20th Century-Fox, N.Y.C., 1951-61; story editor various cos., N.Y.C., 1961-67; story editor, chief of prodn. Bryna Pictures, Los Angeles, 1967-71; story editor McDermott Prodns., Los Angeles, 1971-72; writer Harpers mag., N.Y.C., 1973; writer for Hume Cronyn and Jessica Tandy, N.Y.C.; writer CBS-TV, N.Y.C., 1976; freelance writer, 1980—; writer Baxter Enterprises, Inc., Easton, Conn., 1984-86. Scriptwriter, playwright The Many Faces of Love, 1975; screenwriter King of the Rainy Country, 1979; writer for The Bicentennial Minutes, CBS (Emmy award Acad. TV Arts and Scis. 1976). Speechwriter Dem. Nat. Conv., N.Y.C. and Los Angeles, 1952, 56, 60, 72; bd. dirs. Washington Sq. Outdoor Art Show, N.Y.C., 1976—. Served as lt. USNR, 1943-47. Mem. Writers Guild Am. West, Dramatists Guild, Mensa.

WOLVERTON, LINDA MAY, healthcare company executive; b. Abington, Pa., Apr. 9, 1943; d. James Charles and Gladys Elizabeth (McCarraher) Costello. Student, Pasco Hernando Coll., 1974-77, U. Ala., 1979-80, St. Petersburg Jr. Coll., 1981-82. Diplomate Am. Bd. Quality Assurance and Utilization Rev.; cert. med. staff coordinator. Med. records dir. Community Meml. Hosp., Hamilton, N.Y., 1963-76, Riverside Hosp., New Port Richey, Fla., 1976-77; quality assurance coordinator Shelby Meml. Hosp., Alabaster, Ala., 1977-80; clin. instr. quality assurance U. Ala., Birmingham, 1978-79; quality assurance coordinator Profl. Found. Healthcare, Tampa, Fla., 1980-81; mgr. quality assurance/utilization mgmt. Tampa Gen. Hosp., 1981-82; mgr. health info. Palms of Pasadena Hosp., St. Petersburg, Fla., 1982-84; quality assurance coordinator Seton Med. Ctr., Daly City, Calif., 1984-85; healthcare cons. Coopers & Lybrand, San Francisco, 1985-86; corp. dir. managed care services Parcelsus Healthcare Corp., Pasadena, Calif., 1986—. Treas. Mountain Meadows Homeowners Assn., Pomona, Calif., 1987—. Mem. Nat. Assn. Quality Assurance Profls. (cert., del. 1986-87, region III rep. nat. bd. 1983-84), Am. Med. Records Assn. (accredited), Calif. Assn. Quality Assurance Profls. (nominating com. 1987). Republican. Home: 1715 Calle De Oro Pomona CA 91768 Office: 155 N. Lake Ave. Suite 1100 Pasadena CA 91768

WOLYNIEC, CONSTANCE, business executive, consultant; b. N.Y.C., Jan. 17, 1954; d. Adolph B. and Marion (Jankowsky) W. B.S. cum laude in Bus. Adminstrn., Ithaca Coll., 1974; M.B.A., Babson Coll., 1978. Systems mktg. rep. Control Data Corp., Boston, 1974-78, sales trainer, Greenwich, Conn., 1978-80; dir. Strategic Projects, internat. market entry and devel. co., St. John, V.I., 1980—; pres. The Clothing Studio Inc., Mongoose Jct., St. John, 1984—. Mem. Mensa. Lutheran. Home: Cruz Bay Saint John VI 00830 Office: Strategic Projects Saint John VI 00830

WOMACK, BETTY JEAN, credit union executive; b. Houston, Jan. 29, 1935; d. Leslie Owen and Mary Jane (Raybourn) Spears; m. William R. Womack, Mar. 21, 1981; stepchildren: Glenn, Vicki; children from previous marriage: Jeanne, Kathy, Wesley. Grad. high sch., Spring, Tex. Owner, ptnr. Bounds Florist, Houston, 1965-67; asst. mgr. SPCO Fed. credit Union, Houston, 1971-77; mgr., pres. Rockwell Credit Union, Houston, 1977-79; owner Lady Bug Florist, Houston, 1979-81; pres., mgr. Meml. Employment Credit Union, Houston, 1979—. Campaign v.p. Am. Legion Aux., Houston, 1969-70. Office: Meml Employees Credit Union 7777 Southwest Hwy Houston TX 77074

WOMACK, CHARLOTTE CATHERINE, small business owner; b. Jackson, Miss., Dec. 31, 1952; d. Robert Emmett and Charlotte (Tolley) W. BA in Polit. Sci., Milsaps Coll., 1974. Pres., owner Be-Bop Record Shop, Inc., Jackson, 1974—; dir. Be-Bop Prodns., Inc., 1974—. Democrat. Episcopalian. Office: Be-Bop Record Shop Inc 900 E County Line Rd Ridgeland MS 39157

WOMACK, JUDY RAE SHUMWAY, advertising executive; b. Topeka, Mar. 16, 1945; d. Claude Benson and Violet Mae (Bearde) Shumway; m. Albert Neil Womack, Feb. a5, 1964 (div. Aug. 1984); children: Albert Neil Jr., Jason Scott. A, South Cen. Career Coll., 1983. Dist. tng. mgr. Sunbelt Airlines, Little Rock, 1983-84; lead agt. Exec. Travel, Little Rock, 1984-85; mgr. Exec. Travel West, Little Rock, 1985-86; tng. coordinator, promotions coordinator Dillard's Travel, North Little Rock, Ark., 1986-87; advt. mgr. corp. office, with pub. relations Dillard's Travel, Little Rock, 1987—. Presch. tchr. First United Meth. Ch., Jacksonville, Ark., 1983. Recipient Civil Recognition Gov.'s Support Group, 1987. Republican. Club: Newcomers (pres. 1973).

WOMACK, SHARON G., librarian. Dir. Ariz. Library, Archives and Pub. Records Dept., Phoenix. Office: Ariz State Capitol Mus 1700 W Washington Phoenix AZ 85007

WOMBLE, MELODIE LYNN, utilities executive; b. Rockville Centre, N.Y., Mar. 19, 1945; d. Harold and Sylvia (Ross) Lisses; m. Gary W. Womble, June 10, 1967 (dec. 1978). BA in English and Journalism, Fla. State U., 1967; MEd, U. Miami, 1970; postgrad., Nova U., 1978. Tchr. Dade County (Fla.) Pub. Schs., 1967-69, specialist evaluations, 1975-77; asst. communications research Dallas Ind. Sch. Dist., 1970-73; editor Sports Digest, Miami, Fla., 1974; supr. dept. corp. communications Fla. Power and Light Co., 1977—; instr. U. Miami, 1979, 86—; officer dir. Abba El Prodns., 1984—. Author profl. papers. Charter mem., chair Fla. AWARE Com., 1978-87, program chair state meetings, 1979-80, 83, 85; mem. steering com. Downtown Prayer Breakfast. NDEA fellow, 1970. Mem. Internat. Assn. Bus. Communication (co-chair regional meeting 1979), Women in Communication (moderator seminar 1980-81, 84, panelist 1988), LWV (bd. dirs. legis. liaison 1980-83), Greater Miami C. of C., Fla. C. of C. (adviser, energy task force com. 1983-84), Leadership Miami Alumni Assn. Office: PO Box 029100 Miami FL 33102

WOMBLE, SUSAN ELIZABETH, consumer safety official; b. Wilmington, Del., Dec. 28, 1951; d. Thomas IV and Ruthmary (Mason) Alderson; m. Melvin Eugene Womble, Mar. 26, 1977. BS in Chemistry, Grove City (Pa.) Coll., 1973. Cert. tchr., Pa. Chemist Nat. Bur. Standards, Gaithersburg, Md., 1973-79; chemist Consumer Product Safety Commn., Bethesda, Md., 1979-84, project mgr., 1984—. Contbr. articles to profl. jours. Mem. Am. Chem. Soc., Nat. Assn. Female Execs. Episcopalian. Office: Consumer Product Safety Commn 5401 Westbard Ave Washington DC 20207

WONG, ANGELINE ON-KI, controller; b. Hong Kong, Jan. 31, 1951; came to U.S., 1975; d. Edward Peter and Louise (Young) W. Diploma, Hong Kong Bapt. Coll., 1975; BS in Bus. Adminstrn., NW Okla. State U., 1976; M in Econs., Calif. State U., 1979. Economist U. Wis., Menomonie, 1980-83; lectr. econs. Calif. State U., San Jose, 1983-84; instr. econs. Evergreen Coll., San Jose, 1984; controller Applied Tech. Assn., Inc., Mountain View, Calif., 1983—; ind. researcher in govt. contracting cost and impact, 1986—. Mem. Am. Econ. Assn., Nat. Contract Mgmt. Assn., Am. Payroll Assn., Nat. Assn. Accts. Home: 207 Goodwin St Hayward CA 94544 Office: Applied Tech Assn 1320 Villa St Mountain View CA 94041

WONG, ELAINE DANG, foundation executive; b. Canton, China, June 3, 1936 (parents Am. citizens); d. Robert G. and Fung Heong (Woo) Dang; A.A. (Rotary scholar), Coalinga Coll., 1956; B.S. (AAUW scholar, Grad. Resident scholar), U. Calif., Berkeley, 1958, teaching credential, 1959; m. Philip Wong, Nov. 8, 1959; children—Elizabeth, Russell, Roger, Edith, Valerie. Tchr. acctg. San Mateo (Calif.) High Sch., 1959-60; acct., 1960-75; substitute tchr. Richmond County Schs., Augusta, Ga., 1975-77; comptroller Central Savannah River Area, United Way, Augusta, 1977-82; asst. controller Hammermill Hardwoods div. Hammermill Paper Co., Augusta, 1982-84; controller SFN Communications of Augusta, Inc. (WJBF-TV), 1984-85; acct. Med. Coll. Ga. Found., Inc., 1986—; cons. small bus.; pvt. tutor acctg. Mem. adv. bd. Richmond County Bd. Edn., 1985-87; bd. dirs. Cen. Savannah River chpt. Girl Scouts US, 1986—. Panel judge Jr. Achievement Treas. award, 1980, 81; treas. Chinese Lang. Sch., 1973-75, Merry Neighborhood Sch., 1974-75. Recipient Achievement award Bank of Am., 1954. Mem. Nat. Assn. Accts. (dir. 1978-85, treas. 1982-84), Chinese Assn. Republican. Presbyterian.

WONG, HELEN WANSEE YAU, travel and trade company executive; b. Hong Kong, July 19, 1949; came to U.S., 1969; d. Man C. Yau and Siu C. Ho; m. Lap J. Wong; children: Augustinus, Andrea. BA, Hunter Coll., 1976; MA, NYU, 1987. Patient adv. Gouverneur Hosp., N.Y.C., 1972-76; dir., founder Young Peoples Chinese Cultural Ctr., N.Y.C., 1976—, also bd. dirs.; v.p. Kuo Feng Corp.-China Tours & Trade Co., N.Y.C., 1978—. Recipient Duke of Edinburgh award Gold Medal Award Assn., 1967. Mem.

Asian Fin. Soc. Home: 820 Red Rd Teaneck NJ 07666 Office: Kuo Feng Corp 15 Mercer St New York NY 10013

WONG, MARTHA JEE, educator; b. Houston, Jan. 20, 1939; d. J.T. Jee and B.S. Joe. BS, U. Tex., 1960, M, 1977; EdD, U. Houston, 1983. Tchr. Houston Ind. Sch. Dist., 1973-76, prin., 1978-82, mgr. III, 1982-87; assoc. prof. Baylor U., Waco, Tex., 1987—; cons. Tex. Ednl. Agency, Austin, 1983-86, SW Tech. Asst., Nacadoches, Tex., 1985-86. Contbr. articles to profl. jours. Bd. dirs. Leadership Houston, 1985-88, Meyerland Improvement Assn., Houston 1987-88. Mem. Tex. Council Women Sch. Execs. (chmn. career opportunities), Inst. for Chinese Culture and Language (bd. dirs.), Tex. Assn. Sch. Adminstrs., U. Houston Coll. Ednl. Alumni Assn. (bd. dirs.), Delta Kappa Gamma (v.p. 1985-87, scholar), Phi Delta Kappa, Phi Kappa Phi Honor Soc. Baptist. Clubs: Pink Pink Rose, Chinese Profl.

WONG, SUZANNE CRAWBUCK, librarian; b. Englewood, N.J., July 13, 1957; d. George Austin and Marion Elizabeth (Fournier) Crawbuck; m. Thomas Kay Wong, June 7, 1986. BA in Humanities, St. Peter's Coll., Englewood Cliffs, N.J., 1980. Resources control clk. Arthur Young, N.Y.C., 1982-85, library asst., 1985—. Mem. Amateur Press Assns. (contbr. assn. jour. 1979-86), Cesarean Prevention Movement, Nat. Audbon Soc. Yonkers chpt., Am. Film Inst. Democrat. Mem. Christian Sci. Ch.

WONG, XENIA ZENAIDA, mortgage consultant; b. Panama City, Panama, June 11, 1949; came to U.S., 1979; d. Ernesto Wong and Paulina A. Hendricks; m. Rolando Chang (div. 1975); 1 child, Rolando Jr. BA in Econs., U. Panama, 1972; MBA, U. N.H., 1982. Asst. mgr. Panama Nat. Bank, Panama City, 1976-78; credit mgr. Nat. Fin. Corp., Panama City, 1978-79; project mgr. Merrimack Valley Regional Transit Authority, Haverhill, Mass., 1983-85; mgr. Consumers Mortgage, Inc., Portsmouth, N.H., 1985-87; ind. mortgage cons. Portsmouth, 1988—. Mem. Assn. MBA's, Assn. Female Execs. Home and Office: PO Box 5667 Portsmouth NH 03801

WOO, OLGA FOON, pharmacist, toxicologist, educator; b. San Francisco, Apr. 8, 1949; d. Robert Duck and Foon (Wong) Woo. AB in Art History, U. Calif.-Berkeley, 1970; PharmD, U. Calif.-San Francisco, 1974. Registered pharmacologist, Calif. Asst. prof. Med. Coll. Va., Richmond, 1975-78; asst. prof. and pediatric drugs specialist U. Wash. Children's Hosp. and Med. Ctr., Seattle, 1979-81; pediatric and poison info. cons. and specialist San Francisco Bay Area Regional Poison Control Ctr., 1981—; clin. prof. U. Calif.-San Francisco, 1981—; mem. quality assurance rev. com. Med. Coll. Va., 1975-78; reviewer. Author, editor: Guidebook to OTC Drugs, 1974; editor: The Pharmacy Script (newsletter), 1978-80. Active docent Asian Art Mus., San Francisco, 1981—, Art Mus. Soc. San Francisco, 1981—, Graphics Art Council San Francisco, 1982—. Mem. Am. Assn. Colls. Pharmacy, Am. Pharm. Assn., Calif. Pharm. Assn., N.Y. Acad. Sci., AAAS. Contbr. articles to profl. jours. Office: San Francisco Poison Control Ctr 1001 Potrero Ave 1E86 San Francisco CA 94110

WOOD, BETTY A., utilities executive; b. Atlanta, May 22, 1943; d. William Robert and Ethleen (Beard) W. BS, U. Ga., 1965. Home economist Ga. Power Co., Lawrenceville, 1965-75; sr. home economist Ga. Power Co., Athens, Ga., 1975-77, customer edn. rep., 1977-79, residential rep., 1979-81, sr. residential rep., 1981-85, field mktg. rep., 1985—; coordinator div. speaker's bur. Ga. Power Co, 1985—, Adopt-A Sch. chmn., 1987. Chmn. pub. edn. Clarke-Oconee unit Am. Cancer Soc., 1986—; mem. Women of Ga. Power. Recipient Woman of Achievement award Athens Bus. and Profl. Women's Club, 1977. Mem. UGA Alumni Soc., Am. Home Econ. Assn., Ga. Home Econ. Assn. Democrat. Home: 100 Woodhaven Circle Athens GA 30606 Office: Ga Power Co 1001 Prince Ave PO Box 1312 Athens GA 30613

WOOD, DONNA KAY, healthcare executive; b. Macon, Ga., Aug. 4, 1951; d. Emory Ellis and Josephine (Mitchell) Simpson; m. Johnnie Michael Cowart, June 29, 1969 (div. Jan. 1982); children: Tiffany Lynn Cowart, Michael Todd Cowart; m. Orman Jeffrey Wood, Feb. 21, 1987. Grad. high sch., Warner Robins, Ga., 1969. Bookkeeper Electric Motor & Supply Co., Inc., Tuscaloosa, Ala., 1970-74; adminstrv. v.p. U. Orthopaedic Clinic, PC, Tuscaloosa, 1975—; sec., treas. U. Orthopaedic Clinic, PC, Tuscaloosa, 1979—. Active membership com. YMCA of Tuscaloosa, 1987. Mem. C. of C. of West Ala. (ambassador 1984, membership com. 1985), Med. Group Mgmt. Assn. (pres. Tuscaloosa 1986, Ala. 1987-88). Baptist. Club: Internat. Mgmt. Council. Home: 7503 Spinnaker Ave NE Tuscaloosa AL 35406 Office: U Orthopaedic Clinic PC PO Box 2447 Tuscaloosa AL 35403

WOOD, DORIS JEAN, health science association administrator; b. Chgo., July 2, 1932; d. Joseph and Dorothy (Richardson) Schneider; m. James Albert Wood, July 23, 1960; children: Robert James, Elizabeth Annette. B in Music Edn., Tex. Christian U., 1955. Ch. sec. Presbyn. Ch. of Covenant, Houston, 1954; airline hostess Trans World Airlines, Kansas City and Chgo., 1955-56; tchr. Chgo. Pub. Schs., 1956-57; elem. sch. music tchr. Houston Ind. Schs., 1957-63; bookkeeper, sec. James A. Wood Co., Houston, 1959-74; co-owner, sec., treas. Southwestern Biols., Inc., Pearland, Tex., 1974—; sec., treas. Southwestern Biol. Service Corp, Pearland, Tex., 1981—. Pres. Friends of the Library, Pearland, 1975; del. County and State Rep. Conventions, Angleton, Tex., Austin, Tex., Dallas, 1982, 84, 86; mem. exec. com. Elect Jack Harris for State Rep., Pearland, 1984. Named Notable Woman of Tex. Awards and Honor Soc. of Am., 1984-85. Mem. Am. Bus. Women's Assn. (sec., treas., v.p. 1984-87, pres. 1987-88), Nat. Assn. Female Execs., Pearland/ Hobby Area C. of C., Alpha Xi Delta (chmn. mothers club 1986-87). Presbyterian. Clubs: Pearland Rep. Women's, Golfcrest Country, Bay Area Mil. Officers Wives. Lodge: Rotary. Office: Southwestern Biologicals Inc PO Box 2000 Pearland TX 77588-2000

WOOD, EDNA LUELLA (SELBE), retired nurse, educator; b. Phillipsburg, Kans., Apr. 24, 1925; d. John Carlyle and Cora Jane (Reese) Selbe; R.N. diploma St. Francis Hosp. Sch. Nursing, Topeka, 1946; B.S. in Nursing Edn. (Coll. fellow), St. Mary Coll., Leavenworth, Kans., 1948; M.S. in Health Edn., So. Ill. U., Carbondale, 1972; m. Elmer Leroy Wood, June 6, 1948; children—Carolyn Ann, Wanda Lee, John Leslie. Sch. nurse St. Mary Coll., 1946-48; supr. Meml. Hosp. Cheyenne, Wyo., 1947, 48, staff nurse obstetrics, 1951-55; staff nurse Invenson Meml. Hosp., Laramie, Wyo., 1949-51; with VA Nursing Service, 1955-85, asst. chief nursing service VA Med. Center, Cheyenne 1962-66, chief nursing service, Grand Junction, Colo., 1967-70, Marion, Ill., 1970-76, asso. chief nursing service for edn. Colmery-O'Neil VA Med. Center, Topeka, 1976-85; mem. numerous health-related coms.; mem. Task Force Continuing Edn. for Nurses in Kans., 1980; mem. Kans. Planning Com. for Nurses, 1982; mem. adj. faculty U. Kans. Sch. Nursing, Ft. Hays State U. Sch. Nursing. Mem. Gov.'s Com. for Nurses in Wyo., 1960-66, adv. com. ARC; pres. Wyo. League for Nursing, 1962-66; mem. consumer planning com. U. So. Ill. Sch. Medicine, 1970-72. Recipient Dir.'s commendation for superior performance VA Med. Center, Cheyenne, 1964; hon. recognition plaque So. Ill. Nurses, 1976, Washburn U. Honor Soc. for Nursing, 1980, Eta Kappa chpt. Sigma Theta Tau, 1983; hon. plaque Task Force Continuing Edn. for Nurses, 1982. Mem. Am. Nurses Assn., Kans. State Nurses Assn., Nat. League Nursing, Am. Hosp. Assn. for Health Manpower, Nursing Orgn. VA. Am. Assn. Ret. Persons, Nat. Assn. Ret. Fed. Employees. Mem. Christian Ch. (Disciples of Christ). Clubs: Toastmistress (Cheyenne); Wider Horizons Toastmistress (Grand Junction). Contbr. articles to profl. jours. Home: 730 NW 35th Topeka KS 66617

WOOD, ELIZABETH MARGARET, infosystems specialist, marketing professional; b. Lynwood, Calif., Nov. 5, 1953; d. Roberta Carrie (Pray) W. BA in History cum laude, U. Calif., Irvine, 1975; MBA, UCLA, 1979. Claims rep. Social Security Adminstrn., Downey, Calif., 1975-77; market adminstr. Pacific Telephone, Orange, Calif., 1979-80, acct. exec., 1980-82; product mgr. Pacific Bell, San Francisco, 1982-85; sr. product specialist No. Telecom, San Ramon, Calif., 1985-87, mgr. market support, 1987; mgr. Integrated Systems Digital Equipment Corp., Irvine, Calif., 1987—; dir. communications Women in Mgmt., Los Angeles, 1978-79. Pres. Pleasant Heights Homeowners Assn., Pleasant Hill, Calif., 1987. Mem. U. Calif. at Irvine Alumni Assn. Democrat. Club: Valley Vista Tennis. Office: Digital Equipment Corp 24 Executive Park Irvine CA 92714

WOOD, EVELYN NIELSEN, educator; b. Logan, Utah, Jan. 8, 1909; d. Elias and Rose (Stirland) Nielsen; m. Myron Douglas Wood, June 12, 1929 (dec. May 1987); 1 child, Carolyn Wood Evans. BA, U. Utah, 1929, MA, 1947; postgrad., Columbia U., 1956-57. Tchr. Weber Coll., Ogden, Utah, 1931-32; girls counselor Jordan High Sch., Sandy, Utah, 1948-57, tchr. jr. and sr. high schs., 1948-59; instr. U. Utah, 1957-59; founder, originator Evelyn Wood Reading Dynamics, 1959—; tchr. rapid reading U. Del., 1961; guest lectr. NEA, 1961, Internat. Reading Assn., Tex. Christian U., 1962; faculty Brigham Young U., research specialist for reading, 1973-74. Author, conductor radio programs, 1947; author: (With Marjory Barrows) Reading Skills, 1958, A Breakthrough in Reading, 1961, A New Approach to Speed Reading, 1962, Speed Reading for Comprehension, 1962, also articles. Home: 6024 E Wenduco Ln Tucson AZ 85711

WOOD, FAY S., marketing executive; b. Phila., Aug. 22; d. Paul and Dorothy (Berkowitz) Wiener; children: Deborah, Esther. BA in English, Pa. State U.; grad. exec. mgmt. course RCA Corp. Real estate sales rep., 1968-70; cons. Hearing Centers, Inc., 1970-72; dist. sales mgr. Beltone Hearing Aid Centers, Inc., 1972-76; v.p. PhD Hearing Centers, Inc.; with RCA Service Co., 1976-79, sales mgr., 1977-79, regional sales mgr., N.Y. dist., 1979; v.p. sales and mktg. Full Line Repair Centers, Inc., 1979-81, pres., 1981—; v.p. sales and mktg. Quantech Electronics Corp., Freeport, N.Y., 1981-85; v.p., gen. mgr. Elite Group, Inc., Torrance, Calif., 1985-87, exec. v.p., 1987-88; chief operating officer Prestige Mktg., Inc., Palos Verdes, Calif., 1988—. Mem. adv. bd. Dept. Consumer Affairs, mem. N.Y.C. Commn. on Status of Women. Recipient audiology cert. Dahlberg Electronics, Master Cons. award Beltone Electronics; 1st degree Black Belt in Tae Kwon Do Karate; named Regional Mgr. of Yr., RCA Service Co. Mem. AAUW, LWV, Nat. Assn. Female Execs., Nat. Fedn. Bus. and Profl. Women. Club: B'nai Brith. Office: Prestige Mktg Inc PO Box 2901 Palos Verdes CA 90274

WOOD, HILARY ANN, data processing executive; b. New Bedford, Mass., June 20, 1963; d. Harold Jr. and Arlene Nancy (Tinkham) Wood. AS, New Eng. Inst. Tech., 1985. Computer programmer New Eng. Plastics Corp., New Bedford, 1984-85, cons., 1985—; programmer/analyst Appraisal Services New Eng., Cranton, R.I., 1985-86, The Boston Globe, Dorchester, Mass., 1986—. Home: 29 Pershing Ave Acushnet MA 02743 Office: The Boston Globe 135 Morrissey Blvd Dorchester MA 02127

WOOD, IONA DALE, banker; b. Sweetwater, Tex., Mar. 23, 1934; d. William Manse and Garnet Iona (Keeney) W. Degree in bsnking, So. Meth. U., 1982. Traffic dir. Sta. KXOX, Sweetwater, 1951-53; sec. Valley Nat. Bank, Prescott, Ariz., 1953-77; br. mgr. Valley Nat. Bank, Prescott, 1977-81; br. mgr., v.p. Valley Nat. Bank, Sun City West, Ariz., 1981—. Mem. Sun Cities Symphony Guild, Sun City, 1981—; bd. dirs. Sun City Fine Arts Assn., Sun City, 1984—, Sun Cities Symphony. Recipient First City of Hope Nat. Spirit of Life award Sun Cities chpt., 1988. Mem. Bus. Assn. Sun City West (pres. 1986—), Sun Cities Art Mus. Mem. Ch. of Christ. Lodge: Lioness. Home: 12309 Banyan Dr Sun City West AZ 85375 Office: Valley Nat Bank 13501 Camino Del Sol Sun City West AZ 85375

WOOD, JACALYN KAY, educational consultant; b. Columbus, Ohio, May 25, 1949; d. Carleston John and Grace Anna (Schumacher) W. B.A., Georgetown Coll., 1971; M.S., Ohio State U., 1976; Ph.D., Miami U., 1981. Elem. tchr. Bethel-Tate Schs., Ohio, 1971-73, Columbus (Ohio) Christian Sch., 1973-74, Franklin (Ohio) Schs., 1974-79; teaching fellow Miami U., Oxford, Ohio, 1979-81; cons. intermediate grades Erie County Schs., Sandusky, Ohio, 1981— presenter tchr. inservice tng. Mem. council Sta. WVIZ-TV, 1981—; mem. exec. com. Perkins Community Schs., 1981-85; mem. community adv. bd. Sandusky Vols. Am., Sandusky Sec. Bank, vol. Firelands Community Hosp. Mem. Am. Businesswomen's Assn. (local pres. 1985), Assn. Supervision and Curriculum Devel., Internat. Reading Assn., Ohio Sch. Suprs. Assn. (regional pres. 1986, state pres. 1986-87), Phi Delta Kappa (local sec. 1985, 86). Baptist. Home: 320 Fremont Ave Apt #4 Sandusky OH 44870 Office: 2902 Columbus Ave Sandusky OH 44870

WOOD, JANE ELLEN RUTLEDGE, hospital administrator; b. Milw., May 4, 1943; d. Harold and Helen Frances (Hyde) Rutledge; m. Francis E. (Pete) Wood, June 19, 1965. BS, U. Wis., 1966. Social dir. U. Wis. Meml. Student Union, Madison, 1967-69; dir. vol. service Luth. Hosp., Milw., 1973-80; adminstrv. dir. vols. Good Samaritan Med. Ctr., Milw., 1980-83; dir. community relations Sinai Samaritan Med. Ctr., Milw., 1983—; cons. to vols. YMCA, Milw., 1982; bd. dirs. Avenues West Assn., Milw. Editor (med. newsletter): Med. Staff Briefs, 1985—. Bd. govs., com. chair Am. Heart Assn. of Wis., Milw., 1984-87. Mem. Wis. Student Assn. (sec. 1964-65), Wis. Assn. Dirs. Hosp. Vols. (pres. 1980). Office: Sinai Samaritan Med Ctr Good Samaritan Campus 2000 W Kilbourn Ave Milwaukee WI 53233

WOOD, JAYNEE SMITH, real estate developer; b. Beaumont, Tex., July 26, 1954; d. John Sterling and Mildred (Sumerow) Smith; m. Samuel Eugene Wood, Apr. 5, 1980; children—Samantha, Stephanie, Amanda, Samuel Smith, Baker Sterling. BSBA Okla. State U., 1976. Lic. engr. N.C. Territory rep. Armstrong World Industries, Raleigh, N.C., 1976-80; owner, developer J.S. Wood Broker Assoc., Raleigh, 1980-85; v.p. Sam Wood Assocs., Inc., Raleigh, 1981-85, dir., sec., 1981—; ptnr. SAJA Assocs., Raleigh, 1982—; owner, cons. Splty. Products, Raleigh, 1983-85. Contbr. articles and designs to profl. jours. Vice pres. Breakfast Club Constrn., Raleigh, 1983-85; mem. various coms. United Methodist Ch., Raleigh, 1984-85, spl. com. United Way, Raleigh, 1985. Recipient sales awards and Outstanding Achievement award Integrated Ceiling Systems, 1985. Mem. Illumination Engrs. Soc. Republican. Baptist. Avocations: golf; boating; tennis; skiing. Home: PO Box 31506 Raleigh NC 27622 Office: Sam Wood Assocs Inc 8909 Midway Rd W PO Box 31506 Raleigh NC 27612

WOOD, KATHLEEN DORAN, producer, performer, communications educator; b. Morristown, N.J., June 27, 1946; d. Arthur Francis and Blanche Evaline (Knapp) Ringwood; m. Peter J. Doran, Jan. 25, 1969 (div. Nov. 1977); 1 child, Peter Shawn. BS in Elem. Edn., West Chester U. (Pa.), 1975; MA in Speech Communications and Pub. Relations Mgmt., U. Houston, 1982. Cert. tchr. Caseworker Montgomery County Bd. Assistance, Norristown, Pa., 1972-80, adminstrv. asst. Montgomery County Drug and Alcohol, 1979-80; tchr. spl. edn. Jeanne Pfeifer Sch., Houston, 1980-81; prodn. coordinator Sta. KUHT-TV, Houston, 1981, D.W. Frederickson, Inc., Houston, 1981-82; producer Storer Cable TV, Houston, 1982-85; coordinator Vols. in Pub. Schs., Houston, 1983-84; producer, cons. Columbia Cable TV, Rosenberg, Tex., 1983; cons. pub. relations Retinitis Pigmentosa & Lion's Eye Bank, Houston, 1981-84; lectr. speech, communications U. St. Thomas, Houston, 1984; instr. San Jacinto Coll., 1986-88, Alvin Community Coll., 1986-87, Houston Community Coll., 1986-88, North Harris County Coll., 1987-88; adj. prof. U. Houston, 1986-88, Clear Lake (Tex.) campus, 1987—. Editor, writer (newsletter) Access, 1982-84; reporter asst. editor: (newsletter) Hotline, 1982-84; host, producer Access, Dear Subscriber, Community News, 1983-84. Press asst. Jack Heard for Mayor Campaign, Houston, 1981; mem. Atkinson Sch. PTA, Houston, 1981-86; spokesperson sta. KUHT-TV auction, 1981-84; disc jockey Sta. KSBJ-FM, 1987-88; radio talk show host Access Stas. KACC-FM and KFMK-FM, 1987; actress Pasadena Little Theatre, 1984-86; mem. exec. com., newsletter coordinator Cub Scouts Am. pack 773, 1984-86; mem. U.S.A. Sports Assn., Houston, 1983; founding mem., steering com. Houston Theatre Alliance, 1985-86, exec. bd. 1986-87, founding mem. steering com., 1st v.p., 1987-88; founding editor Cath. Guild of Performing Arts (founder, dir. publicity, exec. bd. 1987-88). Named hon. sheriff's dep. Harris County Sheriff's Office, Houston, 1981. Mem. Women in Cable (exec. bd. 1982-84, chmn. publicity 1982-84), Women in Theatre Network Houston (founding mem., pres. 1985-86, v.p. 1986-87chairperson co-ednl. com. 1987-88), Houston Bus. Com. for Ednl. Excellence (co-chmn. publicity 1985-86), Cath. Guild for the Performing Arts (founder, dir. publicity, editor newsletter, 1987-88). Republican. Roman Catholic. Clubs: Towering Texans, Clear Lake Area Ski (publicity asst. 1982-84) (Houston) Office: U Houston Downtown One Main St Houston TX 77002

WOOD, KATHLEEN OLIVER, writer and editor; b. Mt. Kisco, N.Y., Sept. 17, 1921; d. Eli Leslie and Melba Antoinette (Gislason) Oliver; student Swarthmore Coll., 1938-39, Antioch Coll., 1940-41, U. N.Mex., 1949, Cleve. Coll., 1960-61; m. John Thornton Wood, June, 1941 (div. 1947); children—Mark Thornton, Jonna Grim; m. 2d, Clifford Emanuel Huff, June, 1948 (div. 1955); 1 child, Karen Weston. Tech. sec. Gray Iron Founders Soc., Cleve., 1955-57; tchr. Whiting Bus. Coll., Cleve., 1957-62; editorial asst. Chem. Rubber Co., Cleve., 1966; editor, writer Jefferson Ency., World Pub. Co., Cleve., 1967-68; disc jockey, announcer Sta. WCLV-FM, Cleve., 1968-69; communications coordinator, writer, editor Highlights newsletter University Circle, Inc., Cleve., 1971-81; talk-show hostess, announcer Sta. WERE-AM, Cleve., 1972-73; free-lance writer, editor, cons., 1981—; publicity specialist Am. Assn. Retired Persons, Ohio, 1987-88; tchr. Project LEARN; tutor VIP program. Hostess weekly radio show, CRRS, Cleve. Soc. for Blind; taper books for Library of Congress Service for Visually Handicapped; treas. Cleve. Beautiful Com., 1980, sec., 1982; v.p. Cleve. Cultural Garden Fedn.; trustee E. Cleve. Community Theatre. Mem. Pub. Relations Soc. Am., Internat. Assn. Bus. Communicators, Women's Advt. Club Cleve. (past pres., editor Weathervane 1982-83), Women in Communication, World Assn. Women Journalists and Writers (congress coordinator 1982-83, v.p. U.S. chpt. 1988—), Mensa, Early Settlers. Quaker. Clubs: Zonta Internat. (past pres. Cleve., dir. Area 3 Dist. V, 1984-86), Women's City, Esperanto League of North Am., Universal Esperanto Assn. Author: Greenwood, 1967; editor, pub. Frog in the Milk Pan (Marie Wallace), 1963; editor Graffiti Mag., 1967, Office Gal Mag., 1962-63, Smorgasbrain Mag., 1968. Home: 3118 E Overlook Rd Cleveland Heights OH 44118 Office: PO Box 5612 Cleveland OH 44101

WOOD, LARRY (MARY LAIRD), journalist, author, university educator, public relations executive; b. Sandpoint, Idaho; d. Edward Hayes and Alice (McNeel) Small; children: Mary, Marcia, Barry. BA magna cum laude, U. Wash., 1938, MA with highest honors, 1940; postgrad., Stanford U., 1941-42, U. Calif., Berkeley, 1946-47; cert. in photography, U. Calif., Berkeley, 1971; postgrad. journalism, U. Wis., 1971-72, U. Minn., 1971-72, U. Ga., 1972-73; postgrad. in art, architecture and marine biology, U. Calif., Santa Cruz, 1974-76, Stanford Hopkins Marine Sta., Santa Cruz, 1977-80. Feature writer and columnist 1939—; prof. pub. relations and journalism San Diego State U., 1974, 75; vis. prof. journalism San Jose State U., 1976; assoc. prof. journalism Calif. State U., Hayward, 1978; prof. sci. and environ. journalism U. Calif. Berkeley Extension, 1979—. Contbr. over 3,000 articles on real estate, architecture, edn., oceanography, science, environment, bus. and travel for newspapers, nat. mags., popular sci. mags., nat. and internat. newspaper syndicates, inflight mags., city mags., travel and architecture mags. including Oakland Tribune, Seattle Times, San Francisco Chronicle, Parade, San Jose Mercury News, Christian Sci. Monitor, MonitoRadio, Sports Illus., Mechanix Illus., Popular Mechanics, Parents, House Beautiful, Oceans, Sea Frontiers, PSA Mag., AAA Westways, AAA Motorland, Hawaiian Airlines in Paradise, Linguapress, Travel & Leisure, Family Handyman, Chevron USA. Significant works include home and garden columnist and editor, 5-part series Pacific Coast Ports, 5-part series Railroads of the West, San Francisco Cultural Scene, Endangered Species, Megamouth New Species of Shark, Columbia Receding Glacier, Calif. Underwater Parks, Ebey's Landing Nat. Hist. Preserve, Los Angeles Youth Gangs, Hist. Carousels, Idaho's Big Lakes. Co-author over 20 books including: McGraw-Hill English for Social Living, 1944, Fawcett Boating Books, 1956-66, Fodor's San Francisco, 1982—, Fodor's California, 1984—, Charles Merrill Focus on Life Science, Focus on Physical Science, 1983, 87, Social Issues Research Inc.'s Earth Science, 1988, Woltors-Nordoff-Longman English Language Texts, 1988. Reviewer for Charles Merrill texts, 1983-84; book reviewer for Professional Communicator, 1987—. Nat. chmn. travel writing contest for U.S. univ. journalism students Assn. for Edn. in Journalism/Soc. Am. Travel Writers, 1979-83; judge writing contest for Nat. Assn. Real Estate Editors, 1982-84; mem. adv. bd. KRON/TV, 1986—. Numerous awards, honors, citations, speaking engagements including induction into Broadway Hall of Fame, Seattle, 1984, citations for environ. writing from Nat. Park Service, U.S. Forest Service, Bur. Land Mgmt., Oakland Mus. Assn., Oakland C. of C.; co-recipient Nat. Headliner award for Best Sunday Newspaper Mag. Mem. Pub. Relations Soc. Am. (charter mem. travel and tourism div.), Nat. Sch. Pub. Relations Assn., Environ. Cons. N.Am., Assn. Edn. in Journalism (exec. bd. nat. mag. div. 1978, panel chmn. 1979, 80), Women in Communications (nat. bd. officer 1975-77), Soc. Profl. Journalists (nat. bd. for hist. sites 1980—), Nat. Press Photographers Assn., Nat. Assn. Sci. Writers, Calif. Writers Club (officer 1967, 72), Am. Assn. Med. Writers, Soc. Am. Travel Writers, Internat. Oceanographic Found., Oceanic Soc., Calif. Acad. Environ. News Writers, U. Wash. Alumni (life, charter mem. ocean scis. alumni), U. Calif.-Berkeley Alumni (life), Stanford Alumni, Mortar Board Alumnae Assn., Phi Beta Kappa, Theta Sigma Phi. Home: 6161 Castle Dr Oakland CA 94611

WOOD, LESLIE ANN, retail administrator; b. Chgo., Apr. 9, 1957; d. Howard Arnold and Anita Eleanor (Andler) W. AA, Harper Coll., 1977; BS in Communication Scis., Ill. State U., 1979. Advt. asst. Harry Alter Co., Chgo., 1979-80; clk. typist Career Guild, Evanston, Ill., 1980-81; reporter Aparacor, Evanston, Ill., 1981-82; sales mgmt. trainee Prudential Ins. Co. Am., Millburn, N.J., 1983-84; fin. cons. Summit Fin. Resources, Livingston, N.J., 1984; mgr. Chgo. area Renault Inc. div. AMC/Jeep/Renault, Elk Grove Village, Ill., 1985-87; dist. parts and service mgr. Chrysler Motors, Itasca, Ill., 1987, mgr. customer relations, 1987—. Mem. Nat. Assn. Female Execs. Home: 6822 Northwest Hwy Chicago IL 60631

WOOD, LINDA DORIS, manufacturing company executive; b. Westfield, Mass., Dec. 17, 1953; d. Arthur James Wood and Catherine Margaret (Stinehour) Clark. AB in Biochem., Brown U., 1976; postgrad., Lowell U., 1978-81. Chemist Gen. Electric Co., Wilmington, Mass., 1976-79; program adminstr./program analyst Gen. Electric Co., Wilmington, 1979-81, program mgr., 1981-85; program mgr. Northrop Corp., Norwood, Mass., 1985-87; sr. program mgr. Northrop Corp., Norwood, 1987—. Patentee in field. Mem. Northrop Mgmt. Orgn. (officer). Home: 2 Birch Ln Norton MA 02766 Office: Northrop Corp 100 Morse St Norwood MA 02062

WOOD, LINDA GAYE, real estate development company executive; b. South Haven, Mich., May 12, 1959; d. Gene A. and Beatrice (McKamey) W.; m. Terry M. Shaw, July 20, 1980 (div. 1982). Corr. student broker registration U. San Francisco, 1985. Sr. loan processor Shearson Am Express Mktg., San Diego, 1977-80; office mgr. Lomas & Nettleton Mfg. Co., San Diego, 1980-81; escrow coordinator Barratt Developers, San Diego, 1981-83, Tara Escrow Inc., 1983-84; sales mgr. real estate devel. Watt Industries Inc., Rancho Sante Fe, Calif, 1984-85; asst. v.p., dir. sales and mktg. The Buie Corp., Laguna Niguel, Calif., 1985—. Mem. Orange County Sales and Mktg. Council (bd. dirs. 1985—, mem. exec. bd. 1988—), Assn. Profl. Mktg. Women (rec. sec. 1984-85), Nat. Assn. Female Execs. Republican. Avocations: Swimming; walking; hiking; travel; cycling.

WOOD, MARY LOU, realtor; b. Franklin, Ky., Dec. 17, 1933; d. George Phillip and Clara (Wilkens) Taylor; m. Dewey E. Wood, Aug. 17, 1958 (div. 1983); children: Elizabeth, Pamela, Diane, Christopher. BS in Home Econs. Edn., Western Ky. U., Bowling Green, 1956. Lic. in real estate, Ky. Apprentice home agt. U. Ky., Lexington, 1955; tchr. Huntingburg Sch., Ind., 1956-57, Seneca High Sch., Louisville, 1957-60; decorator Sherwin Williams Co., Russellville, Ky., 1983-85; realtor Shaker Realty and Auction Co., Russellville, 1987—. Mem. beautification com. First Bapt. Ch., Russellville, 1985-87. Ky. Col., Gov. Wendell Ford, State of Ky., 1972. Mem. Nat. Soc. Colonial Dames, Nat. Bd. Realtors, Ky. Bd. Realtors, Logan County Bd. Realtors. Democrat. Baptist. Club: Logan County Home Economist (past pres.). Home: 201 Lynnwood Dr Russellville KY 42276 Office: Shaker Realty West Fourth St Russellville KY 42276

WOOD, MONICA LONGMORE, packaged goods executive; b. Fountainbleau, France, Apr. 3, 1955 (parents Am. citizens); d. Floyd Thenford and Marion (Longmore) Wood; m. Edward Louis Hibshman, Aug. 12, 1983. A.A. with highest honors, Dade Community Coll., 1974; B.S. magna cum laude, U. Fla., 1976; M.B.A. magna cum laude, U. Miami, 1979. Elem. tchr. Dade County Sch. System, Miami, Fla., 1976-78; analyst mktg. research Burger King Corp., Miami, 1979-80, sr. analyst mktg. research, 1980-82, asst. mgr. consumer research, 1982-83, mgr. nat. advt. and sales promotions, 1983-85; mgr. market research Campbell's Soup Co., Camden, N.J., 1985—. Mem. exec. com. Republican party, 1984—. Mem. Am. Mktg. Assn. (pres.-elect 1984-85). Home: 1500 Locust St 3309 Philadelphia PA 19102 Office: Campbell Soup Co 1 Campbell Pl Camden NJ 08101

WOOD, NANCY ELIZABETH, psychologist, educator. d. Donald Sterret and Orne Louise (Erwin) W. B.S., Ohio U., 1943, M.A., 1947; Ph.D., Northwestern U., Evanston, Ill., 1952. Prof. Case-Western Res. U., Cleve., 1952-60; specialist, expert Dept. HEW, Washington, 1960-62; chief of research Pub. Health, Washington, 1962-64; prof. U. So. Calif., Los Angeles, 1965—; learning disabilities cons., 1960-70; assoc. dir. Cleve. Hearing and Speech Ctr., 1952-60; dir. licensing program Brit. Nat. Trust, London. Author: Language Disorders, 1964, Language Development, 1970, Verbal Learning, 1975 (monograph) Auditory Disorders, 1978. Pres. faculty senate U. So. Calif., 1987-88. Recipient Outstanding Faculty award Trojan Fourth Estate, 1982. Fellow Am. Speech and Hearing Assn. (elected, legis. council 1965-68), Am. Psychol. Assn. (cert.), AAAS; mem. Internat. Assn. of Scientists. Republican. Methodist. Office: U So Calif University Park Los Angeles CA 90089

WOOD, ROBERTA SUSAN, foreign service officer; b. Clarksdale, Miss., Oct. 4, 1948; d. Robert Larkin and Dorothy Eloise (Shelton) Wood; B.A. with distinction, Southwestern U., Memphis, 1970; postgrad. Nat. U. Cuyo, Mendoza, Argentina, 1970-71; M.P.A., Harvard U., 1980. Joined U.S. Fgn. Service, 1972; service in Manila, Naples and Turin, Italy and Port-au-Prince, Haiti; mgmt. analyst Dept. State, Washington, 1980-84; U.S. consul gen., Jakarta, Indonesia, 1984-87, NATO Def. Coll., Rome, 1987-88; U.S. Consul Gen. Marseilles, France, 1988—. Fulbright scholar, 1970-71. Mem. Am. Fgn. Service Assn., Consular Officers Assn., Friends of Nat. Zoo, Friends of Kennedy Center, Planned Parenthood Washington, Phi Beta Kappa. Office: Consulat Gen Des Etats-Unis, 9 Rue Armeny, 13006 Marseille France

WOOD, SHARON, mountaineer; b. Halifax, N.S., Can., May 18, 1957; d. Stan and Peggy Wood. Climbed peaks Mt. McKinley (Alaska), Mt. Logan (Can.), Mt. Aconcagua (Argentina), Mt. Makalu (Himalayas), Mt. Everest (Himalayas); Can. Light Everest Expedition, 1986; lectr. in field. Recipient Tenzing Norgay Trophy, 1987. Address: Canmore, AB Canada T0L 0M0 *

WOOD, SHEILA KAY, chemist; b. Phoenix, June 29, 1959; d. Ralph E. And Anna E. (Leuning) Danielson; m. Daniel Steven Wood, Nov. 12, 1983. BS, Ariz. State U., 1981. Lab technician City of Phoenix, 1981-83, chemist, 1983-87, lead chemist, 1987—. Recipient Productivity Improvement award City of Phoenix, 1985. Mem. Nat. Assn. Female Execs., Nat. Assn. Environ Profls., Internat. Platform Assn. Republican. Home: 311 W Stella Ln Phoenix AZ 85013 Office: City of Phoenix 5615 S 91st Ave Phoenix AZ 85353

WOOD, VIRGINIA MARGARET, nurse; b. N.Y.C., Jan. 1, 1936; d. Ivan Smyrna and Louise Catherine (Straub) W.; adopted children—Margaret Theresa, Christine Louise. Diploma Capital City Sch. Nursing, 1957; B.S. in Nursing, U. Nev., 1970; M.Ed. in Allied Health, U. Fla., 1979; Ph.D. in Nursing Adminstrn., Columbia Pacific U., 1983. Staff nurse D.C. Gen. Hosp., Washington, 1957-58, USPHS Indian Health Service, Whiteriver and Phoenix, Ariz., 1958-61, U.S. Air Force, Nellis AFB, Las Vegas, Nev., 1961-63; staff nurse, supr. VA Hosp., Phoenix, 1970-72; nurse instr. VA Hosp., Columbia, Mo. and Gainesville, Fla., 1972-79; nurse educator USPHS Indian Health Service, Whiteriver, 1979-80, dir. nurses, San Carlos, Ariz., 1980—. Served to capt. USAF, 1963-68; maj. U.S. Army, 1975-79. Recipient Supr. of Yr. award USPHS Indian Health Service, 1983. Mem. Am. Nurses Assn., Nat. League Nursing, Ariz. Soc. Ariz. Nursing Service Adminstrs. (nominating com. 1983-84), Phi Kappa Phi, Pi Lambda Theta. Republican. Roman Catholic. Avocations: reading; sewing; walking. Home: Box N San Carlos AZ 85550 Office: USPHS Indian Health Service Hosp Box 208 San Carlos AZ 85550

WOOD, VIVIAN POATES, mezzo soprano, educator, author; b. Washington, Aug. 19, 1923; d. Harold Poates and Mildred Georgette (Patterson) W. studies with Walter Anderson, Antioch Coll., 1953-55, Denise Restout, Saint-Leu-La-Fôret, France and Lakeville, Conn., 1960-62, 64-70, Paul A. Pisk, 1968-71, Paul Ulanowsky, N.Y.C., 1958-68, Elemer Nagy, 1965-68, Vyautas Marijosius, 1967-68; MusB Hartt Coll. Music, 1968; postgrad. (fellow) Yale U., 1968; MusM (fellow), Washington U., St. Louis, 1971, PhD (fellow), 1973. Debut in recital series Internat. Jeunesse Musicals Arts Festival, 1953, solo fellowship Boston Symphony Orch., Berkshire Music Center, Tanglewood, 1964, St. Louis Symphony Orch., 1969, Washington Orch., 1949, Bach Cantata Series Berkshire Chamber Orch., 1964, Yale Symphony Orch., 1968; appearances in U.S. and European recitals, oratorios, operas, radio and TV, 1953-68; appeared as soloist in Internat. Harpsichord Festival, Westminister Choir Coll., Princeton, N.J., 1973; appeared as soloist in meml. concert, Landowska Center, Lakeville, 1969; prof. voice U. So. Miss., Hattiesburg, 1971—, asst. dean Coll. Fine Arts, 1974-76, acting dean, 1976-77; guest prof. Hochschule für Musik, Munich, 1978-79; prof. Italian Internat. Studies Program, Rome, 1986; Miss. coordinator Alliance for Arts Edn., Kennedy Center Performing Arts, 1974—; mem. Miss. Gov.'s Adv. Panel for Gifted and Talented Children, 1974—; mem. 1st Miss. Gov.'s Conf. on the Arts, 1974—; bd. dirs. Miss. Opera Assn. Author: Polenc's Songs: An Analysis of Style, 1971. Recipient Young Am. Artists Concert award N.Y.C., 1955; Wanda Landowska fellow, 1968-72. Mem. Nat. Assn. Tchrs. of Singing, Music Tchrs. Nat. Assn., Am. Musicolog. Soc., Golden Key, Mu Phi Epsilon, Delta Kappa Gamma, Tau Beta Kappa (hon.), Pi Kappa Lambda. Democrat. Episcopalian. Avocation: sailing. Office: U So Miss Sch Music South Sta Box 8264 Hattiesburg MS 39401

WOODARD, ANNE TAYLOR, librarian, insurance agent; b. Rocky Mount, N.C., Jan. 27, 1953; d. Sam Pierce and Doris (Satterwhite) Taylor; m. Calvin Staton Woodard Jr., June 4, 1972 (div. Nov. 1981). BS in Library Sci., East Carolina U., 1974; MS in Library and Info. Sci., Cath. U. Am., 1981. Media specialist G.R. Whitfield Elem. Sch., Grimesland, N.C., 1974-76; library asst. Tidewater Community Coll., Virginia Beach, Va., 1976-82; librarian Louise Obici Meml. Hosp., Suffolk, Va., 1982-83, U.S. Geol. Survey, Reston, Va., 1983—; dog breeder, Reston and Virginia Beach, 1977—; ins. agt. various cos., 1986—. Mem. Alpha Beta Alpha (pres. 1973-74). Methodist. Clubs: Potomac Valley Pekingese (Adelphi, Md.) (bd. dirs. 1986—, Championship Plaque 1986); Greater Pitts. Pekingese; Pekingese Club of Am. (N.Y.C.). Home: 1650 Parkcrest Circle #200 Reston VA 22090

WOODARD, CAROL JANE, early childhood education educator; b. Buffalo, Jan. 19, 1929; d. Harold August and Violet Maybelle (Landsittel) Young; m. Ralph Arthur Woodard, Aug. 19, 1950; children—Camaron Jane, Carsen Jane, Cooper Ralph. BA, Hartwick Coll., 1950; MA, Syracuse U., 1952; PhD, SUNY, Buffalo, 1972; postgrad., Bank St. Coll., Harvard U. Cert. tchr., N.Y. State. Tchr. Orchard Park, N.Y., 1950-51, Danville, Ind., 1951-52, Akron, N.Y., 1952-54; Tchr. Amherst (N.Y.) Coop. Nursery Sch., 1967-69; dir. Garden Nursery Sch., Williamsville, N.Y., 1955-65; asst. prof. early childhood edn. SUNY Coll., Buffalo, 1969-72; lab. demonstration tchr. and student teaching supr. SUNY Coll., 1969-76, assoc. prof., 1972-79, prof., 1979—; cons. Lutheran Ch. Am., Villa Maria Coll., Buffalo Pub. Schs., Headstart Tng. Programs, Erie Community Coll., N.Y. State Dept. Edn., numerous workshops.; cons. sch. systems, indsl. firms, pubs., civic orgns. in child devel.; vis. prof. The Netherlands and East China Univ., Shanghai, People's Republic of China, 1986. Author 7 books for young children, 2 textbooks in field; co-author Physical Science in Early Childhood, 1987; coauthor nat. curriculum for ch. sch. for 3-yr.-olds; author: booklet You Can Help Your Baby Learn; author/coordinator TAKE CARE child protection project, 1987; contbr. chpt. to When Children Play, 1985; contbr. numerous articles in field to profl. jours. Bd. trustees Hartwick Coll., Oneonta, N.Y., 1978-87. Mem. Nat. Assn. Edn. Young Children, Early Childhood Edn. Council Western N.Y., Assn. Childhood Edn. Internat., Phi Delta Kappa, Pi Lambda Theta. Home: 1776 Sweet Rd East Aurora NY 14052 Office: SUNY Coll 1300 Elmwood Ave 301 Bacon Hall Buffalo NY 14222

WOODARD, DOROTHY MARIE, insurance broker; b. Houston, Feb. 7, 1932; d. Gerald Edgar and Bessie Katherine (Crain) Floeck; student N.Mex. State U., 1950; m. Jack W. Woodard; June 19, 1950 (dec.); m. Norman W. Libby, July 19, 1982. Partner, Western Oil Co., Tucumcari, N.Mex., 1950—; owner, mgr. Woodard & Co., Las Cruces, N.Mex., 1959-67; agt., dist. mgr. United Nations Ins. Co., Denver, 1968-74; agt. Western Nat. Life Ins. Co., Amarillo, Tex., 1976—. Exec. dir. Tucumcari Indsl. Commn., 1979—; dir. Bravo Dome Study Com., 1979—; owner Libby Cattle Co., Libby Ranch Co.; regional bd. dirs. N.Mex., Eastern Plains Council Govts., 1979—. Mem. Tucumcari C. of C. Club: Mesa Country. Home: PO Box 823 Tucumcari NM 88401 Home: 415 E Washington St Bueyeros Ranch NM 88412 Office: PO Box 1003 Tucumcari NM 88401

WOODARD, JUNE CAROL, service executive; b. Nashville, Nov. 9, 1952; d. Wallace Daniel Sr. and Maurine F. (Vantrease) Johnson; m. C. Ray Bell, Feb. 29, 1984 (div. Dec. 1984); 1 child, Sutton Mina. Student, U. Tenn., Nashville, 1974. Lic. real estate broker. Sec., treas. Ray Bell Constrn. Co., Inc., Brentwood, Tenn., 1971-83; mgr. bus. ops. Park HealthCare Co. (formerly United HealthCare, Inc.), Nashville, 1983—; cons. acctg. Ray Bell Constrn. Co., Inc., 1983-85. Recipient Fin. and Credit Evaluation award Dun & Bradstreet, Nashville, 1981. Mem. Nat. Beta Club. Baptist. Club: Women in Constrn. (Nashville). Home: 5549 Trousdale Dr Brentwood TN 37027

WOODARD, KATHRYN DELORIS, social services administrator; b. Kearney, Nebr., Jan. 10, 1951; d. Bernard Brunson and Deloris Mae Hiner; stepfather, Eddie Hiner; m. Ronnie Duwayne Adams, Dec. 23, 1966 (div. June 1968); 1 child, Kevin Glenn; m. Otis David Woodard, Feb. 19, 1983; 1 child, Otis Le Andrew; stepchildren: Otis Le' Analdo, Otis Le Antoni, Otis Le' Andre. Student, Kearney State Coll.; AA in Bus. Adminstrn., Cen. Community Coll. Community devel. dir. City of Harvard, Nebr., 1977-79; dir. food stamp ctr. H.D.C., Kansas City, 1981-83; grant cons. Luth. Family and Children's Services, St. Louis, 1984-85; dir. Contact Helpline, St. Louis, 1984—; v.p. Luth. North St. Louis Outreach, 1987—; founding mem. Nebr. State Task Force on Domestic Violence Intervention, 1976-78; founder, facilitator Clay County (Nebr.) Domestic Violence Intervention Project, 1978-79; adj. coordinator Clay County Domestice Violence Project, 1978-79. Active Freedom Inc. Black Polit. Orgn., Kansas City, 1980-83; bd. dirs. So. Christian Leadership Conf., Kansas City, 1980-83. Mem. NOW (pres. Kearny chpt. 1972-75, sec. Hastings, Nebr. chpt. 1977-79), Phi Beta Lambda (2d place Nebr. Ms. Bus. Exec. 1978). Democrat. Lutheran. Home: 2023 Bissell Saint Louis MO 63107 Office: Luth North St Louis Outreach 2023 Bissell Saint Louis MO 63107

WOODARD, MELISSA JOY, banker; b. Yaeger, W.Va., Dec. 26, 1952; d. Roscoe and Jerusha (Robinette) Muncy; m. Craig Woodard, Oct. 15, 1978 (div. June 1984). Student in bus., psychology and English, Spokane (Wash.) Community Coll., 1978-80; student in human relations and communications, Diablo Valley Community Coll., Pleasant Hill, Calif., 1980; student, San Francisco U., 1981-82, U. Md., 1982-83; student in bus. adminstrn., Nat. U., Los Angeles, 1986-88. Retail and photography specialist U.S. Army and USAF Exchange, Spokane, 1970-76; fin. adminstr. Wash. Mut. Savs., Spokane, 1976-78; br. service mgr. Great Western Savs., Walnut Creek, Calif., 1978-81; relations specialist U.S. Govt., Bremerhaven, Fed. Republic of Germany, 1982-83; br. v.p. Great Western Bank, Venice, Calif., 1983—; mgr. Fed. Women's Program, Bremerhaven, 1982-83; trainer fed. employees, Bremerhaven, 1982-83; motivational speaker Toastmasters, Walnut Creek, 1981-82, Venice Skills Ctr., 1985—. Adminstrv. asst. Oakland (Calif.) Spl. Olympics, 1980-82. Century City Congrl. scholar, 1987. Mem. Venice C. of C. (bd. dirs. 1984—). Office: Great Western Bank 1415 Lincoln Blvd Venice CA 90291

WOODARD, NINA ELIZABETH, banker; b. Los Angeles, Apr. 3, 1947; d. Alexander Rhodes and Harriette Jane (Power) Mathews; m. John David Woodard, Mar. 17, 1966; children—Regina M., James D. Grad. Pacific Coast Banking Sch., 1987. Dental asst. Los Angeles, 1965-66; with Security Pacific Nat. Bank, Marina Del Rey, Calif., 1968-69; with First Interstate Bank, Casper, Wyo., 1971—, adminstr. asst. personnel, 1975-78, asst. v.p., asst. mgr. personnel, 1978-82, v.p., dir. mktg. and personnel, 1982-84, v.p., mgr. human resources, 1984—; instr. mktg. Am. Inst. Banking, 1983, Casper Coll., 1982. Mem. Civil Service Commn., City of Casper, 1983—; bd. dirs. YMCA, 1984-87, Downtown Devel. Assn.; pres. Downtown Casper Assn. Named Bus. Woman of Yr., Bus. and Profl. Women, 1982, Young Career Woman, 1975. Mem. Nat. Assn. Bank Women, Bus. and Profl. Women (dist. dir.), Am. Soc. Personnel Adminstrn. (regional v.p., accredited sr. profl. in human resources, state council Wyo. 1987—), Cen. Wyo. Soroptimist. Republican. Roman Catholic. Lodge: Order Eastern Star.

WOODARD, PEGGY LYNN, biomechanical engineer; b. Charleston, S.C., Jan. 9, 1959; d. James Quinton and Jessie Mae (Byrnes) W.; m. René Romero Thibodaux, May 11, 1985. BS in Biomedical Engring., La. Tech. U., 1982. Intern of biomedical engring. Charity Hosp. of New Orleans, 1980; biochem. research technician U. Tex. Med. Br., Galveston, 1982-84; biomechanical engr. II U. Tex. Med. Br., 1984—. Contbr. articles to profl. jours.; co-inventor orthotic brace; patentee in field. Mem. Am. Soc. Mech. Engrs. Office: Univ Tex Med Br Child Health Ctr C-53 Galveston TX 77550

WOODBRIDGE, ANNIE SMITH, emerita librarian, foreign language educator; b. Wingo, Ky., July 7, 1915; d. Ernest Herbert and Flora Susan (Parrish) Smith; B.A., Murray State Coll., 1935; M.A., Peabody Coll., 1936; postgrad. U. Wis., Tex. State Coll. for Women, U. Ky., Sorbonne, Universidad Interamericana; m. Hensley C. Woodbridge, Aug. 28, 1953; 1 dau., Ruby Susan Woodbridge Jung. Tchr. Cadiz High Sch., 1936-37, David Lipscomb Coll., 1937-43, Bethel Coll., 1943-46, Murray State Coll., 1946-54, 59-65; instr. So. Ill. U., Carbondale, 1966-74, researcher Morris Library, 1974-85. Mem. NOW, Midwest Latin Am. Studies Assn., Ellen Glasgow Soc., Soc. Study of Midwestern Lit. Democrat. Mem. Ch. of Christ. Editor: (with others) Collected Short Stories of Mary Johnston; contbr. articles jours. and newsletters. Home: 1804 W Freeman St Carbondale IL 62901

WOODBURY, MARGARET CLAYTOR, physician, university administrator; b. Roanoke, Va., Oct. 30, 1937; d. John Bunyan and Roberta Morris (Woodfin) Claytor; m. Lawrence DeWitt Young, 1959 (div.); children—Laura Ruth, Lawrence DeWitt Jr.; m. 2d, David Henry Woodbury, Jr., Nov. 30, 1968; 1 child, David Henry III. A.B. cum laude, Mt. Holyoke Coll., 1958; postgrad. Albany Med. Coll., 1958-60; M.D., Meharry Med. Coll., 1962. Diplomate Am. Bd. Internal Medicine, Nat. Bd. Med. Examiners. Asst. chief medicine-endocrinology USPHS, S.I., N.Y., 1967-68; chief out-patient clinic USPHS Hosp., Detroit, 1968-69; med. officer-in-charge USPHS Out-patient Clinic, Detroit, 1969-71; instr. internal medicine-endocrinology U. Mich., Ann Arbor, 1969-80, asst. prof. internal medicine-endocrinology and metabolism, 1980—, asst. dean student and minority affairs, 1983—; project dir. Health Careers Opportunity Program/Assistance to Increase Matriculation and Earn Degrees, 1984—; cons. Bryant Neighborhood Clinic, Ann Arbor, 1978; vis. lectr. Morehouse Med. Coll., Atlanta, 1980-82; minority recruitment officer Admissions U. Mich. Med. Sch., Ann Arbor, 1975-83; mem. Adv. Com. on Affirmative Actions Program, 1982-85, chair, 1984-85. Contbr. chpts. to books, articles to profl. jours. Vol. Democratic Party, Ann Arbor, 1972—, co-chair precinct, 1973; parent rep. Engring. Indsl. Support Program, Ann Arbor, 1978-82; vol. Nat. Council Negro Women, Ann Arbor, 1974-76; mentor Ann Arbor Alliance for Achievement in Acads. and the Arts, sec., 1982-83; trustee Mt. Holyoke Coll., 1985—; mem. State of Mich. Dr. Martin Luther King, Jr. Holiday Commn., 1985—; mem. Health Braintrust, Congl. Black Caucus, 1985—. Recipient Biochemistry award Albany Med. Coll. (N.Y.), 1958-60; pediatrics prize Meharry Med. Coll., Nashville, 1960-62; Alumni medal of honor Mt. Holyoke Coll., 1983, Mount Holyoke Alumnae Med. Honor, 1983; fellow Bryn Mawr/HERS Summer Inst. for Women in Higher Edn. Adminstrn., 1987. Mem. Nat. Med. Assn., Am. Med. Women's Assn., Nat. Minority Health Assn. (charter), Alpha Omega Alpha, Sigma Gamma Rho. Presbyterian. Club: Mt. Holyoke (press rep. 1973-76, pres. 1976-80). Office: U Mich Furstenberg Ctr PO Box 0611 Ann Arbor MI 48109

WOODBURY, VIRGINIA PETERSEN, accountant; b. St. Joseph, Mo., Mar. 26, 1938; d. Harold E. and Eulalia E. (Geiger) Petersen; m. Reid A. Woodbury, Aug. 24, 1957; children: Reid A. Jr., Charles E. Student, Lindenwood Coll., 1955-57, U. Mo., 1957-58; BS in Acctg., Mo. Western State Coll., 1974-77. Bookkeeper High Seasons, Inc., Hideaway Park, Colo., 1969-74; acct. Reid Woodbury, Inc., St. Joseph, Mo., 1977-81; mgr. Garfield Lumber Co., St. Joseph, Mo., 1981-82; staff acct. Heartland Hosp. West, St. Joseph, Mo., 1982-85; acct. Reid Woodbury-Chocolate Country, St. Joseph, Mo., 1985-87, Chocolate Country Internat. Inc., St. Joseph, Mo., 1987—; mgr. MMCE Fed. Credit Union, 1982-84. Treas. Heartland Hosp. West Gift Shop, 1977—. Mem. Nat. Assn. Accts. (St. Joseph Pony Express chpt. bd. dirs. 1983-88, sec. 1984-85), Jr. League. Republican. Mem. Christian Church (Disciples of Christ). Lodge: Side by Side Sertoma (charter pres. 1987-88). Office: Chocolate Country Internat Inc 524 Albemarle Saint Joseph MO 64501

WOODBY, HILDA MARIE, psychotherapist, nurse, consultant; b. Abingdon, Va., Nov. 23, 1948; d. Roy Ernest and Mary Bell (Arden) W. BS, U. Va., 1971; MS, Va. Commonwealth, 1976. RN U. Va. Hosp., Charlottesville, 1971-73; teaching asst. Med. Coll. Va., Richmond, 1975-76; nurse educator Radford (Va.) U., 1976-78, John Tyler Community Coll., Chester, Va., 1978-80; RN McGuire Vets. Hosp., Richmond, 1980-87; pres., owner Nurse Adv., Richmond, 1987—; mem. Va. Med. Malpractice Rev. Panel, Richmond, 1980—. Bd. dirs. Vietnam Vets. Am. #78, Richmond, 1981—. Mem. Sigma Theta Tau. Home: 1407 Greystone Ave Richmond VA 23224 Office: Nurse Adv 7629 Hull St Richmond VA 23224

WOODCOCK, CYNTHIA HARDIN, foundation officer; b. Jacksonville, Fla., Oct. 2, 1953; d. Jack Bealle and Doris Jane (Peebles) Hardin; m. Charles Edwin Woodcock III, June 21, 1975. BE, U. N.C., 1975; MBA in Fin., Columbia U., 1979. Asst. program officer The Robert Wood Johnson Foundation, Princeton, N.J., 1976-78; fin. analyst N.J. Dept. Health, Tenton, 1979-80; program officer The Commonwealth Fund, N.Y.C., 1980-85, sr. program officer, 1985-87, asst. v.p. program fin. and mgmt., 1987—. Mem. Sigma Delta Pi, Phi Beta Kappa. Methodist. Office: The Commonwealth Fund One E 75th St New York NY 10021

WOODFORK, NANCY ANN, telephone company executive; b. Boston, Jan. 16, 1948; d. Nelson Carter and Millicent Iona (Beckford) W. BA, U. Mass., 1970; MSW, Boston Coll., 1976. Social worker Adoption Placement Unit Dept. Social Services Dept. Pub. Welfare, Boston, 1970-73, sr. social worker, 1973-76, supt. social services, 1976-79; adminstr. market New Eng. Telephone Co., Boston, 1979-80, account exec., 1980-83; account exec. Nynex, Boston, 1983-84; cons. network New Eng. Telephone Co., Boston, 1984—; interviewer Child Welfare League Am., N.Y.C., 1974-76; trainer, supr. Rainbow Distrs. Inc., Waltham, Mass., 1976-77; interviewer Community Devel. Corp., Roxbury, Mass., 1977; chmn. Black Recruitment Com. Adoption and Foster Care Inc., Boston, 1983-84. Coordinator Com. to Elect Jimmy Carter Pres., Boston, 1976; bd. dirs. Cooper Community Ctr., 1978-82. Mem. Nat. Assn. Black Social Workers, Mass. Adoption Resource Exchange (bd. dirs.). Democrat. Episcopalian. Home: 12 Schuyler St Dorchester MA 02121 Office: New Eng Telephone Co 31 St James Ave Boston MA 02116

WOODHAM, JEAN, sculptor; b. Midland City, Ala., Aug. 16, 1925; d. Marcus Morton and Alma (Clements) W.; m. James Lee Caraway, Nov. 18, 1949 (div. 1968); children: Susan Melissa, Elizabeth Leigh; m. Harold L. Freidman, July 13, 1986. BA, Auburn U., 1946; student, Sculpture Ctr., N.Y.C., 1946-49. vis. lectr. Ga. Inst. Tech, Atlanta, 1971; vis. assoc. prof. Auburn U., 1971, assoc. prof. 1974-75; vis. critic Cornell U., Ithaca, N.Y., 1980; artist-in-residence Djerassi Found., Woodside, Calif., 1983. Commd. sculpture Internat. Bank, Washington, 1964, Flintkote Corp., White Plains, N.Y., 1968-69, Gen. Electric Credit Corp., Stamford, Conn., 1971-72, G.T.E. Corp. hdqrs., Stamford, 1973, Tex. Eastern Transmission, Houston, 1974-75, N.Y.C. Bd. Edn. Truman High Sch., 1975-76, Cooper Meml. Library and Art Ctr., Opelika, Ala., 1977, Auburn (Ala.) U., 1978-79, Norwalk (Conn.) Pub. Library, 1980-81, Temple Beth Or, Montgomery, Ala., 1982, Westport (Conn.) Town Hall, 1982, Cen. Conn. State U., New Britain, 1986-87; one woman shows include Cen. Conn. State U., New Britain, 1987; subject TV film Arts: Themes & Variations, 1984 acquired by Smithsonian Inst., pub. TV film Conn. Profiles, 1979, others. Mem. Westport Symbolic Heritage Preservation Com., 1983-87; mem. liberal arts adv. com., fine arts council Auburn U., Ala., 1987-88; pres.' com. Auburn Generations Fund, 1983-85; chmn. visual arts Westport Arts Ctr., 1981, bd. dirs. 1982-86; charter mem. Coll. Liberal Arts Adv. Council, Fine Arts Council Auburn U., Ala. Recipient 37 awards including Finch award Art of Northeast U.S.A., New Canaan, Conn., 1985, Citation for Contbn. to Arts Gen. Assembly, Hartford, Conn., 1986, Outstanding Profl. and Community Achievements award YWCA Greater Bridgeport: Salute to Women, 1986, Citation, Gov. Conn., 1987; named one of Outstanding Women of Conn., UN, 1987. Mem. Sculptors Guild, Inc. (exec. bd.1966-86, v.p. membership 1983, 84, treas. 1962-67, sec. 1971-73), Silvermine Guild Artists (bd. trustees 1982-84, chmn. admissions 1983). Studio: 26 Pin Oak Ln Westport CT 06880

WOOD PARRISH, VICTORIA ANN, pastor; b. Norwood, Mass., June 21, 1950; d. Ernest O. and Martha Lou (Foreman) Wood; m. w. Keith Parrish, Aug. 15, 1982; children: Heather, Kathleen, W. James. B in Music Edn., DePauw U., 1972; MDiv, Princeton Theol. Sem., 1976. Asst. pastor Arlington Ave. Presbyn. Ch., East Orange, N.J., 1973-74; chaplain Memphis City Hosp., 1974-75; asst. pastor Pearson Meml. United Meth. Ch., Trenton, N.J., 1975-76; assoc. pastor First United Meth. Ch., Franklin, Pa., 1977-79, Erie, Pa., 1979-85; pastor 10th St. United Meth. Ch., Erie, 1985—; clergy team mem. Erie Hospice, 1983—. Mem. Coll. of Chaplains (profl. affiliate), Am. Assn. Pastoral Counselors, Assn. for Clin. Pastoral Edn., AAUW. Republican. United Methodist. Home: 526 E 10th St Erie PA 16503 Office: 10th St United Meth Ch 538 E 10th St Erie PA 16503

WOODRICK, VALERIE PAIGE, management consultant; b. Milw., May 3, 1963; d. Ronald Burdell and Carolyn Jo (Dale) W. BS in Econs., U. Pa., 1983; MBA, U. N.C., Chapel Hill, 1986. Asst. buyer John Wanamaker, Phila., 1983-84; assoc. cons. McKinsey & Co., N.Y.C., 1986—. Mem. Nat. Assn. Female Execs., Assn. MBA Execs., Beta Gamma Sigma. Lutheran. Home: 1203 River Rd 8A Hudson Harbour Edgewater NJ 07020

WOODRING, CAROLE LYN, psychologist, consultant; b. State College, Pa., Nov. 7, 1945; d. Charles Elmer and Helen Pauline W.; m. Eric Marvin Berg, May 30, 1970; children—Nicole Leslie Woodring, Adam Trevor Woodring, Jessica Lynne Woodring. BA Pa. State U., 1967; MA Columbia U., 1969. Foster caseworker Dauphin County Child Care Agy., Harrisburg, Pa., 1967-68; personnel asst. dir. Conf. Bd., Inc., N.Y.C., 1969-70; mgr. tng. design and validation Chem. Bank N.Y. Trust Inc., N.Y.C., 1970-73; tng. cons. 1st Union Corp., Charlotte, N.C., 1978-79; adj. prof. Sacred Heart Coll., Belmont, N.C., 1978-80; dir., officer Fortune Cons., 1977-84; pvt. cons., Matthews, N.C., 1979—; officer pres. J.N. Adams & Assos., 1982—. Trustee, Charlotte Montessori Sch., 1980-83, pres., 1981-83; mem. parent council bd. Charlotte Latin Sch., 1984-85. Mem. Assn. for Psychol. Type, AAUW (past dir.), Am. Psychol. Assn. (assoc.), Sigma Sigma Sigma (past chpt. pres.). Presbyterian. Home: 2528 Sleepy Hollow Dr State College PA 16803 Office: 315 S Allen St Suite 222 State College PA 16801

WOODRUFF, MARIAN DAVIS, former state legislator, art gallery official; b. Boston, Dec. 15, 1922; d. Harvey Nathaniel and Alice Marion (Rohde) Davis; m. Bliss Woodruff, Sept. 27, 1952; children—Nathaniel Rohde, William Watts, Davis Miller, Charlotte Bliss. B.A., Smith Coll., 1945. Guide, Met. Mus. Art, N.Y.C., 1945-46; lectr. Mus. Art, R.I. Sch. Design, Providence, 1946-51; dir. edn. Currier Gallery Art, Manchester, N.H., 1962-66, 70—; program dir. Nashua Arts and Sci. Center, N.H., 1968-69; mem. N.H. Ho. of Reps. from 18th Dist., 1973-76; instr. White Pines Coll., Chester, N.H., 1979-81, 86; field reviewer Inst. Mus. Services, 1985—; bd. dirs. Barn Gallery Assocs., Ogunquit, Maine. Mem. visual arts com. N.H. Commn. Arts; mem. White Mountain Environment Com., Nat. Alliance Arts Edn., Arts Advocacy Com., Nashua Conservation Commn., 1978-80; bd. dirs. Daniel Clark Found., pres., 1977-81; bd. dirs. United Health Systems Agy., 1978-81, Studio Potter, Inc., 1985—; mem. council Nashua League Craftsmen; mem. council League N.H. Craftsmen, 1979—, 84, bd. dirs., 1984-87; founding mem. Nashua LWV; bd. dirs. Nashua Headstart. Mem. Am. Assn. Mus., Order Women Legislators, N.H. Micological Soc. (pres. 1978-80). Democrat. Unitarian-Universalist. Clubs: Appalachian Mountain, Randolph Mountain. Home: 587 Maple St Manchester NH 03104 Office: 192 Orange St Manchester NH 03104

WOODRUFF, MARTHA JOYCE, temporary nursing service executive; b. Unadilla, Ga., Jan. 3, 1941; d. Metz Loy and Helen (McCorvey) Woodruff. BA, Shorter Coll., 1963; MA, U. Tenn.-Knoxville, 1972. Tchr., Albany High Sch. (Ga.), 1963-69; instr. U. Tenn.-Knoxville, 1970-72; asst. prof. Valdosta State Coll. (Ga.), 1972-76; coordinator Staff Builders, Atlanta, 1976-78; pres., owner Med. Personnel Pool, Knoxville, 1978—, Personnel Pool of

Knoxville, Inc., 1985-87; mem., adviser Owners Adv. Council, Personnel Pool of Am., Ft. Lauderdale, Fla., 1980-82. Mem. Nat. League for Nursing, Franchise Owners Assn., Knoxville C. of C. (com. for cost containment 1982-85), Blount County C. of C. (retirement com. 1983, mem. indsl. relations com. 1983). Republican. Methodist.

WOODRUFF, VIRGINIA, television and radio host, producer; b. Morrisville, Pa.; d. Edwin Nichols and Louise (Meredith) W.; m. Raymond F. Beagle Jr. (div.); m. Albert Plaut II (div.); 1 child, Elise Meredith. Past student, Rutgers U. News corr. Sta. WNEW-TV Metromedia, N.Y.C., 1967; nat., internat. critic-at-large Mut. Broadcasting System, 1968-75; lectr. circ. Leigh Bur., 1969-71; byline columnist N.Y. Daily Mirror, N.Y.C., 1971; first arts critic CATV, Telepromter and Westinghouse, 1977-84; host/producer The First Nighter N.Y. Times Primetime Cable Highlight program, 1977-84; pres., chief exec. officer Starpower, Inc., 1984—; affiliate news corr. ABC Radio Network, N.Y.C., 1984-86; perennial critic Off-Off Broadway Short Play Festival, N.Y.C., 1984—. Mem. celebrity panel Arthritis Telethon, N.Y.C., 1976. Selected episodes First Nighter program in archives N.Y. Pub. Library, Billy Rose Theatre Collection, Rodgers and Hammerstein Collection, Performing Arts Research Ctr. Mem. Drama Desk. Presbyterian. Office: Starpower 35 E 10th St New York NY 10003

WOODRUM, PATRICIA ANN, librarian; b. Hutchinson, Kans., Oct. 11, 1941; d. Donald Jewell and Ruby Pauline (Shuman) Hoffman; m. Clayton Eugene Woodrum, Mar. 31, 1962; 1 child, Clayton Eugene, II. BA, Kans. State Coll., Pittsburg, 1963; MLS, U. Okla., 1966. Br. librarian Tulsa City-County Library System, 1964-65, head brs., 1965-66, head reference dept., 1966-67, chief extension, chief pub. service, 1967-73, asst. dir., 1973-76, dir., 1976—. Contbr. articles to profl. jours. Mem. Tulsa Area Council on Aging; mem. exec. com. Downtown Tulsa Unltd.; mem. Friends of Tulsa Library; mem. Leadership Tulsa Alumni; mem. bd. Tulsa Council Internat. Visitors, Tulsa Area Library Coop; mem. community service council bd. Girl Scouts U.S.; trustee Univ. Ctr. at Tulsa Found. Recipient Disting. Librarian award Okla. Library Assn., 1979, Leadership Tulsa Paragon award. Mem. ALA (com. on accreditation), Okla. Library Assn. (pres. 1978-79), Met. C. of C., LWV. Republican. Episcopalian. Office: Tulsa City-County Library 400 Civic Center Tulsa OK 74103

WOODS, ARLEIGH MADDOX, judge; b. Los Angeles, Aug. 31, 1929; d. Benjamin Harris and Ida Lota (Evans) Maddox; m. William T. Woods, Aug. 3, 1952. BA, Chapman Coll., 1949; LLB, Southwestern U., 1952; LLM, U. Va., 1984; LLD (hon.), U. West Los Angeles, 1984. Bar: Calif. 1952, U.S. Supreme Ct. 1965, U.S. Dist. Ct. (9th Cir.) 1952. Sole practice Los Angeles, 1953-57; sr. ptnr. Levy, Kosz & Woods, Los Angeles, 1957-76; judge Los Angeles Superior Ct., 1976-80; assoc. justice Calif. Ct. Appeal, Los Angeles, 1980-82, presiding justice, 1982—; mem. Jud. Council of Calif., San Francisco, 1985-87, Com. on Jud. Performance, San Francisco, 1986—. V.p., mem. Constitutional Rights Found., 1982—. Named Appellate Justice of Yr., Calif. Trial Lawyers Assn., 1983. Mem. Am. Cancer Research Found., Southwestern U. (bd. trustees 1986—). Office: Calif Ct Appeals 3580 Wilshire Blvd Suite 433 Los Angeles CA 90010

WOODS, BARBARA LEE, lithograph company executive; b. Phoenix, Nov. 13, 1942; d. Samuel Thomas and Eunice Kathryn (Looney) Staggs; m. Frank B. Woods, Apr. 19, 1963; 1 child, Stephen Craig. Cert., Durham Bus. Coll., 1964; grad. Plaza Three Modelling Sch., 1983. Sec., First Nat. Life Ins. Co., Phoenix, 1963-65; escrow sec. Stewart Title Co., Phoenix, 1966-69; escrow sec. Minn. Title Co., Phoenix, 1970-72, escrow officer, br. mgr., 1972-75; sec. Franklin Press, Phoenix, 1976-78; co-owner, dir. corp. communications Woods Lithographics, Phoenix, 1978—. Vol. Phoenix Children's Hosp.; bd. dirs., mem. celebrity auction com. Cystic Fibrosis Found., Phoenix, chmn. celebrity auction, 1987-88, chmn. merchandise celebrity auction, 1986, co-chmn. com., 1986; mem. steering com. Women for Warner, Phoenix, 1986. Mem. Phoenix Soc. Communicating Arts, Phoenix Ad Club (bd. rep., programs com., mem. com. to select the man or woman of the year, mem. 50 Yr. Reunion com.), Nat. Assn. Women Bus. Owners, Nat. Assn. Female Execs. (co-chmn. Market '87 com.). Republican. Baptist. Clubs: Arizona, Moon Valley Country (Phoenix). Avocations: walking, piano, calligraphy, hiking. Office: Woods Lithographics Inc 3433 W Earll Dr Phoenix AZ 85017

WOODS, DIANE HOLLIS, university official; b. Altadena, Calif., Apr. 17, 1956; d. Richard Owen and Barbara (Hoffman) Hollis; m. Michael Gage Woods, Aug. 16, 1980; children: Thomas Michael and Kathryn Elizabeth (twins). BA, Ottawa U., 1978; postgrad., U. So. Calif., 1984—. Exec. asst. Fuller Theol. Sem., Pasadena, Calif., 1979-80; corp. legal sec. Barger and Wolen, Los Angeles, 1980-81; employment counselor Lynn Carol Employment Agy., Pasadena, 1981-82; asst. to dean Annenberg Sch. Communications, U. So. Calif., Los Angeles, 1982-85, asst. dir. continuing legal edn. programs Law Ctr., 1985-87, dir. insts. and confs., 1987—. Sec.-treas. sanctuary choir Pasadena Covenant Ch., 1984—, editor newsletter, 1987—. Mem. Am. Mgmt. Assn., Nat. Assn. Female Execs., Women in Mgmt. Democrat. Avocations: writing, photography, travel. Office: U So Calif Law Ctr Office Insts and Confs Law 105-D University Park Los Angeles CA 90089-0071

WOODS, ELAINE MARIE, health clinic administrator; b. Abilene, Tex., Jan. 13, 1948; d. Clifford Utah and Christine Clair (Walter) Woods. B.S., Loyola U., 1970, M.S., 1974, Ph.D., 1979. Wardmaster Gen. Lenord Wood Army Hosp., St. Roberts, Mo., 1979-80; non-commd. officer in charge Finten Army Air Field Dispensary, Finten, Germany, 1980-82; wardmaster HSC 8th Med. Bn., Bad Kreuznach, Germany, 1982-83; non-commd. officer in charge outpatient clinic USA Health Clinic, Dugway, Utah, 1983—. Served with U.S. Army, 1976-83. Decorated Army Commendation medal (3). Democrat. Roman Catholic. Home: Route 7 Box 356 Abilene TX 79605

WOODS, HARRIETT RUTH, state official; b. Cleve., June 2, 1927; d. Armin and Ruth (Wise) Friedman; student U. Chgo., 1945; B.A., U. Mich., 1949; m. James B. Woods, Jan. 2, 1953; children—Christopher, Peter, Andrew. Reporter, Chgo. Herald-Am., 1948, St. Louis Globe-Democrat, 1949-51; producer Star. KPLR-TV, St. Louis, 1964-74; moderator, writer Sta. KETC-TV, St. Louis, 1962-64; council mem. University City, Mo., 1967-74; mem. Mo. Hwy. Commn., 1974, Mo. Transp. Commn., 1974-76; mem. Mo. Senate, 1976-84, lt. gov. State of Mo., 1985—. Bd. dirs. LWV of Mo., 1963, Nat. League of Cities, 1972-74; Democratic nominee for U.S. Senate, 1982, 86. Jewish. Office: PO Box 563 Jefferson City MO 65102

WOODS, KAREN MARGUERITE, psychologist, human development, institute executive; b. Columbus, Ga., Sept. 17, 1945; d. O. Norman and Nan Catherine (Land) Shands; m. Carl Allen Oberkrom, Sept. 3, 1966 (div. Aug. 1974); children: Kristi Lynn, Jeffrey Michael; m. James Wallace Woods II, Aug. 19, 1978 (div. Feb. 1986); 1 child, Jamie Elizabeth. Student, Mercer U., 1963; BA, William Jewell Coll., 1975; MA, U. Mo., Kansas City, 1976. Lic. psychologist, Mo. Counselor, juvenile officer Platte County Juvenile Ct., Platte City, Mo., 1976-78; sch. psychologist North Kansas City Sch. Dist., Mo., 1978-80; counselor Platte Med. Clinic, Platte City, 1981-84; co-founder/dir. north office Counseling Ctr. for Human Devel., Kansas City, 1984-87; founder, pres. Inst. for Human Devel., Kansas City, 1987—; cons. Platte Valley Spl. Edn. Coop., Smithville, Mo., 1984-88; speaker to area schs. and bus., 1976—, Northland Child Abuse Speakers Bur., 1976-78; dir. Northland Women's Resource Ctr., Kansas City. Mem. adv. bd. Mo. Div. Family Services, 1981-83; mem. Northland Child Abuse Task Force, Gladstone, Mo., 1981-83. PEO grantee, 1976; named one of Outstanding Young Women in Am., 1978. Mem. Am. Assn. for Counseling and Guidance, Kansas City Mental Health Assn., Nat. Assn. Female Execs., Zeta Tau Alpha. Democrat. Methodist. Club: Clayview Country. Office: Inst for Human Devel 4444 N Belleview Ste 210 Kansas City MO 64116

WOODS, KATHLEEN MARY, psychologist; b. N.Y.C., July 29, 1946; d. Eugene Joseph and Mary Eileen (Geismar) W. BA, Trinity Coll., 1968; MSW, Catholic U., 1970; MA, Fielding Inst., 1987. Diplomate Clin. Social Work; lic. psychologist, Vt.; cert. social worker, Vt. Social worker Prince William County Community Mental Health Ctr., Manassas, Va., 1970-74; pvt. practice social worker Springfield, Va., 1972-75; alt. care dir. Counseling Service of Addison County, Middlebury, Vt., 1975-78, Asst. dir., 1978-82; social worker Psychotherapy Assocs., Rutland, Vt., 1982-87, psychologist, 1987—; lectr. Adelphi Vt. Sch. Social Work, Burlington, 1980-86. Mem. Nat. Assn. Social Workers, Acad. Cert. Social Workers (diplomate clin. social work), Am. Psychol. Assn. (student affiliate). Democrat. Buddhist.

WOODS, LAURIE, lawyer; b. N.Y.C., Nov. 18, 1947; d. William M. and Sylvia Leona (Bottstein) W.; m. John W. Corwin, June 1, 1968; children—Robert Woods-Corwin, James Woods-Corwin. B.A., New Sch.-N.Y.C., 1969; J.D., Boston U., 1973. Bar: N.Y., 1974. Staff atty. MFY Legal Services, N.Y.C., 1973-79; exec. dir. Nat. Ctr. on Women and Family Law, N.Y.C., 1979—; bd. dirs. N.Y. Women Against Rape, 1982—, Feminist Legal Strategies Project, Washington, 1983—. Contbr. articles in field to publs. Bd. dirs. Gingerbread Day Care Ctr., N.Y.C., 1982-83. Mem. ABA, N.Y. State Bar Assn., Assn. Bar City N.Y., N.Y. Women's Bar Assn. Office: Nat Ctr on Women & Family Law 799 Broadway Room 402 New York NY 10003

WOODS, LINDSAY ELIZABETH, marketing executive; b. Pontiac, Mich., Aug. 2, 1948; d. George Edward Woods and Beth Yvonne (Tucker) Segula. Student, U. Mich., 1966-68; BA in Edn., Lang., Queens Coll., 1970; postgrad., Oakland U., 1975; student, Long Island U., 1981. French, German instr. Union Free Sch. Dist. #1, Mamaroneck, N.Y., 1970-75; dir. sales Nassau Gold Coast News, Suffolk, N.Y., 1976; exec. v.p. LIN-Z Stables, LTD., Old Westbury, N.Y., 1978-82; chief exec. officer, pres., founder Tyler-Woods, Ltd., Locust Valley, N.Y., 1982—; cons. Murray Electronics, Balt., 1982-83; bd. dirs. animal health div. Luitpold Pharms., Inc., Shirley, N.Y. Author (newsletter) Luitpold Letter, 1985—. Mem. Standardbred Owners Assn., U.S. Trotting Assn., Old Westbury Horsemans Assn. (v.p. 1980, trustee 1981—), N.Y. State Tchrs. Assn., Nat. Assn. Female Execs.

WOODS, MARY CAROLINE MCGONAGILL, geologist, editor; b. Amarillo, Tex., Jan. 29, 1921; d. Frank Ellis and Willie Mae (Stroud) McGonagill; Student in geology Tex. Christian U., 1938-40; B.A. in Geology, U. Tex., 1942; postgrad. U. Mex., Mexico City, summer 1947, U. Calif.-Davis, 1971, 75, 76. Registered geologist. Geol. technician Pure Oil Co., Ft. Worth, 1943-47;' geol. sec. dept. geology U. So. Calif., Los Angeles, 1947-49; ground water geologist U.S. Bur. Reclamation, Sacramento, 1964-73; geologist, editor Calif. Div. Mines and Geology, Sacramento, 1974—, editor-in-chief Calif. Geology mag., 1976—; com. mem. Calif. Gov.'s Emergency Task Force on Earthquake Preparedness, Sacramento, 1981-84. Contbr. numerous articles to Calif. Geology. Mem. Assn. Engring. Geologists, Assn. Earth Sci. Editors, Nat. Assn. Geology Tchrs., AAUW, Assn. Women Geologists, Geol. Soc. of Am. Office: Dept Conservation Calif Div Mines and Geology 1516 9th St 4th Floor Sacramento CA 95814

WOODS, NANCY S., personnel executive; b. Bklyn., Feb. 18, 1946; d. Simon and Hanna (Peskin) Burnett; m. Bergen Woods, June 18, 1967 (div. 1981); 1 child, Eric Alan. BA, Rutgers Coll., 1967; postgrad., Temple U., 1969-74. Adminstrv. asst. Becker Co., East Orange, N.J., 1975-76; mgr. pension div. Schechner Corp., Millburn, N.J., 1976-81; profit sharing adminstr. Ziff-Davis Pub. Co., N.Y.C., 1981-86, dir. benefits, 1986—. Mem. social action com. Temple Emanuel, Livingston, N.J., 1985—. Recipient Bus. and Profl. Womens Club scholarship, Westfield, N.J., 1963. Mem. Mag. Pub. Assn. (human resources com.), Assn. Bus. Pub. (chair human resources com. 1988—). Jewish.

WOODS, SANDRA KARLENE, veterinarian; b. Akron, Ohio, Apr. 5, 1946; d. Karl Phillip and Vivian (Poole) Woods. B.S. in Biology, U. Akron, 1970; B.S. in Animal Sci., Tuskegee Inst. (Ala.), 1972, D.V.M., 1974. Supervisory vet. Ohio Dept. Agr., Reynoldsburg, 1974-75; vet. reviewer Ctr. for Vet. Medicine, Rockville, Md., 1975-82, supervisory vet. med. officer, 1982—; also gen. practice veterinary medicine, propr. dog obedience sch. Contbr. articles to jours. Mem. Nat. Assn. Fed. Vets., Am. Soc. Clin. Pathologists (cert. med. technologist), D.C. Acad. Vet. Medicine. Democrat. Methodist. Office: Ctr for Vet Medicine 5600 Fishers Ln Rockville MD 20857

WOODS, SANDRA KAY, brewing company real estate executive; b. Loveland, Colo., Oct. 11, 1944; d. Ivan H. and Florence L. (Betz) Harris; m. Gary A. Woods, June 11, 1967; children—Stephanie Michelle, Michael Harris. B.A., U. Colo., 1966, M.A., 1967. Personnel mgmt. specialist CSC, Denver, 1967; asst. to regional dir. HEW, Denver, 1968-69; urban renewal rep. HUD, Denver, 1970-73, dir. program analysis, 1974-75, asst. regional dir. community planning and devel., 1976-77, regional dir. fair housing, 1978-79; mgr. ea. facility project Adolph Coors Co., Golden Colo., 1980, dir. real estate, 1981, v.p. corp. real estate, 1982—; pres. Industries for Jefferson County (Colo.), 1985. Mem. Exec. Exchange, The White House, 1980; bd. dirs. Golden Local Devel. Corp. (Colo.), 1981-82; fundraising dir. Coll. Arts and Scis., U. Colo., Boulder, 1982-83; mem. U. Colo. Found.; mem. exec. bd. NCCJ, Denver, 1982—; v.p. Women in Bus., Inc., Denver, 1982-83; mem. steering com. 1984 Yr. for All Denver Women, 1983-84. Named one of Outstanding Young Women Am., U.S. Jaycees, 1974, 78, Fifty Women to Watch, Businessweek, 1987. Mem. Indsl. Devel. Resources Council (bd. dirs. 1986—), Am. Mgmt. Assn., Denver C. of C. (co-chairperson steering com. for water 1982-84, Disting. Young Exec. award 1974, mem. Leadership Denver, 1976-77), Denver Women's Forum, Colo. Women's Forum, Assn. of Office and Indsl. Park Developers, Beta Kappa, Pi Alpha Alpha. Republican. Presbyterian. Club: PEO (Loveland, Colo.). Office: Adolph Coors Co Corp Real Estate 807 Golden CO 80401

WOODS, SUSANNE, university dean; b. Honolulu, May 12, 1943; d. Samuel Ernest and Gertrude (Cullom) W. B.A. in Polit. Sci., UCLA, 1964, M.A. in English, 1965; Ph.D. in English and Comparative Lit., Columbia U., 1970; M.A. (hon.), Brown U., 1978. Asst. editor Rand Corp., Calif., 1963-65; instr. Ventura Coll., Calif., 1965-66; lectr. CUNY, 1967-69; asst. prof. U. Hawaii, 1969-72; asst. prof. English Brown U., Providence, 1972-77, assoc. prof., 1977-83, prof., 1983—, dir. grad. studies, 1986-88, assoc. dean faculty, 1987—; vis. assoc. prof. U. Calif., 1981-82. Author: Natural Emphasis, 1984, Donne's Versification, 1988; contbr. numerous articles to profl. jours.; reviewer for various profl. jours. including Renaissance Quar., Jour. English and Germanic Philology; reader for PMLA jour., SEL jour., also others. Active various polit. campaigns, 1960-64, 68-76, 84; mem. staff Senator Daniel K. Inouye, 1963. Bronson fellow, 1976, Huntington Library, 1979-80, 81, Clark Library, 1981, Huntington-NEH, 1984-85, Woodrow Wilson Found., 1968-70. Mem. MLA (chmn. div. 17th Century English lit. 1982), N.E. MLA (chmn. English Renaissance sect. 1978, Milton sect. 1983), Renaissance Soc. Am., Milton Soc. (exec. com. 1987—), Lyrica Soc. (pres. 1987—), Spenser Soc., John Donne Soc. (exec. com. 1987—), Alpha Gamma Delta. Democrat. Episcopalian. Club: Athenaeum (Pasadena, Calif.). Home: 179 University Ave Providence RI 02906 Office: Brown U PO Box 1857 Providence RI 02912

WOODS, WENDY, reporter, editor; b. Newark, Nov. 16, 1952; d. Julian Jonathan and Eileen Margaret (Woods) A.; m. Nicholas Cobalt Gorski, May 29, 1983. Student Wilkes Coll., Wilkes-Barre, Pa., 1970-72; B.A. in Film, Syracuse U., 1976. News reporter Sta. WILK, Wilkes-Barre, 1971-72; reporter, anchor Sta. WIXT-TV, Syracuse, N.Y., 1975-81; corr. Cable News Network, San Francisco, 1981-82; news reporter Sta. KGO-TV (ABC), San Francisco, 1982-84; reporter Computer Chronicles (PBS TV show), 1984—. Editor in chief newsletter Newsbytes, 1983—(Best Online Publ. award Computer Press Assn. 1985). . Recipient best environ. reporting award Central N.Y. Environ. Assn., 1979; best reporting under deadline pressure award Syracuse Press Club, 1980, best investigative reporting award, 1981. Mem. Computer Press Assn. (pres. 1987, v.p. 1988).

WOODS, WILLIE G., English and education educator; b. Yazoo City, Miss.; d. John Wesley and Jessie Willie Mae Woods; B.A., Shaw U., Raleigh, N.C., 1965; M.Ed., Duke U., 1968; postgrad. Temple U., Pa. State U., U. N.H. N.Y.U. Tchr. schs. in N.C. and Md., 1965-69; mem. faculty Harrisburg (Pa.) Area Community Coll., 1969—, assoc. prof. English/edn., 1976-82, prof., 1982—, supr. Writing Center, 1975-78, coordinator Act 101/Basic Studies Program, 1978-83, dir. Acad. Founds. program 1983-87, asst. dean acad. affairs, Acad. Found. and Basic Edn. Div., 1987—, chmn. dirs. council, 1981-82; tchr. Community Resources Inst., 1975—; moderator workshops, cons. in field. Sec., exec. com. People for Progress, 1971-73; bd. mgrs., exec. com. Camp Curtin br. YMCA, 1971-79; bd. dirs. Alternative Rehab. Communities, 1978—; bd. mgrs. Youth Urban Services, Harrisburg Area YMCA, 1981—; bd. dirs. Dauphin Residences, Inc., 1981—. Recipient cert. of merit for community services City of Harrisburg, 1971; Youth Urban Services Vol. of Yr. award, 1983; Black Student Union award Harrisburg Area Community Coll., 1984. Mem. Pa. Assn. Devel. Educators (chmn. conf. 1980, sec. 1981-82, v.p. 1986-87, pres. 1987-88), Pa. Black Conf. Higher Edn. (Outstanding Service award 1980, Central Region award 1982), Nat. Council Tchrs. English, Pa. Edn. Assn., Am. Assn. Community and Jr. Colls. (instl. rep. Nat. Council on Black Am. affairs 1983—), AAUP, Alpha Kappa Alpha (Outstanding Service award 1983, Basileus award 1984), Alpha Kappa Mu. Baptist. Asst. editor Black Conf. Higher Edn. Jour., 1980. Home: 226 Brian Drive Enola PA 17025 Office: 3300 Cameron St Rd Harrisburg PA 17110

WOODSIDE, LISA NICOLE, college dean; b. Portland, Oreg., Sept. 7, 1944; d. Lee and Emma (Wenstrom) W.; student Reed Coll., 1962-65; M.A., U. Chgo., 1968; Ph.D. (Am. Assn. Papyrology grantee, S. Maude Kaemmerling fellow), Bryn Mawr Coll., 1972; cert. Harvard U. Inst. for Ednl. Mgmt., 1979; m. John S. Bilinski, Jr., June 8, 1973. Mem. dean's staff Bryn Mawr Coll., 1970-72; asst. prof. Widener U., Chester, Pa., 1972-77, asso. prof. humanities, 1978-83, asst. dean student services, 1972-76, asso. dean, 1976-79, dean, 1979-83; acad. dean Holy Family Coll., Phila., 1983—; accreditor Commn. on Higher Edn., Middle States Assn., 1979-83. City commr. for community relations Chester, 1980-83; mem. Adult Edn. Council Phila. Mem. Am. Assn. Higher Edn., Council Ind. Colls., Eastern Assn. Coll. Deans, Pa. Assn. Colls. and Tchr. Educators, AAUW (univ. rep. 1975-83), Phi Eta Sigma, Alpha Sigma Lambda. Episcopalian. Club: Am. Fox Terrier. Home: 217 Avondale Rd Wallingford PA 19086 Office: Holy Family Coll Torresdale Philadelphia PA 19114

WOODSON, MARLENE ERDLEY, state legislator; b. Ford City, Pa., Mar. 8, 1937; d. James and Susie (Lettrich) Erdley; div.; children: George, Bert, Robert, Daniel, David. BS, Ind. U. of Pa., 1958; MA, U. South Fla., 1968; EdD, Nova U., 1981. Prof. math. Manatee Community Coll., 1970-82, dir., Inst. Advancement, 1982-86; exec. dir. Manatee Community Coll. Foundation, 1982-86; dir. Pegasus Enterprises, Inc., 1986—; state senator Fla., 1986—. Bd. dirs. Salvation Army. Mem. Manatee Symphony Assn. (past pres.), Sarasota, Manatee C. of C. Republican. Episcopalian. Address: 4815 Manatee Ave W Bradenton FL 33529 *

WOODSON, WILBERTA, small business owner; b. Tecumseh, Nebr., Sept. 7, 1939; d. Charles Wilber and Edith Mildred Woodson; children: Rebecca Louise. Student, Coll. of Emporia, 1957-61; BA, Wichita State U., 1963; MA, U. Hawaii, 1966; postgrad., U. Conn., 1968, U. Ill., 1969-70; MS, U. San Francisco, 1981. Research asst., computer programmer U. Hawaii, Honolulu, 1964-66; computer programmer Newport News (Va.) Shipbldg., 1967; computer programmer econ. research U. Ill., Urbana, 1969-70; cons. Ventura County Mental Health, Ventura, Calif., 1973-78; tech. writer Mohawk Data Scis., Los Gatos, Calif., 1978-79; documentation specialist Tandem Computers, Cupertino, Calif., 1979-84; documentation specialist Oracle Corp., Menlo Park, Calif., 1984-85; cons., 1985-86; pres. Woodtech, Inc., Denver, 1986—. Mem. Nat. Assn. Female Execs., Soc. Tech. Communication, Profl. and Tech. Cons. Assn. Democrat. Unitarian. Home and Office: 2 Adams St #1002 Denver CO 80206

WOODSWORTH, ANNE, librarian, university official; b. Fredericia, Denmark, Feb. 10, 1941; d. Thorvald Ernst and Roma Yrsa (Jensen) Lindner; m. Sverre E. Lunder; 1 dau., Yrsa Anne. B.F.A., U. Man., 1962; B.L.S., U. Toronto, 1964, M.L.S., 1969; PhD, U. Pitts., 1987. Edn. librarian U. Man., 1964-65; reference librarian Winnipeg Public Library, 1965-67; reference librarian Sci. and medicine dept. U. Toronto, 1967-68; med. librarian Toronto Western Hosp., 1969-70; research asst. to chief librarian U. Toronto, 1970-71, head reference dept., 1971-74; personnel dir. Toronto Public Library, 1975-78; dir. libraries York U., Toronto, 1978-83; assoc. provost for libraries U. Pitts., 1983—; pres. Anne Lindner Ltd., 1974-83; bd. dirs. Population Research Found., Toronto, 1980-83, Ctr. for Research Libraries, 1987—; mem. research libraries adv. council OCLC, 1984-87;. Author: The Alternative Press in Canada, 1972, Leadership for Research Libraries, 1988. Can. Council grantee, 1974, Ont. Arts Council grantee, 1974, Council on Library Resources grantee, 1986, 88; UCLA sr. fellow, 1985; Council on Library Resources grantee, 1986. Mem. ALA, Can. Library Assn., Can. Assn. Research Libraries (pres. 1981-83), Assn. Research Libraries (dir. 1981-84, v.p. 1984-85, pres. 1985-86), Pa. Library Assn., Am. Soc. Info. Sci. Office: Univ of Pitts University Libraries 271 Hillman Pittsburgh PA 15260

WOODWARD, BARBARA ANN, financial services representative; b. Buffalo, Jan. 14, 1953; d. John and Claire (Pearman) Zablotny; m. Frederick Howland Woodward, May 18, 1974 (div. Feb. 1981); m. Norbert Bernard Bach, Sept. 1987. BA, SUNY, Buffalo, 1974; MA, U. Toronto, 1976. Resource devel. coodinator Community Congress of San Diego, 1979-81; asst. dir. Sunset Community Edn. Ctr., San Francisco, 1981; exec. dir. Advocates for Women, San Francisco, 1982-85; fin. sales rep. The Equitable, San Francisco, 1986-87; fin. cons. CIGNA Fin. Services, San Francisco, 1987—; regional leader Women's Work Force Network, Washington, 1984-86; sec., treas. No. Calif. Women for Bus. Ownership, San Francisco, 1984-86. U. Toronto fellow, 1975-76. Mem. Nat. Assn. Life Underwriters, Nat. Assn. Female Execs., Am. Mgmt. Assn., Nat. Women's Polit. Caucus, Phi Beta Kappa. Democrat. Office: CIGNA 333 Market St Suite 2400 San Francisco CA 94105

WOODWARD, FAE BLANCHE, journalist; b. Santa Ana, Calif., Nov. 15, 1925; d. Louis George and Rhoda Miranda (Morris) Willits; m. Billy J. Woodward, Nov. 24, 1947; children—Billy, Bobby, Tonni, Clarissa, Kevin, Woodra. Cub reporter, society editor Progress Bull., Pomona, Calif., 1944-48; society editor Telegram Tribune, San Luis Obispo, Calif., 1948-49; Corcoran corr. Fresno Bee (Calif.), 1953-54; corr. Ukiah (Calif.) Daily Jour., 1956-58, 61-64, teletypesetter, 1960, 71, lifestyles editor, 1971—. Tenderfoot leader, mem. tng. com. Sonoma-Mendocino council Boy Scouts Am., 1967—; mem. young women's program Ch. of Jesus Christ of Latter-day Saints, Ukiah, 1981—; mem. sch. adv. com. compensatory edn. Ukiah Unified Sch. Dist., 1974-77, also adv. com. photography, 1979—. Recipient Golden Rule award Calif. Assn. for Retarded, 1980; Disting. Achievement Pub. Info. award North Coast Coordinating Council Devel. Disabilities, 1980, Silver Beaver award Boy Scouts Am., 1983. Mem. Calif. Press Women's Assn. Republican. Home: 6785 W Hwy 20 Star Route 2 Ukiah CA 95482 Office: Ukiah Daily Jour 590 S School St Ukiah CA 95482

WOODWARD, GRETA CHARMAINE, construction company executive, rental and investment property manager; b. Congress, Ohio, Oct. 28, 1930; d. Richard Thomas and Grace Lucetta (Palmer) Duffey; m. John Jay Woodward, Oct. 29, 1949; children: Kirk Jay, Brad Ewing, Clay William. Bookkeeper Kaufman's Texaco, Wooster, Ohio, 1948-49; office mgr. Holland Furnace Co., Wooster, 1948-49; acctg. clk. Columbus and So. Ohio Electric, 1949-50; interviewer, clk. State Ohio Bur. Employment Services, Columbus, 1950-51; clk. Def. Constrn. Supply Ctr. (U.S. Govt.) (formerly Columbus Gen. Depot), 1951-52; treas. Woodward Co., Inc., Reynoldsburg, Ohio, 1963—. Newspaper columnist Briarcliff News, 1960-63. Active Reynoldsburg PTA, 1960-67; adminstrv. bd. mem. Reynoldsburg United Meth. Ch.; mem. women's service bd. Grant Hosp. Avocations: bikeriding, crocheting, writing poetry, stock market, financial mags. Office: Woodward Excavating Co Inc 7320 Tussing Rd Reynoldsburg OH 43068

WOODWARD, JOANNE GIGNILLIAT, actress; b. Thomasville, Ga., Feb. 27, 1930; d. Wade and Elinor (Trimmier) W.; m. Paul Newman, Jan. 29, 1958; children—Elinor Terese, Melissa Stewart, Clea Olivia. Student, La. State U., 1947-49; grad., Neighborhood Playhouse Dramatic Sch., N.Y.C. First TV appearance in Penny, Robert Montgomery Presents, 1952; understudy broadway play Picnic, 1953; appeared in plays Baby Want a Kiss, 1964, Candida, 1982, The Glass Menagerie, Williamstown Theatre Festival, 1985; motion pictures include Three Faces of Eve, 1957 (Acad. award Best Actress, Nat. Bd. Rev. award, Fgn. Press award), Count Three and Pray, 1955, Long Hot Summer, 1958, No Down Payment, 1957, Sound and the Fury, 1959, A Kiss Before Dying, 1956, Rally Round the Flag Boys, 1958, The Fugitive Kind, 1960, Paris Blues, 1961, The Stripper, 1963, A New Kind of Love, 1963, A Big Hand for the Little Lady, 1965, A Fine Madness, 1965, Rachel, Rachel, 1968, Winning, 1969, WUSA, 1970, They Might Be Giants,

1971, The Effect of Gamma Rays on Man-in-the-Moon Marigolds, 1972 (Cannes Film Festival award), Summer Wishes, Winter Dreams, 1973 (N.Y. Film Critics award), The Drowning Pool, 1975, The End, 1978, Harry and Son, 1984, Glass Menagerie, 1987; TV appearances include All the Way Home; TV-film appearances in Sybil, 1976, Come Back, Little Sheba, 1977, See How She Runs, 1978 (Emmy award), Streets of L.A., 1979, The Shadow Box, 1980, Crisis at Central High, 1981, Do You Remember Love?, 1985 (Emmy award); narrator: film documentary Angel Dust. Democrat. Episcopalian. Office: William Morris Agency care Toni Howard 151 El Camino Beverly Hills CA 90212 *

WOODWARD, MELINDA ELLICE, state mental health administrator; b. Atlanta, May 8, 1943; d. Richard Lewis and Helen (Beal) W.; m. James Merwyn Burke, Dec. 11, 1972 (div. 1976); m. Franklin M. Meyer, Feb. 14, 1987. AB, Radcliffe Coll. Harvard U., 1965; M in Pub. Adminstrn., Princeton U., 1969. Planner Vera Inst. Justice, N.Y.C., 1969-71; planner/cons. Oreg. Corrections Div., Salem, 1971-72; planner/cons. Oreg. Mental Health Div., Salem, 1972-78, dep. asst. adminstr., 1978-80, asst. adminstr., 1980-85; dir. support services Fairview Tng. Ctr., Salem, 1985—. A.P. Gordon traveling fellow, Mexico, 1964; Fulbright scholar, Argentina, 1965-66. Democrat. Office: Fairview Tng Ctr 2250 Strong Rd SE Salem OR 97310

WOODWARD, PATRICIA A., lawyer; b. Willimantic, Conn., Oct. 15, 1955; d. Edmond Freeman and Eileen May (Swanson) W.; m. Mark E. Sharp, Sept. 13, 1980; children: Matthew Freeman, Grace Eileen. AA, Hartford Coll. Women, 1975; BA, Williams Coll., 1977; JD, Washington & Lee U., 1980. Bar: Va., U.S. Bankruptcy Ct., U.S. Dist. Ct (ea. dist., western dist.). Assoc. Jud A. Fischel & Assocs., Warrenton, Va., 1980-81; ptnr. Fischl & Woodward, Warrenton, 1981-86; sole practice Warrenton, 1986—. Mem., actor Fauquier Community Theatre, Warrenton, 1981—; mem. Warrenton Chorale, 1983—; bd. dirs. Literacy Vols. Fauquier County, Warrenton, 1986—. Mem. ABA, Va. Bar Assn., Vauquier County Bar Assn., Va. Trial Lawyers Assn., Altrusa (pres. 1982-84, bd. dirs. 1986—). Home: Rt 4 Box 117 Warrenton VA 22186 Office: PO Box 1037 31 S Second St Warrenton VA 22186

WOODWELL, MARGOT BELL, broadcasting executive; b. Pitts., Mar. 5, 1936; d. Davitt Stranahan and Marian (Whieldon) Bell; m. William Herron Woodwell, June 24, 1960; children—Davitt Bell, William Herron, James Ross. A.B., Vassar Coll., 1957. Dir. community support Sta. WQED, Pitts., 1978-84, v.p., sta. mgr., 1984—. Pres. bd. trustees St. Edmunds Acad., Pitts., 1972-75; pres. bd. trustees Episcopal Diocese Pitts., 1975-78; bd. dirs. Union Nat. Bank of Pitts., Cen. Blood Bank, County Bd. of Health, Lemington Home for Aged, Greater Pitts. Literacy Council, Pitts. Literacy Initiative; mem. standing com., 1982—; chmn. Episcopal Diocese Renewal Fund, Pitts., 1980—; trustee Vassar Coll., Poughkeepsie, N.Y., 1982—. Office: Sta-WQED 4802 5th Ave Pittsburgh PA 15217

WOODWORTH, DOROTHY ELIZABETH, economist, administrator; b. Syracuse, N.Y.; d. Melville Anton and Dorothy (Speich) Clark; children: Lynn, David. MPA, Syracuse U., 1945; MA, Stanford U., 1963. Spl. investigator econ. cases Nurnberg Trials, Fed. Republic of Germany; personnel adminstrn. Fgn. Econ. Adminstrn., Fed. Republic of Germany and Austria; chief adminstrn. Decartelization br. Office of Mil. Govt. of U.S., Berlin, Fed. Republic of Germany; pres. Sis Enterprises, Palo Alto, Calif.; chmn. bd. Sis Enterprises, Palo Alto; dir., sec. Clark Harp Co., dir., asst. sec., treas. Clark Music Co.; cons. in field; expert witness on women's econ. issues; lectr. in field. Author: This I Can Do; contbr. articles to profl. jours.; inventor measurement instruments to record progress and achievement of women locally, nationally, internationally. Founder Inter-Allied Cultural Council, OMGUS Employees Suggestion System for Austria, Ger., Women's Heritage Mus.; mem. Carnegie Found. pilot project on Making Ams. Abroad Effective; participant UN Decade for Women Tribune, Mexico City, 1975. Recipient English Speaking Union award, Bernays Found. awards; Syracuse U. scholar, Wellesley U. scholar, Radcliffe U. scholar, Principia U. scholar, others; grantee, Ford Found., AAUW; recipient Commendation, Women of Achievement, Santa Clara County Suprs., many others. Mem. NOW, LWV, AAUW, Nat. Women's Polit. Caucus, Am. Women in Sci., Older Women's League. Club: Radcliffe of the Peninsula, Little House.

WOODWORTH, LESLIE MEREDITH, clergyman; b. Winona, Minn., Mar. 12, 1957; d. Leslie Rufus and Doradelle (Meredith) W. AA in Theology, Christ for The Nations, 1979; BA in Bible, Biola U., 1986—. Tchr. Bible and English Bible Sch. for The Deaf, Manila, 1982-84; dir. music Praising Hands Deaf Ch., Lakewood, Calif., 1986-87; home group leader Emmanuel Episcopal Ch., 1987-88. Republican. Episcopalian. Home: 14615 Rosecrans La Mirada CA 90638

WOODY, CAROL CLAYMAN, data processing executive; b. Bristol, Va., May 20, 1949; d. George Neal and Ida Mae (Nelms) Clayman; B.S. in Math., Coll. William and Mary, Williamsburg, Va., 1971; M.B.A. with distinction (IBM Corp. fellow 1978, Stephen Bufton Meml. Ednl. Found. grantee, 1978-79), Babcock Sch., Wake Forest U., 1979; m. Robert William Woody, Aug. 19, 1972. Programmer trainee GSA, 1971-72; systems engr. Citizens Fidelity Bank & Trust Co., Louisville, 1972-75; programmer/analyst-tng. coordinator Blue Bell, Inc., Greensboro, N.C., 1975-79; supr. programming and tech. services J.E. Baker Co., York, Pa., 1979-82, fin. design supr. bus. systems Lycoming div. AVCO, Stratford, Conn., 1982-83; project mgr. Yale U., 1984—; co-owner Sign of the Sycamore, antiques; mem. Data Processing Standards Bd., 1977, CICS/VS Adv. Council, 1975. Mem. Am. Bus. Woman's Assn. (chpt. v.p. 1978-79; Merit award 1978), Nat. Assn. Female Execs., Delta Omicron (alumni pres. 1973-75, regional chmn. 1979-82). Republican. Presbyterian. Author various manuals. Home: PO Box 1450 Guilford CT 06437 Office: 155 Whitney Ave New Haven CT 06510

WOODY, KATHLEEN JOANNA, lawyer; b. Honolulu, May 3, 1949; d. Edward Franklin and Norma Lee (Harris) W.; m. Martin G. Baker, 1984; 1 child, Mark G. A.B. magna cum laude, U. Miami, 1973, J.D., 1976; LL.M., Columbia U., 1981, now postgrad. Bar: Fla. 1976, D.C. 1977, U.S. Supreme Ct. 1980. Vice pres., tax cons. Franklin Tax Service, Inc., Silver Spring, Md., 1967-76; real estate agt., sales mgr. Pershing Real Estate Co., Silver Spring, 1972-76; atty. U.S. Office Comptroller of Currency, Washington, 1976-78, regional atty. N.Y.C., 1979-80; mem. faculty New Sch. for Social Research, N.Y.C., 1980; teaching fellow, dir. tng. internat. tax program Harvard Law Sch., 1981-82; mem. faculty Inst. Comparative Law in Paris, France for U. San Diego, 1982; ind. research Oxford U., 1982; partner Woody & Woody, 1983—; adj. prof. Georgetown Law Sch., 1983—. Author: Soviet Finance and International Banking and Finance; Legal Ethics and Informed Consent for Medical Research. Mem. Internat. Bar Assn., ABA, D.C. Bar Assn., Fed. Bar Assn., Assn. Bar City N.Y. Baptist. Author: Soviet Finance, International Banking and Finance, Medical Ethics (Informed Consent), Legal Education; contbr. articles to profl. jours. Home: 9131 Sligo Creek Pkwy Silver Spring MD 20901

WOODY, MARSHA, dance educator; b. Oklahoma City, Dec. 25, 1935; d. Doyle L. and Paulene (Lambert) W.; m. Marion Frank Zummo, Dec. 30, 1956; 1 child, Monique Woody. Student Lamar U., 1954-55, Joffrey Sch., N.Y.C., 1956-58, Sch. Am. Ballet, N.Y.C., 1977, David Howard Sch., N.Y.C., 1975, Harkness Sch., N.Y.C., 1968. Cert. Dance Masters Am., Tex. Assn. Tchrs. Dance. Tchr. dance sch., Beaumont, Tex., 1952-55; owner, dance dir. Marsha Woody Acad., Beaumont, 1956—; founder, artistic dir. Beaumont Civic Ballet, 1971—; lectr. in field, performing mem. Southwest Regional Ballet, 1981, mem. Honor Co., 1982; field judge Am. Ballet Competition, 1983. Produced (profl. dancers) Robert La Fosse, Am. Ballet Theatre, N.Y.C., Edmund La Fosse, Royal Winnipeg Ballet of Can., Kristine Richmond, Houston Ballet, Margo McCann, Ft. Worth Ballet, Jennifer Mattingly, Joffrey Ballet, Allison Odom, Tulsa Ballet. Bd. dirs. Beaumont Arts Related Curriculum, Beaumont Med. Surg. Hosp., 1985—; panel advisor Tex. Commn. Arts in Austin, 1984-85. Mem. Beaumont Symphony Guild, Beaumont Community Theatre, Beaumont Opera Buffs, Beaumont Ballet Soc. Republican. Roman Catholic. Clubs: Beaumont Country, Tower (Beaumont). Avocations: travel; collecting antiques; knitting; swimming; skiing. Office: Beaumont Civic Ballet Co 3717 Calder Beaumont TX 77706

WOOLDRIDGE, MARY JANE, writer, photo-stylist; b. Raleigh, N.C., Apr. 3, 1958; d. Oscar Bailey Wooldridge, Jr. and Martha Jane (Clarke) Wooldridge Jordan. AB in History, Duke U., 1980; summer study New Coll., Oxford, England, 1979. Gen. reporter, intern News & Observer, Raleigh, 1979-80; fashion writer N.Y. Times Mag., N.Y.C., 1980-81; free-lance writer N.Y.C., 1981-82; asst. Eliot Janeway, Economist, N.Y.C., 1982-83; fashion and social writer, photo stylist Miami Herald, Fla., 1983—. Author (with others) Best Publications, 1982, also articles. Recipient Atrium award 1986, Fla. Med. Assn. award, 1987. Mem. N.C. Youth Adv. Bd., Raleigh, 1975-76; chmn. N.C. State Youth Councils, 1975-76. Angier B. Duke scholar Duke U., 1978-80. Democrat. Mem. Interdenominational Ch. Avocations: photography, travel. Office: Miami Herald 1 Herald Plaza Miami FL 33101

WOOLFE, ELIZABETH ARMSTRONG, educational administrator; b. Orlando, Fla., Jan. 18, 1929; d. William and Alice Lucy (Metcalf) Armstrong; B.S., Fla. State U., 1950, M.S., 1967; Ed.D. (Charles S. Mott fellow 1974), Fla. Atlantic U., 1979; m. Robert Cecil Woolfe, July 30, 1950; children—Robert Craig, Richard Stephen (dec.), Randall Clark, Russell Cameron. Home service rep. Fla. Power & Light Co., 1960-62; extension home econs. agt. Palm Beach County (Fla.), also U. Fla., 1964-66; from program specialist to tchr. Palm Beach County Sch. Bd., 1966-70, county staff resource tchr. dept. adult and community edn., 1972-74; asst. prof. Indian River Community Coll., 1970-72; part-time instr., then coordinator continuing edn. Palm Beach Jr. Coll., 1976-81, dir. continuing edn. II, North Campus, 1981-86, acting asst. to pres., 1987—. Deacon, Immanuel Presbyn. Ch., Palm Beach Gardens, Fla., 1959-82. Named Woman of Year Bus. and Profl. Women, 1985. Mem. Am. Assn. Community and Jr. Colls., Fla. Assn. Community Colls. (chmn. region 1986-88), Am. Assn. Women Community and Jr. Colls., Assn. Continuing Higher Edn., Am. Soc. Tng. and Devel., AAUW, (mem. div. bd. 1986—), Fla. Assn. Community Colls., Fla. Assn. Community Edn., Fla. Fedn. Women's Clubs (jr. dist. dir. 1962-64), Palm Beach County Panhellenic (pres. 1959-60), Greater W. Palm Beach C. of C., No. Palm Beach C. of C., RSVP (bd. dirs. 1985-88). Alpha Lambda Delta, Kappa Delta Pi, Omicron Nu, Phi Delta Kappa, Alpha Chi Omega. Democrat. Club: Palm Beach Gardens Soroptomist (chmn. youth citizenship com. 1980-82, dir. 1982-84, v.p. 1985-86, pres. 1986-87). Home: 59 Ironwood Way N Palm Beach Gardens FL 33418 Office: 3160 PGA Blvd Palm Beach Gardens FL 33410

WOOLLEY, CATHERINE (JANE THAYER), author; b. Chgo., Aug. 11, 1904; d. Edward Mott and Anna L. (Thayer) W. AB, UCLA, 1927. Advt. copywriter Am. Radiator Co., N.Y.C., 1927-31; freelance writer 1931-33; copywriter, editor house organ Am. Radiator & Standard San. Corp., N.Y.C., 1933-40; desk editor Archtl. Record, 1940-42; prodn. editor SAE Jour., N.Y.C., 1942-43; pub. relations writer NAM, N.Y.C., 1943-47; condr. workshop in juvenile writing Truro Center for Arts, 1977, 78; instr. juvenile writing Cape Cod Writers Conf., 1965, 66. Author: juvenile books (under name Catherine Woolley) I Like Trains, 1944, rev., 1965, Two Hundred Pennies, 1947, Ginnie and Geneva, 1948, David's Railroad, 1949, Schoolroom Zoo, 1950, Railroad Cowboy, 1951, Ginnie Joins In, 1951, David's Hundred Dollars, 1952, Lunch for Lennie, 1952 (pub. as L'Incontentabile Gigi in Italy), The Little Car That Wanted a Garage, 1952, The Animal Train and Other Stories, 1953, Holiday on Wheels, 1953, Ginnie and the New Girl, 1954, Ellie's Problem Dog, 1955, A Room for Cathy, 1956, Ginnie and the Mystery House, 1957, Miss Cathy Leonard, 1958, David's Campaign Buttons, 1959, Ginnie and the Mystery Doll, 1960, Cathy Leonard Calling, 1961, Look Alive, Libby!, 1962, Ginnie and Her Juniors, 1963, Cathy's Little Sister, 1964, Libby Looks for a Spy, 1965, The Shiny Red Rubber Boots, 1965, Ginnie and the Cooking Contest, 1966 (paperback 1979), Ginnie and the Wedding Bells, 1967, Chris in Trouble, 1968, Ginnie and the Mystery Cat, 1969, Libby's Uninvited Guest, 1970, Cathy and the Beautiful People, 1971, Cathy Uncovers a Secret, 1972, Ginnie and the Mystery Light, 1973, Libby Shadows a Lady, 1974, Ginnie and Geneva Cookbook, 1975; under name Jane Thayer juvenile books. The Horse with the Easter Bonnet, 1953, The Popcorn Dragon, 1953, Where's Andy?, 1954, Mrs. Perrywinkle's Pets, 1955, Sandy and the Seventeen Balloons, 1955, The Chicken in the Tunnel, 1956, The Outside Cat, 1957, English edit., 1958, 83, Charley and the New Car, 1957, Funny Stories To Read Aloud, 1958, Andy Wouldn't Talk, 1958, The Puppy Who Wanted a Boy, 1958, rev., 1986, paperback edit., 1988, The Second-Story Giraffe, 1959, Little Monkey, 1959, Andy and His Fine Friends, 1960, The Pussy Who Went To the Moon, 1960, English edit., 1961, A Little Dog Called Kitty, 1961, English edit., 1962, 75, The Blueberry Pie Elf, 1961, English edit., 1962, Andy's Square Blue Animal, 1962, Gus Was a Friendly Ghost, 1962, English edit., 1971, Japanese edit., 1982, A Drink for Little Red Diker, 1963, Andy and the Runaway Horse, 1963, A House for Mrs. Hopper; the Cat that Wanted to Go Home, 1963, Quiet on Account of Dinosaur, 1964, English edit., 1965, 74, paperback edit., 1988, Emerald Enjoyed the Moonlight, 1964, English edition, 1965, The Bunny in the Honeysuckle Patch, 1965, English edit., 1966, Part-Time Dog, 1965 (English edit. 1966), The Light Hearted Wolf, 1966, What's a Ghost Going to Do?, 1966, English edit. 1972, Japanese edit., 1982, The Cat that Joined the Club, 1967 (English edit. 1968), Rockets Don't Go To Chicago, Andy, 1967, A Contrary Little Quail, 1968, Little Mr. Greenthumb, 1968, English edit., 1969, Andy and Mr. Cunningham, 1969, Curious, Furious Chipmunk, 1969, I'm Not a Cat, Said Emerald, 1970 (English edit. 1971), Gus Was A Christmas Ghost, 1970, English edit. 1973, Japanese edit., 1982, Mr. Turtle's Magic Glasses, 1971, Timothy And Madam Mouse, 1971, English edit., 1972, Gus And The Baby Ghost, 1972, English edit. 1973, Japanese edit., 1982, The Little House, 1972, Andy and the Wild Worm, 1973, Gus Was a Mexican Ghost, 1974, English edit. 1975, Japanese edit., 1982, I Don't Believe in Elves, 1975, The Mouse on the Fourteenth Floor, 1977, Gus Was a Gorgeous Ghost, 1978, English edit., 1979, Where Is Squirrel?, 1979, Try Your Hand, 1980, Applebaums Have a Robot, 1980, Clever Raccoon, 1981, Gus Was a Real Dumb Ghost, 1982; contbr. stories to juvenile anthologies, sch. readers, juvenile mags. Trustee Truro Pub. Libraries, 1974-84; Mem. Passaic (N.J.) Bd. Edn., 1953-56, Passaic Redevel. Agy., 1952-53; pres. Passaic LWV, 1949-52. Named mem. N.J. Literary Hall of Fame, 1987. Mem. Authors League Am., Friends of Truro Libraries, Truro Hist. Soc., Amnesty Internat. U.S.A., Kenilworth Soc. Democrat. Home: Higgins Hollow Rd Truro MA 02666

WOOLMAN, MARY ANN, management consultant; b. Portland, Oreg., Nov. 23, 1947; d. Harold Clifford and Anne Kozlowski Wakefield; m. Jeremiah Lawrence, Nov. 11, 1971 (div. Apr. 1987). BS in Edn., No. State Coll., 1970. Art, humanities tchr. Webster (S.D.) High Sch., 1971-72; with repair dept. Zenith Radio Corp. of Iowa, Sioux City, Iowa, 1973-78; from assembly technician to quality circle facilitator Electro Scientific Industries, Portland, Oreg., 1978-86; asst. facilitator Three Mountain Found., Lone Pine, Calif., 1987—. Co-author (tng. manual) People Action Links Working in a Group, 1983. Mem. Internat. Assn. Quality Circles (lectr. 1986), Assn. for Productivity and Inventory Control (instr. 1986-87). Home and Office: Three Mountain Found PO Box 1180 Lone Pine CA 93545

WOOLSTON, EVELYN DORIS, arts administrator, public relations specialist; b. Boston, Nov. 8, 1925; d. Paul Hermann and Louise Martha (Gesch) Franz; m. John Woolston, Apr. 7, 1945; (div. 1967); 1 son, Peter Christopher; m. 2d Robert Franklin May, Feb. 1, 1984. B.A., Emerson Coll., 1947. Asst. merchandising mgr. Sta. WCSC-TV-AM, Charleston, S.C., 1954-57; mgr. promotions and merchandising, Knight Broadcasting, Inc., Portsmouth, N.H., 1957-61; asst. advt. dir. Hahn Shoes, Landover, Md., 1961-70; advt. dir. W & J Sloane, Inc., Washington, 1970-76; exec. dir. Capitol Ballet, Inc., Washington, 1977-80; freelance arts adminstr., Washington, 1980—. Exec. dir. Off the Circle Theatre Co., Washington, 1982-84; chmn., coordinator fund-raising project League of Washington Theatres, 1984-85; bd. dirs. D.C. Contemporary Dance Theatre, 1985—, Washington Stage Guild, 1986— . League Washington Theatres, Helen Hayes Awards, co-chmn. Washington Theatre Fortnight, 1986 ; fund raiser various arts orgns., Washington, 1961—; Mem. Emerson Coll. Alumni Assn. (mem. exec. bd. 1984-86). Republican. Club: ARTS Club of Washington (chmn. drama 1982-83, chmn. outreach 1985—). Avocations: theatre; travel; reading; Japanese literature; swimming. Home and Office: 2734 34th Pl NW Washington DC 20007

WORBOIS, LOIS EVELYN, writer; b. Mt. Pleasant, Pa., June 30, 1930; d. Edwin Thomas and Louvina Elizabeth (May) Butler; m. Robert John Worbois, Feb. 3, 1951; children: James, Cheryl, John (dec.), Susanne, Allen. Student in English edn., Seton Hill Coll., Greensburg, Pa., 1986-88. Free-lance writer Light and Life Press, Winona Lake, Ind., 1969-71; soc. editor News Dispatch, Jeannette, Pa., 1972-75; reporter Standard Observer, Irwin, Pa., 1976-79, woman's editor, 1979-86; free-lance writer, 1986—. Author: The Thorn, 1977. Mem. adv. bd. Sr. Community Service Projects, Westmoreland County Community Coll., 1976-86; mem. Health and Welfare Council, Westmoreland County, 1980-86. Mem. DAR, Soc. Profl. Journalists. Republican. Methodist. Club: Gideons Internat. Aux. (v.p. 1972, sec. 1979) (Westmoreland County). Home: 2849 Schade Hill Rd North Huntingdon PA 15642 Office: Standard Observer Westmoreland Jours Inc PO Box 280 Irwin PA 15642

WORCESTER, PATRICE HERZIG, hotel manager; b. Winchester, Mass., Apr. 28, 1960; d. John Duncan and Margaret (Herzig) W. BS in Hotel Adminstrn., Cornell U., 1984. Asst. hotel mgr. Harrah's Lake Tahoe Hotel/Casino, Stateline, Nev., 1986, hotel mgr., 1986—. Vol. Planned Parenthood of No. Nev., Stateline, 1986-87; cons. Project Bus./Jr. Achievement, Reno, 1984-85. Mem. Nev. Hotel/Motel Assn., Calif. Hotel/Motel Assn., Cornell Soc. Hotelmen, Nat. Assn. Female Execs., Assn. Rep. Women. Home: PO Box 2572 Stateline NV 89449 Office: Harrah's Lake Tahoe Hotel and Casino PO Box 8 Stateline NV 89449

WORCESTER, TONI ELIZABETH, fundraiser; b. N.Y.C., Sept. 22, 1940; d. John Carroll and Lillian Eldora (Smith) Larson; m. Theodore Evarts Worcester, Sept. 2, 1965 (div. Apr. 26, 1984); children: Scott Edward, Geoffrey Eric, Jennipher Elizabeth, Heather Emily. BA, Colo. Coll., 1962. Adminstrv. sec. U.S. Army, France, 1963-64, secondary tchr., 1964-65; lobbyist LWV, Denver, 1984, Colo. Environ. Lobby, Denver, 1985; fund raiser Ind. Coll. Fund of Colo., Denver, 1985—; coordinator Leadership Denver City Scope Project, 1986-87. Contbr. articles to profl. jours. Trustee Colo. Coll., Colo. Springs, 1981-87; chmn. Lowry Landfill Monitoring Com., Denver, 1983-87; bd. dirs. Met. Sewage Disposal Dist., Denver, 1984-88; mem. Denver Com. Fgn. Relations, 1984-88, Colo. Social Legislation com., 1986-88; legis. monitor Girl Scouts U.S., Denver, 1985-88; chmn. Environ. Caucus, Denver, 1987—. Recipient Disting. Service award Denver Regional Council Govts., 1980. Mem. Colo. Assn. Fund-Raisers (legis. chmn. 1986-88), Assn. Governing Bd. Democrat. Congregationalist. Club: Colo. Roundtable (v.p. 1986-87). Home: 460 S Marion Parkway Denver CO 80209 Office: Ind Coll Fund of Colo 387 Denver Club Building Denver CO 80202

WORDEN, KATHARINE COLE, sculptor; b. N.Y.C., May 4, 1925; d. Philip Gillette and Katharine (Pyle) Cole; student Potters Sch., Tucson, 1940-42, Sarah Lawrence Coll., 1942-44; m. Frederic G. Worden, Jan. 8, 1944; children—Rick, Dwight, Philip, Barbara, Katharine. Sculptor; works exhibited Royce Galleries, Galerie Francoise Besnard (Paris), Cooling Gallery (London), Galerie Schumacher (Munich), Selected Artists Gallery, N.Y.C., Art Inst. Boston, Reid Gallery, Nashville, Weiner Gallery, N.Y.C., Boston Athanaeum, House of Humor and Satire, Gabrovo, Bulgaria, 1983, Newport Bay Club, 1984; pvt. collections Grand Palais (Paris), Dakar and Bathurst, Africa; dir. Stride Rite Corp., 1980-85; occupational therapist psychopathic ward Los Angeles County Gen. Hosp., 1953-57; Headstart vol., Watts, Calif., 1965-67; tchr. sculpture Watts Towers Art Center, 1967-69; participant White House Women Doers Luncheon meeting, 1968; dir. Cambridgeport Problem Center, Cambridge, Mass., 1969-71; mem. Jud. Nominating Commn., 1976-79; bd. overseers Boston Mus. Fine Arts, 1980-83; trustee Communication Research Inst., Miami, Fla., 1960-69, chmn. bd., 1966-69; trustee Newport Art Mus., 1984-86, Newport Health Found., 1986—; bd. dirs. Boston Center for Arts, 1976-80, Child and Family Services of Newport County, 1983—. Mem. Common Cause (Mass. adv. bd. 1971-72, dir. 1974-75), Mass. Civil Liberties Union (exec. bd. 1973-74, dir. 1976-77). Home: 24 Ft Wetherill Rd Jamestown RI 02835

WORDEN, MERRILL ELLEN, communications administrator; b. Washington, Jan. 16, 1958; d. Alfred Merrill Worden and Pamela Alison (Van Der Beek) Clinton; m. Craig Rodney Kuecker (div. Jan. 1987). Student, Stephen F. Austin Coll., 1977-80, U. Houston, 1987—. From trainer to software analyst Fisk Telephone Systems, Houston, 1978-80; mgr. customer support United Techs. Corp., Houston, 1980-82; from service analyst to mgr. customer service Rolm Corp. subs. IBM, Houston, 1982-87, mem. customer satisfaction project team, 1987—. Mem. Nat. Assn. Female Execs. Republican. Episcopalian. Office: IBM/Rolm Systems 2450 NASA Rd 1 Houston TX 77058

WORK, JANE ALLEN, psychologist; b. Phila., May 17, 1920; d. Robert Louis and Lois (McKinney) Allen; m. Homer R. Allen (dec. 1963); children: Robert M., Emily Allen Berg, Homer G.; m. William McClean Work. BA, Westminster Coll., 1965; MA, Case Western Res. U., 1967, PhD, 1973. Lic. psychologist, Penn., Ohio. Sch. psychologist City of Cleve., 1968-70; psychologist spl. edn. dist. Lake County, Ill., 1970-73, Cooperative Ednl. Service Agy. 18, Burlington, Wis., 1974-76; dir. psychol. services Marion (Ohio) Area Counseling Ctr., 1976-78; pvt. practice psychology Pitts., 1978-87; free-lance writer Pittsburgh, 1987—; instr. Loyola U., Chgo., Roosevelt U., Chgo., 1973-74, Nat. Sch. Edn., Evanston, Ill., 1974. Mem. Pa. Task Force for Women, Harrisburg, 1986. Mem. Am. Psychol. Assn., Pa. Psychol. Assn., Nat. Writers Club, N.Y. Acad. Scis., NOW (pres. South Hills chpt. 1987-88). Democrat. Presbyterian. Clubs: Sylvania Hills Hound and Hunt (Pitts.); Entre Nous (New Castle, Pa.). Home and Office: 718 Robinwood Dr Pittsburgh PA 15220

WORK, JANE MAGRUDER, manufacturing legislative analyst; b. Owensboro, Ky., Mar. 30, 1927; d. Orion Noel and Willie May (Stallings) Magruder; m. William Work, Nov. 26, 1960; children: Paul McGregor, Jeffrey William. BA, Furman U., 1947; MA, U. Wis., 1948; PhD, Ohio State U., 1959. Dir. radio U. South Miss., Hattisburg, 1948-51; pub. relations assoc. Ohio Fuel Gas Co./Columbia Gas, Columbus, 1952-62; adj. prof. communications Pace U., N.Y.C., 1963-75; dir. speech ERIC, Washington, 1975-76; mgr. orgn. liaison, dir. legis analysis Nat. Assn. Mfgs., Washington, 1977-84, asst. v.p. legis. analysis, 1984-87, v.p. legis. analysis, 1987—; adv. bd. public affairs NYU Grad. Sch., 1983—; adv. bd. ProEdn. Mag., 1984—; cons. IBM, Xerox, 1963-77. Contbr. articles to profl. jours. Transition team Consumer Product Safety Commn., Washington, 1979-80; mem., chmn. No. Va. Pvt. Industry Council, Fairfax County, 1979-85; co-chair Va. Gov.'s Employment & Tng. Task Force, Richmond, 1983; active in other civic activities. Named to Acad. Women Achievers YWCA, 1987. Mem. Future Homemakers of Am. (bd. dirs. 1985-88), Issue Mgmt. Assn. (bd. dirs. 1985-88), Nat. Assn. Industry-Edn. Coop. (bd. dirs. 1983—), Pub. Relations Soc. Am., Speech Communication Assn. (section chmn. 1980-82), World Future Soc., Alpha Psi Omega (hon.), Pi Kappa Delta (hon.). Republican. Presbyterian. Home: 6245 Cheryl Dr Falls Church VA 22044 Office: Nat Assn Mfrs 1331 Pennsylvania Ave NW Suite 1500/North Washington DC 20004-1703

WORKMAN, LAURAL ANN, retail association executive; b. Monrovia, Calif., Feb. 13, 1960; d. Albert Robert and Laura Louise (Benton) W. BMus, U. Oreg., 1983. Acctg. clk. Renfield Importers, N.Y.C., 1981-82; adminstrv. asst. Internat. Council Shopping Ctrs., N.Y.C., 1983-84, meetings mgr., 1984-85, western meetings dir., San Francisco, 1986—. Co-author: Guide to ICSC Idea Exchanges, 1985. Mem. NOW, Nat. Assn. Female Execs., Phi Beta (pres. 1981-82). Democrat. Avocations: classical musician, tennis, travel, swimming. Home: 5401 Diamond Heights Blvd Apt 4 San Francisco CA 94131 Office: Internat Council Shopping Ctrs 353 Sacramento St Suite 400 San Francisco CA 94111

WORKMAN SMITH, ROSE MARIE, nurse; b. Boston, May 2, 1953; d. Henry and Bessie Cornelis (McDonald) Workman; m. Larry Gene McClure, July 21, 1972 (div. Feb. 1975); 1 child, Bobbi Gene; m. L.C. Smith, Dec. 31, 1976 (div. Feb. 1987); children: Leslie Christopher, Johnathan King. BS in Nursing, Boston U., 1975; MS in Human Resources, Golden Gate U., 1987. RN. Asst. mgr., nurse Community Hosp. Monterey (Calif.) Peninsula, 1979—. Served to capt. USAR, 1976-79. Mem. Am. Nurses Assn., Calif. Nurses Assn., NAACP, Alpha Kappa Alpha. Democrat. Baptist. Office: Community Hosp Monterey Peninsula PO Box HH Monterey CA 93940

WORLDS, ANNIE LOIS, educator, police officer; b. Donalsonville, Ga., May 16, 1949; d. Allen and Edith M. (Daniels) W. BS in Biology, Albany (Ga.) State U., 1977. Cert. tchr., Ga., Fla. Tchr. Terrell County High Sch., Dawson, Ga., 1972-75; officer St. Petersburg (Fla.) Police Dept., 1979-78, tng. officer patrol bur., 1978-80, burglary detective investigative bur., 1980-82, sgt. patrol bur., 1982-83, detective sgt. internal affairs, 1983-85, lt., 1985-86, dist. commdr. patrol bur., 1986—; mem. Gen. Order Rev. Com., St. Petersburg, 1983-85; Expert Info. Rev. Com., St. Petersburg, 1987—. Mem. Dem. Women of St. Petersburg, 1984-85. Named one of Outstanding Young Women of Am., 1985; recipient Citizen for the Day award Sta. WPLP, St. Petersburg, 1983, Ned March award 1980. Mem. Nat. Orgn. Black Law Enforcement Execs. (sec. 1981-83), Internal Assn. Women Police. Baptist. Home: 845 65th Ave S Saint Petersburg FL 33705 Office: St Petersburg Police Dept 1300 First Ave N Saint Petersburg FL 33705

WORLEY, CHRISTINE ROWE, radioactive waste technology and nuclear chemistry educator; b. Concord, N.C., Apr. 13, 1955; d. Robert Nolan and Josephine Carolyn (Ritchie) Rowe; m. Michael Baxter Worley, Sept. 11, 1982. BA in Biology, U. N.C., 1978. Radioactive waste technician specialist Duke Power Co. McGuire Nuclear Sta., Cornelius, N.C., 1980-85; assoc. instr. radioactive waste chemistry Duke Power Co. Nat. Acad. Nuclear Tng.-Lake Norman Br., Huntersville, N.C., 1985—. Mem. Am. Nuclear Soc. (nat. and local brs.). Democrat. Lutheran. Office: Duke Power Co Nat Acad for Nuclear Tng Rt 4 Box 531 Huntersville NC 28078

WORLOW, CATHY, human resource executive; b. Peoria, Ill., Sept. 27, 1949; d. Thomas William and W. LaVonne (Deavers) Endres; m. Andy Lee Worlow, May 31, 1975; 1 child, Leah Danielle. AA, Ill. Cen. Coll., East Peoria, 1970; BA, Sangamon State U., 1980; postgrad., Bradley U., 1987—. With acctg. dept. Ruppman Adminstrv. Services, Peoria, 1971-72; sec. Ruppman Mktg. Services, Inc., Peoria, 1972-74, asst. to v.p., 1974-76, dir. purchasing, 1976-80, mgr. bldg. services, 1980-87, mgr. human resources, 1987—. Mem. AAUW (former mem. publicity com.), Cen. Ill. Employee Assn. (v.p. personnel club 1987, pres. 1988—), Nat. Assn. Female Execs. Lutheran. Lodges: Order Ea. Star, Internat. Order Job's Daus.

WORMAN, ROBIN ANN, military officer; b. Greenville, Ohio, Apr. 12, 1953; d. Paul Richard and Miriam Ellen (Jenkins) Getter; m. Ernest William Worman III, Sept. 23, 1977; children: Amanda Beth, Elizabeth Kate. BA in Psychology, Wittenberg U., 1980. Enlisted USN, 1976, commd. ensign, 1981, advanced through grades to lt., 1985; project mgr. data processing service ctr. Pacific command USN, Pearl Harbor, Hawaii, 1981-83, chief naval data ctr. Pacific fleet, 1983-84; analyst operating planning br. Washington, 1984-85; chief ops. support br. Joint Data Systems Support Ctr. Ft. Ritchie, Md., 1985—. 1st v.p., acting pres. Pearl City (Hawaii) Peninsula Community Assn., 1982; active Girl Scouts U.S., Gettysburg, Pa., 1986-87. Mem. USN Inst., Armed Forces Communication and Electronics Assn. Lutheran. Office: USN Joint Data Systems Support Ctr C732 Fort Ritchie MD 21719

WORRELL, AUDREY MARTINY, psychiatrist, state official; b. Phila., Aug. 12, 1935; d. Francis Aloysius and Dorothy (Rawley) Martiny; m. Richard Vernon Worrell, June 14, 1958; children: Philip Vernon, Amy Elizabeth. MD, Meharry Med. Coll., 1960. Diplomate Am. Bd. Psychiatry and Neurology. Dir. capitol region Mental Health Ctr., Hartford, Conn., 1974-77; acting regional dir. Region IV, State Dept. Mental Health, 1976-77; asst. chief psychiatry VA Med. Ctr., Newington, Conn., 1977-78, acting chief psychiatry, 1978-79, chief psychiatry, 1978-80; dir. Capitol Regional Mental Health Facilities, Hartford, Conn., 1980-81; clin. prof. psychiatry U. Conn., 1981—; commr. State Dept. Mental Health, Hartford, 1981-86; chief exec. officer and med. dir. Vista Sandia Hosp., Albuquerque, 1986-88; dir. consultation liason Lovelace Med. Ctr., Albuqueque, 1988—. Contbr. articles to profl. jours. Bd. dirs. Transitional Services, Buffalo, 1973-74, ARC, Buffalo, 1973-74, Child and Family Services, Hartford, 1972-73; co-chmn. United Way/Combined Health Appeal, State of Conn., 1983, 84; active Child Welfare Inst. Adv. Bd., Hartford, 1983—, Conn. Prison Bd., Hartford, 1984-85. Recipient Leadership award Conn. Council Mental Health Ctrs., 1983; Outstanding Contbn. award to Health Services YWCA, Hartford, 1983; chmn. Gov.'s Task Force on Mental Health Policy, 1982-85; mem. Gov.'s Task Force on Homeless, 1983-85. Mem. New Eng. Mental Health Commrs. Assn., Am. Med. Women's Assn., Conn. Assn. Mental Health and Aging, Conn. Coalition for Homeless Inc., Conn. Rehab. Assn., Am. Assn. Psychiat. Adminstrs., Am. Hosp. Assn., AMA, Am. Orthopsychiat. Assn., Am. Pub. Health Assn., Assn. Mental Health Adminstrs., Hosp. and Community Psychiatry Service, Corporators of Inst. of Living of Hartford, Am. Psychiat. Assn., Conn. Psychiat. Soc., NASMHPD (sec., bd. dirs. 1982-86), Am. Coll. Psychiatrists, Am. Coll. Mental Health Adminstrs. Democrat. Office: Lovelace Med Ctr 1314 Madeira SE Albuquerque NM 87108

WORRELL, JUDY SUE, product design company executive; b. Marion, Ind., May 3, 1949; d. Joseph Corwin and Martha Louise (Nall) Mendenhall; m. W. Robert Worrell, Sept. 6, 1969; children: Kedron, Kasey, Kai, Kit, Katie. Student respiratory medicine, Marion Gen. Hosp., 1966-67; student, Ball State U., 1967-68. Staff therapist Marion Gen. Hosp., 1966-69; head respiratory medicine dept. Home Hosp., Purdue U., West Lafayette, Ind., 1969-70; v.p., fin. mgr. Worrell Design, Inc., Mpls., 1976—. Precinct chmn. Ind. Republican com., Hopkins, Minn., 1986—. Home: 148 Interlachen Rd Hopkins MN 55343 Office: Worrell Design Inc 43 Main St SE Suite 506 Minneapolis MN 55414-1029

WORSLEY, RUTH EARNESTINE, deputy federal marshal; b. Bethel, N.C., Feb. 4, 1943; d. Lonnie and Lizzie (Edwards) Wilson; divorced; children: John F. Jr., Jacqueline, Gwendolyn. BS, Rutgers U., 1982, postgrad.; diploma in legal secretarial skills, Essex Coll. Bus., Newark, 1970. Licensed real estate salesperson. Stenographer U.S. Dept. Immigration, Newark, 1970-72; legal sec. U.S. Atty's Office, Newark, 1972-77; correctional officer U.S. Bur. Prisons, N.Y.C., 1977-79; dep. U.S. Marshals Service, Washington, 1979-81, Bklyn., 1981-82; inspector U.S. Marshals Service, N.Y.C., 1983-85; supr., dep. U.S. Marshals Service, Newark, 1985—. Trustee Cen United Presbyn. Ch., Newark, 1986. Served with Army Nat. Guard, 1974-79. Mem. Nat. Assn. Female Execs. (bd. dirs. Montclair, N.J. chpt., 1984—), Nat. Orgn. Black Law Enforcement Execs., Rutgers Alumni Assn., Interagency Com. Women Fed. Law Enforcement, Coalition 100 Black Women. Democrat. Home: 657 Park Ave East Orange NJ 07017 Office: Dept Justice US Marshal's Service 500 US PO & Courthouse Newark NJ 07101

WORTHAM, JUDY MARIE, hospital administrator; b. Evansville, Ind., May 6, 1952; d. Clarence Edward and Elsie Maureen (Scott) Skelton; m. Robert Wayne Wortham; 1 child, Melissa Marie. BA, Miami U., Oxford, Ohio, 1974; M of Adminstrn., Ohio State U., 1988. Social worker Dayton (Ohio) Children's Psychiat. Hosp.; clin. coordinator children's acute care unit Dayton Mental Health Ctr.; asst. adminstr. The Dartmouth Hosp., Dayton, 1986-87, assoc. adminstr., 1987, chief ops. officer, adminstr., 1987—; v.p. Ohio Psychiat. Insts.; presenter networking materials nat. conv. Nat. Assn. Pvt. Psychiat. Hosps., New Orleans, 1986; trainer networking local hosp., Las Cruces, N.Mex., 1987. Mem. Beavercreek Women's League. Mem. Nat. Assn. for Exec. Women, Nat. Assn. Female Execs. Democrat. Baptist. Clubs: Century (Green County, Ohio), Greene County Recreational.

WORTHEN, ANGELA ANNE, insurance agent; b. Phila., Jan. 3, 1960; d. William Ray and Dorothy Mae (Ford) W. AA, Community Coll. of Phila., 1981; BS, York Coll. of Pa., 1982; MEd, Va. Commonwealth U., 1985. Adminstr. Women in Community Service, Phila., 1985; ednl. rep. P.F. Collier, Inc., Phila., 1986; career cons. Career Starters, Inc., Phila., 1986; budget adminstr. Andre Desmond's Beauty Ctrs., Phila., 1987; rep. mktg. Hensley Group/Century 21, Phila., 1987; agt. life/health, telemktg. dept. Colonial Penn Group, Phila., 1987—. Mem. Nat. Assn. Female Execs., Phi Theta Kappa. Democrat. Baptist. Home: 6720 North Gratz St Philadelphia PA 19126

WORTHING, MARCIA LYNN, cosmetics company executive; b. Columbus, Ohio, Jan. 8, 1943; d. Ford Buxton and Dorothy Jean (Leonard) W.; m. Ronald Martin Foster, Jr., Dec. 15, 1973; children—Christopher Worthing, Geoffrey Worthing. B.A., San Francisco State U., 1965. Tchr., San Francisco, 1966-67; editorial asst. Am. Mgmt. Assn., N.Y.C., 1967-69; publs. editor Merrill Lynch Pierce Fenner & Smith, N.Y.C., 1969-72; publs. editor Avon Products, Inc., N.Y.C., 1972-73, supr. personnel, 1973-74, mgr. employment, 1974-76, mgr. tng., 1976-78, dir. personnel, 1978-81, gen. mgr. hqrs., 1981-82, v.p. adminstrn., 1982-84, v.p. human resources, 1984—; bd. dirs. United Water Resources, Paget's Disease Found.; vice chmn. N.Y. Bd. Trade. Office: Avon Products Inc 9 W 57th St New York NY 10019

WORTHINGTON, MARY EMMONS, clinical psychologist; b. San Jose, Calif., Apr. 17, 1922; d. Grover Carlton and Helen Keith (Boulware) Emmons; B.A., Vanderbilt U., 1942; M.L.A., U. So. Calif., 1972; M.A., Pepperdine U., 1975; Ph.D., Fla. Inst. Tech., 1981; m. John Worthington, July 4, 1942; children—Jon, Gina. Librarian, Internat. Grad. U., Lugano, Switzerland, 1976-77; dir. and clin. psychologist High Plains Comprehensive Community Mental Health Center, Osborne, Kans., 1978—; lectr. Pepperdine U., UCLA, Ft. Hays U., Internat. Grad. U. Founder and pres. Friends of Long Beach Library; neighborhood chmn. Girl Scouts U.S.A., 1978-82; mem. Area Agy. on Aging, Osborne, 1981-82; chair bd. trustees UTESA Med. Sch., Dominican Republic; mem. Gov.'s Com. on Drunk Driving. Lic. marriage, family and child therapist, Calif. Mem. Am. Psychol. Assn., Osborne C. of C., Hospice, Osborne County Hosp. Aux., Gamma Phi Beta, Sigma Beta Pi, Psi Chi. Democrat. Methodist. Clubs: PEO (chpt. CR), Fidelia (pres. 1981-82). Home: 318 S 2d St Osborne KS 67473 Office: High Plains Comprehensive Community Mental Health Cent er 121 W Main St Osborne KS 67473

WOS, SUSAN MARIE, microbiologist, researcher; b. Buffalo, Dec. 2, 1955; d. Anthony Lucas and Florence Angeline (Woloszyn) W. BA, SUNY, Buffalo, 1977, MA, 1980, PhD, 1983. Med. lab. technician Erie County Med. Ctr., Buffalo, 1974-79; research technician N.Y. State Dept. Health, Albany, 1979-83; postdoctoral fellow Wadsworth Ctr. Labs./Research, Albany, 1983-84; research microbiologist E.I. duPont de Nemours & Co., Wilmington, Del., 1984-87; staff scientist Integrated Genetics, Inc., Framingham, Mass., 1987—; presentor nat. sci. meetings, 1980—. Author column Infectious Disease Inst. News, 1982; also articles, chpts. Vol. E.J. Meyer Meml. Hosp., Buffalo, 1973-74, Friends of Saratoga Performing Arts Ctr., N.Y., 1981-82. N.Y. State Regents scholar SUNY, Buffalo, 1973-77. Mem. Am. Soc. Microbiology, N.Y. Acad. Sci., Buffalo Collegium of Immunology, Am. Soc. Virology, Sigma Xi. Avocations: travel, microcomputers, photography. Office: Integrated Genetics Inc 31 New York Ave Framingham MA 01701

WOYTHAL, CONSTANCE LEE, psychologist, consultant; b. Milw., Nov. 6, 1954; d. Gerald Clarence and Shirley Estelle (Gross) W.; m. John Francis Neisius, Mar. 20, 1982; 1 child, Adam. BS, U. Wis., Milw., 1976; MS in Edn., U. Wis., River Falls, 1978; postgrad., Alfred Adler Inst., Chgo., 1980, George Williams Coll., 1984, Marquette U., 1984, Cardinal Stritch Coll., 1987. Cert. sch. psychologist, Wis. Psychologist Sch. Dist. of Marshfield, Wis., 1978-81; psychologist Sheboygan County Handicapped Children's Edn. Bd., Sheboygan Falls, Wis., 1981—, devel. and coordinator wellness program, 1984—; workshop facilitator Marshfield Clinic, 1981; cons. wellness lifestyle program Schs. of Sheboygan County, 1985—; lectr. profl. groups. Mem. Nat. Assn. Sch. Psychologists, Nat. Wellness Assn., N.Am. Soc. Adlerian Psychologists, Wis. Sch. Psychology Assn., Sheboygan Wellness Assn. (bd. dirs. 1984—), Mental Health Assn. Home: 2239 N 27th Pl Sheboygan WI 53083 Office: Sheboygan County Handicapped Edn Bd 111 1st St Sheboygan Falls WI 53085 also: Riverview Sch Smith St Plymouth WI 53073

WOZNICKI, LINDA ANN, operations programm analyst; b. Cicero, Ill., Apr. 2, 1962; d. John Joseph Jr. and Pauline (Stieber) Ivaska; m. James Robert Heidmann, July 3, 1982 (div. Feb. 1984); m. Daniel P. Woznicki, May 11, 1985; stepchildren: Andy, Sarah. A in Data Processing, North Central Tech. Inst., 1986. Adminstrv. asst. Wausau (Wis.) Ins. Cos., 1980-82, client service asst., 1982-83, data processing support technician, 1983-85; computer operator Wausau Med. Ctr., 1985; sr. programmer Mortgage Guarantee Ins. Cos., Milw., 1985-88, assocs. systems analyst, 1987—; fitness instr. North suburban YMCA, Brown Deer, Wis., 1987—. Mem. Fathers for Equal Rights, Milw., 1987. Mem. Nat. Assn. for Female Execs. Republican. Roman Catholic. Home: W269 N6980 Hickory Chasm Ct Sussex WI 53089

WRAGG, JOANNA DICARLO, newspaper editor; b. Batavia, N.Y., Nov. 3, 1941; d. Anthony Joseph and Josephine (Ruffino) DiCarlo; m. Otis O. Wragg, III, Dec. 21, 1963; children—Otis O. IV, LaMae. B.A., Fla. State U., 1963. Tchr., Nova Sch., Ft. Lauderdale, Fla., 1963, Pinellas Schs., Safety Harbor, Fla., 1965-68; social worker State of Fla., Lakeland, 1968-70; journalist Lakeland Ledger, 1969-72; editorial writer, then chief editorial writer Miami News, 1972-78; editorial dir. Sta. WPLG-TV, Miami, 1978; editorial writer Miami Herald, 1978-80, assoc. editor, 1980—; pub. speaker. Contbr. articles newspapers. Recipient Pulitzer prize, 1983, Robert F. Kennedy award Robert F. Kennedy Journalism Found., 1971, Disting. Service award Sigma Delta Chi, 1971. Mem. Nat. Conf. Editorial Writers (treas.), Women in Communications. Unitarian. Clubs: Zonta, Miami Forum. Office: Miami Herald 1 Herald Plaza Miami FL 33101

WREGE, JULIA BOUCHELLE, tennis professional; b. Charleston, W.Va., Apr. 11, 1944; d. Dallas Payne and Mary Louise (Hagan) Bouchelle; m. Douglas Ewart Wrege, July 13, 1968; children—Dallas Ewart, Shannon Bouchelle. B.S. in Physics, Ga. Inst. Tech., 1965, M.S. in Physics, 1967. Systems analyst Gen. Electric Apollo Systems, Daytona Beach, Fla., 1967-68; med. scientist Space Instruments Research, Atlanta, 1968-70; head tennis profl. Riverside Tennis Club, Atlanta, 1971-72, Am. Adventures, Roswell, Ga., 1972-75, Hampton Farms Tennis Club, Marietta, Ga., 1975-79; head women's tennis coach Georgia Inst. Tech., Atlanta, 1979-86; stadium chmn., umpire, referee U.S. Tennis Assn., Atlanta, 1977—. Author: Tournament Manual, 1977. Pres. Dickerson Middle Sch. Parent-Tchr.-Student Assn., Marietta, Ga., 1982-85. Named Umpire of Yr., Ga. Tennis Assn., 1978, So. Tennis Assn., 1978; Ga. Tennis Coach of Yr., Assn. Intercollegiate Athletics for Women-Ga. Tennis Coaches Assn., 1981, 82, 83. Mem. U.S. Profl. Tennis Assn. (pres. 1980), U.S. Tennis Assn., Intercollegiate Tennis Coaches Assn., Ga. Tennis Assn. (pres. 1976-81), Atlanta Lawn Tennis Assn., Atlanta Profl. Tennis Assn., Alpha Xi Delta, Sigma Pi Sigma. Republican. Episcopalian. Home: 1366 Little Willeo Rd NE Marietta GA 30068

WREN, CHARLOTTE, real estate broker, consultant; b. Bklyn., July 22, 1947; d. George and Mary Courdy. Student Jones Real Estate Coll., 1981, U. Colo., 1982, 85. Lic. real estate broker, investment specialist. Realtor assoc. Bauer's Brokerage, Grand Junction, Colo., 1981-82, Century 21 Hallmark, Grand Junction, 1982-83; broker assoc. Century 21 Old Homestead Realty, Grand Junction, 1983-86; property mgr., project coordinator, leasing Kroh Bros. Devel. Co., Englwood, Colo., 1983-85; asset mgr. asst. Valley Fed. Savs. & Loan, Grand Junction, 1985; broker-owner Real Estate Services Co., Grand Junction, 1986—; exchanger Colo. West Exchanger, Grand Junction, 1982-85. Commr. City of Grand Junction Housing Authority, 1981-82; bd. dirs. Mesa County Women's Network. Recipient Top Residential Sales Assn. award Century 21 Western Slope Broker's Council, 1983. Mem. Nat. Assn. Realtors, Inst. Creative Mktg., USSA Ski Assn./Powderhorn Racing Club (bd. dirs. 1982, 85). Avocations: travel, skiing, water sports. Office: Real Estate Services Co 718 Horizon Dr Suite 18A Grand Junction CO 81506

WREN, JILL ROBINSON, lawyer, author, editor; b. Summit, N.J., Apr. 30, 1954; d. William and Myrtle Irene (Bennett) Robinson; m. Christopher Gove Wren, June 12, 1976. Student, U. Del., 1972-74; BA, George Washington U., 1976; JD, Boston U., 1980. Bar: Wis. 1980, U.S. Dist. Ct. (ea. and we. dists.) Wis. 1980, U.S. Ct. Appeals (7th cir.) 1980. Jud. law clk. Dane County Cir. Ct., Madison, 1981-83; editor continuing edn. State Bar of Wis., Madison, 1984-86; editor Adams & Ambrose Pub. (formerly Am. Acad. Press), Madison, 1986—; free-lance author, Madison, 1982—; speaker on legal research edn. to various nat. and local orgns., 1983—. Co-author: The Legal Research Manual: A Game Plan for Legal Research and Analysis, 1983, 2d edit., 1986; contbr. articles to profl. jours. Mem. ABA, Wis. State Bar, Assn. Am. Law Schs., Soc. Profl. Journalists, Authors Guild, ACLU, Am. Assn. Law Libraries, Wis. Civil Liberties Union. Democrat. Office: Adams & Ambrose Pub PO Box 9684 Madison WI 53715

WREN, RUTH AVIS, art educator; b. Bethlehem, Pa., Aug. 15, 1945; d. Thomas Benjamin (Morgan) W. BS in Art Edn., Kutztown (Pa.) U., 1968; MEd, Millersville U., 1972; postgrad., Salzburg, Austria and Florence, Italy. Art tchr., artist-in-residence Octorara Area Sch. Dist., Atglen, Pa., 1968—; actress, scene designer various theatres, movie cos., 1975—. Artist, hostess Young Reps., Bethlehem, Pa., 1962-66. Mem. Am. Fedn. TV and Radio Artists. Republican. Unitarian. Club: Swarthmore (Pa.) Players, Barley-Sheaf Players. Office: Octorara Sch Dist Atglen PA 19560

WRENTMORE, ANITA KAY, computer specialist; b. Logan, Ohio, Dec. 3, 1955; d. Lloyd Earl and Gayle Irene (Daubenmire) W. BS, Ohio U., Lancaster, 1978; MS, Ohio U., Athens, 1979; postgrad., Ohio State U., 1985, Cen. Ohio Tech. Coll., 1987. Cert. tchr. Vis. lectr. Denison U., Granville, Ohio, 1980; lectr. Ohio State U., Newark, 1980-83; instr. Cen. Ohio Tech. Coll., Newark, 1983-86; substitute tchr. Newark City Schs., 1986-87, Northfork Sch. Dist., Utica, Ohio, 1987, Lakewood Sch. Dist., Hebron, Ohio, 1987; with Kelly Services, Reynoldsburg, Ohio, 1986-87; computer specialist Def. Constrn. Supply Ctr., Columbus, 1987—; mem. exec. bd. Newark-Licking County Council Tchrs. Math., Newark, 1985—. Mem. Nat. Council Tchrs. Math., Ohio Council Tchrs. Math., Math. Assn. Am., Am. Math. Soc., Nat. Assn. Female Execs., Phi Kappa Phi, Kappa Delta Pi. Democrat. Methodist. Home: 103 Ramona Ave Newark OH 43055

WRIDE, ANH THU, electrical engineer; b. Saigon, Vietnam, Sept. 28, 1955; came to U.S., 1975; d. Lieu V. and Thinh T. (Duong) Doan; m. Bernard R. Wride, Apr. 29, 1978; 1 child, Eric S. B.A. magna cum laude, Brigham Young U., 1977; B.S. in Elec. Engring. magna cum laude, Weber State U., 1984. Electronic technician Communication Certification Lab., Salt Lake City, 1980-81, tech. project leader, 1981-83, engring. mgr., 1984—. Mem. IEEE, Pi Delta Phi. Office: Communication Cert Lab 1940 W Alexander St Salt Lake City UT 84119-2039

WRIGHT, ANN ELIZABETH, physicist, educator; b. Mooringsport, La., Feb. 20, 1922; d. James Aloysius and Mary Louise (Ghenning) Foley; 1 child, Charles Wright Jr. BS in Physics cum laude, U. Houston, 1965; MS in Med. Physics, U. Tex., Houston, 1967; PhD in Radiol. Physics, U. Tex., 1970. Supr. treasury Shell Oil Co., Houston, 1944-59; asst. prof. Baylor Coll. of Medicine, Houston, 1970-75; assoc. prof. U. Tex. Med. Br., Galveston, 1975-82, prof., 1982—; cons. physicist various hosps. nationwide, 1970—. Nat. Cancer Inst. fellow, 1965-70. Mem. Am. Assn. Physicists in Medicine (pres. 1982), Am. Coll. Med. Physics (chmn. bd. chancellors 1984), Am. Inst. Physics (bd. dirs. 1982-86). Office: Univ Tex Med Br 301 University Blvd D-11 Galveston TX 77550

WRIGHT, BOBBIE JEAN, sociology educator; b. Oklahoma City, Apr. 3, 1933; d. Loy Conda and Lanelta (Stalcup) Knight; m. Donald K. Wright, Sept. 30, 1955 (div. 1969); children: Sheryl Ann McLaughlin, Terri Lynn Walton, Karie Kaye. BA in Sociology, Okla. State U., 1954; MRE, So. Bapt. Theol. Sem., 1957; EdD, Nova U., 1976. Dir. student nurses Highland Bapt. Hosp., Louisville, 1954-55; counselor Ormsby Village Delinquent Home, Louisville, 1955-56; asst. exec. dir., teenage dir. YWCA, Allentown, Pa., 1961-64; nat. teenage cons. nat. bd. YWCA, N.Y.C., 1964-65; nat. recruiter YWCA, Tex., 1965-68; owner Char-Burger Restaurant, Sherman, Tex., 1965-67; co-owner Manhattan Janitorial Services, Hampton, Va., 1969-77; asst. prof. Sociology Cen. Va. Community Coll., Lynchburg, Va., 1967-68; prof. sociology Thomas Nelson Community Coll., Hampton, 1968—; with research and devel. United Way, Hampton, 1975-80. Co-author: Instructor Study Guide, Sociology, Horton and Hunt; mem. editorial bd. Annual Editions, 1981—. Judge sci. fairs Hampton, Newport News (Va.) Pub. Schs., 1980—; tng. leader Contact Peninsula, Hampton, Newport News, 1983—; vol. Va. Spl. Olympics, 1984—; Ident-I-Kid, Hampton, Newport News, 1985-86; v.p. Treadmill Civic Assn, Hampton, 1986—. Mem. World Futurist Soc., World Population Soc., Am. Sociological Assn., Va. Sociological Assn. (pres. 1980-81), Delta Kappa Gamma (v.p.). Baptist. Home: 213 Deerfield Blvd Hampton VA 23666

WRIGHT, BRENDA SHIRLENE, transportation company executive; b. Jacksboro, Tex., Dec. 28, 1946; d. James R. and Vera (Cook) Williams; m. Robert H. Garmon (div. June 1981); children: Henry, Holly, Honey; m. George W. Wright, Dec. 28, 1983. Student, East Tex. State U., 1977-78, 81-82, Am. Inst. Banking. V.p., bd. dirs. 1st State Bank, Point, Tex., 1966-83; v.p. Tex. Commerce Bank, Garland, 1983-85; mgr. fin. R.D. Evans Pontiac, Dallas, 1986, Lone Star Dodge, Dallas, 1986; with collections, fin. depts. Jim Allee Olds and Jeep, Dallas, 1987—; pres. B & C Corp., Point, 1981—, Point Pecan Valley, 1982-85. Treas. W.O.W., Point, 1979-86. Mem. Nat. Assn. for Female Execs., Point C. of C. (indsl. com. 1983). Democrat. Baptist. Home: PO Box 305 Point TX 75472 Office: 12277 Shiloh Rd Dallas TX 75228

WRIGHT, CAROLE YVONNE, chiropractor, consultant; b. Long Beach, Calif., July 12, 1932; d. Paul Burt and Mary Leoan (Staley) Fickes; 1 dau., Morgan Michelle. D. Chiropractic, Palmer Coll., Davenport, Iowa, 1975. Instr. Palmer Coll., 1975-76; dir., owner Wright Chiropractic Clinic, Rocklin, Calif., 1978—, Woodland, Calif., 1980-81; dir., co-owner Ft. Sutter Chiropractic Clinic, Sacramento, 1985—; cons. in field; lectr., speaker on radio programs, at seminars. Contbr. articles to profl. jours. Co-chmn. Harold Michaels for Congress campaign, Alameda, Calif., 1972; dist. dir. 14th Congl. Dist., 1983—. Mem. Internat. Chiropractic Assn. Calif. (bd. dirs. 1978-81, pres. 1983-85), Palmer Coll. Alumni Assn. (Calif. state pres. 1981-83), Rocklin C. of C. (bd. dirs. 1979-81), Rocklin-Loomis Bus. and Profl. Women. Republican. Avocations: reading; travel. Home: 4270 Cavitt Stallman Rd Roseville CA 95661 Office: Wright Chiropractic Clinic 3175 Sunset Blvd Suite 105 Rocklin CA 95677

WRIGHT, CATHERINE IRENE, horticulturist; b. Liberal, Kans., Sept. 7, 1953; d. Leonard E. and Edith June (Light) W. BS, Kans. State U., 1975; postgrad., U. Alaska, 1981—. Edn. supr. Cox Arboretum, Dayton, Ohio, 1976-79; grower, supr. P&M Garden Services, Eagle River, Alaska, 1979-80; plant propagator Alaska Plant Materials Ctr., Palmer, Alaska, 1980-81, horticulturist, 1981—; pres. Alaska Botanical Garden, Anchorage, 1986-87. Mem. Am. Soc. Horticulture Sci., Internat. Soc. Horticulture Sci., Alaska Native Plant Soc. (sec. 1984-85, seed exchange chair 1985-86), We. Canadian Soc. Horticulture Sci., Alaska Horticulture Assn., Alaska Horticulture Assn. (treas. 1983-84, sec. 1985-86). Methodist. Home: 18811 Upper Skyline Dr Eagle River AK 99577 Office: Alaska Plant Materials Ctr SRB Box 7440 Palmer AK 99645

WRIGHT, DIANA LOUISE, employment agency owner; b. Bklyn., Oct. 25, 1946; d. Eugene and Lula (Owens) W. B.A. in Psychology, Plattsburgh State U., 1968. Asst. youth service coordinator Clinton County Youth Commn., Plattsburgh, N.Y., 1968; tng. and devel. mgr. AT&T, N.Y.C., 1969-72, asst. editor, 1973-77, mgr. pub. relations, 1978-80, account exec., 1981-83; nat. account mgr., 1984-86; pres. Help Finders Unltd., Inc., Englewood, N.J., 1987—. Mem. Household Services and Nurses Registry Assn., Am. Woman's Econ. Devel. Corp., Nat. Assn. Female Execs., Am. Entrepreneurs Assn. Avocations: interior decorating, antiques, travel. Home: 24 Grant Ave Cresskill NJ 07626 Office: 16 W Palisade Ave Englewood NJ 07631

WRIGHT, ELEANORE REIDELL, retired physician; b. Mattoon, Ill., June 17, 1915; d. Joseph Emanual and Mabel Edna (Eckerly) Reidell; B.S., U. Ill., 1938, B.M., 1940, M.D., 1941, cert. hosp. adminstr., 1959; m. Curtis Wright, Mar. 21, 1941; m. 2d, Arthur O. Hecker, Feb. 11, 1955 (dec.); children—Carolyn Pearson, Eleanore H., Sarah Lawrence, Deborah O'Connell, Curtis. Intern, Augustana Hosp., Chgo., 1940-41; resident Ypsilanti (Mich.) State Hosp., 1950-52, Trenton (N.J.) State Hosp., 1952-54; mem. staff Friends Hosp., Phila., 1954-55; asst. supt. Embreeville (Pa.) Hosp., 1955-70, supt., 1970-71; dir. Eastern Pa. Mental Health programs, 1962-65; lectr. U. Ill., 1941-43, Women's Med. Coll., Phila., 1954-68. Chmn. Cecil Republicans, Inc., 1973; pres. Cecil County Soc. Prevention Cruelty to Animals, 1973-75, 76-78, 79-81; bd. dirs. Foster Care, Cecil County; sec. found. Cecil Community Coll. Grantee in field. Cert. hosp. adminstr. Md. Mem. AMA, Am. Psychiat. Assn., Pa. Psychiat. Assn., Chester County Med. Soc., Am. Coll. Neurol. Psychiatry. Presbyterian. Contbr. articles to profl. jours. Home: 1657 Elk Forest Elkton MD 21921

WRIGHT, ERMA NAOMI, special education educator, dance and music instructor, performer; b. Detroit, Oct. 18, 1930; d. Herman DeWitt Wright and Lillian (Walker-McClellan) Barclay; m. Edward Holsey, Aug. 1948 (div. 1959); children: Edward, Elaine, William, Robert, Erma Gina. AA, Wayne County Community Coll., Detroit, 1976; BA, U. Mich., 1979, MA, 1980. Lyric soprano Edward M. Boatner Sch. Music, N.Y.C., 1954-67; dance instr.

Detroit Dept. Parks and Recreation, 1957-59; recreation specialist, treatment counselor Los Angeles County, 1984-85; fitness instr. Wayne County Community Coll., Detroit, 1986-87; spl. edn. tchr. Detroit Bd. Edn., 1986—; profl. chauffeur Detroit, 1988—; artistic dir. Detroit Council for Arts, 1980. Dir. and choreographer numerous variety shows; singer, dancer throughout Midwest states, 1959—. Youth counselor Washtenaw County, Ypsilanti, Mich., 1981; bd. dirs. Larocque-Bey Sch. Dance and Theater, N.Y.C., 1961-87; pres. Wayne County Community Coll. Soc. for the Preservation of Jazz, 1975-76; bd. dirs. United Mothers Civic League, Detroit, 1957-59. Mem. Am. Guild Variety Artists, Nat. Conf. Artists, Womens' Conf. of Concerns, Los Angeles Area Dance Alliance, Nat. Assn. Female Execs., U. Mich. Alumni Assn. Home: 246 Madison Ave Apt #431 Detroit MI 48226

WRIGHT, FRANCES JANE, educational psychologist; b. Los Angeles, Dec. 22, 1943; d. step-father John David and Evelyn Jane (Dale) Brinegar. BA, Long Beach State U., 1965, secondary tchr. cert., 1966; MA, Brigham Young U., 1968, EdD, 1980; postgrad. U. Nev., 1970, U. Utah, 1972-73; postdoctoral Utah State U., 1985-86. Cert. tchr., adminstr. Utah. Asst. dir. Teenpost Project, San Pedro, Calif., 1966; caseworker Los Angeles County, 1966-67; self-care inservice dir. Utah State Tng. Sch., American Fork, Utah, 1968, vocat. project designer, 1968; tchr. mentally handicapped Santa Ana Unified Schs., Calif., 1968-69; state specialist intellectually handicapped State Office Edn., Salt Lake City, 1969-70; vocat. counselor Manpower, Salt Lake City, 1970-71; tchr. severely handicapped Davis County Schs., Farmington, Utah, 1971-73, diagnostician, 1973-74, resource elem. tchr., 1974-78; instr. Brigham Young U., Salt Lake City, 1976-83; resource tchr. jr. high Davis County Schs., Farmington, 1978—; ednl. cons., Murray, Utah, 1973—; cons. and lectr. in field. Author curriculums in spl. edn.; contbr. articles to profl. jours. Named Profl. of Yr., Utah Assn. for Children with Learning Disabilities, 1985. Mem. Assn. Children/Adults with Learning Disabilities (del. 1979-85, 87, nat. nominating com. 1985-86, nat. bd. dirs. 1988—), NEA, Nat. Assn. Female Execs., Utah Assn. Children/Adults with Learning Disabilities (exec. bd. 1978-84, profl. adv. bd. 1985—), Council Exceptional Children (div. learning disabilities, ednl. diagnostics, behavioral disorders), Utah Ednl. Assn., Davis County Edn. Assn., Council Learning Disabilities, Windstar Found., Smithsonian Found., Nat. Hist. Preservation Found., Cousteau Soc., Nat. Assn. Sch. Adminstrs. Democrat. Mormon. Lodge: Job's Daughters. Avocations: geneology research, horseback riding, sketching, crafts, reading. Home: 5212 Gravenstein Park Murray UT 84123 Office: Kaysville Jr High Sch Kaysville UT 84037

WRIGHT, GARDENIA MARCELLA CRIM, social services administrator; b. Sumter, S.C., Jan. 9, 1958; d. Manning Thomas and Ammie (Dennis) Crim; m. Donald Clyde Wright, Oct. 19, 1985. BA, Columbia (S.C.) Coll., 1978; MSW, U. Ga., 1980. Cert. social worker. Social worker N.E. Ga. Mental Health Ctr., Gainesville, 1980-81, East Cen. Ga. Mental Health Ctr., Augusta, 1981-82; exec. dir. Berry Children's Ctr., Augusta, 1982-84; social worker St. Joseph's Hosp., Augusta, 1984-85; exec. dir. Exchange Club Ctr. for Prevention Child Abuse, Augusta, 1985—; therapist Family Counseling Ctr., Augusta, 1983. Mem. Ga. Chpt. Nat. Assn. Social Workers (sec. 1986-88), Children and Youth Coalition (bd. dirs. 1987-88), Council on Child Abuse, Profl. Women's Assn., Sigma Gamma Rho. Baptist. Club: Key Women (program chair 1986-87). Home: 544 Whitehead Dr Augusta GA 30909

WRIGHT, GERALDINE HATHAWAY (JERE), public relations consultant; b. Salem, Oreg., Aug. 25, 1926; Gail A. and Mary R. (Peterson) H.; BA, U. Md., 1947; postgrad. YWCA Profl. Sch., 1950; children: Gaile Rosamond, Winfield Grant, Carter Lee. Assoc. dir. Internat. Festival of Mime, 1981; cons. United Cable TV, 1981, Fairfax Symphony Orch., 1979-81, STRAIGHT, Inc., 1981-83, Clews Comminication, 1985-86, Children's Hospice Internat.; devel. cons. Wolf Trap Found. for Performing Arts, Wolf Trap Farm Park, 1975-79; pub. relations cons. to Mrs. Jouett Shouse, founder, chmn. Wolf Trap Farm Park for the Performing Arts, 1969-72; acting dir. Fairfax County Council of the Arts, 1973-74; public relations cons. So. Rural Action, 1971-73; YWCA Teen-Age dir., Washington, 1949-54; guest lectr. arts mgmt. Am. U., Washington, 1981—. Vice pres. Fairfax County Council of the Arts, 1969-70, adv. bd., 1972-76, bd. dirs. 1981—; bd. dirs. YWCA of Fairfax County, 1960-66, program chmn. and children's theatre chmn., 1962-65; chmn. Leopold Stokowski's No. Va. Concert, 1963; v.p. Fairfax Symphony Orch., 1986; co-chmn. Community Communications Conf., Washington, 1973; chmn. No. Va. Communications Conf., 1975; bd. dirs. No. Va. Community Found., 1979-88, others; co-chmn. Internat. Children's Festival at Wolf Trap, 1983, mem. gala commn., 1986—; co-chair Women of Yr., Nat. Capital Area YWCA's, 1985; mem. Fairfax County Fair Com., 1985. Recipient Nat. Public Relations Service award Public Relations Soc. Am., 1974, Pres.'s Citation and Thoth award, 1973, Cert. of Appreciation for service Fairfax Council Council of Arts, 1974, Communications award Fairfax C. of C., 1983. Mem. ASCE (bd. trustees scholarship program), Nat. Collegiate Players, No. Va. Press Club, Capital Speakers Club, Delta Delta Delta, Alpha Psi Omega. Episcopalian. Clubs: Fairfax Symphony Assn., Wolf Trap Assn., Cosmos. Author: (with Harold M. Shaw) Smokey Bear and Ranger Hal, LP, 1970; producer; Tribute to Freedom with Senator Everett M. Dirksen, 1972; lyricist, author, various children's stories. Address: 11060 Thrush Ridge Rd Reston VA 22090

WRIGHT, GLADYS STONE, music educator; b. Wasco, Oreg., Mar. 8, 1925; d. Murvel Stuart and Daisy Violet (Warren) Stone; m. Alfred George Wright, June 28, 1953. BS, U. Oreg., MS. Dir. bands Elmira (Oreg.) U-4 High Sch., 1948-53, Otterbein (Ind.) High Sch., 1954-61, Klondike High Sch., West Lafayette, Ind., 1962-70, Harrison High Sch., West Lafayette, 1970-84; organizer, condr. Musical Friendship Tours, Cen. Am., 1967-79; v.p., condr. U.S. Collegiate Wind Band, 1975—; bd. dirs. John Philip Sousa Found. 1984—; chmn. Sudler Cup, 1986—. Editor: Woman Conductor, 1986—; composer: marches Big Bowl and Trumpets and Tabards, 1987. Bd. dirs. N. Am. Wildlife Park, Battleground, Ind. 1985. Recipient Medal of the Order John Philip Sousa Found., 1988. Mem. Am. Bandmasters Assn., Women Band Dirs. Nat. Assn. (founding pres. 1967, sec. 1985, recipient Silver Baton 1974), Am. Sch. Band Dirs. Assn., Nat. Band Assn. (recipient citation excellence 1970), Tippecanoe Arts Fedn. (bd. dirs. 1986), Tippecanoe Fife and Drum Corps. (bd. dirs. 1984), Tau Beta Sigma (Outstanding Service to Music award 1970), Phi Beta Mu (1st hon. woman mem. 1972). Home: 344 Overlook Dr West Lafayette IN 47906

WRIGHT, HELEN KENNEDY, editor, librarian; b. Indpls., Sept. 23, 1927; d. William Henry and Ida Louise (Crosby) Kennedy; m. Samuel A. Wright, Sept. 5, 1970; 1 child, Carl F. Prince II (dec.). BA, Butler U., 1945, MS, 1950; MS, Columbia U., 1952. Reference librarian N.Y. Pub. Library, N.Y.C., 1952-53, Bklyn. Pub. Library, 1953-54; cataloger U. Utah, 1954-57; librarian Chgo. Pub. Library; asst. dir. pub. dept. ALA, Chgo., 1958-62, editor Reference Books Bull., 1962-85; asst. dir. for new product planning, pub. services, 1985-87; asst. editor ALA Yearbook, 1987—. Contbr. to Ency. of Careers, Ency. of Library and Info. Sci., New Book of Knowledge Ency., Bulletin of Bibliography, New Golden Book Encyclopedia. Mem. Phi Kappa Phi, Kappa Delta Pi, Sigma Gamma Rho. Roman Catholic. Home: 1138 W 111th St Chicago IL 60643 Office: Am Library Assn 50 E Huron Chicago IL 60611

WRIGHT, HELENE SEGAL, editor; b. Los Angeles, Jan. 31, 1955; d. Alan and Lila E. (Hambro) Segal; m. David Scott Wright, May 6, 1979. Student, Calif. State U., Fullerton, 1973-75; BA in English, U. Calif., Santa Barbara, 1978. Library asst. ABC-CLIO, Santa Barbara, 1979-80, editorial asst., 1980-81, asst. editor, 1981-83, mng. editor, 1983—. Home: 142 La Vista Grande Santa Barbara CA 93103 Office: ABC-CLIO 2040 Alameda Padre Serra Santa Barbara CA 93103

WRIGHT, JACQUELINE STUCKER, law librarian; b. Euclid, Ohio, Nov. 5, 1933; d. John H. and Betsy (Delaney) Stucker; children: Robert R., John F., David S. BA, U. Ark., 1955, MLIS, 1985; JD, U. Okla., 1973. Bar: Okla. 1974, Ark. 1978. Asst. gen. counsel Okla. Assn. Mcpl. Attys., Norman, 1974-76; law clk. Okla. Ct. Appeals, Oklahoma City, 1975-76, Ark. Supreme Ct., Little Rock, 1976-77; instr. U. Ark. Sch. Law, Little Rock, 1977-78; law clk. U.S. Dist. Ct., Little Rock, 1979; librarian Ark. Supreme Ct., Little Rock, 1979—; chair employees ins. adv. com. State of Ark., 1979—, mem., 1979—. Author: Handbook for Appellate Advocacy, 1980. Mem. Ark. Assn. Women Lawyers (treas. 1978-79, rec. sec. 1980-81, pres. 1981-82), Democrat. Episcopalian. Club: Altrusa (v.p. 1982-84) (Little Rock). Office: Supreme Ct Library Justice Bldg Little Rock AR 72201

WRIGHT, JANET H., management company executive; b. Lansing, Mich., May 5, 1936; d. Alfred E. and Olive (Woody) H.; m. Paul E. Peterson, Dec. 20, 1959 (div. Dec. 1971); Andrew, Russell, Timothy; m. Thompson T. Wright, May 12, 1973; stepchildren—Robert, William, Debra, Holly, Diane, Donna, Thompson. Ed. Mich. State U., 1954-58. Cert. expn. mgr. Engaged in radio, TV and ice show prodn. and pub. relations, 1958-73; asst. dir. convs. Profl. Photographers Am., Des Plaines, Ill., 1975-78; pres. The Wright Orgn., Inc., Des Plaines, 1978—. Officer Des Plaines Sister Cities Internat., 1983-87; active Des Plaines Econ. Devel. Commn., 1987—; rec. sec. Des Plaines Sesquicentennial, 1984-85; judge U.S. Figure Skating Assn., 1978—; mem., recording sec. DuPage Figure Skating Club, 1984-88, v.p., 1988—. Mem. Nat. Assn. Expn. Mgrs. (bd. dirs. 1985—, chpt. pres. 1983, chpt. bd. dirs. 1979-84, nat. chmn. industry and govt. relations com. 1985-88), Meeting Planners Internat., Trade Show Bur., LWV (chpt. officer), P.E.O. (organizing chpt. pres. 1962), Profl. Conv. Mgrs. Assn. Avocation: figure skating. Office: The Wright Orgn 716 Lee St Des Plaines IL 60016

WRIGHT, JEAN VERLICH, writer, public relations executive; b. McKeesport, Pa., July 5, 1950; d. Matthew Louis and Irene (Tomko) Verlich; student Bucknell U., 1968-69; B.A., U. Pitts., 1971; m. S(tanley) Wayne Wright, Sept. 29, 1979. Press sec. Com. to Re-elect President, S.W. Pa., 1972; adminstrv. asst. Pa. Rep. James B. Kelly III, 1972-73; reporter Beaver (Pa.) County Times, 1973-74; proofreader Ketchum, MacLeod & Grove, Pitts., 1975-76; community relations specialist, PPG Industries, Pitts., 1976-77, editor PPG News, 1977-79, sr. staff writer, 1979-84, communications coordinator, 1984-85; pub. relations assoc. Glass Group, 1986—. Mem. Internat. Assn. Bus. Communicators (dir. Pitts. chpt. 1981, v.p. public relations Pitts. chpt. 1982, v.p. Pitts. chpt. 1985, pres. Pitts. chpt. 1986), Aviation/Space Writers Assn., Phi Beta Kappa, Delta Zeta. Office: One PPG Pl 32 E Pittsburgh PA 15272

WRIGHT, JEANNE ELIZABETH JASON, advertising executive; b. Washington, June 24, 1934; d. Robert Stewart and Elizabeth (Gaddis) Jason; m. Benjamin Hickman Wright, Oct. 30, 1965; stepchildren: Benjamin, Deborah, David, Patricia. B.A., Radcliffe Coll., 1956; M.A., U. Chgo., 1958. Psychiat. social worker Lake County Mental Health Clinic, Gary, Ind., Psychiat. and Psychosomatic Inst., Michael Reese Hosp., Chgo., Jewish Child Care Assn., N.Y.C., 1958-70; gen. mgr. Black Media, Inc. (advt. rep. co.), N.Y.C., 1970-74; pres. Black Media, Inc. (advt. rep. co.), 1974-75, Black Resources, Inc., also pres., exec. editor Nat. Black Monitor, N.Y.C., 1975—; also syndicator weekly editorial features. Mem. planning com. First Black Power Conf., Newark, 1966, Second Black Power Conf., Phila., 1967, First Internat. Black Cultural and Bus. Expn., N.Y.C., 1971; nat. bd. dirs. Family Service Assn. Am., 1968-70; bd. dirs. Afro-Am. Family & Community Services, Inc., Chgo., 1971-75; founding council mem. Nat. Assault on Illiteracy Program, 1980—; pres. Metro-N.Y. chpt. Nat. Assn. Media Women Inc., 1986—. Recipient Pres.'s award Nat. Assn. Black Women Attys., 1977, 2d Ann. Freedom's Jour. award Journalism Students and Faculty of U. D.C. Dept. Communicative and Performing Arts, 1979; named Disting. Black Woman in Industry Nat. Council Negro Women, 1981; recipient Spl. award Beta Omicron chpt. Phi Delta Kappa, 1982. Mem. Nat. Assn. Social Workers, AAAS, Acad. Cert. Social Workers, NAACP, Nat. Assn. Media Women (Nat. Media Woman of Yr. award 1984, 86, Founders award 1986), Newswomen's Club N.Y., Inc., U. Chgo. Alumni Assn., Alpha Kappa Alpha. Democrat. Clubs: Radcliffe, Harvard (N.Y.C.). Office: 410 Central Park W Penthouse C New York NY 10025

WRIGHT, JOAN W., personnel director; b. Houma, La., Mar. 18, 1943; d. Purl P. and Almeda (Chitwood) Berger; m. Jess W. Wright, Sept. 17, 1961 (div.); children: Jason T., Lance A.; m. Kelly F. Rice, Dec. 28, 1984. Student, Wichita State U., Boise State U. Personnel specialist U.S. Postal Service, Wichita, Kans., 1962-72; supr. employment and services U.S. Postal Service, Boise, Idaho, 1972—; owner Town & Country, Boise, 1983—. Owner, sec.-treas. Sports Rev. Mem. Garden Club, Nampa, Idaho, 1981-82; vol. Big Bro./Big Sister, 1980-82. Mem. Nat. Assn. Female Execs., Profl. Sec. Assn. Club: Toastmasters. Home: 1723 Jackson Boise ID 83705

WRIGHT, JOSEPHINE ROSA BEATRICE, musicologist; b. Detroit, Sept. 5, 1942; d. Joseph Le Vander and Eva Lee Garrison W.; Mus.B., U. Mo., Columbia, 1963, M.A., 1967; Mus.M., Pius XII Acad., Florence, Italy, 1964; Ph.D., N.Y.U., 1975. Instr. music York Coll., CUNY, 1972-75, asst. prof., 1975; asst. prof. Afro-Am. studies in musicology Harvard U., Cambridge, Mass., 1976-81; asso. dir. integration of Afro-Am. folk arts with music project, Nat. Endowment Humanities, 1979-82; assoc. prof. music Coll. of Wooster, 1981—; interim chair black studies, 1988—; panelist, cons. on music Mass. Council of Arts and Humanities, 1978-80; cons. Nat. Endowment Humanities, 1982-83, 87, Ohio Humanities Council, 1986. Mem. AAUW, Am. Musicol. Soc., Internat. Musicol. Assn., Coll. Music Soc., Assn. for Study of Afro-Am. Life and History, Sonneck Soc., U. Mo. Faculty of Arts and Sci. Alumni Assn. (trustee 1982-85), Pi Kappa Lambda. Democrat. Episcopalian (vestry). Author: Ignatius Sancho (1729-1780), An Early African Composer in England: The Collected Edition of His Music in Facsimile, 1981; editor of new music: The Black Perspective in Music, 1979—; co-editor: The Bicentennial Issue of The Black Perspective in Music, 1976. Contbr. articles to profl. jours. Office: Coll Wooster Dept Music Wooster OH 44691

WRIGHT, JOYCE LOUISE, lawyer; b. Boston, June 28, 1947; d. Louis Elwin Wright Jr. and M. Shirley (Joyce) Benttinen; m. John Ernest Toffling Jr., June 22, 1968 (div. Sept. 1979); children: Kristen Wright, Jamie Beth. BA with highest distinction, U. Maine, 1968; JD, U. Md., 1982. Bar: Md. 1982. Spl. research analyst Dept. Def., Ft. Meade, Md., 1968-72; personnel analyst Anne Arundel County, Annapolis, Md., 1978, tng. dir., 1978-79; community resources coordinator, assoc. commr. Anne Arundel County Commn. for Women, Edgewater, Md., 1979; computer programmer, research analyst Adminstrv. Office of Cts., Annapolis, 1979-81; law clk. State's Atty. Juvenile Cts., Balt., 1981-82, asst. state's atty., 1982-86, dep. div. chief, 1986—. Mem. Citizens' Adv. Group to Howard County Sch. Bd., Md., 1985—; exec. bd. Running Brook Elem. Sch. PTA, Columbia, Md., 1985—, Wilde Lake High Sch. PTA, 1986—; mem. exec. bd. Ruunning Brook, 1985-87; vice chmn. Citizens Adv. Group, 1987—. Invited to participate as Maine del. Model United Nations, 1968. Mem. Phi Beta Kappa, Phi Kappa Phi, Pi Sigma Alpha. Democrat. Home: 5054 Whetstone Rd Columbia MD 21044 Office: Office of State's Atty Suite 300 Clarence Mitchell Jr Ct House Baltimore MD 21202

WRIGHT, JUDITH MITCHELL, management consultant; b. Balt.; d. John Armitage and Mary (Bowen) Mitchell; R.N., Church Home and Hosp. Sch. Nursing, 1970; m. Harold Russell Wright, Jr., Aug. 15, 1970; children—Alexander Bowen, Morgan du Val Watkins Team leader Good Samaritan Hosp., Balt., 1970-73; patient care coordinator Keswick Home for Incurables, Balt., 1974-76; owner, pres. The Wright Group. Co chmn. Druid Hill tennis project Jr. League Balt., 1977, 78, bd. dirs., 1980-84, asst. treas., 1982-83, treas., 1983-84, also mem. exec. bd.; chmn. security Balt. Internat. Indoor Tennis Championships, 1978; co-chmn. ops. 1st Nat. Grand Prix Tennis Classic, 1979, chmn. ops., 1980, asst. chmn., 1981; com. chmn. Troop 500, Boy Scouts Am., 1985-86; v.p. Brooke Army Med. Ctr. Women's Aux., 1985-86. Republican. Episcopalian. Club: Woman's of Roland Park (pres. jr. dept. 1982-83, bd. govs. 1982-84). Home and Office: 510 Hampton Ln Baltimore MD 21204

WRIGHT, JUDITH RAE, accountant; b. Paoli, Ind., Feb. 16, 1929; d. Samuel Earl and Bernice Louise (Lomax) Hudelson; m. James Edward Walters, July 11, 1947 (div. June 1971); children—Jamie Jo, Jennifer Rae; m. 2d, George Ralph Wright, Feb. 20, 1972 (dec. Apr. 1977). Student Northwood Inst., West Baden, Ind., 1968-69, Ind.-U.-Purdue U., Indpls., 1973-74. Acct., Ind. Hwy. Commn., Indpls., 1969-75, Ind. Dept. Correction, Indpls., 1975-76, Ind. Dept. Pub. Welfare, Indpls., 1976-78, Ind. Office Social Services, Indpls., 1978-79; acct. supr. Ind. Dept. Pub. Welfare, Indpls., 1979-84. Mem. Assn. Govt. Accts., Am. Legion Aux., Kappa Kappa Kappa. Republican. Mem. Christian Ch. Office: Ind Dept Pub Welfare 100 N Senate Ave Rm 708 Indianapolis IN 46204

WRIGHT, KAREN MARQUERITE, production engineer, mechanical engineer technologist; b. Iserlohm, Germany, Feb. 7, 1964; came to Can., 1966; d. John Bernard and Margaret Anne (Odell) Dutton; m. Robert Jeffrey Wright, July 12, 1986. Diploma in Mech. Engring. Tech., St. Lawrence Coll., Kingston, Ont., 1984. Research asst. Royal Mil. Coll., Kingston, 1984; lab technician Cen. Wire Industries Ltd., Perth, Ont., 1984-85; prodn. engr. Lisi Aero-Guide Inc., Smiths Falls, Ont., 1985—. Mem. Ont. Assn. Cert. Engring. Technicians and Technologists. Home: Box 527 RR 5, Perth Can K7H 3C7 Office: Lisi Aero-Guide Inc, PO Box 861, 2 Air Care Dr, Smith Falls Can K7A 4W7

WRIGHT, KATIE HARPER, educational administrator, journalist; b. Crawfordsville, Ark., Oct. 5, 1923; d. James Hale and Connie Mary (Locke) Harper; B.A., U. Ill., 1944; M.Ed., 1959; Ed.D., St. Louis U., 1979; m. Marvin Wright, Mar. 21, 1952; 1 dau., Virginia K. Jordan. Elem. and spl. edn. tchr. East St. Louis (Ill.) Pub. Schs., 1944-65, dir. Dist. 189 Instructional Materials Program, 1965-71, dir. spl. edn. Dists. 188, 189, 1971-77, asst. supt. programs, 1977-79; adj. faculty Harris/Stowe State Coll., 1980; cons. to numerous workshops, seminars in field; mem. study tour People's Republic of China, 1984. Mem. Ill. Commn. on Children, 1973-85, East St. Louis Bd. Election Commrs.; pres. bd. dirs. St. Clair County Mental Health Center, 1970-72, 87—; bd. dirs. River Bluff council Girl Scouts, 1979—, nat. bd. dirs., 1981-84; bd. dirs. United Way, 1979—, Urban League, 1979—; pres. bd. trustees East St. Louis Pub. Library, 1972-77; pres., bd. dirs. St. Clair County Mental Health Ctrs., 1987; adv. bd. Landmark Bank; charter mem. Coalition of 100 Black Women; mem. coordinating council ethnic affairs Synod of Mid-Am., Presbyn. Ch. U.S.A; charter mem. Metro East Links Group; charter mem. Gateway chpt. The Links, Inc. Recipient Lamp of Learning award East St. Louis Jr. Wednesday Club, 1965, Journalist award Sigma Gamma Rho, 1986; named woman of the yr. in edn. St. Clair County YWCA, 1987; Outstanding Working Woman award Downtown St. Louis, Inc., 1967; Ill. State citation for ednl. document Love is Not Enough, 1974; Delta Sigma Theta citation for document Good Works, 1979; award Nat. Council Negro Women, 1983; Girl Scout Thanks badge, 1982; Community Service award Met. East Bar Assn., 1983; named Woman of Achievement, St. Louis Globe Democrat, 1974, Outstanding Adminstr. So. region Ill. Office Edn., 1975, named Woman of Yr. in Edn. St. Clair County YWCA, 1987. Mem. Am. Libraries Trustees Assn. (regional v.p. 1978-79, nat. sec. 1979-80), Ill. Commn. on Children, Mensa, Council for Exceptional Children, Top Ladies of Distinction (pres. 1987—), Delta Sigma Theta (chpt. pres. 1960-62), Kappa Delta Pi (pres. So. Ill. U. chpt. 1973-74), Phi Delta Kappa (Service Key award 1984, chpt. pres. 1984-85), Iota Phi Lambda, Pi Lambda Theta (chpt. pres. 1985—). Republican. Presbyterian. Club: East St. Louis Women's (pres. 1973-75). Contbr. articles to profl. jours.; feature writer St. Louis Argus Newspaper, 1979—. Home: 733 N 40th St East Saint Louis IL 62205

WRIGHT, KAY MORROW, computer educator; b. Baytown, Tex., Sept. 28, 1942; d. Morris Robinson and Martha (Whiteman) Morrow; m. Terry Frank Wright, June 4, 1966; children—Stephanie Lynn, Stacie Cole. BA in Math., U. Tex., 1964. Programmer, Bankers Life, Des Moines, 1966-68; programmer analyst Enjay Fibers and Laminates Co., Odenton, Md., 1968-69; dir. data processing Mercy Hosp. Med. Ctr., 1975-78, planning coordinator, 1978-79, computer planning coordinator, 1979-81, systems cons., 1981-82; mktg. assoc. XL-DP, Inc., Des Moines, 1982-84; instr. Coll. Bus. Adminstrn., Drake U., Des Moines, 1984—. Bd. dirs. Iowa Soc. To Prevent Blindness, 1977-83, Mercy Hosp. Credit Union, 1978-80; benefit chmn. Flip for Sight, 1977-81. Mem. Data Processing Mgmt. Assn., Iowa Health Computer Assn. (founding pres. 1978-79), Electronic Computing Health Oriented, Province Alumnae Iowa, Wis. (bd. dirs. 1979-84), League Attys. Wives, Delta Zeta (nat. networking chmn. 1984-86), Delta Sigma Pi (faculty advisor 1987—, Prof. of Yr. 1985-86). Democrat. Methodist. Office: Drake U 351 Aliber Hall Des Moines IA 50311

WRIGHT, LAURALI R. (BUNNY), writer; b. Saskatoon, Sask., Can., June 5, 1939; d. Sidney Victor and Evelyn Jane (Barber) Appleby; m. John Herbert, Jan. 6, 1962 (separated 1985); children: Victoria Kathleen, Johnna Margaret. Student, U. B.C., Carleton U., Banff Sch. Fine Arts, U. Calgary. Journalist The Calgary Herald, 1968-77; freelance writer Calgary, 1977—. Author: (novels) Neighbors, 1979 (Alta. Novelist award 1978), The Favorite, 1982, Among Friends, 1984, The Suspect, 1985 (Edgar Allan Poe Best Novel award Mystery Writers of Am. 1986), Sleep While I Sing, 1986, Love in the Temperate Zone, 1987. Mem. Writers Union Can., Authors' Guild of U.S. Office: care Viking Penguin Inc 40 W 23rd St New York NY 10010 *

WRIGHT, LILYAN BOYD, educator; b. Upland, Pa., May 11, 1920; d. Albert Verlenden and Mabel (Warburton) Boyd; B.S., Temple U., 1942, M.Ed., 1946; Ed.D., Rutgers U., 1972; m. Richard P. Wright, Oct. 23, 1942; 1 dau., Nicki Warburton (Mrs. Arthur Scott Vanek). Tchr. health and phys. edn. Woodbury (N.J.) High Sch., 1942-43, Glen-Nor High Sch., Glenolden, Pa., 1944-46, Chester (Pa.) High Sch., 1946-54; chmn. women's dept. health and phys. edn. Union (N.J.) High Sch., 1954-61; with Trenton State Coll., 1961—, head women's program health and phys. edn., 1967-77, chmn. dept. health, phys. edn. and recreation, 1977-86; mem. N.J. State Com. Div. Girls and Women's Sports, 1958-80; chmn. New Atlantic Field Hockey Sectional Umpiring, 1981-85; chmn. New Atlantic Field Hockey Assn., 1985—. Active Chester United Fund; water safety, first aid instr. ARC Scholarship in her honor N.J. Athletic Assn. Girls, 1971; named to Hall of Fame, Temple U., 1976. Mem. AAHPER (chmn. Eastern dist. assn. div. girls and women's sports, sec. to council for services Eastern dist. 1979-80, chmn. 1980-81, N.J. rep. to council for convs. 1984-85, Honor Fellow award 1986), N.J. AHPER (pres. 1974-75, past pres. 1975-76, v.p. phys. edn. div., Disting. Service and Leadership award 1969, Honor Fellow award 1977), N.J. Women's Lacrosse Assn. (umpiring chmn. 1972-76), Nat. Assn. Phys. Edn. in Higher Edn., Eastern Assn. Phys. Edn. Coll. Women, AAUP, North Jersey, Central Jersey bds. women's ofcls., Am., Pa. (v.p. 1953-54), Chester (pres. 1949-54) fedns. tchrs., U.S. (exec. com.), North Jersey (past pres.) field hockey assns., Kappa Delta Epsilon, Delta Psi Kappa (past pres. Phila. alumni chpt.), Kappa Delta Pi. Episcopalian (vestry St. Luke's Episc. Ch. 1988—). Home: 260 Green Valley Rd Langhorne PA 19047 Office: Trenton State Coll Trenton NJ 08650

WRIGHT, LINDA ANN, brewing company executive; b. Monte Vista, Colo., Mar. 12, 1954; d. Robert E. and Mary Ann (Ress) W.; divorced. BS in Microbiology, Colo. State U., 1977; postgrad., Wake Forest U., 1988—. Asst. mgr. NAFPA, Lincoln, Nebr., 1978-80; lab. mgr. Colo. Agro-Energy Inc., Monte Vista, 1980-82; brewing supr. Strohs Brewing Co., Winston-Salem, N.C., 1983—; cons. NAFPA, 1978-80. Mem. Nat. Assn. Female Execs., Am. Soc. Brewing Co., Am. Soc. Brewing Chemists, Master Brewers Am. Assn., MBA Assn., DAR (asst. regent 1982). Club: Ski (Winston-Salem). Home: 4328 Maranda Rd Winston-Salem NC 27107 Office: Strohs Brewery Barnes Rd Winston-Salem NC 27284

WRIGHT, LINDA DIANE, stockbroker; b. Toledo, May 6, 1948; d. Horace Osband and Peggy Joanne (Perkins) Loomis; m. Sammy Ross Dewyer, Feb. 24, 1968 (div. Apr. 1976); children: Jayme, Jeremy; m. C. Thomas Wright, July 30, 1977; 1 child, Christopher. Student, Bowling Green State U., 1966-67, Kent State U., 1971; grad., Investment Tng. Inst., Atlanta, 1979. Teller Mid-Am. Bank & Trust Co., Bowling Green, Ohio, 1966-71; br. mgr., loan officer Huntington Bank Inc., Bowling Green, 1971-78; rep. Ohio Co., Clearwater, Fla., 1979-82, Raymond, James & Assocs., St. Petersburg, Fla., 1982-84; fin. cons. Cert. Fin. Services, Tampa, Fla., 1984-86; investment exec. Pamco Securities and Ins. Services, St. Petersburg, 1986-88; sr. fin. cons. Integrated Resources Equity Corp., Clearwater, 1988—. Mem. adv. bd. Women's Ctr. of Morton Plant Hosp., Clearwater, 1987. Mem. Nat. Assn. for Profl. Saleswomen, Am. Bus. Women's Assn. Republican. Club: Stock and Bond (St. Petersburg). Home: 3860 Anglers Ln Largo FL 34644 Office: Integrated Resources Equity Corp 2900 US 19 N Suite #102 Clearwater FL 34623

WRIGHT, LINDA JEAN, banker; b. Chgo., Dec. 14, 1949; d. Eugene P. and Rosemary Margaret (Kiley) Kemph; student Loretto Heights Coll., 1967-69, U. Ill.-Urbana, 1970-71; m. Kelly W. Wright, Jr., Feb. 1979 (div. 1984); m. Samuel Neuwirth Klewans, Aug. 28, 1986. Asst. to v.p. Busey 1st Nat. Bank, Urbana, 1969-72; spa mgr., supr. sales tng. Venus and Apollo Health Club, San Antonio, 1973-76; owner Plant Shop, San Antonio, 1976-

77; with Enterprise Bank, Falls Church, Va., 1977-84, comml. lending officer, 1978-84, sr. v.p., 1979-84, corp. sec. of bd. dirs., 1980-84; pres., chief exec. officer Fairfax Savs. Bank, 1984-87; pres., chief exec. officer Bank 2000 of Reston, N.A., 1988— Apptd. pub. official State of Va. Chmn. exec. com. Fairfax-Falls Ch. United Way, United Way Capital Area, Washington, 1984-85; Fairfax County Spl. Task Force, 1986; mem. Fairfax Com. of 100, 1987; mem., bd. dirs. Hospice No. Va., Arlington, 1985-86, chmn. No. Va. Local Devel. Corp., Va. Small Bus. Fin. Authority, Richmond, 1984—; mem. operating bd. Fairfax Hosp., 1987—; pres. No. Va. Transp. Alliance, 1987—. Mem. Fairfax County C. of C. (dir., v.p., pres. 1987—), Nat. Assn. Bank Women (chmn. No. Va. group 1980-81). Roman Catholic. Club: Fairfax Hunt. Avocations: aviation, fox hunting.

WRIGHT, MARGARET ADA BENNETT, business executive; b. Camden, N.J., Dec. 20, 1918; d. John Henry and Margaret Catherine (Blossom) Bennett. B.S., Glassboro State Coll., 1940; M.A., St. Mary's U., 1970; Ph.D., U. Tex., 1976. Cert. elem., secondary tchr., N.J., Tex.; lic. profl. counselor, Tex.; nat. cert. counselor. Tchr. elem. and secondary schs., N.J., 1940-42, 46-48, Tex., 1966-70; adminstr. Student Aid Library and Counseling Ctr., Minnie Stevens Piper Found., San Antonio, 1970-73; counselor Incarnate Word Coll., San Antonio, 1974-75; exec. dir. Tex. Personnel and Guidance Assn., Austin, 1976-79; pres. New Outlook Inc., 1979-86; asst. prof. dept. counseling and human services Grad. Sch., St. Mary's U., 1981-85; producer/dir. ann. conf. Women of 80's, 1980-82. Editor, mng. editor counselor's newsletters and profl. jours. Contbr. articles to profl. jours. Author: Programs Emphasizing Positive Personal Development, 1981. Editor newsletter Women in Bus. Active grad. com. instl. self-study St. Mary's U., 1970-72; bd. dirs. St. Mary's Alumni Assn., 1974-77, Las Palmas YWCA, San Antonio, 1982-84, San Antonio Women's Law Ctr., 1974-78, pres. 1978. Served with USNR (WAVES), 1942-46. Mem. Am. Assn. Counseling and Devel. Republican. Episcopalian. Home: PO Box 29221 San Antonio TX 78229

WRIGHT, MARGARET TAYLOR, marketing consultant; b. Wilmington, N.C., Nov. 8, 1949; d. Thomas Henry Jr. and Margaret (Taylor) W. BA, U. N.C., 1972; MBA, Wake Forest U., 1978. Specialist child advocacy Dept. Human Resources Child Advocacy Council, Raleigh, N.C., 1973-74; dir. region Dept. Human Resources N.C. Office Children, Winston-Salem, 1974-76; asst. mgr., then mgr. brand Food Div. Am. Home Products, N.Y.C., 1978-80; mgr. brand C.F. Mueller Div. Mueller Pasta Foremost McKesson, Jersey City, 1981-83; mgr. brand, new products Popsicle Div. Sara Lee Corp., Englewood, N.J., 1983-86; sr. mgr. product, new products and acquisitions Am. Home Food Products Corp., N.Y.C., 1986-87; pres. Wright Mktg. Blueprint, N.Y.C., 1987—. Youth chmn., campaign com. Holshouser for Gov. Campaign, Wilmington, N.C., 1972; mem. N.C. Jr. League, N.Y.C. Jr. League. Mem. Am. Mktg. Assn., Colonial Dames Soc. Republican. Episcopalian. Club: Princeton. Home: 400 E 54th St New York City NY 10022

WRIGHT, MARY RUTH (MRS. WILLIAM KEMP WRIGHT), psychologist; b. St. Louis, Apr. 2, 1922; d. Leon Carl and Gwendolyn (Travis) Brown; R.N., Washington U., St. Louis, 1944; B.S., U. Houston, 1966, M.A., 1967; Ph.D., Union Grad. Sch., 1978; m. William Kemp Wright, Feb. 10, 1945; children—Gwendolyn, Veronica, Victoria, Jennifer. Instr. surgery Washington U. Sch. Nursing, 1944-45, U.S. Cadet Nurse Corps, USPHS, 1944; instr. pediatrics Children's Meml. Hosp., Chgo., 1945-46; teaching fellow U. Houston, 1965-66; instr. S. Tex. Jr. Coll., Houston, 1967-70; mental health cons. St. Joseph Mental Hosp., Houston, 1966-67; staff psychol. services Almeda Clinic, Houston, 1966-70; pvt. practice marriage and family counselor, Houston, 1970—; med.-psychol. researcher and writer, 1970—; psychologist Vasectomy Clinic, Houston Dept. Health, 1971—; clin. asst. prof. psychology, dept. otorhinolaryngology and communicative scis. Baylor Coll. Medicine, Houston, 1979. Recipient spl. award Security Agy., 1945. Mem. Am. Psychol. Assn., Am. Assn. Marriage and Family Counselors, Am. Assn. Sex Educators and Counselors, Internat. Council Psychologists, Nat. Council Family Relations, Nat. Assn. Social Workers, Mental Health Assn. Houston and Harris County (dir.). Contbr. articles to profl. jours. Home: 3671 Del Monte St Houston TX 77019 Office: 4200 Westheimer Suite 160 Houston TX 77027

WRIGHT, MORGAN MISCHAUNE HAMMARSKJÖLD, banker; b. Rochester, Minn., Aug. 13, 1961; d. Richard William and Avis Iris (Sutherland) W. Student, Winona (Minn.) State U., 1979-81; BS in Physics, U. Minn., 1984, AA in Physiology/Psychology, 1984. Lic. securities profl., Minn.; lic. ins. profl., Minn. Elec. engr. asst. Protronix, Inc., Mpls., 1983-84; with trading desk/research asst. Dougherty, Dawkins, Strand & Yost, Inc., Mpls., 1984-85; stockbroker John Kinnard, Inc., Mpls., 1986-87; registered rep. Midwest Fed. Bank, Mpls., 1987-88, First Bank of Mpls., 1988—; instr. fin. Mpls. Community Coll., 1987—, Inver Hills Community Coll., Inver Grove, Minn., 1987—, Normandale Community Coll., Edina, Minn., 1987 . Mem. Am. Swedish Inst. Republican. Office: First Bank Mpls 120 S 6th St Minneapolis MN 55402

WRIGHT, NADINE ANOHIN, data processing executive; b. Harbin, Hailongjiang, Peoples Rep. China, Sept. 30, 1945; came to U.S., 1960; d. Feoran Firsovitch and Tamara Viacheslavouna (Firsova) Anohin; m. Harry Franklin Wright, Nov. 22, 1978; children: Adrian Christopher, Devon Brhett. AA, City Coll. San Francisco, 1966; diplomas in French and internat. econs., U. Strasbourg, France, 1967, 69; BA, San Francisco State U., 1972, MBA, 1976. Programmer, auditor electronic and data processing Bechtel Corp., San Francisco, 1973-76; specialist electronic data processing Levi Strauss and Co., Frankfurt, Brussels, 1976-78; chief analyst/tech. advisor Calif. State Automobile Assn., San Francisco, 1978-79; supr. electronic data processing audit Crocker Bank, San Francisco, 1979-80, Ampex Corp., Redwood City, Calif., 1980-81; sr. staff analyst, sr. electronic data processing auditor Safeway Stores Corp., Oakland, Calif., 1981-86; cons. Breuners Inc., San Ramon, Calif., 1987—, Bay Area Remodeling and Construction, San Francisco, 1987—; systems engr. IBM Corp., San Francisco 1972-73. Chmn. Community Chest VFW, San Francisco, 1965. Mem. Inst. Internal Auditors (bd. dirs. 1987—, chmn. electronic data processing audit 1983-84), Nat. Assn. Accts. (scholarship com. 1982-83), Electronic Data Processing Auditor Assn. Democrat.

WRIGHT, NANCY HOWELL, interior designer; b. Detroit, Sept. 6, 1932; d. David Austin and Catherine (Bradley) Howell; BFA Ohio Wesleyan U.; student Parsons Sch. Design, 1977; m. Hastings Kemper Wright, June 19, 1954; children—Mark, Kenneth, Barbara, Donald. Interior decorator Country Manor of Branford (Conn.), 1971-75, design mgr., 1976—. Sec. Branford Art League, 1977; chmn. Harrison House Hist. House, Branford, Conn., 1983-84. Allied mem. Am. Soc. Interior Designers (award for best Conn. retail store design, 1980); mem. Delta Phi Delta. Republican. Episcopalian. Home: 35 Wood Rd Branford CT 06405 Office: 312 E Main St Branford CT 06405

WRIGHT, PAMELA CAROL, marketing executive; b. Trenton, N.J., July 8, 1952; d. Harold F. and Mildred D. (Reichent) W.; m. Michael S. Toorock, June 20, 1987. Certificat, University Dijon, France, 1973; BA, Otterbein Coll., 1974. Mgr. Voyager Travel, Lawrenceville, N.J., 1974-78; staff v.p. sales and membership The Am. Soc. Travel Agts., Washington, 1978-84; staff v.p. market devel. The Hertz Corp., N.Y.C., 1984—. Home: 333 E 66th St New York NY 10021

WRIGHT, PAMELA MARIE, banker; b. New Albany, Ind., Mar. 2, 1954. BS in Bus., Ind. U., 1976; MBA, Bellarmine Coll., 1980. Lic. assoc. realtor, Fla. Asst. to dir. fin. CSX Transp., Jacksonville, Fla., 1977-85; assoc. realtor Century 21 Real Estate, Jacksonville, Fla., 1985-86; mortgage adminstr. Mortgage Funding Services, Jacksonville, Fla., 1986-87; ops. analyst Barnett Bank, Jacksonville, 1987—. Mem. supervisory com. Credit Union, Jacksonville, 1984, 87. Mem. Fla. Assn. Realtors, Nat. Assn. Realtors, Jacksonville Bd. Realtors. Roman Catholic. Home: 2544 Ebersol Rd Jacksonville FL 32216

WRIGHT, PATRICIA, state legislator; b. South Bend, Ind., Feb. 28, 1931; m. Paul J. Wright, 1951; children: Timothy, Patrick M. Mem. Ariz. State Senate. Republican. Home: 5818 W Northern Ave Glendale AZ 85302 Office: Office of the State Senate State Capitol Phoenix AZ 85007 *

WRIGHT, PAULA CHRISTINE, educator; b. Cleve., Jan. 2, 1955; d. Paul R. and Gertrude R. (Christman) W. A.B. in French, John Carroll U., 1978, postgrad in edn., 1980—; postgrad. Cleve. Music Sch. Settlement. French and Spanish tchr. Glen Oak Sch. for Girls, Gates Mills, Ohio, 1978-79, Upward Bound Project, Case Western Res. U., Cleve., 1980—, Kirk Middle Sch., East Cleveland, Ohio, 1980-81, Shaw High Sch., East Cleve., 1981-84, Shaker Heights High Sch., Ohio, 1984-85; Midwest del. Fgn. Lang. Tchrs. Inst., NEH, Purdue U., summer 1985; contralto Duffy Liturgical Dance Ensemble, 1985—; owner Booties by Paula, 1987—. Recipient excellence in teaching award Case Western Res. U., 1983; named Tchr. of Yr., Univ. Project Upward Bound, 1984. Vice-pres., treas. St. Dominic Choir, 1984-85. Democrat. Roman Catholic. Club: Fortuna Investment II (treas 1976-83) (Cleve.). Avocations: reading, needlework, singing. Office: 15911 Aldersyde Rd Shaker Heights OH 44120

WRIGHT, PHALA MURRAY, health science association administrator; b. Natchez, Miss., Aug. 5, 1942; d. Therrell Chamberlain Sr. and Phala (Cavin) Murray; m. Gerald Allen Green, July 17, 1960 (div. Apr. 1967); children: Kelly Green Taylor, Karen Green Gregg; m. George William Wright, Jr., May 1971. Student, N.E. La. U., 1967-69. Legal sec. Spencer & Spencer, El Dorado, Ark., 1965-67; exec. sec. Quachita Nat. Bank, Monroe, La., 1967-71; dir. Quachita Med. Soc., Monroe, La., 1981—. Contbr. articles to profl. jours. Bd. dirs. Silver Waters Girl Scout Council, Monroe, 1978-85, Health Care Coalition, Monroe, West Monroe, 1986—; bd. dirs., sec. Quachita Council on Aging, Monroe 1986—; cons. La. Med. Polit. Action com., Baton Rouge, 1985-87; organizer Northeast La. Ladies Tennis League, Monroe 1978-79. Mem. Quachita Med. Soc. Aux. (pres. 1978-79), La. State Med. Soc. Aux. (pres. 1985-86), La. State Med. Soc. (pub. relations com. 1985—), Am. Med. Writers Assn., AMA Aux. Democrat. Episcopalian. Club: So. Investors of Monroe (portfolio mgr. 1987, v.p.). Home: 2702 Birchwood Dr Monroe LA 71201 Office: Quachita Med Soc Inc PO Box 2884 Monroe LA 71201

WRIGHT, RITA CECILIA, nurse; b. Grundy, Va., Aug. 20, 1942; d. John Kinzer and Lois (Pruett) Crawford; m. John P. Frankenburg (div. Oct. 1970); 1 child, John; m. Edward B. Wright III. BEd, U. Toledo, 1977. RN. Health occupations instrn. Whitmer High Sch., Toledo, Ohio, 1974-76; health occupations coordinator Sylvania Northview High Sch., Toledo, 1974-80; realtor Century 21, Toledo, 1980-81; admitting mgr. Flower Hosp., Sylvania, Ohio, 1981-85; med. adminstr. NW Physicians Health Maintenance Orgn., Sylvania, 1985-87; asst. clin. mgr. The Toledo Hosp., 1987—; pres. Health Orgns. Ohio, 1978-79. Mem. Toledo Exec. Network, Toledo Hosp. Alumni Assn. Lutheran. Home: 5365 Silica Sylvania OH 43560 Office: The Toledo Hosp N Cove Blvd Toledo OH 43606

WRIGHT, ROSALIE MULLER, newspaper and magazine editor; b. Newark, June 20, 1942; d. Charles and Angela (Fortunata) Muller; m. Lynn Wright, Jan. 13, 1962; children: James Anthony Meador, Geoffrey Shepard. B.A. in English, Temple U., 1965. Mng. editor Suburban Life mag., Orange, N.J., 1960-62; assoc. editor Phila. mag., 1962-64, mng. editor, 1969-73; founding editor Womensports mag., San Mateo, Calif., 1973-75; editor scene sect. San Francisco Examiner, 1975-77; exec. editor New West mag., San Francisco and Beverly Hills, Calif., 1977-81; features and Sunday editor San Francisco Chronicle, 1981-87, asst. mng. editor features, 1987—; tchr. mag. writing U. Calif.-Berkeley, 1975-76; participant pub. procedure's course Stanford U., 1977-79; chmn. mag. judges Council Advancement and Support Edn. Conf., 1980, judge, 1984. Contbr. numerous mag. articles, critiques, revs., Compton's Ency. Mem. Am. Assn. Sunday and Feature Editors (treas. 1984, sec. 1985, 1st v.p. 1986, pres. 1987). Office: Chronicle Pub Co 901 Mission St San Francisco CA 94119

WRIGHT, SANDRA ELEANOR, university administrator; b. Chgo., Aug. 8, 1946; d. Earl Walter (dec.) and Helen Erna (Flick) Hallgren; m. John Lewis Wright, Aug. 23, 1969; 1 child, Zachary Charles. BA with highest honors, Ill. Coll., 1967; MA, U. Ill., 1968, Sangamon State U., 1971; PhD, Bowling Green State U., 1980. Dir. ctr. continued learning Bowling Green (Ohio) State U., 1974-76, assoc. dir. continuing edn/, 1976-78; dir. continuing edn. Eastern Mich. U., Ypsilanti, 1978-81, dir. internat. studies, 1979-85; devel. dir. U. Mich., Dearborn, 1986—; vis. lectr. Sch. Bus. Eastern Mich. U., 1981-83; instr. English U. Toledo, 1972-73, Lincoln Land Community Coll., Springfield, Ill, 1968-70, instr. experimental studies Bowling Green State U., 1974; ptnr. Change Assoc., Bowling Green, 1986—. Contbr. articles to profl. jours. Mem. Nat. Univ. Continuing Edn. (treas. region IV 1984-86), Council Advancement and Support of Edn., Nat. Soc. Fund Raising Execs. (exec. bd. Mich. chpt. 1987—, editor newsletter 1987), Phi Beta Kappa. Office: U Mich 4901 Evergreen Rd Dearborn MI 48128

WRIGHT, SHIRLEY, organizational consultant; b. Tyler, Tex., June 30, 1943; d. James Benton Payne and Helen Ann (Henley) Payne; m. James Claud Wright, Aug. 31, 1962; Tamorah Ann, Deborah Dawn, Kimorah Kai. BS in Edn., Cen. State U., 1967. Owner, pres. The Organizing Touch, Inc., Edmoond, 1983—. vol. chairperson food cupboard Hope Community Ctr., Edmond, 1984-86; v.p. Performing Arts Council of Edmond, 1985-86. Named Spl. Samaritan Hope Ctr., Edmond, 1986. MEM. Nat. Assn. Female Execs., Edmond C. of C. Republican. Methodist. Clubs: ZTA Parents, Edmond Womens (named spl. community vol. 1986), Nightingales Homemaker (1986-87). Home: 1908 Whipporwill Ct Edmond OK 73013 Office: The Organizing Touch Inc PO Box 994 Edmond OK 73083

WRIGHT, SUSAN KLEIN, hospital administrator, nurse; b. Kearny, N.J., Dec. 24, 1941; d. Ivan John Klein and Winnie (Glancy) Klein Cheasley; m. Robert Francis Wright, Oct. 20, 1962 (div. 1983); children: Daniel Martin, Jennifer Nicole. Diploma in Nursing, John Hopkins U., 1962, BS, 1987, postgrad., 1987—. RN, Md. Staff nurse gen. operating room John Hopkins Hosp., Balt., 1962-63; staff nurse operating room Peninsula Gen. Hosp., Salisbury, Md., 1963-64; staff nurse pediatrics Anne Arundel Gen. Hosp., Annapolis, Md., 1970-72; staff nurse hemopheresis John Hopkins Oncology Ctr., Balt., 1972-74, supr. hemopheresis, 1974-79, mgr. hemopheresis, 1979—; cons. City of Hope Hosp., Duarte, Calif., 1980, Travenol Labs., Deerfield, Ill., 1981-83, Med. Coll. U. S.C., Charleston, 1987. Author: (with others) Fundamentals of A Pheresis Program, 1979, Experimental Hematology Today, 1979, Therapeutic Hemopheresis, 1984, Transfusion Therapy, 1985. Mem. Soc. Hemopheresis Specialists (founder 1979, 1st pres. 1979-81, bd. dirs. 1981-84, chmn. program com. 1981-85, cert. com. 1984—), Am. Assn. Blood Banks (pheresis com. 1979-85), Hopkins U. Nurses Alumni (nominating com. 1977). office: John Hopkins Oncology Ctr 600 N Wolfe St Baltimore MD 21205

WRIGHT, SUSAN WEBBER, law educator; b. Texarkana, Ark., Aug. 22, 1948; d. Thomas Edward and Betty Jane (Gary) Webber; m. Robert Ross Wright, III, May 21, 1983; 1 child, Robin Elizabeth. BA, Randolph-Macon Woman's Coll., 1970; MPA, U. Ark., 1972, JD with high honors, 1975. Bar: Ark. 1975. Law clk. U.S. Ct. Appeals 8th Circuit, 1975-76; asst. prof. law U. Ark.-Little Rock, 1976-78, assoc. prof., 1978-83, prof., 1983—, asst. dean, 1976-78; vis. assoc. prof. Ohio State U., Columbus, 1981, La. State U., Baton Rouge, 1982-83; mem. adv. com. U.S. Ct. Appeals 8th Circuit, St. Louis, 1983—. Author: (with R. Wright) Land Use in a Nutshell, 1978, 2d edit., 1985; editor-in-chief Ark. Law Rev., 1975; contbr. articles to profl. jours. Mem. Ark. Bar Assn., Pulaski County Bar Assn., Ark. Assn. Women Lawyers (v.p. 1977-78). Episcopalian. Office: U Ark Sch Law 400 W Markham St Little Rock AR 72201

WRIGHT-BRUNACHE, PAMELA DENISE, senior buyer; b. Nassawadox, Va., Oct. 26, 1956; d. Jenever Eroscus and Leona (Smith) Wright; m. Jean Claude Brunache, April 3, 1981; 1 child, Jean Yves. BA in Polit. Sci., Va. Wesleyan Coll., 1978. Buyer United Airlines, San Francisco, 1978-82, Litton Industries, San Carlos, Calif., 1982—. Democrat. African Methodist Episcopalian.

WRIGLEY, ELIZABETH SPRINGER (MRS. OLIVER K. WRIGLEY), found. exec.; b. Pitts., Oct. 4, 1915; d. Charles Woodward and Sarah Maria (Roberts) Springer; B.A. U. Pitts., 1935; B.S., Carnegie Inst. Tech., 1936; m. Oliver Kenneth Wrigley, June 16, 1936 (dec. July 1978). Procedure analyst U.S. Steel Corp., Pitts., 1941-43; research asst. The Francis Bacon Found., Inc., Los Angeles, 1944, exec., 1945-50, trustee, 1950—, dir. research, 1951-53, pres., 1954—, dir. Francis Bacon Library; mem. adv. council Royal Skakespeare Revels in the Ojai; mem. regional Fine Arts adv. council Calif. State Poly. U., Pomona. Mem. ALA, Calif. Library Assn., Renaissance Soc. Am., Modern Humanities Research Assn., Cryptogram Assn., Alpha Delta Pi. Presbyn. Mem. Order Eastern Star, Damascus Shrine. Editor: The Skeleton Text of the Shakespeare Folio L.A. (by W.C. Arensberg), 1952. Compiler: Short Title Catalogue Numbers in the Library of the Francis Bacon Foundation, 1958; Wing Numbers in the Library of the Francis Bacon Foundation, 1959; Supplement To Francis Bacon Library Holdings in the STC of English Books, 1967; (with David W. Davies) A Concordance to the Essays of Francis Bacon, 1973. Home: 4805 N Pal Mal Ave Temple City CA 91780 Office: Francis Bacon Library 655 N Dartmouth Ave Claremont CA 91711

WRINGER, PAULA HARMON, educator; b. Princeton, Ind., Aug. 23, 1945; d. Roderick Allen and Emily Lou (Williams) Harmon; B.Nursing, U. Evansville, 1967, M.S., 1975; m. Ralph Dean Wringer, Dec. 9, 1967; children—Brian Allen, Edra Lynn. Unit supr. Norman Beatty Psychiat. Hosp., Westville, Ind., 1967-70; instr. nursing Purdue-North Central Campus, Westville, 1970-73; instr. nursing U. Evansville (Ind.), 1973-75, Olney (Ill.) Community Coll., 1975-76; asst. prof. nursing Purdue U., West Lafayette, Ind., 1976—, acting head baccalaureate program, 1982-83, dir. div. family centered nursing, 1983-88; psychiat. clin. nurse specialist, Logansport (Ind.) State Hosp., 1986—; cons. Lafayette Home Hosp., 1978. Sec. Am. Heart Assn., Tippecanoe unit, 1979-82, v.p., 1982—; mem. adv. bd. Tippecanoe County Elderly Ombudsman, 1979—. Mem. Nat. League Nursing, Am. Nurses Assn., Ind. State Nurse's Assn., Cen. Ind. Health Systems Agy., Sigma Theta Tau, Alpha Tau Delta. Baptist. Lodge: Order Eastern Star. Office: Purdue U Sch Nursing West Lafayette IN 47907

WRISTON, BARBARA, educational consultant; b. Middletown, Conn., June 29, 1917; d. Henry Merritt and Ruth Colton (Bigelow) W. A.B., Oberlin Coll., 1939; A.M., Brown U., 1942; Litt.D. (hon.), Lawrence U., 1977. Mus. asst. Mus. Art, R.I. Sch. Design, Providence, 1939-44; lectr. to schs. Mus. Fine Arts, Boston, 1944-61; exec. dir. mus. edn. Art Inst. Chgo., 1961-78; cons. on edn. The Planting Fields Found., Oyster Bay, N.Y., 1979-82; also bd. dirs. The Planting Fields Found.; bd. dirs. Met. Hist. Structures Assn., N.Y.C. Author: Rare Doings at Bath, 1979. Mem. adv. bd. Hist. Am. Bldgs. Survey, 1972-78; trustee Frontier Nursing Service, 1979. Benjamin Franklin fellow Royal Soc. Arts. Mem. Soc. Archtl. Historians (pres. 1959-62, dir. 1961-64), Furniture History Soc. Home: 30 Waterside Plaza Apt 2D New York NY 10010

WRISTON, KATHRYN DINEEN, coprorate executive; b. Syracuse, N.Y.; d. Robert Emmet and Carolyn (Bareham) Dineen; m. Walter B. Wriston, Mar. 14, 1968. Student, U. Geneva, 1958-59; BA cum laude, Smith Coll., 1960; LLB, U. Mich., 1963. Bar: N.Y.,1964, U.S. Ct. Appeals (2nd cir.), U.S. Supreme Ct., 1968. Assoc. Shearman Sterling, N.Y.C., 1963-68; pres., bd. dirs. Santa Fe So. Pacific Corp., Chicago, 1983—; trustee Northwestern Mut. Life Ins. Co., Milw., 1986— Practising Law Inst., 1975— (v.p. 1985—); bd. dirs. Federated Dept. Stores Inc., Cin., 1975-88. Mem. Pres. Com. White House Fellows; mem. devel. com. U. Mich. Law Sch. Fellow Am. Bar Found.; mem. Am. Inst. CPAs (pres. 1986), Nat. Assn. Accts., Am. Arbitration Assn. (bd. dirs. 1982), Fin. Women's Assn. N.Y., N.Y. County Lawyers Assn. (legal aid com. 1973-76), Rand Inst. Civil Justice (pres. 1985, bd. overseers), Am. Bar Assn., N.Y. State Bar Assn., Assn. Bar of City N.Y.

WROBLESKI, JEANNE PAULINE, lawyer; b. Phila., Feb. 14, 1942; d. Edward Joseph and Pauline (Popelak) Wrobleski; m. Robert J. Klein, Dec. 3, 1979. B.A., Immaculata Coll., 1964; M.A., U. Pa., 1966; J.D., Temple U., 1975. Bar: Pa. 1975. Pvt. practice law, Phila., 1975—. Mem. Commn. on Women and the Legal Profession, 1986; v.p. Center City Residents' Assn. Rhea Liebman scholar, 1974; bd. dirs. South St. Dance Co. Mem. AAUW, ABA, Phila. Bar Assn. (chmn. women's rights com. 1986, com. on jud. selection and reform 1986-87), Pa. Bar Assn., Am. Judicature Soc., Jagiellonian Law Soc., Alpha Psi Omega, Lambda Iota Tau. Democrat. Clubs: Lawyers, Peale. Office: Kohn Savett Klein & Graf PC 2400 One Reading Ctr 1101 Market St Philadelphia PA 19107

WROBLOWA, HALINA STEFANIA, electrochemist; b. Gdansk, Poland, July 5, 1925; came to U.S., 1960, naturalized, 1970; M.Sc., U. Lodz (Poland), 1949; Ph.D., Warsaw Inst. Tech., 1958; 1 dau., Krystyna Wrobel-Knight. Chmn. dept. prep. studies U. Lodz, 1950-53; adj. Inst. for Phys. Chemistry, Acad. Scis., Warsaw, Poland, 1958-60; dep. dir. electrochemistry lab. Energy Inst., U. Pa., Phila., 1960-67, dir. electrochemistry lab., 1968-75; prin. research scientist Ford Motor Co., Dearborn, Mich., 1978—. Served with Polish Underground Army, 1943-45. Decorated Silver Cross of Merit with Swords. Mem. Electrochem. Soc., Internat. Electrochem. Soc., Mensa, Sigma Xi. Contbr. chpts. to books, articles to profl. jours., patent lit. Office: Ford Motor Co SRL S-2079 PO Box 2053 Dearborn MI 48322

WU, FELICIA YING-HSIUEH, biochemist, educator; b. Taipei, Taiwan, Feb. 27, 1939; came to U.S., 1961, naturalized, 1976; d. I-Sung and Ti (Yen) Chen; m. Cheng-Wen Wu, Nov. 10, 1963; children—David, Faith, Albert. B.S., Nat. Taiwan U., 1961; M.S., U. Minn., 1963; Ph.D., Case Western Res. U., 1969. Med. technician dept. biochemistry U.S. Naval Med. Research Unit No. 2, Taipei, Taiwan, 1963-65; research assoc. in biochemistry and molecular biology Cornell U., Ithaca, N.Y., 1969-71; research assoc. dept. pharmacology Yale U., New Haven, 1971-72; assoc. dept. biophysics Albert Einstein Coll. Medicine, Bronx, N.Y., 1972-73, instr., 1973-78, asst. prof. dept. biochemistry, 1978-79; vis. prof. dept. molecular biology Institut Pasteur, Paris, and Unite de physicochimie macromoleculaire Institut Gustave-Roussy, Villejuif, France, 1979-80; assoc. prof. pharm. sci. SUNY-Stony Brook, 1980—, W.J. and F.M. Catacosinos prof., 1980. Contbr. articles to profl. jours. Mem. Am. Soc. Biochemistry and Molecular Biology, Am. Biophys. Soc., Am. Chem. Soc., Am. Inst. Chemists, Am. Soc. Pharmaceutical and Experimental Therapy, Soc. Chinese Bioscientists in Am., Assn. Women in Sci., Internat. Assn. for Women in Bioscis. Office: SUNY Dept Pharmacological Scis HSC 7T-182 Stony Brook NY 11794

WU, MARGARET ANNE, computer scientist, educator; b. Chgo., Apr. 11, 1935; d. Aloys Joseph and Beatrice Rose (Kubal) Schlosser; B.S. in Math., Ill. Inst. Tech., 1956; M.S. in Math., Northwestern U., 1958; Ph.D. in Computer Sci., U. Iowa, 1980; m. Shih-Yen Wu, June 24, 1967; children—Jennifer, Gregory. Research computer scientist IIT Research Inst., Chgo., 1958-67; research assoc. U. Iowa, 1967-71, vis. asst. prof. mgmt. sci., 1979—. Mem. Assn. Computing Machinery, IEEE Computer Soc. Author: Computers and Programming: An Introduction, 1973; Introduction to Computer Data Processing, 1975, 2d edit., 1979; Introduction to Computer Data Processing with Basic, 1980. Office: U Iowa Phillips Hall Iowa City IA 52242

WU, MARY, entrepreneur; b. Orange, N.J., Aug. 19, 1931; d. George Frederick and Helen (James) Drum; divorced, 1968; children: Helen, Stephen. BA with high honors, Ohio U., 1953; MS, Ohio State U., 1957. Analytical chemist Eastman Kodak Co., Rochester, N.Y., 1953-54; asst. editor Chemical Abstracts, Columbus, Ohio, 1957-62; adminstrv. editor Chemical Rubber Co., Cleve., 1968-72; research asst. Case Western Res. U., Cleve., 1976-87. Mem. Phi Beta Kappa, Phi Mu. Home: 195 High St Chagrin Falls OH 44022

WU, TERESITA GO, physician; b. Tarlac, Philippines, Oct. 31, 1946; came to U.S., 1974, naturalized, 1983; d. Li and Virginia (Co) Go; m. Raymond K. Wu, Nov. 21, 1978; children—Tonna, Andrew. B.A., Southwestern U., Philippines, 1967; M.D., U. of East, Quezon City, Philippines, 1972. Resident physician Met. Hosp., Manila, 1972-74; pediatric resident Lincoln Med. Ctr., Bronx, 1974-76; psychiat. resident Kingsboro Psychiat. Ctr., Bklyn., 1976-79; staff physician Brookhaven Hosp., Patchogue, N.Y., 1980; part-time gen. practice medicine, Dix Hills, N.Y., 1979—; psychiatrist, Community Outreach Clinic, 1985—. Contbr. articles to med. and religious jours. Recipient award for Acad. Superiority, Most Honorable Sorority of the Squirette of Hippocrates, 1969. Mem. AMA, Internat. Assn. Med. Specialists, Am. Psychiatric Assn., N.Y. Acad. Scis. Home: 486 Wolf Hill Rd Dix Hills NY 11746

WUESTE, PATRICIA, lawyer; b. San Antonio, Dec. 11, 1953; d. Gus Michael and W. Cecelia (Goodwin) Wueste. B.A., Incarnate Word Coll., 1975; J.D., St. Mary's U., 1978. Bar: Tex. 1978, U.S. Dist. Ct. (we. dist.) Tex. 1982. Mem. Law Office R. Ritter, San Antonio, Tex., 1978—; bd. dirs. Bexar County Mediation Ctr. Named Outstanding Adv. St. Mary's Sch. Law, 1978. Mem. ABA, Tex. Bar Assn., San Antonio Bar Assn. (bd. dirs. Found.), Bexar County Women's Bar Assn. (past pres.), St. Mary's Law Alumni Assn. (past pres.), San Antonio Young Lawyers, Nat. Order Barristers, Delta Theta Phi. Democrat. Roman Catholic. Club: Altrusa. Home: 215 Northcrest San Antonio TX 78201 Office: Law Office Robert Ritter 1026 W Hildebrand San Antonio TX 78201

WULF, SHARON ANN, manufacturing company strategic planning executive; b. New Bedford, Mass., Aug 23, 1954; d. Daniel Thomas and Norma Dorothy (McCabe) Vieira; m. Stanley A. Wulf, 1983. BS in Acctg. cum laude, Providence Coll., 1976; MBA, Northeastern U., 1977; PhD, Columbia Pacific U., 1984. Staff acct., intern Laventhol & Horwath, Providence, 1977; jr. fin. analyst Polaroid Corp., Waltham, Mass., 1977-78, fin. analyst, Freetown, Mass., 1978-79, Cambridge, 1979-81; sr. fin. cons., mktg. strategic planner Digital Equipment Corp., Stow, Mass., 1981-82, Maynard, Mass., 1982-83, mgr. fin. devel. program, 1983-84, strategic fin. cons. engring. div., 1984-86, group mgr. planning and strategic ops., Hudson, Mass., 1986-87, mgr. strategic programs semiconductor ops., 1987—; lectr. in fin. acctg. Southeastern Mass. U., 1979-81; adj. prof. acctg., mgmt. and fin., Northeastern U., Boston, 1980—; cons. in field. Chairperson pub. support and fund raising ARC, New Bedford, Mass., 1974-84. Mem. Nat. Assn. Female Execs. (bd. dirs. 1978-81), Univ. Coll. Faculty Soc., Phi Sigma Tau. Home: 902 Salen End Rd Framingham MA 01701 Office: Digital Equipment Corp HL02-2L9 77 Reed Rd Hudson MA 01756

WULFF, LOIS YVONNE, librarian; b. Seattle, Nov. 23, 1940; d. Arthur Ray and Audrey June (Carpenter) Roark; B.S., Washington State U., 1962; M.L.S., U. Wash., 1963; postgrad. Syracuse U., 1969-70; m. Barry Kahn, Dec. 18, 1971 (dec. 1982). Intern, then head documents div. Ohio State U., 1963-67; spl. project investigator U. Wash., 1968-69; staff asst., head search unit Johns Hopkins Med. Instns., 1971-72; project coordinator, asst. to dir., coordinator health sci. libraries U. Minn., 1973-77; head librarian Alfred Taubman Med. Library, U. Mich., 1978-87, coordinator Med. and Sci./Tech. Libraries, 1981-87, asst. dir. for collection mgmt. Gaylord fellow, 1969-70. Mem. Med. Library Assn., ALA, Assn. Acad. Health Sci. Library Dirs., Assn. Coll. and Research Libraries. Office: U Mich 818 Harlan Hatcher Grad Library Ann Arbor MI 48109

WUNDER, JEAN BAKER, social service director; b. Bklyn., Oct. 1, 1934; d. William Michael and Lillian Jane (Trill) B.; m. Theodore Henry Wunder, Sept. 28, 1957 (div. July 1971); children: Susan Baker Armstrong, William Henry, Robert Theodore. Grad. high sch., Bklyn., 1952. Founder, exec. dir. Family Support Group, Inc., Glen Rock, N.J., 1983—; lectr. Bergen County Dept. Health Service, Paramus, N.J., 1973—, Bergen County Respiratory Soc., Paramus, 1973—; community liaison Future Health Systems, Paramus, 1986—; chairperson Human Resource Coordinating Council, Ridgewood, N.J., 1986—. Leader Cub Scouts Am., Glen Rock, 1972-74; founder, dir. Glen Rock Toughlove, 1981; lectr. substance abuse ministry Archdiocese N.Y.C., 1983—; mem. Bergen County Com. on Youth Substance Abuse, Paramus, 1985—, United Parents Ridgewood, N.J., 1985—; founder, dir. Bergen County Coalition Against Drug Abuse, Glen Rock, 1986. Recipient Jefferson award Pub. Inst., 1983, Gov.'s Vol. award State of N.J. 1987; named Vol. of Yr. Suburban Newspapers, 1984; Bergen County Freeholders grantee, 1986. Mem. Nat. Fedn. for Drug Free Youth, N.J. Fedn. Parents for Drug Free Communities. Home: 178 Harding Rd Glen Rock NJ 07452 Office: Family Support Group Inc West Plaza Glen Rock NJ 07452

WURSTER, THELMA PAULINE, nurse; b. Celina, Ohio, June 9, 1932; d. Francis Q. and Mary Lee (Kindel) Wade; R.N., Miami Valley Hosp., Dayton, Ohio, 1953; B.S. in Nursing, Marquette U., Milw., 1961; M.Ed. in Profl. Devel., U. Wis., Whitewater, 1982; postgrad. Coll. St. Joseph, Joliet, Ill.; m. Charles Wayne Wurster, Aug. 18, 1952. Staff and head nurse hosps. in Ohio and Wis., 1953-80; dir. operating rm. Milw. Children's Hosp., 1966-78, asst. dir. nursing, 1979-80; supr. operating room Eye Inst., Milw. County Med. Complex, Wauwatosa, Wis., 1980-87. R.N., Ohio, Wis. Mem. Assn. Operating Room Nurses, AAUW, Phi Delta Kappa. Republican. Club: Kettle Moraine Curling (Hartland, Wis.). Contbr. articles to profl. jours.

WURZBERGER, SUZANNE ALICE WELLS, shop owner; b. Bridgeport, Conn., June 7, 1938; d. Daniel Marcus and Sarah Evelyn (French) Wells; m. Albert George Wurzberger, May 2, 1959; children—Carolsue, Albert John. A.S., Vt. Coll., 1958; diploma Internat. Corr. Sch., 1979. Owner, operator Norton House, Wilmington, Vt., 1966—; gen. mgr. The New Eng. Plantation, Inc., Wilmington. Author Living History Assn. Jour., 1982. Pres. Parent Tchrs. Club, Wilmington, Vt., 1974-75; troop leader brownies Girl Scouts U.S.A., Wilmington, 1967. Mem. Women Bus. Owners of Vt., Nat. Assn. Female Execs., Am./Internat. Quilt Assn. Republican. Congregationalist. Clubs: Ch. Guild (pres.), Green Mt. Quilters Guild. Avocations: sewing; snowshoeing. Home: Stowe Hill Rd RFD 1 Box 105 Wilmington VT 05363 Office: Norton House 1836 Country Store Village Wilmington VT 05363

WYATT, DEBORAH DENISE, publisher; b. Highland Park, Mich., Aug. 28, 1956; d. Joseph Herbert and Maxine Winnefred (Armstrong) W. B.A. in English and Sociology, Albion Coll., 1978. Products editor Scranton-Gillette Communications, Chgo., 1978, mng. editor, 1979; writer, researcher Interlochen Ctr. for Arts, Mich., 1980; founder, pres., pub., editor Prism Publs., Inc., Traverse City, Mich., 1981—; regional corr. The Mich. Woman, 1984-85; exec. editor Sleeping Bear Dunes Nat. Lakeshore, 1984; pub., editor Leukemia: A Family's Challenge, 1987. Mem. Human Rights Commn., Traverse City, 1984. Mem. Traverse City, C. of C., Phi Beta Kappa. Pub., editor: Leukemia: A Family's Challenge, 1987. Avocations: fiction writing; reading; cross-country skiing; bicycling; swimming. Home: 3005 County Rd 651 Cedar MI 49621 Office: Prism Publs Inc 121 S Union St Traverse City MI 49684

WYATT, JENTA RAE, home economist; b. Chrisman, Ill., July 25, 1935; d. Edwin Boone and Maerene (Mason) Kendall; children: Kerry R., Charissa W. Leintz, Elizabeth R. BS, Rutgers U., 1967, MEd, 1973. Home econs. tchr. South Brunswick High Sch., Monmouth Junction, N.J., 1970-74; vocat. instr. VOTEC, Danville, Ill., 1974-78; extension home econs. agt. Fla. Coop. Extension Services, Wauchula, Fla., 1978-82; extension home econs. tchr. Fla. Coop. Extension Services, Ocala, Fla., 1982—; bd. dirs., chmn. bd. Consumer Credit Counseling Service, Ocala, 1986—. Pres. Village North Homeowners Assn., Ocala, 1986-87. Mem. Fla. Assn. Extension Home Economists (treas. 1983-84, bd. dirs. 1984-85, 2d v.p. 1985-86, 1st v.p. 1987—, pres.-elect 1987-88), Fla. Home Econs. Assn., Epsilon Sigma Phi. Clubs: Pilot (Ocala and Wauchula) (bd. dirs. 1986-87), Woman's. Home: 3823 NE 19th Circle Ocala FL 32670

WYATT, KATHLEEN ANN, publishing executive; b. Nelsonville, Ohio, June 23, 1951; d. Charles Edward and Ella Mae (Johnston) Covelle; m. Larry Gene Wyatt, May 12, 1972; children: Joel Andrew, Christopher Neal. Student, Ea. Ky. U., 1969-72; BS, U. Cin., 1975; MBA, Xavier U., 1987. Dir. subscription services Anderson Pub. Co., Cin., 1972—, also mem. employee recognition com., 1985—. Elected mem. community affairs com. St. Mary's Ch. of Hyde Park, Cin., 1985—; den leader St. Mary's Cub Scouts Am., Cin., 1987—. Mem. Nat. Assn. Female Execs., Xavier MBA Alumni Assn. (trustee 1987—), Alpha Phi Si. Republican. Clubs: Turpin Swim (Cin.); Xavier Blue Chips Investment (founder, pres. 1987—). Lodge: United Order True Sisters. Home: 2943 Erie Ave Cincinnati OH 45208 Office: Anderson Pub Co 2035 Reading Rd Cincinnati OH 45202

WYATT, KATHRYN ELIZABETH BENTON, psychologist, educator; b. Danville, Va., May 11, 1928; d. Joseph Nelson and Margaret (Davis) Benton; B.A., Randolph Macon Woman's Coll., Lynchburg, Va., 1949; M.Ed., U. Va., 1952; M.A., U. N.C., Greensboro, 1974, Ph.D., 1977; m. Landon Russell Wyatt, Aug. 30, 1952; children—Margaret Wyatt Scott, Landon Russell, III, Elizabeth Wyatt Ashe. Instr., then asst. prof. psychology Stratford Coll., Danville, 1949-74, chmn. dept., 1963-74; prof. psychology Danville Community Coll., 1977—. Mem. Danville Sch. Bd.; deacon, tchr. 1st Bapt. Ch., Danville; pres. so. region Va. Sch. Bds. Assn. Mem. Am. Psychol. Assn., Soc. Research Child Devel., Southeastern Psychol. Assn., Va. Psychol. Assn., Va. Acad. Sci. Clubs: Friends Danville Pub. Library (pres.), Jr. Wednesday (pres.), The Wednesday Club (pres.), Gabriella, Wayside Garden, Shakespeare. Author articles in field. Home: 301 Magnolia St Danville VA 24541 Office: Danville Community Coll Danville VA 24541

WYATT, ROSE MARIE, psychiatric and medical social worker, financial planner; b. San Angelo, Tex., Feb. 16; d. James Odis and Annie LaVernia (Lott) W.; B.A. (Ford Found. scholar, 1953-57), Fisk U., 1957; M.S., U. So. Calif., 1963; M.A., M.S.W. (univ. scholar 1970-72, United Charities scholar 1970-72), U. Chgo., 1972; postgrad. in indsl. psychology Ill. Inst. Tech., 1976—. Elem. tchr. Chgo. Bd. Edn., 1959-63, clin. social worker, 1979—; adult program dir. Chgo. YWCA, 1963-64; youth counselor Chgo. Commn. on Youth Welfare, 1964-66; supervising social worker for Head Start, Chgo. Com. on Urban Opportunity, 1966; social worker Chgo. Commn. on Youth Welfare, 1966-68, Jewish Vocat. Service, 1968; social worker Sch. Community Relations, Detroit Public Schs., 1968-70; social worker United Charities, 1972-74; clin. social worker Rosman-Wyatt and Assos., Chgo., 1980—, pres., 1981—; instr. dept. corrections Chgo. State U., 1972—. Adv. bd. United Charities, Calumet Area, program com. chmn., 1974-80; vol. bd. Assn. of Community Agts. 1968-70, Southside Sr. Citizens Coalition, Chgo., 1963-66, Roseland Health Planning Com., 1974-76, Teen Pregnancy Caucus, 1978-82; mem. social work adv. council Chgo. Bd. Edn., 1976. Recipient Outstanding Employee award for med.-social work services Maternal and Child Health Services div. HEW; 1971. Mem. Nat. Assn. Social Workers, Acad. Cert. Social Workers, Ill. Cert. Social Workers, Chgo. Psychol. Club, Ill Acad. Criminology, NEA, Ill. Assn. Sch. Social Workers, Am. Assn. Mental Deficiency, Qualified Mental Retardation Profls., Fisk U. Alumni Assn., Alpha Kappa Alpha. Roman Catholic. Clubs: Am. Bridge Assn., Civenos Bridge.

WYATT, SUSAN MELINDA CLOUGH, human resource development specialist; b. Ft. Worth, Feb. 6, 1943; d. Forrest Weldon and Mildred (Wyatt) Clough; m. David W. McClintock, Apr. 11, 1932 (div. Mar. 1987); children: Lesley Karen, Nathan Crane. BA in Polit. Sci., Whittier Coll., 1965; MA in Lit., Sci., and Arts, U. Mich., 1966; MAT in Secondary Edn., Antioch-Putney Grad. Sch. Edn., 1968; student, Berry Coll., 1983-84, N.C. State U., 1987-88. Research asst. U. Mich., Ann Arbor, 1969-70; fgn. service sec., researcher U.S. Dept. State, Sanaa, Yemen, Washington, 1966-68, 70-72; English tchr. U. Jordan, Amman, 1972-74; cons. various orgns. Washington, 1974-78; personnel officer U.S. Dept. State, Washington, 1978-82; pvt. practice cons., trainer Rome, Ga., 1982-84; dir. career services The Women's Ctr., Raleigh, N.C., 1985-86; dir. edn. Hospice of N.C., Raleigh, 1986; placement counselor N.C. State U., Raleigh, 1987—; cons., trainer various orgns., Raleigh, 1985—; Woodrow Wilson vis. fellow, 1978-82. Recipient Mentor of Distinction award Women in Bus. Adv. Council, 1988. Mem. Am. Soc. Tng. and Devel. (chmn. community affairs 1988). Democrat. Unitarian-Universalist. Home: 2220 The Circle Raleigh NC 27608

WYCKOFF, BEVERLY A., banker, lawyer; b. Williams AFB, Ariz., May 13, 1956; d. Daniel McCoy and Betty Jean (Stumpf) Wyckoff. B.A., Yale U., 1978; J.D., U. Miami (Fla.), 1981. Bar: Ill. 1981. Trust adminstr. Am. Nat. Bank & Trust Co., Chgo., 1981-82, trust officer, 1982-84, 2d v.p., 1984-86; v.p., mgr. Chgo. br., The Sanwa Bank Ltd., 1986—. Mem. Women's Bar Assn. Ill. (mem. com. rights of women 1983-86), Chgo. Bar Assn., Ill. Bar Assn., Friends Lincoln Park Boat Club (treas., dir. 1983—). Republican. Home: 429 W Wellington Ave Chicago IL 60657

WYCKOFF, JUANITA CHARLENE, retired textiles educator; b. Luray, Kans., Sept. 24, 1915; d. William S. and Bertha (McKanna) W.; B.S., Kans. State U., 1940; M.S., Colo. State U., 1959. Tchr., Gove (Kans.) Rural High Sch., 1940, Luray (Kans.) Community High Sch., 1941-42, Decatur Community High Sch., Oberlin, Kans., 1944-46, Oswego (Kans.) High Sch., 1946-48, Cherryvale (Kans.) High Sch., 1948-57; asst. prof. textiles and clothing Mankato (Minn.) State U., 1959-82, ret., 1982; mem. adv. bd. Secondary Home Econs. Dist. No. 77, Mankato. Mem. Centenary Meth. Choir. Mem. NEA, Minn. Edn. Assn., Mankato State U. Interfaculty Assn., Am. Home Econs. Assn., Minn. Home Econs. Assn., Assn. Coll. Prof. Textiles and Clothing, United Meth. Women, Delta Kappa Gamma, Phi Upsilon Omicron, Methodist. Home: 225 Heather Ln Apt 6 Mankato MN 56001

WYCKOFF, SUSAN, astronomy researcher; b. Santa Cruz, Calif., Mar. 18, 1941; d. Stephen and Jean (Taft) W.; m. Peter Augustus Wehinger, July 29, 1967. BA in Astronomy, Mount Holyoke, 1962; postgrad., Swarthmore Coll., 1962-63; PhD in Astronomy, Case Inst. Technology, 1967. Postdoctoral fellow U. Mich., Ann Arbor, 1967-68; asst. prof. Albion (Mich.) Coll., 1968-70; research assoc. U. Kans., Lawrence, 1970-72; sr. lectr. Tel-Aviv U., Israel, 1972-75; prin. research fellow Royal Greenwich Observatory, Sussex, Eng., 1975-78; vis. prof. Ohio State U., Columbus, 1978-79; assoc. prof. Ariz. State U., Tempe, 1979-82, prof., 1982—; adj. prof. Sussex U., 1975-77, U. Heidelberg Theoretical Astrophysics Inst., 1980, U. Ariz., Tucson, 1984—; vis. astronomer Royal Grennwich Observatory, Sussex, Eng., 1983, Mt. Stromlo Observatory, Australian Nat. U., Canberra, 1987; NSF Shapley lectr., 1985-86; vis. com. Aura, Inc., Tucson, 1985-88. Contbr. articles profl. jours. Mem. Gov.'s Disease Control Commn., Phoenix, 1985-87. Fellow Royal Astronomical Soc. (Eng.); mem. NSF adv. com. 1983—, Nat. Acad. Sci. space sci. bd. 1984—, Ariz. State U. Faculty Women's Assn. (pres. 1983-84, exec. bd. 1983—), Am. Astron. Soc. (A.J. Cannon award comm. 1982—), Internat. Astron. Union, Sigma Xi. Home: 2135 E Loma Vista Dr Tempe AZ 85282 Office: Ariz State U Physics/Astronomy Dept Tempe AZ 85287

WYGODA, SYLVIA ANN, association executive; b. Chattanooga, Feb. 24, 1948; d. Hermann and Rae (Raider) W. BS, Ind. U., 1970; MEd, Ga. State U., 1972, postgrad., 1977-78. Cert. tchr., Ga. Tchr. Atlanta Pub. Sch. System, 1970-74; adminstv. asst. Emory U., Atlanta, 1974-76; coordinator Chattanooga State Community Coll., 1976-81, Dekalb Community Coll., Atlanta, 1978-81; asst. commr. Dept. Human Resources State Ga., Atlanta, 1981-83; exec. dir. Sales Mktg. Execs., Atlanta, 1983—. Chmn. Gov.'s Com. Employment Handicapped, Chattanooga 1980-81; bd. dirs. Ga. Spl. Olympics 1981—, sec./treas. 1985-87, bd.dirs. Ind. Living Programs, Atlanta, 1984—, Zachor Holocaust Com., Atlanta, 1985—, Chattanooga Opera, 1979-81, Chattanooga Area Literacy Movement, 1979-81, Chattanooga Girls Club, 1979-81; mem. Ga. Commn. on the Holocaust, 1985—; Private Industry Council (mem. exec. com. 1979-81). Mem. Ga. Soc. Assn. Execs. (com. chmn. 1984-88), Meeting Planners Internat., Phi Delta Kappa (v.p. 1977-78). Lodge: Civitan. Office: Sales and Mktg Execs 4360 Georgetown Sq Suite 805 Atlanta GA 30338

WYLIE, DANNA D., small business owner; b. Newark, Dec. 29, 1944; d. Thomas Heyes and Doris (Bennett) Donnelly; m. William Henry Wylie, June 24, 1978. Assoc.'s degree, Lasell Jr. Coll., 1965; BS, Fla. So. Coll., 1967. Tchr. Howell Twp. (N.J.) Schs., 1968-69; conv. coordinator McGraw Hill Book Co., N.Y.C., 1969-71; sales rep. McGraw Hill Book Co., Bloomington, Ind., 1971-77, L.G. Balfour, Bloomington, 1978-79, 81-83, Wadsworth Pub. Co., Bloomington, 1979-81; owner University Spirit, Bloomington, 1983—. Mem. Univ. Spirit of Am., Delta Zeta (advisor 1984—). Office: University Spirit PO Box 1265 Bloomington IN 47402

WYLIE, HAZEL RUSSELL, continuing education administrator; b. Denison, Tex., Oct. 24, 1919; d. George Dewey and Bertha (Higdon) Hagans; m. John Coakey Russell, Oct. 11, 1941 (dec. Dec. 1951); 1 dau., K. Jayne Russell Larkin; m. 2d O.D. Wylie, July 30, 1966. B.S., North Tex. State U., 1940, M.Ed., 1953; postgrad. So. Meth. U., 1968, U. Del., 1957, others. Tchr., Nacogdoches (Tex.) Ind. Sch. Dist., 1940-42, Liberty Common Sch. Dist., Bowie County, Tex., 1946-52; tchr., adminstr. Dallas Ind. Sch. Dist., 1952-80, short course instr., 1980—; real estate broker, Dallas, 1980—. Mem. Classroom Tchrs. Dallas (pres. 1957-58), Tex. Classroom Tchrs. (dir. 1957-59), Tex. State Tchrs. Assn., NEA, Ret. Tchrs. Assn. Democrat. Presbyterian. Club: Zonta Internat. (pres. Dallas II chpt. 1982-83).

WYLIE, NETA EVANGELINE, psychologist; b. Grapeland, Tex., Sept. 5, 1921; d. Pat and Edith Estelle (Bean) Taylor; m. Roger Wylie, Dec. 16, 1944 (div. Feb. 1976); children: Pat Wylie (dec.), Beth Wylie Hutchinson. MusB, Baylor U., 1942; MA, U. Houston, 1975; PhD, Tex. A&M U., 1976. Lic. psychologist, Tex. Instr. music Temple (Tex.) Jr. Coll., Temple High Sch., 1941-44, East Tex. Bapt. Coll., Marshall, 1944-45; free-lance instr. violin and piano Baytown, Tex., 1945-69; asst. prof. psychology Tex. A&M U., Prairie View, 1975-77; pvt. practice psychology Baytown and Galveston, Tex., 1978—. Pianist First Bapt. Ch., Baytown, 1944-79, organist, First Presbyn. Ch., Galveston, 1980—. Mem. Am. Psychol. Assn., Am. Guild Organists, Mensa, Mu Phi Epsilon. Republican. Presbyterian. Home: 16 Colony Park Circle Galveston TX 77551 Office: C-104 Humana Medical Plaza Baytown TX 77520

WYMAN, IRMA MARIAN, diversified corporation executive; b. Detroit, Jan. 31, 1928; d. Max Carroll and Marie Matilda (Breitenstein) W. BS in Engring., U. Mich., 1949. With Honeywell Inc., 1955—, various positions in mktg., engring., sales support, 1955-77; dir. cen. staff Honeywell Info. Systems, Waltham, Mass., 1977-80; dir. corp. info. services and planning Honeywell Inc., Mpls., 1980-82, v.p. info. mgmt., 1982—. Patentee computer apparatus (award 1963). Named Woman of Yr. in Bus., Minn. YWCA, 1983. Mem. Minn. Women's Econ. Roundtable, St. Paul Chamber Orch. Bd. (bd. dirs. 1981—). Club: Horizon 100. Home: 306 Selby Ave Saint Paul MN 55102 Office: Honeywell Inc Honeywell Plaza 12-5320 Minneapolis MN 55408

WYMAN, LOTTE ANN NOVAK, civic worker; b. Vienna, Austria, Aug. 15, 1925; d. Josef and Hertha (Wallnstorfer) Novak; B.A., Barnard Coll., 1947; 1 dau., Leslie Andrea. Grey Lady, ARC, 1947-55; treas. Women's Assn. First Presbyn. Ch., Greenwich, Conn., 1963-65, chmn. mission interpretation program, 1975-77; bd. dirs. Friends of Sunny Hill Sch. for Phys. and Emotionally Handicapped Children, Greenwich, 1960-78 ; bd. dirs. YWCA, Greenwich, 1963-78, 81-87 , chmn. world fellowship, 1965, mem. bldg. com., 1965-70, pres., 1967-70; bd. dirs. Drug Liberation Program of Greater Stamford, 1970-74, Community Chest, Greenwich, 1967-70, Community Forum, Greenwich, 1970—; bd. dirs. Turtle Bay Music Sch., N.Y.C., 1970-80; bd. dirs. Greenwich Arts Council, 1974-79, pres., 1976-79; bd. dirs. Neuberger Mus., SUNY, 1979-85 , M.I.T. Council for the Arts, 1980—, World Service Council YWCA, 1983—; bd. dirs. Met. Opera Assn., 1980—, adv. dir., 1982—; mem. Purchase Coll. Found., 1983—; cons. Nat. Exec. Service Corps, 1984—; elder 1st Presbyn. Ch. Greenwich, 1986—; mem. Bd. Parks and Recreation, Greenwich, 1986-88; vice chmn. bd. trustees, Bruce Mus., Greenwich, 1986—. Mem. N.Y. Zool. Soc., Ch. Women United (v.p. 1971-72), Stratton Mountain C. of C. Republican. Presbyterian. Clubs: Greenwich Country; Stratton Mountain (Vt.) Country. Home: Baldwin Farms North Greenwich CT 06830

WYNN, SUSAN KATHERINE ARNETT, transportation executive; b. Louisville, Ky., Apr. 29, 1950; d. Deweese Shea and Lurline (Burton) Arnett; m. Lloyd John Wynn, June 24, 1986. Student, Broward Community Coll., 1975-76; BBA in Fin., Fla. State U., 1979; postgrad., Savannah State, 1986—. Sr. acct. Edkerd Found., Clearwater, Fla., 1980-83; acctg. mgr. Pinellas Suncoast Transit Authority, Clearwater, 1983-87; fin. dir. Chatham Area Transit Authority, Savannah, Ga., 1987—; sec., treas. Chatham Transit Pension Fund, Chatham Transit Bd. Dirs., Savannah, 1987—. Mem. Clearwater Jr. Women's Club, Oglethorpe Bus. and Profl. Women's Club, Govt. Fin. Officers Assn., Phi Theta Kappa, Phi Chi Theta (pres. 1978-79, nat. councilor 1978). Democrat. Office: Chatham Area Transit Authority 900 E Gwinnett St Savannah GA 31412

WYNSTRA, NANCY ANN, lawyer; b. Seattle, June 25, 1941; d. Walter S. and Gaile E. (Cogley) W. B.A. cum laude, Whitman Coll., 1963; LL.B. cum laude, Columbia U., 1966. Bar: Wash. 1966, D.C. 1969, Ill. 1979, Pa. 1984. With appellate sect., civil div. U.S. Dept. Justice, Washington, 1966-67; TV corr.-legal news Sta. WRC, NBC and Sta. WTOP, CBS, Washington, 1967-68; spl. asst. Corp. Counsel, D.C., Washington, 1968-70; dir. planning and research D.C. Superior Ct., Washington, 1970-78; spl. advisor White House Spl. Action Office for Drug Abuse Prevention, Washington, 1973-74; fellow Drug Abuse Council, 1974-75; gen. counsel Michael Reese Hosp. and Med. Center, Chgo., 1978-83; sr. v.p., gen. counsel Allegheny Health Services, Inc., Pitts., 1983-87, exec. v.p., gen. counsel, 1987—; pres. Allegheny Health Services Providers Ins. Co., Grand Canyon, 1986— ; cons. to various drug abuse programs, 1971-78. Mem. ABA, Nat. Health Lawyers Assn. (bd. dirs. 1985—), Am. Soc. Hosp. Attys., others. Presbyterian. Contbr. articles to profl. jours. Office: Allegheny Gen Hosp 320 E North Ave Pittsburgh PA 15208

WYSS, DIANNE DUNLOP, coal fuel company executive; b. Kingsport, Tenn., May 1, 1950; d. Donald D. and Maxine (Hooker) Dunlop; m. John Benedict Wyss, Aug. 12, 1978; children: John Christian, Kirsten Dunlop. BS in Phys. Therapy, U. Okla., 1973; MBA in Finance, Va. Poly. and State U., 1980. Chief fin. and adminstrv. officer Slurrytech Inc., Miami, Fla., 1980-83; pres. Fuels Mgmt. subs. Slurrytech Inc., Miami, Fla., 1982-83; v.p. Fuels Mgmt. Inc., Miami, 1983—. Mem. fair share fundraising com. Sidwell Friends Sch., Washington, 1986-87; bd. dirs. Native Am. Model Resource Edn. Program. Mem. Vis. Nurse Assn. (profl. adv. com. 1979—), D.C. LWV (treas. 1980-81, v.p. 1982-83, 86-87). Democrat. Mem. Soc. Friends. Club: Washington Coal. Office: FMI/Slurrytech 7027 SW 148 Terr Miami FL 33158

XETHALIS, EILEEN SCANLON, accountant; b. New Castle, Pa., May 8, 1943; d. Thomas Edward and Martha Irene (Posivach) Scanlon; BA, NYU, 1982; m. Demetrios L. Xethalis, July 11, 1966; children: Sofia Demetria, Lambros Demetrios. Pres. Woodfield Collections , Hightstown, N.J., 1967—. Key leader Capital Funds campaign Princeton Day Sch., 1976-77; v.p. Arts and Exhibits Parents Assn., 1977-79, class parent, 1981. Mem. Am. Mgmt. Assn., Nat. Assn. Accts., Controllers Council, Bus. Planning Bd., Direct Mktg. Assn. Republican. Greek Orthodox. Club: Skyview Country. Home: 182 Stockton St Hightstown NJ 08520 Office: 633 Route 130 East Windsor NJ 08520

YABLON, ANDREA RICE ROZRAN, health care company executive; b. Chgo., Dec. 17, 1941; d. Robert W. and Vivian Hope (Elstein) Rice; m. Jack L. Rozran, Sept. 6, 1965 (div. 1980); m. Marshall Stewart Yablon, Feb. 12, 1981; 1 child, Alexis. BA, U. Mich., 1962; MA, UCLA, 1967; postgrad. U. Chgo., 1965-71. Statis. cons. dept. edn. U. Chgo., 1967-69, Scott, Foresman and Co., Glenview, Ill., 1970; staff assoc. Woodstock Inst., Chgo., 1977-79; pres. Andrea R. Rozran and Assocs., Chgo., 1979-80, Diversified Health Resources, Inc., Chgo., 1980—; cons. City of Chgo., 1979; corp. bd. mem. Blue Cross of Ill., Chgo., 1981—. Author: (monograph) The Planner's Role in Facilitating Private Sector Reinvestment, 1979. Mem. Ill. Health Facilities Planning Bd., Springfield, 1974-79; mem. Ill. adv. com. to U.S. Civil Rights Commn., Chgo., 1979-84; co-chmn. Profl. Health Services div. Jewish United Fund, Chgo., 1985—; mem. priorities com. United Way of Met. Chgo., 1976-79; Mem. LWV (v.p., chmn. various coms., 1972-77), Am. Health Planning Assn., Soc. for Hosp. Planning and Mktg., Women's Health Execs. Network (chmn. by-laws com. 1981-83), Am.-Israel C. of C. (bd. dirs. Met. Chgo. chpt. 1983—). Home: 1209 N Astor St Chicago IL 60610 Office: Diversified Health Resources Inc 520 N Michigan Ave Suite 550 Chicago IL 60611

YACCARINO, MARIE ELAINE, social services director; b. Montclair, N.J., Aug. 28, 1941; d. James Edward and Mary Agnes (Ferrera) Grande; m. Michael Ralph Yaccarino, May 28, 1961; children: Susan, Michael, Daniel. BA magna cum laude, Montclair State Coll., 1988. Exec. sec. Hoffman-LaRoche, Nutley, N.J., 1959-61; v.p. Michelangelo, Inc., North Arlington, N.J., 1969—; cons. Drop-In Ctr., Montclair State Coll., Upper Montclair, N.J., 1988—. Mem. North Arlington Restoration, 1985—. Roman Catholic. Office: Michelangelo Inc 7 Ridge Rd North Arlington NJ 07032

YACHER, NANCY TERRELL STEERE, educator; b. McMinnville, Oreg., Mar. 22, 1935; d. Horace Clifford and Mary Margaret (Newsom) Terrell; student Linfield Coll., 1953-55; B.A. summa cum laude in English, Lewis and Clark Coll., 1957; M.A. in Am. Studies (Danforth fellow, scholar), U. Pa., 1960; postgrad. (Danforth Grad. Woman fellow), U. Kans., 1972-78; m. Sherman L. Yacher, Oct. 5, 1979; children by previous marriage—John Tierney Steere, Robert Terrell Steere. Program asst. Am. Friends Service Com., Phila., 1957-58, 60-61; asst. instr. English dept. U. Kans., Lawrence, 1975-78, lectr., 1985—; asst. prof. English, Washburn U., Topeka, 1980—.

Mem. regional selection com. Danforth Assocs. Program, 1972-74; bd. dirs. Gainesville (Fla.) Women for Equal Civil Rights, 1962-67; chmn. Lawrence Community Nursery, 1968-69; v.p. Schwegler Sch. PTA, Lawrence, 1970-71; bd. dirs. Lawrence Environ. Improvement Assn., 1970-72. Danforth Assoc., 1963-75. Mem. Nat. Council Tchrs. of English, Soc. for Values in Higher Edn., Internat. Platform Assn., Assocs. Religion and Intellectual Life, Inst. for Theol. Encounter with Sci. and Tech., Sigma Tau Delta. Home: 1749 W 20th St Lawrence KS 66046 Office: 157 Morgan Hall Washburn U Topeka KS 66621

YACOBIAN, SONIA SIMONE, metals company executive; b. Cairo, Egypt, Feb. 13, 1943; came to U.S., 1966, naturalized, 1971; d. Simon and Lucy (Guendimian) Samsonian; divorced; children: Tatiana, Richard. BS, Lycee of Cairo, 1962; BBA, U. Cairo, Egypt, 1965; student Pace U., 1978-80. Asst. mgr. new accounts Lincoln Savs. & Loan, Los Angeles, 1973-77; sr. acct. U.S. Industries, N.Y.C., 1977-81; dep. mgr. French C. of C., N.Y.C., 1981-82; mgr. mktg. Samancor Metals, New Rochelle, N.Y., 1982-84; pres. NIDDAM Inc., Dix Hills, N.Y., 1984—. Mem. Assn. Profl. Women in Metal. Republican. Orthodox Christian. Home: 37 Wintergreen Dr Dix Hills Long Island NY 11746 Office: NIDDAM Inc PO Box 877 Melville NY 11747

YACOVONE, ELLEN ELAINE, bank executive; b. Ithaca, N.Y., Aug. 4, 1951; d. Wilfred Elliott and Charlotte Frances (Fox) Drew; m. Richard Daniel Yacovone, June 2, 1979; stepchildren: Christopher Daniel, Kimberly Marie. Student Broome Community Coll., 1973-80; cert. Inst. Fin. Edn., Chgo., 1974. Sec. to exec. v.p. Ithaca Savs., N.Y., summer 1968; mortgage clk. Citizens Savs. Bank, 1968-69; with Lincoln Bank, Van Nuys, Calif., 1970-71; asst. bookkeeper Henry's Jewelers, Binghamton, N.Y., 1971-74; teller, br. supt., br. mgr. First Fed. Savs., Binghamton, N.Y., 1974-82, v.p., central regional sales mgr., 1982-86, dist. sales mgr., 1986-88; br. mgr. Great Western Bank, Pensacola, Fla., 1988—. Mem. Gov.'s Commn. on Domestic Violence, Albany, N.Y., 1983-87; bd. dirs. S.O.S. Shelter, Inc., Endicott, N.Y., 1979-88, pres., 1982-83, treas., 1985-86; vol. United Way of Broome County, Binghamton, 1976-88, WSKG Pub. TV, Conklin, N.Y., 1974-88; mem. Found. State U. Ctr. at Binghamton. Named Woman of Achievement, Broome County Status of Women Council, 1981. Mem. Triple Cities Bus. and Profl. Women (pres. 1979-81, young careerist award 1977), Sales and Mktg. Execs., Broome County C. of C., Broome County Bankers Assn. (bd. dirs. 1979-88, pres. 1983-84), Inst. Fin. Edn. (bd. dirs. 1976-88, pres. 1984-85). Republican. Methodist. Avocations: exercise, camping, wood working, gardening, needlecrafts. Home: 1822 Donegal Way Cantonment FL 32533 Office: Great Western Bank 440 Navy Blvd N Pensacola FL 32507

YAEGER, BILLIE PATRICIA, advertising sales executive; b. Boston, Mar. 17, 1949; d. Harold Stern and Marie Frances (Levenson) Y. Student, Logos Bible Coll. Office mgr., NE rep. Ticketron, Inc., Boston, 1968-73; owner, mgr. Performance King, Natick, Mass., 1973-74, House of Portraits, Lakeland, Fla., 1974-75; employment counselor Snelling & Snelling, Lakeland, 1975-77; advt. sales account exec. The Ledger/N.Y. Times, Lakeland, 1977—. Recipient Chmn. of Bd. award N.Y. Times, 1984-85, 10 Yr. Service award The Ledger/N.Y. Times, 1987, Commendation award Fla. Dept. Law Enforcement, 1986; named Salesperson of Yr., 1987. Mem. Nat. Assn. Female Execs. Republican. Avocations: photography, writing, waterskiing.

YAES, JOYCE IRIS, educator, musician; b. N.Y.C., July 18, 1944; d. William Johnson and Jean (Brander) Idelson; m. Robert Yaes, Nov. 16, 1986. BA, Bklyn. Coll., 1966, MA, 1972; postgrad., Juilliard Sch., 1971-75, Mannes Coll., 1975, Manhattan Sch. Music, 1974-75, U. Neuchatel, Switzerland, 1967, U. San Miguel, Mex., 1969. Cert. tchr., N.Y., Ky. Tchr. art and music N.Y.C., 1966-86; tchr. music Emerson Sch., N.Y.C., 1976-80; agt. ins. N.Y.C., 1982-87; tchr. Living Arts and Sci. Ctr., Lexington, Ky., 1987—; pvt. tchr. music. Author: Humanities and Arts Perspectives, Microphishe Education Perspectives; violinist various orchs., N.Y. and Ky.; dir. various art show. Mem. United Fedn. Tchrs., Music Tchrs. Assn. (mem. exec. com.), Music Educators Nat. Conf., Port Educators Assn., Nat. Assn. Female Execs., Lexington Art League, Federated Music Club, U. Ky. Woman's Club. Office: Living Arts and Sci Ctr 362 Walnut St Lexington KY 40508

YALE, PHYLLIS, management consultant; b. N.Y.C., June 7, 1957; d. William H. and Elaine (Klein) Y.; m. S. Tucker Taft, June 27, 1982; 1 child, Rebecca. AB, Harvard U., 1978, MBA, 1982. Account officer Citibank, N.Y.C., 1978-79, Cleve., 1979-80; cons., mgr., v.p. Bain & Co., Boston, 1982-87; adj. faculty Am. Coll. Healthcare Execs., Chgo., 1985-87. Co-chmn. Harvard- Radcliffe Fund, 1982-85, capital campaign Class '78, Harvard U., 1982-85. Office: Bain & Co 2 Copley Pl Boston MA 02116

YALOW, ROSALYN SUSSMAN, medical physicist; b. N.Y.C., July 19, 1921; d. Simon and Clara (Zipper) Sussman; m. A. Aaron Yalow, June 6, 1943; children: Benjamin, Elanna. A.B., Hunter Coll., 1941; M.S., U. Ill., Urbana, 1942, Ph.D., 1945; D.Sc. (hon.), U. Ill., Chgo., 1974, Phila. Coll. Pharmacy and Sci., 1976, N.Y. Med. Coll., 1976, Med. Coll. Wis., Milw., 1977, Yeshiva U., 1977, Southampton (N.Y.) Coll., 1978, Bucknell U., 1978, Princeton U., 1978, Jersey City State Coll., 1979, Med. Coll. Pa., 1979, Manhattan Coll., 1979, U. Vt., 1980, U. Hartford, 1980, Rutgers U., 1980, Rensselaer Poly. Inst., 1980, Colgate U., 1981, U. So. Calif., 1981, Clarkson Coll., 1982, U. Miami, 1983, Washington U., St. Louis, 1983, Adelphi U., 1983, U. Alta. (Can.), 1983, Columbia U., 1984, SUNY, 1984, Tel Aviv U., 1985, Claremont (Calif.) U., 1986, Mills Coll., Oakland, Calif., 1986; L.H.D. (hon.), Hunter Coll., 1978, Sacred Heart U., Conn., 1978, St. Michael's Coll., Winooski Park, Vt., 1979, Johns Hopkins U., 1979; D. honoris causa, U. Rosario, Argentina, 1980, U. Ghent, Belgium, 1984; D. Humanities and Letters (hon.), Columbia U., 1984; D. Philosophy (hon.), Bar-Ilan U., Israel, 1987. Diplomate: Am. Bd. Scis. Lectr., asst. prof. physics Hunter Coll., 1946-50; physicist, asst. chief radioisotope service VA Hosp., Bronx, N.Y., 1950-70, chief nuclear medicine, 1970-80, acting chief radioisotope service, 1968-70; research prof. Mt. Sinai Sch. Medicine, CUNY, 1968-74, Disting. Service prof., 1974-79, Solomon A. Berson Disting. prof.-at-large, 1986—; Disting. prof.-at-large Albert Einstein Coll. Medicine, Yeshiva U., 1979-85, prof. emeritus, 1986—; chmn. dept. clin. scis. Montefiore Med. Ctr., Bronx, 1980-85; cons. Lenox Hill Hosp., N.Y.C., 1956-62, WHO, Bombay, 1978; sec. U.S. Nat. Com. on Med. Physics, 1963-67; mem. nat. com. Radiation Protection, Subcom. 13, 1957; mem. Pres.'s Study Group on Careers for Women, 1966-72; sr. med. investigator VA, 1972—; dir. Solomon A. Berson Research Lab., VA Hosp., Bronx, N.Y., 1973—. Co-editor: Hormone and Metabolic Research, 1973-79; editorial adv. council: Acta Diabetologica Latina, 1975-77, Ency. Universalis, 1978—; editorial bd.: Mt. Sinai Jour. Medicine, 1976-79, Diabetes, 1976, Endocrinology, 1967-72; contbr. numerous articles to profl. jours. Bd. dirs. N.Y. Diabetes Assn., 1974. Recipient VA William S. Middleton Med. Research award, 1960; Eli Lilly award Am. Diabetes Assn., 1961; Van Slyke award N.Y. met. sect. Am. Assn. Clin. Chemists, 1968; award A.C.P., 1971; Dickson prize U. Pitts., 1971; Howard Taylor Ricketts award U. Chgo., 1971; Gairdner Found. Internat. award, 1971; Commemorative medallion Am. Diabetes Assn., 1972; Bernstein award Med. Soc. State N.Y., 1974; Boehringer-Mannheim Corp. award Am. Assn. Clin. Chemists, 1975; Sci. Achievement award AMA, 1975; Exceptional Service award VA, 1975; A. Cressy Morrison award N.Y. Acad. Scis., 1975; sustaining membership award Assn. Mil. Surgeons, 1975; Distinguished Achievement award Modern Medicine, 1976; Albert Lasker Basic Med. Research award, 1976; La Madonnina Internat. prize Milan, 1977; Golden Plate award Am. Acad. Achievement, 1977; Nobel prize for medicine and physiology, 1977; citation of esteem St. John's U., 1979; G. von Hevesy medal, 1978; Rosalyn S. Yalow Research and Devel. award established Am. Diabetes Assn., 1978; Banting medal, 1978; Torch of Learning award Am. Friends Hebrew U., 1978; Virchow gold medal Virchow-Pirquet Med. Soc., 1978; Gratum Genus Humanum gold medal World Fedn. Nuclear Medicine or Biology, 1978; Jacobi medallion Assn. Alumni Mt. Sinai Sch. Medicine, 1978; Jubilee medal Coll. of New Rochelle, 1978, VA Exceptional Service award, 1978; Fed. Woman's award, 1961; Harvey lectr., 1966; Am. Gastroenterol. Assn. Meml. lectr., 1972; Joslin lectr. New Eng. Diabetes Assn., 1972; Franklin I. Harris Meml. lectr., 1973; 1st Hagedorn Meml. lectr. Acta Endocrinologica Congress, 1973; Sarasota Med. award for achievement and excellence, 1979; gold medal Phi Lambda Kappa, 1980; Achievement in Life award Ency. Brit., 1980; Theobald Smith award, 1982; Pres.'s Cabinet award U. Detroit, 1982; John and Samuel Bard award in medicine and sci. Bard Coll., 1982; Disting. Research award Dallas Assn. Retarded Citizens, 1982; numerous others. Fellow N.Y. Acad. Scis. (chmn. biophysics div. 1964-65), Am. Coll. Radiology (asso. in physics), Clin. Soc. N.Y. Diabetes Assn.; mem. Nat. Acad. Scis., Am. Acad. Arts and Scis., Am. Phys. Soc., Radiation Research Soc., Am. Assn. Physicists in Medicine, Biophys. Soc., Soc. Nuclear Medicine, Endocrine Soc. (Koch award 1972, pres. 1978), Am. Physiol. Soc., (hon.) Harvey Soc., (hon.) Med. Assn. Argentina, (hon.) Diabetes Soc. Argentina, (hon.) Am. Coll. Nuclear Physicians, (hon.) The N.Y. Acad. Medicine, (hon.) Am. Gastroent. Assn., (hon.) N.Y. Roentgen Soc., (hon.) Soc. Nuclear Medicine, Phi Beta Kappa, Sigma Xi, Sigma Pi Sigma, Pi Mu Epsilon, Sigma Delta Epsilon. Office: VA Med Ctr 130 W Kingsbridge Rd Bronx NY 10468

YAMAKOSHI, LOIS, mathematics educator; b. Reedley, Calif., May 9, 1954; d. Frank Kazuo and Helen Shigeko (Kuwada) Y. BS, Pepperdine U., 1976; MA, Calif. State U.-Northridge, 1980; postgrad., UCLA, 1977-81, Calif. State U.-Hayward, 1983-88. Math. tchr. Malibu Park Jr. High Sch., Malibu, Calif., 1976-80, Southgate Lower Sch., London, 1980; math. instr. Los Medanos Coll., Pittsburg, Calif., 1981—; tax preparation instr. H&R Block Co., Walnut Creek, Calif., 1984; speaker in field. Contbr. articles to profl. publs. Project dir. Calif. Chancellor's Office, Sacramento, 1988. Elks Nat. Found. scholar, 1972. Mem. Nat. Council Tchrs. Math. (presider 1985), Math. Assn. Am., Calif. Math. Council Community Colls., United Faculty, Alameda Contra Costa County Math. Educators (sec. 1982—), Kappa Delta Pi, Kappa Kappa. Democrat. Buddhist. Club: Asians on Campus (Pittsburg). Office: Los Medanos Coll 2700 E Leland Rd Box 107 Pittsburg CA 94565

YAMANAKA, WENDI SUZUKO, pharmacist; b. Stockton, Calif., July 27, 1957; d. Noboru and Dorothy Chisato (Kaneko) Y. AA in Natural Scis., San Joaquin Delta Coll., 1977; BS in Chemistry and Biology, U. Pacific, 1980, D in Pharmacy, 1983. Lic. pharmacist Calif., Nev. Intern Campus Pharmacy, Stockton, 1981; clin. intern in pharmacy San Joaquin Gen. Hosp., Stockton, 1982; intern pharmacist Drs. Med. Ctr., Modesto, Calif., 1983; pharmacist Payless Drug Stores, Menlo Park, Calif., 1984—. Mem. Calif. Pharm. Assn., Am. Soc. Hosp. Pharmacists. Buddhist. Home: 125 E Jefferson St Stockton CA 95206

YAMANI, ELAINE REIKO, computer-peripherial company executive; b. Ogden, Utah, Apr. 2, 1945; d. Joe and Chieko (Kato) Yamani; m. Victor G. Sugihara, Aug. 10, 1970 (div. June 1973); 1 dau., Jo Ann Renae. B.S. in English and Psychology, Weber State U., 1965, A.A., 1967; M in Human Resource Mgmt., U. Utah, 1975-79. Personnel generalist Weber State U., Odgen, Utah, 1973-78; personnel specialist Cutter Lab., Ogden, 1978-81; human resource mgr. Iomega, Ogden, 1981-83, compensation and benefits mgr., 1983-85; dir. human resources Cericor Inc., 1983; personnel mgr., Hewlett-Packard, 1983—. Mem. Utah Personnel Assn. (pres. 1988), No. Utah Personnel Assn. (pres. 1980-81). Lodge: Soroptimist (sec. 1981). Office: Hewlett Packard Lake Side Plaza One Suite200 Salt Lake City UT 84116

YANCEY, ANNE RICHARDSON, civic worker; b. Brookline, Mass., Feb. 12, 1913; d. Otis Weld and Lucile (Johnston) Richardson; B.A., Vassar Coll., 1936; m. Charles Stephen Yancey, Apr. 9, 1942; children—Sherod Anne, Charles Stephen. Researcher, asst. sec. Mass. Investors Trust, Boston, 1937-40; researcher Harvard Sch. Pub. Health, 1942-45; partner, co-adminstr. Fairlawn Nursing Home, 1963-73; pres. Dalmin Devel. Corp., Dallas, 1973-84. Mem. Boston Jr. League, 1932-45; mem. Dallas Jr. League, 1945—, 1st v.p., 1952-54; pres. Dallas Vis. Nurse Assn., 1952-54; 1st v.p. Children's Bur., Dallas, 1945-47; bd. dirs. Dallas Planned Parenthood, 1956-58, Dallas Soc. Crippled Children, 1954-60; exec. bd. Community Council Greater Dallas, 1955-65, 1st v.p., 1959-61, chmn. family and children's div., 1957-59; Gov.'s Com. White House Conf. Children and Youth, 1960; mem. Linz Award Com., Dallas, 1961; bd. dirs. Dallas Civic Opera Guild, 1965-72, Council World Affairs, 1964-65, Island Nursing Home, Deer Isle, Maine, 1975-82, Nat. Conservancy, 1977—; class fund chmn. Vassar Coll., Poughkeepsie, N.Y., 1977-81, active Dallas Mus. Fine Arts, Dallas Symphony Orch. League, Friends of Library. Licensed nursing home adminstr., Tex. Mem. Am. Coll. Nursing Home Adminstrs., Nat. Assn. Jr. Leagues Am., Nat. Soc. Colonial Dames Am., Pan Am. Round Table (dir. 1964-65), Am. Hort. Soc. Episcopalian. Clubs: Dallas Women's, Dallas Garden, Garden Club Fedn. Maine (dir.), Evergreen Garden (pres. 1964-65), Boston Vassar, Harpswell Garden, Dallas Vassar. Home: Route 1 Box 827 South Harpswell ME 04079

YANCEY, GLORIA P., telephone company executive; b. Louisville, Apr. 26, 1948; d. Joe T. and Mossie Lee (Wheeler) White; m. Ronald E. Yancey, July 30, 1970 (div. Sept. 1986); 1 child, Angela Pearl. BA, U. Louisville, 1970, MA, 1974. Tchr. Louisville Pub. Schs., 1970-75; instr. Jefferson Community Coll., Louisville, 1974-75; tchr. Ministry of Edn., Kuru Jos, Nigeria, 1975-76; residence ctr. mgr. South Cen. Bell Telephone Co., Louisville, 1976—. Mem. LWV, Friends of Library, Louisville Urban League, Nat. Conf. Negro Women, Water Tower Art Assn. Democrat. Baptist. Home: PO Box 1282 Louisville KY 40202

YANCEY, LAUREL GUILD, lawyer; b. Santa Rosa, Calif., Dec. 12, 1953; d. George Prescott and Helen Elizabeth (Branker) Guild. B.A., Simmons Coll., 1975; J.D., Boston Coll., 1978. Bar: Mass. 1979, D.C. 1985. Law clk. Office Atty. Gen., Boston, 1977-78, Dept. Justice, Washington, summer 1977; sr. atty. Fed. Commns. Com., Washington, 1978—. Assoc. editor UCLA Black Law Jour., 1978. Recipient Community Service award FCC, Washington, 1979, Women in FCC, 1983. Roman Catholic. Home: 15544 Brandywine Rd Brandywine MD 20613 Office: FCC 1919 M St NW Washington DC 20554

YANICKE, GEORGIA ANN, educational administrator; b. Milw., July 10, 1945; d. George Elmer and Lucille Sylvia (Schroeder) Y. Student Goethe Inst., Murnau,-W.Ger., 1966, U. Innsbruck (Austria), 1966; B.A., Cornell Coll., 1967; M.S., U. Wis. Milw., 1970; Ph.D., U. Wis., Madison, 1975. Cert. spl. edn. supr., tchr., Wis. Tchr. mentally retarded McKinley Sch., West Allis, Wis., 1967-69; lectr. U. Wis.-Milw., 1970-74, 77-79, 84-85; practicum supr. U. Wis.-Madison, 1974-75; asst. prof. Creighton U., Omaha, 1975-77; supr. programs for emotionally disturbed and generic early childhood Milw. Pub. Schs., 1977-85, early childhood: exceptional edn. needs, 1985—; cons. Sitters for Handicapped Children Project, Milw. area Girl Scouts U.S., 1973-74, Milw. Pub. Schs., 1976, Creighton U. Inst. for Bus., Law and Social Research, 1976-77; inservice coordinator for Blessed Sacrament St. Richards and St. Philip Neri Cath. Schs., Omaha, Nebr., 1975-76; developer, adminstr. pre-kindergarten screening instrument, 1976-77; mem. child care adv. com. Milw. Area Tech. Coll., 1979-80; mem. edn. study group Wis. Dept. Pub. Instrn., Madison, 1981; condr. workshops in field; speaker profl. meetings. Active Greater Milw. Girl Scouts U.S., 1961-77, bd. dirs., 1971-75; mem. ad hoc study com. Children's Day Services, Planning Council for Mental Health and Social Services, Inc., Milw., 1981-82; mem. ad hoc early childhood aquatics Greater Milw. chpt. ARC, mem. adaptive aquatics com., 1983-85; mem. vol. day care com. for ednl. programming, Milw. County Zoo, 1984. U.S. Office Edn. fellow, 1969-70; U. Wis.-Madison Grad. Sch. fellow, 1974. Mem. Council for Exceptional Children (div. children with learning disabilities state and province com. 1976-77), Am. Assn. on Mental Retardation, Internat. Reading Assn., Wis. State Reading Assn. (emergent reading com. 1986—), Autism Soc. Am. (bd. dirs. Milw. Assn. 1983—), Nat. Council Tchrs. of English, Wis. Assn. for Children with Behavior Disorders (adv. bd. 1977-82, 84—, pres. 1983-84), Wis. Assn. Infant/Toddler Devel. (sec. 1982—), Phi Delta Kappa, Pi Lambda Theta, Delta Kappa Gamma (sec. 1985-86). Home: 9085 N 85th St Milwaukee WI 53224 Office: Elem Zone Milw Pub Schs 3620 N 18th St Milwaukee WI 53206

YANISH, ELIZABETH YAFFE, sculptor; b. St. Louis; d. Sam and Fannie May (Weil) Yaffe; student Washington U., 1941, Denver U., 1960; pvt. studies; m. Nathan Yanish, July 5, 1944; children—Ronald, Marilyn Ginsburg, Mindy. One-woman shows: Woodstock Gallery, London, 1973, Internat. House, Denver, 1963, Colo. Women's Coll., Denver, 1975, Contemporaries Gallery, Santa Fe, 1963, So. Colo. State Coll. Pueblo, 1967, others; exhibited in group shows: Salt Lake City Mus., 1964, 71, Denver Art Mus., 1961-75, Oklahoma City Mus., 1969, Joslyn Mus., Omaha, 1964-68, Lucca (Italy) Invitational, 1971, others; represented in permanent collections: Colo. State Bank, Bmh Synagogue, Denver, Denver Womens Coll., Har Ha Shem Congregation, Boulder, Colo., Faith Bible Chapel, Denver, others. Chmn. visual arts Colo. Centennial-Bicentennial, 1974-75; pres. Denver Council Arts and Humanities, 1973-75; mem. Mayor's Com. on Child Abuse, 1974-75; co-chmn. visual arts spree Denver Pub. Schs., 1975; trustee Denver Center for the Performing Arts, 1973-75; chmn. Concerned Citizens for Arts, 1976; pres. Beth Israel Hosp. Aux., 1985-87; organizer Coat Drive for the Needy, 1982-87; bd. dirs. Srs., Inc. Recipient McCormick award Ball State U., Muncie, Ind., 1964, Purchase award Colo. Women's Coll., Denver, 1963, Tyler (Tex.) Mus., 1963, 1st prize in sculpture 1st Nat. Space Art Show, 1971; Humanities scholar Auraria Libraries, U. Colo., Denver. Mem. Artists Equity Assn., Rocky Mountain Liturgical Arts, Allied Sculptors Colo., Allied Arts Inc. Hist. Denver, Symphony Guild, Parks People, Beth Israel Aux. Jewish. Home: 131 Fairfax St Denver CO 80220

YANKEE, HELEN MARIE, educator, publishing executive; b. Detroit, July 31, 1925; d. Lester G. and Irene Maude (McGinness) Auberlin; m. J.R. Yankee, June 6, 1956; children: Michael, David, Stephen, Jennifer. Diploma Montessori edn., Montessori Inst. Am., 1968; MS, Southeastern U., Greenville, S.C., 1980, PhD, 1981. Chief exec. officer The Fernhaven Studio, Los Angeles, 1966—, Montessori Ednl. Environment, Los Angeles, 1974—, Yankee Montessori Mfg., Los Angeles, 1980-86; pres. Inst. Montessori Internat. Tchr. Tng., Long Beach, Calif., 1980—; research editor Edn. Systems Pub., Los Angeles, 1982—; dir. EEI, Inc., Los Angeles, 1987—; cons. Calif. pub. schs., 1976—. Author: Montessori Curriculum, 1982, Reading Program, 1981, Science for Preschool, 1981, Geography for Preschool, 1982. Mem. Am. Montessori Soc., Montessori Inst. Am. Home: 38395 Trifone Rd Sage CA 92343-9693 Office: Edn Systems Pub PO Box 536 Hemet CA 92343

YANKO, MARGARET MARY, data processing executive; b. West Hazleton, Pa., Nov. 28, 1948; m. William F. Yanko; children: Kasandra Lee, William A. Student, E. Stroudsburg U., Pa., Temple U., Inst. Computer Mgmt. With U.S. Govt. Social Security Adminstrn., Phila., 1969-80; tech. cons. U.S. Govt. Social Security Adminstrn., ops. analyst; sr. MIS trainer Harrah's Marina Casino/Hotel, Atlantic City, N.J., 1980-82; programmer, analyst Harrah's Marina Casino/Hotel, Atlantic City, 1982-84; data processing mgr. Trump Casino/Hotel, Atlantic City, 1984-86; systems cons. CAP Gemini Am., Bala Cynwyd, Pa., 1986; asst.dir.. Cigna Systems, Voorhees, N.J., 1986—; lectr. in field. Contbr. articles to profl. jours. Mem. Data Processing Mgmt. Assn. (N.J. chpt.), Nat. Assn. Female Execs.

YANNELLO, CHERYL ANNETTE, candy company executive, lawyer; b. Buffalo, Jan. 29, 1947; d. Guy Raymond and Grace Alberta (Barone) Y. B.A., Lynchburg Coll., 1968; M.A., SUNY-Stonybrook, 1973; cert. of study N.Y. State Sch. Indsl. and Labor Relations, 1977; J.D., Ohio No. U., 1980. Bar: Ill. 1981. Tchr., West Islip Pub. Sch. (N.Y.), 1968-78; assoc. Klein, Thrope & Jenkins, Ltd., Chgo., 1980-82; indsl. relations mgr. E.J. Brach & Sons, Chgo., 1982-83, asst. v.p. indsl. relations, 1984-86; v.p. personnel, Jacobs Suchard/Brach, Inc., 1987—; counselor Cornell-N.Y. State Sch. Indsl. and Labor Relations, Farmingdale, 1976-77. Officer, pres. West Islip Tchrs. Assn., 1968-78. Mem. ABA, Ill. Bar Assn., Delta Kappa Gamma (Ruth Mack Haven scholar 1979). Office: Jacobs Suchard/Brach Inc 4656 W Kinzie St Chicago IL 60644

YANNELLO, KAREN MARIE, lawyer; b. Buffalo, May 8, 1952; d. Guy R. and Grace A. (Barone) Y. BA, Coll. William and Mary, 1974; JD, U. Va., 1977. Bar: Va. 1977, D.C. 1979. Sr. editor Michie-Bobbs Merrill Law Pub. Co., Charlottesville, Va., 1977-80; lawyer Office of Gen. Counsel, U.S. Dept. Def., Washington, 1980—; pres. sr. profl. women's group Office of Sec. Def., 1983-86. Mem. ABA (pub. contracts sect.), Va. State Bar, D.C. Bar, Phi Beta Kappa.

YANNUZZI, ELAINE VICTORIA, food products executive; b. Summit, N.J., Aug. 14, 1933; d. Emil and Alice (Vance) Y. BA, Seton Hall U., 1968. Pres. Expression Unltd., Warren, N.J., 1971—; presenter seminar N.Y. Food and Wine Show; lectr. NYU, Rutgers U.; moderator Am. Women's Econ. Devel., N.Y.C., 1985-87; speaker Women Bus. Owners of N.J., Princeton, 1986. Author: Gift Wrapping Food, 1985; editorial advisor Fancy Food mag., 1985—; editorial cons. Family Circle Gt. Ideas mag., 1987—. Named Entrepreneur of Yr. N.J. Living mag., 1983, Woman of Yr. NYU, 1986. Mem. Roundtable for Women (bd. dirs. 1986—, Pacesetter award 1985), Nat. Assn. for Splty. Food Trade (steering com. 1986). Home: 4 Timberline Dr Bridgewater NJ 08807 Office: Expression unltd 165 Washington Valley Rd Warren NJ 07060

YANOFSKY, BRENDA LEE, psychologist; b. Boston, May 10, 1950; d. Abraham and Martha (Yakus) Y.; BA cum laude, U. Mass., 1971; MEd cum laude, Tufts U., 1973; cert. advanced grad. studies Boston U., 1974, EdD, 1985. Counselor, Newton North High Sch., Newtonville, Mass., 1972-76; psychologist State of Mass., 1974-76, Oak Park (Mich.) Schs., 1976—; instr. Ea. Mich. U., 1977-81, Mercy Coll., 1982-85; psychologist Jensen Counseling, Farmington Hills, Mich., 1980-86; psychologist Lakewood Clinic, Birmingham, Mich., 1984—; bd. dirs. Multi-Service Ctr., Newton, Mass., 1974-76. Mem. Am. Psychol. Assn., Am. Personnel and Guidance Assn., Mental Health Profs. Assn., Mich. Alcohol and Addiction Assn.

YAP, SALLY SO, quilt artist, designer; b. Manila, Dec. 11, 1954; d. See and Norma (So) Y.; m. Stephen Michael Akey, Jan. 9, 1981; 1 child, David Yap Akey. BS in Architecture, U. Santo Tomas, Manila, 1976; postgrad., Columbia U., 1980-81. Lic. profl. architect, Philippines. Architecture editor Vision mag., Coll. Architecture and Fine Arts, U. Santo Tomas, 1974-76; asst. to sr. ptnr. Gabriel Formoso and Ptnrs., Manila, 1976-78; free-lance archtl. designer Allen, Brown and Sheriff, Toronto, Ont., Can., 1978; urban planning intern Dept. Housing, Preservation and Devel. City of N.Y., 1979-80; architect Human Resources Adminstrn. div. City N.Y., 1981-85, assoc. space analyst, 1985-87; free-lance archtl. designer N.Y.C., 1987—; free-lance quilt artist Bklyn., 1987—. Etching printmaker Postage Stamp series exhibited Bklyn Mus. Sch. Ann. Exhibit, 1983; quilts exhibited at Schweinfurth Art Ctr., Auburn, N.Y., Galeria Mesa, Ariz., New Eng. Quilt Mus., Lowell, Mass., 1987-88. Democrat. Club: Bklyn. Bird. Home and Studio: 211 8th Ave #4D Brooklyn NY 11215

YAQUINTO, KATHLEEN MORAN, teacher, consultant; b. Fanwood, N.J., May 24, 1953; d. Joseph Kevin and Marjorie (Foley) Moran; m. Gary Dennis Yaquinto, Aug. 6, 1977; children: Carlee Ann, Lauren Moran. BS, U. Steubenville (Ohio), 1975. Tchr. John F. Kennedy Sch., Washington, Pa., 1975-77, 79-80; tutor, researcher Marist Coll., Poughkeepsie, N.Y., 1977; tchr. Regina Coeli Sch., Hyde Park, N.Y., 1978-79; supr. Assn. for Retarded Citizens, Meadowlands, Pa., 1982-86; counselor Physicians Weight Loss Ctrs., Washington, Pa., 1985-86; substitute tchr. various SE Pa. sch. dists., 1985—. Fellow Girl Scouts Am.; mem. PTA. Roman Catholic. Office: c/o Gary D Yaquinto 50 E Cherry Ave Washington PA 15301

YARABEK, JENNIFER JOHNSON, food products company executive; b. White Plains, N.Y., May 21, 1961; d. Donald Ferguson and Susanna (Siegrist) Johnson; m. John Andrew Yarabek, Jr., Sept. 6, 1986. BS in Resource Devel., U. Rhode Island, 1983; MBA in Mgmt., Mktg., Pace U., 1987. Consumer rep. Gen. Foods Corp., White Plains, 1984-86, mgr. telemktg., 1986-87; consumer affairs analyst Pepsi-Cola Co., Somers, N.Y., 1987—; bd. dirs. Merritt Promotion Devel. Group, Inc., Stamford, Conn., 1986—. Mem. Soc. Consumer Affairs Profls. (N.Y. Metro chpt.), Home Economists in Bus. Republican. Lutheran. Club: Norwalk Newcomers (Conn.). Home: 45 Deerwood Manor Norwalk CT 06851 Office: Pepsi Cola Co Rts 35 & 100 Somers NY 10589-0905

YARBOROUGH, N. PATRICIA, human resources executive; b. Beckville, Tex., Dec. 7, 1936; d. James Lamar and Del (Davis) Y. B.Mus., North Tex. State U., 1958, Ed.D., 1969; M.Ed., U. Md., 1963. Edn. cons. Prentice-Hall, Inc., Englewood Cliffs, N.J., 1963-65; tchr. Dallas Ind. Sch. Dist., 1965-67, supr. music, 1968-69, coordinator staff devel., 1969-70; dean instrn. Mountain View Coll. of Dallas County Community Coll. Dist., 1976-77, chmn. div. humanities, 1970-73, dean instrn. and student devel., 1973-76; v.p. instrn. Brookhaven Coll. of Dallas County Community Coll. Dist., 1977-80; pres. Mattatuck Community Coll., Waterbury, Conn., 1980-82; dir. human resources devel. Scovill Inc., Scovill World Hdqrs., Waterbury, Conn., 1982-

86; pres. Post Coll., Waterbury, 1986—; also trustee; proposal evaluator NEH, 1981; corporator The Banking Ctr. Bd. dirs. St. Mary's Hosp., Waterbury, 1981—; pub. mem. Conn. Humanities Council, NEH, 1982-84; bd. dirs. ARC, Waterbury chpt., 1982-85. U.S. Office Edn. grantee, N. Tex. State U., 1967. Mem. Sigma Alpha Iota, Alpha Chi, Phi Kappa Lambda. Home: Tyler Crossing Middlebury CT 06762 Office: Post Coll Office of Pres 800 Country Club Rd Waterbury CT 06708 *

YARBOROUGH, VALERIE LOUISE, internal auditor, consultant; b. San Antonio, Aug. 24, 1928; d. Wilbur G. and Grace Helen (Davis) Y.; m. Richard L. Storey (div. Nov. 1971); children: Christopher L., Dianna L., Paula L. Student, Colo. Woman's Coll., Santa Clarita Coll.; BA, Calif. State U., 1973. Mgr. Adams & Assocs., Seattle, 1973-76; staff acct. Helwig & Buttler, 1976-77, George Branley, CPA, Seattle, 1977-78; corp. acct. Westin Hotel Co., Seattle, 1978-79, staff auditor, 1979-85, sr. internal auditor, 1985—; bd. dirs. Christopher & Assocs., Seattle. Mem. Nat. Fedn. Womens Clubs (pres. Seville, Spain chpt. 1967), NOW, League Women Voters, Am. Soc. Women Accts., Nat. Mgmt. Accts. Home: 10019 Densmore N Seattle WA 98133 Office: Westin Bldg 20001 6th Ave Seattle WA 98121

YARBROUGH, JANIS COLEMAN, financial director; b. Athens, Ala., Oct. 20, 1955; d. William Thomas and Charlotte Ann (Turner) Y. Staff acct. Foley's, Houston, 1979-80, asst. mgr. acctg., 1980-81, mgr. fin. acctg., 1981-83, mgr. fin. reporting, 1983-86, mgr. fin. planning, expense control, 1987—. Mem. Phi Mu. Methodist. Avocations: tennis, reading, golf, bridge.

YARBROUGH, JOYCE LENORE, management consultant; b. Bowling Green, Ky., Oct. 7, 1948; d. William S. Yarbrough and Hortense Lenore (Bullock) Jackson; B.A., Fisk U., 1970; M.B.A., Golden Gate U., 1977. Spl. projects coordinator Econ. Opportunity Council, San Francisco, 1971-77; sales/statistician Macy's of Calif., San Francisco, 1971—; mgmt. cons. C.J. & Assos. Enterprises Inc., San Francisco, 1977-78; pres. Le Nore Co., Inc., 1978—; adminstrv. ops. supr. Bur. Census, U.S. Dept. Commerce, 1980; market researcher Western Pacific Industries, 1981—; dist. sales rep. Calif. State Lottery, 1985—. Co-founder Scott-Wada Youth Fund; bd. dirs. Urban League San Francisco, 1973-79, Mental Assn. San Francisco, 1972-79; panelist United Way of Bay Area, 1971-76; treas. Westside Community Mental Health Center, 1976-79; sec. Cath. Youth Orgn., 1977—; sec. Black Agenda Council San Francisco, 1984—. Mem. Mortar Bd. Home: 100 Font Blvd Apt 1K San Francisco CA 94132 Office: PO Box 15117 San Francisco CA 94115

YARBROUGH, LAURA MARIE BRADSHAW, corporate meeting planner; b. Vicksburg, Miss., May 26, 1957; d. Cyrus Joe and Louise Ann (Leonard) Bradshaw; m. Patrick Feldon Yarbrough, July 16, 1977. BS, East Tex. State U., 1979. Cert. meeting profl., 1987. Media dir. Sundance Prodns. Inc., Dallas, 1979; sales promotion specialist Southland Life Ins. Co., Dallas, 1979-83; corp. meeting planner Electronic Data Systems Corp., Dallas, 1983—; Contbr. articles to newsletter and mags. Named Planner of the Year Dallas Chpt. Meetings Planners Internat., 1987. Mem. Meeting Planners Internat. (bd. dirs. 1986—, v.p., adminstr. 1987—). Republican. Roman Catholic.

YARBROUGH, MARTHA CORNELIA, music educator; b. Waycross, Ga., Feb. 8, 1940; d. Henry Elliott and Jessie (Sirmans) Y.; B.M.E., Stetson U., 1962; M.M.E., Fla. State U., 1968, Ph.D., 1973. Choral dir. Ware County High Sch., Waycross, Ga., 1962-64, Glynn Acad., Brunswick, Ga., 1964-70; asst. choral dir. Fla. State U., 1970-72; cons. in music Muscogee County Sch. Dist., Columbus, Ga., 1972-73; cons. in tchr. edn. Psycho-Edno. Cons., Inc., Tallahassee, 1972-73; asst. prof. music edn., dir. univs. choruses and oratorio soc. Syracuse U., 1973-76, assoc. prof. music edn., 1976-83, prof., 1983-86, acting asst. dean Coll. Visual and Performing Arts, 1980-82, acting dir. Sch. Music, 1980-82, chmn. music edn., 1982-86; prof. music La. State U., Baton Rouge, 1986—, coordinator music, edn., 1986—. Mem. Music Educators Nat. Conf., N.Y. State Sch. Music Assn., Am. Ednl. Research Assn., AAUP, Pi Kappa Lambda, Phi Beta, Kappa Delta Pi. Co-author: Competency-Based Music Education, 1980; mem. editorial com. Jour. Research in Music Edn.; contbr. articles to profl. jours., chpts. in books. Office: La State U Sch Music Baton Rouge LA 70803

YARBROUGH, MARY GALE, hospital administrator; b. Ellis County, Tex., Feb. 15, 1946; d. Emmitt Ward and Ruthie Lee (McBrayer) McClendon; m. Orville Leon Yarbrough, Feb. 20, 1936; 1 child, Kyle William. B in Nursing, San Jose State U., 1975; M in Sci., U. Calif., 1977. Infection control practitioner VA Hosp., Palo Alto, Calif., 1970-78; dir. nursing O'Connor Hosp., San Jose, Calif., 1978-83; assoc. adminstr. City of Hope Nat. Med. Ctr., Duarte, Calif., 1983-86; exec. v.p., chief ops. officer Mercy Hosp. and Med. Ctr., San Diego, 1986—; clin. faculty UCLA, 1983—, U. Calif., San Francisco, 1978-83, U. San Diego, 1986—. Editor: Infection Control: An Integrated Approach, 1983; author, contributor Contemporary Strategies for Human Resource Mgmt., 1987, Nursing Skills and Evaluation, 1983, APIC Curriculum for Infection Control Practitioner, 1983. Sec., bd. dirs. Arcadia (Calif.) Jr. All Am. Football League, 1984-85. Recipient Tribute to Women in Industry award YWCA, 1987. Mem. Am. Soc. for Nursing Adminstrs., Calif. Soc. for Nursing Service (chmn.), Assn. for Practitioners in Infection Control (pres. 1976). Lodge: Rotary. Office: Mercy Hosp and Med Ctr 4077 5th Ave San Diego CA 92117

YARBROUGH, ROSE SOMRATY, consulting geologist company executive; b. E. St. Louis, Aug. 8, 1936; d. John Pap and Gertrude (Powers) Somraty; m. James John Chiste, 1957 (div. 1974); children: James John Jr., Deanna Marie Kasich; m. Ronald E. Yarbrough, July 23, 1977; stepchildren: Henry Edward Yarbrough, Scott Richard Yarbrough. BA in Earth Sci., So. Ill. U., 1974. Cert. secondary edn. earth sci., Mo., Ill. Supr. student union ops. So. Ill. U., Edwardsville, 1964=70; secondary edn. earth sci. tchr. Ferguson Florissant Sch. Dist., St. Louis, 1974-78, Fort Zumwalt Sch. Dist., O'Fallon, Mo., 1978-80; cartographer, programmer analyst Def. Mapping Agy. Aerospace Ctr., St. Louis, 1980-84, cartographer, quality assurance mgr., 1984-87; exec. v.p. Geo-Technical Assocs. Inc., Collinsville, Ill., 1987—; cons. Ill. State Office on Landfill Project for local environ. group, Edwardsville, Ill., 1973; bd. mem. Greater St. Louis Gateway Chpt. of Internat. Assn. of Quality Circles, St. Louis, 1984—. Co-author: (manual)Assn. of Am. Geologists Field Manual, Physical Regions of the American Bottoms, 1972. Mem. funding com. YMCA and Sch. Bond Issues, Edwardsville, Ill, 1968, Anderson Hosp., Edwardsville, 1969; bd. dirs. Prelude Civic Ballet Co., Collinsville, Ill., 1969. Mem. Am. Soc. Quality Control, Aassn. of Quality & Participation, Geol. Soc. of Am., So. Ill. Alumni Assn., Phi Kappa Phi, Gamma Theta Upsilon, Gamma Sigma Sigma. Clubs: So. Ill. U. Geography, Media (St. Louis), People to People Internat. (St. Louis). Home: 11040 Sugar Trail Rd Saint Louis MO 63136 Office: Geo-Technical Assocs Inc 2926 Maryville Rd Collinsville IL 62234

YARDIS, PAMELA HINTZ, management computer consulting company executive; b. N.Y.C., Sept. 23, 1944; d. Edward F. and Isabella (Sawers) Hintz; m. J.A. Yardis, Apr. 2, 1966 (div. July 1980); children: Bradley, Brent, Tricia, Todd, Ryan, Kara, Melissa. BA, Bethany Coll., 1966; MA, Columbia U., 1983, MEd, 1983. Tchr. Yonkers (N.Y.) Pub. Schs., 1966-68; cons. PHY, Inc., Stamford, Conn., 1978-83; account exec. Mgmt. Systems, Stamford, 1982-84; sr. account exec., cons. Mgmt. Dynamics, Yonkers, 1984-86; v.p. GMW Assn., Inc., N.Y.C., 1986-87; pres. Chestnut Hill Cons. Group, Inc., Stamford, 1987—. chmn. Mayor's Commn. Prevention Youth Drug and Alcohol Abuse, Stamford, 1986—; mem. Dem. Com., Stamford, Conn., 1984—. Mem. Women in Mgmt. (v.p. 1986-88), Data Processing Mgmt. Assn., Advt. Research Found. Presbyterian. Home: 125 Chestnut Hill Rd Stamford CT 06903 Office: Chestnut Hill Cons Group PO Box 15755 Stamford CT 06901

YAROSZ, DIANE ROEMER, human resources executive; b. N.Y.C., Dec. 25, 1946; d. Leonard Peter and Teresa (Bruno) Roemer; m. Edward Joseph Yarosz; 1 child, Sandra Anne. BA, Hunter Coll., 1968; MEd, Rutgers U., 1977, EdD, 1985. Assoc. dir. Ctr. for Adult Devel. Rutgers U., New Brunswick, N.J., 1977-79; mgr. contract services Tng. House, Inc., Princeton, N.J., 1980-82; mgr. program design and devel. E.R. Squibb & Co., Inc., Princeton, 1982-85, mgr. mgmt. and career devel., 1985-87, dir. human resources planning and devel., 1987—. Named one of 50 people to watch N.J. Bus. Jour., 1988; featured in On the Rise column Fortune mag., 1988. Mem. Am. Soc. Tng. and Devel., Nat. Soc. Performance and Instrn., NOW (pres. Monmouth County chpt. 1975-76). Democrat. Roman Catholic. Home: 17 E Welling Ave Pennington NJ 08534 Office: ER Squibb & Co Rt 206 at Province Line Rd Princeton NJ 08540

YARRIGLE, CHARLENE SANDRA SHUEY, real estate executive and investment counselor; b. Redlands, Calif., July 25, 1940; d. Troy Frank and Anna (Miskew) Shuey; m. Robert Charles Yarrigle, Oct. 16, 1965 (div. July 1985); children: Stephanie Ann, Steven Charles. AA, San Bernardino (Calif.) Coll., 1965; student, Ariz. State U., 1965-66; BS, Northern Mich. U., 1976, postgrad., 1976-77. Clk. Bungalow Grocery, Redlands, 1957-59; operator Pacific Telephone Co., San Bernardino, 1958-61; service rep. So. Calif. Gas, San Bernardino, 1961-66; tchr. bus. Gwinn (Tex.) High Sch., 1976-78; salesperson Century 21-A&M Realtors, Citrus Heights, Calif., 1978—; tchr. Project 100,000, Sheppard AFB, Wichita Falls, Tex., 1966-70. Mem. steering com., adv. bd. Sacramento (Calif.) Bd. Realtors, 1981—; vol. Easter Seal Soc., ARC San Bernardino, 1968-72. Mem. Nat. Assn. Realtors, Calif. Assn. Realtors, Nat. Assn. Female Execs., Sierra Club. Republican. Lodge: Eagles. Office: Century 21 Curragh Downs 4401 Hazel Ave Suite 115 Fair Oaks CA 95628

YASUDA, CATHY TOMI, real estate developer; b. Tokyo, May 2, 1957; d. Takeshi and Teruko (Saito) Y. BA, UCLA, 1979, MBA, 1983. Corp. banking officer 1st Interstate Bank, Ltd., Los Angeles, 1983-85; asst. sec. Mfrs. Hanover Trust Co., N.Y.C., 1985-86; asst. v.p. L.F. Rothschild & Co., N.Y.C., 1986-87; assoc. Morgan Stanley Internat., London, 1987-88; chief investment officer Takao Bldg. Devel. Co., Ltd., N.Y.C., 1988—. Mem. Nat. Assn. Female Execs. Republican. Home: 515 E 72d St Apt 20E New York NY 10021 Office: Takao Bldg Devel Co Ltd 55 E 59th St Suite 1629 New York NY 10022

YATES, DIANE GREINER, librarian; b. Lancaster, Pa., Nov. 16, 1939; d. Arthur Kreider and Catherine Mae (Hersh) Greiner; m. Robert James Yates, Aug. 13, 1960; children—Robert, Andrew, Karen. B.A., Grove City Coll., 1961; M.L.S., U. Pitts., 1972. Cert. med. librarian, Pa. Hotel rep. Glenn Fawcett, Inc., San Francisco, 1961-63; bookmobile librarian Carnegie Library, Pitts., 1963; reference librarian North Hills Library, Glenshaw, Pa., 1969-81, library dir., 1981—. Contbr. articles to mags., book revs. to local newspapers and Voice of Youth Advocates. Bd. dirs. Zoar Home. Mem. Pa. Library Assn. (chmn. various coms. and task forces), ALA, AAUW, Victorian Soc. In Am., Musical Box Soc. Republican. Office: North Hills Library 1822 Mount Royal Blvd Glenshaw PA 15116

YATES, ELINOR KAY, cost engineer; b. Teinsin, Peoples Republic of China, Mar. 9, 1948; d. Sam Lincoln and Yvette (Knickerbocker) Y.; m. Cecil William Lee, June 4, 1976. AS in Bus., N. Va. Community Coll., 1978; BA in Econs., Hood Coll., 1988. Ops. mgr. Elizabeth Condo, Chevy Chase, Md., 1979-81; cost engr. Bechtel Power Corp., Gaithersburg, Md., 1981—. Mem. Am. Assn. Cost Engrs. (assoc.), Am. Planning Assn. (student), Am. Econ. Assn. (jr.), Onicron Delta Epsilon. Club: Toastmasters (v.p. 1985-86).

YATES, ELLA GAINES (MAE), librarian, state official; b. Atlanta, June 14, 1927; d. Fred Douglas and Laura (Moore) Gaines; m. Joseph L. Syndor (dec.); 1 child, Jerri Gaines Sydnor Lee; m. Clayton R. Yates (dec.). A.B., Spelman Coll., Atlanta, 1949; M.S. in L.S, Atlanta U., 1951; J.D., Atlanta Law Sch., 1979. Asst. br. librarian Bklyn. Pub. Library, 1951-54; head children's dept. Orange (N.J.) Pub. Library, 1956-59; br. librarian E. Orange (N.J.) Pub. Library, 1960-69; med. librarian Orange Meml. Hosp., 1967-69; asst. dir. Montclair (N.J.) Pub. Library, 1970-72; asst. dir. Atlanta Pub. Library, 1972-76, dir., 1976-81; dir. learning resource ctr. S/OIC, Seattle, 1982-84; asst. dir. adminstrn. Friendship Force, Atlanta, 1984-86; state librarian Commonwealth of Va., 1986—; adv. bd. Library of Congress Center for the Book, 1977-85; cons. in field; vis. lectr. U. Wash., Seattle, 1981-83; mem. Va. Records Avd. Bd., 1986—; mem. Nagara Exec. Bd., 1987—. Contbr. to profl. jours. Vice chmn. N.J. Women's Council Human Relations, 1957-59; chmn. Friends of Fulton County Jail, 1973-81; bd. dirs. United Cerebral Palsy Greater Atlanta, Inc., Wash., 1979-81; Coalition Against Censorship, 1981-84, YMCA Met. Atlanta, 1979-81, Exec. Women's Network, 1979-82, Freedom to Read Found., 1979-85; sec., exec. officer Va. Library Found. Bd., 1986—. Named Profl. Woman of Yr. N.J. chpt. Nat. Assn. Negro Bus. and Profl. Women's Club, 1964, Profl. Woman of Yr. NAACP, N.J., 1972; Outstanding Chum of Yr., 1976; Outstanding Alumni Spelman Coll., 1977; recipient Meritorious award Atlanta U., 1977; Phoenix award City of Atlanta, 1980; others. Mem. ALA (exec. bd. 1977-83, commn. freedom and access to info.), NAACP, Va. Hist. Landmarks Bd., Va. Bd. for Cert. Librarians, Va. Library Assn., Southeastern Library Assn., Chief Officers of State Library Agys., Delta Theta Phi, Delta Sigma Theta. Baptist. Address: 5216 Beddington Rd Richmond VA 23234

YATES, GAYLE GRAHAM, educator, writer; b. Wayne County, Miss., May 6, 1940; d. Robert C. and Gleta (Jones) Graham; B.A., Millsaps Coll., 1961; M.A.T., Vanderbilt U., 1962; Ph.D., U. Minn., 1973; m. Herschel Wilson Yates, Jr., July 21, 1961; children—Natasha, Stiles. Mem. Faculty English dept. Boston U., 1964-67; vis. scholar Cambridge U., 1973-74, 78; chmn. women's studies U. Minn., Mpls., 1976-81, assoc. prof. women's studies and Am. studies, 1981—, founding mem. Big Ten panel on women's studies. Mem. Minn. Gov.'s Adv. Com. on Families, 1980-82. Named Alumna of Yr., Millsaps Coll., 1976. Mem. Am. Studies Assn. (chmn. women's com. 1981-83), Women Historians of Midwest, Nat. Women's Studies Assn. Democrat. Methodist. Author: What Women Want: The Ideas of the Movement, 1975; editor: Harriet Martineau on Women, 1984. Home: 4105 Vincent Ave S Minneapolis MN 55410 Office: U Minn Am Studies 104 Scott Hall 72 Pleasant Ave SE Minneapolis MN 55455

YATES, JO ANN RUTH, communications educator; b. Chgo., Jan. 7, 1931; m. William R. Yates; children: James William, Douglas Andrew. BA in Speech, U. Ill., Urbana, 1952; MA in Audiology, Hunter Coll., 1962; PhD in Communications Disorders, U. So. Calif., 1971. Cert. lang. pathologist, Calif. Fellow Nat. Inst. Sensory and Neurol. Diseases U. So. Calif., Los Angeles, 1964-66; founder, supr. Pre-sch. Land. Devel. Clinic Calif. State U., Long Beach, 1968—, assoc. prof. communication disorders, 1966-78, prof., 1978-87, dept. chair, speech and hearing dir., 1982-85. Adv. bd. Head Start, 1977—. Recipient Grad. Rehab. Lit. award, 1964, Outstanding Prof. award Calif. State U. Long Beach, 1981-82. Fellow Am. Speech and Hearing Assn. (legis. council 1975-85); mem. Calif. Speech and Hearing Assn. (regional v.p. 1972-74, pres. elect 1981-83, pres. 1983-85, Honors of Assn. 1986), Council of Exceptional Children (Outstandin Achievement award 1985), Assn. State Coll. Univ. Profs. (pres. Calif. State U. Long Beach chpt. 1986). Office: Calif State U Dept Communication Disorders 6101 7th St Long Beach CA 90840

YATES, SANDRA, publishing company executive. Formerly pres. John Fairfax (U.S.) Ltd., N.Y.C; now pres., chief exec. officer Matilda Publications Inc., N.Y.C. Office: Matilda Publs Inc 1 Times Sq New York NY 10036 *

YEAGER, JUDITH JEANNE, crime prevention practitioner; b. Chgo., Feb. 16, 1942; d. Frederic John and Gertrude Mary (Leadroot) Guderian; m. Robert Frederick Yeager, Aug. 22, 1964; children: Jennifer Alyson, Catherine Therese. BA, Mundelein Coll., 1965. Dir. vols. Americana Healthcare Ctrs., Champaign and Urbana, Ill., 1974-76; exec. dir. United Cerebral Palsy, Champaign, 1976-78, Champaign County Crime Prevention Council, 1978-83; corp. sec., treas. Intercom, Inc., Champaign, 1978=85; dep. chief Ill. Atty. Gen.'s Office, Springfield and Chgo. Ill. 1983-85; planner, trainer Ill. Criminal Justice Info. Authority, Chgo., 1986—; trainer, practitioner Ill. Local Govtl. Law Enforcement Officer's Tng. Board, Springfield, 1985—. Bd. dirs. Appeal Selective Service System, Great Lakes, Ill, 1983—; bd. dirs., mem. animal care com. U. Ill. Coll. Vet. Medicine, Urbana, Ill., 1986—; mem. Champaign City Council, 1983—. Named Vol. of Yr. Champaign/Urbana Jaycees, 1980. Mem. Internat. Soc. Crime Prevention Practitioners, Inc. (treas. 1983-85), Ill. Crime Prevention Assn. (sec. 1978-80), Ill. Law Enforcement Exploring (fin. chmn. 1983-83), Nat. Assn. Vols. Criminal Justice (regional chmn. 1980-82). Democrat. Roman Catholic. Home: 508 West John Champaign IL 61820-5810 Office: 102 N Neil Champaign IL 61820

YEAGER, LEONA BRANDES, physician, educator; b. Manville, Ill., June 24, 1908; d. Alberta and Augusta (Irrgang) Brandes; m. Edwin Macy Yeager, June 20, 1936; children: Georgia, Jans. BA, North Central Coll., 1929; MA, Northwestern U., 1943, MD, 1944. Diplomate Am. Bd. Internal Medicine. Dir. student health Northwestern U., Evanston, Ill., 1946-77; prof. clin. medicine Northwestern U., Evanston, 1970-77, emeritus prof. clin. medicine, 1977—; sr. physician Evanston Twp. Hosp., 1946-77, emeritus physician, 1977—; attending physician Cook County Hosp., Chgo., 1946-77. Contbr. articles to profl. jours. Pres. Sun City (Ariz.) Area Interfaith, 1985, Sun City Interfaith Services Aux., 1987—; dir. Coll. Health Nurse Practitioner Program, Evanston, 1975-79; alumni regent Northwestern U., 1986—. Recipient Disting. Alumnus award North Cen. Coll., 1963. Fellow Am. Coll. Health Assn. (pres. 1964, Hitchcock award 1970, Boynton award 1976); mem. AMA, Inst. of Medicine, Geriatric Soc., Nat. Conf. on Aging. Clubs: Lakes (Sun City); Mich. Shores (Wilmette, Ill.). Home: 10606 Emerald Point Sun City AZ 85351

YEAGER, MARIAN LILLIAN ENETE, clinical psychologist, educator; b. New Orleans; d. Albert Grant and Aldie Evelyn (Johnson) Barrientos; m. Noble Enete; 1 child, Noel. MusB, Loyola U., New Orleans, 1945; MA, U. Houston, 1955, PhD, 1957. Asst. prof. dept. psychology U. Houston, 1955-57; assoc. prof. dept. psychiatry Baylor Coll. Medicine, Houston, 1965—; clinical assoc. Tex. Children's Hosp., Houston, 1971; asst. prof. dept. psychiatry U. Tex. Med. Sch. of Houston, 1981; practice psychology Enete & Yeager Psychol. Service, Houston, 1959—. Adv. Bd. Houston Grand Opera, 1984—; bd. dirs. Houston Symphony League, 1985—. Fellow Internat. Group Psychotherapy Assn. (bd. dirs. 1985—) Am. Group Psychotherapy Assn. (treas. 1978—, bd. dirs 1969-73), Houston Group Psychotherapy Assn. (pres. 1979—, sr. adv. 1980—); mem. Am. Psychol. Assn., Am. Acad. Psychotherapy Houston Psychol. Assn. (pres. 1973). Republican. Episcopalian. Home: 3711 Olympia Houston TX 77019 Office: Enete & Yeager Psychol Service Inc Scurlock Towers Suite 1506 Houston TX 77030

YEATTS, NANCY MAE, school system administrator; b. Altoona, Pa., June 9, 1947; d. Charles E. and Dorothy B. (Shull) Y. AAS, Harrisburg (Pa.) Area Community Coll., 1967; B Elem. Edn., Pa. State U., 1969, M Elem. Edn., 1971; EdD, Temple U., 1985. Cert. tchr., Pa. Tchr. Camp Hill (Pa.) Elem. Sch. and Cumberland County, 1969-74; instructional advisor Capital/Area Intermediate Unit Sch. Dist. #15, Dauphin, Cumberland and Perry Counties, Pa., 1974-79; dir. Capital/Area Intermediate Unit Sch. Dist. #15, Lemoyne, Pa., 1979—; mem. Council of Exceptional Children, 1970s-80s, Children's Lit. Council Cen. Pa., 1985—. Mem. Camp Hill Jr. Civic Club, 1970s—; life mem. Humane Soc. Harrisburg, 1985—. Millersville (Pa.) Coll. grantee, 1970. Mem. Pa. State U. Alumni (life), Temple U. Alumni (life), Harrisburg Area Community (life, former bd. dirs.), Harrisburg Bd. Realtors, Phi Delta Kappa (life mem. Harrisburg chpt.). Office: Capital Area Intermediate Unit #15 26 N 9th St Lemoyne PA 17043

YEAZELL, RUTH BERNARD, educator; b. N.Y.C., Apr. 4, 1947; d. Walter and Annabelle (Reich) Bernard; B.A. with high honors, Swarthmore Coll., 1967; M.Phil. (Woodrow Wilson fellow), Yale U., 1970, Ph.D., 1971; m. Stephen C. Yeazell, Aug. 14, 1969 (div. 1980). Asst. prof. English, Boston U., 1971-74; asst. prof. English, UCLA, 1975-77, asso. prof., 1977-80, prof., 1980—. Fellow Guggenheim, 1979-80, NEH, 1988—. Mem. MLA (exec. council 1985—), AAUP (supervising com. English Inst. 1983-86). Author: Language and Knowledge in the Late Novels of Henry James, 1976; Death and Letters of Alice James, 1981; asso. editor Nineteenth-Century Fiction, 1977-80; editor: Sex, Politics, and Science in the 19th Century Novel, 1986. Home: 329 Veteran Ave Los Angeles CA 90024 Office: UCLA Dept English Los Angeles CA 90024

YEFIMOV, MARINA, editor, publisher; b. Leningrad, USSR, Nov. 15, 1937; came to U.S., 1978; d. Mikhail Brisker and Galina Rachko; m. Igor Yefimov; children: Lena, Natasha. M of Engring., Leningrad Poly. Inst., 1960. Engring. researcher Steam and Hydro-Turbines Research Ctr., Leningrad, 1960-64; author Leningrad Radio, 1964-66; free-lance journalist Avrora, Koster, Iskorka mags., Leningrad, 1966-78; TV and radio commentator Leningrad, 1966-78; editor, co-owner Hermitage Pub. Co., Englewood, N.J., 1981—. Contbr. articles and essays to mags. Office: Hermitage Pub Co PO Box 410 Tenafly NJ 07670

YELENICK, MARY THERESE, lawyer; b. Denver, May 17, 1954; d. John Andrew and Maesel Joyce (Reed) Y. B.A. magna cum laude, Colo. Coll., 1976; J.D. cum laude, Georgetown U., 1979. Bar: D.C. 1979, U.S. Dist. Ct. D.C. 1980, U.S. Ct. Appeals (D.C. cir.) 1981, N.Y. 1982, U.S. Dist. Ct. (so. and ea. dists.) N.Y. 1982. Law clk. to presiding justices Superior Ct. D.C., 1979-81; assoc. Chadbourne & Parke, N.Y.C., 1981—. Editor Jour. of Law and Policy Internat. Bus., 1978-79. Mem. Phi Beta Kappa. Democrat. Roman Catholic. Home: 310 E 46th St New York NY 10017 Office: Chadbourne & Parke 30 Rockefeller Plaza New York NY 10112

YELLEN, LINDA, film director, writer, producer; b. Forest Hills, N.Y., July 13, 1949; d. Seymour and Bernice (Mittelman) Y. BA magna cum laude, Barnard Coll., 1969; MFA in Film, Columbia U., 1971, PhD in Lang., Lit. and Communications, 1975. Mem. film faculty Columbia U., N.Y.C., 1971-73, Barnard Coll., 1971-73, Yale U., 1970-71, CUNY, 1974; prin. Chrysalis-Yellen Prodns., Inc., N.Y.C., 1982—; pres. The Linda Yellen Co., N.Y.C., 1988—. Producer, dir. films: Prospera, 1969; Come Out, Come Out, 1971; Looking Up, 1978; producer, dir., co-writer film: Prisoner Without a Name, Cell Without A Number, NCB-TV, 1983 (Peabody award; Writers Guild nominee for best screenplay); exec. producer, producer CBS network spls.: Hard Hat and Legs, 1980; Mayflower: The Pilgrims Adventure, 1979; Playing For Time, 1980 (Emmy award for best dramatic spl., Peabody award, Christopher award); exec. producer, producer, co-writer CBS network spl.: The Royal Romance of Charles and Diana, 1982; exec. producer, producer CBS-TV movie: Second Serve: The Renee Richards Story, 1986 (Luminous award); contbr. articles to N.Y. Times, Village Voice, Interview, Hollywood Reporter. Mem. Dirs. Guild Am. (exec. council), Writers Guild Am., Acad. TV Arts and Scis. Office: Triad Artists Inc 10100 Santa Monica Blvd 16th Fl Los Angeles CA 90067

YELLIN, JUDITH, electrologist; b. Balt., Feb. 21, 1930; d. Jack and Sarah (Grebow) Levin; m. Sidney Yellin, Jan. 1, 1950; children—David, Paul, Tamar. Student U. Md., 1948-50, Catonsville Community Coll., 1969-71. Mgr. credit dept. Lincoln Co., Balt., 1956-59; office mgr. Seaview Constrn. Co., 1960-62; owner, operator Yellin Telephone Soliciting Agy., 1963-65; mgr. Liberty Antique Shop, 1967-69; owner, mgr. Judith Yellin Electrology, 1973—; chief examiner Md. State Bd. Electrology, 1978-81. Fellow Internat. Biog. Assn.; mem. Am. Electrolysis Assn., Md. Assn. Profl. Electrologists. Avocations: travel, reading, collecting Haitian and art deco-nouveau art and jewelry, poetry, inventing. Home: 6232 Blackstone Ave Baltimore MD 21209 Office: Judith Yellin Electrology 1401 Reisterstown Rd Baltimore MD 21208

YELLIN, SHARI BETH, financial analyst; b. Little Neck, N.Y., May 21, 1959; d. Joseph and Phyllis Nancy (Kravatz) Hilton; m. Matthew Scott Yellin, Sept. 30, 1984. BA in Communications, CUNY, Flushing, 1981. Exec. sec. Showtime/The Movie Channel, N.Y.C., 1981-82, statis. coordinator, 1982-84, data base adminstr., 1984, supr., 1984-87, supr., fin. analyst, 1987—. Mem. Nat. Assn. for Female Execs., Inc. Office: Showtime/The Movie Channel 1633 Broadway New York NY 10019

YEO, URSULA MURIEL, industrial engineer; b. Bad Kreuznach, Fed. Republic Germany, May 24, 1957; came to U.S., 1958; d. Kenneth Daniel and Hanna Beate (Leven) Moore; m. Steven Brent Yeo, May 3, 1979; 1 child, Robert Michael. A.A., Harrisburg Area Community Coll., 1977; B.S. in Indsl. Engring., Pa. State U., 1979. Looper (trainee) Bethlehem Steel Corp., Balt., 1979-82; chief indsl. engring. staff U.S. Coast Guard Yard, Balt., 1983—. Mem. Inst. Indsl. Engrs. (rec. sec. 1978-79, treas. 1981-82, v.p. membership 1982-83, bd. dirs. 1983-84, v.p. membership 1986). Republican. Lutheran. Avocations: needlework; sewing; quilting; photography; travel. Home: 373 Phirne Rd Glen Burnie MD 21061

YETS, PAMELA SCHEEL, advertising executive; b. Milw., Nov. 24, 1963; d. Larry John and Donna Jean (Liddell) Scheel; m. Steven Howard Yets, July 26, 1986. A in Mktg., WCTI, 1985. Telemktg. rep. Trane Co., New

Berlin, Wis., 1979-81; sales rep., customer service rep., advt. mktg. asst. Selectv of Wis., Brookfield, 1981-84; coordinator publicity/promotions Santa-ville, Pewaukee, Wis., 1984-85; dir. pub. relations Stadiumfest, Milw., 1985; advt. exec. Staples/Hutchinson & Assoc., Butler, Wis., 1985-87; media buyer William Eisner, Milw., 1987-88; advt. exec. The Artworks, Milw., 1988—. Mem. Nat. Assn. Female Execs., Milw. Advt. Club (media carnival com.), Distributive Edn. Clubs Am., Wis. Hosp. Pub. Relations and Mktg. Soc., Wis. DECA (1st place state and 4th place nat. Mktg. awards 1985). Home: 17501 W Rogers Dr New Berlin WI 53146 Office: 1011 N Mayfair Rd Suite 206 Milwaukee WI 53226

YIH, MAE DUNN, state legislator; b. Shanghai, China, May 24, 1928; d. Chung Woo and Fung Wen (Feng) Dunn; m. Stephen W.H. Yih, 1953; children—Donald, Daniel. B.A., Barnard Coll., 1951; postgrad. Columbia U., 1951-52. Asst. to bursar Barnard Coll., N.Y.C., 1952-54; mem. Oreg. Ho. of Reps. from 36th dist., 1977-83, Oreg. Senate from 19th dist., 1983—. State Democratic precinct woman; mem. Clover Ridge Elem. Sch. Bd., Albany, Oreg., from 1969-78, Albany Union High Sch. Bd., from 1975-79. Mem. AAUW, LWV, Linn County Citizens for Retarded, Linn County Mental Health Assn. Episcopalian. Office: Office State Senate State Capitol Salem OR 97310 also: 34465 Yih Ln NE Albany OR 97321

YIM, MARY ANCILLA, school principal, library director, educator; b. Honolulu, Feb. 17, 1927; d. Ernest K. and Wai Shan (Ching) Y.; student St. Francis Normal Sch., Maria Regina Coll., 1948-52; B.S. in Edn., U. Dayton, 1957; M.S. in L.S., Cath. U. Am., 1962; postgrad. U. Hawaii, Honolulu, 1961-69; cert. advanced studies in instructional adminstrn. SUNY, Oswego, 1975. Joined Third Order of St. Francis, 1948; sec., receptionist, real estate, ins. and law office, Honolulu, 1944-48; tchr. St. Paul's Ch., Whitesboro, N.Y., 1950-52; tchr.-librarian St. Joseph's High Sch., Hilo, Hawaii, 1952-65, prin., 1965-71; asst. prin. Oswego (N.Y.) Cath. High Sch., 1971-75; dir. library Maria Regina Coll., Syracuse, N.Y., 1975-88, instr., 1976-79, asst. prof., 1979-82, assoc. prof., 1982-88; prin. St. Daniel Sch., Syracuse, 1988—. NDEA grantee in English, U. Hawaii, 1964. Mem. ALA, Cath. (chpt. pres. 1980-82; facilitator continuing edn. program 1982—), N.Y. library assns., Assn. Coll. and Research Libraries, Nat. Cath. Edn. Assn. Office: 611 S Roxford Rd Syracuse NY 13208

YINGLING, ADRIENNE E(LIZABETH), communications company executive; b. Hershey, Pa., June 10, 1959; d. Richard Terry Yingling and Dolores Jean (Ott) Brown. Student N.C. State U., Raleigh, 1983—. Lic. real estate assoc., N.C. Asst. mgr. Fast Fare, Raleigh, 1979-80; statis. analyst S.P.A.R., Elmsford, N.Y., 1980-81; relocation dir., sales assoc. Realty World, Cary, N.C., 1981-83; product mgr. Southeastern Electronics, Raleigh, 1983-84; results acct. No. Telecom, Research Triangle Park, N.C., 1984—. Mem. Nat. Assn. Female Execs., Nat. Assn. Accts., N.C. State U. Acctg. Soc., Ayn Rand Inst., Phi Kappa Phi, Gamma Beta Phi, Omicron Delta Epsilon. Avocations: photography; painting; reading; aerobics; dance; golf. Home: 1341 Chester Rd Apt C Raleigh NC 27608 Office: No Telecom 4600 Emperor Blvd Morrisville NC 27560

YINGST, BEVERLY A., corporate professional; b. Effingham, Ill., Mar. 6, 1955; d. William Eugene and Lois Eileen (Gloyd) Myers; 1 child, Ramona. Grad. high sch., Effingham. With Dixie Truckers Home, Effingham, 1973-74; nurses aid Rolling Hills Nursing Home, Effingham, 1974; with Crossroads Press, Effingham, 1974-81; leadperson handmailing Vern-Wood Press, Mt. Vernon, Ill., 1981—. Baptist. Lodge: Women of the Moose (charter). Home: Colonial Dr Apt 3B Mount Vernon IL 62864 Office: Vern-Wood Press PO Box 1628 #1 Vern-wood Dr Mount Vernon IL 62864

YIP, PAMELA MARY, news reporter; b. Hong Kong, Sept. 21, 1956; came to U.S., 1958; d. Kam Chun and Margaret Mary (Shen) Y. BA, Calif. State U., 1979. Radio news reporter Sta. KGNR-KCRA, Sacramento, Calif., 1975-76; reporter UPI, Sacramento, 1976-79, Los Angeles, 1979-80; fin. writer Stockton (Calif.) Record, 1984-88, Los Angeles Herald, 1988—. Recipient Investigative Reporting award AP News Execs. Council, 1982, Pub. Service award Gannett Co., 1982, Bus. Reporting award Calif. Newspaper Pub. Assn., 1986, Well Done award Gannett Co., 1983. Mem. Soc. Profl. Journalists, Am. Soc. Bus. and Econ. Writers, Asian-Am. Journalists Assn., NOW. Democrat. Roman Catholic.

YOCHELSON, KATHRYN MERSEY, art researcher; b. N.Y.C., Oct. 22, 1910; d. Nathan and Esther Mary Mersey; m. Samuel Yochelson, June 21, 1930 (dec. Nov. 1976); children: John Norman, Bonnie Ellen. BA in Art Edn., New Haven Tchrs. Coll., 1930; postgrad., Yale U., Columbia U., Albright Art Sch., Am. U., U. Md. Art tchr. New Haven Sch. System, 1930-39. Researcher on artistic roots of Jewish people, 1940—. Organized permanent art collection at Buffalo Jewish Ctr., 1952; chmn. Seven Painters of Israel exhibition, Albright-Knox Art Gallery, 1953, 20 Artists for Israel, George Washington U., Washington, 1968, Personal Vision: Yochelson Collection of Israeli Art, George Washington U., 1987; author: Israeli Art: Golden Threads; lectr. and contbr. articles in field; reviewed books in field. Vol. edn. dept. Albright-Knox Art Gallery, Buffalo, 1940-60; internat. bd. govs. Tel Aviv Mus. Art, 1977. Mem. Sunday Scholar Series Com., Albright-Knox Art Gallery (life), Brandeis Women's Com. (life), Washington Watercolor Soc. (sec. 1971-72), Nat. Am. Pen Women. Home: 4201 Cathedral Ave Apt 824 East Washington DC 20016

YOCHEM, BARBARA JUNE, sales executive; b. Knox, Ind., Aug. 22, 1945; d. Harley Albert and Rosie (King) Runyan; m. Donald A. Yochem (div. 1979); 1 child, Morgan Lee; m. Don Heard, Dec. 12, 1987. Grad. high school, Knox, Ind., 1963. Sales rep. Hunter Woodworks, Carson, Calif., 1979-84, sales mgr., 1984-87; sales rep. Comml. Lumber and Pallet, Industry, Calif., 1987—; owner By By Prodns., Glendora, Calif., 1976—. Contbr. articles to profl. jours. Recipient U.S. Bronze medal U.S. Olympic Com., 1976, World Bronze Medal U.S. Olympic Com., 1980. Office: By By Prodns PO Box 1676 Glendora CA 91740

YOCHIM, MARIE HIRST, retired association executive; b. Washington; d. Herbert Nelson and Ellen (Mankin) Hirst; m. Eldred Martin Yochim, Dec. 24, 1942. Student, Strayer Coll., 1939-40. Exec. officer Jesse Johnson, Inc., Lakewood Builders & Glenbrook Corp., Arlington, Va., 1940-56; regent DAR Falls Ch. (Va.) Chpt., 1956-59; dir. dist. V Va. DAR, 1962-65, state regent, 1977-80, mem. fin. com. bd. trustees, 1987—; chief of Corresponding Gen.'s Office Nat. Soc. DAR, Washington, 1962-77, organizing sec. gen., 1980-83, 1st v.p. gen., 1983-86, 1983-86. Recipient bronze medal Chapel of Four Chaplains, 1980, Medal of Appreciation Va. Chtp. SAR, 1980, Va. Honor Pin Children of Revolution Va. Chpt., 1981. Lutheran. Clubs: Jamestown Soc., U.S. Daus. of 1812, Colonial Dames of XVII Century, Order of Eastern Star. Home and Office: 7314 Hughes Ct Falls Church VA 22046

YODER, CAROLYN PATRICIA, editor; b. Greenwich, Conn., July 2, 1953; d. Rufus Wayne and Kathryn Louise (Mulhollen) Y. B.A., Washington U., St. Louis, 1975; M.A., U. Iowa-Iowa City, 1979. Editorial asst. D.C. Heath & Co., Lexington, 1979-81; publs. asst. Internat. Human Resources Devel. Corp., Boston, 1981-82, prodn. editor, 1982-83; asst. editor Cobblestone, Cobblestone Pub., Inc., Peterborough, N.H., 1983, editor, 1983-84, editor-in-chief, 1984—, editor-in-chief Faces, 1984—, Classical Calliope, 1984—. Contbr. illustrations to Sojourner, Women, Lake Hope, Off Our Backs. Mem. Bookbuilders of Boston (prodn. coordinator winning book and cover New England Book Show 1983), Assn. Earth Sci. Editors, Greater Boston Rights and Permissions Group, Soc. Scholarly Pub., Ednl. Press Assn. Am. Democrat. Office: Cobblestone Publishing Inc 20 Grove St Peterborough NH 03458

YODER, EILEEN RHUDE, nutrition and health management executive, consultant; b. Evergreen Park, Ill., Aug. 20, 1946; d. Howard Vernon and Diana Joan (Lemon) Rhude; m. Bernard J. Yoder, Oct. 9, 1965 (div. Nov. 1985); children—Laura Joyce, Patricia Carolyn. Lic. nurse Triton Coll., 1966; lic. health facility adminstr. Ball State U., 1979; B.A., Govs. State U., Park Forest, Ill., 1981; MS., PhD Columbia-Pacific U., 1984. Dir. E. Yoder & Assocs., Goshen, Ind., 1966-79; exec. dir. Healthful Living, N.Y.C., 1979-83; pres. Med. Diet Systems, Tinley Park, Ill., 1983—; cons. and writer for various orgns. Author: Allergy-Free Cooking, 1982, 2d rev. edit. 1987; Milk, Egg, and Wheat Free Cooking, 1984; Maintaining Patient Compliance, 1985; also articles. Mem. Asthma and Allergy Found. (bd. dirs., exec. v.p.), AAAS, Am. Heart Assn. (bd. dirs.), Am. Home Econs. Assn. (bd. dirs.). Office: Med Diet Systems Inc PO Box 1124 Tinley Park IL 60477

YOHANN, PRISCILLA ANN, small business owner; b. Fond du Lac, Wis., Mar. 27, 1953; d. James Balcom and Bernice Adeline (Wegner) Hatch; m. Larry R. Wegner, Apr. 14, 1973 (div. 1976); m. Daniel A. Yohann, Sept. 23, 1978; children: Aaron D., Corrine L. AS, Moraine Park Tech. Inst. Clk. Giddings & Lewis, Fond du Lac, Wis., 1976-80; v.p., sec. Dutch's Trading Post Inc., Fond du Lac, 1981—; skin care cons. Mary Kay Cosmetics Inc., 1985. Mem. Ambassador's Club, Assn. Commerce. Mem. United Ch. of Christ. Club: Altrusa (recording sec.). Home: N8187 Deadwood Point Rd Fond du Lac WI 54935 Office: Dutch's Trading Post Inc 258 N Main St Fond du Lac WI 54935

YOPP, JOHANNA FUTCHS, medical office administrator; b. Wilmington, N.C., Sept. 6, 1938; d. Richard and Louise (Friedman) Futchs; m. James D. Yopp Jr., Dec. 26, 1959; children: Beverly, Lynn, James III, Sara Katherine. BA, U. N.C., Greensboro, 1960. Tchr. New Hanover County Schs., Wilmington, N.C., 1960-62, Winston-Salem (N.C.) Forsyth County Schs., 1962-68; mgr. James D. Yopp Jr. MD, Winston-Salem, 1971—. Vol. Winston-Salem/Forsyth County Schs., Winston-Salem Optimist Soccer Club, 1970-73; leader Girl Scouts U.S., Winston-Salem, 1970-73; pres. Mt. Tabor High Sch. PTA, WInston-Salem, 1986-87, 87-88; mem. Forsyth-Stokes Med. Aux., Bowman Gray Med. Ctr. Aux. (Winston-Salem), Winston-Salem-Forsyth County PTA Pres.'s Council Centennial Com., U. N.C., Greensboro. Mem. Nat. Assn. Female Execs., Am. Mgmt. Assn. Republican. Lutheran. Home: 3410 Thoresby Ct Winston-Salem NC 27104 Office: 602 Forsyth Med Park Winston-Salem NC 27103

YOQUELET, LINDA GALE GORDON, human resources administrator; b. Midland, Mich., Apr. 13, 1958; d. David A. and Harriet S. (Sobel) Gordon; m. Michael P. Yoquelet, Aug. 6, 1983; 1 child, Craig Alexander. BS, Miami (Oxford) U., 1980; MBA, Ind. U., 1982. Wage and salary adminstr. L.S. Ayres, Indpls., 1983-84; analyst compensation and benefits First Ind. Fed., Indpls., 1984-86; dir. human resources, asst. v.p. Lincoln Savs. and Loan, Richmond, Va., 1986-87; v.p., dir. human resources Cardinal Savs. and Loan, Richmond, 1987—. Mem. Am. Soc. Personnel Adminstrs., Va. Assn. Human Resource Mgmt. (pres. 1987—), Am. Soc. Profl. and Exec. Women, Nat. Assn. Female Execs., Inst. Fin. Edn. (bd. dirs. Richmond chpt. 1986—), Sigma Delta Pi, Pi Delta Phi. Unitarian. Home: 4103 Ketcham Dr Chesterfield VA 23832 Office: Cardinal Savs & Loan 900 E Main St Richmond VA 23219

YORBURG, BETTY (MRS. LEON YORBURG), educator; b. Chgo., Aug. 27, 1926; d. Max and Hannah (Bernstein) Gitelman; Ph.B., U. Chgo., 1945, M.A., 1948; Ph.D., New Sch. Social Research, 1968; m. Leon Yorburg, June 23, 1946; children—Harriet, Robert. Instr., Coll. New Rochelle, 1966-67; lectr. City Coll. and Grad. Center, City U. N.Y., 1967-69, asst. prof., 1969-73, asso. prof. sociology dept., 1973-77, prof., 1978—; research asst. Prof. Clifford Shaw, Chgo. Area Project, 1946-47. Mem. Am., Eastern sociol. assns., Am. Council Family Relations, AAAS, N.Y. Acad. of Scis. Author: Utopia and Reality, 1969; The Changing Family, 1973; Sexual Identity: Sex Roles and Social Change, 1974; The New Women, 1976; Introduction to Sociology, 1982; Families and Societies, 1983. Home: 20 Earley St City Island NY 10464 Office: CCNY Sociology Dept 138th & Convent Ave New York NY 10031

YORK, BERYL ROXANNE, management consultant; b. N.Y.C., Apr. 22, 1938; d. Joseph and Jean (Goldman) Y.; m. Donald Malawsky, Aug. 23, 1960; 1 child, Douglas. BS, U. Wis., 1960; MS, U. Denver, 1966; PhD, Union Grad Sch., 1976. Fellow U. Denver, 1966-68; instr. Colo. Woman's Coll., Denver, 1968-69; prof. CUNY, 1969-78; assoc. Human Systems Inc., Morristown, N.J., 1978-81; pres. York Assocs., Upper Montclair, N.J., 1981—. Author: Changing Role of Personnel Assistant, 1985, Role of Personnel Assistant, 1986, Assertiveness Training for Women In Business, 1987; contbr. articles to profl. jours. Mem. Nat. Assn. Female Execs., Am. Mgmt. Assn., Am. Soc. Tng. Devel., Phi Beta Kappa. Club: Princeton (N.Y.C.). Home and Office: York Assocs 24 Norwood Ave Upper Montclair NJ 07043

YORK, DEBRA GAIL, insurance company executive; b. Tullahoma, Tenn., Apr. 17, 1949; d. John Leslie and Dorothy Louise (Scott) McElyea; m. William F. York III, Oct. 1967 (div. Oct. 1969); 1 child, Aprill Balina. Grad. high sch., Tullahoma. With sales dept. Electrolux Co., Murfreesboro, Tenn., 1968, Grant's Dept. Store, Tullahoma, 1969; teller, clk. 1st Fed. Savs. and Loan, Tullahoma, 1969-71; with ins. and escrow dept. Home Fed. Savs. and Loan, Memphis, 1971-73; employment counselor Snelling & Snelling, Memphis, 1973; sr. account agt. Allstate Ins. Co., Memphis, 1973—. Active Ams. United for Separation of Ch. and State, Mothers Against Drunk Driving, Pub. Citizen Orgn., Ams. for Non-Smoker's Rights, People for the Am. Way, Nat. Women's Health Network, Common Cause, Nat. Women's Polit. Caucus; bd. dirs. Unity Truth Ch. Mem. NOW, ACLU, LWV. Home: 4506 Crump Rd Memphis TN 38115 Office: Allstate Ins Co 5240 Poplar Ave Memphis TN 38119

YORK, ELIZABETH JANE, innkeeper; b. Camden, N.J., July 27, 1934; d. Charles Evans and Christine (Taggart) Yorke; m. Anthony Neil Gaeta, April 2, 1960 (div. Jan. 1986); children: Greg, Anthony, Anne. BA, Wheaton (Ill.) Coll., Ill., 1957; postgrad., U. N.C., 1957-58. Owner Designing Woman, Minot, Mass., 1976-81; broker Vin Doyle Real Estate, Scituate, Mass., 1978-81; owner, innkeeper The Four Chimneys, Nantucket Island, Mass., 1981—. Group dir. Scituate Newcomers Club, 1976-81; vol. Hosp. Thrift Shop, Nantucket, 1982—, Second Shop, Nantucket, 1982—; mem. Nantucket Conservation Found. Mem. Nantucket C. of C., Cape Cod C. of C., Nantucket Hist. Soc., Nantucket Lodging Assn. Republican. Episcopalian. Club: Cliffside Beach. Home and Office: 38 Orange St Nantucket Island MA 02554

YORK, JANET BREWSTER, nurse, family and sex therapist; b. N.Y.C., Mar. 5, 1941; d. Edward Cox and Janet Stone Brewster; A.A. with honors, Briarclif Coll., 1961; R.N. with highest honors, U. Iowa, 1965; B.A. summa cum laude, Marymount Manhattan Coll., 1975; M.A. with honors, N.Y. U., 1978; m. Albert Thompson York, Mar. 31, 1962 (dec.); children—Clifton Gaston, Torrance Brewster; 1 adopted child, Justin Brigham. Nurse, Manhattan Eye, Ear and Throat Hosp., N.Y.C., 1966-74; nurse, counselor Washington Free Clinic, 1969-71; family therapist Ackerman Family Inst., N.Y.C., 1976-80; sex therapist N.Y. Med. Coll., Flower Fifth Ave Hosp., N.Y.C., 1976-80; individual practice family and sex therapy, N.Y.C., 1978—; supervisory staff grad. edn. program in human sexuality N.Y.U. Med. Center, 1982—. Bd. dirs. Spence/Chapin Adoption Agy. Fellow Internat. Council of Sex Edn. and Parenthood, Am. U., 1981. Mem. Am. Soc. for Sex Therapy and Research, Am. Assn. Sex Edn., Counseling and Therapy, Soc. for Sci. Study Sex, Sex Info. and Edn. Council U.S., Am. Assn. Marriage and Family Therapists. Clubs: Lawrence Beach, Rockaway Hunting, N.Y.U, Millbrook. Contbr. articles to profl. jours.; also videotape Death as a Part of Life. Home: 155 E 72d St New York NY 10021

YORK, JULIE ALEXANDRA, public relations executive; b. Mpls., Feb. 5, 1962; s. Mervyn Allen and Marlene Honey (Grossman) Y. BA, Macalester Coll., St. Paul, 1984. Researcher, supr. Our Office, Inc., St. Paul, 1983-84; with pub. relations dept. The Michelson Co., Los Angeles, from 1984; now owner, prin. Julie York Pub. Relations, Sherman Oaks, Calif. Home: 15354 Weddington #25 Sherman Oaks CA 91411

YORK, SUSAN REBECCA, accountant; b. Pensacola, Fla., Nov. 28, 1956; d. Avin Huey and Peggy Laura (Jernigan) York. B.S. in Phys. Edn., U. Fla., 1977; M.S. in Accountancy, U. Houston, 1983. C.P.A. Sci. tchr., swimming and softball coach Hampton City Schs. (Va.), 1977-79; phys. edn. tchr., volleyball and basketball coach North Forest Ind. Sch. Dist., Houston, 1979-81; sr. tax acct. Arthur Andersen & Co., Houston, 1983-85, Gibraltar Savs. Assn., Houston, 1986—. Mem. Am. Inst. C.P.A.s, Tex. Soc. C.P.A.s, Houston Soc. C.P.A.s, Beta Alpha Psi, Sigma Kappa. Baptist. Home: 5463 Oak Haven Ln Houston TX 77091 Office: Gibraltar Savs Assn 13401 N Freeway Houston TX 77060

YORKE, EDIE ADRIENNE, accountant; b. Ohio, Mar. 22, 1964; d. William Joseph and Bonnie (Weltman) Y. BS in Acctg., Pa. State U., 1985; postgrad., Syracuse U. Jr. acct. Hess Keeley & Co., Millburn, N.J., 1985-86, RODCO, Paramus, N.J., 1986-87; staff acct. J. Josephson Inc., South Hackensack, N.J., 1987—. Jewish. Home: 151 Sadler Rd Bloomfield NJ 07003

YORKE, MARIANNE, lawyer, real estate executive; b. Ridley Park, Pa., Nov. 4, 1948; d. Joseph George and Catherine Veronica (Friel) Y. BA, West Chester U., 1970; JD, Temple U., 1980; MS, U. Pa., 1987. Bar: Pa. 1981. Real estate mgr. CIGNA Service Co., Phila., 1981-85, asst. dir., Phila., 1985—; cons., 1981-82; real estate atty. Garfinkel & Volpicelli, Phila., 1980-81; prin., mng. ptnr. Yorke/Eisenman, Real Estate, Phila., 1976—; lectr. Women in the Arts, 1982—. Contbr. articles to profl. jours. Solicitor Pa. Ballet, Phila., 1983—, United Way, Phila., 1983—; mem. steering com. U. Pa., 1986—, dir. alumni assn., 1987—; mem. adv. com. for econ. devel. Luth. Settlement House Adv. Mem. ABA (forum on constrn.), Pa. Bar Assn. (condominium and zoning coms.), Phila. Bar Assn., Phila. Women Real Estate Attys., Nat. Assn. Corp. Real Estate Execs. (comml. council, surplus properties com.), Atty's Roundtable, Women's Law Caucus, German Soc., Phi Alpha Delta. Democrat. Roman Catholic. Home: 1910 Nectarine St Philadelphia PA 19130 Office: CIGNA Service Co Real Estate Dept 1600 Arch St 17T Philadelphia PA 19103

YORKE-SNEED, KATHRYN, optometrist; b. Pitts., Jan. 12, 1954; d. James M. and Dawn (Disney) Yorke; m. Loyd William Sneed, July 29, 1984; children: Jonathan William, Jessica Dawn; BA in Biopsychology, Vassar Coll., 1975; OD, U. Houston, 1981. Practice optometry, Pasadena, Tex. 1981-82, College Station, Tex., 1982—; indsl. vision cons. Westinghouse Electric Corp., College Station, 1982—; dir. vision screening program Brushy Day Care Ctr., Tex., 1983. Troop leader Bluebonnet council Girl Scouts U.S., 1982-83; bd. dirs. Cen. Tex. area March of Dimes, Bryan, Tex., 1983—. Kuhlman Optometry scholar U. Houston, 1977. Mem. C. of C., Tex. Assn. Optometrists, Better Vision Inst. (Merit award 1978), Am. Bus. Women's Assn. (recording sec. 1983-84, pres. 1984-85, Woman of Yr. award 1985), Phi Kappa Phi, Beta Sigma Kappa, Beta Beta Beta. Avocations: music, backpacking, bicycling. Office: 1010A Post Oak Mall College Station TX 77840

YORK-LONGWORTH, CAROLYN KAYE, writer; b. Greenfield, Ohio, May 21, 1929; d. James Mortimer and Michal Oviatt (Porter) Y.; m. Earl J. Hicks, Oct. 28, 1950 (dec. 1974); children—Sharon Lee Hicks Szymanski, Warren York (dec.), Diana Marie; m. J. Harold Longworth, Aug. 22, 1987. BA, Miami U., Oxford, Ohio, 1950. Copywriter, broadcaster sta. WMOH-AM, Hamilton, Ohio, 1950-56; exec. sec. newsletter First Presbyn. Ch., Middletown, Ohio, 1957-58; traffic dir., broadcaster sta. WPFB and WPBF-FM, Middletown, 1958-62; account exec., broadcasters news sta. WFOL-FM and WENW, Fairfield, Ohio, 1962-68; asst. editor Miami Alumnus, Miami U. 1968-82, editorial asst., alumni affairs univ. relations, 1982—; editor newsletter Ohio Community Theatre Assn., 1972-74. Actress, soprano Miami U. Summer Theatre, 1969—, bd. dirs., 1967-85; co-founder Big Bros. and Sisters of Hamilton and Vicinity, Inc., 1968, chmn. bd., 1976-78; co-founder Oxford Area Community Theatre, 1979, Hamilton chpt. Parents Without Ptnrs., 1966; elder Presbyn. Ch.; sec. Oxford Friends Love Pub. Library Bd.; charter mem. Oxford Community Band; county officer Rep. Party, 1976-82. Mem. Women in Communications (profl. advisor Miami U., Nat. Advisor of Yr. 1977, co-founder Miami U. chpt. 1977), Alpha Epsilon Rho, Delta Zeta Alumnae (pres. Oxford 1970, 81). Home: 808 Clover Circle Oxford OH 45056 also: 47 Reed St Milford Center OH 43045 Office: Miami Univ Oxford OH 45056

YOSHIMOTO, NAOMI, nurse; b. Puunene, Hawaii, Feb. 2, 1951; d. Herbert Toshio and Lillian Mitsue (Yakabe) Y. BS, Brigham Young U., 1973; MS, U. Hawaii, 1983. RN, Utah, Hawaii. Staff nurse Kaiser Med. Found., Honolulu, 1973-75, Latter-Day Saints Hosp., Salt Lake City, 1975-78, Queen's Med. Cen., Honolulu, 1979, 1985; mgr. health service Brigham Young U., Laie, Hawaii, 1979-80; staff nurse Straub Clinics and Hosp. Inc., Honolulu, 1980-83, 1984-87; clin. nurse specialist Kuakini Med. Cen., Honolulu, 1983-84; instr. nursing Sch. Nursing U. Hawaii, Honolulu, 1985; quality assurance and health edn. coordinator Best Care, Honolulu, 1987—. Various positions Ch. Jesus Christ Latter-Day Saints, Honolulu. Mem. Am. Nursing Assn., Am. Assn. Critical Care Nurses, Am. Assn. Nuerosci. Nurses, N. Am. Nursing Diagnosis Assn., Sigma Theta Tau, Phi Kappa Phi. Home: 1532 Halekoa Dr Honolulu HI 96821

YOSHIMURA-SMITH, DAWN AIKO, occupational therapist; b. Honolulu, Sept. 21, 1961; d. Donald A. and Elsie M. (Kuroiwa) Yoshimura; m. Larry M. Smith, July 12, 1986. BS in Occupational Therapy, U. Puget Sound, 1983. Lic. occupational therapist, Wash. Occupational therapist Pacific Med. Ctr., Seattle, 1984-87, St. Francis Hosp., Federal Way, Wash., 1987—. Vol. ARC. Mem. Am. Occupational Therapy Assn. (cert.), Wash. Occupational Therapy Assn.. Home: St Francis Hosp 34515 9th Ave S Federal Way WA 98003

YOST, HELEN MARGUERITE, religious organization social worker; b. San Diego, Oct. 16, 1918; d. Don Merlin Lee and Susie Marguerite (Sims) Y. A.A., Pasadena Jr. Coll., 1939; B.S., UCLA, 1948, postgrad., 1950-52. Girls worker Pasadena Settlement, 1948-52; program dir. YWCA, 1952-56; field dir., div. dir. CYO, Archdiocese of Los Angeles, 1956-84; dir., coordinator dept. aging Catholic Charities, Los Angeles, 1980-86, spl. asst. to adminstrn., 1986-88. Del. Calif. Council Statehouse Conf. Children and Youth, 1980, Statehouse Conf. on Aging, 1981; mem. spl. task force on elder abuse Los Angeles County Area Agy. Aging, 1985—; chmn. evaluation com. Calif. Sr. Legis., 1984—. Served with U.S. Navy, 1943-45. Recipient Genemerenti medal Pope John Paul II, 1985, Friend of Youth award CYO, Los Angeles, 1982, commendation for work as historian and rec. sec. adv. council Los Angeles County Bd. Suprs., Horace N. Mays award for outstanding contbn. to aging through religious community, 1987. Mem. Am. Camping Assn. (Disting. Service award 1980), Am. Area Agy. Aging (adv. council, historian 1983-85, rec. sec. 1985-86), Calif. Conf. Cath. Charities, Nat. Conf. Cath. Charities, Nat. Assn. Female Execs., So. Calif. Interfaith Coalition Aging (pres. 1983-84, v.p. 1984-86). Delta Zeta. Club: Soroptimist (rec. sec. 1977). Avocations: dancing; reading. Home: 1425 E Orange Grove Blvd Apt 10 Pasadena CA 91104 Office: Cath Charities 1400 W 9th St Los Angeles CA 90015

YOUNATHAN, MARGARET TIMS, nutritionist, educator; b. Clinton, Miss., Apr. 25, 1926; d. Peter Asbury and Eula Lee (Tatum) Tims; BA, U. So. Miss., 1946, BS, 1950; MS, U. Tenn., 1951; PhD, Fla. State U., 1958; m. Ezzat S. Younathan, Aug. 11, 1958; children: Janet Nadya, Carol Miriam. Instr., food and nutrition Oreg. State U., 1951-55; postdoctoral research asso. Fla. State U., 1958-59; sr. nutritional cons. Ark. Dept. Health, Little Rock, 1962-68; instr. pediatrics U. Ark. Sch. Medicine, Little Rock, 1962-65, asst. prof. pediatrics, 1965-68; asso. prof. food and nutrition Sch. Home Econs., La. State U., 1971-79, prof., 1979—; internat. nutrition work in Sierra Leone, 1984, Jamaica, 1987. Am. Inst. Nutrition grantee, 1965; La. State U. Council on Research summer faculty grantee, 1980; research grantee Lou Ana Foods, Inc., 1987. Mem. Inst. Food Technologists, Am. Inst. Nutrition, Am. Dietetic Assn., Am. Home Econs. Assn., La. Home Econs. Assn. (pres. dist. D. 1981-82, Disting. Home Economist award 1988), Sigma Xi, Phi Kappa Phi, Gamma Sigma Delta, Omicron Nu, Phi Upsilon Omicron. Mem. Christian Ch. (Disciples of Christ). Contbr. articles on food and nutrition research to profl. jours. Home: 1048 Castle Kirk Dr Baton Rouge LA 70808 Office: La State U Sch Home Econs Baton Rouge LA 70803

YOUNG, ADDIE BELLE, counselor; b. Bastrop, La., Dec. 14, 1930; d. Thomas and Mary (Johnson) Dilworth; m. Leo G. Young, July 18, 1953; children: Leo G., Sherri L. Young Brewer, Pamela L. Young Davis. AA, Contra Costa Coll., 1978; postgrad., Sonoma State U., 1979, Ohlone Coll., 1981, 83-85. Home/sch. liaison investigator PTA, Pinole, Calif., 1978-79; counselor Calif. Dept. Edn., Fremont, Calif., 1978—, Seneca Residential and Day Treatment Ctr., Oakland, Calif., 1986—; mem. Unit 20 Spl. Schs. Task Force, 1988. Active Child-Parent Media Art, Contra Costa County, Calif.,

1986, Contra Costa County Stroke Support Unit; leader Girl Scouts USA, Pinole, 1987-88. Mem. Calif. State Employee Assn. (sec. 1982-83, del. gen. council 1983-84, bargaining unit council 1985-87), Coalition of Labor Union Women. Democrat. Club: Bus. and Profl. (Richmond, Calif.) (sec. 1972-74). Home: 1133 Alberdan Circle Pinole CA 94564

YOUNG, ANN ELIZABETH O'QUINN, historian, educator; b. Waycross, Ga.; d. James Foster and Pearl Elizabeth (Sasser) O'Quinn; student Shorter Coll.; B.A., M.A., U. Ga., Ph.D., 1965; m. Robert William Young, Aug. 18, 1968; children—Abigail Ann, Leslie Lynn. Asst. prof. history Kearney (Nebr.) State Coll., 1965-69, assoc. prof., 1969-72, prof., 1972—; participant Inst. on Islam, Middle East and World Politics, U. Mich., summer 1984. Mem. Am. Hist. Assn., NEA, PEO, World History Assn., Phi Alpha Theta, Delta Kappa Gamma (chpt. pres. 1978-79), Phi Mu. Republican. Presbyterian. Contbg. author Dictionary of Georgia Biography; contbr. articles to profl. revs. Office: Kearney State Coll Dept History Kearney NE 68849

YOUNG, BETTY BIGBY, educational administrator, consultant; b. N.Y.C.; d. Lucius and Dorothy (Hazard) Bigby; m. Haskell Inwood Young, May 6, 1973; children: Haskell I. II, Jessica Melissa. BA, CUNY, Bklyn., 1971, MS, 1973; EdD in Higher Edn. Adminstrn., Nova U., 1987. Exec. sec. U.S. Fgn. Service Dept. State, Washington, 1959-66; asst. dir. Coney Island Community Family Ctr., Bklyn., 1967; community relations specialist Robert Mitchell Cons., N.Y.C., 1968-71; dir. tng. program Sta. CBMC-TV, N.Y.C., 1972-73; pub. relations specialist Model City program of Dade County, Miami, Fla., 1973-75; program mgr. Dept. of Human Resources, Miami, 1975-77; asst. to provost community services Fla. Internat. U., North Miami, 1977-81, dir. univ. relations, 1977-83, dir. acad. support program, 1983-87, dir. minority programs, 1987—. Editor Model City News. Pres. Dade County Sickle Cell Found., Inc., 1980-82, Dade County Pub. Sch. Magnet Adv. Bd., 1987—; v.p. Fla. State Sickle Cell Found., Inc., 1978-83; adv. bd. New Century Devel. Corp., 1985—, Fla. Internat. U. Black Student Union, 1978—, YMCA summer camp, 1985; profl. advisor Pub. Relations Student Soc. of Am., Fla. Internat. U.; adv. com. Magnet Sch. Program, 1987—; active Art in Pub. Places Trust. Mem. AAUW, Pub. Relations Soc. Am. (accredited), Nat. Assn. Female Execs., Kappa Delta Pi (counselor), Omicron Theta, Alpha Epsilon Rho (life). Democrat. Office: Fla Internat U 151st and Biscayne Blvd North Miami FL 33181

YOUNG, BRENDA LEE, editor; b. Evansville, Ind., Oct. 20, 1957; d. Milton Ray and Elizabeth Anne (Waugh) Y.; married (div. 1987); children: Steven Wayne Kempf, Katherine Lee Kempf. BS in Communications, U. So. Ind., 1979. Office mgr. Patrick Communications, Evansville, 1979-80; editor Newburgh (Ind.) Register, 1980-83; mng. editor Warrick Pub., Inc., Boonville, Ind., 1986—. Mem. Boonville Bus. and Profl. Women's Club (pres. 1984-86, named Young Careerist 1987); sec. Main St. United Meth. Ch., Boonville, 1986-87; advisor Boonville Internat. Order of the Rainbow for Girls. Named One of Outstanding Young Women of Am., 1984. Office: Warrick Pub PO Box 71 Boonville IN 47601

YOUNG, CATHERINE ELIZABETH, airline executive; b. Montreal, Can., May 28, 1957; d. Frank Leonard and Shirley Mary (Charlesworth) Croft; m. Robert Brock Young, May 12, 1978; 1 child, Cristin Anne. BA with hon., Queens U., Kingston, Ont., 1979. Sales sec. Mexicana Airlines, Toronto, 1979-82, sales rep., 1982-84, dist. sales mgr., 1984—. Mem. Toronto Bus. Travel Assn., Alliance Can. Travel Assn., Toronto Airline Rep. Bd. Office: Mexicana Airlines, 60 Bloor St W #1206, Toronto CAN M4W3B8

YOUNG, COLLEEN MARA, sales manager; b. Jacksonville, N.C., Feb. 18, 1962; d. Martin Victor and Joyce Josephine (McManus) Y. BA in Econs., U. Calif.-Davis, 1983, BA in Internat. Relations, 1983. Staff writer Pub. Affairs, U. Calif., Davis, 1981-82; career counselor Advt. Services, U. Calif., Davis, 1982-83; computer system mgr. Pacific Bell, San Francisco, 1983-84, sales mgr., 1984-85; writer, Boise, Idaho, 1985—; dir. data processing Mercy Hosp., Nampa, Idaho, 1985—. Author: A Little Mischief, 1985. Vol., Sta. KAID Pub. TV, 1985-86. Mem. Nat. Assn. Female Execs., AHA Healthcare Info. and Mgmt. Systems Soc., Omicron Delta Epsilon, Pi Sigma Alpha. Republican. Roman Catholic. Club: U. Calif. Women's Honor Soc. Avocations: book collecting; the arts; equestrian.

YOUNG, DANA WEBER, finance counseling company executive; b. Cleve., Apr. 29, 1951; d. Donald Alphonse Sr. and Annamae (Edwards) Weber; 1 child, Brie. BA in Pub. Adminstn., St. Cloud (Minn.) State U., 1976; MA, U. Minn., 1978. Lic. SEC broker. Field assoc. Brookings Inst., Washington, 1977-78; aid to mayor City of St. Paul, 1977-78; instr. St. Thomas Coll., St. Paul, 1978-79; asst. city mgr. City of Golden Valley, Minn., 1978-79; dir. devel. resources State of Minn., St. Paul, 1980-82, dir. bus. devel., 1982-84; dir. econ. devel. City of Oxnard, Calif., 1984-85; v.p., regional mgr. Allison-Williams Co., Oxnard, 1985-87; ptnr., mng. dir. Talley, McNeil and Tormey, Inc., Oxnard, 1987-88; chief exec. officer D.W. Young and Assocs., Oxnard, 1988—. Area dir. United Way of Ventura Couty, 1984—; fund raising com. mem. Santa Clara Parrish, Oxnard; mem. Community Redevel. Assn., 1986—, Industrial Devel. Research Council, 1987—, Transp. and Econ. Devel. Com. of Ventura County Econ. Devel. Orgn., 1986—; bd. dirs. Boys and Girls Clubs, 1986—, Calif. Assn. for Local Econ. Devel., 1987—, Ventura County Econ. Devel. Orgn., 1987—. Founder Channel Islands Venture Assn., Ventura County, 1986; mem. Am. Mgmt. Assn., Calif. Soc. Fin. Officers, Oxnard C. of C. (pres. 1987—, v.p. bus. devel. 1986-88, bd. dirs. 1986—). Republican. Roman Catholic. Club: Oxnard Beautiful. Lodge: Optimists. Office: DW Young and Assocs 2073 N Oxnard Blvd Suite 259 Oxnard CA 93030

YOUNG, DIANNE, police officer; b. Memphis, Sept. 1, 1956; d. John Henry Tunstall and Rebecca T. (Taylor) Tunstall Young. Student U. Miss., 1975-78; BS in Criminal Justice, U. Houston, 1987. Peace officer, Tex. With J.C. Penney Co., Detroit, 1977-78, Houston, 1979-80; patrol officer Houston Police Dept., 1980-81; juvenile investigator, 1982—; mem. dispute resolution mediation team Houston Police Officers. Mem. Afro-Am. Police Officers Houston (Officer of Month 1982), Houston Police Patrolmen Union, Stanza Peterson Dancers. Baptist. Home: 1201 Wilcrest St Apt 14 Houston TX 77042 Office: 61 Riesner St Houston TX 77042

YOUNG, DOLORES SALLY, advertising photography company executive; b. Camden, N.J., Mar. 4, 1932; d. Herman Carl and Rayetta (Glading) Brandt; m. Robert Arthur Young, July 17, 1959. BA in Journalism and Advt. with honors, Douglass Coll., Rutgers U., 1954. Chief copywriter Koos Bros. Furniture Showplace, Rahway, N.J., 1954-62; co-owner, sec.-treas. Bob Young Photography, Inc., Colonia, N.J., 1962—; N.J. account exec. Graphics 3, Inc., Jupiter, Fla., 1974-78; trustee Jal-Con, Inc., conv. chmn., 1981; mgr. advt. sales Hosp. News N.J., 1987—. Trustee, 1st Unitarian Soc., Plainfield, N.J., v.p., 1983-84. Recipient Advt. award Asbury Park (N.J.) Press, 1954, Best Lamp Ad award Nat. Lamp Council, 1959, Socrates award for furniture advt., 1956; N.J. State scholar, 1951-54; Desi award, 1978. Mem. AAUW, NOW, Art Dirs. Club N.J. (co-chmn. communications art seminar 1978), N.J. Schola Cantorum (bd. govs.), ACLU. Home: 116 Cleveland Ave Colonia NJ 07067 Office: 15 Prospect Ln Colonia NJ 07067

YOUNG, DONNA DEAN, nurse; b. Missoula, Mont., Nov. 1, 1938; d. Wilbur Dean and Dorothy Frances (Olsen) Brown; m. Leo Edward Young, Dec. 28, 1959; children: Whitney Michelle, Guy Gregory. RN, Sacred Heart Hosp., Spokane, Wash., 1959; B in Health Sci., U. Redlands, 1984, M in Mgmt., 1986. Staff nurse Sacred Heart Med. Ctr., Spokane, 1959-60, 65-66; office mgr. Dr. Paul Nutter, M.D., Spokane, 1960-64; staff nurse/supr. Kootenai Meml. Hosp., Coeur d'Alene, Idaho, 1966-67, Douglas Community Hosp., Roseburg, Oreg., 1967-70; staff nurse St. Patrick Hosp., Missoula, Mont., 1969-70; staff nurse, supr. emergency room Gresham (Oreg.) Community Hosp., 1970-73; tchr.'s aide Irvine (Calif.) Unified Sch. Dist., 1978-80; staff nurse/supr. Healthcare Med. Ctr., Tustin, Calif., 1980—. Pres. PTO, Irvine, 1974-77. Recipient Achievement award Career Leadership Council, 1988.

YOUNG, ELIZABETH ANN, finance executive; b. Clarksdale, Miss., Mar. 24, 1942; d. Hardy Charles Allen and Etherine (Paige) Garrett; m. James E. Young, June 19, 1965 (div. Oct. 1982); children: Charles J. Thompson, Felicia A. Thompson, James L. Student, Crane Jr. Coll., 1959-60, Am. River Coll., 1973-74; cert. mid. mgmt., City Coll. Chgo., 1976. Clk. United Services Advisors Inc., San Antonio, 1977-78, supr., 1978-80, mgr., 1980-85, v.p., 1985—. Mem. Investment Co. Inst., No Load Mut. Fund Assn., Nat. Assn. for Women Execs. Democrat. Episcopalian.

YOUNG, ERNESTINA MUNOZ, insurance sales representative; b. Manila, July 6, 1954; came to U.S., 1978, naturalized 1985; d. Ireneo A. and Marcelina (Catabas) Munoz; m. Carl E. Young, Jr., July 30, 1980, children: Carl E. III, Alyssa M.R. BA in Econs., U. Santo Tomas, Manila, 1975, MBA, 1977. Sales rep. Prudential Life Ins. Co., Los Angeles, 1982-84, Mut. of Omaha, Los Angeles, 1984-85, Met. Life Ins. Co., Los Angeles, 1985—. Roman Catholic. Office: Met Life Ins Co 9300 Flair Dr Suite 105 El Monte CA 91731

YOUNG, ETHEL RUTH, educator; b. Havelock, N.S., Can., Aug. 15, 1934; d. Handley Chipman and Ethel Ring (Sabine) Mullen; m. Harold Edwin Young, June 7, 1955; children: Jennifer Lorraine, Patricia Elaine. AB in Lit., Eastern Nazarene Coll., Quincy, Mass., 1955; MA, Pasadena (Calif.) Coll. (now Point Loma Nazarene Coll.), 1971; teaching credentials, Calif. State U., Fullerton, 1964; postgrad., UCLA, 1965-67, Claremont (Calif.) Grad. Sch., 1980—. Cert. lifetime elem. tchr., Calif.; cert. elem. sch. adminstr., cert. jr. coll. instr., cert. Miller-Unruh reading specialist, Calif. Tchr. pub. schs. Kans., Ohio, and Calif., 1955—; chmn. english dept. Green Twp. High Sch., Franklin Furnace, Ohio, 1961-62; spl. edn. tchr. Centralia Sch. Dist., Buena Park, Calif., 1965-67, 79-81, reading specialist, 1967-79, elem. tchr., 1981—; instr. children's lit. Santa Ana (Calif.) Coll., 1973-75; adj. prof. edn. Point Loma Nazarene Coll., 1975—; speaker nat. conv. Nat. Elem. Edn. Assn., 1981, 82. Author curricula for ch. sch. pubs., 1976-83. Mem. NEA, Calif. Tchrs. Assn., Centralia Edn. Assn. (sec. 1970-72), Pi Lambda Theta, Phi Delta Lambda. Mem. Ch. of the Nazarene. Home: 2437 Deerpark Dr Fullerton CA 92635 Office: Buena Terra Sch 8299 Holder St Buena Park CA 90620

YOUNG, GAIL ADALINE, association executive; b. N.Y.C., June 8, 1948; d. Robert William and Virginia Adaline (Guy) Y. BS in Speech, Emerson Coll., 1971. Asst. to alumni dir. Adelphi Coll., Garden City, N.Y., 1973; asst. to sr. v.p. Hill & Knowlton Inc., N.Y.C., 1973-81; account exec. Glick Lorwin, Inc., N.Y.C., 1981-88; assoc. dir. for pub. affairs and program devel. USO Met. N.Y., N.Y.C., 1982-88, dep. dir. Va. Peninsula USO, Hampton, 1988—; pub. relations cons. New Yorkers for Dearie, N.Y.C., 1981; mem. alumni adv. bd. dirs. Floating Hosp., N.Y.C., 1979-81. Mem. Emerson Coll. Alumni Assn. (v.p. N.Y. chpt. 1983-86), Pub. Relations Soc. Am. (co-chmn. publicity com. N.Y.C. 1979-80). Club: N.Y. Press (by-line ball com. 1980-83, co-chmn. Christmas fundraising program 1982-83). Produced USO show for Pres. and Mrs. Reagan at Statue of Liberty Celebration aboard USS Kennedy, July 4, 1986. Home: 811 Cameo Dr Hampton VA 23666

YOUNG, HOLLY PEACOCK, lawyer; b. Indpls., Sept. 21, 1949; d. John Edward and Sylvia (Griffith) Peacock; m. Gregory Glenn Young, Sept. 2, 1972; children—Reagan Wheelock, Trevor Griffith. Student Dartmouth Coll., 1969-70; B.A., Conn. Coll., 1971; M.A., U. Tex., 1973; J.D., So. Meth. U., 1982. Bar: Tex. 1983; state water program mgr. EPA, Dallas, 1973-75, 75-77; asst. mgr. Menlo Sport, Menlo Park, Calif., 1977-79; dir. Hindostan Whetstone Co., Bedford, Ind.; with Jour. Air Law and Commerce, 1980-82. Bd. dirs. Montessori Sch. of Park Cities, 1983-87; bd. advisors Cottonwood Gulch Found., 1982—. Recipient Bronze medal EPA, 1974. Mem. ABA, Tex. Bar Assn., Dallas Bar Assn. Episcopalian. Home: 4711 Cherokee Trail Dallas TX 75209

YOUNG, JACKIE MERLE, nurse, consultant; b. Knox City, Tex., Aug. 26, 1952; d. J. A. and JoAnn (Tackitt) Maddox; m. William Bruce Young, Aug. 6, 1971 (div. Oct. 1979). Cert., St. Joseph's Sch. Vocat. Nursing, 1972; cert. in emergency med. treatment, Vernon (Tex.) Regional Coll., 1980, student health scis. dept., Tex. Tech U., Lubbock, 1987—. Charge nurse Bapt. Meml. Med. Ctr., San Angelo, Tex., 1972-73; nurse ob/gyn Clinic Hosp., San Angelo, 1973; technician critical care unit Shannon West Tex. Meml. Hosp., San Angelo, 1974; nurse Caprock Hosp., Ploydada, Tex., 1977; & Bay Area Hosp., Coos Bay, Oreg., 1979, Knox County, Knox City, 1979-86; adminstr. Knox City Emergency Med. Services, 1979-86, cons., 1986—; nurse ob/gyn St. Mary's Hosp., Lubbock, Tex., 1986—; cons. Breastfeeding Your Baby, Lubbock, 1986—. Author poems. Mem. Tex. Assn. Emergency Med. Technicians, Lic. Vocat. Nurses Assn. Democrat. Baptist. Home: care of AC Tackitt RR1 Munday TX 76371

YOUNG, JOAN CRAWFORD, advertising executive; b. Hobbs, N.Mex., July 30, 1931; d. William Bill and Ora Maydelle (Boone) Crawford; m. Herchelle B. Young, Nov. 23, 1971 (div.). B.A., Hardin Simmons U., 1952; postgrad. Tex. Tech. U., 1953-54. Reporter, Lubbock (Tex.) Avalanche-Jour., 1952-54; promotion dir. KCBD-TV, Lubbock, 1954-62; account exec. Ward Hicks Advt., Albuquerque, 1962-70; v.p. Mellekas & Assocs., Advt., Albuquerque, 1970-78; pres. J. Young Advt., Albuquerque, 1978—. Bd. dirs. N.Mex. Symphony Orch., 1970-73, United Way of Greater Albuquerque, 1985—. Recipient Silver medal N.Mex. Advt. Fedn., 1977. Mem. N.Mex. Advt. Fedn. (dir. 1975-76), Am. Advt. Fedn., Greater Albuquerque C. of C. (dir. 1984). Republican. Author: (with Louise Allen and Audre Lipscomb) Radio and TV Continuity Writing, 1962. Home: 3425 Avenida Charada NW Albuquerque NM 87107 Also: 303 Roma NW Albuquerque NM 87102

YOUNG, JUDITH GAIL, sales company executive, import executive; b. Chgo., Nov. 6, 1942; d. Ben and Ruth (Golberg) Young; m. Dennis A. Bell, Nov. 6, 1977. B.A., Roosevelt U., 1964. Tchr. Chgo. Bd. Edn., 1965-73; sales rep. T.E. Simmons & Assocs., Chgo., 1973-77; owner, pres. Joy Internat. Corp., Chgo., 1977—; pres. Lyric Internat. Corp., Chgo., 1983—; v.p. Herald Internat. Travel Service, Hong Kong, 1982—, Chefmate Housewares, 1985—; design cons. Taipan Herald Ltd., Hong Kong, 1983—. Mem. vocat. bus. com. Rich Daley for Mayor, Chgo., 1983; mem. women's com. Ann Stephan for Ward Committeeman, Chgo., 1983; fundraiser Mental Health Assn. Chgo., 1982-83, Chgo. Council Fgn. Relations, 1977—. Recipient Outstanding Performance award Randix Industries Ltd., 1980. Mem. Nat. Assn. Female Execs. Democrat. Jewish. Clubs: Internat., Variety (Chgo.). Office: Joy Internat Corp 3928 N Rockwell St Chicago IL 60618

YOUNG, JUNE MAGNA, guidance counselor; b. Chippewa Falls, Wis., Feb. 12, 1936; d. Allen Hans and Hazel Cleone (LaRonge) Y. BS, Macalester Coll., 1959; MEd, U. Minn., 1967, specialist degree, 1978; MA, Coll. of St. Thomas, St. Paul, 1971. Cert. in phys. edn., coaching, secondary and vocat. guidance and counseling, Minn.; cert. nat. counselor. Tchr. Mpls. Pub. Schs., 1959-60; tchr. St. Paul Pub. Schs., 1960-65, 68-72, guidance counselor, 1972—; teaching assoc. U. Minn., Mpls., 1965-67; inst. U. N.Mex., Albuquerque, 1967-68. Mem. edn. com., elder Cen. Presbyn. Ch., St. Paul, 1984-85. Wis. Leadership scholar, 1955-56, Wis. Dept. Rehab. scholar, 1955-56. Mem. Nat. Cert. Counselors Assn., Am. Fedn. Tchrs., Minn. Sch. Counselors Assn., St. Paul Counselors Assn. (bd. dirs. 1978-79, 82-83). Republican. Office: Highland Park Sr High Sch 1015 Snelling Ave S Saint Paul MN 55116

YOUNG, KAREN LEIGH, advertising executive; b. Wilmington, Del., Aug. 11, 1949; d. William Nelson and Patricia (Patton) Y. Student, Skidmore Coll., 1968-69, U. Hull, Eng., 1970-71. Display sales person Evening Standard, London, 1972; advt. dir. Rolling Stone Mag., London, 1973-76; media staff person BBDO, San Francisco, 1977-85; dir. account mgmt. Gardner Communications, San Francisco, 1985-87, v.p., gen. mgr., 1987—. Office: Gardner Communications 27 Maiden Ln San Francisco CA 94108

YOUNG, LESLIE ANN, writer, editor, educator; b. Casper, Wyo., Oct. 4, 1960; d. Earl Allen and Floy Ella (Muender) Young. AA in Psychology with honors, Mesa Coll., Grand Junction, Colo., 1980; BA in Advt. and Pub. Relations, (with honors, U. Tulsa, 1981; MA in Communication with honors, U. Utah, 1987, postgrad., 1987—. Summer intern Quarter Horse Jour., Amarillo, Tex., 1981; publs. editor Autumn Revolution, Tulsa, 1982; bus. and oil writer Tulsa World, 1982; editor Calgary (Alta.) Alumni Mag., U. Calgary, 1983-85; grad. teaching fellow dept. communication U. Utah, 1985—; free-lance writer Horse Sense, Toronto, Colo. Cowboy, Palisade, Colo., Eastern/Western Quarter Horse Jour., Middleboro, Mass., Wild Rose Quarter Horse Jour., Calgary, Quarter Horse News. Conf. scholar Council Advancement and Support of Edn., 1984, Scripps-Howard scholar, 1981, Gannett Found. scholar, 1986-87, M. Neff Smart/Soc. Profl. Jours. scholar, 1987-88. Mem. Internat. Assn. Bus. Communicators, Women in Communications, Sigma Delta Chi, Phi Kappa Phi, Tau Kappa Alpha. Roman Catholic. Office: Univ Utah Dept Communication Salt Lake City UT 84112

YOUNG, LINDA KATHLEEN, health science association executive; b. Fowler, Kans., Apr. 30, 1954; d. Ralph Edward and Ruth Evelyn (Cornelson) Y.; m. Andre Fountain. BS in Nursing, Cen. State U., Edmond, Okla., 1976. RN. Staff nurse med./surg. and coronary care unit Presbyn. Hosp., Oklahoma City, 1976-79; mgr. nursing Hillcrest Osteo. Hosp., Oklahoma City, 1979-80; staff nurse, mgr. Oklahoma U. Teaching Hosp., Oklahoma City, 1981-82; pres. New Life Programs, Oklahoma City, 1981-88, Nursing Entrepreneurs, Ltd., Oklahoma City, 1988—; coordinator lactation cons. program, State of Okla., 1981—, new life car seat rental program at various hosps., 1983—. Named Mentor of Yr., Okla. Metroplex Childbirth Network, Oklahoma City, 1984. Mem. Am. Nurses Assn., Internat. Childbirth Edn. Assn., Internat. Lactation Cons. Assn. Office: New Life Programs PO Box 75393 Oklahoma City OK 73107

YOUNG, LOIS CATHERINE, public administrator, consultant; b. Wakeman, Ohio, Mar. 10, 1930; d. William McKinley and Leona Catherine (Woods) Williams; m. William Walton Young; children: Ralph, Catherine, William. BS, NYU, 1957; MS, Hofstra U., 1962, profl. diploma, 1967, EdD, 1981; M Pub. Adminstrn., Fla. Internat. U., 1988. Cert. tchr., sch. supr., N.Y. Tchr. Copiague (N.Y.) Schs., 1957-59; research assoc. Columbia and Hofstra Univs., Hempstead, N.Y., 1964-69; tchr. Half Hollow Hills Pub. Schs., Dix Hills, N.Y., 1970-72; instr. Conn. Coll., New London, 1972-73; tchr., supr., reading coordinator Hempstead (N.Y.) Pub. Schs., 1975-85; cons. AID, Miami, Fla., 1987—; clinician Hofstra U., Hempstead, 1962-64; tchr. trainer Amityville (N.Y.) Pub. Schs., 1965, Hofstra Univ., 1982; key speaker Internat. Reading Assn., N.Y., Calif., Caribbean Islands, 1982-86. Author numerous poems. Sec. Jack and Jill of Am. Chpt., Nassau County, N.Y., 1960-62; pres. PTA, Uniondale, N.Y., 1962-68; active Boy Scouts Am., Uniondale, 1963-65; bd. dirs. United Nations Assn. Miami Chpt., 1987—. Recipient research grant N.Y. State Fed. Programs, 1978, Laurel Wreath award Doctoral Assn. of N.Y. Educators, 1982; fellow Fla. Internat. U., 1987. Mem. NYU Alumni Assn. (bd. dirs. 1983—), Phi Delta Kappa, Alpha Kappa Alpha (global affairs chmn. 1986—), Kappa Delta Phi. Home: 14320 SW 105 Terr Miami FL 33186

YOUNG, LORETTA, actress; b. Salt Lake City, Jan. 6, 1913. Grad., Ramona Convent, Alhambra, Calif.; student, Immaculate Heart Coll., Hollywood, Calif. Appeared in films, including Laugh Clown Laugh, 1928, Loose Ankles, 1929, The Squall, 1930, Kismet, 1930, The Devil to Pay, 1930, I Like Your Nerve, 1931, Platinum Blonde, 1932, The Hatchet Man, 1932, Big Business Girl, 1932, Life Begins, 1932, Zoo in Budapest, 1933, Man's Castle, 1933, The House of Rothschild, 1934, Midnight Mary, 1935, The Crusaders, 1935, Clive of India, 1935, Call of the Wild, 1935, Shanghai, 1936, Ramona, 1936, Ladies in Love, 1937, Wife, Doctor and Nurse, 1937, Second Honeymoon, 1938, Four Men and a Prayer, 1938, Suez, 1938, Kentucky, 1938, Three Blind Mice, 1938, The Story of Alexander Graham Bell, 1939, The Doctor Takes a Wife, 1939, He Stayed for Breakfast, 1940, Lady from Cheyenne, 1941, The Men in Her Life, 1941, A Night to Remember, 1942, China, 1943, Ladies Courageous, 1944, And Now Tomorrow, 1944, The Stranger, 1945, Along Came Jones, 1946, The Perfect Marriage, 1946, The Farmer's Daughter, 1947 (Acad. award 1947), The Bishop's Wife, 1948, Rachel and the Stranger, 1948, Come to the Stable, 1949, Cause for Alarm, 1951, Half Angel, 1951, Paula, 1952, Because of You, 1952, It Happens Every Thursday, 1953, others; appeared in TV series Loretta Young Show (Emmy awards 1954, 56, 59, Acad. Television Arts & Scis.), 1953-61, in TV film Christmas Eve (Golden Globe Award for best actress in a TV movie), 1986. Office: care Screen Actors Guild 7750 Sunset Blvd Hollywood CA 90046 *

YOUNG, LUCY CLEAVER, physician; b. Wheeling, W.Va., Aug. 8, 1943. B.S. in Chemistry, Wheaton Coll. (Ill.), 1965; M.D., Ohio State U., 1969. Diplomate Am. Bd. Family Practice, Bd. of Ins. Medicine. Rotating intern Riverside Meth. Hosp., Columbus, Ohio, 1969-70; resident Trumbull Meml. Hosp., Warren, Ohio, 1970-71; practice medicine specializing in family practice, West Chicago, Ill., 1971-73, Paw Paw and Mendota, Ill., 1973-78; co-founder and med. dir. Wholistic Health Ctr. of Mendota, 1976-78; asst. med. dir. Met. Life Ins. Co., Gt. Lakes Head Office, Aurora, Ill., 1979-80; med. dir. Commonwealth Life Ins. Co., Louisville, 1980-85; assoc. prof. U. Ill. Abraham Lincoln Sch. Medicine, 1976-79; faculty monitor MacNeal Meml. Hosp. Family Practice Ctr. (Ill.), 1979-80; faculty preceptor U. Louisville Family Practice Dept., 1981-85; Locum Tenens Family Practice for Kron Med. Corp. of Chapel Hill, N.C., 1986—, mem. staffs Central DuPage Hosp., Winfield, Ill., 1971-73, Mendota Community Hosp., 1973-80, Red Bird Mtn. Med. Ctr., Beverly, Ky., 1985—. Fellow Am. Acad. Family Practice; mem. Am. Med. Women's Assn., Christian Med. Soc. Office: PO Box 1300 Chalmette LA 70044

YOUNG, MARGARET ALETHA McMULLEN (MRS. HERBERT WILSON YOUNG), social worker; b. Vossburg, Miss., June 13, 1916; d. Grady Garland and Virgie Aletha (Moore) McMullen; B.A. cum laude, Columbia Bible Coll., 1949; grad. Massey Bus. Coll., 1958; M.S.W., Fla. State U., 1965; postgrad. Jacksonville U., 1961-62, Tulane U., 1967; m. Herbert Wilson Young, Aug. 19, 1959. Dir. Christian edn. Eau Claire Presbyn. Ch., Columbia, S.C., 1946-51; tchr. Massey Bus. Coll., Jacksonville, Fla., 1954-57, office mgr., 1957-59; social worker, unit supr. Fla. div. Family Services, St. Petersburg, 1960-66, dist. casework supr., 1966-71; social worker, project supr., program supr. Project Playpen, Inc., 1971-81, pres. bd., 1982-83, cons., 1986—; mem. council Child Devel. Ctr., 1983—; mem. transitional housing com., Religious Community Services, 1984—. Mem. Acad. Cert. Social Workers, Nat. Assn. Social Workers (pres. Tampa Bay chpt. 1973-74), Fla. Assn. for Health and Social Services (pres. chpt. 1971), Nature conservancy, Fla. Assn. for Children Under Six. Democrat. Presbyn. Rotary Ann (pres. 1970-71). Home: 330 Roebling Rd N Belleair FL 34616

YOUNG, MARGARET BUCKNER, civic worker, author; b. Campbellsville, Ky.; d. Frank W. and Eva (Carter) Buckner; B.A., Ky. State Coll., 1942; M.A., U. Minn., 1946; m. Whitney M. Young, Jr., Jan. 2, 1944 (dec. Mar. 1971); children—Marcia Elaine, Lauren Lee. Instr., Ky. State Coll., 1942-44; instr. edn. and psychology Spelman Coll., Atlanta, 1957-60; dir. Philip Morris, Inc., N.Y. Life Ins. Co. Alternate del. UN Gen. Assembly, 1973. Mem. pub. policy com. Advt. Council. Trustee Lincoln Center for Performing Arts; chmn. Whitney M. Young, Jr. Meml. Found.; trustee Met. Mus. Art; bd. govs. UN Assn., 1975-82; bd. visitors U.S. Mil. Acad., 1978-80. Author: The First Book of American Negroes, 1966; The Picture Life of Martin Luther King, Jr., 1968; The Picture Life of Ralph J. Bunche, 1968; Black American Leaders-Watts, 1969; The Picture Life of Thurgood Marshall, 1970; pub. affairs phamphlet. Home: 330 Oxford Rd New Rochelle NY 10804 Office: 100 Park Ave New York NY 10017

YOUNG, MARJORIE WILLIS, writer, journalist, lecturer; b. Mansfield, Ohio; d. John Edgar and Mary Adelle (Reiter) Willis; student agr. Cornell U., 1924; student Art Students League, 1925-27, Cooper Union, 1925-27, Columbia U., 1927, 43, Sorbonne, U. Paris, 1928-30, Japanese Lang. Sch., Tokyo, 1934-35, N.Y. U., 1944; m. James Russell Young, Oct. 2, 1934; 1 son, Willis Patterson. Columnist in Far East, Internat. News Service, 1938-41; feature writer King Features Syndicate, 1939, Saturday Pictorial Rev., 1941-45; asst. tech. dir. motion picture Behind the Rising Sun, 1943; research dept. Believe It or Not, 1946-48; feature editor and columnist The Sunday Star, Wilmington, Del., 1946-48, promotion dir. David McKay Pub. Co., 1945-48; lectr. Nat. Concert and Artists Corp., 1942-43; feature writer Anderson (S.C.) Independent, 1949-73; feature writer Anderson Daily Mail, 1949-73, asso. editor The New South, ann. spl. edit. of Daily Mail, 1966-73; editor The Safety Jour., Anderson, 1953—; program moderator Decorating for a Holiday, Sta. WAIM-TV, 1953-55, safety program moderator WAIM-TV, 1953—, program moderator How to Cut and Sew, 1954-55, travel feature program WAIM-WCAC-FM, 1973-82; travel editor Quote mag., 1977-80; editor Vets. of Safety news page, What's What monthly; dir. Capitol City Communications, Inc. Spl. scroll dir. Chinese War Orphans Relief, 1941-45; publicity dir. Crusade for Children, State of Del., 1948; publicity chmn. S.C. Indsl. Nurses Assn., 1953; dir. S.C. 4-H Club TV Safety

Program, 1953; coordinator Ann. S.C. State Landmark Conf., 1979. Bd. dirs. Anderson Heritage, Inc. Recipient various awards for safety activities including Disting. Service award S.C. Occupational Safety Council, 1973. Mem. U. S.C. Caroliniana Soc., Writers Assn. Am., Am. Women in Radio and TV, Nat. Recreation Assn., S.C. Recreation Soc. (v.p. and program dir. 1954-56), Anderson County Hist. Soc. (pres. 1978-80), Am. Soc. Safety Engrs., Vets. Safety Internat., (pres. 1979), DAR, Colonial Dames of the XVII Century. Episcopalian. Clubs: Am. News Women's, Nat. Press (Washington); Overseas Press of Am.; Cornell Women's (N.Y.C.). Author: Decorating for Joyful Occasions, 1952; It's Time for Christmas Decorations, 1957; Fodor's Tour Guide of South Carolina, 1966-68, Tour Guide of Georgia, 1966-67; Japanese American Cook Book, 1972; The Cateechee Trail, 1975; South Carolina's Women Patriots of the American Revolution, 1975; Mystery of the Ivory Eagle, 1980. Editor: Textile Leaders, 1963. Home: 2003 Laurel Dr Anderson SC 29621 Office: Safety Jour PO Box 4189 Anderson SC 29622

YOUNG, MARLENE ANNETTE, lawyer, consultant; b. Portland, Oreg., Mar. 3, 1946; d. Hardy Shelby and Eunice Jean (Gregory) Y.; m. Abdullah Samir Rifai, June 3, 1973 (div. May 1981); m. John Hollister Stein, Jan. 1, 1986. BS, Portland State U., 1967; PhD, Georgetown U., 1973; JD, Willamette U., 1975. Bar: Oreg. 1975. Dir. research Multnomah County Sheriff's Office, Portland, 1975-77; sole practice Wilsonville, Oreg., 1975-81; exec. dir. Applied Systems Research & Data, Wilsonville, 1976-81, Nat. Orgn. Victim Assistance, Washington, 1981—; instr. Essex Community Coll., 1971-73, U. Utah, 1976-78, Portland State U., 1979; cons. U. Research Corp., Washington, 1979-83, ABT Assocs., Boston, 1984—. Author: Victim Service System, 1983; (manuals) Patrol Officers and Crime Victims, 1984, Prosecutors: Attorneys for the People, Advocates for the Victims, 1984; editor: Justice and Older Americans, 1977; contbr. articles to profl. jours. Mem. Ways and Means Com., Wilsonville City, 1977-79, planning commn., 1979-81; Bd. visitors Willamette Coll. Law, Salem, Oreg., 1981-83; bd. dirs. Chemeketa Community Coll., Salem, 1979. Recipient Presdl. award Nat. Orgn. Victim Assistance, Washington, 1981, Pub. Policy award World Fedn. Mental Health, Washington, 1983. Mem. ABA (criminal justice sect., adv. bd. 1981—), Nat. Criminal Justice Assn., Soc. Traumatic Stress Studies (bd. dirs. 1985—), World Soc. Victimology (adv. bd. 1979—, Hans Von Hentig award 1985), Gerontol. Soc. Democrat. Methodist. Office: Nat Orgn Victim Assistance 717 D St NW Washington DC 20004 *

YOUNG, MARY BARTLETT, academic administrator; b. Brunswick, Maine, Oct. 15, 1948; d. Phillip Taylor and Nancy Allen (MacKay) Y.; m. Thomas Wendell McMurray, Jan. 28, 1967 (div. Oct. 1975). BA, Case Western Res. U., 1972. Tchr. Black River High Sch., Ludlow, Utah, 1972-74; free-lance writer newspapers and mags. 1974-82; staff writer Contact mag. U. Mass., Amherst, 1982-83, asst. to vice chancellor, 1983-85, dir. communications, 1985—; adj. faculty Hampshire Coll., Amherst, 1980-81. Contbr. articles to profl jours, mags. and newspapers. Bd. dirs. Porter-Phelps-Huntington Mus., Hadley, Mass., 1987—, sta. WFCR-FM, Amherst, 1984-85. Mem. Council for Advancement and Support of Edn. (Silver Excellence award 1984, 87), U. Women's Profl. Network, Women in Devel. Home: 6 Kensington Ave Northampton MA 01060 Office: U Mass 390 Whitmore Bldg Amherst MA 01003

YOUNG, MARY ELIZABETH, educator; b. Utica, N.Y., Dec. 16, 1929; d. Clarence Whitford and Mary Tippit Y. B.A., Oberlin Coll., 1950; Ph.D. (Robert Shalkenbach Found. grantee, Ezra Cornell fellow), Cornell U., 1955. Instr. dept. history Ohio State U., Columbus, 1955-58; asst. prof. Ohio State U., 1958-63, assoc. prof., 1963-69, prof., 1969-73; prof. history U. Rochester, N.Y., 1973—; cons. in field. Author: Redskins, Ruffleshirts, and Rednecks: Indian Allotments in Alabama and Mississippi, 1830-1860, 1961; co-editor, contbr.: The Frontier in American Development: Essays in Honor of Paul Wallace Gates, 1969. Recipient Pelzer award Miss. Valley Hist. Assn., 1955, Award Am. Studies Assn., 1982, Ray A. Billington award, 1982; Social Sci. Research Council grantee, 1968-69. Mem. Am. Hist. Assn., Orgn. Am. Historians, Am. Studies Assn., Am. Soc. Ethnic History, Soc. for Historians of the Early Am. Republic, Am. Antiquarian Soc. Home: 2230 Clover St Rochester NY 14618 Office: U Rochester Dept History Rochester NY 14627

YOUNG, MARY SUE, housing administrator, social worker; b. Clovis, N.Mex., Aug. 18, 1939; d. Leland L. and Louise (Miller) McMillon; m. Abraham Young, Nov. 26, 1969 (div. 1977); children—Luana Elizabeth, Malia Diane. Student Ill. Wesleyan U., 1957-58; B.S., Okla. State U., 1961; M.S.W., St. Louis U., 1967. Vol., Peace Corps, Colombia, 1963-65; sch. social worker State of Ill., East St. Louis, 1967-69; social worker III, State of Hawaii, Honolulu, 1969-72; social work sr. State of Ga., Macon, 1977-79; adminstr. St. Paul Apts., Inc., Macon, 1979—, St. Paul Village, Inc., 1982—. Foster parent, 1972-77; assault team vol. Crisis Line, Macon, 1983—. HEW grantee, 1965-67. Mem. Ga. Gerontol. Soc. (edn. com. 1984), Ga. Assn. Homes and Services for Aging (sec. 1982—), Am. Assn. Homes for Aging (del. 1985—), Episcopal Soc. Ministry for Aging, Nat. Assn. Social Workers. Democrat. Episcopalian. Avocations: swimming; travel. Home: 634 Woodridge Dr Macon GA 31204 Office: 1330 Forsyth St Macon GA 31201

YOUNG, MAXINE JOIDA, professional society administrator; b. Gary, Ind., Feb. 29, 1948; d. Thomas and Rodesia (Hunter) S.; m. Edward Green Young, Dec. 24, 1965; children: Stephanie LaVon, Tamara KenYetta, Edward Green III. Student, U. Ind., 1966, U. Colo., 1967. Sec. pub. affairs dept. Greater Gary C. of C., 1970-73, bookkeeper, 1974-75, adminstv. asst., 1975-83, exec. dir., 1983—; adv. bd. Post-Tribune, Gary, 1986-87; bd. dirs. Lake County Jobs Tng. Corp., Gary, 1986-87. Bd. dirs. Cath. Youth Orgn., Merrillville, Ind., 1985, Gary Hist. and Cultural Soc., 1985; mem. Miller Citizens Corp., Gary, 1986—; adv. bd. Gary Hall of Fame, 1987, Bicentennial on U.S. Constn., 1987; treas. Greater Gary Arts Council, 1980; pres. St. Monica PTA, Gary, 1983-85; active Holy Angels PTA, 1986. Mem. Nat. Assn. Female Execs., NAACP, Nat. Notorial Assn., Ind. Chamber Execs. Assn., NW Ind. Chamber Execs., Urban League NW Ind. Democrat. Roman Catholic. Club: Toastmasters (Merrillville) (charter, sec. 1986—). Lodge: Rotary. Office: Greater Gary C of C 504 Broadway Suite 324 Gary IN 46402

YOUNG, MELBA LECORNU, personnel director; b. Greenfield, Tenn., Mar. 20, 1934; d. Lynn Grooms and Ella May LeCornu; m. Marvin Anderson Young, Aug. 30, 1959; children: Anderson Lynn, Melinda Lea. AA, U. Tenn., Martin, 1954. With employee relations dept. Jackson (Tenn.) Utility Div., 1973-80, personnel dir., 1980—. Bd. dirs. Jackson Area Council on Drugs and Alcohol, 1986—; active United Way of West Tenn. Mem. Am. Pub. Power Assn. (personnel com. Tenn.), Tenn. Valley Pub. Power Assn. (planning com.), Am. Soc. Personnel Dirs. (treas. Jackson chpt. 1987). Baptist. Office: Jackson Utility Div PO Box 68 119 E College Jackson TN 38302

YOUNG, NANCY, lawyer; b. Washington, Dec. 3, 1954; d. John Young and Byounghye Chang; m. Paul Brendan Ford Jr., May 28, 1983; children: Paul Brendan Ford III, Ian Ford. BA, Yale U., 1975, MA, 1976; JD, Columbia U., 1979. Bar: N.Y. 1981. Assoc. Simpson, Thacher & Bartlett, N.Y.C., 1979-82, Richards, O'Neil & Allegaert, N.Y.C., 1982-86; ptnr. Richards and O'Neil, N.Y.C., 1986—. Mem. ABA, Assn. of Bar of City of N.Y., Council on Fgn. Relations. Democrat. Home: 945 Fifth Ave New York NY 10021 Office: Richards & O'Neil 885 3d Ave New York NY 10022-4802

YOUNG, PATSY KIKUE, state legislator; b. Maui, Hawaii, Oct. 29, 1929. Ed. U. Hawaii. Mem. adv. council Leeward Sch., 1966-70; rep. State Constl. Conv., 1968; bd. regents U. Hawaii, 1971; mem. staff Hawaii Senate, 1966-71; mem. Hawaii Ho. of Reps., from 1972; now mem. Hawaii Senate from 23d dist., also sgt.-at-arms. Democrat. Office: Office State Senate State Capitol Honolulu HI 96813 *

YOUNG, PAULA LYNN, advertising executive; b. Valetta, Malta, Dec. 29, 1955; came to U.S., 1956; d. Robert And Method Ann (Barlar) Y. Student, Ga. State U., 1981-86, Emory U., 1986; cert., Ga. Inst. of Home Bldg., 1986. Asst. supr. Prudential Medicare, Atlanta, 1975-79; adminstrv. asst. Showcase Photographics, Atlanta, 1979-80; asst. fin. analyst, vendor co-coordinator Richway div. Federated Dept. Stores, Atlanta, 1980-83; office mgr., designer Beauticraft, Atlanta, 1983-85; designer, pres. Avante Interiors, Inc., Lexington, Ga., 1985—; land devel. adminstrv. asst. Cohn Communities, Inc., Decatur, Ga., 1986-87; advt. rep. Athens Newspapers, 1987—; free-lance design cons., 1986—; campaign project mem. Seagram's Seven, 1984. Co-author accounting manual, 1978. Rep. United Way, Atlanta, 1976; counselor Council on Battered Women, Atlanta, 1985-86. Mem. Nat. Assn. Female Execs. Episcopalian. Office: Athens Banner-Herald One Press Pl Athens GA 30613

YOUNG, REBECCA CONRAD, state legislator; b. Clairton, Pa., Feb. 28, 1934; d. Walter Emerson and Harriet Averill (Colcord) Conrad; m. Merwin Crawford Young, Aug. 17, 1957; children: Eve, Louise, Estelle Merwin, Emily Harriet. BA, U. Mich., 1955; MA in Teaching, Harvard U., 1963; JD, U. Wis., 1983. Commr. State Hwy. Commn., Madison, Wis., 1974-76; dep. sec. Wis. Dept. of Adminstrn., Madison, 1976-77; assoc. Wadsack, Julian & Lawton, Madison, 1983-84; elected rep. Wis. State Assembly, Madison, 1984—. Translator: Katanga Secession, 1965. Supr. Dane County Bd., Madison, 1970-74; v.p. Madison Sch. Bd., 1979-85. Recipient Pub. Interest award Ctr. for Pub. Representation, 1980, Clean 16 Environ. award WI Environ. Decade, Inc., 1985-86, Congress for A Working Am. award, 1986; named YWCA Woman of Distinction, 1981. Mem. ABA. Democrat. Home: 639 Crandall St Madison WI 53711 Office: Wis State Legislature-Assembly State Capitol PO Box 8953 Madison WI 53708

YOUNG, ROSE RAMEY, university security director; b. Washington Court House, Ohio, May 11, 1944; d. Harold Ray Burris and Amanda Frances (Johnson) Dowden; m. Paul Leon Ramey, June 29, 1960 (div. 1974); children: Paul David, Richard Lee, Rebecca Darlene, Terry Lee; m. Robert Thomas Young, Dec. 12, 1983. Grad. high sch., Circleville, Ohio. With quality control dept. Columbus (Ohio) Coated Fabrics, 1969-71; sec. Big Bear Inc., Columbus, 1971-72; security coordinator Capital U., Columbus, 1972—. Mem. Am. Soc. Indsl. Security, Ohio Pvt. Coll. Security Assn. Democrat. Home: 18 Erie Ct Westerville OH 43081 Office: Capital U 2199 E Main St Columbus OH 43209

YOUNG, RUTH LILLIAN, career planning administrator; b. Savannah, Ga., Dec. 19, 1943; d. Henry Joseph and Sarah Frances (Chapman) Y. Student, CUNY, 1970-71, Adelphi U., 1982-83. Sec., bookkeeper Originals of Jamaica (N.Y.), Inc., 1972-74; asst. state dir. Vets. Employment and Tng. Service U.S. Dept. Labor, N.Y.C., 1974-86; adminstrv. asst. Job Opportunities for Women, Hempstead, N.Y., 1987—; advisor Vets. Employment and Tng. Program N.Y. State Legis. Conf.; trustee Prepared Recruitment Employment Plan, U.S. Dept. Labor. Past commr. N.Y. State Temporary Commn. on Dioxin Exposure. Served as cpl. U.S. Army, 1962-65, France and Fed. Republic of Germany. Mem. VFW (life), NOW, NAACP, N.Y.C. Coalition for Fairness to Vets., Inc. (chairperson 1985—), Am. Vets. Com. (nat. bd. dirs. 1980—), Queens Womens Network (bd. dirs. 1986-87), Am. Legion (women's post), Disabled Am. Vets. (life), Vietnam Vets. Am., Cath. War Vets., 369th Vets. Assn., Inc., WAC Vets. Assn., Nat. Assn. Uniformed Services, N.Y. Urban League. Democrat. Home: 145-27 175th St Jamaica NY 11434 Office: Job Opportunities for Women 600 Ave C at Stewart Rd Westbury NY 11550

YOUNG, RUTH (MARIE), elementary educator, consultant; b. Pitts., Pa., Jan. 14, 1939; d. Harry Theodore and Helen Marie (Windeknecht) McR.; m. Arthur Young, Aug. 6, 1960 (div. 1977); children: Gregory, Bruce. BA, Allegheny Coll., 1960; MS, Ind. U., 1965; postgrad., San Diego State U., 1973, 75-78, 83, Calif. State U., 1974, 77, SUNY, Albany, 1976, U. Calif., San Diego, 1978-79, 83, U. Wyo., 1980. Cert. elem. tchr. (life) Calif., N.Y., ednl. adminstr., Calif. Tchr. pub. schs. Niagara Falls, N.Y., 1960-63, Mooresville and Spencer, Ind., 1963-65; elem. tchr. Ind. U. Lab. Sch., Bloomington, 1965-67; tchr. pub. schs. Chula Vista, Calif., 1967-74; coordinator GATE programs Chula Vista City Schs., 1974-78, sci. resource tchr., 1978—, prin. summer sch., 1975-78; dir. GATE Summer Sch. Chula Vista Assn. for Gifted Students, 1981-85; mem. writing team Challenger Ctr. for Space Sci., 1986-87; sci. resource specialist and presenter staff devel. programs at various sch. dists. throughout San Diego County, 1980—; mem. ednl. adv. bd. Reuben H. Fleet Space Theater, San Diego and Balboa Park, Calif., 1985—, Coll. for Kids program, Southwestern Coll., Chula Vista, 1974—, also tchr. astronomy, 1974, 79-83; ednl. cons. Casper, Wyo., 1977. Co-author (tchr.'s guide) Halley HO, 1985, Ways to Effective Teaching (WEFT), 1987. Active Halecrest, Bonita Vista Jr. and Sr. High Sch. chpts. PTA, 1978—. Recipient Hon. Service award Halecrest PTA, Chula Vista, 1982. Mem. Nat. Sci. Tchrs. Assn., Greater San Diego Sci. Tchrs. Assn. (excellence in elem. sch. award 1985), Chula Vista Assn. for Gifted Children (treas. 1981—), Delta Kappa Gamma (pres. Omicron chpt. 1982-84, grantee 1983). Office: Halecrest Sch 475 E J St Chula Vista CA 92010

YOUNG, SHIRLEY JEAN, small business owner; b. Galveston, Tex., Mar. 18, 1944; d. Rufus H. and Ena I. (Carter) Y. Diploma in computers, basic programming, Halix Inst., 1988. Histologic technician, med. sec. St. Mary's Hosp., Galveston, 1963-66; clk.-typist Am. Oil Co., Texas City, 1967-68, Am. Nat. Ins. Co., Galveston, 1969-75; med. sec. U. Tex. Med. Br., Galveston, 1975-83; owner WORDS ETC (Computer Programming), Galveston, 1983—; cons. Art From The Heart, Livingston, Tex., 1984—. Author: Winning Words, 1987; contbr. articles to bus. publs. Mem. Nat. Fedn. for Decency, 1984—. Mem. Nat. Assn. Female Execs., Computer Entrepreneur Assn. Am., Am. Soc. Clin. Pathologists (assoc.). Baptist. Clubs: 700, 1000 (Virginia Beach, Va.). Home: 2311 71st St Galveston TX 77551 Office: WORDS ETC (Computer Programming) 6608 Stewart Rd Suite 308 Galveston TX 77551-1838

YOUNG, SUSAN FRANCES, financial representative; b. Rochelle, Ill., Feb. 5, 1954; d. Robert Ellison and Frances Louise (Naylor) Y. BS, Western Ill. U., 1976. Asst. mgmt. trainee Associated Milk Producers, Inc., Chgo., 1977-78, health care asst. adminstr., 1978-80; health care assoc. adminstr. Associated Milk Producers, Inc., Fond Du Lac, Wis., 1980-82; health care adminstr. Associated Milk Producers, Inc., Schaumburg, Ill., 1982-86; registered rep. Waddell & Reed, Inc., Sterling, Ill., 1987-88; supr., interviewer Pub. Opinion Lab. No. Ill. U., DeKalb, 1988—; cons. credit mgmt. program Chgo. Midwest Credit Mgmt. Assn., Park Ridge, Ill., 1977-79, 83, health care basic tng. sch. Arthur Andersen & Co., Dallas, Tex., 1984, Women in Mgmt. program, office politics program Harper Coll., Palatine, Ill., 1984. Mem. Nat. Wildlife Fedn. (assoc.), Am. Mus. Nat. History (assoc.); charter mem. Rep. Task Force, Statue Liberty Ellis Island Found; apptd. sec. Adv. Bd. Health, Rochelle, 1987—. Mem. Nat. Assn. Female Execs., Am. Mus. Natural History (assoc.), Nat. Wildlife Fedn. (assoc.), Nat. Rifle Assn., Western Ill. U. Alumni Club., Audubon Soc. Home: 1030 Parkview Dr Rochelle IL 61068

YOUNG, TERRIE L., theatrical company executive; b. Lincoln, Ill., Apr. 24, 1957; d. Neal R. and Trella J. (Robinson) Y. BS, Ill. State U., 1982. Adminstrv. analyst Eaton/Cutler-Hammer Inc., Lincoln, 1976-79; prodn., shipping asst. B.F. Goodrich Chem. Co., Henry, Ill., 1979-80; office mgr. Am. Soc. for Med. Technology, Washington, 1982-85; legal sec. Keller & Heckman, Washington, 1985-86; adminstrv. mgr. CACI Internat. Inc., Fairfax, Va., 1986—. Emergency med. technician Sandy Spring Vol. Fire Dept., 1986—, firefighter, 1986—; mem. com. Champlain at Environ Homeowners Assn., Olney, Md., 1987. Mem. Nat. Assn. Female Execs. Democrat. Office: CACI Internat Inc 8260 Willow Oaks Corp Dr Fairfax VA 22031

YOUNG, TOMMIE MORTON, social psychology educator; b. Nashville. B.A. cum laude, Tenn. State U., 1951; M.L.S., George Peabody Coll. for Tchrs., 1955; Ph.D., Duke U., 1977; postgrad. U. Okla., 1967, U. Nebr., 1968. Coordinator, Young Adult Program, Lucy Thurman br. YWCA, 1951-52; instr. edn. Tenn. State U., Nashville, 1956-59; instr., coordinator media program Prairie View Coll. (Tex.), 1959-61; asst. prof. edn., assoc. prof. English, dir. IMC Ctr., U. Ark.-Pine Bluff, 1965-69; asst. prof. English and edn., dir. learning lab., N.C. Central U., Durhan, 1969-74; prof., dir./chairperson library media services and dept. ednl. media, dir. Afro-Am. Family Project, N.C. Agrl. and Tech. State U., Greensboro, 1975—; pres. World Assocs., Inc., Greensboro: dir. workshops, grants. Contbr. research papers, articles to profl. jours. Nat. chmn. Com. to Re-Elect the Pres.; past sec. Fedn. Colored Women's Clubs; bd. dirs. southwestern div. ARC, dir. Volun-Teens; chairperson learning resources com. Task Force Durham Day Care Assn.; bd. dirs., chairperson schs. div. Durham County Unit Am. Cancer Soc.; past mem. adv. bd., bd. dirs. YMCA, Atlanta; 1st v.p. Durham br. NAACP; mem. U.S. Civil Rights Commn.; bd. dirs. NIH, N.C. Council of the Arts; mem. Guilford County Involvement Council; chmn. N.C. adv. com. U.S. Civil Rights Com., N.C. Civil Rights Network; N.C. chmn. Civil Rights Commn.; pres. Women Organized for Self-Realization and Leadership Devel.; mem. exec. planning com. Greensboro. Recipient awards ARC, 1968, 73, NAACP, 1973, HEW, 1978, U.S. Commn. on Civil Rights, 1982. Mem. Assn. Childhood Ednl. Internat., Comparative and Internat. Edn. Assn., Archives Assoc., ALA (past pres.), N.C. Assn. Coll. and Research Librarians, Internat. Platform Assn., Nat. Hist. Soc., NEA, AAUW (honor award 1983, pres. Greensboro br., chairperson internat. relations com.), Zeta Phi Beta (chairperson polit. action com. eastern region, nat. grammateus, Polit. and Civic Service award 1974, Outstanding Social-Polit. Service award 1982, Woman of Yr. 1977). Author: Afro-American Genealogy Sourcebook, 1987. Home: 4303 King Arthur Pl Greensboro NC 27405

YOUNG-BEEDE, RUTH ANN, real estate developer; b. Palo Alto, Calif., July 2, 1951; d. C. Williams and Ruth E. Young; m. Stephen J. Beede, Aug. 11, 1978; children: Christina, Alexander. BS, U. Oreg., 1972, MS, 1973; Cert. Advanced Study, Northeastern U., 1975. Fgn. student counselor Northeastern U., Boston, 1973-75; advisor East-West Ctr., Honolulu, 1975; dir. Grahm Jr. Coll., Boston, 1975-76; career advisor Boston Coll., 1975-76; owner First Investment Trust, Boston, 1979-83, Sacremento, 1983—; owner U Sell Am., Sacremento, 1988—; pvt. practice cons. Boston, 1977-79. Rep. Mayor's Task Force-Urban Design Study, Sacramento, 1987; mem. Sacramento Valley Apt. Assn., Sierra Foothills Rose Soc., 1987; co-founder coalition of Sacramento Women's Orgn., 1987—. Individual Devel. grantee Bus. and Profl. Women, Sacremento, 1986. Mem. Nat. Assn. Student Personnel (bd. dirs. 1977-78), Income Property Investors Assn., Downtown Capitol Bus. and Profl. Women (pres. 1987), Sacramento C. of C.(chmn. 1986), Leadership Sacramento. Republican. Club: Comstock (Sacramento). Lodge: Soroptomist (chmn. Greater Sacramento club 1987, leadership participant 1987-88). Office: First Investment Trust PO Box 938 Orangevale CA 95662

YOUNGBERG, RUTH MAE, nurse; b. Clearwater, Nebr., Sept. 30, 1921; d. Byron DeForest and Mary Jane (Kletke) Brown; R.N., Lincoln Gen. Hosp. Sch. Nursing, 1943; m. Ira Burnell Youngberg, Sept. 13, 1969; children—Carol Hall Anderson, Mary Hall Hughes, Janet Hall Hays. Office nurse, Lincoln, Nebr., 1947-58; staff nurse Porters Hosp., Denver, 1958-59; head nurse, obstetrical supr. Lincoln Gen. Hosp., 1959-74; maternal child health nurse cons. Nebr. State Health Dept., Lincoln, 1974-77; head nurse labor and delivery Lincoln Gen. Hosp., 1977-85. Mem. Nurses Assn. Am. Coll. Obstetricians and Gynecologists (past vice-chmn. Nebr., past membership chmn. Nebr.), Am. Nurse Assn., Nebr. Perinatal Orgn. (dir., past pres.), Great Plains Orgn. Perinatal Health Care (past sec.), Lincoln Gen. Hosp. Alumni Assn. Republican. Methodist. Home: 400 S 46th St Lincoln NE 68510

YOUNGBLOOD, DEBORAH SUE, speech and language pathologist; b. Fairview, Okla., July 29, 1954; d. G. Dean and Beatrice J. (Hiebert) W. BS with honors, Okla. State U., 1976, MA with honors, 1979. Speech-lang. pathologist Mesa Sch. Dist. 51, Grand Junction, Colo., 1979-82, Fed. Migrant Presch., Grand Junction, 1980-81; dir. clin. services, acting exec. dir. Idaho Easter Seal Soc., Boise, 1982-84; chief audiology and speech pathology Boise VA Med. Ctr., 1984-86; pvt. practice speech-lang. pathology Colorado Springs, 1987—; grad. asst. Okla. State U., Stillwater, 1976-78; speech-lang. cons. Boise Cleft Lip-Palate Team, 1982-84, Idaho Migrant Health Adv. Council, Boise, 1982-86; speech pathology cons. St. Alphonsus Med. Ctr., Boise, 1984—. Recipient Superior Performance award VA, 1985. Mem. Am. Speech-Lang.-Hearing Assn. (cert.), Idaho Speech Hearing Assn., Colo. Speech-Hearing Assn. (mem. exec. council 1981, polit. action and peer review com. 1987—), Council Exptl. Children (recording sec. 1981-82, speaker state conv. 1982), Internat. High IQ Soc., Mensa, Phi Kappa Phi. Mailing Address: PO Box 547 Green Mountain Falls CO 80819

YOUNGBLOOD, ELAINE MICHELE, lawyer; b. Schenectady, N.Y., Jan. 9, 1944; d. Roy W. and Mary Louise (Read) Ortoleva; m. William Gerald Youngblood, Feb. 14, 1970; children—Flagg Khristian, Megan Michele. B.A., Wake Forest Coll., 1965; J.D., Albany Law Sch., 1969. Bar: Tex. 1970, U.S. Dist. Ct. (no. dist.) Tex. 1971, U.S. Dist. Ct. (so. dist.) Tex. 1972, Tenn. 1978, U.S. Dist. Ct. (mid. dist.) Tenn. 1978. Assoc., Fanning & Harper, Dallas, 1969, Crocker & Murphy, Dallas, 1970-71, McClure & Burch, Houston, 1972-75, Brown, Bradshaw & Plummer, Houston, 1975-76; ptnr. Seligmann & Youngblood, Nashville, 1977-88; sole practice, Nashville, 1988—. Mem. Com. for Women in Govt., Dallas, 1969-71, Law Day com. of Dallas Bar Assn., 1970-71. Mem. ABA, Tex. Bar Assn., Tenn. Bar Assn., Nashville Bar Assn., Tenn. Trial Lawyers Assn., Nat. Assn. Women Lawyers. Republican. Episcopalian. Club: Cable of Nashville (charter). Address: PO Box 17466 Nashville TN 37217

YOUNGE, LEE HANLE, environmentalist, consultant; b. N.Y.C., Feb. 9, 1943; d. Adolf Ludwig and Eva (Haaga) Hanle; m. P. Dennis Younge, Dec. 18, 1963; children: Allison, Jennifer, Meredith. BS in Edn., U. Bridgeport, Conn., 1964. Tchr. kindergarten Fairfield (Conn.) Bd. Edn., 1964-65; energy asst. Coop. Extension, Elmira, N.Y., 1981-82; cons. Environ. Mgmt. Council, Elmira, 1985—; bd. dirs. Coop. Extension, mem. community resource devel. com., 1982—. Chmn. environ. conservation com., Big Flats, N.Y., 1978—; mem. planning bd., Big Flats, 1984—, groundwater protection com., 1986—. Recipient Pres.'s award Pres. Jimmy Carter, 1980. Mem. AAUW (chmn. literary 1973-80), N.Y. State Assn. Environ. Mgmt. Councils, N.Y. State Assn. Environ. Conservation Commns. (bd. dirs. 1980—). Roman Catholic. Home: 707 Algonquin Dr Horseheads NY 14845 Office: Environ Mgmt Council 425-447 Pennsylvania Ave Elmira NY 14914

YOUNGER, DORIS ANNE, church association executive; b. Allentown, PA, June 30, 1924; d. W. Chester and Esther M. (Peters) Hill; m. George Dana Younger, June 4, 1949; children—Judith Anne Younger Laspesa, Dana Reed, Stephen Peters, Samuel Hill. B.S. in Edn., U. Pa., Phila., 1946; diploma, Phila. Sch. Occupational Therapy, 1947; M.Div., Yale U., 1950; D.Min., N.Y. Theol. Sem., 1978. Mem. faculty Coll. for Human Services, N.Y.C., 1967-71; mem. faculty Kennedy King Coll., Chgo., 1972-76; exec. dir. Am. Baptist Women, Valley Forge, Pa, 1976-83; gen. dir. Ch. Women United, N.Y.C., 1983—. Mem. Yale U. Council, New Haven, 1984—. Democrat. Baptist. Home: 50 Warren Ct South Orange NJ 07079

YOUNGER, JUDITH TESS, lawyer, educator; b. N.Y.C., Dec. 20, 1933; d. Sidney and Kate (Greenbaum) Weintraub; m. Irving Younger, Jan. 21, 1955; children: Rebecca, Abigail M. B.S., Cornell U., 1954; J.D., NYU, 1958; LL.D. (hon.), Hofstra U., 1974. Bar: N.Y. 1958, U.S. Supreme Ct 1962, D.C. 1983, Minn. 1985. Law clk. to judge U.S. Dist. Ct., 1958-60; asso. firm Chadbourne, Parke, Whiteside & Wolff, N.Y.C., 1960-62; mem. firm Younger and Younger, and (successors), 1962-67; adj. asst. prof. N.Y. U. Sch. Law, 1967-69; asst. atty. gen. State of N.Y., 1969-70; assoc. prof. Hofstra U. Sch. Law, 1970-72, prof., assoc. dean, 1972-74; dean, prof. Syracuse Coll. Law, 1974-75; dep. dean, prof. law Cornell Law Sch., 1975-78, prof. law, 1978-85; vis. prof. U. Minn. Law Sch., Mpls., 1984-85; prof. law U. Minn. Law Sch., 1985—; Trustee Cornell U., 1974-78; cons. NOW, 1972-74, Suffolk County for Revision of Its Real Property Tax Act, 1972-73; mem. Gov. Rockefeller's Panel to Screen Candidates of Ct. of Claims Judges, 1973-74. Contbr. articles to profl. jours. Mem. ABA (council legal edn. 1975-79), Am. Law Inst. (adv. restatement property 1982-84), AAUP (v.p. Cornell U. chpt. 1978-79), N.Y. State Bar Assn., Assn. of Bar of City of N.Y., Minn. Bar Assn. Home: 3520 W Calhoun Pkwy Minneapolis MN 55416 Office: U Minn Law Sch Minneapolis MN 55455

YOUNGER, SHARON RANAE, marketing educator, consultant; b. Melemoresville, Tenn., May 28, 1959; d. William B. and Barbara (Burke) Y. BS in Acctg., Union U., 1981; MBA in Mgmt., Memphis State U., 1985; postgrad., Union for Experimenting Colls. and Univs., Cin., 1985—. Fin. analyst Allied-Signal Corp., Jackson, Tenn., 1981-83; mktg. services mgr. 1983-86; prin. Younger Assocs., Jackson, 1986—; instr. mktg. Union U., Jackson, 1986—; lectr. SBA, 1986; trainer TVA, Jackson, 1986-87. Chairperson Leadership Jackson Found., 1987—. Grantee So. Bapt. Edn. Commn., 1987. Mem. Nat. Assn. Female Execs., Bus. and Profl. Women (scholarship chair 1985-86), Jackson C. of C. (chair small bus. exposition

1988-89), Zeta Tau Alpha (pres. alumni chpt. 1987-88). Office: Union U Hwy 45 Bypass Jackson TN 38305

YOUNGINER, DOROTHY PETERSON, respiratory therapist, small business owner; b. Shelby, Mont., June 8, 1942; d. Norman Oscar and Emma Lucille (Luckenbill) Peterson; m. Huey P. Williamson, Apr. 2, 1958 (div. May 1967); children: Frank Paul, Norman Albert, Wendy Kaye; m. Murray Jacob Younginer Jr., June 7, 1969. AS, Shelby State Community Coll., Memphis, 1981; BS in Allied Health Adminstrn., Christian Bros. Coll., Memphis, 1983. Cert. respiratory therapist. Chief technician respiratory therapy St. Francis Hosp., Charleston, S.C., 1971-75; respiratory therapy coordinator Wesley Long Community Hosp., Greensboro, N.C., 1975-77; asst. dir. respiratory therapy St. Joseph Hosp., Memphis, 1977-78, dir. respiratory care services, 1978—; owner Quilts by Dot, Memphis, 1983—; Mem. profl. adv. bd. ContinuCare Home Health Agy., Memphis, 1985—; speaker in field. Mem. Am. Assn Respiratory Care, Tenn. Soc. Respiratory Care, Am. Coll. Healthcare Execs., Am. Quilter's Soc. Republican. Lutheran. Home: 3559 Voltaire Memphis TN 38128 Office: St Joseph Hosp 220 Overton Memphis TN 38105

YOUNG LIVELY, SANDRA LEE, nurse; b. Rockport, Ind., Dec. 31, 1943; d. William Cody and Flora Juanita (Carver) Thorpe; m. Kenneth Leon Doom, May 4, 1962 (div. 1975); children—Patricia, Anita, Elizabeth. A.S., Vincennes U., 1979, student, U. So. Ind., 1987—. Nursing aide, nurse Forest Del Nursing Home, Princeton, Ind., 1975-80; charge nurse Welborn Bapt. Hosp., Evansville, Ind., 1979-80, 82-83; staff nurse Longview Regional Hosp., Tex., 1980-82; dir. home health Roy H. Laird Meml. Hosp., Kilgore, Tex., 1984-86; med. post-coronary nurse Mercy Hosp., Owensboro, Ky., 1987, Dept. of Corrections charge nurse, Branchville Trg. Ctr., Tell City, Ind, 1987— ; staff nurse, asst. dir. Leisure Lodge Home Health, Overton, Tex., 1983-84. Grantee Roy H. Laird Meml. Hosp., 1986. Mem. Nat. Assn. Female Execs., Menniger Found., Vincennes U. Alumni Assn., Smithsonian Inst. Avocations: writing, research, cake decorating, house plants. Home: 435 S Lincoln Ave PO Box 431 Rockport IN 47635 Office: Branchville Tng Ctr Dept of Corrections PO Box 500 Tell City IN 47586

YOUNGSTER, ARDITHE, sales and service manager, independent contractor; b. Summit, N.J., Jan. 25, 1947; d. William Andrew and Mildred (Kutik) Y. BS in Biolog. Sci., Colo. State U., 1968; postgrad., Calif. State U., Long Beach, 1970. Cert. clin. lab. technologist. Clin. lab. technologist, sect. head St. John's Hosp. and Health Ctr., Santa Monica, Calif., 1970-75; product info. supr. Ortho Pharm. Corp., Raritan, N.J., 1975-76; client services chemist Nichols Inst., San Pedro, Calif., 1976; dept. supr. Morton Maxwell Lab., Los Angeles, 1977-79; sales rep. Metpath Labs., Inc., Teterboro, N.J., 1979-81; sales and customer service mgr. Los Angeles, 1981—; quality assurance analyst Pacific Southwest Airlines, San Diego, 1985-88; clin. lab. tng. mgr. Electro-Nucleonics, Inc., Fairfield, N.J., 1987—; coordinator ednl. programs QualiMedTech, Inc., Long Beach, 1982-83. Vol. Health Fair Expo, Los Angeles, 1980-84. Mem. Colo. State U. Alumni Assn. (alumni ambassador 1984—), Nat. Notary Assn., Pacific Palisades C. of C., AAUW, Am. Assn. Clin. Chemists, Ninety Nines, Gamma Phi Beta, Alpha Mu Gamma. Republican. Presbyterian. Office: 845 Via de la Paz Suite 8 Pacific Palisades CA 90272

YOUNT, FLORENCE JANE, lawyer; b. Enid, Okla., Dec. 13, 1926; d. William Edward and Florence Evelyn (McCully) Y. B.A., State U. Iowa, 1948; J.D., S. Tex. Coll. Law, 1958; certificate, Parker Sch. Fgn. and Comparative Law, Columbia U., 1976. Bar: Tex. bar 1958. Atty. Ginther, Warren & Co., Houston, 1959-70; supr. internat. contracts Ea. Hemisphere div. CONOCO, Inc., N.Y.C., Stamford, Conn., 1970-75; sr. atty. Cities Service Co., Houston, 1975-83; contracts supr. Marathon, Houston, 1984—; adviser to Internat. Law Socs. of three Houston law schs.; bd. dirs. S. Tex. Law Jour., Inc., v.p., 1969, 77, 84-87, pres., 1970, 78, 79. Contbr. articles to law jours. Bd. dirs. Park Ave. Christian Ch., N.Y.C., 1971-73, First Christian Ch., Houston, 1977-78; active Vols. of Shelter, N.Y.C., 1973-75; precinct chmn., asso. legal counsel, chmn. rules com. Harris County (Tex.) Republican Com., 1958-68. Recipient Distinguished Alumnus award South Tex. Coll. Law, 1976, Houston Matrix award, 1978, award Bus. and Profl. Women's Club Houston, 1976; named One of 100 Top Corporate Women Bus. Week, 1976. Mem. ABA, Tex. Bar Assn. (contbg. editor Internat. Law Newsletter), Houston Bar Assn., S. Tex. Coll. Law Alumni Assn. (dir. 1977-80), Zool. Soc. Houston. Mem. Christian Ch. Address: 701 Bering Dr 2003 Houston TX 77057

YOUNTS, PATTY LOU, interior design executive, researcher; b. Lexington, N.C., Feb. 20, 1950; d. Wayne Lohr and Rosetta Mae (Myers) Y. B.S., U. N.C.-Greensboro, 1972; postgrad. in Mktg., Wake Forest U., Winston-Salem, N.C., 1976. Apprentice draftsman and interior designer Paul T. Briggs, AIA, Lexington, 1971, in-house designer, specifer, 1972-74; part-time interior designer Watkins Office Interiors, Winston-Salem, 1972-74; ptnr. IN-Ex Designs, Inc., 1974-75, corp. officer, head, 1975-81, pres., owner, 1981—. dir. Industry Gen. Tire, GF Bus. Systems, Armstrong Industries, Mid-State Tile; guest speaker univs. Adv. bd. Lexington Meml Hosp., 1984—, Western Carolina U., 1983—. Recipient N.C. AIA awards for Sch. Planning, 1977, 79. Sperry and Hutchinson scholar, 1968-72, honorary scholar, U. N.C.-Greensboro, 1971-72. Mem. Inst. Bus. Designers (mem., chmn. various coms., pres. Carolinas chpt. 1977-80, 82-84), Am. Soc. Interior Designers, Color Mktg. Group (chairholder 1985). Lexington C. of C. (com. chmn. 1980, bd. dirs. 1981-84). Democrat. Mem. United Ch. of Christ. Avocations: water skiing, golf. Office: Design Cons 302 W Center St Lexington NC 27292

YOUTZ, CAROL ANN, banker attorney; b. Canton, Ohio, June 17, 1953; d. Charles Burton and Florence Nancy (Parks) Youtz; student Baldwin-Wallace Coll., 1971-72; B.S. magna cum laude in Acctg., U. Akron, 1979, J.D. U. Akron Sch. Law., 1985. New accounts counselor The Harter Bank & Trust Co., Canton, Ohio, 1973-75; litigation, corp. and pension paralegal Krugliak, Wilkins, Griffiths & Dougherty Co., Canton, 1975-80; tax and ins. analyst Diebold, Inc., Canton, 1980-81; trust adminstr. Bank One of Akron, N.A., 1981-82, asst. trust officer, 1983-84; sr. employee benefits officer Fidelity Bank, 1984-87; v.p. Equibank, 1987—; mem. Akron Pension Council, 1979-82. Mem. Tuscarawas Philharmonic Orch., 1978-80, Main Line Symphony Orch., 1985-87. Mem. Am. Bar Assn., Akron Pension Council, Beta Alpha Psi, Beta Gamma Sigma, Alpha Sigma Lambda. Mem. United Ch. of Christ. Club: Order of Eastern Star. Home: 2001 Saint James Pl Wexford PA 15090 Office: Two Oliver Plaza Pittsburgh PA 15211-2705

YU, ANNE RAMONA WING-MUI, psychologist, b. Hong Kong, Apr. 9, 1948; came to U.S., 1968, naturalized, 1974; d. Hing-wan and Sin-wah (Yau) Yu; B.A. with honors in Psychology, Ohio U., 1971; M.A., So. Ill. U., 1975. Psychol. examiner Delta Counseling and Guidance Center, Monticello, Ark., 1975-76; psychologist Mid-Nebr. Community Mental Health Center, Grand Island, Nebr., 1977—; supr. satellite clinic Loup Valley Mental Health Center, Loup City, Nebr., 1978-79; project dir. Protection from Domestic Abuse, 1978-79; pres. Taskforce on Domestic Violence and Sexual Assault, Grand Island, 1980-82. Mem. Mental Health Bd. Hall County, 1979; mem. fellows Menninger Found., 1983-84; bd. dirs. YWCA, 1984—. Ohio U. Psi Chi scholar, 1968-71. Mem. Am. Psychol. Assn., Nebr. Assn. for Marriage and Family Therapy (legis. chmn. 1988—, v.p. 1981-84, pres. elect 1984-85, pres. 1985-87), Am. Assn. Sex Educators, Counselors, and Therapists, Am. Assn. Univ. Women (pres. Grand Island chpt. 1984-86, v.p. Nebr. div. 1986—), Grand Island Assn. for Child AbusA Prevention (bd. dirs. 1983—, v.p. 1988—), International Platform Assn., Asian-Am. Psychol. Assn. Home: Apt 101 1524 Coventry Ln Grand Island NE 68801 Office: Mid-Plains Ctr Profl Services 911 Baumann Dr Grand Island NE 68801

YU, LINDA, newswoman, television anchorwoman; b. Xian, China, Dec. 1, 1946; B.A. in Journalism, U. So. Calif., 1968; m. Richard K. Baer, June 1982. With Sta. KTLA-TV, Los Angeles, Sta. KABC-TV, Los Angeles; news anchor, reporter Sta. KATU-TV, Portland, Oreg.; gen. assignment reporter Sta. KGO-TV, San Francisco; with Sta. WMAQ-TV, Chgo., 1979-84, gen. assignment reporter, weekend anchor, 1979-80, co-anchor Monday-Friday edit. NEWSCENTER5, 4:30 PM, 1980-81, co-anchor NEWSCENTER5, 10:00 PM, 1981-84; co-anchor Eyewitness News, WLS-TV, Chgo., 1984—; spl.: Linda Yu in China, 1980; anchor WLS-TV, Chgo., 1984—. Recipient Chgo. Emmy award, 1981, 82, 87. Office: WLS-TV 190 N State St Chicago IL 60601 *

YU HUSSEIN, PATTIE, public relations agency executive; b. Washington, Nov. 15, 1956; d. Michael Yung-An and Maria (Chang) Yu; m. Sharif R. Hussein, June 21, 1980. BS in Journalism, U. Md., 1977, MA in Communications, 1982; cert. in journalism, NYU, 1977. Editorial intern Redbook Mag., 1977; editorial asst. Washington Star Newspaper, 1977-79; media coordinator U. Md. Univ. Relations, College Park, 1979-82; communications freelancer IBM, Bethesda, Md., 1981-82; assoc. Porter/NovelliOmnicom Pub. Relations Network, Washington, 1983-84, sr. assoc., 1984-86, v.p., 1987—; judge United Way corp. campaigns, Alexandria, Va., 1986, World Inst. for Black Communications, 1986; guest lectr. U. Md., Howard U., George Washington U., 1986-87. Freelance editorial writer Mt. Vernon Coll. Alumnae mag., 1982; contbr. articles to profl. jours. Co-chair devel. and pub. relations Regina High Sch., Hyattsville, Md., 1987; pub. relations advisor Beautiful Babies campaign March of Dimes, Washington, 1987; alumni adviser The M Space, U. Md. Journalism Alumni mag., 1981. Recipient awards of excellence Communications Excellence to Black Audiences, 1983, 84, 87, Gold Screen award Nat. Assn. Govt. Communicators, 1984, Addy Cert. of Excellence Washington Advt. Club, 1985, 87. Mem. Pub. Relations Soc. Am. (Nat. capitol chpt., Thoth award), Washington Women in Pub. Relations (bd. dirs.), U. Md. Journalism Alumni Chpt., U. Md. Alumni Assn. Internat., Sigma Delta Chi, Soc. Profl. Journalists. Democrat. Roman Catholic. Clubs: BCC Toastmaster's (Bethesda); Silver Spring Bus. and Profl. Women (corr. chmn. 1981). Office: Porter/Novelli 1001 30th St NW Washington DC 20007

YUKL, TRUDY ANN, psychologist, medical social worker; b. Portsmouth, N.H., Feb. 5, 1947; d. Francis Joseph and Dorothy Helen (Pluff) Y. B.A. in psychology, U. Ky., 1969; M.S. in Counseling, Suffolk U., 1984; postgrad. in counseling psychology, Harvard U., 1984-85, Boston U., 1985—. Med. social worker Mass. Gen. Hosp., Boston, 1969-86, clin. fellow in psychology, 1986-87 clin. internship VA Outpatient clinic, Honolulu, 1987-88; co-founder, dir. Indian Clinic, 1973-86; cons. Boston Indian Council, 1973-86; lectr. in field. Contbr. articles to profl. jours. Health adv. bd. Tecumseh House, Boston, 1980-86; active Homeless Coalition, Boston, 1984-85, community service activities, Lunalilo Home, Kalaupapa Moloka'i, Leahi Hosp. Outpatient dept., office Hawaiian Affairs. Recipient Outstanding Prof. Human Services award, 1974-75, Disting. Leadership award, 1987 88, Acad. All-Am. Achievement award, 1988; nominated Disting. Alumni, U. Ky., 1985. Mem. Nat. Assn. Social Workers, Am. Psychol. Assn., Mass. Psychol. Assn., Phi Delta Kappa. Avocations: travel; photography; music; native American culture; dancing; swimming. Mailing Address: 427 Pau St #302 Honolulu HI 96815

YULINSKY, KRISTINA ANNA VARENAIS, banker; b. Boston, Sept. 3, 1955; d. Andrejs and Mirdza (Kalnins) Varenais; m. Corwin Mark Yulinsky, Mar. 20, 1982. BA in Econs., Smith Coll., 1977; MBA in Fin. and Mktg., Boston U., 1982. Assoc. HEW, Washington, 1975-76; analyst ABT Assocs., Inc., Cambridge, Mass., 1977-80; study dir. Booz Allen & Hamilton, Phila., 1982-84; with mktg. devel. Dun & Bradstreet Corp., N.Y.C., 1984-86; fin. cons. N.Y.C., 1986; v.p. Citicorp N. Am., Harrison, N.Y., 1986-87, N.Y.C., 1987—. Contbr. articles to profl. jours. Mem. Am. Mktg. Assn. Democrat. Jewish. Office: Citicorp N Am 641 Lexington Ave 5th Floor Zone 1 New York NY 10043

YUNG-FATAH, ELLEN MEEFONG, nurse consultant; b. Hong Kong, Jan. 15, 1953; d. James Yorkshing and Kwaifun (Chan) Young; m. Ali Ahmed Fatah, June 4, 1983. BS in Nursing, SUNY, 1980; MPH, Johns Hopkins U., 1983. Asst. educator health Chinatown Health Clinic, N.Y.C., 1978-80; clin. nurse Luth. Med. Ctr., Bklyn., 1980-81, Johns Hopkins Hosp., Balt., 1981-83; cons. nurse D.C. Dept. Consumer & Regulatory Affairs, 1983—; pub. health nurse Balt. City Health Dept., 1981; mem. task force, steering com. for health care regulations D.C., Washington, 1984—; advisor D.C. Health Planning & Devel. Agy., Washington, 1985—; resource person Senate Spl. Com. Aging, House Select Com. Aging, Am. Assn. Retired Persons, others; mem. profl. adv. com. Home Health Agy. Study Georgetown U., 1985-86; mem. Nat. Task Force for Hemodialysis User Edn., 1984—. Contbr. articles to profl. jours. Mem. Am. Pub. Health Assn., Johns Hopkins U. Alumni Soc. Democrat. Moslem. Office: Dept Consumer & Regulatory Affairs 614 H St NW Washington DC 20001

ZABACK, CAROL FAY, food company executive; b. Dillon, Mont., June 12, 1942; d. George H. and Fay (Ellis) Whittaker; m. Edward T. Zaback, Dec. 6, 1964; children: Jodi Ann, Lori Lin, Tedi Jo. Student, Idaho State U., 1960-62; BA, U. Mont., 1963. Sales rep. retail food group Kraft, Inc., Hillside, N.J., 1976-78; account rep. Kraft, Inc., Edison, N.J., 1978-79, sr. account exec., 1979-81, sales supr., 1981—, tng. specialist parent co., 1983—. Mem. Am. Mgmt. Assn., NOW, Am. Humane Soc., Animal Protection Inst. Am., Nat. Assn. Female Execs. Home: Rt 2 Box 780 Campbell Hall NY 10916 Office: Kraft Inc 4 Mayfield Ave Edison NJ 08837

ZABAL, REBECCA ABBY, advertising agency executive; b. N.Y.C., Jan. 30, 1951; d. Max Schain and Shirley Harriet (Pomeranz) Litsky; m. Joseph Raymond, Jan. 18, 1973 (div. 1982). Cert. de Langs. and Arts, U. Barcelona, Spain, 1970; BA, Emerson Coll., 1972. Product devel. mgr. Revlon Inc., N.Y.C., 1972-74; broadcast sales Petry TV Inc., N.Y.C., 1974-76, ABC TV, Los Angeles and N.Y.C., 1976-80; broadcast buyer Doyle Dane Bernbach, N.Y.C., 1980-83; broadcast buyer J. Walter Thompson, N.Y.C., 1983-84, sr. negotiator, 1984-85, 86—; broadcast supr. J. Walter Thompson, Washington, 1985-86. Office: J Walter Thompson USA Inc 466 Lexington Ave New York NY 10017

ZABLE, MARIAN MAGDELEN, physician assistant, consultant; b. Beaver Dam, Wis., Oct. 13, 1933; d. John Joseph and Agatha Mary (Eschlie) Fernbach; m. Jerome Edward Zable, July 30, 1960 (div. 1970); children: Terrence, Andrea, Michael. BS, U. Wis., 1964; Physician Asst., U. Fla., 1975. Tchr. Brown Deer (Wis.) Sch. System, 1964, Orange County (Fla.) Schs., 1965-70; curriculum devel., adminstr. So. Coll., Orlando, Fla., 1970-72; physician asst., asst. dir. Longevity Ctr., Orlando, 1977; physician asst. Pritikin Longevity Ctr., Miami, Fla., 1978-83, Cardiovascular Assocs., Kissimmee, Fla., 1984—; pres., physician asst., cons. Physician's Services, Inc., Orlando, 1986—. Mem. Am. Acad. Physician Assts., Fla. Acad. Physician Assts. Home: 3407 Trentwood Blvd Orlando FL 32812 Office: Cardivascular Assocs 110 W Drury Kissimmee FL 32471

ZACCONE, SUZANNE MARIA, sales executive; b. Chgo., Oct. 23, 1957; d. Dominic Robert and Lorretta F. (Urban) Z. Grad. high sch., Downers Grove, Ill. Sales sec. Brookeridge Realty, Downers Grove, 1975-76; sales cons. Kafka Estates Inc., Downers Grove, 1975-76; adminstrv. asst. Chem. Dist., Inc., Oakbrook, Ill., 1976-77; sales rep., mgr. Anographics Corp., Burr Ridge, Ill., 1977-85; pres., owner Graphic Solutions, Inc., Downers Grove, 1985—. Mem. Women in Mgmt., Nat. Assn. Female Execs., Sales and Mktg. Execs. of Chgo., Women Entrepreneurs of DuPage County. Avocations: reading, sailing, cooking, needlepoint, scuba diving. Office: Graphic Solutions Inc 5117 Main St Downers Grove IL 60515

ZACHARY, ANDREA ANNE, geneticist; b. Cleve., Sept. 25, 1946; d. Anthony A. and Audrey J. (Klaus) Z. BS, Ohio State U., 1967, MS, 1969; PhD, Case Western Res. U., 1982. Research asst. Ohio State U., Columbus, 1969-70; technologist Cleve. Clinic Found., 1970-74, supr. lab., 1974-81, project scientist, 1981-82, staff, 82-84, assoc. lab. dir., 1984-86, co-dir. lab., 1986—; faculty histocompatibility specialist course South-Eastern Organ Procurement Found., 1983, 84, 86, 88; ad hoc cons. NIH, 1985-86. Co-editor: AACHT Lab. Manual, 1981. Author audio-visual program on immunogenetics, 1983. Contbr. articles to profl. jours. and chpts. to scholarly tests. Grantee Kidney Found. of Ohio, 1984, 88, Cleve. Clinic Found., 1985-87. Mem. United Network for Organ Sharing (bd. govs. 1987-88), Am. Soc. for Histocompatibility and Immunogenetics (councillor 1977-78, 83-86, edn. program faculty 1971-83, 85, 88, invited speaker sci. symposium 1988, chairperson tech. affairs com. 1982-84, chairperson accreditation com. 1986-88, editor Lab. Manual 1987), Am. Soc. Human Genetics, Am. Soc. Transplant Physicians (invited speaker 1988), Transplant Soc. of Northeast Ohio (mem. editorial bd. Transplantation), Audubon Soc., Nat. Wildlife Fedn., N.Y. Acad. Scis., Sierra Club. Avocations: nature photography, cross-country skiing, music, leather carving. Office: Cleve Clinic Found 9500 Euclid Ave Cleveland OH 44106

ZACHERL, ANITA MARIE, clinical instructor; b. Brookville, Pa., Sept. 13, 1946; d. Francis Augustine and Hilda Clara (Schill) Z. Diploma in Nursing, St. Vincent Hosp. Sch. of Nursing, 1967. Staff nurse NYU Med. Ctr., N.Y.C., 1967-71, Aspen (Colo.) Valley Hosp., 1971-79; dir. nursing services Med. Personnel Pool, Dallas, 1979-80; clin. specialist Datamedix, Inc., Dallas, 1981-82; nurse cons. Xanar, Inc., Dallas, 1982-87; clin. instr. Xanar/Coherent Med. Group, 1987—; speaker nursing seminars, 1984, 85, 87. Mem. Assn. of Operating Room Nurses, Nat. Assn. of Female Execs., Am. Soc. of Profl. and Exec. Women. Roman Catholic. Home: 2888 Harbinger Ln Dallas TX 75252

ZACHERT, VIRGINIA, psychologist, educator; b. Jacksonville, Ala., Mar. 1, 1920; d. R.E. and Cora H. (Massee) Z. Student, Norman Jr. Coll., 1937; A.B., Ga. State Woman's Coll., 1940; M.A., Emory U., 1947; Ph.D., Purdue U., 1949. Diplomate: Am. Bd. Profl. Psychologists. Statistician Davison-Paxon Co., Atlanta, 1941-44; research psychologist Mil. Contracts, Auburn Research Found., Ala. Poly. Inst.; indsl. and research psychologist Sturm & O'Brien (cons. engrs.), 1958-59; research project dir. Western Design, Biloxi, Miss., 1960-61; self-employed cons. psychologist Norman Park, Ga., 1961-71, Good Hope, Ga., 1971—; research assoc. med. edn. Med. Coll. Ga., Augusta, 1963-65, assoc. prof., 1965-70, research prof., 1970-84, research prof. emeritus, 1984—, chief learning materials div., 1973-84, mem. faculty senate, 1976-84, mem. acad. council, 1976-82, pres. acad. council, 1983, sec., 1978; mem. Ga. Bd. Examiners of Psychologists, 1974-79, v.p., 1977, pres., 1978; mem. adv. bd. Comdr. Gen. ATC USAF, 1967-70; cons. Ga. Silver Haired Legislature, 1980, senator, 1987—, pres. protem, 1987. Author: (with P.L. Wilds) Essentials of Gynecology-Oncology, 1967, Applications of Gynecology-Oncology, 1967. Del. White House Conf. on Aging, 1981. Served as aerologist USN, 1944-46; aviation psychologist USAF, 1949-54. Fellow Am. Psychol. Assn., AAAS; mem. AAUP (chpt. pres. 1977-80), Sigma Xi. (chpt. pres. 1980-81). Baptist. Home: 1126 Highland Ave Augusta GA 30904-4628 Office: Med Coll Ga Dept Ob-Gyn Augusta GA 30912

ZACKY, DOLORES, advertising executive; b. Mexico City, Sept. 22, 1947; came to U.S., 1976; d. German and Dolores (Menendez) Valdes; m. Ralf George Zacky, July 15, 1978; children: Lorena, Denise, Daphne. BA in Spanish and Latin Am. Studies, U. of the Ams., Mexico City, 1970; postgrad., Inst. Latin Am. Studies, London, 1970-71; MA in Spanish with distinction, UCLA, 1978. Producer McCann Erickson, Mexico City, 1971-72; copywriter Manin Display Internat., Mexico City, 1972-74; prof. lit. Colegio Columbia, Mexico City, 1974-76; account exec. Latmark Advt., Los Angeles, 1980-81; assoc. creative dir. Bermudez and Assocs., Los Angeles, 1981-82; v.p., creative dir. J. Walter Thompson/Hispania, Los Angeles, 1982—. Creative dir. (TV commls.) Nature, 1987 (Don Belding award), Te Quiero Mucho, 1987 (Don Belding award 1987). Named one of 4 top women in advt. Adweek mag., 1986. Republican. Roman Catholic. Office: J Walter Thompson USA Inc 10100 Santa Monica Blvd Los Angeles CA 90067

ZAFFIRINI, JUDITH, state senator; b. Laredo, Tex., Feb. 13, 1946; d. George and Nieves Pappas; m. Carlos Zaffirini, 1965; 1 child, Carlos Jr. BS, U. Tex., 1967, MA, 1970, PhD, 1978. Committeewoman Tex. State Dem. Exec. Com., 1978-84; state senator Tex. 1987—; del. Dem. Nat. Conv., 1980, 84. Bd. dirs., dir. pub. relations Laredo Civic Music Assn., 1968—. Named Woman of Achievement Tex. Press Women. Democrat. Roman Catholic. Address: 1407 Washington St Laredo TX 78040 *

ZAGAME, MARIE GRACE, commercial artist and illustrator; b. N.Y.C., Apr. 30, 1927; d. Joseph and Rose (Lo Schiavo) Di Stefano; m. Victor J. T. Zagame, Apr. 8, 1956. Student, Cen. Park Sch. of Art, N.Y.C., 1945, Art Students League, 1946-47, NYU, 1946-48; student in pharmacy, St. John U., 1974-75. Lettering and display artist Abramson's Dept. Store, N.Y.C., 1943-45; home furnishings and shoes artist Gimbels Dept. Store, N.Y.C., 1946; free lance artist Marie Zagame, N.Y.C., 1947—; sec.-treas. Nicholson-Zagame Inc., N.Y.C., 1963-64; pres. Marie Zagame Inc., N.Y.C., 1965—; vol. art tchr. St. Thomas Acad., Whitestone, N.Y., 1974-75. Advt. cons., account exec. Belton Copp for Congress, 2d Congl. Dist., Conn., 1964. Recipient Alexander medal Bd. Edn. N.Y.C., 1944, Good Citizenship medal DAR, 1940, Foster medal Am. Legion, 1940. Democrat. Roman Catholic. Clubs: Poodle of Am., Hudson Valley Poodle. Home and Office: 111 Davis Ave Northfield NJ 08225

ZAGORZYCKI, MARIA TERESA, physician; b. Trenton, N.J., Dec. 18, 1953; d. John M. and Janina Zofia (Jaworski) Z.; B.A. in Biochemistry with distinction in all subjects, Cornell U., 1975; M.D., George Washington U., 1979. Diplomate Am. Bd. Ob-Gyn. Intern, UCLA Hosp., 1979-80, resident in ob-gyn., 1980-82, chief resident in ob-gyn., 1982-83, asst. clin. prof. ob-gyn, 1983—. Fellow Am. Coll. Ob-Gyn, Inter-Am. Coll. Physicians and Surgeons; mem. Am. Fertility Soc., Am. Med. Women's Assn., Am. Assn. Gynecologic Laproscopists, Los Angeles County Obstetrical and Gynecol. Soc., Phi Delta Epsilon. Club: Cornell of So. Calif. Office: 14624 Sherman Way Suite 408 Van Van Nuys CA 91405

ZAHM, BERNICE SCHULTZ, educational administrator; b. Cleve., May 25, 1919; d. Sam and Lillian (Levin) Schultz; B.A., Ohio State U., 1941; M.A. in Ednl. Guidance, Calif. State U., Los Angeles; Ph.D. in Human Behavior, U.S. Internat. U., San Diego, 1972; m. Nathan R. Zahm, 1939 (dec. 1979); children—Stephen, Barbara. Tchr. pub. schs., Los Angeles, 1952-53; pvt. remedial educator, 1953—; founder Zahm Sch. and Ednl. Guidance Center, Los Angeles, 1956—; speaker, lectr. profl. assns., 1965—; cons. to pvt. and pub. schs., 1965—. Recipient award for contbn. to remedial edn. County of Los Angeles, 1964, Outstanding Leadership award Los Angeles Soc. Clin. Psychologists, 1984. Mem. Am. Psychol. Assn., Calif. Psychol. Assn. (chmn. ednl. div., named Disting. Humanitarian 1984). Calif. Assn. Sch. Psychologists, Calif. Assn. Marriage and Family Counselors, Am. Personnel and Guidance Assn. Psychologists for Social Responsibility (co-chmn., steering com. 1984). Contbr. articles to profl. jours. Originator multilectic approach to edn. Address: 4422 Sherman Oaks Circle Sherman Oaks CA 91403

ZAISER, SALLY SOLEMMA VANN, retail book company executive; b. Birmingham, Ala., Jan. 18, 1917; d. Carl Waldo and Einnan (Herndon) Vann; student Birmingham-So. Coll., 1933-36, Akron Coll. Bus., 1937; m. Foster E. Zaiser, Nov. 11, 1939. Acct., A. Simionato, San Francisco, 1958-65; head acctg. dept. Richard T. Clarke Co., San Francisco, 1966; acct. John Howell-Books, San Francisco, 1967-72, sec., treas., 1972-83, 84-85, dir., 1982-85; sec. Great Eastern Mines, Inc., Albuquerque, 1969-81, dir., 1980-85. Braille transcriber for ARC, Kansas City, Mo. 1941-45; vol. worker ARC Hosp. Program, São Paulo, Brazil, 1952. Mem. Book Club Calif., Calif. Hist. Soc., Soc. Lit. and Arts, Gleeson Library Assocs. (dir. 1984-87, editor GLA newsletter 1984-87), Nat. Notary Assn., Theta Upsilon. Republican. Episcopalian. Club: Capitol Hill. Home: 355 Serrano Dr Apt 4-C San Francisco CA 94132 Office: 434 Post St San Francisco CA 94102

ZAITZ, JOAN SALWEN, lawyer; b. N.Y.C., June 29, 1951; d. Sidney and Ruth (Starr) Salwen; m. Alan S. Zaitz, Oct. 18, 1980; children: Jacob Salwen, Jessica Sidney. A.B. cum laude, Syracuse U., 1973; J.D., U. Pa., 1976. Bar: N.Y. 1977. Assoc. Louis E. Cherico, White Plains, N.Y., 1977-80, Joel Martin Aurnou, White Plains, 1980-82; sole practice, Hartsdale, N.Y., 1983-84, Scarsdale, N.Y., 1984—. Mem. N.Y. State Bar Assn., White Plains Bar Assn. (bd. dirs. 1983—), Westchester County Bar Assn. (bd. dirs. lawyer referral service 1983-84), Pi Sigma Alpha. Home and Office: 2 Crawford Ln Scarsdale NY 10583

ZAJICEK (ZEE), BARBARA JEANNE, health care association executive; b. Peoria, Ill., Jan. 12, 1932; d. Gale Edward and Thelma Beatrice (Drury) Allen; student pub. schs.; m. Albert F. Zajicek, July 5, 1973 (dec.); children: Gregg Hahn, Lisa Hahn, Dana Hahn. Office supr., then exec. asst. to pres. Larry Smith & Co., Northfield, Ill., 1970-74, 76-78; asst. to pres., leasing agt. Devel. Control Corp., Northfield, 1974-76; bus. mgr. EMSCO, Ltd., Des Plaines, Ill., 1978-85; v.p./asst. sec.-treas. Midwest Med. Mgmt., 1982-85; exec. dir. Fla. chpt. Am. Coll. Emergency Physicians, Orlando,

1985—. Mem. Emergency Medicine Mgmt. Assn. (past pres., exec. dir. 1985-88), ASAE, FSAE, Meeting Planners Internat., Republican. Lutheran. Home: 3689 Jericho Dr Casselberry FL 32707-6203 Office: Am Coll Emergency Physicians Fla Chapter 5824 S Semoran Blvd Orlando FL 32822-4812

ZAK, DOROTHY ZERYKIER, psychologist; b. Katowice, Poland, Jan. 11, 1950; came to U.S., 1969; d. Mieczystaw and Helena (Stahl) Zerykier; m. Jesse Cooper Brake (dec.); m. Sheldon Jerry Zak, July 6, 1986. BA, Queens Coll., 1973; MA, New Sch. Social Research, 1975. Clin. intern Bergen Pines Hosp., Paramus, N.J., 1976-77; psychologist State Sch. Mentally Retarded, Kinston, N.C., 1977-78, Dorothea Dix Hosp., Raleigh, N.C., 1978-83; pvt. practice cons. N.Y.C., 1983-84; psychologist Fed. Employment and Guidance Services, N.Y.C., 1984-85; vocat. counselor N.Y. Assn. for New Ams. Inc., N.Y.C., 1985-88; ednl. counselor B'nai Brith Career and Counseling Services, N.Y.C., 1988—; part-time cons. St. John's Hosp.-Cath. Med. Ctr. Bklyn. and Queens Weight Loss Program, 1987—. Mem. Am. Psychol. Assn., Polish Inst. Arts and Scis. Office: B'nai Brith 823 UN Plaza New York NY 10017

ZALESKI, JEAN, artist; b. Malta; d. John M. and Carolina (Micallef) Busuttil; children: Jeffrey, Philip, Susan. Student, Art Students League, N.Y.C., 1956-59, New Sch. Social Research, 1967-69, Moore Coll. Art, 1970-71, Parsons Sch. Design, 1974-75, Pratt Inst., 1975-76. Dir. art Studio 733, Great Neck, N.Y., 1963-67; dir. Naples (Itlay) Art Studio, 1972-73; corp. sec. Women in Arts, 1974-75, exec. coordinator, 1976-78; adj. lectr. Bklyn. Coll., 1974-75, Hofstra U., 1977—, Cooper Union, 1986-88. One-woman shows include: Galleria Stuciv, Florence, Italy, 1976, Adelphi U., 1975, Women in Arts Gallery, N.Y.C., 1975, Il Gabbiano Gallery, Naples, 1973, Wallnuts Gallery, Phila., 1971, Neikrug Gallery, N.Y.C., 1970, Alonzo Gallery, 1979, Va. Ctr. for Creative Arts, Sweet Briar, 1981, Hodgell Galleries, Sarasota, Fla., 1982, Elaine Starkman Gallery, N.Y.C., 1986, Romano Gallery, Barnegat Light, N.J., 1987, 88; group exhbns. include Art: U.S.A., N.Y.C., 1969, Internat. Art Exhbn., Cannes, France, 1969, Frick Mus., Pitts., 1970, NAD, N.Y.C., 1970-71, Phila. Mus. Art, 1971, Am. Women Artists, Palazzo Vecchio, Florence, 1972, Internat. Women's Arts Festival, Milan, Italy, 1973 (Gold medal), Bklyn. Mus., 1975, Sweet Briar Coll., 1977, CUNY, 1978, Mus. Hudson Highlands, 1982, Pace U. Gallery, 1982, Bayly Mus., Charlottesville, Va., 1986, Allbright Knox Mus., Buffalo, 1986; represented in permanent collections Easter Seal Human Resource Ctr., N.Y., Hofstra U., N.Y. Pub. Library, Bklyn. Poly. Inst., Met. Mus. Art, Va. Ctr. for Creative Arts, Nat. Mus. Women in Arts. Recipient Susan B. Anthony award NOW, N.Y.C., 1986. Mem. Artists Equity, Women in Arts, Women's Caucus for Art.

ZALKIND, DEBRA, dancer; b. N.Y.C., Mar. 30, 1953; d. Sidney J. and Vivian (Zemachoff) Z.; m. Gary E. Donatelli, Aug. 1, 1982; children: Rayna, Tanya. BFA, Juilliard Sch., 1973; postgrad., Adelphi U., 1969-70. Prin. dancer Pearl Lang Co., N.Y.C., 1974-82, Lar Lubovitch, N.Y.C., 1975-76; choreographer Zalkind/Burke, N.Y.C., 1976-78; producer, pres. The Talking Dance Found., N.Y.C., 1980—; dancer Am. Ballet Comedy, N.Y.C., 1982—; bus. mgr. Hav Cam Inc., N.Y.C., 1982—; instr. dance Pace U., N.Y.C., 1983—. Dancer, appeared in Hair, 1977, The Best Little Whorehouse in Texas, 1978-81; producer: (film) Elegy, 1980, (video) Inner Light, 1982, (video) Intermediate Ballet with David Howard, 1983. Grantee N.Y. State Council of Arts, 1982, N.J. State Council on Arts, 1987. Mem. Actors Equity, Screen Actors Guild. Home: 187 Buena Vista Dr Ringwood NJ 07456 Office: Hav Cam Inc 752 West End Ave New York NY 10025

ZAMBO, CINDRA GAYLE, freight company executive; b. Bonn, Fed. Republic Germany, May 31, 1952; d. William Carl and Una Mae (Nilsson) Henschel; m. James William Harbin, Aug. 31, 1970 (div. 1973); 1 child, Alysia May; m. Stephen John Zambo, Aug. 27, 1982. Lic. fed. maritime commn. Mgr. Bowl and Board Inc., Washington, 1970-73; sec. Howar Devel. Corp., Chevy Chase, Md., 1973; paralegal Pickett, Houlon and Berman, Hyattsville, Md., 1974-77; legal sec. Stevens Davis Miller and Mosher, Arlington, Va., 1977-78; paralegal Flavin, Corcoran and Sulla, Quincy, Mass., 1978-79; cargo broker Hub Shipping Co., Cohasset, Mass., 1979-83; traffic mgr. Dietrich Hide Corp., Boston, 1983—; pres. Aces Ltd., Boston, 1984—. Mem. Nat. Customs Brokers and Freight Forwarders Am. Inc., Boston Customs Brokers and Freight Forwarders Assn., World Trade Club R.I., Fgn. Commerce Club, Greater Boston C. of C. Democrat. Episcopalian. Office: Aces Ltd 186 South St Suite 200 Boston MA 02111

ZAMBOUKOS, CYNTHIA SOTERIA, administrative assistant, travel consultant; b. San Francisco, June 17, 1957; d. James Neal and Nafsika Vasiliki (Katsoulos) Z. B.A. in French and Italian, San Francisco State U., 1980. Asst. sec.-treas. Pacific Am. Group, Inc., San Francisco, 1980-84; freelance travel cons. and legal asst., San Francisco, 1984-86, adminstrv. asst. Wells Fargo Bank, 1986—. Mem. Nat. Assn. Female Execs., Nat. Notary Assn., Alliance Francaise, Hellenic Am. Profl. Soc. Democrat. Greek Orthodox.

ZAMER, BELINDA ROSE, psychologist, educator; b. Washington, Oct. 26, 1953; d. Fred Elias and Yvonne Rose (Habib) Z. AA, Prince George's Coll., Largo, Md., 1973; BA, Cath. U. Am., 1974; MA, George Washington U., 1976, EdD, 1983. Asst. dir., sr. therapist Navy Dept., Washington, 1976-78; employee relations staff EPA, Washington, 1978-82, psychologist, 1982-84; asst. prof. George Washington U., 1983—; instr. Central Mich. U., Washington, 1984—, U. Md., College Park, 1984, John Hopkins U., U. So. Calif., NVA and Marymount U.; cons. WHO, NIMH Study Ctr., Washington; instr. U. Va., Marymount U., U. So. Calif. Bd. dirs. Prince George's Mental Health Assn., Cheverly, Md., 1974; exec. adv. bd. County Council Mental Health, Upper Marlboro, Md., 1975; bd. dirs. NIMH, Adelphi, Md., 1975. Catholic U. Bd. Trustees fellow, 1975, Health and Human Services of Washington grantee, 1976. Mem. AAUW, Nat. Council Exec. Women, Literacy Council Prince George County, Prince George's County Bus. and Profl. Women (exec. bd. 1983), So. Prince George's Bus. and Profl. Women, Phi Beta Kappa (v.p. 1975-76), Psi Chi (v.p. 1976).

ZANETOS, JOANNE MARIE, nurse; b. Columbus, Ohio, Aug. 30, 1956; d. Robert Norman and Joan Cecilia (Mauck) Troyer; m. Timothy James Zanetos, May 13, 1978; 1 child, Thomas William. A.A. in Nursing, Columbus Tech. Inst., 1976, cert. in Am. sign lang. of blind and deaf; cert. John Robert Powers Modeling and Finishing Sch., 1982. R.N. Nurse Doctors Hosp., Columbus, 1976-78, Convacare, Inc., Columbus, 1978-80, Health Care Personnel, Columbus, 1980—. Painter forget-me-knot porcelain plate, 1979 (Gammie award, blue ribbon Columbus Ceramics Festival), porcelain cardinals, 1981 (Gammie award, blue ribbon), Bd. dirs. Women's Assn. of Columbus Symphony Orch., 1984—, chmn. publicity chmn., 1986-87, mem. Young Assocs. of Women's Assn., 1981—, treas., 1985, mem. numerous coms., chmn. property acquisitions for auction Columbus Symphony Orch. League, 1985—, mem. social com., 1984-85; active mem. Condr.'s Club, 1983—; charter mem. Zephyrus League Central Ohio Lung Assn., 1983—, chmn. various coms.; pub. relations chmn. Columbus Greats We Love Exec. Com., 1984-85. Recipient meritorious commendation Doctors Hosp. West, 1978. Roman Catholic. Avocations: china painting; playing piano; water skiing; ceramics; dancing. Home: 4620 Elan Ct Columbus OH 43220

ZANNIE, PATRICIA, economist, artist; b. Rochester, N.Y., Mar. 17, 1941; d. Sabatino Zannie and Elissa (Aschettino) Martone; m. Simon T. King, Nov. 17, 1964 (div. Oct. 1983); 1 child, Simon T. Jr. BS in Social Studies, Le Moyne Coll., 1963; A in Fine Arts, Montgomery County Community Coll., 1983. Economist U.S Dept. Labor, Washington, 1963—. Various one-man shows 1982—; exhibited at Embassy Art Showcase, 1980, Washington Women's Art Ctr., 1981. Vol. So Others May Eat (S.O.M.E.), Washington, 1974—; counselor Montgomery County Crisis Ctr., Md., 1984-86. Recipient Citizenship award VFW, 1958, 59. Mem. Toastmasters (pres. 1979), Pi Gamma Mu, Phi Theta Kappa. Democrat. Roman Catholic. Home: 10109 McKenney Ave Apt 101 Silver Spring MD 20902 Office: US Dept Labor 601 D St NW Room 6004 Washington DC 20213

ZAPATA, CELIA CORREAS, Hispanic literature educator; b. Mendoza, Argentina; married; children—Carol, Martin. BA summa cum laude, Escuela Normal, Tomas Gody Cruz, Mendoza, 1951; BA summa cum laude, U. Cuyo, Mendoza, 1965; Ph.D. summa cum laude in Hispanic Literatures, U. Calif.-Irvine, 1971. Instr. Spanish, Santa Ana Jr. Coll., Calif., 1964-65; assoc. Spanish, U. Calif.-Irvine, 1965-68; educator in Hispanic lit. and culture San Jose State U., Calif., 1969—, prof., 1978—; participant seminars in field; dir. Com. Inter-Am. Women Writers, 1976. Author: Cantos, 1968; Cruz del Sur, 1976; Ensayos Hispanoamericanos, 1978; Tiempo Ajeno, 1980; Detrás de la Reja, 1980; El Trascender Cristiano en la Poética de Leopoldo Panero, 1983; numerous poems, short stories. Contbr. articles, revs. to profl. publs. Founding mem. Council Latin Am. Studies, Calif. State U. System, 1978; panelist, reviewer NEH, 1981—; mem. com. Mex. Am. Heritage of Santa Clara County, 1982; coordinator first conf.. Inter-Am. Women Writers, spl. guest third conf. Universidad Autonoma de Mex., 1981; invited guest Library of Congress, Washington, 1978. Mem. Assn. Tchrs. of Spanish and Portuguese, Pacific Coast Council on Latin Am. Studies, Phological Assn. of Pacific Coast, Ctr. Inter-Am. Women Writers (founder), Latin Am. Studies Assn., Council of Latin Am. Studies. Office: San Jose State U Fgn Lang Dept Washington Sq San Jose CA 95192

ZAPATA, ELSSY-FEDORA, international banker; b. Bogota, Colombia, Nov. 17, 1950; came to U.S., 1973; d. Nelson Zapata-Fergusson and Ines Gonzalez-Crossway. BSBA in Internat. Bus., The Am. U., 1985. Staff on spl. assignment Inter-Am. Devel. Bank, Washington, 1975-80; research asst. Ctr. for Strategic and Internat. Studies, Washington, 1983-85; sr. credit analyst Mfrs. Hanover Trust Co., N.Y.C., 1986-87. Vol. Children's Hosp., Washington, 1979. Recipient scholarship League of United Latin Am. Citizens, 1981, 85, Charlotte Newcombe Foundation, 1982, Hurst and Marion Anderson scholar, 1982, 83, Am. U. Gen. 1984, 85; named one of Outstanding Young Women Am., 1985. Mem. Nat. Assn. Female Execs.

ZAPATA, ZOANNE ELIZABETH, sales professional; b. Havre, Mont., Aug. 22, 1959; d. Thomas Joseph Sr. and Nadine (Lorentzen) Wynne; m. Robert Zapata, Aug. 30, 1986. BS in Chem. Engring., Montana State U., 1981. Environ. engr. Anaconda Copper Co., Great Falls, Mont., 1980; process engr. Celanese Chem. Co., Pampa, Tex., 1981-82; tech. rep. Hercules Inc., Water Mgmt. Div., Amarillo, Tex., 1982-83; tech. sales rep. Hercules Inc., Water Mgmt. Div., Amarillo, 1984-86; sr. tech. sales rep. Hercules Inc., Water Mgmt. Div., Houston, 1986; sales specialist Calgon Corp., Houston, 1986—. Mem. Am. Inst. Chem. Engrs. (treas. 1984-86), Nat. Assn. Female Execs., Soc. Women Engrs., Order of the Engr., Mont. State U. Lifetime Alumnae Orgn. Bozeman. Roman Catholic. Office: Calgon Corp 3300 Bingle Rd Houston TX 77055

ZARATE, LENORE BEATRICE, non-profit administrator; b. N.Y.C., Sept. 21, 1937; d. Saul and Ida Sarah (Friedman) Trushin; m. Alvan O'Neil Zarate, Aug. 31, 1958 (div. Aug. 1971); children: Steven A., Jeffrey T., Jason R. BS with distinction, U. Conn., 1958; postgrad., U. Tex., 1965-66; MA, Cen. Mich. U., Mt. Pleasant, 1981. Adminstrv. asst. U. Conn., Storrs, 1959-60; research asst. U. R.I., Kingston, 1960-61, U. Tex., Austin, 1965-66, 66-67, Dept. of Mental Health and Mental Retardation, Austin, 1966; adminstrv. asst. Am. Social Health Assn., Columbus, Ohio, 1971-75, dir. midwest region, 1976-82, dir. no. region, 1982-87, dir. so. region, 1987, dir. United Way activities, 1988—. Author curriculum guide VD: Getting the Right Answers, 1976. Steering com. Venereal Disease Action Coalition, Detroit, 1978—; bd. dirs. Columbus VD Hotline, 1976-86. Mem. Am. Pub. Health Assn., Am. Venereal Disease Assn. Democrat. Jewish. Office: Am Social Health Assn 1080 Kings Mill Pkwy #150 Columbus OH 43229

ZARNEGAR, ZOHREH TAHEREH, medical educator, researcher, psychologist; b. Ghazvin, Iran, Aug. 27, 1951; d. Gholam-Ali and Esmat (Sadband) Z. B.A. in Psychology, Tehran U. (Iran), 1972; M.A. in Devel. Psychology, Mich. State U., 1976; Ph.D. in Ednl. Psychology, U. So. Calif., 1982. Research asst. UNESCO, Tehran, 1969-73; asst. psychologist Razi Mental Hosp., Tehran, 1970-72; asst. dir. tribal mobile libraries Inst. Intellectual Devel. of Children and Young Adults, Tehran, 1973-74; asst. prof. Tchrs. U., Tehran, 1972-74; pvt. practice research cons., Los Angeles, 1976—; clin. asst. prof. U. So. Calif. Sch. Medicine, Los Angeles, 1981-85, student counselor, 1981-85; v.p. Corp. Researcher, 1984-87; postdoctoral fellow dept. preventive medicine U. So. Calif., 1987—, coordinator, research assoc., 1985—; speaker in field. Author: (with Ahmad Fattahi Pour) Theories of Adult Education, 1973; published and presented many papers in the field of med. edn. and psychology, 1983—. Scholar U. Tehran, 1968-72, 75-80. Mem. Am. Ednl. Research Assn.; mem. Am. Psychol. Assn., Am. Studies Assn., Union of Concerned Scientists, N.Y. Acad. Scis., Bus. Vols. for Arts, Alliance Businesses for Child Devel. (quality assurance com.). Office: U So Calif Sch Medicine Dept Preventive Medicine 35 N Lake Suite 200 Pasadena CA 91101

ZAWACKI, EDNA MARIE, medical company executive, nurse; b. Perce, Que., Can., Dec. 4, 1933; came to U.S., 1951; d. Fred Cain and Winifred LaFlamme; m. Sigmund G. Zawacki, Feb. 15, 1975. Cert. RN, Providence Hosp., Detroit, 1954; BS, Siena Heights Coll., 1986. Nurse operating room San Francisco Gen. Hosp., 1954-56, Outer Dr. Hosp., Lincoln Park, Mich., 1957-75, Seaway Hosp., Trenton, Mich., 1975—; pres. Med. Innovations, Grosse Ile, Mich., 1982—. Patentee bili mask. Mem. Operating Nurses Assn. Republican. Roman Catholic. Clubs: Grosse Ile Country, Grosse Ile Yacht. Home: 29408 E River Rd Grosse Isle MI 48138 Office: 29408 E River Rd Grosse Ile MI 48138

ZAWLOCKI, LOUISE FRANCES, military officer; b. Chgo., Dec. 8, 1940; d. Joseph Tony and Josephine Pauline (Szymusiak) Z.; m. Robert Lawrence Brucks (div. 1970). BS in Agr., U. Minn., 1983. Office mgr. Murtaugh, King, Neiman & Grais, Chgo., 1965-72; sec. 1st Nat. Bank St. Paul, Minn., 1975-77; regional economist (c.e.) U.S. Army, St. Paul, 1980-85, Balt., 1985-87; regional economist logistics agy. U.S. Army, New Cumberland, Pa., 1987—. Columnist, Organic Garden, 1979-83. Mem. Falcon Heights (Minn.) Human Rights Commn., 1981-83; dir. Minn. League of Human Rights Commn., New Ulm, Minn., 1982-83. Mem. Am. Water Resources Assn., Soil Conservation Soc.

ZAYDON, JEMILLE ANN, educator; b. Peckville, Pa., Feb. 21, 1940; d. Joseph and Catherine Ann (Hazzouri) Z.; student Barry Coll. for Women, 1957-59; B.S., Marywood Coll., 1963; M.S. in Edn., Wilkes Coll., 1978; doctoral candidate Temple U. Tchr. St. Hugh Elementary Sch., Coconut Grove, Fla., 1963-64; Allapattah Elementary Sch., Miami, 1964-65, Columbus Elementary Sch., Westfield, N.J., 1965-66; communications instr. Keystone Job Corps, Drums, Pa., 1966-73; vol. instr. Keystone Rehab. Center, Scranton, Pa., 1970-71; curriculum cons. for mentally retarded, Vienna, Austria, 1974; prof. English and reading Lackawanna Jr. Coll., Scranton, 1974—, head dept. English, speech and reading, 1976—, chmn. dept. arts, humanities and social studies, 1977—; adj. prof. English, U. Scranton, 1980—; communications instr. Lackawanna County Vocat. Tech. Sch., 1974—. Supr. recreation program, Hazleton, Pa., summer 1968; founder, adviser Keystone Kourier, 1967-69. Sec. Fedn. Youth, William W. Scranton, 1963; coordinator annual Christmas for Mentally Retarded Keeptone City Residence, Scranton, 1975—; supr. students Heart Fund campaign, 1968-71; developer program mentally retarded Allied Services for Handicapped Scranton, 1973; Class rep. Marywood Coll. Fund Dr., 1978; gen. coordinator Christmas party Keystone City Residence, Scranton, 1975—; coordinator ann. party for mentally retarded at Keystone City residence, Scranton, Pa., 1980—; active ARC, March of Dimes, Heart Fund, Leukemia and United Fund drives, also Sickle Cell Anemia Found. Bd. dirs. Michael F. Harrity Meml. Fund., 1969-73; mem. exec. bd. Northeastern Pa. Environ. Council, also co-chmn. public edn. and funding. Recipient Staff Mem. of Year award, Job Corps, 1969, Humanitarian award, 1980; Educators award Dade County, 1973, 75; named Tchr. of Yr., 1973; Service scholar, Barry Coll., 1958; Mem. Nat., Pa. State edn. assns., Beta Lambda Tau, Sigma Tau Delta, Theta Chi Beta (charter pres. 1961-63), Lambda Iota Tau (life). Democrat. Roman Catholic (instr. Confraternity Christian Doctrine 1956-71). Editor Lebanese Am. Jour., 1957-63. Home: 608 N Main Ave Scranton PA 18504

ZBOROWSKI, BEVERLY JEAN, school administrator, educator; b. Gary, Ind., Apr. 23, 1948; d. Stephen Joseph and Mary Helen (Petrovich) Soohey; m. Joseph Richard Zborowski, Aug. 10, 1968; children—Annemarie Nicole, Natalie Joelle, Nicholas Joseph. B.S., Ind. U., Gary, 1970; M.S., Purdue U., 1975. Life lic. elem. edn. Elem. tchr. Portage Twp. Sch. Corp., Portage, Ind., 1970-73, pres. Portage Twp. Sch. Corp. Bd. Edn., Hebron, Ind., sec. Porter County Vocat. Edn. Com., Valparaiso, Ind., 1984-85; tchr. Washington Twp. Sch. Pres. Porter County Extension Homemakers, 1981-83; mem. Assn. County Neighbors Group, Hebron. Mem. Sigma Beta (chpt. sec. 1982-84). Republican. Roman Catholic. Avocations: gourmet cooking; creative needlework; photography; reading. Office: Porter Twp Sch Corp 208 S 725 W Hebron IN 46341

ZEA, KRISTINA GWYN, costume and production designer; b. N.Y.C., Oct. 24, 1948; d. James Gwyn and Alice Joy (Karl) Z. BS, Columbia U., 1972. Costume designer MGM, N.Y.C., 1979-80, Mabou Mines, N.Y.C., 1982-83, Tristar Pictures, Phila. and San Jose, Calif., 1983-84, Columbia Pictures, Santa Fe, 1984-85; prodn. designer, assoc. producer 20th Century Fox, Chgo., 1985-86; art dir. Tristar Pictures, N.Y.C. and New Orleans, 1986, 20th Century Fox, Washington, 1986-87; production designer Orion Pictures, N.Y.C., 1987—. Named Outstanding Working Woman Glamour Mag., 1982. Mem. Phi Beta Kappa.

ZECKMEISTER, CYNTHIA HANSON, marketing specialist; b. Greenville, S.C., Sept. 24, 1957; d. Charles Wesley and Sylvia Jean (Boone) Hanson; m. Richard Robert Zeckmeister, Mar. 1, 1986. BA in Bus. Adminstrn., Bethel Coll., 1979. Corp. buyer Western Pub. Co., Racine, Wis., 1979-82; traffic mgr., purchasing agt., prodn. scheduler Ruud Lighting Inc., Racine, 1982-85, telemktg. and traffic mgr., 1985-88; buyer Gen. Elec. Corp. Med. Systems, Milw., 1988—. Mem. Concerned Women Am., Milw., 1986—. Mem. Nat. Assn. Female Execs., Nat. Assns. Purchasing Mgrs., Am. Prodn. Inventory Control Soc. Republican.

ZEEMAN, JOAN JAVITS, writer, inventor; b. N.Y.C., Aug. 17, 1928; d. Benjamin Abraham and Lily (Braxton) Javits; m. John Huibert Zeeman III, Mar. 20, 1954; children—Jonathan, Andrea Zeeman Deane, Eloise Zeeman Scharff, Phoebe, Merrily Margaret. B.A., Vassar Coll., 1949; M.Ed., U. Vt., 1976. Pub. relations exec. Benjamin Sonnenberg, N.Y.C., 1949-51; freelance writer, 1952—. Trustee TheatreWorks(formerly Performing Arts Repertory Theatre), N.Y.C., 1953-83, Profl. Childrens Sch., N.Y.C., 1980—. Author: The Compleat Child, 1964. Lyricist musical plays: Young Abe Lincoln, 1961; Hotel Passionato, 1965; song lyricist: Santa Baby, 1953. Patentee Alphocube. Mem. ASCAP, Dramatists Guild. Club: Vassar (sec. 1978-84, v.p. 1984-86) (Westchester, N.Y.). Home: 230 Palmo Way Palm Beach FL 33480 Office: 520 Hommocks Rd Larchmont NY 10538

ZEIDLER, MARIANNA VIRGINIA CLARA, advertising executive; b. Lima, Peru, Aug. 12, 1954; came to U.S., 1980; m. Andy G. Zeidler, Aug. 18, 1980. Student, Pontifica U. Catolica, Peru, 1972-74; BA, English Lang. Acad., Pub. Relations and Adminstrn. Inst., Peru, 1975; degree in German, Goethe Inst., Peru, 1971; degree in French, Alliance Français, Peru, 1980. Cert. corp. adminstr. Adminstrv. trainee Braniff Inc., Lima, 1974; mgr. coordination OCL Holding Co., Lima, 1975-76; with China Airlines, Lima, 1976; with credit dept. Bank of Am., Lima, 1976-80; owner, mgr. Scope Design, Boulder, Colo., 1980—; speaker, translator Inst. Peruano Adminstrn. de Empresas, Lima, 1978-80; tchr. TRANSLEX, Lima, 1978-80; translator Econs. Inst., Lima, 1978-80. Roman Catholic. Office: Scope Design PO Box 3196 Boulder CO 80307

ZEIF, SUZANNE ROSE, psychotherapist; b. Trani, Italy, Jan. 16, 1948; d. Morris Mordechai and Rachel (Lederman) Z. BA, Queens Coll., Flushing, N.Y., 1971; MA in Rehab. Counseling, NYU, 1976. Adminstrv. asst. Fedn. Employment and Guidance Service, N.Y.C., 1974-75; rehab. cons. N.Y. State Office of Vocat. Rehab., N.Y.C., 1976-78; vocat. rehab. counselor South Beach Psychiat. Ctr., S.I., N.Y., 1978-79; dir. program Westchester County Office for the Aging, White Plains, N.Y., 1979-82; vocat., addictions counselor United Hosp., New Rochelle, N.Y., 1982-86; dir. employee assistance program Nyack (N.Y.) Hosp., 1986—; founder, dir. Inst. for Personal and Profl. Devel., Monsey, N.Y., 1981—; presenter, speaker various orgns., 1981—; cons. Freeport Assocs., Scarsdale, N.Y., 1982-84, Meridian Ctr., Stamford, Conn., 1984—, and faculty Rockland Community Coll., Suffern, N.Y., 1986—. Advisor, coordinator Am. Cancer Soc., Westchester, 1981-84; mem. adv. com. N.Y. State Select Com. on Disabled, Albany, 1985—, N.Y. State Standing Com. on Alcoholism and Drug Abuse, Westchester, 1981; forum chairperson Am. Ostomy Assn., Westchester, 1987; founder Nat. Found. of Ileitis and Colitis Support Group Rocklandand Orange Counties. Mem. Assn. Labor Mgmt. and Cons. on Alcoholism (bd. dirs. 1984-86), Am. Psychol. Assn., Aircraft Owners and Pilots Assn., Nat. Rifle Assn., Nat. Assn. Female Execs.

ZEIGLER, CYNTHIA WALKER, zoological association executive; b. Washington, Feb. 16, 1953; d. Henry Gary and Alma Jane (Eichinger) Walker; m. Frank William Zeigler, Sept. 14, 1984. AA in Mass Communications, Miami Dade Community Coll., 1973. Dir. promotion Sportsview, Inc., Miami, Fla., 1975; asst. promotion mgr. Sta. WCIX-TV, Miami, 1975-77; asst. dir. Fla. office CARE, Miami, 1977-85; dir. devel. and membership Zool. Soc. Fla., Miami, 1985-87, asst. exec. dir., 1987—. Producer 12 part TV series Discover Metrozoo, 1986. Chmn. Jr. Orange Bowl, Miami, 1983—. Named one of Outstanding Young Women Am., 1981. Mem. Nat. Assn. Fundraising Execs., Fla. Assn. Wildlife Rehabilitators (pres. 1977—), Children's Respiratory and Nutrition Assn. (trustee 1978—), South Fla. Bus. Communicators (v.p. 1978), Nat. Assn. TV Arts (sec., bd. dirs. 1983, 84). Office: Zool Soc Fla 12400 SW 152 St Miami FL 33177

ZEIGLER, JEANINE BAHRAM PATTON, guidance counselor; b. Chgo., Nov. 9, 1928; d. Lester H. and Florence (Toney) Bahram; m. Daniel J. Patton, Jr. (dec.); children—Daniel J., Deborah J., Denise J.; m. Lamar Henry Zeigler, June 19, 1971. BA, Mich. State U., 1965, MA, 1969. Successively elementary tchr., sch. social worker, elementary sch. prin. Battle Creek (Mich.) public schs., 1965-77; guidance counselor So. U., New Orleans, 1977—, asst. prof., chmn. bd. dirs. Bethany Day Care Ctr., New Orleans, 1978—; hon. chmn. Battle Creek Cancer Crusade, 1976; bd. dirs. Y Ctr., Battle Creek, 1974-77. Recipient various service awards. Mem. Assn. Supervision and Curriculum Devel., Am. Personnel and Guidance Assn., Am. Coll. Personnel Assn., Am. Assn. Non-White Concerns, AAUW (pres. Battle Creek br. 1974-76 membership v.p. La. div. 1981—, pres. New Orleans br. 1984-86, nat. membership com., pres. La. div. 1986), Am. Assn. Counseling and Devel., Am. Assn. Multicultural Counseling Devel. (v.p. membership div. 1981-83, pres. La. div. 1987—), La. Assn. Coll. and Univ. Student Personnel Adminstrs., Urban League, Nat. Council Negro Women (bd. dirs.), Moneychangers Investment Club (pres. 1981—), Delta Sigma Theta. Methodist. Clubs: Nat. Smart Set, Internat. Y Men's (New Orleans). Office: 6400 Press Dr New Orleans LA 70126

ZEIGLER, JUDY ROSE, managament and marketing consultant; b. Monte Vista, Colo., Aug. 26, 1946; d. Orville Edgar Zeigler and Kathryn Genevieve (Parsons) Duncan. BA, U. Oreg., 1968. Asst. v.p., mgr. staff planning and devel. Rainier Nat. Bank, Seattle, 1979-81, asst. v.p., mgr. staff devel., 1981-83; v.p., mgr. staff planning Blue Cross of Washington and Alaska, Seattle, 1983-85, mgr. market research, 1985-86; cons. Strategies Unltd., Seattle, 1986—; workshop presenter Gov.'s Conf. Women on the Move, Seattle, 1984, Women Plus Bus. Conf., Seattle, 1984, 85, 86, 88; pres. Natalie Skeels Meml. Found. Trustees, Seattle, 1987—. Vice chair Blue Ribbon Citizen's Task Force of King County Assessor's Office, Seattle, 1984; chair mktg. com. Bellevue Community Coll. Telecommunications Ctr. Task Force, Seattle, 1985-87; mem. Women's Polit. Caucus, Seattle, 1987—, co-chair fundraising com. Mem. Women's Profl. and Managerial Newtork (pres. 1987-88), Am. Soc. Tng. and Devel. (Puget Sound chpt. pres. 1983-84), Northwest Women's Law Ctr. (bd. dirs. 1988—). Democrat. Home: 1523 11th Ave W Seattle WA 98119 Office: Strategies Unltd 609 Terminal Sales Bldg Seattle WA 98101

ZEILIG, NANCY MEEKS, magazine editor; b. Nashville, Apr. 28, 1943; d. Edward Harvey and Nancy Evelyn (Self) Meeks; m. Lanny Kenneth Fielder, Aug. 20, 1964 (div. Dec. 1970); m. Charles Elliot Zeilig, Jan. 6, 1974; 1 child, Sasha Rebecca. BA, Birmingham-So. Coll., 1964; postgrad., Vanderbilt U., 1971-73. Editorial asst. Reuben H. Donnelley, N.Y.C., 1969-70; asst. editor Vanderbilt U., Nashville, 1970-74; editor U. Minn., St. Paul, 1975; asst. editor McGraw-Hill Inc., Mpls., 1975-76; mng. editor Denver mag., 1976-80; editor Jour. Am. Water Works Assn., Denver, 1981—. Editor, co-pub.: WomanSource, 1982, rev. edit. 1984; editor: 100 Years, 1975; contbr. articles to consumer mags. Office: Jour Am Water Works Assn 6666 W Quincy Denver CO 80235

ZEILINGER, ELNA RAE, educator; b. Tempe, Ariz., Mar. 24, 1937; d. Clayborn Eddie and Ruby Elna (Laird) Simpson; B.A. in Edn., Ariz. State U., 1958, M.A. in Edn., 1966, Ed.S., 1980; m. Philip Thomas Zeilinger, June 13, 1970; children—Shari, Chris. Bookkeeper, First Nat. Bank of Tempe, 1955-56; with registrar's office Ariz. State U., 1956-58; piano tchr., recreation dir. City of Tempe, tchr. Thew Sch., Tempe, 1958-61, elem. tchr. Mitchell Sch., 1962-74, intern prin., 1976, personnel intern, 1977; specialist in gifted edn. Tempe Elem. Schs., 1977-87; elem. tchr. Holdeman Sch., Tempe, 1988—; grad. asst. ednl. adminstrn., Iota Workshop coordinator Ariz. State U., 1978; presenter Ariz. Gifted Conf., 1978-81; condr. survey of gifted programs, 1980; reporter public relations Tempe Sch. Dist., 1978-80, Access com. for gifted programs, 1981-83. Freedom Train com. Ariz. Bicentennial Commn., 1975-76. Named Outstanding Leader in Elem. and Secondary Schs., 1976' Ariz. Cattle Growers scholar, 1954-55; Elks scholar, 1954-55; recipient Judges award Tempe Art League, 1970, Best of Show, Scottsdale Art League, 1976. Mem. Council Exceptional Children, Ariz. Assn. Gifted and Talented, Ariz. Sch. Adminstrs., Tempe Hist. Assn. (liaison 1975), Scottsdale Artists League, Tempe Art League, Am. Bus. Women's Assn. (Woman of Yr. 1983), Phi Kappa Phi, Pi Lambda Theta, Kappa Delta Pi, Phi Delta Kappa, Kappa Delta. Democrat. Congregationalist. Club: Eastern Star. Author: Leadership Role of the Principal in Gifted Programs: A Handbook, 1980; Classified Personnel Handbook, 1977, also reports and monographs. Home: 610 E Colgate St Tempe AZ 85283 Office: Tempe Elem Schs 1326 W 18th St Tempe AZ 85281

ZEITLAN, MARILYN LABB, lawyer; b. N.Y.C., Sept. 17, 1938; d. Charles and Florence (Geller) Labb; m. Barrett M. Zeitlan, Apr. 14, 1957; children—Adam Scott, Daniel Craig. B.A., Queens Coll., 1958, M.S., 1970; J.D., Hofstra U., 1978. Bar: N.Y., 1979. Tchr. N.Y.C., 1958-61; sole practice, Roslyn, N.Y. Mem. Law Rev., Hofstra U., 1976-78. Contbr. articles to profl. jours. Commr. East Hills Environ. Commn., 1971-75; co-founder Roslyn Environ. Assn., 1970; v.p. Roslyn LWV, 1974-75. Hofstra U. Sch. Law fellow, 1976. Mem. ABA, Nassau County Bar Assn., N.Y. State Bar Assn., Nassau-Suffolk Women's Bar Assn., Phi Beta Kappa. Avocation: horseback riding. Office: 1025 Northern Blvd Suite 201 Roslyn NY 11576

ZEKMAN, TERRI MARGARET, graphic designer; b. Chgo., Sept. 13, 1950; d. Theodore Nathan and Lois (Bernstein) Z.; m. Alan Daniels, Apr. 12, 1980; 1 child, Jesse Logan. BFA, Washington U., St. Louis, 1971; postgrad, Art Inst. Chgo., 1974-75. Graphic designer (on retainer) greeting cards and related products Recycled Paper Products Co., Chgo., 1970—; apprenticed graphic designer Helmuth, Obata & Kassabaum, St. Louis, 1970-71; graphic designer Container Corp., Chgo., 1971; graphic designer, art dir., photographer Cuerden Advt. Design, Denver, 1971-74; art dir. D'Arcy, McManus & Masius Advt., Chgo., 1975-76; freelance graphic designer Chgo., 1976-77; art dir. Garfield Linn Advt., Chgo., 1977-78; graphic designer Keiser Design Group, Van Noy & Co., Los Angeles, 1978-79; owner and operator graphic design studio Los Angeles, 1979—. Recipient cert. of merit St. Louis Outdoor Poster Contest, 1970, Denver Art Dirs. Club, 1973.

ZELEI, RITA ANNETTE, educational administrator; b. Barberton, Ohio, Dec. 19, 1938; d. Joseph Emil and Kathryn (Novacic) Z.; 1 child, Bernadette Veronica. BS, U. Akron, Ohio, 1960, MS, 1966, EdD, 1971. Music tchr. Hudson (Ohio) Local Schs., 1960, Akron Pub. Schs., 1960-68; staff Ohio Dept. of Edn., Columbus, 1968-69; spl. crew leader U.S. Bur. of Census, Washington, 1970; ednl. cons. N.J. Dept. Edn., Trenton, 1972; prin. Geneva (Ohio) Elem. Sch., 1972—; adj. prof. Lake Erie Coll., Painesville, 1976-83; cons. Ohio Dept. Edn., Columbus, 1986—. V.P. Geneva Civic Ctr. Bd., 1982—; pres. Geneva Area Grape JAMboree, 1983—; bd. dirs. Ashtabula County Scouts Council, 1979—, Geneva Area Human Services, 1982—; mem. Gov.'s Travel and Tourism Bd., 1987—; del. to China, People to People Ohio Edn., 1986. Named Trendsetter New Cleve. Woman Mag., 1988; recipient Akron Crime Clinic, 1988. Mem. Am. Assn. Sch. Adminstrs., Am. Ednl. Research Assn., AAUW, Geneva Area C. of C. (Citizen of Yr. 1987), Phi Delta Kappa (pres. 1986—). Home: 308 Centennial St Geneva OH 44041 Office: Geneva Elem Sch 119 S Eagle St Geneva OH 44041

ZELENY, MARJORIE PFEIFFER (MRS. CHARLES ELLINGSON ZELENY), psychologist; b. Balt., Mar. 31, 1924; d. Lloyd Armitage and Mable (Willian) Pfeiffer; B.A., U. Md., 1947; M.S., U. Ill., 1949, postgrad., 1951-54; m. Charles Ellingson Zeleny, Dec. 11, 1950 (dec.); children—Ann Douglas, Charles Timberlake. Vocational counseling psychologist VA, Balt., 1947-48; asst. U. Ill. at Urbana, 1948-50, research asso. Bur. Research, 1952-53; chief psychologist dept. neurology and psychiatry Ohio State U. Coll. Medicine, Columbus, 1950-51; research psychologist, cons., Tucson, Washington, 1954—. Mem. Am., D.C. psychol. assns., A.A.A.S., Soc. for Psychol. Study Social Issues, D.A.R., Mortar Bd., Delta Delta Delta, Sigma Delta Epsilon, Psi Chi, Sigma Tau Epsilon. Roman Catholic. Home: 6825 Wemberly Way McLean VA 22101

ZELEPSKY, ANNETTE MARIE, data processing executive; b. Fort Wayne, Ind., Aug. 9, 1958; d. Paul Joseph and Catherine Anne (Amato) Findlay; m. Sept. 26, 1981 (div. Dec. 1985); 1 child, Jacqueline Anne. AAS in Data Processing, 1978; BS in Mgmt., U. Akron, 1980. System programmer Diebold, Inc., North Canton, Ohio, 1980-81; mgr. operating systems Cen. Nat. Bank, Cleve., 1981-85; mgr. system software AAA Mich., Dearborn, 1985—; project officer Share/TSM project, Chgo., 1985—; tutor Akron/Summit Tutorial Program, 1977, Detroit Pub. Schs., 1987-88. Mem. Nat. Assn. Female Execs. Avocations: music, aerobics, sports cars. Home: 20095 Parker Livonia MI 48152 Office: AAA Mich 1 Auto Club Dr Dearborn MI 48126

ZELIK, JOSEPHINE ANN, computer educator; b. Pitts., Mar. 1, 1947; d. Thaddeus and Clara Wanda (Matuszewski) Szczerba; m. Bernard John Zelik, Aug. 12, 1972; 1 child, Maria Beth. BS, Clarion U., 1969; [illegible], Ind. U., Pa., 1973. Cert. ednl. specialist, Pa. Elem. tchr. West Mifflin (Pa.) Area Sch. Dist., 1969—; computer instr. Community Coll. Allegheny County, West Mifflin, 1986—. Mem. Am. Fedn. Tchrs., Nat. Assn. Female Execs. Roman Catholic. Club: S. Suburbia Women's (past newsletter editor). Home: 211 Delano Dr Pittsburgh PA 15236

ZELLAR, KAREN JEAN, nurse; b. Baraga, Mich., Jan. 20, 1948; d. Smerta Reino and Ruth Sylvia (Ylinen) Luukkonen; m. Robert Arthur Zellar, Nov. 21, 1964 (div. Nov. 1984); children: Todd A., Robert Arthur Jr. AA in Nursing, Lake Superior State Coll., 1974. Attendant, then RN State of Mich. Newberry Regional Mental Health Ctr., Newberry, 1966—; adult foster care owner-operator Mich. Dept. Social Services, 1970—. Active Seney (Mich.) Hist. Soc., 1980-82. Mem. Mich. Residential Care Assn. Republican. Home and Office: Seney Ave Seney MI 49883

ZELLINGER, MARGARET MONROE, psychologist; b. Evanston, Ill., July 27, 1956; d. Andrew Perrine and Mary Elizabeth (McCoun) Monroe; m. David Alan Zellinger, Feb. 25, 1948; children: Anita, Sarah, Louis. AB magna cum laude, Princeton U., 1978; MS, Purdue U., 1980, PhD, 1983. Psychologist Augusta (Maine) Mental Health Inst., 1983—; cons. State Maine Dept. Human Services, Augusta, 1986—; adj. prof. in psychology, U. Maine, Orono, 1984—. Contbr. articles to profl. jours. Mem. State Maine Mental Health Rights Adv. Bd., 1986—. NIMH fellow, Purdue U., 1979. Mem. Am. Psychol. Assn., Maine Psychol. Assn. (chmn. div. Pub. Service Psychologists) Assn. for Advancement of Behavior Therapy. Democrat. Office: Augusta Mental Health Inst PO Box 724 Augusta ME 04330

ZELNA, DIANE, accountant; b. Los Angeles, Jan. 13, 1941; d. John S. and Katherine Zelna. Diploma, Life Bible Coll., 1965, A.A. in Bus. Mgmt., Fullerton Coll., 1978; postgrad. U. Calif.-Fullerton, 1979-83. Mgr., Am. Telecom, Inc., Anaheim, Calif., 1978-79; assoc. Edward Tuck & Co., Inc., W. Covina, Calif., 1979-81; pres., owner Assoc. Bus. Services Co., Placentia, Calif., 1981—, owner Gold Medal Sales, Orange, 1984—; corp. sec. Briarcrest, Inc., Covina, 1981; corp. sec., dir. Creative Frameworks, Inc., Santa Ana, Calif., 1982-83; v.p., corp. sec. bd. dirs. Creative Fundraising, Inc., Orange, 1985—; ptnr. Good Time Tickets, Orange County, 1986—. Mem. Am. Soc. Tng. and Devel., Alpha Gamma Sigma. Republican. Christian Ch. Office: Gold Medal Sales 108 W Katella Ave Suite F Orange CA 92667

ZEMANS, JOYCE PEARL, dean; b. Toronto, Ont., Can., Apr. 21, 1940; m. Frederick H. Zemans; children: Deborah, David, Marcia. BA in French, U. Toronto, 1962, MA in Art History, 1966. Co-chair dept. art history Ont. Coll. Art, Toronto, 1970-71, chair dept. liberal arts, 1973-75; chair dept. visual arts York U., Toronto, 1975-81, assoc. prof. art history, 1975—, dean faculty fine arts, 1985—; lectr. art history Ont. Coll. Art, Toronto, 1966-75. Author: (book) Jock Macdonald, 1986; (catalogue) J.W.G. Macdonald: The Inner Landscape, 1981, Christopher Pratt, 1985; (career series) Art, 1971; contbr. articles to profl., acad. jours. Bd. dirs. Nat. Council Art Adminstrn., 1979-82. Mem. Can. Assn. Fine Art Deans (exec.), Univ. Art Assn. Can. (v.p.), Internat. Council Fine Art Deans (bd. dirs.), Internat. Assn. Art Critics, Coll. Art Assn. Office: York U, Faculty Fine Arts, 4700 Keele St, Downsview, ON Canada M3J 1P3

ZEMBA, DOROTHY IRENE, oil and mining company executive; b. Cuyahoga Falls, Ohio, Nov. 20, 1928; d. Raymond Clarence and Anna Frances (Knapp) Dorner; m. John Zemba, Mar. 10, 1951 (dec. Nov. 1978); children: John Raymond, Joel Dennis. Student pub. schs., Akron, Ohio. Sec. Akron Bd. Edn., 1946-47; with printing office Ohio Match Co., Wadsworth, 1947-48; payroll clk. Akron Parcel Co., 1948-50; payroll clk. Ace Rubber Co., Akron, 1950-53, acct., 1953-77; exec. v.p. Gasoil Energy, Inc., Canton, Ohio, 1977-82; corp. sec. Davage Oil & Gas Co., Phoenix, 1982—, also dir.; dir. Profile Mgmt., Inc., Canton; bd. dirs., sec. Davage Tech. Inc., Chandler, Ariz., 1987—; cons. Sq. Circle Devel. Corp., Phoenix, 1985; sec., dir. Paragon Steel Structures, Inc., Chandler, Ariz., 1986—. Mem. Nat. Assn. Female Execs., Am. Soc. Profl. and Exec. Women, Precious Moments Club, Goebel Collectors. Republican. Lutheran. Club: Riker-Bartlett (Ft. Collins, Colo.). Avocations: collecting antiques, art and limited editions of pewter, glass and porcelain. Home: 4826 E Winnebago St Phoenix AZ 85044

ZEMEL, HELENE LEVEY, educator, career consultant; b. N.Y.C., Jan. 3, 1947; d. Theodore Abraham and Sylvia Leah (Bernbach) Levey; BA cum laude, Hofstra U., 1968; MA, Queens Coll., 1972; MBA with distinction, N.Y. Inst. Tech., 1987; m. Leonard S. Zemel, Nov. 27, 1974, 1 child, Tara Michelle. Piano instr., concert artist, 1968-77; asst. adminstr. society, group and council activities IEEE, 1977-78, adminstr. conf. activities and publs., 1978-83; instr. Adelphi Inst., Astoria, N.Y., 1985-87; adj. lectr. York Coll., Jamaica, N.Y., 1987—, La Guardia Community Coll., L.I., 1988—; instr. Royal Bus. Sch., Forest Hills, N.Y., 1987-88, H.A.N.A.C. Skills Devel. Ctr., Astoria, 1988—; pres. The Career Ctr., Forest Hills, 1987—. Teaching fellow Queens Coll., 1972. Mem. N.Y. League Bus. and Profl. Women (rec. sec. 1981-82, treas. 1982-83), Delta Mu Delta. Democrat. Jewish. Home and Office: 102-40 67th Rd Forest Hills NY 11375

ZEMKE, CAROL MARY, college administrator; b. Rochester, Minn., Mar. 12, 1936; d. Kenneth Norman and Anna Matilda (Evjen) Molde; m. Leonard Henry Zemke, Mar. 15, 1958; children—Thomas Leonard, Jay David. A.A., North Hennipen Coll., 1973; BA Concordia Coll., 1987 . Lab. technician Mayo Clinic, Rochester, Minn., 1954-58; tchr. of arts and crafts to handicapped, Div. of Vocat. Adminstrn., Mankato, Minn., 1958-62; dir. Lutheran Ctr., U. Minn.-Mpls., 1983; dir. pub. relations Concordia Coll., St. Paul, 1983-87; devel. officer, 1987— . Author, shortstory book, 1985. Contbr. articles to profl. jours. Editor, sch. quarterly, 1983. Sec. Midway Civic and Commerce Assn., St. Paul, 1985, bd. dirs. 1985—; pres. Lutheran Women's Missionary League, Minn., 1978-82, v.p., 1974-84; chmn. promotion com. Midway Civic & Commerce Assn., 1984-88; sec. Twin Cities Chpt. Religious Pub. Relations Council, Mpls., St. Paul, 1985-86, pres. 1986-87 . Recipient Silver Angel award, Religion in Media, Hollywood, Calif., 1984, Appreciation for Promotion award Midway Civic & Commerce Assn., St. Paul, 1985. Republican. Clubs: Fed. Women's (Rapidan, Minn.) (pres. 1960-64), U. of Minn. Extension (Mpls.) (pres. 1968-70). Avocations: tennis; golfing; swimming; boating; sewing; reading. Home: 4395 Juneau Ln N Plymouth MN 55427 Office: Concordia Coll Hamline & Marshall Sts Saint Paul MN 55104

ZENO, JO ANN, sales executive; b. Akron, Ohio, Sept. 25, 1952; d. Ross and Mary Francis (Gerbec) Z. BA in French and Edn., BS in Spanish, U. Akron, 1975. Tchr. French, Spanish S.E. Local, Ravenna, Ohio, 1975-77, Akron Pub. Schs., 1977-80; sales rep. Xerox Corp., Akron, Cleve., 1980-83; cert. stapling technician U.S. Surg. Corp., Norwalk, Conn., 1983—. Home: 272 Somerset Rd Akron OH 44313

ZENOFF, KATHRYN E., lawyer; b. Chgo., July 30, 1946; d. A.J. and Dorothy J. (Raftenberg) Z.; m. Arthur Rettig, July 30, 1972; children—Rebecca Lauren, Max Louis. B.A. cum laude, Stanford U., 1968; J.D., Columbia U., 1971. Bar: N.Y. 1972, Ill. 1972. Assoc. Aranow, Brodsky, Bohlinger, Benetar & Einhorn, N.Y.C., 1971-75, Zenoff, Westler & Zenoff, Chgo., 1975-77, 78-81; asst. states atty. Cook County, Ill., Chgo., 1977-78; chief juvenile (asst. states atty.) Winnebago County, Rockford, Ill., 1982-85, chief misdemeanor unit, 1985-86, sr. felony prosecutor, 1986—; part-time instr. in law Ill. Inst. Tech., Chgo. Kent Coll. Law, 1976-77; vol. atty. Child Adv. Assn. Chgo., 1976-77, Community Law Office, Harlem, N.Y.C., 1971-74. Bd. dirs. Local Planning Bd. Youth Services, Rockford, 1984—; mem. LWV, Rockford, 1981—. Participant Internat. Fellows Program, Columbia U., 1970. Mem. Chgo. Bar Assn. (chmn. juvenile law com. 1980-81, bench bar relations com., evaluation of jud. candidates com., consumer and credit com. 1975-81), Winnebago County Bar Assn., N.Y. County Lawyers Assn. (spl. com. women's rights 1974-75).

ZEPLIN, JUNE DALTON, bank systems officer; b. Dundee, Scotland, June 4, 1948; came to U.S., 1968; d. John Wilson and Alexandrina Richardson (McComb) Dalton; m. Gary Wayne Zeplin, July 25, 1970; children: Scott Edward, Kimberly Diane. AS in Gen. Bus. Adminstrn., Chaminade U., 1978; BS in Bus. Adminstrn. summa cum laude, U. Houston, 1981. Cert. secondary tchr. Teller Bank of Montreal (Can.), 1966-68, Bank of Am., Inglewood, Calif., 1968-70, Ga. R.R. Bank, Augusta, 1972-73; note teller Victoria (Tex.) Bank & Trust Co., 1978-79; mgmt. trainee Tex., 1981-82; savings supr. Victoria Bank & Trust Co., Tex., 1982-83; systems officer Victoria Bank & Trust Co., 1983—. Den leader, treas. Boy Scouts Am., Victoria, 1980-81; Sunday sch. tchr. First English Luth. Ch., 1978—, chmn. youth com. 1984. Named one of Outstanding Young Women of Am., 1983. Mem. Nat. Assn. Bank Women, Nat. Assn. Female Execs. Office: Victoria Bank & Trust Co 120 Main Victoria TX 77902

ZEPPETELLO, ANGELA MARIE, health maintenance organization administrator; b. Syracuse, N.Y., May 13, 1947; d. Gerald J. and Carmella R. (Carfagno) Z. BA, LeMoyne Coll., 1969. Patient resource agt. N.Y. State Office Mental Health, Syracuse, N.Y., 1969-75; sr. patient resource agt. N.Y. State Office Mental Health, Syracuse, 1975-78; fed. program coordinator N.Y. State Office Mental Health, Albany, 1978-80, dep. dir. patient resources, 1980-86; dir. internal ops. Empire Blue Cross and Blue Shield HEALTHNET, Albany, 1986—; cons. Home Health Care of Am., Newport Beach, Calif., 1985-86. Office: Empire Blue Cross Blue Shield HEALTHNET PO Box 8650 Albany NY 12208

ZERBA, JANET ANN, home health care company administrator; b. Lansing, Mich., Sept. 29, 1941; d. Clare Jay and Thelma Marie (Hollenbeck) Reynolds; m. Jimmy A. Zerba, Mar. 21, 1959; divorced; remarried, Feb. 3, 1979; children: Michael Russell, Jeffrey (dec.), Melinda (dec.); m. Winton Erwin Walker, Nov. 27, 1975 (dec. Nov. 1976). LPN, Lansing Community Coll., 1970, AS in Nursing, 1976. RN, charge nurse Hayes Green Beach Hosp., Charlotte, Mich., 1976-78; RN, nursing supr. Kelly Health Care, Lansing, 1978-84; adminstr. Comprehensive Med. Home Care, Lansing, 1984-86; v.p. home care services Medair Equipment Supply, Lansing, 1986-87; dir. clin. services Americor Home Health Services, Lansing, 1987-88; adminstr. Upjohn Health-Care Services, Lansing, 1988—; profl. adv. and clin. record rev. bds., Americor Home Health Services, Lansing, 1984—; cons. Home Health Services of Mid-Mich., Midland, 1986. Mem. Assn. Career Women (bd. dirs. 1983-84), Capitol Area Discharge Planners (co-chmn. 1980-81, 84-85). Home: 4914 Hudson Dimondale MI 48821

ZERBO, DONNA MARIE, lawyer, accountant; b. N.Y.C., July 28, 1952; d. Albert James and Frances Rose (Piccio) LaSalvia; m. Louis Nicholas Zerbo, May 17, 1975; children—Matthew Joseph, Nicholas Louis. B.A. in Acctg. and Econs. magna cum laude, Queens Coll., 1974; J.D. cum laude, Fordham U., 1979; LL.M. in Taxation, NYU, 1985. Bar: N.Y. 1980; C.P.A., N.J. Sr. asst. tax acct. Deloitte Haskins & Sells, N.Y.C., 1974-76; lectr. bus. law, taxation and acctg. Bloomfield Coll. (N.J.), 1977-78; law clk. U.S. Dist. Ct., Newark, 1978; assoc. Cleary Gottlieb Steen & Hamilton, N.Y.C., 1979-82; assoc. Morgan Lewis & Bockius, N.Y.C., 1982-84; founding ptnr., cons. Zerbo & Co., C.P.A., Fairfield, N.J., 1983—; assoc. Cadwalader, Wickersham & Taft, N.Y.C., 1984-87; tax ptnr. Healy & Baillie, N.Y.C., 1988—; researcher N.Y. State Legis. Law Revision Com., N.Y.C., 1978. Bd. dirs. Cath. Guardian Soc., 1984. Recipient Francis X. Thaddeus award Fordham U., 1979. Mem. ABA, N.Y. State Bar Assn., AAUP. Republican. Roman Catholic.

ZERBO, RITA MICHAELLE, small business owner; b. Indpls., Aug. 13, 1946; d. Robert Cherry Day and Rose Mary Margaret (Anderson) Phillabaum; m. Joseph Nels Zerbo, Feb. 11, 1966 (div. Feb. 1979); children: Phillip Brian, Andrea Michaelle. Student, Howard Community Coll., 1978-82. Clk. Blue Cross/Blue Shield, Indpls., 1964-66; advt. rep. The Post Register, Idaho Falls, 1969-71; real estate sales rep. Grempler Real Estate, Columbia, Md., 1977—; advt. coordinator real estate mag. Stromberg Pubs., Elliott City, Md., 1977-79; advt. sales rep. Army Times Publ. Co., Washington, 1979-80, The News Am., Balt., 1980; owner, pres. Classy Maids Inc., Elliott City, 1980—. Founder, pub. Sagebrush News, Idaho Falls, 1969-71. co-dir. exposition Nat. Housing Mgmt., Washington, 1977. Episcopalian. Club: Navy Wives (Idaho Falls) (pres. 1969-70). Office: Classy Maids Inc 10744 Frederick Rd Ellicott City MD 21043

ZERKEL, JACKIE WADE, computer software executive; b. Birmingham, Ala., Oct. 4, 1961; d. James Ansley and Barbara Jacqulyn (Lassetter) Wade; m. Danny J. Zerkel Jr., Nov. 24, 1984. BS cum laude, Ohio U., 1983. Software design and implimentation engr. CHC, Orlando, Fla., 1984-86; database applications programmer Dublin, Ohio, 1986-87; software adminstr. CHC, Columbus, Ohio, 1987—. Mem. Assn. Women in Computing, Nat. Assn. Female Execs., Dalmatian Club Am. Office: Bell Labs Columbus Works 6200 E Broad St 3D354N Columbus OH 43213

ZERQUERA-FISCHER, CYNTHIA, computer professional; b. Coral Gables, Fla., Sept. 19, 1959; d. Roberto Emilio Zerquera and Dorothy Arline (Owen) Rogers; m. Thomas Gerard Fischer; Apr. 6, 1985. A in Physician Assistance, Sawyer U., 1979. Physician's asst. R.I. Hosp., Providence, 1979-83; mental health asst. Commonwealth of Mass., Framingham, 1983-84; adminstrv. asst. MicroAm., Inc., Framingham, 1984-85, ops. mgr., 1985-87; mgmt. info. systems trainer MicroAm., Inc., Marlboro, Mass., 1987—. Bd. dirs. R.I. State Council on the Arts, Providence, 1978; pres. Young Adult Ministry Southeastern Conf. United Methodist Ch., Framingham, 1986-87; adv. Commn. on Edn. Wesley United Methodist Ch., Framingham, 1983-87, youth ministry First United Methodist Ch., Milford, Mass., 1987. Mem. Nat. Assn. Female Execs. Home: 339 Purchase St Milford MA 01757

ZETT-OTTE, MARY LOUISE, pharmaceutical company executive, quality engineering consultant; b. Wilkes-Barre, Pa., May 16, 1944; d. George E. and Catherine F. (Vitale) Z.; m. Douglas C. Otte, Dec. 30, 1975; 1 child, Douglas A. BS in Med. Tech., Marywood Coll., 1966; MS in Biochemistry, Fairleigh Dickinson U., 1977, MBA in Product Mgmt., 1982; PhD in Mgmt., Fielding Inst., 1988. Cert. quality engr.; registered med. technologist. Supr. clin. chemistry/biochemistry Morristown Meml. Hosp., N.J., 1966-69; scientist Warner Lambert Co., Morris Plains, N.J., 1969-78; quality engr. C.R. Bard, Inc., Murray Hill, N.J., 1978-79; sr. quality engr. Ethicon, Inc., Bridgewater, N.J., 1979-81; sr. research scientist Ortho Pharm. Corp., Raritan, N.J., 1981—. Inventor med. device component intraluminal stapler, 1981. Recipient awards in immunology Sigma Xi, 1977. Mem. Am. Soc. Quality Control (regional councillor food, drug and cosmetic div. 1983-85, sec. 1986-87, treas. 1987-88, chair-woman elect 1988-89, Regional Councillor award 1986), Licensing Exec. Soc. Home: 63A Reinman Rd Warren NJ 07060 Office: Advanced Care Products Rt 202 Raritan NJ 07060

ZICCARDI, MADELINE THERESA, financial consultant; b. Bklyn., June 25, 1955; d. Benjamin Franklin and Carmen (Cuevas) Gicobbe; m. Nicholas Joseph Ziccardi, Dec. 20, 1980; 1 child, Vincent Michael. BA in Criminal Justice, U. Cen. Fla., 1977; M of Pub. Adminstrn., Fla. State U., 1978. Fundraiser March of Dimes, Miami, Fla., 1979; crime analyst City of Miami Police Dept., 1979-81; police planner Metro-Dade Police Dept., Miami, 1981-86; fin. cons. Ziccardi, Inc., Boca Raton, Fla., 1986—. Republican. Roman Catholic. Home and Office: Ziccardi Inc 21374 Summertrace Circle Boca Raton FL 33428

ZICH, SUE SCHAAB, nursing administrator, consultant; b. Buffalo, Oct. 18, 1946; d. Milan Harvey and Mary Margaret (Olmsted) Schaab; B.S. in Nursing, Villa Maria Coll., 1968; m. Timothy John Zich, Nov. 25, 1976; children—John Paul Trottman, Scott Francis Trottman. Staff nurse, charge nurse, team leader Children's Hosp., Buffalo, 1968-71; staff nurse plasmapheresis unit Roswell Park Meml. Inst., Buffalo, 1971-72, 73-75; staff devel. coordinator Episcopal Ch. Home, Buffalo, 1975-77; pediatric unit charge nurse Loudoun Meml. Hosp., Leesburg, Va., 1977; nursing instr. No. Va. Mental Health Inst., Falls Church, 1977-78; dir. nursing service Barcroft Inst., Falls Church, Va., 1978—; cons. nursing home design and remodeling systems, 1986—. Troop com. mem. Troop 884, den leader, 1980-85, den leader coach Pack 1182, 1983-88, dist. mem. Prince William Dist. Boy Scouts Am., day camp dir. Cub Scout Camp Tomahawk, 1983-87, asst. cub roundtable commr., 1986—; Prince William Dist. tng. team, 1981-87, v. chmn. membership, 1988. Recipient Key Leader award Prince William dist. Boy Scouts Am., 1982, Den Leader Tng. award Boy Scouts Am., 1982, Dist. Merit award Boy Scouts Am., 1985, Den Leader Coach Tng. award Boy Scouts Am., 1986, Scouter's Tng. award Boy Scouts Am., 1986. Mem. Dir. Nurses Group No. Va. (sec.-treas. 1980-81, v.p. 1981-87), Nat. Campers and Hikers Assn., Friends of Nat. Zoo, Smithsonian Assocs., Met. Washington Soccer Referees Assn., Va. High Sch. League Ofcl., Commonwealth Indoor/Outdoor Soccer Ofcls. Assn., D.C./Nova Soccer Referees Assn., NIFOA, Villa Maria Coll. Alumnae Assn. (life, past. pres. Buffalo chpt.), St. Edmund's Ladies Guild (pres. 1972-73, advisor 1973-74). Roman Catholic. Home: 9709 Evans Ford Rd Manassas VA 22111 Office: 2960 Sleepy Hollow Rd Falls Church VA 22044

ZIEGEL, BARI A(NN), marketing professional; b. N.Y.C., Nov. 25, 1959; d. Leonard and Norma (Nemeth) Z.; m. Steven M. Rosman, Sept. 8, 1984. BBA, Hofstra U., 1980. Ops., sales rep. Unitours, Inc., N.Y.C., 1980-82; adminstrv. asst. Bozell and Jacobs, Inc., N.Y.C., 1982-83, Parfums Stern, Inc., N.Y.C., 1983-85; mgmt. assoc. Citicorp Indsl. Credit, Inc., Harrison, N.Y., 1985-87; mktg. officer Citicorp Indsl. Credit, Inc., Rye, N.Y., 1987-88; mgr. area AT&T Credit Corp., Valhalla, N.Y., 1988—. Mem. Nat. Assn. Female Execs. Jewish. Office: AT&T Credit Corp 115 Stevens Ave Valhalla NY 10595

ZIEGLER, JANET CASSARO, nurse; b. Bklyn., Oct. 26, 1946; d. Dominic Michael and Rose (Locascio) Cassaro; m. Paul Dennis Ziegler, Nov. 1, 1970; children: Paul Dennis, Daniel Peter, Michael Tyson. BS in Nursing, D'Youville Coll., 1968; M in Nursing, U. Pitts., 1975. Instr. Norfolk (Va.) State Coll., 1970-72; pvt. practice in childbirth edn. Va., 1971-72, Pitts., 1972-81; clin. nurse specialist Vis. Nurse Assn. Allegheny County, Pitts., 1975-83; nurse-healer Therapeutic Rehab. Services, Pitts., 1982—; educator, cons. Am. Soc. Psychoprophylatis in Obstetrics, Pitts., 1971-81; practitioner, educator Clin. Hypnosis, Pitts., 1982—; Biofeedback Inst. Am., Wheat Ridge, Colo., 1983—; practitioner, cons., educator Therapeutic Touch, Pitts., 1981—. Served to lt. USN, 1968-70. Mem. Am. Holistic Nurses Assn., Nurse Healer's Profl. Assocs., Biofeedback and Behavioral Medicine Assn. of Western Pa., Assn. Clin. Nurse Specialists, Aloha Internat., People's Med. Soc., Inst. Noetic Scis. Republican. Roman Catholic. Home: 4566 Dogwood Dr Allison Park PA 15101

ZIEGLER, LAURA J., military officer; b. Norfolk, Va., Dec. 30, 1952; d. George Franklyn Smith and Flossie Jeannette (McLean) Butler; m. Paul Michael Ziegler, Sept. 5, 1981. BA in English, Old Dominion U., 1979; student, Officer Candidate Sch., Newport, R.I., 1980. Commd. ensign USN,

1980, advanced through grades to lt., 1984; configuration control prodn. officer USN, Virginia Beach, Va., 1980-82, computer systems analyst, 1982-83; manpower requirement determination officer USN, Norfolk, 1983-84, 84-86, flag personal protocol officer, 1986—. Contbr. articles to profl. jours. Mem. Tidewater Women Officers Profl. Network Steering Com., Internat. Inst. Indsl., Engrs. Republican. Office: USN SACLANT/USCINCLANT J-0042 Norfolk VA 23511-5100

ZIEGLER, LORRAINE CANEPA, school system administrator; b. N.Y.C., June 7, 1931; d. Rinaldo and Sevarina (Calligaris) Canepa; m. Henry Ziegler, April 12, 1952 (div. 1972; 1 child, William Henry. BA, Hunter Coll., 1952; MEd, Am. U., 1967. Tchr. New London (Conn.) Pub. Schs., 1952-53, Nassau County Pub. Schs., Franklin Square, N.Y., 1953-57, Montgomery County Pub. Schs., Clarksburg, Md., 1960-63; tchr., reading instr. Montgomery County Pub. Schs., Rockville, Md., 1963-66, tchr. specialist, 1966-67, supr. evaluation, 1967-81, asst. dir. Chpt. 1, ECIA, 1981-84, dir. Chpt. 1, ECIA, 1984—. Office: Montgomery County Pub Schs 850 Hungerford Dr Rockville MD 20850

ZIEGLER, SHIRLEY MELAT, nurse, educator; b. Oil City, Pa., Mar. 2, 1935; d. Leon Morrison and Grace Lucina (Lewis) Melat; 1 child, Amy Sue. BS in Nursing Edn., U. Pitts., 1959; MA, N.Y. U., 1964; PhD, U. Tex., Austin, 1977. Instr. Western Psychiatric Inst. and Clinic, Pitts., 1959-62, Ill. Wesleyan U., Bloomington, 1964-65; assoc. prof. nursing Pa. State U., Pitts., 1965-71, Edinboro (Pa.) State U., 1971-73; prof. nursing Tex. Woman's U., Dallas, 1977—. Author: (book) Autonomy in Nursing, 1986; contbr. chapters to books: Health Care Systems Model, 1982, 5th N.A.N.D.A. Summary, 1984; contbr. articles to profl. jours., 1964-65. Mem. Am. Nurses' Assn., North Am. Assn. Nursing Diagnosis, Phi Lambda Theta, Phi Kappa Phi, Phi Delta Gamma. Home: 1620 Banbury Carrollton TX 75006 Office: Tex Woman's U 1810 Inwood Dallas TX 75235

ZIELEN, WENDY LEIGH, purchasing professional; b. Ft. Knox, Ky., Aug. 19, 1960; d. Albin W. and Sandra J. (Horey) . AA, Jackson (Mich.) Community Coll., 1980; BA, U. Mich., 1985. Salesperson Jacobson's, Jackson, 1980-81, dept. mgr., 1981-86, asst. buyer, 1986-88, buyer, 1988—. Mem. Nat. Assn. Female Execs., Jaycees (IDVP Pinckney, Mich. chpt.). Office: Jacobson's 3333 Sargent Rd Jackson MI 49201

ZIELINSKI, NANCY SCHUPPER, sales executive; b. Orange, N.J., May 30, 1947; d. Irving Samuel and Patricia S. (Goldberg) Schupper; m. Clement A. Zielinski, July 7, 1968; children: Jeffrey A., Andrew R., Kimberly R. BA, Boston U., 1968; student, George Washington U., 1969; postgrad., Boston U., 1970-72. Tchr. Prince William County (Va.) Schs., Woodbridge, 1968-69; asst. to presdl. study team on long range planning Boston U., 1969-71; nutritional counselor Diet Control Ctrs., Union, N.J., 1974-78; technician, office adminstr. Dr. Donald Hersh, Maplewood, N.J., 1979-82; sr. account rep. The Holden Group, Los Angeles, 1982-85, regional sales dir., 1985—; selected to write nat. tng. program The Holden Group, 1987. Pres. Playhouse Inc., West Orange, N.J., 1981-82.

ZIERCHER, JULIA ANN, managing editor; b. St. Louis, June 28, 1937; d. Herbert William and Elizabeth Ziercher. B.A., Washington U., St. Louis, 1959; M.S. in English Lit., U. Wis.-Madison, 1962. Jr. high sch. English tchr. Huntington, N.Y., 1960-63, Ladue, Mo., 1963-65; copy editor Surgery jour., C.V. Mosby Co., St. Louis, 1965-66; sr. editing supr. McGraw-Hill Book Co., St. Louis and N.Y.C., 1966-72; sales rep. Alex Taylor & Co. Inc., N.Y.C., 1972-74; copy editing supr. Harper & Row, N.Y.C., 1974-77; mng. editor children's books, E.P. Dutton, N.Y.C., 1977—. Office: EP Dutton 2 Park Ave New York NY 10016

ZIFF, RUTH, advertising agency executive; b. N.Y.C., May 26, 1924; d. Herman and Lena (Medoff) Baron; m. Solomon Ziff, Mar. 29, 1942; children: Charles Elliot, Ellen Barbara. BA, Hunter Coll., 1944; MA (Acad. scholar), Columbia U., 1948; PhD, CUNY, 1975. Dir. psychol. barometer and link audit pub. attitudes Psychol. Corp., N.Y.C., 1944-49; v.p., mgr. research Benton & Bowles, Inc., N.Y.C., 1950-75; exec. v.p., dir. research and mktg. services Doyle Dane Bernbach, Inc. (now DDB Needham Worldwide, Inc.), N.Y.C., 1975—. Contbr. articles to profl. jours. Named Advt. Woman of Yr., Am. Advt. Fedn., 1973. Mem. Advt. Women of N.Y., Am. Mktg. Assn. (past. pres. N.Y. chpt.), Market Research Council (past pres.), Copy Research Council (past pres.), Phi Beta Kappa, Alpha Chi Alpha. Office: DDB Needham Worldwide Inc 437 Madison Ave New York NY 10022 •

ZIGUN, SYLVIA HELENE, psychotherapist, health educator; b. N.Y.C., July 28, 1934; d. David J. and Anna (Felenstein) Moscovitz; m. Charles Zigun, June 9, 1957; children—Jeffrey, Benjamin. B.A., Brown U., 1954; M.N., Yale U., 1957; M.S., U. Bridgeport, 1980; postgrad. Union Grad. Sch., 1981—. R.N., Conn. Psychotherapist, Psychotherapy Assocs. of Fairfield, Conn., 1979—; cons. State of Conn. div. ARC health nursing programs, 1974-75; chmn. nursing services Southeastern Fairfield chpt. ARC, 1974-76, childbirth educator, 1974-76. Mem. Internat. Acad. Preventive Medicine, Internat. Acad. Bariatric Medicine, Sigma Xi, Phi Beta Kappa. Office: Psychotherapy Assocs of Fairfield 400 Post Rd Fairfield CT 06430

ZIKMUND, BARBARA BROWN, minister, educator; b. Ann Arbor, Mich., Oct. 16, 1939; d. Henry Daniels and Helen (Langworthy) Brown; m. Joseph Zikmund II, Aug. 26, 1961; 1 child, Brian Joseph. BA, Beloit Coll., 1961; BDiv, Duke U., 1964, PhD, 1969; D in Div (hon.), Doane Coll., 1984, Chgo. Theol. Sem., 1985. Ordained to ministry United Ch. of Christ, 1964. Instr. Albright Coll., Reading, Pa., 1966-67, Temple U., Phila., 1967-68, Ursinus Coll., Collegeville, Pa., 1968-69; asst. prof. religion studies Albion Coll., Mich., 1970-75; asst. prof. ch. history, dir. studies Chgo. Theol. Sem., 1975-80; dean and assoc. prof. ch. history Pacific Sch. Religion, Berkeley, Calif., 1981-85, dean and prof. ch. history, 1985—; chmn. United Ch. of Christ Hist. Council, 1983-85, mem. council for ecumenism, 1983—; mem. Nat. Council Chs. Commn. on Faith and Order, 1979-87, World Council of Chs. Programme Theol. Edn., 1984—. Author: Discovering the Church, 1983. Editor: Hidden Histories in the UCC, 1984, vol. 2, 1987: (with Manschreck) American Religious Experience, 1976; editorial bd. Jour. Ecumenical Studies, 1987—; contbr. articles to profl. jours. Mem. City Council, Albion, Mich., 1972-75. Woodrow Wilson fellow, 1964-66; NEH grantee, 1974-75. Mem. Assn. Theol. Schs. (v.p. 1984-86, pres. 1986—, issues implementation grantee 1983-84), Am. Soc. Ch. History (council 1983-85), Internat. Assn. Women Ministers (v.p. 1977-79), AAUW (v.p. 1973-75). Democrat. Home: 1281 Peachwood Ct San Bruno CA 94066 Office: Pacific Sch Religion 1798 Scenic Ave Berkeley CA 94709

ZILBERBERG, BARBARA, psychologist; b. Nairobi, Kenya, Sept. 15, 1943; came to U.S., 1950, naturalized, 1957; d. Isidore and Sophie (Werner) Zysman; B.A. cum laude, City U. N.Y., 1964; M.A., New Sch. Social Research, 1966; cert. in sch. psychology Montclair State Coll., 1979-81; m. Charles Zilberberg, Sept. 2, 1965; 1 dau., Julie. Intern in psychology Central Islip (N.Y.) State Hosp., 1965-66; sr. clin. psychologist Kings Park (N.Y.) State Hosp., 1966-68; psychologist Bonnie Brae Residential Treatment Center, Millington, N.J., 1977-78, Sayreville (N.J.) Pub. Schs., 1981—. Mem. Nat. Assn. Sch. Psychologists, Am. Psychol. Assn., N.J. Assn. Sch. Psychologists, Psi Chi. Club: Mensa. Office: Sayreville Pub Schs One Taft Pl Parlin NJ 08859

ZILCZER, JUDITH KATY, museum curator, art historian, writer; b. Waterbury, Conn., Nov. 6, 1948; d. Paul and Rose (Merkler) Z. B.A. with distinction, George Washington U., 1969, M.A., 1971; Ph.D., U. Del., 1975. Teaching fellow George Washington U., 1969-71; Smithsonian fellow Nat. Mus. of Am. Art, Washington, 1973-74; research asst. Hirshhorn Mus., Washington, 1974-75, historian, 1976—; asst. professorial lectr. George Washington U., 1976, assoc. professorial lectr., 1979-80; guest curator Phila. Mus. Art, 1979-80; cons. High Mus. Art, Atlanta, 1985-86. Author: The Noble Buyer, 1978, Joseph Stella, 1983; co-author: The Advent of Modernism, 1986;contbr. articles to profl. jour. Recipient Spl. Commendation David Lloyd Kreeger Art History Competition, 1970; Fluid Research award Smithsonian Instn., 1977; Unidel fellow U. Del., 1971-73, Smithsonian fellow, 1973-74; Penrose grantee Philos. Soc. Phila. Am. Philos. Soc. grantee, 1976-77. Mem. Coll. Art Assn. Am., Women's Caucus for Art, Nat. Trust Historic Preservation, Am. Assn. Mus., Archives of Am. Art, Assn. Historians of Am. Art. Democrat. Jewish. Office: Hirshhorn Mus and Sculpture Garden 8th St and Independence Ave SW Washington DC 20560

ZILHAVER, LORI ANN, small business owner; b. Meadville, Pa., Mar. 17, 1959; d. James Allen and Myra June (Jeffrey) Z. Grad. high sch., Cambridge Springs, Pa. Waitress Holiday Inn, Edinboro, Pa., 1976-78; asst. mgr. Arby's, Erie, Pa., 1977—; sec. Erie Cotton Products, 1979-81; mgr. Zilhaver's County Store, Erie, 1981-85; clk., bookkeeper Ca-Ro Dress Shoppe, Erie, 1978-81, owner, 1985—. Lodge: Zonta. Office: Ca-Ro Dress Shoppe 2304 W 8th Erie PA 16505

ZIMARDI, JOSELYN T., communications professional; b. Manila, June 26, 1949; d. Ricardo Bautista and Corazon (Torres) Ignacio; m. Ronald S. Zimardi, Jan. 31, 1981; 1 child, Daniel Ricardo. BA in English Lit., Calif. State U., San Francisco, 1972. Workshop instr. U. Calif., Berkeley, 1978-80; archtl. edit. writer Bolles Assocs., San Francisco, 1981-82; publicist Sta. KPIX-TV, San Francisco, 1982-83; dir. pub. relations, advt. Boca Investors, Inc., Boca Raton, Fla., 1984-86; writer Entry Systems div. IBM, Boca Raton, 1986—; pub. relations cons. Muir Cornelius Moore, Inc., Boca Raton, 1984. Author: (poetry anthology) Kunyaku-Ragged Bowels, 1978, Collection of Asian American Writings, 1984; contbg. writer numerous poems and short stories. Mem. Pub. Relations Soc. Am., Am. Mktg. Assn. Republican.

ZIMMER, JANET ROSE, lawyer; b. Lancaster, Pa., Apr. 14, 1949; d. Robert Clare and Rose Evelyn (Williams) Zimmer; m. Gene D'Agostino. AB magna cum laude, Duke U., 1971; JD, Georgetown U., 1975. Bar: D.C. 1975, N.Y. 1986. Tchr. English, Ea. Lancaster County Sch. Dist., Pa., 1971-72; atty./advisor Div. Corp. Fin. U.S. SEC, Washington, 1975-78, spl. counsel and br. chief Div. Market Regulation, 1978-80; assoc. Rogers & Wells, Washington, 1980-82; assoc. Seward & Kissel, Washington, 1982-85, ptnr., 1986—. D.C. chmn. Robert L. Burch for (Ohio) State Senate, 1984. Mem. ABA (sect. corp., banking and bus. law, com. on fed. regulation of securities), D.C. Bar Assn., Women's Bar Assn. D.C., Kappa Delta Pi. Club: Sierra (No. Va. conservation com. mem. 1980). Office: Seward & Kissel 818 Connecticut Ave NW Suite 800 Washington DC 20006

ZIMMER, MARY JO, pediatrician; b. Milw., Mar. 19, 1955; d. Joseph John and Alberta (Pyzyk) Z. BS, U. Wis., Milw., 1977; MD, U. Wis., Madison, 1981. Diplomate Am. Bd. Pediatrics. Intern in pediatrics Children's Hosp. Med. Ctr., Cin., 1981-82, resident in pediatrics, 1982-84, 1981-84; pediatrician Milw. Med. Clinic, 1984—. Speaker Woman to Woman Conf., Milw., 1985, vol., 1986. Fellow Am. Acad. Pediatrics; mem. Milw. Pediatric Soc., Phi Beta Kappa. Roman Catholic. Office: Milw Med Clinic 3003 W Good Hope Rd Milwaukee WI 53217

ZIMMERMAN, BEVERLY MAY MCKAY, nursing educator; b. Rochester, N.Y., Mar. 2, 1939; d. James Kenneth and Gertrude Florence (Ritchie) McKay; m. Abraham Abba Zimmerman, Oct. 5, 1968; children—Lisa Marie, Sarah Ritchie. Cert. Pediatric Nurse, Rutgers U., 1975; cert. in Family Therapy, N.J. Ctr. Family Studies, 1983; B.S., Cornell U., 1963; M.Ed., Columbia, 1968, Ed.D., 1980. Instr. N.Y. Hosp., White Plains, 1964-66, Cornell U., N.Y.C., 1968-69; asst. prof. Seton Hall U., South Orange, N.J., 1976-81; assoc. prof. nursing, Fairleigh Dickinson U., Rutherford, N.J., 1981—, asst. dean Maxwell Becton Coll. Liberal Arts, 1985—. Bd. dirs., treas. New Providence LWV, New Providence, N.J., 1970-76; bd. dirs., pres. Jefferson Sch. PTA, Summit N.J., 1976-81. Computer grantee Fairleigh Dickinson U., 1983, 1984. Mem. Am. Nurses Assn., N.J. State Nurses Assn., Am. Orthopsychiat. Assn., N.J. Soc. Cert. Clin. Specialists Psychiat. Mental Health Nursing. Democrat. Presbyterian. Home: 1 Canterbury Ct Warren NJ 07060 Office: Fairleigh Dickinson U 188 Montross Ave Rutherford NJ 07070

ZIMMERMAN, BRENDA GAIL, association executive, word processing consultant; b. Peoria, Ill., Jan. 25, 1950; d. Charles Franklin and Mary Jeanette (Hardy) Hendrickson. Assoc. Applied Sci., Ill. Central Coll., 1974; cert. Adminstr.'s Guide to Word Processing, 1980, Personnel Law Seminar, 1985; postgrad. Inst. Orgn. Mgmt., 1986—. Adminstrv. asst. Greater Detroit C. of C., 1978, word processing supr., 1978-83, office mgr., 1983—; instr. Word Processing, Detroit, 1978—, Art of Dictation, Detroit, 1978—. Author Supervisors Guide to Word Processing, 1980, Word Processing Training Course, 1983. Mem. Internat. Soc. Wang Users, Assn. Info. Systems Profls., Wang Office Systems Users Soc., Phi Theta Kappa. Republican. Baptist. Avocations: baseball; reading; writing. Home: 1204 E Harwood St Madison Heights MI 48071 Office: Greater Detroit C of C 600 W Lafayette St Detroit MI 48226

ZIMMERMAN, EVELYN NELLIE, county supervisor; b. Pittsville, Wis., Jan. 8, 1922; d. Herman John and Margaret Johanna (Cook) Christensen; m. George Glen Zimmerman, Mar. 26, 1938 (dec. Apr. 1976); children—Nancy Zimmerman Wyman, Dorene Zimmerman Russell, Kathleen Zimmerman Chansley, George Herman; m. Don. C. Peterson, Apr. 9, 1988; stepchildren: Dorothy Goygrich, Franklynn. Student Mid-State Tech., Wisconsin Rapids, 1977-78, 85-86, U. Wis.-Stevens Point, 1978-79. Pvt. practice sewing and designing, Wisconsin Rapids, 1962-81; mem. Wood County Bd. Supervision, Wisconsin Rapids, 1978-90; Welfare Fraud Coalition, 1978-90, Wis. Pub. Health Affiliate, 1986-88 clk. Family Natural Foods, Wisconsin Rapids, 1981-85, election bd. Wood County, 1949-62, 73-80; chmn. child support and veterans services Bd. Social Services, Wisconsin Rapids, 1978-90, Area Comprehensive Health, Wood County, 1979-83, Community Options Program, 1978-88; sec. Wood County Health Com., 1978-88, vice-chair, 1988-90. Transp. Com., 1980-82; chmn. Community Options Program, 1978-90; trustee Moravian Ch., Wisconsin Rapids, 1976-83; pres., bd. dirs. Wis. Human Services Assn., 1986-88; . Recipient Presdl. Recognition award Wis. Human Services Bd. Mems. and Dirs. Assn., 1988. Mem. Wis. Social Services Assn. (county bd. mem. Recognition award 1988), Wisconsin Rapids Bus. & Profl. Women's Club (treas. 1973-75, 2d vice chmn. 1975-77, 1st vice chmn. 1977-79, bd. dirs. 1979-82, Woman of Achievement award 1986), North Central Dist. Social Services Assn. (pres. 1985-86), Wis. Child Support Enforcement Assn. Democrat. Avocations: creative writing; sewing; reading; swimming. Home: 2330 6th St S Wisconsin Rapids WI 54494

ZIMMERMAN, FRANCES ADDIE HOWELL, government official, business and employment consultant; b. Kansas City, Mo., Oct. 10; d. Dewey J. and Louise Frances (Wydick) Howell; Asso. Degree, Park Coll., Parkville, Mo., 1944; student Rockhurst Coll., 1970, U. Mo., Kansas City, 1972, U. Mich., 1976, 77, U. Houston, 1977, U. Kans., 1979; m. Eugene R. Zimmerman, Aug. 10, 1945 (dec. Nov. 1982); children—Donald, Nancy Zimmerman Giller, Robert J., Laura. Dir. public relations program, county organizer Am. Cancer Soc., Kansas City, Mo., 1959-60; public relations Mo. Employment Service, 1962-75; instr., art dir. Regional Tng. Center, U.S. Dept. Labor, Overland Park, Kans., 1975-80, public relations and employer com. coordinator, Kansas, Mo., 1980—, pres. Zimmerman & Assocs. Cons., 1988— ; instr. Mo. Div. Employment Security, 1983—, Johnson County Community coll.; cons. in field. Pres., Scarritt Sch. PTA, 1950; bd. dirs. Shawnee Mission (Kans.) High Sch., 1960; v.p. Jefferson City Women's Polit. Caucus, 1983; mem. Mo. Commn. on Status of Women, 1983. Mem. Internat. Assn. Personnel (v.p. Mo. 1975, exec. bd. internat. award of merit Mo. 1975), Am. Soc. Trainers and Developers (charter mem. orgnl. devel. media div., program com.), Nat. Assn. Female Execs., Mid-Am. Soc. Assn. Execs., Nelson Gallery Art, Kansas City C. of C., Urban League Greater Kansas City, Personal Dynamics Assn., Park Coll. Alumni Assn. Art Dirs. Club Kansas City, Nelson Gallery Art Soc. Baptist. Clubs: Kansas City Art Dirs., Overland Park Lioness. Lodge: Soroptimist. Home: 10568 Century Ln Overland Park KS 66215

ZIMMERMAN, JACQUELYN, infosystems specialist; b. Rahway, N.J., Jan. 12, 1951; d. Alfred Francis Zimmerman and Laura Morgan. AA in Data Processing, Coll. San Mateo, 1984. Data control clk. Supermarket Distribrs., South Boston, Mass., 1973, Met. Data, Hyde Park, Mass., 1974; programmer The Gap, San Bruno, Calif., 1974-79; sr. analyst Ampex, Redwood City, Calif., 1979-83; project mgr. GTE/U.S. Sprint, Burlingame, Calif., 1983-87; MIS mgr. Xidex, Santa Clara, Calif., 1987—; co-chmn. Order and Billing Forum, 1985-87. Author: (poetry) The Poet, 1982; editor Burlingame Hist. Soc., 1986—. Democrat. Roman Catholic. Office: Xidex 5201 Patrick Henry Santa Clara CA 95050

ZIMMERMAN, JANICE MARIE, savings and loan executive; b. Chgo., June 27, 1958; d. Edward Chester and Frances (Baranowski) Pawlowski; m. Michael Scott Daniel, May 25, 1980 (div. Oct. 1983); m. Daniel Victor Zimmerman, Sept. 7. 1985. B.S. in Fin., Eastern Ill. U., 1980; M.S. in Fin., St. Louis U., 1987. Asst. examiner Fed. Res. Bank, Chgo., 1980-82; fin. analyst Fed. Res. Bank St. Louis, 1982-84; v.p., treas. Illini Fed., Fairview Heights, Ill., 1984-87; asst. v.p. Community Fed., St. Louis, 1987—. Mem. Fin. Mgrs. Soc., Nat. Assn. Female Execs., Internat. Platform Assn. Republican. Jewish. Club: Creve Coeur Racquet (Mo.). Avocations: reading; golfing; writing. Office: Community Fed One Community Ctr Saint Louis MO 63131

ZIMMERMAN, JEAN, lawyer; b. Berkeley, Calif., Dec. 3, 1947; d. Donald Scheel Zimmerman and Phebe Jean (Reed) Doan; m. Gilson Berryman Gray III, Nov. 25, 1982; children: Charles Donald Buffum, Catherine Elisabeth Phebe (twins); stepchildren: Alison Travis, Laura Rebecca, Gilson Berryman. BSBA, U. Md., 1970; JD, Emory U., 1975. Bar: Ga. 1975, D.C. 1976, N.Y. 1980. Asst. mgr. investments FNMA, Washington, D.C., 1970-73; assoc. counsel Fuqua Industries Inc., Atlanta, 1976-79; assoc. Sage Gray Todd & Sims, N.Y.C., 1979-84; assoc. counsel J. Henry Schroder Bank and Trust Co., N.Y.C., 1984-85, asst. gen. counsel, 1985-86; assoc. gen. counsel IBJ Schroder Bank & Trust Co., N.Y.C., 1987—, also sec., 1988—. Founder, officer ERA Ga., Atlanta, 1977-79. Mem. ABA, N.Y. State Bar Assn., Ga. Assn. Women Lawyers (bd. dirs. 1977-79), LWV, DAR. Democrat. Office: IBJ Schroder Bank & Trust Co One State St New York NY 10004

ZIMMERMAN, JO ANN, lieutenant governor, nurse; b. Van Buren County, Iowa, Dec. 24, 1936; d. Russell and Hazel (Ward) McIntosh; m. A. Tom Zimmerman, Aug. 26, 1956; children: Andrew, Lisa, Don and Ron (twins), Beth. Diploma in Nursing, Broadlawns Sch. of Nursing, Des Moines, 1958; BA with honors, Drake U., 1973; postgrad., Iowa State U., 1973-75. RN, Iowa. Asst. head nurse maternity dept. Broadlawns Med. Ctr., Des Moines, 1958-59, weekend supr. nursing services, 1960-61, supr. maternity dept., 1966-68; instr. maternity nursing Broadlawns Sch. Nursing, Des Moines, 1968-71; health planner, community relations assoc. Iowa Health Systems Agy., Des Moines, 1978-82; mem. Iowa Ho. Reps., 1982-86; lt. gov. State of Iowa, 1986—. Contbr. articles to profl. jours. Mem. advanced registered nurse practitioner task force on cert. nurse midwives Iowa Bd. Nursing, 1980-81, Waukee, Polk County, Iowa Health Edn. Coordinating Council, Iowa Women's Polit. Caucus, Dallas County Women's Polit. Caucus; chmn. Des Moines Area Maternity Nursing Conf. Group, 1969-70, task force on sch. health services Iowa Dept. Health, 1982, task force health edn. Iowa Dept. Pub. Instruction, 1979, adv. com. health edn. assessment tool, 1980-81, Nat. Lt. Govs. Conf. Task Force on Agrl. and Rural Devel.; Dallas County Dem. Cen. Com., 1979-84; bd. dirs. Iowa PTA, 1979-83; chairperson Health Com., 1980-84; bd. dirs. Waukee Community Sch. Bd., 1976-79, pres., 1978-79. Mem. Am. Nursing Assn., Iowa Nurses Assn., Iowa League for Nursing (bd. dirs. 1979-83), Family Centered Childbirth Edn. Assn. (childbirth instr., advisor), LWV, Met. Des Moines LWV (health chmn.), Iowa Cattlemen's Assn. Mem. Christian Ch. Office: Office of Lt Gov State Capitol Bldg Des Moines IA 50319

ZIMMERMAN, MARGARET HANSON, accountant, educator; b. Phila., June 27, 1928; d. Edwin M.T. and Ednamay (LaChappele) Hanson; m. Albright G. Zimmerman. BS in Commerce, Drexel U., 1950; MBA, Temple U., 1958. CPA, Pa. Prin. Margaret H. Zimmerman, CPA, Yardley, Pa., 1962—; prof. Rider Coll., Lawrenceville, N.J., 1955-88; com. mem. Pa. Inst. CPA's; past prof. Drexel U., Phila., Trenton (N.J.) State Coll., Bucks County Community Coll., Newton, Pa. Auditor Twp. of Lower Makefield, Phila., 1963-81. Recipient Outstanding Alumnae Chpt. award Gamma Sigma Sigma; named to Temple U. Acctg. Hall of Fame, 1987. Home and Office: 1361 River Rd Yardley PA 19067

ZIMMERMAN, MARION HARRIET, medical consultant; b. Malden, Mass., Aug. 30, 1941; d. Jack and Anna (Alexenberg) Friend; m. Richard Zimmerman, Aug. 1, 1965 (div. July 1976); children: Joel, Jill. AA, Mt. Ida Coll., 1960. Med. mgr. dept. orthopedic surgery Tufts U., Boston, 1976—; pvt. practice med. mgmt. cons. Lexington, Mass., 1983—; reimbursement mgr. Health Stop Med. Mgmt., Wellesley, Mass., 1984—; cons. Multiply Med. Groups, 1984—; lectr. Boston U. Grad. Sch. Pub. Health. Author, editor: Massachusetts Orthopedic Guide, 1984. Trustee, exec. bd. dirs. Green Acres Day Sch., Waltham, Mass., 1986—. Mem. Mass. Med. Soc. (medicare/medicaid com. 1986-87), Mass. Med. Group Mgrs. (medicaid com., other coms. 1980-87). Jewish. Club: New Eng. Backgammon (Cambridge, Mass.) (bd. dirs.). Home and Office: 85 Kendall Rd Lexington MA 02173

ZIMMERMAN, MURIEL, psychotherapist, psychoanalyst; b. N.Y.C., Aug. 17, 1920. BA, Bklyn. Coll., 1941; PhD, New Sch. Social Research, 1944. Faculty psychology Bklyn. Coll., 1944-50; psychotherapist research Bklyn. State Hosp., 1950-51; psychoanalyst, psychotherapist N.Y.C., 1951—; clin. assoc. prof. Cornell Med. Sch., N.Y.C., 1970—. Co-editor: Object and Self: A Developmental Approach, 1981; contbr. articles to profl. jours. Mem. Am. Psychol. Assn., EPA, N.Y. State Psychol. Assn., Inst. Psychoanalytic Tng. and Research, N.Y. Freudian Soc., CPP. Home: 55 E 86th ST New York NY 10028

ZIMMERMAN, SUSAN G., sales executive; b. Lincoln, Nebr., Aug. 3, 1952; d. Robert Loyal and Marion Lucille (Brown) Mueller; m. Steven D. Zimmerman, Jan., 1988; children: Kathryn, Jamison, Sari, Desiree. BS, U. Minn., 1974. Traffic coordinator Barrickman Red Barron Advt., Mpls., 1974-75; high sch. tchr. Robbinsdale, Osseo and Blaine Schs., Mpls., 1974-83; adult edn. instr. Osseo, Robbinsdale Sch. Dist., Mpls., 1983; conf. coordinator Lakewood Pub./Tng. Mag., Mpls., 1983-84; from project mgr. to dir. sales Cardinal Health Systems, Mpls., 1984-87, exec. dir. sales, 1987; now with Equitable Fin. Cos., St. Paul; pres. Mgmt. Edn. Cons. Corp. of Am., Mpls., 1984—. Free-lance writer Mpls. Star & Tribune, 1982-83. Mem. Nat. Assn. Female Execs., Minn. Alumni Assn., Am. Soc. Tng. and Devel., Community Edn. Assn., Am. Mgmt. Assn. Presbyterian. Club: Flagship (Eden Prairie, Minn.). Home: 7142 Upper 139th St W Apple Valley MN 55124 Office: Equitable Fin Cos 325 Cedar Suite 300 Saint Paul MN 55101-3636

ZIMMERMAN, VERNDELL GINA (VERNIE), utility administrator; b. Sacramento, Calif., Aug. 31, 1943; d. Vernon H. and Fontella (Carroll) Carpenter; m. John R. Zimmerman, Sept. 11, 1965 (div. Feb. 1984); children: Paige Lee, Jon Paul. Student, Reno Bus. Coll., 1963, U. Nev., 1973-77; AS, Truckee Meadows Community Coll., 1985; BS in Mgmt. Sci., Sierra Nev. Coll., 1986. Various office positions Beck Corp., Reno, 1962-64; sr. rep. Sierra Pacific Power Co., Reno, 1964-65, with accounts payable dept., 1971-72, rates analyst, 1972-78, billing analyst, 1978-79, supr. customer contacts, 1979-86, adminstr. customer acctg., 1986—; loan officer Sierra Pacific Credit Union, 1980-85, mem. supervisory com., 1985-87. Assoc. advisor Explorers Boy Scouts Am., Reno, 1975—; arbitrator Better Bus. Bur., Reno, 1980—. Mem. Nat. Assn. Female Execs., Bus. Women's Inst. Clubs: Toastmistress (Reno); Rainbow Girls (bd. dirs. 1978-83, Grand Cross of Color 1982). Office: Sierra Pacific Power Co PO Box 10100 Reno NV 89520

ZIMMERMAN-MCLEOD, KAREN MICHELLE, psychotherapist; b. East Greenwich, R.I., Jan. 5, 1957. BA, U. S.C., 1979, St. Leo Coll., 1979; postgrad., U. S.C., 1980-82, MSW, 1982. Cert. marriage family therapist, clin. counselor; lic. therapist. Computer operator, programmer USAF, 1975-79; tchr. Furman High Sch., Sumter, S.C., 1975-80; psychiat. social worker Crafts Farrow State Hosp., Columbia, 1982-83, C.M. Tucker Human Resources Ctr., Columbia, 1983-84; tchr. Sumter Sch. Dist #2, 1979-82, 84-85; dir. clin. ops. Psychiat. Health Services, Columbia, 1984-87; prin., dir. Associated Psychotherapists, Sumter, 1987—; owner, therapist Vocat. Transfer Services East, Sumter, 1982—; cons. area attys., physicians, industries, Sumter, Columbia, 1983—; instr. Sumter Area Tech, 1980-82; EAP Counselor, Sumter, 1984—; adj. asst. prof. U. S.C., 1987—. Contbr. articles to profl. jours. Bd. dirs. YWCA, Sumter, 1984—, Drug and Alcohol Commn. Sumter County, 1986—; campaign worker local polit. entities,

Sumter, Pinewood, S.C., 1983—; area coordinator Cystic Fibrosis, Pinewood, 1984, 85. Mem. Am. Bus. Womens Assn. (pres. 1986—), Soc. Clin. Social Workers, Nat. Assn. Social Workers (cert.), Nat. Assn. Rehab. Counselors, Nat. Assn. Family Mediators, S.C. Soc. Clin. Social Work, Nat. Assn. Female Execs. (network dir. 1985—). Lodge: Civitan (twin honoree 1987). Home: 1975 Coral Way Sumter SC 29150 Office: Associated Psychotherapists 7 E Calhoun St Sumter SC 29150

ZIMMERMANN, CHERYL DIANE, horse breeder, consultant; b. Phila., Oct. 16, 1952; d. John Raymond and Edna May (Rosenbaum) Z. Student, Slippery Rock State Coll. Asst. prof. Slippery Rock (Pa.) State Coll., 1971-72; with IRS, Phila., 1973-74; stable mgr. Fox Willow Farm, Newtown, Pa., 1974-75; horse trainer Glenn View Farms, Washington Crossing, Pa., 1975; hot walker to groom Keystone Racetrack, Bensalem, Pa., 1976-77; clk. to asst. mgr. Nashamins Valley Fruit & Produce, Bensalem, 1977-81; owner, mgr. and sales agt. Cherlance Arabians Assocs. Breeders, Pineville, Pa., 1981—, photographer, video editor, 1981—; photogrpaher and video editor Cherlance Arabians Assocs. Breeders, 1981—; tax cons., Pineville, 1981—. Co-author numerous scripts. Mem. Mid-Atlantic Arabian Horse Assn., Pa. Arabian Horse Assn., Arabian Horse Registry Am., Am. Horse Show Assn., Blue Ridge Arabian Horse Assn. (editor newsletter 1985-86). Home and Office: Cherlance Arabians PO Box 82 Holicong Rd Pineville PA 18946-0082

ZINDEL, BONNIE, writer; b. N.Y.C., May 3, 1943; d. Jack and Claire (Bromberg) Hildebrand; m. Paul Zindel, Oct. 25, 1973; children: David, Lizabeth. BA in Psychology, Hofstra U., 1964. Dir. pub. relations The Cleveland Play House, Cleve., 1969-72; producer show Intermission Feature, Boston Symphony, sta. WCLV-FM, Cleve., 1970-72. Author: A Star for the Latecomer, 1980; Hollywood Dream Machine, 1984; playwright I Am A Zoo-Jewish Repetory Theatre-The Troupe Theatre, 1976; Lemons in the Morning, A.M. Back Alley Theatre, 1983, The Latecomer, 1985, Adriana Earthlight-Student Shrink, 1987. Mem. Playwrights Unit-Actors Studio, Women in Film. Office: care Curtis Brown 10 Astor Pl New York NY 10003

ZINGALE, MARY GENEVIEVE, social services administrative supervisor; b. Bklyn., Oct. 14, 1928; d. Salvatore and Mary (Fornito) Z. Vocat. edn. cert., SUNY, Albany, 1961; BA in Social Studies, Coll. St. Rose, Albany, 1966; MSW, Adelphi U., 1977; cert., Suffolk County Inst. for Psychoanalytic Psychotherapy, 1986. Entered Congregation of Religious of Good Shepherd of Angers, 1946; child care worker Euphrasian Residence, N.Y.C., 1950-51; child care worker St. Anne Inst., Albany, 1951-72, trade sewing tchr., 1952-61, tchr. social studies and religion, 1963-72, children's clothing buyer, purchasing agt., adminstr. campus shop, 1951-72, tchr. bus., case aide, 1972-76, social worker, 1976-81, purchasing agt., 1976—, casework supr., 1981—; field instr. Adelphi U., 1983—. Mem. Nat. Assn. Social Workers, N.Y. State Soc. Clin. Social Work Psychotherapists Inc. (cert. 1986). Roman Catholic. Address: Madonna Heights Burrs Ln Huntington NY 11743

ZINGARO, KATHLEEN GAIL, human resources executive; b. Phila., Sept. 21, 1953; d. Joseph C. and Connie (Chiarizio) Z. Payroll/personnel adminstr. Star Sprinkler Co., Phila., 1974-77; personnel mgr. Star Porcelain Co., Trenton, N.J., 1977-81, Heinemann Electric Co., Lawrenceville, N.J., 1981-87; pres. The Zingaro Group, 1987— . Adv. bd. pub. relations com. Salvation Army, Trenton, N.J., 1982-85; loaned exec. Delaware Valley United Way, Trenton, 1983-84, div. co-chairperson, 1985, div. chairperson, 1986; mem. bus. adv. council Assn. Advancement Mental Health, Princeton, N.J., 1983—, chairperson, 1984-87; indsl. relations com. N.J. Bus. & Industry Assn., Trenton, 1983-84, vocat. guidance adv. com. N.J. Dept. Edn., Trenton, 1983-84. Recipient Superior Merit award Am. Soc. Personnel Adminstrn., 1983, 84. Mem. Delaware Valley Personnel Assn. (v.p. membership 1980-81, pres. 1982-84, chair adv. bd. 1984-86), Indsl. Relations Research Assn., Am. Soc. Personnel Adminstrn. (dir. pub. affairs 1984-87). Office: 21 Greene St Newtown PA 18940

ZINK, ELIZABETH BARNES, industrial health specialist; b. Princeton, N.J., Sept. 30, 1957; d. Charles Albert and Marie Diggins (Dey) Z. BS, Elmira (N.Y.) Coll., 1979, MS in Pub. Health, 1981. Cert. indsl. hygienist. Indsl. hygienist Allied Chem. Co. subs. Allied Corp., Baton Rouge, 1981-82, foreman lab. indsl. hygiene, 1982-84; specialist occupational health Allied Corp., Morristown, N.J., 1984-86; mgr. occupational health Allied-Signal Corp., Morristown, N.J., 1986—. Mem. Am. Indsl. Hygiene Assn., Am. Acad. Indsl. Hygiene, Am. Welding Soc., Nat. Assn. Female Execs. Republican. Roman Catholic. Office: Allied-Signal Corp PO Box 1139R Morristown NJ 07960

ZINN, BARBARA LYNNE, department store executive; b. Jersey City, June 4, 1951; d. Sidney and Ruth Jean (Riker) Genser; m. David H. Zinn, Jan. 15, 1972 (div. 1984). Student Douglass Coll., Rutgers U., 1969-72. Buyer better sportswear Abraham & Straus, Bklyn., 1973-76; buyer Miss Bergdorf Sportswear dept. Bergdorf Goodman, N.Y.C., 1976-77; buyer better dresses and suits Bambergers, Newark, 1977-79, buyer moderate shoes, 1979-82, mdse. councillor/buyer jr. and moderate shoes, 1982-84, mdse. councillor moderate shoes, 1984-85, divisional mdse. adminstr. for women's shoes, 1985-86, div. mdse. adminstr. for cosmetics, 1986—, v.p., 1987—. Recipient Outstanding Corp. Group Performance award Brown Shoe Co., 1980, 81, 82. Mem. Fragrance Found., Women's Accessory Council.

ZINN, MINDY, sales and marketing professional; b. N.Y.C., Sept. 30, 1952; d. Norman and Leonora (Gerstein) Z.; m. James Elliot Garner, Aug. 26, 1979 (div. 1982). BA, CUNY, 1974; MA, Kean Coll., 1977; MBA, William Paterson Coll., 1987. Cert. psychology and social studies tchr. Dir. sr. citizen's program St. Clare's Hosp., Denville, N.J., 1977—; vis. faculty Coll. St. Elizabeth, Convent Station, N.J., 1982, Seton Hall U., South Orange, N.J., 1983; sales and marketing person Roche Biomedical Labs., Raritan, N.J., 1987—; cons. Theresa Grotta Rehab. Ctr., West Orange, N.J., 1987, Johnson and Johnson, New Brunswick, N.J., 1987; media appearances and presentations on behalf of senior citizens. Contbr. articles to profl. jours. and mags. Chairperson Com. on the Aging Network, Morris County, N.J. Mem. Am. Mgmt. Assn., Gerontol. Soc. Am., Nat. Assn. Female Execs. Home and Office: Kingswick Apts B-8 Thorofare NJ 08086

ZINTZ, ANDREA CAREN, human resources executive; b. Englewood, N.J., July 17, 1953; d. Dexter Harold and Arlyne Carol (Wenzelberg) Z.; m. Barry Salvatore Levatino, June 7, 1987. BS, Emerson Coll., 1975; MA, Fielding Inst., 1986, PhD, 1988. Tng. specialist Macys & Co., N.Y.C., 1976-77; adminstr. tng. missile and surface radar RCA, Moorestown, N.J., 1977-79; mgr. tng. Personal Products Corp., Milltown, N.J., 1980-81; mgr. tng. and orgn. devel. Ortho Pharm. Corp., Raritan, N.J., 1981-85, mgr. employee relations and devel., 1986—. Mem. Orgn. Devel. Network. Office: Ortho Pharm Corp Rt 202 Box 300 Raritan NJ 08869

ZIZELMAN, MARY ANN ELIZABETH, educator; b. Cleve., Dec. 9, 1933; d. Emil William and Pauline (Krisko) Hansh; m. Robert Frederick Zizelman, Jun. 8, 1957; children: Debra Ann, Sharyl Ann. BS in Philosophy, Notre Dame Coll., South Euclid, Ohio, 1956; postgrad., Cleve. State U. Cert. elem., high sch. tchr., Ohio. Tchr. Hoban-Dominican High Sch., Cleve., 1956-58; elem. tchr. Hodge Sch. Cleve. Bd. Edn., 1964-79, Oliver Hazard Perry Sch. Cleve. Bd. Edn., 1979—. Martha Holden Jennings scholar. Mem. Cleve. Tchrs. Union (chmn. pub. relations 1986—, mem. exec. bd., 1986—), Ohio Fed. Tchrs. (mem. publicity and service com. 1986—), Am. Fedn. Tchrs., Coalition Labor Union Women, Notre Dame Coll. Alumnae Assn. Roman Catholic. Clubs: St. William Ladies Guild (v.p. 1978-80), Madison Country. Home: 338 Halle Dr Euclid OH 44132 Office: Oliver Hazard Perry Sch 18400 Schenely Ave Cleveland OH 44132

ZLOTOLOW, PAULINE RICH, plant company executive; b. Cleve., Aug. 24, 1922; d. Isadore and Rebecca (Oppenheim) Rich; m. Sherman Zlotolow, June 1, 1943 (dec. 1986); children: Ian, Steve, Marsha. Student, U. Fla., Sarasota, 1983. Pres. Exhibition Enterprises, Louisville, 1966-76, Florasota Tropical Plants, Sarasota, 1986-87; advt. mgr. Burdines, 1976-86; pres. Skylight Prodn. Co., 1988. Author, producer (TV program) Sarasota Cares, 1983. V.p. Children's Hosp., Louisville, 1968; chair-person Council Mentally Retarded of Jefferson County, 1969; exec. producer (films) We Can Do It for Pinellas Assn. for Retarded Children, 1985, Finnish Line for Manatee County United Way, 1988. Mem. Downtown Merchants Assn. (chair-person), United Way Sarasota (bd. dirs., film producer 1983), Sarasota and Manatee Press Club, Ky. Press Assn., Am. Women Radio and T.V. Democrat. Jewish. Home: 1087 Peppertree Rd Sarasota FL 33581

ZOBEL, RYA W., judge; b. Germany, Dec. 18, 1931. A.B., Radcliffe Coll., 1953; LL.B., Harvard U., 1956. Bar: Mass. bar 1956, U.S. Dist. Ct., Mass., 1956, U.S. Ct. Appeals (1st cir.) 1967. Mem. Hill & Barlow, Boston, 1967-73; mem. Goodwin, Procter & Hoar, Boston, 1973-79; U.S. dist. judge of Mass. Boston, 1979—. Mem. ABA, Boston Bar Assn., Am. Bar Found., Mass. Bar Assn., Am. Law Inst. Office: US Dist Ct Room 1802 McCormack PO & Cthouse Boston MA 02109 *

ZOHAR, ZITA, pianist, artistic director, lecturer; b. Bucharest, Romania, May 11, 1949; arrived in Israel, 1962, came to U.S., 1966; d. Marcel and Cecile (Shapira) Finkelstein; m. Adrian Smilovici, Dec. 22, 1972. Diploma, Rubin Acad. Mus., Ramat-Aviv, Israel, 1966; hon. diploma, Chigiana Shc., Siena, Italy, 1970; BS, MS, The Juilliard Sch., 1971. Founder, artistic dir. Festival Chamber Players, L.I., N.Y., 1981—; music dir. Hecksher Series, L.I., 1985—; conductor Vanderbilt Orch., L.I., 1985-86; lectr., instr. various schs., 1979—; asst. Dorothy Taubman Sch. at Amherst, 1978-82. Bd. dirs. Musician's Group, Bucharest, Romania, 1961, Music for All, Tel-Aviv, 1968, Festical Chamber Players, N.Y.C., 1985. Recipient First Prize Rep. Commn., 1959, First Prize Bach Competition Israeli Acad., 1965, Silver medal Busoni Competition, 1970. Mem. Chamber Music Am., Juilliard Sch. Alumni Assn., N.Y. Exec. Women. Home and Office: 205 W 57 #3DB New York NY 10019

ZOLBER, KATHLEEN KEEN, nutrition educator, management consultant; b. Walla Walla, Wash., Dec. 9, 1916; d. Wildie H. and Alice (Johnson) Keen; m. Melvin L. Zolber, Sept. 19, 1937. BS in Foods and Nutrition, Walla Walla Coll., 1941; MA, Wash. State U., 1961; PhD, U. Wis., 1968. Registered dietitian. Dir. food service Walla Walla Coll., 1941-50, mgr. coll. store, 1951-59, asst. prof. food and nutrition, 1959-62, assoc. prof., 1962-64; assoc. prof. nutrition Loma Linda (Calif.) U., 1964-72, prof. nutrition, 1973—, dir. dietetic edn., 1967-84, dir. dietetics Med. Ctr., 1972-84, dir. nutrition program, 1984—. Mead Johnson grantee, 1965-67; recipient Alumna of Yr. award Walla Walla Coll., 1977; Delores Nyhus award Calif. Dietetic Assn., 1978. Mem. Am. Dietetic Assn. (pres. 1982—), Am. Pub. Health Assn., Am. Home Econs. Assn., Am. Mgmt. Assn., AAUP, Soc. Food Service Research, Soc. Personnel Adminstrn., Omicron Nu, Delta Omega. Office: Loma Linda U Sch Pub Health Dept Nutrition Loma Linda CA 93354

ZOLOTOW, CHARLOTTE SHAPIRO, author, editor; b. Norfolk, Va., June 26, 1915; d. Louis J. and Ella F. (Bernstein) Shapiro; m. Maurice Zolotow, Apr. 14, 1938 (div. 1969); children: Stephen, Ellen. Student, U. Wis., 1933-36. Editor children's book dept. Harper & Row, N.Y.C., 1938-44; sr. editor Harper & Row, 1962-70; v.p., asso. pub. Harper Jr. Books, 1976-81; editorial cons., editorial dir. Charlotte Zolotow Books, 1981—; tchr. U. Colo. Writers Conf. on Children's Books, U. Ind. Writers Conf.; also lectr. children's books. Author: The Park Book, 1944, Big Brother, 1960, The Sky Was Blue, 1963, The Magic Words, 1952, Indian Indian, 1952, The Bunny Who Found Easter, 1959, In My Garden, 1960, Not a Little Monkey, 1957, The Man With The Purple Eyes, 1961, Mr. Rabbit and the Lovely Present, 1962, The White Marble, 1963, A Rose, A Bridge and A Wild Black Horse, 1964, Someday, 1965, When I Have a Little Girl, 1965, If It Weren't for You, 1966, 2d edit. 1987, Big Sister, Little Sister, 1966, All That Sunlight, 1967, When I Have A Son, 1967, My Friend John, 1968, Summer Is, 1968, Some Things Go Together, 1969, The Hating Book, 1969, The New Friend, 1969, River Winding, 1970, 79, Lateef and His World, 1970, Yani and His World, 1970, You and Me, 1971, Wake Up and Goodnight, 1971, William's Doll, 1972, Hold My Hand, 1972, 2d edit. 1987, The Beautiful Christmas Tree, 1972, Janie, 1973, My Grandson Lew, 1974, The Summer Night, 1974, 2d edit. 1987, The Unfriendly Book, 1975, It's Not Fair, 1976, 2d edit. 1987, Someone New, 1978, Say It, 1980, If You Listen, 1980, 2d edit. 1987, The New Friend, 1981, One Step, Two ..., 1981, The Song, 1982, I Know a Lady, 1984, Timothy Tool., 1986, Everything Glistens, Everything Sings, 1987, I Like to be Little, 1987, The Poodle Who Barked at the Wind, 1987, A Rose, a Bridge, and a Wild Black Horse, 1987; others; compiler An Overpraised Season, Early Sorrow. Mem. PEN, Authors League. Home: 29 Elm Pl Hastings-on-Hudson NY 10706 Office: 10 E 53d St New York NY 10022

ZONKA, CONSTANCE ZIPPRODT, public relations executive; b Evanston, Ill., May 23, 1937; d. Herbert Edward and Agnes Irene (Turpin) Zipprodt; m. Leif B. Sorensen, June 29, 1959 (div. Mar. 1964); 1 child, Heidi Liselotte; m. Robert F. Zonka, Aug. 5, 1970 (div. June 1982) 1 son, Milo Matthew. B.A., U. Fla., 1958; student Smith Coll., 1955-56; postgrad U. Chgo., 1958-59. Dir. publicity WIND Radio, Chgo., 1962-64; Midwest asst. pub. relations dir. Time Inc., Chgo., 1964-66; account exec. D.J. Edelman, Inc., Chgo., 1966-69; pres. Connie Zonka & Assocs., Chgo., 1970-87; dir. Facets Multimedia, Chgo., 1983—; coordinator Chgo. Communications, 1974—; dir. pub. relations, Columbia Coll., Chgo.; cons. Newsweek Mag., Wisdom Bridge Theatre. Mem. benefit com. Midwest Women's Ctr., Chgo., 1983—; mem. Met. Planning Council, Chgo. Mem. NOW, Nat. Assn. Female Execs., Nat. Assn Women Bus. Owners., Pub. Relations Soc. Am., Publicity Club Chgo. (Golden Trumpet award 1980, Merit award 1982). Democrat. Clubs: Arts, East Bank, City (Chgo.). Home: 901 S Plymouth Ct Chicago IL 60605 Office: Columbia Coll 600 S Michigan Ave Chicago IL 60605

ZOOK, MARTHA FRANCES HARRIS, retired nursing administrator; b. Topeka, Nov. 15, 1921; d. Dwight Thacher and Helen Muriel (Houston) Harris; R.N., Meriden (Conn.) Hosp. Sch. Nursing, 1947; student U. Kans., 1948-49, Kans. State U., 1960-61, Barton County Community Coll., 1970-73; B.A., Stephens Coll., 1977; postgrad. Ft. Hays State U., 1978-79; m. Paul Warren Zook, July 2, 1948; children—Mark Warren, Mary Elizabeth Zook Hughey. Staff nurse Stormont Hosp., Topeka, 1947-48; staff nurse Watkins Meml. Hosp., Lawrence, Kans., 1948-49; nursing supr. Larned State Hosp., 1949-53, sect. supr., 1956-57, dir. nursing, 1958-61, 83-86; sect. nurse Sedgewick Sect., 1961-76, clin. instr. nursing edn., 1976-77, dir. nursing edn., 1977-83; clinic nurse for podiatrist; sect. supr. Dillon Bldg., Larned, 1957-58; Vol. Am. Cancer Soc. Republican. Roman Catholic. Home: 1109 Johnson St Larned KS 67550

ZOON, KATHRYN EGLOFF, biochemist; b. Yonkers, N.Y., Nov. 6, 1948; d. August R. and Violet T. (Pollock) Egloff; B.S. (N.Y. State Regents fellow), Rensselaer Poly. Inst., 1970; Ph.D. (fellow), Johns Hopkins U., 1975; m. Robert A. Zoon, Aug. 22, 1970; children—Christine K, Jennifer R. Interferon research fellow NIH, Bethesda, Md., 1975-77, staff fellow, 1977-79, sr. staff fellow, 1979-80; sr. staff fellow div. biochem. biophysics Bur. Biologics, FDA, Bethesda, 1980-83; research chemist div. virology Office of Biologics Research and Rev., FDA, 1983—, now also chief immunology lab., dep. dir. virology div. Mem. Internat. Soc. Interferon Research. Roman Catholic. Contbr. numerous articles on research in biol. chemistry to sci. jours.; editor Interferon Research, 1980—. Office: Virology Office of Biologics and Rev Bldg 29A Room 2A17 8800 Rockville Pike Bethesda MD 20892

ZOPF, EVELYN LANOEL MONTGOMERY, guidance counselor; b. Laurel, Miss., July 10, 1932; d. Arthur LaNoel and Ruby Lee (Lewis) Montgomery; m. Paul Edward Zopf Jr., Aug. 5, 1956; 1 child, Eric Paul. MusB in Edn., U. So. Miss., 1953, MA, 1954. Guidance counselor U. So. Miss., 1953-54, U. Fla., 1954-56; tchr. New Orleans City Schs., 1956-57; pub. sch. music tchr., band dir., choral dir. Putnam County Schs., Fla., 1957-59; pvt. music tchr. voice, piano, clarinet and trumpet, 1953-61; substitute tchr. Guilford County Schs., 1959—; mem. arts series com. Guilford Coll., 1973-77; interim choir dir. New Garden Friends Meeting, 1961, chmn. music com., 1974-76; adviser to fgn. students, 1954-56, 59-62; mem. First Internat. Congress on Quaker Edn. Com., 1987-88, Guilford Coll.'s Sesquicentennial Com., 1985-87; speaker various religious and art groups. Vol. ARC, Boy Scouts Am.; mem. U. Fla. Union Bd., 1955-56; precinct del. County Dem. Conv., 1977, 79, precinct worker, 1980, campaign worker, 1980; bd. dirs. Greensboro Friends of Music, 1970-71, Greensboro chpt. N.C. Symphony Bd., 1979—. Mem. United Soc. of Friends Women (pres. 1979-81), Internat. Fellowship Quaker Women, Guilford Coll. Community Chorus, Phi Mu. Clubs: Women's Soc. (dir. 1978—), Guilford Coll. Arts Appreciation (v.p. 1980-81, pres. 1981-82), Guilford Gourmet. Home: 815 George White Rd Greensboro NC 27410

ZORSCH, CATHERINE MARY, physical therapist; b. Rochester, N.Y., Apr. 18, 1959; d. Charles Shelby Jr. and Mary Margaret (Mattle) Z. BS, U. Buffalo, 1981. Staff, chief phys. therapist Restorative Services Inc., Hobart, Ind., 1981-83; dir. phys. therapy Highland (Ind.) Med. Ctr., 1982-83; staff phys. therapy Park Ridge Hosp., Rochester, 1983-85; dir. phys. therapy Wesley on East, Rochester, 1985—; pvt. practice phys. therapy Gates Chili Sch. Dist., Rochester, 1983—, Home Health, Rochester, 1983—. Music leader St. Monica's Cath. Ch., Rochester, 1986—, Charismatic Renewal Office, Rochester, 1984—. Mem. Am. Phys. Therapy Assn., Assn. Christian Therapists, Nat. Assn. Female Execs. Roman Catholic. Home: 175 Willowbrook Rd Rochester NY 14616 Office: Park Ridge Hosp 1555 Long Pond Rd Rochester NY 14626

ZOTTOLA, CARLA JEAN, insurance executive; b. Pitts., Oct. 21, 1959; d. Henry and Sheila Naomi (Cataldo) Z. AAS in Mktg. and Retailing Sales, Cen. Piedmont Community Coll. Lic. broker, N.C. Rep. sales Western-So. Ins., Charlotte, N.C., 1981-87; owner, proprietor 'Z' Best Ins. Services, Charlotte, N.C., 1986—. Mem. Nat. Assn. Life Underwriters, Women Life Underwriters, Nat. Assn. for Female Execs. Methodist. Office: 'Z' Best Ins Services 401 S Independence Blvd Suite 521 Charlotte NC 28204

ZOUHARY, KATHLEEN MAHER, lawyer; b. Greenville, Ohio, June 28, 1951; d. Thomas Richard and Mary (Brown) Maher; b. Jack Zouhary, Oct. 21, 1978; children—Kathleen Marie, Alexis Jacqueline. B.A. in Polit. Sci. cum laude, Miami U., Oxford, Ohio, 1973; J.D. cum laude, U. Notre Dame, 1976. Bar: Ohio 1976. Assoc., Fuller & Henry, Toledo, 1976-81, ptnr., 1981-85; v.p., gen. counsel St. Luke's Hosp., Maumee, Ohio, 1985—. Gen. chmn. Tribute to Women and Industry, Toledo, 1984, honoree, 1982; bd. dirs. Women Involved in Toledo, 1981-83; trustee Toledo Legal Aid Soc., 1977—. Mem. Am. Acad. Hosp. Attys., ABA, Ohio Bar Assn., Toledo Bar Assn., Miami Presidents Club, St. Luke's Hosp. Pacesetter Club, Phi Beta Kappa. Lodge: Zonta. Office: St Luke's Hosp 5901 Monclova Rd Maumee OH 43537

ZOZAYA, JULIA SOTO, media consultant; b. Kingman, Ariz., Mar. 23, 1926; d. Francisco Cuesta and Maria (Blanca) Soto; m. Steve Mike Zozaya, Jan. 3, 1945; 1 child, Steve Mike. Student Lamson Bus. Coll., Phoenix, 1959-60, Phoenix Coll., 1960. Adminstr. employee relations Zozaya Constrn. Co., 1960-66; state info. specialist Ariz. Dept. Econ. Security, 1966-82; pres. Am. Internat. Devel. Corp., Inc., Phoenix, 1972-83; owner, gen. mgr. Sta.-KNNN-FM, Phoenix, 1982-84; media cons. Am. Internat. Diversified, Phoenix, 1984—; spl. Ariz. del. White House Conf. on Aging, 1971, Mich. Com. on Employment Handicapped, 1976-78; cons. White House Conf. on Small Bus., 1978-80. Bd. dirs. Nat. Caucus on Aging, 1971; bd. dirs. Dept. Labor Spl. Com. on Women, 1967-69, Ariz. Health Planning Com., 1976-79, Pres.'s Com. for Employment Handicapped, 1978-81, Project SER, 1979-81, Nat. Health Planning Council, 1977-82, Ariz. Dept. Edn. Div. Handicapped; 1st v.p. Ariz. Fedn. of Blind, 1964; state publicity chairperson League United Latin Am. Citizens, 1967-68, nat. v.p., 1969-71, past bd. dirs., past newsletter editor, nat. dir. aging and housing, women's affairs, 1972-74; mem. Phoenix Arts Commn., 1987. Recipient citation of merit, Gov. Ariz., 1968, 78, 83, Traditional Dress and Jewelry award Apache Tribe, 1968; various awards League United Latin Am. Citizens, including Woman of Yr. award, 1969, 80; Ring award Hopi Tribe, 1970, Outstanding Citizen award Image, Inc., 1977, cert. appreciation Epsilon Sigma Alpha Internat., 1978, Diana award Epsilon Sigma Alpha Internat., 1979, Goodwill Ambassador's award Ariz. Lion's Club, 1979, cert. appreciation Ariz. Adv. Council on Vocat. Edn., 1980, 82. Mem. Am. Assn. Tng. and Devel., Am. Women in Radio and TV, Nat. Assn. Broadcasters, Statewide Reading Service for Blind and Handicapped-Sun Sounds, Ariz. Town Halls, Chicano Por la Causa, Mujer (outstanding citizen award 1976), Nat. Hispanic C. of C. (founder, 1st v.p. 1977), Ariz. Mexican C. of C. (incorporator, pres. 1972-80, Disting. Service award 1971, 50th Anniversary Service award 1979). Democrat. Roman Catholic. Avocations: music; dance; history and culture. Home: 4548 W Osborn Rd Phoenix AZ 85031

ZOZOM, ELIZABETH, graphic designer, sculptor; b. Bayonne, N.J., June 12, 1955; d. Andrew Zozom and Ada (Cooper) Smith. Assoc. in Specialized Tech., Art Inst. Phila., 1975; student Pa. Acad. Fine Arts, 1977-78. Asst. art dir. Phila. Mag., 1975-76; designer, proofreader Stephenson Bros. Printers, Phila., 1980-81; designer, proofreader Running Press Book Pubs., Phila., 1981-82, design dir., 1982-83, dir. prodn. and design, 1983—. Exhibited group shows including: Pratt Inst., N.Y.C., 1972, Provident Bank, Phila., 1974, Women's Art League Phila., 1976, Gallery 3 1/2 & 4, Phila., 1976, Etage, Phila., 1977, Art Inst. Phila., 1977, Old City Art Spring Festival, Phila., 1978, Race Gallery, Phila., 1979. Mem. Phila. Book Clinic, Art Dirs. Club Phila. Office: Running Press Book Pubs PO Box 15862 Philadelphia PA 19103

ZUBILLAGA, PRISCILLA CROTTS, bank administrator; b. Gastonia, N.C., Feb. 13, 1959. BA, Newberry Coll., 1980; M in Pub. Adminstrn., Brenau Coll., 1987. Teller, savs. counselor 1st Carolina Fed. Savs. and Loan, Columbia, S.C., 1981-82, account rep., 1982-83; supr. NOW accounts, automatic teller Security Fed. Savs. and Loan, Columbia, 1983-84; supr. accounts payable Niggel Assocs., Columbia, 1984-85; mem. staff bus. devel. Bankers 1st Fed. Savs. and Loan, Augusta, Ga., 1985-87, adminstrv. asst., adminstr. returns, 1987—. Scholar Robert Abrams Fgn. Lang., 1977-80, Newberry Coll. Alumni, 1977-80, Internat. Playtex, 1977. Mem. Image Nat. Hispanic Orgn., Nat. Assn. Female Execs., Network Augusta. Republican. Roman Catholic.

ZUBRACK, RODIE LINDA, financial executive; b. Woodbury, N.J., Oct. 1, 1942; d. Paul and Wilhelmina Julia (Koehler) Steffens; m. Henry Martin Buza, Nov. 9, 1963 (div. 1978); children: Deneen Marie, Clark, Jeffrey Leonard; m. Fred Zubrack, July 18, 1986. AA, Gloucester County Coll., 1980; BS, Temple U., 1982. Asst. to controller Ritz Hotel, Atlantic City, N.J., 1980-82; asst. controller Sheraton Poste Inn, Cherry Hill, N.J, 1982-86; v.p. CBC Assocs., Inc., Sterling, Va., 1986—. Mem. Profl. Bus. Women Assn. Roman Catholic. Office: CBC Assocs Inc 109 N King St Leesburg VA 22075

ZUCK, WYNONA COLLEEN, editor; b. Kansas City, Mo., Sept. 30, 1939; d. Earl Albert and Bertha (Drake) Howell; m. James Daniel Bardwell (div. 1967); 1 child, John Albert; m. Willard Alonzo Zuck; step-children: Cathy, Dawn, Sherrie, Linda. Student, Longview Community Coll. Paste-up artist Western Auto, Kansas City, Mo., 1957-60; keyline artist Trainor, Christianson & Barclay, Kansas City, 1960-61, Art, Inc., Kansas City, 1961-62, Nat. Bellas Hess, N. Kansas City, Mo., 1965-69, Unity Sch. Christianity, 1969-72; assoc. editor Wee Wisdom, Unity Village, Mo., 1972, editor, 1977-85; assoc. editor Daily Word, Unity Village, 1985, editor, 1985—; mem. editorial adv. com. Unity Sch., Unity Village, 1986—. Office: Daily Word Unity School of Christianity Unity Village MO 64065

ZUCKER, FAYE, book editor; b. N.Y.C., June 1, 1951; d. Irving and Esther (Katz) Z. BA, U. Chgo., 1972, MA, 1975. Writer, editor Lassiter & Co., Inc., Chgo., 1974-75; editor Frederick Ungar Pub. Co., N.Y.C., 1976-77; mng. editor Springer Pub. Co., N.Y.C., 1977-79, Haworth Press, N.Y.C., 1980-85, Harrington Park Press, N.Y.C., 1983-85; mng. editor books Raven Press, Ltd., N.Y.C., 1987—; cons. Tchrs. Coll. Press, N.Y.C., 1985-86, Chelsea Video Studios, Hollywood, Calif., 1986—. Recipient Rittenhouse award Med. Library Assn. Office: Raven Press Ltd 1185 Ave of Americas New York NY 10036

ZUCKER, JEAN MAXSON, nurse; b. Dunmore, Pa., Aug. 9, 1925; d. Earl L. and Florence M. (Cromwell) Maxson; R.N., Kings County Hosp. Center, 1948; cert. gerontol. nurse; children—Lawrence F., Pamela J., Diane K. Pvt. duty nurse various locations, N.Y., N.J., 1959-64; indsl. nurse Bendix Corp., Eatontown, N.J., 1955; asst. head nurse Point Pleasant Hosp., N.J., 1964-66; head nurse intensive and coronary care unit VA Hosp., Ft. Howard, Md., 1974-78; clin. nurse USPHS Hosp., Balt., 1978-81; nursing supr. VA Hosp.

Center, Ft. Howard, 1981—; tchr. in field. Mem. Am., Md. nurses assns., Am. Assn. Critical Care Nurses. Democrat. Methodist. Address: 2013 Barry Rd Baltimore MD 21222

ZUKIN, MARYANN, pediatrician; b. Los Angeles, Apr. 27, 1955; d. Arthur Samuel and Bernice (Friedel) Z. BA in Biology, U. Calif. at San Diego, La Jolla, 1976; MD, UCLA, 1980. Diplomate Am. Bd. Pediatrics. Intern Kaiser Permanente, Los Angeles, 1980-81, residency, 1981-84, pediatrician, 1984—. Vol. physician Flying Samaritans, Los Angeles, 1983—. Calif. Gov.'s scholar, 1972, Calif. Fedn. Gold Seal scholar, 1972; recipient Santa Monica (Calif.) Police Dept. Involvement award, 1983. Fellow Am. Acad. Pediatrics. Office: Kaiser Permanente 5220 Telford Los Angeles CA 90022

ZULLO, LORETTA JO, dietitian; b. Vernal, Utah, Mar. 5, 1955; d. Louis John and Beulah Merle (Richens) Z.; m. Joseph Stephen Wall, Sept. 25, 1982; 1 child, Daniel Joseph. BS, Ariz. State U., 1977. Registered dietitian. Food service dir. Howards Grove (Wis.) Pub. Schs., 1978-79; exec. dir. Dairy Council Wis., Milw., 1979-82; healthcare services mgr. CFS Continental, Phoenix, 1982-87; dir. bus. devel. Sand Dollar Food Cos., Inc., 1987—. Mem. Am. Dietetic Assn., Ariz. Dietetic Assn., Cen. Dist. Dietetic Assn. (pres. 1985-86), Wis. Nutrition Council (sec. 1979-80). Republican. Office: Sand Dollar Cos Inc 1255 W Baseline Suite 124 Mesa AZ 85203

ZUPANCIC, CHRISTINE ANN, furniture company executive; b. Maple Heights, Ohio, July 5, 1957; d. Joseph John and Eva Marie (Sudick) Z. A.A., Art. Inst. Pitts., 1978; student, Florence, Italy, 1977. Layout artist, artist Gordon's Jewelers, Houston, 1978-79; art dir., artist Weiner's Clothing, Houston, 1979-81; art dir. Finger's Furniture, Houston, 1981—. Mem. Mus. Fine Arts, Houston Opera Guild. Roman Catholic. Club: Slovenian/American (Houston). Avocations: painting; plastic casting jewelry; photography. Office: Finger's Furniture Co PO Box 194 Houston TX 77001

ZUPON, KAREN ELIZABETH, state official; b. Salinas, Calif., Jan. 17, 1944; d. Charles Edward and Muriel Scott (Barber) Kneib. B.A., U. Calif., Davis, 1972, also postgrad. Courtroom artist, writer KMGH-TV, Denver, 1978-79; news reporter, anchor, producer, courtroom artist KCRL-TV, Reno, Nev., 1979-81; news reporter, anchor, producer KGUN-TV, Tucson, 1981-83, KTVN-TV, Reno, 1983-84, KOLO-TV, Reno, 1984-85; exec. aide, press sec. Office of Gov. Nev., Carson City, 1985—. Mem. Nev. State Press Assn. Democrat. Office: Office Gov Exec Chambers Capitol Complex Carson City NV 89710

ZUR, JANICE MAE, relocation company executive; b. N.Y.C., July 11, 1942; d. Charles and Roslyn (Zemon) Epand; m. Harvey Namm, Jan. 21, 1961 (div. 1980); children: Frederick Michael, Audra Aileen; m. Eitan Zur, Mar. 14, 1985. Degree in Interior Design, Wilsey Inst., 1966. Lic. real estate broker and gen. contractor. Comptroller Island Floor Installers, L.I., N.Y., 1970-79; pres. Distinctive Concepts, Inc., N.Y.C., 1979-84, Distinctive Concepts West, Los Angeles, 1985—. Mem. Nat. Assn. Realtors, Los Angeles Bd. Realtors, Nat. Assn. Contractors, Century City Bus. Group, Los Angeles C. of C., Westchester County (N.Y.) C. of C., Swiss Am. Bus. Assn., German-Am. C. of C., Australian-Am. C. of C., Brit.-Am. C. of C., French-Am. C. of C. Republican. Jewish. Clubs: Braemar (Reseda, Calif.); Monterey (Palm Desert, Calif.). Office: Distinctive Concepts West 1888 Century Park East Suite #1208 Los Angeles CA 90067

ZURBUCHEN, SUSAN JANE, arts consultant; b. Madison, Wis., June 28, 1949; d. Herbert August and Ruth Helen (Pfaffenbach) Z. BA in Speech and Theatre, Lakeland Coll., Sheboygan, Wis., 1970; MA in Theatre Arts, U. Minn., 1972. Salesperson Keebler Co., Elmhurst, Ill., 1975; regional coordinator Office Criminal Justice Programs, Traverse City, Mich., 1976-77; bus. mgr. Old Town Playhouse, Traverse City, 1978-81; dir. adminstrn. Ind. Arts Commn., Indpls., 1982-85; arts cons. 10th Pan Am. Games, Indpls., 1985-87, Arts Co. of Indpls., 1988—; actress, dir. Traverse City Civic Players, 1976-81; grantsmanship Cons. Grand Traverse County (Mich.), 1977-81; spl. events cons. LWV, Traverse City, 1980-81. Puppeteer syndicated TV show Time for Timothy: PuppetVision, 1982—. Bd. dirs. Criminal Justice Adv. Council, Traverse City, 1976-82, Rainbow House, Inc., Cadillac, Mich., 1977-79; pres. bd. dirs Women's Resource Ctr., Traverse City, 1977-80; bd. dirs. Very Spl. Arts Ind.,, 1986—. Mem. LWV (bd. dirs. 1981-82), Nat. Assn. Female Execs., Am. Theatre Assn. Mem. United Ch. of Christ.

ZURYLO, BEVERLY ANISOWICZ, bursar, sports columnist, city official; b. Northampton, Mass., Oct. 18, 1947; d. Chester Stanley and Christine Constance (Szarkowski) Anisowicz. AA, Greenfield Community Coll., 1971; BA magna cum laude, U. Mass., 1973; MS, Antioch-New Eng. Grad. Sch. 1988; postgrad. U. Mass., 1988—. Bursar, Smith Coll., Northampton, Mass., 1977—, instr. Antioch-New Eng. Grad. Sch., Greenfield Community Coll., 1987—; columnist Pro Football Weekly, Chgo., 1979—; free-lance writer, 1981—; pres. Investments Unlimited, Northampton, 1976, 78-80; treas. Town of Whately, Mass., 1988—; sports talk show host various Mass. radio stas., 1982-84. Author: Beefcake and Lifeslices, 1986. Mem. Nat. Assn. Accts. (v.p. communications 1975-78), Phi Beta Kappa. Avocations: whale watching, interspecies communication, scuba diving, photography. Home: RFD 1 16 Laurel Mountain Rd Haydenville MA 01039 Office: Smith Coll College Hall 5 Northampton MA 01063

ZUSSY, NANCY LOUISE, librarian; b. Tampa, Fla., Mar. 4, 1947; d. John David and Patsy Ruth (Stone) Roche; m. R. Mark Allen, Dec. 20, 1986. B.A. in Edn., U. Fla., 1969; MLS, U. So. Fla., 1977, M.S. in Pub. Mgmt., 1980. Cert. librarian, Wash. Ednl. evaluator State of Ga., Atlanta, 1969-70; media specialist DeKalb County Schs., Decatur, Ga., 1970-71; researcher Ga. State Library, Atlanta, 1971; asst. to dir. reference Clearwater (Fla.) Pub. Library, 1972-78, dir. libraries, 1978-81; dep. state librarian Wash. State Library, Olympia, 1981-86, state librarian, 1986—; chmn. Consortium Automated Libraries, Olympia, 1982—; cons. various pub. libraries, Wash., 1981—; exec. officer Wash. Library Network, 1986—. Contbr. articles to profl. jours. Treas. Thurston-Mason Community Mental Health Bd., Olympia, 1983-85, dir., 1982-85; mem. race com. Seafair Hydroplane Race, Seattle, 1986. Mem. ALA (Assn. Specialized and Coop. Library Agys. legis. com. 1983—, chmn. legis. com. 1985-87, vice chmn. state library agys. sect. 1985-86, chmn. state ibrary agys. sect. 1986-87, chmn. govt. affairs com. Library Adminstrn. and Mgmt. Assn. 1986-87), Freedom to Read Found. (bd. dirs. 1988—), Chief Officers of State Library Agys. (dir.-at-large 1986—), Wash. Library Assn. (co-founder legis. planning com. 1982—, fed. relations coordinator 1984—), Fla. Library Assn. (legis. and planning com. 1978-81), Pacific Northwest Library Assn., Phi Kappa Phi, Phi Beta Mu. Home: 904 E Bay Dr #B-404 Olympia WA 98506 Office: Wash State Library AJ-11 Olympia WA 98504-0111

ZWEIGENTHAL, GAIL, magazine editor; b. N.Y.C., Feb. 27, 1944; d. Joseph and Bessie (Lang) Z. B.A., Tufts U., 1965. Editorial asst. Gourmet mag., N.Y.C., then assoc. editor, sr. editor, mng. editor, now exec. editor. Office: Gourmet Mag 560 Lexington Ave New York NY 10022 *

ZWICKL, JUDITH ELLEN, computer consultant; b. Denver, June 13, 1949; d. Arthur Hoober and Julia Lorraine (Koester) Neumann; m. Ronald Dean Zwickl, June 13, 1970. BS, Colo. State U., 1971; MBA, U. N.H., 1976. Service rep. New Eng. Telephone Co., Dover, N.H., 1972-75; account rep. ADP Network Services, Balt., 1977-79, cons. Western div., San Francisco, 1979-80; mem. staff Los Alamos Nat. Lab., 1983-86, assoc. group leader, 1984-86; software specialist III, Digital Equipment Corp., 1986-87, software specialist IV, 1987—; Mem. credit com. Los Alamos Credit Union, 1981-83, chmn., 1982-83, mem. supervisory com., 1983-85, chmn., 1984-85, bd. dirs., 1985—, sec. bd. dirs., 1986-87; vice chmn. Lacu Bd. Dirs., 1987-88. Mem. Balt. Econ. Soc. (rec. sec. 1978-79). Home: 314 Potrillo Dr Los Alamos NM 87544

ZWILICH, ELLEN TAAFFE, composer; b. Miami, Fla., Apr. 30, 1939; d. Edward Porter and Ruth (Howard) Taaffe; m. Joseph Zwilich, June 22, 1969 (dec. June 1979). MusB, Fla. State U., 1960, MusM, 1962: D Mus. Arts. Juilliard Sch., 1975; studies with Roger Sessions and Elliott Carter; MusD (hon.), Oberlin Coll., 1987. Premier Symposium for Orch., Pierre Boulez, N.Y.C., 1975, Chamber Symphony and Passages, Boston Musica Viva, 1979, 82. Symphony 1. Gunther Schuller. Am. Composers Orch., 1982; violinist Am. Symphony, N.Y.C., 1965-73; composer: Sonata in Three Movements, 1973-74; String Quartet, 1974; Clarino Quartet, 1977; Chamber Symphony, 1979; Passages (for Sorprano and Chamber Ensemble), 1981; String Trio, 1982; Symphony 1:3 Movements for Orch., 1982 (Grammy nomination New World Records, 1987); Divertimento, 1983; Einsame Nacht, 1971; Emlekezet, 1978; Im Nebel, 1972; Passages for Soprano and Orch., 1982; Trompeten, 1974; Fantasy for Harpsichord, 1983; Intrada, 1983; Prologue and Variations, 1983; Double Quartet for Strings, Chamber Music Soc. of Lincoln Ctr., 1984; Celebration for Orch., Indpls. Symphony, John Nelson, 1984; Symphony #2 (Cello Symphony) San Francisco Symphony, Edo De Waart, 1985; Concerto Grosso 1985, Handel Festival Orch., Steven Simon, 1986; Concerto for Piano and Orch., Detroit Symphony, Gunther Herbig, Marc-André Hamelin, 1986; Images for 2 Pianos and Orch., Nat. Symphony Orch., F. Machetti, 1987; Tanzspiel, Peter Martins N.Y.C. Ballet, 1987; Praeludium Boston chpt. AGO, 1987; Piano Trio, Kalichstein, Laredo and Robinson trio, 1987; Symbolon, Zubin Mehta and the N.Y. Philharm., Leningrad, Moscow, N.Y.C., 1988. Recipient Elizabeth Sprague Coolidge Chamber Music prize, 1974, Gold medal G.B. Viotti, Vercelli, Italy, 1975, citation Ernst von Dohnani, 1981, Pulitizer prize, 1983, Nat. Inst. Arts and Letters award, 1984, Composers award Lancaster Symphony Orch., Arturo Toscanini Music Critics award, 1987; Martha Baird Rockefeller Fund rec. grantee, 1977, 79, 82, Guggenheim fellow, 1981. Mem. Am. Fedn. Musicians (hon. life). Am. Music Ctr. (bd. dirs., v.p. 1982-84), Internat. League Women Composers. Home: 600 W 246th St Riverdale NY 10471 Office: care Music Assocs Am 224 King St Englewood NJ 07631

ZWILLING, JANE RIEGELHAUPT, psychologist; b. Bklyn., July 10, 1957; d. Jack and Eileen (Pullman) Riegelhaupt; m. Howard Zwilling, July 26, 1980; 1 child, Amanda. BS, CUNY, 1978, MS, cert. in sch. psychology, 1980; D of Psychology, Pace U., 1983. Lic. psychologist, N.Y. Intern in clin. psychology The Children's Village, Dobbs Ferry, N.Y., 1982-83; psychologist Blythedale Children's Hosp., Valhalla, N.Y., 1983-84; sch. psychologist Half Hollow Hills Sch. Dist., Dix Hills, N.Y., 1984—; pvt. practice psychologist Woodbury and Plainview, N.Y., 1984—. Author: (with others) Advances In Therapies for Children, 1986. Mem. Am. Psychol. Assn., Suffolk County Psychol. Assn., Nassau County Psychol. Assn., Assn. Play Therapy (editor newsletter 1982-83, 83-84, v.p. 1982-83, 83-84), Assn. Sch. Psychology (pres. Bklyn. Coll. chpt. 1979-80). Office: 1117 Old Country Rd Plainview NY 11803

ZYKAN, MARY SUSAN, solid waste disposal company owner; b. St. Louis, Oct. 7, 1946; d. Edward Patrick and Edna Elenora (Showalter) Schneider; m. Robert Walter Zykan, Mar. 27, 1965; children—Robert, Ronald, Steven, Karen. Grad. high sch., Overland, Mo. Sec. Greater St. Louis Foster Parent Assn., 1969-72, v.p., 1973-76; treas. Met. San. Haulers Assn., 1975-78; owner R & Z Hauling Service, St. Ann, Mo., 1965—; waste industry advisor Bi-State Devel. Agy., St. Louis, 1977-78; com. mem. St. Louis County Solid Waste Adv. Com., 1977-78; waste industry advisor Mo. Dept. Natural Resources Task Force, 1982-83. Editor newsletter Greater St. Louis Foster Parent Assn., 1970-76. Vol. Emergency Foster Home, St. Louis County Welfare Agy., Mo., 1972-74; planner, guest speaker Forest Park Community Coll. Waste Conf., 1980. Recipient Service awards St. Louis County Juvenile Ct., 1973, 78, Community Service award St. Charles County Solid Waste Task Force, 1986-87. Mem. Nat. Solid Waste Mgmt. Assn. (pres. Mo. chpt. 1981-82, legis. sec. 1985, chmn. solid waste legis. com. 1984-85), Met. San. Haulers Assn. (pres. 1985, bd. dirs. 1974-85, service award 1979), Nat. Fedn. Ind. Bus., Mo. Waste Coalition (conf. exhibit com. 1982, Achievement award 1985). Lutheran. Club: Am. Bdll. Avocations: bowling; swimming; bell colleclting; writing. Home: 10319 Millwood St Saint Ann MO 63074 Office: R & Z Hauling Service 10319 Millwood St Saint Ann MO 53074